FA

As the 2009 *Thoroughbred Times Racing Almanac* goes to press, the North American racing industry is in the midst of one of the most traumatic periods in its history, no less significant and potentially damaging than the antigambling sentiment that virtually shut down the sport a century ago. Back then, a group of people and politicians imposed their vision of morality on others. Racing came back within a few years in New York, but the restoration process took much longer in other states.

The threat to racing this time concerns the welfare of the horse and how well the industry takes care of its athletes. The anguish associated with Barbaro's injury and death had barely faded when the filly Eight Belles broke down fatally after finishing a gallant second to Big Brown in the 2008 Kentucky Derby Presented by Yum! Brands (G1). Within hours, racing was widely portrayed in the media as brutal and insensitive; some called for an outright ban.

The situation was exacerbated by the admission by Richard Dutrow Jr., trainer of Derby and Preakness Stakes (G1) Big Brown, that he routinely had steroids administered to all the horses in his stable, including the classic winner. Although legal, administering steroids to racehorses ran counter to an accelerating industry movement to ban all steroids from the racetrack environment. Big Brown's owners subsequently declared that all horses in the stable, including the dual classic winner, would no longer receive steroids.

The latest trauma made clear how much America cares about its horses, even if it largely has lost interest in racing as a sport. The concern that resulted from Barbaro's unexplained injury in the 2006 Preakness Stakes morphed into outrage when Eight Belles broke both front ankles while galloping out after the Derby finish. True, no one loves these horses more than the people who work with them, but it was not clear that the sport as a whole shared that love and concern. Racing, long known as the Teflon sport because all scandals and criticisms did not seem to stick, appeared to be losing some of its nonstick coating.

At base, the tremors shaking the sport represent a husbandry issue. Are we taking as good care of our horses as we should? What can we do to make racing safer for the horses? Is it good husbandry to race horses that are medicated? These are questions that will extend through 2009 and beyond. To be sure, some forward-looking steps have been taken. One of them was the Racing Medication and Testing Consortium, an industry initiative that had its roots in 2001 and has advocated coast-to-coast standards that are scientifically based. Barbaro's death in early 2007 from laminitis fostered another initiative, the Welfare and Safety of the Racehorse Summit, which had its second session shortly before the 2008 Derby. The Jockey Club formed the Thoroughbred Safety Committee shortly after Eight Belles's breakdown and called for a ban on steroids, limits on the size of toe grabs on racing plates, and new restrictions on whip use by jockeys.

Eight Belles's death also stirred political fires that reflected the anger and anguish felt by the American public. A congressional subcommittee hearing was held in June 2008, and the deck appeared to be stacked toward those seeking federal control over horse racing. How both the industry and the Congress respond in 2009 will be one of the issues covered by THOROUGHBRED TIMES, in the weekly magazine, on the website *www.thoroughbredtimes.com*, and in the 2010 *Thoroughbred Times Racing Almanac*.

Just as changes happened in the sport, so have changes occurred in the THOROUGHBRED TIMES family. Aylett Melton, who handled all matters related to public auctions for the magazine and *Almanac*, was very seriously injured in an automobile accident in December 2007. With boundless courage, she continues to make progress, and we all wish her well in her recovery. Gail Allensworth, who was the *Thoroughbred Times Stallion Directory* editor for 20 years, departed to attend to family matters, and we also wish her well. Assuming the *Stallion Directory* position is Melissa Humphrey, a 12-year THOROUGHBRED TIMES veteran who also becomes the *Thoroughbred Times Racing Almanac* editor.

The Almanac is a team effort, and several members of the team merit special thanks. In the Research Department, Patrick Reed assumed more *Almanac* responsibilities, and Colleen Jonsson ably handled auction sales for all publications. In the Art Department, *Almanac* Production Coordinator Betty Gee stayed a step ahead of everyone and made sure that everything was in order and completed on time. Art Director Jeanette Vance never hesitated to pitch in when the pace quickened. Deanna Bowden, chief copy editor, assured both accuracy and consistency. The *Thoroughbred Times Racing Almanac* provides a unique picture of the industry, and this ever-growing publication would not exist without them.

Don Clippinger, Editorial Director
Lexington, Kentucky
June 26, 2008

TABLE OF CONTENTS

State of the Industry
- Thoroughbred Economy in 2007-'08 1
- Pari-Mutuel Wagering by State in 2005 5
- Claiming Activity by State, Province in 2007 8
- Auction Sales by State, Province in 2007 11
- All About Purses 2007 16
- Purse Distribution by Track in 2007 23
- Racinos and Racing 25

Year in Review
- Top Ten Stories of 2007 28
- Leaders of 2007 31
- Chronology of 2007 and 2008 33
- 2007-2008 Obituaries 36
- 2007-2008 Horse Deaths 44

History of Racing
- History of Racing, Decade by Decade 57
- Key Dates in American Racing History 65
- Notable Horses in Racing 74
- Oldest Notable Horses of All Time 93

Eclipse Awards
- History of the Eclipse Awards 95
- Eclipse Award-Winning Horses 95
- Eclipse Award-Winning Individuals 97
- Eclipse Award Media Winners 99
- Owners of Eclipse Award Winners 101
- Breeders of Eclipse Award Winners 103
- Trainers of Eclipse Award Winners 105
- Sires of Eclipse Award Winners 106
- 2007 Eclipse Award Winners 108
- Champions Before Eclipse Awards 110

Racing Hall of Fame
- History of Racing Hall of Fame 112
- Members of Racing Hall of Fame 112
- Owners of Racing Hall of Fame Members 114
- Breeders of Racing Hall of Fame Members 115
- Trainers of Racing Hall of Fame Members 116
- Sires of Racing Hall of Fame Members.................117
- Regional Halls of Fame 118

Triple Crown
- History of the Triple Crown 121
- Triple Crown Productions 122
- Road to the Triple Crown 127
- Triple Crown Winners 128
- Near Triple Crown Winners 134
- Owners of Triple Crown Race Winners 135
- Breeders of Triple Crown Race Winners 136
- Trainers of Triple Crown Race Winners 137
- Jockeys of Triple Crown Race Winners 138
- Sires of Triple Crown Race Winners 139
- Kentucky Derby History 140
- Preakness Stakes History 156
- Belmont Stakes History 167
- 2008 Kentucky Derby 178
- 2008 Preakness Stakes 180
- 2008 Belmont Stakes 182

Breeders' Cup
- History 184
- Leaders 188
- Breeders' Cup Classic 196
- Breeders' Cup Turf 199
- Breeders' Cup Juvenile 202
- Breeders' Cup Filly and Mare Turf 205
- Breeders' Cup Sprint 207
- Breeders' Cup Mile 210
- Breeders' Cup Juvenile Fillies 212
- Breeders' Cup Distaff 215
- 2007 Classic 218
- 2007 Turf 220
- 2007 Juvenile 222
- 2007 Filly and Mare Turf 224
- 2007 Sprint 226
- 2007 Mile 228
- 2007 Juvenile Fillies 230
- 2007 Distaff 232
- 2007 Filly and Mare Sprint 234
- 2007 Juvenile Turf 234
- 2007 Dirt Mile 235

Racing
- Review of 2007 Season 236
- Richest North American Stakes Races of 2007 239
- Chronology of Richest North American Race 240
- How American Races are Graded 241
- Graded Stakes Histories 244
- Previously Graded Stakes 496
- 2007 North American Stakes Races 498
- Oldest Stakes Races 545
- Fastest Times of 2007 548
- North American Records 549
- Progression of Track Records 550
- Leading Earners of All Time 552
- All-Time Earners by Deflated Dollars 570
- Leading Earners by Foal Crop 573
- All-Time Earners by State Where Bred 574
- Leading 2007 Earners by State Where Bred 583
- Performance Rates for 2007 584
- Experimental Free Handicap 587
- American Match Races 591
- Notable Walkovers Since 1930 593
- Scale of Weights 593
- Oldest Grade 1 Stakes Winners 594
- The Claiming Game 599
- North American Claiming Races in 2007 600
- Claiming Crown 608
- Best Claimers 610

Racetracks
- Racetracks of North America 613
- Racetrack Locations and Abbreviations 708
- Purse Distribution by Year 710
- Top 25 Tracks by Average Attendance in 2007 710
- Top 25 Tracks by Average 2007 Handle 711
- Revenues to States from Horse Racing 712

The Original

THOROUGHBRED TIMES
Racing Almanac™
2009

THOROUGHBRED TIMES BOOKS

The Original
THOROUGHBRED TIMES
Racing Almanac™

2009
A Thoroughbred Times Book™

Editor in Chief: Mark Simon
Editorial Director: Don Clippinger
Editors: Ed DeRosa, Tom Law, John P. Sparkman
Information Technology: Jason Crane, Alan Johnson, Keith Thompson
Editorial Research: Frank Angst, Jeff Apel, Steve Bailey, Liane Crossley, Mike Curry, Pete Denk, Sarah Dorroh, Myra Lewyn, Jeff Lowe, Tom Musgrave, Joe Nevills, Mary Simon, Denise Steffanus
Statistical Research: Gail Allensworth, Melissa Humphrey, Colleen Jonsson, Aylett Melton, Carlos Peña-Rivera, Patrick Reed
Editorial Assistants: Deanna Bowden, Kelly McAninch, Katie Mudd
Art Director: Jeanette Vance
Production Coordinator: Betty Gee
Production Staff: Nicole Elliott, Laura Lacy, Amy McLean, LaDonna Murphy, Tami Zigo
Cover Photo: Photo by Z/Vincent Dusovic

Thoroughbred Times Co. Inc.
Chairman: Norman Ridker
President: Mark Simon
Publisher: Joe Morris
Editorial Office: 2008 Mercer Rd., Lexington, KY 40511

THOROUGHBRED TIMES RACING ALMANAC welcomes comments and suggestions from readers. Every communication is read by the editors and receives consideration and attention.
THOROUGHBRED TIMES RACING ALMANAC does not decide wagers.

THOROUGHBRED TIMES RACING ALMANAC OF 2009™
Copyright © 2008 Thoroughbred Times Co. Inc.
All rights reserved. No part of this book may be reproduced in any form or by any electronic or mechanical means, including information storage and retrieval systems, without permission in writing from the publisher.

Statistics provided herein are compiled by Thoroughbred Times Co. Inc. from data supplied by Jockey Club Information Systems Inc., Daily Racing Form Inc., and Equibase Co. Data provided or compiled by Jockey Club Information Systems Inc. generally are accurate but occasionally errors and omissions occur as a result of incorrect data received from others, mistakes in processing, and other causes. The Jockey Club Information Systems Inc. disclaims responsibility for the consequences, if any, of such errors, but would appreciate any errors or omissions being called to its attention. Information as to races, race results, earnings, and other statistical data for races run subsequent to December 31, 1990, was obtained from Equibase Co. and is utilized only with permission of the copyright owner. Such information for periods prior to January 1, 1991, was obtained from Daily Racing Form Inc. Information pertaining to pedigree and production records contained herein copyright the Jockey Club Information Systems Inc.

THOROUGHBRED TIMES RACING ALMANAC™ and THOROUGHBRED TIMES®
are registered trademarks of Thoroughbred Times Co. Inc.
International Standard Serial Number (ISSN) 1540-5486
ISBN Number 978-193395876-7

THOROUGHBRED TIMES RACING ALMANAC ™
Thoroughbred Times Books™
An imprint of BowTie Press™
www.thoroughbredtimes.com
e-mail: letters@thoroughbredtimes.com

Table of Contents

People
- Leading Owners of 2007 713
- Leading Breeders of 2007 719
- Leading Trainers of 2007 724
- Leading Jockeys of 2007 731
- Notable Names of the Past 738
- Contemporary Individuals 753
- Industry Awards 767

Breeding
- Development of the Breeding Industry 775
- Registration Rules for Breeding 777
- Foal Registration 781
- Evolution of the Breed 782
- Breeding Theories 784

Sires
- Leading Sires by Progeny Earnings in 2007 789
- Leading Juvenile Sires by Progeny Earnings in 2007 794
- Leading Freshman Sires by Progeny Earnings in 2007 796
- Leading Broodmare Sires by Progeny Earnings in 2007 798
- Leading Sires by Progeny Earnings in North America in 2007 800
- Leading Juvenile Sires by Progeny Earnings in North America in 2007 802
- Leading Freshman Sires by Progeny Earnings in North America in 2007 804
- Leading Broodmare Sires by Progeny Earnings in North America in 2007 806
- Leading Worldwide Sires by 2007 Progeny Earnings 808
- Leading General Sire by Year 809
- Leading Juvenile Sire by Year 809
- Leading Freshman Sire by Year 810
- Leading Broodmare Sire by Year 810
- Profiles of Leading Sires by Year 811
- All-Time Leading Sires 820
- Leading 2007 Sires by State or Province 825
- Stallion Syndications 830
- Leading Stud Farms of 2007 832
- Live Foal Report for 2007 834
- Report of Mares Bred for 2007 842
- Stallions Bred in 2007 844

Broodmares
- Broodmares of the Year 851
- Leading Broodmares by 2007 Progeny Earnings 855
- Most Group/Graded Stakes Winners for a Broodmare 856
- Most Stakes Winners for a Broodmare 856
- Most Foals for a Broodmare 857
- Most Wins by Broodmare's Offspring 858
- Most Starts by Broodmare's Offspring 859
- Oldest Broodmares to Produce a Winner 859
- Most Millionaires Produced by a Broodmare 860
- Consecutive Generations of Producing Graded Stakes Winners 861
- Champions Who Produced Champions 861

Auctions
- History of Thoroughbred Auctions 862
- Auction Review of 2007 863
- Highest Auction Prices of 2007 866
- Chronological Review of 2007 Sales 870
- Histories of Major Sales 871
- Highest-Priced Horses of All Time 875
- Leading Buyers of 2007 882
- Leading Consignors of 2007 884
- Pinhooking 887

Organizations
- Jockey Club 895
- National Thoroughbred Racing Association 897
- Thoroughbred Racing Associations 898
- Thoroughbred Racing Protective Bureau 899
- American Horse Council 899
- Association of Racing Commissioners International 900
- Equibase 900
- Jockeys' Guild 901
- Keeneland Association 902
- Thoroughbred Owners and Breeders Association 902
- National Horsemen's Benevolent and Protective Association 903
- National Industry Organizations 904
- State and Provincial Racing Organizations 905
- Charitable Organizations 912
- Thoroughbred Retirement and Rescue 912
- Sales Companies 917
- Publicly Owned Companies 918

International
- Review of 2007 Racing Season 922
- Richest International Races of 2007 923
- Chronology of Richest International Race 924
- Major International Stakes Races 924
- English Triple Crown 932
- 2007 World Racehorse Rankings 935
- Cartier Awards 939
- Major International Racetracks 941
- International Sire Lists 956
- Sovereign Awards 960
- Canadian Horse Racing Hall of Fame 963

Reference
- Rules of Racing 964
- Preference Date System 969
- How to Handicap a Race 971
- How to Read a Race Chart 982
- Pari-Mutuel Wagering 983
- Betting Odds and Payouts 984
- Distance Equivalents 985
- Glossary of Common Racing and Breeding Terms 986
- Conformation and Anatomy Terms 998
- Common Veterinary Terms 1001

GENERAL INDEX

Abbreviations
Racetracks and Locations 708
Track Conditions 971
Used in This Book 1005
Ack Ack H. 244
Acorn S. 244
Adena Stallions' Miss Preakness S. 245
Adirondack S. 245
Aegon Turf Sprint S. 246
Affirmed H. 246
Age Definitions 779
Age, Legal to Attend Races 712
A Gleam Invitational H. 247
Alabama S. 247
Alcibiades S. 248
Alfred G. Vanderbilt H. 248
Allaire duPont Distaff S. 248
All Along S. 249
All American S. 249
All-Sources Wagering, Top 25 Meets by Average 711
All-Time Leading Sires 820
Broodmare Sires by Group 1 or Grade 1 Stakes Winners 823
Broodmare Sires by Group or Graded Stakes Winners 823
Broodmare Sires by Progeny Earnings 822
Broodmare Sires by Stakes Winners 823
General Sires by Group 1 or Grade 1 Stakes Winners 821
General Sires by Group or Graded Stakes Winners 821
General Sires by Percentage of Stakes Winners 821
General Sires by Stakes Winners 820
General Sires by Winners 820
North American General Sires by Progeny Earnings 820
Alysheba S. 250
American Classic Winners, Dams of Multiple ...139
American Derby 250
American Horse Council 899
American Invitational H. 251
American Invitational Oaks 251
American Turf S. 251
Amsterdam S. 251
Anatomy and Conformation Terms 998
Ancient Title S. 252
Anthony Downs, Ks. 646
Apache County Fair, Az. 613
Appalachian S. 252
Apple Blossom H. 253
Appleton H. 253
Aqueduct, N.Y. 674
Arapahoe Park, Co. 631
Arcadia H. 254
Aristides S. 254
Arkansas Derby 255
Arlington H. 255
Arlington Matron H. 256
Arlington Million S. 256
Arlington Park, Il.
Hall of Fame 118
Profile 639
Arlington-Washington Futurity 257
Arlington-Washington Lassie S. 258
Ashland S. 258
Assiniboia Downs, Mb. 703
Association of Racing Commissioners International 900
Athenia H. 259
Atlantic City Race Course, N.J. 667
Attendance
Belmont Stakes 167
Breeders' Cup 184
Kentucky Derby 140
Preakness Stakes 156
Top 25 Meets by On-Track Average 710
Auction Prices
Average by State and Province in 2007 11
Highest Yearling, Through the Years 879
Median by State and Province in 2007 12
Nominal and Deflated Dollars, 1990-2007 10
Progression of Highest Yearling 879
Auction Review of 2007 863
Broodmares 865
Two-Year-Olds 864
Weanlings 864
Yearlings 863
Auction Sales 862
By State and Province in 2007 11
Biggest Bargains Since 1980 893
Chronological Review of Major 2007 Sales 870
Highest-Priced Broodmares of 2007 869
Highest-Priced Horses of All Time 875
Highest-Priced Two-Year-Olds of 2007 868
Highest-Priced Weanlings of 2007 867
Highest-Priced Yearlings of 2007 866
Highest Yearling Prices Through the Years 879
Histories of Major Sales 871
History of Thoroughbred Auctions 862
Leading Buyers by Broodmare Purchases in 2007 883
Leading Buyers by Total Purchases in 2007 ...882
Leading Buyers by Two-Year-Old Purchases in 2007 883
Leading Buyers by Weanling Purchases in 2007 883
Leading Buyers by Yearling Purchases in 2007 882
Leading Buyers of Top-Priced Yearlings 882
Leading Consignors by Average Receipts in 2007 885
Leading Consignors by Broodmare Receipts in 2007 885
Leading Consignors by Percent Sold in 2007 886
Leading Consignors by Total Receipts in 2007 884
Leading Consignors by Two-Year-Old Receipts in 2007 885
Leading Consignors by Weanling Receipts in 2007 884
Leading Consignors by Yearling Receipts in 2007 884
Leading Consignors of Top-Priced Yearlings 882
Leading Sires of Top-Priced Yearlings 882
Nominal and Deflated Dollars, 1990-2007 10
Progression of Top-Priced Yearlings 879
Top-Priced Broodmares in North America 878
Top-Priced Two-Year-Olds in North America 876
Top-Priced Weanlings in North America 877
Top-Priced Yearlings by Year 880
Top-Priced Yearlings in North America 875
Yearling Sales Average by Year 886
Auctions, Leading
Barretts Equine Ltd. Selected Two-Year-Olds in Training 874
Fasig-Tipton Calder Selected Two-Year-Olds in Training 873
Fasig-Tipton Kentucky July Selected Yearlings 872
Fasig-Tipton Saratoga Selected Yearlings 872
Keeneland April Two-Year-Olds in Training 873
Keeneland January Horses of All Ages 875
Keeneland July Selected Yearlings 872
Keeneland November Breeding Stock 874
Keeneland September Yearlings 871
Ocala Breeders' Sales Co. February Two-Year-Olds in Training 874
Average
Auction Prices by State and Province in 2007 ..11
Broodmare Prices by State and Province in 2007 11
Broodmare Sales, by Year 887
Earnings per Runner, 1998-2007 16
Field Size, 1998-2007 22
Leading Consignors by Average Receipts in 2007 885
Number of Starts, 1998-2007 22
Purses, 1998-2007 16
Purses in North America, 1996-2007 1
Sales of All Horses, by Year 886
Stud Fees by State and Province, 2003-2007 ..15
Two-Year-Old Prices by State and Province in 2007 11
Two-Year-Olds in Training Sales, by Year 886
Weanling Prices by State and Province in 2007 11
Weanling Sales, by Year 886
Yearling Prices by State and Province in 2007 11
Yearling Sales, by Year 886
Average Earnings of Sires
Leading Broodmare Sires per Starter in North America in 2007 807
Leading Broodmare Sires per Starter Worldwide in 2007 799
Leading Freshman Sires per Starter in North America in 2007 805
Leading Freshman Sires per Starter Worldwide in 2007 797
Leading General Sires per Starter in North America in 2007 801
Leading General Sires per Starter Worldwide in 2007 792
Leading Juvenile Sires per Starter in North America in 2007 803
Leading Juvenile Sires per Starter Worldwide in 2007 795
Averages for the Breed 783
Awards, International
Cartier Awards 939
Lord Derby Awards 940
Sovereign Awards 960
Awards, North American 767
Eric Beitia Memorial Award 767
Big Sport of Turfdom 767
F. Ambrose Clark Award 767
Coman Humanitarian Award 767
Dogwood Dominion Award 768
Charles W. Engelhard Award 768
Jerry Frutkoff Preakness Photography Award 768
John W. Galbreath Award 768
Avelino Gomez Memorial Award 768
John K. Goodman Alumni Award 768
Walter Haight Award 769
Hardboot Award 769
Joe Hirsch Breeders' Cup Newspaper Writing Award 769
Jockey Club Medal of Honor 769
Lavin Cup 769
Bill Leggett Breeders' Cup Magazine Writing Award 769
William H. May Award 770
Mr. Fitz Award 770
Isaac Murphy Award 770
Old Hilltop Award 770
Joe Palmer Award 771
Joan F. Pew Award 771
Clay Puett Award 771
Red Smith Award 771
Sovereign Awards 960
University of Arizona RTIP Distinguished Senior Award 772
University of Arizona RTIP Distinguished Service Award 772
UTTA Outstanding Trainer of the Year Award ..772
Alfred Gwynne Vanderbilt Award 773
Mike Venezia Memorial Award 773
White Horse Award 773
P.A.B. Widener II Trophy 773
David F. Woods Memorial Award 774
George Woolf Memorial Jockey Award 774
Azalea S. 259
Azeri S. 260
Baldwin S. 260
Ballerina S. 261

General Index v

Ballston Spa H. 261
Barbara Fritchie H. 262
Barbaro S. 263
Barretts Equine Ltd. Selected Two-Year-Olds in Training 874
Bashford Manor S. 263
Bayakoa H. 264
Bay Meadows Sprint H. 264
Bay Meadows Fair, Ca. 618
Bay Meadows Race Course, Ca. 619
Bay Shore S. 264
Beaugay H. 265
Beaumont S. 266
Bed o' Roses H. 266
Eric Beitia Memorial Award 767
Beldame S. 266
Belmont Park, N.Y.
Belmont Stakes 167
Profile 675
Belmont Stakes 167
Attendance 167
Beaten Favorites, Odds-On 173
Birthplaces of Winners 174
Breeders, Leading by Wins 170
Carnation Blanket 169
Derby, Preakness Winners Not Favored in 172
Fillies in 174
Fractions, Fastest 172
Front-Running Winners 173
Geldings in 174
Graded History 267
History 167
Jockeys, Leading by Wins 171
Jockeys, Most Mounts 171
Longest-Priced Winners 173
Margins, Largest Winning 173
Margins, Smallest Winning 174
"New York, New York" 169
Owners, Leading by Wins 170
Owners, Most Starts 170
Post Positions, Winning 173
Race Conditions 126
Review of 2008 Belmont 182
Shortest-Priced Winners 173
"Sidewalks of New York" 169
Sires, Leading by Wins 172
Status of Winners Since 1970 177
Tabular History 175
Trainers, Leading by Wins 171
Trainers, Most Starts 171
Trivia 170
Trophy and Tray 168
Wagering 169
Winners Who Sired Winners 172
Winning Time, Evolution of Record 172
Winning Time, Fastest 172
Winning Time, Slowest 172
Ben Ali S. 268
Berkeley S. 268
Bernard Baruch H. 269
Bessemer Trust Breeders' Cup Juvenile 269
Best Pal S. 270
Bets, Types of 973
Betting, Odds and Payouts 984
Beulah Park, Oh. 679
Beverly D. S. 271
Beverly Hills H. 271
Bewitch S. 271
Big Sport of Turfdom 767
Bill Hartack Memorial H. 272
Bing Crosby H. 272
Black-Eyed Susan S. 273
Bloodstock Sales, Relationship of, 1982-2007 2
Blue Grass S. 273
Blue Ribbon Downs, Ok. 682
Boiling Springs S. 273
Bold Ruler H. 274
Bonnie Miss S. 275
Bourbonette Oaks 275
Bowling Green H. 276
Boyd Gaming Corp. 918
Boyd Gaming's Delta Jackpot S. 276
Boyd Gaming's Delta Princess Powered by Youbet.com S. 277
Breed
Averages for 783
Evolution of 782
Breeders
Eclipse Award Winners 97
Leading Belmont Stakes by Wins 170
Leading by Average Earnings per Starter in 2007 721
Leading by Breeders' Cup Purses 189
Leading by Breeders' Cup Wins 188
Leading by Earnings, 1997-2007 719
Leading by Earnings in 2007 719
Leading by Eclipse Award Winners 103
Leading by Number of Grade 1 Stakes Winners in 2007 723
Leading by Number of Grade 1 Stakes Wins in 2007 722
Leading by Number of Graded Stakes Winners in 2007 722
Leading by Number of Graded Stakes Wins in 2007 722
Leading by Number of Stakes Winners in 2007 721
Leading by Number of Stakes Wins in 2007 721
Leading by Number of Winners in 2007 723
Leading by Number of Wins in 2007 723
Leading Kentucky Derby by Wins 144
Leading of 2007 719
Leading of Racing Hall of Fame Members 115
Leading of Triple Crown Race Winners 136
Leading Preakness Stakes by Wins 159
Of Eclipse Award Winners 103
Of Racing Hall of Fame Members 115
Breeders' Cup 184
Attendance, by Year 184
Attendance, Largest 194
Attendance, Smallest 194
Betting, Largest On-Track 194
Betting, Smallest On-Track 195
Breeders, Leading by Purses Won 189
Breeders, Leading by Wins 188
Earnings, Highest in Races 192
Entries, by Year 193
Entries, Supplemental 186
Field Size, Average by Race 193
Field Size, Average by Year 193
History 184
Jockeys, Leading by Most Mounts on Program 191
Jockeys, Leading by Most Wins on Program 190
Jockeys, Leading by Mounts 190
Jockeys, Leading by Purses 190
Jockeys, Leading by Wins 188
Leaders 188
Location of Races 184
Margins, Largest Winning 192
Margins, Smallest Winning 192
Most Pre-Entries for a Race 194
Nominations 193
Oldest Race Winners 194
Oldest Starters 195
Oldest Surviving Winners 193
Owners, Leading by Most Starts on Program 189
Owners, Leading by Purses 189
Owners, Leading by Starts 189
Owners, Leading by Wins 188
Pari-Mutuel Odds, Average by Year 192
Pre-Entries, by Year 193
Purses 187
Purses, Largest 187
Review of 2007 Classic 218
Review of 2007 Dirt Mile 235
Review of 2007 Distaff 232
Review of 2007 Filly and Mare Sprint 234
Review of 2007 Filly and Mare Turf 224
Review of 2007 Juvenile 222
Review of 2007 Juvenile Fillies 230
Review of 2007 Juvenile Turf 234
Review of 2007 Mile 228
Review of 2007 Sprint 226
Review of 2007 Turf 220
Sires, Leading by Most Placings 191
Sires, Leading by Most Starts 191
Sires, Leading by Purses 191
Sires, Leading by Wins 189
Starters, by Year 193
Supplemental Entries 186
Television Ratings 185
Trainers, Leading by Most Starts on Program 190
Trainers, Leading by Most Wins on Program 190
Trainers, Leading by Purses 190
Trainers, Leading by Starts 190
Trainers, Leading by Wins 188
Trophy 187
Wagering, by Year 184
Winners, by Career Earnings 192
Winners, by Place Where Bred 192
Winners, Favored by Race 192
Winners, Favored by Year 192
Winners, Longest-Priced 195
Winners, Shortest-Priced 195
Winners Who Produced Winners 191
Winners Who Sired Winners 191
Breeders' Cup Classic 196
Breeders, by Wins 197
Champions from Race 198
Changes in Classic 199
Graded History 277
History 196
Jockeys, by Wins 197
Margins, Largest Winning 198
Margins, Smallest Winning 198
Owners, by Wins 197
Post Positions, Winning 199
Review of 2007 Classic 218
Sires, by Wins 197
Starters, Fewest 198
Starters, Most 198
Supplemental Entries 198
Tabular History 196
Trainers, by Wins 197
Winners, by Place Where Bred 197
Winners, Fastest 198
Winners, Longest-Priced 198
Winners, Shortest-Priced 198
Winners, Slowest 198
Breeders' Cup Distaff 215
Beaten Odds-On Favorites 217
Breeders, by Wins 216
Champions from Race 216
Changes in Distaff 217
Graded History 313
History 215
Jockeys, by Wins 216
Margins, Largest Winning 217
Margins, Smallest Winning 217
Owners, by Wins 216
Post Positions, Winning 217
Review of 2007 Distaff 232
Sires, by Wins 216
Starters, Fewest 217
Starters, Most 217
Supplemental Entries 216
Tabular History 215
Trainers, by Wins 216
Winners, by Place Where Bred 216
Winners, Fastest 217
Winners, Longest-Priced 217
Winners, Shortest-Priced 217
Winners, Slowest 217
Breeders' Cup Filly and Mare Turf 205
Breeders, by Wins 205
Champions from Race 206
Changes in Filly and Mare Turf 206
Graded History 314
History 205
Jockeys, by Wins 206
Margins, Largest Winning 206
Margins, Smallest 206
Owners, by Wins 205
Post Positions, Winning 206
Review of 2007 Filly and Mare Turf 224
Sires, by Wins 206

vi General Index

Starters in Filly and Mare Turf....206
Supplemental Entries....206
Tabular History....205
Trainers, by Wins....206
Winners, by Place Where Bred....206
Winners, Fastest....206
Winners, Slowest....206
Breeders' Cup Juvenile....202
Beaten Odds-On Favorites....204
Breeders, by Wins....203
Champions from Race....204
Changes in Juvenile....205
Graded History....269
History....202
Jockeys, by Wins....203
Margins, Largest Winning....204
Margins, Smallest Winning....204
Owners, by Wins....203
Post Positions, Winning....205
Review of 2007 Juvenile....222
Sires, by Wins....204
Starters, Fewest....204
Starters, Most....204
Supplemental Entries....204
Tabular History....202
Trainers, by Wins....203
Winners, by Place Where Bred....204
Winners, Fastest....204
Winners, Longest-Priced....204
Winners, Shortest-Priced....204
Winners, Slowest....204
Breeders' Cup Juvenile Fillies....212
Beaten Odds-On Favorites....214
Breeders, by Wins....213
Champions from Race....214
Changes in Juvenile Fillies....215
Graded History....277
History....212
Jockeys, by Wins....214
Margins, Largest Winning....214
Margins, Smallest Winning....214
Owners, by Wins....213
Post Positions, Winning....215
Review of 2007 Juvenile Fillies....230
Sires, by Wins....214
Starters, Fewest....215
Starters, Most....215
Supplemental Entries....214
Tabular History....213
Trainers, by Wins....214
Winners, by Place Where Bred....214
Winners, Fastest....214
Winners, Longest-Priced....214
Winners, Shortest-Priced....214
Winners, Slowest....214
Breeders' Cup Mile....210
Beaten Odds-On Favorites....212
Breeders, by Wins....211
Champions from Race....211
Changes in Mile....212
Graded History....400
History....210
Jockeys, by Wins....211
Margins, Largest Winning....211
Margins, Smallest Winning....211
Owners, by Wins....210
Post Positions, Winning....212
Review of 2007 Mile....228
Sires, by Wins....211
Starters, Fewest....212
Starters, Most....212
Supplemental Entries....211
Tabular History....210
Trainers, by Wins....211
Winners, by Place Where Bred....211
Winners, Fastest....212
Winners, Longest-Priced....211
Winners, Shortest-Priced....211
Winners, Slowest....212
Breeders' Cup Sprint....207
Beaten Odds-On Favorites....209
Breeders, by Wins....208
Champions from Race....209
Changes in Sprint....209
Graded History....481
History....207
Jockeys, by Wins....208
Margins, Largest Winning....209
Margins, Smallest Winning....209
Owners, by Wins....208
Post Positions, Winning....209
Review of 2007 Sprint....226
Sires, by Wins....208
Starters, Fewest....209
Starters, Most....209
Supplemental Entries....208
Tabular History....207
Trainers, by Wins....208
Winners, by Place Where Bred....208
Winners, Fastest....209
Winners, Longest-Priced....209
Winners, Shortest-Priced....209
Winners, Slowest....209
Breeders' Cup Turf....199
Beaten Odds-On Favorites....201
Breeders, by Wins....200
Champions from Race....201
Changes in Turf....202
Graded History....361
History....199
Jockeys, by Wins....200
Margins, Largest Winning....201
Margins, Smallest Winning....201
Owners, by Wins....200
Post Positions, Winning....202
Review of 2007 Turf....220
Sires, by Wins....200
Starters, Fewest....202
Starters, Most....201
Supplemental Entries....201
Tabular History....199
Trainers, by Wins....200
Winners, by Place Where Bred....201
Winners, Fastest....201
Winners, Longest-Priced....201
Winners, Shortest-Priced....201
Winners, Slowest....201
Breeders' Futurity....278
Breeding....775
Deadlines....780
Development of Industry....775
Fees....780
Notable Contemporary Individuals....753
Notable Names in Racing's Past....738
Relationships of Important Sires....782
Terminology....779
Breeding and Racing Glossary....986
Breeding Theories....784
Breeding to Best Performers....784
Bruce Lowe Numbers....786
Inbred Horses, Famous....785
Inbreeding....785
Modern Genetics....788
Nicks....786
Roman Dosage....788
Varola Dosage....787
Vuillier Dosage....787
Vuillier Dosages of Selected Horses....787
Broodmares....851
Auction Sales by State and Province in 2007....11
Average Prices by State and Province in 2007....11
Champions Who Produced Champions....861
Graded Stakes Producers of Graded Stakes Producers....861
Highest-Priced in North America....878
Highest-Priced of 2007....869
Leading Buyers by Purchases in 2007....883
Leading by 2007 Earnings in North America....855
Leading by Progeny Earnings....855
Leading Consignors by Receipts in 2007....885
Median Prices by State and Province in 2007....12
Most Consecutive Foals for....857
Most Foals for....857
Most Group or Graded Stakes Winners for....856
Most Millionaires Produced by....860
Most Stakes Winners for....856
Most Starts by Offspring....859
Most Winners for....858
Most Wins by Offspring....858
Oldest to Produce a Named Foal....859
Oldest to Produce a Stakes Winner....860
Oldest to Produce a Winner....859
Sales Average by Year....887
Broodmare Sire List, Most Times Headed....810
Broodmare Sire List, Most Times Headed Consecutively....810
Broodmare Sires
All-Time Leading by Group 1 or Grade 1 Stakes Winners....823
All-Time Leading by Group or Graded Stakes Winners....823
All-Time Leading by Progeny Earnings....822
All-Time Leading by Stakes Winners....823
By Average Earnings per Starter in North America in 2007....807
By Average Earnings per Starter Worldwide in 2007....799
By Median Earnings per Starter in North America in 2007....807
By Median Earnings per Starter Worldwide in 2007....799
By Number of Graded Stakes Winners in North America in 2007....807
By Number of Graded Stakes Winners Worldwide in 2007....799
By Number of Stakes Winners in North America in 2007....807
By Number of Stakes Winners Worldwide in 2007....799
By Number of Winners in North America in 2007....807
By Number of Winners Worldwide in 2007....799
By Number of Wins in North America in 2007....807
By Number of Wins Worldwide in 2007....799
Leading by North American Earnings in 2007....806
Leading by Worldwide Earnings in 2007....798
Leading by Year....810
Broodmares of the Year
1946-2007....851
Profiles of....851
Brooklyn H.....278
Brown County Fair, S.D.....690
Bryan Station S.....279
Buena Vista H.....279
Bulleit Bourbon Palm Beach S.....279
Buyers
Leading by Broodmare Purchases in 2007....883
Leading by Total Purchases in 2007....882
Leading by Two-Year-Old Purchases in 2007....883
Leading by Weanling Purchases in 2007....883
Leading by Yearling Purchases in 2007....882
Leading of Top-Priced Yearlings....882
Calder Derby....280
Calder Race Course, Fl.
Hall of Fame....118
Profile....633
Californian S.....281
California Thoroughbred Breeders Association Hall of Fame....118
Canadian Horse Racing Hall of Fame....963
Canadian Triple Crown Winners....962
Canadian Turf H.....281
Canterbury Park Holding Corp.....918
Canterbury Park, Mn.
Hall of Fame....119
Profile....662
Cardinal H.....282
Carleton F. Burke H.....283
Carry Back S.....283
Carter H.....284
Cartier Awards....939
CashCall Futurity....284
CashCall Mile Invitational S.....285
Central Bank Transylvania S.....285
Champagne S.....286
Champions Before Eclipse Awards....110
Handicap Female....111
Handicap Male....111

General Index vii

Horse of the Year 110
Sprinter 111
Steeplechase 111
Three-Year-Old Filly 110
Three-Year-Old Male 110
Turf Horse 111
Two-Year-Old Filly 110
Two-Year-Old Male 110
Champions, Eclipse Award-Winning 95
Apprentice Jockey 98
Breeder 97
Female Sprinter 97
Horse of the Year 95
Jockey 98
Male Sprinter 97
Man of the Year 98
Older Female 96
Older Male 96
Owner 97
Owner-Breeder 97
Sprinter 97
Steeplechaser 97
Three-Year-Old Filly 96
Three-Year-Old Male 96
Trainer 97
Turf Female 96
Turf Horse 96
Turf Male 96
Two-Year-Old Filly 95
Two-Year-Old Male 95
Champions Who Produced Champions 861
Charitable Organizations 912
Charles Town Races, W.V.
Profile 697
Racino 27
Charles Whittingham Memorial H. 286
Charts, How to Read 982
Chicago H. 287
Chilukki S. 287
Chronology
Of 2007-2008 33
Of Record Stallion Syndications 830
Of Richest International Race 924
Of Richest North American Race 240
Churchill Distaff Turf Mile S. 288
Churchill Downs, Ky.
Corporate Profile 918
Kentucky Derby 140
Profile 647
Twin Spires 142
Churchill Downs S. 288
Cicada S. 289
Cigar Mile H. 289
Cinema H. 289
Citation H. 290
Claimed
Most Consecutive Times, 1991-2007 607
Most Consecutive Times in 2007 607
Most Times, 1991-2007 606
Most Times in 2007 606
Claimers, Profiles of Best 610
Claiming
Activity by State and Track in 2007 601
Activity by State or Province in 2007 8
Canadian, Activity by Province and Track in 2007 602
Most Claiming Wins, 1991-2007 605
Most Claiming Wins in 2007 605
Most Wins After First Claim, 1991-2007 604
Most Wins After First Claim in 2007 604
Purses, by Claiming Category 21
Claiming Crown
History 608
Tabular History of Races 608
Claiming Races 599
Claimed Most Consecutive Times, 1991-2007 607
Claimed Most Consecutive Times in 2007 607
Claimed Most Times, 1991-2007 606
Claimed Most Times in 2007 606
Claiming Activity by State and Track 601
Claims by Category, Canada 601
Claims by Category, United States 601
Highest Earnings After First Claim in 2007 603
History of Claiming Races 599
Leading Earners After First Claim, 1991-2007 603
Most Claiming Wins, 1991-2007 605
Most Claiming Wins in 2007 605
Most Wins After First Claim, 1991-2007 604
Most Wins After First Claim in 2007 604
North American in 2007 600
Claims
by Category, Canada 601
by Category, United States 601
F. Ambrose Clark Award 767
Clark H. 290
Clement L. Hirsch H. 291
Clement L. Hirsch Memorial Turf Championship S. 292
Cliff Hanger S. 292
Coaching Club American Oaks 293
Cochise County Fair, Az. 613
Coconino County Fair, Az. 613
Colonel E. R. Bradley H. 294
Colonial Downs, Va. 694
Colonial Turf Cup S. 294
Color Definitions 779
Columbus Races, Ne. 663
Coman Humanitarian Award 767
Comely S. 294
Commonwealth S. 295
Commonwealth Turf S. 295
Companies, Publicly Owned 918
Boyd Gaming Corp. 918
Canterbury Park Holding Corp. 918
Churchill Downs Inc. 918
Harrah's Entertainment 919
Macrovision Solutions Corp. 919
Magna Entertainment Corp. 919
MAXXAM Inc. 920
MTR Gaming Group Inc. 920
Penn National Gaming Inc. 920
Scientific Games Corp. 921
Youbet.com Inc. 921
Conformation and Anatomy Terms 998
Consignors
Leading by Average Receipts in 2007 885
Leading by Broodmare Receipts in 2007 885
Leading by Percent Sold in 2007 886
Leading by Total Receipts in 2007 884
Leading by Two-Year-Old Receipts in 2007 885
Leading by Weanling Receipts in 2007 884
Leading by Yearling Receipts in 2007 884
Leading of Top-Priced Yearlings 882
Contemporary Individuals 753
Coolmore Lexington S. 295
Cotillion Breeders' Cup H. 296
Count Fleet Sprint H. 296
Crown Royal American Turf S. 296
Dahlia H. 297
***Daily Racing Form*/NTRA National Handicapping Championship 100**
Dallas Turf Cup H. 297
Dams of Multiple American Classic Winners 139
Darley Alcibiades S. 297
Darley Arabian 782
Darley Test S. 298
Dates, Key in American Racing History 65
Davona Dale S. 299
Dayton Days, Wa. 695
Deaths, Horses 2007-2008 44
Deaths, Human 2007-2008 36
Debutante S. 299
Deflated Earnings, Leaders by 570
Deflated Earnings, Leading Females by 572
Delaware H. 300
Delaware Oaks 300
Delaware Park, De.
Profile 632
Racino 26
Del Mar, Ca. 620
Del Mar Debutante S. 301
Del Mar Derby 301
Del Mar Futurity 302
Del Mar H. 303
Del Mar Mile H. 303
Del Mar Oaks 303
Delta Downs, La.
Profile 652
Racino 26
Delta Jackpot S. 304
Delta Princess S. 304
Demoiselle S. 304
Deputy Minister H. 305
Diana S. 305
Discovery H. 306
Dispersals, Notable 894
Distaff H. 306
Distance Equivalents 985
Dixie S. 307
Dogwood Dominion Award 768
Dogwood S. 308
Donn H. 308
Doubledogdare S. 309
Downs at Albuquerque, N.M.
Profile 672
Racino 26
Dwyer S. 309
Early Times Mint Julep H. 310
Earners
Chronology of All-Time International Leading 554
Chronology of All-Time Leading 553
Leading After First Claim, 1991-2007 603
Leading by Category 557
Leading by Foal Crop 573
Leading by Province Where Bred in 2007 583
Leading by State Where Bred, 1954-2007 574
Leading by State Where Bred in 2007 583
Leading Female in North America 557
Leading in North America 557
Leading International of All Time 554
Leading of All Time 552
North American Leading by Year 556
World's Leading 555
Earnings
Aggregate Purse by State Where Bred in 2007 7
Average per Runner, 1998-2007 16
By Number of Wins for 2007 18
Distribution by Age and Sex for 2007 19
Highest After First Claim in 2007 603
Highest in Breeders' Cup Races 192
Leaders by Deflated 570
Leading Breeders by in 2007 719
Leading Broodmares by Progeny 855
Leading Females by Deflated 572
Leading Jockeys by, 1982-2007 731
Leading Jockeys by, in 2007 731
Leading Owners by, in 2007 713
Leading Trainers by, in 2007 724
Median per Runner, 1998-2007 16
Most by a Jockey in a Year, 1994-2007 737
Most by an Owner in a Year, 1986-2007 718
Most by a Trainer in a Year, 1985-2007 730
North American Leaders in Grade 1 Stakes 558
North American Leaders in Graded Stakes 557
North American Leading Females on Turf 559
North American Leading Males on Turf 558
North American Leading Two-Year-Old Females 559
North American Leading Two-Year-Old Males 559
North American Older Females, Single Season 561
North American Older Males, Single Season 561
North American Three-Year-Old Females, Single Season 560
North American Three-Year-Old Males, Single Season 560
Per Starter, Leading Jockeys by Average in 2007 733
Per Starter, Leading Trainers by Average in 2007 726
Earnings by Sires' Progeny
All-Time Leading Broodmare Sires by 822
All-Time Leading General Sires by 822

viii General Index

Leading Broodmare Sires by Average per Starter in North America in 2007 807
Leading Broodmare Sires by Average per Starter Worldwide in 2007 799
Leading Broodmare Sires by in North America in 2007 806
Leading Broodmare Sires by Median per Starter in North America in 2007 807
Leading Broodmare Sires by Median per Starter Worldwide in 2007 799
Leading Broodmare Sires by Worldwide in 2007 798
Leading Freshman Sires by Average per Starter in North America in 2007 805
Leading Freshman Sires by Average per Starter Worldwide in 2007 797
Leading Freshman Sires by in North America in 2007 804
Leading Freshman Sires by Median per Starter in North America in 2007 805
Leading Freshman Sires by Median per Starter Worldwide in 2007 797
Leading Freshman Sires by Worldwide in 2007 796
Leading Juvenile Sires by Average per Starter in North America in 2007 803
Leading Juvenile Sires by Average per Starter Worldwide in 2007 795
Leading Juvenile Sires by in North America in 2007 802
Leading Juvenile Sires by Median per Starter in North America in 2007 803
Leading Juvenile Sires by Median per Starter Worldwide in 2007 795
Leading Juvenile Sires by Worldwide in 2007 794
Leading Sires by Average per Starter in North America in 2007 801
Leading Sires by Average per Starter Worldwide in 2007 792
Leading Sires by in North America in 2007 800
Leading Sires by Median per Starter in North America in 2007 801
Leading Sires by Median per Starter Worldwide in 2007 792
Leading Sires by Worldwide in 2007 789

Eastern Idaho State Fair, Id. 638
Eastern Oregon Livestock Show, Or. 685
Eatontown S. 310
Eclipse Awards 95
Apprentice Jockey 98
Audio-Multimedia-Internet 100
Award of Merit 98
Breeder 97
Breeders, Leading of Winners 103
Breeders of Winners 103
Curlin 108
English Channel 109
Feature and Enterprise Writing 99
Feature Writing 99
Female Sprinter 97
Film Achievement 100
Ginger Punch 108
Good Night Shirt 109
History of 95
Horse of the Year 95
Horses 95
Indian Blessing 108
Individuals 97
Jockey 98
Lahudood (GB) 109
Lawyer Ron 108
Live Racing Programming 100
Local Television Achievement 99
Magazine Writing 99
Male Sprinter 97
Man of the Year 98
Maryfield 109
Media 99
Midnight Lute 109
National Television Achievement 99
News and Commentary Writing 99
Newspaper Writing 99
News Writing 99
Older Female 96
Older Male 96
Outstanding Achievement 98
Owner 97
Owner-Breeder 97
Owners, Leading of Winners 101
Owners of Winners 101
Photography Achievement 100
Radio Achievement 100
Rags to Riches 108
Sires, Leading of Winners 106
Sires of Winners 106
Special Award 98
Sprinter 97
Steeplechaser 97
Television Feature 100
Three-Year-Old Filly 96
Three-Year-Old Male 96
Trainer 97
Trainers, Leading of Winners 105
Trainers of Winners 105
Turf Female 96
Turf Horse 96
Turf Male 96
Two-Year-Old Filly 95
Two-Year-Old Male 95
War Pass 108

Eddie Read H. 311
El Camino Real Derby 311
El Conejo H. 312
El Encino S. 312
Elkhorn S. 313
Elko County Fair, Nv. 666
Ellis Park, Ky. 648
Emerald Downs, Wa. 696
Emirates Airline Breeders' Cup Distaff 313
Emirates Airline Breeders' Cup Filly and Mare Turf 314
Endeavour S. 314
Endine H. 314
Charles W. Engelhard Award 768
English Triple Crown 932
History of 932
Influence of 934
Winners of 932
Equibase 900
Eureka Downs, KS. 646
Evangeline Downs, La. 653
Evergreen Park (Grand Prairie), Ab. 700
Evolution of the Breed 782
Excelsior H. 314
Experimental Free Handicap 587
Colts, Geldings of 2007 588
Fillies of 2007 589
Highweights, by Year 587
History 587
Fair Grounds, La.
Hall of Fame 119
Profile 654
Racino 27
Fair Grounds H. 315
Fair Grounds Oaks 315
Fair Meadows at Tulsa, Ok. 683
Fairmount Park, Il. 641
Fairplex Park, Ca. 621
Falls City H. 316
Fantasy S. 317
Fasig-Tipton Calder Selected Two-Year-Olds in Training 873
Fasig-Tipton Kentucky July Selected Yearlings 872
Fasig-Tipton Saratoga Selected Yearlings 872
Fayette S. 317
Female Jockeys
In the Belmont Stakes 172
In the Kentucky Derby 146
In the Preakness Stakes 160
With More Than 1,000 Wins 736
Female Trainers
In the Belmont Stakes 171
In the Kentucky Derby 145
In the Preakness Stakes 159

Ferndale, Ca. 622
Field Size, Average, 1998-2007 22
Fifth Third Elkhorn S. 318
Fillies
In the Belmont Stakes 174
In the Kentucky Derby 149
In the Preakness Stakes 163
Finger Lakes Gaming and Race Track, N.Y.
Profile 676
Racino 27
Firecracker H. 318
First Flight H. 319
First Lady H. 319
First Lady S. 320
Fitz Dixon Cotillion H. 320
Fleur de Lis H. 320
Florida Derby 321
Flower Bowl Invitational S. 322
Foal Crop, Leading Earners by 573
Foals
Annual Registration in North America 781
Identification 780
Live by State and Province, 2003-2007 14
Live in North America, 1997-2007 13
Most Consecutive for a Broodmare 857
Most for a Broodmare 857
Registration 781
Registrations by State in 2006 781
Registrations, Trend of in North America 781
Fonner Park, Ne. 664
Forego S. 322
Fort Erie, On.
Profile 704
Racino 27
Fort Marcy H. 323
Fort Pierre Races, S.D. 690
Forward Gal S. 323
Fountain of Youth S. 324
Fourstardave H. 324
Frances A. Genter S. 325
Frank E. Kilroe Mile H. 325
Frank J. De Francis Memorial Dash S. 326
Fred W. Hooper H. 326
Freshman Sires
By Average Earnings per Starter in North America in 2007 805
By Average Earnings per Starter Worldwide in 2007 797
By Median Earnings per Starter in North America in 2007 805
By Median Earnings per Starter Worldwide in 2007 797
By Number of Graded Stakes Winners in North America in 2007 805
By Number of Graded Stakes Winners Worldwide in 2007 797
By Number of Stakes Winners in North America in 2007 805
By Number of Stakes Winners Worldwide in 2007 797
By Number of Winners in North America in 2007 805
By Number of Winners Worldwide in 2007 797
By Number of Wins in North America in 2007 ..805
By Number of Wins Worldwide in 2007 797
Leading by North American Earnings in 2007 804
Leading by Worldwide Earnings in 2007 796
Leading by Year 810
Fresno, Ca. 622
Frizette S. 327
Jerry Frutkoff Preakness Photography Award 768
Future Wager, Kentucky Derby 143
Futurity S. 327
John W. Galbreath Award 768
Gallant Bloom H. 328
Gallorette H. 328
Gamely S. 329
Garden City S. 330
Gardenia H. 330
Gazelle S. 331

General Index ix

Geldings
In the Belmont Stakes 174
In the Kentucky Derby 149
In the Preakness Stakes....163
Gender Terminology 780
General George H. 331
General Sire List, Most Times Headed....810
General Sire List, Most Times Headed Consecutively....810
Generous S. 332
Genetics, Modern....788
Gila County Fair, Az. 614
Gillespie County Fairgrounds, Tx. 690
Glens Falls H. 332
Glossaries
Common Racing and Breeding Terms....986
Common Veterinary Terms....1001
Conformation and Anatomy Terms....998
Go for Wand H. 333
Golden Gate Fields, Ca. 623
Golden Gate Fields S. 333
Golden Rod S. 334
Avelino Gomez Memorial Award....768
John K. Goodman Alumni Award....768
Goodwood S. 334
Gotham S. 335
Grade 1 Stakes Races
Earnings, North American Leaders by....558
Leading Sires by Number of Winners in North America in 2007....801
Leading Sires by Number of Winners Worldwide in 2007....793
Oldest Female Winners of Since 1976....594
Oldest Male Winners of Since 1976....594
Grade 1 Stakes Winners, All-Time Leading Broodmare Sires by....823
Graded Stakes
American....244
by State in 2008....243
by Track in 2008....241
Changes for 2008....243
Earnings, North American Leaders by....557
How Graded....241
Leading Breeders by Wins in 2007....722
Leading Jockeys by Wins in 2007....734
Leading Owners by Wins in 2007....716
Leading Trainers by Wins in 2007....727
Leading Winners of in North America....565
Oldest Female Winners of Since 1976....596
Oldest Male Winners of Since 1976....595
Previously Graded....496
Producers of Graded Stakes Producers....861
Purse Comparison of Graded and Group Stakes....242
Summary of 2008 Changes....242
Graded Stakes Histories
An alphabetical list of all graded stakes races in North America, reporting conditions, distance, stakes record, winner, winning jockey, second- and third-place horses, number of starters, final time, and first-place purse....244
Graded Stakes Winners
All-Time Leading Sires of....820
Leading Broodmare Sires by Number of in North America in 2007....807
Leading Broodmare Sires by Number of Worldwide in 2007....799
Leading Freshman Sires by Number of in North America in 2007....805
Leading Freshman Sires by Number of Worldwide in 2007....797
Leading Juvenile Sires by Number of in North America in 2007....803
Leading Juvenile Sires by Number of Worldwide in 2007....795
Leading Sires by Number of in North America in 2007....801
Leading Sires by Number of Worldwide in 2007....793
Most for a Broodmare....856
Graded Stakes Winners, All-Time Leading Sires of....821
Graham County Fair, Az. 614
Grants Pass, Or. 685
Gravesend H. 336
Great Falls, Mt. 663
Great Lakes Downs, Mi. 661
Greenlee County Fair, Az. 614
Grey Goose Bewitch S. 336
Group Stakes, Purse Comparison with Graded Stakes....242
Gulfstream Park, Fl.
Garden of Champions....119
Profile....634
Gulfstream Park H. 337
Gulfstream Park Turf S. 337
Walter Haight Award....769
Hall of Fame, American Racing....112
Breeders, Leading of Members....115
Breeders of Members....115
Eligibility....112
Exemplars of Racing....112
History....112
Horses....113
Jockeys....112
Members of....112
Owners, Leading of Members....114
Owners of Members....114
Sires, Leading of Members....117
Sires of Members....117
Trainers....113
Trainers, Leading of Members....116
Trainers of Members....116
Hall of Fame, Canadian Horse Racing....963
Halls of Fame, Regional....118
Arlington Park....118
Calder Race Course....118
California Thoroughbred Breeders Association....118
Canterbury Park....119
Fair Grounds....119
Gulfstream Park Garden of Champions....119
Hawthorne Race Course....119
Lone Star Park....119
Monmouth Park Hall of Champions....120
Nebraska Racing Hall of Fame....120
Prairie Meadows Racetrack....120
Remington Park....120
Texas Horse Racing Hall of Fame....120
Virginia Thoroughbred Hall of Fame....120
Washington Racing Hall of Fame....120
Hal's Hope H. 338
Handicapping
Championships, National, *Daily Racing Form*/NTRA....100
How-To Guide....971
How to Improve....975
Sample Race....979
Hanshin Cup H. 338
Hardboot Award....769
Harold C. Ramser Sr. H. 339
Harrah's Entertainment....919
Haskell Invitational S. 339
Hastings Race Course, B.C. 702
Hawthorne Derby 340
Hawthorne Gold Cup H. 341
Hawthorne H. 341
Hawthorne Race Course, Il.
Hall of Fame....119
Profile....642
Herecomesthebride S. 342
Hill 'n' Dale Cigar Mile H. 342
Hill Prince S. 343
Hillsborough S. 343
Hipodromo Camarero, P.R. 707
Joe Hirsch Breeders' Cup Newspaper Writing Award....769
Hirsch Jacobs S. 343
Historical Dates in American Racing History....65
History of Racing....57
1901-'10....58
1911-'20....58
1921-'30....59
1931-'40....59
1941-'50....60
1951-'60....60
1961-'70....61
1971-'80....61
1981-'90....62
1991-2000....62
19th century....57
2001-'08....63
Hollywood Derby....344
Hollywood Gold Cup S. 345
Hollywood Juvenile Championship S. 345
Hollywood Oaks....346
Hollywood Park, Ca. 624
Hollywood Prevue S. 346
Hollywood Starlet S. 347
Hollywood Turf Cup S. 347
Hollywood Turf Express H. 348
Holy Bull S. 348
Honeybee S. 349
Honey Fox H. 349
Honeymoon H. 350
Honorable Miss H. 350
Hoosier Park, In. 643
Hopeful S. 351
Horse Deaths, 2007-2008....44
Horsemen's Atokad Downs, Ne. 665
Horsemen's Park, Ne. 665
Horses
All-Time Leading by Starts....568
Deaths, 2007-2008....44
Eclipse Award Winners, Historical....95
Eclipse Award Winners of 2007....108
Highest-Priced of All Time....875
Leading Unbeaten....564
Losingest of All Time....568
Notable in Racing History....74
Oldest Notable of All Time....93
Racing Hall of Fame....113
Winningest by Decade by Year of Birth....562
Winningest of All Time....562
Humana Distaff H. 351
Hurricane Bertie H. 352
Hutcheson S. 352
Illinois Derby....353
Imported Horses, How Designated....776
Inbred Horses, Famous....785
Inbreeding....785
Indiana Derby....353
Indiana Downs, In. 644
Indiana Oaks....353
Individuals
Contemporary Notable....753
Eclipse Award-Winning....97
Notable of the Past....738
Industry Awards....767
Eric Beitia Memorial Award....767
Big Sport of Turfdom....767
F. Ambrose Clark Award....767
Coman Humanitarian Award....767
Dogwood Dominion Award....768
Charles W. Engelhard Award....768
Jerry Frutkoff Preakness Photography Award....768
John W. Galbreath Award....768
Avelino Gomez Memorial Award....768
John K. Goodman Alumni Award....768
Walter Haight Award....769
Hardboot Award....769
Joe Hirsch Breeders' Cup Newspaper Writing Award....769
Jockey Club Medal of Honor....769
Lavin Cup....769
Bill Leggett Breeders' Cup Magazine Writing Award....769
William H. May Award....770
Mr. Fitz Award....770
Isaac Murphy Award....770
Old Hilltop Award....770
Joe Palmer Award....771
Joan F. Pew Award....771
Clay Puett Award....771
Red Smith Award....771
University of Arizona RTIP Distinguished Senior Award....772

General Index

University of Arizona RTIP
  Distinguished Service Award......772
UTTA Outstanding Trainer
  of the Year Award......772
Alfred Gwynne Vanderbilt Award......773
Mike Venezia Memorial Award......773
White Horse Award......773
P.A.B. Widener II Trophy......773
David F. Woods Memorial Award......774
George Woolf Memorial Jockey Award......774
Industry Organizations, National......904
Inglewood H.......354
International Racing......922
  Progression of Richest Race, 1980-2007......924
  Review of 2007......922
  Richest Races of 2007......923
International Sires
  2007 Leading by Earnings by Country......956
  Leading......808
Iowa Oaks......354
Iroquois S.......355
Jaipur S.......355
Jamaica H.......356
Jefferson Cup S.......356
Jenny Wiley S.......357
Jerome H.......357
Jerome Racing, Id.......638
Jersey Act......775
Jersey Shore S.......358
Jim Dandy S.......358
Jim Murray Memorial H.......359
Jockey Club......895
  Contact Information......780
Jockey Club Gold Cup S.......359
Jockey Club Medal of Honor......769
Jockeys
  African-American in Kentucky Derby......146
  Fees......970
  Female in Kentucky Derby......146
  Female With More Than 1,000 Wins......736
  How Paid......970
  Leading by Average Earnings per
    Starter in 2007......733
  Leading by Belmont Stakes Wins......171
  Leading by Breeders' Cup Mounts......190
  Leading by Breeders' Cup Purses......190
  Leading by Breeders' Cup Wins......188
  Leading by Career Purses......735
  Leading by Career Wins......736
  Leading by Earnings, 1982-2007......731
  Leading by Earnings in 2007......731
  Leading by Earnings in a Year, 1994-2007......737
  Leading by Kentucky Derby Wins......145
  Leading by Most Mounts on
    Breeders' Cup Program......191
  Leading by Most Wins on Breeders'
    Cup Program......190
  Leading by Number of Grade 1 Stakes
    Winners in 2007......735
  Leading by Number of Grade 1 Stakes
    Wins in 2007......734
  Leading by Number of Graded Stakes
    Winners in 2007......734
  Leading by Number of Graded Stakes
    Wins in 2007......734
  Leading by Number of Stakes
    Winners in 2007......733
  Leading by Number of Stakes Wins in 2007......733
  Leading by Number of Winners in 2007......735
  Leading by Number of Wins in 2007......735
  Leading by Percent Stakes Wins in 2007......733
  Leading by Preakness Stakes Wins......159
  Leading by Triple Crown Race Winners......138
  Leading of 2007......731
  Most Belmont Stakes Mounts......171
  Most Consecutive Wins in 2007......737
  Most Consecutive Wins Since 1976......737
  Most Kentucky Derby Mounts......145
  Most Preakness Stakes Mounts......160
  Most Wins on One Day in 2007......736
  Most Wins on One Program in 2007......736
  Racing Hall of Fame Members......112
Jockeys' Guild......901

Joe Hirsch Turf Classic Invitational S.......360
John B. Connally Turf H.......360
John C. Mabee H.......361
John Deere Breeders' Cup Turf......361
Juddmonte Spinster S.......362
Just a Game S.......362
Juvenile Sire List, Most Times Headed......810
Juvenile Sire List, Most Times
  Headed Consecutively......810
Juvenile Sires
  By Average Earnings per Starter
    in North America in 2007......803
  By Average Earnings per
    Starter Worldwide in 2007......795
  By Median Earnings per Starter
    in North America in 2007......803
  By Median Earnings per
    Starter Worldwide in 2007......795
  By Number of Graded Stakes Winners
    in North America in 2007......803
  By Number of Graded Stakes Winners
    Worldwide in 2007......795
  By Number of Stakes Winners
    in North America in 2007......803
  By Number of Stakes Winners
    Worldwide in 2007......795
  By Number of Winners
    in North America in 2007......803
  By Number of Winners Worldwide
    in 2007......795
  By Number of Wins
    in North America in 2007......803
  By Number of Wins Worldwide in 2007......795
  Leading by North American
    Earnings in 2007......802
  Leading by Worldwide Earnings in 2007......794
  Leading by Year......809
Kamloops, B.C.......703
Keeneland April Two-Year-Olds in Training......873
Keeneland Association......902
Keeneland January Horses of All Ages......875
Keeneland July Selected Yearlings......872
Keeneland November Breeding Stock......874
Keeneland Race Course, Ky.......649
Keeneland September Yearlings......871
Kelso H.......363
Kenny Noe Jr. H.......363
Kent S.......364
Kentucky Cup Classic S.......364
Kentucky Cup Distaff S.......365
Kentucky Cup Juvenile S.......365
Kentucky Cup Sprint S.......365
Kentucky Cup Turf S.......366
Kentucky Derby......140
  Attendance......140
  Beaten Favorites, Shortest-Priced......148
  Birthplaces of Winners......149
  Breeders, Leading by Wins......144
  Fewest Starts by Winner Before Derby......152
  Fillies in......149
  Final Quarter-Mile Times Since 1950......147
  Foreign-Based Runners......150
  Fractions, Fastest......147
  Front-Running Winners......150
  Future Pool Payoffs......143
  Future Wager......143
  Garland of Roses......143
  Geldings in......149
  Gelding Winners of......149
  Glasses and Mint Julep Cups......142
  Graded History......366
  History......140
  How Favorites Fared Since 1930......147
  Jockeys, African-American in......146
  Jockeys, Female in......146
  Jockeys, Leading by Wins......145
  Jockeys, Most Mounts......145
  Kentucky Derby Festival......142
  Longest-Priced Winners......148
  Maiden Starters in......149
  Maiden Winners of......149
  Margins, Largest Winning......148
  Margins, Smallest Winning......148

"My Old Kentucky Home"......142
Owners, Leading by Wins......144
Post Positions, Winning......150
Pre-Derby Starts at Three, by Decade......152
Pre-Derby Starts, Average by Decade......152
Prep Race Before......152
Presidents at......141
Race Conditions......125
Review of 2008 Derby......178
Shortest-Priced Winners......148
Sires, Leading by Wins......146
Starts Before......152
Tabular History......154
Track Conditions......144
Trainers, Leading by Wins......145
Trainers, Most Starts......145
Trivia......143
Trophy......141
Twin Spires......142
Undefeated Starters......150
Wagering Handle, 1981-2008......141
Wagering Handle, Record......142
Weather Conditions......144
Winners' Fewest Starts Before Derby......152
Winners' Most Starts Before Derby......152
Winners Sold at Auction......151
Winners' Starts at Three Before Derby......152
Winners' Starts at Two......152
Winners, Status of......151
Winners' Total Starts Before Derby......152
Winners Unraced at Two......151
Winners Who Sired Winners......146
Winning Time, Evolution of Record......148
Winning Time, Fastest......146
Winning Time, Slowest......146
Kentucky Derby Festival......142
Kentucky Downs, Ky.......651
Kentucky Jockey Club S.......367
Kentucky Oaks......367
Kentucky S.......368
Key Dates in American Racing History......65
King's Bishop S.......368
Kin Park, B.C.......703
Knickerbocker H.......369
La Brea S.......369
La Canada S.......370
Lady's Secret S.......371
La Habra S.......371
La Jolla H.......372
Lake George S.......372
Lake Placid S.......373
Lane's End Breeders' Futurity......373
Lane's End S.......374
La Prevoyante H.......374
Las Cienegas H.......375
Las Flores H.......376
Las Palmas H.......376
Las Virgenes S.......377
La Troienne S.......377
Laurel Park, Md.......657
Lavin Cup......769
Lazaro Barrera Memorial S.......378
Leaders of 2007......31
Leading Sires......789
  Broodmare Sire by Year......810
  Broodmare Sires by North American
    Earnings in 2007......806
  Broodmare Sires Worldwide in 2007......798
  By Average Earnings per Starter
    in North America in 2007......801
  By Average Earnings per
    Starter Worldwide in 2007......792
  By Median Earnings per
    Starter in North America in 2007......801
  By Median Earnings per
    Starter Worldwide in 2007......792
  By North American Earnings in 2007......800
  By Number of Grade 1 Stakes Winners
    in North America in 2007......801
  By Number of Grade 1 Stakes Winners
    Worldwide in 2007......793
  By Number of Graded Stakes Winners
    in North America in 2007......801

General Index xi

By Number of Graded Stakes Winners
Worldwide in 2007 793
By Number of Millionaires All-Time 824
By Number of Stakes Winners
in North America in 2007 801
By Number of Stakes Winners
Worldwide in 2007 793
By Number of Winners
in North America in 2007 801
By Number of Winners Worldwide in 2007 792
By Number of Wins in North America
in 2007 801
By Number of Wins Worldwide in 2007 793
By State and Province in 2007 825
By Worldwide Earnings in 2007 808
Freshman Sire by Year 810
Freshman Sires by North American
Earnings in 2007 804
Freshman Sires Worldwide in 2007 796
Juvenile Sire by Year 809
Juvenile Sires by North American
Earnings in 2007 802
Juvenile Sires by Worldwide
Earnings in 2007 794
North American General Sire by Year 809
Profiles of Leading by Year 811
Stallions by 2007 Foals 834
Stallions by Mares Bred in 2007 842
With Only One Crop to Race Worldwide,
All-Time 824
Leading Stud Farms by 2007
Stallion Earnings 832
Lecomte S. 378
Legal Age to Attend Races 712
Bill Leggett Breeders' Cup
Magazine Writing Award 769
Les Bois Park, Id. 638
Lethbridge, Ab. 700
Lexus Raven Run S. 379
Live Foals
By Stallions by State and Province in 2007 835
By State and Province, 2003-2007 14
North American, 1997-2007 13
Report of 2007 834
Stallions with, in 2007 835
Locations, Racetracks 708
Locust Grove H. 379
Lone Star Derby 380
Lone Star Park H. 380
Lone Star Park, Tx.
Hall of Fame 119
Profile 690
Longacres Mile H. 380
Long Island H. 381
Lord Derby Awards 940
Los Alamitos Race Course, Ca. 626
Los Angeles H. 382
Losingest Horses of All Time 568
Louisiana Derby 382
Louisiana Downs, La.
Profile 656
Racino 26
Louisville H. 383
Louisville S. 384
Lowe, Bruce 786
Mac Diarmida H. 384
Macrovision Solutions Corp. 919
Madison S. 384
Magna Entertainment Corp. 919
Maker's Mark Mile S. 384
Malibu S. 385
Manor Downs, Tx. 692
Man o' War S. 385
Mares Bred
By State and Province, 2003-2007 12
North American Mares Bred, 1997-2007 13
Report of 2007 842
Marquis Downs, Sk. 706
Maryland Lottery Pimlico Special H. 386
"Maryland, My Maryland" 158
Maryland Sprint H. 386
Matchmaker S. 387
Match Races, American 591
Matriarch S. 387
Matron S. 387
MAXXAM Inc. 920
William H. May Award 770
Meadowlands Cup S. 388
Meadowlands, N.J. 669
Media Awards, Eclipse 99
Median
Broodmare Prices by State and Province
in 2007 12
Earnings per Runner, 1998-2007 16
Two-Year-Old Prices by State and
Province in 2007 12
Weanling Prices by State and
Province in 2007 12
Yearling Prices by State and
Province in 2007 12
Median Earnings of Sires
Leading Broodmare Sires per
Starter in North America in 2007 807
Leading Broodmare Sires per
Starter Worldwide in 2007 799
Leading Freshman Sires per
Starter in North America in 2007 805
Leading Freshman Sires per
Starter Worldwide in 2007 797
Leading Juvenile Sires per
Starter in North America in 2007 803
Leading Juvenile Sires per
Starter Worldwide in 2007 795
Leading Sires per Starter
in North America in 2007 801
Leading Sires per Starter Worldwide in 2007 792
Memorial Day H. 389
Mervin H. Muniz Jr. Memorial H. 389
Mervyn LeRoy H. 389
Metropolitan H. 390
Miami Mile H. 391
Miesque S. 391
Milady H. 391
Millarville Race Society, Ab. 700
Millionaires
All-Time Leading Sires by Number of 824
Most Produced by a Broodmare 860
Mineshaft H. 392
Mint Julep H. 392
Miss Grillo S. 392
Miss Preakness S. 393
Modesty H. 393
Mohave County Fair, Az. 614
Molly Pitcher H. 393
Monmouth Oaks 394
Monmouth Park, N.J.
Hall of Champions 120
Profile 668
Monrovia H. 395
Morvich H. 395
Most Consecutive Times
Heading Broodmare Sire List 810
Most Consecutive Times
Heading General Sire List 810
Most Consecutive Times
Heading Juvenile Sire List 810
Most Consecutive Victories 563
Most Stakes Wins by Decade
by Year of Birth 566
Most Times Heading Broodmare Sire List 810
Most Times Heading General Sire List 810
Most Times Heading Juvenile Sire List 810
Mother Goose S. 396
Mountaineer Casino Racetrack
and Resort, W.V.
Profile 698
Racino 26
Mr. Fitz Award 770
Mr. Prospector H. 396
Mrs. Revere S. 397
Mt. Pleasant Meadows, Mi. 661
MTR Gaming Group Inc. 920
Isaac Murphy Award 770
My Charmer H. 397
"My Old Kentucky Home" 142
Naming a Thoroughbred 778
Nashua S. 398
Nassau County S. 398
National Horsemen's Benevolent
and Protective Association 903
National Museum of Racing
Hall of Fame S. 399
National Thoroughbred Racing Association
Daily Racing Form/NTRA National
Handicapping Championship 100
Profile 897
Native Diver H. 399
NetJets Breeders' Cup Mile 400
New Orleans H. 400
News Stories, Leading of 2007 28
New York Racing Association 28
New York S. 401
Next Move H. 401
Nicks 786
Noble Damsel H. 402
Norfolk S. 402
North American
Industry Organizations 904
Leading, Raced Horses of 2007 546
Pari-Mutuel Wagering in 2007 1
Purses, 1996-2007 1
Racetrack Locations 708
Stakes Races in 2007 498
North Dakota Horse Park, N.D. 679
Northern Dancer S. 403
Northlands Park, Ab. 701
Notable
Contemporary Individuals 753
Horses in Racing 74
Names in Racing's Past 738
Oldest Horses of All Time 93
Oaklawn H. 403
Oaklawn Park, Ar. 618
Oak Leaf S. 404
Oak Tree Derby 404
Oak Tree Mile S. 405
Oak Tree Racing Association
at Santa Anita, Ca. 626
Obeah H. 405
Obituaries, 2007-2008 36
Ocala Breeders' Sales Co. February
Two-Year-Olds 874
Ocala Training Center, Fl. 635
Oceanport S. 406
Odds and Payouts 984
Ogden Phipps H. 406
Ohio Derby 407
Oldest
Breeders' Cup Race Winners 194
Breeders' Cup Starters 195
Broodmares to Produce a Named Foal 859
Broodmares to Produce a Stakes Winner 860
Broodmares to Produce a Winner 859
Grade 1 Stakes Winners, Female
Since 1976 594
Grade 1 Stakes Winners, Male Since 1976 594
Graded Stakes Winners, Female
Since 1976 596
Graded Stakes Winners, Males Since 1976 595
Notable Horses of All Time 93
Notable Horses of All Time, Profiles of 93
Stakes Winners, Female Since 1976 596
Stakes Winners, Male Since 1976 596
Surviving Breeders' Cup Winners 193
Winners, 1987-2007 598
Winners Female Since 1976 597
Winners Male Since 1976 597
Winners of 2007 598
Old Hat S. 408
Old Hilltop Award 770
Oneida County Fair, Id. 639
On-Track Wagering, Top 25 Meets
by Average 711
Orchid H. 408
Organizations 895
American Horse Council 899
Association of Racing Commissioners
International 900
Charitable Organizations 912

General Index

Equibase 900
Jockey Club 895
Jockeys' Guild 901
Keeneland Association 902
National Horsemen's Benevolent
 and Protective Association 903
National Thoroughbred Racing Association 897
North American Industry Organizations 904
Sales Companies 917
State and Provincial Racing Organizations 905
Thoroughbred Owners and
 Breeders Association 902
Thoroughbred Racing Associations ... 898
Thoroughbred Racing Protective Bureau 899
Thoroughbred Retirement and Rescue 912
Ouija Board H. 409
Owners
 Eclipse Award Winners 97
 Leading by Average Earnings per
  Starter in 2007 715
 Leading by Belmont Stakes Wins 170
 Leading by Breeders' Cup Purses 189
 Leading by Breeders' Cup Starts 189
 Leading by Breeders' Cup Wins 188
 Leading by Earnings, 1983-2007 713
 Leading by Earnings in 2007 713
 Leading by Earnings in a Year,
  1986-2007 718
 Leading by Kentucky Derby Wins 144
 Leading by Most Starters on
  Breeders' Cup Program 189
 Leading by Number of Grade 1 Stakes
  Winners in 2007 717
 Leading by Number of Grade 1 Stakes
  Wins in 2007 717
 Leading by Number of Graded
  Stakes Winners in 2007 716
 Leading by Number of Graded
  Stakes Wins in 2007 716
 Leading by Number of Stakes
  Winners in 2007 715
 Leading by Number of Stakes
  Wins in 2007 715
 Leading by Number of Wins in 2007 . 717
 Leading by Percent Stakes Winners in 2007 ... 716
 Leading by Preakness Stakes Wins .. 158
 Leading of 2007 713
 Leading of Eclipse Award Winners ... 101
 Leading of Hall of Fame Members 114
 Leading of Triple Crown Race Winners 135
 Most Belmont Stakes Starters 170
 Most Kentucky Derby Starters 144
 Most Preakness Stakes Starters 159
 Most Wins on One Day in 2007 717
 Most Wins on One Program in 2007 . 718
 Of Eclipse Award Winners 101
 Of Racing Hall of Fame Members 114
Pacific Classic S. 409
Palm Beach H. 409
Joe Palmer Award 771
Palomar H. 409
Palos Verdes H. 410
Pan American H. 411
Pari-Mutuel Wagering
 By State in 2005 5
 How It Began 983
 Odds and Payouts 984
 Racetrack, 1996-2007 1
 Takeout by State 6
Pat O'Brien H. 411
Pegasus S. 412
Penn National Gaming Inc. 920
Penn National Race Course, Pa. 687
Pennsylvania Derby 412
People 713
Performance Rates
 For 2007 584
 Top, 1997-2007 586
Perryville S. 413
Personal Ensign S. 413
Peter Pan S. 414
Joan F. Pew Award 771

Philadelphia Park, Pa.
 Profile 688
 Racino 27
Philip H. Iselin S. 414
Phoenix S. 415
Pilgrim S. 415
Pimlico Race Course, Md.
 Alibi Breakfast 158
 Cupola, Painting of After Preakness 157
 Preakness Stakes 156
 Profile 658
Pinhooking, Defined 887
Pinhooks
 Least Successful Weanling to Juvenile
  by Percentage Loss 893
 Least Successful Weanling to Juvenile
  by Total Loss 892
 Least Successful Weanling to Yearling
  by Percentage Loss 891
 Least Successful Weanling to Yearling
  by Total Loss 890
 Least Successful Yearling to Juvenile
  by Percentage Loss 889
 Least Successful Yearling to Juvenile
  by Total Loss 888
 Most Successful Weanling to Juvenile
  by Percentage Gain 892
 Most Successful Weanling to Juvenile
  by Total Gain 891
 Most Successful Weanling to Yearling
  by Percentage Gain 890
 Most Successful Weanling to Yearling
  by Total Gain 889
 Most Successful Yearling to Juvenile
  by Percentage Gain 888
 Most Successful Yearling to Juvenile
  by Total Gain 887
Pinnacle Race Course, Mi. 661
Pin Oak Valley View S. 416
Pleasanton, Ca. 628
Pocahontas S. 416
Pocatello Downs, Id. 639
Poker H. 417
Portland Meadows, Or. 685
Potrero Grande H. 417
Prairie Meadows Cornhusker H. 418
Prairie Meadows Racetrack, Ia.
 Hall of Fame 120
 Profile 645
 Racino 26
Preakness Stakes 156
 Added Value of 157
 Alibi Breakfast 158
 Attendance 156
 Beaten Favorites, Odds-On 161
 Birthplaces of Winners 164
 Black-Eyed Susans 157
 Breeders, Leading by Wins 159
 Cupola, Painting of Pimlico 157
 Fillies in 163
 Fractions, Fastest 161
 Front-Running Winners 162
 Geldings in 163
 Gelding Winners of 163
 Graded History 419
 History 156
 Jockeys, Leading by Wins 159
 Jockeys, Most Mounts 160
 Longest-Priced Winners 162
 Margins, Largest Winning 161
 Margins, Smallest Winning 161
 "Maryland, My Maryland" 158
 Owners, Leading by Wins 158
 Owners, Most Starters 159
 Post Positions, Winning 163
 Race Conditions 126
 Review of 2008 Preakness 180
 Shortest-Priced Winners 162
 Sires, Leading by Wins 160
 Status of Winners 164
 Supplemental Nominees 160
 Tabular History 165
 Trainers, Leading by Wins 159

Trainers, Most Starters 159
Trivia 158
Wagering 162
Winners Who Sired Winners 160
Winning Favorites Since 1979 163
Winning Time, Evolution of Record ... 161
Winning Time, Fastest 161
Winning Time, Slowest 161
Woodlawn Vase 157
Preference Date System 969
Presque Isle Downs, Pa.
 Profile 689
 Racino 27
Previously Graded Stakes Races 496
Princess Rooney H. 419
Prioress S. 420
Profiles of Leading Sires 811
Profiles of Leading Stud Farms of 2007 832
Progression of Fastest Times on Dirt 550
Progression of Leading Earner 553
Providencia S. 420
Pucker Up S. 421
Clay Puett Award 771
Purses
 All About Purses 2007 16
 Aggregate Earnings by State Where Bred
  in 2007 7
 Average, 1998-2007 16
 Average North American, 1996-2007 .. 1
 Breeders' Cup 187
 Breeders' Cup Distribution of $2-million .. 187
 By Claiming Category 21
 By Racetrack in 2007 23
 By State and Province in 2007 3
 Comparisons of Graded and Group Stakes 242
 Distribution by Age and Sex for 2007 . 19
 Distribution by Best Finish Position ... 20
 Distribution by Class of Races for 2007 ... 21
 Distribution by Distance for 2007 22
 Distribution by Year, 1972-2007 710
 Distribution of Earnings of Runners
  by Age and Sex for 2007 20
 Distribution of Races by Purse for 2007 21
 Function of Number of Wins for 2007 . 18
 Jockey for Career 735
 Largest Breeders' Cup 187
 Leading Breeders by, 1997-2007 719
 Leading Breeders by, in 2007 719
 Leading Jockeys by, 1982-2007 731
 Leading Jockeys by, in 2007 731
 Leading Owners by, 1983-2007 713
 Leading Owners by, in 2007 713
 Leading Trainers by, 1980-2007 724
 Leading Trainers by, in 2007 724
 Most by a Jockey in a Year, 1994-2007 737
 Most by an Owner in a Year, 1986-2007 718
 Most by a Trainer in a Year, 1985-2007 730
 Relationships of, 1982-2007 2
 North American, 1996-2007 1
 North American Races, 1998-2007 .. 16
 Races by Age and Sex for 2007 19
 Racinos, 2000-2007 26
 Runners by Age and Sex for 2007 ... 20
 Selected Racing Statistics, 1998-2007 ... 16
 Total, 1998-2007 16
Queen Elizabeth II Challenge Cup S. 421
Queens County H. 422
Races
 Number by State and Province in 2007 3
 Number of, 1998-2007 16
 Percentage of Best by Country 243
 Richest of 2007 239
 Types of 977
Racetrack Locations 708
Racetracks
 Abbreviations and Locations 708
 Purse Distribution in 2007 23
 Wagering, 1996-2007 1
Racetracks, International 941
 Aintree 945
 Argentino de Palermo 941
 Ascot 945
 Ascot (Australia) 942

General Index xiii

Avondale 952
Baden-Baden 950
Canterbury 942
Caulfield 942
Chantilly 948
Cheltenham 946
Cidade Jardim 944
Clairwood 954
Club Hipico de Santiago 945
Curragh, The 951
Deauville 949
Doncaster 946
Doomben 942
Dusseldorf 950
Eagle Farm 943
Ellerslie 953
Epsom Downs 946
Flemington 943
Goodwood 947
Greyville 954
Hamburg 950
Hanshin 952
Happy Valley 951
Hawke's Bay 953
Haydock Park 947
Hipodromo Chile 945
Kempton Park 947
Kenilworth 954
Koln 950
Kyoto 952
La Gavea 944
La Plata 941
Leopardstown 951
Lingfield Park 947
Longchamp 949
Maisons-Laffitte 949
Maronas National Racetrack 955
Monterrico 954
Moonee Valley 943
Morphettville 943
Mulheim 950
Nad al Sheba 955
Nakayama 952
Newbury 947
Newmarket 948
Otaki 953
Riccarton Park 953
Roma Capannelle 951
Rosehill Gardens 944
Royal Randwick 944
Saint-Cloud 949
Sandown Park 948
San Isidro 942
San Siro 952
Scottsville 955
Sha Tin 951
Singapore Racecourse 954
Taruma 945
Te Rapa 953
Tokyo 952
Trentham 953
Turffontein 955
Vina del Mar 945
Warwick Farm 944
York 948

Racetracks, North American 613
Anthony Downs, Ks. 646
Apache County Fair, Az. 613
Aqueduct, N.Y. 674
Arapahoe Park, Co. 631
Arlington Park, Il. 639
Assiniboia Downs, Mb. 703
Atlantic City Race Course, N.J. 667
Bay Meadows Fair, Ca. 618
Bay Meadows Race Course, Ca. 619
Belmont Park, N.Y. 675
Beulah Park, Oh. 679
Blue Ribbon Downs, Ok. 682
Brown County Fair, S.D. 690
Calder Race Course, Fl. 633
Canterbury Park, Mn. 662
Charles Town Races, W.V. 697
Churchill Downs, Ky. 647
Cochise County Fair, Az. 613
Coconino County Fair, Az. 613
Colonial Downs, Va. 694
Columbus Races, Ne. 663
Dayton Days, Wa. 695
Delaware Park, De. 632
Del Mar, Ca. 620
Delta Downs, La. 652
Downs at Albuquerque, N.M. 672
Eastern Idaho State Fair, Id. 638
Eastern Oregon Livestock Show, Or. 685
Elko County Fair, Ne. 666
Ellis Park, Ky. 648
Emerald Downs, Wa. 696
Eureka Downs, Ks. 646
Evangeline Downs, La. 653
Evergreen Park (Grand Prairie), Ab. 700
Fair Grounds, La. 654
Fair Meadows at Tulsa, Ok. 683
Fairmount Park, Il. 641
Fairplex Park, Ca. 621
Ferndale, Ca. 622
Finger Lakes Gaming and Race Track, N.Y. 676
Fonner Park, Ne. 664
Fort Erie, On. 704
Fort Pierre Races, S.D. 690
Fresno, Ca. 622
Gila County Fair, Az. 614
Gillespie County Fairgrounds, Tx. 690
Golden Gate Fields, Ca. 623
Graham County Fair, Az. 614
Grants Pass, Or. 685
Great Falls, Mt. 663
Great Lakes Downs, Mi. 661
Greenlee County Fair, Az. 614
Gulfstream Park, Fl. 634
Hastings Race Course, B.C. 702
Hawthorne Race Course, Il. 642
Hipodromo Camarero, P.R. 707
Hollywood Park, Ca. 624
Hoosier Park, In. 643
Horsemen's Atokad Downs, Ne. 665
Horsemen's Park, Ne. 665
Indiana Downs, In. 644
Jerome Racing, Id. 638
Kamloops, B.C. 703
Keeneland Race Course, Ky. 649
Kentucky Downs, Ky. 651
Kin Park, B.C. 703
Laurel Park, Md. 657
Les Bois Park, Id. 638
Lethbridge, Ab. 700
Lone Star Park, Tx. 690
Los Alamitos Race Course, Ca. 626
Louisiana Downs, La. 656
Manor Downs, Tx. 692
Marquis Downs, Sk. 706
Meadowlands, N.J. 669
Millarville Race Society, Ab. 700
Mohave County Fair, Az. 614
Monmouth Park, N.J. 668
Mountaineer Casino Racetrack and Resort, W.V. 698
Mt. Pleasant Meadows, Mi. 661
North Dakota Horse Park, N.D. 679
Northlands Park, Ab. 701
Oaklawn Park, Ar. 618
Oak Tree Racing Association at Santa Anita, Ca. 626
Ocala Training Center, Fl. 635
Oneida County Fair, Id. 639
Penn National Race Course, Pa. 687
Philadelphia Park, Pa. 688
Pimlico Race Course, Md. 658
Pinnacle Race Course, Mi. 661
Pleasanton, Ca. 628
Pocatello Downs, Id. 639
Portland Meadows, Or. 685
Prairie Meadows Racetrack, Ia. 645
Presque Isle Downs, Pa. 689
Remington Park, Ok. 683
Retama Park, Tx. 692
Rillito Park, Az. 615
River Downs, Oh. 680
Ruidoso Downs, N.M. 670
Rupert Downs, Id. 639
Sacramento, Ca. 628
Sam Houston Race Park, Tx. 693
Santa Anita Park, Ca. 628
Santa Cruz County Fair, Az. 615
Santa Rosa, Ca. 630
Saratoga Race Course, N.Y. 677
Stampede Park, Ab. 701
State Fair Park, Ne. 666
Stockton, Ca. 630
Suffolk Downs, Ma. 660
Sun Downs, Wa. 696
Sunflower Downs, B.C. 703
Sunland Park, N.M. 671
SunRay Park, N.M. 671
Tampa Bay Downs, Fl. 635
Thistledown, Oh. 681
Tillamook County Fair, Or. 686
Timonium, Md. 659
Tropical Park, Fl. 637
Turf Paradise, Az. 616
Turfway Park, Ky. 651
Vallejo, Ca. 631
Waitsburg Race Track, Wa. 697
Walla Walla, Wa. 697
Will Rogers Downs, Ok. 684
Woodbine, On. 705
Woodlands, Ks. 646
Wyoming Downs, Wy. 699
Yavapai Downs, Az. 617
Yellowstone Downs, Mt. 663
Zia Park, N.M. 673

Racetrack Stocks, North American
Revenues and Profit or Loss in 2007 921
Stock Performance, 2002-2007 921

Racing 236
Glossary of Common Terms 986
History of 57
International 922
Names in Racing's Past 738
Notable Contemporary Individuals 753
Older Female 238
Older Male 238
Review of 2007 Season 236
Rules of 964
Sprint Divisions 238
Steeplechaser 238
Terms and Comments 974
Three-Year-Old Fillies 237
Turf Divisions 238
Two-Year-Old Fillies 237
Two-Year-Old Males 237

Racing Dates by State and Province in 2007 3
Racing Dates, Races, Runners, Starts, Purses by State and Province in 2007 3
Racing Hall of Fame, American 112
Breeders, Leading of Members 115
Breeders of Members 115
Eligibility 112
Exemplars of Racing 112
History 112
Horses 113
Jockeys 112
Members of 112
Owners, Leading of Members 114
Owners of Members 114
Sires, Leading of Members 117
Sires of Members 117
Trainers 113
Trainers, Leading of Members 116
Trainers of Members 116

Racinos 25
Effect on Thoroughbred Economy 1

Records, North American Track 549
Railbird S. 422
Rampart H. 423
Rancho Bernardo H. 423
Raven Run S. 424
Razorback H. 424
Rebel S. 425
Red Bank S. 425

xiv General Index

Red Smith H. 426
Reference 964
Registration Rules
History of 777
How to Name a Thoroughbred 778
How to Register a Thoroughbred 777
Regret S. 427
Remington Park, Ok.
Hall of Fame 120
Profile 683
Remsen S. 427
Report of Live Foals of 2007 834
Report of Mares Bred for 2007 842
Retama Park, Tx. 692
Revenues to States From Racing, 2005 5
Revenues to the States From Racing, Historical 4
Revenue to Government 712
Richest
International Stakes Races of 2007 923
North American Race, Chronology of 240
North American Stakes Races of 2007 239
Richter Scale Sprint Championship H. 428
Rillito Park, Az. 615
Risen Star S. 428
River City H. 429
River Downs, Oh. 680
Robert B. Lewis S. 429
Robert F. Carey Memorial H. 430
Robert G. Dick Memorial H. 430
Roman, Steven A., Ph.D. 788
Ruffian H. 431
Ruidoso Downs, N.M.
Profile 670
Racino 27
Rules
Of Racing 964
Of Thoroughbred Registration 777
Runners
Distribution of Races and Purses by Age and Sex for 2007 19
Distribution of Earnings for 2007 17
Earnings by Age and Sex for 2007 20
Number of, 1998-2007 16
Percentage Earning Purses, 1998-2007 16
Rupert Downs, Id. 639
Sabin H. 431
Sacramento, Ca. 628
Safely Kept S. 432
Sales Companies 917
Salvator Mile S. 432
Sam Houston Race Park, Tx. 693
San Antonio H. 433
San Carlos H. 433
San Clemente H. 434
San Diego H. 435
Sands Point S. 435
San Felipe S. 436
San Fernando S. 436
Sanford S. 437
San Francisco Mile S. 437
San Gabriel H. 438
San Gorgonio H. 439
San Juan Capistrano Invitational H. 439
San Luis Obispo H. 440
San Luis Rey H. 441
San Marcos S. 441
San Pasqual H. 442
San Rafael S. 443
San Simeon H. 443
Santa Ana H. 444
Santa Anita Derby 445
Santa Anita H. 445
Santa Anita Oaks 446
Santa Anita Park, Ca. 628
Santa Barbara H. 446
Santa Cruz County Fair, Az. 615
Santa Margarita Invitational H. 447
Santa Maria H. 448
Santa Monica H. 448
Santa Paula S. 449
Santa Rosa, Ca. 630
Santa Ynez S. 449
Santa Ysabel S. 450
San Vicente S. 451
Sapling S. 451
Saranac S. 452
Saratoga Race Course, N.Y. 677
Saratoga Special S. 452
Scale of Weights 593
Schuylerville S. 453
Scientific Games Corp. 921
Secretariat S. 454
Senator Ken Maddy H. 454
Senorita S. 455
Shadwell Turf Mile S. 456
Shakertown S. 456
Sham S. 456
Sheepshead Bay H. 456
Shirley Jones H. 457
Shoemaker Mile S. 458
Shuvee H. 458
Silks, History of 64
Silverbulletday S. 459
Sir Beaufort S. 459
Sires 789
All-Time Leading Broodmare by Group 1 or Grade 1 Stakes Winners 823
All-Time Leading Broodmare by Progeny Earnings 822
All-Time Leading by Group 1 or Grade 1 Stakes Winners 821
All-Time Leading by Group or Graded Stakes Winners 821
All-Time Leading by Number of Millionaires 824
All-Time Leading by Percentage of Stakes Winners 821
All-Time Leading by Stakes Winners 820
All-Time Leading by Winners 820
All-Time Leading North American General by Progeny Earnings 820
All-Time Leading with Only One Crop to Race Worldwide 824
By 2007 Foals 834
By Average Earnings per Starter in North America in 2007 801
By Average Earnings per Starter Worldwide in 2007 792
By Mares Bred in 2007 842
By Median Earnings per Starter in North America in 2007 801
By Median Earnings per Starter Worldwide in 2007 792
By North American Earnings in 2007 800
By Number of Graded Stakes Winners in North America in 2007 801
By Number of Graded Stakes Winners Worldwide in 2007 793
By Number of Stakes Winners in North America in 2007 801
By Number of Stakes Winners Worldwide in 2007 793
By Number of Winners in North America in 2007 801
By Number of Winners Worldwide in 2007 792
By Number of Wins in North America in 2007 801
By Number of Wins Worldwide in 2007 793
By State and Province Where Bred 825
By Worldwide Earnings in 2007 808
Leading Belmont Stakes by Wins 172
Leading Broodmare by Average Earnings per Starter in North America in 2007 807
Leading Broodmare by Average Earnings per Starter Worldwide in 2007 799
Leading Broodmare by Median Earnings per Starter in North America in 2007 807
Leading Broodmare by Median Earnings per Starter Worldwide in 2007 799
Leading Broodmare by Number of Graded Stakes Winners in North America in 2007 807
Leading Broodmare by Number of Graded Stakes Winners Worldwide in 2007 799
Leading Broodmare by Number of Stakes Winners in North America in 2007 807
Leading Broodmare by Number of Stakes Winners Worldwide in 2007 799
Leading Broodmare by Number of Winners in North America in 2007 807
Leading Broodmare by Number of Winners Worldwide in 2007 799
Leading Broodmare by Number of Wins in North America in 2007 807
Leading Broodmare by Number of Wins Worldwide in 2007 799
Leading Broodmare Sires, by North American Earnings in 2007 806
Leading Broodmare by Worldwide Earnings in 2007 798
Leading Broodmare, by Year 810
Leading by Breeders' Cup Purses 191
Leading by Breeders' Cup Wins 189
Leading by Most Breeders' Cup Placings 191
Leading by Most Breeders' Cup Starts 191
Leading by Number of Grade 1 Stakes Winners in North America in 2007 801
Leading by Number of Grade 1 Stakes Winners Worldwide in 2007 793
Leading Freshman by Earnings in North America in 2007 804
Leading Freshman by Earnings Worldwide in 2007 796
Leading Freshman by Number of Graded Stakes Winners in North America in 2007 805
Leading Freshman by Number of Graded Stakes Winners Worldwide in 2007 797
Leading Freshman by Number of Stakes Winners in North America in 2007 805
Leading Freshman by Number of Stakes Winners Worldwide in 2007 797
Leading Freshman by Number of Winners in North America in 2007 805
Leading Freshman by Number of Winners Worldwide in 2007 797
Leading Freshman by Number of Wins in North America in 2007 805
Leading Freshman by Number of Wins Worldwide in 2007 797
Leading Freshman by Year 810
Leading Juvenile by Earnings in North America in 2007 802
Leading Juvenile by Earnings Worldwide in 2007 794
Leading Juvenile by Number of Graded Stakes Winners in North America in 2007 803
Leading Juvenile by Number of Graded Stakes Winners Worldwide in 2007 795
Leading Juvenile by Number of Stakes Winners in North America in 2007 803
Leading Juvenile by Number of Stakes Winners Worldwide in 2007 795
Leading Juvenile by Number of Winners in North America in 2007 803
Leading Juvenile by Number of Winners Worldwide in 2007 795
Leading Juvenile by Number of Wins in North America in 2007 803
Leading Juvenile by Number of Wins Worldwide in 2007 795
Leading Juvenile by Year 809
Leading Kentucky Derby by Wins 146
Leading North American General by Year 809
Leading of Eclipse Award Winners 106
Leading of Racing Hall of Fame Members 117
Leading of Top-Priced Yearlings 882
Leading of Triple Crown Race Winners 139
Leading Preakness Stakes by Wins 160
Of Eclipse Award Winners 106
Of Racing Hall of Fame Members 117
Profiles of Leading by Year 811
Worldwide Leading in 2007 808
Sires, Leading International of 2007 956
Argentina 956
Australia 956
Brazil 956
Canada 956
England 956
England/Ireland 956
France 957
Germany 957

General Index xv

Hong Kong ... 957
Ireland ... 957
Italy ... 957
Japan ... 958
Puerto Rico ... 958
Saudi Arabia ... 958
United Arab Emirates ... 958

Sires, Leading International by Year ... 958
Argentina ... 958
Australia ... 958
Brazil ... 958
Canada ... 959
England ... 959
England/Ireland ... 959
France ... 959
Germany ... 959
Hong Kong ... 959
Ireland ... 959
Italy ... 959
Japan ... 959
United Arab Emirates ... 959

Sixty Sails H. ... 460
Skip Away H. ... 460
Smile Sprint H. ... 461
Red Smith Award ... 771
Sorrento S. ... 461
Southwest S. ... 462
Sovereign Awards ... 960
History of ... 960
Profiles of 2007 Sovereign Award Winners ... 962

Spend a Buck H. ... 462
Spinaway S. ... 463
Spinster S. ... 463
Sport Page H. ... 463
Stage Door Betty H. ... 464
Stakes Placings, Most in North America ... 567
Stakes Placings, Most in North America Without Stakes Win ... 567
Stakes Races
American Graded Histories ... 244
International ... 924
Leading Winners of, in North America ... 565
Of 2007 ... 498
Oldest ... 545
Oldest Continuously Run ... 545
Previously Graded ... 496
Richest International of 2007 ... 923
Richest of 2007 ... 239

Stakes Winners
Leading Breeders by, in 2007 ... 721
Leading Jockeys by, in 2007 ... 733
Leading Owners by Percentage of in 2007 ... 716
Leading Trainers by, in 2007 ... 726
Leading Trainers by Percentage of in 2007 ... 727
Most for a Broodmare ... 856
Oldest Female Since 1976 ... 596
Oldest Male Since 1976 ... 596

Stakes Winners of Sires
All-Time Leading Broodmare Sires by ... 823
All-Time Leading Sires by Percentage of ... 821
All-Time Leading Sires of ... 820
Leading Broodmare Sires by Number of, in North America in 2007 ... 807
Leading Broodmare Sires by Number of Worldwide in 2007 ... 799
Leading Freshman Sires by Number of, in North America in 2007 ... 805
Leading Freshman Sires by Number of Worldwide in 2007 ... 797
Leading Juvenile Sires by Number of, in North America in 2007 ... 803
Leading Juvenile Sires by Number of Worldwide in 2007 ... 795
Leading Sires by Number of, in North America in 2007 ... 801
Leading Sires by Number of Worldwide in 2007 ... 793

Stakes Wins
Leading Breeders by, in 2007 ... 721
Leading Jockeys by, in 2007 ... 733
Leading Owners by, in 2007 ... 715
Leading Trainers by, in 2007 ... 726

Stallions
And Mares Bred in the U.S., Canada, and North America, 1992-2007 ... 843
Bred in 2007 ... 844
By State and Province, 2003-2007 ... 13
Leading by 2007 Foals ... 834
Leading by Mares Bred in 2007 ... 842
Mares Bred by State and Province in 2007 ... 843
North American in Production, 1997-2007 ... 13

Stallion Syndications ... 830
Chronology of Record Stallion Syndications ... 830
Top North American Stallion Syndications of All Time ... 831

Stampede Park, Ab. ... 701
Stars and Stripes Turf H. ... 464
Starts
All-Time Leading Horses by ... 568
Average Number of, 1998-2007 ... 22
Most by Broodmare's Offspring ... 859
Most by Decade by Year of Birth ... 569
Number of by State and Province in 2007 ... 3

State and Provincial Organizations ... 905
State Fair Park, Ne. ... 666
States
Aggregate Purse Earnings by, in 2007 ... 7
Aggregate Stud Fees, 2003-2007 ... 14
Aggregate Stud Fees by Year 2001-2007 ... 14
Auction Sales in 2007 ... 11
Average Auction Prices in 2007 ... 11
Average Stud Fees, 2003-2007 ... 15
Average Stud Fees by Year, 2001-2007 ... 14
Broodmare Auction Prices ... 11
Claiming Activity in 2007 ... 8
Foal Registration by, in 2006 ... 781
Leading Sires by ... 825
Live Foals, 2003-2007 ... 14
Mares Bred, 2003-2007 ... 12
Median Auction Prices in 2007 ... 12
Pari-Mutuel Takeout ... 6
Pari-Mutuel Wagering in 2005 ... 5
Races, Number of in 2007 ... 3
Racing Dates in 2007 ... 3
Racing Organizations ... 895
Racinos and Daily Purses ... 26
Revenues from Horse Racing in 2005 ... 5
Revenue to from Horse Racing, Historical ... 4
Stallions in Production, 2003-2007 ... 13
Starts, Number of in 2007 ... 3
Two-Year-Old Auction Prices ... 11
Weanling Auction Prices ... 11
Yearling Auction Prices ... 11

State Where Bred
Leading Earners by ... 574
Leading Earners by in 2007 ... 583

Stephen Foster H. ... 465
Stockton, Ca. ... 630
Stonerside Beaumont S. ... 465
Stories, Top News of 2007 ... 28
Strub S. ... 466
Stud Farms
Leading by 2007 Progeny Earnings ... 832
Profiles of Leading in 2007 ... 832

Stud Fees
Aggregate by State and Province, 2003-2007 ... 14
Aggregate by Year, 2001-2007 ... 14
Average by State and Province, 2003-2007 ... 15
Average by Year, 2001-2007 ... 14

Stuyvesant H. ... 466
Suburban H. ... 467
Suffolk Downs, Ma. ... 660
Sun Downs, Wa. ... 696
Sunflower Downs, B.C. ... 703
Sunland Park, N.M.
Profile ... 671
Racino ... 27

SunRay Park, N.M.
Profile ... 671
Racino ... 27

Sunset H. ... 467
Super Derby ... 468
Suwannee River H. ... 469
Swale S. ... 469
Swaps S. ... 470
Sword Dancer Invitational S. ... 470
Sycamore S. ... 471
Takeout by State ... 6
Tampa Bay Derby ... 471
Tampa Bay Downs, Fl. ... 635
Taylor Made Matchmaker S. ... 472
Tempted S. ... 472
Test S. ... 473
Texas Mile S. ... 473
The Very One H. ... 473
Thistledown, OH. ... 681
Thoroughbred Club of America S. ... 474
Thoroughbred Economy in 2007-'08 ... 1
Thoroughbred Owners and Breeders Association ... 902
Thoroughbred Racing Associations ... 898
Thoroughbred Racing Protective Bureau ... 899
Thoroughbred Retirement and Rescue ... 912
Tillamook County Fair, Or. ... 686
Times
Fastest of 2007 ... 548
North American Track Records ... 549
Progression of Fastest on Dirt ... 550

Timonium, Md. ... 659
Toboggan H. ... 474
Tokyo City H. ... 475
Tom Fool H. ... 475
Top Flight H. ... 476
Top Stories of 2007 ... 28
Toyota Blue Grass S. ... 477
Track Condition Abbreviations ... 971
Track Records, North American ... 549
Trainers
Eclipse Award Winners ... 97
Leading by Average Earnings per Starter in 2007 ... 726
Leading by Belmont Stakes Wins ... 171
Leading by Breeders' Cup Purses ... 190
Leading by Breeders' Cup Starts ... 190
Leading by Breeders' Cup Wins ... 188
Leading by Earnings, 1980-2007 ... 724
Leading by Earnings in 2007 ... 724
Leading by Earnings in a Year, 1985-2007 ... 730
Leading by Kentucky Derby Wins ... 145
Leading by Most Starts on Breeders' Cup Program ... 190
Leading by Number of Grade 1 Stakes Winners in 2007 ... 728
Leading by Number of Grade 1 Stakes Wins in 2007 ... 728
Leading by Number of Graded Stakes Winners in 2007 ... 728
Leading by Number of Graded Stakes Wins in 2007 ... 727
Leading by Number of Stakes Winners in 2007 ... 726
Leading by Number of Stakes Wins in 2007 ... 726
Leading by Number of Wins in 2007 ... 728
Leading by Percent Stakes Winners in 2007 ... 727
Leading by Preakness Stakes Wins ... 159
Leading of 2007 ... 724
Leading of Eclipse Award Winners ... 105
Leading of Racing Hall of Fame Members ... 116
Leading of Triple Crown Race Winners ... 137
Most Belmont Stakes Starters ... 171
Most Kentucky Derby Starters ... 145
Most Preakness Stakes Starters ... 159
Most Wins on One Day in 2007 ... 729
Most Wins on One Program in 2007 ... 729
Of Eclipse Award Winners ... 105
Of Racing Hall of Fame Members ... 116
Racing Hall of Fame ... 113

Transylvania S. ... 477
Travers S. ... 477
Triple Bend Invitational H. ... 478
Triple Crown, American ... 121
Affirmed ... 133
Assault ... 131
Birthplaces of Winners ... 121

xvi General Index

Breeders, Leading of Winners.....136
Citation.....132
Count Fleet.....131
Definition of Applicant.....125
Gallant Fox.....129
History of American.....121
Jockeys, Leading of Winners.....138
Nominations by Year.....122
Omaha.....129
Origins of.....121
Owners, Leading of Winners.....135
Race Conditions.....123
Release and Indemnification.....124
Reservation of Rights.....124
Road to.....127
Seattle Slew.....133
Secretariat.....132
Sir Barton.....128
Sires, Leading of Winners.....139
Television Ratings and Share.....121
Trainers, Leading of Winners.....137
Triple Crown Productions.....122
Trophy.....128
War Admiral.....130
Whirlaway.....130
Winners.....128
Winners by State or Country Where Bred.....121
Winners of Two Races.....134
Winners, Profiles of.....128
Triple Crown, Canadian.....962
Triple Crown, English.....932
Tropical Park Derby.....479
Tropical Park, Fl......637
Tropical Turf H......479
True North H......480
Turf Classic Invitational S......480
Turf Classic S......480
Turf Paradise, Az......616
Turf Sprint S......480
Turfway Park Fall Championship S......480
Turfway Park, Ky......651
Turnback the Alarm H......481
Tuzla H......481
TVG Breeders' Cup Sprint.....481
Twin Spires.....142
Two-Year-Olds
Auction Sales by State and Province in 2007...11
Average Prices by State and Province in 2007.....11
Highest-Priced in North America.....876
Highest-Priced of 2007.....868
Leading Buyers by Purchases in 2007.....883
Leading Consignors by Receipts in 2007.....885
Median Prices by State and Province in 2007.....12
Sales Average by Year.....886
Unbeaten Horses, Leading.....564
United Nations S......482
University of Arizona RTIP Distinguished Senior Award.....772
University of Arizona RTIP Distinguished Service Award.....772
UTTA Outstanding Trainer of the Year Award.....772
Vagrancy H......483
Vallejo, Ca......631
Valley View S......483
Alfred Gwynne Vanderbilt Award.....773
Vanity Invitational H......483
Varola, Francesco.....787
Mike Venezia Memorial Award.....773
Vernon O. Underwood S......484
Veterinary, Common Terms.....1001
Victory Ride S......484
Vinery Madison S......485
Violet S......485
Virginia Derby.....485
Virginia Oaks.....486
Vosburgh S......486
Vuillier, Col. Jean-Joseph.....787
Wagering Handle
Belmont Stakes.....169
Breeders' Cup.....184
Kentucky Derby.....141
Preakness Stakes.....162
Top 25 Meets by Average All-Sources in 2007.....711
Top 25 Meets by Average On-Track in 2007...711
Total North American in 2007.....1
Wagering, Pari-Mutuel
By State in 2005.....5
How Pari-Mutuel Began.....983
Odds and Payouts.....984
Racetrack, 1996-2007.....1
Relationship of, 1982-2007.....2
Takeout by State.....6
Wagers, Type of.....973
Waitsburg Race Track, Wa......697
Walkovers.....593
Walla Walla, Wa......697
Washington Park H......486
Weanlings
Auction Sales by State and Province in 2007...11
Average Prices by State and Province in 2007.....11
Highest-Priced in North America.....877
Highest-Priced of 2007.....867
Leading Buyers by Purchases in 2007.....883
Leading Consignors by Receipts in 2007.....884
Median Prices by State and Province in 2007.....12
Sales Average by Year.....886
Weights, Scale of.....593
Westchester H......487
West Virginia Derby.....488
White Horse Award.....773
Whitney H......488
P.A.B. Widener II Trophy.....773
William Donald Schaefer H......489
Will Rogers Downs, Ok......684
Will Rogers S......489
Wilshire H......490
Winners
American Triple Crown.....128
Canadian Triple Crown.....962
English Triple Crown.....932
Leading of Grade 1 Races in North America.....565
Leading of Graded Stakes in North America.....565
Leading of Stakes Races in North America.....565
Most for a Broodmare.....858
Of Two Triple Crown Races.....134
Oldest 1987-2007.....598
Oldest Female Grade 1 Stakes Since 1976.....594
Oldest Female Graded Stakes Since 1976.....596
Oldest Female Since 1976.....597
Oldest Female Stakes Since 1976.....596
Oldest Male Grade 1 Stakes Since 1976.....594
Oldest Male Graded Stakes Since 1976.....595
Oldest Male Since 1976.....597
Oldest Male Stakes Since 1976.....596
Oldest of 2007.....598
Oldest of Breeders' Cup Race.....194
Oldest Surviving Breeders' Cup.....193
With Highest All-Time Odds.....984
Winners by Sires' Progeny
All-Time Leading Sires by.....820
Leading Broodmare Sires by Number of in North America in 2007.....807
Leading Broodmare Sires by Number of Worldwide in 2007.....799
Leading Freshman Sires by Number of in North America in 2007.....805
Leading Freshman Sires by Number of Worldwide in 2007.....797
Leading Juvenile Sires by Number of in North America in 2007.....803
Leading Juvenile Sires by Number of Worldwide in 2007.....795
Leading Sires by Number of in North America in 2007.....801
Leading Sires by Number of Worldwide in 2007.....792
Winning Colors S......490
Winningest
Horses by Decade by Year of Birth.....562
Horses of All Time.....562
Wins
Earnings as Function of for 2007.....18
Jockey for Career.....736
Leaders by Grade 1 Races.....565
Leaders by Graded Stakes Races.....565
Leaders by Stakes Races.....565
Leaders of Million-Dollar Races.....564
Leading Breeders by, in 2007.....723
Leading Jockeys by, in 2007.....735
Leading Owners by, in 2007.....717
Leading Trainers by, in 2007.....728
Most After First Claim, 1991-2007.....604
Most After First Claim in 2007.....604
Most by Broodmare's Offspring.....858
Most by Decade by Year of Birth.....562
Most Claiming, 1991-2007.....605
Most Claiming in 2007.....605
Most Consecutive.....563
Most Stakes by Decade by Year of Birth.....566
Wins by Sires' Progeny
Leading Broodmare Sires by Number of in North America in 2007.....807
Leading Broodmare Sires by Number of Worldwide in 2007.....799
Leading Freshman Sires by Number of in North America in 2007.....805
Leading Freshman Sires by Number of Worldwide in 2007.....797
Leading Juvenile Sires by Number of in North America in 2007.....803
Leading Juvenile Sires by Number of Worldwide in 2007.....795
Leading Sires by Number of in North America in 2007.....801
Leading Sires by Number of Worldwide in 2007.....793
Withers S......490
W. L. McKnight H......491
Woodbine, On.
Profile.....705
Racino.....27
Woodford Reserve Bourbon S......492
Woodford Reserve Manhattan H......492
Woodford Reserve Turf Classic S......493
Woodlands, Ks......646
Woodlawn Vase.....157
Wood Memorial S......493
David F. Woods Memorial Award.....774
Woodward S......494
Woody Stephens S......495
George Woolf Memorial Jockey Award.....774
World Thoroughbred Racehorse Rankings of 2007.....935
Wyoming Downs, Wy......699
Yavapai Downs, Az......617
Year in Review.....28
Yearlings
Auction Sales by State and Province in 2007...11
Average Prices by State and Province in 2007.....11
Highest-Priced of 2007.....866
Highest-Priced of All Time.....875
Highest Prices Through the Years.....879
Leading Buyers by Purchases in 2007.....882
Leading Buyers of Top-Priced.....882
Leading Consignors by Receipts in 2007.....884
Leading Consignors of Top-Priced.....882
Leading Sires of Top-Priced.....882
Median Prices by State and Province in 2007.....12
Most Expensive North American by Year.....880
Progression of Highest Prices.....879
Sales Average by Year.....886
Yellow Ribbon S......495
Yellowstone Downs, Mt......663
Youbet.com Inc......921
Zia Park, N.M.
Profile.....673
Racino.....27

STATE OF THE INDUSTRY
Thoroughbred Economy in 2007-'08

For as long as just about anyone can remember, North American racing purses and the pari-mutuel wagering on those races have had a direct relationship. Handle goes up, purses go up. Handle goes down, purses go down. That relationship began to get a little fuzzy in the 1990s, as a few racetracks added slot machines to their betting repertoires. Thus, with a revenue stream from video lottery terminals or slots, purses could go up even if the wagering handle dipped. Racetracks effectively became slots casinos, and the racino era began.

At first, the gaming supplements were largely limited to smaller tracks, such as those in West Virginia and Delaware that had been in danger of closing their doors without a boost from alternative gaming. But then more states added other forms of gaming, and some of those racing states—such as Louisiana and Pennsylvania—were not so small. Track by track as slot machines took over floor space in the grandstands, the racino effect on purses grew stronger while the relationship of purses and wagering handle became weaker.

That process is by no means complete—after all, Aqueduct most likely will have video lottery terminals before this decade is over—but 2007 may be viewed in retrospect as the year in which the direct link between purses and handle was broken, perhaps irretrievably. The process appeared to be continuing in the first half of 2008.

The new trend is pari-mutuel wagering handle down, purses up—maybe. In 2007, purses increased 5.2% while wagering handle declined 0.5%. For the first quarter of 2008, both wagering and purses declined, although the decline in purses was significantly smaller than a stunning 3.1% drop in wagering on United States races for the three-month period. (More information on 2007 purses can be found in "All About Purses" beginning on page 16.)

North American Purses

Year	Total Purses	Average Purse
2007	$1,251,579,551	$22,269
2006	1,189,277,214	20,964
2005	1,149,003,138	20,051
2004	1,177,769,765	20,069
2003	1,154,238,845	19,626
2002	1,170,169,267	19,597
2001	1,146,337,367	18,936
2000	1,093,661,241	18,053
1999	1,008,162,608	6,770
1998	968,366,929	15,838
1997	888,667,752	13,997
1996	845,916,706	13,163

The increases in purses in 2006 and '07 after a decrease in '05 came as a result of revenue sources other than pari-mutuel wagering, notably slot machines at tracks. The effects of this seismic change in the sport are worrisome for two reasons. First, they are not spread evenly over the continent. Formerly weak jurisdictions have become economic powerhouses in terms of the purses they offer, but they have not necessarily become powerhouse racing venues—just rich ones.

That change is beneficial to the sport in one sense because it provides more money to owners in regional markets. However, the newly strong markets bleed betting dollars from markets that lack political authorization for slot machines. Louisiana, for instance, has been taking pari-mutuel and bloodstock business away from Texas because its purses are heavily underwritten by slot-machine revenues. In 2007, before Fair Grounds began to derive substantial purse revenue from slots, machine gaming furnished 62.6% of purses. In Delaware, the percentage was even higher, 72.4%.

Without question, a notable chunk of the new purse money in 2007 came from Pennsylvania, where the slot machines began producing purse dollars in late '06. Almost the entire $10.7-million

North American Thoroughbred Pari-Mutuel Wagering
(Millions of Dollars)

	United States			Canada			Total	
Year	On-Track	Off-Track	Total	On-Track	Off-Track	Total	Total	Change
2007	$1,670	$13,055	$14,725	$132	$375	$506	$15,231	−0.5%
2006	1,688	13,097	14,785	109	419	529	15,313	+1.2%
2005	1,741	12,819	14,561	144	423	568	15,129	−3.0%
2004	1,860	13,239	15,099	137	364	502	15,601	−0.7%
2003	1,902	13,278	15,180	139	394	534	15,714	0.5%
2002	2,029	13,033	15,062	153	414	567	15,629	3.2%
2001	2,112	12,487	14,599	153	387	540	15,139	2.3%
2000	2,270	12,051	14,321	150	325	475	14,796	4.5%
1999	2,359	11,365	13,724	161	278	439	14,163	4.0%
1998	2,498	10,617	13,115	188	310	498	13,613	4.2%
1997	2,703	9,839	12,542	217	310	527	13,069	6.5%
1996	2,944	8,683	11,627	259	383	642	12,269	9.3%

purse structure for the new Presque Isle Downs came from its slot machines. By year's end, nearly 60% of all Pennsylvania purse money was derived from slot machines—and that was before Penn National Race Course opened its lavish casino.

Another issue is that some of the strongest racing circuits in the U.S.—the ones where the best horses now compete—remain have-nots. Aqueduct is projected to have slots in 2009 or '10 to bolster purses in the metropolitan New York market, but slot machines most likely are on a distant horizon for tracks in Illinois and Kentucky, and California probably will never have slots because Native American casinos and their political influence are pervasive.

The second reason for concern is that the reliance on nonpari-mutuel sources diminishes the importance of the money bet on the horses and the attention that should be accorded to trends in pari-mutuel wagering. Racetrack gambling has become a very small part of the overall gambling market, but little attention has been given to the fact that the racing market itself has declined in real terms.

Ever since bookmakers were booted from U.S. racetracks, pari-mutuel wagering handle has been the most important determinant of the Thoroughbred industry's health. First, wagering levels determine purse levels. Taking a long view, purses have grown enormously in more than 40 years. Less than $150-million in 1968, purses surpassed $1.2-billion in 2007. With very few hiccups (albeit two in the current decade), purses have increased just about every year.

In terms of buying power, purses have increased by more than three-quarters in that period. Adjusted for inflation using the U.S. Commerce Department's implicit price deflator, real purses increased from $592.8-million in 1968 to $1.046-billion in 2007, a 76.4% boost in buying power.

Why did an almost 2% increase in annual real purses occur? Most likely, several factors were at work. First, horsemen became more aggressive in demanding a fair share of the proceeds from racing. Second, state taxes on pari-mutuel handle have plummeted over those 40 years as racing's economics became ragged. Third, takeout—especially with the advent of exotic wagers—has increased sharply.

Pari-mutuel wagering on Thoroughbred racing has not fared as well as purses. According to *American Racing Manual*, pari-mutuel wagering totaled $3.847-billion in 1968. By 2007, the betting total had risen to $15.231-billion in the U.S. and Canada, the Jockey Club and Equibase reported. That is a sizable increase, up nearly fourfold over 40 years.

But, when the inflation is wrung from that increase, the picture darkens. The 1968 handle when adjusted for inflation totaled $15.440-billion. The 2007 wagering in real, inflation-adjusted dollars was $12.728-billion. In short, Thoroughbred wagering in real terms has actually declined 17.6% in 40 years.

While changes in wagering patterns and the

Relationship of Wagering, Purses, and Bloodstock Sales, 1982-2007

Year	Wagering	Change	Purses	Change	Bloodstock	Change	Purse/Wagering	Bloodstock/Purse
2007	$15,231,000,000	−0.5%	$1,251,579,551	5.2%	$1,234,601,842	−2.6%	8.2%	98.6%
2006	15,313,000,000	1.2%	1,189,277,214	3.5%	1,267,054,866	11.3%	7.8%	106.5%
2005	15,129,000,000	−3.0%	1,149,003,138	−2.4%	1,138,751,345	8.0%	7.6%	99.1%
2004	15,601,000,000	−0.7%	1,177,769,765	2.0%	1,054,384,913	23.3%	7.5%	89.5%
2003	15,714,000,000	0.5%	1,154,238,845	−1.4%	855,123,171	11.5%	7.3%	74.1%
2002	15,629,000,000	3.2%	1,170,169,267	2.1%	767,048,402	−9.4%	7.5%	65.6%
2001	15,139,000,000	2.3%	1,146,337,367	4.8%	846,478,571	−22.5%	7.6%	73.8%
2000	14,796,000,000	4.5%	1,093,661,241	8.5%	1,091,872,249	9.0%	7.4%	99.8%
1999	14,163,000,000	4.0%	1,008,162,608	4.1%	1,001,718,775	20.9%	7.1%	99.4%
1998	13,613,000,000	4.2%	968,366,929	9.0%	828,664,233	18.3%	7.1%	85.6%
1997	13,069,000,000	6.5%	888,667,752	5.1%	700,362,250	12.8%	6.8%	78.8%
1996	12,269,000,000	9.3%	845,916,706	3.7%	620,712,382	17.9%	6.9%	73.4%
1995	11,224,000,000	6.1%	815,987,125	5.9%	526,647,938	20.9%	7.3%	64.5%
1994	10,578,000,000	4.8%	770,326,193	2.9%	435,690,484	21.5%	7.3%	56.6%
1993	10,091,421,346	−1.0%	748,415,925	−2.9%	358,718,349	8.1%	7.4%	47.9%
1992	10,198,201,240	1.2%	771,136,296	1.3%	331,736,278	−13.3%	7.6%	43.0%
1991	10,072,337,897	0.1%	761,446,198	−1.7%	382,547,681	−16.3%	7.6%	50.2%
1990	10,057,909,767	1.2%	775,006,519	0.5%	457,182,271	−11.7%	7.7%	59.0%
1989	9,933,984,517	4.1%	771,421,230	4.7%	517,653,394	−2.1%	7.8%	67.1%
1988	9,538,956,529	7.2%	736,698,230	4.6%	528,620,037	−5.8%	7.7%	71.8%
1987	8,900,457,788	6.2%	704,372,435	6.4%	561,197,988	9.5%	7.9%	79.7%
1986	8,378,383,989	1.5%	661,826,092	3.1%	512,300,043	−20.7%	7.9%	77.4%
1985	8,254,612,623	1.9%	641,658,553	7.1%	645,768,989	−3.2%	7.8%	100.6%
1984	8,104,018,644	5.7%	599,348,425	10.1%	667,312,715	−1.6%	7.4%	111.3%
1983	7,668,055,765	−0.7%	544,260,167	3.4%	678,288,175	24.3%	7.1%	124.6%
1982	7,723,476,101	1.4%	526,587,096	3.9%	545,587,527	−0.1%	6.8%	103.6%

Source: Pari-Mutuel Handle 1982-'93, *American Racing Manual*; 1994-2007, Equibase Co.

rise of offshore betting sites have been blamed for the actual, current-dollar declines in 2004, '05, and '07, pari-mutuel wagering has been declining for a very long time in inflation-adjusted dollars. While the peak in current-dollar wagering occurred in 2003, at the peak of full-card simulcast wagering, the inflation-adjusted peak was in 1970, at $15.698-billion. The only time since the 1970s that the inflation-adjusted wagering handle breached the $15-billion mark was in 2002, also at the apex of full-card simulcasting, and it has fallen every year since then.

Bloodstock sales, the other major component of the Thoroughbred industry, also declined in 2007, by 2.6% at all public auctions in North America. In principle, racetrack purses are an influence on bloodstock prices because relatively few male horses end up with significant residual value as a stallion, and most broodmare prospects must earn their way into the breeding shed.

On average, bloodstock sales at public auctions each year are about 80% of wagering handle. Sometimes, however, the relationship varies widely from that norm and usually results in corrections to the bloodstock market. In 1983, bloodstock prices were nearly 125% of purses, and that distortion preceded a long and painful recession in the auction markets, where annual revenues fell to as low as 43% of purses a decade later.

A long, relatively stable recovery followed, until bloodstock prices were 106.5% of purses in 2006. Last year's modest correction of 2.6% lowered public-auction sales to 98.6% of annual purses.—*Don Clippinger*

Racing Dates, Races, Runners, Starts, Purses by State and Province in 2007

	Racing Dates	Races	Runners	Starts	Purses
NORTH AMERICA	**6,714**	**56,356**	**72,991**	**460,477**	**$1,256,815,949**
Arizona	247	1,867	3,099	14,968	16,281,108
Arkansas	52	515	1,642	4,222	14,991,250
California	731	5,055	8,439	40,047	166,056,979
Colorado	35	243	507	1,697	1,888,253
Delaware	135	1,113	2,983	7,516	35,105,277
Florida	356	3,659	7,582	30,413	86,091,512
Georgia	2	10	62	67	374,250
Idaho	48	277	545	1,864	1,110,569
Illinois	301	2,699	4,650	21,475	53,993,840
Indiana	109	1,020	2,684	9,232	12,667,450
Iowa	86	662	1,438	5,047	14,899,192
Kansas	41	220	777	1,751	1,161,664
Kentucky	270	2,658	7,663	23,184	80,090,433
Louisiana	357	3,548	7,658	32,245	91,134,737
Maryland	191	1,774	4,482	14,083	42,779,420
Massachusetts	101	903	1,181	7,057	11,568,028
Michigan	126	891	1,093	6,587	9,150,718
Minnesota	68	565	1,158	4,348	8,521,015
Montana	19	92	242	583	211,714
Nebraska	104	899	1,272	6,907	6,369,259
Nevada	9	65	256	446	277,229
New Jersey	125	1,167	2,909	8,730	65,617,206
New Mexico	270	1,571	2,846	13,575	30,898,976
New York	406	3,664	6,554	29,321	141,617,480
North Carolina	3	13	78	99	241,250
North Dakota	26	120	319	850	432,797
Ohio	360	2,805	4,846	22,860	21,722,300
Oklahoma	203	1,238	2,976	11,441	18,890,410
Oregon	95	760	1,245	5,406	3,445,985
Pennsylvania	408	3,748	7,401	30,215	73,623,366
South Carolina	4	20	128	155	583,510
South Dakota	2	10	70	71	22,700
Tennessee	1	6	66	66	385,000
Texas	192	1,713	3,653	14,995	25,605,950
Virginia	50	414	1,875	3,673	10,030,352
Washington	110	937	1,665	6,963	10,320,818
West Virginia	452	4,358	8,820	37,591	73,173,824
Wyoming	11	20	67	118	41,515
UNITED STATES	**6,106**	**51,299**	**67,294**	**419,868**	**$1,131,377,336**
Alberta	177	1,242	1,719	9,044	$ 15,464,342
British Columbia	78	669	1,011	4,967	9,498,067
Manitoba	69	554	881	4,339	5,281,501
Ontario	253	2,357	3,687	20,374	94,362,336
Saskatchewan	31	235	454	1,885	832,367
CANADA	**608**	**5,057**	**7,356**	**40,609**	**$125,438,613**

Revenues to Government From Horse Racing

Through much of the 20th century and into the 21st century, government has looked to gambling as a tax upon the willing, a way to ease the burden of most taxpayers by levying a heavy tax load on all gambling wagers. In the 1940s, the tax burden on racetracks exploded. In the 1970s and '80s, the states created lotteries, which had a heavy tax burden but nonetheless drew patrons through slick advertising and hefty jackpots. In the 1990s and beyond, the attention of state government shifted to slot machines and casino games. Some of the machine wagering was authorized for racetracks.

The following table, compiled by the Association of Racing Commissioners International, illustrates very clearly the rise of horse racing—principally Thoroughbred racing but also Quarter Horse and Standardbred racing—as a source of government income and its decline. In the depths of the Great Depression, the horse-racing industry was not taxed heavily, either in current dollars or inflation-adjusted dollars. That circumstance began to change in the late 1930s, as the nation began to emerge from the Depression and, with war on the horizon, to change to a military economy. For the first time in 1939, revenues to government passed the $10-million level. By 1942, the tax had more than doubled, and it doubled again by '44.

After World War II, demands on states and local governments for schools and other services grew exponentially, and so did the taxes on horse racing. By 1951, horse racing contributed more than $100-million in taxes; by '56, the tax had doubled again. Also in 1956, the tax on racing surpassed $1-billion in inflation-adjusted dollars for the first time. It peaked at more than $2-billion in deflated dollars in 1975.

At approximately that time, Thoroughbred racing began a slow, steady slide. As racing lost patrons to other sports—all of which had, unlike racing, embraced television as a way to enlarge their fan bases—racetracks were transformed from monopolist profit centers to marginally profitable or even losing operations. The tracks made compelling arguments to state governments that unless pari-mutuel taxes were reduced drastically, the racetracks would be unable to remain in business, and the state would lose both jobs and revenue on wagers placed at the track. The argument that a small tax was better than nothing carried the day, and subsequently some states eliminated the pari-mutuel tax altogether.

Revenue to States from Horse Racing

Year	Current Dollars	Deflated Dollars	Year	Current Dollars	Deflated Dollars
2005	$325,919,323	$288,424,180	1969	$461,498,886	$1,764,881,586
2004	338,885,365	313,144,858	1968	426,856,448	1,713,388,384
2003	343,588,382	325,152,249	1967	394,381,913	1,650,616,971
2002	346,799,090	333,637,106	1966	388,452,125	1,676,096,501
2001	351,511,182	343,363,174	1965	369,892,036	1,641,411,298
2000	367,786,590	367,786,590	1964	350,095,928	1,581,925,480
1999	392,201,085	400,744,968	1963	316,570,791	1,452,292,830
1998	431,722,361	447,510,533	1962	287,930,030	1,334,925,263
1997	441,768,972	463,002,255	1961	264,853,077	1,244,727,310
1996	443,882,538	472,960,127	1960	258,039,385	1,226,364,645
1995	455,764,292	494,825,844	1959	243,388,655	1,172,900,848
1994	451,546,549	500,278,697	1958	222,049,651	1,083,274,715
1993	471,735,474	533,752,135	1957	216,747,621	1,081,682,907
1992	491,259,606	568,686,237	1956	207,456,272	1,069,748,218
1991	523,249,392	619,640,699	1955	186,989,588	997,650,259
1990	623,839,806	764,603,268	1954	178,015,828	966,584,286
1989	584,888,183	744,549,344	1953	167,426,465	917,757,304
1988	596,202,319	787,648,055	1952	142,489,696	790,643,081
1987	608,351,461	831,126,648	1951	117,250,564	661,759,589
1986	587,357,677	824,361,652	1950	98,366,167	601,591,138
1985	625,159,697	896,762,006	1949	95,327,053	582,968,768
1984	650,262,852	961,145,299	1948	95,803,364	584,808,717
1983	641,387,176	983,617,060	1947	97,926,984	631,542,525
1982	652,888,463	1,040,857,799	1946	94,035,859	672,357,064
1981	680,199,584	1,150,560,030	1945	65,265,405	522,541,273
1980	712,727,523	1,318,815,615	1944	55,971,233	460,062,740
1979	680,919,798	1,374,262,933	1943	38,194,727	321,342,142
1978	673,063,831	1,470,952,709	1942	22,005,278	195,099,548
1977	700,239,986	1,637,911,644	1941	21,128,173	201,893,674
1976	714,629,120	1,777,861,280	1940	16,145,182	164,612,378
1975	780,081,431	2,052,737,832	1939	10,369,807	106,960,361
1974	645,980,984	1,860,276,412	1938	9,576,335	97,817,518
1973	585,201,524	1,837,425,112	1937	8,434,792	83,653,595
1972	531,404,550	1,761,600,975	1936	8,611,538	89,100,238
1971	512,838,417	1,773,852,226	1935	8,386,255	87,740,688
1970	486,403,097	1,766,554,431	1934	6,024,193	64,292,348

Total Reported Pari-Mutuel Handle From Thoroughbred Racing and All Forms of Racing in 2005

State	Thoroughbred	Mixed	Total	State	Thoroughbred	Mixed	Total
Alabama	$ 44,974,727		$ 44,974,727	Nevada	$ 471,425,704	$ 7,712,861	$ 520,119,725
Arizona		$182,962,479	182,962,479	New Hampshire	140,464,114		165,258,456
Arkansas	57,867,109	223,221,235	281,088,344	New Jersey	660,456,773	97,961,339	1,032,469,282
California	1,670,731,712	201,600,694	2,143,744,029	New Mexico		102,072,445	102,072,445
Colorado		64,024,525	64,024,525	New York	2,256,778,155		2,644,523,292
Connecticut		240,312,537	240,312,537	North Dakota		35,393,495	35,393,495
Delaware	19,344,115	70,388,340	89,732,455	Ohio	29,977,790	381,876,346	456,730,940
Florida	820,193,655		922,806,353	Oklahoma		110,748,023	110,748,023
Idaho		12,275,701	12,275,701	Oregon		966,055,829	966,055,829
Illinois	718,002,087		1,002,819,877	Pennsylvania	786,964,634		1,001,786,691
Indiana		146,059,357	189,742,927	Rhode Island		55,528,030	55,528,030
Iowa		30,093,135	30,093,135	South Dakota		5,245,548	5,245,548
Kansas		44,784,260	44,784,260	Texas		408,787,581	408,787,581
Kentucky	230,431,811	297,843,726	531,480,928	Virginia	117,637,398		151,758,202
Louisiana	324,452,372		341,816,989	Washington	154,172,316	3,412,248	157,584,564
Maine		54,738,918	61,630,144	West Virginia	37,441,008	60,872,991	98,313,999
Maryland	69,722,614	427,559,134	505,256,563	Wisconsin		39,989,587	39,989,587
Massachusetts	169,855,963	8,642,686	196,468,006	Wyoming		22,840,698	22,840,698
Michigan	2,613,420	287,240,920	310,993,746	**Totals**	**$8,940,764,978**	**$4,616,919,883**	**$15,360,771,018**
Minnesota	53,863,940	17,764,529	76,219,527				
Montana		8,910,689	8,910,689				
Nebraska	103,426,690		103,426,690				

Note: Quarter Horse and Harness racing data is not noted in table but their handle is included in state totals.
Source: Association of Racing Commissioners International

Pari-Mutuel Wagering by State in 2005

State	On-Track	Intertrack	Off-Track	Total
Alabama			$ 44,974,727	$ 44,974,727
Arizona	$ 18,675,490	$ 17,495,117	146,791,872	182,962,479
Arkansas	57,867,109	223,221,235		281,088,344
California	467,366,358	1,057,278,137	619,099,534	2,143,744,029
Colorado	1,730,736	561,885	61,731,904	64,024,525
Connecticut			240,312,537	240,312,537
Delaware	18,568,775		71,163,680	89,732,455
Florida	165,203,980	121,217,295	636,385,078	922,806,353
Idaho	883,458		11,392,243	12,275,701
Illinois	120,287,813	183,317,298	699,214,766	1,002,819,877
Indiana	10,122,685	4,221,094	175,399,148	189,742,927
Iowa	6,718,332		23,374,803	30,093,135
Kansas	1,842,888		42,941,372	44,784,260
Kentucky	168,467,362	65,169,841	297,843,726	531,480,929
Louisiana	54,532,900	56,857,814	230,426,275	341,816,989
Maine	5,704,268	1,186,958	54,738,918	61,630,144
Maryland	47,956,112	30,939,708	426,360,743	505,256,563
Massachusetts	19,926,091	2,692,802	173,849,113	196,468,006
Michigan	23,934,235			310,993,746
Minnesota	17,590,704		58,628,823	76,219,527
Montana	1,923,975		6,986,714	8,910,689
Nebraska	8,614,324	5,155,279	89,657,087	103,426,690
Nevada	366,468		519,753,257	520,119,725
New Hampshire	3,260,266			165,258,456
New Jersey	193,080,492	70,361,550	769,027,240	1,032,469,282
New Mexico	26,550,227	7,212,736	68,309,482	102,072,445
New York	355,664,040	835,529,034	1,453,330,218	2,644,523,292
North Dakota	492,567		34,900,928	35,393,495
Ohio	74,854,594			456,730,940
Oklahoma	11,089,564	2,591,071	97,067,388	110,748,023
Oregon	4,526,700	1,008,987	960,520,142	966,055,829
Pennsylvania	48,806,383			1,001,786,691
Rhode Island			55,528,030	55,528,030
South Dakota	353,031		4,892,517	5,245,548
Texas	59,135,927	17,125,400	332,526,254	408,787,581
Virginia	6,295,404	1,774,779	143,688,019	151,758,202
Washington	27,458,569	106,833	130,019,162	157,584,564
West Virginia	37,441,008	5,566,057	55,306,934	98,313,999
Wisconsin			39,989,587	39,989,587
Wyoming	1,253,405		21,587,293	22,840,698
Totals	**$2,068,546,240**	**$2,710,590,910**	**$8,797,719,514**	**$15,360,771,018**

Intertrack and off-track totals are incomplete because breakdown was unavailable.
Source: Association of Racing Commissioners International.

Pari-Mutuel Takeout by State

Pari-mutuel takeout is the amount deducted from wagers before odds are calculated and payments are made to winning bettors.

The money taken out from the wagers goes to state taxes, horsemen as purses, the racetrack operators, breed enhancement funds, and other funds.

Arizona—Up to 25% on win-place-show wagers; up to 30% on two-horse wagers; up to 35% on multiple-horse wagers.

Arkansas—17% on win-place-show wagers; 21% on multiple wagers.

California—15.43% on win-place-show wagers; 20.1% on exotic wagers.

Colorado—18.5% on win-place-show wagers; 28% on exotic wagers.

Delaware—17% on win-place-show wagers; 19% on daily doubles and exactas; 27% on all other exotic wagers.

Florida—Individual tracks determine takeout rate.

Idaho—23% on win-place-show wagers; 23.75% on exotic wagers.

Illinois—17% on total handle; 20.5% on two-horse wagers; 25% on wagers involving three or more horses.

Indiana—18% on win-place-show wagers; 21.5% on exotic wagers.

Iowa—Up to 18% on win-place-show wagers; up to 24% on two-horse wagers; up to 25% on all other wagers.

Kansas—18% on win-place-show wagers; up to 22% on multiple wagers.

Kentucky—At tracks above $1,200,000 daily average: 16% on win-place-show wagers; 19% on exotic wagers. At tracks below $1,200,000 daily average: 17.5% on win-place-show wagers; 19% on exotic wagers.

Louisiana—17% on win-place-show wagers; 20.5% on two-horse wagers; 25% on multiple-horse wagers.

Maryland—At mile tracks, 18% on win-place-show wagers; 21% on two-horse multiple wagers; 25.75% on three-horse multiple wagers.

Massachusetts—19% on win-place-show wagers; 26% on exotic wagers (24% at fairs).

Michigan—17% on win-place-show wagers; up to 28% on multiples; up to 35% on multiple wagers with permission of racing commissioner.

Minnesota—Up to 17% on win-place-show wagers; 23% on exotic wagers.

Montana—20% on win-place-show wagers; up to 25% on exotic wagers.

Nebraska—15% to 18% on win-place-show wagers; up to 24% on exotic wagers.

Nevada—Not more than 20% of gross handle.

New Jersey—17% on win-place-show wagers; 19% on two-horse wagers; 25% on all other wagers.

New Mexico—Class A tracks: 19% on win-place-show wagers; 21% to 25% on exotic wagers. Class B tracks: 18.75% to 25% on win-place-show wagers; 21% to 30% on exotic wagers.

New York—At NYRA racetracks, 15% on win-place-show wagers; 17.5% on multiple wagers; 25% on exotics and super exotics. At Finger Lakes, 18% on win-place-show wagers, 20% on multiple wagers, 25% on exotics and super exotics.

North Dakota—20% on win-place-show wagers; 25% on exotics.

Ohio—18% on win-place-show wagers; 22.5% on exotic wagers.

Oklahoma—18% on win-place-show wagers; 20% on multiple-horse wagers; 20% on up to three-race wagers (such as Pick Three); 25% on multiple-race wagers (more than three races, such as Pick Six).

Oregon—19% on win-place-show wagers; 22% on multiple wagers. At fairs, up to 22% on all wagers.

Pennsylvania—17% on regular wagering pools; 19% if average daily handle is less than $300,000; 20% on exactas, daily doubles and quinellas; 26% to 35% on trifectas.

Texas—18% on win-place-show wagers; up to 21% on two-horse wagers; up to 25% on three-horse wagers.

Virginia—18% on win-place-show wagers; 22% on all other wagers.

Washington—16.1% on win-place-show wagers; 22.1% on all other wagers.

West Virginia—17.25% on win-place-show wagers; 19% on two-horse wagers; 25% on three horses or more.

Wyoming—20.9% on win-place-show wagers; 25.9% on exotic wagers.

2007 Aggregate Purse Earnings by State Where Bred

United States

State Where Bred	Starters Worldwide	Starts Worldwide	Winners Worldwide	Wins Worldwide	Earnings Worldwide
Alabama	102	578	28	47	$ 651,783
Arizona	604	3,731	262	421	4,226,553
Arkansas	592	3,857	263	438	6,031,020
California	6,435	39,188	2,937	4,941	93,279,973
Colorado	353	1,822	150	215	2,140,771
Connecticut	2	12	0	0	6,695
Delaware	1	8	1	2	20,506
Florida	9,860	69,930	5,070	8,899	184,203,045
Georgia	70	388	24	32	450,898
Idaho	265	1,517	114	177	1,492,466
Illinois	2,004	13,853	985	1,635	29,160,005
Indiana	1,013	6,819	427	679	8,718,459
Iowa	768	4,979	345	564	9,584,943
Kansas	167	795	61	82	722,981
Kentucky	18,942	117,145	9,516	16,142	433,875,328
Louisiana	3,746	20,193	1,330	1,995	50,677,257
Maryland	2,130	14,229	1,040	1,773	40,243,556
Massachusetts	115	778	45	73	1,476,564
Michigan	758	5,723	404	696	9,060,278
Minnesota	507	3,000	222	320	4,993,518
Mississippi	38	208	14	23	286,527
Missouri	40	207	12	17	231,208
Montana	95	473	42	58	689,398
Nebraska	321	1,997	155	246	2,371,768
Nevada	4	20	2	3	10,746
New Hampshire	3	11	1	1	7,665
New Jersey	799	5,490	353	562	17,726,214
New Mexico	1,376	7,628	519	802	16,702,192
New York	3,923	26,262	1,839	2,973	76,749,382
North Carolina	27	194	12	16	212,165
North Dakota	87	414	33	46	308,842
Ohio	1,236	8,883	614	1,047	12,694,198
Oklahoma	1,512	8,531	566	885	14,740,724
Oregon	457	3,004	216	388	2,240,189
Pennsylvania	1,883	12,375	888	1,457	39,482,255
South Carolina	84	526	37	61	848,247
South Dakota	39	126	7	10	59,989
Tennessee	28	204	13	19	274,407
Texas	2,988	18,385	1,209	1,965	27,543,780
Utah	52	242	15	19	123,121
Virginia	752	4,603	310	518	12,000,287
Washington	1,513	9,332	695	1,180	12,320,709
West Virginia	988	5,980	355	538	12,396,408
Wisconsin	7	64	3	3	37,041
Wyoming	3	11	1	2	4,168

Canada

Province Where Bred	Starters Worldwide	Starts Worldwide	Winners Worldwide	Wins Worldwide	Earnings Worldwide
Alberta	886	5,005	373	593	$ 7,697,726
British Columbia	1,024	6,015	492	773	9,708,459
Manitoba	183	1,052	68	95	1,504,506
Ontario	2,808	18,362	1,353	2,248	70,196,791
Saskatchewan	109	547	32	46	343,360

Totals

Where Bred	Starters Worldwide	Starts Worldwide	Winners Worldwide	Wins Worldwide	Earnings Worldwide
United States	66,689	423,715	31,135	51,970	$1,131,078,229
Canada	5,010	30,981	2,318	3,755	89,450,842
North America	**71,699**	**454,696**	**33,453**	**55,725**	**$1,220,529,071**

Claiming Activity by State or Province and Claiming Category in 2007

	No. Claims	Value	Average
North America			
Maiden Claiming	1,951	$ 39,763,700	$20,381
$0-$4,999	2,035	7,228,650	3,552
$5,000-$9,999	4,584	27,979,250	6,104
$10,000-$19,999	4,392	56,596,000	12,886
$20,000 and up	3,385	108,441,000	32,036
Total	14,396	200,244,900	13,910
United States			
Maiden Claiming	1,800	36,858,200	20,477
$0-$4,999	1,920	6,806,450	3,545
$5,000-$9,999	4,353	26,438,250	6,074
$10,000-$19,999	4,117	52,976,500	12,868
$20,000 and up	3,094	99,661,000	32,211
Total	13,484	185,882,200	13,785
Arizona			
Maiden Claiming	54	374,000	6,926
$0-$4,999	233	756,700	3,248
$5,000-$9,999	176	1,111,750	6,317
$10,000-$19,999	68	879,500	12,934
$20,000 and up	8	190,000	23,750
Total	485	2,937,950	6,058
Arkansas			
Maiden Claiming	38	730,000	19,211
$0-$4,999	0	0	0
$5,000-$9,999	69	395,000	5,725
$10,000-$19,999	68	838,500	12,331
$20,000 and up	74	2,073,000	28,014
Total	211	3,306,500	15,671
California			
Maiden Claiming	389	11,299,500	29,048
$0-$4,999	399	1,226,800	3,075
$5,000-$9,999	342	2,211,750	6,467
$10,000-$19,999	568	7,183,000	12,646
$20,000 and up	887	30,855,500	34,786
Total	2,196	41,477,050	18,888
Colorado			
Maiden Claiming	1	5,000	5,000
$0-$4,999	7	23,200	3,314
$5,000-$9,999	4	20,000	5,000
$10,000-$19,999	0	0	0
$20,000 and up	0	0	0
Total	11	43,200	3,927
Delaware			
Maiden Claiming	36	765,000	21,250
$0-$4,999	0	0	0
$5,000-$9,999	113	643,000	5,690
$10,000-$19,999	118	1,540,500	13,055
$20,000 and up	69	2,083,000	30,188
Total	300	4,266,500	14,222
Florida			
Maiden Claiming	246	6,526,500	26,530
$0-$4,999	0	$ 0	$ 0
$5,000-$9,999	274	1,808,750	6,601
$10,000-$19,999	469	6,306,000	13,446
$20,000 and up	411	13,953,500	33,950
Total	1,154	22,068,250	19,123
Idaho			
Maiden Claiming	1	2,500	2,500
$0-$4,999	29	84,900	2,928
$5,000-$9,999	2	11,250	5,625
$10,000-$19,999	0	0	0
$20,000 and up	0	0	0
Total	31	96,150	3,102
Illinois			
Maiden Claiming	78	1,261,500	16,173
$0-$4,999	108	420,800	3,896
$5,000-$9,999	216	1,294,750	5,994
$10,000-$19,999	387	5,158,000	13,328
$20,000 and up	165	4,757,500	28,833
Total	876	11,631,050	13,277
Indiana			
Maiden Claiming	9	52,500	5,833
$0-$4,999	62	248,000	4,000
$5,000-$9,999	66	363,750	5,511
$10,000-$19,999	5	57,500	11,500
$20,000 and up	0	0	0
Total	133	669,250	5,032
Iowa			
Maiden Claiming	14	212,500	15,179
$0-$4,999	22	88,000	4,000
$5,000-$9,999	64	395,000	6,172
$10,000-$19,999	54	688,000	12,741
$20,000 and up	13	325,000	25,000
Total	153	1,496,000	9,778
Kansas			
Maiden Claiming	0	0	0
$0-$4,999	10	29,000	2,900
$5,000-$9,999	2	10,000	5,000
$10,000-$19,999	1	10,000	10,000
$20,000 and up	0	0	0
Total	13	49,000	3,769
Kentucky			
Maiden Claiming	183	3,992,000	21,814
$0-$4,999	21	84,000	4,000
$5,000-$9,999	340	2,103,500	6,187
$10,000-$19,999	347	4,824,500	13,903
$20,000 and up	322	11,235,000	34,891
Total	1,030	18,247,000	17,716
Louisiana			
Maiden Claiming	169	2,281,500	13,500
$0-$4,999	133	517,000	3,887
$5,000-$9,999	547	3,114,750	5,694

State of the Industry — Claiming Activity in 2007

	No. Claims	Value	Average
$10,000-$19,999	426	$ 5,240,000	$12,300
$20,000 and up	190	5,142,500	27,066
Total	1,296	14,014,250	10,813
Maryland			
Maiden Claiming	83	1,485,000	17,892
$0-$4,999	12	49,500	4,125
$5,000-$9,999	206	1,303,500	6,328
$10,000-$19,999	225	3,002,500	13,344
$20,000 and up	150	3,915,500	26,103
Total	593	8,271,000	13,948
Massachusetts			
Maiden Claiming	4	27,500	6,875
$0-$4,999	37	148,500	4,014
$5,000-$9,999	54	314,250	5,819
$10,000-$19,999	37	430,500	11,635
$20,000 and up	0	0	0
Total	128	893,250	6,979
Michigan			
Maiden Claiming	0	0	0
$0-$4,999	9	34,500	3,833
$5,000-$9,999	3	17,500	5,833
$10,000-$19,999	11	122,000	11,091
$20,000 and up	0	0	0
Total	23	174,000	7,565
Minnesota			
Maiden Claiming	7	75,000	10,714
$0-$4,999	14	56,000	4,000
$5,000-$9,999	41	270,000	6,585
$10,000-$19,999	34	418,000	12,294
$20,000 and up	11	250,000	22,727
Total	100	994,000	9,940
Montana			
Maiden Claiming	0	0	0
$0-$4,999	1	1,600	1,600
$5,000-$9,999	0	0	0
$10,000-$19,999	0	0	0
$20,000 and up	0	0	0
Total	1	1,600	1,600
Nebraska			
Maiden Claiming	1	10,000	10,000
$0-$4,999	60	167,000	2,783
$5,000-$9,999	23	123,000	5,348
$10,000-$19,999	4	45,000	11,250
$20,000 and up	0	0	0
Total	87	335,000	3,851
Nevada			
Maiden Claiming	0	0	0
$0-$4,999	6	14,000	2,333
$5,000-$9,999	0	0	0
$10,000-$19,999	0	0	0
$20,000 and up	0	0	0
Total	6	14,000	2,333
New Jersey			
Maiden Claiming	38	847,000	22,289

	No. Claims	Value	Average
$0-$4,999	0	$ 0	$ 0
$5,000-$9,999	106	656,500	6,193
$10,000-$19,999	186	2,391,500	12,858
$20,000 and up	144	3,980,000	27,639
Total	436	7,028,000	16,119
New Mexico			
Maiden Claiming	20	217,250	10,863
$0-$4,999	11	44,000	4,000
$5,000-$9,999	180	1,159,500	6,442
$10,000-$19,999	91	1,142,500	12,555
$20,000 and up	16	385,000	24,063
Total	298	2,731,000	9,164
New York			
Maiden Claiming	82	2,895,000	35,305
$0-$4,999	97	388,000	4,000
$5,000-$9,999	61	412,500	6,762
$10,000-$19,999	183	2,445,000	13,361
$20,000 and up	449	15,722,500	35,017
Total	790	18,968,000	24,010
North Carolina			
Maiden Claiming	1	10,000	10,000
$0-$4,999	0	0	0
$5,000-$9,999	0	0	0
$10,000-$19,999	1	10,000	10,000
$20,000 and up	0	0	0
Total	1	10,000	10,000
Ohio			
Maiden Claiming	15	73,500	4,900
$0-$4,999	105	409,000	3,895
$5,000-$9,999	51	290,250	5,691
$10,000-$19,999	8	95,500	11,938
$20,000 and up	0	0	0
Total	164	794,750	4,846
Oklahoma			
Maiden Claiming	12	122,500	10,208
$0-$4,999	62	220,000	3,548
$5,000-$9,999	84	550,500	6,554
$10,000-$19,999	44	523,000	11,886
$20,000 and up	17	405,000	23,824
Total	207	1,698,500	8,205
Oregon			
Maiden Claiming	2	11,200	5,600
$0-$4,999	90	266,200	2,958
$5,000-$9,999	12	76,500	6,375
$10,000-$19,999	1	10,000	10,000
$20,000 and up	0	0	0
Total	103	352,700	3,424
Pennsylvania			
Maiden Claiming	114	1,641,500	14,399
$0-$4,999	129	489,000	3,791
$5,000-$9,999	485	2,887,750	5,954
$10,000-$19,999	362	4,647,000	12,837
$20,000 and up	105	2,750,000	26,190
Total	1,081	10,773,750	9,966

State of the Industry — Auction Activity in 2007

	No. Claims	Value	Average		No. Claims	Value	Average
Texas				**Alberta**			
Maiden Claiming	24	$325,000	$13,542	Maiden Claiming	24	$272,000	$11,333
$0-$4,999	38	147,000	3,868	$0-$4,999	15	44,600	2,973
$5,000-$9,999	89	580,000	6,517	$5,000-$9,999	65	419,500	6,454
$10,000-$19,999	114	1,264,000	11,088	$10,000-$19,999	96	1,347,500	14,036
$20,000 and up	27	645,000	23,889	$20,000 and up	41	1,034,000	25,220
Total	268	2,636,000	9,836	Total	217	2,845,600	13,113
Virginia				**British Columbia**			
Maiden Claiming	12	164,000	13,667	Maiden Claiming	22	355,500	16,159
$0-$4,999	0	0	0	$0-$4,999	1	4,500	4,500
$5,000-$9,999	15	94,000	6,267	$5,000-$9,999	54	375,000	6,944
$10,000-$19,999	18	250,000	13,889	$10,000-$19,999	36	473,000	13,139
$20,000 and up	4	112,000	28,000	$20,000 and up	30	715,000	23,833
Total	37	456,000	12,324	Total	121	1,567,500	12,955
Washington				**Manitoba**			
Maiden Claiming	44	557,500	12,670	Maiden Claiming	8	50,000	6,250
$0-$4,999	33	123,000	3,727	$0-$4,999	39	150,000	3,846
$5,000-$9,999	79	540,000	6,835	$5,000-$9,999	34	216,500	6,368
$10,000-$19,999	56	777,500	13,884	$10,000-$19,999	11	115,000	10,455
$20,000 and up	23	626,000	27,217	$20,000 and up	0	0	0
Total	191	2,066,500	10,819	Total	84	481,500	5,732
West Virginia				**Ontario**			
Maiden Claiming	123	893,750	7,266	Maiden Claiming	97	2,228,000	22,969
$0-$4,999	192	770,750	4,014	$0-$4,999	44	183,500	4,170
$5,000-$9,999	649	3,679,250	5,669	$5,000-$9,999	76	518,000	6,816
$10,000-$19,999	231	2,677,000	11,589	$10,000-$19,999	132	1,684,000	12,758
$20,000 and up	9	255,000	28,333	$20,000 and up	220	7,031,000	31,959
Total	1,081	7,382,000	6,829	Total	472	9,416,500	19,950
Canada				**Saskatchewan**			
Maiden Claiming	151	2,905,500	19,242	Maiden Claiming	0	0	0
$0-$4,999	115	422,200	3,671	$0-$4,999	16	39,600	2,475
$5,000-$9,999	231	1,541,000	6,671	$5,000-$9,999	2	12,000	6,000
$10,000-$19,999	275	3,619,500	13,162	$10,000-$19,999	0	0	0
$20,000 and up	291	8,780,000	30,172	$20,000 and up	0	0	0
Total	912	14,362,700	15,749	Total	18	51,600	2,867

Auction Prices in Current and Deflated Dollars, 1990-2007

	All Horses			Yearlings		
Year	No. Sold	Nominal Dollars	Deflated Dollars	No. Sold	Nominal Dollars	Deflated Dollars
2007	21,209	$1,234,601,872	$1,031,637,509	10,215	$562,026,375	$469,631,144
2006	21,407	1,267,054,866	1,086,975,616	10,216	579,476,050	497,118,438
2005	20,737	1,138,739,345	1,007,733,934	10,127	554,087,873	490,343,250
2004	20,290	1,054,852,803	963,987,355	9,427	496,948,119	454,140,807
2003	19,110	855,725,521	804,223,075	8,840	424,884,038	399,312,092
2002	18,473	767,816,102	736,959,603	8,928	391,472,126	375,739,897
2001	19,191	846,478,571	826,647,302	9,081	473,487,556	462,394,707
2000	21,225	1,091,872,249	1,091,872,249	9,527	519,775,432	519,775,432
1999	20,184	1,002,587,575	1,024,428,388	8,705	439,800,627	449,381,439
1998	19,653	828,664,233	858,968,647	8,260	354,191,040	367,143,876
1997	18,444	687,534,250	720,580,051	8,057	307,689,262	322,478,108
1996	18,871	620,712,382	661,373,633	8,026	277,221,538	295,381,599
1995	18,518	526,647,938	571,784,616	7,882	243,392,908	264,253,043
1994	17,972	448,685,293	497,108,646	7,744	210,460,233	233,173,681
1993	16,605	364,519,425	412,440,938	7,460	187,232,894	211,847,449

Year	No. Sold	Nominal Dollars	Deflated Dollars	No. Sold	Nominal Dollars	Deflated Dollars
1992	17,504	$348,995,344	$403,999,935	7,933	$176,825,683	$204,694,893
1991	18,977	401,102,091	474,991,818	8,179	213,940,466	253,351,885
1990	21,153	500,167,261	613,025,200	8,937	268,378,588	328,935,639

Auction Sales by State and Province in 2007

	Yearling	Two-Year-Old	Weanling	Broodmare	Others	Total
North America	$562,026,375	$193,064,064	$86,771,752	$384,674,148	$8,065,533	$1,234,601,872
Arizona	783,250	0	800	16,400	2,000	802,450
California	5,545,000	32,115,900	219,200	4,348,900	2,389,900	44,618,900
Florida	22,360,700	117,543,600	5,891,200	7,025,600	113,600	152,934,700
Illinois	0	368,200	0	0	0	368,200
Indiana	19,600	37,500	0	22,000	4,500	83,600
Iowa	203,600	113,000	0	2,200	0	318,800
Kentucky	451,723,500	17,487,000	77,877,400	370,173,700	5,270,400	922,532,000
Louisiana	2,419,750	1,500,900	41,850	429,600	40,150	4,432,250
Maryland	13,502,000	20,314,600	1,092,300	1,020,100	90,600	36,019,600
Michigan	85,900	9,400	0	2,200	500	98,000
Minnesota	368,200	0	0	0	0	368,200
New Mexico	1,233,250	0	0	0	0	1,233,250
New York	47,504,400	0	1,314,400	397,000	0	49,215,800
Oklahoma	435,550	125,850	1,300	275,100	38,350	876,150
Oregon	26,200	0	12,250	11,900	0	50,350
Pennsylvania	144,950	125,400	3,400	94,450	65,625	433,825
Texas	3,373,500	3,298,000	112,200	336,000	1,400	7,121,100
Washington	2,517,000	0	45,500	105,000	7,100	2,674,600
West Virginia	34,250	5,600	250	32,100	5,850	78,050
United States	**$552,280,600**	**$193,044,950**	**$86,612,050**	**$384,292,250**	**$8,029,975**	**$1,224,259,825**
Alberta	$1,273,362	$ 8,114	$ 1,402	$ 47,481	$34,558	$ 1,364,917
British Columbia	1,056,060	0	0	16,817	0	1,072,877
Manitoba	97,627	0	0	0	0	97,627
Ontario	7,318,726	11,000	158,300	317,600	1,000	7,806,626
Canada	**$9,745,775**	**$19,114**	**$159,702**	**$381,898**	**$35,558**	**$10,342,047**

Average Auction Prices by State and Province in 2007

	Yearling	Two-Year-Old	Weanling	Broodmare	Others	Total
North America	$ 55,019	$ 61,820	$44,384	$ 69,548	$20,949	$58,211
Arizona	5,554	0	800	1,822	1,000	5,244
California	10,725	74,170	4,215	10,208	28,793	29,529
Florida	18,743	69,717	18,182	11,728	14,200	40,140
Illinois	0	13,150	0	0	0	13,150
Indiana	1,781	6,250	0	1,222	2,250	2,259
Iowa	3,770	7,062	0	550	0	4,308
Kentucky	83,037	174,870	61,807	101,779	28,335	86,842
Louisiana	6,125	8,479	1,819	2,309	1,911	5,526
Maryland	22,243	49,790	9,256	6,072	5,662	27,349
Michigan	4,295	1,566	0	2,200	500	3,500
Minnesota	7,670	0	0	0	0	7,670
New Mexico	6,389	0	0	0	0	6,389
New York	139,309	0	17,525	4,841	0	98,826
Oklahoma	5,513	3,813	650	1,965	1,534	3,140
Oregon	1,310	0	1,361	626	0	1,048
Pennsylvania	3,370	4,478	1,700	2,196	3,453	3,213
Texas	12,925	17,000	3,619	5,419	1,400	12,971
Washington	10,991	0	2,676	3,281	887	9,351
West Virginia	2,140	2,800	250	1,605	1,170	1,773
United States	**$57,481**	**$61,932**	**$45,228**	**$70,564**	**$21,299**	**$59,827**
Alberta	$ 8,268	$2,028	$ 701	$1,637	$4,936	$ 6,963
British Columbia	10,776	0	0	4,204	0	10,518
Manitoba	4,244	0	0	0	0	4,244
Ontario	22,044	5,500	4,165	6,107	1,000	18,368
Canada	**$16,055**	**$3,185**	**$3,992**	**$4,492**	**$4,444**	**$13,863**

Median Auction Prices by State and Province in 2007

	Yearling	Two-Year-Old	Weanling	Broodmare	Others	Total
North America	**$15,000**	**$ 20,000**	**$17,000**	**$12,000**	**$ 6,500**	**$15,000**
Arizona	2,500	0	0	1,300	1,000	2,500
California	5,000	17,000	2,600	4,000	5,500	5,500
Florida	9,000	25,000	10,000	5,000	5,850	14,000
Illinois	0	9,600	0	0	0	9,600
Indiana	1,300	1,450	0	950	2,250	1,100
Iowa	1,450	3,000	0	500	0	1,500
Kentucky	32,000	127,500	30,000	26,000	15,000	30,000
Louisiana	3,000	4,500	850	1,200	1,200	2,500
Maryland	9,000	28,000	5,000	3,450	2,750	10,500
Michigan	2,350	1,400	0	0	0	1,800
Minnesota	5,100	0	0	0	0	5,100
New Mexico	3,000	0	0	0	0	3,000
New York	60,000	0	10,000	2,000	0	25,000
Oklahoma	2,500	1,300	650	900	850	1,300
Oregon	1,050	0	700	450	0	675
Pennsylvania	2,000	2,975	1,700	1,150	2,100	2,000
Texas	5,500	9,750	1,900	1,750	0	6,000
Washington	7,000	0	900	650	800	5,000
West Virginia	1,650	2,800	0	900	750	1,200
United States	**$15,000**	**$20,000**	**$18,000**	**$12,000**	**$6,500**	**$15,000**
Alberta	$ 4,774	$2,004	$ 701	1,102	$2,504	$3,324
British Columbia	5,107	0	0	4,038	0	4,988
Manitoba	1,899	0	0	0	0	1,899
Ontario	10,447	5,500	1,500	4,100	0	8,000
Canada	**$ 7,212**	**$3,403**	**$1,500**	**$2,404**	**$1,752**	**$5,720**

Yearling Auction Prices, 1990-2007

Year	Average	Change	Median	Change
2007	$55,019	–3%	$15,000	7%
2006	56,722	4%	14,000	6%
2005	54,713	4%	13,206	2%
2004	52,715	10%	13,000	8%
2003	48,063	10%	12,000	9%
2002	43,847	–16%	11,000	22%
2001	52,140	–4%	9,000	–22%
2000	54,558	8%	11,538	–4%
1999	50,522	18%	12,000	1%
1998	42,880	12%	11,900	8%
1997	38,189	11%	11,000	16%
1996	34,540	12%	9,500	–5%
1995	30,879	14%	10,000	11%
1994	27,177	8%	9,000	13%
1993	25,098	13%	8,000	14%
1992	22,289	–15%	7,000	17%
1991	26,157	–13%	6,000	–14%
1990	30,030	–7%	7,000	8%

North American Mares Bred, 2003-2007

	2007	2006	2005	2004	2003
North America	**59,310**	**61,674**	**61,998**	**61,625**	**60,278**
Alabama	96	117	122	136	112
Alaska	0	0	1	3	2
Arizona	458	543	535	485	513
Arkansas	603	538	551	593	546
California	4,597	4,811	5,150	5,747	5,725
Colorado	290	336	423	431	448
Connecticut	1	6	0	1	5
Delaware	1	2	0	0	0
Florida	6,467	7,088	7,220	6,935	6,609
Georgia	83	68	82	116	87
Idaho	219	234	218	308	268
Illinois	840	986	928	1,067	1,106
Indiana	552	451	543	685	800
Iowa	411	422	470	505	595
Kansas	133	133	155	189	150
Kentucky	21,911	21,413	20,899	20,346	20,156
Louisiana	4,128	3,921	3,554	3,090	2,617
Maine	0	0	0	0	5
Maryland	1,416	1,620	1,727	1,603	1,646
Massachusetts	32	28	30	68	81
Michigan	415	536	432	544	482
Minnesota	313	361	407	341	324
Mississippi	41	39	48	72	66
Missouri	69	62	89	73	77
Montana	108	153	145	181	172
Nebraska	305	354	318	360	331
Nevada	18	10	16	15	9
New Hampshire	4	0	0	0	0
New Jersey	370	440	299	257	318
New Mexico	1,918	1,992	1,781	1,528	1,393
New York	2,051	2,240	2,405	2,591	2,683
North Carolina	36	61	53	61	58
North Dakota	134	125	102	110	67
Ohio	339	445	449	515	580
Oklahoma	1,614	1,505	1,484	1,488	1,449
Oregon	367	451	458	449	406
Pennsylvania	1,076	1,139	1,213	1,003	966
Rhode Island	0	2	4	1	2
South Carolina	129	124	130	140	146
South Dakota	107	111	126	111	104
Tennessee	86	101	103	56	78
Texas	2,200	2,564	2,827	2,882	3,044
Utah	194	267	195	216	88

State of the Industry — Stallion Production

	2007	2006	2005	2004	2003
Vermont	1	3	2	4	2
Virginia	129	200	227	387	415
Washington	871	1,001	1,175	1,160	1,090
West Virginia	973	1,130	1,220	1,048	981
Wisconsin	24	34	29	22	41
Wyoming	7	15	26	19	27
Puerto Rico	843	862	796	775	714
United States	**56,137**	**58,182**	**58,371**	**57,942**	**56,870**
Alberta	751	903	944	914	821
British Columbia	716	772	856	786	739
Manitoba	125	152	165	184	193
New Brunswick	1	1	2	3	1
Nova Scotia	0	0	0	1	1
Ontario	1,418	1,491	1,493	1,619	1,530
Prince Edward Island	4	0	0	0	0
Quebec	5	11	14	13	0
Saskatchewan	153	162	153	163	123
Canada	**3,173**	**3,492**	**3,627**	**3,683**	**3,408**

	2007	2006	2005	2004	2003
New Hampshire	1	0	0	0	0
New Jersey	24	30	24	25	33
New Mexico	166	166	166	148	141
New York	106	114	115	142	145
North Carolina	9	11	12	17	15
North Dakota	20	16	16	19	14
Ohio	61	69	78	83	89
Oklahoma	162	192	188	171	176
Oregon	51	52	52	46	44
Pennsylvania	88	113	118	109	104
Rhode Island	0	1	1	1	2
South Carolina	22	18	23	24	23
South Dakota	12	14	16	9	13
Tennessee	19	23	22	13	17
Texas	264	288	310	319	335
Utah	22	34	26	27	24
Vermont	1	2	1	3	2
Virginia	38	55	55	53	53
Washington	68	78	89	94	79
West Virginia	76	75	88	77	73
Wisconsin	4	9	10	7	12
Wyoming	4	7	7	6	11
Puerto Rico	69	69	57	53	58
United States	**3,052**	**3,250**	**3,321**	**3,407**	**3,374**
Alberta	75	76	83	71	80
British Columbia	53	59	57	58	54
Manitoba	18	22	21	21	20
New Brunswick	1	1	1	2	1
Nova Scotia	0	0	0	1	1
Ontario	88	95	96	102	111
Prince Edward Island	2	0	0	0	0
Quebec	3	3	3	4	0
Saskatchewan	22	21	20	20	20
Canada	**262**	**277**	**281**	**279**	**287**

Mares Bred in North America, 1997-2007

Year	Mares Bred	Change
2007	59,310	−3.8%
2006	61,674	−0.5%
2005	61,998	+0.6%
2004	61,625	+2.2%
2003	60,278	−1.7%
2002	61,299	+0.2%
2001	61,185	+4.0%
2000	58,856	+3.6%
1999	56,790	+2.2%
1998	55,543	−2.2%
1997	56,791	

North American Stallions in Production, 2003-2007

	2007	2006	2005	2004	2003
North America	3,314	3,527	3,602	3,686	3,661
Alabama	20	19	19	25	19
Alaska	0	0	1	1	1
Arizona	49	61	50	53	51
Arkansas	63	61	57	68	60
California	280	293	319	376	363
Colorado	46	47	49	62	69
Connecticut	1	3	0	1	1
Delaware	1	1	0	0	0
Florida	233	226	235	228	238
Georgia	13	12	18	20	15
Idaho	31	35	34	45	42
Illinois	88	101	95	111	105
Indiana	69	73	80	86	89
Iowa	37	40	39	45	42
Kansas	23	22	20	25	25
Kentucky	354	357	349	352	364
Louisiana	289	273	270	228	194
Maine	0	0	0	0	2
Maryland	54	64	71	67	73
Massachusetts	9	8	10	17	19
Michigan	52	54	47	57	61
Minnesota	33	36	35	32	30
Mississippi	10	9	13	14	14
Missouri	17	16	17	17	17
Montana	28	33	34	42	33
Nebraska	28	34	37	36	38
Nevada	6	5	5	6	4

North American Stallions in Production, 1997-2007

Year	Stallions Standing	Change
2007	3,314	−6.0%
2006	3,527	−2.1%
2005	3,602	−2.3%
2004	3,686	+0.7%
2003	3,661	−2.8%
2002	3,766	−4.5%
2001	3,945	+11.5%
2000	3,539	−3.6%
1999	3,672	−3.3%
1998	3,797	−9.1%
1997	4,178	

North American Live Foals, 1997-2007

Year	Live Foals	Change
2007	40,106	−2.5%
2006	41,115	+1.3%
2005	40,607	+2.0%
2004	39,812	+2.6%
2003	38,793	+2.6%
2002	37,796	−6.2%
2001	40,309	+10.2%
2000	36,567	+5.7%
1999	34,594	+1.7%
1998	34,030	+1.8%
1997	33,443	

North American Live Foals, 2003-2007

	2007	2006	2005	2004	2003
North America	40,106	41,115	40,607	39,812	38,793
Alabama	42	66	60	58	53
Alaska	0	2	1	1	1
Arizona	326	333	317	338	316
Arkansas	281	302	335	306	353
California	3,354	3,632	3,960	4,045	4,043
Colorado	177	227	253	264	225
Connecticut	5	0	0	0	0
Delaware	2	0	1	1	2
Florida	4,426	4,474	4,290	4,229	4,595
Georgia	37	59	51	55	68
Hawaii	0	0	1	0	0
Idaho	125	144	165	151	128
Illinois	499	536	621	600	593
Indiana	209	277	346	420	408
Iowa	230	282	285	342	314
Kansas	61	84	80	84	72
Kentucky	15,463	15,393	14,748	14,476	13,076
Louisiana	2,266	2,101	1,880	1,598	1,275
Maine	0	0	2	0	3
Maryland	1,078	1,152	1,076	1,081	1,231
Massachusetts	15	20	37	50	76
Michigan	306	278	330	318	284
Minnesota	200	231	169	194	168
Mississippi	17	22	35	33	33
Missouri	23	53	49	51	65
Montana	78	89	107	103	119
Nebraska	189	171	204	169	179
Nevada	8	8	7	11	9
New Hampshire	0	0	1	1	0
New Jersey	267	191	163	208	271
New Mexico	1,184	1,083	932	808	771
New York	1,423	1,452	1,656	1,703	1,587
North Carolina	37	32	31	33	37
North Dakota	70	50	43	42	43
Ohio	196	253	293	343	459
Oklahoma	767	895	845	814	897
Oregon	266	282	302	274	255
Pennsylvania	665	709	574	574	607
Puerto Rico	602	555	552	530	512
Rhode Island	2	2	1	1	0
South Carolina	62	58	67	51	76
South Dakota	49	53	54	40	46
Tennessee	60	45	35	44	54
Texas	1,495	1,652	1,710	1,835	1,881
Utah	142	96	112	58	55
Vermont	3	1	3	1	6
Virginia	135	133	240	285	311
Washington	607	727	738	603	706
West Virginia	659	654	542	548	468
Wisconsin	14	17	7	22	16
Wyoming	10	11	13	13	20
United States	**38,132**	**38,887**	**38,324**	**37,809**	**36,767**
Alberta	414	545	524	449	456
British Columbia	462	523	502	452	441
Manitoba	62	76	95	82	91
New Brunswick	1	4	1	1	0
Nova Scotia	0	0	0	1	4
Ontario	949	995	1,067	958	941
Prince Edward Island	0	0	0	0	12
Quebec	5	0	3	0	8
Saskatchewan	81	85	91	60	73
Canada	**1,974**	**2,228**	**2,283**	**2,003**	**2,026**

Aggregate Revenues From Stud Fees by Year, 2001-2007

Year	Aggregate	Change
2007	$634,416,950	8.9%
2006	582,765,900	10.9%
2005	525,556,950	6.0%
2004	495,898,625	–4.8%
2003	520,932,750	10.8%
2002	470,076,700	5.4%
2001	445,861,075	

Average North American Stud Fees by Year, 2001-2007

Year	Average	Change
2007	$18,378	10.0%
2006	16,714	10.0%
2005	15,189	3.3%
2004	14,710	–9.5%
2003	16,258	8.3%
2002	15,028	11.1%
2001	13,531	

Aggregate Revenues From Stud Fees, 2003-2007

Calculated by multiplying actual number of live foals by stallion times the stud fee in preceding year.

	2007	2006	2005	2004	2003
North America	**$634,416,950**	**$582,765,900**	**$525,556,950**	**$495,898,625**	**$520,932,750**
Alabama	37,250	38,350	26,100	33,500	48,700
Arizona	276,550	188,300	191,600	179,250	151,350
Arkansas	300,400	254,300	332,500	309,250	295,250
California	13,508,450	14,776,700	16,399,200	17,631,950	15,087,850
Colorado	395,600	133,050	215,250	207,000	184,300
Florida	24,915,250	23,524,050	22,145,000	21,602,950	20,760,800
Georgia	27,800	43,950	18,100	28,450	27,400
Idaho	55,750	106,000	127,450	77,300	110,000
Illinois	576,350	409,700	815,750	698,950	668,950
Indiana	123,200	279,750	373,450	443,600	322,100
Iowa	358,850	399,800	472,650	499,450	349,300
Kansas	31,750	45,000	17,100	16,450	27,750
Kentucky	557,704,750	506,187,050	448,619,300	420,514,550	448,111,500
Louisiana	3,131,900	3,003,850	2,714,950	1,927,700	1,334,350
Maine	0	0	0	0	1,000

State of the Industry — Stud Fees by State

	2007	2006	2005	2004	2003
Maryland	$ 6,971,750	$ 7,843,500	$ 7,785,250	$ 7,031,850	$ 8,488,400
Massachusetts	8,000	9,000	21,500	31,000	41,500
Michigan	305,300	265,700	319,700	317,650	284,900
Minnesota	333,800	355,950	232,650	221,350	142,100
Mississippi	1,000	1,000	3,500	6,750	5,050
Missouri	15,500	21,100	22,000	9,500	13,700
Montana	26,350	47,200	51,050	32,600	45,700
Nebraska	214,000	130,750	143,750	112,000	132,500
Nevada	0	0	5,000	0	2,500
New Jersey	700,500	421,000	411,000	505,250	658,500
New Mexico	2,429,850	1,826,950	1,560,000	924,000	669,350
New York	7,100,000	7,161,250	8,092,350	8,960,050	8,581,750
North Carolina	37,750	36,750	2,000	19,800	25,800
North Dakota	31,800	27,250	16,700	14,500	28,600
Ohio	161,500	182,350	203,900	210,450	360,100
Oklahoma	606,800	737,200	619,400	706,675	664,800
Oregon	293,250	282,300	327,500	294,800	264,000
Pennsylvania	1,779,250	1,546,750	1,174,250	998,750	960,250
Puerto Rico	438,500	392,000	152,000	331,000	117,500
South Carolina	41,250	26,500	30,500	17,850	22,500
South Dakota	12,100	33,300	41,600	27,900	20,100
Tennessee	8,400	12,750	7,550	9,800	13,000
Texas	2,921,000	3,360,900	3,565,850	3,916,550	4,238,000
Utah	253,500	13,500	34,500	8,800	10,100
Virginia	38,100	67,750	780,800	746,750	795,500
Washington	1,245,150	1,243,550	1,179,450	808,300	1,104,450
West Virginia	1,245,500	1,434,600	763,350	837,200	596,000
Wisconsin	1,000	0	600	2,800	0
Wyoming	1,000	1,000	5,000	2,950	0
United States	**$628,665,750**	**$576,871,700**	**$520,021,100**	**$491,277,225**	**$515,767,250**
Alberta	$ 769,000	$ 859,450	$ 690,000	$ 637,000	$ 701,250
British Columbia	1,041,700	1,051,000	1,034,850	1,032,000	940,350
Manitoba	50,000	35,750	76,400	45,800	55,800
Ontario	3,842,500	3,914,500	3,654,700	2,856,700	3,438,250
Saskatchewan	48,000	33,500	79,900	49,900	29,850
Canada	**$5,751,200**	**$5,894,200**	**$5,535,850**	**$4,621,400**	**$5,165,500**

Average North American Stud Fees, 2003-2007

	2007	2006	2005	2004	2003
NORTH AMERICA	$18,380	$16,715	$15,190	$14,711	$16,259
Alabama	1,490	1,370	1,305	1,288	1,571
Arizona	1,323	1,088	1,228	1,080	1,173
Arkansas	1,589	1,278	1,205	1,222	1,140
California	4,871	4,856	5,109	5,221	5,019
Colorado	3,297	1,109	1,321	1,310	1,631
Florida	6,077	5,670	5,543	5,297	4,979
Georgia	1,264	1,831	1,207	1,355	1,442
Idaho	1,014	1,359	1,225	1,017	1,467
Illinois	1,597	1,576	1,728	1,652	1,604
Indiana	1,400	1,655	1,675	1,680	1,220
Iowa	1,940	1,834	1,921	1,777	1,397
Kansas	962	918	900	823	816
Kentucky	36,609	33,773	31,107	30,030	34,930
Louisiana	1,842	1,745	1,774	1,493	1,333
Maine					500
Maryland	6,723	7,269	7,443	6,801	7,175
Massachusetts	1,000	1,000	1,433	1,409	1,297
Michigan	1,696	1,954	1,816	1,755	1,737
Minnesota	1,677	1,663	1,723	1,570	1,366
Mississippi	1,000	1,000	700	563	561
Missouri	1,107	1,055	1,158	950	913
Montana	850	1,098	865	776	879
Nebraska	1,659	1,308	1,188	1,287	1,366
Nevada			2,500		2,500
New Jersey	3,019	2,665	2,834	2,871	2,953
New Mexico	2,721	2,407	2,604	2,281	1,875
New York	$5,160	$4,918	$5,218	$5,938	$6,099
North Carolina	2,221	2,297	1,000	990	1,032
North Dakota	935	908	928	630	894
Ohio	1,242	1,436	1,324	1,291	1,349
Oklahoma	1,395	1,443	1,153	1,260	1,227
Oregon	1,298	1,357	1,300	1,254	1,195
Pennsylvania	3,031	2,451	2,207	2,094	2,017
Puerto Rico	2,707	2,631	1,854	2,399	1,780
South Carolina	1,115	1,060	1,220	939	833
South Dakota	864	925	904	900	874
Tennessee	764	911	755	700	929
Texas	3,052	3,003	2,848	2,916	3,273
Utah	3,292	1,227	1,190	800	481
Virginia	2,117	1,232	4,109	3,539	3,414
Washington	2,521	2,396	2,176	2,138	2,004
West Virginia	2,328	2,594	1,739	1,800	1,509
Wisconsin	500		300	933	
Wyoming	1,000	1,000	1,000	738	
UNITED STATES	**$19,090**	**$17,376**	**$15,835**	**$15,280**	**$16,949**
Alberta	$2,323	$2,170	$1,971	$1,954	$2,021
British Columbia	2,815	3,055	2,835	2,723	2,718
Manitoba	1,111	993	1,124	935	858
Ontario	4,797	4,531	3,955	3,700	4,152
Saskatchewan	1,263	1,288	1,567	1,559	1,298
CANADA	**$3,629**	**$3,538**	**$3,149**	**$2,966**	**$3,210**

All About Purses 2007

by Don Clippinger

Purses in 2007 clearly reflected the effects of new money from sources other than pari-mutuel wagering. As reported in the *2008 Jockey Club Fact Book* based on Equibase figures, pari-mutuel wagering on Thoroughbred racing declined 0.5% in '07, to $15.23-billion in the United States and Canada. At the same time, North American purses climbed to a record $1,251,579,551.

For the first time, purses in the U.S. and Canada passed the $1.2-billion milestone in 2007, and total payments to horse owners were up 5.2% from '06. Average earnings per starter, average purse per race, and median earnings per runner also were records in current dollars, although not in inflation-adjusted dollars.

While 5.2% is most certainly a very healthy number, the sheer magnitude of the increase in dollars is striking. Purse payments to horse owners increased $62.3-million in 2007 from the previous year. Eliminating such effects as three new $1-million Breeders' Cup races and a stronger Canadian dollar, the sport had more than $50-million in new purse money, a huge amount by any measure.

When purses increase more than $50-million while pari-mutuel play is essentially flat, the effects of other forms of gaming on Thoroughbred racing become obvious. The direct relationship of pari-mutuel wagering to purses has been broken as gaming's contribution to purses now approaches 25%.

Still, the 2007 purse numbers were something to crow about, although it must be noted that it remains difficult for the horse owner to break even, much less produce a substantial profit. Here are some highlights of the 2007 purses report:

- Purses in the U.S. and Canada totaled $1,251,579,551, up 5.2% from a record $1,189,277,214 in 2006. The percentage increase was the largest since an 8.5% jump in 2000, when the full-card simulcasting revolution was at its peak;
- Purses were paid in 56,202 races, a nearly 1% decline from 2006 and the fewest races held in North America since 1970;
- Average purse per race soared to a record $22,269, up 6.2% because substantially more money was spread over fewer races;
- The total number of runners increased slightly to 72,691 after two years of fewer starters;
- Average earnings per runner rose 4.9% to a record $17,218;
- Real average earnings per runner—adjusted for inflation—increased 2.2% to $14,387, the second increase in a row but still well below the high-water mark of $15,798 in 2000;
- The midpoint of all purses, known as the median, increased in current dollars but not in inflation-adjusted dollars. The current-dollar median earnings per runner, $6,680, was a record but remained far below the amount needed to pay for a horse's upkeep for a year;
- A total of 3,720 runners—5.1% of all starters—failed to earn any part of a purse. It was the lowest percentage of nonearners in recent history;
- Even though more horses collected a piece of a purse, fewer than half of all starters, 46.5%, won a race in 2007;
- Horses that won at least one race earned an average of $32,537; horses that failed to win a race earned an average of $3,881;
- Horses that won a stakes race earned an average of $161,527;

Table 1
Selected Racing Statistics, North American Thoroughbred Racing, 1998-2007

Year	No. of Runners	No. of Races	Total Purses	Average Purse	Earnings per Runner Average	Earnings per Runner Median	Percentage of Runners Earning Purses
2007	72,691	56,202	$ 1,251,579,551	$22,269	$17,218	$6,680	94.9%
2006	72,445	56,730	1,189,277,214	20,964	16,416	6,520	92.8%
2005	72,487	57,305	1,149,003,138	20,051	15,851	6,135	92.2%
2004	73,915	58,686	1,177,769,765	20,069	15,934	5,877	91.5%
2003	73,614	58,813	1,154,238,845	19,626	15,680	5,714	90.3%
2002	72,504	59,712	1,170,169,267	19,597	16,139	6,003	89.6%
2001	70,942	60,538	1,146,337,367	18,936	16,159	6,010	90.6%
2000	69,230	60,579	1,093,661,241	18,053	15,798	5,796	90.2%
1999	68,435	60,118	1,008,162,608	16,770	14,732	5,310	89.1%
1998	68,419	61,141	968,366,929	15,838	14,153	4,939	88.8%
Change:							
2006-2007	0.3%	−0.9%	5.2%	6.2%	4.9%	2.4%	
1998-2007	6.2%	−8.1%	29.3%	40.6%	21.7%	35.2%	
Average Change:							
1998-2007	0.6%	−0.8%	2.9%	4.1%	2.2%	3.5%	

Table 2
Distribution of Earnings of Runners for 2007

Earnings Range	No. of Runners	Percent of Runners	Earnings	Percent of Earnings	Average Earnings
$300,000 or more	197	0.3%	122,980,619	9.8%	624,267
$200,000 - 299,999	203	0.3%	49,008,531	3.9%	241,421
$100,000 - 199,999	1,077	1.5%	143,910,077	11.5%	133,621
$75,000 - 99,999	1,135	1.6%	97,206,444	7.8%	85,644
$50,000 - 74,999	2,711	3.7%	163,986,426	13.1%	60,489
$25,000 - 49,999	8,369	11.5%	292,438,264	23.4%	34,943
$20,000 - 24,999	3,606	5.0%	80,595,362	6.4%	22,350
$15,000 - 19,999	5,093	7.0%	88,402,520	7.1%	17,358
$10,000 - 14,999	7,338	10.1%	90,414,237	7.2%	12,321
$9,000 - 9,999	1,856	2.6%	17,587,508	1.4%	9,476
$8,000 - 8,999	1,934	2.7%	16,400,860	1.3%	8,480
$7,000 - 7,999	2,108	2.9%	15,796,006	1.3%	7,493
$6,000 - 6,999	2,293	3.2%	14,871,647	1.2%	6,486
$5,000 - 5,999	2,440	3.4%	13,382,912	1.1%	5,485
$4,000 - 4,999	2,584	3.6%	11,610,140	0.9%	4,493
$3,000 - 3,999	2,982	4.1%	10,391,787	0.8%	3,485
$2,000 - 2,999	3,686	5.1%	9,114,034	0.7%	2,473
$1,000 - 1,999	5,367	7.4%	7,773,677	0.6%	1,448
$1 - 999	13,992	19.2%	5,708,500	0.5%	408
None	3,720	5.1%	0	0.0%	0
Totals	**72,691**	**100.0%**	**1,251,579,551**	**100.0%**	**17,218**

- Race winners collectively earned 88% of all purse money, unchanged from 2006;
- Stakes races constituted 4.8% of all races and offered 24.9% of all purses. Optional claiming races continued to increase in popularity, and they remained the second-best-paid category of races by average purse per race;
- Claiming races accounted for 66.1% of all races but distributed just 37% of all purses;
- The average number of starts per horse continued its long slide to 6.3 in 2007, the fewest ever; and
- Average field size inched up to 8.2 starters per race and remained in the narrow range that statistic has occupied since the mid-1990s.

This is the 35th year that "All About Purses" has been published. As in the past, the statistics encompass all Thoroughbred purses distributed to racehorses in North America in 2007, excluding Mexico and Puerto Rico, and were provided to THOROUGHBRED TIMES based on data obtained from the Jockey Club Information Services Inc. Steeplechase races are excluded.

Record Purses in 2007

The broadest measures of North American purses are contained in **Table 1**, which also contains some of the brightest highlights of the year. Total purses—defined as the money actually paid to horse owners rather than the advertised purses of races—surged 5.2% to a record $1,251,579,551.

The other significant measures were also records. Average purse per race climbed to $22,269, a 6.2% increase with the assistance of fewer races. In general, races have been declining since a peak of 82,726 in 1989.

The larger number of runners, 72,691, is by no means a record. That statistic topped out at 91,436 in 1989, at the end of a bloodstock-market bubble that resulted in extreme overproduction.

The average earnings per starter of $17,218 was a record, and the record median—half above that earnings level and half below—provided further illustration of how difficult it is to make a profit with racehorses. The midpoint of racetrack earnings in 2007 was $6,680 per runner, up 2.5% from '06.

Even in the most economical markets, a horse that earns the median is making only roughly one-quarter of its upkeep, and a horse making the average is unprofitable in most markets.

Over the landscape of two decades, year-to-year statistics illustrate the industry's trajectory from a time when most wagering was conducted on live races at the racetrack, to a period when full-card simulcast racing reigned, to the present time when revenues generated outside the racing enclosure have become a significant contributor to purses.

Going back 20 years to 1988, purses totaled $736.7-million, which reflected an anemic industry that was almost entirely dependent upon the money gambled at the track on live racing for its purses. Beginning in 1994, full-card simulcasting began to pick up steam, after purses had declined nearly 3% in the preceding year. Over the next few years, full-card wagering revitalized the industry. Total purses climbed above $1-billion for the first time in 1999, and they have remained above that benchmark.

Table 3
Earnings as a Function of Number of Wins for 2007

Races Won	No. of Runners	Percent of Runners	Total Earnings	Percent of Earnings	Average Earnings
More than 13	1	0.0%	$ 150,144	0.0%	$150,144
13	0	0.0%	0	0.0%	0
12	0	0.0%	0	0.0%	0
11	2	0.0%	221,715	0.0%	110,858
10	1	0.0%	63,166	0.0%	63,166
9	1	0.0%	65,044	0.0%	65,044
8	18	0.0%	2,028,065	0.2%	112,670
7	39	0.1%	5,376,023	0.4%	137,847
6	146	0.2%	19,361,983	1.5%	132,616
5	407	0.6%	40,596,306	3.2%	99,745
4	1,345	1.9%	113,432,388	9.1%	84,336
3	3,510	4.8%	200,264,922	16.0%	57,056
2	8,649	11.9%	327,637,458	26.2%	37,882
1	19,712	27.1%	391,569,346	31.3%	19,865
0	38,860	53.5%	150,812,991	12.0%	3,881
Totals	72,691	100.0%	$1,251,579,551	100.0%	$ 17,218

In 2000, purses increased 8.5% to nearly $1.1-billion. But as the betting market became saturated, the increases slowed and then stopped before the trend line turned upward in 2006 as more and more non-pari-mutuel money fed into purses. In all likelihood, that trend will continue for the foreseeable future.

Table 2 shows purses according to the annual earnings of all runners, and 3,720 horses had no earnings, which represented 5.1% of all starters. That number is most notable for the change from 2006, when 5,194 horses, or 7.2% of all starters, did not earn any purse money. In one year, more than 2% of all starters moved from zero earnings to at least a few dollars on their earnings tabs.

To be sure, the percentage of purse earners has been moving up steadily over the last 20 years. In 1998, the percentage of horses that earned purses was 88.8%, or a full 6.1 percentage points lower than the 2007 tally of 94.9% earners. Most of the change in the distribution of earnings occurred at the lower earnings levels. The next level up, horses that earned between $1 and $999, contained 13,992 horses, or 19.2% of all starters in 2007. A year earlier, 12,947 horses, or 17.9% of all starters, fell into that category. Taken together, the horses earning less than $1,000 in 2007 totaled 24.4%, while the same group amounted to 25.1% a year earlier. Exactly 400 runners earned $200,000 or more, and their earnings totaled $172,018,150, or 13.7% of all purses.

Inflation Effects

Total purses in real terms—with the effects of inflation removed—were up 2.5% to $1,045,824,536 in 2007. Average purse per race was an inflation-adjusted $18,608, a 3.5% increase over 2006.

Those numbers are good but not great. Real total purses topped out at $1,123,143,259 in 2002, and they have not been within hailing distance of that level since. The deflated average purse per race also topped out in 2002, at $18,809.

The numbers turn slightly sour when earnings per runner are adjusted for inflationary effects. To be sure, real average earnings per runner rose in 2007, to $14,387, a 2.2% increase because of more runners competing for the available purse dollars. But the median per runner declined, albeit less than one-quarter of a percentage point.

Looking over the span of a decade, inflation-adjusted numbers reveal that, while the sport has made some notable progress, it has not zoomed ahead. In ten years, inflation-adjusted total purses grew by a modest 4.2%, which means that the year-to-year increase was less than one-half percent. In real terms, even with new money entering the sport, the industry has been standing still.

Real average earnings per runner actually declined, by 1.9% over the decade since 1998, while inflation-adjusted median earnings per runner rose 9%, or less than 1% a year. The most significant growth has been in real average purse per race, but its 13.3% increase in ten years is largely attributable to 8.1% fewer races over that period.

Starting and Winning

To win, you must start. To win a lot of purse money, you must be sound enough to make a significant number of starts—up to a point where the rule of diminishing returns begins to take hold. A horse that managed only one start in 2007 earned an average of $2,151. As the number of starts increases, the average earnings of those runners increased, too. At ten starts, average earnings rose to $29,702. The upward progression of average earnings was steady to nine starts, which had a modest dip from eight starts.

Horses that start more than ten times in a year often race at lower levels and must try to compensate for smaller pots by making more starts. The 85 horses that made more than 21 starts were, on a start-by-start basis, the worst paid in the sport. Taken together, they earned barely $2-million, and their earnings per start were $1,030, the lowest of any category.

Starting certainly is important, but winning is just about everything. As shown in **Table 3**, 53.5% of all runners never found their way to the winner's circle in 2007. Those 38,860 starters earned 12% of all purses in 2007, but their average earnings were a paltry $3,881, or less than one-quarter of the year's average earnings per runner of $17,218.

One win boosts the horse above the average earnings per runner, to $19,865. Slightly more than one-quarter of all starters in 2007 were able to manage a single victory. Those two groups, nonwinners and those with only victory, accounted for four of every five starters (80.6%).

Win by win, the numbers grow smaller and the share of purses grows larger—again, up to a point. In 2007, 11.9% of all starters managed two victories, and their average earnings rose to $37,882. No wins through two wins account for more than nine of every ten starters.

Thus, a horse that can win three or more races is rare. Only 3,510 horses won three races in 2007, and their average earnings were $57,056. The upward progression continues to the 39 horses that won seven races in 2007; their average earnings were $137,847.

In most years, average earnings trend downward after seven wins, but not in 2007. The highest average earnings belonged to Golden Hare, who won an amazing 14 races in 2007 and earned $150,144. The Gilded Time gelding won three more races than any other starter. The two horses to win 11 races in 2007, Fortunate Trail and Princess

Table 4
Distribution of Races and Purses by Age and Sex for 2007

Sex	No. of Races	Percent of Races	Purses	Percent of Purses	Average Purse per Race
TWO-YEAR-OLDS					
Females	2,051	3.6%	$ 67,600,444	5.4%	$32,960
Males	56	0.1%	4,842,011	0.4%	86,464
Either Sex	2,389	4.3%	74,077,686	5.9%	31,008
Overall	4,496	8.0%	146,520,141	11.7%	32,589
THREE-YEAR-OLDS					
Females	2,756	4.9%	88,400,682	7.1%	32,076
Males	44	0.1%	2,355,573	0.2%	53,536
Either Sex	2,967	5.3%	110,928,463	8.9%	37,387
Overall	5,767	10.3%	201,684,718	16.1%	34,972
THREE-YEAR-OLDS AND UP					
Females	15,333	27.3%	300,447,101	24.0%	19,595
Males	92	0.2%	1,374,277	0.1%	14,938
Either Sex	22,861	40.7%	429,770,437	34.3%	18,799
Overall	38,286	68.1%	731,591,815	58.5%	19,109
FOUR-YEAR-OLDS					
Females	45	0.1%	1,561,323	0.1%	34,696
Males	0	0.0%	0	0.0%	0
Either sex	81	0.1%	2,560,292	0.2%	31,609
Overall	126	0.2%	4,121,615	0.3%	32,711
FOUR-YEAR-OLDS AND UP					
Females	2,846	5.1%	64,411,133	5.1%	22,632
Males	10	0.0%	380,530	0.0%	38,053
Either sex	4,662	8.3%	102,772,657	8.2%	22,045
Overall	7,518	13.4%	167,564,320	13.4%	22,288
FIVE-YEAR-OLDS AND UP					
Females	0	0.0%	0	0.0%	0
Males	0	0.0%	0	0.0%	0
Either Sex	9	0.0%	96,942	0.0%	10,771
Overall	9	0.0%	96,942	0.0%	10,771
TOTALS					
Females	23,031	41.0%	$ 522,420,683	41.7%	$22,683
Males	202	0.4%	$ 8,952,391	0.7%	$44,319
Either Sex	32,969	58.7%	$ 720,206,477	57.5%	$21,845
Overall	56,202	100.0%	$1,251,579,551	100.0%	$22,269

Composer, each won more than $100,000.

Winners collected 88% of all purse money in 2007, unchanged from the previous year (**Figure 1**). By contrast, a horse that could not win but finished second at least once received just 8.5% of all purse money. The horses whose best finish was second had average earnings of $9,940, which would not come close to paying its annual training fees.

For lower finishers, the shares of the purse and average earnings become truly paltry. A horse that could finish no better than sixth in 2007 had average earnings of $272.

Age and Sex

Table 4 demonstrates how the racetrack is very much a male's world. They have more opportunities, and that advantage translates into more purse money. Because of fewer chances to race for purse money, races limited to fillies and mares sometimes have a higher average purse.

In the big picture, fillies and mares lost a little ground in 2007. Racing secretaries wrote

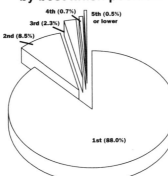

Figure 1
Distribution of purses by best finish position

23,031 races for females in 2007, down from 23,319 in '06. The percentage of female-only races slipped very slightly from 41.1% in 2006 to 41% in '07.

To be sure, the total purses available to fillies and mares increased, to $522,420,683 from $498,364,046 a year earlier, but the percentage of purse money allotted to fillies and mares declined to 41.7% from 41.9%.

The only bright spot for females was that overall they had a higher purse per race, $22,683, than the open races, which averaged $21,845.

Table 5 looks at the disparities between males and females from another perspective, by the number of runners of each sex on the racetrack and the purses they earn. At younger ages, males and females have similar numbers of starters. For two-year-old races in 2007, 5,735 runners were female and 5,937 were male. That is a difference of only 202 runners, but the money was not divided proportionately. Thus, juvenile males averaged $12,892 to $12,205 for fillies.

For three-year-olds in 2007, male runners out-

Table 5
Distribution of Runners and Earnings by Age and Sex for 2007

Sex	No. of Runners	Percent of Runners	Earnings	Percent of Earnings	Avg. Earnings
			TWO-YEAR-OLDS		
Females	5,735	7.9%	$ 69,992,835	5.6%	$12,205
Males	5,937	8.2%	76,537,760	6.1%	12,892
Overall	11,674	16.1%	146,540,505	11.7%	12,553
			THREE-YEAR-OLDS		
Females	10,493	14.4%	200,987,888	16.1%	19,154
Males	10,908	15.0%	235,271,967	18.8%	21,569
Overall	21,402	29.4%	436,271,411	34.9%	20,385
			FOUR-YEAR-OLDS		
Females	7,777	10.7%	150,870,818	12.1%	19,400
Males	8,980	12.4%	179,276,383	14.3%	19,964
Overall	16,757	23.1%	330,147,201	26.4%	19,702
			FIVE-YEAR-OLDS		
Females	4,182	5.8%	65,957,513	5.3%	15,772
Males	5,980	8.2%	107,572,363	8.6%	17,989
Overall	10,163	14.0%	173,530,954	13.9%	17,075
			SIX-YEAR-OLDS AND UP		
Females	3,698	5.1%	40,164,537	3.2%	10,861
Males	8,996	12.4%	124,917,222	10.0%	13,886
Overall	12,695	17.5%	165,084,309	13.2%	13,004
			TOTALS		
Females	**31,885**	**43.9%**	**$ 527,973,591**	**42.2%**	**$16,559**
Males	**40,801**	**56.1%**	**$ 723,580,866**	**57.8%**	**$17,734**
Overall	**72,691**	**100.0%**	**$1,251,579,551**	**100.0%**	**$17,218**

Table 6
Distribution of Races by Class for 2007

CLAIMING	No. of Races	Percent of Races	No. of Starts	Average Starters	Purses	Percent of Purses	Avg. Purse per Race
CLAIMING	26,808	47.7%	216,456	8.1	$331,465,170	26.5%	$12,364
$0 to 999	0	0.0%	0	0.0	0	0.0%	0
$1,000 to 1,999	97	0.2%	674	6.9	228,133	0.0%	2,352
$2,000 to 2,999	1,372	2.4%	10,578	7.7	5,711,714	0.5%	4,163
$3,000 to 3,999	1,856	3.3%	15,160	8.2	10,175,234	0.8%	5,482
$4,000 to 4,999	4,529	8.1%	37,662	8.3	35,343,264	2.8%	7,804
$5,000 to 5,999	5,414	9.6%	46,138	8.5	51,885,638	4.1%	9,584
$6,000 to 6,999	1,224	2.2%	9,800	8.0	13,568,485	1.1%	11,085
$7,000 to 7,999	2,120	3.8%	17,114	8.1	22,712,941	1.8%	10,714
$8,000 to 8,999	693	1.2%	5,478	7.9	7,290,130	0.6%	10,520
$9,000 to 9,999	12	0.0%	86	7.2	105,701	0.0%	8,808
$10,000 to 14,999	3,861	6.9%	30,426	7.9	55,406,526	4.4%	14,350
$15,000 to 19,999	2,179	3.9%	16,728	7.7	36,003,959	2.9%	16,523
$20,000 and up	3,451	6.1%	26,612	7.7	93,033,445	7.4%	26,958
TOTAL CLAIMING	**37,150**	**66.1%**	**307,598**	**8.3**	**462,560,424**	**37.0%**	**12,451**
Optional Claiming	2,856	5.1%	20,679	7.2	99,856,039	8.0%	34,964
Starter Allowance	1,250	2.2%	9,150	7.3	22,229,565	1.8%	17,784
Starter Handicap	104	0.2%	811	7.8	2,680,086	0.2%	25,770
Maiden	6,293	11.2%	54,836	8.7	178,409,459	14.3%	28,350
Allowance	5,813	10.3%	45,234	7.8	173,189,569	13.8%	29,793
Handicap	56	0.1%	350	6.3	939,390	0.1%	16,775
Stakes	2,680	4.8%	20,614	7.7	311,715,019	24.9%	116,312
TOTAL NONCLAIMING	**19,052**	**33.9%**	**151,674**	**8.0**	**789,019,127**	**63.0%**	**41,414**
TOTAL ALL RACES	**56,202**	**100.0%**	**459,272**	**8.2**	**$1,251,579,551**	**100.0%**	**$22,269**

numbered fillies by slightly more than 400 starters. But the males earned purses of $235,271,967 compared with $200,987,888 for fillies. Males had average earnings of $21,569 compared with $19,154 for fillies.

Distribution of Races

Higher purse levels in 2007 benefited all races, but some received a bigger boost than others. Some changes in how purse money is distributed are contained in **Table 6**, which looks at the classes of races and the purse money distributed in them.

Claimers long have been the bedrock of American racing, and they continue to account for roughly two-thirds of all races. The percentage, once higher than 70%, has moved up and down within a fairly narrow range in the last decade. In 2007, 66.1% of all races were claimers, up from 65.6% the previous year.

Those races were paid 37% of all purses in both years, so claiming races lost a little ground in 2007 with a larger percentage of races and the same proportion of purse money. The number of claiming races actually slipped, to 37,150 from 37,208 in 2006.

The average purse paid to claimers increased to $12,451 from $11,815, a 5.4% increase. Stakes races accounted for only 4.8% of races (up mod-

Table 7
Distribution of all North American Races by Purse for 2007

Range of Purses	No. of Races	Total Purses
$499 or less	3	$ 0
$500-999	2	1,600
$1,000-1,999	264	441,387
$2,000-2,999	690	1,716,741
$3,000-3,999	1,004	3,439,596
$4,000-4,999	2,083	9,161,002
$5,000-5,999	1,732	9,367,804
$6,000-6,999	3,898	25,074,475
$7,000-7,999	2,493	18,460,079
$8,000-8,999	3,373	28,275,436
$9,000-9,999	3,594	33,495,198
$10,000-12,499	6,725	74,321,929
$12,500-14,999	4,212	57,486,855
$15,000-19,999	7,729	132,050,090
$20,000-24,999	4,190	92,934,224
$25,000-29,999	3,603	97,175,626
$30,000-39,999	3,400	114,207,315
$40,000-49,999	3,151	140,481,845
$50,000-74,999	2,651	154,040,037
$75,000-99,999	426	35,008,902
$100,000-199,999	657	82,316,386
$200,000-299,999	157	36,829,282
$300,000-399,999	50	15,798,519
$400,000-499,999	27	11,382,852
$500,000-749,999	44	23,661,056
$750,000-999,999	17	13,649,414
$1,000,000 and up	27	40,801,901
Totals	**56,202**	**$1,251,579,551**

Table 8
Average Field Size and Number of Starts

Year	Avg. Number of Starts	Avg. Field Size	Year	Avg. Number of Starts	Avg. Field Size
2007	6.3	8.2	1997	7.6	8.2
2006	6.4	8.1	1996	7.6	8.3
2005	6.5	8.2	1995	7.7	8.2
2004	6.6	8.3	1994	7.8	8.3
2003	6.6	8.3	1993	7.9	8.6
2002	6.8	8.3	1992	7.9	8.6
2001	7.0	8.2	1991	7.9	8.7
2000	7.1	8.1	1990	7.9	8.9
1999	7.2	8.2	1989	8.0	8.8
1998	7.6	8.5	1988	8.0	9.1

estly from 4.7% in 2006), but they distributed 24.9% of all purse money, up from 24.6% in the previous year. The average stakes purse was $116,312, up 6% from $109,741 in 2006.

Table 7 presents the distribution of purses in North America in 2007 by value. Reflecting in part higher purse levels across the board, the largest category of races was between $15,000 and $19,999. That level had 7,729 races and purses totaling $132,050,090. In 2006, the largest category was $10,000 to $12,499, which had 7,469 races worth a total of $82,505,651. In 2007, 27 races worth $1-million or more were run—including 11 Breeders' Cup races—and their payments totaled $40,801,901.

Field Size

Field size is a constant worry for racing secretaries and mutuel managers, and it continued to be a cause for concern in 2007. One piece of good news in **Table 8** was that field size was up, albeit by a modest 0.1 starters per race. The not-so-good news is that the uptick was from a record low for field size, 8.1 starters per race in 2006, and such modest increases in the past have not been sustained. Average field size was 8.9 starters per race in 1990.

One truly bad piece of news was that the average number of starts per year declined yet again, to a record low of 6.3 starts per runner in 2007. Even the advent of synthetic racing surfaces in several jurisdictions has not been able to stem the declines in average starts.

Average starts are an indication of overall racing soundness, and the indisputable conclusion is that the Thoroughbred in North American racing continues to grow less sound. In 1989, the average number of starts was eight, and that figure has fallen steadily without an increase in even one year. In the span of a decade, the average Thoroughbred makes 1.3 fewer starts annually.

Some racing traditionalists decry the loss of the long-distance race, and Breeders' Cup Ltd. is giving them a long-winded race this year, the Breeders' Cup Marathon at 1½ miles on the main track in 2008.

One indisputable conclusion from **Table 9** is that it pays to have a horse that runs long. With 28.5% of all races, six-furlong contests were the most common in North American racing in 2007. They paid out 24.1% of all purses, with an average pot of $18,032. Rising average purses for distance races begin at 1¹⁄₁₆ miles ($31,427) and continue through 1¼ miles ($209,121).

Don Clippinger is editorial director of Thoroughbred Times.

Table 9
Distribution of Races and Purses by Distance for 2007
(All Two-Year-Old Races Omitted)

Distance	Number of Races	Percent of Races	Purses	Percent of Purses	Avg. Purse per Race
Less than 5 furlongs	2,415	4.7%	$ 25,476,804	2.3%	$ 10,549
5 furlongs	2,956	5.7%	47,337,038	4.3%	16,014
Between 5 and 6 furlongs	6,124	11.8%	82,848,310	7.5%	13,528
6 furlongs	14,745	28.5%	265,886,513	24.1%	18,032
Between 6 and 7 furlongs	4,297	8.3%	84,557,630	7.7%	19,678
7 furlongs	2,942	5.7%	72,745,084	6.6%	24,726
Between 7 and 8 furlongs	539	1.0%	11,244,196	1.0%	20,861
1 mile	7,843	15.2%	167,849,542	15.2%	21,401
1 mile 40 yds.	136	0.3%	3,167,375	0.3%	23,290
1 mile 70 yds.	3,220	6.2%	51,383,782	4.6%	15,958
1¹⁄₁₆ miles	4,910	9.5%	154,305,737	14.0%	31,427
1⅛ miles	1,204	2.3%	81,718,048	7.4%	67,872
1³⁄₁₆ miles	41	0.1%	5,674,522	0.5%	138,403
1¼ miles	132	0.3%	27,603,949	2.5%	209,121
1⁵⁄₁₆–1⅜ miles	76	0.1%	8,011,233	0.7%	105,411
1⁷⁄₁₆ miles	0	0.0%	0	0.0%	
1½ miles	83	0.2%	13,684,920	1.2%	164,879
More than 1½ miles	43	0.1%	1,564,727	0.1%	36,389
Totals	**51,706**	**100.0%**	**$1,105,059,410**	**100.0%**	**$ 21,372**

… State of the Industry — Racetrack Purses 23

Purse Distribution by Track in 2007

Northeast

Track, State	Average Daily Racing Days	Average Purse Distribution (Change from Previous Year)	Average Purse	Stakes Purses (% Total Purse)
Aqueduct, N.Y.	118	$372,931 (6%)	$42,111	$105,012 (22%)
Atlantic City Race Course, N.J.	4	153,584 (–4%)	21,184	52,950 (9%)
Belmont Park, N.Y.	92	547,529 (7%)	59,054	162,303 (41%)
Finger Lakes, N.Y.	158	121,882 (8%)	13,609	84,309 (7%)
Meadowlands, N.J.	41	292,735 (–7%)	32,615	86,427 (24%)
Monmouth Park, N.J.	79	627,629 (66%)	65,155	317,141 (59%)
Saratoga Race Course, N.Y.	37	755,481 (12%)	80,094	184,746 (44%)
Suffolk Downs, Ma.	101	114,535 (14%)	12,811	76,819 (11%)

Mid-Atlantic

Track, State	Average Daily Racing Days	Average Purse Distribution (Change from Previous Year)	Average Purse	Stakes Purses (% Total Purse)
Charles Town Races, W.V.	229	$181,699 (–8%)	$18,551	$ 72,723 (8%)
Colonial Downs, Va.	41	221,803 (5%)	24,779	153,555 (34%)
Delaware Park, De.	135	260,039 (4%)	31,541	124,344 (18%)
Laurel Park, Md.	148	215,935 (–1%)	23,041	94,623 (16%)
Mountaineer Race Track, W.V.	223	141,546 (–14%)	14,924	107,784 (10%)
Penn National Race Course, Pa.	177	82,433 (8%)	9,299	46,767 (2%)
Philadelphia Park, Pa.	203	236,252 (68%)	24,419	148,359 (10%)
Pimlico Race Course, Md.	31	311,257 (–10%)	31,636	139,168 (36%)
Presque Isle Downs, Pa.	25	430,260	53,782	133,333 (15%)
Timonium, Md.	7	118,419 (–8%)	12,753	45,000 (11%)

Midwest

Track, State	Average Daily Racing Days	Average Purse Distribution (Change from Previous Year)	Average Purse	Stakes Purses (% Total Purse)
Anthony Downs, Ks.	6	$ 10,300 (24%)	$ 3,090	$ 5,897 (57%)
Arlington Park, Il.	94	277,280 (2%)	28,423	135,174 (25%)
Beulah Park, Oh	119	49,395 (–2%)	5,797	61,154 (14%)
Canterbury Park, Mn.	68	125,309 (–6%)	15,081	47,727 (18%)
Chippewa Downs, N.D.	6	11,212 (41%)	2,320	3,769 (22%)
Churchill Downs, Ky.	73	486,112 (0%)	47,761	251,800 (36%)
Columbus Races, Ne.	24	49,592 (–11%)	5,668	12,069 (11%)
Ellis Park, Ky.	46	139,880 (2%)	14,267	72,088 (19%)
Eureka Downs, Ks.	11	11,209 (58%)	3,425	0 (0%)
Fairmount Park, Il.	89	54,486 (–18%)	6,661	45,800 (6%)
Fonner Park, Ne.	36	62,385 (–7%)	6,645	26,762 (17%)
Fort Pierre, S.D.	2	11,350 (269%)	2,270	0 (0%)
Great Lakes Downs, Mi.	99	91,075 (0%)	10,620	66,061 (21%)
Hawthorne Race Course, Il.	118	195,596 (–3%)	21,898	113,808 (18%)
Hoosier Park, In.	61	131,468 (–9%)	13,756	104,103 (19%)
Horsemen's Atokad Downs, Ne.	3	79,021 (13%)	12,477	0 (0%)
Horsemen's Park, Ne.	4	111,834 (–8%)	24,852	33,640 (38%)
Indiana Downs, In.	48	96,831 (1%)	10,636	45,000 (6%)
Keeneland Race Course, Ky.	32	645,774 (0%)	68,654	258,103 (47%)
Kentucky Downs, Ky.	6	218,500 (–21%)	28,500	99,000 (38%)
Lincoln State Fair, Ne.	37	60,778 (–4%)	7,162	19,797 (10%)
Mt. Pleasant Meadows, Mi.	27	4,975 (2%)	3,198	0 (0%)
North Dakota Horse Park, N.D.	20	18,276 (15%)	4,017	13,503 (37%)
Prairie Meadows Racetrack, Ia.	86	173,246 (–4%)	22,506	81,726 (22%)
River Downs, Oh.	105	63,226 (–4%)	8,468	73,636 (12%)
The Woodlands, Ks.	24	40,690 (–2%)	5,955	19,100 (23%)
Thistledown, Oh.	136	67,688 (–7%)	9,142	76,923 (11%)
Turfway Park, Ky.	112	144,015 (3%)	14,492	93,677 (18%)

Southeast

Track, State	Average Daily Racing Days	Average Purse Distribution (Change from Previous Year)	Average Purse	Stakes Purses (% Total Purse)
Calder Race Course, Fl.	172	$237,766 (–3%)	$22,384	$ 94,583 (30%)
Gulfstream Park, Fl.	88	334,627 (14%)	36,176	194,565 (30%)
Ocala Training Center, Fl.	1	390,000 (3%)	65,000	65,000 (100%)
Percy Warner, Tn.	1	385,000 (5%)	64,167	81,250 (84%)
Tampa Bay Downs, Fl.	94	162,340 (2%)	15,154	92,398 (16%)

Southwest

Track, State	Average Daily Racing Days	Average Purse Distribution (Change from Previous Year)	Average Purse	Stakes Purses (% Total Purse)
Blue Ribbon Downs, Ok.	64	$ 13,133 (8%)	$ 6,226	$ 15,675 (4%)
Delta Downs, La.	93	240,381 (7%)	23,987	111,289 (18%)
Evangeline Downs, La.	89	194,646 (–9%)	19,421	84,316 (11%)
Fair Grounds, La.	84	382,409 (314%)	38,424	122,575 (23%)
Fair Meadows at Tulsa, Ok.	31	51,099 (–1%)	9,963	45,000 (6%)
Gillespie County Fairgrounds, Tx.	8	19,000 (38%)	5,630	15,600 (21%)

State of the Industry — Racetrack Purses

Track, State	Average Daily Racing Days	Average Purse Distribution (Change from Previous Year)	Average Purse	Stakes Purses (% Total Purse)
Lone Star Park, Tx.	67	$194,871 (–4%)	$20,087	$106,060 (26%)
Louisiana Downs, La.	91	212,455 (–21%)	21,772	94,642 (19%)
Manor Downs, Tx.	16	27,989 (27%)	8,142	45,000 (30%)
Oaklawn Park, Ar.	52	288,293 (5%)	29,109	165,528 (30%)
Remington Park, Ok.	69	185,499 (4%)	20,252	70,819 (17%)
Retama Park, Tx.	32	121,203 (36%)	12,158	70,000 (23%)
Ruidoso Downs, N.M.	56	49,594 (–8%)	11,768	56,772 (31%)
Sam Houston Race Park, Tx.	69	116,975 (14%)	12,192	61,606 (20%)
Sunland Park, N.M.	79	175,261 (–20%)	25,037	112,675 (24%)
SunRay Park, N.M.	44	73,156 (19%)	13,468	60,400 (19%)
The Downs at Albuquerque, N.M.	43	90,939 (121%)	16,226	50,477 (30%)
Will Rogers Downs, Ok.	39	94,010 (29%)	11,751	0 (0%)
Zia Park, N.M.	48	148,894 (–8%)	23,665	117,203 (30%)

West Coast

Track, State	Average Daily Racing Days	Average Purse Distribution (Change from Previous Year)	Average Purse	Stakes Purses (% Total Purse)
Apache County Fair, Az.	4	$ 9,614 (–2%)	$ 2,024	$ 4,640 (12%)
Arapahoe Park, Co.	35	53,950 (7%)	7,771	31,671 (32%)
Bay Meadows Fair, Ca.	11	130,913 (–1%)	16,180	0 (0%)
Bay Meadows Race Course, Ca.	100	156,196 (–5%)	18,485	82,504 (10%)
Cochise County Fair, Az.	3	12,158 (75%)	2,026	0 (0%)
Cow Capital Turf Club, Mt.	2	4,586 (21%)	2,293	3,000 (33%)
Crooked River Roundup, Or.	4	16,667 (17%)	3,030	3,688 (11%)
Dayton, Wa.	2	13,285 (44%)	2,214	0 (0%)
Del Mar, Ca.	43	539,133 (1%)	62,487	194,436 (38%)
Eastern Oregon Livestock Show, Or.	3	15,500 (54%)	2,583	0 (0%)
Elko County Fair, Nv.	7	31,854 (27%)	4,551	12,723 (34%)
Emerald Downs, Wa.	91	111,253 (0%)	12,286	63,919 (22%)
Fairplex Park, Ca.	16	281,338 (–1%)	27,448	80,686 (29%)
Ferndale, Ca.	10	27,200 (0%)	6,476	8,286 (9%)
Flagstaff, Az.	4	32,340 (12%)	4,975	7,228 (6%)
Fresno, Ca.	11	69,205 (1%)	11,895	58,338 (15%)
Gila County Fair, Az.	4	10,419 (28%)	2,084	0 (0%)
Golden Gate Fields, Ca.	98	171,302 (4%)	19,914	89,705 (13%)
Graham County Fair, Az.	3	10,548 (7%)	1,978	0 (0%)
Grants Pass, Or.	9	17,921 (16%)	2,372	3,520 (15%)
Great Falls, Mt.	7	11,151 (–12%)	2,110	2,950 (8%)
Greenlee County Fair, Az.	4	12,671 (19%)	2,204	8,183 (16%)
Hollywood Park, Ca.	95	440,926 (5%)	50,589	180,619 (37%)
Les Bois Park, Id.	45	24,644 (9%)	4,047	16,445 (37%)
Los Alamitos Race Course, Ca.	188	16,590 (10%)	7,203	0 (0%)
Mohave County Fair, Az.	4	13,080 (58%)	2,378	3,495 (13%)
Oak Tree at Santa Anita, Ca.	31	429,534 (0%)	48,597	152,268 (39%)
Pleasanton, Ca.	11	167,583 (11%)	18,252	51,461 (14%)
Portland Meadows, Or.	76	40,916 (15%)	4,936	17,627 (16%)
Rillito Park, Az.	8	13,369 (8%)	2,431	6,343 (18%)
Santa Anita Park, Ca.	85	463,230 (0%)	53,065	176,723 (35%)
Santa Cruz County Fair, Az.	4	10,169 (22%)	2,034	0 (0%)
Santa Rosa, Ca.	18	133,861 (–16%)	16,503	57,290 (10%)
Solano County Fair, Ca.	5	105,368 (–13%)	13,171	59,100 (11%)
Stockton, Ca.	9	112,859 (43%)	13,914	50,758 (15%)
Sun Downs, Wa.	10	10,113 (1%)	1,714	3,032 (12%)
Tillamook County Fair, Or.	3	20,638 (46%)	2,814	4,250 (14%)
Turf Paradise, Az.	153	89,571 (11%)	10,469	40,243 (27%)
Waitsburg Race Track, Wa.	2	10,188 (4%)	1,852	0 (0%)
Walla Walla, Wa.	5	9,750 (–11%)	1,573	2,000 (4%)
White Pine County Horse Races, Nv.	2	27,125	3,391	4,625 (17%)
Wyoming Downs, Wy.	11	3,774 (0%)	2,076	3,812 (18%)
Yavapai Downs, Az.	56	36,580 (–1%)	5,853	15,151 (17%)
Yellowstone Downs, Mt.	10	12,448 (1%)	2,441	7,392 (12%)

Canada

Track, Province	Average Daily Racing Days	Average Purse Distribution (Change from Previous Year)	Average Purse	Stakes Purses (% Total Purse)
Assiniboia Downs, Mb.	69	$ 76,543 (11%)	$ 9,533	$ 39,881 (23%)
Fort Erie, On.	84	104,419 (1%)	11,289	73,663 (10%)
Grand Prairie, Ab.	21	18,457 (31%)	3,996	8,136 (19%)
Hastings Race Course, B.C.	68	136,352 (–7%)	15,200	71,499 (29%)
Kamloops, B.C.	6	19,863 (–6%)	3,612	5,942 (25%)
Kin Park, B.C.	3	21,617 (–15%)	3,603	8,000 (25%)
Lethbridge, Ab.	44	30,385 (9%)	6,428	15,875 (44%)
Marquis Downs, Sk.	29	28,291 (14%)	3,646	9,925 (27%)
Melville District Agripar, Sk.	2	5,960	1,192	1,661 (14%)
Millarville Race Society, Ab.	1	29,563 (–3%)	7,391	14,077 (48%)
Northlands Park, Ab.	61	135,230 (16%)	15,803	67,143 (28%)
Stampede Park, Ab.	50	109,224 (6%)	13,288	55,670 (14%)
Sunflower Downs, B.C.	1	42,105 (5%)	5,263	6,749 (64%)
Woodbine, On.	169	506,456 (9%)	54,172	198,085 (27%)

Racing Enters the Racino Era

Racino is a highly descriptive new word, created by combining a racetrack with a casino. The concept also is relatively new, dating from the 1990s. Initially, the racino concept—which essentially puts video lottery terminals or slot machines into racetracks or free-standing facilities at racetracks—rescued three racing operations, Mountaineer Race Track in West Virginia, Prairie Meadows Racetrack in Iowa, and historic Delaware Park. Gaming machines have spread from those three locations to Louisiana, New Mexico, New York, and Oklahoma. In 2006, electronic gaming began in Pennsylvania and Florida. In some cases, the gaming machines have saved racetracks from possible closure. In other jurisdictions, the machines have transformed marginal tracks into highly profitable businesses paying race purses near or above the North American average.

Governmental bodies such as state legislatures have passed electronic-gaming legislation over the opposition of antigambling organizations, and politicians have been willing to risk the wrath of these groups because slots and VLTs represent a tax upon the willing—that is, those individuals who go to the track or some other site to play the slots. Like the state's cut from lotteries, casino taxes tend to be high. Until the 1980s, horse racing represented a tax on the willing horseplayer who went to the track despite takeouts that included a hefty state tax. As horse racing began to be marginalized as a major sport and wagering handle stagnated or declined in the 1980s and '90s, states were forced to cut taxes sharply on horse-racing wagers.

Like most revolutions in the horse-racing industry, the era of racinos began with little notice and far from the recognized centers of the sport. The racino revolution began on June 8, 1990, at Mountaineer in Chester, West Virginia. Mountaineer, which was known as Waterford Park from its founding in 1951 until '87, certainly needed help. It paid very low purses, and its horses occupied racing's bottom rung. The West Virginia lottery, which began operation in 1986, put 160 voucher-spitting video lottery terminals at Mountaineer to help the track and to help itself. A dispute over the machines went to the state Supreme Court, which ruled that the video lottery terminals had to be authorized by the Legislature or shut down. With no interruption in play, the Legislature approved video lottery terminals in 1994, local voters endorsed the machines, and the newly legitimate VLTs began operating on May 10, 1994. Mountaineer changed its name to Mountaineer Race Track and Gaming Resort in 2001.

The state's other Thoroughbred track, Charles Town Races, was purchased in 1996 by Penn National Gaming Inc. after voters in Jefferson County, West Virginia, approved machine gaming. While successful from the start, Mountaineer and Charles Town received a significant boost when the state Legislature authorized the tracks to install coin-drop video lottery terminals in fall 1999. Like tracks elsewhere, purses have increased tremendously in the years since the machines were installed, but both tracks have experienced declines in later years.

The second significant launch of video lottery terminals occurred on April 1, 1995, when the first slot machines began operation at Prairie Meadows Racetrack in Altoona, Iowa. Prairie Meadows had struggled from its first days in 1989. Even full-card simulcasting could not save the track from a bankruptcy filing in 1991, and the facility closed its doors on September 2, 1991. Because Polk County, which includes the track, had underwritten the $40-million in bonds to build the track, the county ended up owning the track in 1993, and racing resumed that May. Acting on a positive recommendation of a gambling task force, the Legislature and local voters authorized slot machines at the state's horse and dog tracks in 1994, and the machines began spewing revenues. The total play for 1995 totaled nearly $1-billion.

From the start, however, the county and horsemen were locked in a battle over who should get the lion's share of the slots revenue. The horsemen thought that they should; the county and several prominent citizens argued for minimal contribution to purses and maximum contribution to local government and civic projects. The issue has never been completely resolved, although the balance of power has tilted toward the property owner, Polk County. While Prairie Meadows's purses climbed toward the North American per-race average for several years, a new contract between the county and the track's operator in 2002 resulted in a purse cut beginning in '03. Purses fell further in 2004. This pattern—an initial sharp increase in purses followed by, for a number of reasons, stagnant or declining purses—has been repeated elsewhere.

Delaware Park followed a pattern similar to Prairie Meadows. Built in the later years of the Great Depression by William duPont Jr. and associates, the track near Wilmington opened in June 1937 and for many years was a magnet for racing fans in the Philadelphia area. In the 1970s and '80s, new competitors arose, and the Maryland tracks—which had used Delaware as a summer base—began racing year-round. In 1982, the track closed and was dormant until William Rickman Sr. bought it in late '83. The track reopened in 1984 and survived on creative management and fan loyalty for the next decade. Full-card simulcasting helped, but Delaware Park turned the corner with passage of the Horse Racing Redevelopment Act in June 1994. Delaware Park's slot machines began operation on December 29, 1995. To be sure, the racetrack and its purses received a generous portion of the slots revenue, but most

money went to the state. In 2005, the state's share from Delaware Park and two Standardbred tracks was $199-million, or 7.1% of state revenue.

With the slots money, Delaware Park was able to rebuild its purse structure and its stakes program, and its purses are now well above the North American average. The track also has encountered changes in the purse payouts as events unrelated to the racetrack have affected slots play. For instance, after the state of Delaware banned smoking in public places in late 2002, slots play declined for a while, and as a result purses declined in '03, although they rose again in '04.

In the mid-1990s, New Mexico's racetracks were on the ropes. But the tracks and horsemen lobbied for slots, won approval for them, and entered the racino age in February 1999 at Sunland Park, which is just across the Texas border from El Paso. The state's other tracks followed suit, and all have experienced sizable increases in purses. The casino boom proved so alluring that a new track, Zia Park, was built in Hobbs. Its casino began operation in November 2004, and racing at the $54-million facility began in 2005. The track was sold to Penn National Gaming Inc. for $200-million in 2006.

Riverboat gambling began in Louisiana in 1993, video poker machines were added to the gambling mix in '98, and land-based casinos opened in '99. Slot machines arrived at the track on February 13, 2002, in sleepy Vinton, not far from the Texas border at Delta Downs. Las Vegas speculator Shawn Scott bought the track for $10-million in 1999; Boyd Gaming Corp. bought it for a reported $125-million two years later. Louisiana Gaming Control Board reports make clear why the price went through the roof. By the end of 2002, Delta's slots had generated $60-million in net win—after the 652,038 slots players had gotten their share—with the state receiving $9.1-million in taxes.

Purses and breeders' funds received $10.8-million.

Louisiana Downs, purchased by Harrah's Inc., opened its slots operation on May 21, 2003, and Evangeline Downs, relocated to St. Landry Parish after local voters rejected slots at its former site, began casino operations on December 19, 2003. Fair Grounds traded its video-poker machines for slots in 2007. Without question, Louisiana's purses have benefited greatly from slots. At Delta, purses increased from an average of $8,783 for its 2001-'02 meet to $19,675 per race for the 2003-'04 season. End-of-year figures indicate how profitable the machines are. In all, 6.5-million slots players went to Louisiana track facilities in fiscal 2007, and the net taxable win was $300-million. After deductions for purses, breeders' funds, and community grants, Louisiana's tax was $55.5-million.

Slot machines also were installed in Ontario's two Thoroughbred tracks, at Fort Erie in 1999 and Woodbine in 2000, with positive results initially. However, reduced play on the machines resulted in lower purses at both tracks in 2004 and '05. Canada was not the only location with a mixed picture from the slot machines. Although New York approved video lottery terminals at racetracks in the wake of the September 11, 2001, terrorist attack on the World Trade Center's twin towers, the first slots operation did not open until January 2003 at Saratoga Raceway, a Standardbred track, and Finger Lakes became the first Thoroughbred track in New York with VLTs on February 18, 2004. A proposed VLT operation at Aqueduct is likely to open in late 2009 or '10.

Video lottery terminals were authorized in both Pennsylvania and Oklahoma in 2004; Oklahoma began operations in '05 and Pennsylvania followed in late '06. Video lottery terminals at Gulfstream Park in Florida began operating in late 2006.

—*Don Clippinger*

Racinos and Daily Purses, 2000-2007

Delaware
Delaware Park

Year	Types of Gaming	Racing Days	Avg. Daily Purse Distribution	Avg. Purse Change
2007	Pari-Mutuel, Slot Machines	135	$260,039	(4%)
2006	Pari-Mutuel, Slot Machines	136	250,309	(–7%)
2005	Pari-Mutuel, Slot Machines	138	269,165	(6%)
2004	Pari-Mutuel, Slot Machines	134	253,345	(8%)
2003	Pari-Mutuel, Slot Machines	141	233,813	(–20%)
2002	Pari-Mutuel, Slot Machines	141	291,204	(14%)
2001	Pari-Mutuel, Slot Machines	139	255,018	(4%)
2000	Pari-Mutuel, Slot Machines	149	245,466	(5%)

Iowa
Prairie Meadows Racetrack

Year	Types of Gaming	Racing Days	Avg. Daily Purse Distribution	Avg. Purse Change
2007	Pari-Mutuel, Slots, Table Games	86	$173,246	(–4%)
2006	Pari-Mutuel, Slots, Table Games	81	180,261	(31%)
2005	Pari-Mutuel, Slot Machines	95	137,965	(2%)
2004	Pari-Mutuel, Slot Machines	96	135,639	(–4%)
2003	Pari-Mutuel, Slot Machines	100	141,619	(–15%)
2002	Pari-Mutuel, Slot Machines	98	166,172	(4%)
2001	Pari-Mutuel, Slot Machines	97	160,447	(10%)
2000	Pari-Mutuel, Slot Machines	98	146,500	(17%)

Louisiana
Delta Downs

Year	Types of Gaming	Racing Days	Avg. Daily Purse Distribution	Avg. Purse Change
2007	Pari-Mutuel, Slot Machines	93	$240,381	(7%)
2006	Pari-Mutuel, Slot Machines	36	224,659	(30%)
2005	Pari-Mutuel, Slot Machines	53	172,616	(–13%)
2004	Pari-Mutuel, Slot Machines	99	197,760	(0%)
2003	Pari-Mutuel, Slot Machines	82	196,899	(85%)
2002	Pari-Mutuel, Slot Machines	88	106,421	(115%)
2001	Pari-Mutuel	85	49,404	(–4%)
2000	Pari-Mutuel	52	51,200	(32%)

Evangeline Downs

Year	Types of Gaming	Racing Days	Avg. Daily Purse Distribution	Avg. Purse Change
2007	Pari-Mutuel, Slot Machines	89	$194,646	(–9%)
2006	Pari-Mutuel, Slot Machines	142	212,754	(19%)
2005	Pari-Mutuel, Slot Machines	100	179,298	(48%)
2004	Pari-Mutuel, Slot Machines	92	121,317	(67%)
2003	Pari-Mutuel	87	72,805	(–8%)
2002	Pari-Mutuel	82	79,104	(4%)
2001	Pari-Mutuel	82	75,848	(–4%)
2000	Pari-Mutuel	82	78,779	(–1%)

State of the Industry — Racinos

Fair Grounds

Year	Types of Gaming	Racing Days	Avg. Daily Purse Distribution	Avg. Purse Change
2007	Pari-Mutuel, Video Poker	84	$382,409	(19%)
2006	Pari-Mutuel, Video Poker	11	92,322	(−61%)
2005	Pari-Mutuel, Video Poker	36	238,932	(−5%)
2004	Pari-Mutuel, Video Poker	82	251,513	(−2%)
2003	Pari-Mutuel, Video Poker	83	256,249	(−4%)
2002	Pari-Mutuel, Video Poker	80	265,740	(−2%)
2001	Pari-Mutuel, Video Poker	89	271,595	(2%)
2000	Pari-Mutuel, Video Poker	90	266,958	(−2%)

Louisiana Downs

Year	Types of Gaming	Racing Days	Avg. Daily Purse Distribution	Avg. Purse Change
2007	Pari-Mutuel, Slot Machines	91	$212,455	(−11%)
2006	Pari-Mutuel, Slot Machines	105	239,217	(5%)
2005	Pari-Mutuel, Slot Machines	141	241,596	(31%)
2004	Pari-Mutuel, Slot Machines	102	183,924	(2%)
2003	Pari-Mutuel, Slot Machines	80	180,934	(14%)
2002	Pari-Mutuel	80	158,176	(27%)
2001	Pari-Mutuel	89	124,801	(−15%)
2000	Pari-Mutuel	83	146,226	(2%)

New Mexico
Ruidoso Downs

Year	Types of Gaming	Racing Days	Avg. Daily Purse Distribution	Avg. Purse Change
2007	Pari-Mutuel, Slot Machines	56	$49,594	(−8%)
2006	Pari-Mutuel, Slot Machines	55	54,003	(19%)
2005	Pari-Mutuel, Slot Machines	56	45,480	(0%)
2004	Pari-Mutuel, Slot Machines	57	45,582	(−16%)
2003	Pari-Mutuel, Slot Machines	57	54,420	(25%)
2002	Pari-Mutuel, Slot Machines	57	43,458	(4%)
2001	Pari-Mutuel, Slot Machines	57	41,615	(7%)
2000	Pari-Mutuel, Slot Machines	57	38,890	(34%)

Sunland Park

Year	Types of Gaming	Racing Days	Avg. Daily Purse Distribution	Avg. Purse Change
2007	Pari-Mutuel, Slot Machines	79	$175,261	(−20%)
2006	Pari-Mutuel, Slot Machines	57	220,350	(31%)
2005	Pari-Mutuel, Slot Machines	67	167,608	(8%)
2004	Pari-Mutuel, Slot Machines	92	155,473	(−5%)
2003	Pari-Mutuel, Slot Machines	75	162,876	(59%)
2002	Pari-Mutuel, Slot Machines	78	102,135	(31%)
2001	Pari-Mutuel, Slot Machines	79	78,144	(28%)
2000	Pari-Mutuel, Slot Machines	86	60,852	(116%)

SunRay Park

Year	Types of Gaming	Racing Days	Avg. Daily Purse Distribution	Avg. Purse Change
2007	Pari-Mutuel, Slot Machines	44	$73,156	(19%)
2006	Pari-Mutuel, Slot Machines	48	61,558	(25%)
2005	Pari-Mutuel, Slot Machines	38	49,439	(−6%)
2004	Pari-Mutuel, Slot Machines	44	52,611	(−28%)
2003	Pari-Mutuel, Slot Machines	40	73,074	(−5%)
2002	Pari-Mutuel, Slot Machines	35	76,840	(65%)
2001	Pari-Mutuel, Slot Machines	46	46,621	(14%)
2000	Pari-Mutuel, Slot Machines	41	41,063	(26%)

The Downs at Albuquerque

Year	Types of Gaming	Racing Days	Avg. Daily Purse Distribution	Avg. Purse Change
2007	Pari-Mutuel, Slot Machines	43	$90,939	(121%)
2006	Pari-Mutuel, Slot Machines	67	41,182	(−8%)
2005	Pari-Mutuel, Slot Machines	59	44,940	(−8%)
2004	Pari-Mutuel, Slot Machines	69	48,663	(−12%)
2003	Pari-Mutuel, Slot Machines	67	55,118	(−8%)
2002	Pari-Mutuel, Slot Machines	64	59,890	(13%)
2001	Pari-Mutuel, Slot Machines	63	52,892	(17%)
2000	Pari-Mutuel, Slot Machines	69	45,256	(30%)

Zia Park

Year	Types of Gaming	Racing Days	Avg. Daily Purse Distribution	Avg. Purse Change
2007	Pari-Mutuel, Slot Machines	48	$148,894	(−8%)
2006	Pari-Mutuel, Slot Machines	49	162,508	(20%)
2005	Pari-Mutuel, Slot Machines	42	135,377	

New York
Finger Lakes Gaming

Year	Types of Gaming	Racing Days	Avg. Daily Purse Distribution	Avg. Purse Change
2007	Pari-Mutuel, Slot Machines	158	$121,882	(8%)
2006	Pari-Mutuel, Slot Machines	156	112,470	(5%)
2005	Pari-Mutuel, Slot Machines	160	107,550	(2%)
2004	Pari-Mutuel, Slot Machines	157	105,755	(40%)
2003	Pari-Mutuel	154	75,282	(−4%)
2002	Pari-Mutuel	161	78,223	(0%)
2001	Pari-Mutuel	165	78,302	(−3%)
2000	Pari-Mutuel	167	80,655	(1%)

Ontario
Fort Erie

Year	Types of Gaming	Racing Days	Avg. Daily Purse Distribution	Avg. Purse Change
2007	Pari-Mutuel, Slot Machines	84	$104,419	(−13%)
2006	Pari-Mutuel, Slot Machines	101	119,601	(16%)
2005	Pari-Mutuel, Slot Machines	104	103,046	(−46%)
2004	Pari-Mutuel, Slot Machines	81	191,755	(−4%)
2003	Pari-Mutuel, Slot Machines	114	200,504	(1%)
2002	Pari-Mutuel, Slot Machines	116	197,936	(16%)
2001	Pari-Mutuel, Slot Machines	116	170,310	(52%)
2000	Pari-Mutuel, Slot Machines	107	111,681	(32%)

Woodbine

Year	Types of Gaming	Racing Days	Avg. Daily Purse Distribution	Avg. Purse Change
2007	Pari-Mutuel, Slot Machines	169	$506,456	(9%)
2006	Pari-Mutuel, Slot Machines	162	464,326	(8%)
2005	Pari-Mutuel, Slot Machines	164	430,916	(−13%)
2004	Pari-Mutuel, Slot Machines	167	498,136	(−13%)
2003	Pari-Mutuel, Slot Machines	162	571,514	(2%)
2002	Pari-Mutuel, Slot Machines	166	558,598	(13%)
2001	Pari-Mutuel, Slot Machines	165	494,595	(2%)
2000	Pari-Mutuel, Slot Machines	160	483,979	(53%)

Pennsylvania
Philadelphia Park

Year	Types of Gaming	Racing Days	Avg. Daily Purse Distribution	Avg. Purse Change
2007	Pari-Mutuel, Slot Machines	203	$236,252	(68%)
2006	Pari-Mutuel, Slot Machines	203	140,885	(−9%)
2005	Pari-Mutuel	210	154,195	(10%)
2004	Pari-Mutuel	216	140,737	(0%)
2003	Pari-Mutuel	213	140,056	(−3%)
2002	Pari-Mutuel	216	144,153	(−3%)
2001	Pari-Mutuel	220	149,248	

Presque Isle Downs

Year	Types of Gaming	Racing Days	Avg. Daily Purse Distribution	Avg. Purse Change
2007	Pari-Mutuel, Slot Machines	25	$430,260	

West Virginia
Charles Town Races

Year	Types of Gaming	Racing Days	Avg. Daily Purse Distribution	Avg. Purse Change
2007	Pari-Mutuel, Slot Machines	229	$181,699	(−8%)
2006	Pari-Mutuel, Slot Machines	224	196,961	(18%)
2005	Pari-Mutuel, Video Lottery	243	166,355	(−26%)
2004	Pari-Mutuel, Video Lottery	231	224,692	(52%)
2003	Pari-Mutuel, Video Lottery	235	148,243	(13%)
2002	Pari-Mutuel, Video Lottery	254	131,273	(−8%)
2001	Pari-Mutuel, Video Lottery	233	142,154	(48%)
2000	Pari-Mutuel, Video Lottery	208	96,022	(25%)

Mountaineer Race Track

Year	Types of Gaming	Racing Days	Avg. Daily Purse Distribution	Avg. Purse Change
2007	Pari-Mutuel, Slot Machines	223	$141,546	(−14%)
2006	Pari-Mutuel, Slot Machines	229	164,241	(8%)
2005	Pari-Mutuel, Video Lottery	216	151,642	(−12%)
2004	Pari-Mutuel, Video Lottery	219	171,818	(−2%)
2003	Pari-Mutuel, Video Lottery	222	175,244	(5%)
2002	Pari-Mutuel, Video Lottery	230	166,383	(14%)
2001	Pari-Mutuel, Video Lottery	228	145,463	(30%)
2000	Pari-Mutuel, Video Lottery	221	111,797	(32%)

YEAR IN REVIEW
Review of 2007: *Big Trouble in the Big Apple*

New York racing grabs the headlines throughout the year, and the battle over the franchise held by the New York Racing Association extends into 2008

Soap-opera viewers feel as though they cannot miss a day of their favorite show's daily stories and twisting plotlines. Then again, if viewers miss a year or two of the shows, upon return, they find few substantial changes.

Those who have followed the saga of the New York racing franchise can relate. At the end of 2006, the current franchise holder—the New York Racing Association—was bankrupt, and a state ad hoc committee had just rated NYRA the worst of three potential franchise bidders.

At the beginning of 2007, Eliot Spitzer became the Empire State's governor and, though regarded as no friend of NYRA while serving as the state's attorney general, recommended in September that NYRA continue to operate the state's three largest Thoroughbred tracks—Aqueduct, Belmont Park, and Saratoga Race Course.

But nothing is simple or straightforward in New York, and a dispute over other issues between the Democratic governor and Joseph Bruno, the powerful Republican who then led the state Senate, spilled over into the racing debate, and the year ended with no agreement. To make matters more complicated, NYRA officials had said that they would not allow racing to continue without a franchisee in place.

In early 2008, NYRA agreed to two short extensions before an agreement was worked out on the racing franchise with NYRA gaining another 25 years at the helm. Left unsettled at that point was which entity would run the 4,500 video lottery terminals that eventually will be installed at Aqueduct.

While the twists and turns have seemed endless, it is important to remember how important the franchise decision will be for the industry. The issues include:

The future of Aqueduct: NYRA envisioned New York's winter track as its main racino with 4,500 VLTs. Excelsior Racing Associates, one of three bidders in competition with NYRA, wanted gaming at Aqueduct and Belmont. Spitzer, who resigned in early 2008 over a sex scandal, suggested closing Aqueduct altogether and moving winter racing to Belmont. In all likelihood, Aqueduct will remain open.

National racing: The health of the New York circuit is critical to Thoroughbred racing. In 2007, Belmont paid average daily purses of $484,808 (up 4% compared with '06) at its spring meeting and $659,330 (up 12%) at its fall meet. Saratoga Race Course's average daily purses registered at $775,077 (up 15%) and Aqueduct purses rose substantially.

Regional issues: Delaware, Pennsylvania, West Virginia, and other tracks in New York already offer alternative gaming, and slots at Aqueduct, and possibly Belmont, would surely affect neighboring businesses.

Delaware Park suffered decreased handle in 2007 and blamed a shortage of horses despite slots-fueled purses.

In addition to many slots throughout the region, neighboring states Connecticut and New Jersey offer full-service casino gambling, and some experts say estimates that Aqueduct gaming could generate $660-million a year are too high because of this competition.

Simulcasts: As big as the franchise decision is for New York racing, it will no doubt affect the industry as a whole, particularly those segments that handle wagers. NYRA's exclusive agreement with Television Games Network expired on December 31, and NYRA made its signal available to all major advance-deposit wagering sites. The signal also is heavily prized among brick-and-mortar wagering outlets throughout North America.

1½ Years Ago

Under then-Governor George Pataki, the ad hoc committee accepted bids from three organizations in August 2006 to operate the state's three major tracks. The organizations had changed and been reshaped prior to that deadline.

Excelsior Racing Associates, a group then

led by New York Yankees General Partner Steve Swindal, led the way by scoring a 97 on the committee's weighted scoring system. In second, at 92.5, was Empire Racing Associates, which at that point included Churchill Downs Inc., Magna Entertainment Corp., Woodbine Entertainment Group, New York horsemen, and many other investors.

NYRA came in a well-beaten third, collecting the show spot with a 76.5 rating.

Writing the next plotline would be the state Legislature and Spitzer, who became governor in 2007. As attorney general, Spitzer found many problems with NYRA. In a 2003 report, Spitzer documented:

• Track tellers handling large amounts of cash without proper oversight and regularly incurring huge shortages in their accounts that effectively slashed their taxable income;
• Track tellers betting on races, a violation of NYRA rules;
• Track teller schemes to cheat patrons out of their winnings;
• Parking lot attendants charging four times the maximum on-track parking rates and pocketing the difference; and
• Poorly trained track security personnel.

Also in the report, Spitzer accused NYRA officials of withholding information and misleading state regulators on repeated occasions. It said senior management abused expense accounts and spent thousands of dollars at a time on food, drink, and entertainment.

Ranked third by the previous governor's committee and seemingly not favored by the new governor, NYRA's fate seemed sealed, but soap opera viewers know that a terminal main character is always just a miracle cure away from revival.

NYRA Back in Hunt

Spitzer formed his own committee, which reviewed four bidders, with Australia-based Capital Play Inc. joining the fray. (As if things are not strange enough in New York, NYRA had stopped accepting wagers from Capital Play's secondary pari-mutuel outlet in 2005 because of integrity concerns.)

By September, NYRA suddenly looked appealing to Spitzer. NYRA agreed to drop ownership claims of track land—valued by some at $1-billion—and the state would forgive $130-million in NYRA debt.

As part of the agreement, a separate gaming franchise would be established while not-for-profit NYRA would receive the state's racing franchise for another 30 years, a franchise it has held since 1955.

Just more than four years after documenting NYRA's problems, Spitzer was singing its praises.

"NYRA is the best entity to operate Thoroughbred racing in New York state," Spitzer said. "The state, in consultation with NYRA, will choose an experienced gaming operator to operate the [VLT] franchise at Aqueduct. This will ensure that we have the best possible operator for both racing and the gaming franchise."

NYRA Chairman Steven Duncker trumpeted NYRA's efforts in winning approval. Each organization spent an estimated $2-million preparing bids and an additional $1-million complying with an independent integrity review required by Spitzer. Under the plan, Aqueduct would receive 4,500 VLT machines.

"[This] is the culmination of NYRA's efforts over the past several years to reinvent itself," Duncker said. "The governor's support is a testament to the efforts undertaken by NYRA to become the racing industry leader in integrity and corporate governance."

A Good Year

Oddly enough, as politicians deliberated New York racing's future, the circuit registered a memorable season in 2007.

Rags to Riches became the first filly to win the $1-million Belmont Stakes (G1) in more than 100 years. Four eventual Breeders' Cup World Championships race winners prepped at Belmont Park on September 29-30: Jockey Club Gold Cup Stakes (G1) and Breeders' Cup Classic Powered by Dodge (G1) winner Curlin, Joe Hirsch Turf Classic Invitational Stakes (G1) and John Deere Breeders' Cup Turf (G1) winner English Channel, Beldame Stakes (G1) third-place finisher and Emirates Airline Breeders' Cup Distaff (G1) winner Ginger Punch, and Flower Bowl Invitational Stakes (G1) and Emirates Airline Breeders' Cup Filly and Mare Turf (G1) winner Lahudood (GB).

Bessemer Trust Breeders' Cup Juvenile (G1) winner War Pass and Grey Goose Breeders' Cup Juvenile Fillies (G1) winner Indian Blessing both prepped with Grade 1 victories at Belmont as well.

Moreover, all six of the above-mentioned

horses won Eclipse Awards in their respective divisions and Curlin was voted Horse of the Year.

With stars at the Saratoga meeting like Street Sense, Midnight Lute, Lawyer Ron, and Hard Spun, the circuit's signature meeting generated record on-track handle of $123,018,041 and its total all-sources handle, $582,656,106, was up 6.2% compared with 2006. Average daily purses at NYRA tracks increased in 2007.

"NYRA remains committed to continuing this effort while at the same time retaining its position as the producer of the best racing product in North America, as exhibited by the recently concluded Saratoga race meeting," Duncker said.

Alas, the decision by Spitzer, a Democrat, only resulted in more maneuvering in Albany. Bruno, a Republican, questioned the decision.

"The governor's handling of the process to select a new racing franchise has had several false starts and now has a questionable finish," Bruno said. "His announcement still leaves more questions than answers."

Bruno suggested that the franchise is big enough to include more than one operator. Nonetheless, NYRA's franchise expired on December 31 and the organization threatened a shutdown if a new franchisee was not awarded.

Former New York Yankee Yogi Berra is credited with saying, "It's not over until it's over," but NYRA received its franchise extension for 25 years and was poised to exit bankruptcy in mid-2008.

Other Top Stories of 2007

Thoroughbred racing began the year saying goodbye to one of its biggest stars in recent years in 2006 Kentucky Derby Presented by Yum! Brands (G1) winner Barbaro. While the killer "B"s of Barbaro and Bernardini dominated the Triple Crown in 2006, a more balanced—and some might argue more competitive crop—contested the 2007 series.

Uncertainty was common theme for several of this year's biggest stories, including long-term effects of synthetic surfaces and the future of Magna Entertainment Corp. racetracks.

Meanwhile, change was the key word for segments of the industry related to account wagering, the Breeders' Cup World Championships, and sales integrity reform.

These top stories have as much to do with 2007 as '08, as the aftereffects of these stories figure to shape the Thoroughbred racing landscape for some time.

2. Powerful Crop

An unusually strong group of three-year-olds graced the American racing scene and created an indelible impact in 2007.

Street Sense, Curlin, and Rags to Riches were the key players in a thrilling Triple Crown series that ended up as just the first stage in a powerful season for the crop of 2004.

Street Sense became the first Bessemer Trust Breeders' Cup Juvenile (G1) winner to succeed in the Kentucky Derby when he rallied past 18 horses on May 5, thus dispelling the supposed "Juvenile jinx."

Curlin continued his meteoric rise by chasing down Street Sense in the Preakness Stakes (G1) on May 19, pushing ahead in the final stride to win by a head in razor-sharp time.

Kentucky Oaks (G1) winner Rags to Riches challenged males in the Belmont Stakes (G1) and came through in brilliant style to win by a head over Curlin and become the first female to win the race since Tanya in 1905.

Rags to Riches suffered a season-ending leg injury in the Gazelle Stakes (G1) on September 15, but Street Sense and Curlin carried on as standard-bearers for the three-year-old division the rest of the season.

Street Sense added victories in the Jim Dandy (G2) and Travers (G1) Stakes to his already impressive résumé.

Curlin reached a new level of success with his victories in the Jockey Club Gold Cup Stakes (G1) and Breeders' Cup Classic Powered by Dodge (G1), leading a powerful showing by members of the 2004 crop in major races across the country against older rivals this fall.

Other Grade 1 winners from the crop included Derby and Breeders' Cup Classic runner-up Hard Spun, Any Given Saturday, Nobiz Like Shobiz, and Dream Rush.

3. Barbaro's Battle Ends

The racing industry celebrated the legacy of 2006 Kentucky Derby winner Barbaro on January 22 at the Eclipse Awards ceremony in Beverly Hills, California.

The colt's owners and breeders, Roy and Gretchen Jackson, made two trips to the stage

to accept the outstanding owner title as well as a Special Eclipse Award. Four of the seven winners of the Media Eclipse Award were honored for work directly or indirectly tied to Barbaro.

Just one week later, the Jacksons faced the decision they had been dreading for eight months. They decided to euthanize Barbaro rather than allow him to suffer from laminitis.

Barbaro's condition deteriorated progressively in the final weeks of his life. The National Thoroughbred Racing Association created a fund in Barbaro's memory that will support two projects focusing on laminitis.

4. Synthetic Surfaces Spread

The spread of synthetic surfaces continued to transform North American racing in 2007, with Arlington Park, Del Mar, Golden Gate Fields, and Santa Anita Park all replacing their conventional dirt tracks.

Presque Isle Downs also began its inaugural season in September with a Tapeta Footings track, one of three brands of synthetic surfaces in place for live racing at nine racetracks in North America. In November, Golden Gate hosted the first races over its new Tapeta surface.

Santa Anita and parent company Magna Entertainment elected to install Cushion Track, the same surface that is in use at nearby Hollywood Park. It experienced drainage problems in 2008, and Santa Anita replaced it with a Pro Ride surface.

Arlington and Del Mar opted for Polytrack, which is the main surface at Keeneland Race Course, Turfway Park, and Woodbine.

The influx of new surfaces has not come without problems. Catastrophic injuries tripled at Keeneland during the 2007 fall meet compared with 2006. Del Mar dealt with criticism

Leaders of 2007

Category	Leader	Leading Statistic
Owner by Wins	Louis O'Brien	221
Owner by Earnings	Stronach Stables	$7,076,134
Owner by Grade 1 Wins	Stronach Stables	5
Owner by Grade 1 Earnings	Stonestreet Stables, Padua Stables, George Bolton, and Midnight Cry Stables	$4,300,000
Owner by Graded Stakes Winners	Zayat Stables	7
Breeder by Wins	Adena Springs	527
Breeder by Earnings	Adena Springs	$17,618,475
Breeder by Grade 1 Wins	Adena Springs	6
Breeder by Grade 1 Earnings	Fares Farm	$4,300,000
Breeder by Graded Stakes Winners	Adena Springs	8
Trainer by Wins	Steve Asmussen	488
Trainer by Earnings	Todd Pletcher	$28,115,697
Trainer by Grade 1 Wins	Todd Pletcher	17
Trainer by Grade 1 Earnings	Todd Pletcher	$10,647,852
Trainer by Graded Stakes Winners	Todd Pletcher	33
Jockey by Wins	Russell Baze	399
Jockey by Earnings	Garrett Gomez	$22,800,074
Jockey by Grade 1 Wins	Garrett Gomez	13
Jockey by Grade 1 Earnings	Garrett Gomez	$7,115,692
Jockey by Graded Stakes Winners	Garrett Gomez	35
Sire by Wins	Langfuhr	243
Sire by Earnings	Smart Strike	$14,477,651
Sire by Grade 1 Wins	Smart Strike	7
Sire by Grade 1 Earnings	Smart Strike	$7,496,573
Sire by Winners	Langfuhr	131
Sire by Graded Stakes Winners	A.P. Indy	10
Horse by Wins	Golden Hare	14
Horse by Earnings	Curlin	$5,102,800
Horse by Graded Stakes Wins	(tie) Citronnade, Curlin, Nobiz Like Shobiz, Rutherienne	5
Horse by Grade 1 Wins	Rags to Riches	4
Horse by Starts	I'm an Evil One	29
Oldest Stakes Winner	(tie) Be My Friend, Caller One, Chief Swan, D D Dot Comm, Larry the Longshot, Tender Offer (Ire)	10
Oldest Graded Stakes Winner	(tie) Evening Attire, The Tin Man	9
Broodmare by Earnings	Sherriff's Deputy	$5,103,600

over the difference in the consistency of the Polytrack surface between morning training and afternoon racing.

Woodbine altered the mix of its Polytrack surface after the track froze in late February and early March.

5. Shift in Account Wagering

Churchill Downs Inc. and Magna Entertainment dramatically changed the account-wagering landscape in 2007 with the launch of horse racing content distributor TrackNet Media Group.

The bulk of signals controlled by Churchill moved from Television Games Network to HorseRacing TV, and its wagering content shifted to TrackNet outlets TwinSpires.com, XpressBet.com, and AmericaTAB.

Handle through Churchill outlets declined in the first two quarters after the divide, while TVG fared better with an emphasis on top tracks it offers like Del Mar and Saratoga Race Course.

Youbet.com Inc. struggled in 2007, primarily because of problems at International Racing Group, its offshore rebate outlet. Youbet.com Chief Executive Officer Chuck Champion stepped down in December.

6. John Henry Dies at 32

Two-time Horse of the Year John Henry was euthanized on October 8 because of kidney problems. The popular gelding was 32.

A seven-time Eclipse Award winner, John Henry resided for 22 years in the Hall of Champions at the Kentucky Horse Park in Lexington.

Champion sprinter Kona Gold took up residence at the Horse Park.

7. Breeders' Cup Evolution Continues

Breeders' Cup Ltd. embarked on a dramatic season of change with the introduction of a two-day format in 2007.

The Breeders' Cup board of directors added three new races for the inaugural Friday card on October 26 at Monmouth Park. The results were encouraging enough for the board to tack on three more races for 2008 at Santa Anita. The Dirt Mile, Filly and Mare Sprint, and Juvenile Turf will be joined in 2008 by the Dirt Marathon, Juvenile Filly Turf, and Turf Sprint.

Breeders' Cup also launched the "Win and You're In" Breeders' Cup Challenge series to help promote the World Championships.

8. Prominent Trainers Serve Suspensions

Medication issues maintained a familiar position hanging over the North American racing industry in 2007.

Todd Pletcher and Steve Asmussen ended the year comfortably ahead of all other trainers in purse earnings, 11 months after both were detached from racing while suspended for medication violations.

Upon returning, Pletcher and Asmussen both enjoyed career-best seasons.

Another top trainer, Patrick Biancone, finished the year with 9½ months remaining on a one-year penalty from the Kentucky Horse Racing Authority for multiple violations stemming from the discovery of cobra venom in his barn at Keeneland.

9. Sales Integrity Moves Foward

The Sales Integrity Task Force recommended in October that the Kentucky auction industry police itself through modifications of conditions of sale rather than through legislative changes.

The task force's proposal included a ban on anabolic steroids within 45 days of sale, a code of conduct for bloodstock agents, and voluntary disclosure of ownership and medical issues.

Keeneland Association and Fasig-Tipton Co., both members of the task force, subsequently agreed on a joint policy prohibiting the use of exogenous anabolic steroids for weanlings and yearlings within 45 days of their sales in 2008.

10. Magna Regroups

After accruing hundreds of millions of dollars in losses, Magna Entertainment put on the brakes in 2007 and began to focus on debt reduction.

The company announced plans in September 2007 to sell Great Lakes Downs, Thistledown, and Portland Meadows. Magna also abandoned plans to build a new racetrack in Dixon, California, and completed its purchase of the Maryland Jockey Club.

The revolving door continued turning in Magna's leadership, with Michael Neuman becoming the fifth chief executive officer to depart the company since 2000.—*Jeff Lowe*

Chronology of 2007 and 2008

2007

January 8, 2007—Breeders' Cup Ltd. announces an expanded two-day 2007 World Championships event, with the addition of Juvenile Turf, Filly and Mare Sprint, and Dirt Mile races.

January 9—Injured Kentucky Derby Presented by Yum! Brands (G1) winner Barbaro suffers a serious setback in his recovery when another separation is discovered in his foundered left hind foot.

January 16—Breeders' Cup Classic Powered by Dodge (G1) winner Invasor (Arg) tops the 2006 World Thoroughbred Racehorse Rankings.

January 17—It is announced that Barbaro owners Roy and Gretchen Jackson, and the University of Pennsylvania's New Bolton Center, will receive 2006 Special Eclipse Award for contributions to racing.

January 21—A record 470 horses are nominated early to the 2007 Triple Crown races, topped by champions Street Sense and Dreaming of Anna.

January 22—Invasor (Arg) is named Horse of the Year for 2006 at the Eclipse Awards ceremony in California.

January 25—Maryland Jockey Club officials announce that the historic Pimlico Special Handicap (G1) will not be run in 2007 due to financial considerations. Juvenile champions Street Sense and Dreaming of Anna top the 2006 Experimental Free Handicap assignments.

January 26—Noble Threewitt, America's oldest active trainer at age 95, saddles his final starter after a 75-year career. He is honored with a retirement ceremony at Santa Anita Park on February 24.

January 27—A high-risk surgery is performed on Barbaro to insert steel pins through his cannon bone to eliminate weight-bearing on his injured right hind ankle.

January 29—Barbaro is euthanized.

January 31—Longtime industry leader John A. Bell III passes away at age 88.

February 1—NTRA announces that it will create a Barbaro Memorial Fund to raise awareness and money for equine laminitis research.

February 5—Argentine-based jockey Jorge Ricardo notches his 9,591st career win, surpassing Russell Baze as the world's all-time winningest rider.

February 16—Officials of NTRA, *Daily Racing Form*, and the National Turf Writers Association announce the establishment of an Eclipse Award for champion female sprinter.

February 20—The Maryland Racing Commission denies a request by former Kentucky Derby-winning jockey Ronnie Franklin to reinstate his license.

March 3—Lava Man becomes only the third horse in 70 years to win back-to-back runnings of the Santa Anita Handicap (G1).

March 7—The National Turf Writers Association announces that Russell Baze will receive his 11th Isaac Murphy award honoring the North American jockey with the highest winning percentage for 2006.

March 9—Two-time Horse of the Year and Racing Hall of Fame member John Henry celebrates his 32nd birthday at the Kentucky Horse Park.

March 10—Bobby Frankel becomes Santa Anita Park's winningest trainer of all time, after scoring victory number 870.

March 22—The California Horse Racing Board declines to grant a waiver to Bay Meadows Race Course of a requirement to install a synthetic racing surface by 2008 and denies the 73-year-old San Francisco-area track an operating license for '08.

March 25—Jon Court receives the George Woolf Memorial Jockey Award at Santa Anita Park.

March 31—2006 Horse of the Year Invasor (Arg) scores a victory in the $6-million Emirates Airline Dubai World Cup (UAE-G1).

April 14—Author Joe Drape wins the inaugural $10,000 Castleton Lyons-THOROUGHBRED TIMES Book Award, for *Black Maestro*, a biography of African-American jockey Jimmy Winkfield.

April 16—Former NTRA Group Purchasing President Joe Morris is named publisher of Thoroughbred Times Co.

April 17—The American Graded Stakes Committee denies Breeders' Cup Ltd.'s request for immediate Grade 1 status for its new Dirt Mile, Filly and Mare Sprint, and Juvenile Turf races.

April 18—The Illinois House of Representatives passes a bill outlawing horse slaughter for human consumption.

April 25—Cara Rafaela, dam of champion Bernardini, is named 2006 Broodmare of the Year by the Kentucky Thoroughbred Owners and Breeders.

April 30—Kentucky Derby (G1) sponsor Yum! Brands announces a $1-million bonus to this year's winner if he beats Barbaro's 6½-length victory margin.

May 4—Rags to Riches romps in the 133rd running of the Kentucky Oaks (G1). Jockey Mark Guidry scores his 5,000th career victory at Churchill Downs.

May 5—Favored Street Sense scores a come-from-behind victory in the Kentucky Derby Presented by Yums! Brands (G1). NBC Sports premieres the documentary "Barbaro: A Nation's Horse," postponed from April 29, which would have been Barbaro's fourth birthday.

May 19—Curlin catches Street Sense in the final stride to win the Preakness Stakes (G1).

May 24—Illinois Governor Rod Blagojevich signs legislation that closes the last remaining horse slaughterhouse in America.

May 28—The Tin Man becomes the fourth nine-year-old to win a Grade 1 race, with his victory in Hollywood Park's Shoemaker Mile Stakes.

May 29—The Racing Hall of Fame announces that its 2007 inductees will include trainers Henry Forrest, Frank McCabe, and John Veitch; jockeys Jose Santos and John Sellers; and horses Silver Charm, Swoon's Son, and Mom's Command.

June 9—Rags to Riches becomes the first filly in 102 years to win the Belmont Stakes (G1) and the third of her sex ever to win the New York classic.

June 13—Millionaire Grade 1 winner Wallenda returns from Japan to live as a pensioner at Old Friends Thoroughbred retirement facility in Georgetown, Kentucky.

June 23—2006 Horse of the Year Invasor (Arg) is retired from racing after injuring an ankle in a workout.

June 24—Emma-Jayne Wilson becomes the first female rider to win Canada's classic Queen's Plate Stakes, aboard 15.20-to-1 longshot Mike Fox.

June 30—Lava Man joins Racing Hall of Famer Native Diver as the only three-time consecutive winners of the Hollywood Gold Cup Stakes (G1).

July 4—Jockey Joe Bravo scores his 4,000th career victory.

Year in Review — Chronology of 2007 and 2008

July 11—Calvin Borel receives the 2007 ESPY award as America's best jockey.

July 13—Champion three-year-old and 2003 dual classic winner Funny Cide is retired from racing.

July 18—Del Mar racetrack unveils its new Polytrack surface before a record opening-day crowd of 42,842.

July 25—Saratoga Race Course sets an opening-day record for on-track wagering of more than $3.8-million.

July 30—Jockey Jose Santos, winner of more than 4,600 races, announces his retirement one week before his induction into the Racing Hall of Fame.

August 6—The Racing Hall of Fame inducts largest class of members since 1978 at ceremony held in Saratoga Springs, New York.

August 7—1982 Kentucky Derby (G1) winner Gato Del Sol dies of old age in Kentucky.

August 10—Two of Preakness Stakes (G1) winner Curlin's owners, lawyers Shirley Cunningham Jr. and William Gallion, are ordered to prison by a federal judge to await trial on charges of conspiracy to commit wire fraud in their handling of a fen-phen settlement.

August 20—Wicks Group announces it will sell *Daily Racing Form* for about $190-million to the private equity firm Arlington Capital Partners.

August 21—Jockey Perry Ouzts scores his 5,000th career victory, aboard Kandinsky, at River Downs.

August 22—James "Jimmy" Bell and W. Cothran "Cot" Campbell are elected to the Jockey Club.

August 23—More than 30 well-known shuttle stallions are quarantined in Australia after several horses show signs of equine influenza.

August 25—Australian racing is canceled due to equine influenza outbreak. Kentucky Derby Presented by Yum! Brands (G1) winner Street Sense wins the Travers Stakes (G1).

August 26—Jockey Terry Houghton rides his 4,000th career winner.

August 30—Kentucky stewards order trainer Patrick Biancone to serve a 15-day suspension after one of his horses tests positive for an illegal drug.

September 1—Presque Isle Downs opens, becoming the first Thoroughbred track to operate in the Erie area of Northwest Pennsylvania since 1987.

September 4—New York Governor Eliot Spitzer recommends that NYRA continue operating Saratoga Race Course, Belmont Park, and Aqueduct for a 30-year period, with video lottery terminal operation at Aqueduct to be handled by another entity.

September 8—Racing resumes in Australia under strict restrictions.

September 15—Belmont Stakes (G1) winner Rags to Riches suffers a hairline fracture in the Gazelle Stakes (G1) and is out for the year. The Green Monkey, who sold at auction in 2006 for a world-record $16-million, finishes third in his debut at Belmont Park.

September 16—Jockey Randy Meier rides career winner number 4,000, at Arlington Park.

September 21—America's last horse slaughter plant closes when the United States Court of Appeals rules that an Illinois law banning such slaughter is constitutional.

September 25—Keeneland's September yearling sale concludes with 3,799 racing prospects sold for an average price of $101,347, down 9.9% from 2006. Total receipts drop 3.7% to $385,018,600.

September 27—Keeneland announces it has cataloged a record 5,415 horses for its November 5-19 breeding stock sale.

October 8—Two-time Horse of the Year and Racing Hall of Fame member John Henry is euthanized at the Kentucky Horse Park at the age of 32.

October 12—A world-record price for a yearling filly is set when a daughter of Sadler's Wells brings $5.53-million at Tattersalls. The Jockeys' Guild files for Chapter 11 bankruptcy protection.

October 17—Trainer Patrick Biancone agrees to a one-year suspension from training, beginning November 1, for a violation of Kentucky medication rules.

October 18—The Jockey Club releases its 2007 report of mares bred data, with Stormy Atlantic covering a season-high 199 mares.

October 19—A crowd estimated at 500 attends a memorial service for John Henry at the Kentucky Horse Park. Arlington Capital Partners becomes the seventh owner of *Daily Racing Form* when it completes the purchase of the 113-year-old publication.

October 20—Ten-year-old steeplechaser McDynamo scores his fifth consecutive victory in the Grand National Hurdle Stakes.

October 21—Del Mar racetrack is used as an evacuation center for both horses and people during the devastating San Diego wildfires.

October 24—Noted owner Cynthia Phipps dies as a result of a fire in her Manhattan residence.

October 26-27—The first two-day Breeders' Cup World Championships is held at rain-swept Monmouth Park, and Curlin easily wins the $5-million Breeders' Cup Classic Powered by Dodge (G1).

October 31—Trainer Scott Lake saddles his 4,000th career winner.

November 1—A Kentucky judge rules that a part-interest in Curlin must be turned over to more than 400 plaintiffs involved in a fen-phen drug lawsuit against two of the colt's owners, suspended lawyers Shirley Cunningham Jr. and William Gallion.

November 2—WinStar Farm announces that Distorted Humor will stand for a $300,000 fee in 2008, the co-highest in North America with Storm Cat and A.P. Indy.

November 3—Jockey Patrick Valenzuela returns from an injury after 11 months to win two races at Zia Park.

November 5—English champion Playful Act (Ire) brings a world-record $10.5-million for a broodmare or broodmare prospect on the opening day of Keeneland's November breeding stock sale.

November 6—Efficient wins the two-mile, $5-million Emirates Melbourne Cup (Aus-G1).

November 7—Jockey Mario Pino becomes the 15th North American jockey to reach the 6,000-win milestone, aboard Pass Play, at Laurel Park.

November 10—Jockey Mark Guidry retires after 33 years in the saddle and 5,043 victories, 21st on North America's all-time list of winningest riders.

November 11—Jockey Garrett Gomez sets a North American record for stakes wins during a single season scoring his 71st aboard Spring Awakening in the Moccasin Stakes at Hollywood Park.

November 13—Keeneland's November breeding stock sale establishes a new all-time auction record for gross revenue, with $322-million in sales midway through the marathon event.

November 14—Prix de l'Arc de Triomphe Lucien Barriere (Fr-G1) winner Dylan Thomas (Ire) receives the Cartier Award as Europe's Horse of the Year.

November 19—Keeneland's 15-day November breeding stock sale ends, establishing a record $340,877,200 in total receipts.

Year in Review — Chronology of 2007 and 2008

November 21—The Green Monkey, who sold for a world-record $16-million in 2006, remains a maiden after finishing fourth in his third career start and turf debut at Hollywood Park.

November 23—Trainer Todd Pletcher establishes a single-season earnings record of $26,850,873, surpassing his own record set in 2006.

November 26—Racing Hall of Fame jockey Bill Hartack dies of a heart attack at age 74 while on a Texas hunting trip.

November 30—Kona Gold, champion sprinter of 2000, takes up residence at the Kentucky Horse Park.

December 7—Williamstown, a graded stakes-winning 1:32.79 miler by Seattle Slew, is saved from euthanization and is pensioned at the Old Friends retirement home near Georgetown, Kentucky.

December 10—Breeders' Cup Ltd. adds three new races for 2008: the Turf Sprint, Juvenile Fillies Turf, and Dirt Marathon. The World Championships will be held October 24-25 at the Oak Tree Meet at Santa Anita.

December 14—Sealy Hill is named Canada's 2007 Horse of the Year, becoming only the third filly or mare to be so honored within the current voting system.

December 16—New Mexican sensation Peppers Pride wraps up her third season of racing with a perfect 14-for-14 lifetime record.

December 18—The Preservation League of New York State adds Saratoga Race Course to its list of endangered historic sites.

December 22—Jerry Hollendorfer becomes the fourth North American trainer to saddle 5,000 winners.

December 23—All-time winningest trainer Dale Baird is killed in a car accident in Indiana at age 72.

December 30—Longtime leading North American owner-breeder Louis Wolfson passes away at age 95.

December 31—New York Racing Association's franchise expires, but racing in New York continues when the association agrees to a three-week temporary extension from the state.

2008

January 5-7—After heavy rainstorms pummel Southern California, Santa Anita Park cancels live racing because of drainage problems with its new Cushion Track surface.

January 9—Argentine-based jockey Jorge Ricardo becomes the first to ride 10,000 winners.

January 13—Trainer Todd Pletcher saddles his 2,000th career winner, at Santa Anita Park. Keeneland January horses of all ages sale ends with a 21% increase in average and with an all-time record sale median of $17,000.

January 17—Rags to Riches's Belmont Stakes (G1) victory over Curlin is named the National Thoroughbred Racing Association's "Moment of the Year" for 2007.

January 21—Curlin is crowned 2007 Horse of the Year at the 37th annual Eclipse Awards dinner, in Beverly Hills. New York Racing Association is granted an extension that will permit racing to continue at Aqueduct until February 13.

January 22—Principal owner Jess Jackson states that 2007 Horse of the Year Curlin will race at four in '08.

January 23—Grade 1 winner Will's Way is pensioned to Old Friends retirement home, near Georgetown, Kentucky.

January 24—Champion juveniles War Pass and Indian Blessing receive top weights among males and females, respectively, on the 2007 Experimental Free Handicap.

January 29—Roy and Gretchen Jackson announce the remains of 2006 Kentucky Derby (G1) winner Barbaro will be interred at Churchill Downs.

February 1—Jockey Russell Baze becomes the first North American rider to score 10,000 career victories.

February 10—Jockey Edgar Prado scores his 6,000th victory, at Gulfstream Park.

February 12—The Green Monkey, at $16-million the most expensive horse ever sold at auction, retires winless in three starts.

February 13—New York's Legislature approves a bill giving NYRA a 25-year franchise to operate state racetracks, averting a possible shutdown.

February 17—Winning Colors, a member of the Racing Hall of Fame and one of only three filly Kentucky Derby winners, dies from complications of colic.

February 29—Magna Entertainment Corp. announces it lost more than $113-million in 2007.

March 24—Belmont Stakes (G1) winner and 2007 champion three-year-old filly Rags to Riches is retired after injuring her right fore pastern.

March 29—Horse of the Year Curlin runs off with the $6-million Dubai World Cup (UAE-G1) by 7½ lengths.

April 7—T. D. Thornton, author of *Not By a Long Shot—A Season at a Hard-Luck Horse Track*, wins the second annual $10,000 Castleton Lyons-THOROUGHBRED TIMES Book Award.

April 10—Synergy Investments Ltd., a Dubai-based company, acquires Fasig-Tipton Co.

April 19—2007 juvenile male champion War Pass is knocked off the Derby trail with an ankle injury.

April 21—The Racing Hall of Fame reveals its 2008 induction class will include trainer Carl Nafzger, jockeys Edgar Prado and Ismael Valenzuela; champions Inside Information and Manila; and Ancient Title.

April 23—Better Than Honour, dam of 2006 and '07 Belmont Stakes (G1) winners Jazil and Rags to Riches, is named Broodmare of the Year.

April 26—Undefeated Pepper's Pride ties an American record with her 16th consecutive victory.

April 29—Jockey Russell Baze earns his 12th Isaac Murphy Award from the National Turf Writers Association for the North American rider with the year's highest winning percentage.

May 3—Undefeated Big Brown captures the Kentucky Derby Presented by Yum! Brands (G1); runner-up Eight Belles breaks down fatally after the finish.

May 6—People for the Ethical Treatment of Animals (PETA) demonstrates outside the offices of the Kentucky Horse Racing Authority, protesting alleged cruelty in racing.

May 12—Legendary European sire Sadler's Wells, sire of 296 stakes winners and 18 champions, is pensioned from stud duty at age 27.

May 13—Two-time leading American sire Storm Cat, sire of 162 stakes winners, is pensioned at age 25.

May 17—Big Brown scores an easy victory in the Preakness Stakes (G1).

May 25—Triple Crown hopeful Big Brown develops a quarter crack in his left fore foot.

June 3—It is announced that the remains of ill-fated Kentucky Derby runner-up Eight Belles will be interred at the Kentucky Derby Museum.

June 7—Big Brown fails to finish in the Belmont Stakes (G1), but no problem is detected. Da' Tara wins the race at odds of 38.50-to-1.

2007-2008 Obituaries

Tom Ainslie (Richard Carter), 89, noted handicapper and author, whose books included *Ainslie's Complete Guide to Thoroughbred Racing*; on September 1, 2007, in New York City.

Dr. George Allen, 67, longtime University of Kentucky professor of veterinary science, considered a leading authority on equine herpesvirus and equine rhinopneumonitis; on April 6, 2008, in Kentucky.

Arthur I. Appleton, 92, noted Florida-based breeder, owner of Bridlewood Farm; 1991 Florida breeder of the year; a North American top-ten breeder in 2007; several-term director of the Florida Thoroughbred Breeders' and Owners' Association, whose top runners included 2002 Florida horse of the year Forbidden Apple and Grade 1 winner Jolie's Halo; on January 15, 2008, in Ocala.

Robert Atkins, Australian-based stud adviser who worked with the Sangster family's Swettenham Stud for 30 years; on January 30, 2007, in Australia.

Steve Austin, 57, former jockey, who scored 612 wins at racetracks primarily in Washington state between 1967 and '79; of a heart attack, on December 8, 2007, in Washington.

Dale Baird, 72, Eclipse Award-winning trainer, who holds the all-time record for winners with 9,445 and reigned 15 times as America's leading conditioner by annual winners; of injuries sustained in a car accident, on December 23, 2007, in Hancock County, Indiana.

Daniel Baker, 23, Australian jockey; of injuries sustained in a fall at Grafton racecourse, on December 2, 2007, in New South Wales, Australia.

Dr. Howard Baker, 68, breeder of six stakes winners, including Racing Hall of Fame inductee Serena's Song; of cancer, on February 10, 2007, in Encino, California.

Dr. Robert Baker, 78, renowned Southern California veterinary surgeon, who established the noted Chino Valley Equine Hospital in 1970; of complications from orthopedic surgeries, on January 5, 2008, in Solana Beach, California.

Diane Banks, 65, former jockey, trainer, and breeder, owner of Y Bar Ranch; longtime member of the Texas Thoroughbred Breeders Association; of cancer, on March 31, 2007, in Texas.

Tony Barnard, 77, a former farm trainer for Tartan Stable, who developed such champions as Unbridled, Cozzene, and Smile; of congestive heart failure, on October 1, 2007, in Ocala.

William Battaglia, 75, former publicity director at Latonia Race Course, brother of the late Latonia and River Downs general manager John Battaglia, and uncle of veteran Kentucky oddsmaker and racetrack announcer Mike Battaglia; of heart failure, on July 24, 2007, in Milford, Ohio.

Jim Bausch, 70, twice leading owner at Sam Houston Race Park, leading owner at Retama Park; of pneumonia, on May 10, 2008, in Houston.

John A. Bell III, 88, well-known owner and breeder, industry leader, founder of Jonabell Farm, and key figure in formation of the American Horse Council, who raced 1987 champion juvenile filly Epitome and raised '54 Epsom Derby winner Never Say Die; of pulmonary fibrosis, on January 31, 2007, in Lexington.

Richard Bellasis, 91, former trainer, father of Northern California trainer Tim Bellasis; on February 28, 2007, in California.

Alfred Bellew, 95, Thoroughbred racing's oldest licensed official, who served as a state steward, clerk of scales, and paddock judge at River Downs prior to his retirement in 2004; on January 12, 2007, in Kentucky.

Brandon Benson, 21, award-winning equine photographer, assistant New York Racing Association track photographer, whose work had been featured in THOROUGHBRED TIMES and *Daily Racing Form*; on May 22, 2008.

Bruce Bessonett, 64, Remington Park trainer, who saddled runners for nearly 40 years; in late January 2008, in Oklahoma.

William T. "Buddy" Bishop III, 64, a trustee and attorney for the Keeneland Association; son of W. T. Bishop, Keeneland's first general manager; member of the Jockey Club; past president of the Thoroughbred Club of America; of a stroke, on April 3, 2008, in Kentucky.

Wayne Blackwell, 70, longtime Florida-based owner and breeder, owner of Wile-a-Way Farm near Ocala; member of the Florida Thoroughbred Breeders' and Owners' Association; on August 9, 2007, in Ocala.

Wayne Blue, 73, Midwest-based trainer, who conditioned racehorses for nearly 60 years; in mid-March 2007, in Lincoln, Nebraska.

Muriel Bowes, 76, longtime tack shop owner at Hastings Park, backstretch learning center volunteer, widow of trainer Wilf Bowes; in October 2007, in Canada.

Neil Boyce, 83, retired Chicago-based trainer, who saddled 29 stakes winners, including Grade 3 winner Valid Vixen and 12-time stakes winner Calestoga; on March 8, 2008, in Oregon.

James Bracken, 90, retired jockey agent and four-time leading trainer at Calder Race Course, member of the Calder hall of fame, whose runners included Grade 1 winner Primal; on April 19, 2008, in Florida.

Errol Bradford, 69, longtime Kentucky-based farrier, whose equine clients had included 2002 Belmont Stakes (G1) winner Sarava and multiple G1 winner Harlan's Holiday; of cancer, on February 20, 2007, in Kentucky.

Frances Breede, 68, owner and president of Morrissey's Horse Pullmans horse transport business; on March 25, 2007, at her home in New Jersey.

Barbara Brewer, 80, longtime board member and past secretary-treasurer of the New York Thoroughbred Breeders, founder of Onteora Farm, who raced two-time Finger Lakes horse of the year Lordofthemountain and Runaway Tiger; on January 3, 2008, in Canandaigua, New York.

Lucy Burch, 28, Louisiana-based jockey, who had ridden 20 winners from 369 mounts since 2001; in a car accident, on August 15, 2007, near Shreveport, Louisiana.

Dr. Steve Buttgenbach, 64, longtime Southern California-based racetrack veterinarian, whose equine patients included champions A.P. Indy and Princess Rooney; of cancer, on May 15, 2007, in La Canada, California.

Alfredo Callejas, 71, New York-based trainer for nearly 30 years, whose noted runners included multiple graded stakes winners Cupecoy's Joy and Senor

Speedy, and classic-placed El Bakan; on January 12, 2008, in Beverly Hills, Florida.

Fermo Cambianica, 79, longtime Southern California Turf writer, handicapper, and former publicity director at Los Alamitos racetrack; of cancer, on April 21, 2007, in California.

Elmer Campbell, 83, well-known blacksmith at East Coast racetracks, whose clients included Racing Hall of Fame horsemen Laz Barrera and T. J. Kelly; on January 31, 2007, in Miami.

Manuel Caraballo, 65, Puerto Rican-based jockey who won more than 1,400 races in four decades of riding; of injuries sustained after falling from his mount, on February 18, 2007, at the Randall "Doc" James racetrack, in the U.S. Virgin Islands.

Kellie Cerin, 51, horsewoman, wife of trainer Vladimir Cerin; of an apparent heart attack, on February 1, 2007, while on vacation in Puerto Vallarta, Mexico.

Hernan Ceriani Cernadas, 73, leading Argentine breeder, owner of the famed Haras La Quebrada, breeder of more than 170 Grade 1 or Group 1 winners; following a long illness, on January 17, 2007, in Argentina.

Dr. Ronald Chak, 70, breeder, owner of Newchance Farm in Ocala, where he bred 24 stakes winners, including Grade 1 winners Mister Frisky and Peace Rules; after a long illness, on January 19, 2008, in Florida.

John Ciechanowski, 86, former European champion amateur jockey and later a private trainer to the Maktoum family; of cancer, on April 23, 2008, near Lambourn, England.

Jorge Ciscerno, 29, exercise rider for trainer Kelly Von Hemel at Oaklawn Park; in a car accident, on February 16, 2008, in Hot Springs, Arkansas.

Ted Cleveland, 76, trainer for nearly 50 years, who saddled major black-type winners Hoist Emy's Flag, Bold Jessie, and Convenient, and bred graded stakes winner Faster Than Sound; of cancer, on December 21, 2007, in Lexington.

Al Coffman, 85, longtime handicapper for the Detroit *Free Press* and Detroit *News*, who wrote under the pen name "Al Speedy;" on November 21, 2007, in Michigan.

Frank Colee, longtime trainer based in the Southwest, who saddled more than 200 winners between 1976 and 2008, including 1977 California-bred champion two-year-old male and Grade 3 winner Chance Dancer; in early 2008.

Con Collins, 82, longtime Irish trainer, who saddled his first winner in 1952 and won the 1984 Irish Oaks (Ire-G1); following a brief illness, on January 30, 2007, in Dublin, Ireland.

William Condren, 74, owner, who in partnerships won the 1991 and '94 Kentucky Derby (G1) with Strike the Gold and Go for Gin, respectively, and the '96 Preakness Stakes (G1) with Louis Quatorze; board member of the Grayson-Jockey Club Research Foundation; on October 29, 2007, in Boston.

Guy Contrada, 74, retired jockey who rode for nearly 25 years in Canada and the United States whose wins included the Winnipeg and Manitoba Derbys; on March 9, 2008, in Pawtucket, Rhode Island.

Dreabon Copeland, 84, owner and breeder who campaigned homebred stakes winners Saucy Mae, Lakeside Cup, and Angel Trumpet; of heart problems, on February 25, 2007, in Houston.

John Corbett, 69, well-known English bloodstock agent, who co-founded Heron Bloodstock Agency in the late 1960s; after a short illness, in January 2008, in England.

Elmer Cowen, 77, trainer, whose career spanned six decades during which he won training titles at Beulah Park and Thistledown, and whose top runner was two-time Ohio Horse of the Year Crypto's Redjet; on July 13, 2007, in Columbus, Ohio.

Howard Craig, 78, former jockey, whose biggest win came aboard Timely Tip in the 1954 Arkansas Derby. Also served as a trainer, patrol judge, clerk of scales, and an employee of Darby Dan Farm's Ohio division; on October 31, 2007.

Warren A. "Jimmy" Croll Jr., 88, Racing Hall of Fame. Trained 1994 Horse of the Year Holy Bull; divisional champions Housebuster, Forward Gal, and Parka; and stakes winner Mr. Prospector; on June 6, 2008, in Long Branch, New Jersey.

Harvey Culp, longtime trainer, who saddled stakes winners Speedy Cure and Conte Di Savoya; of heart failure, on August 21, 2007, in Ocala.

Marguerite Finney Dance, 74, former editor of *The Maryland Horse* and *Mid-Atlantic Thoroughbred* magazines, daughter and sister, respectively, of the late industry leaders Humphrey and John Finney; following a lengthy illness, on June 24, 2007, in Maryland.

Sam David Jr., 81, longtime trainer and one-time All-American football player, figured prominently in getting summer racing dates in Florida; on July 26, 2007, in Louisiana.

Doug Deisley, 59, trainer; unexpectedly, while traveling to a sale in Arkansas, on February 10, 2007.

Gary Demorest, 54, noted Canadian trainer, who led the standings at Hastings Park in 2005 and whose top runners included 2005 British Columbia Derby winner Spaghetti Mouse; of kidney failure, on April 29, 2007, near Vancouver, British Columbia.

David Dennis, 81, breeder, owner, and trainer; 1998 owner of the year in Montana; trained homebred '98 Montana horse of the year G. R.'s Dream; of natural causes, on February 4, 2008, in Helena, Montana.

Dennis Diaz, 64, owner, who purchased Spend a Buck for $12,500 and later won the Kentucky Derby (G1) and more than $4.2-million with him; of cancer, on July 2, 2007, in Tampa, Florida.

Bruce Donaldson, 87, former president of the Pennsylvania Horse Breeders Association and the Pennsylvania Breeding Fund program; on March 4, 2007, in Unionville, Pennsylvania.

Harmon Drake, 73, nine-time leading trainer at Thistledown racetrack between 1984 and '90, husband of trainer Shirley Girten; of pulmonary disease, on June 26, 2007, in Garfield Heights, Ohio.

Patricia Dudley, 77, longtime owner, breeder, and trainer in New England; member of the Massachusetts Horse Breeders Association; owned and conditioned stakes winner Jody's Way; after a long illness, on March 22, 2007, in Lawrence, Massachusetts.

Lois Duffy, 96, owner, whose top runners included 1990 Seagram Grand National Handicap Steeplechase winner Mr Frisk. Daughter of noted American breeder Walter Salmon Jr., owner of Mereworth Farm; on October 6, 2007, in Chestertown, Maryland.

Don Dunn, 84, longtime Western Canadian racing secretary and steward, member of the British Columbia Horse Racing hall of fame; on June 25, 2007, in Canada.

Robert Durr, 88, member of the Kentucky Horse Racing Commission between 1980 and '91, breeder of several stakes winners in various partnerships, including Grade 3 winners Your Tent Or Mine and Savedbythelight; of cardiac arrest, on May 21, 2007, in Edgewood, Kentucky.

Robert Durso, 68, East Coast-based trainer for nearly half a century, whose top runners included graded stakes-winning millionaire Frisk Me Now and 1999 Sapling Stakes (G3) winner Dont Tell the Kids; after a short illness, on January 31, 2007, in Hallandale, Florida.

Harold Elkind, 86, owner, whose runners included stakes winner Mr. Paul; of natural causes, on February 21, 2007, in California.

Jack Elliott, 85, well-known Australian racing journalist, who covered nearly 50 Melbourne Cups and founded the Australian Racing Writers Association; after a long illness, on November 4, 2007, in Australia.

Jim Fleming, 75, Australian owner and breeder, former chairman of the Sydney Turf Club; raced 1999 Entenmanns Irish One Thousand Guineas (Ire-G1) winner Hula Angel; owner of Tyreel Stud and breeder of more than 40 group stakes winners; on December 1, 2007, in Sydney, Australia.

Clem Florio, 78, longtime Turf writer, handicapper, and former Maryland Jockey Club oddsmaker; of lung and pancreatic cancer, on May 25, 2008, in Hollywood, Florida.

Eve Fout, 78, noted equine artist, winner of two perpetual trophies awarded by the National Steeplechase Association, co-founder of the American Academy of Equine Art. Widow of the late trainer Paul Fout; on December 5, 2007, in The Plains, Virginia.

Kenneth Franzheim II, 82, owner and breeder, who bred 1983 Hawthorne Derby (G3) winner St. Forbes; former United States ambassador to New Zealand; on October 29, 2007, in Houston.

Milton Friedman, 85, owner, who campaigned stakes winners Stutz Blackhawk, My Turbulent Beau, and Lansing Cut Off; on March 18, 2007, in Los Angeles.

Ed Friendly, 85, founder and past president of Thoroughbred Owners of California; creator and producer of such hit television series as "Laugh-In" and "Little House on the Prairie;" of cancer, on June 17, 2007, in Rancho Santa Fe, California.

Leonard Fruchtman, 86, owner for more than 30 years, whose runners included 1960 Preakness winner Bally Ache and eight-time stakes winner Our Michael, and who also owned Miles Park and Santa Fe Downs racetracks during the 1970s; on December 22, 2007, in Toledo, Ohio.

Richard Galpin, 71, international bloodstock agent for nearly a half-century, whose auction purchases included eventual Belmont Stakes (G1) winner Sarava and Bessemer Trust Breeders' Cup Juvenile (G1) winner Wilko; of a stroke, on February 27, 2008, in Miami.

Hugo Garibay, 33, groom; found stabbed to death in the hallway of a backstretch dormitory, on March 27, 2007, at Gulfstream Park, in Florida.

Orlando Garrido, 43, retired jockey, who rode Thoroughbreds and Quarter Horses to approximately 950 wins, mostly at Southwestern racetracks; of injuries sustained when he fell from a ladder, on January 15, 2008, in Scottsdale, Arizona.

Gus George, 77, Thoroughbred owner, breeder, and trainer, who served as president of the Ohio Horsemen's Benevolent and Protective Association from 2000-'05; on March 17, 2008, at his home in Sunbury, Ohio.

Martha Gerry, 88, owner and breeder of three-time Horse of the Year Forego; Jockey Club member; chairman emeritus of the National Museum of Racing and Hall of Fame board of trustees; aunt of Lane's End principal William Farish; following heart surgery, on September 17, 2007, in New York City.

Clyde Gholson, 77, longtime trainer based at Woodbine; following a brief illness, on May 13, 2008, in Canada.

Lenny Giardelli, 67, groom and assistant to trainer Merrill Scherer for 40 years; of a heart attack, on April 1, 2008, in Florida.

Wes Gilbert, 79, West Coast- and Canadian-based trainer for 50 years, whose trainee Hap Logue scored 11 consecutive victories in 1973; on May 20, 2008, in Hayward, California.

Tom Gilcoyne, 91, volunteer historian for the National Museum of Racing and Hall of Fame from 1989 to 2004; on January 3, 2008, in New York.

Richard Goetz, 71, owner, breeder, and proprietor of Richard J. Goetz Horse Transportation; on January 6, 2007, in Louisiana.

Frank Gomez, 78, retired Florida-based trainer and member of the Calder Race Course hall of fame, whose outstanding runners included eventual champions Smile, Princess Rooney, and Cherokee Run; on December 23, 2007, in Pembroke Pines, Florida.

Archie Gookstetter, 92, retired trainer and bloodstock agent, who in 1965 founded the North Idaho Racing Association; on January 14, 2007, in Spokane, Washington.

Dale Gress, 62, retired Mid-Atlantic-based jockey, who rode to nearly 1,500 wins during a 30-year career and reigned as one of Penn National Race Course's leading riders; on March 27, 2008, in Chambersburg, Pennsylvania.

Carl Grether, 80, owner, who campaigned graded stakes winners Crafty C. T. and Madame Pietra; from complications of Parkinson's disease, on July 1, 2007, in California.

Merv Griffin, 82, owner, noted game show producer, and former Hollywood Park director, who campaigned 2005 champion two-year-old male Stevie Wonderboy; of prostate cancer, on August 12, 2007, in Los Angeles.

Keith Gudsell, 83, major New Zealand-based agent, whose Dominion Bloodstock Agency also served clients in South Africa, Hong Kong, and Japan; after a brief illness, on July 7, 2007.

Cliff Guilliams, 52, writer, handicapper, and longtime chartcaller for *Daily Racing Form* and Equibase, who helped to produce the annual Kentucky Derby (G1) chart, and whose namesake, The Cliff's Edge, won the 2004 Blue Grass Stakes (G1); unexpectedly, on April 12, 2008, in Louisville.

Alma Headley Haggin, 96, daughter of Keeneland co-founder Hal Price Headley, widow of the late Keeneland President and Chairman Louis Lee Haggin II, sister of Mill Ridge Farm owner Alice Headley Chan-

dler, and mother of Keeneland director-trustee Louis Haggin III; on January 23, 2008, in Lexington.

James Halket, 92, former trainer, member of the British Columbia Horse Racing hall of fame, whose best runners included 15-time stakes winner Westbury Road and 1975 Longacres Mile Stakes (G3) winner Jim; on June 17, 2007, in Vancouver, British Columbia.

Oscar Hall Sr., 78, trainer, who saddled more than 300 career winners on the New England and Kentucky circuits; on March 3, 2007, in Cincinnati.

Leslie Harrison, 63, longtime racing and breeding manager for Plantation Stud in Newmarket, England; of a brain hemorrhage, on February 11, 2007, in England.

Bill Hartack, 74, Racing Hall of Fame jockey, whose 4,272 winning rides included five in the Kentucky Derby and three in the Preakness Stakes; ranked twice as America's leading rider by purse earnings; of a heart attack, on November 26, 2007, near Freer, Texas.

Bruce Haynes, 46, steeplechase trainer, whose best runner was multiple stakes winner Rowdy Irishman and who saddled earners of more than $1-million, co-owner with his wife, Anne, of Holston Hollow Farm; of a heart attack, on January 24, 2008, in Tennessee.

Alison Hershbell, 30, former jockey, who won 275 races at East Coast racetracks, between 1994 and 2003; following a long illness, on February 17, 2007, in Philadelphia.

Barry Holmes, 46, jockey agent, leading Thoroughbred trainer at Los Alamitos Race Course in 2001; of a heart attack, on May 27, 2008, in California.

Danny Holmes, 71, co-host of the Santa Rosa Fair racing seminars for more than 20 years; on September 2, 2007, in California.

Roger Hoysted, 61, Australian-based trainer, whose top runners included millionaire Group 1 winner Lad Of The Manor; of prostate cancer, in September 2007, in Australia.

Jerry Howe, retired trainer, who saddled horses during the 1970s and '80s on the West Coast and at Caliente; in May 2007, in Florida.

Max Hugel, 81, successful owner and breeder, board chairman of Rockingham Park, former deputy director of the Central Intelligence Agency; of cancer, on February 19, 2007, in Ocala.

Dr. Tadashi Iida, 80, noted owner, breeder, and veterinarian in Japan; developer and chief executive of successful Chiyoda Farm breeding and training center, whose top runners included 2002 Japanese champion Peace of World; of a heart attack, on November 14, 2007, in Japan.

Ethel Imprescia, 94, longtime owner; wife of retired trainer Dominic Imprescia, who saddled multiple Grade 1 winner Timely Writer; on October 10, 2007, in Aventura, Florida.

Leonard Iwan, 68, trainer, based at Great Lakes Downs, husband of trainer Marilyn Iwan; of a heart attack, in September 2007, in Michigan.

Laurie Jaffee, 85, legendary South African owner and racing official, whose champions included Empress Club (Arg), London News, and Bush Telegraph; of cancer, on March 27, 2008, in Johannesburg, South Africa.

Linda Javid, 45, former administrator for the Kentucky Thoroughbred Farm Managers' Club and former Jockey Club employee; on October 17, 2007, in Lexington.

Ron Jewell, 74, well-known trainer based in Western Canada; on May 10, 2007, in Canada.

Joe Johnson, 77, owner, who developed the Kentucky Training Center and who raced 1978 Canadian champion Giboulee and '70s stakes winners Mickey McGuire and Romeo; of a brain hemorrhage, on March 28, 2008, in Bal Harbour, Florida.

E. C. Johnston Jr., 85, Texas oilman, who raised both Thoroughbreds and Quarter Horses at his Rafter J Ranch, and whose homebred runners included stakes-winning half sister to Affirmed Won't She Tell; on March 28, 2008, in Longview, Texas.

Farrell W. Jones, 84, prominent former Southern California-based trainer, who led the Santa Anita Park standings eight times and whose top runners included 1971 Santa Margarita Handicap winner Manta. Father of noted trainer Gary Jones; following a lengthy illness, on March 12, 2007, near Hemet, California.

Richard I. G. Jones, 68, prominent Pennsylvania horseman; member of the Jockey Club; former co-owner of Walnut Green Bloodstock, which in 1983 sold a then-world record $5.25-million broodmare at auction; of a brain tumor, on January 11, 2007, in Wilmington, Delaware.

Hamilton Jordan, 63, White House chief of staff for President Jimmy Carter, who assisted during the mid-1990s in promoting the idea for the National Thoroughbred Association, precursor to the NTRA; of cancer, on May 20, 2008, in Atlanta.

Michael Kahn, 58, Sweden's most successful trainer, whose runners included 1985 Swedish Triple Crown winner Homosassa; of cancer, in May 2007, in Sweden.

Dr. Wallace Stanley Karutz, 85, owner of Bourbon Hills Farm in Paris, Kentucky, breeder of 1986 champion two-year-old filly Brave Raj; of a stroke, on January 31, 2008, in Ocala.

Shig Katayama, 82, owner, who raced under the name Clear Valley Stable, often in partnership with Santa Anita Park President Ron Charles, and whose best runners included graded stakes winners Champion Lodge (Ire), Abaginone, and Uraib (Ire); of cancer, on June 23, 2007.

Barbara "Bobby" Kees, 86, Maryland-based trainer, who owned, bred, and conditioned stakes winners Waited, Mr. Moby Dick, and South Bend, and who in 1963 became the first woman to top the trainer standings at a North American racetrack, Green Mountain Park in Vermont; on February 25, 2008, in Maryland.

Roger King, 63, owner, breeder, and television producer of the "Oprah Winfrey Show" and "Jeopardy," who raced stakes winner Courageous King and bred graded stakes-placed Atswhatimtalknbout; of a stroke, on December 8, 2007, in Boca Raton, Florida.

Jeanette Kellam, 72, Arizona-based owner and breeder for 35 years, whose top homebreds included 2005 stakes winner Desert Glory; on October 29, 2007, at her Chino Valley Ranch, in Chino Valley, Arizona.

Richard Kelley, 91, racing enthusiast, stepfather of former President Bill Clinton; after a lengthy illness, on January 31, 2007, in Hot Springs, Arkansas.

Palmer Knapp, 72, owner, who raced graded stakes winner Icantgoforthat in partnership, and father of trainer Steve Knapp; of a heart problem, on April 8, 2008, in Idaho.

Ted Labanowich, 74, Turf writer, who served as the *Daily Racing Form*'s Fort Erie correspondent and

as a racing columnist for the Hamilton *Spectator*; of stomach cancer, on October 11, 2007, in Ontario, Canada.

Rene Lambert, 88, owner and breeder, whose best homebred was millionaire Grade 1 winner Sky Jack; of natural causes, on October 12, 2007, in Toluca Lake, California.

Elizabeth Whitcomb Lampton, 74, co-owner of Elmendorf Farm with her husband, Dinwiddie Lampton Jr.; of injuries sustained in a carriage accident on the farm, on March 22, 2008, near Lexington.

Oskar Langer, 84, two-time champion German jockey and later the trainer of 473 winners; on March 10, 2007, in Germany.

Bernice Lavin, 81, owner, who with husband Leonard Lavin developed the Alberto-Culver Co. and owned Glen Hill Farm in Florida, where they bred and raced such Grade 1 winners as 1994 Breeders' Cup Distaff (G1) winner One Dreamer and Convenience; following a long illness, on October 29, 2007, in Glencoe, Illinois.

Dale Leach, 72, longtime manager of Northwest Farms; on September 16, 2007, in Yakima, Washington.

Eve Mortimer Ledyard, 89, breeder of Japanese Group 1 winner Nobo Jack and North American graded stakes winners Rhoman Rule, Wonders Delight, and Tina's Ten; of heart failure, on October 1, 2007, in West Grove, Pennsylvania.

Kenneth Lennox, 88, former director of racing at Monmouth Park, and previously a paddock judge, patrol and placing judge, steward, and racing secretary at the New Jersey track; on December 18, 2007, in Long Branch, New Jersey.

Buddy LeRoux, 77, owner of Suffolk Downs racetrack from 1986 to '89, and former part owner of the Boston Red Sox baseball team; of natural causes, on January 7, 2008, in New Hampshire.

William Levin, 84, owner and breeder, past chairman of the New York Breeding and Development Fund, whose racing stable once included stakes winners Bold Reason, Sir Ack, and Sir Keys; on January 26, 2008, in Florida.

Bob Logan, 68, well-known Australian bloodstock insurance agent; after collapsing from a brain hemorrhage at the Inglis Broodmare Sales, on April 23, 2007, in Sydney, Australia.

Brian Long, 45, jockey, who rode the winners of more than 1,000 races during a nearly 30-year career and who reigned as leading rider at Les Bois Park in 2007; found dead in his apartment, on January 12, 2008, in El Paso, Texas.

William Lucas, 82, retired jockey and member of the Jockeys' Guild, whose career victories included the 1963 Alcibiades Stakes at Keeneland and 1963 Breeders' Futurity at Churchill Downs; on April 30, 2008, in Lexington.

David L. MacLean, 49, longtime Canadian-based trainer, who had trained more than 175 winners for clientele that included Frank Stronach and Richard Duchossois, including graded stakes winner Katahaula County; of pancreatic cancer, on August 17, 2007, in Ontario, Canada.

Ron MacLeod, 66, advertising executive and consultant, who co-founded the successful advertising agency MacLeod and Hopper; on September 15, 2007, in Lexington.

Gerald Magee, 76, New Mexico-based owner and breeder, who with his wife, Avon, bred stakes winners Macho Ego and Dusk Patrol, and who operated Magee Transportation for 22 years; on February 16, 2008, in Bloomfield, New Mexico.

Charles "Buddy" Martens, 77, retired New York-based jockey and contract rider for Brookmeade Stable during the 1940s and '50s, father of jockey George Martens, who won the '81 Belmont Stakes (G1) with Summing; of cancer, on January 25, 2008, in Edmond, Oklahoma.

Samuel Martin, 77, one-time foreman for Greentree Stable, who also worked for Calumet Farm and Rokeby Stables; on January 16, 2008.

Trudy McCaffery, 62, co-owner of West Coast Grade 1 winners Free House, Came Home, and Pacific Squall, served on the board of Oak Tree Racing Association and the California Thoroughbred Breeders Association; of cancer, on February 12, 2007, in Rancho Santa Fe, California.

William McCollum, 83, authority on equine infectious diseases, who developed a vaccine for equine viral arteritis; on July 1, 2007, in Lexington.

Art McCready, 83, longtime starter at Longacres racetrack; after a lengthy illness, on June 13, 2007, in Washington.

Dorothy McCutcheon, 80, former trainer who saddled runners at Golden Gate Fields, Turf Paradise, Suffolk Downs, and Finger Lakes during the 1970s. Wife of retired trainer J. R. McCutcheon; of congestive heart failure, on April 25, 2007, in California.

J. R. McCutcheon, 83, owner and trainer, who saddled 319 winners over a 39-year career. Widower of trainer Dorothy McCutcheon; of Lou Gehrig's Disease, on November 30, 2007, in California.

Jim McKay, 86, Emmy-winning broadcaster, longtime host of "ABC Wide World of Sports," and co-founder of the Maryland Million, on June 7, 2008, in Monkton, Maryland.

John McKinnon, 86, former stable agent for Racing Hall of Fame trainer Jack Van Berg and farm manager of Alice Ann Farm in Florida; in December 2007, in Michigan.

Lee McLaughlin, 71, longtime racehorse owner, actor, and stuntman, whose wife, Anita, makes stakes saddlecloths for Santa Anita Park; on September 20, 2007, in Northridge, California.

Rolland McMaster, 93, longtime Michigan breeder and owner of McMaster Farm, which stands leading state sire Demaloot Demashoot; former director of the Michigan Thoroughbred Breeders and Owners Association; in October 2007, in Fenton, Michigan.

William McMeans, 69, successful Washington-based trainer, whose top runners included Washington hall of fame member Table Run and major stakes winner Times Rush; following a long illness, on March 6, 2007, in Sunnyside, Washington.

Mary Mehok, 65, wife of trainer Bill Mehok, member of the Arizona Thoroughbred Breeders Association, who was involved with the backstretch church at Turf Paradise; on January 25, 2008, in Arizona.

George Moore, 84, legendary Australian jockey who won 2,278 races and 35 Derbys during a 33-year career, including the 1967 Epsom Derby on Royal Palace. Father of successful trainers Gary and John Moore; on January 8, 2008, in Sydney, Australia.

James Moran Jr., Maryland-based owner and breeder, who operated Elk Manor Farm and whose homebreds included 2006 English highweight Les Arcs and Maryland champion Richetta; after a short illness, on April 9, 2008, in Maryland.

Henry Moreno, 77, retired jockey, who rode Dark Star to a 24-to-1 upset over Native Dancer in the 1953 Kentucky Derby; of pancreatic cancer, on February 1, 2007, in Florence, Oregon.

John Morgan, 76, retired trainer whose career spanned nearly 35 years, and who saddled future Racing Hall of Fame jockey Earlie Fires's first winner; of cancer, on December 16, 2007, in Hot Springs, Arkansas.

Ross Morton, 74, track announcer at Finger Lakes for nearly a half-century and for 23 years at Gulfstream Park, whose calls included races with Seattle Slew, Forego, John Henry, and Spectacular Bid; on February 20, 2008, in Hollywood, Florida.

Damien Murphy, 23, Irish jockey; of injuries sustained in a fall at Wellington racetrack, on January 28, 2007, in Australia.

Ed Nahem, 64, California-based owner and breeder, whose best runners included 1993 champion older male Bertrando and Grade 1 winner Bilo; of liver failure, on October 31, 2007, in Beverly Hills, California.

Robert Narvell, 62, longtime horseman, who owned and operated Iron Bridge Farm near Parkesburg, Pennsylvania; on February 23, 2007, in Unionville, Pennsylvania.

Eugene Navarro, 92, retired trainer, member of Calder Race Course's Oriental Park Hall of Fame, whose top runners included multiple graded stakes winners Charon and Youmadeyourpoint; on November 27, 2007, in Hallandale, Florida.

John Nazareth Sr., 77, horseman, who spent half a century in racing as a jockey and trainer, associated with such runners as Graustark, Genuine Risk, Kauai King, and Foolish Pleasure; on November 2, 2007, in Indiantown, Florida.

Harold "Whitey" Nolen, 67, Southwest-based trainer during the 1980s and '90s, auctioneer, member of the Race Track Chaplaincy of Texas council based at Lone Star Park; of heart failure, on April 22, 2008, in Fort Worth, Texas.

Louis Olah, 79, longtime keeper of the silks in the jockeys' rooms at New York Racing Association racetracks and a former jockey, who won nearly 200 races; of a staphylococcus infection, on March 8, 2008, in New York.

Jose Olivares, 66, retired jockey, member of the Oriental Park Hall of Fame at Calder Race Course, leading rider of 1959 in Cuba, a leading rider at Finger Lakes until paralyzed in a 1970 fall; of a heart attack, on January 17, 2007, in Tampa, Florida.

Robert O'Malley, 69, longtime executive at Suffolk Downs, where over 30 years his offices included general manager, chief operating officer, and vice president of planning and development; of cancer, on February 25, 2007, in Milton, Massachusetts.

Vic Oppegard, 87, retired Southern California trainer, whose runners included 1987 Hollywood Oaks (G1) winner Perchance to Dream; on March 2, 2008, in Kentucky.

Beach Opperman, 49, trainer, based at Lone Star Park in Texas; on January 21, 2007, in Metairie, Louisiana.

Peggy Oster, owner, trainer, and outrider, based at Turf Paradise; on December 9, 2007, in Arizona.

Mario Padovani, 96, retired trainer, who saddled runners in New York and Florida from the 1940s through the '60s; on March 19, 2008, in Ocala.

David Parks, 54, Washington-based owner and breeder, member of the Washington Thoroughbred Breeders Association, and co-owner of Fell Hill Farm with wife, Elaine, where they bred state-bred champions Spanish Highway and Judicature; of a heart attack, on February 10, 2007, in Auburn, Washington.

Brigid Payne, 36, Australian-based jockey, daughter of trainer Patrick Payne and one of eight sibling riders; of heart seizures, on January 8, 2007, in Australia.

Sir Philip Payne-Gallwey, 72, a former director of the British Bloodstock Agency, who purchased French champion Nureyev as a yearling for $1.3-million for Stavros Niarchos, and who sent influential sire *Sir Tristram to the Southern Hemisphere in 1975; on February 3, 2008, in Newbury, England.

William Pearce, 80, longtime Canadian-based trainer; of leukemia, on April 28, 2008, in Ontario.

Rebecca Peters, 31, New Zealand-based jockey; of injuries sustained in a training accident at Riccarton Park, on June 6, 2007, in New Zealand.

Peter Petro, 73, longtime owner, father of trainers Mike Petro and Kathy Ritvo, and of jockey Nick Petro; in early June 2007, in Florida.

John Petty, 97, retired Texas breeder, founder of Paradise Farms, near Longview, whose top homebred runners included Texas Derby winner Day Time Tudor; on August 9, 2007.

Joan Phillips, 83, owner-breeder of champions Sunshine Forever and Soaring Softly, daughter of the late Darby Dan Farm founder John Galbreath, and mother of the farm's current co-managing partner John Phillips; on April 21, 2008, in Columbus, Ohio.

Cynthia Phipps, 62, noted owner, who campaigned homebred champion Christmas Past and Grade 1 winners Versailles Treaty and Gold Fever; daughter of famed owner-breeder Ogden Phipps and sister of current Jockey Club Chairman Ogden Mills "Dinny" Phipps; of injuries sustained in an apartment fire, on October 24, 2007, in New York.

Hubert Pilcher, 71, Florida-based horseman, owner of Shade Tree Farm, and former manager at Meadowbrook, Waldemar, and Gateway Farms, who worked with such prominent stallions as What a Pleasure, L'Enjoleur, and Norcliffe; on February 6, 2008, in Florida.

William Pindell, 69, retired jockey, who rode at Charles Town Races for 17 years and later served as a jockeys' valet there for more than a quarter-century; on May 19, 2007, in Virginia.

Sidney Port, 96, longtime Chicago-based owner, whose top runners included two-time Stars and Stripes Breeders' Cup Turf Handicap (G3) winner Ballingarry (Ire) and 2004 Arlington Classic Stakes (G2) winner Toasted; on June 11, 2007, in Chicago.

Chuck Potter, 52, simulcast coordinator at Emerald Downs since 1996, former jockey's agent and longtime owner; of a heart attack, on January 11, 2007, in Washington.

Anthony Presti, 76, former jockey, who rode competitively between 1957 and '72 before retiring to become a trainer; on February 20, 2007.

Jack Proctor, 81, trainer, brother of the late Texas horse racing hall of fame trainer Willard Proctor, uncle to successful trainers Hap and Tom Proctor; on April 6, 2008, in Gilmer, Texas.

Frank Rappa, 75, retired Southern California-based trainer, whose runners included Grade 3 winner First Advance; after an illness, on April 1, 2007, in Henderson, Nevada.

Gwen Reading, 89, owner for six decades with her husband, John; in September 2007, in Michigan.

Don Rice, 72, an eight-time leading trainer at Tampa Bay Downs, who saddled more than 1,400 winners in a 30-year career; of an injury sustained at his Central Florida farm, on January 6, 2008, in Gainesville, Florida.

Tony Richards, 80, European-based owner and founder of Ewar Stud Farm, whose 1985 champion French juvenile Bold Arrangement (GB) finished second in the Kentucky Derby (G1) the following spring; on January 2, 2008, in England.

Sir Tristram Ricketts, 61, racing executive, chief executive of Britain's Horserace Betting Levy Board; former chief executive and secretary of the British Horseracing Board; chairman of the European Pattern Committee; of pancreatic cancer, on November 7, 2007, in England.

Dr. Gerry Rose, well-known Australian veterinarian and owner, whose runners included 1999 Australian highweight filly and Group 1 winner Belle Du Jour; of cancer, in June 2007, in Australia.

Baron Guy de Rothschild, 98, one of France's leading owners and breeders for more than a half-century, whose runners included 1963 English and French Horse of the Year Exbury; on June 12, 2007, in France.

George "Jeep" Ryan, 78, retired jockey, who won more than 900 races while riding primarily in Ohio and Kentucky; of a stroke, on February 19, 2007, in Amelia, Ohio.

Tony Ryan, 71, co-founder of Ireland-based Ryanair, owner of Castleton Lyons Farm in Lexington, co-sponsor with THOROUGHBRED TIMES of a $10,000 book award competition; of cancer, on October 3, 2007, in County Kildare, Ireland.

Elizabeth Samuel, 74, co-founder of multiple Sovereign Award-winning Sam-Son Farm with her late husband, Ernie, breeder of such champions as Dance Smartly and Chief Bearhart, and of leading 2007 North American sire Smart Strike; of cancer and emphysema, in March 2008, in Canada.

Tammy Samuel-Balaz, 47, owner and breeder who ran her family's Sovereign Award-winning Sam-Son Farm, where Racing Hall of Fame filly Dance Smartly and leading sire Smart Strike were bred and raised; of cancer, on January 5, 2008, in Canada.

Joseph Scafidi, 65, prominent New England owner, who raced stakes winner Malaika and 2005 New England champion older male Itsawonderfulife; of cancer, on April 8, 2007, in Massachusetts.

Al Schwizer, 71, former trainer and Southern California-based exercise rider, who worked for Racing Hall of Fame trainer Bobby Frankel for 30 years; on January 7, 2008, in Monrovia, California.

Jane Clark Scott, owner and breeder, former exercise rider; board member of the Race Track Chaplaincy of America and Women's Thoroughbred Action League; in November 2007, in Florida.

Angelo J. "Bill" Segale, 83, owner, whose top runners included Washington-bred champions Jumron Won and T. V. Patient; at his home, on January 1, 2007, in Federal Way, Washington.

Rol Shaal, 76, longtime racing official at Nebraska racetracks, member of the Nebraska racing hall of fame; after a long illness, on March 12, 2007, in Gordon, Nebraska.

Mary McLeod Shoemaker, 85, owner, six-term member of the Arizona Thoroughbred Breeders Association board, raced three-time stakes winner Strategically; on August 19, 2007, in Tucson, Arizona.

Freida Shuffett, 65, a longtime member of the Keeneland Association sales department; on October 17, 2007, in Kentucky.

John Silvertand, 62, breeder of 2005 champion and double classic winner Afleet Alex; of cancer, on January 7, 2007, in West Palm Beach, Florida.

Richard Sinkler, 63, breeder, who bred and raced 1986 Massachusetts horse of the year Isadorable and was honored that year as that state's top owner-breeder; of cancer, on October 10, 2007, at his home near Charlestown, Rhode Island.

Bob Sinne, 86, retired trainer who saddled more than 1,000 winners in a 50-year career; following a long illness, on March 12, 2007, in San Dimas, California.

Ronald Sladon, 78, president and spokesman for Calumet Farm during the 1990s, who in '92 received the Ambassador of Racing Award from the Kentucky Thoroughbred Media; of cancer, on January 14, 2008, in Daytona Beach, Florida.

Dr. John Steiner, 64, equine veterinarian at Hagyard Equine Medical Institute for 16 years; of a head injury sustained while working with a horse at Rhinebeck Equine Hospital, on May 26, 2008, in New York.

James Stone, 82, owner, chairman of New Orleans-based Stone Energy Corp., whose runners included Grade 1 winner and classic-placed Menifee and two-time Gold Cup (Eng-G1) winner Ardross; on January 14, 2008.

Allan Stubbs, 80, eight-time leading Tasmanian trainer between 1974 and '91; of cancer, early in 2007, in Australia.

Warren Stute, 85, longtime California-based trainer, whose top runners included major stakes winners *Figonero, June Darling, and Grey Memo; brother of noted trainer Mel Stute; of complications from a stroke, on August 9, 2007, in Arcadia, California.

Gerald Sutton, 84, owner and breeder, who raised both Thoroughbreds and Quarter Horses at his Florida farm, Sutton Place, and whose construction business developed many Ocala-area farms; in August 2007, in Florida.

Teddy Tamer, 76, former *Daily Racing Form* clocker, who at Hialeah Park in 1972 recorded Secretariat's first official workout; of cancer, on July 3, 2007, at his home in Cocoa Beach, Florida.

Shirley Taylor, 83, former two-term president of the Thoroughbred Owners and Breeders Association; member of the Jockey Club; part-owner of European champion Alleged; of complications from a stroke, on February 27, 2007, in Billings, Montana.

Ralph Theroux Sr., 86, longtime jockey's agent, whose clients had included Racing Hall of Fame riders Pat Day, Walter Blum, and Bill Boland; on September 15, 2007, in New York.

Year in Review — 2007-2008 Obituaries

Dave Thompson, 82, retired longtime jockey's agent, who represented future Racing Hall of Fame rider Pat Day briefly during the early 1970s; on May 26, 2008, in Sun City, Arizona.

Jackie Thompson, 80, farrier, who shod Kentucky Derby (G1) winners Dark Star, Proud Clarion, Dust Commander, Gato Del Sol, and Swale; following a long illness, on September 4, 2007, in Lexington.

Thomas Thompson, 35, founder and managing partner of Southern California-based Owner's Stable, which assembled racing and breeding partnerships; after a long illness, on January 8, 2007, in California.

Ron Thomson, 76, Canadian trainer for nearly a half-century; on May 10, 2008, in Canada.

Susannah Hodges Thurston, 44, graphic design artist, who was instrumental in launching THOROUGHBRED TIMES as its first production manager from 1985 to '92; on May 2, 2008, in Frankfort, Kentucky.

Donna Trant, 52, longtime executive secretary to Oaklawn Park President Charles Cella, member of senior management at Oaklawn; of cancer, on June 1, 2007, in Arkansas.

Tic Tic Trinidad, 61, longtime bloodstock manager for Australia-based owner Eduardo Cojuangco; of a heart attack, in early February 2007, in the Philippines.

Lou Tuck, 89, longtime owner-breeder, who campaigned 1980 Hollywood Gold Cup (G1) winner Go West Young Man, and who with his wife, Libby, owned Wild Plum Farm in Colorado; on April 13, 2008, in Littleton, Colorado.

Terry Turner, 54, trainer and former jockey, who also operated a rehabilitation and layup facility; on May 16, 2007, in Canon City, Colorado.

Hector Ventura Jr., 31, former jockey based at Emerald Downs, who won 365 races and $3.1-million in prize money between 1995 and 2006; of an apparent drug overdose, on December 3, 2007, in Auburn, Washington.

Charlie Vinci, 83, retired Chicago-based trainer for more than 50 years, who saddled 895 winners and was inducted into the Illinois Thoroughbred Horsemen's Association; on May 31, 2007, in Hinsdale, Illinois.

Carlo Vittadini, 92, noted European owner and breeder, who raced 1975 English Horse of the Year Grundy and champions Orange Bay, Brook, and *Ortis III; on September 2, 2007, in Milan, Italy.

Elmo Walker, 72, trainer, breeder; on February 3, 2007, in Tyler, Texas.

Donald Q. Wallace, 75, lead architect for the Kentucky Horse Park and many Central Kentucky horse farms; on January 21, 2007, in Lexington.

Sidney Watters Jr., 90, Racing Hall of Fame trainer, whose runners included champions Hoist the Flag and Slew o' Gold, as well as steeplechase champions Amber Diver and Shadow Brook; on February 14, 2008, in Maryland.

Chuck Werstler, 86, retired trainer, who saddled runners for Dixiana Stable for three decades and whose best included major stakes winners Golden Ruler, Hard Work, and Flying Target; on April 5, 2007, in Hermitage, Tennessee.

Ed Westendorf, 57, owner and co-host of "The Regular Guy Handicapping Show" at River Downs; on November 5, 2007, in Beavercreek, Ohio.

Frank Whiteley Jr., 93, Racing Hall of Fame trainer, who in a nearly 50-year career conditioned Hall of Fame performers Forego, Ruffian, and Damascus, and champion Tom Rolfe; after a long illness, on May 2, 2008, in Camden, South Carolina.

Peter Whiting, 76, longtime West Coast breeder, sales consignor-agent, and former director of the California Thoroughbred Breeders Association, who, with his wife, Judy, owned The Anvil ranch in Solvang; of cancer, on March 20, 2007, in Fort Bragg, California.

Thomas Whitney, 90, owner and breeder and noted author-translator, who bred 1985 Goffs Irish One Thousand Guineas (Ire-G1) winner Al Bahathri, plus Grade and Group 1 winners Aptostar and Duke of Marmalade; on December 2, 2007, in New York.

Helen Hickman Wickes, 83, owner and breeder for more than a half-century, who with her late husband, Walter, raced multiple stakes winner Aonbarr; after a short illness, on August 11, 2007, near Unionville, Pennsylvania.

Alec Wildenstein, 67, French owner and breeder, who campaigned Group 1 winners Westerner and Aquarelliste; son of renowned owner-breeder Daniel Wildenstein; on February 18, 2008, in Paris.

Tony Wildman, 60, Australian trainer, whose runners included group winners Timbourina, Gentle Genius, and Cinque Cento; after a long battle with cancer, on June 3, 2008, in Australia.

Les Wiley Jr., 74, longtime Kentucky-based trainer, who saddled more than 600 winners since 1971; following a long illness, on February 19, 2008, in Kentucky.

Augustine "Gus" Williams, 81, owner, who campaigned 2003 champion three-year-old male and dual classic winner Funny Cide as a member of Sackatoga Stable; of a stroke, on April 12, 2007, in Albany, New York.

Louis Wolfson, 95, financier, whose Harbor View Farm ranked as America's leading breeder by wins three times during the 1970s and as leading owner between '78-'80. Owner-breeder with wife, Patrice, of Racing Hall of Fame inductee Affirmed and champions Outstandingly, Flawlessly, and It's in the Air; on December 30, 2007, in Bal Harbour, Florida.

H. L. Womack, 75, a former leading trainer at River Downs and Latonia Race Course, who saddled more than 600 winners between 1976 and 2007; on January 17, 2008, in Edgewood, Kentucky.

Alan Woods, 62, well-known handicapper, who was said to have accounted for up to 2% of Hong Kong's total racing handle of $64-billion; on January 26, 2008, in Hong Kong.

Dick Worsley, 73, former English-based jockey who rode both on the flat and over jumps during the 1940s and '50s, and later became a trainer in the United States; of stomach cancer, on January 7, 2007, in Newark, Delaware.

Roy Yaka, 75, retired successful Northern California-based jockey and trainer; after a long illness, on February 21, 2007, in California.

David Yount, 56, former vice president and director of racing at Evangeline Downs racetrack; of cancer, on April 2, 2008, at his home in Sunset, Louisiana.

Philippe Zanotti, 44, exercise rider and sale-horse showman; of injuries sustained in a car accident, on June 9, 2007, in Lexington.

Horse Deaths 2007 and 2008

AARON THE HAT, 1995 b. h., Glitterman—Love Cut, by Cutlass. 35-3-3-4, $50,650. Won the 2000 Magic City Classic S. Sire of winners; in 2007, in Alabama.

ABBONDANZA, 2001 ch. g., Alphabet Soup—Katie McLaury, by Centrust. 28-8-4-4, $378,355. Won the 2004 Hirsch Jacobs S.; of a heart attack following a workout, in early February 2007.

ABSOLUTE CHAMPION, 2001 b. g., Marauding—Beauty Belle, by Ideal Planet. 32-7-6-3, $2,857,572. Champion sprinter of 2007 in Hong Kong. Won the 2006 Cathay Pacific Hong Kong Sprint (HK-G1); after breaking down in the Krisflyer International Sprint, on May 18, 2008, in Singapore.

AETOLIAN, 1982 gr. h., Danzig—Flying Fur, by *Sky High II. 3-2-1-0, $30,040. Sire of four known stakes winners, including 1996 Uruguayan champion grass mare La Riviana; of old age, in April 2007, in Argentina.

A FLEETS DANCER, 1995 ch. h., Afleet—My Dream Come True, by Vice Regent. 45-12-6-8, $1,036,649. Canadian champion older male of 2001. Sire of 16 winners from first two crops racing; in 2007, at Anson Stud Farm, in Ontario.

AL AKBAR, 1990 b. h., Success Express—Gala Night, by Blakeney. 9-6-1-2, $159,226. Won the 1993 Bayer Classic (NZ-G1). Sire of eight stakes winners, including New Zealand classic winner and highweight Hustler; of a hoof injury, in July 2007, at Grangewilliam Stud, in New Zealand.

ALEXANDER TANGO (IRE), 2004 ch. f., Danehill Dancer—House in Wood, by Woodman. 12-4-2-1, $357,012. Won the 2007 Garden City S. (G1); of injuries sustained in a freak accident, in October 2007, at Woods Edge Farm, in Lexington.

ALKALDE, 1985 dk. b. or br. h., Konigsstuhl—Astra, by Kaiseradler. German highweight at three. Won the 1988 Mehl-Muelhens-Rennen (Ger-G1) (German Two Thousand Guineas). Sire of nine stakes winners, including German highweight Wild Romance; of heart failure, in January 2007, in Germany.

ALL AT SEA, 1989 ch. m., Riverman—Lost Virtue, by Cloudy Dawn. 9-5-3-0, $555,643. Won the 1992 Prix du Moulin de Longchamp (Fr-G1). Dam of stakes winner Insinuate; in 2007.

AL MAMOON, 1981 ch. h., Believe It—Lady Winborne, by Secretariat. 32-11-7-3, $1,249,906. Won the 1987 John Henry H. (G1). Sire of nine stakes winners, including Grade 2 winner Onceinabluemamoon; of old age, on May 18, 2007, at Cardiff Stud Farms, in Creston, California.

ALMUTAWAKEL (GB), 1995 b. h., Machiavellian—Elfaslah, by Green Desert. 19-4-4-1, $3,643,021. Won the 1999 Dubai World Cup (UAE-G1). Sire of eight stakes winners, including New Zealand champion Wahid and 2007 Mercedes-Benz Hong Kong Derby (HK-G1) winner Izzat; from chronic arthrosis, in November 2007, at Derrinstown Stud, in Ireland.

ALOHA PROSPECTOR, 1985 b. h., Native Prospector—Ms. Hapa Haole, by *Hawaii. 7-4-0-3, $203,393. Won the 1988 Swift S. (G3). Sire of three stakes winners, including multiple Grade 2 winner Unfinished Symph; in 2007, at Ackel Thoroughbred Farm, in Sulphur, Louisiana.

AQUILEGIA, 1989 ch. m., Alydar—Courtly Dee, by Never Bend. 30-8-5-9, $446,081. Won the 1993 New York H. (G2). Dam of a $2.4-million yearling and three stakes winners, including English Group 3 winner Bertolini; of foaling complications, in March 2007, at Middlebrook Farm, in Lexington.

ARBUCKLE BANDIT, 2003 b. g., Service Stripe—Sombra En El Cielo, by Marquetry. 13-5-2-4, $218,158. Won the 2006 Commonwealth Turf S.; of a heart attack during a race, on January 13, 2007, at Fair Grounds, in New Orleans.

ARWON, 1973 b. g., Aritzo—Fair Flash, by Resurgent. Won the 1978 and '79 Melbourne Cup (Aus-G1); due to infirmities of age, on May 19, 2007, in Australia.

ARYENNE, 1977 b. m., Green Dancer—Americaine, by Cambremont. 10-5-1-1, $283,098. Won the 1980 Poule d'Essai des Pouliches (French One Thousand Guineas). Dam of 1990 Ever Ready Epsom Derby (Eng-G1) winner Quest for Fame (GB) and Grade 2 winner Yenda (GB); on July 9, 2007, in England.

ASCOT KNIGHT, 1984 b. h., Danzig—Bambee T. T., by Better Bee. 10-2-3-2, $200,232. Won the 1987 Mecca Bookmakers' Scottish Derby. Canada's leading sire of 2000. Sire of 33 stakes winners, including Canadian champion Pennyhill Park and Grade 1 winner Influent; euthanized due to declining health, on February 8, 2007, at Windfields Farm, near Toronto.

ASHBY HILL, 2002 ch. g., Cahill Road—Prado's Joy, by El Prado (Ire). 12-4-1-2, $70,274. Won the 2005 Lea County Sprint S.; after he collapsed near the finish of a $6,250 claiming race at Golden Gate Fields, on November 15, 2007, in California.

ASTRA, 1996 b. m., Theatrical (Ire)—Savannah Slew, by Seattle Slew. 16-11-1-2, $1,378,424. Winner of four Grade 1 stakes; of colic, in June 2007, at Hagyard Equine Medical Institute, in Lexington.

BADTOTHEBONEANDREW, 2002 ch. h., On the Sauce—Singular Mischief, by Singular. 34-4-7-6, $351,162. Louisiana-bred champion three-year-old male of 2005. Won the 2005 Louisiana Champions Day Classic S.; in early 2007, in Louisiana.

BANKER'S GOLD, 1994 ch. h., Forty Niner—Banker's Lady, by Nijinsky II. 15-6-3-1, $461,420. Won the 1998 Tom Fool H. (G2). Sire of 11 stakes winners, including Panamanian champions Daphne and Distintoydiferente; euthanized after breaking a leg, in April 2008, in Cyprus.

BANKER'S JET, 1982 b. g., Tri Jet—Weezie, by Final Ruling. 106-28-22-15, $679,381. Winner of seven stakes, including the 1987 A Phenomenon S. Rescued by Thoroughbred Retirement Foundation in the early 1990s, when found starving at a New York riding stable; from arthritis, on July 23, 2007, at the Connecticut farm of TRF Treasurer Ray Roy.

BARBARO, 2003 dk. b. or br. c., Dynaformer—La Ville Rouge, by Carson City. 7-6-0-0, $2,302,200. Won the 2006 Kentucky Derby Presented by Yum! Brands (G1), Florida Derby (G1); of injuries sustained in the 2006 Preakness Stakes (G1) and laminitis; on January 29, 2007, at the New Bolton Center, in Kennett Square, Pennsylvania.

BARKLEY SOUND, 2004 b. c., Dixieland Band—Class On Class, by Jolie's Halo. 7-3-0-1, $79,696. Won the 2007 Pasco S.; after breaking down in the Derby Trial S., on April 28, 2007, at Churchill Downs, in Louisville.

BECAME A LARK, 1974 b. m., T. V. Lark—*Blow Up II, by Abdos. 30-6-3-9, $135,550. Won the 1979 Golden Poppy H. Dam of 1989 Hollywood Derby (G1) winner Live the Dream and Grade 3 winner Warcraft. Grandam of Grade 1 winner Kicken Kris; of old age, on December 12, 2007, at Crestwood Farm, in Lexington.

BLAZING SWORD, 1994 dk. b. or br. g., Sword Dance (Ire)—Demetroula, by Singular. 45-11-7-7, $1,184,055. Florida-bred champion, who won the 2000 Washington Park H. (G2), Widener H. (G3); of an aneurysm, in April 2008, at Stonehedge Farm South, in Williston, Florida.

BLUE DAKOTA, 2002 b. h., Namid—Touraya, by Tap On Wood. 7-4-0-0, $103,146. Won the 2004 Norfolk S. (Eng-G3); of injuries sustained in a farm accident, in 2007, at Hedgeholme Stud, in Australia.

BLUEGRASS WARRIOR, 1985 ch. g., Navajo—Kentucky Lucky, by *Relian. 125-21-15-10, $231,533. Ran through the age of 13 and set three track records at Turfway Park in 1990 and '91; in August 2007, in Kentucky.

BLUE ON BLUES, 2001 ch. g., Lode—Blue Baby Blue, by Forever Sparkle. 34-6-6-3, $248,046. Won the 2004 Asociacion de Propietarios de Caballos de Carrera de Buenos Aires (Arg-G3); of a heart attack, in early March 2007, at Nad al Sheba racecourse, in Dubai.

BO CHIME, 2003 dk. b. or br. f., Chimes Band—Bountiful Table, by Pirate's Bounty. 18-4-3-3, $141,287. Won the 2005 Dessie and Fern Sawyer Futurity and the Sorie S.; after breaking down following a race, on March 6, 2007, at Sunland Park, in New Mexico.

BOLD GIRL, 2004 b. f., Red Ransom—Bold Bold (Ire), by Sadler's Wells. 6-2-1-0, $57,913. Won the 2007 Prix Policeman-Federation Equestre de la Principaute de Monaco; after breaking down in the Prix Cleopatre (Fr-G3), on May 1, 2007, at Saint-Cloud, in France.

Bondage, 2003 b. f., Broad Brush—Vow That Binds, by Miswaki. 19-5-6-3, $187,470. Stakes-placed; after breaking down in the Ladies Handicap, on December 15, 2007, at Aqueduct, in New York.

BREGAWN, 1974 ch. g., Saint Denys—Miss Society, by Choral Society. 74-20-0-0, $286,460. Won the 1983 Cheltenham Gold Cup; of old age, in the fall of 2007, in Ireland.

BRIGHT CANDLES, 1987 ch. m., El Gran Senor—Christmas Bonus, by Key to the Mint. 34-5-6-8, $405,091. Won the 1990 Santa Ysabel S. Dam of Grade 1 winner and noted sire Grand Slam, and stakes-winning Leestown; of foaling complications, in March 2007, at Overbrook Farm, in Lexington.

BRIGHT ONE, 2003 ch. c., Dance Brightly—Twinkle, by Lively One. 8-4-1-0, $594,294. Won the 2006 West Virginia Derby (G3); after breaking down in the Richter Scale Breeders' Cup Championship Stakes (G2), on March 3, 2007, at Gulfstream Park, in Florida.

Bucksplasher, 1977 ch. h., Buckpasser—Victoria Star, by Northern Dancer. 45-5-7-9, $126,454. Grade 2-placed. Sire of 31 stakes winners, including 1998 champion grass male Buck's Boy; in early October 2007, at Irish Acres Farm, in Ocala.

BUROOJ, 1990 br. h., Danzig—Princess Sucree, by Roberto. 21-7-5-4, $185,398. Won the 1995 Bonusprint September S. (Eng-G3). Sire of 13 known stakes winners, including 2005 Brazilian champion two-year-old colt Eumsonho and Group 1 winner Baccarat; colic, in February 2007, in Brazil.

CADOUDAL, 1979 dk. b. or br. h., Green Dancer—Come to Sea, by Sea Hawk II. 9-2-2-1, $120,618. Won the 1982 Prix Hocquart (Fr-G2). Sire of 49 stakes winners, including millionaire French steeplechasers Kotkijet and Earl Grant; of old age, on February 9, 2007, in France.

CAMDEN PARK, 1998 b. h., A.P. Indy—Danzig Island, by Danzig. 6-2-0-1, $78,710. South Africa's leading freshman sire of 2006-'07. Sire of two stakes winners, including multiple Group 1 winner Jay Peg; of toxic shock, on June 21, 2007, in South Africa.

CANADIAN SILVER, 1988 gr. h., Geiger Counter—Cheerily, by Drone. 29-11-7-4, $536,803. Five-time stakes winner in Canada. Sire of three stakes winners, including Australian Group 2 winner Make Mine Magic; in April 2008, in Australia.

CANDY BOX, 2002 dk. b. or br. m., Running Stag—Miners Mirage, by Mining. 13-4-5-0, $205,520. Won the 2007 Stormy Krissy S., Grade 2-placed; after breaking down in a workout, on May 7, 2007, at Belmont Park, in New York.

Candy Stripes, 1982 ch. h., Blushing Groom (Fr)—Bubble Company (Fr), by Lyphard. 6-2-1-0, $47,357. Classic-placed in France. Two-time leading sire in Argentina. Sire of 61 stakes winners and ten champions, including 2006 U.S. Horse of the Year Invasor (Arg); of colic, on February 28, 2007, at Haras Carampagne, in Argentina.

CANTREL, 2004 ch. f., Gulch—Red Satin Slippers, by Peteski. 9-5-1-1, $146,790. Won the 2007 Wonders Delight S.; after breaking down in the Inaugural S., on September 1, 2001, at Presque Isle Downs, in Pennsylvania.

CAPOTE, 1984 dk. b. or br. h., Seattle Slew—Too Bald, by Bald Eagle. 10-3-0-1, $714,470. Champion at two. Won the 1986 Breeders' Cup Juvenile (G1). Sire of 62 stakes winners, including champion Boston Harbor and Grade 1 winner Capote Belle; euthanized due to spinal cord problems, on August 24, 2007, at Three Chimneys Farm, in Midway, Kentucky.

CARLINGFORD CASTLE, 1980 ch. h., Le Bevard—Rachel Ruysch, by Skymaster. Won the 1983 Gallinule S. (Ire-G2), second in the '83 Epsom Derby (Eng-G1). Sire of five stakes winners; of heart attack, in early 2007, at Astley Grange Stud, in England.

CARNIVALAY, 1981 b. h., Northern Dancer—Obeah, by Cyane. 4-1-1-1, $18,480. Maryland's leading sire of 1992. Sire of 38 stakes winners, including steeplechase stakes winner Mixed Up; of a heart attack, on January 9, 2007, at Country Life Farm, in Bel Air, Maryland.

CASINO EVIL, 2003 b. c., Salt Lake—Code of Love, by Cryptoclearance. 22-6-5-3, $309,906. Won the 2006 Round Table S.; after breaking down in the Ack Ack

H. (G3), on November 3, 2007, at Churchill Downs, in Louisville.

CATBIRD, 1996 b. h., Danehill—Fitting, by Marscay. 14-5-1-0, $1,114,553. Australian champion at two. Won the 1999 Golden Slipper S. (Aus-G1). Sire of ten stakes winners, including Group 1 winner Cats Fun; of laminitis, on June 9, 2007, in Australia.

CAT'S AT HOME, 1997 b. h., Tabasco Cat—Homewrecker, by Buckaroo. 31-9-4-3, $708,575. Won the 2002 Philip H. Iselin H. (G2). Sire of stakes winners Spread the News and House Mouse; unexpectedly, on March 24, 2007, at Windfields Farm, in Ontario.

CEFIS, 1985 ch. h., Caveat—Ring Dancer, by Dancing Champ. 67-6-8-9, $785,314. Won the 1988 Pennsylvania Derby (G2). Sire of winners; of a heart attack, in January 2007, at Middle Creek Farm, in Woodhull, New York.

CELESTIAL DANCER, 1979 b. h., Godswalk—Oulanova, by Nijinsky II. 26-6-0-1, $92,402. Won the 1984 Prix de Meautry (Fr-G3). Sire of 15 stakes winners, including Singaporean highweight Bojack; euthanized due to failing health, in May 2007, at Lyndhurst Stud, in Australia.

CHACE CITY, 2004 b. c., Carson City—General Jeanne, by Honour and Glory. 4-3-0-0, $219,783. Won the 2006 Saratoga Special Breeders' Cup S. (G2); of colic, in January 2007, at Peterson and Smith Equine Hospital, in Ocala.

CHARMING HOSTESS, 2005 dk. b. or br. f., Cape Town—Charming Gal, by Slew's Royalty. Unraced. Sold for $800,000 at the 2007 Barretts March two-year-olds in training sale; after breaking down in a workout, on November 22, 2007, at Hollywood Park, in California.

CHEEKY LADY, 1997 b. m., Roselier—Railstown Cheeky, by Strong Gale. 17-3-2-3, $83,230. Stakes-winning Irish hurdler; of injuries sustained in a fall during the Irish Grand National, on April 9, 2007, in Ireland.

CHELSEY FLOWER, 1991 b. m., His Majesty—Chelsey Dancer, by Affirmed. 34-8-3-7, $568,305. Won the 1996 Flower Bowl Invitational H. (G1). Dam of French group winner Kentucky Dynamite; of foaling complications, on March 14, 2007, at Rood & Riddle Equine Clinic, in Lexington.

CHILUKKI, 1997 b. m., Cherokee Run—Song of Syria, by Damascus. 17-11-3-0, $1,201,828. Champion two-year-old filly of 1999. Won the 1999 Vinery Del Mar Debutante S. (G1), Oak Leaf S. (G1); of foaling complications, on May 7, 2007, at Hagyard Equine Medical Institute, in Lexington.

CLEVER BERTIE, 1991 b. m., Timeless Native—Clever But Costly, by Clever Trick. Unraced. Dam of multiple graded stakes winners Hurricane Bertie and Allamerican Bertie; from arthritic complications, on May 30, 2008, at Clarkland Farm, in Lexington.

COMMANDER IN CHIEF, 1990 b. h., Dancing Brave—Slightly Dangerous, by Roberto. 6-5-0-1, $1,311,514. European champion three-year-old colt. Won the 1993 Ever Ready Epsom Derby (Eng-G1) and Budweiser Irish Derby (Ire-G1). Sire of 15 stakes winners, including Japanese champion Ein Bride; in a farm accident, on June 12, 2007, at Yushun Stallion Station, in Japan.

CORMORANT, 1974 b. h., His Majesty—Song Sparrow, by *Tudor Minstrel. 12-8-2-0, $243,174. Won the 1977 Jersey Derby (G1). Twice leading New York sire. Sire of 47 stakes winners, including champion Saratoga Dew and 1994 Kentucky Derby (G1) winner Go for Gin; broodmare sire of 2005 TVG Breeders' Cup Sprint (G1) winner Silver Train; of old age, on May 4, 2007, at Waldorf Farm, in North Chatham, New York.

CRAFTY RIDAN, 1986 dk. b. or br. h., Crafty Prospector—Lady Ridanilustros, by Illustrious. 59-13-5-16, $174,454. Won the 1991 Grasmick H. Two-time leading South Dakota sire. Sire of seven stakes winners, including Mr. Zooha; of a heart attack, in March 2008, at Dick Kellem Farm, in Belle Fourshce, South Dakota.

CRITIKOLA (ARG), 1995 ch. m., Tough Critic—Hola Keats, by *Keats. 22-8-3-3, $170,539. Won the 2000 Marcos Levalle (Arg-G2). Grade 1-placed in the U.S. Dam of 2006 Kentucky Oaks (G1) winner Lemons Forever; in April 2008.

CUTLASS REALITY, 1982 ch. h., Cutlass—Landera, by In Reality. 66-14-12-9, $1,405,660. Won the 1988 Hollywood Gold Cup H. (G1) and Californian S. (G1). Sire of ten stakes winners, including Cantua Creek; of laminitis, on October 5, 2007, at Harris Farms, in Coalinga, California.

DANCE SMARTLY, 1988 dk. b. or br. m., Danzig—Classy 'n Smart, by Smarten. 17-12-2-3, $3,263,835. Racing Hall of Fame. Canadian Horse of the Year in 1991. Eclipse Award winner at three. Canadian Broodmare of the Year in 2001. Dam of champion Dancethruthedawn and Queen's Plate S. winner Scatter the Gold; as a result of a paddock injury, on August 18, 2007, in Canada.

DANCING PIRATE, 1983 b. h., Pirate's Bounty—Fire Dance, by Bold Hitter. 13-3-2-3, $164,765. Won the 1985 San Miguel S. Sire of three stakes winners, including Fancy Pirate; in 2007, in California.

DANCING WITH WINGS, 1988 b. m., Danzig—Loudrangle, by Quadrangle. 11-5-1-0, $137,276. Won the 1991 Ontario Damsel S. Dam of 2004 Canadian Horse of the Year Soaring Free; in 2007.

DANTRELLE LIGHT, 2004 ch. f., Colony Light—Rainbow Fame, by Quest for Fame (GB). 16-4-2-3, $189,130. Won the 2007 Lulu's Ransom S.; after breaking down in the Stormy Frolic S. at Calder Race Course, on November 18, 2007, in Florida.

DANZIG DARLING, 1982 b. m., Danzig—Middlemarch, by Buckpasser. 22-4-6-2, $80,263. Won the 1985 Miss Woodford S. Dam of stakes winners Misnomer and Darling Danzig; in 2007.

DEFENSIVE PLAY, 1987 dk. b. or br. h., Fappiano—Safe Play, by Sham. 26-6-4-5. $1,688,631. Won the 1991 Charles H. Strub S. (G1). Sire of 13 stakes winners, including South African champion Mythical Play. Broodmare sire of 2007 Emirates Melbourne Cup (Aus-G1) winner Efficient; on November 20, 2007, at JDL Farm, in Vaughn, Montana.

Deploy, 1987 b. h., Shirley Heights—Slightly Dangerous, by Roberto. 5-2-2-1, $197,536. Classic-placed. Half brother to champions Warning (GB) and Commander in Chief. Sire of 15 stakes winners, including European highweight Zomaradah (GB); of a heart attack, in February 2008, at Scarvagh House, in Ireland.

Deputy Regent, 1980 dk. b. or br. h., Vice Regent—Tarpaper Alley, by Canadian Champ. 8-2-0-4, $26,994. Stakes-placed, Woodbine course-record-setter. Sire of three stakes winners, including Dusty Deputy; in 2007, in Canada.

DETROIT CITY, 2002 gr. or ro. h., Kingmambo—Seattle Victory, by Seattle Song. 20-12-1-0, $781,199. Won the 2006 Boylesports.com International Hurdle; of a heart attack during the Coral Ascot Hurdle, on November 24, 2007, at Ascot Race Course, in England.

DIAMOND LOVER, 1982 br. m., Sticks And Stones—Eight Carat, by *Pieces of Eight II. Winner of the 1987 Clearwood Railway H. (NZ-G1). Dam of four stakes winners, including champion Tristalove and Australian Derby (Aus-G1) winner Don Eduardo; euthanized due to failing health, on August 28, 2007, at Cambridge Stud, in Australia.

DIMITROVA, 2000 b. f., Swain (Ire)—The Caretaker (Ire), by Caerleon. 14-4-2-1, $1,142,696. Won the 2003 Flower Bowl Invitational S. (G1). Sold for $2-million in 2004 as a broodmare prospect at the Keeneland November breeding stock sale; in 2007.

DIXIE DOT COM, 1995 b. h., Dixie Brass—Sky Meadows, by Conquistador Cielo. 23-8-6-1, $1,332,775. Won the 1999 San Fernando Breeders' Cup S. (G2). Sire of winners; of a heart attack, on April 26, 2007, at Willow Tree Farm, in Burson, California.

DIXIELAND BRASS, 1986 ch. h., Dixieland Band—Windmill Gal, by Gallant Romeo. 8-5-0-1, $175,290. Won the 1989 Fountain of Youth S. (G2). Sire of 22 stakes winners, including Grade 2 winner Brass Scale; in 2007, at Flying Horse Farm, in British Columbia.

DREAM OF ANGELS, 2004 ch. c., Trippi—Burn Brightly, by American Chance. 9-5-2-2, $227,090. Won the 2006 Jack Price Juvenile and Middleground Breeders' Cup S.; of injuries sustained in a paddock accident, on October 6, 2007, at Keeneland Race Course, in Kentucky.

ECLIPTICAL, 1982 ch. h., Exclusive Native—Minnetonka, by Chieftain. 10-1-1-0, $9,482. Sire of five stakes winners, including 1994 Ohio Derby (G2) winner Exclusive Praline; of intestinal problems, on January 2, 2008, at Nandi Farm, in New Freedom, Pennsylvania.

EIGHT BELLES, 2005 gr. or ro. f., Unbridled's Song—Away, by Dixieland Band. 10-5-3-1, $708,650. Won the 2008 Fantasy S. (G2); broke down while pulling up after finishing second in the Kentucky Derby Presented by Yum! Brands (G1), on May 3, 2008, at Churchill Downs. Became cause celebre with PETA.

ELECTRIC LIGHT, 2002 gr. or ro. g., Silver Ghost—Aesthete, by Nijinsky II. 23-4-4-4, $159,732. Won the 2005 Pasco S.; after breaking down in a $50,000 optional claiming race, on September 14, 2007, at Belmont Park, in New York.

Elisa's Energy, 2002 dk. b. or br. f., Chester House—Merion Miss, by Halo. 13-4-3-3, $175,108. Multiple stakes-placed. Half sister to Arkansas Derby (G2) winner Private Emblem; of colic, in 2007.

ENVOY, 1998 b. g., Personal Escort—Sovereign Command, by Bold Venture. 48-9-3-3, $429,574. Won the 2006 Dulux New Zealand Colour Map Wellington Cup (NZ-G1); after breaking down in the Skycity Auckland Cup (NZ-G1), on March 7, 2007, at Ellerslie racecourse, in New Zealand.

ETERNAL SEARCH, 1978 dk. b. or br. m., Northern Answer—Bon Debarras, by Ruritania. 44-18-11-2, $642,177. Three-time Canadian champion. Winner of 15 stakes. Dam of six winners, including three stakes-placed; of cancer, in 2007, at Curraghmore Farm, in Ontario.

EVENING PERFORMANCE, 1991 b. m., Night Shift—Classic Design, by Busted. 27-7-4-2, $251,917. European and English highweighted older female sprinter of 1996. Won the 1996 Flying Five S. (Ire-G3); after colic surgery, in 2007, in England.

EXPENSE ACCOUNT, 1988 gr. or ro. h., Private Account—Expressive Dance, by Riva Ridge. 16-2-0-2, $38,296. Sire of five stakes winners, including $200,000-earners Solingen and Red Hawkeye; in a paddock accident, on January 25, 2007, at B-T Ranch, in Collinsville, Oklahoma.

FAPPIANO'S STAR, 1988 b. h., Fappiano—Star Hawaii, by *Hawaii. 49-13-5-4, $212,041. Won the 1995 Louisiana Handicap. Leading sire of 2003 and '05 in Puerto Rico. Sire of Puerto Rican horses of the year Bricola and Borrascoso; of a kidney ailment, on February 21, 2007, at Potrero Los Llanos, in Puerto Rico.

FAYR JAG, 1999 b. g., Fayruz—Lominda, by Lomond. 64-11-7-5, $742,360. Won the 2004 Golden Jubilee S. (Eng-G1); of injuries sustained in a starting gate accident, on April 21, 2008, at Pontefract racecourse, in England.

FIFTY STARS, 1998 b. h., Quiet American—My Bubbling Belle, by Tsunami Slew. 20-4-2-0, $706,222. Won the 2001 Louisiana Derby (G2). Sire of two first-crop winners; of a heart attack, on July 14, 2007, at a farm in Rockwall, Texas.

Finocchio, 1984 ro. h., Tap Shoes—By Law, by Drone. 46-15-7-8, $114,514. Stakes-placed. Sire of seven winners from seven starters; of old age, on August 27, 2007, at D & R Racing Stables, in Pinckney, Michigan.

FIT TO FIGHT, 1979 b. h., Chieftain—Hasty Queen II, by One Count. 26-14-3-3, $1,042,075. Won the 1984 New York handicap triple crown. Sire of 40 stakes winners, including Grade 1 winners Key Contender and Fit to Scout; of old age, on May 30, 2008, at Blue Ridge Farm, in Virginia.

FLAWLESS TREASURE, 2002 b. m., War Chant—Rose Diamond, by Diamond Shoal (GB). 18-3-1-1, $151,587. Won the 2008 Sabin S.; after breaking down in the Sheepshead Bay H. (G2), on May 24, 2008, at Belmont Park, in New York.

FLIGHT FORTY NINE, 1991 ch. h., Forty Niner—Fun Flight, by Full Pocket. 14-5-1-0, $126,768. Won the 1994 Bachelor S. Sire of stakes winners Flighty Forty Nine and Just in Flight; in 2007, at La Vista Farms, in Bonnerdale, Arkansas.

FLIPPY DIANE, 1994 gr. or ro. m., Aaron's Concorde—Elegant Edythe, by North Sea. 23-5-5-4, $202,250. Won the 1999 Maryland Million Distaff H.; of foaling complications, in April 2007.

FLIRTATIOUS, 1997 b. m., A.P. Indy—Grand Charmer, by Lord Avie. 12-4-5-1, $171,266. Dam of 2006 champion three-year-old filly Wait a While; euthanized due to wobbler syndrome, on July 20, 2007, in Kentucky.

FLY CRY, 1991 b. h., On to Glory—Good Routes,

by Pass Catcher. 29-12-8-3, $479,460. Won nine stakes, including the 1994 Risen Star S. Sire of winners; in 2007, at Simpson Farm, in Loranger, Louisiana.

FLYING CHEVRON, 1992 dk. b. or br. h., Carson City—Fly Me First, by *Herbager. 12-5-1-1, $383,610. Won the 1995 NYRA Mile H. (G1). Sire of six stakes winners, including millionaire Grade 1 winner Captain Squire; of a ruptured tumor, on March 6, 2007, at Woodvale Farm, in Lewisville, Pennsylvania.

FLY NORTH, 1993 b. m., Pleasant Colony—Dry North, by Temperence Hill. 8-3-1-1, $114,027. Won the 1995 Ontario Debutante S. Dam of 2002 champion three-year-old filly Farda Amiga; euthanized on July 11, 2007, at Payson Stud, in Lexington.

FRAN'S VALENTINE, 1982 dk. b. or br. m., Saros (GB)—Iza Valentine, by Bicker. 34-13-4-5, $1,375,465. Grade 1 winner. In inaugural Breeders' Cup Juvenile Fillies (G1) in 1984, became only horse to be disqualified from first in a Breeders' Cup event; dam of multiple Grade 1 winner With Anticipation and French group winner With Fascination; of old age, in October 2007, at Derry Meeting Farm, in Cochranville, Pennsylvania.

FRIEL'S FOR REAL, 2000 dk. b. or br. m., Sword Dance (Ire)—Beaties for Real, by Unreal Zeal. 33-13-5-4, $674,544. Won the 2004 Pimlico Breeders' Cup Distaff H. (G3); during a thunderstorm, on July 18, 2007, at Overbrook Farm, in Lexington.

GATO DEL SOL, 1979 gr. h., *Cougar II—Peacefully, by Jacinto. 39-7-9-7, $1,340,107. Won the 1982 Kentucky Derby (G1). Sire of two known stakes winners, including Panamanian champion Redactora; of old age, on August 7, 2007, at Stone Farm, in Paris, Kentucky.

GEORGE WASHINGTON (IRE), 2003 b. c., Danehill—Bordighera, by Alysheba. 14-6-1-4, $1,475,816. Europe's champion two- and three-year-old male; won the 2006 Stan James Two Thousand Guineas (Eng-G1); euthanized after breaking down in the Breeders' Cup Classic Powered by Dodge (G1), on October 27, 2007, at Monmouth Park, in New Jersey.

GIBSON COUNTY, 1997 b. h., In Excess (Ire)—Miss Gibson County, by Winrightt. 25-5-3-5, $376,465. California-bred 1999 champion juvenile male. Sire of two stakes winners, including 2008 Sunshine Millions Oaks winner American County; of an aneurysm, on March 12, 2008, at Ocala Stud Farm, in Florida.

GOLD TRAIN, 2005 ch. c., Gold Case—Sablena, by Mongol Warrior. 2-1-0-0, $12,625; after breaking down in the Lane's End Breeders' Futurity (G1), on October 6, 2007, at Keeneland Race Course, in Lexington.

GOWER, 2002 b. h., Mecke—Hidden Intent, by Pentelicus. 17-5-4-1, $162,825. Won the 2005 Ocala Breeders' Sales Sprint S.; of an apparent heart attack, after a workout at Calder Race Course, on June 5, 2007, in Florida.

GRACEFUL MINISTER, 1992 dk. b. or br. m., Deputy Minister—Cagey Exuberance, by Exuberant. 42-11-4-6, $446,445. Won the 1997 and '98 Wishing Well S. Dam of stakes-placed Uncontrollable; in 2007.

GROOM DANCER, 1984 b. h., Blushing Groom (Fr)—Featherhill (Fr), by Lyphard. 13-8-0-1, $255,205. Highweight at three in France. Won the 1987 Prix Lupin (Fr-G1). Sire of 40 stakes winners, including English, French, and European highweight Pursuit of Love; in early 2007, at Cheveley Park Stud, in England.

HALF FAMOUS, 2004 ch. c., Tribal Rule—Love Token, by Cox's Ridge. 10-2-3-1, $81,150. Won the 2006 Lost in the Fog Juvenile S., Grade 2-placed; after breaking down in the Palo Verde S., on March 4, 2007, at Turf Paradise, in Phoenix, Arizona.

HALLO DANDY, 1974 b. g., Menelek—Dandy Hall, by Last of the Dandies. 53-10-0-0, $143,741. Won England's Grand National Steeplechase in 1984; of old age, in January 2007, in England.

HALORY HUNTER, 1995 ch. h., Jade Hunter—Halory, by Halo. 10-3-2-3, $713,120. Won the 1998 Toyota Blue Grass S. (G2). Sire of five stakes winners, including Puerto Rican champion Forbidden Queen and multiple Grade 2 winner Halory Leigh; of laminitis, on August 20, 2007, at Double LL Farm, in Bosque, New Mexico.

HALO STEVEN, 2003 b. g., Halo's Image—Talullah, by Twining. 12-6-3-1, $341,819. Won the 2006 British Columbia Derby (Can-G3); of a heart attack, following a workout on January 28, 2007, at Hollywood Park, in California.

Hendrix, 2001 b. h., Sultry Song—Fluttery Danseur, by Wavering Monarch. 26-5-3-5, $389,150. Grade 1-placed; after breaking down in the Arcadia Handicap (G2), on April 7, 2007, at Santa Anita Park, in California.

HENNESSY, 1993 ch. h., Storm Cat—Island Kitty, by *Hawaii. 9-4-3-0, $580,400. Won the 1995 Hopeful S. (G1). Leading juvenile sire of 2001. Sire of 63 stakes winners, including champion Johannesburg and Grade 1 winners Henny Hughes and Madcap Escapade; of a heart attack, in August 2007, in Argentina.

HESANOLDSALT, 2003 dk. b. or br. h., Broad Brush—Salty Gal, by Cox's Ridge. 22-4-7-3, $514,938. Won the 2006 Fred W. Hooper H. (G3); of injuries sustained in a backstretch accident, on January 16, 2008, at Palm Meadows Training Center, in Florida.

HE'S NO PIE EATER, 2003 br. c., Canny Lad—Ladies' Day, by Ascot Knight. 16-5-2-3, $595,837. Won the 2007 Dubai Rosehill Guineas (Aus-G1); after breaking down in a workout, on April 16, 2007, at Randwick racecourse, in Australia.

HIGH ACCOLADE, 2000 b. h., Mark of Esteem (Ire)—Generous Lady, by Generous. 21-6-5-4, $684,788. Won the 2003 King Edward VII S. (Eng-G2), classic-placed; after breaking down in a workout, in late June 2007, in England.

HIGH AGAIN, 2004 ch. f., High Yield—Miss Belle O, by Olympio. 12-3-2-2, $270,546. Won the 2007 Bonnie Miss S. (G2); of a heart attack during a workout on December 13, 2007, at Payson Park Training Center, in Florida.

HIGH DICE, 1995 b. g., Lytrump—Sand Wedge, by Affirmed. 81-21-16-16, $350,590. Winner of 16 stakes in Nebraska; of a bladder blockage, in August 2007, in Nebraska.

HIGHLAND BUD, 1985 b. g., Northern Baby—Fleur d'Or, by Exclusive Native. 27-10-10-3, $514,796. Champion steeplechaser of 1989. Won the 1989 and '92 Breeders' Cup Steeplechase; euthanized due to a debilitating sinus condition, on May 20, 2008, at

Charles and Sherry Fenwick Jr.'s farm, in Butler, Maryland.

HIGHLAND CHIEFTAIN, 1983 b. h., Kampala—La Primavera, by Northfields. 35-16-5-3, $334,896. Italian highweight at four and five. Sire of stakes winner Golden Flower; of old age, in 2007, in Germany.

HIGH YIELD, 1997 ch. h., Storm Cat—Scoop the Gold, by Forty Niner. 14-4-4-3, $1,170,196. Won the 2000 Toyota Blue Grass S. (G1). Sire of 16 stakes winners, including Canadian champion and classic winner Alezzandro; of a heart infection, in early December 2007, at Haras de la Haie Neuve, in Mondevert, France.

HOIST HER FLAG, 1982 ro. m., Aferd—Su La Con, by Beauquillo. 43-19-9-5, $290,849. Winner of 11 stakes at Canterbury Downs. Dam of stakes winner First Flag; of melanoma, on July 30, 2007, at Barrington Hills Farm, in Barrington, Illinois.

HOT NOVEL, 1986 dk. b. or br. m., Mari's Book—Quite Honestly, by Believe It. 17-6-4-4, $380,227. Won the 1990 Rancho Bernardo Breeders' Cup H. (G3). Dam of $4.5-million-earning multiple Grade 1 winner Behrens; on May 30, 2008, at Norfields Farm, in Versailles, Kentucky.

HUMPTY'S HOEDOWN, 1990 ch. h., Mt. Livermore—Squawker, by Bold Lad. 32-12-3-5, $385,740. Won nine stakes, including the 1993 British Columbia Derby. Sire of winners; in 2007, at Chambers Ranch, in Bancroft, Idaho.

ICE PEARL, 1984 b. m., Flatbush—Ice Blossom, by Spartan General. Unraced. Dam of $1,358,659 European steeplechase stakes winner Florida Pearl; of foaling complications, on March 5, 2007, in England.

IKTITAF, 2001 b. g., Alhaarth—Istibshar, by Mr. Prospector. 22-9-2-3, $406,595. One of Ireland's outstanding hurdlers; of a tendon injury and an infection, on December 17, 2007, in Ireland.

IMAGINA (CHI), 2002 b. m., Great Regent—Lujuriosa, by Lord Florey. 25-6-6-0, $157,088. Won the 2008 Carolina First Carolina Cup Hurdle S.; after falling in the National Hunt Cup Hurdle S., on May 17, 2008, in Malvern, Pennsylvania.

INDIAN FLARE, 2002 b. m., Cherokee Run—True Flare, by Capote. 20-7-5-3, $444,486. Won the 2007 Vagrancy H. (G2); of cardiovascular shock after fracturing her pelvis during the running of the Ballerina S. (G1), on August 26, 2007, at Saratoga Race Course, in New York.

INESPERADO (FR), 1999 b. h., Zayyani (Ire)—Ile Mamou, by Ela-Mana-Mou. 37-9-7-3, $688,580. Won the 2002 Del Mar Derby (G2), Cinema Breeders' Cup H. (G3); after breaking down in a $4,000 claiming race, on May 18, 2007, at Golden Gate Fields, in California.

INJUSTICE, 2001 gr. or ro. m., Lit de Justice—Mello But Bold, by Nasty and Bold. 29-10-5-3, $446,540. Won the 2005 Azeri Breeders' Cup S. (G3); of injuries sustained in a farm accident, in early March 2007.

IRISH OPEN, 1984 b. h., Irish Tower—No Opening, by Buckpasser. 39-17-10-5, $463,221. Stakes winner. Three-time leading sire in Texas. Sire of 13 stakes winners. Broodmare sire of Grade 1 winners Spun Sugar and Daaher; of a heart attack, on March 31, 2007, at Double S Thoroughbreds, in Poyner, Texas.

IRON COUNTY XMAS, 1994 dk. b. or br. g., Cox's Ridge—Christmas Bonus, by Key to the Mint. 50-10-6-5, $140,035. Won the 1998 Spring Juvenile Hurdle in Ireland; of a heart attack, during a race at Willowdale Steeplechase in Unionville, Pennsylvania.

IS IT TRUE, 1986 b. h., Raja Baba—Roman Rockette, by Proudest Roman. 15-5-2-2, $819,999. Won the 1988 Breeders' Cup Juvenile (G1). Sire of 27 stakes winners, including Grade 1 millionaire Yes It's True; of a heart attack, on February 22, 2007, at Walmac Farm, in Lexington.

Island Storm, 1994 ch. h., Island Whirl—Mimi's Valentine, by Fire Dancer. 26-7-3-4, $139,859. Stakes-placed. Sire of stakes winners Weatherstorm and Q Fortunate Sun; of a leg injury suffered in a stall accident, on February 25, 2007, at Northwin Stables, in Michigan.

ITSALLGREEKTOME, 1987 gr. g., Sovereign Dancer—Sans Supplement, by *Grey Dawn II. 29-8-10-2, $1,994,618. Champion turf male of 1990. Won the 1990 Hollywood Derby (G1), Hollywood Turf Cup H. (G1); due to infirmities of age, on February 15, 2007, at Cardiff Stud, in California.

ITTY BITTY PRETTY, 2003 b. f., El Corredor—Tipsy Girl, by Raise a Cup. 9-2-1-3, $189,768. Won the 2006 Santa Ysabel S. (G3); after breaking down in a workout, on May 20, 2007, at Hollywood Park, in California.

JEFF'S COMPANION, 1980 ch. h., *Noholme II—Noble Madame, by *Vaguely Noble. 13-2-1-3, $60,898. Won the 1983 Count Fleet S. Sire of 13 stakes winners, including Solda Holme; in 2007, in Oregon.

JETS FAN, 2000 dk. b. or br. g., Gold Token—Sarah's Lady, by Saratoga Six. 24-7-6-0, $172,561. Won the 2004 San Carlos H.; after breaking down in a $4,000 claiming race, on August 13, 2007, at Suffolk Downs, in Massachusetts.

JILBAB, 1999 dk. b. or br. m., A.P. Indy—Headline (GB), by Machiavellian. 9-3-2-2, $347,880. Won the 2002 Coaching Club American Oaks (G1); of colic, on June 27, 2007, in Kentucky.

Jimka, 1978 b. m., Jim French—Kastueuse, by Kashmir II. 76-7-3-10, $92,540. Stakes-placed in France. Dam of French highweight and $5-million-earner Jim and Tonic; of heart failure, in April 2007, in France.

JIMMY O, 2000 dk. b. or br. g., Stormy Atlantic—Pat On the Back, by Unreal Zeal. 33-5-4-6, $207,386. Won the 2002 Beau Brummel S.; after breaking his neck in a racing accident, on February 3, 2007, at Aqueduct, in New York.

JOE GOT EVEN, 2004 b. c., Stephen Got Even—Expedicionaria (Ven), by Inland Voyager. 9-3-2-1, $167,589. Won the 2007 WEBN S.; of laminitis, in May 2007, at Rood & Riddle Equine Hospital, in Lexington.

JOHN HENRY, 1975 b. g., Ole Bob Bowers—Once Double, by Double Jay. 83-39-15-9, $6,591,860. Racing Hall of Fame. Two-time Horse of the Year and four-time grass champion. Winner of 30 stakes, including 16 Grade 1s, on both dirt and grass; due to infirmities of age, on October 8, 2007, at the Kentucky Horse Park, in Lexington.

JOINT EFFORT, 2003 ch. f., Runaway Groom—C. C. Princess, by Conquistador Cielo. 18-6-5-1, $791,465. Won the 2006 Dogwood Breeders' Cup S. (G3), La Troienne S. (G3); after breaking down in a workout, on July 29, 2007, at Churchill Downs, in Louisville.

JOKERS WILD, 2003 b. h., Black Minnaloushe—Miss Rory, by Rory's Jester. 19-6-4-1, $365,340. Champion New Zealand two-year-old of 2006. Won the 2006 Ford Diamond S. (NZ-G1); of an infection, on January 17, 2008, in Melbourne, Australia.

JUGAH, 1981 b. h., Northern Dancer—Highest Trump, by Bold Bidder. 12-3-2-2, $18,277. Stakes-placed in Ireland. Five-time leading sire in Victoria, Australia. Sire of 18 stakes winners, including Australian Group 1-winning millionaire Juggler; euthanized due to arthritis, in March 2007, at Bombara Downs, in Australia.

KENDOR, 1986 g. h., Kenmare—Belle Mecene, by Gay Mecene. 9-5-2-0, $574,588. Champion at two in France. Won the 1989 Dubai Poule d'Essai des Poulains (Fr-G1) (French Two Thousand Guineas). Sire of 35 stakes winners, including French highweights Keltos and Nombre Premier; of a massive hemorrhage, on June 6, 2007, at Haras de la Reboursiere et de Montaigu, in France.

KETTLE HILL, 2004 gr. or ro. g., Pleasant Tap—Butterfield, by Unbridled's Song. 14-3-3-3, $151,986. Won the 2007 Prairie Bayou S.; of colic, early in 2008.

KID GRINDSTONE, 2002 gr. or ro. g., Grindstone—Lady in Waiting, by Woodman. 27-9-4-3, $341,492. Won the 2006 Fifth Season S. (G3); after breaking down in a $25,000 claiming race, on August 16, 2007, at Arlington Park, in Illinois.

KING'S DRAMA (IRE), 2000 b. g., King's Theatre (Ire)—Last Drama, by Last Tycoon (Ire). 31-10-7-6, $1,157,916. Won the 2005 Sword Dancer Invitational S. (G1); of an injury suffered immediately following ligament surgery; in the spring of 2007.

KLEVEN, 1981 ch. h., Alydar—Strings Attached, by *Tudor Minstrel. 3-1-1-1, $20,700. Sire of six stakes winners, including $1.8-million-earning UAE highweight Big Jag; in 2007, in California.

KRIBENSIS, 1984 gr. g., Henbit—Aquaria, by *Double-U-Jay. 27-13-2-1, $345,114. Champion English hurdler in 1990. Won the 1990 Waterford Crystal Champion Challenge Trophy; in mid-October 2007, at Freemason Lodge, in England.

LADIES DIN, 1995 b. g., Din's Dancer—Ladies Double, by Kris S. 37-12-6-6, $1,966,754. Won the 2000 Eddie Read H. (G1) and '02 Shoemaker Breeders' Cup Mile S. (G1); of a heart attack while show jumping, in the summer of 2007.

LAGUNAS, 1981 b. h., Ile de Bourbon—Liranga, by Literat. Champion at two in Germany. Won the 1984 Deutsches Derby (Ger-G1). Leading 1996 sire in Slovakia. Sire of 24 stakes winners and three Eastern European champions. Broodmare sire of 2002 Vodafone Epsom Oaks (Eng-G1) winner Kazzia (Ger); of colic, in early 2007.

LAKE AUSTIN, 1997 dk. b. or br. h., Storm Cat—Lakeway, by Seattle Slew. 13-3-3-0, $124,373. Sire of 2007 Kentucky Cup Sprint S. (G3) winner Piratesonthelake and stakes winner Capt. Joe Blow; following colic surgery, in December 2007, at Delta Equine Center, in Vinton, Louisiana.

LATIN RHYTHMS, 2004 b. c., King Cugat—Chris' Rocket Girl, by Seattle Dancer. 5-3-2-0, $164,240. Won the 2007 El Cajon S. Grade 2-placed; after breaking down in a workout, on September 23, 2007, at Hollywood Park, in California.

LAUREL QUEEN, 1988 ch. m., Viking—Prima Bella by High Hat. 53-22-6-3, $112,079. In 1993 became England's most prolific distaff winner in the postwar era with her 22nd career victory; of colic, in June 2007, in England.

LETHAL GRANDE, 1999 dk. b. or br. g., Corslew—La Bardot, by Somethingfabulous. 80-26-18-13, $409,788. Multiple Oregon-bred champion, leading Oregon-bred money winner of all time; after breaking down in the Invitational H., on November 5, 2007, at Portland Meadows, in Oregon.

LE VIE DEI COLORI, 2000 b. h., Efisio—Mystic Tempo, by El Gran Senor. 24-14-2-2, $897,953. Italian highweight at two and three. Group winner in France, England, and Italy; in a farm accident, in May 2008, at Rathbarry Stud, in County Cork, Ireland.

LIFE'S MAGIC, 1981 b. m., Cox's Ridge—Fire Water, by Tom Rolfe. 32-8-11-6, $2,255,218. Champion at three and four. Won the 1985 Breeders' Cup Distaff (G1). Dam of three stakes-placed runners; of old age, on August 21, 2007, at Trackside Farm, in Versailles, Kentucky.

LIKE MOM LIKE SONS, 2004 ch. c., Carson City—Mycuptofea, by Williamstown. 5-4-0-0, $154,532. Won the 2007 Woodstock S.; of laminitis, on July 7, 2007, at the University of Guelph veterinary clinic, in Ontario.

LITE LIGHT, 1988 b. m., Majestic Light—Printing Press, by In Reality. 26-8-4-4, $1,231,596. Won the 1991 Kentucky Oaks (G1), Coaching Club American Oaks (G1). Dam of three stakes winners, including English group winner Saddad and Japanese stakes winner Gaily Egret; of foaling complications, on May 5, 2007, at Spring Hill Farm, in Casanova, Virginia.

LITERATI, 1985 ch. h., Nureyev—*Lovelight II, by Bleep-Bleep. 9-3-2-3, $53,472. Stakes winner in Ireland, Grade 3-placed in the U.S. Sire of stakes winners Literal Prowler and Ready Eddie; in 2007, in California.

LOVEONTHEROAD, 1995 dk. b. or br. f., Jahafil (GB)—Ona Lucky Road, by Kennedy Road. 11-4-4-0, $214,172. Won the 1998 Santa Paula S. Dam of two winners from two starters; in 2007, in California.

LT. SAMPSON, 2001 gr. or ro. g., Wolf Power (SAf)—Lucy'spicksix, by Saratoga Six. 37-9-6-4, $226,231. Won the 2005 Minnesota Turf Championship S.; of a heart attack, in late September 2007.

LUCKY NORTH, 1981 b. h., Northern Dancer—Lucky Ole Me, by Olden Times. 20-4-6-2, $117,362. Won the 1986 Phoenix H. Sire of 18 stakes winners, including Grade 2 winner My Luck Runs North. Broodmare sire of Grade 1 millionaire Lady Tak; of natural causes, in the summer of 2007, at Ziprick Thoroughbreds, in Manitoba.

LYTRUMP, 1985 dk. b. or br. h., Lypheor (GB)—Highest Trump, by Bold Bidder. 45-1-2-6, $24,161. One of Nebraska's leading sires. Sire of 19 stakes winners, including Nebraska-bred champion High Dice and 18-time winner Fantango Lady; in August 2007, in Nebraska.

MACH GLORY (ARG), 2004 dk. b. or br. c., Honour and Glory—Mucci Baby, by Cozzene. 9-2-2-0, $69,182. Champion Argentine two-year-old of 2006-'07. Won the 2007 Estrellas Juvenile (Arg-G1); in spring of 2008.

MAGIC MYTH, 2005 dk. b. or br. f., Johannesburg—Magnificent Crown, by The Irish Lord. Half sister to three stakes winners. 3-1-0-0, $32,200; after breaking down in the Hidden Light S., on October 26, 2007, at the Oak Tree meet at Santa Anita, in California.

MARIA'S MON, 1993 gr. or r. h., Wavering Monarch—Carlotta Maria, by Caro (Ire). 7-4-1-1, $507,140. Champion at two. Won the 1995 Moet Champagne S. (G1). Sire of 34 stakes winners, including champion Wait a While and Kentucky Derby (G1) winner Monarchos; of multiple organ failure, on September 14, 2007, at Hagyard Equine Medical Institute, in Lexington.

MAT-BOY (ARG), 1979 ch. h., *Matun—Boyera (Arg), by Pastiche. 13-9-0-1, $202,002. Argentina's Horse of the Year in 1983. Won the 1984 Widener H. (G1). Sire of 24 stakes winners, including champion Victim Boy and U.S. Grade 1 winner Festin (Arg); of colic, in early March 2007, at Haras La Biznaga, in Argentina.

Mayor Bozarth, 2004 dk. b. or br. c., Deputy Commander—Unique Millie R., by Olden Times. 8-2-2-1, $92,784. Grade 3-placed in 2007; after breaking down in a division of the Oceanside Stakes, on July 18, 2007, at Del Mar racetrack, in California.

MCKELVEY, 1999 b. g., Anshan (GB)—Chatty Actress, by Le Bavard. 22-6-5-2, $478,644. Won the 2006 Britannia Building Society English Summer National; of injuries sustained in an accident during the John Smiths Grand National Steeplechase, on April 5, 2008, at Aintree racecourse, in England.

MENDING FENCES, 2002 dk. b. or br. h., Forestry—Mended Heart, by *Le Fabuleux. 27-7-5-3, $231,400. Won the 2007 John B. Connally Breeders' Cup Turf H. (G3); after breaking down in the Dixie S. (G2), on May 19, 2007, at Pimlico Race Course, in Maryland.

MERCANTILE, 2004 b. g., Golden Missile—Silverdew, by Silver Deputy. 11-3-2-2, $83,160. Sold for $2-million at the 2006 Fasig-Tipton Calder sale of selected two-year-olds in training; after breaking down in an optional claiming race, on January 20, 2008, at Fair Grounds, in New Orleans.

MERTZON, 1982 ch. h., Mr. Prospector—Sarsar, by Damascus. 14-1-2-2, $16,065. Sire of five stakes winners, including $332,821-earner Noztrem; in 2007, at Bobby Hall Farm, in Hot Springs, Arkansas.

MEURICE, 2004 b. c., Strategic—Espadon, by Danehill. 7-3-2-2, $784,535; Champion Australian two-year-old of 2006-'07. Won the Salinger Champagne Stakes (Aus-G1). Purchased by Darley Stud in 2006 for $12-million as a stallion prospect; after breaking down in a workout, on January 31, 2008, at Randwick racecourse, in Australia.

MI JUBILEE, 2002 b. m., Howbaddouwantit—Mi Steel, by Mi Preferido. 47-9-8-2, $164,664. New Zealand highweighted filly three. Won the 2005 Ford Ellerslie Sires' Produce S. (NZ-G1); after breaking down in the Attwood Marshall Lawyers Silk Stocking H., on May 3, 2008, at Gold Coast racecourse, in Australia.

MIKKI STREET, 2001 br. h., Cape Cross (Ire)—Ocean Pearl, by Crested Wave. Won the 2006 Zabeel Classic (NZ-G1); after breaking down in a workout, on January 23, 2007, at Awapuni, in New Zealand.

MISS ALLEGED, 1987 b. m., Alleged—Miss Tusculum, by Boldnesian. 15-5-4-3, $1,757,342. Champion grass female of 1991; highweighted older female in France in '91. Won the 1991 Breeders' Cup Turf (G1). Dam of stakes winner Zghorta; of foaling complications, on February 28, 2008, at Coolmore Ireland.

MISSED THE STORM, 1990 dk. b. or br. m., Storm Cat—Missed the Wedding, by Blushing Groom (Fr). 15-6-4-2, $334,986. Won the 1993 Test S. (G1). Dam of winners; in 2008.

MOM'S COMMAND, 1982 ch. m., Top Command—Star Mommy, by Pia Star. 16-11-2-1, $902,972. Racing Hall of Fame. Champion filly at three. Won the 1985 filly triple crown. Dam of 11 winners, including Grade 3 winner Jonesboro; of laminitis, on February 3, 2007, at Runnymede Farm, in North Hampton, New Hampshire.

MOSCOW BALLET, 1982 b. h., Nijinsky II—Millicent, by Cornish Prince. 4-2-0-0, $16,349. Won the 1984 P. J. Prendergast Railway S. (Ire-G3). Sire of 20 stakes winners, including Grade 1 winners Dancing Edie, Golden Ballet, and Dominant Dancer; of a degenerative condition in his hindquarters, on April 4, 2008, at Harris Farms, in Coalinga, California.

MULTIPLY, 1992 b. m., Easy Goer—Add, by Spectacular Bid. Unraced. Dam of 2007 Breeders' Cup Dirt Mile winner Corinthian and Grade 2 winner Desert Hero; of laminitis, on May 20, 2007, in England.

NASHOBA'S KEY, 2003 b. m., Silver Hawk—Nashoba (Ire), by Caerleon. 10-8-1-0, $1,252,090. Won the 2008 Santa Margarita Invitational H. (G1) and '07 Yellow Ribbon S. (G1); of injuries sustained in a stall accident; on May 28, 2008, in California.

NIGHT FAX, 1991 dk. b. or br. m., Known Fact—Night Letter (Ger), by *Marduk II. 21-7-4-3, $242,486. Won the 1995 Delaware H. (G2). Dam of 2006 Virginia-bred champion juvenile filly Miss Goodnight; of foaling complications, on April 7, 2007, at Audley Farm, in Berryville, Virginia.

NIGHTSTORM, 1994 dk. b. m., Storm Cat—Halo's Daughter, by Halo. 6-1-2-2, $39,310. Dam of 2007 Wood Memorial S. (G1) winner Nobiz Like Shobiz; of injuries sustained in a paddock accident, on November 20, 2007.

NINE KEYS, 1990 b. m., Forty Niner—Clef d'Argent, by Key to the Mint. 11-7-3-1, $637,320. Won the 1994 Apple Blossom H.; of foaling complications, on March 22, 2008, at Claiborne Farm, in Paris, Kentucky.

NORTHERN BABY, 1976 b. h., Northern Dancer—Two Rings, by Round Table. 17-5-2-5, $329,983. Won the 1979 Champion S. (Eng-G1). Sire of 47 stakes winners, including champion grass female Possibly Perfect and champion steeplechasers Highland Bud and Warm Spell; of old age, on February 21, 2007, at Stone Farm, in Paris, Kentucky.

OCALA SLEW, 1986 b. h., Seattle Slew—Golden Way, by Diplomat Way. Unraced. Sold for $500,000 as a Saratoga yearling. Sire of four stakes winners, including triple Grade 3 winner Arthur L.; in 2007, in Michigan.

OLYMPIC NATIVE, 1985 ch. h., Raise a Native—Olympic Moment, by Olympiad King. 10-5-1-0, $138,050. Won the 1989 Pat O'Brien H. Sire of more than 40 winners; in 2007, in California.

OLYMPIC PROSPECT, 1984 ch. g., Northern Jove—Brilliant Future, by *Forli. 32-14-3-3, $725,320. Won the 1990 Potrero Grande H. (G3); euthanized due to severe arthritis, in February 2007, in Alpine, California.

OMI, 1993 dk. b. or br. m., Wild Again—Flying Heat, by Private Account. 16-7-4-1, $319,718. Won the 1997 Arlington Matron H. (G3). Dam of stakes-winning Brushed Bayou and a $4.2-million 2000 Saratoga yearling; of colic, in May 2007, in Florida.

ONE WAY STREET, 1981 b. m., Habitat—Guillotina, by Busted. 6-4-0-0, $46,032. Won the 1984 Princess Royal S. (Eng-G3). Dam of three group winners, including French highweight Grape Tree Road (GB); of foaling complications, in May 2007, in England.

Oregon, 1988 dk. b. or br. h., Halo—Three Troikas (Fr), by Lyphard. 7-2-2-0, $60,529. Grade 3-placed. Sire of 19 stakes winners, including Singaporean stakes winners Dreyfuss and Ouzo. Broodmare sire of 2005 Conrad Treasury Cup (Aus-G1) winner Portland Singa; of laminitis, in May 2007, in Australia.

OUTOFTHEBLUEBELL, 1985 b. m., Red Ryder—Natchez Bluebell, by Star Envoy. 36-8-7-6, $195,966. Won the 1988 Matt Winn H. Washington's 2000 broodmare of the year. Dam of Grade 1 winner Rings a Chime; of a strangulated intestine, on August 23, 2007, at Griffin Place, in Buckley, Washington.

PALACE MUSIC, 1981 ch. h., The Minstrel—Come My Prince, by Prince John. 21-7-5-3, $918,750. Grade 1-Group 1 winner in England and the U.S. North America's leading sire of 1995. Sire of 33 stakes winners, including 1995-'96 Horse of the Year and $9,999,815-earner Cigar; of old age, on January 7, 2008, at Rangal Park Stud, in Australia.

PARADISUS, 2000 b. g., Numerous—Hyfiver, by Irish Tower. 21-13-5-1, $63,529. Champion Peruvian sprinter of 2004 and champion grass horse of '05; broke down in a workout, on February 14, 2007.

PAROSE, 1994 ch. g., Parlay Me—Roses for Classy, by Son of Briartic. 11-4-24-26-23, $1,167,855. Won the 2002 Woodbine Slots Cup H. (Can-G3). Retired at 12 to Long Run Thoroughbred Retirement Foundation; of colic, in October 2007.

PERFECTING, 1985 dk. b. or br. h., Affirmed—Cornish Colleen, by Cornish Prince. 14-3-5-1, $190,869. Won the 1988 La Jolla Handicap (G3). Sire of three stakes winners, including Maryland Million Turf S. winner Elberton; of cancer, on September 7, 2007, at Elberton Hill, in Maryland.

PERSONAL BID, 1990 b. m., Personal Flag—Kemp, by Spectacular Bid. 16-5-2-2, $163,298. Won the 1993 Cicada S.; of a heart attack, in November 2007, in Kentucky.

PLATINUM PAWS, 1988 ro. m., Vice Regent—Catcando, by Al Hattab. 38-4-7-10, $348,799. Won the 1991 Woodbine Sales S. Dam of multiple stakes winner Daddy Cool; of foaling complications, in March 2008, at Margaux Farm, in Kentucky.

POLISH GIFT, 2000 dk. b. or br. h., Danzig—Miner's Game, by Mr. Prospector. 7-1-0-0, $30,600. Full brother to Grade 3 winner Survivalist. First-crop two-year-olds of 2007 included four-time stakes winner Margo's Gift; of colic, in January 2007, at Allaire Farms, in Poulsbo, Washington.

POSIDONAS (GB), 1992 b. h., Slip Anchor—Tamassos, by Dance in Time. 27-8-4-5, $765,516. Won the 1995 Gran Premio d'Italia (Ity-G1). Sire of winners; in January 2008, at Sweet Wall Stud, in Ireland.

POST INVADER, 2004 dk. b. or br. f., Salt Lake—Post Marked, by Stop the Music. 8-2-1-1, $94,280. Won the 2006 Cassidy S.; of injuries sustained when she flipped in the paddock at Calder Race Course, on November 18, 2007, in Florida.

PRESIDENTIAL ORDER, 1993 b. h., Danzig—Mitterand, by Hold Your Peace. 1-0-0-0, $850. Among the leading sires in Indiana. Sire of five stakes winners, including Indy Energy and Sir Travel; of injuries sustained in a farm accident, on April 23, 2008, at M. C. Roberts Farms, in Mooresville, Indiana.

PRIDE OF TAHNEE, 1984 ch. m., Best Western—Tahnee's Pride, by Boucher. Unraced. Dam of three Australian Group 1 winners, including $2.6-million-earner Shogun Lodge and Referral; euthanized in May 2008, at Woodlands Stud, in Australia.

PRIVATE SCHOOL, 1987 dk. b. or br. h., Bates Motel—Never Wood, by Torsion. 42-15-10-1, $737,762. Won the 1990 Ohio Derby (G2). Sire of stakes winner Coed Ruth E.; of an aneurysm, on December 17, 2007, at Eutrophia Farms, in Chesterland, Ohio.

PROSPECTIVE JOY, 1991 ro. m., Allen's Prospect—Jovial Joy, by Rollicking. 6-3-2-1, $68,620. Won the 1994 Jameela S. Dam of Grade 1 winner Hookedonthefeelin; of foaling complications, on March 16, 2007.

PROSPECTOR JONES, 1992 b. h., Mr. Prospector—Jeanne Jones, by Nijinsky II. Unraced. Sire of 17 stakes winners, including three-time New Mexico champion Ciento, Skirt Alert, and Hat Creek; of colic, in January 2007, at Brunacini Farms, in Belen, New Mexico.

QUEENA, 1986 b. m., Mr. Prospector—Too Chic, by Blushing Groom (Fr). 17-10-2-1, $565,024. Champion older female of 1991. Dam of three million-dollar-plus yearlings, including Grade 1 winner Brahms and Grade 3 winner La Reina; of colic, in December 2007, at Middlebrook Farm, in Lexington.

QUEENLEDO, 2002 dk. b. or br. m., Slewdledo—Tenderness, by Wronsky. 18-7-7-0, $242,824. Washington-bred champion. Won six stakes, including the 2006 Emerald Breeders' Cup Distaff H.; of colic, in December 2007.

QUIET RESOLVE, 1995 b. g., Affirmed—Quiet Cleo, by No Louder. 31-10-6-4, $2,346,768. Canadian Horse of the Year and champion grass male in 2000. Won the 1999 Atto Mile S. (Can-G1); of injuries suffered following colic surgery, on February 1, 2007, in Canada.

QUIZ THE MAID, 2001 dk. b. or br. m., Basket Weave—Appease, by Apalachee. 48-13-12-5, $106,741. Five-time stakes winner in Washington state; after breaking down in a $5,000 claiming race, on December 11, 2007, at Mountaineer Race Track, in West Virginia.

RACEY DREAMER, 1999 ch. g., A.P. Indy—Dahlia's Dreamer, by Theatrical (Ire). 13-8-0-1, $180,400. Won the 2004 National Hunt Cup Hurdle S. in course-record time; of injuries sustained in the Royal Chase for the

Sport of Kings Hurdle S., on April 20, 2007, at Keeneland Race Course, in Lexington.

RAINBOW QUEST, 1981 b. h., Blushing Groom (Fr)—I Will Follow, by *Herbager. 14-6-4-2, $592,716. Champion at four in England and France. Sire of 103 stakes winners and five champions. Twice England's leading broodmare sire; euthanized following colic surgery, on July 7, 2007, in England.

RAISE A MAN, 1977 ch. h., Raise a Native—Delta Sal, by Delta Judge. 12-6-1-1, $257,450. Won the 1980 San Felipe H. (G2). Sire of 24 stakes winners, including two South African champions and major U.S. graded winner Vinnie the Viper; of natural causes, on July 22, 2007, at Milfer Farm, in Unadilla, New York.

RAKEEN, 1987 b. h., Northern Dancer—Glorious Song, by Halo. 12-6-1-4, $11,239. Won the 1991 Allen Snijman S. (SAf-G2). Sire of 23 stakes winners, including South African champions Jet Master and Young Rake; euthanized due to a hock injury, in May 2007, at Lammerskraal Stud, in South Africa.

REBEL REBEL (IRE), 2002 b. h., Revoque—French Quarter (Ire), by Ile de Bourbon. 22-5-4-2, $603,072. Won the 2006 Poker H. (G3); of injuries sustained in the 2006 Hong Kong Mile (HK-G1), in April 2007, in Hong Kong.

REGAL BAND, 1987 b. m., Dixieland Band—Regal Roberta, by Roberto. 18-3-7-3, $86,865. Dam of 2001 Kentucky Derby (G1) winner Monarchos; of liver failure, on April 9, 2007, at Rood & Riddle Equine Hospital, in Lexington.

RHYTHM, 1987 b. h., Mr. Prospector—Dance Number, by Northern Dancer. 20-6-3-4, $1,592,532. Champion at two. Won the 1989 Breeders' Cup Juvenile (G1). Sire of 24 stakes winners, including Australian champion Ethereal; of injuries sustained in a paddock accident, on September 4, 2007, at Diamond F Ranch, in Grass Valley, California.

RIVERINA CHARM, 1985 b. m., *Sir Tristram—Country Charm, by Northfields. 22-7-2-3, $59.391. Highweighted filly at three and four in Australia. Won the 1988 One Thousand Guineas (Aus-G1). Dam of Group 2 winners Sarwatch and Paolino; in May 2007, in New Zealand.

ROBELLINO, 1978 b. h., Roberto—Isobelline, by *Pronto. 14-5-3-0, $136,984. Won the 1980 Royal Lodge S. (Eng-G2). Sire of 42 stakes winners, including English and Irish highweight Royal Rebel and English classic winner Mister Baileys (GB); of old age, on July 4, 2007, at Littleton Stud, in England.

ROI NORMAND, 1983 dk. b. or br. h., Exclusive Native—Luth de Saron (Fr), by Luthier. 17-5-2-1, $390,466. Won the 1988 Sunset H. (G1). Leading Brazilian sire of 2000. Sire of 51 stakes winners, including Eclipse Award winner Riboletta (Brz); of colic, on February 20, 2007, at Haras Santa Ana do Rio Grande, in Brazil.

RORY'S JESTER, 1982 ch. h., Crown Jester—Rory's Rocket, by Roan Rocket. Won the 1985 Golden Slipper S. (Aus-G1). Sire of 76 stakes winners, including champion Isca; on March 27, 2007, at Swettenham Stud, in Victoria, Australia.

RUNAWAY GROOM, 1979 gr. h., Blushing Groom (Fr)—Yonnie Girl, by Call the Witness. 18-6-5-1, $347,537. Canadian champion at three. Won the 1982 Travers S. (G1). Sire of 74 stakes winners, including champion sprinter Cherokee Run and millionaire Grade 1 winners Wekiva Springs and Down the Aisle; of old age, on June 8, 2007, at Vinery, in Lexington.

RUN PRISSY RUN, 1991 b. m., Bayou Hebert—Jannis Jan, by *Tudor Grey. Unraced. Louisiana's 2002 broodmare of the year. Dam of three stakes winners, including $503,799-earner Doctor Mike; of a heart attack, on March 5, 2007, at Clear Creek Stud, in Folsom, Louisiana.

RUSSIAN TANGO, 1990 dk. b. or br. m., Nijinsky II—Brave Raj, by Rajab. 15-4-1-3, $92,390. Won the 1994 The Very One H. Dam of Grade 2 winner Eurosilver; after colic surgery, in early 2007, at Hagyard Equine Medical Institute, in Lexington.

SAHM, 1994 dk. b. or br. h., Mr. Prospector—Salsabil (Ire), by Sadler's Wells. 11-5-4-0, $198,879. Won the 1998 Knickerbocker H. (G2). Sire of ten stakes winners, including Irish group winner Mustameet; of an intestinal illness, on March 20, 2007, at Rood & Riddle Equine Hospital, in Lexington.

SALIERI, 1980 ch. h., Accipiter—Hogan's Sister, by Speak John. 11-6-3-0, $164,208. Won the 1982 Mill Reef S. (Eng-G2). Sire of 19 stakes winners, including Australian champion Schillaci and multiple Group 1 winner Shaftesbury Avenue; of old age, in March 2008, at Widden Stud, in Australia.

SAN LUIS, 1998 b. h., Flying Spur—Star Style Girl, by Without Fear. 12-3-5-0, $60,379. New Zealand highweight at two. Won the 2001 Ford Manawatu Sires' Produce S. (NZ-G1). Sire of stakes winner Star Of Luis; of laminitis, in October 2007, at Grangewilliam Stud, in New Zealand.

Savethelastdance, 1988 dk. b. or br. m., Nureyev—Bon Debarras, by Ruritania. 28-4-6-9, $204,389. Multiple stakes-placed. Dam of millionaire and 2004 Queen's Plate winner Niigon; of a lymphatic condition, on January 17, 2007.

SAYYEDATI (GB), 1990 b. m., Shadeed—Dubian (GB), by High Line. 22-6-5-3, $1,408,616. Multiple European highweight. Won the 1993 Madagans One Thousand Guineas (Eng-G1). Dam of Group 2 winner Almushahar; in August 2007.

SCOTTSVILLE, 1988 dk. b. or br. h., by Deputy Minister—Tricot, by The Axe II. 25-7-4-1, $195,339. Won the 1991 Maryland Million Turf. Sire of multiple stakes winner White Star; in 2007, in Louisiana.

SEATTLE DANCER, 1984 b. h., Nijinsky II—My Charmer, by Poker. Former record-priced auction yearling at $13.1-million. 5-2-1-1, $152,413. Won the 1987 Windfields Farm Gallinule S. (Ire-G2). Sire of 37 stakes winners, including Italian highweight Happy Dancer; of a heart attack, in June 2007, in Germany.

SECRET CLAIM, 1985 b. h., Mr. Prospector—Secrettame, by Secretariat. 11-3-3-2, $67,240. Full brother to Gone West. Sire of six stakes winners, including Arctic Squall and Casino Prince; of an injury sustained in a breeding shed accident, in March 2008, at Heartlines Ranch, in Normangee, Texas.

SEEKING SLEW, 2002 dk. b. or br. h., Seeking the Gold—Borodislew, by Seattle Slew. 4-2-0-0, $327,265. Won the 2005 Kent Breeders' Cup S. (G3); in 2007.

SHADEA, 1988 br. m., Straight Strike—Concia, by First Consul. 5-1-2-2, $130,243. Won the 1991 Sweet

Embrace S. (Aus-G3). Dam of 2004 Australian Horse of the Year Lonhro and Group 1 winner Niello; found dead in her paddock, on July 17, 2007, at Woodlands Stud, in Australia.

SHARKY'S REVIEW, 1998 b. m., Sharkey—Irish Review, by Sir Harry Lewis. 36-15-5-7, $685,425. Ten-time stakes winner at Prairie Meadows Racetrack; of Potomac fever, in July 2007.

SHARON BROWN, 1980 gr. m., Al Hattab—Agathea's Dawn, by *Grey Dawn II. 32-3-6-5, $45,860. Dam of 1994 Horse of the Year Holy Bull and stakes winner Winnie D.; of old age, on July 28, 2007, at Kinsman Farm, in Ocala.

SHARP CAT, 1994 ch. m., Storm Cat—In Neon, by Ack Ack. 22-15-3-0, $2,032,575. Won the 1997 Acorn S. (G1) and '98 Beldame S. (G1). Sold for $3.1-million as a broodmare; of foaling complications, on April 21, 2008, at Darley at Gainsborough, in Versailles, Kentucky.

SHEEZAWILDKAT, 1996 b. m., Clever Champ—Ceefrancis Run, by Century Prince. 30-7-3-5, $50,270. Dam of multiple 2007 stakes winner Heezafrequentflyer; of foaling complications, in the spring of 2007, at Windy Willows Farm, in Libertytown, Maryland.

SILVER BUCK, 1978 gr. h., Buckpasser—Silver True, by Hail to Reason. 16-7-2-2, $421,906. Won the 1982 Suburban H. (G1). Sire of 40 stakes winners, including champion and Racing Hall of Fame member Silver Charm; of old age, on October 4, 2007, at Bridlewood Farm, in Ocala.

SINISTER G, 2001 dk. b. or br. h., Matty G—Sinister Punch, by Two Punch. 37-8-4-5, $599,469. Won the 2004 Lane's End S. (G2); of a ruptured bowel, on May 8, 2007, at New Bolton Center, in Pennsylvania.

SLEW O' GOLD, 1980 b. h., Seattle Slew—Alluvial, by Buckpasser. 21-12-5-1, $3,533,534. Champion at three and four. Won the 1983 and '84 Jockey Club Gold Cup (G1). Sire of 28 stakes winners, including seven U.S. Grade 1 winners. Broodmare sire of champion sprinter Kona Gold; of old age, on October 14, 2007, at Three Chimneys Farm, in Midway, Kentucky.

SNAADEE, 1987 dk. b. or br. h., Danzig—Somfas, by What a Pleasure. 8-4-0-0, $99,976. Won the 1992 UB Group Temple S. (Eng-G2). Sire of 13 stakes winners, including Group 1 winner Bedouin; of injuries sustained in a paddock accident, in September 2007, in Australia.

SO SEDULOUS, 1991 b. m., The Minstrel—Sedulous (Ire), by Tap On Wood. 11-2-2-1, $21,457. Two-time German Broodmare of the Year. Dam of five stakes winners, including 2005 John Deere Breeders' Cup Turf (G1) winner Shirocco (Ger) and group winner Subiaco; in February 2008, in Germany.

SOUGHT OUT, 1988 b. m., Rainbow Quest—Edinburgh, by Charlottown. 20-5-7-3, $402,366. Twice Europe's highweighted distance mare. Won the 1992 Ciga Prix du Cadran (Fr-G1). Dam of three stakes winners, including 2004 Vodafone Epsom Derby (Eng-G1) winner North Light (Ire); of foaling complications, on May 23, 2008, at Ballymacoll Stud, in Ireland.

SOVIET LAD, 1985 b. h., Nureyev—*Green Valley II, by *Val de Loir. 17-3-4-4, $152,586. Won the 1988 Prix de Pontarme. Sire of six stakes winners, including Turkish stakes winner Manas; of a heart attack, in February 2007, at Park Crest Stud, in Australia.

SPANISH HIGHWAY, 2001 ch. g., Cahill Road—Prado's Joy, by El Prado (Ire). 44-5-8-9, $196,848. Won the 2004 Tempe H., '06 Fox Sports Network H.; after breaking down in an optional claiming race, on August 19, 2007, at Emerald Downs, in Washington.

SPORTS TOWN, 2004 b. c., Belong to Me—Answer to Me, by Peteski. 6-3-0-2, $104,007. Won the 2007 Ogygian S. at Belmont Park; of laminitis, on June 29, 2007, at New Bolton Center, in Pennsylvania.

STARBOROUGH, 1994 ch. h., Soviet Star—Flamenco Wave, by Desert Wine. 12-4-1-1, $434,651. Won the 1997 St. James's Palace S. (Eng-G1) and Prix Jean Prat (Fr-G1). Sire of four stakes winners, including Scandinavian champion Appel Au Maitre; euthanized following leg surgery, early in 2007, in France.

STAR WAY, 1977 ch. h., *Star Appeal—New Way, by *Klairon. Won the 1979 Chesham S., Group 1-placed. Sire of 59 stakes winners, including New Zealand champions Smiling Like and Nimue; of old age, in April 2008, at Windsor Park Stud, in New Zealand.

Storm Boot, 1989 ch. h., Storm Cat—Aliata, by Mr. Prospector. 14-4-3-1, $70,510. Stakes-placed. Sire of 51 stakes winners, including Bourbon Belle and Hurricane Bertie; of degenerative tendonitis and laminitis, on May 10, 2007, at Hagyard Equine Medical Institute, in Lexington.

STORM MARCOPOLO (ARG), 2003 dk. b. or br. h., Bernstein—Marplatense Soy, by Mountdrago. 13-7-3-1, $79,788. Argentina's 2007 champion sprinter; of complications from anesthesia used to perform an MRI on his right front foot, on May 16, 2008, at Hagyard Equine Medical Institute, in Lexington.

STRAIGHT FLUSH, 1975 b. h., Riva Ridge—Somethingroyal, by *Princequillo. 28-3-4-3, $49,820. Half brother to champions Secretariat and Sir Gaylord. Rescued from a Texas cattle feed lot in 1999. Sire of 54 winners; of old age, on September 3, 2007, in Hemet, California.

STRIKE A BALANCE, 1983 ro. m., Green Dancer—Strike a Pose, by Iron Ruler. 3-2-1-0, $30,720. Dam of 1995 Canadian Horse of the Year Peaks and Valleys and stakes winner Alternate; of foaling complications, on April 12, 2007, at Pin Oak Stud, in Versailles, Kentucky.

STRODES CREEK, 1991 b. h., Halo—Bottle Top, by Topsider. 9-3-2-2, $430,006. Won the 1994 J. O. Tobin S., second in the Kentucky Derby (G1). Sire of six stakes winners, including Slovakian champion Mona Say and Doc D; of a leg injury suffered in January 2008, at Gumak Farm, in South Korea.

STUTZ BEARCAT, 1975 b. g., First Landing—Sunny Morning, by Amber Morn. 86-23-14-12, $271,181. Winner of seven stakes, including the 1980 Vigil H. and Fair Play S.; of injuries sustained in a farm accident, in 2008.

SUL LAGO, 2004 b. g., Include—Explosive Glow, by American Standard. 15-4-5-1, $136,025. Won the 2006 Northern Lights Futurity; broke down past the finish line after winning an allowance race at Remington Park, on September 23, 2007, in Oklahoma.

SULTRY SUN, 1980 dk. b. or br. m., Buckfinder—Sunny Dame, by Damascus. 14-9-0-2, $222,277. Won the 1984 Molly Pitcher H. (G2). Dam of Grade 1-winning millionaires Sultry Song and Solar Splendor, and graded

stakes winner Strategic Mission. Grandam of Grade 1 winner Mass Media; on March 7, 2008, at Live Oak Stud, in Ocala.

SUN BOAT (GB), 2002 b. g., Machiavellian—One So Wonderful, by Nashwan. 13-4-3-1, $334,345. Won the 2007 San Diego H. (G2); of laminitis, on September 18, 2007, at Bonnie Acres Farm, in Hemet, California.

SUPER FROLIC, 2000 ch. h., Pine Bluff—Lindsay Frolic, by Mt. Livermore. 43-11-5-7, $1,457,209. Won the 2005 Hawthorne Gold Cup H. (G2); after breaking down in the Presque Isle Mile Stakes, on September 15, 2007, at Presque Isle Downs, in Pennsylvania.

SUPERVISOR, 2000 b. g., Skip Trial—Silver Doe, by Silver Buck. 57-5-7-8, $460,979. Won the 2005 Spend a Buck H. (G3); collapsed after finishing sixth in the Spend a Buck H., on October 13, 2007, at Calder Race Course, in Florida.

SWEET ANNATIVO, 1993 gr. or ro. m., Puntivo—Sweet Anna M., by Prove Out. 17-1-0-2, $4,661. Dam of Grade 2 winner Mister Fotis; of colic, on June 13, 2007, at Blue Sink Farm, in Ocala.

TAKE A BOW, 2001 b. h., Royal Applause (GB)—Giant Nipper, by Nashwan. 26-5-7-6, $309,338. Won the 2007 Betfair Brigadier Gerard S. (Eng-G3); after breaking down in the Totesport.com Winter Hill S. (Eng-G3), on August 25, 2007, at Windsor racecourse, in England.

Ten Cents a Shine, 2000 dk. b. or br. g., Devil His Due—Aunt Mottz, by Honey Jay. 17-4-2-0, $144,644. Grade 2-placed, finished eighth in the 2003 Kentucky Derby (G1); after breaking down in a training race, on May 6, 2007, in Winterthur, Delaware.

TERLINGUA, 1976 ch. f., Secretariat—Crimson Saint, by Crimson Satan. 17-7-4-1, $423,896. Won the 1978 Hollywood Juvenile Championship S. (G2). Dam of leading sire Storm Cat and graded stakes winner Chapel of Dreams; of old age, on April 30, 2008, at Overbrook Farm, in Lexington.

TEXAS CITY, 1988 dk. b. or br. h., Mr. Prospector—Miss Betty, by Buckpasser. Unraced. Sire of five stakes winners, including Grade 3 winner Baytown; of complications from a breeding shed injury, on May 25, 2007, at Our Pleasure Farm, in Nacogdoches, Texas.

THREE DEGREES (IRE), 2002 gr. or ro. m., Singspiel (Ire)—Miss University, by Beau Genius. 16-3-6-3, $490,241. Won the 2005 Honeymoon Breeders' Cup H. (G2); after breaking down at the finish of the Gamely S. (G1), on May 28, 2007, at Hollywood Park, in California.

THREE WONDERS, 1997 b. h., Storm Cat—Wood of Binn, by Woodman. 30-4-2-2, $318,032. Won the 2000 Kent Breeders' Cup S. (G3). Florida's leading freshman and second-crop sire of 2006 and '07, respectively; euthanized due to a wobbler-like syndrome, on May 16, 2008, in Florida.

TIDAL LIGHT, 1983 br. m., Diagramatic—Azores, by King of Babylon. Multiple New Zealand Group 1 winner. Dam of six winners, including one group-placed; in March 2007, at Woodlands Stud, in Australia.

TIFFANY ICE, 1982 gr. h., Icecapade—Auntie's Niece, by Chieftain. 19-5-4-1, $188,095. Won the 1984 Sanford S. (G2). Sire of 14 stakes winners, including two-time Mexican Horse of the Year Dilic and Canadian champion Buckys Solution; of cancer and old age, in April 2007, in Oregon.

TINCHEN'S PRINCE, 1983 gr. g., Cornish Prince—Tinchen, by *Grey Dawn II. 95-14-21-14, $953,463. Won the 1988 Gen. Douglas MacArthur H., Ashley T. Cole S., etc.; due to infirmities of age, on April 27, 2007.

TIP OF THE ICEBERG, 2001 br. g., Nediym (Ire)—Ice Column, by Pillaster. 28-4-5-1, $36,287; first Thoroughbred casualty of Australia's equine influenza outbreak, in early September 2007, in New South Wales, Australia.

TIROL, 1987 br. h., Thatching—Alpine Niece, by Great Nephew. 9-5-1-2, $521,159. Won the 1990 General Accident Two Thousand Guineas (Eng-G1) and Airlie Coolmore Irish Two Thousand Guineas. Sire of 22 stakes winners, including Irish classic winner Tarascon; in 2007, at Capricorn Stud Farm, in India.

T. J.'S LUCKY MOON, 1999 dk. b. or br. g., Tejabo—Moonland Princess, by Key to the Moon. 10-2-1-0, $671,505. Won the 2002 Queen's Plate S.; on March 30, 2008, at Molinaro Stable, in Canada.

TRAKI TRAKI, 1987 ch. m., Mo Power—Ride the Rainbow, by True Colors. 18-6-2-2, $68,941. Won the 1990 Old Hat S. Dam of four stakes winners, including Grade 1 winner Bushfire; of a ruptured uterine artery, on April 14, 2007, in Florida.

Tribunal, 1997 ch. h., Deputy Minister—Six Crowns, by Secretariat. Half brother to champion Chief's Crown. 18-3-3-4, $315,140. Grade 1-placed. Washington's 2006 leading freshman sire. Sire of 2007 Emerald Downs Derby winner Mulcahy; after surgery for a leg injury, on January 8, 2008, at Washington State University in Pullman, Washington.

TROPICAL STAR (IRE), 2000 b. g., Machiavellian—Tropical, by Green Desert. 21-7-5-2, $1,055,228. Won the 2007 Najah al Shindagha Sprint (UAE-G3); euthanized due to injuries suffered in a paddock accident, on February 24, 2007, in the United Arab Emirates.

TUDO AZUL (BRZ), 2003 b. c., Boatman—One Flashblue, by Blue Diamond II. 5-4-0-1, $70,146. Champion at two in Brazil. Won the 2006 Grande Premio Ipiranga (Brz-G1) (Brazilian Two Thousand Guineas); of an intestinal infection, in late February 2007, in the United Arab Emirates.

TURBO LAUNCH, 1985 ch. m., Relaunch—David's Tobin, by *Tobin Bronze. 8-4-1-0, $126,325. Won the 1987 Canterbury Debutante S. Dam of two stakes winners, including 2001 Broodmare of the Year Turko's Turn. Grandam of 2001 Horse of the Year Point Given; unexpectedly, two weeks after foaling, on June 5, 2007, in Maryland.

TYROLEAN EMPRESS, 2003 ch. f., Swiss Yodeler—Queen of Synastry, by Synastry. 21-2-5-0, $91,700. Won the 2006 Magali Farms S.; after breaking down in a race at Santa Anita Park, on February 10, 2007, in California.

VALID'S VALID, 2002 ch. m., Valid Wager—Florida Cracker, by Prospectors Gamble. 23-5-2-4, $233,177. Won the 2007 Valid S.; after breaking down in the Pio Pico Stakes at Fairplex Park, on September 14, 2007, in Pomona, California.

VALID WAGER, 1992 b. h., Valid Appeal—Bid Gal,

by Bold Bidder. 16-5-5-0, $306,020. Won the 1996 Westchester H. (G3). Sire of 15 stakes winners, including Grade 1 winner Valid Video; of cancer, on May 15, 2007, in California.

VAL'S PRINCE, 1992 ch. g., Eternal Prince—Key Buy, by Valid Appeal. 52-13-12-5, $2,118,785. Won the 1997 and '99 Turf Classic Invitational S. (G1); of colic, on August 19, 2007.

VAUDEVILLE, 1991 b. h., Theatrical (Ire)—S'Nice, by Riverman. 15-4-3-0, $604,350. Won the 1994 Secretariat S. (G1). Sire of stakes winner Night Dash; euthanized due to a leg condition, in February 2007, at Hidden Springs Ranch, in Yarnell, Arizona.

VERNON CASTLE, 1983 dk. b. or br. h., Seattle Slew—Rullian's Princess, by Prince John. 13-4-3-2, $390,258. Won the 1986 California Derby (G2). Sire of stakes winners First Journey and Cesi (Mex); in 2007.

VICTORY SMILE, 1996 b. g., Victory Dance (Ire)—Fluoride, by Crested Wave. 54-8-9-6, $349,401. Won the 2002 Metropolitan H. (Aus-G1); euthanized following a paddock accident, in February 2007, in New Zealand.

VOULEZ VOUS, 2004 dk. b. or br. f., Elusive Quality—Gather the Storm, by Storm Cat. 3-1-0-1, $31,850. Sold for $775,000 as a two-year-old; after breaking down in the La Habra S., on March 4, 2007, at Santa Anita Park, in California.

WAQUOIT, 1983 gr. h., Relaunch—Grey Parlo, by *Grey Dawn II. 30-19-4-3, $2,225,360. Won the 1988 Jockey Club Gold Cup S. (G1). Sire of 32 stakes winners, including Grade 1-winning millionaire Halo America; of infirmities of age, on June 14, 2007, at Northview Stallion Station, in Chesapeake City, Maryland.

WAR, 1984 b. h., Majestic Light—Victorian Queen, by Victoria Park. 31-5-4-5, $377,832. Won the 1987 Blue Grass S. (G1). Sire of Grade 3 winner Gulf Reckoning; in 2007, in Florida.

WAR OF THE WORLDS, 2002 br. g., Commands—Conquered, by Star Watch. Raced in Hong Kong as Royal Delight. 15-6-1-2, $657,326. Won the 2007 HSBC Premier Bowl; after breaking down in a workout, in January 2008, at Sha Tin racecourse, in Hong Kong.

WESTERN PLAYBOY, 1986 ch. h., Play Fellow—Westward Hope, by Daniel Boone. 45-8-7-7, $1,128,449. Illinois horse of the year in 1989. Won the 1989 Blue Grass S. (G1). Sire of four stakes winners, including graded winners Southern Playgirl and Wade for Me; of a heart attack, in April 2007, at Fairberry Farm, in Waterloo, Illinois.

WESTERN PRIZE, 2004 ch. c., Pure Prize—Marfa's Squall, by Marfa. 17-5-4-3, $261,900. Won the 2007 Ruidoso Thoroughbred Derby and Charles Taylor Derby; after breaking down past the finish line following a third-place finish in the Hawthorne Derby (G3), on October 13, 2007, at Hawthorne Race Course, in Illinois.

WHAT A QUESTION, 2002 b. h., Qui Danzig—Waseela, by Ahonoora. 10-3-3-1, $58,636. Won the 2006 Sunday Tribune Byerly Turk Plate (SAf-G3); of injuries sustained in a road accident, on November 3, 2007, in South Africa.

WHO DOCTOR WHO, 1983 dk. b. or br. g., Doctor Stat—The Girl Who, by Barnstorming. 64-33-16-5, $813,870. Winner of 26 stakes, including the 1986 President's Cup S. (G3); of laminitis, on February 22, 2007, at trainer Herb Riecken's farm, in Fremont, Nebraska.

WHO WHAT WIN, 2003 dk. b. or br. g., Dance Brightly—Charms Way, by Salt Lake. 23-7-9-1, $382,445. Won the 2007 Mellow Roll S. and Sherpa Guide S.; after breaking down in the Alex M. Robb H., on December 30, 2007, at Aqueduct, in New York.

WICKED WITCHCRAFT, 1980 dk. b. or br. m., Good Behaving—Surrogate, by *Yatasto. 33-10-5-4, $218,559. Won the 1985 Marion H. Van Berg Memorial H. Dam of three graded stakes winners, including champion The Wicked North; of natural causes, on March 13, 2007, at Randal Farm, in Fallbrook, California.

WILD FIT, 2003 gr. or ro. f., Wild Wonder—Grannies Feather, by At Full Feather. 10-2-3-1, $555,079. Won the 2005 Del Mar Debutante S. (G1); of colic, in January 2007, in California.

WINNING COLORS, 1985 ro. m., Caro (Ire)—All Rainbows, by Bold Hour. 19-8-3-1, $1,526,837. Racing Hall of Fame. Won the 1988 Kentucky Derby (G1), Santa Anita Derby (G1). Dam of five winners, including stakes-placed Golden Colors; of colic, on February 17, 2008, at Hagyard Equine Medical Institute, in Lexington.

WISE MANDATE, 2005 b. c., Perfect Mandate—Baroness V Ullmann, by Bold Badgett. 8-2-1-0, $108,060. Won the 2007 Jack Goodman S. at Oak Tree; after breaking down in a workout, on December 11, 2007, at Hollywood Park, in California.

WOODLANDER, 2002 b. h., Forestry—Madam Lagonza, by Kingmambo. 25-5-3-3, $330,374. Won the 2007 Fort Marcy H. (G3); after breaking down in the Cozzene S., on October 19, 2007, at the Meadowlands, in New Jersey.

WOODMAN, 1983 ch. h., Mr. Prospector—Playmate, by Buckpasser. 5-3-0-1, $28,045. Champion at two in Ireland. Sire of 110 stakes winners, including champions Hansel and Timber Country. Broodmare sire of 118 stakes winners and leading broodmare sire of 2007; of old age, on July 19, 2007, at Ashford Stud, in Versailles, Kentucky.

ZACCIO, 1976 ch. g., *Lorenzaccio—Delray Dancer, by Chateaugay. 42-22-7-3, $288,124. Three-time champion steeplechaser and member of the Racing Hall of Fame; of old age, on September 19, 2007, in Peapack, New Jersey.

ZATO, 2003 ch. g., Zafonic—Top Table, by Shirley Heights. 28-4-3-3, $125,620. Won the 2005 Prix des Jouvenceaux et des Jouvencelles; collapsed following a race at Ascot, on November 23, 2007, in England.

ZOMAN, 1987 ch. h., Affirmed—A Little Affection, by King Emperor. 24-7-5-3, $1,040,372. English highweight and Irish champion. Won the 1992 Budweiser International S. (G1); in 2007.

ZUPPARDO'S PRINCE, 1976 dk. b. or br. h., Cornish Prince—Prim Lady, by Primate. 28-12-7-2, $181,547. Won the 1980 and 1981 Phoenix H. Nine-time leading sire in Louisiana. Sire of 34 stakes winners, including Grade 2 winners Zuppardo Ardo and Astas Foxy Lady; of old age, on August 24, 2007, at Clear Creek Stud, in Folsom, Louisiana.

HISTORY OF RACING

by Mary Simon

Horse racing officially appeared in the annals of history in approximately 1000 B.C. when Greeks started racing horses with chariots drawn behind them, a dangerous game that subsequently was adopted by the Romans and Egyptians. For the 33rd Olympiad in 644 B.C., formal competition began with riders astride the horses. The Romans, who conquered England in 43 A.D. under Emperor Claudius and ruled it until 410 A.D., carried their horses and their sport to the island nation, where a millennium later it would blossom into the sport known as Thoroughbred racing.

By the late 1500s, racing had become a favorite pastime of English noblemen. King Henry VIII and his daughter Queen Elizabeth I both maintained racing stables, and Elizabeth's cousin King James I established Newmarket racecourse early in the 17th century. His son Charles I also was a racing enthusiast, but he was overthrown and beheaded in 1649, and Lord Protector Oliver Cromwell banned horse racing. After the restoration of the monarchy in 1660, racing flourished under its ardent devotee King Charles II.

Because of Charles II's love for the sport, racing became known as the sport of kings, and during his rule the first of three imported Arabian stallions began the genetic progression toward the Thoroughbred of today. In 1688, Capt. Robert Byerly purportedly returned from Hungary with a captured stallion who became known as the Byerly Turk. Sixteen years later, British consul Thomas Darley smuggled an Arabian stallion out of Syria and transplanted him to Yorkshire; he became known as the Darley Arabian. In approximately 1730, an Arabian stallion of unknown lineage appeared in the stable of the Earl of Godolphin and became known as the Godolphin Arabian. These three stallions would become the foundation sires of the Thoroughbred. The Darley Arabian sired Flying Childers, generally regarded as the first great Thoroughbred, in 1714. (For more on the development of the Thoroughbred, see Evolution of the Breed.)

In the late 18th century, racing began to assume a formal structure. Racecourses were established, and the first of the English classics, the St. Leger Stakes, was run in 1776. The Epsom Derby followed four years later, and the Two Thousand Guineas had its first running in 1809. As racing developed in England, it found its way to the American colonies. In 1665, New York Governor Richard Nicholls gave the name Newmarket to America's first racetrack. Although the first track was located in New York, horse racing tended to be frowned upon by religious leaders and communities in the North, but the sport flourished in the South. The first known Thoroughbred sire imported to North America from England was *Bulle Rock, an aged son of the Darley Arabian. Although *Bulle Rock had no lasting influence, pre-Revolution imports such as *Fearnought, pint-sized *Janus, and the *Cub mare influenced the breed's development.

19th Century

Early American presidents, particularly those from the South, were racing fans. Thomas Jefferson approved the Senate's practice of adjourning early to attend local meets. Senators of the day might have marveled at the fabled 28-foot stride of the great colt Florizel or witnessed the unbeatable brilliance of First Consul during his 21-race winning streak.

It was an era of often unrecorded and disputed genealogies, and races were crudely timed, if at all. The 1823 victory of American Eclipse over Henry in the North-South match at Long Island's Union Course proved a milestone in post-Colonial racing. The $20,000-a-side event drew a significant portion of the New York populace and helped American Eclipse stake his claim as the first American earnings champion, with $56,700. At the same time, *Leviathan was standing for America's highest known fee—$75—but he was not the most notable stallion of the period. That honor went to *Diomed, a British castoff after the Revolutionary War. The inaugural Epsom Derby winner in 1780, he arrived on American shores in Virginia in '98, acquired for a meager $250. *Diomed proceeded over 11 seasons to reshape the American Thoroughbred in his own remarkable image, getting runners that were uniformly taller, heavier of bone, stouter, stronger, and faster than their contemporaries.

Unlike England, where the Epsom Derby and St. Leger heralded a trend toward shorter races, America maintained its long heat races for the first half of the century. While the style of racing evolved over time, change of another kind arrived on March 17, 1850, when *Diomed's great-great grandson Lexington was born on a Central Kentucky farm. Brilliant on the racecourse and even more accomplished at stud, Lexington would reign 16 times—including 14 in succession—as the country's leading sire.

As the century progressed, races became shorter, purses rose, and racing began to become organized. Saratoga Race Course, Pim-

lico Race Course, Churchill Downs, and Fair Grounds opened for business. The Travers Stakes had its first running in 1864, and the Belmont Stakes was run for the first time in 1867. The Preakness Stakes followed in 1873, and the Kentucky Derby was staged for the first time in '75. Late in the century, the Jockey Club was established to oversee the growing sport, and it soon assumed control of the *American Stud Book*. In 1889, Miss Woodford became the first American Thoroughbred to top $100,000 in career earnings. Two-year-old racing gained popularity with the inaugural 1888 Futurity, worth $40,000 to the winner; five years later, a juvenile named Domino set a single-season earnings record of $170,790 that would stand for decades. Kingston—last of the great iron horses of a dying era—retired in 1894 with 89 victories, a record to this day. By the end of the 19th century, Kentucky had become the heart of America's Thoroughbred business, with more professional horsemen than any other region. America and its Thoroughbred industry were thus poised to enter a modern era of even greater change.

1901-'10

The American century's first decade was one of promise and turmoil for the Thoroughbred racing industry. Trouble brewed even as financier James R. Keene's great Commando blistered the track at the dawn of the century and as Commando's unbeatable son Colin carried the Keene colors to victory after brilliant victory a few years later. Even as Keene's stable racked up unprecedented earnings, as record purses were dispensed, and as Belmont Park opened its glorious gates, a dark cloud was settling ominously on racing's horizon.

Racing may have been the sport of kings, but it was also part of a larger gambling industry. Increasingly, the taint of corruption eroded public confidence in the sport as high-profile incidents were exposed. Keene's Sysonby, one of the sport's all-time greats, suffered his only loss in the 1904 Futurity after being drugged by a groom. Delhi, the 1904 Belmont Stakes winner, later ran sluggishly and was found to have sponges inserted far up into his nostrils. Electric prods, dopings, ringers, crooked jockeys, and diverse gambling scams involving track bookmakers were daily journalistic fodder.

By 1907, anti-racetrack wagering laws had been simmering for some time on legislative back burners across America. In June 1908, New York passed the Agnew-Hart bill with the ardent blessing of Governor Charles Evans Hughes, who used the legislation as a weapon against the Tammany Hall political machine, a major beneficiary of racing in the New York metropolitan area. Without revenues from legalized gambling, racing soon found it impossible to support itself. In 1910, historic Saratoga was among the racetracks that ceased operation, and E. J. "Lucky" Baldwin's original Santa Anita Park was forced to close.

A domino effect occurred as other states rushed to pass similar legislation. The national purse structure collapsed, declining from a 1907 average of $949 per race to $643 in '09. Top stables, including Keene's, shipped overseas in a European invasion so successful that it would pave the way for the next great blow to the American Thoroughbred industry—the English Jockey Club's 1913 passage of the "Jersey Act" banning most American-breds from their Stud Book. In 1908, Churchill Downs's energetic general manager, Col. Matt Winn, pulled some old pari-mutuel machines out of storage, dusted them off, and put them back into use. When racing resumed in the next decade, the pari-mutuel wagering system quickly would become dominant.

Despite all, several great competitors appeared on racing's stage to illuminate the era. Colin was one of nine future Racing Hall of Fame members who campaigned during the decade. Man o' War's fiery sire, Fair Play, was another, along with Commando, Sysonby, Artful, Beldame, Roseben, Broomstick, and Peter Pan.

1911-'20

As indignation among the American populace swelled over the puritan campaigners' assault on gambling and alcohol consumption, a group of wealthy horsemen began to stockpile a fund with which to hold future race meets. The future came quickly. Although the Agnew-Hart legislation moldered on the books until 1934, the penalties associated with it were stripped away by May 30, 1913, when Belmont Park opened for the first time since 1910. Between 1908 and '13, however, American breeders had sent overseas more than 1,500 horses, among them at least 24 champions. Some eventually came back, but many did not. Leading sires *Rock Sand and *Meddler, also part of the exodus, were lost forever to American breeding.

The British responded with the Jersey Act in 1913, which effectively barred many old American lines from England's *General Stud Book,* but the first shots of World War I one year later quickly changed the United States from an exporter of bloodstock into an aggressive importer. Between 1916-'20, numerous English-breds and French-breds became American champions, including *Short Grass, *Sun Briar, *Hourless, *Omar Khayyam, *Johren, *Sunbonnet, *Enfilade, and *Constancy.

Even in the shadow of war, the decade was memorable for its outstanding runners, includ-

ing future Racing Hall of Fame geldings Roamer, Old Rosebud, and Exterminator. Together, they won 129 races and set or equaled 29 records from five furlongs to 2¼ miles at 14 different racetracks. Iron Mask set a North American record for 5½ furlongs that would stand for 30 years, and the mare Pan Zareta took a back seat to no male in the realm of blazing speed. H. P. Whitney's Regret routinely whipped the boys and in 1915 became the first filly to win the Kentucky Derby. The Triple Crown was won for the first time in 1919 by Sir Barton, although the sweep did not take on its popular name until the '30s.

Sir Barton won the Belmont on June 11, five days after the decade's finest specimen made his first career start at Belmont Park. Man o' War, considered the greatest American horse of all time, was ineligible for admission to the *General Stud Book*, but in 16 months of competition redefined greatness. He lost one race at two that he should have won, failing to overcome a bad start in the Sanford Stakes at Saratoga Race Course and losing to Upset, but he never lost again. In 1920, "Big Red" established five American and two track records in 11 starts and won his races by a combined 164 lengths. Man o' War capped his extraordinary career on October 12, 1920, by galloping away from Sir Barton in a winner-take-all race at Kenilworth Park in Canada. The $80,000 purse sent him to stud as the richest American Thoroughbred in history with $249,465.

1921-'30

On the surface at least, the Roaring Twenties were a time of outrageous fun—flappers and the fox trot are indelible images of the era—and horse racing rode the crest of this postwar celebration. Elaborate new racetracks were the overt symbol of this prosperity—at least 15 of note were constructed in the United States during the 1920s, including Arlington and Washington Parks in Chicago and Hialeah Park in Florida. Purses went through the roof. In 1923, Zev became the first American racehorse to bank $200,000 in a season and, by '30, Gallant Fox—the second Triple Crown winner and the first to be recognized for sweeping the three American classics—had raised that bar to $300,000. Jockey Earle Sande, trainer James Fitzsimmons, breeder Harry Payne Whitney, and owner Harry Sinclair each established earnings records that would stand for years. Bloodstock prices also went into orbit, with a yearling commanding a record $75,000 in 1928.

Because the Jersey Act remained in force, horses mostly migrated to the west. Future leading sires *St. Germans, *Sickle, and *Challenger II were among the importees, as was the great matron *La Troienne. In late 1925, *Sir Gallahad III arrived at Claiborne Farm, where he would reign four times as America's premier sire and 12 times as its leading broodmare sire. *Sir Gallahad III's American-bred counterpart was Man o' War, a private stallion who had seven of his eight champions in his first four crops and in 1926—with only three crops racing—set a progeny earnings record of $409,927.

No single racehorse towered above all others in the 1920s as Man o' War and Colin had before, but the decade nonetheless yielded 15 Racing Hall of Fame members. Foremost among them was Exterminator, the wonderful gelding who scored a 20th-century record 34 stakes victories and retired as America's richest Thoroughbred. Grey Lag flirted with greatness, as did champions Sarazen, Blue Larkspur, Reigh Count, and Gallant Fox. Zev, Crusader, and Sun Beau were big money winners. Princess Doreen won 34 races and broke Miss Woodford's 40-year female earnings record with $174,745. Other notable fillies included 1924 Preakness winner Nellie Morse; multiple champions Black Maria and Bateau; and Rose of Sharon, considered best of either sex at three in 1929. For a time, it appeared the good times would go on forever, but the stock market crashed in October 1929, which led to events that caused the Great Depression.

1931-'40

As the Depression shrunk race purses 40%, the average yearling price slumped to $570 in 1932. But, as the Depression eased, the Thoroughbred industry entered one of its healthiest eras. Purses rose by decade's end to record heights, and yearling sales gained strength. Racing also had some wealthy, influential leaders. Joseph E. Widener, vice chairman of the New York Jockey Club, crusaded tirelessly to return the sport in the Empire State to its former glory. Jockey Club Chairman William Woodward campaigned 1935 Triple Crown winner Omaha, but more importantly that year he fired some of the angriest, most articulate words at England's discriminatory Jersey Act. During the decade, increasingly sophisticated stall starting gates were developed, photo-finish cameras were installed, and saliva testing for drugs gained widespread use. Keeneland Race Course, Del Mar Thoroughbred Club, Santa Anita Park, and Hollywood Park opened for business.

Although the 1930s featured many standout racehorses, including 17 future Racing Hall of Fame members and two Triple Crown winners, three in particular captured the hearts of America—C. V. Whitney's Equipoise, Australasian wonder *Phar Lap, and claimer-turned-champion Seabiscuit. Although bred in the purple and owned by one of America's wealthiest

bluebloods, there was nothing pretentious about Equipoise, a son of Pennant who was a champion at two in 1930, a three-time handicap champion, and a world-record miler. Seabiscuit, an undersized Wheatley Stable reject, developed into a megastar, reigning as '38 Horse of the Year and twice as America's handicap champion. In one of the decade's greatest moments, Seabiscuit defeated 1937 Triple Crown winner War Admiral in the two-horse '38 Pimlico Special Stakes. *Phar Lap illuminated the Depression's darkest hour by winning the 1932 Agua Caliente Handicap in record time, but the huge New Zealander died just 17 days later under suspicious circumstances.

The 1930s launched a feminine revolution of sorts. Top Flight defeated males in the 1931 Futurity to become the first $200,000 juvenile earner and richest American female. Mrs. Payne Whitney's Twenty Grand won that year's Kentucky Derby, and Isabel Dodge Sloane became America's leading owner in 1934. As war in Europe approached, America imported several top stallions. In 1936, Hancock organized a syndicate to purchase *Blenheim II, for $250,000; four years later, C. V. Whitney acquired the stallion's classic-winning son, *Mahmoud.

1941-'50

Despite a world at war for half the decade, the 1940s very well may have been racing's finest hour, with four Triple Crown winners crowning the decade. The war years were grim for the sport, however. Southern California's tracks were shut down—Santa Anita was an internment camp for Japanese-Americans, Hollywood was an army storage unit, and Del Mar was used for assembling aircraft wings. Travel restrictions crippled the Saratoga yearling sale and led to the creation of the Breeders' Sales Co., precursor of Keeneland Sales. In late 1944, the government banned racing, and only victory in Europe saved the '45 Triple Crown.

Leavening the somber news from overseas were the exploits of Whirlaway, Calumet's "Mr. Longtail," winner of the 1941 Triple Crown. Then there was Alsab, a $700 yearling of peasant lineage who outgamed Whirlaway by a nose in a famous 1942 match race at Narragansett Park. Mrs. John D. Hertz's 1943 Triple Crown winner, Count Fleet, habitually crushed his opposition and romped to a 25-length Belmont Stakes victory, despite a career-ending injury. High-headed, flame-coated Stymie was not the best, but he was nevertheless beloved by fans who made him the people's horse. Claimed for $1,500 from King Ranch by trainer Hirsch Jacobs, Stymie became the first Thoroughbred to surpass $900,000 in career earnings. King Ranch had Assault, who overcame a deformed right fore foot to win the 1946 Triple Crown. The 1940s also produced several top fillies, including Racing Hall of Fame members Twilight Tear, Busher, Gallorette, Bewitch, Two Lea, and Bed o' Roses. Argentine-bred *Miss Grillo set a 2½-mile world record in the 1948 Pimlico Cup Handicap.

The decade virtually belonged to Warren Wright's magnificent Calumet Stable, whose champions were trained by Ben and Jimmy Jones and in many cases ridden by Eddie Arcaro—all Racing Hall of Fame members. Calumet reigned as America's top owner seven times during the decade, edged only by a trio of prominent women—Mrs. Payne Whitney (1942), Elizabeth Graham ('45), and Isabel Dodge Sloane ('50). Runners who carried the feared devil's red and blue silks during the 1940s included Racing Hall of Fame members Whirlaway, Twilight Tear, Armed, Citation, Bewitch, Coaltown, and Two Lea, and father-son Kentucky Derby winners Pensive and Ponder. Citation was not only Calumet's best but also one of the century's most talented runners. Champion at two and three, American Triple Crown hero, and winner of 16 consecutive races, Citation would become the sport's first millionaire in 1951.

Late in the decade, Claiborne Farm acquired *Nasrullah, a rogue stallion who would transform the American bloodstock industry. Also in 1949, England's Jockey Club backed down after 36 years and rescinded the despised Jersey Act, by now long outdated and hindering rather than helping the British breeding industry. America thus regained its former stature as a respected source of international bloodstock.

1951-'60

As it entered the second half of the 20th century, the U.S. confronted a rapidly changing world. It was at war in Korea, the threat of Nazism had been replaced by the peril of nuclear cataclysm, television was helping to create a truly national society, and polio had been conquered. America's appetite for racing seemed utterly insatiable; attendance and handle records were established almost annually. Perhaps it was too successful. In this decade, racing failed to build a lasting partnership with television—an arrogant decision that the industry would regret into the 21st century.

The 1950s were a time of rising incomes and rising expectations. In 1956, Nashua became the first million-dollar stallion syndication. Also that year, jockey Bill Hartack became the first to ride winners of $2-million in a single season; he topped $3-million the following year. The 1950s witnessed a growing interest in early competition—particularly after the spectacular 1953 debut of the world's richest race, the $270,000 Garden State Stakes for two-year-olds at Gar-

den State Park in New Jersey. Soundness became an issue in the 1950s, with the high-profile breakdowns of such stars as Hail to Reason and Swaps. In the late 1950s, phenylbutazone—an anti-inflammatory drug popularly known as Bute—came into wide use to ease the aches and pains of thoroughbreds, though not legal for racing.

Racing in the 1950s had several stars but no Triple Crown winner. (Jockey Eddie Arcaro blamed himself for Nashua's loss to Swaps in the 1955 Derby. Nashua subsequently won the Preakness and Belmont.) The first equine superhero of the TV age was Native Dancer—the "Gray Ghost of Sagamore," whose only loss in 22 starts was by a head in the 1953 Kentucky Derby. Also racing at that time was Tom Fool, who carried heavy imposts to ten straight victories. As Native Dancer and Tom Fool exited the stage, the prodigiously talented pair of Nashua and Swaps took their place. They met twice, with Swaps winning the 1955 Derby and Nashua the '55 $100,000 Washington Park match race. The foal crop of 1954 contained Bold Ruler, Round Table, and *Gallant Man, all Racing Hall of Fame members. Round Table lasted the longest, 66 races, and was America's first great grass horse. Talent was so widespread that no one noticed an ordinary-looking bay gelding who won only a maiden race in 1959. But Kelso went on to become one of the major heroes of the 1960s.

1961-'70

The 1960s were a watershed for America and American racing. Inaugurated in January 1961 was John F. Kennedy, the first president born in the 20th century. Racial segregation was overthrown in the South, but lives were lost in the battle. Kennedy's assassination in 1963 shook America to its core, and soon the collective conformism of the '50s crumbled. As men walked on the moon, young soldiers were dying in an unpopular Vietnam war.

Racing increasingly became a game of haves and have-nots. In 1967, Damascus banked a single-season record $817,941. That same year, North America's earnings per runner averaged $3,359, or about half of training costs for a year. Medication also became an issue, especially when Dancer's Image was disqualified from his 1968 Kentucky Derby victory over a Bute positive.

State legislators looked to racing to plug budget gaps; at the end of the decade, proposed federal tax changes led to the creation of the American Horse Council to help lobby on behalf of horse racing and breeding interests. Simultaneously, racing was losing some of its audience as other professional sports and entertainment forms gained popularity. National attendance declined in 1967 for the first time since World War II, despite nearly 100 added racing days. During the 1960s, total racing days increased 35%, while average daily attendance declined 3%. At decade's end, off-track betting was approved in New York, which would lead to even larger attendance declines.

Against this chaotic and disquieting backdrop, Kelso—and others like him—redeemed this troubled era and made it one of the most remarkable in 200 years. Allaire duPont's Kelso tore through the handicap ranks, ruling as Horse of the Year from 1960 through '64. Carry Back emerged from Florida to win the 1961 Kentucky Derby and Preakness Stakes. Other outstanding performers of the era were Arts and Letters, Majestic Prince, Nodouble, Northern Dancer, and Fort Marcy, but the second half of the decade belonged to Buckpasser, Damascus, and Dr. Fager. Together, they started 85 times and compiled a 64-13-5 record.

Fillies of the 1960s deserve special mention. Cicada, Old Hat, Affectionately, Straight Deal, Tosmah, Politely, Gamely, and Shuvee averaged 56 career starts. Cicada set an earnings record; Moccasin became the first juvenile filly to take Horse of the Year honors in the 1965 Thoroughbred Racing Associations poll; Dark Mirage was first to sweep New York's filly triple crown in 1968; Dr. Fager's younger half sister, Ta Wee, toted an average of 136 pounds in 1970. Women gained the right to ride in races in 1969, and trailblazer Diane Crump rode in the '70 Derby. Bloodstock prices were heating up, and Nijinsky II was syndicated for a record $5.44-million in 1970.

1971-'80

In some respects, the decade between 1971 and '80 was one of the century's most satisfying periods for American Thoroughbred racing. Great runners and big money energized the era, but they also disguised some troubling problems, such as race fixing, increasingly lenient medication rules, and a declining audience. The 1970s were racing's best years since the '40s, with three Triple Crown winners within five years. The bloodstock markets were supercharged as well, with the beginning of the Northern Dancer era and the speculative buying that eventually damaged the markets in the 1980s.

Secretariat, Seattle Slew, and Affirmed, the three Triple Crown winners, attracted most of the attention, and they shared the limelight with Forego, Ruffian, and Spectacular Bid, among others. It has been said that Secretariat appeared at the precise moment when America and racing needed him most. A transcendent, larger-than-life figure bursting with almost supernatural vitality, he streaked across racing's

stage in 1972 and '73, leaving behind an impression of pure greatness unrivaled since Man o' War. After he won the 1973 Kentucky Derby (G1) in record time (1:59⅖, a mark that still stands) and the Preakness Stakes (G1) with consummate ease (also probably a record even though the timing was botched), Secretariat quieted every skeptic with his 31-length triumph in the Belmont Stakes (G1) in 2:24, 2⅕ seconds—11 lengths—faster than the existing world record. Seattle Slew blazed through the Triple Crown, becoming the first to complete the sweep with an unbeaten record, and one year later Affirmed won the Triple Crown over his nemesis Alydar, who was second in all three races.

The Triple Crown winners did not stand alone in the spotlight. Twenty-two future Racing Hall of Fame members campaigned during this decade, including six from a remarkable 1970 foal crop. Among them were the first distaff millionaire, Dahlia, 12-for-12 juvenile La Prevoyante, and Forego, who was Horse of the Year three times. Ruffian cruised unbeaten through ten starts until the ill-fated 1975 match race with Kentucky Derby winner Foolish Pleasure that took her life. The era closed with yet another performer for the ages. The Triple Crown eluded Spectacular Bid, but not much else did between 1978 and '80. The compact gray colt set nine track, American, and world standards. In 1980, Genuine Risk became only the second filly in 106 years to win the Kentucky Derby.

The 1970s signaled the dramatic rise of top Hispanic jockeys, with none more prominent than Laffit Pincay Jr. Among trainers, the torch passed to Charlie Whittingham and Laz Barrera, whose West Coast-based stables also hailed the arrival of California as a centerpiece of American racing. The industry was changing in other ways, due in part to the 1971 introduction of off-track betting in New York. By 1977, OTB wagers finally exceeded money wagered on track in New York, and the gap would widen thereafter.

1981-'90

The breeding industry follows the fortunes of the racetrack, but for a few years in the 1980s that relationship became temporarily detached, or so it seemed, as rich foreign buyers pursued yearlings by Northern Dancer and his sons. In 1985, a Nijinsky II colt was sold for a record $13.1-million at the Keeneland July sale of selected yearlings, but by then the bloodstock markets had entered a slide that would last into the 1990s. Stud fees climbed to unsupportable levels on the fantasy, and everything came crashing down. On the track, attendance was falling while wagering and purses stagnated.

In 1982, at the peak of the bloodstock boom, horseman John Gaines worried over the industry's fundamentals and came up with an idea to market it. One year earlier, the Budweiser Arlington Million had been inaugurated at Arlington Park as the world's first $1-million Thoroughbred race. Enthusiastically received, it had drawn a field of international grass stars and was won by John Henry. Gaines envisioned a single championship day of racing, offering millions of dollars in purse money, paid for by stallion and foal nomination fees. In November 1984 at Hollywood Park, his dream became reality at the first Breeders' Cup championship day, arguably the sport's greatest innovation since the Triple Crown.

Although he missed the first Breeders' Cup and never raced again, Dotsam Stable's John Henry proved once again that the American Dream was alive and well. He was a gelded son of an obscure sire, and he earned more than $6.5-million. In the 1980s, fillies shined brightest. Eight of the decade's 13 Racing Hall of Fame performers thus far have been members of the distaff set, including Horses of the Year All Along (Fr) and Lady's Secret, 1988 Kentucky Derby winner Winning Colors, undefeated champions Personal Ensign (13-for-13) and Landaluce (5-for-5 before her death), and two-time champion Go for Wand, who died on the track in the 1990 Breeders' Cup Distaff (G1). Also notable were two-time champions Bayakoa (Arg) and Miesque.

Although males of the 1980s lacked the brilliance of their female counterparts, they did provide memorable moments. Ferdinand gave Whittingham his first Kentucky Derby victory at age 73 in 1986, and in '87 he fought to the bitter end under Racing Hall of Fame member Bill Shoemaker to edge Derby winner Alysheba in the Breeders' Cup Classic (G1). The fierce 1989 rivalry between Sunday Silence and Easy Goer ranks among the sport's best, and also memorable was Conquistador Cielo's 14-length triumph in the 1982 Belmont Stakes, the first of trainer Woody Stephens's historic five straight wins in that classic. One of the decade's most poignant moments was trainer Carl Nafzger's spontaneous televised description of Unbridled's 1990 Kentucky Derby stretch run for 92-year-old owner Frances Genter. Trainer D. Wayne Lukas rewrote the record books repeatedly during these years, setting and breaking his own earnings standards.

1991-2000

The century's final decade was a breakthrough for America's racetracks, which built a solid foundation first on intrastate intertrack wagering and then on the true bonanza, interstate full-card wagering. The full-card explosion forever altered

the sport. By mid-decade, off-site wagering accounted for 74% of racing's handle, a figure that jumped to 82% by 1999. Some tracks added slot machines to boost both purses and profits without putting any new patrons in the stands. The bloodstock markets recovered from a prolonged recession and rose to new heights as the decade ended.

Lexington ad executive Fred Pope, with counsel from John Gaines, in 1996 proposed an industry alliance to revitalize the sport and create a "major league of racing." Their National Thoroughbred Association, an owner-driven organization, soon was swallowed up by the National Thoroughbred Racing Association (NTRA), which was launched in April 1998 and reached into every corner of the sport. Racing series added hours of television coverage, and in 1999 Television Games Network (TVG) debuted on satellite and a few cable systems.

In the bloodstock market, stallion owners began breeding their stars to large books of mares and sent them to the Southern Hemisphere for double duty. A record for a stallion syndication was set in 2000 when Fusaichi Pegasus commanded a record $60-million to $70-million price tag.

A trio of sensational grays—Holy Bull, Silver Charm, and Skip Away—and Allen Paulson's marvelous bay Cigar captured the imagination of the racing public in the 1990s. Together they won classics, championships, and $30-million, but they were sired by stallions with average stud fees of $7,800. Among females, Serena's Song and Dance Smartly were the decade's standouts.

It was an exciting classics decade, with the Triple Crown on the line each year between 1997 and '99, with Silver Charm, Real Quiet, and Charismatic winning the Derby and Preakness before coming up short in the Belmont. Silver Charm and Real Quiet were trained by Bob Baffert, but the classics of the 1990s virtually belonged to Lukas, who won six consecutive classic races with five different horses and also trained Charismatic for Robert and Beverly Lewis, Californians who owned Silver Charm and Serena's Song. Cigar, a two-time Horse of the Year, won 16 consecutive races but proved sterile.

Class I racing returned to Texas, but the first two tracks to open, Sam Houston Race Park and Retama Park, struggled initially. Lone Star Park in the populous Dallas-Fort Worth area was a success from its opening in April 1997. An important trend that began toward the end of the decade was the consolidation of racetrack ownership under Magna Entertainment Corp. and Churchill Downs Inc. That consolidation would continue into the 21st century.

2001-'08

The beginning of the new century was indelibly scarred by an act of unspeakable horror, a terrorist attack with commercial jetliners that killed approximately 3,000 innocent people in New York's World Trade Center towers, at the Pentagon, and in a rural Pennsylvania field, where passengers sacrificed their lives to protect American institutions from Islamist terrorists who had hijacked their plane. September 11, 2001, forever will be seared on the American psyche, along with December 7, 1941, and November 22, 1963. In 2001, a racing event, the Breeders' Cup World Thoroughbred Championships, marked the first international sporting event in the New York region following the attacks.

In the 21st century's first decade, Thoroughbred racing experienced triumphs and it engaged in self-evaluation as the gambling element of the sport began to change. It also had to deal with an attempt to fix the outcome of a bet on the 2002 Breeders' Cup. Meanwhile, the consolidation of American racing into the hands of a few publicly traded companies grew and then ebbed. On the track, the dominant news events were three rags-to-riches horses who stepped out of obscurity and stood on the brink of the sport's ultimate prize, the Triple Crown. War Emblem was the first Derby-Preakness winner of the 21st century in 2002, and he was followed by Funny Cide, a crowd-pleasing gelding owned by a group of fun-loving friends. Smarty Jones, who won the 2004 Derby as the favorite and scored in the Preakness by a record margin, finished second in the Belmont. America's love of the horse was epitomized by the saga of Barbaro, who won the 2006 Derby but broke down in the Preakness. His fight for life became international news, and the nation grieved his death due to laminitis in early 2007.

In the new century's first decade, the sport began to come to grips with a new phenomenon, offshore betting operations known as rebaters (because they rebated part of every bet to their high-dollar players). Some rebaters paid money to purses and others did not. As a result, total North American wagering rose in 2003 while purses declined. The following year, purses rose while wagering declined, a sign of the emergence of racinos—racetracks with slot-machine casinos attached to them—and the trend became pronounced in 2007.

The sport began an evaluation of its wagering systems in 2002 when three former fraternity brothers fixed the Breeders' Cup Ultra Pick Six wager. The fix was quickly uncovered when 43.50-to-1 Volponi won the Breeders' Cup Classic (G1). Industry officials came together with the tote companies to strengthen safeguards,

although implementation of new wagering protocols moved forward very slowly. In a stroke for the sport's integrity, the Racing Medication and Testing Consortium developed model rules on racing drugs and lobbied successfully for their adoption in most racing states. Also, the industry mobilized against alkalizing agents, known as milkshakes, which reputedly delayed the onset of muscle fatigue, and anabolic steroids.

The Kentucky commercial breeding industry, plunged into recession after the 2001 terrorist attacks, sustained a significant blow in '01 and subsequent years from mare reproductive loss syndrome (MRLS), which caused the loss of more than 500 late-term fetuses and almost 3,000 early-term fetuses in Central Kentucky. Attributed to Eastern tent caterpillars, MRLS cost the Kentucky Thoroughbred industry an estimated $300-million and contributed to the demise of the Keeneland July sale of selected yearlings. The bloodstock markets recovered in 2003 and '04.

The sport's stewardship toward its racehorses came into question with Barbaro and intensified when the filly Eight Belles broke down after finishing second in the 2008 Derby. To improve safety, California mandated synthetic surfaces by 2008.

Condensed from "Racing Through the Century," for which Mary Simon was awarded the 2000 Eclipse Award for outstanding features-enterprise writing and which was later published as a book with additional material.

History of Racing Silks

Worn by each jockey to represent a horse's owner, racing silks have been associated with horse racing for nearly two millennia. *Kennets Roman Antiquities* (1696) cites colors worn at chariot races: "At these races, the Romans rode in different colours, particularly the companies of Charioteers, to distinguish themselves." Nero was so fond of his green colors that he often wore a green toga when he attended the races during the first century.

The records of England's King Henry VIII mention jockeys' attire in the first half of the 16th century. His 1530 purse accounts show payments for "doublets [shirts] of Bruges Satin for the boys that runne the gueldings" and for "ryding cappes of Black Satin lyned with black vellute [velvet]." Silk, though expensive, was used for jockeys' jackets and caps because of its light weight and soft, smooth texture. Velvet also was used through the first half of the 19th century.

On October 4, 1762, 19 members of the English Jockey Club registered their colors at Newmarket "for the greater convenience of distinguishing the horses in running." Across the Atlantic Ocean just four years later, Philadelphia horsemen registered their silks with the Philadelphia Jockey Club. Registering yellow silks was Lewis Morris Jr., a signer of the Declaration of Independence.

One of the longest-used silks in America belonged to Howell E. Jackson, a relative of President Andrew Jackson who chose all-maroon colors first used in the early 1820s. The all-scarlet silks of Francis Morris (no relation to Lewis) were first worn in 1862 at the Union Course on Long Island. The Morris family used those colors for four generations through John A. Morris.

Rules published for the October 17-19, 1826, race meeting in Lexington required jockeys to wear a silk jacket and cap. The American Jockey Club, founded in 1894, registered silks for $1 annually or $25 lifetime. The most famous silks in American racing have been those of prominent, private stables—the devil's red and blue of Calumet Farm, the plain black jacket with cherry cap of the late Ogden Phipps, and the all-orange silks of Claiborne Farm.

Sporadically, racetracks have experimented with color-coded silks and jockeys' caps. In 1947, Portland Meadows assigned silks colors by post positions, an idea that was copied at Sportsman's Park and Prescott Downs. Narragansett Park matched the colors of jockeys' caps with post positions. Neither experiment caught on nationally.

In the evolution of Thoroughbred racing in the United States, silk has mostly yielded to nylon or Lycra as the preferred fabric of jockeys' colors. Aerodynamic silks have become commonplace in American racing. First unveiled in 1988 when trainer D. Wayne Lukas used them on all 12 of his horses in the Breeders' Cup, aerodynamic silks, though more costly, are widely available today.

Approximately 28,000 sets of silks are registered with the Jockey Club. Owners pay an annual fee of $15 or $60 every five years. The Jockey Club ceased registering lifetime silks in 1964 while perpetually reserving 3,500 designs.

The Jockey Club has registered silks with various punctuation marks, geometric figures, riding equipment, racetracks, vegetables, musical notes, instruments, birds, dogs, horses, foxes, and even an elephant. Though silks can vary from state to state, roughly 95% of all silks designs are registered with the Jockey Club.

—*Bill Heller*

Key Dates in American Racing History

1665	New York Governor Richard Nicolls establishes America's first formal racecourse on Long Island, names it "New Market."
1730	The Darley Arabian's son *Bulle Rock becomes the first recognized Thoroughbred imported to America, into the Virginia colony.
1752	The great racemare *Selima wins an intercolonial race in Virginia worth $10,000 **(December)**.
1764	Undefeated racehorse and foundation sire Eclipse is born in England during a solar eclipse. Future influential sire *Fearnought is imported to America.
1780	The inaugural Epsom Derby is won by Sir Charles Bunbury's *Diomed **(May 4)**.
1798	*Diomed is imported to Virginia at age 21 for the equivalent of $250; he becomes America's most important early sire. *Spread Eagle, 1795 Epsom Derby winner, is imported into Virginia.
1801	*Spread Eagle reportedly covers 234 mares. Leviathan, American racing's first great gelding, concludes a 23-race win streak, which remains an American record for more than two centuries.
1802	Leviathan wins a five-mile race carrying 180 pounds.
1804	*Sir Harry, 1798 Epsom Derby winner, is imported into Virginia.
1805	American foundation sire Sir Archy is foaled.
1806	Northern champion First Consul runs his undefeated streak to 21.
1808	*Diomed dies in Virginia at age 31 **(March 10)**.
1810	Maria runs five four-mile heats to win a $500 purse at Fairfield, Virginia **(October 3)**.
1820	American Eclipse covers 87 mares for a $12.50 fee.
1821	Union Course opens on Long Island, becomes America's first famous racetrack **(October 15)**.
1823	American Eclipse defeats Henry in North-South match over the Union Course; he becomes America's leading earner, with $56,700 **(May 27)**.
1833	Leading sires Sir Archy and his best son, Sir Charles, die on same day **(June 7)**.
1836	*Glencoe, winner of the 1834 Two Thousand Guineas, is imported into Alabama.
1842	Fashion defeats Boston in a Union Course match race before a crowd of more than 50,000 **(May 10)**.
1845	Peytona defeats Fashion in a $20,000 match race over two four-mile heats at the Union Course and surpasses American Eclipse as the leading American money winner, with $62,400 **(May 13)**. Fashion defeats Peytona in two four-mile heats at Camden, New Jersey **(May 28)**.
1850	Lexington is born **(March 17)**.
1852	Black Swan defeats Governor Pio Pico's non-Thoroughbred stallion Sarco in a nine-mile match race at Los Angeles for a $2,000 purse and 1,000 head of cattle **(March)**.
1855	Lexington sets a four-mile world record of 7:19¾ **(April 2)**. Lexington defeats Lecomte in a match race at New Orleans **(April 14)**.
1856	Lexington sells for an American record $15,000 to Robert A. Alexander.
1857	American-bred Prioress wins England's Cesarewitch Handicap at Newmarket **(October 13)**. Lexington retires to Woodburn Stud in Kentucky.
1860	Don Juan wins the first running of Canada's Queen's Plate **(June 27)**. Revenue becomes America's first leading sire based on progeny earnings instead of winners.
1861	Lexington leads the American sire list for the first of a record 16 times. Planet surpasses Peytona as America's leading money winner, with $69,700.
1864	Lexington's unbeaten son Norfolk wins America's first Derby—the $1,000 Jersey Derby at Paterson **(June 7)**. Saratoga Race Course opens; the inaugural Travers Stakes is won by Lexington's son Kentucky **(August 2)**. Asteroid, another undefeated son of Lexington, is stolen from Woodburn Stud by Confederate guerillas **(October 22)**, recovered a week later. Norfolk is sold for an American record $15,001.
1866	Jerome Park opens in New York **(September 25)**.
1867	The inaugural Belmont Stakes is won by the filly Ruthless at Jerome Park **(June 19)**. Robert A. Alexander dies at Woodburn at age 48 **(December)**.
1868	The Ladies Handicap is inaugurated at Jerome Park, becoming the first major American race to be carded annually for fillies and mares **(June 16)**.
1870	Monmouth Park opens in New Jersey **(July 30)**. Pimlico Race Course opens in Maryland **(October 25)**.
1872	Fair Grounds racetrack opens in New Orleans **(April 13)**.
1873	The inaugural Preakness Stakes at Pimlico is won by Survivor **(May 27)**. Volume I of the *American Stud Book* is published.
1874	Pari-mutuel wagering is introduced at Jerome Park.
1875	*Kentucky Livestock Record* begins publication **(February 5)**, with a subscription cost of $3 per year. Churchill Downs opens; the inaugural Kentucky Derby is won by Aristides **(May 17)**. Lexington dies **(July 1)**.
1877	Congress adjourns to watch Parole defeat Tom Ochiltree and Ten Broeck at Pimlico **(October 24)**.
1878	Ten Broeck defeats Mollie McCarthy in East-West match at Louisville **(July 4)**.
1880	America's first recorded post parade is held before the Belmont Stakes **(June 14)**. Sheepshead Bay racecourse opens in New York **(June 19)**. Blue Gown, the 1868 Epsom Derby winner, dies en route to America.
1881	Pierre Lorillard's Iroquois becomes the first American-owned and -bred Epsom Derby winner **(June 1)**. Hindoo wins his 18th consecutive race **(September 1)**. Parole retires as the leading American money winner, with $82,816.

History of Racing — Key Dates

1882 Fair Grounds racetrack installs electric lights in its grandstand.
1883 The Louisville Jockey Club racetrack is renamed Churchill Downs.
1884 Buchanan becomes the first maiden Kentucky Derby winner **(May 16)**.
1886 Miss Woodford becomes the first American Thoroughbred to top $100,000 in earnings **(June 2)**. Two-year-old Tremont wins each of his 13 career starts in a ten-week span that ends on **August 7**.
1887 Hanover wins 17 consecutive races.
1888 Trainer R. Wyndham Walden saddles a record seventh Preakness Stakes winner, Refund **(May 11)**. King Thomas brings an American yearling auction record of $40,000 **(June 26)**. The inaugural Futurity Stakes at Sheepshead Bay is worth $40,900 to winner Proctor Knott **(September 3)**.
1889 Hanover ends Miss Woodford's reign as the leading American money winner **(August 29)**, retiring with earnings of $118,887. U.S. purse distribution is $2.4-million; 4,820 races are run.
1890 The Preakness Stakes is run at Morris Park in New York **(June 10)**. Salvator runs a world-record 1:35½ mile down the straightaway at Monmouth Park **(August 28)**.
1891 Hawthorne Race Course opens near Chicago **(May 20)**. *St. Blaise sells for a world auction record $100,000 at the August Belmont I estate dispersal **(October 16)**.
1892 Kingston surpasses Hanover as America's top earner, with $138,917, on his way to $140,195.
1893 Boundless wins the American Derby at Washington Park, after an hour and 40-minute delay at the starting post **(June 24)**. *Ormonde, regarded as Europe's best horse of the 19th century, arrives for stud duty in California **(September 8)**. Two-year-old Domino sets a single-season earnings record of $170,890 and becomes America's leading money winner **(September 29)**. Himyar sets a single-season progeny earnings record of $249,502.
1894 The Jockey Club is incorporated **(February 9)**. Kingston scores a record 89th career victory **(August 21)**. Aqueduct racetrack opens in New York **(September 27)**. *Daily Racing Form* begins publication **(November 17)**. *Sir Modred becomes the only California-based stallion to lead the American year-end sire list.
1895 *Livestock Record* changes its name to *The Thoroughbred Record* **(February 2)**. August Belmont II heads the new Westchester Racing Association, the controlling body of New York racing **(August 14)**. Domino retires with record American earnings of $193,550 **(September 17)**.
1896 Domino arrives in Lexington and makes his last public appearance before entering stud **(February 3)**.
1897 Jockey Club buys the *American Stud Book* from H. Sanders Bruce for $35,000 **(May 17)**. Lucretia Borgia races against time at Oakland, California, setting a world four-mile record of 7:11 that remains on the books today. Domino dies of meningitis at age six **(July 29)**.
1898 Fasig-Tipton auction company is incorporated. American-born jockey Tod Sloan introduces his high-stirrup, crouched ("monkey-on-a-stick") riding style to England.
1899 Fasig-Tipton Co. conducts its first Thoroughbred auction, under electric lights at Madison Square Garden, New York **(June 19)**. Champion and four-time leading sire Hanover dies **(March 23)**.
1900 Pari-mutuel wagering is introduced at Fair Grounds. The Jockey Club registers 3,476 foals. Johnny Reiff becomes the first American to top the English jockey standings, with 143 victories.
1901 William Collins Whitney becomes the second American owner to win the Epsom Derby, with Volodyovski **(June 5)**. James R. Keene's American-bred Cap and Bells, by Domino, wins the Epsom Oaks **(June 7)**. Racing Hall of Fame racehorse and leading sire Hindoo dies at age 23 **(July 4)**. Champion Hamburg sells for $60,000 at the Marcus Daly estate dispersal **(October 1)**. Future five-time leading sire *Star Shoot is imported.
1902 Savable earns the decade's largest winner's purse, $44,500, in the Futurity Stakes **(August 30)**.
1903 Flocarline is the first filly to win the Preakness Stakes **(May 30)**. Africander is the first three-year-old Suburban Handicap winner **(June 18)**.
1904 Oaklawn Park opens in Arkansas **(February 24)**. Leading owner W. C. Whitney dies **(March 7)**. Elwood becomes the first Kentucky Derby winner owned and bred by women **(May 2)**. Hamburg sells for $70,000 at the W. C. Whitney estate dispersal **(October 10)**.
1905 Champion Commando dies of tetanus at age seven **(March 13)**. Belmont Park opens **(May 4)**. Tanya becomes the second filly to win the Belmont Stakes **(May 24)**. Artful hands Sysonby his only defeat, in the Futurity Stakes **(August 27)**. Roseben sets an American six-furlong record of 1:11⅗ under 147 pounds in the Manhattan Handicap **(October 6)**.
1906 An earthquake destroys San Francisco's Ingleside racetrack **(April 18)**. Sysonby dies of septic poisoning at age four **(June 17)**. Roseben wins the Manhattan Handicap for a second time under 147 pounds **(October 12)**. Kentucky appoints the first state racing commission.
1907 Colin launches his perfect 15-for-15 career with a maiden victory at Belmont Park **(May 29)**. The original Santa Anita Park opens in California **(December 7)**. Commando posthumously breaks his grandsire Himyar's single-season progeny earnings record, with $270,345.
1908 California-bred Rubio wins England's Grand National Steeplechase **(March 26)**. Bookmakers are barred from Churchill Downs and 15 pari-mutuel machines are installed **(March)**. Agnew-Hart legislation outlaws public betting in New York, though racing continues without wagering **(June 13)**. Colin ends his career in the Tidal Stakes, a betless exhibition at Sheepshead Bay **(June 20)**. The Locke Law ends racing in New Orleans.
1909 The Walker-Otis Anti-Racetrack Gambling Bill is passed in California, effectively blacking out racing there for a quarter-century **(February 19)**. The Preakness winner's silks are painted on the Pimlico Clubhouse's weathervane for the first time **(May 12)**.

1910 New York passes the Director's Criminal Liability Act, making racetrack operators and executives subject to imprisonment if gambling is found to occur on track premises. All New York tracks cease operation. A mass exodus of American breeding stock and racehorses to Europe begins.

1911 Laurel Race Course opens in Maryland **(October 2)**. Three-hundred ninety yearlings average $230 at U.S. auctions. The average U.S. purse reaches a 20th-century low $371.

1912 Wishing Ring wins at Latonia, paying a record $1,885.50 for a $2 wager **(June 17)**. James R. Keene sells Castleton Stud in Kentucky for $225 an acre. Star Charter is the season's leading money winner, with $14,655. Influential sire *Rock Sand and champion Tanya are included in the mass exportation of bloodstock to Europe.

1913 The English Jockey Club passes the Jersey Act, excluding most American pedigrees from admission to the *General Stud Book* **(April)**. Donerail wins the Kentucky Derby at record odds of 91.45-to-1 **(May 10)**. Belmont Park reopens without legal wagering **(May 30)**. Whisk Broom II becomes the first to sweep New York's handicap triple crown—the Metropolitan, Brooklyn, and Suburban Handicaps **(June 28)**. James R. Keene's estate dispersal is conducted at Madison Square Garden, and future Racing Hall of Fame member Peter Pan tops the sale at $38,000 **(September 2)**.

1914 Iron Mask carries 150 pounds to victory at Juarez, Mexico, setting a 5$\frac{1}{2}$-furlong world record of 1:03$\frac{2}{5}$ that stands for 30 years **(March 8)**. Old Rosebud sets a Kentucky Derby record of 2:03$\frac{2}{5}$ that stands for 17 years **(May 9)**.

1915 Pan Zareta gives ten pounds to Joe Blair and beats him in a match race at Juarez, setting a five-furlong world record of :57$\frac{1}{5}$ that stands for 36 years **(February 10)**. Pan Zareta carries 146 pounds to victory at Juarez, giving rivals from 31 to 54 pounds **(March 26)**. Regret becomes the first filly to win the Kentucky Derby **(May 8)**. The Preakness Stakes is run in two divisions for the only time **(May 15)**.

1916 *Star Shoot sires a record 27 juvenile winners.

1917 The New York State Racing Commission recommends to the Legislature that pari-mutuel wagering be legalized **(January)**. Man o' War is born **(March 29)**. *Omar Khayyam becomes the first foreign-bred Kentucky Derby winner **(May 12)**. Borrow wins the Brooklyn Handicap over Kentucky Derby winners Regret, Old Rosebud, and *Omar Khayyam **(June 25)**.

1918 Exterminator wins the Kentucky Derby at 29.60-to-1 odds **(May 11)**. Man o' War is sold to Samuel D. Riddle for $5,000 at the Saratoga yearling sale **(August 17)**. Roamer is the first to crack a 1:35 mile, running in 1:34$\frac{4}{5}$ at Saratoga **(August 21)**.

1919 Sir Barton, a maiden, wins the Kentucky Derby **(May 10)**; he becomes the first American Triple Crown winner in winning the Belmont Stakes **(June 18)**. Man o' War wins his first start, at Belmont Park **(June 6)**; he suffers his only career defeat, to Upset, in Saratoga's Sanford Memorial **(August 13)**. Purchase walks over in the inaugural Jockey Club Gold Cup **(September 13)**. The American Jockey Club registers a century-low 1,665 foals.

1920 Man o' War smashes the world record for 1$\frac{3}{8}$ miles in winning the Belmont Stakes by 20 lengths **(June 12)**; wins the Lawrence Realization Stakes by approximately 100 lengths **(September 4)**; carries 138 pounds to win the Potomac Handicap at Havre de Grace while setting a 1$\frac{1}{16}$-mile track record **(September 18)**; defeats Sir Barton in an $80,000 match race at Kenilworth Park in Canada **(October 12)**; retires as America's leading earner, with $249,465.

1921 Man o' War makes a farewell public gallop around the Kentucky Association racetrack in Lexington **(January 28)**. Counterclockwise racing begins at Belmont Park.

1922 Morvich scores his 11th victory in 11 starts in the Kentucky Derby **(May 13)**, joining Regret as the only undefeated Derby winners to that time. Kentucky Derby winner and future Racing Hall of Fame member Old Rosebud breaks down in a race at Jamaica racetrack and dies at age 11 **(May 23)**.

1923 Exterminator scores a record 34th stakes victory **(April 21)**. Kentucky Derby winner Zev defeats Epsom Derby winner *Papyrus in a Belmont Park match **(October 20)**. Zev becomes the first American racehorse to top $200,000 in single-season earnings ($272,008). Earl Sande rides the winners of $569,394, a record that stands for 20 years.

1924 Nellie Morse is the fourth and final filly Preakness winner **(May 12)**. Nine-year-old Exterminator finishes third in his 100th and final career start **(June 21)**. Three "international specials" are staged in the U.S. and are won by American-breds Wise Counsellor at Belmont Park **(September 1)**, Ladkin at Aqueduct **(September 27)**, and Sarazen at Latonia **(October 11)**. French star *Epinard finishes second in all three. Man o' War is represented by his first stakes winner when By Hisself wins the Autumn Days Stakes at Empire City **(October 20)**.

1925 Hialeah Park opens in Florida, ushering in an era of big-time winter racing **(January 15)**. Network radio's first broadcast of a Kentucky Derby is aired from Louisville's WHAS **(May 16)**. River Downs opens near Cincinnati **(July 6)**. War Feathers, a Man o' War–*Tuscan Red filly, sells at Saratoga for $50,500, an American yearling auction record **(August 10)**. *Sir Gallahad III arrives at Claiborne Farm from France, becoming the first major American stallion syndication **(December 15)**.

1926 Boot to Boot wins Washington Park's American Derby, the first U.S. race to offer a $100,000-added purse **(July 31)**. Man o' War sets a single-season progeny earnings record of $408,137 with just two crops racing. North American yearling sales average is $2,640.

1927 John Longden scores the first of his 6,032 career victories aboard Hugo K. Asher at Salt Lake City **(October 4)**. Arlington Park racetrack opens near Chicago **(October 13)**.

1928 New Broom, a yearling son of Whisk Broom II, sells for $75,000, an auction record that stands for 26 years **(August 7)**. Wirt G. Bowman becomes America's first flying Thoroughbred, traveling by airplane from San Diego to San Francisco **(October)**.

History of Racing — Key Dates

1929 The $100,000 Coffroth Handicap at Tijuana, Mexico, is won by Golden Prince **(March 17)**. Clyde Van Dusen becomes the eighth gelding to win the Kentucky Derby **(May 18)**. Whichone wins the Futurity Stakes, earning America's first six-figure winner's purse, $105,730 **(September 14)**.

1930 The Preakness Stakes is the first American classic to be started from a gate **(May 9)**. Gallant Fox sweeps the Triple Crown **(June 7)**. Jim Dandy defeats Gallant Fox at 100-to-1 odds in the Travers Stakes **(August 16)**. Gallant Fox becomes the first racehorse to surpass $300,000 in single-season earnings **(September 17)**.

1931 Hawthorne Park is the first track in the U.S. to use an electronic timer **(August 3)**. Top Flight becomes the leading distaff money winner and the first juvenile to top $200,000 in earnings **(November 7)**. Tropical Park racetrack opens in Florida **(December 26)**. Influential broodmare *La Troienne is imported.

1932 Eddie Arcaro rides his first winner, at Agua Caliente **(January 14)**. Australian wonder horse *Phar Lap wins the $50,000 Agua Caliente Handicap **(March 20)**; dies in California under mysterious circumstances **(April 5)**. Sportsman's Park opens near Chicago **(May 2)**. The North American yearling sales average declines to $570.

1933 The Woolwine-Maloney Bill legalizes pari-mutuel wagering in California **(February 19)**. Brokers Tip, a maiden, wins the Kentucky Derby in a "fighting finish" involving jockeys Don Meade and Herb Fisher, aboard Head Play **(May 6)**. Longacres racetrack opens in Washington state **(August 3)**. Saliva drug testing instituted at Hialeah Park. Legal bookmaking returns to New York. Walter Vosburgh compiles weights for the first Experimental Free Handicap.

1934 Bay Meadows Race Course opens in Northern California and is the first in America to use a photo-finish camera **(November 3)**. Santa Anita Park opens in Southern California **(December 25)**. The Kentucky Derby purse is reduced from $50,000 to $30,000. Hialeah Park builds the first modern American grass course.

1935 The inaugural $100,000 Santa Anita Handicap is won by *Azucar, with Twenty Grand and Equipoise in the beaten field **(February 23)**. Mary Hirsch is the first woman awarded a trainer's license from the Jockey Club **(April)**. Omaha becomes the third Triple Crown winner **(June 8)**. Suffolk Downs opens in Massachusetts **(July 10)**.

1936 Jockey Ralph Neves pronounced "dead" after a racing accident at Bay Meadows; he returns to the track that day **(May 12)**. Keeneland Race Course opens in Kentucky **(October 15)**. *Daily Racing Form* begins formal recognition of annual divisional champions, names Granville the first Horse of the Year. Black Toney stands for an American-high $2,000 fee.

1937 Stagehand receives 30 pounds from Seabiscuit and beats him by a nose in the Santa Anita Handicap **(March 5)**. War Admiral becomes the fourth Triple Crown winner **(June 5)**. Delaware Park opens **(June 26)**. Bing Crosby and Pat O'Brien open Del Mar racetrack in California **(July 3)**. Sir Barton, America's first Triple Crown winner, dies in Wyoming **(October 30)**.

1938 Hollywood Park opens in California **(June 10)**. Equipoise dies at age ten **(August 10)**. Seabiscuit defeats *Ligaroti in a Del Mar match race **(August 12)**; Seabiscuit defeats War Admiral in a two-horse Pimlico Special **(November 1)**.

1939 Gulfstream Park opens in Florida **(February 1)**. Ben A. Jones becomes Calumet Farm's trainer **(July)**. The Grayson Foundation is established to finance equine research **(August 12)**. Bay Meadows Race Course installs America's first electric, enclosed starting gate, developed by Clay Puett.

1940 In his third try, Seabiscuit wins the Santa Anita Handicap and retires as the world's leading money winner, with $437,730 **(March 2)**. Pari-mutuel wagering is legalized in New York **(April 1)**; Jamaica racetrack opens in New York with pari-mutuel wagering **(April 15)**.

1941 Golden Gate Fields opens in California **(February 1)**. Merrick dies at age 38, as the oldest known Thoroughbred **(March 13)**. Whirlaway becomes the fifth American Triple Crown winner **(June 7)**.

1942 Thoroughbred Racing Associations is formed **(March 19)**. Garden State Park opens in New Jersey **(July 18)**. Future leading American sire and broodmare sire *Princequillo is claimed for $2,500 **(August 20)**. Alsab defeats Whirlaway in a $25,000 match at Narragansett Park **(September 19)**. Jockey Eddie Arcaro is suspended by Jockey Club stewards for one year for dangerous riding in the Cowdin Stakes **(September 26)**. Whirlaway becomes the first $500,000 earner **(October 3)**. Santa Anita is used as an internment center for Japanese-Americans. Co. North American yearlings average $638, about half the 1941 average.

1943 Man o' War is pensioned from stud duty at age 26 **(March)**. Stymie is claimed by trainer Hirsch Jacobs for $1,500 **(June 2)**. Tanforan racetrack in California is utilized as a naval training base **(June 3)**. Count Fleet wins the Belmont Stakes by 25 lengths to become the sixth Triple Crown winner **(June 5)**. The Breeders' Sales Co. is organized in Kentucky **(September)**. A wartime ban on "pleasure driving" causes the cancellation or relocation of several race meetings.

1944 The only triple dead-heat in a North American stakes race occurs in Aqueduct's Carter Handicap, between Bossuet, Wait a Bit, and Brownie **(June 10)**. The Breeders' Sales Co. conducts its first yearling auction, at Keeneland **(July 31-August 3)**.

1945 Horse racing in the United States is called off by order of the War Mobilization Board **(January 3)**. American racing resumes four days after Nazi Germany surrenders **(May 12)**. Owner Fred Hooper wins the Kentucky Derby with his first horse, Hoop, Jr. **(June 9)**. North American yearling average soars to $5,146.

1946 Jockey George "The Iceman" Woolf dies following a spill at Santa Anita **(January 4)**. The first transcontinental flight with a Thoroughbred passenger is recorded when Historian flies from Chicago to Los Angeles **(May 29)**. Assault becomes the seventh Triple Crown winner **(June 1)**. Atlantic City Race Course opens **(July 22)**. *Fair Truckle is first to break 1:09 for six furlongs, running 1:08⅖ at Golden Gate Fields **(October 4)**. Assault becomes the first $400,000 single-season earner **(November 9)**. The first transatlantic flight with racehorses on board takes place, from Ireland to New Jersey **(November 26-27)**. Lip tattoos are adopted as a method of identifying racehorses.

1947 Stepfather brings a world auction record of $200,000 at the Louis B. Mayer dispersal **(February 27)**. Seabiscuit dies at age 14 **(May 17)**. Armed defeats Assault at Belmont Park in the first $100,000 winner-take-all match race **(September 27)**. Man o' War dies at age 30 **(November 1)**. Stymie retires with record earnings of $918,485. Calumet is the first stable to top $1-million in a season. Automatic hotwalking machines are introduced.

1948 *Alibhai is syndicated for a record $500,000. Citation becomes the eighth Triple Crown winner **(June 12)**. Gallorette is the first racemare to top $400,000 in career earnings **(July 17)**. Citation ends his campaign with a new single-season earnings record of $709,470 **(December 11)**. *Shannon II becomes the first to crack 2:00 for 1¼ miles, running the distance in 1:59⅘ at Golden Gate Fields **(October 23)**.

1949 Apprentice Bill Shoemaker rides his first winner, at Golden Gate Fields **(April 20)**. Hollywood Park's grandstand and clubhouse are destroyed by fire **(May 6)**. England's Jockey Club rescinds the Jersey Act after 36 years **(June)**. *Nasrullah is purchased by an American syndicate for $340,000. Keeneland installs America's first aluminum rail.

1950 Detroit Race Course opens **(May 25)**. Future five-time leading American sire *Nasrullah arrives at Claiborne Farm in Kentucky **(July)**. The National Museum of Racing is chartered at Saratoga Springs, New York **(October)**. Gordon Glisson wins the first George Woolf Memorial Jockey Award.

1951 The Santa Anita Maturity offers a record $205,700 purse, with a record winner's share of $144,325 going to Great Circle **(February 3)**. Citation becomes racing's first equine millionaire, winning the Hollywood Gold Cup in his final start **(July 14)**. Bewitch passes Gallorette as leading distaff earner with $462,605. **(July 14)**. The Pimlico Special, won by Bryan G., becomes the first nationally televised race **(November 16)**. Lloyd's of London pays off a $250,000 insurance claim on gravely injured Your Host, who survives to sire Kelso.

1952 The Kentucky Derby is broadcast for the first time on national television, by CBS, and is won by Hill Gail, Ben Jones's record sixth winner **(May 3)**. English representative *Wilwyn wins the inaugural Washington, D.C., International at Laurel Park **(October 18)**. Apprentice jockey Tony DeSpirito scores a single-season record 390 victories **(December 31)**.

1953 Dark Star, 24.90-to-1, hands Native Dancer his only defeat, in the Kentucky Derby **(May 2)**. Charlie Whittingham saddles his first career stakes winner, Porterhouse **(June 10)**. Tom Fool is the second New York handicap triple crown winner, taking the Brooklyn Handicap under 136 pounds **(July 11)**. The Garden State Stakes is inaugurated as the world's richest race, worth $239,000 **(October 31)**. R. H. "Red" McDaniel becomes the first trainer to saddle 200 winners in a season **(December 1)**. Santa Anita opens its Camino Real grass course **(December 26)**. Bill Shoemaker smashes the single-season win record, with 485 victories **(December)**. *Royal Charger is advertised at an American record $10,000 stud fee.

1954 The San Juan Capistrano Handicap is America's first $100,000 grass race **(March 6)**. Bold Ruler and Round Table are foaled at Claiborne Farm in Kentucky **(April 6)**. Determine becomes the first gray Kentucky Derby winner **(May 1)**. Never Say Die is the second American-bred Epsom Derby winner, 73 years after Iroquois **(June 2)**.

1955 The National Museum of Racing opens at Saratoga Springs; the Racing Hall of Fame is instituted **(August 6)**. Camarero's undefeated streak concludes after a world-record 56 consecutive victories, in Puerto Rico **(August)**. Nashua defeats Swaps in a $100,000 match race at Washington Park **(August 31)**. Nashua becomes the first $1-million stallion syndication, for $1,251,000. **(December 15)**. New York Racing Association Inc. is established. *Sir Gallahad III leads the American broodmare sire list for a record 12th time.

1956 Turf Paradise opens in Arizona **(January 7)**. Nashua becomes racing's second equine millionaire **(February 18)**. Woodbine opens in Canada **(June 12)**. John Longden becomes the world's winningest jockey, with 4,871 victories **(September 3)**. Bill Shoemaker and Bill Hartack become the first to ride winners of $2-million in a season. Swaps carries 130 pounds to a 1:39 clocking for 1¹⁄₁₆ miles, a mark that stands as a dirt record for 27 years **(June 23)**. The original Aqueduct racetrack is torn down.

1957 Florida Breeders' Sales Co. conducts the first two-year-olds in training sale, at Hialeah **(January 28)**. Bold Ruler defeats Round Table and *Gallant Man in the three-horse Trenton Handicap, described as the race of the year **(November 9)**. Bill Hartack is the first jockey to top $3-million in single-season earnings. The American foal crop tops 10,000 for the first time.

1958 Round Table becomes racing's third equine millionaire **(May 11)**. Future Hall of Fame jockey Jack Westrope is killed in a spill during the Hollywood Oaks **(June 19)**. Round Table supplants Nashua as the world's all-time leading money winner **(October 11)**.

History of Racing — Key Dates

1959 *Tomy Lee is the second foreign-bred winner of the Kentucky Derby **(May 2)**. Jamaica racetrack in New York is torn down to make way for a housing development **(August)**. Modern $32-million Aqueduct racetrack opens in New York **(September 14)**.

1960 Undefeated *Ribot arrives in the U.S. for stud duty **(June 23)**. Kelso wins the first of five Horse of the Year titles. The Animal Insurance Co. of America pays off a $1-million policy on Bally Ache, who died on October 28 **(December)**.

1961 Northern Dancer is born **(May 27)**. Ben A. Jones, Racing Hall of Fame trainer, dies **(June 13)**. A son of Swaps, Swapson, becomes the first six-figure American auction yearling, selling for $130,000 at Keeneland July **(July 24)**. National Association of State Racing Commissioners recommends a general ban on all drugs, narcotics, anesthetics, and analgesics. Kelso becomes the third winner of New York's handicap triple crown **(July 22)**. Racing Hall of Fame jockey Eddie Arcaro retires **(November 18)**.

1962 Champion Crimson Satan is the first high-profile positive finding for phenylbutazone after winning the Leonard Richards Handicap at Delaware Park **(July 23)**. Angel Cordero Jr. rides his first North American winner **(July 26)**. Crazy Kid is first to break 1:08 for six furlongs, clocking 1:07⅘ at Del Mar **(August 18)**. Never Say Die becomes the first American-bred to lead the English sire list.

1963 Bold Ruler leads the American sire list for the first of eight times.

1964 Northern Dancer wins the Kentucky Derby in track-record time of 2:00 **(May 2)**. Laffit Pincay Jr. scores his first career victory, in Panama **(May 19)**. Seven-year-old Kelso wins a fifth Jockey Club Gold Cup **(October 31)** and earns a record fifth Horse of the Year title. Wagering in the United States tops $3-billion.

1965 Affectionately wins the Vagrancy Handicap under 137 pounds, the most weight successfully carried by a filly in 49 years **(July 26)**. Buckpasser breaks the juvenile earnings record, with $568,096 **(October 16)**. Northern Dancer stands his first season for a $10,000 stud fee. Moccasin becomes the first juvenile filly to be named Horse of the Year, in the Thoroughbred Racing Associations poll.

1966 Graustark is syndicated for a record $2.4-million **(June)**. Kelso retires as the world's leading money winner, with $1,977,165 **(March 2)**. John Longden wins the San Juan Capistrano aboard George Royal in his final career ride and retires with a world record 6,032 victories **(March 12)**. Three-year-old Buckpasser becomes the youngest equine millionaire **(August 20)**. American foal registrations top 20,000 for the first time.

1967 Buckpasser concludes a 15-race win streak in the Metropolitan Handicap at Aqueduct **(May 30)**. Damascus defeats Buckpasser and Dr. Fager by ten lengths in the Woodward Stakes **(September 30)**; banks record single-season earnings of $817,941. Future double classic winner Majestic Prince brings a yearling auction record of $250,000 at Keeneland July **(July 24)**. National racetrack attendance declines for the first time since World War II. Buckpasser is syndicated for a record $4.8-million. Bold Ruler becomes the first to sire juvenile winners of more than $1-million in a season.

1968 Dancer's Image becomes the only disqualified Kentucky Derby winner, after the then-illegal phenylbutazone shows up in his post-race test **(May 4)**. American-bred Sir Ivor wins the Epsom Derby **(May 29)**. Dark Mirage is the first New York filly triple crown winner **(June 22)**. A *Sea-Bird filly sets a world auction record of $405,000 at Keeneland July **(July 23)**. Native Diver becomes the first California-bred millionaire **(July 15)**. Dr. Fager wins the Washington Park Handicap with 134 pounds, in a world-record 1:32⅕ mile **(August 24)**. Dr. Fager carries 139 pounds to victory in the Vosburgh Handicap, his final career start **(November 2)**. *Vaguely Noble is syndicated for $5-million.

1969 Male riders boycott a race at Tropical Park in which Barbara Jo Rubin was scheduled to ride **(January 15)**. Diane Crump becomes the first female to compete in an American Thoroughbred pari-mutuel race, finishing tenth at Hialeah **(February 7)**. Rubin becomes the first of her sex to win a pari-mutuel Thoroughbred race in America, at Charles Town Races **(February 22)**; Diane Crump is the first female rider to win a stakes, on Easy Lime in Fair Grounds's Spring Fiesta Cup **(March 29)**. Richard Nixon is the first sitting 20th-century president to attend the Kentucky Derby **(May 3)**. Not-for-profit Oak Tree Racing Association launches its first meeting, at Santa Anita **(October 7)**.

1970 Secretariat is foaled in Virginia **(March 30)**. The New York Legislature votes to legalize city-operated off-track betting parlors **(April 8)**. New York Governor Nelson Rockefeller signs a bill legalizing OTB in the Empire State **(April 22)**. Diane Crump finishes 15th as the first female to ride in the Kentucky Derby **(May 2)**. Exacta wagering is introduced in New York and New Jersey **(June)**. Crowned Prince sets a $510,000 world yearling record at Keeneland July **(July 20)**. Citation dies at age 25 **(August 8)**. Bill Shoemaker passes John Longden as the all-time winning jockey, with victory number 6,033 **(September 7)**. Canadian-bred Nijinsky II sweeps undefeated through the English Triple Crown **(September 12)**. Nijinsky II is syndicated for a record $5.44-million.

1971 Eclipse Awards are instituted by Thoroughbred Racing Associations, *Daily Racing Form*, and National Turf Writers Association. Off-track betting begins in New York **(April 8)**. Canonero II, a $1,200 auction yearling, wins the Kentucky Derby **(May 1)** and Preakness Stakes **(May 15)**. Eight-time leading sire Bold Ruler dies at age 17 **(July 12)**. Former Illinois Governor Otto Kerner is indicted on federal charges that included bribery to influence racing matters **(December)**. National purse distribution tops $200-million.

History of Racing — Key Dates

1972 European racing authorities institute pattern system to rate best races. Jockey Bill Shoemaker sets an all-time stakes record with win number 555 **(March 2)**. What a Treat brings a $450,000 auction record for a female Thoroughbred **(March 6)**. *Morning Telegraph* daily racing newspaper suspends publication after 139 years **(April 10)**. Kentucky's Court of Appeals awards Forward Pass the winner's purse from the 1968 Kentucky Derby, making him Calumet Farm's eighth Derby winner **(April 28)**. American-owned and -bred Roberto wins the Epsom Derby (Eng-G1) **(June 7)**. Convenience defeats Typecast in a $250,000 Hollywood match race **(June 17)**. Secretariat finishes fourth in his debut **(July 4)** but goes on to win seven of nine starts and is voted Horse of the Year at the conclusion of his two-year-old season. Roberto ends Brigadier Gerard's 15-race win streak, in the Benson and Hedges Gold Cup (Eng-G1) **(August 15)**. Four-time leading breeder Arthur B. "Bull" Hancock Jr. dies **(September 14)**.

1973 At urging of European racing authorities, North American Graded Stakes Committee is formed and begins grading of North American races. Champion mare Typecast brings a world auction record of $725,000 **(January 28)**. Secretariat's record $6.08-million syndication is announced **(February 26)**. Sunday racing begins in California at Hollywood Park **(April 15)**. Secretariat sets a Kentucky Derby (G1) record of 1:59⅖ **(May 5)**. *Cougar II becomes the first foreign-bred millionaire **(May 5)**. Secretariat wins the Belmont Stakes (G1) by 31 lengths in a world record 2:24 for 1½ miles, becoming the ninth Triple Crown winner **(June 9)**. Secretariat is featured simultaneously on the covers of *Time*, *Newsweek*, and *Sports Illustrated* **(June 11)**. Wajima, from the last crop of Bold Ruler, brings a world record yearling price of $600,000 at Keeneland July **(July)**. Secretariat defeats stablemate Riva Ridge in the inaugural Marlboro Cup, setting a world record of 1:45⅖ for 1⅛ miles **(September 15)**. Secretariat ends his career triumphantly in the Canadian International Championship (G2) **(October 28)**. Count Fleet dies at age 33 **(December 3)**. Sandy Hawley is the first jockey to ride 500 winners in a season **(December 15)**.

1974 The centennial Kentucky Derby (G1) is won by Cannonade before a record crowd of 163,628 **(May 4)**. Chris Evert defeats Miss Musket by approximately 50 lengths in a $350,000 match race at Hollywood **(July 20)**. Dahlia is the first distaff millionaire **(August 20)**. D. Wayne Lukas saddles his first Thoroughbred stakes winner, Harbor Hauler, in a division of the Foothill Stakes at Pomona **(September 13)**. Dahlia becomes a stakes winner in five countries **(October 27)**. Louisiana Downs opens **(October 30)**. Apprentice jockey Chris McCarron sets a single-season win record of 546. Dan Lasater nearly doubles the previous single-season earnings record for an owner, with $3,020,521.

1975 Ruffian breaks down in Belmont Park's "battle of the sexes" match race against Foolish Pleasure **(July 6)**; dies following surgery and is buried in the Belmont infield **(July 7)**. Seattle Slew sells as a yearling for $17,500 at the Fasig-Tipton Kentucky July sale **(July 19)**. Two yearling colts are stolen from their stalls at the Keeneland fall sale **(September 7)** and are never recovered. On-track betting in the United States tops $5-billion for the first time. On-track attendance tops 50-million for the first time. Champion Wajima is syndicated for a world-record $7.2-million.

1976 Secretariat's son Canadian Bound is the world's first seven-figure auction yearling, bringing $1.5-million at Keeneland July **(July 20)**. Connecticut opens its Teletrack satellite wagering site. Forego wins his third straight Horse of the Year title. What a Pleasure is syndicated for a world-record $8-million.

1977 Washington Park is destroyed by fire **(February 5)**. Garden State Park's grandstand and clubhouse are destroyed by fire **(April 14)**. Seattle Slew becomes the first undefeated American Triple Crown winner **(June 11)**. Champion Fanfreluche is stolen from a pasture at Claiborne Farm **(June 24)**; recovered unharmed six months later. Seattle Slew suffers his first career loss in the Swaps Stakes at Hollywood Park **(July 3)**. Maryland Governor Marvin Mandel is convicted on racing-related racketeering and mail fraud charges **(August 23)**. The Meadowlands in New Jersey opens its first Thoroughbred meet **(September 6)**. American foal registrations top 30,000 for the first time. Lebon-*Cinzano ringer scandal breaks in New York **(September 23)**. Steve Cauthen becomes the first to ride winners of $6-million in a single season **(December 10)** and is later named *Sports Illustrated*'s Sportsman of the Year and Professional Athlete of the Year by the Associated Press. The Minstrel is syndicated for a world-record $9-million.

1978 John Henry wins a $25,000 claiming race **(May 21)**; switches to turf and wins for $35,000 claiming tag at Belmont Park **(June 1)**. Affirmed becomes the 11th Triple Crown winner **(June 10)**. Triple Crown winners meet for the first time, with Seattle Slew defeating Affirmed in the Marlboro Cup Handicap (G1) **(September 16)**. Affirmed is syndicated for a world-record $14.4-million.

1979 Affirmed becomes the first career $2-million earner **(June 24)**. Affirmed defeats Kentucky Derby (G1) and Preakness Stakes (G1) victor Spectacular Bid in the Jockey Club Gold Cup (G1); becomes the first to earn $1-million in a single season **(October 6)**. Hollywood Park introduces pick-six wagering **(April 23)**. Turf female division added to annual North American championships.

1980 Genuine Risk becomes the second filly Kentucky Derby winner **(May 3)**. Ex-jockey Con Errico is convicted of race fixing in New York **(May 19)**, is sentenced to ten years in prison. Spectacular Bid walks over in Woodward Stakes (G1) **(September 20)**. Prerace drug testing of horses begins at Aqueduct **(October 14)**. Spectacular Bid is syndicated for a record $22-million.

1981 Julie Krone rides her first winner, at Tampa Bay Downs **(February 12)**. The Arlington Million is inaugurated at Arlington Park as the world's first $1-million Thoroughbred race, with John Henry defeating The Bart by a nose. **(August 30)**. Storm Bird is syndicated for a record $30-million.

1982 Mary Russ becomes the first female jockey to win a North American Grade 1 race, with Lord Darnley in the Widener Handicap **(February 27)**. Trainer Woody Stephens saddles the first of five con-

History of Racing — Key Dates

secutive Belmont Stakes (G1) winners, Conquistador Cielo **(June 5)**. A son of Nijinsky II—Spearfish brings a record $4.25-million at Keeneland July. Simulcasting begins at Woodbine and Fort Erie in Canada. John Gaines conceives the idea for the Breeders' Cup. Conquistador Cielo is syndicated for a record $36.4-million.

1983 European champion Shergar is stolen from Ballymany Stud in Ireland **(February 8)**; he was never recovered. Genuine Risk produces a stillborn colt by Secretariat, the first offspring of two Kentucky Derby (G1) winners **(April 4)**. Shareef Dancer is syndicated for a record $40-million. Jockey Angel Cordero Jr. rides to a record $10-million season. All Along (Fr) becomes America's first foreign-bred Horse of the Year. Simulcasting begins from the Meadowlands to Atlantic City Race Course **(September 28)**. John Henry becomes the first $4-million earner **(December 11)**. Fourteen Northern Dancer sales yearlings average $3,320,357. The Hollywood Futurity (G1) is carded as racing's first $1-million event for two-year-olds **(December 18)**.

1984 A share in Seattle Slew sells for $3-million **(May)**. Swale collapses and dies eight days after winning the Belmont Stakes **(June 17)**. Equine viral arteritis (EVA) halts Kentucky breeding season two weeks early **(June)**. Fit to Fight becomes the fourth horse to sweep New York's handicap triple crown **(July 21)**. The inaugural Breeders' Cup is run at Hollywood Park before 64,625 on-track fans and 50-million television viewers; Wild Again wins the $3-million Breeders' Cup Classic (G1) **(November 10)**. Nine-year-old John Henry retires with record earnings of $6,597,947.

1985 Bill Shoemaker is the first jockey to reach $100-million in purse winnings **(March 3)**. Garden State Park, rebuilt at a cost of approximately $200-million, reopens **(April 1)**. Spend a Buck earns $2.6-million in purse and bonus money following his Jersey Derby (G3) victory **(May 27)**. Steve Cauthen becomes the first American jockey to win both a Kentucky Derby (G1) and Epsom Derby (Eng-G1) **(June 5)**. Creme Fraiche becomes the first gelding to win the Belmont Stakes **(June 8)**. Seattle Dancer sells for a world auction record of $13.1-million at Keeneland July **(July 23)**. Arlington Park's grandstand is destroyed by fire **(July 31)**. Teleprompter (GB) wins the Arlington Million (G1) in front of a razed grandstand and an on-track crowd of 35,651 **(August 25)**. THOROUGHBRED TIMES weekly news magazine publishes its inaugural edition **(September 20)**. Miss Oceana brings a world-record broodmare price of $7-million at the Newstead Farm dispersal **(November 10)**. American foal registrations top 50,000 for the first time.

1986 A season to 25-year-old Northern Dancer sells at auction for $710,000 **(January)**. The Santa Anita Handicap (G1) becomes the first $1-million-guaranteed handicap, won by Greinton (GB) **(March 2)**. Jan Ciochetti is the first woman to call a race at a major track (Hialeah) **(March 21)**. Woody Stephens saddles his fifth straight Belmont Stakes (G1) winner, Danzig Connection **(June 7)**. Laurel Park inaugurates the Maryland Million **(October 18)**. Lawmaker breaks *Star Shoot's 70-year-old record by siring his 28th juvenile winner **(December 12)**; ends the year with 30 two-year-old winners. Jockey Club foal registrations reach an all-time annual high of 51,293. The Jockey Club launches a mandatory blood-typing program. Joint nomination to Triple Crown races begins.

1987 Jockey Chris Antley wins a record nine races in a single day, at Aqueduct and Meadowlands **(October 31)**. Tejano becomes the first juvenile millionaire **(December 12)**. Northern Dancer retires from breeding. Chrysler Corp. becomes first sponsor of the $5-million Triple Crown Challenge.

1988 Winning Colors is the third filly Kentucky Derby (G1) winner **(May 7)**. Personal Ensign ends her 13-for-13 career with a thrilling victory over Winning Colors in the Breeders' Cup Distaff (G1) **(November 5)**. Alysheba wins the Breeders' Cup Classic (G1) and retires as the leading American money earner, with $6,679,242 **(November 5)**.

1989 E. P. Taylor, breeder of Northern Dancer and Nijinsky II, dies at age 88 **(May 14)**. Belmont Park is the first American racetrack to time races in hundredths of a second. Arlington International Racecourse opens **(June 28)**. Northern Park, the last Northern Dancer yearling sold at auction, brings $2.8-million at Keeneland **(July 18)**. Secretariat dies at age 19 **(October 4)**. Pari-mutuel wagering on horse racing returns to Texas for the first time since 1937 **(October 6)**. Jockey Kent Desormeaux establishes a single-season win record of 547 **(November 30)**; ends the year with 598 winners.

1990 Bill Shoemaker retires as the world's winningest jockey, with 8,833 victories **(February 3)**. D. Wayne Lukas becomes the first trainer to saddle career winners of $100-million **(May 12)**. Champion Go for Wand breaks down fatally in the Breeders' Cup Distaff (G1) **(October 27)**. Northern Dancer dies at age 29 **(November 16)**. Alydar dies at Calumet Farm under suspicious circumstances **(November 17)**.

1991 The American Championship Racing Series is launched as a designed-for-television event. Bill Shoemaker is paralyzed in a California car accident **(April 8)**. Equibase, a joint venture of the Jockey Club and Thoroughbred Racing Associations, is formed and begins gathering past-performance data in competition with *Daily Racing Form*.

1992 Henryk de Kwiatkowski buys Calumet Farm for $17-million at a bankruptcy auction **(March 26)**. Gilded Time runs the fastest six furlongs ever recorded by a two-year-old, 1:07.84, in the Sapling Stakes at Monmouth Park **(August 8)**.

1993 At age 16, Kentucky Derby (G1) winner Genuine Risk produces her first live foal, a colt by Rahy **(May 15)**. Julie Krone becomes the first female jockey to win an American classic, with Colonial Affair in the Belmont Stakes **(June 5)**. Claude R. "Shug" McGaughey III saddles five graded stakes winners at Belmont Park in single day **(October 16)**. Arcangues wins the Breeders' Cup Classic at record 133.60-to-1 odds **(November 6)**. Fair Grounds's grandstand is destroyed by fire **(December 17)**.

History of Racing — Key Dates

1994 Thoroughbred Racing Associations appoints Brian McGrath as its first and only commissioner **(January 17)**. The American Championship Racing Series is canceled. Class 1 racing begins in Texas at Sam Houston Race Park **(April 29)**. Thoroughbred Owners of California is launched.

1995 New York becomes the last North American racing jurisdiction to legalize race-day use of the antibleeder medication furosemide **(September 1)**. Hoosier Park opens **(September 1)**. Delaware Park and Prairie Meadows Racetrack install slot machines.

1996 Cigar scores his 16th consecutive victory, tying Citation's modern record **(July 13)**. Cigar retires as the world's leading money winner, with $9,999,815 **(October 26)**. Serena's Song becomes the top North American distaff earner, with $3,283,388.

1997 A $25-million infertility insurance claim is paid off on Cigar **(March 24)**. Racing Hall of Fame member Exceller is killed in a Swedish slaughterhouse at age 24 **(April 7)**. Keeneland utilizes a public address system for the first time, at its spring meeting. Colonial Downs opens as Virginia's first parimutuel racetrack **(September 1)**. Arlington International announces that it will suspend racing because of financial losses, political climate in Illinois **(September 8)**. Racing Hall of Fame jockey Eddie Arcaro dies at age 81 **(November 14)**.

1998 The National Thoroughbred Racing Association (NTRA) is launched **(April 1)**. Tim Smith is named NTRA commissioner **(April 21)**. Real Quiet fails by a nose in his quest for the Triple Crown **(June 6)**. Elusive Quality clocks a world-record 1:31.63 mile on Belmont Park's grass **(July 4)**. Company controlled by Frank Stronach buys Santa Anita Park. Equibase becomes the sport's sole provider of past-performance data and acquires *Daily Racing Form* database.

1999 Julie Krone retires as the all-time winningest female jockey, with 3,546 victories **(April 18)**. Mr. Prospector dies at age 29 **(June 1)**. Television Games Network (TVG) debuts **(July 14)**. Dale Baird becomes the first trainer to saddle 8,000 winners **(July 22)**. Churchill Downs Inc. purchases Hollywood Park for $140-million **(September 10)**. Laffit Pincay Jr. passes Bill Shoemaker as the world's winningest jockey **(December 10)**, with 8,834 victories. Frank Stronach-controlled Magna Entertainment Corp. buys Gulfstream Park, Golden Gate Fields, Thistledown, and Remington Park. Churchill Downs Inc. acquires Calder Race Course.

2000 Julie Krone becomes the first female elected to the Racing Hall of Fame **(May 2)**. Arlington Park reopens after a two-year hiatus **(May 14)**. NTRA and Breeders' Cup Ltd. consolidate **(May 18)**. Fusaichi Pegasus becomes the first favorite to win the Kentucky Derby in 21 years **(May 6)**; syndicated for a reported record $60-million to $70-million **(June 25)**. Leading breeder Allen Paulson dies at 78 **(July 19)**. Breeder Fred Hooper dies at 102 **(August 3)**. Churchill Downs Inc. buys Arlington Park.

2001 Triple Crown winner Affirmed dies at 26 **(January 12)**. The Breeders' Cup becomes formally known as the Breeders' Cup World Thoroughbred Championships **(June 26)**. Jerry Bailey becomes the first jockey to ride winners of $20-million in a season **(October 7)**. Tiznow becomes the first two-time winner of the Breeders' Cup Classic **(October 27)**. Laura Hillenbrand's *Seabiscuit: An American Legend* tops the New York *Times* bestseller list for nonfiction.

2002 Japan-based T.M.Opera O, the world's richest Thoroughbred, retires with earnings of $16,200,337 **(January 25)**. Seattle Slew, the last living American Triple Crown winner, dies at age 28 **(May 7)**. Racing Hall of Fame jockey Chris McCarron retires after career victory number 7,139 **(June 23)**. Volponi scores the second-biggest upset in Breeders' Cup Classic (G1) history, with an $89 payoff **(October 26)**. Ultra Pick Six wager on Breeders' Cup races is found to have been fixed. Magna International buys Lone Star Park **(October 30)** and the controlling interest in Maryland tracks **(November 13)**.

2003 Johnny Longden dies on his 96th birthday **(February 14)**. Laffit Pincay Jr. retires as all-time leading jockey by wins, with 9,530 **(April 29)**. Funny Cide becomes first gelding to win Kentucky Derby since Clyde Van Dusen in 1929 **(May 3)**. Bill Shoemaker dies at age 72 **(October 12)**. Richard Mandella wins a record four Breeders' cup races **(October 25)**. Trainer Bobby Frankel set records for single-season earnings and Grade 1 victories.

2004 Owner-breeder William T. Young dies at age 85 **(January 12)**. Smarty Jones wins the Preakness by a record 11½ lengths **(May 15)**. Churchill Downs buys Fair Grounds **(October 15)**.

2005 John R. Gaines, creator of the Breeders' Cup, dies at age 76 **(February 11)**. Churchill Downs Inc. sells Hollywood Park **(July 6)**. Hurricane Katrina damages Fair Grounds, and shortened 2005-'06 meet is moved to Louisiana Downs **(August 29)**. Ashado sells for record $9-million as broodmare prospect **(November 7)**. Jockeys' Guild ousts President L. Wayne Gertmenian **(November 15)**.

2006 Breeders' Cup Ltd. increases World Championships purses to $20-million **(May 2)**. Barbaro wins Kentucky Derby **(May 6)** but breaks down in Preakness **(May 20)**. Breeders' Cup announces schedule of "Win and You're In" races to qualify for championship races **(October 31)**.

2007 Breeders' Cup announces expansion to a second day with three new $1-million races **(January 15)**. Barbaro is euthanized due to laminitis **(January 29)**. Breeders' Cup Juvenile winner and champion Street Sense wins the Kentucky Derby **(May 5)**. Rags to Riches becomes third filly to win Belmont Stakes **(June 9)**. First two-day Breeders' Cup World Championships is held **(October 26-27)**. Todd Pletcher establishes earning record for a trainer.

2008 Horse of the Year Curlin wins Dubai World Cup **(March 29)**. Derby-Preakness winner Big Brown is syndicated for more than $50-million **(May 17)**. Big Brown does not complete the Triple Crown as he fails to finish in the Belmont Stakes **(June 7)**. Death of filly Eight Belles after finishing second in the Derby prompts congressional hearings **(June 19)**.

Notable Horses in Racing
Racing Hall of Fame members are listed in italics

The name of each horse is followed by year of birth and year of death, if known. Color and sex (colt, filly, or gelding) are followed by sire, dam, and broodmare sire. The horse's race record is detailed by number of starts, wins, seconds, thirds, and earnings, followed by championship honors and most important wins. Records from the 18th and 19th centuries may be incomplete, and earnings may be impossible to determine. If the horse sired or produced significant stakes winners, that information follows the race record. A sire's or dam's place in important male or female lines is noted when pertinent.

ACK ACK, 1966-1990. B. c., Battle Joined—Fast Turn, by *Turn-to. 27-19-6-0, $636,641, Horse of the Year in 1971, champion sprinter, champion older male, Santa Anita H., Hollywood Gold Cup H., etc. Sire of 54 stakes winners, including Youth, Broad Brush, Ack's Secret, Rascal Lass, Caline. Broodmare sire of Sharp Cat, Royal Anthem, Benny the Dip, North Sider, Lost Code.

AFFECTIONATELY, 1960-1979. Dk. b. or br. f., Swaps—Searching, by War Admiral. 52-28-8-6, $546,659, champion two-year-old filly, champion sprinter, champion older mare, Top Flight H., Spinaway S., etc. Dam of Personality.

AFFIRMED, 1975-2001. Ch. c., Exclusive Native—Won't Tell You, by Crafty Admiral. 29-22-5-1, $2,393,818, Horse of the Year in 1978-'79, champion two- and three-year-old male, champion older male, Triple Crown, Jockey Club Gold Cup (G1), etc. Sire of more than 80 stakes winners, including Flawlessly, Quiet Resolve, Affirmed Success, Peteski. Broodmare sire of Chelsey Flower, Harlan's Holiday, Balancheine.

AFLEET ALEX, 2002-. B. c., Northern Afleet—Maggy Hawk, by Hawkster. 12-8-2-1, $2,765,800, champion three-year-old male, Preakness S. (G1), Belmont S. (G1), Hopeful S. (G1), etc. Best known for recovering from a near fall in 2005 Preakness Stakes before 4¾-length victory.

AFRICANDER, 1900-unknown. B. c. *Star Ruby—Afric Queen, by *Darebin. 60-19-15-8, $102,325, champion three-year-old, Belmont S., Suburban H., etc.

ALARM, 1869-1895. B. c., *Eclipse—*Maud, by Stockwell. 9-6-2-1, $12,500, match race with Inverary. Sire of Himyar, Panique, Danger, Ann Fief, Fidele. First American male-line ancestor of Domino, Plaudit lines.

ALCIBIADES, 1927-1957. Ch. f., Supremus—*Regal Roman, by Roi Herode. 23-7-2-4, $47,860, champion two-year-old filly, Kentucky Oaks, etc. Dam of Menow, Lithe, Salaminia. Foundation mare of family that includes Sir Ivor, Firm Policy, Rash Statement, Twice the Vice, Shine Again, Halo America.

ALL ALONG (FR), 1979-2005. B. f., Targowice—Agujita (Fr), by Vieux Manoir. 21-9-4-2, $2,125,809, Horse of the Year in 1983, champion older female, champion older horse in France, Prix de l'Arc de Triomphe (Fr-G1), Turf Classic S. (G1), etc. Dam of Along All, Arnaqueur.

ALLEGED, 1974-2000. B. c., Hoist the Flag—Princess Pout, by Prince John. 10-9-1-0, $623,187, champion three-year-old in England and France, champion older horse in Europe, Prix de l'Arc de Triomphe (Fr-G1) twice, etc. One of only five horses to win consecutive runnings of the Prix de l'Arc de Triomphe. Sire of 100 stakes winners, including Miss Alleged, Law Society, Midway Lady, Shantou. Broodmare sire of Suave Dancer, Dr Devious (Ire), Dream Well (Fr).

ALLEZ FRANCE, 1970-1989. B. f., *Sea-Bird—Priceless Gem, by Hail to Reason. 21-13-3-1, $1,262,801, Horse of the Year in France in 1974, champion two- and three-year-old filly, champion older mare twice, Prix de l'Arc de Triomphe (Fr-G1), etc. Dam of Action Francaise. Considered greatest filly ever trained in France.

ALMAHMOUD, 1947-1971. Ch. f., *Mahmoud—Arbitrator, by Peace Chance. 11-4-0-1, $32,760, Vineland H., etc. Dam of Cosmah, Natalma. Foundation mare of family that includes Northern Dancer, Halo, Danehill, Tosmah, Flawlessly, Arctic Tern, Machiavellian, Bago, L'Emigrant, Cannonade, La Prevoyante.

ALSAB, 1939-1963. B. c., Good Goods—Winds Chant, by Wildair. 51-25-11-5, $350,015, champion two- and three-year-old colt, Preakness S., American Derby, etc. Sire of 17 stakes winners, including Myrtle Charm, Armageddon, Sabette. Defeated Triple Crown winner Whirlaway in match race. Tail-male ancestor of line that leads to Broad Brush.

ALYDAR, 1975-1990. Ch. c., Raise a Native—Sweet Tooth, by On-and-On. 26-14-9-1, $957,195, Travers S. (G1), Florida Derby (G1), etc. Leading sire in 1990. Sire of 77 stakes winners, including Alysheba, Easy Goer, Criminal Type, Turkoman, Althea, Strike the Gold, Miss Oceana. Broodmare sire of Ajina, Anees, Cat Thief, General Meeting, Lakeway, Lure, Peintre Celebre.

ALYSHEBA, 1984- . B. c., Alydar—Bel Sheba, by Lt. Stevens. 26-11-8-2, $6,679,242, Horse of the Year in 1988, champion three-year-old male, champion older male, Kentucky Derby (G1), Preakness S. (G1), Breeders' Cup Classic (G1), etc. Sire of more than 15 stakes winners, including Alywow, Bright Moon, Moonlight Dance.

AMERICAN ECLIPSE, 1814-1847. Ch. c., Duroc—Millers Damsel, by *Messenger. 8-8-0-0, $56,700, North-South Match Race with (Sir) Henry. Sire of Black Maria, Ariel, Medoc, Fanny, Lance. First great American champion.

AMERICAN FLAG, 1922-1942. Ch. c., Man o' War—*Lady Comfey, by Roi Herode. 17-8-1-1, $82,725, champion three-year-old colt, Belmont S., Withers S., etc. Sire of 16 stakes winners including Nellie Flag, Gusto. Broodmare sire of Raise You, Mar-Kell.

ANCIENT TITLE, 1970-1981. Dk. b. or br. g., Gummo—Hi Little Gal, by Bar Le Duc. 57-24-11-9, $1,252,791, Hollywood Gold Cup Invitational H. (G1), Charles H. Strub S. (G1), etc. Won 20 stakes; leading California-bred money earner at the time of his death.

ANITA PEABODY, 1925-1934. B. or br. f., Luke McLuke—*La Dauphine, by The Tetrarch. 8-7-0-1, $113,105, champion two-year-old filly, Futurity S., Debutante S., etc. Dam of Our Count.

A.P. INDY, 1989- . Dk. b. or br. c., Seattle Slew—Weekend Surprise, by Secretariat. 11-8-0-1, $2,979,815, Horse of the Year in 1992, champion three-year-old male, Belmont S. (G1), Breeders' Cup Classic (G1), etc. Sire of more than 100 stakes winners, including Mineshaft, Rags to Riches, Tempera, Golden Missile, Aptitude, Lu Ravi, Secret Status, A P Valentine, Old Trieste.

ARAZI, 1989-. Ch. c., Blushing Groom (Fr)—Danseur Fabuleux, by Northern Dancer. 14-9-1-1, $1,212,351,

champion two-year-old male, Horse of the Year in Europe. Breeders' Cup Juvenile (G1), Grand Criterium (Fr-G1), etc. Sire of 15 stakes winners, including Congaree, First Magnitude (Ire), America (Ire).

ARISTIDES, 1872-1893. Ch. c., *Leamington—Sarong, by Lexington. 21-9-5-1, $18,325, Kentucky Derby, Withers S., Jerome S., etc. First winner of Kentucky Derby in 1875.

ARMED, 1941-1964. Br. g., Bull Lea—Armful, by Chance Shot. 81-41-20-10, $817,475, Horse of the Year in 1947, champion handicap horse twice, Suburban H., Widener H. twice, Gulfstream Park H., etc.

ARTFUL, 1902-1927. B. f., Hamburg—Martha II, by Dandie Dinmont. 8-6-2-0, $81,125, Futurity S., etc. Only horse to defeat Sysonby. Tail-female ancestor of family that includes Runaway Groom.

ARTS AND LETTERS, 1966-1998. Ch. c., *Ribot—All Beautiful, by Battlefield. 23-11-6-1, $632,404, Horse of the Year in 1969, champion three-year-old colt, champion handicap horse, Belmont S., Jockey Club Gold Cup, etc. Sire of 30 stakes winners, including Codex, Winter's Tale, Illiterate.

ASSAULT, 1943-1971. Ch. c., Bold Venture—Igual, by Equipoise. 42-18-6-7, $675,470, Horse of the Year in 1946, champion three-year-old colt, Triple Crown, Suburban H., Brooklyn H. twice, etc. Sterile at stud.

ASTEROID, 1861-1886. B. c., Lexington—Nebula, by *Glencoe. 12-12-0-0, $12,800, Woodlawn Vase, etc. One of three sons of Lexington, along with Kentucky and Norfolk, to be considered the best racehorses of the 1860s, called the "great triumvirate." Sire of Creedmoor, Ballankeel.

*AUSTRALIAN, 1858-1879. Ch. c. West Australian—*Emilia, by Young Emilius. 10-3-3-3, $12,150, Doswell S., Galt House S. Sire of Spendthrift, Wildidle, Baden Baden, Fellowcraft, Joe Daniels, Springbok. American founder of male line that includes Man o' War, War Admiral, In Reality, Tiznow.

AZERI, 1998- . Ch. f., Jade Hunter—Zodiac Miss (Aus), by Ahonoora. 24-17-4-0, $4,079,820, Horse of the Year in 2002, champion older female 2002, '03, '04, Breeders' Cup Distaff (G1), Apple Blossom H. (G1) 2002-'04, etc. Leading North American distaff earner.

BALD EAGLE, 1955-1977. B. c., *Nasrullah—Siama, by Tiger. 29-12-5-4, $692,946, champion older horse, Metropolitan H., Suburban H., etc. Sire of 12 stakes winners, including Too Bald, San San. Broodmare sire of 33 stakes winners, including Exceller, Capote.

BALLOT, 1904-1937. Ch. c., *Voter—*Cerito, by Lowland Chief. 38-20-6-6, $154,545, Suburban H., etc. Sire of Midway, Chilhowee, Star Voter. Broodmare sire of Bull Lea.

BARBARO, 2003-2007. Dk. b. or br. c., Dynaformer—La Ville Rouge, by Carson City. 7-6-0-0, $2,302,200. Winner of the 2006 Kentucky Derby Presented by Yum! Brands (G1) who broke down severely in the Preakness Stakes (G1); survived surgery to repair his injured right hind leg but succumbed to effects of laminitis; his injury and treatment attracted international attention, and charitable funds for equine research were created in his name.

BATTLEFIELD, 1948-1964. Ch. c., War Relic—Dark Display, by Display. 44-22-14-2, $474,727, champion two-year-old colt, Futurity S., Hopeful S., Travers S., etc. Sire of Yorktown. Broodmare sire of Arts and Letters, Steeple Jill.

BATTLESHIP, 1927-1958. Ch. c., Man o' War—*Quarantaine, by Sea Sick. 55-24-6-4, $71,641, Grand National Steeplechase in England and U.S., etc. Sire of Shipboard, War Battle.

BAYAKOA (ARG), 1984-1997. B. f., Consultant's Bid—Arlucea (Arg), by Good Manners. 39-21-9-0, $2,861,701, champion older female twice, Breeders' Cup Distaff (G1) twice, Spinster S. (G1) twice, etc.

BED O' ROSES, 1947-1953. B. f., Rosemont—Good Thing, by Discovery. 46-18-8-6, $383,925, champion two-year-old filly, champion handicap mare, Santa Margarita H., Matron S., etc.

BELDAME, 1901-1923. Ch. f., Octagon—*Bella Donna, by Octavian. 31-17-6-4, $102,135, Suburban H., Alabama S., Ladies H., etc. Dam of Belvale. Tail-female ancestor of family that includes Revoked, Lion Heart.

BEN ALI, 1883-unknown. Br. c., Virgil—Ulrica, by Lexington. 40-12-3-5, $25,090, Kentucky Derby, Hopeful S., etc.

BEN BRUSH, 1893-1918. B. c., Bramble—Roseville, by Reform. 40-25-5-5, $65,208, Kentucky Derby, Suburban H., etc. Leading sire in 1909. Sire of Broomstick, Sweep, Delhi, Meridian, Pebbles, Theo Cook, Von Tromp.

BEND OR, 1877-1903. Ch. c., Doncaster—Rouge Rose, by Thormanby. 14-10-2-0, $90,304, Epsom Derby, Champion S., etc. Sire of *Ormonde, Bona Vista, Kendal, Orvieto. Tail-male ancestor of Phalaris, *Teddy lines.

BEST PAL, 1988-1998. B. g., *Habitony—Ubetshedid, by King Pellinore. 47-18-11-4, $5,668,245, Santa Anita H. (G1), Hollywood Gold Cup H. (G1), etc. Leading California-bred money earner at retirement.

BEWITCH, 1945-1959. Br. f., Bull Lea—Potheen, by Wildair. 55-20-10-11, $462,605, champion two-year-old filly, champion handicap mare, Arlington Lassie S., Vanity H., etc. Defeated stablemate Citation in 1947 Washington Park Futurity.

BIG BROWN, 2005- . B. c., Boundary—Mien, by Nureyev. 6-5-0-0, $2,714,500. Kentucky Derby (G1), Preakness S. (G1), Florida Derby (G1), etc. First undefeated horse since Smarty Jones to win the Kentucky Derby. Syndicated for more than $50-million.

BIMELECH, 1937-1966. B. c., Black Toney—*La Troienne, by *Teddy. 15-11-2-1, $248,745, champion two- and three-year-old colt, Preakness S., Belmont S., etc. Sire of 30 stakes winners, including Better Self, Be Faithful, Guillotine, Hilarious, Brookfield. Broodmare sire of Lalun, No Robbery. Full brother to Black Helen.

BIRDCATCHER, 1833-1860. Ch. c., Sir Hercules—Guiccioli, by Bob Booty. 18-6-4-4, $6,666 in Ireland, Madrid Plate, Peel Cup, etc. Sire of *Alfred, The Baron, Bird on the Wing, Chanticleer, Daniel O'Rourke, Kingfisher. Tail-male ancestor of Phalaris, *Teddy, Blandford male lines. Famous for passing on white spots in his chestnut coat, known as "Birdcatcher spots."

BLACK GOLD, 1921-1928. Bl. c., Black Toney—Useeit, by Bonnie Joe. 35-18-5-4, $110,553, champion three-year-old colt, Kentucky Derby, Ohio Derby, etc. Broke down fatally at seven and buried in the infield at Fair Grounds.

BLACK HELEN, 1932-1957. B. f., Black Toney—*La Troienne, by *Teddy. 22-15-0-2, $61,800, champion three-year-old filly, Coaching Club American Oaks, Florida Derby, etc. Tail-female ancestor of family that includes Pleasant Tap, Go for Gin, But Why Not, Princess Rooney. Full sister to Bimelech.

BLACK MARIA, 1826-1840. Bl. f., American Eclipse—Lady Lightfoot, by Sir Archy. 26-13-(placings unknown), $14,900, Jockey Club Purse, etc. Ran 17 times in four-mile heats. Won a five-heat, four-mile heat race that caused death of one opponent from exhaustion.

History of Racing — Notable Horses

BLACK MARIA, 1923-1932. Bl. f., Black Toney—*Bird Loose, by Sardanapale. 52-18-14-6, $110,350, champion three-year-old filly, champion older mare twice, Kentucky Oaks, Metropolitan H., Ladies H. twice, etc. Tail-female ancestor of family that includes Polynesian, Air Forbes Won.

BLACK TIE AFFAIR (IRE), 1986- . Gr. or ro. c., Miswaki—Hat Tab Girl, by Al Hattab. 45-18-9-6, $3,370,694, Horse of the Year in 1991, champion older male, Breeders' Cup Classic (G1), Philip H. Iselin H. (G1), etc. Sire of more than 30 stakes winners, including Formal Gold, Evening Attire. Exported from the United States to Japan in 1997; returned in 2003.

BLACK TONEY, 1911-1938. Br. c., Peter Pan—Belgravia, by Ben Brush. 37-12-10-7, $12,815, Independence H., Valuation S., etc. Sire of more than 35 stakes winners, including Balladier, Big Hurry, Bimelech, Black Gold, Black Helen, Black Maria, Black Servant, Brokers Tip, Miss Jemima. Broodmare sire of more than 25 stakes winners, including Bridal Flower, Elkridge, Relic, Searching. Foundation sire of Col. E. R. Bradley's Idle Hour Farm.

BLANDFORD, 1919-1935. Br. c., Swynford—Blanche, by White Eagle. 4-3-1-0, $16,041, Princess of Wales's S., etc. Leading sire three times in England. Sire of *Blenheim II, *Bahram, Brantome, Windsor Lad, Campanula, Trigo, Dalmary, Mistress Ford, Pasch, Udaipur, Umidwar. Tail-male ancestor of line leading to The Axe II, Quadrangle, Crepello, Mtoto.

***BLENHEIM II**, 1927-1958. Br. c., Blandford—Malva, by Charles O'Malley. 10-5-3-0, $73,060, Epsom Derby, etc. Leading sire in 1941. Sire of more than 45 stakes winners, including Whirlaway, *Mahmoud, Donatello II, Mar-Kell, Fervent, A Gleam, Jet Pilot. Broodmare sire of A Glitter, Coaltown, Hill Gail, Kauai King, Le Paillon, *Nasrullah, Wistful. Tail-male ancestor of line leading to The Axe II, Quadrangle, Crepello, Mtoto.

BLUE LARKSPUR, 1926-1947. B. c., Black Servant—Blossom Time, by *North Star III. 16-10-3-1, $272,070, regarded as Horse of the Year in 1929, champion three-year-old colt, champion handicap horse, Belmont S., Classic S., etc. Sire of 44 stakes winners, including But Why Not, Myrtlewood, Painted Veil, Blue Swords, Alablue, Revoked, Blue Delight, Bee Ann Mac. Broodmare sire of Alanesian, Be Faithful, Busanda, By Jimminy, Cohoes, Durazna, Real Delight, Twilight Tear.

BLUSHING GROOM (FR), 1974-1992. Ch. c., Red God—Runaway Bride (GB), by Wild Risk. 10-7-1-2, $407,153, champion two-year-old in France, champion miler in France, Grand Criterium (Fr-G1), Poule d'Essai des Poulains (French Two Thousand Guineas) (Fr-G1), etc. Leading sire in England in 1989. Sire of 92 stakes winners, including Nashwan, Rainbow Quest, Arazi, Sky Beauty, Rahy, Blushing John, Runaway Groom, Al Bahathri, Blush With Pride, Mt. Livermore. Broodmare sire of Awesome Again, Flute, Kahyasi, Lammtarra, Macho Uno, Stravinsky, T.M.Opera O.

BOLD FORBES, 1973-2000. Dk. b. or br. c., Irish Castle—Comely Nell, by Commodore M. 18-13-1-4, $546,536, champion three-year-old male, champion two-year-old in Puerto Rico, Kentucky Derby (G1), Belmont S. (G1), etc. Sire of 29 stakes winners, including Tiffany Lass, Air Forbes Won.

BOLD LAD, 1962-1986. Ch. c., Bold Ruler—Misty Morn, by *Princequillo. 19-14-2-1, $516,465, champion two-year-old, Metropolitan H., Futurity S., Hopeful S., etc. Sire of 29 stakes winners, including Sirlad (Ire), Bold Fascinator, Gentle Thoughts, Rube the Great.

BOLD 'N DETERMINED, 1977-1997. B. f., Bold and Brave—Pidi, by Determine. 20-16-2-0, $949,599, Coaching Club American Oaks (G1), Kentucky Oaks (G1), etc. Winner of six Grade 1 races at three in 1980, she had the misfortune of being in the same crop as Kentucky Derby (G1) winner and champion three-year-old filly Genuine Risk. Defeated Genuine Risk in the 1980 Maskette Stakes (G2).

BOLD RULER, 1954-1971. Dk. b. c., *Nasrullah—Miss Disco, by Discovery. 33-23-4-2, $764,204, Horse of the Year in 1957, champion three-year-old colt, champion sprinter, Preakness S., Futurity S., Suburban H., etc. Leading sire eight times, seven in succession (1963-'69). Sire of 82 stakes winners, including Secretariat, Gamely, Lamb Chop, Bold Lad (out of Misty Morn), Bold Lad (out of *Barn Pride), Bold Bidder, Wajima, Queen Empress, Queen of the Stage, Boldnesian, Chieftain, Dewan, Reviewer. Broodmare sire of Autobiography, Christmas Past, Private Terms, Sensational. Tail-male ancestor of Seattle Slew line.

BOLD VENTURE, 1933-1958. Ch. c., *St. Germans—Possible, by Ultimus. 11-6-2-0, $68,300, champion three-year-old colt, Kentucky Derby, Preakness S. Sire of 12 stakes winners, including Assault, Middleground. Broodmare sire of Miss Cavandish, Prove Out.

BON NOUVEL, 1960-unknown. B. g., Duc de Fer—Good News, by *Happy Argo. 51-16-11-7, $176,148, champion steeplechaser three times, Temple Gwathmey Stp. H., Brook Stp. H. twice, etc.

BORROW, 1908-unknown. Ch. g., Hamburg—Forget, by Exile. 91-24-20-12. $87,275, Middle Park Plate (in England), Brooklyn H., etc. Defeated three Kentucky Derby winners in 1917 Brooklyn H.

BOSTON, 1833-1850. Ch. c., Timoleon—Sister to Tuckahoe, by Ball's Florizel. 45-40-2-1, $51,700, champion of his era. Leading sire three times. Sire of Lexington, Lecomte, Commodore, Madeline, Nina, Ringgold, Red Eye. Won 70 of 81 heats, 47 at 4 miles. Lost famous match race with Fashion.

BOURTAI, 1942-1970. B. f., Stimulus—Escutcheon, by *Sir Gallahad III. 12-2-1-2, $3,850, 3rd Pimlico Nursery S. Dam of Bayou, Levee, Delta, Banta, Ambassador. Tail-female ancestor of Aptitude, Big Spruce, Coastal, Dike, Sacahuista, Shuvee, Sleepytime, Slew o' Gold, Talking Picture.

BOWL OF FLOWERS, 1958-unknown. Ch. f., Sailor—Flower Bowl, by *Alibhai. 16-10-3-3, $398,504, champion two- and three-year-old filly, Coaching Club American Oaks, Spinster S., etc. Dam of sires Whiskey Road, Big Burn.

BRIGADIER GERARD, 1968-'89. B. c., Queen's Hussar—La Paiva, by Prince Chevalier. 18-17-1-0, $631,199, Horse of the Year in England, champion miler twice, champion older horse, Two Thousand Guineas, King George VI and Queen Elizabeth II S., etc. Sire of 28 stakes winners, including Light Cavalry, Vayrann, Comrade in Arms, General (Fr). One of the greatest English horses of the 20th century and grandsire of Lord At War (Arg), one of the last representatives of the Fairway male line.

BROAD BRUSH, 1983- . B. c., Ack Ack—Hay Patcher, by Hoist the Flag. 27-14-5-5, $2,656,793, Santa Anita H. (G1), Suburban H. (G1), etc. Leading sire in 1994. Sire of more than 90 stakes winners, including Farda Amiga, Concern, Include, Broad Appeal, Pompeii, Nobo True.

BROOMSTICK, 1901-1931. B. c., Ben Brush—*Elf, by Galliard. 39-14-11-5, $74,730, Travers S., Brighton H.,

etc. Leading sire 1913-'15; leading broodmare sire 1932-'33. Sire of 69 stakes winners, including Regret, Whisk Broom II, Bostonian, Broomspun, Cudgel, Halcyon, Sweeper, Traffic, Transmute, Wildair, Escoba, Flying Witch, Remembrance. Broodmare sire of Equipoise, Mother Goose, Whichone.

BROWN BESS, 1982- . Dk. b. or br. f., *Petrone—Chickadee, by Windy Sands. 36-16-8-6, $1,300,920, champion grass female, Santa Barbara H. (G1), Ramona H. (G1), Yellow Ribbon Inv. S. (G1), etc.

BUCKPASSER, 1963-1978. B. c., Tom Fool—Busanda, by War Admiral. 31-25-4-1, $1,462,014, Horse of the Year in 1966, champion two- and three-year-old colt, champion handicap horse twice, Jockey Club Gold Cup, Metropolitan H., etc. Leading broodmare sire 1983-'84, '88-'89. Sire of 35 stakes winners, including Numbered Account, Relaxing, La Prevoyante, L'Enjoleur, Norcliffe, State Dinner, Silver Buck, Buckaroo, Lassie Dear, Passing Mood. Broodmare sire of Slew o' Gold, Seeking the Gold, Coastal, Woodman, Private Account, Easy Goer, El Gran Senor, Miswaki, Touch Gold.

BULL DOG, 1927-1954. Dk. b. or br. c., *Teddy—Plucky Liege, by Spearmint. 8-2-1-0, $7,802 Prix Daphnis, etc. Leading sire in 1943; leading broodmare sire in 1953, '54, '56. Sire of 52 stakes winners, including Bull Lea, Occupy, Our Boots, Occupation, Johns Joy, The Doge, Canina, Miss Dogwood, Miss Mommy, Tiger. Broodmare sire of Tom Fool, Decathlon, Dark Star, Rough'n Tumble. Full brother to *Sir Gallahad III; half brother to Bois Roussel, Admiral Drake.

BULLE ROCK, 1709-unknown. B. c., Darley Arabian—Byerley Turk mare, by Byerley Turk. Earliest Thoroughbred recorded as imported (in 1730) to the United States in the *American Stud Book*. No horse matching his description and pedigree appears in the *General Stud Book*, but he is generally accepted as America's first Thoroughbred.

BULL LEA, 1935-1964. Br. c., *Bull Dog—Rose Leaves, by Ballot. 27-10-7-3, $94,825, Widener H., Blue Grass S., etc. Leading sire in 1947, '48, '49, '52, '53; leading broodmare sire 1958-'61. Sire of 57 stakes winners, ten champions, including Citation, Coaltown, Hill Gail, Two Lea, Twilight Tear, Bewitch, Real Delight, Iron Liege, Armed, Durazna, Next Move. Broodmare sire of Barbizon, Bramalea, Gate Dancer, Idun, Leallah, Pucker Up, Quadrangle, Tim Tam.

BUSHER, 1942-1955. Ch. f., War Admiral—Baby League, by Bubbling Over. 21-15-3-1, $334,035, Horse of the Year in 1945, champion two- and three-year-old filly, champion handicap mare, Hollywood Derby, Santa Margarita H., etc. Dam of Jet Action. Tail-female ancestor of family that includes Beau's Eagle, Play On.

BUSHRANGER, 1930-1937. Ch. g., *Stefan the Great—War Path, by Man o' War. 21-11-3-1, $20,635, champion steeplechaser, Grand National Stp. H., Broad Hollow Stp. H. twice, etc.

BYERLEY TURK, ca. 1680. Bl. c. of unknown parentage. Sire of Jigg, Basto, Black Hearty. One of three Thoroughbred male-line foundation sires. Tail-male ancestor of the Herod line leading to *Ambiorix, The Tetrarch, Dr Devious (Ire), Indian Ridge.

CAFE PRINCE, 1970-unknown. B. g., Creme dela Creme—Princess Blair, by Blue Prince. 52-18-5-4, $228,238, champion steeplechaser twice, Colonial Cup International Stp. twice, etc.

CANONERO II, 1968-1981. B. c., *Pretendre—Dixieland II, by Nantallah. 23-9-3-4, $360,933, champion three-year-old male, Kentucky Derby, Preakness S.-ntr, etc. Sire of five stakes winners, including Cannon Boy. First foreign-trained horse to win Kentucky Derby.

CAPOT, 1946-1974. Br. c., Menow—Piquet, by *St. Germans. 28-12-4-7, $347,260, Horse of the Year in 1949, champion three-year-old colt, Preakness S., Belmont S., etc. Sired 13 foals, no stakes winners.

CARBINE, 1885-1913. B. c., Musket—Mersey, by Knowsley. 43-33-6-3, $143,982, Melbourne Cup twice, Sydney Cup twice, etc.. Sire of Amberite, *Bomba, Fowling-Piece, Greatorex, Miss Gunning, Ramrod, Spearmint, Wallace. Won 1890 Melbourne Cup under 145 pounds. Still widely considered best New Zealand-bred of all time.

CARRY BACK, 1958-1983. Br. c., Saggy—Joppy, by Star Blen. 62-21-11-11, $1,241,165, champion three-year-old colt, Kentucky Derby, Preakness S., etc. Sire of ten stakes winners, including Taken Aback, Sharp Gary, Back in Paris.

CAVALCADE, 1931-1940. Br. c., *Lancegaye—*Hastily, by Hurry On. 22-8-5-3, $127,165, Horse of the Year in 1934, champion two- and three-year-old colt, Kentucky Derby, American Derby, etc. Sire of three stakes winners.

CHALLEDON, 1936-1958. B. c., *Challenger II—Laura Gal, by *Sir Gallahad III. 44-20-7-6, $334,660, Horse of the Year in 1939 and '40, champion three-year-old colt, champion handicap horse, Preakness S., Whitney S., etc. Sire of 13 stakes winners, including Ancestor, Tenacious, Donor.

CHARISMATIC, 1996- . Ch. c., Summer Squall—Bali Babe, by Drone. 17-5-2-4, $2,038,064, Horse of the Year in 1999, champion three-year-old male, Kentucky Derby (G1), Preakness S. (G1), etc. Exported to Japan in 2002.

CHIEF'S CROWN, 1982-1997. B. c., Danzig—Six Crowns, by Secretariat. 21-12-3-3, $2,191,168, champion two-year-old male, Breeders' Cup Juvenile (G1), Travers S. (G1), etc. Sire of more than 50 stakes winners, including Erhaab, Grand Lodge, Chief Bearhart, Concerto, Chief Honcho.

CHRIS EVERT, 1971-2001. Ch. f., Swoon's Son—Miss Carmie, by T. V. Lark. 15-10-2-2, $679,475, champion three-year-old filly, filly triple crown, Coaching Club American Oaks (G1), Hollywood Special S. (match race with Miss Musket), etc. Dam of Six Crowns, Wimbledon Star. Second dam of Chief's Crown.

CICADA, 1959-1981. B. f., Bryan G.—Satsuma, by Bossuet. 42-23-8-6, $783,674, champion two- and three-year-old filly, champion older mare, Kentucky Oaks, Beldame S., etc. Dam of Cicada's Pride. Retired as world's leading money-winning female.

CIGAR, 1990- . B. c., Palace Music—Solar Slew, by Seattle Slew. 33-19-4-5, $9,999,815, Horse of the Year in 1995 and '96, champion older horse twice, Breeders' Cup Classic (G1), Dubai World Cup, etc. Leading earner of all-time in North America. Sterile at stud. Resides at Kentucky Horse Park.

CITATION, 1945-1970. B. c., Bull Lea—*Hydroplane II, by Hyperion. 45-32-10-2, $1,085,760, Horse of the Year in 1948, champion two- and three-year-old colt, champion handicap horse, Triple Crown, Jockey Club Gold Cup, Hollywood Gold Cup, etc. First $1-million earner. Sire of 12 stakes winners, including Silver Spoon, Fabius.

CLEOPATRA, 1917-1932. Ch. f., Corcyra—*Gallice, by Gallinule. 26-8-10-4, $55,937, champion three-year-old filly, Coaching Club American Oaks, Alabama S.,

etc. Dam of Pompey, Laughing Queen; third dam of Tom Fool. Tail-female ancestor of family that includes Ambiopoise, Dust Commander.

COALTOWN, 1945-1965. B. c., Bull Lea—Easy Lass, by *Blenheim II. 39-23-6-3, $415,675, Horse of the Year in 1949, champion sprinter, champion handicap horse, Jerome H., Blue Grass S., etc. Never sired a stakes winner. Exported to France in 1955.

COLIN, 1905-1932. Br. c., Commando—*Pastorella, by Springfield. 15-15-0-0, $178,110, champion two- and three-year-old colt, Belmont S., Futurity S., etc. Sire of Jock, Neddie, On Watch. Shy breeder. Tail-male ancestor of line that leads to Broad Brush.

COMMANDO, 1898-1905. B. c., Domino—Emma C., by *Darebin. 9-7-2-0, $58,196, champion two- and three-year-old colt, Belmont S., Junior Champion S., etc. Leading sire in 1907. Sire of ten stakes winners from 27 foals, including Colin, Peter Pan, Celt, Hippodrome, Superman, Transvaal, and of Ultimus.

CONQUISTADOR CIELO, 1979-2002. B. c., Mr. Prospector—K D Princess, by Bold Commander. 13-9-0-2, $474,328, Horse of the Year in 1982, champion three-year-old male, Belmont S. (G1), Metropolitan H. (G1), etc. Sire of more than 65 stakes winners, including Marquetry, Forty Niner Days, Wagon Limit. Broodmare sire of more than 80 stakes winners, including Apelia, Dixie Dot Com, Thornfield.

CORRECTION, 1888-1911. B. f., Himyar—Mannie Gray, by Enquirer. 122-38-35-22, $45,600, Toboggan Slide H., etc. Dam of Yankee, Miss Malaprop, Nature. Tail-female ancestor of family that includes Affirmed, Lil E. Tee, Ghostzapper. Full sister to Domino.

COSMAH, 1953-1979. B. f., Cosmic Bomb—Almahmoud, by *Mahmoud. 30-9-5-2, $86,525, Astarita S., etc. Broodmare of the Year in 1974. Dam of Tosmah, Halo, Fathers Image, Maribeau. Foundation mare of family that includes Flawlessly, L'Emigrant, Cannonade, Stephan's Odyssey.

***COUGAR II**, 1966-1989. Dk b. or br. c., Tale of Two Cities—*Cindy Lou II, by Madara. 50-20-7-17, $1,172,625, champion grass horse, Santa Anita H. (G1), Sunset H. (G1), etc. Sire of 24 stakes winners, including Gato Del Sol, Exploded.

COUNTERPOINT, 1948-1970. Ch. c., Count Fleet—Jabot, by *Sickle. 21-10-3-1, $284,575, Horse of the Year in 1951, champion three-year-old colt, Belmont S., Jockey Club Gold Cup, etc. Sire of 11 stakes winners, including Dotted Swiss, Harmonizing, Honey Dear, Snow White.

COUNT FLEET, 1940-1973. Br. c., Reigh Count—Quickly, by Haste. 21-16-4-1, $250,300, Horse of the Year in 1943, champion two- and three-year-old colt, Triple Crown, Champagne S., Withers S., etc. Leading sire in 1951; leading broodmare sire in 1963. Sire of 39 stakes winners, including Counterpoint, One Count, Kiss Me Kate, Count Turf, Count of Honor, Juliets Nurse. Broodmare sire of Kelso, Prince John, Quill, Fleet Nasrullah, Gallant Romeo, Lamb Chop.

CREME FRAICHE, 1982-2003. B. g., Rich Cream—Likely Exchange, by Terrible Tiger. 64-17-12-13, $4,024,727, Belmont S. (G1), Jockey Club Gold Cup (G1) twice, Super Derby (G1), etc.

CRIMINAL TYPE, 1985-2005. Ch. c., Alydar—Klepto, by No Robbery. 24-10-5-3, $2,351,274, Horse of the Year in 1990, champion older male, Hollywood Gold Cup (G1), Pimlico Special H. (G1), Metropolitan H. (G1), etc. Sire of seven stakes winners, including Hoolie. Exported to Japan in 1992.

CRIMSON SATAN, 1959-1982. Ch. c., Spy Song—*Papila, by Requiebro. 58-18-9-9, $796,077, champion two-year-old colt, Garden State S., Charles H. Strub S., etc. Sire of 33 stakes winners, including Crimson Saint, Krislin, Whitesburg.

CRUSADER, 1923-1940. Ch. c., Man o' War—Star Fancy, by *Star Shoot. 42-18-8-4, $203,261, consensus Horse of the Year in 1926, champion three-year-old colt, Belmont S., Jockey Club Gold Cup, Suburban H. twice, etc. Sire of six stakes winners, including *Crossbow II.

CURLIN, 2004- . Ch. c., Smart Strike—Sherriff's Deputy, by Deputy Minister. 11-8-1-2, $9,936,800. Horse of the Year 2007, champion three-year-old male, Breeders' Cup Classic (G1), Preakness S. (G1), Dubai World Cup (UAE-G1), Jockey Club Gold Cup (G1), etc.

DAHLIA, 1970-2001. Ch. f., *Vaguely Noble—Charming Alibi, by Honeys Alibi. 48-15-3-7, $1,489,105, Horse of the Year in England in 1974 and '75, champion three-year-old in Ireland, champion three-year-old in England, champion grass horse in U.S., champion older mare twice in England, King George VI and Queen Elizabeth S. (Eng-G1) twice, Washington, D.C., International (G1), etc. Dam of Dahar, Rivlia, Delegant, Dahlia's Dreamer, Wajd, Llandaff. First distaff millionaire.

DALAKHANI, 2000- . Gr. c., Darshaan—Daltawa, by Miswaki. 9-8-1-0, $2,496,059, European Horse of the Year and champion three-year-old in 2003, Prix de l'Arc de Triomphe (Fr-G1), Prix du Jockey-Club (Fr-G1) (French Derby), etc.

DAMASCUS, 1964-1995. B. c., Sword Dancer—Kerala, by *My Babu. 32-21-7-3, $1,176,781, Horse of the Year in 1967, champion three-year-old colt, champion handicap horse, Preakness S., Belmont S., Jockey Club Gold Cup S., etc. Sire of 71 stakes winners, including Private Account, Desert Wine, Highland Blade, Ogygian, Honorable Miss, Time for a Change, Judger, Bailjumper, Timeless Moment, Cutlass. Broodmare sire of more than 155 stakes winners, including Boundary, Chilukki, Coronado's Quest, Shadeed.

DANCE SMARTLY, 1988-2007 . Dk. b. or br. f., Danzig—Classy 'n Smart, by Smarten. 17-12-2-3, $3,263,835, champion three-year-old filly in U.S., Canadian Horse of the Year, champion two- and three-year-old filly in Canada, Canadian Triple Crown, Breeders' Cup Distaff (G1), Queen's Plate S., etc. Dam of Queen's Plate winners Scatter the Gold, Dancethruthedawn.

DANEHILL, 1986-2003. B. c., Danzig—Razyana, by His Majesty. 9-4-1-2, $321,064, Ladbroke Sprint S. (Eng-G1), etc. Brother to Eagle Eyed, Harpia, Shibboleth, half brother to Euphonic. Leading sire in Australia eight times, leading sire in France twice, leading sire in U.S. Sire of more than 345 stakes winners, including Rock of Gibraltar (Ire), Flying Spur, Danewin, Fairy King Prawn, Dane Ripper, Banks Hill (GB), Intercontinental (GB).

DANZIG, 1977-2006. B. c., Northern Dancer—Pas de Nom, by Admiral's Voyage. 3-3-0-0, $32,400. Leading sire 1991-'93. Sire of more than 185 stakes winners, including Chief's Crown, Polish Precedent, Dayjur, Danehill, Dance Smartly, Langfuhr, Anabaa, Green Desert, Pine Bluff. Broodmare sire of more than 125 stakes winners, including Caller One, Fusaichi Pegasus.

DARK MIRAGE, 1965-1969. Dk. b. or br. f., *Persian Road II—Home by Dark, by Hill Prince. 27-12-3-2, $362,788, champion three-year-old filly, first winner of the filly triple crown in New York, Kentucky Oaks,

Delaware Oaks, etc. Won nine consecutive stakes and broke down trying for tenth. Died at four.

DARK STAR, 1950-1972. Br. c., *Royal Gem II—Isolde, by *Bull Dog. 13-6-2-2, $131,337, Kentucky Derby, Derby Trial, etc. Only horse to defeat Native Dancer. Sire of 26 stakes winners, including My Dad George, Hidden Treasure. Broodmare sire of Youth, Mississipian, Too Bald.

DARLEY ARABIAN, 1700. B. c. of unknown parentage. Sire of Flying Childers, Aleppo, Almanzor, Bartlett's Childers. One of three male-line foundation sires of the Thoroughbred breed. Tail-male ancestor of the Eclipse male line leading to Phalaris, Blandford, Hyperion, *Teddy, Domino lines.

DARSHAAN, 1981-2001. Br. c., Shirley Heights—Delsy, by Abdos. 8-5-0-1, $226,979, champion three-year-old in France, Prix du Jockey-Club (Fr-G1) (French Derby), etc. Leading sire in France in 2003, leading broodmare sire in England twice, leading broodmare sire in France. Sire of more than 90 stakes winners, including Dalakhani, Kotashaan (Fr), Aliysa (Ire), Mark of Esteem (Ire). Broodmare sire of High Chaparral (Ire), Ebadiyla, Islington (Ire), Yesterday (Ire).

DAVONA DALE, 1976-1997. B. f., Best Turn—Royal Entrance, by Tim Tam. 18-11-2-1, $641,612, champion three-year-old filly, filly triple crown, Kentucky Oaks (G1), etc.

DECATHLON, 1953-1972. B. c., Olympia—Dog Blessed, by *Bull Dog. 42-25-8-1, $269,530, champion sprinter twice, Oceanport H. twice, Hutcheson S., etc. Sire of 12 stakes winners, including Juanita.

DELANCEY'S CUB MARE, 1762. F., Cub—Second mare (dam of Amaranthus), by Second. One of the first great imported American foundation mares. Dam of (Maria) Slamerkin. Tail-female ancestor of family that includes Nearco, Neckar, Golden Trail, Parole, Imp, Black Gold, Mad Hatter, Sun Beau, Flirtilla, Sumpter, Artful, Delhi, Falsetto, Halma.

DEPUTY MINISTER, 1979-2004. Dk. b. or br. c., Vice Regent—Mint Copy, by Bunty's Flight. 22-12-2-2, $696,964, champion two-year-old male in U.S., Horse of the Year in Canada in 1981, champion two-year-old male in Canada, Laurel Futurity (G1), Donn H. (G2), etc. Leading sire in 1997 and '98. Sire of more than 80 stakes winners, including Go for Wand, Open Mind, Awesome Again, Dehere, Touch Gold. Broodmare sire of more than 105 stakes winners, including Halfbridled.

DESERT VIXEN, 1970-1982. Dk. b. or br. f., In Reality—Desert Trial, by Moslem Chief. 28-13-6-3, $421,538, champion three-year-old filly, champion older female, Alabama S. (G1), Beldame S. (G1) twice, etc. Dam of Real Shadai; full sister to Valid Appeal.

DETERMINE, 1951-1972. Gr. c., *Alibhai—Koubis, by *Mahmoud. 44-18-7-9, $573,360, Kentucky Derby, Santa Anita Derby, etc. First gray winner of the Kentucky Derby. Sire of 21 stakes winners, including Decidedly, Warfare, Donut King. Broodmare sire of Bold 'n Determined, Gummo, Princess Pout.

DEVIL DIVER, 1939-1961. B. c., *St. Germans—Dabchick, by *Royal Minstrel. 47-22-12-3, $261,064, champion handicap horse twice, Metropolitan H. twice, Suburban H., Whitney S., etc. Sire of 17 stakes winners, including Beau Diable, Call Over, Ruddy.

DIOMED, 1777-1808. Ch. c., Florizel—Spectator mare (sister to Juno), by Spectator. 20-11-5-3, $38,200, champion three-year-old in England. First winner of the Epsom Derby. Sire of Sir Archy, Haynie's Maria, Ball's Florizel, Duroc, Fanny, Young Giantess, Potomac, Virginius. Imported to U.S. in 1798. Tail-male ancestor of Boston, Lexington.

DISCOVERY, 1931-1958. Ch. c., Display—Ariadne, by *Light Brigade. 63-27-10-10, $195,287, Horse of the Year in 1935, champion handicap horse twice, Whitney S. three times, Brooklyn H. three times, etc. Famed as a weight carrier. Sire of 25 stakes winners, including Conniver, Miss Disco, Find, Loser Weeper, Traffic Court. Broodmare sire of Bold Ruler, Native Dancer, Intentionally, Hasty Road, Traffic Judge, Bed o' Roses.

DISGUISE, 1897-1927. B. c., Domino—*Bonnie Gal, by Galopin. 8-3-0-4, $40,275, Jockey Club S., 3rd Epsom Derby, etc. Sire of Maskette, Court Dress, Harmonicon, Helmet, Miss Puzzle, Wonder, Comely.

DISPLAY, 1923-1944. B. c., Fair Play—*Cicuta, by *Nassovian. 103-23-25-27, $256,326, Preakness S., Hawthorne Gold Cup, etc. Sire of 11 stakes winners, including Discovery, Parade Girl.

DOMINO, 1891-1897. Br. c., Himyar—Mannie Gray, by Enquirer. 25-19-2-1, $193,550, Champion two-year-old, Futurity S., Withers S., etc. Sire of Commando, Cap and Bells, Disguise, Noonday, Running Stream, Pink Domino. Sired only 20 foals in two crops, eight stakes winners, two classic winners.

DR. FAGER, 1964-1976. B. c., Rough'n Tumble—Aspidistra, by Better Self. 22-18-2-1, $1,002,642, Horse of the Year in 1968, champion older horse, champion sprinter twice, champion grass horse, Whitney S., Vosburgh H. twice, etc. Leading sire in 1977. Sire of 35 stakes winners, including Dr. Patches, Dearly Precious, L'Alezane, Dr. Blum, Tree of Knowledge, Lie Low, Lady Love. Broodmare sire of Cure the Blues, Equalize, Fappiano, Quiet American, Sewickley. Won every championship for which he was eligible in 1968.

DUKE OF MAGENTA, 1875-1899. B. c., Lexington—Magenta, by *Yorkshire. 19-15-3-1, $45,913, Belmont S., Preakness S., Travers S., etc. Sire of Duke, Eric, Ballyhoo. Sent to England with Parole after three-year-old season, but became a roarer and never raced again.

EASY GOER, 1986-1994. Ch. c., Alydar—Relaxing, by Buckpasser. 20-14-5-1, $4,873,770, champion two-year-old male, Belmont S. (G1), Jockey Club Gold Cup (G1), etc. Sire of nine stakes winners, including Will's Way, My Flag, Furlough. Broodmare sire of champion Storm Flag Flying.

ECLIPSE, 1764-1789. Ch. c., Marske—Spiletta, by Regulus. 18-18-0-0, undefeated champion in England, won 11 King's Plates. Never leading sire but runner-up 11 times. Sire of Pot8O's, King Fergus, Serjeant, Dungannon, Alexander, Joe Andrews, Mercury, Meteor, Saltram, Volunteer. Tail-male line ancestor of more than 95% of modern Thoroughbreds, including Phalaris, Hyperion, Blandford lines.

ECLIPSE, 1855-1878. B. c., Orlando—Gaze, by Bay Middleton. 9-4-0-1, $9,015, Newmarket S., Clearwell S. Sire of Alarm, Ruthless. Tail-male line ancestor of Domino, Plaudit, Dr. Fager, Holy Bull, Broad Brush.

EIGHT THIRTY, 1936-1965. Ch. c., Pilate—Dinner Time, by High Time. 27-16-3-5, $155,475, Travers S., Whitney S., Metropolitan H., etc. Sire of 45 stakes winners, including Sailor, Bolero, Royal Coinage, Rare Perfume, Sunday Evening, Make Tracks, Anyoldtime. Broodmare sire of Cornish Prince, Evening Out, Hold Your Peace, Jaipur, Rare Treat.

ELKRIDGE, 1938-1961. B. g., Mate—Best by Test, by Black Toney. 123-31-18-15, $230,680, champion steeplechaser twice, North American Stp. H. four times, Indian River Stp. H. four times, etc.

EMPEROR OF NORFOLK, 1885-1907. B. c., Norfolk—Marian, by Malcolm. 29-21-2-4, $72,400, American Derby, Brooklyn Derby, etc. Sire of Americus (Rey del Carreras), Cruzados. Buried at Santa Anita Park.

ENDURANCE BY RIGHT, 1899-1908. B. f., Inspector B.—*Early Morn, by Silvester. 18-16-0-2, $27,645, champion two-year-old filly, Champagne S., Clipsetta S., etc. Dam of Stamina. Tail-female ancestor of family that includes Plucky Play, Windjammer, Racing Room.

*EPINARD, 1920-1942. Ch. c., Badajoz—Epine Blanche, by *Rock Sand. 20-12-6-0, $46,688, champion two-year-old in France, Grand Criterium, Prix d'Ispahan, etc. Great French champion who ran second in each of three international races in U.S. in 1925. Sire of Rodosto, Marica, Epithet.

EQUIPOISE, 1928-1938. Ch. c., Pennant—Swinging, by Broomstick. 51-29-10-4, $338,610, Horse of the Year in 1932 and '33, champion handicap horse three times, champion two-year-old colt, Metropolitan H. twice, Whitney S., etc. Leading sire in 1942. Sire of nine stakes winners, including Shut Out, Level Best, Bolingbroke, Attention, Swing and Sway. Broodmare sire of Assault, Myrtle Charm.

EXCELLER, 1973-1997. B. c., *Vaguely Noble—Too Bald, by Bald Eagle. 33-15-5-6, $1,674,587, Jockey Club Gold Cup (G1), Grand Prix de Paris (Fr-G1), etc. Sire of 19 stakes winners, including Slew's Exceller, Squan Song. Died in a slaughterhouse in Sweden.

EXTERMINATOR, 1915-1945. Ch. g., *McGee—Fair Empress, by Jim Gore. 100-50-17-17, $252,596, Kentucky Derby, Saratoga Cup twice, etc. Won record 34 stakes races. Won 19 times carrying 130 pounds or more.

FAIRMOUNT, 1921-unknown. Ch. g., Fair Play—Sunflower, by *Rock Sand. 22-12-5-0, $74,075, Temple Gwathmey Memorial Steeplechase H. three times, Manley Memorial Steeplechase H., etc.

FAIR PLAY, 1905-1929. Ch. c., Hastings—*Fairy Gold, by Bend Or. 32-10-11-3, $86,950, Flash S., Coney Island Jockey Club S., etc. Leading sire in 1920, '24, '27; leading broodmare sire in 1931, '34, '38. Sire of Man o' War, Chance Play, Mad Hatter, Display, Chance Shot, Mad Play, Ladkin, Chatterton, Olambala, Stagecraft, Masda, Native Wit, Oval. Broodmare sire of High Quest, Jamestown, Stagehand, Sun Beau. Tail-male ancestor of line leading to In Reality, Valid Appeal, Tiznow.

FAIRWAY, 1925-1948. B. c., Phalaris—Scapa Flow, by Chaucer. 15-12-1-0, $194,685, champion three-year-old in England, St. Leger S., Champion S. twice, etc. Leading sire in England four times; leading broodmare sire in England in 1946 and '47. Sire of Blue Peter, Fair Copy, Fair Trial, Full Sail, Garden Path, Honeyway, Ribbon, Tide-Way, *Watling Street. Founder of sire line that leads to Shergar, Troy, Ela-Mana-Mou, Brigadier Gerard, Lord At War (Arg).

FALL ASPEN, 1976-1998. Ch. f., Pretense—Change Water, by Swaps. 20-8-3-0, $198,037, Matron S. (G1), Prioress S., etc. Broodmare of the Year in 1994. Dam of nine stakes winners, including Timber Country, Northern Aspen, Hamas (Ire), Elle Seule, Colorado Dancer (Ire), Fort Wood. Tail-female ancestor of family that includes Dubai Millennium, Charnwood Forest (Ire), El-nadim, Mehthaaf, Occupandiste.

FASHION, 1837-1860. Ch. f., *Trustee—Bonnets o' Blue, by Sir Charles. 36-32-0-0, $41,500, won match race with Boston, etc. Dam of A la Mode. Greatest of four-mile heat fillies.

FAVORITE TRICK, 1995-2006. Dk. b. or br. c., Phone Trick—Evil Elaine, by Medieval Man. 16-12-0-1, $1,726,793, Horse of the Year in 1997, champion two-year-old male, Breeders' Cup Juvenile (G1), Hopeful S. (G1), etc. First two-year-old since Secretariat in 1972 to be voted Horse of the Year.

*FEARNOUGHT, 1755-1776. B. c., Regulus—Silvertail, by Heneage's Whitenose. Five wins in England, won three King's Plates. Early American foundation sire. Sire of Symme's Wildair, Fitzhugh's Regulus, Spotswood's Apollo, Eden's Whynot, Gallant, Othello, Harris's Eclipse, Goldfinder.

FERDINAND, 1983-2002. Ch. c., Nijinsky II—Banja Luka, by Double Jay. 29-8-9-6, $3,777,978, Horse of the Year in 1987, champion older male, Kentucky Derby (G1), Breeders' Cup Classic (G1), etc. Sire of eight stakes winners, including Bull Inthe Heather. Exported to Japan in 1995 and slaughtered there.

FIRENZE (FIRENZI), 1884-1902. B. f., Glenelg—Florida, by Virgil. 82-47-21-9, $112,471, Gazelle S., Monmouth H., Jerome S. (beating Hanover), etc. Tail-female ancestor of family that includes Carry Back, Paul Jones.

FIRST FLIGHT, 1944-1975. B. f., *Mahmoud—Fly Swatter, by *Dis Donc. 24-11-3-3, $197,965, champion two-year-old filly, Matron S., Monmouth Oaks, etc. Defeated Jet Pilot in Futurity S.

FIRST LANDING, 1956-1987. B. c., *Turn-to—Hildene, by Bubbling Over. 37-19-9-2, $779,577, champion two-year-old colt, Champagne S., Hopeful S., etc. Sire of 27 stakes winners, including Riva Ridge, First Family, Gladwin.

FLATTERER, 1979- . Dk. b. or br. g., Mo Bay—Horizontal, by Nade. 51-24-7-5, $534,854, four-time champion steeplechaser 1983-'86, Marion duPont Scott Colonial Cup International Stp. three times, Temple Gwathmey Steeplechase H. twice, etc.

FLAWLESSLY, 1988-2002. B. f., Affirmed—La Confidence, by Nijinsky II. 28-16-4-3, $2,572,536, champion grass female twice, Beverly D. S. (G1), Matriarch S. (G1) three times, etc.

FLOWER BOWL, 1952-1968. B. f., *Alibhai—Flower Bed, by *Beau Pere. 32-7-4-3, $174,625, Ladies H., Delaware H., etc. Dam of Bowl of Flowers, Graustark, His Majesty.

FOOLISH PLEASURE, 1972-1994. B. c., What a Pleasure—Fool-Me-Not, by Tom Fool. 26-16-4-3, $1,216,705, champion two-year-old male, Kentucky Derby (G1), Suburban H. (G1), Great Match S. (with Ruffian), etc. Sire of 43 stakes winners, including Baiser Vole, Marfa, Kiri's Clown, Maudlin, Prayers'n Promises.

FOREGO, 1970-1997. B. g., *Forli—Lady Golconda, by Hasty Road. 57-34-9-7, $1,938,957, three-time Horse of the Year 1974-'76, champion older male 1974-'77, champion sprinter, Marlboro Cup H. (G1), Metropolitan H. (G1) twice, Woodward H. (G1) three times, etc. Last of the great weight carriers.

*FORLI, 1963-1988. Ch. c., Aristophanes—Trevisa, by Advocate. 10-9-1-0, $156,648, Horse of the Year in Argentina, Quadruple Crown, Gran Premio Carlos Pellegrini, Gran Premio Nacional (Argentine Derby), Coronado S.-ncr, etc. Brother to *Tirreno, Tibur. Sire of 60 stakes winners, including Forego, Thatch, Intrepid Hero, Sadeem, Formidable. Broodmare sire of Swale, Nureyev, Precisionist.

FORT MARCY, 1964-1991. B. g., *Amerigo—Key Bridge, by *Princequillo. 75-21-18-14, $1,109,791, Horse

History of Racing — Notable Horses

of the Year in 1970, champion grass horse twice, champion handicap horse, Washington, D.C., International S. twice, Man o' War S., etc. Half-brother to Key to the Mint.

FORWARD GAL, 1968-1984. Ch. f., Native Charger—Forward Thrust, by Jet Action. 26-12-4-6, $438,933, champion two-year-old filly, Frizette S., Monmouth Oaks, etc. Third dam of Freedom Cry (GB).

FOURSTARDAVE, 1985-2002. Ch. g., Compliance—Broadway Joan, by Bold Arian. 100-21-18-16, $1,636,737, St. Paul Derby (G2), Daryl's Joy S. (G3) twice, etc. Won a race at Saratoga Race Course for eight consecutive years. Full brother to Irish classic winner Fourstars Allstar.

FREE FOR ALL, 1942-1964. Br. c., Questionnaire—Panay, by *Chicle. 7-6-0-0, $111,225, Arlington Futurity, Washington Park Futurity, etc. Sire of Rough'n Tumble. Tail-male ancestor of Dr. Fager, Holy Bull.

FRIAR ROCK, 1913-1928. Ch. c., *Rock Sand—*Fairy Gold, by Bend Or. 21-9-1-3, $20,365, champion three-year-old, Belmont S., Suburban H., Brooklyn H., etc. Sire of Pilate, Friar's Carse, Apprehension, Inchcape, Black Curl, Emotion, Heloise, Tenez.

FRIZETTE, 1905-1929. B. f., Hamburg—*Ondulee, by St. Simon. 36-12-8-7, $16,135, Rosedale S., Laureate S., etc. Dam of Banshee, Durzetta, *Lespedeza II. Foundation mare of family that includes Myrtlewood, Seattle Slew, Mr. Prospector, Tourbillon, Sinndar, Cordova, Darshaan, Corejada, *Apollonia, Akiyda, Acamas, Akarad, *Priam II, *Djeddah, Sing Sing, Jet Pilot, Shecky Greene, Typecast, Bahri, Forestry, Chief Bearhart, Escena, Dahlia, Vitriolic, Vagrancy, Anees, Truly Bound, Baldric, Honorable Miss. Exported to France and sent to slaughter at age 24.

FUSAICHI PEGASUS, 1997- . B. c., Mr. Prospector—Angel Fever, by Danzig. 9-6-2-0, $1,994,400, Kentucky Derby (G1), Wood Memorial S. (G2), etc. Syndicated for a world-record $60-million to $70-million in 2000. Sire of more than 25 stakes winners, including Roman Ruler, Bandini.

GALLANT BLOOM, 1966-1991. B. f., *Gallant Man—Multiflora, by Beau Max. 22-16-1-1, $535,739, champion two- and three-year-old filly, champion handicap mare, Santa Margarita Invitational H., Spinster S., Monmouth Oaks, etc.

GALLANT FOX, 1927-1954. B. c., *Sir Gallahad III—Marguerite, by Celt. 17-11-3-2, $328,165, consensus Horse of the Year in 1930, champion three-year-old colt, Triple Crown, Jockey Club Gold Cup, etc. Sire of 18 stakes winners, including Omaha, Granville, Flares.

***GALLANT MAN**, 1954-1988. B. c., *Migoli—*Majideh, by *Mahmoud. 26-14-4-1, $510,355, Belmont S.-ntr, Jockey Club Gold Cup, etc. Sire of 51 stakes winners, including Gallant Bloom, Gallant Romeo, War Censor, Spicy Living, Ring Twice. Broodmare sire of Genuine Risk, *Habitony, Lord Avie.

GALLORETTE, 1942-1959. Ch. f., *Challenger II—Gallette, by *Sir Gallahad III. 72-21-20-13, $445,535, champion handicap mare, Metropolitan H., Whitney S., Beldame H., etc. World's leading money-earning female at retirement. Dam of Mlle. Lorette, Courbette. Foundation mare of family that includes Minstrella, Misty Gallore, Silver Ghost, White Gloves, Greenwood Lake, Dancing Moss.

GAMELY, 1964-1975. B. f., Bold Ruler—Gambetta, by *My Babu. 41-16-9-6, $574,961, champion three-year-old filly, champion older mare twice, Alabama S., Beldame S. twice, etc. Dam of Cellini.

GENUINE RISK, 1977- . Ch. f., Exclusive Native—Virtuous, by *Gallant Man. 15-10-3-2, $646,587, champion three-year-old filly, Kentucky Derby (G1), Ruffian H. (G1), etc. Second filly to win Kentucky Derby.

GHOSTZAPPER, 2000- . B. h., Awesome Again—Baby Zip, by Relaunch. 11-9-0-1, $3,446,120, 2004 Horse of the Year and champion older male, Breeders' Cup Classic (G1) in track and stakes record, Metropolitan H. (G1), Vosburgh H. (G1), Woodward S. (G1), etc.

***GLENCOE**, 1831-1858. Ch. c., Sultan—Trampoline, by Tramp. 10-8-1-1, $33,459, Two Thousand Guineas, Ascot Gold Cup, etc. Sire of Pocahontas, Peytona, Reel, Pryor, Star Davis, Vandal. Male-line ancestor of Hanover, Hamburg.

GODOLPHIN ARABIAN, 1724-1753. Br. c. of unknown parentage. Leading sire in England three times. Sire of Cade, Lath, Dismal, Regulus, Babraham, Blank. One of three male-line foundation sires of the Thoroughbred breed. Tail-male ancestor of Matchem line leading to Man o' War, In Reality, Tiznow.

***GO FOR WAND**, 1987-1990. B. f., Deputy Minister—Obeah, by Cyane. 13-10-2-0, $1,373,338, champion two- and three-year-old filly, Alabama S. (G1), Breeders' Cup Juvenile Fillies (G1), etc. Died at three in Breeders' Cup Distaff (G1). Buried in infield at Saratoga Race Course.

GOOD AND PLENTY, 1900-1907. B. g., Rossington—Famine, by Jils Johnson. 21-14-4-1, $45,815, Grand National Steeplechase H., Westbury Steeplechase H., etc.

GRANVILLE, 1933-1951. B. c., Gallant Fox—Gravita, by *Sarmatian. 18-8-4-3, $111,820, Horse of the Year in 1936, champion three-year-old colt, Belmont S., Travers S., etc. Sired only two stakes winners.

GREY LAG, 1918-1942. Ch. c., *Star Shoot—Miss Minnie, by *Meddler. 47-25-9-3, $136,715, Horse of the Year in 1921, champion three-year-old colt, champion handicap horse twice, Belmont S., Metropolitan H., Suburban H., etc. Shy breeder, sired only one stakes winner from 17 foals.

GUN BOW, 1960-1979. B. c., Gun Shot—Ribbons and Bows, by War Admiral. 42-17-8-4, $798,722, Metropolitan H., Whitney S., etc. Sire of six stakes winners, including Pistol Packer. Exported to Japan in 1973.

HAIL TO REASON, 1958-1976. Br. c., *Turn-to—Nothirdchance, by Blue Swords. 18-9-2-2, $328,434, champion two-year-old colt, Hopeful S., Sanford S., etc. Broke down and retired at end of two-year-old season. Leading sire in 1970. Sire of 43 stakes winners, including Roberto, Halo, Stop the Music, Mr. Leader, Bold Reason, Trillion, Priceless Gem, Straight Deal, Hail to All, Regal Gleam, Personality, Proud Clarion, Admiring. Broodmare sire of Allez France, Escaline (Fr), Royal Glint, Silver Buck, Triptych. Tail-male ancestor of line that includes Saint Ballado, Sunday Silence, Red Ransom, Brian's Time.

HALO, 1969-2000. Dk. b. or br. c., Hail to Reason—Cosmah, by Cosmic Bomb. 31-9-8-5, $259,553, United Nations H. (G1), Tidal H. (G2), etc. Leading sire in 1983 and '89. Sire of 63 stakes winners, including Sunday Silence, Sunny's Halo, Glorious Song, Devil's Bag, Saint Ballado, Rainbow Connection, Goodbye Halo, Lively One, Jolie's Halo, Coup de Folie. Broodmare sire of Halo America, Machiavellian, Pine Bluff, Rahy, Singspiel (Ire).

HAMBURG, 1895-1915. B. c., Hanover—Lady Reel, by Fellowcraft. 21-16-3-2, $60,380, consensus champion three-year-old colt, Lawrence Realization, Brighton Cup,

etc. Leading sire in 1905. Sire of Artful, Borrow, Burgomaster, Frizette, Prince Eugene, Lady Hamburg II, Biturica, Jersey Lightning, Rosie O'Grady.

HANOVER, 1884-1899. Ch. c., Hindoo—Bourbon Belle, by *Bonnie Scotland. 50-32-14-2, $118,887, consensus champion three-year-old colt, Belmont S., Lawrence Realization, etc. Won 17 consecutive races. Leading sire 1895-'98. Sire of Hamburg, Abe Frank, Blackstock, David Garrick, Halma, Handspun, Rhoda B., Tea's Over, The Commoner, Urania, Yankee.

HARRY BASSETT, 1868-1878. Ch. c., Lexington—Canary Bird, by *Albion. 36-23-6-3 $59,450, consensus champion three-year-old colt, Belmont S., Travers S., etc.

HASTINGS, 1893-1917. Br. c., Spendthrift—*Cinderella, by Tomahawk or Blue Ruin. 21-10-8-0, $16,340, Belmont S., Toboggan H., etc. Leading sire 1902, '08. Sire of Fair Play, Gunfire, Don Enrique, Flittergold, Masterman. Notorious for his savage temperament.

HAYNIE'S MARIA, 1808-unknown. Ch. f., *Diomed—Bellair mare, by Bellair. 9-8-1-0. Won at distances from four furlongs to four-mile heats. Famed as the nemesis of the stable of Andrew Jackson who said, "I could not beat her."

HELIOPOLIS, 1936-1959. B. c., Hyperion—Drift, by Swynford. 15-5-2-1, $71,216, Prince of Wales's S., Imperial Produce S., etc. Leading sire in 1950, '54. Sire of 53 stakes winners, including High Gun, Olympia, Helioscope, Grecian Queen, Parlo, Berlo, Aunt Jinny, Summer Tan, Princess Turia, Camargo. Broodmare sire of Riva Ridge, Summer Guest.

HENRY (SIR HENRY), 1819-1837. Ch. c., Sir Archy—Diomed mare, by *Diomed. Southern representative in first great North-South four-mile heat match race against American Eclipse at the Union Course, New York, in 1823. Won first heat, but beaten in second and third. Won four-mile and three-mile heat races, including 1823 Jockey Club Purse at Petersburg, Virginia. Sire of Post Boy, Decatur, Alice Grey.

HENRY OF NAVARRE, 1891-1917. Ch. c., Knight of Ellerslie—Moss Rose, by *The Ill-Used. 42-29-8-3, $68,985, champion three-year-old colt, Belmont S., Travers S., etc. Sire of Grave and Gay, Orienta.

HEROD, 1758-1780. B. c., Tartar—Cypron, by Blaze. 10-6-3-0, Match against Antinous, etc. Leading sire in England eight times. Sire of Highflyer, Florizel, Woodpecker, Bridget, Bagot, Maid Of The Oaks, Phenomenom. Tail-male line ancestor of The Tetrarch, Tourbillon, *Ambiorix, Ahonoora, Dr Devious (Ire), Indian Ridge.

HIGHFLYER, 1774-1793. B. c., Herod—Rachel, by Blank. 12-12-0-0, Grosvenor S., Great Subscription Race, etc. Leading sire in England a record 13 times, record 12 in succession. Sire of Sir Peter Teazle, Delpini, Huncamunca, Noble, Rockingham, Skyscraper, Maid Of All Work, Prunella.

HIGH GUN, 1951-1962. Br. c., *Heliopolis—Rocket Gun, by Brazado. 24-11-5-4, $486,025, champion three-year-old colt, champion handicap horse, Belmont S., Jockey Club Gold Cup, etc. Virtually sterile; sired only four foals.

HILL PRINCE, 1947-1970. B. c., *Princequillo—Hildene, by Bubbling Over. 30-17-5-4, $422,140, Horse of the Year in 1950, champion two- and three-year-old colt, champion handicap horse, Preakness S., Jockey Club Gold Cup, etc. Sire of 23 stakes winners, including Bayou, Levee, Royal Living, Middle Brother. Broodmare sire of Dark Mirage, Shuvee.

HILLSDALE, 1955-1972. B. c., Take Away—Johann, by Johnstown. 41-23-6-4, $646,935, Hollywood Gold Cup H., Californian S., etc. Sire of nine stakes winners, including Bravery II and Hi Q.

HINDOO, 1878-1901. B. c., Virgil—Florence, by Lexington. 35-30-3-2, $71,875, champion two- and three-year-old colt, Kentucky Derby, Travers S., etc. Won 18 consecutive races at two and three. Sire of Hanover, Buddhist, Hindoo Rose, Jim Gore, Sallie McClelland.

HIS MAJESTY, 1968-1995. B. c., *Ribot—Flower Bowl, by *Alibhai. 22-5-6-3, $99,430, Everglades S., Leading sire in 1982. Sire of 59 stakes winners, including Pleasant Colony, Tight Spot, Majesty's Prince, Cetewayo, Mehmet. Broodmare sire of Danehill, Dynaformer, Midway Lady, Risen Star. Brother to Graustark, half brother to Bowl of Flowers.

HOLY BULL, 1991- . Gr. c., Great Above—Sharon Brown, by Al Hattab. 16-13-0-0, $2,481,760, Horse of the Year in 1994, champion three-year-old male, Travers S. (G1), Metropolitan H. (G1), etc. Sire of more than 25 stakes winners, including Macho Uno, Giacomo.

HYPERION, 1930-1960. Ch. c., Gainsborough—Selene, by Chaucer. 13-9-1-2, $124,386, champion three-year-old in England, Epsom Derby, St. Leger S., etc. Leading sire in England six times; leading broodmare sire in England four times. Sire of *Alibhai, Aristophanes, Aureole, Godiva, Gulf Stream, *Heliopolis, High Hat, *Khaled, Owen Tudor, Pensive, Sun Chariot. Broodmare sire of Alycidon, *Aunt Edith II, *Carrozza, Citation, Nearctic, Pretense. Foundation sire of line that leads to *Forli, Star Kingdom, *Vaguely Noble, Marscay, Nodouble, Efisio.

IMP, 1894-1909. Br. f., Wagner—Fondling, by Fonso. 171-62-35-29, $70,069, champion older mare twice, Suburban H., etc. Immortalized in verse as "My Coal Black Lady."

IN REALITY, 1964-1989. B. c., Intentionally—My Dear Girl, by Rough'n Tumble. 27-14-9-2, $795,824. Pimlico Futurity, Florida Derby, Metropolitan H., etc. Sire of 81 stakes winners, including 28 graded stakes winners and champions Smile, Desert Vixen, and Known Fact.

INSIDE INFORMATION, 1991-. B. m., Private Account—Pure Profit, by Key to the Mint. 17-14-1-2, $1,641,806. Champion older female in 1995 and winner of that year's Breeders' Cup Distaff (G1) by a Breeders' Cup record 13½ lengths. Also won Spinster S. (G1), Ashland S. (G1), Ruffian H. (G1), Acorn S. (G1), etc. Dam of 2005 champion three-year-old filly Smuggler.

INVASOR (ARG), 2002- . B. h., Candy Stripes—Quendom (Arg), by Interprete. 12-11-0-0, $7,804,070. North American Horse of the Year in 2006 after season that culminated in Breeders' Cup Classic Powered by Dodge (G1) victory; also won the 2007 Emirates Airline Dubai World Cup (UAE-G1); Uruguayan Horse of the Year in 2005.

IROQUOIS, 1878-1899. B. c., *Leamington—Maggie B.B., by *Australian. 26-12-4-3, $99,707, champion three-year-old in England, Epsom Derby, St. Leger S., etc. First American-bred winner of the Epsom Derby in 1881. Leading sire in 1892. Sire of Tammany, Huron.

JAIPUR, 1959-1987. Dk. b. c., *Nasrullah—Rare Perfume, by Eight Thirty. 19-10-6-0, $618,926, champion three-year-old colt, Belmont S., Travers S., etc. Sire of Amber Rama, Mansingh, Pontifex.

JANUS (LITTLE JANUS), 1746-1780. Ch. c., Janus—Fox mare, by Fox. Won twice in England and once in the U.S. at four-mile heats. Sire of Meade's Celer, Clodius, Goode's Old Twigg. Early Colonial Thorough-

bred foundation sire and foundation sire of the original Virginia Quarter Horse.

JAY TRUMP, 1957-1988. Dk. b. or br. g., Tonga Prince—Be Trump, by *Bernborough. 29-13-5-2, Grand National Steeplechase H. in England, etc. Also won three Maryland Hunt Cups.

JIM DANDY, 1927-unknown. Ch. g., Jim Gaffney—Thunderbird, by *Star Shoot. 141-7-6-8, $49,570, Travers S., Grand Union Hotel S., etc. Upset Gallant Fox and Whichone in 1930 Travers S. at 100-to-1.

JOHN HENRY, 1975-2007. B. g., Ole Bob Bowers—Once Double, by Double Jay. 83-39-15-9, $6,591,860, Horse of the Year 1981, '83, champion grass male four times, champion older male in '81; Santa Anita H. (G1) twice, Jockey Club Gold Cup (G1), Oak Tree Invitational (G1) three times, Hollywood Invitational H. (G1) three times, etc.

JOHN P. GRIER, 1917-1943. Ch. c., Whisk Broom II—Wonder, by Disguise. 17-10-4-2, $37,006, Queens County H., Aqueduct H., etc. Sire of more than 25 stakes winners, including Boojum, El Chico, Jack High, White Lies. Pressed Man o' War to narrowest victory in 1920 Dwyer S.

JOHNSTOWN, 1936-1950. B. c., Jamestown—La France, by *Sir Gallahad III. 21-14-0-3, $169,315, Kentucky Derby, Belmont S., etc. Sire of Flood Town, Acoma. Broodmare sire of Nashua.

JOLLY ROGER, 1922-1948. Ch. g., Pennant—Lethe, by *All Gold. 49-18-9-9, $143,240, Grand National Steeplechase H. twice, Brook Stp. H., etc.

***KAYAK II**, 1935-1946. Dk. br. c., Congreve—Mosquita, by Your Majesty. 26-14-8-1, $213,205, champion handicap horse, Santa Anita H., Hollywood Gold Cup, etc. Shy breeder.

KELSO, 1957-1983. Dk. b. or br. g., Your Host—Maid of Flight, by Count Fleet. 63-39-12-2, $1,977,896, Horse of the Year 1960-'64, champion three-year-old male, champion older horse four times, handicap triple crown, Jockey Club Gold Cup five times, Woodward S. three times, etc. Only five-time Horse of the Year.

KENTUCKY, 1861-1875. B. c., Lexington—Magnolia, by *Glencoe. 23-21-0-0, $33,700, Travers S., Saratoga Cup twice, etc. Won 20 consecutive races; first winner of the Travers S. Sire of Nina, Woodbine. Along with Norfolk and Asteroid, one of three dominant sons of Lexington, called the "great triumvirate."

***KHALED**, 1943-1968. Br. c., Hyperion—Eclair, by Ethnarch. 12-6-1-1, $38,860, Middle Park S., Coventry S., etc. Sire of 61 stakes winners, including Swaps, Terrang, Going Abroad, New Policy, Correspondent, A Glitter, Bushel-n-Peck. Broodmare sire of Candy Spots, Outing Class, Prove It.

KINCSEM, 1874-unknown. B. f., Cambuscan—Waternymph, by Cotswold. 54-54-0-0, Goodwood Cup, etc. All-time leader by number of wins among unbeaten horses. Greatest horse ever bred in Hungary. Raced all over Europe and in England.

KING'S BISHOP, 1969-1981. B. c., Round Table—Spearfish, by Fleet Nasrullah. 28-11-4-3, $308,079, Carter H. (G2), Fall Highweight H. (G3), etc. Sire of 30 stakes winners, including King's Swan, Possible Mate, Queen to Conquer, Queen Lib, Bishop's Ring.

KINGSTON, 1884-1912. Br. c., Spendthrift—*Kapanga, by Victorious. 138-89-33-12, $140,195, First Special S., etc. Leading sire in 1900, '10. Sire of Novelty, Wild Mint, Lida B. Holds American record for most races won at 89.

KINGSTON TOWN, 1976-1991. Dk.b. or br. g.,

Bletchingly—Ada Hunter (Ger), by Andrea Mantegna. 42-32-6-2, $1,565,015, Horse of the Year in Australia, champion miler, champion older horse, W. S. Cox Plate (Aus-G1) three times, AJC Derby (Aus-G1), Sydney Cup (Aus-G1), etc. Greatest Australian racehorse of second half of 20th century.

KOTASHAAN (FR), 1988- . Dk. b. or br. c., Darshaan—Haute Autorite, by Elocutionist. 22-10-5-2, Horse of the Year in 1993, champion grass male, Breeders' Cup Turf (G1), Eddie Read H. (G1), etc. Exported to Japan in 1994.

LADY LIGHTFOOT, 1812-1834. Br. f., Sir Archy—Black Maria, by *Shark. Won at least 23 races, 15 at four-mile heats. Dam of Black Maria, Terror.

LADY'S SECRET, 1982-2003. Gr. f., Secretariat—Great Lady M., by Icecapade. 45-25-9-3, $3,021,325, Horse of the Year in 1986, champion older female, Breeders' Cup Distaff (G1), Whitney H. (G1), etc. All-time distaff leading earner at time of retirement.

LANDALUCE, 1980-1982. Dk. b. or br. f., Seattle Slew—Strip Poker, by Bold Bidder. 5-5-0-0, $372,365, champion two-year-old filly, Oak Leaf S. (G1), Del Mar Debutante S. (G2), etc. Died at two.

LA PREVOYANTE, 1970-1974. B. f., Buckpasser—Arctic Dancer, by Nearctic. 39-25-5-3, $572,417, champion two-year-old filly in U.S., Horse of the Year in Canada in 1972, champion two-year-old filly in Canada, champion older female in Canada, Frizette S., Spinaway S., etc. Won all 12 of her starts at two. Died at four.

***LA TROIENNE**, 1926-1954. B. f., *Teddy—Helene de Troie, by Helicon. 7-0-1-1, $146. Greatest American foundation mare of the 20th century. Dam of Bimelech, Black Helen. Foundation mare of family that includes Buckpasser, Easy Goer, Allez France, Affectionately, Busher, Glamour, Numbered Account, Private Account, Woodman, Bee Ann Mac, Autobiography, Cohoes, The Axe II, Big Hurry, Searching, Relaxing, Bridal Flower, Caerleon, Straight Deal, Glowing Tribute, Sea Hero, Lite Light, Go for Gin, Pleasant Tap, Princess Rooney, Prairie Bayou.

LECOMTE, 1850-1856. Ch. c., Boston—Reel, by *Glencoe. 16-11-5-0, $12,630, Jockey Club Purse, etc. Only horse to defeat Lexington. Sire of Umpire, Sherrod.

***L'ESCARGOT**, 1963-1984. Ch. g., Escart III—What a Daisy, by Grand Inquisitor. 63-14-15-8, $237,572, champion steeplechaser, Cheltenham Gold Cup Steeplechase H. twice, Meadow Brook Steeplechase H., etc.

LEXINGTON, 1850-1875. B. c., Boston—Alice Carneal, by *Sarpedon. 7-6-1-0, $56,600, Great State Post S., etc. Leading sire 1861-'74, '76, '78. Sire of Asteroid, Norfolk, Kentucky, Tom Ochiltree, Duke of Magenta, Tom Bowling, Harry Bassett, Sultana, Maiden, Florence, General Duke, Hira, Idlewild, Lida, Preakness, Salina, Ulrica, War Dance. Leading sire record 16 times, 14 in succession.

LONESOME GLORY, 1988-2002. Ch. g., Transworld—Stronghold (Fr), by Green Dancer. 44-24-5-6, $1,325,868, champion steeplechaser five times, Carolina Cup Hurdle S. twice, Colonial Cup Steeplechase S. twice, etc. First steeplechase millionaire.

LONGFELLOW, 1867-1893. Br. c., *Leamington—Nantura, by Brawner's Eclipse. 16-13-2-0, $11,200, Monmouth Cup twice, Saratoga Cup, etc. Leading sire in 1891. Sire of Freeland, The Bard, Thora, Longstreet, Leonatus, Riley.

LUKE BLACKBURN, 1877-1904. B. c., *Bonnie Scotland—Nevada, by Lexington. 39-25-6-2, $49,460,

Champion S., Kenner S., etc. Won 22 of 24 races at three. Sire of Proctor Knott.

LYPHARD, 1969-2005. B. c., Northern Dancer—Goofed, by *Court Martial. 12-6-1-0, $195,427, Prix Jacques le Marois, Prix de la Foret, etc. Leading sire in U.S. in 1986, leading sire in France 1978 and '79; leading broodmare sire in France in 1985 and '86. Sire of 115 stakes winners, including Dancing Brave, Manila, Three Troikas (Fr), Reine de Saba (Fr), Jolypha, Dancing Maid (Fr), Pharly, Bellypha (Ire), Sangue (Ire), Sabin, Al Nasr (Fr), Elliodor, Featherhill (Fr), Lypheor (GB), Skimble. Broodmare sire of Bering (GB), Groom Dancer, Hatoof.

MAD HATTER, 1916-1935. B. or br. c., Fair Play—Madcap, by *Rock Sand. 98-32-22-15, $194,525, consensus champion handicap horse, Jockey Club Gold Cup twice, Toboggan H., etc. Sire of 22 stakes winners, including Snowflake, The Nut.

MAGGIE B.B., 1867-1889. B. f., *Australian—Madeline, by Boston. 7-3-4-0, $2,950, Sequel S. Greatest American broodmare of 19th century. Dam of Iroquois, Harold, Jaconet, Pera, Panique, Red and Blue. Tail-female ancestor of family that includes Alanesian, Boldnesian, Lawrin, Idun, Top Flight, Whisk Broom II, Life's Magic, Bald Eagle, Dubai Millennium.

***MAHMOUD**, 1933-1962. Gr. c., *Blenheim II—Mah Mahal, by Gainsborough. 11-4-2-3, $85,413, champion three-year-old in England, Epsom Derby, Champagne S., etc. Leading sire in 1946; leading broodmare sire in 1957. Sire of 66 stakes winners, including The Axe II, Oil Capitol, Cohoes, First Flight, Vulcan's Forge, Mount Marcy, Adile, Snow Goose, Almahmoud, Happy Mood, Mahmoudess. Broodmare sire of Cosmah, Determine, *Gallant Man, *Grey Dawn II, Misty Morn, Silver Spoon, Your Host. Made the gray coat color popular in America.

MAIDEN, 1862-1880. B. f., Lexington—Kitty Clark, by *Glencoe. 15-5-8-3, $5,500, Travers S., Produce S., etc. Second Travers S. winner. Dam of Parole, sixth dam of Nearco.

MAJESTIC PRINCE, 1966-1981. Ch. c., Raise a Native—Gay Hostess, by *Royal Charger. 10-9-1-0, $414,200, Kentucky Derby, Preakness S., etc. Sire of 33 stakes winners, including Majestic Light, Coastal, Sensitive Prince, Eternal Prince.

MAKYBE DIVA, 1999-. B. m., Desert King—Tugela, by Riverman. 36-15-4-3, $10,767,186. 2005 Horse of the Year in Australia, Melbourne Cup (Aus-G1) three times, W. S. Cox Plate (Aus-G1), etc. Retired as world's leading female earner after winning record third Melbourne Cup.

MANILA, 1983-. B. h., Lyphard—Dona Ysidra, by *Le Fabuleux. 18-12-5-0, $2,692,799. Champion grass male in 1986, when he won the Breeders' Cup Turf (G1). Also won Arlington Million (G1), Turf Classic (G1), United Nations H. (G1) (twice), etc. Sire of Bien Bien; leading broodmare sire in Turkey in 2003.

MAN O' WAR, 1917-1947. Ch. c., Fair Play—Mahubah, by *Rock Sand. 21-20-1-0, $249,465, consensus champion two- and three-year-old colt, Belmont S., Travers S., etc. Leading sire in 1926. Sire of 62 stakes winners, including War Admiral, Crusader, American Flag, War Relic, Bateau, Scapa Flow, Edith Cavell, Maid at Arms, Florence Nightingale, Battleship, Clyde Van Dusen, Hard Tack. Broodmare sire of Blue Swords, Helioscope, Mata Hari, Pavot, Vagrancy. Tail-male ancestor of line that leads to In Reality, Tiznow. Still considered by many to be the greatest racehorse of all time.

MASKETTE, 1906-c.1930. B. f., Disguise—Biturica, by Hamburg. 17-12-3-0, $77,090, consensus champion two- and three-year-old filly, Futurity S., Alabama S., Matron S., Spinaway S., etc.

MATA HARI, 1931-1957. Br. f., Peter Hastings—War Woman, by Man o' War. 16-7-0-2, $66,699, consensus champion two- and three-year-old filly, Breeders' Futurity, Kentucky Jockey Club S., Illinois Derby, etc. Dam of Spy Song, Mr. Music.

MATCHEM, 1748-1781. B. c., Cade—Partner mare, by Partner. 8 wins, The Whip, etc. Leading sire three times in England. Sire of Conductor, Pantaloon, Alfred, Hollandaise, Tetotum. Male-line ancestor of Man o' War, In Reality, Tiznow, Hurry On, Sassafras (Fr).

MATE, 1928-1953. Ch. c., Prince Pal—Killashandra, by *Ambassador IV. 75-20-14-19, $301,810, Preakness S., American Derby, etc. Great rival of Equipoise, Twenty Grand. Sire of five stakes winners, including two-time champion steeplechaser Elkridge.

***MEDLEY**, 1776-1792. Gr. c., Gimcrack—Arminda, by Snap. 13 wins. Sire of Bellair, Calypso, Grey Diomed, Grey Medley, Lamplighter. Early American foundation sire.

***MESSENGER**, 1780-1808. Gr. c., Mambrino—Turf mare, by Turf. 10 wins, $7,365. Sire of Miller's Damsel, Tippoo Saib, Potomac, Bright Phoebus, Mambrino. Early American foundation sire; also foundation sire of the American Standardbred breed.

MIDDLEGROUND, 1947-1972. Ch. c., Bold Venture—Verguenza, by Chicaro. 15-6-6-2, $237,725, Kentucky Derby, Belmont S., Hopeful S., etc. Sire of seven stakes winners, including Resaca. Shy breeder.

MIESQUE, 1984- . B. f., Nureyev—Pasadoble, by Prove Out. 16-12-3-1, $2,070,163, champion grass female twice in U.S., champion two-year-old in France, champion miler in England, champion older mare in France, Breeders' Cup Mile (G1) twice, One Thousand Guineas (Eng-G1), etc. Dam of Kingmambo, East of the Moon, Miesque's Son, Moon Is Up.

MILL REEF, 1968-1986. B. c., Never Bend—Milan Mill, by *Princequillo. 14-12-2-0, $450,533, Horse of the Year in Europe, champion three-year-old in England and France, champion older horse in France, Epsom Derby, Prix de l'Arc de Triomphe, etc. Leading sire in England twice. Sire of 62 stakes winners, including Reference Point, Shirley Heights, Acamas, Glint of Gold, Ibn Bey (GB). Broodmare sire of Last Tycoon (Ire), Pentire. Tail-male ancestor of line that includes Darshaan, Dalakhani, Daylami (Ire).

MINESHAFT, 1999- . Dk.b. or br. c., A. P. Indy–Propectors Delite, by Mr. Prospector. 18-10-3-1, $2,283,402. Horse of the Year in 2003, champion older male, Jockey Club Gold Cup (G1), etc.

MISS WOODFORD, 1880-1899. Br. f., *Billet—Fancy Jane, by Neil Robinson. 48-37-2-1, $118,270, Alabama S., Spinaway S., Pimlico S., etc. First American horse to earn $100,000.

MOCCASIN, 1963-1986. Ch. f., Nantallah—*Rough Shod II, by Gold Bridge. 21-11-2-4, $388,075, Horse of the Year in 1965 Thoroughbred Racing Associations poll, champion two-year-old filly, Gardenia S., Test S., etc. Dam of Apalachee, Scuff, Flippers.

MODESTY, 1881-unknown. Ch. f., War Dance—Ballet, by Planet. 82-35-8-11, $49,135, Kentucky Oaks, American Derby, etc. First filly winner of the American Derby. Tail-female ancestor of family that includes Regret, Thunderer, First Fiddle.

MOLLIE MCCARTHY, 1873-unknown. B. f.,

Monday—Hennie Farrow, by Shamrock. 17-15-0-0, $18,750, Winter S., Garden City Cup, etc. One of the last great four-mile heat fillies.

MOM'S COMMAND, 1982-2007. Ch. f., Top Command—Star Mommy, by Pia Star. 16-11-2-1, $902,972, champion three-year-old filly, filly triple crown.

MONSIEUR TONSON, 1822-unknown. B. c., Pacolet—Madame Tonson, by Top Gallant. 12-11-0-0. Leading sire in 1834. Sire of Argyle. First horse bred west of the Appalachians to win in the East.

MORVICH, 1919-1946. Bl. c., Runnymede—Hymir, by Dr. Leggo. 16-12-2-1, $172,909, Kentucky Derby, Hopeful S., etc. First California-bred winner of the Kentucky Derby in 1922, won first 12 starts. Sire of 12 stakes winners.

MOTHER GOOSE, 1922-unknown. Br. f., *Chicle—Flying Witch, by Broomstick. 10-3-1-3, $72,755, consensus champion two-year-old filly, Futurity S. (defeated 28 others in a record field), Fashion S., etc. Dam of Arbitrator. Full sister to Whichone. Tail-female ancestor of family that includes Northern Dancer, Halo, Arctic Tern, Machiavellian, La Prevoyante, Tosmah, Danehill.

MR. PROSPECTOR, 1970-1999. B. c., Raise a Native—Gold Digger, by Nashua. 14-7-4-2, $112,171, Gravesend H., Whirlaway S., etc. Leading sire in 1987-'88; leading broodmare sire in 1997-2004. Sire of 180 stakes winners, including Forty Niner, Fusaichi Pegasus, Seeking the Gold, It's in the Air, Fappiano, Woodman, Gulch, Carson City, Conquistador Cielo, Gone West, Gold Beauty, Kingmambo, Machiavellian, Miswaki. Broodmare sire of Dayjur, Fasliyev, Hollywood Wildcat, Pulpit, Mineshaft.

MUMTAZ MAHAL, 1921-1945. Gr. f., The Tetrarch—Lady Josephine, by Sundridge. 10-7-2-0, $67,421, champion two-year-old, champion sprinter, Champagne S., Nunthorpe S., etc. Dam of Mirza II, Badruddin. Tail-female ancestor of *Nasrullah, *Royal Charger, Abernant, Petite Etoile, Shergar, Octagonal, Oh So Sharp (GB), *Migoli, Aliya, Risen Star, Left Bank, Kalamoun. Known as "the Flying Filly." Still considered by many the fastest filly ever to race in England.

MY CHARMER, 1969-1993. B. f., Poker—Fair Charmer, by Jet Action. 32-6-4-2, $34,133, Fair Grounds Oaks. Dam of Seattle Slew, Lomond, Seattle Dancer (record $13.1-million yearling).

MYRTLEWOOD, 1932-1950. B. f., Blue Larkspur—*Frizeur, by *Sweeper. 22-15-4-2, $40,620, champion sprinter, champion handicap mare, Ashland S., Hawthorne Sprint H., etc. Set five track records and equaled three. Dam of Durazna, Miss Dogwood. Foundation mare of family that includes Seattle Slew, Mr. Prospector, Myrtle Charm, Lomond, Typecast, Siberian Express, Highest Trump, Bahri, Ajina, Escena, Sewickley, Forestry, Chief Bearhart.

NASHUA, 1952-1982. B. c., *Nasrullah—Segula, by Johnstown. 30-22-4-1, $1,288,565, Horse of the Year in 1955, champion two- and three-year-old colt, Preakness S., Belmont S., Jockey Club Gold Cup twice, etc. Sire of 77 stakes winners, including Shuvee, Noble Nashua, Diplomat Way, Producer, Marshua, Bramalea, Bombay Duck, Good Manners, Nalee. Broodmare sire of Mr. Prospector, Roberto. First $1-million syndicated stallion.

***NASRULLAH**, 1940-1959. B. c., Nearco—Mumtaz Begum, by *Blenheim II. 10-5-1-2, $15,259, champion two-year-old colt in England, Champion S., Coventry S., etc. Leading sire in 1955-'56, '59-'60, '62 in U.S.; leading sire in England. Sire of 93 stakes winners, including Bold Ruler, Nashua, Never Bend, Nearula, *Musidora, Never Say Die, Jaipur, Bald Eagle, Red God, Delta, Grey Sovereign. Broodmare sire of Drumtop, Natashka, *Sovereign II, Talking Picture, Turkish Trousers. Tail-male ancestor of Bold Ruler, Never Bend, Blushing Groom (Fr), Caro (Ire) lines.

NATIVE DANCER, 1950-1967. Gr. c., Polynesian—Geisha, by Discovery. 22-21-1-0, $785,240, Horse of the Year in 1952, '54, champion two- and three-year-old colt, champion handicap horse, Belmont S., Preakness S., Travers S., Futurity S., etc. Sire of 43 stakes winners, including Raise a Native, Hula Dancer, Dan Cupid, Secret Step, Kauai King, Dancer's Image, Native Charger, Native Street, Exclusive Dancer. Broodmare sire of Northern Dancer, General Assembly, Icecapade, Ruffian. Founder of male line that includes Mr. Prospector, Alydar, *Sea-Bird, Forty Niner, Seeking the Gold, Woodman, Thunder Gulch.

NATIVE DIVER, 1959-1967. Br. g., Imbros—Fleet Diver, by Devil Diver. 81-37-7-12, $1,026,500, Hollywood Gold Cup three times, San Carlos H. twice, etc. Won 33 stakes. Became the first California-bred millionaire.

NEARCO, 1935-1957. B. c., Pharos—Nogara, by Havresac II. 14-14-0-0, $85,974, champion two- and three-year-old in Italy, Grand Prix de Paris, Derby Italiano, etc. Leading sire three times in England; leading broodmare sire three times in England. Sire of *Nasrullah, Dante, *Masaka, *Amerigo, Mossborough, Narrator, Nimbus, *Royal Charger, Sayajirao, Infatuation, *Malindi, Neasham Belle, Netherton Maid, *Rivaz. Broodmare sire of *Arctic Prince, Charlottesville, Saint Crespin III, Sheshoon, *Tulyar, *Vaguely Noble. Tail-male ancestor of Northern Dancer, Bold Ruler, Blushing Groom (Fr), Never Bend, Caro (Ire) male lines.

NEARCTIC, 1954-1973. Br. c., Nearco—*Lady Angela, by Hyperion. 47-21-5-3, $152,384, Horse of the Year in Canada in 1958, Michigan Mile, Saratoga Special S., Canadian Maturity, etc. Sire of 49 stakes winners, including Northern Dancer, Icecapade, Nonoalco, Briartic, Cool Reception, Cold Comfort, Cool Moon, Arctic Dancer, Christmas Wind. Broodmare sire of Kennedy Road, La Prevoyante.

NEEDLES, 1953-1984. B. c., Ponder—Noodle Soup, by Jack High. 21-11-3-3, $600,355, champion two- and three-year-old colt, Kentucky Derby, Belmont S., etc. Sire of 21 stakes winners, including Irish Rebellion. First Florida-bred winner of the Kentucky Derby.

NEJI, 1950-1982. Ch. g., *Hunters Moon IV—Accra, by Annapolis. 46-17-11-8, $270,694, champion steeplechaser three times, Temple Gwathmey Steeplechase H. twice, Grand National Steeplechase H. twice, etc.

NELLIE FLAG, 1932-1953. Ch. f., American Flag—Nellie Morse, by Luke McLuke. 22-6-5-1, $59,665, champion two-year-old filly, Kentucky Jockey Club S., Matron S., etc. Dam of Mar-Kell, Sunshine Nell, Nellie L. Foundation mare of family that includes Forego, Bold Forbes, Bet Twice, Lakeway, Mark-Ye-Well, Saratoga Six.

NELLIE MORSE, 1921-1941. B. f., Luke McLuke—La Venganza, by Abercorn. 34-7-9-3, $73,565, consensus champion three-year-old filly, Preakness S., Fashion S., etc. Dam of Nellie Flag, Count Morse.

NEVER SAY DIE, 1951-1975. Ch. c., *Nasrullah—Singing Grass, by War Admiral. 12-3-1-3, $89,200, champion three-year-old in England, Epsom Derby, St. Leger S., etc. Leading sire in England in 1962. Sire of 41 stakes winners, including Never Too Late, Saidam, Die Hard. Broodmare sire of 95 stakes winners. Second American-bred to win the Epsom Derby. First American-bred to lead English sire list.

NEXT MOVE, 1947-1968. Br. f., Bull Lea—Now What, by Chance Play. 46-17-11-3, $398,550, champion three-year-old filly, champion older mare, Coaching Club American Oaks, Beldame H. twice, etc. Dam of Good Move, Restless Native. Fourth dam of Peteski.

NIJINSKY II, 1967-1992. B. c., Northern Dancer—Flaming Page, by Bull Page. 13-11-2-0, $667,220, Horse of the Year in Europe in 1970, champion two- and three-year-old in England and Ireland, English Triple Crown, King George VI and Queen Elizabeth S., etc. Last winner of the English Triple Crown. Leading sire in England in 1986; leading broodmare sire in U.S. in 1993-'94. Sire of 155 stakes winners, including Caerleon, Lammtarra, Ferdinand, Ile de Bourbon, Sky Classic, Golden Fleece, Royal Academy, Green Dancer, Number, Javamine, Maplejinsky. Broodmare sire of more than 245 stakes winners, including Fantastic Light, Flawlessly, Forest Flower, Heavenly Prize, Java Gold, Rubiano, Sky Beauty.

NODOUBLE, 1965-1990. Ch. c., *Noholme II—AblaJay, by Double Jay. 42-13-11-5, $846,749, champion handicap horse twice, Santa Anita H., Metropolitan H., etc. Leading sire in 1981. Sire of 91 stakes winners, including Overskate, Mairzy Doates, Coolawin, Chain Store. Broodmare sire of 89 stakes winners, including Sky Classic, Regal Classic.

***NOOR**, 1945-1974. Br. c., *Nasrullah—Queen of Baghdad, by *Bahram. 31-12-5-3, $356,940, champion handicap horse, Santa Anita H., Hollywood Gold Cup H., etc. Sire of Yours, Flutterby, Noureddin. Broodmare sire of Dancer's Image, Delta Judge. Defeated Citation four times at five.

NORFOLK, 1861-1890. B. c., Lexington—Novice, by *Glencoe. 5-5-0-0, $10,550, Jersey Derby, etc. Sire of Emperor of Norfolk, El Rio Rey, Flood, Ralston. Member of sire Lexington's "great triumvirate" with Asteroid and Kentucky.

NORTHERN DANCER, 1961-1990. B. c. Nearctic—Natalma, by Native Dancer. 18-14-2-2, $580,647, champion three-year-old colt, Horse of the Year in 1964 in Canada, champion two-year-old colt in Canada, Kentucky Derby, Preakness S., etc. Leading sire in U.S. in 1971, leading broodmare sire in U.S. in 1991; leading sire in England four times. Sire of 146 stakes winners, including Nijinsky II, Sadler's Wells, Nureyev, The Minstrel, El Gran Senor, Storm Bird, Lyphard, Northern Taste, Northfields, Unfuwain, Northernette, Fanfreluche, Shareef Dancer, Try My Best, Be My Guest, Cool Mood, Dixieland Band. Broodmare sire of more than 240 stakes winners, including Arazi, Eillo, L'Alezane, L'Enjoleur, Narita Brian, Noverre, Rhythm, Ryafan, Southern Halo.

NUREYEV, 1977-2001. B. c., Northern Dancer—Special, by *Forli. 3-2-0-0, $42,522, champion miler in France, Prix Thomas Bryon (Fr-G3), Prix Djebel. Disqualified from victory in 1980 Two Thousand Guineas (Eng-G1). Leading sire twice in France. Sire of more than 135 stakes winners, including Miesque, Peintre Celebre, Theatrical (Ire), Soviet Star, Sonic Lady, Fasliyev. Broodmare sire of more than 135 stakes winners, including Desert King, East of the Moon, Kingmambo, Peteski, Zabeel.

OEDIPUS, 1946-1978. Br. g., Blue Larkspur—Be Like Mom, by *Sickle. 58-14-12-9, $132,405, champion steeplechaser three times, Grand National Steeplechase H., Brook Steeplechase H. twice, etc.

OLD ROSEBUD, 1911-1922. B. g., Uncle—Ivory Bells, by Himyar. 80-40-13-8, $74,729, Kentucky Derby, Carter H., Flash S., etc. Set Kentucky Derby record that stood for 17 years.

OMAHA, 1932-1959. Ch. c., Gallant Fox—Flambino, by *Wrack. 22-9-7-2, $154,705, champion three-year-old colt, Triple Crown, Dwyer S., Classic S., etc. Sire of seven stakes winners, including Prevaricator. Broodmare sire of Summer Tan.

ONE COUNT, 1949-1966. Dk. br. c., Count Fleet—Ace Card, by Case Ace. 23-9-3-3, $245,625, Horse of the Year in 1952, champion three-year-old colt, Belmont S., Travers S., etc. Sire of 12 stakes winners, including Airmans Guide. Broodmare sire of Fit to Fight, Obeah.

***ORMONDE**, 1883-1904. B. c., Bend Or—Lily Agnes, by Macaroni. 16-16-0-0, $138,340, Champion at two, three, and four in England, English Triple Crown. Sire of Orme, Ormondale, *Gold Finch, Ossary. Progressively sterile. Tail-male ancestor of *Teddy line. Widely considered the greatest English racehorse of 19th century; he was a roarer.

OUIJA BOARD (GB), 2001- . Dk. b. or br. m., Cape Cross (Ire)—Selection Board, by Welsh Pageant. 22-10-3-5, $6,312,552. Two-time Cartier Award winner as European Horse of the Year, 2004 and '06, and champion turf female in North America in those years after winning the '04 and '06 Breeders' Cup Filly and Mare Turf (G1); also won the Vodafone Epsom Oaks (Eng-G1) and Darley Irish Oaks (Ire-G1).

PAN ZARETA, 1910-1918. Ch. f., Abe Frank—Caddie Griffith, by Rancocas. 151-76-31-21, $39,082, Juarez H., Rio Grande H., etc. Won carrying 140 pounds or more five times. Died at eight and is buried in infield at Fair Grounds. Holds record for most wins by American distaffer.

***PAPYRUS**, 1920-1941. Br. c., Tracery—Miss Matty, by Marcovil. 18-9-5-1, $110,068, Epsom Derby, Chester Vase, etc. First Epsom Derby winner to race in the U.S. in international match race against Zev in 1923. Sire of Barbara Burrini, *Cosquilla, *Osiris II, Honey Buzzard.

PARLO, 1951-1978. Ch. f., *Heliopolis—Fairy Palace, by Pilate. 34-8-6-3, $309,240, champion three-year-old filly, champion handicap mare twice, Alabama S., Beldame H., etc. Tail-female ancestor of Arts and Letters, Silverbulletday, Saudi Poetry, Zaccio, Waquoit.

PAROLE, 1873-1903. Br. g., *Leamington—Maiden, by Lexington. 127-59-22-16, $82,111, Saratoga Cup, Epsom Gold Cup (in England), etc. Leading American money winner 1881-1885.

PASEANA (ARG), 1987-2006. B. f., Ahmad—Pasiflin (Arg), by Flintham. 36-19-10-2, $3,317,427, champion older female twice, Breeders' Cup Distaff (G1), Milady H. (G1) twice, Apple Blossom H. (G1) twice, etc.

PAVOT, 1942-1975. Br. c., Case Ace—Coquelicot, by Man o' War. 32-14-6-2, $373,365, undefeated champion two-year-old colt, Belmont S., Futurity S., etc. Sire of 14 stakes winners, including Andre, Cigar Maid.

PEPPERS PRIDE, 2003- . Dk. b. or br. f., Desert God—Lady Pepper, by Chili Pepper Pie. 16-16-0-0, $861,665. Undefeated winner of record-tying 16 consecutive races, 12 stakes wins.

PERSONAL ENSIGN, 1984- . B. f., Private Account—Grecian Banner, by Hoist the Flag. 13-13-0-0, $1,679,880, champion older female, Breeders' Cup Distaff (G1), Beldame S. (G1) twice, etc. Broodmare of the Year in 1996. Dam of My Flag, Miner's Mark, Traditionally; grandam of Storm Flag Flying.

PETER PAN, 1904-1933. B. c., Commando—*Cinderella, by Hermit. 17-10-3-1, $115,450, Belmont S.,

History of Racing — Notable Horses

Hopeful S., etc. Sire of Black Toney, Pennant, Peter Hastings, Tryster, Prudery, Vexatious, Panoply, Wendy.

PEYTONA, 1839-1858. Ch. f., *Glencoe—Giantess, by *Leviathan. 8-6-1-0, $62,400, Peyton S., North-South Match, etc. One-time leading American money earner; defeated Fashion in last great North-South match race.

PHALARIS, 1913-1931. B. c., Polymelus—Bromus, by Sainfoin. 24-16-2-1, $26,376, Challenge S. twice, Stud Produce S., etc. Leading sire twice in England. Sire of 65 stakes winners, including Pharos, Fairway, Colorado, Manna, Fair Isle, *Sickle, *Pharamond II, Chatelaine. Broodmare sire of *Easton, Godiva, Mid-day Sun, Picture Play. Tail-male ancestor of *Nasrullah, Northern Dancer, Native Dancer, Buckpasser sire lines.

PHARIS, 1936-1957. Br. c., Pharos—Carissima, by Clarissimus. 3-3-0 0, $47,531, champion three-year-old in France, Prix du Jockey-Club (French Derby), Grand Prix de Paris, etc. Leading sire in France four times. Sire of *Ardan, Auriban, Philius, Dynamiter, *Priam II, Asterblute. Greatest horse bred in France in first half of 20th century. Racing career cut short by World War II; confiscated by the Nazis during the war and spent five years in Germany.

***PHAR LAP**, 1926-1932. Ch. g., Night Raid—Entreaty, by Winkie. 51-37-3-2, $305,921, AJC Derby, Victoria Derby, W. S. Cox Plate twice; won Agua Caliente H. in only start in North America; died shortly after under mysterious circumstances. Considered Australia's greatest racehorse.

PLANET, 1855-1875. Ch. c., Revenue—Nina, by Boston. 31-27-4-0, $69,700, Great Post S. twice, etc. Sire of Katy Pease, Hubbard, Ballet. Replaced Peytona as America's leading money earner.

PLAUDIT, 1895-1919 B. c., Himyar—*Cinderella, by Tomahawk or Blue Ruin. 20-8-5-0, $32,715, Kentucky Derby, Champagne S., etc. Sire of King James, Casuarina, Rosa Mundi, Spoonful. Tail-male ancestor of Dr. Fager, Holy Bull, Giacomo.

POCAHONTAS, 1837-1870. B. f., *Glencoe—Marpessa, by Muley. 9-0-3-0, $0. Greatest English broodmare of 19th century, dam of Stockwell, King Tom, Rataplan. Ancestress of modern families that include foundation mares Rosy Legend, Kizil-Kourgan, Traverse, Traffic Court, Segula as well as racehorses and sires Dante, Sayajirao, *Ksar, *Kantar, Traffic Judge, Hasty Road, Nashua, Louis Quatorze.

POINT GIVEN, 1998- . Ch. c., Thunder Gulch—Turko's Turn, by Turkoman. 13-9-3-0, $3,968,500, Horse of the Year in 2001, champion three-year-old male, Belmont S. (G1), Preakness S. (G1), etc.

POT8O'S, 1773-unknown. Ch. c., Eclipse—Sportsmistress, by Sportsman. 30 wins in England, Craven S., Jockey Club Plate three times, etc. Sire of Champion, Coriander, Mandane, Waxy. Tail-male line ancestor of Phalaris, Hyperion, Blandford, Domino lines.

PREAKNESS, 1867-1881. B. c., Lexington—Bayleaf, by *Yorkshire. 39-18-11-5, $43,679, Dinner Party S., Saratoga Cup, etc. Sire in England of Fiddler, Piccadilly.

PRECISIONIST, 1981-2006. Ch. c., Crozier—Excellently, by *Forli. 46-20-10-4, $3,485,398, champion sprinter, Breeders' Cup Sprint (G1), Woodward S. (G1), etc. Virtually sterile. Sired only four foals.

PRETTY POLLY, 1901-1931. Ch. f., Gallinule—Admiration, by Saraband. 24-22-2-0, $187,780, champion two- and three-year-old in England, Epsom Oaks, St. Leger S., Coronation Cup twice, etc. Dam of Molly Desmond, Polly Flinders. Tail-female ancestor of Abadan, Arabella, Brigadier Gerard, Carroll House, *Daumier,

Donatello II, Flute Enchantee, Flying Water, Luthier, Marwell, Nearctic, Northern Taste, Premonition, Psidium, St. Paddy, Supreme Court, Swain (Ire). Widely regarded as the greatest English racemare of all time; known as "the peerless Pretty Polly."

PRIMONETTA, 1958-1993. Ch. f., Swaps—Banquet Bell, by Polynesian. 25-17-2-2, $306,690, champion older mare, Alabama S., Spinster S. twice, etc. Broodmare of the Year in 1978; dam of Prince Thou Art, Maud Muller, Cum Laude Laurie, Grenfall. Sister to Chateaugay.

***PRINCEQUILLO**, 1940-1964. B. c., Prince Rose—*Cosquilla, by *Papyrus. 33-12-5-7, $96,550, Jockey Club Gold Cup, Saratoga Cup, etc. Leading sire 1957-'58; leading broodmare sire 1966-'70, '72, '73, '76. Sire of 65 stakes winners, including Round Table, Dedicate, Prince John, How, Quill, Hill Prince, Misty Morn, Princessnesian, Discipline. Broodmare sire of Bold Lad, *Comtesse de Loir, Fort Marcy, Key to the Mint, Kris S., Mill Reef, Secretariat, Sham, Sir Gaylord.

PRINCESS DOREEN, 1921-1952. B. f., *Spanish Prince II—Lady Doreen, by Ogden. 94-34-15-17, $174,754, Coaching Club American Oaks, Saratoga H., etc. Dam of Miss Doreen. Tail-female ancestor of Brown Bess, Caller I. D.

PRINCESS ROONEY, 1980- . Gr. f., Verbatim—Parrish Princess, by Drone. 21-17-2-1, $1,343,339, champion older female, Breeders' Cup Distaff (G1), Spinster S. (G1), etc.

PRIORESS, 1853-1868. B. f., *Sovereign—Reel, by *Glencoe. 24-10-1-3, $22,637, Cesarewitch H., two Queen's Plates, etc. First American-bred to win in England, victorious in a runoff after a dead heat in the 1857 Cesarewitch H.

PROCTOR KNOTT, 1886-unknown. Ch. g., Luke Blackburn—Tallapoosa, by *Great Tom. 26-11-6-4, $80,040, Futurity S., Junior Champion S., 2nd Kentucky Derby, etc. First winner of the Futurity Stakes (now at Belmont Park) in 1888, the race that swung the pendulum of American racing toward two-year-old speed because of its large purse.

PRUDERY, 1918-1930. B. f., Peter Pan—Polly Flinders, by Burgomaster. 22-7-6-5, $47,625, consensus champion two-year-old filly, Alabama S., Spinaway S., etc. Dam of Whiskery, Victorian, Halcyon. Tail-female ancestor of Taylor's Special.

QUESTIONNAIRE, 1927-1950. B. c., Sting—Miss Puzzle, by Disguise. 45-19-8-4, $89,611, Metropolitan H., Brooklyn H., etc. Sire of 24 stakes winners, including Requested, Free For All, Carolyn A., Hash, Stefanita, Third Degree. Tail-male line ancestor of Dr. Fager, Holy Bull, Giacomo.

RAISE A NATIVE, 1961-1988. Ch. c., Native Dancer—Raise You, by Case Ace. 4-4-0-0, $45,955, champion two-year-old colt, Juvenile S., Great American S. Sire of 78 stakes winners, including Alydar, Mr. Prospector, Exclusive Native, Majestic Prince, Laomedonte, Crowned Prince, Native Royalty, Marshua's Dancer, Native Partner, Where You Lead. Broodmare sire of Ajdal, Meadowlake, Slightly Dangerous.

REAL DELIGHT, 1949-1969. B. f., Bull Lea—Blue Delight, by Blue Larkspur. 15-12-1-0, $261,822, champion three-year-old filly, champion handicap mare, Coaching Club American Oaks, Kentucky Oaks, etc. Dam of Plum Cake, No Fooling, Spring Sunshine. Foundation mare of family that includes Alydar, Our Mims, Codex, Rich Cream, Christmas Bonus, Grand Slam, Sugar and Spice, Christmas Past.

REAL QUIET, 1995- . B. c., Quiet American—

Really Blue, by Believe It. 20-6-5-6, $3,271,802, champion three-year-old male, Kentucky Derby (G1), Preakness S. (G1), Hollywood Gold Cup S. (G1), etc. Came within a nose of winning Triple Crown in 1998 Belmont S. (G1). Sire of No Place Like It.

REEL, 1838-unknown. Gr. f., *Glencoe—*Gallopade, by Catton. 8-7-1-0. Dam of Lecomte, Prioress, Starke, War Dance. Tail-female ancestor of modern family that includes Two Lea, Tim Tam, Miz Clementine, Best Turn, Chris Evert, Chief's Crown, Winning Colors.

REGRET, 1912-1934. Ch. f., Broomstick—Jersey Lightning, by Hamburg. 11-9-1-0, $35,093, Kentucky Derby, Hopeful S., etc. First filly to win the Kentucky Derby. Tail-female ancestor of family that includes First Fiddle, Divine Comedy.

REIGH COUNT, 1925-1948. Ch. c., *Sunreigh—*Contessina, by Count Schomberg. 27-12-4-0, $178,170, champion two- and three-year-old colt, Kentucky Derby, Jockey Club Gold Cup S., Coronation Cup (in England), etc. Sire of 22 stakes winners, including Count Fleet, Triplicate, Count Arthur. Broodmare sire of Gallahadion.

REVENUE, 1843-unknown. B. c., *Trustee—Rosalie Somers, by Sir Charles. 21-16-5-0. Jockey Club Purse, Proprietor's Purse, etc. Leading sire in 1860. Sire of Planet, Fanny Washington, Revolver.

***RIBOT**, 1952-1972. B. c., Tenerani—Romanella, by El Greco. 16-16-0-0, $288,648, champion at two, three, and four in Italy, champion at four in England and France, Prix de l'Arc de Triomphe twice, King George VI and Queen Elizabeth S., etc. Leading sire three times in England. Sire of 65 stakes winners, including Arts and Letters, Tom Rolfe, Graustark, His Majesty, Ragusa, Molvedo, *Prince Royal II. Broodmare sire of more than 100 stakes winners, including Cannonade, Cascapedia, Majestic Light, Grandsire of Pleasant Colony.

RIVA RIDGE, 1969-1985. B. c., First Landing—Iberia, by *Heliopolis. 30-17-3-1, $1,111,497, champion two-year-old male, champion handicap male, Kentucky Derby, Belmont S., etc. Sire of 29 stakes winners, including Tap Shoes, Rivalero, Blitey. Broodmare sire of more than 45 stakes winners, including Life At the Top.

RIVERMAN, 1969-1999. B. c., Never Bend—River Lady, by Prince John. 8-5-2-1, $223,960, Poule d'Essai des Poulains (French Two Thousand Guineas), etc. Leading sire in France in 1980-'81. Sire of 128 stakes winners, including Irish River (Fr), Triptych, Bahri, Gold River (Fr), Detroit (Fr), Imperfect Circle, Korveya. Broodmare sire of Bosra Sham, Carnegie (Ire), Erhaab, Hector Protector, Highest Honor (Fr), Saint Cyrien, Spinning World.

ROAMER, 1911-1919. B. g., *Knight Errant—*Rose Tree II, by Bona Vista. 98-39-26-9, $98,828, Travers S., Carter H., Saratoga H. three times, etc.

ROBERTO, 1969-1988. B. c., Hail to Reason—Bramalea, by Nashua. 14-7-4-0, $332,272, champion three-year-old in England in 1972, champion two-year-old in Ireland in 1971, Epsom Derby, etc. Sire of 85 stakes winners, including Sunshine Forever, Brian's Time, Plenty of Grace, Dynaformer, and Red Ransom. Broodmare sire of more than 145 stakes winners, including Blushing K. D., Commander in Chief, Warning (GB).

ROCK OF GIBRALTAR (Ire), 1999- . B. c., Danehill—Offshore Boom, by Be My Guest. 13-10-2-0, $1,888,048, Horse of the Year in Europe, champion three-year-old colt, highweighted colt at three on International Classification at 7-9½ furlongs, Two Thousand Guineas (Eng-G1), Sussex S. (Eng-G1), Prix du Moulin de Longchamp (Fr-G1), etc. Won record seven Group 1 races in succession in 2001-'02.

ROSEBEN, 1901-1918. B. g., *Ben Strome—Rose Leaf, by Duke of Montrose. 111-52-25-12, $75,110, Carter H., Manhattan H. twice, etc. Great sprinter who won 14 races under 140 pounds or more, known as "the big train."

ROUGH'N TUMBLE, 1948-1968. B. c., Free For All—Roused, by *Bull Dog. 16-4-5-4, $126,980, Santa Anita Derby, Primer S., etc. Sire of 24 stakes winners, including Dr. Fager, My Dear Girl, Flag Raiser, Ruffled Feathers, Minnesota Mac, Treasure Chest. Florida foundation sire.

***ROUGH SHOD II**, 1944-1965. B. f., Gold Bridge—Dalmary, by Blandford. 7-1-1-1, $1,306. Dam of Moccasin, Ridan, Lt. Stevens, Gambetta, Thong. Foundation mare of family that includes Sadler's Wells, Nureyev, Thatch, Gamely, Drumtop, Fairy King, King Pellinore, El Condor Pasa, Number, Bienamado.

ROUND TABLE, 1954-1987. B. c., *Princequillo—*Knight's Daughter, by Sir Cosmo. 66-43-8-5, $1,749,869, Horse of the Year in 1958, champion grass horse three times, champion handicap horse twice, Santa Anita H., Hollywood Gold Cup H., etc. Leading sire in 1972. Sire of 83 stakes winners, including Baldric, Apalachee, Flirting Around, Targowice, Royal Glint, King Pellinore, Drumtop, Knightly Manner, Advocator, King's Bishop, Artaius, Dancealot, Foreseer, Poker, Tell. Broodmare sire of 125 stakes winners, including Bowl Game, Caerleon, Hidden Lake, Outstandingly, Topsider.

***ROYAL CHARGER**, 1942-1961. Ch. c., Nearco—Sun Princess by Solario. 20-6-7-2, $20,291, Queen Anne S., Ayr Gold Cup, etc. Sire of 54 stakes winners, including *Turn-to, Mongo, *Royal Serenade, Royal Native, Idun, Royal Orbit, Gilles de Retz, Happy Laughter, Royal Palm, *Banri an Oir. Broodmare sire of Majestic Prince, Tudor Queen. Tail-male ancestor of Roberto, Halo lines.

RUFFIAN, 1972-1975. Dk. b. or br. f., Reviewer—Shenanigans, by Native Dancer. 11-10-0-0, $313,428, champion two- and three-year-old filly, filly triple crown, Spinaway S. (G1), etc. Broke down in match race with Foolish Pleasure and euthanized when she reinjured leg after surgery. Buried in infield at Belmont Park.

RUTHLESS, 1864-1876. B. f., *Eclipse—Barbarity, by *Simoom. 11-7-4-0, $11,000, Belmont S., Travers S., etc. Won first Belmont S. Best of five high-class sisters out of Barbarity nicknamed "the barbarous battalion."

SABIN, 1980- . Ch. f., Lyphard—Beaconaire, by *Vaguely Noble. 25-18-0-2, $1,098,341, Yellow Ribbon Invitational S. (G1), etc. Dam of Sabina, Al Sabin.

SADLER'S WELLS, 1981- . B. c., Northern Dancer—Fairy Bridge, by Bold Reason. 11-6-3-0, $713,690, Irish Two Thousand Guineas (Ire-G1), Eclipse S. (Eng-G1), etc. Leading sire in England-Ireland 14 times. Sire of more than 295 stakes winners, including Galileo (Ire), High Chaparral (Ire), In the Wings (GB), Salsabil (Ire), Old Vic, Northern Spur (Ire), El Prado (Ire), Montjeu (Ire), Carnegie (Ire), Barathea (Ire), Imagine, King of Kings (Ire), Fort Wood. Broodmare sire of at least 199 stakes winners. Pensioned in 2008.

SAFELY KEPT, 1986- . B. f., Horatius—Safely Home, by Winning Hit. 31-24-2-3, $2,194,206, champion sprinter, Breeders' Cup Sprint (G1), Test S. (G1), etc.

SAINT LIAM, 2000-2006. B. h., Saint Ballado—Quiet Dance, by Quiet American. 20-9-6-1, 2005 Horse of the Year and champion older male, Breeders' Cup Classic

(G1), Stephen Foster H. (G1), Donn H. (G1), Woodward S. (G1), etc.

SALVATOR, 1886-1909. Ch. c., *Prince Charlie—Salina, by Lexington. 19-16-1-1, $113,240, consensus champion three-year-old, Suburban H., Lawrence Realization, etc. Sire of Salvation. Subject of the Ella Wheeler Wilcox poem "How Salvator Won."

SARAZEN, 1921-1940. Ch. g., High Time—Rush Box, by Box. 55-27-2-6, $225,000, Champagne S., Carter H., Dixie H. twice, etc. Defeated *Epinard in third race of the International Series of 1924.

SCEPTRE, 1899-1927. Br. f., Persimmon—Ornament, by Bend Or. 25-13-4-4, $192,544, champion three-year-old, champion older horse, Epsom Oaks, Two Thousand Guineas, One Thousand Guineas, St. Leger S., etc. Dam of Curia, Grosvenor. Tail-female ancestor of Buchan, Commanche Run, Craig an Eran, Relko, Reliance, *Match II, *Noor, *St. Germans, Sunny Jane, Torbido. One of two fillies to win four of the five English classics.

*SEA-BIRD, 1962-1973. Ch. c., Dan Cupid—Sicalade, by Sicambre. 8-7-1-0, $645,283, Horse of the Year in France and England, Epsom Derby, Prix de l'Arc de Triomphe, etc. Sire of 33 stakes winners, including Allez France, Little Current, Gyr, Arctic Tern. Broodmare sire of Alydar's Best, Assert (Ire), Bikala, Miss Oceana. Considered France's greatest racehorse.

SEABISCUIT, 1933-1947. B. c., Hard Tack—Swing On, by Whisk Broom II. 89-33-15-13, $437,730, Horse of the Year in 1938, champion handicap male twice, Pimlico Special, Santa Anita H., etc. Sire of four stakes winners, including Sea Swallow.

SEARCHING, 1952-1973. B. f., War Admiral—Big Hurry, by Black Toney. 89-25-14-16, $327,381, Maskette H., Diana H. twice, etc. Dam of Affectionately, Priceless Gem, Admiring. Foundation mare of family that includes Allez France, Sea Hero, Lite Light, Personality, Al Mamoon.

SEATTLE SLEW, 1974-2002. Dk. b. or br. c., Bold Reasoning—My Charmer, by Poker. 17-14-2-0, $1,208,726, Horse of the Year in 1977, champion two- and three-year-old colt, champion older horse, Triple Crown, Woodward S. (G1), etc. Leading sire in 1984; leading broodmare sire 1995-'96. Sire of more than 110 stakes winners, including A.P. Indy, Swale, Slew o' Gold, Surfside, Capote, Landaluce, Vindication, Slew City Slew, Taiki Blizzard, Lakeway, Honest Lady, General Meeting, Avenue of Flags, Slewvescent, Slewacide. Broodmare sire of more than 135 stakes winners, including Cigar, Agnes World, Escena, Lemon Drop Kid, Golden Attraction, Seeking the Pearl. Only horse to win Triple Crown while undefeated.

SECRETARIAT, 1970-1989. Ch. c., Bold Ruler—Somethingroyal, by *Princequillo. 21-16-3-1, $1,316,808, Horse of the Year in 1972-'73, champion two- and three-year-old male, champion grass horse, Triple Crown, Marlboro Cup H., etc. Leading broodmare sire in 1992. Sire of 56 stakes winners, including Lady's Secret, Risen Star, Medaille d'Or, Terlingua, General Assembly, Tinners Way, Weekend Surprise, Secrettame, Six Crowns. Broodmare sire of more than 160 stakes winners, including A.P. Indy, Chief's Crown, Dehere, Gone West, Secreto, Storm Cat, Summer Squall.

*SELIMA, 1745-1766. B. f., Godolphin Arabian—Shireborn mare, by Hobgoblin. 2-2-0-0, $10,200, Great Intercolonial Match Race with Tryal. Dam of Ariel, Selim, Ebony, Bellair, Lightfoot's Partner. Tail-female ancestor of family that includes Hanover, Inspector B.,

Peytona, Foxhall, The Vid, Pirate's Revenge, Cherokee Run.

SENSATION, 1877-1899. Br. c., *Leamington—Susan Beane, by Lexington. 8-8-0-0, $20,250, champion two-year-old colt, Flash S., Nursery S., etc. Sire of Democrat.

SERENA'S SONG, 1992- . B. f., Rahy—Imagining, by Northfields. 38-18-11-3, $3,283,388, champion three-year-old filly, Mother Goose S. (G1), Beldame S. (G1), etc. Leading North American money-earning female at time of retirement. Dam of Serena's Tune, Sophisticat, Grand Reward.

SHIRLEY JONES, 1956-1978. B. f., Double Jay—L'Omelette, by *Alibhai. 49-18-9-5, $282,313, Test S., Maskette H., etc.

SHUVEE, 1966-1986. Ch. f., Nashua—Levee, by Hill Prince. 44-16-10-6, $890,445, champion handicap mare, champion older female, filly triple crown, Jockey Club Gold Cup twice, etc. Dam of Tom Swift, Shukey, Benefice.

*SICKLE, 1924-1943. Br. c., Phalaris—Selene, by Chaucer. 10-3-4-2, $23,629, Prince of Wales's S., etc. Leading sire in 1936, '38. Sire of 41 stakes winners, including Stagehand, Brevity, Unbreakable, Star Pilot, Cravat, Reaping Reward, Misty Isle, Jabot. Broodmare sire of Bornastar, Counterpoint, Dan Cupid, How, Social Outcast. Tail-male ancestor of Native Dancer sire line.

SILENT WITNESS, 1999- . B. g., El Moxie—Jade Tiara, by Bureaucracy. 20-18-1-1, $5,885,654, Hong Kong Horse of the Year and champion sprinter in 2004-'05, Sprinters S., Hong Kong Sprint (HK-G1) twice, etc. Australian-bred won first 17 races, 2002-'05, and never defeated in 18 starts at 1,400 meters (6.96 furlongs) or shorter through 2005.

SILVERBULLETDAY, 1996- . B. f., Silver Deputy—Rokeby Rose, by Tom Rolfe. 23-15-3-1, $3,093,207, champion two- and three-year-old filly, Breeders' Cup Juvenile Fillies (G1), Kentucky Oaks (G1), etc.

SILVER CHARM, 1994- . Gr. or ro. c., Silver Buck—Bonnie's Poker, by Poker. 24-12-7-2, $6,944,369, champion three-year-old male, Kentucky Derby (G1), Preakness S. (G1), Dubai World Cup (UAE-G1), etc.

SILVER SPOON, 1956-1978. Ch. f., Citation—Silver Fog, by *Mahmoud. 27-13-3-4, $313,930, champion three-year-old filly, Santa Anita Derby, Milady H., etc. Dam of Inca Queen. Tail-female ancestor of family that includes Catinca, Metfield.

SIR ARCHY, 1805-1833. Ch. c., *Diomed—*Castianira, by Rockingham. 7-4-1-0, Post S. Leading Colonial sire. Sire of Sir Charles, Timoleon, Flirtilla, Bertrand, Henry, Kosciusko, Lady Lightfoot, Sumpter, Reality. Oldest member of the Racing Hall of Fame.

SIR BARTON, 1916-1937. Ch. c., *Star Shoot—Lady Sterling, by Hanover. 31-13-6-5, $116,857, consensus champion three-year-old colt, Triple Crown, Saratoga H., etc. First winner of the American Triple Crown. Sire of seven stakes winners, including Easter Stockings.

*SIR GALLAHAD III, 1920-1949. B. c., *Teddy—Plucky Liege, by Spearmint. 24-11-3-3, $17,009, Poule d'Essai des Poulains (French Two Thousand Guineas), Prix Jacques le Marois, match race with *Epinard, etc. Leading sire 1930, '33-'34, '40; leading broodmare sire '39, '43-'52, '55. Sire of 56 stakes winners, including Gallant Fox, Gallahadion, High Quest, Vagrancy, Foxbrough, Fighting Fox, Hoop, Jr., Roman. Broodmare sire of 180 stakes winners, including Beaugay, Challedon, *Galatea II, Gallorette, Johnstown, Royal Native. Greatest American broodmare sire of the 20th century. First major American stallion syndication.

SKIP AWAY, 1993- . Gr. or ro. c., Skip Trial—Ingot Way, by Diplomat Way. 38-18-10-6, $9,616,360, Horse of the Year in 1998, champion three-year-old male, champion older male twice, Breeders' Cup Classic (G1), Jockey Club Gold Cup (G1) twice, etc. Sire of 11 stakes winners.

SKY BEAUTY, 1990- 2004. B. f., Blushing Groom (Fr)—Maplejinsky, by Nijinsky II. 21-15-2-2, $1,336,000, champion older female, filly triple crown, Alabama S. (G1), Ruffian H. (G1), etc.

SLEW O' GOLD, 1980-2007. B. c., Seattle Slew—Alluvial, by Buckpasser. 21-12-5-1, $3,533,534, champion three-year-old male, champion older male, Jockey Club Gold Cup (G1) twice, Woodward S. (G1) twice, etc. Sire of 29 stakes winners, including Golden Opinion, Gorgeous, Dramatic Gold, Thirty Six Red, Awe Inspiring. Broodmare sire of Kona Gold.

SMARTY JONES, 2001-. Ch. h., Elusive Quality—I'll Get Along, by Smile. 9-8-1-0, $7,613,155, champion three-year-old male, Kentucky Derby (G1), Preakness S. (G1), Arkansas Derby (G2), etc. First undefeated horse since Seattle Slew to win the Kentucky Derby; received $5-million bonus for winning Derby and two Oaklawn Park races.

SOMETHINGROYAL, 1952-1983. B. f., *Princequillo—Imperatrice, by Caruso. 1-0-0-0, $0. Broodmare of the Year in 1973. Dam of Secretariat, Sir Gaylord, First Family, Syrian Sea, Somethingfabulous. Foundation mare of family that includes Saratoga Dew, Alada, John Cherry, Personal Business.

SPECTACULAR BID, 1976-2003. Gr. or ro. c., Bold Bidder—Spectacular, by Promised Land. 30-26-2-1, $2,781,608, Horse of the Year in 1980, champion two- and three-year-old male, champion older male, Kentucky Derby (G1), Preakness S. (G1), etc. Sire of more than 40 stakes winners, including Lotus Pool, Double Feint, Spectacular Love. Broodmare sire of more than 85 stakes winners.

SPEND A BUCK, 1982-2002. B. c., Buckaroo—Belle de Jour, by Speak John. 15-10-3-2, $4,220,689, Horse of the Year in 1985, champion three-year-old male, Kentucky Derby (G1), Monmouth H. (G1), etc. Sire of more than 30 stakes winners, including Antespend, Hard Buck (Brz). Exported to Brazil in 1997.

SPENDTHRIFT, 1876-1900. Ch. c., *Australian—Aerolite, by Lexington. 13-10-5-0, $27,250, Belmont S., Jersey Derby, etc. Sire of Kingston, Hastings, Lamplighter. Tail-male ancestor of line that leads to Fair Play, Man o' War, War Admiral, In Reality, Tiznow.

SPINAWAY, 1878-1904. Ch. f., *Leamington—Megara, by *Eclipse. 9-7-2-0, $16,225, champion two-year-old filly, Hopeful S., Juvenile S., etc. Dam of Lazzarone. Tail-female ancestor of family that includes Giant's Causeway, Tanya, Floradora, Star Pilot, By Land By Sea, Gummo, Spearfish, Gaily, King's Bishop.

SPY SONG, 1943-1973. Br. c., Balladier—Mata Hari, by Peter Hastings. 36-15-9-4, $206,325, Arlington Futurity, Clang H., etc. Sire of 28 stakes winners, including Crimson Satan, Sly Pola, Sari's Song. Broodmare sire of 91 stakes winners, including Blue Tom, Faraway Son, Liloy (Fr), Singh.

***STAR SHOOT**, 1898-1919. B. c., Isinglass—Astrology, by Hermit. 10-3-1-1, $34,747 in England, National Breeders' Produce S., etc. Leading sire 1911-'12, '16-'17, '19; leading broodmare sire 1924-'26, '28-'29. Sire of Sir Barton, Grey Lag, Uncle, Wistful, Daylight Saving, Mindful, Priscilla. Broodmare sire of Blazes, Crusader, Gusto, Jack High. Sired a record 27 juvenile winners in 1916 that stood for 70 years.

STOCKWELL, 1849-1870. Ch. c., The Baron—Pocahontas, by *Glencoe. 16-11-3-0, $48,457, champion three-year-old in England, Two Thousand Guineas, St. Leger S., etc. Leading sire in England seven times. Sire of Doncaster, Achievement, Caller Ou, Cantiniere, Chevisaunce, Lord Lyon, Regalia, St. Albans, The Marquis. Known as the "Emperor of Stallions." Tail-male ancestor of Phalaris, *Teddy male lines.

STRAIGHT DEAL, 1962-1982. B. f., Hail to Reason—No Fiddling, by King Cole. 99-21-21-9, $733,020, champion handicap mare, Delaware H., Santa Margarita H., etc. Dam of Desiree, Reminiscing.

STREET SENSE, 2004- . Dk. b. or br. c., Street Cry (Ire)—Bedazzle, by Dixieland Band. 8-4-2-2, $2,958,200. First Breeders' Cup Juvenile (G1) winner to win the Kentucky Derby (G1); first juvenile male champion since Spectacular Bid to win the Derby; won the 2006 Bessemer Trust Breeders' Cup Juvenile by a record ten lengths.

ST. SIMON, 1881-1908. Br. c., Galopin—St. Angela, by King Tom. 9-9-0-0, $23,121, Ascot Gold Cup, Epsom Gold Cup, Goodwood Cup, etc. Leading sire in England nine times. Sire of Persimmon, Diamond Jubilee, St. Frusquin, Rabelais, Chaucer, Memoir, La Fleche. Tail-male ancestor of *Ribot, *Princequillo male lines.

STYMIE, 1941-1962. Ch. c., Equestrian—Stop Watch, by On Watch. 131-35-33-28, $918,485, champion handicap horse, Metropolitan H. twice, Whitney S., etc. Sire of 12 stakes winners, including Rare Treat, Joe Jones, Paper Tiger. Broodmare sire of Regal Gleam, What a Treat. Retired as world's leading money earner in 1950.

SUN BEAU, 1925-1944. B. c., *Sun Briar—Beautiful Lady, by Fair Play. 74-33-12-10, $376,744, consensus champion handicap horse three times, Hawthorne Gold Cup three times, Aqueduct H., etc. Sire of six stakes winners, including Sun Lover. Leading money earner at his retirement in 1931.

***SUN BRIAR**, 1915-1943. B. c., Sundridge—*Sweet Briar II, by St. Frusquin. 22-8-4-5, $74,355, consensus champion two-year-old colt, Travers S., Hopeful S., etc. Sire of more than 30 stakes winners, including Sun Beau, Pompey, Firethorn.

SUNDAY SILENCE, 1986-2002. Dk. b. or br. c., Halo—Wishing Well, by Understanding. 14-9-5-0, $4,968,554, Horse of the Year in 1989, champion three-year-old male, Kentucky Derby (G1), Preakness S. (G1), Breeders' Cup Classic (G1), etc. Leading sire in Japan 1995-2004. Sire of more than 135 stakes winners, including Air Shakur, Dance Partner, Marvelous Sunday, Dance in the Dark, Bubble Gum Fellow, Fuji Kiseki, Special Week, Stay Gold, Genuine, Tayasu Tsuyoshi. All-time leading sire by earnings, exceeding $530-million.

SUNLINE, 1995. B. f., Desert Sun (GB)—Songline, by Western Symphony. 48-32-9-3, $6,625,105, Horse of the Year three times in Australia, Cox Plate (Aus-G1) twice, Flight S. (Aus-G1), Doncaster H. (Aus-G1) twice, etc.

SUSAN'S GIRL, 1969-1988. B. f., Quadrangle—Quaze, by *Quibu. 63-29-14-11, $1,251,668, champion three-year-old filly, champion older female twice, Spinster S. (G1) twice, Delaware H. (G1) twice, etc. Dam of Copelan, Paramount Jet.

SWALE, 1981-1984. Dk. b. or br. c., Seattle Slew—Tuerta, by *Forli. 14-9-2-2, $1,583,660, champion three-year-old male, Kentucky Derby (G1), Belmont S. (G1), etc. Died eight days after winning Belmont Stakes.

SWAPS, 1952-1972. Ch. c., *Khaled—Iron Reward, by *Beau Pere. 25-19-2-2, $848,900, Horse of the Year in 1956, champion handicap horse, Kentucky Derby, Hollywood Gold Cup H., etc. Sire of 35 stakes winners, including Affectionately, Chateaugay, Primonetta, No Robbery. Broodmare sire of Best Turn, Fall Aspen, Numbered Account, Personality.

SWOON'S SON, 1953-1977. B. c., The Doge—Swoon, by Sweep Like. 51-30-10-3, $970,605, American Derby, Arlington Classic, etc. Sire of 22 stakes winners, including Chris Evert, Loom, Mr. Washington. Won 22 stakes.

SWORD DANCER, 1956-1984. Ch. c., Sunglow—Highland Fling, by By Jimminy. 39-15-7-4, $829,610, Horse of the Year in 1959, champion three-year-old colt, champion handicap horse, Belmont S., Jockey Club Gold Cup, etc. Sire of 15 stakes winners, including Damascus, Lady Pitt.

SYSONBY, 1902-1906. B. c., *Melton—*Optime, by Orme. 15-14-0-1, $184,438, champion two- and three-year-old colt, Metropolitan H., Saratoga Special, etc. Died at four.

TANYA, 1902-1929. Ch. f., *Meddler—Handspun, by Hanover. 10-6-1-1, $73,127, Belmont S., Hopeful S., Spinaway S., etc. Second filly to win the Belmont S.

TA WEE, 1966-1980. Dk. b. or br. f., Intentionally—Aspidistra, by Better Self. 21-15-2-1, $284,941, champion sprinter twice, Vosburgh H., Fall Highweight H. twice, etc. Dam of Great Above, Tax Holiday, Entropy, Tweak.

***TEDDY**, 1913-1936. B. c., Ajax—Rondeau, by Bay Ronald. 8-5-1-2, Gran Premio de San Sebastian, Prix des Trois Ans, etc. Leading sire in France twice. Sire of *Sir Gallahad III, *Bull Dog, *La Troienne, *Ortello, Aethelstan, Asterus, Rose of England, Brumeux, Case Ace, Sun Teddy, Anne de Bretagne, Anna Bolena, Assignation, Boxeuse, Coeur a Coeur, La Moqueuse. Tail-male ancestor of line leading to Damascus, Private Account, Captain Steve.

TEMPTED, 1955-unknown. Ch. f., *Half Crown—Enchanted Eve, by Lovely Night. 45-18-4-9, $330,760, champion handicap mare, Alabama S., Ladies H., etc. Dam of Lead Me On.

TEN BROECK, 1872-1887. B. c., *Phaeton—Fanny Holton, by Lexington. 30-23-3-1, $27,550, Phoenix Hotel S., Louisville Cup, etc. Sire of Jim Gray. Once held every major American record from one to four miles.

TENNY, 1886-1909. B. c., *Rayon d'Or—Belle of Maywood, by Hunter's Lexington. 65-25-15-12, $88,442, Brooklyn H., First Special S., etc. Defeated Racing Hall of Fame members Firenze, Hanover, and Kingston, but consistently beaten by Racing Hall of Famer Salvator.

THE TETRARCH, 1911-1935. Gr. c., Roi Herode—Vahren, by Bona Vista. 7-7-0-0, $55,206, Champagne S., Coventry S., etc. Leading sire in England in 1924. Sire of Mumtaz Mahal, Tetratema, Salmon Trout, *Stefan the Great, Caligula, Polemarch, Paola, Snow Maiden, *The Satrap. Called "the Spotted Wonder"; revived the Herod male line in England and popularized the gray coat color.

THE VERY ONE, 1975-1992. B. f., One for All—*Veruschka, by Venture. 71-22-12-9, $1,104,623, Santa Barbara H. (G1), Black Helen H. (G2), etc.

THUNDER GULCH, 1992- . Ch. c., Gulch—Line of Thunder, by Storm Bird. 16-9-2-2, $2,915,086, champion three-year-old male, Kentucky Derby (G1), Belmont S. (G1), etc. Sire of more than 35 stakes winners, including Point Given, Spain, Tweedside.

TIMOLEON, 1813-1836. Ch. c., Sir Archy—Saltram mare, by *Saltram. 16-14-0-0. Sire of Boston, Hotspur, Sally Walker, Saluda, Omega, Washington.

TIM TAM, 1955-1982. Dk. b. c., Tom Fool—Two Lea, by Bull Lea. 14-10-1-2, $467,475, champion three-year-old colt, Kentucky Derby, Preakness S., etc. Sire of 14 stakes winners, including Tosmah, Timmy Lad, Nancy Jr. Broodmare sire of Before Dawn, Davona Dale, Known Fact, Mac Diarmida, Tentam.

TIPPITY WITCHET, 1915-unknown. B. g., Broomstick—*Lady Frivoles, by St. Simon. 266-78-52-42, $88,241. Raced to age 14, beginning his career in stakes but descending to the claiming ranks.

TIZNOW, 1997- . B. c., Cee's Tizzy—Cee's Song, by Seattle Song. 15-8-4-2, $6,427,830, Horse of the Year in 2000, champion three-year-old colt, champion older male, Breeders' Cup Classic (G1) twice, Santa Anita H. (G1), etc. Only dual winner of the Breeders' Cup Classic. Sire of champion Folklore.

T.M. OPERA O, 1996- . Ch. c., Opera House (GB)—Once Wed, by Blushing Groom (Fr). 26-14-6-3, $16,200,337, Horse of the Year in Japan, champion three-year-old colt in Japan, Japan Cup (Jpn-G1), etc. World's leading money-winning Thoroughbred.

TOM BOWLING, 1870-unknown. B. c., Lexington—Lucy Fowler, by *Albion. 17-14-3-0, $35,000, champion three-year-old colt, Travers S., Jersey Derby, Jerome S., Monmouth Cup, etc. Sire of General Monroe.

TOM FOOL, 1949-1976. B. c., Menow—Gaga, by *Bull Dog. 30-21-7-1, $570,165, Horse of the Year in 1953, champion two-year-old colt, champion handicap horse, champion sprinter, handicap triple crown, Futurity S., etc. Leading broodmare sire in England in 1965. Sire of 36 stakes winners, including Buckpasser, Tim Tam, Silly Season, Tompion, Dunce, Jester, Funloving, Sweet Folly, Dinner Partner, Dunce Cap II. Broodmare sire of 90 stakes winners, including Foolish Pleasure, Hatchet Man, Late Bloomer, *Meadow Court, Stop the Music, Majesty's Prince.

TOM ROLFE, 1962-1989. B. c., *Ribot—Pocahontas, by Roman. 32-16-5-5, $671,297, champion three-year-old colt, Preakness S., American Derby-ntr, etc. Sire of 49 stakes winners, including Hoist the Flag, Run the Gantlet, Droll Role, Bowl Game. Broodmare sire of more than 105 stakes winners, including Diminuendo, Environment Friend, Forty Niner, Life's Magic, Niniski, Notebook, Silverbulletday.

TOP FLIGHT, 1929-1949. Dk. br. f., *Dis Donc—Flyatit, by Peter Pan. 16-12-0-0, $275,900, champion two- and three-year-old filly, Coaching Club American Oaks, Futurity S., etc. Dam of Flight Command. Tail-female ancestor of family that includes Watch Fob, Sikeston. World's leading money-winning female at time of retirement.

TOSMAH, 1961-1992. B. f., Tim Tam—Cosmah, by Cosmic Bomb. 39-23-6-2, $612,588, champion two- and three-year-old filly, champion handicap mare, Frizette S., Beldame S., etc. Dam of La Guidecca.

TREMONT, 1884-1901. Bl. c., Virgil—Ann Fief, by Alarm. 13-13-0-0, $39,135, champion two-year-old colt, Great American S., etc.

***TURN-TO**, 1951-1973. B. c., *Royal Charger—*Source Sucree, by Admiral Drake. 8-6-1-1, $280,032, Garden State S., Flamingo S., etc. Sire of 25 stakes winners, including First Landing, Hail to Reason, Sir Gaylord, Best Turn, Cyane. Broodmare sire of 63 stakes winners, including Ack Ack, Bessarabian, Chinook Pass. Male line ancestor of Halo, Roberto lines.

T. V. LARK, 1957-1975. B. c., *Indian Hemp—Miss Larksfly, by Heelfly. 72-19-13-6, $902,194, champion grass horse, Washington, D.C., International S., United Nations H., etc. Leading sire in 1974. Sire of 53 stakes win-

ners, including Quack, T. V. Commercial, Pink Pigeon, Buffalo Lark, Golden Don, T. V. Vixen, Romeo. Broodmare sire of 85 stakes winners, including Bates Motel, Chris Evert.

TWENTY GRAND, 1928-1948. B. c., *St. Germans—Bonus, by *All Gold. 23-14-4-3, $261,790, Horse of the Year in 1931, champion three-year-old colt, Kentucky Derby, Belmont S., etc. Sterile at stud.

TWILIGHT TEAR, 1941-1954. B. f., Bull Lea—Lady Lark, by Blue Larkspur. 24-18-2-2, $202,165, Horse of the Year in 1944, champion two- and three-year-old filly, champion handicap mare, Coaching Club American Oaks, Pimlico Special, etc. Dam of A Gleam, Bardstown, Coiner. Tail-female ancestor of family that includes Before Dawn, Gleaming, A Glitter.

TWO LEA, 1946-1973. B. f., Bull Lea—Two Bob, by The Porter. 26-15-6-3, $309,250, champion three-year-old filly, champion handicap mare, Hollywood Gold Cup H., Santa Margarita H., etc. Dam of Tim Tam, On-and-On, Pied d'Or.

ULTIMUS, 1906-1921. Ch c., Commando—Running Stream, by Domino. Unraced. Sire of Luke McLuke, High Time, High Cloud, Infinite, Stimulus, Supremus. Broodmare sire of Bold Venture, Case Ace, Flying Heels. One of the very few unraced successful sires; inbred 2x2 to Domino.

UNBRIDLED, 1987-2001. B. c., Fappiano—Gana Facil, by *Le Fabuleux. 24-8-6-6, $4,489,475, champion three-year-old male, Kentucky Derby (G1), Breeders' Cup Classic (G1), etc. Sire of more than 40 stakes winners, including Banshee Breeze, Anees, Unbridled's Song, Halfbridled, Empire Maker, Red Bullet.

UPSET, 1917-1941. Ch. c., Whisk Broom II—Pankhurst, by *Voter. 17-5-7-1, $37,504, Sanford S., etc. Only horse to defeat Man o' War. Sire of 11 stakes winners, including Misstep.

VAGRANCY, 1939-1964. Dk. b. f., *Sir Gallahad III—Valkyr, by Man o' War. 42-15-8-8, $102,480, champion three-year-old filly, champion handicap mare, Coaching Club American Oaks, Alabama S., etc. Dam of Black Tarquin, Vulcania. Tail-female ancestor of family that includes Ferdinand, Fiddle Isle, Natashka, Tallahto, Hidden Light, Truly Bound, Anees.

VANDAL, 1850-1872. B. c., *Glencoe—Tranby mare, by *Tranby. 6-4-1-1. Sire of Vandalite, Survivor, Virgil, Capitola, Vicksburg, Mollie Jackson, Ella D.

VERTEX, 1954-1981. Ch. c., The Rhymer—Kanace, by Case Ace. 25-17-3-1, $453,424, Pimlico Special, Gulfstream Park H., etc. Sire of 25 stakes winners, including Lucky Debonair, Top Knight, Vertee. Broodmare sire of 50 stakes winners.

VICTORIA PARK, 1957-1985. B. c., Chop Chop—Victoriana, by Windfields. 19-10-4-2, $250,076, Horse of the Year in Canada, Queen's Plate, Remsen S., etc. Sire of 25 stakes winners, including Kennedy Road, Solometeor, Victorian Era, Floral Victory. Broodmare sire of Northern Taste, The Minstrel.

***VOTER**, 1894-unknown. Ch. c., Friar's Balsam—*Mavourneen, by Barcaldine. 49-26-6-7, $34,217, Metropolitan H., Toboggan H., etc. Sire of Ballot, Runnymede, Curiosity, Inaugural, Pankhurst.

WAGNER, 1834-1862. Ch. c., Sir Charles—Maria West, by Marion. 18-12-6-0, $34,150, Jockey Club Purse, etc. Sire of Starke, Lavender, Rhynodyne, Neil Robinson, Endorser.

WANDA, 1882-1905. Ch. f., *Mortemer—Minnie Minor, by Lexington. 24-12-8-0, $58,160, Monmouth Oaks, Champion Stallion S., etc. Tail-female ancestor of family that includes Swaps, Iron Liege, Flying Ebony, Creme dela Creme, Cascapedia, Althea, Green Desert, *Durbar II, Kauai King.

WAR ADMIRAL, 1934-1959. Br. c., Man o' War—Brushup, by Sweep. 26-21-3-1, $273,240, Horse of the Year in 1937, champion three-year-old colt, Triple Crown, Jockey Club Gold Cup, Whitney S., etc. Leading sire in 1945; leading broodmare sire '62, '64. Sire of 40 stakes winners, including Busher, Blue Peter, Searching, Admiral Vee, Busanda, War Date, Blue Banner, Mr. Busher, Bee Mac, Striking. Broodmare sire of 112 stakes winners, including Affectionately, Better Self, Buckpasser, Crafty Admiral, Gun Bow, Hoist the Flag, Iron Liege, Never Say Die, Priceless Gem.

WAR RELIC, 1938-1963. Ch. c., Man o' War—Friar's Carse, by Friar Rock. 20-9-4-2, $89,495, Massachusetts H., Kenner S., etc. Sire of Battlefield, Intent, Relic, Missile. Broodmare sire of Hail to All, My Dear Girl. Tail-male ancestor of male line that includes Tiznow, In Reality, Relaunch.

WEEKEND SURPRISE, 1980-2001. B. f., Secretariat—Lassie Dear, by Buckpasser. 31-7-5-10, $402,892, Golden Rod S. (G3), Schuylerville S. (G3), etc. Broodmare of the Year in 1992. Dam of A.P. Indy, Summer Squall, Welcome Surprise, Honor Grades.

WHICHONE, 1927-1944. Br. c., *Chicle—Flying Witch, by Broomstick. 14-10-2-1, $192,705, consensus champion two-year-old colt, Futurity S., Champagne S., etc. Sire of ten stakes winners, including Handcuff, Today. Rival of Gallant Fox; first winner of $100,000 first-prize purse in 1929 Futurity. Broodmare sire of Lord Boswell, Vulcan's Forge. Full brother to Mother Goose.

WHIRLAWAY, 1938-1953. Ch. c., *Blenheim II—Dustwhirl, by Sweep. 60-32-15-9, $561,161, Horse of the Year in 1941-'42, champion two- and three-year-old colt, champion handicap horse, Triple Crown, Jockey Club Gold Cup, Travers S., etc. Sire of 18 stakes winners, including Scattered, Kurun, Whirl Some. Broodmare sire of Lady Pitt, Beau Prince. Exported to France in 1950.

WHISK BROOM II, 1907-1928. Ch. c., Broomstick—Audience, by Sir Dixon. 26-10-8-0, $38,776, first winner of America's handicap triple crown, Victoria Cup (in England), etc. Sire of Whiskery, Diavolo, Victorian, Whiskaway, John P. Grier, Broomshot, Swing On, Upset, Weno. Broodmare sire of Seabiscuit, Double Jay.

WINNING COLORS, 1985-2008. Ro. f., Caro (Ire)—All Rainbows, by Bold Hour. 19-8-3-1, $1,526,837, champion three-year-old filly, Kentucky Derby (G1), Santa Anita Derby (G1), etc. Third filly to win Kentucky Derby.

YO TAMBIEN, 1889-1896. Ch. f., Joe Hooker—Marian, by Malcolm. 73-44-11-9, $89,480, Garfield Park Derby, etc. Half sister to Emperor of Norfolk, El Rio Rey.

YOUR HOST, 1947-1961. Ch. c., *Alibhai—*Boudoir II, by *Mahmoud. 23-13-5-2, $384,795, Santa Anita Derby, Del Mar Futurity, etc. Sire of 16 stakes winners, including Kelso, Social Climber, Windy Sands. Broodmare sire of Tosho Boy, Terry's Secret, Ruken.

ZACCIO, 1976-2007. Ch. g., *Lorenzaccio—Delray Dancer, by Chateaugay. 42-22-7-3, $288,124, champion steeplechaser three times, Colonial Cup International Steeplechase twice, Temple Gwathmey Steeplechase H., etc.

ZEV, 1920-1943. Br. c., The Finn—Miss Kearney, by *Planudes. 43-23-8-5, $313,639, champion two- and three-year-old colt, Kentucky Derby, Belmont S., International Race S., etc. Sire of two stakes winners. Defeated *Papyrus in first international race in U.S. Retired as world's leading money earner.

Profiles of Oldest Notable Horses
Listed alphabetically by age

MERRICK (38), 1903-1941. Ch. g., *Golden Garter—Bianca, by Wildidle. 205-61-40-24, $26,785. Won Pontchartrain Selling S. Died on March 13, 1941, at Merrick Place in Lexington, where he was buried.

BARGAIN DAY (37), 1965-2002. B. h., Prove It—Special Price, by *Toulouse Lautrec. 43-13-3-7, $146,575. Won 1970 Bing Crosby H. at Del Mar in course record 1:27.60 for 7½ furlongs on grass. Sire of 24 stakes winners, including 1⅛-mile course-record-setter Hoedown's Day (1:38.40). Died of natural causes on June 24, 2002, at Van Mar Farm, in Galt, California.

LYPHARD (36), 1969-2005. See Notable Horses in Racing in this chapter.

PRIMONETTA (35), 1958-1993. See Notable Horses in Racing in this chapter.

STOP THE MUSIC (35), 1970-2005. B. h., Hail to Reason—Bebopper, by Tom Fool. 30-11-10-4, $448,922. Won 1972 Champagne S. (on disqualification of Secretariat), 1973 Dwyer S. (G2). Sire of 46 stakes winners, including champion and classic winner Temperence Hill and Grade 1 winners Music Merci, Dontstop Themusic, Cure the Blues, etc. Broodmare sire of at least 86 stakes winners including Giacomo. Pensioned at Gainesway, in Lexington.

***GALLANT MAN (34)**, 1954-1988. See Notable Horses in Racing in this chapter.

***GREEN VALLEY II (34)**, 1967-2001. Dk. b. or br. m., *Val de Loir—Sly Pola, by Spy Song. Unraced. Dam of six stakes winners, including French classic winner and leading sire Green Dancer and graded/group winners Val Danseur and Ercolano. Died on July 22, 2001, at Haras de Saint-Leonard, in France.

IMPERATRICE (34), 1938-1972. Dk. b. or br. m., Caruso—Cinquepace, by Brown Bud. 31-11-7-2, $37,255. Won the 1941 Test S., 1942 Fall Highweight H. Dam of six stakes winners, including Scattered, Squared Away, and Imperium. Grandam of Secretariat. Euthanized in October 1972 at The Meadow, in Doswell, Virginia, where she was buried.

Oldest Notable Horses of All Time

Age	Horse, YOB Sex, Sire	Record	Earnings
39	Mercian Queen, 1929 m., by Mercian King	No record	
38	Merrick, 1903 g., by *Golden Garter	205-61-40-24	$ 26,785
37	Bargain Day, 1965 h., by Prove It	43-13-3-7	146,575
36	Lyphard, 1969 h., by Northern Dancer	12-6-1-0	195,402
35	*Daylight Prince, 1973 g., by Hail the Prince*	*64-9-14-5*	*80,636*
	Mary's Fantasy, 1973 m., by Olympian King	*36-8-5-4*	*82,093*
	Plains Gal, 1962 m., by *Nirgal	24-1-0-3	2,300
	Primonetta, 1958 m., by Swaps	25-17-2-2	306,690
	Stop the Music, 1970 h., by Hail to Reason	30-11-10-4	448,922
	Young Langford, 1840 h., by *Langford	No record	
34	Eternal, 1971 m., by Raimondo	Unraced	
	Float Me, 1903 g., by Menow	122-19-21-17	72,055
	*Gallant Man, 1954 h., by *Migoli	26-14-4-1	510,355
	*Green Valley II, 1967 m., by *Val de Loir	Unraced	
	Imperatrice, 1938 m., by Caruso	31-11-7-2	37,255
	*Janus, 1746 h., by Janus	3 wins	
	Kenilworth, 1898 h., by *Sir Modred	163, 61 wins	31,270
	Lucky Spell, 1971 m., by Lucky Mel	69-12-8-11	253,655
	Nicosia, 1972 m., by Gallant Romeo	19-8-2-0	254,495
	Raja Baba, 1968 h., by Bold Ruler	41-7-12-9	123,287
	Vieux Manoir, 1947 h., by Brantome	No record	
33	American Eclipse, 1814 h., by Duroc	8-8-0-0	56,700
	Arwon, 1973 g., by Aritzo	11-4-5-2	206,436
	Ballot, 1904 h., by *Voter	38-20-6-6	154,545
	Became a Lark, 1974 m., by T. V. Lark	30-6-3-9	135,550
	Billy Barton, 1918 g., by *Huon	No record	43,040
	Brown Berry, 1960 m., by Mount Marcy	29-6-3-3	53,625
	Chateaucreek, 1970 m., by Chateaugay	29-6-1-2	24,203
	Cormorant, 1974 h., by His Majesty	12-8-2-0	243,174
	Count Fleet, 1940 h., by Reigh Count	21-16-4-1	250,300
	Dogoon, 1952 h., by The Doge	74-28-15-4	220,360
	Ga Hai, 1971 h., by Determine	43-13-2-5	257,548
	Green Finger, 1958 m., by Better Self	18-1-3-1	5,935
	Halo Dandy, 1974 g., by Menelek	No record	
	Inseparable, 1945 g., by Unbreakable	135-22-26-22	239,542
	*Inspirado, 1964 h., by Souepi	37-4-10-5	9,932
	Lucky Mel, 1954 h., by Olympia	12-7-0-1	106,450
	Matchem, 1748 h., by Cade	8 wins	
	Miss Debbie Lee, 1966 m., by Accomplish	14-1-5-1	6,152
	Mr. Leader, 1966 h., by Hail to Reason	25-10-3-3	219,803
	Napalm, 1963 m., by *Nilo	17-2-2-5	9,575
	Northern Taste, 1971 h., by Northern Dancer	23-5-3-4	154,177
	Old Friendship, 1783 h., by Apollo	No record	
	Pocahontas, 1837 m., by *Glencoe	9-0-3-0	0
	Round Table, 1954 h., by *Princequillo	66-43-8-5	1,749,869
	*September Child, 1933 m., by The Porter	68-4-2-3	2,110
	*Stan, 1950 g., by *Kingsway II	40-18-2-4	241,880
	Stutz Bearcat, 1975 g., by First Landing	86-23-14-12	271,181
33	Susquehanna, 1874 m. by *Leamington	No record	
	Sweepida, 1937 g., by Sweepster	65-18-12-10	$111,640
	Tameretti, 1962 m., by Tim Tam	35-4-6-10	25,415
	Tripping, 1908 m., by Delhi	No record	
	Twosy, 1942 m., by Bull Lea	52-21-17-3	101,375
	Victorian Heiress, 1968 m., by Northern Dancer	12-3-0-1	20,590
	What a Myth, 1957 g., by Coup de Myth	(Steeplechaser in England)	
32	Arts and Letters, 1966 h., by *Ribot	23-11-6-1	632,404
	Big Spruce, 1969 h., by *Herbager	40-9-9-7	673,117
	Blue Fleet, 1940 m., by Count Fleet	5-2-0-1	1,350
	Bold Bikini, 1969 m., by Boldnesian	21-6-5-4	57,528
	Bowl Game, 1974 g., by Tom Rolfe	23-11-6-5	907,083
	Come My Prince, 1972 m., by Prince John	Unraced	
	Crimson Saint, 1969 m., by Crimson Satan	11-7-0-2	91,770
	Dreamville, 1960 m., by Hilarious	39-4-6-5	12,930
	Ela-Mana-Mou, 1976 h., by Pitcairn	*16-10-2-2*	*810,247*
	Exclusive Ribot, 1972 h., by *Ribot	32-6-4-3	43,974
	Fanfreluche, 1967 m., by Northern Dancer	21-11-6-2	238,688
	Gay Serenade, 1960 m., by *Royal Serenade	26-8-5-2	90,531
	Hamette, 1973 m., by Hametus	Unraced	
	Honey Jay, 1968 h., by Double Jay	63-24-10-11	223,853
	Hope of Glory, 1972 m., by Mr. Leader	35-9-3-5	168,421
	Introductivo, 1969 h., by *Sensitivo	54-6-10-15	107,128
	Jazzman, 1973 h., by Hasty Road	20-2-1-1	8,139
	John Henry, 1975 g., by Ole Bob Bowers	83-39-15-9	6,591,860
	Kittiwake, 1968 m., by *Sea-Bird	54-18-12-9	338,086
	Knightly Manner, 1961 h., by Round Table	67-16-13-10	436,676
	Legendra, 1944 m., by *Challenger II	32-6-2-5	23,220
	Little Current, 1971 h., by *Sea-Bird	16-4-3-1	354,704
	Little Hut, 1952 m., by Occupy	55-5-7-14	22,220
	Mill George, 1975 h., by Mill Reef	4-2-0-1	17,350
	Minnesota Mac, 1964 h., by Rough'n Tumble	11-4-2-2	63,275
	Miss Justice (GB), 1961 m., by King's Bench	4-1-0-1	970
	*Monade, 1959 m., by *Klairon	35-10-5-4	252,016
	Oracle II, 1910 g., by Oxford	No record	
	*Philomela, 1954 m., by *Tudor Minstrel	23-1-2-2	560
	Queen Sucree, 1966 m., by *Ribot	4-1-0-0	3,925
	Sampson, 1745 h., by Blaze	No record	
	*Slady Castle, 1969 h., by *Tudor Melody	19-4-3-3	20,835
	S. S. Bellstar, 1966 h., by Eagle Admiral	36-10-10-5	40,637
	Star Fiddle, 1946 h., by High Strung	99-24-20-14	129,945
	Straight Flush, 1975 h., by Riva Ridge	28-3-4-3	49,820
	Taba (Arg), 1973 m., by Table Play	8-3-0-1	20,609
	Terlingua, 1976 m., by Secretariat	17-7-4-1	423,896
	The Ghizeh, 1948 m., by Questionnaire	47-4-8-7	13,610
	*Tobin Bronze, 1962 h., by Arctic Explorer	60-28-10-5	391,447
	Why Me Lord, 1974 m., by Bold Reasoning	11-1-1-0	3,613

Bold Italic=Still living.

*JANUS (34), 1746-1780. See Notable Horses in Racing in this chapter.

KENILWORTH (34), 1898-1932. Br. h., *Sir Modred—*Queen Bess, by Gilroy or St. Martin. 168-61-18-22, $31,270. Sire. Died of a ruptured artery, on December 16, 1932, at the ranch of owner L. M. Bugeia, in Marin County, California.

LUCKY SPELL (34), 1971-2005. B. m., Lucky Mel—Incantation, by Prince Blessed. 69-12-8-11, $253,655. Won 1974 Princess S. (G3) and Las Palmas H. (G3). Dam of three stakes winners, including English Group 3 winner Merlins Charm. Grandam of 1995 Breeders' Cup Juvenile (G1) winner Unbridled's Song. Pensioned in California.

MISS DEBBIE LEE (34), 1966-2000. B. m., Accomplish—Lucky Gay, by Blue Gay. 14-1-5-1, $6,152. Dam of four stakes winners, including Strate Sunshine and Strate Miss. Died in December 2000 at Dash Goff's ranch in Arkansas.

RAJA BABA (34), 1968-2002. B. h., Bold Ruler—Missy Baba, by *My Babu. 41-7-12-9, $123,287. Stakes winner. Leading American sire, juvenile sire of 1980. Leading 1976 freshman sire. Sire of 62 stakes winners, including champion Sacahuista and Grade 1 winners Is It True, Junius, Well Decorated, etc. Broodmare sire of more than 75 stakes winners. Euthanized on October 9, 2002, at Hermitage Farm, in Goshen, Kentucky, where he stood his entire career. Buried on the farm.

VIEUX MANOIR (34), 1947-1981. B. h., Brantome—Vieille Canaille, by Finglas. Champion at three in France. Leading French sire of 1958. Among the leading French broodmare sires. Sire of 26 stakes winners, including French champion and leading sire *Val de Loir. Died November 19, 1981, at Haras de Meautry in Normandy, France.

AMERICAN ECLIPSE (33), 1814-1847. See Notable Horses in Racing in this chapter.

BALLOT (33), 1904-1937. See Notable Horses in Racing in this chapter.

BILLY BARTON (33), 1918-1951. Br. g., *Huon—Mary Le Bus, by *St. Savin. Great American steeplechaser. Second to Tipperary Tim in the 1928 Grand National at Aintree, England—the only two horses to finish that year. Died March 11, 1951, at Belmont Farm, in Elkridge, Maryland.

BROWN BERRY (33), 1960-1993. B. m., Mount Marcy—Brown Baby, by Phalanx. 29-6-3-3, $53,625. Won 1962 Del Mar Debutante. Dam of 1975 Belmont Stakes (G1) winner Avatar, 1988 French Derby (Fr-G1) winner Hours After, and 1972 Charles H. Strub S. winner Unconscious. Died May 18, 1993, at Brookdale Farm, in Versailles, Kentucky. Buried on the farm.

CHATEAUCREEK (33), 1970-2003. Ch. m., Chateaugay—Mooncreek, by Sailor. 29-6-1-2, $24,203. Stakes winner. Dam of 1980 champion and Epsom Derby (Eng-G1) winner Henbit. Grandam of Grade 1 winners Mr Purple and Queens Court Queen. Euthanized due to infirmities of age on August 7, 2003, at Mineola Farm, in Lexington. Buried on the farm.

COUNT FLEET (33), 1940-1973. See Notable Horses in Racing in this chapter.

GA HAI (33), 1971-2004. Gr. h., Determine—Goyala, by Goyamo. 43-13-2-5, $257,548. Won 1975 and 1976 Arcadia H. (G3). Sire of seven stakes winners. Pensioned in 1995. Died on March 17, 2004, at Reigle Heir Farms, in Grantville, Pennsylvania. Buried on the farm.

GREEN FINGER (33), 1958-1991. Dk. b. or br. m., Better Self—Flower Bed, by *Beau Pere. 18-1-3-1, $5,935. Dam of two stakes winners, including Grade 2 winner Free Hand. Died in 1991 and buried at Old Frankfort Stud (formerly King Ranch), near Lexington.

LUCKY MEL (33), 1954-1987. Ch. h., Olympia—*Royal Mink, by *Royal Charger. 12-7-0-1, $106,450. Stakes winner at two. Set five-furlong world record of :56.60, at Hollywood Park. Sire of 23 stakes winners, including graded winners Copper Mel and Lucky Spell. Broodmare sire of 44 stakes winners. Died at Old English Rancho, in Fresno, California.

MATCHEM (33), 1748-1781. See Notable Horses in Racing in this chapter.

MR. LEADER (33), 1966-1999. B. h., Hail to Reason—Jolie Deja, by *Djeddah. 25-10-3-3, $219,803. Won 1970 Tidal H., Stars and Stripes H. Sire of 83 stakes winners, including Grade 1 winners Ruhlmann, Hurry Up Blue, Wise Times, Quiet Little Table, Martial Law. Broodmare sire of more than 110 stakes winners, including champion Epitome. Euthanized on April 20, 1999, at Nuckols Farm in Midway, Kentucky, and buried at the farm.

NAPALM (33), 1963-1996. Ch. m., *Nilo—Fire Falls, by *Bull Dog. 17-2-2-5, $9,575. Dam of millionaire Grade 2 winner Fighting Fit and stakes winner Hot Words. Euthanized on February 9, 1996, at Nuckols Farm in Midway, Kentucky.

NORTHERN TASTE (33), 1971-2004. Ch. h., Northern Dancer—Lady Victoria, by Victoria Park. 23-5-3-4, $154,177. Won 1974 Prix de la Foret (Fr-G1). Nine-time leading sire in Japan, four-time leading Japanese broodmare sire. Sire of 48 stakes winners and six champions. Died in December 2004 at Shadai Stallion Station, on Hokkaido, Japan. Cremated and buried at the farm.

POCAHONTAS (33), 1837-1870. See Notable Horses in Racing in this chapter.

ROUND TABLE (33), 1954-1987. See Notable Horses in Racing in this chapter.

SWEEPIDA (33), 1937-1970. Br. g., Sweepster—Rapida, by *Hand Grenade. 65-18-12-10, $111,640. Won 1940 Santa Anita Derby, Bay Meadows H., etc. Died May 8, 1970, at the San Joaquin County Fair in Stockton, California, where he had lived as a pensioner. Buried in front of the racetrack grandstand.

TAMERETT (33), 1962-1995. Dk. b. or br. m., Tim Tam—*Mixed Marriage, by *Tudor Minstrel. 35-4-6-10, $25,415. Dam of five stakes winners, including English champion miler Known Fact and Grade 1 winner Tentam. Grandam of noted sire Gone West. Died September 15, 1995, at Mare Haven Farm, in Lexington and buried on the farm.

TRIPPING (33), 1908-1941. B. m., Delhi—*Fairy Slipper, by St. Serf. 20-2-0-4, $950. Dam of two stakes winners, including 1920 Futurity S. winner Step Lightly. Died September 21, 1941, at Haylands Farm, in Lexington.

TWOSY (33), 1942-1975. B. m., Bull Lea—Two Bob, by The Porter. 52-21-17-3, $101,375. Multiple stakes winner. Sister to Racing Hall of Fame member Two Lea and to major stakes winner Miz Clementine. Dam of four winners and one stakes-placed runner. Died and was buried at Calumet Farm in Lexington.

VICTORIAN HEIRESS (33), 1968-2001. B. m, Northern Dancer—Victoriana, by Windfields. 12-3-0-1, $20,590. Dam of Canadian champion Northern Blossom. Half sister to 1960 Canadian Horse of the Year Victoria Park. Died in fall 2001 at Tranquility Farm in Tehachapi, California.

ECLIPSE AWARDS
History of the Eclipse Awards

Thoroughbred racing's first official champions were recognized for the 1936 racing season by *Daily Racing Form*, which named Granville as Horse of the Year and selected champions in six divisions.

Beginning in the 1950 racing season, Thoroughbred Racing Associations, formed eight years earlier, announced its own set of champions. Usually the *Form*'s and TRA's separate lists of champions coincided, but sometimes they did not. For example, Horse of the Year titles went separately to One Count and Native Dancer in 1952, Bold Ruler and Dedicate in '57, Roman Brother and Moccasin in '65, and Fort Marcy and Personality in '70.

In 1971, J. B. Faulconer, then president of the Turf Publicists of America, an organization of marketing and public-relations representatives from racetrack and industry organizations, was asked by Monmouth Park executive Philip H. Iselin to head a committee to consolidate the year-end championship honors. Faulconer brought together the *Form*, TRA, and the National Turf Writers Association to select one set of champions.

Faulconer is credited with naming the Eclipse Award, which honors the great 18th-century English racehorse and sire from whom most modern-day Thoroughbreds descend in male line. He selected Lexington artist Adalin Wichman to design the award statuette of a lone Thoroughbred tacked in preparation for a race, and he served as master of ceremonies at the inaugural awards dinner on January 26, 1972, at New York's Waldorf Astoria. Faulconer was the host through 1976.

Today, the National Thoroughbred Racing Association has replaced the TRA in the three voting groups. Members of the three eligible organizations vote on winners of the 11 divisional categories and then select the Horse of the Year. In addition, the groups vote on the outstanding breeder, owner, trainer, jockey, and apprentice jockey.

For the first time in 2003, Eclipse Award winners were determined on a one-person, one-vote basis. Formerly, the Eclipse Award winners were determined by bloc voting, one vote for each group.

Since the awards were founded, a few notable events have occurred. In 1978, a tie in the voting for outstanding two-year-old filly resulted in It's in the Air and Candy Eclair being named co-champions, while Dr. Patches and J. O. Tobin were voted co-champion sprinters. Voting procedures were changed to eliminate ties. In 1979, the champion turf horse division was divided into male and female categories, and the sprinter category was split in 2007. In Eclipse Award history, two-year-olds have been voted Horse of the Year just twice: Secretariat (1972) and Favorite Trick ('97).

Eclipse Award-Winning Horses

Horse of the Year
2007 Curlin
2006 Invasor (Arg)
2005 Saint Liam
2004 Ghostzapper
2003 Mineshaft
2002 Azeri (female)
2001 Point Given
2000 Tiznow
1999 Charismatic
1998 Skip Away
1997 Favorite Trick
1996 Cigar
1995 Cigar
1994 Holy Bull
1993 Kotashaan (Fr)
1992 A.P. Indy
1991 Black Tie Affair (Ire)
1990 Criminal Type
1989 Sunday Silence
1988 Alysheba
1987 Ferdinand
1986 Lady's Secret (female)
1985 Spend a Buck
1984 John Henry
1983 All Along (Fr) (female)
1982 Conquistador Cielo
1981 John Henry
1980 Spectacular Bid
1979 Affirmed
1978 Affirmed
1977 Seattle Slew
1976 Forego
1975 Forego
1974 Forego
1973 Secretariat
1972 Secretariat
1971 Ack Ack

Two-Year-Old Male
2007 War Pass
2006 Street Sense
2005 Stevie Wonderboy
2004 Declan's Moon
2003 Action This Day
2002 Vindication
2001 Johannesburg
2000 Macho Uno
1999 Anees
1998 Answer Lively
1997 Favorite Trick
1996 Boston Harbor
1995 Maria's Mon
1994 Timber Country
1993 Dehere
1992 Gilded Time
1991 Arazi
1990 Fly So Free
1989 Rhythm
1988 Easy Goer
1987 Forty Niner
1986 Capote
1985 Tasso
1984 Chief's Crown
1983 Devil's Bag
1982 Roving Boy
1981 Deputy Minister
1980 Lord Avie
1979 Rockhill Native
1978 Spectacular Bid
1977 Affirmed
1976 Seattle Slew
1975 Honest Pleasure
1974 Foolish Pleasure
1973 Protagonist
1972 Secretariat
1971 Riva Ridge

Two-Year-Old Filly
2007 Indian Blessing
2006 Dreaming of Anna
2005 Folklore
2004 Sweet Catomine
2003 Halfbridled
2002 Storm Flag Flying
2001 Tempera
2000 Caressing
1999 Chilukki

Eclipse Awards — Past Champions

1998 Silverbulletday
1997 Countess Diana
1996 Storm Song
1995 Golden Attraction
1994 Flanders
1993 Phone Chatter
1992 Eliza
1991 Pleasant Stage
1990 Meadow Star
1989 Go for Wand
1988 Open Mind
1987 Epitome
1986 Brave Raj
1985 Family Style
1984 Outstandingly
1983 Althea
1982 Landaluce
1981 Before Dawn
1980 Heavenly Cause
1979 Smart Angle
1978 †It's in the Air
     †Candy Eclair
1977 Lakeville Miss
1976 Sensational
1975 Dearly Precious
1974 Ruffian
1973 Talking Picture
1972 La Prevoyante
1971 Numbered Account
†Tied in voting, named
  co-champions

Three-Year-Old Male
2007 Curlin
2006 Bernardini
2005 Afleet Alex
2004 Smarty Jones
2003 Funny Cide
2002 War Emblem
2001 Point Given
2000 Tiznow
1999 Charismatic
1998 Real Quiet
1997 Silver Charm
1996 Skip Away
1995 Thunder Gulch
1994 Holy Bull
1993 Prairie Bayou
1992 A.P. Indy
1991 Hansel
1990 Unbridled
1989 Sunday Silence
1988 Risen Star
1987 Alysheba
1986 Snow Chief
1985 Spend a Buck
1984 Swale
1983 Slew o' Gold
1982 Conquistador Cielo
1981 Pleasant Colony
1980 Temperence Hill
1979 Spectacular Bid
1978 Affirmed
1977 Seattle Slew

1976 Bold Forbes
1975 Wajima
1974 Little Current
1973 Secretariat
1972 Key to the Mint
1971 Canonero II

Three-Year-Old Filly
2007 Rags to Riches
2006 Wait a While
2005 Smuggler
2004 Ashado
2003 Bird Town
2002 Farda Amiga
2001 Xtra Heat
2000 Surfside
1999 Silverbulletday
1998 Banshee Breeze
1997 Ajina
1996 Yanks Music
1995 Serena's Song
1994 Heavenly Prize
1993 Hollywood Wildcat
1992 Saratoga Dew
1991 Dance Smartly
1990 Go for Wand
1989 Open Mind
1988 Winning Colors
1987 Sacahuista
1986 Tiffany Lass
1985 Mom's Command
1984 Life's Magic
1983 Heartlight No. One
1982 Christmas Past
1981 Wayward Lass
1980 Genuine Risk
1979 Davona Dale
1978 Tempest Queen
1977 Our Mims
1976 Revidere
1975 Ruffian
1974 Chris Evert
1973 Desert Vixen
1972 Susan's Girl
1971 Turkish Trousers

Older Male
2007 Lawyer Ron
2006 Invasor (Arg)
2005 Saint Liam
2004 Ghostzapper
2003 Mineshaft
2002 Left Bank
2001 Tiznow
2000 Lemon Drop Kid
1999 Victory Gallop
1998 Skip Away
1997 Skip Away
1996 Cigar
1995 Cigar
1994 The Wicked North
1993 Bertrando
1992 Pleasant Tap
1991 Black Tie Affair (Ire)

1990 Criminal Type
1989 Blushing John
1988 Alysheba
1987 Ferdinand
1986 Turkoman
1985 Vanlandingham
1984 Slew o' Gold
1983 Bates Motel
1982 Lemhi Gold
1981 John Henry
1980 Spectacular Bid
1979 Affirmed
1978 Seattle Slew
1977 Forego
1976 Forego
1975 Forego
1974 Forego
1973 Riva Ridge
1972 Autobiography
1971 Ack Ack

Older Female
2007 Ginger Punch
2006 Fleet Indian
2005 Ashado
2004 Azeri
2003 Azeri
2002 Azeri
2001 Gourmet Girl
2000 Riboletta (Brz)
1999 Beautiful Pleasure
1998 Escena
1997 Hidden Lake
1996 Jewel Princess
1995 Inside Information
1994 Sky Beauty
1993 Paseana (Arg)
1992 Paseana (Arg)
1991 Queena
1990 Bayakoa (Arg)
1989 Bayakoa (Arg)
1988 Personal Ensign
1987 North Sider
1986 Lady's Secret
1985 Life's Magic
1984 Princess Rooney
1983 Ambassador of Luck
1982 Track Robbery
1981 Relaxing
1980 Glorious Song
1979 Waya (Fr)
1978 Late Bloomer
1977 Cascapedia
1976 Proud Delta
1975 Susan's Girl
1974 Desert Vixen
1973 Susan's Girl
1972 Typecast
1971 Shuvee

Turf Male[1]
2007 English Channel
2006 Miesque's Approval

2005 Leroidesanimaux (Brz)
2004 Kitten's Joy
2003 High Chaparral (Ire)
2002 High Chaparral (Ire)
2001 Fantastic Light
2000 Kalanisi (Ire)
1999 Daylami (Ire)
1998 Buck's Boy
1997 Chief Bearhart
1996 Singspiel (Ire)
1995 Northern Spur (Ire)
1994 Paradise Creek
1993 Kotashaan (Fr)
1992 Sky Classic
1991 Tight Spot
1990 Itsallgreektome
1989 Steinlen (GB)
1988 Sunshine Forever
1987 Theatrical (Ire)
1986 Manila
1985 Cozzene
1984 John Henry
1983 John Henry
1982 Perrault (GB)
1981 John Henry
1980 John Henry
1979 Bowl Game

Turf Female[1]
2007 Lahudood (GB)
2006 Ouija Board (GB)
2005 Intercontinental (GB)
2004 Ouija Board (GB)
2003 Islington (Ire)
2002 Golden Apples (Ire)
2001 Banks Hill (GB)
2000 Perfect Sting
1999 Soaring Softly
1998 Fiji (GB)
1997 Ryafan
1996 Wandesta (GB)
1995 Possibly Perfect
1994 Hatoof
1993 Flawlessly
1992 Flawlessly
1991 Miss Alleged
1990 Laugh and Be Merry
1989 Brown Bess
1988 Miesque
1987 Miesque
1986 Estrapade
1985 Pebbles (GB)
1984 Royal Heroine (Ire)
1983 All Along (Fr)
1982 April Run (Ire)
1981 De La Rose
1980 Just a Game (Ire)
1979 Trillion

Turf Horse[1]
1978 Mac Diarmida
1977 Johnny D.
1976 Youth

Eclipse Awards — Past Champions

1975 *Snow Knight	1996 Lit de Justice	1975 Gallant Bob	1993 Lonesome Glory
1974 Dahlia (female)	1995 Not Surprising	1974 Forego	1992 Lonesome Glory
1973 Secretariat	1994 Cherokee Run	1973 Shecky Greene	1991 Morley Street (Ire)
1972 *Cougar II	1993 Cardmania	1972 Chou Croute (female)	1990 Morley Street (Ire)
1971 Run the Gantlet	1992 Rubiano	1971 Ack Ack	1989 Highland Bud
	1991 Housebuster	†Tied in voting, named co-champions	1988 Jimmy Lorenzo (GB)
Male Sprinter²	1990 Housebuster		1987 Inlander (GB)
2007 Midnight Lute	1989 Safely Kept (female)		1986 Flatterer
	1988 Gulch	**Steeplechaser**	1985 Flatterer
Female Sprinter²	1987 Groovy	2007 Good Night Shirt	1984 Flatterer
2007 Maryfield	1986 Smile	2006 McDynamo	1983 Flatterer
	1985 Precisionist	2005 McDynamo	1982 Zaccio
Sprinter²	1984 Eillo	2004 Hirapour (Ire)	1981 Zaccio
2006 Thor's Echo	1983 Chinook Pass	2003 McDynamo	1980 Zaccio
2005 Lost in the Fog	1982 Gold Beauty (female)	2002 Flat Top	1979 Martie's Anger
2004 Speightstown	1981 Guilty Conscience	2001 Pompeyo (Chi)	1978 Cafe Prince
2003 Aldebaran	1980 Plugged Nickle	2000 All Gong (GB)	1977 Cafe Prince
2002 Orientate	1979 Star de Naskra	1999 Lonesome Glory	1976 Straight and True
2001 Squirtle Squirt	1978 †Dr. Patches	1998 Flat Top	1975 Life's Illusion
2000 Kona Gold	†J. O. Tobin	1997 Lonesome Glory	1974 *Gran Kan
1999 Artax	1977 What a Summer	1996 Correggio (Ire)	1973 Athenian Idol
1998 Reraise	(female)	1995 Lonesome Glory	1972 Soothsayer
1997 Smoke Glacken	1976 My Juliet (female)	1994 Warm Spell	1971 Shadow Brook

¹One turf category prior to 1979; ²One sprinter category prior to 2007.

Eclipse Award-Winning Individuals

Owner	1974 Dan Lasater	1979 Claiborne Farm	
2007 Shadwell Stable	1973 Not awarded	1978 Harbor View Farm	
2006 Darley Stable	1972 Not awarded	1977 E. P. Taylor	
Roy and Gretchen Jackson	1971 Mr. and Mrs. E. E. Fogelson	1976 Nelson Bunker Hunt	
2005 Michael Gill		1975 Fred W. Hooper	
2004 Kenneth and Sarah Ramsey	**Breeder**	1974 John W. Galbreath	
2003 Juddmonte Farms	2007 Adena Springs	1973 Not awarded	
2002 Richard Englander	(Frank Stronach)	1972 Not awarded	
2001 Richard Englander	2006 Adena Springs	1971 Not awarded	
2000 Frank Stronach	2005 Adena Springs		
1999 Frank Stronach	2004 Adena Springs	**Owner-Breeder**	
1998 Frank Stronach	2003 Juddmonte Farms	1973 Meadow Stable-Meadow Stud	
1997 Carolyn Hine	2002 Juddmonte Farms	(C. T. Chenery)	
1996 Allen E. Paulson	2001 Juddmonte Farms	1972 Meadow Stable-Meadow Stud	
1995 Allen E. Paulson	2000 Frank Stronach	(C. T. Chenery)	
1994 John Franks	1999 William S. Farish & Partners	1971 Paul Mellon	
1993 John Franks	1998 John and Betty Mabee		
1992 Juddmonte Farms	1997 John and Betty Mabee	**Trainer**	
1991 Sam-Son Farm	1996 Farnsworth Farms	2007 Todd Pletcher	
1990 Mrs. Frances Genter	1995 Juddmonte Farms	2006 Todd Pletcher	
1989 Ogden Phipps	1994 William T. Young	2005 Todd Pletcher	
1988 Ogden Phipps	1993 Allen E. Paulson	2004 Todd Pletcher	
1987 Mr. and Mrs. Eugene Klein	1992 William S. Farish	2003 Bobby Frankel	
1986 Mr. and Mrs. Eugene Klein	1991 John and Betty Mabee	2002 Bobby Frankel	
1985 Mr. and Mrs. Eugene Klein	1990 Calumet Farm	2001 Bobby Frankel	
1984 John Franks	1989 North Ridge Farm	2000 Bobby Frankel	
1983 John Franks	1988 Ogden Phipps	1999 Bob Baffert	
1982 Viola Sommer	1987 Nelson Bunker Hunt	1998 Bob Baffert	
1981 Dotsam Stable	1986 Paul Mellon	1997 Bob Baffert	
1980 Mr. and Mrs. Bertram Firestone	1985 Nelson Bunker Hunt	1996 Bill Mott	
1979 Harbor View Farm	1984 Claiborne Farm	1995 Bill Mott	
1978 Harbor View Farm	1983 E. P. Taylor	1994 D. Wayne Lukas	
1977 Maxwell Gluck	1982 Fred W. Hooper	1993 Bobby Frankel	
1976 Dan Lasater	1981 Golden Chance Farm	1992 Ron McAnally	
1975 Dan Lasater	1980 Adele Paxson	1991 Ron McAnally	

Eclipse Awards — Past Champions

1990 Carl Nafzger
1989 Charles Whittingham
1988 C. R. McGaughey
1987 D. Wayne Lukas
1986 D. Wayne Lukas
1985 D. Wayne Lukas
1984 Jack Van Berg
1983 Woody Stephens
1982 Charles Whittingham
1981 Ron McAnally
1980 Grover G. "Buddy" Delp
1979 Lazaro Barrera
1978 Lazaro Barrera
1977 Lazaro Barrera
1976 Lazaro Barrera
1975 Steve DiMauro
1974 Sherrill Ward
1973 H. Allen Jerkens
1972 Lucien Laurin
1971 Charles Whittingham

Jockey
2007 Garrett Gomez
2006 Edgar Prado
2005 John Velazquez
2004 John Velazquez
2003 Jerry Bailey
2002 Jerry Bailey
2001 Jerry Bailey
2000 Jerry Bailey
1999 Jorge Chavez
1998 Gary Stevens
1997 Jerry Bailey
1996 Jerry Bailey
1995 Jerry Bailey
1994 Mike Smith
1993 Mike Smith
1992 Kent Desormeaux
1991 Pat Day
1990 Craig Perret
1989 Kent Desormeaux
1988 Jose Santos
1987 Pat Day
1986 Pat Day
1985 Laffit Pincay Jr.
1984 Pat Day
1983 Angel Cordero Jr.
1982 Angel Cordero Jr.
1981 William Shoemaker
1980 Chris McCarron
1979 Laffit Pincay Jr.
1978 Darrel McHargue
1977 Steve Cauthen
1976 Sandy Hawley
1975 Braulio Baeza
1974 Laffit Pincay Jr.
1973 Laffit Pincay Jr.
1972 Braulio Baeza
1971 Laffit Pincay Jr.

Apprentice Jockey
2007 Joe Talamo
2006 Julien Leparoux
2005 Emma-Jayne Wilson
2004 Brian Hernandez Jr.
2003 Eddie Castro
2002 Ryan Fogelsonger
2001 Jeremy Rose
2000 Tyler Baze
1999 Ariel Smith
1998 Shaun Bridgmohan
1997 Roberto Rosado
       Philip Teator (tie)
1996 Neil Poznansky
1995 Ramon Perez
1994 Dale Beckner
1993 Juan L. Umana
1992 †Rosemary Homeister Jr.
1991 Mickey Walls
1990 Mark Johnston
1989 Michael Luzzi
1988 Steve Capanas
1987 Kent Desormeaux
1986 Allen Stacy
1985 Art Madrid Jr.
1984 Wesley Ward
1983 Declan Murphy
1982 Alberto Delgado
1981 Richard Migliore
1980 Frank Lovato Jr.
1979 Cash Asmussen
1978 Ron Franklin
1977 Steve Cauthen
1976 George Martens
1975 Jimmy Edwards
1974 Chris McCarron
1973 Steve Valdez
1972 Thomas Wallis
1971 Gene St. Leon

†Jesus Bracho was originally awarded the title but relinquished it in 1994.

Eclipse Award of Merit
2006 John Nerud
2005 Helen "Penny" Chenery
2004 Oaklawn Park and Cella Family
2003 Richard L. Duchossois
2002 Ogden Phipps
       Howard Battle
2001 Harry T. Mangurian Jr.
       Pete Pedersen
2000 Jim McKay
1999 Not awarded
1998 D. G. Van Clief Jr.
1997 Bob and Beverly Lewis
1996 Allen E. Paulson
1995 James E. "Ted" Bassett III
1994 Alfred G. Vanderbilt
1993 Paul Mellon
1992 Robert P. Strub
       Joe Hirsch
1991 Fred W. Hooper
1990 Warner L. Jones
1989 Michael Sandler
1988 John Forsythe
1987 J. B. Faulconer
1986 Herman Cohen
1985 Keene Daingerfield
1984 John Gaines
1983 Not awarded
1982 Not awarded
1981 William Shoemaker
1980 John D. Schapiro
1979 Frank E. "Jimmy" Kilroe
1978 Ogden Mills "Dinny" Phipps
1977 Steve Cauthen
1976 Jack J. Dreyfus Jr.

Special Award
2007 Kentucky Horse Park
2006 Team Barbaro
2005 Cash is King Stable
2004 Dale Baird
2003 Not awarded
2002 Keeneland Library
2001 Sheikh Mohammed bin Rashid al Maktoum
2000 John Hettinger
1999 Laffit Pincay Jr.
1998 Oak Tree Racing Association
1997 Not awarded
1996 Not awarded
1995 Russell Baze
1994 Eddie Arcaro
       John Longden
1993 Not awarded
1992 Not awarded
1991 Not awarded
1990 Not awarded
1989 Richard L. Duchossois
1988 Edward J. DeBartolo Sr.
1987 Anheuser-Busch
1986 Not awarded
1985 Arlington Park
1984 C. V. Whitney
1983 Not awarded
1982 Not awarded
1981 Not awarded
1980 John T. Landry
       Pierre E. Bellocq
1979 Not awarded
1978 Not awarded
1977 Not awarded
1976 William Shoemaker
1975 Not awarded
1974 Charles Hatton
1973 Not awarded
1972 Not awarded
1971 Robert J. Kleberg

Man of the Year
1975 John A. Morris
1974 William L. McKnight
1973 Edward P. Taylor
1972 John W. Galbreath

Outstanding Achievement
1972 Arthur B. Hancock Jr.
       (posthumously)
1971 Charles Engelhard
       (posthumously)

Eclipse Award Media Winners

Outstanding Newspaper Writing

1999 Maryjean Wall, Lexington *Herald-Leader*
1998 Tom Keyser, Baltimore *Sun*
1997 Maryjean Wall, Lexington *Herald-Leader*
1996 Tom Keyser, Baltimore *Sun*
1995 Stephanie Diaz, Riverside *Press-Enterprise*
1994 Mike Downey, Los Angeles *Times*
1993 Jennie Rees, Louisville *Courier-Journal*
1992 James Wallace, Seattle *Post Intelligencer*
1990 Paul Moran, *Newsday*
1989 Ronnie Virgets, *Gambit*
1988 Billy Reed, Lexington *Herald-Leader*
1987 Tim Layden, Capital Newspapers
1986 Edwin Pope, Miami *Herald*
1985 Paul Moran, *Newsday*
1984 Bill Christine, Los Angeles *Times*
     Eddie Donnally, Dallas *Morning News*
1983 Dave Koemer, Louisville *Times*
1982 Edwin Pope, Miami *Herald*
1981 Dave Kindred, Washington *Post*
1980 Maryjean Wall, Lexington *Herald*
1979 Billy Reed, Louisville *Courier-Journal*
1978 Joe Hirsch, *Daily Racing Form*
1977 Skip Bayless, Los Angeles *Times*
1976 Edwin Pope, Miami *Herald*
1975 Bob Harding, Newark *Star-Ledger*
1974 William H. Rudy, New York *Post*
1973 Red Smith, New York *Times*
1972 Phil Ranallo, Buffalo *Courier Express*
1971 Scott Young, Toronto *Telegram*

Outstanding Magazine Writing

1999 Tom Keyser, Baltimore *Sun*
1998 Laura Hillenbrand, *American Heritage*
1997 Bill Heller, *The Backstretch*
1996 Don Clippinger, *Mid-Atlantic Thoroughbred*
1995 Not awarded
1994 Jay Hovdey, *The Blood-Horse*
1993 Stephanie Diaz, *The Backstretch*
1992 Joseph P. Pons Jr., *The Blood-Horse*
1990 Bill Nack, *Sports Illustrated*
1989 Bill Nack, *Sports Illustrated*
1988 Jennie Rees, Louisville *Courier-Journal* (Sunday Magazine)
1987 Jack Mann, *Spur*
1986 Bill Nack, *Sports Illustrated*
1985 Bill Mooney, *The Thoroughbred Record*
1984 Frank Deford, *Sports Illustrated*
1983 Arnold Kirkpatrick, *Keeneland*
1982 Jay Hovdey, *Horsemen's Journal*
1981 Joseph P. Pons Jr., *The Blood-Horse*
1980 Clive Gammon, *Sports Illustrated*
1979 William Leggett, *Sports Illustrated*
1978 Bill Nack, *Sports Illustrated*
1977 Whitney Tower, *Classic*
1976 Whitney Tower, *Classic*
1975 Frank Deford, *Sports Illustrated*
1974 Chet Hagan, *Spur*
1973 Pete Axthelm, *Newsweek*
1972 Edward L. Bowen, *The Blood-Horse*
1971 Bill Surface, *Reader's Digest*

Outstanding Feature and Enterprise Writing

2007 Brian Hiro, North County *Times*
2006 Mike Jensen, Philadelphia *Inquirer*
2005 Janet Patton, Lexington *Herald-Leader*
2004 Mike Jensen, Philadelphia *Inquirer*
2003 Bill Nack, *GQ*
2002 John Jeremiah Sullivan, *Harper's*
2001 Laura Hillenbrand, *EQUUS*
2000 Mary Simon, Thoroughbred Times

Outstanding Feature Writing

1991 Bill Nack, *Sports Illustrated*

Outstanding News Writing

1991 Bill Nack, *Sports Illustrated*

Outstanding News and Commentary Writing

2007 Bill Mooney, *Post Time USA*
2006 Dick Jerardi, Philadelphia *Daily News*
2005 Bob Ford, Philadelphia *Inquirer*
2004 Bill Christine, Los Angeles *Times*
2003 Jay Hovdey, *Daily Racing Form*
2002 Joe Drape, New York *Times*
2001 Janet Patton, Lexington *Herald-Leader*
2000 Jay Hovdey, *Daily Racing Form*

Local Television Achievement

2007 Horse Racing Alberta, CTV Calgary
2006 WLKY-TV, Louisville
2005 WAVE-TV, Louisville
2004 WAVE-TV, Louisville
2003 WKYT, Lexington
2002 Fox Sports Net Southwest
2001 WTVI, Charlotte, NC
2000 WMAR-TV, Baltimore
1999 Amy Zimmerman & Michael Ewing, Fox-TV Sports West
1998 Jeff Lifson, WHAS-TV, Louisville
1997 Brian Blessing, Ontario Jockey Club
1996 Kenny Rice, WTVQ-TV, Lexington
1995 JCM Productions, New York
1994 Ronnie Virgets, WNXO, New Orleans
1993 Stephen Sadis, KBTC, Tacoma
1992 Rick Cushing, WKPC-TV, Louisville
1991 WABC-TV, New York
1990 Philip Von Borries, WKPC-TV, Louisville
1989 Chris Thomas, WFLA-TV, Tampa
1988 Joseph Kwong, KCET-TV, Los Angeles
1987 Arlington Park
1986 Louisiana Downs
1985 Oak Tree Racing Association
1984 NYRA/Cinema Mistral
1983 Cawood Ledford Productions
1982 ON-TV, Los Angeles
1981 WHAS, Louisville
1980 WCAU, Philadelphia
1979 Dave Johnson, ON-TV
1978 Cawood Ledford, WHAS, Louisville
1977 Jane Chastain, KABC, Los Angeles
1976 NYRA-OTB Race of the Week
1975 Cawood Ledford, WHAS, Louisville

National Television Achievement

1999 Mark Shapiro and William Rapaport, ESPN
1998 E. S. Lamoreaux III, *CBS News Sunday Morning*
1997 E. S. Lamoreaux III, *CBS News Sunday Morning*
1996 NBC Sports
1995 ABC's Wide World of Sports
1994 ABC's Wide World of Sports
1993 E. S. Lamoreaux III, CBS News, *Sunday Morning with Charles Kuralt*
1992 ABC Sports
1991 CBS News, *Sunday Morning with Charles Kuralt*
1990 ABC Sports
1989 ABC Sports
1988 Thoroughbred Sports, *Racing Across America*
1987 ABC
1986 ABC
1985 CBS

Eclipse Awards — Media Winners

1984 NBC
1983 CBS
1982 ESPN
1981 Canadian Broadcasting Corp.
1980 ABC
1979 Don Ohlmeyer, NBC
1978 Roger Murphy, Public Broadcasting System
1977 Jack Whitaker, CBS
1976 CBS
1975 CBS
1974 Pen Densham, John Watson, Insight Productions
1973 Chuck Milton, Tony Verna, CBS
1972 Chuck Milton, Tony Verna, CBS
1971 Burt Bacharach, CBS

National Television— Live Racing Programming

2007 NBC Sports
2006 NBC Sports
2005 NBC Sports
2004 NBC Sports
2003 NBC Sports
2002 NBC Sports
2001 NBC
2000 ABC Sports
1999 Curt Gowdy Jr., Craig Janoff, Howard Katz, and John Filippelli, ABC Sports

National Television— Features

2007 HBO Sports
2006 HRTV and Pony Highway Productions
2005 NBC Sports
2004 ESPN
2003 MSNBC and ESPN Classic
2002 NBC Sports
2001 ESPN Classic

Audio–Multimedia–Internet

2007 www.heraldleaderphoto.com
2006 WBAL, Baltimore
2005 Sirius Satellite Radio
2004 Premiere Radio Networks
2003 KSPN/ESPN Radio, Los Angeles; WBAL, Baltimore
2002 Shelby Whitfield, Premiere Radio

Radio Achievement

2001 WBAL, Baltimore
2000 Shelby Whitfield, Premiere Radio
1999 Tom Leach, WVLK-AM, Lexington
1998 Not awarded
1997 John Patti, WBAL, Baltimore
1996 Robin Dawson, CJCL, Toronto
1995 Vic Stauffer, KKAR, Omaha
1994 John Asher, WHAS, Louisville
1993 Tom Leach, WVLK, Lexington
1992 John Asher, WHAS, Louisville
1991 Julia McEvoy, National Public Radio
1990 John Asher, WHAS, Louisville
1989 John Asher, WAVG, Louisville
1988 John Asher, WAVG, Louisville
1987 Bob Lauder, WHAS. Louisville
1986 ABC Radio Network
1985 Bob Lauder, WHAS Louisville
1984 WBAL, Baltimore
1983 Tom Davis, WCBM, Baltimore
1982 ABC Radio Network
1981 WBAL, Baltimore
1980 Not awarded
1979 Dick Woolley, WITH, Baltimore
1978 Ted Patterson, WBAL, Baltimore
1977 Not awarded
1976 Win Elliot, CBS
1975 Not awarded
1974 Not awarded
1973 Not awarded
1972 Not awarded
1971 Win Elliot, CBS

Film Achievement

1972 Joseph Burnham

Photography Achievement

2007 Douglas Lees, Fauquier *Times Democrat*
2006 Matt Goins, Lexington *Herald-Leader*
2005 Lynn Roberts, Fair Grounds
2004 Cindy Pierson Dulay, *Mid-Atlantic Thoroughbred*
2003 Frank Anderson, THOROUGHBRED TIMES
2002 Michael Clevenger, Louisville *Courier-Journal*
2001 Barbara Livingston, *The Thoroughbred Chronicle*
2000 Dave Landry, *Canadian Thoroughbred*
1999 Michael J. Marten, *Daily Racing Form*
1998 Ryan Haynes, Northlands Park
1997 Jean Raftery, Calder Race Course
1996 Skip Dickstein, *The Blood-Horse*
1995 Michael J. Marten, *Daily Racing Form*
1994 Tony Leonard, THOROUGHBRED TIMES
1993 Michael Burns, Ontario Jockey Club
1992 Barbara Livingston, *The Blood-Horse*
1991 Rayetta Burr, Benoit & Associates
1990 Michael Cartee, *Thoroughbred of California*
1989 Ron Cortes, Philadelphia *Inquirer*
1988 Ben Van Hook, Louisville *Courier-Journal*
1987 Dan Farrell, New York *Daily News*
1986 Janice Wilkman, Los Angeles *Times*
1985 Kim Pratt, Garden State Park
1984 Bill Straus, *The Thoroughbred Record*
1983 Rayetta Burr, *Paddock*
1982 Kay Coyte, *Horsemen's Journal*
1981 Tom Baker, River Downs
1980 Bob Coglianese, New York Racing Association
1979 Skip Ball, *Maryland Horse*
1978 Douglas Lees, Fauquier *Democrat*
1977 John Walther, Miami *Herald*
1976 John J. Vasile, Covina (California) *Sentinel*
1975 John Pineda, Miami *Herald*
1974 Michael Burns, Ontario Jockey Club
1973 Harry Leder, United Press International
1972 Bob Coglianese, New York Racing Association
1971 Art Rogers, Los Angeles *Times*

Daily Racing Form/NTRA National Handicapping Championship

Year	Winner	Residence	Winning Total
2008	Richard Goodall	Las Vegas, Nv.	$272.30
2007	Stanley Bavlish	Virginia Beach, Va.	189.20
2006	Ron Rippey	Wayne, N.J.	237.20
2005	Jamie Michelson Jr.	West Bloomfield, Mi.	240.40
2004	Kent Meyer	Sioux City, Ia.	238.40
2003	Steve Wolfson Jr.	Port Orange, Fl.	279.60
2002	Herman Miller	Oakland, Ca.	205.30
2001	Judy Wagner	New Orleans, La.	237.70
2000	Steve Walker	Lincoln, Ne.	305.40

Owners of Eclipse Award Winners

Aga Khan—Kalanisi (Ire).
Aleo, Harry—Lost in the Fog.
Alexander, Helen, David Aykroyd, and Helen Groves—Althea.
Allbritton, Joseph—Hansel.
Anderson, Frank, Verne H. Winchell, and Rick Carradini—Tight Spot.
Arindel Farm—Wait a While.
Augustin Stables—Cafe Prince (1977, '78), Pompeyo (Chi).
Bacharach, Burt C.—Heartlight No. One.
Bailey, Richard E.—Dearly Precious.
Beal, Barry and L. R. French—Landaluce, Sacahuista.
Beal, Barry, L. R. French, and Eugene Klein—Capote.
Bell III, John A.—Epitome.
Blue Vista—Possibly Perfect.
Brant, Peter M.—Gulch, Just a Game (Ire), Waya (Fr).
Bray Jr., Dana S.—Johnny D.
Buckland Farm—Pleasant Colony, Pleasant Stage, Pleasant Tap.
Caibett, Edgar—Canonero II.
Calabrese, Frank—Dreaming of Anna.
Calbourne Farm—Brown Bess.
Calumet Farm—Before Dawn, Davona Dale, Our Mims.
Calumet Farm and Jurgen Arnemann—Criminal Type.
Cash is King Stable—Afleet Alex.
Cee's Stable—Tiznow (2001).
Cella, Charles—Northern Spur (Ire).
Centennial Farms—Rubiano.
Christiana Stables—Go for Wand (1989, '90).
Claiborne Farm—Forty Niner, Swale.
Clark Jr., Mrs. F. Ambrose—*Gran Kan.
Clark Jr., Stephen C.—Shadow Brook.
Clay, Robert and Tracy Farmer—Hidden Lake.
Cooper, Audrey H. and Michael Fennessy—Yanks Music.
Couvercelle, Jean—Cardmania.
Cowan, Irving and Marjorie—Hollywood Wildcat.
Craig, Sidney and Jenny—Paseana (Arg) (1992, '93).
Croll Jr., Warren A.—Holy Bull.
Crown Stable—Eillo.
Darby Dan Farm—Little Current, Sunshine Forever, Tempest Queen.
Darley—Bernardini.
Davison, Mrs. Richard—Guilty Conscience.
De Camargo, Jose, Winner Silk Inc., and Old Friends Inc.—Farda Amiga.
De Kwiatkowski, Henryk—Conquistador Cielo, De La Rose.
Lord Derby—Ouija Board (GB) (2004, '06).
Dogwood Stable—Inlander (GB), Storm Song.
Dotsam Stable—John Henry (1980, '81, '83, '84).
Due Process Stables—Dehere.
Earnhardt, Hal and Patti—Indian Blessing.

East-West Stable—Wajima.
Eldon Farm—Hirapour (Ire).
Elmendorf Farm—Protagonist, Talking Picture.
Engel, Charles F.—Saratoga Dew.
Envoy Stable—Ambassador of Luck.
Equusequity Stable—Slew o' Gold (1983, '84).
Evergreen Farm—Lit de Justice.
Fares, Issam M.—Miss Alleged.
Farish, William S., James Elkins, and Temple Webber Jr.—Mineshaft.
Farish, Will, William Kilroy, Harold Goodman, and Tomonori Tsurumaki—A.P. Indy.
Fey, Barry, Moon Han, Class Racing Stable, Larry Opas, Frank Sinatra, and Craig Dollase—Reraise.
Firestone, Mr. and Mrs. Bertram R.—April Run (Ire), Genuine Risk, Honest Pleasure, Jimmy Lorenzo (GB), What a Summer.
505 Farms and Ed Nahem—Bertrando.
Flaxman Holdings—Aldebaran.
Flying Zee Stables—Wayward Lass.
Folsom Farm and J. Merrick Jones Jr.—Chou Croute.
Forked Lightning Ranch—Ack Ack.
Fradkoff, Serge and Baron Thierry Van Zuylen de Nyevelt—Perrault (GB).
Franks, John—Answer Lively.
Fuller, Peter—Mom's Command.
Genter, Frances A. Stable—Smile, Unbridled.
Gerry, Nancy—Flat Top (1998, 2002).
Godolphin Racing—Daylami (Ire), Fantastic Light, Tempera.
Gorman, Mark, Nick J. Mestrandrea, and Jim Perry—Maryfield.
Green, Dolly—Brave Raj.
Greentree Stable—Bowl Game, Late Bloomer.
Greer, John L.—Foolish Pleasure.
Griffin, Merv Ranch Co.—Stevie Wonderboy.
Griggs, John K.—Warm Spell.
Grinstead, Carl and Ben Rochelle—Snow Chief.
Guest, Virginia—Life's Illusion.
Hamilton, Emory Alexander—Queena.
Hancock III, Arthur, Charlie Whittingham, and Dr. Ernest Gaillard—Sunday Silence.
Harbor View Farm—Affirmed (1977, '78, '79), Flawlessly (1992, '93), It's in the Air, Outstandingly.
Hatley, Melvin E. and Eugene V. Klein—Life's Magic.
Hawksworth Farm—Spectacular Bid (1978, '79, '80).
Henley Jr., Mrs. Jesse H.—Highland Bud.
Hersh, Trust of Philip and Sophie—The Wicked North.
Hibbert, Robert E.—Roving Boy.
Hickory Tree Stable—Devil's Bag.

Leading Owners
Wholly or in partnership, by number of titles won, including Horse of the Year

12—Allen E. Paulson
9—Harbor View Farm
8—Eugene V. Klein
7—Lazy F Ranch
7—Robert and Beverly Lewis
6—Dotsam Stable
6—Mr. and Mrs. Bertram Firestone
6—William L. Pape
6—Stronach Stables
6—Michael Tabor
5—Calumet Farm
5—Mrs. Walter M. Jeffords Jr.
5—Meadow Stable
5—Overbrook Farm
5—Ogden Phipps
5—The Thoroughbred Corp.

By Individual Winners

9—Allen E. Paulson
5—Mr. and Mrs. Bertram Firestone
5—Eugene V. Klein
5—Bob and Beverly Lewis
5—Overbrook Farm
5—Ogden Phipps
4—Calumet Farm
4—Harbor View Farm
4—Juddmonte Farms
4—Sheikh Mohammed bin Rashid al Maktoum
4—Ogden Mills Phipps
4—Stronach Stables
4—The Thoroughbred Corp.

Hine, Carolyn H.—Skip Away (1996, '97, '98).
Hi Yu Stable—Chinook Pass.
Hofmann, Mrs. Philip B.—Gold Beauty, Sky Beauty.
Hooper Sr., Fred W.—Precisionist, Susan's Girl (1972, '73, 1975).
Horton, Robert P.—Gallant Bob.
Houghland, Calvin—All Gong (GB).
Hughes, B. Wayne—Action This Day.
Hunter Farm—Spend a Buck.
Hunt, Nelson Bunker—Dahlia, Youth.
Hunt, Nelson Bunker and Edward L. Stephenson—Trillion.
Icahn, Carl—Meadow Star.
Jackson, Michael—Morley Street (Ire) (1990, '91).
Jaime, Royce S. Racing Stable and Suarez Racing—Thor's Echo.
Jayeff B Stables and Barry Weisbord—Safely Kept.
Jay Em Ess Stable—Declan's Moon.
Jeffords Jr., Mrs. Walter M.—Lonesome Glory (1992, '93, '95, '97, '99).
Jhayare Stables—Itsallgreektome.
Jones, Aaron and Marie—Ribolletta (Brz).
Jones, Aaron U.—Lemhi Gold, Tiffany Lass.
Jones Jr., J. Merrick and Folsom Farm—Chou Croute.

Jones, Mrs. Mary F.—*Cougar II.
Juddmonte Farms—Banks Hill (GB), Intercontinental (GB), Ryafan, Wandesta (GB).
Kaster, Mr. and Mrs. Richard and Mr. and Mrs. Donald Propson—Countess Diana.
Keck, Mrs. Howard B.—Ferdinand, Turkish Trousers.
Kellman, Joseph—Shecky Greene.
Klein, Eugene V.—Family Style, Open Mind (1988, '89), Winning Colors.
Klein, Eugene, L. R. French, and Barry Beal—Capote.
Klein, Eugene V. and Melvin E. Hatley—Life's Magic.
Klein, Mr. and Mrs. Eugene V.—Lady's Secret.
LaCombe, Joseph—Favorite Trick.
Lamarque Racing Stable and Louis J. Roussel III—Risen Star.
Lancaster Jr., Carlyle, et al.—Star de Naskra.
Lanzman, David—Squirtle Squirt.
LaPenta, Robert—War Pass.
La Presle Farm—Kotashaan (Fr).
Lazy F Ranch—Forego (1974, '75, '76, '77).
Levesque, Jean-Louis—La Prevoyante.
Levy, Morton and Marjoh and Donald and David Willmot—Deputy Minister.
Levy, Robert P.—Housebuster (1990, '91).
Levy, Robert, William Roberts, and Alex Karkenny—Smoke Glacken.
Lewis, Robert and Beverly—Charismatic, Folklore, Orientate, Serena's Song, Silver Charm.
Lewis, Robert and Beverly, Gainesway Farm, and Overbrook Farm—Timber Country.
Lickle, William C.—Correggio (Ire).
Live Oak Plantation—Miesque's Approval.
Loblolly Stable—Prairie Bayou, Temperence Hill, Vanlandingham.
Locust Hill Farm—Ruffian (1974, '75).
Maktoum, Sheikh Maktoum bin Rashid al—Hatoof.
Maktoum, Sheikh Mohammed bin Rashid al—Pebbles (GB), Singspiel (Ire).
Maktoum, Sheikh Mohammed bin Rashid al and Allen E. Paulson—Arazi.
Mangurian Jr., Harry T.—Desert Vixen.
Meadow Stable—Riva Ridge, Secretariat (1972, '73).
Melnyk, Eugene and Laura—Speightstown.
Milch, David, Marc Silverman, and Jack Silverman—Gilded Time.
Mill House—Sensational.
Molasky, Irwin and Andrew, Bruce Headley, and High Tech Stable (Michael Singh)—Kona Gold.
Montpelier—Proud Delta, Soothsayer.
Moran, Michael—McDynamo (2003, '05, '06).

Murdock, Mrs. Lewis C.—Zaccio (1980, '81, '82).
Nerud, John A.—Cozzene.
Niarchos, Stavros—Miesque (1987, '88).
Nishiyama, Masayuki—Paradise Creek.
Oak, Harry A.—Rockhill Native.
Overbrook Farm—Boston Harbor, Flanders, Golden Attraction, Surfside.
Oxley, John C.—Beautiful Pleasure.
Padua Stables—Vindication.
Pape, William L.—Athenian Idol, Martie's Anger.
Pape, William L., George Harris, and Jonathan Sheppard—Flatterer (1983, '84, '85, '86).
Paraneck Stable—Artax.
Paternostro, Paul and D. Wayne Lukas—North Sider.
Paulson, Allen E.—Ajina, Blushing John, Cigar (1995, '96), Eliza, Escena, Estrapade.
Paulson, Allen E. and Bertram R. Firestone—Theatrical (Ire).
Paulson, Allen E. Living Trust—Azeri (2002, '03, '04).
Paulson, Allen E. and Sheikh Mohammed bin Rashid al Maktoum—Arazi.
Paxson, Adele—Candy Eclair.
Pegram, Mike—Real Quiet, Silverbulletday (1998, '99).
Pegram, Mike, Paul Weitman, and Carl Watson—Midnight Lute.
Perry, William H.—Revidere.
Phillips Racing Partnership—Soaring Softly.
Phipps, Cynthia—Christmas Past.
Phipps, Mrs. Ogden—Straight and True.
Phipps, Ogden—Easy Goer, Heavenly Prize, Numbered Account, Personal Ensign, Relaxing.
Phipps, Ogden Mills—Inside Information, Rhythm, Smuggler, Storm Flag Flying.
Pin Oak Stable—Laugh and Be Merry.
Pollard, Carl F.—Caressing.
Pope Jr., George A.—J. O. Tobin.
Prestonwood Farm—Groovy, Victory Gallop.
Quarter B. Farm—Buck's Boy.
Ramsey, Ken and Sarah—Kitten's Joy.
Ridder, Bernard R.—Cascapedia.
Riordan, Michael D.—Bates Motel.
Robins, Gerald W. and Timothy Sams—Tasso.
Robinson, Jill E.—Cherokee Run.
Rokeby Stable—Key to the Mint, Run the Gantlet.
Rosen, Carl—Chris Evert.
Rosenthal, Mrs. Morton—Maria's Mon.
Ryehill Farm—Heavenly Cause, Smart Angle.
Sackatoga Stable—Funny Cide.
Salman, Prince Fahd bin—Fiji (GB).
Sams, Timothy and Gerald W. Robins—Tasso.
Sam-Son Farm—Chief Bearhart, Dance Smartly, Sky Classic.
Sangster, Robert E.—Royal Heroine (Ire).
Sarkowsky, Herman—Phone Chatter.

Saron Stable—Turkoman.
Saylor, Paul—Fleet Indian.
Scatuorchio, James—English Channel.
Scharbauer, Dorothy and Pamela—Alysheba (1987, '88).
Schiff, John M.—Plugged Nickle.
Shadwell Stable—Invasor (Arg), Lahudood (GB).
Shannon, Bradley M.—Manila.
SKS Stable—Lord Avie.
Someday Farm—Smarty Jones.
Sommer, Sigmund—Autobiography.
Star Crown Stable—Chief's Crown.
Starlight Stables, Paul Saylor, and Johns Martin—Ashado (2004, '05).
Stephen, Martha and Richard and The Thoroughbred Corp.—Jewel Princess.
Stone, Mrs. Whitney—Shuvee.
Stonerside Stable—Chilukki.
Stonestreet Stables, Padua Stables, George Bolton, and Midnight Cry Stables—Curlin.
Stonewall Farms Racing Division and Estate of James T. Hines Jr.—Lawyer Ron.
Straub-Rubens, Cecilia and Michael Cooper—Tiznow (2000).
Stronach, Frank and Nelson Bunker Hunt—Glorious Song.
Stronach Stables—Ghostzapper, Ginger Punch, Macho Uno, Perfect Sting.
Stud TNT and Stonewall Farm Stallions—Leroidesanimaux (Brz).
Sullivan, Jeffrey—Black Tie Affair (Ire).
Summa Stable—Track Robbery.
Tabor, Michael—Left Bank, Thunder Gulch.
Tabor, Michael and Susan Magnier—High Chaparral (Ire) (2002, '03), Johannesburg.
Tabor, Michael and Derek Smith—Rags to Riches.
Tafel, James B.—Street Sense.
Tafel, James, Richard Santulli, and Jayeff B Stables—Banshee Breeze.
Tanaka, Gary—Golden Apples (Ire), Gourmet Girl.
Tartan Stable—Dr. Patches.
Tayhill Stable—Seattle Slew (1978).
Taylor, Mrs. Karen L.—Seattle Slew (1976, '77).
The Thoroughbred Corp.—Anees, Point Given.
The Thoroughbred Corp. and Russell Reineman—War Emblem.
Tizol, E. Rodriguez—Bold Forbes.
Torsney, Dr. Jerome M.—Mac Diarmida.
Tucker, Paula—Princess Rooney.
Valando, Thomas—Fly So Free.
Vance, Jeanne—Lemon Drop Kid.
Van Worp, Robert—Not Surprising.
Via, Harold A. Jr.—Good Night Shirt.
Warren, Mr. and Mrs. William Jr.—Saint Liam.
Weasel Jr., George—My Juliet.
Weinsier, Randolph—Lakeville Miss.
Lord Weinstock, Executors of the late—Islington (Ire).

Wertheimer Farm—Halfbridled.
Westerly Stud—Typecast.
Whitham, Mr. and Mrs. Frank E.—Bayakoa (Arg) (1989, '90).

Whitney, Marylou—Bird Town.
Wildenstein, Daniel—All Along (Fr).
Wildenstein Stable—Steinlen (GB).

Windfields Farm and Neil Phillips—*Snow Knight.
Wygod, Martin and Pamela—Sweet Catomine.

Breeders of Eclipse Award Winners

Adams, Mrs. Vanderbilt—Desert Vixen.
Adena Springs—Ghostzapper, Ginger Punch, Macho Uno, Perfect Sting.
Aga Khan—Daylami (Ire), Hirapour (Ire), Kalanisi (Ire).
Alexander, Emory—Queena.
Allez France Stables—Steinlen (GB).
Augustus, Peggy—Johnny D.
Baker, Dr. Howard—Serena's Song.
Ballydoyle Stud—Correggio (Ire).
Ballymacoll Stud Farm—Islington (Ire).
Barnhart, Anna Marie—Skip Away (1996, '97, '98).
Bell, H. Bennett and Jessica Bell Nicholson—Epitome.
Benjamin, Edward Bernard—Canonero II (Ire).
Benjamin, E. V. III and William G. Clark—Chou Croute.
Bettersworth, J. R.—My Juliet.
Blue Bear Stud—Zaccio (1980, '81, '82).
Blue Diamond Ranch—Snow Chief.
Blue Seas Music Inc.—Heartlight No. One.
Bowman, Dr. and Mrs. Thomas—Good Night Shirt.
Brant, Peter M.—Gulch, Thunder Gulch.
Calabrese, Frank C.—Dreaming of Anna.
Calbourne Farm—Brown Bess.
Calumet Farm—Before Dawn, Criminal Type, Davona Dale, Our Mims.
Cannata, Carl and Olivia—Gourmet Girl.
Carrion, Jaime S.—Action This Day, Meadow Star.
Carroll, Mike and John C. Harvey Jr.—Maryfield.
Castleman, Ben S.—Seattle Slew (1976, '77, '78).
Centurion Farms—Deputy Minister.
Chenery, Helen B.—Saratoga Dew.
Cherry Valley Farm—War Pass.
Christiana Stables—Go for Wand (1989, '90).
Claiborne Farm—Forty Niner, Revidere, Slew o' Gold (1983, '84), Swale, Wajima.
Cleaboy Farms Co.—Inlander (GB).
Cohen, Ollie A.—Eillo.
Cojuangco, Edwardo M. Jr.—Manila.
Coughlan, Sean—High Chaparral (Ire) (2002, '03).
Cowan, Irving and Marjorie—Hollywood Wildcat.
Danada Farm—Proud Delta.
Darley—Bernardini, Tempera.
Davison, Mrs. Richard—Guilty Conscience.
Dayton Ltd.—All Along (Fr), Waya (Fr).
Delta Thoroughbreds Inc.—Cardmania.
De Mestre, J. W.—Jimmy Lorenzo (GB).
Due Process Stables—Dehere, Open Mind (1988, '89).

Earnhardt, Hal and Patti—Indian Blessing.
Eaton Farms Inc. and Red Bull Stable—Bold Forbes.
Echo Valley Horse Farm Inc.—Chris Evert, Winning Colors.
Egan, James and David Hanley—Golden Apples (Ire).
Elmendorf Farm—Protagonist, Shadow Brook, Talking Picture.
Evans, Edward P.—Saint Liam.
Evans, Mrs. Thomas Mellon—Pleasant Stage.
Evans, Thomas Mellon—Pleasant Colony, Pleasant Tap.
Evans, Tom, Macon Wilmil Equines, and Marjac Farm—Midnight Lute.
Fares Farm—Curlin.
Farfellow Farms Ltd.—Anees.
Farish, William S., James Elkins, and Temple Webber Jr.—Mineshaft.
Farish, William S. and Ogden Mills Phipps—Storm Song.
Farish, William S. and W. S. Kilroy—A.P. Indy, Lemon Drop Kid.
Farish, William S. and W. Temple Webber Jr.—Wait a While.
Farnsworth Farms—Beautiful Pleasure, Jewel Princess.
Fast Lane Farms and Block & Forman—Thor's Echo.
Feeney, F.—April Run (Ire).
Firestone, Mr. and Mrs. Bertram R.—Paradise Creek, Theatrical (Ire).
Flaxman Holdings Ltd.—Aldebaran, Miesque (1987, '88).
Floyd, William—Highland Bud.
Fox, Richard and Nathan and Richard Kaster—McDynamo (2003, '05, '06).
Franks, John—Answer Lively.
Freeman, Carl M.—Miss Alleged.
Fuller, C. T.—Ambassador of Luck.
Fuller, Peter—Mom's Command.
Gainesway Thoroughbreds Ltd.—Orientate.
Gainsborough Farm—Fantastic Light, Hatoof.
Galbreath, John W.—Little Current, Sunshine Forever.
Galbreath, Mrs. John W.—Tempest Queen.
Galbreath/Phillips Racing Partnership—Soaring Softly.
Genter Stable, Frances A.—Smile.
Golden Chance Farm Inc.—John Henry (1980, '81, '83, '84).
Greentree Stud—Bowl Game, Late Bloomer.
Groves, Helen, Helen Alexander, and David Aykroyd—Althea.
Guest, Raymond R.—Cascapedia.
Guest, Virginia D.—Life's Illusion.

Leading Breeders
Wholly or in partnership,
by number of titles won,
including Horse of the Year
11—Allen E. Paulson
9—Harbor View Farm
7—William S. Farish and Partners
7—Lazy F Ranch
6—Claiborne Farm
6—Golden Chance Farm
6—Ogden Phipps
5—Adena Springs
5—Calumet Farm
5—Walter M. Jeffords Jr.
5—Aaron U. Jones
5—Meadow Stud
5—William L. Pape and Jonathan Sheppard

By Individual Winners
6—Ogden Phipps
5—Claiborne Farm
5—William Farish and Partners
5—Allen E. Paulson
4—Adena Springs
4—Calumet Farm
4—Overbrook Farm
4—Harbor View Farm
4—Juddmonte Farms
4—Nelson Bunker Hunt

Gunther, John, Tony Holmes, Walter Zent—Stevie Wonderboy.
Guggenheim, Harry F.—Ack Ack.
Hancock, Arthur B. III and Leone J. Peters—Risen Star.
Happy Valley Farm—It's in the Air.
Haras Bage do Sul—Leroidesanimaux (Brz).
Haras Clausan—Invasor (Arg).
Haras El Huerton—*Gran Kan.
Haras General Cruz—*Cougar II.
Haras Principal—Bayakoa (Arg) (1989, '90).
Haras Santa Amelia—Pompeyo (Chi).
Haras Santa Ana do Rio Grande—Riboletta (Brz).
Haras Vacacion—Paseana (Arg) (1992, '93).
Harbor View Farm—Affirmed (1977-'79), Athenian Idol, Outstandingly, Flawlessly (1992, '93).
Hartigan, John H.—Mac Diarmida.
Hayden, Mr. and Mrs. David—Safely Kept.
Hibbert, Robert E.—Roving Boy.
Hickey, P. Noel—Buck's Boy.
Highclere Inc. and Clear Creek—Silverbulletday (1998, '99).
Hines, James T. Jr.—Lawyer Ron.
Hi Yu Stables—Chinook Pass.
Hofmann, Mr. and Mrs. Philip B.—Gold Beauty.

Homan, J. L.—Gallant Bob.
Hooper, Fred W.—Precisionist.
Hooper Jr., Fred W.—Susan's Girl (1972, '73, '75).
Humphrey, G. Watts Jr., and William S. Farish III—Sacahuista.
Humphrey, Mrs. G. Watts Jr.—Genuine Risk.
Hundley, Bruce and Wayne Garrison—Fly So Free.
Hunt, Nelson Bunker—Dahlia, Estrapade, Trillion, Youth.
Iandoli, Lewis E.—Conquistador Cielo.
Irish American Bloodstock Agency Ltd.—Yanks Music.
Irish Hill Farm and Rowe W. Harper—Spend a Buck.
Janney, Mr. and Mrs. Stuart S. Jr.—Ruffian (1974, '75).
Jason, Mrs. William M. and Mrs. William Gilmore—Spectacular Bid (1978, '79, '80).
Jeffords, Walter M. Jr.—Lonesome Glory (1992, '93, '95, '97, '99).
Jones, Aaron U.—Lemhi Gold, Tiffany Lass.
Jones, Aaron U. and Marie D.—Ashado (2004, '05), Speightstown.
Jones, Brereton C.—Caressing.
Juddmonte Farms—Banks Hill (GB), Intercontinental (GB), Ryafan, Wandesta (GB).
Karutz, Dr. Wallace—Brave Raj.
Kaster, Richard S.—Countess Diana.
Keck, Howard B.—Ferdinand, Turkish Trousers.
Keene Ridge Farm—English Channel.
Kellman, Joseph—Shecky Greene.
Kitchen, Edgar—Track Robbery.
Kluener, Robert G.—Warm Spell.
Knight, Landon—Flat Top (1998, 2002).
Kris Syndicate and Kirtlington Stud Ltd.—All Gong (GB).
Lancaster, Carlyle J.—Star de Naskra.
Lazy F Ranch—Forego (1974, '75, '76, '77).
Levesque, Jean-Louis—La Prevoyante.
Levy, Blanche P. and Murphy Stable—Housebuster (1990, '91).
Levy, Robert P. and Cisley Stable—North Sider.
Lewis, Robert and Beverly—Folklore.
Lilley, J. A. C.—*Snow Knight.
Little Hill Farm—Real Quiet.
Little, Marvin A. Jr.—Hansel.
Live Oak Stud—Miesque's Approval.
Loblolly Stable—Prairie Bayou, Vanlandingham.
Lowquest Ltd.—Timber Country.
Luro, Horatio A.—Wayward Lass.
Lyster III, W. G. and Jayeff B Stables—Johannesburg.
Madden, Preston—Alysheba (1987, '88).
Maktoum, Sheikh Mohammed bin Rashid al—Singspiel (Ire).
Mangurian, Mr. and Mrs. Harry T. Jr.—Gilded Time.
Maynard, Richard D.—Chief Bearhart.
Meadow Stud—Riva Ridge, Secretariat (1972, '73).
Mellon, Paul—Key to the Mint, Run the Gantlet.
Mill House—Sensational.
Nahem, Ed—Bertrando.
Narducci, M.D., Audrey—Squirtle Squirt.
Nerud, John A.—Cozzene.
Newgate Stud Company—Fiji (GB).
North Ridge Farm—Blushing John, Capote.
Nuckols Brothers—Typecast.
Nuckols, Charles Jr. and Sons—Hidden Lake, War Emblem.
Oak Cliff Thoroughbreds Ltd.—Sunday Silence.
Onett, George C.—Cherokee Run.
Overbrook Farm—Boston Harbor, Flanders, Golden Attraction, Surfside.
Pancoast, Mrs. Jean R.—Dearly Precious.
Pape, William L. and Jonathan Sheppard—Flatterer (1983, '84, '85, '86), Martie's Anger.
Parkhill, Marshall—Morley Street (Ire) (1990, '91).
Parrish, Douglas, Estate of Emma Haggin Parrish, and Dr. David C. Parrish III—Life's Magic.
Parrish Hill Farm and William S. Farish—Charismatic.
Paulson, Allen E.—Ajina, Azeri (2002, '03, '04), Cigar (1995, '96), Eliza, Escena.
Paxson, Adele—Candy Eclair.
Payson Stud—Farda Amiga, Vindication.
Pelican Stable—Holy Bull.
Perez, Carlos—Kona Gold.
Peskoff, Stephen D.—Black Tie Affair (Ire).
Phillips, Mrs. Jacqueline Getty—Bates Motel.
Phillips Racing Partnership/Galbreath—Soaring Softly.
Phipps, Cynthia—Christmas Past.
Phipps, Mrs. Ogden—Straight and True.
Phipps, Ogden—Easy Goer, Heavenly Prize, Numbered Account, Personal Ensign, Relaxing, Storm Flag Flying.
Phipps, Ogden Mills—Inside Information, Rhythm, Smuggler.
Pin Oak Farm—Laugh and Be Merry.
Polinger, Milton—What a Summer.
Polk, Dr. Albert F. Jr.—Temperence Hill.
Pope, George A. Jr.—J. O. Tobin.
Ramsey, Kenneth and Sarah—Kitten's Joy.
Rathvale Stud—Just a Game (Ire).
Ravenbrook Farm Inc.—Not Surprising.
Ridgely, Brice—Declan's Moon.
Roach, Dr. Ben and Tom Roach—Princess Rooney.
Robertson, Corbin—Turkoman.
Robins, Gerald W. and Timothy H. Sams—Tasso.
Robinson, Marshall T.—Groovy.
Rosebrock, Perry M.—Smoke Glacken.
Rosen, Carl—Chief's Crown.
Rosenthal, Morton—Maria's Mon.
Ryan, B. L.—Royal Heroine (Ire).
Ryehill Farm—Heavenly Cause, Smart Angle.
Sam-Son Farm—Dance Smartly, Sky Classic.
Sarkowski, Herman—Phone Chatter.
Schiff, John M.—Plugged Nickle.
Scott, Mrs. Marion duPont—Soothsayer.
Selective Seasons—Family Style.
Seper, Susan—Lost in the Fog.
Sergent, Willard—Reraise.
Shadwell Estate Co.—Lahudood (GB).
Shead, A. D. and F. H. Sasse—Perrault (GB).
Silvertand, John Martin—Afleet Alex.
Skara Glen Stables—Rags to Riches.
Someday Farm—Smarty Jones.
Spendthrift Farm and Francis Kernan—Landaluce.
Spreen, Robert H.—Lady's Secret.
Stanley Estate and Stud Co.—Ouija Board (GB), (2004, '06).
Stone, Whitney—Shuvee.
Straub-Rubens, Cecilia—Tiznow (2000, '01).
Sugar Maple Farm—Itsallgreektome, Sky Beauty.
Swettenham Stud—Lit de Justice.
Swettenham Stud and Partners—Northern Spur (Ire).
Tafel, James B.—Banshee Breeze, Street Sense.
Tall Oaks Farm—Victory Gallop.
Tartan Farms Corp.—Dr. Patches, Unbridled.
Taylor, E. P.—Devil's Bag, Glorious Song.
The Thoroughbred Corp.—Point Given.
Third Kirsmith Racing Associates—Rubiano.
Thomas, Dr. E. W. and Carolaine Farm—Rockhill Native.
Thomas/Lakin—Fleet Indian.
Viking Farms Ltd.—Lord Avie.
Vinery and Carondelet Farm—Artax.
Waldemar Farms Inc.—Foolish Pleasure, Honest Pleasure.
Warren Hill Stud and Mimika Financiera—Pebbles (GB).
Weinsier, Randolph—Lakeville Miss.
Wertheimer and Brother—Halfbridled, Kotashaan (Fr).
West, Dr. and Mrs. R. Smiser and MacKenzie Miller—De La Rose.
West, Dr. and Mrs. R. Smiser, and Mr. and Mrs. MacKenzie Miller—Chilukki.
Wheatley Stable—Autobiography.
Whitney, Marylou—Bird Town.
Wilson, Ralph C. Jr.—Arazi.
Winchell, Verne H.—Cafe Prince (1977-'78), Tight Spot.
WinStar Farm—Funny Cide.
Witt, Mr. and Mrs. Robert—Possibly Perfect.
Wood, Mr. and Mrs. M. L.—Favorite Trick.
Wootton, Mary Lou—Silver Charm.
Wygod, Martin and Pamela—Sweet Catomine.
Youngblood, John and Fletcher Gray—Left Bank.
Zurek, Edward N.—The Wicked North.

Trainers of Eclipse Award Winners

Albertrani, Louis—Artax.
Albertrani, Thomas—Bernardini.
Alexander, Frank—Cherokee Run.
Allard, Edward T.—Mom's Command.
Anderson, Laurie—Chinook Pass.
Arias, Juan—Canonero II.
Asmussen, Steve—Curlin.
Badgett Jr., William—Go for Wand (1989, '90).
Baffert, Bob—Chilukki, Indian Blessing, Midnight Lute, Point Given, Real Quiet, Silverbulletday (1998, '99), Silver Charm, Vindication, War Emblem.
Balding, Gerald B. "Toby"—Morley Street (Ire) (1990, '91).
Barnett, Robert—Answer Lively.
Barrera, Lazaro S.—Affirmed (1977, '78, '79), Bold Forbes, It's in the Air, J. O. Tobin, Lemhi Gold, Tiffany Lass.
Bary, Pascal—Miss Alleged (with Charles Whittingham).
Belanger Jr., Gerald W.—Glorious Song.
Bernstein, David—The Wicked North.
Biancone, Patrick L.—All Along (Fr).
bin Suroor, Saeed—Daylami (Ire), Fantastic Light.
Bohannan, Thomas—Prairie Bayou.
Boutin, Francois—April Run (Ire) Arazi, Miesque (1987, '88).
Brittain, Clive E.—Pebbles (GB).
Brothers, Frank—Hansel.
Burch, J. Elliot—Key to the Mint, Run the Gantlet.
Byrne, Patrick—Countess Diana, Favorite Trick.
Campbell, Gordon C.—Cascapedia.
Campo, John P.—Pleasant Colony, Protagonist, Talking Picture.
Canani, Julio—Sweet Catomine.
Cantey, Joseph B.—Temperence Hill.
Carroll, Henry—Smoke Glacken.
Catalano, Wayne—Dreaming of Anna.
Cecil, Ben—Golden Apples (Ire).
Cocks, W. Burling—Zaccio (1980, '81, '82).
Croll Jr., Warren A.—Holy Bull, Housebuster (1990, '91).
Curtis Jr., William—Gold Beauty.
Day, Jim—Dance Smartly, Sky Classic.
de Seroux, Laura—Azeri (2002, '03).
DiMauro, Steve—Dearly Precious, Wajima.
Dollase, Craig—Reraise.
Dollase, Wallace—Itsallgreektome, Jewel Princess.
Doyle, A. T.—Typecast.
Drysdale, Neil—A.P. Indy, Fiji (GB), Hollywood Wildcat, Princess Rooney, Tasso.
Dunham, Robert G.—Chou Croute.
Dunlop, Edward—Ouija Board (GB) (2004, '06).
Dutrow, Richard Jr.—Saint Liam.
Elliot, Janet E.—Correggio (Ire), Flat Top (1998, 2002).
Ellis, Ron—Declan's Moon.
Euster, Eugene—My Juliet.
Fabre, Andre—Banks Hill (GB).
Fenstermaker, L. Ross—Precisionist, Susan's Girl (1975).
Fenwick, Charles—Inlander (GB).
Ferris, Richard D.—Star de Naskra.
Fisher, Jack—Good Night Shirt.
Fout, Douglas—Hirapour (Ire).
Fout, Paul R.—Life's Illusion.
Frankel, Bobby—Aldebaran, Bertrando, Ghostzapper, Ginger Punch, Intercontinental (GB), Leroidesanimaux (Brz), Possibly Perfect, Ryafan, Squirtle Squirt, Wandesta (GB).
Freeman, W. C.—Shuvee.
Frostad, Mark—Chief Bearhart.
Furr, C.—*Gran Kan.
Gambolati, Cam—Spend a Buck.
Gaver, John M.—Late Bloomer.
Gaver Jr., John M.—Bowl Game.
Gilchrist, Greg—Lost in the Fog.
Goldberg, Alan E.—Safely Kept.
Goldfine, Lou M.—Shecky Greene.
Gosden, John H. M.—Bates Motel, Royal Heroine (Ire).
Griggs, John K.—Warm Spell.
Harty, Eoin—Tempera.
Hassinger Jr., Alex—Anees, Eliza.
Hauswald, Phil—Epitome.
Head, Christiane—Hatoof.
Headley, Bruce—Kona Gold.
Hendriks, Sanna Neilson—McDynamo (2003, '05, '06), Pomeyo (Chi).
Hertler, John O.—Slew o' Gold (1983, '84).
Hickey, P. Noel—Buck's Boy.
Hine, Hubert—Guilty Conscience, Skip Away (1996, '97, '98).
Howard, Neil—Mineshaft.
Howe, Peter M.—Proud Delta, Soothsayer.
Inda, Eduardo—Riboletta (Brz).
Jenda, Charles J.—Brown Bess.
Jerkens, H. Allen—Sky Beauty.
Jolley, LeRoy—Foolish Pleasure, Genuine Risk, Honest Pleasure, Manila, Meadow Star, What a Summer.
Jones, Gary—Turkoman.
Kay, Michael—Johnny D.
Kelly, Thomas J.—Plugged Nickle.
Kimmel, John—Hidden Lake.
King Jr., S. Allen—Candy Eclair.
Laurin, Lucien—Riva Ridge, Secretariat (1972, '73).
Laurin, Roger—Chief's Crown, Numbered Account.
Lepman, Budd—Eillo.
Lobo, Paulo—Farda Amiga.
Lukas, D. Wayne—Althea, Azeri (2004), Boston Harbor, Capote, Charismatic, Criminal Type, Family Style, Flanders, Folklore, Golden Attraction, Gulch, Lady's Secret, Landaluce, Life's Magic (1984, '85), North Sider, Open Mind (1988, '89), Orientate, Sacahuista, Serena's Song, Steinlen (GB), Surfside, Thunder Gulch, Timber Country, Winning Colors.
Lundy, Richard J.—Blushing John.
Mandella, Richard—Action This Day, Halfbridled, Kotashaan (Fr), Phone Chatter.
Manzi, Joseph—Roving Boy.
Marquette, Joseph D.—Gallant Bob.
Marti, Pedro—Heartlight No. One.
Martin, Frank—Autobiography, Outstandingly.
Martin, Jose—Groovy, Lakeville Miss, Wayward Lass.
McAnally, Ronald—Bayakoa (Arg) (1989, '90), John Henry (1980, '81, '83, '84), Northern Spur (Ire), Paseana (Arg) (1992, '93), Tight Spot.
McGaughey III, Claude R.—Easy Goer, Heavenly Prize, Inside Information, Personal Ensign, Queena, Rhythm, Smuggler, Storm Flag Flying, Vanlandingham.
McLaughlin, Kiaran—Invasor (Arg), Lahudoud (GB).

Leading Trainers

By number of titles won, including Horse of the Year

29—D. Wayne Lukas
13—Charlie Whittingham
12—Ron McAnally
11—Bob Baffert
10—Lazaro Barrera
10—Bobby Frankel
10—Jonathan Sheppard
9—Claude McGaughey III
9—Todd Pletcher
9—Woody Stephens
8—Bill Mott
7—Frank Y. Whiteley Jr.
6—LeRoy Jolley
6—F. Bruce Miller
5—Neil Drysdale
5—Hubert Hine
5—Lucien Laurin
5—Richard Mandella
5—Flint S. Schulhofer

By Individual Winners

24—D. Wayne Lukas
10—Bobby Frankel
9—Bob Baffert
9—Claude McGaughey III
9—Charles Whittingham
8—Todd Pletcher
8—Woody Stephens
6—Laz Barrera
6—LeRoy Jolley
6—Jonathan Sheppard
5—Ron McAnally
5—Bill Mott
5—Flint S. Schulhofer

Meredith, Derek—Cardmania.
Miller, F. Bruce—All Gong (GB), Lonesome Glory (1992, '93, '95, '97, '99).
Miller, MacKenzie—*Snow Knight.
Mott, Bill—Ajina, Cigar (1995, '96), Escena, Paradise Creek, Theatrical (Ire).
Nafzger, Carl A.—Banshee Breeze, Street Sense, Unbridled.
Nerud, Jan H.—Cozzene.
Nerud, John A.—Dr. Patches.
Nickerson, Victor J.—John Henry (1981).
Nobles, Reynaldo—Dehere.
O'Brien, Aidan—High Chaparral (Ire) (2002, '03), Johannesburg.
O'Brien, Leo—Yanks Music.
O'Neill, Doug—Maryfield, Stevie Wonderboy, Thor's Echo.
Orseno, Joseph F.—Macho Uno, Perfect Sting.
Penna, Angel—Relaxing.
Penna Jr., Angel—Christmas Past, Laugh and Be Merry.
Perdomo, Pico—Gourmet Girl.
Perlsweig, Daniel—Lord Avie.
Peterson, Douglas—Seattle Slew (1978).
Pletcher, Todd—Ashado (2004, '05), English Channel, Fleet Indian, Lawyer Ron, Left Bank, Rags to Riches, Speightstown, Wait a While.
Poulos, Ernie—Black Tie Affair (Ire).
Preger, Mitchell C.—Ambassador of Luck.
Ritchey, Tim—Afleet Alex.
Robbins, Jay—Tiznow (2000, '01).
Romans Dale L.—Kitten's Joy.
Rondinello, Thomas L.—Little Current, Tempest Queen.
Root Sr., T. F.—Desert Vixen.
Roussel III, Louis J.—Risen Star.
Russell, John W.—Susan's Girl (1972, '73).
Sahadi, Jenine—Lit de Justice.
Schosberg, Richard—Maria's Mon.
Schulhofer, Flint S.—Fly So Free, Lemon Drop Kid, Mac Diarmida, Rubiano, Smile.
Sciacca, Gary—Saratoga Dew.
Servis, John—Smarty Jones.
Sheppard, Jonathan E.—Athenian Idol, Cafe Prince (1977, '78), Flatterer (1983, '84, '85, '86), Highland Bud, Jimmy Lorenzo (GB), Martie's Anger.
Smithwick, D. Michael—Straight and True.
Speckert, Chris—Pleasant Stage, Pleasant Tap.
Starr, John—La Prevoyante.
Stephens, Woodford C.—Conquistador Cielo, De La Rose, Devil's Bag, Forty Niner, Heavenly Cause, Sensational, Smart Angle, Swale.
Stevens, Herbert—Rockhill Native.
Stoute, Sir Michael—Islington (Ire), Kalanisi (Ire), Singspiel (Ire).
Stute, Mel—Brave Raj, Snow Chief.
Tagg, Barclay—Funny Cide.
Tammaro, John—Deputy Minister.
Toner, James J.—Soaring Softly.
Trovato, Joseph A.—Chris Evert.
Turner Jr., William H.—Seattle Slew (1976-'77).
Van Berg, Jack—Alysheba (1987-'88).
Vance, David R.—Caressing.
Van Worp, Judson—Not Surprising.
Veitch, John M.—Before Dawn, Davona Dale, Our Mims, Sunshine Forever.
Vienna, Darrell—Gilded Time.
Walden, W. Elliott—Victory Gallop.
Ward, John T.—Beautiful Pleasure.
Ward, Sherrill W.—Forego (1974, '75).
Watters Jr., Sidney—Shadow Brook, Slew o' Gold (1983, '84).
Wheeler, Robert L. and John W. Russell—Track Robbery.
Whiteley, David A.—Just a Game (Ire), Revidere, Waya (Fr).
Whiteley Jr., Frank Y.—Forego (1976, '77), Ruffian (1974, '75).
Whittingham, Charles—Ack Ack, *Cougar II, Estrapade, Ferdinand, Flawlessly (1992, '93), Miss Alleged (with Pascal Bary), Perrault (GB), Sunday Silence, Turkish Trousers.
Wolfson, Martin—Miesque's Approval.
Zilber, Maurice—Youth, Dahlia, Trillion.
Zito, Nicholas P.—Bird Town, Storm Song, War Pass.

Sires of Eclipse Award Winners

Ack Ack—Youth.
Affirmed—Flawlessly (1992, '93).
Ahmad—Paseana (Arg) (1992, '93).
Air Forbes Won—Yanks Music.
***Alcibiades II**—Athenian Idol.
Alleged—Flat Top (1998, 2002), Miss Alleged.
Alydar—Althea, Alysheba (1987, '88), Criminal Type, Easy Goer, Turkoman.
A.P. Indy—Bernardini, Mineshaft, Rags to Riches, Tempera.
Awesome Again—Ghostzapper, Ginger Punch.
Bagdad—Turkish Trousers.
Battle Joined—Ack Ack.
Best Turn—Davona Dale.
Better Than Honour—Rags to Riches.
Blushing Groom (Fr)—Arazi, Blushing John, Sky Beauty.
Bold Bidder—Spectacular Bid (1978, '79, '80).
Bold Forbes—Tiffany Lass.
Bold Reasoning—Seattle Slew (1976, '77, '78).
Bold Ruler—Secretariat (1972, '73), Wajima.
Broad Brush—Farda Amiga.
Buckaroo—Spend a Buck.
Buckpasser—La Prevoyante, Numbered Account, Relaxing.
Bucksplasher—Buck's Boy.
Candy Stripes—Invasor (Arg), Leroidesanimaux (Brz).
Cape Cross (Ire)—Ouija Board (GB) (2004, '06).
Cape Town—Bird Town.
Capote—Boston Harbor.
Caro (Ire)—Cozzene, Winning Colors.
Cee's Tizzy—Gourmet Girl, Tiznow (2000, '01).
Cherokee Run—Chilukki, War Pass.
Chief's Crown—Chief Bearhart.
Chieftain—Cascapedia.
Cohoes—Shadow Brook.
Concern—Good Night Shirt.
Consultant's Bid—Bayakoa (Arg) (1989, '90).
Cormorant—Saratoga Dew.
Court Ruling—Guilty Conscience.
Cox's Ridge—Cardmania, Life's Magic 1984, '85), Vanlandingham.
Creme dela Creme—Cafe Prince (1977, '78).
Crozier—Precisionist.
Cryptoclearance—Victory Gallop.
Danehill—Banks Hill (GB), Intercontinental (GB).
Danzatore—Reraise.
Danzig—Chief's Crown, Dance Smartly.
Darshaan—Kotashaan (Fr).
Deep Run—Morley Street (Ire) (1990, '91).

Leading Sires
By number of titles won, including Horse of the Year
11—Mr. Prospector
9—Seattle Slew
8—Alydar
7—Exclusive Native
7—*Forli
6—Bold Ruler
6—Ole Bob Bowers
5—Deputy Minister
5—Sadler's Wells
5—Transworld

By Individual Winners
10—Mr. Prospector
6—Seattle Slew
5—Alydar
4—Sadler's Wells
4—Unbridled

Deerhound—Countess Diana.
Delta Judge—Proud Delta.
Deputy Minister—Dehere, Go for Wand (1989, '90), Open Mind (1988, '89).
Distorted Humor—Funny Cide.
Djakao—Perrault (GB).
Doyoun—Daylami (Ire), Kalanisi (Ire).
Dr. Fager—Dearly Precious, Dr. Patches.

Eclipse Awards — Sires of Champions

Dynaformer—McDynamo (2003, '05, '06).
El Gran Senor—Lit de Justice.
El Prado (Ire)—Kitten's Joy.
Elusive Quality—Maryfield, Smarty Jones.
Erins Isle (Ire)—Laugh and Be Merry.
Exclusive Native—Affirmed (1977, '78, '79), Genuine Risk, Outstandingly.
Fappiano—Tasso, Unbridled, Rubiano.
Faraway Son—Waya (Fr).
Far North—The Wicked North.
Firestreak—*Snow Knight.
First Landing—Riva Ridge.
***Forli**—Forego (1974, '75, '76, '77).
French Deputy—Left Bank.
Gallant Romeo—Gallant Bob, My Juliet.
Gone West—Speightstown.
Graustark—Key to the Mint, Tempest Queen.
Great Above—Holy Bull.
***Grey Dawn II**—Christmas Past, Heavenly Cause.
Gulch—Thunder Gulch.
Habitat—Steinlen (GB).
Hail the Pirates—Wayward Lass.
Hail to Reason—Trillion.
Halo—Devil's Bag, Glorious Song, Sunday Silence.
Hennessy—Johannesburg.
***Herbager**—Our Mims.
His Majesty—Pleasant Colony, Tight Spot.
Hoist the Flag—Sensational.
Holy Bull—Macho Uno.
Honour and Glory—Caressing.
Horatius—Safely Kept.
Ile de Bourbon—Inlander (GB).
Indian Charlie—Fleet Indian, Indian Blessing.
In Reality—Desert Vixen, Smile.
In the Wings (GB)—Singspiel (Ire).
Irish Castle—Bold Forbes.
Irish River (Fr)—Hatoof, Paradise Creek.
Jade Hunter—Azeri (2002, '03, '04).
Java Gold—Kona Gold.
Kahyasi—Hirapour (Ire).
Key to the Mint—Jewel Princess, Plugged Nickle.
Kingmambo—Lemon Drop Kid.
Kris—All Gong (GB).
Kris S.—Action This Day, Hollywood Wildcat, Soaring Softly.
Langfuhr—Lawyer Ron.
Lear Fan—Ryafan.
Licencioso—*Gran Kan.
Little Missouri—Prairie Bayou.
Lively One—Answer Lively.
Lord Gaylord—Lord Avie.
***Lorenzaccio**—Zaccio (1980, '81, '82).
Lost Soldier—Lost in the Fog.
Lt. Stevens—Chou Croute.
Lyphard—Manila.
Lypheor (GB)—Royal Heroine (Ire).
Malibu Moon—Declan's Moon.
Maria's Mon—Wait a While.
Marquetry—Artax, Squirtle Squirt.
Maudlin—Beautiful Pleasure.

Meadowlake—Meadow Star.
Medieval Man—Not Surprising.
Miesque's Son—Miesque's Approval.
Minnesota Mac—Mac Diarmida.
Miswaki—Black Tie Affair (Ire).
Mo Bay—Flatterer (1983, '84, '85, '86).
Mr. Prospector—Aldebaran, Conquistador Cielo, Eillo, Forty Niner, Gold Beauty, Golden Attraction, Gulch, It's in the Air, Queena, Rhythm.
Mt. Livermore—Housebuster (1990, '91), Eliza, Orientate.
***Mystic II**—Life's Illusion, Soothsayer.
Nashua—Shuvee.
Nashwan—Wandesta (GB).
Naskra—Star de Naskra.
Native Born—Chinook Pass.
Never Bend—J. O. Tobin, Straight and True.
Nijinsky II—De La Rose, Ferdinand, Sky Classic.
***Noholme II**—Shecky Greene.
Norcliffe—Groovy.
No Robbery—Track Robbery.
Northern Afleet—Afleet Alex.
Northern Baby—Highland Bud, Possibly Perfect, Warm Spell.
Northern Jove—Candy Eclair.
Nureyev—Miesque (1987, '88), Theatrical (Ire).
Nureyev Dancer—Pompeyo (Chi).
Olden Times—Roving Boy.
Ole Bob Bowers—John Henry (1980, '81, '83, '84).
Our Emblem—War Emblem.
Our Jimmy—Jimmy Lorenzo (GB).
Our Native—Rockhill Native.
Palace Music—Cigar (1995, '96).
***Petrone**—Brown Bess.
PhoneTrick—Favorite Trick, Phone Chatter.
Pivotal—Golden Apples (Ire).
Pleasant Colony—Pleasant Stage, Pleasant Tap.
***Pretendre**—Canonero II.
Prince John—Protagonist, Typecast.
Private Account—Inside Information, Personal Ensign.
Quadrangle—Smart Angle, Susan's Girl (1972, '73, '75).
Quiet American—Hidden Lake, Real Quiet.
Rahy—Dreaming of Anna, Fantastic Light, Serena's Song.
Rainbow Quest—Fiji (GB).
Rainy Lake—Lakeville Miss.
Raise a Cup—Before Dawn.
Rajab—Brave Raj.
Raja Baba—Sacahuista.
Real Quiet—Midnight Lute.
Red Ransom—Perfect Sting.
Reflected Glory—Snow Chief.
Reviewer—Revidere, Ruffian (1974, '75).
Roberto—Sunshine Forever.
Rock Talk—Heartlight No. One.
Roi Normand—Riboletta (Brz).
Runaway Groom—Cherokee Run.

Run the Gantlet—April Run (Ire).
Sadler's Wells—Correggio (Ire), High Chaparral (Ire) (2002, '03), Islington (Ire), Northern Spur (Ire).
Saint Ballado—Ashado (2004, '05), Saint Liam.
***Sea-Bird**—Little Current.
Seattle Slew—A.P. Indy, Capote, Landaluce, Slew o' Gold (1983, '84), Surfside, Swale, Vindication.
Secretariat—Lady's Secret, Risen Star.
Seeking the Gold—Flanders, Heavenly Prize.
Sharpen Up (GB)—Pebbles (GB).
Silver Buck—Silver Charm.
Silver Deputy—Silverbulletday (1998, '99).
Singspiel (Ire)—Lahudood (GB).
Sir Ivor—Bates Motel.
Skip Trial—Skip Away (1996, '97, '98).
***Sky High II**—Autobiography.
Skywalker—Bertrando.
Smart Strike—Curlin, English Channel.
Sovereign Dancer—Itsallgreektome.
Speak John—Talking Picture.
Spring Double—Martie's Anger.
Stage Door Johnny—Johnny D., Late Bloomer.
State Dinner—Family Style.
Stephen Got Even—Stevie Wonderboy.
Stop the Music—Temperence Hill.
Storm Cat—Storm Flag Flying, Sweet Catomine.
Strawberry Road (Aus)—Ajina, Escena.
Street Cry (Ire)—Street Sense.
Summer Squall—Charismatic, Storm Song.
Summing—Epitome.
Swiss Yodeler—Thor's Echo.
Swoon's Son—Chris Evert.
Tale of Two Cities—*Cougar II.
Tarboosh—Just a Game (Ire).
Targowice—All Along (Fr).
Thunder Gulch—Point Given.
Time for a Change—Fly So Free.
Timeless Moment—Gilded Time.
Tiznow—Folklore.
Tom Rolfe—Bowl Game, Run the Gantlet.
Top Command—Mom's Command.
Topsider—North Sider.
Transworld—Lonesome Glory (1992, '93, '95, '97, '99).
Two Punch—Smoke Glacken.
Unbridled—Anees, Banshee Breeze, Halfbridled, Smuggler.
***Vaguely Noble**—Dahlia, Estrapade, Lemhi Gold.
Verbatim—Princess Rooney.
Vice Regent—Deputy Minister.
Wavering Monarch—Maria's Mon.
What a Pleasure—Foolish Pleasure, Honest Pleasure.
What Luck—Ambassador of Luck, What a Summer.
Woodman—Hansel, Timber Country.

2007 Eclipse Award Winners

CURLIN
Horse of the Year, Three-Year-Old Male
2004 ch. c., Smart Strike—Sherriff's Deputy, by Deputy Minister
Breeder: Fares Farm (Ky.)
Owners: Stonestreet Stables, Padua Stables, George Bolton, and Midnight Cry Stables
Trainer: Steve Asmussen
2007 and Career Record: 9-6-1-2, $5,102,800
2007 Stakes Victories: Breeders' Cup Classic Powered by Dodge (G1), Jockey Club Gold Cup S. (G1), Preakness S. (G1), Arkansas Derby (G2), Rebel S. (G3)

In less than nine months, Curlin went from an unraced three-year-old to the undisputed champion of North American racing. His maiden start at Gulfstream Park, which he won by 12¾ lengths on February 3, raised eyebrows and a lot of cash. Bloodstock agent John Moynihan put together a group of clients who paid a reported $3.5-million for 80% of Curlin from Midnight Cry Stables, the racing operation of two Kentucky lawyers who would be in jail by the time of his title-clinching victory. Turned over to Steve Asmussen—Helen Pitts had trained him for the maiden win—Curlin followed the Smarty Jones path from Oaklawn Park but came up short in the Kentucky Derby Presented by Yum! Brands (G1). He nailed Derby winner Street Sense at the finish line of the Preakness Stakes (G1) but then was defeated a head by filly Rags to Riches in a historic Belmont Stakes (G1). After a short break, Asmussen brought the Smart Strike colt back with a third-place finish in the Haskell Invitational Stakes (G1), and he bested Lawyer Ron in the Jockey Club Gold Cup Stakes (G1) before soundly defeating his opponents in the Breeders' Cup Classic Powered by Dodge (G1). After the season's end, Stonestreet Stables owner Jess Jackson bought out all his partners except Midnight Cry, whose ownership was the subject of litigation.

WAR PASS
Two-Year-Old Male
2005 dk. b. or br. c., Cherokee Run—Vue, by Mr. Prospector
Breeder: Cherry Valley Farm (Ky.)
Owner: Robert LaPenta
Trainer: Nick Zito
2007 and Career Record: 4-4-0-0, $1,397,400
2007 Stakes Victories: Bessemer Trust Breeders' Cup Juvenile (G1), Champagne S. (G1)

In 2001, owner Robert LaPenta and trainer Nick Zito developed a pinhooking strategy to support LaPenta's racing stable. They bought promising yearlings and offered them for sale the following year as two-year-olds in training. Among those they sold was Fusaichi Samurai, a $270,000 yearling who was purchased for $4.5-million in 2004. They kept and raced the ones that did not reach their reserve price (The Cliff's Edge, a buy-back, was LaPenta's first Grade 1 winner) or missed the sale because of injury. War Pass fell into the latter category. A $180,000 purchase, he missed the spring sales because of an ankle chip, but the Cherokee Run colt did not miss anything else. A front-runner, he was never headed and won all four starts by daylight. He sealed his title with a 4¾-length victory in the Bessemer Trust Breeders' Cup Juvenile (G1).

INDIAN BLESSING
Two-Year-Old Filly
2005 dk. b. or br. f., Indian Charlie—Shameful, by Flying Chevron
Owners-Breeders: Hal and Patti Earnhardt (Ky.)
Trainer: Bob Baffert
2007 and Career Record: 3-3-0-0, $1,357,200
2007 Stakes Victories: Breeders' Cup Juvenile Fillies (G1), Frizette S. (G1)

Despite making only three starts, the fewest ever for a champion, Indian Blessing blazed to an unbeaten season for her owners-breeders, Hal and Patti Earnhardt of Phoenix. When trainer Bob Baffert departed Del Mar in midsummer, Indian Blessing accompanied him and carried her speed to open-length victories. After scoring her maiden victory in her August 30 debut at Saratoga Race Course, the Indian Charlie filly drew clear to a 4½-length victory in the Frizette Stakes (G1) at Belmont Park. Monmouth Park's slop posed no impediment, and she won the Breeders' Cup Juvenile Fillies (G1) by 3½ lengths to lock up her championship.

RAGS TO RICHES
Three-Year-Old Filly
2004 ch. f., A.P. Indy—Better Than Honour, by Deputy Minister
Breeder: Skara Glen Stables (Ky.)
Owners: Michael Tabor and Derrick Smith
Trainer: Todd Pletcher
2007 Record: 6-5-1-0, $1,340,028
2007 Stakes Victories: Belmont S. (G1), Kentucky Oaks (G1), Santa Anita Oaks (G1), Las Virgenes S. (G1)
Lifetime Record Through 2007: 7-5-1-0, $1,342,528

A maiden when the year opened, Rags to Riches charged to four Grade 1 victories and a place in the history books before she went to the sidelines last summer. Her most notable accomplishment was beating eventual Horse of the Year Curlin in a thrilling stretch drive in the Belmont Stakes (G1). She was only the third filly to win the Belmont and the first since Tanya in 1905. She was also the second straight foal of Better Than Honour to win the Belmont; her half brother Jazil won in 2006. The head victory in the Belmont was atypical for the A.P. Indy filly, who won the Santa Anita Oaks (G1) by 5½ lengths and the Kentucky Oaks by 4¼ lengths.

LAWYER RON
Older Male
2003 ch. c., Langfuhr—Donation, by Lord Avie
Breeder: James T. Hines Jr. (Ky.)
Owners: Stonewall Farms Racing Division 1 and the estate of James T. Hines Jr.
Trainer: Todd Pletcher
2007 Record: 8-4-2-1, $1,320,000
2007 Stakes Victories: Woodward S. (G1), Whitney H. (G1), Oaklawn H. (G2)
Lifetime Record Through 2007: 26-12-4-4, $2,790,008

A classics contender in 2006, Lawyer Ron remained in training at four and secured a championship with three notable victories. After a Gulfstream Park tuneup victory, Lawyer Ron won the Oaklawn Handicap (G2) before defeats in the Metropolitan Handicap (G1) (third) at Belmont Park and the Salvator Mile Handicap (G3) (second) at Monmouth Park. He found his best form at Saratoga Race Course, where he set a track record in winning the Whitney Handicap (G1) and scored a runaway victory in the Woodward Stakes (G1). He subsequently finished second to Curlin in the Jockey Club Gold Cup Stakes (G1) and did not handle the sloppy track at Monmouth for the Breeders' Cup Classic Powered by Dodge (G1).

GINGER PUNCH
Older Female
2003 ch. f., Awesome Again—Nappelon, by Bold Revenue
Breeder: Adena Springs (Fl.)
Owner: Stronach Stables

Trainer: Bobby Frankel
2007 Record: 8-5-2-1, $1,827,060
2007 Stakes Victories: Emirates Airline Breeders' Cup Distaff (G1), Ruffian H. (G1), Go for Wand H. (G1), First Flight H. (G2)
Lifetime Record Through 2007: 14-7-5-1, $1,901,679

Unraced at two, Ginger Punch won two of six starts at three, and the Awesome Again filly saved the best to date for her four-year-old season, which culminated with a victory in the Emirates Airline Breeders' Cup Distaff (G1) and a championship. After finishing second in two graded stakes races, the Florida-bred filly collected her first stakes win in the First Flight Handicap (G2) at Belmont Park. She became a Grade 1 winner with a six-length score in the Go for Wand Handicap at Saratoga Race Course, and added another in the Ruffian Handicap at Belmont. Third in the Beldame Stakes (G1), Ginger Punch savored the sloppy going at Monmouth Park and stared down Hystericalady to take the Breeders' Cup Distaff by a neck.

ENGLISH CHANNEL
Turf Male

2002 ch. h., Smart Strike—Belva, by Theatrical (Ire)
Breeder: Keene Ridge Farm (Ky.)
Owner: James Scatuorchio
Trainer: Todd Pletcher
2007 Record: 7-4-2-0, $2,640,000
2007 Stakes Victories: John Deere Breeders' Cup Turf (G1), Joe Hirsch Turf Classic Invitational S. (G1), United Nations S. (G1)
Lifetime Record Through 2007: 23-13-4-1, $5,319,028

For three seasons, English Channel had been knocking on the door of a championship, and he finally achieved the long-sought title in 2007, a year in which he went halfway around the world for little purpose and then sealed the deal for his Eclipse Award a few miles from owner James Scatuorchio's Rumson, New Jersey, home. After a win at Gulfstream Park, English Channel went to the Persian Gulf for the Dubai Duty Free (UAE-G1), only to finish a distant 12th behind eventual Japanese Horse of the Year Admire Moon. The trip did not take too much out of him, however. After finishing second to Better Talk Now in Belmont Park's Manhattan Handicap (G1), the Smart Strike horse scored a second straight victory in the United Nations Stakes (G1) at Monmouth Park. After another second, in Saratoga Race Course's Sword Dancer Invitational Stakes (G1), English Channel won Belmont's Joe Hirsch Turf Classic Invitational Stakes (G1) and then ran away to a seven-length score in the John Deere Breeders' Cup Turf (G1) at Monmouth.

LAHUDOOD (GB)
Turf Female

2003 b. m., Singspiel (Ire)—Rahayeb (GB), by Arazi
Breeder: Shadwell Estate Co. Ltd. (GB)
Owners: Shadwell Stable
Trainer: Kiaran McLaughlin
2007 Record: 5-3-1-0, $1,560,500
2007 Stakes Victories: Emirates Airline Breeders' Cup Filly and Mare Turf (G1), Flower Bowl Invitational S. (G1)
Lifetime Record Through 2007: 12-4-5-1, $1,695,370

For Sheikh Hamdan bin Rashid al Maktoum and his Shadwell Stable operation, the hits kept rolling in 2007. Invasor (Arg), his 2006 Horse of the Year, won the Donn Handicap (G1) in the United States and the Emirates Airline Dubai World Cup (UAE-G1) in his homeland. He had secured his first American classic winner in 2006 when Jazil won the Belmont Stakes (G1). Lahudood (GB) gave the Dubai prince his first homebred North American champion when she concluded the season with victories in the Flower Bowl Invitational Stakes (G1) and the Emirates Airline Filly and Mare Turf (G1) on soft ground at Monmouth Park.

MIDNIGHT LUTE
Male Sprinter

2003 dk. b. or br. c., Real Quiet—Candytuft, by Dehere
Breeder: Tom Evans, Macon Wilmil Equines, and Marjac Farms (Ky.)
Owners: Mike Pegram, Paul Weitman, and Carl Watson
Trainer: Bob Baffert
2007 Record: 6-2-2-0, $1,368,000
2007 Stakes Victories: TVG Breeders' Cup Sprint (G1), Forego S. (G1)
Lifetime Record Through 2007: 11-5-3-1, $1,610,600

Breathing problems affected Midnight Lute's career and required three surgeries, but the Real Quiet colt found his wind at just the right time, in the late summer and fall of 2007. After going winless in his first three starts at four, Midnight Lute broke through with his first Grade 1 victory, in the Forego Stakes at Saratoga Race Course on September 1. After an eight-week break, he powered to a decisive victory in the TVG Breeders' Cup Sprint (G1) and secured an Eclipse Award as champion male sprinter, the first year the sprinting title had been separated by gender.

MARYFIELD
Female Sprinter

2001 b. m., Elusive Quality—Sly Maid, by Desert Wine
Breeder: Mike Carroll and John C. Harvey Jr. (On.)
Owners: Mark Gorman, Nick J. Mestrandrea, and Jim Perry
Trainer: Doug O'Neill
2007 Record: 8-3-0-0, $896,330
2007 Stakes Victories: Ballerina S. (G1), Distaff Breeders' Cup H. (G2), Breeders' Cup Filly and Mare Sprint
Lifetime Record Through 2007: 28-9-5-1, $1,360,835

Doug O'Neill built his reputation in the claiming ranks, and he pulled off the greatest claim of all, Lava Man, who earned more than $5.1-million after O'Neill took him for $50,000 in 2004. Maryfield was a good claim, too. Claimed for $50,000 in 2006, the Elusive Quality mare came into her own in '07 with three stakes victories, including a Grade 1 win and a score in the first Breeders' Cup Filly and Mare Sprint. At Saratoga Race Course in August, she won a head bob over Baroness Thatcher to take the Ballerina Stakes (G1), and she prevailed by a half-length in the slop at Monmouth Park to win her Breeders' Cup race and secure the first female sprinter title.

GOOD NIGHT SHIRT
Steeplechase

2001 ch. g., Concern—Hot Story, by Two Punch
Breeder: Dr. and Mrs. Thomas Bowman (Md.)
Owner: Harold A. Via Jr.
Trainer: Jack Fisher
2007 Record: 5-3-1-0, $314,163
2007 Stakes Victories: Marion duPont Scott Colonial Cup Hurdle S., Iroquois Hurdle S., Lonesome Glory Hurdle S.
Lifetime Record Through 2007: 26-8-4-3, $483,563

As the 2007 steeplechase season opened, Good Night Shirt was in peril of being converted into a timber horse, the fate of jumpers who do not possess enough speed to compete over hurdles. But the Concern gelding delivered a pleasant surprise, finding his stride over National Fences—the American equivalent of brush hurdles—and culminating his season with a victory in the Marion duPont Scott Colonial Cup Hurdle Stakes that clinched his title.

Champions Before Eclipse Awards

Daily Racing Form (DRF) began naming champions in 1936. Beginning in 1950, the Thoroughbred Racing Associations (TRA) began naming its own champions. The following table contains the horses named champions by those two organizations. Where neither the letter (D) nor (T) follows the name of the horse, both the DRF and the TRA named that horse champion. When there were different champions named in any category, the DRF champion is noted with the letter (D) and the TRA with the letter (T). *Daily Racing Form*, the TRA, and the National Turf Writers Association joined forces in 1971 to create the Eclipse Awards, which now recognize the champions of racing in North America.

†-filly, *-imported horse; (D) *Daily Racing Form*; (T) Thoroughbred Racing Associations

Horse of the Year
1970	Fort Marcy (D)
	Personality (T)
1969	Arts and Letters
1968	Dr. Fager
1967	Damascus
1966	Buckpasser
1965	Roman Brother (D)
	†Moccasin (T)
1964	Kelso
1963	Kelso
1962	Kelso
1961	Kelso
1960	Kelso
1959	Sword Dancer
1958	Round Table
1957	Bold Ruler (D)
	Dedicate (T)
1956	Swaps
1955	Nashua
1954	Native Dancer
1953	Tom Fool
1952	One Count (D)
	Native Dancer (T)
1951	Counterpoint
1950	Hill Prince
1949	Capot
1948	Citation
1947	Armed
1946	Assault
1945	†Busher
1944	†Twilight Tear
1943	Count Fleet
1942	Whirlaway
1941	Whirlaway
1940	Challedon
1939	Challedon
1938	Seabiscuit
1937	War Admiral
1936	Granville

Two-Year-Old Male
1970	Hoist the Flag
1969	Silent Screen
1968	Top Knight
1967	Vitriolic
1966	Successor
1965	Buckpasser
1964	Bold Lad
1963	Hurry to Market
1962	Never Bend
1961	Crimson Satan
1960	Hail to Reason
1959	Warfare
1958	First Landing
1957	Nadir (D)
	Jewel's Reward (T)
1956	Barbizon
1955	Needles
1954	Nashua
1953	Porterhouse
1952	Native Dancer
1951	Tom Fool
1950	Battlefield
1949	Hill Prince
1948	Blue Peter
1947	Citation
1946	Double Jay
1945	Star Pilot
1944	Pavot
1943	Platter
1942	Count Fleet
1941	Alsab
1940	Our Boots
1939	Bimelech
1938	El Chico
1937	Menow
1936	Pompoon

Two-Year-Old Filly
1970	Forward Gal
1969	Fast Attack (D)
	Tudor Queen (T)
1968	Gallant Bloom (D)
	Process Shot (T)
1967	Queen of the Stage
1966	Regal Gleam
1965	Moccasin
1964	Queen Empress
1963	Tosmah (D)
	Castle Forbes (T)
1962	Smart Deb
1961	Cicada
1960	Bowl of Flowers
1959	My Dear Girl
1958	Quill
1957	Idun
1956	Leallah (D)
	Romanita (T)
1955	Doubledogdare (D)
	Nasrina (T)
1954	High Voltage
1953	Evening Out
1952	Sweet Patootie
1951	Rose Jet
1950	Aunt Jinny
1949	Bed o' Roses
1948	Myrtle Charm
1947	Bewitch
1946	First Flight
1945	Beaugay
1944	Busher
1943	Durazna
1942	Askmenow
1941	Petrify
1940	Level Best
1939	Now What
1938	Incoselda
1937	Jacola
1936	Apogee

Three-Year-Old Male
1970	Personality
1969	Arts and Letters
1968	Stage Door Johnny
1967	Damascus
1966	Buckpasser
1965	Tom Rolfe
1964	Northern Dancer
1963	Chateaugay
1962	Jaipur
1961	Carry Back
1960	Kelso
1959	Sword Dancer
1958	Tim Tam
1957	Bold Ruler
1956	Needles
1955	Nashua
1954	High Gun
1953	Native Dancer
1952	One Count
1951	Counterpoint
1950	Hill Prince
1949	Capot
1948	Citation
1947	Phalanx
1946	Assault
1945	Fighting Step
1944	By Jimminy
1943	Count Fleet
1942	Alsab
1941	Whirlaway
1940	Bimelech
1939	Challedon
1938	Stagehand
1937	War Admiral
1936	Granville

Three-Year-Old Filly
1970	Office Queen (D)
	Fanfreluche (T)
1969	Gallant Bloom
1968	Dark Mirage
1967	Furl Sail (D)
	Gamely (T)
1966	Lady Pitt
1965	What a Treat
1964	Tosmah
1963	Lamb Chop
1962	Cicada
1961	Bowl of Flowers

1960	Berlo
1959	Royal Native (D)
	Silver Spoon (T)
1958	Idun
1957	Bayou
1956	Doubledogdare
1955	Misty Morn
1954	Parlo
1953	Grecian Queen
1952	Real Delight
1951	Kiss Me Kate
1950	Next Move
1949	‡Two Lea
	‡Wistful
1948	Miss Request
1947	But Why Not
1946	Bridal Flower
1945	Busher
1944	Twilight Tear
1943	Stefanita
1942	Vagrancy
1941	Painted Veil
1940	Not awarded
1939	Unerring
1938	Not awarded
1937	Not awarded
1936	Not awarded

‡ (D) co-champions

Handicap Male

1970	Fort Marcy (D)
	Nodouble (T)
1969	Arts and Letters (D)
	Nodouble (T)
1968	Dr. Fager
1967	Damascus (D)
	Buckpasser (T)
1966	Buckpasser (D)
	Bold Bidder (T)
1965	Roman Brother
1964	Kelso
1963	Kelso
1962	Kelso
1961	Kelso
1960	Bald Eagle
1959	Sword Dancer (D)
	Round Table (T)
1958	Round Table
1957	Dedicate
1956	Swaps
1955	High Gun
1954	Native Dancer
1953	Tom Fool
1952	Crafty Admiral
1951	Hill Prince
1950	*Noor
1949	Coaltown
1948	Citation
1947	Armed
1946	Armed
1945	Stymie
1944	Devil Diver
1943	Market Wise
	Devil Diver
1942	Whirlaway
1941	Mioland
1940	Challedon
1939	*Kayak II
1938	Seabiscuit
1937	Seabiscuit
1936	Discovery

Handicap Female

1970	Shuvee
1969	Gallant Bloom (D)
	Gamely (T)
1968	Gamely
1967	Straight Deal
1966	Open Fire (D)
	Summer Scandal (T)
1965	Old Hat
1964	Tosmah (D)
	Old Hat (T)
1963	Cicada
1962	Primonetta
1961	Airmans Guide
1960	Royal Native
1959	Tempted
1958	Bornastar
1957	Pucker Up
1956	Blue Sparkler
1955	Misty Morn (D)
	Parlo (T)
1954	Parlo (D)
	Lavender Hill (T)
1953	Sickle's Image
1952	Real Delight (D)
	Next Move (T)
1951	Bed o' Roses
1950	Two Lea
1949	Bewitch
1948	Conniver
1947	But Why Not
1946	Gallorette
1945	Busher
1944	Twilight Tear
1943	Mar-Kell
1942	Vagrancy
1941	Fairy Chant
1940	War Plumage
1939	Lady Maryland
1938	Marica
1937	Not awarded
1936	Myrtlewood

Sprinter

1970	†Ta Wee
1969	†Ta Wee
1968	Dr. Fager
1967	Dr. Fager
1966	Impressive
1965	†Affectionately
1964	Ahoy
1963	Not awarded
1962	Not awarded
1961	Not awarded
1960	Not awarded
1959	Intentionally
1958	Bold Ruler
1957	Decathlon
1956	Decathlon
1955	Berseem
1954	White Skies
1953	Tom Fool
1952	Tea-Maker
1951	Sheilas Reward
1950	Sheilas Reward

1949	Delegate
	Royal Governor
1948	Coaltown
1947	Polynesian

1947: first year category included

Turf Horse

1970	Fort Marcy
1969	*Hawaii
1968	Dr. Fager (D)
	Fort Marcy (T)
1967	Fort Marcy
1966	Assagai
1965	Parka
1964	*Turbo Jet II
1963	Mongo
1962	Not awarded
1961	T. V. Lark
1960	Not awarded
1959	Round Table
1958	Round Table
1957	Round Table
1956	Career Boy
1955	*St. Vincent
1954	*Stan
1953	*Iceberg II

1953: first year category included

Steeplechase

1970	Top Bid
1969	*L'Escargot
1968	Bon Nouvel
1967	Quick Pitch
1966	Mako (D)
	Tuscalee (T)
1965	Bon Nouvel
1964	Bon Nouvel
1963	Amber Diver
1962	Barnabys Bluff
1961	Peal
1960	Benguala
1959	Ancestor
1958	Neji
1957	Neji
1956	Shipboard
1955	Neji
1954	King Commander
1953	The Mast
1952	Jam (D)
	Oedipus (T)
1951	Oedipus
1950	Oedipus
1949	Trough Hill
1948	American Way
1947	War Battle
1946	Elkridge
1945	Mercator
1944	Rouge Dragon
1943	Brother Jones
1942	Elkridge
1941	Speculate
1940	Not awarded
1939	Not awarded
1938	Not awarded
1937	Jungle King
1936	Bushranger

RACING HALL OF FAME
History of Racing Hall of Fame

The Racing Hall of Fame was founded in 1955 to honor the all-time greats of the sport, though it is largely limited to horses, jockeys, and trainers. Housed in the National Museum of Racing in Saratoga Springs, New York, the Racing Hall of Fame contains plaques that summarize the accomplishments of each inductee.

Each spring, a panel votes on the horses and people nominated for induction into the Hall of Fame. The results are announced in late April, and the induction ceremony takes place the first Monday of August in Saratoga Springs. Categories under consideration each year are contemporary male, contemporary female, jockey, and trainer.

Nominees for induction into the Hall of Fame are first obtained from the 125 members of the Hall of Fame voting panel. Unsuccessful candidates who appeared on the final ballot in the previous three years automatically are added to the initial list of candidates. The suggestions then go before a nomination committee, which narrows the names down to three for each category for that year's ballots.

Names of the three finalists in each division then go before the entire voting panel. Before 2005, the top vote-getter in each category was selected as that year's inductee. Beginning in 2005, members of the voting panel cast yes-or-no votes on the three candidates. A candidate had to receive at least 75% of the votes cast to be eligible for induction. When the 75% requirement produced only one inductee in 2005 and none in '06, the Hall of Fame reverted to plurality voting in '07.

From time to time, the Historical Review Committee and the Steeplechase Committee make additional selections to the Hall of Fame.

Hall of Fame Eligibility Criteria:

1. Thoroughbreds become eligible when five calendar years have elapsed between their final racing year and their year of nomination.

2. Eligible Thoroughbreds are classified as contemporary male or female if they have been retired between five and 25 years. Horses that have been retired for more than 25 years are classified as horses of yesteryear and are considered by the Historical Review Committee.

3. Beginning in 2006, active jockeys become eligible after riding Thoroughbreds for 20 years (any interruptions in their careers for injury are not counted against them). Before 2006, the requirement was 15 years.

4. Active trainers become eligible after 25 years as licensed Thoroughbred trainers.

5. The 20- and 25-year requirements may be waived for retired jockeys and trainers, but a five-year waiting period is then observed before they become eligible. In cases of fragile health, the Hall of Fame Committee may request that the five-year waiting period be waived at the discretion of the Executive Committee.

Members of the National Museum of Racing Hall of Fame
Exemplars of Racing (Year Inducted)

John W. Hanes (1982)
C. V. Whitney (1991)

Walter M. Jeffords (1973)
Paul Mellon (1989)

George D. Widener (1971)

Jockeys (Year Inducted)

Frank D. "Dooley" Adams (1970)
John Adams (1965)
Joe Aitcheson Jr. (1978)
Edward Arcaro (1958)
Ted Atkinson (1957)
Braulio Baeza (1976)
Jerry Bailey (1995)
George Barbee (1996)
Carroll K. Bassett (1972)
Russell Baze (1999)
Walter Blum (1987)
Bill Boland (2006)
George "Pete" Bostwick (1968)
Sam Boulmetis Sr. (1973)
Steve Brooks (1963)
Don Brumfield (1996)
Thomas H. Burns (1983)
James H. Butwell (1984)

J. Dallett "Dolly" Byers (1967)
Steve Cauthen (1994)
Frank Coltiletti (1970)
Angel Cordero Jr. (1988)
Robert H. "Specs" Crawford (1973)
Pat Day (1991)
Eddie Delahoussaye (1993)
Kent Desormeaux (2004)
Lavelle "Buddy" Ensor (1962)
Laverne Fator (1955)
Earlie Fires (2001)
Jerry Fishback (1992)
Andrew "Mack" Garner (1969)
Edward "Snapper" Garrison (1955)
Avelino Gomez (1982)
Henry F. Griffin (1956)
Eric Guerin (1972)
William J. Hartack (1959)

Sandy Hawley (1992)
Albert Johnson (1971)
William J. Knapp (1969)
Julie Krone (2000)
Clarence Kummer (1972)
Charles Kurtsinger (1967)
John P. Loftus (1959)
John Longden (1958)
Daniel A. Maher (1955)
J. Linus McAtee (1956)
Chris McCarron (1989)
Conn McCreary (1975)
Rigan McKinney (1968)
James McLaughlin (1955)
Walter Miller (1955)
Isaac B. Murphy (1955)
Ralph Neves (1960)
Joe Notter (1963)

George M. Odom (1955)
Winfield "Winnie" O'Connor (1956)
Frank O'Neill (1956)
Ivan H. Parke (1978)
Gilbert W. Patrick (1970)
Laffit Pincay Jr. (1975)
Edgar Prado (2008)
Samuel Purdy (1970)
John Reiff (1956)
Alfred Robertson (1971)
John L. Rotz (1983)
Earl Sande (1955)

Jose Santos (2007)
Carroll H. Schilling (1970)
John Sellers (2007)
William Shoemaker (1958)
Willie Simms (1977)
James "Tod" Sloan (1955)
Mike Smith (2003)
Alfred P. "Paddy" Smithwick (1973)
Gary Stevens (1997)
James Stout (1968)
Fred Taral (1955)
Bayard Tuckerman Jr. (1973)

Ron Turcotte (1979)
Nash Turner (1955)
Robert N. Ussery (1980)
Ismael "Milo" Valenzuela (2008)
Jacinto Vasquez (1998)
Jorge Velasquez (1990)
Thomas Walsh (2005)
Jack Westrope (2002)
George M. Woolf (1955)
Raymond Workman (1956)
Manuel Ycaza (1977)

Trainers (Year Inducted)

Lazaro S. Barrera (1979)
H. Guy Bedwell (1971)
Edward D. Brown (1984)
J. Elliott Burch (1980)
Preston M. Burch (1963)
William P. Burch (1955)
Fred Burlew (1973)
Frank E. Childs (1968)
Henry S. Clark (1982)
W. Burling Cocks (1985)
James P. Conway (1996)
Warren A. "Jimmy" Croll Jr. (1994)
Grover G. "Buddy" Delp (2002)
Neil Drysdale (2000)
William Duke (1956)
Louis Feustel (1964)
James Fitzsimmons (1958)
Henry Forrest (2007)
Robert Frankel (1995)
John M. Gaver Sr. (1966)
Carl Hanford (2006)
Thomas J. Healey (1955)
Sam C. Hildreth (1955)
Hubert "Sonny" Hine (2003)
Max Hirsch (1959)
William J. "Buddy" Hirsch (1982)
Thomas Hitchcock Sr. (1973)
Hollie Hughes (1973)
John J. Hyland (1956)

Hirsch Jacobs (1958)
H. Allen Jerkens (1975)
Philip G. Johnson (1997)
William R. Johnson (1986)
LeRoy Jolley (1987)
Ben A. Jones (1958)
Horace A. "Jimmy" Jones (1959)
Andrew Jackson Joyner (1955)
Thomas J. Kelly (1993)
Lucien Laurin (1977)
J. Howard Lewis (1969)
D. Wayne Lukas (1999)
Horatio Luro (1980)
John E. Madden (1983)
James W. Maloney (1989)
Richard Mandella (2001)
Frank "Pancho" Martin (1981)
Ron McAnally (1990)
Frank McCabe (2007)
Henry McDaniel (1956)
Claude R. "Shug" McGaughey III (2004)
MacKenzie "Mack" Miller (1987)
William Molter Jr. (1960)
William I. Mott (1998)
Winbert Mulholland (1967)
Carl Nafzger (2008)
Edward A. Neloy (1983)
John A. Nerud (1972)

Burley Parke (1986)
Angel Penna Sr. (1988)
Jacob Pincus (1988)
John W. Rogers (1955)
James G. Rowe Sr. (1955)
Flint S. "Scotty" Schulhofer (1992)
Jonathan Sheppard (1990)
Robert A. Smith (1976)
Tom Smith (2001)
D. M. "Mike" Smithwick (1971)
Woodford C. "Woody" Stephens (1976)
Meshach "Mesh" Tenney (1991)
Henry J. Thompson (1969)
Harry Trotsek (1984)
Jack C. Van Berg (1985)
Marion H. Van Berg (1970)
John Veitch (2007)
Sylvester Veitch (1977)
Robert W. Walden (1970)
Michael Walsh (1997)
Sherrill Ward (1978)
Sidney Watters Sr. (2005)
Frank Whiteley Jr. (1978)
Charles Whittingham (1974)
Ansel Williamson (1998)
G. Carey Winfrey (1975)
William C. Winfrey (1971)
Nicholas P. Zito (2005)

Horses (Year Inducted, Year Foaled)

Ack Ack (1986, 1966)
Affectionately (1989, 1960)
Affirmed (1980, 1975)
All Along (Fr) (1990, 1979)
Alsab (1976, 1939)
Alydar (1989, 1975)
Alysheba (1993, 1984)
American Eclipse (1970, 1814)
Ancient Title (2008, 1970)
A.P. Indy (2000, 1989)
Armed (1963, 1941)
Artful (1956, 1902)
Arts and Letters (1994, 1966)
Assault (1964, 1943)
Battleship (1969, 1927)
Bayakoa (Arg) (1998, 1984)
Bed o' Roses (1976, 1947)
Beldame (1956, 1901)
Ben Brush (1955, 1893)
Bewitch (1977, 1945)
Bimelech (1990, 1937)
Black Gold (1989, 1921)

Black Helen (1991, 1932)
Blue Larkspur (1957, 1926)
Bold 'n Determined (1997, 1977)
Bold Ruler (1973, 1954)
Bon Nouvel (1976, 1960)
Boston (1955, 1833)
Bowl of Flowers (2004, 1958)
Broomstick (1956, 1901)
Buckpasser (1970, 1963)
Busher (1964, 1942)
Bushranger (1967, 1930)
Cafe Prince (1985, 1970)
Carry Back (1975, 1958)
Cavalcade (1993, 1931)
Challedon (1977, 1936)
Chris Evert (1988, 1971)
Cicada (1967, 1959)
Cigar (2002, 1990)
Citation (1959, 1945)
Coaltown (1983, 1945)
Colin (1956, 1905)
Commando (1956, 1898)

*Cougar II (2006, 1966)
Count Fleet (1961, 1940)
Crusader (1995, 1923)
Dahlia (1981, 1970)
Damascus (1974, 1964)
Dance Smartly (2003, 1988)
Dark Mirage (1974, 1965)
Davona Dale (1985, 1976)
Desert Vixen (1979, 1970)
Devil Diver (1980, 1939)
Discovery (1969, 1931)
Domino (1955, 1891)
Dr. Fager (1971, 1964)
Easy Goer (1997, 1986)
Eight Thirty (1994, 1936)
Elkridge (1966, 1938)
Emperor of Norfolk (1988, 1885)
Equipoise (1957, 1928)
Exceller (1999, 1973)
Exterminator (1957, 1915)
Fairmount (1985, 1921)
Fair Play (1956, 1905)

Fashion (1980, 1837)
Firenze (1981, 1884)
Flatterer (1994, 1979)
Flawlessly (2004, 1988)
Foolish Pleasure (1995, 1972)
Forego (1979, 1970)
Fort Marcy (1998, 1964)
Gallant Bloom (1977, 1966)
Gallant Fox (1957, 1927)
*Gallant Man (1987, 1954)
Gallorette (1962, 1942)
Gamely (1980, 1964)
Genuine Risk (1986, 1977)
Go for Wand (1996, 1987)
Good and Plenty (1956, 1900)
Granville (1997, 1933)
Grey Lag (1957, 1918)
Gun Bow (1999, 1960)
Hamburg (1986, 1895)
Hanover (1955, 1884)
Henry of Navarre (1985, 1891)
Hill Prince (1991, 1947)
Hindoo (1955, 1878)
Holy Bull (2001, 1991)
Imp (1965, 1894)
Inside Information (2008, 1991)
Jay Trump (1971, 1957)
John Henry (1990, 1975)
Johnstown (1992, 1936)
Jolly Roger (1965, 1922)
Kelso (1967, 1957)
Kentucky (1983, 1861)
Kingston (1955, 1884)
Lady's Secret (1992, 1982)
La Prevoyante (1995, 1970)
*L'Escargot (1977, 1963)
Lexington (1955, 1850)
Lonesome Glory (2005, 1988)

Longfellow (1971, 1867)
Luke Blackburn (1955, 1877)
Majestic Prince (1988, 1966)
Manila (2008, 1983)
Man o' War (1957, 1917)
Maskette (2001, 1906)
Miesque (1999, 1984)
Miss Woodford (1967, 1880)
Mom's Command (2007, 1982)
Myrtlewood (1979, 1932)
Nashua (1965, 1952)
Native Dancer (1963, 1950)
Native Diver (1978, 1959)
Needles (2000, 1953)
Neji (1966, 1950)
*Noor (2002, 1945)
Northern Dancer (1976, 1961)
Oedipus (1978, 1946)
Old Rosebud (1968, 1911)
Omaha (1965, 1932)
Pan Zareta (1972, 1910)
Parole (1984, 1873)
Paseana (Arg) (2001, 1987)
Personal Ensign (1993, 1984)
Peter Pan (1956, 1904)
Precisionist (2003,1981)
Princess Doreen (1982, 1921)
Princess Rooney (1991, 1980)
Real Delight (1987, 1949)
Regret (1957, 1912)
Reigh Count (1978, 1925)
Riva Ridge (1998, 1969)
Roamer (1981, 1911)
Roseben (1956, 1901)
Round Table (1972, 1954)
Ruffian (1976, 1972)
Ruthless (1975, 1864)
Salvator (1955, 1886)

Sarazen (1957, 1921)
Seabiscuit (1958, 1933)
Searching (1978, 1952)
Seattle Slew (1981, 1974)
Secretariat (1974, 1970)
Serena's Song (2002, 1992)
Shuvee (1975, 1966)
Silver Charm (2007, 1994)
Silver Spoon (1978, 1956)
Sir Archy (1955, 1805)
Sir Barton (1957, 1916)
Skip Away (2004, 1993)
Slew o' Gold (1992, 1980)
Spectacular Bid (1982, 1976)
Stymie (1975, 1941)
Sun Beau (1996, 1925)
Sunday Silence (1996, 1986)
Susan's Girl (1976, 1969)
Swaps (1966, 1952)
Swoon's Son (2007, 1953)
Sword Dancer (1977, 1956)
Sysonby (1956, 1902)
Ta Wee (1994, 1966)
Ten Broeck (1982, 1872)
Tim Tam (1985, 1955)
Tom Fool (1960, 1949)
Top Flight (1966, 1929)
Tosmah (1984, 1961)
Twenty Grand (1957, 1928)
Twilight Tear (1963, 1941)
Two Lea (1982, 1946)
War Admiral (1958, 1934)
Whirlaway (1959, 1938)
Whisk Broom II (1979, 1907)
Winning Colors (2000, 1985)
Zaccio (1990, 1976)
Zev (1983, 1920)

Owners of Racing Hall of Fame Members

H. C. Applegate—Old Rosebud
Augustin Stables—Cafe Prince
E.J. "Lucky" Baldwin—Emperor of Norfolk
Edith W. Bancroft—Damascus
Belair Stud—Gallant Fox, Granville, Johnstown, Nashua, Omaha
August Belmont II—Beldame, Fair Play, Henry of Navarre
Col. E. R. Bradley—Bimelech, Black Helen, Blue Larkspur, Busher
William Brann—Challedon, Gallorette
Briardale Farm—Tosmah
Brookmeade Stable—Bowl of Flowers, Cavalcade, Sword Dancer
S. S. Brown—Broomstick
Calumet Farm—Alydar, Armed, Bewitch, Citation, Coaltown, Davona Dale, Real Delight, Tim Tam, Twilight Tear, Two Lea, Whirlaway
Christopher T. Chenery (Meadow Stable)—Hill Prince
Christiana Stable—Go for Wand
Claiborne Farm—Round Table
Edwardo Cojuangco Jr.—Manila
Gen. Nathaniel Coles—American Eclipse
E. T. Colton—Pan Zareta

Brownell Combs—Myrtlewood
Sidney H. Craig—Paseana (Arg)
Warren A. "Jimmy" Croll Jr.—Holy Bull
J. F. Cushman and E. V. Snedeker—Kingston
D & H Stable—Needles
Marcus Daly—Hamburg
Dotsam Stable—John Henry

Leading Owners of Racing Hall of Fame Horses

11— Calumet Farm
6— James R. Keene*
5— Belair Stud
    Dwyer Brothers
4— Col. Edward R. Bradley
    Meadow Stable
3— August Belmont II
    Glen Riddle Farm
    Brookmeade Stable
    Ethel D. Jacobs
    Greentree Stable
    Ogden Phipps
    Alfred G. Vanderbilt
    C. V. Whitney
    Harry Payne Whitney
*Includes partnerships

E. Gay Drake—Swoon's Son
Allaire duPont—Kelso
Mike Dwyer—Ben Brush
Phil and Mike Dwyer—Hanover, Hindoo, Kingston, Luke Blackburn, Miss Woodford
Rex Ellsworth—Swaps
Equusequity Stable—Slew o' Gold
Diana Firestone—Genuine Risk
Mr. and Mrs. E. E. Fogelson—Ack Ack
Peter Fuller—Mom's Command
Dr. Ernest Gaillard, Arthur B. Hancock III, and Charles Whittingham—Sunday Silence
Gedney Farm—Gun Bow
Martha F. Gerry—Forego
William Gibbons—Fashion
Greentree Stable—Devil Diver, Tom Fool, Twenty Grand
John L. Greer—Foolish Pleasure
Harry Guggenheim—Ack Ack
James Ben Ali Haggin—Firenze, Salvator
Harbor View Farm—Affirmed, Flawlessly
Dan Harness—Imp
Frank Harper—Ten Broeck
John Harper—Longfellow
Hawksworth Farm—Spectacular Bid

Mrs. John D. Hertz—Count Fleet, Reigh Count
Carolyn Hine—Skip Away
Max Hirsch—Grey Lag
Thomas Hitchcock—Elkridge, Good and Plenty
Fred Hooper—Precisionist, Susan's Girl
Rosa M. Hoots—Black Gold
Charles S. Howard—*Noor, Seabiscuit
Nelson Bunker Hunt—Dahlia, Exceller
John Hunter, George Osgood, and William Travers—Kentucky
Ethel Jacobs—Affectionately, Searching, Stymie
Kay Jeffords—Lonesome Glory
Col. William R. Johnson—Boston, Sir Archy
Davy C. Johnson—Roseben
B. B. and Monfort Jones—Princess Doreen
Mary Jones—*Cougar II
James R. Keene—Colin, Commando, Maskette, Peter Pan, Sysonby
James R. and Foxhall Keene—Domino
Kerr Stable—Round Table
Willis Sharpe Kilmer—Exterminator, Sun Beau
King Ranch—Assault, Gallant Bloom
William and Ethel Kirkland—Ancient Title
Eugene Klein—Winning Colors
Mr. and Mrs. Eugene Klein—Lady's Secret
Eugene Leigh and Ed Brown—Ben Brush
Jean-Louis Levesque—La Prevoyante
Robert and Beverly Lewis—Serena's Song, Silver Charm
Locust Hill Farm—Ruffian

Pierre Lorillard—Parole
Ralph Lowe—*Gallant Man
John E. Madden—Hamburg
Harry Mangurian Jr.—Desert Vixen
Louis B. Mayer—Busher
Bryon McClelland—Henry of Navarre
Frank McMahon—Majestic Prince
Meadow Stable (Christopher T. Chenery)—Cicada, Riva Ridge, Secretariat
Paul Mellon (Rokeby Stable)—Arts and Letters
J. Cal Milam—Exterminator
Andrew Miller—Roamer
Kent Miller—Elkridge
Lloyd Miller—Dark Mirage
Francis Morris—Ruthless
Mrs. Lewis C. Murdock—Zaccio
J. F. Newman—Pan Zareta
Stavros Niarchos—Miesque
Jonathan Sheppard, William Pape, and George Harris—Flatterer
Allen E. Paulson—Cigar
William Haggin Perry—Gamely
Lillian Bostwick Phipps—Neji, Oedipus
Ogden Phipps—Buckpasser, Easy Goer, Personal Ensign
Ogden Mills Phipps—Inside Information
Powhatan—*L'Escargot
Jack Price—Carry Back
Rancocas Stable—Zev
Mrs. Theodore Randolph—Bon Nouvel
Glen Riddle Farm—Crusader, Man o' War, War Admiral
Nathaniel Rives—Boston
Rokeby Stable (Paul Mellon)—Fort Marcy

Carl Rosen—Chris Evert
Commander J. K. L. Ross—Sir Barton
Albert Sabath—Alsab
Walter J. Salmon Jr.—Battleship
Sam-Son Farm—Dance Smartly
Saron Stable—Bold 'n Determined
Dorothy and Pamela Scharbauer—Alysheba
Marion duPont Scott—Battleship
Bradley M. "Mike" Shannon—Manila
Mr. and Mrs. L. K. Shapiro—Native Diver
Harry Sinclair—Grey Lag
Mrs. Mary Stephenson—Jay Trump
Mrs. Whitney Stone—Shuvee
Tartan Farms—Dr. Fager, Ta Wee
Tayhill Stable—Seattle Slew
E. P. Taylor—Northern Dancer
Richard Ten Broeck—Lexington
Tomonori Tsurumaki and Farish-Goodman-Kilroy—A.P. Indy
Paula Tucker—Princess Rooney
Cornelius W. Van Ranst—American Eclipse
Alfred G. Vanderbilt—Bed o' Roses, Discovery, Native Dancer
Mrs. W. K. Vanderbilt III—Sarazen
Wheatley Stable—Bold Ruler
Frank and Janis Whitham—Bayakoa (Arg)
C. V. Whitney—Equipoise, Silver Spoon, Top Flight
Harry Payne Whitney—Artful, Regret, Whisk Broom II
Mrs. Payne Whitney—Jolly Roger
George D. Widener—Eight Thirty
Joseph E. Widener—Bushranger, Fairmount
Daniel Wildenstein—All Along (Fr)
Capt. Jim Williams—Luke Blackburn

Breeders of Racing Hall of Fame Members

Muriel Vanderbilt Adams—Desert Vixen
H. H. Aga Khan—*Noor
H. H. Aga Khan and Prince Aly Khan—*Gallant Man
Lucien O. Appleby—Henry of Navarre
F. Wallis Armstrong—Cavalcade
Dr. Howard Baker—Serena's Song
Mrs. Thomas Bancroft—Damascus
Anna Marie Barnhart—Skip Away
Belair Stud—Gallant Fox, Granville, Nashua, Omaha
August Belmont II—Beldame, Fair Play, Man o' War
Bieber-Jacobs Stables—Affectionately
Blue Bear Stud—Zaccio
E. R. Bradley/Idle Hour Stock Farm—Bimelech, Black Helen, Blue Larkspur, Busher, Oedipus
William L. Brann—Challedon
Brookmeade Stable—Bowl of Flowers, Sword Dancer
S. S. Brown—Whisk Broom II
Preston Burch—Gallorette
Calumet Farm—Alydar, Armed, Bewitch, Citation, Coaltown, Davona Dale, Real Delight, Tim Tam, Twilight Tear, Two Lea, Whirlaway

Mrs. Thomas J. Carson—Roseben
Ben Castleman—Seattle Slew
Christopher T. Chenery—Hill Prince
Christiana Stables—Go for Wand
Claiborne Farm—Gamely, Round Table, Slew o' Gold
John Clay—Kentucky
Clay Brothers—Roamer
Edwardo Cojuangco Jr.—Manila

Leading Breeders of Racing Hall of Fame Horses

11— Calumet Farm
6— James R. Keene
5— Idle Hour Stock Farm
 John Madden*
4— Belair Stud
 Ogden Phipps
3— August Belmont II
 Claiborne Farm
 Greentree Stable
 Meadow Stud
 Daniel Swigert
 Harry Payne Whitney

*Includes partnerships

Gen. Nathaniel Coles—American Eclipse
Brownell Combs—Myrtlewood
Leslie Combs II—Majestic Prince
Dayton Ltd.—All Along (Fr)
E. Gay Drake—Swoon's Son
Allaire duPont—Kelso
Echo Valley Farm—Chris Evert, Winning Colors
Rex Ellsworth—Swaps
Mrs. Charles W. Engelhard—Exceller
Con Enright—Hamburg
William S. Farish and W. S. Kilroy—A.P. Indy
Joseph F. Flanagan—Elkridge
Flaxman Holdings Ltd.—Miesque
Capt. James and A. C. Franklin—Luke Blackburn
Peter Fuller—Mom's Command
William Gibbons—Fashion
Mrs. William Gilmore and Mrs. William Jason—Spectacular Bid
Golden Chance Farm—John Henry
Greentree Stable—Devil Diver, Jolly Roger, Twenty Grand
Harry Guggenheim—Ack Ack
Arthur B. Hancock Sr.—Johnstown

Haras General Cruz—*Cougar II
Haras Principal—Bayakoa (Arg)
Haras Vacacion—Paseana (Arg)
Harbor View Farm—Affirmed, Flawlessly
Dan Harness—Imp
Frank B. Harper—Good and Plenty
John Harper—Ten Broeck, Longfellow
Duval Headley—Dark Mirage, Tom Fool
Mrs. John D. Hertz—Count Fleet
Max Hirsch and King Ranch—Stymie
Fred Hooper—Precisionist, Susan's Girl
Rosa M. Hoots—Black Gold
Mrs. G. Watts Humphrey Jr.—Genuine Risk
Nelson Bunker Hunt—Dahlia
Mr. and Mrs. Stuart S. Janney Jr.—Ruffian
Mrs. William Jason and Mrs. William Gilmore—Spectacular Bid
Walter Jeffords Jr.—Lonesome Glory
Marius E. Johnston—Sarazen
James R. Keene—Colin, Commando, Maskette, Peter Pan, Kingston, Sysonby
Willis Sharpe Kilmer—Reigh Count, Sun Beau
King Ranch—Assault ,Gallant Bloom, Stymie
William and Ethel Kirkland—Ancient Title
Dixie Knight—Exterminator
Gordon E. Layton—Bold 'n Determined
Lazy F Ranch—Forego
W. E. Leach—Needles
Jean-Louis Levesque—La Prevoyante

John E. Madden—Grey Lag, Old Rosebud, Princess Doreen, Zev
John E. Madden and Vivian A. Gooch—Sir Barton
Preston Madden—Alysheba
Maine Chance Farm—Gun Bow
Meadow Stud—Cicada, Riva Ridge, Secretariat
Paul Mellon—Arts and Letters, Fort Marcy
Mereworth Farm—Discovery
Eugene Mori—Tosmah
Francis Morris—Ruthless
J. F. Newman—Pan Zareta
Oak Cliff Thoroughbreds—Sunday Silence
Mrs. B. O'Neill—L'Escargot
William Pape and Jonathan Sheppard—Flatterer
Allen E. Paulson—Cigar
Pelican Stable—Holy Bull
Ogden Phipps—Buckpasser, Easy Goer, Personal Ensign, Searching
Ogden Mills Phipps—Inside Information
Thomas Piatt—Alsab
Jack Price—Carry Back
Dr. A. C. Randolph—Bon Nouvel
Capt. Archibald Randolph and Col. John Tayloe III—Sir Archy
Samuel D. Riddle—Crusader, War Admiral
Ben Roach and Tom Roach—Princess Rooney
Runnymede Farm—Ben Brush, Hanover

Walter J. Salmon—Discovery, Battleship
Sam-Son Farm—Dance Smartly
Marion duPont Scott—Neji
Jan Sensenich—Jay Trump
Mr. and Mrs. L. K. Shapiro—Native Diver
Robert H. Spreen—Lady's Secret
Whitney Stone—Shuvee
Daniel Swigert—Firenze, Hindoo, Salvator
Tartan Farms—Dr. Fager, Ta Wee
E. P. Taylor—Northern Dancer
Maj. Barak Thomas—Domino
Alfred G. Vanderbilt—Bed o' Roses, Native Dancer
Waldemar Farms—Foolish Pleasure
Elisha Warfield—Lexington
Aristides Welch—Parole
Wheatley Stable—Bold Ruler, Seabiscuit
C. V. Whitney—Silver Spoon
Harry Payne Whitney—Equipoise, Regret, Top Flight
William C. Whitney—Artful
John Wickham—Boston
George D. Widener—Eight Thirty
Joseph E. Widener—Bushranger, Fairmount
Verne H. Winchell—Cafe Prince
Theodore Winters—Emperor of Norfolk
Woodford and Clay—Miss Woodford
Mary Lou Wootton—Silver Charm
Col. Milton Young—Broomstick

Trainers of Racing Hall of Fame Members

Note: In instances when more than one trainer had a Hall of Fame horse during the horse's career, all are credited.

Edward T. "Ned" Allard—Mom's Command
William Badgett—Go for Wand
Bob Baffert—Silver Charm
Lazaro Barrera—Affirmed
Guy Bedwell—Sir Barton

Leading Trainers of Racing Hall of Fame Horses

10— James Rowe Sr.
8— Ben A. Jones
6— James "Sunny Jim" Fitzsimmons
     Charlie Whittingham
5— Horace A. "Jimmy" Jones
4— J. Elliott Burch
3— Neil Drysdale
     Max Hirsch
     Hirsch Jacobs
     LeRoy Jolley
     D. Wayne Lukas
     Ron McAnally
     Claude R. "Shug" McGaughey III
     John Nerud
     Frank Whiteley Jr.
     William C. Winfrey

John Belcher—Boston
Patrick Biancone—All Along (Fr)
Frank A. Bonsal—Ack Ack
George H. "Pete" Bostwick—Oedipus, Neji
Francois Boutin—Miesque
William Brennan—Twenty Grand
Charles Brossman—Imp
Ed Brown—Ben Brush
Henry Brown—Lexington
William Brown—Parole
J. Elliott Burch—Arts and Letters, Bowl of Flowers, Fort Marcy, Sword Dancer
Fred Burlew—Beldame
Matt Byrnes—Firenze, Salvator
Don Cameron—Count Fleet
Hardy Campbell—Kingston
Edward A. Christmas—Gallorette
W. Burling Cocks—Zaccio
Harry Colston—Ten Broeck
E. T. Colton—Pan Zareta
George Conway—Crusader, War Admiral
Warren A. "Jimmy" Croll—Holy Bull
James E. Day—Dance Smartly
Grover G. "Bud" Delp—Spectacular Bid
Neil Drysdale—A.P. Indy, Bold 'n Determined, Princess Rooney
Richard Dutrow Sr.—Flawlessly
Ross Fenstermaker—Precisionist, Susan's Girl
Louis Feustel—Man o' War

James "Sunny Jim" Fitzsimmons—Bold Ruler, Gallant Fox, Granville, Johnstown, Nashua, Omaha
Hugh Fontaine—Needles
E. Foucon—Pan Zareta
Willard C. Freeman—Shuvee
John M. Gaver Sr.—Devil Diver, Tom Fool
Jack Goldsborough—Roamer
Carl Hanford—Kelso
John Harper—Longfellow
J. H. "Casey" Hayes—Cicada, Hill Prince
Thomas J. Healey—Equipoise, Top Flight
S. M. Henderson—Princess Doreen
John Hertler—Slew o' Gold
Sam Hildreth—Grey Lag, Zev
Hubert "Sonny" Hine—Skip Away
Max Hirsch—Assault, Gallant Bloom, Sarazen
William Hirsch—Gallant Bloom
Reg Hobbs—Battleship
Freddy Hopkins—Equipoise
Will Hurley—Bimelech, Black Helen
John Hyland—Beldame, Henry of Navarre
Hirsch Jacobs—Affectionately, Searching, Stymie
William H. Johnson—Boston, Sir Archy
LeRoy Jolley—Foolish Pleasure, Genuine Risk, Manila
Ben A. Jones—Armed, Bewitch, Cita-

Racing Hall of Fame — Sires of Members

tion, Coaltown, Real Delight, Twilight Tear, Two Lea, Whirlaway
Horace A. "Jimmy" Jones—Bewitch, Citation, Coaltown, Tim Tam, Two Lea
Andrew J. Joyner—Fair Play, Whisk Broom II
Charles Kiernan—Good and Plenty
Ray Kindred—Myrtlewood
Everett King—Dark Mirage
Billy Lakeland—Domino, Hamburg
Thomas Larkin—Sir Archy
Lucien Laurin—Riva Ridge, Secretariat
John Lee—Kelso
J. Howard Lewis—Bushranger, Fairmount
John Longden—Majestic Prince
D. Wayne Lukas—Lady's Secret, Serena's Song, Winning Colors
Horatio Luro—Northern Dancer
John E. Madden—Hamburg
James W. Maloney—Gamely
Francois Mathet—Exceller
Ron McAnally—Bayakoa (Arg), John Henry, Paseana (Arg)
Frank McCabe—Hanover
Byron McClelland—Henry of Navarre
John McClelland—Emperor of Norfolk
Henry McDaniel—Exterminator, Reigh Count
Claude R. "Shug" McGaughey III—Easy Goer, Inside Information, Personal Ensign
Joe Mergler—Tosmah
B. S. Michell—Reigh Count
Bruce Miller—Lonesome Glory
Kent Miller—Elkridge
Buster Millerick—Native Diver

A. J. Minor—Ruthless
William Molter—Round Table
D. L. Moore—Neji, *L'Escargot
William I. Mott—Cigar
W. F. "Bert" Mulholland—Eight Thirty
Tom Murphy—Twenty Grand
Edward Neloy—Buckpasser, Gun Bow
John Nerud—Dr. Fager, *Gallant Man, Ta Wee
H. S. Newman—Pan Zareta
J. L. Newman—Susan's Girl
Victor J. "Lefty" Nickerson—John Henry
George Odom—Busher
Burley Parke—*Noor
Chuck Parke—Susan's Girl
Douglas R. Peterson—Seattle Slew
Vincent Powers—Jolly Roger
Jack Price—Carry Back
John B. Pryor—Lexington
John W. Rogers—Artful
Tommy Root Sr.—Desert Vixen
James Rowe Jr.—Twenty Grand
James Rowe Sr.—Colin, Commando, Hindoo, Luke Blackburn, Maskette, Miss Woodford, Peter Pan, Regret, Sysonby, Whisk Broom II
John Russell—Precisionist, Susan's Girl
Louis J. Schaefer—Challedon
Flint S. "Scotty" Schulhofer—Ta Wee
Jonathan Sheppard—Cafe Prince, Flatterer
A. Shuttinger—Sun Beau
Robert A. Smith—Cavalcade
Thomas Smith—Seabiscuit
Crompton "Tommy" Smith Jr.—Jay Trump

D. Michael Smithwick—Bon Nouvel, Neji
E. V. Snedeker—Kingston
John Starr—La Prevoyante
J. H. Stotler—Discovery
Keith Stucki—Ancient Title
August "Sarge" Swenke—Alsab
Arthur Taylor—Boston, Sir Archy
M. A. "Mesh" Tenney—Swaps
Bob Thomas—Emperor of Norfolk
H. J. Thompson—Blue Larkspur
G. R. Tompkins—Crusader
Joseph Trovato—Chris Evert
Bob Tucker—Broomstick
William H. Turner Jr.—Seattle Slew
Jack Van Berg—Alysheba
John Veitch—Alydar, Davona Dale
Sherrill Ward—Forego
Sidney Watters Jr.—Slew o' Gold
Hanley Webb—Black Gold
Frank D. Weir—Old Rosebud, Roseben
R. L. Wheeler—Silver Spoon
Frank Whiteley Jr.—Damascus, Forego, Ruffian
Charles Whittingham—Ack Ack, *Cougar II, Dahlia, Exceller, Flawlessly, Sunday Silence
J. Whyte—Sun Beau
Capt. Jim Williams—Luke Blackburn
Lex Wilson—Swoon's Son
Peter Wimmer—Broomstick, Imp
William C. Winfrey—Bed o' Roses, Buckpasser, Native Dancer
Maurice Zilber—Dahlia, Exceller
Unknown—American Eclipse, Fashion, Kentucky

Sires of Racing Hall of Fame Members

Abe Frank—Pan Zareta
Affirmed—Flawlessly
Ahmad—Paseana (Arg)
Alydar—Alysheba, Easy Goer
***Amerigo**—Fort Marcy
Battle Joined—Ack Ack
Ben Brush—Broomstick
***Ben Strome**—Roseben
Best Turn—Davona Dale
***Billet**—Miss Woodford
Black Servant—Blue Larkspur
Black Toney—Bimelech, Black Gold, Black Helen
***Blenheim II**—Whirlaway
Blue Larkspur—Myrtlewood, Oedipus
Bold and Brave—Bold 'n Determined
Bold Bidder—Spectacular Bid
Bold Reasoning—Seattle Slew
Bold Ruler—Gamely, Secretariat
Bold Venture—Assault
***Bonnie Scotland**—Luke Blackburn
Boston—Lexington
Bramble—Ben Brush
Broomstick—Regret, Whisk Broom II
Bryan G.—Cicada
Buckpasser—La Prevoyante
Bull Lea—Armed, Bewitch, Citation, Coaltown, Real Delight, Twilight Tear, Two Lea

Caro (Ire)—Winning Colors
***Challenger II**—Challedon, Gallorette
Citation—Silver Spoon
Commando—Colin, Peter Pan
Consultant's Bid—Bayakoa (Arg)
Creme dela Creme—Cafe Prince
Crozier—Precisionist
Danzig—Dance Smartly
Deputy Minister—Go for Wand
***Diomed**—Sir Archy
***Dis Donc**—Top Flight
Disguise—Maskette
Display—Discovery
Domino—Commando
Duc de Fer—Bon Nouvel
Duroc—American Eclipse
***Eclipse**—Ruthless
Equestrian—Stymie
Escart III—*L'Escargot
Exclusive Native—Affirmed, Genuine Risk
Fair Play—Fairmount, Man o' War
First Landing—Riva Ridge
***Forli**—Forego
Gallant Fox—Granville, Omaha
***Gallant Man**—Gallant Bloom
Glenelg—Firenze
Good Goods—Alsab
Great Above—Holy Bull

Leading Sires of Racing Hall of Fame Horses

7— Bull Lea

3— Black Toney
   Man o' War
   *Nasrullah

2— Alydar
   Blue Larkspur
   Bold Ruler
   Broomstick
   *Challenger II
   Commando
   Exclusive Native
   Fair Play
   Gallant Fox
   *Leamington
   Pennant
   *Princequillo
   Private Account
   Raise a Native
   Seattle Slew
   *St. Germans
   *Star Shoot
   Tom Fool
   *Vaguely Noble
   War Admiral

Gummo—Ancient Title
Gun Shot—Gun Bow
Halo—Sunday Silence
Hamburg—Artful
Hanover—Hamburg
Hard Tack—Seabiscuit
Hastings—Fair Play
High Time—Sarazen
Himyar—Domino
Hindoo—Hanover
*Hunters Moon IV—Neji
Imbros—Native Diver
In Reality—Desert Vixen
Intentionally—Ta Wee
Jamestown—Johnstown
*Khaled—Swaps
*Knight Errant—Roamer
Knight of Ellerslie—Henry of Navarre
*Lancegaye—Cavalcade
*Leamington—Longfellow, Parole
Lexington—Kentucky
*Lorenzaccio—Zaccio
Lyphard—Manila
Man o' War—Battleship, Crusader, War Admiral
Mate—Elkridge
*McGee—Exterminator
*Melton—Sysonby
Menow—Tom Fool
*Migoli—*Gallant Man
Mo Bay—Flatterer
*Nasrullah—Bold Ruler, Nashua, *Noor

Nearctic—Northern Dancer
Norfolk—Emperor of Norfolk
Nureyev—Miesque
Octagon—Beldame
Ole Bob Bowers—John Henry
Palace Music—Cigar
Pennant—Equipoise, Jolly Roger
*Persian Road II—Dark Mirage
*Phaeton—Ten Broeck
Pilate—Eight Thirty
Polynesian—Native Dancer
Ponder—Needles
*Prince Charlie—Salvator
*Princequillo—Hill Prince, Round Table
Private Account—Inside Information, Personal Ensign
Quadrangle—Susan's Girl
Rahy—Serena's Song
Raise a Native—Alydar, Majestic Prince
Reign Count—Count Fleet
Reviewer—Ruffian
*Ribot—Arts and Letters
Rosemont—Bed o' Roses
Rossington—Good and Plenty
Rough'n Tumble—Dr. Fager
Saggy—Carry Back
Sailor—Bowl of Flowers
Seattle Slew—A.P. Indy, Slew o' Gold
Secretariat—Lady's Secret
Silver Buck—Silver Charm
*Sir Gallahad III—Gallant Fox
Skip Trial—Skip Away

*Spanish Prince II—Princess Doreen
Spendthrift—Kingston
*St. Germans—Devil Diver, Twenty Grand
*Star Shoot—Grey Lag, Sir Barton
*Stefan the Great—Bushranger
*Sun Briar—Sun Beau
Sunglow—Sword Dancer
*Sunreigh—Reigh Count
Swaps—Affectionately
Swoon's Son—Chris Evert
Sword Dancer—Damascus
Tale of Two Cities—*Cougar II
Targowice—All Along (Fr)
The Doge—Swoon's Son
The Finn—Zev
Tim Tam—Tosmah
Timoleon—Boston
Tom Fool—Buckpasser, Tim Tam
Tonga Prince—Jay Trump
Top Command—Mom's Command
Transworld—Lonesome Glory
*Trustee—Fashion
Uncle—Old Rosebud
*Vaguely Noble—Dahlia, Exceller
Verbatim—Princess Rooney
Virgil—Hindoo
Wagner—Imp
War Admiral—Busher, Searching
What a Pleasure—Foolish Pleasure
Your Host—Kelso

Regional Halls of Fame

Arlington Park
No new members have been inducted since 1989.

Horses
Armed
Buckpasser
Candy Spots
Citation
Coaltown
Dr. Fager
Equipoise
Nashua
Native Dancer
Round Table
Secretariat
Tom Rolfe
T. V. Lark
Twilight Tear
Jockeys
Eddie Arcaro
Braulio Baeza
Steve Brooks
Doug Dodson
Bill Hartack
Johnny Sellers
Bill Shoemaker
Trainers
William Hal Bishop
Ben Jones
H. A. "Jimmy" Jones
Harry Trotsek
Arnold Winick
Stables
Calumet Farm
Hasty House Farm
William Hal Bishop Stable

Calder Race Course
Calder Race Course created its Hall of Fame in 1995 and annually inducts at least one new member in each of four categories. No members were inducted in 2007.

Horses (Year Inducted)
Boots 'n Jackie (2005)
Brave Raj (1995)
Carterista (2004)
Chaposa Springs (2003)
Cherokee Run (1998)
Flying Pidgeon (2000)
Hollywood Wildcat (2002)
Judy's Red Shoes (1996)
Mecke (1999)
Princess Rooney (1995)
Shocker T. (2006)
Smile (1995)
Spend a Buck (1995)
Spirit of Fighter (1997)
The Vid (2001)
Jockeys (Year Inducted)
Eibar Coa (2004)
Mike Gonzalez (2001)
Walter Guerra (1998)
Rosemary Homeister Jr. (2006)
Michael Lee (1996)
Gene St. Leon (1995)
Miguel Rivera (2000)
Pedro Rodriguez (2005)
Mary Russ (2003)
Alex Solis (2002)
Jacinto Vasquez (1999)
Jose Velez Jr. (1997)
Owners-Breeders (Year Inducted)
Arthur Appleton (1999)
Bee Bee Stable (2005)
Gilbert Campbell (2004)
Cobble View Stable (2001)
Herb and Ione Elkins (2006)
Farnsworth Farms (1997)
John Franks (2003)
Frances Genter Stable (1998)
Fred Hooper (1995)
James Lewis Jr. (2000)
Harry T. Mangurian Jr. (1995)
Ocala Stud Farm (2002)
Tartan Farms (1996)
Trainers (Year Inducted)
James Bracken (2000)
Frank Gomez (1995)
Stanley Hough (1996)
Jose "Pepe" Mendez (2004)
Luis Olivares (2002)
Edward Plesa Jr. (2006)
Harold Rose (1997)
John Tammaro (1999)
Emanuel Tortora (1998)
Bill White (2005)
Martin D. Wolfson (2003)
Ralph Ziadie (2001)

California Thoroughbred Breeders Association
The California Thoroughbred Breeders Association Hall of Fame, created to salute those instrumental to the state's breeding and racing, revived its membership in 2006 after making no new inductions since 1988.

California-Breds (Year Inducted)
Ancient Title (1988)
Best Pal (2006)
Emperor of Norfolk (1988)
Flying Paster (2007)
Free House (2006)
Honeymoon (1987)
Morvich (1988)
Native Diver (1987)
Swaps (1987)
Stallions (Year Inducted)
Alibhai (1987)
Decidedly (2007)
Determine (1988)
Fleet Nasrullah (1988)
Khaled (1987)
Breeders (Year Inducted)
Elias J. "Lucky" Baldwin (1988)
Rex Ellsworth (1987)
John Harris (2007)
Ellwood B. Johnston (1987)
John and Betty Mabee (2006)
Louis B. Mayer (1987)
George A. Pope Jr. (1988)
Connie M. Ring (1988)
Owners (Year Inducted)
Fred W. Hooper (1988)
Charles S. Howard (1987)
Trainers (Year Inducted)
Farrell W. Jones (1988)
R. H. "Red" McDaniel (1988)
M. E. "Buster" Millerick (1988)

William Molter (1987)
Mel Stute (2007)
Meshach Tenney (1987)
Charlie Whittingham (1987)
Jockeys (Year Inducted)
Johnny Adams (1988)
Russell Baze (2007)
John Longden (1987)
Laffit Pincay Jr. (1988)
Bill Shoemaker (1987)
Jack Westrope (1988)
George Woolf (1987)

Management and Promotion (Year Inducted)
Bing Crosby (1988)
Joe Hernandez (1987)
Mervyn LeRoy (1988)
Dr. Charles H. Strub (1987)
Special Recognition (Year Inducted)
Kenneth Maddy (2006)
Col. F. W. "Bill" Koester (1988)
Louis R. Rowan (1987)

Canterbury Park

Created to honor those who contributed to the track and Minnesota racing, the Canterbury Park Hall of Fame inducts from one to three new members each year.

Horses
Blair's Cove
Come Summer
Hoist Her Flag
Honor the Hero
John Bullit (NZ)
K Z Bay
Little Bro Lantis
Northbound Pride
Princess Elaine
Timeless Prince
Valid Leader
Who Doctor Who
Jockeys
Sandy Hawley

Dean Kutz
Luis Quinonez
Mike Smith
Scott Stevens
Trainers
Carl Nafzger
Doug Oliver
Bernell Rhone
David Van Winkle
Owners
Chuck Bellingham
Frances Genter
Bobbi Knapper
Paul Knapper
Dan Mjolsness

Breeders
Almar Farms
Art and Gretchen Eaton
Robert Morehouse
Others
Paul Allen
Brooks Fields
Tom Metzen
Tom Ryther Sr.
Curtis, Randy, Russ, and Paul Sampson
Dale Shenian
Dark Star
Jim Wells

Fair Grounds

Fair Grounds established its Hall of Fame in 1971 to honor those who made lasting contributions to racing on both the local and national levels. No new inductions since 1995.

Horses
A Letter to Harry
Black Gold
Blushing K. D.
Cabildo
Chou Croute
Colonel Power
Concern
Davona Dale
Diplomat Way
Dixie Poker Ace
Furl Sail
Grindstone
Lecomte
Lexington
Marriage
Master Derby
Mike's Red
Mineshaft
Monarchist
Monique Rene
No Le Hace
Pan Zareta
*Princequillo
Quatrain
Reel
Risen Star
Scott's Scoundrel
Silverbulletday
Spanish Play
Taylor's Special
Tenacious
Tiffany Lass
Tippety Witchet
Whirlaway
Yorktown
Jockeys
Eddie Arcaro
Robby Albarado
Ron Ardoin
Robert L. Baird
Raymond Broussard

Pat Day
Eddie Delahoussaye
Andrew Garner
Edward "Snapper" Garrison
Eric Guerin
Abe Hawkins
Johnny Heckmann
John Longden
J. D. Mooney
Jimmy Nichols
Winnie O'Connor
Craig Perret
Randy Romero
Earle Sande
Bill Shoemaker
James Forman "Tod" Sloan
Larry Snyder
David Whited
Trainers
Tom Amoss
Bobby Barnett
Angel Barrera
W. Hal Bishop
Frank Brothers
Joseph Broussard
Grover "Bud" Delp
Joey Dorignac III
Henry Forrest
Norman "Butsy" Hernandez
Neil Howard
Ben Jones
Jack Lohman
J. O. Meaux
Bill Mott
Homer Pardue
Anthony Pelleteri
Louie Roussel III
Clifford Scott
Dewey Smith

Harry Trotsek
Jack Van Berg
Marion H. Van Berg
C. W. "Cracker" Walker
Vester R. Wright
Owners-Breeders
Col. Edward R. Bradley
Dorothy Brown
Jack DeFee
Joseph P. Dorignac Jr.
John Franks
T. A. Grissom
William G. Helis Sr.
Samuel Clay Hildreth
Duncan Farrar Kenner
Lane's End
Harvey Peltier
J. R. Strauss Sr.
Thomas Jefferson Wells
Roger W. Wilson
Anthony Zupparado
Others
Frank "Buddy" Abadie
Eric Wolfson Blind
Richard Ten Broeck
John Blanks Campbell
John F. Clark Jr.
Capt. William Cottrill
Francis Dunne
Marie Krantz
Sylvester W. Labrot Jr.
Allen LaCombe
John S. Letellier
John G. Masoni
Claude Mauberret Jr.
Gardere "Gar" Moore
Mervin H. Muniz Jr.
Joseph A. Murphy
John Kenneth "Jack" O'Hara
Thomas P. Scott
Albert Stall Sr.

Gulfstream Park

Gulfstream Park's Garden of Champions inductees must be retired, have competed at Gulfstream at least once, and have been named divisional champions or have competed against the highest caliber of competition. The garden no longer exists because of massive renovations in 2002.

Horses
Ajina
Alydar
A.P. Indy
Armed
Artax
Arts and Letters
Bald Eagle
Banshee Breeze
Battlefield
Bayakoa (Arg)
Beautiful Pleasure
Black Tie Affair (Ire)
Blushing John
Bold Ruler
Bowl Game
Buck's Boy
Candy Eclair
Carry Back
Cherokee Run
Chief's Crown
Christmas Past
Cicada
Cigar
Coaltown
Counterpoint
Crafty Admiral
Cryptoclearance
Dark Star
Davona Dale
Daylami (Ire)
Decathlon
Dehere
De La Rose
Deputy Minister
Easy Goer
Eillo
Eliza
Escena

Favorite Trick
Fly So Free
Foolish Pleasure
Forego
Fort Marcy
Forty Niner
Forward Gal
Fraise
Funny Cide
Genuine Risk
Gilded Time
Go for Wand
Groovy
Hansel
Heavenly Prize
Hollywood Wildcat
Holy Bull
Honest Pleasure
Housebuster
Inside Information
Izvestia
Kelso
Lady's Secret
La Prevoyante
Late Bloomer
Left Bank
Lemon Drop Kid
Little Current
Lord Avie
Mac Diarmida
Nashua
Needles
Nodouble
Northern Dancer
Office Queen
Old Hat
Open Mind
Paradise Creek
Parka

Paseana (Arg)
Perfect Sting
Pleasant Colony
Pleasant Tap
Plugged Nickle
Princess Rooney
Roman Brother
Round Table
Rubiano
Sabin
Safely Kept
Sailor
Shecky Greene
Silverbulletday
Silver Charm
Skip Away
Sky Beauty
Sky Classic
Smile
Snow Chief
Soaring Softly
Spectacular Bid
Steinlen (GB)
Sunday Silence
Sunshine Forever
Swale
Swaps
Swoon's Son
Sword Dancer
Thunder Gulch
Tim Tam
Unbridled
Vanlandingham
Victory Gallop
Winning Colors
White Skies
With Approval

Hawthorne Race Course

Hawthorne Race Course launched its Hall of Fame on November 10, 1996, with a tribute to 21 jockey inductees. No new members have been inducted since trainers were honored for the first time in 1998.

Jockeys (Year Inducted)
Johnny Adams (1996)
Eddie Arcaro (1996)
Ted Atkinson (1996)
Braulio Baeza (1996)
Jerry Bailey (1996)
Robert L. Baird (1997)
Steve Brooks (1996)
Steve Cauthen (1996)
Angel Cordero Jr. (1996)
Pat Day (1996)
Eddie Delahoussaye (1996)
Juvenal Diaz (1998)
Earlie Fires (1997)
Gerland Gallitano (1997)
Chris McCarron (1996)

Randall Meier (1997)
Isaac Murphy (1996)
Laffit Pincay Jr. (1996)
Earle Sande (1996)
Shane Sellers (1997)
Bill Shoemaker (1996)
Ray Sibille (1998)
Carlos Silva (1998)
Ron Turcotte (1996)
Jorge Velasquez (1996)
George Woolf (1996)
Trainers (Year Inducted)
Ernie Poulos (1998)
Jere Smith Sr. (1998)
Other (Year Inducted)
Phil Georgeff (1996)

Lone Star Park Hall of Fame

Lone Star Park founded its Hall of Fame in 2007 as part of a yearlong celebration of the track's ten-year anniversary. Names of original inductees will be enshrined in the saddling paddock.

Horses (Year Inducted)
Anet (2007)
Mocha Express (2007)
Trainers (Year Inducted)
Steve Asmussen (2007)
Bob Baffert (2007)

Jockey (Year Inducted)
Ronald Ardoin (2007)
Owner (Year Inducted)
Tom Durant (2007)
Breeders (Year Inducted)
Jim and Marilyn Helzer (2007)

Monmouth Park

The Hall of Champions was established in 1986 to honor local horses that achieved success on the national level.

Affectionately
Alydar
Alysheba
Bet Twice
Black Tie Affair (Ire)
Blue Sparkler
Bold Ruler
Buckpasser
Carry Back
Damascus
Dan Horn
Dearly Precious
Decathlon
Dehere
Desert Vixen
English Channel
First Flight
Forego
Formal Gold
Forty Niner
Friendly Lover
Frisk Me Now
Ghostzapper
Hansel
Helioscope
Holy Bull
Inside Information
John Henry
Kelso
Lady's Secret
Lion Heart
Lord Avie
Lost Code
Majestic Light
Misty Morn
Mongo
Nashua
Needles
Open Mind
Personal Ensign
Point Given
Politely
Polynesian
Riva Ridge
Ruffian
Safely Kept
Serena's Song
Silverbulletday
Skip Away
Smoke Glacken
Spectacular Bid
Spend a Buck
Stymie
Sword Dancer
Ta Wee
Teddy Drone
Touch Gold
War Emblem
With Anticipation

Nebraska Racing Hall of Fame

The Nebraska Racing Hall of Fame was established in 1966. No inductions were made in 1995-2005.

Horses (Year Inducted)
Amadevil
Dazzling Falls (2007)
Gate Dancer (1991)
Omaha (1969)
Rose's Gem (1971)
Vale of Tears (2007)
Who Doctor Who (1993)
Jockeys (Year Inducted)
Irving Anderson (1976)
Steve Brooks (1971)
Perry Compton (2006)
Earl Dew (1978)
Fred Ecoffey (1981)
Dave Erb (1972)
Ira Hanford (1968)
John Lively (1979)
Charley Thorpe (1978)
R. D. Williams (2007)
Trainers (Year Inducted)
Earl Beezley (1972)
Carl Hanford (1968)
Hoss Inman (1992)
C. B. Irwin (1979)
Robert Irwin (1973)
Bob Lee
John Nerud (1970)
Lyman Rollins (1992)
J. D. Taylor (2007)
Jack Van Berg (1976)
Marion H. Van Berg (1966)
Don Von Hemel (1991)
Robert L. Wheeler (1972)

Owners-Breeders (Year Inducted)
Mr. and Mrs. Al Cascio (1993)
Omer "Pete" Hall (1970)
Jack Fickler (1985)
Barton Ford (1978)
Mike Ford (1967)
William Fudge (1973)
Orville Kemling (1981)
Paul Kemling (1981)
Ken Opstein (1985)
Herb and Nancy Riecken
Gary and Mary West (2007)
Others (Year Inducted)
Warren Albert (1978)
Dale Becker (1985)
James E. "Tom" Bock (1973)
Ralph Boomer (1971)
Don Fair (1979)
Harry Farnham (1971)
Leon Hall (2007)
J. J. "Jake" Isaacson (1969)
Don Lee (1992)
Hugh Miner
Earl Moyer (1967)
Murdock Platner (1979)
Grover Porter (1969)
Roland Shaal
Al Swihart (1992)
Terry Wallace (2007)
Dean Williams (1995)
Howard Wolff (1969)

Prairie Meadows Racetrack

Iowa's first horse-racing facility established its Hall of Fame in 1998.

Horses (Year Inducted)
Dontforgethisname (1999)
Lady Tamworth (2003)
Nut N Better (2003)
Railroad Red (1998)
Prince Ariba (1999)
Sharky's Review (2005)
Sure Hot Biscuit (2004)
Vaguely Who (2001)
Owners-Breeders (Year Inducted)
Jim Bader (1998)
Jack Bishop (2002)

Bob and Marlene Bryant (2002)
Jim and Sandra Rasmussen (2000)
Others (Year Inducted)
Dick Clark (2004)
Ken Grandquist (2005)
Keith Hopkins (2001)
Dan Johnson (2006)
Gary Lucas (2005)
Berl Priebe (2005)
Ed Skinner (1999)
Jim Woodward (1999)

Remington Park

The Remington Hall of Fame was established in 1999. No others have been inducted since the original group.

Jockey
Pat Steinberg
Trainer
Donnie K. Von Hemel
Owner-Breeder
Ran Ricks Jr.
Horse
Clever Trevor

Texas Horse Racing Hall of Fame

The Texas Horse Racing Hall of Fame was created in 1999 at Retama Park to pay tribute to the people and horses who have influenced the state's racing industry.

Horses (Year Inducted)
Assault (1999)
Groovy (2001)
Middleground (2000)
Pan Zareta (1999)
Staunch Avenger (2002)
Stymie (2000)
Two Altazano (2003)
Jockeys (Year Inducted)
Cash Asmussen (2003)
Jerry Bailey (2000)
Bill Shoemaker (1999)
Trainer (Year Inducted)
Max Hirsch (2000)
D. Wayne Lukas (2005)
Carl Nafzger (2007)
Willard Proctor (2003)

Owners-Breeders (Year Inducted)
Josephine Abercrombie (2005)
Williams S. Farish (2004)
Nelson Bunker Hunt (2004)
Jim Helzer (2005)
Robert Kleberg Jr. (1999)
Walter Merrick (2000)
Clarence Scharbauer Jr. (2001)
Hilmer and Faye Schmidt (2006)
Joe R. Straus Sr. (2001)
Emerson Woodward (2001)
Others (Year Inducted)
Allen Bogan (2003)
Charles "Doc" Graham (2002)
Herbert Graham (2005)
Robert Johnson Sr. (2006)
Patricia Link (2004)
B. F. Phillips (1999)
W. T. Waggoner (2001)

Virginia Equine Hall of Fame

The Virginia Thoroughbred Hall of Fame began inducting members in 1978. No new members since 2000.

Horses
Cicada
Cyane
First Landing
Fort Marcy
Genuine Risk
Hansel
Hagley
Hildene
Legendra
Lexington
Majesty's Prince
Miss Oceana
Mill Reef
Mongo
Norfolk
Paradise Creek
Pilate
Pleasant Colony
Quadrangle
Reigh Count
Rubiano
Saluter
Sea Hero
Secretariat
Seeking the Pearl
Sir Archy
Somethingroyal
Sword Dancer
Sun Beau
People
Ted Atkinson
Christopher Chenery
Melville Church II
Thomas Mellon Evans
Bertram and Diana Firestone
J. Jorth Fletcher
Kenneth Gilpin
Tyson Gilpin
Gordon Grayson
Richard Hancock
Taylor Hardin
Abram S. Hewitt
Dr. Fritz Howard
Howell E. Jackson
Mrs. J. P. Jones
Keswick Stables
Dorothy N. Lee
Paul Mellon
James P. Mills
Dr. Frank O'Keefe
George L. Ohrstrom Jr.
William Haggin Perry
Mrs. A. C. Randolph
Marion duPont Scott
Isabell Dodge Sloan
Whitney Stone
Liz Whitney Tippett
D. G. Van Clief Sr.
Orme Wilson Jr.

Washington Racing Hall of Fame

The first Washington Racing Hall of Fame members were inducted in 2004.

Special Lifetime Achievement (Year Inducted)
Joe Gottstein (2003)
Breeders (Year Inducted)
Dan Agnew (2007)
Herb Armstrong (2003)
George Drumheller (2004)
Jerre Paxton (2003)
Guy and Barbara Roberts (2005)
C. J. Sebastian (2006)
Jockeys (Year Inducted)
John Adams (2007)
Gary Baze (2005)
Russell Baze (2004)
Basil James (2005)
Albert Johnson (2006)
Ralph Neves (2003)
Gary Stevens (2003)
Trainers (Year Inducted)
Allen Drumheller Sr. (2003)
Francis Keller (2006)
Bud Klokstad (2005)
R. H. "Red" McDaniel (2007)
Jim Penney (2003)
Tom Smith (2003)
Charlie Whittingham (2004)
Horses (Year Inducted)
Captain Condo (2003)
Chinook Pass (2003)
Saratoga Passage (2004)
Sir William (2006)
Smogy Dew (2005)
Trooper Seven (2003)
Turbulator (2004)

TRIPLE CROWN
History of the Triple Crown

As with other great sporting events such as the Olympics and the World Series, the Triple Crown has a rich tradition and history. While modern memory places the Triple Crown in a fixed format—the Kentucky Derby (G1) on the first Saturday in May, the Preakness Stakes (G1) two weeks later, and the Belmont Stakes (G1) three weeks after the Preakness—the series has undergone changes ranging from subtle to seismic in its history.

Origins

The Triple Crown did not start with the inauguration of the three races—the Belmont in 1867, the Preakness six years later, and the Derby in '75. Of the three races, only the Derby has been run continuously, with gaps in the history of the Preakness (1891-'93) and the Belmont (1911 and '12, when antigambling legislation shut down New York racing). In some years, the Derby and Preakness were run within days of each other, and in two years (1917 and '22) they were run on the same day. In some years, the Preakness was run before the Derby.

Far from its current summit as the most prestigious race for American three-year-olds, the Derby in the early 20th century was a struggling regional race. The marketing and showmanship genius of Churchill Downs track executive Col. Matt J. Winn elevated the race to national and international prominence during the first quarter of the century.

When Sir Barton became the first Triple Crown winner in 1919, he was not recognized as a Triple Crown winner, only as a fast-developing three-year-old who went from maiden to multiple major stakes winner within two months.

In fact, the origin of the term "Triple Crown" (which had been in use in England for decades) has been disputed for many years. For decades, credit for coining the expression generally was accorded to legendary *Daily Racing Form* columnist Charlie Hatton. While Hatton's stature and repeated use of the term closely associated him with the Triple Crown, the phrase arguably was first put in print by New York *Times* writer Bryan Field, who used the expression in 1930 after Gallant Fox won the Belmont.

The Triple Crown has been characterized by clusters of winners, especially in the 1930s, '40s, and '70s, and long droughts in between. After Gallant Fox won the 1930 Triple Crown for owner-breeder Belair Stud, only five years passed before Gallant Fox's son Omaha won for Belair. Two years later in 1937, Man o' War's son War Admiral took the Triple Crown for Glen Riddle Farm.

The Triple Crown sweep was achieved four times in the 1940s. First, Calumet Farm and jockey Eddie Arcaro won in 1941 with Whirlaway, and Mrs. John D. Hertz's Count Fleet rolled to victory two years later with Johnny Longden in the saddle. In 1946, King Ranch's homebred Assault scored the triple, and two years later Arcaro and Calumet collected their second Triple Crown sweep with Citation.

In 1950, the Thoroughbred Racing Associations formally recognized the three-race series as the Triple Crown and commissioned Cartier to craft a three-sided trophy, one side for each race. The trophy was in storage many years before Secretariat breezed to a Triple Crown victory in 1973, the first sweep in a quarter-century. Four years later, the brilliant Seattle Slew became the first to win the series without a defeat on his record. In 1978, the first back-to-back Triple Crown sweep occurred when Affirmed defeated Alydar in three classic battles. Harbor View Farm's Affirmed would be the last Triple Crown

Triple Crown Television Ratings and Share

Year	Kentucky Derby Rating	Kentucky Derby Share	Preakness Stakes Rating	Preakness Stakes Share	Belmont Stakes Rating	Belmont Stakes Share
2008	7.3	18	4.7	12	7.2	17
2007	7.5	18	4.9	13	2.9	8
2006	7.0	18	5.4	14	3.5	9
2005	7.3	18	5.1	13	4.5	11
2004	7.4	18	6.1	15	11.3	26
2003	6.4	17	5.6	13	9.5	23
2002	7.1	18	5.7	14	7.6	21
2001	8.1	21	5.6	16	4.5	13
2000	5.8	17	3.6	10	2.8	9
1999	6.3	19	3.4	10	6.0	17
1998	6.1	18	3.6	11	5.9	18
1997	7.1	19	4.8	14	5.3	16
1996	7.4	21	3.7	11	2.9	9
1995	6.0	17	3.2	10	3.5	11
1994	7.5	21	4.4	14	3.9	12
1993	7.3	22	4.7	15	4.2	11

Each rating point represents 1,102,000 viewers as of June 2007. Share is the percentage of televisions tuned to that program.

Birthplaces of Triple Crown Race Winners

Place of Birth	TC Race Wins	Place of Birth	TC Race Wins
Kentucky	281	New York	7
Virginia	21	Canada	4
Florida	19	Texas	4
New Jersey	13	Ireland	2
Maryland	11	Montana	2
Pennsylvania	11	Ohio	2
California	9	Illinois	1
United Kingdom	9	Kansas	1
Tennessee	8	Missouri	1

winner of the 20th century as another long drought took hold.

Through the remainder of the 20th century, five horses came within one race of winning the Triple Crown, but none collected the prize. Alysheba won the first two races in 1987 but was a distant fourth to Bet Twice in the Belmont. Sunday Silence won two spirited battles with Easy Goer in 1989 and finished a well-beaten second to his nemesis in the Belmont. The Triple Crown bids of the 1990s occurred in three consecutive years, 1997-'99. In 1997, Derby and Preakness winner Silver Charm could not repel the late charge of Touch Gold in the Belmont. The following year, Real Quiet appeared to have the Belmont won but lost by a nose in the last stride to Victory Gallop. Charismatic, the 1999 Derby and Preakness winner, finished third by less than two lengths despite sustaining a leg fracture in the Belmont's late stages.

At the start of the 21st century, War Emblem won the first two legs in 2002, only to finish eighth in the Belmont. In 2003, Funny Cide won the Derby and Preakness but finished third in the Belmont; in '04, Smarty Jones came within one length of becoming the 12th Triple Crown winner. Afleet Alex won the 2005 Preakness and Belmont after finishing third in the Derby.

The 2006 Triple Crown was a story of triumph and tragedy. Barbaro won the Kentucky Derby Presented by Yum! Brands (G1) by a dominant 6½ lengths. Bred and owned by the Lael Stables of Roy and Gretchen Jackson, the Dynaformer colt was trained to victory by Michael Matz off a five-week break after his Florida Derby (G1) win. Barbaro broke down shortly after the start of the Preakness and ultimately died of the effects of laminitis in early 2007. The Preakness winner, Bernardini, went on to win the Jockey Club Gold Cup Stakes (G1) and was voted champion three-year-old male. The following year, Street Sense broke the jinx associated with Breeders' Cup Juvenile (G1) winners when he won the Derby by 2¼ lengths but lost the Preakness by a head to Curlin. In the Belmont Stakes, Rags to Riches became the first filly winner in 102 years. She was the second consecutive Belmont winner out of the Deputy Minister mare Better Than Honour.

Triple Crown Productions

Charged with marketing the Kentucky Derby (G1), Preakness Stakes (G1), and Belmont Stakes (G1), Triple Crown Productions was created at a time of turmoil within the industry and especially at the three tracks that stage the races. Threatened with a hostile takeover, Churchill Downs Inc. reorganized in 1984 and hired Thomas Meeker, a lawyer, as its president. The following year, Garden State Park reopened and lured the Derby winner, Spend a Buck, off the Triple Crown trail to the Jersey Derby (G3) with a $2-million bonus. Robert E. Brennan, then Garden State's chairman, spoke of the Jersey Derby taking the place of the Preakness at Pimlico Race Course in the Triple Crown. The New York Racing Association also was mired in internal turmoil.

Incorporated in September 1985, Triple Crown Productions opened its office at Churchill Downs in January '86, with Audrey R. Korotkin as its first executive director. In addition to its marketing function, Triple Crown Productions inaugurated a common nomination form and fees for the races, with early nominations of $600 each closing in mid-January and late nominations, originally $3,000 and now $6,000, closing six weeks before the Derby. Previously, each track obtained nominations for its own races. Supplemental entries (initially $150,000 for the Derby and $100,000 each for the Preakness and Belmont) were permitted beginning in 1990. The Derby supplementary fee was increased to $200,000 in 2005, and Greeley's Galaxy became the first supplemental nominee.

In 1987, the company offered the first Triple Crown Challenge—$5-million in purse money and bonuses to a Triple Crown winner and a $1-million bonus to the horse with the best overall performances in all three races. Triple Crown Productions financed the first bonus year (Bet

Nominations Since Unified Under Triple Crown Productions

Year	Early	Late	Total	Total Fees	Each Track's Share
2008	449	11	460	$335,400	$111,800
2007	450	10	460	330,000	110,000
2006	426	14	440	339,600	113,200
2005	358	13	371	292,800	97,600
2004	434	14	448	344,400	114,800
2003	446	8	454	315,600	105,200
2002	405	12	417	315,000	105,000
2001	440	7	447	306,000	102,000
2000	387	13	400	310,200	103,400
1999	396	11	407	303,600	101,200
1998	384	6	390	266,800	88,933
1997	375	13	388	303,000	101,000
1996	354	7	361	254,800	84,800
1995	317	7	324	232,400	77,400
1994	354	9	363	266,400	88,800
1993	342	25	367	317,700	105,900
1992	389	18	407	314,400	104,800
1991	369	8	377	257,400	85,800
1990	315	33	348	282,000	94,000
1989	381	13	394	267,600	89,200
1988	381	20	401	288,600	96,200
1987	398	24	422	310,800	103,600
1986	422	30	452	343,200	144,400

Early nomination fee has been $600 since 1986; late nomination fee: 1986-'90, $3,000; 1991-'93, $4,500; 1994-present, $6,000.

Twice collected $1-million after he finished second to Alysheba in the Derby and Preakness and won the Belmont). Chrysler Corp. became the sponsor of the bonus in 1988.

Meeker, chairman of Triple Crown Productions, eliminated the executive director position in August 1989, but media attention the following winter led to hiring Edward Seigenfeld, a former NYRA marketing vice president, as the organization's executive director. In 1993, the $1-million bonus for the best overall finish was eliminated.

Chrysler bowed out as the Triple Crown Challenge sponsor after 1995 and was replaced by Visa USA, the credit-card marketing company. Beginning in 1998, a Triple Crown sweep would earn a $5-million bonus in addition to purse earnings from the three races. Visa ended its sponsorship in 2005. In 2004, NYRA abandoned the Triple Crown's joint television contract with NBC in a dispute over revenue splits. NYRA signed up with ABC beginning in 2006.

For the first time since the inception of Triple Crown Productions, no bonus of any kind was offered in 2006, and no bonus was offered in subsequent years. Visa ended its Triple Crown sponsorship in 2005 as well as its sponsorship of a $5-million bonus to any horse that wins the Triple Crown. Visa reduced its sponsorship in 2006 to the Kentucky Derby. Following are the conditions for the 2008 races.

Triple Crown 2008 Conditions
1. General.

Entries to the Races are received only upon the condition that the Applicant will comply with the rules and regulations governing Thoroughbred horse races adopted by the state where each Race is run and the rules and regulations of each Association and will comply with and abide by any decision of the state racing officials and/or the officers of the Association regarding the interpretation and application of such rules and regulations. To the extent of any inconsistency between these conditions and the rules and regulations of the state regulatory agency in the state in which a Race is run, such rules and regulations shall control in that state for the Race. The Applicant consents and agrees to all provisions of each Association's current application, entry form, condition book, conditions and/or other application or agreement regarding the use of stall space (collectively, the "Stall Agreement"), the terms of which are specifically incorporated herein by reference, and upon request shall execute all such applications and/or agreements before bringing any horse upon the respective Association's grounds. In the event of a conflict between these conditions and an Association's Stall Agreement, the provisions of the Association's Stall Agreement shall govern. Without limiting the generality of this paragraph, the Applicant consents and agrees to abide by all provisions of the Rules for Advertising (including, without limiting, Rules for Jockey Advertising) for each Race as promulgated by the Association hosting that Race.

In making this application to participate in Thoroughbred racing, it is understood that an investigative report may be requested whereby information is obtained through personal interviews with third parties. The request may include information as to the Applicant's character, general reputation, personal characteristics, mode of living or such other information as may be relevant to the Applicant's integrity as a racing participant. The Applicant shall have the right to make a written request to an Association within a reasonable period of time for a complete and accurate disclosure of additional information concerning the nature and scope of the investigation.

Each Association reserves the right to start all Races with or without a stall gate starting machine. Each Association reserves the right to cancel any Race, without notice, at any time prior to the actual running thereof, without liability, except for the return by the canceling Association of fees as described herein.

In the event of cancellation of a Race or the revocation of, or refusal to accept an Applicant's nomination, entry or stall application, or denial of the right to start a Race, the Association taking such action shall return to the Applicant all entry, starting and supplemental fees received by the Association and one-third (1/3) of the nomination fee paid by the Applicant and shall have no further liability to the Applicant as a result of such action.

Each Association reserves the right to make all decisions regarding preferences and conditions with regard to its respective Race and its decision shall be final. Each Association reserves the right, in its sole and absolute discretion, to refuse, cancel or revoke any nomination or entry, stall application or Stall Agreement or the transfer thereof and reserves the right to deny the right to start in a Race, without notice to the Applicant and for any reason, including but not limited to, the Applicant's failure to fully perform or abide by all provisions and conditions hereof. The Applicant hereby consents to and agrees that in the event any litigation is instituted which involves Churchill Downs Incorporated or Triple Crown Productions LLC, the Applicant is subject to jurisdiction and venue in the courts of Jefferson County, Kentucky, and in the Federal Courts of the Western District of Kentucky. In the event any litigation is instituted which involves The Maryland Jockey Club of Baltimore City Inc., the Applicant hereby consents to and agrees that the Applicant is subject to jurisdiction and venue in the Circuit Court for Baltimore City, and in the Federal Courts for the District of Maryland. In the event litigation is instituted which involves The New York Racing Association Inc., the Applicant hereby consents to and agrees that the Applicant is subject to jurisdiction and venue in the Supreme Court of New York, County of Nassau, and the Federal Courts for the Eastern District of New York.

Triple Crown Productions LLC reserves the right, in its sole and absolute discretion, to accept nominations without timely payment of required nomination fees or receipt of an executed nomination form. Facsimile nomination forms must be followed by timely payment of all nomination fees and

subsequent delivery of an originally executed nomination form. The inclusion by Triple Crown Productions LLC of a horse's name in the publicly released list of nominees to the Races shall constitute prima facie evidence of the Applicant's nomination and liability for nomination fees. The Applicant shall be responsible for payment of all fees including, without limitation, the nomination fee. The Applicant is liable to and shall reimburse Triple Crown Productions LLC for any costs, damages or expenses incurred by it, including reasonable attorneys' fees, in collecting any unpaid nomination or other fees.

The Kentucky Derby post position shall be determined as follows: A nontransferable lot number shall be drawn for each horse named as a starter at the Closing. The lot number drawn for each starter shall determine the numerical order for selection of post position. Selection of post position shall be made by each owner of a horse (or, if more than one, the owners collectively) or the authorized agent of the horse's owner(s). Horses having common ties through ownership or training shall each be treated separately for purposes of selecting post position. Detailed rules governing the post position draw process are available from the Racing Secretary's office and will be distributed prior to the Closing. These rules shall control.

2. Release and Indemnification.

In consideration of the Applicant's admission to each Association's facility, the Applicant hereby releases the Association from all claims for loss or damage of, or injury to, or death of any persons or property (including horses as well as loss of use of property) sustained by the Applicant and/or its invitees and/or the property owned or under the control of the Applicant located at the Association's facilities. The Applicant recognizes the risks of its activities to be undertaken at the Association's facilities and it has inspected and is familiar with each Association's facilities and does voluntarily and fully assume all risk of loss, injury, damage, death or destruction to any person or property. This release and assumption of risk provision shall not be effective as to any cause of loss attributable to any intentional, willful, gross, or reckless conduct of the Association.

The Applicant further agrees to protect, indemnify and hold harmless the Association (or if indemnification is not available, to contribute to the Association's losses) from and against any loss, damage, claims or expenses (including reasonable attorneys' and other fees), arising directly or indirectly from any acts or omissions of the Applicant, or any of the Applicant's horses, or any agent, employee or invitee of the Applicant, arising out of or in connection with the Applicant's activities at the Association's facilities.

The foregoing release and indemnification provisions shall be construed in a manner consistent with the limitations set forth herein to be as broad and inclusive as permitted by and in a manner consistent with the laws and regulations of the Association's jurisdiction and shall be binding upon the Applicant, its successors and/or assignees. The maintenance by the Association of insurance relating to the claims released and/or indemnified hereby shall not affect the terms or interpretation of this Agreement and the Applicant agrees that any and all insurers of the Applicant, whether insurers of property, personal injury or any other loss, if their insurance policies do not already so provide, agree that they waive and will not exercise any rights of subrogation in the event of loss of or damage to the subject property, as well as the loss of use thereof, except that any waiver of subrogation will not be effective where such waiver will result in such liability policy becoming null and void. For purposes of this Agreement, the Association shall mean and include the Association and its owners, officers, directors, trustees, agents, employees, contractors, servants and licensees.

Responsibility for the maintenance of general liability and horse mortality insurance to cover the risks outlined above rests with the Applicant. Consultation with a competent insurance advisor is strongly recommended. Failure to maintain adequate insurance may subject the Applicant to the risks outlined above.

3. Reservation of Rights.

As the organizer, host and sponsor of Thoroughbred horse races, each Association hereby reserves unto itself, its agents, assigns and licensees and the Applicant hereby assigns to the Association all interest it may have in the Host Rights, as herein defined. The Host Rights shall mean the sole and exclusive right to: (a) produce, exhibit, sell, license, transfer or transmit in any manner still or motion pictures, radio and television broadcasts, interactive computer including Internet, mobile phones or any other media transmission, now known or hereafter developed, of all events which occur on the Association's property, including without limitation, all activities occurring before, during and after Thoroughbred horse races; (b) utilize the race and the results thereof, all for any purpose or use as the Association shall determine; (c) limit, prohibit or regulate the display of any commercial advertising symbols, or other identification, other than an Applicant's registered silks, in connection with any race or related activities; and (d) develop, produce and sell, by or through any licensee, goods using the Applicant's name or likeness, the name or likeness of any horse owned by the Applicant brought onto the Association's grounds, or any other identifying feature, silks, trademark or copyrighted material which is used in connection with the race. The submission of a nomination or making of an entry in any race shall mean that the Applicant consents to the above reservation of the Host Rights and consents to be photographed or to otherwise be a subject of still or moving pictures, radio or television programs, without remuneration except for contributions to horsemen's purses from wagering on the races as established by contract or legislation. The Applicant agrees that he has not and will not execute any documents or take any other action, which purports to assign or otherwise transfer any interest in the Host Rights or assert any claim, demand or cause of action against the Association which is inconsistent with the full and exclusive exercise by the Association of its Host Rights.

4. Definition of Applicant.

As used herein, "Applicant" shall mean and include the nominating owner(s) and the owner's agents, trainers and jockeys and their agents, heirs, representatives, successors, next of kin and assigns; provided, however, that the rights and benefits of the Applicant under this Agreement are personal and no such right or benefit shall be subject to voluntary or involuntary alienation, assignment or transfer. The Applicant covenants that all of the above persons have agreed to the foregoing conditions and further agrees that it will deliver their written consent and agreement to such conditions upon request of the Association. The Applicant shall indemnify and hold the Association harmless from and against any claim or cause of action (including any expense incurred in connection therewith, including reasonable attorneys' and other fees) that may be asserted by or on behalf of any person which is inconsistent with the release and indemnification provisions set forth in the foregoing paragraph.

The Triple Crown
First Closing, January 19, 2008 — $600
Second Closing, March 29, 2008 — $6,000

Nominations to each and all of the Triple Crown races, The Kentucky Derby, The Preakness Stakes and The Belmont Stakes (the "Races") may be made by payment of a single nomination fee to Triple Crown Productions LLC as agent for Churchill Downs Incorporated, The Maryland Jockey Club of Baltimore City Inc. and The New York Racing Association Inc. (the "Association" or "Associations" as the case may be). The nomination fee for nominations postmarked or hand delivered by January 19, 2008, is $600 and for nominations postmarked or hand delivered from January 20 through March 29, 2008, is $6,000. Horses nominated on or before March 29, 2008, shall be considered original nominees ("Original Nominees").

At any time, prior to the Closing for The Kentucky Derby, as defined below, additional nominations to all three Races may be made upon payment of a supplementary fee of $200,000 to Churchill Downs Incorporated. Following the running of The Kentucky Derby, horses may be nominated at any time prior to Closing for The Preakness Stakes or The Belmont Stakes (time of Closing being defined below).

The supplementary fee payable for such nomination shall be $100,000 payable to The Maryland Jockey Club of Baltimore City Inc. for supplemental nomination to The Preakness Stakes and The Belmont Stakes or $100,000 payable to The New York Racing Association Inc. for supplemental nomination to The Belmont Stakes only. All supplemental fees will be included in the purse distribution for the Race run by the Association to which the supplemental nomination is paid, unless otherwise specified in the specific Race rules below. The ability of horses nominated by payment of the foregoing supplementary fees ("Supplemental Nominees") to enter any Race will be determined in accordance with the conditions of that Race. All nominees, original, supplemental or otherwise, will be required to pay entry and starting fees for the Race or Races in which they participate before they may start.

134th Running of Kentucky Derby
$2,000,000 Guaranteed
Minimum Gross (Grade 1)
To Be Run Saturday, May 3, 2008
One Mile and a Quarter

For three-year-olds, with an entry fee of $25,000 each and a starting fee of $25,000 each. Supplemental nominations may be made upon payment of $200,000 and in accordance with the rules set forth herein. All fees, including supplemental nominations, in excess of $900,000 in the aggregate shall be paid to the winner. Churchill Downs Incorporated shall guarantee a minimum gross purse of $2,000,000 (the "Guaranteed Purse"). The winner shall receive $1,240,000, second place shall receive $400,000, third place shall receive $200,000, fourth place shall receive $100,000 and fifth place shall receive $60,000 from the Guaranteed Purse (the Guaranteed Purse to each place to be divided equally in the event of a dead heat). Starters shall be named through the entry box on Wednesday, April 30, 2008, at 10:00 a.m. Eastern Daylight Time (the "Closing"). The maximum number of starters shall be limited to twenty (20). Colts and Geldings shall each carry a weight of one hundred twenty six (126) pounds; Fillies shall each carry one hundred twenty one (121) pounds. Supplemental Nominees will be allowed to enter but will not have preference over any Original Nominee and will not be allowed to start the Race if the maximum number of starters has otherwise been reached by Original Nominees prior to the Closing. If the number of nominees exceeds the number of available starting positions at the Closing, these conditions shall be applied to determine which nominees will be allowed to start. In the event that more than twenty (20) entries pass through the entry box at the Closing, the starters shall be determined at the Closing from Original Nominees first, then Supplemental Nominees if starting positions are still available with preference given to those horses that have accumulated the highest earnings in the Graded Stakes races, including all monies actually paid for performance in such Graded Stakes races. For purposes of this preference, the graded status of each race shall be the graded status assigned to the race by the International Cataloguing Standards Committee in Part I of the International Cataloguing Standards as published by The Jockey Club Information Systems, Inc. each year. Should additional starters be needed to bring the field to twenty (20), the remaining starters shall be determined at the Closing with preference given to those horses that have accumulated the highest earnings in non-restricted sweepstakes. For purposes of this preference, a "non-restricted sweepstakes" shall mean those sweepstakes whose conditions contain no restrictions other than that of age or sex. In the case of ties resulting from preferences or otherwise, the additional starter(s) shall be determined by lot. Any horse excluded from running because of the aforementioned preference(s) shall be refunded the $25,000 entry fee and the $200,000 supplemental fee, if applicable. An "also-eligible" list will not be maintained and in no event will starters be added or allowed to run in the Race which are not determined to be starters at the Closing. Post position shall be

determined as follows: a nontransferable lot number shall be drawn for each horse named as a starter at the Closing. The lot number drawn for each starter shall determine the numerical order for selection of post position. Selection of post position shall be made by each owner of a horse (or, if more than one, the owners collectively) or the authorized agent of the horse's owner(s). Horses having common ties through ownership or training shall each be treated separately for purposes of selecting post position. In the event of one or more scratches after the selection of post position, then starters with the post position higher than the post position of the scratched starter will be moved to the lowest empty post position (i.e., toward the inside rail of the race track) so that there are no empty post positions in-between horses at the start of The Kentucky Derby. Detailed rules governing the post position draw process are available from the Racing Secretary's office and will be distributed prior to the Closing. These rules shall control. The owner of the winner of the Race shall receive a gold trophy. In the event of one or more scratches after the selection of post position, then starters with the post position higher than the scratched starter will be moved to the lowest empty post position so there will be no empty post position at the start of the Kentucky Derby.

133rd Running of Preakness Stakes
$1,000,000 Guaranteed (Grade 1)
To Be Run Saturday, May 17, 2008
One Mile and Three-Sixteenths

For three-year-olds, $10,000 to pass the entry box, starters to pay $10,000 additional. Supplemental nominations may be made in accordance with the rules, upon payment of $100,000, 60% of the purse to the winner, 20% to second, 11% to third, 6% to fourth and 3% to fifth. Weight 126 pounds for Colts and Geldings, 121 pounds for Fillies. Starters to be named through the entry box on Wednesday, May 14, 2008, three days before the race by the usual time of closing (the "Closing"). The Preakness field will be limited to fourteen (14) entries and shall be determined on the Wednesday immediately preceding the day of the race. In the event that more than fourteen (14) horses are properly nominated and pass through the entry box by the usual time of Closing, the starters will be determined at the Closing with the first seven (7) horses given preference by accumulating the highest earnings in Graded Stakes (lifetime); for purposes of this preference, the graded status of each race shall be the graded status assigned to the race by the International Cataloguing Standards Committee in Part 1 of the International Cataloguing Standards as published by The Jockey Club Information Systems, Inc. each year. The next four (4) starters will be determined by accumulating the highest earnings (lifetime) in all non-restricted stakes. "Non-restricted stakes" shall mean those stakes whose conditions contain no restrictions other than that of age or sex. The remaining three (3) starters shall be determined by accumulating the highest earnings (lifetime) in all races. Should this preference produce any ties, the additional starter(s) shall be determined by lot. In application of the above described rule, each horse will be separately considered without regard to identity of its owner. If the rules described in this paragraph result in the exclusion of any horse, the $10,000 entry fee previously paid will be refunded to the owner of said horse. The above conditions notwithstanding, no horse which earns purse money in The Kentucky Derby shall be denied the opportunity to enter and start in The Preakness Stakes. A replica of the Woodlawn Vase will be presented to the winning owner to remain his or her personal property.

140th Running of Belmont Stakes
$1,000,000 (Grade 1)
To Be Run Saturday, June 7, 2008
One Mile and a Half

For three-year-olds, by subscription of $600 each, to accompany the nomination, if made on or before January 19, 2008, or $6,000, if made on or before March 29, 2008, $10,000 to pass the entry box and $10,000 additional, to start. At any time prior to the closing time of entries, horses may be nominated to The Belmont Stakes upon payment of a supplemental fee of $100,000 to The New York Racing Association Inc. All entrants, supplemental or otherwise, will be required to pay entry and starting fees; but, no fees, supplemental or otherwise, shall be added to the purse. The purse for The Belmont Stakes shall be one million dollars ($1,000,000.00) divided as follows: sixty percent (60%) to the winner, twenty percent (20%) to the second place winner, eleven percent (11%) to the third place winner, six percent (6%) to the fourth place winner, and three percent (3%) to the fifth place winner. Colts and Geldings, 126 lbs. Fillies, 121 lbs. Starters to be named at the closing time of entries. The Belmont field will be limited to sixteen (16) starters. In the event more than 16 entries pass through the entry box at the closing, the starters will be determined at the closing with the first eight (8) starters given preference by accumulating the highest earnings in Graded Sweepstakes at a mile or over. For purposes of this preference, the graded status of each race shall be the Grade assigned by the International Cataloguing Standards Committee in Part 1 of The International Cataloguing Standards as published annually by The Jockey Club Information Systems, Incorporated. The next five (5) starters will be determined by accumulating the highest earnings in all non-restricted sweepstakes. "Non-restricted sweepstakes" shall mean those sweepstakes whose conditions contain no restrictions other than age or sex. The remaining three (3) starters shall be determined by accumulating the highest earnings in all races. Should this preference produce any ties, the additional starter(s) shall be determined by lot. If the rules described result in the exclusion of any horse, the $10,000 entry fee will be refunded to the owner of said horse. The above conditions notwithstanding, any horse, which earns purse money in either The Kentucky Derby or The Preakness Stakes shall be included in the initial eight (8) starters of The Belmont Stakes. The winning owner will be presented with the August Belmont Memorial Cup, to be retained for one year, as well as a trophy for permanent possession and trophies to the winning trainer and jockey.

Road to the 2008 Triple Crown

The following races are traditionally used as preps for the Triple Crown races. The table includes the dates and winners of the races in 2008.

Date	Race	Trk	Dist.	Time	First three finishers
1/1	Tropical Park Derby (G3)	Crc	1⅛mT	1:46.95	**COWBOY CAL, Why Tonto, Cannonball**
1/5	Count Fleet S.	Aqu	1m70yds	1:41.14	**GIANT MOON, Spanky Fischbein, Roman Emperor**
1/5	Hutcheson S. (G2)	GP	7f	1:23.21	**SMOOTH AIR, Silver Edition, Halo Najib**
1/12	Lecomte S. (G3)	FG	1m	1:37.79	**Z FORTUNE, Blackberry Road, Mad Flatter**
1/12	San Rafael S. (G2)	SA	1mAW	1:33.37	**EL GATO MALO, Indian Sun, Massive Drama**
1/20	San Pedro S.	SA	6½fAW	1:13.07	**GAYEGO, Sea of Pleasure, Cardinal Zin**
1/26	Sunshine Millions Dash S.	SA	6fAW	1:06.53	**BOB BLACK JACK**, Winsome Charm, **Afleet Ruler**
1/27	California Derby	GG	1 1/16mAW	1:44.57	**YANKEE BRAVO**, Cafe Tortoni, **Victory Pete**
2/2	Black Gold S.	FG	abt5½fT	1:06.12	AMAZING RESULTS, General G, Excessive Heat
2/2	Robert B. Lewis S. (G2)	SA	1 1/16mAW	1:40.76	**CROWN OF THORNS, Coast Guard, Reflect Times (Jpn)**
2/2	Swale S. (G2)	GP	6½f	1:15.63	**EATON'S GIFT**, Surrealdeal, **Wincat**
2/2	Whirlaway S.	Aqu	1 1/16m	1:44.47	**BARRIER REEF, Roman Emperor, Texas Wildcatter**
2/9	Risen Star S. (G3)	FG	1 1/16m	1:44.68	**PYRO, Z Fortune, Visionaire**
2/9	Turf Paradise Derby	TuP	1 1/16m	1:42.81	**NIKKI'SGOLDENSTEED**, Ez Dreamer, **Meer Kat (Ire)**
2/10	San Vicente S. (G2)	SA	7fAW	1:20.01	**GEORGIE BOY, Into Mischief, Massive Drama**
2/11	Darley OBS Championship S.	OTC	1 1/16mAW	1:46.40	**HALO NAJIB, Hello From Heaven,** Ghostly Thunder
2/16	Borderland Derby	Sun	1 1/16m	1:47.19	**PONI COLADA, Cape Time, No Jepordy**
2/16	Sam F. Davis S.	Tam	1 1/16m	1:44.13	**FIERCE WIND, Big Truck, Smooth Air**
2/18	Southwest S. (G3)	OP	1m	1:37.89	**DENIS OF CORK, Sierra Sunset, dh-Sacred Journey/ dh-Liberty Bull**
2/24	Fountain of Youth S. (G2)	GP	1⅛m	1:50.07	**COOL COAL MAN, Elysium Fields, Court Vision**
3/1	John Battaglia Memorial S.	TP	1 1/16mAW	1:44.69	ABSOLUTELY CINDY, **Your Round**, Dixie Decision
3/1	Sham S. (G3)	SA	1⅛mAW	1:50.15	**COLONEL JOHN, El Gato Malo, Victory Pete**
3/2	Baldwin S. (G3)	SA	abt6½fT	1:13.09	TEN MEROPA, **Sky Cape**, D. Double You
3/8	El Camino Real Derby (G3)	BM	1 1/16m	1:43.17	AUTISM AWARENESS, **Nikki'sgoldensteed, Tres Borrachos**
3/8	Gotham S. (G3)	Aqu	1 1/16m	1:44.60	**VISIONAIRE, Texas Wildcatter**, Larrys Revenge
3/8	Louisiana Derby (G2)	FG	1 1/16m	1:44.44	**PYRO, My Pal Charlie, Yankee Bravo**
3/15	Rebel S. (G2)	OP	1 1/16m	1:43.88	**SIERRA SUNSET, King's Silver Son, Isabull**
3/15	San Felipe S. (G2)	SA	1 1/16mAW	1:42.35	**GEORGIE BOY, Gayego, Bob Black Jack**
3/15	Tampa Bay Derby (G3)	Tam	1 1/16m	1:44.25	**BIG TRUCK, Atoned**, Dynamic Wayne
3/16	WinStar Derby	Sun	1⅛m	1:49.82	**LIBERTY BULL, Screen to Screen**, Ablaze With Spirit
3/22	Hansel S.	TP	6fAW	1:10.03	MITIGATION, **U. S. Cavalry**, Stormin Yank
3/22	Lane's End S. (G2)	TP	1⅛mAW	1:50.20	**ADRIANO, Halo Najib, Medjool**
3/22	Rushaway S.	TP	1 1/16mAW	1:44.55	**BIG GLEN, Miner's Claim, Icabad Crane**
3/29	Florida Derby (G1)	GP	1⅛m	1:48.16	**BIG BROWN, Smooth Air, Tomcito**
3/29	Bulleit Bourbon Palm Beach S. (G3)	GP	1⅛mT	1:45.98	**SPORTING ART**, Flying Dismount, Moral Compass
3/29	San Miguel S.	SA	6fAW	1:09.07	**SALUTE THE SARGE**, Leonides, **Sea of Pleasure**
3/29	UAE Derby (UAE-G2)	Nad	1,800m	1:48.60	=HONOUR DEVIL (Arg), =Royal Vintage (SAf), =Cocoa Beach (Chi)
4/4	Central Bank Transylvania S. (G3)	Kee	1 1/16mAW	1:44.43	**BOSS LAFITTE, Riley Tucker**, Budge Man
4/5	Bay Shore S. (G3)	Aqu	7f	1:23.67	**J BE K, Gattopardo, Jockey Ridge**
4/5	Illinois Derby (G2)	Haw	1⅛m	1:49.01	**RECAPTURETHEGLORY, Golden Spikes, Z Humor**
4/5	Santa Anita Derby (G1)	SA	1⅛mAW	1:48.16	**COLONEL JOHN, Bob Black Jack, Coast Guard**
4/5	Wood Memorial S. (G1)	Aqu	1⅛m	1:52.35	**TALE OF EKATI, War Pass, Court Vision**
4/6	Lafayette S.	Kee	7fAW	1:22.26	**KEEP LAUGHING**, Hatta Fort (GB), **Eaton's Gift**
4/12	Arkansas Derby (G2)	OP	1⅛m	1:49.63	**GAYEGO, Z Fortune, Tres Borrachos**
4/12	Holy Bull S. (G3)	GP	1 3/16m	1:58.14	**HEY BYRN**, Dream Maestro, Famous Patriot
4/12	Toyota Blue Grass S. (G1)	Kee	1⅛mAW	1:49.71	**MONBA, Cowboy Cal, Kentucky Bear**
4/19	Coolmore Lexington S. (G2)	Kee	1 1/16mAW	1:42.14	**BEHINDATTHEBAR**, Samba Rooster, **Riley Tucker**
4/26	Derby Trial S.	CD	7½f	1:28.45	**MACHO AGAIN, Kodiak Kowboy**, Fujita
4/26	Withers S. (G3)	Aqu	1m	1:34.50	**HARLEM ROCKER, J Be K**, Double or Nothing
5/3	Kentucky Derby Presented by Yum! Brands (G1)	CD	1¼m	2:01.82	**BIG BROWN, Eight Belles, Denis of Cork**
5/10	Peter Pan S. (G2)	Bel	1⅛m	1:47.87	**CASINO DRIVE, Mint Lane, Ready's Echo**
5/17	Preakness S. (G1)	Pim	1 3/16m	1:54.80	**BIG BROWN, Macho Again, Icabad Crane**
6/7	Belmont S. (G1)	Bel	1½m	2:29.65	**DA' TARA, Denis of Cork, dh-Anak Nakal/Ready's Echo**

Triple Crown nominees are listed in bold.

Triple Crown Winners

America's Triple Crown Winners

Year	Horse	Owner	Trainer	Jockey
1978	Affirmed	Harbor View Farm	Lazaro Barrera	Steve Cauthen
1977	Seattle Slew	Karen L. Taylor	William Turner Jr.	Jean Cruguet
1973	Secretariat	Meadow Stable	Lucien Laurin	Ron Turcotte
1948	Citation	Calumet Farm	H. A. "Jimmy" Jones	Eddie Arcaro
1946	Assault	King Ranch	Max Hirsch	Warren Mehrtens
1943	Count Fleet	Mrs. John D. Hertz	Don Cameron	John Longden
1941	Whirlaway	Calumet Farm	Ben A. Jones	Eddie Arcaro
1937	War Admiral	Samuel D. Riddle	George Conway	Charles Kurtsinger
1935	Omaha	Belair Stud	James Fitzsimmons	William Saunders
1930	Gallant Fox	Belair Stud	James Fitzsimmons	Earle Sande
1919	Sir Barton	J. K. L. Ross	H. Guy Bedwell	John Loftus

Triple Crown Trophy

The Triple Crown trophy was commissioned in 1950 by the Thoroughbred Racing Associations, which copyrighted the term Triple Crown, and has three sides to symbolize the three races in the series. The trophy was presented retroactively to the eight previous winners of the three races.

The first three-year-old with a chance to claim the silver Triple Crown trophy was Tim Tam, who won the 1958 Kentucky Derby and Preakness Stakes but finished second to *Cavan in the Belmont Stakes. Secretariat in 1973 was the first horse to be presented the trophy after sweeping the three races.

Sir Barton

At the start of 1919, Sir Barton was far down the pecking order in trainer H. Guy Bedwell's stable. Commander J.K.L. Ross had purchased the *Star Shoot colt at Saratoga for $10,000 in 1918, but Sir Barton was winless in his six starts as a two-year-old and made his three-year-old debut in the '19 Kentucky Derby. His role in the Derby on May 10, 1919, was to serve as a pacemaker for his highly fancied stablemate, Billy Kelly. They went off at 2.60-to-1, second choice behind the 2.10-to-1 entry of Sailor and Eternal. Ridden by Johnny Loftus, Sir Barton bucked the odds, leading all the way and winning the Derby by five lengths over his stablemate. He was immediately shipped to Baltimore and won the Preakness Stakes on May 14 (a Wednesday) by four lengths over Eternal as the 7-to-5 favorite. In the Belmont Stakes on June 11, Sir Barton was 2-to-5 against the entry of Sweep On, third in the Preakness, and Natural Bridge. Sir Barton allowed Natural Bridge to set the pace for three-quarters of a mile before taking the lead and winning by five lengths. Between his Preakness and Belmont victories, Sir Barton won the Withers Stakes.

Sir Barton's achievement was unprecedented, but he was overshadowed by the appearance of Man o' War, who sustained the only defeat of his career in that year's Sanford Memorial Stakes at Saratoga Race Course.

As a four-year-old in 1920, Sir Barton alternated

Ch. c., 1916, by *Star Shoot—Lady Sterling, by Hanover

Owner: Commander J. K. L. Ross
Breeders: Madden and Gooch (Ky.)
Trainer: H. Guy Bedwell
Jockey: Johnny Loftus

		Race Record			
Year	Starts	1st	2nd	3rd	Earnings
1918	6	0	1 (1)	0	$ 4,113
1919	13	8 (8)	3 (2)	2 (1)	88,250
1920	12	5 (5)	2 (2)	3 (3)	24,494
	31	13 (13)	6 (5)	5 (4)	$116,857

1919—1st Kentucky Derby, Preakness S., Belmont S., Withers S., Potomac H., Maryland H., Pimlico Fall Series No. 2, Pimlico Fall Series No. 3
1920—1st Saratoga H., Merchants' and Citizens' H., Dominion H., Climax H., Rennert H.

between brilliant and ordinary, winning five of 12 starts but finishing off the board twice. Because of his chronically sore feet and difficult temperament, he lost several races that he should have won against less talented opponents.

After losing a match race to Man o' War, Sir Barton faded from view. Retired to stud at the end of the 1920 season, he enjoyed only moderate success, was sold to the United States Cavalry Remount Station, and lived on a Wyoming ranch until his death in '37.

Gallant Fox

Bred and owned by the Belair Stud of William Woodward, Gallant Fox marked a shift in the standards of American breeding. The introduction of *Sir Gallahad III to the United States from France in the late 1920s represented an important step forward for the American breeding industry. For the next several decades, American breeders went to Europe for proven stallions or prospects, particularly in England. The result was a significant increase in the quality of American racehorses. Woodward was one of the syndicate members involved in the purchase of *Sir Gallahad III, who stood at Claiborne Farm in Kentucky.

Gallant Fox was a good but not outstanding two-year-old, winning the Flash and Junior Champion Stakes and placing in three other stakes in his seven starts in 1929. In the care of trainer James "Sunny Jim" Fitzsimmons, Gallant Fox developed into an imposing physical specimen at three.

A four-length winner in Aqueduct's 1930 Wood Memorial Stakes, Gallant Fox hurtled through the Triple Crown, winning the Preakness on May 9 by three-quarters of a length, the Kentucky Derby eight days later by two lengths, and the Belmont on June 7 by three lengths over Whichone, his leading rival. Three weeks later,

B. c., 1927, by *Sir Gallahad III— Marguerite, by Celt

Owner-Breeder: Belair Stud (Ky.)
Trainer: James Fitzsimmons
Jockey: Earl Sande

Year	Starts	Race Record 1st	2nd	3rd	Earnings
1929	7	2 (2)	2 (1)	2 (2)	$ 19,890
1930	10	9 (9)	1 (1)	0	308,275
	17	11 (11)	3 (2)	2 (2)	$328,165

1929—1st Flash S., Junior Champion S.
1930—1st Kentucky Derby, Preakness S., Belmont S., Wood Memorial S., Dwyer S., Classic S., Saratoga Cup, Lawrence Realization S., Jockey Cup Gold Cup

Gallant Fox added the Dwyer Stakes to his list of triumphs.

His only loss of the year occurred in the Travers Stakes at Saratoga Race Course, where he ran second to 100-to-1 longshot Jim Dandy.

At the end of the year, Gallant Fox was retired to stud at Claiborne, where he sired 1935 Triple Crown winner Omaha and '36 Belmont Stakes winner Granville. Gallant Fox died on November 13, 1954, and was buried at Claiborne alongside his sire and dam.

Omaha

Five years after his Gallant Fox became the second Triple Crown winner, William Woodward saw his decision to participate in the syndication of French runner *Sir Gallahad III for stud duty in the United States pay off with a second Triple Crown winner. Omaha, a son of Gallant Fox and grandson of *Sir Gallahad III, won nine of 22 starts, but his career did not measure up to that of his sire. At two, Omaha won only once in nine starts, although he finished second in the Sanford and Champagne Stakes.

Once again, trainer James "Sunny Jim" Fitzsimmons's patient hand allowed the chestnut colt to fill out nicely over the winter between his two- and three-year-old years. On May 4, 1935, Omaha stepped onto an off track at Churchill Downs as the 4-to-1 second choice for the Kentucky Derby (favored at 3.80-to-1 was the filly Nellie Flag). Omaha made his move for the lead on the far turn, led by two lengths at the top of the stretch, and won by a relatively easy 1½ lengths over Roman Soldier.

One week later, Omaha was a runaway, six-length winner of the Preakness Stakes over Firethorn, who had skipped the Derby. Despite losing two weeks later in the Withers Stakes, Omaha won the Belmont Stakes by 1½ lengths

Ch. c., 1932, by Gallant Fox— Flambino, by *Wrack

Owner-Breeder: Belair Stud (Ky.)
Trainer: James Fitzsimmons
Jockey: Willie Saunders

Year	Starts	Race Record 1st	2nd	3rd	Earnings
1934 (U.S.)	9	1	4 (3)	0	$ 3,850
1935 (U.S.)	9	6 (5)	1 (1)	2 (2)	142,255
1936 (Eng.)	4	2 (2)	2 (2)	0	8,650
	22	9 (7)	7 (6)	2 (2)	$154,705

1935—1st Kentucky Derby, Preakness S., Belmont S., Dwyer S., Classic S.
1936—(In England) 1st Victor Wild S., Queen's Plate

on June 8. Omaha finished third in the Brooklyn Handicap in his next start but won his next two starts, the Dwyer Stakes and the Arlington Classic, before an injury ended his season.

As a four-year-old, Omaha was shipped to England and finished second in the Ascot Gold Cup. Omaha failed at stud, and Claiborne in 1943 sent him to a New York farm. Moved to a farm in Nebraska in 1950, Omaha died in '59 and was buried at Ak-Sar-Ben racetrack in Omaha.

War Admiral

Glen Riddle Farms owner Samuel Riddle owned War Admiral's famous sire, Man o' War, but chose to skip the Kentucky Derby with him in 1920. In Riddle's estimation, Churchill Downs was too far west, and the Derby was too early in the year for his comfort.

War Admiral, a striking brown colt out of the Sweep mare Brushup, had won three of six starts as a two-year-old, and his one stakes victory was in the minor Eastern Shore Handicap at Havre de Grace in Maryland. He returned to Havre de Grace for his first start of 1937 and won the Chesapeake Stakes. Riddle then decided to give War Admiral a shot at the Kentucky Derby.

Sent off as the 8-to-5 favorite in a Derby field of 20, War Admiral led at every point of call and easily held off champion two-year-old Pompoon in the final furlong to win by 1¾ lengths.

One week later, War Admiral was put to a much sterner test in the Preakness Stakes by Pompoon, who battled the Derby winner from the top of Pimlico Race Course's stretch. War Admiral won by a head. In the Belmont Stakes on June 5, War Admiral stumbled at the start, injuring his right foreleg, but the diminutive colt cruised to an easy, three-length victory over Sceneshifter.

Br. c., 1934, by Man o' War—Brushup, by Sweep

Owner: Glen Riddle Farms
Breeder: Samuel Riddle (Ky.)
Trainer: George Conway
Jockey: Charles Kurtsinger

Year	Starts	1st	2nd	3rd	Earnings
1936	6	3 (1)	2 (2)	1 (1)	$ 14,800
1937	8	8 (6)	0	0	166,500
1938	11	9 (8)	1 (1)	0	90,840
1939	1	1	0	0	1,100
	26	21 (15)	3 (3)	1 (1)	$273,240

1936—1st Eastern Shore H.
1937—1st Kentucky Derby, Preakness S., Belmont S., Chesapeake S., Pimlico Special, Washington H.
1938—1st Whitney S., Jockey Club Gold Cup, Saratoga Cup, Saratoga H., Wilson S., Queens County H., Rhode Island H., Widener H.

Voted Horse of the Year and champion three-year-old, War Admiral lost a 1938 match race to Seabiscuit in the Pimlico Special.

At stud, War Admiral sired 40 stakes winners and two champions from 320 starters, 12.5% of starters, in his 20-year stud career. He died in 1959.

Whirlaway

Prone to wild trips around the racetrack, Whirlaway could be a danger to himself and those around him, but he was worth the risk to train and run. In his three- and four-year-old seasons, he made 42 starts, won 25 times, finished second 13 times, and was third in his other four starts. Handled patiently by Racing Hall of Fame trainer Ben Jones, Whirlaway became the first of eight Kentucky Derby winners and two Triple Crown winners for Calumet Farm.

For the Derby on May 3, 1941, Jones fashioned new blinkers for Whirlaway, cutting away the left cup but leaving the right cup intact. He also made a rider change, with Eddie Arcaro replacing Wendall Eads. On Derby day, Whirlaway displayed his customary tendency to run near the back of the pack early. With a quarter-mile left, Whirlaway had moved up to fourth place and was flying. He exploded through a final quarter-mile, running it in :24, and won by eight lengths.

Despite walking out of the gate and trailing by more than nine lengths after a half-mile of the Preakness on May 10, Whirlaway again came on late and won by 5½ lengths. Nearly one month later in the Belmont Stakes, Whirlaway stunned his three rivals by taking off after a half-mile and opening up a seven-length lead after six furlongs. Despite entering the stretch a bit wide, he won

Ch. c., 1938, by *Blenheim II—Dustwhirl, by Sweep

Owner-Breeder: Calumet Farm (Ky.)
Trainer: Ben A. Jones
Jockey: Eddie Arcaro

Year	Starts	1st	2nd	3rd	Earnings
1940	16	7 (4)	2 (2)	4 (3)	$77,275
1941	20	13 (8)	5 (5)	2	272,386
1942	22	12 (10)	8 (6)	2 (2)	211,250
1943	2	0	0	1	250
	60	32 (22)	15 (13)	9 (5)	$561,161

1940—1st Saratoga Special, Hopeful S., Breeders' Futurity, Walden S.
1941—1st Kentucky Derby, Preakness S., Belmont S., Travers S., Lawrence Realization S., Saranac H., Dwyer S., American Derby
1942—1st Brooklyn H., Jockey Club Gold Cup, Massachusetts H., Narragansett Special, Dixie H., Washington H., Louisiana H., Trenton H., Governor Bowie H., Clark H.

by 2½ lengths to become the fifth Triple Crown winner.

The colt maintained his brilliance through 1942, when he was named Horse of the Year a second time.

Sold to French interests, Whirlaway died in southern Normandy on April 6, 1953.

Count Fleet

In 1927, Yellow Cab founder John D. Hertz watched a two-year-old race in which one of the runners reached out and bit another horse dueling with him for the lead. It was a remarkable display of aggression and a single-minded will to win. Hertz was sufficiently impressed to buy the colt, Reigh Count, who won the 1928 Kentucky Derby. Hertz never had much faith in Reigh Count as a stallion and bred him to only a few mares each year, including Quickly, who on March 24, 1940, gave birth to a gangly brown package named Count Fleet. The youngster was so clumsy and awkward that Hertz considered selling him as a yearling and again early in his two-year-old campaign. At two, Count Fleet won ten of 15 starts, was voted champion two-year-old colt, and on the Experimental Free Handicap was accorded highweight of 132 pounds, still the highest weight ever assigned.

As a three-year-old, Count Fleet had no equal. He usually went to the lead early, discouraged his competition by the stretch, and won as he pleased.

In the Kentucky Derby on May 1, Count Fleet went off as the 2-to-5 favorite in the field of ten. He broke sharply under John Longden, went

Br. c., 1940, by Reigh Count—Quickly, by Haste				
Owner-Breeder: Mrs. John D. Hertz (Ky.)				
Trainer: Don Cameron				
Jockey: John Longden				
Race Record				
Year	Starts	1st	2nd	3rd	Earnings
1942	15	10 (4)	4 (2)	1 (1)	$ 76,245
1943	6	6 (5)	0	0	174,055
	21	16 (9)	4 (2)	1 (1)	$250,300

1942—1st Champagne S., Pimlico Futurity, Walden S., Wakefield S.
1943—1st Kentucky Derby, Preakness S., Belmont S., Wood Memorial S., Withers S.

immediately to the lead, opened two lengths after six furlongs, and won by an easy three lengths over Blue Swords. One week later, Count Fleet won the Preakness by eight lengths. In the Belmont Stakes on June 5, Count Fleet, at odds of 1-to-20, won by 25 lengths in 2:28¼.

A seemingly minor injury to Count Fleet's left front ankle did not respond to treatment and ended his career. At stud, he sired champions Counterpoint and Kiss Me Kate as well as Count Turf, upset winner of the 1951 Kentucky Derby. Count Fleet died on December 3, 1973.

Assault

As a foal, Assault stepped on a surveyor's stake at King Ranch, which left him with a malformed right front hoof. As a result, he was called the club-footed comet.

Trainer Max Hirsch initially was unsure that Assault could withstand training because of the injury, but the Bold Venture colt won two of nine starts at two in 1945. He went off at 8.20-to-1 in the Kentucky Derby on May 4, 1946. Assault, with jockey Warren Mehrtens up, blew past Spy Song and Knockdown early in the stretch and won by eight lengths.

One week later in the Preakness Stakes, Assault's Triple Crown dreams nearly ended. Mehrtens decided to go for the knockout punch and sent Assault after the leaders going into the far turn. Assault tired and staggered home, winning by a fast-diminishing neck over Lord Boswell.

When the Belmont Stakes came around on June 1, many racing fans believed the 1½ miles would expose Assault. Lord Boswell was sent off as the 1.35-to-1 favorite, with Assault the second choice at 7-to-5. Mehrtens allowed Assault to reach contention gradually. Trailing Natchez by two lengths in midstretch, Assault exploded past him in the final 200 yards and won by three lengths.

Horse of the Year in 1946, Assault won five of

Ch. c., 1943, by Bold Venture—Igual, by Equipoise					
Owner-Breeder: King Ranch (Tx.)					
Trainer: Max Hirsch					
Jockey: Warren Mehrtens					
Race Record					
Year	Starts	1st	2nd	3rd	Earnings
1945	9	2 (1)	2	1 (1)	$ 17,250
1946	15	8 (8)	2 (2)	3 (3)	424,195
1947	7	5 (5)	1	1 (1)	181,925
1948	2	1	0	0	3,250
1949	6	1 (1)	1	1 (1)	45,900
1950	3	1	0	1	2,950
	42	18 (15)	6 (2)	7 (6)	$675,470

1945—1st Flash S.
1946—1st Kentucky Derby, Preakness S., Belmont S., Wood Memorial S., Dwyer S., Westchester H., Pimlico Special, Experimental Free H. No. 1
1947—1st Suburban H., Brooklyn H., Butler H., Grey Lag H., Dixie H.
1949—1st Brooklyn H.

seven starts in '47 and spent much of the year battling fellow handicappers Stymie and Armed for the all-time earnings crown.

Assault was retired to stud in early 1948 but proved to be sterile. Returned to the racetrack, he ran until he was seven. Pensioned at King Ranch, he was euthanized in 1971 after fracturing a leg.

Citation

Citation resulted from a mating of Calumet Farm's premier sire, Bull Lea, with *Hydroplane II, whom Warren Wright purchased from Lord Derby in the spring of 1941. Citation was foaled on April 11, 1945, and joined trainer H. A. "Jimmy" Jones's Maryland division in the spring of '47 to begin his racing career.

At two, his only loss was in the Washington Park Futurity to stablemate Bewitch.

Citation began his three-year-old season with two victories over older horses at Hialeah Park before winning the Everglades and Flamingo Stakes. His jockey, Al Snider, died in a boating accident after the Flamingo, and Jones induced Eddie Arcaro to take the mount.

In the Kentucky Derby against only five opponents on May 1, Citation spotted stablemate Coaltown six lengths in the opening half-mile and ran him down to win by 3½ lengths.

In the Preakness Stakes two weeks later, Citation set the pace and won by 5½ lengths as the 1-to-10 favorite. With four weeks between the Preakness and Belmont Stakes, Jones sent out Citation for an 11-length victory in the Jersey Stakes. On June 12 in the Belmont, Citation, at 1-to-5 odds, scored an eight-length triumph over Better Self.

Citation won 19 times in 1948, including a walkover in the Pimlico Special. At the end of his three-year-old season, Citation had 27 victories and two seconds in 29 starts, with earnings of $865,150.

In 1951, Citation won the Hollywood Gold Cup, becoming racing's first $1-million earner. Immediately retired to Calumet, he was an undistinguished sire. He died on August 8, 1970.

B. c., 1945, by Bull Lea—*Hydroplane II, by Hyperion

Owner-Breeder: Calumet Farm (Ky.)
Trainers: Ben A. Jones and H. A. "Jimmy" Jones
Jockey: Eddie Arcaro

Year	Starts	1st	2nd	3rd	Earnings
1947	9	8 (3)	1 (1)	0	$ 155,680
1948	20	19 (16)	1 (1)	0	709,470
1949	—	—	—	—	—
1950	9	2 (1)	7 (5)	0	73,480
1951	7	3 (2)	1 (1)	2	147,130
	45	32 (22)	10 (8)	2	$1,085,760

1947—1st Futurity S., Pimlico Futurity, Elementary S.
1948—1st Kentucky Derby, Preakness S., Belmont S., Jockey Club Gold Cup, Pimlico Special, Belmont Gold Cup, American Derby, Flamingo S., Jersey S., Stars and Stripes H., Tanforan H., Sysonby Mile, Chesapeake S., Seminole H., Derby Trial, Everglades H.
1950—1st Golden Gate Mile H.
1951—1st American H., Hollywood Gold Cup

Secretariat

Like Man o' War, Secretariat was known as Big Red, and both were big in accomplishments. Secretariat, by leading sire Bold Ruler out of the *Princequillo mare Somethingroyal, made his career debut on July 4, 1972, in a 5½-furlong maiden race at Aqueduct and finished fourth with a late surge. Secretariat subsequently won five stakes impressively and was voted Horse of the Year.

In February 1973, as Secretariat was being prepared for the Triple Crown campaign, he was syndicated by Claiborne Farm for a record $6.08-million. Secretariat easily won his first two starts of the year, the Bay Shore (G3) and the Gotham (G2) Stakes, but the colt ran third in the Wood Memorial Stakes (G1) on April 20, most likely due to a lip abscess. His Kentucky Derby (G1) was one that will forever be remembered. After breaking near the back of the pack, Secretariat began picking up horses on the first turn, collared Sham at the top of the lane, and drew away to a 2½-length victory in a Derby record 1:59⅖ for 1¼ miles.

In the Preakness Stakes (G1), jockey Ron Turcotte sensed a slow early pace and allowed Secretariat to surge to the lead as the six-horse field entered the backstretch. Secretariat dominated the rest of the race and again won by 2½ lengths over Sham. A timer malfunction effectively nullified what should have been a track record.

Only Sham and three others showed up to oppose Secretariat in the Belmont Stakes (G1) on June 9. Secretariat and Sham dueled through the first six furlongs in 1:09⅖ before Sham surrendered. Secretariat steadily pulled away to win by 31 lengths while running 1½ miles in 2:24, an American record.

Retired to Claiborne, Secretariat was a good but not great sire. He died of complications from laminitis on October 4, 1989.

Ch. c., 1970, by Bold Ruler—Somethingroyal, by *Princequillo

Owner: Meadow Stable
Breeder: Meadow Stud (Va.)
Trainer: Lucien Laurin
Jockey: Ron Turcotte

Year	Starts	1st	2nd	3rd	Earnings
1972	9	7 (5)	1 (1)	0	$ 456,404
1973	12	9 (9)	2 (2)	1 (1)	860,404
	21	16 (14)	3 (3)	1 (1)	$1,316,808

1972—1st Hopeful S., Futurity S., Garden State S., Laurel Futurity, Sanford S.,
1973—1st Kentucky Derby (G1), Preakness S. (G1), Belmont S. (G1), Man o' War S. (G1), Canadian International Championship S. (G2), Marlboro Cup H., Arlington Invitational S., Gotham S. (G2), Bay Shore S. (G3)

Seattle Slew

A son of Bold Reasoning out of My Charmer, by Poker, Seattle Slew was brought along patiently by his young trainer, Billy Turner Jr. He was voted champion two-year-old male after a stunning Champagne Stakes (G1) win in just his third start.

At three, Seattle Slew won Hialeah Park's Flamingo Stakes (G1) by four lengths on March 26 and took Aqueduct's Wood Memorial Stakes (G1) by 3¼ lengths on April 23.

For the Derby on May 7, Seattle Slew went off as the 1-to-2 favorite. Disaster nearly struck at the start when he swerved out and was sharply taken up by jockey Jean Cruguet. At the top of the stretch, Seattle Slew put away For The Moment and then cruised home by 1¾ lengths over Run Dusty Run.

Two weeks later in the Preakness Stakes (G1), 2-to-5 Seattle Slew took command leaving the backstretch and won by 1½ lengths over Iron Constitution. Seattle Slew then dominated the Belmont Stakes (G1), winning by four lengths over Run Dusty Run. Seattle Slew was the first to complete the series without a defeat. Turner suggested a rest, but owners Karen and Mickey Taylor and Sally and Jim Hill insisted on running in Hollywood Park's Swaps Stakes (G1). Slew finished fourth and did not race again in 1977.

Seattle Slew made seven starts as a four-year-old for trainer Doug Peterson, and his five victories included an epic win over Affirmed in the Marlboro Cup Invitational Handicap (G1), the first meeting of Triple Crown winners. Standing first at Spendthrift Farm and then at Three Chimneys Farm, he sired A.P. Indy, 1992 Horse of the Year, and more than 100 stakes winners. He died on May 7, 2002, at Hill 'n' Dale Farm, where he was moved shortly before his death.

Dk. b. or br. c., 1974, by Bold Reasoning—My Charmer, by Poker

Owners: Mickey and Karen L. Taylor, Dr. Jim and Sally Hill
Breeder: Ben S. Castleman (Ky.)
Trainers: William H. Turner Jr. (1976-'77); Doug Peterson (1978)
Jockey: Jean Cruguet

Race Record

Year	Starts	1st	2nd	3rd	Earnings
1976	3	3 (1)	0	0	$ 94,350
1977	7	6 (5)	0	0	641,370
1978	7	5 (3)	2 (2)	0	473,006
	17	14 (9)	2 (2)	0	$1,208,726

1976—1st Champagne S. (G1)
1977—1st Kentucky Derby (G1), Preakness S. (G1), Belmont S. (G1), Wood Memorial S. (G1), Flamingo S. (G1)
1978—1st Marlboro Cup Invitational H. (G1), Woodward S. (G1), Stuyvesant S. (G3)

Affirmed

The 1978 Triple Crown, the first won in back-to-back years, belonged to Affirmed, but his name will forever be linked with Alydar, the first horse to finish second in all three races to a Triple Crown winner.

Both colts dominated their arenas at three, and the Kentucky Derby (G1), in which Alydar went off as the 6-to-5 favorite with Affirmed at 9-to-5, was a clash of titans. Third early under jockey Steve Cauthen, Affirmed surged past Believe It early in the stretch and opened a two-length lead in midstretch. Alydar made a late charge but finished second, beaten 1½ lengths.

Two weeks later on May 20, the two would stage an epic duel in the Preakness Stakes (G1). Affirmed, 1-to-2, once again stalked the early pace and inherited the lead after a quarter-mile. Jorge Velasquez asked Alydar for speed on the backstretch, and the Raise a Native colt reached Affirmed's side leaving the turn. They fought to the wire, with Affirmed winning by a neck.

In the Belmont Stakes (G1) three weeks later, 3-to-5 Affirmed was the only speed in a field of five, and 11-to-10 Alydar shadowed him practically from the start. After a half-mile, Affirmed led by one length, and by the top of Belmont Park's stretch they were a head apart. Alydar appeared to take a narrow lead inside the furlong pole, but Affirmed fought back and won by a head. He was voted Horse of the Year and repeated in 1979 with six consecutive Grade 1 victories. The sport's first $2-million earner, he sired more than 80 stakes winners. He died on January 12, 2001, at Jonabell Farm.

Ch. c., 1975, by Exclusive Native—Won't Tell You, by Crafty Admiral

Owner-Breeder: Harbor View Farm (Fl.)
Trainer: Lazaro Barrera
Jockey: Steve Cauthen

Race Record

Year	Starts	1st	2nd	3rd	Earnings
1977	9	7 (6)	2 (2)	0	$ 343,477
1978	11	8 (7)	2 (2)	0	901,541
1979	9	7 (6)	1 (1)	1 (1)	1,148,800
	29	22 (19)	5 (5)	1 (1)	$2,393,818

1977—1st Hopeful S. (G1), Futurity S. (G1), Laurel Futurity (G1), Sanford S. (G2), Hollywood Juvenile Championship S. (G2), Youthful S.
1978—1st Kentucky Derby (G1), Preakness S. (G1), Belmont S. (G1), Santa Anita Derby (G1), Hollywood Derby (G1), San Felipe H. (G2), Jim Dandy S. (G3)
1979—1st Jockey Club Gold Cup (G1), Hollywood Gold Cup (G1), Santa Anita H. (G1), Woodward S. (G1), Californian S. (G1), Charles H. Strub S. (G1)

Near Triple Crown Winners

While the Triple Crown has been swept on 11 occasions, in 50 other years three-year-olds have won two legs of the Triple Crown. Among the 50 near successes were 21 horses who won the Kentucky Derby and Preakness Stakes but not the Belmont Stakes.

Of those 21, injury felled several in the Belmont (including Tim Tam and Charismatic), several have come agonizingly close (Silver Charm, Real Quiet, Smarty Jones), and two did not run in the Belmont (Burgoo King, Bold Venture) because of injuries before the race.

Following are the 50 horses who won two of the three races. Winner of the race the Triple Crown hopeful lost is in parentheses.

Year	Horse	Kentucky Derby	Preakness	Belmont
2008	Big Brown	Won	Won	DNF (Da' Tara)
2005	Afleet Alex	3rd (Giacomo)	Won	Won
2004	Smarty Jones	Won	Won	2nd (Birdstone)
2003	Funny Cide	Won	Won	3rd (Empire Maker)
2002	War Emblem	Won	Won	8th (Sarava)
2001	Point Given	5th (Monarchos)	Won	Won
1999	Charismatic	Won	Won	3rd (Lemon Drop Kid)
1998	Real Quiet	Won	Won	2nd (Victory Gallop)
1997	Silver Charm	Won	Won	2nd (Touch Gold)
1995	Thunder Gulch	Won	3rd (Timber Country)	Won
1994	Tabasco Cat	6th (Go for Gin)	Won	Won
1991	Hansel	10th (Strike the Gold)	Won	Won
1989	Sunday Silence	Won	Won	2nd (Easy Goer)
1988	Risen Star	3rd (Winning Colors)	Won	Won
1987	Alysheba	Won	Won	4th (Bet Twice)
1984	Swale	Won	7th (Gate Dancer)	Won
1981	Pleasant Colony	Won	Won	3rd (Summing)
1979	Spectacular Bid	Won	Won	3rd (Coastal)
1976	Bold Forbes	Won	3rd (Elocutionist)	Won
1974	Little Current	5th (Cannonade)	Won	Won
1972	Riva Ridge	Won	4th (Bee Bee Bee)	Won
1971	Canonero II	Won	Won	4th (Pass Catcher)
1969	Majestic Prince	Won	Won	2nd (Arts and Letters)
1968	Forward Pass	Won†	Won	2nd (Stage Door Johnny)
1967	Damascus	3rd (Proud Clarion)	Won	Won
1966	Kauai King	Won	Won	4th (Amberoid)
1964	Northern Dancer	Won	Won	3rd (Quadrangle)
1963	Chateaugay	Won	2nd (Candy Spots)	Won
1961	Carry Back	Won	Won	7th (Sherluck)
1958	Tim Tam	Won	Won	2nd (*Cavan)
1956	Needles	Won	2nd (Fabius)	Won
1955	Nashua	2nd (Swaps)	Won	Won
1953	Native Dancer	2nd (Dark Star)	Won	Won
1950	Middleground	Won	2nd (Hill Prince)	Won
1949	Capot	2nd (Ponder)	Won	Won
1944	Pensive	Won	Won	2nd (Bounding Home)
1942	Shut Out	Won	5th (Alsab)	Won
1940	Bimelech	2nd (Gallahadion)	Won	Won
1939	Johnstown	Won	5th (Challedon)	Won
1936	Bold Venture	Won	Won	Did not start
1932	Burgoo King	Won	Won	Did not start
1931	Twenty Grand	Won	2nd (Mate)	Won
1923	Zev	Won	12th (Vigil)	Won
1922	Pillory	Did not start	Won	Won
1920	Man o' War	Did not start	Won	Won
1895	Belmar	Did not start	Won	Won
1881	Saunterer	Did not start	Won	Won
1880	Grenada	Did not start	Won	Won
1878	Duke of Magenta	Did not start	Won	Won
1877	Cloverbrook	Did not start	Won	Won

†Won on disqualification of Dancer's Image. Winner of race is in parentheses.

Leading Owners of Triple Crown Race Winners

17 Calumet Farm: Kentucky Derby: Whirlaway (1941), Pensive ('44), Citation ('48), Ponder ('49), Hill Gail ('52), Iron Liege ('57), Tim Tam ('58), Forward Pass ('68); Preakness: Whirlaway ('41), Pensive ('44), Faultless ('47), Citation ('48), Fabius ('56), Tim Tam ('58), Forward Pass ('68); Belmont: Whirlaway ('41), Citation ('48)

12 Belair Stud: Kentucky Derby: Gallant Fox (1930), Omaha ('35), Johnstown ('39); Preakness: Gallant Fox ('30), Omaha ('35), Nashua ('55); Belmont: Gallant Fox ('30), Faireno ('32), Omaha ('35), Granville ('36), Johnstown ('39), Nashua ('55)

10 Harry P. Whitney: Kentucky Derby: Regret (1915), Whiskery ('27); Preakness: Royal Tourist ('08), Broomspun ('21), Bostonian ('27), Victorian ('28); Belmont: Tanya ('05), Burgomaster ('06), Prince Eugene ('13), *Johren ('18)

9 E. R. Bradley (Idle Hour Stock Farm): Kentucky Derby: Behave Yourself (1921), Bubbling Over ('26), Burgoo King ('32), Brokers Tip ('33); Preakness: Kalitan ('17), Burgoo King ('32), Bimelech ('40); Belmont: Blue Larkspur ('29), Bimelech ('40)

8 Dwyer Brothers:
6—Dwyer Brothers (M. F. and Phil J.): Kentucky Derby: Hindoo (1881); Belmont: George Kinney ('83), Panique ('84), Inspector B. ('86), Hanover ('87), Sir Dixon ('88)
1—M. F. Dwyer: Kentucky Derby: Ben Brush (1896)
1—Phil J. Dwyer: Preakness: Half Time (1899)
George L. Lorillard: Preakness: Duke of Magenta (1878), Harold ('79), Grenada ('80), Saunterer ('81), Vanguard ('82); Belmont: Duke of Magenta ('78), Grenada ('80), Saunterer ('81)

7 August Belmont II: Preakness: Margrave (1896), Don Enrique (1907), Watervale ('11); Belmont: Hastings (1896), Masterman (1902), Friar Rock ('16), *Hourless ('17)
Glen Riddle Farms: Kentucky Derby: War Admiral (1937); Preakness: Man o'War ('20), War Admiral ('37); Belmont: Man o' War ('20), American Flag ('25), Crusader (1926), War Admiral ('37)
Greentree Stable: Kentucky Derby: Twenty Grand (1931), Shut Out ('42); Preakness: Capot ('49); Belmont: Twenty Grand ('31), Shut Out ('42), Capot ('49), Stage Door Johnny ('68)
James R. Keene:
6—James R. Keene: Belmont: Spendthrift (1879), Commando (1901), Delhi ('04), Peter Pan ('07), Colin ('08), Sweep ('10)
1—James R. Keene and Foxhall P. Keene: Preakness: Assignee (1894)

6 Robert and Beverly Lewis:
5—Robert and Beverly Lewis: Kentucky Derby: Silver Charm (1997), Charismatic ('99); Preakness: Silver Charm ('97), Charismatic ('99); Belmont: Commendable (2000)
1—Gainesway Farm, Robert and Beverly Lewis, and Overbrook Farm: Preakness: Timber Country (1995)
Meadow Stable (C. T. and Penny Chenery): Kentucky Derby: Riva Ridge (1972), Secretariat ('73); Preakness: Hill Prince ('50), Secretariat ('73); Belmont: Riva Ridge ('72), Secretariat ('73)

5 Overbrook Farm (W. T. Young):
2—Overbrook Farm: Kentucky Derby: Grindstone (1996); Belmont: Editor's Note ('96)
2—Overbrook Farm and David Reynolds: Preakness: Tabasco Cat (1994); Belmont: Tabasco Cat ('94)
1—Gainesway Farm, Robert and Beverly Lewis, and Overbrook Farm: Preakness: Timber Country (1995)
King Ranch: Kentucky Derby: Assault (1946), Middleground ('50); Preakness: Assault ('46); Belmont: Assault ('46), Middleground ('50), High Gun ('54)
Darby Dan Farm: Kentucky Derby: Chateaugay (1963), Proud Clarion ('67); Preakness: Little Current ('74); Belmont: Chateaugay ('63), Little Current ('74)

4 Brookmeade Stable: Kentucky Derby: Cavalcade (1934); Preakness: High Quest ('34), Bold ('51); Belmont: Sword Dancer ('59)
Mrs. John D. Hertz: Kentucky Derby: Reigh Count (1928), Count Fleet ('43); Preakness: Count Fleet ('43); Belmont: Count Fleet ('43)
J.K.L. Ross: Kentucky Derby: Sir Barton (1919); Preakness: Damrosch ('16), Sir Barton ('19); Belmont: Sir Barton ('19)
The Thoroughbred Corp: Kentucky Derby: War Emblem (2002); Preakness: Point Given ('01), War Emblem ('02); Belmont: Point Given ('01)

3 William Condren:
1—B. Giles Brophy, William Condren, and Joseph Cornacchia: Kentucky Derby: Strike the Gold (1991)
1—William Condren and Joseph Cornacchia: Kentucky Derby: Go for Gin (1994)
1—William Condren, Georgia Hofmann, and Joseph Cornacchia: Preakness: Louis Quatorze (1996)
Joseph Cornacchia:
1—B. Giles Brophy, William Condren, and Joseph Cornacchia: Kentucky Derby: Strike the Gold (1991)
1—William Condren and Joseph Cornacchia: Kentucky Derby: Go for Gin (1994)
1—William Condren, Georgia Hofmann, and Joseph Cornacchia: Preakness: Louis Quatorze (1996)
Arthur B. Hancock III:
1—Arthur B. Hancock III and Leone J. Peters: Kentucky Derby: Gato Del Sol (1982)
2—Arthur B. Hancock III, Ernest Gaillard, and Charlie Whittingham: Kentucky Derby: Sunday Silence (1989); Preakness: Sunday Silence ('89)
Harbor View Farm: Kentucky Derby: Affirmed (1978); Preakness: Affirmed ('78); Belmont: Affirmed ('78)
Loblolly Stable: Preakness: Pine Bluff (1992), Prairie Bayou ('93); Belmont: Temperence Hill ('80)
David McDaniel: Belmont: Harry Bassett (1871), Joe Daniels ('72), Springbok ('73)
Preakness Stable (James Galway): Preakness: Montague (1890), Belmar ('95); Belmont: Belmar ('95)
Rokeby Stable: Kentucky Derby: Sea Hero (1993); Belmont: Quadrangle ('64), Arts and Letters ('69)

Triple Crown — Leaders

3 **Walter J. Salmon:** Preakness: Vigil (1923), Display ('26), Dr. Freeland ('29)
H. F. Sinclair: Belmont: Grey Lag (1921), Zev ('23), Mad Play ('24)
Karen and Mickey Taylor and Sally and James Hill: Kentucky Derby: Seattle Slew (1977); Preakness: Seattle Slew ('77); Belmont: Seattle Slew ('77)
Joseph E. Widener: Belmont: Chance Shot (1927), Hurryoff ('33), Peace Chance ('34)
Richard T. Wilson Jr.: Preakness: The Parader (1901), Pillory ('22); Belmont: Pillory ('22)

Leading Breeders of Triple Crown Race Winners

18 **Calumet Farm:** Kentucky Derby: Whirlaway (1941), Pensive ('44), Citation ('48), Ponder ('49), Hill Gail ('52), Iron Liege ('57), Tim Tam ('58), Forward Pass ('68), Strike the Gold ('91); Preakness: Whirlaway ('41), Pensive ('44), Faultless ('47), Citation ('48), Fabius ('56), Tim Tam ('58), Forward Pass ('68); Belmont: Whirlaway ('41), Citation ('48)

15 **A. J. Alexander:** Kentucky Derby: Baden-Baden (1877), Fonso ('80), Joe Cotton ('85), Chant ('94); Preakness: Tom Ochiltree ('75), Shirley ('76), Grenada ('80), Duke of Magenta ('90); Belmont: Harry Bassett ('71), Joe Daniels ('72), Springbok ('73), Duke of Magenta ('78), Spendthrift ('79), Grenada ('80), Burlington ('90)

12 **Harry P. Whitney:** Kentucky Derby: Regret (1915), Whiskery ('27); Preakness: Royal Tourist ('08), Buskin ('13), Holiday ('14), Broomspun ('21), Bostonian ('27), Victorian ('28); Belmont: Tanya ('05), Burgomaster ('06), Prince Eugene ('13), *Johren ('18)

11 **John E. Madden**
8—John E. Madden: Kentucky Derby: Old Rosebud (1914), Paul Jones ('20), Zev ('23), Flying Ebony ('25); Belmont: Joe Madden ('09), The Finn ('15), Grey Lag ('21), Zev ('23)
3—John E. Madden and Vivian A. Gooch: Kentucky Derby: Sir Barton (1919); Preakness: Sir Barton ('19); Belmont: Sir Barton ('19)

10 **Belair Stud:** Kentucky Derby: Gallant Fox (1930), Omaha ('35); Preakness: Gallant Fox ('30), Omaha ('35), Nashua ('55); Belmont: Gallant Fox ('30), Faireno ('32), Omaha ('35), Granville ('36), Nashua ('55)

August Belmont II: Preakness: Margrave (1896), Don Enrique (1907), Watervale ('11), Damrosch ('16), Man o' War ('20); Belmont: Masterman ('02), Friar Rock ('16), *Hourless ('17), Man o' War ('20), Chance Shot ('27)

8 **E. R. Bradley (Idle Hour Stock Farm):** Kentucky Derby: Behave Yourself (1921), Bubbling Over ('26), Burgoo King ('32), Brokers Tip ('33); Preakness: Burgoo King ('32), Bimelech ('40); Belmont: Blue Larkspur ('29), Bimelech ('40)

7 **Greentree Stud:** Kentucky Derby: Twenty Grand (1931), Shut Out ('42); Preakness: Capot ('49); Belmont: Twenty Grand ('31), Shut Out ('42), Capot ('49), Stage Door Johnny ('68)

6 **William S. Farish**
3—William S. Farish and William S. Kilroy: Preakness: Summer Squall (1990); Belmont: A.P. Indy ('90), Lemon Drop Kid ('99)
2—Parrish Hill Farm and William S. Farish: Kentucky Derby: Charismatic (1999); Preakness: Charismatic ('99)
1—William S. Farish and E. J. Hudson: Belmont: Bet Twice (1987)

6 **James Ben Ali Haggin:** Kentucky Derby: Stone Street (1908); Preakness: Old England ('02), Cairngorm ('05), Rhine Maiden ('15); Belmont: Commanche (1893), Africander (1903)
Meadow Stud (C. T. Chenery): Kentucky Derby: Riva Ridge (1972), Secretariat ('73); Preakness: Hill Prince ('50), Secretariat ('73); Belmont: Riva Ridge ('72), Secretariat ('73)

5 **Ezekiel F. Clay**
4—Clay and Woodford: Kentucky Derby: Ben Brush (1896); Preakness: Buddhist ('89); Belmont: Hanover ('87), Sir Dixon ('88)
1—Ezekiel F. Clay: Kentucky Derby: Agile (1905)
John W. Galbreath: Kentucky Derby: Chateaugay (1963), Proud Clarion ('67); Preakness: Little Current ('74); Belmont: Chateaugay ('63), Little Current ('74)
James R. Keene: Belmont: Commando (1901), Delhi ('04), Peter Pan ('07), Colin ('08), Sweep ('10)
King Ranch: Kentucky Derby: Assault (1946), Middleground ('50); Preakness: Assault ('46); Belmont: Assault ('46), Middleground ('50)
Samuel D. Riddle: Kentucky Derby: War Admiral (1937); Preakness: War Admiral ('37); Belmont: American Flag ('25), Crusader ('26), War Admiral ('37)

4 **Arthur B. Hancock III**
3—Arthur B. Hancock III and Leone J. Peters: Kentucky Derby: Gato Del Sol (1982); Preakness: Risen Star ('88); Belmont: Risen Star ('88)
1—Arthur B. Hancock III and Stonerside Ltd.: Kentucky Derby: Fusaichi Pegasus (2000)
Arthur B. Hancock Sr.
3—Arthur B. Hancock: Kentucky Derby: Johnstown (1939); Preakness: Vigil ('23); Belmont: Johnstown ('39)
1—Arthur B. Hancock and Mrs. R. A. Van Clief: Kentucky Derby: Jet Pilot (1947)
Aristides Welch: Preakness: Harold (1879), Saunterer ('81); Belmont: Saunterer ('81), Panique ('84)

3 **August Belmont I:** Preakness: Jacobus (1883); Belmont: Fenian ('69), Forester ('82)
A. J. Cassatt: Preakness: Montague (1890); Belmont: Foxford ('91), Patron ('92)
Ben S. Castleman: Kentucky Derby: Seattle Slew (1977), Preakness: Seattle Slew ('77), Belmont: Seattle Slew ('77)
Claiborne Farm: Kentucky Derby: Swale (1984); Belmont: Coastal ('79), Swale ('84)
Harbor View Farm: Kentucky Derby: Affirmed (1978); Preakness: Affirmed ('78); Belmont: Affirmed ('78)
Mrs. John D. Hertz: Kentucky Derby: Count Fleet (1943); Preakness: Count Fleet ('43); Belmont: Count Fleet ('43)

Triple Crown — Leaders

3   **George J. Long:** Kentucky Derby: Azra (1892), Manuel (1899), Sir Huon (1906)
    H. Price McGrath (McGrathiana Stud): Kentucky Derby: Aristides (1875); Preakness: Paul Kauvar ('97); Belmont: Calvin ('75)
    Paul Mellon: Kentucky Derby: Sea Hero (1993); Belmont: Quadrangle ('64), Arts and Letters ('69)

3   **Overbrook Farm**
    2—Overbrook Farm and David Reynolds: Preakness: Tabasco Cat (1994); Belmont: Tabasco Cat ('94)
    1—Overbrook Farm: Kentucky Derby: Grindstone (1996)
    Daniel Swigert: Kentucky Derby: Hindoo (1881), Apollo ('82), Ben Ali ('86)

Leading Trainers of Triple Crown Race Winners

13 **James "Sunny Jim" Fitzsimmons:** Kentucky Derby: Gallant Fox (1930), Omaha ('35), Johnstown ('39); Preakness: Gallant Fox ('30), Omaha ('35), Nashua ('55), Bold Ruler ('57); Belmont: Gallant Fox ('30), Faireno ('32), Omaha ('35), Granville ('36), Johnstown ('39), Nashua ('55)
    D. Wayne Lukas: Kentucky Derby: Winning Colors (1988), Thunder Gulch ('95), Grindstone ('96), Charismatic ('99); Preakness: Codex ('80), Tank's Prospect ('85), Tabasco Cat ('94), Timber Country ('95), Charismatic ('99); Belmont: Tabasco Cat ('94), Thunder Gulch ('95), Editor's Note ('96), Commendable (2000)

11 **James Rowe Sr.:** Kentucky Derby: Hindoo (1881), Regret (1915); Preakness: Broomspun (1921); Belmont: George Kinney (1883), Panique (1884), Commando (1901), Delhi ('04), Peter Pan ('07), Colin ('08), Sweep ('10), Prince Eugene ('13)
    R. Wyndham Walden: Preakness: Tom Ochiltree (1875), Duke of Magenta ('78), Harold ('79), Grenada ('80), Saunterer ('81), Vanguard ('82), Refund ('88); Belmont: Duke of Magenta ('78), Grenada ('80), Saunterer ('81), *Bowling Brook ('98)

9   **Max Hirsch:** Kentucky Derby: Bold Venture (1936), Assault ('46), Middleground ('50); Preakness: Bold Venture ('36), Assault ('46); Belmont: Vito ('28), Assault ('46), Middleground ('50), High Gun ('54)
    B. A. "Ben" Jones: Kentucky Derby: Lawrin (1938), Whirlaway ('41), Pensive ('44), Citation ('48), Ponder ('49), Hill Gail ('52); Preakness: Whirlaway ('41), Pensive ('44); Belmont: Whirlaway ('41)

8   **Bob Baffert:** Kentucky Derby: Silver Charm (1997), Real Quiet ('98), War Emblem (2002); Preakness: Silver Charm ('97), Real Quiet ('98), Point Given (2001), War Emblem ('02); Belmont: Point Given ('01)
    Woodford C. "Woody" Stephens: Kentucky Derby: Cannonade (1974), Swale ('84); Preakness: Blue Man ('52); Belmont: Conquistador Cielo ('82), Caveat ('83), Swale ('84), Creme Fraiche ('85), Danzig Connection ('86)

7   **H. A. "Jimmy" Jones:** Kentucky Derby: Iron Liege (1957), Tim Tam ('58); Preakness: Faultless ('47), Citation ('48), Fabius ('56), Tim Tam ('58); Belmont: Citation ('48)
    Sam Hildreth: Belmont: Jean Bereaud (1899), Joe Madden (1909), Friar Rock ('16), *Hourless ('17), Grey Lag ('21), Zev ('23), Mad Play ('24)

6   **Thomas J. Healy:** Preakness: The Parader (1901), Pillory ('22), Vigil ('23), Display ('26), Dr. Freeland ('29); Belmont: Pillory ('22)
    Lucien Laurin: Kentucky Derby: Riva Ridge (1972), Secretariat ('73); Preakness: Secretariat ('73); Belmont: Amberoid ('66), Riva Ridge ('72), Secretariat ('73)

5   **John M. Gaver:** Kentucky Derby: Shut Out (1942); Preakness: Capot ('49); Belmont: Shut Out ('42), Capot ('49), Stage Door Johnny ('68)
    Lazaro Barrera: Kentucky Derby: Bold Forbes (1976), Affirmed ('78); Preakness: Affirmed ('78); Belmont: Bold Forbes ('76), Affirmed ('78)
    H. J. "Dick" Thompson: Kentucky Derby: Behave Yourself (1921), Bubbling Over ('26), Burgoo King ('32), Brokers Tip ('33); Preakness: Burgoo King ('32)
    Nicholas P. Zito: Kentucky Derby: Strike the Gold (1991), Go for Gin ('94); Preakness: Louis Quatorze ('96); Belmont: Birdstone (2004), Da' Tara (2008)

4   **Henry Forrest:** Kentucky Derby: Kauai King (1966), Forward Pass ('68); Preakness: Kauai King ('66), Forward Pass ('68)
    George Conway: Kentucky Derby: War Admiral (1937); Preakness: War Admiral ('37); Belmont: Crusader ('26), War Admiral ('37)
    Frank McCabe: Preakness: Half Time (1899); Belmont: Inspector B. ('86), Hanover ('87), Sir Dixon ('88)

3   **H. Guy Bedwell:** Kentucky Derby: Sir Barton (1919); Preakness: Sir Barton ('19); Belmont: Sir Barton ('19)
    J. Elliott Burch: Belmont: Sword Dancer (1959), Quadrangle ('64), Arts and Letters ('69)
    G. D. Cameron: Kentucky Derby: Count Fleet (1943); Preakness: Count Fleet ('43); Belmont: Count Fleet ('43)
    Peter Coyne: Kentucky Derby: Sir Huon (1906); Belmont: Chance Shot ('27), Peace Chance ('34)
    Edward Feakes: Preakness: Montague (1890), Belmar ('95); Belmont: Belmar ('95)
    Thomas P. Hayes: Kentucky Derby: Donerail (1913); Preakness: Paul Kauvar (1897), Head Play (1933)
    William Hurley: Preakness: Kalitan (1917), Bimelech ('40); Belmont: Bimelech ('40)
    Horatio Luro: Kentucky Derby: Decidedly (1962), Northern Dancer ('64); Preakness: Northern Dancer ('64)
    David McDaniel: Belmont: Harry Bassett (1871), Joe Daniels ('72), Springbok ('73)
    James Rowe Jr.: Kentucky Derby: Twenty Grand (1931); Preakness: Victorian ('28); Belmont: Twenty Grand ('31)
    William H. Turner Jr.: Kentucky Derby: Seattle Slew (1977); Preakness: Seattle Slew ('77); Belmont: ('77)
    James Whalen: Preakness: Don Enrique (1907), Watervale ('11), Buskin ('13)
    Frank Y. Whiteley Jr.: Preakness: Tom Rolfe (1965), Damascus ('67); Belmont: Damascus ('67)
    Charles Whittingham: Kentucky Derby: Ferdinand (1986), Sunday Silence ('89); Preakness: Sunday Silence ('89)

Leading Jockeys of Triple Crown Race Winners

17 Eddie Arcaro: Kentucky Derby: Lawrin (1938), Whirlaway ('41), Hoop, Jr. ('45), Citation ('48), Hill Gail ('52); Preakness: Whirlaway ('41), Citation ('48), Hill Prince ('50), Bold ('51), Nashua ('55), Bold Ruler ('57); Belmont: Whirlaway ('41), Shut Out ('42), Pavot ('45), Citation ('48), One Count ('52), Nashua ('55)

11 William Shoemaker: Kentucky Derby: Swaps (1955), *Tomy Lee ('59), Lucky Debonair ('65), Ferdinand ('86); Preakness: Candy Spots ('63), Damascus ('67); Belmont: *Gallant Man ('57), Sword Dancer ('59), Jaipur ('62), Damascus ('67), Avatar ('75)

9 Pat Day: Kentucky Derby: Lil E. Tee (1992); Preakness: Tank's Prospect ('85), Summer Squall ('90), Tabasco Cat ('94), Timber Country ('95), Louis Quatorze ('96); Belmont: Easy Goer ('89), Tabasco Cat ('94), Commendable (2000)

William J. Hartack: Kentucky Derby: Iron Liege (1957), Venetian Way ('60), Decidedly ('62), Northern Dancer ('64), Majestic Prince ('69); Preakness: Fabius ('56), Northern Dancer ('64), Majestic Prince ('69); Belmont: *Celtic Ash ('60)

Earl Sande: Kentucky Derby: Zev (1923), Flying Ebony ('25), Gallant Fox ('30); Preakness: Gallant Fox ('30); Belmont: Grey Lag ('21), Zev ('23), Mad Play ('24), Chance Shot ('27), Gallant Fox ('30)

8 James McLaughlin: Kentucky Derby: Hindoo (1881); Preakness: Tecumseh ('85); Belmont: Forester ('82), George Kinney ('83), Panique ('84), Inspector B. ('86), Hanover ('87), Sir Dixon ('88)

Gary Stevens: Kentucky Derby: Winning Colors (1988), Thunder Gulch ('95), Silver Charm ('97); Preakness: Silver Charm ('97), Point Given (2001); Belmont: Thunder Gulch (1995), Victory Gallop ('98), Point Given (2001)

6 Jerry Bailey: Kentucky Derby: Sea Hero (1993), Grindstone ('96); Preakness: Hansel ('91), Red Bullet (2000); Belmont: Hansel (1991), Empire Maker (2003)

Angel Cordero Jr.: Kentucky Derby: Cannonade (1974), Bold Forbes ('76), Spend a Buck ('85); Preakness: Codex ('80), Gate Dancer ('84); Belmont: Bold Forbes ('76)

Charles Kurtsinger: Kentucky Derby: Twenty Grand (1931), War Admiral ('37); Preakness: Head Play ('33), War Admiral ('37); Belmont: Twenty Grand ('31), War Admiral ('37)

Chris McCarron: Kentucky Derby: Alysheba (1987), Go for Gin ('94); Preakness: Alysheba ('87), Pine Bluff ('92), Belmont: Danzig Connection ('86), Touch Gold ('97)

Ron Turcotte: Kentucky Derby: Riva Ridge (1972), Secretariat ('73); Preakness: Tom Rolfe ('65), Secretariat ('73); Belmont: Riva Ridge ('72), Secretariat ('73)

5 Eddie Delahoussaye: Kentucky Derby: Gato Del Sol (1982), Sunny's Halo ('83); Preakness: Risen Star ('88); Belmont: Risen Star ('88), A.P. Indy ('92)

Kent Desormeaux: Kentucky Derby: Real Quiet (1998), Fusaichi Pegasus (2000), Big Brown ('08); Preakness: Real Quiet (1998), Big Brown (2008)

Lloyd Hughes: Preakness: Tom Ochiltree (1875), Harold ('79), Grenada ('80); Belmont: Duke of Magenta ('78), Grenada ('80)

John Loftus: Kentucky Derby: George Smith (1916), Sir Barton ('19); Preakness: *War Cloud ('18), Sir Barton ('19); Belmont: Sir Barton ('19)

Willie Simms: Kentucky Derby: Ben Brush (1898), Plaudit ('98); Preakness: Sly Fox ('98); Belmont: Comanche ('93), Henry Of Navarre ('94)

4 Braulio Baeza: Kentucky Derby: Chateaugay (1963); Belmont: Sherluck ('61), Chateaugay ('63), Arts and Letters ('69)

George Barbee: Preakness: Survivor (1873), Shirley ('76), Jacobus ('83); Belmont: Saxon ('74)

William "Billy" Donohue: Kentucky Derby: Leonatus (1883); Preakness: Culpepper ('74), Dunboyne ('87); Belmont: Algerine ('76)

Eric Guerin: Kentucky Derby: Jet Pilot (1947); Preakness: Native Dancer ('53); Belmont: Native Dancer ('53), High Gun ('54)

Albert Johnson: Kentucky Derby: Morvich (1922), Bubbling Over ('26); Belmont: American Flag ('25), Crusader ('26)

Clarence Kummer: Preakness: Man o' War (1920), Coventry ('25); Belmont: Man o' War ('20), Vito ('28)

Conn McCreary: Kentucky Derby: Pensive (1944), Count Turf ('51); Preakness: Pensive ('44), Blue Man ('52)

Laffit Pincay Jr.: Kentucky Derby: Swale (1984); Belmont: Conquistador Cielo ('82), Caveat ('83), Swale ('84)

James Stout: Kentucky Derby: Johnstown (1939); Belmont: Granville ('36), Pasteurized ('38), Johnstown ('39)

Fred Taral: Kentucky Derby: Manuel (1899); Preakness: Assignee ('94), Belmar ('95); Belmont: Belmar ('95)

Ismael "Milo" Valenzuela: Kentucky Derby: Tim Tam (1958), Forward Pass ('68); Preakness: Tim Tam ('58), Forward Pass ('68)

3 Chris Antley: Kentucky Derby: Strike the Gold (1991), Charismatic ('99); Preakness: Charismatic ('99)

William Boland: Kentucky Derby: Middleground (1950); Belmont: Middleground ('50), Amberoid ('66)

James H. "Jimmy" Butwell: Preakness: Buskin (1913); Belmont: Sweep ('10), *Hourless ('17)

Steve Cauthen: Kentucky Derby: Affirmed (1978); Preakness: Affirmed ('78); Belmont: Affirmed ('78)

T. Costello: Preakness: Saunterer (1881), Vanguard ('82); Belmont: Saunterer ('81)

Jean Cruguet: Kentucky Derby: Seattle Slew (1977), Preakness: Seattle Slew ('77); Belmont: Seattle Slew ('77)

Eddie Dugan: Preakness: Royal Tourist (1908), Watervale ('11); Belmont: Joe Madden ('09)

Mack Garner: Kentucky Derby: Cavalcade (1934); Preakness: Blue Larkspur ('29), Hurryoff ('33)

C. Holloway: Preakness: Cloverbrook (1877), Duke of Magenta ('78); Belmont: Cloverbrook ('77)

John Longden: Kentucky Derby: Count Fleet (1943); Preakness: Count Fleet ('43); Belmont: Count Fleet ('43)

3   **J. Linus "Pony" McAtee:** Kentucky Derby: Whiskery (1927), Clyde Van Dusen ('29); Preakness: Damrosch ('16)
    Warren Mehrtens: Kentucky Derby: Assault (1946); Preakness: Assault ('46), Belmont: Assault ('46)
    Isaac Murphy: Kentucky Derby: Buchanan (1884), Riley ('90), Kingman ('91)
    Edgar Prado: Kentucky Derby: Barbaro (2006); Belmont: Sarava (2002), Birdstone ('04)
    Jose Santos: Kentucky Derby: Funny Cide (2003); Preakness: Funny Cide (2003); Belmont: Lemon Drop Kid (1999)

3   **William "Smokey" Saunders:** Kentucky Derby: Omaha (1935); Preakness: Omaha ('35); Belmont: Omaha ('35)
    John Sellers: Kentucky Derby: Carry Back (1961); Preakness: Carry Back ('61); Belmont: Hail to All ('65)
    Bobby Swim: Kentucky Derby: Vagrant (1876); Belmont: General Duke ('68), Calvin ('75)
    Wayne D. Wright: Kentucky Derby: Shut Out (1942); Preakness: Polynesian ('45); Belmont: Peace Chance ('34)

Leading Sires of Triple Crown Race Winners

7   **Lexington:** Preakness Stakes: Tom Ochiltree (1875), Shirley ('76), Duke of Magenta ('78); Belmont: General Duke ('68), Kingfisher ('70), Harry Bassett ('71), Duke of Magenta ('78)
6   **Bull Lea:** Kentucky Derby: Citation (1948), Hill Gail ('52), Iron Liege ('57); Preakness: Faultless ('47), Citation ('48); Belmont: Citation ('48)
    Man o' War: Kentucky Derby: Clyde Van Dusen (1929); War Admiral ('37); Preakness: War Admiral ('37); Belmont: American Flag ('25), Crusader ('26), War Admiral ('37)
    ***Sir Gallahad III:** Kentucky Derby: Gallant Fox (1930), Gallahadion ('40), Hoop, Jr. ('45); Preakness: Gallant Fox ('30), High Quest, ('34); Belmont: Gallant Fox ('30)
5   **Bold Venture:** Kentucky Derby: Assault (1946), Middleground ('50); Preakness: Assault ('46); Belmont: Assault ('46), Middleground ('50)
    Broomstick: Kentucky Derby: Meridian (1911), Regret ('15); Preakness: Holiday ('14), Broomspun ('21), Bostonian ('27)
    Fair Play: Preakness: Man o'War (1920), Display ('26); Belmont: Man o'War ('20), Mad Play ('24), Chance Shot ('27)
4   ***Australian:** Kentucky Derby: Baden-Baden (1877); Belmont: Joe Daniels ('72), Springbok ('73), Spendthrift ('79)
    Alydar: Kentucky Derby: Alysheba (1987), Strike the Gold ('91); Preakness: Alysheba ('87); Belmont: Easy Goer ('89)
4   **Black Toney:** Kentucky Derby: Black Gold (1924), Brokers Tip ('33); Preakness: Bimelech ('40); Belmont: Bimelech ('40)
    ***Blenheim II:** Kentucky Derby: Whirlaway (1941), Jet Pilot ('47); Preakness: Whirlaway ('41); Belmont: Whirlaway ('41)
    Exclusive Native: Kentucky Derby: Affirmed (1978); Genuine Risk ('80); Preakness: Affirmed ('78); Belmont: Affirmed ('78)
    Falsetto: Kentucky Derby: Chant (1894), His Eminence (1901); Sir Huon ('06); Belmont: Patron ('92)
    Gallant Fox: Kentucky Derby: Omaha (1935); Preakness: Omaha ('35); Belmont: Omaha ('35), Granville ('36)
    King Alfonso: Kentucky Derby: Fonso (1880); Joe Cotton ('85); Preakness: Grenada ('80); Belmont: Grenada ('80)
    ***Leamington:** Kentucky Derby: Aristides (1875); Preakness: Harold ('79), Saunterer ('81); Belmont: Saunterer ('81)
    ***Nasrullah:** Preakness: Nashua (1955), Bold Ruler ('57); Belmont: Nashua ('55), Jaipur ('62)
    ***Star Shoot:** Kentucky Derby: Sir Barton (1919); Preakness: Sir Barton ('19); Belmont: Sir Barton ('19), Grey Lag ('21)
    ***St. Germans:** Kentucky Derby: Twenty Grand (1931); Bold Venture ('36); Preakness: Bold Venture ('36); Belmont: Twenty Grand ('31)
    Virgil: Kentucky Derby: Vagrant (1876), Hindoo ('81), Ben Ali ('86); Preakness: Vanguard ('82)

Dams of Multiple American Classic Winners

Broodmare	Offspring	Race	Year
Better Than Honour	Rags to Riches	Belmont Stakes	2007
	Jazil	Belmont Stakes	2006
Weekend Surprise	A.P. Indy	Belmont Stakes	1992
	Summer Squall	Preakness Stakes	1990
Prudery	Victorian	Preakness Stakes	1928
	Whiskery	Kentucky Derby	1927
Leisure	Holiday	Preakness Stakes	1914
	Royal Tourist	Preakness Stakes	1908
Ignite	Sir Huon	Kentucky Derby	1906
	Hindus	Preakness Stakes	1900
*Cinderella	Plaudit	Kentucky Derby	1898
	Hastings	Belmont Stakes	1896
Lady Margaret	Masterman	Belmont Stakes	1902
	Margrave	Preakness Stakes	1896
Maggie B. B.	Panique	Belmont Stakes	1884
	Harold	Preakness Stakes	1879

Kentucky Derby History

The Kentucky Derby was the dream of Col. Meriwether Lewis Clark Jr., grandson of William Clark of Lewis and Clark Expedition fame. Just 29 when the first Derby was run in 1875, Meriwether Clark had the family's sense of adventure and ambition but devoted his energies to equine pursuits.

Racing in Louisville was essentially dead in the early 1870s following the closure in '70 of Woodlawn Course, located east of the city. In 1872, Clark traveled to England to observe its racing scene.

He returned with grand ambitions of creating a racing palace in Louisville with races modeled on such leading events in England as the Epsom Derby, Epsom Oaks, and St. Leger Stakes. With $32,000 in investment capital, Clark set about building Louisville's new racetrack in 1874. The facility, built on 80 acres of land leased from Clark's uncles, John and Henry Churchill, was called the Louisville Jockey Club.

The Louisville Jockey Club opened on Monday, May 17, 1875, with four races. It was a sunny day with a crisp breeze, according to an account in the *Live Stock Record* (precursor of *The Thoroughbred Record* and THOROUGHBRED TIMES), and the "course was in splendid order, and all the appurtenances requisite for the comfort and convenience of racing was ready to hand."

All 42 nominees for the inaugural Derby were listed in the program and 15 started, with H. P. McGrath's nobly named Aristides becoming the first Derby winner.

One week after the first meet ended, the *Live Stock Record*'s editor, Benjamin G. Bruce, noted that, while he had attended the inaugural meet at Jerome Park and had visited Saratoga Race Course and Long Branch, "never have we seen such a grand success, taking it from its beginning to its close, as the late inaugural meeting of the Louisville Jockey Club."

While the first race meet was an artistic success, at least in Bruce's view, the financial situation of the Louisville Jockey Club was perilous almost from its start. For most of its first 40 years, the Derby would be regarded as a strong regional race at best and an embarrassing farce at worst. There were many reasons for the race's decline. Louisville was still considered western territory to many leading Eastern stables, and the situation grew worse when a track official insulted leading owner James Ben Ali Haggin in 1886. The race's initial 1½-mile distance was considered too taxing for three-year-olds in the spring.

The revival of the track and its signature race began in 1902. Col. Matt Winn, a Louisville tailor with no racetrack management experience but an undying love for the track—he attended every Kentucky Derby from 1875 to 1949—recruited a group of Louisvillians to purchase the track for

Kentucky Derby Attendance

Year	Attendance	Year	Attendance
2008	157,770	1988	137,694
2007	156,635	1987	130,532
2006	157,536	1986	123,819
2005	156,435	1985	108,573
2004	140,054	1984	126,453
2003	148,530	1983	134,444
2002	145,033	1982	141,009
2001	154,210	1981	139,195
2000	153,204	1980	131,859
1999	151,051	1979	128,488
1998	143,215	1978	131,004
1997	141,981	1977	124,038
1996	142,668	1976	115,387
1995	144,110	1975	113,324
1994	130,594	1974	163,628
1993	136,817	1973	134,476
1992	132,543	1972	130,564
1991	135,554	1971	123,284
1990	128,257	1970	105,087
1989	122,653		

$40,000. Winn spent a decade straightening out the financial mess at the track, which by then was known as Churchill Downs. Then, he set out to revive the Kentucky Derby.

The years 1913-'15 would establish the race's credentials from both a romantic and qualitative standpoint. The 1913 running was won by 91.45-to-1 longshot Donerail, who remains the race's longest-priced winner. The race also picked up an unofficial ambassador in winning rider Roscoe Goose, who lived for a half-century mere blocks from the track, dispensing wisdom and schooling such prospective jockeys as two-time Derby winner Charlie Kurtsinger.

The next year, the gallant gelding Old Rosebud won, enhancing the race's reputation. And, in 1915, New York owner Harry Payne Whitney shipped his marvelous, unbeaten filly Regret to Louisville, where she became the first filly to win the Derby. While some Eastern stables still shied away from shipping west for the Derby—most notably Samuel Riddle's decision not to run Man o' War in 1920—the Derby's reputation was set after 1915.

Winn was a showman who combined a promoter's instincts with a passion for the Derby. The Kentucky Derby benefited from Winn's skill until he died on October 6, 1949. By the time of his death, the Derby had become a national racing institution, traditionally run on the first Saturday in May and part of the Triple Crown, a three-race series for three-year-olds considered as the ultimate test for young horses. The track's twin spires, constructed in 1895 when the physical plant was rebuilt on what had been the backstretch side of the original track, were transformed from a unique architectural feature to an iconic symbol.

Before he died, however, Winn witnessed some

amazing Derbys. Longshot Exterminator won the 1918 Derby in his three-year-old debut after he was purchased to help train another horse who did not make the race. There were two famous victories by maidens: Sir Barton's 1919 victory launched the first successful Triple Crown campaign, while Brokers Tip won in '33 after his jockey, Don Meade, fought with Head Play's rider, Herb Fisher, down the stretch.

Winn also had to adjust to the circumstances of World War II. Travel restrictions in 1943 gave that Derby a distinctly local flavor, and it became known as the "Street Car Derby." Further war restrictions shut down the sport in early 1945; when the restrictions were lifted after V-E Day, the Derby was scheduled for June 9, the only time the race has been run in June. Three years later, Citation won the Triple Crown—the eighth during Winn's tenure at Churchill.

History flows easily through the Kentucky Derby. Each year seems to bring an amazing, astounding, or simply amusing story. From the sublime (Bill Shoemaker standing up at the sixteenth pole and possibly costing *Gallant Man the 1957 Derby) to the ridiculous (the antics of unraced Nevada gelding One Eyed Tom, who failed to make it to the starting gate in 1972), the Derby has something to offer every racing fan.

Over the past 30 years, the Derby's story has been about the growth of the event as a local and international event. Attendance rose from the 120,000-to-130,000 level in the late 1980s to more than 150,000 starting in 1999. (Security restrictions following the September 11, 2001, terrorist attacks and Churchill's rebuilding program held attendance below 150,000 from 2002 through '04.) Unsuccessful Triple Crown bids by Silver Charm, Real Quiet, and Charismatic from 1997-'99 and by War Emblem, Funny Cide, and Smarty Jones from 2002-'04 created a heightened level of awareness in the Triple Crown races. The efforts of Godolphin Racing (Dubai), The Thoroughbred Corp. (Saudi Arabia and owner of War Emblem), and Michael Tabor and John Magnier (Monaco and Ireland, respectively) to win the race in the late 1990s and early 2000s have given the race an international flavor.—*John Harrell*

Presidents at the Derby

Since World War II, attending the Kentucky Derby has become a pastime of United States presidents. Getting them to attend while they are actually in office, however, has proved to be a challenge. Eight U.S. presidents have been seen under the twin spires on the first Saturday in May, but Richard Nixon is the only one to attend the race while in office. He attended the event in 1968 while he was running for his first term and then fulfilled a promise when he returned the next year, his first in the Oval Office.

Also attending the Derby in 1969 were two future presidents, Gerald Ford and Ronald Reagan. Ford returned in 1983, along with Jimmy Carter, who defeated him in the 1976 presidential race, and future President George H. W. Bush. Bush returned in 2000, along with his son and future President George W. Bush.

Other presidents who attended the race—though they were not in the Oval Office at the time—were Harry Truman and Lyndon B. Johnson.

Kentucky Derby Trophy

The Kentucky Derby trophy, featuring a simple but classic design with a horse and garland of roses on top, was first presented in 1924, when Black Gold won the 50th running of the Derby.

The trophy had been commissioned for the golden anniversary Derby by Churchill Downs President Col. Matt Winn, who wanted a standard trophy for the connections of each Derby winner. The original design remains to this day, except for one change, when the horseshoe on the trophy was inverted upward starting with the 1999 Derby. The horseshoe had been pointed down for 75 years, according to ancient belief that an upside-down shoe afforded protection. But, since racing superstition maintains that luck runs out of horseshoes that are pointed down, the shoe was inverted.

Kentucky Derby Handle

Year	On-Track	Off-Track	Total
2008	$12,118,527	$102,438,837	$114,557,364
2007	12,076,490	106,241,224	118,317,714
2006	12,075,504	106,351,370	118,426,874
2005	10,706,881	93,278,493	103,985,374
2004	9,488,539	89,875,549	99,364,088
2003	9,135,919	78,832,118	87,968,037
2002	8,630,408	70,464,398	79,094,806
2001	8,360,273	59,192,483	67,552,756
2000	8,737,659	53,059,793	61,797,452
1999	8,025,318	46,171,266	54,196,586
1998	7,890,907	44,586,385	52,477,292
1997	7,401,141	41,891,506	49,292,647
1996	7,488,725	37,734,438	45,223,163
1995	7,297,050	37,518,438	44,815,488
1994	7,449,744	37,289,274	44,739,018
1993	6,811,130	33,458,735	40,269,865
1992	6,690,746	28,250,209	34,940,955
1991	6,744,979	27,499,222	34,244,201
1990	6,948,762	27,452,177	34,400,939
1989	6,751,067	23,089,515	29,840,582
1988	7,346,411	25,525,312	32,871,723
1987	6,362,673	20,829,236	27,191,909
1986	6,165,119	19,932,231	26,097,350
1985	5,770,074	14,474,555	20,244,629
1984	5,420,787	13,521,146	18,941,933
1983	5,546,977	—	5,546,977
1982	5,011,575	—	5,011,575
1981	4,566,179	455,163	5,021,342

Kentucky Derby simulcast wagering began in 1981, when three tracks (Longacres, Yakima Meadows, and Centennial) wagered a total of $455,163. Simulcast wagering was shelved for two years and resumed in 1984. Off-track wagering includes interstate and intrastate wagering.

The only other changes made to the Derby trophy were for the 75th (1949), 100th ('74), and 125th ('99) runnings, when additional jewels were added. Several Derby trophies are on display at the Kentucky Derby Museum; the oldest is Flying Ebony's trophy from the 1925 Derby.

Glasses and Mint Julep Cups

The popularity of the mint julep as the official Kentucky Derby drink grew in proportion with the introduction of Derby glasses and sterling silver julep cups as Derby souvenirs in the middle years of the 20th century.

The Derby glass made its introduction in 1938 after Churchill officials noted that patrons took water glasses from their tables on Derby day as souvenirs. In 1939, glass manufacturers were encouraged to add color to the glasses, making them as attractive as mint julep glasses. Sales of mint juleps increased threefold, according to track officials, and the glasses have gone on to become the most popular Derby souvenirs.

The sterling silver cups were introduced in 1951 as part of the legacy of Col. Matt Winn, who had died two years earlier. Winn wished to make the cups an official Derby souvenir, and they have been part of Derby lore now for more than a half-century. The cups, which hold 12 fluid ounces, were unchanged in design until 1984, when noted owner-breeder Leslie Combs II pointed out that the horseshoe on the glass pointed down, a superstitious sign of bad luck in racing, although an upside-down shoe was regarded in folklore as affording protection. The horseshoe was turned upright and remains so to this day.

Although some relatively minor errors have occurred in the printing on the glasses, two significant mistakes occurred on approximately 100,400 of the half-million Derby glasses manufactured for the 2002 Derby. The erroneous glasses had Burgoo King winning the Triple Crown in 1932 (he won the Derby and Preakness but did not compete in the Belmont Stakes) and War Admiral failing to win the 1937 Triple Crown (he did). These erroneous glasses immediately became collectors' items.

Enduring Twin Spires

The twin spires atop Churchill Downs's grandstand are arguably the best-known architectural feature of any racetrack in the world. They date from the reconstruction of the Louisville track in 1894-'95. Designed by 24-year-old Louisville architect Joseph D. Baldez, the twin spires were intended only as an ornamental feature of the new grandstand, which was constructed at a cost of $100,000. Col. Matt Winn, Churchill's longtime president, once told Baldez, "Joe, when you die there's one monument that will never be taken down, the twin spires."

The spires are checked periodically for structural soundness, and they underwent a renovation in 2002 as part of the $27-million first phase of Churchill's $121-million renewal project. Workmen inspecting the spires found a copy of the Louisville *Courier-Journal* from 1907 and a flag wrapped around a '08 copy of the *Courier-Journal*.

Kentucky Derby Wagering

Each year, the Kentucky Derby attracts the largest crowd in North American racing, usually in excess of 140,000. The Derby also is the sport's biggest day for wagering in North America. In 2006, the Derby set a North American record for most money bet on a single race. Wagering on the Derby totaled $118,426,874, which was 14.6% above the 2005 record total of $103,985,374 from all sources. In 2008, on-track wagering on the Derby was a record $12,118,527.

Kentucky Derby Festival

Conducted annually since 1956, the Kentucky Derby Festival has grown into a weeks-long celebration of Louisville's premier attraction. A not-for-profit community organization, the Kentucky Derby Festival recruits 4,000 volunteers for 70 special events that annually attract approximately 1.5-million people to venues in and around Louisville. Financed by 325 corporate sponsors and the sale of Pegasus Pins, the festival contributes an estimated $93-million to the local economy.

Three of the best-known events of the Kentucky Derby Festival are the Pegasus Parade, the Great Balloon Race, and the Great Steamboat Race. In 1990, the Kentucky Derby Festival added a new attraction, Thunder Over Louisville. Held three weeks before the Derby, it is billed as the nation's largest fireworks display and attracts thousands to the banks of the Ohio River each April.

The schedule of events for the 2008 Kentucky Derby Festival included:

They're Off! Luncheon	April 11
Thunder Over Louisville	April 12
Fillies' Derby Ball	April 18
Basketball Classic	April 19
Great Balloon Race	April 24-26
Great Bed Races	April 28
Knights of Columbus Charity Dinner	April 28
Run for the Rosé	April 29
Derby Trainers Dinner	April 29
Great Steamboat Race	April 30
Pegasus Parade	May 1

"My Old Kentucky Home"

As the Kentucky Derby field parades onto the racetrack from the paddock, the University of Louisville Marching Band plays "My Old Kentucky Home," a song whose meaning and involvement with the Derby are shrouded in some mystery. Stephen Collins Foster (1826-'64) wrote the song in 1853, while visiting cousins at

Federal Hill in Bardstown, Kentucky, a short distance from Louisville.

According to contemporary accounts, the song was first played at the Derby in 1921, and Damon Runyon reported in '29 that the song was played several times on Derby day. The following year, according to the Philadelphia *Public Ledger*, the song was played as the field came onto the track for the Derby.

The sentimental melody and its lyrics may well have foreshadowed the sadness that would fall upon the nation in the Civil War. A Pittsburgh native who lived many years of his brief life there, Foster began writing minstrel songs and had a national hit with "Oh, Susanna" in 1848. His view of slaves and slavery apparently changed in the next few years. According to some accounts, Foster may have been inspired to write "My Old Kentucky Home" after reading Harriet Beecher Stowe's *Uncle Tom's Cabin*, published in 1851. Foster's first draft in his song workbook was entitled "Poor Uncle Tome, Good Night."

"My Old Kentucky Home" came in the midst of Foster's most productive period. He wrote "Old Folks at Home" in 1851 and "Jeannie With the Light Brown Hair" in '54. Foster died in January 1864 after sustaining a cut, probably alcohol-related, at a New York boarding house. One of his best-known songs, "Beautiful Dreamer," was published posthumously.

"My Old Kentucky Home, Good-Night!" was adopted by Kentucky as its state song in 1928. The official lyrics were subsequently changed to remove references to "darkies" in the original version. The song had three verses, but only the first is now sung. Here are the modern lyrics:

The sun shines bright in the old Kentucky home
'Tis summer, the people are gay;
The corn top's ripe and the meadow's in the bloom,
While the birds make music all the day;
The young folks roll on the little cabin floor,
All merry, all happy, and bright,
By'n by hard times comes a-knocking at the door,
Then my old Kentucky home, good night!
Chorus
Weep no more, my lady,
Oh weep no more today!
We will sing one song for the old Kentucky home,
For the old Kentucky home far away.

Kentucky Derby Future Wager

For years, future-book wagers on the Kentucky Derby have enriched Las Vegas casinos, and Churchill Downs tapped into that bet in 1999 with the Kentucky Derby Future Wager. The bet is offered three times each year, with four days in each wagering period.

Bettors choose the horse they believe will win, with the final pool being offered approximately four weeks before the Derby. From modest beginnings, the wager gained popularity and achieved a record mark of $1,655,034 in 2005.

Here are the amounts wagered by year:

Year	Pool 1	Pool 2	Pool 3	Total
2008	$439,379	$325,306	$291,835	$1,056,520
2007	520,688	379,613	465,123	1,365,424
2006	552,627	464,236	454,743	1,471,606
2005	620,535	511,655	522,844	1,655,034
2004	536,958	358,966	386,244	1,282,168
2003	516,906	391,002	222,261	1,130,169
2002	577,889	401,070	524,847	1,503,806
2001	510,815	372,961	425,871	1,309,647
2000	465,454	306,259	387,206	1,158,919
1999	267,748	178,811	229,674	676,233

Future Pool Payoffs

Year	Winner	Pool 1 Win Price	Pool 2 Win Price	Pool 3 Win Price	Derby Day Win Price
2008	Big Brown	$ 8.60	$ 15.00	$ 8.60	$ 2.40
2007	Street Sense	22.80	18.20	15.40	11.80
2006	Barbaro	40.20	32.20	20.80	14.20
2005	Giacomo	52.00	54.20	103.60	102.60
2004	Smarty Jones	5.60†	10.80†	23.60	10.20
2003	Funny Cide	188.00	120.80	107.40	27.60
2002	War Emblem	7.60†	16.00†	24.00†	43.00
2001	Monarchos	36.60	13.00	15.80	23.00
2000	Fusaichi Pegasus	27.80	26.40	8.00	6.60
1999	Charismatic	10.20†	30.20†	26.60†	64.60

† Part of mutuel field

Derby Winner's Garland of Roses

Run for the roses, the popular nickname of the Kentucky Derby, derives from the garland of roses that is laid over the winner's withers. By 1925, the rose garland was so much a part of the race's pageantry that New York sports columnist Bill Corum coined the "run for the roses" phrase. Corum would serve as Churchill Downs's president from 1950 to '58.

According to Derby lore, the rose was designated as the Derby's official flower in 1884 by Col. M. Lewis Clark, the race's founder. News articles reported that Ben Brush was presented with a collar of pink and white roses after his 1896 Derby win.

In 1931, Churchill commissioned Mrs. Kingsley Walker to create a rose garland for the Derby winner. Her design placed 500 dark-red roses and greenery on a cloth-backed blanket. Burgoo King wore the first Walker-designed garland in 1932, and she continued to craft the garlands until '74. Her daughter, Betty Korfhage, continued the tradition into the 1980s. Beginning in 1987, Kroger Co., a Cincinnati-based grocery chain, took over the task of creating the Derby winner's garland of roses.

Derby Trivia

Largest Field: 23 in 1974.
Smallest Field: Three in 1892 and 1905.
Longest-Priced Runner Since 1908: A Dragon Killer, seventh in 1958 at 294.40-to-1.
Most Maidens in One Race: Six in 1882 (Highflyer, seventh; Pat Malloy colt, ninth; Wallensee, tenth; Newsboy, 11th; Mistral, 12th; Robert Bruce, 14th).
Most Lifetime Starts Going into Derby: 66, Florizar, 1900 (second).

Fewest Lifetime Starts Going into Derby: Zero, 11 times, most recently by Col. Hogan, 1911 (seventh).

Mutuel Field Horses Who Won the Derby: Canonero II, 1971; Count Turf, 1951; Flying Ebony, 1925.

Derby Winners Who Never Started Again: Grindstone, 1996; Bubbling Over, 1926.

Derby Winner as Both Jockey and Trainer: Johnny Longden, rider of Count Fleet in 1943 and trainer of Majestic Prince in '69.

Longest-Priced Derby Favorite: Harlan's Holiday, 6-to-1, in 2002.

Derby Weather, Track Condition, and Temperature Since 1940

Year	Winner	Weather	Track Condition	Temp
2008	Big Brown	Clear	Fast	68
2007	Street Sense	Mostly cloudy	Fast	78
2006	Barbaro	Clear	Fast	68
2005	Giacomo	Clear	Fast	79
2004	Smarty Jones	Thunderstorm	Sloppy	68
2003	Funny Cide	Partly cloudy	Fast	67
2002	War Emblem	Clear	Fast	71
2001	Monarchos	Clear	Fast	83
2000	Fusaichi Pegasus	Clear	Fast	82
1999	Charismatic	Clear	Fast	72
1998	Real Quiet	Clear	Fast	70
1997	Silver Charm	Overcast	Fast	51
1996	Grindstone	Thunderstorm	Fast	75
1995	Thunder Gulch	Partly cloudy	Fast	72
1994	Go for Gin	Thunderstorm	Sloppy	57
1993	Sea Hero	Overcast	Fast	69
1992	Lil E. Tee	Overcast	Fast	78
1991	Strike the Gold	Overcast	Fast	80
1990	Unbridled	Mostly cloudy	Good	63
1989	Sunday Silence	Overcast	Muddy	51
1988	Winning Colors	Clear	Fast	72
1987	Alysheba	Mostly cloudy	Fast	79
1986	Ferdinand	Partly cloudy	Fast	63
1985	Spend a Buck	Partly cloudy	Fast	72
1984	Swale	Overcast	Fast	71
1983	Sunny's Halo	Thunderstorm	Fast	81
1982	Gato Del Sol	Partly cloudy	Fast	75
1981	Pleasant Colony	Clear	Fast	55
1980	Genuine Risk	Clear	Fast	72
1979	Spectacular Bid	Clear	Fast	55
1978	Affirmed	Clear	Fast	67
1977	Seattle Slew	Partly cloudy	Fast	69
1976	Bold Forbes	Overcast	Fast	62
1975	Foolish Pleasure	Overcast	Fast	63
1974	Cannonade	Partly cloudy	Fast	68
1973	Secretariat	Partly cloudy	Fast	69
1972	Riva Ridge	Partly cloudy	Fast	75
1971	Canonero II	Partly cloudy	Fast	73
1970	Dust Commander	Partly cloudy	Good	64
1969	Majestic Prince	Partly cloudy	Fast	87
1968	Forward Pass	Partly cloudy	Fast	71
1967	Proud Clarion	Overcast	Fast	61
1966	Kauai King	Partly cloudy	Fast	67
1965	Lucky Debonair	Clear	Fast	84
1964	Northern Dancer	Overcast	Fast	76
1963	Chateaugay	Partly cloudy	Fast	80
1962	Decidedly	Partly cloudy	Fast	81
1961	Carry Back	Overcast	Good	81
1960	Venetian Way	Partly cloudy	Good	64
1959	*Tomy Lee	Partly cloudy	Fast	94
1958	Tim Tam	Partly cloudy	Muddy	86
1957	Iron Liege	Overcast	Fast	47
1956	Needles	Clear	Fast	82
1955	Swaps	Overcast	Fast	85
1954	Determine	Overcast	Fast	84
1953	Dark Star	Clear	Fast	76
1952	Hill Gail	Clear	Fast	79
1951	Count Turf	Partly cloudy	Fast	67
1950	Middleground	Overcast	Fast	70
1949	Ponder	Partly cloudy	Fast	57
1948	Citation	Overcast	Sloppy	72
1947	Jet Pilot	Overcast	Fast	57
1946	Assault	Overcast	Slow	68
1945	Hoop, Jr.	Partly cloudy	Muddy	77
1944	Pensive	Partly cloudy	Good	54
1943	Count Fleet	Clear	Fast	54
1942	Shut Out	Partly cloudy	Fast	87
1941	Whirlaway	Partly cloudy	Fast	76
1940	Gallahadion	Clear	Fast	62

Leading Derby Owners by Wins

8 **Calumet Farm:** Whirlaway, 1941; Pensive, 1944; Citation, 1948; Ponder, 1949; Hill Gail, 1952; Iron Liege, 1957; Tim Tam, 1958; Forward Pass, 1968.

4 **Col. E. R. Bradley:** Behave Yourself, 1921; Bubbling Over, 1926; Burgoo King, 1932; Brokers Tip, 1933.

3 **Belair Stud:** Gallant Fox, 1930; Omaha, 1935; Johnstown, 1939.

2 **Bashford Manor Stable:** Azra, 1892; Sir Huon, 1906.
Harry Payne Whitney: Regret, 1915; Whiskery, 1927.
Mrs. John D. Hertz: Reigh Count, 1928; Count Fleet, 1943.
Greentree Stable: Twenty Grand, 1931; Shut Out, 1942.
King Ranch: Assault, 1946; Middleground, 1950.
Darby Dan Farm: Chateaugay, 1963; Proud Clarion, 1967.
Meadow Stable: Riva Ridge, 1972; Secretariat, 1973.
William Condren and Joseph Cornacchia: Strike the Gold, 1991; Go for Gin, 1994.
Robert and Beverly Lewis: Silver Charm, 1997; Charismatic, 1999.

Owners With Most Derby Starters

Name	Strs.	Wins	2nd	3rd	Unplaced
Col. E. R. Bradley/ Idle Hour Stock Farm	28	4	4	1	19
Calumet Farm	20	8	4	2	7
Greentree Stable	19	2	2	1	14
Harry Payne Whitney	19	2	1	1	15
C. V. Whitney	15	0	1	1	13
Bashford Manor	11	2	2	1	6
† Overbrook Farm	11	1	0	2	8
† Michael Tabor	11	1	1	0	9
Milky Way Farm	10	1	0	2	7
Dixiana Farm	9	0	3	0	6
†Robert and Beverly Lewis	9	2	0	1	6
Belair Stud	8	3	1	0	4
Elmendorf Farm	8	0	0	0	8
Hal Price Headley	8	0	0	0	8
Three D's Stock Farm	8	0	0	1	7

†Includes partnerships

Leading Derby Breeders by Wins

9 **Calumet Farm:** Whirlaway, 1941; Pensive, 1944; Citation, 1948; Ponder, 1949; Hill Gail, 1952; Iron Liege, 1957; Tim Tam, 1958; Forward Pass, 1968; Strike the Gold, 1991.

5 **John Madden:** Old Rosebud, 1914; Sir Barton, 1919; Paul Jones, 1920; Zev, 1923; Flying Ebony, 1925.

4	**A. J. Alexander:** Baden-Baden, 1877; Fonso, 1880; Joe Cotton, 1885; Chant, 1894.
	E. R. Bradley (Idle Hour Stock Farm):
	1 E. R. Bradley: Behave Yourself, 1921.
	2 Idle Hour Stock Farm: Bubbling Over, 1926; Brokers Tip, 1933.
	1 H. N. Davis and Idle Hour Stock Farm: Burgoo King, 1932.
3	**Bashford Manor Stable (George J. Long):** Azra, 1892, Manuel, 1899; Sir Huon, 1906.
	Daniel Swigert: Hindoo, 1881; Apollo, 1882; Ben Ali, 1886.
2	**Belair Stud:** Gallant Fox, 1930; Omaha, 1935.
	Claiborne Farm: Johnstown, 1939; Swale, 1984.
	R. A. Fairbairn: Gallahadion, 1940; Hoop, Jr., 1945.
	John W. Galbreath: Chateaugay, 1963; Proud Clarion, 1967.
	Greentree Stable: Twenty Grand, 1931; Shut Out, 1942.
	Arthur B. Hancock III:
	1 A. B. Hancock III and Leone J. Peters: Gato Del Sol, 1982.
	1 A. B. Hancock III and Stonerside Ltd.: Fusaichi Pegasus, 2000.
	King Ranch: Assault, 1946; Middleground, 1950.
	Meadow Stud: Riva Ridge, 1972; Secretariat, 1973.
	Harry Payne Whitney: Regret, 1915; Whiskey, 1927.
	Milton Young: Montrose, 1887; Donau, 1910.

Leading Derby Trainers by Wins

6	**Ben A. Jones:** Lawrin, 1938; Whirlaway, 1941; Pensive, 1944; Citation, 1948; Ponder, 1949; Hill Gail, 1952.
4	**H. J. "Dick" Thompson:** Behave Yourself, 1921; Bubbling Over, 1926; Burgoo King, 1932; Brokers Tip, 1933.
	D. Wayne Lukas: Winning Colors, 1988; Thunder Gulch, 1995; Grindstone, 1996; Charismatic, 1999.
3	**Bob Baffert:** Silver Charm, 1997; Real Quiet, 1998; War Emblem, 2002.
	James "Sunny Jim" Fitzsimmons: Gallant Fox, 1930; Omaha, 1935; Johnstown, 1939.
	Max Hirsch: Bold Venture, 1936; Assault, 1946; Middleground, 1950.
2	**John McGinty:** Leonatus, 1883; Montrose, 1887.
	James Rowe Sr.: Hindoo, 1881; Regret, 1915.
	H. A. "Jimmy" Jones: Iron Liege, 1957; Tim Tam, 1958.
	Horatio Luro: Decidedly, 1962; Northern Dancer, 1964.
	Henry Forrest: Kauai King, 1966; Forward Pass, 1968.
	Lucien Laurin: Riva Ridge, 1972; Secretariat, 1973.
	W. C. "Woody" Stephens: Cannonade, 1974; Swale, 1984.
	LeRoy Jolley: Foolish Pleasure, 1975; Genuine Risk, 1980.
	Lazaro Barrera: Bold Forbes, 1976; Affirmed, 1978.
	Charlie Whittingham: Ferdinand, 1986; Sunday Silence, 1989.
	Nicholas P. Zito: Strike the Gold, 1991; Go for Gin, 1994.
	Carl Nafzger: Unbridled, 1990; Street Sense, 2007.

Female Trainers in the Derby

A woman has yet to win the Kentucky Derby as either a jockey or a trainer, but several female trainers have come close to landing one of racing's biggest prizes.

Northern California-based trainer Shelley Riley came closest to notching a Kentucky Derby victory when her 29.90-to-1 longshot, Casual Lies, finished second to Lil E. Tee in 1992.

Mary Hirsch, daughter of Racing Hall of Fame trainer Max Hirsch, was the first female trainer to saddle a Derby starter. No Sir, also owned by Mary Hirsch, finished 13th in 1937.

The women who have trained Derby starters:

Trainer	Horse	Year	Finish
Jamie Sanders	Teuflesberg	2007	17th
Kristin Mulhall	Imperialism	2004	3rd
Jennifer Pederson	Song of the Sword	2004	11th
Jenine Sahadi	The Deputy (Ire)	2000	14th
Akiko Gothard	K One King	1999	8th
Kathy Walsh	Hanuman Highway	1998	7th
Cynthia Reese	In Contention	1996	15th
Shelly Riley	Casual Lies	1992	2nd
Patti Johnson	Fast Account	1985	4th
Dianne Carpenter	Kingpost	1988	14th
	Biloxi Indian	1984	12th
Mary Keim	Mr. Pak	1965	6th
Mrs. Albert Roth	Senecas Coin	1949	DNF
Mary Hirsch	No Sir	1937	13th

Trainers With Most Derby Starters

Trainer	Strs.	Wins	2nd	3rd	Unplaced
D. Wayne Lukas	42	4	1	5	32
H. J. Thompson	24	4	2	1	17
Nicholas P. Zito	21	2	0	0	17
James Rowe Sr.*	18	2	1	1	14
Bob Baffert	17	3	1	2	11
Todd Pletcher	15	0	2	1	10
Max Hirsch	14	3	0	2	9
W. C. Stephens	14	2	3	3	6
LeRoy Jolley	13	2	2	1	8
James Fitzsimmons	11	3	1	0	7
Ben A. Jones	11	6	2	1	2

*Information on James Rowe Sr. is incomplete

Leading Derby Jockeys by Wins

5	**Eddie Arcaro:** Lawrin, 1938; Whirlaway, 1941; Hoop, Jr., 1945; Citation, 1948; Hill Gail, 1952.
	Bill Hartack: Iron Liege, 1957; Venetian Way, 1960; Decidedly, 1962; Northern Dancer, 1964; Majestic Prince, 1969.
4	**Bill Shoemaker:** Swaps, 1955; *Tomy Lee, 1959; Lucky Debonair, 1965; Ferdinand, 1986.
3	**Isaac Murphy:** Buchanan, 1884; Riley, 1890; Kingman, 1891.
	Earl Sande: Zev, 1923; Flying Ebony, 1925; Gallant Fox, 1930.
	Angel Cordero Jr.: Cannonade, 1974; Bold Forbes, 1976; Spend a Buck, 1985.
	Gary Stevens: Winning Colors, 1988; Thunder Gulch, 1995; Silver Charm, 1997.
	Kent Desormeaux: Real Quiet, 1998; Fusaichi Pegasus, 2000; Big Brown, 2008.

Jockeys With Most Derby Mounts

Jockey	Strs.	Wins	2nd	3rd	Unplaced
Bill Shoemaker	26	4	3	4	15
Pat Day	22	1	4	2	15
Eddie Arcaro	21	5	3	2	11
Laffit Pincay Jr.	21	1	4	2	14
Chris McCarron	18	2	3	0	13
Gary Stevens	18	3	2	1	12
Jerry Bailey	17	2	2	1	12
Angel Cordero Jr.	17	3	1	0	13

Jockey	Strs.	Wins	2nd	3rd	Unplaced
Kent Desormeaux	15	3	0	2	10
Mike Smith	15	1	3	1	10
Mack Garner	14	1	0	1	12
Corey Nakatani	14	0	0	0	14
Jorge Velasquez	14	1	1	2	10
Johnny Adams	13	0	2	0	11
Don Brumfield	13	1	0	1	11

African-American Jockeys in the Derby

African-American jockeys dominated the Kentucky Derby during the race's first quarter-century. Between 1875 and 1902, 11 African-American riders won 15 runnings of the Derby. The most famous were Isaac Murphy, the first jockey to win the Derby three times, and Jimmy Winkfield, who won the Derby in 1901 and '02.

Marlon St. Julien became the first African-American rider in the Derby in 79 years when he finished seventh aboard Curule in the 2000 renewal.

African-American riders who have won the Derby:

Jockey	Year	Mount
Jimmy Winkfield	1902	Alan-a-Dale
	1901	His Eminence
Willie Simms	1898	Plaudit
	1896	Ben Brush
James "Soup" Perkins	1895	Halma
Alonzo "Lonnie" Clayton	1892	Azra
Isaac Murphy	1891	Kingman
	1890	Riley
	1884	Buchanan
Isaac Lewis	1887	Montrose
Erskine Henderson	1885	Joe Cotton
Babe Hurd	1882	Apollo
George Garret Lewis	1880	Fonso
William Walker	1877	Baden-Baden
Oliver Lewis	1875	Aristides

Female Jockeys in the Derby

Jockey	Mount	Year	Finish
Rosemary Homeister	Supah Blitz	2003	13th
Julie Krone	Suave Prospect	1995	11th
	Ecstatic Ride	1992	14th
Andrea Seefeldt	Forty Something	1991	16th
Patricia Cooksey	So Vague	1984	11th
Diane Crump	Fathom	1970	15th

Leading Derby Sires by Wins

3 **Virgil:** Vagrant, 1876; Hindoo, 1881; Ben Ali, 1886.
Falsetto: Chant, 1894; His Eminence, 1901; Sir Huon, 1906.
*****Gallahad III:** Gallant Fox, 1930; Gallahadion, 1940; Hoop, Jr., 1945.
Bull Lea: Citation, 1948; Hill Gail, 1952; Iron Liege, 1957.
2 **King Alfonso:** Fonso, 1880; Joe Cotton, 1885.
Longfellow: Leonatus, 1883; Riley, 1890.
Broomstick: Meridian, 1911; Regret, 1915.
*****McGee:** Donerail, 1913; Exterminator, 1918.
The Finn: Zev, 1923; Flying Ebony, 1925.
Black Toney: Black Gold, 1924; Brokers Tip, 1933.
Man o' War: Clyde Van Dusen, 1929; War Admiral, 1937.
*****St. Germans:** Twenty Grand, 1931; Bold Venture, 1936.
*****Blenheim II:** Whirlaway, 1941; Jet Pilot, 1947.
2 **Bold Venture:** Assault, 1946; Middleground, 1950.
Bold Bidder: Cannonade, 1974; Spectacular Bid, 1979.
Exclusive Native: Affirmed, 1978; Genuine Risk, 1980.
Halo: Sunny's Halo, 1983; Sunday Silence, 1989.
Alydar: Alysheba, 1987; Strike the Gold, 1991.

Derby Winners Who Sired Derby Winners

2 **Bold Venture (1936):** Assault, 1946; Middleground, 1950.
1 **Halma (1895):** Alan-a-Dale, 1902.
Bubbling Over (1926): Burgoo King, 1932.
Reigh Count (1928): Count Fleet, 1943.
Gallant Fox (1930): Omaha, 1935.
Count Fleet (1943): Count Turf, 1951.
Pensive (1944): Ponder, 1949.
Ponder (1949): Needles, 1956.
Determine (1954): Decidedly, 1962.
Swaps (1955): Chateaugay, 1963.
Seattle Slew (1977): Swale, 1984.
Unbridled (1990): Grindstone, 1996.

Fastest Derby Winning Times

1¼ miles

Year	Winner	Time	Cond.
1973	Secretariat	1:59⅖	Fast
2001	Monarchos	1:59.97	Fast
1964	Northern Dancer	2:00	Fast
1985	Spend a Buck	2:00⅕	Fast
1962	Decidedly	2:00⅖	Fast
1967	Proud Clarion	2:00⅗	Fast
1996	Grindstone	2:01.06	Fast
2000	Fusaichi Pegasus	2:01.12	Fast
2002	War Emblem	2:01.13	Fast
2003	Funny Cide	2:01.19	Fast
1978	Affirmed	2:01⅕	Fast
1965	Lucky Debonair	2:01⅕	Fast
1995	Thunder Gulch	2:01.27	Fast

Time recorded in hundredths of a second beginning in 1991

1½ miles

Year	Winner	Time	Cond.
1889	Spokane	2:34½	Fast
1886	Ben Ali	2:36½	Fast
1879	Lord Murphy	2:37	Fast
1878	Day Star	2:37¼	Dusty
1885	Joe Cotton	2:37¼	Good

Slowest Derby Winning Times

1¼ miles

Year	Winner	Time	Cond.
1908	Stone Street	2:15⅕	Heavy
1907	Pink Star	2:12⅗	Heavy
1897	Typhoon II	2:12½	Heavy
1899	Manuel	2:12	Fast
1918	Exterminator	2:10⅘	Muddy
1929	Clyde Van Dusen	2:10⅘	Muddy
1905	Agile	2:10¾	Heavy
1928	Reigh Count	2:10⅖	Heavy
1919	Sir Barton	2:09⅘	Heavy
1912	Worth	2:09⅖	Muddy

1½ miles

Year	Winner	Time	Cond.
1891	Kingman	2:52¼	Slow
1890	Riley	2:45	Muddy
1883	Leonatus	2:43	Heavy
1892	Azra	2:41½	Heavy
1894	Chant	2:41	Fast

How Derby Favorites Fared Since 1930

Year	Favorite	Odds (to $1)	Finish
2008	**Big Brown**	**2.40**	**1**
2007	**Street Sense**	4.90	**1**
2006	Sweetnorthernsaint	5.50	7
2005	Bellamy Road	2.60	7
2004	**Smarty Jones**	**4.10**	**1**
2003	Empire Maker	2.50	2
2002	Harlan's Holiday	6.00	7
2001	Point Given	1.80	5
2000	**Fusaichi Pegasus**	**2.30**	**1**
1999	Excellent Meeting	e4.80	5
	General Challenge		11
1998	Indian Charlie	2.70	3
1997	Captain Bodgit	3.10	2
1996	Unbridled's Song	3.50	5
1995	Timber Country	e3.40	3
	Serena's Song		16
1994	Holy Bull	2.20	12
1993	Prairie Bayou	4.40	2
1992	Arazi	0.90	8
1991	Hansel	2.50	10
1990	Mister Frisky	1.90	8
1989	Easy Goer	e0.80	2
	Awe Inspiring		3
1988	Private Terms	3.40	9
1987	Demons Begone	2.20	Eased
1986	Snow Chief	2.10	11
1985	Chief's Crown	1.20	3
1984	Life's Magic	e2.80	8
	Althea		19
1983	Marfa	e2.40	5
	Balboa Native		9
	Total Departure		20
1982	Air Forbes Won	2.70	7
1981	Proud Appeal	e2.30	18
	Golden Derby		21
1980	Rockhill Native	2.10	5
1979	**Spectacular Bid**	**0.60**	**1**
1978	Alydar	1.20	2
1977	**Seattle Slew**	**0.50**	**1**
1976	Honest Pleasure	0.40	2
1975	**Foolish Pleasure**	**1.90**	**1**
1974	**Cannonade**	**e1.50**	**1**
	Judger		8
1973	**Secretariat**	**e1.50**	**1**
	Angle Light		10
1972	**Riva Ridge**	**1.50**	**1**
1971	Unconscious	2.80	5
1970	My Dad George	2.80	2
1969	**Majestic Prince**	**1.40**	**1**
1968	Forward Pass	2.20	†
1967	Damascus	1.70	3
1966	**Kauai King**	**2.40**	**1**
1965	Bold Lad	2.00	10
1964	Hill Rise	1.40	2
1963	Candy Spots	1.50	3
1962	Ridan	1.10	3
1961	**Carry Back**	**2.50**	**1**
1960	Tompion	1.10	4
1959	First Landing	3.60	3
1958	Jewel's Reward	e2.00	4
	Ebony Pearl		10
1957	Bold Ruler	1.20	4
1956	**Needles**	**1.60**	**1**
1955	Nashua	1.30	2
1954	Correlation	3.00	6
1953	Native Dancer	e0.70	2
	Social Outcast		7
1952	**Hill Gail**	**1.10**	**1**
1951	Battle Morn	2.80	6
1950	Your Host	1.60	9
1949	Olympia	0.80	6
1948	**Citation**	**e0.40**	**1**
	Coaltown		2
1947	Phalanx	2.00	2
1946	Lord Boswell	e1.10	4
	Knockdown		5
	Perfect Bahram		9
1945	Pot o' Luck	3.30	2
1944	Stir Up	1.40	3
1943	**Count Fleet**	**0.40**	**1**
1942	**Shut Out**	**e1.90**	**1**
	Devil Diver		6
1941	**Whirlaway**	**2.90**	**1**
1940	Bimelech	0.40	2
1939	**Johnstown**	**0.60**	**1**
1938	Fighting Fox	1.40	6
1937	**War Admiral**	**1.60**	**1**
1936	Brevity	0.80	2
1935	Nellie Flag	3.80	4
1934	**Cavalcade**	**e1.50**	**1**
	Time Clock		7
1933	Ladysman	e1.43	4
	Pomponius		5
1932	Tick On	1.84	6
1931	**Twenty Grand**	**e0.88**	**1**
	Anchors Aweigh		10
	Surf Board		11
1930	**Gallant Fox**	**1.19**	**1**

e—entry; †Placed first through disqualification but did not affect mutuel payments.

Fastest Derby Fractions

Quarter-Mile: :21⁴⁄₅, Top Avenger (1981)
Half-Mile: :44.86, Songandaprayer (2001)
Six Furlongs: 1:09.25, Songandaprayer (2001)
One Mile: 1:34⁴⁄₅, Spend a Buck (1985)

Final Quarter-Mile Times in Derby Since 1950

Year	Final Quarter Time	Winner	Position After 1 Mile
2008	:25.26	Big Brown	1
2007	:25.13	Street Sense	3
2006	:24.34	Barbaro	1
2005	:26.87	Giacomo	11
2004	:26.71	Smarty Jones	2
2003	:25.44	Funny Cide	2
2002	:24.43	War Emblem	1
2001	:24.97	Monarchos	6
2000	:25.38	Fusaichi Pegasus	6
1999	:25.71	Charismatic	3
1998	:26.77	Real Quiet	1
1997	:25.13	Silver Charm	3
1996	:25.90	Grindstone	1
1995	:25.55	Thunder Gulch	3
1994	:26	Go for Gin	1
1993	:25.46	Sea Hero	7
1992	:25.32	Lil E. Tee	5
1991	:25.57	Strike the Gold	6
1990	:24²⁄₅	Unbridled	2
1989	:27¹⁄₅	Sunday Silence	3

Year	Final Quarter Time	Winner	Position After 1 Mile
1988	:26⅕	Winning Colors	1
1987	:26⅗	Alysheba	3
1986	:25⅘	Ferdinand	5
1985	:25⅖	Spend a Buck	1
1984	:25⅘	Swale	1
1983	:25⅖	Sunny's Halo	1
1982	:25⅕	Gato Del Sol	5
1981	:26	Pleasant Colony	4
1980	:24⅖	Genuine Risk	1
1979	:24⅘	Spectacular Bid	2
1978	:25⅖	Affirmed	2
1977	:26⅕	Seattle Slew	1
1976	:26	Bold Forbes	1
1975	:26	Foolish Pleasure	4
1974	:25⅖	Cannonade	1
1973	:23⅕	Secretariat	2
1972	:25⅘	Riva Ridge	1
1971	:27	Canonero II	4
1970	:26	Dust Commander	7
1969	:24⅕	Majestic Prince	2
1968	:26	Forward Pass	2
1967	:24⅗	Proud Clarion	5
1966	:26⅖	Kauai King	1
1965	:24⅕	Lucky Debonair	2
1964	:24	Northern Dancer	1
1963	:26⅖	Chateaugay	4
1962	:25⅕	Decidedly	5
1961	:27⅘	Carry Back	6
1960	:25⅘	Venetian Way	2
1959	:26⅕	*Tomy Lee	2
1958	:26⅗	Tim Tam	4
1957	:25⅖	Iron Liege	2
1956	:26⅗	Needles	7
1955	:24⅘	Swaps	1
1954	:26	Determine	2
1953	:25⅖	Dark Star	1
1952	:26⅕	Hill Gail	1
1951	:25⅗	Count Turf	4
1950	:24⅘	Middleground	2

Evolution of Derby Stakes Record at 1¼ miles

Year	Winner	Time
1896	Ben Brush	2:07¾
1900	Lieut. Gibson	2:06¼
1911	Meridian	2:05
1913	Donerail	2:04⅘
1914	Old Rosebud	2:03⅖
1931	Twenty Grand	2:01⅘
1941	Whirlaway	2:01⅖
1962	Decidedly	2:00⅖
1964	Northern Dancer	2:00
1973	Secretariat	1:59⅖

Shortest-Priced Derby Beaten Favorites

Year	Horse	Odds	Finish
1976	Honest Pleasure	0.40-to-1	2nd
1940	Bimelech	0.40-to-1	2nd
1953	Native Dancer	0.70-to-1	2nd
1989	Easy Goer	0.80-to-1	2nd
1949	Olympia	0.80-to-1	6th
1936	Brevity	0.80-to-1	2nd
1992	Arazi	0.90-to-1	8th
1911	Governor Gray	1-to-1	2nd
1916	Thunderer	1.05-to-1	5th
1960	Tompion	1.10-to-1	4th
1962	Ridan	1.10-to-1	3rd
1946	Lord Boswell	1.10-to-1	4th
1921	Prudery	1.10-to-1	3rd

Shortest-Priced Derby Winners

Year	Winner	Odds
1948	Citation	0.40-to-1
1943	Count Fleet	0.40-to-1
1977	Seattle Slew	0.50-to-1
1979	Spectacular Bid	0.60-to-1
1939	Johnstown	0.60-to-1
1912	Worth	0.80-to-1
1914	Old Rosebud	0.85-to-1
1931	Twenty Grand	0.88-to-1
1952	Hill Gail	1.10-to-1
1906	Sir Huon	1.10-to-1
1930	Gallant Fox	1.19-to-1

Longest-Priced Derby Winners

Year	Horse	Odds
1913	Donerail	91.45-to-1
2005	Giacomo	50.30-to-1
1940	Gallahadion	35.20-to-1
1999	Charismatic	31.30-to-1
1967	Proud Clarion	30.10-to-1
1918	Exterminator	29.60-to-1
1953	Dark Star	24.90-to-1
1995	Thunder Gulch	24.50-to-1
1908	Stone Street	23.72-to-1
1982	Gato Del Sol	21.20-to-1
2002	War Emblem	20.50-to-1
1936	Bold Venture	20.50-to-1
1923	Zev	19.20-to-1
1986	Ferdinand	17.70-to-1

Largest Winning Margins

Year	Winner	Lengths
1946	Assault	8
1941	Whirlaway	8
1939	Johnstown	8
1914	Old Rosebud	8
2006	Barbaro	6½
1945	Hoop, Jr.	6
1894	Chant	6
1985	Spend a Buck	5¼
1970	Dust Commander	5
1932	Burgoo King	5
1926	Bubbling Over	5
1919	Sir Barton	5
1895	Halma	5

Smallest Winning Margins

Year	Winner	Margin
1996	Grindstone	nose
1959	*Tomy Lee	nose
1957	Iron Liege	nose
1933	Brokers Tip	nose
1902	Alan-a-Dale	nose
1898	Plaudit	nose
1896	Ben Brush	nose
1892	Azra	nose
1889	Spokane	nose
1997	Silver Charm	head
1953	Dark Star	head
1947	Jet Pilot	head
1936	Bold Venture	head
1927	Whiskery	head
1921	Behave Yourself	head
1920	Paul Jones	head

Triple Crown — Kentucky Derby

Birthplaces of Derby Winners

State	Winners
Kentucky	101
Florida	6
Virginia	4
California	3
Tennessee	3
New Jersey	2
Pennsylvania	2
Texas	2
Canada	2
Great Britain	2
Illinois	1
Kansas	1
Maryland	1
Missouri	1
Montana	1
New York	1
Ohio	1

Fillies in the Derby

In the long history of the Kentucky Derby, only three fillies have won the 1¼-mile classic: Regret in 1915, Genuine Risk in '80, and Winning Colors in '88.

Fillies to start in the Derby:

Year	Filly	Finish
2008	Eight Belles	2nd
1999	Excellent Meeting	5th
	Three Ring	19th
1995	Serena's Song	16th
1988	**Winning Colors**	1st
1984	Life's Magic	8th
	Althea	19th
1982	Cupecoy's Joy	10th
1980	**Genuine Risk**	1st
1959	Silver Spoon	5th
1945	Misweet	12th
1936	Gold Seeker	9th
1935	Nellie Flag	4th
1934	Mata Hari	4th
	Bazaar	9th
1932	Oscillation	13th
1930	Alcibiades	10th
1929	Ben Machree	18th
1922	Startle	8th
1921	Prudery	3rd
	Careful	5th
1920	Cleopatra	15th
1919	Regalo	9th
1918	Viva America	3rd
1915	**Regret**	1st
1914	Bronzewing	3rd
	Watermelon	7th
1913	Gowell	3rd
1912	Flamma	3rd
1911	Round the World	6th
1906	Lady Navarre	2nd
1883	Pike's Pride	6th
1879	Ada Glenn	7th
	Wissahickon	9th
1877	Early Light	8th
1876	Lizzie Stone	6th
	Marie Michon	7th
1875	Ascension	10th
	Gold Mine	15th

Maiden Winners of the Derby

Year	Winner
Brokers Tip	1933
Sir Barton	1919
Buchanan	1884

Maiden Starters Since 1950

Maidens in the Derby were a common occurrence until the mid-1930s. Since 1950, only seven maidens have run in the Derby, and none came close to winning. The connections of several runners, most notably Great Redeemer in 1979, were harshly criticized for running.

Year	Horse	Finish
1998	Nationalore	9th
1990	Pendleton Ridge	13
1979	Great Redeemer	10th
1971	Fourulla	19th
1959	The Chosen One	14
1958	Flamingo	13th
1950	On the Mark	8th

Geldings in the Derby

In all, 106 geldings have started in the Derby since 1908. Before then, records of starters were incomplete. The geldings that have started in the Kentucky Derby since 1980:

Year	Gelding	Finish
2007	Imawildandcrazyguy	4th
	Dominican	11th
2006	Sweetnorthernsaint	7th
2003	**Funny Cide**	1st
	Buddy Gil	6th
2002	Perfect Drift	3rd
	Easy Grades	13th
2001	Balto Star	14th
1999	General Challenge	11th
1998	Hanuman Highway (Ire)	7th
1997	Celtic Warrior	10th
1996	Cavonnier	2nd
	Alyrob	8th
	Zarb's Magic	13th
1993	Prairie Bayou	2nd
	Truth of It All	10th
1991	Best Pal	2nd
1989	Wind Splitter	11th
	Clever Trevor	13th
1988	Kingpost	14th
1986	Bachelor Beau	14th
1984	Raja's Shark	14th
1983	My Mac	14th
1982	Real Dare	19th
1981	Television Studio	5th
	Beau Rit	13th
1980	Rockhill Native	5th
	Execution's Reason	11th

Gelding Winners of the Derby

With Funny Cide's victory in the 2003 Derby, the losing streak for geldings ended after 74 years, dating to Clyde Van Dusen in 1929. In the 1990s, three geldings finished second: Best Pal ('91), Prairie Bayou ('93), and Cavonnier ('96). The winning geldings:

Year	Gelding
2003	Funny Cide
1929	Clyde Van Dusen

Year	Gelding
1920	Paul Jones
1918	Exterminator
1914	Old Rosebud
1888	Macbeth II
1882	Apollo
1876	Vagrant

Foreign-Based Runners in the Kentucky Derby

Following are horses that were trained primarily outside the U.S. prior to their start in the Kentucky Derby. Horses that made more than one U.S. start at three prior to their start in the Derby are not included.

Derby	Starter	Derby Finish	Country Where Based or Last Started
2002	Johannesburg	8	Ireland
	Essence of Dubai	9	United Arab Emirates
	Castle Gandolfo	12	Ireland
2001	Express Tour	8	United Arab Emirates
2000	China Visit	6	United Arab Emirates
	Curule	7	United Arab Emirates
1999	Worldly Manner	7	United Arab Emirates
1995	Eltish	6	England
	Citadeed	9	England
	Ski Captain	14	Japan
1994	Ulises[1]	14	Panama
1993	El Bakan[2]	18	Panama
1992	Dr Devious (Ire)	7	England
	Arazi	8	France
	Thyer	13	England
1986	Bold Arrangement (GB)[3]	2	England
1974	*Sir Tristram[4]	11	France
	Set n' Go[5]	15	Venezuela
	Lexico	22	Venezuela
1972	Pacallo[6]	16	Puerto Rico
1971	**Canonero II**	1	Venezuela

[1] Ulises started in the Lexington Stakes (G2) at Keeneland 13 days prior to the Derby.
[2] El Bakan started in the Lexington Stakes (G2) at Keeneland 13 days prior to the Derby.
[3] Bold Arrangement started in the Blue Grass Stakes (G1) at Keeneland nine days prior to the Derby.
[4] *Sir Tristram started in the Stepping Stone Purse at Churchill seven days prior to the Derby.
[5] Set n' Go started in the Carl G. Rose Memorial Handicap at Hialeah 24 days prior to the Derby.
[6] Pacallo started in the Stepping Stone Purse at Churchill seven days prior to the Derby.

Front-Running Derby Winners

The following Kentucky Derby winners were on the lead at all points of call.

Year	Winner	Winning Margin
2002	War Emblem	4
1988	Winning Colors	neck
1985	Spend a Buck	5¼
1976	Bold Forbes	1
1972	Riva Ridge	3¼
1966	Kauai King	½
1955	Swaps	1½
1953	Dark Star	head
1947	Jet Pilot	head
1945	Hoop, Jr.	6
1943	Count Fleet	3
1939	Johnstown	8
1937	War Admiral	1¾
1929	Clyde Van Dusen	2
1926	Bubbling Over	5
1923	Zev	1½
1922	Morvich	1½

Year	Winner	Winning Margin
1920	Paul Jones	head
1919	Sir Barton	5
1915	Regret	2
1914	Old Rosebud	8
1912	Worth	neck
1911	Meridian	¾
1910	Donau	½
1909	Wintergreen	4
1905	Agile	3
1902	Alan-a-Dale	nose
1901	His Eminence	1½
1900	Lieut. Gibson	3
1897	Typhoon II	neck
1895	Halma	5
1894	Chant	6
1893	Lookout	4
1887	Montrose	2
1883	Leonatus	3
1881	Hindoo	4
1880	Fonso	1
1878	Day Star	1
1875	Aristides	2

Winning Derby Post Positions

Winning Derby post positions since 1900:

Post	Winners	Post	Winners
1	12	11	3
2	9	12	3
3	8	13	4
4	10	14	2
5	12	15	3
6	6	16	3
7	8	17	0
8	9	18	1
9	4	19	0
10	10	20	2

Undefeated Starters

Big Brown, the 2008 Kentucky Derby winner, was only the seventh undefeated horse to win the Derby. The other five were Regret in 1915, Morvich in '22, Majestic Prince in '69, Triple Crown winner Seattle Slew in '77, Smarty Jones in 2004, and Barbaro in '06.

The undefeated Derby starters since Regret in 1915:

Year	Horse	Pre-Derby Starts	Derby Finish
2008	**Big Brown**	3	**1st**
	Showing Up	3	6th
2007	Curlin	3	3rd
2006	**Barbaro**	5	**1st**
2004	**Smarty Jones**	6	**1st**
2000	China Visit	2	6th
	Trippi	4	11th
1998	Indian Charlie	4	3rd
1990	Mister Frisky	16	8th
1988	Private Terms	7	9th
1982	Air Forbes Won	4	7th
1978	Sensitive Prince	6	6th
1977	**Seattle Slew**	6	**1st**
1969	**Majestic Prince**	7	**1st**
1963	Candy Spots	6	3rd
	No Robbery	5	5th
1953	Native Dancer	11	2nd
1948	Coaltown	4	2nd
1940	Bimelech	8	2nd
1922	**Morvich**	11	**1st**
1916	Thunderer	3	5th
1915	**Regret**	3	**1st**

Derby Winners Sold at Public Auction and Privately

Derby	Winner	Year	Sale	Price
2008	Big Brown	2006	FT Oct	$ 60,000
		2007	Kee April	190,000
2003	Funny Cide	2001	FT Saratoga	22,000
		2002	Private	75,000
2002	War Emblem	2000	Kee Sept	20,000
		2002	Private	900,000
2001	Monarchos	1999	FT Saratoga	90,000 (RNA)
		2000	FT Calder	170,000
2000	Fusaichi Pegasus	1998	Kee July	4,000,000
1999	Charismatic	1996	Private	200,000
1998	Real Quiet	1996	Kee Sept	17,000
1997	Silver Charm	1995	OBSC Aug	16,500
		1996	OBSC April	100,000
1995	Thunder Gulch	1993	Kee July	40,000
		1994	Kee April	120,000 (RNA)
1994	Go for Gin	1991	FT Ky	32,000
		1992	FT Saratoga	150,000
1992	Lil E. Tee	1991	OBSC April	25,000
1990	Unbridled	1987	Tartan dispersal	90,000
1989	Sunday Silence	1987	Kee July	17,000 (RNA)
		1988	CTS March	32,000
1988	Winning Colors	1986	Kee July	575,000
1987	Alysheba	1985	Kee July	500,000
1985	Spend a Buck	1983	Private	12,500
1980	Genuine Risk	1978	FT Ky	32,000

Derby	Winner	Year	Sale	Price
1979	Spectacular Bid	1977	Kee Sept.	$ 37,000
1977	Seattle Slew	1975	FT Ky	17,500
1976	Bold Forbes	1974	FT Ky	15,200
1975	Foolish Pleasure	1973	FT Saratoga	20,000
1971	Canonero II	1969	Kee Sept	1,200
1970	Dust Commander	1968	Kee Sept	6,500
1969	Majestic Prince	1967	Kee July	250,000
1966	Kauai King	1968	FT Saratoga	42,000
1960	Venetian Way	1958	Kee July	10,500
1959	*Tomy Lee	1956	Tatt Dec	6,762
1954	Determine	1952	Kee July	12,500
1953	Dark Star	1951	Kee July	6,500
1951	Count Turf	1949	FT Saratoga	3,700
1947	Jet Pilot	1945	Kee July	41,000
1945	Hoop, Jr.	1943	Kee July	10,200
1940	Gallahadion	1938	FT Saratoga	5,000
1934	Cavalcade	1932	FT Saratoga	1,200

FT Fasig-Tipton; CTS California Thoroughbred Sale; RNA Reserve Not Attained

Derby Winners Unraced at Two

A juvenile campaign of some sort is virtually a prerequisite for winning the Kentucky Derby. Only one horse, Apollo, has won the Derby without racing as a two-year-old, and he accomplished that feat in 1882, in the eighth running.

In recent years, only four horses have won the Derby after making only one start as a two-year-old.

Status of Kentucky Derby Winners Since 1970

Year	Winner	Birthdate	Status	Where Stands/Stood	Location	Death Date
2008	Big Brown	4/10/2005	In training			
2007	Street Sense	2/23/2004	Stallion	Darley	Lexington, Ky.	
2006	Barbaro	4/29/2003	Deceased			1/29/2007
2005	Giacomo	2/16/2002	Stallion	Adena Springs Kentucky	Midway, Ky.	
2004	Smarty Jones	2/28/2001	Stallion	Three Chimneys Farm	Midway, Ky.	
2003	Funny Cide	4/20/2000	Retired			
2002	War Emblem	2/20/1999	Stallion	Shadai Stallion Station	Hokkaido, Japan	
2001	Monarchos	2/9/1998	Stallion	Nuckols Farm	Midway, Ky.	
2000	Fusaichi Pegasus	4/12/1997	Stallion	Ashford Stud	Versailles, Ky.	
1999	Charismatic	3/13/1996	Stallion	JBBA Shizunai Stallion Station	Hokkaido, Japan	
1998	Real Quiet	3/7/1995	Stallion	Penn Ridge Farms	Harrisburg, Pa.	
1997	Silver Charm	2/22/1994	Stallion	JBBA Shizunai Stallion Station	Hokkaido, Japan	
1996	Grindstone	1/23/1993	Stallion	Overbrook Farm	Lexington, Ky.	
1995	Thunder Gulch	5/23/1992	Stallion	Ashford Stud	Versailles, Ky.	
1994	Go for Gin	4/18/1991	Stallion	Bonita Farm	Darlington, Md.	
1993	Sea Hero	3/4/1990	Stallion	Karacabey Pension Stud	Izmit, Turkey	
1992	Lil E. Tee	3/29/1989	Stallion	Old Frankfort Stud	Lexington, Ky.	
1991	Strike the Gold	3/21/1988	Stallion	Karacabey Pension Stud	Izmit, Turkey	
1990	Unbridled	3/5/1987	Deceased	Claiborne Farm	Paris, Ky.	10/18/2001
1989	Sunday Silence	3/25/1986	Deceased	Shadai Stallion Station	Hokkaido, Japan	8/19/2002
1988	Winning Colors	3/14/1985	Deceased			2/17/2008
1987	Alysheba	3/3/1984	Stallion	Janadriyah Stud Farm	Riyadh, Saudi Arabia	
1986	Ferdinand	3/12/1983	Deceased	Arrow Stud	Hokkaido, Japan	2002
1985	Spend a Buck	5/15/1982	Deceased	Haras Bage do Sul	Sao Paulo, Brazil	11/24/2002
1984	Swale	4/21/1981	Deceased			6/17/1984
1983	Sunny's Halo	2/11/1980	Deceased	Double S Thoroughbred Farm	Tyler, Tx.	6/3/2003
1982	Gato Del Sol	2/23/1979	Deceased			8/7/2007
1981	Pleasant Colony	5/4/1978	Deceased	Lane's End	Versailles, Ky.	12/31/2002
1980	Genuine Risk	2/15/1977	Pensioned	Newstead Farm	Upperville, Va.	
1979	Spectacular Bid	2/17/1976	Deceased	Milfer Farm	Unadilla, N.Y.	6/9/2003
1978	Affirmed	2/21/1975	Deceased	Jonabell Farm	Lexington, Ky.	1/12/2001
1977	Seattle Slew	2/15/1974	Deceased	Three Chimneys Farm	Midway, Ky.	5/7/2002
1976	Bold Forbes	3/31/1973	Deceased	Stone Farm	Paris, Ky.	8/9/2000
1975	Foolish Pleasure	3/23/1972	Deceased	Horseshoe Ranch	Dayton, Wy.	11/17/1994
1974	Cannonade	5/12/1971	Deceased	Gainesway	Lexington, Ky.	8/3/1993
1973	Secretariat	3/30/1970	Deceased	Claiborne Farm	Paris, Ky.	10/4/1989
1972	Riva Ridge	4/13/1969	Deceased	Claiborne Farm	Paris, Ky.	4/21/1985
1971	Canonero II	4/24/1968	Deceased	Gainesway	Lexington, Ky.	11/11/1981
1970	Dust Commander	2/8/1967	Deceased	Springland Farm	Paris, Ky.	10/7/1991

Tim Tam, trained by H. A. "Jimmy" Jones, won in 1958 after finishing unplaced in his only start at two. Also unplaced in his only juvenile start was Lucky Debonair, who won the 1965 Derby. Fusaichi Pegasus finished second in his only start as a two-year-old and won the Derby as the 2.30-to-1 favorite in 2000, and Big Brown won his only start at two prior to winning the Derby in '08.

Winners' Total Starts Before Derby

Decade	Total Starts Before Derby	Average No. Starts
2000-'08	52	5.8
1990-'99	90	9.0
1980-'89	93	9.3
1970-'79	136	13.6
1960-'69	129	12.9
1950-'59	137	13.7
1940-'49	138	13.8

Derby Winners' Starts at Two

Decade	Total Starts at Two	Average No. Starts
2000-'08	23	2.6
1990-'99	52	5.2
1980-'89	60	6.0
1970-'79	89	8.9
1960-'69	72	7.2
1950-'59	75	7.5
1940-'49	89	8.9

Winners' Starts at Three Before Derby

Decade	Total Starts at Three Before Derby	Average No. Starts
2000-'08	29	3.2
1990-'99	38	3.8
1980-'89	33	3.3
1970-'79	47	4.7
1960-'69	57	5.7
1950-'59	62	6.2
1940-'49	49	4.9

Total Pre-Derby Starts

Decade	Starters	Starts	Avg. No. Starts
2000-'08	168	1,191	7.09
1990-'99	167	1,387	8.31
1980-'89	171	1,720	10.06
1970-'79	149	1,945	13.05
1960-'69	126	2,151	17.07
1950-'59	145	2,316	15.97
1940-'49	126	1,805	14.33

Derby Starters' Starts at Two

Decade	Starters	Starts at 2	Avg. No. Starts
2000-'08	168	637	3.79
1990-'99	167	749	4.49
1980-'89	171	954	5.58
1970-'79	149	1,016	6.82
1960-'69	126	1,272	10.1

Decade	Starters	Starts at 2	Avg. No. Starts
1950-'59	145	1,405	9.69
1940-'49	126	1,241	9.85

Pre-Derby Starts at Three

Decade	Starters	Starts at 3 Before Derby	Average No. Starts
2000-'08	168	554	3.30
1990-'99	167	638	3.82
1980-'89	171	766	4.48
1970-'79	149	929	6.23
1960-'69	126	879	6.98
1950-'59	145	911	6.28
1940-'49	126	564	4.48

Most Total Starts by Winner Before Derby

Total Starts	Horse	Year	Starts at Two	At Three Before Derby
28	Carry Back	1961	21	7
23	Whirlaway	1941	16	7
22	Dust Commander	1970	14	8
	Determine	1954	14	8
21	Cannonade	1974	17	4
20	Count Turf	1951	10	10
17	Forward Pass	1968	10	7
	Iron Liege	1957	8	9
	Count Fleet	1943	15	2
16	Citation	1948	9	7
14	Charismatic	1999	7	7
	Spectacular Bid	1979	9	5
	Northern Dancer	1964	9	5
	Venetian Way	1960	9	5
	Hill Gail	1952	7	7
	Jet Pilot	1947	12	2
	Gallahadion	1940	5	9

Fewest Total Starts by Winner Before Derby

Total Starts	Horse	Year	Starts at Two	At Three Before Derby
3	Big Brown	2008	1	2
	Regret	1915	3	0
5	Barbaro	2006	2	3
	Fusaichi Pegasus	2000	1	4
	Grindstone	1996	2	3
6	Smarty Jones	2004	2	4
	Funny Cide	2003	3	3
	Monarchos	2001	2	4
	Silver Charm	1997	3	3
	Sunday Silence	1989	3	3
	Winning Colors	1988	2	4
	Seattle Slew	1977	3	3
7	Street Sense	2007	5	2
	Giacomo	2005	4	3
	War Emblem	2002	3	4
	Strike the Gold	1991	3	4
	Genuine Risk	1980	4	3
	Majestic Prince	1969	2	5
	Hoop, Jr.	1945	5	2

Starts by Kentucky Derby Winners at Two and Three

Year	Winner	Starts at 2	Starts Before Derby at 3	Total Pre-Derby Starts	Total Starts at 3	Total Starts at 2-3	Derby Prep	Finish
2008	Big Brown	1	2	3			Florida Derby (G1)	1
2007	Street Sense	5	2	7	8	13	Toyota Blue Grass S. (G1)	2
2006	Barbaro	2	3	5	5	7	Florida Derby (G1)	1
2005	Giacomo	4	3	7	6	10	Santa Anita Derby (G1)	4
2004	Smarty Jones	2	4	6	7	9	Arkansas Derby (G2)	1
2003	Funny Cide	3	3	6	8	11	Wood Memorial S. (G1)	2
2002	War Emblem	3	4	7	10	13	Illinois Derby (G2)	1
2001	Monarchos	2	4	6	7	9	Wood Memorial S. (G2)	2

Triple Crown — Kentucky Derby

Year	Winner	Starts at 2	Starts Before Derby at 3	Total Pre-Derby Starts	Total Starts at 3	Total Starts at 2-3	Derby Prep	Finish
2000	Fusaichi Pegasus	1	4	5	8	9	Wood Memorial S. (G2)	1
1999	Charismatic	7	7	14	10	17	Lexington S. (G2)	1
1998	Real Quiet	9	3	12	6	15	Santa Anita Derby (G1)	2
1997	Silver Charm	3	3	6	7	10	Santa Anita Derby (G1)	2
1996	Grindstone	2	3	5	4	6	Arkansas Derby (G2)	2
1995	Thunder Gulch	6	3	9	10	16	Blue Grass S. (G2)	4
1994	Go for Gin	5	4	9	11	16	Wood Memorial S. (G1)	2
1993	Sea Hero	7	3	10	9	16	Blue Grass S. (G2)	4
1992	Li E. Tee	4	4	8	6	10	Arkansas Derby (G2)	2
1991	Strike the Gold	3	4	7	12	15	Blue Grass S. (G2)	1
1990	Unbridled	6	4	10	11	17	Blue Grass S. (G2)	3
1989	Sunday Silence	3	3	6	9	12	Santa Anita Derby (G1)	1
1988	Winning Colors	2	4	6	10	12	Santa Anita Derby (G1)	1
1987	Alysheba	7	3	10	10	17	Blue Grass S. (G1)	1, pl 3
1986	Ferdinand	5	4	9	8	13	Santa Anita Derby (G1)	3
1985	Spend a Buck	8	3	3	7	15	Garden State S.	1
1984	Swale	7	4	11	7	14	Lexington S.	2
1983	Sunny's Halo	11	2	13	9	20	Arkansas Derby (G1)	1
1982	Gato Del Sol	8	4	12	9	17	Blue Grass S. (G1)	2
1981	Pleasant Colony	5	8	8	9	14	Wood Memorial S. (G1)	1
1980	Genuine Risk	4	3	7	8	12	Wood Memorial S. (G1)	3
1979	Spectacular Bid	9	5	14	12	21	Blue Grass S. (G1)	1
1978	Affirmed	9	4	13	11	20	Hollywood Derby (G1)	1
1977	Seattle Slew	3	3	6	7	10	Wood Memorial S. (G1)	1
1976	Bold Forbes	8	5	13	10	18	Wood Memorial S. (G1)	1
1975	Foolish Pleasure	7	4	11	11	18	Wood Memorial S. (G1)	1
1974	Cannonade	17	4	21	8	25	Churchill allowance	1
1973	Secretariat	9	3	12	12	21	Wood Memorial S. (G1)	3
1972	Riva Ridge	9	3	12	12	21	Blue Grass S.	1
1971	Canonero II	4	8	12	11	15	Series 4A-5A H.	3
1970	Dust Commander	14	8	22	23	37	Blue Grass S.	1
1969	Majestic Prince	2	5	7	8	10	Churchill allowance	1
1968	Forward Pass	10	7	17	13	23	Blue Grass S.	1
1967	Proud Clarion	3	5	8	13	16	Blue Grass S.	2
1966	Kauai King	4	8	12	12	16	Governor's Gold Cup	1
1965	Lucky Debonair	1	8	9	10	11	Blue Grass S.	1
1964	Northern Dancer	9	5	14	9	18	Blue Grass S.	1
1963	Chateaugay	5	3	8	12	17	Blue Grass S.	1
1962	Decidedly	8	4	12	12	20	Blue Grass S.	2
1961	Carry Back	21	7	28	16	37	Wood Memorial S.	2
1960	Venetian Way	9	5	14	11	20	Churchill allowance	2
1959	*Tomy Lee	8	4	12	7	15	Blue Grass S.	1
1958	Tim Tam	1	10	11	13	14	Derby Trial S.	1
1957	Iron Liege	8	9	17	17	25	Derby Trial S.	5
1956	Needles	10	3	13	8	18	Florida Derby	1
1955	Swaps	6	3	9	9	15	Churchill allowance	1
1954	Determine	14	8	22	15	29	Derby Trial S.	2
1953	Dark Star	6	5	11	7	13	Derby Trial S.	1
1952	Hill Gail	7	7	14	8	15	Derby Trial S.	1
1951	Count Turf	10	10	20	14	24	Wood Memorial S.	5
1950	Middleground	5	4	9	10	15	Derby Trial S.	2
1949	Ponder	4	8	12	21	25	Derby Trial S.	2
1948	Citation	9	7	16	20	29	Derby Trial S.	1
1947	Jet Pilot	12	2	14	5	17	Jamaica H.	1
1946	Assault	9	3	12	15	24	Derby Trial S.	4
1945	Hoop, Jr.	5	2	7	4	9	Cedar Manor Purse	2
1944	Pensive	5	7	12	17	22	Chesapeake S.	2
1943	Count Fleet	15	2	17	6	21	Wood Memorial S.	1
1942	Shut Out	9	2	11	12	21	Blue Grass S.	1
1941	Whirlaway	16	7	23	20	36	Derby Trial S.	2
1940	Gallahadion	5	9	14	17	22	Derby Trial S.	2
1939	Johnstown	12	3	15	9	21	Wood Memorial S.	1
1938	Lawrin	15	8	23	11	26	Derby Trial S.	1
1937	War Admiral	6	2	8	8	14	Chesapeake S.	1
1936	Bold Venture	8	1	9	3	11	South Shore Purse	1
1935	Omaha	9	2	11	9	18	Wood Memorial S.	3
1934	Cavalcade	11	2	13	7	18	Chesapeake S.	1
1933	Brokers Tip	4	1	5	5	9	Lexington allowance	2
1932	Burgoo King	12	1	13	4	16	Lexington allowance	2
1931	Twenty Grand	8	2	10	10	18	Preakness S.	2
1930	Gallant Fox	7	2	9	10	17	Preakness S.	1

Kentucky Derby

Grade 1, Churchill Downs, three-year-olds, 1¼ miles, dirt. Held on May 3, 2008, with gross value of $2,211,800. First run in 1875. Weights: colts and geldings, 126 pounds; fillies, 121 pounds.

Year	Winner	Jockey	Second	Third	Strs	Time	Track	1st Purse
2008	**Big Brown**	K. Desormeaux	†Eight Belles	Denis of Cork	20	2:01.82	ft	$1,451,800
2007	**Street Sense**	C. Borel	Hard Spun	Curlin	20	2:02.17	ft	1,450,000
2006	**Barbaro**	E. Prado	Bluegrass Cat	Steppenwolfer	20	2:01.36	ft	1,143,200
2005	**Giacomo**	M. Smith	Closing Argument	Afleet Alex	20	2:02.75	ft	1,639,600
2004	**Smarty Jones**	S. Elliott	Lion Heart	Imperialism	18	2:04.06	sy	**6,184,800**
2003	**‡Funny Cide**	J. Santos	Empire Maker	Peace Rules	16	2:01.19	ft	800,200
2002	**War Emblem**	V. Espinoza	Proud Citizen	Perfect Drift	18	2:01.13	ft	1,875,000
2001	**Monarchos**	J. Chavez	Invisible Ink	Congaree	17	1:59.97	ft	812,000
2000	**Fusaichi Pegasus**	K. Desormeaux	Aptitude	Impeachment	19	2:01.12	ft	888,400
1999	**Charismatic**	C. Antley	Menifee	Cat Thief	19	2:03.29	ft	886,200
1998	**Real Quiet**	K. Desormeaux	Victory Gallop	Indian Charlie	15	2:02.38	ft	738,800
1997	**Silver Charm**	G. Stevens	Captain Bodgit	Free House	13	2:02.44	ft	700,000
1996	**Grindstone**	J. Bailey	‡Cavonnier	Prince of Thieves	19	2:01.06	ft	869,800
1995	**Thunder Gulch**	G. Stevens	Tejano Run	Timber Country	19	2:01.27	ft	707,400
1994	**Go for Gin**	C. McCarron	Strodes Creek	Blumin Affair	14	2:03.72	sy	628,800
1993	**Sea Hero**	J. Bailey	‡Prairie Bayou	Wild Gale	19	2:02.42	ft	735,900
1992	**Lil E. Tee**	P. Day	Casual Lies	Dance Floor	18	2:03.04	ft	724,800
1991	**Strike the Gold**	C. Antley	‡Best Pal	Mane Minister	16	2:03.08	ft	655,800
1990	**Unbridled**	C. Perret	Summer Squall	Pleasant Tap	15	2:02	gd	581,000
1989	**Sunday Silence**	P. Valenzuela	Easy Goer	Awe Inspiring	15	2:05	my	574,200
1988	**†Winning Colors**	G. Stevens	Forty Niner	Risen Star	17	2:02⅕	ft	611,200
1987	**Alysheba**	C. McCarron	Bet Twice	Avies Copy	17	2:03⅖	ft	618,600
1986	**Ferdinand**	W. Shoemaker	Bold Arrangement (GB)	Broad Brush	16	2:02⅘	ft	609,400
1985	**Spend a Buck**	A. Cordero Jr.	Stephan's Odyssey	Chief's Crown	13	2:00⅕	ft	406,800
1984	**Swale**	L. Pincay Jr.	Coax Me Chad	At the Threshold	20	2:02⅖	ft	537,400
1983	**Sunny's Halo**	E. Delahoussaye	Desert Wine	Caveat	20	2:02⅕	ft	426,000
1982	**Gato Del Sol**	E. Delahoussaye	Laser Light	Reinvested	19	2:02⅖	ft	428,850
1981	**Pleasant Colony**	J. Velasquez	Woodchopper	Partez	21	2:02	ft	317,200
1980	**†Genuine Risk**	J. Vasquez	Rumbo	Jaklin Klugman	13	2:02	ft	250,550
1979	**Spectacular Bid**	R. Franklin	General Assembly	Golden Act	10	2:02⅖	ft	228,650
1978	**AFFIRMED**	S. Cauthen	Alydar	Believe It	11	2:01⅕	ft	186,900
1977	**SEATTLE SLEW**	J. Cruguet	Run Dusty Run	Sanhedrin	15	2:02⅕	ft	214,700
1976	**Bold Forbes**	A. Cordero Jr.	Honest Pleasure	Elocutionist	9	2:01⅗	ft	165,200
1975	**Foolish Pleasure**	J. Vasquez	Avatar	Diabolo	15	2:02	ft	209,600
1974	**Cannonade**	A. Cordero Jr.	Hudson County	Agitate	**23**	2:04	ft	274,000
1973	**SECRETARIAT**	R. Turcotte	Sham	Our Native	13	**1:59⅖**	ft	155,050
1972	**Riva Ridge**	R. Turcotte	No Le Hace	Hold Your Peace	16	2:01⅘	ft	140,300
1971	**Canonero II**	G. Avila	Jim French	Bold Reason	20	2:03⅕	ft	145,500
1970	**Dust Commander**	M. Manganello	My Dad George	High Echelon	17	2:03⅖	gd	127,800
1969	**Majestic Prince**	W. Hartack	Arts and Letters	Dike	8	2:01⅘	ft	113,200
1968	**Forward Pass**	I. Valenzuela	Francie's Hat	T. V. Commercial	14	2:02⅕	ft	122,600
1967	**Proud Clarion**	R. Ussery	Barbs Delight	Damascus	14	2:00⅗	ft	119,700
1966	**Kauai King**	D. Brumfield	Advocator	Blue Skyer	15	2:02	ft	120,500
1965	**Lucky Debonair**	W. Shoemaker	Dapper Dan	Tom Rolfe	11	2:01⅕	ft	112,000
1964	**Northern Dancer**	W. Hartack	Hill Rise	The Scoundrel	12	2:00	ft	114,300
1963	**Chateaugay**	B. Baeza	Never Bend	Candy Spots	9	2:01⅘	ft	108,900
1962	**Decidedly**	W. Hartack	Roman Line	Ridan	15	2:00⅖	ft	119,650
1961	**Carry Back**	J. Sellers	Crozier	Bass Clef	15	2:04	gd	120,500
1960	**Venetian Way**	W. Hartack	Bally Ache	Victoria Park	13	2:02⅖	gd	114,850
1959	***Tomy Lee**	W. Shoemaker	Sword Dancer	First Landing	17	2:02⅕	ft	119,650
1958	**Tim Tam**	I. Valenzuela	Lincoln Road	Noureddin	14	2:05	my	116,400
1957	**Iron Liege**	W. Hartack	*Gallant Man	Round Table	9	2:02⅕	ft	107,950
1956	**Needles**	D. Erb	Fabius	Come On Red	17	2:03⅖	ft	123,450
1955	**Swaps**	W. Shoemaker	Nashua	Summer Tan	10	2:01⅘	ft	108,400
1954	**Determine**	R. York	Hasty Road	Hasseyampa	17	2:03	ft	102,050
1953	**Dark Star**	H. Moreno	Native Dancer	Invigorator	11	2:02	ft	90,050
1952	**Hill Gail**	E. Arcaro	Sub Fleet	Blue Man	16	2:01⅗	ft	96,300
1951	**Count Turf**	C. McCreary	Royal Mustang	‡Ruhe	20	2:02⅗	ft	98,050
1950	**Middleground**	W. Boland	Hill Prince	Mr. Trouble	14	2:01⅗	ft	92,650
1949	**Ponder**	S. Brooks	Capot	Palestinian	14	2:04⅕	ft	91,600
1948	**CITATION**	E. Arcaro	Coaltown	My Request	6	2:05⅖	sy	83,400
1947	**Jet Pilot**	E. Guerin	Phalanx	Faultless	13	2:06⅘	sl	92,160
1946	**ASSAULT**	W. Mehrtens	Spy Song	Hampden	17	2:06⅗	sl	96,400
1945	**Hoop, Jr.**	E. Arcaro	Pot o'Luck	‡Darby Dieppe	16	2:07	my	64,850
1944	**Pensive**	C. McCreary	Broadcloth	‡Stir Up	16	2:04⅕	gd	64,675
1943	**COUNT FLEET**	J. Longden	Blue Swords	Slide Rule	10	2:04	ft	60,725
1942	**Shut Out**	W. Wright	Alsab	Valdina Orphan	15	2:04⅖	ft	64,225

Triple Crown — Kentucky Derby

Year	Winner	Jockey	Second	Third	Strs	Time	Track	1st Purse
1941	WHIRLAWAY	E. Arcaro	Staretor	Market Wise	11	2:01 1/5	ft	$61,275
1940	Gallahadion	C. Bierman	Bimelech	‡Dit	8	2:05	ft	60,150
1939	Johnstown	J. Stout	Challedon	Heather Broom	8	2:03 2/5	ft	46,350
1938	Lawrin	E. Arcaro	Dauber	Can't Wait	10	2:04 1/5	ft	47,050
1937	WAR ADMIRAL	C. Kurtsinger	Pompoon	Reaping Reward	20	2:03 1/5	ft	52,050
1936	Bold Venture	I. Hanford	Brevity	Indian Broom	14	2:03 3/5	ft	37,725
1935	OMAHA	W. Saunders	Roman Soldier	Whiskolo	18	2:05	gd	39,525
1934	Cavalcade	M. Garner	Discovery	Agrarian	13	2:04	ft	28,175
1933	Brokers Tip	D. Meade	Head Play	Charley O.	13	2:06 4/5	gd	48,925
1932	Burgoo King	E. James	Economic	Stepenfetchit	20	2:05 1/5	ft	52,350
1931	Twenty Grand	C. Kurtsinger	Sweep All	Mate	12	2:01 4/5	ft	48,725
1930	GALLANT FOX	E. Sande	Gallant Knight	Ned O.	15	2:07 3/5	gd	50,725
1929	‡Clyde Van Dusen	L. McAtee	Naishapur	Panchio	21	2:10 4/5	my	53,950
1928	Reigh Count	C. Lang	Misstep	Toro	22	2:10 2/5	hy	55,375
1927	Whiskery	L. McAtee	‡Osmand	Jock	15	2:06	sl	51,000
1926	Bubbling Over	A. Johnson	Bagenbaggage	Rock Man	13	2:03 4/5	ft	50,075
1925	Flying Ebony	E. Sande	Captain Hal	Son of John	20	2:07 3/5	sy	52,950
1924	Black Gold	J. Mooney	Chilhowee	Beau Butler	19	2:05 1/5	ft	52,775
1923	Zev	E. Sande	Martingale	Vigil	21	2:05 2/5	ft	53,600
1922	Morvich	A. Johnson	Bet Mosie	John Finn	10	2:04 3/5	ft	53,775
1921	Behave Yourself	C. Thompson	Black Servant	†Prudery	12	2:04 1/5	ft	38,450
1920	‡Paul Jones	T. Rice	Upset	On Watch	17	2:09	sl	30,375
1919	SIR BARTON	J. Loftus	‡Billy Kelly	*Under Fire	12	2:09 4/5	hy	20,825
1918	‡Exterminator	W. Knapp	Escoba	†Viva America	8	2:10 4/5	my	14,700
1917	*Omar Khayyam	C. Borel	Ticket	Midway	15	2:04 3/5	ft	16,600
1916	George Smith	J. Loftus	Star Hawk	Franklin	9	2:04	ft	9,750
1915	†Regret	J. Notter	Pebbles	‡Sharpshooter	16	2:05 2/5	ft	11,450
1914	‡Old Rosebud	J. McCabe	‡Hodge	‡Bronzewing	7	2:03 2/5	ft	9,125
1913	Donerail	R. Goose	Ten Point	†Gowell	8	2:04 4/5	ft	5,475
1912	Worth	C. Schilling	Duval	†Flamma	7	2:09 2/5	my	4,850
1911	Meridian	G. Archibald	‡Governor Gray	Colston	7	2:05	ft	4,850
1910	Donau	F. Herbert	Joe Morris	Fighting Bob	7	2:06 2/5	ft	4,850
1909	Wintergreen	V. Powers	‡Miami	Dr. Barkley	10	2:08 1/5	sl	4,850
1908	Stone Street	A. Pickens	‡Sir Cleges	Dunvegan	8	2:15 1/5	hy	4,850
1907	Pink Star	A. Minder	Zal	Ovelando	6	2:12 3/5	hy	4,850
1906	Sir Huon	R. Troxler	†Lady Navarre	James Reddick	6	2:08 4/5	ft	4,850
1905	Agile	J. Martin	Ram's Horn	Layson	3	2:10 3/4	hy	4,850
1904	Elwood	F. Prior	Ed Tierney	Brancas	5	2:08 1/2	ft	4,850
1903	Judge Himes	H. Booker	Early	Bourbon	6	2:09	ft	4,850
1902	Alan-a-Dale	J. Winkfield	Inventor	The Rival	4	2:08 3/4	ft	4,850
1901	His Eminence	J. Winkfield	Sannazarro	Driscoll	5	2:07 3/4	ft	4,850
1900	Lieut. Gibson	J. Boland	Florizar	Thrive	7	2:06 1/4	ft	4,850
1899	Manuel	F. Taral	‡Corsine	Mazo	5	2:12	ft	4,850
1898	Plaudit	W. Simms	Lieber Karl	Isabey	4	2:09	gd	4,850
1897	Typhoon II	F. Garner	Ornament	Dr. Catlett	6	2:12 1/2	hy	4,850
1896	Ben Brush	W. Simms	Ben Eder	Semper Ego	8	2:07 3/4	dy	4,850
1895	Halma	J. Perkins	Basso	Laureate	4	2:37 1/2	ft	2,970
1894	Chant	F. Goodale	Pearl Song	Sigurd	5	2:41	ft	4,020
1893	Lookout	E. Kunze	Plutus	Boundless	6	2:39 1/4	ft	3,840
1892	Azra	A. Clayton	Huron	Phil Dwyer	3	2:41 1/2	hy	4,230
1891	Kingman	I. Murphy	Balgowan	High Tariff	4	2:52 1/4	sl	4,550
1890	Riley	I. Murphy	Bill Letcher	Robespierre	6	2:45	my	5,460
1889	Spokane	T. Kiley	‡Proctor Knott	Once Again	8	2:34 1/2	ft	4,880
1888	‡Macbeth II	G. Covington	Gallifet	White	7	2:38 1/4	ft	4,740
1887	Montrose	I. Lewis	Jim Gore	‡Jacobin	7	2:39 1/4	ft	4,200
1886	Ben Ali	P. Duffy	Blue Wing	Free Knight	10	2:36 1/2	ft	4,890
1885	Joe Cotton	E. Henderson	Bersan	‡Ten Booker	10	2:37 1/4	gd	4,630
1884	Buchanan	I. Murphy	Loftin	Audrain	9	2:40 1/4	gd	3,990
1883	Leonatus	W. Donohue	‡Drake Carter	Lord Raglan	7	2:43	hy	3,760
1882	‡Apollo	B. Hurd	Runnymede	Bengal	14	2:40 1/4	gd	4,560
1881	Hindoo	J. McLaughlin	‡Lelex	Alfambra	6	2:40	ft	4,410
1880	Fonso	G. Lewis	Kimball	‡Bancroft	5	2:37 1/2	dy	3,800
1879	Lord Murphy	C. Shauer	Falsetto	Strathmore	9	2:37	ft	3,550
1878	Day Star	J. Carter	Himyar	Leveller	9	2:37 1/4	dy	4,050
1877	Baden-Baden	W. Walker	Leonard	King William	11	2:38	ft	3,300
1876	‡Vagrant	B. Swim	Creedmore	Harry Hill	11	2:38 1/4	ft	2,950
1875	Aristides	O. Lewis	Volcano	Verdigris	15	2:37 3/4	ft	2,850

†—filly, ‡—gelding, *—imported horse

1875-'95: 1 1/2 miles; 1973-present: Grade 1; 1968: Dancer's Image finished first but was disqualified from purse money; bold indicates records set in number of starters, time, and winning purse; War Emblem's record winning purse includes a $1-million bonus awarded by Sportman's Park for winning the Illinois Derby (G2) and a Triple Crown race. Smarty Jones's 2004 purse includes $5-million bonus from Oaklawn Park. Triple Crown winners are in all capitalized letters.

History of the Preakness Stakes

Born out of a party boast and named for a horse who met an unfortunate end, the Preakness Stakes (G1) is the second jewel of the American Triple Crown and the second-oldest American classic.

Both the Preakness Stakes and Pimlico Race Course, the track where the classic race is staged annually on the third Saturday of May, trace their roots to a party hosted by Milton H. Sanford in Saratoga Springs, New York, in 1868. At the party, Maryland Governor Oden Bowie promised that a new racetrack would open in Baltimore to play host to the Dinner Party Stakes, to which he pledged a hefty purse.

A 70-acre track site, which had been known as Pimlico since the 1850s and had been used for racing since then, was purchased by the Maryland Agricultural Society from Robert Wylie in 1866. The organization held a fair meet at the site in 1869 but failed to raise enough money to complete the track.

Bowie, a horse owner and sportsman, helped another group, the Maryland Jockey Club, to negotiate a lease of the property—$1,000 annual rent for ten years. Gen. John Elliott designed the track, and Pimlico opened on October 25, 1870. Among the amenities was the Pimlico Clubhouse, a Baltimore landmark until it was destroyed by fire in 1966.

Sanford, a New York horseman who made a portion of his fortune by selling blankets to the army in the Civil War, sent his three-year-old colt Preakness to make his only start of that year in the new Dinner Party Stakes. Bred in Kentucky by A. J. Alexander, Sanford bought the colt by Lexington out of Bay Leaf, by *Yorkshire, as a yearling for $2,000. He named the colt after his farms in New Jersey and Kentucky, which also bore the name Preakness. The name is derived from the language of the Minisi Indians in northern New Jersey; in their language, "pra-qua-les" meant "quail woods."

Under English jockey Billy Hayward, Preakness won the first Dinner Party Stakes, which today is known as the Dixie Stakes (G2) and is run on grass. Three years later, in 1873, the Maryland Jockey Club staged its first spring meeting and honored the winner of the first Dinner Party Stakes by naming the 1½-mile race for three-year-olds the Preakness Stakes.

Second race on a three-race program on Tuesday, May 23, 1873, the first Preakness Stakes attracted a field of seven to compete for the $2,050 total purse. A crowd estimated at 12,000 made Bowie's Catesby the favorite, but John Chamberlin's Survivor won by ten lengths, which until 2004 was the race's largest winning margin. In 2004, Roy and Patricia Chapman's Smarty Jones won by 11½ lengths.

Preakness Attendance

Year	On-Track	Total	Year	On-Track	Total
2008	112,222	121,876	1988	81,282	88,654
2007	121,263	132,221	1987		87,945
2006	118,402	128,643	1986		87,652
2005	115,318	125,687	1985		81,235
2004	112,668	124,351	1984		80,566
2003	100,268	109,931	1983		71,768
2002	101,138	117,055	1982		80,724
2001	104,454	118,926	1981		84,133
2000	98,304	111,821	1980		83,455
1999	100,311	116,526	1979		72,607
1998	91,122	103,269	1978		81,261
1997	88,594	102,118	1977		77,346
1996	85,122	97,751	1976		62,256
1995	87,707	100,818	1975		75,216
1994	86,343	99,834	1974		54,911
1993	85,495	97,641	1973		61,657
1992	85,294	96,865	1972		48,721
1991	87,245	96,695	1971		47,221
1990	86,531	96,106	1970		42,474
1989	90,145	98,896			

Total attendance figures from 1988 to 2000 include combined intertrack sites (Laurel, Rosecroft, Delmarva Downs) and exclude Maryland off-track betting sites. Total attendance in 2001-'08 includes Laurel.

Preakness, the horse for whom the race was named, continued to race until age eight, winning the 1875 Baltimore Cup and finishing in a dead heat with Springbok in that year's Saratoga Cup. Sold to England for stud, Preakness became difficult to handle in his later years and was shot to death by his owner, the Duke of Hamilton.

Pimlico staged the first 17 runnings of the Preakness, but the Maryland Jockey Club encountered financial difficulties in 1889, and the race was run the following year at Morris Park in New York. It was not run in 1891, '92, and '93—thus, though two years older than the Kentucky Derby, the Preakness has had one fewer running—and reappeared in 1894 at Gravesend Race Course in Brooklyn, where it would be renewed for 15 years.

Pimlico regained its financial health early in the new century, but the Preakness did not return to Baltimore until May 12, 1909, when Effendi set the pace and won by one length over Fashion Plate while running a mile in 1:39⅕. Unlike the Belmont Stakes, which was not run in 1911 and '12 because of New York antigambling legislation, the Preakness was run with betting through those years.

The race proved so popular that in 1918 the Preakness—then at 1⅛ miles—was run in two divisions, the only American classic race to be split. On May 14 of the following year, J.K.L. Ross's Sir Barton won the Preakness only four days after scoring his maiden victory in the Kentucky Derby. On June 11, 1919, the *Star Shoot colt defeated two opponents in the Belmont Stakes to become the first Triple Crown winner. The feat was noted after the fact when *Daily Racing Form* columnist

Charles Hatton popularized the designation for the three races beginning in 1930.

The Preakness's reputation was sealed in 1920 when the great Man o' War opened his three-year-old season with a 1½-length victory over Upset, the only horse ever to defeat him. The Preakness remained at 1⅛ miles until 1925, when it was changed to its present 1³⁄₁₆ miles.

In 1930, the Preakness was the first race of Gallant Fox's Triple Crown, but after '31 the race took its place as second in the series. In 1945, after victory in Europe led to the lifting of a voluntary ban on racing, the Preakness was run one week after the Derby and one week before the Belmont.

Pimlico was the scene of three memorable Triple Crown efforts in the 1970s: Secretariat's sweeping move to the lead on the clubhouse turn in 1973, Seattle Slew's brilliance in '77, and the stretch-long battle of Affirmed and Alydar in '78.

The race has had its share of controversy as well. In 1962, Greek Money won by a nose over Ridan, whose rider, Manuel Ycaza, claimed foul. A head-on photo, however, disclosed that Ycaza was in fact using his hands and elbows to restrain Greek Money. In 1980, Kentucky Derby winner Genuine Risk was herded wide at the top of the stretch by winner Codex, ridden by Angel Cordero Jr. An objection by Genuine Risk's jockey, Jacinto Vasquez, was disallowed, and Bertram Firestone, the filly's co-owner, forced a long Maryland Racing Commission hearing into the result. The original order of finish was upheld.

The Preakness in the 1980s and '90s was notable for two close finishes: Sunday Silence's 1989 nose victory over Easy Goer and the '97 race, in which Silver Charm won by a head over Free House, with third-place finisher Captain Bodgit another head farther back.

In 2002, '03, and '04, the Derby winners scored victories in the Preakness. War Emblem won in 2002, and Funny Cide romped by 9¾ lengths, then the second-largest margin, in '03. Funny Cide was only the seventh gelding to win the Preakness. Smarty Jones won in 2004 by a record 11½ lengths. In 2005, Afleet Alex overcame a near fall and won by 4¾ lengths.—*Don Clippinger*

Woodlawn Vase

The Woodlawn Vase, said to be the most valuable trophy in sports, is presented annually to the owner of the Preakness Stakes winner. The trophy, 34 inches tall and weighing almost 30 pounds, was created in 1860 by Tiffany and Co. for the Woodlawn Racing Association in Louisville.

After being buried during the Civil War to prevent it from being melted down, the trophy was unearthed and remained in Louisville until 1878, when the Dwyer brothers won it. They presented it to the Coney Island Jockey Club, and it was subsequently presented at two other New York tracks, Jerome Park and Morris Park.

Thomas C. Clyde won the trophy in 1904 and gave it to the Maryland Jockey Club, of which he was a director, in '17. That year, E. R. Bradley's Kalitan was the first horse to win the Woodlawn Vase at Pimlico.

A Preakness Tradition

A Preakness Stakes tradition observed each year is the painting of the winner's silks on a weather vane atop the Preakness presentation stand. The practice dates to 1909, when lightning destroyed a weather vane atop the Members' Clubhouse, which dated to 1870. The track's directors commissioned a new weather vane depicting a horse and rider, and the weather vane was adorned with the colors of Effendi that year.

The clubhouse structure, an ornate Victorian building that contained dining rooms, sleeping rooms, and a library, burned to the ground in June 1966. Since then, winner's colors have been painted on a weather vane atop an infield replica of the old clubhouse's cupola.

Black-Eyed Susans in the Spring

The black-eyed Susan, Maryland's state flower since 1918, blooms each summer and fall in Maryland and other states, but not in the spring. Thus, the black-eyed Susans that adorn the Preakness Stakes (G1) winner's garland are not black-eyed Susans. Actually, they are Viking daisies in disguise.

The ersatz black-eyed Susans were first draped across Bimelech's withers after the 1940 Preakness. Today, the garland is 18" wide and 90" long, and assembling it requires two days. First,

---

Added Value of the Preakness

The purse value of the Preakness Stakes has increased from $1,000 in 1873 to $1-million guaranteed, with the winner currently collecting a check for $650,000. The increase is significant; $1,000 in 1873 would equal only $14,210 today, which is the purse level of a good-quality claiming race.

The Preakness purse has been decreased on occasion, including once during the Great Depression (1933) and in consecutive years, 1949 and 1950. Following is the progression of the Preakness purse:

Year	Added Value	Year	Added Value
1998	*$1,000,000	1918	**$15,000
1989	500,000	1917	5,000
1985	350,000	1912	1,500
1979	200,000	1909	2,000
1959	150,000	1907	2,500
1953	100,000	1904	2,000
1951	75,000	1902	1,500
1950	50,000	1899	1,000
1949	75,000	1895	2,000
1946	100,000	1983	250,000
1937	50,000	1894	1,000
1933	25,000	1890	1,500
1922	50,000	1873	1,000
1921	40,000	* guaranteed purse	
1919	25,000	** each division	

greenery is attached to a spongy rubber base, and then more than 80 bunches of daisies are secured to the base. Heavy felt is then attached to the back to protect the horse. After that, black lacquer is daubed on the center of the daisies to simulate black-eyed Susans.

Origins of the Alibi Breakfast

The Alibi Breakfast, a Preakness-week tradition, is a direct descendant of the informal gatherings on the porch of the historic Old Clubhouse in the 1930s, when trainers, journalists, racing officials, and others would gather during training hours to watch the horses and swap stories.

David Woods, Pimlico Race Course's publicity director in the 1940s, formalized the get-togethers as a Preakness event at which owners and trainers could explain why they believed their horses would win, or take the opportunity to propose an alibi or two in case they did not win.

The track's principal awards—the Old Hilltop Award, Special Award of Merit, and the David F. Woods Memorial Award—are presented during the breakfast.

"Maryland, My Maryland"

While the roots of "My Old Kentucky Home" most likely were opposition to slavery, "Maryland, My Maryland" was originally a nine-stanza poem written in support of the Confederacy.

The author was James Ryder Randall, who wrote it in April 1861 to protest Union troops marching through Baltimore. A Maryland native, Randall was then teaching in Louisiana.

His poem was set to the tune of "Lauriger Horatius" ("O, Tannenbaum"), and the song achieved wide popularity in Maryland and throughout the South before becoming the official state song in 1939.

The two stanzas that are sung:

The despot's heel is on thy shore,
  Maryland!
His torch is at thy temple door,
  Maryland!
Avenge the patriotic gore
That flecked the streets of Baltimore,
And be the battle queen of yore,
  Maryland! My Maryland!
Thou wilt not cower in the dust,
  Maryland!
Thy beaming sword shall never rust,
  Maryland!
Remember Carroll's sacred trust,
Remember Howard's warlike thrust,
And all thy slumberers with the just,
  Maryland! My Maryland!

Preakness Trivia

• Derby winners in recent years were not necessarily favored in the Preakness. Since 1986, the following Derby winners did not go off as the Preakness favorites: Ferdinand, 1986, second; Sunday Silence, 1989, won; Lil E. Tee, 1992, fifth; Sea Hero, 1993, fifth; Silver Charm, 1997, won; Real Quiet, 1998, won; Charismatic, 1999, won; Giacomo, 2005, third.

• Two individuals have won the Preakness both as jockeys and trainers. Louis Schaefer rode Dr. Freeland to victory in 1929 and one decade later trained Challedon to a Preakness win. Johnny Longden rode Count Fleet in 1943 and trained Majestic Prince in '69.

• A starting gate was first used for the Preakness in 1930.

• The Preakness has been run at seven different distances since 1873. The race was as short as one mile in 1909 and '10, as long as 1¾ miles in 1889, and 1 3/16 miles since 1925.

• Two African-American jockeys have won the Preakness: George B. "Spider" Anderson aboard Buddhist in 1889 and Willie Simms on Sly Fox in '98. The only black jockey to ride in the Preakness in modern times was Wayne Barnett, who finished eighth aboard Sparrowvon in 1985.

• The Preakness preceded the Kentucky Derby on the racing calendar 11 times between 1888 and 1931.

• In 1890, the Preakness and the Belmont Stakes were run on the same card at Morris Park.

• From 1910 through '16, the Preakness was run as a handicap. From 1895 through 1907, the race was under allowance conditions, limiting it to horses that had not won a race worth a certain amount.

• The Preakness was run in divisions in 1918, when *War Cloud and Jack Hare Jr. won.

Leading Preakness Owners by Wins

7   **Calumet Farm:** Whirlaway, 1941; Pensive, 1944; Faultless, 1947; Citation, 1948; Fabius, 1956; Tim Tam, 1958; Forward Pass, 1968.

5   **George L. Lorillard:** Duke of Magenta, 1878; Harold, 1879; Grenada, 1880; Saunterer, 1881; Vanguard, 1882.

4   **Harry Payne Whitney:** Royal Tourist, 1908; Broomspun, 1921; Bostonian, 1927; Victorian, 1928.

3   **Belair Stud:** Gallant Fox, 1930; Omaha, 1935; Nashua, 1955.
    E. R. Bradley: Kalitan, 1917; Burgoo King, 1932; Bimelech, 1940.
    Robert and Beverly Lewis: Timber Country (co-owners), 1995; Silver Charm, 1997; Charismatic, 1999.
    Walter J. Salmon: Vigil, 1923; Display, 1926; Dr. Freeland, 1929.

2   **August Belmont II:** Don Enrique, 1907; Watervale, 1911.
    Brookmeade Stable: High Quest, 1934; Bold, 1951.
    J. F. Chamberlin: Survivor, 1873; Tom Ochiltree, 1875.
    Glen Riddle Farm: Man o' War, 1920; War Admiral, 1937.
    Loblolly Stable: Pine Bluff, 1992; Prairie Bayou, 1993.

2   **Overbrook Farm:** Tabasco Cat (co-owner), 1994; Timber Country (co-owner), 1995.
    Preakness Stable: Montague, 1890; Belmar, 1895.
    J. K. L. Ross: Damrosch, 1916; Sir Barton, 1919.
    The Thoroughbred Corp.: Point Given, 2001; War Emblem 2002.

Owners with Most Preakness Starters

Owner	Starters	Wins
Greentree Stable	20	1
Harry Payne Whitney	15	4
Calumet Farm	14	7
August Belmont II	11	2
George L. Lorillard	11	5
Overbrook Farm	11	2
Brookmeade Stable	9	2
King Ranch	8	1
Robert and Beverly Lewis	8	3
Pierre Lorillard	8	1
Wheatley Stable	7	1
Rancocas Stable	6	0
Mrs. Ethel D. Jacobs	6	1

Leading Preakness Breeders by Wins

7   **Calumet Farm:** Whirlaway, 1941; Pensive, 1944; Faultless, 1947; Citation, 1948; Fabius, 1956; Tim Tam, 1958; Forward Pass, 1968.

6   **Harry Payne Whitney:** Royal Tourist, 1908; Buskin, 1913; Holiday, 1914; Broomspun, 1921; Bostonian, 1927; Victorian, 1928.
    August Belmont II: Jacobus, 1883; Margrave, 1896; Don Enrique, 1907; Watervale, 1911; Damrosch, 1916; Man o' War, 1920.

4   **A. J. Alexander:** Tom Ochiltree, 1875; Shirley, 1876; Duke of Magenta, 1878; Grenada, 1880.

3   **Belair Stud:** Gallant Fox, 1930; Omaha, 1935; Nashua, 1955.
    James Ben Ali Haggin: Old England, 1902; Cairngorm, 1905; Rhine Maiden, 1915.

2   **William S. Farish:** Summer Squall (co-breeder), 1990; Charismatic (co-breeder), 1999.
    Idle Hour Stock Farm: Burgoo King (co-breeder), 1932; Bimelech, 1940.
    Loblolly Stable: Pine Bluff, 1992; Prairie Bayou, 1993.
    Raceland Stud: Whimsical, 1906; Colonel Holloway, 1912.
    Walter J. Salmon: Display, 1926; Dr. Freeland, 1929.
    R. W. Walden: Vanguard, 1882; Refund, 1882.
    Aristides Welch: Harold, 1879; Saunterer, 1881.

Leading Preakness Trainers by Wins

7   **R. Wyndham Walden:** Tom Ochiltree, 1875; Duke of Magenta, 1878; Harold, 1879; Grenada, 1880; Saunterer, 1881; Vanguard, 1882; Refund, 1888.

5   **Thomas J. Healey:** The Parader, 1901; Pillory, 1922; Vigil, 1923; Display, 1926; Dr. Freeland, 1929.
    D. Wayne Lukas: Codex, 1980; Tank's Prospect, 1985; Tabasco Cat, 1994; Timber Country, 1995; Charismatic, 1999.

4   **Bob Baffert:** Silver Charm, 1997; Real Quiet, 1998; Point Given, 2001; War Emblem, 2002.
    James E. "Sunny Jim" Fitzsimmons: Gallant Fox, 1930; Omaha, 1935; Nashua, 1955; Bold Ruler, 1957.
    H. A. "Jimmy" Jones: Faultless, 1947; Citation, 1948; Fabius, 1956; Tim Tam, 1958.

3   **James Whalen:** Don Enrique, 1907; Watervale, 1911; Buskin, 1913.

2   **Thomas Bohannan:** Pine Bluff, 1992; Prairie Bayou, 1993.
    Edward Feakes: Montague, 1890; Belmar, 1895.
    Henry Forrest: Kauai King, 1966; Forward Pass, 1968.
    T. P. Hayes: Paul Kauvar, 1897; Head Play, 1933.
    J. S. Healey: Layminster, 1910; Holiday, 1914.
    Max Hirsch: Bold Venture, 1936; Assault, 1946.
    William Hurley: Kalitan, 1917; Bimelech, 1940.
    B. A. "Ben" Jones: Whirlaway, 1941; Pensive, 1944.
    Andrew W. Joyner: Cairngorm, 1905; Royal Tourist, 1908.
    Jack Van Berg: Gate Dancer, 1984; Alysheba, 1987.
    Frank Y. Whiteley Jr.: Tom Rolfe, 1965; Damascus, 1967.

Trainers with Most Starters

Trainer	Starters	Wins
D. Wayne Lukas	32	5
Max Hirsch	19	2
Nicholas Zito	19	1
James E. Fitzsimmons	18	4
James Rowe Sr.	14	1
Bob Baffert	9	4
Woody Stephens	9	1
Preston Burch	8	1
John P. Campo	8	1

Female Trainers in the Preakness

Here are the female trainers with Preakness starters:

Year	Horse	Trainer	Finish
2004	Imperialism	Kristin Mulhall	5th
	Water Cannon	Linda Albert	10th
2003	New York Hero	Jennifer Pedersen	6th
	Kissin Saint	Lisa Lewis	10th
2002	Magic Weisner	Nancy H. Alberts	2nd
2001	Griffinite	Jennifer Leigh-Peterson	5th
1998	Silver's Prospect	Jean Rolfe	10th
1996	In Contention	Cynthia Reese	6th
1993	Hegar	Penny Lewis	9th
1992	Casual Lies	Shelley Riley	3rd
	Speakerphone	Dean Gaudet	14th
1990	Fighting Notion	Nancy Heil	5th
1980	Samoyed	Judith Zouck	6th
1968	Sir Beau	Judy Johnson	7th

Leading Preakness Jockeys by Wins

Eddie Arcaro, known as "The Master," held sway over the Preakness Stakes in his storied career, winning the race six times in 15 starts. His closest challenger is Pat Day, who has won the race three consecutive times, 1994-'96, and has five victories with 17 Preakness starters.

The leading Preakness jockeys with two or more victories:

6   **Eddie Arcaro:** Whirlaway, 1941; Citation, 1948; Hill Prince, 1950; Bold, 1951; Nashua, 1955; Bold Ruler, 1957.

5   **Pat Day:** Tank's Prospect, 1985; Summer Squall, 1990; Tabasco Cat, 1994; Timber Country, 1995; Louis Quatorze, 1996.

3   **George Barbee:** Survivor, 1873; Shirley, 1876; Jacobus, 1883.
    William Hartack: Fabius, 1956; Northern Dancer, 1964; Majestic Prince, 1969.

3 **L. Hughes:** Tom Ochiltree, 1875; Harold, 1879; Grenada, 1880.
2 **Jerry Bailey:** Hansel, 1991; Red Bullet, 2000.
Angel Cordero Jr.: Codex, 1980; Gate Dancer, 1984.
Costello: Saunterer, 1881; Vanguard, 1882.
Kent Desormeaux: Real Quiet, 1998; Big Brown, 2008.
Fisher: Knight of Ellersie, 1884; The Bard, 1886.
C. Holloway: Cloverbrook, 1877; Duke of Magenta, 1878.
Clarence Kummer: Man o' War, 1920; Coventry, 1925.
Charles Kurtsinger: Head Play, 1933; War Admiral, 1937.
John Loftus: War Cloud, 1918; Sir Barton, 1919.
Chris McCarron: Alysheba, 1987; Pine Bluff, 1992.
Conn McCreary: Pensive, 1944; Blue Man, 1952.
Bill Shoemaker: Candy Spots, 1963; Damascus, 1967.
Gary Stevens: Silver Charm, 1997; Point Given, 2001.
Fred Taral: Assignee, 1894; Belmar, 1895.
Ismael Valenzuela: Tim Tam, 1958; Forward Pass, 1968.

Jockeys With Most Preakness Mounts

Jockey	Starts	Wins
Pat Day	17	5
Gary Stevens	16	2
Eddie Arcaro	15	6
Jerry Bailey	15	2
Angel Cordero Jr.	13	2
Chris McCarron	13	2
Bill Shoemaker	12	2
Kent Desormeaux	11	2
William Hartack	11	3
Edgar Prado	11	0
Jorge Velasquez	11	1
Braulio Baeza	10	0
Linus McAtee	10	1
Mike Smith	10	1

Female Jockeys in the Preakness

Only two female jockeys have ridden in the Preakness, and the best finish was by Patricia Cooksey, who was sixth aboard Tajawa in 1985. Andrea Seefeldt, a Maryland-based rider, finished seventh in 1994 aboard Looming.

Jockey	Year	Horse	Finish
Andrea Seefeldt	1994	Looming	7th
Patricia Cooksey	1985	Tajawa	6th

Leading Preakness Sires by Wins

3 **Lexington:** Tom Ochiltree, 1875; Shirley, 1876; Duck of Magenta, 1878.
Broomstick: Holiday, 1914; Broomspun, 1921; Bostonian, 1927.
2 ***Leamington:** Harold, 1879; Saunterer, 1881.
***Watercress:** Watervale, 1911; Rhine Maiden, 1915.
Fair Play: Man o' War, 1920; Display, 1926.
***Sir Gallahad III:** Gallant Fox, 1930; High Quest, 1934.
Bull Lea: Faultless, 1947; Citation, 1948.
***Nasrullah:** Nashua, 1955; Bold Ruler, 1957.
Sovereign Dancer: Gate Dancer, 1984; Louis Quatorze, 1996.
Woodman: Hansel, 1991; Timber Country, 1995.

Preakness in the Pedigree

Preakness winners who have sired other Preakness winners:

Man o' War (1920): War Admiral (1937)
Gallant Fox (1930): Omaha (1935)
Bold Venture (1936): Assault (1946)
Polynesian (1945): Native Dancer (1953)
Citation (1948): Fabius (1956)
Native Dancer (1953): Kauai King (1966)
Bold Ruler (1957): Secretariat (1973)
Secretariat (1973): Risen Star (1988)
Summer Squall (1990): Charismatic (1999)

Supplemental Nominations to the Preakness

When Triple Crown Productions launched a common nomination in 1986, no supplemental entries were permitted. The rules were changed in 1991 to allow supplemental entries, although no horse owner has yet to put up $100,000 to gain a place in the Preakness Stakes starting gate.

Supplemental entries to the Preakness were first permitted in 1938, and the first supplemental entrant to win was Citation, who won the '48 Triple Crown. Calumet Farm owner Warren Wright supplemented both Citation and Coaltown for $3,000 each, but only Citation started. Hill Prince (1950) and Master Derby ('75) were supplemental winners.

Here are the supplemented Preakness starters since 1959:

Year	Horse	Supplement	Finish	Purse Winnings
1985	Tajawa	$20,000	6th	$ 0
	Sport Jet	20,000	10th	0
	Hajji's Treasure	20,000	11th	0
1984	Fight Over	15,000	3rd	30,000
1982	Reinvested	10,000	6th	0
1981	Paristo	10,000	3rd	20,000
1980	Lucky Pluck	10,000	8th	0
1975	**Master Derby**	10,000	1st	158,100
	Native Guest	10,000	7th	0
1974	Super Florin	10,000	10th	0
1970	Dust Commander	10,000	9th	0
1968	Nodouble	10,000	3rd*	15,000
1967	Barb's Delight	10,000	6th	0
1959	Manassah Mauler	10,000	8th	0

* moved up from fourth via disqualification

Fastest Preakness Winning Times

Tank's Prospect and Louis Quatorze share the record for the fastest running of the Preakness Stakes, 1:53⅖. Louis Quatorze, the 1996 winner, was timed in 1:53.43, but Tank's Prospect in 1985 was timed in one-fifths of a second, the standard at that time.

Unofficially, Secretariat ran the Preakness's $1\frac{3}{16}$ miles in the same time. He was caught in 1:53⅖ by *Daily Racing Form* clockers who were hand-timing the race. A malfunctioning official timer recorded a time of 1:55, but that was subsequently adjusted to 1:54⅖.

Year	Winner	Time	Cond.
1985	Tank's Prospect	1:53⅖	Fast
1996	Louis Quatorze	1:53.43	Fast
2007	Curlin	1:53.46	Fast
1984	Gate Dancer	1:53⅗	Fast
1990	Summer Squall	1:53⅗	Fast
1989	Sunday Silence	1:53⅘	Fast
1971	Canonero II	1:54	Fast
1991	Hansel	1:54.05	Fast
1979	Spectacular Bid	1:54⅕	Good
1980	Codex	1:54⅕	Fast
1973	Secretariat	1:54⅖*	Fast
1977	Seattle Slew	1:54⅖	Fast
1978	Affirmed	1:54⅖	Fast
1995	Timber Country	1:54.45	Fast
1981	Pleasant Colony	1:54⅗	Fast
1974	Little Current	1:54⅗	Good
1955	Nashua	1:54⅗	Fast
2006	Bernardini	1:54.65	Fast
2008	Big Brown	1:54.80	Fast

* Hand-timed in 1:53⅖

Evolution of Preakness Stakes Record

Year	Winner	Time
1925	Coventry	1:59
1934	High Quest	1:58⅕
1942	Alsab	1:57
1949	Capot	1:56
1955	Nashua	1:54⅗
1971	Canonero II	1:54
1984	Gate Dancer	1:53⅗
1985	Tank's Prospect	1:53⅖
1996	Louis Quatorze	1:53⅖ (1:53.43)

Fastest Preakness Fractions

First Quarter-Mile: :22⅖ Flag Raiser (1965), Fight Over (1984), Eternal Prince (1985), Vicar (1999).

First Half-Mile: :45, Bold Forbes (1976).

First Six Furlongs: 1:09, Bold Forbes (1976).

Fastest First Mile: 1:34⅕, Chief's Crown (1985), Sunday Silence (1989).

Fastest Final Three-Sixteenths: :18, Summer Squall, 1990.

Slowest Preakness Winning Times

Citation, a Triple Crown winner and regarded as one of the greatest Thoroughbreds of the 20th century, ran the slowest Preakness Stakes ever, 2:02⅖. But the *Daily Racing Form* chart characterized the track as heavy, which would have been considerably slower than today's speed-tuned racing surfaces.

Following are the slowest Preakness runnings since 1925, when the race's distance became $1\frac{3}{16}$ miles.

Year	Winner	Time	Cond.
1948	Citation	2:02⅖	Heavy
1933	Head Play	2:02	Slow
1927	Bostonian	2:01⅗	Good
1929	Dr. Freeland	2:01⅗	Fast
1946	Assault	2:01⅖	Fast
1930	Gallant Fox	2:00⅗	Fast
1928	Victorian	2:00⅕	Fast
1932	Burgoo King	1:59⅘	Fast
1938	Dauber	1:59⅘	Sloppy
1939	Challedon	1:59⅘	Muddy
1926	Display	1:59⅘	Fast
1950	Hill Prince	1:59⅕	Slow
1944	Pensive	1:59⅕	Fast

Largest Winning Margins

Year	Winner	Lengths
2004	Smarty Jones	11½
1873	Survivor	10
2003	Funny Cide	9¾
1943	Count Fleet	8
1889	Buddhist	8
1991	Hansel	7
1974	Little Current	7
1951	Bold	7
1938	Dauber	7
1968	Forward Pass	6
1935	Omaha	6
1878	Duke of Magenta	6
1979	Spectacular Bid	5½
1948	Citation	5½
1941	Whirlaway	5½
2006	Bernardini	5¼
2008	Big Brown	5¼
1950	Hill Prince	5
1912	Colonel Holloway	5

Smallest Winning Margins

Year	Winner	Margin
1989	Sunday Silence	nose
1962	Greek Money	nose
1936	Bold Venture	nose
1934	High Quest	nose
1928	Victorian	nose
1902	Old England	nose
2007	Curlin	head
1997	Silver Charm	head
1985	Tank's Prospect	head
1969	Majestic Prince	head
1949	Capot	head
1937	War Admiral	head
1932	Burgoo King	head
1926	Display	head
1922	Pillory	head
1905	Cairngorm	head
1900	Hindus	head

Preakness Odds-On Beaten Favorites

The shortest-priced beaten favorites in the Preakness Stakes were Riva Ridge in 1972 and Fusaichi Pegasus in 2000. Both entered the

Preakness off Derby victories and both went off at 3-to-10. Riva Ridge fell to Bee Bee Bee on a sloppy track, and Fusaichi Pegasus finished second to Red Bullet.

Here are the odds-on beaten favorites in the Preakness:

Year	Horse	Odds	Finish
2006	Barbaro	0.50-to-1	DNF
2000	Fusaichi Pegasus	0.30-to-1	2nd
1972	Riva Ridge	0.30-to-1	4th
1939	Gilded Knight-Johnstown entry	0.45-to-1	2nd 5th
1982	Linkage	0.50-to-1	2nd
1989	Easy Goer	0.60-to-1	2nd
1956	Needles	0.60-to-1	2nd
1984	Swale	0.80-to-1	7th
1964	Hill Rise	0.80-to-1	3rd
1976	Honest Pleasure	0.90-to-1	5th
1954	Correlation	0.90-to-1	2nd

Shortest-Priced Preakness Winners

Year	Winner	Odds
1979	Spectacular Bid	0.10-to-1
1948	Citation	0.10-to-1
1943	Count Fleet	0.15-to-1
2008	Big Brown	0.20-to-1
1953	Native Dancer	0.20-to-1
1973	Secretariat	0.30-to-1
1955	Nashua	0.30-to-1
1937	War Admiral	0.35-to-1
1977	Seattle Slew	0.40-to-1
1934	High Quest	0.45-to-1
1978	Affirmed	0.50-to-1

Longest-Priced Preakness Winners

Year	Winner	Odds
1975	Master Derby	23.40-to-1
1925	Coventry	21.80-to-1
1926	Display	19.35-to-1
1972	Bee Bee Bee	18.70-to-1
1983	Deputed Testamony	14.50-to-1
1974	Little Current	13.10-to-1
2006	Bernardini	12.90-to-1
1924	Nellie Morse	12.10-to-1
1945	Polynesian	12-to-1
1922	Pillory	11.15-to-1
1962	Greek Money	10.90-to-1
1976	Elocutionist	10.10-to-1

Preakness Front-Running Winners

The following Preakness winners were on the lead at all points of call, beginning at a quarter-mile (approaching the clubhouse turn). Regarded as speed horses, neither Seattle Slew nor Affirmed led the opening quarter-mile in the Preakness.

Year	Winner	Winning Margin
1996	Louis Quatorze	3¼
1982	Aloma's Ruler	½
1972	Bee Bee Bee	1½
1960	Bally Ache	4
1957	Bold Ruler	2
1954	Hasty Road	neck
1951	Bold	7
1948	Citation	5½
1945	Polynesian	2½

Preakness Wagering, 1980-2008

Year	Preakness Winner	Preakness In-State Handle	Preakness Simulcasting	Preakness Total Handle
2008	Big Brown	$2,758,591	$42,930,971	$45,689,562
2007	Curlin	3,624,860	53,428,219	57,053,079
2006	Bernardini	3,710,548	52,684,102	56,394,560
2005	Afleet Alex	4,079,858	56,781,232	60,861,090
2004	Smarty Jones	3,808,863	54,982,543	58,791,406
2003	Funny Cide	3,151,864	38,008,281	41,620,145
2002	War Emblem	3,440,321	44,254,871	47,695,192
2001	Point Given	3,342,237	37,352,557	40,694,884
2000	Red Bullet	2,482,262	26,550,064	29,032,326
1999	Charismatic	3,056,891	26,438,761	34,435,703
1998	Real Quiet	2,103,027	17,624,933	23,640,365
1997	Silver Charm	2,667,000	18,087,214	26,602,245
1996	Louis Quatorze	2,352,900	20,545,618	22,898,518
1995	Timber Country	2,519,388	20,869,915	23,389,303
1994	Tabasco Cat	2,548,282	21,461,540	24,009,822
1993	Prairie Bayou	2,269,946	19,293,287	21,563,233
1992	Pine Bluff	2,365,023	19,338,393	21,703,416
1991	Hansel	2,504,693	18,289,622	20,794,315
1990	Summer Squall	2,257,916	16,625,833	18,883,749
1989	Sunday Silence	2,519,893	17,306,821	19,826,714
1988	Risen Star	2,392,384	18,519,289	20,911,673
1987	Alysheba	1,846,768		
1986	Snow Chief	1,680,923		
1985	Tank's Prospect	1,461,997		
1884	Gate Dancer	1,358,444		
1983	Deputed Testamony	1,251,931		
1982	Aloma's Ruler	1,257,244		
1981	Pleasant Colony	1,387,797		
1980	Codex	1,215,664		

Triple Crown — Preakness Stakes

Year	Winner	Winning Margin
1943	Count Fleet	8
1940	Bimelech	3
1937	War Admiral	head
1934	High Quest	nose
1933	Head Play	4
1920	Man o' War	1½
1919	Sir Barton	4
1918	Jack Hare Jr.	2
1915	Rhine Maiden	1½
1914	Holiday	¾
1911	Watervale	1
1909	Effendi	1
1902	Old England	nose
1899	Half Time	1
1896	Margrave	1
1889	Buddhist	8
1882	Vanguard	neck

Winning Preakness Favorites Since 1979

Year	Winner	Odds
2008	Big Brown	0.20-to-1
2005	Afleet Alex	3.30-to-1
2004	Smarty Jones	0.70-to-1
2003	Funny Cide	1.90-to-1
2002	War Emblem	2.80-to-1
2001	Point Given	2.30-to-1
1995	Timber Country	1.90-to-1
1993	Prairie Bayou	2.20-to-1
1992	Pine Bluff	7-to-2
1987	Alysheba	2-to-1
1981	Pleasant Colony	3-to-2
1979	Spectacular Bid	1-to-10

Winning Preakness Post Positions

Since 1909, Preakness Stakes winners have come out of the sixth post position 16 times. Only two Preakness winners, Display in 1926 and Point Given in 2001, have come out of the 11th starting position.

Thirteen winners have come out of the fourth hole, and 11 each have broken from the second, third, and seventh slots.

Here are the winning post positions since 1909:

Post	Winners	Post	Winners
1	9	7	11
2	11	8	10
3	11	9	3
4	13	10	2
5	10	11	2
6	16	12	3

Preakness Wins by Geldings

Year	Winner
2003	Funny Cide
1993	Prairie Bayou
1914	Holiday
1913	Buskin
1910	Layminster
1907	Don Enrique
1876	Shirley

Geldings were barred from 1920-'34.

Geldings in the Preakness

Year	Gelding	Finish
2008	Tres Borrachos	9
2006	Sweetnorthernsaint	2
	Like Now	7
2005	Scrappy T	2
	Galloping Grocer	13
2004	Water Cannon	10
2003	**Funny Cide**	**1**
	Foufa's Warrior	7
2002	Magic Weisner	2
	Menacing Dennis	10
1999	Valhol	9
1998	Hot Wells	4
1997	Cryp Too	9
1996	Cavonnier	4
	Secreto de Estado	9
1994	Silver Goblin	8
	Polar Expedition	10
1993	**Prairie Bayou**	**1**
	Koluctoo Jimmy Al	10
1992	Dash for Dotty	8
1991	Best Pal	5
1990	Fighting Notion	5
	J. R.'s Horizon	9
1986	Miracle Wood	5
1985	Sparrowvon	8

Fillies in the Preakness

Since Genuine Risk finished second behind Codex in the controversial 1980 Preakness Stakes, only two other fillies have run in the race. Winning Colors finished a valiant third behind Risen Star after Forty Niner pressed her early, and Excellent Meeting did not finish in the 1999 Preakness.

Four fillies have won the Preakness: Flocarline in 1903, Whimsical in '06, Rhine Maiden in '15, and Nellie Morse in '24.

Here are the 52 fillies to compete in the Preakness:

Year	Horse	Owner	Finish
1999	Excellent Meeting	Golden Eagle Farm	DNF
1988	Winning Colors	Mr. & Mrs. Eugene V. Klein	3rd
1980	Genuine Risk	Diana Firestone	2nd
1939	Ciencia	King Ranch	6th
1937	Jewell Dorsett	J. W. Brown	8th
1935	Nellie Flag	Calumet Farm	7th
1930	Snowflake	W J. Salmon	3rd
1928	Bateau	W. M. Jeffords	8th
1927	Fair Star	Foxcatcher Farm	6th
1925	Maid At Arms	Glen Riddle Farm	11th
1924	**Nellie Morse**	H. C. Fisher	1st
1923	Sally's Alley	W. S. Kilmer	11th
1922	Miss Joy	Montford Jones	10th
1921	Polly Ann	S. L. Jenkins	2nd
	Careful	W. J. Salmon	12th
	Lough Storm	E. B. McLean	13th
1919	Milkmaid	J.K.L. Ross	8th
1918	Mary Maud	C. E. Clements	6th
1918	Quietude	A. H. Morris	9th
	Kate Bright	A. Neal	3rd
1917	Fruit Cake	E. T. Zollicoffer	4th
	Fox Trot	J. E. Griffith	14th

Triple Crown — Preakness Stakes

Year	Horse	Owner	Finish
1915	**Rhine Maiden**	E. F. Whitney	1st
1913	Cadeau	J. G. Oxnard	5th
1912	Jeannette B.	C. C. Smithson	5th
1911	Heatherbroom	E. B. Cassatt	6th
1909	Hill Top	R. Angarola	3rd
	Arondack	Mrs. J. McLaughlin	6th
	Sans Souci II	G. J. Kraus	7th
	Grania	A. Garson	8th
1906	**Whimsical**	T. J. Gaynor	1st
	Content	W. Clay	2nd
	Flip Flap	J. A. Bennet	7th
	Fatinitza	Palestine Stable	8th
1905	Kiamesha	Oneck Stable	2nd
	Coy Maid	Kenilworth Stable	3rd
	Bohemia	Albemarle Stable	5th
	Iota	H. B. Duryea	9th
1904	Possession	C. Oxx	7th
	Flammula	W. H. Kraft	8th
1903	**Flocarline**	M. H. Tichenor & Co.	1st
1902	Barouche	W. H. McCorkle	6th
	Sun Shower	Jere Dunn	7th

Year	Horse	Owner	Finish
1901	Sadie S.	P. H. Sullivan	2nd
1896	Intermission	J. E. McDonald	3rd
	Cassette	A. Clason	4th
1895	Sue Kittie	O. A. Jones	3rd
	Bombazette	C. Littlefield Jr.	7th
1894	Flirt	Manhattan Stable	13th
1881	Aella	George L. Lorillard	6th
1880	Emily F.	J. J. Bevins	3rd
1875	Australind	Harbeck & Johnson	7th

Birthplaces of Preakness Winners

State	Winners	State	Winners
Kentucky	90	New York	3
Maryland	8	Tennessee	2
Florida	7	Ohio	1
Pennsylvania	6	Texas	1
Virginia	6	Canada	1
California	4	England	1
New Jersey	4		

Status of Preakness Winners Since 1970

Year	Winner	Birthdate	Status	Where Stands or Stood	Location	Death Date
2008	Big Brown	4/10/2005	In training			
2007	Curlin	3/25/2004	In training			
2006	Bernardini	3/23/2003	Stallion	Darley	Lexington, Ky.	
2005	Afleet Alex	5/9/2002	Stallion	Gainesway	Lexington, Ky.	
2004	Smarty Jones	2/28/2001	Stallion	Three Chimneys Farm	Midway, Ky.	
2003	Funny Cide	4/20/2000	Retired			
2002	War Emblem	2/20/1999	Stallion	Shadai Stallion Station	Hokkaido, Japan	
2001	Point Given	3/27/1998	Stallion	Three Chimneys Farm	Midway, Ky.	
2000	Red Bullet	4/13/1997	Stallion	Adena Springs South	Ocala, Fl.	
1999	Charismatic	3/13/1996	Stallion	JBBA Shizunai Stallion Station	Hokkaido, Japan	
1998	Real Quiet	3/7/1995	Stallion	Penn Ridge Farms	Harrisburg, Pa.	
1997	Silver Charm	2/22/1994	Stallion	JBBA Shizunai Stallion Station	Hokkaido, Japan	
1996	Louis Quatorze	3/13/1993	Stallion	Murmur Farm	Darlington, Md.	
1995	Timber Country	4/12/1992	Stallion	Shadai Stallion Station	Hokkaido, Japan	
1994	Tabasco Cat	4/15/1991	Deceased	JBBA Shizunai Stallion Station	Hokkaido, Japan	3/6/2004
1993	Prairie Bayou	3/14/1990	Deceased			6/5/1993
1992	Pine Bluff	5/10/1989	Stallion	Kilkerry Farm	Royal, Ar.	
1991	Hansel	3/12/1988	Pensioned	Lazy Lane Farms	Upperville, Va.	
1990	Summer Squall	3/12/1987	Pensioned	Lane's End	Versailles, Ky.	
1989	Sunday Silence	3/25/1986	Deceased	Shadai Stallion Station	Hokkaido, Japan	8/19/2002
1988	Risen Star	3/25/1985	Deceased	Walmac International	Lexington, Ky.	3/13/1998
1987	Alysheba	3/3/1984	Stallion	Janadriyah Stud Farm	Aljanadriya, Saudi Arabia	
1986	Snow Chief	3/17/1983	Stallion	Eagle Oak Ranch	Paso Robles, Ca.	
1985	Tank's Prospect	5/2/1982	Deceased	Venture Farms	Pilot Point, Tx.	3/2/1995
1984	Gate Dancer	3/31/1981	Deceased	Silverleaf Farm	Orange Lake, Fl.	3/6/1998
1983	Deputed Testamony	5/7/1980	Pensioned	Bonita Farm	Darlington, Md.	
1982	Aloma's Ruler	4/21/1979	Deceased	B & B Farm	Monee, Il.	6/21/2003
1981	Pleasant Colony	5/4/1978	Deceased	Lane's End	Versailles, Ky.	12/31/2002
1980	Codex	2/28/1977	Deceased	Tartan Farms	Ocala, Fl.	8/20/1984
1979	Spectacular Bid	2/17/1976	Deceased	Milfer Farm	Unadilla, Ny.	6/9/2003
1978	Affirmed	2/21/1975	Deceased	Jonabell Farm	Lexington, Ky.	1/12/2001
1977	Seattle Slew	2/15/1974	Deceased	Three Chimneys Farm	Midway, Ky.	5/7/2002
1976	Elocutionist	3/4/1973	Deceased	Airdrie Stud	Midway, Ky.	3/30/1995
1975	Master Derby	4/24/1972	Deceased	Not Just Another Horse Farm	Chino, Ca.	1/22/1999
1974	Little Current	4/5/1971	Deceased	Pacific Equine Clinic	Monroe, Wa.	1/19/2003
1973	Secretariat	3/30/1970	Deceased	Claiborne Farm	Paris, Ky.	10/4/1989
1972	Bee Bee Bee	4/3/1969	Deceased	JBBA Stallion Station	Hokkaido, Japan	
1971	Canonero II	4/24/1968	Deceased	Gainesway	Lexington, Ky.	11/11/1981
1970	Personality	5/27/1967	Deceased		Japan	1990

Preakness Stakes

Grade 1, Pimlico Race Course, three-year-olds, $1\frac{3}{16}$ miles, dirt. Held on May 17, 2008, with gross value of $1,000,000. First run in 1873. Weights: colts and geldings, 126 pounds; fillies, 121 pounds.

Year	**Winner**	**Jockey**	**Second**	**Third**	**Strs**	**Time**	**Track**	**1st Purse**
2008	**Big Brown**	K. Desormeaux	Macho Again	Icabad Crane	12	1:54.80	ft	$600,000
2007	**Curlin**	R. Albarado	Street Sense	Hard Spun	9	1:53.46	ft	600,000
2006	**Bernardini**	J. Castellano	Sweetnorthernsaint	Hemingway's Key	9	1:54.65	ft	600,000
2005	**Afleet Alex**	J. Rose	Scrappy T	Giacomo	14	1:55.04	ft	650,000
2004	**Smarty Jones**	S. Elliott	Rock Hard Ten	Eddington	10	1:55.59	ft	650,000
2003	**‡Funny Cide**	J. Santos	Midway Road	Scrimshaw	10	1:55.61	gd	650,000
2002	**War Emblem**	V. Espinoza	Magic Weisner	Proud Citizen	13	1:56.36	ft	650,000
2001	**Point Given**	G. Stevens	A P Valentine	Congaree	11	1:55.51	ft	650,000
2000	**Red Bullet**	J. Bailey	Fusaichi Pegasus	Impeachment	8	1:56.04	gd	650,000
1999	**Charismatic**	C. Antley	Menifee	Badge	13	1:55.32	ft	650,000
1998	**Real Quiet**	K. Desormeaux	Victory Gallop	Classic Cat	10	1:54.75	ft	**650,000**
1997	**Silver Charm**	G. Stevens	Free House	Captain Bodgit	10	1:54.84	ft	488,150
1996	**Louis Quatorze**	P. Day	Skip Away	Editor's Note	12	**1:53.43**	ft	458,120
1995	**Timber Country**	P. Day	Oliver's Twist	Thunder Gulch	11	1:54.45	ft	446,810
1994	**Tabasco Cat**	P. Day	Go for Gin	Concern	10	1:56.47	ft	447,720
1993	**‡Prairie Bayou**	M. Smith	Cherokee Run	‡El Bakan	12	1:56.61	ft	471,835
1992	**Pine Bluff**	C. McCarron	Alydeed	Casual Lies	14	1:55.60	gd	484,120
1991	**Hansel**	J. Bailey	Corporate Report	Mane Minister	8	1:54	ft	432,770
1990	**Summer Squall**	P. Day	Unbridled	Mister Frisky	9	1:53⅗	ft	445,900
1989	**Sunday Silence**	P. Valenzuela	Easy Goer	Rock Point	8	1:53⅘	ft	438,230
1988	**Risen Star**	E. Delahoussaye	Brian's Time	†Winning Colors	9	1:56⅕	gd	413,700
1987	**Alysheba**	C. McCarron	Bet Twice	Cryptoclearance	9	1:55⅘	ft	421,100
1986	**Snow Chief**	A. Solis	Ferdinand	Broad Brush	7	1:54⅘	ft	411,900
1985	**Tank's Prospect**	P. Day	Chief's Crown	Eternal Prince	11	**1:53⅖**	ft	423,200
1984	**Gate Dancer**	A. Cordero Jr.	Play On	Fight Over	10	1:53⅗	ft	243,600
1983	**Deputed Testamony**	D. A. Miller Jr.	Desert Wine	High Honors	12	1:55⅖	sy	251,200
1982	**Aloma's Ruler**	J. Kaenel	Linkage	Cut Away	7	1:55⅖	ft	209,900
1981	**Pleasant Colony**	J. Velasquez	Bold Ego	Paristo	13	1:54⅗	ft	200,800
1980	**Codex**	A. Cordero Jr.	†Genuine Risk	Colonel Moran	8	1:54⅕	ft	180,600
1979	**Spectacular Bid**	R. Franklin	Golden Act	Screen King	5	1:54⅕	gd	165,300
1978	**AFFIRMED**	S. Cauthen	Alydar	Believe It	7	1:54⅖	ft	136,200
1977	**SEATTLE SLEW**	J. Cruguet	Iron Constitution	Run Dusty Run	9	1:54⅖	ft	138,600
1976	**Elocutionist**	J. Lively	Play the Red	Bold Forbes	6	1:55	ft	129,700
1975	**Master Derby**	D. G. McHargue	Foolish Pleasure	Diabolo	10	1:56⅖	ft	158,100
1974	**Little Current**	M. A. Rivera	‡Neapolitan Way	Cannonade	13	1:54⅗	gd	156,500
1973	**SECRETARIAT**	R. Turcotte	Sham	Our Native	6	1:54⅖	ft	129,900
1972	**Bee Bee Bee**	E. Nelson	No Le Hace	Key to the Mint	7	1:55⅗	sy	135,300
1971	**Canonero II**	G. Avila	Eastern Fleet	Jim French	11	1:54	ft	137,400
1970	**Personality**	E. Belmonte	My Dad George	Silent Screen	14	1:56⅕	ft	151,300
1969	**Majestic Prince**	W. Hartack	Arts and Letters	Jay Ray	8	1:55⅗	ft	129,500
1968	**Forward Pass**	I. Valenzuela	Out of the Way	Nodouble	10	1:56⅘	ft	142,700
1967	**Damascus**	W. Shoemaker	In Reality	Proud Clarion	10	1:55⅕	ft	151,500
1966	**Kauai King**	D. Brumfield	Stupendous	Amberoid	9	1:55⅖	ft	129,000
1965	**Tom Rolfe**	R. Turcotte	Dapper Dan	Hail to All	9	1:56⅕	ft	128,100
1964	**Northern Dancer**	W. Hartack	The Scoundrel	Hill Rise	6	1:56⅘	ft	124,200
1963	**Candy Spots**	W. Shoemaker	Chateaugay	Never Bend	8	1:56⅕	ft	127,500
1962	**Greek Money**	J. L. Rotz	Ridan	Roman Line	11	1:56⅕	ft	135,800
1961	**Carry Back**	J. Sellers	Globemaster	Crozier	9	1:57⅗	ft	126,200
1960	**Bally Ache**	R. Ussery	Victoria Park	*Celtic Ash	6	1:57⅗	ft	121,000
1959	**Royal Orbit**	W. Harmatz	Sword Dancer	Dunce	11	1:57	ft	136,200
1958	**Tim Tam**	I. Valenzuela	Lincoln Road	Gone Fishin'	12	1:57⅕	ft	97,900
1957	**Bold Ruler**	E. Arcaro	Iron Liege	Inside Tract	7	1:56⅕	ft	66,300
1956	**Fabius**	W. Hartack	Needles	No Regrets	9	1:58⅖	ft	84,250
1955	**Nashua**	E. Arcaro	Saratoga	Traffic Judge	8	1:54⅗	ft	67,550
1954	**Hasty Road**	J. Adams	Correlation	Hasseyampa	11	1:57⅖	ft	91,600
1953	**Native Dancer**	E. Guerin	Jamie K.	Royal Bay Gem	7	1:57⅘	ft	65,200
1952	**Blue Man**	C. McCreary	‡Jampol	One Count	10	1:57⅖	ft	86,135
1951	**Bold**	E. Arcaro	Counterpoint	Alerted	8	1:56⅖	ft	83,110
1950	**Hill Prince**	E. Arcaro	Middleground	Dooly	6	1:59⅕	sl	56,115
1949	**Capot**	T. Atkinson	Palestinian	Noble Impulse	9	1:56	ft	79,985
1948	**CITATION**	E. Arcaro	Vulcan's Forge	Bovard	4	2:02⅖	hy	91,870
1947	**Faultless**	D. Dodson	On Trust	Phalanx	11	1:59	ft	98,005
1946	**ASSAULT**	W. Mehrtens	Lord Boswell	Hampden	10	2:01⅖	ft	96,620
1945	**Polynesian**	W. D. Wright	Hoop, Jr.	‡Darby Dieppe	9	1:58⅘	ft	66,170
1944	**Pensive**	C. McCreary	Platter	‡Stir Up	7	1:59⅕	ft	60,075
1943	**COUNT FLEET**	J. Longden	Blue Swords	Vincentive	4	1:57⅖	gd	43,190
1942	**Alsab**	B. James	dh-Requested	dh-Sun Again	10	1:57	ft	58,175

Year	Winner	Jockey	Second	Third	Strs	Time	Track	1st Purse
1941	**WHIRLAWAY**	E. Arcaro	King Cole	Our Boots	8	1:58⅘	gd	$49,365
1940	**Bimelech**	F. A. Smith	Mioland	Gallahadion	9	1:58⅗	ft	53,230
1939	**Challedon**	G. Seabo	Gilded Knight	Volitant	6	1:59⅘	my	53,710
1938	**Dauber**	M. Peters	Cravat	Menow	9	1:59⅘	sy	51,875
1937	**WAR ADMIRAL**	C. Kurtsinger	Pompoon	Flying Scot	8	1:58⅖	gd	45,600
1936	**Bold Venture**	G. Woolf	Granville	Jean Bart	11	1:59	ft	27,325
1935	**OMAHA**	W. Saunders	Firethorn	Psychic Bid	8	1:58⅖	ft	25,325
1934	**High Quest**	R. Jones	Cavalcade	Discovery	7	1:58⅕	ft	25,175
1933	**Head Play**	C. Kurtsinger	Ladysman	Utopian	10	2:02	sl	26,850
1932	**Burgoo King**	E. James	Tick On	Boatswain	9	1:59⅘	ft	50,375
1931	**Mate**	G. Ellis	Twenty Grand	Ladder	7	1:59	ft	48,225
1930	**GALLANT FOX**	E. Sande	Crack Brigade	†Snowflake	11	2:00⅗	ft	51,925
1929	**Dr. Freeland**	L. Schaefer	Minotaur	African	11	2:01⅗	ft	52,325
1928	**Victorian**	R. Workman	Toro	Solace	**18**	2:00⅕	ft	60,000
1927	**Bostonian**	A. Abel	Sir Harry	Whiskery	12	2:01⅗	gd	53,100
1926	**Display**	J. Malben	Blondin	Mars	13	1:59⅘	ft	53,625
1925	**Coventry**	C. Kummer	‡Backbone	Almadel	12	1:59	ft	52,700
1924	**†Nellie Morse**	J. Merimee	Transmute	Mad Play	15	1:57⅕	sy	54,000
1923	**Vigil**	B. Marinelli	Gen. Thatcher	‡Rialto	13	1:53⅗	ft	52,000
1922	**Pillory**	L. Morris	Hea	June Grass	12	1:51⅗	ft	51,000
1921	**Broomspun**	F. Coltiletti	†Polly Ann	Jeg	14	1:54⅕	sl	43,000
1920	**Man o' War**	C. Kummer	Upset	Wildair	9	1:51⅗	ft	23,000
1919	**SIR BARTON**	J. Loftus	Eternal	Sweep On	12	1:53	ft	24,500
1918	***War Cloud**	J. Loftus	Sunny Slope	*Lanius	10	1:53⅗	gd	12,250
	Jack Hare, Jr.	C. Peak	The Porter	†Kate Bright	6	1:53⅖	gd	11,250
1917	**Kalitan**	E. Haynes	Al. M. Dick	‡Kentucky Boy	14	1:54⅖	ft	4,800
1916	**Damrosch**	L. McAtee	Greenwood	Achievement	9	1:54⅘	ft	1,380
1915	**†Rhine Maiden**	D. Hoffman	Half Rock	Runes	6	1:58	my	1,275
1914	**‡Holiday**	A. Schuttinger	Brave Cunarder	Defendum	6	1:53⅘	ft	1,355
1913	**‡Buskin**	J. Butwell	Kleburne	‡Barnegat	8	1:53⅖	ft	1,670
1912	**Col. Holloway**	C. Turner	Bwana Tumbo	Tipsand	7	1:56⅗	sl	1,450
1911	**Watervale**	E. Dugan	Zeus	‡The Nigger	7	1:51	ft	2,700
1910	**‡Layminster**	R. Estep	Dalhousie	Sager	12	1:40⅕	ft	2,800
1909	**Effendi**	W. Doyle	Fashion Plate	†Hill Top	10	1:39⅘	ft	2,725
1908	**Royal Tourist**	E. Dugan	Live Wire	‡Robert Cooper	4	1:46⅖	ft	2,455
1907	**‡Don Enrique**	G. Mountain	Ethon	Zambesi	7	1:45⅗	hy	2,260
1906	**†Whimsical**	W. Miller	†Content	Larabie	10	1:45	ft	2,355
1905	**Cairngorm**	W. Davis	†Kiamesha	†Coy Maid	10	1:45⅘	ft	2,145
1904	**Bryn Mawr**	E. Hildebrand	Wotan	‡Dolly Spanker	10	1:44⅕	ft	2,355
1903	**†Flocarline**	W. Gannon	Mackey Dwyer	Rightful	6	1:44⅘	ft	1,875
1902	**Old England**	L. Jackson	Major Daingerfield	Namtor	7	1:45⅘	hy	2,240
1901	**The Parader**	F. Landry	†Sadie S.	Dr. Barlow	5	1:47⅕	hy	1,605
1900	**Hindus**	H. Spencer	*Sarmatian	Ten Candles	10	1:48⅖	ft	1,900
1899	**Half Time**	R. Clawson	Filigrane	Lackland	3	1:47	ft	1,580
1898	**Sly Fox**	W. Simms	The Huguenot	Nuto	4	1:49¾	gd	1,450
1897	**Paul Kauvar**	C. Thorpe	Elkin	On Deck	7	1:51¼	sy	1,420
1896	**Margrave**	H. Griffin	Hamilton II	*Intermission	4	1:51	ft	1,350
1895	**Belmar**	F. Taral	‡April Fool	†Sue Kittie	7	1:50½	ft	1,350
1894	**Assignee**	F. Taral	Potentate	‡Ed Kearney	14	1:49¼	ft	1,830
1890	**Montague**	J. Martin	Philosophy	Barrister	4	2:36¾	ft	1,215
1889	**Buddhist**	G. Anderson	Japhet	———	2	2:17½	ft	1,130
1888	**Refund**	F. Littlefield	Judge Murray	Glendale	4	2:49	hy	1,185
1887	**Dunboyne**	W. Donohue	Mahony	Raymond	4	2:39½	ft	1,675
1886	**The Bard**	S. Fisher	Eurus	Elkwood	5	2:45	gd	2,050
1885	**Tecumseh**	J. McLaughlin	Wickham	‡John C.	4	2:49	hy	2,160
1884	**Knight of Ellerslie**	S. Fisher	Welcher	———	2	2:39½	ft	1,905
1883	**Jacobus**	G. Barbee	Parnell	———	2	2:42½	gd	1,635
1882	**Vanguard**	T. Costello	Heck	‡Col. Watson	3	2:44½	gd	1,250
1881	**Saunterer**	T. Costello	‡Compensation	Baltic	6	2:40½	gd	1,950
1880	**Grenada**	L. Hughes	Oden	†Emily F.	5	2:40½	ft	2,000
1879	**Harold**	L. Hughes	Jerico	‡Rochester	6	2:40½	ft	2,550
1878	**Duke of Magenta**	C. Holloway	Bayard	‡Albert	3	2:41¾	gd	2,100
1877	**Cloverbrook**	C. Holloway	Bombast	Lucifer	4	2:45½	sl	1,600
1876	**‡Shirley**	G. Barbee	Rappahannock	Compliments	8	2:44¾	gd	1,950
1875	**Tom Ochiltree**	L. Hughes	Viator	†Bay Final	9	2:43½	sl	1,900
1874	**Culpepper**	W. Donohue	*King Amadeus	Scratch	6	2:56½	my	1,900
1873	**Survivor**	G. Barbee	John Boulger	Artist	7	2:43	sl	1,800

†—filly; ‡—gelding; *—imported horse; dh-dead heat; bold indicates records set in starters, time, and 1st purse; Triple Crown winners are in all capitalized letters.

1894, 1½ miles; 1889, 1¼ miles; 1894-1900,1908, 1 1/16 miles; 1901-'07, 1 mile and 70 yards; 1909,1910, 1 mile; 1911-'24, 1⅛ miles. 1891-'93, not run. 1890 held at Morris Park, New York; 1894-1908 Gravesend, New York. Run in two divisions in 1918. 1973-present, Grade 1. Dancer's Image disqualified from third to eighth in 1968. Secretariat's time in 1973 originally reported as 1:55; hand-timed by *Daily Racing Form* clockers in 1:53⅖

Belmont Stakes History

Unforgettable horses, jockeys, and trainers punctuate the glorious history of the Belmont Stakes, a compelling race if only because two three-year-olds carrying equal weights of 126 pounds can battle its testing 1½-mile distance and be separated at the finish line by inches. It has happened more than once in the final race of the Triple Crown.

First run in 1867, the Belmont Stakes is named for August Belmont I, a prominent investment banker and Thoroughbred owner who was president of the American Jockey Club. The Belmont Stakes preceded the Preakness by six years and the Kentucky Derby by eight.

Francis Morris's filly Ruthless won the first Belmont Stakes, which was contested at Jerome Park in the Bronx on a Thursday afternoon at 1⅝ miles, "cleverly by a head" over De Coursey. The purse was $2,500.

The first 23 runnings of the Belmont Stakes were held on a ribbon-like course at Jerome Park. In 1890, the Belmont Stakes moved to Morris Park, a 1⅜-mile track a few miles east of what is now Van Cortland Park in the Bronx.

Fifteen years later, in 1905, the Belmont Stakes had a new home, Belmont Park, but the race was not run in 1911 and '12 because antigambling legislation shut down racing in New York in those years. Unlike the Belmont's current counterclockwise path, the race was run clockwise—like many English and European races—until 1921. By then, two great champions with a unique link had won the race known as the Test of Champions in strikingly different styles.

Colin is one of only two undefeated American champions with more than five starts in the past 96 years (the other is Personal Ensign).

Colin nearly lost his unbeaten record because of a mistake by Joe Notter, his jockey in the 1908 Belmont Stakes. In a driving rainstorm so intense that no final time was taken, Notter misjudged the finish line on Colin, and his five-length lead was shaved to a head by a fast-closing Fair Play.

Colin continued to a perfect 15-for-15 record. Fair Play sired Man o' War, the once-beaten champion who won the Belmont by 20 lengths over his only challenger, Donnacona, at odds of 0.04-to-1.

Gallant Fox is one of only two Triple Crown winners who was not the favorite in the Belmont Stakes.

The previous year, Whichone had beaten Gallant Fox in the 1929 Futurity and also had won the Champagne and Saratoga Special Stakes. Whichone missed the Kentucky Derby and Preakness Stakes the following spring because of knee problems, but he returned to win the Withers Stakes and went off the 7-to-10 favorite in the 1930 Belmont Stakes.

Gallant Fox had won the Wood Memorial Stakes, Preakness, and Kentucky Derby (in that order), but he went off at odds of 8-to-5 in the field of just four in the Belmont. Gallant Fox uncharacteristically took the lead immediately and scampered to a surprisingly easy three-length victory in a stakes record of 2:31⅗ for 1½ miles.

Gallant Fox's winning Belmont Stakes margin paled next to the 25-length romp of Count Fleet, who completed his 1943 Triple Crown at odds of 1-to-20 "galloping," according to the Belmont chart.

Three years later, Assault went off as the 7-to-5 second choice in the Belmont but, like Gallant Fox, he completed his Triple Crown with a three-length victory. Favored Lord Boswell finished fifth in the field of seven at 1.35-to-1.

In 1948, Citation cruised to an eight-length win in the Belmont to become the fourth Triple Crown winner in eight years. There would not be another for a quarter-century.

Plenty of upsets occurred in those 25 years from Citation to Secretariat, but none was more shocking than Sherluck's 1961 victory over 2-

Belmont Attendance

Year	Attendance	Year	Attendance
2008	94,476	1988	56,223
2007	46,870	1987	64,772
2006	61,168	1986	42,555
2005	62,274	1985	43,446
2004	120,139	1984	46,430
2003	101,864	1983	56,677
2002	103,222	1982	46,050
2001	73,857	1981	61,200
2000	67,810	1980	58,883
1999	85,818	1979	59,073
1998	80,162	1978	65,417
1997	70,682	1977	71,026
1996	40,797	1976	58,788
1995	37,171	1975	60,611
1994	42,695	1974	52,153
1993	45,037	1973	67,605
1992	50,204	1972	54,635
1991	51,766	1971	82,694
1990	50,123	1970	54,299
1989	64,959		

to-5 favorite Carry Back at odds of 65.05-to-1, which resulted in a then-record Belmont Stakes win payout of $132.10.

Carry Back, who finished seventh, joined Pensive (1944) and Tim Tam ('58) as Kentucky Derby and Preakness winners who lost in the Belmont Stakes.

Five more followed Carry Back in the next ten years: Northern Dancer (1964), Kauai King ('66), Forward Pass ('68), Majestic Prince ('69), and Canonero II, who attracted 82,694, then the largest crowd in Belmont Park history, on June 5, 1971, in his fourth-place finish to Pass Catcher, a 34.50-to-1 longshot.

Just when everybody thought there might not ever be another Triple Crown winner—the tremendous growth in the number of foals was frequently cited as a reason—along came Secretariat.

To provide a perspective on his 31-length 1973 Belmont Stakes victory in a world record 2:24, consider that the next-fastest winners, Easy Goer in '89 and A.P. Indy in '92, went in 2:26, the equivalent of ten lengths slower.

Secretariat's 1973 Triple Crown was followed by two more in the ensuing five years: Seattle Slew, who in '77 became the first undefeated Triple Crown winner, and Affirmed one year later.

The Triple Crowns of 1977 and '78 were starkly different. Seattle Slew dominated his generation, while Affirmed was pushed to the limit by his nemesis, Alydar.

The final sixteenth of a mile of the 1978 Belmont Stakes, with Affirmed on the inside under Steve Cauthen and Alydar at his throat under Jorge Velasquez, was a dramatic test of will in which Affirmed prevailed by a head. That was not the closest Belmont Stakes finish. Colin had won by the same margin, and Granville in 1936, Jaipur in '62, and Victory Gallop in '98 prevailed by a nose.

Spectacular Bid had a shot at becoming the third consecutive Triple Crown winner in 1979 but checked in third at 3-to-10 to Coastal in the Belmont after reportedly stepping on a safety pin that morning. Two years later, Kentucky Derby and Preakness winner Pleasant Colony failed to sweep the series, finishing third to Summing.

Then, Woody Stephens took over. People questioned the Racing Hall of Fame trainer's judgment when he announced that Conquistador Cielo, who had just routed older horses by 7¼ lengths in the one-mile Metropolitan Handicap (G1) five days earlier, would start in the Belmont Stakes. Stephens knew his horse, and the colt won the Belmont by 14 lengths under Laffit Pincay Jr.

Stephens-trained Caveat won the 1983 Belmont, and ill-fated Swale won in '84. Then Stephens ran first and second with Creme Fraiche and Stephan's Odyssey in 1985. In 1986, Stephens won his fifth consecutive Belmont Stakes with Danzig Connection, at odds of 8-to-1.

Three consecutive blowouts occurred in the late 1980s, with Bet Twice winning by 14 lengths over Derby and Preakness winner Alysheba (who finished fourth) in '87, Risen Star adding to his Preakness triumph with a 14¾-length Belmont romp, and Easy Goer avenging his Derby and Preakness losses to Sunday Silence by winning the '89 Belmont Stakes by eight lengths.

The middle years of the 1990s were dominated by Racing Hall of Fame trainer D. Wayne Lukas, who secured consecutive victories with Tabasco Cat (1994), Thunder Gulch ('95), and Editor's Note ('96).

Julie Krone became the first female rider to win a Triple Crown race when she guided Colonial Affair to a 2¼-length win in the 1993 Belmont for trainer Flint S. "Scotty" Schulhofer. The Racing Hall of Fame trainer collected his second Belmont victory in 1999 when Lemon Drop Kid denied Lukas-trained Charismatic a Triple Crown before a then-record crowd of 85,818.

Charismatic's loss marked the third straight year that a Triple Crown was on the line. In 1997, Silver Charm, trained by Bob Baffert, led 100 yards before the finish but was passed by Touch Gold, who won by three-quarters of a length. One year later, Baffert-trained Real Quiet looked home free in the Belmont before weakening late and losing by a nose in the final stride to Victory Gallop.

Two years later, Baffert recorded his first Belmont win with Point Given's 2001 victory before 73,857, the largest Belmont Stakes crowd without a Triple Crown on the line.

A Triple Crown was at stake in each of the next three years, but War Emblem, Funny Cide, and Smarty Jones were defeated. A record crowd of 120,139 turned out in 2004 for Smarty Jones's bid.

In 2007, Rags to Riches became the first filly to win the Belmont since Tanya in 1905.

Belmont Trophy and Tray

The Belmont Stakes trophy is a solid silver bowl originally crafted by Tiffany's, and it was the trophy that August Belmont I's Fenian won

in 1869 after taking the third running of the race.

The Belmont family presented it as a perpetual trophy for the Belmont Stakes in 1926, and each winning owner is given the option of keeping the trophy for the year his horse wins. Atop the cover of the trophy is a silver figure of Fenian. The bowl is supported by three horses representing influential sires Eclipse, Herod, and Matchem.

The winning owner also receives a permanent large silver tray with the names of previous Belmont Stakes winners engraved on it. Trays also are presented to the winning trainer, jockey, exercise rider, and groom.

Carnation Blanket

The Kentucky Derby (G1) has its roses, the Preakness Stakes (G1) has ersatz black-eyed Susans, and the carnation is the official flower of the Belmont Stakes (G1). Imported from either California or Colombia, between 300 and 400 carnations are glued onto a green velveteen backing to create the blanket that adorns the Belmont winner.

From "Sidewalks" to "New York, New York"

Until 1997, the song that escorted the Belmont Stakes field onto the track was "Sidewalks of New York," written in 1894 by Charles Lawlor, a vaudevillian, and James W. Blake, a hat salesman and lyricist.

More than one version of the lyrics exist, but the best-known stanza is:

East Side, West Side, all around the town
The kids sang "ring around rosie," "London Bridge is falling down"
Boys and girls together, me and Mamie O'Rourke
We tripped the light fantastic on the sidewalks of New York.

"New York, New York" is of much more recent vintage, written by John Kander and Fred Ebb in 1977 for the movie of the same name. Composer Kander and lyricist Ebb were one of

Belmont Wagering, 1980-2008

Year	Winner	On-Track Handle	OTB Handle	Simulcasting	Total Handle
2008	Da' Tara	$4,283,221		$52,209,679	$56,492,900
2007	Rags to Riches	2,429,354		35,357,028	37,786,382
2006	Jazil	2,324,567		42,781,075	45,105,642
2005	Afleet Alex	2,736,948		45,312,800	48,049,748
2004	Birdstone	4,331,463		59,340,243	63,671,706
2003	Empire Maker	3,440,151		44,642,048	48,082,199
2002	Sarava	3,753,983		54,503,406	58,257,389
2001	Point Given	2,707,574		34,959,635	37,667,209
2000	Commendable	2,046,835		28,354,418	30,401,253
1999	Lemon Drop Kid	3,143,508		40,839,558	43,983,066
1998	Victory Gallop	2,521,457		25,864,228	28,385,685
1997	Touch Gold	2,229,860		22,546,860	24,776,720
1996	Editor's Note	1,639,134		18,714,712	20,353,846
1995	Thunder Gulch	1,571,891	$3,672,079	15,310,597	20,554,567
1994	Tabasco Cat	1,717,684	3,299,616	13,848,321	18,865,621
1993	Colonial Affair	2,793,320	4,567,493	17,472,438	24,833,251
1992	A.P. Indy	2,058,039	4,365,205	12,581,848	19,005,092
1991	Hansel	2,222,049	5,206,757	12,877,258	20,306,064
1990	Go and Go (Ire)	1,588,767	3,832,777	8,985,594	14,407,138
1989	Easy Goer	2,565,156	4,062,020	12,269,211	18,896,387
1988	Risen Star	1,439,045	4,135,493	8,685,408	14,259,946
1987	Bet Twice	2,703,924	6,794,377	8,242,290	17,740,591
1986	Danzig Connection	2,038,445	4,469,831	5,869,281	12,377,557
1985	Creme Fraiche	1,840,198	4,982,800	4,518,679	11,341,677
1884	Swale	2,063,135	5,540,202	4,080,482	11,683,819
1983	Caveat	1,530,010	3,724,455	2,961,256	8,215,721
1982	Conquistador Cielo	1,201,491	2,248,366	2,488,107	5,937,964
1981	Smarten	1,420,517	3,204,415	465,950	5,090,882
1980	Temperence Hill	1,603,057	3,769,868		5,372,925

Beginning in 1996, figures for OTB and simulcasting handle were combined.

Broadway's most successful teams; their credits included *Cabaret, Funny Lady, Woman of the Year,* and *Zorba. New York, New York,* not regarded as one of director Martin Scorsese's better films, starred Liza Minelli, who performed the song in the movie, and Robert de Niro. The song subsequently was recorded by Frank Sinatra and rose to number 32 on the hits chart in 1980.

Its lyrics:

Start spreading the news
I'm leaving today
I want to be a part of it, New York, New York
These vagabond shoes
Are longing to stray
And make a brand new start of it
New York, New York
I want to wake up in the city that never sleeps
To find I'm king of the hill, top of the heap
These little town blues
Are melting away
I'll make a brand new start of it
In old New York
If I can make it there
I'll make it anywhere
It's up to you, New York, New York.

Belmont Trivia

- The Belmont Stakes has not always been contested at 1½ miles. Prior to 1874, the race was run at 1⅝ miles. The Belmont was held at 1¼ miles from 1890 through '92, and in '95, 1904, and 1905. It was 1⅛ miles in 1893 and '94; at 1⅜ miles 1896 through 1903 and from 1906 through '25. The Belmont was run at 1½ miles from 1874 through '89 and from 1926 to the present.

- The Belmont Stakes was run at Aqueduct from 1963 through '67 while Belmont Park was being rebuilt.

- The smallest Belmont Stakes field was two. It happened in 1887, '88, '92, 1910, and '20. The largest Belmont Stakes field was 15 in 1983.

- Jazil was the 53rd bay to win the Belmont. Fifty-one winners have been chestnut, 30 dark bay or brown, three black, two gray, and one roan.

- Thirty-six of the 140 runnings of the Belmont have been run on off tracks, the most recent in 2003 when Empire Maker won.

- The 2001 Belmont drew a crowd of 73,857, the largest for the race without a horse going for the Triple Crown and eighth highest behind 120,139 in 2004, 103,222 in '02, 101,864 in 2003, 94,476 in '08, 85,818 in 1999, 82,694 in '71, and 80,162 in '98.

- Sarava was the 17th Belmont winner whose name began with the letter 'S'. Twenty Belmont winners had names beginning with 'C'.

Leading Belmont Owners by Wins

6 **James R. Keene:** Spendthrift, 1879; Commando, 1901; Delhi, 1904; Peter Pan, 1907; Colin 1908; Sweep, 1910.
Belair Stud: Gallant Fox, 1930; Faireno, 1932; Omaha, 1935; Granville, 1936; Johnstown, 1939; Nashua, 1955.

5 **Mike and Phil Dwyer:** George Kinney, 1883; Panique, 1884; Inspector B., 1886; Hanover, 1887; Sir Dixon, 1888.

4 **Glen Riddle Farms:** Man o'War, 1920; American Flag, 1925; Crusader, 1926; War Admiral, 1937.
Greentree Stable: Twenty Grand, 1931; Shut Out, 1942; Capot, 1949; Stage Door Johnny, 1968.

3 **August Belmont II:** Masterman, 1902; Friar Rock, 1916; *Hourless, 1917.
King Ranch: Assault, 1946; Middleground, 1950; High Gun, 1954.

Owners with Most Belmont Starters

Name	Starts	Wins	2nd	3rd	Unplaced
C. V. Whitney	20	2	2	4	12
August Belmont I	19	2	4	4	9
Greentree Stable	15	4	1	2	8
Belair Stud	14	6	0	1	7
King Ranch	14	3	2	1	8
James R. Keene	12	6	2	1	3
Brookmeade Stable	11	2	1	1	7
Calumet Farm	11	2	5	2	2
Wheatley Stable	11	0	0	3	8
George D. Widener	10	1	3	2	4
Marcus Daly	8	1	1	2	4
George Lorillard	8	3	3	0	2
Pierre Lorillard	8	1	0	3	4
Ogden Phipps	8	1	0	1	6
August Belmont II	7	3	2	0	2
Buckland Stable	7	0	0	1	6
Darby Dan Farm	7	2	0	1	4
Dwyer Brothers	7	5	1	0	1
Walter M. Jeffords	7	1	1	0	5
D. McDaniel	7	3	0	0	4
Meadow Stable	7	2	0	1	4

Leading Belmont Breeders by Wins

7 **A. J. Alexander:** Harry Bassett, 1871; Joe Daniels, 1872; Springbok, 1873; Duke of Magenta, 1878; Spendthrift, 1879; Grenada, 1880; Burlington, 1890.

5 **Belair Stud:** Gallant Fox, 1930; Faireno, 1932; Omaha, 1935; Granville, 1936; Nashua, 1955.
J. R. Keene: Commando, 1901; Delhi, 1904; Peter Pan, 1907; Colin, 1908; Sweep, 1910.
John E. Madden: Joe Madden, 1909; The Finn, 1915; Sir Barton, 1919; Grey Lag, 1921; Zev, 1923.

4 August Belmont II: Masterman, 1902; Friar Rock, 1916; *Hourless, 1917; Man o' War, 1920.
   Greentree: Twenty Grand, 1931; Shut Out, 1942; Capot, 1949; Stage Door Johnny, 1968.
   H. P. Whitney: Tanya, 1905; Burgomaster, 1906; Prince Eugene, 1913; *Johren, 1918.
3 W. S. Farish: Bet Twice, 1987; A.P. Indy, 1991; Lemon Drop Kid, 1999.
   Sam Riddle: American Flag, 1925; Crusader, 1926; War Admiral, 1937.

Leading Belmont Trainers by Wins

8 James Rowe: George Kinney, 1883; Panique, 1884; Commando, 1901; Delhi, 1904; Peter Pan, 1907; Colin, 1908; Sweep, 1910; Prince Eugene, 1913.
7 Sam Hildreth: Jean Bereaud, 1899; Joe Madden, 1909; Friar Rock, 1916; Hourless, 1917; Grey Lag, 1921; Zev, 1923; Mad Play, 1924.
6 James "Sunny Jim" Fitzsimmons: Gallant Fox, 1930; Faireno, 1932; Omaha, 1935; Granville, 1936; Johnstown, 1939; Nashua, 1955.
5 W. C. "Woody" Stephens: Conquistador Cielo, 1982; Caveat, 1983; Swale, 1984; Creme Fraiche, 1985; Danzig Connection, 1986.
4 Max Hirsch: Vito, 1928; Assault, 1946; Middleground, 1950; High Gun, 1954.
   D. Wayne Lukas: Tabasco Cat, 1994; Thunder Gulch, 1995; Editor's Note, 1996; Commendable, 2000.
   R. W. Walden: Duke of Magenta, 1878; Grenada, 1880; Saunterer, 1881; *Bowling Brook, 1898.
3 Elliott Burch: Sword Dancer, 1959; Quadrangle, 1964; Arts and Letters, 1969.
   John M. Gaver: Shut Out, 1942; Capot, 1949; Stage Door Johnny, 1968.
   Lucien Laurin: Amberoid, 1966; Riva Ridge, 1972; Secretariat, 1973.
   Frank McCabe: Inspector B., 1886; Hanover, 1887; Sir Dixon, 1888.
   David McDaniel: Harry Bassett, 1871; Joe Daniels, 1872; Springbok, 1873.
2 Tom Barry: *Cavan, 1958; *Celtic Ash, 1960.
   Flint S. "Scotty" Schulhofer: Colonial Affair, 1993; Lemon Drop Kid, 1999.
   Sylvester Veitch: Phalanx, 1947; Counterpoint, 1951.
   Oscar White: Pavot, 1945; One Count, 1952.
   Nicholas Zito: Birdstone, 2004; Da' Tara, 2008

Trainers with Most Belmont Starters Since 1972

Name	Starts	Wins	2nd	3rd	Unplaced
Nicholas P. Zito	20	2	6	2	10
D. Wayne Lukas	19	4	0	1	14
John P. Campo	10	0	0	1	9
LeRoy Jolley	10	0	2	1	7
Woodford C. Stephens	9	5	1	1	2
Todd Pletcher	8	1	1	2	4
Bob Baffert	7	1	2	0	4
Flint S. Schulhofer	7	2	1	9	4
Lou Rondinello	6	1	0	2	3
Alfredo Callejas	5	0	0	0	5
C. R. McGaughey III	5	1	1	1	2

Female Trainers in the Belmont

Seven women have trained Belmont Stakes starters, and the best finish was that by Dianne Carpenter-trained Kingpost, who finished a distant second behind Risen Star in 1988.

In 2002, owner-breeder-trainer Nancy Alberts saddled Magic Weisner for a fourth-place finish behind upset winner Sarava.

Women who have trained Belmont starters:

Year	Trainer	Horse	Finish
2003	Linda Rice	Supervisor	5th
2002	Nancy Alberts	Magic Weisner	4th
1996	Cynthia Reese	In Contention	9th
1992	Shelley Riley	Casual Lies	5th
1988	Dianne Carpenter	Kingpost	2nd
1985	Patricia Johnson	Fast Account	4th
1984	Sarah Lundy	Minstrel Star	11th

Leading Belmont Jockeys by Wins

6 Eddie Arcaro: Whirlaway, 1941; Shut Out, 1942; Pavot, 1945; Citation, 1948; One Count, 1952; Nashua, 1955.
   James McLaughlin: Forester, 1882; George Kinney, 1883; Panique, 1884; Inspector B., 1886; Hanover, 1887; Sir Dixon, 1888.
5 Earle Sande: Grey Lag, 1921; Zev, 1923; Mad Play, 1924; Chance Shot, 1927; Gallant Fox, 1930.
   Bill Shoemaker: Gallant Man, 1957; Sword Dancer, 1959; Jaipur, 1962; Damascus, 1967; Avatar, 1975.
3 Braulio Baeza: Sherluck, 1961; Chateaugay, 1963; Arts and Letters, 1969.
   Pat Day: Easy Goer, 1989; Tabasco Cat, 1994; Commendable, 2000.
   Laffit Pincay Jr.: Conquistador Cielo, 1982; Caveat, 1983; Swale, 1984.
   James Stout: Granville, 1936; Pasteurized, 1938; Johnstown, 1939.

Jockeys with Most Belmont Mounts Since 1938

Name	Starts	Wins	2nd	3rd	Unplaced
Eddie Arcaro	22	6	3	2	11
Angel Cordero Jr.	21	1	2	4	14
Jerry Bailey	20	2	1	1	16
Pat Day	17	3	2	2	10
Braulio Baeza	14	3	2	0	9
Jose Santos	14	1	2	1	10
Laffit Pincay Jr.	13	3	3	0	7
Jorge Velasquez	13	0	1	5	7
John Velazquez	12	1	1	1	9
Eric Guerin	11	2	2	1	6
Eddie Maple	11	2	1	0	8
Chris McCarron	11	2	1	2	6
Bill Shoemaker	11	5	1	1	4
Mike Smith	11	0	1	2	8
Jacinto Vasquez	10	0	3	1	6
Jorge Chavez	9	0	0	1	8
Gary Stevens	9	3	1	1	4
Ron Turcotte	9	2	1	9	6

Name	Starts	Wins	2nd	3rd	Unplaced
Ruben Hernandez	8	1	0	0	7
Edgar Prado	8	2	0	0	6
Bobby Ussery	8	0	1	0	7
John Sellers	7	1	1	1	4

Only One Female Jockey in Belmont Stakes

Julie Krone, the only female jockey in the Racing Hall of Fame, is the only female rider to have had a mount in the Belmont. Krone won the 1993 Belmont Stakes aboard Colonial Affair. She retired in 1999 but resumed her career in 2002 and retired in 2004.

Krone's Belmont Stakes mounts:

Year	Mount	Finish
1996	South Salem	DNF
1995	Star Standard	2nd
1993	**Colonial Affair**	1st
1992	Colony Light	6th
1991	Subordinated Debt	9th

Leading Belmont Sires by Wins

5 **Lexington:** General Duke, 1868; Kingfisher, 1870; Harry Bassett, 1871; Duke of Magenta, 1878; Saunterer, 1881.

3 ***Australian:** Joe Daniels, 1872; Springbok, 1873; Spendthrift, 1879.

Fair Play: Man o' War, 1920; Mad Play, 1924; Chance Shot, 1927.

Man o' War: American Flag, 1925; Crusader, 1926; War Admiral, 1937.

2 **Commando:** Peter Pan, 1907; Colin, 1908.

Count Fleet: Counterpoint, 1951; One Count, 1952.

Gallant Fox: Omaha, 1935; Granville, 1936.

Hamburg: Burgomaster, 1906; Prince Eugene, 1913.

***Nasrullah:** Nashua, 1955; Jaipur, 1962.

***Negofol:** *Hourless, 1917; Vito, 1928.

Seattle Slew: Swale, 1984; A.P. Indy, 1992.

***Star Shoot:** Sir Barton, 1919; Grey Lag, 1921.

Belmont Winners Who Sired Belmont Winners

3 **Man o' War (1920):** American Flag, 1925; Crusader, 1926; War Admiral, 1937.

2 **Commando (1901):** Peter Pan, 1907; Colin, 1908.

Gallant Fox (1930): Omaha, 1935; Granville, 1936.

Count Fleet (1943): Counterpoint, 1951; One Count, 1952.

Seattle Slew (1977): Swale, 1984; A.P. Indy, 1992.

1 **Duke of Magenta (1878):** Eric, 1889.

Spendthrift (1879): Hastings, 1896.

Hastings (1896): Masterman, 1902.

The Finn (1915): Zev, 1923.

Sword Dancer (1959): Damascus, 1967.

Secretariat (1973): Risen Star, 1988.

A.P. Indy (1992): Rags to Riches, 2007.

Derby-Preakness Winners Not Favored in the Belmont

Thirty-one three-year-olds swept the Kentucky Derby and Preakness to earn a chance at the Triple Crown. Ironically, the only two who were not the betting favorites in the Belmont Stakes became Triple Crown champions.

Gallant Fox in 1930 was the 8-to-5 second choice to 4-to-5 Whichone, who finished second. Assault in 1946 was the 7-to-5 second choice to 1.35-to-1 Lord Boswell, who finished fifth.

Fastest Belmont Winning Times

Year	Winner	Time	Cond.
1973	Secretariat	2:24	Fast
1989	Easy Goer	2:26	Fast
1992	A.P. Indy	2:26	Good
1988	Risen Star	2:26⅖	Fast
2001	Point Given	2:26.56	Fast
1957	Gallant Man	2:26⅗	Fast
1978	Affirmed	2:26⅘	Fast
1994	Tabasco Cat	2:26.82	Fast

Fastest Fractions

Quarter-Mile	:23	Another Review, 1991
Half-Mile	:46⅕	Secretariat, 1973
Six Furlongs	1:09⅘	Secretariat, 1973
One Mile	1:34⅕	Secretariat, 1973
1¼ Miles	1:59	Secretariat, 1973

Slowest Belmont Winning Times

Year	Winner	Time	Cond.
1970	High Echelon	2:34	Sloppy
1928	Vito	2:33⅕	Fast
1932	Faireno	2:32⅘	Fast
1929	Blue Larkspur	2:32⅘	Sloppy
1933	Hurryoff	2:32⅗	Fast
1927	Chance Shot	2:32⅖	Fast
1944	Bounding Home	2:32⅕	Fast
1926	Crusader	2:32⅕	Fast
1995	Thunder Gulch	2:32.02	Good
1930	Gallant Fox	2:31⅗	Fast
2000	Commendable	2:31.19	Fast
1941	Whirlaway	2:31	Fast

Evolution of Belmont Stakes Record at 1½ Miles

Year	Winner	Time	Cond.
1874	Saxon	2:39½	Fast
1926	Crusader	2:32⅕	Sloppy
1930	Gallant Fox	2:31⅗	Good
1931	Twenty Grand	2:29⅗	Fast
1934	Peace Chance	2:29⅕	Fast
1937	War Admiral	2:28⅗	Fast
1943	Count Fleet	2:28⅕	Fast
1957	Gallant Man	2:26⅗	Fast
1973	Secretariat	2:24	Fast

Triple Crown — Belmont Stakes

Shortest-Priced Belmont Winners

Winner	Year	Odds
Man o' War	1920	0.04-to-1
Count Fleet	1943	0.05-to-1
Hanover	1887	0.05-to-1
George Kinney	1883	0.08-to-1
Secretariat	1973	0.10-to-1
Johnstown	1939	0.12-to-1
Sweep	1910	0.12-to-1
Nashua	1955	0.15-to-1
Citation	1948	0.20-to-1
Forester	1882	0.20-to-1
Whirlaway	1941	0.25-to-1
Chance Shot	1927	0.25-to-1
*Hourless	1917	0.25-to-1
Sir Dixon	1888	0.36-to-1
Burgomaster	1906	0.40-to-1
Sir Barton	1919	0.40-to-1
Seattle Slew	1977	0.40-to-1
Native Dancer	1953	0.45-to-1
Colin	1908	0.50-to-1
Jean Bereaud	1899	0.50-to-1
Grenada	1880	0.50-to-1

Longest-Priced Belmont Winners

Year	Horse	Odds
2002	Sarava	70.25-to-1
1961	Sherluck	65.05-to-1
1980	Temperence Hill	53.40-to-1
2008	Da' Tara	38.50-to-1
2004	Birdstone	36.00-to-1
1971	Pass Catcher	34.50-to-1
1999	Lemon Drop Kid	29.75-to-1
2000	Commendable	18.80-to-1
1944	Bounding Home	16.35-to-1

Belmont Odds-On Beaten Favorites

Year	Horse	Odds	Finish
1958	Tim Tam	0.15-to-1	2nd
1979	Spectacular Bid	0.30-to-1	3rd
2008	Big Brown	0.30-to-1	DNF
1938	Dauber	0.33-to-1	2nd
1922	*Snob II	0.33-to-1	2nd
2004	Smarty Jones	0.35-to-1	2nd
1942	Alsab	0.40-to-1	2nd
1928	Victorian	0.40-to-1	5th
1961	Carry Back	0.45-to-1	7th
1963	Candy Spots	0.50-to-1	2nd
1952	Blue Man	0.50-to-1	2nd
1944	Pensive	0.50-to-1	2nd
1900	Missionary	0.50-to-1	3rd
1966	Kauai King	0.60-to-1	4th
1915	Pebbles	0.60-to-1	3rd
1971	Canonero II	0.70-to-1	4th
1913	Rock View	0.70-to-1	2nd
1947	Faultless	0.75-to-1	5th
1998	Real Quiet	0.80-to-1	2nd
1987	Alysheba	0.80-to-1	4th
1981	Pleasant Colony	0.80-to-1	3rd
1964	Northern Dancer	0.80-to-1	3rd
1949	Ponder	0.80-to-1	2nd
1930	Whichone	0.80-to-1	2nd
1895	Counter Tenor	0.80-to-1	2nd
1891	Montana	0.80-to-1	2nd
1889	Diablo	0.80-to-1	2nd
1960	Tompion	0.85-to-1	4th
1957	Bold Ruler	0.85-to-1	3rd
1950	Hill Prince	0.85-to-1	7th
1989	Sunday Silence	0.90-to-1	2nd

Front-Running Belmont Winners

Since Capot in 1949, only seven horses have won the Belmont while leading at every point of call, Da' Tara being the first since Swale in '84. The following Belmont Stakes winners were on the lead at all points of call.

Year	Winner	Winning Margin
2008	Da' Tara	5¼
1984	Swale	4
1978	Affirmed	Head
1977	Seattle Slew	4
1976	Bold Forbes	Neck
1973	Secretariat	31
1972	Riva Ridge	7
1949	Capot	½
1948	Citation	8
1943	Count Fleet	25
1939	Johnstown	5
1937	War Admiral	3
1932	Faireno	1½
1930	Gallant Fox	3
1927	Chance Shot	1½
1923	Zev	1½
1920	Man o' War	20
1917	*Hourless	10
1916	Friar Rock	3
1915	The Finn	4
1910	Sweep	6
1908	Colin	Head
1907	Peter Pan	1
1906	Burgomaster	4
1905	Tanya	½
1904	Delhi	3½
1902	Masterman	2
1901	Commando	½
1898	*Bowling Brook	8

Winning Belmont Post Positions

Post	Winners	Post	Winners
1	23	7	12
2	11	8	6
3	13	9	4
4	9	10	2
5	14	11	2
6	7		

Largest Winning Margins

Year	Horse	Lengths
1973	Secretariat	31
1943	Count Fleet	25
1920	Man o' War	20
1988	Risen Star	14¾
1987	Bet Twice	14

Year	Horse	Lengths
1982	Conquistador Cielo	14
2001	Point Given	12¼
1888	Sir Dixon	12
1931	Twenty Grand	10
1917	*Hourless	10

Smallest Winning Margins

Year	Horse	Margin
1998	Victory Gallop	nose
1962	Jaipur	nose
1936	Granville	nose
2007	Rags to Riches	head
1999	Lemon Drop Kid	head
1991	Hansel	head
1978	Affirmed	head
1908	Colin	head
1900	Ildrim	head
1899	Jean Bereaud	head
1895	Belmar	head
1893	Commanche	head
1889	Eric	head
1876	Algerine	head
1867	Ruthless	head
1981	Summing	neck
1976	Bold Forbes	neck
1975	Avatar	neck
1965	Hail to All	neck
1956	Needles	neck
1954	High Gun	neck
1953	Native Dancer	neck
1938	Pasteurized	neck
1936	Granville	neck
1896	Hastings	neck
1891	Foxford	neck
1881	Saunterer	neck
1874	Saxon	neck

Fillies in the Belmont

Ruthless left a tough act to follow when she won the inaugural Belmont Stakes in 1867. Only 21 other fillies have raced in the Belmont Stakes, and just two others, Tanya in 1905 and Rags to Riches in 2007, have won. Kentucky Derby winner and Preakness runner-up Genuine Risk was second to Temperence Hill in 1980, and six other fillies have finished third, most recently My Flag in '96.

Year	Filly	Finish
2007	**Rags to Riches**	1st
1999	Silverbulletday	7th
1996	My Flag	3rd
1988	Winning Colors	6th
1980	Genuine Risk	2nd
1954	Riverina	7th
1932	Laughing Queen	10th
1927	Flambino	3rd
1923	Miss Smith	8th
1913	Flying Fairy	3rd
1905	**Tanya**	1st
	Flinders	7th
1885	Miss Palmer	6th
1871	Mary Clark	6th
1871	Nellie Gray	10th
1870	Midday	3rd
	Nellie James	4th
	Stamps	6th
1869	Invercauld	3rd
	Viola	7th
1868	Fanny Ludlow	3rd
1867	**Ruthless**	1st

Geldings in the Belmont

Creme Fraiche, owned by Elizabeth Moran's Brushwood Stable, remains the only gelding ever to have won the Belmont Stakes. In its early years, the Belmont conditions allowed geldings to run in the classic race, but America subsequently bowed to European practice, which barred geldings from major races. Lanius, a gelding, ran in the 1918 Belmont, but it was not until '57 that geldings again were permitted in the race. Creme Fraiche was the first gelding to compete in the Belmont since 1979 champion juvenile male Rockhill Native finished third in '80.

Geldings who have started in the Belmont since 1985:

Year	Gelding	Finish
2007	Imawildandcrazyguy	6th
2004	Tap Dancer	6th
2003	Funny Cide	3rd
2002	Magic Weisner	4th
	Perfect Drift	10th
2001	Balto Star	8th
2000	Unshaded	3rd
1998	Thomas Jo	3rd
1997	Irish Silence	5th
1996	Jamies First Punch	8th
	Cavonnier	DNF
1993	Prairie Bayou	DNF
1991	Subordinated Debt	9th
1988	Kingpost	2nd
1985	**Creme Fraiche**	1st

Birthplaces of Belmont Winners

Place of Birth	Winners
Kentucky	91
Virginia	11
New Jersey	7
England	6
Florida	6
New York	3
Pennsylvania	3
Tennessee	3
California	2
Ireland	2
Maryland	2
Texas	2
Canada	1
Montana	1

Belmont Stakes

Grade 1, Belmont Park, three-year-olds, 1½ miles, dirt. Held on June 7, 2008, with gross value of $1,000,000. First run in 1867. Weights: colts and geldings, 126 pounds; fillies, 121 pounds.

Year	Winner	Jockey	Second	Third	Strs	Time	Track	1st Purse
2008	**Da'Tara**	A. Garcia	Denis of Cork	dh-Ready's Echo dh-Anak Nakal	9	2:29.65	ft	$600,000
2007	**†Rags to Riches**	J. Velazquez	Curlin	Tiago	7	2:28.74	ft	600,000
2006	**Jazil**	F. Jara	Bluegrass Cat	Sunriver	12	2:27.86	ft	600,000
2005	**Afleet Alex**	J. Rose	Andromeda's Hero	Nolan's Cat	11	2:28.75	ft	600,000
2004	**Birdstone**	E. Prado	Smarty Jones	Royal Assault	9	2:27.50	ft	600,000
2003	**Empire Maker**	J. Bailey	Ten Most Wanted	Funny Cide	6	2:28.26	sy	600,000
2002	**Sarava**	E. Prado	Medaglia d'Oro	Sunday Break (Jpn)	11	2:29.71	ft	600,000
2001	**Point Given**	G. Stevens	A P Valentine	Monarchos	9	2:26.56	ft	600,000
2000	**Commendable**	P. Day	Aptitude	‡Unshaded	11	2:31.19	ft	600,000
1999	**Lemon Drop Kid**	J. Santos	Vision and Verse	Charismatic	12	2:27.88	ft	600,000
1998	**Victory Gallop**	G. Stevens	Real Quiet	‡Thomas Jo	11	2:29.16	ft	**600,000**
1997	**Touch Gold**	C. McCarron	Silver Charm	Free House	7	2:28.82	ft	432,600
1996	**Editor's Note**	R. Douglas	Skip Away	†My Flag	14	2:28.96	ft	437,880
1995	**Thunder Gulch**	G. Stevens	Star Standard	‡Citadeed	11	2:32.02	ft	415,440
1994	**Tabasco Cat**	P. Day	Go for Gin	Strodes Creek	6	2:26.82	ft	392,280
1993	**Colonial Affair**	J. Krone	Kissin Kris	Wild Gale	13	2:29.97	gd	444,540
1992	**A.P. Indy**	E. Delahoussaye	My Memoirs (GB)	Pine Bluff	11	2:26.13	gd	458,880
1991	**Hansel**	J. Bailey	Strike the Gold	Mane Minister	11	2:28.10	ft	417,480
1990	**Go and Go (Ire)**	M. Kinane	Thirty Six Red	Baron de Vaux	9	2:27⅕	gd	411,600
1989	**Easy Goer**	P. Day	Sunday Silence	Le Voyageur	10	2:26	ft	413,520
1988	**Risen Star**	E. Delahoussaye	‡Kingpost	Brian's Time	6	2:26⅖	ft	303,720
1987	**Bet Twice**	C. Perret	Cryptoclearance	Gulch	9	2:28⅕	ft	329,160
1986	**Danzig Connection**	C. McCarron	Johns Treasure	Ferdinand	10	2:29⅘	sy	338,640
1985	**‡Creme Fraiche**	E. Maple	Stephan's Odyssey	Chief's Crown	11	2:27	my	307,740
1984	**Swale**	L. Pincay Jr.	Pine Circle	Morning Bob	11	2:27⅕	ft	310,020
1983	**Caveat**	L. Pincay Jr.	Slew o' Gold	Barberstown	**15**	2:27⅘	ft	215,100
1982	**Conquistador Cielo**	L. Pincay Jr.	Gato Del Sol	Illuminate	11	2:28⅕	sy	159,720
1981	**Summing**	G. Martens	Highland Blade	Pleasant Colony	11	2:29	ft	170,580
1980	**Temperence Hill**	E. Maple	†Genuine Risk	Rockhill Native	10	2:29⅘	my	176,228
1979	**Coastal**	R. Hernandez	Golden Act	Spectacular Bid	8	2:29⅗	ft	161,400
1978	**AFFIRMED**	S. Cauthen	Alydar	Darby Creek Road	5	2:26⅘	ft	110,580
1977	**SEATTLE SLEW**	J. Cruguet	Run Dusty Run	Sanhedrin	8	2:29⅗	my	109,080
1976	**Bold Forbes**	A. Cordero Jr.	McKenzie Bridge	Great Contractor	10	2:29	ft	117,000
1975	**Avatar**	W. Shoemaker	Foolish Pleasure	Master Derby	9	2:28⅕	ft	116,160
1974	**Little Current**	M. Rivera	Jolly Johu	Cannonade	9	2:29⅕	ft	101,970
1973	**SECRETARIAT**	R. Turcotte	Twice a Prince	My Gallant	5	**2:24**	ft	90,120
1972	**Riva Ridge**	R. Turcotte	Ruritania	Cloudy Dawn	10	2:28	ft	83,540
1971	**Pass Catcher**	W. Blum	Jim French	Bold Reason	13	2:30⅗	ft	97,710
1970	**High Echelon**	J. Rotz	Needles n Pens	Naskra	10	2:34	sy	115,000
1969	**Arts and Letters**	B. Baeza	Majestic Prince	Dike	6	2:28⅘	ft	104,050
1968	**Stage Door Johnny**	H. Gustines	Forward Pass	Call Me Prince	9	2:27⅕	ft	117,700
1967	**Damascus**	W. Shoemaker	Cool Reception	Gentleman James	9	2:28⅘	ft	104,950
1966	**Amberoid**	W. Boland	Buffle	Advocator	11	2:29⅗	ft	117,700
1965	**Hail to All**	J. Sellers	Tom Rolfe	First Family	8	2:28⅖	ft	104,150
1964	**Quadrangle**	M. Ycaza	Roman Brother	Northern Dancer	8	2:28⅖	ft	110,850
1963	**Chateaugay**	B. Baeza	Candy Spots	Choker	7	2:30⅕	gd	101,700
1962	**Jaipur**	W. Shoemaker	Admiral's Voyage	Crimson Satan	8	2:28⅘	ft	109,550
1961	**Sherluck**	B. Baeza	Globemaster	Guadalcanal	9	2:29⅕	ft	104,900
1960	***Celtic Ash**	W. Hartack	Venetian Way	Disperse	7	2:29⅗	ft	96,785
1959	**Sword Dancer**	W. Shoemaker	Bagdad	Royal Orbit	9	2:28⅗	sy	93,525
1958	***Cavan**	P. Anderson	Tim Tam	‡Flamingo	8	2:30⅕	ft	73,440
1957	***Gallant Man**	W. Shoemaker	Inside Tract	Bold Ruler	6	2:26⅗	ft	78,350
1956	**Needles**	D. Erb	Career Boy	Fabius	8	2:29⅘	ft	83,600
1955	**Nashua**	E. Arcaro	Blazing Count	Portersville	8	2:29	ft	83,700
1954	**High Gun**	E. Guerin	Fisherman	*Limelight	13	2:30⅘	ft	89,000
1953	**Native Dancer**	E. Guerin	Jamie K.	Royal Bay Gem	6	2:28⅗	ft	82,500
1952	**One Count**	E. Arcaro	Blue Man	Armageddon	6	2:30⅕	ft	82,400
1951	**Counterpoint**	D. Gorman	Battlefield	Battle Morn	9	2:29	ft	82,000
1950	**Middleground**	W. Boland	Lights Up	Mr. Trouble	9	2:28⅗	ft	61,350
1949	**Capot**	T. Atkinson	Ponder	Palestinian	8	2:30⅕	ft	60,900
1948	**CITATION**	E. Arcaro	Better Self	Escadru	8	2:28⅕	ft	77,700
1947	**Phalanx**	R. Donoso	Tide Rips	Tailspin	9	2:29⅗	ft	78,900

Year	Winner	Jockey	Second	Third	Strs	Time	Track	1st Purse
1946	**ASSAULT**	W. Mehrtens	Natchez	Cable	7	2:30 4/5	ft	$75,400
1945	**Pavot**	E. Arcaro	Wildlife	Jeep	8	2:30 1/5	ft	52,675
1944	**Bounding Home**	G. L. Smith	Pensive	Bull Dandy	7	2:32 1/5	ft	55,000
1943	**COUNT FLEET**	J. Longden	Fairy Manhurst	‡Deseronto	3	2:28 1/5	ft	35,340
1942	**Shut Out**	E. Arcaro	Alsab	Lochinvar	7	2:29 1/5	ft	44,520
1941	**WHIRLAWAY**	E. Arcaro	Robert Morris	‡Yankee Chance	4	2:31	ft	39,770
1940	**Bimelech**	F. Smith	Your Chance	Andy K.	6	2:29 3/5	ft	35,030
1939	**Johnstown**	J. Stout	Belay	Gilded Knight	6	2:29 3/5	ft	37,020
1938	**Pasteurized**	J. Stout	Dauber	Cravat	6	2:29 2/5	ft	34,530
1937	**WAR ADMIRAL**	C. Kurtsinger	Sceneshifter	Vamoose	7	2:28 3/5	ft	38,020
1936	**Granville**	J. Stout	Mr. Bones	Hollyrood	10	2:30	ft	29,800
1935	**OMAHA**	W. Saunders	Firethorn	Rosemont	5	2:30 3/5	sy	35,480
1934	**Peace Chance**	W. Wright	High Quest	Good Goods	8	2:29 1/5	ft	43,410
1933	**Hurryoff**	M. Garner	Nimbus	Union	9	2:32 3/5	ft	49,490
1932	**Faireno**	T. Malley	Osculator	Flag Pole	11	2:32 4/5	ft	55,120
1931	**Twenty Grand**	C. Kurtsinger	Sun Meadow	Jamestown	3	2:29 3/5	ft	58,770
1930	**GALLANT FOX**	E. Sande	Whichone	Questionnaire	4	2:31 3/5	gd	66,040
1929	**Blue Larkspur**	M. Garner	African	Jack High	8	2:32 4/5	sy	59,650
1928	**Vito**	C. Kummer	Genie	Diavolo	6	2:33 1/5	ft	63,430
1927	**Chance Shot**	E. Sande	Bois de Rose	†Flambino	6	2:32 2/5	ft	60,910
1926	**Crusader**	A. Johnson	Espino	Haste	9	2:32 1/5	sy	48,550
1925	**American Flag**	A. Johnson	Dangerous	Swope	7	2:16 4/5	ft	38,500
1924	**Mad Play**	E. Sande	Mr. Mutt	Modest	11	2:18 4/5	gd	42,880
1923	**Zev**	E. Sande	Chickvale	‡Rialto	8	2:19	gd	38,000
1922	**Pillory**	C. H. Miller	*Snob II	Hea	4	2:18 4/5	ft	39,200
1921	**Grey Lag**	E. Sande	Sporting Blood	Leonardo II	4	2:16 4/5	ft	8,650
1920	**Man o' War**	C. Kummer	*Donnacona	————	2	2:14 1/5	ft	7,950
1919	**SIR BARTON**	J. Loftus	Sweep On	Natural Bridge	3	2:17 2/5	ft	11,950
1918	***Johren**	F. Robinson	*War Cloud	‡Cum Sah	4	2:20 2/5	ft	8,950
1917	***Hourless**	J. Butwell	Skeptic	Wonderful	3	2:17 4/5	gd	5,800
1916	**Friar Rock**	E. Haynes	Spur	Churchill	4	2:22	my	4,100
1915	**The Finn**	G. Byrne	Half Rock	Pebbles	3	2:18 2/5	ft	1,825
1914	**Luke McLuke**	M. Buxton	‡Gainer	‡Charlestonian	3	2:20	ft	3,275
1913	**Prince Eugene**	R. Troxler	Rock View	†Flying Fairy	4	2:18	ft	3,075
1910	**Sweep**	J. Butwell	Duke of Ormonde	————	2	2:22	ft	9,700
1909	**Joe Madden**	E. Dugan	Wise Mason	‡Donald Macdonald	5	2:21 3/5	ft	24,550
1908	**Colin**	J. Notter	Fair Play	King James	4	n/a	sy	22,765
1907	**Peter Pan**	G. Mountain	Superman	Frank Gill	5	n/a	ft	22,765
1906	**Burgomaster**	L. Lyne	The Quail	Accountant	6	2:20	gd	22,700
1905	**†Tanya**	E. Hildebrand	Blandy	Hot Shot	7	2:08	ft	17,240
1904	**Delhi**	G. Odom	Graziallo	Rapid Water	8	2:06 3/5	ft	14,685
1903	**Africander**	J. Bullman	Whorler	Red Knight	4	2:21 3/4	ft	12,285
1902	**Masterman**	J. Bullman	Ranald	King Hanover	6	2:22 3/5	ft	12,020
1901	**Commando**	H. Spencer	The Parader	All Green	3	2:21	ft	11,595
1900	**Ildrim**	N. Turner	‡Petruchio	Missionary	7	2:21 1/4	ft	14,790
1899	**Jean Bereaud**	R. Clawson	Half Time	Glengar	4	2:23	ft	10,680
1898	***Bowling Brook**	F. Littlefield	Previous	Hamburg	4	2:32	hy	7,810
1897	**Scottish Chieftain**	J. Scherrer	On Deck	Octagon	6	2:23 1/4	ft	3,350
1896	**Hastings**	H. Griffin	Handspring	Hamilton II	4	2:24 1/2	gd	3,025
1895	**Belmar**	F. Taral	Counter Tenor	Nanki Pooh	5	2:11 1/2	hy	2,700
1894	**Henry of Navarre**	W. Simms	Prig	Assignee	3	1:56 1/2	ft	6,680
1893	**Comanche**	W. Simms	Dr. Rice	Rainbow	5	1:53 1/4	ft	5,310
1892	**Patron**	W. Hayward	Shellbark	————	2	2:12	my	6,610
1891	**Foxford**	E. Garrison	Montana	Laurestan	6	2:08 3/4	gd	5,070
1890	**Burlington**	S. Barnes	Devotee	Padishah	9	2:07 3/4	ft	8,560
1889	**Eric**	W. Hayward	Diablo	Zephyrus	3	2:47 1/4	gd	4,960
1888	**Sir Dixon**	J. McLaughlin	Prince Royal	————	2	2:40 1/4	ft	3,440
1887	**Hanover**	J. McLaughlin	Oneko	————	2	2:43 1/2	hy	2,900
1886	**Inspector B.**	J. McLaughlin	The Bard	Linden	5	2:41	ft	2,720
1885	**Tyrant**	P. Duffy	‡St. Augustine	Tecumseh	6	2:43	gd	2,710
1884	**Panique**	J. McLaughlin	Knight of Ellerslie	Himalaya	4	2:42	gd	3,150
1883	**George Kinney**	J. McLaughlin	‡Trombone	Renegade	4	2:42 1/2	ft	3,070
1882	**Forester**	J. McLaughlin	Babcock	‡Wyoming	3	2:43	ft	2,600
1881	**Saunterer**	T. Costello	Eole	Baltic	6	2:47	hy	3,000
1880	**Grenada**	W. Hughes	Ferncliffe	Turenne	4	2:47	gd	2,800
1879	**Spendthrift**	G. Evans	‡Monitor	Jericho	6	2:24 3/4	sy	4,250
1878	**Duke of Magenta**	W. Hughes	Bramble	Sparta	6	2:43 1/2	my	3,850

Triple Crown — Belmont Stakes

Year	Winner	Jockey	Second	Third	Strs	Time	Track	1st Purse
1877	Cloverbrook	C. Holloway	‡Loiterer	Baden-Baden	13	2:46	hy	$5,200
1876	Algerine	W. Donohue	Fiddlesticks	Barricade	5	2:40½	ft	3,700
1875	Calvin	R. Swim	Aristides	Milner	14	2:42¼	ft	4,450
1874	Saxon	G. Barbee	Grinstead	Aaron Pennington	9	2:39½	ft	4,200
1873	Springbok	J. Rowe	Count d'Orsay	Strachino	10	3:01¾	fr	5,200
1872	Joe Daniels	J. Rowe	‡Meteor	Shylock	9	2:58¼	fr	4,500
1871	Harry Bassett	W. Miller	Stockwood	By the Sea	11	2:56	ft	5,450
1870	Kingfisher	Dick	Foster	†Midday	7	2:59½	ft	3,750
1869	Fenian	C. Miller	Glenelg	†Invercauld	8	3:04¼	hy	3,350
1868	General Duke	R. Swim	Northumberland	†Fanny Ludlow	6	3:02	ft	2,800
1867	†Ruthless	J. Gilpatrick	DeCourcey	Rivoli	4	3:05	hy	1,850

†—filly, ‡—gelding, *—imported horse
1867-'73, 1⅝ miles; 1890-'92, 1895, 1904-'05, 1¼ miles; 1893-'94, 1⅛ miles; 1896-1903, 1906-'25, 1⅜ miles. 1867-'89, held at Jerome Park; 1890-1904, Morris Park; 1963-'67, Aqueduct. Not run 1911 and '12. 1973-present, Grade 1. Hansel (1991), Risen Star (1988), and Bet Twice (1987) earned $1-million bonus from Triple Crown Productions. 1907-'08 no official time recorded; bold-faced type shows records in starters, time, and purse earnings.

Status of Belmont Stakes Winners Since 1970

Year	Winner	Birthdate	Status	Where Stands/Stood	Location	Death Date
2008	Da' Tara	4/26/2005	In Training			
2007	Rags to Riches	2/27/2004	Retired	Ashford Stud	Versailles, Ky.	
2006	Jazil	2/11/2003	Stallion	Shadwell Stud	Lexington, Ky.	
2005	Afleet Alex	3/9/2002	Stallion	Gainesway	Lexington, Ky.	
2004	Birdstone	5/16/2001	Stallion	Gainesway	Lexington, Ky.	
2003	Empire Maker	4/27/2000	Stallion	Juddmonte Farms	Lexington, Ky.	
2002	Sarava	3/2/1999	Stallion	CloverLeaf Farms II	Reddick, Fl.	
2001	Point Given	3/27/1998	Stallion	Three Chimneys Farm	Midway, Ky.	
2000	Commendable	4/13/1997	Stallion	KRA Jeju Stud Farm	South Korea	
1999	Lemon Drop Kid	5/26/1996	Stallion	Lane's End	Versailles, Ky.	
1998	Victory Gallop	5/30/1995	Stallion	Karacabey Pension Stud	Izmit, Turkey	
1997	Touch Gold	5/26/1994	Stallion	Adena Springs Kentucky	Versailles, Ky.	
1996	Editor's Note	4/26/1993	Stallion	Haras Abolengo	Argentina	
1995	Thunder Gulch	5/23/1992	Stallion	Ashford Stud	Versailles, Ky.	
1994	Tabasco Cat	4/15/1991	Deceased	JBBA Shizunai Stallion Station	Hokkaido, Japan	3/6/2004
1993	Colonial Affair	4/19/1990	Stallion	Haras El Paraiso	Capitan Sarmiento, Argentina	
1992	A.P. Indy	3/31/1989	Stallion	Lane's End	Versailles, Ky.	
1991	Hansel	3/12/1988	Pensioned	Lazy Lane Farms	Upperville, Va.	
1990	Go and Go (Ire)	3/21/1987	Deceased	Waldorf Farm	North Chatham, N.Y.	3/2000
1989	Easy Goer	3/21/1986	Deceased	Claiborne Farm	Paris, Ky.	5/1/1994
1988	Risen Star	3/25/1985	Deceased	Walmac International	Lexington, Ky.	3/13/1998
1987	Bet Twice	4/20/1984	Deceased	Muirfield East	Chesapeake City, Md.	3/5/1999
1986	Danzig Connection	4/6/1983	Stallion	Allevamento Al-Ca Torre	Comiso, Italy	
1985	Creme Fraiche	4/7/1982	Deceased	Brushwood Farm	Malvern, Pa.	10/9/2003
1984	Swale	4/21/1981	Deceased			6/17/1984
1983	Caveat	3/16/1980	Deceased	Northview Stallion Station	Chesapeake City, Md.	2/1/1995
1982	Conquistador Cielo	3/20/1979	Deceased	Claiborne Farm	Paris, Ky.	12/17/2002
1981	Summing	4/16/1978	Deceased	Getaway Thoroughbred Farms	Romoland, Ca.	1/2007
1980	Temperence Hill	3/6/1977	Deceased	Swang Jei Farm	Nontaburi, Thailand	6/03/2003
1979	Coastal	4/6/1976	Deceased	Summerhill Stud	Mooi River, South Africa	9/28/2005
1978	Affirmed	2/21/1975	Deceased	Jonabell Farm	Lexington, Ky.	1/12/2001
1977	Seattle Slew	2/15/1974	Deceased	Three Chimneys Farm	Midway, Ky.	5/7/2002
1976	Bold Forbes	3/31/1973	Deceased	Stone Farm	Paris, Ky.	8/9/2000
1975	Avatar	3/10/1972	Deceased	Frisch's Farm	Morrow, Oh.	12/3/1992
1974	Little Current	4/5/1971	Deceased	Pacific Equine Clinic	Monroe, Wa.	1/19/2003
1973	Secretariat	3/30/1970	Deceased	Claiborne Farm	Paris, Ky.	10/4/1989
1972	Riva Ridge	4/13/1969	Deceased	Claiborne Farm	Paris, Ky.	4/21/1985
1971	Pass Catcher	4/6/1968	Deceased	Ocala Stud Farm	Ocala, Fl.	1993
1970	High Echelon	3/22/1967	Deceased	Franks Farms	Ocala, Fl.	5/15/1991

2008 Kentucky Derby: Delivering the Goods

In mid-January, Michael Sherack of IEAH Stables asked trainer Richard Dutrow Jr. whether Big Brown would be a candidate for the Triple Crown races. Big Brown had yet to race for IEAH since being purchased privately after a debut win on the turf at Saratoga Race Course on September 3. Quarter cracks in both front feet had brought his racing career to a standstill and limited his daily activity to walking Dutrow's shedrow. In the entire month of January, Big Brown never stepped foot on a racetrack for training.

Dutrow told Sherack, IEAH's vice president of investor relations, that Big Brown might be ready for the Triple Crown's final leg, the Belmont Stakes (G1) on June 7. Less than four months after that conversation, Big Brown overcame a procession of obstacles and scored a powerful victory in the $2,211,800 Kentucky Derby Presented by Yum! Brands (G1) on May 3 at Churchill Downs.

Before the second-largest crowd in Derby history, Big Brown remained undefeated in becoming the first horse since 1915 to win the classic with just three prior starts, and the first winner since '29 to succeed from post 20. The Derby was marred by the fatal breakdown of the filly Eight Belles, who finished a game second but then broke both front ankles galloping out on the clubhouse turn. She was euthanized on the track.

Big Brown crossed the finish line 4¾ lengths in front as the 2.40-to-1 favorite under Kent Desormeaux, igniting a raucous grandstand celebration from a massive cheering party led by Dutrow and members of IEAH, a New York-based company that organizes and manages racing partnerships.

Dutrow made no effort to contain his enthusiasm over Big Brown leading up to the Derby. Inconsistent form contributed to Dutrow's assessment of Big Brown's Derby competition.

Big Brown's prominence reflected an unlikely climb to racing's premier level by a horse who did not have his first workout of the year until late February. He had battled foot problems since shortly after IEAH purchased a 75% interest in him for approximately $3-million in September 2007 from Paul Pompa Jr., who named Big Brown in honor of United Parcel Service, a longtime client of his trucking company based in Brooklyn, New York. Dutrow and Michael Iavarone, co-president of IEAH, originally hoped to run Big Brown in the Breeders' Cup Juvenile Turf on October 25 at Monmouth Park, but he developed a quarter crack in his left front foot after his first workout with the new stable.

The hoof injury required 45 days of rest before

Owners
IEAH Stables is the racing operation of International Equine Acquisitions Holdings Inc., which is owned and operated by co-presidents Michael Iavarone and Richard Schiavo. Iavarone founded IEAH after working for investment companies specializing in low-cost stocks and trading for his own account as a day trader. Schiavo, former chief administrative officer of Smith Barney, joined the company as an investor in 2003 and moved into an administrative role in early '04. Paul Pompa Jr., the owner of a trucking company, resides in Warren, New Jersey. He sold 75% of Big Brown to IEAH in 2007.

Breeder
Monticule is located in Lexington and is owned by Gary B. Knapp, Ph.D., a marketing professor who owned Park Communications Inc., a diversified media company until its sale in 1997. In 2003, he acquired an interest in Equix, which assesses the biomechanical characteristics of racehorses. The farm has grown to 630 acres.

Dutrow eased Big Brown back into training at Palm Meadows Training Center in Florida. As Big Brown progressed, Dutrow became more and more impressed. Another quarter crack, this time in the right front foot, cost 45 more days of training.

Once the hoof healed, Dutrow proceeded cautiously with three workouts before picking a comeback spot, a one-mile allowance race on Gulfstream Park's turf on March 5. Inclement weather forced the race to be moved from the turf to dirt, which only heightened Dutrow's elation when Big Brown kicked away powerfully to win by 12¾ lengths under Desormeaux.

The performance created enough buzz that Big Brown was installed as the 3-to-1 program-line favorite for the Florida Derby (G1) on March 29 at Gulfstream, even though he drew the outside post in the field of 12. He won by five lengths.

Dutrow chose the outside position in the Derby starting gate, believing that the colt had natural speed to gain position and would not spend much time in the starting gate. He sharpened Big Brown with a three-furlong workout on May 1 at Churchill.

Under regular exercise rider Michelle Nevin, Big Brown covered the distance in :35.40, which was slightly faster than Dutrow intended.

Big Brown overcame all obstacles on the big day. He broke sharply for Desormeaux, who gradually angled him toward the inside rail while rating behind longshot pacemaker Bob Black Jack. Big Brown was four or five wide in the first turn, and he dropped back to sixth while running in the clear along the backstretch.

Approaching the half-mile pole, Big Brown made a quick rally to challenge the leaders, and he took command with authority heading into the stretch, opening up 2½ lengths at the eighth pole and drawing off for the clear victory.

—*Jeff Lowe*

TENTH RACE
Churchill
May 3, 2008

1¼ MILES on dirt. 134th running of the Kentucky Derby Presented by Yum! Brands. Grade 1. Three-year-olds. Purse $2,000,000 guaranteed. Track record: Secretariat, 1:59⅖, May 5, 1973.

Value of race $2,211,800; Winner $1,451,800; second $400,000; third $200,000; fourth $100,000; fifth $60,000. Mutuel WPS Pool $47,956,786. Exacta Pool $22,641,373. Trifecta Pool $27,057,852. Superfecta Pool $9,067,204.

Horse	M/Eqt.	Wt.	PP	¼	½	¾	1 mi.	Str.	Fin.	Jockey	Odds $1
Big Brown, 3, c	Lf	126	20	4½	61½	6½	1hd	12½	14¾	K. Desormeaux	2.40 *
Eight Belles, 3, f	LA	121	5	5hd	5½	52	4½	22	23½	G. Saez	13.10
Denis of Cork, 3, c	LA	126	16	20	20	20	13hd	61	32¾	C. Borel	27.20
Tale of Ekati, 3, c	LA	126	2	9½	7hd	71	51	4½	4¾	E. Coa	37.40
Recapturetheglory, 3, c	LAf	126	8	3½	3hd	3hd	2hd	32	5½	E. Baird	49.00
Colonel John, 3, c	L	126	10	17½	16hd	10½	6½	7½	6¾	C. Nakatani	4.70
Anak Nakal, 3, c	LA	126	3	16½	15½	171	12hd	112	7no	R. Bejarano	53.90
Pyro, 3, c	LA	126	9	18½	17hd	18½	152	9½	8¾	S. Bridgmohan	5.70
Cowboy Cal, 3, c	LA	126	17	2½	2½	21	3½	5½	93¾	J. Velazquez	39.20
Z Fortune, 3, c	LA	126	6	7hd	8½	81	82	8½	101½	R. Albarado	19.20
Smooth Air, 3, c	L	126	12	15½	184	11hd	10½	10hd	111¾	M. Cruz	42.00
Visionaire, 3, c	LA	126	8	194	193	19hd	18½	163	121½	J. Lezcano	25.30
Court Vision, 3, c	LAb	126	4	13½	12½	15½	14½	12hd	13nk	G. Gomez	17.70
Z Humor, 3, c	LA	126	11	141	131½	16½	162	15½	147¼	R. Douglas	63.60
Cool Coal Man, 3, c	LA	126	1	6½	4½	4hd	94	141	15nk	J. Leparoux	44.10
Bob Black Jack, 3, c	Lb	126	13	1½	11	1½	7hd	132	164¾	R. Migliore	29.40
Gayego, 3, c	LA	126	19	81	92	9½	11½	174	1712	M. Smith	18.90
Big Truck, 3, c	LA	126	7	10hd	10½	12½	17½	183	182	J. Castellano	28.60
Adriano, 3, c	LA	126	15	11hd	14½	14½	194	194	198¾	E. Prado	28.90
Monba, 3, c	LAb	126	14	12½	111	13½	20	20	20	R. Dominguez	31.60

L=Salix; LA=Salix and adjunct bleeder medication; b=blinkers; f=front bandages.

OFF AT 6:15. Times: :23.30, :47.04, 1:11.14, 1:36.56, 2:01.82.
Start: Good for all except #8 and #12. Weather: Clear. Track: Fast.

$2 Mutuel Prices:
20—BIG BROWN............................. 6.80 5.00 4.80
5—EIGHT BELLES........................ 10.60 6.40
16—DENIS OF CORK..................... 11.60

$2 EXACTA 20-5 PAID $141.60 $2 TRIFECTA 20-5-16 PAID $3,445.60
$2 SUPERFECTA 20-5-16-2 PAID $58,737.80 $2 DAILY DOUBLE 5-20 PAID $24.80
$2 DAILY DOUBLE CALDER/DERBY 2-20 PAID $15.40; OAKS/DERBY 8-20 PAID $37.80
$2 PICK THREE 9-5-20 (3 CORRECT) PAID $732.80
$2 PICK FOUR 7-9-2/5-20 (4 CORRECT) PAID $14,675.60
$2 PICK SIX 1-2/4/5-7-9-2/5-20 (5 CORRECT) PAID $1,271.00
$2 FUTURE WAGER (POOL 1—24) PAID $8.60; (POOL 2—24) PAID $15.00; (POOL 3—3) PAID $8.60
$2 OVER/UNDER (OVER 32) PAID $2.40 $2 SUPER HIGH FIVE 20-5-16-2-18 PAID $0

B. c., by Boundary out of Mien, by Nureyev. Trainer: Richard Dutrow Jr. Owners: IEAH Stables and Paul P. Pompa Jr. Breeder: Monticule (Ky.).

BIG BROWN rated off the early pace four wide, advanced five wide when ready after five furlongs, ranged up outside the leaders approaching the stretch, took over before angling in near the rail in the stretch, and increased his lead under steady urging. EIGHT BELLES, forwardly placed, was steadied near the three-eighths and quarter poles when lacking a clear path, went out to follow the winner into the stretch, and gamely held on to be second best. She fractured both ankles while galloping out and was euthanized. DENIS OF CORK advanced between rivals with three furlongs to run and moved to the inside in the stretch. TALE OF EKATI, steadied early, came six wide into the stretch, reached a forward position in midstretch, but lacked a further bid. RECAPTURETHEGLORY, close up, surged with the winner into the stretch, but tired in the final furlong. COLONEL JOHN, steadied early, made a bold run to the quarter pole, but could not sustain the bid. ANAK NAKAL, outrun early, improved his position, but was no threat. PYRO angled in after the start, came four wide into the stretch, but could not menace. COWBOY CAL pressed the early pace, but tired in the stetch. Z FORTUNE maintained a good position to the stretch and tired. SMOOTH AIR broke in the air, steadied twice in the first half-mile, and lacked a late bid. VISIONAIRE stumbled at the start, was outrun for five furlongs, and improved his position late. COURT VISION was reserved inside and could not menace. Z HUMOR, carried in early, never threatened. COOL COAL MAN was away alertly, but faded after seven furlongs. BOB BLACK JACK set the early pace and faded after a mile. GAYEGO, sluggish at the start, was through after six furlongs. BIG TRUCK, steadied and bumped early, gave way after six furlongs. ADRIANO took up early and was no factor. MONBA steadied early and was no menace.

2008 Preakness: No Contest

Forget everything you know about Big Brown's connections or this year's Triple Crown season. Forget trainer Richard Dutrow Jr.'s checkered past; forget owner IEAH Stables's reputation for mercilessly acquiring horses; forget the heartbreak of Kentucky Derby Presented by Yum! Brands (G1) runner-up Eight Belles breaking down.

Forget all the questions and take time to enjoy the racehorse that is Big Brown, who made mincemeat of his competition in the 133rd edition of the Preakness Stakes (G1) on May 17 at Pimlico Race Course.

Big Brown is the first Derby-Preakness winner since Smarty Jones in 2004, the fourth dating back to '02, the seventh dating back to 1997, and the 11th dating back to '79. If it is possible for an undefeated Kentucky Derby winner to have a coming-out party, then the Preakness was it. Big Brown not only won the race by 5¼ lengths as the shortest-priced favorite (1-to-5) since Spectacular Bid, but he also decimated his rivals who ran with him, and those who did not never threatened at any point.

Big Brown was third through the early part of the 1³⁄₁₆-mile race with Cubanacan Stables' Arkansas Derby (G2) winner Gayego and Zayat Stables' Coolmore Lexington Stakes (G2) third-place finisher Riley Tucker on the lead through fractions of :23.59, :46.81, and 1:10.48.

Jockey Kent Desormeaux gave Big Brown his cue midway on the far turn, and the Boundary colt exploded to the front in a flash and was already five lengths past his nearest opponent turning for home. Big Brown went on to win the race in 1:54.80, with West Point Thoroughbreds's Derby Trial Stakes winner Macho Again in second and Earle Mack's Federico Tesio Stakes winner Icabad Crane another half-length back in third. Gayego and Riley Tucker finished 11th and 12th, respectively, in the 12-horse field.

"[On the far turn], I looked back under my arms one more time before I asked him to run to see where everybody was," Desormeaux said. "I kissed at [Big Brown], I tapped him on the shoulder, and he just took off; he's got some turn of foot.

"I guess I was knuckling on him for about 100 yards, and then I looked between my legs, and they were eight [lengths] behind me. I stopped pushing. I said, 'That's enough.' I looked one more time at the sixteenth pole, and they were still [many] lengths behind me, so I started slowing him down and watching [the infield matrix board] to make sure nothing crazy happened."

The two weeks between the Derby and Preakness was a tumultuous time for the Thoroughbred industry as it reeled from the Eight Belles breakdown and dealt with mainstream criticism regarding the safety of the sport and the treatment of animals.

Trainer
Richard Dutrow Jr. began his career as an assistant to his father at age 16 and remained in New York when the elder Dutrow returned to Maryland in the late 1990s. Starting with one horse, he gained prominence first as a claiming trainer and added top stakes horses in recent years. His best so far is Saint Liam, Horse of the Year in 2005.

Jockey
Kent Desormeaux rose from the bush tracks of Louisiana and became the nation's top apprentice in 1986 while riding mostly in Maryland. He was honored as outstanding jockey in 1989, when he set a record for most victories, 598. He was voted into the Racing Hall of Fame in 2004.

While those two weeks probably could not have gone by fast enough for some in the industry, they very likely went by too quickly for Dutrow, who lamented in the 14 days leading up to the middle jewel of Thoroughbred racing's Triple Crown that he did not like running horses on two weeks' rest, particularly off a race as taxing as the Derby.

Trainer Bob Baffert, who has won the Preakness four times, including all three times he saddled the Derby winner in the race, said after the 2008 Derby that the Preakness would be the easiest race of the classic races for Big Brown to win.

"Once you win that Derby, you're on cruise control," Baffert said, drawing on his experience with Silver Charm in 1997, Real Quiet in '98, and War Emblem in 2002. "There's not much you can do to mess things up. If you had your horse ready for the Derby, then he'll be ready for the Preakness. The Belmont with that extra week is what can trip you up."

Big Brown stayed in Louisville for 11 days after the Derby, returning to training on May 7 at Churchill Downs and mostly jogging because of wet conditions in Kentucky the week after the Derby. He arrived at Pimlico in Baltimore on May 14, galloped two miles on May 15, jogged one mile on May 16, and worked two furlongs the morning of the race.

The Big Brown camp must have really liked what it saw because the mood around the Pimlico stakes barn in the 24 hours before the race versus the previous 48 hours was noticeably more jocular.

Dutrow joked after the race that his mood change coincided with the arrival of his girlfriend, but Big Brown clearly was telling his team that he was ready to run.

By the morning of the race, after Big Brown worked about 12 hours before the Preakness, Dutrow was convinced he had the winner. "I could see he was full of energy," Dutrow said. "I didn't want to take any of that energy out of him; I just wanted to let him know that he was going to run later on."

The confidence was contagious, as bettors made Big Brown the 1-to-5 favorite. Gayego was the second choice at 9.20-to-1, the second-highest second choice in the history of the race, and the rest of the field had double-digit odds.

Robert and Blythe Clay's Three Chimneys Farm got in on the action with a gamble of its own, securing a deal with IEAH to stand Big Brown at the Midway, Kentucky, farm that also is home to Smarty Jones and the former home of 1977 Triple Crown winner Seattle Slew.

Michael Iavarone, co-president of IEAH, said that he signed the deal on his way to the racetrack on Preakness day. Earlier in the week, he had said an announcement would come on May 15, but there was a hiccup in the process. Two days later, IEAH and Three Chimneys were on the NBC broadcast of the race announcing their reported but undisclosed deal exceeding $50-million.

In becoming the first Derby-Preakness winner since Smarty Jones by winning those two races by a combined ten lengths, Big Brown has defeated 29 rivals, with Gayego being the only foe to challenge the division leader in both races.

—Ed DeRosa

12th RACE
Pimlico
May 17, 2008

1$\frac{3}{16}$ miles on dirt. 133rd running of the Preakness Stakes. Grade 1. Three-year-olds. Purse $1,000,000 guaranteed. Track record: Farma Way, 1:52.55, May 11, 1991.

Value of race $1,000,000; Winner $600,000; second $200,000; third $110,000; fourth $60,000, fifth $30,000. Mutuel WPS Pool $14,313,782. Exacta Pool $10,798,076. Trifecta Pool $13,908,765. Superfecta Pool $6,434,928.

Horse	M/Eqt.	Wt.	PP	¼	½	¾	1 mi.	Str.	Fin.	Jockey	Odds $1
Big Brown, 3, c	Lf	126	6	5	$3^{½}$	$3^{1½}$	3^{2}	$1^{5½}$	$1^{5¼}$	K. Desormeaux	0.20*
Macho Again, 3, c	LAb	126	1	1	6^{hd}	6^{hd}	8^{2}	4^{hd}	$2^{½}$	J. Leparoux	39.90
Icabad Crane, 3, c	LA	126	3	2	10^{hd}	12	9^{hd}	5^{3}	$3^{¾}$	J. Rose	22.20
Racecar Rhapsody, 3, c	LAb	126	5	9	9^{2}	$9^{2½}$	10^{2}	$2^{½}$	$4^{4¼}$	R. Albarado	25.10
Stevil, 3, c	LAb	126	8	3	5^{1}	5^{1}	$4^{½}$	3^{1}	$5^{3¾}$	J. Velazquez	40.60
Kentucky Bear, 3, c	LA	126	7	12	8^{hd}	$8^{½}$	$6^{½}$	$7^{1½}$	$6^{½}$	J. Theriot	13.90
Hey Byrn, 3, c	LA	126	12	6	$4^{1½}$	4^{1}	5^{hd}	6^{1}	$7^{1¾}$	C. Lopez	34.30
Giant Moon, 3, c	LAb	126	10	7	7^{3}	7^{1}	$7^{½}$	$11^{1½}$	$8^{¾}$	R. Dominguez	36.60
Tres Borrachos, 3, g	LA	126	2	11	12	11^{hd}	12	10^{hd}	$9^{1¼}$	T. Baze	43.20
Yankee Bravo, 3, c	LAb	126	4	10	11^{hd}	10^{hd}	11^{hd}	9^{1}	$10^{7¼}$	A. Solis	23.70
Gayego, 3, c	Lb	126	11	8	$1^{1½}$	$1^{1½}$	1^{hd}	12	11^{nk}	M. Smith	9.20
Riley Tucker, 3, c	LAb	126	9	4	$2^{1½}$	$2^{2½}$	2^{1}	8^{1}	12	E. Prado	36.40

Scratched: Behindatthebar

L=Salix; LA=Salix and adjunct bleeder medication; b=blinkers; f=front bandages.

OFF AT: 6:17. Weather: Clear. Track: Fast. Start: Good for all except Tres Borrachos and Kentucky Bear.
Times: :23.59, :46.81, 1:10.48, 1:35.72, 1:54.80.

$2 Mutuel Prices:				
	7—BIG BROWN	2.40	2.60	2.40
	1—MACHO AGAIN		17.20	10.40
	3—ICABAD CRANE			5.60

$2 PICK THREE 5-7-5/7 (3 CORRECT) PAID $415.80
$2 PICK FOUR 3/7-5-7-5/7 (FOUR CORRECT) PAID $1,182.20
$1 PICK SIX 1/2/4-2/9/10/12-3/7-5-7-5/7 (FIVE CORRECT) PAID $19.90
$1 PICK SIX 1/2/4-2/9/10/12-3/7-5-7-5/7 (SIX CORRECT) PAID $3,863.40
$2 DAILY DOUBLE 7-7 PAID $10.40 $2 DAILY DOUBLE SPECIAL/PREAKNESS 3-7 PAID $20.20
$2 EXACTA 7-1 PAID $36.60 $1 SUPERFECTA 7-1-3-6 PAID $1,192.30 $2 TRIFECTA 7-1-3 PAID $336.80

B. c., by Boundary out of Mien, by Nureyev. Trainer: Richard Dutrow Jr. Owners: IEAH Stables and Paul Pompa Jr. Breeder: Monticule (Ky.)

BIG BROWN, in hand along the inside nearing the first turn, was wrangled back and angled five wide leaving the three-quarter pole, stalked the leaders under confident handling, lodged a bid midway on the far turn, charged to the front in upper stretch, moved clear under urging near the eighth pole, and was taken in hand through the final sixteenth. MACHO AGAIN saved ground early, steadied in traffic midway on the far turn, angled out nearing the quarter pole, and continued willingly to gain the place. ICABAD CRANE commenced a rail run leaving the far turn, split horses in upper stretch, and closed late. RACECAR RHAPSODY saved ground to the half-mile pole, moved between rivals near the three-eighths pole, continued his run to midstretch, and flattened out. STEVIL advanced between rivals to reach contention on the far turn, but failed to sustain the bid. KENTUCKY BEAR stumbled at the start, made a sharp move along the rail leaving the far turn, checked behind a wall of horses in upper stretch, and finished evenly. HEY BYRN chased the pace, remained a factor to the quarter pole, and steadily tired. GIANT MOON chased the leaders down the backstretch, swung eight wide leaving the quarter pole, and lacked a late response. TRES BORRACHOS stumbled badly at the start, checked repeatedly in the first quarter-mile, and failed to reach contention. YANKEE BRAVO lacked speed and lacked needed response when called on. GAYEGO bumped GIANT MOON leaving the gate, was hustled to gain a clear advantage, dueled on the far turn to the top of the stretch, gave way, and was not abused. RILEY TUCKER stalked the pace, gained a brief lead between rivals midway on the far turn, and then stopped leaving the three-sixteenths marker.

2008 Belmont: Big Upset

Staring into haze-filtered sunlight, 94,476 fans on a sweltering afternoon at Belmont Park watched a Nick Zito vision become reality, and the Racing Hall of Fame trainer's dream proved a nightmare for previously undefeated Triple Crown hopeful Big Brown.

On the lengthy far turn of the 1½-mile Belmont Stakes (G1), Zito kept one eye on his dice roll of an entrant, Da' Tara, and the other on Big Brown. Da' Tara had enjoyed a clear lead throughout, but Zito was waiting to see if he could hold up against Big Brown's expected late burst, which had powered the undefeated colt to victories in the Kentucky Derby Presented by Yum! Brands (G1) and Preakness Stakes (G1).

"When Big Brown was starting to fade back, I started jumping up and down like a jumping jack," Zito said after Da' Tara posted an improbable 38.50-to-1 upset win in the 140th Belmont on June 7. "I was watching Big Brown, and obviously he was not Big Brown."

For the second time in the last five runnings of the Belmont, Zito thwarted the Triple Crown hopes of an undefeated colt. In 2004, Zito earned his first Belmont win when 36-to-1 Birdstone caught unbeaten Smarty Jones in deep stretch. Big Brown's Triple Crown hopes would never emerge from that hazy far turn, leaving Seattle Slew's feat as the sport's only undefeated Triple Crown winner safe for at least another year, and making it 30 years since a horse last won the Triple Crown.

After jockey Kent Desormeaux attempted to rouse Big Brown from third near the half-mile pole, the Boundary colt was unable to gain any ground on Da' Tara. Big Brown was racing with a patched quarter crack in his left front foot. Just three weeks earlier, he ran down (skinned his heels) in the Preakness. Now in the Belmont turn, he appeared to be climbing, not delivering his usual powerful stride. Near the three-eighths pole, Desormeaux began to ease Big Brown, taking the length of the stretch to finally gather him just past the finish line.

"I was keeping an eye on the horse in front and I thought, 'Okay, let's engage and let's at least keep him honest,'" Desormeaux said. "And then I was done. I had no horse. Fortunately there's no popped tires. He's just out of gas."

Richard Dutrow Jr., Big Brown's trainer who exuded confidence in his colt in the days leading up to the Belmont, said after the race he could not find anything wrong.

While Big Brown was being pulled up, Da' Tara found another gear. The dark bay or brown colt opened a five-length lead at the quarter pole on his way to a 5¼-length victory under Alan Garcia, who scored his first classic win on his first Belmont mount.

In securing the first classic win for sire Tiznow,

Owner
Robert D. LaPenta, a resident of Westport, Connecticut, is chairman and chief executive officer of L-1 Identity Solutions, a provider of services for protecting against identity and asset theft. He ventured into racing with basketball coach Rick Pitino and opened his own stable in 2001 with Nick Zito as his trainer and adviser. LaPenta's strategy has been to buy horses as yearlings and offer them for sale as two-year-olds. He races the ones that do not sell. His best is 2007 champion two-year-old male War Pass.

Breeder
WinStar Farm is the racing and breeding operation of Kenny Troutt and Bill Casner. At the Versailles, Kentucky, farm, they stand Tiznow in partnership with Taylor Made Farm and Michael Cooper. WinStar bred Funny Cide, a dual classic winner in 2003.

Da' Tara completed the race in 2:29.65, the slowest time since Sarava's 2002 upset. Da' Tara is the first Belmont winner since Swale in 1984 to win while setting all the pace.

"I was so happy by the five-eighths pole," said Garcia, 22, and not even alive when Affirmed secured the most recent Triple Crown sweep in 1978. "I was looking and thinking I have a shot, and when I move my horse to the half-mile pole, he takes off and I said, 'Oh, my God, Da' Tara, you can do it.'"

Two mornings before the Belmont, Zito met with a few reporters outside his tidy barn to explain his entry of Da' Tara and Anak Nakal in a race where Big Brown would be an odds-on favorite. He used what is quickly becoming one of his favorite expressions, "You have to play the game," in describing his reasoning.

While the phrase may sound like a cliché, Zito also used it when he saddled Birdstone to victory for Marylou Whitney in the 2004 Belmont. In a sport where win percentages have helped new trainers obtain owners, Zito continues to give his horses more opportunities to race, especially when a new condition—for instance a unique distance like 1½ miles—could change a Thoroughbred's fortunes.

Da' Tara's second-place finish in the Barbaro Stakes on the Preakness undercard encouraged Zito. Da' Tara raced well on the lead there. Even when passed by Roman Emperor, he battled back to finish second and earn his first stakes placing.

Sensing there might not be much early speed in the Belmont, Zito began to consider entering Da' Tara. He liked what he saw in the colt's training over the Oklahoma training track at Saratoga Race Course. He called owner Robert LaPenta, who gave him the go-ahead. Da' Tara had just a maiden win in seven starts.

"Nick called a week ago and said, 'Are we crazy?' And I said, 'Look, we're always crazy,' and we did it," LaPenta said after the race. "Nick just did a phenomenal job here, a really great job."

Still, Da' Tara's previous two starts were at Churchill Downs and Pimlico Race Course, but

his races were the Derby Trial Stakes and the Barbaro, not the Kentucky Derby and Preakness. He had lost his four previous races by a combined 33¼ lengths, including a sound 23½-length thrashing at the hands of Big Brown in the Florida Derby (G1). In the Belmont, he would again face Big Brown, winner of his five career starts by a combined 39 lengths. Going into the race, Zito thought Da' Tara was improving, had a chance to get an easy early lead, and with his breeding, possibly could handle the distance.

None of those qualities were listed on sheets of paper.

"You look at the past performances and you don't see yourself winning," Zito said. "You run a lot of horses and the percentage isn't always there. I'd probably be better off starting fewer horses and being 6-to-5 all the time. But you have to play the game."

Before the $1-million Belmont, Zito made no secret he wanted Da' Tara to seize the lead. Garcia delivered, quickly hustling to the front and moving inside into the first turn. Meanwhile, Big Brown struggled after breaking from the rail, was tugged off the heels of other horses repeatedly, and bumped Anak Nakal to get outside the leaders. When Desormeaux asked him to run, it was clear nothing was happening, and the jockey chose to ease him at the top of the stretch.—*Frank Angst*

11TH RACE
Belmont
June 7, 2008

1½ MILES on dirt. 139th running of the Belmont Stakes. Grade 1. Purse $1,000,000 guaranteed. Three-year-olds. Weight: 126 lbs. Fillies allowed 5 lbs. Track record: Secretariat, 2:24, June 9, 1973.

Value of race $1,000,000; Winner $600,000; second $200,000; third $85,000; third $85,000; fifth $30,000. Mutuel WPS Pool $18,103,512. Exacta Pool $11,126,643. Trifecta Pool $15,176,254. Superfecta Pool: $7,281,649. Daily Double Pool $435,847.

Horse	M/Eqt.	Wt.	PP	¼	½	1 mi.	1¼	Str.	Fin.	Jockey	Odds $1
Da' Tara, 3, c.	Lc	126	5	1³	1¹	1²	1⁵	1⁴	1⁵¼	A. Garcia	38.50
Denis of Cork, 3, c.	L	126	4	6ʰᵈ	6¹	5½	2½	2²	2²¾	R. Albarado	7.20
DH-Anak Nakal, 3, c.	Lc	126	7	4²	4⁶	4²	3½	3½	3³	J. Leparoux	34.25
DH-Ready's Echo, 3, r.	Lf	126	8	8½	8²	8½	6½	5⁴	3³	J. Velazquez	28.75
Macho Again, 3, c.	Lb	126	3	5²	5½	6ʰᵈ	5½	4¹	5⁷¼	G. Gomez	17.40
Tale of Ekati, 3, c.	L	126	6	2¹	2¹	2½	4½	6⁸	6⁶½	E. Coa	14.50
Guadalcanal, 3, c.		126	2	7¹	7ʰᵈ	9	9	8	7½	J. Castellano	25.00
Icabad Crane, 3, c.	L	126	9	9	9	7³	7⁴	7½	8	J. Rose	17.00
Big Brown, 3, c.	Lf	126	1	3½	3²	3²½	8½	—	—	K. Desormeaux	0.30*

L=Salix; b=blinkers; c=mud calks; f=front bandages.

OFF AT 6:31 p.m. Start: Good for all. Weather: Clear. Track: Fast.
Time: :23.82, :48.30, 1:12.90, 1:37.96, 2:03.21, 2:29.65.

$2 Mutuel Prices:

6—DA' TARA	79.00	28.00	14.80
4—DENIS OF CORK		5.40	4.10
8—ANAK NAKAL (DH)			7.60
9—READY's ECHO (DH)			6.20

$2 EXACTA 6-4 PAID $659.00 $2 TRIFECTA 6-4-8 PAID $3,703.00 $2 TRIFECTA 6-4-9 PAID $3,954.00
$2 SUPERFECTA 6-4-8-9 PAID $48,637.00 $2 SUPERFECTA 6-4-9-8 PAID $47,309.00
$2 DAILY DOUBLE 10-6 PAID $1,574.00 $2 DAILY DOUBLE BROOKLYN/BELMONT 2-6 PAID $550.00
$2 PICK THREE 5--10-6 (3 CORRECT) PAID $6,475.00 $2 PICK FOUR 1-5-10-6 (4 CORRECT) PAID $34,287.00
$2 PICK SIX 3/7-4-1-5-10-6 (5 CORRECT) PAID $1,106.00
$2 CONSOLATION DOUBLE BROOKLYN/BELMONT 2-5 PAID $7.30

Dk. b. or br. c., by Tiznow—Torchera, by Pirate's Bounty. Trainer: Nick Zito Owner: Robert V. LaPenta. Breeder: WinStar Farm (Ky.)

DA' TARA angled in after taking the lead, opened a clear advantage on the first turn, raced uncontested on the front down the backstretch, dug in when challenged briefly on the final turn, drifted out when struck left-handed with the whip at the three-sixteenths pole, and edged away under steady urging. DENIS OF CORK raced in the middle of the pack for seven furlongs, split rivals midway on the final turn, took up the chase after the winner in upper stretch, but was no match. ANAK NAKAL was bumped by BIG BROWN and carried out on the first turn, moved between horses when asked to run midway on the final turn, and closed gradually to get a share. READY'S ECHO, outrun for a half-mile, swung six wide at the quarter pole, and improved his position late. MACHO AGAIN lodged a mild rally to gain contention at the top of the stretch, but failed to sustain the bid. TALE OF EKATI pressed the pace, raced just behind the leader into upper stretch, and steadily tired. GUADALCANAL stumbled at the break and never reached contention. ICABAD CRANE was never a factor. BIG BROWN steadied and broke outward, was steadied while rank in the first quarter-mile, was taken outside and bumped ANAK NAKAL on the first turn, stalked the leaders while wide for seven furlongs, was asked to run on the far turn, dropped back abruptly on the turn, and was pulled up approaching the quarter pole.

BREEDERS' CUP
Breeders' Cup History

John R. Gaines, one of the central figures in the North American commercial breeding industry in the last quarter of the 20th century, was renowned for his creativity and his powers of persuasion. In the early 1980s, Gaines needed all his considerable talents to get a fractious industry lined up behind a groundbreaking concept, which he believed would help to define the Thoroughbred industry and give it a centerpiece.

Gaines's creation was the Breeders' Cup. From the perspective of the 21st century, the Breeders' Cup stands as the most successful initiative of the Thoroughbred industry in the last half of the 20th century. Creation of the Breeders' Cup allowed the sport to hold a championship event in late fall for the majority of age and sex divisions, an important element missing from a sport that had its major fall championship races scattered across the nation at several tracks.

Gaines conceived the idea in part out of anger and frustration. He was angered by a television program in the early 1980s that had depicted Thoroughbred racing as a haven of drug abuse. Indeed, permissive medication policies at racetracks had eroded confidence in the sport's integrity, and racing had continued its long, slow slide in popularity—a decline that began shortly after World War II. Even as the commercial bloodstock markets boomed in the early 1980s, race purses in inflation-adjusted dollars were shrinking.

The highly successful owner of Gainesway in Lexington and an innovator in the stallion-station concept, Gaines developed the idea for a championship day of racing with multimillion-dollar purses to attract the world's best runners, with the races being broadcast nationally on a major television network. The racing, as important as it was, would not be an end unto itself. The event would be used to build racing's popularity, with the organization in charge of the event becoming a leader in marketing the sport.

Given the sport's propensity for infighting, it is surprising the Breeders' Cup came into being in very much the form Gaines first envisioned Thoroughbred racing's championship event. But it was not easy.

Gaines had to sell the concept to a skeptical industry in 1982, and he had to do it one person at a time. His first target was John W. Galbreath, owner of Darby Dan Farm and an influential sportsman in the United States and England. (At the time, Galbreath was the only person to have raced both a Kentucky Derby winner [Chateaugay] and an Epsom Derby victor [Roberto].)

Gaines went to Columbus, Ohio, to meet with Galbreath, who initially thought little of the idea. But, as Gaines sketched out his idea in detail, Galbreath came on board. Moving quickly, Gaines lined up other supporters, including Spendthrift Farm's Leslie Combs II, Nelson Bunker Hunt, Windfields Farms' Charles Taylor, Will Farish, Racing Hall of Fame trainer John Nerud, Brereton C. Jones, John T. L. Jones Jr., and Seth Hancock, who a decade earlier had taken over management of his family's Claiborne Farm.

All great ideas have their moments, and Gaines's idea came at just the right time for the Thoroughbred industry. Commercial breeders, who would pay a big part of the program's cost by nominating their stallions and foals, were enjoying un-

Where Championship Days Were Held

Churchill Downs (6): 1988, 1991, 1994, 1998, 2000, 2006
Belmont Park (4): 1990, 1995, 2001, 2005
Hollywood Park (3): 1984, 1987, 1997
Gulfstream Park (3): 1989, 1992, 1999
Santa Anita Park (3): 1986, 1993, 2003
Arlington Park (1): 2002
Aqueduct (1): 1985
Lone Star Park (1): 2004
Monmouth Park (1): 2007
Woodbine (1) 1996

Breeders' Cup Attendance and Wagering by Year

Year	Site	On-Track Attendance	On-Track Wagering*	Total Wagering*
2007	Monmouth	69,584	$14,371,882	$131,306,643
2006	Churchill	75,132	**17,184,919**	134,357,846
2005	Belmont	54,289	13,385,593	116,465,923
2004	Lone Star	53,717	11,274,066	109,838,668
2003	Santa Anita	51,486	13,678,118	107,535,731
2002	Arlington	46,118	12,143,114	108,885,673
2001	Belmont	52,987	12,067,995	98,008,747
2000	Churchill	76,043	13,579,798	101,283,427
1999	Gulfstream	45,124	11,065,973	96,485,255
1998	Churchill	**80,452**	13,544,859	91,338,477
1997	Hollywood	51,161	8,191,459	71,639,333
1996	Woodbine	42,243	5,925,469	67,738,890
1995	Belmont	37,246	7,590,332	64,075,207
1994	Churchill	71,671	10,146,524	78,224,530
1993	Santa Anita	55,130	12,142,750	79,744,742
1992	Gulfstream	45,415	9,915,542	76,876,726
1991	Churchill	66,204	11,945,562	67,588,113
1990	Belmont	51,236	9,107,270	55,328,195
1989	Gulfstream	51,342	10,216,258	55,345,677
1988	Churchill	71,237	9,219,083	42,932,379
1987	Hollywood	57,734	10,202,252	31,864,457
1986	Santa Anita	69,155	12,510,109	31,984,490
1985	Aqueduct	42,568	7,200,175	26,941,288
1984	Hollywood	64,254	8,443,070	16,452,179

*Breeders' Cup races only. Beginning in 2007, combined figures for both days.

precedented prosperity as bloodstock prices rose to record levels and stallion fees climbed.

At the same time, racing was perceived as a sport in trouble, and relatively low purse levels dissuaded some prospective owners from buying horses. Although overseas interests sent the bloodstock markets skyrocketing, many breeders realized the prices they received for their sale offerings and the stallion fees they charged were directly related to purses, which determined how much a sale purchase potentially could earn.

Gaines chose the sport's most prestigious event, the Kentucky Derby (G1), to announce his idea. He was honored at the Kentucky Derby Festival's "They're Off" luncheon on April 23, 1982, and there he outlined his idea, a $13-million afternoon featuring the world's best racehorses. Gaines named it the Breeders' Cup.

He moved quickly to assemble a board of directors and girded for the inevitable naysayers. New York racing interests were opposed because Gaines's proposal would diminish the importance of the New York Racing Association's fall races, which frequently decided year-end titles.

Smaller-scale breeders also voiced their opposition. Gaines said breeders could breed one more mare to a stallion to cover the cost of the stallion nomination fee each year. Such a strategy would work for a breeder with barns filled with desirable stallions whose books were filled, and Gaines was one of those breeders. But, for a small-scale breeder trying to fill the book of a less commercial stallion, the stallion nomination most likely would be paid out of the stallion owner's pocket.

Other breeders raised concerns that Gaines was putting all the money into one event, arguing that the money should be spread throughout the year to supplement purses of existing stakes races. On that point, a compromise was reached, with $10-million earmarked for the championship day and an equal portion going into Breeders' Cup-sponsored races around the country.

By the fall of 1982, the Breeders' Cup was beset with infighting, and Hancock delivered an unexpected blow when he did not nominate Claiborne's stallions on grounds that the organization had not developed a clear game plan. Gaines realized he had become a lightning rod for opponents and resigned the presidency on October 22, becoming chairman. C. Gibson Downing Jr., a Lexington lawyer with a modest-sized stud farm and a reputation for consensus building, became Breeders' Cup president. Hancock signed up after a rules book was written on how the money would be spent, and smaller breeders followed his lead. D. G. Van Clief Jr. came on board that fall as executive director.

For several months, Gaines and Nerud trav-

Television Ratings for Breeders' Cup

Date	Host Track	Rating/Share
2007	Monmouth Park	0.9/NA
2006	Churchill Downs	0.8/2
2005	Belmont Park	1.5/4
2004	Lone Star Park	1.4/4
2003	Santa Anita Park	1.8/5
2002	Arlington Park	2.0/5
2001	Belmont Park	1.7/5
2000	Churchill Downs	1.8/5
1999	Gulfstream Park	1.9/5
1998	Churchill Downs	2.2/6
1997	Hollywood Park	2.2/6
1996	Woodbine	2.5/8
1995	Belmont Park	2.8/9
1994	Churchill Downs	2.7/8
1993	Santa Anita Park	3.4/9
1992	Gulfstream Park	3.0/8
1991	Churchill Downs	3.0/9
1990	Belmont Park	2.7/9
1989	Gulfstream Park	3.7/11
1988	Churchill Downs	4.0/11
1987	Hollywood Park	2.9/7
1986	Santa Anita Park	4.4/12
1985	Aqueduct	4.0/11
1984	Hollywood Park	5.1/13

eled around the country, selling breeders and racetrack operators on the concept. By April 15, 1983, 1,083 stallions had been nominated to the program, and the Breeders' Cup was up and running. Nerud said in 1985 that a decision was made early to hold the first Breeders' Cup in a warm climate so television viewers would see racing in a pleasant setting. Marjorie Everett, chief executive of Hollywood Park, lobbied heavily for the first event, and on February 24, 1983, the Inglewood, California, track was named as host of the first Breeders' Cup, to be held on November 10, 1984. In a bow to New York interests, Aqueduct was host of the second Breeders' Cup in 1985.

At Nerud's suggestion, marketers Mike Letis and Mike Trager of Sports Marketing and Television International were brought in to negotiate a television deal, and a contract with NBC was signed on September 13, 1983. The show would run for four hours on a Saturday afternoon and would include live coverage of all seven Breeders' Cup championship races. In January 1984, all seven races were granted Grade 1 status.

From the first race, won by Chief's Crown in the $1-million Breeders' Cup Juvenile (G1), the Breeders' Cup was an unprecedented success. That afternoon's races attracted a crowd of 64,254, and the day concluded with a breathtaking $3-million Breeders' Cup Classic (G1), in which supplemental entry Wild Again edged Gate Dancer and Slew o' Gold for the biggest race purse ever offered to that time.

An even larger crowd, 69,155, attended the third Breeders' Cup at Santa Anita Park in suburban Los Angeles, but that record lasted only two years until Churchill Downs hosted the fifth Breeders' Cup in 1988 before a crowd of 71,237. On a dreary, rainy, chilly day in Louisville, they were treated to one of the event's most exciting races when undefeated Personal Ensign closed relentlessly in the final yards and caught that year's Kentucky Derby winner, Winning Colors, at the finish line to win the Breeders' Cup Distaff (G1) by a nose. With that victory, Personal Ensign was retired unbeaten in 13 starts.

The Breeders' Cup traveled to Florida for the first time in 1989, and Gulfstream Park was the scene for another monumental struggle in which Sunday Silence fought off the challenge of Easy Goer to win the Breeders' Cup Classic. The event reached its nadir the following year at Belmont Park, when Go for Wand sustained a fatal breakdown near the finish line of the Breeders' Cup Distaff and was euthanized. Subsequently, Breeders' Cup Ltd. instituted prerace examinations in an effort to limit breakdowns.

As rich races became more common, especially internationally, Breeders' Cup Ltd. increased its championship day purses, raising the Classic to $4-million in 1996 and the Distaff to $2-million in '98. In 1999, a new race, the $1-million Filly and Mare Turf (G1), was added, raising the afternoon's total purses to $13-million. In 2001, the championship day was renamed the Breeders' Cup World Thoroughbred Championships, and in '03 total purses increased to $14-million. In 2006, the championship day was renamed again, to the Breeders' Cup World Championships, and total purse money was increased to $20-million, with the Classic carrying a $5-million purse and the Turf raised to $3-million. All other races were allotted a $2-million purse.

In 2003, Breeders' Cup increased total entry fees 50% to 3% of the race purse. Stallion nomination fees were adjusted beginning in 2006. Stallions with 50 to 99 live foals were assessed 1½ times the advertised stud fee, and stallions with more than 100 foals were assessed twice the stud fee.

Some of the most noteworthy changes in Breeders' Cup history occurred in 2006 and early '07. The first change was Van Clief's retirement as president and chief executive officer after more than 23 years with the organization. Announced in April 2006, the change took effect before the World Championships at Churchill Downs. Succeeding Van Clief on an interim basis was Gregory C. Avioli, who also served as interim CEO of the National Thoroughbred Racing Association. In April 2007, Avioli was appointed president and CEO on a permanent basis.

Churchill was host to the World Championships for a record sixth time in 2006, but new to the event was coverage by the ESPN cable sports

Breeders' Cup Supplemental Entries

From its beginning, the Breeders' Cup program has allowed supplemental entries for its championship races, but the supplemental fee was intentionally made expensive to encourage stallion and foal owners to nominate their horses to the program. The supplemental fee was originally 12% of the purse for horses whose sires were nominated to the Breeders' Cup, the European Breeders' Fund, or a common fund of the two organizations. If a stallion was not nominated to the program at the time of the foal's conception, the supplementary fee was 20% of the purse.

For the foal to be nominated, the stallion must first be nominated to the program. Thus, when John Henry was pre-entered for the first $2-million Breeders' Cup Turf (G1) in 1984, owners Sam and Dorothy Rubin had to pay a $400,000 fee to start the gelding because his sire, Ole Bob Bowers, was not nominated to the program. The Rubins paid a $133,000 pre-entry fee, which was nonrefundable, and John Henry did not start because of a minor injury.

The hefty fees for horses whose sires were not nominated to the program worked against Southern Hemisphere horses in particular. Frank and Janis Whitham paid $200,000 to start Bayakoa (Arg) in the 1989 Breeders' Cup Distaff (G1) and again put up a $200,000 supplemental fee to start her the following year. Bayakoa won both times, earning a first-place purse of $450,000 each year. At that time, the supplemental fees did not go into the race purses but were retained by Breeders' Cup Ltd.

The rules were changed for the 1998 Breeders' Cup championship. Beginning with foals of 1996, the supplemental fee for offspring of nominated stallions was reduced to 9%, while the fee remained at 12% for older horses and 20% for horses whose sires were not nominated to the program.

Another change allowed supplemented horses to receive a credit for the net supplementary fees, after pre-entry, entry, and starting fees were taken out. High Chaparral (Ire) started in the 2002 Breeders' Cup Turf with payment of a $180,000 supplemental fee. When he started the following year, he had a $120,000 credit for the supplemental fee—the original $180,000 payment less starting fees of 3% of the total purse, or $60,000. High Chaparral won in 2002 and finished in a dead heat for the win with Johar in '03.

A further change added the net supplemental fees to the race purse, also in 1998. As a result of this change, the Breeders' Cup Classic (G1) in 1998 had a record purse of $4,689,920.

network after 22 years with NBC. The broadcasting change was intended to reach more committed general sports fans, but it did not initially result in higher ratings. During the week leading up to the 2006 World Championships, Breeders' Cup Ltd. officials announced a new program, Win and You're In, which assured starting positions in the championship races to the winners of designated races if all nominating and starting fees were paid. The initial Win and You're In menu constituted 24 races on six programs at six different tracks, starting at Saratoga Race Course in late July 2007. Win and You're In expanded to 57 races in 2008.

In January 2007, Breeders' Cup announced it was expanding to a second day, effective with that year's World Championships at Monmouth Park in New Jersey. Added to the championship series were three $1-million races, the Breeders' Cup Dirt Mile, Breeders' Cup Filly and Mare Sprint, and Breeders' Cup Juvenile Turf. A year later, three more races were added: the $1-million Breeders' Cup Turf Sprint, $1-million Breeders' Cup Juvenile Fillies Turf, and the $500,000 Breeders' Cup Marathon. Also for 2008, all filly and mare races were moved to the Friday card.

—*Don Clippinger*

Breeders' Cup Trophy

The Breeders' Cup trophy is an authentic reproduction of the Torrie horse, created by Giovanni da Bologna in Florence, Italy, most likely in the late 1580s. The sculpture is known as an ecorche or flayed horse and shows the horse's muscles in great detail.

Although its original commission is not known, the sculpture may have been a study made for an equestrian statue of Duke Cosimo I, which was completed in 1591 and stands today in the Piazza della Signoria in Florence.

The sculptor's original ecorche in bronze was acquired by Sir James Erskine of Torrie in the early 1800s. It was bequeathed to the University of Edinburgh in 1836 and today is housed in the university's Museum of Fine Arts in Scotland.

The Breeders' Cup trophy was cast from the original under supervision of University of Edinburgh curators, and the replica is owned by Breeders' Cup Ltd. Smaller replicas are presented to winners of each Breeders' Cup race, and winning breeders, trainers, and jockeys also are presented with replicas.

Breeders' Cup Purses

When John Gaines first proposed the Breeders' Cup in 1982, he envisioned a purse structure of $13-million for the championship day. As the concept was put into final form for the first championship day in 1984, purses and nominator fees totaled $10-million. Five of seven races had $1-million purses (Juvenile, Juvenile Fillies, Sprint, Distaff, Mile); the Turf had a $2-million purse, and the Classic was $3-million.

In 1996, the Classic was increased to $4-million, and the Distaff was raised to $2-million two years later. The $1-million Filly and Mare Turf was added in 1999, and the Juvenile and Mile were increased to $1.5-million each in 2003, raising total purses to $14-million.

A 1997 change in the rules for supplemental nominations has resulted in higher purses. Beginning in 1998, supplemental-nomination money is added to the total purse. Thus, the 1998 Breeders' Cup Classic, which contained supplemental nominees Gentlemen (Arg), Silver Charm, and Skip Away, raised the total purse ($4,689,920) and nominator fees above $5-million, then the biggest race purse ever.

The 2006 purse increases raised the total distribution to $20-million, with the Classic worth $5-million, the Turf worth $3-million, and the six other races at $2-million each. The addition of three new races, each worth $1-million, increased the total distribution to $23-million for 2007 and the total rose to $25-million for 2008.

In addition to purse money paid to the horse's owner or owners, the Breeders' Cup purse structure contains 5% awards for both the stallion nominator and the foal nominator. Here is the 2008 distribution for a $2-million race:

Distribution of $2-Million Purse

Finish	Purse	Owner	Stallion Nominator	Foal Nominator
1st	57.2%	$1,040,000	$52,000	$52,000
2nd	22.0%	400,000	20,000	20,000
3rd	12.1%	220,000	11,000	11,000
4th	5.7%	114,000		
5th	3.0%	60,000		
Total	100.0%	$1,834,000	$83,000	$83,000

Largest Breeders' Cup Purses

(Not including stallion and foal nominator fees)

Year	Race	Purse	Winner	Value to Winner
1998	Classic	**$4,689,920**	Awesome Again	**$2,662,400**
2007	Classic	4,580,000	Curlin	**2,700,000**
2006	Classic	4,580,000	Invasor (Arg)	**2,700,000**
2000	Classic	4,369,320	Tiznow	2,480,400
2005	Classic	4,291,560	Saint Liam	2,433,600
1997	Classic	4,030,400	Skip Away	2,288,000
2004	Classic	3,668,000	Ghostzapper	2,080,000
2003	Classic	3,668,000	Pleasantly Perfect	2,080,000
2002	Classic	3,664,000	Volponi	2,080,000
2001	Classic	3,664,000	Tiznow	2,080,000
1999	Classic	3,664,000	Cat Thief	2,080,000
1996	Classic	3,664,000	Alphabet Soup	2,080,000
1995	Classic	2,798,000	Cigar	1,560,000
1994	Classic	2,748,000	Concern	1,560,000
1993	Classic	2,748,000	Arcangues	1,560,000
1992	Classic	2,748,000	A.P. Indy	1,560,000
1991	Classic	2,748,000	Black Tie Affair (Ire)	1,560,000
1990	Classic	2,739,000	Unbridled	1,350,000
1989	Classic	2,739,000	Sunday Silence	1,350,000
1988	Classic	2,739,000	Alysheba	1,350,000
1987	Classic	2,739,000	Ferdinand	1,350,000
1986	Classic	2,739,000	Skywalker	1,350,000
1985	Classic	2,739,000	Proud Truth	1,350,000
1984	Classic	2,739,000	Wild Again	1,350,000

From 1984 through '90, the Breeders' Cup Classic had a race purse of $2,739,000 and a winner's share of $1.35-million. The next highest purse was $2,271,680 in the 2000 Breeders' Cup Turf, won by Kalanisi (Ire).

Breeders' Cup Leaders

Leading Owners by Wins

6 **Eugene V. Klein** (Is It True, 1988 Juvenile; Open Mind, 1988 Juvenile Fillies; Success Express, 1987 Juvenile; Lady's Secret, 1986 Distaff; Twilight Ridge, 1985 Juvenile Fillies; Life's Magic, 1985 Distaff)
Allen E. Paulson (Escena, 1998 Distaff; Ajina, 1997 Distaff; Cigar, 1995 Classic; Eliza, 1992 Juvenile Fillies; Opening Verse, 1991 Mile; Theatrical [Ire], 1987 Turf)
5 **Flaxman Holdings Ltd.** (Six Perfections [Fr], 2003 Mile; Domedriver [Ire], 2002 Mile; Spinning World, 1997 Mile; Miesque [twice], 1987, '88 Mile)
Stronach Stables (Ginger Punch, 2007 Distaff; Ghostzapper, 2004 Classic; Macho Uno, 2000 Juvenile; Perfect Sting, 2000 Filly and Mare Turf; Awesome Again, 1998 Classic)
4 **Ogden Mills Phipps** (Pleasant Home, 2005 Distaff; Storm Flag Flying, 2002 Juvenile Fillies; Inside Information, 1995 Distaff; Rhythm, 1989 Juvenile)
3 **Godolphin Racing** (Fantastic Light, 2001 Turf; Tempera, 2001 Juvenile Fillies; Daylami [Ire], 1999 Turf)
Overbrook Farm (Cat Thief, 1999 Classic; Boston Harbor, 1996 Juvenile; Flanders, 1994 Juvenile Fillies)
Ogden Phipps (My Flag, 1995 Juvenile Fillies; Dancing Spree, 1989 Sprint; Personal Ensign, 1988 Distaff)
The Thoroughbred Corp. (Johar, 2003 Turf; Spain, 2000 Distaff; Anees, 1999 Juvenile)

Leading Breeders by Wins

6 **Allen E. Paulson** (Azeri, 2002 Distaff; Escena, 1998 Distaff; Ajina, 1997 Distaff; Cigar, 1995 Classic; Fraise, 1992 Turf; Eliza, 1992 Juvenile Fillies)
5 **Flaxman Holdings/Niarchos Family** (Six Perfections [Fr], 2003 Mile; Domedriver [Ire], 2002 Mile; Spinning World, 1997 Mile; Miesque [twice], 1987, '88 Mile)
Frank Stronach/Adena Springs (Ginger Punch, 2007 Distaff; Ghostzapper, 2004 Classic; Macho Uno, 2000 Juvenile; Perfect Sting, 2000 Filly and Mare Turf; Awesome Again, 1998 Classic)
4 **Ogden Mills Phipps/Phipps Stable** (Pleasant Home, 2005 Distaff; Storm Flag Flying, 2002 Juvenile Fillies; Inside Information, 1995 Distaff; Rhythm, 1989 Juvenile)
3 **Aga Khan** (Kalanisi [Ire], 2000 Turf; Daylami [Ire], 1999 Turf; Lashkari [GB], 1984 Turf)
Sean Coughlan (High Chaparral [Ire] [twice], 2002, '03 Turf; Ridgewood Pearl [GB], 1995 Mile)
Fares Farm (Curlin, 2007 Classic; Da Hoss, 1998 Mile; Da Hoss, 1996 Mile)
Overbrook Farm (Cat Thief, 1999 Classic; Boston Harbor, 1996 Juvenile; Flanders, 1994 Juvenile Fillies)
Ogden Phipps (My Flag, 1995 Juvenile Fillies; Dancing Spree, 1989 Sprint; Personal Ensign, 1988 Distaff)

Leading Trainers by Wins

18 **D. Wayne Lukas** (Folklore, 2005 Juvenile Fillies; Orientate, 2002 Sprint; Spain, 2000 Distaff; Cat Thief, 1999 Classic; Cash Run, 1999 Juvenile Fillies; Boston Harbor, 1996 Juvenile; Timber Country, 1994 Juvenile; Flanders, 1994 Juvenile Fillies; Steinlen [GB], 1989 Mile; Is It True, 1988 Juvenile; Gulch, 1988 Sprint; Open Mind, 1988 Juvenile Fillies; Success Express, 1987 Juvenile; Sacahuista, 1987 Distaff; Capote, 1986 Juvenile; Lady's Secret, 1986 Distaff; Life's Magic, 1985 Distaff; Twilight Ridge, 1985 Juvenile Fillies)
9 **Claude R. "Shug" McGaughey III** (Pleasant Home, 2005 Distaff; Storm Flag Flying, 2002 Juvenile Fillies; Inside Information, 1995 Distaff; My Flag, 1995 Juvenile Fillies; Lure [twice], 1992, '93 Mile; Rhythm, 1989 Juvenile; Dancing Spree, 1989 Sprint; Personal Ensign, 1988 Distaff)
6 **Neil Drysdale** (War Chant, 2000 Mile; Hollywood Wildcat, 1993 Distaff; A.P. Indy, 1992 Classic; Prized, 1989 Turf; Tasso, 1985 Juvenile; Princess Rooney, 1984 Distaff)
Richard Mandella (Pleasantly Perfect, 2003 Classic; Johar, 2003 Turf; Action This Day, 2003 Juvenile; Halfbridled, 2003 Juvenile Fillies; Kotashaan [Fr], 1993 Turf; Phone Chatter, 1993 Juvenile Fillies)
5 **Bob Baffert** (Midnight Lute, 2007 Sprint; Indian Blessing, 2007 Juvenile Fillies; Vindication, 2002 Juvenile; Silverbulletday, 1998 Juvenile Fillies; Thirty Slews, 1992 Sprint)
Robert J. Frankel (Ginger Punch, 2007 Distaff; Intercontinental [GB], 2005 Filly & Mare Turf; Ghostzapper, 2004 Classic; Starine [Fr], 2002 Filly and Mare Turf; Squirtle Squirt, 2001 Sprint)
William I. Mott (Escena, 1998 Distaff; Ajina, 1997 Distaff; Cigar, 1995 Classic; Fraise, 1992 Turf; Theatrical [Ire], 1987 Turf)
4 **Andre Fabre** (Shirocco [Ger], 2005 Turf; Banks Hill [GB], 2001 Filly and Mare Turf; In the Wings [GB], 1990 Turf; Arcangues, 1993 Classic)
Ron McAnally (Northern Spur [Ire], 1995 Turf; Paseana [Arg], 1992 Distaff; Bayakoa [Arg] [twice], 1989, '90 Distaff)

Leading Jockeys by Wins

15 **Jerry Bailey** (Saint Liam, 2005 Classic; Six Perfections [Fr], 2003 Mile; Orientate, 2002 Sprint; Squirtle Squirt, 2001 Sprint; Macho Uno, 2000 Juvenile; Perfect Sting, 2000 Filly and Mare Turf; Soaring Softly, 1999 Filly and Mare Turf; Cash Run, 1999 Juvenile Fillies; Answer Lively, 1998 Juvenile; Boston Harbor, 1996 Juvenile; Cigar, 1995 Classic; My Flag, 1995 Juvenile Fillies; Concern, 1994 Classic; Arcangues, 1993 Classic; Black Tie Affair [Ire], 1991 Classic)
12 **Pat Day** (Unbridled Elaine, 2001 Distaff; Cat Thief, 1999 Classic; Awesome Again, 1998 Classic; Favorite Trick, 1997 Juvenile; Timber Country, 1994 Juvenile; Flanders, 1994 Juvenile Fillies; Dance Smartly, 1991 Distaff; Unbridled, 1990 Classic; Theatrical (Ire), 1987 Turf; Epitome, 1987 Juvenile Fillies; Lady's Secret, 1986 Distaff; Wild Again, 1984 Classic)
10 **Mike Smith** (Azeri, 2002 Distaff; Vindication, 2002 Juvenile; Skip Away, 1997 Classic; Ajina, 1997 Distaff; Unbridled's Song, 1995 Juvenile; Inside Information, 1995 Distaff; Tikkanen, 1994 Turf; Cherokee Run, 1994 Sprint; Lure [twice], 1992, '93 Mile)
9 **Chris McCarron** (Tiznow [twice], 2000, '01 Classic; Alphabet Soup, 1996 Classic; Northern Spur [Ire], 1995 Turf; Paseana [Arg], 1992 Distaff; Gilded Time, 1992 Juvenile; Sunday Silence, 1989 Classic; Alysheba, 1988 Classic; Precisionist, 1985 Sprint)
8 **Gary Stevens** (War Chant, 2000 Mile; Anees, 1999 Juvenile; Escena, 1998 Distaff; Silverbulletday, 1998 Juvenile Fillies; Da Hoss, 1996 Mile; One Dreamer, 1994 Distaff; Brocco, 1993 Juvenile; In the Wings [GB], 1990 Turf)
7 **Eddie Delahoussaye** (Hollywood Wildcat, 1993 Distaff; Cardmania, 1993 Sprint; A.P. Indy, 1992 Classic; Thirty Slews, 1992 Sprint; Pleasant Stage, 1991 Juvenile Fil-

lies; Prized, 1989 Turf; Princess Rooney, 1984 Distaff)
Corey Nakatani (Thor's Echo, 2006 Sprint; Sweet Catomine, 2004 Juvenile Fillies; Silic [Fr], 1999 Mile; Reraise, 1998 Sprint; Elmhurst, 1997 Sprint; Lit de Justice, 1996 Sprint; Jewel Princess, 1996 Distaff)
Laffit Pincay Jr. (Phone Chatter, 1993 Juvenile Fillies; Bayakoa [Arg], [twice], 1989, '90 Distaff; Is It True, 1988 Juvenile; Skywalker, 1986 Classic; Capote, 1986 Juvenile; Tasso, 1985 Juvenile)
Jose Santos (Volponi, 2002 Classic; Chief Bearhart, 1997 Turf; Fly So Free, 1990 Juvenile; Meadow Star, 1990 Juvenile Fillies; Steinlen [GB], 1989 Mile; Success Express, 1987 Juvenile; Manila, 1986 Turf)
Patrick Valenzuela (Adoration, 2003 Distaff; Fraise, 1992 Turf; Eliza, 1992 Juvenile Fillies; Arazi, 1991 Juvenile; Opening Verse, 1991 Mile; Very Subtle, 1987 Sprint; Brave Raj, 1986 Juvenile Fillies)
John Velazquez (English Channel, 2007 Turf; Speightstown, 2004 Sprint; Ashado, 2004 Distaff; Storm Flag Flying, 2002 Juvenile Fillies; Starine [Fr], 2002 Filly and Mare Turf; Caressing, 2000 Juvenile Fillies; Da Hoss, 1998 Mile)

Leading Sires by Wins

6 **Sadler's Wells** (High Chaparral [Ire] [twice], 2002, '03 Turf; Islington [Ire], 2003 Filly and Mare Turf; Northern Spur [Ire], 1995 Turf; Barathea [Ire], 1994 Mile; In the Wings [GB], 1990 Turf)
5 **Danzig** (War Chant, 2000 Mile; Lure [twice], 1992, '93 Mile; Dance Smartly, 1991 Distaff; Chief's Crown, 1984 Juvenile)
Kris S. (Action This Day, 2003 Juvenile; Soaring Softly, 1999 Filly and Mare Turf; Brocco, 1993 Juvenile; Hollywood Wildcat, 1993 Distaff; Prized, 1989 Turf)
4 **Awesome Again** (Ginger Punch, 2007 Distaff; Round Pond, 2006 Distaff; Ghostzapper, 2004 Classic; Wilko, 2004 Juvenile)
Gone West (Speightstown, 2004 Sprint; Johar, 2003 Turf; Da Hoss [twice], 1996, '98 Mile)
Nureyev (Spinning World, 1997 Mile; Miesque [twice], 1987, '88 Mile; Theatrical [Ire], 1987 Turf)
Storm Cat (Sweet Catomine, 2004 Juvenile Fillies; Storm Flag Flying, 2002 Juvenile Fillies; Cat Thief, 1999 Classic; Desert Stormer, 1995 Sprint)
3 **Cox's Ridge** (Cardmania, 1993 Sprint; Twilight Ridge, 1985 Juvenile Fillies; Life's Magic, 1985 Distaff)
Deputy Minister (Awesome Again, 1999 Classic; Go for Wand, 1989 Juvenile Fillies; Open Mind, 1988 Juvenile Fillies)
Mr. Prospector (Rhythm, 1989 Juvenile; Gulch, 1988 Sprint; Eillo, 1984 Sprint)
Nijinsky II (Royal Academy, 1990 Mile; Dancing Spree, 1989 Sprint; Ferdinand, 1987 Classic)
Seattle Slew (Vindication, 2002 Juvenile; A.P. Indy, 1992 Classic; Capote, 1986 Juvenile)
Seeking the Gold (Pleasant Home, 2005 Distaff; Cash Run, 1999 Juvenile Fillies; Flanders, 1994 Juvenile Fillies)
Strawberry Road (Aus) (Escena, 1998 Distaff; Ajina, 1997 Distaff; Fraise, 1992 Turf)
Unbridled (Halfbridled, 2003 Juvenile Fillies; Anees, 1999 Juvenile; Unbridled's Song, 1995 Juvenile)

Leading Owners by Purses Won

Owner	Starts	Wins	Earnings
Stronach Stables	16	5	$8,492,400
Allen E. Paulson	30	5	6,670,000
Darley	25	2	5,504,960
Godolphin	36	3	5,218,200
Overbrook Farm	28	3	4,387,000
Shadwell Stable	11	2	4,284,080
Juddmonte Farms	46	2	4,207,820
The Thoroughbred Corp.	22	3	4,164,200
Daniel Wildenstein	19	2	3,917,000
Ogden Phipps	19	3	3,611,000
Eugene V. Klein	18	5	3,043,000
Sam-Son Farm	19	2	3,018,760
Frances A. Genter	8	2	2,835,000
Aga Khan	10	2	2,740,400
Flaxman Holdings Ltd.	16	4	2,662,760

Owners With Most Starts

Owner	Starts	Wins	Earnings
Juddmonte Farms	46	2	$4,207,820
Godolphin	36	3	5,218,200
Allen E. Paulson	30	5	6,670,000
Overbrook Farm	28	3	4,387,000
Darley	25	2	5,504,960
Gainsborough Farm	23	0	1,031,840
The Thoroughbred Corp.	22	3	4,164,200
Ogden Phipps	19	3	3,611,000
Sam-Son Farm	19	2	3,018,760
Daniel Wildenstein	19	2	3,917,000
Eugene V. Klein	18	5	3,043,000
Flaxman Holdings Ltd.	16	4	2,662,760
Stronach Stables	16	5	8,492,400
Golden Eagle Farm	15	0	1,443,800
Edmund Gann	14	0	2,408,800
Mr. and Mrs. Jerome S. Moss	14	0	559,000
Ogden Mills Phipps	14	3	2,258,500
Michael Tabor	14	0	546,600

Owners With Most Starters on a Program

Starters	Owner	Year
8	Godolphin Racing	2001
7	Eugene V. Klein	1987
6	Sheikh Maktoum bin Rashid al Maktoum	1993
5	Juddmonte Farms	1992
4	Juddmonte Farms	2003
	Godolphin Racing	2000
	Juddmonte Farms	2000
	Stronach Stables	2000
	The Thoroughbred Corp.	2000
	Allen E. Paulson	1997
	The Thoroughbred Corp.	1997
	Godolphin Racing	1996
	Overbrook Farm	1996
	Juddmonte Farms	1994
	Eugene V. Klein	1988
	Ogden Phipps	1988
	Eugene V. Klein	1985

Leading Breeders by Purses Won

Breeder	Starts	Wins	Earnings
Allen E. Paulson	28	6	$7,854,800
Overbrook Farm	26	3	4,843,000
Darley	24	2	4,649,600
Juddmonte Farms	46	2	4,145,820
Adena Springs	6	3	3,856,800
Aga Khan	12	3	3,780,400
Fares Farm	7	3	3,760,000
Ogden Phipps	17	3	3,611,000
Wimborne Farm	8	1	2,736,600
The Thoroughbred Corp.	6	2	2,732,400
Sean Coughlan	3	3	2,541,600

Breeder	Starts	Wins	Earnings
Clovelly Farms	3	1	$2,520,000
Edward P. Evans	10	1	2,433,600
Anna Marie Barnhart	2	1	2,288,000
Gainsborough Farm	18	1	2,252,040
Bertram and Diana Firestone	13	1	2,240,000

Leading Trainers by Purses Won

Trainer	Starts	Wins	Earnings
D. Wayne Lukas	146	18	$19,635,520
Robert Frankel	72	5	12,073,420
Claude McGaughey	49	9	8,693,560
William Mott	53	5	8,592,960
Todd Pletcher	51	3	7,911,650
Andre Fabre	39	4	7,621,000
Bob Baffert	47	5	7,509,800
Richard Mandella	28	6	7,116,960
Aidan O'Brien	44	3	6,936,270
Neil Drysdale	33	6	6,529,840
Jay Robbins	6	2	4,938,400
Nicholas Zito	32	2	4,574,820
Richard Dutrow	9	3	4,564,000
Saeed bin Suroor	27	2	4,313,800
Charles Whittingham	24	2	4,298,000

Trainers With Most Starts

Trainer	Starts	Wins	Earnings
D. Wayne Lukas	146	18	$19,635,520
Robert Frankel	72	5	12,073,420
William Mott	53	5	8,592,960
Todd Pletcher	51	3	7,911,650
Claude R. McGaughey III	49	9	8,693,560
Bob Baffert	47	5	7,509,800
Aidan O'Brien	44	3	6,936,270
Andre Fabre	39	4	7,621,000
Neil Drysdale	33	6	6,529,840
Nicholas Zito	32	2	4,574,820
Richard Mandella	28	6	7,116,960
Ronald McAnally	28	4	3,518,000
Michael Stoute	27	3	3,810,650
Saeed bin Suroor	27	2	4,313,800
Flint Schulhofer	26	2	2,841,400

Trainers With Multiple Victories on Breeders' Cup Program

4 Richard Mandella (2003 Classic, Turf, Juvenile, Juvenile Fillies)

3 D. Wayne Lukas (1988 Juvenile, Juvenile Fillies, Sprint)

2 Bob Baffert (2007 Juvenile, Juvenile Fillies, Sprint); **Patrick Byrne** (1998 Juvenile, Juvenile Fillies); **Richard Dutrow Jr.** (2005 Classic, Sprint); **D. Wayne Lukas** (five times) (1985 Distaff, Juvenile Fillies; 1986 Distaff, Juvenile; 1987 Distaff, Juvenile; 1994 Juvenile, Juvenile Fillies; 1999 Classic, Juvenile Fillies); **Richard Mandella** (1993 Turf, Juvenile Fillies); **Claude R. "Shug" McGaughey III** (twice) (1995 Distaff, Juvenile Fillies; 1989 Juvenile, Sprint); **Joseph Orseno** (2000 Juvenile, Filly and Mare Turf); **Todd Pletcher** (2004 Distaff, Sprint)

Trainers With Most Starters on a Program

Starters	Trainer	Year
17	Todd Pletcher	2006
14	D. Wayne Lukas	1987
12	D. Wayne Lukas	1988
11	D. Wayne Lukas	1989
10	Todd Pletcher	2007
10	D. Wayne Lukas	1996
10	D. Wayne Lukas	1985
9	Charles Whittingham	1987
8	Todd Pletcher	2005
	Robert Frankel	2003
	Bob Baffert	1999
	D. Wayne Lukas	1998
	D. Wayne Lukas	1997
	D. Wayne Lukas	1994
	Andre Fabre	1993
	D. Wayne Lukas	1991

Leading Jockeys by Purses Won

Jockey	Mounts	Wins	Earnings
Pat Day	117	12	$23,033,360
Jerry Bailey	102	15	22,006,440
Chris McCarron	101	9	17,669,600
Gary Stevens	99	8	13,723,910
John Velazquez	71	7	11,309,930
Mike Smith	57	10	10,885,760
Corey Nakatani	65	7	9,965,480
Lanfranco Dettori	48	6	9,542,910
Jose Santos	65	7	8,008,800
Eddie Delahoussaye	68	7	7,775,000
Alex Solis	57	3	7,365,960
Edgar Prado	56	3	7,225,680
Garrett Gomez	30	4	7,047,750
Laffit Pincay	61	7	6,811,000
Patrick Valenzuela	53	7	6,559,930
Angel Cordero	48	4	6,010,000

Jockeys With Multiple Victories on Breeders' Cup Program

2 Jerry Bailey (four times) (1995 Classic, Juvenile Fillies; 1996 Juvenile, Mile; 1999 Filly and Mare Turf, Juvenile Fillies; 2000 Juvenile, Filly and Mare Turf); **Jorge Chavez** (1999 Distaff, Sprint); **Angel Cordero Jr.** (1988 Juvenile Fillies, Sprint); **Pat Day** (twice) (1987 Turf, Juvenile Fillies; 1994 Juvenile, Juvenile Fillies); **Eddie Delahoussaye** (twice) (1992 Classic, Sprint; 1993 Distaff, Sprint); **Lanfranco Dettori** (2006 Filly and Mare Turf, Turf); **Garrett Gomez** (2007 Juvenile Fillies, Sprint; 2005 Juvenile, Mile); **Chris McCarron** (1992 Distaff, Juvenile); **Corey Nakatani** (1996 Distaff, Sprint); **Laffit Pincay Jr.** (1986 Classic, Juvenile); **Edgar Prado** (2005 Juvenile Fillies, Sprint); **Jose Santos** (1990 Juvenile, Juvenile Fillies); **Mike Smith** (four times) (1994 Turf, Sprint; 1995 Classic, Distaff; 1997 Classic, 2002 Distaff, Juvenile); **Alex Solis** (2003 Classic, Turf); **Gary Stevens** (1998 Distaff, Juvenile Fillies); **Patrick Valenzuela** (twice) (1991 Juvenile, Mile; 1992 Turf, Juvenile Fillies); **Cornelio Velasquez** (2007 Juvenile, Mile); **Jorge Velasquez** (1985 Classic, Juvenile Fillies); **John Velazquez** (twice) (2002 Filly and Mare Turf, Juvenile Fillies; 2004 Distaff, Sprint)

Jockeys With Most Mounts in Breeders' Cup

Jockey	Mounts	Wins	Earnings
Pat Day	117	12	$23,033,360
Jerry Bailey	102	15	22,006,440
Chris McCarron	101	9	17,669,600
Gary Stevens	99	8	13,723,910
John Velazquez	71	7	11,309,930
Eddie Delahoussaye	68	7	7,775,000
Corey Nakatani	65	7	9,965,480

Breeders' Cup — Leaders

Jockey	Mounts	Wins	Earnings
Jose Santos	65	7	$8,008,800
Kent Desormeaux	61	3	5,470,575
Laffit Pincay	61	7	6,811,000
Mike Smith	57	10	10,885,760
Alex Solis	57	3	7,365,960
Edgar Prado	56	3	7,225,680
Patrick Valenzuela	53	7	6,559,930
Angel Cordero	48	4	6,010,000
Lanfranco Dettori	48	6	9,542,910
Jorge Chavez	40	2	3,488,640

Jockeys with Most Mounts on a Program

Mounts	Jockey	Year
9	Kent Desormeaux	2007
8	Garrett Gomez	2007
	John Velazquez	2007
	Edgar Prado	2006
	John Velazquez	2006
	John Velazquez	2005
	Corey Nakatani	2004
	Edgar Prado	2004
	John Velazquez	2004
	John Velazquez	2003
	John Velazquez	2002
	Jerry Bailey	2001
	Jerry Bailey	2000
	Jerry Bailey	1999

Leading Sires by Purses Won

Sire	Starts	Wins	Earnings
Sadler's Wells	42	6	$7,261,150
Storm Cat	38	4	7,136,300
Awesome Again	8	4	5,800,800
Danzig	48	5	5,657,320
Deputy Minister	26	3	5,370,560
Cee's Tizzy	3	2	5,360,400
Smart Strike	8	2	4,879,160
Seattle Slew	26	3	4,655,400
Pleasant Colony	20	2	4,541,320
Alydar	19	1	4,495,000
Saint Ballado	5	2	3,893,600
Kris S.	13	5	3,721,900
Cozzene	10	2	3,621,000
Mr. Prospector	42	3	3,421,680
Nureyev	23	4	3,408,400

Leading Sires by Most Breeders' Cup Starts

Sire	Starts	Wins	Earnings
Danzig	48	5	$5,657,320
Mr. Prospector	42	3	3,421,680
Sadler's Wells	42	6	7,261,150
Storm Cat	38	4	7,136,300
Deputy Minister	26	3	5,370,560
Seattle Slew	26	3	4,655,400
Dynaformer	23	0	2,500,400
Nureyev	23	4	3,408,400
A.P. Indy	20	1	2,341,600
Pleasant Colony	20	2	4,541,320
Alydar	19	1	4,495,000
Danehill	19	2	2,415,400
Rahy	18	2	2,973,480
Affirmed	17	0	817,880
Gone West	17	4	2,856,000
Cox's Ridge	16	3	2,529,000
Fappiano	15	2	3,386,000
Irish River (Fr)	15	0	1,700,140
Relaunch	15	2	3,004,000

Leading Sires by Most Breeders' Cup Placings

Sire	1st	2nd	3rd	Placings
Danzig	5	6	3	14
Sadler's Wells	6	3	5	14
Storm Cat	4	6	4	14
Seattle Slew	3	4	3	10
Alydar	1	5	3	9
Cox's Ridge	3	2	4	9
Mr. Prospector	3	3	2	8
Nureyev	4	2	2	8
Sovereign Dancer	0	5	3	8
Deputy Minister	3	1	3	7
Nijinsky II	3	2	2	7
Pleasant Colony	2	4	1	7

Breeders' Cup Winners Who Sired Breeders' Cup Winners

Breeders' Cup Winner/Sire	Offspring (Breeders' Cup Victory)
A.P. Indy (1992 Classic)	Tempera (2001 Juvenile Fillies)
Awesome Again (1998 Classic)	Ghostzapper (2004 Classic), Ginger Punch (2007 Distaff), Round Pond (2006 Distaff), Wilko (2004 Juvenile)
Capote (1986 Juvenile)	Boston Harbor (1996 Juvenile)
Cherokee Run (1994 Sprint)	War Pass (2007 Breeders' Cup Juvenile)
Chief's Crown (1984 Juvenile)	Chief Bearhart (1997 Turf)
Cozzene (1995 Mile)	Alphabet Soup (1996 Classic), Tikkanen (1994 Turf)
Royal Academy (1990 Mile)	Val Royal (Fr) (2001 Mile)
Tiznow (2000 and '01 Classic)	Folklore (2005 Juvenile Fillies)
Unbridled (1990 Classic)	Anees (1999 Juvenile), Halfbridled (2003 Juvenile Fillies), Unbridled's Song (1995 Juvenile)
Unbridled's Song (1995 Juvenile)	Unbridled Elaine (2001 Distaff)
Wild Again (1984 Classic)	Elmhurst (1997 Sprint)

Breeders' Cup Winners Who Produced Breeders' Cup Winners

Breeders' Cup Winner/Broodmare	Offspring (Breeders' Cup Victory)
Hollywood Wildcat (1993 Distaff)	War Chant (2000 Mile)
My Flag (1995 Juvenile Fillies)	Storm Flag Flying (2002 Juvenile Fillies)
Personal Ensign (1988 Distaff)	My Flag (1995 Juvenile Fillies)

Sire	1st	2nd	3rd	Placings
Danehill	2	3	1	6
Dynaformer	0	3	3	6
Fappiano	2	2	2	6
Gone West	4	2	0	6
Kris S.	5	0	1	6
Seeking the Gold	3	2	1	6
Unbridled	3	2	1	6

Winners by Country and State Bred

Country	Starters	Winners
Ireland	137	14
Great Britain	112	11
France	46	5
Argentina	10	4
Canada	69	4
Germany	6	1

State	Starters	Winners
Kentucky	1,107	109
Florida	195	20
California	67	3
Maryland	22	3
Pennsylvania	18	3
Oklahoma	2	2
Illinois	9	1
New Jersey	11	1

Breeders' Cup Race Winners by Total Earnings

Horse	Breeders' Cup Victory	Total Earnings
Cigar	1995 Classic	$9,999,815
Skip Away	1997 Classic	9,616,360
Curlin	2007 Classic	9,396,800
Fantastic Light	2001 Turf	8,486,957
Invasor (Arg)	2006 Classic	7,804,070
Pleasantly Perfect	2003 Classic	7,789,880
Alysheba	1988 Classic	6,679,242
Tiznow	2000, '01 Classic	6,427,830
Ouija Board (GB)	2004, '06 Filly and Mare Turf	6,312,552
High Chaparral (Ire)	2002, '03 Turf	5,331,231
English Channel	2007 Turf	5,319,028
Sunday Silence	1989 Classic	4,968,554
Daylami (Ire)	1999 Turf	4,614,762
Unbridled	1990 Classic	4,489,475
Saint Liam	2005 Classic	4,456,995
Street Sense	2006 Juvenile	4,383,200
Awesome Again	1998 Classic	4,374,590
Pilsudski (Ire)	1996 Turf	4,080,297
Azeri	2002 Distaff	4,079,820
Better Talk Now	2004 Turf	4,071,724

Horses With Highest Earnings in Breeders' Cup Races

Horse	Year(s) Started	Earnings
Tiznow	2000, '01	$4,560,400
Curlin	2007	2,700,000
Invasor (Arg)	2006	2,700,000
Awesome Again	1998	2,662,400
Pleasantly Perfect	2003, '04	2,520,000
Saint Liam	2005	2,433,600
Skip Away	1997, '98	2,288,000
Cat Thief	1998, '99, 2000	2,200,000
Ouija Board (GB)	2004-'06	2,133,200
Alysheba	1986, '87, '88	2,133,000
Alphabet Soup	1996	2,080,000
Ghostzapper	2004	2,080,000
Volponi	2002, '03	2,080,000

Horse	Year(s) Started	Earnings
Cigar	1995, '96	$2,040,000
High Chaparral (Ire)	2002, '03	2,021,600
English Channel	2005-'07	1,988,400
Red Rocks (Ire)	2006, '07	1,920,000
Better Talk Now	2004-'07	1,793,000
Spain	1999, 2000, '01	1,755,200
Unbridled	1990, '91	1,710,000

Winning Favorites by Race

Race	Winning Favorites	Race	Winning Favorites
Distaff	41.7%	Turf	33.3%
Juvenile	37.5%	Classic	29.2%
Mile	25.0%	Juvenile Turf	0.0%
Sprint	25.0%	Filly and Mare Sprint	0.0%
Filly and Mare Turf	44.4%	Dirt Mile	0.0%
Juvenile Fillies	58.3%		

Favored Winners and Average Odds by Year

Year	Site	Winning Favorites	Average Winning Odds
2007	Monmouth Park	27.3%	5.68-to-1
2006	Churchill Downs	25.0%	11.31-to-1
2005	Belmont Park	25.0%	10.18-to-1
2004	Lone Star Park	50.0%	10.51-to-1
2003	Santa Anita Park	25.0%	14.90-to-1
2002	Arlington Park	50.0%	11.62-to-1
2001	Belmont Park	12.5%	8.63-to-1
2000	Churchill Downs	25.0%	16.65-to-1
1999	Gulfstream Park	25.0%	12.69-to-1
1998	Churchill Downs	28.6%	4.31-to-1
1997	Hollywood Park	71.4%	4.34-to-1
1996	Woodbine	28.6%	7.48-to-1
1995	Belmont Park	42.9%	4.46-to-1
1994	Churchill Downs	42.9%	12.06-to-1
1993	Santa Anita Park	42.9%	21.19-to-1
1992	Gulfstream Park	42.9%	6.59-to-1
1991	Churchill Downs	28.6%	15.36-to-1
1990	Belmont Park	57.1%	3.74-to-1
1989	Gulfstream Park	28.6%	5.00-to-1
1988	Churchill Downs	42.9%	4.59-to-1
1987	Hollywood Park	28.6%	12.74-to-1
1986	Santa Anita Park	28.6%	10.36-to-1
1985	Aqueduct	42.9%	3.31-to-1
1984	Hollywood Park	57.1%	15.98-to-1

Largest Winning Margins

Year	Winner	Race	Margin
1995	Inside Information	Distaff	13½
2006	Street Sense	Juvenile	10
2005	Pleasant Home	Distaff	9¼
1997	Countess Diana	Juvenile Fillies	8½
2007	English Channel	Turf	7
1984	Princess Rooney	Distaff	7
1990	Bayakoa (Arg)	Distaff	6¾
2007	Corinthian	Dirt Mile	6½
2002	Volponi	Classic	6½
1985	Life's Magic	Distaff	6¼
1997	Skip Away	Classic	6
2006	Round Pond	Distaff	5½
2001	Banks Hill (GB)	Filly and Mare Turf	5½
1997	Favorite Trick	Juvenile	5½
1986	Brave Raj	Juvenile Fillies	5½

Smallest Winning Margins

Year	Winner	Race	Margin
2003	High Chaparral (Ire)	Turf	DH
	Johar	Turf	

Year	Winner	Race	Margin
1996	Alphabet Soup	Classic	nose
1984	Eillo	Sprint	nose
1987	Epitome	Juvenile Fillies	nose
1998	Escena	Distaff	nose
1987	Ferdinand	Classic	nose
1992	Fraise	Turf	nose
1993	Hollywood Wildcat	Distaff	nose
2000	Macho Uno	Juvenile	nose
1988	Personal Ensign	Distaff	nose
1985	Tasso	Juvenile	nose
2001	Tiznow	Classic	nose

Nominations, Pre-Entries, Entries, and Starters by Year

Year	Foal Nominations	Pre-Entries	Entries	Starters
2007	16,090	141	124	117
2006	16,272	121	104	104
2005	16,183	117	100	99
2004	15,947	101	93	91
2003	14,927	101	91	90
2002	13,846	104	92	90
2001	15,015	109	98	94
2000	15,760	135	105	103
1999	15,191	128	102	101
1998	14,081	117	85	82
1997	12,751	94	77	76
1996	11,971	90	85	82
1995	10,543	101	84	81
1994	9,738	126	94	91
1993	9,564	103	82	81
1992	9,392	112	92	91
1991	10,056	116	91	90
1990	11,003	110	91	83
1989	11,734	101	89	81
1988	11,276	87	79	75
1987	12,183	106	91	84
1986	11,494	90	79	76
1985	10,907	110	90	82
1984	10,034	77	69	68

Pre-entries are number of individual horses made eligible. Owners may pre-enter a horse in up to two races. Beginning in 2007, two-day totals.

Average Field Sizes by Race

Race	Average Field	Most Starters	Fewest Starters
Classic	11.5	14	8
Dirt Mile	8.0	8	8
Distaff	9.3	14	6
Filly and Mare Sprint	10.0	10	10
Filly and Mare Turf	12.3	14	10
Juvenile	12.0	14	8
Juvenile Fillies	11.6	14	8
Juvenile Turf	12.0	12	12
Mile	13.2	14	10
Sprint	12.9	14	9
Turf	11.7	14	8

Average Field Sizes by Year

Year	Site	Starters	Avg. Field
2007	Monmouth Park	117	10.64
2006	Churchill Downs	104	13.00
2005	Belmont Park	99	12.38
2004	Lone Star Park	91	11.38
2003	Santa Anita Park	90	11.25
2002	Arlington Park	90	11.25
2001	Belmont Park	94	11.75
2000	Churchill Downs	103	12.88
1999	Gulfstream Park	101	12.63
1998	Churchill Downs	82	11.71
1997	Hollywood Park	76	10.86
1996	Woodbine	82	11.71
1995	Belmont Park	81	11.57
1994	Churchill Downs	91	13.00
1993	Santa Anita Park	81	11.57
1992	Gulfstream Park	91	13.00

Oldest Surviving Breeders' Cup Winners

Age	Horse, YOB, Sex, Sire	Race(s) Won	Status	Current Location
28	**Cozzene**, 1980 c. by Caro (Ire)	1985 Mile	At stud	Gainesway Farm, Ky.
	Princess Rooney, 1980 f. by Verbatim	1984 Distaff	Pensioned	Gentry Farm, Ky.
	Wild Again, 1980 c. by Icecapade	1984 Classic	Pensioned	Three Chimneys Farm, Ky.
26	**Manila**, 1983 c. by Lyphard	1986 Turf	At stud	Karacabey Pension Stud, Tur.
	Theatrical (Ire), 1982 c. by Nureyev	1987 Turf	At stud	Hill 'n' Dale Farm, Ky.
25	**Tasso**, 1983 c. by Fappiano	1985 Juvenile	At stud	Janadriyah Stud Farm, KSA
	Twilight Ridge, 1983 f. by Cox's Ridge	1985 Juvenile Fillies	Broodmare	Manchester Farm, Ky.
24	**Alysheba**, 1984 c. by Alydar	1988 Classic	At stud	Janadriyah Stud Farm, KSA
	Gulch, 1984 c. by Mr. Prospector	1988 Sprint	At stud	Lane's End, Ky.
	Miesque, 1984 f. by Nureyev	1987, '88 Mile	Broodmare	Lane's End, Ky.
	Personal Ensign, 1984 f. by Private Account	1988 Distaff	Pensioned	Claiborne Farm, Ky.
	Sacahuista, 1984 f. by Raja Baba	1987 Distaff	Pensioned	Creekview Farm, Ky.
23	**Dancing Spree**, 1985 c. by Nijinsky II	1989 Sprint	At stud	Manor Farm Stud, Eng.
	Success Express, 1985 c. by Hold Your Peace	1987 Juvenile	Pensioned	Vinery Stud, Aus.
22	**Black Tie Affair (Ire)**, 1986 c. by Miswaki	1991 Classic	At stud	O'Sullivan Farms, W.V.
	Cardmania, 1986 g. by Cox's Ridge	1993 Sprint	Retired	United Pegasus Foundation, Ca.
	Prized, 1986 c. by Kris S.	1989 Turf	At stud	O'Sullivan Farms, W.V.
	Safely Kept, 1986 f. by Horatius	1990 Sprint	Broodmare	Burleson Farms, Ky.
21	**Miss Alleged**, 1987 f. by Alleged	1991 Turf	Broodmare	Haras de Manneville, Fr.
	Royal Academy, 1987 c. by Nijinsky II	1990 Mile	At stud	Ashford Stud, Ky.
	Thirty Slews, 1987 g. by Slewpy	1992 Sprint	Retired	Carla Gaines, Ca. (stable pony/companion)
20	**Arcangues**, 1988 c. by Sagace (Fr)	1993 Classic	At stud	Nakamura Chikusan, Jpn.
	Kotashaan (Fr), 1988 c. by Darshaan	1993 Turf	At stud	Ballycurragh Stud Farm, Ire.
	One Dreamer, 1988 f. by Relaunch	1994 Distaff	Broodmare	Glen Hill Farm, Fl.

Year	Site	Starters	Avg. Field
1991	Churchill Downs	90	12.86
1990	Belmont Park	83	11.86
1989	Gulfstream Park	81	11.57
1988	Churchill Downs	75	10.71
1987	Hollywood Park	84	12.00
1986	Santa Anita Park	76	10.86
1985	Aqueduct	82	11.71
1984	Hollywood Park	68	9.71

Most Pre-Entries for a Breeders' Cup Race

Year	Race	Pre-Entries
2000	Mile	29
1998	Mile	27
1999	Mile	25
1994	Sprint	25
2006	Juvenile Fillies	24
2002	Mile	24
1995	Mile	24
1998	Sprint	24
1994	Turf	24

Largest Breeders' Cup On-Track Attendance

Year	Site	On-Track Attendance
1998	Churchill Downs	80,452
2000	Churchill Downs	76,043
2006	Churchill Downs	75,132
1994	Churchill Downs	71,671
1988	Churchill Downs	71,237
1986	Santa Anita Park	69,155
1991	Churchill Downs	66,204

Smallest Breeders' Cup On-Track Attendance

Year	Site	On-Track Attendance
1995	Belmont Park	37,246
2007	Monmouth Park	41,781
1996	Woodbine	42,243
1985	Aqueduct	42,568
1999	Gulfstream Park	45,124
1992	Gulfstream Park	45,415
2002	Arlington Park	46,118

Largest Breeders' Cup On-Track Wagering

Year	Site	On-Track Wagering
2006	Churchill Downs	$18,259,971
2003	Santa Anita Park	13,678,118
2000	Churchill Downs	13,579,798
1998	Churchill Downs	13,544,859
2005	Belmont Park	13,385,593
2007	Monmouth Park	12,726,622
1986	Santa Anita Park	12,510,109

Oldest Breeders' Cup Race Winners

Age	Horse, YOB Pedigree	Race
7	**Cardmania**, 1986 g. by Cox's Ridge—L'Orangerie, by J. O. Tobin	1993 Sprint
	Elmhurst, 1990 g. by Wild Again—Mimbet, by Raise a Native	1997 Sprint
	Miesque's Approval, 1999 h. by Miesque's Son—Win Approval, by With Approval	2006 Mile
6	**Bayakoa (Arg)**, 1984 m. by Consultant's Bid—Arlucea (Arg), by Good Manners	1990 Distaff
	Da Hoss, 1992 g. by Gone West—Jolly Saint (Ire), by Welsh Saint	1998 Mile
	Kona Gold, 1994 g. by Java Gold—Double Sunrise, by Slew o' Gold	2000 Sprint
	Lit de Justice, 1990 g. by El Gran Senor—Kanmary (Fr), by Kenmare	1996 Sprint
	Maryfield, 2001 f. by Elusive Quality—Sly Maid, by Desert Wine	2007 Filly & Mare Sprint
	One Dreamer, 1988 m. by Relaunch—Creatively, by Pretense	1994 Distaff
	Speightstown, 1998 h. by Gone West—Silken Cat, by Storm Cat	2004 Sprint
	Steinlen (GB), 1983 h. by Habitat—Southern Seas (GB), by Jim French	1989 Mile
5	**Alphabet Soup**, 1991, h. by Cozzene—Illiterate, by Arts and Letters	1996 Classic
	Arcangues, 1988, h. by Sagace (Fr)—Albertine (Fr), by Irish River (Fr)	1993 Classic
	Bayakoa (Arg), 1984 m. by Consultant's Bid—Arlucea (Arg), by Good Manners	1989 Distaff
	Better Talk Now, 1999 g. by Talkin Man—Bendita, by Baldski	2004 Turf
	Black Tie Affair (Ire), 1986 h. by Miswaki—Hat Tab Girl, by Al Hattab	1991 Classic
	Buck's Boy, 1993 g. by Bucksplasher—Molly's Colleen, by Verbatim	1998 Turf
	Cigar, 1990 h. by Palace Music—Solar Slew, by Seattle Slew	1995 Classic
	Cozzene, 1980 h. by Caro (Ire)—Ride the Trails, by Prince John	1985 Mile
	Daylami (Ire), 1994 h. by Doyoun—Daltawa, by Miswaki	1999 Turf
	Desert Stormer, 1990 m. by Storm Cat—Breezy Stories, by Damascus	1995 Sprint
	English Channel, 2002 c. by Smart Strike—Belva, by Theatrical (Ire)	2007 Turf
	Escena, 1993 m. by Strawberry Road (Aus)—Claxton's Slew, by Seattle Slew	1998 Distaff
	Fantastic Light, 1996 h. by Rahy—Jood, by Nijinsky II	2001 Turf
	Great Communicator, 1983 g. by Key to the Kingdom—Blaheen, by Beekeeper	1988 Turf
	Intercontinental (GB), 2000 m. by Danehill—Hasili (Ire), by Kahyasi	2005 Filly & Mare Turf
	Kotashaan (Fr), 1988 h. by Darshaan—Haute Autorite, by Elocutionist	1993 Turf
	Opening Verse, 1986 h. by The Minstrel—Shy Dawn, by *Grey Dawn II	1991 Mile
	Ouija Board (GB), 2001 m. by Cape Cross (Ire)-Selection Board, by Welsh Pageant	2006 Filly & Mare Turf
	Paseana (Arg), 1987 m. by Ahmad—Pasiflin (Arg), by Flintham	1992 Distaff
	Pleasantly Perfect, 1998 h. by Pleasant Colony—Regal State, by Affirmed	2003 Classic
	Saint Liam, 2000 h. by Saint Ballado-Quiet Dance, by Quiet American	2005 Classic
	Starine (Fr), 1997 m. by Mendocino—Grisonnante (Fr), by Kaldoun	2002 Filly & Mare Turf
	Theatrical (Ire), 1982 h. by Nureyev—Tree of Knowledge (Ire), by Sassafras (Fr)	1987 Turf
	Thirty Slews, 1987 g. by Slewpy—Chickery Chick, by Hatchet Man	1992 Sprint
	Val Royal (Fr), 1996 h. by Royal Academy—Vadlava, by Bikala	2001 Mile

Smallest Breeders' Cup On-Track Betting

Year	Site	On-Track Wagering
1996	Woodbine	$5,925,469
1985	Aqueduct	7,200,175
1995	Belmont Park	7,590,332
1997	Hollywood Park	8,191,459
1984	Hollywood Park	8,443,070
1990	Belmont Park	9,107,270

Shortest-Priced Winners

Year	Horse	Race	Odds
1990	Meadow Star	Juvenile Fillies	0.20-to-1
1994	Flanders	Juvenile Fillies	0.40-to-1*
1985	Life's Magic	Distaff	0.40-to-1*
1991	Dance Smartly	Distaff	0.50-to-1*
1986	Lady's Secret	Distaff	0.50-to-1*
1988	Personal Ensign	Distaff	0.50-to-1
1985	Twilight Ridge	Juvenile Fillies	0.60-to-1
1989	Bayakoa (Arg)	Distaff	0.70-to-1
1984	Chief's Crown	Juvenile	0.70-to-1
1995	Cigar	Classic	0.70-to-1
1988	Open Mind	Juvenile Fillies	0.70-to-1
1984	Princess Rooney	Distaff	0.70-to-1

*Part of entry

Longest-Priced Winners

Year	Horse	Race	Odds
1993	Arcangues	Classic	133.60-to-1
2000	Spain	Distaff	55.90-to-1
1984	Lashkari (GB)	Turf	53.40-to-1
1994	One Dreamer	Distaff	47.10-to-1
2000	Caressing	Juvenile Fillies	47.00-to-1
2002	Volponi	Classic	43.50-to-1
1991	Miss Alleged	Turf	42.10-to-1
2003	Adoration	Distaff	40.70-to-1
1986	Last Tycoon (Ire)	Mile	35.90-to-1
1999	Cash Run	Juvenile Fillies	32.50-to-1
1984	Wild Again	Classic	31.30-to-1
2005	Pleasant Home	Distaff	30.75-to-1
1987	Epitome	Juvenile Fillies	30.40-to-1
1999	Anees	Juvenile	30.30-to-1
2004	Wilko	Juvenile	28.30-to-1
2004	Better Talk Now	Turf	27.90-to-1

Oldest Breeders' Cup Starters

Age	Horse, YOB Sex Sire	Race Started	Finish
9	Bet On Sunshine, 1992 g. by Bet Big	2001 Sprint	13th
	John's Call, 1991 g. by Lord At War (Arg)	2000 Turf	3rd
8	Bet On Sunshine, 1992 g. by Bet Big	2000 Sprint	3rd
	Better Talk Now, 1999, g. by Talkin Man	2007 Turf	4th
	Cardmania, 1986 g. by Cox's Ridge	1994 Sprint	3rd
	Chorwon, 1993 g. by Cozzene	2001 Turf	6th
	Friendly Lover, 1988 h. by Cutlass	1996 Sprint	11th
	Kona Gold, 1994 g. by Java Gold	2002 Sprint	4th
	Truce Maker, 1978 h. by Ack Ack	1986 Mile	14th
7	Affirmed Success, 1994 g. by Affirmed	2001 Mile	11th
	A. P. Assay, 1991 m. by A.P. Indy	1998 Sprint	5th
	Awad, 1990 h. by Caveat	1997 Turf	9th
	Better Talk Now, 1999 g. by Talkin Man	2006 Turf	2nd
	Cardmania, 1986 g. by Cox's Ridge	1993 Sprint	**1st**
	Down the Aisle, 1993 h. by Runaway Groom	2000 Turf	12th
	Elmhurst, 1990 g. by Wild Again	1997 Sprint	**1st**
	El Senor, 1984 h. by Valdez	1991 Turf	9th
	Flag Down, 1990 h. by Deputy Minister	1997 Turf	3rd
	Forbidden Apple, 1995 h. by Pleasant Colony	2002 Mile	4th
	Fourstars Allstar, 1988 h. by Compliance	1995 Mile	7th
	Friendly Lover, 1988 h. by Cutlass	1995 Sprint	5th
	Gold Land, 1991 g. by Gone West	1998 Sprint	4th
	Host (Chi), 2000 c., by Hussonet	2007 Mile	5th
	Kona Gold, 1994 g. by Java Gold	2001 Sprint	7th
	Lakota Brave, 1989 g. by Northern Prospect	1996 Sprint	5th
	Little Bold John, 1982 g. by John Alden	1989 Mile	10th
	Miesque's Approval, 1999 h. by Miesque's Son	2006 Mile	**1st**
	Music Merci, 1986 g. by Stop the Music	1993 Sprint	6th
	Nuclear Debate, 1995 g. by Geiger Counter	2002 Mile	12th
	Perfect Drift, 1999 g. by Dynaformer	2006 Classic	8th
	Precisionist, 1981 h. by Crozier	1988 Sprint	5th
	Ricks Natural Star, 1989 g. by Natural Native	1996 Turf	14th
	River Keen (Ire), 1992 h. by Keen	1999 Classic	11th
	Sabona, 1982 h. by Exclusive Native	1989 Mile	2nd
	Savinio, 1990 g. by The Minstrel	1997 Classic	5th
	Son of a Pistol, 1992 g. by Big Pistol	1999 Sprint	13th
	Soviet Line (Ire), 1990 g. by Soviet Star	1997 Mile	7th
	Special Ring, 1997 g. by Nureyev	2004 Mile	13th
	Spook Express (SAf), 1994 m. by Comic Blush	2001 Filly and Mare Turf	2nd
	Steinlen (GB), 1983 h. by Habitat	1990 Mile	4th
	Val's Prince, 1992 g. by Eternal Prince	1999 Turf	11th
	With Anticipation, 1995 g. by Relaunch	2002 Turf	2nd

History of Breeders' Cup Races

Breeders' Cup Classic

America's classic distance is 1¼ miles on dirt, and the Breeders' Cup Classic (G1) has offered some classic, spine-tingling contests. The race has been the kingmaker among the eight Breeders' Cup races, producing 13 Horses of the Year in its 24 runnings. The respective winners in 2004, '05, '06, and '07, Ghostzapper, Saint Liam, Invasor (Arg), and Curlin, were voted Horse of the Year.

Although the year's best horse does not always win the Breeders' Cup Classic, the race has been extremely competitive, with eight of the races decided by less than one length. The only three runaway victories were Volponi's 6½-length upset in the 2002 Classic at Arlington Park, Skip Away's six-length triumph at Hollywood Park in 1997, and Curlin's 4½-length score in 2007 at Monmouth Park.

The series began with a classic finish in the 1984 Breeders' Cup at Hollywood Park, with three horses charging together through the final furlong. Longshot supplemental entry Wild Again set the pace and prevailed by a neck on the inside. Gate Dancer bore in on favorite Slew o' Gold nearing the wire, and jockey Angel Cordero Jr. restrained Slew o' Gold through the final yards to protect the eventual champion older male. Gate Dancer finished second, but Hollywood's stewards disqualified him to third, moving up Slew o' Gold to second.

The race did not yield its first Horse of the Year until 1987, when the Breeders' Cup returned to Hollywood and '86 Kentucky Derby (G1) winner Ferdinand met '87 Derby victor Alysheba. They hooked up inside the sixteenth pole and fought to the wire, with even-money favorite Ferdinand prevailing by a nose under jockey Bill Shoemaker. Ferdinand was voted Horse of the Year and champion older male, while Alysheba was honored as champion three-year-old male. The following year, Alysheba won the Classic at Churchill Downs and was voted Horse of the Year.

The 1989 Breeders' Cup Classic reunited Triple Crown rivals Sunday Silence and Easy Goer, and they battled through deep stretch as they had in the Derby and Preakness Stakes (G1) that year. Sunday Silence, who had won both the Derby and Preakness, proved best and won by a neck over Belmont Stakes (G1) victor Easy Goer. Sunday Silence was voted champion three-year-old male and Horse of the Year. After a truncated four-year-old campaign, Sunday Silence was sold for stud duty in Japan, where he became that country's all-time leading sire.

Tiznow, the race's only two-time winner, pro-

Breeders' Cup Classic

Grade 1, $5-million, three-year-olds and up, 1¼ miles, dirt. Held October 27, 2007, at Monmouth Park with gross value of $4,580,000. First held in 1984. Weights: Northern Hemisphere three-year-olds, 121 pounds; older, 126 pounds. Southern Hemisphere three-year-olds, 116 pounds; older, 126 pounds. Fillies and mares allowed three pounds.

Year	Winner	Jockey	Second	Third	Site	Time	Cond.	1st Purse
2007	**Curlin**, 3	R. Albarado	Hard Spun	Awesome Gem	Mth	2:00.59	sy	**$2,700,000**
2006	**Invasor (Arg)**, 4	F. Jara	Bernardini	Premium Tap	CD	2:02.18	ft	**2,700,000**
2005	**Saint Liam**, 5	J. Bailey	Flower Alley	Perfect Drift	Bel	2:01.49	ft	2,433,600
2004	**Ghostzapper**, 4	J. Castellano	Roses in May	Pleasantly Perfect	LS	**1:59.02**	ft	2,080,000
2003	**Pleasantly Perfect**, 5	A. Solis	Medaglia d'Oro	Dynever	SA	1:59.88	ft	2,080,000
2002	**Volponi**, 4	J. Santos	Medaglia d'Oro	Milwaukee Brew	AP	2:01.39	ft	2,080,000
2001	**Tiznow**, 4	C. McCarron	Sakhee	Albert the Great	Bel	2:00.62	ft	2,080,000
2000	**Tiznow**, 3	C. McCarron	Giant's Causeway	Captain Steve	CD	2:00.75	ft	2,480,400
1999	**Cat Thief**, 3	P. Day	Budroyale	Golden Missile	GP	1:59.52	ft	2,080,000
1998	**Awesome Again**, 4	P. Day	Silver Charm	Swain (Ire)	CD	2:02.16	ft	2,662,400
1997	**Skip Away**, 4	M. Smith	Deputy Commander	Dowty	Hol	1:59.16	ft	2,288,000
1996	**Alphabet Soup**, 5	C. McCarron	Louis Quatorze	Cigar	WO	2:01.00	ft	2,080,000
1995	**Cigar**, 5	J. Bailey	L'Carriere	Unaccounted For	Bel	1:59.58	my	1,560,000
1994	**Concern**, 3	J. Bailey	Tabasco Cat	Dramatic Gold	CD	2:02.41	ft	1,560,000
1993	**Arcangues**, 5	J. Bailey	Bertrando	Kissin Kris	SA	2:00.83	ft	1,560,000
1992	**A.P. Indy**, 3	E. Delahoussaye	Pleasant Tap	Jolypha	GP	2:00.20	ft	1,560,000
1991	**Black Tie Affair (Ire)**, 5	J. Bailey	Twilight Agenda	Unbridled	CD	2:02.95	ft	1,560,000
1990	**Unbridled**, 3	P. Day	Ibn Bey (GB)	Thirty Six Red	Bel	2:02⅕	ft	1,350,000
1989	**Sunday Silence**, 3	C. McCarron	Easy Goer	Blushing John	GP	2:00⅕	ft	1,350,000
1988	**Alysheba**, 4	C. McCarron	Seeking the Gold	Waquoit	CD	2:04⅘	my	1,350,000
1987	**Ferdinand**, 4	W. Shoemaker	Alysheba	Judge Angelucci	Hol	2:01⅖	ft	1,350,000
1986	**Skywalker**, 4	L. Pincay Jr.	Turkoman	Precisionist	SA	2:00⅖	ft	1,350,000
1985	**Proud Truth**, 3	J. Velasquez	Gate Dancer	Turkoman	Aqu	2:00⅘	ft	1,350,000
1984	**Wild Again**, 4	P. Day	Slew o' Gold	Gate Dancer	Hol	2:03⅖	ft	1,350,000

1997: Skip Away supplemental entry, Whiskey Wisdom disqualified from third to fourth; 1984: Gate Dancer disqualified from second to third

vided two scintillating finishes, holding off Giant's Causeway in 2000 by a neck at Churchill and then coming back courageously to best Sakhee by a nose in '01 at Belmont Park.

Three-year-olds have done well in the Classic, winning eight of the first 24 runnings, and two three-year-old winners have become successful sires. The 1990 Classic winner, Derby victor Unbridled, sired winners of the Kentucky Derby and Preakness, as well as two Breeders' Cup Juvenile (G1) victors and a Juvenile Fillies (G1) winner. A.P. Indy, the 1992 winner and Horse of the Year, was North America's leading sire in 2006 and sired '01 Juvenile Fillies (G1) winner Tempera. Tiznow was a three-year-old when he won in 2000 and was voted Horse of the Year.

While the Classic has yielded some classic contests, it also has produced its share of puzzles and one especially bizarre finish. Arcangues won in 1993 at 133.60-to-1, the longest price for any Breeders' Cup winner, and Volponi won at 43.50-to-1 in 2002. The unusual finish came in the 1998 Classic, which featured one of the best fields ever assembled for a Breeders' Cup race. Silver Charm took the lead in the stretch but began to bear out in the final furlong. Swain (Ire), a leading European contender, followed Silver Charm to the far outside under left-handed whipping by his jockey, Frankie Dettori. Awesome Again dashed through the hole they created and won by three-quarters of a length over Silver Charm. Skip Away, the 1.90-to-1 favorite who finished sixth, was voted Horse of the Year.

Owners by Wins

2 **Stronach Stables** (Awesome Again, Ghostzapper)
1 **Amherst Stable and Spruce Pond Stable** (Volponi), **Black Chip Stable** (Wild Again), **Cee's Stable** (Tiznow), **Michael Cooper and Cecilia Straub-Rubens** (Tiznow), **Darby Dan Farm** (Proud Truth), **Diamond A Racing** (Pleasantly Perfect), **William S. Farish, Harold Goodman, William S. Kilroy, and Tomonori Tsurumaki** (A.P. Indy), **Frances Genter** (Unbridled), **Arthur Hancock III, Ernest Gaillard, and Charlie Whittingham** (Sunday Silence), **Carolyn Hine** (Skip Away), **Elizabeth Keck** (Ferdinand), **Robert Meyerhoff** (Concern), **Oak Cliff Stable** (Skywalker), **Overbrook Farm** (Cat Thief), **Allen E. Paulson** (Cigar), **Ridder Thoroughbred Stable** (Alphabet Soup), **Dorothy and Pamela Scharbauer** (Alysheba), **Shadwell Stable** (Invasor [Arg]), **Stonestreet Stables, Padua Stables, George Bolton, and Midnight Cry Stables** (Curlin), **Jeffrey Sullivan** (Black Tie Affair [Ire]), **Mrs. William K. Warren Jr.** (Saint Liam), **Daniel Wildenstein** (Arcangues)

Breeders by Wins

2 **Oak Cliff Thoroughbreds** (Skywalker, Sunday Silence), **Cecilia Straub-Rubens** (Tiznow [twice]), **Frank Stronach/Adena Springs** (Awesome Again, Ghostzapper)
1 **Allez France Stables** (Arcangues), **Amherst Stable** (Volponi), **Anna Marie Barnhart** (Skip Away), **Clovelly Farms** (Pleasantly Perfect), **Edward P. Evans** (Saint Liam), **Fares Farm** (Curlin), **William S. Farish and William S. Kilroy** (A.P. Indy), **Mrs. John W. Galbreath** (Proud Truth), **Haras Clausan** (Invasor [Arg]), **Howard B. Keck** (Ferdinand), **W. Paul Little** (Wild Again), **Preston Madden** (Alysheba), **Robert Meyerhoff** (Concern), **Overbrook Farm** (Cat Thief), **Allen E. Paulson** (Cigar), **Stephen Peskoff** (Black Tie Affair [Ire]), **Southeast Associates** (Alphabet Soup), **Tartan Farms** (Unbridled)

Trainers by Wins

2 **Jay Robbins** (Tiznow [twice]), **Charlie Whittingham** (Ferdinand, Sunday Silence)
1 **Steve Asmussen** (Curlin), **Patrick Byrne** (Awesome Again), **Neil Drysdale** (A.P. Indy), **Richard E. Dutrow Jr.** (Saint Liam), **Andre Fabre** (Arcangues), **Bobby Frankel** (Ghostzapper), **Hubert "Sonny" Hine** (Skip Away), **David Hofmans** (Alphabet Soup), **Philip G. Johnson** (Volponi), **D. Wayne Lukas** (Cat Thief), **Richard Mandella** (Pleasantly Perfect), **Kiaran McLaughlin** (Invasor [Arg]), **Bill Mott** (Cigar), **Carl Nafzger** (Unbridled), **Ernie Poulos** (Black Tie Affair [Ire]), **Richard Small** (Concern), **Vincent Timphony** (Wild Again), **Jack Van Berg** (Alysheba), **John Veitch** (Proud Truth), **Mike Whittingham** (Skywalker)

Jockeys by Wins

5 **Jerry Bailey** (Arcangues, Black Tie Affair [Ire], Cigar, Concern, Saint Liam), **Chris McCarron** (Alphabet Soup, Alysheba, Sunday Silence, Tiznow [twice])
4 **Pat Day** (Awesome Again, Cat Thief, Unbridled, Wild Again)
1 **Robby Albarado** (Curlin), **Javier Castellano** (Ghostzapper), **Eddie Delahoussaye** (A.P. Indy), **Fernando Jara** (Invasor [Arg]), **Laffit Pincay Jr.** (Skywalker), **Jose Santos** (Volponi), **Bill Shoemaker** (Ferdinand), **Mike Smith** (Skip Away), **Alex Solis** (Pleasantly Perfect), **Jorge Velasquez** (Proud Truth)

Sires by Wins

2 **Cee's Tizzy** (Tiznow [twice])
1 **Alydar** (Alysheba), **Awesome Again** (Ghostzapper), **Broad Brush** (Concern), **Candy Stripes** (Invasor [Arg]), **Cozzene** (Alphabet Soup), **Cryptoclearance** (Volponi), **Deputy Minister** (Awesome Again), **Fappiano** (Unbridled), **Graustark** (Proud Truth), **Halo** (Sunday Silence), **Icecapade** (Wild Again), **Miswaki** (Black Tie Affair [Ire]), **Nijinsky II** (Ferdinand), **Palace Music** (Cigar), **Pleasant Colony** (Pleasantly Perfect), **Relaunch** (Skywalker), **Sagace** (Arcangues), **Saint Ballado** (Saint Liam), **Seattle Slew** (A.P. Indy), **Skip Trial** (Skip Away), **Smart Strike** (Curlin), **Storm Cat** (Cat Thief)

Winners by Place Where Bred

Locality	Winners	Locality	Winners
Kentucky	14	Pennsylvania	1
California	2	Argentina	1
Florida	2	Canada	1
Maryland	2	Ireland	1

Breeders' Cup — Classic History

Supplemental Entries

Year	Runner	Fee	Finish	Earnings
2005	Starcraft (NZ)	$800,000	7	$ 0
2001	**Tiznow**	(credit)	1	2,080,000
	Gander	(credit)	9	0
2000	**Tiznow**	360,000	1	2,480,400
	Captain Steve	270,000†	3	562,800
	Gander	360,000	9	0
1998	Silver Charm	480,000	2	1,024,000
	Skip Away	(credit)	6	0
	Gentlemen (Arg)	800,000	10	0
1997	**Skip Away**	480,000	1	2,288,000
1994	Best Pal	360,000	5	60,000
	Bertrando	360,000	6	0
1993	Bertrando	360,000	2	600,000
	Best Pal	360,000	10	0
1988	Waquoit	360,000	3	324,000
	Cutlass Reality	360,000	7	0
1985	Vanlandingham	360,000	7	0
1984	**Wild Again**	360,000	1	1,350,000

†includes credit from 1999

Eclipse Award Winners from Race

Year	Runner	Finish	Title
2007	**Curlin**	1	HOY, 3yo male
	Lawyer Ron	7	Older male
2006	**Invasor (Arg)**	1	HOY, older male
	Bernardini	2	3yo male
2005	**Saint Liam**	1	HOY, older male
2004	**Ghostzapper**	1	HOY, older male
	Azeri	5	Older female
2003	Funny Cide	9	3yo male
2002	War Emblem	8	3yo male
2001	**Tiznow**	1	Older male
2000	**Tiznow**	1	HOY, 3yo male
	Lemon Drop Kid	5	Older male
1998	Skip Away	6	HOY, older male
1997	**Skip Away**	1	Older male
1996	Cigar	3	HOY, older male
1995	**Cigar**	1	HOY, older male
1993	Bertrando	2	Older male
1992	**A.P. Indy**	1	HOY, 3yo male
	Pleasant Tap	2	Older male
1991	**Black Tie Affair (Ire)**	1	HOY, older male
1990	**Unbridled**	1	3yo male
1989	**Sunday Silence**	1	HOY, 3yo male
	Blushing John	3	Older male
1988	**Alysheba**	1	HOY, older male
1987	**Ferdinand**	1	HOY, older male
	Alysheba	2	3yo male
1986	Turkoman	2	Older male
1985	Vanlandingham	7	Older male
1984	Slew o' Gold	2	Older male

HOY = Horse of the Year

Largest Winning Margins

Year	Winner	Margin
2002	Volponi	6½
1997	Skip Away	6
2007	Curlin	4½
2004	Ghostzapper	3
1995	Cigar	2½
1993	Arcangues	2
1992	A.P. Indy	2

Smallest Winning Margins

Year	Winner	Margin
2001	Tiznow	nose
1996	Alphabet Soup	nose
1987	Ferdinand	nose
1985	Proud Truth	head
1984	Wild Again	head
2000	Tiznow	neck
1994	Concern	neck
1989	Sunday Silence	neck

Shortest-Priced Winners

Year	Winner	Odds
1995	Cigar	0.70-to-1
1987	Ferdinand	1.00-to-1
1988	Alysheba	1.50-to-1
1997	Skip Away	1.80-to-1

Longest-Priced Winners

Year	Winner	Odds
1993	Arcangues	133.60-to-1
2002	Volponi	43.50-to-1
1984	Wild Again	31.30-to-1
1996	Alphabet Soup	19.85-to-1
1999	Cat Thief	19.60-to-1

Fastest Winners

Year	Winner	Track	Time	Cond.
2004	Ghostzapper	LS	1:59.02	fast
1997	Skip Away	Hol	1:59.16	fast
1999	Cat Thief	GP	1:59.52	fast
1995	Cigar	Bel	1:59.58	muddy
2003	Pleasantly Perfect	SA	1:59.88	fast
1992	A.P. Indy	GP	2:00.20	fast
1989	Sunday Silence	GP	2:00⅕	fast

Slowest Winners

Year	Winner	Track	Time	Cond.
1988	Alysheba	CD	2:04⅘	muddy
1984	Wild Again	Hol	2:03⅗	fast
1991	Black Tie Affair (Ire)	CD	2:02.95	fast
1994	Concern	CD	2:02.41	fast
1990	Unbridled	Bel	2:02.20	fast
2006	Invasor (Arg)	CD	2:02.18	fast
1998	Awesome Again	CD	2:02.16	fast

Most Starters

Year	Track	Starters
1999	Gulfstream Park	14
1994	Churchill Downs	14
1992	Gulfstream Park	14
1990	Belmont Park	14
2006	Churchill Downs	13
2005	Belmont Park	13
2004	Lone Star Park	13
2001	Belmont Park	13
2000	Churchill Downs	13
1996	Woodbine	13
1993	Santa Anita Park	13
2002	Arlington Park	12
1987	Hollywood Park	12

Fewest Starters

Year	Track	Starters
1989	Gulfstream Park	8
1985	Aqueduct	8
1984	Hollywood Park	8
2007	Monmouth Park	9
1997	Hollywood Park	9
1988	Churchill Downs	9
2003	Santa Anita Park	10
1998	Churchill Downs	10

Winning Post Positions

Post	Starters	Winners	Percent
1	24	2	8.3%
2	24	3	12.5%
3	24	2	8.3%
4	24	2	8.3%
5	24	1	4.2%
6	24	3	12.5%
7	24	0	0.0%
8	24	2	8.3%
9	21	0	0.0%
10	18	2	11.1%
11	15	1	6.7%
12	13	4	30.8%
13	11	0	0.0%
14	4	1	25.0%

Changes in Classic

The only changes in the Breeders' Cup Classic were increases in the purse from $3-million to $4-million in 1996 and to $5-million in 2006.

Breeders' Cup Turf

The race conditions of the Breeders' Cup Turf (G1), 1½ miles on grass at weight for age, constitute the classic standard of European racing, and as a result, overseas runners have won a majority of the contests. But they have not been dominant, probably because running in late October or early November—sometimes in tropical conditions—is not part of the European schedule, which traditionally culminates for top horses in early October with the running of the Prix de l'Arc de Triomphe (Fr-G1).

In fact, American owners and trainers have fielded some outstanding grass runners, and they have defeated top-level European competitors over the years. At times, lesser American runners have prevailed because the Europeans were past their best form or did not adapt well to warm weather at Breeders' Cup sites.

Because of its importance on the world racing calendar, the Breeders' Cup Turf has become the definitive North American championship race. In every year except 1984 (John Henry's last championship season), '89 and 2006 (when the male titles went to Breeders' Cup Mile [G1] winners Steinlen [GB] and Miesque's Approval, respectively), and '05, when Europeans swept the top spots, a North American turf champion has come out of the Turf.

The 2003 edition featured the first dead heat in any Breeders' Cup race when High Chaparral (Ire) and Johar reached the finish line together. High Chaparral became the first—and only—dual Turf winner.

A decade earlier, American-trained Kotashaan (Fr) dominated grass racing in Southern California and scored a half-length victory over fellow Californian Bien Bien in the Turf. With a weak handicap division that year and no domi-

Breeders' Cup Turf

Grade 1, $3-million, three-year-olds and up, 1½ miles, turf. Held October 27, 2007, at Monmouth Park with gross value $2,748,000. First held in 1984. Weights: Northern Hemisphere three-year-olds, 121 pounds; older, 126 pounds; Southern Hemisphere three-year-olds, 116 pounds; older, 125 pounds. Fillies and mares allowed three pounds.

Year	Winner	Jockey	Second	Third	Site	Time	Cond.	1st Purse
2007	**English Channel**, 5	J. Velazquez	Shamdinan (Fr)	Red Rocks (Ire)	Mth	2:36.96	sf	**$1,620,000**
2006	**Red Rocks (Ire)**, 3	L. Dettori	Better Talk Now	English Channel	CD	2:27.32	fm	**1,620,000**
2005	**Shirocco (Ger)**, 4	C. Soumillon	Ace (Ire)	Azamour (Ire)	Bel	2:29.30	gd	1,185,600
2004	**Better Talk Now**, 5	R. Dominguez	Kitten's Joy	Powerscourt (GB)	LS	2:29.70	yl	1,040,000
2003	(DH) **High Chaparral**, 4	M. Kinane		Falbrav (Ire)	SA	2:24.24	fm	763,200
	(DH) **Johar**, 4	A. Solis						763,200
2002	**High Chaparral (Ire)**, 3	M. Kinane	With Anticipation	Falcon Flight (Fr)	AP	2:30.14	yl	1,258,400
2001	**Fantastic Light**, 5	L. Dettori	Milan (GB)	Timboroa (GB)	Bel	2:24.36	fm	1,112,800
2000	**Kalinisi (Ire)**, 4	J. Murtagh	Quiet Resolve	John's Call	CD	2:26.96	fm	1,289,600
1999	**Daylami (Ire)**, 5	L. Dettori	Royal Anthem	Buck's Boy	GP	2:24.73	gd	1,040,000
1998	**Buck's Boy**, 5	S. Sellers	Yagli	Dushyantor	CD	2:28.74	fm	1,040,000
1997	**Chief Bearhart**, 4	J. Santos	Borgia (Ger)	Flag Down	Hol	**2:23.92**	fm	1,040,000
1996	**Pilsudski (Ire)**, 4	W. Swinburn	Singspiel (Ire)	Swain (Ire)	WO	2:30.20	gd	1,040,000
1995	**Northern Spur (Ire)**, 4	C. McCarron	Freedom Cry (GB)	Carnegie (Ire)	Bel	2:42.07	sf	1,040,000
1994	**Tikkanen**, 3	M. Smith	Hatoof	Paradise Creek	CD	2:26.50	fm	1,040,000
1993	**Kotashaan (Fr)**, 5	K. Desormeaux	Bien Bien	Luazur (Fr)	SA	2:25.16	fm	1,040,000
1992	**Fraise**, 4	P. Valenzuela	Sky Classic	Quest for Fame (GB)	GP	2:24.08	fm	1,040,000
1991	**Miss Alleged**, f, 4	E. Legrix	Itsallgreektome	Quest for Fame (GB)	CD	2:30.95	fm	1,040,000
1990	**In the Wings (GB)**, 4	G. Stevens	With Approval	El Senor	Bel	2:29⅗	gd	900,000
1989	**Prized**, 3	E. Delahoussaye	Sierra Roberta (Fr)	Star Lift (GB)	GP	2:28	gd	900,000
1988	**Great Communicator**, 5	R. Sibille	Sunshine Forever	Indian Skimmer	CD	2:35⅕	gd	900,000
1987	**Theatrical (Ire)**, 5	P. Day	Trempolino	Village Star (Fr)	Hol	2:24⅖	fm	900,000
1986	**Manila**, 3	J. Santos	Theatrical (Ire)	Estrapade	SA	2:25⅖	fm	900,000
1985	**Pebbles (GB)**, f, 4	P. Eddery	Strawberry Road (Aus)	Mourjane (Ire)	Aqu	2:27	fm	900,000
1984	**Lashkari (GB)**, 3	Y. Saint-Martin	All Along (Fr)	Raami (GB)	Hol	2:25⅕	fm	900,000

2003: Dead heat. 2002, '03: High Chaparral (Ire), supplemental entry. 1985: Pebbles (GB), supplemental entry.

nant three-year-old coming out of the Triple Crown series, Kotashaan was voted both champion turf male and Horse of the Year. He remains the only Turf winner to earn the top North American honor.

Early in the Turf's history, European runners gave indications they would dominate the race. Unheralded Lashkari (GB) won the inaugural running at Hollywood Park in 1984 at 53.40-to-1, the longest winning odds in the race's history. Lashkari, who never duplicated that effort, was bred and owned by the Aga Khan, who also bred back-to-back Turf winners Daylami (Ire), who was leased to Godolphin Racing, and Kalanisi (Ire), also owned by the Aga Khan. In 2001, Godolphin's Fantastic Light won at 7-to-5.

Pebbles (GB) was supplemented to the race in 1985 and scored a hard-fought victory over Strawberry Road (Aus). The Turf in the following year at Santa Anita Park was expected to showcase Dancing Brave, the Arc winner whose only career defeat was a second-place finish in the Epsom Derby (Eng-G1). But Dancing Brave was clearly over the top and tired to finish fourth as Manila stormed to a neck victory over Theatrical (Ire), who would win the Turf the following year.

California-based runners Great Communicator and Prized won in 1988 and '89, respectively, and the American home-court advantage appeared to be an important factor in the Turf. But European runners won the following two years and subsequently have performed well. In 1996, overseas interests swept the top four spots as Pilsudski (Ire) finished ahead of Singspiel (Ire), Swain (Ire), and Shantou. Shirocco (Ger) led a similar rout in 2005.

Canadian-bred Chief Bearhart scored a popular 1.90-to-1 victory in 1997, and Illinois-bred Buck's Boy led a North American sweep of the top spots at Churchill Downs in '98. The European contingent then asserted itself through 2002, with California-based Johar sharing the winner's circle with High Chaparral in '03. In 2004, Maryland-based Better Talk Now won at 27.90-to-1 over 7-to-10 favorite Kitten's Joy at Lone Star Park.

Owners by Wins

2 **Aga Khan** (Kalanisi [Ire], Lashkari [GB]), **Godolphin Racing** (Daylami [Ire], Fantastic Light), **Susan Magnier and Michael Tabor** (High Chaparral [Ire] [twice]), **Sheikh Mohammed bin Rashid al Maktoum** (In the Wings [GB], Pebbles [GB])
1 **Augustin Stable** (Tikkanen), **Bushwood Racing Partners** (Better Talk Now), **Charles Cella** (Northern Spur [Ire]), **Class Act Stable** (Great Communicator), **Clover Racing Stable and Meadowbrook Farm** (Prized), **Fares Farm** (Miss Alleged), **La Presle Farm** (Kotashaan [Fr]), **Allen E. Paulson and Bertram Firestone** (Theatrical [Ire]), **Madeleine Paulson** (Fraise), **Quarter B. Farm** (Buck's Boy), **J. Paul Reddam** (Red Rocks [Ire]), **Sam-Son Farm** (Chief Bearhart), **James T. Scatuorchio** (English Channel), **Bradley M. "Mike" Shannon** (Manila),

The Thoroughbred Corp. (Johar), **Baron Georg von Ullmann** (Shirocco [Ger]), **Lord Arnold Weinstock and executors of Simon Weinstock** (Pilsudski [Ire])

Breeders by Wins

3 **Aga Khan** (Daylami [Ire], Kalanisi [Ire], Lashkari [GB])
2 **Sean Coughlan** (High Chaparral [Ire] [twice])
1 **Ballylinch Stud** (Red Rocks [Ire]), **Ballymacoll Stud** (Pilsudski [Ire]), **Eduardo Cojuangco Jr.** (Manila), **Bertram and Diana Firestone** (Theatrical [Ire]), **Carl M. Freeman** (Miss Alleged), **Gainsborough Farm** (Fantastic Light), **Irish Acres Farm** (Buck's Boy), **Keene Ridge Farm** (English Channel), **Sheikh Mohammed bin Rashid al Maktoum** (In the Wings [GB]), **Richard Maynard** (Chief Bearhart), **Meadowbrook Farm** (Prized), **Allen E. Paulson** (Fraise), **George Strawbridge Jr.** (Tikkanen), **Swettenham Stud & Partners** (Northern Spur [Ire]), **The Thoroughbred Corp.** (Johar), **Baron Georg von Ullmann** (Shirocco [Ger]), **Warren Hill Stud and Miika Financiera** (Pebbles [GB]), **James B. Watriss** (Great Communicator), **Wertheimer & Frère** (Kotashaan [Fr]), **Wimborne Farm** (Better Talk Now)

Trainers by Wins

2 **Andre Fabre** (In the Wings [GB], Shirocco [Ger]), **Richard Mandella** (Kotashaan [Fr], Johar), **William Mott** (Fraise, Theatrical [Ire]), **Aidan O'Brien** (High Chaparral [Ire] [twice]), **Sir Michael Stoute** (Kalanisi [Ire], Pilsudski [Ire]), **Saeed bin Suroor** (Daylami [Ire], Fantastic Light)
1 **Thad Ackel** (Great Communicator), **Pascal Bary** (Miss Alleged), **Clive Brittain** (Pebbles [GB]), **Neil Drysdale** (Prized), **Mark Frostad** (Chief Bearhart), **P. Noel Hickey** (Buck's Boy), **LeRoy Jolley** (Manila), **Ron McAnally** (Northern Spur [Ire]), **Brian Meehan** (Red Rocks [Ire]), **H. Graham Motion** (Better Talk Now), **Jonathan Pease** (Tikkanen), **Alain de Royer-Dupre** (Lashkari [GB]), **Todd A. Pletcher** (English Channel)

Jockeys by Wins

3 **Lanfranco Dettori** (Daylami [Ire], Fantastic Light, Red Rocks [Ire])
2 **Michael Kinane** (High Chaparral [Ire] [twice]), **Jose Santos** (Chief Bearhart, Manila)
1 **Pat Day** (Theatrical [Ire]), **Eddie Delahoussaye** (Prized), **Kent Desormeaux** (Kotashaan [Fr]), **Ramon Dominguez** (Better Talk Now), **Pat Eddery** (Pebbles [GB]), **Eric Legrix** (Miss Alleged), **Chris McCarron** (Northern Spur [Ire]), **John Murtagh** (Kalanisi [Ire]), **Yves Saint-Martin** (Lashkari [GB]), **Shane Sellers** (Buck's Boy), **Ray Sibille** (Great Communicator), **Mike Smith** (Tikkanen), **Alex Solis** (Johar), **Christophe Soumillon** (Shirocco [Ger]), **Gary Stevens** (In the Wings [GB]), **Walter Swinburn** (Pilsudski [Ire]), **Patrick Valenzuela** (Fraise), **John Velazquez** (English Channel)

Sires by Wins

4 **Sadler's Wells** (High Chaparral [Ire] [twice], In the Wings [GB], Northern Spur [Ire])
2 **Doyoun** (Daylami [Ire], Kalanisi [Ire])
1 **Alleged** (Miss Alleged), **Bucksplasher** (Buck's Boy), **Chief's Crown** (Chief Bearhart), **Cozzene** (Tikkanen), **Darshaan** (Kotashaan [Fr]), **Galileo**

(Ire) (Red Rocks [Ire]), **Gone West** (Johar), **Key to the Kingdom** (Great Communicator), **Kris S.** (Prized), **Lyphard** (Manila), **Mill Reef** (Lashkari [GB]), **Monsun** (Shirocco [Ger]), **Nureyev** (Theatrical [Ire]), **Polish Precedent** (Pilsudski [Ire]), **Rahy** (Fantastic Light), **Sharpen Up (GB)** (Pebbles [GB]), **Smart Strike** (English Channel), **Strawberry Road (Aus)** (Fraise), **Talkin Man** (Better Talk Now)

Winners by Place Where Bred

Locality	Winners	Locality	Winners
Ireland	8	Pennsylvania	1
Kentucky	8	Canada	1
Great Britain	3	France	1
Florida	1	Germany	1
Illinois	1		

Supplemental Entries

Year	Runner	Fee	Finish	Earnings
2005	Shirocco (Ger)	$180,000	1	$1,185,600
	Azamour (Ire)	180,000	3	250,800
2003	High Chaparral (Ire)	(credit)	1	762,200
	Falbrav (Ire)	180,000	3	233,200
2002	High Chaparral (Ire)	180,000	1	1,258,400
	Falcon Flight (Fr)	180,000	3	290,400
	Golan (Ire)	180,000	6	0
2001	Timboroa (GB)	180,000	3	256,800
2000	John's Call	240,000	3	297,600
	Montjeu (Ire)	180,000	7	0
	Subtle Power (Ire)	180,000	10	0
1986	Estrapade	240,000	3	216,000
1985	Pebbles (GB)	240,000	1	900,000
	Greinton (GB)	240,000	7	0

Eclipse Award Winners from Race

Year	Runner	Finish	Title
2007	**English Channel**	1	Turf male
2004	**Kitten's Joy**	2	Turf male
2003	**High Chaparral (Ire)**	1 (dh)	Turf male
2002	**High Chaparral (Ire)**	1	Turf male
2001	**Fantastic Light**	1	Turf male
2000	**Kalanisi (Ire)**	1	Turf male
1999	**Daylami (Ire)**	1	Turf male
1998	**Buck's Boy**	1	Turf male
1997	**Chief Bearhart**	1	Turf male
1996	Singspiel (Ire)	2	Turf male
1995	**Northern Spur (Ire)**	1	Turf male
1994	Hatoof	2	Turf female
	Paradise Creek	3	Turf male
1993	Kotashaan (Fr)	1	Horse of the Year, Turf male
1992	Sky Classic	2	Turf male
1991	**Miss Alleged**	1	Turf female
1988	Sunshine Forever	2	Turf male
1987	**Theatrical (Ire)**	1	Turf male
1986	Manila	1	Turf male
	Estrapade	3	Turf female
1985	**Pebbles (GB)**	1	Turf female

Largest Winning Margins

Year	Winner	Margin
2007	English Channel	7
1999	Daylami (Ire)	2½
2005	Shirocco (Ger)	1¾
2004	Better Talk Now	1¾
1994	Tikkanen	1½
2002	High Chaparral (Ire)	1¼
1998	Buck's Boy	1¼
1996	Pilsudski (Ire)	1¼

Smallest Winning Margins

Year	Winner	Margin
2003	High Chaparral (Ire) Johar	Dead heat
1992	Fraise	nose
1989	Prized	head
1995	Northern Spur (Ire)	neck
1986	Manila	neck
1985	Pebbles (GB)	neck
1984	Lashkari (GB)	neck

Shortest-Priced Winners

Year	Winner	Odds
2002	High Chaparral (Ire)	0.90-to-1
2001	Fantastic Light	1.40-to-1
1993	Kotashaan (Fr)	1.50-to-1
1999	Daylami (Ire)	1.60-to-1
1987	Theatrical (Ire)	1.80-to-1

Longest-Priced Winners

Year	Winner	Odds
1984	Lashkari (GB)	53.40-to-1
1991	Miss Alleged	42.10-to-1
2004	Better Talk Now	27.90-to-1
1994	Tikkanen	16.60-to-1
2003	Johar	14.20-to-1
1992	Fraise	14.00-to-1

Odds-On Beaten Favorites

Year	Favorite	Odds	Finish
2004	Kitten's Joy	7-to-10	2
1994	Paradise Creek	4-to-5	3
1992	Sky Classic	9-to-10	2
1986	Dancing Brave	1-to-2	4

Fastest Winners

Year	Winner	Track	Time	Cond.
1997	Chief Bearhart	Hol	2:23.92	firm
1992	Fraise	GP	2:24.08	firm
2003	(DH) High Chaparral (Ire) (DH) Johar	SA	2:24.24	firm
2001	Fantastic Light	Bel	2:24.36	firm
1987	Theatrical (Ire)	Hol	2:24.40	firm
1999	Daylami (Ire)	GP	2:24.73	good
1993	Kotashaan (Fr)	SA	2:25.16	firm
1984	Lashkari (GB)	Hol	2:25.20	firm
1986	Manila	SA	2:25.40	firm

Slowest Winners

Year	Winner	Track	Time	Cond.
1995	Northern Spur (Ire)	Bel	2:42.07	soft
2007	English Channel	Mth	2:36.96	soft
1988	Great Communicator	CD	2:35⅕	good
1991	Miss Alleged	CD	2:30.95	firm
1996	Pilsudski (Ire)	WO	2:30.20	good
2002	High Chaparral (Ire)	AP	2:30.14	yielding
2004	Better Talk Now	LS	2:29.70	yielding
1990	In the Wings (GB)	Bel	2:29.60	good
2005	Shirocco (Ger)	Bel	2:29.30	good

Most Starters

Year	Track	Starters
1999	Gulfstream Park	14
1996	Woodbine	14

Breeders' Cup — Juvenile History

Year	Track	Starters
1994	Churchill Downs	14
1993	Santa Anita Park	14
1989	Gulfstream Park	14
1987	Hollywood Park	14
1985	Aqueduct	14

Fewest Starters

Year	Track	Starters
2007	Monmouth Park	8
2004	Lone Star Park	8
2002	Arlington Park	8
2003	Santa Anita Park	9
1986	Santa Anita Park	9
1992	Gulfstream Park	10
1988	Churchill Downs	10
2006	Churchill Downs	11
2001	Belmont Park	11
1997	Hollywood Park	11
1990	Belmont Park	11
1984	Hollywood Park	11

Winning Post Positions

Post	Starters	Winners	Percent
1	24	2	8.3%
2	24	6	25.0%
3	24	2	8.3%
4	24	0	0.0%
5	24	3	12.5%
6	24	1	4.2%
7	24	1	4.2%
8	24	1	4.2%
9	21	4	19.0%
10	19	0	0.0%
11	17	0	0.0%
12	12	3	25.0%
13	12	2	16.7%
14	7	0	0.0%

Changes in Turf

For 2006, the purse of the Breeders' Cup Turf was increased to $3-million from $2-million.

Breeders' Cup Juvenile

The Breeders' Cup Juvenile (G1) has been highly productive in deciding divisional champions, trailing only the Breeders' Cup Juvenile Fillies (G1). Nineteen of the first 24 Juvenile winners received Eclipse Awards as champion juvenile male, with one, Favorite Trick, also garnering Horse of the Year honors in 1997.

But after their championship season, the Juvenile winners had a perplexingly difficult time reproducing that form at three and beyond, particularly in the following year's classics. Whether it was because these juvenile champions could not gear back up so quickly in the spring after a fall campaign, the distances at three were too far for them, or these juveniles could not stay sound long enough to contest the spring classics, for 22 years no winner of the Juvenile was able to win the Kentucky Derby (G1). This phenomenon became known as the "Juvenile jinx."

All that changed in 2007, when Street Sense, winner of the '06 Juvenile at Churchill Downs by a race-record ten lengths, returned to Churchill the first Saturday in May and won the Derby in stylish fashion. Street Sense was the second Juvenile winner to take a classic, following Timber Country, who won the 1995 Preakness Stakes (G1).

The first Breeders' Cup Juvenile was won by Chief's Crown, who finished second or third in

Breeders' Cup Juvenile

Grade 1, $2-million, two-year-old colts and geldings, 1 1/16 miles, dirt. Held on October 27, 2007, at Monmouth Park with gross value of $1,832,000. First held in 1984. Weights: 122 pounds.

Year	Winner	Jockey	Second	Third	Site	Time	Cond.	1st Purse
2007	War Pass	C. Velasquez	Pyro	Kodiak Kowboy	Mth	1:42.76	sy	$1,080,000
2006	Street Sense	C. H. Borel	Circular Quay	Great Hunter	CD	1:42.59	ft	1,080,000
2005	Stevie Wonderboy	G. Gomez	Henny Hughes	First Samurai	Bel	1:41.64	ft	826,800
2004	Wilko	L. Dettori	Afleet Alex	Sun King	LS	1:42.09	ft	780,000
2003	Action This Day	D. Flores	Minister Eric	Chapel Royal	SA	1:43.62	ft	780,000
2002	Vindication	M. Smith	Kafwain	Hold That Tiger	AP	1:49.61	ft	556,400
2001	Johannesburg	M. Kinane	Repent	Siphonic	Bel	1:42.27	ft	520,000
2000	Macho Uno	J. Bailey	Point Given	Street Cry (Ire)	CD	1:42.05	ft	556,400
1999	Anees	G. Stevens	Chief Seattle	High Yield	GP	1:42.29	ft	556,400
1998	Answer Lively	J. Bailey	Aly's Alley	Cat Thief	CD	1:44	ft	520,000
1997	Favorite Trick	P. Day	Dawson's Legacy	Nationalore	Hol	**1:41.47**	ft	520,000
1996	Boston Harbor	J. Bailey	Acceptable	Ordway	WO	1:43.40	ft	520,000
1995	Unbridled's Song	M. Smith	Hennessy	Editor's Note	Bel	1:41.60	my	520,000
1994	Timber Country	P. Day	Eltish	Tejano Run	CD	1:44.55	ft	520,000
1993	Brocco	G. Stevens	Blumin Affair	Tabasco Cat	SA	1:42.99	ft	520,000
1992	Gilded Time	C. McCarron	It'sali'lknownfact	River Special	GP	1:43.43	ft	520,000
1991	Arazi	P. Valenzuela	Bertrando	Snappy Landing	CD	1:44.78	ft	520,000
1990	Fly So Free	J. Santos	Take Me Out	Lost Mountain	Bel	1:43 3/5	ft	450,000
1989	Rhythm	C. Perret	Grand Canyon	Slavic	GP	1:43 3/5	ft	450,000
1988	Is It True	L. Pincay Jr.	Easy Goer	Tagel	CD	1:46 3/5	my	450,000
1987	Success Express	J. Santos	Regal Classic	Tejano	Hol	**1:35 1/5**	ft	450,000
1986	Capote	L. Pincay Jr.	Qualify	Alysheba	SA	1:43 1/5	ft	450,000
1985	Tasso	L. Pincay Jr.	Storm Cat	Scat Dancer	Aqu	1:36 1/5	ft	450,000
1984	Chief's Crown	D. MacBeth	Tank's Prospect	Spend a Buck	Hol	1:36 1/5	ft	450,000

2002: Run at 1 1/8 miles. 1984-'85, 1987: run at one mile. 1985: Tasso supplementary entry.

all of the following year's classics, won the Travers Stakes (G1) against three-year-olds, and took the Marlboro Cup Handicap (G1) against older horses. He had the three-year-old title and Horse of the Year honors in his sights until finishing fourth as the favorite in the 1985 Breeders' Cup Classic (G1). Second to Chief's Crown in the 1984 Juvenile was Tank's Prospect, who won the following year's Preakness. Tiring to finish third, beaten only 1½ lengths, was Spend a Buck, the 1985 Derby winner who was voted champion three-year-old male and Horse of the Year.

The pattern would be repeated in subsequent editions of the Juvenile. Alysheba, third in 1986, won the following year's Derby and Preakness and was voted champion three-year-old male. Bet Twice, who conquered him in the Belmont Stakes (G1), finished fourth in the 1986 Juvenile. Pine Bluff was seventh in the 1991 Juvenile but won the Preakness the following year. Sea Hero, seventh in the 1992 Juvenile, won the following year's Derby. Finishing third to Brocco in the 1993 Juvenile was Tabasco Cat, who would become a dual classic winner in '94 for D. Wayne Lukas. Seven years later, Point Given came off a close second-place finish in the Juvenile to win the 2001 Preakness, Belmont, and Travers. Retired with an injury after the Travers, he was voted 2001 Horse of the Year and champion three-year-old male. Afleet Alex, second in the 2004 Juvenile, won the following year's Preakness and Belmont.

Losing a close decision was the best sire of the late 1990s and early 2000s, Storm Cat, who just failed to last the one-mile distance of the Juvenile at Aqueduct in 1985. Capote, winner of the 1986 Juvenile, never won again but became a successful sire, getting '96 Juvenile winner Boston Harbor.

Perhaps the most memorable running of the Juvenile occurred at Churchill Downs in 1991, when French-trained Arazi broke from the outside post position, blew by the field on the final turn, and romped to a five-length victory. Voted champion two-year-old male off that one North American start, Arazi was hampered by knee problems early in his three-year-old season and finished eighth as the favorite in the 1992 Derby.

Another disappointment was Favorite Trick, who was voted 1997 Horse of the Year after an overwhelming victory in the Juvenile. He finished eighth in the Derby.

The following year's Juvenile winner, Answer Lively, ran tenth in the 1999 Derby, and that year's Juvenile victor, Anees, was 13th the following May. Macho Uno, the 2000 Juvenile winner, did not make it to the following year's Derby, and '01 Juvenile winner Johannesburg ran eighth in the '02 Derby. Vindication, an easy winner at Arlington Park in 2002, did not start in the Derby. Action This Day, the 2003 Juvenile victor, finished sixth in '04, and Wilko, the '04 Juvenile winner at Lone Star Park, came home sixth in the '05 Derby.

Owners by Wins

2 **Eugene V. Klein** (Is It True, Success Express)
1 **Barry A. Beal, Lloyd R. "Bob" French Jr., and Eugene V. Klein** (Capote), **Mr. and Mrs. Albert Broccoli** (Brocco), **John Franks** (Answer Lively), **Gainesway Stable, Overbrook Farm, and Robert and Beverly Lewis** (Timber Country), **Merv Griffin Ranch Co.** (Stevie Wonderboy), **B. Wayne Hughes** (Action This Day), **Joseph LaCombe** (Favorite Trick), **Robert LaPenta** (War Pass), **David Milch and Jack and Mark Silverman** (Gilded Time), **Overbrook Farm** (Boston Harbor), **Padua Stables** (Vindication), **Paraneck Stable** (Unbridled's Song), **Allen E. Paulson and Sheikh Mohammed bin Rashid al Maktoum** (Arazi), **Ogden Mills Phipps** (Rhythm), **J. Paul Reddam and Susan Roy** (Wilko), **Gerald Robins** (Tasso), **Stronach Stables** (Macho Uno), **Star Crown Stable** (Chief's Crown), **Michael Tabor and Susan Magnier** (Johannesburg), **James B. Tafel** (Street Sense), **The Thoroughbred Corp.** (Anees), **Thomas Valando** (Fly So Free)

Breeders by Wins

1 **Adena Springs** (Macho Uno), **Jaime Carrion (trustee)** (Action This Day), **Cherry Valley Farm** (War Pass), **Farfellow Farms** (Anees), **John Franks** (Answer Lively), **John Gunther, Tony Holmes, and Walter Zent** (Stevie Wonderboy), **Bruce Hundley and Wayne Garrison** (Fly So Free), **Warner L. Jones Jr.** (Is It True), **Lowquest Ltd.** (Timber Country), **Wayne G. Lyster III and Jayeff B Stables** (Johannesburg), **Mandysland Farm** (Unbridled's Song), **Mr. and Mrs. Harry T. Mangurian Jr.** (Gilded Time), **Meadowbrook Farms** (Brocco), **North Ridge Farm** (Capote), **Overbrook Farm** (Boston Harbor), **Rosenda Parra** (Wilko), **Payson Stud** (Vindication), **Ogden Mills Phipps** (Rhythm), **Gerald L. Robins and Timothy H. Sams** (Tasso), **Carl Rosen** (Chief's Crown), **James B. Tafel** (Street Sense), **Tri Star Stable** (Success Express), **Ralph Wilson Jr.** (Arazi), **Mr. and Mrs. M. L. Wood** (Favorite Trick)

Trainers by Wins

5 **D. Wayne Lukas** (Boston Harbor, Capote, Is It True, Success Express, Timber Country)
1 **Bob Baffert** (Vindication), **Bobby Barnett** (Answer Lively), **Francois Boutin** (Arazi), **Patrick Byrne** (Favorite Trick), **Neil Drysdale** (Tasso), **Alex Hassinger Jr.** (Anees), **Roger Laurin** (Chief's Crown), **Richard Mandella** (Action This Day), **Claude R. "Shug" McGaughey III** (Rhythm), **Carl Nafzger** (Street Sense), **Jeremy Noseda** (Wilko), **Aidan O'Brien** (Johannesburg), **Doug O'Neill** (Stevie Wonderboy), **Joseph Orseno** (Macho Uno), **James Ryerson** (Unbridled's Song), **Flint S. "Scotty" Schulhofer** (Fly So Free), **Darrell Vienna** (Gilded Time), **Randy Winick** (Brocco), **Nicholas Zito** (War Pass)

Jockeys by Wins

3 **Jerry Bailey** (Answer Lively, Boston Harbor, Macho Uno), **Laffit Pincay Jr.** (Capote, Is It True, Success Express)
2 **Pat Day** (Favorite Trick, Timber Country), **Jose Santos** (Fly So Free, Success Express), **Mike Smith** (Vindication, Unbridled's Song), **Gary Stevens** (Anees, Brocco)
1 **Calvin H. Borel** (Street Sense), **Angel Cordero** (Open Mind), **Eddie Delahoussaye** (Pleasant Stage), **Lanfranco Dettori** (Wilko), **Rene Douglas** (Dreaming of Anna), **David Flores** (Action This Day), **Garrett Gomez** (Stevie Wonderboy), **Walter Guerra** (Outstandingly), **Michael Kinane** (Johannesburg), **Julie Krone** (Halfbridled), **Don MacBeth** (Chief's Crown), **Chris McCarron**

(Gilded Time), **Corey Nakatani** (Sweet Catomine), **Craig Perret** (Rhythm), **Edgar Prado** (Folklore), **Randy Romero** (Go for Wand), **Shane Sellers** (Countess Diana), **Patrick Valenzuela** (Arazi), **Cornelio Velasquez** (War Pass), **Jorge Velasquez** (Twilight Ridge)

Sires by Wins

Wins	Sire
2	Kris S. (Action This Day, Brocco), **Seattle Slew** (Capote, Vindication), **Unbridled** (Anees, Unbridled's Song)
1	**Awesome Again** (Wilko), **Blushing Groom (Fr)** (Arazi), Capote (Boston Harbor), **Cherokee Run** (War Pass), Danzig (Chief's Crown), **Fappiano** (Tasso), **Hennessy** (Johannesburg), **Hold Your Peace** (Success Express), Holy Bull (Macho Uno), Lively One (Answer Lively), **Mr. Prospector** (Rhythm), **Phone Trick** (Favorite Trick), **Raja Baba** (Is It True), **Stephen Got Even** (Stevie Wonderboy), **Street Cry (Ire)** (Street Sense), **Time for a Change** (Fly So Free), **Timeless Moment** (Gilded Time), Woodman (Timber Country)

Winners by Place Where Bred

Locality	Winners
Kentucky	21
Florida	3

Supplemental Entries

Year	Runner	Fee	Finish	Earnings
2005	Jealous Profit	$135,000	10	$ 0
2002	Whywhywhy	90,000	10	0
2000	Arabian Light	90,000	5	21,400
1999	Captain Steve	90,000	11	0
1992	Caponostro	120,000	6	0
1991	Bertrando	120,000	2	200,000
	Agincourt	120,000	5	20,000
1990	Best Pal	120,000	6	10,000
1985	**Tasso**	120,000	1	450,000
1984	Spend a Buck	120,000	3	108,000

Eclipse Award Winners from Race

Year	Runner	Finish	Title
2007	**War Pass**	1	Juvenile male
2006	**Street Sense**	1	Juvenile male
2005	**Stevie Wonderboy**	1	Juvenile male
2003	**Action This Day**	1	Juvenile male
2002	**Vindication**	1	Juvenile male
2001	**Johannesburg**	1	Juvenile male
2000	**Macho Uno**	1	Juvenile male
1999	**Anees**	1	Juvenile male
1998	**Answer Lively**	1	Juvenile male
1997	**Favorite Trick**	1	Horse of the Year, Juvenile male
1996	**Boston Harbor**	1	Juvenile male
1994	**Timber Country**	1	Juvenile male
1993	Dehere	8	Juvenile male
1992	**Gilded Time**	1	Juvenile male
1991	**Arazi**	1	Juvenile male
1990	**Fly So Free**	1	Juvenile male
1989	**Rhythm**	1	Juvenile male
1988	Easy Goer	2	Juvenile male
1986	**Capote**	1	Juvenile male
1985	**Tasso**	1	Juvenile male
1984	**Chief's Crown**	1	Juvenile male

Largest Winning Margins

Year	Winner	Margin
2006	Street Sense	10
1997	Favorite Trick	5½
1993	Brocco	5
1991	Arazi	5
2007	War Pass	4¾
1990	Fly So Free	3

Smallest Winning Margins

Year	Winner	Margin
2000	Macho Uno	nose
1985	Tasso	nose
1998	Answer Lively	head
1996	Boston Harbor	neck
1995	Unbridled's Song	neck

Shortest-Priced Winners

Year	Winner	Odds
1984	Chief's Crown	0.70-to-1
1997	Favorite Trick	1.20-to-1
1990	Fly So Free	1.40-to-1
1992	Gilded Time	2.00-to-1

Longest-Priced Winners

Year	Winner	Odds
1999	Anees	30.30-to-1
2004	Wilko	28.30-to-1
2003	Action This Day	26.80-to-1
2006	Street Sense	15.20-to-1
1988	Is It True	9.20-to-1

Odds-On Beaten Favorites

Year	Favorite	Odds	Finish
2001	Officer	0.75-to-1	5
1993	Dehere	7-to-10	8
1988	Easy Goer	3-to-10	2

Fastest Winners

Year	Winner	Track	Time	Cond.
1997	Favorite Trick	Hol	1:41.47	fast
1995	Unbridled's Song	Bel	1:41.60	muddy
2005	Stevie Wonderboy	Bel	1:41.64	fast
2000	Macho Uno	CD	1:42.05	fast
2004	Wilko	LS	1:42.09	fast
2001	Johannesburg	Bel	1:42:27	fast
1999	Anees	GP	1:42.29	fast
2006	Street Sense	CD	1:42.59	fast

Slowest Winners

Year	Winner	Track	Time	Cond.
2002	Vindication	AP	1:49.61	fast
1988	Is It True	CD	1:46⅗	muddy
1991	Arazi	CD	1:44.78	fast
1994	Timber Country	CD	1:44.55	fast
1998	Answer Lively	CD	1:44.00	fast
1986	Capote	SA	1:43.80	fast
2003	Action This Day	SA	1:43.62	fast
1992	Gilded Time	GP	1:43.43	fast

Most Starters

Year	Track	Starters
2006	Churchill Downs	14
2000	Churchill Downs	14
1999	Gulfstream Park	14
1991	Churchill Downs	14

Fewest Starters

Year	Track	Starters
2004	Lone Star Park	8
1997	Hollywood Park	8
1996	Woodbine	10
1988	Churchill Downs	10
1984	Hollywood Park	10

Winning Post Positions

Post	Starters	Winners	Percent
1	24	2	8.3%
2	24	3	12.5%
3	24	6	25.0%
4	24	2	8.3%
5	24	2	8.3%
6	24	1	4.2%
7	24	2	8.3%
8	24	2	8.3%
9	22	1	4.5%
10	22	0	0.0%
11	19	1	5.3%
12	16	1	6.3%
13	13	0	0.0%
14	4	1	25.0%

Changes in Juvenile

The Juvenile purse was increased to $1.5-million in 2003 and $2-million in '06. Originally contested at one mile, the distance was changed to 1 1/16 miles in 1988. It was contested at 1 1/16 miles in 1986 and at 1 1/8 miles in 2002.

Breeders' Cup Filly and Mare Turf

In July 1998, the Breeders' Cup board of directors voted to fill an obvious gap in its championship lineup by creating the $1-million Breeders' Cup Filly and Mare Turf (G1) at 1¼ miles. Until the first Filly and Mare Turf at Gulfstream Park in 1999, the female turf division had no definitive championship race, and distaffers were forced to race in open company.

The new race for fillies and mares, first run at 1⅜ miles because of Gulfstream's grass course configuration, fulfilled its intended function. Phillips Racing Partnership's Soaring Softly locked up an Eclipse Award as champion turf female with a three-quarter-length victory in 1999. The following year, Stronach Stables' Perfect Sting won by the same margin over Tout Charmant at Churchill Downs. Perfect Sting was subsequently voted champion turf female. European interests broke through in 2001 when Juddmonte Farms' French-based Banks Hill (GB) won by 5½ lengths at Belmont Park. For the first time in 2001, the Filly and Mare Turf was run at 1¼ miles, its prescribed distance when course configurations permit.

Beginning with Banks Hill, horses bred overseas dominated the Filly and Mare Turf.

Banks Hill, a Danehill filly trained by Andre Fabre for her 2001 triumph, returned in '02 to seek a second victory, this time in the care of Bobby Frankel. She could manage no better than second, beaten 1½ lengths by Starine (Fr), who was owned and trained by Frankel. Islington (Ire) finished third in the 2002 Filly and Mare Turf, and she returned the following year to score a neck victory over L'Ancresse (Ire) in the Filly and Mare Turf at Santa Anita Park. In an unusual pattern to that race, all North American-bred horses finished behind the top five finishers.

Britain's honor would be upheld in 2004 when Lord Derby's homebred Ouija Board (GB) invaded and scored a 1½-length victory over Film Maker. Europe's Horse of the Year after her victories in the Epsom Oaks (Eng-G1) and Darley Irish Oaks (Ire-G1), the Cape Cross (Ire) filly also was voted an Eclipse Award as North America's outstanding turf female. She returned in 2005 and finished second to eventual champion Intercontinental (GB), Banks Hill's sister. In one of her final career starts, Ouija Board won the 2006 Filly and Mare Turf, again over Film Maker, and was voted her second Eclipse Award. Lahudood (GB), trained in the U.S. by Kiaran McLaughlin, won in 2007 and was voted an Eclipse Award.

Owners by Wins

2 **Lord Derby** (Ouija Board [GB] [twice]), **Juddmonte Farms** (Banks Hill [GB], Intercontinental [GB])
1 **Robert Frankel** (Starine [Fr]), **Phillips Racing Partnership** (Soaring Softly), **Shadwell Stable** (Lahudood [GB]), **Stronach Stables** (Perfect Sting), **Estate of Lord Weinstock** (Islington [Ire])

Breeders by Wins

2 **Juddmonte Farms** (Banks Hill [GB], Intercontinental [GB]), **Stanley Estate and Stud Co.** (Ouija Board [GB] [twice])
1 **Ballymacoll Stud Farm** (Islington [Ire]), **Catherine Dubois** (Starine [Fr]), **Galbreath-Phillips Racing Partnership** (Soaring Softly), **Shadwell Estate Co. Ltd.** (Lahudood [GB]), **Frank Stronach** (Perfect Sting)

Breeders' Cup Filly and Mare Turf

Grade 1, $2-million, fillies and mares, three-year-olds and up, fillies and mares, 1⅜ miles, turf. Held October 27, 2007, at Monmouth Park with gross value of $1,951,080. First held in 1999. Weights: Northern Hemisphere three-year-olds, 118 pounds; older, 123 pounds; Southern Hemisphere three-year-olds, 113 pounds; older, 122 pounds.

Year	Winner	Jockey	Second	Third	Site	Time	Cond.	1st purse
2007	Lahudood (GB), 4	A. Garcia	Honey Ryder	Passage of Time (GB)	Mth	2:22.75	sf	$1,150,200
2006	Ouija Board (GB), 5	L. Dettori	Film Maker	Honey Ryder	CD	2:14.55	fm	1,188,000
2005	Intercontinental (GB), 5	R. Bejarano	Ouija Board (GB)	Film Maker	Bel	2:02.34	gd	551,200
2004	Ouija Board (GB), 3	K. Fallon	Film Maker	Wonder Again	LS	2:18.25	yl	733,200
2003	Islington (Ire), 4	K. Fallon	L'Ancresse (Ire)	Yesterday (Ire)	SA	1:59.13	fm	551,200
2002	Starine (Fr)	J. Velazquez	Banks Hill (GB	Islington (Ire)	AP	2:03.57	yl	665,600
2001	Banks Hill (GB), 3	O. Peslier	Spook Express (SAf)	Spring Oak (GB)	Bel	2:00.36	fm	722,800
2000	Perfect Sting, 4	J. Bailey	Tout Charmant	Catella (Ger)	CD	2:13.07	fm	629,200
1999	Soaring Softly, 4	J. Bailey	Coretta (Ire)	Zomaradah (GB)	GP	2:13.89	gd	556,400

1999-2000, 2004, 2006, 1⅜ miles; 2001-'03, 2005, 1¼ miles

Breeders' Cup — Filly and Mare Turf History

Trainers by Wins
- **2** Edward Dunlop (Ouija Board [GB] [twice]), **Robert Frankel** (Intercontinental [GB], Starine [Fr])
- **1** Andre Fabre (Banks Hill [GB]), **Kiaran McLaughlin** (Lahudood [GB]), **Joseph Orseno** (Perfect Sting), **Sir Michael Stoute** (Islington [Ire]), **James J. Toner** (Soaring Softly)

Jockeys by Wins
- **2** Jerry Bailey (Soaring Softly, Perfect Sting), **Kieren Fallon** (Ouija Board [GB], Islington [Ire])
- **1** Rafael Bejarano (Intercontinental [GB]), **Lanfranco Dettori** (Ouija Board [GB]), **Alan Garcia** (Lahudood [GB]), **Olivier Peslier** (Banks Hill [GB]), **John Velazquez** (Starine [Fr])

Sires by Wins
- **2** Cape Cross (Ire) (Ouija Board [GB] [twice]), **Danehill** (Banks Hill [GB], Intercontinental [GB])
- **1** Kris S. (Soaring Softly), **Mendocino** (Starine [Fr]), **Red Ransom** (Perfect Sting), **Sadler's Wells** (Islington [Ire]), **Singspiel (Ire)** (Lahudood [GB])

Winners by Place Where Bred

Locality	Winners
Great Britain	5
Kentucky	2
France	1
Ireland	1

Supplemental Entries

Year	Runner	Fee	Finish	Earnings
2007	Lahudood (GB)	$180,000	1	$1,150,200
2006	Ouija Board (GB)	(credit)	1	1,188,000
	Satwa Queen (Fr)	180,000	5	55,000
2005	Ouija Board (GB)	(credit)	2	212,000
	Megahertz (GB)	(credit)	8	0
	Flip Flop (Fr)	90,000	12	0
2004	Ouija Board (GB)	90,000	1	$733,200
	Moscow Burning	90,000	4	80,370
	Super Brand (SAf)	200,000	9	0
	Katdogwan (GB)	90,000	10	0
	Megahertz (GB)	(credit)	11	0
	Aubonne (Ger)	90,000	12	0
2003	Islington (Ire)	(credit)	1	551,200
	Megahertz (GB)	90,000	5	31,800
2002	Starine (Fr)	(credit)	1	665,600
	Islington (Ire)	90,000	3	153,600
	Golden Apples (Ire)	90,000	4	71,680
	Kazzia (Ger)	90,000	6	0
	Turtle Bow (Fr)	90,000	9	0
2001	Spook Express (SAf)	200,000	2	278,000
	Kalypso Katie (Ire)	200,000	6	0
	Starine (Fr)	90,000	10	0
	England's Legend (Fr)	90,000	11	0
2000	Caffe Latte (Ire)	(credit)	9	0
	Catella (Ger)	90,000	3	145,200
	Colstar	90,000	7	0
	Petrushka (Ire)	90,000	5	24,200
1999	Caffe Latte (Ire)	90,000	4	59,920

Eclipse Award Winners from Race

Year	Runner	Finish	Title
2007	Lahudood (GB)	1	Turf female
2006	Ouija Board (GB)	1	Turf female
2005	Intercontinental (GB)	1	Turf female
2004	Ouija Board (GB)	1	Turf female
2003	Islington (Ire)	1	Turf female
2002	Golden Apples (Ire)	4	Turf female
2001	Banks Hill (GB)	1	Turf female
2000	Perfect Sting	1	Turf female
1999	Soaring Softly	1	Turf female

Largest Winning Margins

Year	Winner	Margin
2001	Banks Hill (GB)	5½
2006	Ouija Board (GB)	2¼
2004	Ouija Board (GB)	1½
2002	Starine (Fr)	1½
2005	Intercontinental (GB)	1¼

Smallest Winning Margins

Year	Winner	Margin
2003	Islington (Ire)	neck
2007	Lahudood (GB)	¾
2000	Perfect Sting	¾
1999	Soaring Softly	¾

Fastest Winners

Year	Winner	Track	Time	Cond.
2003	Islington (Ire)	SA	1:59.13	firm
2001	Banks Hill (GB)	Bel	2:00.36	firm
2005	Intercontinental (GB)	Bel	2:02.34	good
2002	Starine (Fr)	AP	2:03.57	yielding

Slowest Winners

Year	Winner	Track	Time	Cond.
2007	Lahudood (GB)	Mth	2:22.75	soft
2004	Ouija Board (GB)	LS	2:18.25	yielding
2006	Ouija Board (GB)	CD	2:14.55	firm
1999	Soaring Softly	GP	2:13.89	good
2000	Perfect Sting	CD	2:13.07	firm

Number of Starters

Year	Track	Starters
2007	Monmouth Park	11
2006	Churchill Downs	10
2005	Belmont Park	14
2004	Lone Star Park	12
2003	Santa Anita Park	12
2002	Arlington Park	12
2001	Belmont Park	12
2000	Churchill Downs	14
1999	Gulfstream Park	14

Winning Post Positions

Post	Starters	Winners	Percent
1	9	0	0.0%
2	9	1	11.1%
3	9	0	0.0%
4	9	1	11.1%
5	9	3	33.3%
6	9	0	0.0%
7	9	0	0.0%
8	9	1	11.1%
9	9	0	0.0%
10	9	1	11.1%
11	8	1	12.5%
12	7	1	14.3%
13	3	0	0.0%
14	3	0	0.0%

Changes in Filly and Mare Turf

The Filly and Mare Turf, inaugurated in 1999, has been held at 1⅜ miles four times rather than its prescribed 1¼ miles due to course configurations. Its purse was increased to $2-million in 2006.

Breeders' Cup Sprint

Roughly half of all North American races are run at six furlongs, and thus the $2-million Breeders' Cup Sprint (G1) is the prototypical American race. The six-furlong dash has proved to be a competitive contest, principally among North American runners, and in many years it has been a nightmare for handicappers.

As a championship event, the Breeders' Cup Sprint has been especially decisive in years when no horse clearly dominated the division. In 15 of the 24 runnings of the Sprint, the Eclipse Award for champion sprinter has gone to the winner.

The first Breeders' Cup Sprint in 1984 set the tone for the series, with Eillo desperately holding off Commemorate to win by a nose. Eight runnings of the Breeders' Cup Sprint have been decided by a neck or less. Eillo was favored at 1.30-to-1, and no favorite would again win the Sprint for ten years, until Cherokee Run (2.80-to-1) in 1994. Lit de Justice was a lukewarm 4-to-1 favorite in 1996, Kona Gold won at 1.70-to-1 in 2000, and Orientate prevailed at 2.70-to-1 in '02.

Between Eillo and Cherokee Run, the Sprint was won by two other champions, Precisionist (1985) and Gulch ('88), who could not be characterized as pure sprinters. Fred Hooper's homebred Precisionist won the 1¼-mile Charles H. Strub Stakes (G1) the same year he was sprint champion, and Gulch was really best at one mile, winning the Metropolitan Handicap (G1) twice, 1987 and '88, the latter his championship year.

The Sprint in 1990 remains one of the most memorable in Breeders' Cup history. Safely Kept, the prior year's champion sprinter, fought a spirited, head-to-head battle with English invader Dayjur, the 2.40-to-1 favorite. Inside the furlong pole, Dayjur appeared to take command, but 40 yards from the wire he jumped the shadow of Belmont Park's grandstand and briefly lost his action. Those missteps proved sufficient for 12.20-to-1 Safely Kept to regain the lead.

Although Dayjur failed to become the first overseas horse to win the Sprint, the European contingent broke through the following year when Sheikh Albadou (GB) won at Churchill Downs. At 26.30-to-1, Sheikh Albadou remains the longest-priced winner of the Sprint. Average odds of Sprint winners were a healthy 10-to-1.

Kona Gold, the 2000 winner, proved that top-quality sprinters could be durable as well as fast. Carefully managed by co-owner and trainer Bruce Headley, the Java Gold gelding ran third in 1998, second in '99, and finally won at age six. In winning at Churchill Downs, Kona Gold set a track record, 1:07.77, still the fastest time ever for the Sprint. Kona Gold was the 7-to-2 favorite when seeking a second straight win in 2001 but finished seventh behind winner Squirtle Squirt. In 2002, his record fifth start in the race, he finished fourth.

Racing Hall of Fame trainer D. Wayne Lukas may be best known for his classic horses, but he collected his second Sprint victory with favored Orientate in 2002 at Arlington Park. The following year, Cajun Beat stormed to a 22.80-to-1 victory over a talented field at Santa Anita

Breeders' Cup Sprint

Grade 1, $2-million, three-year-olds and up, 6 furlongs. Held on October 27, 2007, at Monmouth Park with gross value of $1,832,000. First held in 1984. Weights: Northern Hemisphere three-year-olds, 123 pounds; older, 126 pounds; Southern Hemisphere three-year-olds, 121 pounds; older, 126 pounds; fillies and mares allowed three pounds.

Year	Winner	Jockey	Second	Third	Site	Time	Cond.	1st Purse
2007	Midnight Lute, 4	G. Gomez	Idiot Proof	Talent Search	Mth	1:09.18	sy	$1,080,000
2006	Thor's Echo, 4	C. Nakatani	Friendly Island	Nightmare Affair	CD	1:08.80	ft	1,150,200
2005	Silver Train, 3	E. Prado	Taste of Paradise	Lion Tamer	Bel	1:08.86	ft	551,200
2004	Speightstown, 6	J. Velazquez	Kela	My Cousin Matt	LS	1:08.11	ft	551,200
2003	Cajun Beat, 3	C. Velasquez	Bluesthestandard	Shake You Down	SA	1:07.95	ft	613,600
2002	Orientate, 4	J. Bailey	Thunderello	Crafty C. T.	AP	1:08.89	ft	592,800
2001	Squirtle Squirt, 3	J. Bailey	Xtra Heat	Caller One	Bel	1:08.41	ft	520,000
2000	Kona Gold, 6	A. Solis	Honest Lady	Bet On Sunshine	CD	1:07.77	ft	520,000
1999	Artax, 4	J. Chavez	Kona Gold	Big Jag	GP	1:07.89	ft	624,000
1998	Reraise, 3	C. Nakatani	Grand Slam	Kona Gold	CD	1:09.07	ft	572,000
1997	Elmhurst, 7	C. Nakatani	Hesabull	Bet On Sunshine	Hol	1:08.01	ft	613,600
1996	Lit de Justice, 6	C. Nakatani	Paying Dues	Honour and Glory	WO	1:08.60	ft	520,000
1995	Desert Stormer, m, 5	K. Desormeaux	Mr. Greeley	Lit de Justice	Bel	1:09.14	my	520,000
1994	Cherokee Run, 4	M. Smith	Soviet Problem	Cardmania	CD	1:09.54	ft	520,000
1993	Cardmania, 7	E. Delahoussaye	Meafara	Gilded Time	SA	1:08.76	ft	520,000
1992	Thirty Slews, 5	E. Delahoussaye	Meafara	Rubiano	GP	1:08.21	ft	520,000
1991	Sheikh Albadou (GB), 3	P. Eddery	Pleasant Tap	Robyn Dancer	CD	1:09.36	ft	520,000
1990	Safely Kept, f, 4	C. Perret	Dayjur	Black Tie Affair (Ire)	Bel	1:09 3/5	ft	450,000
1989	Dancing Spree, 4	A. Cordero Jr.	Safely Kept	Dispersal	GP	1:09	ft	450,000
1988	Gulch, 4	A. Cordero Jr.	Play the King	Afleet	CD	1:10 2/5	sy	450,000
1987	Very Subtle, f, 3	P. Valenzuela	Groovy	Exclusive Enough	Hol	1:08 4/5	ft	450,000
1986	Smile, 4	J. Vasquez	Pine Tree Lane	Bedside Promise	SA	1:08 2/5	ft	450,000
1985	Precisionist, 4	C. McCarron	Smile	Mt. Livermore	Aqu	1:08 2/5	ft	450,000
1984	Eillo, 4	C. Perret	Commemorate	Fighting Fit	Hol	1:10 1/5	ft	450,000

Park, and the Eclipse Award went to race favorite Aldebaran, who finished sixth at 2.10-to-1. In 2004, Speightstown secured an Eclipse Award with a 1¼-length victory over Kela. The 2005 race was marked by unbeaten Lost in the Fog's bid for the three-year-old championship (Xtra Heat had gotten her divisional title with a second to Squirtle Squirt in 1999) but he finished seventh at 7-to-10 behind another three-year-old, Silver Train.

In the 1980s, the Sprint was a graveyard for one of the era's most talented sprinters, Groovy. He went off at 2-to-5 in the 1986 Sprint and finished fourth, 4¼ lengths behind front-running winner Smile. At Hollywood Park the following year, Groovy went off at 4-to-5 and ran second to another front-runner, Ben Rochelle's filly Very Subtle. Groovy was voted an Eclipse Award as outstanding sprinter in 1987. The only other Sprint starter to lose at odds-on besides Groovy and Lost in the Fog was two-time champion Housebuster, who finished ninth at 2-to-5 odds in 1991.

Owners by Wins

1 Peter M. Brant (Gulch), Buckram Oak Farm (Silver Train), Jean Couvercelle (Cardmania), Crown Stable (Eillo), Mitch DeGroot, Dutch Masters III, and Mike Pegram (Thirty Slews), Craig Dollase, Barry Fey, Moon Han, and Frank Sinatra (Reraise), Evergreen Farm (Lit de Justice), Evergreen Farm and Jenine Sahadi (Elmhurst), Frances Genter Stable (Smile), Bruce Headley, Irwin and Andrew Molasky, and High Tech Stable (Kona Gold), Fred Hooper (Precisionist), Royce S. Jaime Racing Stable and Suarez Racing (Thor's Echo), Jayeff B Stable and Barry Weisbord (Safely Kept), David J. Lanzman (Squirtle Squirt), Robert and Beverly Lewis (Orientate), Eugene and Laura Melnyk (Speightstown), Joanne Nor (Desert Stormer), Padua Stables, John Iracane, and Joseph Iracane (Cajun Beat), Paraneck Stable (Artax), Ogden Phipps (Dancing Spree), Jill Robinson (Cherokee Run), Ben Rochelle (Very Subtle), Hilal Salem (Sheikh Albadou [GB]), and Watson and Weitman Performance LLC and Mike Pegram (Midnight Lute)

Breeders by Wins

1 Peter M. Brant (Gulch), Calumet Farm (Elmhurst), Carondelet Farm and Vinery (Artax), Ollie A. Cohen (Eillo), Delta Thoroughbreds (Cardmania), Tom Evans, Macon Wilmil Equine, and Marjac Farm (Midnight Lute), Fast Lane Farms and Block & Forman (Thor's Echo), Gainesway Thoroughbreds Ltd. (Orientate), Frances Genter Stable (Smile), Grousemont Farm (Thirty Slews), Mr. and Mrs. David Hayden (Safely Kept), Highclere Stud (Sheikh Albadou [GB]), Fred Hooper (Precisionist), Aaron and Marie Jones (Speightstown), John T. L. Jones Jr. and H. Smoot Fahlgren (Cajun Beat), John Howard King (Very Subtle), Joe Mulholland Sr., Joe Mulholland Jr., et al. (Silver Train), Audrey Narducci (Squirtle Squirt), Joanne Nor (Desert Stormer), George Onett (Cherokee Run), Carlos Perez (Kona Gold), Ogden Phipps (Dancing Spree), Willard Sergent (Reraise), Swettenham Stud and Julian G. Rogers (Lit de Justice)

Trainers by Wins

2 Bob Baffert (Midnight Lute, Thirty Slews), D. Wayne Lukas (Gulch, Orientate), Jenine Sahadi (Elmhurst, Lit de Justice)
1 Louis Albertrani (Artax), Frank Alexander (Cherokee Run), Craig Dollase (Reraise), Richard Dutrow Jr. (Silver Train), Ross Fenstermaker (Precisionist), Robert Frankel (Squirtle Squirt), Alan Goldberg (Safely Kept), Bruce Headley (Kona Gold), Budd Lepman (Eillo), Frank Lyons (Desert Stormer), Steve Margolis (Cajun Beat), Claude R. "Shug" McGaughey III (Dancing Spree), Derek Meredith (Cardmania), Doug O'Neill (Thor's Echo), Todd Pletcher (Speightstown), Flint S. "Scotty" Schulhofer (Smile), Alexander Scott (Sheikh Albadou [GB]), Mel Stute (Very Subtle)

Jockeys by Wins

4 Corey Nakatani (Elmhurst, Lit de Justice, Reraise, Thor's Echo)
2 Jerry Bailey (Orientate, Squirtle Squirt), Angel Cordero Jr. (Dancing Spree, Gulch), Eddie Delahoussaye (Cardmania, Thirty Slews), Craig Perret (Eillo, Safely Kept)
1 Jorge Chavez (Artax), Kent Desormeaux (Desert Stormer), Pat Eddery (Sheikh Albadou [GB]), Garrett Gomez (Midnight Lute), Chris McCarron (Precisionist), Edgar Prado (Silver Train), Mike Smith (Cherokee Run), Alex Solis (Kona Gold), Patrick Valenzuela (Very Subtle), Jacinto Vasquez (Smile), Cornelio Velasquez (Cajun Beat), John Velazquez (Speightstown)

Sires of Winners

2 Marquetry (Artax, Squirtle Squirt), Mr. Prospector (Eillo, Gulch)
1 Cox's Ridge (Cardmania), Crozier (Precisionist), Danzatore (Reraise), El Gran Senor (Lit de Justice), Gone West (Speightstown), Grand Slam (Cajun Beat), Green Desert (Sheikh Albadou [GB]), Hoist the Silver (Very Subtle), Horatius (Safely Kept), In Reality (Smile), Java Gold (Kona Gold), Mt. Livermore (Orientate), Nijinsky II (Dancing Spree), Old Trieste (Silver Train), Real Quiet (Midnight Lute), Runaway Groom (Cherokee Run), Slewpy (Thirty Slews), Storm Cat (Desert Stormer), Swiss Yodeler (Thor's Echo), Wild Again (Elmhurst)

Winners by Place Where Bred

Locality	Winners
Kentucky	17
Florida	4
California	1
Maryland	1
Great Britain	1

Supplemental Entries

Year	Runner	Fee	Finish	Earnings
2006	Nightmare Affair	$180,000	3	$213,000
2005	Lost in the Fog	90,000	7	0
2004	PT's Grey Eagle	90,000	8	0
2003	Bluesthestandard	90,000	2	236,000
	Shake You Down	90,000	3	129,800
	Private Horde	90,000	9	0
2002	Disturbingthepeace	90,000	7	0
	Bonapaw	90,000	10	0
1999	Son of a Pistol	120,000	13	0
	Enjoy the Moment	120,000	14	0
1998	Reraise	120,000	1	572,000
1997	Men's Exclusive	200,000	6	0
1996	Criollito (Arg)	200,000	12	0
1994	Cherokee Run	120,000	1	520,000
	Soviet Problem	120,000	2	200,000

Year	Runner	Fee	Finish	Earnings
1994	Exclusive Praline	120,000	9	$ 0
1989	Sewickley	120,000	5	50,000
1987	Zabaleta	120,000	4	70,000
	Zany Tactics	120,000	9	0
1985	Committed	200,000	7	0
1984	Pac Mania	200,000	9	0

Eclipse Award Winners from Race

Year	Runner	Finish	Title
2007	**Midnight Lute**	1	Sprinter
2006	**Thor's Echo**	1	Sprinter
2005	Lost in the Fog	7	Sprinter
2004	**Speightstown**	1	Sprinter
2003	Aldebaran	6	Sprinter
2002	**Orientate**	1	Sprinter
2001	**Squirtle Squirt**	1	Sprinter
	Xtra Heat	2	3yo filly
2000	**Kona Gold**	1	Sprinter
1999	**Artax**	1	Sprinter
1998	**Reraise**	1	Sprinter
1996	**Lit de Justice**	1	Sprinter
1995	Not Surprising	4	Sprinter
1994	**Cherokee Run**	1	Sprinter
1993	**Cardmania**	1	Sprinter
1992	Rubiano	3	Sprinter
1991	Housebuster	9	Sprinter
1989	Safely Kept	2	Sprinter
1988	**Gulch**	1	Sprinter
1987	Groovy	2	Sprinter
1986	**Smile**	1	Sprinter
1985	**Precisionist**	1	Sprinter
1984	**Eillo**	1	Sprinter

Largest Winning Margins

Year	Winner	Margin
2007	Midnight Lute	4¾
2006	Thor's Echo	4
1987	Very Subtle	4
1991	Sheikh Albadou (GB)	3
2003	Cajun Beat	2¼
1998	Reraise	2

Smallest Winning Margins

Year	Winner	Margin
1984	Eillo	nose
2005	Silver Train	head
1994	Cherokee Run	head
1995	Desert Stormer	neck
1993	Cardmania	neck
1992	Thirty Slews	neck
1990	Safely Kept	neck
1989	Dancing Spree	neck

Shortest-Priced Winners

Year	Winner	Odds
1984	Eillo	1.30-to-1
2000	Kona Gold	1.70-to-1
2007	Midnight Lute	2.50-to-1
2002	Orientate	2.70-to-1
1994	Cherokee Run	2.80-to-1

Longest-Priced Winners

Year	Winner	Odds
1991	Sheikh Albadou (GB)	26.30-to-1
2003	Cajun Beat	22.80-to-1
1992	Thirty Slews	18.70-to-1
1997	Elmhurst	16.60-to-1
1989	Dancing Spree	16.60-to-1

Odds-On Beaten Favorites

Year	Favorite	Odds	Finish
2005	Lost in the Fog	7-to-10	7
1991	Housebuster	2-to-5	9
1987	Groovy	4-to-5	2
1986	Groovy	2-to-5	4

Fastest Winners

Year	Winner	Track	Time	Cond.
2000	Kona Gold	CD	1:07.77	fast
1999	Artax	GP	1:07.89	fast
2003	Cajun Beat	SA	1:07.95	fast
1997	Elmhurst	Hol	1:08.01	fast
2004	Speightstown	LS	1:08.11	fast
1992	Thirty Slews	GP	1:08.21	fast
1987	Very Subtle	Hol	1:08⅖	fast
1986	Smile	SA	1:08⅖	fast
1985	Precisionist	Aqu	1:08⅖	fast

Slowest Winners

Year	Winner	Track	Time	Cond.
1988	Gulch	CD	1:10⅖	sloppy
1984	Eillo	Hol	1:10⅕	fast
1990	Safely Kept	Bel	1:09⅗	fast
1994	Cherokee Run	CD	1:09.54	fast
1991	Sheikh Albadou (GB)	CD	1:09.36	fast
2007	Midnight Lute	Mth	1:09.18	sloppy
1995	Desert Stormer	Bel	1:09.14	muddy

Most Starters

Year	Track	Starters
2006	Churchill Downs	14
2001	Belmont Park	14
2000	Churchill Downs	14
1999	Gulfstream Park	14
1998	Churchill Downs	14
1997	Hollywood Park	14
1994	Churchill Downs	14
1993	Santa Anita Park	14
1992	Gulfstream Park	14
1990	Belmont Park	14
1985	Aqueduct	14

Fewest Starters

Year	Track	Starters
1986	Santa Anita Park	9
2007	Monmouth Park	10
2005	Belmont Park	11
1991	Churchill Downs	11
1984	Hollywood Park	11

Winning Post Positions

Post	Starters	Winners	Percent
1	24	2	8.3%
2	24	4	16.7%
3	24	3	12.5%
4	24	2	8.3%
5	24	4	16.7%
6	24	0	0.0%
7	24	0	0.0%
8	24	1	4.2%
9	24	1	4.2%
10	23	3	13.0%
11	23	3	13.0%
12	20	0	0.0%
13	20	0	0.0%
14	12	0	0.0%

Changes in Sprint

The purse for the Sprint was doubled to $2-million in 2006.

Breeders' Cup Mile

In the Breeders' Cup Mile (G1), good things have come in twos. Five Breeders' Cup races have had repeat winners, and the Breeders' Cup Mile has had three horses who have posted two victories each.

Miesque, bred by owner Stavros Niarchos's Flaxman Holdings Ltd., sparkled in the Mile on turf at Hollywood Park in 1987 and conquered a slower surface at Churchill Downs the following year. The remarkable Francois Boutin-trained filly won by 3½ lengths in California and by four lengths in Kentucky—the largest winning margin in the race's history. On the strength of her single North American victories, Miesque was voted champion grass female in 1987 and '88. Her stakes-winning colt Miesque's Son was the sire of 2006 Mile winner Miesque's Approval, that year's champion turf male. He also won by four lengths.

The Niarchos family also campaigned Mile winners Spinning World (1997), Domedriver (Ire) (2002), and Six Perfections (Fr) ('03) in the name of Flaxman Holdings.

Claiborne Farm's homebred Lure, arguably one of the most accomplished horses never to win an end-of-year championship, also scored two daylight victories, winning by three lengths at Gulfstream Park in 1992 and by 2¼ lengths the following year at Santa Anita Park for trainer Claude R. "Shug" McGaughey III.

Da Hoss became a two-time Mile winner by virtue of his courage and the innovative training regimen of Michael Dickinson. In 1996, Dickinson had his assistant, Joan Wakefield, tested the Woodbine turf course in high heels to determine the best path for the Gone West gelding, who won by 1½ lengths. Da Hoss missed the following season due to injury and came back to run in the 1998 Mile with only one start in two years. He rallied on a firm Churchill turf course to overtake Hawksley Hill (Ire) and win by a head.

European-based horses have had consistent success in the Mile. Nine of the first 24 winners were based with European trainers prior to their wins.

Most remarkable about the Mile has been the domination of the Northern Dancer sire line. Although the great Windfields Farm stallion did not sire a winner himself, six of his sons and three of his grandsons have sired winners, accounting for 13 victories in the first 24 years. His sons Danzig and Nureyev each have sired three winners.

Owners by Wins

5 **Flaxman Holdings Ltd./Stavros Niarchos** (Domedriver [Ire], Miesque [twice], Six Perfections [Fr], Spinning World)

2 **Claiborne Farm** (Lure [twice]), **Prestonwood Farm and Wall Street Stable** (Da Hoss, [twice])

1 **Classic Thoroughbreds PLC** (Royal Academy), **Anne Coughlan** (Ridgewood Pearl [GB]), **Marjorie and Irving Cowan** (War Chant), **IEAH Stables, Andrew and John A. Cohen, Steve Cobb, and Doug Robertson** (Kip Deville), **J. Terrence Lanni, Bernard Schiappa, Kenneth Poslosky, et al.** (Silic [Fr]), **Little Red Feather Racing** (Singletary), **David S. Milch** (Val Royal [Fr]), **Sheikh Mohammed bin Rashid al Maktoum and Gerald Leigh** (Barathea [Ire]), **Live Oak Plantation** (Miesque's

Breeders' Cup Mile

Grade 1, $2-million, three-year-olds and up, 1 mile, turf. Held October 27, 2007, at Monmouth Park with gross value of $2,409,080. First held in 1984. Weights: Northern Hemisphere three-year-olds, 122 pounds; older, 126 pounds. Southern Hemisphere three-year-olds, 119 pounds; older, 126 pounds. Fillies and mares allowed three pounds.

Year	Winner	Jockey	Second	Third	Site	Time	Cond.	1st Purse
2007	**Kip Deville**, 4	C. Velasquez	Excellent Art (GB)	Cosmonaut	Mth	1:39.78	sf	**$1,420,200**
2006	**Miesque's Approval**, 7	E. Castro	Aragorn (Ire)	Badge of Silver	CD	1:34.75	fm	1,171,800
2005	**Artie Schiller**, 4	G. Gomez	Leroidesanimaux (Brz)	Gorella (Fr)	Bel	1:36.10	gd	1,053,000
2004	**Singletary**, 4	D. Flores	Antonius Pius	Six Perfections (Fr)	LS	1:36.90	yl	873,600
2003	**Six Perfections (Fr)**, f, 3	J. Bailey	Touch of the Blues (Fr)	Century City (Ire)	SA	1:33.86	fm	780,000
2002	**Domedriver (Ire)**	T. Thulliez	Rock of Gibraltar (Ire)	Good Journey	AP	1:36.92	yl	556,400
2001	**Val Royal (Fr)**, 5	J. Valdivia Jr.	Forbidden Apple	Bach (Ire)	Bel	**1:32.05**	fm	592,800
2000	**War Chant**, 3	G. Stevens	North East Bound	Dansili (GB)	CD	1:34.67	fm	608,400
1999	**Silic (Fr)**, 4	C. Nakatani	Tuzla (Fr)	Docksider	GP	1:34.26	gd	520,000
1998	**Da Hoss**, 6	J. Velazquez	Hawksley Hill (Ire)	Labeeb (GB)	CD	1:35.27	fm	520,000
1997	**Spinning World**, 4	C. Asmussen	Geri	Decorated Hero (GB)	Hol	1:32.77	fm	572,000
1996	**Da Hoss**, 4	G. Stevens	Spinning World	Same Old Wish	WO	1:35.80	gd	520,000
1995	**Ridgewood Pearl (GB)**, f, 3	J. Murtagh	Fastness (Ire)	Sayyedati (GB)	Bel	1:43.65	sf	520,000
1994	**Barathea (Ire)**, 4	L. Dettori	Johann Quatz (Fr)	Unfinished Symph	CD	1:34.50	fm	520,000
1993	**Lure**, 4	M. Smith	Ski Paradise	Fourstars Allstar	SA	1:33.58	fm	520,000
1992	**Lure**, 3	M. Smith	Paradise Creek	Brief Truce	GP	1:32.90	fm	520,000
1991	**Opening Verse**, 5	P. Valenzuela	Val des Bois (Fr)	Star of Cozzene	CD	1:37.59	fm	520,000
1990	**Royal Academy**, 3	L. Piggott	Itsallgreektome	Priolo	Bel	1:35⅕	gd	450,000
1989	**Steinlen (GB)**, 6	J. Santos	Sabona	Most Welcome (GB)	GP	1:37⅕	gd	450,000
1988	**Miesque**, f, 4	F. Head	Steinlen (GB)	Simply Majestic	CD	1:38⅗	gd	450,000
1987	**Miesque**, f, 3	F. Head	Show Dancer	Sonic Lady	Hol	1:32⅘	fm	450,000
1986	**Last Tycoon (Ire)**, 3	Y. Saint-Martin	Palace Music	Fred Astaire	SA	1:35⅕	fm	450,000
1985	**Cozzene**, 5	W. Guerra	Al Mamoon	Shadeed	Aqu	1:35	fm	450,000
1984	**Royal Heroine (Ire)**, f, 4	F. Toro	Star Choice	Cozzene	Hol	1:32⅗	fm	450,000

1985—Palace Music disqualified from second to ninth.

Approval), **John Nerud** (Cozzene), **Allen E. Paulson** (Opening Verse), **Robert Sangster** (Royal Heroine [Ire]), **Richard C. Strauss** (Last Tycoon [Ire]), **Mrs. Thomas J. Walsh and Timber Bay Farm** (Artie Schiller), **Wildenstein Stable** (Steinlen [GB])

Breeders by Wins

5 Flaxman Holdings Ltd./Niarchos Family (Domedriver [Ire], Miesque [twice], Six Perfections [Fr], Spinning World)
2 Claiborne Farm and Gamely Corp. (Lure [twice]), Fares Farm (Da Hoss [twice])
1 Allez France Stables Ltd. (Steinlen [GB]), **Center Hills Farm** (Kip Deville), **Sean Coughlan** (Ridgewood Pearl [GB]), **Marjorie and Irving Cowan** (War Chant), **M. Armenio Simoes de Almeida** (Silic [Fr]), **Disler Farms** (Singletary), **Tom Gentry** (Royal Academy), **Haras du Mezeray** (Artie Schiller), **Kilfrush Stud Ltd.** (Last Tycoon [Ire]), **Jean-Luc Lagardere** (Val Royal [Fr]), **Gerald Leigh** (Barathea [Ire]), **Live Oak Stud** (Miesque's Approval), **John Nerud** (Cozzene), **B. L. Ryan** (Royal Heroine [Ire]), **Jacques D. Wimpfheimer** (Opening Verse)

Trainers by Wins

2 Pascal Bary (Domedriver [Ire], Six Perfections [Fr]), **Francois Boutin** (Miesque [twice]), **Julio Canani** (Silic [Fr]), **Val Royal** [Fr]), **Michael Dickinson** (Da Hoss [twice]), **Claude R. "Shug" McGaughey III** (Lure [twice])
1 Don Chatlos (Singletary), Robert Collet (Last Tycoon [Ire]), Luca Cumani (Barathea [Ire]), Neil Drysdale (War Chant), Richard E. Dutrow Jr. (Kip Deville), John Gosden (Royal Heroine [Ire]), James A. Jerkens (Artie Schiller), D. Wayne Lukas (Steinlen [GB]), Richard Lundy (Opening Verse), Jan Nerud (Cozzene), Michael O'Brien (Royal Academy), John Oxx (Ridgewood Pearl [GB]), Jonathan Pease (Spinning World), Martin Wolfson (Miesque's Approval)

Jockeys by Wins

2 Freddie Head (Miesque [twice]), Mike Smith (Lure [twice]), Gary Stevens (Da Hoss, War Chant)
1 Cash Asmussen (Spinning World), Jerry Bailey (Six Perfections [Fr]), Eddie Castro (Miesque's Approval), Lanfranco Dettori (Barathea [Ire]), David Flores (Singletary), Garrett Gomez (Artie Schiller), Walter Guerra (Cozzene), John Murtagh (Ridgewood Pearl [GB]), Corey Nakatani (Silic [Fr]), Lester Piggott (Royal Academy), Yves Saint-Martin (Last Tycoon [Ire]), Jose Santos (Steinlen [GB]), Thierry Thulliez (Domedriver [Ire]), Fernando Toro (Royal Heroine [Ire]), Jose Valdivia Jr. (Val Royal [Fr]), Patrick Valenzuela (Opening Verse), Cornelio Velasquez (Kip Deville), John Velazquez (Da Hoss)

Sires by Wins

3 Danzig (Lure [twice], War Chant), Nureyev (Miesque [twice], Spinning World)
2 Gone West (Da Hoss [twice]), Indian Ridge (Domedriver [Ire], Ridgewood Pearl [GB])
1 Caro (Ire) (Cozzene), Celtic Swing (Six Perfections [Fr]), El Prado (Ire) (Artie Schiller), Habitat (Steinlen [GB]), Kipling (Kip Deville), Lypheor (GB) (Royal Heroine [Ire]), Miesque's Son (Miesque's Approval), Nijinsky II (Royal Academy), Royal Academy (Val Royal [Fr]), Sadler's Wells (Barathea [Ire]), Sillery (Silic [Fr]), Sultry Song (Singletary), The Minstrel (Opening Verse), Try My Best (Last Tycoon [Ire])

Winners by Place Where Bred

Locality	Winners	Locality	Winners
Kentucky	12	Florida	2
Ireland	4	Great Britain	2
France	3	Oklahoma	1

Supplemental Entries

Year	Runner	Fee	Finish	Earnings
2007	Kip Deville	$300,000	1	$1,420,200
	Excellent Art (GB)	180,000	2	526,000
	Host (Chi)	50,000	5	65,750
	Remarkable News (Ven)	300,000	7	0
2006	Gorella (Fr)	(credit)	7	0
	Araafa (Ire)	180,000	9	0
2005	Leroidesanimaux (Brz)	135,000	2	405,000
	Gorella (Fr)	135,000	3	222,750
	Majors Cast (Ire)	135,000	5	60,750
	Host (Chi)	300,000	7	0
2004	Blackdoun (Fr)	135,000	7	0
	Mr. O'Brien (Ire)	135,000	9	0
2002	Landseer (GB)	90,000	DNF	0
2001	Val Royal (Fr)	90,000	1	592,800
	Express Tour	90,000	10	0
2000	Ladies Din	120,000	8	0
	Indian Lodge (Ire)	90,000	13	0
1997	Lucky Coin	120,000	4	61,600
1992	Bistro Garden	120,000	14	0
1991	Star of Cozzene	120,000	3	120,000
1986	Hatim	120,000	13	0
	Truce Maker	120,000	14	0
1985	Rousillon	120,000	9	0
1984	Night Mover	120,000	8	0

DNF Did not finish

Eclipse Award Winners from Race

Year	Runner	Finish	Title
2006	**Miesque's Approval**	1	Turf male
2005	Leroidesanimaux (Brz)	2	Turf male
1993	Flawlessly	9	Turf female
1991	Tight Spot	9	Turf male
1990	Itsallgreektome	2	Turf male
1989	**Steinlen (GB)**	1	Turf male
1988	**Miesque**	1	Turf female
1987	**Miesque**	1	Turf female
1985	**Cozzene**	1	Turf male
1984	**Royal Heroine (Ire)**	1	Turf female

Largest Winning Margins

Year	Winner	Margin
2006	Miesque's Approval	4
1988	Miesque	4
1987	Miesque	3½
1994	Barathea (Ire)	3
1992	Lure	3

Smallest Winning Margins

Year	Winner	Margin
1998	Da Hoss	head
1986	Last Tycoon (Ire)	head
2000	War Chant	neck
1999	Silic (Fr)	neck
1990	Royal Academy	neck

Shortest-Priced Winners

Year	Winner	Odds
1993	Lure	1.30-to-1
1984	Royal Heroine (Ire)	1.70-to-1*
1989	Steinlen (GB)	1.80-to-1
1988	Miesque	2.00-to-1*

*Part of entry

Longest-Priced Winners

Year	Winner	Odds
1986	Last Tycoon (Ire)	35.90-to-1

Odds-On Beaten Favorites

Year	Winner	Odds
1991	Opening Verse	26.70-to-1
2002	Domedriver (Ire)	26.00-to-1
2006	Miesque's Approval	24.30-to-1
2004	Singletary	16.50-to-1

Odds-On Beaten Favorites

Year	Favorite	Odds	Finish
2002	Rock of Gibraltar (Ire)	4-to-5	2
1994	Lure	9-to-10	9

Fastest Winners

Year	Winner	Track	Time	Cond.
2001	Val Royal (Fr)	Bel	1:32.05	firm
1984	Royal Heroine (Ire)	Hol	1:32⅗	firm
1997	Spinning World	Hol	1:32.77	firm
1987	Miesque	Hol	1:32⅘	firm
1992	Lure	GP	1:32.90	firm

Slowest Winners

Year	Winner	Track	Time	Cond.
1995	Ridgewood Pearl (GB)	Bel	1:43.65	soft
2007	Kip Deville	Mth	1:39.78	soft
1988	Miesque	CD	1:38⅗	good
1991	Opening Verse	CD	1:37.59	firm
1989	Steinlen (GB)	GP	1:37⅕	good
2002	Domedriver (Ire)	AP	1:36.92	yielding

Most Starters

Year	Track	Starters
2006	Churchill Downs	14
2004	Lone Star Park	14
2002	Arlington Park	14
2000	Churchill Downs	14
1999	Gulfstream Park	14
1998	Churchill Downs	14
1996	Woodbine	14

Year	Track	Starters
1994	Churchill Downs	14
1992	Gulfstream Park	14
1991	Churchill Downs	14
1987	Hollywood Park	14
1986	Santa Anita Park	14
1985	Aqueduct	14

Fewest Starters

Year	Track	Starters
1984	Hollywood Park	10
1989	Gulfstream Park	11
2005	Belmont Park	12
2001	Belmont Park	12
1997	Hollywood Park	12
1988	Churchill Downs	12

Winning Post Positions

Post	Starters	Winners	Percent
1	24	3	12.5%
2	24	4	16.7%
3	24	1	4.2%
4	24	2	8.3%
5	24	1	4.2%
6	24	2	8.3%
7	24	2	8.3%
8	24	1	4.2%
9	24	0	0.0%
10	24	3	12.5%
11	23	2	9.1%
12	22	3	13.0%
13	18	0	0.0%
14	13	0	0.0%

Changes in Mile

The purse of the Breeders' Cup Mile was increased to $1.5-million from $1-million in 2003 and to $2-million in '06.

Breeders' Cup Juvenile Fillies

One of the most all-American of the Breeders' Cup races, the Breeders' Cup Juvenile Fillies (G1) has produced the most champions in year-end Eclipse Award balloting among Breeders' Cup races. Twenty-one of the 24 winners were subsequently voted year-end champions, and the other three placed in the race.

The first Breeders' Cup Juvenile Fillies, the second race on the inaugural card in 1984, produced the afternoon's first bit of controversy. In making a winning move at the top of the stretch, Fran's Valentine knocked Pirate's Glow off stride and pushed her into Canadian star Bessarabian. Fran's Valentine held off Outstandingly to reach the finish line first, but stewards disqualified Fran's Valentine to tenth for causing interference. After Outstandingly followed with a win in the Hollywood Starlet Stakes (G1), she was voted an Eclipse Award as champion two-year-old filly, a title that would be earned by all but three of the succeeding Juvenile Fillies winners.

The Juvenile Fillies at Aqueduct in 1985 launched a dominating run by D. Wayne Lukas, who took the first two spots that year with Twilight Ridge and Family Style. Lukas saddled the top three finishers in 1988, with Open Mind the winner. In 1994, he sent out Flanders and Serena's Song to finish one-two. Flanders pulled up lame after the race and subsequently was retired. Serena's Song, second by a head, was champion three-year-old filly the following year and retired as North America's then-leading female earner with $3,283,388. Lukas also won in 1999 with longshot Cash Run and in 2005 with Folklore, the 12th favorite to win the race. Favorites also won in 2006 and '07.

In addition to Open Mind, who was voted champion at two and three, Juvenile Fillies winners who earned two championship titles were Go for Wand and Silverbulletday. Go for Wand took the two-year-old title with a triumph at Gulfstream Park in 1989 and won an Eclipse Award as champion three-year-old filly posthumously after a fatal breakdown in the 1990 Breeders' Cup Distaff (G1). Silverbulletday scored a half-length victory over stablemate Excellent Meeting in the 1998 Juvenile Fillies and won four Grade 1 races the following year to wrap up the three-year-old filly title.

Ashado, second to Halfbridled in 2003, went on to win the Breeders' Cup Distaff (G1) in '04

and collect an Eclipse Award as champion three-year-old filly. She was voted champion older female of 2005 after another stellar campaign that ended with a third-place finish in the Distaff. She subsequently was sold for a record $9-million as a broodmare prospect.

Even more than the Breeders' Cup Juvenile (G1), the Juvenile Fillies in recent years has been noteworthy for the inability of its winners to maintain their form at age three. Storm Flag Flying, a daughter of 1995 Juvenile Fillies winner My Flag and unbeaten in 2002, failed to win at three, although she was a Grade 1 winner at four in '04 and finished second to Ashado in the '04 Distaff. Halfbridled, also unbeaten at two, failed to win her two starts at three in 2004 and was retired. Sweet Catomine, an impressive Juvenile Fillies winner and a near-unanimous Eclipse Award champion, won twice at three, including an easy victory in the Santa Anita Oaks (G1), but was retired after running fifth in the Santa Anita Derby (G1).

The Juvenile Fillies also is notable for its number of odds-on winners. Lukas's three-horse entry was 3-to-5 in 1985, and in '88 his five-horse coupling was 7-to-10. Two years later at Belmont Park, LeRoy Jolley-trained Meadow Star went off at 1-to-5 and won by five lengths. Lukas struck again at Churchill in 1994, when Flanders won at 2-to-5 in an entry with Cat Appeal. Silverbulletday, trained by Bob Baffert, won at 4-to-5 in 1998, and Ogden Mills Phipps's Storm Flag Flying won at 4-to-5 in 2002. The only filly beaten at odds-on was 0.95-to-1 You, who finished fourth in 2001.

Through 2007, only 13 overseas-based fillies have competed in the Juvenile Fillies, with their best finishes a pair of fourths in 1993 and '94. Godolphin Racing won in 2001 with Tempera, who was trained in the United States by Eoin Harty.

Owners by Wins

2 **Eugene V. Klein** (Open Mind, Twilight Ridge)

1 **John A. Bell III** (Epitome), **Buckland Farm** (Pleasant Stage), **Frank Calabrese** (Dreaming of Anna), **Christiana Stable** (Go for Wand), **Dogwood Stable** (Storm Song), **Hal and Patti Earnhardt** (Indian Blessing), **Godolphin Racing** (Tempera), **Dolly Green** (Brave Raj), **Harbor View Farm** (Outstandingly), **Carl Icahn** (Meadow Star), **Richard A., Nancy R., and Nancy A. Kaster and Donald Propson** (Countess Diana), **Robert and Beverly Lewis** (Folklore), **Overbrook Farm** (Flanders), **Padua Stables** (Cash Run), **Allen E. Paulson** (Eliza), **Mike Pegram** (Silverbulletday), **Ogden Phipps** (My Flag), **Ogden Mills Phipps** (Storm Flag Flying), **Carl F. Pollard** (Caressing), **Herman Sarkowsky** (Phone Chatter), **Wertheimer Farm** (Halfbridled), **Martin and Pamela Wygod** (Sweet Catomine)

Breeders by Wins

1 **Thomas E. Burrow** (Twilight Ridge), **Frank Calabrese** (Dreaming of Anna), **Jaime S. Carrion** (Meadow Star), **Christiana Stable** (Go for Wand), **Darley Stud Management** (Tempera), **Due Process Stable** (Open Mind), **Hal and Patti Earnhardt** (Indian Blessing), **Robert S. Evans** (Cash Run), **Mrs. Thomas M. Evans** (Pleasant Stage), **William S. Farish and Ogden Mills Phipps** (Storm Song), **Harbor View Farm** (Outstandingly), **Highclere Inc. and Clear Creek** (Silverbulletday), **Brereton C. Jones** (Caressing), **Wallace S. Karutz** (Brave Raj), **Richard S. Kaster** (Countess Diana), **Robert and Beverly Lewis** (Folklore), **Jessica Bell Nicholson and H. Bennett Bell** (Epitome), **Overbrook Farm** (Flanders), **Allen E. Paulson** (Eliza), **Ogden Phipps** (My Flag), **Phipps Stable/Ogden Mills Phipps** (Storm Flag Flying), **Herman Sarkowsky** (Phone Chatter),

Breeders' Cup Juvenile Fillies

Grade 1, $2-million, two-year-old fillies, 1 1/16 miles, dirt. Held on October 27, 2007, at Monmouth Park with gross value of $1,832,000. First held in 1984. Weights: 119 pounds.

Year	Winner	Jockey	Second	Third	Site	Time	Cond.	1st Purse
2007	**Indian Blessing**	G. Gomez	Proud Spell	Backseat Rhythm	Mth	1:44.73	sy	**$1,080,000**
2006	**Dreaming of Anna**	R. Douglas	Octave	Cotton Blossom	CD	1:43.81	ft	**1,080,000**
2005	**Folklore**	E. Prado	Wild Fit	Original Spin	Bel	1:43.85	ft	551,200
2004	**Sweet Catomine**	C. Nakatani	Balletto (UAE)	Runway Model	LS	1:41.65	ft	520,000
2003	**Halfbridled**	J. Krone	Ashado	Victory U. S. A.	SA	1:42.75	ft	520,000
2002	**Storm Flag Flying**	J. Velazquez	Composure	Santa Catarina	AP	1:49.60	gd	520,000
2001	**Tempera**	D. Flores	Imperial Gesture	Bella Bellucci	Bel	1:41.49	ft	520,000
2000	**Caressing**	J. Velazquez	Platinum Tiara	She's a Devil Due	CD	1:42.77	ft	592,800
1999	**Cash Run**	J. Bailey	Chilukki	Surfside	GP	1:43.31	ft	520,000
1998	**Silverbulletday**	G. Stevens	Excellent Meeting	Three Ring	CD	1:43.68	ft	520,000
1997	**Countess Diana**	S. Sellers	Career Collection	Primaly	Hol	**1:42.11**	ft	535,600
1996	**Storm Song**	C. Perret	Love That Jazz	Critical Factor	WO	1:43.60	ft	520,000
1995	**My Flag**	J. Bailey	Cara Rafaela	Golden Attraction	Bel	1:42.55	my	520,000
1994	**Flanders**	P. Day	Serena's Song	Stormy Blues	CD	1:45.28	ft	520,000
1993	**Phone Chatter**	L. Pincay	Sardula	Heavenly Prize	SA	1:43.08	ft	520,000
1992	**Eliza**	P. Valenzuela	Educated Risk	Boots 'n Jackie	GP	1:42.93	ft	520,000
1991	**Pleasant Stage**	E. Delahoussaye	La Spia	Cadillac Women	CD	1:46.48	ft	520,000
1990	**Meadow Star**	J. Santos	Private Treasure	Dance Smartly	Bel	1:44	ft	450,000
1989	**Go for Wand**	R. Romero	Sweet Roberta	Stella Madrid	GP	1:44 1/5	ft	450,000
1988	**Open Mind**	A. Cordero Jr.	Darby Shuffle	Lea Lucinda	CD	1:46 3/5	my	450,000
1987	**Epitome**	P. Day	Jeanne Jones	Dream Team	Hol	1:36 2/5	ft	450,000
1986	**Brave Raj**	P. Valenzuela	Tappiano	Saros Brig	SA	1:43 1/5	ft	450,000
1985	**Twilight Ridge**	J. Velasquez	Family Style	Steal a Kiss	Aqu	1:35 4/5	ft	450,000
1984	**Outstandingly**	W. Guerra	Dusty Heart	Fine Spirit	Hol	1:37 4/5	ft	450,000

1984-'85, '87—run at one mile; 2002—run at 1 1/8 miles; 1984—Fran's Valentine disqualified from first to tenth.

Wertheimer Farm et Frere (Halfbridled), **Martin and Pamela Wygod** (Sweet Catomine)

Trainers by Wins

5 D. Wayne Lukas (Cash Run, Flanders, Folklore, Open Mind, Twilight Ridge)
2 Bob Baffert (Indian Blessing, Silverbulletday), **Richard Mandella** (Halfbridled, Phone Chatter), **Claude R. "Shug" McGaughey III** (My Flag, Storm Flag Flying)
1 William Badgett Jr. (Go for Wand), **Patrick Byrne** (Countess Diana), **Julio Canani** (Sweet Catomine), Wayne Catalano (Dreaming of Anna), **Eoin Harty** (Tempera), Alex Hassinger Jr. (Eliza), Philip Hauswald (Epitome), LeRoy Jolley (Meadow Star), **Frank Martin** (Outstandingly), Christopher Speckert (Pleasant Stage), Mel Stute (Brave Raj), David Vance (Caressing), Nick Zito (Storm Song)

Jockeys by Wins

2 Jerry Bailey (Cash Run, My Flag), **Pat Day** (Epitome, Flanders), **Patrick Valenzuela** (Brave Raj, Eliza), John Velazquez (Caressing, Storm Flag Flying)
1 Angel Cordero Jr. (Open Mind), **Eddie Delahoussaye** (Pleasant Stage), Rene Douglas (Brave Raj), Craig Perret (Storm Song), **Laffit Pincay Jr.** (Phone Chatter), Edgar Prado (Folklore), **Randy Romero** (Go for Wand), Jose Santos (Meadow Star), **Shane Sellers** (Countess Diana), Gary Stevens (Silverbulletday), Jorge Velasquez (Twilight Ridge)

Sires by Wins

2 Deputy Minister (Go for Wand, Open Mind), **Seeking the Gold** (Cash Run, Flanders), **Storm Cat** (Storm Flag Flying, Sweet Catomine)
1 A.P. Indy (Tempera), **Cox's Ridge** (Twilight Ridge), Deerhound (Countess Diana), **Easy Goer** (My Flag), Exclusive Native (Outstandingly), **Honour and Glory** (Caressing), Indian Charlie (Indian Blessing), **Meadowlake** (Meadow Star), Mt. Livermore (Eliza), **Phone Trick** (Phone Chatter), Pleasant Colony (Pleasant Stage), Rahy (Dreaming of Anna), Rajab (Brave Raj), Silver Deputy (Silverbulletday), **Summer Squall** (Storm Song), Summing (Epitome), Tiznow (Folklore), **Unbridled** (Halfbridled)

Winners by Place Where Bred

Locality	Winners	Locality	Winners
Kentucky	19	New Jersey	1
Florida	3	Pennsylvania	1

Supplemental Entries

Year	Runner	Fee	Finish	Earnings
2005	Wild Fit	$90,000	2	$212,000
2000	Cindy's Hero	90,000	4	63,840
	Out of Sync	90,000	9	0
1995	Tipically Irish	120,000	6	0
1994	Post It	120,000	6	0

Eclipse Award Winnners from Race

Year	Runner	Finish	Title
2007	Indian Blessing	1	Juvenile filly
2006	Dreaming of Anna	1	Juvenile filly
2005	Folklore	1	Juvenile filly
2004	Sweet Catomine	1	Juvenile filly
2003	Halfbridled	1	Juvenile filly
2002	Storm Flag Flying	1	Juvenile filly
2001	Tempera	1	Juvenile filly
2000	Caressing	1	Juvenile filly
1999	Chilukki	2	Juvenile filly
1998	Silverbulletday	1	Juvenile filly
1997	Countess Diana	1	Juvenile filly
1996	Storm Song	1	Juvenile filly
1995	Golden Attraction	3	Juvenile filly
1994	Flanders	1	Juvenile filly
1993	Phone Chatter	1	Juvenile filly
1992	Eliza	1	Juvenile filly
1991	Pleasant Stage	1	Juvenile filly
1990	Meadow Star	1	Juvenile filly
1989	Go for Wand	1	Juvenile filly
1988	Open Mind	1	Juvenile filly
1987	Epitome	1	Juvenile filly
1986	Brave Raj	1	Juvenile filly
1985	Family Style	2	Juvenile filly
1984	Outstandingly	1	Juvenile filly

Largest Winning Margins

Year	Winner	Margin
1997	Countess Diana	8½
1986	Brave Raj	5½
1990	Meadow Star	5
1996	Storm Song	4½
2004	Sweet Catomine	3¾
2007	Indian Blessing	3½

Smallest Winning Margins

Year	Winner	Margin
1987	Epitome	nose
1994	Flanders	head
1993	Phone Chatter	head
1991	Pleasant Stage	head

Shortest-Priced Winners

Year	Winner	Odds
1990	Meadow Star	0.20-to-1
1994	Flanders	0.40-to-1*
1985	Twilight Ridge	0.60-to-1*
1988	Open Mind	0.70-to-1*
2002	Storm Flag Flying	0.80-to-1
1998	Silverbulletday	0.80-to-1

*Part of entry

Longest-Priced Winners

Year	Winner	Odds
2000	Caressing	47.00-to-1
1999	Cash Run	32.50-to-1
1987	Epitome	30.40-to-1
1984	Outstandingly	22.80-to-1

Odds-On Beaten Favorites

Year	Favorite	Odds
2001	You	0.95-to-1

Fastest Winners at 1 1/16 Miles

Year	Winner	Track	Time	Cond.
2001	Tempera	Bel	1:41.49	fast
2004	Sweet Catomine	LS	1:41.65	fast
1997	Countess Diana	Hol	1:42.11	fast
1995	My Flag	Bel	1:42.55	muddy
2003	Halfbridled	SA	1:42.75	fast
2000	Caressing	CD	1:42.77	fast

Slowest Winners at 1 1/16 Miles

Year	Winner	Track	Time	Cond.
1988	Open Mind	CD	1:46⅗	muddy

Year	Winner	Track	Time	Cond.
1991	Pleasant Stage	CD	1:46.48	fast
1994	Flanders	CD	1:45.28	fast
2007	Indian Blessing	Mth	1:44.73	sloppy
1989	Go for Wand	GP	1:44⅕	fast
1990	Meadow Star	Bel	1:44	fast

Most Starters

Year	Track	Starters
2006	Churchill Downs	14
2003	Santa Anita Park	14
1997	Hollywood Park	14
1991	Churchill Downs	14
2007	Monmouth Park	13
1994	Churchill Downs	13
1990	Belmont Park	13

Fewest Starters

Year	Track	Starters
1995	Belmont Park	8
1993	Santa Anita Park	8
2001	Belmont Park	9
1999	Gulfstream Park	9

Winning Post Positions

Post	Starters	Winners	Percent
1	24	3	12.5%
2	24	1	4.2%
3	24	1	4.2%
4	24	4	16.7%
5	24	1	4.2%
6	24	3	12.5%
7	24	0	0.0%
8	24	4	16.7%
9	22	4	18.2%
10	20	0	0.0%
11	17	1	5.9%
12	16	0	0.0%
13	7	0	0.0%
14	4	2	50.0%

Changes in Juvenile Fillies

Originally at one mile, the distance was changed to 1 1/16 miles in 1988. It was contested at 1 1/16 miles in 1986 and at 1⅛ miles in 2002. The purse was doubled to $2-million in 2006.

Breeders' Cup Distaff

Although the Breeders' Cup Distaff (G1) has produced three of the eight highest-priced winners in the event's history, the race for fillies and mares has in fact been one of the most consistent of the original seven races.

That record of consistency began with the inaugural Breeders' Cup Distaff at Hollywood Park in 1984. Princess Rooney, winner of the Vanity Handicap (G1) and Spinster Stakes (G1) in prior starts, went off as the 7-to-10 favorite and rolled to a seven-length victory.

In subsequent editions, the Distaff generally was characterized by dominant winners scoring by open lengths. In fact, Inside Information's 13½-length win in 1995 remains the series' largest winning margin. Azeri waltzed away to a five-length victory in 2002 to lock up a Horse of the Year title, and Lady's Secret won by 2½ lengths in 1986, her Horse of the Year season. Round Pond, overlooked at 13.90-to-1, won by 5½ lengths in 2006. Odds-on favorites have won the race seven times.

The 1988 running remains one of the most memorable of all Breeders' Cup races. Undefeated Personal Ensign, seemingly beaten at the

Breeders' Cup Distaff

Grade 1, $2-million, three-year-olds and up, fillies and mares, 1⅛ miles. Held October 27, 2007, at Monmouth Park with gross value of $2,070,160. First held in 1984. Weights: Northern Hemisphere three-year-olds, 119 pounds; older, 123 pounds. Southern Hemisphere three-year-olds, 114 pounds; older, 123 pounds.

Year	Winner	Jockey	Second	Third	Site	Time	Cond.	1st Purse
2007	**Ginger Punch**, 4	R. Bejarano	Hystericalady	Octave	Mth	1:50.11	sy	$1,220,400
2006	**Round Pond**, 4	E. Prado	Happy Ticket	Balletto (UAE)	CD	1:50.50	ft	1,220,400
2005	**Pleasant Home**, 4	C. Velazquez	Society Selection	Ashado	Bel	1:48.34	ft	1,040,000
2004	**Ashado**, 4	J. Velazquez	Storm Flag Flying	Stellar Jayne	LS	1:48.26	ft	1,080,000
2003	**Adoration**, 4	P. Valenzuela	Elloluv	Got Koko	SA	1:49.17	ft	1,040,000
2002	**Azeri**	M. Smith	Farda Amiga	Imperial Gesture	AP	1:48.64	gd	1,040,000
2001	**Unbridled Elaine**, 3	P. Day	Spain	Two Item Limit	Bel	1:49.21	ft	**1,227,200**
2000	**Spain**, 3	V. Espinoza	Surfside	Heritage of Gold	CD	1:47.66	ft	**1,227,200**
1999	**Beautiful Pleasure**, 4	J. Chavez	Banshee Breeze	Heritage of Gold	GP	1:47.56	ft	1,040,000
1998	**Escena**, 5	G. Stevens	Banshee Breeze	Keeper Hill	CD	1:49.89	ft	1,040,000
1997	**Ajina**, 3	M. Smith	Sharp Cat	Escena	Hol	1:47.30	ft	520,000
1996	**Jewel Princess**, 4	C. Nakatani	Serena's Song	Different (Arg)	WO	1:48.40	ft	520,000
1995	**Inside Information**, 4	M. Smith	Heavenly Prize	Lakeway	Bel	**1:46.15**	my	520,000
1994	**One Dreamer**, 6	G. Stevens	Heavenly Prize	Miss Dominique	CD	1:50.70	ft	520,000
1993	**Hollywood Wildcat**, 3	E. Delahoussaye	Paseana (Arg)	Re Toss (Arg)	SA	1:48.35	ft	520,000
1992	**Paseana (Arg)**, 5	C. McCarron	Versailles Treaty	Magical Maiden	GP	1:48.17	ft	520,000
1991	**Dance Smartly**, 3	P. Day	Versailles Treaty	Brought to Mind	CD	1:50.95	ft	520,000
1990	**Bayakoa (Arg)**, 6	L. Pincay Jr.	Colonial Waters	Valay Maid	Bel	1:49⅕	ft	450,000
1989	**Bayakoa (Arg)**, 5	L. Pincay Jr.	Gorgeous	Open Mind	GP	1:47⅖	ft	450,000
1988	**Personal Ensign**, 4	R. Romero	Winning Colors	Goodbye Halo	CD	1:52	my	450,000
1987	**Sacahuista**, 3	R. Romero	Clabber Girl	Oueee Bebe	Hol	2:02⅘	ft	450,000
1986	**Lady's Secret**, 4	P. Day	Fran's Valentine	Outstandingly	SA	**2:01⅕**	ft	450,000
1985	**Life's Magic**, 4	A. Cordero Jr.	Lady's Secret	Dontstop Themusic	Aqu	2:02	ft	450,000
1984	**Princess Rooney**, 4	E. Delahoussaye	Life's Magic	Adored	Hol	2:02⅖	ft	450,000

1984-'87—run at 1¼ miles; 1989 and '90—Bayakoa (Arg) supplementary entry; 1992—Paseana (Arg) supplemental entry.

sixteenth pole, closed relentlessly on Winning Colors, that year's Kentucky Derby (G1) winner, and put her nose in front at the wire to close out her career undefeated in 13 starts.

In 15 of 24 years, both the champion three-year-old filly and older female have competed in the Distaff.

Supplemental entries have had excellent success in the Distaff. Bayakoa (Arg), supplemented for $200,000 in 1989 and '90, won both years. Paseana (Arg), supplemented in 1992 and '93, won in her first try and finished second in '93.

The biggest upset in Distaff history occurred in 2000, when dominant West Coast mare Riboletta (Brz) ran seventh as the 2-to-5 favorite.

Racing Hall of Fame members who have contested the race are Princess Rooney, Lady's Secret, Personal Ensign, Winning Colors, Bayakoa, Go for Wand, Dance Smartly, Paseana, Inside Information, and Serena's Song.

Owners by Wins

2 **Allen E. Paulson** (Ajina, Escena), **Ogden Mills Phipps** (Inside Information, Pleasant Home), **Frank and Janis Whitham** (Bayakoa [Arg] [twice])

1 **Amerman Racing Stable** (Adoration), **Barry A. Beal and L. R. French Jr.** (Sacahuista), **Irving and Marjorie Cowan** (Hollywood Wildcat), **Sidney Craig** (Paseana [Arg]), **Roger J. Devenport** (Unbridled Elaine), **Fox Hill Farms** (Round Pond), **Glen Hill Farm** (One Dreamer), **Mel Hatley and Eugene V. Klein** (Life's Magic), **Mr. and Mrs. Eugene V. Klein** (Lady's Secret), **John Oxley** (Beautiful Pleasure), **Allen E. Paulson Living Trust** (Azeri), **Ogden Phipps** (Personal Ensign), **Sam-Son Farm** (Dance Smartly), **Starlight Stables, Paul Saylor, and Johns Martin** (Ashado), **Stronach Stables** (Ginger Punch), **The Thoroughbred Corp.** (Spain), **The Thoroughbred Corp. and Martha and Richard Stephen** (Jewel Princess), **Paula Tucker** (Princess Rooney)

Breeders by Wins

3 **Allen E. Paulson** (Ajina, Azeri, Escena)

2 **Farnsworth Farms** (Beautiful Pleasure, Jewel Princess), **Haras Principal** (Bayakoa [Arg], twice), **Ogden Mills Phipps** (Inside Information, Pleasant Home)

1 **Adena Springs** (Ginger Punch), **Lucy G. Bassett** (Adoration), **Irving and Marjorie Cowan** (Hollywood Wildcat), **Glen Hill Farm** (One Dreamer), **Golden Orb Farm and K. David Schwartz** (Unbridled Elaine), **Haras Vacacion** (Paseana [Arg]), **G. Watts Humphrey and William S. Farish** (Sacahuista), **Aaron and Marie Jones** (Ashado), **Mr. and Mrs. Douglas Parrish and David Parrish III** (Life's Magic), **Ogden Phipps** (Personal Ensign), **Ben and Tom Roach** (Princess Rooney), **Sam-Son Farm** (Dance Smartly), **Robert H. Spreen** (Lady's Secret), **The Thoroughbred Corp.** (Spain), **John Toffan and Trudy McCaffery** (Round Pond)

Trainers by Wins

4 **D. Wayne Lukas** (Lady's Secret, Life's Magic, Sacahuista, Spain)

3 **Ron McAnally** (Bayakoa [Arg] [twice], Paseana [Arg]), **Claude R. "Shug" McGaughey III** (Inside Information, Personal Ensign, Pleasant Home)

2 **Neil Drysdale** (Hollywood Wildcat, Princess Rooney), **William I. Mott** (Ajina, Escena)

1 **James Day** (Dance Smartly), **Laura de Seroux** (Azeri), **Wallace Dollase** (Jewel Princess), **Robert Frankel** (Ginger Punch), **David Hofmans** (Adoration), **Michael Matz** (Round Pond), **Todd Pletcher** (Ashado), **Tom Proctor** (One Dreamer), **Dallas Stewart** (Unbridled Elaine), **John T. Ward Jr.** (Beautiful Pleasure)

Jockeys by Wins

3 **Pat Day** (Dance Smartly, Lady's Secret, Unbridled Elaine), **Mike Smith** (Azeri, Ajina, Inside Information)

2 **Eddie Delahoussaye** (Hollywood Wildcat, Princess Rooney), **Laffit Pincay Jr.** (Bayakoa [Arg] [twice]), **Randy Romero** (Personal Ensign, Sacahuista), **Gary Stevens** (Escena, One Dreamer)

1 **Rafael Bejarano** (Ginger Punch), **Jorge Chavez** (Beautiful Pleasure), **Angel Cordero** (Life's Magic), **Victor Espinoza** (Spain), **Chris McCarron** (Paseana [Arg]), **Corey Nakatani** (Jewel Princess), **Edgar Prado** (Round Pond), **Patrick Valenzuela** (Adoration), **Cornelio Velasquez** (Pleasant Home), **John Velazquez** (Ashado)

Sires by Wins

2 **Awesome Again** (Ginger Punch, Round Pond), **Consultant's Bid** (Bayakoa [Arg], twice), **Private Account** (Inside Information, Personal Ensign), **Strawberry Road (Aus)** (Ajina, Escena)

1 **Ahmad** (Paseana [Arg]), **Cox's Ridge** (Life's Magic), **Danzig** (Dance Smartly), **Honor Grades** (Adoration), **Jade Hunter** (Azeri), **Key to the Mint** (Jewel Princess), **Kris S.** (Hollywood Wildcat), **Maudlin** (Beautiful Pleasure), **Raja Baba** (Sacahuista), **Relaunch** (One Dreamer), **Saint Ballado** (Ashado), **Secretariat** (Lady's Secret), **Seeking the Gold** (Pleasant Home), **Thunder Gulch** (Spain), **Unbridled's Song** (Unbridled Elaine), **Verbatim** (Princess Rooney)

Winners by Place Where Bred

Locality	Winners
Kentucky	14
Florida	5
Argentina	3
Oklahoma	1
Ontario	1

Supplemental Entries

Year	Runner	Fee	Finish	Earnings
2007	Ginger Punch	$180,000	1	$1,220,400
	Tough Tiz's Sis	180,000	7	0
2006	Asi Siempre	180,000	2 pl. 4	115,260
2001	Miss Linda (Arg)	400,000	6	0
2000	Riboletta (Brz)	400,000	7	0
1996	Different (Arg)	200,000	3	120,000
1993	Paseana (Arg)	200,000	2	200,000
1992	**Paseana (Arg)**	200,000	1	520,000
1990	**Bayakoa (Arg)**	200,000	1	450,000
1989	**Bayakoa (Arg)**	200,000	1	450,000
1986	Classy Cathy	120,000	4	70,000
1985	Dontstop Themusic	120,000	3	108,000
	Isayso	120,000	6	10,000

Eclipse Award Winners from Race

Year	Runner	Finish	Title
2007	Ginger Punch	1	Older female
2006	**Fleet Indian**	DNF	Older female
2005	Ashado	3	Older female
2004	**Ashado**	1	3yo filly
2002	**Azeri**	1	Horse of the Year, Older female
	Farda Amiga	2	3yo filly
2000	Surfside	2	3yo filly
	Riboletta (Brz)	7	Older female

Breeders' Cup — Distaff History

Year	Runner	Finish	Title
1999	**Beautiful Pleasure**	1	Older female
	Silverbulletday	6	3yo filly
1998	**Escena**	1	Older female
	Banshee Breeze	2	3yo filly
1997	**Ajina**	1	3yo filly
	Hidden Lake	7	Older female
1996	**Jewel Princess**	1	Older female
1995	**Inside Information**	1	Older female
	Serena's Song	5	3yo filly
1994	Heavenly Prize	2	3yo filly
	Sky Beauty	9	Older female
1993	**Hollywood Wildcat**	1	3yo filly
	Paseana (Arg)	2	Older female
1992	**Paseana (Arg)**	1	Older female
	Saratoga Dew	12	3yo filly
1991	**Dance Smartly**	1	3yo filly
	Queena	5	Older female
1990	**Bayakoa (Arg)**	1	Older female
	Go for Wand	DNF	3yo filly
1989	**Bayakoa (Arg)**	1	Older female
	Open Mind	3	3yo female
1988	**Personal Ensign**	1	Older female
	Winning Colors	2	3yo filly
1987	**Sacahuista**	1	3yo filly
	North Sider	6	Older female
1986	**Lady's Secret**	1	Horse of the Year, Older female
1985	**Life's Magic**	1	Older female
1984	**Princess Rooney**	1	Older female
	Life's Magic	2	3yo filly

Largest Winning Margins

Year	Winner	Margin
1995	Inside Information	13½
2005	Pleasant Home	9¼
1984	Princess Rooney	7
1990	Bayakoa (Arg)	6¾
1985	Life's Magic	6¼
2002	Azeri	5

Smallest Winning Margins

Year	Winner	Margin
1998	Escena	nose
1993	Hollywood Wildcat	nose
1988	Personal Ensign	nose
2001	Unbridled Elaine	head
2007	Ginger Punch	neck
1994	One Dreamer	neck

Shortest-Priced Winners

Year	Winner	Odds
1985	Life's Magic	0.40-to-1*
1991	Dance Smartly	0.50-to-1*
1988	Personal Ensign	0.50-to-1
1986	Lady's Secret	0.50-to-1*
1989	Bayakoa (Arg)	0.70-to-1
1984	Princess Rooney	0.70-to-1

*Part of entry

Longest-Priced Winners

Year	Winner	Odds
2000	Spain	55.90-to-1
1994	One Dreamer	47.10-to-1
2003	Adoration	40.70-to-1
2005	Pleasant Home	30.75-to-1
2006	Round Pond	13.90-to-1
2001	Unbridled Elaine	12.30-to-1

*Part of entry

Odds-On Beaten Favorites

Year	Winner	Odds	Finish
2006	Fleet Indian	2.70-to-1	DNF
2003	Sightseek	0.60-to-1	4
2000	Riboletta (Brz)	0.40-to-1	7
1998	Banshee Breeze	0.80-to-1	2
1990	Go for Wand	0.70-to-1	DNF
1987	Infinidad (Chi)	0.70-to-1	4

Fastest Winners at 1⅛ Miles

Year	Winner	Track	Time	Cond.
1995	Inside Information	Bel	1:46.15	muddy
1997	Ajina	Hol	1:47.30	fast
1989	Bayakoa (Arg)	GP	1:47⅖	fast
1999	Beautiful Pleasure	GP	1:47.56	fast
2000	Spain	CD	1:47.66	fast

Slowest Winners at 1⅛ Miles

Year	Winner	Track	Time	Cond.
1988	Personal Ensign	CD	1:52	muddy
1991	Dance Smartly	CD	1:50.95	fast
1994	One Dreamer	CD	1:50.70	fast
2006	Round Pond	CD	1:50.50	fast
2007	Ginger Punch	Mth	1:50.11	sloppy
1998	Escena	CD	1:49.89	fast

Most Starters

Year	Track	Starters
2006	Churchill Downs	14
1992	Gulfstream Park	14
2005	Belmont Park	13
1991	Churchill Downs	13
2007	Monmouth Park	12
2004	Lone Star Park	11
2001	Belmont Park	11

Fewest Starters

Year	Track	Starters
1996	Woodbine	6
1987	Hollywood Park	6
2003	Santa Anita Park	7
1990	Belmont Park	7
1985	Aqueduct	7
1984	Hollywood Park	7

Winning Post Positions

Post	Starters	Winners	Percent
1	24	6	25.0%
2	24	1	4.2%
3	24	0	0.0%
4	24	6	25.0%
5	24	4	16.7%
6	24	3	12.5%
7	22	1	4.5%
8	18	0	0.0%
9	12	0	0.0%
10	9	1	11.1%
11	7	1	14.3%
12	5	0	0.0%
13	4	0	0.0%
14	2	1	50.0%

Changes in Distaff

Two significant changes have occurred in the conditions of the Breeders' Cup Distaff: For the 1988 running, the distance was shortened to 1⅛ miles from 1¼ miles, and in '98 the purse was increased to $2-million from $1-million.

2007 Classic: Curlin's Best Shot

The field for the 24th edition of the Breeders' Cup Classic Powered by Dodge (G1) was so rich with talent, so deep with consistent performers, and so packed with the saltiest competitors that an absolutely flawless performance would be required to land the ultimate prize that essentially meant a Horse of the Year title.

Seven of the nine starters in the Classic field were Grade 1 or Group 1 winners, led by an extremely talented quintet of three-year-olds who already waged some tenacious battles during the spring classics, North America's leading older male sporting a pair of razor-sharp victories in two of New York's best summer stakes, and a classy European import seeking improvement from a strong run a year ago.

The other two combatants were overachieving Grade 2 winners. Throw in the fact the Classic would be contested over a racetrack so saturated it was a sea of slop, and it was evident that none of the nine starters had any room for error.

A perfect performance was ordered for the $4.58-million Classic, and it was Curlin who once again delivered a spectacular effort in front of 41,781 rain-soaked fans who turned out for the second soggy day of the two-day Breeders' Cup World Championships program on October 27 at Monmouth Park.

Curlin not only fired his best shot, unleashing what has become a patented and expected strong middle move and powerful finishing kick to win the 1¼-mile Classic, but he also locked up the Horse of the Year and champion three-year-old male titles. The three-year-old Smart Strike colt officially won by 4½ lengths from the ever-gallant Hard Spun, with Awesome Gem third and Street Sense fourth in track-record-equaling time of 2:00.59.

"The horse has spoiled us with his consistency," said winning trainer Steve Asmussen. "You're looking to compare him with something else, and there's just not another horse to compare him with."

In the days leading up to the Classic, attention focused on the three-year-old crop of 2007, led by Curlin, Preakness Stakes (G1) and Jockey Club Gold Cup Stakes (G1) winner, and Street Sense, '06 champion two-year-old male and '07 Kentucky Derby Presented by Yum! Brands (G1) and Travers Stakes (G1) winner. Hard Spun, Any Given Saturday, and Tiago were also in the mix with victories in such important events as the King's Bishop (G1), Haskell Invitational (G1), and Goodwood (G1) Stakes, respectively.

Asmussen relished the chance to take on that group again, along with a rematch with Whitney Handicap (G1) and Woodward Stakes (G1) winner Lawyer Ron, whom Curlin had edged in the Jockey Club Gold Cup four weeks earlier at Belmont Park.

Curlin finished third in the Kentucky Derby in just his fourth career start and then narrowly defeated Street Sense in the Preakness. In turn, he sustained a narrow loss to the talented filly Rags to Riches in the Belmont Stakes (G1).

Asmussen freshened the massive, muscular chestnut briefly after the spring classics, mapping out a program that featured training at Churchill Downs, Saratoga Race Course's Oklahoma training track, Keeneland Race Course's Polytrack, and two prep races.

The entire program was in the hands of Asmussen, who had the full support of the ownership team of Jess Jackson's Stonestreet Stables, Satish and Anne Sanan's Padua Stables, George Bolton, and Shirley Cunningham's and Bill Gallion's Midnight Cry Stables. (Cunningham and Gallion could not attend the race; the suspended lawyers were sentenced to prison in Kentucky while awaiting trial on federal fraud charges related to alleged misappropriation of funds from the fen-phen class-action settlement.)

"This has been a team effort from the beginning led by Steve and John Moynihan," Jackson said of the trainer and bloodstock agent who helped secure the purchase of Curlin shortly after he won a seven-furlong maiden race at Gulfstream Park by 12¾ lengths in early February.

In the Breeders' Cup, Curlin had little trouble negotiating the turns at Monmouth, something he did not do particularly well in his only poor performance of the season, a third-place finish in the Haskell.

Curlin, fourth choice at 4.40-to-1 at post time,

Owners

Stonestreet Stables is the racing and breeding operation of Jess Jackson, a Sonoma, California, resident who is best known as the owner of Kendall-Jackson Wineries. **Padua Stables** is the racing and breeding operation of Satish and Anne Sanan and their children. A native of India and a Breeders' Cup Ltd. board member, Satish Sanan has built and sold several successful companies, including IMR Global. **George Bolton** is chief investment officer of WestEnd Capital Management in San Francisco. **Midnight Cry Stables** is the racing entity of suspended lawyers William Gallion and Shirley Cunningham Jr., both of whom were jailed while awaiting trial on federal fraud charges related to the fen-phen class-action lawsuit settlement.

Breeder

Fares Farms in Lexington is owned by Issam Fares, a native of Lebanon who served as that nation's deputy prime minister until early 2005. Fares, who conducted a dispersal of nearly all his bloodstock in 1998 to concentrate on his political activities, won the 1991 Breeders' Cup Turf with Miss Alleged as part of the 42.10-to-1 mutuel field. Fares Farm also bred two-time Breeders' Cup Mile (G1) winner Da Hoss in 1996 and in '98.

broke cleanly under jockey Robby Albarado and ran in tandem with 5-to-2 favorite Street Sense over the slick and shiny surface past the stands and finish post the first time. Hard Spun and jockey Mario Pino took their customary position at the front of the field and led a group of five runners that also included Lawyer Ron, Diamond Stripes, Any Given Saturday, and George Washington (Ire) through the opening quarter-mile in :23.11 and a sharp half-mile in :45.85.

As the field approached the head of the stretch, only Hard Spun, Lawyer Ron, and Any Given Saturday were in front of Street Sense and Curlin, who had little trouble dispatching Any Given Saturday before quickly overtaking a tiring Lawyer Ron. Albarado and Curlin got the jump on Street Sense as they set sail for Hard Spun at the head of the lane.

With less than a quarter-mile to run and the Horse of the Year prize awaiting at the finish, Curlin made his final move, a decisive thrust past a determined Hard Spun that left that rival alone in second, with Street Sense unable to counter down on the inside. "Curlin is the genuine article, and I just couldn't go with him," said Calvin Borel, Street Sense's jockey.—*Tom Law*

ELEVENTH RACE
Monmouth Park
October 27, 2007

1¼ miles on dirt. 24th running of the Breeders' Cup Classic Powered by Dodge (G1). Purse $5-million guaranteed. Three-year-olds and up. Weights (Northern Hemisphere): Three-year-olds, 121 lbs. Older, 126 lbs. (Southern Hemisphere): Three-year-olds, 116 lbs. Older, 126 lbs. Fillies and mares allowed 3 lbs.

Value of race: $4,580,000. Value to winner: $2,700,000; second: $1,000,000; third: $500,000; fourth: $255,000; fifth: $125,000. Mutuel Pool $9,276,636.

Horse	Wt.	M/Eqt	PP	¼	½	¾	1m.	Str.	Fin.	Jockey	Odds $1
Curlin, 3, c.	121	L	4	6^{hd}	6^1	5^½	2^2	1^1	1^{4½}	R. Albarado	4.40
Hard Spun, 3, c.	121	LAc	8	1^1	1^{1½}	1^{2½}	1^2	2^{2½}	2^{4¾}	M. Pino	8.10
Awesome Gem, 4, c.	126	Lbc	6	8^4	8^2	8^2	6^{2½}	4^4	3^1	D. Flores	28.30
Street Sense, 3, c.	121	Lf	2	7^{2½}	7^7	6^1	3^2	3^5	4^{8¼}	C. Borel	2.50*
Tiago, 3, c.	121	LAf	9	9	9	9	7^4	5^5	5^{10}	M. Smith	12.80
Any Given Saturday, 3, c.	121	LAc	3	4^½	4^2	3^{1½}	5^4	6^{1½}	6^{hd}	G. Gomez	3.90
Lawyer Ron, 4, c.	126	LA	1	2^½	2^1	2^{1½}	4^½	7^5	7^{8¼}	J. Velazquez	3.90
Diamond Stripes, 4, c.	126	Lb	7	3^1	3^1	4^{1½}	9	9	8	C. Velasquez	38.80
George Washington (Ire), 4, c.	126	L	5	5^4	5^{4½}	7^{4½}	8^{2½}	8^½	—	M. Kinane	9.00

L=Salix; LA=Salix and adjunct bleeder medication; c=mud calks; f=front bandages.

OFF AT 5:44. Start: Good for all. Weather: Cloudy. Track: Sloppy (Sealed).
Time: :23.11, :45.85, 1:10.67, 1:35.86, 2:00.59.

$2 Mutuel Prices:	4—CURLIN	10.80	5.20	4.20
	8—HARD SPUN		7.60	5.80
	6—AWESOME GEM			9.40

$2 EXACTA 4-8 PAID $70.80 $1 TRIFECTA 4-8-6 PAID $645.30
$1 SUPERFECTA 4-8-6-2 PAID $2,146.20 $2 DAILY DOUBLE 6-4 PAID $55.60
$1 PICK THREE 4-6-4 PAID $166.40 $1 PICK FOUR 8-4-6-4 PAID $1,506.50
$2 PICK SIX 6-2/3-8-4-6-4 (5 CORRECT) PAID $1,536.40
$2 PICK SIX 6-2/3-8-4-6-4 (6 CORRECT) PAID $321,813.20

Ch. c., by Smart Strike—Sherriff's Deputy, by Deputy Minister. Trainer: Steven Asmussen. Owner: Stonestreet Stables, Padua Stables, George Bolton, and Midnight Cry Stables. Bred by Fares Farm Inc. (Ky.).

CURLIN was unhurried for five furlongs while racing outside STREET SENSE along the backstretch, got the jump on that one while splitting horses to make his move on the turn, rapidly closed the gap angling three wide at the quarter pole, drew alongside HARD SPUN to challenge in upper stretch, surged to the front opening a clear advantage a furlong out, then drew away with authority under steady right hand urging to win going away. HARD SPUN sprinted clear on the first turn, set a rapid pace while saving ground, raced uncontested on the lead to the top of the stretch, yielded to the winner nearing the furlong marker, then continued on well to clearly best the others. AWESOME GEM raced far back for seven furlongs, advanced a bit from outside midway on the turn, swung three wide, then closed late to gain a share. STREET SENSE tucked in along the rail in the early stages, raced in hand while saving ground along the backstretch, made his move with the winner midway on the turn, was unable to stay with that one approaching the quarter pole, then flattened out. TIAGO was outrun while trailing to the far turn, lodged a mild move while saving ground on the turn, then lacked a strong closing response. ANY GIVEN SATURDAY chased along the inside in the early stages, moved out slightly along the backstretch, tracked the leaders to the far turn, and dropped back midway on the turn. LAWYER RON steadied slightly along the rail while a bit rank leaving the first turn, angled outside HARD SPUN approaching the backstretch, pressed the pace from outside for five furlongs, lagged behind on the far turn, and gave way nearing the stretch. DIAMOND STRIPES bobbled a bit at the start, stalked the leaders while three wide, dropped well back on the far turn, and was never close thereafter. GEORGE WASHINGTON (IRE) raced in midpack for a half, was finished leaving the three-eighths pole, then broke down inside the furlong marker and was euthanized.

2007 Turf: Home-Course Advantage

English Channel's rise to the top of the turf division was not as meteoric as Curlin's eight-month Horse of the Year campaign, but that progress suited owner James Scatuorchio just fine as he watched his most successful horse cap a four-year career with a dominating victory in the $2,748,000 John Deere Breeders' Cup Turf (G1) on October 27 at Monmouth Park.

The win took on special meaning for Scatuorchio, 60, who lives about 15 minutes north of Monmouth in Rumson, New Jersey, and maintains two boxes at the Oceanport racetrack. The Breeders' Cup crowd responded enthusiastically when track announcer Larry Collmus said as English Channel entered the winner's circle that the Kentucky-bred Smart Strike horse is owned by a New Jersey resident.

"I don't know if you can script it any better," Scatuorchio said. "That's the stuff you dream about. When we came back this year knowing the race was going to be at Monmouth, we always had in the back of our mind how excited we would be to get him to that race."

Of course, they did not just get him into "that race," they won "that race." And they did not just win "that race" but won it by a record seven lengths while defeating Prix de l'Arc de Triomphe Lucien Barriere (Fr-G1) winner and European champion Dylan Thomas (Ire) as well as two previous Breeders' Cup Turf winners in Red Rocks (Ire) and Better Talk Now.

"He's run a lot of great races in a lot of big spots, but certainly never like that," trainer Todd Pletcher said. "That would have to be his crowning moment to dominate a world-class group of horses like he did."

The world-class group included four foreign-bred horses, though only Dylan Thomas and Red Rocks trained in Europe—the smallest European contingent for the race since 2004 at Lone Star Park, where Better Talk Now pulled a 27.90-to-1 upset.

English Channel's win capped a sweep of the Breeders' Cup grass races by North American-based horses, the first time that has been accomplished since the Breeders' Cup added the Filly and Mare Turf (G1) in 1999.

English Channel entered this year's Breeders' Cup having already won consecutive editions of the United Nations Stakes (G1) at Monmouth, first setting a course record of 2:13.24 for 1⅜ miles in 2006 and then lowering it 0.35 seconds to 2:12.89 in '07.

Those victories, however, came on good and firm turf, respectively—conditions far different from the soft footing that awaited this year's Turf participants after 48 hours of steady rain saturated the Jersey Shore.

"No one has run in the type of condition Monmouth was in yesterday," said Pletcher, who maintains a stable there during the annual summer meet. "My take on it is that English Channel is one of those horses who doesn't like a little bit of softness, but yesterday was a real bog, and his size and agility helped him get over it."

English Channel, sent off as the 3-to-1 second betting choice, was never far away from the leaders through the opening stages of the 1½-mile race, as jockey John Velazquez sat two lengths off pacesetter Fri Guy through an opening half-mile in a dawdling :53.20. Secretariat Stakes (G1) winner Shamdinan (Fr) pressed Fri Guy but never made the lead as English Channel passed the top two when they rounded the far turn for the second time and opened up seven lengths on the field within a quarter-mile. Final time of the race was 2:36.96.

"We got the perfect trip," Velazquez said. "Our plan was to save ground and wait as long as possible before we made our move. Everything was perfect."

Shamdinan stayed on for second while Fri Guy faded to seventh, beating just Transduction Gold. Red Rocks finished third after getting the jump on Better Talk Now entering the final turn. Dylan Thomas was never a factor in the race but managed fifth, with Grand Couturier (GB) sixth of eight starters, equaling the race's smallest field.

English Channel had become a Breeders' Cup mainstay, finishing fifth to eventual champion Shirocco (Ger) in the Turf as a three-year-old in 2005 at Belmont Park and third in '06 at

---

Owner
James T. Scatuorchio, a resident of Rumson, New Jersey, is a stockbroker who retired from Donaldson, Lufkin, and Jenrette in 1998. He was part of the syndicate that owned Tale of the Cat, and he raced More Than Ready, a top two-year-old in 1999 and a Grade 1-winning sprinter the following year.

Breeder
Keene Ridge Farm is owned by Ann McBrayer, president of Kentucky Eagle Beer in Lexington. She bought the 170-acre property near Keeneland Race Course in 1994 and maintains a broodmare band of approximately 12.

Churchill Downs. Pletcher acknowledged English Channel was a cut below the world's best grass horses in 2005 but said he felt the horse was unlucky to be third behind Red Rocks and Better Talk Now in the '06 race.

"Last year we had an outside post, and he never relaxed," Velazquez said. "This year he's older, and he has learned to relax. That was the key today."

It was in defeat in Saratoga Race Course's Sword Dancer Invitational Handicap (G1) in August that both Pletcher and Velazquez discovered English Channel had begun to relax in the early stages of his races and did not need to be pressured when he was off the bit.

Dylan Thomas went off as the shortest priced favorite of the day at 9-to-10, and he failed to give his backers even the slightest thrill. He broke slowly, failed to get within two lengths of the leader at any point in the race, and finished fifth, beaten 8½ lengths.

"It was not turf racing," jockey Johnny Murtagh said as he pointed to his mud-covered silks. "He was spinning his wheels out there. He even hated the warm-up, and this is a horse who loves his racing and everything about it."

English Channel, who concluded his racing career with earnings of $5,319,028, was voted champion turf male. He retired to Hurricane Hall in Lexington and stood the 2008 season for a $25,000 fee.—*Ed DeRosa*

TENTH RACE
Monmouth Park
October 27, 2007

1½ miles on turf. 24th running of the John Deere Breeders' Cup Turf (G1). Purse $3-million guaranteed. Three-year-olds and up. Weights (Northern Hemisphere): Three-year-olds, 121 lbs. Older, 126 lbs. (Southern Hemisphere): Three-year-olds, 116 lbs. Older, 125 lbs. Fillies and mares allowed 3 lbs.

Value of race: $2,748,000. Value to winner: $1,620,000; second: $600,000; third: $300,000; fourth: $153,000; fifth: $75,000. Mutuel Pool $4,361,506.

Horse	Wt.	M/Eqt	PP	¼	½	1m	1¼	Str.	Fin.	Jockey	Odds $1
English Channel, 5, h.	126	LA	6	3¹	3¹	2½	1¹	1³	1⁷	J. Velazquez	3.00
Shamdinan (Fr), 3, c.	121	L	4	2²	2¹	3²	2½	2²	2¾	J. Leparoux	25.60
Red Rocks (Ire), 4, c.	126	L	2	5½	5½	4½	4½	3ʰᵈ	3¾	L. Dettori	5.60
Better Talk Now, 8, g.	126	LAbf	3	7²	7²	7⁸	6⁴	6²½	4ʰᵈ	R. Dominguez	8.10
Dylan Thomas (Ire), 4, c.	126	L	7	6³½	6³	5ʰᵈ	5²	5²	5¹¼	J. Murtagh	0.90*
Grand Couturier (GB), 4, c.	126	Lf	5	8	8	8	8	7³	6¹¼	C. Borel	8.90
Fri Guy, 4, c.	126	LA	1	1¹½	1¹	1¹	3½	4ʰᵈ	7²⁴½	K. Desormeaux	29.10
Transduction Gold, 4, c.	126	L	8	4ʰᵈ	4¹	6³½	7⁶	8	8	J. Graham	58.10

L=Salix; LA=Salix and adjunct bleeder medication; b=blinkers; f=front bandages.

OFF AT 4:54. Start: Good for all. Weather: Clear. Track: Soft.
Time: :26.07, :53.20, 1:19.91, 1:46.01, 2:11.25, 2:36.96.

$2 Mutuel Prices:	6—ENGLISH CHANNEL	8.00	4.40	3.00
	4—SHAMDINAN (FR)		17.60	9.40
	2—RED ROCKS (IRE)			4.60

$2 EXACTA 6-4 PAID $152.00 $1 TRIFECTA 6-4-2 PAID $282.70
$1 SUPERFECTA 6-4-2-3 PAID $1,234.60 $1 PICK THREE 8-4-6 PAID $238.70

Ch. h., by Smart Strike—Belva, by Theatrical (Ire). Trainer: Todd Pletcher. Owner: James T. Scatuorchio. Bred by Keene Ridge Farm (Ky.).

ENGLISH CHANNEL was hard held early along the inside, moved between horses along the backstretch, took charge leaving the far turn, opened a clear advantage in upper stretch, then steadily increased his advantage under steady right-hand encouragement. SHAMDINAN (FR) stalked the pace in the three path to the far turn, moved outside the winner to threaten midway on the turn, but was no match for that rival while continuing on well to best the others. RED ROCKS (IRE) was taken well in hand early while saving ground, was rated just off the pace for a mile, angled between horses leaving the turn, and finished evenly. BETTER TALK NOW raced far back most of the way while saving ground, angled wide leaving the turn, failed to threaten, and passed tiring rivals. DYLAN THOMAS (IRE), away slowly, saved ground early, raced between horses along the backstretch, angled out at the quarter pole and lacked a strong closing response. GRAND COUTURIER (GB) dropped back early and never reached contention while saving ground. FRI GUY set the pace to the far turn and gave way. TRANSDUCTION GOLD stalked in two path and gave way on far turn.

2007 Juvenile: War Pass in Front

The last remnants of three days of persistent rain fell softly as owner Robert LaPenta and trainer Nick Zito stepped out of the Monmouth Park press conference that followed War Pass's resounding victory in the Bessemer Trust Breeders' Cup Juvenile (G1) on October 27. As they embraced, LaPenta said four emphatic words: "This was the one."

War Pass had assured himself an Eclipse Award as champion two-year-old male and had remained undefeated in four starts and essentially unchallenged with a dominant performance at Monmouth's soaked main track in the $1,832,000 Juvenile. In a visual duplicate of Indian Blessing's runaway triumph in the Grey Goose Breeders' Cup Juvenile Fillies (G1) 39 minutes earlier, War Pass carried his dazzling speed to the finish to win by 4¾ lengths under Cornelio Velasquez.

War Pass completed the Juvenile's 1 1/16 miles in 1:42.76 on a sloppy and sealed track, nearly two seconds faster than Indian Blessing's final time in controlling nearly every step of the Juvenile Fillies. The Cherokee Run colt out of Vue, by Mr. Prospector, also had led at every call when he scored in the Champagne Stakes (G1) on October 6 at Belmont Park in his stakes debut. The Juvenile was his first start around two turns.

The Juvenile was the richest victory in Zito's Racing Hall of Fame career, which is most indelibly defined by his Kentucky Derby (G1) wins with Strike the Gold in 1991 and Go for Gin in '94. War Pass also ended a slow period for Zito's stable. After winning 19 stakes races in 2005, including four Grade 1 races, Zito dropped to six stakes wins and no Grade 1s in '06. The barn registered four stakes victories in 2007 before War Pass broke through in the Champagne for Zito's first Grade 1 win in nearly 24 months.

War Pass put himself on the map as a strong two-year-old prospect with a victory in his debut at six furlongs on July 28 at Saratoga Race Course. Instead of jumping him into top company in the Hopeful (G1) or Saratoga Special (G2) Stakes, Zito elected to target an optional claiming race on August 26 at Saratoga. War Pass delivered a five-length victory.

"Years ago we used to do that—prepare the two-year-olds properly," said Zito, ever the traditionalist. "You'd break your maiden, you'd run in [an entry-level allowance race] at Saratoga, and then you'd go on to a race like the Champagne." LaPenta suggested they might want to pass up the Juvenile, but Zito advised him the opportunity was too big to pass up. "Which is unusual, because I can be conservative," Zito said. "When you have the horse like this, it's easy."

LaPenta opened his own stable in 2001 after getting into racing as a partner with Rick Pitino, the University of Louisville basketball coach who raced under the banner of Ol Memorial Stable. LaPenta has about 30 horses in training, the vast majority of them with Zito.

The president and founder of a company that provides personal identity and asset protection, LaPenta occasionally has pinhooked some of his top prospects. He sold a Fusaichi Pegasus colt out of Hidden Storm, by Storm Cat, to Fusao Sekiguchi at the 2004 Fasig-Tipton Calder sale of selected two-year-olds in training for $4.5-million, at the time a world record for a juvenile in training.

After buying War Pass for $180,000 from Claiborne Farm's consignment at the 2006 Keeneland September yearling sale, LaPenta entered the colt in the Calder sale through Scanlon Training Center, agent. An ankle chip was discovered, however, and he was withdrawn. LaPenta said he did not consider selling War Pass once the colt joined Zito's barn after recovering from surgery to remove the chip. "Once they get to the tracks, once they prove they are racehorses, we don't sell them," said LaPenta, who turned down an offer from Ahmed Zayat prior to the Champagne to buy an interest in the colt.

In the Juvenile, Velasquez sat motionless as War Pass quickly opened a four-length advantage on the far turn and continued to open up daylight at the top of the lane. Pyro was the only

Owner
Robert LaPenta is chairman and chief executive officer of L-1 Identity Solutions, a provider of services to prevent identity theft. He previously was a vice president of Lockheed Martin Corp. He entered racing in a partnership managed by University of Louisville basketball coach Rick Pitino and started on his stable in 2001. With trainer Nick Zito, he developed a strategy to pinhook yearlings and to race those that did not sell.

Breeder
Owned by Claiborne Farm President Seth Hancock, **Cherry Valley Farm** owns seven broodmares. Cherry Valley bred stakes winners Sintra, Country Light, and Pomeroy, among others, and in partnership with The Gamely Corp. bred and sold European stakes winner Shadeed.

horse to gain any ground in the final quarter-mile, rallying to take second, 12 lengths ahead of stablemate Kodiak Kowboy in third.

Pyro, the second choice at 4.10-to-1, had finished third to War Pass in the Saratoga optional claiming race and second in the Champagne. Kodiak Kowboy won two graded stakes over the summer and finished second to Tale of Ekati in the Futurity Stakes (G2) at Belmont Park. "[Pyro and Kodiak Kowboy] are both really good horses," said Steve Asmussen, trainer of both colts. "The Breeders' Cup was a great opportunity for them, but the winner has beaten us three times in a row now."

Tale of Ekati, the third choice at 4.80-to-1, finished fourth, and Champagne third-place finisher Z Humor followed in fifth. Horses who raced on the dirt at Belmont in their final prep swept the top five positions.

The win ended a dubious streak in the Breeders' Cup for Zito, who had only one victory from 29 previous starts. His best finish from nine Juvenile starters was a second place with Acceptable in 1996, the same year Storm Song provided him with his lone victory, in the Breeders' Cup Juvenile Fillies (G1). "Sometimes luck just isn't on your side," Zito said. "Today it was."—*Jeff Lowe*

FIFTH RACE
Monmouth Park
October 27, 2007

1 1/16 miles on dirt. 24th running of the Bessemer Trust Breeders' Cup Juvenile (G1). Purse $2-million guaranteed. Colts and geldings, 2-year-olds. Weight: 122 lbs.

Value of race: $1,832,000. Value to winner: $1,080,000; second: $400,000; third: $200,000; fourth: $102,000; fifth: $50,000.
Mutuel Pool $3,258,133.

Horse	Wt.	M/Eqt	PP	St.	1/4	1/2	3/4	Str.	Fin.	Jockey	Odds $1
War Pass, 2, c.	122	Lc	2	2	1$1\frac{1}{2}$	1$2\frac{1}{2}$	1^4	1^7	1$4\frac{3}{4}$	C. Velasquez	2.20*
Pyro, 2, c.	122	L	6	7	8^2	8$1\frac{1}{2}$	7$1\frac{1}{2}$	2^3	2^{12}	S. Bridgmohan	4.10
Kodiak Kowboy, 2, c.	122	L	3	1	5$1\frac{1}{2}$	3$\frac{1}{2}$	2^1	4^2	3$\frac{3}{4}$	J. Velazquez	11.90
Tale of Ekati, 2, c.	122	LA	9	8	6$\frac{1}{2}$	6$\frac{1}{2}$	5^1	3^{hd}	4$1\frac{3}{4}$	E. Coa	4.80
Z Humor, 2, c.	122	LAb	1	6	4^{hd}	5^1	6^1	5$\frac{1}{2}$	5^{hd}	K. Desormeaux	6.90
Old Man Buck, 2, c.	122	LAb	8	9	10$2\frac{1}{2}$	11	10$\frac{1}{2}$	7$\frac{1}{2}$	6$2\frac{1}{4}$	R. Bejarano	17.80
Overextended, 2, c.	122	L	5	11	11	9^2	8^2	6^{hd}	7$4\frac{1}{2}$	L Dettori	35.30
Shore Do, 2, c.	122	Lb	4	10	9$\frac{1}{2}$	10$\frac{1}{2}$	9$\frac{1}{2}$	8$\frac{1}{2}$	8$7\frac{1}{2}$	M. Smith	27.20
Salute the Sarge, 2, c.	122	Lc	10	3	3^{hd}	4$1\frac{1}{2}$	3$\frac{1}{2}$	9^6	9$7\frac{1}{2}$	D. Flores	15.70
Wicked Style, 2, c.	122	LA	11	4	7^2	7^4	11	10^3	10^{28}	R. Albarado	7.20
Globalization, 2, c.	122	LA	7	5	2^1	2^1	4^1	11	11	J. Castellano	30.10

L=Salix; LA=Salix and adjunct bleeder medication; b=blinkers; c=mud calks.

OFF AT 1:13. Start: Good for all. Weather: Cloudy. Track: Sloppy (sealed).
Time: :22.76, :45.56, 1:09.65, 1:35.64, 1:42.76.

$2 Mutuel Prices:	2—WAR PASS............	6.40	3.80	2.80
	7—PYRO		4.60	3.60
	3—KODIAK KOWBOY			6.40

$2 EXACTA 2-7 PAID $25.20 $1 TRIFECTA 2-7-3 PAID $73.00
$1 SUPERFECTA 2-7-3-10 PAID $275.60 $1 PICK THREE 3-4-2 PAID $152.00
$0.50 PICK FIVE 1-11-3-4/13-2/4/11 PAID $22,099.60

Dk. b. or br. c., by Cherokee Run—Vue, by Mr. Prospector. Trainer: Nick Zito. Owner: Robert V. LaPenta. Bred by Cherry Valley Farm (Ky.).

WAR PASS sprinted clear along the rail, raced uncontested on the lead on the backstretch, extended his advantage on the turn, opened a comfortable lead in upper stretch, and was never threatened while being kept to the task under steady left-hand encouragement. PYRO fractious in the gate, was bumped at the start, checked between horses on the first turn, was unhurried for a half, moved around horses while gaining on the turn, angled three wide entering the stretch, and finished willingly to clearly best the others. KODIAK KOWBOY steadied between horses on the first turn, chased the leaders four wide to the turn, and lacked a strong closing bid. TALE OF EKATI angled to the rail on the first turn, raced evenly in midpack for six furlongs, lodged a mild bid on the turn, and flattened out. Z HUMOR failed to mount a serious rally while saving ground. OLD MAN BUCK was outrun for six furlongs and circled six wide at the quarter pole. OVEREXTENDED was shuffled back soon after the start and never reached contention. SHORE DO was never a factor. SALUTE THE SARGE drifted out on the first turn, and raced wide throughout while lacking a rally. WICKED STYLE was finished after going five furlongs while wide throughout. GLOBALIZATION stumbled and broke inward at the start, prompted the pace in the two path, and gave way on the turn.

2007 Filly and Mare Turf: No Boundaries

Lahudood (GB)—meaning "No boundaries." The optimistic Arabic name certainly proved appropriate when four-year-old filly Lahudood opened a two-length lead in the stretch of the Emirates Airline Breeders' Cup Filly and Mare Turf (G1) and then gamely held off charges from Passage of Time (GB) and Honey Ryder to secure an upset victory in the $1,951,080 race on a turf course her trainer believed she might not handle. Just two races earlier, she had struggled home last of seven in the Beverly D. Stakes (G1) on good turf at Arlington Park.

As rain fell at Monmouth, trainer Kiaran McLaughlin contacted Rick Nichols, general manager for owner Sheikh Hamdan bin Rashid al Maktoum's Shadwell Farm. Nichols contacted Sheikh Hamdan, who encouraged everyone involved to move forward with the Breeders' Cup start. "We talked with Sheikh Hamdan, and he said she was okay on soft turf in Europe, but just that she was much better on firm turf," McLaughlin said. With the decision made, Lahudood delivered, giving Sheikh Hamdan a Breeders' Cup victory for the second consecutive year, after Invasor (Arg) in the 2006 Breeders' Cup Classic Powered by Dodge (G1), and his first with a homebred.

In the Filly and Mare Turf, Lahudood thrived, deftly holding her position between horses early for jockey Alan Garcia before surging to the front midway on the far turn. The winning Breeders' Cup performance again reminded McLaughlin and Nichols of the astute horsemanship of Sheikh Hamdan. "He's very seldom ever wrong," Nichols said. "He knows his horses and he knows the game. So when he says something, you listen."

Lahudood, a homebred by Singspiel (Ire) out of the Arazi mare Rahayeb (GB), was sent to the United States with Makderah (Ire), a Danehill filly whom McLaughlin initially favored because she picked things up well during training. But Sheikh Hamdan maintained Lahudood was more talented, even after she lost her North American debut in a Belmont Park allowance race and Makderah won the New York Stakes (G2) there on June 23.

Nichols understood McLaughlin's assessment. "Quite honestly, I saw her the first time in January, went down to Palm Meadows [Training Center in Florida], right after she came in," Nichols said. "She's quite a different filly now than what she was then. She was very light and spindly looking. You really wouldn't have thought that day that we would be sitting here today."

Nichols and McLaughlin told a similar ugly duckling story about Invasor, who also appeared slight after extensive travel following his 2005 campaign, when he earned Horse of the Year honors in Uruguay. Nichols gestured a thumb toward McLaughlin when asked how such horses are able to eventually blossom on the racetrack. "It's mainly due to Kiaran's excellent horsemanship, his staff. They have built her up and made her stronger, into a gorgeous filly," Nichols said.

Besides growing physically, Lahudood also matured through attentive training. "She just has been training and getting better the last 60 days, and we have top exercise riders because she's a little temperamental and difficult. They have done a great job," McLaughlin said. "Lorenzo Morales has been getting on her the last 45 days and really has settled her down. I really have a great team of people, and she's a top filly."

McLaughlin said Lahudood lifted his confidence when she squeezed through along the hedge to win the Flower Bowl Invitational Stakes (G1) on September 29 at Belmont Park, upsetting 2006's champion three-year-old filly, Wait a While.

With 11 horses and riders battling for position before the fast-approaching first of three turns in the Filly and Mare Turf, Lahudood would need all of that maturity in the roughly run, 1⅜-mile test.

After briefly racing in last place, two-time Group 1 winner Simply Perfect (GB) passed the entire field on the outside of the first turn and took the lead the first time through the stretch. Simply Perfect bolted to the outside on the second turn, taking early contenders Precious Kitten and Arravale with her before

---

Owner-Breeder

Shadwell Stable is the racing operation of Sheikh Hamdan bin Rashid al Maktoum, deputy ruler of Dubai and minister of finance and industry for the United Arab Emirates. He owns approximately 200 broodmares worldwide and seven farms, including 1,350-acre Shadwell Farm in Lexington. He had initial success in England, where his runners have won the Epsom Derby (Eng-G1) twice and the One Thousand Guineas (Eng-G1) four times. He owned Invasor (Arg), North America's Horse of the Year in 2006 after winning the Breeders' Cup Classic Powered by Dodge (G1) and subsequent winner of the '07 Emirates Airline Dubai World Cup (UAE-G1).

being eased near the outside rail.

Lahudood raced inside of that trouble as Argentina (Ire) with Kent Desormeaux up soon took over the role of leader through six furlongs in 1:18.95. Passage of Time, favored at 2.80-to-1, raced between horses before launching her bid in the far turn. Undefeated Nashoba's Key followed Argentina closely and had to steady several times as Argentina kept shifting gears. The Southern California standout finally found a bit of room in the final turn but was boxed in and would settle for fourth.

While other horses found trouble, Lahudood seemed to create her own luck, holding position before opening a clear advantage and completing the 1⅜ miles in 2:22.75 on soft turf. Glencrest Farm's Honey Ryder, trained by Todd Pletcher, strongly rallied to claim second, a neck in front of Passage of Time.

—Frank Angst

SIXTH RACE
Monmouth Park
October 27, 2007

1⅜ miles on turf. 9th running of the Emirates Airline Breeders' Cup Filly and Mare Turf (G1). Purse $2-million guaranteed. Fillies and mares three years old and up. Weights (Northern Hemisphere): Three-year-olds, 118 lbs. Older, 123 lbs. (Southern Hemisphere): Three-year-olds, 113 lbs. Older, 122 lbs. Supplemented: Lahudood.

Value of race: $1,951,080. Value to winner: $1,150,200; second: $426,000; third: $213,000; fourth: $108,630; fifth: $53,250. Mutuel Pool $3,798,895.

Horse	Wt	M/Eqt	PP	¼	½	¾	1m	Str.	Fin.	Jockey	Odds $1
Lahudood (GB), 4, f.	123	LA	5	4^{hd}	7^{hd}	$4^{\frac{1}{2}}$	$3^{\frac{1}{2}}$	1^{2}	$1^{\frac{3}{4}}$	A. Garcia	11.70
Honey Ryder, 6, m.	123	LA	2	11	9^{hd}	6^{hd}	$7^{\frac{1}{2}}$	4^{hd}	2^{nk}	J. Velazquez	6.10
Passage of Time (GB), 3, f.	118		4	$8^{1\frac{1}{2}}$	8^{2}	5^{1}	4^{1}	2^{1}	3^{1}	R. Dominguez	2.80*
Nashoba's Key, 4, f.	123	L	3	$7^{\frac{1}{2}}$	6^{hd}	3^{hd}	5^{hd}	$5^{1\frac{1}{2}}$	$4^{\frac{1}{2}}$	J. Talamo	3.30
All My Loving (Ire), 3, f.	118	Lb	1	$10^{\frac{1}{2}}$	11	$7^{\frac{1}{2}}$	6^{hd}	6^{hd}	$5^{3\frac{1}{4}}$	P. Smullen	17.80
Timarwa (Ire), 3, f.	118		7	3^{1}	5^{1}	2^{hd}	2^{hd}	7^{2}	$6^{2\frac{1}{4}}$	M. Kinane	25.00
Arravale, 4, f.	123	L	9	5^{hd}	$4^{\frac{1}{2}}$	10	10	8^{3}	$7^{3\frac{1}{4}}$	J. Valdivia Jr.	27.00
Precious Kitten, 4, f.	123	LA	11	1^{1}	$2^{\frac{1}{2}}$	9^{2}	9^{hd}	10	8^{2}	R. Bejarano	10.00
Argentina (Ire), 5, m.	123	LA	6	$2^{\frac{1}{2}}$	$3^{\frac{1}{2}}$	1^{1}	1^{hd}	3^{hd}	$9^{1\frac{3}{4}}$	K. Desormeaux	7.90
Danzon, 4, f.	123	L	8	$9^{\frac{1}{2}}$	10^{hd}	8^{2}	8^{6}	$9^{\frac{1}{2}}$	10	J. Leparoux	10.90
Simply Perfect (GB), 3, f.	118	L	10	$6^{1\frac{1}{2}}$	1^{1}	—	—	—	—	J. Murtagh	10.70

L=Salix; LA=Salix and adjunct bleeder medication; b=blinkers.

OFF AT 1:57. Start: Good for all. Weather: Showery. Turf: Soft.
Time: :25.99, :52.06, 1:18.95, 1:44.60, 2:09.72, 2:22.75.

$2 Mutuel Prices:				
	6—LAHUDOOD (GB)	**25.40**	**11.40**	**6.40**
	2—HONEY RYDER		**6.60**	**4.60**
	4—PASSAGE OF TIME (GB)			**3.40**

$2 EXACTA 6-2 PAID $167.60 **$1 TRIFECTA 6-2-4 PAID $384.90**
$1 SUPERFECTA 6-2-4-3 PAID $1,185.60 **$1 PICK THREE 4-2-6 PAID $168.00**

B. f., by Singspiel (Ire)—Rahayeb (GB), by Arazi. Trainer: Kiaran McLaughlin. Owner: Shadwell Stable. Bred by Shadwell Estate Co. Ltd. (GB).

LAHUDOOD (GB) steadied in tight between horses in the early stages, was hard held while racing in good position between rivals along the backstretch, closed the gap to threaten on the far turn, surged to the front midway on the turn, opened clear advantage in upper stretch, edged away, then held off runner-up under steady right-hand urging. HONEY RYDER checked early, raced well back, gained between horses on the far turn, angled four wide, then finished well from outside. PASSAGE OF TIME (GB) rated between horses, lodged a bid three wide on the turn, made a run to threaten, then weakened late. NASHOBA'S KEY tucked in along the rail in the early stages, steadied while lacking room before going a half, was boxed in on inside through the turn, saved ground to the top of the stretch, lodged a mild bid, and weakened late. ALL MY LOVING (IRE) broke awkwardly, checked after hitting gate, rushed up along the rail, steadied sharply along the rail while being wrangled back through opening half-mile, lacked room while saving ground, steadied in traffic on the turn, angled five wide, then rallied belatedly. TIMARWA (IRE) contested pace after going a half, raced in close contention between horses while three wide, lodged a bid from outside nearing the quarter pole, but could not sustain rally. ARRAVALE was carried extremely wide midway on the first turn and was never close. PRECIOUS KITTEN was carried out badly on the first turn and failed to threaten thereafter. ARGENTINA (IRE) steadied along the inside, took the lead along the backstretch, battled inside to the turn and tired. DANZON failed to mount a serious rally. SIMPLY PERFECT (GB) bolted on first turn and was pulled up.

2007 Sprint: Midnight Dash

Midnight Lute is an unconventional sprinter who took an unconventional route to the Breeders' Cup World Championships. So, it should come as little surprise he won the $1,832,000 TVG Breeders' Cup Sprint (G1) in a most unconventional fashion. The son of Kentucky Derby (G1) and Preakness Stakes (G1) winner Real Quiet came from far off the pace in a splashy display of pure speed, torpedoed down the sloppy homestretch, and won by 4¾ lengths, the largest winning margin in the 24-year history of the six-furlong race.

The Sprint victory, coupled with an astonishing performance in the Forego Stakes (G1) in his prior start eight weeks earlier, earned Midnight Lute championship honors in the sprint division. Trainer Bob Baffert was supremely confident in Midnight Lute through the week preceding the Sprint on October 27 at Monmouth Park, but he knew luck would need to fall his way in a race that often ends in a blanket finish, and the slightest of bobbles can leave a runner way out from under the blanket. He knew the first few seconds would be the key to his chances, and he knew his colt has a well-documented record of indifference in that department.

"He's not a quick sort," Baffert said days before the race. "The break is going to be very crucial. If he gets away, he's good enough, he should do it. He's getting better with age. He's like a big kid; he was kind of awkward." When the gate opened, Baffert thought all was lost. Midnight Lute was whacked from the outside, steadied, and then pinched back from both sides.

Rider Garrett Gomez kept Midnight Lute, the Sprint's 5-to-2 favorite, just off the rail and well behind pacesetter Talent Search, who posted fractions of :21.56 for the first quarter-mile, and :44.06 for the half, the latter split in company with Idiot Proof. Gomez improved his position slightly around the turn and then swung Midnight Lute out six paths off the rail for the winning run.

"I made the decision to come around horses," said Gomez, who was on his way to the AIG Bill Shoemaker Award as the top jockey at the Breeders' Cup. "Commentator took us out a little farther than I would have liked, but once I got him clear, he came on."

Like a freight train. Make that a torpedo. Full speed ahead. Midnight Lute came splashing down the middle of the track and swallowed up the field in a performance that reminded his trainer of Arazi in the 1991 Breeders' Cup Juvenile (G1). Midnight Lute completed the six furlongs in 1:09.18, well off the track record of 1:07.47 set in July by Idiot Proof, who finished second. The winner earned $1.08-million, nearly tripling his lifetime earnings to $1,550,600.

The progeny of Real Quiet show only an average affinity for off tracks, a 16% win rate from 254 starts. Midnight Lute may love the slop, or he may have been so much the best on a gray New Jersey afternoon that the surface simply did not matter. "You always worry about the mud," Baffert said. "But one thing I've learned through the years, the good ones always come through. You'd better lead a good one up there because you're running against the best, and they shine."

There was never a doubt about the winner, but the next two spots were a matter of some contention. Ryan Fogelsonger, who crossed the finish line third aboard Talent Search, claimed foul against second-place finisher Idiot Proof, with David Flores in the saddle. "It was nothing," said Flores, and the stewards agreed.

Smokey Stover, winner of Monmouth's Icecapade Stakes in his previous start, ran a disappointing race, finishing ninth as the 3.90-to-1 second betting choice. "I knew at the half-mile pole he was done," said trainer Greg Gilchrist. "Aaron [Gryder] was riding him like he was on the front side instead of the backside. I've got to take my hat off to the winner." Also running less than his best race was Greg's Gold, who finished eighth after leaving the gate at odds of 6.10-to-1.

Owners

Watson & Weitman Performances is the racing operation of Karl Watson and Paul Weitman, who are car dealers in Tucson, Arizona. In partnerships, they own ten horses, all trained by Bob Baffert. Their Breeders' Cup winner was named for a nickname of University of Arizona basketball coach Lute Olson. **Mike Pegram** is a longtime Baffert client who owns 22 McDonald's restaurant franchises in Arizona. He raced two-time champion Silverbulletday and Real Quiet, winner of the 1998 Kentucky Derby (G1) and Preakness Stakes (G1).

Breeders

Tom Evans owns Trackside Farm in Versailles, Kentucky, in partnership with Pat Clark. Evans, honored as 2002 farm manager of the year by the Kentucky Thoroughbred Farm Managers' Club, is the brother of Robert Evans, chief executive officer of Churchill Downs Inc. **Macon Wilmil Equines** is the racing and breeding operation of Dr. Ted Forrest of Louisville. Marjac Farms is the breeding operation of Rich Burke, owner of Marjac Capital Partners in Richmond, Virginia. Each owns one-third of Candy Candyturf, dam of Midnight Lute.

Out of the Dehere mare Candytuft, Midnight Lute was bred in Kentucky by Tom Evans, Macon Wilmil Equines, and Marjac Farms. That partnership sold him at auction as a yearling for $70,000 to Tom McGreevy of Caldera Racing. He was offered at auction as a two-year-old but did not reach his reserve price. Baffert said he later purchased the colt privately for $300,000 for owners Karl Watson, Paul Weitman, and Mike Pegram, all longtime clients.

Breathing problems bumped Midnight Lute off the Triple Crown trail before he ever got on it. The colt required throat surgery to keep his air passageways clear, according to Baffert. It proved unsuccessful, so the colt had the same surgery again, requiring a yearlong layoff. In the fall of 2006, he won Keeneland Race Course's Perryville Stakes (G3) decisively. He ran well in Santa Anita Park's Strub series, but had a third throat surgery after a subpar Commonwealth Breeders' Cup Stakes (G2) at Keeneland in the spring of 2007.

After 4½ months of rest and recuperation, Midnight Lute came back with a monster effort in the seven-furlong Forego at Saratoga Race Course, with exactly the same kind of move he would make in the TVG Breeders' Cup Sprint eight weeks later.—*Steve Myrick*

SEVENTH RACE
Monmouth Park
October 27, 2007

6 furlongs on dirt. 24th running of the TVG Breeders' Cup Sprint (G1). Purse $2-million guaranteed. 3-year-olds and up. Weights (Northern Hemisphere): Three-year-olds, 123 lbs. Older, 126 lbs. (Southern Hemisphere): Three-year-olds, 121 lbs. Older, 126 lbs. Fillies and mares allowed 3 lbs. Track record: Idiot Proof, 1:07.47, July 4, 2007.

Value of race: $1,832,000. Value to winner: $1,080,000; second: $400,000; third: $200,000; fourth: $102,000; fifth: $50,000.
Mutuel Pool $4,304,908.

Horse	Wt.	M/Eqt	PP	St.	¼	½	Str.	Fin.	Jockey	Odds $1
Midnight Lute, 4, c.	126	LAb	2	8	8½	7³	31½	1⁴¾	G. Gomez	2.50*
Idiot Proof, 3, c.	123	Lc	6	2	3²½	2²½	1¹	2¹¾	D. Flores	5.80
Talent Search, 4, c.	126	LAbc	3	3	1¹	1ʰᵈ	2⁵	3²½	R. Fogelsonger	17.90
Benny the Bull, 4, c.	126	L	7	10	10	9½	6⁴	4¹½	M. Guidry	7.20
Kelly's Landing, 6, h.	126	LA	4	6	6²	4½	4³	5²	L. Dettori	10.40
Bordonaro, 6, h.	126	LA	8	5	9³½	10	7²	6ʰᵈ	R. Migliore	30.10
Commentator, 6, h.	126	Lc	5	4	2½	3³	5½	7⁴	J. Bravo	9.00
Greg's Gold, 6, h.	126	LA	9	7	7¹½	8¹	8½	8¹⁸	V. Espinoza	6.10
Smokey Stover, 4, c.	126	L	1	9	5³	6¹½	10	9¹¹	A. Gryder	3.90
Forefathers, 3, c.	123	LA	10	1	4ʰᵈ	5¹	9ʰᵈ	10	K. Desormeaux	19.80

L=Salix; LA=Salix and adjunct bleeder medication; b=blinkers; c=mud calks.

OFF AT 2:38. Start: Good for all. Weather: Cloudy. Track: Sloppy (sealed).
Time: :21.56, :44.06, :56.58, 1:09.18.

$2 Mutuel Prices:	2—MIDNIGHT LUTE	7.00	4.00	3.00
	7—IDIOT PROOF		6.60	4.60
	4—TALENT SEARCH			8.60

$2 EXACTA 2-7 PAID $49.80 $1 TRIFECTA 2-7-4 PAID $242.60
$1 SUPERFECTA 2-7-4-8 PAID $1,374.40 $1 PICK THREE 2-6-2 PAID $203.90
$1 PICK FOUR 4/13-2/4/11-6-2/3 PAID $1,032.80

Dk. b. or br. c., by Real Quiet—Candytuft, by Dehere. Trainer: Bob Baffert. Owners: Watson and Weitman Performance LLC and Mike Pegram. Bred by Tom Evans, Macon Wilmil Equine, and Marjac Farm (Ky.).

MIDNIGHT LUTE steadied after being bumped and pinched back, raced far back for a half, began to angle out midway on the turn, rapidly closed the gap while swinging six wide leaving the quarter pole, then unleashed a strong late run under right-hand urging. IDIOT PROOF pressed the pace three wide along the backstretch, drew on even terms for the lead at the quarter pole, drifted in a bit after opening a clear lead in midstretch, relinquished the lead to the winner a sixteenth out, then held well to best the others. TALENT SEARCH broke inward at the start, was hustled up along the rail, dueled along the inside in upper stretch, steadied and altered course to the outside in midstretch, and weakened. BENNY THE BULL hit the side of the gate, checked, dropped back early, raced well back for a half, advanced between horses on the turn, then rallied belatedly. KELLY'S LANDING settled in midpack, lodged a mild five-wide move at the quarter pole then lacked a strong response. BORDONARO checked and was bumped at the start. COMMENTATOR popped open the gate prior to the start, pressed the early pace, dropped back nearing the quarter pole and steadily tired. GREG'S GOLD failed to mount a serious rally. SMOKEY STOVER raced just off the pace, swung three wide on the turn and lacked further response. FOREFATHERS checked slightly, showed speed while three wide, and gave way. Following a stewards' inquiry as well as a claim of foul lodged by the rider of TALENT SEARCH against IDIOT PROOF for interference in the stretch, there was no change in the order of finish.

2007 Mile: Oklahoma's Pride

Trainer Richard Dutrow Jr. appeared on "The Oprah Winfrey Show" on the Tuesday of Breeders' Cup World Championships week for a segment on his Breeders' Cup Filly and Mare Sprint contender, Oprah Winney. An audible roar arose from the rain-soaked Monmouth Park crowd on October 26 when Oprah Winney moved into second at the quarter pole, but she tired and finished eighth, disappointing her fans and the exalted talk-show host after whom she was named.

Also in Dutrow's barn, although receiving much less media attention in the days leading up to the Breeders' Cup, was a strapping gray or roan four-year-old colt named Kip Deville, a top contender for the NetJets Breeders' Cup Mile (G1) on October 27. Bred on an advertised stud fee of $1,500 in Oklahoma—a state that previously produced one Breeders' Cup winner, 1986 Breeders' Cup Distaff (G1) winner and Horse of the Year Lady's Secret—Kip Deville already had proved his mettle with victories in races such as the Frank E. Kilroe Mile Handicap (G1) and Maker's Mark Mile Stakes (G1).

"He's all horse," Dutrow said the day before the Breeders' Cup. "He don't want to make friends with nobody. He just wants to go out there and do what he can do. He wants to be left alone. He's all racehorse. He's sitting on a big race."

Talk-show material Kip Deville was not, but he proved Dutrow's words correct. Getting a perfect trip under Cornelio Velasquez, Kip Deville broke well, angled to the rail, and settled directly behind pacesetter Cosmonaut, tracking sensible fractions of :49.54 and 1:14.65 on the soft turf.

Angling out and splitting horses turning for home, 8.20-to-1 Kip Deville was full of run while under hand urging from Velasquez. Excellent Art (GB), an accomplished European invader who was favored at 2.10-to-1, rallied stoutly to finish second, a length behind the winner and a length in front of third-place Cosmonaut.

"I wait, wait, wait, and he was relaxing behind horses," Velasquez said. "At the quarter pole, I found room. I didn't want to go to the lead, but he took me there, and in the final three-sixteenths, he broke away from them." He completed the mile in 1:39.78.

Kip Deville's victory set off a jubilant celebration from IEAH Stables, which purchased him privately for $500,000 last year and owns him in partnership with Andrew and John Cohen, Steve Cobb, and Doug Robertson. Because he was not nominated to the Breeders' Cup program, it cost the owners $300,000 to supplement Kip Deville to the Mile.

"The last hundred yards, if I could capture it and carry it on the rest of my life, I'd like to," said IEAH Co-President Michael Iavarone. "Fortunately we have it on tape, because I have to look back on this, because it's like we're living a dream here. Rick has done an amazing job."

South Wind Ranch and Wayne Cobb bought Kip Deville for $20,000 at the 2004 Fasig-Tipton Texas summer yearling sale. Entered in the 2005 Fasig-Tipton Midlantic two-year-olds in training sale by consignor Mike Neatherlin, agent, Kip Deville was bought back for $32,000.

Trained by Neatherlin and owned by the Cobb and Neatherlin families, Kip Deville won four of his first eight starts in Texas, Oklahoma, Louisiana, and Arkansas. Following a four-length victory in the $75,000 Grand Prairie Turf Challenge Stakes, a one-mile turf race at Lone Star Park on April 29, 2006, agent Ron Freitas contacted IEAH about buying the horse.

"Iavarone called me up when me, Bobby Frankel, and my best friend Louie were going up to Saratoga," Dutrow said. "Bobby's got his computer, and he's sitting in the front seat, so I said, 'Bobby, bring up this race.'

"We watched it, and Bobby looked back, and said, 'Rick, if you don't buy him, I will.'"

Kip Deville's first race for his new connections was the $1-million Colonial Turf Cup Stakes, a 1 3/16-mile grass race for three-year-olds at Colonial Downs in which he set fast early fractions and faded late to finish second to Lael Stable's Showing Up. Following off-the-board finishes in the Virginia Derby (G2) and Kent Breeders' Cup Stakes (G3), Dutrow put Julien Leparoux on Kip Deville for the $150,000 Bryan Station Stakes at Keeneland Race Course on October 15, 2006.

The French-born rider's patient style opened

Owner
IEAH Stables is the racing subsidiary of International Equine Acquisitions Holdings Inc., which is operated by New Yorkers Michael Iavarone and Richard J. Schiavo, who share the titles of co-president and co-chief executive officer. Iavarone, who worked on Wall Street, started IEAH, and Schiavo joined the company as an investor in 2003 and as a management member the following year. The company maintains about 50 horses in training, including top sprinter Benny the Bull.

Breeder
Center Hills Farm, which has been renamed Mighty Acres, is owned by dentist Warren Center in Pryor, Oklahoma. The Center family owns and stands Kip Deville's sire, Kipling, a regally bred $1.4-million yearling purchase originally campaigned by Michael Tabor and Susan Magnier. Center also owned Kip Deville's dam, Klondike Kaytie, by Encino, who died in 2005 while foaling the Mile winner's full sister Kip Seville. Center's wife, Linda, bottle-raised Kip Seville.

a new dimension for Kip Deville, who rated early in the mile race, stalking the pace from close range, before powering home through his final quarter in :22.80 to win by 1¼ lengths. Following a sixth-place finish behind Showing Up in the 1¼-mile Hollywood Derby (G1), Kip Deville cut back to a mile and closed his three-year-old season with a one-length victory in the $114,300 Sir Beaufort Stakes (G3) on Hollywood Park's turf.

Having found Kip Deville's preferred running style and distance, Dutrow ambitiously entered him in the $300,000 Kilroe Mile at Santa Anita Park on March 3. He responded with a game neck victory over Bayeux in 1:33.88. For his second start of 2007, Kip Deville shipped to Keeneland Race Course for the $250,000 Maker's Mark. The race featured a rematch with Showing Up, and Kip Deville won by a neck.

Kip Deville experienced a midsummer slump that Dutrow attributed soreness in hind-end muscles, and the four-year-old finished a good second to Shakespeare in the $1,003,600 Woodbine Mile Stakes (Can-G1). Kip Deville has won nine of 21 starts and earned $2,434,422.

—Pete Denk

EIGHTH RACE
Monmouth Park
October 27, 2007

1 mile on turf. 24th running of the NetJets Breeders' Cup Mile (G1). Purse $2-million guaranteed. Three-year-olds and up. Weights (Northern Hemisphere): Three-year-olds, 122 lbs. Older, 126 lbs. (Southern Hemisphere): Three-year-olds, 119 lbs. Older, 126 lbs. Fillies and mares allowed 3 lbs. Supplemented: Excellent Art, Host, Kip Deville, Remarkable News.

Value of race: $2,409,080. Value to winner: $1,420,200; second: $526,000; third: $263,000; fourth: $134,130; fifth: $65,750. Mutuel Pool $4,085,095.

Horse	Wt.	M/Eqt	PP	St.	¼	½	¾	Str.	Fin.	Jockey	Odds $1
Kip Deville, 4, c.	126	Lb	7	4	2hd	4½	3hd	2²	1¹	C. Velasquez	8.20
Excellent Art (GB), 3, c.	122	L	12	12	12⁵	11hd	10hd	5²	2¹	J. Murtagh	2.10*
Cosmonaut, 5, h.	126	L	6	6	1¹	1¹	1hd	1½	3nk	J. Leparoux	14.20
Nobiz Like Shobiz, 3, c.	122	LA	8	5	10½	10²	4hd	3hd	4½	J. Velazquez	3.90
Host (Chi), 7, h.	126	LA	3	1	13	13	13	10hd	5¾	G. Gomez	15.60
Trippi's Storm, 4, c.	126	LA	5	3	7hd	9½	9hd	7½	6³½	J. Castellano	9.30
Remarkable News (Ven), 5, h.	126	L	13	11	6¹	3¹	2¹	4hd	7nk	R. Dominguez	16.20
Rebellion (GB), 4, c.	126	LA	1	2	4hd	7hd	8½	9½	8¹¾	E. Coa	44.80
Icy Atlantic, 6, h.	126	LA	2	13	11hd	12⁵	12⁴	11¹	9¹	C. DeCarlo	39.30
Jeremy, 4, c.	126	- -	4	7	9¹	8½	7½	6½	10¹½	L. Dettori	7.30
Purim, 5, h.	126	LAf	11	10	8½	6½	11½	8¹	11⁶	J. Theriot	20.80
Silent Name (Jpn), 5, h.	126	LA	10	9	5hd	5½	5hd	12¹	12³¾	K. Desormeaux	18.20
My Typhoon (Ire), 5, m.	123	LA	9	8	3½	2hd	6hd	13	13	E. Castro	29.70

L=Salix; LA=Salix and adjunct bleeder medication; b=blinkers; f=front bandages.

OFF AT 3:24. Start: Good for all. Weather: Showery. Turf: Soft.
Time: :24.26, :49.54, 1:14.65, 1:39.78.

$2 Mutuel Prices:	8—KIP DEVILLE................................	18.40	7.20	5.20
	13—EXCELLENT ART (GB).............		4.20	3.00
	7—COSMONAUT..............................			6.60

$2 EXACTA 8-13 PAID $70.80 $1 TRIFECTA 8-13-7 PAID $376.90
$1 SUPERFECTA 8-13-7-9 PAID $1,750.30 $1 PICK THREE 6-2-8 PAID $574.90

Gr. or ro. c., by Kipling—Klondike Kaytie, by Encino. Trainer: Richard Dutrow Jr. Owners: IEAH Stables, Andrew Cohen, John A. Cohen, Steve Cobb, and Doug Robertson. Bred by Center Hills Farm (Ok).

KIP DEVILLE tucked in along the rail on the first turn, settled along the inside while well placed along the backstretch, edged a bit closer while saving ground on the turn, split horses while rallying at the three-sixteenths pole, charged to the front inside the furlong marker, and drew clear. EXCELLENT ART (GB) was unhurried while racing behind horses in the five path along the backstretch, launched a bid on turn, closed the gap in upper stretch, lugged in nearing the furlong marker, then finished well from outside. COSMONAUT sprinted clear in the early stages, raced uncontested to the lead to the far turn, dug in when challenged, fought gamely into midstretch, then yielded grudgingly. NOBIZ LIKE SHOBIZ was unhurried for a half-mile, unleashed a steady four-wide move nearing the quarter pole, lodged a bid to threaten at the top of the stretch, then flattened out a bit in the late stages. HOST (CHI) broke awkwardly, trailed for six furlongs, circled eight wide entering the stretch and rallied belatedly. TRIPPI'S STORM steadied sharply on the first turn, raced in traffic along the backstretch, steadied behind horses on the turn, angled out at the top of the stretch and finished well late. REMARKABLE NEWS (VEN) chased the pace three wide to the turn and tired. REBELLION (GB) steadied on the first turn, raced in traffic, steadied midway on the turn, angled five wide and lacked strong closing response. ICY ATLANTIC was outrun while saving ground, swung six wide at the quarter pole, and failed to menace. JEREMY checked early, steadied in tight on first turn, saved ground and steadied on the turn. PURIM chased three wide and tired. SILENT NAME (JPN) gave way. MY TYPHOON (IRE) pressed the pace for a half and steadily tired.

2007 Juvenile Fillies: Brilliant Blessing

Bob Baffert, who loves a stage, was front and center for the $1,832,000 Grey Goose Breeders' Cup Juvenile Fillies (G1), for which he trained favored Indian Blessing. He was the leading character even though he had had to scratch Cry and Catch Me just three days before the October 27 race. Winner of the Oak Leaf Stakes (G1) on September 29 at Oak Tree at Santa Anita, Cry and Catch Me had developed a fever after shipping to Monmouth Park and was scratched. A front-runner, Cry and Catch Me would have been one of the favorites in the Juvenile Fillies, and her defection changed the complexion of the race.

Patti and Hal Earnhardt III's homebred Indian Blessing, undefeated in two starts, now possessed all the early speed in the race. Without her stablemate in the starting gate, it appeared she would be able to dictate early pace without pressure.

Baffert heard a lot of the talk about scratching Cry and Catch Me to help the chances of Indian Blessing, but he dismissed such speculation out of hand.

"She got sick, and we had to scratch her," Baffert said. "She was training extremely well. Thank God she did not get very sick, and we got it under control in time, so she'll be back to race again."

Privately, Baffert knew Indian Blessing was more talented than Cry and Catch Me—at least at this stage of their careers—and he was confident Indian Blessing would win with or without Cry and Catch Me in the field.

"When I worked the two together," he said, "Indian Blessing would just put her away."

The only question surrounding Indian Blessing was not her talent or speed, but her ability to negotiate two turns. She had made just two starts, winning a 5½-furlong maiden race at Saratoga Race Course in front-running fashion, and then the one-mile Frizette Stakes (G1) at Belmont Park on October 6 around one turn. In the Frizette, Indian Blessing took the lead early and sprinted out to a commanding eight-length advantage in the stretch before winning by 4½ lengths.

"She's a very talented filly," Baffert said. "But you never know about two turns until they do it."

The connections of the 12 fillies lining up against Indian Blessing, a daughter of Indian Charlie out of Shameful, by Flying Chevron, hoped her Achilles' heel would indeed be two turns in the 1 1/16-mile race, because the race was

Owners-Breeders
Hal J. Earnhardt III and his wife, **Patti**, reside in Queen Creek, Arizona. Hal Earnhardt is president of Earnhardt Automotive, owner of ten dealerships in the Phoenix area. The Earnhardts are longtime clients of trainer Bob Baffert and began racing Quarter Horses with him at Los Alamitos. Earnhardt was the breeder and co-owner of Indian Charlie, winner of the 1998 Santa Anita Derby and the sire of Indian Blessing. The Earnhardts also raced multiple stakes winner Behaving Badly.

not shaping up in their favor. The steady rain over two days had made the track sloppy, and early speed was faring well in the first three races of the day, with the Juvenile Fillies kicking off the Breeders' Cup card as the fourth race.

The bettors made Indian Blessing the 1.70-to-1 favorite. Since Indian Blessing was the best of the East and Cry and Catch Me the best of the West, bettors looked around for a new candidate to beat Indian Blessing, and for a time, surprisingly settled on Smarty Deb, an undefeated filly by Smart Strike who had made all four of her starts at Emerald Downs.

In early betting, Smarty Deb, who was 30-to-1 on the morning line, was 4-to-1 for a long time before finally drifting to third choice at 8.40-to-1. Northwest Farms' homebred had defeated colts twice, including in her previous start in the 1 1/16-mile Gottstein Futurity. Her connections were delighted with just being there.

"When they announced that we had gotten into the field," said Smarty Deb's trainer, Doris Harwood, "tears welled up in my eyes. I was so thrilled."

Second choice at 5.60-to-1 was Janis Whitham's homebred Izarra, second to Cry and Catch Me in the Oak Leaf, and the 9.40-to-1 fourth choice was Brereton C. Jones's homebred Proud Spell, undefeated winner of the Matron Stakes (G2).

When the gates sprung, Indian Blessing fulfilled expectations by going right to the front from the fourth post position under Garrett Gomez.

"She left the gate really good for us, and my main concern with her [was to get her to relax]," Gomez said. "The other day [in the Frizette], in the one-turn mile, she got a little aggressive with me, so I tried not to warm her up too much.

"She's a very tactical filly, and you can put her where you want. The idea wasn't to make the lead. It was just to get a good forward position, but once she made it up to the first turn, she was really rolling and I let her go."

Heading into the first turn, Indian Blessing was flanked by A to the Croft, a confirmed stretch runner who surprisingly went to the front after breaking from the extreme outside post position. Proud Spell raced in third, with the rest of the field strung out behind them.

Indian Blessing maintained a short lead under pressure through an opening half-mile in :46.44, with A to the Croft still pressing on the outside.

At the half-mile pole, Indian Blessing sprinted clear, and she appeared to settle the field. She negotiated the first six furlongs in 1:10.61 while owning a three-length lead, and she then widened her advantage to six lengths in midstretch. As had occurred in the Frizette, she labored late in the race, shortening her stride, but still had enough in reserve to win by 3½ lengths. Proud Spell, ridden by Gabriel Saez, ran well the entire race to finish second, a half-length ahead of 19-to-1 Backseat Rhythm in third.

Baffert, who won the 1998 Juvenile Fillies with Silverbulletday, became the fourth trainer to send out multiple winners of the race, joining Racing Hall of Famers D. Wayne Lukas (five winners), Richard Mandella (two winners), and Shug McGaughey (two winners).—*Mark Simon*

FOURTH RACE
Monmouth Park
October 27, 2007

1 1/16 miles on dirt. 24th running of the Breeders' Cup Juvenile Fillies (G1). Purse $2-million guaranteed. Fillies, 2-year-olds. Weight: 119 lbs.

Value of race: $1,832,000. Value to winner: $1,080,000; second: $400,000; third: $200,000; fourth: $102,000; fifth: $50,000. Mutuel Pool $3,302,388.

Horse	Wgt.	M/Eqt	PP	St.	¼	½	¾	Str.	Fin.	Jockey	Odds $1
Indian Blessing, 2, f.	119	LAb	4	2	$1^{1/2}$	$1^{1/2}$	1^{3}	1^{6}	$1^{3 1/2}$	G. Gomez	1.70*
Proud Spell, 2, f.	119	LAc	10	3	3^{1}	3^{1}	3^{1}	$3^{1 1/2}$	$2^{1/2}$	G. Saez	9.40
Backseat Rhythm, 2, f.	119	Lc	7	13	13	12^{1}	8^{3}	2^{hd}	3^{4}	J. Castellano	19.00
Tasha's Miracle, 2, f.	119	Lbc	3	9	$6^{1/2}$	$6^{1/2}$	4^{1}	4^{2}	$4^{2 1/4}$	D. Flores	16.80
Smarty Deb, 2, f.	119	LA	9	5	5^{2}	4^{hd}	5^{1}	5^{2}	5^{hd}	R. Frazier	8.40
Clearly Foxy, 2, f.	119	LA	2	4	12^{hd}	13	$10^{1/2}$	$6^{1/2}$	$6^{7 3/4}$	P. Husbands	16.80
Grace Anatomy, 2, f.	119	L	12	12	11^{3}	7^{1}	7^{hd}	$8^{1/2}$	$7^{4 1/2}$	L. Dettori	11.40
Zee Zee, 2, f.	119	LA	11	6	$9^{1/2}$	$9^{1 1/2}$	11^{hd}	10^{1}	8^{2}	R. Albarado	19.00
A to the Croft, 2, f.	119	LAbf	13	7	$2^{1/2}$	2^{2}	2^{1}	$7^{1/2}$	$9^{1 3/4}$	K. Desormeaux	12.80
Izarra, 2, f.	119	L	8	10	8^{1}	8^{1}	12^{5}	$9^{1/2}$	10^{1}	V. Espinoza	5.60
Set Play, 2, f.	119	L	6	11	10^{hd}	$11^{1/2}$	6^{hd}	11^{8}	11^{21}	B. Blanc	41.20
Irish Smoke, 2, f.	119	L	5	8	7^{1}	$10^{1 1/2}$	13	13	12^{4}	J. Leparoux	12.50
Phantom Income, 2, f.	119	LA	1	1	4^{hd}	5^{2}	$9^{1/2}$	$12^{1/2}$	13	E. Coa	30.00

L=Salix; LA=Salix and adjunct bleeder medication; b=blinkers; c=mud calks; f=front bandages.

OFF AT 12:34. Start: Good for all. Weather: Cloudy. Track: Sloppy (sealed).
Time: :23.55, :46.44, 1:10.61, 1:37.72, 1:44.73.

$2 Mutuel Prices:				
	4—INDIAN BLESSING	**5.40**	**4.80**	**3.20**
	10—PROUD SPELL		**8.80**	**5.80**
	7—BACKSEAT RHYTHM			**9.60**

$2 EXACTA 4-10 PAID $54.20 $1 TRIFECTA 4-10-7 PAID $243.00
$1 SUPERFECTA 4-10-7-3 PAID $3,280.80 $1 PICK THREE 11-3-4 PAID $320.20

Dk. b. or br. f., by Indian Charlie—Shameful, by Flying Chevron. Trainer: Bob Baffert. Owners-breeders: Patti and Hal Earnhardt III (Ky.).

INDIAN BLESSING outsprinted rivals for the early advantage, set the pace while in hand along the backstretch, saved ground while extending her lead on the turn, opened a wide gap in upper stretch, and edged away under strong right-hand encouragement. PROUD SPELL was bumped between horses on the first turn, raced three wide for six furlongs, took up chase from outside on the turn, drifted out when struck left-handed in upper stretch, then closed gradually through the stretch but couldn't threaten the winner. BACKSEAT RHYTHM bobbled and shuffled back at the start, was unhurried for a half while saving ground, split horses while gaining on the turn, moved back to the rail and rallied belatedly to gain a share. TASHA'S MIRACLE steadied in tight and was brushed along the rail on the first turn, advanced five wide at the five-eighths pole, made a steady run while continuing wide midway on the turn, lodged a bid leaving the quarter pole and flattened out. SMARTY DEB steadied between horses in tight on the first turn, steadied sharply approaching the backstretch, raced in good position between horses for six furlongs and lacked a strong closing response. CLEARLY FOXY was in tight along the rail on the first turn, dropped back while saving ground along the backstretch and lacked the needed response when called upon. GRACE ANATOMY was bumped and carried wide on the first turn and failed to threaten thereafter. ZEE ZEE failed to rally. A TO THE CROFT pressed the winner from outside for six furlongs and dropped back on the turn. IZARRA broke inward at the start, bore out six wide on the first turn, continued six wide to the top of the stretch, and drifted out in the upper stretch. SET PLAY saved ground to no avail. IRISH SMOKE steadied in tight though the first turn. PHANTOM INCOME gave way.

2007 Distaff: Ginger Punches

Owner Frank Stronach did not hesitate once he got the word from trainer Bobby Frankel that multiple Grade 1 winner Ginger Punch should be supplemented at a cost of $180,000 into the $2,070,160 Emirates Airline Breeders' Cup Distaff (G1).

The four-year-old Awesome Again filly had finished third in her previous start in Belmont Park's Beldame Stakes (G1) on September 30, but it was back-to-back victories in the Go for Wand (G1) and Ruffian (G1) Handicaps by a combined 6¾ lengths in her prior two starts that gave them the confidence to pay her way into the field of 12 that included seven other Grade 1 winners.

The move paid off handsomely for Stronach, a perennial Eclipse Award finalist as North America's top owner and breeder, as Ginger Punch survived a long, physical duel with Hystericalady down the length of Monmouth Park's stretch to prevail by a neck on October 27.

With Frankel choosing to remain at his Southern California home to care for his cancer-stricken eight-year-old Australian sheepdog, Happy, training duties for the day fell to 28-year-old assistant Chad Brown, who developed emotional ties to the muscular chestnut filly as she overcame a series of setbacks to put herself in position to capture a season-ending championship.

"She's had her share of issues—from not running as a two-year-old to several surgeries to correct breathing problems—but Bobby always knew she could be special," Brown said. "Most trainers would have given up and retired her last year. Instead, he was patient, managed her perfectly, and here we are." Stronach said the filly was not nominated to the Breeders' Cup because the sheer numbers in his massive breeding operation made it difficult to put up the money to include every foal.

Ginger Punch did not arrive at Monmouth Park until 48 hours before the race, as Brown and fellow assistant Jose Cuevas chose to do much of her prerace preparation at Belmont. Meanwhile, Northern California-based trainer Jerry Hollendorfer, who would saddle Humana Distaff Stakes (G1) winner Hystericalady, was giddy at the thought of an off track for the four-year-old Distorted Humor filly, who won her career debut by 3½ lengths on a wet-fast track at Golden Gate Fields in May 2005.

Hollendorfer had other reasons to be confident. Hystericalady, winner of three of seven starts on the season prior to the Breeders' Cup, captured the Molly Pitcher Breeders' Cup Handicap (G2) by 6¼ lengths on August 25 over the Monmouth main track.

At the same time, Todd Pletcher was trying to develop a strategy for his three Distaff starters: Grade 1 winners Octave and Unbridled Belle and Grade 2 winner Indian Vale, the 3-to-1 morning-line favorite.

Bettors at Monmouth and across North America pretty much dismissed the program betting line and made Gazelle Stakes (G1) winner Lear's Princess the slight 9-to-2 favorite over Ginger Punch, also at 9-to-2. Indian Vale went off at 8.30-to-1.

In the Distaff, Ginger Punch received a patient, ground-saving, stalking trip under Rafael Bejarano, positioned in fourth while Bear Now, pressured by 9.20-to-1 Hystericalady, led the field through a quarter-mile in :22.68 and a half-mile in :46.64.

Entering the far turn, Bear Now weakened and began to drop back as Ginger Punch and Hystericalady hooked up for a three-furlong, side-by-side sprint to the wire.

Hystericalady, ridden by Eddie Castro, had a short lead turning for home and came in on Ginger Punch, bumping her near the eighth pole. Ginger Punch fought back gamely, however, and dug in to edge her rival at the line by a neck. Her winning time was 1:50.11 for the Distaff's 1⅛ miles.

"I saw a lot of speed on the upside, so the best I could do was stay clear and keep dirt out of her face," Bejarano said. "When we got to the three-eighths [pole], [Hystericalady] was in the third lane and I was in the first. When he [jockey Eddie Castro] saw me, he tried to push me into the rail and intimidate me."

Octave made a powerful late run down the center of the track to finish third, another neck

---

Owner-Breeder

Stronach Stables is the operation of Magna International Inc. Chairman Frank Stronach, an Austrian native who built the successful auto-parts company in Canada and then pursued his Thoroughbred interests with characteristic verve. A multiple Eclipse Award winner as both outstanding owner and breeder, Stronach has raced four Breeders' Cup winners bred by his Adena Springs operation, which has bases in Canada, Florida, and Kentucky. Ghostzapper, the 2004 Horse of the Year after winning the Breeders' Cup Classic, was sired by Awesome Again, who carried Stronach's colors to victory in the 1998 Breeders' Cup. He also is chairman of racetrack company Magna Entertainment Corp.

farther back and 4¼ lengths in front of Lady Joanne in fourth. Indian Vale finished ninth, and Lear's Princess was tenth.

For Brown, a Breeders' Cup victory was a perfect end to a thrilling week. "It's really been exciting," Brown said. "I think too much has been made of Bobby not being here because he has full trust and confidence in all of his assistants to get the job done when he's not around. He basically gives us the keys to the car and tells us to drive, and I can't thank him enough for that opportunity."

Asked one more time whether there was any hesitation before putting up such a large chunk of money to get Ginger Punch into the race, Stronach grinned.

"In hindsight, no," he said with a chuckle, content in the knowledge that his $180,000 gamble had more than paid off. It also had purchased a championship. Ginger Punch subsequently was voted North America's champion older female. Ginger Punch remained in training in 2008 and won Churchill's Louisville Handicap (G2) and Belmont's Ogden Phipps Handicap (G1) to raise her career earnings above $2.5-million.—*Steve Bailey*

NINTH RACE
Monmouth Park
October 27, 2007

1⅛ miles, dirt. 24th running of the Emirates Airline Breeders' Cup Distaff (G1). Purse $2-million guaranteed. Fillies and mares three years old and upward. Weights (Northern Hemisphere): Three-year-olds, 119 lbs. Older, 123 lbs. (Southern Hemisphere): Three-year-olds, 114 lbs. Older, 123 lbs. Track record: Spend a Buck, 1:46.80, August 17, 1985.

Value of race: $2,070,160. Value to winner: $1,220,400; second: $452,000; third: $226,000; fourth: $115,260; fifth: $56,500. Mutuel Pool $3,751,116.

Horse	Wt.	M/Eqt	PP	St.	¼	½	¾	Str.	Fin.	Jockey	Odds $1
Ginger Punch, 4, f.	123	LA	4	6	5 1½	3 hd	1 hd	2 3	1 nk	R. Bejarano	4.50
Hystericalady, 4, f.	123	LAc	12	11	2 hd	2 1	3 1½	1 hd	2 nk	E. Castro	9.20
Octave, 3, f.	119	LAc	8	10	12	12	10 hd	3 2	3 4¼	G. Gomez	7.80
Lady Joanne, 3, f.	119	Lf	5	1	4 hd	4 hd	4½	4 1½	4 2	C. Borel	6.90
Unbridled Belle, 4, f.	123	LAbc	11	12	10 1	10 hd	5 1	5 4	5 7¾	R. Dominguez	6.20
Balance, 4, f.	123	LAb	1	2	6 hd	7½	7 2½	7 hd	6 2¼	V. Espinoza	12.10
Tough Tiz's Sis, 3, f.	119	LAb	3	4	11 4	11 4	8 hd	8 hd	7 4	M. Smith	22.90
Bear Now, 3, f.	119	LA	6	3	1½	1 1	2 hd	6½	8 1¾	J. Baird	13.00
Indian Vale, 5, m.	123	LAc	10	7	3 hd	5 1½	6 1	9 2½	9 ½	J. Velazquez	8.30
Lear's Princess, 3, f.	119	LAbc	7	8	8 hd	9½	12	10 4	10 25¼	E. Coa	4.50*
Teammate, 4, f.	123	L	9	9	9 1½	8½	11 2	11 hd	11 4¼	C. Velasquez	22.40
Prop Me Up, 5, m.	123	LAb	2	5	7½	6 hd	9 1	12	12	J. Bravo	30.00

L=Salix; LA=Salix and adjunct bleeder medication; c=mud calks; f=front bandages; b=blinkers.

OFF AT 4:07. Start: Good for all. Weather: Showery. Track: Sloppy (sealed).
Time: :22.68, :46.64, 1:11.11, 1:36.35, 1:50.11.

$2 Mutuel Prices:	4—GINGER PUNCH	11.00	6.20	4.40
	12—HYSTERICALADY		9.60	7.20
	8—OCTAVE			5.00

$2 EXACTA 4-12 PAID $141.60 $1 TRIFECTA 4-12-8 PAID $534.70
$1 SUPERFECTA 4-12-8-5 PAID $3,418.50 $1 PICK THREE 2-8-4 PAID $241.00

Ch. f., by Awesome Again—Nappelon, by Bold Revenue. Trainer: Robert Frankel. Owner: Stronach Stables. Bred by Adena Springs (Fla.).

GINGER PUNCH settled just off the pace while saving ground, moved through on the rail to challenge on the far turn, battled heads apart inside HYSTERICALADY leaving the quarter pole, was bumped off stride by that one inside the furlong pole, and then fought back gamely under left-handed urging to prevail. HYSTERICALADY pressed the pace, bumped the winner in midstretch, and then yielded grudgingly. OCTAVE, outrun for six furlongs, closed the gap on the turn, split rivals in upper stretch, and then closed steadily from the outside. LADY JOANNE raced just off the pace between horses into upper stretch and lacked a strong closing bid. UNBRIDLED BELLE bobbled a few strides away from the gate, steadied while lacking room for a half-mile, made a sharp move to reach contention on the far turn but could not sustain her bid. BALANCE saved ground and lacked the needed response. TOUGH TIZ'S SIS raced well back for six furlongs and passed mostly tiring horses. BEAR NOW set the pace to the far turn and steadily tired thereafter. INDIAN VALE stalked the pace on the backstretch and faded in the stretch. LEAR'S PRINCESS bumped with TEAMMATE on the first turn, steadied in traffic at the five-eighths pole, and was never close thereafter. TEAMMATE was never a factor. PROP ME UP failed to mount a serious rally. After a stewards' inquiry into the stretch run, there was no change in the order of finish.

2007 Filly and Mare Sprint: Mayfield pays off

Venerable racing destinations such as Keeneland Race Course and Saratoga Race Course were foreign territory for entertainment industry caterer Nick Mestrandrea just a few years ago. But then the company of the Syosset, New York, native and Burbank, California, resident was hired to provide meals for the cast and crew of the 2003 movie *Seabiscuit* during location filming. The logistics were likely to prove difficult, but Mestrandrea took the job despite his initial hesitation.

Little did Mestrandrea know how working behind the scenes on a movie portraying the champion Thoroughbred of the Great Depression era would lay the foundation for a life-changing journey. Mestrandrea was introduced to Racing Hall of Fame jockey Gary Stevens, who portrayed rider George Woolf in the film. Stevens, along with several other jockeys and agents on the movie set, conversed with Mestrandrea during meal breaks, urging him to visit the racetrack and start enjoying the experience. Eventually, Mestrandrea and partners Jim Perry and Mark Gorman—brought together by trainer Doug O'Neill—claimed Court Shenanigans in 2004. When the horse won his first start for his new owners, a total of 118 people crammed into the Hollywood Park winner's circle for the photo.

It was a precursor of bigger triumphs. On October 26, the trio along with partner Mark Verge and a host of family, friends, and guests ran shrieking through the rain to Monmouth Park's winner's circle in raucous celebration after their six-year-old mare Mayfield charged six wide in an exhilarating stretch drive to best rail-skimming longshot Miraculous Miss by a half-length in the inaugural running of the $1,030,500 Breeders' Cup Filly and Mare Sprint. Mayfield, at 8-to-1, ran six furlongs in 1:09.85 on a sealed, sloppy track.

O'Neill claimed Mayfield for $50,000 out of a one-mile turf race on January 16, 2006, at Santa Anita Park and dropped her in for a $40,000 tag four weeks later. "We were lucky we didn't lose her then," O'Neill said. "[Trainer] Josie Carroll, who had her before, had her in miraculous condition. She had great pedigree. I've got some friends that help me out watching morning workouts, and they said she was training really well. We claim so many kinds of horses, and so many of them don't turn out. This just happened to be the one that turned the right way."

The first running of the Breeders' Cup Filly and Mare Sprint was the third career Breeders' Cup victory for O'Neill, and the first for jockey Elvis Trujillo, who rode the Elusive Quality mare to a nose decision over Baroness Thatcher in the Ballerina Stakes (G1) on August 26 at Saratoga.

Previously undefeated Grade 3 winner La Traviata, the 2.10-to-1 favorite, and two-time Grade 1 winner Dream Rush, the 3.10-to-1 second choice, both got off to quick starts in the sloppy going. Dream Rush scorched an opening half-mile with fractions of :21.29 and :44.19, with La Traviata tracking her. La Traviata stopped first, but Dream Rush and jockey Eibar Coa gamely battled on while a bevy of closers took dead aim. While Mayfield and Trujillo took the outside route, jockey Jeremy Rose had 43.50-to-1 longshot Miraculous Miss on the rail. The four-year-old Mr. Greeley filly closed strongly inside the furlong pole, but Mayfield was moving fastest of all to secure the victory and an Eclipse Award as champion female sprinter.—*Tom De Martini*

2007 Juvenile Turf: The Now Horse

It was wait, wait, wait for Nownownow in the inaugural $916,000 Breeders' Cup Juvenile Turf on October 26 at Monmouth Park. While Prussian slugged it out on the front end and ultimately faded to tenth, jockey Julien Leparoux patiently waited at the back of the 12-horse field with 12.60-to-1 Nownownow to make his run in the final quarter of the one-mile turf race for two-year-olds.

The strategy paid off with a stunning half-length victory over lukewarm 2.80-to-1 favorite Achill Island (Ire). It was another 1¾ lengths back to 15.10-to-1 Cannonball in third. Unrelenting rain had earned the Monmouth turf course a rating of yielding, but it caused no hardship for Nownownow, a son of freshman sire Whywhywhy. He covered the mile in 1:40.48.

"I moved at the quarter pole, and I knew I was going to get it in the stretch," said Leparoux, a 24-year-old from Senlis, France, who relocated to the United States in 2003 and enjoyed extensive success with trainer Patrick Biancone. "The turf is not too deep; it's just wet.

"Patrick [Biancone] told me to make him relax and take him back a little," said Leparoux, who won the Eclipse Award as outstanding apprentice jockey in 2006. "He was relaxing when I came outside in the straight, and he took off."

Biancone's shadow clearly hung over the victory despite his absence from post-race festivities. On October 21, he had transferred the colt, one of his seven Breeders' Cup entrants, and all his East Coast horses into the hands of his assistant, Francois Parisel. Biancone relinquished all the horses in his care in advance of serving a negotiated six-month suspension, which was to begin on November 1, for violations of Kentucky's horse racing drug rules.

Biancone ignited further controversy when

he was spotted on Monmouth's backstretch on October 25, was reminded by racing commission officials of his trainer-transfer agreement, and was asked to leave. He also had been at Parisel's barn the previous day, although he referred all questions to the trainer of record.

Fabien Ouaki, who owns the Tati clothing stores and races as the Fab Oak Stable, said his longtime friend Biancone would not share in the Breeders' Cup first-place purse of $540,000.

Although he has enjoyed success racing in Europe, Ouaki now has committed himself to race in the United States. "I am a breeder for 20 years, and every year I sell my best horses to America," Ouaki said. "So after 15 years, I tried to sell a horse [privately] whose name is Bonapartiste (Fr), [but he did not sell]. So I send it to [trainer] Ron McAnally, [and he] was a very successful horse in California. So I launched an operation there, and I don't [race] in France." Bonapartiste would go on to win the Del Mar Handicap (G2) in 1998.

Nownownow provided a first Breeders' Cup trophy not only for his owner-breeder but also for Leparoux, whose late father, Robert, was a jockey and assistant trainer in France. Parisel is another transplanted native of France, arriving in 1979.

When Nownownow got up in the final 50 yards, he snatched victory from the Irish-bred Achill Island, the Sadler's Wells colt also had made a come-from-behind bid with a five-wide move in the final sixteenth of a mile. "He ran a stormer," said Aidan O'Brien, Achill Island's trainer. "We're delighted. He came to win this race, and just got nabbed on the line."—*Carol Hodes*

2007 Dirt Mile: Corinthian rules

On the afternoon of the first two-day Breeders' Cup World Championships on October 26, just as persistent rain appeared to have turned form on its head, the inaugural Breeders' Cup Dirt Mile dished up a race that made perfect sense.

Corinthian prevailed as the 3.70-to-1 second betting choice in the Dirt Mile, the final race on the inaugural Friday program. Race favorite Discreet Cat finished third, although bettors at Monmouth Park and elsewhere were basing his 3-to-2 odds much more on what he had been rather than the horse that he had become.

Centennial Farms' Corinthian was the Dirt Mile's only 2007 Grade 1 winner at a mile, after his victory in the Metropolitan Handicap (G1) on May 28, and the Pulpit colt out of the Easy Goer mare Multiply dramatically proved his superiority with a 6½-length victory under Kent Desormeaux in the $916,000 Breeders' Cup Dirt Mile.

Gottcha Gold, sent off at 7.30-to-1 despite an obvious affinity for the Monmouth main track, finished second, 8¼ lengths ahead of Discreet Cat. Wanderin Boy, the one horse in the race with a proven liking for the slop, finished fourth, a head farther back, after weakening in the final furlong.

The one big question about Corinthian (in addition to his frequently difficult temperament) was his ability to handle a sloppy track. Monmouth's track had become wet two days before the Dirt Mile, so trainer Jimmy Jerkens had gotten a reading on how he handled a wet track the day before the race, after shipping from his Belmont Park base.

"Down here, we galloped him and gave him a good, strong blowout down the backstretch [on October 25], and he seemed to handle it really good," Jerkens said. "I always thought the mare being by Easy Goer, I always thought they excelled in the slop. Looking at the pedigrees, I thought there was no problem there. And with Pulpit, they seemed like they could do anything."

Corinthian certainly took to the slop and the distance in his final race before retiring to Antony Beck's Gainesway Farm in Lexington. Corinthian ran the one mile and 70 yards in 1:39.06, slightly off Cable Boy's 1:38.78 track record, which was set in May.

While the Monmouth track accommodates mile races, Breeders' Cup officials had feared that a full field of 14 would lead to a potentially dangerous cavalry charge to the clubhouse turn, so they extended the distance to a mile and 70 yards, a common distance for mile tracks with a short run into the turn.

As it turned out, only nine runners of varying accomplishment were entered for the Dirt Mile, and that number dropped to eight when trainer Bill Mott scratched Zayat Stables' Forefathers in favor of a run in the TVG Breeders' Cup Sprint (G1) the following day.

Corinthian was a well-deserved second betting choice, although his record was spotty after the Met Mile. "After the Met Mile, we thought he could do anything. It didn't work out," the trainer said of a well-beaten sixth-place finish in the Suburban Handicap (G1) and a fourth in the Woodward. "He goes in and out of form. It's just the kind of horse he is."

Although Corinthian has good speed, Desormeaux restrained him as his opponents flew away from the starting gate. On a track that had been producing startlingly fast early fractions, Gottcha Gold completed the first quarter-mile in :22.58 and the half in :45.94. Corinthian and Desormeaux moved up on the backstretch, with Discreet Cat outside them, and advanced toward the lead on the final turn. Entering the stretch, Corinthian attacked Gottcha Gold under strong handling and quickly opened a 2½-length advantage at the furlong pole.—*Don Clippinger*

RACING
Review of 2007 Racing Season

by Don Clippinger

Opera had its three tenors—Jose Carreras, Placido Domingo, and the late Luciano Pavarotti—and North American Thoroughbred racing in 2007 had its three three-year-olds. Actually, the sport had more than three—especially if the classic-winning filly Rags to Riches is thrown into the mix—but Curlin, Street Sense, and Hard Spun grabbed most of the headlines through much of the year. With a weak handicap division, Curlin eventually rose to the top of the sport in 2007, and he remained there with a dominant victory in the '08 Emirates Airline Dubai World Cup (UAE-G1).

Before Curlin ever made a start, Street Sense emerged from his championship juvenile season to accomplish something that had never before been achieved. James Tafel's homebred Street Cry (Ire) colt was attempting to become the first Bessemer Trust Breeders' Cup Juvenile (G1) victor to win the Kentucky Derby (G1). Carl Nafzger, who had trained Unbridled to Derby and Breeders' Cup Classic (G1) victories in 1990, took an unconventional first step toward the first Saturday in May by running Street Sense in the Tampa Bay Derby (G3) on March 17. Street Sense won, but only by a nostril over Todd Pletcher-trained Any Given Saturday.

The champion was perceived as vulnerable, and a raft of challengers prepared to take him on in Kentucky. Even before the Tampa Bay race, Hard Spun had kept alive his unbeaten record by winning Fair Grounds's LeComte Stakes (G3) in January by 6½ lengths, with Teuflesberg finishing third. When they next met, Teuflesberg turned the tables by winning the Southwest Stakes in February at Oaklawn Park, while Hard Spun checked in fourth as the 1-to-2 favorite.

With the talented maiden winner Curlin targeting the Rebel Stakes (G3) on March 17 at Oaklawn—he would win by 5¼ lengths—trainer Larry Jones steered Hard Spun toward Turfway Park's Polytrack and the Lane's End Stakes (G2) on March 24, which he won by 3¼ lengths.

In South Florida, Scat Daddy was Gulfstream Park's top Derby prospect, with victories in the Fountain of Youth Stakes (G2) and the Florida Derby (G1), both in March. Out West, maiden Tiago, a half brother to Derby winner Giacomo, ran a poor seventh to Great Hunter in the Robert B. Lewis Stakes (G2) at Santa Anita Park in March, but experience and added distance helped him to a half-length victory in the Santa Anita Derby (G1) on April 7.

Nafzger targeted the Toyota Blue Grass Stakes (G1) on April 14, and Street Sense was overtaken by 8-to-1 Dominican, who would not win another race in 2007. On the same afternoon, Curlin proved he was a serious contender with a 10½-length romp in the Arkansas Derby (G2). Thus was the stage set for a memorable Derby on May 5 at Churchill Downs, with Street Sense favored at 4.90-to-1, Curlin at 5-to-1, and Hard Spun at 10-to-1. Nafzger had Street Sense tuned precisely, and jockey Calvin Borel took the rail route to a 2¼-length victory over Hard Spun, while Curlin checked in third, eight lengths behind the winner.

The three three-year-olds then decamped for Baltimore, where they fired up again for the Preakness Stakes (G1) on May 19. The trifecta box still paid off, but the numbers were scrambled. Curlin won in the last jump over Street Sense, with Hard Spun a tenacious third. Street Sense then bowed out of the Triple Crown chase, and in the June 9 Belmont Stakes (G1) Rags to Riches nailed Curlin on the money, with Tiago third and Hard Spun fourth.

Saratoga Race Course's Jim Dandy Stakes (G2) on July 29 and Monmouth Park's Haskell Invitational Handicap (G1) on August 5 traditionally open the post-classics season, and Street Sense prepped for the Travers Stakes (G1) with a victory in the Jim Dandy, while Any Given Saturday notched a dominant score in the Haskell. Hard Spun finished second, and Curlin, short of full condition but favored at 9-to-10, finished third.

Hard Spun, a Danzig colt bred in Pennsylvania by Michael Moran and the Brushwood Stable of his mother, Betty Moran, dropped back in distance and collected his first Grade 1 victory in the King's Bishop Stakes on August 25 at Saratoga, where Street Sense defeated a game Grasshopper in the Travers on the same card. After those races, all the leading three-year-olds targeted the Breeders' Cup Classic Powered by Dodge, to be held at Monmouth on October 25. Any Given Saturday struck first, winning the Brooklyn Handicap (G2) against an undistinguished group of older horses at 0.15-to-1 odds on September 22. A week later, Hard Spun defeated Street Sense in the Kentucky Cup Classic Stakes (G2) on Turfway's Polytrack.

Curlin, clearly coming to his best form, defeated the year's best older males in the Jockey Club Gold Cup Stakes (G1) on September 30 and was awesome in winning the Breeders' Cup Clas-

sic, in which the tenacious Hard Spun finished second and Street Sense was fourth on a very sloppy track. Street Sense, Hard Spun, and Any Given Saturday were retired to Darley in Lexington, while Curlin collected his Horse of the Year statuette and launched an effort to become North America's all-time leading earner in 2008.

Two-Year-Old Males

The competition among juveniles usually is a case of East versus West, but the West Coast had little to offer in the 2007 campaign to the Breeders' Cup Juvenile or the Eclipse Award. The East, however, was a hotbed of two-year-old activity. The championship season effectively begins at Saratoga, and first out of the gate was Ready's Image, a Keeneland Race Course winner who won Belmont Park's Tremont Stakes on July 1 before taking the Sanford Stakes (G2) in late July at Saratoga. His mastery lasted only a few weeks, until Majestic Warrior defeated him by 2¼ lengths in the Hopeful Stakes (G1) on September 3, Saratoga's centerpiece race for two-year-old males.

Trainer Nick Zito likes to start his two-year-olds slowly and allow them to build their confidence in soft company, away from the rigors of the major stakes races. Thus, he sent out Robert LaPenta's War Pass to win a Saratoga maiden race in late July and an optional claiming race four weeks later.

As the action returned to Belmont, Charles Fipke's homebred Tale of Ekati took the Futurity Stakes (G2) on September 15, defeating Kodiak Kowboy by a length. While trainer Barclay Tagg decided to train Tale of Ekati up to the Breeders' Cup Juvenile, most other top juveniles headed into the Champagne Stakes (G1) on October 6. Majestic Warrior was favored at 1.05-to-1, but front-running War Pass took the lead and never looked back, easily fending off Pyro to win the mile race in 1:36. Neither Majestic Warrior (sixth) nor Ready's Image (eighth) started again in 2007. Even with the ranks of top two-year-old diminished, War Pass faced ten opponents in the Breeders' Cup Juvenile on a sloppy Monmouth track and won by 4¾ lengths over Pyro to earn the championship.

Two-Year-Old Fillies

The leading two-year-old fillies of 2007 were rising stars with brief résumés; the most starts for any of the top contenders was four. The division had a reasonable distribution of horses between East and West, but trainer Bob Baffert fled an inconsistent Polytrack surface at Del Mar and headed to Saratoga and its rich juvenile races. He struck first when More Happy won the Adirondack Stakes (G2) on August 15. Several races earlier that month, Patrick Biancone sent out Irish Smoke for a maiden victory. They met in Saratoga's Spinaway Stakes (G1) on September 2, with Irish Smoke winning by 3¼ lengths over A to the Croft.

Toward the end of the Saratoga season, Baffert sent out Patti and Hal Earnhardt's homebred Indian Blessing for an effortless maiden victory, and he brought her back in a Grade 1 race, Belmont's Frizette Stakes on October 6. The huge step up in class proved no deterrent, and the Indian Charlie filly won by 4½ lengths. Taking a slightly different path to Monmouth was trainer Larry Jones, who gave Brereton Jones's Proud Spell two easy races in Delaware before shipping to New York, where the Proud Citizen filly easily won Belmont's Matron Stakes (G2) on September 15. They met again in the Grey Goose Breeders' Cup Juvenile Fillies (G1), in which Indian Blessing set all the pace and won by 3½ lengths, and Indian Blessing was voted champion juvenile filly at year-end.

Three-Year-Old Fillies

The division featured only the third filly to win the Belmont Stakes, but she was by no means the only star in a group almost as deep as their male counterparts. Still, the star of the year was Rags to Riches, who never wore any rags. By A.P. Indy and out of the dam of 2006 Belmont winner Jazil, Michael Tabor's and Derrick Smith's filly went from maiden winner on January 7 to Grade 1 winner in the Las Virgenes Stakes (G1) on February 10 at Santa Anita. For trainer Pletcher, she then waltzed through the Santa Anita (G1) and Kentucky (G1) Oaks before her historic victory in the Belmont. Physical problems led to her only career defeat, in the Gazelle Stakes (G1) in September, and she subsequently was retired and bred to Giant's Causeway.

Rags to Riches had plenty of high-class company in Pletcher's barn. Octave finished second in the May 4 Kentucky Oaks to her stablemate and then won the June 30 Mother Goose Stakes (G1) and July 21 Coaching Club American Oaks (G1), both by a half-length. She did not win again for the remainder of the year although she ran a strong third in the Emirates Airline Breeders' Cup Distaff (G1). In eight 2007 starts, she finished no worse than third.

Another Pletcher standout was Panty Raid, who jumped from a Keeneland allowance win on Polytrack on April 13 to a victory in the Black-Eyed Susan Stakes (G2) on the dirt at Pimlico Race Course on May 18, and then triumphed on grass in the American Oaks Invitational Stakes (G1) on July 7 at Hollywood Park. After finish-

ing fifth in the August 18 Alabama Stakes (G1), she won Keeneland's Juddmonte Spinster Stakes (G1) on October 7.

Nafzger trains only a handful of horses each year for longtime clients, and residing in his stable with Street Sense was Lady Joanne, who performed well in top company in both the Midwest and New York. In early June, she won Churchill's Dogwood Stakes (G3), finished second in the Mother Goose, won the restricted Banshee Breeze Stakes (named for a Nafzger-trained champion) at Saratoga, and then collected a Grade 1 victory in the Alabama. She was second to Panty Raid in the Spinster and fourth in the Breeders' Cup Distaff. Rags to Riches was voted champion three-year-old filly.

Older Male

The season of 2006 spilled over into '07, with Invasor (Arg), the reigning North American Horse of the Year, taking the Donn Handicap (G1) on February 3 and then triumphing in the Dubai World Cup on March 31. But he never started again, and no one picked up his mantle. Lawyer Ron, a Triple Crown hopeful in 2006, put everything together for Pletcher for a few races, and they were enough to collect a championship title. In the spring, he won the Oaklawn Handicap (G2), and he owned Saratoga with runaway victories in the Whitney Handicap (G1) on July 28 and Woodward Stakes (G1) on September 1. But he was no match for Curlin in the Jockey Club Gold Cup and Breeders' Cup Classic.

Lava Man's six-year-old season started out with victories in the Sunshine Millions San Manuel Indian Bingo and Casino Turf Stakes on January 27 and the Santa Anita Handicap (G1) on March 3. After a wasted trip to Dubai, he won the Hollywood Gold Cup Stakes (G1) on June 30 for a third time but was not a factor in two subsequent graded stakes starts. Student Council rewarded a new owner, Millennium Farms, with back-to-back victories in the Pacific Classic Stakes (G1) on August 19 and Hawthorne Gold Cup Handicap (G2) on September 29 before an unproductive trip to the Japan Cup Dirt (Jpn-G1) in November.

Older Female

Unlike their male counterparts, this division was highly talented and competitive. Frank Stronach's Ginger Punch collected the Eclipse Award with three Grade 1 victories, culminating in the Breeders' Cup Distaff. But right beside her on the Monmouth finish line, beaten a neck, was Hystericalady, who won Churchill's Humana Distaff Stakes (G1) in the spring and Monmouth's Molly Pitcher Handicap (G2) in the summer.

Emerging from the West for the Breeders' Cup was undefeated Nashoba's Key, who prospered on both synthetic surfaces and turf. Before finishing fourth to Lahudood (GB) in the Emirates Airline Breeders' Cup Filly and Mare Turf (G1), she won Hollywood's Vanity Invitational Handicap (G1) in July and Del Mar's Clement L. Hirsch Handicap (G2) in August on synthetic surfaces and the Yellow Ribbon Stakes (G1) on turf at Oak Tree at Santa Anita in September.

Turf Divisions

Although both male and female divisions contained some talented runners, neither could be described as vintage. English Channel came back from a wasted trip to Dubai to win three Grade 1 races, culminating with an easy victory in the John Deere Breeders' Cup Turf (G1) and an Eclipse Award as best turf male. After Market was a strong factor on the West Coast, with four consecutive graded victories, two of them Grade 1. Also in California, durable Daytona (Ire) scored back-to-back wins in the Oak Tree (G2) and Hollywood (G1) Derbys at the end of the season.

Among the females, Lahudood collected the Eclipse Award with back-to-back Grade 1 victories. One of the most intriguing female turf specialists was Bettina Jenney's Mrs. Lindsay, who was second in the Prix de Diane Hermes (Fr-G1) (French Oaks) in June before winning the Prix Vermeille Lucien Barriere (Fr-G1) in September and the E. P. Taylor Stakes (Can-G1) in October at Woodbine.

Sprint Divisions

Both sprint divisions were competitive without being top shelf. Midnight Lute had two Grade 1 victories, and his score in the TVG Breeders' Cup Sprint (G1) was enough to earn him an Eclipse Award. Maryfield's two end-of-season victories, in the Ballerina Stakes (G1) and the Breeders' Cup Filly and Mare Sprint, earned her the first-ever female sprint title. Also noteworthy was three-year-old Dream Rush, who collected Grade 1 victories in the Prioress and Test Stakes but finished fifth in the Breeders' Cup contest.

Steeplechaser

McDynamo closed out his illustrious career with his fifth score in the Breeders' Cup Steeplechase Stakes (which reverted to its original name, the Grand National Hurdle Stakes, in 2007), but the three-time Eclipse winner was literally overtaken by Sonny Via's Good Night Shirt, who clinched a first Eclipse Award for trainer Jack Fisher with a clear victory in the Marion duPont Scott Colonial Cup Hurdle Stakes.

Richest North American Stakes Races of 2007

Race (Grade)	Purse	Track	Distance (Miles)	Winner	Value to Winner
Breeders' Cup Classic Powered by Dodge (G1)	$4,580,000	Monmouth Park	1¼	Curlin	$2,700,000
John Deere Breeders' Cup Turf (G1)	2,748,000	Monmouth Park	1½T	English Channel	1,620,000
NetJets Breeders' Cup Mile (G1)	2,409,080	Monmouth Park	1T	Kip Deville	1,420,200
Kentucky Derby Presented by Yum! Brands (G1)	2,210,000	Churchill Downs	1¼	Street Sense	1,450,000
Pattison Canadian International S. (Can-G1)	2,073,699	Woodbine	1½T	Cloudy's Knight	1,242,480
Emirates Airline Breeders' Cup Distaff (G1)	2,070,160	Monmouth Park	1⅛	Ginger Punch	1,220,400
Emirates Airline Breeders' Cup Filly and Mare Turf (G1)	1,951,080	Monmouth Park	1⅜T	Lahudood (GB)	1,150,200
Bessemer Trust Breeders' Cup Juvenile (G1)	1,832,000	Monmouth Park	1 1/16	War Pass	1,080,000
Breeders' Cup Juvenile Fillies (G1)	1,832,000	Monmouth Park	1 1/16	Indian Blessing	1,080,000
TVG Breeders' Cup Sprint (G1)	1,832,000	Monmouth Park	6f	Midnight Lute	1,080,000
Pacific Classic S. (G1)	1,120,000	Del Mar	1¼AW	Student Council	600,000
Haskell Invitational S. (G1)	1,060,000	Monmouth Park	1⅛	Any Given Saturday	600,000
E. P. Taylor S. (Can-G1)	1,052,484	Woodbine	1¼T	Mrs. Lindsay	621,240
Breeders' Cup Filly & Mare Sprint	1,030,500	Monmouth Park	6f	Maryfield	607,500
Delaware H. (G2)	1,000,900	Delaware Park	1¼	Unbridled Belle	600,000
Arkansas Derby (G2)	1,000,000	Oaklawn Park	1⅛	Curlin	600,000
Arlington Million S. (G1)	1,000,000	Arlington Park	1¼T	Jambalaya	594,000
Belmont S. (G1)	1,000,000	Belmont Park	1½	Rags to Riches	600,000
Boyd Gaming's Delta Jackpot S. (G3)	1,000,000	Delta Downs	1 1/16	dh-Turf War dh-Z Humor	400,000
CashCall Mile Invitational S. (G2)	1,000,000	Hollywood Park	1T	Lady of Venice (Fr)	525,000
Florida Derby (G1)	1,000,000	Gulfstream Park	1⅛	Scat Daddy	600,000
Pennsylvania Derby (G2)	1,000,000	Philadelphia Park	1⅛	Timber Reserve	544,000
Preakness S. (G1)	1,000,000	Pimlico	1 3/16	Curlin	600,000
Santa Anita H. (G1)	1,000,000	Santa Anita Park	1¼	Lava Man	600,000
Sunshine Millions Classic S.	1,000,000	Gulfstream Park	1⅛	McCann's Mojave	550,000
Travers S. (G1)	1,000,000	Saratoga	1¼	Street Sense	600,000
Virginia Derby (G2)	1,000,000	Colonial Downs	1¼T	Red Giant	600,000
Woodbine Mile S. (Can-G1)	973,893	Woodbine	1T	Shakespeare	582,240
Queen's Plate S.	936,022	Woodbine	1¼AW	Mike Fox	560,940
Breeders' Cup Dirt Mile	916,000	Monmouth Park	1m 70y	Corinthian	540,000
Breeders' Cup Juvenile Turf	916,000	Monmouth Park	1T	Nownownow	540,000
Stephen Foster H. (G1)	829,500	Churchill Downs	1⅛	Flashy Bull	498,863
Whitney H. (G1)	810,000	Saratoga	1⅛	Lawyer Ron	450,000
Jockey Club Gold Cup S. (G1)	765,000	Belmont Park	1¼	Curlin	450,000
CashCall Futurity (G1)	753,000	Hollywood Park	1 1/16 AW	Into Mischief	403,000
American Oaks Invitational S. (G1)	750,000	Hollywood Park	1¼T	Panty Raid	450,000
Beverly D. S. (G1)	750,000	Arlington Park	1 3/16 T	Royal Highness (Ger)	445,500
Colonial Turf Cup S. (G3)	750,000	Colonial Downs	1 3/16 T	Summer Doldrums	450,000
Fitz Dixon Cotillion H. (G2)	750,000	Philadelphia Park	1 1/16	Bear Now	426,000
Hollywood Gold Cup S. (G1)	750,000	Hollywood Park	1¼AW	Lava Man	450,000
Santa Anita Derby (G1)	750,000	Santa Anita Park	1⅛	Tiago	450,000
Toyota Blue Grass S. (G1)	750,000	Keeneland	1⅛AW	Dominican	465,000
West Virginia Derby (G3)	750,000	Mountaineer	1⅛	Zanjero	450,000
Wood Memorial S. (G1)	750,000	Aqueduct	1⅛	Nobiz Like Shobiz	450,000
United Nations S. (G1)	742,500	Monmouth Park	1⅜T	English Channel	450,000
Northern Dancer Breeders' Cup Turf S. (Can-G2)	666,013	Woodbine	1½T	Sky Conqueror	400,638
Shadwell Turf Mile S. (G1)	648,000	Keeneland	1T	Purim	372,000
Beldame S. (G1)	612,000	Belmont Park	1⅛	Unbridled Belle	360,000
Joe Hirsch Turf Classic Invitational S. (G1)	612,000	Belmont Park	1½T	English Channel	360,000
Alabama S. (G1)	600,000	Saratoga	1¼	Lady Joanne	360,000
Flower Bowl Invitational S. (G1)	600,000	Belmont Park	1¼T	Lahudood (GB)	360,000
Metropolitan H. (G1)	600,000	Belmont Park	1	Corinthian	360,000
WinStar Derby	600,000	Sunland Park	1⅛	Song of Navarone	300,000
Louisiana Derby (G2)	594,000	Fair Grounds	1 1/16	Circular Quay	360,000
Kentucky Oaks (G1)	589,200	Churchill Downs	1⅛	Rags to Riches	332,428

Race (Grade)	Purse	Track	Distance (Miles)	Winner	Value to Winner
Woodford Reserve Turf Classic S. (G1)	$561,000	Churchill Downs	$1\frac{1}{8}$T	Sky Conqueror	$330,430
Lane's End Breeders' Futurity (G1)	560,000	Keeneland	$1\frac{1}{16}$AW	Wicked Style	310,000
Clark H. (G2)	554,000	Churchill Downs	$1\frac{1}{8}$	A. P. Arrow	329,741
Juddmonte Spinster S. (G1)	540,000	Keeneland	$1\frac{1}{8}$AW	Panty Raid	310,000
Diana S. (G1)	520,000	Saratoga	$1\frac{1}{8}$T	My Typhoon (Ire)	300,000
Goodwood S. (G1)	520,000	Oak Tree at Santa Anita	$1\frac{1}{8}$AW	Tiago	300,000
Nearctic S. (Can-G2)	518,942	Woodbine	6fT	Heros Reward	310,620
Super Derby (G2)	515,000	Louisiana Downs	$1\frac{1}{8}$	Going Ballistic	275,000
Indiana Derby (G2)	510,600	Hoosier Park	$1\frac{1}{16}$	Zanjero	294,360
Delaware Oaks (G2)	505,600	Delaware Park	$1\frac{1}{16}$	Moon Catcher	305,000
Kent Breeders' Cup S. (G3)	501,200	Delaware Park	$1\frac{1}{8}$T	Nobiz Like Shobiz	300,000
Apple Blossom H. (G1)	500,000	Oaklawn Park	$1\frac{1}{16}$	Ermine	300,000
Ashland S. (G1)	500,000	Keeneland	$1\frac{1}{16}$AW	Christmas Kid	310,000
Darley Alcibiades S. (G1)	500,000	Keeneland	$1\frac{1}{16}$AW	Country Star	310,000
Donn H. (G1)	500,000	Gulfstream Park	$1\frac{1}{8}$	Invasor (Arg)	300,000
Hawthorne Gold Cup H. (G2)	500,000	Hawthorne	$1\frac{1}{4}$	Student Council	300,000
Hollywood Derby (G1)	500,000	Hollywood Park	$1\frac{1}{4}$T	Daytona (Ire)	300,000
Illinois Derby (G2)	500,000	Hawthorne	$1\frac{1}{8}$	Cowtown Cat	300,000
Jim Dandy S. (G2)	500,000	Saratoga	$1\frac{1}{8}$	Street Sense	300,000
Lane's End S. (G2)	500,000	Turfway Park	$1\frac{1}{8}$AW	Hard Spun	300,000
Man o' War S. (G1)	500,000	Belmont Park	$1\frac{3}{8}$T	Doctor Dino (Fr)	300,000
Massachusetts H.	500,000	Suffolk Downs	$1\frac{1}{8}$	Brass Hat	300,000
Matriarch S. (G1)	500,000	Hollywood Park	1T	Precious Kitten	300,000
Mervin H. Muniz Jr. Memorial H. (G2)	500,000	Fair Grounds	$1\frac{1}{8}$T	Einstein (Brz)	300,000
Oaklawn H. (G2)	500,000	Oaklawn Park	$1\frac{1}{8}$	Lawyer Ron	300,000
Princess Rooney H. (G1)	500,000	Calder	6f	River's Prayer	285,200
Queen Elizabeth II Challenge Cup S. (G1)	500,000	Keeneland	$1\frac{1}{8}$T	Bit of Whimsy	310,000
Smile Sprint H. (G2)	500,000	Calder	6f	Mach Ride	303,800
Sunshine Millions Distaff S.	500,000	Santa Anita Park	$1\frac{1}{16}$	Joint Effort	275,000
Sunshine Millions Filly and Mare Turf S.	500,000	Gulfstream Park	$1\frac{1}{8}$T	Miss Shop	275,000
Sunshine Millions San Manuel Indian Bingo and Casino Turf S.	500,000	Santa Anita Park	$1\frac{1}{8}$T	Lava Man	275,000
Sword Dancer Invitational S. (G1)	500,000	Saratoga	$1\frac{1}{2}$T	Grand Couturier (GB)	300,000
Woodward S. (G1)	500,000	Saratoga	$1\frac{1}{8}$	Lawyer Ron	300,000
Meadowlands Cup H. (G2)	499,000	Meadowlands	$1\frac{1}{8}$	Diamond Stripes	300,000
New Orleans H. (G2)	485,000	Fair Grounds	$1\frac{1}{8}$	Master Command	300,000
Prince of Wales S.	476,850	Fort Erie	$1\frac{3}{16}$	Alezzandro	286,110
Breeders' S.	475,617	Woodbine	$1\frac{1}{2}$T	Marchfield	284,460
Labatt Woodbine Oaks	473,486	Woodbine	$1\frac{1}{8}$AW	Sealy Hill	282,960
West Virginia Breeders' Classic S.	450,000	Charles Town Races	$1\frac{1}{8}$	Eastern Delite	225,000
First Lady S. (G2)	432,000	Keeneland	1T	Vacare	248,000

Chronology of Richest North American Race

Purse	Race	Track	Year	Winner	Value to Winner
$4,689,920	Breeders' Cup Classic (G1)	Churchill Downs	1998	Awesome Again	$2,662,400
4,030,400	Breeders' Cup Classic (G1)	Hollywood Park	1997	Skip Away	2,288,000
3,664,000	Breeders' Cup Classic (G1)	Woodbine	1996	Alphabet Soup	2,080,000
2,798,000	Breeders' Cup Classic (G1)	Belmont Park	1995	Cigar	1,560,000
2,748,000	Breeders' Cup Classic (G1)	Churchill Downs	1991	Black Tie Affair (Ire)	1,560,000
2,739,000	Breeders' Cup Classic (G1)	Hollywood Park	1984	Wild Again	1,350,000
1,049,725	Hollywood Futurity (G1)	Hollywood Park	1983	Fali Time	549,849
1,000,000	Arlington Million S. (G1)	Arlington Park	1981	John Henry	600,000
549,000	Jockey Club Gold Cup S. (G1)	Belmont Park	1980	Temperence Hill	329,400
500,000	Hollywood Gold Cup H. (G1)	Hollywood Park	1979	Affirmed	275,000
385,350	Arlington-Washington Futurity	Arlington Park	1968	Strong Strong	212,850
367,700	Arlington-Washington Futurity	Arlington Park	1966	Diplomat Way	195,200
357,250	Arlington-Washington Futurity	Arlington Park	1962	Candy Spots	142,250
319,210	Garden State S.	Garden State Park	1956	Barbizon	168,430
282,370	Garden State S.	Garden State Park	1955	Prince John	157,918
269,965	Garden State S.	Garden State Park	1954	Summer Tan	151,096
269,395	Garden State S.	Garden State Park	1953	*Turn-to	151,282
205,700	Santa Anita Maturity	Santa Anita Park	1951	Great Circle	144,325

How American Races Are Graded

At the urging of European racing officials who in 1972 had created the pattern race system to identify and grade the best-quality races in Europe, the Thoroughbred Owners and Breeders Association created the North American Graded Stakes Committee and implemented a similar grading system for the '73 racing season. The gradings were principally designed to assist bloodstock buyers by identifying the North American races that in the recent past had consistently attracted the highest levels of competition. Grade 1 would be the highest level, followed by Grade 2 and Grade 3, the latter being the lowest level of stakes race accorded a grade.

The first North American gradings, totaling 330 races, were announced in January 1973, and the English Jockey Club immediately accepted them. Fasig-Tipton Co. began to publish the gradings in its catalogs in 1975, and Keeneland Association followed in '76. In 1998, Canadian racing authorities began to grade that nation's races, and the name of the TOBA-led organization was changed to the American Graded Stakes Committee and dealt only with United States stakes races.

Grades of America's best races are reviewed annually by the American Graded Stakes Committee because stakes programs are dynamic and ever-changing products of conditions. The quality of any race's contestants may differ markedly from one year to the next. When a trend in the quality of the field of a race is established, be it improving or deteriorating, the race is reevaluated for grading. Members have said they take a five-year view of each race when considering the gradings.

Committee

The committee has 11 voting members: six TOBA members serving five-year terms and five racing official members elected by the TOBA committee members and serving three-year terms. In addition, the committee's grading sessions have guest observers and invited guests. To be considered for membership on the committee, a candidate must have served as a guest observer for at least one grading session.

Members of the committee for the November 27, 2007, session at which '08 gradings were determined:

TOBA: Dell Hancock (chairperson), John Amerman, Rollin W. Baugh, Bill Heiligbrodt, Fred Seitz, and Peter Willmott.

Racing official members: Rogers Beasley, P. J. Campo, Michael Dempsey, Michael Harlow, and Thomas S. Robbins.

Guest observers: Georganne Hale, Seth Hancock, Todd Pletcher, Ismael Trejo, and Rose Mary Williams.

Invited guests: Robert Bork, Norman Case, Bill Farish, Carl Hamilton, and Nobutoshi Mochizuki.

Criteria

To be eligible for grading, a race must meet several criteria for being graded and for retaining the status. Among the criteria are:

Purse: The race must have a minimum purse, excluding state-bred supplements, of $250,000 for Grade 1, $150,000 for Grade 2, and $100,000 for Grade 3.

Continuity: In general, a race must have two prior runnings under essentially the same conditions to be graded, although in rare circumstances Grade 1 status has been accorded immediately to races of special note, such as the

2008 Graded Stakes by Racetrack

Track	G1	G2	G3	Total
Belmont Park	21	19	13	53
Santa Anita Park	10	24	14	48
Hollywood Park	13	14	18	45
Churchill Downs	5	11	22	38
Gulfstream Park	3	12	17	32
Saratoga Race Course	14	13	4	31
Keeneland Race Course	9	7	14	30
Aqueduct	3	7	16	26
Oak Tree at Santa Anita	15	3	4	22
Del Mar	7	10	2	19
Calder Race Course	1	4	12	17
Arlington Park	3	1	11	15
Monmouth Park	2	1	10	13
Fair Grounds	0	4	6	10
Oaklawn Park	1	4	5	10
Pimlico Race Course	2	3	5	10
Delaware Park	0	2	5	7
Turfway Park	0	2	5	7
Hawthorne Race Course	0	2	4	6
Lone Star Park	0	0	5	5
Colonial Downs	0	1	3	4
Golden Gate Fields	0	1	3	4
Laurel Park	1	2	1	4
Meadowlands	0	1	3	4
Tampa Bay Downs	0	0	4	4
Bay Meadows Race Course	0	0	2	2
Delta Downs	0	0	2	2
Hoosier Park	0	2	0	2
Philadelphia Park	0	2	0	2
Prairie Meadows	0	1	1	2
Ellis Park	0	0	1	1
Emerald Downs	0	0	1	1
Kentucky Downs	0	0	1	1
Louisiana Downs	0	1	0	1
Mountaineer Park	0	0	1	1
Sam Houston Race Park	0	0	1	1
Thistledown	0	1	0	1
Totals	**110**	**155**	**216**	**481**

Breeders' Cup races. Races with restrictions other than sex or age are not eligible.

Drug testing: Post-race tests must meet or exceed guidelines in the committee's drug testing protocol.

In addition, if track management changes a graded race from dirt to grass, or vice versa, or changes the race's distance by more than one-quarter mile or from less than one mile to more than one mile, or vice versa, the race will be considered a new race and ineligible for grading until it has been run twice under the same conditions. If a race's place on the calendar is changed substantially, such as from July to January, the race's grading may be reviewed.

Seven votes are required to raise any grading, and six votes are needed to downgrade a race.

In determining a grading, the committee considers the quality of its field over the prior five years as measured by several statistical yardsticks. Among the considerations are:

- Points based on number of in-the-money finishes in unrestricted black-type races;
- Percentage of graded stakes winners in the field;
- Quality points assigned to the race based on the number of graded stakes winners in the field; and

Summary of Grade Changes

	No.	% Graded Stakes	Change from 2007
Grade 1	110	22.9%	2.8%
Grade 2	155	32.2%	-1.3%
Grade 3	216	44.9%	2.9%

- Ratings of the North American Rating Committee, a panel composed of racing secretaries that each week assigns a hypothetical weight to every horse running in American black-type races.

Beginning in 1999, graded turf races moved to the main track because of course conditions were automatically downgraded one grade, although the American Graded Stakes Committee reviews each such race within five days of the running and can restore the original grading. The change in grading affects only that year's running and is not considered in the grading process.

The American Graded Stakes Committee notifies racetracks with races in the lowest echelons of their respective gradings that the races may be downgraded, but the race will not be considered for downgrading until it has been run another time.

More graded stakes are offered in the U.S. than all group races throughout Europe, which

Purse Comparison of Graded and Group Races by Country

	Grade 1		Grade 2		Grade 3		Total	
Country	Races	Average First Money	Races	Average First Money	Races	Average First Money	Races	Average First Money
2006 Racing Season								
Canada	3	$800,000	9	$213,333	25	$111,214	37	$191,902
Ireland	12	367,928	8	98,168	28	63,614	48	139,156
Great Britain	31	330,081	43	100,859	65	52,221	139	129,442
France	26	303,139	27	92,731	54	47,360	107	120,957
Italy	9	169,969	4	85,543	13	45,752	26	94,872
Germany	7	203,109	13	67,331	28	42,731	48	72,782
United States	104	377,715	151	151,789	205	94,484	460	177,330
2005 Racing Season								
Canada	3	$800,000	9	$205,793	25	$123,606	37	$198,440
Ireland	12	406,671	8	112,487	28	70,514	48	161,549
Great Britain	31	354,172	40	109,297	65	57,066	136	140,146
France	26	324,997	27	95,946	54	50,876	107	128,859
Italy	9	194,761	5	93,120	13	50,363	27	106,414
Germany	7	249,333	12	83,889	29	49,823	48	87,435
United States	96	373,784	152	157,548	199	92,242	447	174,914
2004 Racing Season								
Canada	3	$650,000	10	$178,296	25	$114,418	38	$173,511
Ireland	12	378,076	8	107,627	26	65,516	46	154,376
Great Britain	31	326,886	40	104,883	62	53,718	133	133,476
France	27	254,844	27	78,387	54	45,786	108	106,197
Italy	8	225,094	5	101,293	13	52,081	27	106,414
Germany	7	244,733	13	80,378	28	47,892	48	85,396
United States	100	402,694	154	153,891	219	86,285	473	175,190

has evoked criticism among some Europeans who contend that American black type is cheapened by the plentiful graded races. However, less than 1% of all American races are graded, a smaller percentage than Ireland, Great Britain, or France.

2008 Grade Changes
Upgrades
Grade 2 to Grade 1: First Lady Stakes (Keeneland Race Course), Just a Game Stakes (Belmont Park), Maker's Mark Mile Stakes (Keeneland).

Grade 3 to Grade 2: Fifth Third Elkhorn Stakes (Keeneland), Indiana Oaks (Hoosier Park), Lake George Stakes (Saratoga Race Course), Old Hat Stakes (Gulfstream Park), Providencia Stakes (Santa Anita Park), Rebel Stakes (Oaklawn Park), Sands Point Stakes (Belmont).

Ungraded to Grade 3: Appalachian Stakes (Keeneland), Boyd Gaming's Delta Princess Stakes (Delta Downs), Bryan Station Stakes (Keeneland), Colonel E. R. Bradley Handicap (Fair Grounds), Commonwealth Turf Stakes (Churchill Downs), Endeavour Stakes (Tampa Bay Downs), Florida Oaks (Tampa Bay), Harold C. Ramser Sr. Handicap (Oak Tree at Santa Anita), Honeybee Stakes (Oaklawn), La Habra Stakes (Santa Anita), Miss Grillo Stakes (Belmont), Obeah Handicap (Delaware Park), Pilgrim Stakes (Belmont), Robert G. Dick Memorial Handicap (Delaware), Southwest Stakes (Oaklawn), Tuzla Handicap (Santa Anita), Virginia Oaks (Colonial Downs), Woodford Reserve Bourbon Stakes (Keeneland).

Downgrades
Grade 2 to Grade 3: Nassau County Stakes (Belmont), San Rafael Stakes (Santa Anita), Washington Park Handicap (Arlington Park).

Grade 3 to ungraded: Aqueduct Handicap (Aqueduct), Arlington Classic Stakes (Arlington), Bay Meadows Handicap (Bay Meadows Race Course), Bayou Handicap (Fair Grounds), Essex Handicap (Oaklawn).

2008 Graded Stakes by State

State	G1	G2	G3	Total
California	45	52	43	140
New York	38	39	33	110
Kentucky	14	20	43	77
Florida	4	16	33	53
Illinois	3	3	15	21
New Jersey	2	2	13	17
Maryland	3	5	6	14
Louisiana	0	5	8	13
Arkansas	1	4	5	10
Delaware	0	2	5	7
Texas	0	0	6	6
Virginia	0	1	3	4
Indiana	0	2	0	2
Iowa	0	1	1	2
Pennsylvania	0	2	0	2
Ohio	0	1	0	1
Washington	0	0	1	1
West Virginia	0	0	1	1
Totals	**110**	**155**	**216**	**481**

Percentages of Best Races by Country

	Total Races	Stakes	Graded Stakes	G1 Stakes
2006 Racing Season				
Canada	5,234	238 (4.5%)	37 (0.7%)	3 (0.1%)
Ireland	874	102 (11.7%)	52 (5.9%)	12 (1.4%)
Great Britain	5,554	285 (5.1%)	138 (2.5%)	31 (0.6%)
France	4,102	233 (5.7%)	107 (2.6%)	26 (0.6%)
Italy	4,814	82 (1.7%)	26 (0.5%)	9 (0.2%)
Germany	1,720	110 (6.4%)	48 (2.8%)	7 (0.4%)
United States	51,491	1,965 (3.8%)	460 (0.9%)	104 (0.2%)
2005 Racing Season				
Canada	5,238	243 (4.7%)	37 (0.7%)	3 (0.1%)
Ireland	868	99 (11.4%)	48 (5.5%)	12 (1.4%)
Great Britain	5,301	283 (5.3%)	136 (2.6%)	31 (0.6%)
France	4,058	232 (5.7%)	107 (2.6%)	26 (0.6%)
Italy	4,801	81 (1.7%)	27 (0.6%)	9 (0.2%)
Germany	1,840	110 (6.0%)	48 (2.6%)	7 (0.4%)
United States	52,061	1,942 (3.7%)	447 (0.9%)	96 (0.2%)
2004 Racing Season				
Canada	5,263	249 (4.7%)	38 (0.7%)	3 (0.1%)
Ireland	845	97 (11.5%)	46 (5.4%)	12 (1.4%)
Great Britain	5,241	279 (5.3%)	133 (2.5%)	31 (0.6%)
France	4,026	232 (5.7%)	108 (2.6%)	27 (0.6%)
Italy	4,898	78 (1.6%)	27 (0.5%)	9 (0.2%)
Germany	1,891	110 (5.8%)	48 (2.5%)	7 (0.2%)
United States	53,403	1,879 (2.5%)	473 (0.9%)	100 (0.2%)

American Graded Stakes

Ack Ack Handicap

Grade 3 in 2008. Churchill Downs, three-year-olds and up, 1 mile, dirt. Held November 3, 2007, with a gross value of $221,600. First held in 1991. First graded in 1997. Stakes record 1:34.08 (2007 Istan).

Year	Winner	Jockey	Second	Third	Strs	Time	1st Purse
2007	Istan, 5, 118	K. J. Desormeaux	Sun King, 5, 121	Ryan's for Real, 4, 115	8	**1:34.08**	$133,272
2006	It's No Joke, 4, 119	R. Albarado	Irene's Mon, 3, 111	Level Playingfield, 5, 113	12	1:34.77	134,234
2005	Straight Line, 3, 114	S. Bridgmohan	Vicarage, 3, 117	Level Playingfield, 4, 115	9	1:28.34	69,564
2004	Sir Cherokee, 4, 114	C. H. Borel	Fire Slam, 3, 117	Slate Run, 4, 106	6	1:29.48	102,436
2003	Cappuchino, 4, 117	J. K. Court	Pass Rush, 4, 116	Twilight Road, 6, 116	7	1:31.66	102,579
2002	Twilight Road, 5, 113	P. Day	Mountain General, 4, 116	Binthebest, 5, 113	9	1:29.39	69,874
2001	Illusioned, 3, 118	P. Day	Strawberry Affair, 3, 112	Fappie's Notebook, 4, 116	11	1:28.63	70,866
2000	Chindi, 6, 113	T. T. Doocy	Smolderin Heart, 5, 113	Millencolin, 3, 113	10	1:29.30	70,494
1999	Littlebitlively, 5, 119	C. H. Borel	Run Johnny, 7, 117	Tactical Cat, 3, 117	11	1:28.97	71,672
1998	Distorted Humor, 5, 120	C. H. Borel	Crafty Friend, 5, 113	Chindi, 4, 113	6	1:29.61	68,262
1997	Cat's Career, 4, 108	W. Martinez	Rare Rock, 4, 112	Victor Cooley, 4, 122	6	1:34.64	69,130
1996	Western Trader, 5, 113	C. H. Borel	Top Account, 4, 117	Strategic Intent, 4, 113	8	1:29.84	70,308
1995	Mystery Storm, 3, 112	C. Gonzalez	I'm Very Irish, 4, 113	Tarzans Blade, 4, 116	10	1:29.10	75,660
1994	Lost Pan, 4, 114	D. M. Barton	Sir Vixen, 6, 112	Groovy Jett, 3, 112	8	1:30.27	54,795
1991	Seven Spades, 4, 108	D. W. Cox	Discover, 3, 114	Senator to Be, 4, 115	12	1:37.62	38,513

Named for Forked Lightning Ranch's Racing Hall of Fame member, 1971 Horse of the Year, and '69 Derby Trial winner Ack Ack (1966 c. by Battle Joined). Formerly sponsored by Emirates Airline of Dubai, United Arab Emirates 2006. Not held 1992-'93. 7½ furlongs 1994-'96, 1998-2005. Equaled track record 1995. Track record 2001.

Ack Ack Handicap

Grade 3 in 2008. Hollywood Park, three-year-olds and up, 7½ furlongs, all weather. Held June 7, 2008, with a gross value of $111,700. First held in 2001. First graded in 2006. Stakes record 1:27.15 (2003 Joey Franco).

Year	Winner	Jockey	Second	Third	Strs	Time	1st Purse
2008	Rebellion (GB), 5, 120	R. Bejarano	Tropic Storm, 4, 116	Stoneside (Ire), 4, 116	10	1:27.68	$67,020
2007	El Roblar, 5, 117	V. Espinoza	Siren Lure, 6, 121	Publication, 8, 116	8	1:28.51	65,820
2006	Lucky J. H., 4, 119	P. A. Valenzuela	Captain Squire, 7, 119	Primerica, 8, 115	7	1:29.66	60,000
2005	McCann's Mojave, 5, 116	J. Valdivia Jr.	Congrats, 5, 121	St Averil, 4, 115	8	1:27.23	60,210
2004	Taste of Paradise, 5, 116	J. K. Court	Buddy Gil, 4, 122	Black Bart, 5, 116	6	1:28.02	46,845
2003	Joey Franco, 4, 118	P. A. Valenzuela	Kela, 5, 117	Publication, 4, 116	7	**1:27.15**	60,275
2001	Grey Memo, 4, 122	G. K. Gomez	National Saint, 5, 116	Elaborate, 6, 122	8	1:28.19	59,460

Named for Forked Lightning Ranch's Racing Hall of Fame member, 1971 Horse of the Year, and '71 Hollywood Gold Cup winner Ack Ack (1966 c. by Battle Joined). Not held 2002. Ack Ack S. 2001. Dirt 2001-'06. Four-year-olds and up 2001.

Acorn Stakes

Grade 1 in 2008. Belmont Park, three-year-olds, fillies, 1 mile, dirt. Held June 7, 2008, with a gross value of $237,500. First held in 1931. First graded in 1973. Stakes record 1:34.05 (2002 You).

Year	Winner	Jockey	Second	Third	Strs	Time	1st Purse
2008	Zaftig, 3, 121	J. R. Velazquez	Indian Blessing, 3, 121	Game Face, 3, 121	4	1:34.50	$150,000
2007	Cotton Blossom, 3, 121	J. R. Velazquez	Dream Rush, 3, 121	Christmas Kid, 3, 121	6	1:34.70	150,000
2006	Bushfire, 3, 121	A. O. Solis	Hello Liberty, 3, 121	Last Romance, 3, 121	7	1:35.89	150,000
2005	Round Pond, 3, 121	S. Elliott	Smuggler, 3, 121	In the Gold, 3, 121	6	1:35.33	150,000
2004	Island Sand, 3, 121	T. J. Thompson	Society Selection, 3, 121	Friendly Michelle, 3, 121	9	1:34.89	150,000
2003	Bird Town, 3, 121	E. S. Prado	Lady Tak, 3, 121	Final Round, 3, 121	7	1:35.29	150,000
2002	You, 3, 121	J. D. Bailey	Willa On the Move, 3, 121	Bella Bellucci, 3, 121	5	**1:34.05**	150,000
2001	Forest Secrets, 3, 121	C. J. McCarron	Victory Ride, 3, 121	Real Cozzy, 3, 121	8	1:34.92	120,000
2000	Finder's Fee, 3, 121	J. R. Velazquez	C'Est L' Amour, 3, 121	Roxelana, 3, 121	10	1:37.38	120,000
1999	Three Ring, 3, 121	J. D. Bailey	Better Than Honour, 3, 121	Madison's Charm, 3, 121	8	1:36.16	120,000
1998	Jersey Girl, 3, 121	M. E. Smith	Santaria, 3, 121	Brave Deed, 3, 121	10	1:36.32	90,000
1997	Sharp Cat, 3, 121	G. L. Stevens	Dixie Flag, 3, 121	Ajina, 3, 121	7	1:34.41	90,000
1996	Star de Lady Ann, 3, 121	M. E. Smith	Yanks Music, 3, 121	Stop Traffic, 3, 121	12	1:34.62	90,000
1995	Cat's Cradle, 3, 121	C. W. Antley	Country Cat, 3, 121	Lucky Lavender Gal, 3, 121	7	1:37.53	90,000
1994	Inside Information, 3, 121	M. E. Smith	Cinnamon Sugar (Ire), 3, 121	Sovereign Kitty, 3, 121	5	1:34.26	90,000
1993	Sky Beauty, 3, 121	M. E. Smith	Educated Risk, 3, 121	In Her Glory, 3, 121	6	1:35.50	90,000
1992	Prospectors Delite, 3, 121	P. Day	Pleasant Stage, 3, 121	Turnback the Alarm, 3, 121	12	1:35.10	113,400
1991	Meadow Star, 3, 121	J. D. Bailey	Versailles Treaty, 3, 121	Dazzle Me Jolie, 3, 121	6	1:37.42	103,680
1990	Stella Madrid, 3, 121	A. T. Cordero Jr.	Danzig's Beauty, 3, 121	Seaside Attraction, 3, 121	7	1:36.00	104,580
1989	Open Mind, 3, 121	A. T. Cordero Jr.	Hot Novel, 3, 121	Triple Strike, 3, 121	11	1:35.40	111,960
1988	Aptostar, 3, 121	R. G. Davis	Topicount, 3, 121	Avie's Gal, 3, 121	9	1:34.80	109,980
1987	Grecian Flight, 3, 121	C. Perret	Fiesta Gal, 3, 121	Bound, 3, 121	13	1:35.20	113,580
1986	Lotka, 3, 121	J. D. Bailey	Dynamic Star, 3, 121	Life At the Top, 3, 121	8	1:35.20	136,080
1985	Mom's Command, 3, 121	A. Fuller	Le l'Argent, 3, 121	Diplomette, 3, 121	8	1:35.80	113,040
1984	Miss Oceana, 3, 121	E. Maple	Life's Magic, 3, 121	Proud Clarioness, 3, 121	9	1:35.80	135,720
1983	Ski Goggle, 3, 121	C. J. McCarron	Princess Rooney, 3, 121	Thirty Flags, 3, 121	9	1:35.00	69,360
1982	Cupecoy's Joy, 3, 121	A. Santiago	Nancy Huang, 3, 121	Vestris, 3, 121	9	1:34.20	51,750
1981	Heavenly Cause, 3, 121	L. A. Pincay Jr.	Dame Mysterieuse, 3, 121	Autumn Glory, 3, 121	7	1:35.20	50,850
1980	Bold 'n Determined, 3, 121	E. Delahoussaye	Mitey Lively, 3, 121	Sugar and Spice, 3, 121	8	1:36.80	50,400

Year	Winner	Jockey	Second	Third	Strs	Time	1st Purse
1979	Davona Dale, 3, 121	J. Velasquez	Eloquent, 3, 121	Plankton, 3, 121	8	1:36.00	$50,130
1978	Tempest Queen, 3, 121	J. Velasquez	Lakeville Miss, 3, 121	White Star Line, 3, 121	6	1:35.40	31,920
1977	Bring Out the Band, 3, 121	D. Brumfield	Your Place Or Mine, 3, 121	Mrs. Warren, 3, 121	11	1:36.80	33,690
1976	Dearly Precious, 3, 121	J. Velasquez	Optimistic Gal, 3, 121	Tell Me All, 3, 121	8	1:35.80	33,390
1975	Ruffian, 3, 121	J. Vasquez	Somethingregal, 3, 121	Gallant Trial, 3, 121	7	1:34.80	33,660
1974	Special Team, 3, 121	M. A. Rivera	Stage Door Betty, 3, 121	Raisela, 3, 121	9	1:35.40	33,960
	Chris Evert, 3, 121	J. Velasquez	Clear Copy, 3, 121	Fiesta Libre, 3, 121	9	1:36.00	33,960
1973	Windy's Daughter, 3, 121	B. Baeza	Poker Night, 3, 121	Voler, 3, 121	11	1:35.40	36,540

Named for the phrase, "Great oaks from little acorns grow"; in the past the Acorn preceded the Coaching Club American Oaks. Held at Aqueduct 1960-'67, 1969-'75. Two divisions 1951, '70, '74. Dead heat for first 1954, '56.

Adena Stallions' Miss Preakness Stakes

Grade 3 in 2008. Pimlico Race Course, three-year-olds, fillies, 6 furlongs, dirt. Held May 16, 2008, with a gross value of $100,000. First held in 1986. First graded in 2002. Stakes record 1:10 (2000 Lucky Livi).

Year	Winner	Jockey	Second	Third	Strs	Time	1st Purse
2008	Palanka City, 3, 122	C. A. Emigh	Casanova Killer, 3, 116	Beau's Valentine, 3, 116	5	1:10.90	$60,000
2007	Time's Mistress, 3, 122	M. Guidry	Silver Knockers, 3, 116	Richwoman, 3, 122	7	1:10.23	75,000
2006	Wildcat Bettie B, 3, 118	R. A. Dominguez	Press Camp, 3, 116	G City Gal, 3, 118	7	1:10.05	75,000
2005	Burnish, 3, 118	R. Bejarano	Partners Due, 3, 116	Hot Storm, 3, 122	7	1:12.40	60,000
2004	Forest Music, 3, 115	R. A. Dominguez	Stephan's Angel, 3, 119	Fall Fashion, 3, 119	11	1:10.97	60,000
2003	Belong to Sea, 3, 117	J. Castellano	Chimichurri, 3, 122	Forever Partners, 3, 119	5	1:11.10	60,000
2002	Vesta, 3, 117	M. G. Pino	Willa On the Move, 3, 117	Shameful, 3, 119	6	1:10.25	60,000
2001	Kimbralata, 3, 117	T. Dunkelberger	Carafe, 3, 117	Stormy Pick, 3, 122	5	1:11.20	60,000
2000	Lucky Livi, 3, 119	R. Wilson	Big Bambu, 3, 117	Swept Away, 3, 119	5	**1:10.00**	60,000
1999	Hookedonthefeelin, 3, 122	G. L. Stevens	Silent Valay, 3, 122	Paula's Girl, 3, 122	4	1:11.26	60,000
1998	Storm Beauty, 3, 119	C. R. Woods Jr.	Brac Drifter, 3, 115	Hair Spray, 3, 122	5	1:10.81	45,000
1997	Weather Vane, 3, 122	M. G. Pino	Move, 3, 122	Cayman Sunset, 3, 122	8	1:11.94	64,740
1996	Nic's Halo, 3, 117	R. Wilson	Palette Knife, 3, 115	Crafty But Sweet, 3, 122	4	1:11.55	32,655
1995	Lilly Capote, 3, 122	G. L. Stevens	Broad Smile, 3, 122	Norstep, 3, 122	7	1:10.90	32,640
1994	Foolish Kisses, 3, 113	E. S. Prado	Aly's Conquest, 3, 114	Platinum Punch, 3, 113	8	1:12.45	32,730
1993	My Rosa, 3, 113	E. S. Prado	Fighting Jet, 3, 121	Code Blum, 3, 121	5	1:11.33	32,175
1992	Toots La Mae, 3, 113	J. Bravo	Missy White Oak, 3, 118	Jazzy One, 3, 121	6	1:11.97	26,505
1991	Missy's Music, 3, 114	M. G. Pino	Dixie Rouge, 3, 113	Accent Knightly, 3, 113	6	1:11.48	15,975
1990	Love Me a Lot, 3, 115	C. J. McCarron	Dixie Landera, 3, 113	Tabs, 3, 116	6	1:11.40	19,170
1989	Montoya, 3, 118	L. A. Pincay Jr.	dh-Another Boom, 3, 121 dh-Cojinx, 3, 121		7	1:10.60	22,470
1988	Caromine, 3, 115	C. J. McCarron	Light Beat, 3, 118	Saved by Grace, 3, 118	9	1:13.00	24,911
1987	Cutlasee, 3, 116	C. J. McCarron	I'm Out, 3, 114	Pelican Bay, 3, 115	8	1:12.60	21,158
1986	Marion's Madel, 3, 115	C. J. McCarron	Zigbelle, 3, 115	Babbling Brook, 3, 116	8	1:12.80	21,060

Held day before the Preakness S. (G1). Sponsored by Adena Springs, which is owned by Magna Entertainment Corp. chairman Frank Stronach 2004-'08. Miss Preakness S. 1986-2003. Dead heat for second 1989.

Adirondack Stakes

Grade 2 in 2008. Saratoga Race Course, two-year-olds, fillies, 6½ furlongs, dirt. Held August 15, 2007, with a gross value of $150,000. First held in 1901. First graded in 1973. Stakes record 1:15.16 (2001 You).

Year	Winner	Jockey	Second	Third	Strs	Time	1st Purse
2007	More Happy, 2, 118	R. Bejarano	A to the Croft, 2, 118	Passion, 2, 118	9	1:17.51	$90,000
2006	Octave, 2, 118	G. K. Gomez	True Addiction, 2, 118	Magical Ride, 2, 118	9	1:19.04	120,000
2005	Folklore, 2, 117	C. H. Velasquez	Fifth Avenue, 2, 121	Truart, 2, 117	7	1:13.66	90,000
2003	Whoopi Cat, 2, 116	E. S. Prado	Unbridled Beauty, 2, 116	Eye Dazzler, 2, 116	7	1:17.51	90,000
2002	Awesome Humor, 2, 122	P. Day	Stellar, 2, 117	Holiday Runner, 2, 122	6	1:17.75	90,000
2001	You, 2, 115	E. S. Prado	Cashier's Dream, 2, 122	Magic Storm, 2, 115	7	**1:15.16**	90,000
2000	Raging Fever, 2, 122	J. D. Bailey	Two Item Limit, 2, 117	Secret Lover, 2, 117	6	1:17.47	90,000
1999	Regally Appealing, 2, 114	E. S. Prado	Miss Wineshine, 2, 122	Trump My Heart, 2, 114	6	1:16.86	90,000
1998	Things Change, 2, 114	J. A. Santos	Extended Applause, 2, 117	Brittons Hill, 2, 114	9	1:18.14	90,000
1997	Salty Perfume, 2, 114	S. J. Sellers	Brac Drifter, 2, 114	Joustabout, 2, 114	6	1:17.94	90,000
1996	Storm Song, 2, 113	P. Day	Last Two States, 2, 113	dh-Exclusive Hold, 2, 113 dh-Larkwhistle, 2, 116	9	1:17.60	84,075
1995	Flat Fleet Feet, 2, 113	M. E. Smith	Steady Cat, 2, 112	Western Dreamer, 2, 120	7	1:16.74	65,760
1994	Seeking Regina, 2, 114	J. D. Bailey	Changing Ways, 2, 119	Phone Bird, 2, 114	7	1:18.51	66,600
1993	Astas Foxy Lady, 2, 119	R. P. Romero	Footing, 2, 114	Casa Eire, 2, 119	6	1:10.11	68,520
1992	Sky Beauty, 2, 116	E. Maple	Missed the Storm, 2, 114	Distinct Habit, 2, 121	7	1:10.16	70,560
1991	American Royale, 2, 119	A. T. Gryder	Bless Our Home, 2, 114	Turnback the Alarm, 2, 119	8	1:10.72	71,640
1990	Really Quick, 2, 114	A. T. Cordero Jr.	Devilish Touch, 2, 119	Ferber's Follies, 2, 114	9	1:11.40	54,270
1989	Dance Colony, 2, 116	J. A. Santos	In Full Cry, 2, 114	Saratoga Sizzle, 2, 114	6	1:11.80	52,200
1988	Pat Copelan, 2, 114	P. Day	Channel Three, 2, 116	Premier Playmate, 2, 116	6	1:10.80	66,780
1987	Over All, 2, 121	A. T. Cordero Jr.	Flashy Runner, 2, 114	Careless Flirt, 2, 114	5	1:10.60	64,890
1986	Sacahuista, 2, 119	C. J. McCarron	Collins, 2, 114	Release the Lyd, 2, 116	7	1:11.60	53,280
1985	Nervous Baba, 2, 114	J. Velasquez	Family Style, 2, 114	Steal a Kiss, 2, 114	7	1:09.60	54,450
1984	Contredance, 2, 119	E. Maple	Outstandingly, 2, 114	Oriental, 2, 114	7	1:10.40	53,100
1983	Buzz My Bell, 2, 114	J. Velasquez	Upturning, 2, 116	Mrs. Flagler, 2, 116	6	1:12.40	33,720
1982	Jelly Bean Holiday, 2, 116	J. Fell	Midnight Rapture, 2, 114	Flying Lassie, 2, 114	7	1:10.80	34,920

Racing — Graded Stakes

Year	Winner	Jockey	Second	Third	Strs	Time	1st Purse
1981	**Thrilld n Delightd**, 2, 114	J. Velasquez	Apalachee Honey, 2, 119	Trove, 2, 116	9	1:10.80	$35,160
1980	**Sweet Revenge**, 2, 119	J. Velasquez	Companionship, 2, 114	Honey's Appeal, 2, 114	7	1:10.40	34,080
1979	**Smart Angle**, 2, 119	S. Maple	Lucky My Way, 2, 114	Andrea F., 2, 114	9	1:11.00	26,835
1978	**Whisper Fleet**, 2, 119	J. Cruguet	Island Kitty, 2, 114	Golferette, 2, 114	8	1:10.60	22,410
1977	**L'Alezane**, 2, 121	R. Turcotte	Sunny Bay, 2, 121	Misgivings, 2, 114	7	1:10.60	22,335
1976	**Harvest Girl**, 2, 114	J. Cruguet	Bonnie Empress, 2, 114	Drama Critic, 2, 119	7	1:11.00	22,545
1975	**Optimistic Gal**, 2, 120	B. Baeza	Glory Glory, 2, 120	Against all Flags, 2, 120	5	1:11.20	22,515
1974	**Laughing Bridge**, 2, 120	L. A. Pincay Jr.	Stulcer, 2, 120	Some Swinger, 2, 120	6	1:10.80	16,950
1973	**Talking Picture**, 2, 120	B. Baeza	In Hot Pursuit, 2, 120	Bedknob, 2, 120	10	1:11.00	17,625

Named for the Adirondack mountain region of New York. Grade 3 1975-'83. Adirondack H. 1901-'45. Adirondack Breeders' Cup S. 2006. Held at Belmont Park 1943-'45. Held at Jamaica 1953-'54. Not held 1911-'12, 1946-'52, 1956-'61, 2004. 6 furlongs 1901-'45, 1962-'93, 2005. 5½ furlongs 1953-'55. Both sexes 1901-'29. Dead heat for third 1996.

Aegon Turf Sprint Stakes

Grade 3 in 2008. Churchill Downs, three-year-olds and up, 5 furlongs, turf. Held May 2, 2008, with a gross value of $126,400. First held in 1995. First graded in 2001. Stakes record :56.01 (2003 Fiscally Speaking).

Year	Winner	Jockey	Second	Third	Strs	Time	1st Purse
2008	**Mr. Nightlinger**, 4, 121	J. Theriot	Salute the Count, 8, 118	Atticus Kristy, 7, 118	8	:56.18	$76,019
2007	**Gaff**, 5, 121	J. R. Velazquez	Ellwood and Jake, 4, 118	Congo King, 4, 118	8	:56.84	101,671
2006	**Man Of Illusion (Aus)**, 5, 118	J. R. Leparoux	Justice for Auston, 7, 118	Atticus Kristy, 5, 124	12	:56.28	66,886
2005	**Mighty Beau**, 6, 121	P. A. Valenzuela	Chosen Chief, 6, 119	Sgt. Bert, 4, 119	10	:56.18	70,370
2004	**Lydgate**, 4, 114	P. Day	Mighty Beau, 5, 117	Banned in Boston, 4, 114	11	:56.56	71,114
2003	**Fiscally Speaking**, 4, 114	J. K. Court	Morluc, 7, 122	Testify, 6, 122	11	**:56.01**	71,486
2002	**Testify**, 5, 119	E. Delahoussaye	Texas Glitter, 6, 122	Gone Fishin, 6, 116	10	:57.39	75,206
2001	**Morluc**, 5, 122	R. Albarado	Testify, 4, 119	Texas Glitter, 5, 122	9	:57.60	70,494
2000	**Bold Fact**, 5, 120	R. Migliore	Howbaddouwantit, 5, 123	Fantastic Finish, 4, 114	12	:56.37	75,330
1999	**Howbaddouwantit**, 4, 123	M. E. Smith	Mr Fessus, 4, 114	Three Card Willie, 4, 118	11	:56.90	71,486
1998	**Indian Rocket (GB)**, 4, 116	G. L. Stevens	G H's Pleasure, 6, 120	Claire's Honor, 4, 114	12	:57.32	75,950
1997	**Sandtrap**, 4, 123	A. O. Solis	Appealing Skier, 4, 114	G H's Pleasure, 5, 120	11	:56.51	71,734
1996	**Danjur**, 4, 114	J. D. Bailey	Hello Paradise, 5, 117	Linear, 6, 123	10	:56.09	57,281
1995	**Long Suit**, 4, 114	W. Martinez	Bold n' Flashy, 6, 120	†Scottish Fantasy, 7, 111	11	:56.90	57,086

Sponsored by the AEGON Group N.V. of The Hague, the Netherlands 1999-2008. Churchill Downs Turf Sprint S. 1995-'98. Established course record 1995. Course record 1996, 2003. †Denotes female.

Affirmed Handicap

Grade 3 in 2008. Hollywood Park, three-year-olds, 1 1/16 miles, all weather. Held June 17, 2007, with a gross value of $106,600. First held in 1940. First graded in 1973. Stakes record 1:40.83 (1999 General Challenge).

Year	Winner	Jockey	Second	Third	Strs	Time	1st Purse
2007	**Desert Code**, 3, 118	R. Migliore	Albertus Maximus, 3, 117	Cobalt Blue, 3, 121	5	1:44.21	$63,960
2006	**Point Determined**, 3, 121	V. Espinoza	A. P. Warrior, 3, 120	Arson Squad, 3, 116	5	1:42.55	60,000
2005	**Indian Ocean**, 3, 115	J. K. Court	Surf Cat, 3, 116	Dover Dere, 3, 118	4	1:42.53	63,060
2004	**Boomzeeboom**, 3, 115	V. Espinoza	Twice as Bad, 3, 121	Wimplestiltskin, 3, 116	3	1:42.11	66,120
2003	**Eye of the Tiger**, 3, 119	A. O. Solis	Ministers Wild Cat, 3, 118	Bullistic, 3, 115	4	1:42.30	63,120
2002	**Came Home**, 3, 124	C. J. McCarron	Tracemark, 3, 120	Calkins Road, 3, 117	6	1:41.99	64,500
2001	**Until Sundown**, 3, 117	G. L. Stevens	Top Hit, 3, 114	Bayou the Moon, 3, 118	5	1:43.10	60,000
2000	**Tiznow**, 3, 111	V. Espinoza	Dixie Union, 3, 122	Millencolin, 3, 114	6	1:42.35	80,550
1999	**General Challenge**, 3, 124	D. R. Flores	Desert Hero, 3, 120	Crowning Storm, 3, 116	5	**1:40.83**	75,000
1998	**Old Trieste**, 3, 118	C. J. McCarron	Old Topper, 3, 117	Kraal, 3, 116	6	1:41.84	62,340
1997	**Deputy Commander**, 3, 117	C. S. Nakatani	Hello (Ire), 3, 121	Holzmeister, 3, 121	6	1:42.80	61,500
1996	**Hesabull**, 3, 117	E. Delahoussaye	Benton Creek, 3, 116	Semoran, 3, 118	7	1:43.25	61,050
1995	**Mr Purple**, 3, 120	C. S. Nakatani	Pumpkin House, 3, 115	Oncefortheroad, 3, 114	6	1:42.37	77,050
1994	**R Friar Tuck**, 3, 113	J. D. Bailey	Pollock's Luck, 3, 114	Wild Invader, 3, 115	8	1:49.08	96,100
1993	**Codified**, 3, 117	G. L. Stevens	Roman Image, 3, 117	Future Storm, 3, 118	7	1:48.85	94,100
1992	**Natural Nine**, 3, 117	L. A. Pincay Jr.	Prospect for Four, 3, 114	Never Round, 3, 117	8	1:49.42	95,500
1991	**Compelling Sound**, 3, 118	G. L. Stevens	Best Pal, 3, 123	Caliche's Secret, 3, 117	5	1:47.90	91,300
1990	**Stalwart Charger**, 3, 120	L. A. Pincay Jr.	Toby Jug, 3, 112	Kentucky Jazz, 3, 120	5	1:48.40	91,100
1989	**Raise a Stanza**, 3, 115	C. A. Black	Broke the Mold, 3, 112	Prized, 3, 116	12	1:48.40	102,200
1988	**Iz a Saros**, 3, 113	A. T. Gryder	Stalwars, 3, 119	Bel Air Dancer, 3, 117	8	1:49.00	95,900
1987	**Candi's Gold**, 3, 116	G. L. Stevens	On the Line, 3, 116	The Medic, 3, 116	7	1:47.60	93,500
1986	**†Melair**, 3, 115	P. A. Valenzuela	Southern Halo, 3, 113	Snow Chief, 3, 127	12	1:32.80	220,000
1985	**Pancho Villa**, 3, 118	L. A. Pincay Jr.	Proudest Doon, 3, 118	Nostalgia's Star, 3, 118	9	1:33.80	64,050
1984	**Tights**, 3, 119	L. A. Pincay Jr.	M. Double M., 3, 116	Precisionist, 3, 121	8	1:48.60	46,850
1983	**My Habitony**, 3, 115	D. Pierce	Tanks Brigade, 3, 119	Hyperborean, 3, 115	6	1:48.60	47,250
1982	**Journey At Sea**, 3, 122	C. J. McCarron	Cassaleria, 3, 120	Guachan, 3, 112	5	1:46.80	49,650
1981	**Stancharry**, 3, 117	P. A. Valenzuela	Dusty Hula, 3, 116	Seafood, 3, 117	6	1:51.00	47,150
1980	**Score Twenty Four**, 3, 114	D. G. McHargue	dh-First Albert, 3, 116 dh-Loto Canada, 3, 119		6	1:48.20	37,200
1979	**Valdez**, 3, 119	L. A. Pincay Jr.	Pole Position, 3, 118	Beau's Eagle, 3, 123	5	1:47.40	37,500
1978	**Radar Ahead**, 3, 123	D. G. McHargue	Double Win, 3, 114	Think Snow, 3, 122	6	1:48.40	38,200
1977	**Text**, 3, 119	D. G. McHargue	Bad 'n Big, 3, 120	Sonny Collins, 3, 118	5	1:47.20	37,000
1976	**L'Heureux**, 3, 119	D. Pierce	Romeo, 3, 115	Crystal Water, 3, 125	7	1:47.40	38,600
1975	**Forcetan**, 3, 119	D. Pierce	Sibirri, 3, 114	Larrikin, 3, 121	5	1:48.80	37,300

Racing — Graded Stakes 247

Year	Winner	Jockey	Second	Third	Strs	Time	1st Purse
1974	Battery E., 3, 117	L. A. Pincay Jr.	Stardust Mel, 3, 120	Agitate, 3, 124	5	1:47.80	$36,800
1973	Carry the Banner, 3, 115	A. Pineda	Rod, 3, 119	Out of the East, 3, 120	8	1:41.20	39,200

Named for Harbor View Farm's Racing Hall of Fame member, '78 Triple Crown winner, and '79 Hollywood Gold Cup H. (G1) winner Affirmed (1975 c. by Exclusive Native). Formerly named in honor of Hollywood's film industry. Formerly named in honor of the Forty-niners ("argonauts") who went west to California in search of gold. Grade 2 1973-'89. Argonaut H. 1940-'60, 1973-'78. Argonaut S. 1961-'72. Silver Screen H. 1979-'92. Held at Santa Anita Park 1949. Not held 1942-'43. 1¹/₁₆ miles 1940, '44, '46-'53, '60-'73. 1 mile 1941, '45, '54-'59, '85-'86. 1¹/₈ miles 1979-'84, '87-'94. Turf 1968-'72. Dirt 1973-2006. Four-year-olds and up 1940-'41. Three-year-olds and up 1944-'59, '86. Two divisions 1963, '67, '70. Dead heat for second 1980. †Denotes female.

A Gleam Invitational Handicap

Grade 2 in 2008. Hollywood Park, three-year-olds and up, fillies and mares, 7 furlongs, all weather. Held July 6, 2007, with a gross value of $150,000. First held in 1941. First graded in 1973. Stakes record 1:20.53 (1998 A. P. Assay).

Year	Winner	Jockey	Second	Third	Strs	Time	1st Purse
2007	Somethinaboutlaura, 5, 122	V. Espinoza	Strong Faith, 6, 114	Theverythoughtof U, 4, 112	10	1:21.93	$90,000
2006	Somethinaboutlaura, 4, 116	V. Espinoza	Maryfield, 5, 119	Allswellthatnswell, 5, 117	6	1:20.88	90,000
2005	Alphabet Kisses, 4, 119	G. L. Stevens	Valentine Dancer, 5, 118	Muir Beach, 4, 114	9	1:21.67	90,000
2004	Dream of Summer, 5, 114	M. E. Smith	Tucked Away, 4, 116	Elusive Diva, 3, 112	9	1:21.16	90,000
2003	Cee's Elegance, 6, 116	V. Espinoza	You, 4, 121	Affluent, 5, 119	5	1:21.47	150,000
2002	Irguns Angel, 4, 116	E. Delahoussaye	Secret Liaison, 4, 116	Kalookan Queen, 6, 122	10	1:22.50	120,000
2001	Go Go, 4, 124	E. Delahoussaye	Kitty On the Track, 4, 115	Nany's Sweep, 5, 117	5	1:22.19	120,000
2000	Honest Lady, 4, 121	K. Desormeaux	Seth's Choice, 4, 115	Hookedonthefeelin, 4, 116	5	1:21.47	120,000
1999	Enjoy the Moment, 4, 117	D. R. Flores	Snowberg, 4, 115	Woodman's Dancer, 5, 117	6	1:21.35	120,000
1998	A. P. Assay, 4, 116	E. Delahoussaye	Exotic Wood, 6, 124	Closed Escrow, 5, 114	7	**1:20.53**	150,000
1997	Toga Toga Toga, 5, 119	G. L. Stevens	Our Summer Bid, 5, 115	Radu Cool, 5, 116	7	1:22.75	65,040
1996	Igotrhythm, 4, 116	E. Delahoussaye	Klassy Kim, 5, 116	Cat's Cradle, 4, 118	5	1:21.54	63,840
1995	Angi Go, 5, 117	G. L. Stevens	Desert Stormer, 5, 118	Dancing Mirage, 4, 115	6	1:21.45	62,700
1994	Golden Klair (GB), 4, 117	C. J. McCarron	Cargo, 5, 117	Minidar, 4, 117	4	1:22.00	60,400
1993	Bold Windy, 4, 115	G. L. Stevens	La Spia, 4, 115	Bountiful Native, 5, 122	9	1:21.62	65,700
1992	Forest Fealty, 5, 116	M. A. Pedroza	Brought to Mind, 5, 120	Devil's Orchid, 5, 120	8	1:22.13	64,800
1991	Survive, 7, 119	R. A. Baze	Stormy But Valid, 5, 121	Brought to Mind, 4, 117	6	1:22.10	62,400
1990	Stormy But Valid, 4, 120	G. L. Stevens	Hot Novel, 4, 118	Tis Juliet, 4, 114	5	1:21.20	61,300
1989	Daloma (Fr), 5, 115	C. J. McCarron	Survive, 5, 116	Behind the Scenes, 5, 116	7	1:21.60	47,900
1988	Integra, 4, 118	G. L. Stevens	Behind the Scenes, 4, 116	Carol's Wonder, 4, 117	5	1:23.00	46,100
1987	Le l'Argent, 5, 118	D. G. McHargue	Sari's Heroine, 4, 117	Rare Starlet, 4, 115	4	1:23.00	48,650
1986	Outstandingly, 4, 120	G. L. Stevens	Eloquack, 4, 110	Shywing, 4, 120	5	1:21.80	46,100
1985	Dontstop Themusic, 5, 121	L. A. Pincay Jr.	Lovlier Linda, 5, 122	Mimi Baker, 4, 110	4	1:21.40	36,500
1984	Lass Trump, 4, 116	C. J. McCarron	Pleasure Cay, 4, 116	Angel Savage (Mex), 4, 112	9	1:21.20	39,400
1983	Matching, 5, 121	R. Sibille	Sierva (Arg), 5, 116	Bara Lass, 4, 117	7	1:22.40	31,800
1982	Happy Bride (Ire), 4, 113	W. A. Guerra	Lucky Lady Ellen, 3, 117	Jones Time Machine, 3, 112	5	1:08.40	30,700
1981	She Can't Miss, 4, 117	P. A. Valenzuela	Cherokee Frolic, 3, 114	Shine High, 5, 122	6	1:09.00	32,050
1980	Great Lady M., 5, 115	P. A. Valenzuela	Double Deceit, 4, 116	Splendid Girl, 4, 120	5	1:08.40	30,550
1979	Delice, 4, 116	E. Delahoussaye	Great Lady M., 4, 117	Sateen, 3, 111	7	1:08.80	25,100
1978	Reminiscing, 4, 124	L. A. Pincay Jr.	Sing Back, 5, 122	Thirteenth Hope, 5, 113	9	1:09.60	25,450
1977	Just a Kick, 5, 121	S. Hawley	Cornish Colleen, 4, 113	Winter Solstice, 5, 122	5	1:09.40	18,450
1976	Winter Solstice, 4, 119	J. Lambert	Vol Au Vent, 4, 120	Powerful Lady, 4, 118	8	1:09.00	19,700
1975	Viva La Vivi, 5, 125	L. A. Pincay Jr.	Modus Vivendi, 4, 122	Fleet Gazelle, 4, 112	6	1:08.40	18,800
1974	Lt.'s Joy, 4, 117	L. A. Pincay Jr.	Viva La Vivi, 4, 123	Shadycroft Gal, 5, 115	7	1:09.00	16,000
1973	Wingo Belle, 5, 118	R. Nono	Convenience, 5, 126	Veneke, 6, 116	8	1:08.60	19,150

Named for Calumet Farm's 1952, '53 Milady H. winner A Gleam (1949 f. by *Blenheim II). Formerly named for California's redwood, the sequoia. Grade 3 1986-'89. A Gleam H. 1997-2003. Sequoia H. 1959-'78. Not held 1942-'43, 1947-'58. 6 furlongs 1944, 1959-'82. Dirt 1941-2006. Two-year-olds 1944. Equaled track record 1998.

Alabama Stakes

Grade 1 in 2008. Saratoga Race Course, three-year-olds, fillies, 1¹/₄ miles, dirt. Held August 18, 2007, with a gross value of $600,000. First held in 1872. First graded in 1973. Stakes record 2:00.80 (1990 Go for Wand).

Year	Winner	Jockey	Second	Third	Strs	Time	1st Purse
2007	Lady Joanne, 3, 121	C. H. Borel	Lear's Princess, 3, 121	Octave, 3, 121	7	2:03.62	$360,000
2006	Pine Island, 3, 121	J. Castellano	Teammate, 3, 121	Lemons Forever, 3, 121	9	2:02.87	360,000
2005	Sweet Symphony, 3, 121	J. D. Bailey	Spun Sugar, 3, 121	R Lady Joy, 3, 121	7	2:04.45	450,000
2004	Society Selection, 3, 121	C. H. Velasquez	Stellar Jayne, 3, 121	Ashado, 3, 121	8	2:02.70	450,000
2003	Island Fashion, 3, 121	J. R. Velazquez	Awesome Humor, 3, 121	Spoken Fur, 3, 121	6	2:05.08	450,000
2002	Farda Amiga, 3, 121	P. Day	Allamerican Bertie, 3, 121	You, 3, 121	6	2:04.68	450,000
2001	Flute, 3, 121	E. S. Prado	Exogenous, 3, 121	Two Item Limit, 3, 121	7	2:01.88	450,000
2000	Jostle, 3, 121	M. E. Smith	Secret Status, 3, 121	Spain, 3, 121	6	2:04.72	450,000
1999	Silverbulletday, 3, 121	J. D. Bailey	Strolling Belle, 3, 121	Gandria, 3, 121	7	2:02.71	240,000
1998	Banshee Breeze, 3, 121	J. D. Bailey	Lu Ravi, 3, 121	Manistique, 3, 121	6	2:03.41	150,000
1997	Runup the Colors, 3, 121	J. D. Bailey	Ajina, 3, 121	Tomisue's Delight, 3, 121	6	2:02.28	150,000
1996	Yanks Music, 3, 121	J. R. Velazquez	Escena, 3, 121	My Flag, 3, 121	7	2:03.06	150,000
1995	Pretty Discreet, 3, 121	M. E. Smith	Friendly Beauty, 3, 121	Rogues Walk, 3, 121	9	2:02.14	120,000
1994	Heavenly Prize, 3, 121	M. E. Smith	Lakeway, 3, 121	Sovereign Kitty, 3, 121	7	2:03.25	120,000
1993	Sky Beauty, 3, 121	M. E. Smith	Future Pretense, 3, 121	Silky Feather, 3, 121	5	2:03.49	120,000
1992	November Snow, 3, 121	C. W. Antley	Saratoga Dew, 3, 121	Pacific Squall, 3, 121	7	2:02.75	120,000

Year	Winner	Jockey	Second	Third	Strs	Time	1st Purse
1991	Versailles Treaty, 3, 121	A. T. Cordero Jr.	Til Forbid, 3, 121	Designated Dancer, 3, 121	6	2:02.57	$120,000
1990	Go for Wand, 3, 121	R. P. Romero	Charon, 3, 121	Pampered Star, 3, 121	3	2:00.80	130,560
1989	Open Mind, 3, 121	A. T. Cordero Jr.	Dearly Loved, 3, 121	Dream Deal, 3, 121	7	2:04.20	139,440
1988	Maplejinsky, 3, 121	A. T. Cordero Jr.	Make Change, 3, 121	Willa On the Move, 3, 121	5	2:01.80	136,320
1987	Up the Apalachee, 3, 121	J. Velasquez	Without Feathers, 3, 121	Fiesta Gal, 3, 121	7	2:04.00	138,240
1986	Classy Cathy, 3, 121	E. Fires	Valley Victory (Ire), 3, 121	Life At the Top, 3, 121	7	2:04.20	138,720
1985	Mom's Command, 3, 121	A. Fuller	Fran's Valentine, 3, 121	Foxy Deen, 3, 121	5	2:03.20	84,000
1984	Life's Magic, 3, 121	J. Velasquez	Lucky Lucky Lucky, 3, 121	Class Play, 3, 121	5	2:02.60	98,100
1983	Spit Curl, 3, 121	J. Cruguet	Lady Norcliffe, 3, 121	Sabin, 3, 121	5	2:02.40	65,880
1982	Broom Dance, 3, 121	G. McCarron	Too Chic, 3, 121	Mademoiselle Forli, 3, 121	7	2:02.20	67,680
1981	Prismatical, 3, 121	E. Maple	Banner Gala, 3, 121	Discorama, 3, 121	6	2:02.40	66,000
1980	Love Sign, 3, 121	R. Hernandez	Weber City Miss, 3, 121	Sugar and Spice, 3, 121	6	2:01.00	65,880
1979	It's in the Air, 3, 121	J. Fell	Davona Dale, 3, 121	Mairzy Doates, 3, 121	5	2:01.40	64,980
1978	White Star Line, 3, 121	M. Venezia	Summer Fling, 3, 121	Tempest Queen, 3, 121	6	2:04.00	64,920
1977	Our Mims, 3, 121	J. Velasquez	Sensational, 3, 121	Cum Laude Laurie, 3, 121	11	2:03.00	66,060
1976	Optimistic Gal, 3, 121	E. Maple	‡Javamine, 3, 121	Moontee, 3, 121	7	2:01.60	48,555
1975	Spout, 3, 121	J. Cruguet	Aunt Jin, 3, 121	Funalon, 3, 121	10	2:04.00	49,170
1974	Quaze Quilt, 3, 121	H. Gustines	Chris Evert, 3, 121	Fiesta Libre, 3, 115	8	2:02.60	33,660
1973	Desert Vixen, 3, 119	J. Velasquez	Bag of Tunes, 3, 119	Summer Festival, 3, 116	9	2:04.20	34,620

Named for the home state of Confederate Capt. Cottrill of Mobile, Alabama, the race's originator. Held at Belmont Park 1943-'45. Not held 1893-'96, 1898-1900, 1911-'12. 1¹⁄₈ miles 1872-'97, 1904, 1906-'16. 1¹⁄₁₆ miles 1901-'03, 1905.
‡Dona Maya finished second, DQ to fourth, 1976.

Alcibiades Stakes —*See* Darley Alcibiades Stakes

Alfred G. Vanderbilt Handicap

Grade 2 in 2008. Saratoga Race Course, three-year-olds and up, 6 furlongs, dirt. Held July 28, 2007, with a gross value of $260,000. First held in 1985. First graded in 1990. Stakes record 1:08.04 (2004 Speightstown).

Year	Winner	Jockey	Second	Third	Strs	Time	1st Purse
2007	Diabolical, 4, 120	M. G. Pino	Attila's Storm, 5, 117	Simon Pure, 4, 114	8	1:08.67	$150,000
2006	War Front, 4, 115	J. A. Santos	Judiths Wild Rush, 5, 116	Mass Media, 5, 117	6	1:10.21	124,920
2005	Pomeroy, 4, 117	E. Coa	I'm the Tiger, 5, 114	Voodoo, 7, 112	7	1:08.69	120,000
2004	Speightstown, 6, 120	J. R. Velazquez	Clock Stopper, 4, 115	Gators N Bears, 4, 118	6	1:08.04	120,000
2003	Private Horde, 4, 115	J. P. Lumpkins	Mountain General, 5, 118	Mike's Classic, 4, 114	5	1:09.18	120,000
2002	Orientate, 4, 121	J. D. Bailey	Say Florida Sandy, 8, 115	Multiple Choice, 4, 112	6	1:09.72	120,000
2001	Five Star Day, 5, 117	G. K. Gomez	Delaware Township, 5, 116	Bonapaw, 5, 117	7	1:08.57	120,000
2000	‡Successful Appeal, 4, 118	E. S. Prado	Intidab, 7, 117	Chasin' Wimmin, 5, 112	8	1:09.21	120,000
1999	Intidab, 6, 113	R. G. Davis	Artax, 4, 117	Yes It's True, 3, 117	7	1:09.03	90,000
1998	Kelly Kip, 4, 117	J. Samyn	Trafalger, 4, 114	Receiver, 5, 113	7	1:09.60	82,545
1997	Royal Haven, 5, 116	R. Migliore	Cold Execution, 6, 116	Punch Line, 7, 120	7	1:09.65	65,220
1996	Prospect Bay, 4, 113	J. D. Bailey	Honour and Glory, 3, 119	Lite the Fuse, 5, 123	7	1:08.29	65,760
1995	Not Surprising, 5, 115	R. G. Davis	Chimes Band, 4, 119	Mining Burrah, 5, 116	10	1:09.60	67,140
1994	Boundary, 4, 117	J. R. Velazquez	Cherokee Run, 4, 120	I Can't Believe, 6, 113	7	1:08.61	65,880
1993	Gold Spring (Arg), 5, 119	P. Day	Friendly Lover, 5, 122	Detox, 4, 115	9	1:09.31	70,680
1992	For Really, 5, 115	P. Day	Burn Fair, 5, 115	Drummond Lane, 5, 122	9	1:08.61	71,520
1991	Kid Russell, 5, 115	R. Mojica Jr.	Mr. Nasty, 4, 122	To Freedom, 3, 117	8	1:09.52	71,400
1990	Prospectors Gamble, 5, 122	J. A. Garcia	Sewickley, 5, 115	Mr. Nickerson, 4, 122	4	1:09.20	50,400
1989	Mr. Nickerson, 3, 112	J. A. Santos	Quick Call, 5, 115	Miami Slick, 4, 119	6	1:08.80	52,650
1988	High Brite, 4, 122	A. T. Cordero Jr.	Abject, 4, 115	Uncle Ho, 5, 115	4	1:10.20	50,400
1987	Banker's Jet, 5, 115	J. L. Vargas	Royal Pennant, 4, 115	Sun Master, 6, 122	6	1:09.20	49,230
1986	Cognizant, 5, 117	P. Day	Royal Pennant, 3, 112	Cullendale, 4, 115	7	1:09.60	33,060
1985	Cognizant, 4, 117	P. Day	Mayanesian, 6, 117	Spender, 4, 117	7	1:09.60	33,360

Named for Alfred Gwynne Vanderbilt (1912-'99), chairman of NYRA, and president of Belmont and Pimlico. Formerly named for Brownell Combs II's 1983 Jim Dandy S. (G3) winner A Phenomenon (1980 c. by Tentam), who broke down while leading in the '84 Forego H. (G2); A Phenomenon is one of four horses buried on the Saratoga grounds. Grade 3 1992-'94. A Phenomenon S. 1985-'93, 1996-'97. A Phenomenon H. 1994-'95, 1998-'99. A. G. Vanderbilt H. 2000-'02. Alfred G. Vanderbilt Breeders' Cup H. 2006. ‡Intidab finished first, DQ to second, 2000.

Allaire duPont Distaff Stakes

Grade 2 in 2008. Pimlico Race Course, three-year-olds and up, fillies and mares, 1¹⁄₁₆ miles, dirt. Held May 17, 2008, with a gross value of $150,000. First held in 1992. First graded in 1994. Stakes record 1:42.43 (2008 Buy the Barrel).

Year	Winner	Jockey	Second	Third	Strs	Time	1st Purse
2008	Buy the Barrel, 4, 120	G. Saez	Lexi Star, 6, 118	Bear Now, 4, 118	8	1:42.43	$90,000
2007	Rolling Sea, 4, 118	G. K. Gomez	Leah's Secret, 4, 120	Kettleoneup, 4, 124	7	1:42.88	60,000
2006	Pool Land, 4, 120	G. K. Gomez	Josh's Madelyn, 5, 118	In the Gold, 4, 124	9	1:42.71	120,000
2005	Silmaril, 4, 115	R. Fogelsonger	Ashado, 4, 123	Friel's for Real, 5, 114	4	1:44.87	60,000
2004	Friel's for Real, 4, 115	A. Castellano Jr.	Saintly Action, 5, 114	Nonsuch Bay, 5, 116	8	1:45.03	90,000
2003	Mandy's Gold, 5, 117	J. D. Bailey	Summer Colony, 5, 121	Stormy Frolic, 4, 114	4	1:46.32	90,000
2002	Summer Colony, 4, 119	J. R. Velazquez	Dancethruthedawn, 4, 119	Happily Unbridled, 4, 115	7	1:42.90	90,000
2001	Serra Lake, 4, 112	P. Day	Jostle, 4, 119	Prized Stamp, 4, 114	5	1:50.22	120,000
2000	Roza Robata, 5, 114	P. Day	Bella Chiarra, 5, 118	On a Soapbox, 4, 116	5	1:49.82	120,000
1999	Mil Kilates, 6, 113	S. J. Sellers	Merengue, 4, 121	Unbridled Hope, 5, 116	8	1:49.05	120,000

Racing — Graded Stakes 249

Year	Winner	Jockey	Second	Third	Strs	Time	1st Purse
1998	Ajina, 4, 120	J. D. Bailey	Naskra Colors, 6, 112	Pocho's Dream Girl, 4, 113	8	1:48.70	$120,000
1997	Rare Blend, 4, 114	J. D. Bailey	Scenic Point, 4, 114	Aileen's Countess, 5, 114	5	1:51.51	120,000
1996	Serena's Song, 4, 123	G. L. Stevens	Shoop, 5, 116	Churchbell Chimes, 5, 114	4	1:49.75	120,000
1995	Pennyhill Park, 5, 115	M. E. Smith	Halo America, 5, 117	Calipha, 4, 121	6	1:49.32	120,000
1994	Double Sixes, 4, 112	E. S. Prado	Broad Gains, 4, 118	Mz. Zill Bear, 5, 118	6	1:51.19	120,000
1993	Deputation, 4, 114	C. W. Antley	D. Theatrical Gal, 4, 112	Low Tolerance, 4, 115	6	1:49.12	120,000
1992	Wilderness Song, 4, 121	C. Perret	Harbour Club, 5, 110	Brilliant Brass, 5, 117	7	1:49.06	150,000

Named for prominent Maryland owner and breeder Allaire C. duPont (1913-2006); duPont bred and raced five-time Horse of the Year Kelso. Races for females are typically referred to as distaff races. Grade 3 1994-2006. Pimlico Distaff H. 1992-2001. Pimlico Breeders' Cup Distaff H. 2002-'05. Allaire duPont Breeders' Cup Distaff S. 2006-'07. 1 1/8 miles 1992-2001.

All Along Stakes

Grade 3 in 2008. Colonial Downs, three-year-olds and up, fillies and mares, 1 1/8 miles, turf. Held June 16, 2007, with a gross value of $197,000. First held in 1985. First graded in 1990. Stakes record 1:46.58 (2006 Film Maker).

Year	Winner	Jockey	Second	Third	Strs	Time	1st Purse
2007	Silver Charades, 5, 120	J. Valdivia Jr.	Humoristic, 6, 120	Bridge Game, 4, 120	11	1:49.62	$120,000
2006	Film Maker, 6, 120	R. A. Dominguez	Latice (Ire), 5, 120	Art Fan, 5, 120	6	1:46.58	120,000
2005	Stupendous Miss, 4, 120	G. L. Stevens	Humoristic, 4, 120	Dynamia, 4, 120	10	1:51.10	120,000
2004	Film Maker, 4, 119	E. S. Prado	Noisette, 4, 119	Lady Linda, 6, 119	7	1:50.08	120,000
2003	Dress To Thrill (Ire), 4, 117	E. S. Prado	Lady Linda, 5, 117	Lady of the Future, 5, 117	9	1:49.16	120,000
2002	Secret River, 5, 117	H. Karamanos	Golden Corona, 4, 117	Cayman Sunset (Ire), 5, 117	6	1:50.76	90,000
2001	Colstar, 5, 121	J. K. Court	Lucky Lune (Fr), 4, 119	Crystal Sea, 4, 119	8	1:47.53	90,000
2000	Idle Rich, 5, 115	A. T. Gryder	Emanating, 4, 115	Orange Sunset (Ire), 4, 115	11	1:55.95	60,000
1999	Tampico, 6, 122	E. S. Prado	Heavenly Advice, 5, 115	Absolutely Queenie, 6, 115	10	1:47.63	60,000
1998	Bursting Forth, 4, 122	E. S. Prado	The Unforgiven, 4, 117	Be Elusive, 4, 115	8	1:49.05	60,000
1997	Beyrouth, 5, 115	D. Rice	Hero's Pride (Fr), 4, 117	Palliser Bay, 5, 122	10	1:49.27	67,830
1996	Another Legend, 4, 115	C. O. Klinger	Brushing Gloom, 4, 119	Short Time, 4, 115	7	1:58.80	60,000
1994	Alice Springs, 4, 120	R. R. Douglas	Via Borghese, 5, 120	Mz. Zill Bear, 5, 116	6	1:47.34	150,000
1993	Lady Blessington (Fr), 5, 116	C. A. Black	Via Borghese, 4, 118	Logan's Mist, 4, 116	5	1:51.58	150,000
1992	Marble Maiden (GB), 3, 114	T. Jarnet	Wedding Ring (Ire), 3, 122	Sheba Dancer (Fr), 3, 114	7	1:49.89	180,000
1991	Sha Tha, 3, 113	M. E. Smith	Julie La Rousse (Ire), 3, 113	Once in My Life (Ire), 3, 114	11	1:52.49	180,000
1990	Foresta, 4, 120	A. T. Cordero Jr.	Miss Josh, 4, 120	Vijaya, 3, 114	10	1:49.40	180,000
1989	Lady Winner (Fr), 3, 112	K. Desormeaux	Capades, 3, 116	Betty Lobelia, 5, 116	8	1:53.60	180,000
1988	Ravinella, 3, 120	G. Guignard	Chapel of Dreams, 4, 120	Betty Lobelia, 3, 116	12	1:49.80	150,000
1985	Bug Eyed Betty, 2, 118	V. A. Bracciale Jr.	Cosmic Tiger, 2, 118	Eleanor's Best, 2, 118	7	1:36.60	29,185

Named for Daniel Wildenstein's Racing Hall of Fame member, 1983 Horse of the Year, and '83 Washington, D.C. International (G1) winner All Along (Fr) (1979 f. by Targowice). Formerly sponsored by Mignon C. Smith's Mede Cahaba Stable of Washington, D.C. 2005. Grade 2 1990-'97. All Along Breeders' Cup S. 2001-'04, 2006-'07. Mede Cahaba All Along Breeders' Cup S. 2005. Held at Laurel Park 1988-'94, 1996. Held at Delaware Park 1997. Held at Pimlico 1999. Not held 1995, 1986-'87. 1 9/16 miles 2000. Equaled course record 2001. Course record 2006.

All American Stakes

Grade 3 in 2008. Golden Gate Fields, three-year-olds and up, 1 1/8 miles, all weather. Held November 17, 2007, with a gross value of $150,000. First held in 1968. First graded in 1985. Stakes record 1:47.11 (2006 Buzzards Bay).

Year	Winner	Jockey	Second	Third	Strs	Time	1st Purse
2007	McCann's Mojave, 7, 122	F. T. Alvarado	Putmeinyourwill, 4, 122	Hello Sunday (Fr), 4, 122	9	1:50.04	$90,000
2006	Buzzards Bay, 4, 117	J. Valdivia Jr.	Melanyhasthepapers, 5, 113	Ace Blue (Brz), 6, 116	6	1:47.11	82,500
2005	Yougottawanna, 6, 118	J. P. Lumpkins	Jake Skate, 5, 119	Adreamisborn, 6, 119	7	1:41.42	41,250
2004	Yougottawanna, 5, 116	R. A. Baze	Gold Ruckus, 6, 115	Snorter, 4, 118	5	1:40.08	41,250
2003	Reba's Gold, 6, 118	C. J. Rollins	Free Corona, 5, 116	Truly a Judge, 5, 117	6	1:41.63	55,000
2002	Palmeiro, 4, 115	J. P. Lumpkins	Moonlight Meeting, 7, 116	Prodigious, 5, 117	9	1:42.31	82,500
2001	Euchre, 5, 118	J. P. Lumpkins	Irisheyesareflying, 5, 118	Moonlight Charger, 6, 115	8	1:41.69	82,500
2000	Peach Flat, 6, 114	J. Valdivia Jr.	Boss Ego, 4, 115	Casey Griffin, 4, 115	5	1:42.48	75,000
1999	Worldly Ways (GB), 5, 116	R. A. Baze	Barter Town, 4, 112	dh-Highland Gold, 4, 115 dh-Scooter Brown, 4, 114	8	1:40.62	60,000
1998	Wild Wonder, 4, 121	R. A. Baze	Crypto Star, 4, 118	General Royal, 4, 115	6	1:41.33	60,000
1997	Mister Fire Eyes (Ire), 5, 115	R. J. Warren Jr.	Region, 8, 115	Tolomeo, 4, 113	6	1:41.28	60,000
1996	Tzar Rodney (Fr), 4, 114	T. M. Chapman	Joy of Glory, 7, 115	Opera Score, 5, 115	5	1:49.74	60,000
1995	Bluegrass Prince (Ire), 4, 114	T. M. Chapman	Lord Shirldor (SAf), 6, 116	Kinema Red, 5, 113	7	1:49.01	68,750
1994	Slew of Damascus, 6, 122	T. M. Chapman	Fast Cure, 5, 114	The Tender Track, 7, 116	6	1:43.75	55,000
1993	Never Black, 6, 115	C. S. Nakatani	Stark South, 5, 115	Daros (GB), 4, 114	6	1:42.53	55,000
1992	Gum, 6, 112	G. Boulanger	Forty Niner Days, 5, 116	Prudent Manner (Ire), 5, 113	7	1:41.73	55,000
1991	Forty Niner Days, 4, 115	T. T. Doocy	Neptuno (Arg), 5, 116	Trebizond, 5, 115	6	1:42.70	55,000
1990	River Master, 4, 116	R. G. Davis	Miswaki Tern, 5, 116	Exclusive Partner, 8, 117	8	1:43.20	55,000
1989	Simply Majestic, 5, 121	R. D. Hansen	Ongoing Mister, 4, 113	Astronaut Prince, 5, 114	6	1:42.40	55,000
1988	Ifrad, 6, 117	T. M. Chapman	Stop the Fighting (Ire), 5, 115	Nickle Band, 4, 113	7	1:43.40	55,000
1987	Mangaki, 6, 115	T. T. Doocy	Barbery, 6, 116	Santella Mac (Ire), 4, 115	12	1:34.40	84,410
1986	Clever Song, 4, 122	F. Toro	Truce Maker, 4, 114	Ocean View, 5, 117	7	1:28.00	63,000
1985	Hegemony (Ire), 4, 121	D. G. McHargue	Champion Pilot, 4, 121	Nak Ack, 4, 117	5	1:28.40	71,740
1984	Ancestral (Ire), 4, 115	R. Sibille	Otter Slide, 5, 116	dh-Famous Star (GB), 5, 115 dh-Silveyville, 6, 124	10	1:29.20	49,750
1983	Major Sport, 6, 115	T. M. Chapman	Aristocratical, 6, 114	Take the Floor, 4, 115	11	1:29.40	50,300

Year	Winner	Jockey	Second	Third	Strs	Time	1st Purse
1982	Crews Hill (GB), 6, 118	R. A. Baze	Shagbark, 7, 122	Hallowed Envoy, 5, 116	7	1:29.40	$64,800
1981	Borrego Sun, 4, 114	R. A. Baze	Prenotion, 6, 116	Kane County, 4, 113	7	1:29.60	25,550
1980	California Express, 5, 110	J. Aragon	Kamehameha, 5, 121	Miami Sun, 6, 120	7	1:29.60	19,000
1979	Struttin' George, 5, 122	T. M. Chapman	Don Alberto, 4, 119	Charley Sutton, 5, 114	8	1:28.00	13,100
1978	Maheras, 5, 132	W. Mahorney	Charley Sutton, 4, 115	Oriental Magic, 6, 113	5	:56.20	15,550
1977	L'Natural, 4, 114	R. Caballero	Maheras, 4, 126	Sporting Goods, 7, 122	7	:56.00	15,800
1976	Shirley's Champion, 5, 114	F. Olivares	King Charly, 6, 113	Oriental Magic, 4, 114	7	:56.80	15,800
1975	Cherry River, 5, 126	W. Mahorney	El Potrero, 4, 115	Black Tornado, 5, 116	9	:56.80	16,200
1974	Tragic Isle, 5, 124	F. Mena	Prince Rameses, 5, 113	Times Rush, 6, 113	6	1:08.80	15,000
1973	Selecting, 4, 112	R. Yaka	I'm Ed, 4, 111	Goalie, 4, 120	7	1:09.00	15,150

In the past was a traditional Memorial Day weekend race. Formerly named for Charles S. Howard's 1938 Horse of the Year and '37, '38 Bay Meadows H. winner Seabiscuit (1933 c. by Hard Tack). Renamed in 2003 to coincide with the release of the movie *Seabiscuit*. All American H. 1968-2002, 2006. Seabiscuit H. 2003. Seabiscuit Breeders' Cup H. 2004-'05. Held at Bay Meadows 2001-'05. 6 furlongs 1968-'74. 5 furlongs 1975-'78. 7 1/2 furlongs 1979-'86. 1 mile 1987. 1 1/16 miles 1988-'94, 1997-2005. Dirt 1968-'74, 1997-2006. Turf 1975-'96. Four-year-olds and up 2005-'06. Dead heat for third 1984, '99.

Alysheba Stakes

Grade 3 in 2008. Churchill Downs, three-year-olds and up, 1 1/16 miles, dirt. Held May 2, 2008, with a gross value of $166,050. First held in 2004. First graded in 2007. Stakes record 1:42.32 (2005 Limehouse).

Year	Winner	Jockey	Second	Third	Strs	Time	1st Purse
2008	Giant Gizmo, 4, 118	R. Bejarano	Better Than Bonds, 6, 118	Wanderin Boy, 7, 119	7	1:43.96	$100,896
2007	Wanderin Boy, 6, 124	C. S. Nakatani	Half Ours, 4, 118	Student Council, 5, 120	7	1:43.45	68,236
2006	Gouldings Green, 5, 118	C. J. Lanerie	Wild Desert, 4, 118	Andromeda's Hero, 4, 118	8	1:42.37	68,861
2005	Limehouse, 4, 117	J. R. Velazquez	Skipaslew, 4, 117	Missme, 6, 117	8	**1:42.32**	69,998
2004	Congrats, 4, 116	J. R. Velazquez	Perfect Drift, 5, 114	Kodema, 5, 120	8	1:44.31	70,432

Named for Dorothy and Pamela Scarbauer's Racing Hall of Fame member, 1988 Horse of the Year, and '87 Kentucky Derby (G1) winner Alysheba (1984 c. by Alydar).

American Derby

Grade 2 in 2008. Arlington Park, three-year-olds, 1 3/16 miles, turf. Held July 21, 2007, with a gross value of $250,000. First held in 1884. First graded in 1973. Stakes record 1:54.60 (1955 Swaps).

Year	Winner	Jockey	Second	Third	Strs	Time	1st Purse
2007	Lattice, 3, 119	R. Albarado	Going Ballistic, 3, 121	Eighteenthofmarch, 3, 119	9	1:54.85	$144,000
2006	Union Avenue, 3, 119	L. Melancon	Can't Beat It, 3, 119	Amigoni (Ire), 3, 119	14	1:57.20	150,000
2005	Gun Salute, 3, 121	C. H. Velasquez	Purim, 3, 121	Exceptional Ride, 3, 119	8	1:55.31	150,000
2004	Simple Exchange (Ire), 3, 119	P. Smullen	Cool Conductor, 3, 119	Toasted, 3, 123	8	1:54.93	150,000
2003	Evolving Tactics (Ire), 3, 117	P. Smullen	Californian (GB), 3, 121	Scottago, 3, 116	5	1:59.04	150,000
2002	Mananan McLir, 3, 116	R. R. Douglas	Jazz Beat (Ire), 3, 117	Extra Check, 3, 116	8	1:57.11	135,000
2001	Fan Club's Mister, 3, 121	R. A. Meier	Monsieur Cat, 3, 116	Royal Spy, 3, 123	7	2:03.27	150,000
2000	Pine Dance, 3, 114	E. Ahern	Hymn (Ire), 3, 114	Del Mar Show, 3, 114	4	1:55.46	120,000
1997	Honor Glide, 3, 120	G. K. Gomez	Worldly Ways (GB), 3, 120	Daylight Savings, 3, 114	8	1:55.94	120,000
1996	‡Jaunatxo, 3, 114	J. L. Diaz	Trail City, 3, 120	Marlin, 3, 114	12	1:55.82	150,000
1995	Gold and Steel (Fr), 3, 114	A. T. Gryder	Torrential, 3, 120	Unanimous Vote (Ire), 3, 120	7	1:55.02	180,000
1994	dh-Overbury (Ire), 3, 114	S. J. Sellers		Star Campaigner, 3, 114	10	1:55.29	120,000
	dh-Vaudeville, 3, 114	A. D. Lopez					
1993	Explosive Red, 3, 120	S. J. Sellers	Earl of Barking (Ire), 3, 120	Newton's Law (Ire), 3, 114	9	1:59.92	180,000
1992	The Name's Jimmy, 3, 120	P. Day	Standiford, 3, 114	May I Inquire, 3, 114	14	1:59.41	180,000
1991	Olympio, 3, 126	E. Delahoussaye	Discover, 3, 114	Jackie Wackie, 3, 123	8	2:00.99	180,000
1990	Real Cash, 3, 123	P. A. Valenzuela	Home At Last, 3, 123	Adjudicating, 3, 117	6	2:02.00	180,000
1989	Awe Inspiring, 3, 126	C. Perret	Dispersal, 3, 123	Caesar, 3, 114	8	2:02.40	124,500
1987	Fortunate Moment, 3, 126	E. Fires	Fast Forward, 3, 114	Gem Master, 3, 118	9	2:03.80	100,350
1985	Creme Fraiche, 3, 123	E. Maple	Red Attack, 3, 114	Smile, 3, 123	5	2:01.60	96,000
1984	dh-At the Threshold, 3, 126	P. Day		Par Flite, 3, 114	7	2:04.00	46,800
	dh-High Alexander, 3, 120	G. Gallitano					
1983	Play Fellow, 3, 123	P. Day	Le Cou Cou, 3, 114	Brother, 3, 114	8	2:04.40	65,100
1982	Wolfie's Rascal, 3, 123	R. Hernandez	Dew Line, 3, 114	Northern Majesty, 3, 120	8	2:05.60	65,100
1981	Pocket Zipper, 3, 120	R. Sibille	Fairway Phantom, 3, 123	Double Sonic, 3, 123	11	2:03.80	84,000
1980	Hurry Up Blue, 3, 114	G. Gallitano	Tizon, 3, 114	Spruce Needles, 3, 123	6	2:04.40	83,400
1979	Smarten, 3, 126	S. Maple	Super Hit, 3, 114	Weather Tamer, 3, 114	6	2:05.20	63,600
1978	Nasty and Bold, 3, 114	J. Samyn	Star de Naskra, 3, 114	Beau Sham, 3, 114	13	2:03.40	68,100
1977	Silver Series, 3, 126	L. Snyder	Run Dusty Run, 3, 126	Brach's Hilarious, 3, 112	6	2:02.40	68,880
1976	Fifth Marine, 3, 121	R. Turcotte	Majestic Light, 3, 121	Play the Red, 3, 121	11	1:49.20	93,400
1975	Honey Mark, 3, 116	G. Patterson	High Steel, 3, 112	Go to the Bank, 3, 111	14	1:44.40	93,400
1974	Determined King, 3, 112	D. Montoya	Orders, 3, 114	Sr. Diplomat, 3, 111	13	1:47.80	92,000
1973	Bemo, 3, 117	W. J. Passmore	Golden Don, 3, 116	Buffalo Lark, 3, 114	12	1:49.60	69,400

Formerly sponsored by PrimeCo Communications 1997. Grade 1 1973-'74, 1981-'89. PrimeCo American Derby 1997. Held at Washington Park 1884-1904, 1926-'27, 1929-'57. Held at Hawthorne Race Course 1916. Not held 1895-'97, 1899, 1905-'15, 1917-'25, 1936, 1938-'39, 1986, 1988, 1998-'99. 1 1/2 miles 1884-1904, 1926-'27. 1 1/4 miles 1916, 1928-'51, 1962-'65, 1977-'91. 1 1/8 miles 1952-'54, 1958-'61, 1966-'74, 1976. 1 1/16 miles 1975. Dirt 1884-1954, 1958-'69, 1977-'91. Dead heat for first 1984, 1994. ‡Trail City finished first, DQ to second, 1996.

American Invitational Handicap

Grade 2 in 2008. Hollywood Park, three-year-olds and up, 1 1/8 miles, turf. Held June 30, 2007, with a gross value of $250,000. First held in 1938. First graded in 1973. Stakes record 1:45.60 (1987 Clever Song).

Year	Winner	Jockey	Second	Third	Strs	Time	1st Purse
2007	Out of Control (Brz), 4, 113	M. C. Baze	The Tin Man, 9, 123	Fast and Furious (Fr), 6, 116	6	1:46.89	$150,000
2006	The Tin Man, 8, 121	V. Espinoza	Hendrix, 5, 116	Fourty Niners Son, 5, 120	5	1:46.24	150,000
2005	Whilly (Ire), 4, 117	F. F. Martinez	King of Happiness, 6, 120	Fourty Niners Son, 4, 115	8	1:46.30	150,000
2004	Bayamo (Ire), 5, 117	D. R. Flores	Sarafan, 7, 119	Night Patrol, 8, 114	5	1:46.60	90,000
2003	Candy Ride (Arg), 4, 120	G. L. Stevens	Special Ring, 6, 118	Irish Warrior, 5, 116	5	1:46.20	90,000
2002	The Tin Man, 4, 115	M. E. Smith	Devine Wind, 6, 115	Kappa King, 5, 116	7	1:46.82	90,000
2001	Takarian (Ire), 6, 114	G. K. Gomez	Fighting Falcon, 5, 114	Fateful Dream, 4, 116	7	1:48.19	90,000
2000	Dark Moondancer (GB), 5, 122	C. J. McCarron	Sardaukar (GB), 4, 113	Sunshine Street, 5, 119	6	1:46.74	90,000
1999	Takarian (Ire), 4, 114	G. K. Gomez	Montemiro (Fr), 5, 112	Special Quest (Fr), 4, 115	6	1:47.37	90,000
1998	Magellan, 5, 116	G. L. Stevens	Bonapartiste (Fr), 4, 116	Sharekann (Ire), 6, 112	8	1:47.05	90,000
1997	El Angelo, 5, 118	A. O. Solis	Naninja, 4, 114	Wavy Run (Ire), 6, 117	6	1:46.99	96,360
1996	Labeeb (GB), 4, 119	E. Delahoussaye	Gold and Steel (Fr), 4, 118	Earl of Barking (Ire), 6, 116	8	1:45.78	66,120
1995	Silver Wizard, 5, 118	G. L. Stevens	Romarin (Brz), 5, 120	Savinio, 5, 118	5	1:46.02	91,900
1994	Blues Traveller (Ire), 4, 115	C. W. Antley	Gothland (Fr), 5, 119	Johann Quatz (Fr), 5, 116	7	1:46.50	128,000
1993	†Toussaud, 4, 114	K. Desormeaux	Man From Eldorado, 5, 115	Journalism, 5, 117	6	1:46.87	126,000
1992	Man From Eldorado, 4, 114	K. Desormeaux	Bold Russian (GB), 5, 116	Golden Pheasant, 6, 123	4	1:47.11	122,000
1991	Tight Spot, 4, 123	L. A. Pincay Jr.	Exbourne, 5, 122	Super May, 5, 118	8	1:46.00	129,400
1990	Classic Fame, 4, 117	E. Delahoussaye	Steinlen (GB), 7, 125	Pleasant Variety, 6, 116	7	1:47.80	126,800
1989	Mister Wonderful (GB), 6, 115	F. Toro	Steinlen (GB), 6, 121	Pranke (Arg), 5, 117	4	1:47.20	183,600
1988	Skip Out Front, 6, 115	C. J. McCarron	Steinlen (GB), 5, 121	World Court, 5, 113	4	1:46.40	120,800
1987	Clever Song, 5, 118	L. A. Pincay Jr.	Skip Out Front, 5, 114	Barbery, 6, 115	7	1:45.60	127,800
1986	Al Mamoon, 5, 119	P. A. Valenzuela	Truce Maker, 8, 111	Will Dancer (Fr), 4, 114	6	1:39.20	107,000
1985	Tsunami Slew, 4, 117	G. L. Stevens	Al Mamoon, 4, 117	Dahar, 4, 123	7	1:46.20	122,300
1984	Bel Bolide, 6, 121	T. Lipham	Silveyville, 6, 118	Vin St Benet (GB), 5, 118	8	1:46.80	123,600
1983	John Henry, 8, 127	C. J. McCarron	Prince Florimund (SAf), 5, 120	Tonzarun, 5, 114	8	1:48.40	97,100
1982	Spence Bay (Ire), 7, 122	F. Toro	The Bart, 6, 124	Peter Jones, 4, 113	10	1:47.20	100,300
1981	Bold Tropic (SAf), 6, 126	W. Shoemaker	The Bart, 5, 117	Don Roberto, 4, 112	9	1:46.80	98,100
1980	Bold Tropic (SAf), 5, 124	W. Shoemaker	Inkerman, 5, 115	Borzoi, 4, 117	8	1:46.40	65,700
1979	Smoggy (GB), 5, 114	D. G. McHargue	Dom Alaric (Fr), 5, 120	Inkerman, 4, 119	8	1:47.40	65,500
1978	Effervescing, 5, 119	L. A. Pincay Jr.	Diagramatic, 5, 123	April Axe, 3, 113	4	1:47.20	65,500
1977	Hunza Dancer, 5, 120	J. Cruguet	Anne's Pretender, 5, 121	Legendaire, 4, 115	11	1:47.20	68,900
1976	King Pellinore, 4, 121	W. Shoemaker	Riot in Paris, 5, 123	Caucasus, 4, 120	7	1:48.00	48,200
1975	Pass the Glass, 4, 115	F. Toro	Big Band, 5, 116	Against the Snow, 5, 114	11	1:48.20	53,800
	Montmartre, 5, 115	F. Toro	Top Crowd, 4, 115	Ancient Title, 5, 128	9	1:49.60	51,800
1974	Plunk, 4, 117	L. A. Pincay Jr.	Scantling, 4, 115	Mr. Cockatoo, 5, 114	11	1:48.20	51,900
1973	Kentuckian, 4, 114	R. Campas	Life Cycle, 4, 121	Wing Out, 5, 118	9	1:48.00	50,400

Traditionally held during the July 4 holiday. Grade 1 1988-'89. American H. 1938-2004. Held at Santa Anita Park 1949. Not held 1942-'43. 1 1/16 miles 1945-'46, 1986. 1 1/4 miles 1950. Dirt 1938-'67. Four-year-olds and up 1945. Two divisions 1975. †Denotes female.

American Invitational Oaks

Grade 1 in 2008. Hollywood Park, three-year olds (Northern and Southern Hemisphere), fillies, 1 1/4 miles, turf. Held July 7, 2007, with a gross value of $750,000. First held in 2002. First graded in 2004. Stakes record 1:59.03 (2005 Cesario [Jpn]).

Year	Winner	Jockey	Second	Third	Strs	Time	1st Purse
2007	Panty Raid, 3, 121	E. S. Prado	Valbenny (Ire), 3, 121	Anamato (Aus), 4, 125	9	2:01.53	$450,000
2006	Wait a While, 3, 121	G. K. Gomez	Asahi Rising (Jpn), 3, 121	Arravale, 3, 121	8	1:59.38	450,000
2005	Cesario (Jpn), 3, 121	Y. Fukunaga	Melhor Ainda, 3, 121	Singhalese (GB), 3, 121	12	1:59.03	450,000
2004	Ticker Tape (GB), 3, 121	K. Desormeaux	Dance in the Mood (Jpn), 3, 121	Hollywood Story, 3, 121	13	2:01.54	450,000
2003	Dimitrova, 3, 119	D. R. Flores	Sand Springs, 3, 121	Atlantic Ocean, 3, 121	14	1:59.98	450,000
2002	‡Megahertz (GB), 3, 121	A. O. Solis	Dublino, 3, 121	Alozaina (Ire), 3, 121	14	2:00.46	300,000

Held during the July 4 holiday. Formerly sponsored by American Airlines of Dallas/Ft. Worth, Texas 2006. ‡Dublino finished first, DQ to second, 2002.

American Turf Stakes — See Crown Royal American Turf Stakes

Amsterdam Stakes

Grade 2 in 2008. Saratoga Race Course, three-year-olds, 6 1/2 furlongs, dirt. Held July 30, 2007, with a gross value of $150,000. First held in 1901. First graded in 1998. Stakes record 1:15.97 (2007 Most Distinguished).

Year	Winner	Jockey	Second	Third	Strs	Time	1st Purse
2007	Most Distinguished, 3, 115	R. Bejarano	Americanus, 3, 115	Starbase, 3, 116	9	**1:15.97**	$90,000
2006	Court Folly, 3, 115	C. H. Borel	Songster, 3, 123	El Nino, 3, 117	4	1:16.14	90,000
2005	Santana Strings, 3, 121	E. Coa	Social Probation, 3, 116	Silver Train, 3, 115	9	1:10.18	90,000
2004	Bwana Charlie, 3, 123	S. J. Sellers	Pomeroy, 3, 123	Weigelia, 3, 123	7	1:09.40	90,000
2003	Zavata, 3, 119	J. D. Bailey	Great Notion, 3, 121	Trust N Luck, 3, 123	7	1:08.64	90,000
2002	Listen Here, 3, 121	P. Day	Boston Common, 3, 123	Bold Truth, 3, 115	8	1:09.58	90,000
2001	City Zip, 3, 123	J. F. Chavez	Speightstown, 3, 118	Smile My Lord, 3, 118	6	1:11.03	81,420
2000	Personal First, 3, 120	P. Day	Disco Rico, 3, 123	Trippi, 3, 123	6	1:09.33	66,000
1999	Successful Appeal, 3, 122	E. S. Prado	Lion Hearted, 3, 114	Silver Season, 3, 119	9	1:10.25	50,340

Year	Winner	Jockey	Second	Third	Strs	Time	1st Purse
1998	dh-Mint, 3, 119	E. Coa		Southern Bostonion, 3, 119	8	1:10.28	$33,060
	dh-Secret Firm, 3, 117	E. S. Prado					
1997	Oro de Mexico, 3, 117	C. W. Antley	Trafalger, 3, 122	Kelly Kip, 3, 122	7	1:10.58	16,425
1996	Distorted Humor, 3, 115	P. Day	Gold Fever, 3, 121	Stu's Choice, 3, 115	7	1:09.13	32,820
1995	Kings Fiction, 3, 112	P. Day	Lord Carson, 3, 115	Ft. Stockton, 3, 115	5	1:09.75	32,250
1994	Chimes Band, 3, 117	J. D. Bailey	Ledford, 3, 115	Halo's Image, 3, 115	6	1:09.90	32,325
	Mr. Shawklit, 3, 115	W. H. McCauley	Scarlet Rage, 3, 115	Groovy Jett, 3, 117	5	1:10.89	32,325
1993	Evil Bear, 3, 117	J. A. Santos	Punch Line, 3, 122	Digging In, 3, 119	5	1:22.09	28,800

Named for Amsterdam, New York, located in Montgomery County. Formerly named for Flying Zee Stable's G2 SW Screen King (1976 c. by Silent Screen); Screen King broke his maiden at Belmont Park and ended his career at Saratoga in the Travers S. (G1). Grade 3 1998-2000. Screen King S. 1993-'97. Held at Belmont Park 1993. Not held 1911-'12, 1924-'92. 1 mile 1901-'23. 7 furlongs 1993. 6 furlongs 1901-'10, 1913-'23, 1994-2005. Three-year-olds and up 1901-'23. Two divisions 1994. Dead heat for first 1998.

Ancient Title Stakes

Grade 1 in 2008. Oak Tree at Santa Anita, three-year-olds and up, 6 furlongs, all weather. Held October 7, 2007, with a gross value of $300,000. First held in 1985. First graded in 1990. Stakes record 1:07.57 (2007 Idiot Proof).

Year	Winner	Jockey	Second	Third	Strs	Time	1st Purse
2007	Idiot Proof, 3, 123	D. R. Flores	Greg's Gold, 6, 124	Barbecue Eddie, 3, 123	5	**1:07.57**	$180,000
2006	Bordonaro, 5, 124	P. A. Valenzuela	Thor's Echo, 4, 124	Jungle Prince, 5, 124	6	1:07.93	120,000
2005	Captain Squire, 6, 124	A. O. Solis	Zanzibar (Arg), 4, 124	Indian Country, 4, 124	7	1:08.85	150,000
2004	Pt's Grey Eagle, 3, 109	A. Bisono	Pohave, 4, 118	Hombre Rapido, 7, 114	8	1:08.84	120,000
2003	Avanzado (Arg), 6, 116	T. Baze	Captain Squire, 4, 117	Bluesthestandard, 6, 115	6	1:08.12	81,375
2002	†Kalookan Queen, 6, 119	A. O. Solis	Crafty C. T., 4, 116	Mellow Fellow, 7, 117	6	1:08.26	125,625
2001	Swept Overboard, 4, 116	E. Delahoussaye	Kona Gold, 7, 127	I Love Silver, 3, 116	7	1:07.67	124,260
2000	Kona Gold, 6, 124	A. O. Solis	Regal Thunder, 6, 117	Elaborate, 5, 116	4	1:08.11	123,060
1999	Lexicon, 4, 116	K. Desormeaux	Kona Gold, 5, 120	Regal Thunder, 5, 117	8	1:07.84	125,400
1998	Gold Land, 7, 117	K. Desormeaux	†A. P. Assay, 4, 116	Swiss Yodeler, 4, 114	8	1:08.50	94,020
1997	Elmhurst, 7, 114	C. S. Nakatani	Swiss Yodeler, 3, 114	Larry the Legend, 5, 115	7	1:08.62	95,000
1996	Lakota Brave, 7, 117	E. Delahoussaye	Letthebighossroll, 8, 119	‡Paying Dues, 4, 118	5	1:08.16	93,700
1995	†Track Gal, 4, 116	G. L. Stevens	Siphon (Brz), 4, 117	Forest Gazelle, 4, 116	6	1:08.32	59,150
1994	Saratoga Gambler, 6, 113	M. A. Pedroza	Uncaged Fury, 3, 114	Concept Win, 4, 117	8	1:08.67	62,500
1993	Cardmania, 7, 116	E. Delahoussaye	Music Merci, 7, 117	Bahatur, 4, 114	8	1:08.04	61,975
1992	Gray Slewpy, 4, 118	K. Desormeaux	Trick Me, 4, 114	Light of Morn, 6, 117	9	1:08.48	59,372
1991	Frost Free, 6, 118	C. J. McCarron	Answer Do, 5, 118	Sir Beaufort, 4, 113	7	1:08.66	61,525
1990	Corwyn Bay (Ire), 4, 118	E. Delahoussaye	Sensational Star, 6, 119	Yes I'm Blue, 4, 117	7	1:08.40	61,375
1989	Sam Who, 4, 120	L. A. Pincay Jr.	Sunny Blossom, 4, 116	Don's Irish Melody, 6, 114	5	1:08.00	46,050
1988	Olympic Prospect, 4, 123	L. A. Pincay Jr.	Sebrof, 4, 118	Reconnoitering, 4, 114	6	1:09.00	55,630
1987	Zany Tactics, 6, 123	J. L. Kaenel	On the Line, 3, 117	Carload, 5, 117	3	1:09.00	35,500
1986	Groovy, 3, 123	J. A. Santos	Rosie's K. T., 5, 117	Sun Master, 5, 114	8	1:08.20	49,450
1985	Temerity Prince, 5, 120	W. A. Ward	Debonaire Junior, 4, 124	Bid Us, 5, 115	6	1:09.20	37,150

Named for Kirkland Stable's 1975, '76 Californian S. (G1) winner Ancient Title (1970 g. by Gummo). Grade 3 1990-'98. Grade 2 1999-2000. Ancient Title H. 1985-'89. Ancient Title Breeders' Cup H. 1990-2004. Ancient Title Breeders' Cup S. 2005-'06. Dirt 1985-2006. ‡Criollito (Arg) finished third, DQ to fourth, 1996. Track record 2001. †Denotes female.

Appalachian Stakes

Grade 3 in 2008. Keeneland Race Course, three-year-olds, fillies, 1 mile, turf. Held April 16, 2008, with a gross value of $125,000. First held in 1989. First graded in 2008. Stakes record 1:34.80 (1998 Halo River).

Year	Winner	Jockey	Second	Third	Strs	Time	1st Purse
2008	Alwajeeha, 3, 117	J. R. Velazquez	Sweepstake (Ire), 3, 117	I Lost My Choo, 3, 119	10	1:37.37	$77,500
2007	Audacious Chloe, 3, 121	J. R. Velazquez	Classic Neel, 3, 119	Red Birkin, 3, 117	12	1:36.39	71,734
2006	Lady of Venice (Fr), 3, 117	J. R. Leparoux	May Night, 3, 117	J'ray, 3, 121	5	1:35.85	67,642
2005	Melhor Ainda, 3, 121	J. R. Velazquez	Paddy's Daisy, 3, 123	Sweet Talker, 3, 121	8	1:37.69	69,936
2004	Lucifer's Stone, 3, 120	J. A. Santos	Western Ransom, 3, 116	Honey Ryder, 3, 116	7	1:37.58	70,370
2003	Ocean Drive, 3, 120	J. D. Bailey	Tangle (Ire), 3, 117	Cheryl's Myth, 3, 116	8	1:36.13	69,005
2002	Stylelistick, 3, 120	P. Day	Lush Soldier, 3, 120	August Storm, 3, 120	9	1:36.62	69,502
2001	Bold Answer, 3, 116	M. Guidry	Voodoo Dancer, 3, 120	Word Puzzle, 3, 120	9	1:35.22	70,370
2000	Impending Bear, 3, 116	P. Day	Ever After, 3, 116	Hummingbird Red, 3, 116	10	1:36.24	70,246
1999	Tres Coronas, 3, 114	J. F. Chavez	Perfect Sting, 3, 114	Seducer, 3, 119	9	1:35.26	69,254
1998	Halo River, 3, 116	C. Perret	Adel, 3, 114	Shires Ende, 3, 114	9	**1:34.80**	45,096
1997	Witchful Thinking, 3, 118	S. J. Sellers	Starry Dreamer, 3, 118	St Lucinda, 3, 113	8	1:35.19	44,733
1996	Dyna Whirl, 3, 112	R. G. Davis	Vashon, 3, 112	Cymbala (Fr), 3, 114	6	1:38.22	44,169
1995	Bail Out Becky, 3, 121	S. J. Sellers	Christmas Gift, 3, 118	Appointed One, 3, 113	9	1:41.74	42,110
1994	Bedroom Blues, 3, 115	M. E. Smith	Promised Legacy, 3, 113	Fred's Affair, 3, 121	9	1:45.11	34,271
1993	Harlan Honey, 3, 115	P. Day	Foxy Ferdie, 3, 121	Heavenliness, 3, 114	6	1:45.38	37,976
1992	White Corners, 3, 115	C. Perret	Sing For Free, 3, 113	Shes Just Super, 3, 121	9	1:44.49	39,260
1991	Radiant Ring, 3, 121	P. Day	Wavering Wandy, 3, 112	Maria Balastiere, 3, 115	10	1:43.74	36,741
1990	Super Fan, 3, 115	J. A. Santos	Southern Tradition, 3, 121	Wavering Girl, 3, 121	9	1:44.00	36,254
1989	To the Lighthouse, 3, 115	R. P. Romero	Darby Shuffle, 3, 121	Fairway Style, 3, 115	10	1:46.20	36,465

Named for the Appalachian mountain region located in Eastern Kentucky. 1¹/₁₆ miles 1989-'95.

Apple Blossom Handicap

Grade 1 in 2008. Oaklawn Park, four-year-olds and up, fillies and mares, 1 1/16 miles, dirt. Held April 5, 2008, with a gross value of $500,000. First held in 1973. First graded in 1977. Stakes record 1:40.20 (1984 Heatherten).

Year	Winner	Jockey	Second	Third	Strs	Time	1st Purse
2008	Zenyatta, 4, 116	M. E. Smith	Brownie Points, 5, 115	Ginger Punch, 5, 122	6	1:42.64	$300,000
2007	Ermine, 4, 116	E. Castro	Take D' Tour, 6, 118	Round Pond, 5, 120	8	1:44.02	300,000
2006	Spun Sugar, 4, 116	M. J. Luzzi	Happy Ticket, 5, 119	La Reason, 6, 114	6	1:42.59	300,000
2005	Dream of Summer, 6, 117	P. A. Valenzuela	Star Parade (Arg), 6, 116	Shadow Cast, 4, 116	7	1:43.86	300,000
2004	Azeri, 6, 123	M. E. Smith	‡Star Parade (Arg), 5, 114	Wild Spirit (Chi), 5, 119	6	1:41.24	300,000
2003	Azeri, 5, 123	M. E. Smith	Take Charge Lady, 4, 118	Mandy's Gold, 5, 116	7	1:43.00	300,000
2002	Azeri, 4, 117	M. E. Smith	Affluent, 4, 118	Miss Linda (Arg), 5, 118	5	1:42.75	300,000
2001	Gourmet Girl, 6, 113	C. H. Borel	Lu Ravi, 6, 114	Lazy Slusan, 6, 116	11	1:42.15	300,000
2000	Heritage of Gold, 5, 118	S. J. Sellers	Lu Ravi, 5, 114	Bordelaise (Arg), 5, 113	7	1:42.22	300,000
1999	Banshee Breeze, 4, 122	J. D. Bailey	Sister Act, 4, 114	Silent Eskimo, 4, 112	6	1:41.64	300,000
1998	Escena, 5, 117	J. D. Bailey	Glitter Woman, 4, 119	Toda Una Dama (Arg), 5, 115	7	1:40.95	300,000
1997	Halo America, 7, 117	C. H. Borel	Jewel Princess, 5, 124	Different (Arg), 5, 121	8	1:41.65	300,000
1996	Twice the Vice, 5, 117	C. J. McCarron	Halo America, 6, 115	Serena's Song, 4, 124	7	1:41.71	300,000
1995	Heavenly Prize, 4, 120	P. Day	Halo America, 5, 116	Paseana (Arg), 8, 122	6	1:42.76	300,000
1994	Nine Keys, 4, 116	M. E. Smith	Mamselle Bebette, 4, 116	Re Toss (Arg), 7, 117	10	1:42.15	300,000
1993	Paseana (Arg), 6, 124	C. J. McCarron	Looie Capote, 4, 115	Luv Me Luv Me Not, 4, 114	9	1:41.80	300,000
1992	Paseana (Arg), 5, 124	C. J. McCarron	Fit for a Queen, 6, 121	Slide Out Front, 4, 109	8	1:42.13	300,000
1991	Degenerate Gal, 6, 115	P. Day	Charon, 4, 121	Fit to Scout, 4, 116	6	1:41.25	300,000
1990	Gorgeous, 4, 122	E. Delahoussaye	Bayakoa (Arg), 6, 126	Affirmed Classic, 4, 112	4	1:40.40	210,000
1989	Bayakoa (Arg), 5, 120	L. A. Pincay Jr.	Goodbye Halo, 4, 125	Invited Guest (Ire), 5, 116	6	1:41.60	150,000
1988	By Land by Sea, 4, 121	F. Toro	Invited Guest (Ire), 4, 116	Hail a Cab, 5, 113	10	1:41.20	150,000
1987	North Sider, 5, 122	A. T. Cordero Jr.	Family Style, 4, 120	Queen Alexandra, 5, 119	7	1:41.20	162,300
1986	Love Smitten, 5, 119	C. J. McCarron	Lady's Secret, 4, 127	Sefa's Beauty, 7, 122	7	1:40.40	162,180
1985	Sefa's Beauty, 6, 120	P. Day	Heatherten, 6, 127	Life's Magic, 4, 123	7	1:42.20	161,700
1984	Heatherten, 5, 116	S. Maple	Try Something New, 5, 121	Holiday Dancer, 4, 115	10	1:40.20	167,400
1983	Miss Huntington, 6, 118	J. Velasquez	‡Sefa's Beauty, 4, 117	Queen of Song, 4, 114	13	1:44.80	172,620
1982	Track Robbery, 6, 124	E. Delahoussaye	Andover Way, 4, 120	Jameela, 6, 123	6	1:45.20	161,040
1981	Bold 'n Determined, 4, 124	E. Delahoussaye	La Bonzo, 5, 111	Karla's Enough, 4, 119	7	1:44.20	131,820
1980	Billy Jane, 4, 113	J. Lively	Jameela, 4, 118	Miss Baja, 5, 121	11	1:43.60	106,290
1979	Miss Baja, 4, 113	E. Maple	Kit's Double, 5, 114	Navajo Princess, 4, 121	10	1:43.00	106,800
1978	Northernette, 4, 119	D. Brumfield	Taisez Vous, 4, 124	Cum Laude Laurie, 4, 121	9	1:42.00	74,130
1977	Hail Hilarious, 4, 121	D. Pierce	Kittyluck, 4, 112	Summertime Promise, 5, 119	15	1:41.40	82,290
1976	Summertime Promise, 4, 119	D. G. McHargue	Baygo, 7, 114	Costly Dream, 5, 113	9	1:40.60	35,760
1975	Susan's Girl, 6, 124	J. Nichols	Truchas, 6, 116	Matuta, 4, 114	12	1:42.40	36,720
1974	Big Dare, 4, 116	R. N. Ussery	Gallant Davelle, 4, 122	Sixty Sails, 4, 115	11	1:41.80	19,050

Named for the apple trees typically in bloom during the Oaklawn Park meet. Grade 3 1977. Grade 2 1978-'81, 1990-'91. 6 furlongs 1974. 1 mile 70 yards 1975-'79. Three-year-olds and up 1974. ‡Number finished second, DQ to fourth, 1983. ‡Wild Spirit (Chi) finished second, DQ to third on an Arkansas Racing Commission decision, 2004. Held as an overnight handicap 1973.

Appleton Handicap

Grade 3 in 2008. Gulfstream Park, four-year-olds and up, 1 mile, turf. Held January 27, 2008, with a gross value of $125,000. First held in 1952. First graded in 1973. Stakes record 1:32.12 (2007 Silver Tree).

Year	Winner	Jockey	Second	Third	Strs	Time	1st Purse
2008	Buffalo Man, 4, 117	E. S. Prado	Elusive Fort (SAf), 6, 117	Jet Propulsion, 5, 115	10	1:34.86	$75,000
2007	Silver Tree, 7, 118	E. S. Prado	Steel Light, 6, 117	Old Dodge (Brz), 6, 117	8	1:32.12	75,000
2006	Gulch Approval, 6, 115	R. E. Alvarado Jr.	Old Dodge (Brz), 5, 115	Drum Major, 4, 115	9	1:32.80	60,000
2005	Mr. Light (Arg), 6, 114	C. H. Velasquez	Host (Chi), 5, 119	Millennium Dragon (GB), 6, 120	8	1:32.98	60,000
2004	Millennium Dragon (GB), 5, 116	R. Migliore	Political Attack, 5, 118	Proud Man, 6, 118	12	1:34.40	90,000
2003	Point Prince, 4, 115	M. R. Cruz	Krieger, 5, 115	Red Sea (GB), 7, 114	9	1:37.84	90,000
2002	Pisces, 5, 113	R. I. Velez	North East Bound, 6, 117	Capsized, 6, 114	10	1:39.41	90,000
2001	Associate, 6, 114	J. F. Chavez	Band Is Passing, 5, 119	El Mirasol, 6, 115	12	1:33.69	90,000
2000	Band Is Passing, 4, 115	E. Coa	Hibernian Rhapsody (Ire), 5, 119	Shamrock City, 5, 114	11	1:40.11	60,000
1999	Behaviour (GB), 7, 113	S. J. Sellers	Notoriety, 6, 112	Legs Galore, 4, 113	6	1:45.77	60,000
1998	Sir Cat, 5, 119	J. D. Bailey	Wild Event, 5, 114	Kingcanrunallday, 5, 116	5	1:42.69	60,000
1997	Montjoy, 5, 116	M. E. Smith	Mighty Forum (GB), 6, 114	Elite Jeblar, 7, 114	12	1:39.88	60,000
1996	The Vid, 6, 122	W. H. McCauley	Dove Hunt, 5, 120	Montreal Red, 4, 115	11	1:41.79	60,000
1995	Dusty Screen, 7, 116	W. H. McCauley	The Vid, 5, 114	Dove Hunt, 4, 114	7	1:42.72	60,000
1994	Paradise Creek, 5, 121	M. E. Smith	Fourstars Allstar, 4, 117	Elite Jeblar, 4, 111	8	1:40.57	60,000
1993	Cigar Toss (Arg), 6, 112	B. G. Moore	Bidding Proud, 4, 113	Archies Laughter, 5, 114	9	1:43.55	60,000
1992	Royal Ninja, 6, 112	J. D. Bailey	Archies Laughter, 4, 114	Native Boundary, 4, 116	12	1:42.49	60,000
1991	Jolie's Halo, 4, 110	R. Platts	Rowdy Regal, 4, 110	Shot Gun Scott, 4, 118	11	1:40.50	60,000
1990	Highland Springs, 6, 118	C. Perret	Prince Randi, 4, 115	Wanderkin, 7, 116	9	1:35.20	60,000
1989	Fabulous Indian, 4, 109	E. O. Nunez	Equalize, 7, 125	Simply Majestic, 5, 121	11	1:35.00	60,000
1988	Yankee Affair, 6, 116	R. P. Romero	Performing Pappy, 4, 114	Kings River (Ire), 6, 114	14	1:35.00	60,000
1987	Regal Flier, 6, 113	J. Vasquez	Wollaston, 5, 117	Hi Ideal, 5, 113	9	1:35.60	27,375
	Racing Star, 5, 111	S. B. Soto	Trubulare, 4, 111	Onyxly, 6, 116	10	1:35.60	27,975
1986	Cool, 5, 116	J. Vasquez	Dr. Schwartzman, 5, 120	Smart and Sharp, 7, 115	11	1:39.60	39,690
1985	Smart and Sharp, 6, 117	M. Russ	Amerilad, 4, 112	Dr. Schwartzman, 4, 117	11	1:34.60	31,740
	Star Choice, 6, 118	J. McKnight	Late Act, 4, 121	Solidified, 4, 114	10	1:34.40	31,440

Racing — Graded Stakes

Year	Winner	Jockey	Second	Third	Strs	Time	1st Purse
1984	Super Sunrise (GB), 5, 118	C. Perret	Smart and Sharp, 5, 110	Guston (Arg), 6, 115	11	1:34.40	$23,628
	Great Substence, 6, 113	G. St. Leon	Dr. Schwartzman, 3, 109	Rising Raja, 4, 113	10	1:35.00	23,418
1983	Northrop, 4, 116	J. Velasquez	Forkali, 5, 114	North Course, 8, 113	6	1:22.00	26,754
1982	Gleaming Channel, 4, 116	C. Perret	Double Cadet, 4, 111	Victorian Double, 4, 112	9	1:36.00	18,375
	King of Mardi Gras, 6, 113	A. Smith Jr.	Some One Frisky, 6, 114	Explosive Bid, 4, 115	9	1:36.40	18,225
1981	North Course, 6, 115	B. Thornburg	Proctor, 4, 120	Royal Centurion, 4, 113	11	1:34.80	23,292
	Drum's Captain (Ire), 6, 114	A. Gilbert	Foretake, 5, 116	Poverty Boy, 6, 114	10	1:35.00	23,082
1980	Morning Frolic, 5, 117	A. T. Cordero Jr.	Match the Hatch, 4, 111	Nar, 5, 113	12	1:35.40	19,365
	Pipedreamer (GB), 5, 113	J. Cruguet	Houdini, 5, 119	Once Over Lightly, 7, 114	10	1:34.40	18,915
1979	Fleet Gar, 4, 114	J. Fell	Romeo, 6, 118	Vic's Magic, 6, 121	11	1:36.40	19,005
	Regal and Royal, 4, 120	J. Fell	North Course, 4, 114	Bob's Dusty, 5, 121	11	1:37.00	19,155
1978	Qui Native, 4, 117	D. MacBeth	All Friends (Ire), 6, 115	Tablao (Chi), 5, 114	10	1:36.40	19,350
	Do Lishus, 4, 110	J. D. Bailey	Haverty, 4, 113	Leader of the Band, 6, 113	11	1:37.20	19,500
1977	Gay Jitterbug, 4, 118	L. Saumell	What a Threat, 5, 110	Riverside Sam, 4, 109	9	1:36.40	16,185
	Cinteelo, 4, 115	B. Thornburg	Commanding Lead, 6, 110	*El Guindo, 6, 111	10	1:36.20	16,335
1976	Step Forward, 4, 114	M. Solomone	Faithful Diplomat, 4, 111	Passionate Pirate, 5, 111	9	1:34.00	20,775
	Improviser, 4, 113	J. Cruguet	Odd Man, 5, 112	Peppy Addy, 4, 113	11	1:35.60	21,195
1975	Duke Tom, 5, 113	P. I. Grimm	Dartsum, 6, 116	Return to Reality, 6, 110	14	1:36.20	17,460
	Beau Bugle, 5, 116	M. Hole	The Grok, 4, 114	Mr. Door, 4, 115	13	1:36.20	16,860
1974	Right On, 5, 112	E. Maple	*Rey Maya, 7, 112	Rapid Sage, 4, 114	13	1:37.80	21,930
1973	Windtex, 4, 113	J. L. Rotz	Getajetholme, 4, 112	Prince of Truth, 5, 114	9	1:35.20	16,140
	Life Cycle, 4, 112	F. Iannelli	Roundhouse, 5, 108	Hope Eternal, 5, 112	10	1:35.40	16,290

Named for Arthur I. Appleton (1915-2008), owner of Bridlewood Farm in Florida. Not graded 1975-'84. Grade 2 1998, 2000-'03. 1 1/16 miles 1952, 1992-2000. 1 1/8 miles 1953-'64. 7 furlongs 1965-'66, 1972, 1983. 1 mile 70 yards 1991. Dirt 1952-'66, 1972, 1983, 1991, 1993, 1995, 1998-'99. Three-year-olds and up 1952-2006. Two divisions 1973, 1975-'82, 1984-'85, 1987.

Arcadia Handicap

Grade 2 in 2008. Santa Anita Park, four-year-olds and up, 1 mile, turf. Held April 5, 2008, with a gross value of $150,000. First held in 1988. First graded in 1990. Stakes record 1:33.13 (2008 Daytona [Ire]).

Year	Winner	Jockey	Second	Third	Strs	Time	1st Purse
2008	Daytona (Ire), 4, 120	A. O. Solis	Hyperbaric, 5, 113	Golden Balls (Ire), 4, 116	6	**1:33.13**	$90,000
2007	Icy Atlantic, 6, 115	R. A. Dominguez	El Roblar, 5, 115	Willow O Wisp, 5, 117	9	1:35.18	90,000
2006	Silent Name (Jpn), 4, 116	R. Bejarano	Chinese Dragon, 4, 119	Milk It Mick (GB), 5, 117	10	1:33.72	90,000
2005	Singletary, 5, 120	A. O. Solis	Sweet Return (GB), 5, 117	Buckland Manor, 5, 117	5	1:33.52	90,000
2004	Diplomatic Bag, 4, 116	D. R. Flores	Statement, 6, 114	Seinne (Chi), 7, 115	7	1:47.90	90,000
2003	Century City (Ire), 4, 116	J. Valdivia Jr.	Gondolieri (Chi), 4, 116	Sunday Break (Jpn), 4, 117	9	1:47.84	90,000
2002	Seinne (Chi), 5, 115	C. J. McCarron	Irish Prize, 6, 122	Kerrygold (Fr), 6, 116	9	1:47.16	90,000
2001	Lazy Lode (Arg), 7, 121	L. A. Pincay Jr.	Night Patrol, 5, 116	Wake the Tiger, 5, 114	5	1:49.74	90,000
2000	Falcon Flight (Fr), 4, 114	B. Blanc	Bonapartiste (Fr), 4, 118	Otavalo (Ire), 5, 114	7	1:47.88	97,950
1999	Commitisize, 4, 117	D. R. Flores	Majorien (GB), 5, 117	Ladies Din, 4, 119	7	1:48.25	90,000
1998	Hawksley Hill (Ire), 5, 117	G. L. Stevens	Precious Ring, 5, 114	Kirkwall (GB), 4, 117	8	1:49.96	167,350
1997	Labeeb (GB), 5, 118	E. Delahoussaye	Talloires, 7, 118	Pinfloron (Fr), 5, 115	5	1:35.80	80,100
1996	Tychonic (GB), 6, 118	G. L. Stevens	Debutant Trick, 6, 117	Savinio, 6, 117	6	1:35.84	80,300
1995	Savinio, 5, 116	C. J. McCarron	River Flyer, 4, 121	Romarin (Brz), 5, 120	7	1:34.74	91,800
1994	Norwich (GB), 7, 117	P. A. Valenzuela	Megan's Interco, 5, 119	Gothland (Fr), 5, 118	7	1:34.14	75,850
1993	Val des Bois (Fr), 7, 118	P. A. Valenzuela	Star of Cozzene, 5, 122	C. Sam Maggio, 7, 113	7	1:35.07	77,750
1992	Exbourne, 5, 119	G. L. Stevens	Repriced, 4, 113	Madjaristan, 6, 115	6	1:33.21	95,000
1991	Pharisien (Fr), 4, 113	C. S. Nakatani	Exbourne, 5, 118	Tartas (Fr), 5, 112	11	1:33.30	102,500
1990	Steinlen (GB), 7, 125	J. A. Santos	Bruho, 4, 117	Wonder Dancer, 4, 111	6	1:33.40	63,200
1989	Political Ambition, 5, 121	E. Delahoussaye	Patchy Groundfog, 6, 118	Steinlen (GB), 6, 122	5	1:34.60	62,600
1988	Steinlen (GB), 5, 117	G. L. Stevens	Political Ambition, 4, 120	Neshad, 4, 117	9	1:34.80	88,760

Named for Arcadia, California, city in which Santa Anita Park is located. Formerly named for two California land grants called Rancho El Rincon. Grade 3 1990-'94. El Rincon H. 1988-2000. 1 1/8 miles 1998-2004.

Aristides Stakes

Grade 3 in 2008. Churchill Downs, three-year-olds and up, 6 furlongs, dirt. Held May 31, 2008, with a gross value of $119,125. First held in 1989. First graded in 1999. Stakes record 1:07.59 (2005 Kelly's Landing).

Year	Winner	Jockey	Second	Third	Strs	Time	1st Purse
2008	Indian Chant, 5, 118	J. Theriot	Noonmark, 5, 122	Elite Squadron, 4, 124	6	1:08.40	$67,828
2007	Fabulous Strike, 4, 120	R. A. Dominguez	Cougar Cat, 5, 118	Gaff, 5, 122	5	1:07.64	99,882
2006	Lost in the Fog, 4, 124	R. A. Baze	Kelly's Landing, 5, 117	Level Playingfield, 5, 114	6	1:08.52	69,024
2005	Kelly's Landing, 4, 116	G. L. Stevens	Battle Won, 5, 117	Jet Prospector, 4, 116	6	**1:07.59**	100,719
2004	Champali, 4, 116	R. Bejarano	Beau's Town, 6, 121	Battle Won, 4, 114	6	1:09.04	100,533
2003	Mountain General, 5, 116	C. J. Lanerie	Beau's Town, 5, 123	Pass Rush, 4, 118	7	1:16.01	67,580
2002	Orientate, 4, 116	R. Albarado	Binthebest, 5, 114	No Armistice, 5, 116	7	1:14.41	66,650
2001	Bet On Sunshine, 9, 120	C. H. Borel	Alannan, 5, 119	Dash for Daylight, 4, 110	6	1:14.79	67,208
2000	Bet On Sunshine, 8, 119	F. C. Torres	Proven Cure, 6, 117	Sun Bull, 4, 111	7	1:15.11	68,014
1999	Run Johnny, 7, 116	P. Day	Squall Valley, 4, 112	Neon Shadow, 5, 114	8	1:16.27	68,572
1998	Thisnearlywasmine, 4, 115	S. J. Sellers	Partner's Hero, 4, 115	El Amante, 5, 118	7	1:15.72	67,518
1997	High Stakes Player, 5, 119	S. J. Sellers	Trafalger, 3, 106	Bet On Sunshine, 5, 122	7	1:15.81	21,800
1996	Lord Carson, 4, 115	D. M. Barton	Criollito (Arg), 5, 117	Bet On Sunshine, 4, 110	5	1:15.94	70,525
1995	Boone's Mill, 3, 106	D. M. Barton	Ojai, 6, 113	Hot Jaws, 5, 118	7	1:15.90	69,924

Year	Winner	Jockey	Second	Third	Strs	Time	1st Purse
1994	**Never Wavering**, 5, 116	S. J. Sellers	Demaloot Demashoot, 4, 119	American Chance, 5, 117	8	1:16.55	$53,479
1993	**Gold Spring (Arg)**, 5, 115	F. A. Arguello Jr.	Take Me Out, 5, 119	In the Zone, 4, 113	6	1:16.43	35,718
1992	**Tricky Fun**, 4, 113	P. Day	Guns of Cielo, 5, 112	Richman, 4, 118	6	1:16.35	44,720
1991	**Bio**, 5, 117	B. E. Bartram	Bratt's Choice, 4, 117	Guns of Cielo, 4, 112	6	1:16.62	44,668
1990	**Beau Genius**, 5, 122	R. D. Lopez	Bio, 4, 113	Launch a Dream, 5, 111	9	1:16.20	45,240
1989	**Bet the Pot**, 4, 115	C. R. Woods Jr.	Temptation Time, 5, 115	Good Roar, 5, 113	5	1:16.00	33,703

Named for the first winner of the Kentucky Derby, H. P. McGrath's Aristides (1872 c. by *Leamington). Aristides H. 1996-2003. Aristides Breeders' Cup H. 2004-'06. 6½ furlongs 1989-2003. Track record 2000, '05.

Arkansas Derby

Grade 2 in 2008. Oaklawn Park, three-year-olds, 1⅛ miles, dirt. Held April 12, 2008, with a gross value of $1,000,000. First held in 1936. First graded in 1973. Stakes record 1:46.80 (1984 †Althea).

Year	Winner	Jockey	Second	Third	Strs	Time	1st Purse
2008	**Gayego**, 3, 122	M. E. Smith	Z Fortune, 3, 122	Tres Borrachos, 3, 118	13	1:49.63	$600,000
2007	**Curlin**, 3, 122	R. Albarado	Storm in May, 3, 122	Deadly Dealer, 3, 118	9	1:50.09	600,000
2006	**Lawyer Ron**, 3, 122	J. McKee	Steppenwolfer, 3, 118	Private Vow, 3, 122	13	1:51.38	600,000
2005	**Afleet Alex**, 3, 122	J. Rose	Flower Alley, 3, 122	Andromeda's Hero, 3, 122	10	1:48.80	600,000
2004	**Smarty Jones**, 3, 122	S. Elliott	Borrego, 3, 118	Pro Prado, 3, 122	11	1:49.41	600,000
2003	**Sir Cherokee**, 3, 118	T. J. Thompson	Eugene's Third Son, 3, 118	Christine's Outlaw, 3, 118	12	1:48.39	300,000
2002	**Private Emblem**, 3, 122	D. J. Meche	Wild Horses, 3, 118	dh-Bay Monster, 3, 118 dh-Windward Passage, 3, 122	11	1:52.20	300,000
2001	**Balto Star**, 3, 122	M. Guidry	Jamaican Rum, 3, 122	Son of Rocket, 3, 122	11	1:49.04	300,000
2000	**Graeme Hall**, 3, 118	R. Albarado	Snuck In, 3, 122	Impeachment, 3, 118	14	1:49.49	300,000
1999	**‡Certain**, 3, 122	K. Desormeaux	Torrid Sand, 3, 118	Ecton Park, 3, 122	7	1:49.30	300,000
1998	**Victory Gallop**, 3, 118	A. O. Solis	Hanuman Highway (Ire), 3, 118	Favorite Trick, 3, 122	9	1:49.86	300,000
1997	**Crypto Star**, 3, 122	P. Day	Phantom On Tour, 3, 122	Pacificbounty, 3, 122	11	1:49.20	300,000
1996	**Zarb's Magic**, 3, 122	R. D. Ardoin	Grindstone, 3, 122	Halo Sunshine, 3, 122	12	1:49.21	300,000
1995	**Dazzling Falls**, 3, 122	G. K. Gomez	Flitch, 3, 118	On Target, 3, 122	8	1:50.60	300,000
1994	**Concern**, 3, 118	G. K. Gomez	Blumin Affair, 3, 118	Silver Goblin, 3, 122	9	1:48.16	300,000
1993	**Rockamundo**, 3, 118	C. H. Borel	Kissin Kris, 3, 122	Foxtrail, 3, 122	10	1:48.17	300,000
1992	**Pine Bluff**, 3, 122	J. D. Bailey	Lil E. Tee, 3, 122	Desert Force, 3, 122	6	1:49.49	300,000
1991	**Olympio**, 3, 122	E. Delahoussaye	Corporate Report, 3, 118	Richman, 3, 122	11	1:47.67	300,000
1990	**Silver Ending**, 3, 122	G. L. Stevens	Real Cash, 3, 122	Power Lunch, 3, 118	13	1:48.00	300,000
1989	**Dansil**, 3, 121	L. Snyder	Clever Trevor, 3, 126	Advocate Training, 3, 115	11	1:49.20	240,000
1988	**Proper Reality**, 3, 118	J. D. Bailey	Primal, 3, 115	Sea Trek, 3, 123	8	1:48.40	300,000
1987	**Demons Begone**, 3, 123	P. Day	Lookinforthebigone, 3, 118	You're No Bargain, 3, 115	6	1:47.60	300,000
1986	**Rampage**, 3, 118	P. Day	Wheatly Hall, 3, 115	†Family Style, 3, 121	14	1:48.20	300,000
1985	**Tank's Prospect**, 3, 123	G. L. Stevens	Encolure, 3, 126	Irish Fighter, 3, 115	9	1:48.40	349,650
1984	**†Althea**, 3, 121	P. A. Valenzuela	Pine Circle, 3, 118	Gate Dancer, 3, 118	11	1:46.80	360,150
1983	**Sunny's Halo**, 3, 126	E. Delahoussaye	Caveat, 3, 120	Exile King, 3, 117	14	1:49.40	176,340
1982	**Hostage**, 3, 117	J. Fell	El Baba, 3, 126	Bold Style, 3, 123	10	1:51.60	170,580
1981	**Bold Ego**, 3, 123	J. Lively	Top Avenger, 3, 120	Woodchopper, 3, 123	9	1:50.40	137,160
1980	**Temperence Hill**, 3, 123	D. Haire	Bold 'n Rulling, 3, 117	Sun Catcher, 3, 120	10	1:50.60	107,160
1979	**Golden Act**, 3, 126	S. Hawley	Smarten, 3, 120	Strike the Main, 3, 115	10	1:50.00	107,280
1978	**Esops Foibles**, 3, 126	C. J. McCarron	Chief of Dixieland, 3, 117	Special Honor, 3, 120	13	1:52.20	82,470
1977	**Clev Er Tell**, 3, 126	R. Broussard	Kodiack, 3, 117	Best Person, 3, 117	12	1:50.60	80,520
1976	**Elocutionist**, 3, 126	J. Lively	New Collection, 3, 117	Klen Klitso, 3, 120	12	1:49.20	81,480
1975	**Promised City**, 3, 126	D. E. Whited	Bold Chapeau, 3, 117	My Friend Gus, 3, 120	14	1:51.80	82,140
1974	**J. R.'s Pet**, 3, 123	D. G. McHargue	Silver Florin, 3, 120	Nick's Folly, 3, 120	17	1:50.60	86,910
1973	**Impecunious**, 3, 126	J. Velasquez	Vodika, 3, 123	Warbucks, 3, 123	10	1:49.60	74,130

Formerly named Arkansas Centennial Derby in honor of the 100th anniversary of the founding of the state of Arkansas in 1836. Grade 1 1981-'88. Not held 1945. Dead heat for third 2002. ‡Valhol finished first, DQ to seventh for jockey's use of an illegal electrical stimulation device, 1999. †Denotes female.

Arlington Handicap

Grade 3 in 2008. Arlington Park, three-year-olds and up, 1¼ miles, turf. Held July 21, 2007, with a gross value of $200,000. First held in 1929. First graded in 1973. Stakes record 2:00.40 (1985 Pass the Line).

Year	Winner	Jockey	Second	Third	Strs	Time	1st Purse
2007	**Cosmonaut**, 5, 121	J. R. Leparoux	Revved Up, 9, 117	Go Between, 4, 116	9	2:01.32	$115,200
2006	**Cosmonaut**, 4, 115	J. R. Leparoux	Load a Chronic, 6, 112	Artiste Royal (Ire), 5, 117	6	2:03.10	120,000
2005	**Cool Conductor**, 4, 120	C. H. Velasquez	Vangelis, 6, 119	Major Rhythm, 6, 116	7	2:02.26	120,000
2004	**Senor Swinger**, 4, 118	B. Blanc	Mystery Giver, 6, 120	Ballingarry (Ire), 5, 121	7	2:03.38	150,000
2003	**Honor in War**, 4, 120	D. R. Flores	Better Talk Now, 4, 115	Mystery Giver, 5, 118	10	2:02.71	150,000
2002	**Falcon Flight (Fr)**, 6, 115	R. R. Douglas	Kappa King, 5, 117	Gretchen's Star, 7, 115	10	2:03.13	135,000
2001	**Make No Mistake (Ire)**, 6, 116	R. Albarado	Takarian (Ire), 6, 116	El Gran Papa, 4, 115	7	2:02.53	150,000
2000	**Northern Quest (Fr)**, 5, 113	R. Albarado	Profit Option, 5, 112	Where's Taylor, 4, 114	11	2:02.13	90,000
1997	**Wild Event**, 4, 114	M. Guidry	Storm Trooper, 4, 114	Chorwon, 4, 113	8	2:01.52	90,000
1996	**Torch Rouge (GB)**, 5, 116	M. Guidry	Sentimental Moi, 6, 113	Volochine (Ire), 5, 115	6	2:03.32	120,000
1995	**Manilaman**, 4, 114	R. P. Romero	Snake Eyes, 5, 117	Bluegrass Prince (Ire), 4, 117	7	2:02.82	120,000
1994	**Fanmore**, 6, 119	P. Day	Marastani, 4, 114	Split Run, 6, 114	7	2:01.72	150,000
1993	**Evanescent**, 6, 114	A. T. Gryder	Split Run, 5, 113	Magesterial Cheer, 5, 112	10	2:00.93	150,000
1992	**Sky Classic**, 5, 125	P. Day	‡Duckaroo, 6, 111	Glity, 4, 116	9	2:00.62	150,000
1991	**Filago**, 4, 116	P. A. Valenzuela	Super Abound, 4, 113	Izvestia, 4, 114	12	2:01.40	150,000

Racing — Graded Stakes

Year	Winner	Jockey	Second	Third	Strs	Time	1st Purse
1990	Pleasant Variety, 6, 115	E. Fires	Double Booked, 5, 114	Ten Keys, 6, 121	7	2:04.00	$180,000
1989	Unknown Quantity (GB), 4, 112	J. Velasquez	Frosty the Snowman, 4, 122	Delegant, 5, 113	5	2:11.20	120,000
1987	Ifrad, 5, 114	G. Baze	Storm On the Loose, 4, 115	Grey Classic, 4, 114	8	2:12.20	90,360
1986	Mourjane (Ire), 6, 117	J. A. Santos	Will Dancer (Fr), 4, 115	Clever Song, 4, 118	9	2:01.40	112,350
1985	Pass the Line, 4, 113	J. L. Diaz	The Noble Player, 5, 118	Executive Pride (Ire), 4, 113	7	**2:00.40**	82,050
1984	Who's for Dinner, 5, 109	M. Venezia	Nijinsky's Secret, 6, 127	Star Choice, 5, 112	7	2:04.00	70,800
1983	Palikaraki (Fr), 5, 116	W. Shoemaker	Rossi Gold, 7, 122	Late Act, 4, 113	11	2:35.80	76,200
1982	Flying Target, 5, 115	R. W. Cox	Rossi Gold, 6, 125	Don Roberto, 5, 118	8	2:32.40	71,640
1981	Spruce Needles, 4, 115	J. C. Espinoza	Summer Advocate, 4, 117	Sea Chimes (Ire), 5, 116	8	2:35.00	72,060
1980	Yvonand (Fr), 4, 111	E. Beitia	Rossi Gold, 4, 120	Lyphard's Wish (Fr), 4, 121	8	2:31.40	71,700
1979	Bowl Game, 5, 124	J. Velasquez	Young Bob, 4, 110	†Liveinthesunshine, 4, 105	14	2:32.20	79,260
1978	Romeo, 5, 116	E. Fires	Fluorescent Light, 4, 118	Improviser, 6, 118	9	2:32.00	73,080
1977	Cunning Trick, 4, 110	B. Fann	‡*Vadim, 7, 118	No Turning, 4, 118	8	2:33.80	72,480
1976	Victorian Prince, 6, 118	R. Platts	Improviser, 4, 118	Bold Roll, 4, 112	12	1:58.20	90,000
1975	Royal Glint, 5, 125	J. E. Tejeira	*Zografos, 7, 113	Buffalo Lark, 5, 122	9	1:55.80	87,400
1974	Buffalo Lark, 4, 118	L. Snyder	Royal Glint, 4, 112	Spot T V, 7, 111	13	1:54.40	91,800
1973	Dubassoff, 4, 117	J. Vasquez	Jogging, 6, 114	Red Reality, 7, 118	14	1:58.60	72,750

Grade 2 1973-'80, 1990-'97. Grade 1 1981-'89. Arlington Park H. 1963, '72, '74. Held at Washington Park 1943-'45. Held at Hawthorne 1985. Not held 1940, 1969-'71, 1988, 1998-'99. 1⅛ miles 1929, '52, '65. 1⁷⁄₁₆ miles 1941, 1953-'62, 1964, 1973-'76. 1 mile 1963, 1966-'67. 7 furlongs 1968. 1½ miles 1972, 1977-'83. Dirt 1929-'39, 1942-'53, 1963, 1965-'72. Originally scheduled on turf 1975. ‡No Turning finished second, DQ to third, 1977. ‡Plate Dancer finished second, DQ to fifth, 1992. Track record 1975. *Denotes female.

Arlington Matron Handicap

Grade 3 in 2008. Arlington Park, three-year-olds and up, fillies and mares, 1⅛ miles, all weather. Held May 26, 2008, with a gross value of $150,000. First held in 1930. First graded in 1973. Stakes record 1:48.40 (1986 Queen Alexandra; 1989 Between the Hedges).

Year	Winner	Jockey	Second	Third	Strs	Time	1st Purse
2008	Indescribable, 4, 115	J. Rose	Leah's Secret, 5, 117	Lady Carlock, 4, 114	7	1:49.82	$88,200
2007	Solo Survivor, 5, 117	M. Guidry	Ms. Lydonia, 6, 114	Round Heels (Ire), 6, 115	6	1:49.94	89,550
2006	Sea Siren, 4, 116	M. Guidry	Stop a Train, 4, 117	Sunset Kisses, 6, 116	5	1:49.19	90,000
2005	‡Quick Temper, 4, 114	S. Bridgmohan	Diavla, 4, 116	For Gillian, 4, 116	7	1:49.75	90,000
2004	Adoration, 5, 123	V. Espinoza	Tamweel, 4, 116	Indy Groove, 4, 116	7	1:49.75	90,000
2003	Take Charge Lady, 4, 123	S. J. Sellers	Lakenheath, 5, 116	To the Queen, 4, 117	6	1:50.19	90,000
2002	Lakenheath, 4, 115	C. A. Emigh	With Ability, 4, 116	Your Out, 4, 115	5	1:50.78	90,000
2001	Humble Clerk, 4, 114	L. J. Melancon	Maltese Superb, 4, 115	Lakenheath, 3, 115	7	1:51.53	90,000
2000	Megans Bluff, 3, 111	C. R. Woods Jr.	On a Soapbox, 4, 115	Tutorial, 4, 113	8	1:51.41	90,000
1997	Omi, 4, 114	M. Guidry	Gold Memory, 4, 115	Trick Attack, 6, 114	5	1:51.93	60,000
1996	Belle of Cozzene, 4, 115	D. R. Pettinger	War Thief, 4, 113	Your Ladyship, 6, 116	9	1:49.34	75,000
1995	Mariah's Storm, 4, 117	R. N. Lester	Mysteriously, 4, 117	Minority Dater, 4, 114	9	1:50.60	60,000
1994	Hey Hazel, 4, 115	M. G. Pino	Passing Vice, 4, 114	Pennyhill Park, 4, 116	8	1:49.58	60,000
1993	Erica's Dream, 5, 115	W. Martinez	Pleasant Jolie, 5, 114	Meafara, 4, 123	6	1:50.09	60,000
1992	Lemhi Go, 4, 114	E. Fires	Beth Believes, 6, 112	Diamond City, 4, 113	8	1:49.67	45,000
1991	Lucky Lady Lauren, 4, 112	J. Velasquez	Beth Believes, 5, 113	Bungalow, 4, 112	6	1:49.21	45,000
1990	Degenerate Gal, 5, 117	R. P. Romero	Evangelical, 4, 115	Confirmed Dancer, 4, 113	6	1:49.20	48,555
1989	Between the Hedges, 5, 112	P. A. Johnson	Topicount, 4, 116	Stoneleigh's Hope, 4, 114	10	**1:48.40**	65,010
1987	Family Style, 4, 123	S. Hawley	Royal Cielo, 3, 113	Tide, 5, 114	7	1:52.20	49,320
1986	Queen Alexandra, 4, 122	D. Brumfield	Mr. T.'s Tune, 5, 113	Bessarabian, 4, 121	6	**1:48.40**	92,220
1985	Heatherten, 6, 126	R. P. Romero	Solo Skater, 5, 112	Mr. T.'s Tune, 4, 114	8	2:04.00	49,410
1984	Choose a Partner, 4, 116	D. Brumfield	First Flurry, 5, 113	Silvered Silk, 4, 117	7	2:04.00	62,595
1983	May Day Eighty, 4, 115	J. Vasquez	Sefa's Beauty, 4, 125	Stay a Leader, 4, 113	10	2:04.40	50,355
1982	Sweetest Chant, 4, 115	E. Fires	Miss Huntington, 5, 119	Turnablade, 5, 115	7	2:02.60	48,960
1981	La Bonzo, 5, 110	J. Lively	Wistful, 4, 123	Weber City Miss, 4, 123	8	2:02.60	66,360
1980	Impetuous Gal, 5, 115	E. Fires	Salzburg, 5, 112	Liveinthesunshine, 5, 108	10	2:01.40	67,200
1979	Amerigirl, 4, 115	B. Swatuk	Frosty Skater, 4, 118	Calderina (Ity), 4, 122	10	1:51.20	52,800
1978	Rich Soil, 4, 117	C. H. Silva	Satan's Cheer, 6, 112	Sans Arc, 4, 113	11	1:51.20	38,340
1977	Javamine, 4, 119	J. Velasquez	*Star Ball, 5, 119	Ivory Castle, 3, 110	9	1:53.20	52,620
1976	Nicosia, 4, 118	W. Gavidia	B. J. King, 4, 111	Hope of Glory, 4, 109	9	1:49.40	45,450
	Cyclyla Zee, 3, 110	H. Arroyo	Sugar Plum Time, 4, 115	True Reality, 3, 109	9	1:49.60	46,200
1975	*Polynesienne, 4, 110	L. Snyder	Princesse Grey, 4, 110	Pass a Glance, 4, 116	9	1:51.80	45,050
	Sixty Sails, 5, 114	L. Snyder	Victorian Queen, 4, 118	Princess Ormea, 3, 110	8	1:52.80	45,050
1974	Sixty Sails, 4, 121	D. E. Whited	*Protectora, 5, 117	What Will Be, 4, 118	14	1:50.60	46,300
1973	*Last Home, 4, 112	F. Alvarez	North Broadway, 3, 115	Ziba Blue, 6, 114	12	1:50.00	35,800

Matron races are traditionally held for older fillies and mares. Grade 2 1973-'89. Matron H. 1964-'83. Held at Washington Park 1943-'45. Held at Hawthorne Race Course 1985. Not held 1933-'36, 1988, 1998-'99. 1 mile 1930-'57. 1¼ miles 1980-'85. Dirt 1930-'65, 1980-2006. Turf 1966-'79. Three-year-olds and up 1952. Fillies 1952. Two divisions 1975-'76. ‡Indy Groove finished first, DQ to seventh for a positive drug test, 2005.

Arlington Million Stakes

Grade 1 in 2008. Arlington Park, three-year-olds and up, 1¼ miles, turf. Held August 11, 2007, with a gross value of $1,000,000. First held in 1981. First graded in 1983. Stakes record 1:58.69 (1995 Awad).

Year	Winner	Jockey	Second	Third	Strs	Time	1st Purse
2007	Jambalaya, 5, 126	R. Albarado	The Tin Man, 9, 126	Doctor Dino (Fr), 5, 126	7	2:04.76	$594,000

Racing — Graded Stakes

Year	Winner	Jockey	Second	Third	Strs	Time	1st Purse
2006	The Tin Man, 8, 126	V. Espinoza	Cacique (Ire), 5, 126	Soldier Hollow (GB), 6, 126	10	2:01.35	$600,000
2005	Powerscourt (GB), 5, 126	K. Fallon	Kitten's Joy, 4, 126	Fourty Niners Son, 4, 126	10	2:03.38	600,000
2004	‡Kicken Kris, 4, 126	K. Desormeaux	Magistretti, 4, 126	Epalo (Ger), 5, 126	13	2:00.08	600,000
2003	‡Sulamani (Ire), 4, 126	D. R. Flores	dh-Kaieteur, 4, 126 dh-Paolini (Ger), 6, 126		13	2:02.29	600,000
2002	Beat Hollow (GB), 5, 126	J. D. Bailey	Sarafan, 5, 126	Forbidden Apple, 7, 126	9	2:02.94	600,000
2001	Silvano (Ger), 5, 126	A. Suborics	Hap, 5, 126	Redattore (Brz), 6, 126	12	2:02.64	600,000
2000	Chester House, 5, 126	J. D. Bailey	Manndar (Ire), 4, 126	Mula Gula, 4, 126	7	2:01.37	1,200,000
1997	Marlin, 4, 126	G. L. Stevens	Sandpit (Brz), 8, 126	Percuntait (GB), 4, 126	8	2:02.54	600,000
1996	Mecke, 4, 126	R. G. Davis	Awad, 6, 126	Sandpit (Brz), 7, 126	9	2:00.49	600,000
1995	Awad, 5, 126	E. Maple	Sandpit (Brz), 6, 126	The Vid, 5, 126	11	1:58.69	600,000
1994	Paradise Creek, 5, 126	P. Day	Fanmore, 6, 126	Muhtarram, 5, 126	14	1:59.78	600,000
1993	Star of Cozzene, 5, 126	J. A. Santos	Evanescent, 6, 126	Johann Quatz (Fr), 4, 126	8	2:07.50	600,000
1992	Dear Doctor (Fr), 5, 126	C. B. Asmussen	Sky Classic, 5, 126	Golden Pheasant, 6, 126	12	1:59.84	600,000
1991	Tight Spot, 4, 126	L. A. Pincay Jr.	Algenib (Arg), 4, 122	†Kartajana (Ire), 4, 123	10	1:59.55	600,000
1990	Golden Pheasant, 4, 126	G. L. Stevens	With Approval, 4, 126	Steinlen (GB), 7, 126	11	1:59.60	600,000
1989	Steinlen (GB), 6, 126	J. A. Santos	†Lady in Silver, 3, 117	Yankee Affair, 7, 126	13	2:03.60	600,000
1988	Mill Native, 4, 126	C. B. Asmussen	Equalize, 6, 126	Sunshine Forever, 3, 118	14	2:00.00	600,000
1987	Manila, 4, 126	A. T. Cordero Jr.	Sharrood, 4, 126	Theatrical (Ire), 5, 126	8	2:02.40	600,000
1986	†Estrapade, 6, 122	F. Toro	Divulge, 4, 126	Pennine Walk (Ire), 4, 126	14	2:00.80	600,000
1985	Teleprompter (GB), 5, 126	T. A. Ives	Greinton (GB), 4, 126	Flying Pidgeon, 4, 126	13	2:03.40	600,000
1984	John Henry, 9, 126	C. J. McCarron	†Royal Heroine (Ire), 4, 122	Gato Del Sol, 5, 126	12	2:01.40	600,000
1983	Tolomeo (Ire), 3, 118	P. Eddery	John Henry, 8, 126	Nijinsky's Secret, 5, 126	14	2:04.40	600,000
1982	Perrault (GB), 5, 126	L. A. Pincay Jr.	Be My Native, 3, 118	Motavato, 4, 126	14	1:58.80	600,000
1981	John Henry, 6, 126	W. Shoemaker	The Bart, 5, 126	†Madam Gay (GB), 3, 117	12	2:07.60	600,000

First million-dollar Thoroughbred race in North America. Formerly sponsored by the Anheuser-Busch Co. of St. Louis, Missouri 1982-'87. Arlington Million Invitational S. 1981. Budweiser Million S. 1982-'84. Budweiser-Arlington Million 1985-'87. Held at Woodbine Race Course 1989. Not held 1998-'99. Dead heat for second 2003. ‡Storming Home (GB) finished first, DQ to fourth, 2003. ‡Powerscourt (GB) finished first, DQ to fourth, 2004. Course record 1995. †Denotes female.

Arlington-Washington Futurity

Grade 3 in 2008. Arlington Park, two-year-olds, 1 mile, all weather. Held September 1, 2007, with a gross value of $198,500. First held in 1927. First graded in 1973. Stakes record 1:35.16 (2005 Sorcerer's Stone).

Year	Winner	Jockey	Second	Third	Strs	Time	1st Purse
2007	Wicked Style, 2, 117	R. Albarado	Riley Tucker, 2, 117	Sebastian County, 2, 119	7	1:36.52	$118,200
2006	dh-Got the Last Laugh, 2, 119 dh-Officer Rocket (GB), 2, 119	R. R. Douglas M. Guidry	Street Sense, 2, 117		10	1:36.71	80,000
2005	Sorcerer's Stone, 2, 119	M. Guidry	Charley Tango, 2, 119	Red Raymond, 2, 119	9	1:35.16	120,000
2004	Three Hour Nap, 2, 119	E. Razo Jr.	dh-Elusive Chris, 2, 122 dh-Straight Line, 2, 119		6	1:38.56	120,000
2003	Cactus Ridge, 2, 122	E. M. Martin Jr.	Glittergem, 2, 117	Texas Deputy, 2, 119	6	1:35.44	90,000
2002	Most Feared, 2, 122	M. Guidry	Anasheed, 2, 122	Unleash the Power, 2, 122	10	1:37.52	90,000
2001	Publication, 2, 122	R. A. Meier	It'sallinthechase, 2, 122	Dubai Squire, 2, 122	7	1:38.78	90,000
2000	Trailthefox, 2, 121	S. J. Sellers	Starbury, 2, 121	Blame It On Ruby, 2, 121	11	1:37.25	90,000
1997	Cowboy Dan, 2, 121	D. Kutz	Captain Maestri, 2, 121	Fiamma, 2, 121	9	1:36.68	90,000
1996	Night in Reno, 2, 121	M. Guidry	Flying With Eagles, 2, 121	Thisnearlywasmine, 2, 121	8	1:36.67	120,000
1994	Evansville Slew, 2, 121	P. Compton	Valid Wager, 2, 121	Mr Purple, 2, 121	9	1:37.84	120,000
1993	Polar Expedition, 2, 121	C. C. Bourque	Gimme Glory, 2, 121	Delicate Cure, 2, 121	6	1:39.28	120,000
1992	Gilded Time, 2, 121	C. J. McCarron	Boundlessly, 2, 121	Rockamundo, 2, 121	6	1:37.84	200,580
1991	Caller I. D., 2, 121	J. D. Bailey	Count the Time, 2, 121	West by West, 2, 121	9	1:36.01	188,880
1990	Hansel, 2, 122	P. Day	Walesa, 2, 122	Discover, 2, 122	7	1:36.40	220,440
1989	Secret Hello, 2, 122	A. T. Gryder	Richard R., 2, 122	Bite the Bullet, 2, 122	6	1:35.80	220,860
1987	Tejano, 2, 122	J. Vasquez	Jim's Orbit, 2, 122	Native Stalwart, 2, 122	7	1:36.20	247,080
1986	Eet Twice, 2, 122	C. Perret	Conquistarose, 2, 122	Jazzing Around, 2, 122	11	1:37.20	300,420
1985	Meadowlake, 2, 122	J. L. Diaz	Bar Tender, 2, 122	Papal Power, 2, 122	6	1:16.20	286,320
1984	Spend a Buck, 2, 122	C. Hussey	Dusty's Darby, 2, 122	Viva Maxi, 2, 122	7	1:38.00	355,320
1983	All Fired Up, 2, 122	R. D. Evans	Holme On Top, 2, 122	Smart n Slick, 2, 122	17	1:27.00	330,135
1982	Total Departure, 2, 122	E. Fires	Coax Me Matt, 2, 122	Highland Park, 2, 122	8	1:23.60	271,515
1981	Lets Dont Fight, 2, 122	J. Lively	Tropic Ruler, 2, 122	Music Leader, 2, 122	15	1:29.20	305,385
1980	Well Decorated, 2, 122	L. A. Pincay Jr.	Lord Avie, 2, 122	Fairway Phantom, 2, 122	15	1:23.80	240,885
1979	Execution's Reason, 2, 122	E. Delahoussaye	Preemptive, 2, 122	Brent's Trans Am, 2, 122	9	1:22.40	89,790
1978	Jose Binn, 2, 122	A. T. Cordero Jr.	Exuberant, 2, 122	Strike Your Colors, 2, 122	12	1:17.40	120,660
1977	Sauce Boat, 2, 122	S. Cauthen	Gonquin, 2, 122	Forever Casting, 2, 122	14	1:16.60	130,665
1976	Run Dusty Run, 2, 122	D. G. McHargue	Royal Ski, 2, 122	Eagletar, 2, 122	11	1:16.40	120,465
1975	Honest Pleasure, 2, 122	D. G. McHargue	Khyber Rules, 2, 122	Rule the Ridge, 2, 122	19	1:18.40	140,610
1974	Greek Answer, 2, 122	M. A. Castaneda	Colonel Power, 2, 122	The Bagel Prince, 2, 122	7	1:17.80	122,505
1973	Lover John, 2, 122	R. N. Ussery	Beau Groton, 2, 122	Hula Chief, 2, 122	11	1:11.60	97,470

Merged with old Washington Park Futurity, renamed after closure of Washington Park. Grade 1 1973-'89. Grade 2 1990-2001. American National Futurity 1927-'28. Arlington Futurity 1932-'61. Arlington-Washington Breeders' Cup Futurity 2004-'06. Held at Washington Park 1943-'45. Held at Hawthorne Race Course 1985. Not held 1929-'31, 1970, 1988, 1995, 1998-'99. 6 furlongs 1927-'61, 1971-'73. 7 furlongs 1962-'69, 1979-'83. 6½ furlongs 1974-'78, 1985. Dirt 1927-2006. Colts and geldings 1973-'83. Dead heat for second 2004. Dead heat for first 2006.

Arlington-Washington Lassie Stakes

Grade 3 in 2008. Arlington Park, two-year-olds, fillies, 1 mile, all weather. Held September 8, 2007, with a gross value of $150,000. First held in 1929. First graded in 1973. Stakes record 1:35.93 (2005 Original Spin).

Year	Winner	Jockey	Second	Third	Strs	Time	1st Purse
2007	Dreaming of Liz, 2, 116	E. T. Baird	Rasierra, 2, 117	Minewander, 2, 118	11	1:37.08	$86,400
2006	Lisa M, 2, 116	C. H. Marquez Jr.	Sutra, 2, 116	Call the Kitty, 2, 118	8	1:38.90	60,000
2005	Original Spin, 2, 116	J. M. Campbell	Ex Caelis, 2, 116	Coolwind, 2, 116	9	1:35.93	90,000
2004	Culinary, 2, 116	C. H. Marquez Jr.	Runway Model, 2, 118	Kota, 2, 118	8	1:36.98	60,000
2003	Zosima, 2, 118	P. Day	Everyday Angel, 2, 116	Cryptos' Best, 2, 118	10	1:36.02	60,000
2002	Moonlight Sonata, 2, 121	S. Laviolette	Parting, 2, 121	Souris, 2, 121	13	1:37.82	60,000
2001	Joanies Bella, 2, 121	M. St. Julien	Brief Bliss, 2, 121	First Again, 2, 121	9	1:39.34	60,000
2000	Thunder Bertie, 2, 119	J. Beasley	Caressing, 2, 119	Zahwah, 2, 119	10	1:36.91	60,000
1997	Silver Maiden, 2, 119	B. S. Laviolette	Arctic Lady, 2, 119	So Generous, 2, 119	6	1:37.54	60,000
1996	Southern Playgirl, 2, 119	R. P. Romero	Leo's Gypsy Dancer, 2, 119	Broad Dynamite, 2, 119	7	1:38.27	90,000
1994	Shining Light, 2, 119	J. L. Diaz	She's a Lively One, 2, 119	Alltheway Bertie, 2, 119	5	1:41.70	90,000
1993	Mariah's Storm, 2, 119	R. N. Lester	Shapely Scrapper, 2, 119	Minority Dater, 2, 119	14	1:38.95	90,000
1992	Eliza, 2, 119	P. A. Valenzuela	Banshee Winds, 2, 119	Tourney, 2, 119	6	1:39.58	134,850
1991	Speed Dialer, 2, 119	P. Day	Cadillac Women, 2, 119	Mystic Hawk, 2, 119	7	1:36.58	141,390
1990	Through Flight, 2, 120	J. M. Johnson	Good Potential, 2, 120	Wild for Traci, 2, 120	6	1:39.00	138,870
1989	Trumpet's Blare, 2, 122	L. A. Pincay Jr.	Special Happening, 2, 122	Puffy Doodle, 2, 122	6	1:38.60	128,040
1987	Joe's Tammie, 2, 122	C. Perret	Tomorrow's Child, 2, 122	Pearlie Gold, 2, 122	6	1:25.00	186,840
1986	Delicate Vine, 2, 122	G. L. Stevens	Sacahuista, 2, 122	Ruling Angel, 2, 122	6	1:23.40	165,660
1985	Family Style, 2, 119	L. A. Pincay Jr.	Deep Silver, 2, 119	Pamela Kay, 2, 119	8	1:18.00	250,200
1984	Contredance, 2, 119	P. Day	Tiltalating, 2, 119	Miss Delice, 2, 119	5	1:26.00	211,560
1983	Miss Oceana, 2, 119	E. Maple	Life's Magic, 2, 119	Bottle Top, 2, 119	11	1:23.40	112,146
1982	For Once'n My Life, 2, 119	E. Maple	Some Kinda Flirt, 2, 119	How Clever, 2, 119	8	1:23.40	106,461
1981	Milingo, 2, 119	R. Sibille	Maniches, 2, 119	Justa Little One, 2, 119	15	1:25.20	129,798
1980	Truly Bound, 2, 119	W. Shoemaker	Safe Play, 2, 119	Masters Dream, 2, 119	11	1:25.20	83,022
1979	Sissy's Time, 2, 119	E. Fires	Ellie Milove, 2, 119	Vogue Folks, 2, 119	6	1:11.00	63,399
1978	It's in the Air, 2, 119	E. Delahoussaye	Angel Island, 2, 119	Bequa, 2, 119	8	1:09.60	71,394
1977	Stub, 2, 119	R. Turcotte	Rainy Princess, 2, 119	Go Line, 2, 119	13	1:10.40	70,329
1976	Special Warmth, 2, 119	S. Maple	Wavy Waves, 2, 119	Drama Critic, 2, 119	10	1:10.40	68,700
1975	Dearly Precious, 2, 119	M. Hole	Free Journey, 2, 119	Head Spy, 2, 119	12	1:11.20	67,938
1974	Hot n Nasty, 2, 119	D. G. McHargue	Sharm a Sheikh, 2, 119	Mystery Mood, 2, 119	10	1:11.40	64,386
1973	Special Team, 2, 119	A. Pineda	Thirty One Jewels, 2, 119	Two Timing Lass, 2, 119	9	1:11.40	59,574

Merged with old Washington Park Lassie S., renamed after closure of Washington Park. Grade 2 1976-'80, 1990-'97. Grade 1 1981-'89. Lassie S. 1929-'31. Arlington Lassie S. 1932-'62. Arlington-Washington Breeders' Cup Lassie S. 2005-'06. Held at Washington Park 1943-'45. Not held 1970-'71, 1988, 1995, 1998-'99. 5½ furlongs 1929-'31. 7 furlongs 1932, 1980-'84, 1986-'87. 6 furlongs 1933-'61, 1972-'79. 6½ furlongs 1962-'69, 1985. Dirt 1929-2006.

Ashland Stakes

Grade 1 in 2008. Keeneland Race Course, three-year-olds, fillies, 1 1/16 miles, all weather. Held April 5, 2008, with a gross value of $500,000. First held in 1879. First graded in 1973. Stakes record 1:41.72 (1999 Silverbulletday).

Year	Winner	Jockey	Second	Third	Strs	Time	1st Purse
2008	Little Belle, 3, 121	R. Maragh	Bsharpsonata, 3, 121	Proud Spell, 3, 121	7	1:43.69	$310,000
2007	Christmas Kid, 3, 121	R. R. Douglas	Octave, 3, 121	Dawn After Dawn, 3, 121	8	1:42.90	310,000
2006	Bushfire, 3, 121	C. H. Velasquez	Wait a While, 3, 121	Balance, 3, 121	8	1:45.16	310,000
2005	Sis City, 3, 121	E. S. Prado	Runway Model, 3, 121	Memorette, 3, 121	6	1:46.35	310,000
2004	Madcap Escapade, 3, 118	R. R. Douglas	Ashado, 3, 123	Last Song, 3, 120	4	1:44.55	310,000
2003	Elloluv, 3, 120	R. Albarado	Lady Tak, 3, 123	Holiday Lady, 3, 116	7	1:43.58	342,085
2002	Take Charge Lady, 3, 123	A. J. D'Amico	Take the Cake, 3, 118	Belterra, 3, 120	8	1:43.29	345,805
2001	Fleet Renee, 3, 116	J. R. Velazquez	Golden Ballet, 3, 123	Latour, 3, 120	11	1:43.77	357,275
2000	Rings a Chime, 3, 116	S. J. Sellers	Zoftig, 3, 116	Circle of Life, 3, 116	6	1:44.43	341,155
1999	Silverbulletday, 3, 123	J. D. Bailey	Marley Vale, 3, 115	Gold From the West, 3, 115	6	1:41.72	337,280
1998	Well Chosen, 3, 115	C. R. Woods Jr.	Let, 3, 115	Banshee Breeze, 3, 120	7	1:43.00	344,410
1997	Glitter Woman, 3, 121	M. E. Smith	Anklet, 3, 121	Storm Song, 3, 121	8	1:43.80	337,125
1996	My Flag, 3, 121	J. D. Bailey	Cara Rafaela, 3, 121	Mackie, 3, 118	5	1:42.69	335,265
1995	Urbane, 3, 115	E. Delahoussaye	Conquistadoress, 3, 115	Post It, 3, 121	6	1:43.41	207,483
1994	Inside Information, 3, 121	M. E. Smith	Bunting, 3, 115	Private Status, 3, 118	6	1:46.99	171,198
1993	Lunar Spook, 3, 121	S. J. Sellers	Avie's Shadow, 3, 115	Roamin Rachel, 3, 115	7	1:43.43	171,973
1992	Prospectors Delite, 3, 121	C. Perret	Spinning Round, 3, 121	Luv Me Luv Me Not, 3, 121	10	1:42.65	186,063
1991	Do It With Style, 3, 115	S. J. Sellers	Private Treasure, 3, 121	Til Forbid, 3, 112	7	1:43.67	182,894
1990	Go for Wand, 3, 121	R. P. Romero	Charon, 3, 121	Piper Piper, 3, 112	5	1:43.60	145,665
1989	Gorgeous, 3, 118	E. Delahoussaye	Blondeinamotel, 3, 115	Some Romance, 3, 121	8	1:43.20	157,430
1988	Willa On the Move, 3, 118	C. J. McCarron	On to Royalty, 3, 121	Colonial Waters, 3, 121	11	1:45.80	151,125
1987	Chic Shirine, 3, 118	S. Hawley	Buryyourbelief, 3, 112	Our Little Margie, 3, 113	12	1:44.60	117,683
1986	Classy Cathy, 3, 116	E. Fires	She's a Mystery, 3, 116	Patricia J. K., 3, 121	11	1:44.00	116,513
1985	Koluctoo's Jill, 3, 118	R. P. Romero	Lucy Manette, 3, 121	Foxy Deen, 3, 121	7	1:44.40	74,718
1984	Enumerating, 3, 114	D. Brumfield	Miss Oceana, 3, 121	Rose of Ashes, 3, 113	4	1:49.20	88,707
1983	Princess Rooney, 3, 121	J. Vasquez	Shamivor, 3, 114	Decision, 3, 116	5	1:45.40	74,133
1982	Blush With Pride, 3, 118	W. Shoemaker	Exclusive Love, 3, 116	Delicate Ice, 3, 113	10	1:45.00	83,070
1981	Truly Bound, 3, 121	W. Shoemaker	Wayward Lass, 3, 121	Dame Mysterieuse, 3, 121	5	1:44.00	56,778

Racing — Graded Stakes

Year	Winner	Jockey	Second	Third	Strs	Time	1st Purse
1980	Flos Florum, 3, 112	R. P. Romero	Cerada Ridge, 3, 114	Lady Taurian Peace, 3, 116	8	1:26.40	$41,210
	Sugar and Spice, 3, 113	J. Fell	Nice and Sharp, 3, 114	Satin Ribera, 3, 116	9	1:27.20	41,210
1979	Candy Eclair, 3, 121	A. S. Black	Himalayan, 3, 114	Countess North, 3, 115	7	1:27.00	39,618
1978	Mucchina, 3, 113	J. Amy	Grenzen, 3, 121	Bold Rendezvous, 3, 118	10	1:27.20	40,527
1977	Sound of Summer, 3, 118	F. Toro	Mrs. Warren, 3, 121	Our Mims, 3, 118	9	1:26.80	40,333
1976	Optimistic Gal, 3, 121	B. Baeza	Alvarada, 3, 116	Confort Zone, 3, 113	6	1:26.80	37,895
1975	Sun and Snow, 3, 116	G. Patterson	My Juliet, 3, 116	Red Cross, 3, 114	8	1:26.60	39,488
1974	Maud Muller, 3, 114	D. Brumfield	Clemanna, 3, 113	Irish Sonnet, 3, 119	9	1:27.00	29,834
	Winged Wishes, 3, 116	D. Brumfield	Cherished Moment, 3, 117	Jay Bar Pet, 3, 113	8	1:28.80	29,786
1973	Raging Whirl, 3, 113	W. Soirez	Protest, 3, 116	A Little Lovin, 3, 110	12	1:10.80	23,611

Named for Henry Clay's home, Ashland, located in Lexington. Sponsored by Ashland Inc. of Covington, Kentucky 1986-2008. Grade 3 1973-'78. Grade 2 1979-'85. Ashland Oaks 1879-1932. Held at Kentucky Association 1932. Held at Churchill Downs 1943-'45. Not held 1897-1911, 1933-'35, 1938-'39. 1 1/2 miles 1879-'82. 1 1/4 miles 1883-'89. 1 mile 1890-1926. 1 mile 70 yards 1932. 6 furlongs 1940-'73. About 7 furlongs 1974-'80. Dirt 1879-2006. Three-year-olds and up 1936-'37. Fillies and mares 1936-'37. Two divisions 1974, '80.

Athenia Handicap

Grade 3 in 2008. Belmont Park, three-year-olds and up, fillies and mares, 1 1/16 miles, turf. Held October 13, 2007, with a gross value of $109,100. First held in 1978. First graded in 1980. Stakes record 1:40.53 (2001 Babae [Chi] [2nd Div.]).

Year	Winner	Jockey	Second	Third	Strs	Time	1st Purse
2007	Criminologist, 4, 115	J. R. Velazquez	I'm in Love, 4, 115	Dance Away Capote, 5, 117	6	1:45.09	$65,460
2006	Pommes Frites, 4, 118	J. A. Santos	Chaibia (Ire), 3, 113	Dream Lady, 4, 115	8	1:42.95	67,380
2005	Asti (Ire), 4, 114	J. F. Chavez	Bohemian Lady, 4, 120	Zosima, 4, 117	6	1:42.57	66,780
2004	Finery, 4, 113	P. Fragoso	Madeira Mist (Ire), 5, 118	With Patience, 5, 114	11	1:43.73	69,420
2003	Caught in the Rain, 4, 115	R. Migliore	Lojo, 4, 114	Coney Kitty (Ire), 5, 113	8	1:45.05	67,800
2002	Babae (Chi), 6, 120	J. F. Chavez	Strawberry Blonde (Ire), 4, 116	Silver Rail, 5, 112	12	1:44.90	70,020
2001	Verruma (Brz), 5, 114	J. R. Velazquez	Siringas (Ire), 3, 112	Freefourracing, 5, 113	8	1:42.09	82,725
	Babae (Chi), 5, 116	J. F. Chavez	Batique, 5, 117	Sweet Prospect (GB), 3, 110	8	**1:40.53**	82,725
2000	Wild Heart Dancing, 4, 115	J. F. Chavez	Fickle Friends, 4, 114	Silken (GB), 4, 114	8	1:43.40	67,500
1999	Antoniette, 4, 119	J. F. Chavez	Dominique's Joy, 4, 113	Prospectress, 4, 115	4	1:41.89	66,840
1998	Tampico, 5, 114	J. Bravo	Irish Daisy, 5, 113	Rumpipumpy (GB), 5, 115	10	1:42.90	51,210
1997	Rapid Selection, 4, 113	J. Bravo	Dynasty, 4, 114	Preachersnightmare, 4, 111	6	1:47.11	65,940
1996	Sixieme Sens, 4, 116	J. D. Bailey	Rapunzel Runz, 5, 115	Fashion Star, 4, 113	7	1:37.92	66,660
1995	Caress, 4, 114	R. G. Davis	Manila Lila, 5, 115	Vinista, 5, 119	6	1:54.18	68,340
1994	Lady Affirmed, 3, 111	J. F. Chavez	Irving's Girl, 4, 110	Cox Orange, 4, 116	11	1:48.66	52,245
1993	Trampoli, 4, 117	M. E. Smith	Kirov Premiere (GB), 3, 114	Dahlia's Dreamer, 4, 110	8	2:17.16	54,000
1992	Fairy Garden, 4, 112	J. A. Krone	Passagere du Soir (GB), 5, 117	Seewillo, 4, 113	5	2:13.62	52,020
1991	Flaming Torch (Ire), 4, 117	P. A. Valenzuela	Plenty of Grace, 4, 114	Highland Penny, 6, 116	9	2:13.99	55,800
1990	Buy the Firm, 4, 111	J. D. Bailey	Rigamajig, 4, 111	Igmaar (Fr), 4, 111	4	2:18.20	52,650
1989	Capades, 3, 115	A. T. Cordero Jr.	Miss Unnameable, 5, 114	Key Flyer, 4, 110	8	2:13.20	54,360
1988	High Browser, 3, 108	P. Day	Miss Unnameable, 4, 109	Gaily Gaily (Ire), 5, 110	10	2:18.60	57,780
1987	Lead Kindly Light, 4, 110	J. M. Pezua	Barbara's Moment, 3, 111	Spectacular Bev, 3, 114	7	2:23.80	70,920
1986	Dawn's Curtsey, 4, 111	E. Maple	Festivity, 3, 113	Perfect Point, 4, 115	8	2:16.00	55,440
1985	Videogenic, 3, 114	J. Cruguet	Persian Tiara (Ire), 5, 119	Key Witness, 3, 108	13	2:15.40	61,020
1984	Key Dancer, 3, 111	A. T. Cordero Jr.	Surely Georgie's, 3, 107	Rossard (Den), 4, 123	11	2:14.80	56,700
1983	Rose Crescent, 4, 108	R. G. Davis	Lady Norcliffe, 3, 111	Infinite, 3, 112	9	2:22.00	34,380
1982	Mintage (Fr), 3, 114	J. Samyn	Doodle, 3, 119	Street Dance, 3, 112	8	2:17.80	32,790
	Middle Stage, 3, 112	J. J. Miranda	Realms Reason (Ire), 3, 114	Vocal, 3, 115	6	2:17.40	32,790
1981	De La Rose, 3, 125	E. Maple	Noble Damsel, 3, 111	Andover Way, 3, 113	8	2:00.40	51,120
1980	Love Sign, 3, 121	R. Hernandez	Rokeby Rose, 3, 111	Classic Curves, 3, 111	10	2:00.40	50,490
1979	Poppycock, 3, 114	J. Velasquez	Fourdrinier, 3, 114	Six Crowns, 3, 114	10	2:05.60	52,470
1978	Terpsichorist, 3, 114	M. Venezia	Consort, 3, 110	Bonnie Blue Flag, 3, 110	12	2:03.20	33,300

Named for Hal Price Headley's 1946 Ladies H. winner Athenia (1943 f. by *Pharamond II). Not graded 2005. Held at Aqueduct 1982, 1994-'95, 1999-2000, 2002-'04. 1 1/4 miles 1978-'81. 1 3/8 miles 1982-'93. 1 1/8 miles 1994-'95, 1997. 1 mile 1996. Dirt 1979, '90, '95, 2005. Originally scheduled on turf 2005. Three-year-olds 1978-'83. Fillies 1978-'83. Two divisions 1982, 2001.

Azalea Stakes

Grade 3 in 2008. Calder Race Course, three-year-olds, fillies, 6 furlongs, dirt. Held July 7, 2007, with a gross value of $291,750. First held in 1972. First graded in 1996. Stakes record 1:10.32 (2005 Leave Me Alone).

Year	Winner	Jockey	Second	Third	Strs	Time	1st Purse
2007	Sheets, 3, 117	R. Albarado	Sindy With an S, 3, 116	Holly Torque Tango, 3, 116	9	1:10.40	$176,000
2006	Victorina, 3, 118	R. A. Baze	‡G City Gal, 3, 115	Frolicing, 3, 114	8	1:11.51	176,000
2005	Leave Me Alone, 3, 118	K. Desormeaux	Hide and Chic, 3, 114	Midtown Miss, 3, 114	6	**1:10.32**	132,000
2004	Dazzle Me, 3, 115	S. J. Sellers	Reforest, 3, 114	Boston Express, 3, 114	7	1:11.40	177,000
2003	Ebony Breeze, 3, 118	C. H. Velasquez	Storm Flag, 3, 116	Crafty Brat, 3, 116	13	1:10.82	176,000
2002	Bold World, 3, 118	C. H. Borel	Willa On the Move, 3, 114	Tchula Miss, 3, 114	10	1:10.86	105,000
2001	Hattiesburg, 3, 118	M. Guidry	Southern Tour, 3, 114	Spanish Glitter, 3, 115	11	1:11.81	150,000
2000	Swept Away, 3, 116	P. Day	Precious Feather, 3, 112	Watchfull, 3, 116	8	1:11.53	120,000
1999	Show Me the Stage, 3, 116	R. J. Courville	Could Be, 3, 116	Exact, 3, 116	9	1:11.91	75,000
1998	Cassidy, 3, 114	J. A. Rivera II	Holy Capote, 3, 114	Fantasy Angel, 3, 118	8	1:11.93	75,000
1997	Little Sister, 3, 116	F. Lovato Jr.	Princess Pietrina, 3, 112	Maggie Auxier, 3, 114	7	1:13.08	120,000

Racing — Graded Stakes

Year	Winner	Jockey	Second	Third	Strs	Time	1st Purse
1996	J J'sdream, 3, 118	H. Castillo Jr.	Supah Avalanche, 3, 112	Race Artist, 3, 114	7	1:23.87	$65,100
1995	Lucky Lavender Gal, 3, 116	R. R. Douglas	Chaposa Springs, 3, 117	Dancin Renee, 3, 116	6	1:23.50	60,000
1994	Cut the Charm, 3, 121	H. Castillo Jr.	Just a Little Kiss, 3, 114	Tasso Bee, 3, 112	11	1:25.51	60,000
1993	Kimscountrydiamond, 3, 115	J. Vasquez	Nijivision, 3, 113	Hollywood Wildcat, 3, 117	10	1:23.44	60,000
1992	C. C.'s Return, 3, 113	R. J. Thibeau Jr.	Fortune Forty Four, 3, 114	Subtle Dancer, 3, 113	7	1:25.33	30,000
1991	Ranch Ragout, 3, 113	E. O. Nunez	Parisian Flight, 3, 115	Foolishly Wild, 3, 110	8	1:18.53	33,120
1990	Sweet Proud Polly, 3, 115	P. A. Rodriguez	Highway Lady, 3, 115	Bald Cat, 3, 112	7	1:26.20	32,790
1989	Princess Mora, 3, 112	S. Gaffalione	Georgies Doctor, 3, 118	Silk Stocks, 3, 117	7	1:25.60	32,790
1988	Grand Splash, 3, 114	R. N. Lester	Myfavorite Charity, 3, 114	Hi Maudie, 3, 116	8	1:25.60	46,500
1987	My Sweet Replica, 3, 115	S. B. Soto	Shot Gun Bonnie, 3, 114	Ches Pie, 3, 116	10	1:25.20	33,990
1986	Classy Tricks, 3, 112	M. C. Suckie	Janjac, 3, 112	Thirty Zip, 3, 119	13	1:25.40	30,410
1985	Jackie McCleaf, 3, 120	C. Hussey	Nahema, 3, 118	Nyama, 3, 118	10	1:25.80	33,840
1984	Birdie Belle, 3, 120	H. A. Valdivieso	Sugar's Image, 3, 120	Scorched Panties, 3, 120	10	1:25.80	33,990
1983	Current Gal, 3, 112	E. Cardone	Silvered Silk, 3, 115	Paris Roulette, 3, 115	12	1:25.60	17,295
1982	Here's to Peg, 3, 116	J. A. Velez Jr.	Cut, 3, 114	Bad Dancin Rita, 3, 116	10	1:26.00	16,905
1981	Ange Gal, 3, 113	G. Cohen	Float Upstream, 3, 115	Whoop It, 3, 114	8	1:26:00	16,515
	Kaylem Ho, 3, 115	A. Smith Jr.	Toga Toga, 3, 119	Secret Kingdom, 3, 115	8	1:25.80	16,515
1980	She Can't Miss, 3, 122	W. A. Guerra	Nice and Sharp, 3, 119	Karla's Enough, 3, 119	7	1:11.20	16,515
1979	Burn's Return, 3, 115	M. A. Rivera	Solo Haina, 3, 120	Speier's Hope, 3, 115	9	1:24.00	16,860
1978	Lucy Belle, 3, 113	A. Smith Jr.	We Believe in You, 3, 113	Wings of Destiny, 3, 122	8	1:25.20	14,040
1977	Countess Pruner, 3, 116	J. S. Rodriguez	Delphic Oracle, 3, 113	White Goddess, 3, 119	5	1:11.20	13,440
1976	Forty Nine Sunsets, 3, 122	G. St. Leon	Head Spy, 3, 113	Noble Royalty, 3, 113	6	1:11.80	13,560
1975	Solo Royal, 3, 113	G. St. Leon	My Mom Nullah, 3, 119	Finery, 3, 119	11	1:12.40	14,640

Named for the azalea of the rhododendron family common to South Florida. Azalea H. 1972, 1992-'93. Azalea Breeders' Cup S. 1996-'98, 2000-'07. Azalea Breeders' Cup H. 1999. Not held 1973-'74. 1¹/₁₆ miles 1972. 7 furlongs 1978-'79, 1981-'90, 1992-'96. Three-year-olds and up 1972. Fillies and mares 1972. Two divisions 1981. ‡Frolicing finished second, DQ to third, 2006.

Azeri Stakes

Grade 3 in 2008. Oaklawn Park, four-year-olds and up, fillies and mares, 1¹/₁₆ miles, dirt. Held March 9, 2008, with a gross value of $171,500. First held in 1987. First graded in 1990. Stakes record 1:42.01 (1999 Sister Act).

Year	Winner	Jockey	Second	Third	Strs	Time	1st Purse
2008	Hystericalady, 5, 117	R. Albarado	Brownie Points, 5, 115	Clever Strike, 4, 118	5	1:43.86	$105,000
2007	India, 4, 115	C. P. DeCarlo	Kettleoneup, 4, 117	A True Pussycat, 4, 117	4	1:44.37	105,000
2006	Round Pond, 4, 113	S. Elliott	Happy Ticket, 5, 119	Platinum Ballet, 5, 115	6	1:43.93	105,000
2005	Injustice, 4, 115	L. S. Quinonez	Colony Band, 4, 113	Island Sand, 4, 113	6	1:43.40	105,000
2004	Golden Sonata, 5, 117	C. H. Marquez Jr.	Keys to the Heart, 5, 117	Mayo On the Side, 5, 113	10	1:44.32	120,000
2003	Bien Nicole, 5, 118	D. R. Pettinger	Red n'Gold, 5, 117	Mandy's Gold, 5, 117	9	1:44.19	120,000
2002	Ask Me No Secrets, 4, 116	M. E. Smith	Red n'Gold, 4, 116	Descapate, 4, 118	5	1:44.56	120,000
2001	Heritage of Gold, 6, 116	R. Albarado	Lu Ravi, 6, 118	Ive Gota Bad Liver, 4, 114	8	1:44.30	120,000
2000	Heritage of Gold, 5, 112	S. J. Sellers	Lu Ravi, 5, 118	Light Line, 5, 112	4	1:44.15	120,000
1999	Sister Act, 4, 113	C. H. Borel	Glitter Woman, 5, 114	Mil Kilates, 6, 114	6	**1:42.01**	60,000
1998	Turn to the Queen, 5, 112	T. T. Doocy	Danzalert, 4, 112	Leo's Gypsy Dancer, 4, 118	7	1:44.76	90,000
1997	Halo America, 7, 118	C. H. Borel	Gold n Delicious, 4, 112	Capote Belle, 4, 117	5	1:42.18	90,000
1996	Belle of Cozzene, 4, 113	D. R. Pettinger	Halo America, 6, 120	Little May, 6, 115	5	1:43.32	94,350
1995	Halo America, 5, 115	W. T. Cloninger Jr.	Heavenly Prize, 4, 121	Biolage, 6, 111	4	1:42.59	92,700
1994	Morning Meadow, 4, 116	S. P. Romero	Gravette, 4, 113	Her Valentine, 4, 113	10	1:44.60	94,650
1993	Guiza, 6, 118	C. S. Nakatani	Teddy's Top Ten, 4, 113	Fappies Cosy Miss, 5, 112	8	1:44.79	93,600
1992	Cuddles, 4, 118	D. Guillory	Rare Guest, 5, 112	Dixie Splash, 4, 113	10	1:43.82	94,500
1991	A Wild Ride, 4, 120	P. Day	Timber Ribbon, 4, 114	Topsa, 4, 107	9	1:42.31	94,770
1990	A Penny Is a Penny, 5, 116	A. T. Gryder	Affirmed Classic, 4, 114	Fit for a Queen, 4, 113	8	1:43.60	95,340
1989	Savannah's Honor, 4, 117	J. D. Bailey	Invited Guest (Ire), 5, 120	Barbara Sue, 5, 114	7	1:45.00	94,920
1988	Ms. Margi, 4, 116	J. D. Bailey	Queen Alexandra, 6, 121	Hail a Cab, 5, 116	7	1:44.20	94,890
1987	North Sider, 5, 121	A. T. Cordero Jr.	Queen Alexandra, 5, 122	Ann's Bid, 4, 123	7	1:42.20	79,872

Named for the Allen E. Paulson Living Trust's 2002 Horse of the Year and '02, '03, '04 Apple Blossom H. (G1) winner Azeri (1998 f. by Jade Hunter). Not graded 1995, 1997-'99. Oaklawn Budweiser Breeders' Cup H. 1987-'91, 1993-'95. Oaklawn Breeders' Cup H. 1992, 1996-'97. Oaklawn Breeders' Cup S. 1998-2004. Azeri Breeders' Cup S. 2005-'07. Three-year-olds and up 1987-'94, 1996-2005.

Baldwin Stakes

Grade 3 in 2008. Santa Anita Park, three-year-olds, about 6¹/₂ furlongs, turf. Held March 2, 2008, with a gross value of $110,050. First held in 1968. First graded in 1973. Stakes record 1:11.96 (2007 Desert Code).

Year	Winner	Jockey	Second	Third	Strs	Time	1st Purse
2008	Ten Meropa, 3, 115	T. Baze	Sky Cape, 3, 119	D. Double You, 3, 117	8	1:13.09	$66,030
2007	Desert Code, 3, 117	R. Migliore	Bitter Bill, 3, 114	Vaunt (GB), 3, 115	5	**1:11.96**	63,960
2006	Fast Parade, 3, 115	G. K. Gomez	The Pharaoh, 3, 114	Da Stoops, 3, 122	7	1:15.11	66,300
2005	High Standards, 3, 117	E. S. Prado	Talking to John, 3, 117	Run Thruthe Sun, 3, 117	7	1:16.16	66,270
2004	Seattle Borders, 3, 114	A. O. Solis	Stalking Tiger, 3, 117	Jungle Prince, 3, 114	10	1:14.09	68,010
2003	Buddy Gil, 3, 117	G. L. Stevens	King Robyn, 3, 116	Flirt With Fortune, 3, 116	11	1:12.56	68,730
2002	Shuffling Kid (GB), 3, 115	P. A. Valenzuela	Red Briar (Ire), 3, 116	Dark Sorcerer (GB), 3, 114	12	1:13.30	68,640
2001	Skip to the Stone, 3, 117	C. S. Nakatani	Trailthefox, 3, 122	Bills Paid, 3, 114	6	1:16.29	66,000
2000	Fortifier, 3, 114	B. Blanc	Performing Magic, 3, 116	Joopy Doopy, 3, 117	8	1:16.79	66,870
1999	American Spirit, 3, 114	E. Ramsammy	Chomper (Ire), 3, 115	Impressive Grades, 3, 119	13	1:13.93	69,300

Year	Winner	Jockey	Second	Third	Strs	Time	1st Purse
1998	**Wrekin Pilot (GB)**, 3, 116	E. Delahoussaye	Commitisize, 3, 122	Tenbyssimo (Ire), 3, 117	8	1:13.32	$66,240
1997	**Latin Dancer**, 3, 116	C. A. Black	King of Swing, 3, 116	Swiss Yodeler, 3, 122	11	1:14.48	67,850
1996	**Sandtrap**, 3, 114	C. S. Nakatani	Strangelove, 3, 115	Benton Creek, 3, 117	6	1:15.03	64,300
1995	**Sierra Diablo**, 3, 116	E. Delahoussaye	Raji, 3, 117	Huge Gator, 3, 116	6	1:15.36	47,300
1994	**Silver Music**, 3, 114	C. W. Antley	Eagle Eyed, 3, 117	Makinanhonestbuck, 3, 117	8	1:13.76	48,375
1993	**Future Storm**, 3, 117	K. Desormeaux	Concept Win, 3, 119	Siebe, 3, 117	11	1:15.02	51,550
1992	**Reckless Ruckus**, 3, 116	P. A. Valenzuela	Fabulous Champ, 3, 114	Slerp, 3, 115	8	1:17.28	49,850
1991	**What a Spell**, 3, 117	D. R. Flores	Broadway's Top Gun, 3, 122	Shining Prince, 3, 114	7	1:16.30	49,875
1990	**Farma Way**, 3, 115	R. Sibille	Iam the Iceman, 3, 117	Robyn Dancer, 3, 117	12	1:13.80	52,975
1989	**Tenacious Tom**, 3, 119	E. Delahoussaye	Mountain Ghost, 3, 122	Gum, 3, 119	11	1:14.80	51,900
1988	**Exclusive Nureyev**, 3, 116	E. Delahoussaye	Prospectors Gamble, 3, 117	Mehmetski, 3, 114	9	1:14.40	39,162
	Dr. Brent, 3, 117	A. O. Solis	Accomplish Ridge, 3, 117	Glad Music, 3, 114	9	1:15.00	39,262
1987	**Chime Time (GB)**, 3, 116	P. A. Valenzuela	Sweetwater Springs, 3, 117	McKenzie Prince, 3, 114	11	1:15.00	40,750
1986	**Jetting Home**, 3, 116	D. G. McHargue	Royal Treasure, 3, 114	El Corazon, 3, 114	6	1:17.40	38,350
1985	**Knighthood (Fr)**, 3, 114	G. L. Stevens	Full Honor, 3, 117	Infantryman, 3, 114	8	1:14.80	39,900
1984	**Debonaire Junior**, 3, 117	C. J. McCarron	Fortunate Prospect, 3, 119	Distant Ryder, 3, 117	11	1:14.40	41,700
1983	**Total Departure**, 3, 117	L. A. Pincay Jr.	Paris Prince, 3, 117	Morry's Champ, 3, 114	9	1:15.20	40,950
1982	**Remember John**, 3, 117	E. Delahoussaye	Time to Explode, 3, 120	Crystal Star, 3, 114	7	1:15.20	39,200
1981	**Descaro**, 3, 115	D. G. McHargue	Motivity, 3, 120	Steelinctive (GB), 3, 114	13	1:14.60	36,700
1980	**Corvette Chris**, 3, 115	F. Toro	Executive Counsel, 3, 114	Moorish Star, 3, 114	10	1:13.60	28,550
1979	**To B. Or Not**, 3, 114	C. Baltazar	Debonair Roger, 3, 116	Young Driver, 3, 114	7	1:15.60	27,000
1978	**B. W. Turner**, 3, 117	D. Pierce	O Big Al, 3, 120	Princely Lark, 3, 114	9	1:14.00	27,550
1977	**Current Concept**, 3, 120	S. Hawley	Bad 'n Big, 3, 114	Text, 3, 120	10	1:13.20	24,900
1976	**Gaelic Christian**, 3, 114	R. Rosales	El Portugues, 3, 117	Grandaries, 3, 114	9	1:13.60	20,750
1975	**Uniformity**, 3, 114	S. Hawley	Crumbs, 3, 114	Wine Nipper, 3, 114	7	1:14.20	20,050
1974	**Battery E.**, 3, 116	L. A. Pincay Jr.	Wedge Shot, 3, 117	Ride Off, 3, 117	5	1:14.00	19,150
1973	**Bensadream**, 3, 115	D. Pierce	Princely Axe, 3, 114	Gold Bag, 3, 115	9	1:14.00	21,350

Named for Elias J. "Lucky" Baldwin (1828-1909), builder of the original Santa Anita Park. Not graded 1975-'94, 2000, '06. 6½ furlongs 1979, 1982-'83, '86, 1991-'92, '95, 2000-'01. Dirt 1979, 1982-'83, '86, '91-'92, '95, 2000-'01, 2005-'06. Originally scheduled on turf 2005-'06. Colts and geldings 1978-'87. Two divisions 1988.

Ballerina Stakes

Grade 1 in 2008. Saratoga Race Course, three-year-olds and up, fillies and mares, 7 furlongs, dirt. Held August 26, 2007, with a gross value of $250,000. First held in 1979. First graded in 1981. Stakes record 1:21.09 (2004 Lady Tak).

Year	Winner	Jockey	Second	Third	Strs	Time	1st Purse
2007	**Maryfield**, 6, 119	E. Trujillo	Baroness Thatcher, 3, 114	Miraculous Miss, 4, 117	9	1:22.78	$150,000
2006	**Dubai Escapade**, 4, 122	E. S. Prado	Nothing But Fun, 4, 117	Stormy Kiss (Arg), 4, 119	7	1:23.07	150,000
2005	**Happy Ticket**, 4, 117	J. R. Velazquez	Pleasant Home, 4, 117	Molto Vita, 5, 117	7	1:24.53	150,000
2004	**Lady Tak**, 4, 119	J. D. Bailey	My Trusty Cat, 4, 116	Harmony Lodge, 6, 119	7	**1:21.09**	150,000
2003	**Harmony Lodge**, 4, 115	R. Migliore	Shine Again, 6, 120	Gold Mover, 5, 118	8	1:22.23	150,000
2002	**Shine Again**, 5, 116	J. Samyn	Raging Fever, 4, 121	Mandy's Gold, 4, 118	7	1:22.26	150,000
2001	**Shine Again**, 4, 113	J. Samyn	Country Hideaway, 5, 118	Dream Supreme, 4, 122	5	1:22.33	150,000
2000	**Dream Supreme**, 3, 113	P. Day	Country Hideaway, 4, 117	Bourbon Belle, 5, 118	9	1:22.97	150,000
1999	**Furlough**, 5, 114	M. E. Smith	Bourbon Belle, 4, 117	dh-Catinca, 4, 121	10	1:23.04	120,000
				dh-Hurricane Bertie, 4, 117			
1998	**Stop Traffic**, 5, 118	S. J. Sellers	Runup the Colors, 4, 116	U Can Do It, 5, 115	5	1:22.23	120,000
1997	**Pearl City**, 3, 110	J. Bravo	Ashboro, 4, 115	Flashy n Smart, 4, 112	5	1:22.39	90,000
1996	**Chaposa Springs**, 4, 120	S. J. Sellers	Capote Belle, 3, 117	Broad Smile, 4, 114	6	1:21.88	90,000
1995	**Classy Mirage**, 5, 119	J. A. Krone	Inside Information, 4, 126	Laura's Pistolette, 4, 112	6	1:22.55	90,000
1994	**Roamin Rachel**, 4, 118	P. Day	Classy Mirage, 4, 123	Twist Afleet, 3, 113	6	1:21.85	65,040
1993	**Spinning Round**, 4, 119	J. F. Chavez	November Snow, 4, 119	Apelia, 4, 117	7	1:21.49	69,120
1992	**Serape**, 4, 116	C. W. Antley	Harbour Club, 5, 116	Nannerl, 5, 122	9	1:21.22	71,160
1991	**Queena**, 5, 119	M. E. Smith	Missy's Mirage, 3, 111	Dream Touch, 4, 110	9	1:22.00	72,240
1990	**Feel the Beat**, 5, 119	J. A. Santos	Fantastic Find, 4, 116	Proper Evidence, 5, 119	8	1:22.00	71,880
1989	**Proper Evidence**, 4, 116	C. W. Antley	Aptostar, 4, 119	Lake Valley, 4, 114	11	1:23.20	73,080
1988	**Cadillacing**, 4, 116	A. T. Cordero Jr.	Thirty Zip, 5, 116	Ready Jet Go, 3, 111	6	1:21.60	69,000
1987	**I'm Sweets**, 4, 119	E. Maple	Storm and Sunshine, 4, 116	Pine Tree Lane, 5, 122	5	1:22.60	82,260
1986	**Gene's Lady**, 5, 119	R. P. Romero	Le Slew, 5, 116	Tea Room, 4, 110	8	1:22.40	81,420
1985	**Lady's Secret**, 3, 117	D. MacBeth	Mrs. Revere, 4, 116	Solar Halo, 4, 116	9	1:22.60	67,680
1984	**Lass Trump**, 4, 122	P. Day	Adored, 4, 122	Sultry Sun, 4, 116	5	1:21.80	51,840
1983	**Ambassador of Luck**, 4, 124	A. Graell	Number, 4, 119	Broom Dance, 4, 122	4	1:22.20	32,640
1982	**Expressive Dance**, 4, 122	D. MacBeth	Tell a Secret, 5, 116	Sprouted Rye, 5, 113	8	1:22.80	35,160
1981	**Love Sign**, 4, 119	R. Hernandez	Jameela, 5, 122	Tell a Secret, 4, 113	4	1:22.60	32,400
1980	**Davona Dale**, 4, 119	J. Velasquez	Misty Gallore, 4, 124	It's in the Air, 4, 119	4	1:22.20	33,780
1979	**Blitey**, 3, 111	A. T. Cordero Jr.	Shukey, 4, 116	Bold Rendezvous, 4, 116	5	1:23.20	25,770

Named for Howell E. Jackson's Ballerina (1950 f. by Rosemont), first winner of the Maskette S. Grade 3 1981-'83. Grade 2 1984-'87. Ballerina S. 1979-1994, 2005. Ballerina H. 1994-2004. Ballerina Breeders' Cup S. 2006. Dead heat for third 1999.

Ballston Spa Handicap

Grade 2 in 2008. Saratoga Race Course, three-year-olds and up, fillies and mares, 1 1/16 miles, turf. Held August 23, 2007, with a gross value of $200,000. First held in 1983. First graded in 1994. Stakes record 1:39.47 (1997 Valor Lady).

Year	Winner	Jockey	Second	Third	Strs	Time	1st Purse
2007	**Wait a While**, 4, 121	G. K. Gomez	Vacare, 4, 119	Meribel, 4, 117	7	1:40.00	$120,000

Racing — Graded Stakes

Year	Winner	Jockey	Second	Third	Strs	Time	1st Purse
2006	My Typhoon (Ire), 4, 118	G. K. Gomez	Karen's Caper, 4, 115	Asi Siempre, 4, 117	7	1:41.72	$120,000
2005	Alinghi (Aus), 4, 119	E. S. Prado	Que Puntual (Arg), 5, 118	Delta Princess, 6, 118	11	1:40.30	69,780
2004	Ocean Drive, 4, 119	J. R. Velazquez	Personal Legend, 4, 115	High Court (Brz), 4, 114	10	1:43.92	128,400
2003	Stylish, 5, 116	J. R. Velazquez	Snow Dance, 5, 117	Cozzy Corner, 5, 112	9	1:41.03	120,000
2002	Surya, 4, 114	J. D. Bailey	Shooting Party, 4, 118	Solvig, 5, 114	3	1:52.29	126,409
2001	Penny's Gold, 4, 118	J. D. Bailey	Babae (Chi), 5, 114	Chaste, 5, 113	6	1:40.69	126,120
2000	License Fee, 5, 116	P. Day	Pico Teneriffe, 4, 116	Hello Soso (Ire), 4, 114	7	1:43.53	125,700
1999	Pleasant Temper, 5, 118	J. D. Bailey	Cuanto Es, 4, 113	Lets Get Cozzy, 5, 114	5	1:41.84	124,680
1998	Memories of Silver, 5, 122	J. D. Bailey	Witchful Thinking, 4, 118	Ashford Castle, 4, 114	7	1:40.93	126,600
1997	Valor Lady, 5, 112	J. R. Velazquez	Antespend, 4, 116	Rumpipumpy (GB), 4, 114	6	**1:39.47**	130,200
1996	Danish (Ire), 5, 115	J. A. Santos	Apolda, 5, 121	dh-Caress, 5, 113	3	1:41.50	126,360
				dh-Upper Noosh, 4, 111			
1995	Weekend Madness (Ire), 5, 117	S. J. Sellers	Irish Linnet, 7, 120	Allez Les Trois, 4, 115	7	1:40.34	93,300
1994	Weekend Madness (Ire), 4, 115	S. J. Sellers	You'd Be Surprised, 5, 120	Heed, 5, 110	8	1:43.77	93,510
1993	One Dreamer, 5, 116	E. Fires	Eenie Meenie Miney, 4, 111	Irish Linnet, 5, 116	10	1:39.38	94,440
1992	Aurora, 4, 114	C. Perret	Olden Rijn, 4, 112	Irish Linnet, 4, 113	7	1:36.94	93,870
1991	Paris Opera, 5, 116	G. L. Stevens	Daring Doone (GB), 8, 114	Le Famo, 5, 114	10	1:37.41	94,470
1990	Fire the Groom, 3, 114	L. Dettori	Sally Rous (Ire), 3, 114	Christiecat, 3, 115	12	1:35.20	95,820
1989	Wakonda, 5, 116	A. T. Cordero Jr.	Foresta, 3, 108	Toll Fee, 4, 111	5	1:33.80	93,900
1983	Subversive Chick, 3, 114	D. J. Murphy	Soft Morning, 4, 119	It Takes Only One, 3, 114	11	1:24.20	22,380

Named for Ballston Spa, New York, located south of Saratoga Springs. Grade 3 1994-2001, 2003-'05. Not graded 2002. Aqueduct Breeders' Cup H. 1989-'92. Aqueduct Budweiser Breeders' Cup H. 1993. Saratoga Budweiser Breeders' Cup H. 1994-'95. Saratoga Breeders' Cup H. 1996. Ballston Spa Breeders' Cup H. 1997-2005. Held at Aqueduct 1992-'93. Not held 1984-'88. 1 mile 1989-'93. 1 1/8 miles 2002. Dirt 1989, 2002. Originally scheduled on turf 2002. Dead heat for third 1996.

Barbara Fritchie Handicap

Grade 2 in 2008. Laurel Park, three-year-olds and up, fillies and mares, 7 furlongs, dirt. Held February 16, 2008, with a gross value of $276,750. First held in 1952. First graded in 1973. Stakes record 1:21.40 (1989 Tappiano).

Year	Winner	Jockey	Second	Third	Strs	Time	1st Purse
2008	Golden Dawn, 4, 114	C. Hill	Control System, 4, 120	For Kisses, 5, 114	8	1:23.24	$180,000
2007	Oprah Winney, 4, 116	M. E. Smith	Silmaril, 6, 117	Smart and Fancy, 4, 115	8	1:24.92	180,000
2005	Cativa, 5, 114	E. S. Prado	Sensibly Chic, 5, 115	Silmaril, 4, 114	10	1:23.64	120,000
2004	Bear Fan, 5, 116	R. Fogelsonger	Gazillion, 5, 116	Bronze Abe, 5, 117	9	1:23.55	120,000
2003	Xtra Heat, 5, 125	R. Wilson	Carson Hollow, 4, 119	Spelling, 4, 113	7	1:24.76	120,000
2002	Xtra Heat, 4, 128	H. Vega	Prized Stamp, 5, 114	Kimbralata, 4, 114	8	1:22.70	120,000
2001	Prized Stamp, 4, 113	T. Dunkelberger	Superduper Miss, 5, 114	Tax Affair, 4, 113	6	1:23.74	120,000
2000	Tap to Music, 5, 115	J. Bravo	Her She Kisses, 4, 114	Di's Turn, 5, 114	13	1:24.75	120,000
1999	Passeggiata (Arg), 6, 113	M. G. Pino	Catinca, 4, 121	Nothing Special, 5, 108	8	1:23.55	150,000
1998	J J'sdream, 5, 115	L. C. Reynolds	Palette Knife, 5, 113	Stylish Encore, 5, 114	10	1:24.21	150,000
1997	Miss Golden Circle, 5, 118	R. Migliore	Lottsa Talc, 7, 119	Whaleneck, 4, 113	12	1:23.05	120,000
1996	Lottsa Talc, 6, 117	F. T. Alvarado	Up an Eighth, 5, 114	Evil's Pic, 4, 116	14	1:22.61	120,000
1995	Smart 'N Noble, 4, 117	M. G. Pino	Dust Bucket, 4, 114	Gooni Goo Hoo, 5, 110	10	1:24.13	120,000
1994	Mixed Appeal, 6, 111	A. C. Salazar	Known as Nancy, 4, 111	Winka, 4, 115	12	1:23.31	120,000
1993	Moon Mist, 4, 112	T. G. Turner	Ritchie Trail, 5, 113	Femma, 5, 114	9	1:23.50	120,000
1992	Wood So, 5, 113	M. G. Pino	Wide Country, 4, 120	Wait for the Lady, 5, 111	7	1:24.56	120,000
1991	Fappabrust, 4, 114	A. T. Cordero Jr.	Devil's Orchid, 4, 118	Diva's Debut, 5, 116	10	1:23.30	120,000
1990	Amy Be Good, 4, 112	M. E. Smith	Channel Three, 4, 111	Banbury Fair, 5, 110	10	1:23.40	120,000
1989	Tappiano, 5, 123	K. Desormeaux	Very Subtle, 5, 124	Tops in Taps, 6, 114	12	**1:21.40**	120,000
1988	Psyched, 5, 113	K. Desormeaux	Spring Beauty, 5, 116	Kerygma, 4, 115	10	1:22.60	81,250
1987	Spring Beauty, 4, 115	J. A. Santos	Notches Trace, 4, 110	Pine Tree Lane, 5, 126	8	1:25.40	88,770
1986	Willowy Mood, 4, 115	B. Thornburg	Aerturas (Fr), 5, 116	Alabama Nana (Ire), 5, 119	10	1:25.40	73,840
1985	Dumdedumdum, 4, 115	D. A. Miller Jr.	Kattegat's Pride, 6, 119	Sharp Little Girl, 4, 110	8	1:25.00	87,993
	Flip's Pleasure, 5, 115	J. Samyn	Applause, 5, 120	Gene's Lady, 4, 109	8	1:24.00	71,793
1984	Pleasure Cay, 4, 115	D. A. Miller Jr.	Kattegat's Pride, 5, 117	Amanti, 5, 117	9	1:22.80	56,325
	Bara Lass, 5, 125	D. A. Miller Jr.	Owned by All, 4, 109	Willamae, 4, 113	7	1:24.00	55,025
1983	Stellarette, 5, 114	A. Delgado	Hoist Emy's Flag, 4, 116	Cheap Seats, 4, 122	10	1:24.40	74,100
1982	Lady Dean, 4, 119	D. A. Miller Jr.	Sweet Revenge, 4, 114	Sinister Queen, 4, 113	10	1:24.20	46,768
	The Wheel Turns, 5, 121	G. McCarron	Island Charm, 5, 122	Up the Flagpole, 4, 119	9	1:23.60	46,118
1981	Skipat, 7, 124	C. B. Asmussen	Whispy's Lass, 6, 114	Secret Emotion, 4, 113	8	1:23.00	72,865
1980	Misty Gallore, 4, 121	D. MacBeth	Gladiolus, 6, 122	Silver Ice, 5, 116	10	1:23.60	55,770
1979	Skipat, 5, 125	J. W. Edwards	Pearl Necklace, 5, 122	The Very One, 4, 113	8	1:22.40	53,755
1978	Bold Brat, 5, 115	J. W. Moseley	Spot Two, 4, 116	Satin Dancer, 5, 114	7	1:23.40	37,375
1977	Mt. Airy Queen, 4, 114	D. R. Wright	Avum, 4, 109	Forty Nine Sunsets, 4, 118	6	1:23.80	36,270
1976	Donetta, 5, 119	J. W. Moseley	Pinch Pie, 5, 117	Heydairya, 5, 108	11	1:24.60	37,765
1975	Twixt, 6, 126	W. J. Passmore	Crackerfax, 4, 109	Donetta, 4, 112	11	1:25.40	38,350
1974	Twixt, 5, 124	W. J. Passmore	Groton Miss, 5, 112	In the Mattress, 4, 114	10	1:24.40	38,350
1973	First Bloom, 5, 117	A. Gomez	Pas de Nom, 5, 116	Winged Affair, 5, 111	12	1:23.40	38,350

Named for Barbara Fritchie, a 95-year-old woman who, according to legend, waved her Union flag as Confederate Gen. Thomas "Stonewall" Jackson passed through Frederick, Maryland. Grade 3 1973-'91. Barbara Fritchie Breeders' Cup H. 2007. Held at Bowie 1952-'84. Not held 1960, '72, 2006. 1 1/16 miles 1952-'54. 6 furlongs 1957-'59, 1963. 1 mile 1961. Two divisions 1982, 1984-'85.

Barbaro Stakes

Grade 3 in 2008. Delaware Park, three-year-olds, 1 1/16 miles, dirt. Held July 15, 2007, with a gross value of $300,600. First held in 1937. First graded in 1973. Stakes record 1:42.41 (2001 Burning Roma).

Year	Winner	Jockey	Second	Third	Strs	Time	1st Purse
2007	Xchanger, 3, 118	E. S. Prado	King of the Roxy, 3, 116	Phone Home, 3, 116	7	1:43.40	$180,000
2006	Awfully Smart, 3, 116	R. A. Dominguez	Ah Day, 3, 118	Little Cliff, 3, 116	6	1:43.23	180,000
2005	Sun King, 3, 122	R. Bejarano	Golden Man, 3, 115	High Limit, 3, 122	5	1:43.33	180,000
2004	Pollard's Vision, 3, 122	J. D. Bailey	Britt's Jules, 3, 116	Pies Prospect, 3, 115	7	1:43.85	150,000
2003	Awesome Time, 3, 115	A. S. Black	Christine's Outlaw, 3, 115	Cherokee's Boy, 3, 122	8	1:43.26	150,000
2002	Running Tide, 3, 115	R. A. Dominguez	Nothing Flat, 3, 115	The Sewickley Kid, 3, 115	8	1:45.10	150,000
2001	Burning Roma, 3, 122	R. Wilson	Marciano, 3, 122	Bay Eagle, 3, 115	5	**1:42.41**	120,000
2000	Grundlefoot, 3, 113	T. Dunkelberger	Perfect Cat, 3, 114	Mercaldo, 3, 114	8	1:44.04	120,000
1999	Stellar Brush, 3, 114	M. J. McCarthy	Smart Guy, 3, 115	Successful Appeal, 3, 122	8	1:42.78	120,000
1998	Scatmandu, 3, 114	R. Migliore	Hot Wells, 3, 115	True Silver, 3, 113	7	1:42.43	90,000
1997	Leestown, 3, 116	J. A. Velez Jr.	Universe, 3, 115	Bleu Madura, 3, 116	8	1:43.46	90,000
1982	Northrop, 3, 113	L. Moyers	Majesty's Prince, 3, 126	Victory Zone, 3, 113	6	1:50.00	14,755
1981	Sportin' Life, 3, 116	K. D. Black	Main Stem, 3, 116	Aspro, 3, 113	7	1:49.00	18,801
1980	Proctor, 3, 113	V. A. Bracciale Jr.	Poor Dad, 3, 122	Colossal Apostle, 3, 113	12	1:50.20	30,778
1979	Lucy's Axe, 3, 126	R. B. Gilbert	Buck's Chief, 3, 114	Idle Jack, 3, 113	8	1:50.80	21,450
1978	Mac Diarmida, 3, 122	J. Cruguet	Prince Misko, 3, 122	Strange Proposal, 3, 116	10	1:46.80	22,653
1977	True Colors, 3, 113	S. Cauthen	Singleton, 3, 113	Best Person, 3, 113	13	1:43.20	19,663
1976	Cinteelo, 3, 117	B. Thornburg	Chati, 3, 117	Babas Fables, 3, 114	12	1:43.40	28,500
1975	My Friend Gus, 3, 117	B. Fann	Talc, 3, 120	Too Easy, 3, 114	10	1:42.20	30,290
1974	Silver Florin, 3, 122	R. Wilson	Ground Breaker, 3, 116	Clyde William, 3, 116	13	1:47.40	34,450
1973	London Company, 3, 122	C. Barrera	Bemo, 3, 119	Warbucks, 3, 119	8	1:47.80	41,798

Named for Lael Stables's 2006 Kentucky Derby Presented by Yum! Brands (G1) winner Barbaro (2003 c. by Dynaformer); Barbaro broke his maiden at Delaware Park in his first start. Formerly named for Leonard P. Richards, second chairman of the Delaware Racing Commission. Formerly named for the Delaware state nickname, the Diamond State. Grade 2 1973-'74. Not graded 1980-'82, 1997-2001. Diamond State S. 1937-'47. Leonard Richards S. 1948-'82, 1997-2006. Not held 1943, 1983-'96. 1 1/8 miles 1937-'68, 1979-'82. Turf 1970-'80.

Bashford Manor Stakes

Grade 3 in 2008. Churchill Downs, two-year-olds, 6 furlongs, dirt. Held July 7, 2007, with a gross value of $165,150. First held in 1902. First graded in 1991. Stakes record 1:09.15 (2007 Kodiak Kowboy).

Year	Winner	Jockey	Second	Third	Strs	Time	1st Purse
2007	Kodiak Kowboy, 2, 122	C. J. Lanerie	Dr. Nick, 2, 118	Crackalackin, 2, 118	6	**1:09.15**	$101,373
2006	Circular Quay, 2, 118	R. Bejarano	Shermanesque, 2, 118	Run Alex Run, 2, 118	8	1:09.96	100,134
2005	Deputy G, 2, 117	G. L. Stevens	R Loyal Man, 2, 117	Honor Due, 2, 117	10	1:11.38	109,275
2004	Lunarpal, 2, 121	S. J. Sellers	Storm Surge, 2, 117	Maximus C, 2, 117	7	1:11.11	101,184
2003	Limehouse, 2, 121	R. Albarado	First Money, 2, 117	Cuvee, 2, 121	6	1:10.62	100,905
2002	Lone Star Sky, 2, 115	M. Guidry	Posse, 2, 121	Cooper Crossing, 2, 115	7	1:09.68	84,475
2001	Lunar Bounty, 2, 115	F. Lovato Jr.	Binyamin, 2, 115	Storm Passage, 2, 115	5	1:09.90	82,925
2000	Duality, 2, 115	C. H. Borel	Strait Cat, 2, 114	Take Arms, 2, 115	9	1:10.09	86,258
1999	Dance Master, 2, 115	B. Peck	Sky Dweller, 2, 115	Snuck In, 2, 115	8	1:10.38	89,280
1998	Time Bandit, 2, 115	C. R. Woods Jr.	Yes It's True, 2, 121	Haus of Dehere, 2, 115	8	1:10.78	68,262
1997	Favorite Trick, 2, 121	P. Day	Double Honor, 2, 115	Cowboy Dan, 2, 118	8	1:09.92	68,696
1996	Boston Harbor, 2, 115	M. J. Luzzi	Prairie Junction, 2, 115	Nobel Talent, 2, 115	8	1:09.96	72,150
1995	A. V. Eight, 2, 115	A. J. Trosclair	Aggie Southpaw, 2, 115	Seeker's Reward, 2, 115	8	1:11.40	71,630
1994	Hyroglyphic, 2, 116	G. K. Gomez	Boone's Mill, 2, 116	Hobgoblin, 2, 116	13	1:10.25	75,660
1993	†Miss Ra He Ra, 2, 113	W. Martinez	Ramblin Guy, 2, 116	Riverinn, 2, 112	13	1:12.98	76,180
1992	Mountain Cat, 2, 116	C. R. Woods Jr.	Tempered Halo, 2, 121	Storm Flight, 2, 116	7	1:10.62	53,869
1991	Pick Up the Phone, 2, 116	J. C. Espinoza	Sprintmaster, 2, 116	Thanatopsis, 2, 112	7	1:12.08	35,815
1990	To Freedom, 2, 121	J. C. Espinoza	Richman, 2, 121	Discover, 2, 116	7	1:10.20	35,555
1989	Summer Squall, 2, 121	P. Day	Table Limit, 2, 118	Appealing Breeze, 2, 121	6	1:10.20	35,068
1988	Bio, 2, 118	P. A. Johnson	Revive, 2, 112	Curtis John, 2, 114	11	1:11.80	37,148
1987	Blair's Cove, 2, 114	S. J. Sellers	Endurance, 2, 118	Mr. Igloo, 2, 116	11	1:11.80	37,310
1986	Faster Than Sound, 2, 118	C. Perret	Renumeration, 2, 115	Arunti, 2, 121	7	1:11.20	46,648
1985	Tile, 2, 115	L. J. Melancon	Tug, 2, 115	Sir Grandeur, 2, 115	12	1:04.40	30,896
1984	Jerry F., 2, 112	P. Day	Storm Scope, 2, 115	Wet My Whistle, 2, 115	3	1:05.80	17,241
1983	Betwixt n' Between, 2, 115	P. Day	Real Sharp Dancer, 2, 121	Biloxi Indian, 2, 118	13	1:05.00	22,896
1982	Willow Drive, 2, 115	J. Neagle	Stepping E. J., 2, 118	Mindboggling, 2, 115	11	1:05.00	20,264
1981	T. V. Mark, 2, 122	P. Nicolo	Shilling, 2, 122	Good Ole Master, 2, 122	10	:59.60	18,103
1980	Golden Derby, 2, 117	J. C. Espinoza	Wrong Impression, 2, 122	Stubilem, 2, 117	9	:59.00	19,338
1979	Rajohn Greco, 2, 122	J. C. Espinoza	Egg's Dynamite, 2, 122	Native Amber, 2, 122	8	1:00.20	19,451
1978	Spy Charger, 2, 127	G. Mahon	Uncle Fudge, 2, 122	Vennie Redberry, 2, 122	6	:58.40	14,089
1977	Going Investor, 2, 122	B. Sayler	Old Jake, 2, 117	Chwesboken, 2, 122	7	:58.40	14,235
1976	Judge John Boone, 2, 122	E. Delahoussaye	Wishem Well, 2, 122	Golden Trade, 2, 117	8	:58.60	14,625
1975	Khyber King, 2, 122	E. Delahoussaye	Bold Laddie, 2, 122	Right On Mike, 2, 122	5	:58.60	15,633
1974	Pac Quick, 2, 125	G. Patterson	Paris Dust, 2, 121	Kaanapali, 2, 122	9	:59.60	16,608
1973	Tisab, 2, 122	M. Manganello	No Advance, 2, 122	To the Rescue, 2, 122	6	:59.00	16,965

Named for an old Louisville-area plantation and neighborhood, Bashford Manor. Grade 2 1999-2001. 4 1/2 furlongs 1902-'25. 5 furlongs 1926-'81. 5 1/2 furlongs 1982-'85. Colts and geldings 1940-'81. †Denotes female.

Bayakoa Handicap

Grade 2 in 2008. Hollywood Park, three-year-olds and up, fillies and mares, 1 1/16 miles, all weather. Held December 1, 2007, with a gross value of $150,000. First held in 1981. First graded in 1983. Stakes record 1:40.90 (2007 Romance Is Diane).

Year	Winner	Jockey	Second	Third	Strs	Time	1st Purse
2007	**Romance Is Diane**, 3, 115	M. C. Baze	Tough Tiz's Sis, 3, 120	Fonce De (Fr), 5, 117	5	**1:40.90**	$90,000
2006	**Foxysox (GB)**, 3, 118	V. Espinoza	Round Heels (Ire), 5, 115	Dona Amelia (Chi), 4, 116	12	1:41.84	90,000
2005	**Star Parade (Arg)**, 6, 116	M. A. Pedroza	Dream of Summer, 6, 122	Island Fashion, 5, 119	9	1:41.96	90,000
2004	**Hollywood Story**, 3, 115	V. Espinoza	Royally Chosen, 6, 116	A. P. Adventure, 3, 117	7	1:41.11	90,000
2003	**Star Parade (Arg)**, 4, 112	V. Espinoza	Adoration, 4, 121	Bare Necessities, 4, 119	6	1:41.02	90,000
2002	**Starrer**, 4, 118	P. A. Valenzuela	Cee's Elegance, 5, 113	Angel Gift, 4, 115	6	1:41.74	90,000
2001	**Starrer**, 3, 118	J. D. Bailey	Queenie Belle, 4, 118	Tropical Lady (Brz), 4, 115	7	1:42.52	90,000
2000	**Feverish**, 5, 119	E. Delahoussaye	Gourmet Girl, 5, 118	Lazy Slusan, 5, 117	9	1:42.26	90,000
1999	**Manistique**, 4, 124	C. S. Nakatani	Snowberg, 4, 115	Riboletta (Brz), 4, 116	7	1:43.16	90,000
1998	**Manistique**, 3, 119	G. L. Stevens	India Divina (Chi), 4, 114	Numero Uno, 4, 115	4	1:42.51	60,000
1997	**Sharp Cat**, 3, 121	A. O. Solis			1	1:42.68	60,000
1996	**Listening**, 4, 120	C. J. McCarron	Cat's Cradle, 4, 120	Belle's Flag, 3, 117	7	1:42.66	64,920
1995	**Pirate's Revenge**, 4, 119	C. W. Antley	Urbane, 3, 120	Ashtabula, 4, 116	5	1:41.80	61,960
1994	**Thirst for Peace**, 5, 115	A. O. Solis	Glass Ceiling, 4, 117	Dancing Mirage, 3, 119	7	1:42.28	63,500
1993	**Golden Klair (GB)**, 3, 115	C. J. McCarron	Pacific Squall, 4, 118	Cargo, 4, 116	7	1:41.20	63,500
1992	**Brought to Mind**, 5, 120	P. A. Valenzuela	Re Toss (Arg), 5, 115	Interactive, 3, 112	8	1:42.62	65,200
1991	**Paseana (Arg)**, 4, 117	C. J. McCarron	Darnewood, 3, 116	Luna Elegante (Arg), 5, 117	6	1:42.70	62,700
1990	**Fantastic Look**, 4, 118	C. J. McCarron	Spanish Dior, 3, 112	Tis Juliet, 4, 115	6	1:42.40	62,200
1989	**Approved to Fly**, 3, 115	A. O. Solis	Saros Brig, 5, 115	Lucky Song, 3, 114	7	1:48.20	63,400
1988	**Nastique**, 4, 119	W. Shoemaker	Miss Brio (Chi), 4, 116	T. V. of Crystal, 3, 117	6	1:48.00	76,800
1986	**Family Style**, 3, 115	G. L. Stevens	Infinidad (Chi), 4, 114	Waterside, 4, 113	7	1:50.00	82,700
1985	**Love Smitten**, 4, 116	C. J. McCarron	Mimi Baker, 4, 111	Dontstop Themusic, 5, 125	7	1:47.80	61,600
1984	**Dontstop Themusic**, 4, 118	T. Lipham	Paradies (Arg), 4, 114	Fancy Wings, 4, 116	8	1:50.20	64,500
1983	**Sweet Diane**, 3, 115	R. Sibille	Miss Huntington, 6, 117	Bersid, 5, 118	11	1:48.00	67,900
1982	**Sierva (Arg)**, 4, 117	L. A. Pincay Jr.	Miss Huntington, 5, 117	Plenty O'Toole, 5, 115	11	1:48.20	68,900
1981	**Happy Guess (Arg)**, 5, 117	W. Shoemaker	Track Robbery, 5, 123	Targa, 4, 112	6	1:49.60	62,100

Named for Mr. and Mrs. Frank E. Whitham's 1989, '90 champion older female and '89 Vanity H. (G1) winner Bayakoa (Arg) (1984 f. by Consultant's Bid). Grade 3 1983-'85. Silver Belles H. 1981-'93. Not held 1987. 1 1/8 miles 1981-'89. Dirt 1981-2005. Won in a walkover 1997.

Bay Meadows Sprint Handicap

Grade 3 in 2008. Bay Meadows Race Course, four-year-olds and up, 6 furlongs, dirt. Held March 15, 2008, with a gross value of $98,000. First held in 1986. First graded in 2000. Stakes record 1:07.94 (2001 Lexicon).

Year	Winner	Jockey	Second	Third	Strs	Time	1st Purse
2008	**Bonfante**, 7, 117	F. T. Alvarado	Jack Hes Tops, 4, 114	Vicarino, 4, 121	4	1:09.39	$60,000
2007	**Smokey Stover**, 4, 123	A. T. Gryder	Britt's Jules, 6, 116	Areyoutalkintome, 6, 117	4	1:08.40	55,000
2006	**Carthage**, 6, 120	D. Carr	Trickey Trevor, 7, 120	Areyoutalkintome, 5, 116	4	1:09.33	68,750
2004	**Court's in Session**, 5, 115	R. M. Gonzalez	Debonair Joe, 5, 117	Hombre Rapido, 7, 118	9	1:08.91	41,250
2003	**El Dorado Shooter**, 6, 120	C. P. Schvaneveldt	Halo Cat, 5, 118	Radar Contact, 7, 116	6	1:08.63	82,500
2002	**Mellow Fellow**, 7, 119	R. A. Baze	Explicit, 5, 120	Swept Overboard, 5, 122	6	1:08.35	110,000
2001	**Lexicon**, 6, 117	R. A. Baze	Swept Overboard, 4, 117	You and You Alone, 4, 115	4	**1:07.94**	82,500
2000	**Lexicon**, 5, 115	R. A. Baze	Men's Exclusive, 7, 116	Dixie Dot Com, 5, 116	5	1:09.19	110,000
1999	**Big Jag**, 6, 118	J. Valdivia Jr.	Men's Exclusive, 6, 117	Lexicon, 4, 116	6	1:08.87	110,000
1998	**Musafi**, 4, 116	D. R. Flores	dh-The Barking Shark, 5, 116 dh-Mr. Doubledown, 4, 116		7	1:08.59	110,000
1997	**Tres Paraiso**, 5, 116	C. S. Nakatani	Mashaka's Pride, 4, 112	Boundless Moment, 5, 117	5	1:07.98	110,000
1996	**Boundless Moment**, 4, 116	K. Desormeaux	Concept Win, 6, 115	Paying Dues, 4, 119	11	1:08.81	110,000
1995	**Lucky Forever**, 6, 116	G. F. Almeida	Wild Gold, 5, 115	Uncaged Fury, 4, 116	6	1:08.71	117,700
1994	**†Soviet Problem**, 4, 120	R. A. Baze	Wild Gold, 4, 115	Concept Win, 4, 119	8	1:08.58	31,200
1993	**Lucky Forever**, 4, 114	A. L. Castanon	Cardmania, 7, 116	Scherando, 4, 115	9	1:08.98	87,750
1992	**Superstrike (GB)**, 5, 118	D. Sorenson	Anjiz, 4, 114	Naevus Star, 6, 111	7	1:08.83	86,950
1991	**Robyn Dancer**, 4, 119	L. A. Pincay Jr.	Blue Eyed Danny, 5, 115	Letthebighossroll, 3, 116	7	1:09.30	84,728
1990	**Earn Your Stripes**, 6, 117	P. A. Valenzuela	Frost Free, 5, 116	Just Deeds, 4, 113	6	1:08.40	84,700
1989	**Happy Toss (Arg)**, 4, 115	F. Toro	No Marker, 5, 111	Hot Operator, 4, 113	6	1:39.80	86,250
1988	**Good Command**, 5, 117	R. A. Baze	Slyly Gifted, 5, 113	Miracle Horse (Fr), 4, 117	5	1:42.00	85,950
1987	**Judge Angelucci**, 4, 122	G. Baze	He's a Saros, 4, 115	Show Dancer, 5, 117	4	1:48.20	85,350
1986	**Hopeful Word**, 5, 116	F. Toro	Armin, 5, 114	Bozina, 5, 115	8	1:40.40	87,350

Bay Meadows Budweiser Breeders' Cup H. 1986-'95. Bay Meadows Breeders' Cup Sprint H. 1996-'01, 2004-'07. Bay Meadows Breeders' Cup Sprint S. 2002-'03. Not held 2005. 1 1/16 miles 1986, 1988-'89. 1 1/8 miles 1987. Three-year-olds and up 1986-2006. Dead heat for second 1998. †Denotes female.

Bay Shore Stakes

Grade 3 in 2008. Aqueduct, three-year-olds, 7 furlongs, dirt. Held April 5, 2008, with a gross value of $150,000. First held in 1894. First graded in 1973. Stakes record 1:20.54 (1998 Limit Out).

Year	Winner	Jockey	Second	Third	Strs	Time	1st Purse
2008	**J Be K**, 3, 116	G. K. Gomez	Gattopardo, 3, 118	Jockey Ridge, 3, 116	7	1:23.67	$90,000
2007	**Bill Place**, 3, 120	C. H. Velasquez	Hobbitontherocks, 3, 116	Les Grands Trois, 3, 116	7	1:22.99	90,000
2006	**Too Much Bling**, 3, 120	G. K. Gomez	Songster, 3, 116	One Way Flight, 3, 120	5	1:22.40	90,000

Racing — Graded Stakes

Year	Winner	Jockey	Second	Third	Strs	Time	1st Purse
2005	Lost in the Fog, 3, 123	R. A. Baze	White Socks, 3, 116	Big Top Cat, 3, 116	6	1:21.33	$90,000
2004	Forest Danger, 3, 116	J. R. Velazquez	Abbondanza, 3, 116	Indian War Dance, 3, 116	8	1:20.67	90,000
2003	Halo Homewrecker, 3, 116	J. R. Velazquez	Don Six, 3, 116	Stanislavsky, 3, 116	11	1:23.19	90,000
2002	Roman Dancer, 3, 120	K. Desormeaux	Warners, 3, 116	Monthir, 3, 116	10	1:22.21	90,000
2001	Skip to the Stone, 3, 120	V. Espinoza	Multiple Choice, 3, 116	Friday's a Comin', 3, 120	8	1:22.46	90,000
2000	Precise End, 3, 116	J. F. Chavez	Turnofthecentury, 3, 114	Port Herman, 3, 114	7	1:22.27	66,000
1999	Perfect Score, 3, 118	E. S. Prado	Royal Ruby, 3, 114	Prince Monty, 3, 116	8	1:22.98	66,120
1998	Limit Out, 3, 115	J. Samyn	Good and Tough, 3, 113	Diamond Studs, 3, 113	6	**1:20.54**	65,460
1997	Hawks Landing, 3, 114	R. Migliore	Adverse, 3, 113	Standing On Edge, 3, 113	7	1:22.00	66,480
1996	Jamies First Punch, 3, 115	J. R. Velazquez	Gold Fever, 3, 115	Firey Jennifer, 3, 115	9	1:22.13	67,200
1995	Blissful State, 3, 118	M. J. Luzzi	Northern Ensign, 3, 114	Pat n Jac, 3, 115	6	1:23.92	64,680
1994	Prank Call, 3, 113	J. R. Velazquez	Mr. Shawklit, 3, 117	Popol's Gold, 3, 122	7	1:09.84	65,940
1992	Three Peat, 3, 114	C. W. Antley	Goldwater, 3, 117	Best Decorated, 3, 114	10	1:21.68	75,600
1991	Stately Wager, 3, 119	J. F. Chavez	Mineral Ice, 3, 119	Vouch for Me, 3, 117	7	1:23.95	71,040
1990	Richard R., 3, 117	J. A. Santos	For Really, 3, 114	Cielo, 3, 114	7	1:22.80	70,080
1989	Houston, 3, 116	L. A. Pincay Jr.	Mr. Nickerson, 3, 114	Wee Stark, 3, 119	6	1:22.40	69,000
1988	Perfect Spy, 3, 119	R. G. Davis	Success Express, 3, 123	Proud and Valid, 3, 117	5	1:22.60	98,460
1987	Gulch, 3, 123	J. A. Santos	High Brite, 3, 119	Shawklit Won, 3, 114	9	1:23.20	124,800
1986	Zabaleta, 3, 114	D. G. McHargue	Groovy, 3, 117	Belocolus, 3, 114	8	1:22.00	95,250
	Buck Aly, 3, 117	N. Santagata	Landing Plot, 3, 119	Raja's Revenge, 3, 119	8	1:23.80	95,250
1985	Pancho Villa, 3, 114	F. Lovato Jr.	El Basco, 3, 114	Spend a Buck, 3, 123	9	1:22.20	97,020
1984	Secret Prince, 3, 114	C. Perret	The Wedding Guest, 3, 126	I'm a Rounder, 3, 114	9	1:11.20	95,580
1983	Strike Gold, 3, 114	E. Maple	Assault Landing, 3, 114	Chas Conerly, 3, 114	9	1:22.60	34,620
1982	Shimatoree, 3, 114	A. T. Cordero Jr.	Big Brave Rock, 3, 114	John's Gold, 3, 114	7	1:23.20	33,000
1981	Proud Appeal, 3, 121	J. Fell	Willow Hour, 3, 114	Royal Pavilion, 3, 114	4	1:22.20	32,940
1980	Colonel Moran, 3, 121	J. Velasquez	Son of a Dodo, 3, 115	Dunham's Gift, 3, 114	7	1:23.80	34,260
1979	Belle's Gold, 3, 114	G. Martens	Screen King, 3, 121	General Assembly, 3, 123	4	1:21.80	32,040
1978	Piece of Heaven, 3, 119	R. Hernandez	Just Right Classi, 3, 114	Slap Jack, 3, 114	8	1:11.00	32,460
1977	Cormorant, 3, 121	D. R. Wright	Medieval Man, 3, 119	Hey Hey J. P., 3, 114	6	1:10.80	32,460
1976	Bold Forbes, 3, 119	A. T. Cordero Jr.	Eustace, 3, 121	Full Out, 3, 124	8	1:20.80	33,780
1975	Laramie Trail, 3, 113	M. Venezia	T. V. Charger, 3, 113	Ascetic, 3, 121	5	1:23.60	26,910
	Lefty, 3, 113	R. Turcotte	Tass, 3, 113	Gallant Bob, 3, 119	8	1:23.80	27,360
1974	Hudson County, 3, 113	M. Miceli	Frankie Adams, 3, 119	Instead of Roses, 3, 116	11	1:22.60	34,680
1973	Secretariat, 3, 126	R. Turcotte	Champagne Charlie, 3, 118	Impecunious, 3, 126	6	1:23.20	16,650

Named for Bay Shore, a hamlet located on Long Island, New York. Grade 2 1985-'92. Bayshore S. 1894-1909. Bay Shore H. 1925-'62, 1979-'80. Held at Gravesend 1894-1909. Not held 1910-'24, 1956-'59, 1993. 1 1/16 miles 1894. 1 mile 1895, 1933, 1960-'63. 6 furlongs 1896-'98, 1934-'35, 1977-'78, 1984, 1994. About 6 furlongs 1899-1909. 6 1/2 furlongs 1936-'39. Three-year-olds and up 1894-1960. Two divisions 1975, '86.

Beaugay Handicap

Grade 3 in 2008. Aqueduct, three-year-olds and up, fillies and mares, 1 1/16 miles, turf. Held April 26, 2008, with a gross value of $106,200. First held in 1978. First graded in 1986. Stakes record 1:40.16 (1991 Summer Secretary).

Year	Winner	Jockey	Second	Third	Strs	Time	1st Purse
2008	Criminologist, 5, 119	J. R. Velazquez	All Is Vanity (Fr), 4, 117	Factual Contender, 7, 115	5	1:41.44	$64,920
2007	Masseuse, 5, 115	E. S. Prado	Stormy Kiss (Arg), 5, 115	Finlandia, 5, 116	7	1:47.43	68,160
2006	Pommes Frites, 4, 115	C. H. Velasquez	Naissance Royale (Ire), 4, 117	Brunilda (Arg), 6, 115	8	1:43.15	67,380
2005	Finery, 5, 116	P. Fragoso	Changing World, 5, 118	Asti (Ire), 4, 117	9	1:44.56	67,680
2004	Dedication (Fr), 5, 118	J. Castellano	Aud, 4, 117	Caught in the Rain, 5, 114	7	1:46.38	66,000
2003	Delta Princess, 4, 113	M. J. Luzzi	Wonder Again, 4, 118	Voodoo Dancer, 5, 120	9	1:42.36	67,440
2002	Voodoo Dancer, 4, 119	J. D. Bailey	Golden Corona, 4, 115	Babae (Chi), 6, 116	10	1:43.10	67,920
2001	Gaviola, 4, 120	J. D. Bailey	Truebreadpudding, 6, 113	Efficient Frontier, 4, 114	6	1:41.74	65,940
2000	Perfect Sting, 4, 119	J. D. Bailey	License Fee, 5, 114	Fictitious (GB), 4, 114	7	1:42.30	65,820
1999	Tampico, 4, 113	J. R. Velazquez	U R Unforgetable, 5, 115	Shashobegon, 4, 114	7	1:44.32	67,020
1998	National Treasure, 5, 117	R. Migliore	Aspiring, 5, 113	Dixie Ghost, 4, 111	7	1:37.94	67,740
1997	Careless Heiress, 4, 116	J. Bravo	Song of Africa, 4, 113	Gastronomical, 4, 115	6	1:46.28	65,760
1996	Christmas Gift, 4, 118	J. D. Bailey	Caress, 5, 119	Aucilla, 5, 113	9	1:42.89	50,805
1995	Caress, 4, 113	R. G. Davis	Shir Dar (Fr), 5, 113	Statuette, 5, 116	8	1:42.06	49,905
1994	Cox Orange, 4, 112	J. D. Bailey	Irish Linnet, 6, 116	Statuette, 4, 116	5	1:43.32	49,395
1993	McKaymackenna, 4, 113	J. Velasquez	Aurora, 5, 113	Chinese Empress, 4, 114	10	1:44.80	57,240
1992	Christiecat, 5, 116	J. Samyn	Metamorphose, 4, 113	Navarra, 4, 109	10	1:46.84	56,520
1991	Summer Secretary, 6, 116	J. Velasquez	Virgin Michael, 4, 113	Christiecat, 4, 115	7	**1:40.16**	54,270
1990	Fieldy (Ire), 7, 119	C. Perret	Summer Secretary, 5, 114	Lady Talc, 6, 110	5	1:45.80	52,740
1989	Summer Secretary, 4, 109	J. Samyn	Far East, 6, 110	Fieldy (Ire), 6, 116	9	1:43.40	56,880
1988	Key to the Bridge, 4, 112	E. Maple	Marimascus, 4, 112	Just Class (Ire), 4, 115	5	1:51.80	65,160
1987	Give a Toast, 4, 111	R. G. Davis	Videogenic, 5, 117	Small Virtue, 4, 113	8	1:44.20	68,940
1986	Duty Dance, 4, 115	J. Cruguet	Possible Mate, 5, 124	Lucky Touch, 4, 109	10	1:40.20	55,800
1985	Possible Mate, 4, 119	J. Vasquez	Make the Magic, 4, 109	Annie Edge (Ire), 5, 114	8	1:40.60	42,600
1984	Thirty Flags, 4, 113	A. T. Cordero Jr.	Jubilous, 4, 114	Nany, 4, 111	12	1:42.00	45,840
1983	Trevita (Ire), 6, 119	J. Velasquez	Beech Island, 5, 108	Top of the Barrel, 5, 105	12	1:47.80	37,020
1982	Cheap Seats, 3, 113	A. T. Cordero Jr.	Tina Tina Too, 4, 115	Fancy Naskra, 4, 112	7	1:45.20	33,780
1981	Andover Way, 3, 120	A. T. Cordero Jr.	Water Dance, 4, 117	Tournament Star, 3, 109	9	1:44.00	34,440
1980	Samarta Dancer, 4, 114	L. Saumell	Plankton, 4, 121	Bien Fait, 4, 109	8	1:43.60	33,540

Year	Winner	Jockey	Second	Third	Strs	Time	1st Purse
1979	Plankton, 3, 113	R. Hernandez	Miss Baja, 4, 114	Reflection Pool, 5, 112	6	1:46.00	$25,612
	Heavenly Ade, 3, 114	M. Solomone	Propitiate, 4, 112	Gladiolus, 5, 122	5	1:45.60	25,613
1978	Shukey, 3, 113	J. Velasquez	Sans Critique, 4, 118	Whodatorsay, 4, 109	6	1:45.20	25,755

Named for Maine Chance Farm's 1945 champion two-year-old filly Beaugay (1943 f. by Stimulus). Held at Belmont Park 1983-'92. 1 mile 1998. Dirt 1978-'82, 1998. Two divisions 1979.

Beaumont Stakes — *See* Stonerside Beaumont Stakes

Bed o' Roses Handicap

Grade 2 in 2008. Aqueduct, three-year-olds and up, fillies and mares, 7 furlongs, dirt. Held April 19, 2008, with a gross value of $158,100. First held in 1957. First graded in 1973. Stakes record 1:22.66 (2008 Rite Moment).

Year	Winner	Jockey	Second	Third	Strs	Time	1st Purse
2008	Rite Moment, 4, 117	R. Maragh	Lady Marlboro, 4, 118	Cowgirls Don't Cry, 4, 113	6	1:22.66	$94,860
2007	Carmandia, 5, 116	M. J. Luzzi	Magnolia Jackson, 5, 118	Swap Fliparoo, 4, 116	5	1:22.98	94,140
2006	Magnolia Jackson, 4, 115	N. Arroyo Jr.	Grecian Lover, 4, 115	Annika Lass, 5, 114	5	1:23.87	95,040
2005	Pleasant Home, 4, 114	C. H. Velasquez	Traci Girl, 6, 114	Cativa, 5, 117	7	1:36.72	95,220
2004	Passing Shot, 5, 115	J. A. Santos	Smok'n Frolic, 5, 119	Nonsuch Bay, 5, 116	6	1:35.50	95,040
2003	Raging Fever, 5, 119	A. T. Gryder	Smok'n Frolic, 4, 120	Nonsuch Bay, 4, 117	5	1:34.86	93,960
2002	Raging Fever, 4, 121	J. R. Velazquez	Atelier, 5, 119	Shiny Band, 4, 112	6	1:34.96	94,980
2001	Country Hideaway, 5, 117	J. R. Velazquez	Critical Eye, 4, 115	Jostle, 4, 117	7	1:34.98	95,520
2000	Ruby Rubles, 5, 113	C. C. Lopez	Up We Go, 4, 114	Go to the Ink, 4, 111	7	1:36.96	65,580
1999	Catinca, 4, 120	R. Migliore	Foil, 4, 113	License Fee, 4, 113	6	1:34.95	94,620
1998	Dixie Flag, 4, 117	M. J. Luzzi	Hidden Reserve, 4, 113	U Can Do It, 5, 118	9	1:33.60	96,780
1997	Flat Fleet Feet, 4, 119	M. E. Smith	Mama Dean, 4, 113	Ashboro, 4, 116	6	1:34.00	95,940
1996	Punkin Pie, 6, 110	J. C. Trejo	Incinerate, 6, 115	Lottsa Talc, 6, 121	6	1:35.13	65,220
1995	Incinerate, 5, 113	F. Leon	Imah, 5, 114	Beckys Shirt, 4, 113	5	1:35.86	63,960
1994	Classy Mirage, 4, 117	R. G. Davis	For all Seasons, 4, 115	Dispute, 4, 122	6	1:34.00	64,680
1993	Lady d'Accord, 6, 111	J. F. Chavez	Missy's Mirage, 5, 123	Buck Some Belle, 4, 106	5	1:36.76	67,320
1992	Nannerl, 5, 115	J. A. Krone	English Charm, 6, 111	Spy Leader Lady, 4, 115	7	1:37.27	68,100
	Lady d'Accord, 5, 114	J. F. Chavez	My Treasure, 5, 112	Crystal Vous, 4, 112	7	1:37.86	68,580
1991	Devil's Orchid, 4, 120	R. A. Baze	Colonial Waters, 6, 119	Sharp Dance, 5, 114	6	1:35.93	68,520
1990	Survive, 6, 117	J. A. Santos	Amy Be Good, 4, 114	Warfie, 4, 111	6	1:34.20	68,640
1989	Banker's Lady, 4, 118	A. T. Cordero Jr.	Aptostar, 4, 118	Avie's Gal, 4, 114	5	1:35.40	68,400
1988	Aptostar, 3, 103	J. A. Krone	Clabber Girl, 5, 117	Psyched, 5, 114	8	1:35.40	70,680
1987	Ms. Eloise, 4, 115	R. G. Davis	Spring Beauty, 4, 116	Tricky Squaw, 4, 115	9	1:36.60	84,660
1986	Chaldea, 6, 110	J. Samyn	Add Mint, 4, 111	Lady On the Run, 4, 120	9	1:36.00	75,120
1985	Nany, 5, 120	J. Vasquez	Flip's Pleasure, 5, 118	Sintrillium, 7, 120	6	1:36.00	50,850
1984	Pleasure Cay, 4, 115	R. G. Davis	Sweet Missus, 4, 103	Sintrillium, 6, 113	8	1:42.00	54,090
1983	Broom Dance, 4, 118	G. McCarron	Adept, 4, 109	Viva Sec, 5, 112	7	1:35.40	33,420
1982	Who's to Answer, 4, 108	E. Beitia	Real Prize, 4, 114	Faisana (Arg), 5, 110	9	1:36.60	33,180
1981	Chain Bracelet, 4, 114	F. Lovato Jr.	Lady Oakley (Ire), 4, 116	Contrary Rose, 5, 115	7	1:35.40	33,960
1980	Misty Gallore, 4, 125	D. MacBeth	Propitiate, 5, 115	Gueniviere, 4, 111	6	1:36.40	33,600
1979	Lady Lonsdale, 4, 111	C. B. Asmussen	Hagany, 5, 112	Back to Stay, 4, 107	7	1:36.80	31,980
	One Sum, 5, 118	J. Fell	Reflection Pool, 5, 113	Pearl Necklace, 5, 121	7	1:37.80	31,980
1978	Fearless Queen, 5, 108	M. Venezia	Notably, 5, 110	One Sum, 4, 123	7	1:46.20	25,785
1977	Shawi, 4, 109	M. Venezia	Proud Delta, 5, 125	Secret Lanvin, 4, 111	8	1:45.80	25,770
1976	Imminence, 4, 115	E. Maple	Spring Is Here, 4, 108	Land Girl, 4, 114	9	1:35.40	23,040
1975	Shy Dawn, 4, 121	D. Montoya	Something Super, 5, 118	Flo's Pleasure, 5, 115	7	1:36.20	16,860
1974	Klepto, 4, 123	D. Montoya	Ladies Agreement, 4, 112	Summer Guest, 5, 122	6	1:35.40	16,410
1973	Poker Night, 3, 108	R. Woodhouse	Numbered Account, 4, 123	Ferly, 5, 114	7	1:35.40	16,605

Named for Alfred G. Vanderbilt's Racing Hall of Fame member, 1949 champion two-year-old filly, '51 champion older female, and '49 Demoiselle S. winner Bed o' Roses (1947 f. by Rosemont). Grade 3 1975-'87, 1997-2005. Bed o' Roses H. 1957-'95. Bed o' Roses Breeders' Cup H. 1996-2007. Held at Jamaica 1957-'59. 1 1/16 miles 1957-'59, 1977-'78. 1 mile 70 yards 1984. 1 mile 1960-'76, 1979-'83, 1985-2005. Two divisions 1979, 1992.

Beldame Stakes

Grade 1 in 2008. Belmont Park, three-year-olds and up, fillies and mares, 1 1/8 miles, dirt. Held September 30, 2007, with a gross value of $612,000. First held in 1905. First graded in 1973. Stakes record 1:45.80 (1990 Go for Wand).

Year	Winner	Jockey	Second	Third	Strs	Time	1st Purse
2007	Unbridled Belle, 4, 123	R. A. Dominguez	Indian Vale, 5, 123	Ginger Punch, 4, 123	7	1:48.63	$360,000
2006	Fleet Indian, 5, 123	J. A. Santos	Balletto (UAE), 4, 123	Round Pond, 4, 123	6	1:48.69	360,000
2005	Ashado, 4, 123	J. R. Velazquez	Happy Ticket, 4, 123	Society Selection, 4, 123	7	1:48.88	450,000
2004	Sightseek, 5, 123	J. Castellano	Society Selection, 3, 120	Storm Flag Flying, 4, 123	5	1:49.60	450,000
2003	Sightseek, 4, 123	J. D. Bailey	Bird Town, 3, 120	Buy the Sport, 3, 120	7	1:49.27	450,000
2002	Imperial Gesture, 3, 120	J. D. Bailey	Mandy's Gold, 4, 123	Summer Colony, 4, 123	7	1:50.63	450,000
2001	Exogenous, 3, 120	J. Castellano	Flute, 3, 120	Spain, 4, 123	8	1:49.20	450,000
2000	Riboletta (Brz), 5, 123	C. J. McCarron	Beautiful Pleasure, 5, 123	Pentatonic, 5, 123	5	1:46.14	450,000
1999	Beautiful Pleasure, 4, 123	J. F. Chavez	Silverbulletday, 3, 119	Catinca, 4, 123	5	1:47.74	300,000
1998	Sharp Cat, 4, 123	C. S. Nakatani	Tomisue's Delight, 4, 123	Pocho's Dream Girl, 4, 123	7	1:46.20	240,000
1997	Hidden Lake, 4, 123	R. Migliore	Ajina, 3, 119	Jewel Princess, 5, 123	8	1:48.26	240,000
1996	Yanks Music, 3, 119	J. R. Velazquez	Serena's Song, 4, 123	Clear Mandate, 4, 123	6	1:47.02	240,000
1995	Serena's Song, 3, 119	G. L. Stevens	Heavenly Prize, 4, 123	Lakeway, 4, 123	5	1:48.75	150,000

Racing — Graded Stakes

Year	Winner	Jockey	Second	Third	Strs	Time	1st Purse
1994	Heavenly Prize, 3, 119	P. Day	Educated Risk, 4, 123	Classy Mirage, 4, 123	4	1:48.86	$150,000
1993	Dispute, 3, 119	J. D. Bailey	Shared Interest, 5, 123	Vivano, 4, 123	6	1:47.22	150,000
1992	Saratoga Dew, 3, 119	W. H. McCauley	Versailles Treaty, 4, 123	Coxwold, 4, 123	5	1:46.99	150,000
1991	Sharp Dance, 5, 123	M. E. Smith	Versailles Treaty, 3, 119	Lady d'Accord, 4, 123	6	1:48.01	150,000
1990	Go for Wand, 3, 119	R. P. Romero	Colonial Waters, 5, 123	Buy the Firm, 4, 123	5	**1:45.80**	167,700
1989	Tactile, 3, 118	R. Migliore	Colonial Waters, 4, 123	Rose's Cantina, 5, 123	6	2:05.20	170,100
1988	Personal Ensign, 4, 123	R. P. Romero	Classic Crown, 3, 118	Sham Say, 3, 118	5	2:01.20	199,440
1987	Personal Ensign, 3, 118	R. P. Romero	Coup de Fusil, 5, 123	Silent Turn, 3, 118	10	2:04.40	182,100
1986	Lady's Secret, 4, 123	P. Day	Coup de Fusil, 4, 123	Classy Cathy, 3, 118	4	2:01.60	189,600
1985	Lady's Secret, 3, 118	J. Velasquez	Isayso, 6, 123	Kamikaze Rick, 3, 118	5	2:03.60	160,920
1984	Life's Magic, 3, 118	J. Velasquez	Miss Oceana, 3, 118	Key Dancer, 3, 118	4	2:03.20	158,280
1983	Dance Number, 4, 123	A. T. Cordero Jr.	Heartlight No. One, 3, 118	Mochila, 4, 123	7	2:00.60	133,200
1982	Weber City Miss, 5, 123	A. T. Cordero Jr.	Mademoiselle Forli, 3, 118	Love Sign, 5, 123	9	2:04.20	134,100
1981	Love Sign, 4, 123	W. Shoemaker	dh-Glorious Song, 5, 123		7	2:01.80	131,100
			dh-Jameela, 5, 123				
1980	Love Sign, 3, 118	R. Hernandez	Misty Gallore, 4, 123	It's in the Air, 4, 123	4	2:02.80	96,300
1979	Waya (Fr), 5, 123	C. B. Asmussen	Fourdrinier, 3, 118	Kit's Double, 6, 123	7	2:06.20	97,050
1978	Late Bloomer, 4, 123	J. Velasquez	Pearl Necklace, 4, 123	Cum Laude Laurie, 4, 123	4	2:02.20	78,150
1977	Cum Laude Laurie, 3, 118	A. T. Cordero Jr.	What a Summer, 4, 123	Charming Story, 3, 118	7	2:01.80	80,025
1976	Proud Delta, 4, 123	J. Velasquez	Revidere, 3, 118	*Bastonera II, 5, 120	8	1:46.80	64,920
1975	Susan's Girl, 6, 123	B. Baeza	*Tizna, 6, 123	Pass a Glance, 4, 123	9	1:48.40	67,980
1974	Desert Vixen, 4, 123	L. A. Pincay Jr.	Poker Night, 4, 123	*Tizna, 5, 123	9	1:46.60	68,760
1973	Desert Vixen, 3, 118	J. Velasquez	Poker Night, 3, 118	Susan's Girl, 4, 123	7	1:46.20	65,880

Named for August Belmont II's Racing Hall of Fame member, consensus champion racemare, and 1904 Carter H. winner Beldame (1901 f. by Octagon). Beldame H. 1905-'59. Held at Aqueduct 1905-'56, 1959, 1962-'68. Not held 1908, 1910-'16, 1933-'38. 5 furlongs 1905-'32. 1 1/16 miles 1939. 1 1/4 miles 1977-'89. Two-year-olds 1905-'32. Fillies 1905-'32. Dead heat for second 1981. Equaled track record 1973. Equaled world record 1973.

Belmont Stakes

Grade 1 in 2008. Belmont Park, three-year-olds, 1 1/2 miles, dirt. Held June 7, 2008, with a gross value of $1,000,000. First held in 1867. First graded in 1973. Stakes record 2:24 (1973 Secretariat [current world and track record]).

(See Triple Crown section for complete history of the Belmont Stakes)

Year	Winner	Jockey	Second	Third	Strs	Time	1st Purse
2008	Da' Tara, 3, 126	A. Garcia	Denis of Cork, 3, 126	dh- Anak Nakal, 3, 126	9	2:29.65	$600,000
				dh- Ready's Echo, 3, 126			
2007	†Rags to Riches, 3, 121	J. R. Velazquez	Curlin, 3, 126	Tiago, 3, 126	7	2:28.74	600,000
2006	Jazil, 3, 126	F. Jara	Bluegrass Cat, 3, 126	Sunriver, 3, 126	12	2:27.86	600,000
2005	Afleet Alex, 3, 126	J. Rose	Andromeda's Hero, 3, 126	Nolan's Cat, 3, 126	11	2:28.75	600,000
2004	Birdstone, 3, 126	E. S. Prado	Smarty Jones, 3, 126	Royal Assault, 3, 126	9	2:27.50	600,000
2003	Empire Maker, 3, 126	J. D. Bailey	Ten Most Wanted, 3, 126	Funny Cide, 3, 126	6	2:28.26	600,000
2002	Sarava, 3, 126	E. S. Prado	Medaglia d'Oro, 3, 126	Sunday Break (Jpn), 3, 126	11	2:29.71	600,000
2001	Point Given, 3, 126	G. L. Stevens	A P Valentine, 3, 126	Monarchos, 3, 126	9	2:26.56	600,000
2000	Commendable, 3, 126	P. Day	Aptitude, 3, 126	Unshaded, 3, 126	11	2:31.19	600,000
1999	Lemon Drop Kid, 3, 126	J. A. Santos	Vision and Verse, 3, 126	Charismatic, 3, 126	12	2:27.88	600,000
1998	Victory Gallop, 3, 126	G. L. Stevens	Real Quiet, 3, 126	Thomas Jo, 3, 126	11	2:29.16	600,000
1997	Touch Gold, 3, 126	C. J. McCarron	Silver Charm, 3, 126	Free House, 3, 126	7	2:28.82	432,660
1996	Editor's Note, 3, 126	R. R. Douglas	Skip Away, 3, 126	†My Flag, 3, 121	14	2:28.96	437,880
1995	Thunder Gulch, 3, 126	G. L. Stevens	Star Standard, 3, 126	Citadeed, 3, 126	11	2:32.02	415,440
1994	Tabasco Cat, 3, 126	P. Day	Go for Gin, 3, 126	Strodes Creek, 3, 126	6	2:26.82	392,280
1993	Colonial Affair, 3, 126	J. A. Krone	Kissin Kris, 3, 126	Wild Gale, 3, 126	13	2:29.97	444,540
1992	A.P. Indy, 3, 126	E. Delahoussaye	My Memoirs (GB), 3, 126	Pine Bluff, 3, 126	11	2:26.13	458,880
1991	Hansel, 3, 126	J. D. Bailey	Strike the Gold, 3, 126	Mane Minister, 3, 126	11	2:28.10	1,417,480
1990	Go and Go (Ire), 3, 126	M. J. Kinane	Thirty Six Red, 3, 126	Baron de Vaux, 3, 126	9	2:27.20	411,600
1989	Easy Goer, 3, 126	P. Day	Sunday Silence, 3, 126	Le Voyageur, 3, 126	10	2:26.00	413,520
1988	Risen Star, 3, 126	E. Delahoussaye	Kingpost, 3, 126	Brian's Time, 3, 126	8	2:26.40	1,303,720
1987	Bet Twice, 3, 126	C. Perret	Cryptoclearance, 3, 126	Gulch, 3, 126	9	2:28.20	1,329,160
1986	Danzig Connection, 3, 126	C. J. McCarron	Johns Treasure, 3, 126	Ferdinand, 3, 126	10	2:29.80	338,640
1985	Creme Fraiche, 3, 126	E. Maple	Stephan's Odyssey, 3, 126	Chief's Crown, 3, 126	11	2:27.00	307,740
1984	Swale, 3, 126	L. A. Pincay Jr.	Pine Circle, 3, 126	Morning Bob, 3, 126	11	2:27.20	310,020
1983	Caveat, 3, 126	L. A. Pincay Jr.	Slew o' Gold, 3, 126	Barberstown, 3, 126	15	2:27.80	215,100
1982	Conquistador Cielo, 3, 126	L. A. Pincay Jr.	Gato Del Sol, 3, 126	Illuminate, 3, 126	11	2:28.20	159,720
1981	Summing, 3, 126	G. Martens	Highland Blade, 3, 126	Pleasant Colony, 3, 126	11	2:29.00	170,580
1980	Temperence Hill, 3, 126	E. Maple	†Genuine Risk, 3, 121	Rockhill Native, 3, 126	12	2:29.80	176,220
1979	Coastal, 3, 126	R. Hernandez	Golden Act, 3, 126	Spectacular Bid, 3, 126	8	2:28.60	161,400
1978	Affirmed, 3, 126	S. Cauthen	Alydar, 3, 126	Darby Creek Road, 3, 126	5	2:26.80	110,580
1977	Seattle Slew, 3, 126	J. Cruguet	Run Dusty Run, 3, 126	Sanhedrin, 3, 126	8	2:29.60	109,080
1976	Bold Forbes, 3, 126	A. T. Cordero Jr.	McKenzie Bridge, 3, 126	Great Contractor, 3, 126	10	2:29.00	117,000
1975	Avatar, 3, 126	W. Shoemaker	Foolish Pleasure, 3, 126	Master Derby, 3, 126	9	2:28.20	116,160
1974	Little Current, 3, 126	M. A. Rivera	Jolly Johu, 3, 126	Cannonade, 3, 126	9	2:29.20	101,970
1973	Secretariat, 3, 126	R. Turcotte	Twice a Prince, 3, 126	My Gallant, 3, 126	5	**2:24.00**	90,120

Named for August Belmont I (1816-'90), president of Jerome Park. Belmont H. 1895, 1913. Held at Jerome Park 1867-'89. Held at Morris Park 1890-1904. Held at Aqueduct 1963-'67. Not held 1911-'12. 1 5/8 miles 1867-'73. 1 1/4 miles 1890-'92, 1895, 1904-'05. 1 1/8 miles 1893-'94. 1 3/8 miles 1896-1903, 1906-'25. Colts and fillies 1919-'56. World record 1973. Track record 1973. †Denotes female. $1-million Triple Crown bonus awarded on a points basis 1987-'88, 1991.

Ben Ali Stakes

Grade 3 in 2008. Keeneland Race Course, four-year-olds and up, 1¹/₈ miles, all weather. Held April 20, 2008, with a gross value of $150,000. First held in 1917. First graded in 1973. Stakes record 1:46.78 (2004 Midway Road).

Year	Winner	Jockey	Second	Third	Strs	Time	1st Purse
2008	Sterwins, 5, 117	S. Bridgmohan	Go Between, 5, 123	Sir Whimsey, 4, 121	6	1:48.53	$93,000
2007	Jade's Revenge, 4, 117	K. J. Desormeaux	Minister's Joy, 5, 117	Mustanfar, 6, 117	11	1:49.93	93,000
2006	Wanderin Boy, 5, 117	J. Castellano	Alumni Hall, 7, 117	Noble Causeway, 4, 117	6	1:49.18	93,000
2005	Alumni Hall, 6, 121	R. Albarado	Pies Prospect, 4, 123	Go Now, 4, 117	8	1:51.29	93,000
2004	Midway Road, 4, 116	R. Albarado	Evening Attire, 6, 116	Sir Cherokee, 4, 120	5	**1:46.78**	93,000
2003	Mineshaft, 4, 120	R. Albarado	American Style, 4, 116	Metatron, 4, 116	4	1:48.52	68,386
2002	Duckhorn, 5, 116	J. F. Chavez	Parade Leader, 5, 120	Connected, 5, 118	4	1:50.18	66,464
2001	Broken Vow, 4, 116	E. S. Prado	Perfect Cat, 4, 116	Jadada, 6, 116	5	1:48.47	66,216
2000	Midway Magistrate, 6, 116	S. J. Sellers	Liberty Gold, 6, 116	Early Warning, 5, 118	7	1:49.15	67,518
1999	Jazz Club, 4, 115	P. Day	Smile Again, 4, 115	Early Warning, 4, 115	6	1:48.16	67,456
1998	Storm Broker, 4, 114	R. Albarado	Delay of Game, 5, 119	Gator Dancer, 5, 114	6	1:48.23	67,208
1997	Louis Quatorze, 4, 119	P. Day	Knockadoon, 5, 113	King James, 5, 113	5	1:49.60	66,526
1996	Knockadoon, 4, 112	J. D. Bailey	Halo's Image, 5, 117	Thorny Crown, 5, 113	4	1:48.92	66,216
1995	Wildly Joyous, 4, 114	M. Walls	Danville, 4, 117	Powerful Punch, 6, 113	7	1:49.68	50,406
1994	Pistols and Roses, 5, 123	M. E. Smith	Sunny Sunrise, 7, 119	Compadre, 4, 113	6	1:51.77	50,251
1993	Sunny Sunrise, 6, 119	R. Wilson	Conte Di Savoya, 4, 113	Prize Fight, 4, 112	8	1:48.90	50,933
1992	dh-Loach, 4, 117	P. A. Valenzuela		Out of Place, 5, 119	6	1:49.95	34,212
	dh-Profit Key, 5, 113	S. J. Sellers					
1991	Sports View, 4, 119	C. Perret	Bright Again, 4, 113	Exemplary Leader, 5, 112	6	1:49.67	53,495
1990	Master Speaker, 5, 121	J. D. Bailey	Lac Ouimet, 7, 114	Silver Survivor, 4, 119	7	1:49.00	54,893
1989	Classic Account, 4, 114	P. Day	Regal Classic, 4, 117	Brian's Time, 4, 121	5	1:50.60	53,885
1988	Homebuilder, 4, 119	D. Brumfield	Bet Twice, 4, 126	Blue Buckaroo, 5, 117	4	1:51.40	52,293
1987	Intrusion, 5, 111	S. Hawley	Coaxing Mark, 4, 114	Blue Buckaroo, 4, 117	5	1:49.60	34,678
1986	Czar Nijinsky, 4, 119	W. H. McCauley	Little Missouri, 4, 114	Minneapple, 4, 117	8	1:50.20	43,542
1985	Bello, 4, 116	G. Gallitano	Silent King, 4, 117	Hi Pi, 6, 113	7	1:48.80	35,295
1984	Aspro, 6, 116	D. Brumfield	Play Fellow, 4, 123	Jack Slade, 4, 115	5	1:50.80	34,564
1983	Aspro, 5, 115	V. A. Bracciale Jr.	Thirty Eight Paces, 5, 115	Rivalero, 7, 121	8	1:49.60	35,588
1982	Withholding, 5, 121	L. J. Melancon	Aspro, 4, 122	Swinging Light, 4, 113	8	1:49.60	35,880
1981	Withholding, 4, 113	B. Sayler	Summer Advocate, 4, 113	Two's a Plenty, 4, 115	6	1:50.20	34,986
1980	Architect, 4, 120	S. A. Spencer	Revivalist, 6, 116	All the More, 7, 116	5	1:48.80	27,999
1979	Kodiack, 5, 114	G. Gallitano	Hot Words, 4, 113	Morning Frolic, 4, 115	8	1:49.60	31,054
1978	Prince Majestic, 4, 118	E. Delahoussaye	Inca Roca, 5, 114	All the More, 6, 122	9	1:41.80	21,824
1977	Honest Pleasure, 4, 124	C. Perret	Inca Roca, 4, 118	Packer Captain, 5, 113	9	1:42.40	18,623
1976	My Friend Gus, 4, 114	D. G. McHargue	Packer Captain, 4, 116	Dragset, 5, 113	8	1:42.40	18,116
1975	Navajo, 5, 122	J. Nichols	L. Grant Jr., 5, 118	Hasty Flyer, 4, 115	12	1:43.80	19,419
1974	Knight Counter, 6, 119	E. Fires	Model Husband, 5, 117	Jim's Alibhi, 7, 113	6	1:41.80	17,648
1973	Knight Counter, 5, 120	D. Brumfield	‡Guitar Player, 5, 118	Introductivo, 4, 114	12	1:43.00	18,785

Named for James Ben Ali Haggin (1821-1914), native Kentuckian and owner of Elmendorf Farm, and his 1886 Kentucky Derby winner Ben Ali (1883 c. by Virgil). Ben Ali H. 1917-'89. Held at Kentucky Association 1917-'31. Held at Churchill Downs 1943-'45. Not held 1923-'27, 1932-'36. 1¹/₁₆ miles 1937-'30, 1937-'53, 1963-'78. About 6 furlongs 1931. About 7 furlongs 1946-'62. Dirt 1917-2006. Three-year-olds and up 1917-'85. Dead heat for first 1992. ‡Hustlin Greek finished second, DQ to 12th for a positive drug test, 1973. Track record 2004.

Berkeley Stakes

Grade 3 in 2008. Golden Gate Fields, three-year-olds and up, 1¹/₁₆ miles, dirt. Held May 26, 2008, with a gross value of $150,000. First held in 1933. First graded in 2000. Stakes record 1:40.94 (2005 Desert Boom).

Year	Winner	Jockey	Second	Third	Strs	Time	1st Purse
2008	McCann's Mojave, 8, 123	F. T. Alvarado	Desert Code, 4, 123	Pass the Heat, 5, 123	6	1:43.06	$90,000
2007	My Creed, 6, 119	M. Linares	Visa Parade (Arg), 4, 117	Desert Boom, 7, 118	8	1:43.46	55,000
2006	Spellbinder, 5, 118	R. M. Gonzalez	Sharp Writer, 4, 117	Cooperation, 5, 113	6	1:43.07	82,500
2005	Desert Boom, 5, 113	R. M. Gonzalez	Easy Million, 5, 116	Yougottawanna, 6, 118	7	**1:40.94**	55,000
2004	Snorter, 4, 116	R. A. Baze	Yougottawanna, 5, 116	Taste of Paradise, 5, 116	5	1:33.92	55,000
2003	I'madrifter, 5, 115	R. M. Gonzalez	Palmeiro, 5, 117	Skip to the Stone, 5, 116	5	1:35.13	55,000
2002	Irisheyesareflying, 6, 120	J. Valdivia Jr.	Boss Ego, 6, 116	Palmeiro, 4, 116	11	1:35.41	55,000
2001	Blade Prospector (Brz), 6, 118	O. A. Berrio	Dixie Dot Com, 6, 119	Milk Wood (GB), 6, 115	6	1:34.18	55,000
2000	Voice of Destiny, 4, 113	R. Q. Meza	Mr. Doubledown, 6, 115	Twilight Affair, 6, 115	8	1:35.67	75,000
1999	Hal's Pal (GB), 6, 117	B. Blanc	Wild Wonder, 5, 122	Worldly Ways (GB), 5, 115	7	1:34.96	75,000
1998	Wild Wonder, 4, 115	R. A. Baze	General Royal, 4, 115	March of Kings, 5, 117	8	1:35.19	47,700
1997	Houston Fleet M D, 2, 118	D. Carr	Slewp'a Doop, 2, 116	Big Find, 2, 116	5	1:36.67	26,600
1996	Double Jab, 4, 115	R. A. Baze	Corslew, 5, 116	Cleante (Arg), 6, 115	8	1:35.18	49,725
1995	River Special, 4, 115	T. M. Chapman	He's Illustrious, 7, 116	Misty Wind (Ire), 6, 114	5	1:34.33	32,600
1994	Infamous Deed, 5, 115	R. J. Warren Jr.	Misty Wind (Ire), 5, 115	J. F. Williams, 4, 115	7	1:35.67	25,960
1993	Music Prospector, 5, 118	R. D. Hansen	Michael's Flyer, 6, 115	Flying Continental, 6, 124	5	1:35.29	31,450
1992	High Energy, 4, 115	R. J. Warren Jr.	Bold Current, 4, 114	Beau's Alliance, 5, 115	3	1:35.70	32,800
1991	On the Menu, 4, 112	C. L. Davenport	Crackedbell, 5, 116	Ongoing Mister, 5, 117	5	1:34.80	31,600
1990	Ongoing Mister, 4, 114	T. T. Doocy	Present Value, 5, 113	Lucky Harold H., 5, 110	8	1:34.20	33,600
1989	Sanger Chief, 5, 114	T. T. Doocy	Lucky Harold H., 4, 114	Power Forward, 5, 119	7	1:35.60	31,900
1988	Rocky Marriage, 7, 116	R. A. Baze	Dormello (Arg), 6, 115	Bagdad Dawn, 5, 112	7	1:36.80	32,250
1987	Sun Master, 5, 117	M. Castaneda	Beldale Lear, 5, 123	Prairie Breaker, 6, 114	6	1:34.60	25,400

Racing — Graded Stakes

Year	Winner	Jockey	Second	Third	Strs	Time	1st Purse
1985	Nak Ack, 4, 114	J. C. Judice	Holmbury, 5, 113	Chum Salmon, 5, 116	9	1:36.20	$26,600
1984	Songhay, 5, 114	J. C. Judice	Grand Balcony, 5, 113	The Jandy Man, 4, 113	11	1:35.40	27,300
1983	Pleasant Power, 5, 115	J. R. Anderson	Lord Advocate, 4, 117	Red Crescent, 7, 119	13	1:40.60	27,800
1982	Foyt's Ack, 7, 115	R. M. Gonzalez	Borrego Sun, 5, 118	Pleasant Power, 4, 112	8	1:38.00	25,650
1981	Head Hawk, 5, 111	D. Sorenson	His Honor, 6, 115	Beau Moro, 6, 117	7	1:45.60	25,750
1979	Gustoso, 4, 120	R. Campas	Rassendyll, 5, 113	Rescator, 5, 117	7	1:34.40	20,500
1978	Boy Tike, 5, 114	A. L. Diaz	Dr. Krohn, 5, 120	Miami Sun, 4, 120	7	1:36.20	19,250
1977	Lino, 5, 112	R. Caballero	Crafty Native, 4, 114	Classy Surgeon, 4, 116	7	1:37.40	16,050
1976	Branford Court, 6, 113	A. L. Diaz	Austin Mittler, 4, 117	Carry the Banner, 6, 113	7	1:35.00	15,700
1975	Star of Kuwait, 7, 118	W. Mahorney	Willie Pleasant, 4, 116	Mac's L., 4, 111	10	1:44.80	16,450
1974	*Yvetot, 6, 120	F. Olivares	Sensitive Music, 5, 114	*Larkal II, 6, 113	8	1:43.80	17,800
1973	*Yvetot, 5, 112	V. Tejada	Cabin, 5, 121	Masked, 4, 120	10	1:44.20	18,050

Named for Berkeley, California, located near San Francisco. Berkeley H. 1933, 1938, 1949-2003, 2005-'06. Berkeley H. 1933-2003, 2005-'07. Berkeley Breeders' Cup H. 2004. Held at Tanforan 1933. Held at Bay Meadows 1938. Not held 1934-'37, 1939-'47, 1961-'62, 1980, 1997. About 6 furlongs 1938-'50, 1952-'55, 1957-'59. 1 mile 1951, 1956, 1964, 1976-'80, 1982-2004. 1¼ miles 1966-'70. 1⅛ miles 1971. Turf 1972-'74, 1976. Originally scheduled on turf 1975. Two-year-olds and up 1933. Two-year-olds 1948, '57, '96. Three-year-olds 1949-'56, 1958-'65. Four-year-olds and up 1968. Colts and geldings 1948. Fillies 1956-'58, 1964. Nonwinners of a race worth $12,500 to the winner 1973. Nonwinners of a race worth $35,000 to the winner at one mile or over 1990, '92.

Bernard Baruch Handicap

Grade 2 in 2008. Saratoga Race Course, three-year-olds and up, 1⅛ miles, turf. Held August 25, 2007, with a gross value of $200,000. First held in 1959. First graded in 1973. Stakes record 1:45.33 (2007 Shakis [Ire]).

Year	Winner	Jockey	Second	Third	Strs	Time	1st Purse
2007	Shakis (Ire), 7, 116	A. Garcia	Big Prairie, 5, 115	Drum Major, 5, 116	10	1:45.33	$120,000
2006	Ashkal Way (Ire), 4, 115	G. K. Gomez	Dreadnaught, 6, 116	Interpatation, 4, 113	8	1:46.78	120,000
2005	Artie Schiller, 4, 122	R. Migliore	Silver Tree, 5, 117	America Alive, 4, 119	5	1:45.67	90,000
2004	Silver Tree, 4, 116	J. D. Bailey	Nothing to Lose, 4, 117	Irish Colonial, 5, 113	7	1:49.66	90,000
2003	Trademark (SAf), 7, 114	R. Migliore	Rouvres (Fr), 4, 116	Slew Valley, 6, 113	7	1:49.06	90,000
2002	Del Mar Show, 5, 120	J. D. Bailey	Volponi, 4, 116	Forbidden Apple, 7, 121	7	1:48.51	90,000
2001	Hap, 5, 121	J. D. Bailey	Royal Strand (Ire), 7, 115	Dr. Kashnikow, 4, 114	7	1:47.06	90,000
2000	Hap, 4, 115	J. D. Bailey	Inexplicable, 5, 115	Draw Shot, 7, 114	13	1:45.82	90,000
1999	Middlesex Drive, 4, 117	S. J. Sellers	Tangazi, 4, 114	Comic Strip, 4, 116	8	1:46.55	90,000
1998	Yagli, 5, 121	J. D. Bailey	Tamhid, 5, 113	Jambalaya Jazz, 6, 115	9	1:46.22	85,380
1997	Sentimental Moi, 7, 112	C. P. DeCarlo	Jambalaya Jazz, 5, 115	Boyce, 6, 120	8	1:46.11	66,480
1996	Volochine (Ire), 5, 113	P. Day	Green Means Go, 4, 116	Compadre, 6, 108	9	1:47.58	68,700
1995	Fourstars Allstar, 7, 120	J. A. Santos	Turk Passer, 5, 114	Compadre, 5, 112	7	1:47.67	66,240
1994	Lure, 5, 125	M. E. Smith	Paradise Creek, 5, 126	Fourstardave, 9, 114	5	1:46.10	64,920
1993	Furiously, 4, 119	J. D. Bailey	Star of Cozzene, 5, 123	Royal Mountain Inn, 4, 114	5	1:45.46	70,320
1992	Fourstars Allstar, 4, 113	M. E. Smith	Lotus Pool, 5, 113	Maxigroom, 4, 114	6	1:46.06	70,680
1991	Double Booked, 6, 122	A. Madrid Jr.	Who's to Pay, 5, 118	Solar Splendor, 4, 113	8	1:49.14	71,400
1990	Who's to Pay, 4, 110	J. Samyn	Steinlen (GB), 7, 126	River of Sin, 6, 115	9	1:48.40	52,920
1989	Steinlen (GB), 6, 121	J. A. Santos	Soviet Lad, 4, 111	Brian's Time, 4, 112	8	1:51.00	73,920
1988	My Big Boy, 5, 113	R. P. Romero	Steinlen (GB), 5, 120	Wanderkin, 5, 115	9	1:46.80	72,600
1987	Talakeno, 7, 115	A. T. Cordero Jr.	Manila, 4, 127	Duluth, 5, 114	4	1:47.40	85,380
1986	Exclusive Partner, 4, 112	J. Velasquez	I'm a Banker, 4, 111	Creme Fraiche, 4, 117	12	1:50.80	82,200
1985	Win, 5, 124	R. Migliore	Cozzene, 5, 120	Sitzmark, 5, 112	9	1:47.00	59,400
1984	Win, 4, 112	A. Graell	Intensify, 4, 113	Cozzene, 4, 114	9	1:47.40	57,510
1983	Tantalizing, 4, 115	J. D. Bailey	Ten Below, 4, 114	Acaroid, 4, 115	9	1:48.80	34,140
	Fray Star (Arg), 5, 114	O. Vergara	Fortnightly, 3, 113	Who's for Dinner, 4, 109	9	1:48.40	34,380
1982	Pair of Deuces, 4, 115	R. Hernandez	Native Courier, 7, 117	McCann, 4, 112	11	1:47.80	36,540
1981	Native Courier, 6, 114	E. Maple	Manguin, 5, 105	Proctor, 4, 118	7	1:47.40	33,450
	Great Neck, 5, 119	A. T. Cordero Jr.	War of Words, 4, 111	Match the Hatch, 5, 114	5	1:47.60	33,690
1980	Premier Ministre, 4, 116	R. I. Encinas	Great Neck, 4, 112	Tiller, 6, 126	11	2:13.60	35,700
1979	Overskate, 4, 128	R. Platts	Timbo, 3, 108	Native Courier, 4, 115	11	1:51.80	35,610
1978	Dominion (GB), 6, 115	J. Samyn	Bill Brill, 4, 111	Upper Nile, 4, 119	11	1:49.00	24,480
1977	Majestic Light, 4, 126	S. Hawley	Alias Smith, 4, 112	Clout, 5, 114	11	1:46.20	23,175
1976	Intrepid Hero, 4, 123	E. Maple	Modred, 3, 118	Erwin Boy, 5, 126	8	1:50.40	22,530
1975	dh-Salt Marsh, 5, 116	E. Maple		Drollery, 5, 112	8	1:49.80	18,061
	dh-Ward McAllister, 4, 110	D. Montoya					
1974	Golden Don, 4, 113	V. A. Bracciale Jr.	Halo, 5, 119	Scantling, 4, 117	10	1:46.00	23,580
1973	Tentam, 4, 118	J. Velasquez	Scrimshaw, 5, 111	Astray, 4, 114	10	1:45.40	14,265
	Red Reality, 7, 120	J. Velasquez	Tri Jet, 4, 121	Ruritania, 4, 113	9	1:46.60	14,190

Named for Bernard Baruch (1870-1965), avid racing fan and adviser to presidents. Grade 3 1973-'82. Grade 1 1988-'89. Bernard Baruch S. 1959-'60. 1 1/16 miles 1962-'71. 1⅜ miles 1980. Dirt 1959-'60, 1979. Three-year-olds 1959-'60. Two divisions 1973, '81, '83. Equaled course record 1993. Course record 2007.

Bessemer Trust Breeders' Cup Juvenile

Grade 1 in 2008. Monmouth Park, two-year-olds, colts and geldings, 1 1/16 miles, dirt. Held October 27, 2007, with a gross value of $1,832,000. First held in 1984. First graded in 1984. Stakes record 1:41.47 (1997 Favorite Trick).

Year	Winner	Jockey	Second	Third	Strs	Time	1st Purse
2007	War Pass, 2, 122	C. H. Velasquez	Pyro, 2, 122	Kodiak Kowboy, 2, 122	11	1:42.76	$1,080,000
2006	Street Sense, 2, 122	C. H. Borel	Circular Quay, 2, 122	Great Hunter, 2, 122	14	1:42.59	1,080,000

Racing — Graded Stakes

Year	Winner	Jockey	Second	Third	Strs	Time	1st Purse
2005	Stevie Wonderboy, 2, 122	G. K. Gomez	Henny Hughes, 2, 122	First Samurai, 2, 122	14	1:41.64	$826,800
2004	Wilko, 2, 122	L. Dettori	Afleet Alex, 2, 122	Sun King, 2, 122	8	1:42.09	780,000
2003	Action This Day, 2, 122	D. R. Flores	Minister Eric, 2, 122	Chapel Royal, 2, 122	12	1:43.62	780,000
2002	Vindication, 2, 122	M. E. Smith	Kafwain, 2, 122	Hold That Tiger, 2, 122	13	1:49.61	556,400
2001	Johannesburg, 2, 122	M. J. Kinane	Repent, 2, 122	Siphonic, 2, 122	12	1:42.27	520,000
2000	Macho Uno, 2, 122	J. D. Bailey	Point Given, 2, 122	Street Cry (Ire), 2, 122	14	1:42.05	556,400
1999	Anees, 2, 122	G. L. Stevens	Chief Seattle, 2, 122	High Yield, 2, 122	14	1:42.29	556,400
1998	Answer Lively, 2, 122	J. D. Bailey	Aly's Alley, 2, 122	Cat Thief, 2, 122	13	1:44.00	520,000
1997	Favorite Trick, 2, 122	P. Day	Dawson's Legacy, 2, 122	Nationalore, 2, 122	8	1:41.47	520,000
1996	Boston Harbor, 2, 122	J. D. Bailey	Acceptable, 2, 122	Ordway, 2, 122	10	1:43.40	520,000
1995	Unbridled's Song, 2, 122	M. E. Smith	Hennessy, 2, 122	Editor's Note, 2, 122	13	1:41.60	520,000
1994	Timber Country, 2, 122	P. Day	Eltish, 2, 122	Tejano Run, 2, 122	13	1:44.55	520,000
1993	Brocco, 2, 122	G. L. Stevens	Blumin Affair, 2, 122	Tabasco Cat, 2, 122	11	1:42.99	520,000
1992	Gilded Time, 2, 122	C. J. McCarron	It'sali'lknownfact, 2, 122	River Special, 2, 122	13	1:43.43	520,000
1991	Arazi, 2, 122	P. A. Valenzuela	Bertrando, 2, 122	Snappy Landing, 2, 122	14	1:44.78	520,000
1990	Fly So Free, 2, 122	J. A. Santos	Take Me Out, 2, 122	Lost Mountain, 2, 122	11	1:43.40	450,000
1989	Rhythm, 2, 122	C. Perret	Grand Canyon, 2, 122	Slavic, 2, 122	12	1:43.60	450,000
1988	Is It True, 2, 122	L. A. Pincay Jr.	Easy Goer, 2, 122	Tagel, 2, 122	10	1:46.60	450,000
1987	Success Express, 2, 122	J. A. Santos	Regal Classic, 2, 122	Tejano, 2, 122	13	1:35.20	450,000
1986	Capote, 2, 122	L. A. Pincay Jr.	Qualify, 2, 122	Alysheba, 2, 122	13	1:43.80	450,000
1985	Tasso, 2, 122	L. A. Pincay Jr.	Storm Cat, 2, 122	Scat Dancer, 2, 122	13	1:36.20	450,000
1984	Chief's Crown, 2, 122	D. MacBeth	Tank's Prospect, 2, 122	Spend a Buck, 2, 122	10	1:36.20	450,000

Sponsored by Bessemer Trust of New York City 2001-'07. Held at Hollywood Park 1984, '87, '97. Held at Aqueduct 1985. Held at Santa Anita Park 1986, '93, 2003. Held at Churchill Downs 1988, '91, '94, '98, 2000, '06. Held at Gulfstream Park 1989, '92, '99. Held at Belmont Park 1990, '95, 2001, '05. Held at Woodbine 1996. Held at Arlington Park 2002. Held at Lone Star Park 2004. 1 mile 1984-'85, 1987. 1 1/8 miles 2002.

Best Pal Stakes

Grade 2 in 2008. Del Mar, two-year-olds, 6 1/2 furlongs, all weather. Held August 12, 2007, with a gross value of $147,000. First held in 1967. First graded in 1983. Stakes record 1:15.08 (2001 Officer).

Year	Winner	Jockey	Second	Third	Strs	Time	1st Purse
2007	Salute the Sarge, 2, 123	M. C. Baze	Georgie Boy, 2, 123	Sky Cape, 2, 119	4	1:19.43	$90,000
2006	Principle Secret, 2, 119	A. O. Solis	Great Hunter, 2, 119	Stormello, 2, 119	8	1:16.15	90,000
2005	What a Song, 2, 123	V. Espinoza	Bashert, 2, 119	Plug Me In, 2, 117	4	1:15.64	90,000
2004	Roman Ruler, 2, 118	C. S. Nakatani	Actxecutive, 2, 118	Slewsbag, 2, 116	5	1:15.93	90,000
2003	Perfect Moon, 2, 122	P. A. Valenzuela	Capitano, 2, 118	Military Mandate, 2, 118	10	1:16.90	90,000
2002	Kafwain, 2, 117	V. Espinoza	Chief Planner, 2, 117	Outta Here, 2, 117	7	1:17.00	90,000
2001	Officer, 2, 121	V. Espinoza	Metatron, 2, 117	Essence of Dubai, 2, 117	3	1:15.08	90,000
2000	Flame Thrower, 2, 117	C. S. Nakatani	Trailthefox, 2, 121	Legendary Weave, 2, 117	7	1:16.51	90,000
1999	Dixie Union, 2, 121	A. O. Solis	Exchange Rate, 2, 119	Captain Steve, 2, 117	5	1:16.40	90,000
1998	Worldly Manner, 2, 117	G. L. Stevens	Domination, 2, 117	Waki American, 2, 115	8	1:16.78	65,580
1997	Old Topper, 2, 117	A. O. Solis	King of the Wild, 2, 117	Souvenir Copy, 2, 117	8	1:16.57	68,825
1996	Swiss Yodeler, 2, 121	A. O. Solis	Golden Bronze, 2, 117	Deeds Not Words, 2, 117	8	1:16.12	65,550
1995	Cobra King, 2, 117	R. A. Baze	Northern Afleet, 2, 117	Desert Native, 2, 117	8	1:15.89	60,350
1994	Timber Country, 2, 117	A. O. Solis	Desert Mirage, 2, 115	Supremo, 2, 117	7	1:16.60	46,575
1993	Creston, 2, 117	C. A. Black	Troyalty, 2, 121	Flying Sensation, 2, 115	6	1:16.35	45,900
1992	Devil Diamond, 2, 117	K. Desormeaux	Wheeler Oil, 2, 119	Crafty, 2, 117	6	1:22.60	45,900
1991	Scherando, 2, 121	F. Mena	Star Recruit, 2, 117	Prince Wild, 2, 119	9	1:22.47	47,625
1990	Best Pal, 2, 119	P. A. Valenzuela	Xray, 2, 117	Sunshine Machine, 2, 117	7	1:22.20	46,575
1989	A. Sir Dancer, 2, 117	E. Delahoussaye	Drag Race, 2, 115	†Patches, 2, 113	7	1:23.00	47,550
1988	Rob an Plunder, 2, 119	C. J. McCarron	Mountain Ghost, 2, 117	Pokarito, 2, 117	8	1:23.00	48,050
1987	Purdue King, 2, 121	C. J. McCarron	Accomplish Ridge, 2, 117	Mixed Pleasure, 2, 119	8	1:23.20	38,550
1986	Temperate Sil, 2, 117	W. Shoemaker	Polar Jet, 2, 117	Gold On Green, 2, 115	8	1:23.00	32,250
1985	Swear, 2, 116	E. Delahoussaye	Bright Tom, 2, 116	Smokey Orbit, 2, 114	9	1:36.60	32,750
1984	Saratoga Six, 2, 120	A. T. Cordero Jr.	Private Jungle, 2, 117	Indigenous, 2, 116	7	1:36.80	31,650
1983	Party Leader, 2, 116	R. Sibille	Juliet's Pride, 2, 115	Gumboy, 2, 116	7	1:37.20	31,550
1982	Roving Boy, 2, 115	E. Delahoussaye	Encourager, 2, 115	Full Choke, 2, 117	5	1:35.40	30,650
1981	The Captain, 2, 117	L. A. Pincay Jr.	Distant Heart, 2, 115	Gato Del Sol, 2, 115	9	1:36.80	26,400
1980	Bold and Gold, 2, 113	D. C. Hall	Splendid Spruce, 2, 115	Sir Dancer, 2, 113	7	1:37.40	22,550
1979	Doonesbury, 2, 113	S. Hawley	Executive Counsel, 2, 115	Defiance, 2, 117	5	1:35.40	19,300
1978	Flying Paster, 2, 117	D. Pierce	Roman Oblisk, 2, 117	Runaway Hit, 2, 114	9	1:35.60	19,500
1977	Spanish Way, 2, 117	L. A. Pincay Jr.	Tampoy, 2, 117	Misrepresentation, 2, 114	10	1:36.00	16,700
1976	Visible, 2, 117	L. A. Pincay Jr.	*Habitony, 2, 114	Replant, 2, 115	7	1:35.80	16,200
1975	Crazy Channon, 2, 115	D. Pierce	Classy Surgeon, 2, 114	Lexington Laugh, 2, 117	9	1:37.20	13,700
1974	Diabolo, 2, 120	W. Shoemaker	Trond Sang, 2, 114	Neat Claim, 2, 114	7	1:35.60	13,050
1973	Battery E., 2, 115	W. Harris	Jenny's Boy, 2, 120	Marchen McTavish, 2, 115	5	1:30.60	12,750

Named for Golden Eagle Farm's multiple Grade 1 stakes winner and 1990 Balboa S. (G3) winner Best Pal (1988 g. by *Habitony); Best Pal retired as the leading California-bred earner. Formerly named for Vasco Nunez de Balboa, first European to see the Pacific Ocean. Grade 3 1983-2002. Balboa H. 1967. Balboa S. 1972-'95. Not held 1968-'71. About 7 1/2 furlongs 1972-'73. 1 mile 1974-'85. 7 furlongs 1986-'92. Dirt 1967-'71, 1974-2006. Turf 1972-'73. †Denotes female. Nonwinners of a race worth $10,000 to the winner 1974-'75.

Beverly D. Stakes

Grade 1 in 2008. Arlington Park, three-year-olds and up, fillies and mares, 1³/₁₆ miles, turf. Held August 11, 2007, with a gross value of $750,000. First held in 1987. First graded in 1991. Stakes record 1:53.20 (1990 Reluctant Guest).

Year	Winner	Jockey	Second	Third	Strs	Time	1st Purse
2007	Royal Highness (Ger), 5, 123	R. R. Douglas	Irridescence (SAf), 6, 123	Lady of Venice (Fr), 4, 123	7	1:56.68	$445,500
2006	Gorella (Fr), 4, 123	J. R. Leparoux	Film Maker, 6, 123	Live Life (Fr), 4, 123	10	1:53.71	450,000
2005	Angara (GB), 4, 123	G. L. Stevens	Megahertz (GB), 5, 124	Melhor Ainda, 3, 117	9	1:58.30	450,000
2004	Crimson Palace (SAf), 5, 123	L. Dettori	Riskaverse, 5, 123	Necklace (GB), 3, 117	11	1:56.58	450,000
2003	Heat Haze (GB), 4, 123	J. Valdivia Jr.	Bien Nicole, 5, 123	Riskaverse, 4, 123	7	1:55.94	420,000
2002	Golden Apples (Ire), 4, 123	P. A. Valenzuela	Astra, 6, 123	England's Legend (Fr), 5, 123	6	1:54.86	420,000
2001	England's Legend (Fr), 4, 123	C. S. Nakatani	The Seven Seas, 5, 123	Spook Express (SAf), 7, 123	9	1:56.75	420,000
2000	Snow Polina, 5, 123	J. D. Bailey	Happyanunoit (NZ), 5, 123	Country Garden (GB), 5, 123	10	1:55.87	300,000
1997	Memories of Silver, 4, 123	J. D. Bailey	Maxzene, 4, 123	Dance Design (Ire), 4, 123	6	1:54.38	300,000
1996	Timarida (Ire), 4, 123	J. P. Murtagh	Perfect Arc, 4, 123	Alpride (Ire), 5, 123	11	1:54.06	300,000
1995	Possibly Perfect, 5, 123	C. S. Nakatani	Alice Springs, 5, 123	Alpride (Ire), 4, 123	7	1:54.95	300,000
1994	Hatoof, 5, 123	W. R. Swinburn	Flawlessly, 6, 123	Potridee (Arg), 5, 123	8	1:55.59	300,000
1993	‡Flawlessly, 5, 123	C. J. McCarron	Via Borghese, 4, 123	Let's Elope (NZ), 6, 123	7	1:55.61	300,000
1992	Kostroma (Ire), 6, 123	K. Desormeaux	Ruby Tiger (Ire), 5, 123	Dance Smartly, 4, 123	13	1:54.10	300,000
1991	Fire the Groom, 4, 123	G. L. Stevens	Colour Chart, 4, 123	Miss Josh, 5, 123	7	1:53.58	300,000
1990	Reluctant Guest, 4, 123	R. G. Davis	Lady Winner (Fr), 4, 123	Royal Touch (Ire), 5, 123	12	**1:53.20**	300,000
1989	Claire Marine (Ire), 4, 123	C. J. McCarron	Capades, 3, 117	Gaily Gaily (Ire), 6, 123	8	2:01.80	300,000
1987	Dancing On a Cloud, 4, 114	J. M. Lauzon	Spruce Luck, 6, 114	Caitie Kisses, 4, 112	10	1:55.00	34,650

Named for Beverly Duchossois, the late wife of Arlington Park Chairman Richard Duchossois. Not held 1988, 1998-'99. 1¹/₁₆ miles 1987. ‡Let's Elope (NZ) finished first, DQ to third, 1993.

Beverly Hills Handicap

Grade 2 in 2008. Hollywood Park, three-year-olds and up, fillies and mares, 1¼ miles, turf. Held July 1, 2007, with a gross value of $150,000. First held in 1938. First graded in 1973. Stakes record 1:58.56 (2002 Astra).

Year	Winner	Jockey	Second	Third	Strs	Time	1st Purse
2007	Citronnade, 4, 122	D. R. Flores	Andrea (NZ), 6, 113	Naughty Rafaela (Brz), 5, 117	5	2:01.47	$90,000
2006	Memorette, 4, 115	V. Espinoza	Live Life (Fr), 4, 119	Moscow Burning, 6, 121	9	2:00.16	90,000
2005	Megahertz (GB), 6, 124	A. O. Solis	Winendynme, 4, 117	Halo Ola (Arg), 5, 115	6	2:01.78	120,000
2004	Light Jig (GB), 4, 114	A. O. Solis	Moscow Burning, 4, 117	Noches De Rosa (Chi), 6, 118	6	2:01.52	120,000
2003	Voodoo Dancer, 5, 120	C. S. Nakatani	Dublino, 4, 122	Megahertz (GB), 4, 117	5	2:00.80	120,000
2002	Astra, 6, 124	K. Desormeaux	Peu a Peu (Ger), 4, 116	Crazy Ensign (Arg), 6, 117	5	**1:58.56**	150,000
2001	Astra, 5, 121	K. Desormeaux	Happyanunoit (NZ), 6, 122	Kalypso Katie (Ire), 4, 116	5	1:59.61	120,000
2000	Happyanunoit (NZ), 5, 120	B. Blanc	Sweet Life, 4, 115	Polaire (Fr), 5, 114	5	1:59.32	150,000
1999	Virginie (Brz), 5, 118	L. A. Pincay Jr.	Tranquility Lake, 4, 122	Keeper Hill, 4, 118	6	2:00.21	150,000
1998	Squeak (GB), 4, 115	G. L. Stevens	Sixy Saint, 4, 115	Freeport Flight, 4, 114	7	2:01.56	180,000
1997	Windsharp, 6, 122	C. S. Nakatani	Different (Arg), 5, 121	Donna Viola (GB), 5, 122	6	2:00.60	180,000
1996	Different (Arg), 4, 117	C. J. McCarron	Bail Out Becky, 4, 118	Flagbird, 5, 118	8	2:00.74	163,800
1995	Alpride (Ire), 4, 115	C. J. McCarron	Possibly Perfect, 5, 124	Wandesta (GB), 4, 119	6	1:46.67	185,000
1994	Corrazona, 4, 119	G. L. Stevens	Hollywood Wildcat, 4, 124	Flawlessly, 6, 124	7	1:47.40	188,400
1993	Flawlessly, 5, 123	C. J. McCarron	Jolypha, 4, 121	Party Cited, 4, 117	4	1:47.00	180,200
1992	Flawlessly, 4, 122	C. J. McCarron	Kostroma (Ire), 6, 124	Alcando (Ire), 6, 113	5	1:47.13	184,000
1991	Alcando (Ire), 5, 113	J. A. Garcia	Fire the Groom, 4, 120	Countus In, 6, 117	8	1:46.50	130,200
1990	dh-Beautiful Melody, 4, 115	K. Desormeaux		Stylish Star, 4, 116	6	1:47.00	82,300
	dh-Reluctant Guest, 4, 115	R. G. Davis					
1989	Claire Marine (Ire), 4, 120	C. J. McCarron	Fitzwilliam Place (Ire), 5, 121	No Review, 4, 116	6	1:47.20	93,100
1988	Fitzwilliam Place (Ire), 4, 119	A. T. Gryder	Ladanum, 4, 114	Chapel of Dreams, 4, 117	9	1:47.20	98,200
1987	Auspiciante (Arg), 6, 117	P. A. Valenzuela	Reloy, 4, 120	Festivity, 4, 114	8	1:46.20	64,600
1986	Estrapade, 6, 122	F. Toro	Treizieme, 5, 115	Sauna (Aus), 5, 117	7	1:59.00	63,800
1985	Johnica, 4, 115	G. L. Stevens	Estrapade, 5, 125	L'Attrayante (Fr), 5, 118	5	1:48.20	61,900
1984	Royal Heroine (Ire), 4, 123	F. Toro	Adored, 4, 121	Comedy Act, 5, 118	9	1:47.20	93,200
1983	Absentia, 4, 115	F. Toro	Latrone, 6, 110	Triple Tipple, 4, 118	11	1:49.00	68,500
1982	Sangue (Ire), 4, 119	W. Shoemaker	Ack's Secret, 6, 123	Miss Huntington, 5, 117	6	1:47.40	63,300
1981	Track Robbery, 5, 120	P. A. Valenzuela	Princess Karenda, 4, 121	Save Wild Life, 4, 115	5	1:46.80	61,800
1980	Country Queen, 5, 122	L. A. Pincay Jr.	Wishing Well, 5, 122	The Very One, 5, 117	10	1:47.40	50,550
1979	Giggling Girl, 5, 117	C. J. McCarron	Country Queen, 4, 123	More So (Ire), 4, 116	9	1:47.60	50,100
1978	Swingtime, 6, 119	F. Toro	Grande Brisa, 4, 115	Drama Critic, 4, 118	7	1:48.40	48,000
1977	Swingtime, 5, 120	F. Toro	Fortunate Betty, 4, 115	*Bastonera II, 6, 126	7	1:48.40	48,000
1976	*Bastonera II, 5, 121	L. A. Pincay Jr.	Miss Toshiba, 4, 124	Miss Tokyo, 4, 110	7	1:50.20	38,800
1975	*La Zanzara, 5, 122	D. Pierce	*Dulcia, 6, 123	Mercy Dee, 4, 110	5	2:14.80	46,500
1974	*La Zanzara, 4, 120	D. Pierce	Mon Miel, 4, 114	Dogtooth Violet, 4, 116	6	2:14.20	38,000
1973	Le Cle, 4, 119	W. Shoemaker	Pallisima, 4, 115	Convenience, 5, 124	9	2:14.80	49,900

Named for Beverly Hills, California. Grade 1 1973-2002. Not held 1940-'67. 1¹/₁₆ miles 1938. 1 mile 1939. 1⅜ miles 1968-'75. 1¹/₁₆ miles 1976-'85, 1987-'95. Dirt 1938-'39. Three-year-olds 1939. Both sexes 1939. Dead heat for first 1990. California-breds 1938-'39.

Bewitch Stakes — *see* Grey Goose Bewitch Stakes

Bill Hartack Memorial Handicap

Grade 3 in 2008. Hawthorne Race Course, three-year-olds and up, 1 1/8 miles, dirt. Held April 19, 2008, with a gross value of $200,000. First held in 1956. First graded in 1984. Stakes record 1:47.60 (1999 Baytown).

Year	Winner	Jockey	Second	Third	Strs	Time	1st Purse
2008	Ryan's for Real, 5, 114	E. D. Rodriguez	Fairbanks, 5, 116	Mr. Champ, 4, 111	5	1:51.18	$120,000
2007	Master Command, 5, 123	J. R. Velazquez	Sweetnorthernsaint, 4, 120	Le Jester, 7, 114	4	1:49.47	151,875
2006	Three Hour Nap, 4, 113	F. C. Torres	Summer Book, 5, 115	Courthouse, 5, 110	6	1:52.48	150,000
2005	Pollard's Vision, 4, 118	J. R. Velazquez	Badge of Silver, 5, 120	Lord of the Game, 4, 117	4	1:49.12	150,000
2004	Ten Most Wanted, 4, 121	D. R. Flores	Colonial Colony, 6, 113	New York Hero, 4, 113	6	1:49.54	150,000
2003	Fight for Ally, 6, 116	E. Razo Jr.	Colonial Colony, 5, 114	Parrott Bay, 6, 115	8	1:53.46	150,000
2002	Hail The Chief (GB), 5, 114	J. F. Chavez	E Z Glory, 5, 115	Ubiquity, 5, 115	7	1:51.72	120,000
2001	Chicago Six, 6, 117	A. J. Juarez Jr.	Guided Tour, 5, 118	Glacial, 6, 114	5	1:48.28	120,000
2000	Take Note of Me, 6, 120	R. Albarado	Glacial, 5, 113	Nite Dreamer, 5, 118	8	1:49.91	120,000
1999	Baytown, 5, 114	M. Guidry	Precocity, 5, 120	Fred Bear Claw, 5, 116	7	1:47.60	120,000
1998	Polar Expedition, 7, 117	M. Guidry	Bucks Nephew, 8, 115	Shed Some Light, 6, 114	9	1:49.91	120,000
1997	Bucks Nephew, 7, 118	G. K. Gomez	Natural Selection, 4, 114	Gotha, 5, 112	8	1:49.87	120,000
1996	‡Prory, 4, 113	C. H. Silva	Polar Expedition, 5, 116	Shed Some Light, 4, 114	9	1:50.83	150,000
1995	Dusty Screen, 7, 116	E. Maple	Come On Flip, 4, 114	Adhocracy, 5, 113	8	1:51.57	150,000
1994	Recoup the Cash, 4, 113	J. L. Diaz	Dread Me Not, 4, 114	Danc'n Jake, 5, 112	7	1:49.03	150,000
1993	Stalwars, 8, 118	J. L. Diaz	Count the Time, 4, 115	Richman, 5, 119	8	1:49.46	150,000
1992	Stalwars, 7, 115	M. Guidry	Richman, 4, 122	Sunny Prince, 5, 113	6	1:48.15	156,300
1991	Allijeba, 5, 116	S. J. Sellers	Whiz Along, 6, 110	Sound of Cannons, 4, 115	8	1:50.43	157,680
1990	Dual Elements, 4, 118	J. L. Diaz	Tricky Creek, 4, 120	Blue Buckaroo, 7, 115	11	1:49.60	143,730
1989	Present Value, 5, 112	W. Shoemaker	Super Roberto, 4, 113	Honor Medal, 8, 121	9	1:49.20	126,510
1988	Lost Code, 4, 129	C. Perret	Honor Medal, 7, 122	Outlaws Sham, 5, 114	7	1:49.60	125,640
1987	Honor Medal, 6, 118	L. E. Ortega	Blue Buckaroo, 4, 115	Coffer Dam, 6, 113	9	1:49.80	95,490
1986	Magic Notch, 4, 117	J. L. Diaz	Rocky Knave, 6, 121	Tuner Jr., 4, 113	7	1:50.00	65,220
1985	Norwick, 6, 117	K. Skinner	Harham's Sizzler, 6, 121	Badwagon Harry, 5, 116	9	1:51.20	67,440
1984	Prince Forli, 4, 118	R. A. Meier	Full Flame, 8, 119	Spare Card, 4, 117	8	1:52.60	64,080
1983	Determined Bidder, 4, 114	C. H. Silva	Thumbsucker, 4, 117	John's Gold, 4, 115	9	1:52.00	64,710
1982	Frost King, 4, 127	R. Platts	Dusky Duke, 6, 114	Recusant, 4, 115	12	1:49.80	66,750
1981	Dusky Duke, 5, 118	G. E. Louviere	Boyne Valley (Ire), 5, 119	Good and Early, 5, 120	6	1:49.00	46,350
1980	All the More, 7, 119	L. Snyder	Hold Your Tricks, 5, 114	Young Bob, 5, 117	9	1:46.20	46,890
1979	Once Over Lightly, 6, 113	S. A. Spencer	‡Batonnier, 4, 114	Hold Your Tricks, 4, 114	9	1:45.60	46,680
1978	Auberge, 5, 112	O. Sanchez	Bill Bonbright, 5, 121	Brown Cabildo, 4, 116	9	1:41.00	19,305
1977	Yallah Native, 4, 112	J. P. Powell	Dare to Command, 5, 119	Brown Cabildo, 3, 109	8	1:37.80	31,860
1976	Honey Mark, 4, 124	R. Sibille	Heathen Ways, 6, 114	Chateauvira, 8, 111	7	1:46.80	46,680
1975	*Zografos, 7, 120	H. Arroyo	Sr. Diplomat, 4, 116	‡Sharp Gary, 4, 118	6	1:44.20	34,410
1974	Tom Tulle, 4, 120	L. Snyder	Smooth Dancer, 4, 111	Chateauvira, 6, 117	8	1:43.40	37,800
1973	Fame and Power, 4, 118	A. Rini	Full Pocket, 4, 122	Chateauvira, 5, 113	9	1:37.80	21,285

Named for Racing Hall of Fame jockey and five-time Kentucky Derby winner Bill Hartack (1932-2007). Formerly named for the National Jockey Club, parent company of Sportsman's Park until 2002, when it allied with Hawthorne Race Course to become Hawthorne National LLC. National Jockey Club H. 1956-2007. Held at Sportsman's Park 1956-'98, 2000-'02. 1 1/16 miles 1956-'73, 1974-'76, 1979-'80. 6 1/2 furlongs 1972. 1 mile 1973, 1977-'78. Four-year-olds and up 1984-2002. ‡Christopher R. finished third, DQ to fourth, 1975. ‡Hold Your Tricks finished second, DQ to third, 1979. ‡Bucks Nephew finished first, DQ to fourth, 1996. Track record 1992, '93.

Bing Crosby Handicap

Grade 1 in 2008. Del Mar, three-year-olds and up, 6 furlongs, all weather. Held July 29, 2007, with a gross value of $300,000. First held in 1946. First graded in 1985. Stakes record 1:07.80 (1962 Crazy Kid; 1968 Pretense; 1969 Kissin' George; 1978 Bad 'n Big).

Year	Winner	Jockey	Second	Third	Strs	Time	1st Purse
2007	In Summation, 4, 119	C. S. Nakatani	Greg's Gold, 6, 117	Bordonaro, 6, 120	9	1:11.06	$180,000
2006	Pure as Gold, 4, 113	J. K. Court	Bordonaro, 5, 120	Battle Won, 6, 114	6	1:08.79	180,000
2005	Greg's Gold, 4, 115	D. R. Flores	Battle Won, 5, 117	Taste of Paradise, 6, 115	9	1:08.64	180,000
2004	Kela, 6, 113	T. Baze	Pohave, 6, 118	Hombre Rapido, 7, 115	10	1:08.51	150,000
2003	Beau's Town, 5, 119	P. A. Valenzuela	Captain Squire, 4, 117	Bluesthestandard, 6, 117	9	1:07.96	120,000
2002	Disturbingthepeace, 4, 116	V. Espinoza	Freespool, 6, 115	Mellow Fellow, 7, 118	9	1:09.21	90,000
2001	Kona Gold, 7, 126	A. O. Solis	Caller One, 4, 124	Swept Overboard, 4, 115	4	1:08.22	120,000
2000	Kona Gold, 6, 123	A. O. Solis	Love That Red, 4, 118	Lexicon, 5, 117	6	1:08.50	124,200
1999	Christmas Boy, 6, 114	C. S. Nakatani	Son of a Pistol, 7, 123	Expressionist, 4, 116	6	1:08.11	96,360
1998	Son of a Pistol, 6, 120	A. O. Solis	Gold Land, 7, 117	Boundless Moment, 6, 116	7	1:08.10	97,200
1997	First Intent, 6, 115	R. R. Douglas	Boundless Moment, 5, 118	High Stakes Player, 5, 120	7	1:08.80	102,000
1996	Lit de Justice, 6, 121	C. S. Nakatani	Concept Win, 6, 116	Gold Land, 5, 116	6	1:08.19	126,750
1995	Gold Land, 4, 116	E. Delahoussaye	Lucky Forever, 6, 118	G Malleah, 4, 116	8	1:08.07	89,300
1994	King's Blade, 3, 112	C. S. Nakatani	Memo (Chi), 7, 121	Gundaghia, 7, 118	8	1:08.64	62,400
1993	The Wicked North, 4, 116	C. A. Black	Thirty Slews, 6, 121	Black Jack Road, 9, 115	8	1:08.52	61,200
1992	Thirty Slews, 5, 116	E. Delahoussaye	Slerp, 3, 115	Anjiz, 4, 114	10	1:08.20	64,900
1991	Bruho, 5, 117	C. S. Nakatani	Thirty Slews, 4, 115	Due to the King, 4, 116	8	1:08.25	62,900
1990	Sensational Star, 6, 113	R. Q. Meza	Frost Free, 5, 116	Timeless Answer, 4, 116	5	1:08.00	60,150
1989	On the Line, 5, 124	G. L. Stevens	Speedratic, 4, 117	Cresting Water, 4, 115	7	1:08.00	63,800
1988	Olympic Prospect, 4, 124	A. O. Solis	Faro, 6, 118	Sebrof, 4, 119	6	1:08.80	59,410
1987	Zany Tactics, 6, 120	J. L. Kaenel	Bolder Than Bold, 5, 118	My Favorite Moment, 6, 115	8	1:09.00	38,600
1986	American Legion, 6, 119	E. Delahoussaye	Bold Brawley, 3, 113	‡Ondarty, 4, 112	7	1:08.20	38,000

Year	Winner	Jockey	Second	Third	Strs	Time	1st Purse
1985	My Favorite Moment, 4, 116	E. Delahoussaye	Rosie's K. T., 4, 116	Fifty Six Ina Row, 4, 119	10	1:09.80	$33,350
1984	Night Mover, 4, 120	L. E. Ortega	Premiership, 4, 119	Pac Mania, 4, 115	7	1:08.60	31,800
1983	Chinook Pass, 4, 125	L. A. Pincay Jr.	Vagabond Song, 4, 116	Haughty But Nice, 5, 115	7	1:08.60	32,000
1982	Pencil Point (Ire), 4, 114	C. J. McCarron	Terresto's Singer, 5, 114	Shanekite, 4, 115	8	1:09.00	32,650
1981	Syncopate, 6, 120	E. Delahoussaye	Reb's Golden Ale, 6, 119	To B. Or Not, 5, 122	6	1:08.60	31,100
1980	Reb's Golden Ale, 5, 117	S. Hawley	Bolger, 4, 114	Bad 'n Big, 6, 118	4	1:08.80	24,400
1979	Syncopate, 4, 116	S. Hawley	White Rammer, 5, 122	Fleet Twist, 5, 116	7	1:08.40	22,750
1978	Bad 'n Big, 4, 124	W. Shoemaker	Amadevil, 4, 121	Decoded, 4, 115	8	**1:07.80**	19,400
1977	Cherry River, 7, 120	L. A. Pincay Jr.	*Leinster House, 4, 111	Mark's Place, 5, 124	7	1:08.40	15,800
1976	Cherry River, 6, 120	L. A. Pincay Jr.	Sawtooth, 5, 111	Fast Spot, 6, 115	7	1:09.40	15,900
1975	Messenger of Song, 3, 119	J. Lambert	‡Stake Driver, 5, 114	Century's Envoy, 4, 122	5	1:08.80	12,450
1974	Rise High, 4, 113	J. E. Tejeira	Tragic Isle, 5, 116	Against the Snow, 4, 115	8	1:09.00	13,250
1973	Pataha Prince, 8, 114	W. Shoemaker	King of Cricket, 6, 114	Rough Night, 5, 120	9	1:08.00	13,700

Named for movie star and singer H. L. "Bing" Crosby (1903-'77), first president of Del Mar Turf Club. Grade 3 1985-'98. Grade 2 1999-2003. Bing Crosby Breeders' Cup H. 1996-2004. About 7½ furlongs 1970. Dirt 1946-'69, 1971-2006. Turf 1970. ‡Beira finished second, DQ to fifth, 1975. ‡Triple Sec finished third, DQ to fourth, 1986.

Black-Eyed Susan Stakes

Grade 2 in 2008. Pimlico Race Course, three-year-olds, fillies, 1⅛ miles, dirt. Held May 16, 2008, with a gross value of $200,000. First held in 1919. First graded in 1973. Stakes record 1:47.83 (1999 Silverbulletday).

Year	Winner	Jockey	Second	Third	Strs	Time	1st Purse
2008	Sweet Vendetta, 3, 122	C. Hill	Shes All Eltish, 3, 122	Seattle Smooth, 3, 122	8	1:49.60	$120,000
2007	Panty Raid, 3, 116	E. S. Prado	Winning Point, 3, 116	Baroness Thatcher, 3, 120	8	1:50.07	150,000
2006	‡Regal Engagement, 3, 116	R. A. Dominguez	Smart N Pretty, 3, 116	Baghdaria, 3, 122	7	1:50.11	150,000
2005	Spun Sugar, 3, 116	J. R. Velazquez	R Lady Joy, 3, 122	Pleasant Chimes, 3, 116	6	1:53.27	120,000
2004	Yearly Report, 3, 122	J. D. Bailey	Pawyne Princess, 3, 115	Rare Gift, 3, 115	7	1:52.65	120,000
2003	Roar Emotion, 3, 122	J. R. Velazquez	Fircroft, 3, 119	Santa Catarina, 3, 117	8	1:52.33	120,000
2002	Chamrousse, 3, 115	J. D. Bailey	Shop Till You Drop, 3, 117	Autumn Creek, 3, 115	6	1:51.61	120,000
2001	Two Item Limit, 3, 122	R. Migliore	Indy Glory, 3, 117	Tap Dance, 3, 122	5	1:50.84	120,000
2000	Jostle, 3, 122	K. Desormeaux	March Magic, 3, 122	Impending Bear, 3, 122	7	1:52.56	120,000
1999	Silverbulletday, 3, 122	G. L. Stevens	Dreams Gallore, 3, 117	Vee Vee Star, 3, 115	7	**1:47.83**	120,000
1998	Added Gold, 3, 115	J. R. Velazquez	Tappin' Ginger, 3, 115	Hansel's Girl, 3, 117	8	1:49.75	120,000
1997	Salt It, 3, 117	C. H. Marquez Jr.	Buckeye Search, 3, 122	Holiday Ball, 3, 115	7	1:50.52	120,000
1996	Mesabi Maiden, 3, 115	M. E. Smith	Cara Rafaela, 3, 122	Ginny Lynn, 3, 122	8	1:51.00	120,000
1995	Serena's Song, 3, 122	G. L. Stevens	Conquistadoress, 3, 115	Rare Opportunity, 3, 115	7	1:48.45	120,000
1994	Calipha, 3, 114	R. Wilson	Bunting, 3, 114	Golden Braids, 3, 114	13	1:51.12	120,000
1993	Aztec Hill, 3, 122	M. E. Smith	Traverse City, 3, 114	Jacody, 3, 117	10	1:49.78	120,000
1992	Miss Legality, 3, 122	C. J. McCarron	Known Feminist, 3, 114	Diamond Duo, 3, 114	8	1:51.11	150,000
1991	Wide Country, 3, 122	S. N. Chavez	John's Decision, 3, 117	Nalees Pin, 3, 117	9	1:51.26	150,000
1990	Charon, 3, 122	C. Perret	Valay Maid, 3, 122	Bright Candles, 3, 122	9	1:48.40	150,000
1989	Imaginary Lady, 3, 122	G. L. Stevens	Some Romance, 3, 122	Moonlight Martini, 3, 117	9	1:48.20	150,000
1988	Costly Shoes, 3, 121	P. Day	Thirty Eight Go Go, 3, 121	Lost Kitty, 3, 121	6	1:44.80	97,915
1987	Grecian Flight, 3, 121	C. Perret	Bal Du Bois, 3, 121	Arctic Cloud, 3, 121	10	1:44.20	101,750
1986	Family Style, 3, 121	C. J. McCarron	Steel Maiden, 3, 121	Firgie's Jule, 3, 121	8	1:44.60	100,385
1985	Koluctoo's Jill, 3, 121	C. J. McCarron	Denver Express, 3, 116	A Joyful Spray, 3, 121	7	1:43.00	74,295
1984	Lucky Lucky Lucky, 3, 121	A. T. Cordero Jr.	Sintra, 3, 116	Duo Disco, 3, 121	7	1:41.20	100,060
1983	Batna, 3, 121	L. D. Ruch	Lovin Touch, 3, 116	Weekend Surprise, 3, 121	10	1:42.40	75,400
1982	Delicate Ice, 3, 114	D. Brumfield	Trove, 3, 121	Milingo, 3, 121	10	1:44.60	74,945
1981	Dame Mysterieuse, 3, 121	E. Maple	Wayward Lass, 3, 121	Real Prize, 3, 121	7	1:44.20	72,800
1980	Weber City Miss, 3, 118	V. A. Bracciale Jr.	Bishop's Ring, 3, 111	Champagne Star, 3, 114	6	1:44.40	74,620
1979	Davona Dale, 3, 121	J. Velasquez	Phoebe's Donkey, 3, 118	Plankton, 3, 121	6	1:42.60	72,670
1978	Caesar's Wish, 3, 121	D. R. Wright	Jevalin, 3, 116	Miss Baja, 3, 121	8	1:44.20	55,120
1977	Small Raja, 3, 114	A. T. Cordero Jr.	Northern Sea, 3, 121	Enthused, 3, 116	5	1:42.80	54,503
1976	What a Summer, 3, 111	C. J. McCarron	Dearly Precious, 3, 121	Artfully, 3, 114	10	1:42.40	37,895
1975	My Juliet, 3, 116	A. Hill	Gala Lil, 3, 114	Funalon, 3, 121	6	1:44.00	37,635
1974	Blowing Rock, 3, 111	A. Agnello	Heydairya, 3, 111	Shantung Silk, 3, 116	8	1:43.00	22,425
1973	Fish Wife, 3, 111	D. Gargan	Guided Missle, 3, 112	Out Cold, 3, 116	6	1:44.00	22,685

Named for the Maryland state flower. Grade 3 1973-'75. Pimlico Oaks 1937-'49. Black-Eyed Susan H. 1951. Not held 1932-'36, 1950. 1 1/16 miles 1919-'29, 1931, 1937-'49, 1953-'88. 1 mile 70 yards 1930. 1 3/16 miles 1951. ‡Smart N Pretty finished first, DQ to second, 2006.

Blue Grass Stakes — *See* Toyota Blue Grass Stakes

Boiling Springs Stakes

Grade 3 in 2008. Monmouth Park, three-year-olds, fillies, 1 1/16 miles, turf. Held June 30, 2007, with a gross value of $150,000. First held in 1977. First graded in 1980. Stakes record 1:40.09 (1998 Mysterious Moll).

Year	Winner	Jockey	Second	Third	Strs	Time	1st Purse
2007	‡Rutherienne, 3, 118	J. Bravo	Sharp Susan, 3, 120	Red Birkin, 3, 116	6	1:40.60	$90,000
2006	Quite a Bride, 3, 118	C. H. Velasquez	Ebony Rose, 3, 120	Perilous Pursuit, 3, 118	8	1:41.37	90,000
2005	Toll Taker, 3, 118	A. T. Gryder	Pleasant Lyrics, 3, 116	Ruby Martini, 3, 116	7	1:41.10	90,000
2004	Seducer's Song, 3, 119	J. Bravo	Go Robin, 3, 117	River Belle (GB), 3, 117	9	1:45.66	90,000
2002	Showlady, 3, 114	R. Migliore	Dreamers Glory, 3, 116	With Patience, 3, 117	9	1:42.27	120,000

Racing — Graded Stakes

Year	Winner	Jockey	Second	Third	Strs	Time	1st Purse
2001	Mystic Lady, 3, 120	E. Coa	Shooting Party, 3, 114	Plunderthepeasants, 3, 115	4	1:42.63	$120,000
2000	Storm Dream (Ire), 3, 116	J. Samyn	Watch, 3, 117	Lady Dora, 3, 114	11	1:47.09	60,000
1999	Wild Heart Dancing, 3, 116	J. F. Chavez	Confessional, 3, 118	Petunia, 3, 114	8	1:43.08	120,000
1998	Mysterious Moll, 3, 116	J. L. Espinoza	Who Did It and Run, 3, 120	Thunder Kitten, 3, 116	12	**1:40.09**	120,000
1997	Stoneleigh, 3, 114	J. A. Santos	Majestic Sunlight, 3, 114	Dancing Water, 3, 115	6	1:41.13	60,000
	Victory Chime, 3, 114	M. E. Smith	Miss Pop Carn, 3, 111	Colonial Play, 3, 113	9	1:41.99	60,000
1996	Careless Heiress, 3, 118	C. Perret	Briarcliff, 3, 114	Dathuil (Ire), 3, 115	9	1:50.54	60,000
1995	Christmas Gift, 3, 116	W. H. McCauley	Ring by Spring, 3, 114	Transient Trend, 3, 114	7	1:43.49	48,000
	Class Kris, 3, 118	R. Wilson	Twilight Encounter, 3, 112	Appointed One, 3, 114	7	1:43.27	48,000
1994	Avie's Fancy, 3, 119	J. C. Ferrer	Teasing Charm, 3, 114	Knocknock, 3, 115	7	1:41.41	45,000
1993	Tribulation, 3, 110	J. Samyn	Exotic Sea, 3, 114	Bright Penny, 3, 115	11	1:42.70	45,000
1992	Captive Miss, 3, 120	J. Bravo	Logan's Mist, 3, 116	Aquilegia, 3, 113	9	1:40.78	45,000
1991	Dance O'My Life, 3, 114	C. W. Antley	Monica Faye, 3, 110	Verbasle, 3, 115	11	1:41.44	45,000
1990	Memories of Pam, 3, 112	J. D. Bailey	Hot Marshmellow, 3, 114	Baltic Chill, 3, 118	8	1:41.00	41,550
	Plenty of Grace, 3, 112	J. D. Bailey	Southern Tradition, 3, 120	Sabina, 3, 114	6	1:42.20	40,950
1989	Darby Shuffle, 3, 116	J. A. Krone	To the Lighthouse, 3, 116	Warranty Applied, 3, 115	9	1:40.60	53,730
1988	Siggebo, 3, 119	R. Wilson	Flashy Runner, 3, 115	Lusty Lady, 3, 113	7	1:43.20	51,930
1987	Rullah Runner, 3, 109	W. A. Guerra	Tappiano, 3, 119	Key Bid, 3, 120	12	1:41.40	35,460
1986	Small Virtue, 3, 114	J. A. Santos	Sweet Velocity, 3, 115	Country Recital, 3, 121	11	1:41.60	47,985
	Spruce Fir, 3, 119	D. B. Thomas	Ala Mahlik (Ire), 3, 116	Spring Innocence, 3, 113	11	1:41.60	47,985
1985	Jolly Saint (Ire), 3, 114	J. A. Santos	Miss Hardwick, 3, 115	Dawn's Curtsey, 3, 115	13	1:41.00	49,620
1984	Possible Mate, 3, 116	D. MacBeth	Distaff Magic, 3, 113	Miss Audimar, 3, 112	13	1:41.80	33,930
1983	Sabin, 3, 124	E. Maple	Aspen Rose, 3, 114	Propositioning, 3, 117	11	1:47.80	33,480
1982	Sunny Sparkler, 3, 113	J. Samyn	Fact Finder, 3, 113	Milingo, 3, 117	10	1:41.40	26,895
	Larida, 3, 119	E. Maple	Doodle, 3, 115	Distinctive Moon, 3, 114	11	1:41.40	27,075
1981	Irish Joy, 3, 114	C. C. Lopez	First Approach, 3, 113	Dance Forth, 3, 114	11	1:42.40	26,925
	Wings of Grace, 3, 112	J. Velasquez	Andover Way, 3, 114	Pukka Princess, 3, 120	8	1:41.40	26,385
1980	Champagne Ginny, 3, 114	J. Velasquez	Qui Royalty, 3, 112	Classic Curves, 3, 111	9	1:42.00	26,505
	Refinish, 3, 113	C. J. McCarron	Keep Off (Ire), 3, 111	Cannon Boy, 3, 113	9	1:41.60	26,505
1979	Jameela, 3, 118	V. A. Bracciale Jr.	Fanny Saperstein, 3, 119	Whydidju, 3, 119	6	1:41.60	27,934
	Gala Regatta, 3, 122	E. Maple	dh-Record Acclaim, 3, 114 dh-Tweak, 3, 113		6	1:41.00	27,934
1978	Key to the Saga, 3, 118	J. Samyn	Terpsichorist, 3, 117	Amerigirl, 3, 112	9	1:41.40	28,519
	Sisterhood, 3, 112	B. Gonzalez	Island Kiss, 3, 108	White Star Line, 3, 122	9	1:41.40	28,519
1977	Council House, 3, 116	C. Perret	Rich Soil, 3, 119	Pressing Date, 3, 115	10	1:42.40	28,633
	Critical Cousin, 3, 119	A. T. Cordero Jr.	Sans Arc, 3, 116	Small Raja, 3, 123	6	1:42.40	28,243

Named for former name of East Rutherford, New Jersey, home of the Meadowlands, the race's original location. Not graded 2001, '05. Boiling Springs H. 1977-'78, 1981-'97. Boiling Springs Breeders' Cup H. 1998-2002. Held at the Meadowlands 1977-2002. Not held 2003. Dirt 1998, 2001, '05. Originally scheduled on turf 2001, '05. Two divisions 1977-'82, 1986, 1990, 1995, 1997. Dead heat for second 1979 (2nd Div.). ‡Red Birkin finished first, DQ to third, 2007.

Bold Ruler Handicap

Grade 3 in 2008. Belmont Park, three-year-olds and up, 6 furlongs, dirt. Held May 10, 2008, with a gross value of $109,100. First held in 1976. First graded in 1982. Stakes record 1:07.54 (1999 Kelly Kip).

Year	Winner	Jockey	Second	Third	Strs	Time	1st Purse
2008	Lucky Island (Arg), 4, 115	A. Garcia	Man of Danger, 6, 115	Forefathers, 4, 116	7	1:09.14	$65,460
2007	Songster, 4, 117	E. S. Prado	Dashboard Drummer, 6, 116	Dark Cheetah, 5, 114	5	1:08.80	64,440
2006	Tiger, 5, 117	E. Coa	Dark Cheetah, 4, 115	Bishop Court Hill, 6, 119	5	1:08.49	64,020
2005	Uncle Camie, 5, 115	R. Migliore	Don Six, 5, 120	Thunder Touch, 4, 114	5	1:08.67	63,960
2004	Canadian Frontier, 5, 111	J. Castellano	Key Deputy, 4, 114	First Blush, 4, 113	6	1:08.97	64,620
2003	Shake You Down, 5, 115	M. J. Luzzi	Here's Zealous, 6, 114	Peeping Tom, 6, 117	5	1:08.47	65,040
2002	Left Bank, 5, 121	J. R. Velazquez	Silky Sweep, 5, 114	Say Florida Sandy, 8, 116	4	1:09.30	63,646
2001	Say Florida Sandy, 7, 117	J. Bravo	Delaware Township, 5, 117	Lake Pontchartrain, 6, 113	7	1:08.67	65,520
2000	Brutally Frank, 6, 115	S. Bridgmohan	Kelly Kip, 6, 121	Kashatreya, 6, 115	7	1:08.64	65,880
1999	Kelly Kip, 5, 123	J. Samyn	Artax, 4, 115	Brushed On, 4, 115	5	**1:07.54**	64,440
1998	Kelly Kip, 4, 117	J. Samyn	Say Florida Sandy, 4, 111	Johnny Legit, 4, 114	8	1:07.61	66,120
1997	Punch Line, 7, 122	R. G. Davis	Golden Tent, 8, 111	Blissful State, 5, 116	6	1:08.80	64,980
1996	Lite the Fuse, 5, 119	J. A. Krone	Cold Execution, 5, 119	Splendid Sprinter, 4, 115	5	1:09.51	64,500
1995	Rizzi, 4, 117	D. V. Beckner	Lite the Fuse, 4, 111	Evil Bear, 5, 116	6	1:08.91	64,560
1994	Chief Desire, 4, 117	J. R. Velazquez	Boom Towner, 4, 120	Won Song, 4, 112	6	1:08.76	66,300
1993	Slerp, 4, 119	J. A. Santos	Argyle Lake, 7, 121	Big Jewel, 5, 121	8	1:09.17	70,200
1992	Jolies Appeal, 4, 119	W. H. McCauley	Reappeal, 6, 119	Fiercely, 4, 119	5	1:09.29	67,560
1991	Rousing Past, 4, 119	N. Santagata	True and Blue, 6, 121	Sunshine Jimmy, 4, 119	5	1:09.96	67,200
1990	Mr. Nickerson, 4, 119	C. W. Antley	Dancing Pretense, 5, 119	Diamond Donnie, 4, 119	5	1:09.20	66,240
1989	Pok Ta Pok, 4, 121	R. Migliore	Teddy Drone, 4, 119	Claim, 4, 119	6	1:09.80	67,560
1988	King's Swan, 8, 123	C. W. Antley	Seattle Knight, 4, 119	Faster Than Sound, 4, 123	7	1:10.20	103,680
1987	†Pine Tree Lane, 5, 118	A. T. Cordero Jr.	Love That Mac, 5, 123	Play the King, 4, 121	7	1:09.00	103,680
1986	Phone Trick, 4, 123	J. Velasquez	Love That Mac, 4, 119	Rexson's Bishop, 4, 121	7	1:08.80	70,680
1985	Rocky Marriage, 5, 119	A. T. Cordero Jr.	Entropy, 5, 121	Majestic Venture, 4, 119	6	1:08.80	51,390
1984	Top Avenger, 6, 121	A. Graell	Believe the Queen, 4, 119	Au Point, 4, 123	10	1:09.20	55,350
1983	Maudlin, 5, 119	J. D. Bailey	Top Avenger, 5, 123	Singh Tu, 4, 121	4	1:11.60	49,500
1982	Always Run Lucky, 4, 123	J. J. Miranda	King's Fashion, 7, 119	Band Practice, 4, 119	4	1:09.40	49,050

Racing — Graded Stakes

Year	Winner	Jockey	Second	Third	Strs	Time	1st Purse
1981	Dave's Friend, 6, 123	A. S. Black	Naughty Jimmy, 4, 119	Fappiano, 4, 119	6	1:09.60	$48,510
1980	Dave's Friend, 5, 123	V. A. Bracciale Jr.	Tilt Up, 5, 121	Double Zeus, 5, 121	6	1:09.80	48,690
1979	Star de Naskra, 4, 119	J. Fell	Vencedor, 5, 126	Big John Taylor, 5, 119	8	1:09.20	48,420
1978	Half High, 5, 115	A. Santiago	Great Above, 6, 121	Cruise On In, 4, 110	6	1:09.40	25,665
1977	Jaipur's Gem, 4, 113	J. Samyn	Expletive Deleted, 4, 107	Cojak, 4, 126	6	1:09.60	22,050
1976	Chief Tamanaco, 3, 114	A. T. Cordero Jr.	Relent, 5, 114	Jackson Square, 4, 116	4	1:09.80	21,750

Named for Wheatley Stable's Racing Hall of Fame member, 1957 Horse of the Year, and eight-time leading North American sire Bold Ruler (1954 c. by *Nasrullah). Grade 2 1985-'89. Bold Ruler S. 1979-'93. Held at Aqueduct 1976-2001. Track record 1998, '99. †Denotes female.

Bonnie Miss Stakes

Grade 2 in 2008. Gulfstream Park, three-year-olds, fillies, 1⅛ miles, dirt. Held March 29, 2008, with a gross value of $150,000. First held in 1971. First graded in 1982. Stakes record 1:48.25 (2006 Teammate).

Year	Winner	Jockey	Second	Third	Strs	Time	1st Purse
2008	Shes All Eltish, 3, 118	E. Castro	Robbie's Gal, 3, 118	Highest Class, 3, 118	6	1:51.80	$90,000
2007	High Again, 3, 118	C. H. Velasquez	Christmas Kid, 3, 120	Fee Fi Fo Fum, 3, 116	8	1:50.87	90,000
2006	Teammate, 3, 116	C. H. Velasquez	Wonder Lady Anne L, 3, 120	Wait a While, 3, 120	7	**1:48.25**	90,000
2005	Jill Robin L, 3, 116	J. D. Bailey	In the Gold, 3, 118	Holy Trinity, 3, 116	7	1:53.12	90,000
2004	Last Song, 3, 118	E. S. Prado	Society Selection, 3, 120	Rare Gift, 3, 116	5	1:50.60	120,000
2003	Ivanavinalot, 3, 122	J. R. Velazquez	My Boston Gal, 3, 120	Holiday Lady, 3, 118	7	1:50.72	120,000
2002	Dust Me Off, 3, 116	M. Guidry	Nonsuch Bay, 3, 116	Belterra, 3, 120	6	1:49.67	150,000
2001	Tap Dance, 3, 114	J. D. Bailey	Halo Reality, 3, 117	Unbridled Lassie, 3, 114	7	1:52.05	150,000
2000	Cash Run, 3, 119	J. D. Bailey	Deed I Do, 3, 114	Bejoyfulandrejoyce, 3, 114	6	1:44.11	120,000
1999	Three Ring, 3, 122	J. R. Velazquez	Olympic Charmer, 3, 117	Marley Vale, 3, 117	5	1:43.75	120,000
1998	Banshee Breeze, 3, 114	R. P. Romero	Santaria, 3, 114	Cotton House Bay, 3, 114	8	1:46.57	120,000
1997	Glitter Woman, 3, 117	M. E. Smith	Southern Playgirl, 3, 119	Dixie Flag, 3, 114	5	1:43.20	120,000
1996	My Flag, 3, 117	J. D. Bailey	Escena, 3, 114	La Rosa, 3, 117	5	1:45.77	120,000
1995	Mia's Hope, 3, 117	K. L. Chapman	Minister Wife, 3, 119	Incredible Blues, 3, 117	9	1:44.85	120,000
1994	Inside Information, 3, 114	M. E. Smith	Cinnamon Sugar (Ire), 3, 113	Jade Flush, 3, 114	10	1:42.94	120,000
1993	Dispute, 3, 114	J. D. Bailey	Sky Beauty, 3, 114	Lunar Spook, 3, 117	6	1:43.67	120,000
1992	Spectacular Sue, 3, 114	W. S. Ramos	Spinning Round, 3, 117	Tricky Cinderella, 3, 112	6	1:44.14	120,000
1991	Withallprobability, 3, 117	C. Perret	Fancy Ribbons, 3, 117	Outlasting, 3, 114	6	1:43.30	120,000
1990	Charon, 3, 121	E. Fires	Trumpet's Blare, 3, 121	De La Devil, 3, 121	7	1:44.60	120,000
1989	Open Mind, 3, 121	A. T. Cordero Jr.	Seattle Meteor, 3, 121	Surging, 3, 114	6	1:43.80	120,000
1988	On to Royalty, 3, 121	C. Perret	Tomorrow's Child, 3, 121	Make Change, 3, 112	12	1:45.60	120,000
1987	Mar Mar, 3, 121	W. A. Guerra	Super Cook, 3, 121	Without Feathers, 3, 118	12	1:44.60	90,000
1986	Patricia J. K., 3, 121	J. A. Santos	Noranc, 3, 121	Family Style, 3, 121	11	1:45.20	135,570
1985	Lucy Manette, 3, 121	C. Perret	Outstandingly, 3, 121	Micki Bracken, 3, 121	9	1:44.80	72,240
1984	Miss Oceana, 3, 121	E. Maple	Enumerating, 3, 114	Katrinka, 3, 121	9	1:42.40	70,605
1983	Unaccompanied, 3, 116	R. Woodhouse	‡Bright Crocus, 3, 114	Dewl Reason, 3, 112	12	1:45.40	58,320
1982	Christmas Past, 3, 121	J. Vasquez	Norsan, 3, 113	Our Darling, 3, 112	6	1:44.20	34,830
1981	Dame Mysterieuse, 3, 118	J. Samyn	Banner Gala, 3, 113	Heavenly Cause, 3, 121	7	1:44.40	52,335
1980	Lien, 3, 112	E. Maple	Wistful, 3, 115	Champagne Ginny, 3, 114	9	1:22.00	18,510
1979	Davona Dale, 3, 122	J. Velasquez	Candy Eclair, 3, 122	Prove Me Special, 3, 114	4	1:21.00	17,545
1978	Jevalin, 3, 114	M. Solomone	‡Raise a Companion, 3, 110	Sharp Belle, 3, 110	10	1:23.80	18,600
1977	Herecomesthebride, 3, 114	L. Saumell	Grand Luxe, 3, 114	Rich Soil, 3, 112	9	1:21.80	20,970
1976	Get Swinging, 5, 111	A. Ramos	Twenty Six Girl, 4, 112	North of Boston, 4, 114	8	1:45.80	17,400
1975	Cheers Marion, 4, 113	M. Castaneda	Hinterland, 5, 116	Summer Sprite, 5, 114	8	1:42.20	10,207
	Diomedia, 4, 116	M. Castaneda	Gems and Roses, 5, 122	Exclusive Lady, 5, 113	8	1:42.00	10,207
1974	City Girl, 3, 112	E. Maple	Maud Muller, 3, 112	Double Bend, 3, 112	12	1:22.60	21,540
1973	Fun Palace, 4, 111	E. Fires	Hasty Jude, 4, 119	Viewpoise, 5, 112	12	1:44.40	14,145

Named for Bonnie Donn, daughter of James Donn Jr., president of Gulfstream Park from 1972-'78. Grade 3 1982-'87. Bonnie Miss H. 1976. About 1 1/16 miles 1971. 7 furlongs 1972, 1974, 1977-'80. 1 1/16 miles 1973, 1975-'76, 1981-2000. Turf 1971, 1975-'76. Originally scheduled on turf 1973. Three-year-olds and up 1971, 1973, 1975-'76. Fillies and mares 1971, 1973, 1975-'76. Two divisions 1975. ‡Cornish Queen finished second, DQ to fourth, 1978. ‡Miss Molly finished second, DQ to 12th, 1983.

Bourbonette Oaks

Grade 3 in 2008. Turfway Park, three-year-olds, fillies, 1 mile, all weather. Held March 22, 2008, with a gross value of $150,000. First held in 1983. First graded in 2006. Stakes record 1:35.03 (1997 Buckeye Search).

Year	Winner	Jockey	Second	Third	Strs	Time	1st Purse
2008	Maren's Meadow, 3, 115	G. Saez	Valentine Fever, 3, 121	A to the Croft, 3, 115	8	1:38.15	$91,605
2007	Sealy Hill, 3, 118	P. Husbands	Panty Raid, 3, 115	Aspiring, 3, 115	12	1:37.51	93,000
2006	Top Notch Lady, 3, 115	R. Albarado	Coronado's Vision, 3, 117	Lemons Forever, 3, 117	9	1:39.26	93,000
2005	Dance Away Capote, 3, 121	R. Bejarano	Gallant Secret, 3, 114	Amazing Buy, 3, 121	11	1:37.52	93,000
2004	Class Above, 3, 121	J. D. Bailey	Susan's Angel, 3, 114	Native Annie, 3, 121	6	1:37.98	93,000
2003	‡Adopted Daughter, 3, 114	D. P. Butler	Golden Marlin, 3, 114	Unbridled Femme, 3, 121	11	1:37.41	93,000
2002	Colonial Glitter, 3, 112	P. Day	Southey, 3, 112	Madame X Ski, 3, 114	9	1:37.06	93,000
2001	Sweet Nanette, 3, 112	P. Day	Upside, 3, 115	Heathers Promise, 3, 114	7	1:37.55	62,600
2000	Trip, 3, 112	W. Martinez	Lorie Darlin, 3, 112	Upon a Thron, 3, 112	9	1:36.25	93,600
1999	Sweeping Story, 3, 112	J. F. Chavez	Elaines Reason, 3, 112	Bag Lady Jane, 3, 112	9	1:37.72	99,634
1998	Nurse Goodbody, 3, 112	W. Martinez	Victorica, 3, 112	Swoop City, 3, 112	7	1:36.05	62,600
1997	Buckeye Search, 3, 112	B. Peck	City Band, 3, 112	Fountain Square, 3, 112	7	**1:35.03**	62,600

Year	Winner	Jockey	Second	Third	Strs	Time	1st Purse
1996	**Clamorosa**, 3, 113	J. D. Bailey	Ginny Lynn, 3, 112	Pledged, 3, 115	12	1:37.17	$65,000
1995	**Sherzarcat**, 3, 115	K. Desormeaux	Minister Wife, 3, 118	Grand Charmer, 3, 115	9	1:38.98	65,000
1994	**Private Status**, 3, 112	P. Day	Princess Nana, 3, 112	Simply Nijinsky, 3, 112	10	1:38.09	39,000
1993	**Sentimentaldiamond**, 3, 121	M. T. Johnston	Ruggles, 3, 112	Clarwithaflare, 3, 121	7	1:38.23	32,500
1992	**Preach**, 3, 121	J. A. Krone	Pleasureconnection, 3, 121	Pleasant Baby, 3, 114	9	1:40.95	39,000
1991	**Saratoga Dame**, 3, 121	M. McDowell	Promising Preppy, 3, 118	Flashing Eyes, 3, 121	11	1:37.10	35,149
1990	**Appella**, 3, 112	W. D. Troilo	Arm the Natives, 3, 112	Will Never Tell, 3, 115	9	1:41.00	34,580
	Joannie Banannie, 3, 121	P. Day	Coax Me Linn, 3, 110	Ioya, 3, 114	9	1:40.00	34,515
1989	**Gorgeous**, 3, 121	P. Day	Up, 3, 118	Blondeinamotel, 3, 121	9	1:36.20	28,681
1988	**Stolie**, 3, 112	M. McDowell	International Gal, 3, 114	Fun Ticket, 3, 111	8	1:40.80	28,048
	Darien Miss, 3, 121	R. P. Romero	Jump With Joy, 3, 112	Angry Angel, 3, 112	8	1:39.00	34,977
1987	**Combative**, 3, 112	P. Day	After the Show, 3, 118	Queen's Highness, 3, 112	10	1:38.60	27,630
1986	**Hail a Cab**, 3, 112	L. J. Melancon	Close Tolerance, 3, 110	Silver Saucer, 3, 112	12	1:40.40	25,680
	Pretty Sham, 3, 121	F. Lovato Jr.	Prime Union, 3, 121	Hagley's Relic, 3, 121	9	1:40.20	19,841
	Classy Carlotta, 3, 115	R. D. Fielding	Penalty Declared, 3, 113	Bold Princesa, 3, 112	11	1:40.00	20,004
1985	**Wealthy and Wise**, 3, 113	E. J. Sipus Jr.	Box of Birds, 3, 112	Delta Star, 3, 113	8	1:37.40	13,341
	Mahalia, 3, 113	C. Schwing	Sally Shark, 3, 114	Trops Gal, 3, 110	10	1:40.40	13,471
1984	**Dusty Gloves**, 3, 112	A. T. Cordero Jr.	Sean's Sommer, 3, 112	Rose of Ashes, 3, 115	12	1:38.80	12,450
1983	**Push On**, 3, 112	J. McKnight	Keep On Dancing, 3, 122	Shecky's Song, 3, 116	9	1:40.80	7,719
	Fiesty Belle, 3, 111	J. Velasquez	Talk About Home, 3, 122	Country Dust, 3, 111	9	1:39.00	9,376

The Bourbonette Oaks is traditionally run the same day as the Lane's End S. (G2), formerly the Jim Beam S., and was named as a comparable distaff race. Bourbonette S. 1983-'98. Bourbonette Breeders' Cup S. 1999-2006. Host track known as Latonia Race Course 1983-'86. Dirt 1983-2005. Two divisions 1983, '85, '88, '90. Three divisions 1986.
‡Golden Marlin finished first, DQ to second, 2003.

Bowling Green Handicap

Grade 2 in 2008. Belmont Park, three-year-olds and up, 1 3/8 miles, turf. Held July 15, 2007, with a gross value of $150,000. First held in 1958. First graded in 1973. Stakes record 2:10.20 (1990 With Approval).

Year	Winner	Jockey	Second	Third	Strs	Time	1st Purse
2007	**Sunriver**, 4, 116	G. K. Gomez	Trippi's Storm, 4, 114	Silver Whistle, 5, 116	8	2:12.68	$90,000
2006	**Go Deputy**, 6, 117	F. Jara	Crown Point, 4, 112	Leadwithyourchin, 4, 112	5	2:17.49	90,000
2005	**Cacht Wells (Arg)**, 5, 114	E. Coa	Relaxed Gesture (Ire), 4, 117	Dreadnaught, 5, 117	7	2:15.49	90,000
2004	**Kicken Kris**, 4, 117	E. S. Prado	Better Talk Now, 5, 115	Gigli (Brz), 6, 113	10	2:12.19	90,000
2003	**Whitmore's Conn**, 5, 116	J. Samyn	Quest Star, 4, 117	Macaw (Ire), 4, 116	9	2:15.92	90,000
2002	**Whitmore's Conn**, 4, 112	S. Bridgmohan	Staging Post, 4, 115	Moon Solitaire (Ire), 5, 116	9	2:13.43	90,000
2001	**King Cugat**, 4, 119	J. D. Bailey	Slew Valley, 4, 112	Man From Wicklow, 4, 112	7	2:10.62	90,000
2000	**Elhayq (Ire)**, 5, 113	S. Bridgmohan	Yankee Dollar, 4, 110	Carpenter's Halo, 4, 115	9	2:13.81	90,000
1999	**Honor Glide**, 5, 114	J. A. Santos	Parade Ground, 4, 118	‡Fahris (Ire), 5, 116	6	2:11.07	90,000
1998	**Cetewayo**, 4, 112	J. R. Velazquez	Officious, 5, 113	Chief Bearhart, 5, 124	6	2:13.45	90,000
1997	**Influent**, 6, 120	J. Samyn	Flag Down, 7, 118	Notoriety, 4, 108	8	2:11.00	90,000
1996	**Flag Down**, 6, 118	J. A. Santos	Broadway Flyer, 5, 118	Diplomatic Jet, 4, 119	9	2:13.29	90,000
1995	**Sentimental Moi**, 5, 111	R. B. Perez	Awad, 5, 121	Proceeded, 4, 108	8	2:15.48	90,000
1994	**Turk Passer**, 4, 110	J. R. Velazquez	Sea Hero, 4, 117	Fraise, 6, 124	6	2:13.25	90,000
1993	**Dr. Kiernan**, 4, 114	C. W. Antley	Spectacular Tide, 4, 111	Lomitas (GB), 5, 117	8	2:17.70	90,000
1992	**Wall Street Dancer**, 4, 114	P. Day	Fraise, 4, 113	Libor, 5, 109	7	2:12.92	120,000
1991	**Three Coins Up**, 3, 111	J. D. Bailey	Phantom Breeze (Ire), 5, 117	Beyond the Lake (Ire), 5, 115	12	2:16.50	120,000
1990	**With Approval**, 4, 118	C. Perret	Chenin Blanc, 4, 113	El Senor, 6, 121	9	2:10.20	113,280
1989	**El Senor**, 5, 117	W. H. McCauley	Coeur de Lion (Fr), 5, 121	Pay the Butler, 5, 116	10	2:18.60	144,960
1988	**Coeur de Lion (Fr)**, 4, 117	C. Perret	Pay the Butler, 4, 112	Milesius, 4, 115	13	2:13.40	151,680
1987	**Theatrical (Ire)**, 5, 123	P. Day	Akabir, 6, 121	Dance of Life, 4, 121	12	2:14.00	144,960
1986	**Uptown Swell**, 4, 114	E. Maple	Palace Panther (Ire), 5, 116	Equalize, 4, 116	13	2:14.84	147,690
1985	**Sharannpour (Ire)**, 5, 114	A. T. Cordero Jr.	Flying Pidgeon, 4, 117	Long Mick (Fr), 4, 121	14	2:13.20	156,300
1984	**Hero's Honor**, 4, 120	J. D. Bailey	Nassipour, 4, 110	Super Sunrise (GB), 5, 123	11	2:14.00	144,120
1983	**Tantalizing**, 4, 113	J. Vasquez	Sprink, 5, 113	Majesty's Prince, 4, 122	7	2:14.80	105,120
1982	**Open Call**, 4, 124	J. Velasquez	Johnny Dance, 4, 114	Baltimore Canyon, 4, 116	10	2:24.80	89,850
1981	**Great Neck**, 5, 114	A. T. Cordero Jr.	Key to Content, 4, 119	Match the Hatch, 5, 115	8	2:12.00	84,450
1980	**Sten**, 5, 114	J. Fell	John Henry, 5, 128	Lyphard's Wish (Fr), 4, 120	9	2:13.20	86,550
1979	**Overskate**, 4, 117	R. Platts	†Waya (Fr), 5, 125	Bowl Game, 5, 123	7	2:11.40	84,525
1978	**Tiller**, 4, 117	J. Fell	Proud Arion, 4, 111	Bowl Game, 4, 124	10	2:12.40	70,260
1977	**Hunza Dancer**, 5, 117	J. Cruguet	Improviser, 5, 122	Noble Dancer (GB), 5, 117	13	1:58.80	68,580
1976	**Erwin Boy**, 5, 120	R. Turcotte	Drollery, 6, 111	Trumpeter Swan, 5, 111	9	2:26.00	34,740
1975	**Barcas**, 4, 113	M. Castaneda	Drollery, 5, 113	*Telefonico, 4, 124	6	2:32.20	33,240
1974	**Take Off**, 5, 120	R. Turcotte	†Garland of Roses, 5, 109	Astray, 5, 126	9	2:26.40	34,260
1973	**†Summer Guest**, 4, 119	J. Vasquez	Red Reality, 7, 124	Astray, 4, 113	9	2:29.20	34,200

Named for the lower tip of Manhattan Island, New York, where there was once a green for lawn bowling. Grade 1 1983-'89. Held at Aqueduct 1963-'67. 1 1/2 miles 1960-'62, 1968-'76. 1 5/8 miles 1963-'67. 1 1/4 miles 1977. Course record 1977.
‡Federal Trial finished third, DQ to fourth, 1999. †Denotes female.

Boyd Gaming's Delta Jackpot Stakes

Grade 3 in 2008. Delta Downs, two-year-olds, 1 1/16 miles, dirt. Held December 7, 2007, with a gross value of $1,000,000. First held in 2002. First graded in 2006. Stakes record 1:45.34 (2003 Mr. Jester).

Year	Winner	Jockey	Second	Third	Strs	Time	1st Purse
2007	**dh-Turf War**, 2, 119	C. H. Borel		Golden Yank, 2, 119	10	1:45.43	$400,000
	dh-Z Humor, 2, 117	G. K. Gomez					

Racing — Graded Stakes 277

Year	Winner	Jockey	Second	Third	Strs	Time	1st Purse
2006	Birdbirdistheword, 2, 119	R. Albarado	Pirates Deputy, 2, 119	Xchanger, 2, 122	10	1:45.42	$600,000
2004	Texcess, 2, 119	V. Espinoza	Closing Argument, 2, 119	Anthony J., 2, 117	10	1:48.20	600,000
2003	Mr. Jester, 2, 115	R. Chapa	Fire Slam, 2, 115	Perfect Moon, 2, 115	10	**1:45.34**	600,000
2002	Outta Here, 2, 116	K. Desormeaux	Comic Truth, 2, 117	Cherokee's Boy, 2, 116	10	1:37.77	300,000

Boyd Gaming's Delta Jackpot S. (G3) is the second-richest race for juveniles in North America. Sponsored by Boyd Gaming Corp. of Henderson, Nevada, parent company of Delta Downs 2003-'04, 2006-'07. Not held 2005. Dead heat for first 2007.

Boyd Gaming's Delta Princess Powered by Youbet.com Stakes

Grade 3 in 2008. Delta Downs, two-year-olds, fillies, 1 mile, dirt. Held December 7, 2007, with a gross value of $300,000. First held in 2002. First graded in 2008. Stakes record 1:39.17 (2003 Salty Romance).

Year	Winner	Jockey	Second	Third	Strs	Time	1st Purse
2007	By the Light, 2, 121	R. Bejarano	Miss Missile, 2, 121	Lady On Holiday, 2, 116	10	1:40.21	$180,000
2006	Miss Atlantic City, 2, 121	K. J. Desormeaux	Appealing Zophie, 2, 121	Stage Stop, 2, 121	6	1:40.40	180,000
2004	Punch Appeal, 2, 121	D. J. Meche	Summer Raven, 2, 121	Snipper Lou, 2, 118	6	1:40.42	150,000
2003	Salty Romance, 2, 114	M. E. Smith	Questionable Past, 2, 114	Turn to Lass, 2, 114	10	**1:39.17**	150,000
2002	My Trusty Cat, 2, 114	T. J. Thompson	Souris, 2, 114	Miss Mary Apples, 2, 116	8	1:39.54	150,000

Sponsored by Boyd Gaming Corp. of Henderson, Nevada, parent company of Delta Downs 2003-'04, 2006-'07. Presented by Youbet.com Inc. of Woodland Hills, California 2007. Not held 2005.

Breeders' Cup Classic Powered by Dodge

Grade 1 in 2008. Monmouth Park, three-year-olds and up, 1 1/4 miles, dirt. Held October 27, 2007, with a gross value of $4,580,000. First held in 1984. First graded in 1984. Stakes record 1:59.02 (2004 Ghostzapper).

Year	Winner	Jockey	Second	Third	Strs	Time	1st Purse
2007	Curlin, 3, 121	R. Albarado	Hard Spun, 3, 121	Awesome Gem, 4, 126	9	2:00.59	$2,700,000
2006	Invasor (Arg), 4, 126	F. Jara	Bernardini, 3, 122	Premium Tap, 4, 126	13	2:02.18	2,700,000
2005	Saint Liam, 5, 126	J. D. Bailey	Flower Alley, 3, 122	Perfect Drift, 6, 126	13	2:01.49	2,433,600
2004	Ghostzapper, 4, 126	J. Castellano	Roses in May, 4, 126	Pleasantly Perfect, 6, 126	13	**1:59.02**	2,080,000
2003	Pleasantly Perfect, 5, 126	A. O. Solis	Medaglia d'Oro, 4, 126	Dynever, 3, 121	10	1:59.88	2,080,000
2002	Volponi, 4, 126	J. A. Santos	Medaglia d'Oro, 3, 121	Milwaukee Brew, 5, 126	12	2:01.39	2,080,000
2001	Tiznow, 4, 126	C. J. McCarron	Sakhee, 4, 126	Albert the Great, 4, 126	13	2:00.62	2,080,000
2000	Tiznow, 3, 122	C. J. McCarron	Giant's Causeway, 3, 122	Captain Steve, 3, 122	13	2:00.75	2,480,400
1999	Cat Thief, 3, 122	P. Day	Budroyale, 6, 126	Golden Missile, 4, 126	14	1:59.52	2,080,000
1998	Awesome Again, 4, 126	P. Day	Silver Charm, 4, 126	Swain (Ire), 6, 126	10	2:02.16	2,662,400
1997	Skip Away, 4, 126	M. E. Smith	Deputy Commander, 3, 122	‡Dowty, 5, 126	9	1:59.16	2,288,500
1996	Alphabet Soup, 5, 126	C. J. McCarron	Louis Quatorze, 3, 121	Cigar, 6, 126	13	2:01.00	2,080,000
1995	Cigar, 5, 126	J. D. Bailey	L'Carriere, 4, 126	Unaccounted For, 4, 126	11	1:59.58	1,560,000
1994	Concern, 3, 122	J. D. Bailey	Tabasco Cat, 3, 122	Dramatic Gold, 3, 122	14	2:02.41	1,560,000
1993	Arcangues, 5, 126	J. D. Bailey	Bertrando, 4, 126	Kissin Kris, 3, 122	13	2:00.83	1,560,000
1992	A.P. Indy, 3, 121	E. Delahoussaye	Pleasant Tap, 5, 126	†Jolypha, 3, 118	14	2:00.20	1,560,000
1991	Black Tie Affair (Ire), 5, 126	J. D. Bailey	Twilight Agenda, 5, 126	Unbridled, 4, 126	11	2:02.80	1,560,000
1990	Unbridled, 3, 121	P. Day	Ibn Bey (GB), 6, 126	Thirty Six Red, 3, 121	14	2:02.20	1,350,000
1989	Sunday Silence, 3, 122	C. J. McCarron	Easy Goer, 3, 122	Blushing John, 4, 126	8	2:00.20	1,350,000
1988	Alysheba, 4, 126	C. J. McCarron	Seeking the Gold, 3, 122	Waquoit, 5, 126	9	2:04.80	1,350,000
1987	Ferdinand, 4, 126	W. Shoemaker	Alysheba, 3, 122	Judge Angelucci, 4, 126	12	2:01.40	1,350,000
1986	Skywalker, 4, 126	L. A. Pincay Jr.	Turkoman, 4, 126	Precisionist, 5, 126	11	2:00.40	1,350,000
1985	Proud Truth, 3, 122	J. Velasquez	Gate Dancer, 4, 126	Turkoman, 3, 122	8	2:00.80	1,350,000
1984	Wild Again, 4, 126	P. Day	‡Slew o' Gold, 4, 126	Gate Dancer, 3, 122	8	2:03.40	1,350,000

Sponsored by the Dodge division of Chrysler LLC of Detroit, Michigan 2003-'07. Held at Hollywood Park 1984, '87, '97. Held at Aqueduct 1985. Held at Santa Anita Park 1986, '93, 2003. Held at Churchill Downs 1988, '91, '94, '98, 2000, '06. Held at Gulfstream Park 1989, '92, '99. Held at Belmont Park 1990, '95, 2001, '05. Held at Woodbine 1996. Held at Arlington Park 2002. Held at Lone Star Park 2004. Track record 1996. ‡Gate Dancer finished second, DQ to third, 1984. ‡Whiskey Wisdom finished third, DQ to fourth, 1997. †Denotes female.

Breeders' Cup Distaff — *See* Emirates Airline Breeders' Cup Distaff

Breeders' Cup Filly and Mare Turf — *See* Emirates Airline Breeders' Cup Filly and Mare Turf

Breeders' Cup Juvenile — *See* Bessemer Trust Breeders' Cup Juvenile

Breeders' Cup Juvenile Fillies

Grade 1 in 2008. Monmouth Park, two-year-olds, fillies, 1 1/16 miles, dirt. Held October 27, 2007, with a gross value of $1,832,000. First held in 1984. First graded in 1984. Stakes record 1:41.49 (2001 Tempera).

Year	Winner	Jockey	Second	Third	Strs	Time	1st Purse
2007	Indian Blessing, 2, 119	G. K. Gomez	Proud Spell, 2, 119	Backseat Rhythm, 2, 119	13	1:44.73	$1,080,000
2006	Dreaming of Anna, 2, 119	R. R. Douglas	Octave, 2, 119	Cotton Blossom, 2, 119	14	1:43.81	1,080,000
2005	Folklore, 2, 119	E. S. Prado	Wild Fit, 2, 119	Original Spin, 2, 119	10	1:43.85	551,200
2004	Sweet Catomine, 2, 119	C. S. Nakatani	Balletto (UAE), 2, 119	Runway Model, 2, 119	12	1:41.65	520,000
2003	Halfbridled, 2, 119	J. A. Krone	Ashado, 2, 119	Victory U. S. A., 2, 119	14	1:42.75	520,000

Year	Winner	Jockey	Second	Third	Strs	Time	1st Purse
2002	Storm Flag Flying, 2, 119	J. R. Velazquez	Composure, 2, 119	Santa Catarina, 2, 119	10	1:49.60	$520,000
2001	Tempera, 2, 119	D. R. Flores	Imperial Gesture, 2, 119	Bella Bellucci, 2, 119	9	1:41.49	520,000
2000	Caressing, 2, 119	J. R. Velazquez	Platinum Tiara, 2, 119	She's a Devil Due, 2, 119	12	1:42.77	592,800
1999	Cash Run, 2, 119	J. D. Bailey	Chilukki, 2, 119	Surfside, 2, 119	9	1:43.31	520,000
1998	Silverbulletday, 2, 119	G. L. Stevens	Excellent Meeting, 2, 119	Three Ring, 2, 119	10	1:43.68	520,000
1997	Countess Diana, 2, 119	S. J. Sellers	Career Collection, 2, 119	Primaly, 2, 119	14	1:42.11	535,600
1996	Storm Song, 2, 119	C. Perret	Love That Jazz, 2, 119	Critical Factor, 2, 119	12	1:43.60	520,000
1995	My Flag, 2, 119	J. D. Bailey	Cara Rafaela, 2, 119	Golden Attraction, 2, 119	8	1:42.55	520,000
1994	Flanders, 2, 119	P. Day	Serena's Song, 2, 119	Stormy Blues, 2, 119	13	1:45.28	520,000
1993	Phone Chatter, 2, 119	L. A. Pincay Jr.	Sardula, 2, 119	Heavenly Prize, 2, 119	8	1:43.08	520,000
1992	Eliza, 2, 119	P. A. Valenzuela	Educated Risk, 2, 119	Boots 'n Jackie, 2, 119	12	1:42.93	520,000
1991	Pleasant Stage, 2, 119	E. Delahoussaye	La Spia, 2, 119	Cadillac Women, 2, 119	14	1:46.48	520,000
1990	Meadow Star, 2, 119	J. A. Santos	Private Treasure, 2, 119	Dance Smartly, 2, 119	13	1:44.00	450,000
1989	Go for Wand, 2, 119	R. P. Romero	Sweet Roberta, 2, 119	Stella Madrid, 2, 119	12	1:44.20	450,000
1988	Open Mind, 2, 119	A. T. Cordero Jr.	Darby Shuffle, 2, 119	Lea Lucinda, 2, 119	12	1:46.60	450,000
1987	Epitome, 2, 119	P. Day	Jeanne Jones, 2, 119	Dream Team, 2, 119	12	1:36.40	450,000
1986	Brave Raj, 2, 119	P. A. Valenzuela	Tappiano, 2, 119	Saros Brig, 2, 119	12	1:43.20	450,000
1985	Twilight Ridge, 2, 119	J. Velasquez	Family Style, 2, 119	Steal a Kiss, 2, 119	12	1:35.80	450,000
1984	‡Outstandingly, 2, 119	W. A. Guerra	Dusty Heart, 2, 119	Fine Spirit, 2, 119	11	1:37.80	450,000

Formerly sponsored by the Alberto-Culver Co. of Chicago, Illinois 2005. Formerly sponsored by Long John Silver's of Louisville, Kentucky 2002. Held at Hollywood Park 1984, '87, '97. Held at Aqueduct 1985. Held at Santa Anita Park 1986, '93, 2003. Held at Churchill Downs 1988, '91, '94, '98, 2000, '06. Held at Gulfstream Park 1989, '92, '99. Held at Belmont Park 1990, '95, 2001, '05. Held at Woodbine 1996. Held at Arlington Park 2002. Held at Lone Star Park 2004. 1 mile 1984-'85, 1987. 1 1/8 miles 2002. ‡Fran's Valentine finished first, DQ to tenth, 1984.

Breeders' Cup Mile — *See* NetJets Breeders' Cup Mile

Breeders' Cup Sprint — *See* TVG Breeders' Cup Sprint

Breeders' Cup Turf — *See* John Deere Breeders' Cup Turf

Breeders' Futurity — *See* Lane's End Breeders' Futurity

Brooklyn Handicap

Grade 2 in 2008. Belmont Park, three-year-olds and up, 1 1/2 miles, dirt. Held June 6, 2008, with a gross value of $199,000. First held in 1887. First graded in 1973. Stakes record 2:26 (1978 Nasty and Bold; 1981 Hechizado [Arg]).

Year	Winner	Jockey	Second	Third	Strs	Time	1st Purse
2008	Delosvientos, 5, 116	E. Coa	Evening Attire, 10, 115	Angliana, 6, 115	6	2:30.96	$120,000
2007	Any Given Saturday, 3, 118	G. K. Gomez	Tasteyville, 4, 114	Helsinki, 3, 112	5	1:48.31	94,320
2006	Wanderin Boy, 5, 117	J. Castellano	Awesome Twist, 4, 114	Reverberate, 4, 115	6	1:47.94	95,700
2005	Limehouse, 4, 115	J. R. Velazquez	Gygistar, 6, 117	‡Royal Assault, 4, 112	9	1:46.69	150,000
2004	Seattle Fitz (Arg), 5, 116	R. Migliore	Dynever, 4, 117	Newfoundland, 4, 115	6	1:46.30	150,000
2003	Iron Deputy, 4, 114	R. Migliore	Volponi, 5, 122	Saarland, 4, 115	5	1:47.84	150,000
2002	Seeking Daylight, 4, 113	E. S. Prado	Country Be Gold, 5, 113	Griffinite, 4, 114	8	1:46.35	150,000
2001	Albert the Great, 4, 122	J. F. Chavez	Perfect Cat, 4, 115	Top Official, 6, 113	7	1:47.41	150,000
2000	Lemon Drop Kid, 4, 120	E. S. Prado	Lager, 6, 114	Down the Aisle, 7, 112	7	1:49.93	150,000
1999	Running Stag, 5, 117	S. J. Sellers	Deputy Diamond, 4, 113	Sir Bear, 6, 119	8	1:46.39	210,000
1998	Subordination, 4, 114	E. Coa	Sir Bear, 5, 118	Mr. Sinatra, 4, 115	11	1:46.64	180,000
1997	Formal Gold, 4, 119	J. D. Bailey	Stephanotis, 4, 116	Circle of Light, 4, 111	8	1:46.21	180,000
1996	Wekiva Springs, 5, 120	M. E. Smith	Mahogany Hall, 5, 114	Admiralty, 4, 111	6	1:46.78	180,000
1995	You and I, 4, 115	J. F. Chavez	Key Contender, 7, 112	Slick Horn, 5, 113	9	1:49.02	150,000
1994	Devil His Due, 5, 120	M. E. Smith	Wallenda, 4, 118	Sea Hero, 4, 119	7	1:46.71	150,000
1993	Living Vicariously, 3, 111	R. G. Davis	Michelle Can Pass, 5, 116	Jacksonport, 4, 111	8	2:17.80	150,000
1992	Chief Honcho, 5, 117	R. P. Romero	‡Valley Crossing, 4, 114	Lost Mountain, 4, 114	11	2:16.91	210,000
1991	Timely Warning, 6, 112	M. J. Luzzi	Chief Honcho, 4, 121	De Roche, 5, 115	8	2:14.03	210,000
1990	‡Montubio (Arg), 5, 113	J. Vasquez	Mi Selecto, 5, 114	De Roche, 4, 113	7	2:28.60	241,920
1989	Forever Silver, 4, 116	J. Vasquez	Drapeau Tricolore, 4, 112	Jack of Clubs, 6, 112	8	2:28.60	238,560
1988	Waquoit, 5, 121	J. A. Santos	Personal Flag, 5, 120	Creme Fraiche, 6, 118	4	2:28.80	229,740
1987	Waquoit, 4, 123	C. J. McCarron	Bordeaux Bob, 4, 112	Full Courage, 4, 108	9	2:28.40	249,480
1986	Little Missouri, 4, 109	J. Samyn	Roo Art, 4, 118	Creme Fraiche, 4, 118	6	2:26.40	195,900
1985	Bounding Basque, 5, 111	A. Graell	†Life's Magic, 4, 114	Pine Circle, 4, 115	10	2:28.40	207,300
1984	Fit to Fight, 5, 129	J. D. Bailey	Vision, 3, 109	Dew Line, 5, 116	8	2:27.40	201,600
1983	Highland Blade, 5, 117	J. Vasquez	Sing Sing, 5, 118	Silver Supreme, 5, 113	13	2:31.00	172,800
1982	Silver Supreme, 4, 111	A. T. Cordero Jr.	Princelet, 4, 112	Baltimore Canyon, 4, 113	6	2:29.40	131,700
1981	Hechizado (Arg), 5, 116	R. Hernandez	The Liberal Member, 6, 113	Peat Moss, 6, 111	10	2:26.00	138,300
1980	Winter's Tale, 4, 112	J. Fell	State Dinner, 5, 121	Ring of Light, 5, 114	5	2:28.60	130,200
1979	The Liberal Member, 4, 114	R. I. Encinas	Bowl Game, 5, 119	State Dinner, 4, 123	8	2:28.80	99,000
1978	Nasty and Bold, 3, 112	J. Samyn	Father Hogan, 5, 118	Great Contractor, 5, 122	7	2:26.00	63,900
1977	Great Contractor, 4, 112	A. T. Cordero Jr.	Forego, 7, 137	American History, 5, 112	13	2:26.20	66,660
1976	Forego, 6, 134	H. Gustines	Lord Rebeau, 5, 114	Foolish Pleasure, 4, 126	8	2:01.20	67,860
1975	Forego, 5, 132	H. Gustines	Monetary Principle, 5, 109	Stop the Music, 5, 121	8	1:59.80	66,780

Racing — Graded Stakes 279

Year	Winner	Jockey	Second	Third	Strs	Time	1st Purse
1974	Forego, 4, 129	H. Gustines	Billy Come Lately, 4, 114	Arbees Boy, 4, 116	7	1:54.80	$66,600
1973	Riva Ridge, 4, 127	R. Turcotte	True Knight, 4, 117	Tentam, 4, 119	7	1:52.40	67,200

Named for the Brooklyn borough of New York City. Grade 1 1973-'92. Held at Gravesend Park 1887-1910. Held at Aqueduct 1914-'44, 1946-'55, 1960-'74, 1991-'93. Held at Jamaica 1956-'59. Not held 1911-'12. Brooklyn Breeders' Cup H. 2006. 1¼ miles 1887-1914, 1940-'55, 1960-'71, 1975-'76. 1³⁄₁₆ miles 1956-'59, 1972-'74. 1³⁄₈ miles 1991-'93. 1¹⁄₈ miles 1915-'39, 1994-2007. ‡Mi Selecto finished first, DQ to second, 1990. ‡Lost Mountain finished second, DQ to third, 1992. ‡Cuba finished third, DQ to fifth, 2005. World record 1973. Track record 1973, '75. †Denotes female.

Bryan Station Stakes

Grade 3 in 2008. Keeneland Race Course, three-year-olds, 1 mile, turf. Held October 14, 2007, with a gross value of $150,000. First held in 1993. First graded in 2008. Stakes record 1:33.60 (1995 Very Special Lite).

Year	Winner	Jockey	Second	Third	Strs	Time	1st Purse
2007	Inca King, 3, 123	S. Bridgmohan	Distorted Reality, 3, 120	Admiral Bird, 3, 117	10	1:35.88	$93,000
2006	Kip Deville, 3, 120	J. R. Leparoux	Storm Treasure, 3, 117	Smart Enough, 3, 120	9	1:35.36	93,000
2005	T. D. Vance, 3, 123	E. S. Prado	Rey de Cafe, 3, 123	Therecomesatiger, 3, 117	8	1:34.65	93,000
2001	Gino's Spirits (GB), 5, 124	P. Day	Watch, 4, 119	Binalegend, 5, 119	10	1:36.06	52,545
2000	White Beauty, 5, 120	T. T. Doocy	Pratella, 5, 124	Solar Bound, 4, 118	7	1:35.00	47,275
1999	Mingling Glances, 5, 123	L. Melancon	Red Cat, 4, 123	Cuanto Es, 4, 119	7	1:36.39	47,187
	Pratella, 4, 119	L. Melancon	License Fee, 4, 117	White Beauty, 4, 117	7	1:34.93	40,362
1998	Mingling Glances, 4, 115	P. Day	My Own Lovely Lee, 6, 116	Dance Design (Ire), 5, 115	9	1:34.44	44,780
1997	Cut the Cuteness, 5, 115	M. F. Rowland	Duck Trap, 4, 118	Totally Naughty, 7, 118	6	1:35.63	35,030
1996	Mariuka, 3, 114	W. Martinez	Romy, 5, 117	Valor Lady, 4, 114	9	1:35.64	43,850
	Vice On Ice, 5, 117	S. J. Sellers	Memories (Ire), 5, 123	Alive With Hope, 5, 114	9	1:35.71	34,100
1995	Very Special Lite, 5, 114	A. T. Gryder	Camlan, 4, 117	Romy, 4, 123	10	**1:33.60**	39,408
1994	Vinista, 4, 116	S. J. Sellers	Assert Oneself, 4, 126	Bobbycom, 4, 116	10	1:46.21	33,780
1993	Gray Cashmere, 4, 113	J. A. Santos	Auto Dial, 5, 121	River Bank Kid, 4, 113	6	1:44.44	33,294

Named in honor of the first settlement in Lexington, Bryan's Station, founded in 1779. Not held 2002-'04. 1¹⁄₁₆ miles 1993-'94. Dirt 1993. Four-year-olds and up 1993. Three-year-olds and up 1994-2001. Fillies and mares 1993-2001. Two divisions 1996, '99.

Buena Vista Handicap

Grade 2 in 2008. Santa Anita Park, four-year-olds and up, fillies and mares, 1 mile, turf. Held February 18, 2008, with a gross value of $150,000. First held in 1988. First graded in 1990. Stakes record 1:33.48 (1992 Gold Fleece [1st Div]; 1997 Media Nox [GB]).

Year	Winner	Jockey	Second	Third	Strs	Time	1st Purse
2008	Costume (GB), 4, 114	G. K. Gomez	Black Mamba (NZ), 5, 116	Kris' Sis, 5, 114	9	1:34.57	$90,000
2007	Conveyor's Angel, 5, 114	S. Arias	Singalong (GB), 5, 115	Attima (GB), 4, 120	8	1:35.77	90,000
2006	Silver Cup (Ire), 4, 116	V. Espinoza	Elusive Diva, 5, 118	Mirabilis, 4, 118	11	1:34.92	90,000
2005	Uraib (Ire), 5, 115	J. K. Court	Resplendency, 4, 117	Elusive Diva, 4, 116	5	1:33.72	90,000
2004	Fun House, 5, 116	G. L. Stevens	Katdogawn (GB), 4, 117	Fudge Parade, 4, 116	7	1:36.13	90,000
2003	Final Destination (NZ), 5, 115	V. Espinoza	Garden in the Rain (Fr), 6, 115	Embassy Belle (Ire), 5, 116	7	1:35.99	90,000
2002	Blue Moon (Fr), 5, 113	B. Blanc	Queen of Wilshire, 6, 116	Old Money (Aus), 5, 118	7	1:35.54	90,000
2001	Rare Charmer, 6, 115	L. A. Pincay Jr.	Elegant Ridge (Ire), 6, 117	Uncharted Haven (GB), 4, 116	11	1:36.67	90,000
2000	Lexa (Fr), 6, 115	B. Blanc	Here's to You, 4, 114	Sierra Virgen, 5, 114	6	1:36.17	97,250
1999	Tuzla (Fr), 5, 120	C. S. Nakatani	Supercilious, 6, 117	Green Jewel (GB), 5, 116	5	1:35.79	90,000
1998	Dance Parade, 4, 116	K. Desormeaux	Shake the Yoke (GB), 5, 118	Donna Viola (GB), 6, 121	10	1:36.03	101,524
1997	Media Nox (GB), 4, 115	C. S. Nakatani	Traces of Gold, 5, 115	Grafin, 6, 116	12	**1:33.48**	85,250
1996	Matiara, 4, 119	G. L. Stevens	Real Connection, 5, 114	Dirca (Ire), 4, 116	8	1:35.74	81,800
1995	Lyin to the Moon, 6, 116	K. Desormeaux	Jacodra's Devil, 4, 115	Exchange, 7, 122	5	1:36.77	61,700
1994	‡Skimble, 5, 118	C. S. Nakatani	Hero's Love, 6, 121	Possibly Perfect, 4, 120	11	1:34.85	66,300
1993	Marble Maiden (GB), 4, 118	K. Desormeaux	Suivi, 4, 117	Party Cited, 4, 116	7	1:36.23	65,000
1992	Gold Fleece, 4, 114	A. O. Solis	Elegance, 5, 115	Danzante, 4, 114	9	**1:33.48**	52,100
	Appealing Missy, 5, 117	C. J. McCarron	Exchange, 4, 120	Re Toss (Arg), 5, 117	9	1:34.25	52,100
1991	Taffeta and Tulle, 5, 120	C. J. McCarron	Bequest, 5, 117	Somethingmerry, 4, 114	9	1:34.30	67,200
1990	Saros Brig, 6, 116	P. A. Valenzuela	Royal Touch (Ire), 5, 123	Nikishka, 5, 118	10	1:34.20	68,100
1989	Annoconnor, 5, 121	C. A. Black	Daring Doone (GB), 6, 112	Daloma (Fr), 5, 116	8	1:36.40	65,800
1988	Davie's Lamb, 4, 117	F. Toro	Sly Charmer, 5, 114	Pen Bal Lady (GB), 4, 119	9	1:39.00	63,050

Named for two 19th-century California ranchos named Buena Vista Rancho; buena vista means "good view." Grade 3 1990-'94, 2005. Dirt 2005. Originally scheduled on turf 2005. Two divisions 1992. ‡Lady Blessington (Fr) finished first, DQ to ninth, 1994.

Bulleit Bourbon Palm Beach Stakes

Grade 3 in 2008. Gulfstream Park, three-year-olds, 1¹⁄₈ miles, turf. Held March 29, 2008, with a gross value of $100,000. First held in 1987. First graded in 1990. Stakes record 1:45.94 (2006 Go Between).

Year	Winner	Jockey	Second	Third	Strs	Time	1st Purse
2008	Sporting Art, 3, 116	J. Castellano	Flying Dismount, 3, 117	Moral Compass, 3, 120	11	1:45.98	$60,000
2007	Duveen, 3, 118	M. Guidry	Soldier's Dancer, 3, 122	Storm in May, 3, 120	7	1:47.48	60,000
2006	Go Between, 3, 118	E. S. Prado	Up an Octave, 3, 122	Papal Crown, 3, 118	7	**1:45.94**	60,000
2005	Interpatation, 3, 116	T. G. Turner	Tadreeb, 3, 118	Fishy Advice, 3, 118	8	1:47.12	60,000
2004	Kitten's Joy, 3, 122	J. D. Bailey	Prince Arch, 3, 118	Pa Pa Da, 3, 118	7	1:48.76	60,000
2003	Nothing to Lose, 3, 122	J. D. Bailey	White Cat, 3, 118	Imitation, 3, 118	12	1:48.28	60,000

Racing — Graded Stakes

Year	Winner	Jockey	Second	Third	Strs	Time	1st Purse
2002	Orchard Park, 3, 118	J. D. Bailey	Lord Juban, 3, 118	Red's Top Gun, 3, 116	12	1:49.80	$60,000
2001	Proud Man, 3, 119	R. R. Douglas	One Eyed Joker, 3, 114	Strategic Partner, 3, 112	12	1:48.32	90,000
2000	Mr. Livingston, 3, 114	S. J. Sellers	Powerful Appeal, 3, 114	Gateman (GB), 3, 117	11	1:48.04	45,000
1999	Swamp, 3, 114	R. Migliore	Marquette, 3, 114	Valid Reprized, 3, 119	12	1:48.38	45,000
1998	Cryptic Rascal, 3, 119	M. E. Smith	The Kaiser, 3, 113	American Odyssey, 3, 114	8	1:55.01	45,000
1997	Unite's Big Red, 3, 117	R. A. Hernandez	Trample, 3, 112	Tekken (Ire), 3, 117	7	1:47.32	45,000
1996	Harrowman, 3, 114	M. E. Smith	A Real Zipper, 3, 117	Ok by Me, 3, 119	6	1:49.22	45,000
1995	Admiralty, 3, 114	J. A. Krone	Nostra, 3, 114	Smells and Bells, 3, 114	4	1:51.03	30,000
1994	Mr. Angel, 3, 112	W. H. McCauley	Clint Essential, 3, 114	Fabulous Frolic, 3, 119	9	1:44.66	30,000
1993	Kissin Kris, 3, 112	D. Penna	Pride Prevails, 3, 112	Awad, 3, 119	10	1:46.41	38,760
1992	Preferences, 3, 114	J. C. Duarte Jr.	Doo You, 3, 112	Stress Buster, 3, 114	12	1:42.64	38,940
1991	Magic Interlude, 3, 114	C. W. Antley	Island Delay, 3, 117	Explosive Jeff, 3, 114	11	1:43.10	38,310
1990	Dawn Quixote, 3, 119	C. Perret	Rowdy Regal, 3, 119	Always Running, 3, 115	9	1:23.40	30,000
1989	Shy Tom, 3, 113	R. P. Romero	Verbatree, 3, 114	Group Process, 3, 114	8	1:37.20	29,835
	Storm Predictions, 3, 119	S. Gaffalione	Mercedes Won, 3, 122	Ocean Mistery, 3, 113	10	1:36.20	30,735
1988	Tanzanid, 3, 115	D. Valiente	Cefis, 3, 113	Denomination (GB), 3, 113	12	1:35.60	39,420
1987	Racing Star, 5, 114	S. B. Soto	Explosive Darling, 5, 118	New Colony, 4, 109	9	1:34.80	36,390

Named in honor of the residents of West Palm Beach and Palm Beach County, Florida. Sponsored by the Bulleit Distilling Co. of Lawrenceburg, Kentucky 2008. Palm Beach H. 1987. Palm Beach S. 1988-2007. 1 mile 1987-'89. 7 furlongs 1990. 1 1/16 miles 1991-'93. About 1 1/16 miles 1994. About 1 1/8 miles 1998. Dirt 1990, '93, '95. Three-year-olds and up 1987. Two divisions 1989.

Calder Derby

Grade 3 in 2008. Calder Race Course, three-year-olds, 1 1/8 miles, turf. Held April 26, 2008, with a gross value of $400,000. First held in 1972. First graded in 1996. Stakes record 1:47.70 (1998 Crowd Pleaser).

Year	Winner	Jockey	Second	Third	Strs	Time	1st Purse
2008	Sporting Art, 3, 119	J. Castellano	Tour Ireland, 3, 115	El Sultry Sun, 3, 119	11	1:47.93	$233,120
2007	Soldier's Dancer, 3, 119	C. H. Velasquez	Imawildandcrazyguy, 3, 117	Fair Weather Stan, 3, 119	11	1:52.21	116,560
2006	Can't Beat It, 3, 117	R. R. Douglas	Croton Road, 3, 117	Elizabul, 3, 115	11	1:48.79	120,000
2005	Dazzling Dr. Cevin, 3, 115	J. A. Garcia	Dream On Dream On, 3, 117	Talented Prince, 3, 115	7	1:52.44	120,000
2004	Eddington, 3, 114	E. Coa	Bob's Proud Moment, 3, 118	‡Caballero Negro, 3, 114	12	1:51.25	120,000
2003	Stroll, 3, 122	J. D. Bailey	Certifiably Crazy, 3, 115	Super Frolic, 3, 119	9	1:48.39	120,000
2002	Union Place, 3, 115	E. Coa	Miesque's Approval, 3, 122	The Judge Sez Who, 3, 122	11	1:47.76	120,000
2001	Western Pride, 3, 122	D. G. Whitney	Tour of the Cat, 3, 113	Built Up, 3, 117	10	1:51.12	120,000
2000	Whata Brainstorm, 3, 122	R. Homeister Jr.	Muntej (GB), 3, 122	Womble, 3, 117	12	1:47.80	120,000
1999	Isaypete, 3, 122	J. C. Ferrer	Rhythmean, 3, 117	Phi Beta Doc, 3, 122	12	1:50.01	120,000
1998	Crowd Pleaser, 3, 122	J. Samyn	Stay Sound, 3, 122	The Kaiser, 3, 117	10	1:47.70	120,000
1997	Blazing Sword, 3, 117	G. Boulanger	dh-Royal Tuneup, 3, 117		10	1:53.15	90,000
			dh-Topaz Runner, 3, 117				
1996	Laughing Dan, 3, 117	P. A. Rodriguez	Sea Horse, 3, 117	†Flying Concert, 3, 114	11	1:50.75	66,300
1995	Pineing Patty, 3, 122	L. J. Melancon	Sea Emperor, 3, 122	Mucha Mosca, 3, 117	7	1:51.40	60,000
1994	Halo's Image, 3, 117	G. Boulanger	Honest Colors, 3, 117	Rocky's Halo, 3, 117	10	1:52.38	90,000
1993	Medieval Mac, 3, 113	M. Russ	Raise an Alarm, 3, 113	Fight for Love, 3, 116	9	1:41.79	30,000
1992	Birdonthewire, 3, 112	M. T. Hunter	Shahpour, 3, 113	Ponche, 3, 111	7	1:44.36	30,000
1991	Scottish Ice, 3, 113	R. N. Lester	Chihuahua, 3, 120	Jackie Wackie, 3, 121	9	1:46.10	33,450
1990	Zalipour, 3, 118	D. A. Acevedo	Country Isle, 3, 115	Rowdy Regal, 3, 114	7	1:46.60	32,580
1989	‡Silver Sunsets, 3, 114	M. A. Gonzalez	Compuquine, 3, 114	Run for Your Honey, 3, 111	6	1:45.80	32,190
1988	Frosty the Snowman, 3, 116	D. Valiente	In the Slammer, 3, 116	Distinctintentions, 3, 112	7	1:44.40	30,750
1987	Schism, 3, 117	R. N. Lester	Slewdonza, 3, 112	Fabulous Devotion, 3, 114	6	1:47.20	32,640
1986	Annapolis John, 3, 120	J. A. Velez Jr.	Kid Colin, 3, 115	Real Forest, 3, 118	7	1:46.20	28,160
1985	Gray Haze, 3, 115	F. A. Pennisi	Alfred, 3, 115	Jeblar, 3, 115	11	1:46.00	33,780
1984	Opening Lead, 4, 114	J. A. Santos	Ward Off Trouble, 4, 114	Darn That Alarm, 3, 112	14	1:47.60	34,860
1983	Opening Lead, 3, 117	B. Gonzalez	The Cerfer, 3, 112	Neutral Player, 3, 112	12	1:48.20	20,640
1982	Glorious Past, 3, 115	A. Smith Jr.	Count Rebeau, 3, 115	Ell's New Canaan, 3, 112	9	1:45.80	19,905
1981	Poking, 5, 117	G. Cohen	Yosi Boy, 5, 114	Pair of Deuces, 3, 112	10	1:53.40	23,415
1980	J. Rodney G., 5, 113	F. Verardi	Two's a Plenty, 3, 109	Cherry Pop, 4, 125	8	1:53.20	23,040
1979	Breezy Fire, 4, 118	M. A. Rivera	Abba Cap, 5, 115	Selma's Boy, 4, 117	9	1:52.00	16,665
1978	Ole Wilk, 4, 114	I. J. Jimenez	America Brave, 4, 110	Classy State, 5, 115	10	1:42.60	18,600
1977	What a Threat, 5, 117	R. Gaffalione	†Noble Royalty, 4, 116	Lightning Thrust, 4, 122	8	1:42.60	17,400
1976	Chilean Chief, 5, 118	J. Imparato	El Rosillo, 3, 112	L. Grant Jr., 6, 116	9	1:45.80	17,700
1975	dh-*Rimsky II, 4, 116	A. Haldar		Plagiarize, 4, 112	12	1:42.20	12,400
	dh-Strand of Gold, 5, 112	P. Nicolo					
1974	‡Amberbee, 6, 117	J. Garrido	Enchanted Ruler, 3, 112	Seminole Joe, 6, 113	9	1:46.60	14,280
1973	Willmar, 5, 122	G. St. Leon	Sea Phantom, 5, 118	†Hickory Gray, 4, 115	8	1:25.20	7,020

Formerly named for Hollywood, Florida, hometown of real-estate developer Stephen Calder, who built Calder Race Course. Not graded 1998-'99, 2001, 2005. Hollywood H. 1972-'81, 1984, 1987-'93. Hollywood S. 1982-'83, 1985-'86. Calder Breeders' Cup Derby 1996. 7 furlongs 1972-'73. 1 1/16 miles 1974-'78, 1982-'92. 1 mile 70 yards 1993. Dirt 1972-'74, 1976, 1979-'97, 2001, 2005. Originally scheduled on turf 2001, '05. Three-year-olds and up 1972-'81, 1984. Dead heat for first 1975. Dead heat for second 1997. ‡Snurb finished first, DQ to seventh, 1974. ‡Big Stanley finished first, DQ to sixth, 1989. ‡Capias finished third, DQ to 12th, 2004. Track record 1993. †Denotes female.

Californian Stakes

Grade 2 in 2008. Hollywood Park, three-year-olds and up, 1 1/8 miles, all weather. Held May 31, 2008, with a gross value of $245,000. First held in 1954. First graded in 1973. Stakes record 1:45.80 (1980 Spectacular Bid).

Year	Winner	Jockey	Second	Third	Strs	Time	1st Purse
2008	Heatseeker (Ire), 5, 122	R. Bejarano	Tiago, 4, 126	Surf Cat, 6, 118	4	1:47.06	$150,000
2007	Buzzards Bay, 5, 116	J. Valdivia Jr.	Sun Boat (GB), 5, 116	A. P. Xcellent, 4, 116	10	1:49.72	150,000
2006	Dixie Meister, 4, 116	D. R. Flores	Super Frolic, 6, 118	That's an Outrage, 5, 116	8	1:49.53	150,000
2005	Lava Man, 4, 118	P. A. Valenzuela	Anziyan Royalty, 5, 117	Skukuza, 5, 116	7	1:47.83	150,000
2004	Even the Score, 6, 118	D. R. Flores	Total Impact (Chi), 6, 116	Nose The Trade (GB), 6, 118	8	1:47.64	150,000
2003	Kudos, 6, 116	A. O. Solis	Piensa Sonando (Chi), 5, 118	Reba's Gold, 6, 118	7	1:47.91	240,000
2002	Milwaukee Brew, 5, 122	K. Desormeaux	Bosque Redondo, 5, 118	Momentum, 4, 118	8	1:48.06	300,000
2001	Skimming, 5, 116	G. K. Gomez	Futural, 5, 120	Aptitude, 4, 116	5	1:48.12	300,000
2000	Big Ten (Chi), 5, 116	A. O. Solis	Early Pioneer, 5, 118	Mojave Moon, 4, 116	5	1:49.22	150,000
1999	Old Trieste, 4, 116	C. J. McCarron	Budroyale, 6, 120	Puerto Madero (Chi), 5, 122	7	1:46.55	180,000
1998	Mud Route, 4, 116	C. J. McCarron	Deputy Commander, 4, 122	Worldly Ways (GB), 4, 117	6	1:48.00	150,000
1997	River Keen (Ire), 5, 117	K. Desormeaux	Hesabull, 4, 118	Benchmark, 6, 118	6	1:47.38	150,000
1996	Tinners Way, 6, 116	E. Delahoussaye	Helmsman, 4, 122	Mr Purple, 4, 122	4	1:46.60	151,980
1995	Concern, 4, 122	M. E. Smith	Tossofthecoin, 5, 118	Tinners Way, 5, 116	8	1:47.74	160,900
1994	The Wicked North, 5, 120	K. Desormeaux	Kingdom Found, 4, 116	Slew of Damascus, 6, 116	8	1:46.68	165,000
1993	Latin American, 5, 116	G. L. Stevens	Missionary Ridge (GB), 6, 116	Memo (Chi), 6, 118	7	1:46.92	220,000
1992	Another Review, 4, 119	K. Desormeaux	Defensive Play, 5, 120	Ibero (Arg), 5, 119	7	1:48.11	119,400
1991	Roanoke, 4, 116	E. Delahoussaye	Anshan (GB), 4, 118	Marquetry, 4, 113	10	1:48.30	175,600
1990	Sunday Silence, 4, 126	P. A. Valenzuela	Stylish Winner, 6, 115	Charlatan (Chi), 5, 111	3	1:48.00	168,400
1989	Sabona, 7, 115	C. J. McCarron	Blushing John, 4, 124	Lively One, 4, 118	6	1:46.80	185,800
1988	Cutlass Reality, 6, 115	C. J. McCarron	Gulch, 4, 126	Judge Angelucci, 4, 126	4	1:47.60	180,200
1987	Judge Angelucci, 4, 118	G. Baze	Iron Eyes, 4, 115	Snow Chief, 4, 126	8	1:48.20	193,200
1986	Precisionist, 5, 126	C. J. McCarron	Super Diamond, 6, 117	Skywalker, 4, 121	7	1:33.60	188,400
1985	Greinton (GB), 4, 119	L. A. Pincay Jr.	Precisionist, 4, 126	Lord At War (Arg), 5, 118	4	1:32.60	179,600
1984	Desert Wine, 4, 121	E. Delahoussaye	Interco, 4, 122	Sari's Dreamer, 5, 116	8	1:47.60	193,600
1983	The Wonder (Fr), 5, 119	W. Shoemaker	Prince Spellbound, 4, 122	Poley, 4, 117	8	1:48.40	192,000
1982	Erins Isle (Ire), 4, 117	L. A. Pincay Jr.	It's the One, 4, 128	Major Sport, 5, 118	10	1:48.00	200,200
1981	Eleven Stitches, 4, 122	S. Hawley	Temperence Hill, 4, 130	†Kilijaro (Ire), 5, 123	12	1:48.40	207,600
1980	Spectacular Bid, 4, 130	W. Shoemaker	Paint King, 4, 115	Caro Bambino (Ire), 5, 118	7	**1:45.80**	184,450
1979	Affirmed, 4, 130	L. A. Pincay Jr.	Syncopate, 4, 114	Harry's Love, 4, 117	8	1:41.20	159,900
1978	J. O. Tobin, 4, 126	S. Cauthen	Replant, 4, 120	Cox's Ridge, 4, 127	6	1:41.00	124,550
1977	Crystal Water, 4, 128	L. A. Pincay Jr.	Mark's Place, 5, 121	Ancient Title, 7, 123	6	1:41.20	65,300
1976	Ancient Title, 6, 127	S. Hawley	Pay Tribute, 4, 117	Austin Mittler, 4, 116	6	1:41.20	65,300
1975	Ancient Title, 5, 126	L. A. Pincay Jr.	Big Band, 5, 117	Century's Envoy, 4, 117	10	1:40.20	73,100
1974	Quack, 5, 126	D. Pierce	Ancient Title, 4, 126	Woodland Pines, 5, 120	9	1:40.20	70,900
1973	Quack, 4, 126	D. Pierce	Royal Owl, 4, 125	Tri Jet, 4, 118	6	1:41.40	65,300

Named in honor of the residents of the state of California. Grade 1 1973-'96. 1 1/16 miles 1954-'79. Dirt 1954-2006. Track record 1980. †Denotes female.

Canadian Turf Handicap

Grade 3 in 2008. Gulfstream Park, four-year-olds and up, 1 1/16 miles, turf. Held January 4, 2008, with a gross value of $100,000. First held in 1967. First graded in 1973. Stakes record 1:38.20 (2005 Old Forester).

Year	Winner	Jockey	Second	Third	Strs	Time	1st Purse
2008	Host (Chi), 8, 116	J. R. Velazquez	Yate's Black Cat, 5, 115	National Captain (SAf), 6, 114	12	1:39.95	$60,000
2007	Giant Wrecker, 5, 114	J. Castellano	Host (Chi), 7, 117	Jambalaya, 5, 117	7	1:39.70	60,000
2006	English Channel, 4, 119	J. R. Velazquez	Miesque's Approval, 7, 116	Silver Tree, 6, 117	9	1:39.13	60,000
2005	Old Forester, 4, 114	E. Coa	Gulch Approval, 5, 114	Muqbil, 5, 114	11	**1:38.20**	60,000
2004	Newfoundland, 4, 115	J. R. Velazquez	Millennium Dragon (GB), 5, 118	Everything to Gain, 5, 113	6	1:44.90	60,000
2003	Political Attack, 4, 114	M. Guidry	Miesque's Approval, 4, 116	Strategic Partner, 4, 114	7	1:40.43	60,000
2002	North East Bound, 6, 116	J. A. Velez Jr.	Capsized, 6, 114	Flying Avie, 6, 114	4	1:44.01	90,000
2001	Inexplicable, 6, 115	J. A. Santos	Band Is Passing, 5, 118	David Copperfield, 4, 114	8	1:39.43	90,000
2000	Shamrock City, 5, 114	E. S. Prado	Rhythmean, 4, 113	Sharp Appeal, 7, 115	10	1:47.15	60,000
1999	Federal Trial, 4, 114	R. G. Davis	Deep Dive, 4, 114	Unite's Big Red, 5, 116	11	1:47.90	60,000
1998	Subordination, 4, 112	J. D. Bailey	Cimarron Secret, 7, 117	Tour's Big Red, 5, 113	7	1:50.87	60,000
1997	Devil's Cup, 4, 114	R. Wilson	Da Bull, 5, 113	Green Means Go, 5, 115	12	1:47.01	60,000
1996	The Vid, 6, 124	W. H. McCauley	Gone for Real, 5, 114	Warning Glance, 5, 115	5	1:47.05	60,000
1995	The Vid, 5, 117	J. D. Bailey	Star of Manila, 4, 118	Country Coy, 5, 113	9	1:47.19	60,000
1994	Paradise Creek, 5, 123	M. E. Smith	Glenfiddich Lad, 5, 118	Nijinsky's Gold, 5, 113	8	1:47.84	60,000
1993	Stagecraft (GB), 6, 112	J. D. Bailey	Roman Envoy, 5, 121	Carterista, 4, 114	10	1:47.80	60,000
1992	Buckhar, 4, 113	J. Cruguet	Tin Can Ali, 4, 113	Archies Laughter, 4, 114	13	1:48.49	60,000
1991	Izvestia, 4, 122	R. Platts	†Miss Josh, 5, 112	Bye Union Ave., 5, 113	14	1:41.50	60,000
1990	Youmadeyourpoint, 4, 114	D. Valiente	Wanderkin, 7, 116	Maceo, 6, 113	7	1:44.60	60,000
1989	Equalize, 7, 126	J. A. Santos	Sunshine Forever, 4, 126	Mi Selecto, 4, 116	7	1:41.00	71,280
1988	Equalize, 6, 112	J. D. Bailey	Yankee Affair, 6, 118	San's the Shadow, 4, 117	16	1:41.20	99,180
1987	Racing Star, 5, 112	S. B. Soto	Glaros (Fr), 5, 112	Salem Drive, 5, 113	9	1:40.80	54,420
	New Colony, 4, 109	V. H. Molina	Tri for Size, 6, 110	Trubulare, 4, 111	9	1:42.00	55,020
1986	Amerilad, 5, 113	J. A. Velez Jr.	Flying Pidgeon, 5, 119	Uptown Swell, 4, 115	8	1:40.80	57,060
	Vanlandingham, 5, 126	D. MacBeth	Ends Well, 5, 115	Dr. Schwartzman, 5, 118	8	1:40.00	56,460
1985	Solidified, 4, 113	J. Cruguet	Selous Scout, 4, 113	Jack Slade, 5, 122	13	1:40.60	62,010
	Nepal, 5, 112	J. D. Bailey	Dr. Schwartzman, 4, 116	Roving Minstrel, 4, 116	12	1:40.00	61,410

Year	Winner	Jockey	Second	Third	Strs	Time	1st Purse
1984	Ayman, 4, 112	J. Cruguet	Smart and Sharp, 5, 110	Guston (Arg), 6, 114	11	1:40.00	$57,555
1983	Data Swap, 6, 115	M. Solomone	Northrop, 4, 118	Wicked Will (GB), 5, 116	12	1:47.20	42,105
	Super Sunrise (GB), 4, 112	E. Maple	Summer Advocate, 6, 118	Pin Puller, 4, 112	10	1:46.60	40,755
1982	Robsphere, 5, 115	D. Brumfield	Dom Menotti (Fr), 5, 111	King of Mardi Gras, 6, 115	13	1:41.00	39,690
1981	Proctor, 4, 119	C. Perret	Imperial Dilemma, 4, 113	Foretake, 5, 115	15	1:41.00	61,290
1980	Morning Frolic, 5, 118	A. T. Cordero Jr.	Pearlescent (GB), 4, 114	Dickens Hill (Ire), 4, 122	13	1:41.20	41,220
1979	Roan Star, 6, 115	C. Perret	Fleet Gar, 4, 117	Family Doctor, 6, 113	11	1:40.80	31,590
	Noble Dancer (GB), 7, 128	J. Vasquez	Scythian Gold, 4, 118	River Warrior, 4, 114	10	1:41.00	31,290
1978	Practitioner, 5, 119	J. S. Rodriguez	Haverty, 4, 112	That's a Nice, 4, 116	11	1:41.60	29,820
	Court Open, 4, 109	R. Woodhouse	All Friends (Ire), 6, 114	Oilfield, 5, 114	11	1:40.80	29,520
1977	Gravelines (Fr), 5, 122	J. D. Bailey	Proponent, 5, 114	Lord Layabout, 4, 112	11	1:44.40	33,420
	Gay Jitterbug, 4, 121	L. Saumell	Riverside Sam, 4, 110	Blacksmith, 5, 110	10	1:44.00	32,820
1976	Step Forward, 4, 117	M. Solomone	*Lord Henham, 4, 112	Conesaba, 5, 113	9	1:40.20	40,320
1975	Sir Jason, 4, 113	M. A. Rivera	Westgate Mall, 6, 109	Mr. Door, 4, 114	14	1:40.80	30,677
1974	Baccalaureate, 4, 110	R. Woodhouse	*Rey Maya, 7, 112	Jogging, 7, 117	15	1:42.20	43,800
1973	Windtex, 4, 116	J. L. Rotz	Dubassoff, 4, 117	dh-Getajetholme, 4, 112	9	1:41.40	23,835
				dh-Super Sail, 5, 112			
	Life Cycle, 4, 115	F. Iannelli	Roundhouse, 5, 113	Hope Eternal, 5, 112	7	1:42.80	23,415

Named in honor of the numerous Canadian tourists who visit South Florida. Grade 2 1985-'97. Not graded 2002, 2005-'06. Canadian Club Turf H. 1991. About 1 1/16 miles 1983. 1 1/8 miles 1992-2000. Dirt 1972, '90, '98, 2002, '04. Originally scheduled on turf 2004. Three-year-olds and up 1967-2006. Two divisions 1973, 1977-'79, 1983, 1985-'87. Dead heat for third 1973. Course record 1992. †Denotes female.

Cardinal Handicap

Grade 3 in 2008. Churchill Downs, three-year-olds and up, fillies and mares, 1 1/8 miles, turf. Held November 17, 2007, with a gross value of $164,550. First held in 1974. First graded in 1995. Stakes record 1:47.81 (1996 Bail Out Becky [DQ to second]).

Year	Winner	Jockey	Second	Third	Strs	Time	1st Purse
2007	Criminologist, 4, 119	J. R. Velazquez	Argentina (Ire), 5, 120	Nottawasaga, 4, 116	8	1:51.06	$98,964
2006	Sabellina, 5, 115	J. R. Leparoux	Silca's Sister (GB), 3, 116	Royal Copenhagen (Fr), 4, 115	11	1:49.96	100,100
2005	Sundrop (Jpn), 4, 117	M. Guidry	Delta Princess, 6, 118	Finery, 5, 116	12	1:50.10	108,531
2004	Aud, 4, 115	B. Blanc	May Gator, 5, 117	Angela's Love, 4, 114	11	1:53.94	107,601
2003	Riskaverse, 4, 118	C. H. Velasquez	Bien Nicole, 5, 120	Firth of Lorne (Ire), 4, 116	12	1:50.53	108,624
2002	Quick Tip, 4, 114	R. Albarado	San Dare, 4, 114	Bien Nicole, 4, 118	10	1:51.08	107,322
2001	Watch, 4, 114	C. Perret	Sitka, 4, 111	Gino's Spirits (GB), 5, 118	9	1:49.12	104,997
2000	Illiquidity, 4, 115	J. K. Court	License Fee, 5, 118	Miss of Wales (Chi), 5, 114	12	1:49.72	109,182
1999	Pratella, 4, 114	B. Peck	Mingling Glances, 5, 116	Uanme, 4, 112	9	1:48.88	106,299
1998	B. A. Valentine, 5, 115	J. F. Chavez	Mingling Glances, 4, 112	Cuando, 4, 116	13	1:48.62	111,693
1997	Colcon, 4, 114	J. D. Bailey	Dance Clear (Ire), 4, 112	Sagar Pride (Ire), 4, 113	12	1:51.89	108,903
1996	‡Miss Caerleona (Fr), 4, 114	L. J. Melancon	Bail Out Becky, 4, 121	Striesen, 4, 113	7	**1:47.81**	72,850
1995	Apolda, 4, 114	P. Day	Alive With Hope, 4, 114	Lady Reiko (Ire), 4, 115	11	1:49.59	75,530
1994	Bold Ruritana, 4, 116	P. Day	Eternal Reve, 3, 117	Monaassabaat, 3, 113	11	1:48.25	76,375
1993	River Ball (Arg), 7, 109	J. Parsley	Marshua's River, 6, 112	Logan's Mist, 4, 118	9	1:55.79	74,945
1992	Auto Dial, 4, 113	S. J. Sellers	Radiant Ring, 4, 119	Red Journey, 4, 114	5	1:52.04	71,500
1991	Christiecat, 4, 118	A. T. Cordero Jr.	Super Fan, 4, 115	Screen Prospect, 4, 113	9	1:51.10	75,010
1990	Dance for Lucy, 4, 113	D. Penna	Betty Lobelia, 5, 114	Phoenix Sunshine, 5, 113	10	1:51.80	39,033
	Lady in Silver, 4, 122	P. Day	Coolawin, 4, 121	Splendid Try, 4, 112	8	1:51.40	38,789
1989	Townsend Lass, 4, 114	K. K. Allen	Bangkok Lady, 3, 112	Bearly Cooking, 6, 114	8	1:52.00	57,233
1988	Top Corsage, 5, 118	P. A. Valenzuela	Savannah's Honor, 3, 116	Graceful Darby, 4, 119	8	1:52.40	36,823
1987	Lake Champlain (Ire), 4, 119	P. Day	Marianna's Girl, 4, 113	Shot Gun Bonnie, 3, 119	10	1:46.20	37,440
1986	Oriental, 4, 123	K. K. Allen	Kapalua Butterfly, 4, 120	Glorious View, 4, 120	13	1:45.80	31,281
1985	Mrs. Revere, 4, 112	L. J. Melancon	Wealthy and Wise, 3, 113	My Inheritance, 3, 112	8	1:48.20	22,219
	Mr. T.'s Tune, 4, 118	K. K. Allen	Gerrie Singer, 4, 115	Adaptable, 4, 112	8	1:47.40	22,219
1984	Electric Fanny, 3, 112	J. C. Espinoza	Straight Edition, 4, 115	Mickey's Echo, 5, 120	8	1:48.00	21,271
1983	Charge My Account, 4, 112	P. Day	Heatherten, 4, 123	Etoile Du Matin, 4, 115	10	1:47.20	18,801
1982	Betty Money, 3, 116	B. Sayler	Raja's Delight, 4, 112	Mezimica, 4, 112	15	1:38.80	20,792
	Promising Native, 3, 114	S. Maple	What Glitter, 4, 112	Sweetest Chant, 4, 123	13	1:39.60	20,629
1981	Knights Beauty, 4, 115	T. W. Hightower	Deuces Over Seven, 4, 117	Roger's Turn, 3, 115	15	1:24.80	20,768
	Safe Play, 3, 122	S. A. Spencer	Lillian Russell, 4, 122	La Vue, 4, 119	10	1:24.20	18,330
1980	Vite View, 4, 120	D. Brumfield	Doing It My Way, 4, 120	Jeanie's Fancy, 4, 117	9	1:24.80	19,581
	Champagne Ginny, 3, 119	D. Brumfield	Impetuous Gal, 5, 122	Red Chiffon, 3, 114	9	1:24.60	18,119
1979	Impetuous Gal, 4, 116	E. Fires	Billy Jane, 3, 114	Cookie Puddin, 3, 113	9	1:24.80	18,021
	Gap Axe, 4, 115	D. Brumfield	Unreality, 5, 120	Honey Blonde, 4, 112	8	1:24.80	19,484
1978	Love to Tell, 3, 116	E. Delahoussaye	Selari's Choice, 4, 112	Bit of Sunshine, 4, 112	8	1:24.40	17,883
	Unreality, 4, 123	L. P. Suire	Navajo Princess, 4, 123	Irish Agate, 3, 111	9	1:24.20	18,046
1977	Likely Exchange, 3, 114	J. McKnight	My Compliments, 5, 113	My Bold Beauty, 3, 114	8	1:24.80	14,675
	Famed Princess, 4, 113	C. Ledezma	Chatta, 3, 112	Leigh Simms, 4, 113	9	1:24.80	14,836
1976	Hope of Glory, 4, 114	D. Brumfield	Bronze Point, 3, 115	Straight, 4, 116	8	1:25.00	14,666
	Vivacious Meg, 4, 114	R. Breen	Regal Gal, 3, 115	Regal Rumor, 4, 119	8	1:25.40	14,666
1975	Visier, 3, 116	R. Riera Jr.	Slade's Prospect, 3, 116	Ski Run, 3, 116	8	1:45.80	17,225
1974	Cut the Talk, 3, 116	D. Brown	Holding Pattern, 3, 126	Sturdy Steel, 3, 116	7	1:45.20	14,349

Named for Kentucky's state bird. Kentucky Cardinal S. 1974-'75, 1983-'85. Kentucky Cardinal H. 1976-'82. Cardinal S. 1986. 1 1/16 miles 1974-'75, 1983-'87. 7 furlongs 1976-'81. 1 mile 1982. Dirt 1974-'86, 1988, 1992. Three-year-olds 1974-'75. Both sexes 1974-'75. Two divisions 1976-'82, 1985, 1990. ‡Bail Out Becky finished first, DQ to second, 1996.

Racing — Graded Stakes 283

Carleton F. Burke Handicap

Grade 3 in 2008. Oak Tree at Santa Anita, three-year-olds and up, 1½ miles, turf. Held October 28, 2007, with a gross value of $111,300. First held in 1969. First graded in 1973. Stakes record 2:24.13 (2007 Spring House).

Year	Winner	Jockey	Second	Third	Strs	Time	1st Purse
2007	Spring House, 5, 115	G. K. Gomez	Isipingo, 4, 116	Runaway Dancer, 8, 117	10	**2:24.13**	$66,780
2006	Symphony Sid, 6, 111	M. C. Baze	Artiste Royal (Ire), 5, 119	Runaway Dancer, 7, 117	7	2:24.18	60,000
2005	Golden Rahy, 6, 115	A. O. Solis	Wild Buddy, 6, 114	†Stage Shy, 5, 118	6	2:27.02	60,000
2004	Habaneros, 5, 116	D. R. Flores	Pellegrino (Brz), 5, 116	Gallant (GB), 7, 113	8	2:26.91	60,000
2003	Runaway Dancer, 4, 112	M. E. Smith	Labirinto, 5, 116	Senor Swinger, 3, 114	9	2:28.38	83,550
2002	Special Matter, 4, 110	T. Baze	Alyzig, 5, 113	Dance Dreamer, 4, 117	5	2:28.47	90,000
2001	Cagney (Brz), 4, 116	M. E. Smith	Kerrygold (Fr), 5, 116	Northern Quest (Fr), 6, 118	9	2:26.10	90,000
2000	Timboroa (GB), 4, 114	D. R. Flores	dh-Kerrygold (Fr), 4, 116 dh-Res Judicata (GB), 5, 115		9	2:27.91	84,990
1999	Public Purse, 5, 119	A. O. Solis	Star Performance, 6, 115	Achilles (GB), 4, 115	8	2:25.83	90,000
1998	Perim (Fr), 5, 113	B. Blanc	Single Empire (Ire), 4, 116	Rate Cut, 4, 114	9	2:29.29	75,000
1997	Prussian Blue, 5, 117	K. Desormeaux	Embraceable You (Fr), 4, 116	Kessem Power (NZ), 5, 114	7	2:31.37	75,000
1996	Dernier Empereur, 6, 118	C. J. McCarron	Bon Point (GB), 6, 118	Party Season (GB), 5, 116	8	2:24.24	98,750
1995	Varadavour (Ire), 6, 115	A. O. Solis	Patio de Naranjos (Chi), 4, 117	Raintrap (GB), 5, 114	7	2:30.27	90,350
1994	Savinio, 4, 114	C. J. McCarron	Square Cut, 5, 114	Sir Mark Sykes (Ire), 4, 117	8	2:02.69	95,700
1993	Know Heights (Ire), 4, 117	K. Desormeaux	Fanmore, 5, 116	Myrakalu (Fr), 5, 114	7	2:00.07	96,000
1992	Missionary Ridge (GB), 5, 117	K. Desormeaux	Carnival Baby, 4, 112	Myrakalu (Fr), 4, 113	9	2:00.89	98,000
1991	Super May, 5, 117	C. S. Nakatani	Algenib (Arg), 4, 121	Pride of Araby, 5, 112	9	1:58.58	103,700
1990	‡Ultrasonido (Arg), 5, 114	C. J. McCarron	Rial (Arg), 5, 118	Eradicate (GB), 5, 117	8	1:59.80	129,400
1989	Alwuhush, 4, 120	J. A. Santos	Frankly Perfect, 4, 122	Speedratic, 4, 115	10	1:58.00	134,400
1988	Nasr El Arab, 3, 121	G. L. Stevens	Northern Provider, 6, 112	Trokhos, 5, 115	9	2:01.04	133,000
1987	Rivlia, 5, 121	L. A. Pincay Jr.	Captain Vigors, 5, 116	Circus Prince, 4, 115	10	2:03.20	102,550
1986	Louis Le Grand, 4, 115	W. Shoemaker	Schiller, 4, 114	Silveyville, 8, 120	10	2:01.20	133,700
1985	Tsunami Slew, 4, 121	G. L. Stevens	Yashgan (GB), 4, 121	Best of Both, 5, 115	7	1:59.60	78,550
1984	Silveyville, 6, 117	C. J. McCarron	Gordian (GB), 4, 115	Gato Del Sol, 5, 121	7	1:59.60	64,100
1983	Bel Bolide, 5, 122	T. Lipham	Travelling Victor, 4, 118	Bold Run (Fr), 4, 118	2	2:01.20	64,200
1982	Mehmet, 4, 117	E. Delahoussaye	Craelius, 3, 114	It's the One, 4, 124	7	1:58.60	63,600
1981	Spence Bay (Ire), 6, 120	F. Toro	Providential (Ire), 4, 121	Super Moment, 4, 121	10	2:00.60	67,200
1980	Bold Tropic (SAf), 5, 125	W. Shoemaker	Balzac, 5, 121	Shagbark, 5, 116	7	1:58.20	49,300
1979	Silver Eagle (Ire), 5, 125	F. Toro	John Henry, 4, 118	Shagbark, 4, 118	9	1:59.20	50,200
1978	Star of Erin (Ire), 4, 113	W. Shoemaker	Improviser, 6, 115	Mr. Redoy, 4, 118	9	1:59.00	38,400
	Palton (Chi), 5, 122	H. E. Moreno	Star Spangled, 4, 118	Lunar Probe (NZ), 4, 114	9	1:59.00	38,400
1977	Double Discount, 4, 116	F. Mena	No Turning, 4, 118	Vigors, 4, 120	8	1:57.40	33,000
1976	King Pellinore, 4, 124	W. Shoemaker	*Royal Derby II, 7, 116	George Navonod, 4, 115	8	1:57.60	33,300
1975	Top Command, 4, 113	W. Shoemaker	Against the Snow, 5, 116	Top Crowd, 4, 116	6	2:01.20	24,875
	Kirrary, 5, 114	F. Mena	Buffalo Lark, 5, 121	†*Dulcia, 6, 117	6	2:00.40	24,875
1974	†Tallahto, 4, 120	L. A. Pincay Jr.	High Protein, 4, 117	Scantling, 4, 117	6	1:59.00	32,300
1973	‡Kentuckian, 4, 117	D. Pierce	Wing Out, 5, 119	†Le Cle, 4, 116	9	1:59.00	33,400

Named for Carleton F. Burke (1882-1962), first chairman of the California Horse Racing Board. Grade 2 1973-'84, 1990-'97. Grade 1 1985-'89. Carleton F. Burke Invitational H. 1969-'70. 1¼ miles 1969-'94. About 1½ miles 2000. Two divisions 1975, '78. Dead heat for second 2000. ‡Groshawk finished first, DQ to fifth, 1973. ‡Rial (Arg) finished first, DQ to second, 1990. †Denotes female.

Carry Back Stakes

Grade 2 in 2008. Calder Race Course, three-year-olds, 6 furlongs, dirt. Held July 7, 2007, with a gross value of $300,000. First held in 1970. First graded in 2003. Stakes record 1:09.30 (2005 Lost in the Fog).

Year	Winner	Jockey	Second	Third	Strs	Time	1st Purse
2007	Black Seventeen, 3, 117	C. L. Potts	Teuflesberg, 3, 117	Yesbyjimminy, 3, 115	9	1:09.84	$178,560
2006	Too Much Bling, 3, 122	E. S. Prado	Mach Ride, 3, 115	Blazing Rate, 3, 122	6	1:10.48	177,000
2005	Lost in the Fog, 3, 122	R. A. Baze	Qureall, 3, 115	Hot Space, 3, 115	6	**1:09.30**	177,000
2004	Weigelia, 3, 117	A. O. Solis Jr.	Classy Migration, 3, 112	Bwana Charlie, 3, 119	11	1:10.50	177,000
2003	Valid Video, 3, 122	J. Bravo	Cajun Beat, 3, 117	Super Fuse, 3, 117	6	1:10.15	177,000
2002	Royal Lad, 3, 117	J. D. Bailey	Captain Squire, 3, 122	Friendly Frolic, 3, 114	9	1:10.73	150,000
2001	Illusioned, 3, 117	J. F. Chavez	Beyond Brilliant, 3, 117	Gallant Frolic, 3, 115	10	1:11.08	150,000
2000	Caller One, 3, 122	C. S. Nakatani	Fappie's Notebook, 3, 115	Malagot, 3, 115	9	1:10.35	120,000
1999	Silver Season, 3, 112	E. Coa	Deep Gold, 3, 117	Night Patrol, 3, 117	9	1:11.32	120,000
1998	Mint, 3, 115	E. Coa	Diamond Studs, 3, 115	Mt. Laurel, 3, 112	8	1:11.38	120,000
1997	Renteria, 3, 115	E. Coa	Red, 3, 122	Willow Skips Trial, 3, 115	11	1:11.28	120,000
1996	Fortunate Review, 3, 117	A. Toribio	Betweenhereorthere, 3, 115	Night Runner, 3, 113	12	1:23.27	60,000
1995	Sonic Signal, 3, 115	R. R. Douglas	Leave'm Inthedark, 3, 117	Too Great, 3, 113	10	1:24.79	60,000
1994	Score a Birdie, 3, 115	H. Castillo Jr.	Fortunate Joe, 3, 112	Ali'lbito'reality, 3, 114	7	1:24.09	60,000
1993	Humbugaboo, 3, 112	M. Russ	Signoir Valery, 3, 112	Kassee, 3, 113	8	1:22.74	60,000
1992	Always Silver, 3, 116	M. A. Lee	Appealtothechief, 3, 114	Dr Arne, 3, 114	7	1:25.00	30,000
1991	Ocala Flame, 3, 113	R. N. Lester	Sunny and Pleasant, 3, 113	Jacquelyn's Groom, 3, 113	9	1:19.02	33,180
1990	Country Isle, 3, 114	H. Castillo Jr.	Run Turn, 3, 120	Ultimate Swale, 3, 112	10	1:24.80	33,840
1989	Big Stanley, 3, 120	D. Valiente	Valid Space, 3, 114	Jabotinsky, 3, 117	6	1:23.60	32,490
1988	In the Slammer, 3, 114	M. A. Gonzalez	Lover's Trust, 3, 122	Ashmint, 3, 115	6	1:23.80	32,220
1987	You're No Bargain, 3, 117	O. J. Londono	Right Rudder, 3, 117	Jilsie's Gigalo, 3, 118	9	1:25.60	44,010
1986	Kid Colin, 3, 116	G. St. Leon	Big Jolt, 3, 116	Lucky Rebeau, 3, 116	13	1:25.80	38,610

Year	Winner	Jockey	Second	Third	Strs	Time	1st Purse
1985	Smile, 3, 123	J. Vasquez	Paravon, 3, 112	Hickory Hill Flyer, 3, 114	7	1:23.80	46,260
1984	Bowmans Express, 3, 117	O. J. Londono	Mo Exception, 3, 114	No Room, 3, 119	12	1:25.40	19,305
1983	Opening Lead, 3, 112	B. Gonzalez	El Perico, 3, 117	Neutral Player, 3, 112	9	1:25.80	16,785
1982	Rex's Profile, 3, 115	E. Cardone	Libra Moon, 3, 118	Center Cut, 3, 123	7	1:11.40	16,395
1981	Face the Moment, 3, 115	E. Cardone	†Toga Toga, 3, 113	Incredible John, 3, 118	8	1:11.00	16,530
1980	Diplomatic Note, 3, 112	J. D. Bailey	Buckn' Shoe, 3, 115	Fast Fast Freddie, 3, 113	9	1:12.00	16,785
1979	Breezy Fire, 4, 120	M. A. Rivera	Cherry Pop, 3, 113	Noble Heart, 3, 111	9	1:24.60	16,770
1978	Admiral Rix, 2, 116	T. Barrow	Tartan Tam, 2, 116	Cherry Pop, 2, 116	9	1:07.40	14,160
1977	Chwesboken, 2, 119	D. Hidalgo	Noon Time Spender, 2, 122	Ski's Never Bend, 2, 116	5	1:05.40	13,320
1976	Winners Hit, 2, 119	R. Broussard	My Budget, 2, 119	Time for Fun, 2, 116	11	1:07.00	14,640
1975	†Precipitory, 2, 116	J. Salinas	Chic Ruler, 2, 116	Upper Current, 2, 119	10	1:06.80	14,400

Named for Dorchester Farm Stable's Racing Hall of Fame member and 1961 champion three-year-old male Carry Back (1958 c. by Saggy); Carry Back was the all-time leading Florida-bred earner at his retirement. Grade 3 2003-'04. Carry Back H. 1981-'93. Held at Tropical Park 1970. Not held 1972-'74. 5½ furlongs 1975-'78. 7 furlongs 1979, 1984-'90, 1992-'96. 6½ furlongs 1991. Two-year-olds and up 1979. †Denotes female.

Carter Handicap

Grade 1 in 2008. Aqueduct, three-year-olds and up, 7 furlongs, dirt. Held April 5, 2008, with a gross value of $300,000. First held in 1895. First graded in 1973. Stakes record 1:20.04 (1999 Artax).

Year	Winner	Jockey	Second	Third	Strs	Time	1st Purse
2008	Bustin Stones, 4, 116	E. S. Prado	Executive Fleet, 5, 114	Premium Wine, 4, 115	9	1:22.91	$180,000
2007	Silver Wagon, 6, 118	J. Castellano	Diabolical, 4, 117	Ah Day, 4, 115	6	1:21.46	180,000
2006	Bishop Court Hill, 6, 115	J. A. Santos	Sir Greeley, 4, 116	Big Apple Daddy, 4, 114	6	1:23.27	180,000
2005	Forest Danger, 4, 117	R. Bejarano	Medallist, 4, 117	Don Six, 5, 116	6	1:20.46	210,000
2004	Pico Central (Brz), 5, 117	A. O. Solis	Strong Hope, 4, 119	Eye of the Tiger, 4, 114	9	1:20.22	210,000
2003	Congaree, 5, 122	G. L. Stevens	Aldebaran, 5, 118	Peeping Tom, 6, 114	5	1:21.48	210,000
2002	Affirmed Success, 8, 119	R. Migliore	Voodoo, 4, 113	Burning Roma, 4, 117	10	1:21.84	210,000
2001	Peeping Tom, 4, 118	S. Bridgmohan	Say Florida Sandy, 7, 116	Hook and Ladder, 4, 118	7	1:21.33	180,000
2000	Brutally Frank, 6, 116	S. Bridgmohan	Western Expression, 4, 113	Affirmed Success, 6, 122	7	1:21.66	120,000
1999	Artax, 4, 114	J. F. Chavez	Affirmed Success, 5, 119	Western Borders, 5, 113	9	**1:20.04**	120,000
1998	Wild Rush, 4, 117	K. Desormeaux	Banker's Gold, 5, 114	Western Borders, 4, 115	10	1:21.16	120,000
1997	Langfuhr, 5, 122	J. F. Chavez	Stalwart Member, 4, 113	Western Winter, 5, 112	9	1:22.99	90,000
1996	Lite the Fuse, 5, 121	J. A. Krone	Flying Chevron, 4, 115	Placid Fund, 4, 114	10	1:20.92	90,000
1995	Lite the Fuse, 4, 111	R. B. Perez	Our Emblem, 4, 114	You and I, 4, 113	9	1:21.40	90,000
1994	Virginia Rapids, 4, 118	J. Samyn	Punch Line, 4, 114	Cherokee Run, 4, 113	11	1:21.45	90,000
1993	Alydeed, 4, 122	C. Perret	Loach, 5, 112	Argyle Lake, 7, 113	10	1:22.70	90,000
1992	Rubiano, 5, 118	J. A. Santos	Kid Russell, 6, 112	In Excess (Ire), 5, 122	9	1:21.41	120,000
1991	Housebuster, 4, 122	C. Perret	Black Tie Affair (Ire), 5, 123	Gervazy, 4, 116	8	1:21.31	120,000
1990	Dancing Spree, 5, 123	C. W. Antley	Dancing Pretense, 5, 115	Sewickley, 5, 119	7	1:22.00	137,280
1989	On the Line, 5, 125	G. L. Stevens	True and Blue, 4, 114	Dr. Carrington, 4, 110	8	1:21.40	140,880
1988	Gulch, 4, 124	J. A. Santos	Afleet, 4, 124	Its Academic, 4, 108	8	1:20.40	174,300
1987	†Pine Tree Lane, 5, 119	R. P. Romero	King's Swan, 7, 123	Zany Tactics, 6, 119	6	1:21.20	170,400
1986	Love That Mac, 4, 117	E. Maple	Ziggy's Boy, 4, 118	King's Swan, 6, 120	7	1:21.60	116,160
1985	Mt. Livermore, 4, 117	J. D. Bailey	Rocky Marriage, 5, 122	Carr de Naskra, 4, 125	6	1:20.80	83,340
1984	Bet Big, 4, 115	J. Samyn	Cannon Shell, 5, 109	A Phenomenon, 4, 126	10	1:21.80	73,200
1983	Vittorioso, 4, 113	A. Smith Jr.	Sing Sing, 5, 122	Fit to Fight, 4, 116	9	1:22.80	67,800
1982	Pass the Tab, 4, 118	A. Graell	Royal Hierarchy, 5, 115	Maudlin, 4, 114	12	1:22.40	52,110
1981	Amber Pass, 4, 114	E. Maple	Guilty Conscience, 5, 111	Dunham's Gift, 4, 116	7	1:23.00	49,410
1980	Czaravich, 4, 126	L. Adams	Tanthem, 5, 122	Nice Catch, 6, 120	6	1:21.00	49,050
1979	Star de Naskra, 4, 122	J. Fell	Alydar, 4, 126	Sensitive Prince, 4, 126	6	1:21.80	48,690
1978	Jaipur's Gem, 5, 115	J. Samyn	Vencedor, 4, 111	Half High, 5, 118	7	1:21.60	32,070
	Pumpkin Moonshine, 4, 107	D. A. Borden	Prefontaine, 4, 112	Big John Taylor, 4, 113	6	1:22.20	31,920
1977	dh-Gentle King, 4, 110	D. Montoya		Full Out, 4, 117	8	1:22.00	21,914
	dh-Quiet Little Table, 4, 119	E. Maple					
	Soy Numero Uno, 4, 126	R. Broussard	Barrera, 4, 119	Gallant Bob, 5, 116	6	1:22.20	31,770
1976	Due Diligence, 4, 111	J. Amy	†Honorable Miss, 6, 122	Amerrico, 4, 112	8	1:22.40	33,810
1975	Forego, 5, 134	H. Gustines	Stop the Music, 5, 123	Orders, 4, 114	10	1:21.60	34,860
1974	Forego, 4, 129	H. Gustines	Mr. Prospector, 4, 124	Timeless Moment, 4, 113	8	1:22.20	33,900
1973	King's Bishop, 4, 114	E. Maple	Onion, 4, 114	Petrograd, 4, 118	10	1:20.40	35,220

Named for Capt. William Carter of Brooklyn, New York, who contributed $500 of the first $600 purse. Grade 2 1973-'87. Held at Belmont Park 1946, 1956-'59, 1968-'69, 1972-'74, 1986, 1994-'96. Not held 1909, 1911-'13. 1¼ miles 1895. 1⅛ miles 1896. 1 1/16 miles 1897. About 7 furlongs 1898. 6½ furlongs 1899-1902. Two divisions 1977-'78. Dead heat for first 1977 (1st Div.). Track record 1973, '99. †Denotes female. Held as an allowance race 1933-'34.

CashCall Futurity

Grade 1 in 2008. Hollywood Park, two-year-olds, 1 1/16 miles, all weather. Held December 22, 2007, with a gross value of $753,000. First held in 1981. First graded in 1983. Stakes record 1:40.74 (1994 Afternoon Deelites).

Year	Winner	Jockey	Second	Third	Strs	Time	1st Purse
2007	Into Mischief, 2, 121	V. Espinoza	Colonel John, 2, 121	Massive Drama, 2, 121	12	1:40.82	$403,000
2006	Stormello, 2, 121	K. Desormeaux	Liquidity, 2, 121	Roman Commander, 2, 121	10	1:42.19	264,900
2005	Brother Derek, 2, 121	A. O. Solis	Your Tent Or Mine, 2, 121	Bob and John, 2, 121	8	1:42.02	244,350
2004	Declan's Moon, 2, 121	V. Espinoza	Giacomo, 2, 121	Wilko, 2, 121	7	1:41.63	269,700
2003	Lion Heart, 2, 121	M. E. Smith	St Averil, 2, 121	That's an Outrage, 2, 121	5	1:42.80	225,600

Racing — Graded Stakes 285

Year	Winner	Jockey	Second	Third	Strs	Time	1st Purse
2002	Toccet, 2, 121	J. F. Chavez	‡Domestic Dispute, 2, 121	Coax Kid, 2, 121	6	1:41.26	$243,900
2001	Siphonic, 2, 121	J. D. Bailey	Fonz's, 2, 121	Officer, 2, 121	8	1:42.09	274,050
2000	Point Given, 2, 121	G. L. Stevens	Millennium Wind, 2, 121	Golden Ticket, 2, 121	4	1:42.21	204,300
1999	Captain Steve, 2, 121	R. Albarado	High Yield, 2, 121	Cosine, 2, 121	6	1:43.27	245,400
1998	Tactical Cat, 2, 121	L. A. Pincay Jr.	Prime Timber, 2, 121	Premier Property, 2, 121	5	1:42.63	235,800
1997	Real Quiet, 2, 121	K. Desormeaux	Artax, 2, 121	Nationalore, 2, 121	11	1:41.34	282,120
1996	Swiss Yodeler, 2, 121	A. O. Solis	Stolen Gold, 2, 121	In Excessive Bull, 2, 121	13	1:42.70	348,510
1995	Matty G, 2, 121	A. O. Solis	Odyle, 2, 121	Ayrton S, 2, 121	7	1:41.75	275,000
1994	Afternoon Deelites, 2, 121	K. Desormeaux	Thunder Gulch, 2, 121	A. J. Jett, 2, 121	5	1:40.74	275,000
1993	Valiant Nature, 2, 121	L. A. Pincay Jr.	Brocco, 2, 121	Flying Sensation, 2, 121	6	1:40.78	275,000
1992	River Special, 2, 121	L. A. Pincay Jr.	Stuka, 2, 121	Earl of Barking (Ire), 2, 121	6	1:43.27	275,000
1991	A.P. Indy, 2, 121	E. Delahoussaye	Dance Floor, 2, 121	Casual Lies, 2, 121	14	1:42.85	329,780
1990	Best Pal, 2, 121	J. A. Santos	General Meeting, 2, 121	Reign Road, 2, 121	9	1:35.40	495,000
1989	Grand Canyon, 2, 121	A. T. Cordero Jr.	Farma Way, 2, 121	Silver Ending, 2, 121	9	1:33.00	495,000
1988	King Glorious, 2, 121	C. J. McCarron	Music Merci, 2, 121	Hawkster, 2, 121	10	1:35.60	495,000
1987	Tejano, 2, 121	L. A. Pincay Jr.	Purdue King, 2, 121	Regal Classic, 2, 121	8	1:34.60	495,000
1986	Temperate Sil, 2, 121	W. Shoemaker	Alysheba, 2, 121	Masterful Advocate, 2, 121	12	1:36.20	495,000
1985	Snow Chief, 2, 121	A. O. Solis	Electric Blue, 2, 121	Ferdinand, 2, 121	10	1:34.20	589,600
1984	Stephan's Odyssey, 2, 121	E. Maple	First Norman, 2, 121	Right Con, 2, 121	13	1:43.40	627,000
1983	Fali Time, 2, 121	S. Hawley	Bold T. Jay, 2, 121	†Life's Magic, 2, 118	12	1:41.60	549,849
1982	Roving Boy, 2, 121	E. Delahoussaye	Desert Wine, 2, 121	Fifth Division, 2, 121	9	1:41.80	418,770
1981	Stalwart, 2, 121	C. J. McCarron	Cassaleria, 2, 121	†Header Card, 2, 118	12	1:47.80	365,805

Sponsored by CashCall Inc. of Fountain Valley, California 2007. Hollywood Futurity 1981-2006. 1 mile 1985-'90. Dirt 1981-2005. ‡Kafwain finished second, DQ to fourth, 2002. †Denotes female.

CashCall Mile Invitational Stakes

Grade 2 in 2008. Hollywood Park, three-year-olds and up, fillies and mares, 1 mile, turf. Held July 6, 2007, with a gross value of $1,000,000. First held in 1998. First graded in 2001. Stakes record 1:33.33 (2006 Dance in the Mood [Jpn]).

Year	Winner	Jockey	Second	Third	Strs	Time	1st Purse
2007	Lady of Venice (Fr), 4, 119	J. R. Leparoux	Precious Kitten, 4, 121	Price Tag (GB), 4, 123	9	1:33.56	$525,000
2006	Dance in the Mood (Jpn), 5, 123	V. Espinoza	Sweet Talker, 4, 123	Luas Line (Ire), 4, 123	8	1:33.33	400,000
2005	Intercontinental (GB), 5, 123	J. D. Bailey	Ticker Tape (GB), 4, 121	Navaja (NZ), 5, 117	3	1:34.33	120,000
2004	Janeian (NZ), 6, 121	K. Desormeaux	Katdogawn (GB), 4, 123	Makeup Artist, 4, 121	6	1:34.79	65,820
2003	Magic Mission (GB), 4, 115	C. S. Nakatani	Little Treasure (Fr), 4, 121	Belleski, 4, 115	9	1:34.25	67,320
2002	Surya, 4, 117	K. Desormeaux	Angel Gift, 4, 117	Reine de Romance (Ire), 4, 121	12	1:34.73	68,880
2001	Kalatiara (Aus), 4, 114	C. J. McCarron	Dianehill (Ire), 5, 121	Al Desima (GB), 4, 116	7	1:34.41	65,940
2000	Tranquility Lake, 5, 121	E. Delahoussaye	Dianehill (Ire), 4, 119	Reciclada (Chi), 5, 119	6	1:33.98	46,590
1999	Tuzla (Fr), 5, 123	C. S. Nakatani	Isle de France, 4, 119	Chime After Chime, 4, 113	5	1:34.32	42,240
1998	Tuzla (Fr), 4, 115	C. S. Nakatani	Sonja's Faith (Ire), 4, 119	Plus (Chi), 5, 115	7	1:34.33	42,990

Formerly named for Robert E. Sangster's 1984 champion grass mare and '84 Breeders' Cup Mile (at Hollywood Park) winner Royal Heroine (Ire) (1980 f. by Lypheor [GB]). Sponsored by CashCall Inc. of Fountain Valley, California 2006-'07. Grade 3 2001-'06. Royal Heroine S. 1998-2004. Royal Heroine Invitational S. 2005. CashCall Invitational S. 2006.

Central Bank Transylvania Stakes

Grade 3 in 2008. Keeneland Race Course, three-year-olds, 1 1/16 miles, all weather. Held April 4, 2008, with a gross value of $150,000. First held in 1989. First graded in 2003. Stakes record 1:44.43 (2008 Boss Lafitte).

Year	Winner	Jockey	Second	Third	Strs	Time	1st Purse
2008	Boss Lafitte, 3, 117	R. Albarado	Riley Tucker, 3, 117	Budge Man, 3, 117	8	1:44.43	$93,000
2007	Marcavelly, 3, 117	E. S. Prado	In Jest, 3, 117	Cobrador, 3, 117	9	1:36.98	93,000
2006	Chin High, 3, 117	S. Bridgmohan	Le Plaix (Fr), 3, 117	Wherethewestbegins, 3, 117	10	1:37.87	93,000
2005	Chattahoochee War, 3, 121	J. D. Bailey	Guillaume Tell (Ire), 3, 117	Rey de Cafe, 3, 121	8	1:35.28	93,000
2004	Timo, 3, 117	E. S. Prado	Mr. J. T. L., 3, 116	America Alive, 3, 116	9	1:36.52	70,308
2003	White Cat, 3, 116	S. J. Sellers	Deep Shadow, 3, 118	Christmas Away, 3, 116	9	1:34.98	62,000
2002	Flying Dash (Ger), 3, 116	J. D. Bailey	Back Packer, 3, 116	Political Attack, 3, 120	8	1:35.69	62,000
2001	Baptize, 3, 120	J. D. Bailey	Dynameaux, 3, 116	Act of Reform, 3, 116	7	1:35.28	70,556
2000	Field Cat, 3, 116	M. E. Smith	Lendell Ray, 3, 116	Go Lib Go, 3, 123	9	1:35.19	70,618
1999	Good Night, 3, 114	S. J. Sellers	Air Rocket, 3, 114	Make Your Mark, 3, 114	10	1:35.00	70,308
1998	Dog Watch (GB), 3, 116	R. G. Davis	Reformer Rally, 3, 118	American Odyssey, 3, 114	10	1:34.65	45,781
1997	Near the Bank, 3, 118	P. Day	Daylight Savings, 3, 114	Song for James, 3, 113	6	1:36.40	44,249
1996	More Royal, 3, 112	J. A. Krone	Defacto, 3, 121	Rough Opening, 3, 121	9	1:35.92	43,202
1995	‡Crimson Guard, 3, 118	M. E. Smith	Dixie Dynasty, 3, 114	‡Nostra, 3, 118	9	1:44.04	42,259
1994	Star of Manila, 3, 121	S. J. Sellers	Prix de Crouton, 3, 118	Carpet, 3, 114	6	1:42.87	43,555
1993	Proud Shot, 3, 118	W. H. McCauley	Explosive Red, 3, 121	Awad, 3, 121	7	1:44.17	34,364
1992	Casino Magistrate, 3, 121	R. D. Lopez	Coaxing Matt, 3, 112	Trans Caribbean, 3, 115	7	1:46.62	35,636
1991	Eastern Dude, 3, 121	S. J. Sellers	Magic Interlude, 3, 121	January Man, 3, 112	10	1:42.94	36,514
1990	Izvestia, 3, 112	R. P. Romero	Scattered, 3, 115	Divine Warning, 3, 112	9	1:43.80	36,043
1989	Shy Tom, 3, 121	R. P. Romero	Once Over Knightly, 3, 118	Ringerman, 3, 121	6	1:50.00	35,133

Named for Transylvania University, the oldest college west of the Allegheny Mountains, founded in 1780 in Lexington. Sponsored by Central Bank of Lexington 2005-'08. 1 mile 1996-2007. Turf 1989-2007. ‡Ops Smile finished first, DQ to eighth, 1995. ‡Hawk Attack finished third, DQ to seventh, 1995.

Champagne Stakes

Grade 1 in 2008. Belmont Park, two-year-olds, 1 mile, dirt. Held October 6, 2007, with a gross value of $416,000. First held in 1867. First graded in 1973. Stakes record 1:34.20 (1983 Devil's Bag).

Year	Winner	Jockey	Second	Third	Strs	Time	1st Purse
2007	War Pass, 2, 122	C. H. Velasquez	Pyro, 2, 122	Z Humor, 2, 122	8	1:36.12	$240,000
2006	Scat Daddy, 2, 122	J. R. Velazquez	Nobiz Like Shobiz, 2, 122	Pegasus Wind, 2, 122	10	1:36.97	240,000
2005	First Samurai, 2, 122	J. D. Bailey	Henny Hughes, 2, 122	Superfly, 2, 122	6	1:36.29	300,000
2004	Proud Accolade, 2, 122	J. R. Velazquez	Afleet Alex, 2, 122	Sun King, 2, 122	8	1:42.30	300,000
2003	Birdstone, 2, 122	J. D. Bailey	Chapel Royal, 2, 122	Dashboard Drummer, 2, 122	7	1:44.05	300,000
2002	Toccet, 2, 122	J. F. Chavez	Icecoldbeeratreds, 2, 122	Erinsouthernman, 2, 122	9	1:44.45	300,000
2001	Officer, 2, 122	V. Espinoza	Jump Start, 2, 122	Heavyweight Champ, 2, 122	5	1:43.39	300,000
2000	A P Valentine, 2, 122	J. F. Chavez	Point Given, 2, 122	Yonaguska, 2, 122	10	1:41.45	300,000
1999	Greenwood Lake, 2, 122	J. Samyn	Chief Seattle, 2, 122	High Yield, 2, 122	7	1:43.70	240,000
1998	The Groom Is Red, 2, 122	C. S. Nakatani	Lemon Drop Kid, 2, 122	Weekend Money, 2, 122	7	1:42.91	240,000
1997	Grand Slam, 2, 122	G. L. Stevens	Lil's Lad, 2, 122	Halory Hunter, 2, 122	8	1:40.59	240,000
1996	Ordway, 2, 122	J. R. Velazquez	Traitor, 2, 122	Gold Tribute, 2, 122	12	1:42.09	240,000
1995	Maria's Mon, 2, 122	R. G. Davis	Diligence, 2, 122	Devil's Honor, 2, 122	8	1:43.29	300,000
1994	Timber Country, 2, 122	P. Day	Sierra Diablo, 2, 122	On Target, 2, 122	11	1:44.01	300,000
1993	Dehere, 2, 122	C. J. McCarron	Crary, 2, 122	Amathos, 2, 122	6	1:35.91	300,000
1992	Sea Hero, 2, 122	J. D. Bailey	Secret Odds, 2, 122	Press Card, 2, 122	10	1:34.87	300,000
1991	Tri to Watch, 2, 122	A. T. Cordero Jr.	Snappy Landing, 2, 122	Pine Bluff, 2, 122	15	1:36.61	300,000
1990	Fly So Free, 2, 122	J. A. Santos	Happy Jazz Band, 2, 122	Subordinated Debt, 2, 122	13	1:35.60	381,600
1989	Adjudicating, 2, 122	J. Vasquez	Rhythm, 2, 122	Senor Pete, 2, 122	6	1:37.60	343,220
1988	Easy Goer, 2, 122	P. Day	Is It True, 2, 122	Irish Actor, 2, 122	4	1:34.80	334,200
1987	Forty Niner, 2, 122	E. Maple	Parlay Me, 2, 122	Tejano, 2, 122	11	1:36.80	370,860
1986	Polish Navy, 2, 122	R. P. Romero	Demons Begone, 2, 122	Bet Twice, 2, 122	7	1:35.20	199,500
1985	Mogambo, 2, 122	A. T. Cordero Jr.	Groovy, 2, 122	Mr. Classic, 2, 122	5	1:37.20	194,700
1984	For Certain Doc, 2, 122	M. Zuniga	Mighty Appealing, 2, 122	Tank's Prospect, 2, 122	6	1:49.20	171,600
1983	Devil's Bag, 2, 122	E. Maple	Dr. Carter, 2, 122	Our Casey's Boy, 2, 122	12	**1:34.20**	142,200
1982	Copelan, 2, 122	J. D. Bailey	Pappa Riccio, 2, 122	El Cubanaso, 2, 122	13	1:37.80	144,000
1981	Timely Writer, 2, 122	J. Fell	†Before Dawn, 2, 119	New Discovery, 2, 122	13	1:36.40	90,150
1980	Lord Avie, 2, 122	J. Velasquez	Noble Nashua, 2, 122	Sezyou, 2, 122	9	1:37.20	85,350
1979	Joanie's Chief, 2, 122	R. Hernandez	Rockhill Native, 2, 122	Googolplex, 2, 122	8	1:38.20	81,750
1978	Spectacular Bid, 2, 122	J. Velasquez	General Assembly, 2, 122	Crested Wave, 2, 122	6	1:34.80	80,250
1977	Alydar, 2, 122	J. Velasquez	Affirmed, 2, 122	Darby Creek Road, 2, 122	6	1:36.60	80,400
1976	Seattle Slew, 2, 122	J. Cruguet	For The Moment, 2, 122	Sail to Rome, 2, 122	10	1:34.40	82,350
1975	Honest Pleasure, 2, 122	B. Baeza	Dance Spell, 2, 122	Whatsyourpleasure, 2, 122	14	1:36.40	89,625
1974	Foolish Pleasure, 2, 122	J. Vasquez	Harvard Man, 2, 122	Ramahorn, 2, 122	9	1:36.00	86,850
1973	Holding Pattern, 2, 122	M. Miceli	Green Gambados, 2, 122	Hosiery, 2, 122	10	1:36.00	55,425
	Protagonist, 2, 122	A. Santiago	Prince of Reason, 2, 122	Cannonade, 2, 122	10	1:36.00	55,425

Named after the Champagne S. (Eng-G2) in England, held at Doncaster. Sponsored by Moet & Chandon Champagne of Epernay, France 1994-'97. Held at Jerome Park 1867-'89. Held at Morris Park 1890-1904. Held at Aqueduct 1959, 1961, 1963-'67, 1984. Not held 1910-'13, 1956. 1 mile 1867-'70, 1890, 1940-'83, 1985-'93. 6 furlongs 1871-'89. 7 furlongs 1891-1904. About 7 furlongs 1905-'32. 6½ furlongs 1933-'39. 1⅛ miles 1984. 1 1/16 miles 1994-2004. Two divisions 1973. †Denotes female.

Charles Whittingham Memorial Handicap

Grade 1 in 2008. Hollywood Park, three-year-olds and up, 1¼ miles, turf. Held June 7, 2008, with a gross value of $300,000. First held in 1969. First graded in 1973. Stakes record 1:57.75 (1993 Bien Bien).

Year	Winner	Jockey	Second	Third	Strs	Time	1st Purse
2008	Artiste Royal (Ire), 7, 117	D. R. Flores	Monzante, 4, 113	Lava Man, 7, 121	7	1:59.99	$180,000
2007	After Market, 4, 118	A. O. Solis	Lava Man, 6, 124	Obrigado (Fr), 4, 118	8	1:58.77	180,000
2006	Lava Man, 5, 122	C. S. Nakatani	King's Drama (Ire), 6, 122	Red Fort (Ire), 6, 118	9	2:00.29	180,000
2005	Sweet Return (GB), 5, 123	A. O. Solis	Red Fort (Ire), 5, 117	Vangelis, 6, 118	9	2:01.35	210,000
2004	Sabiango (Ger), 6, 116	T. Baze	Bayamo (Ire), 5, 116	Just Wonder (GB), 4, 116	11	2:01.52	210,000
2003	Storming Home (GB), 5, 124	G. L. Stevens	Mister Acpen (Chi), 5, 115	Cagney (Brz), 6, 114	6	2:00.66	210,000
2002	Denon, 4, 116	G. K. Gomez	Night Patrol, 6, 114	Skipping (GB), 5, 117	9	2:01.47	210,000
2001	Bienamado, 5, 124	C. J. McCarron	Senure, 5, 117	Timboroa (GB), 5, 116	9	1:59.34	210,000
2000	White Heart (GB), 5, 117	K. Desormeaux	Self Feeder (Ire), 6, 116	Deploy Venture (GB), 4, 112	6	2:00.83	180,000
1999	River Bay, 6, 119	A. O. Solis	Majorien (GB), 5, 117	Alvo Certo (Brz), 6, 118	9	2:00.66	240,000
1998	Storm Trooper, 5, 117	K. Desormeaux	River Bay, 5, 121	Prize Giving (GB), 5, 116	7	2:03.05	240,000
1997	Rainbow Dancer (Fr), 6, 123	A. O. Solis	Sunshack (GB), 6, 118	Marlin, 4, 120	8	2:00.00	240,000
1996	Sandpit (Brz), 7, 122	C. S. Nakatani	Northern Spur (Ire), 5, 123	Awad, 6, 119	6	1:59.52	300,000
1995	Earl of Barking (Ire), 5, 115	G. F. Almeida	Sandpit (Brz), 6, 122	Savinio, 5, 117	10	1:59.78	275,000
1994	Grand Flotilla, 7, 116	G. L. Stevens	Bien Bien, 5, 122	Blues Traveller (Ire), 4, 117	8	1:59.23	275,000
1993	Bien Bien, 4, 119	C. J. McCarron	Best Pal, 5, 122	Leger Cat (Arg), 7, 116	8	**1:57.75**	275,000
1992	Quest for Fame (GB), 5, 122	G. L. Stevens	Classic Fame, 6, 120	River Traffic, 4, 114	9	1:58.99	275,000
1991	Exbourne, 5, 119	G. L. Stevens	ItsalIgreektome, 4, 123	Prized, 5, 123	6	2:00.10	275,000
1990	Steinlen (GB), 7, 124	L. A. Pincay Jr.	Hawkster, 4, 122	Santangelo (Arg), 6, 110	9	2:03.00	275,000
1989	Great Communicator, 6, 123	R. Sibille	Nasr El Arab, 4, 124	Equalize, 7, 120	9	1:59.40	275,000
1988	Political Ambition, 4, 119	E. Delahoussaye	Baba Karam (Ire), 4, 116	dh-Great Communicator, 5, 120 dh-Skip Out Front, 5, 117	7	1:58.60	165,000
1987	Rivlia, 5, 117	C. J. McCarron	Great Communicator, 4, 112	Schiller, 5, 116	6	2:24.20	165,000

Racing — Graded Stakes 287

Year	Winner	Jockey	Second	Third	Strs	Time	1st Purse
1986	**Flying Pidgeon**, 5, 120	S. B. Soto	Dahar, 5, 126	Both Ends Burning, 6, 122	6	2:27.00	$165,000
1985	**Both Ends Burning**, 5, 121	E. Delahoussaye	Dahar, 4, 123	Swoon, 7, 114	5	2:25.00	165,000
1984	**John Henry**, 9, 126	C. J. McCarron	Galant Vert (Fr), 4, 116	Load the Cannons, 4, 120	9	2:25.00	165,000
1983	**Erins Isle (Ire)**, 5, 127	L. A. Pincay Jr.	Exploded, 6, 115	Prince Spellbound, 4, 120	12	2:25.80	165,000
1982	**Exploded**, 5, 117	L. A. Pincay Jr.	Lemhi Gold, 4, 123	The Bart, 6, 125	6	2:25.20	165,000
1981	**John Henry**, 6, 130	L. A. Pincay Jr.	Caterman (NZ), 5, 122	Galaxy Libra (Ire), 5, 118	7	2:27.80	110,000
1980	**John Henry**, 5, 128	D. G. McHargue	Balzac, 5, 120	Go West Young Man, 5, 117	10	2:25.40	137,500
1979	**Johnny's Image**, 4, 123	S. Hawley	Star Spangled, 5, 122	Dom Alaric (Fr), 5, 119	11	2:25.20	137,500
1978	**Exceller**, 5, 127	W. Shoemaker	Bowl Game, 4, 123	Noble Dancer (GB), 6, 126	12	2:25.80	110,000
1977	**Vigors**, 4, 117	J. Lambert	Caucasus, 5, 126	Anne's Pretender, 5, 122	12	2:26.80	120,000
1976	**†Dahlia**, 6, 117	W. Shoemaker	Caucasus, 4, 119	Pass the Glass, 5, 121	12	2:26.80	120,000
1975	***Barclay Joy**, 5, 113	A. L. Diaz	Captain Cee Jay, 5, 117	Chief Hawk Ear, 7, 119	10	2:27.00	75,000
1974	**Court Ruling**, 4, 117	W. Mahorney	Outdoors, 5, 113	London Company, 4, 123	10	2:27.00	75,000
1973	**Life Cycle**, 4, 115	L. A. Pincay Jr.	Wing Out, 5, 118	*Cougar II, 7, 130	10	2:25.60	75,000

Named for Racing Hall of Fame trainer Charles Whittingham (1913-'99). Formerly sponsored by Ford Motor Co. of Detroit, Michigan 1971. Hollywood Park Invitational Turf H. 1969-'70, 1972. Ford Pinto Invitational Turf H. 1971. Hollywood Invitational H. 1973-'88. Hollywood Turf H. 1989-'98. Charles Whittingham H. 1999-2002. 1½ miles 1969-'87. Dead heat for third 1988. Equaled course record 1973. Course record 1993. †Denotes female.

Chicago Handicap

Grade 3 in 2008. Arlington Park, three-year-olds and up, fillies and mares, 7 furlongs, all weather. Held June 16, 2007, with a gross value of $175,000. First held in 1986. First graded in 1992. Stakes record 1:21.24 (1992 Withallprobability).

Year	Winner	Jockey	Second	Third	Strs	Time	1st Purse
2007	**Lady Belsara**, 4, 116	E. T. Baird	Trendy Lady, 4, 116	Dimple Pinch, 5, 115	10	1:23.10	$102,000
2006	**Ebony Breeze**, 6, 115	J. Jacinto	Pentelicus Dance (Ecu), 5, 111	Annika Lass, 5, 119	7	1:22.02	105,000
2005	**Happy Ticket**, 4, 116	E. Razo Jr.	Savorthetime, 6, 117	Injustice, 4, 116	7	1:22.54	105,000
2004	**My Trusty Cat**, 4, 116	R. R. Douglas	Our Josephina, 4, 112	Smoke Chaser, 5, 116	5	1:23.54	105,000
2003	**For Rubies**, 4, 116	C. Perret	Raging Fever, 5, 120	Oglala Sue, 5, 113	8	1:24.21	69,450
2002	**Mandy's Gold**, 4, 116	R. R. Douglas	Cat and the Hat, 4, 116	Caressing, 4, 115	6	1:22.86	98,664
2001	**Trip**, 4, 114	C. Perret	Hidden Assets, 4, 115	Rose of Zollern (Ire), 5, 115	7	1:22.18	99,312
2000	**Saoirse**, 4, 118	D. Clark	The Happy Hopper, 4, 115	Dif a Dot, 5, 114	7	1:23.09	102,195
1997	**J J'sdream**, 4, 118	M. Guidry	Capote Belle, 4, 120	Eseni, 4, 117	7	1:22.20	101,625
1996	**Bunbeg**, 4, 114	M. Walls	Morris Code, 4, 118	Rhapsodic, 5, 114	8	1:23.86	102,990
1995	**Low Key Affair**, 4, 113	A. T. Gryder	Morning Meadow, 5, 115	Marina Park (GB), 5, 120	9	1:24.64	93,840
1994	**Minidar**, 4, 116	V. Belvoir	Spinning Round, 5, 118	Traverse City, 4, 113	10	1:22.49	93,960
1993	**Meafara**, 4, 121	J. L. Diaz	Shared Interest, 5, 115	Real Display, 4, 114	11	1:22.12	93,870
1992	**Withallprobability**, 4, 115	G. K. Gomez	Fit for a Queen, 6, 120	Madam Bear, 4, 114	9	**1:21.24**	93,450
1991	**Safely Kept**, 5, 126	C. Perret	Nurse Dopey, 4, 118	Token Dance, 4, 114	7	1:23.05	93,060
1990	**Fit for a Queen**, 4, 112	P. Day	Channel Three, 4, 113	Sexy Slew, 4, 113	12	1:23.00	94,650
1989	**Rose's Record**, 5, 114	J. Velasquez	Sunshine Always, 5, 114	‡Daloma (Fr), 5, 116	7	1:24.60	93,120
1987	**Lazer Show**, 4, 123	P. Day	Very Subtle, 3, 120	Moonbeam McQueen, 4, 111	6	1:22.80	46,275
1986	**Lazer Show**, 3, 115	P. Day	Balladry, 4, 115	Gene's Lady, 5, 122	8	1:21.40	93,360

Named for the city of Chicago, near suburban Arlington Heights, location of Arlington Park. Chicago Budweiser Breeders' Cup H. 1986-'91, 1993-'95. Chicago Breeders' Cup H. 1992, 1996-2006. Not held 1988, 1998-'99. Dirt 1986-2006. ‡Josette finished third, DQ to fourth, 1989.

Chilukki Stakes

Grade 2 in 2008. Churchill Downs, three-year-olds and up, fillies and mares, 1 mile, dirt. Held November 3, 2007, with a gross value of $221,000. First held in 1986. First graded in 1988. Stakes record 1:33.57 (2000 Chilukki).

Year	Winner	Jockey	Second	Third	Strs	Time	1st Purse
2007	**Rolling Sea**, 4, 122	R. Albarado	High Heels, 3, 120	My Chickadee, 4, 118	8	1:36.02	$132,910
2006	**Sangrita**, 3, 116	E. S. Prado	Joint Effort, 3, 118	Indian Flare, 4, 118	9	1:36.65	101,335
2005	**Bending Strings**, 4, 117	R. Albarado	Prospective Saint, 4, 121	Miss Fortunate, 5, 121	11	1:35.19	104,997
2004	**Halory Leigh**, 4, 115	C. Perret	Lady Tak, 4, 113	Susan's Angel, 3, 115	12	1:35.05	142,848
2003	**Lead Story**, 4, 114	C. H. Borel	Awesome Humor, 3, 118	Born to Dance, 4, 113	10	1:36.55	139,748
2002	**Softly**, 4, 114	J. K. Court	Bare Necessities, 3, 115	Victory Ride, 4, 118	9	1:35.07	138,632
2001	**Nasty Storm**, 3, 115	P. Day	Forest Secrets, 5, 113	Trip, 4, 117	8	1:35.30	137,764
2000	**Chilukki**, 3, 116	G. L. Stevens	Reciclada (Chi), 5, 113	Rose of Zollern (Ire), 4, 114	10	**1:33.57**	154,008
1999	**Let**, 4, 113	C. H. Borel	Roza Robata, 4, 114	Dif a Dot, 4, 115	9	1:34.41	138,880
1998	**Dream Scheme**, 5, 113	C. H. Borel	Sister Act, 3, 111	Beautiful Pleasure, 3, 110	9	1:34.41	139,624
1997	**Feasibility Study**, 5, 120	R. Albarado	J J'sdream, 4, 113	Mama's Pro, 4, 115	14	1:37.61	146,196
1996	**Fast Catch**, 4, 109	W. Martinez	Serena's Song, 4, 125	Bedroom Blues, 5, 112	9	1:36.55	139,624
1995	**Lakeway**, 4, 122	K. Desormeaux	Alcovy, 5, 113	Laura's Pistolette, 4, 116	8	1:35.94	137,280
1994	**Educated Risk**, 4, 118	P. Day	Pennyhill Park, 4, 117	Alcovy, 4, 116	8	1:35.74	138,125
1993	**Miss Indy Anna**, 3, 111	P. Day	One Dreamer, 5, 115	Deputation, 4, 119	13	1:37.72	141,960
1992	**Wilderness Song**, 4, 120	C. Perret	Miss Jealski, 3, 110	Dance Colony, 5, 113	11	1:36.22	102,440
1991	**Fit for a Queen**, 5, 121	R. D. Lopez	Wilderness Song, 3, 118	Summer Matinee, 4, 113	10	1:38.60	100,555
1990	**Oh My Jessica Pie**, 3, 114	M. A. Gonzalez	Seaside Attraction, 3, 115	Sweet Nostalgia, 3, 111	10	1:36.80	102,993
1989	**Classic Value**, 3, 114	P. Day	Coastal Connection, 4, 115	Rose's Record, 5, 117	12	1:35.40	102,960
1988	**Darien Miss**, 3, 116	P. A. Johnson	Sheena Native, 4, 117	Coastal Connection, 3, 112	13	1:36.80	102,928

Year	Winner	Jockey	Second	Third	Strs	Time	1st Purse
1987	Bound, 3, 113	E. Maple	Miss Bid, 4, 115	Intently, 4, 114	14	1:37.00	$103,253
1986	Lazer Show, 3, 120	C. R. Woods Jr.	Balladry, 4, 116	Mrs. Revere, 5, 120	11	1:22.60	102,473

Named for Stonerside Stable's 1999 champion two-year-old filly and 2000 Churchill Downs Distaff H. (G2) winner Chilukki (f. by Cherokee Run). Grade 3 1988-'91. Churchill Downs Budweiser Breeders' Cup H. 1986-'91, 1993-'95. Churchill Downs Breeders' Cup H. 1992. Churchill Downs Distaff H. 1996-2004. 7 furlongs 1986. Track record 2000.

Churchill Distaff Turf Mile Stakes

Grade 3 in 2008. Churchill Downs, three-year-olds and up, fillies and mares, 1 mile, turf. Held May 3, 2008, with a gross value of $169,050. First held in 1983. First graded in 1997. Stakes record 1:33.96 (2003 Heat Haze [GB]).

Year	Winner	Jockey	Second	Third	Strs	Time	1st Purse
2008	Bayou's Lassie, 5, 118	E. S. Prado	Dreaming of Anna, 4, 124	Ventura, 4, 118	8	1:37.70	$101,671
2007	Take the Ribbon, 4, 118	R. Bejarano	Quite a Bride, 4, 122	Rich Fantasy, 4, 118	5	1:36.89	103,138
2006	Mirabilis, 4, 122	P. A. Valenzuela	Special Grayce, 4, 118	More Than Promised, 4, 122	10	1:35.93	67,794
2005	Miss Terrible (Arg), 6, 117	A. O. Solis	Sand Springs, 5, 123	Shaconage, 5, 121	7	1:35.89	69,564
2004	Shaconage, 4, 121	B. Blanc	Etoile Montante, 4, 123	Chance Dance, 4, 117	10	1:36.10	70,246
2003	Heat Haze (GB), 4, 123	J. Valdivia Jr.	Quick Tip, 5, 123	Sentimental Value, 4, 121	11	1:33.96	72,540
2002	Stylish, 4, 116	J. D. Bailey	La Recherche, 4, 123	Dianehill (Ire), 6, 123	10	1:35.72	71,424
2001	Iftiraas (GB), 4, 118	J. D. Bailey	Gino's Spirits (GB), 5, 118	Solvig, 4, 120	7	1:36.69	70,432
2000	Don't Be Silly, 5, 116	J. F. Chavez	Really Polish, 5, 114	Pricearose, 4, 116	8	1:34.78	71,548
1999	Shires Ende, 4, 118	J. R. Velazquez	Ashford Castle, 5, 120	Sophie My Love, 4, 123	9	1:35.43	74,152
1998	Witchful Thinking, 4, 120	S. J. Sellers	Colcon, 5, 123	Swearingen, 4, 123	10	1:37.23	74,896
1997	B. A. Valentine, 4, 114	S. J. Sellers	Striesen, 5, 116	Romy, 6, 123	10	1:36.98	71,796
1996	Apolda, 5, 123	J. D. Bailey	Country Cat, 4, 123	Bold Ruritana, 6, 123	8	1:36.50	55,283
1995	Bold Ruritana, 5, 123	P. Day	Icy Warning, 5, 116	Rapunzel Runz, 4, 114	10	1:34.64	56,111
1994	Weekend Madness (Ire), 4, 123	C. R. Woods Jr.	Russian Bride, 4, 120	Suspect Terrain, 5, 114	9	1:38.58	55,770
1993	Lady Blessington (Fr), 5, 120	P. Day	You'd Be Surprised, 4, 118	Wassifa (GB), 5, 116	9	1:34.96	37,570
1992	Quilma (Chi), 5, 120	E. Delahoussaye	Behaving Dancer, 5, 123	Radiant Ring, 4, 123	10	1:35.36	38,285
1991	Foresta, 5, 123	A. T. Cordero Jr.	Coolawin, 5, 118	Primetime North, 4, 120	10	1:36.30	38,870
1990	Foresta, 4, 114	A. T. Cordero Jr.	Saros Brig, 6, 123	Bearly Cooking, 7, 114	5	1:37.20	36,205
1989	Classic Account, 4, 116	P. Day	Fast Forward, 5, 116	R. B. McCurry, 4, 112	4	1:51.20	35,132
1988	Buoy, 3, 123	P. Day	Frosty the Snowman, 3, 115	Cougarized, 3, 123	7	1:43.40	36,725
1987	Fast Forward, 3, 115	P. Day	Sooner Showers, 3, 115	Homebuilder, 3, 115	5	1:43.20	36,043
1983	‡Le Cou Cou, 3, 121	D. L. Howard	High Honors, 3, 121	Common Sense, 3, 121	10	1:49.60	34,125

Formerly named for Churchill Downs's most recognized feature (and corporate logo), the twin spires atop its grandstand. Formerly sponsored by CompUSA Management Co. of Dallas 2005. Formerly sponsored by Argent Mortgage Co., of Orange, California 2004. Formerly sponsored by CITGO Petroleum Corp. of Tulsa, Oklahoma 2001-'03. Formerly sponsored by Ashland Inc. of Covington, Kentucky 1999. Formerly sponsored by AEGON Group N.V. of The Hague, the Netherlands 1998. Formerly sponsored by Providian Corp. of Louisville 1995-'97. Formerly sponsored by Capital Holding Corp. (predecessor of Providian Corp.) of Louisville 1988-'94. Twin Spires S. 1983-'87. Capital Holding Twin Spires S. 1988. Capital Holding Twin Spires H. 1989. Capital Holding Mile S. 1990-'91, 1993-'94. Capital Holding S. 1992. Providian Mile S. 1995-'97. Aegon Mile S. 1998. Ashland Mile S. 1999. Churchill Downs Distaff Turf Mile S. 2000. CITGO Distaff Turf Mile S. 2001-'03. Argent Mortgage Distaff Turf Mile S. 2004. CompUSA Turf Mile S. 2005. Not held 1984-'86. 1 1/8 miles 1983, 1989. 1 1/16 miles 1987-'88. Dirt 1983-'89. Three-year-olds 1983-'88. Both sexes 1983-'88. ‡High Honors finished first, DQ to second, 1983. Equaled course record 1992. Course record 1993.

Churchill Downs Stakes

Grade 2 in 2008. Churchill Downs, four-year-olds and up, 7 furlongs, dirt. Held May 3, 2008, with a gross value of $282,000. First held in 1911. First graded in 1992. Stakes record 1:20.50 (2001 Alannan).

Year	Winner	Jockey	Second	Third	Strs	Time	1st Purse
2008	Elite Squadron, 4, 118	J. R. Velazquez	Noonmark, 5, 120	Hewitts, 4, 118	8	1:21.53	$169,595
2007	Saint Anddan, 5, 120	R. Bejarano	Ah Day, 4, 118	Will He Shine, 5, 118	6	1:22.31	170,485
2006	Trickey Trevor, 7, 117	R. A. Baze	With Distinction, 5, 116	Level Playingfield, 5, 113	10	1:21.68	134,881
2005	Battle Won, 5, 115	R. A. Dominguez	Level Playingfield, 4, 112	Pomeroy, 4, 118	11	1:20.56	143,220
2004	Speightstown, 6, 115	J. R. Velazquez	McCann's Mojave, 4, 117	Publication, 5, 116	7	1:21.38	137,516
2003	Aldebaran, 5, 120	J. D. Bailey	Pass Rush, 4, 117	Cappuchino, 4, 115	12	1:21.80	144,956
2002	‡D'wildcat, 4, 115	K. Desormeaux	Snow Ridge, 4, 119	Binthebest, 5, 113	10	1:22.37	106,299
2001	Alannan, 4, 118	E. S. Prado	Bonapaw, 5, 116	Exchange Rate, 4, 113	10	1:20.50	111,321
2000	Straight Man, 4, 112	J. F. Chavez	Mula Gula, 4, 114	Patience Game, 4, 114	7	1:21.53	104,904
1999	Rock and Roll, 4, 112	P. Day	Liberty Gold, 5, 114	Run Johnny, 7, 113	7	1:22.81	103,137
1998	Distorted Humor, 5, 119	G. L. Stevens	Gold Land, 7, 116	El Amante, 5, 113	7	1:21.18	103,509
1997	Diligence, 4, 114	M. E. Smith	Victor Cooley, 4, 115	Criollito (Arg), 6, 115	9	1:22.37	70,432
1996	Criollito (Arg), 5, 115	C. J. McCarron	Forty Won, 5, 115	Powis Castle, 5, 114	9	1:21.01	74,620
1995	Goldseeker Bud, 4, 109	W. Martinez	Level Sands, 4, 112	Go for Gin, 4, 115	11	1:21.75	75,205
1994	Honor the Hero, 6, 115	G. K. Gomez	Memo (Chi), 7, 121	Saratoga Gambler, 6, 116	6	1:23.05	71,370
1993	Callide Valley, 5, 116	G. L. Stevens	Furiously, 4, 117	Ojai, 4, 110	11	1:22.01	56,063
1992	Pleasant Tap, 5, 120	E. Delahoussaye	Take Me Out, 4, 120	Cantrell Road, 6, 113	9	1:22.32	55,526
1991	Thirty Six Red, 4, 117	J. D. Bailey	Private School, 4, 113	Bratt's Choice, 4, 115	7	1:22.15	37,635
1990	Beau Genius, 4, 119	R. D. Lopez	Traskwood, 4, 113	Learn by Heart, 5, 115	12	1:23.20	37,830
1989	Dancing Spree, 4, 116	P. Day	Carborundum, 5, 117	Broadway Chief, 4, 115	13	1:24.00	38,253
1988	Conquer, 4, 117	G. L. Stevens	Homebuilder, 4, 117	Carborundum, 4, 117	9	1:23.20	36,823
1987	Sovereign's Ace, 5, 117	L. A. Pincay Jr.	Sun Master, 6, 123	Savings, 4, 114	5	1:22.00	21,236
1986	Sovereign's Ace, 4, 117	P. Rubbicco	Artichoke, 5, 120	Clever Wake, 4, 116	9	1:22.60	21,957

Racing — Graded Stakes

Year	Winner	Jockey	Second	Third	Strs	Time	1st Purse
1985	Rapid Gray, 6, 120	P. Day	Roxbury Park, 4, 114	Steel Robbing, 5, 115	7	1:24.00	$24,391
	Bayou Hebert, 4, 111	J. McKnight	Harry 'n Bill, 5, 117	Never Company, 5, 117	6	1:23.40	24,196
1984	Habitonia, 4, 118	P. Day	Roman Jamboree, 4, 114	Euathlos, 4, 113	5	1:23.00	20,914
1983	Shot n' Missed, 6, 118	L. Moyers	Vodika Collins, 5, 112	Gallant Gentleman, 4, 115	6	1:23.60	21,239
1982	Top Avenger, 4, 114	R. P. Romero	It's a Rerun, 6, 110	Shot n' Missed, 5, 117	9	1:23.00	21,661
	Bayou Black, 6, 119	R. D. Ardoin	Vodika Collins, 4, 118	Prince Crimson, 5, 116	6	1:22.80	23,433
1981	Dreadnought, 4, 112	J. C. Espinoza	Tiger Lure, 7, 113	Turbulence, 5, 119	12	1:23.60	19,874
1980	Dr. Riddick, 6, 114	D. Brumfield	Cregan's Cap, 5, 112	Silent Dignity, 4, 119	8	1:23.20	17,615
1979	Trimlea, 5, 113	J. Velasquez	Dr. Riddick, 5, 119	Cabrini Green, 4, 118	8	1:24.60	19,240
1978	To the Quick, 4, 116	J. Amy	It's Freezing, 6, 120	Prince Majestic, 4, 121	9	1:25.00	14,511
1977	It's Freezing, 5, 120	E. Delahoussaye	Buddy Larosa, 4, 112	Silver Hope, 6, 119	8	1:23.40	14,528
1976	Yamanin, 4, 115	G. Patterson	It's Freezing, 4, 117	Easter Island, 4, 115	9	1:23.80	14,495
1975	Navajo, 5, 123	J. Nichols	Silver Hope, 4, 116	Silver Badge, 4, 110	10	1:24.40	14,804
1974	Barbizon Streak, 6, 115	R. Wilson	Grocery List, 5, 117	Jim's Alibhi, 7, 114	11	1:25.40	15,015
1973	Code of Honor, 5, 115	E. Fires	Knight Counter, 5, 122	Hook It Up, 5, 115	10	1:23.00	15,096

Formerly sponsored by W. S. Farish's Lane's End, located near Versailles, Kentucky 2001. Formerly sponsored by Winner Communications, a telecommunications company involved in televised horse racing 2000. Grade 3 1992-'97. Churchill Downs H. 1911-'13, 1938-'82, 1988-'99, 2002-'06. Winnercomm H. 2000. Lane's End Churchill Downs H. 2001. Not held 1914-'37. 1 1/8 miles 1911-'13. Three-year-olds and up 1911-'13, 1938-'43, 1947-'88. Two divisions 1982, '85. ‡Snow Ridge finished first, DQ to second, 2002. Track record 1998, 2001.

Cicada Stakes

Grade 3 in 2008. Aqueduct, three-year-olds, fillies, 6 furlongs, dirt. Held March 15, 2008, with a gross value of $106,000. First held in 1975. First graded in 1996. Stakes record 1:09.66 (2006 Wild Gams).

Year	Winner	Jockey	Second	Third	Strs	Time	1st Purse
2008	Carolyn's Cat, 3, 118	A. Garcia	Ready for Fortune, 3, 118	Dill Or No Dill, 3, 120	5	1:10.16	$64,800
2007	Control System, 3, 116	J. Pimentel	Golden Dreamer, 3, 122	Special Dream, 3, 122	7	1:10.43	65,760
2006	Wild Gams, 3, 118	E. Coa	Celestial Legend, 3, 122	Oprah Winney, 3, 116	7	1:09.66	66,360
2005	Dixie Talking, 3, 116	A. Garcia	Acey Deucey, 3, 122	Alfonsina, 3, 116	8	1:23.04	65,880
2004	Bohemian Lady, 3, 116	E. S. Prado	Whoopi Cat, 3, 116	Baldomera, 3, 122	6	1:23.22	65,460
2003	Cyber Secret, 3, 122	S. Bridgmohan	Roar Emotion, 3, 116	Boxer Girl, 3, 118	6	1:22.55	64,980
2002	Proper Gamble, 3, 122	J. Castellano	Short Note, 3, 118	Forest Heiress, 3, 120	6	1:23.32	65,160
2001	Xtra Heat, 3, 122	R. Wilson	Erin Moor, 3, 116	Chasm, 3, 116	4	1:23.39	63,770
2000	Finder's Fee, 3, 118	J. D. Bailey	Apollo Cat, 3, 116	Southern Sandra, 3, 121	6	1:23.07	65,100
1999	Potomac Bend, 3, 118	M. T. Johnston	Carleaville, 3, 114	Jane, 3, 112	7	1:23.18	48,915
1998	Jersey Girl, 3, 116	R. Migliore	Vienna Blues, 3, 114	Babai Danzig, 3, 116	9	1:22.95	50,175
1997	Vegas Prospector, 3, 116	M. J. McCarthy	Ormsby County, 3, 112	Valid Affect, 3, 118	6	1:26.23	48,375
1996	J J'sdream, 3, 121	G. Boulanger	Dahl, 3, 114	Mystic Rhythms, 3, 118	9	1:23.44	50,310
1995	Lucky Lavender Gal, 3, 114	R. G. Davis	Stormy Blues, 3, 118	Dancin Renee, 3, 116	7	1:23.45	48,870
1994	Our Royal Blue, 3, 114	R. Wilson	Sovereign Kitty, 3, 118	Princess Joanne, 3, 113	5	1:22.38	48,375
1993	Personal Bid, 3, 118	J. A. Santos	Sheila's Revenge, 3, 118	In Excelcis Deo, 3, 116	4	1:23.52	31,800
1988	Feel the Beat, 3, 114	J. A. Santos	Bold Lady Anne, 3, 121	Dear Dusty, 3, 114	6	1:11.00	41,220
1983	May Day Eighty, 4, 117	J. Fell	Viva Sec, 5, 117	Clever Guest, 4, 117	9	1:42.80	26,430
1982	Bold Ribbons, 3, 116	A. T. Cordero Jr.	Cupecoy's Joy, 3, 121	Adept, 3, 114	11	1:11.00	34,980
1981	In True Form, 3, 114	A. Santiago	Wading Power, 3, 114	Hawkeye Express, 3, 114	12	1:12.80	34,800
1980	The Wheel Turns, 3, 114	M. Venezia	Darlin Momma, 3, 121	Remote Ruler, 3, 118	8	1:11.20	33,180
1979	Spanish Fake, 3, 114	J. Amy	Shirley the Queen, 3, 114	Quadrangles Plum, 3, 114	11	1:13.20	32,790
1978	New Rinkle, 3, 114	R. Hernandez	Star Gala, 3, 114	Idmon, 3, 114	6	1:13.00	25,440
1977	Ring O'Bells, 3, 118	A. T. Cordero Jr.	Shufleur, 3, 114	Maria's Baby, 3, 116	5	1:10.80	21,855
1976	Tough Elsie, 3, 116	J. Imparato	Light Frost, 3, 114	Quintas Vicki, 3, 118	13	1:10.20	23,610
1975	Cast the Die, 2, 116	R. Turcotte	Artfully, 2, 116	Veroom Maid, 2, 116	9	1:10.40	27,240

Named for Meadow Stable's Racing Hall of Fame member and '62 Beldame H. winner Cicada (1959 f. by Bryan G.). Held at Belmont Park 1983, '93. Not held 1984-'87, 1989-'92. 1 1/16 miles 1983. 7 furlongs 1993-2005. Two-year-olds 1975. Three-year-olds and up 1983. Fillies and mares 1983.

Cigar Mile Handicap — See Hill 'n' Dale Cigar Mile Handicap

Cinema Handicap

Grade 3 in 2008. Hollywood Park, three-year-olds, 1 1/8 miles, turf. Held June 23, 2007, with a gross value of $113,500. First held in 1946. First graded in 1973. Stakes record 1:46.56 (1994 Unfinished Symph).

Year	Winner	Jockey	Second	Third	Strs	Time	1st Purse
2007	Worldly (GB), 3, 120	V. Espinoza	Golden Balls (Ire), 3, 119	Tycoon Doby, 3, 116	5	1:47.40	$63,900
2006	Genre (GB), 3, 118	M. A. Pedroza	Niagara Causeway, 3, 114	Film Fortune, 3, 113	8	1:47.73	65,520
2005	Willow O Wisp, 3, 119	G. K. Gomez	Osidy, 3, 114	Honorable Coach, 3, 113	5	1:48.59	95,670
2004	Greek Sun, 3, 120	A. O. Solis	Laura's Lucky Boy, 3, 122	Whilly (Ire), 3, 117	7	1:48.40	97,470
2003	Just Wonder (GB), 3, 117	K. Desormeaux	Bis Repetitas, 3, 115	Slew City Citadel, 3, 115	8	1:47.41	98,730
2002	Inesperado (Fr), 3, 116	K. Desormeaux	Regiment, 3, 122	Johar, 3, 118	7	1:47.63	97,560
2001	Sligo Bay (Ire), 3, 118	L. A. Pincay Jr.	Learing At Kathy, 3, 117	Marine (GB), 3, 119	7	1:48.40	65,160
2000	David Copperfield, 3, 116	V. Espinoza	Duke of Green (GB), 3, 117	Silver Axe, 3, 119	7	1:47.73	64,560
1999	Fighting Falcon, 3, 119	B. Blanc	Eagleton, 3, 120	Major Hero, 3, 113	8	1:48.06	66,000
1998	Commitisize, 3, 118	D. R. Flores	Killer Image, 3, 115	Lord Smith (GB), 3, 116	7	1:48.03	65,220
1997	Worldly Ways (GB), 3, 115	C. S. Nakatani	P. T. Indy, 3, 118	Brave Act (GB), 3, 120	9	1:48.43	66,180

Year	Winner	Jockey	Second	Third	Strs	Time	1st Purse
1996	Let Bob Do It, 3, 120	K. Desormeaux	Dr. Sardonica, 3, 115	Winter Quarters, 3, 115	8	1:47.58	$81,660
1995	Via Lombardia (Ire), 3, 119	E. Delahoussaye	Bryntirion, 3, 113	Oncefortheroad, 3, 115	9	1:47.22	65,400
1994	Unfinished Symph, 3, 118	G. Baze	Vaudeville, 3, 115	Fumo Di Londra (Ire), 3, 121	7	1:46.56	63,100
1993	Earl of Barking (Ire), 3, 121	C. J. McCarron	Manny's Prospect, 3, 115	Minks Law, 3, 113	5	1:47.45	61,100
1992	Bien Bien, 3, 113	C. J. McCarron	Fax News, 3, 114	Prospect for Four, 3, 112	8	1:47.10	65,600
1991	Character (GB), 3, 114	G. L. Stevens	River Traffic, 3, 117	Kalgrey (Fr), 3, 114	6	1:47.10	62,600
1990	Jovial (GB), 3, 115	G. L. Stevens	Mehmetori, 3, 113	Itsallgreektome, 3, 117	10	1:47.80	67,400
1989	‡Raise a Stanza, 3, 114	G. L. Stevens	Exemplary Leader, 3, 116	Notorious Pleasure, 3, 120	6	1:47.80	62,100
1988	Peace, 3, 117	A. O. Solis	Blade of the Ball, 3, 113	Roberto's Dancer, 3, 115	8	1:46.80	78,400
1987	Something Lucky, 3, 119	L. A. Pincay Jr.	The Medic, 3, 117	Savona Tower, 3, 115	6	1:46.80	62,400
1986	Manila, 3, 117	F. Toro	Vernon Castle, 3, 120	Full of Stars, 3, 115	10	1:47.00	80,400
1985	Don't Say Halo, 3, 116	D. G. McHargue	Derby Dawning, 3, 115	Emperdori, 3, 115	9	1:47.60	65,800
1984	Prince True, 3, 117	P. A. Valenzuela	M. Double M., 3, 116	Majestic Shore, 3, 115	7	1:40.20	63,700
1983	Baron O'Dublin, 3, 115	E. Delahoussaye	Tanks Brigade, 3, 119	Re Ack, 3, 116	9	1:43.00	66,300
1982	Give Me Strength, 3, 121	J. Samyn	Journey At Sea, 3, 122	Bargain Balcony, 3, 118	8	1:40.60	64,600
1981	Minnesota Chief, 3, 119	C. J. McCarron	Stancharry, 3, 117	Splendid Spruce, 3, 125	12	1:40.60	69,900
1980	First Albert, 3, 113	F. Mena	Big Doug, 3, 115	Kenderboun, 3, 117	12	1:48.00	68,800
1979	Beau's Eagle, 3, 121	S. Hawley	Ibacache (Chi), 3, 122	Paint King, 3, 113	8	1:47.00	64,500
1978	Kamehameha, 3, 120	T. M. Chapman	El Fantastico, 3, 114	Singular, 3, 118	12	1:47.40	102,800
1977	Bad 'n Big, 3, 121	L. A. Pincay Jr.	Iron Constitution, 3, 124	Minnesota Gus, 3, 112	8	1:48.00	96,450
1976	Majestic Light, 3, 121	S. Hawley	L'Heureux, 3, 120	*Bynoderm, 3, 116	10	1:48.20	67,200
1975	Terete, 3, 113	W. Shoemaker	Larrikin, 3, 125	Dusty County, 3, 117	6	1:48.60	46,400
1973	*Amen II, 3, 115	E. Belmonte	Kirrary, 3, 114	†Card Table, 3, 110	12	1:49.00	52,350

Named for Los Angeles's best-known industry. Grade 2 1973-'93. Cinema Breeders' Cup H. 2002-'07. Held at Santa Anita Park 1949. Not held 1974. 1 1/16 miles 1946-'49, 1951-'55, 1981-'84. 1 mile 1950. Dirt 1946-'67. ‡Notorious Pleasure finished first, DQ to third, 1989. †Denotes female.

Citation Handicap

Grade 1 in 2008. Hollywood Park, three-year-olds and up, 1 1/16 miles, turf. Held November 23, 2007, with a gross value of $400,000. First held in 1977. First graded in 1979. Stakes record 1:39.67 (2006 Ashkal Way [Ire]).

Year	Winner	Jockey	Second	Third	Strs	Time	1st Purse
2007	Lang Field, 4, 115	J. K. Court	Zann, 4, 115	Proudinho (Ger), 4, 114	9	1:39.72	$240,000
2006	Ashkal Way (Ire), 4, 119	G. K. Gomez	Hendrix, 5, 116	Three Valleys, 5, 117	13	1:39.67	240,000
2004	Leroidesanimaux (Brz), 4, 117	J. K. Court	A to the Z, 4, 115	Three Valleys, 3, 115	10	1:41.36	240,000
2003	Redattore (Brz), 8, 120	J. A. Krone	Irish Warrior, 5, 117	Mister Acpen (Chi), 5, 116	6	1:40.74	240,000
2002	Good Journey, 6, 123	P. Day	Seinne (Chi), 5, 115	White Heart (GB), 7, 115	10	1:41.45	300,000
2001	Good Journey, 5, 115	C. J. McCarron	Decarchy, 4, 117	Irish Prize, 5, 122	8	1:44.30	300,000
2000	Charge d'Affaires (GB), 5, 116	J. A. Santos	Ladies Din, 5, 122	Native Desert, 7, 116	10	1:40.30	300,000
1999	Brave Act (GB), 5, 119	A. O. Solis	Native Desert, 6, 116	Bouccaneer (Fr), 4, 119	11	1:39.69	300,000
1998	Military, 4, 118	G. K. Gomez	Mr Lightfoot (Ire), 4, 117	Worldly Ways (GB), 4, 114	8	1:50.58	180,000
1997	Geri, 5, 121	J. D. Bailey	Mufattish, 4, 116	Martiniquais (Ire), 4, 116	6	1:48.35	180,000
1996	Gentlemen (Arg), 4, 119	G. L. Stevens	Smooth Runner, 5, 115	Via Lombardia (Ire), 4, 116	7	1:45.55	180,000
1995	Fastness (Ire), 5, 120	G. L. Stevens	Earl of Barking (Ire), 5, 116	Silver Wizard, 5, 117	7	1:44.78	165,000
1994	Southern Wish, 5, 115	C. S. Nakatani	Square Cut, 5, 114	Jeune Homme, 4, 117	7	2:00.20	137,500
1993	Jeune Homme, 3, 114	T. Jarnet	Paradise Creek, 4, 120	Johann Quatz (Fr), 4, 120	8	1:45.84	137,500
1992	Leger Cat (Arg), 6, 114	C. S. Nakatani	†Trishyde, 3, 111	Luthier Enchanteur, 4, 117	8	1:46.48	137,500
1991	Notorious Pleasure, 5, 118	L. A. Pincay Jr.	Somethingdifferent, 4, 114	Classic Fame, 5, 118	8	1:45.78	102,600
	Fly Till Dawn, 5, 119	L. A. Pincay Jr.	Best Pal, 3, 119	Wolf (Chi), 4, 119		1:45.86	102,600
1990	Colway Rally (GB), 6, 114	C. A. Black	Exclusive Partner, 8, 117	The Medic, 6, 116	5	1:47.80	62,300
1989	Fair Judgment, 5, 117	E. Delahoussaye	Quiet Boy, 4, 113	Skip Out Front, 7, 117	6	1:50.00	63,300
1988	Forlitano (Arg), 7, 118	P. A. Valenzuela	Precisionist, 7, 121	Skip Out Front, 6, 117	11	1:46.60	69,200
1987	Forlitano (Arg), 6, 120	P. A. Valenzuela	Conquering Hero, 4, 115	Ifrad, 5, 115	12	1:47.40	71,500
1986	Al Mamoon, 5, 122	G. L. Stevens	Silveyville, 8, 118	Will Dancer (Fr), 4, 115	8	1:48.00	123,700
1985	Zoffany, 5, 115	E. Delahoussaye	Lord At War (Arg), 5, 125	Foscarini (Ire), 4, 115	9	1:44.80	69,100
1984	Lord At War (Arg), 4, 117	W. Shoemaker	Executive Pride (Ire), 3, 116	Prairie Breaker, 4, 116	8	1:50.60	68,300
1983	Beldale Lustre, 4, 113	C. J. McCarron	The Hague, 4, 115	Sir Pele, 4, 114	10	1:49.40	53,000
	Pewter Grey, 4, 115	R. Sibille	Belmont Bay (Ire), 6, 119	Lucence, 4, 115	10	1:49.60	53,500
1982	Caterman (NZ), 6, 121	C. J. McCarron	Cajun Prince, 5, 118	Island Whirl, 4, 123	5	1:41.00	46,700
1981	Tahitian King (Ire), 5, 120	W. Shoemaker	King Go Go, 6, 115	Cajun Prince, 4, 113	11	1:48.80	136,000
1980	Caro Bambino (Ire), 5, 118	P. A. Valenzuela	Life's Hope, 7, 116	Island Sultan, 5, 111	6	1:33.20	36,950
1979	Text, 5, 122	W. Shoemaker	Farnesio (Arg), 5, 117	Bad 'n Big, 5, 119	7	1:40.70	63,600
1978	Effervescing, 5, 120	L. A. Pincay Jr.	Dr. Patches, 4, 116	Text, 4, 122	6	1:40.20	62,700
1977	Painted Wagon, 4, 117	C. Baltazar	Legendaire, 4, 114	Pay Tribute, 5, 118	7	1:40.40	48,500

Named for Calumet Farm's Racing Hall of Fame member, 1948 Horse of the Year, '48 Triple Crown winner, and '51 Hollywood Gold Cup winner Citation (1945 c. by Bull Lea). Grade 3 1979-'80, 1984-'86. Not graded 1981-'83. Grade 2 1987-2003. Not held 2005. 1 mile 1980. 1 1/8 miles 1981, 1983-'84, 1986-'93, 1995-'98. About 1 1/8 miles 1985. 1 1/4 miles 1994. Dirt 1977-'82, 1984. Two divisions 1983, '91. Course record 1995. †Denotes female.

Clark Handicap

Grade 2 in 2008. Churchill Downs, three-year-olds and up, 1 1/8 miles, dirt. Held November 23, 2007, with a gross value of $554,000. First held in 1875. First graded in 1973. Stakes record 1:47.39 (2006 Premium Tap).

Year	Winner	Jockey	Second	Third	Strs	Time	1st Purse
2007	A. P. Arrow, 5, 115	R. A. Dominguez	Brass Hat, 6, 118	Diamond Stripes, 4, 120	9	1:48.66	$329,741

Racing — Graded Stakes

Year	Winner	Jockey	Second	Third	Strs	Time	1st Purse
2006	**Premium Tap**, 4, 122	K. Desormeaux	Wild Desert, 4, 118	A. P. Arrow, 4, 113	12	1:**47.39**	$329,816
2005	**Magna Graduate**, 3, 116	J. R. Velazquez	Suave, 4, 118	Perfect Drift, 6, 122	12	1:50.89	355,570
2004	**Saint Liam**, 4, 117	E. S. Prado	Seek Gold, 4, 111	Perfect Drift, 5, 118	9	1:50.81	345,960
2003	**‡Quest**, 4, 114	J. Castellano	Evening Attire, 5, 118	Aeneas, 4, 114	14	1:52.42	360,840
2002	**Lido Palace (Chi)**, 5, 121	J. F. Chavez	Crafty Shaw, 4, 115	Hero's Tribute, 4, 114	11	1:49.13	283,464
2001	**Ubiquity**, 4, 113	C. Perret	Include, 4, 120	Mr Ross, 6, 114	10	1:48.26	280,240
2000	**†Surfside**, 3, 113	P. Day	Guided Tour, 4, 114	Maysville Slew, 4, 113	9	1:48.75	276,272
1999	**Littlebitlively**, 5, 118	C. H. Borel	Pleasant Breeze, 4, 112	Nite Dreamer, 4, 114	12	1:50.88	284,456
1998	**Silver Charm**, 4, 124	G. L. Stevens	Littlebitlively, 4, 113	Wild Rush, 4, 117	8	1:49.07	275,776
1997	**Concerto**, 3, 113	J. D. Bailey	Terremoto, 6, 114	Rod and Staff, 4, 107	11	1:49.72	284,704
1996	**Isitingood**, 5, 120	D. R. Flores	Savinio, 6, 119	Coup D' Argent, 4, 110	9	1:48.99	174,220
1995	**Judge T C**, 4, 115	J. M. Johnson	Tyus, 5, 113	Alphabet Soup, 4, 117	14	1:49.82	153,140
1994	**Sir Vixen**, 6, 112	D. Kutz	Danville, 3, 113	Prize Fight, 5, 115	7	1:51.36	143,150
1993	**Mi Cielo**, 3, 117	M. E. Smith	Take Me Out, 5, 115	Forry Cow How, 5, 115	13	1:51.43	150,540
1992	**Zeeruler**, 4, 113	G. K. Gomez	Flying Continental, 6, 118	Echelon's Ice Man, 4, 109	13	1:50.11	76,050
1991	**Out of Place**, 4, 119	W. H. McCauley	Echelon's Ice Man, 3, 110	British Banker, 3, 111	11	1:52.29	74,230
1990	**Secret Hello**, 3, 115	P. Day	Din's Dancer, 5, 119	De Roche, 4, 121	7	1:50.60	72,410
1989	**No Marker**, 5, 113	D. W. Cox	Set a Record, 5, 114	Stop the Stage, 4, 111	12	1:51.20	75,205
1988	**Balthazar B.**, 5, 112	K. Desormeaux	Clever Secret, 4, 115	Slew City Slew, 4, 123	9	1:51.20	80,835
1987	**Intrusion**, 5, 114	L. J. Melancon	Savings, 4, 116	Mister C., 4, 116	9	1:51.40	47,655
1986	**Come Summer**, 4, 112	P. A. Johnson	Taylor's Special, 5, 126	Sumptious, 3, 120	9	1:49.80	47,363
1985	**Hopeful Word**, 4, 118	P. Day	Dramatic Desire, 4, 113	Big Bobcat, 5, 111	9	1:51.00	49,510
1984	**Eminency**, 6, 121	P. Day	Jack Slade, 4, 122	Bayou Hebert, 3, 114	10	1:49.00	36,400
1983	**Jack Slade**, 3, 117	J. McKnight	Northern Majesty, 4, 122	Cad, 5, 118	8	1:49.80	35,912
1982	**Hechizado (Arg)**, 6, 117	R. P. Romero	Withholding, 5, 116	Pleasing Times, 3, 115	10	1:52.40	36,823
1981	**Withholding**, 4, 121	L. J. Melancon	Recusant, 3, 111	Hard Up, 5, 115	11	1:52.00	37,213
1980	**Sun Catcher**, 3, 117	D. Brumfield	Belle's Ruler, 5, 116	Withholding, 3, 116	10	1:53.40	35,636
1979	**Lot o' Gold**, 3, 123	J. C. Espinoza	Poverty Boy, 4, 114	Capital Idea, 6, 114	9	1:50.80	38,383
1978	**Bob's Dusty**, 4, 116	R. DePass	Kodiack, 4, 114	Raymond Earl, 3, 117	7	1:49.60	34,629
1977	**Bob's Dusty**, 3, 118	R. DePass	Packer Captain, 5, 116	Almost Grown, 5, 113	12	1:49.80	21,889
1976	**Yamanin**, 4, 120	G. Patterson	Warbucks, 6, 115	Play Boy, 3, 113	10	1:54.40	21,661
1975	**Warbucks**, 5, 124	L. J. Melancon	Silver Badge, 4, 118	†Shoo Dear, 4, 111	7	1:54.40	17,761
1974	**Mr. Door**, 3, 114	W. Gavidia	†Fairway Flyer, 5, 116	Cut the Talk, 3, 115	8	1:52.20	17,989
1973	**Golden Don**, 3, 122	M. Manganello	Amber Prey, 4, 115	Rastaferian, 4, 118	13	1:52.80	22,392

Named for Meriwether Lewis Clark (1846-'99), founder of the Kentucky Derby. Grade 3 1973-'97. Grade 1 2006. Clark S. 1875-1901. 2 miles 1875-'80. 1¼ miles 1881-'95. 1¹/₁₆ miles 1902-'21, 1925-'54. Three-year-olds 1875-1901. ‡Evening Attire finished first, DQ to second, 2003. †Denotes female.

Clement L. Hirsch Handicap

Grade 2 in 2008. Del Mar, three-year-olds and up, fillies and mares, 1¹/₁₆ miles, all weather. Held August 5, 2007, with a gross value of $294,000. First held in 1937. First graded in 1983. Stakes record 1:40 (1982 Matching).

Year	Winner	Jockey	Second	Third	Strs	Time	1st Purse
2007	**Nashoba's Key**, 4, 120	J. Talamo	Bai and Bai, 4, 114	Balance, 4, 122	4	1:48.29	$180,000
2006	**Healthy Addiction**, 5, 118	V. Espinoza	Happy Ticket, 5, 120	Star Parade (Arg), 7, 118	5	1:42.92	180,000
2005	**Tucked Away**, 5, 118	A. O. Solis	Hollywood Story, 4, 119	Valentine Dancer, 5, 117	8	1:42.80	180,000
2004	**Miss Loren (Arg)**, 6, 114	J. K. Court	House of Fortune, 3, 113	Royally Chosen, 6, 116	8	1:42.93	180,000
2003	**Azeri**, 5, 127	M. E. Smith	Got Koko, 4, 118	Tropical Blossom, 5, 108	5	1:42.12	180,000
2002	**Azeri**, 4, 126	M. E. Smith	Angel Gift, 4, 114	Se Me Acabo (Chi), 4, 114	5	1:42.66	180,000
2001	**Tranquility Lake**, 6, 120	E. Delahoussaye	Gourmet Girl, 6, 122	Nany's Sweep, 5, 116	4	1:41.78	180,000
2000	**Riboletta (Brz)**, 5, 125	C. J. McCarron	Bordelaise (Arg), 5, 115	Gourmet Girl, 5, 115	6	1:42.06	180,000
1999	**A Lady From Dixie**, 4, 116	C. W. Antley	Manistique, 4, 124	Yolo Lady, 4, 116	5	1:43.58	180,000
1998	**Sharp Cat**, 4, 124	C. S. Nakatani	Supercilious, 5, 115	Numero Uno, 4, 116	4	1:42.16	180,000
1997	**Radu Cool**, 5, 117	C. J. McCarron	Supercilious, 4, 113	Swoon River, 5, 110	6	1:42.66	180,000
1996	**Different (Arg)**, 4, 120	C. J. McCarron	Top Rung, 5, 115	Borodislew, 6, 117	4	1:42.48	189,200
1995	**Borodislew**, 5, 118	C. J. McCarron	Lakeway, 4, 121	Golden Klair (GB), 5, 118	6	1:41.87	178,150
1994	**Paseana (Arg)**, 7, 123	C. J. McCarron	Exchange, 6, 120	Magical Maiden, 5, 118	4	1:40.59	117,150
1993	**Magical Maiden**, 4, 120	G. L. Stevens	Vieille Vigne (Fr), 6, 111	Party Cited, 4, 117	8	1:42.68	123,600
1992	**Exchange**, 4, 120	L. A. Pincay Jr.	Fowda, 4, 120	Brought to Mind, 5, 119	8	1:42.00	123,100
1991	**Vieille Vigne (Fr)**, 4, 116	M. A. Pedroza	Formidable Lady, 4, 115	Lite Light, 3, 121	4	1:42.67	120,300
1990	**Bayakoa (Arg)**, 6, 127	L. A. Pincay Jr.	Fantastic Look, 4, 113	Formidable Lady, 4, 112	5	1:40.60	88,500
1989	**Goodbye Halo**, 4, 120	C. A. Black	Flying Julia, 6, 112	Kool Arrival, 3, 115	4	1:41.80	77,450
1988	**Clabber Girl**, 5, 120	C. J. McCarron	Annoconnor, 4, 118	Integra, 4, 119	3	1:41.60	75,100
1987	**Infinidad (Chi)**, 5, 118	C. A. Black	Margaret Booth, 4, 117	Le l'Argent, 5, 117	9	1:41.40	63,540
1986	**Fran's Valentine**, 4, 119	W. Shoemaker	Cenyak's Star, 4, 116	Dontstop Themusic, 6, 123	5	1:41.40	59,590
1985	**Dontstop Themusic**, 5, 122	D. G. McHargue	Golden Screen, 5, 112	Lovlier Linda, 5, 119	4	1:41.80	45,650
1984	**Princess Rooney**, 4, 123	P. A. Valenzuela	Flag de Lune, 4, 115	Moment to Buy, 3, 116	5	1:40.40	60,100
1983	**Sangue (Ire)**, 5, 121	W. Shoemaker	Avigaition, 4, 122	Skillful Joy, 4, 117	5	1:42.20	46,600
1982	**Matching**, 4, 116	R. Sibille	Miss Huntington, 5, 116	Cat Girl, 4, 117	4	**1:40.00**	45,850
1981	**Save Wild Life**, 4, 118	C. J. McCarron	Princess Karenda, 4, 120	Track Robbery, 5, 125	4	1:41.60	47,650
1980	**Wayside Station**, 5, 113	P. A. Valenzuela	Concussion, 6, 117	Mike Fogarty (Ire), 5, 115	7	1:28.80	19,775
	Galaxy Libra (Ire), 4, 118	W. Shoemaker	Wickerr, 5, 117	To B. Or Not, 4, 116	5	1:29.00	19,375
1979	**He's Dewan**, 4, 119	D. G. McHargue	Caro Bambino (Ire), 4, 119	No No, 4, 115	10	1:29.00	23,950

Year	Winner	Jockey	Second	Third	Strs	Time	1st Purse
1978	Nantequos, 5, 120	D. G. McHargue	Lunar Probe (NZ), 4, 118	dh-Around We Go, 5, 117	10	1:29.40	$20,250
				dh-Crew of Ocala, 4, 114			
1977	Notably Different, 4, 113	C. Baltazar	Key Account, 5, 114	Pikehall, 3, 109	8	1:29.40	13,375
	Authorization, 5, 113	D. G. McHargue	Cherry River, 7, 112	Mister Dan, 4, 114	7	1:29.20	13,175
1976	Uniformity, 4, 115	R. Campas	White Fir, 4, 118	*Royal Derby II, 7, 119	9	1:28.20	16,900
1975	Bahia Key, 5, 119	W. Harris	Fair Test, 7, 119	Top Command, 4, 117	5	1:34.00	12,750
1974	Bahia Key, 4, 120	A. Pineda	*Trotteur, 4, 117	Soft Victory, 6, 122	9	1:34.20	13,650
1973	Grotonian, 4, 117	W. Shoemaker	Expediter, 4, 115	China Silk, 4, 114	5	1:50.60	12,600

Named for Clement L. Hirsch (1914-2000), an original Del Mar director. Formerly named for the city of Chula Vista, California. Grade 3 1983-'85. Chula Vista H. 1937-'99. Not held 1938-'66, 1968-'72. 5½ furlongs 1937. 1 mile 1967, 1974-'75. 1⅛ miles 1973. 7½ furlongs 1976-'80. Dirt 1937-'72, 1974-'75, 1981-2006. Turf 1973, 1976-'80. Two-year-olds 1937. Both sexes 1973-'80. Two divisions 1977, '80. Dead heat for third 1978. Nonwinners of a race worth $12,500 to the winner other than claiming 1974. California-breds 1937.

Clement L. Hirsch Memorial Turf Championship Stakes

Grade 1 in 2008. Oak Tree at Santa Anita, three-year-olds and up, 1¼ miles, turf. Held October 6, 2007, with a gross value of $250,000. First held in 1969. First graded in 1973. Stakes record 1:58.48 (1996 Bon Point [GB] [DQ to fifth]).

Year	Winner	Jockey	Second	Third	Strs	Time	1st Purse
2007	Artiste Royal (Ire), 6, 124	J. Talamo	The Tin Man, 9, 124	Isipingo, 4, 124	7	1:59.89	$150,000
2006	The Tin Man, 8, 124	V. Espinoza	T. H. Approval, 5, 124	Artiste Royal (Ire), 5, 124	6	2:00.12	150,000
2005	Fourty Niners Son, 4, 124	C. S. Nakatani	‡Leprechaun Kid, 6, 124	Laura's Lucky Boy, 4, 124	8	2:01.17	150,000
2004	Star Over the Bay, 6, 124	T. Baze	Sarafan, 7, 124	Vangelis, 5, 124	7	1:58.70	150,000
2003	Storming Home (GB), 5, 124	G. L. Stevens	Johar, 4, 124	Irish Warrior, 5, 124	4	2:01.64	150,000
2002	The Tin Man, 4, 124	M. E. Smith	Sarafan, 5, 124	Blue Steller (Ire), 4, 124	6	1:58.93	180,000
2001	Senure, 5, 124	A. O. Solis	White Heart (GB), 6, 124	Cagney (Brz), 4, 124	6	1:59.47	180,000
2000	Mash One (Chi), 6, 124	D. R. Flores	Boatman, 4, 124	Asidero (Arg), 4, 124	6	2:00.67	180,000
1999	Mash One (Chi), 5, 124	D. R. Flores	Lazy Lode (Arg), 5, 124	Bonapartiste (Fr), 5, 124	6	1:59.07	180,000
1998	Military, 4, 124	C. S. Nakatani	Bonapartiste (Fr), 4, 124	River Bay, 5, 124	5	2:02.04	180,000
1997	Rainbow Dancer (Fr), 6, 124	A. O. Solis	‡Lord Jain (Arg), 5, 124	Sandpit (Brz), 8, 124	9	2:01.80	180,000
1996	‡†Admise (Fr), 4, 121	K. Desormeaux	Khoraz, 6, 124	Golden Post, 6, 124	5	1:58.48	180,000
1995	Northern Spur (Ire), 4, 124	C. J. McCarron	Sandpit (Brz), 6, 124	Royal Chariot, 5, 124	8	2:02.37	180,000
1994	Sandpit (Brz), 5, 124	C. S. Nakatani	Grand Flotilla, 7, 124	Approach the Bench (Ire), 6, 124	5	2:25.12	180,000
1993	Kotashaan (Fr), 5, 124	K. Desormeaux	Luazur (Fr), 4, 124	†Let's Elope (NZ), 6, 121	4	2:25.60	180,000
1992	Navarone, 4, 126	P. A. Valenzuela	Defensive Play, 5, 126	Daros (GB), 3, 121	6	2:24.29	240,000
1991	Filago, 4, 126	P. A. Valenzuela	Missionary Ridge (GB), 4, 126	†Kartajana (Ire), 4, 123	9	2:23.62	300,000
1990	Rial (Arg), 5, 126	R. Q. Meza	Eradicate (Ire), 5, 126	Saratoga Passage, 5, 126	11	2:23.80	300,000
1989	Hawkster, 3, 121	R. A. Baze	Pay the Butler, 5, 126	Saratoga Passage, 4, 126	9	2:22.80	300,000
1988	Nasr El Arab, 3, 121	G. L. Stevens	Great Communicator, 5, 126	Circus Prince, 5, 126	8	2:25.20	240,000
1987	Allez Milord, 4, 126	C. J. McCarron	Louis Le Grand, 5, 126	Rivlia, 5, 126	10	2:36.20	240,000
1986	†Estrapade, 6, 123	F. Toro	Theatrical (Ire), 4, 126	Uptown Swell, 4, 126	10	2:26.00	240,000
1985	Yashgan (GB), 4, 126	C. J. McCarron	Both Ends Burning, 5, 124	Cariellor (Fr), 4, 126	10	2:27.20	240,000
1984	Both Ends Burning, 4, 126	R. A. Baze	Gato Del Sol, 5, 126	Raami (GB), 3, 121	12	2:25.40	240,000
1983	†Zalataia (Fr), 4, 123	F. Head	John Henry, 8, 126	Load the Cannons, 3, 122	9	2:29.20	240,000
1982	John Henry, 7, 126	W. Shoemaker	Craelius, 3, 122	Regalberto, 4, 126	7	2:24.00	180,000
1981	John Henry, 6, 126	W. Shoemaker	Spence Bay (Ire), 6, 126	The Bart, 5, 126	7	2:23.40	180,000
1980	John Henry, 5, 126	L. A. Pincay Jr.	Balzac, 5, 126	Bold Tropic (SAf), 5, 126	10	2:23.40	120,000
1979	Balzac, 4, 126	C. J. McCarron	†Trillion, 5, 123	Silver Eagle (Ire), 5, 126	9	2:25.40	90,000
1978	Exceller, 5, 126	W. Shoemaker	Star of Erin (Ire), 4, 126	dh-As de Copas (Arg), 5, 126	9	2:24.60	90,000
				dh-Good Land (NZ), 7, 126			
1977	Crystal Water, 4, 126	W. Shoemaker	Vigors, 4, 126	Ancient Title, 7, 126	10	2:26.40	60,000
1976	King Pellinore, 4, 126	W. Shoemaker	*Royal Derby II, 7, 126	L'Heureux, 3, 121	9	2:31.40	60,000
1975	Top Command, 4, 126	W. Shoemaker	Top Crowd, 4, 126	Buffalo Lark, 5, 126	8	2:26.00	60,000
1974	†Tallahto, 4, 123	L. A. Pincay Jr.	Within Hail, 3, 122	Montmartre, 4, 126	11	2:25.80	60,000
1973	Portentous, 3, 122	J. Ramirez	Groshawk, 3, 122	dh-Kentuckian, 4, 126	8	2:25.60	60,000
				dh-Kirrary, 3, 122			

Named for Clement L. Hirsch (1914-2000), co-founder and first president of Oak Tree Racing Association. The race is held during the Oak Tree meet at Santa Anita Park. Oak Tree S. 1969-'70. Oak Tree Invitational 1971-'95. Oak Tree Turf Championship 1996-'99. Clement L. Hirsch Turf Championship 2000. 1½ miles 1969-'94. Dead heat for third 1973, '78. ‡Bon Point (GB) finished first, DQ to fifth, 1996. ‡Marlin finished second, DQ to fourth, 1997. ‡Whilly (Ire) finished second, DQ to fifth, 2005. †Denotes female.

Cliff Hanger Stakes

Grade 3 in 2008. Meadowlands, three-year-olds and up, 1⅟₁₆ miles, turf. Held September 21, 2007, with a gross value of $150,000. First held in 1977. First graded in 1985. Stakes record 1:39.40 (1988 Wanderkin).

Year	Winner	Jockey	Second	Third	Strs	Time	1st Purse
2007	Presious Passion, 4, 117	A. Garcia	Touched by Madness, 5, 117	Carnera, 4, 117	7	1:41.48	$90,000
2006	Old Forester, 5, 117	E. S. Prado	Tune of the Spirit, 5, 117	Crown Point, 4, 117	8	1:42.54	90,000
2005	Hotstufanthensome, 5, 119	R. Maragh	Icy Atlantic, 4, 117	Stormy Ray, 6, 117	8	1:54.32	90,000
2004	Dr. Kashnikow, 7, 116	R. Migliore	Tam's Terms, 6, 116	Host (Chi), 4, 117	8	1:42.47	120,000
2002	Saint Verre, 4, 113	J. Samyn	Pinky Pizwaanski, 4, 116	Spruce Run, 4, 115	4	1:42.40	90,000
2001	Crash Course, 5, 114	R. Wilson	Solitary Dancer, 5, 114	Union One, 4, 114	10	1:43.14	90,000
2000	North East Bound, 4, 118	J. A. Velez Jr.	Johnny Dollar, 4, 114	Swamp, 4, 120	11	1:41.78	90,000
1999	Virginia Carnival, 7, 114	J. Samyn	Star Connection, 5, 114	Grapeshot, 5, 116	12	1:42.44	90,000

Year	Winner	Jockey	Second	Third	Strs	Time	1st Purse
1998	Mi Narrow, 4, 111	J. Bravo	Treat Me Doc, 4, 114	Boyce, 7, 114	6	1:43.58	$60,000
1997	Dixie Bayou, 4, 114	J. R. Velazquez	Brave Note (Ire), 6, 115	Joker, 5, 116	10	1:39.45	60,000
1996	Thorny Crown, 5, 115	M. J. Luzzi	Ihtiraz (GB), 6, 114	Winnetou, 6, 112	5	1:44.71	60,000
1995	‡Mighty Forum (GB), 4, 114	W. H. McCauley	Joker, 3, 106	Fourstars Allstar, 7, 120	7	1:41.09	60,000
1994	Binary Light, 5, 112	J. Samyn	Brazany, 4, 112	Burst of Applause, 5, 109	5	1:41.41	45,000
1993	Excellent Tipper, 5, 117	C. Perret	Rinka Das, 4, 115	First and Only, 6, 115	6	1:43.69	45,000
1992	Roman Envoy, 4, 116	C. Perret	Futurist, 4, 116	Royal Ninja, 6, 115	8	1:39.92	45,000
1991	Finder's Choice, 6, 114	R. Aviles	Royal Rue, 5, 113	Great Normand, 6, 117	8	1:40.31	45,000
1990	Chas' Whim, 3, 115	A. T. Stacy	Kali High, 6, 115	Royal Ninja, 4, 112	11	1:46.40	45,000
1989	Ten Keys, 5, 114	K. Desormeaux	Wanderkin, 6, 121	Soviet Lad, 4, 112	7	1:42.20	52,290
1988	Wanderkin, 5, 118	R. G. Davis	Salem Drive, 6, 117	San's the Shadow, 4, 117	9	**1:39.40**	53,730
1987	Foligno, 5, 115	J. A. Santos	Cost Conscious, 5, 116	Air Display, 4, 113	7	1:41.40	46,995
	Silver Comet, 4, 117	W. H. McCauley	Broadway Tommy, 5, 112	Prince Daniel, 4, 114	3	1:43.80	31,831
1986	Explosive Darling, 4, 118	R. P. Romero	Equalize, 4, 114	Lieutenant's Lark, 4, 120	7	1:40.00	48,360
1985	Late Act, 6, 117	J. D. Bailey	Silver Surfer, 4, 116	Pax Nobiscum, 5, 116	7	1:45.00	47,790
1984	Late Act, 5, 113	E. Maple	Sitzmark, 4, 111	Quick Dip, 4, 112	10	1:40.80	46,020
	Cozzene, 4, 115	W. A. Guerra	Ayman, 4, 112	Pin Puller, 5, 114	6	1:40.40	45,300
1983	Erin's Tiger, 5, 112	J. Velasquez	Who's for Dinner, 4, 113	Kentucky River, 5, 112	9	1:41.20	33,450
1982	Erin's Tiger, 4, 114	J. Velasquez	Santo's Joe, 5, 116	Dew Line, 3, 114	8	1:44.60	26,295
	Acaroid, 4, 114	A. T. Cordero Jr.	North Course, 7, 114	Thirty Eight Paces, 4, 116	7	1:44.60	26,115
1981	Bill Wheeler, 4, 119	W. H. McCauley	Mannerism, 4, 113	Brahmin, 5, 115	15	1:43.60	33,510
1980	Quality T. V., 3, 114	J. Velasquez	Conservatoire, 3, 109	Bill Wheeler, 3, 112	10	1:43.80	32,640
1979	Exclusively Mine, 3, 114	W. Nemeti	Telly Hill, 5, 126	Picturesque, 3, 116	7	1:44.20	34,678
1978	Mr. Lincroft, 4, 117	V. A. Bracciale Jr.	Telly Hill, 4, 119	†Forbidden Isle, 3, 109	15	1:44.20	36,270
1977	Dan Horn, 5, 125	D. MacBeth	Shore Patrol, 7, 113	Popular Victory, 5, 118	9	1:43.60	34,873

Named to honor the early movie industry in New Jersey, referring to suspenseful silent film serials. Grade 3 1985-2001. Not graded 2002. Cliff Hanger H. 1977-'81, 1983-2002, donors. Not held 2003. Dirt 1978-'81, 1985, '87, '93, '96, '98, 2002. Originally scheduled on turf 2002. Two divisions 1982, '84, '87. Equaled course record 1997. ‡Joker finished first, DQ to second, 1995. †Denotes female.

Coaching Club American Oaks

Grade 1 in 2008. Belmont Park, three-year-olds, fillies, 1¼ miles, dirt. Held July 21, 2007, with a gross value of $300,000. First held in 1917. First graded in 1973. Stakes record 2:00.40 (1997 Ajina).

Year	Winner	Jockey	Second	Third	Strs	Time	1st Purse
2007	Octave, 3, 121	J. R. Velazquez	Lear's Princess, 3, 121	Folk, 3, 121	7	2:02.17	$180,000
2006	Wonder Lady Anne L, 3, 121	E. S. Prado	Pine Island, 3, 121	Miss Shop, 3, 121	9	2:04.63	180,000
2005	Smuggler, 3, 121	E. S. Prado	Summerly, 3, 121	Spun Sugar, 3, 121	7	2:04.39	300,000
2004	Ashado, 3, 121	J. R. Velazquez	Stellar Jayne, 3, 121	Magical Illusion, 3, 121	6	2:02.43	300,000
2003	Spoken Fur, 3, 121	J. D. Bailey	Fircroft, 3, 121	Savedbythelight, 3, 121	7	2:31.02	300,000
2002	Jilbab, 3, 121	M. J. Luzzi	Tarnished Lady, 3, 121	Shop Till You Drop, 3, 121	7	2:31.48	210,000
2001	Tweedside, 3, 121	J. R. Velazquez	Exogenous, 3, 121	Unbridled Lassie, 3, 121	8	2:30.70	210,000
2000	Jostle, 3, 121	M. E. Smith	Resort, 3, 121	Secret Status, 3, 121	7	2:29.99	210,000
1999	On a Soapbox, 3, 121	J. D. Bailey	Dreams Gallore, 3, 121	Strolling Belle, 3, 121	8	2:29.31	210,000
1998	Banshee Breeze, 3, 121	J. D. Bailey	Keeper Hill, 3, 121	Best Friend Stro, 3, 121	6	2:31.56	180,000
1997	Ajina, 3, 121	M. E. Smith	Tomisue's Delight, 3, 121	Key Hunter, 3, 121	5	**2:00.40**	150,000
1996	My Flag, 3, 121	J. D. Bailey	Gold n Delicious, 3, 121	Weekend in Seattle, 3, 121	7	2:04.64	150,000
1995	Golden Bri, 3, 121	J. A. Santos	Serena's Song, 3, 121	Change Fora Dollar, 3, 121	6	2:03.86	150,000
1994	Two Altazano, 3, 121	J. A. Santos	Plenty of Sugar, 3, 121	Sovereign Kitty, 3, 121	7	2:02.88	150,000
1993	Sky Beauty, 3, 121	M. E. Smith	Future Pretense, 3, 121	Silky Feather, 3, 121	5	2:01.56	150,000
1992	Turnback the Alarm, 3, 121	C. W. Antley	Easy Now, 3, 121	Pleasant Stage, 3, 121	6	2:03.53	150,000
1991	Lite Light, 3, 121	C. S. Nakatani	Meadow Star, 3, 121	Car Gal, 3, 121	6	2:00.54	150,000
1990	Charon, 3, 121	C. Perret	Crowned, 3, 121	Paper Money, 3, 121	7	2:02.60	172,500
1989	‡Open Mind, 3, 121	A. T. Cordero Jr.	Nite of Fun, 3, 121	Rose Diamond, 3, 121	6	2:32.40	170,100
1988	Goodbye Halo, 3, 121	J. Velasquez	Aptostar, 3, 121	Make Change, 3, 121	8	2:32.80	170,400
1987	Fiesta Gal, 3, 121	A. T. Cordero Jr.	Mint Cooler, 3, 121	Run Come See, 3, 121	7	2:31.00	172,500
1986	Valley Victory (Ire), 3, 121	R. P. Romero	Life At the Top, 3, 121	Lotka, 3, 121	8	2:28.00	166,680
1985	Mom's Command, 3, 121	A. Fuller	Bessarabian, 3, 121	Foxy Deen, 3, 121	8	2:32.00	142,560
1984	Class Play, 3, 121	J. Cruguet	Life's Magic, 3, 121	Miss Oceana, 3, 121	5	2:29.80	164,520
1983	High Schemes, 3, 121	J. Samyn	Spit Curl, 3, 121	Lady Norcliffe, 3, 121	16	2:30.20	107,460
1982	Christmas Past, 3, 121	J. Vasquez	Cupecoy's Joy, 3, 121	Flying Partner, 3, 121	10	2:28.60	84,900
1981	‡Wayward Lass, 3, 121	C. B. Asmussen	Real Prize, 3, 121	Banner Gala, 3, 121	6	2:28.20	81,750
1980	Bold 'n Determined, 3, 121	E. Delahoussaye	Erin's Word, 3, 121	Farewell Letter, 3, 121	7	2:31.80	84,000
1979	Davona Dale, 3, 121	J. Velasquez	Plankton, 3, 121	Croquis, 3, 121	5	2:30.00	79,575
1978	Lakeville Miss, 3, 121	R. Hernandez	Caesar's Wish, 3, 121	Tempest Queen, 3, 121	5	2:29.40	63,540
1977	Our Mims, 3, 121	J. Velasquez	Road Princess, 3, 121	Fia, 3, 121	7	2:29.40	65,880
1976	Revidere, 3, 121	J. Vasquez	Optimistic Gal, 3, 121	No Duplicate, 3, 121	10	2:28.40	68,640
1975	Ruffian, 3, 121	J. Vasquez	Equal Change, 3, 121	Let Me Linger, 3, 121	7	2:27.80	66,700
1974	Chris Evert, 3, 121	J. Velasquez	Fiesta Libre, 3, 121	Maud Muller, 3, 121	10	2:28.80	68,520
1973	Magazine, 3, 121	A. T. Cordero Jr.	Bag of Tunes, 3, 121	Lady Love, 3, 121	13	2:27.80	70,200

Named in honor of the Coaching Club of America, first sponsor of the race. The Coaching Club preserved the aristocratic traditions of driving four-in-hand coaches (a coach pulled by four horses with a single rein) socially and in competitions—the ability to drive one of these coaches was a condition of membership. Coaching Club American Oaks H. 1917-'27. Held at Aqueduct 1963-'67. 1⅛ miles 1917. 1½ miles 1942-'43, 1971-'89, 1998-2003. 1⅜ miles 1919-'41, 1944-'58. ‡Real Prize finished first, DQ to second, 1981. ‡Nite of Fun finished first, DQ to second, 1989.

Colonel E. R. Bradley Handicap

Grade 3 in 2008. Fair Grounds, four-year-olds and up, about 1 1/16 miles, turf. Held January 12, 2008, with a gross value of $100,000. First held in 1984. First graded in 2008. Stakes record 1:42 (1994 Dixie Poker Ace).

Year	Winner	Jockey	Second	Third	Strs	Time	1st Purse
2008	French Beret, 5, 115	J. Graham	Major Rhythm, 9, 117	Sterwins, 5, 118	9	1:45.83	$60,000
2007	Purim, 5, 117	J. L. Castanon	Fort Prado, 6, 120	Cloudy's Knight, 7, 116	12	1:43.22	60,000
2005	Onthedeanslist, 6, 117	C. J. Lanerie	Fort Prado, 4, 122	Middleweight, 5, 116	6	1:44.17	45,000
	America Alive, 4, 116	R. Albarado	Honor in War, 6, 119	Rapid Proof, 5, 115	11	1:44.43	60,000
2004	Skate Away, 5, 116	G. Melancon	Warleigh, 6, 117	Great Bloom, 6, 117	9	1:45.04	36,000
2003	Royal Spy, 5, 116	R. Albarado	Dynameaux, 5, 115	Freefourinternet, 5, 115	11	1:45.25	45,000
2002	Northcote Road, 7, 120	L. Melancon	Candid Glen, 5, 115	Red Mountain, 5, 117	6	1:46.03	45,000
2001	Cornish Snow, 8, 113	L. Melancon	Royal Strand (Ire), 7, 117	Talkmeister, 5, 113	13	1:42.99	45,000
2000	Rod and Staff, 7, 115	R. Albarado	Phil the Grip, 6, 110	Daylight Savings, 6, 117	6	1:44.50	45,000
1999	Baytown, 5, 114	C. C. Bourque	Western Trader, 8, 118	Stay Sound, 4, 113	3	1:45.95	30,000
1998	Joyeux Danseur, 5, 114	R. Albarado	Jaunatxo, 5, 117	Hollie's Chief, 7, 114	8	1:44.90	30,000
1997	Snake Eyes, 7, 117	R. Albarado	Nijinsky's Gold, 8, 114	Beavers Nose, 5, 113	8	1:47.28	26,100
1996	Kumhwa, 5, 114	G. Melancon	Michislew, 5, 113	Artic Explosion, 4, 113	5	1:46.25	26,040
1995	Pride of Summer, 7, 115	R. King, Jr.	Milt's Overture, 4, 116	Fly Cry, 4, 123	8	1:43.67	25,725
1994	Dixie Poker Ace, 7, 119	C. H. Borel	Yukon Robbery, 5, 113	First and Only, 7, 117	14	**1:42.00**	20,280
1993	Dixie Poker Ace, 6, 120	C. H. Borel	Yukon Robbery, 4, 115	Little Bro Lantis, 5, 116	6	1:44.40	19,680
1992	Dixie Poker Ace, 5, 119	C. H. Borel	Slick Groom, 4, 116	Match Carr, 4, 113	5	1:45.60	19,335
1991	Sangria Time, 4, 117	D. Guillory	Viva Deputy, 6, 112	Motor City Smitty, 5, 110	8	1:46.90	19,635
1990	Majesty's Imp, 4, 115	E. J. Perrodin	Allijeba, 4, 113	La Leroux, 7, 113	9	1:45.60	16,770
1989	Ingot's Ruler, 7, 114	R. D. Ardoin	Zuppardo's Love, 8, 113	Cold Hearted Man, 4, 113	9	1:46.00	16,425
1988	Zuppardo's Love, 7, 114	J. K. Court	Illustrious High, 6, 114	Outlaws Sham, 5, 115	8	1:44.60	13,395
1984	Dugan Knight, 3, 119	R. Migliore	Katie's Bidder, 4, 120	Tellicherry, 3, 116	7	1:47.80	9,840

Named for Colonel Edward R. Bradley (1859-1946), owner of Fair Grounds from 1926-'34; Bradley also owned Idle Hour Stock Farm near Lexington. E. R. Bradley H. 1984. Colonel E. R. Bradley S. 1988-'95. Not held 1985-'87, 2006. Held in January and December 2005. Dirt 1985-'93, 1996. Three-year-olds 1984. Three-year-olds and up 2005. Two divisions 2005.

Colonial Turf Cup Stakes

Grade 3 in 2008. Colonial Downs, three-year-olds, 1 3/16 miles, turf. Held June 16, 2007, with a gross value of $750,000. First held in 2005. First graded in 2007. Stakes record 1:52.98 (2006 Showing Up).

Year	Winner	Jockey	Second	Third	Strs	Time	1st Purse
2007	Summer Doldrums, 3, 126	J. Lezcano	Strike a Deal, 3, 116	Souvenir Slew, 3, 116	9	1:55.68	$450,000
2006	Showing Up, 3, 120	C. H. Velasquez	Kip Deville, 3, 116	Go Between, 3, 118	14	**1:52.98**	600,000
2005	English Channel, 3, 118	J. R. Velazquez	Exceptional Ride, 3, 116	Interpatation, 3, 118	6	1:56.37	300,000

Comely Stakes

Grade 2 in 2008. Aqueduct, three-year-olds, fillies, 1 mile, dirt. Held April 12, 2008, with a gross value of $147,000. First held in 1945. First graded in 1973. Stakes record 1:35.50 (2002 Bella Bellucci).

Year	Winner	Jockey	Second	Third	Strs	Time	1st Purse
2008	Sherine, 3, 118	A. Garcia	Ready for Fortune, 3, 118	Elusive Lady, 3, 122	5	1:37.25	$90,000
2007	Boca Grande, 3, 122	M. E. Smith	Winning Point, 3, 116	Perfect Forest, 3, 116	8	1:36.54	90,000
2006	Miraculous Miss, 3, 122	K. J. Desormeaux	Regal Engagement, 3, 120	Daytime Promise, 3, 120	6	1:36.67	90,000
2005	Acey Deucey, 3, 118	D. Nelson	Seeking the Ante, 3, 116	Pleasant Chimes, 3, 116	8	1:35.95	90,000
2004	Society Selection, 3, 122	J. F. Chavez	Bending Strings, 3, 116	Daydreaming, 3, 116	8	1:35.89	67,200
2003	Cyber Secret, 3, 122	S. Bridgmohan	Storm Flag Flying, 3, 122	Bonay, 3, 116	5	1:35.97	64,740
2002	Bella Bellucci, 3, 122	G. L. Stevens	Short Note, 3, 116	Nonsuch Bay, 3, 116	5	**1:35.50**	64,920
2001	‡Two Item Limit, 3, 122	R. Migliore	Mandy's Gold, 3, 118	It All Adds Up, 3, 116	7	1:36.17	66,060
2000	March Magic, 3, 114	R. Migliore	Jostle, 3, 121	Finder's Fee, 3, 121	6	1:36.79	65,460
1999	Madison's Charm, 3, 112	J. Samyn	Better Than Honour, 3, 121	Oh What a Windfall, 3, 121	7	1:35.54	65,520
1998	Fantasy Angel, 3, 114	J. F. Chavez	Hansel's Girl, 3, 116	Best Friend Stro, 3, 118	12	1:37.44	69,300
1997	Dixie Flag, 3, 114	J. Samyn	Global Star, 3, 114	How About Now, 3, 114	7	1:36.96	66,120
1996	Little Miss Fast, 3, 118	J. F. Chavez	J J'sdream, 3, 118	Stop Traffic, 3, 112	6	1:36.58	65,940
1995	Nappelon, 3, 112	J. F. Chavez	Stormy Blues, 3, 121	Incredible Blues, 3, 114	6	1:36.26	64,440
1994	Dixie Luck, 3, 116	F. Leon	Penny's Reshoot, 3, 116	Our Royal Blue, 3, 112	7	1:37.02	66,240
1993	Private Light, 3, 112	R. G. Davis	Russian Bride, 3, 113	True Affair, 3, 118	6	1:44.19	68,280
1992	Saratoga Dew, 3, 114	W. H. McCauley	City Dance, 3, 113	Looking for a Win, 3, 114	7	1:37.22	69,480
1991	Meadow Star, 3, 121	C. W. Antley	Do It With Style, 3, 114	I'm a Thriller, 3, 118	5	1:38.02	67,560
1990	Fappaburst, 3, 114	J. Vasquez	Miss Spentyouth, 3, 114	Bundle Bits, 3, 118	4	1:21.60	49,770
1989	Surging, 3, 118	A. T. Cordero Jr.	Nite of Fun, 3, 112	Luv That Native, 3, 112	6	1:23.00	52,290
1988	Avie's Gal, 3, 114	J. Velasquez	Topicount, 3, 116	Ready Jet Go, 3, 114	8	1:22.40	66,780
1987	Devil's Bride, 3, 116	R. Q. Meza	Oh So Precious, 3, 116	Valid Line, 3, 114	7	1:23.60	65,790
1986	Misty Drone, 3, 112	J. Vasquez	I'm Splendid, 3, 121	Storm and Sunshine, 3, 114	12	1:24.00	59,940
1985	Mom's Command, 3, 121	A. Fuller	Majestic Folly, 3, 113	Clocks Secret, 3, 121	9	1:22.20	55,170
1984	Wild Applause, 3, 113	P. Day	Suavite, 3, 113	Proud Clarioness, 3, 116	7	1:23.20	50,610
1983	Able Money, 3, 113	A. Graell	Stark Drama, 3, 113	Idle Gossip, 3, 113	10	1:23.80	35,580
1982	Nancy Huang, 3, 113	J. Velasquez	Broom Dance, 3, 113	Dance Number, 3, 113	10	1:24.40	34,860
1981	Expressive Dance, 3, 123	D. MacBeth	Tina Tina Too, 3, 118	Explosive Kingdom, 3, 114	11	1:23.40	35,220
1980	Cybele, 3, 113	C. B. Asmussen	Punta Punta, 3, 113	Kashan, 3, 113	7	1:22.60	27,225
1979	Countess North, 3, 113	A. T. Cordero Jr.	Palm Hut, 3, 116	Run Cosmic Run, 3, 113	5	1:23.40	25,725
1978	Mashteen, 3, 113	R. Hernandez	Tempest Queen, 3, 118	Mucchina, 3, 113	6	1:23.00	25,665
1977	Bring Out the Band, 3, 118	D. Brumfield	Cum Laude Laurie, 3, 113	Emmy, 3, 113	10	1:23.60	22,650

Racing — Graded Stakes

Year	Winner	Jockey	Second	Third	Strs	Time	1st Purse
1976	Tell Me All, 3, 113	J. Ruane	Dearly Precious, 3, 121	Worthyana, 3, 113	5	1:23.20	$22,080
1975	Ruffian, 3, 113	J. Vasquez	Aunt Jin, 3, 113	Point in Time, 3, 113	5	1:21.20	16,755
1974	Clear Copy, 3, 113	D. Montoya	Shy Dawn, 3, 118	Chris Evert, 3, 118	10	1:24.40	17,670
1973	Java Moon, 3, 116	A. T. Cordero Jr.	Windy's Daughter, 3, 121	Voler, 3, 116	11	1:22.80	17,610

Named for James Butler's Comely (1912 f. by Disguise); Butler was the owner of Empire City, where the race originated. Grade 3 1973-'87, 1996-2004. Comely H. 1945-'53. Held at Jamaica 1945-'51, 1959. Held at Empire City 1952-'53. Held at Belmont Park 1976, 1981, 1984-'85. Not held 1954-'58. 1 1/16 miles 1945-'53, 1993. 5 furlongs 1959. 7 furlongs 1960-'90. Three-year-olds and up 1945-'53. Fillies and mares 1945-'53. Two-year-olds 1959. Both sexes 1959. ‡Mandy's Gold finished first, DQ to second, 2001.

Commonwealth Stakes

Grade 2 in 2008. Keeneland Race Course, three-year-olds and up, 7 furlongs, all weather. Held April 12, 2008, with a gross value of $390,000. First held in 1987. First graded in 1990. Stakes record 1:20.50 (1998 Distorted Humor).

Year	Winner	Jockey	Second	Third	Strs	Time	1st Purse
2008	Rebellion (GB), 5, 118	E. S. Prado	Elite Squadron, 4, 118	Medzendeekron, 5, 120	10	1:21.40	$248,000
2007	Silent Name (Jpn), 5, 118	C. S. Nakatani	Lewis Michael, 4, 118	Steel Light, 6, 118	11	1:21.26	248,000
2006	Sun King, 4, 120	C. S. Nakatani	Kazoo, 8, 120	Spanish Chestnut, 4, 118	12	1:23.30	274,784
2005	Clock Stopper, 5, 118	J. D. Bailey	Gators N Bears, 5, 118	Silver Wagon, 4, 118	6	1:22.06	263,438
2004	Lion Tamer, 4, 122	M. E. Smith	Private Horde, 5, 120	Marino Marini, 4, 118	6	1:23.14	167,555
2003	Smooth Jazz, 4, 118	E. S. Prado	Crafty C. T., 5, 118	Multiple Choice, 5, 120	7	1:21.73	169,725
2002	Orientate, 4, 120	P. Day	Aldebaran, 4, 118	Twilight Road, 5, 118	7	1:21.54	168,640
2001	Alannan, 5, 118	E. S. Prado	Valiant Halory, 4, 118	Liberty Gold, 7, 118	8	1:22.39	170,965
2000	Richter Scale, 6, 121	R. Migliore	Son's Corona, 5, 117	Deep Gold, 4, 117	6	1:21.07	128,836
1999	Good and Tough, 4, 115	S. J. Sellers	Purple Passion, 5, 115	Crucible, 4, 115	5	1:22.09	127,906
1998	Distorted Humor, 5, 119	G. L. Stevens	El Amante, 5, 114	Partner's Hero, 4, 121	8	**1:20.50**	130,820
1997	Victor Cooley, 4, 114	E. M. Martin Jr.	Western Winter, 5, 112	Appealing Skier, 4, 121	7	1:22.40	129,332
1996	Afternoon Deelites, 4, 124	K. Desormeaux	Western Winter, 4, 113	Our Emblem, 5, 115	6	1:21.12	131,068
1995	Golden Gear, 4, 118	C. Perret	Turkomatic, 4, 112	Lit de Justice, 5, 121	6	1:22.06	130,758
1994	Memo (Chi), 7, 118	P. Atkinson	American Chance, 5, 115	British Banker, 6, 115	10	1:22.32	69,378
1993	Alydeed, 4, 115	C. Perret	Binalong, 4, 118	Senor Speedy, 6, 115	6	1:21.43	113,057
1992	Pleasant Tap, 5, 116	E. Delahoussaye	To Freedom, 4, 115	Run On the Bank, 5, 118	6	1:22.40	118,188
1991	Black Tie Affair (Ire), 5, 124	J. L. Diaz	Housebuster, 4, 124	Exemplary Leader, 5, 115	6	1:21.86	118,625
1990	Black Tie Affair (Ire), 4, 118	M. Guidry	Shaker Knit, 5, 116	Momsfurrari, 6, 118	9	1:22.00	121,111
1989	Sewickley, 4, 115	R. P. Romero	Irish Open, 5, 118	Dancing Spree, 4, 115	9	1:22.40	36,368
1988	Calestoga, 6, 120	D. Brumfield	You're No Bargain, 4, 117	Carload, 6, 120	10	1:09.40	101,628
1987	Exclusive Enough, 3, 111	M. E. Smith	†Lazer Show, 4, 120	High Brite, 3, 120	8	1:08.40	101,010

Named for the commonwealth of Kentucky. Grade 3 1990-'93. Commonwealth Breeders' Cup S. 1987-'88, 1990-2007. Commonwealth Breeders' Cup H. 1989. 6 furlongs 1987-'88. Dirt 1987-2006. †Denotes female.

Commonwealth Turf Stakes

Grade 3 in 2008. Churchill Downs, three-year-olds, 1 1/16 miles, turf. Held November 11, 2007, with a gross value of $166,500. First held in 2004. First graded in 2008. Stakes record 1:43.17 (2007 Inca King).

Year	Winner	Jockey	Second	Third	Strs	Time	1st Purse
2007	Inca King, 3, 123	S. Bridgmohan	Equitable, 3, 119	Slew's Tizzy, 3, 119	7	**1:43.17**	$101,166
2006	Arbuckle Bandit, 3, 119	B. Blanc	Storm Treasure, 3, 117	Kingship, 3, 123	10	1:44.19	100,013
2005	Therecomesatiger, 3, 117	M. Guidry	Cosmonaut, 3, 117	Drum Major, 3, 115	9	1:43.94	108,438
2004	Broadway View, 3, 114	J. McKee	America Alive, 3, 116	Capo, 3, 114	10	1:44.75	106,113

Named for the commonwealth of Kentucky, one of four commonwealths in the United States; the others are Massachusetts, Pennsylvania, and Virginia.

Coolmore Lexington Stakes

Grade 2 in 2008. Keeneland Race Course, three-year-olds, 1 1/16 miles, all weather. Held April 19, 2008, with a gross value of $325,000. First held in 1936. First graded in 1986. Stakes record 1:41.06 (1999 Charismatic).

Year	Winner	Jockey	Second	Third	Strs	Time	1st Purse
2008	Behindatthebar, 3, 117	D. R. Flores	Samba Rooster, 3, 117	Riley Tucker, 3, 117	11	1:42.14	$201,500
2007	Slew's Tizzy, 3, 117	R. Albarado	Starbase, 3, 117	Forty Grams, 3, 117	9	1:43.20	201,500
2006	Showing Up, 3, 117	C. H. Velasquez	Like Now, 3, 123	Bear Character, 3, 117	10	1:46.42	201,500
2005	Coin Silver, 3, 117	J. Castellano	Sort It Out, 3, 117	Storm Surge, 3, 117	7	1:45.76	201,500
2004	Quintons Gold Rush, 3, 116	J. D. Bailey	Fire Slam, 3, 116	Song of the Sword, 3, 116	14	1:43.82	201,500
2003	Scrimshaw, 3, 116	E. S. Prado	Eye of the Tiger, 3, 116	Domestic Dispute, 3, 116	7	1:45.47	225,479
2002	Proud Citizen, 3, 116	M. E. Smith	Crimson Hero, 3, 116	Easyfromthegitgo, 3, 116	8	1:44.58	226,083
2001	Keats, 3, 116	L. J. Melancon	‡Griffinite, 3, 116	Bay Eagle, 3, 116	10	1:43.54	230,315
2000	Unshaded, 3, 116	S. J. Sellers	Globalize, 3, 120	Harlan Traveler, 3, 116	8	1:43.72	221,588
1999	Charismatic, 3, 115	J. D. Bailey	Yankee Victor, 3, 115	Finder's Gold, 3, 115	12	**1:41.06**	234,794
1998	Classic Cat, 3, 114	R. Albarado	Voyamerican, 3, 114	Grand Slam, 3, 123	8	1:42.85	228,300
1997	Touch Gold, 3, 115	G. L. Stevens	Smoke Glacken, 3, 118	Deeds Not Words, 3, 112	5	1:43.27	116,963
1996	City by Night, 3, 115	S. J. Sellers	Prince of Thieves, 3, 118	Roar, 3, 118	11	1:42.39	123,473
1995	Star Standard, 3, 115	P. Day	Royal Mitch, 3, 118	Guadalcanal, 3, 115	5	1:45.02	99,882
1994	Southern Rhythm, 3, 118	G. K. Gomez	Soul of the Matter, 3, 118	Ulises, 3, 113	5	1:45.72	85,095
1993	Grand Jewel, 3, 118	J. D. Bailey	El Bakan, 3, 113	Truth of It All, 3, 115	9	1:43.61	87,219
1992	My Luck Runs North, 3, 118	R. D. Lopez	Lure, 3, 118	Agincourt, 3, 115	5	1:44.06	89,083
1991	Hansel, 3, 121	J. D. Bailey	Shotgun Harry J., 3, 115	Speedy Cure, 3, 118	4	1:42.66	86,743

Year	Winner	Jockey	Second	Third	Strs	Time	1st Purse
1990	Home At Last, 3, 118	J. D. Bailey	Pleasant Tap, 3, 115	Thirty Slews, 3, 116	9	1:43.40	$73,385
1989	Notation, 3, 115	P. Day	Bionic Prospect, 3, 114	Charlie Barley, 3, 118	8	1:44.40	71,663
1988	Risen Star, 3, 118	J. Vasquez	Forty Niner, 3, 121	Stalwars, 3, 118	5	1:42.80	68,673
1987	War, 3, 115	W. H. McCauley	Candi's Gold, 3, 115	Momentus, 3, 118	6	1:44.40	96,843
1986	Wise Times, 3, 115	K. K. Allen	Country Light, 3, 118	Blue Buckaroo, 3, 112	9	1:44.80	71,793
1985	Stephan's Odyssey, 3, 118	L. A. Pincay Jr.	Tajawa, 3, 112	Northern Bid, 3, 112	7	1:42.60	34,775
1984	He Is a Great Deal, 3, 111	J. C. Espinoza	Swale, 3, 123	Timely Advocate, 3, 112	5	1:45.40	34,450

Named for the city of Lexington, Kentucky. Sponsored by John and Susan Magnier's Coolmore Stud in County Tipperary, Ireland 1998-2006. Grade 3 1986-'87. Not held 1938-'83. 6 furlongs 1936-'37. Dirt 1936-2006. Two-year-olds 1936-'37. ‡Mr. John finished second, DQ to eighth, 2001. Held as overnight handicap 1940.

Cotillion Breeders' Cup Handicap —
See Fitz Dixon Cotillion Breeders' Cup Handicap

Count Fleet Sprint Handicap

Grade 3 in 2008. Oaklawn Park, four-year-olds and up, 6 furlongs, dirt. Held April 10, 2008, with a gross value of $150,000. First held in 1974. First graded in 1986. Stakes record 1:08.18 (2001 Bonapaw).

Year	Winner	Jockey	Second	Third	Strs	Time	1st Purse
2008	Semaphore Man, 6, 118	T. T. Doocy	Junior College, 6, 118	Lovango, 4, 116	7	1:09.78	$90,000
2007	Bordonaro, 6, 121	R. Migliore	Semaphore Man, 5, 115	Off Duty, 4, 116	6	1:09.11	90,000
2006	Bordonaro, 5, 122	P. A. Valenzuela	Friendly Island, 5, 118	Semaphore Man, 4, 115	7	1:08.77	90,000
2005	Top Commander, 5, 113	C. Gonzalez	Forest Grove, 4, 114	That Tat, 7, 119	8	1:08.74	90,000
2004	Shake You Down, 6, 121	R. A. Dominguez	Where's the Ring, 5, 115	Aloha Bold, 6, 114	6	1:09.27	90,000
2003	Beau's Town, 5, 122	J. Theriot	Honor Me, 5, 116	Sand Ridge, 8, 114	6	1:09.01	90,000
2002	Explicit, 5, 116	L. J. Meche	Entepreneur, 5, 115	Junior Deputy, 4, 113	5	1:08.60	90,000
2001	Bonapaw, 5, 118	G. Melancon	Chindi, 7, 114	Bidis, 4, 117	7	1:08.18	75,000
2000	†Show Me the Stage, 4, 116	D. R. Flores	Smoldering Heart, 5, 115	Vinnie's Boy, 4, 114	6	1:09.62	75,000
1999	Reraise, 4, 122	C. S. Nakatani	Run Johnny, 7, 114	E J Harley, 7, 115	6	1:08.59	75,000
1998	Chindi, 4, 113	D. R. Pettinger	E J Harley, 6, 113	Western Fame, 6, 115	8	1:09.77	75,000
1997	High Stakes Player, 5, 120	K. Desormeaux	†Capote Belle, 4, 116	Victor Avenue, 4, 116	7	1:08.86	90,000
1996	Concept Win, 6, 120	G. L. Stevens	Roythelittleone, 4, 114	Spiritbound, 4, 113	7	1:09.06	90,000
1995	Hot Jaws, 5, 113	C. H. Borel	Demaloot Demashoot, 5, 116	Mr. Cooperative, 4, 119	7	1:09.49	90,000
1994	Demaloot Demashoot, 4, 115	M. E. Smith	Honor the Hero, 6, 117	Sir Hutch, 4, 118	6	1:08.39	90,000
1993	Approach, 6, 116	P. Day	Ponche, 4, 113	Never Wavering, 4, 110	13	1:09.64	90,000
1992	Gray Slewpy, 4, 117	K. Desormeaux	Potentiality, 6, 116	Hidden Tomahawk, 4, 115	7	1:08.97	60,000
1991	Overpeer, 7, 122	P. Day	Silent Reflex, 5, 113	Peaked, 6, 118	7	1:08.37	60,000
1990	Malagra, 4, 117	V. L. Smith	Pentelicus, 6, 115	Sunny Blossom, 5, 120	10	1:08.80	60,000
1989	Twice Around, 4, 116	C. H. Borel	Be a Agent, 5, 117	Never Forgotten, 5, 114	10	1:09.20	60,000
1988	Salt Dome, 5, 116	L. Snyder	Pewter, 4, 113	Bold Pac Man, 4, 112	9	1:08.60	60,000
1987	Sun Master, 6, 117	G. L. Stevens	Rocky Marriage, 7, 116	Chief Steward, 6, 118	8	1:09.40	69,540
1986	Mister Gennaro, 5, 115	F. Olivares	Beveled, 4, 114	Charging Falls, 5, 125	9	1:08.80	71,100
1985	Taylor's Special, 4, 123	R. P. Romero	Mt. Livermore, 4, 119	T. H. Bend, 4, 110	10	1:08.40	98,280
1984	Dave's Friend, 9, 122	E. Delahoussaye	†All Sold Out, 5, 114	Lucky Salvation, 4, 113	8	1:09.00	70,260
1983	Dave's Friend, 8, 124	L. Snyder	General Jimmy, 4, 117	Liberty Lane, 5, 113	9	1:10.00	70,320
1982	Sandbagger, 4, 114	D. Haire	Blue Water Line, 4, 117	Lockjaw, 4, 116	10	1:12.00	39,240
1981	General Custer, 5, 111	L. Snyder	Avenging Gossip, 4, 111	Be a Prospect, 4, 112	7	1:10.40	34,470
1980	Silent Dignity, 4, 114	S. Maple	Gustoso, 5, 111	J. Burns, 5, 115	7	1:11.00	34,680
1979	Amadevil, 5, 114	T. G. Greer	Little Reb, 4, 120	Sean's Song, 4, 114	7	1:11.20	34,890
1978	Last Buzz, 5, 126	A. Rini	Best Person, 4, 110	Sucha Pleasure, 4, 118	10	1:11.00	33,390
1977	Silver Hope, 6, 120	R. L. Turcotte	Dr's Enjoy Dollars, 5, 116	Brets Kicker, 6, 113	9	1:10.40	18,480
1976	Brets Kicker, 5, 111	J. D. Bailey	Silver Doctor, 6, 118	Mr. Barb, 4, 110	6	1:10.00	17,640
1975	Prince Astro, 6, 123	D. W. Whited	Silver Doctor, 5, 114	Faneuil Boy, 4, 112	7	1:10.00	18,030
1974	Barbizon Streak, 6, 114	R. Wilson	Pleasure Castle, 4, 120	Pesty Jay, 6, 122	7	1:11.00	17,370

Named for Mrs. John D. Hertz's Racing Hall of Fame member, 1943 Horse of the Year, '43 Triple Crown winner, and '51 leading North American sire Count Fleet (1940 c. by Reigh Count). Grade 2 1988-'89. Count Fleet H. 1974-'82. Three-year-olds and up 1974-'75, 1992, 2006. †Denotes female.

Crown Royal American Turf Stakes

Grade 3 in 2008. Churchill Downs, three-year-olds, 1 1/16 miles, turf. Held May 2, 2008, with a gross value of $181,950. First held in 1992. First graded in 1998. Stakes record 1:40.93 (1997 Royal Strand [Ire]).

Year	Winner	Jockey	Second	Third	Strs	Time	1st Purse
2008	Tizdejavu, 3, 117	G. K. Gomez	Sailor's Cap, 3, 117	Nistle's Crunch, 3, 117	9	1:46.14	$108,300
2007	Duveen, 3, 123	M. Guidry	Whatsthescript (Ire), 3, 123	Jazz Quest, 3, 121	10	1:44.03	111,146
2006	Stream Cat, 3, 122	J. R. Leparoux	Go Between, 3, 122	Gaelic Storm, 3, 117	6	1:42.27	70,158
2005	Rey de Cafe, 3, 122	J. Castellano	Rush Bay, 3, 116	Guillaume Tell (Ire), 3, 122	9	1:42.00	71,114
2004	Kitten's Joy, 3, 123	J. D. Bailey	Prince Arch, 3, 123	Capo, 3, 117	9	1:43.13	70,556
2003	Senor Swinger, 3, 117	P. Day	Remind, 3, 117	Foufa's Warrior, 3, 117	10	1:41.38	75,268
2002	Legislator, 3, 116	E. S. Prado	Stage Call (Ire), 3, 123	Orchard Park, 3, 123	10	1:44.43	72,106
2001	Strategic Partner, 3, 116	J. R. Velazquez	Baptize, 3, 123	Dynameaux, 3, 120	6	1:42.89	73,098
2000	King Cugat, 3, 123	J. D. Bailey	Lendell Ray, 3, 116	Go Lib Go, 3, 120	11	1:41.25	73,222
1999	Air Rocket, 3, 120	J. D. Bailey	Haus of Dehere, 3, 117	Conserve, 3, 118	10	1:42.65	71,548

Racing — Graded Stakes

Year	Winner	Jockey	Second	Third	Strs	Time	1st Purse
1998	Dernier Croise (Fr), 3, 116	G. L. Stevens	Tenbyssimo (Ire), 3, 123	Silver Lord, 3, 114	10	1:44.28	$78,120
1997	Royal Strand (Ire), 3, 116	P. Day	Rob 'n Gin, 3, 118	Deputy Commander, 3, 115	10	**1:40.93**	71,796
1996	Broadway Beau, 3, 114	C. J. McCarron	Trail City, 3, 123	Gotcha, 3, 114	10	1:41.87	76,375
1995	Unanimous Vote (Ire), 3, 120	G. L. Stevens	Nostra, 3, 116	Native Regent, 3, 123	10	1:42.07	76,700
1994	Jaggery John, 3, 123	M. E. Smith	Milt's Overture, 3, 116	Zuno Star, 3, 116	10	1:45.05	56,453
1993	‡Desert Waves, 3, 118	S. J. Sellers	Compadre, 3, 116	Super Snazzie, 3, 116	5	1:42.64	36,628
1992	Senor Tomas, 3, 118	M. E. Smith	Coaxing Matt, 3, 114	Black Question, 3, 123	8	1:43.10	37,440

Sponsored by the Crown Royal Co. of Stamford, Connecticut 1995-2007. American Turf S. 1992-'94. ‡Compadre finished first, DQ to second, 1993. Course record 1997.

Dahlia Handicap

Grade 2 in 2008. Hollywood Park, three-year-olds and up, fillies and mares, 1 1/16 miles, turf. Held December 16, 2007, with a gross value of $150,000. First held in 1982. First graded in 1984. Stakes record 1:40.40 (1989 Stylish Star).

Year	Winner	Jockey	Second	Third	Strs	Time	1st Purse
2007	Citronnade, 4, 122	D. R. Flores	Black Mamba (NZ), 4, 116	Lavender Sky, 3, 116	9	1:41.49	$90,000
2006	Grande Melody (Ire), 3, 114	J. R. Leparoux	Naissance Royale (Ire), 4, 120	Singalong (GB), 4, 114	10	1:40.96	90,000
2004	Festival (Jpn), 5, 111	D. Sorenson	Irgunette (Aus), 5, 113	Belle Ange (Fr), 3, 114	5	1:42.11	90,000
2003	Katdogawn (GB), 3, 116	M. E. Smith	Personal Legend, 3, 115	Betty's Wish, 3, 117	10	1:41.52	90,000
2002	dh-Surya, 4, 118	P. A. Valenzuela		Honestly Darling, 4, 114	9	1:44.55	60,000
	dh-Tout Charmant, 6, 119	A. O. Solis					
2001	Verruma (Brz), 5, 115	G. K. Gomez	Vencera (Fr), 4, 115	Heads Will Roll (GB), 3, 117	8	1:43.24	90,000
2000	Follow the Money, 4, 115	V. Espinoza	Smooth Player, 4, 120	Beautiful Noise, 4, 117	7	1:40.71	90,000
1999	Lady At Peace, 3, 113	G. K. Gomez	Cyrillic, 4, 117	Country Garden (GB), 4, 115	5	1:41.50	90,000
1998	Tuzla (Fr), 4, 119	C. S. Nakatani	Sonja's Faith (Ire), 4, 118	Curitiba, 4, 115	5	1:41.75	60,000
1997	Golden Arches (Fr), 3, 117	C. J. McCarron	Sonja's Faith (Ire), 3, 113	Traces of Gold, 5, 116	8	1:41.09	60,000
1996	Sixieme Sens, 4, 116	C. S. Nakatani	Grafin, 5, 116	Admise (Fr), 4, 121	8	1:42.37	66,600
1995	Didina (GB), 3, 115	E. Delahoussaye	Dirca (Ire), 3, 113	Rapunzel Runz, 4, 116	10	1:45.20	68,300
1994	Skimble, 5, 118	E. Delahoussaye	Queens Court Queen, 5, 118	Shir Dar (Fr), 4, 115	8	1:42.33	66,000
1993	Kalita Melody (GB), 5, 115	C. A. Black	Vinista, 3, 116	Gumpher, 5, 116	7	1:44.73	64,500
1992	Kostroma (Ire), 6, 124	G. L. Stevens	Vijaya, 5, 114	Guiza, 5, 116	8	1:41.40	66,500
1991	Re Toss (Arg), 4, 115	C. S. Nakatani	Elegance, 4, 115	Gaelic Bird (Fr), 4, 114	11	1:40.77	70,400
1990	Petalia, 5, 113	K. Desormeaux	Bequest, 4, 117	Island Jamboree, 4, 113	6	1:41.40	48,900
	Little Brianne, 5, 119	J. A. Garcia	Stylish Star, 4, 119	Girl of France (GB), 4, 115	7	1:40.60	50,900
1989	Stylish Star, 3, 116	C. J. McCarron	Ariosa, 5, 113	Sugarplum Gal, 4, 114	9	**1:40.40**	51,600
	Saros Brig, 5, 114	G. L. Stevens	Nikishka, 4, 120	Beat, 4, 115	7	1:40.40	49,600
1988	Balbonella (Fr), 4, 117	F. Toro	Goodbye Halo, 3, 120	Pen Bal Lady (GB), 4, 117	7	1:42.80	75,100
1987	Invited Guest (Ire), 3, 114	W. Shoemaker	Secuencia (Chi), 5, 115	Smooch (GB), 4, 117	9	1:43.40	71,950
	Top Corsage, 4, 118	J. A. Santos	Any Song (Ire), 4, 116	Aberuschka (Ire), 5, 120	6	1:43.20	48,700
1986	Aberuschka (Ire), 4, 122	P. A. Valenzuela	An Empress, 3, 117	Reloy, 3, 118	7	1:41.60	80,740
1985	Capricorn Belle (GB), 4, 117	C. J. McCarron	Justicara (Ire), 4, 118	Solva (GB), 4, 115	9	1:41.60	66,200
1984	Lina Cavalieri (GB), 4, 117	E. Delahoussaye	Pampas (Ire), 4, 115	Salt Spring (Arg), 5, 117	12	1:44.20	53,050
1983	Geraldine's Store, 4, 118	J. Samyn	Northerly Glow, 4, 111	Satin Ribera, 6, 115	8	1:42.40	32,500
	First Advance, 4, 114	T. Lipham	Absentia, 4, 116	Bersid, 5, 122	6	1:42.00	33,500
1982	Sangue (Ire), 4, 122	L. A. Pincay Jr.	Star Pastures (GB), 4, 118	Pat's Joy, 4, 115	7	1:41.40	31,900
	Milingo, 5, 114	T. Lipham	Pink Safir (Fr), 6, 112	Berry Bush, 5, 119	10	1:42.60	33,400

Named for Nelson Bunker Hunt's Racing Hall of Fame member and '76 Hollywood Invitational H. (G1) winner Dahlia (1970 f. by *Vaguely Noble). Grade 3 1984-'89, 2004. Not held 2005. Dirt 2004. Originally scheduled on turf 2004. Two divisions 1982-'83, 1987, 1989-'90. Dead heat for first 2002.

Dallas Turf Cup Handicap

Grade 3 in 2008. Lone Star Park, three-year-olds and up, 1 3/8 miles, turf. Held May 26, 2008, with a gross value of $200,000. First held in 1997. First graded in 2006. Stakes record 1:45.54 (1998 Yaqthan [Ire]).

Year	Winner	Jockey	Second	Third	Strs	Time	1st Purse
2008	Church Service, 5, 116	B. Blanc	Storm Military (Arg), 6, 115	Red Rock Creek, 7, 114	8	1:50.54	$120,000
2007	Embossed (Ire), 5, 117	G. K. Gomez	Crested (GB), 4, 115	Waupaca, 7, 116	7	1:52.68	120,000
2006	Trial by Jury, 7, 115	A. J. Juarez Jr.	New Export (Brz), 5, 116	Waupaca, 6, 116	6	1:52.69	120,000
2005	Sea Dub, 6, 115	L. Taylor	Fullbridled, 4, 114	Major Rhythm, 6, 116	11	1:48.82	120,000
2004	Maysville Slew, 8, 115	M. C. Berry	Star Over the Bay, 6, 115	A to the Z, 4, 115	7	1:49.89	120,000
2003	Patrol, 4, 116	M. J. Luzzi	Slew the Red, 6, 114	Storybook Kid, 5, 113	10	1:48.75	150,000
2002	Suances (GB), 4, 118	D. R. Flores	Our Main Man, 4, 113	Candid Glen, 5, 114	8	1:49.09	150,000
2001	El Gran Papa, 4, 113	G. K. Gomez	Dignitas Dancer, 5, 114	Nat's Big Party, 7, 114	8	1:49.30	180,000
2000	Gold Nugget, 5, 115	B. J. Walker Jr.	Majestic Jove, 6, 114	Northern Quest (Fr), 5, 112	10	1:53.17	150,000
1999	Martiniquais (Ire), 6, 117	D. R. Flores	Special Moments, 6, 115	Burbank, 6, 115	9	1:49.39	90,000
1998	Yaqthan (Ire), 8, 116	B. D. Peck	Burbank, 5, 116	Scott's Scoundrel, 6, 115	6	**1:45.54**	90,000
1997	Burbank, 4, 113	D. R. Pettinger	Lost Soldier, 7, 118	Hyderabad, 6, 114	8	1:47.55	90,000

Named for the city of Dallas; Lone Star Park is located in nearby Grand Prairie. Dallas Turf Cup S. 1999. Course record 1997, '98.

Darley Alcibiades Stakes

Grade 1 in 2008. Keeneland Race Course, two-year-olds, fillies, 1 1/16 miles, all weather. Held October 5, 2007, with a gross value of $500,000. First held in 1952. First graded in 1973. Stakes record 1:42.24 (1998 Silverbulletday).

Year	Winner	Jockey	Second	Third	Strs	Time	1st Purse
2007	Country Star, 2, 118	R. Bejarano	A to the Croft, 2, 118	Grace Anatomy, 2, 118	10	1:45.85	$310,000

Year	Winner	Jockey	Second	Third	Strs	Time	1st Purse
2006	Bel Air Beauty, 2, 118	F. Jara	Untouched Talent, 2, 118	Her Majesty, 2, 118	14	1:45.32	$248,000
2005	She Says It Best, 2, 118	E. M. Martin Jr.	Ex Caelis, 2, 118	Performing Diva, 2, 118	11	1:49.07	248,000
2004	Runway Model, 2, 118	R. Bejarano	Sharp Lisa, 2, 118	In the Gold, 2, 118	10	1:44.31	248,000
2003	Be Gentle, 2, 118	C. H. Velasquez	Galloping Gal, 2, 118	Deb's Charm, 2, 118	7	1:45.51	248,000
2002	Westerly Breeze, 2, 118	R. Albarado	Ruby's Reception, 2, 118	Final Round, 2, 118	9	1:46.90	276,024
2001	Take Charge Lady, 2, 118	A. J. D'Amico	Never Out, 2, 118	Cunning Play, 2, 118	11	1:44.23	280,736
2000	She's a Devil Due, 2, 118	M. Guidry	Nasty Storm, 2, 118	Cash Deal, 2, 118	7	1:44.86	270,320
1999	Scratch Pad, 2, 118	W. Martinez	Rare Beauty, 2, 118	Cash Run, 2, 118	8	1:44.16	274,288
1998	Silverbulletday, 2, 118	G. L. Stevens	Extended Applause, 2, 118	Grand Deed, 2, 118	11	1:42.24	281,976
1997	Countess Diana, 2, 118	S. J. Sellers	Lily O'Gold, 2, 118	Beautiful Pleasure, 2, 118	6	1:45.39	266,600
1996	Southern Playgirl, 2, 118	R. P. Romero	‡Screamer, 2, 118	Private Pursuit, 2, 118	7	1:46.94	168,330
1995	Cara Rafaela, 2, 118	P. Day	Birr, 2, 118	Gold Sunrise, 2, 118	10	1:44.43	139,252
1994	Post It, 2, 118	S. Maple	Morris Code, 2, 118	Cat Appeal, 2, 118	5	1:46.33	66,650
1993	Stellar Cat, 2, 118	S. J. Sellers	Slew Kitty Slew, 2, 118	Beau Blush, 2, 118	6	1:44.68	122,200
1992	Eliza, 2, 118	P. A. Valenzuela	Avie's Shadow, 2, 118	True Affair, 2, 118	6	1:43.30	122,200
1991	Spinning Round, 2, 118	J. M. Johnson	Queens Court Queen, 2, 118	Midnight Society, 2, 118	5	1:47.38	122,200
1990	Private Treasure, 2, 118	J. D. Bailey	Through Flight, 2, 118	Southern Bar Girl, 2, 118	8	1:43.80	173,420
1989	Special Happening, 2, 118	J. A. Santos	Talltalelady, 2, 118	Fashion Delight, 2, 118	7	1:44.60	141,375
1988	Wonders Delight, 2, 118	G. L. Stevens	Affirmed Classic, 2, 118	Seattle Meteor, 2, 118	7	1:46.40	130,000
1987	Terra Incognita, 2, 118	D. E. Foster	Epitome, 2, 118	Pearlie Gold, 2, 118	8	1:44.60	102,996
1986	Zero Minus, 2, 118	S. Hawley	Bound, 2, 118	Desirous, 2, 118	7	1:45.20	125,567
1985	Silent Account, 2, 118	K. K. Allen	Steal a Kiss, 2, 118	Python, 2, 118	10	1:46.20	132,321
1984	Foxy Deen, 2, 118	D. Montoya	Weekend Delight, 2, 118	Dusty Heart, 2, 118	12	1:45.60	117,224
1983	Lucky Lucky Lucky, 2, 118	J. Vasquez	Flippers, 2, 118	Geevilla, 2, 118	10	1:47.00	119,675
1982	Jelly Bean Holiday, 2, 118	D. Brumfield	Quarrel Over, 2, 118	Issues n' Answers, 2, 118	7	1:45.80	97,825
1981	Apalachee Honey, 2, 118	W. Shoemaker	Chilling Thought, 2, 118	Casual, 2, 118	10	1:45.20	102,034
1980	Sweet Revenge, 2, 118	J. Velasquez	Expressive Dance, 2, 118	Masters Dream, 2, 118	6	1:28.00	99,190
1979	Salud, 2, 118	J. C. Espinoza	Diorama, 2, 118	Sweetest Roman, 2, 118	6	1:28.20	93,503
1978	Angel Island, 2, 119	E. Delahoussaye	Terlingua, 2, 119	Too Many Sweets, 2, 119	7	1:26.40	89,619
1977	L'Alezane, 2, 119	R. Turcotte	Robalea, 2, 119	No No-Nos, 2, 119	5	1:27.20	80,990
1976	Sans Supplement, 2, 119	W. Gavidia	Avilion, 2, 119	Resolver, 2, 119	10	1:27.60	89,733
1975	Optimistic Gal, 2, 119	D. G. McHargue	Old Goat, 2, 119	Answer, 2, 119	9	1:28.00	79,593
1974	Hope of Glory, 2, 119	J. Nichols	Funny Cat, 2, 119	Snow Doll, 2, 119	9	1:27.20	54,197
1973	City Girl, 2, 119	E. Fires	Fairway Fable, 2, 119	Quick Cure, 2, 119	8	1:27.80	44,924

Named for Hal Price Headley's 1929 consensus champion two-year-old filly, '30 champion three-year-old filly, and '30 Kentucky Oaks winner Alcibiades (1927 f. by Supremus). Sponsored by Sheikh Mohammed bin Rashid al Maktoum's Darley 2003-'07. Formerly sponsored by Walmac Int'l. of Lexington 1997-2002. Grade 3 1973-'75. Grade 2 1976-2006. About 7 furlongs 1952-'80. Dirt 1952-2005. ‡Private Pursuit finished second, DQ to third, 1996.

Darley Test Stakes

Grade 1 in 2008. Saratoga Race Course, three-year-olds, fillies, 7 furlongs, dirt. Held August 4, 2007, with a gross value of $250,000. First held in 1922. First graded in 1973. Stakes record 1:20.83 (2003 Lady Tak).

Year	Winner	Jockey	Second	Third	Strs	Time	1st Purse
2007	Dream Rush, 3, 122	E. Coa	Boca Grande, 3, 120	Baroness Thatcher, 3, 118	12	1:22.42	$150,000
2006	Swap Fliparoo, 3, 116	E. Coa	Original Spin, 3, 118	Misty Rosette, 3, 118	13	1:24.13	150,000
2005	Leave Me Alone, 3, 118	K. Desormeaux	Hide and Chic, 3, 116	In the Gold, 3, 120	9	1:22.76	150,000
2004	Society Selection, 3, 120	E. S. Prado	Bending Strings, 3, 120	Forest Music, 3, 118	12	1:23.69	150,000
2003	Lady Tak, 3, 122	J. D. Bailey	Bird Town, 3, 122	House Party, 3, 122	7	1:20.83	150,000
2002	You, 3, 123	J. D. Bailey	Carson Hollow, 3, 120	Spring Meadow, 3, 120	7	1:22.84	150,000
2001	Victory Ride, 3, 116	E. S. Prado	Xtra Heat, 3, 123	Nasty Storm, 3, 120	8	1:21.72	150,000
2000	Dream Supreme, 3, 115	P. Day	Big Bambu, 3, 118	Finder's Fee, 3, 123	11	1:22.66	150,000
1999	Marley Vale, 3, 114	J. R. Velazquez	Awful Smart, 3, 114	Emanating, 3, 114	11	1:22.77	150,000
1998	Jersey Girl, 3, 123	M. E. Smith	Brave Deed, 3, 114	Catinca, 3, 114	11	1:23.02	120,000
1997	Fabulously Fast, 3, 114	J. D. Bailey	Aldiza, 3, 114	Pearl City, 3, 117	9	1:21.65	90,000
1996	Capote Belle, 3, 115	J. R. Velazquez	Flat Fleet Feet, 3, 115	J J'sdream, 3, 123	8	1:21.08	90,000
1995	Chaposa Springs, 3, 120	J. D. Bailey	Miss Golden Circle, 3, 114	Daijin, 3, 123	9	1:21.81	90,000
1994	Twist Afleet, 3, 114	J. D. Bailey	Penny's Reshoot, 3, 118	Heavenly Prize, 3, 121	8	1:22.08	90,000
1993	Missed the Storm, 3, 114	M. E. Smith	Miss Indy Anna, 3, 114	Educated Risk, 3, 114	5	1:22.12	90,000
1992	November Snow, 3, 116	C. W. Antley	Meafara, 3, 114	‡Classy Women, 3, 116	8	1:21.33	105,480
1991	Versailles Treaty, 3, 114	A. T. Cordero Jr.	Ifyoucouldseemenow, 3, 121	‡Classy Women, 3, 116	7	1:22.85	104,240
1990	Go for Wand, 3, 124	R. P. Romero	Screen Prospect, 3, 118	Token Dance, 3, 118	10	1:21.00	73,440
1989	Safely Kept, 3, 121	C. Perret	Fantastic Find, 3, 114	Cojinx, 3, 116	5	1:21.40	101,520
1988	Fara's Team, 3, 121	J. D. Bailey	Lake Valley, 3, 114	Classic Crown, 3, 118	11	1:22.60	109,980
1987	Very Subtle, 3, 121	P. A. Valenzuela	Up the Apalachee, 3, 121	Silent Turn, 3, 121	14	1:21.00	116,280
1986	Storm and Sunshine, 3, 118	C. Perret	Classy Cathy, 3, 121	I'm Sweets, 3, 121	7	1:22.80	103,500
1985	Lady's Secret, 3, 121	J. Velasquez	Mom's Command, 3, 124	Majestic Folly, 3, 118	6	1:21.60	99,600
1984	Sintra, 3, 116	K. K. Allen	Wild Applause, 3, 121	Lucky Lucky Lucky, 3, 124	9	1:22.60	101,404
1983	Lass Trump, 3, 114	P. Day	Medieval Moon, 3, 121	Chic Belle, 3, 114	9	1:22.80	34,380
1982	Gold Beauty, 3, 116	D. Brumfield	Ambassador of Luck, 3, 121	Number, 3, 114	12	1:22.80	35,940
1981	Cherokee Frolic, 3, 121	G. Cohen	Maddy's Tune, 3, 114	Discorama, 3, 118	6	1:23.20	34,140
1980	Love Sign, 3, 116	A. T. Cordero Jr.	Weber City Miss, 3, 121	Andrea F., 3, 114	7	1:22.20	33,900
1979	Blitey, 3, 114	A. T. Cordero Jr.	Jameela, 3, 114	Spanish Fake, 3, 121	10	1:22.60	25,987
	Clef d'Argent, 3, 114	R. Hernandez	Alada, 3, 114	Syncopating Lady, 3, 114	10	1:22.20	25,988

Racing — Graded Stakes 299

Year	Winner	Jockey	Second	Third	Strs	Time	1st Purse
1978	White Star Line, 3, 121	J. Fell	Silken Delight, 3, 114	Zerelda, 3, 114	8	1:21.40	$22,095
	Tingle Stone, 3, 114	R. Hernandez	Mucchina, 3, 121	Summer Fling, 3, 116	7	1:22.00	22,020
1977	Small Raja, 3, 124	M. Solomone	Pressing Date, 3, 114	Pearl Necklace, 3, 116	9	1:21.80	22,275
	Northern Sea, 3, 121	J. Velasquez	Northernette, 3, 121	Flying Above, 3, 114	8	1:22.40	22,200
1976	Ivory Wand, 3, 114	P. Day	Doc Shah's Siren, 3, 116	Pacific Princess, 3, 114	10	1:23.00	22,500
1975	Hot n Nasty, 3, 122	J. E. Tejeira	A Charm, 3, 116	Alpine Lass, 3, 116	7	1:22.00	19,665
	My Juliet, 3, 116	J. Vasquez	Slip Screen, 3, 113	‡Funalon, 3, 113	7	1:22.00	19,590
1974	Quaze Quilt, 3, 121	J. Vasquez	Maud Muller, 3, 113	Clear Copy, 3, 121	11	1:22.40	20,385
	Maybellene, 3, 116	D. Meade Jr.	Raisela, 3, 116	Stage Door Betty, 3, 121	11	1:23.60	20,385
1973	Desert Vixen, 3, 121	J. Velasquez	Full of Hope, 3, 118	Clandenita, 3, 118	5	1:23.00	13,470
	Waltz Fan, 3, 118	J. Velasquez	Gallant Davelle, 3, 116	Tuerta, 3, 116	7	1:23.60	13,545

Sometimes used as a prep or "test" for the Alabama S. (G1) later in the meet. Sponsored by Sheikh Mohammed bin Rashid al Maktoum's Darley 2006–'07. Grade 2 1973–'74, 1979–'87. Grade 3 1975–'78. Test S. 1922–2005. Held at Belmont Park 1943–'45. Not held 1923–'25, 1961. 1 1/4 miles 1922. Two divisions 1973–'75, 1977–'79. ‡Fleet Victress finished third, DQ to fourth, 1975 (2nd Div.). ‡Zama Hummer finished third, DQ to sixth, 1991.

Davona Dale Stakes

Grade 2 in 2008. Gulfstream Park, three-year-olds, fillies, 1 mile, dirt. Held March 2, 2008, with a gross value of $150,000. First held in 1988. First graded in 1993. Stakes record 1:37.34 (2007 Christmas Kid).

Year	Winner	Jockey	Second	Third	Strs	Time	1st Purse
2008	Bsharpsonata, 3, 119	E. Camacho	Game Face, 3, 119	Robbie's Gal, 3, 119	6	1:37.97	$90,000
2007	Christmas Kid, 3, 119	R. R. Douglas	High Again, 3, 117	Lisa M, 3, 119	8	**1:37.34**	90,000
2006	Wait a While, 3, 119	J. R. Velazquez	Teammate, 3, 115	Wonder Lady Anne L, 3, 119	7	1:50.27	90,000
2005	Sis City, 3, 121	J. R. Velazquez	In the Gold, 3, 117	Jill Robin L, 3, 117	6	1:50.20	90,000
2004	Miss Coronado, 3, 117	C. H. Velasquez	Eye Dazzler, 3, 115	Society Selection, 3, 121	7	1:44.62	90,000
2003	Yell, 3, 117	J. R. Velazquez	Ivanavinalot, 3, 121	Gold Player, 3, 115	5	1:44.96	90,000
2002	Ms Brookski, 3, 121	R. Homeister Jr.	Colonial Glitter, 3, 117	French Satin, 3, 115	9	1:45.14	60,000
2001	Latour, 3, 112	J. R. Velazquez	Gold Mover, 3, 116	Courageous Maiden, 3, 113	7	1:45.51	60,000
2000	Cash Run, 3, 118	J. D. Bailey	Regally Appealing, 3, 116	Secret Status, 3, 114	9	1:40.37	60,000
1999	Three Ring, 3, 118	J. R. Velazquez	Golden Temper, 3, 113	Gold From the West, 3, 116	5	1:41.53	60,000
1998	Diamond On the Run, 3, 112	J. R. Velazquez	Uanme, 3, 114	Dixie Melody, 3, 113	10	1:42.65	60,000
1997	Glitter Woman, 3, 114	M. E. Smith	City Band, 3, 121	Southern Playgirl, 3, 121	6	1:39.31	60,000
1996	Plum Country, 3, 118	P. Day	‡My Flag, 3, 118	La Rosa, 3, 118	9	1:42.08	60,000
1995	Mia's Hope, 3, 114	K. L. Chapman	Minister Wife, 3, 113	Culver City, 3, 113	6	1:43.26	60,000
1994	Cut the Charm, 3, 118	J. D. Bailey	She Rides Tonite, 3, 114	Delightful Bet, 3, 113	8	1:41.44	60,000
1993	Lunar Spook, 3, 118	M. Guidry	Boots 'n Jackie, 3, 121	In Her Glory, 3, 112	7	1:42.09	30,000
1992	Miss Legality, 3, 116	J. A. Krone	November Snow, 3, 114	Spectacular Sue, 3, 114	8	1:42.00	30,000
1991	Fancy Ribbons, 3, 118	C. Perret	Hula Pride, 3, 114	Designated Dancer, 3, 116	9	1:41.10	45,420
1990	Big Pride, 3, 112	E. Fires	Crowned, 3, 121	Sonic Gray, 3, 112	6	1:26.00	21,000
1989	Waggley, 6, 122	J. Samyn	Plate Queen, 4, 113	Ataentsic, 5, 113	7	1:27.00	20,640
1988	Charming Tigress, 5, 115	P. Day	Polar Wind, 4, 117	No Doublet, 5, 115	9	1:24.60	21,069
	Cadillacing, 4, 122	R. P. Romero	Easter Mary, 4, 115	Saucey Missy, 5, 117	9	1:23.00	21,249

Named for Calumet Farm's Racing Hall of Fame member, 1979 Filly Triple Crown winner, and '79 Bonnie Miss S. winner Davona Dale (1976 f. by Best Turn). Grade 3 1993–'97. Davona Dale H. 1988. Davona Dale Breeders' Cup S. 1989, '91. 7 furlongs 1988–'90. 1 mile 70 yards 1991–2000. 1 1/16 miles 2001–'04. 1 1/8 miles 2005–'06. Four-year-olds and up 1988. Three-year-olds and up 1989. Fillies and mares 1988, '89. Two divisions 1988. ‡Rare Blend finished second, DQ to sixth, 1996.

Debutante Stakes

Grade 3 in 2008. Churchill Downs, two-year-olds, fillies, 6 furlongs, dirt. Held July 7, 2007, with a gross value of $111,000. First held in 1889. First graded in 1996. Stakes record 1:09.27 (2007 Rated Fiesty).

Year	Winner	Jockey	Second	Third	Strs	Time	1st Purse
2007	Rated Fiesty, 2, 122	S. Bridgmohan	Dreabons Legacy, 2, 118	American County, 2, 118	8	**1:09.27**	$66,756
2006	Richwoman, 2, 122	S. Bridgmohan	Chagall, 2, 118	Lenaro, 2, 118	6	1:10.50	67,335
2005	Effectual, 2, 117	R. Albarado	Joint Effort, 2, 117	Swept Gold, 2, 117	9	1:03.95	69,812
2004	Classic Elegance, 2, 117	P. Day	Paragon Queen, 2, 117	Cool Spell, 2, 117	9	1:04.18	68,696
2003	Be Gentle, 2, 117	C. H. Velasquez	Renaissance Lady, 2, 117	Sweet Jo Jo, 2, 117	8	1:03.96	68,758
2002	Awesome Humor, 2, 115	C. H. Borel	Vibs, 2, 115	Attemptress, 2, 115	7	1:03.45	67,890
2001	Cashier's Dream, 2, 118	D. J. Meche	Lakeside Cup, 2, 115	Colonial Glitter, 2, 115	8	1:02.52	68,510
2000	Gold Mover, 2, 121	C. Perret	Princess Belle, 2, 115	Tricky Elaine, 2, 115	9	1:03.79	69,626
1999	Chilukki, 2, 121	W. Martinez	Miss Wineshine, 2, 112	Cecilia's Crown, 2, 115	9	1:03.66	69,998
1998	Silverbulletday, 2, 115	W. Martinez	The Happy Hopper, 2, 115	Mancari's Rose, 2, 115	9	1:04.70	69,502
1997	Love Lock, 2, 115	P. Day	Countess Diana, 2, 115	Quick Lap, 2, 115	13	1:03.84	72,478
1996	Move, 2, 121	P. Day	Sarah's Prospector, 2, 115	Live Your Best, 2, 115	10	1:05.66	73,840
1995	Golden Attraction, 2, 115	D. M. Barton	Western Dreamer, 2, 121	Tipically Irish, 2, 115	9	1:04.19	70,948
1994	Chargedupsycamore, 2, 121	P. Day	Phone Bird, 2, 116	Our Gem, 2, 116	9	1:05.24	54,405
1993	Fly Love, 2, 116	B. E. Bartram	Miss Ra He Ra, 2, 116	Astas Foxy Lady, 2, 121	11	1:05.23	37,635
1992	Hollywood Wildcat, 2, 116	F. A. Arguello Jr.	Cosmic Speed Queen, 2, 116	Royal Beat, 2, 116	9	1:06.02	38,480
1991	Greenhaven Lane, 2, 112	K. Tsuchiya	Moment of Grace, 2, 114	One for Smoke, 2, 116	11	1:06.23	36,953
1990	Barbara's Nemesis, 2, 116	J. Deegan	Gracielle, 2, 112	Cosmic Music, 2, 112	10	1:12.00	36,693
1989	Icy Folly, 2, 116	K. K. Allen	Hard Freeze, 2, 118	Lucy's Glory, 2, 118	14	1:11.20	37,993
1988	Seaquay, 2, 114	R. M. Ehrlinspiel	Weekend Spree, 2, 118	Coax Chelsie, 2, 112	8	1:11.20	35,718
1987	Bold Lady Anne, 2, 118	J. Davidson	Over All, 2, 118	Penny's Growl, 2, 114	7	1:11.60	25,773
	Dark Silver, 2, 116	M. McDowell	She's Freezing, 2, 116	Saved by Grace, 2, 116	9	1:12.60	26,260

Racing — Graded Stakes

Year	Winner	Jockey	Second	Third	Strs	Time	1st Purse
1986	Burnished Bright, 2, 121	P. Day	Before Sundown, 2, 118	Shivering Gal, 2, 115	7	1:11.20	$46,810
1985	Tricky Fingers, 2, 115	L. J. Melancon	Likker Is Quikker, 2, 118	Time for Honor, 2, 115	12	1:05.20	31,013
1984	Knot, 2, 115	K. K. Allen	Don't Joke, 2, 112	Off Shore Breeze, 2, 115	10	1:06.40	22,393
1983	Arabizon, 2, 115	L. Moyers	Ark, 2, 115	Starafar, 2, 113	9	1:05.80	22,181
1982	Ice Fantasy, 2, 115	P. A. Johnson	Wrong Answer, 2, 115	Fifth Affair, 2, 121	12	1:04.60	20,735
1981	Pure Platinum, 2, 119	P. Day	Miss Preakness, 2, 119	Cypress Bay, 2, 119	10	:58.80	19,939
1980	Excitable Lady, 2, 119	D. Brumfield	Masters Dream, 2, 119	Bend the Times, 2, 119	7	:58.60	19,484
1979	Lissy, 2, 114	M. S. Sellers	Barbizon's Flower, 2, 119	Happy Hollie, 2, 119	13	:59.80	20,426
1978	Nervous John, 2, 122	C. J. McCarron	Porpourie, 2, 114	Rainbow Streak, 2, 122	7	:58.40	14,658
1977	Sweet Little Lady, 2, 122	R. Turcotte	Sahsie, 2, 119	‡Crystalan, 2, 122	8	:58.00	14,706
1976	Olden, 2, 122	R. Breen	Jungle Angel, 2, 119	Every Move, 2, 114	9	:58.80	14,950
1975	Answer, 2, 119	M. Hole	Pink Jade, 2, 122	Turn Over, 2, 119	8	:58.20	16,283
1974	Sun and Snow, 2, 119	E. Guerin	Floral Princess, 2, 114	Classy Note, 2, 119	13	:59.40	17,794
1973	Me and Connie, 2, 124	J. Nichols	Bundler, 2, 119	Shanjar, 2, 114	7	:58.20	16,835

Young women making their first formal appearance in society are known as debutantes. Churchill Downs Debutante S. 1928. Not held 1932-'37. 4 furlongs 1895-1922. 4½ furlongs 1923-'25. 5 furlongs 1926-'81. 6 furlongs 1986-'90. Two divisions 1987. ‡Miss Poodle Pup finished third, DQ to fourth, 1977. Equaled track record 1997, '99. Track record 2001.

Delaware Handicap

Grade 2 in 2008. Delaware Park, three-year-olds and up, fillies and mares, 1¼ miles, dirt. Held July 15, 2007, with a gross value of $1,000,900. First held in 1937. First graded in 1973. Stakes record 1:59.80 (1987 Coup de Fusil).

Year	Winner	Jockey	Second	Third	Strs	Time	1st Purse
2007	Unbridled Belle, 4, 115	R. A. Dominguez	Lila Paige, 6, 113	Promenade Girl, 5, 117	8	2:01.16	$600,000
2006	Fleet Indian, 5, 120	J. A. Santos	Dynamic Deputy, 4, 114	Take a Check, 4, 115	9	2:02.08	600,000
2005	Island Sand, 4, 115	J. D. Bailey	Two Trail Sioux, 4, 117	Personal Legend, 5, 114	11	2:02.89	600,000
2004	Summer Wind Dancer, 4, 116	V. Espinoza	Roar Emotion, 4, 117	Misty Sixes, 6, 116	8	2:03.63	450,000
2003	Wild Spirit (Chi), 4, 117	J. D. Bailey	Take Charge Lady, 4, 120	Shiny Sheet, 5, 112	8	2:02.95	450,000
2002	Summer Colony, 4, 118	J. R. Velazquez	Your Out, 4, 113	Two Item Limit, 4, 115	9	2:04.52	360,000
2001	Irving's Baby, 4, 113	R. A. Dominguez	Under the Rug, 6, 115	Lazy Slusan, 6, 121	6	2:05.21	360,000
2000	Lu Ravi, 5, 117	P. Day	Tap to Music, 5, 116	Silverbulletday, 4, 119	8	2:02.21	360,000
1999	Tap to Music, 4, 116	P. Day	Keeper Hill, 4, 120	Unbridled Hope, 5, 114	13	2:02.15	300,000
1998	Amarillo, 4, 110	J. A. Krone	Tuxedo Junction, 5, 115	Timely Broad, 4, 110	9	2:04.37	300,000
1997	Power Play, 5, 114	L. C. Reynolds	Gold n Delicious, 4, 115	Effectiveness, 4, 113	11	2:03.40	210,000
1996	Urbane, 4, 117	A. O. Solis	Alcovy, 6, 117	Shoop, 5, 115	13	2:01.89	180,000
1995	Night Fax, 4, 108	J. D. Carle	Cavada, 4, 113	It's Personal, 5, 114	9	2:02.98	95,070
1994	With a Wink, 4, 114	R. Migliore	Passing Vice, 4, 115	Alphabulous, 5, 111	9	2:03.37	95,150
1993	Green Darlin, 4, 113	M. J. Luzzi	Girl On a Mission, 4, 116	Starry Val, 4, 112	11	2:03.76	96,300
1992	Brilliant Brass, 5, 117	E. S. Prado	Train Robbery, 5, 111	Risen Colony, 4, 113	6	2:03.11	93,780
1991	Crowned, 4, 117	R. Wilson	Maskra's Lady, 4, 114	Tia Juanita, 5, 113	8	2:04.01	69,420
1990	Seattle Dawn, 4, 115	R. E. Colton	Warfie, 4, 112	Thirty Eight Go Go, 5, 115	7	2:03.00	68,160
1989	Nastique, 5, 120	E. Maple	Colonial Waters, 4, 117	Thirty Eight Go Go, 4, 118	4	2:01.20	64,890
1988	Nastique, 4, 116	E. Maple	Ms. Eloise, 5, 117	Lawyer Talk, 4, 112	7	2:07.60	67,410
1987	Coup de Fusil, 5, 114	A. T. Cordero Jr.	Steal a Kiss, 4, 113	Catatonic, 5, 118	6	1:59.80	68,760
1986	Shocker T., 4, 122	G. St. Leon	Endear, 4, 122	Leecoo, 5, 112	6	2:02.20	69,120
1985	Basie, 4, 110	J. Cruguet	Heatherten, 6, 126	Life's Magic, 4, 122	5	2:02.00	93,360
1984	Adored, 4, 120	L. A. Pincay Jr.	Mademoiselle Forli, 5, 114	Weekend Surprise, 4, 111	6	2:03.20	94,680
1983	May Day Eighty, 4, 115	J. Vasquez	Try Something New, 4, 116	Broom Dance, 4, 113	6	2:03.20	66,722
1982	Jameela, 6, 121	J. L. Kaenel	Zvetlana, 4, 111	Love Sign, 5, 125	9	2:02.60	74,523
1981	Relaxing, 5, 119	A. T. Cordero Jr.	Wistful, 4, 121	Lady of Promise, 4, 111	10	2:01.00	75,075
1980	Heavenly Ade, 4, 112	J. D. Bailey	Croquis, 4, 112	Blitey, 4, 113	9	2:00.00	93,893
1979	Likely Exchange, 5, 112	M. S. Sellers	Sans Critique, 5, 111	Plains and Simple, 4, 110	9	2:03.40	73,938
1978	Late Bloomer, 4, 119	J. Velasquez	Dottie's Doll, 5, 117	Cum Laude Laurie, 4, 119	9	2:02.20	73,938
1977	Our Mims, 3, 117	J. Velasquez	Mississippi Mud, 4, 124	Dottie's Doll, 4, 118	5	2:01.00	70,785
1976	Optimistic Gal, 3, 119	E. Maple	T. V. Vixen, 3, 118	Vodka Time, 4, 115	6	2:01.00	65,040
1975	Susan's Girl, 6, 125	R. Broussard	Pass a Glance, 4, 116	Raisela, 4, 117	6	2:01.80	70,915
1974	Krislin, 5, 115	A. T. Cordero Jr.	Twixt, 5, 124	Summer Guest, 5, 114	9	2:01.60	74,555
1973	Susan's Girl, 4, 127	L. A. Pincay Jr.	Summer Guest, 4, 122	Light Hearted, 4, 125	6	2:00.60	71,305

Formerly named for the city of New Castle, Delaware. Grade 1 1973-'89. Grade 3 1996-2002. New Castle H. 1937-'54. Held at Saratoga 1983-'85. Not held 1943. 1 1/16 miles 1937-'50.

Delaware Oaks

Grade 2 in 2008. Delaware Park, three-year-olds, fillies, 1 1/16 miles, dirt. Held July 14, 2007, with a gross value of $505,600. First held in 1938. First graded in 1973. Stakes record 1:42.39 (2007 Moon Catcher).

Year	Winner	Jockey	Second	Third	Strs	Time	1st Purse
2007	Moon Catcher, 3, 120	C. H. Marquez Jr.	Winning Point, 3, 116	Cotton Blossom, 3, 122	7	1:42.39	$305,000
2006	Adieu, 3, 116	J. R. Velazquez	Amandatude, 3, 116	Gasia, 3, 120	8	1:43.72	300,000
2005	R Lady Joy, 3, 119	J. Lezcano	Round Pond, 3, 122	Dance Away Capote, 3, 116	6	1:43.25	300,000
2004	Yearly Report, 3, 122	J. D. Bailey	Ender's Sister, 3, 119	A Lulu Ofa Menifee, 3, 115	8	1:43.80	300,000
2003	Island Fashion, 3, 122	I. Puglisi	Awesome Humor, 3, 115	Ladyecho, 3, 115	9	1:44.95	300,000
2002	Allamerican Bertie, 3, 115	L. J. Melancon	Alternate, 3, 117	Pass the Virtue, 3, 119	6	1:43.40	150,000
2001	Zonk, 3, 115	M. J. McCarthy	Mystic Lady, 3, 122	Lady Andromeda, 3, 115	11	1:45.27	151,000
2000	Sincerely, 3, 117	M. J. McCarthy	Trip, 3, 119	Valleydar, 3, 117	5	1:43.83	150,000
1999	Brushed Halory, 3, 115	E. M. Martin Jr.	Gold From the West, 3, 115	Queen's Word, 3, 115	5	1:43.42	150,000

Racing — Graded Stakes 301

Year	Winner	Jockey	Second	Third	Strs	Time	1st Purse
1998	**Nickel Classic**, 3, 119	C. H. Borel	Lu Ravi, 3, 122	Taffy Davenport, 3, 117	8	1:42.81	$120,000
1997	**Runup the Colors**, 3, 116	P. Day	Timely Broad, 3, 113	City Band, 3, 113	10	1:44.20	90,000
1996	**Like a Hawk**, 3, 114	R. E. Colton	Mercedes Song, 3, 118	Winter Melody, 3, 118	10	1:37.01	30,000
1982	**Lady Eleanor**, 3, 115	R. Wilson	Sailing Hour, 3, 112	Milingo, 3, 115	10	1:50.20	38,480
1981	**Up the Flagpole**, 3, 112	K. D. Black	Stunning Native, 3, 112	Object d'Art, 3, 113	6	1:49.40	53,820
1980	**Bishop's Ring**, 3, 112	M. G. Pino	Diplomatic Role, 3, 122	Sugar and Spice, 3, 122	7	1:48.60	53,203
1979	**It's in the Air**, 3, 122	W. Shoemaker	Jameela, 3, 115	Himalayan, 3, 114	6	1:49.40	52,780
1978	**White Star Line**, 3, 122	J. Fell	Queen Lib, 3, 119	Silken Delight, 3, 114	6	1:52.60	35,230
1977	**Cum Laude Laurie**, 3, 112	J. Velasquez	Pressing Date, 3, 113	Sweet Alliance, 3, 122	7	1:48.20	35,490
1976	**‡Pacific Princess**, 3, 111	E. Maple	T. V. Vixen, 3, 125	All Rainbows, 3, 114	9	1:49.60	33,660
1975	**Let Me Linger**, 3, 117	C. Barrera	dh-Funalon, 3, 123		9	1:51.40	36,237
			dh-M'lle. Cyanne, 3, 117				
1974	**Plantain**, 3, 114	G. McCarron	Enchanted Native, 3, 111	Knightly Wooing, 3, 114	14	1:50.40	38,350
1973	**Desert Vixen**, 3, 121	J. Velasquez	Bag of Tunes, 3, 121	Ladies Agreement, 3, 112	10	1:49.20	37,083

Grade 3 1999-2003. Not held 1943, 1983-'95. 1¹⁄₈ miles 1938-'82. 1 mile 1996. Turf 1996. Dead heat for second 1975. ‡T. V. Vixen finished first, DQ to second, 1976.

Del Mar Debutante Stakes

Grade 1 in 2008. Del Mar, two-year-olds, fillies, 7 furlongs, all weather. Held September 3, 2007, with a gross value of $250,000. First held in 1951. First graded in 1973. Stakes record 1:21.45 (1994 Call Now).

Year	Winner	Jockey	Second	Third	Strs	Time	1st Purse
2007	**Set Play**, 2, 117	B. Blanc	Spring Awakening, 2, 117	Izarra, 2, 117	12	1:26.79	$150,000
2006	**Point Ashley**, 2, 117	V. Espinoza	Untouched Talent, 2, 121	She's Included, 2, 117	8	1:23.34	150,000
2005	**Wild Fit**, 2, 117	A. O. Solis	Mystery Girl, 2, 117	River's Prayer, 2, 121	11	1:23.20	150,000
2004	**Sweet Catomine**, 2, 114	V. Espinoza	Souvenir Gift, 2, 120	Hello Lucky, 2, 116	9	1:24.18	150,000
2003	**Halfbridled**, 2, 116	J. A. Krone	Hollywood Story, 2, 115	Victory U. S. A., 2, 116	6	1:22.20	150,000
2002	**Miss Houdini**, 2, 116	G. L. Stevens	Santa Catarina, 2, 115	Indy Groove, 2, 115	8	1:23.43	150,000
2001	**Habibti**, 2, 115	V. Espinoza	Who Loves Aleyna, 2, 116	Tempera, 2, 117	5	1:22.22	150,000
2000	**Cindy's Hero**, 2, 114	G. K. Gomez	Notable Career, 2, 119	Euro Empire, 2, 119	5	1:22.61	150,000
1999	**Chilukki**, 2, 121	D. R. Flores	Spain, 2, 115	She's Classy, 2, 116	7	1:23.54	150,000
1998	**Excellent Meeting**, 2, 115	K. Desormeaux	Antahkarana, 2, 115	Colorado Song, 2, 115	9	1:22.34	150,000
1997	**Vivid Angel**, 2, 115	K. Desormeaux	Griselle, 2, 115	Czarina, 2, 117	8	1:24.26	150,000
1996	**Sharp Cat**, 2, 115	R. R. Douglas	Desert Digger, 2, 119	Broad Dynamite, 2, 116	10	1:23.98	150,000
1995	**Batroyale**, 2, 119	M. A. Pedroza	Proud Dixie, 2, 117	General Idea, 2, 116	12	1:22.55	137,500
1994	**Call Now**, 2, 115	A. O. Solis	How So Oiseau, 2, 119	Ski Dancer, 2, 116	9	**1:21.45**	137,500
1993	**Sardula**, 2, 116	E. Delahoussaye	Phone Chatter, 2, 119	Ballerina Gal, 2, 114	8	1:21.61	137,500
1992	**Beal Street Blues**, 2, 116	G. L. Stevens	Fit n Fappy, 2, 114	Zoonaqua, 2, 120	9	1:37.17	137,500
1991	**La Spia**, 2, 114	A. O. Solis	Soviet Sojourn, 2, 120	Wicked Wit, 2, 118	7	1:37.09	161,000
1990	**Beyond Perfection**, 2, 114	A. O. Solis	Lite Light, 2, 120	Title Bought, 2, 116	7	1:34.80	191,400
1989	**Rue de Palm**, 2, 115	R. A. Baze	Dominant Dancer, 2, 118	Cheval Volant, 2, 118	9	1:35.00	202,050
1988	**‡Lea Lucinda**, 2, 114	G. L. Stevens	Approved to Fly, 2, 114	Beware of the Cat, 2, 115	8	1:36.40	193,850
1987	**Lost Kitty**, 2, 117	G. L. Stevens	Royal Weekend, 2, 113	Hasty Pasty, 2, 117	5	1:36.00	128,850
1986	**Brave Raj**, 2, 117	C. A. Black	Road to Happiness, 2, 113	Soft Copy, 2, 115	7	1:35.80	125,325
1985	**Arewehavingfunyet**, 2, 120	P. A. Valenzuela	Python, 2, 117	Wee Lavaliere, 2, 117	6	1:36.00	134,210
1984	**Fiesta Lady**, 2, 117	L. A. Pincay Jr.	Doon's Baby, 2, 119	Trunk, 2, 115	7	1:38.80	93,050
	Full O Wisdom, 2, 113	C. J. McCarron	Pirate's Glow, 2, 115	Wayward Pirate, 2, 119	5	1:37.40	91,050
1983	**Althea**, 2, 119	L. A. Pincay Jr.	Diachrony, 2, 113	Victorious Joy, 2, 113	6	1:36.00	126,190
1982	**Landaluce**, 2, 119	L. A. Pincay Jr.	Issues n' Answers, 2, 116	Granja Reina, 2, 113	6	1:35.60	124,655
1981	**Skillful Joy**, 2, 113	C. J. McCarron	Marl Lee Ann, 2, 113	A Kiss for Luck, 2, 116	12	1:37.40	138,310
1980	**Raja's Delight**, 2, 113	C. J. McCarron	Prestigious Lady, 2, 115	Native Fancy, 2, 119	10	1:37.40	110,225
1979	**Table Hands**, 2, 119	W. Shoemaker	Hazel R., 2, 116	Arcades Ambo, 2, 117	9	1:35.00	106,770
1978	**Terlingua**, 2, 119	D. G. McHargue	Beauty Hour, 2, 116	Blowin' Wild, 2, 113	8	1:36.20	79,140
1977	**Extravagant**, 2, 113	M. Castaneda	Foxy Juliana, 2, 115	Honey Jar, 2, 113	12	1:36.40	81,490
1976	**Telferner**, 2, 116	L. A. Pincay Jr.	Asterisca, 2, 113	Maxine N., 2, 113	7	1:37.20	65,175
1975	**Queen to Be**, 2, 116	D. G. McHargue	T. V. Terese, 2, 113	Awaken, 2, 113	6	1:36.80	57,805
1974	**Bubblewin**, 2, 113	W. Shoemaker	Spout, 2, 116	Cut Class, 2, 114	6	1:36.80	57,445
1973	**Fleet Peach**, 2, 116	D. Pierce	Fresno Star, 2, 113	Divine Grace, 2, 113	8	1:09.60	46,205

Young women making their first formal appearance in society are known as debutantes. Formerly sponsored by Vinery of Lexington, Kentucky 1999. Grade 2 1973-'98. 6 furlongs 1951-'73. 1 mile 1974-'92. Dirt 1951-2006. Two divisions 1984. ‡Approved to Fly finished first, DQ to second, 1988.

Del Mar Derby

Grade 2 in 2008. Del Mar, three-year-olds, 1¹⁄₈ miles, turf. Held September 2, 2007, with a gross value of $400,000. First held in 1945. First graded in 1973. Stakes record 1:45.85 (2005 Willow O Wisp).

Year	Winner	Jockey	Second	Third	Strs	Time	1st Purse
2007	**Medici Code (GB)**, 3, 122	M. A. Pedroza	Augment, 3, 122	Worldly (GB), 3, 122	10	1:47.10	$240,000
2006	**Get Funky**, 3, 122	J. Valdivia Jr.	Obrigado (Fr), 3, 122	Union Avenue, 3, 122	9	1:46.39	240,000
2005	**Willow O Wisp**, 3, 122	G. K. Gomez	Tedo (Ger), 3, 122	Osidy, 3, 122	13	**1:45.85**	240,000
2004	**Blackdoun (Fr)**, 3, 122	C. S. Nakatani	Toasted, 3, 122	Laura's Lucky Boy, 3, 122	10	1:46.75	240,000
2003	**Fairly Ransom**, 3, 122	A. O. Solis	Devious Boy (GB), 3, 122	Sweet Return (GB), 3, 122	9	1:46.45	180,000
2002	**Inesperado (Fr)**, 3, 121	C. S. Nakatani	Johar, 3, 121	Rock Opera, 3, 121	9	1:47.49	180,000
2001	**Romanceishope**, 3, 121	C. J. McCarron	Indygo Shiner, 3, 121	Blue Steller (Ire), 3, 121	10	1:47.93	180,000

Racing — Graded Stakes

Year	Winner	Jockey	Second	Third	Strs	Time	1st Purse
2000	Walkslikeaduck, 3, 121	E. Delahoussaye	Purely Cozzene, 3, 121	†New Story, 3, 118	10	1:46.66	$180,000
1999	Val Royal (Fr), 3, 121	C. S. Nakatani	Fighting Falcon, 3, 121	In Frank's Honor, 3, 121	10	1:48.53	180,000
1998	Ladies Din, 3, 121	K. Desormeaux	Expressionist, 3, 121	Scooter Brown, 3, 121	9	1:48.59	180,000
1997	Anet, 3, 121	G. L. Stevens	Brave Act (GB), 3, 121	Worldly Ways (GB), 3, 121	7	1:48.42	180,000
1996	Rainbow Blues (Ire), 3, 122	C. S. Nakatani	The Barking Shark, 3, 122	Mateo, 3, 122	9	1:50.01	180,000
1995	Da Hoss, 3, 122	R. R. Douglas	Lake George, 3, 122	Tabor, 3, 122	9	1:48.08	165,000
1994	Ocean Crest, 3, 122	L. A. Pincay Jr.	Unfinished Symph, 3, 122	‡Powis Castle, 3, 122	10	1:48.74	165,000
1993	Guide (Fr), 3, 122	K. Desormeaux	Future Storm, 3, 122	The Real Vaslav, 3, 122	12	1:49.73	165,000
1992	Daros (GB), 3, 122	E. Delahoussaye	Smiling and Dancin, 3, 122	Major Impact, 3, 122	12	1:48.80	165,000
1991	Eternity Star, 3, 122	F. T. Alvarado	Stark South, 3, 122	June's Reward, 3, 122	10	1:49.24	165,000
1990	Tight Spot, 3, 122	L. A. Pincay Jr.	Itsallgreektome, 3, 122	Predecessor, 3, 122	10	1:49.60	165,000
1989	Hawkster, 3, 121	P. A. Valenzuela	River Master, 3, 119	Lode, 3, 116	9	1:48.00	130,500
1988	Silver Circus, 3, 118	R. A. Baze	Perfecting, 3, 118	Roberto's Dancer, 3, 116	8	1:49.00	127,900
1987	Deputy Governor, 3, 119	E. Delahoussaye	Stately Don, 3, 120	The Medic, 3, 118	9	1:48.40	98,700
1986	Vernon Castle, 3, 123	E. Delahoussaye	Prince Bobby B., 3, 119	Mazaad (Ire), 3, 119	9	1:48.40	95,500
1985	First Norman, 3, 117	G. L. Stevens	Pretensor, 3, 116	Catane, 3, 112	9	1:48.00	82,300
1984	Tsunami Slew, 3, 119	E. Delahoussaye	Prince True, 3, 119	Majestic Shore, 3, 115	12	1:48.00	99,650
1983	Tanks Brigade, 3, 122	R. Q. Meza	Ansuan, 3, 115	Evening M'lord (Ire), 3, 117	11	1:49.00	85,350
1982	Give Me Strength, 3, 123	L. A. Pincay Jr.	Water Bank, 3, 117	Take the Floor, 3, 117	13	1:49.00	88,100
1981	Juan Barrera, 3, 115	F. Toro	Buen Chico, 3, 114	Rock Softly, 3, 113	10	1:49.00	83,950
1980	Exploded, 3, 117	L. A. Pincay Jr.	Aristocratical, 3, 120	Son of a Dodo, 3, 118	10	1:49.60	70,300
1979	Relaunch, 3, 121	L. A. Pincay Jr.	Kamalii King, 3, 111	Pole Position, 3, 120	8	1:48.80	51,450
1978	Misrepresentation, 3, 119	D. Pierce	Singular, 3, 119	Wayside Station, 3, 115	10	1:49.60	33,450
1977	Text, 3, 122	D. G. McHargue	Pay the Toll, 3, 119	Hill Fox, 3, 115	10	1:49.40	32,750
1976	Montespan, 3, 115	D. G. McHargue	Dr. Krohn, 3, 117	Today 'n Tomorrow, 3, 118	10	1:48.40	26,550
1975	Larrikin, 3, 116	D. Pierce	Messenger of Song, 3, 116	Wood Carver, 3, 115	9	1:48.80	28,900
1974	Lightning Mandate, 3, 116	A. Pineda	Within Hail, 3, 113	Prince Petrone, 3, 113	7	1:50.00	27,900
1973	Right Honorable, 3, 115	J. Lambert	Groshawk, 3, 119	Dancing Papa, 3, 113	10	1:49.20	28,650

Formerly named for William Quigley, a La Jolla, California, stockbroker and co-founder of the Del Mar Turf Club. Grade 3 1973-'80. Quigley Memorial H. 1945-'47. Del Mar Invitational Derby 1991-'96. 1¹⁄₁₆ miles 1945-'48. Dirt 1945-'69. Two divisions 1970. ‡Eagle Eyed finished third, DQ to seventh, 1994. Equaled course record 2000. Course record 2005. †Denotes female.

Del Mar Futurity

Grade 1 in 2008. Del Mar, two-year-olds, 7 furlongs, all weather. Held September 5, 2007, with a gross value of $250,000. First held in 1948. First graded in 1973. Stakes record 1:21.29 (2004 Declan's Moon).

Year	Winner	Jockey	Second	Third	Strs	Time	1st Purse
2007	Georgie Boy, 2, 121	G. K. Gomez	Salute the Sarge, 2, 123	Drill Down, 2, 117	13	1:25.34	$150,000
2006	Horse Greeley, 2, 117	V. Espinoza	Great Hunter, 2, 119	Stormello, 2, 117	7	1:22.93	150,000
2005	Stevie Wonderboy, 2, 117	G. K. Gomez	The Pharaoh, 2, 117	Jealous Profit, 2, 117	11	1:22.43	150,000
2004	Declan's Moon, 2, 116	V. Espinoza	Roman Ruler, 2, 120	Swiss Lad, 2, 116	4	1:21.29	150,000
2003	Siphonizer, 2, 116	J. A. Krone	Minister Eric, 2, 116	Perfect Moon, 2, 122	5	1:23.10	150,000
2002	Icecoldbeeratreds, 2, 119	D. R. Flores	Kafwain, 2, 119	Chief Planner, 2, 115	8	1:22.94	150,000
2001	Officer, 2, 121	V. Espinoza	Kamsack, 2, 115	Metatron, 2, 116	5	1:22.33	150,000
2000	Flame Thrower, 2, 116	J. D. Bailey	Street Cry (Ire), 2, 116	Arabian Light, 2, 119	8	1:22.00	150,000
1999	Forest Camp, 2, 116	D. R. Flores	Dixie Union, 2, 121	Captain Steve, 2, 115	5	1:21.67	150,000
1998	Worldly Manner, 2, 119	K. Desormeaux	Daring General, 2, 119	Waki American, 2, 114	7	1:23.05	150,000
1997	Souvenir Copy, 2, 115	C. J. McCarron	Old Topper, 2, 119	Commitisize, 2, 115	8	1:23.10	150,000
1996	Silver Charm, 2, 116	D. R. Flores	Gold Tribute, 2, 115	Swiss Yodeler, 2, 121	7	1:22.88	150,000
1995	Future Quest, 2, 115	K. Desormeaux	Othello, 2, 115	Cavonnier, 2, 117	8	1:21.81	137,500
1994	On Target, 2, 115	A. O. Solis	Supremo, 2, 115	Timber Country, 2, 119	9	1:22.37	137,500
1993	Winning Pact, 2, 115	C. S. Nakatani	Ramblin Guy, 2, 119	Ferrara, 2, 116	7	1:22.04	137,500
1992	River Special, 2, 115	C. J. McCarron	Sudden Hush, 2, 120	Seattle Sleet, 2, 114	7	1:36.64	137,500
1991	Bertrando, 2, 114	A. O. Solis	Zurich, 2, 114	Star Recruit, 2, 115	10	1:36.45	188,500
1990	Best Pal, 2, 120	P. A. Valenzuela	Pillaring, 2, 116	Got to Fly, 2, 117	11	1:35.40	231,600
1989	Drag Race, 2, 117	F. Olivares	†Rue de Palm, 2, 117	Single Dawn, 2, 114	12	1:35.40	241,600
1988	Music Merci, 2, 118	C. J. McCarron	Bruho, 2, 114	Texian, 2, 117	11	1:35.40	229,300
1987	†Lost Kitty, 2, 117	L. A. Pincay Jr.	Bold Second, 2, 118	Purdue King, 2, 118	9	1:36.20	174,800
1986	Qualify, 2, 114	G. L. Stevens	†Sacahuista, 2, 117	Brevito, 2, 116	7	1:35.60	158,535
1985	Tasso, 2, 117	L. A. Pincay Jr.	†Arewehavingfunyet, 2, 117	Snow Chief, 2, 117	6	1:36.00	155,760
1984	Saratoga Six, 2, 120	A. T. Cordero Jr.	Indigenous, 2, 117	Lomax, 2, 117	7	1:36.00	173,440
1983	†Althea, 2, 117	L. A. Pincay Jr.	Juliet's Pride, 2, 115	Gumboy, 2, 114	5	1:34.80	147,865
1982	Roving Boy, 2, 117	E. Delahoussaye	Desert Wine, 2, 120	Balboa Native, 2, 116	9	1:38.00	159,945
1981	Gato Del Sol, 2, 114	E. Delahoussaye	The Captain, 2, 120	Ring Proud, 2, 115	7	1:37.40	160,720
1980	Bold and Gold, 2, 114	D. C. Hall	Looks Like Rain, 2, 114	Sir Dancer, 2, 117	5	1:36.20	129,630
1979	The Carpenter, 2, 114	C. J. McCarron	Doonesbury, 2, 117	Executive Counsel, 2, 114	6	1:35.20	98,710
1978	Flying Paster, 2, 117	D. Pierce	Priority, 2, 117	Roman Oblisk, 2, 117	8	1:34.80	100,400
1977	Go West Young Man, 2, 114	F. Olivares	Tampoy, 2, 114	Spanish Way, 2, 117	6	1:35.80	85,845
1976	Visible, 2, 117	L. A. Pincay Jr.	*Habitony, 2, 117	Washoe County, 2, 115	10	1:35.40	74,535
1975	Telly's Pop, 2, 117	F. Mena	Lexington Laugh, 2, 119	Body Bend, 2, 114	8	1:36.00	66,275
1974	Diabolo, 2, 116	W. Shoemaker	George Navonod, 2, 119	Dimaggio, 2, 122	7	1:35.40	67,120
1973	Such a Rush, 2, 116	W. Shoemaker	Fast Pappa, 2, 116	The Gay Greek, 2, 117	11	1:29.80	65,740

Grade 2 1973-'83, 1990-2006. 6 furlongs 1948-'70. 7¹⁄₂ furlongs 1971-'73. 1 mile 1974-'92. Dirt 1948-'70, 1974-2006. Turf 1971-'73. Two divisions 1971. †Denotes female.

Del Mar Handicap

Grade 2 in 2008. Del Mar, three-year-olds and up, 1 3/8 miles, turf. Held August 26, 2007, with a gross value of $250,000. First held in 1937. First graded in 1973. Stakes record 2:12.15 (2002 Delta Form [Aus]).

Year	Winner	Jockey	Second	Third	Strs	Time	1st Purse
2007	After Market, 4, 124	A. O. Solis	Runaway Dancer, 8, 118	Spring House, 5, 115	7	2:13.01	$150,000
2006	T. H. Approval, 5, 120	A. O. Solis	Artiste Royal (Ire), 5, 116	Super Strut, 6, 115	10	2:12.34	150,000
2005	Leprechaun Kid, 6, 113	T. Baze	Laura's Lucky Boy, 4, 118	Exterior, 4, 117	10	2:12.81	150,000
2004	Star Over the Bay, 6, 116	T. Baze	Sarafan, 7, 121	†Moscow Burning, 4, 114	9	2:12.71	150,000
2003	Irish Warrior, 5, 116	A. O. Solis	Continental Red, 7, 117	Continuously, 4, 114	9	2:12.28	150,000
2002	Delta Form (Aus), 6, 115	G. F. Almeida	The Tin Man, 4, 117	Blue Steller (Ire), 4, 117	10	**2:12.15**	150,000
2001	Timboroa (GB), 5, 118	L. A. Pincay Jr.	Northern Quest (Fr), 6, 116	Super Quercus (Fr), 5, 117	7	2:12.59	150,000
2000	Northern Quest (Fr), 5, 116	C. J. McCarron	‡Perssonet (Chi), 5, 114	Alvo Certo (Brz), 7, 115	8	2:12.65	150,000
1999	Sayarshan (Fr), 4, 115	B. Blanc	Dancing Place (Chi), 6, 116	Ladies Din, 4, 120	8	2:14.35	150,000
1998	Bonapartiste (Fr), 4, 115	C. J. McCarron	River Bay, 5, 123	Military, 4, 116	6	2:14.18	150,000
1997	Rainbow Dancer (Fr), 6, 118	A. O. Solis	Dowty, 5, 119	Lord Jain (Arg), 5, 114	8	2:13.68	150,000
1996	Dernier Empereur, 6, 116	P. A. Valenzuela	Talloires, 6, 119	Party Season (GB), 5, 117	7	2:13.89	150,000
1995	Royal Chariot, 5, 117	L. A. Pincay Jr.	River Rhythm, 8, 117	Party Season (GB), 4, 116	10	2:13.78	137,500
1994	Navarone, 6, 117	P. A. Valenzuela	Approach the Bench (Ire), 6, 116	Sir Mark Sykes (Ire), 5, 116	8	2:14.37	137,500
1993	Luazur (Fr), 4, 116	P. Day	Kotashaan (Fr), 5, 123	Myrakalu (Fr), 5, 114	7	2:15.11	137,500
1992	Navarone, 4, 117	P. A. Valenzuela	Qathif, 5, 117	Stark South, 4, 117	8	2:15.17	137,500
1991	My Style (Ire), 4, 115	K. Desormeaux	Forty Niner Days, 4, 118	Super May, 5, 117	9	2:13.38	165,000
1990	Live the Dream, 4, 118	A. O. Solis	Mehmetori, 3, 107	Soft Machine, 5, 113	12	2:13.00	165,000
1989	Payant (Arg), 5, 118	R. G. Davis	Saratoga Passage, 4, 118	†No Review, 4, 112	9	2:15.20	165,000
1988	Sword Dance (Ire), 4, 114	C. J. McCarron	Great Communicator, 5, 120	Banda Karam (Ire), 4, 115	11	2:15.80	165,000
1987	Swink, 4, 120	W. Shoemaker	Santella Mac (Ire), 4, 115	Skip Out Front, 5, 115	12	2:13.80	165,000
1986	Raipillan (Chi), 4, 114	R. A. Baze	Schiller, 4, 113	Shulich (GB), 5, 113	12	2:14.40	165,000
1985	Barberstown, 5, 117	F. Toro	My Habitony, 5, 118	First Norman, 3, 114	10	1:58.00	137,000
1984	Precisionist, 3, 116	C. J. McCarron	Pair of Deuces, 6, 116	Super Diamond, 4, 117	10	1:56.80	137,000
1983	Bel Bolide, 5, 117	W. Shoemaker	Gato Del Sol, 4, 123	Egg Toss, 6, 117	9	1:58.20	82,500
1982	Muttering, 3, 117	W. Shoemaker	Regalberto, 4, 119	Exploded, 5, 121	9	1:57.00	82,500
1981	Wickerr, 6, 118	C. J. McCarron	Tahitian King (Ire), 5, 121	Galaxy Libra (Ire), 5, 121	8	1:57.40	82,500
1980	Go West Young Man, 5, 123	E. Delahoussaye	Relaunch, 4, 118	Balzac, 5, 121	9	1:58.20	75,000
1979	Ardiente, 4, 118	C. J. McCarron	Quick Turnover, 4, 122	Sudanes (Arg), 6, 111	10	1:56.80	75,000
1978	Palton (Chi), 5, 114	H. E. Moreno	Farnesio (Arg), 4, 119	Vic's Magic, 5, 119	8	1:57.40	60,000
1977	Ancient Title, 7, 123	D. G. McHargue	Painted Wagon, 4, 118	†Cascapedia, 4, 117	9	1:55.40	60,000
1976	Riot in Paris, 5, 122	W. Shoemaker	Avatar, 4, 122	Good Report, 6, 115	8	1:57.40	60,000
1975	*Cruiser II, 6, 117	F. Olivares	Top Crowd, 4, 115	Against the Snow, 5, 117	9	2:14.40	60,000
1974	*Redtop III, 5, 115	F. Toro	My Old Friend, 5, 118	Nantwice, 5, 111	10	2:16.00	60,000
1973	Red Reality, 7, 122	B. Baeza	Wing Out, 5, 119	Life Cycle, 4, 124	10	2:17.00	60,000

Del Mar Invitational H. 1973, 1975-'87, 1989-'96. Not held 1942-'44. 1 1/16 miles 1937-'48. 1 1/8 miles 1949-'69. 1 3/4 miles 1971. About 1 1/4 miles 1976-'85. Dirt 1937-'69, 1976-'85. Two divisions 1972. ‡Alvo Certo (Brz) finished second, DQ to third, 2000. Course record 1975. †Denotes female.

Del Mar Mile Handicap

Grade 2 in 2008. Del Mar, three-year-olds and up, 1 mile, turf. Held August 19, 2007, with a gross value of $314,000. First held in 1987. First graded in 1989. Stakes record 1:32.21 (2005 Three Valleys).

Year	Winner	Jockey	Second	Third	Strs	Time	1st Purse
2007	Crossing The Line (NZ), 5, 114	G. K. Gomez	Becrux (Ity), 5, 121	Isipingo, 4, 114	9	1:32.59	$180,000
2006	Aragorn (Ire), 4, 123	C. S. Nakatani	Wild Buddy, 7, 114	Hendrix, 5, 116	7	1:32.68	240,000
2005	Three Valleys, 4, 119	P. A. Valenzuela	We All Love Aleyna, 4, 118	Wild Buddy, 6, 114	10	**1:32.21**	210,000
2004	Supah Blitz, 4, 116	V. Espinoza	Domestic Dispute, 4, 117	During, 4, 117	6	1:35.14	150,000
2003	Joey Franco, 4, 116	P. A. Valenzuela	Reba's Gold, 6, 116	Grey Memo, 6, 117	7	1:35.70	90,000
2002	Congaree, 4, 119	M. E. Smith	Kela, 4, 117	Reba's Gold, 5, 116	6	1:36.34	150,000
2001	El Corredor, 4, 121	V. Espinoza	Figlio Mio, 4, 113	Performing Magic, 4, 116	6	1:35.24	150,000
2000	El Corredor, 3, 111	V. Espinoza	Cliquot, 4, 117	Literal Prowler, 6, 112	8	1:35.05	158,160
1999	Hollycombe, 5, 116	G. L. Stevens	Flying With Eagles, 5, 115	Old Trieste, 4, 122	8	1:35.46	126,060
1998	Old Trieste, 3, 116	C. J. McCarron	Grajagan (Arg), 4, 111	Stalwart Tsu, 4, 116	4	1:35.35	123,172
1997	Benchmark, 6, 117	E. Delahoussaye	Crafty Friend, 4, 118	Northern Afleet, 4, 120	5	1:35.57	126,700
1996	Dramatic Gold, 5, 117	K. Desormeaux	Alphabet Soup, 5, 120	Savinio, 6, 118	5	1:34.78	125,650
1995	Alphabet Soup, 4, 115	C. J. McCarron	Lykatill Hil, 5, 117	Luthier Fever, 4, 115	9	1:34.33	117,150
1994	Lykatill Hil, 4, 118	E. Delahoussaye	D'Hallevant, 4, 117	Stuka, 4, 115	6	1:34.01	62,200
1993	Region, 4, 115	C. S. Nakatani	Lottery Winner, 4, 115	L'Express (Chi), 4, 115	10	1:34.98	122,100
1992	Reign Road, 4, 114	D. R. Flores	Sir Beaufort, 5, 116	Charmonnier, 4, 115	10	1:35.29	122,000
1991	Twilight Agenda, 5, 122	K. Desormeaux	Opening Verse, 5, 117	Robyn Dancer, 4, 117	5	1:34.17	116,950
1990	Stalwart Charger, 3, 115	R. M. Gonzalez	Flying Continental, 4, 120	Ruhlmann, 5, 123	4	1:34.60	116,300
1989	On the Line, 5, 124	L. A. Pincay Jr.	Good Taste (Arg), 7, 117	Lively One, 4, 125	5	1:33.40	115,400
1988	Precisionist, 7, 125	C. J. McCarron	Lively One, 3, 114	He's a Saros, 5, 116	4	1:34.60	85,150
1987	Good Command, 4, 114	C. J. McCarron	Stop the Fighting (Ire), 4, 118	Candi's Gold, 3, 113	6	1:34.80	86,250

Grade 3 1989. Del Mar Budweiser Breeders' Cup H. 1987-'95. Del Mar Breeders' Cup H. 1996-2006. Dirt 1987-2004. Course record 2005.

Del Mar Oaks

Grade 1 in 2008. Del Mar, three-year-olds, fillies, 1 1/8 miles, turf. Held August 18, 2007, with a gross value of $400,000. First held in 1957. First graded in 1973. Stakes record 1:46.26 (2004 Amorama [Fr]).

Year	Winner	Jockey	Second	Third	Strs	Time	1st Purse
2007	Rutherienne, 3, 122	C. S. Nakatani	Valbenny (Ire), 3, 122	Super Freaky, 3, 122	10	1:46.79	$240,000

Year	Winner	Jockey	Second	Third	Strs	Time	1st Purse
2006	Arravale, 3, 122	J. Valdivia Jr.	‡Foxysox (GB), 3, 122	Soothsay (Ire), 3, 122	10	1:48.03	$240,000
2005	Singhalese (GB), 3, 122	M. E. Smith	Three Degrees (Ire), 3, 122	Dancing Edie, 3, 122	9	1:46.29	180,000
2004	Amorama (Fr), 3, 122	D. R. Flores	Ticker Tape (GB), 3, 122	Sweet Win, 3, 122	7	**1:46.26**	180,000
2003	Dessert, 3, 122	C. S. Nakatani	Solar Echo, 3, 122	Personal Legend, 3, 122	8	1:47.04	180,000
2002	Dublino, 3, 121	K. Desormeaux	Megahertz (GB), 3, 121	Alozaina (Ire), 3, 121	6	1:47.16	180,000
2001	Golden Apples (Ire), 3, 121	G. K. Gomez	Affluent, 3, 121	Reine de Romance (Ire), 3, 121	8	1:47.98	180,000
2000	No Matter What, 3, 121	V. Espinoza	Theoretically, 3, 121	Premiere Creation (Fr), 3, 121	9	1:50.02	150,000
1999	Tout Charmant, 3, 121	D. R. Flores	Smooth Player, 3, 121	Sweet Ludy (Ire), 3, 121	10	1:48.64	150,000
1998	Sicy d'Alsace (Fr), 3, 121	C. S. Nakatani	‡Adel, 3, 121	Tranquility Lake, 3, 121	10	1:48.26	150,000
1997	Famous Digger, 3, 121	B. Blanc	Golden Arches (Fr), 3, 121	See You Soon (Fr), 3, 121	10	1:49.14	150,000
1996	Antespend, 3, 120	C. W. Antley	Gastronomical, 3, 120	True Flare, 3, 120	8	1:48.93	150,000
1995	Bail Out Becky, 3, 120	S. J. Sellers	Sleep Easy, 3, 120	Top Ruhl, 3, 120	9	1:49.72	137,500
1994	Twice the Vice, 3, 120	G. L. Stevens	Malli Star, 3, 120	Pharma, 3, 120	6	1:47.73	96,250
1993	Hollywood Wildcat, 3, 120	E. Delahoussaye	Possibly Perfect, 3, 120	Miami Sands (Ire), 3, 120	10	1:48.31	96,250
1992	Suivi, 3, 120	A. O. Solis	Race the Wild Wind, 3, 120	Alysbelle, 3, 120	8	1:48.60	96,250
1991	Flawlessly, 3, 120	C. J. McCarron	Seattle Symphony, 3, 120	Fowda, 3, 120	6	1:49.50	96,250
1990	Slew of Pearls, 3, 117	C. A. Black	Adorable Emilie (Fr), 3, 115	Annual Reunion, 3, 117	12	1:49.80	97,900
1989	Stylish Star, 3, 115	C. J. McCarron	Darby's Daughter, 3, 119	General Charge (Ire), 3, 119	9	1:48.60	97,500
1988	No Review, 3, 115	R. Q. Meza	Do So, 3, 124	Jungle Gold, 3, 115	7	1:49.00	96,300
1987	Lizzy Hare, 3, 114	G. L. Stevens	Chapel of Dreams, 3, 114	Down Again, 3, 114	13	1:50.40	104,300
1986	Hidden Light, 3, 124	W. Shoemaker	Kraemer, 3, 114	Shotgun Wedding, 3, 119	7	1:47.80	92,700
1985	Savannah Dancer, 3, 119	W. Shoemaker	‡Magnificent Lindy, 3, 122	Queen of Bronze, 3, 115	8	1:48.80	94,250
1984	Fashionably Late, 3, 119	C. J. McCarron	Lucky Lucky Lucky, 3, 124	Auntie Betty, 3, 114	7	1:49.40	92,400
1983	Heartlight No. One, 3, 122	L. A. Pincay Jr.	Foggy Moon, 3, 115	Fabulous Notion, 3, 122	10	1:50.20	84,100
1982	Castilla, 3, 122	R. Sibille	Avigaition, 3, 119	Skillful Joy, 3, 119	8	1:50.20	81,050
1981	French Charmer, 3, 117	D. G. McHargue	Amber Ever, 3, 119	Shimmy, 3, 119	9	1:49.40	82,200
1980	Movin' Money, 3, 114	P. A. Valenzuela	Princess Karenda, 3, 122	Tobin's Rose, 3, 119	11	1:49.40	71,000
1979	Our Suiti Pie, 3, 113	C. J. McCarron	Caline, 3, 121	Ancient Art, 3, 116	9	1:49.80	52,300
1978	Country Queen, 3, 121	F. Toro	B. Thoughtful, 3, 124	Donna Inez, 3, 113	11	1:49.80	33,450
1977	Taisez Vous, 3, 121	D. Pierce	Drama Critic, 3, 114	Giggling Girl, 3, 113	9	1:48.80	31,550
1976	Go March, 3, 116	L. A. Pincay Jr.	Pennygown, 3, 113	Franmari, 3, 116	7	1:49.20	25,700
1975	Snap Apple, 3, 113	F. Mena	Mia Amore, 3, 115	Miss Francesca, 3, 116	8	1:50.00	21,450
1974	Modus Vivendi, 3, 113	D. Pierce	Move Abroad, 3, 116	Heather Road, 3, 115	9	1:50.20	21,850
1973	Sandy Blue, 3, 121	D. Pierce	Sphere, 3, 112	Meilleur, 3, 118	12	1:49.40	20,850

Grade 3 1973-'78, 1988-'91. Grade 2 1979-'87, 1992-'93. Del Mar Invitational Oaks 1992-'94, 1996. 1 mile 1957-'64. Dirt 1957-'64. Two divisions 1966, '70. ‡Pirate's Glow finished second, DQ to fourth, 1985. ‡Tranquility Lake finished second, DQ to third, 1998. ‡Take the Ribbon finished second, DQ to fourth, 2006.

Delta Jackpot Stakes — *See* Boyd Gaming's Delta Jackpot Stakes
Delta Princess Stakes — *See* Boyd Gaming's Delta Princess Stakes
Demoiselle Stakes

Grade 2 in 2008. Aqueduct, two-year-olds, fillies, 1 1/8 miles, dirt. Held November 24, 2007, with a gross value of $200,000. First held in 1908. First graded in 1973. Stakes record 1:50 (1978 Plankton).

Year	Winner	Jockey	Second	Third	Strs	Time	1st Purse
2007	Mushka, 2, 115	J. R. Velazquez	Elusive Lady, 2, 119	Melissa Jo, 2, 115	7	1:51.61	$120,000
2006	Boca Grande, 2, 115	M. E. Smith	Get Ready Bertie, 2, 116	Successful Outlook, 2, 119	9	1:50.17	120,000
2005	Wonder Lady Anne L, 2, 116	C. H. Velasquez	Cinderella's Dream, 2, 119	Wait a While, 2, 119	5	1:52.85	120,000
2004	Sis City, 2, 119	J. R. Velazquez	Salute, 2, 115	Winning Season, 2, 115	7	1:50.39	120,000
2003	Ashado, 2, 117	J. D. Bailey	La Reina, 2, 121	Dr. Kathy, 2, 115	7	1:52.88	120,000
2002	Roar Emotion, 2, 115	J. R. Velazquez	Savedbythelight, 2, 115	Feisty Step, 2, 115	10	1:51.43	120,000
2001	Smok'n Frolic, 2, 121	J. R. Velazquez	Lady Shari, 2, 121	Proxy Statement, 2, 117	7	1:50.57	120,000
2000	Two Item Limit, 2, 122	R. Migliore	Sweep Dreams, 2, 116	Kingsland, 2, 116	8	1:52.25	120,000
1999	Jostle, 2, 121	S. Elliott	March Magic, 2, 112	Shawnee Country, 2, 121	8	1:51.51	120,000
1998	‡Better Than Honour, 2, 113	R. Migliore	Waltz On By, 2, 115	Oh What a Windfall, 2, 121	9	1:52.70	120,000
1997	Clark Street, 2, 121	M. E. Smith	Soft Senorita, 2, 114	Mercy Me, 2, 121	8	1:53.98	120,000
1996	Ajina, 2, 121	P. Day	Hidden Reserve, 2, 114	Biding Time, 2, 114	9	1:53.74	120,000
1995	La Rosa, 2, 114	J. A. Krone	Quiet Dance, 2, 114	Escena, 2, 112	7	1:50.92	120,000
1994	Minister Wife, 2, 121	J. D. Bailey	Miss Golden Circle, 2, 118	Special Broad, 2, 121	9	1:53.48	120,000
1993	Strategic Maneuver, 2, 116	J. D. Bailey	Sovereign Kitty, 2, 112	‡Princess Tru, 2, 114	6	1:53.62	120,000
1992	Fortunate Faith, 2, 112	A. Madrid Jr.	True Affair, 2, 116	Our Tomboy, 2, 112	8	1:53.59	120,000
1991	Stolen Beauty, 2, 113	C. W. Antley	Turnback the Alarm, 2, 116	Easy Now, 2, 116	9	1:52.08	120,000
1990	Debutant's Halo, 2, 116	C. Perret	Private Treasure, 2, 121	Slept Thru It, 2, 117	7	1:53.80	69,960
1989	Rootentootenwooten, 2, 112	J. D. Bailey	Bookkeeper, 2, 113	Why Go On Dreaming, 2, 113	8	1:51.60	109,440
1988	Open Mind, 2, 121	A. T. Cordero Jr.	Darby's Daughter, 2, 119	Gild, 2, 121	10	1:52.00	147,120
1987	Goodbye Halo, 2, 113	A. T. Cordero Jr.	Tap Your Toes, 2, 112	Galway Song, 2, 119	9	1:53.00	142,080
1986	Tappiano, 2, 121	J. Cruguet	Soaring Princess, 2, 112	Graceful Darby, 2, 112	7	1:53.20	131,940
1985	I'm Sweets, 2, 121	E. Maple	Family Style, 2, 121	Steal a Kiss, 2, 112	8	1:50.20	98,280
1984	Diplomette, 2, 112	R. Hernandez	Golden Silence, 2, 114	Koluctoo's Jill, 2, 112	10	1:54.60	72,360
1983	Qualique, 2, 112	M. Venezia	Lucky Lucky Lucky, 2, 121	Buzz My Bell, 2, 112	6	1:51.20	65,160
1982	Only Queens, 2, 112	M. A. Rivera	Gold Spruce, 2, 113	National Banner, 2, 113	7	1:52.00	49,680
1981	Snow Plow, 2, 121	A. T. Cordero Jr.	Larida, 2, 115	Vain Gold, 2, 121	8	1:53.00	50,220
1980	Rainbow Connection, 2, 119	A. T. Cordero Jr.	De La Rose, 2, 116	Tina Tina Too, 2, 116	6	1:50.80	48,870

Racing — Graded Stakes

Year	Winner	Jockey	Second	Third	Strs	Time	1st Purse
1979	Genuine Risk, 2, 116	L. A. Pincay Jr.	Smart Angle, 2, 121	Spruce Pine, 2, 112	7	1:51.20	$49,185
1978	Plankton, 2, 112	R. Hernandez	Distinct Honor, 2, 113	Belladora, 2, 112	9	1:50.00	48,465
1977	Caesar's Wish, 2, 116	D. R. Wright	Lakeville Miss, 2, 121	Island Kiss, 2, 114	7	1:50.60	47,565
1976	Bring Out the Band, 2, 116	D. Brumfield	Our Mims, 2, 113	Road Princess, 2, 112	12	1:50.80	49,500
1975	Free Journey, 2, 117	L. A. Pincay Jr.	Artfully, 2, 112	Dottie's Doll, 2, 114	11	1:50.20	51,210
1974	Land Girl, 2, 116	J. Vasquez	Alpine Lass, 2, 121	Funalon, 2, 118	14	1:36.20	35,940
1973	Chris Evert, 2, 121	L. A. Pincay Jr.	Amberalero, 2, 116	Khaled's Kaper, 2, 116	11	1:36.40	17,370

Demoiselle in French means young female. Grade 3 1973-'75. Grade 1 1981-'89. Held at Empire City 1908-'14, 1917-'42. Held at Belmont Park 1915-'16, 1958. Held at Jamaica 1944-'53. Not held 1909, 1911-'13, 1933-'35, 1954-'57, 1960-'62. 5½ furlongs 1908-'32. 5¾ furlongs 1936-'42. 6 furlongs 1943-'47. 1¹⁄₁₆ miles 1948-'53. 7 furlongs 1958-'59. 1 mile 1963-'74. ‡Bunting finished third, DQ to fifth, 1993. ‡Tutorial finished first, DQ to fifth, 1998.

Deputy Minister Handicap

Grade 3 in 2008. Gulfstream Park, four-year-olds and up, 6½ furlongs, dirt. Held February 3, 2007, with a gross value of $100,000. First held in 1990. First graded in 2000. Stakes record 1:15.17 (2003 Native Heir).

Year	Winner	Jockey	Second	Third	Strs	Time	1st Purse
2007	Keyed Entry, 4, 113	J. R. Velazquez	Sir Greeley, 5, 117	Nar, 4, 113	5	1:15.72	$60,000
2006	Universal Form, 5, 116	M. R. Cruz	War Front, 4, 115	Judiths Wild Rush, 5, 117	7	1:16.48	60,000
2005	Medallist, 4, 115	J. A. Santos	Mister Fotis, 4, 113	Kela, 7, 119	6	1:15.62	60,000
2004	Alke, 4, 112	J. R. Velazquez	Cajun Beat, 4, 123	Coach Jimi Lee, 4, 115	7	1:15.80	60,000
2003	Native Heir, 5, 114	C. H. Velasquez	Binthebest, 6, 115	Fire and Glory, 4, 114	8	1:15.17	60,000
2002	Fappie's Notebook, 5, 116	J. F. Chavez	Twilight Road, 5, 113	Binthebest, 5, 114	7	1:16.19	60,000
2001	Istintaj, 5, 116	J. D. Bailey	Fappie's Notebook, 4, 114	Fantastic Finish, 5, 114	8	1:16.08	60,000
2000	Deep Gold, 4, 112	J. R. Velazquez	Forty One Carats, 4, 116	Klabin's Gold, 5, 114	8	1:15.89	60,000
1999	Good and Tough, 4, 115	S. J. Sellers	Western Borders, 5, 113	Mint, 4, 113	7	1:21.63	60,000
1998	Irish Conquest, 5, 112	E. Coa	Frisk Me Now, 4, 119	Oro de Mexico, 4, 115	10	1:22.54	60,000
1997	Templado (Ven), 4, 113	J. D. Bailey	Sea Emperor, 5, 114	Punch Line, 7, 119	6	1:09.69	45,000
1996	Jess C's Whirl, 6, 115	J. A. Krone	Buffalo Dan, 5, 117	Patton, 5, 114	6	1:10.67	30,000
1995	Chimes Band, 4, 120	J. D. Bailey	Distinct Reality, 4, 112	Ponche, 6, 113	6	1:09.16	30,000
1994	I Can't Believe, 6, 113	E. Maple	Demaloot Demashoot, 4, 115	Devil On Ice, 5, 115	7	1:08.12	30,000
1993	Loach, 5, 114	J. A. Santos	Hidden Tomahawk, 5, 113	British Banker, 5, 114	6	1:22.51	30,000
1992	Take Me Out, 5, 118	J. D. Bailey	Drummond Lane, 5, 110	Frozen Runway, 5, 114	9	1:22.78	30,000
1991	Unbridled, 4, 119	P. Day	Housebuster, 4, 122	Shuttleman, 5, 114	9	1:21.92	30,000
1990	Beau Genius, 5, 118	C. Perret	The Red Rolls, 6, 112	Joel (Arg), 8, 112	7	1:23.00	30,000

Named for Centurion Farm's, Kinghaven Farm's, and Due Process Stable's 1981 Canadian Horse of the Year, '97, '98 leading North American sire, and '83 Donn H. (G2) winner Deputy Minister (1979 c. by Vice Regent). Not held 2008. 7 furlongs 1990-'93, 1998-'99. 6 furlongs 1994-'97. Three-year-olds and up 1990-2006. Equaled track record 2003.

Diana Stakes

Grade 1 in 2008. Saratoga Race Course, three-year-olds and up, fillies and mares, 1⅛ miles, turf. Held July 28, 2007, with a gross value of $520,000. First held in 1939. First graded in 1973. Stakes record 1:45.40 (1978 Waya [Fr]).

Year	Winner	Jockey	Second	Third	Strs	Time	1st Purse
2007	My Typhoon (Ire), 5, 120	E. Castro	Argentina (Ire), 5, 118	Makderah (Ire), 4, 120	8	1:46.47	$300,000
2006	Angara (GB), 5, 120	F. Jara	Sweet Talker, 4, 120	Argentina (Ire), 4, 118	6	1:49.20	300,000
2005	Sand Springs, 5, 120	J. R. Velazquez	Que Puntual (Arg), 5, 120	Angara (GB), 4, 118	7	1:46.91	300,000
2004	Wonder Again, 5, 120	E. S. Prado	Riskaverse, 5, 118	Ocean Drive, 4, 118	7	1:48.99	300,000
2003	Voodoo Dancer, 5, 120	C. S. Nakatani	Heat Haze (GB), 4, 118	Pertuisane (GB), 4, 115	8	1:47.98	300,000
2002	Tates Creek, 4, 117	J. D. Bailey	Voodoo Dancer, 4, 120	Snow Dance, 4, 117	9	1:48.00	300,000
2001	Starine (Fr), 4, 114	J. R. Velazquez	Babae (Chi), 5, 116	Penny's Gold, 4, 120	9	1:46.17	300,000
2000	Perfect Sting, 4, 123	J. D. Bailey	License Fee, 5, 116	Hello Soso (Ire), 4, 113	7	1:47.01	300,000
1999	Heritage of Gold, 4, 115	S. J. Sellers	Khumba Mela (Ire), 4, 114	Mossflower, 5, 114	9	1:45.93	180,000
1998	Memories of Silver, 5, 123	J. D. Bailey	B. A. Valentine, 5, 114	Auntie Mame, 4, 122	8	1:46.14	180,000
1997	Rumpipumpy (GB), 4, 114	J. A. Santos	B. A. Valentine, 4, 116	Antespend, 4, 117	12	1:48.59	120,000
1996	Electric Society (Ire), 5, 117	M. E. Smith	Powder Bowl, 4, 116	Upper Noosh, 4, 110	9	1:46.56	120,000
1995	Perfect Arc, 3, 113	J. R. Velazquez	Danish, 4, 118	Tiffany's Taylor, 5, 113	6	1:46.85	85,125
1994	Via Borghese, 5, 115	J. A. Santos	Blazing Kadie, 4, 110	Coronation Cup, 3, 108	7	1:52.01	83,010
1993	Ratings, 5, 110	J. A. Krone	Lady Blessington (Fr), 5, 118	Garendare (GB), 4, 113	8	1:49.80	72,240
1992	Plenty of Grace, 5, 114	W. H. McCauley	Ratings, 4, 114	Highland Crystal, 4, 115	12	1:46.66	75,960
1991	Christiecat, 4, 117	J. Samyn	Virgin Michael, 4, 112	Senora Tippy, 5, 111	10	1:47.66	75,360
1990	Foresta, 4, 113	A. T. Cordero Jr.	To the Lighthouse, 4, 113	Songlines, 4, 111	11	1:48.40	56,790
1989	‡Glowing Honor, 4, 115	J. D. Bailey	Wooing, 4, 111	Laugh and Be Merry, 4, 114	9	1:50.20	76,200
1988	Glowing Honor, 3, 106	P. Day	Sunny Roberta, 3, 111	Graceful Darby, 4, 112	9	1:49.40	73,680
1987	Bailrullah, 5, 111	J. Cruguet	Perfect Point, 5, 114	Videogenic, 5, 113	13	1:46.20	91,860
1986	Duty Dance, 4, 118	J. Cruguet	Dismasted, 4, 115	Kapalua Butterfly, 5, 112	11	1:49.80	91,380
1985	Lake Country, 4, 117	J. Fell	Possible Mate, 4, 118	Key Dancer, 4, 120	11	1:48.40	58,230
1984	Wild Applause, 3, 109	W. A. Guerra	Pretty Perfect, 4, 109	Spit Curl, 4, 118	7	1:48.20	70,650
1983	Geraldine's Store, 4, 108	J. Samyn	Trevita (Ire), 6, 120	Infinite, 3, 111	8	1:47.20	33,840
	Hush Dear, 4, 117	J. Vasquez	If Winter Comes, 5, 112	First Approach, 5, 116	9	1:48.40	34,080
1982	Hush Dear, 4, 109	E. Beitia	Larida, 3, 114	So Pleasantly, 4, 113	11	1:47.40	34,170
	If Winter Comes, 4, 110	E. Beitia	Canaille (Ire), 4, 112	Noble Damsel, 4, 114	10	1:47.40	34,170
1981	De La Rose, 3, 114	E. Maple	Rokeby Rose, 4, 115	Euphrosyne, 5, 112	8	1:50.60	36,420
1980	Just a Game (Ire), 4, 123	D. Brumfield	The Very One, 5, 117	Relaxing, 4, 119	6	1:49.00	35,520
1979	Pearl Necklace, 5, 124	J. Fell	Island Kiss, 4, 114	Terpsichorist, 4, 119	9	1:48.80	35,010

Racing — Graded Stakes

Year	Winner	Jockey	Second	Third	Strs	Time	1st Purse
1978	Waya (Fr), 4, 115	A. T. Cordero Jr.	Pearl Necklace, 4, 125	Fia, 4, 110	12	1:45.40	$33,240
1977	Javamine, 4, 114	A. T. Cordero Jr.	Pearl Necklace, 3, 109	Rich Soil, 3, 114	8	1:48.40	32,640
1976	Glowing Tribute, 3, 116	R. Turcotte	Fleet Victress, 4, 117	Nijana, 3, 111	9	1:47.60	32,910
1975	Heloise, 4, 113	M. Venezia	Victorian Queen, 4, 118	Princesse Grey, 4, 112	12	1:47.40	35,250
1974	Fairway Flyer, 5, 118	J. Velasquez	North Broadway, 4, 117	Brindabella, 4, 113	9	1:47.20	35,070
1973	Cathy Baby, 4, 119	J. Velasquez	Something Super, 3, 113	Worldling, 4, 111	8	1:46.80	13,620
	Lightning Lucy, 3, 116	R. Turcotte	Flying Fur, 4, 114	Summer Guest, 4, 122	7	1:46.60	13,545

Named for the mythological Roman goddess of the hunt, Diana. Grade 2 1973-2002. Diana H. 1939-2004. Held at Belmont Park 1943-'45. Dirt 1939-'72. Two divisions 1973, 1982-'83. ‡Wooing finished first, DQ to second, 1989.

Discovery Handicap

Grade 3 in 2008. Aqueduct, three-year-olds, 1 1/8 miles, dirt. Held November 24, 2007, with a gross value of $109,900. First held in 1945. First graded in 1973. Stakes record 1:47.20 (1973 Forego).

Year	Winner	Jockey	Second	Third	Strs	Time	1st Purse
2007	Now a Victor, 3, 118	J. R. Velazquez	Shopton Lane, 3, 115	Dr. V's Magic, 3, 116	7	1:50.15	$65,940
2006	Roman Dynasty, 3, 115	J. R. Velazquez	On Board Again, 3, 117	Valid Notebook, 3, 117	5	1:51.11	64,380
2005	Magna Graduate, 3, 117	J. R. Velazquez	Scrappy T, 3, 119	Buzzards Bay, 3, 121	11	1:41.35	172,350
2004	Zakocity, 3, 116	J. Castellano	Stolen Time, 3, 116	Mahzouz, 3, 115	8	1:49.78	66,060
2003	During, 3, 120	J. A. Santos	Unforgettable Max, 3, 114	Inamorato, 3, 114	8	1:51.18	67,080
2002	Saint Marden, 3, 117	J. D. Bailey	Regency Park, 3, 115	No Parole, 3, 117	10	1:49.13	68,400
2001	Evening Attire, 3, 111	S. Bridgmohan	Street Cry (Ire), 3, 118	Free of Love, 3, 115	7	1:48.62	65,580
2000	Left Bank, 3, 119	J. R. Velazquez	Perfect Cat, 3, 114	Open Sesame, 3, 115	4	1:47.30	64,020
1999	Adonis, 3, 118	J. R. Velazquez	Best of Luck, 3, 118	Waddaan, 3, 113	6	1:50.11	64,980
1998	Early Warning, 3, 115	J. F. Chavez	Deputy Diamond, 3, 117	Gulliver, 3, 115	8	1:48.94	50,010
1997	Mr. Sinatra, 3, 116	M. E. Smith	Concerto, 3, 121	Twin Spires, 3, 116	5	1:49.55	64,626
1996	Gold Fever, 3, 121	M. E. Smith	Crafty Friend, 3, 115	Early Echoes, 3, 111	9	1:49.01	66,720
1995	Michael's Star, 3, 112	J. A. Krone	Hunting Hard, 3, 113	Reality Road, 3, 114	10	1:50.34	67,380
1994	Serious Spender, 3, 113	J. F. Chavez	Unaccounted For, 3, 121	Malmo, 3, 112	4	1:51.24	63,540
1993	Prospector's Flag, 3, 114	J. F. Chavez	Virginia Rapids, 3, 118	Living Vicariously, 3, 114	8	1:52.30	70,320
1992	New Deal, 3, 111	R. G. Davis	Offbeat, 3, 114	Dodsworth, 3, 113	11	1:48.08	74,880
1991	Upon My Soul, 3, 112	J. Samyn	Excellent Tipper, 3, 114	Honest Ensign, 3, 110	11	1:49.62	75,960
1990	Sports View, 3, 113	J. A. Santos	Chief Honcho, 3, 117	dh-Killer Diller, 3, 116	7	1:48.60	52,830
				dh-Out of Place, 3, 112			
1989	Tricky Creek, 3, 117	C. Perret	Traskwood, 3, 113	Farewell Wave, 3, 110	9	1:50.00	71,280
1988	Dynaformer, 3, 116	A. T. Cordero Jr.	Star Attitude, 3, 113	Congeleur, 3, 112	7	1:50.00	104,580
1987	Parochial, 3, 117	J. A. Krone	Homebuilder, 3, 112	Forest Fair, 3, 115	11	1:51.20	109,620
1986	Moment of Hope, 3, 108	M. Venezia	Gold Alert, 3, 109	Clear Choice, 3, 112	9	1:49.60	54,000
1985	Proud Truth, 3, 126	J. Velasquez	Important Business, 3, 113	Romancer, 3, 110	6	1:49.20	51,750
1984	Key to the Moon, 3, 120	D. Beckon	Silver Stark, 3, 110	Raja's Shark, 3, 124	6	1:50.00	42,300
1983	Country Pine, 3, 118	J. D. Bailey	Jacque's Tip, 3, 115	Father Don Juan, 3, 112	6	1:49.60	33,420
1982	Trenchant, 3, 113	J. Samyn	Dew Line, 3, 113	Exclusive Era, 3, 112	5	1:50.80	32,880
1981	Princelet, 3, 113	E. Maple	Accipiter's Hope, 3, 118	Pass the Tab, 3, 126	7	1:51.00	33,240
1980	Fappiano, 3, 114	A. T. Cordero Jr.	Reef Searcher, 3, 114	Royal Hierarchy, 3, 111	11	1:50.00	35,280
1979	Belle's Gold, 3, 121	A. T. Cordero Jr.	Smarten, 3, 122	Gallant Best, 3, 115	7	1:48.00	33,270
1978	Sorry Lookin, 3, 110	R. I. Velez	Silent Cal, 3, 115	Judge Advocate, 3, 114	6	1:49.60	31,740
1977	Cox's Ridge, 3, 126	E. Maple	Broadway Forli, 3, 123	Papelote, 3, 107	9	1:48.60	32,670
1976	Wise Philip, 3, 107	D. Montoya	Teddy's Courage, 3, 115	Patriot's Dream, 3, 112	8	1:48.60	32,460
1975	Dr. Emil, 3, 115	B. Baeza	Rushing Man, 3, 125	Syllabus, 3, 113	7	1:48.60	33,630
1974	Rube the Great, 3, 119	A. T. Cordero Jr.	Holding Pattern, 3, 126	Sharp Gary, 3, 118	5	1:48.20	33,270
	Green Gambados, 3, 120	A. T. Cordero Jr.	Best of It, 3, 116	Jolly Johu, 3, 121	9	1:48.20	33,570
1973	Forego, 3, 127	H. Gustines	My Gallant, 3, 122	‡Arbees Boy, 3, 114	7	**1:47.20**	33,300

Named for Alfred G. Vanderbilt's Racing Hall of Fame member, 1935 Horse of the Year, and three-time Brooklyn H. winner Discovery (1931 c. by Display). Grade 2 1988-'89. Held at Belmont 1960-'61, 1968-'70, 2005. 1 1/16 miles 2005. Two divisions 1974. Dead heat for third 1990. ‡Key to the Kingdom finished third, DQ to seventh, 1973.

Distaff Handicap

Grade 2 in 2008. Aqueduct, three-year-olds and up, fillies and mares, 6 furlongs, dirt. Held March 22, 2008, with a gross value of $143,900. First held in 1954. First graded in 1973. Stakes record 1:09.73 (2007 Maryfield).

Year	Winner	Jockey	Second	Third	Strs	Time	1st Purse
2008	Rite Moment, 4, 115	R. Maragh	Your Flame in Me, 4, 115	Scatkey, 5, 114	6	1:09.86	$94,740
2007	Maryfield, 6, 117	J. F. Chavez	Candy Box, 5, 115	Oprah Winney, 4, 118	7	**1:09.73**	95,100
2006	Smokey Glacken, 5, 120	J. Castellano	Magnolia Jackson, 5, 114	Annika Lass, 5, 114	8	1:10.24	94,800
2005	Bank Audit, 4, 118	R. Migliore	Sensibly Chic, 5, 117	Travelator, 5, 116	7	1:22.07	95,040
2004	Randaroo, 4, 121	R. Migliore	Chirimoya, 5, 110	Storm Flag Flying, 4, 118	4	1:22.64	93,240
2003	Carson Hollow, 4, 120	M. J. Luzzi	Raging Fever, 5, 118	Bonefide Reason, 5, 112	8	1:22.42	94,740
2002	Raging Fever, 4, 120	J. R. Velazquez	Prized Stamp, 5, 114	La Galerie (Arg), 6, 115	7	1:21.78	94,680
2001	Dream Supreme, 4, 119	A. T. Gryder	Folly Dollar, 4, 113	Country Hideaway, 5, 118	5	1:23.66	108,960
2000	Honest Lady, 4, 117	B. Blanc	Her She Kisses, 4, 115	Tap to Music, 5, 118	8	1:22.10	111,300
1999	Furlough, 5, 115	H. Castillo Jr.	Catinca, 4, 121	Tomorrows Sunshine, 5, 113	9	1:23.23	112,260
1998	Parlay, 4, 114	R. Migliore	Lucky Marty, 5, 113	Green Light, 4, 114	9	1:24.10	67,260
1997	Miss Golden Circle, 5, 120	R. Migliore	Inquisitive Look, 4, 110	Punkin Pie, 7, 109	8	1:24.47	65,400
1996	Lottsa Talc, 6, 120	F. T. Alvarado	Traverse City, 6, 120	Dust Bucket, 5, 116	7	1:24.04	75,820
1995	Recognizable, 4, 120	M. E. Smith	Beckys Shirt, 4, 113	Kurofune Mystery, 5, 116	8	1:22.94	66,540
1994	Classy Mirage, 4, 114	R. G. Davis	Jill Miner, 4, 114	Air Port Won, 4, 109	8	1:11.37	66,480

Racing — Graded Stakes

Year	Winner	Jockey	Second	Third	Strs	Time	1st Purse
1992	Nannerl, 5, 112	M. E. Smith	Missy's Mirage, 4, 119	Withallprobability, 4, 117	6	1:24.68	$68,880
1991	Devil's Orchid, 4, 117	R. A. Baze	Your Hope, 6, 112	Fappaburst, 4, 114	5	1:21.18	67,080
1990	Channel Three, 4, 111	J. F. Chavez	Divine Answer, 4, 113	Hedgeabout, 6, 112	10	1:23.20	54,090
1989	Avie's Gal, 4, 112	N. Santagata	Haiati, 4, 111	Topicount, 4, 117	5	1:24.00	51,660
1988	Cadillacing, 4, 112	R. P. Romero	Cagey Exuberance, 4, 118	Bishop's Delight, 5, 111	5	1:22.60	50,670
1987	Pine Tree Lane, 5, 125	A. T. Cordero Jr.	Spring Beauty, 4, 117	Gene's Lady, 6, 117	7	1:22.40	52,650
1986	Ride Sally, 4, 118	W. A. Guerra	Willowy Mood, 4, 116	Clocks Secret, 4, 122	8	1:21.60	54,540
1985	Give Me a Hint, 5, 109	W. A. Ward	Nany, 5, 121	Descent, 5, 106	8	1:25.20	55,080
1984	Am Capable, 4, 125	A. T. Cordero Jr.	Sweet Missus, 4, 104	Fissure, 4, 107	7	1:11.00	52,290
1983	Jones Time Machine, 4, 122	A. T. Cordero Jr.	Fancy Naskra, 5, 113	Adept, 4, 111	6	1:23.20	32,880
1982	Lady Dean, 4, 120	D. A. Miller Jr.	Westport Native, 4, 114	Raise 'n Dance, 4, 107	8	1:23.80	33,000
1981	Lady Oakley (Ire), 4, 118	J. Fell	It's in the Air, 5, 120	Lovin' Lass, 4, 110	8	1:25.40	33,900
1980	Misty Gallore, 4, 124	D. MacBeth	Lady Lonsdale, 5, 114	Spanish Fake, 4, 112	6	1:24.60	33,240
1979	Skipat, 5, 122	J. W. Edwards	Sweet Joyce, 4, 106	Unpossible, 4, 107	10	1:10.40	32,520
1978	Vandy Sue, 4, 112	A. M. Rodriguez	Sea Drone, 4, 108	Dalton Road, 5, 118	7	1:12.00	22,185
1977	What a Summer, 4, 118	E. Maple	Secret Lanvin, 4, 112	Shy Dawn, 6, 120	5	1:11.60	21,975
1976	Shy Dawn, 5, 118	A. T. Cordero Jr.	‡Land Girl, 4, 114	Ladies Agreement, 6, 114	8	1:24.20	22,550
1975	Something Super, 5, 115	J. Cruguet	Shy Dawn, 4, 121	Second Coming, 4, 108	9	1:22.20	16,996
1974	Krislin, 5, 113	V. A. Bracciale Jr.	Batucada, 5, 116	Ladies Agreement, 4, 112	8	1:22.00	16,770
1973	Ferly, 5, 113	R. Turcotte	Wakefield Miss, 5, 115	Twixt, 4, 112	8	1:24.00	16,920

Races for females are typically referred to as distaff races. Grade 3 1973-'88. Distaff Breeders' Cup H. 1999-2007. Held at Belmont Park 1956-'59. Not held 1993. 7 furlongs 1954-'76, 1980-'83, 1985-'92, 1995-2005. ‡Imminence finished second, DQ to fourth, 1976.

Distaff Handicap — *See* Humana Distaff Handicap

Dixie Stakes

Grade 2 in 2008. Pimlico Race Course, three-year-olds and up, 1 1/8 miles, turf. Held May 17, 2008, with a gross value of $250,000. First held in 1870. First graded in 1973. Stakes record 1:46.34 (2004 Mr O'Brien [Ire]).

Year	Winner	Jockey	Second	Third	Strs	Time	1st Purse
2008	Pays to Dream, 4, 118	J. Castellano	Stay Close (GB), 6, 118	Ra Der Dean, 8, 118	9	1:54.74	$150,000
2007	Remarkable News (Ven), 5, 122	R. A. Dominguez	Cosmonaut, 5, 124	Outperformance, 4, 120	11	1:46.36	150,000
2006	Better Talk Now, 7, 124	R. A. Dominguez	Dreadnaught, 6, 118	Artie Schiller, 5, 124	7	1:48.48	150,000
2005	Cool Conductor, 4, 118	C. H. Velasquez	Artie Schiller, 4, 124	Good Reward, 4, 118	5	1:52.79	120,000
2004	Mr O'Brien (Ire), 5, 119	R. A. Dominguez	Millennium Dragon (GB), 5, 121	Warleigh, 6, 124	11	**1:46.34**	120,000
2003	Dr. Brendler, 5, 117	R. A. Dominguez	Perfect Soul (Ire), 5, 117	Sardaukar (GB), 7, 117	6	1:57.78	120,000
2002	Strut the Stage, 4, 117	R. Albarado	Del Mar Show, 5, 119	Slew the Red, 5, 117	7	1:51.70	120,000
2001	Hap, 5, 119	J. D. Bailey	Make No Mistake (Ire), 6, 119	Cynics Beware, 7, 119	8	1:48.56	120,000
2000	Quiet Resolve, 5, 117	R. Albarado	Haami, 5, 117	Holditholditholdit, 4, 117	9	1:50.42	120,000
1999	Middlesex Drive, 4, 115	P. Day	Sky Colony, 6, 115	Divide and Conquer, 5, 115	10	1:48.64	120,000
1998	Yagli, 5, 121	J. D. Bailey	Sky Colony, 5, 115	Blazing Sword, 4, 115	12	1:51.01	120,000
1997	Ops Smile, 5, 115	E. S. Prado	Brave Note (Ire), 4, 115	Sharp Appeal, 4, 121	8	1:48.20	120,000
1996	Gold and Steel (Fr), 4, 121	A. O. Solis	Same Old Wish, 4, 115	Comstock Lode, 4, 115	9	1:52.80	120,000
1995	The Vid, 5, 119	J. D. Bailey	Pennine Ridge, 4, 115	Blues Traveller (Ire), 5, 121	6	1:52.25	120,000
1994	Paradise Creek, 5, 124	P. Day	Lure, 4, 124	Astudillo (Ire), 4, 115	8	1:48.51	90,000
1993	Lure, 4, 124	M. E. Smith	Star of Cozzene, 5, 119	Binary Light, 4, 115	8	1:47.60	90,000
1992	Sky Classic, 5, 122	P. Day	Fourstars Allstar, 4, 116	Social Retiree, 5, 112	10	1:47.83	90,000
1991	Double Booked, 6, 118	P. Day	Chas' Whim, 4, 116	Opening Verse, 5, 118	9	1:47.04	90,000
1990	Two Moccasins, 4, 114	R. P. Romero	My Big Boy, 7, 115	Marksmanship, 5, 113	10	2:35.80	90,000
1989	Coeur de Lion (Fr), 5, 121	J. Cruguet	Dance Card Filled, 6, 115	Dynaformer, 4, 118	10	2:38.40	90,000
1988	Kadial (Ire), 5, 112	G. L. Stevens	Top Guest (Ire), 5, 118	Milesius, 4, 120	5	2:45.00	71,045
1987	Akabir, 6, 115	C. Perret	Little Bold John, 5, 117	Vilzak, 4, 113	9	2:28.60	74,360
1986	Uptown Swell, 4, 117	W. A. Guerra	Southern Sultan, 4, 112	†Carlypha (Ire), 5, 108	13	2:27.40	92,445
1985	Nassipour, 5, 115	V. A. Bracciale Jr.	†Persian Tiara (Ire), 5, 113	‡Computer's Choice, 5, 116	9	2:27.60	72,800
1984	†Persian Tiara (Ire), 4, 109	R. L. Shelton	Crazy Moon, 4, 112	Canadian Factor, 4, 118	8	2:41.00	88,675
1983	Khatango, 4, 114	V. A. Bracciale Jr.	London Times, 5, 108	Super Sunrise (GB), 4, 114	10	2:28.60	75,075
1982	Robsphere, 5, 120	J. Velasquez	Present the Colors, 5, 113	Rich and Ready, 6, 115	13	2:30.20	76,960
1981	El Barril (Chi), 5, 116	J. Vasquez	Buckpoint (Fr), 5, 119	Birthday List, 6, 108	9	2:29.80	73,255
1980	Marquee Universal (Ire), 4, 118	H. Pilar	†The Very One, 5, 113	Match the Hatch, 4, 115	14	2:29.60	77,155
1979	†The Very One, 4, 108	C. Cooke	That's a Nice, 5, 116	Fluorescent Light, 5, 124	8	2:28.60	72,995
1978	Fluorescent Light, 4, 114	V. A. Bracciale Jr.	That's a Nice, 4, 115	Improviser, 6, 118	7	2:33.20	37,343
	Bowl Game, 4, 120	J. Velasquez	Oilfield, 5, 110	Trumpeter Swan, 7, 110	9	2:33.40	37,993
1977	Improviser, 5, 120	M. A. Rivera	Grey Beret, 5, 114	Oilfield, 4, 118	12	2:29.40	56,875
1976	Barcas, 5, 112	V. A. Bracciale Jr.	One On the Aisle, 4, 115	Neapolitan Way, 5, 108	9	2:29.60	37,375
1975	Bemo, 5, 114	C. J. McCarron	Outdoors, 6, 115	Drollery, 5, 114	13	2:33.40	39,325
1974	London Company, 4, 122	A. T. Cordero Jr.	Scrimshaw, 6, 110	Mister Diz, 8, 110	9	2:28.80	38,025
1973	Laplander, 6, 111	V. A. Bracciale Jr.	Chrisaway, 5, 112	*Wustenchef, 8, 112	10	2:30.40	38,675

Named for Maj. Barak G. Thomas's mare Dixie (1859 f. by *Sovereign). Formerly named the Reunion S. to signify a reunion of the original subscribers to the Dinner Party S. Originally named the Dinner Party S. The name originated with a Saratoga Springs dinner party attended by a group of men whose main topic of conversation was the revival of Baltimore racing after the Civil War; all present agreed to support the inaugural running of the race in 1870. Formerly sponsored by CompUSA Management Co. of Dallas 2005-'06. Formerly sponsored by Argent Mortgage Co. of Orange, California 2004. Formerly sponsored by CITGO Petroleum Corp. of Tulsa, Oklahoma 2003. Formerly sponsored by Early Times Distillery Co. of Louisville 1991-'96. Grade 3 1990-'93. Dinner Party S. 1870. Dixie H. 1871, 1902-'04, 1925-'90, 1991-'94, 1996. Reunion S. 1872-'85.

Held at Benning, Washington, D.C. 1902-'04. Not held 1889-1901, 1905-'23. 2 miles 1870-'88. 1³/₄ miles 1902-'04. 1⁷/₁₆ miles 1924. 1³/₈ miles 1955-'59. 1¹/₂ miles 1960-'90. 1⁵/₈ miles 1988. Dirt 1870-1954, 1988. Three-year-olds 1870-1904. Two divisions 1965, '78. ‡Pass the Line finished third, DQ to fourth, 1985. Course record 2004. †Denotes female.

Dogwood Stakes

Grade 3 in 2008. Churchill Downs, three-year-olds, fillies, 1 mile, dirt. Held May 31, 2008, with a gross value of $109,000. First held in 1975. First graded in 1998. Stakes record 1:34.56 (2008 Acoma).

Year	Winner	Jockey	Second	Third	Strs	Time	1st Purse
2008	**Acoma**, 3, 117	R. Albarado	Keep the Peace, 3, 117	Secret Gypsy, 3, 117	6	**1:34.56**	$66,904
2007	Lady Joanne, 3, 123	C. H. Borel	High Again, 3, 123	Upcoming Story, 3, 117	8	1:35.35	101,698
2006	Joint Effort, 3, 116	R. R. Douglas	Ready to Please, 3, 120	Victorina, 3, 116	9	1:35.49	101,148
2005	Miss Matched, 3, 116	S. Bridgmohan	Culinary, 3, 120	Catta Pilosa, 3, 116	7	1:43.49	101,928
2004	Stellar Jayne, 3, 120	R. Albarado	Dynaville, 3, 114	Ender's Sister, 3, 122	5	1:43.14	100,068
2003	Golden Marlin, 3, 115	S. J. Sellers	Double Scoop, 3, 114	Throne, 3, 114	7	1:45.96	67,580
2002	Take Charge Lady, 3, 121	A. J. D'Amico	Charmed Gift, 3, 116	Allamerican Bertie, 3, 114	7	1:42.73	67,890
2001	Nasty Storm, 3, 114	L. J. Meche	Love At Noon, 3, 114	Golly Greeley, 3, 116	7	1:43.41	68,014
2000	Welcome Surprise, 3, 112	F. C. Torres	Lady Melesi, 3, 114	Vivid Sunset, 3, 114	7	1:46.80	68,014
1999	Golden Temper, 3, 116	S. J. Sellers	Boom Town Girl, 3, 121	Honey Hill Lil, 3, 116	8	1:43.73	69,068
1998	Really Polish, 3, 116	P. Day	‡Beat the Play, 3, 114	Victorica, 3, 121	5	1:44.78	67,642
1997	Leo's Gypsy Dancer, 3, 116	P. Day	Buckeye Search, 3, 121	Flying Lauren, 3, 118	7	1:44.95	69,006
1996	Ginny Lynn, 3, 121	L. J. Melancon	Everhope, 3, 121	Hidden Lake, 3, 114	7	1:43.22	53,576
1995	Gal in a Ruckus, 3, 121	W. H. McCauley	Country Cat, 3, 116	Naskra Colors, 3, 114	7	1:43.88	53,528
1994	Briar Road, 3, 114	L. J. Melancon	Stella Cielo, 3, 114	Shadow Miss, 3, 121	6	1:44.78	53,186
1993	With a Wink, 3, 114	C. R. Woods Jr.	Lovat's Lady, 3, 112	Unlaced, 3, 116	8	1:44.21	36,010
1992	Hitch, 3, 121	B. E. Bartram	Bionic Soul, 3, 121	Secretly, 3, 114	8	1:47.68	36,075
1991	Be Cool, 3, 121	A. T. Gryder	Barri Mac, 3, 114	Saratoga Dame, 3, 121	8	1:46.46	36,563
1990	Patches, 3, 118	K. K. Allen	Mrs. K., 3, 116	Mirth, 3, 114	4	1:46.60	34,873
1989	Luthier's Launch, 3, 118	P. Day	Motion in Limine, 3, 116	Dreamy Mimi, 3, 121	9	1:45.20	36,465
1988	Darien Miss, 3, 121	D. Brumfield	Stolie, 3, 118	Most Likely, 3, 116	8	1:43.80	35,848
1987	Lady Gretchen, 3, 112	M. McDowell	Super Cook, 3, 122	Jonowo, 3, 122	7	1:44.00	46,193
1986	Hail a Cab, 3, 119	P. A. Johnson	Tall Poppy, 3, 111	Marshesseaux, 3, 114	8	1:46.60	46,810
1985	Foxy Deen, 3, 118	D. Montoya	Weekend Delight, 3, 120	Clouhalo, 3, 112	8	1:50.00	35,945
1984	Mrs. Revere, 3, 121	L. J. Melancon	Rambling Rhythm, 3, 119	Robin's Rob, 3, 115	8	1:51.20	49,510
1983	Bon Gout, 3, 117	P. Day	Andthebeatgoeson, 3, 112	Workin Girl, 3, 112	8	1:53.00	36,368
1982	Amazing Love, 3, 117	L. J. Melancon	Sefa's Beauty, 3, 117	Bold Siren, 3, 113	8	1:46.60	23,546
1981	Savage Love, 3, 116	P. Nicolo	Westport Native, 3, 118	Brian's Babe, 3, 116	6	1:24.80	19,053
	Fancy Naskra, 3, 118	J. Lively	Contrefaire, 3, 121	Solo Disco, 3, 118	10	1:25.20	17,948
1980	Quality Corner, 3, 121	M. S. Sellers	Forever Cordial, 3, 121	No No Nona, 3, 121	9	1:24.00	19,403
1979	Split the Tab, 3, 121	D. Haire	Shawn's Gal, 3, 121	Safe, 3, 121	10	1:24.00	19,663
1978	Bold Rendezvous, 3, 121	A. Rini	Step in the Circle, 3, 118	Timeforaturn, 3, 118	8	1:23.40	14,446
1977	Unreality, 3, 121	M. Fromin	Shady Lou, 3, 121	Time for Pleasure, 3, 118	12	1:25.40	15,031
1976	T. V. Vixen, 3, 121	M. Manganello	Sunny Romance, 3, 116	Old Goat, 3, 121	6	1:23.40	14,154
1975	My Juliet, 3, 121	A. Hill	Snow Doll, 3, 118	Hope She Does, 3, 118	9	1:24.00	14,999

Named for the dogwood tree, plentiful in Kentucky. Dogwood Breeders' Cup S. 2004-'06. 7 furlongs 1975-'81. 1¹/₁₆ miles 1982, 1986-2005. 1¹/₈ miles 1983-'85. Two divisions 1981. ‡Nickel Classic finished second, DQ to fifth, 1998.

Donn Handicap

Grade 1 in 2008. Gulfstream Park, four-year-olds and up, 1¹/₈ miles, dirt. Held February 2, 2008, with a gross value of $500,000. First held in 1959. First graded in 1973. Stakes record 1:46.40 (1979 Jumping Hill).

Year	Winner	Jockey	Second	Third	Strs	Time	1st Purse
2008	**Spring At Last**, 5, 119	E. Coa	A. P. Arrow, 6, 119	Kiss the Kid, 5, 115	8	1:48.35	$300,000
2007	Invasor (Arg), 5, 123	F. Jara	Hesanoldsalt, 4, 114	A. P. Arrow, 5, 116	8	1:48.43	300,000
2006	Brass Hat, 5, 118	W. Martinez	Pies Prospect, 5, 114	Andromeda's Hero, 4, 115	9	1:47.79	300,000
2005	Saint Liam, 5, 119	E. S. Prado	Roses in May, 5, 121	Eddington, 4, 114	6	1:48.43	300,000
2004	Medaglia d'Oro, 5, 122	J. D. Bailey	Seattle Fitz (Arg), 5, 113	Funny Cide, 4, 119	8	1:47.68	300,000
2003	Harlan's Holiday, 4, 120	J. R. Velazquez	Hero's Tribute, 5, 114	Puzzlement, 4, 114	11	1:49.63	300,000
2002	Mongoose, 4, 114	E. S. Prado	‡Kiss a Native, 5, 114	Rize, 6, 114	14	1:49.63	300,000
2001	Captain Steve, 4, 120	J. D. Bailey	Albert the Great, 4, 119	Gander, 5, 115	7	1:48.95	300,000
2000	Stephen Got Even, 4, 115	S. J. Sellers	Golden Missile, 5, 114	Behrens, 6, 121	10	1:48.50	300,000
1999	Puerto Madero (Chi), 5, 120	K. Desormeaux	Behrens, 5, 113	Silver Charm, 5, 126	12	1:48.34	300,000
1998	Skip Away, 5, 126	J. D. Bailey	Unruled, 5, 112	Sir Bear, 5, 113	10	1:50.17	180,000
1997	Formal Gold, 4, 113	J. Bravo	Skip Away, 4, 123	Mecke, 5, 120	10	1:47.49	180,000
1996	Cigar, 6, 128	J. D. Bailey	Wekiva Springs, 5, 117	†Heavenly Prize, 5, 115	8	1:49.12	180,000
1995	Cigar, 5, 115	J. D. Bailey	Primitive Hall, 6, 112	Bonus Money (GB), 4, 112	9	1:49.68	180,000
1994	Pistols and Roses, 5, 113	H. Castillo Jr.	Eequalsmcsquared, 5, 113	Wallonda, 4, 113	11	1:50.67	180,000
1993	Pistols and Roses, 4, 112	H. Castillo Jr.	Irish Swap, 6, 113	Missionary Ridge (GB), 6, 118	9	1:50.10	240,000
1992	Sea Cadet, 4, 115	A. O. Solis	Out of Place, 5, 114	Sunny Sunrise, 5, 115	8	1:48.14	300,000
1991	Jolie's Halo, 4, 114	R. Platts	Sports View, 4, 116	Secret Hello, 4, 116	12	1:47.50	300,000
1990	Primal, 5, 120	E. Fires	Ole Atocha, 5, 111	Western Playboy, 4, 119	8	1:50.00	120,000
1989	Cryptoclearance, 5, 121	J. A. Santos	Slew City Slew, 5, 118	Primal, 4, 117	12	1:50.20	120,000
1988	Jade Hunter, 4, 112	J. D. Bailey	Cryptoclearance, 4, 123	Personal Flag, 5, 120	8	1:48.80	120,000
1987	Little Bold John, 5, 111	M. A. Gonzalez	Skip Trial, 5, 118	Wise Times, 4, 117	7	1:48.80	96,660
1986	Creme Fraiche, 4, 122	E. Maple	Skip Trial, 4, 122	Minneapple, 4, 115	13	1:51.20	77,280
1985	Mo Exception, 4, 115	R. Breen	Dr. Carter, 4, 120	Key to the Moon, 4, 122	10	1:48.60	74,280
1984	Play Fellow, 4, 122	P. Day	Courteous Majesty, 4, 111	Jack Slade, 4, 114	9	1:49.00	53,955

Racing — Graded Stakes 309

Year	Winner	Jockey	Second	Third	Strs	Time	1st Purse
1983	**Deputy Minister**, 4, 122	D. MacBeth	Key Count, 4, 113	Rivalero, 7, 121	16	1:48.60	$60,840
1982	**Joanie's Chief**, 5, 111	J. Samyn	Double Sonic, 4, 111	Lord Darnley, 4, 113	12	1:49.00	57,330
1981	**Hurry Up Blue**, 4, 116	C. C. Lopez	Tunerup, 5, 126	Joanie's Chief, 4, 107	5	1:49.00	51,345
1980	**Lot o' Gold**, 4, 119	D. Brumfield	Addison, 5, 117	Going Investor, 5, 112	9	1:48.80	54,600
1979	**Jumping Hill**, 7, 122	J. Fell	Bob's Dusty, 5, 120	Silent Cal, 4, 121	14	**1:46.40**	60,150
1978	**Man's Man**, 4, 115	R. Woodhouse	Intercontinent, 4, 116	Adriatico (Arg), 7, 110	11	1:42.20	39,000
1977	**Legion**, 7, 113	L. Saumell	Logical, 5, 114	Yamanin, 5, 124	7	1:48.80	37,440
1976	**Foolish Pleasure**, 4, 129	B. Baeza	Packer Captain, 4, 114	Home Jerome, 6, 112	10	1:21.40	37,980
1975	**Proud and Bold**, 5, 118	G. St. Leon	Holding Pattern, 4, 121	Arbees Boy, 5, 119	6	1:48.00	35,280
1974	**Forego**, 4, 125	H. Gustines	True Knight, 5, 123	Proud and Bold, 4, 122	5	1:48.60	36,000
1973	**Triumphant**, 4, 114	B. Baeza	Second Bar, 4, 121	Gentle Smoke, 4, 113	7	1:47.80	37,560

Named in honor of James Donn Sr. (1887-1972), founder of modern Gulfstream Park. Grade 3 1973-'74. Grade 2 1975-'87. 1½ miles 1959-'64. 7 furlongs 1976. 1 1/16 miles 1978. Turf 1959-'64. ‡Red Bullet finished second, DQ to fourth, 2002. Track record 2006. †Denotes female.

Doubledogdare Stakes

Grade 3 in 2008. Keeneland Race Course, four-year-olds and up, fillies and mares, 1 1/16 miles, all weather. Held April 18, 2008, with a gross value of $125,000. First held in 1992. First graded in 2007. Stakes record 1:41.32 (1999 Lu Ravi).

Year	Winner	Jockey	Second	Third	Strs	Time	1st Purse
2008	**Carriage Trail**, 5, 117	K. J. Desormeaux	Say You Will (Ire), 4, 117	Indescribable, 4, 117	7	1:42.51	$77,500
2007	**Asi Siempre**, 5, 121	G. K. Gomez	Pyramid Love, 4, 117	Warrior Girl, 4, 117	6	1:46.40	67,332
2006	**Pool Land**, 4, 117	J. R. Velazquez	Private Gift, 4, 117	Miss Matched, 4, 117	5	1:44.08	66,526
2005	**Colony Band**, 4, 117	J. R. Velazquez	La Reason, 5, 117	Ender's Sister, 4, 117	7	1:46.15	68,014
2004	**Mayo On the Side**, 5, 116	P. Day	Cat Fighter, 4, 116	Roar Emotion, 4, 116	8	1:43.92	75,826
2003	**Reason to Talk**, 4, 116	P. Day	Salty Farma, 5, 116	Extend, 5, 116	4	1:45.19	67,394
2002	**Dancethruthedawn**, 4, 116	R. Albarado	Maltese Superb, 5, 116	De Bertie, 5, 120	5	1:42.92	66,712
2001	**Darling My Darling**, 4, 116	M. E. Smith	Frankly My Dear, 4, 118	Fast Delivery, 4, 118	6	1:44.38	67,270
2000	**Silverbulletday**, 4, 123	J. D. Bailey	Roza Robata, 5, 116	Pepita Ramoje, 5, 116	3	1:43.76	66,774
1999	**Lu Ravi**, 4, 120	W. Martinez	Pantufla, 4, 115	Biogio's Rose, 5, 118	6	**1:41.32**	67,456
1998	**Top Secret**, 5, 114	J. Bravo	One Rich Lady, 4, 120	Pleasant Temper, 4, 114	5	1:42.60	44,733
1997	**Singing Heart**, 5, 114	C. Perret	Mediation (Ire), 5, 114	Ultimate Strike, 5, 114	10	1:02.49	45,499
1994	**Jeano**, 6, 114	S. J. Sellers	Casual Rendezvous, 3, 112	Clever Act, 3, 112	8	1:24.06	26,784
1993	**How Rare**, 4, 123	B. E. Bartram	Nannerl, 6, 114	Fujitime, 5, 117	8	1:22.02	30,695
1992	**Jeano**, 4, 114	S. J. Sellers	Erica's Dream, 4, 123	Jenny's Playmate, 5, 120	8	1:22.61	23,436

Named for Claiborne Farm's 1955 champion two-year-old filly, '56 champion three-year-old filly, and '56 Spinster S. winner Doubledogdare (1953 f. by Double Jay). Not held 1995-'96. 7 furlongs 1992-'94. 5½ furlongs 1997. Turf 1997. Dirt 1992-'96, 1998-2006. Three-year-olds and up 1992-'97.

Dwyer Stakes

Grade 2 in 2008. Belmont Park, three-year-olds, 1 1/16 miles, dirt. Held July 4, 2007, with a gross value of $147,000. First held in 1887. First graded in 1973. Stakes record 1:40.02 (2004 Medallist).

Year	Winner	Jockey	Second	Third	Strs	Time	1st Purse
2007	**Any Given Saturday**, 3, 121	G. K. Gomez	Nobiz Like Shobiz, 3, 123	Sightseeing, 3, 121	5	1:40.69	$90,000
2006	**Strong Contender**, 3, 115	E. S. Prado	Doc Cheney, 3, 115	Da Stoops, 3, 115	6	1:45.24	90,000
2005	**Roman Ruler**, 3, 119	J. D. Bailey	Flower Alley, 3, 123	Proud Accolade, 3, 119	6	1:40.83	90,000
2004	**Medallist**, 3, 121	J. F. Chavez	The Cliff's Edge, 3, 123	Sir Shackleton, 3, 121	6	**1:40.02**	90,000
2003	**Strong Hope**, 3, 115	J. R. Velazquez	Nacheezmo, 3, 115	Sky Mesa, 3, 119	7	1:41.76	90,000
2002	**Gygistar**, 3, 121	J. R. Velazquez	Nothing Flat, 3, 117	American Style, 3, 115	6	1:42.59	90,000
2001	**E Dubai**, 3, 121	J. D. Bailey	Windsor Castle, 3, 119	Hero's Tribute, 3, 121	4	1:40.38	145,500
2000	**Albert the Great**, 3, 115	R. Migliore	More Than Ready, 3, 119	Red Bullet, 3, 123	4	1:42.62	90,000
1999	**Forestry**, 3, 122	J. D. Bailey	Doneraile Court, 3, 119	Successful Appeal, 3, 122	6	1:41.00	90,000
1998	**Coronado's Quest**, 3, 124	M. E. Smith	Ian's Thunder, 3, 112	Scatmandu, 3, 122	5	1:42.49	90,000
1997	**Behrens**, 3, 117	J. D. Bailey	Glitman, 3, 117	Banker's Gold, 3, 122	6	1:42.26	90,000
1996	**Victory Speech**, 3, 117	J. D. Bailey	Gold Fever, 3, 119	Robb, 3, 117	6	1:41.53	99,000
1995	**Hoolie**, 3, 117	R. G. Davis	Reality Road, 3, 112	Western Larla, 3, 119	6	1:42.74	90,000
1994	**Holy Bull**, 3, 124	M. E. Smith	Twining, 3, 122	Bay Street Star, 3, 119	4	1:41.15	90,000
1993	**Cherokee Run**, 3, 123	P. Day	Miner's Mark, 3, 123	Silver of Silver, 3, 123	6	1:47.62	120,000
1992	‡**Agincourt**, 3, 119	J. F. Chavez	Three Peat, 3, 119	Windundermywings, 3, 114	6	1:47.84	120,000
1991	**Lost Mountain**, 3, 123	C. Perret	Smooth Performance, 3, 114	Fly So Free, 3, 126	7	1:49.20	120,000
1990	**Profit Key**, 3, 123	J. A. Santos	Rhythm, 3, 123	Graf, 3, 114	4	1:47.40	102,960
1989	**Roi Danzig**, 3, 114	E. Maple	Contested Colors, 3, 114	Rampart Road, 3, 114	5	1:49.20	133,680
1988	**Seeking the Gold**, 3, 123	P. Day	Evening Kris, 3, 119	Gay Rights, 3, 123	6	1:48.00	137,040
1987	**Gone West**, 3, 123	E. Maple	Pledge Card, 3, 114	Polish Navy, 3, 123	6	1:48.40	138,240
1986	**Ogygian**, 3, 123	W. A. Guerra	Johns Treasure, 3, 114	Personal Flag, 3, 114	4	1:48.40	112,680
1985	**Stephan's Odyssey**, 3, 123	L. A. Pincay Jr.	Cutlass Reality, 3, 114	Important Business, 3, 126	8	1:49.20	88,500
1984	**Track Barron**, 3, 119	J. Cruguet	Darn That Alarm, 3, 123	Slew the Coup, 3, 114	7	1:47.80	99,600
1983	**Au Point**, 3, 114	J. D. Bailey	Potentiate, 3, 114	Intention, 3, 114	10	1:48.20	67,680
1982	**Conquistador Cielo**, 3, 126	E. Maple	John's Gold, 3, 114	Reinvested, 3, 119	6	1:45.80	67,560
1981	**Noble Nashua**, 3, 119	C. B. Asmussen	Tap Shoes, 3, 126	Silver Express, 3, 114	10	1:49.20	67,680
1980	**Amber Pass**, 3, 114	D. MacBeth	Temperence Hill, 3, 129	Comptroller, 3, 119	6	1:49.00	67,440
1979	**Coastal**, 3, 126	R. Hernandez	Private Account, 3, 114	Quiet Crossing, 3, 119	6	1:47.00	63,840
1978	**Junction**, 3, 120	J. Fell	Buckaroo, 3, 117	Darby Creek Road, 3, 121	3	1:48.80	47,025
1977	**Bailjumper**, 3, 116	A. T. Cordero Jr.	Lynn Davis, 3, 112	Iron Constitution, 3, 121	8	1:47.60	48,870
1976	**Quiet Little Table**, 3, 111	E. Maple	Sir Lister, 3, 116	Dance Spell, 3, 117	8	1:49.00	50,895

Racing — Graded Stakes

Year	Winner	Jockey	Second	Third	Strs	Time	1st Purse
1975	Valid Appeal, 3, 110	J. S. Long	Wajima, 3, 118	Hunka Papa, 3, 116	8	1:48.40	$50,400
1974	Hatchet Man, 3, 114	R. Turcotte	Rube the Great, 3, 124	Kin Run, 3, 112	9	2:01.20	51,120
1973	Stop the Music, 3, 120	H. Gustines	Arbees Boy, 3, 115	Duc de Flanagan, 3, 111	8	2:02.60	50,625

Named in honor of leading 19th-century owners Mike and Phil Dwyer. Formerly named in honor of the city of Brooklyn, New York. Grade 1 1983-'88. Brooklyn Derby 1887-1917. Dwyer H. 1956-'78. Held at Gravesend Park 1887-1910. Held at Aqueduct 1914-'55, 1960-'74, 1976. Held at Jamaica 1956, 1959. Not held 1911-'12. 1½ miles 1887, 1898-1909, 1926-'34. 1⅛ miles 1888-'97, 1915-'24, 1935-'39, 1975-'93. 1¼ miles 1910-'14, 1940-'55, 1960-'74. 1⁵⁄₁₆ miles 1925. 1³⁄₁₆ miles 1956-'59. ‡Three Peat finished first, DQ to second, 1992.

Early Times Mint Julep Handicap

Grade 3 in 2008. Churchill Downs, three-year-olds and up, fillies and mares, 1¹⁄₁₆ miles, turf. Held June 16, 2007, with a gross value of $164,100. First held in 1977. First graded in 2001. Stakes record 1:40.70 (2007 Quite a Bride).

Year	Winner	Jockey	Second	Third	Strs	Time	1st Purse
2007	Quite a Bride, 4, 121	R. Albarado	Magnificent Song, 4, 120	Danzon, 4, 117	6	**1:40.70**	$100,728
2006	My Typhoon (Ire), 4, 119	R. Albarado	Rich in Spirit, 4, 118	Louve Royale (Ire), 5, 124	11	1:41.55	67,022
2005	Delta Princess, 6, 117	R. Albarado	Shaconage, 5, 116	Erhu, 4, 112	7	1:42.43	68,262
2004	Stay Forever, 7, 116	E. Castro	Sand Springs, 4, 120	Eternal Melody (NZ), 4, 115	9	1:42.66	104,346
2003	Kiss the Devil, 5, 115	L. J. Meche	Quick Tip, 5, 119	Cellars Shiraz, 4, 120	9	1:41.73	104,346
2002	Megans Bluff, 5, 118	C. Perret	Cozy Island, 4, 112	Solvig, 5, 117	8	1:42.87	69,998
2001	Megans Bluff, 4, 118	C. Perret	Sitka, 4, 109	Good Game, 4, 116	10	1:42.88	70,432
2000	Pratella, 5, 118	L. J. Melancon	Silver Comic, 4, 115	Histoire Sainte (Fr), 4, 113	8	1:43.08	69,378
1999	Mingling Glances, 5, 113	L. J. Melancon	Formal Tango, 4, 115	Red Cat, 4, 116	11	1:42.59	70,928
1998	B. A. Valentine, 5, 116	F. Torres	Lordy Lordy, 5, 113	Mingling Glances, 4, 112	9	1:41.42	70,804
1997	‡Valor Lady, 5, 114	R. Albarado	My Secret, 5, 114	Everhope, 4, 112	11	1:41.20	71,238
1996	Bail Out Becky, 4, 118	C. Perret	Country Cat, 4, 117	Fluffkins, 4, 115	8	1:41.86	54,698
1995	Romy, 4, 118	J. L. Diaz	Olden Lek, 5, 114	Memories (Ire), 4, 113	6	1:42.69	54,941
1994	Words of War, 5, 117	C. H. Marquez Jr.	Freewheel, 5, 116	Eurostorm, 4, 112	10	1:40.98	55,673
1993	Classic Reign, 4, 115	F. A. Arguello Jr.	Tap Routine, 4, 113	Liz Cee, 5, 114	10	1:42.84	37,375
1992	Lady Shirl, 5, 123	P. A. Johnson	Topsa, 5, 112	Behaving Dancer, 5, 119	7	1:41.41	37,083
1991	Dance for Lucy, 5, 116	L. J. Melancon	Welsh Muffin (Ire), 4, 113	Super Fan, 4, 118	10	1:43.07	37,148
1990	Tunita, 5, 114	R. J. Thibeau Jr.	Port St. Mary (GB), 4, 113	Flags Waving, 4, 112	8	1:43.80	25,821
	Phoenix Sunshine, 5, 116	J. Deegan	Vana Turns, 5, 111	Carousel Baby, 4, 111	8	1:43.20	31,476
1989	Here's Your Silver, 4, 115	M. McDowell	Lt. Lao, 5, 117	Danzig's Bride, 4, 114	10	1:50.40	37,115
1988	How I Wish, 4, 113	E. Fires	Gaily Gaily (Ire), 5, 113	No Choice, 5, 114	10	1:51.00	36,660
1987	Thunderdome, 4, 119	S. H. Bass	Acquire, 5, 119	No Choice, 4, 119	8	1:37.80	26,247
	Innsbruck (GB), 4, 114	S. Hawley	Fantasy Lover, 4, 114	Marianna's Girl, 4, 122	8	1:38.00	21,470
1986	Zenobia Empress, 5, 120	E. Fires	Donut's Pride, 4, 120	Ante, 5, 117	7	1:35.80	28,418
1985	Stave, 4, 112	C. R. Woods Jr.	Gerrie Singer, 4, 120	Switching Trick, 5, 117	10	1:35.00	21,694
1984	Lass Trump, 4, 111	G. Patterson	Lady Hawthorn, 4, 114	Delhousie, 4, 111	7	1:37.00	26,267
1983	Naskra Magic, 4, 114	P. Rubbicco	Excitable Lady, 5, 120	Charge My Account, 4, 112	8	1:36.60	23,433
1982	Kate's Cabin, 4, 115	E. Snell	Mean Martha, 4, 112	Forever Cordial, 5, 112	8	1:25.20	23,855
1981	Lillian Russell, 4, 118	R. J. Hirdes Jr.	Run Ky. Run, 4, 121	Salud, 4, 114	9	1:23.20	19,468
1980	Likely Exchange, 6, 118	D. E. Whited	Nauti Lass, 5, 119	Dearyouloveme, 4, 117	11	1:24.40	19,728
1979	Bold Rendezvous, 4, 115	A. L. Fernandez	Likely Exchange, 5, 116	Popped Corn, 4, 116	10	1:25.00	17,908
1978	Time for Pleasure, 4, 120	T. Barrow	Don't Cry Barbi, 4, 119	Dear Irish, 4, 119	10	1:23.40	14,609
1977	Satan's Cheer, 5, 115	M. Manganello	Confort Zone, 4, 117	Decided Lady, 4, 115	7	1:24.00	14,300

Named for the traditional bourbon drink served at the Kentucky Derby. Sponsored by Early Times Distillery Co. of Louisville 2001-'07. Mint Julep S. 1982-'87, 1995-'96, 1998. 7 furlongs 1977-'82. 1 mile 1983-'87. 1⅛ miles 1988-'89. Three-year-olds and up 1988. Two divisions 1987, '90. ‡Romy finished first, DQ to fourth, 1997. Course record 1992, '94, 2007.

Eatontown Stakes

Grade 3 in 2008. Monmouth Park, three-year-olds and up, fillies and mares, 1¹⁄₁₆ miles, turf. Held June 16, 2007, with a gross value of $150,000. First held in 1971. First graded in 1996. Stakes record 1:39.48 (2007 Karen's Caper).

Year	Winner	Jockey	Second	Third	Strs	Time	1st Purse
2007	Karen's Caper, 5, 117	B. Blanc	Redaspen, 5, 119	Roshani, 4, 117	7	**1:39.48**	$90,000
2006	Brunilda (Arg), 6, 119	E. Castro	Rahys' Appeal, 4, 115	Prop Me Up, 4, 117	6	1:44.00	90,000
2005	Smart N Classy, 5, 115	J. A. Velez Jr.	Lentil, 6, 116	Spotlight (GB), 4, 118	7	1:46.22	90,000
2004	Ocean Drive, 4, 120	E. Coa	Honorable Cat, 5, 114	Fast Cookie, 4, 118	6	1:41.79	60,000
2003	Stylish, 5, 118	H. Castillo Jr.	Something Ventured, 4, 117	Sweet Deimos (GB), 4, 113	9	1:41.69	60,000
2002	Clearly a Queen, 5, 119	E. Coa	Laurica, 5, 114	Presumed Innocent, 5, 117	9	1:44.02	60,000
2001	Cousin Gigi, 4, 115	R. Wilson	Quidnaskra, 6, 116	Crystal Sea, 4, 113	8	1:47.50	60,000
2000	Reciclada (Chi), 5, 118	A. O. Solis	Mumtaz (Fr), 4, 122	Dominique's Joy, 5, 117	8	1:44.34	60,000
1999	Formal Tango, 4, 113	J. D. Bailey	Proud Owner, 4, 115	Natalie Too, 5, 122	7	1:42.62	60,000
1998	Gastronomical, 5, 115	G. L. Stevens	Tampico, 5, 117	dh-Danzica Clear (Ire), 5, 112 dh-Poopsie, 4, 114	10	1:43.39	41,400
1997	B. A. Valentine, 4, 122	C. J. McCarron	Everhope, 4, 112	Vashon, 4, 122	11	1:41.41	41,460
1996	Gail's Brush, 5, 116	G. Boulanger	Plenty of Sugar, 5, 117	Lady Affirmed, 5, 116	7	1:40.40	45,000
1995	Symphony Lady, 5, 119	J. Bravo	Cox Orange, 5, 122	Grafin, 4, 119	6	1:43.64	30,000
1994	Verbal Volley, 4, 119	R. E. Colton	Irving's Girl, 4, 114	Uptown Show, 5, 113	8	1:44.71	24,000
1993	Topsa, 6, 113	L. R. Rivera Jr.	Naked Royalty, 4, 115	Suspect Terrain, 4, 115	7	1:46.39	21,000
1992	Red Journey, 4, 115	N. Santagata	Hot Times Are Here, 4, 113	Flashing Eyes, 4, 113	7	1:45.06	21,000
1991	Jacuzzi Boogie, 4, 119	N. Santagata	Hear the Bells, 4, 113	Be Exclusive (Ire), 5, 113	5	1:41.67	21,000
1990	Miss Unnameable, 6, 113	L. Saumell	Lip Service, 5, 116	Perfect Coin, 4, 112	9	1:48.00	34,110
1989	Highland Penny, 4, 112	D. Carr	Starofanera, 4, 113	River Memories, 5, 114	9	1:50.00	34,770

Racing — Graded Stakes 311

Year	Winner	Jockey	Second	Third	Strs	Time	1st Purse
1988	Hear Music, 5, 115	M. Castaneda	Fancy Pan, 5, 112	Antique Mystique, 4, 111	7	1:49.80	$34,440
1987	Bailrullah, 5, 111	N. Santagata	Princely Proof, 4, 116	Krotz, 4, 118	10	1:44.00	28,590
	Cadabra Abra, 4, 118	W. H. McCauley	Treasure Map, 5, 115	Spruce Fir, 4, 121	6	1:43.80	28,110
1986	Mazatleca (Mex), 6, 117	C. Perret	Cope of Flowers, 4, 114	Darbrielle, 4, 113	8	1:43.20	27,960
	Bharal, 5, 114	J. Velasquez	Thirteen Keys, 4, 114	Dawn's Curtsey, 4, 118	8	1:43.80	28,200
1985	Agacerie, 4, 118	A. T. Cordero Jr.	Meddlin Maggie, 4, 115	Natural Grace, 4, 114	8	1:44.20	34,830
1984	Jubilous, 4, 118	G. McCarron	Maidenhead, 5, 113	High Schemes, 4, 118	13	1:43.40	36,060
1983	Doodle, 4, 118	J. J. Miranda	Olamic, 4, 110	Bright Choice, 4, 112	12	1:44.00	28,410
1982	Kuja Happa, 4, 114	D. R. Wright	Qui Silent, 4, 113	Suave Princess, 4, 113	10	1:44.80	27,465
1981	Wayward Lassie, 4, 112	D. Montoya	Earlham, 5, 114	Paris Press, 4, 114	7	1:44.60	16,957
	Endicotta, 5, 116	D. Brumfield	Dance Troupe, 4, 115	Farewell Letter, 4, 113	5	1:44.80	16,717
1980	Riddle's Reply, 4, 113	E. Cardone	Sharp Zone, 4, 111	Newmarket Lady, 4, 112	8	1:44.20	20,078
	Nasty Jay, 5, 111	R. E. McKnight	T. V. Highlights, 6, 119	O'Connell Street, 4, 113	9	1:44.00	20,288
1979	The Very One, 4, 116	C. Cooke	Frosty Skater, 4, 120	Municipal Bond, 4, 113	8	1:46.20	25,236
1978	Huggle Duggle, 4, 113	B. Gonzalez	All Biz, 6, 118	Navajo Princess, 4, 114	9	1:42.60	22,116
1977	Jolly Song, 5, 112	J. Nied Jr.	T. V. Genie, 4, 112	All Biz, 5, 117	9	1:47.20	18,590
1976	‡Collegiate, 4, 113	J. W. Edwards	Copano, 4, 119	Double Ack, 3, 114	10	1:43.60	14,950
	Stage Luck, 4, 118	J. W. Edwards	Hinterland, 6, 114	*Deesse Du Val, 5, 121	9	1:43.80	14,788
1975	Hinterland, 5, 114	C. Perret	Ringmistress, 5, 114	Kudara, 4, 119	8	1:43.60	18,135
1974	Bird Boots, 5, 119	B. Thornburg	Belle Marie, 4, 117	Shaya, 4, 108	13	1:46.80	19,207
1973	‡Telly, 5, 110	V. A. Bracciale Jr.	Lightning Lucy, 3, 113	Wire Chief, 5, 111	8	1:43.60	14,763
	Cathy Baby, 4, 116	M. A. Rivera	Aglimmer, 4, 116	Bold Place, 4, 117	7	1:42.60	14,633

Named for Eatontown, New Jersey, located in Monmouth County. Eatontown H. 1973-'90, 1996, 2002-'06. 1¹/₁₆ miles 1988-'90, 2001. Dirt 1974, '77, 2006. Two divisions 1972, 1973, 1976, 1980-'81, 1986-'87. Dead heat for third 1998. ‡Lightning Lucy finished first, DQ to second, 1973 (1st Div.). ‡Copano finished first, DQ to second, 1976 (1st Div.). Course record 2007.

Eddie Read Handicap

Grade 1 in 2008. Del Mar, three-year-olds and up, 1⅛ miles, turf. Held July 22, 2007, with a gross value of $400,000. First held in 1974. First graded in 1980. Stakes record 1:44.79 (2006 Aragorn [Ire]).

Year	Winner	Jockey	Second	Third	Strs	Time	1st Purse
2007	After Market, 4, 120	A. O. Solis	Out of Control (Brz), 4, 115	Rob Roy, 5, 117	5	1:47.36	$240,000
2006	Aragorn (Ire), 4, 121	C. S. Nakatani	Sweet Return (GB), 6, 117	Silent Name (Jpn), 4, 118	7	**1:44.79**	240,000
2005	Sweet Return (GB), 5, 120	A. O. Solis	Fourty Niners Son, 4, 117	Singletary, 5, 120	6	1:46.53	240,000
2004	Special Ring, 7, 118	V. Espinoza	Bayamo (Ire), 5, 119	Sweet Return (GB), 4, 119	10	1:45.40	240,000
2003	Special Ring, 6, 117	D. R. Flores	Decarchy, 6, 117	Irish Warrior, 5, 114	6	1:45.87	240,000
2002	Sarafan, 7, 117	C. S. Nakatani	Beat Hollow (GB), 5, 122	Redattore (Brz), 7, 118	6	1:46.77	240,000
2001	Redattore (Brz), 6, 115	A. O. Solis	Native Desert, 8, 116	Super Quercus (Fr), 5, 115	6	1:47.20	240,000
2000	Ladies Din, 5, 120	K. Desormeaux	Chester House, 4, 114	Gold Nugget, 5, 115	8	1:48.64	240,000
1999	Joe Who (Brz), 6, 116	C. W. Antley	Ladies Din, 4, 114	Bouccaneer (Fr), 4, 115	10	1:48.75	240,000
1998	Subordination, 4, 117	D. R. Flores	Bonapartiste (Fr), 4, 115	Hawksky Hill (Ire), 5, 120	7	1:47.40	180,000
1997	Expelled, 5, 113	J. A. Garcia	El Angelo, 5, 119	Marlin, 4, 122	7	1:48.60	180,000
1996	Fastness (Ire), 6, 124	C. S. Nakatani	Smooth Runner, 5, 114	Gold and Steel (Fr), 4, 118	6	1:47.05	193,000
1995	Fastness (Ire), 5, 115	G. L. Stevens	Romarin (Brz), 5, 119	Northern Spur (Ire), 4, 118	8	1:48.42	182,600
1994	Approach the Bench (Ire), 6, 113	C. S. Nakatani	Fastness (Ire), 4, 114	Johann Quatz (Fr), 5, 116	7	1:48.83	187,250
1993	Kotashaan (Fr), 5, 117	K. Desormeaux	Leger Cat (Arg), 7, 116	Rainbow Corner (GB), 4, 114	6	1:48.45	183,750
1992	Marquetry, 5, 118	D. R. Flores	Luthier Enchanteur, 5, 116	Leger Cat (Arg), 6, 115	7	1:47.20	187,250
1991	Tight Spot, 4, 125	L. A. Pincay Jr.	Val des Bois (Fr), 5, 115	Madjaristan, 5, 116	7	1:47.32	188,500
1990	Fly Till Dawn, 4, 112	R. Q. Meza	Classic Fame, 4, 119	Golden Pheasant, 4, 122	8	1:47.20	157,750
1989	Saratoga Passage, 4, 116	E. Delahoussaye	Skip Out Front, 7, 116	Pasakos, 4, 116	8	1:49.00	162,750
1988	Deputy Governor, 4, 120	E. Delahoussaye	Santella Mac (Ire), 5, 118	Simply Majestic, 4, 115	12	1:48.40	176,500
1987	Sharrood, 4, 120	L. A. Pincay Jr.	Santella Mac (Ire), 4, 114	Skip Out Front, 5, 115	9	1:48.00	133,200
1986	Al Mamoon, 5, 121	P. A. Valenzuela	Zoffany, 6, 123	Truce Maker, 8, 115	7	1:46.60	113,400
1985	Tsunami Slew, 4, 119	G. L. Stevens	Al Mamoon, 4, 118	Both Ends Burning, 5, 117	7	1:46.80	112,300
1984	Ten Below, 5, 117	L. A. Pincay Jr.	Silveyville, 6, 117	Desert Wine, 4, 124	6	1:48.20	96,200
1983	Prince Spellbound, 4, 121	C. Lamance	Bel Bolide, 5, 117	Ask Me, 4, 115	11	1:48.40	108,000
1982	Wickerr, 7, 119	E. Delahoussaye	Spence Bay (Ire), 7, 122	Perrault (GB), 5, 129	7	1:48.40	95,300
1981	Wickerr, 6, 115	C. J. McCarron	Super Moment, 4, 117	Mike Fogarty (Ire), 6, 114	7	1:49.80	80,750
1980	Go West Young Man, 5, 120	E. Delahoussaye	The Bart, 4, 118	Bold Tropic (SAf), 5, 124	6	1:47.60	64,250
1979	Good Lord (NZ), 8, 115	W. Shoemaker	Shagbark, 4, 117	True Statement, 5, 115	11	1:48.40	42,450
1978	Effervescing, 5, 124	L. A. Pincay Jr.	Text, 4, 123	Bywayofchicago, 4, 117	9	1:48.60	33,050
1977	No Turning, 4, 115	F. Toro	Today 'n Tomorrow, 4, 119	†*Star Ball, 5, 111	9	1:48.80	32,440
1976	Branford Court, 6, 116	R. Campas	Diode, 4, 114	Austin Mittler, 4, 115	8	1:48.40	26,150
1975	Blue Times, 4, 115	J. Lambert	Portentous, 5, 112	Confederate Yankee, 4, 115	11	1:49.20	28,200
1974	My Old Friend, 5, 115	A. L. Diaz	Montmartre, 4, 116	War Heim, 7, 121	9	1:49.20	22,100

Named in honor of longtime Del Mar publicity director Eddie Read. Grade 3 1980-'81. Grade 2 1982-'87. Course record 2003, '06. †Denotes female.

El Camino Real Derby

Grade 3 in 2008. Bay Meadows Race Course, three-year-olds, 1¹/₁₆ miles, dirt. Held March 8, 2008, with a gross value of $150,000. First held in 1982. First graded in 1986. Stakes record 1:39.40 (1988 Ruhlmann).

Year	Winner	Jockey	Second	Third	Strs	Time	1st Purse
2008	Autism Awareness, 3, 117	L. Contreras	Nikki'sgoldensteed, 3, 117	Tres Borrachos, 3, 115	9	1:43.17	$90,000
2007	Bwana Bull, 3, 120	R. A. Baze	Freesgood, 3, 120	Zoning In, 3, 115	7	1:43.22	110,000
2006	Cause to Believe, 3, 117	R. A. Baze	Objective, 3, 115	Bold Chieftain, 3, 115	6	1:41.81	137,500

Racing — Graded Stakes

Year	Winner	Jockey	Second	Third	Strs	Time	1st Purse
2005	Uncle Denny, 3, 117	R. A. Baze	Wannawinemall, 3, 115	Buzzards Bay, 3, 117	10	1:42.22	$110,000
2004	Kilgowan, 3, 116	C. J. Rollins	dh-Capitano, 3, 116 dh-Seattle Borders, 3, 117		10	1:43.87	110,000
2003	Ocean Terrace, 3, 115	M. E. Smith	Ministers Wild Cat, 3, 117	Ten Most Wanted, 3, 115	10	1:42.26	110,000
2002	Yougottawanna, 3, 120	J. P. Lumpkins	Danthebluegrassman, 3, 117	Lusty Latin, 3, 115	10	1:43.48	110,000
2001	Hoovergetthekeys, 3, 120	R. J. Warren Jr.	Startac, 3, 120	Mo Mon, 3, 115	8	1:40.85	110,000
2000	Remember Sheikh, 3, 117	F. T. Alvarado	True Confidence, 3, 116	Country Coast, 3, 115	14	1:43.47	110,000
1999	Cliquot, 3, 115	D. R. Flores	Charismatic, 3, 115	No Cal Bread, 3, 117	7	1:43.29	110,000
1998	Event of the Year, 3, 115	R. A. Baze	Post a Note, 3, 117	Clover Hunter, 3, 120	5	1:40.27	110,000
1997	Pacificbounty, 3, 120	K. Desormeaux	Wild Wonder, 3, 115	Carmen's Baby, 3, 117	6	1:41.85	110,000
1996	Cavonnier, 3, 115	M. A. Pedroza	Sergeant Stroh, 3, 113	E C's Dream, 3, 116	9	1:43.41	110,000
1995	Jumron (GB), 3, 113	G. F. Almeida	Snow Kidd'n, 3, 113	American Day, 3, 113	8	1:43.73	110,000
1994	Tabasco Cat, 3, 113	P. Day	Flying Sensation, 3, 115	Robannier, 3, 115	7	1:42.78	110,000
1993	El Atroz, 3, 117	R. Q. Meza	Offshore Pirate, 3, 117	Lykatill Hil, 3, 119	9	1:43.77	110,000
1992	Casual Lies, 3, 117	A. Patterson	Seahawk Gold, 3, 115	Silver Ray, 3, 122	11	1:42.00	165,000
1991	Sea Cadet, 3, 117	T. M. Chapman	General Meeting, 3, 118	Mizter Interco, 3, 122	9	1:40.70	165,000
1990	Silver Ending, 3, 115	G. L. Stevens	Individualist, 3, 115	Single Dawn, 3, 122	8	1:43.00	165,000
1989	Double Quick, 3, 115	A. O. Solis	Rob an Plunder, 3, 112	Hawkster, 3, 122	6	1:43.60	165,000
1988	Ruhlmann, 3, 117	P. Day	Havanaffair, 3, 117	Chinese Gold, 3, 119	9	**1:39.40**	137,500
1987	Masterful Advocate, 3, 120	L. A. Pincay Jr.	Fast Delivery, 3, 120	Hot and Smoggy, 3, 115	11	1:42.40	137,500
1986	Snow Chief, 3, 120	A. O. Solis	Badger Land, 3, 120	Darby Fair, 3, 120	6	1:42.60	137,500
1985	Tank's Prospect, 3, 120	J. Velasquez	Right Con, 3, 120	‡Dan's Diablo, 3, 120	9	1:41.00	151,000
1984	French Legionaire, 3, 120	R. A. Baze	Gate Dancer, 3, 120	Heavenly Flash (Ire), 3, 120	11	1:42.40	126,200
1983	Knightly Rapport, 3, 120	F. Toro	Croeso, 3, 120	Twilight Career, 3, 120	9	1:44.80	96,700
1982	Cassaleria, 3, 120	D. G. McHargue	Crystal Star, 3, 120	Tropic Ruler, 3, 120	9	1:42.80	76,100

Named for the El Camino Real, "the Royal Road" through the California frontier. Held at Golden Gate 2001-'04. Dead heat for second 2004. ‡Skywalker finished second, DQ to fourth, 1985.

El Conejo Handicap

Grade 3 in 2008. Santa Anita Park, four-year-olds and up, 5½ furlongs, all weather. Held January 1, 2008, with a gross value of $108,900. First held in 1975. First graded in 2000. Stakes record 1:01.27 (2008 In Summation).

Year	Winner	Jockey	Second	Third	Strs	Time	1st Purse
2008	In Summation, 5, 122	C. S. Nakatani	Barbecue Eddie, 4, 116	Idiot Proof, 4, 122	5	**1:01.27**	$65,340
2007	Harvard Avenue, 6, 118	G. K. Gomez	Areyoutalkintome, 6, 117	Proud Tower Too, 5, 121	9	1:02.68	66,440
2006	With Distinction, 5, 116	J. Santiago	Jungle Prince, 5, 116	Jet West, 5, 117	10	1:02.44	67,260
2005	Areyoutalkintome, 4, 114	T. Baze	Hombre Rapido, 8, 116	Woke Up Dreamin, 5, 115	9	1:02.52	66,300
2004	Boston Common, 5, 117	G. L. Stevens	Summer Service, 4, 112	King Robyn, 4, 119	6	1:02.35	64,560
2003	Kona Gold, 9, 123	A. O. Solis	Radiata, 6, 115	No Armistice, 6, 116	7	1:02.63	65,280
2002	Snow Ridge, 4, 114	M. E. Smith	Explicit, 5, 117	Rio Oro, 7, 117	8	1:03.05	65,700
2000	Freespool, 4, 115	C. J. McCarron	Men's Exclusive, 7, 117	Lexicon, 5, 118	7	1:02.50	65,220
	Freespool, 4, 114	C. J. McCarron	Mellow Fellow, 5, 115	Old Topper, 5, 116	6	1:03.33	64,200
1999	Kona Gold, 5, 119	A. O. Solis	Big Jag, 6, 117	Mr. Doubledown, 5, 115	6	1:01.74	64,380
1998	The Exeter Man, 6, 114	G. K. Gomez	Tower Full, 6, 117	Red, 4, 114	5	1:02.23	64,020
1997	High Stakes Player, 5, 115	C. S. Nakatani	Kern Ridge, 6, 111	Subtle Trouble, 6, 114	5	1:02.89	63,850
1996	Lit de Justice, 6, 119	C. S. Nakatani	A. J. Jett, 4, 112	Fu Man Slew, 5, 116	6	1:01.85	64,250
1995	Phone Roberto, 6, 114	C. J. McCarron	‡Lost Pan, 5, 112	Rotsaluck, 4, 117	8	1:02.34	65,000
1994	Gundaghia, 7, 116	E. Delahoussaye	Sir Hutch, 4, 114	Davy Be Good, 6, 117	8	1:02.01	64,800
1993	Fabulous Champ, 4, 113	C. J. McCarron	Arrowtown, 5, 117	Slerp, 4, 117	7	1:02.66	63,800
1992	Gray Slewpy, 4, 114	K. Desormeaux	Frost Free, 7, 119	Cardmania, 6, 115	8	1:02.01	61,275
1991	Black Jack Road, 7, 115	G. L. Stevens	Laurens Quest, 6, 110	Lee's Tanthem, 4, 117	6	1:05.30	61,975
1990	Frost Free, 5, 115	C. J. McCarron	Sunny Blossom, 5, 119	Prospectors Gamble, 5, 114	5	1:03.00	45,900
1989	Sunny Blossom, 4, 114	F. H. Valenzuela	Sensational Star, 5, 115	Prospectors Gamble, 4, 116	7	1:04.60	47,100
1988	Sylvan Express (Ire), 5, 119	E. Delahoussaye	Carload, 6, 117	High Brite, 4, 120	8	1:03.80	48,100
1986	†Take My Picture, 4, 113	G. L. Stevens	Rosie's K. T., 5, 119	Five North, 5, 114	5	1:03.00	37,300
1985	Debonaire Junior, 4, 126	C. J. McCarron	Much Fine Gold, 4, 112	Fifty Six Ina Row, 4, 119	7	1:02.60	38,950
1984	Premiership, 4, 115	R. Q. Meza	Haughty But Nice, 6, 116	Chip o' Lark, 5, 117	7	1:03.40	30,425
	Night Mover, 4, 117	E. Delahoussaye	Dave's Friend, 9, 120	†Bara Lass, 5, 117	7	1:03.20	30,525
1983	Pompeii Court, 6, 123	L. A. Pincay Jr.	General Jimmy, 4, 115	Kangroo Court, 6, 120	8	1:02.80	39,350
1982	To B. Or Not, 6, 122	C. J. McCarron	Belfort (Fr), 5, 116	Terresto's Singer, 5, 115	8	1:02.20	39,350
1981	To B. Or Not, 5, 122	P. A. Valenzuela	Summer Time Guy, 5, 119	Cool Frenchy, 6, 115	11	1:02.40	35,500
1975	Move Abroad, 4, 113	S. Hawley	Reputation, 5, 115	Mercy Dee, 4, 121	5	1:49.20	11,375

Named for Rancho El Conejo, located in Ventura, California; conejo means rabbit. Not graded 2000 (January). Not held 1976-'80, 1987, 2001. Dirt 1975-2007. Four-year-olds and up 1992-2000. Held in January and December 2000. Two divisions 1984. ‡Lit de Justice finished second, DQ to sixth, 1995. Track record 1992, '96, '99. †Denotes female.

El Encino Stakes

Grade 2 in 2008. Santa Anita Park, four-year-olds, fillies, 1 1/16 miles, all weather. Held January 13, 2008, with a gross value of $150,000. First held in 1954. First graded in 1980. Stakes record 1:40.61 (2008 Zenyatta).

Year	Winner	Jockey	Second	Third	Strs	Time	1st Purse
2008	Zenyatta, 4, 116	D. R. Flores	Tough Tiz's Sis, 4, 122	Romance Is Diane, 4, 122	6	**1:40.61**	$90,000
2007	Sugar Shake, 4, 115	D. R. Flores	Kris' Sis, 4, 117	Wonder Lady Anne L, 4, 119	6	1:43.70	90,000
2006	Proposed, 4, 118	P. A. Valenzuela	Play Ballado, 4, 117	Somethinaboutlaura, 4, 117	5	1:44.32	90,000
2005	Girl Warrior, 4, 115	V. Espinoza	A. P. Adventure, 4, 119	Tarlow, 4, 116	7	1:42.76	90,000

Racing — Graded Stakes

Year	Winner	Jockey	Second	Third	Strs	Time	1st Purse
2004	Victory Encounter, 4, 117	M. E. Smith	Personal Legend, 4, 115	Cat Fighter, 4, 115	7	1:42.52	$90,000
2003	Got Koko, 4, 119	A. O. Solis	Bella Bellucci, 4, 117	Bare Necessities, 4, 119	8	1:42.25	90,000
2002	Affluent, 4, 119	E. Delahoussaye	Royally Chosen, 4, 117	Sea Reel, 4, 115	6	1:42.60	90,000
2001	Chilukki, 4, 119	G. L. Stevens	Spain, 4, 122	Queenie Belle, 4, 119	4	1:42.55	90,000
2000	Olympic Charmer, 4, 119	C. J. McCarron	Her She Kisses, 4, 115	Smooth Player, 4, 117	7	1:42.71	97,470
1999	Manistique, 4, 119	G. L. Stevens	Gourmet Girl, 4, 117	Magical Allure, 4, 119	3	1:43.10	90,000
1998	‡Fleet Lady, 4, 117	G. K. Gomez	Minister's Melody, 4, 117	I Ain't Bluffing, 4, 119	6	1:43.04	96,840
1997	Belle's Flag, 4, 119	C. S. Nakatani	Housa Dancer (Fr), 4, 115	Listening, 4, 119	9	1:41.61	82,650
1996	Jewel Princess, 4, 117	A. O. Solis	Sleep Easy, 4, 119	Urbane, 4, 119	4	1:41.94	78,800
1995	Klassy Kim, 4, 117	K. Desormeaux	Twice the Vice, 4, 119	Crissy Aya, 4, 115	5	1:42.43	61,400
1994	Supah Gem, 4, 117	C. S. Nakatani	Sensational Eyes, 4, 119	Stalcreek, 4, 119	8	1:41.33	64,500
1993	Pacific Squall, 4, 119	C. J. McCarron	Avian Assembly, 4, 117	Magical Maiden, 4, 119	7	1:45.67	63,900
1992	Exchange, 4, 117	L. A. Pincay Jr.	Grand Girlfriend, 4, 115	Damewood, 4, 115	10	1:43.32	67,000
1991	A Wild Ride, 4, 122	C. J. McCarron	Highland Tide, 4, 114	Somethingmerry, 4, 117	7	1:42.50	63,500
1990	Akinemod, 4, 119	G. L. Stevens	Luthier's Launch, 4, 117	Kelly, 4, 116	6	1:41.20	62,900
1989	Goodbye Halo, 4, 124	P. Day	T. V. of Crystal, 4, 117	Savannah's Honor, 4, 114	4	1:41.80	60,200
1988	By Land by Sea, 4, 115	F. Toro	Very Subtle, 4, 122	Annoconnor, 4, 114	8	1:41.60	64,300
1987	Seldom Seen Sue, 4, 114	W. Shoemaker	Miraculous, 4, 117	Top Corsage, 4, 122	6	1:43.00	61,850
1986	Lady's Secret, 4, 124	C. J. McCarron	Shywing, 4, 119	Sharp Ascent, 4, 119	10	1:41.80	65,850
1985	Mitterand, 4, 119	E. Delahoussaye	Percipient, 4, 117	Allusion, 4, 117	6	1:42.00	61,600
1984	Lovlier Linda, 4, 117	W. Shoemaker	Weekend Surprise, 4, 117	Angel Savage (Mex), 4, 115	8	1:42.00	51,250
1983	Beautiful Glass, 4, 119	C. J. McCarron	Header Card, 4, 119	Skillful Joy, 4, 122	11	1:41.20	50,550
1982	Edge, 4, 114	C. B. Asmussen	Safe Play, 4, 119	Northern Fable, 4, 117	12	1:41.20	68,000
1981	Princess Karenda, 4, 122	E. Delahoussaye	Swift Bird, 4, 117	Lisawan, 4, 114	10	1:42.00	49,650
1980	It's in the Air, 4, 124	L. A. Pincay Jr.	Prize Spot, 4, 121	‡Glorious Song, 4, 116	8	1:41.20	38,750
1979	B. Thoughtful, 4, 121	D. Pierce	Queen Yasna, 4, 116	Petron's Love, 4, 114	7	1:41.60	38,250
1978	Taisez Vous, 4, 121	D. Pierce	Little Happiness, 4, 116	Table the Rumor, 4, 121	4	1:41.80	30,200
1977	*Woodsome, 4, 115	M. S. Sellers	*Lucie Manet, 4, 115	Granja Sueno, 4, 115	11	1:42.20	27,450
1976	Fascinating Girl, 4, 115	S. Hawley	Bold Baby, 4, 115	Just a Kick, 4, 121	6	1:42.40	18,850
1975	Triggairo, 6, 119	D. Pierce	*Benson, 6, 116	Lansquinet, 4, 119	7	1:49.40	19,700
1974	Wild World, 5, 118	W. Shoemaker	Class A, 6, 115	Proper Escort, 5, 112	10	1:49.80	18,150
1973	Class A, 5, 122	D. Tierney	Sitka D., 6, 119	Cabin, 5, 119	11	1:44.60	18,950

Named for Rancho El Encino, one of the original Spanish ranchos located in western Los Angeles County, California. Grade 3 1980-'89. El Encino H. 1954-'57, 1974-'75. El Encino Claiming S. 1968-'73. Not held 1958-'67, 1970. 1¼ miles 1955-'63. 1⅛ miles 1974-'75. Turf 1955-'57. Dirt 1954-2007. Four-year-olds and up 1954-'75. Both sexes 1954-'75. ‡Terlingua finished third, DQ to fourth, 1980. ‡I Ain't Bluffing finished first, DQ to third, 1998. Starters for a claiming price of $50,000 or less 1974.

Elkhorn Stakes — See Fifth Third Elkhorn Stakes

Emirates Airline Breeders' Cup Distaff

Grade 1 in 2008. Monmouth Park, three-year-olds and up, fillies and mares, 1⅛ miles, dirt. Held October 27, 2007, with a gross value of $2,070,160. First held in 1984. First graded in 1984. Stakes record 1:46.15 (1995 Inside Information).

Year	Winner	Jockey	Second	Third	Strs	Time	1st Purse
2007	Ginger Punch, 4, 123	R. Bejarano	Hystericalady, 4, 123	Octave, 3, 119	12	1:50.11	$1,220,400
2006	Round Pond, 4, 123	E. S. Prado	‡Happy Ticket, 5, 123	Balletto (UAE), 4, 123	14	1:50.50	1,220,400
2005	Pleasant Home, 4, 123	C. H. Velasquez	Society Selection, 4, 123	Ashado, 4, 123	13	1:48.34	1,040,000
2004	Ashado, 3, 123	J. R. Velazquez	Storm Flag Flying, 4, 123	Stellar Jayne, 3, 119	11	1:48.26	1,040,000
2003	Adoration, 4, 123	P. A. Valenzuela	Elloluv, 3, 119	Got Koko, 4, 123	7	1:49.17	1,040,000
2002	Azeri, 4, 123	M. E. Smith	Farda Amiga, 3, 119	Imperial Gesture, 3, 119	8	1:48.64	1,040,000
2001	Unbridled Elaine, 3, 120	P. Day	Spain, 4, 123	Two Item Limit, 3, 120	11	1:49.21	1,227,200
2000	Spain, 3, 120	V. Espinoza	Surfside, 3, 120	Heritage of Gold, 5, 123	9	1:47.66	1,227,200
1999	Beautiful Pleasure, 4, 123	J. F. Chavez	Banshee Breeze, 4, 123	Heritage of Gold, 4, 123	8	1:47.56	1,040,000
1998	Escena, 5, 123	G. L. Stevens	Banshee Breeze, 3, 120	Keeper Hill, 3, 120	8	1:49.89	1,040,000
1997	Ajina, 3, 120	M. E. Smith	Sharp Cat, 3, 120	Escena, 4, 123	7	1:47.30	520,000
1996	Jewel Princess, 4, 123	C. S. Nakatani	Serena's Song, 4, 123	Different (Arg), 4, 123	6	1:48.40	520,000
1995	Inside Information, 4, 123	M. E. Smith	Heavenly Prize, 4, 123	Lakeway, 4, 123	5	**1:46.15**	520,000
1994	One Dreamer, 6, 123	G. L. Stevens	Heavenly Prize, 3, 120	Miss Dominique, 5, 123	9	1:50.70	520,000
1993	Hollywood Wildcat, 3, 120	E. Delahoussaye	Paseana (Arg), 6, 123	Re Toss (Arg), 6, 123	8	1:48.35	520,000
1992	Paseana (Arg), 5, 123	C. J. McCarron	Versailles Treaty, 4, 123	Magical Maiden, 3, 119	14	1:48.17	520,000
1991	Dance Smartly, 3, 120	P. Day	Versailles Treaty, 3, 120	Brought to Mind, 4, 123	13	1:50.95	520,000
1990	Bayakoa (Arg), 6, 123	L. A. Pincay Jr.	Colonial Waters, 5, 123	Valay Maid, 3, 119	7	1:49.20	450,000
1989	Bayakoa (Arg), 5, 123	L. A. Pincay Jr.	Gorgeous, 4, 119	Open Mind, 3, 119	10	1:47.40	450,000
1988	Personal Ensign, 4, 123	R. P. Romero	Winning Colors, 3, 119	Goodbye Halo, 3, 119	9	1:52.00	450,000
1987	Sacahuista, 3, 119	R. P. Romero	Clabber Girl, 4, 123	Oueee Bebe, 3, 119	8	2:02.80	450,000
1986	Lady's Secret, 4, 123	P. Day	Fran's Valentine, 4, 123	Outstandingly, 4, 123	8	2:01.20	450,000
1985	Life's Magic, 4, 123	A. T. Cordero Jr.	Lady's Secret, 3, 119	Dontstop Themusic, 5, 123	7	2:02.00	450,000
1984	Princess Rooney, 4, 123	E. Delahoussaye	Life's Magic, 3, 119	Adored, 4, 123	7	2:02.40	450,000

Sponsored by Emirates Airline of Dubai, United Arab Emirates 2005-'07. Formerly sponsored by Nextel Communications of Reston, Virginia 2004. Held at Hollywood Park 1984, '87, '97. Held at Aqueduct 1985. Held at Santa Anita Park 1986, '93, 2003. Held at Churchill Downs 1988, '91, '94, '98, 2000, '06. Held at Gulfstream Park 1989, '92, '99. Held at Belmont Park 1990, '95, 2001, '05. Held at Woodbine 1996. Held at Arlington Park 2002. Held at Lone Star Park 2004. 1¼ miles 1984-'87. ‡Asi Siempre finished second, DQ to fourth, 2006.

Emirates Airline Breeders' Cup Filly & Mare Turf

Grade 1 in 2008. Monmouth Park, three-year-olds and up, fillies and mares, 1 3/8 miles, turf. Held October 27, 2007, with a gross value of $1,951,080. First held in 1999. First graded in 1999. Stakes record 2:13.07 (2000 Perfect Sting).

Year	Winner	Jockey	Second	Third	Strs	Time	1st Purse
2007	Lahudood (GB), 4, 123	A. Garcia	Honey Ryder, 6, 123	Passage of Time (GB), 3, 118	11	2:22.75	$1,150,200
2006	Ouija Board (GB), 5, 123	L. Dettori	Film Maker, 6, 123	Honey Ryder, 5, 123	10	2:14.55	1,188,000
2005	Intercontinental (GB), 5, 123	R. Bejarano	Ouija Board (GB), 4, 123	Film Maker, 5, 123	14	2:02.34	551,200
2004	Ouija Board (GB), 3, 118	K. Fallon	Film Maker, 4, 123	Wonder Again, 5, 123	12	2:18.25	733,200
2003	Islington (Ire), 4, 123	K. Fallon	L'Ancresse (Ire), 3, 118	Yesterday (Ire), 3, 118	12	1:59.13	551,200
2002	Starine (Fr), 5, 123	J. R. Velazquez	Banks Hill (GB), 4, 123	Islington (Ire), 3, 118	12	2:03.57	665,600
2001	Banks Hill (GB), 3, 119	O. Peslier	Spook Express (SAf), 7, 123	Spring Oak (GB), 3, 119	12	2:00.36	722,800
2000	Perfect Sting, 4, 123	J. D. Bailey	Tout Charmant, 4, 123	Catella (Ger), 4, 123	14	**2:13.07**	629,200
1999	Soaring Softly, 4, 123	J. D. Bailey	Coretta (Ire), 5, 123	Zomaradah (GB), 4, 123	14	2:13.89	556,400

Sponsored by Emirates Airline of Dubai, United Arab Emirates 2005-'07. Formerly sponsored by the Alberto-Culver Co. of Chicago, Illinois 2004. Held at Gulfstream Park 1999. Held at Churchill Downs 2000, '06. Held at Belmont Park 2001, '05. Held at Santa Anita Park 2003. Held at Lone Star Park 2004. 1 1/4 miles 2001-'03, 2005.

Endeavour Stakes

Grade 3 in 2008. Tampa Bay Downs, four-year-olds and up, fillies and mares, 1 1/16 miles, turf. Held February 16, 2008, with a gross value of $147,500. First held in 2000. First graded in 2008. Stakes record 1:40.26 (2006 My Lordship).

Year	Winner	Jockey	Second	Third	Strs	Time	1st Purse
2008	Dreaming of Anna, 4, 116	C. H. Velasquez	Lear's Princess, 4, 117	Meribel, 5, 116	9	1:42.38	$90,000
2007	Cassydora (GB), 5, 120	J. R. Velazquez	Bright Abundance, 6, 122	Warrior Girl, 4, 120	10	1:43.05	60,000
2006	My Lordship, 5, 122	C. H. Velasquez	Laurafina, 4, 116	Amorama (Fr), 5, 116	10	**1:40.26**	75,000
2005	Delta Princess, 6, 117	H. Castillo Jr.	Fast Cookie, 5, 116	Lentil, 6, 116	11	1:43.54	45,000
2004	Madeira Mist (Ire), 5, 116	E. S. Prado	Something Ventured, 5, 117	Coney Kitty (Ire), 6, 116	12	1:44.97	45,000
2003	Wander Mom, 5, 122	M. R. Cruz	Strait From Texas, 4, 116	Kimster, 4, 116	12	1:50.89	45,000
2002	Chausson Poire, 4, 122	T. L. Pompell	Kelly Bag, 5, 118	Golden Antigua, 5, 116	11	1:50.40	45,000
2001	Cybil, 5, 115	F. L. Ortiz	Megans Bluff, 4, 122	Golden Saint, 4, 119	6	1:48.48	45,000
2000	Office Miss, 6, 122	J. Bravo	Seducer, 4, 115	Diablos First Lady, 4, 122	11	1:48.93	45,000

Named for the space shuttle Endeavour, first launched in May 1992. Endeavour Breeders' Cup S. 2006. 1 1/8 miles 2000-'03. Three-year-olds and up 2000-'01.

Endine Stakes

Grade 3 in 2008. Delaware Park, three-year-olds and up, fillies and mares, 6 furlongs, dirt. Held September 8, 2007, with a gross value of $200,600. First held in 1971. First graded in 2001. Stakes record 1:08.35 (2003 House Party).

Year	Winner	Jockey	Second	Third	Strs	Time	1st Purse
2007	Silmaril, 6, 121	J. Rose	Ticket to Seattle, 3, 117	Sugar Swirl, 4, 121	7	1:09.52	$120,000
2006	Miraculous Miss, 3, 119	R. A. Dominguez	Gilded Gold, 5, 121	Coli Bear, 3, 115	8	1:09.82	120,000
2005	Umpateedle, 6, 116	A. T. Gryder	Sensibly Chic, 5, 117	Ebony Breeze, 5, 118	8	1:10.18	120,000
2004	Ebony Breeze, 4, 119	H. Castillo Jr.	Umpateedle, 5, 117	Bronze Abe, 5, 119	6	1:09.73	120,000
2003	House Party, 3, 117	J. A. Santos	Vision in Flight, 4, 114	Mooji Moo, 4, 115	8	**1:08.35**	120,000
2002	Xtra Heat, 4, 121	H. Vega	Outstanding Info, 4, 118	Urban Dancer, 4, 118	5	1:10.91	90,000
2001	Xtra Heat, 3, 118	R. Wilson	Ivy's Jewel, 4, 118	Big Bambu, 4, 121	5	1:09.64	90,000
2000	Superduper Miss, 4, 114	T. G. Turner	Debby d'Or, 5, 119	Cassidy, 5, 119	7	1:10.22	60,000
1999	Hurricane Bertie, 4, 117	P. Day	Little Sister, 5, 119	Bourbon Belle, 5, 119	4	1:08.75	60,000
1998	Soverign Lady, 4, 115	M. E. Smith	Weather Vane, 4, 122	Little Sister, 4, 117	8	1:09.43	45,000
1997	Dancin Renee, 5, 122	J. A. Velez Jr.	Two Punch Lil, 5, 122	Ana Belen (Chi), 4, 113	6	1:10.04	30,000
1996	Hay Hanne, 4, 114	J. A. Velez Jr.	Know B's, 4, 116	Ayrial Delight, 4, 122	8	1:10.30	22,770
1982	Wading Power, 4, 107	H. Pilar	Bravo Native, 4, 108	Lady Dean, 4, 123	9	1:10.65	14,723
1981	Veiled Look, 5, 120	W. J. Passmore	Rejuvavate, 5, 113	Tequila Sheila, 3, 109	7	1:08.80	17,875
1980	Candy Eclair, 4, 126	J. D. Bailey	‡Wondrous Me, 4, 108	Grecian Victory, 4, 112	9	1:09.80	29,803
1979	Quatre Saisons, 4, 115	V. A. Bracciale Jr.	Shanachie, 3, 112	Order in Court, 6, 115	6	1:12.00	21,580
1978	Dainty Dotsie, 4, 127	B. Phelps	Spot Two, 4, 123	Debby's Turn, 4, 113	5	1:09.60	21,450
1977	My Juliet, 5, 127	A. S. Black	Debby's Turn, 3, 115	Catabias, 5, 113	4	1:09.60	17,973
1976	Donetta, 5, 118	J. W. Moseley	Susie's Last, 4, 112	Crackerfax, 5, 115	10	1:12.00	17,145
1975	Honky Star, 4, 119	J. E. Tejeira	Laraka, 5, 117	Sailingon, 4, 114	5	1:11.00	18,655
1974	Miss Rebound, 6, 123	B. Baeza	Flo's Pleasure, 4, 116	Gallant Davelle, 4, 116	8	1:10.00	19,045
1973	Light Hearted, 4, 118	E. Nelson	Barely Even, 4, 125	Levee Night, 5, 113	7	1:10.00	18,525

Named for Christiana Stable's 1958, '59 Delaware H. winner Endine (1954 f. by *Rico Monte). Endine H. 1971-'82, 2003-'04. Not held 1983-'95. ‡She Can't Miss finished second, DQ to fourth, 1980. Equaled track record 2003.

Excelsior Handicap

Grade 3 in 2008. Aqueduct, three-year-olds and up, 1 1/8 miles, dirt. Held April 5, 2008, with a gross value of $150,533. First held in 1903. First graded in 1973. Stakes record 1:47.69 (1997 Ormsby).

Year	Winner	Jockey	Second	Third	Strs	Time	1st Purse
2008	Temporary Saint, 5, 113	C. C. Lopez	Nite Light, 4, 116	Angliana, 6, 115	8	1:51.13	$66,720
2007	Magna Graduate, 5, 118	J. R. Velazquez	Naughty New Yorker, 5, 115	Accountforthegold, 5, 114	6	1:48.10	125,460
2006	West Virginia, 5, 115	N. Arroyo Jr.	Funny Cide, 6, 115	Colita, 6, 114	9	1:48.28	67,140
2005	Offlee Wild, 5, 121	R. Bejarano	Rogue Agent, 6, 115	Cuba, 4, 113	5	1:50.41	120,000
2004	Funny Cide, 4, 120	J. A. Santos	Evening Attire, 6, 119	Host (Chi), 4, 114	5	1:49.57	120,000
2003	Classic Endeavor, 5, 113	C. C. Lopez	Balto Star, 5, 119	Tempest Fugit, 6, 114	5	1:48.10	90,000
2002	John Little, 4, 111	N. Arroyo Jr.	Windsor Castle, 4, 113	Ground Storm, 6, 114	8	1:49.25	120,000
2001	Cat's At Home, 4, 115	F. Leon	Top Official, 6, 113	Boston Party, 5, 115	8	1:48.92	120,000

Year	Winner	Jockey	Second	Third	Strs	Time	1st Purse
2000	Lager, 6, 113	H. Castillo Jr.	Best of Luck, 4, 114	Chester House, 5, 117	9	1:49.76	$120,000
1999	Smart Coupons, 6, 114	R. R. Douglas	Archers Bay, 4, 118	Pasay, 4, 112	9	1:49.71	120,000
1998	Sir Bear, 5, 117	E. M. Jurado	K. J.'s Appeal, 4, 117	Accelerator, 4, 111	8	1:49.24	120,000
1997	Ormsby, 5, 116	C. C. Lopez	Greatsilverfleet, 7, 112	Circle of Light, 4, 111	9	1:47.69	120,000
1996	May I Inquire, 7, 111	J. Bravo	Personal Merit, 5, 114	Ormsby, 4, 115	8	1:50.67	120,000
1995	Iron Gavel, 5, 111	J. R. Martinez Jr.	Electrojet, 6, 114	Danzig's Dance, 6, 115	7	1:49.28	90,000
1994	Colonial Affair, 4, 121	J. A. Santos	Contract Court, 4, 109	West by West, 5, 116	6	1:49.82	90,000
1993	Devil His Due, 4, 117	M. E. Smith	Exotic Slew, 6, 109	Bill Of Rights, 4, 112	10	2:03.05	72,120
1992	Defensive Play, 5, 117	D. R. Flores	Alyten, 4, 111	Will to Reign, 4, 109	5	2:01.95	102,780
1991	Chief Honcho, 4, 117	M. E. Smith	I'm Sky High, 5, 115	Apple Current, 4, 115	6	2:02.69	102,060
1990	Lay Down, 6, 112	C. W. Antley	Lac Ouimet, 7, 113	Doc's Leader, 4, 112	5	2:02.20	100,980
1989	Forever Silver, 4, 111	J. A. Krone	Its Academic, 5, 113	Jack of Clubs, 6, 113	5	2:02.60	99,720
1988	Lac Ouimet, 5, 116	J. D. Bailey	Personal Flag, 5, 117	Talinum, 4, 116	9	2:00.20	140,880
1987	Lac Ouimet, 4, 114	E. Maple	Alioth, 4, 113	Proud Debonair, 5, 115	9	2:02.00	106,380
1986	Garthorn, 6, 124	R. Q. Meza	Nordance, 4, 110	Broadway Tommy, 4, 107	5	2:02.40	101,340
1985	Morning Bob, 4, 112	J. Vasquez	Lord of the Manor, 4, 112	Last Turn, 5, 110	8	2:04.20	87,750
1984	Canadian Factor, 4, 117	J. Velasquez	Luv a Libra, 4, 117	Canadian Calm, 4, 108	5	2:03.00	102,150
1983	Fast Gold, 4, 114	J. Samyn	Turn Bold, 4, 107	Sing Sing, 5, 124	7	2:04.00	67,200
1982	Globe, 5, 112	M. Venezia	Accipiter's Hope, 4, 116	Bar Dexter, 4, 118	9	2:03.40	66,480
1981	Irish Tower, 4, 127	J. Fell	Ring of Light, 6, 113	†Relaxing, 5, 125	6	2:00.80	64,680
1980	Ring of Light, 5, 114	C. B. Asmussen	Silent Cal, 5, 122	Rivalero, 4, 118	10	2:01.40	67,560
1979	Special Tiger, 4, 113	G. Martens	Mister Brea (Arg), 5, 125	Coverack, 6, 112	6	2:03.80	63,600
1978	Cox's Ridge, 4, 129	E. Maple	Pumpkin Moonshine, 4, 108	Nearly On Time, 4, 113	7	1:50.60	49,005
1977	Turn and Count, 4, 123	S. Cauthen	Festive Mood, 8, 115	Gabe Benzur, 4, 112	6	1:51.00	48,150
1976	Double Edge Sword, 6, 116	A. T. Cordero Jr.	Northerly, 4, 115	Sharp Gary, 5, 119	9	1:48.20	51,120
1975	Step Nicely, 5, 126	A. T. Cordero Jr.	Monetary Principle, 5, 113	Jolly John, 4, 119	8	1:48.40	33,990
1974	*Everton II, 5, 117	M. A. Castaneda	Prince Dantan, 4, 123	Three Or Less, 4, 108	7	1:49.00	33,840
1973	Key to the Mint, 4, 126	R. Turcotte	King's Bishop, 4, 115	North Sea, 4, 120	5	1:47.80	32,640

Named for the state motto of New York, "Excelsior," meaning "upward, ever upward." Grade 2 1973-'97. Excelsior Breeders' Cup H. 1996-2007. Held at Jamaica 1903-'10, 1915-'59. Not held 1909, 1911-'12, 1914, 1933, 1967. 1 1/16 miles 1903-'59. 1 mile 1960. 1 1/4 miles 1979-'93. †Denotes female.

Fair Grounds Handicap

Grade 3 in 2008. Fair Grounds, four-year-olds and up, about 1 1/8 miles, turf. Held February 9, 2008, with a gross value of $140,000. First held in 1988. First graded in 2006. Stakes record 1:49.48 (2007 Cloudy's Knight).

Year	Winner	Jockey	Second	Third	Strs	Time	1st Purse
2008	Daytona (Ire), 4, 119	M. E. Smith	Jazz Quest, 4, 115	Sterwins, 5, 116	10	1:50.09	$90,000
2007	Cloudy's Knight, 7, 115	R. Zimmerman	Devilment, 5, 115	Storm Treasure, 4, 115	9	1:49.48	120,000
2006	Fort Prado, 5, 118	R. Albarado	Onthedeanslist, 7, 118	Waupaca, 6, 116	8	1:43.16	101,880
2005	G P Fleet, 5, 117	J. R. Martinez Jr.	Honor in War, 6, 119	Rapid Proof, 5, 116	9	1:53.79	75,000
2004	Mystery Giver, 6, 120	R. Albarado	Skate Away, 5, 118	Great Bloom, 6, 116	8	1:51.77	75,000
2003	Mystery Giver, 5, 117	R. Albarado	Dynameaux, 5, 115	Freefourinternet, 5, 115	9	1:51.40	90,000
2002	Mystery Giver, 4, 117	E. M. Martin Jr.	Even the Score, 4, 113	Candid Glen, 5, 115	13	1:50.13	90,000
2001	Candid Glen, 4, 113	E. J. Perrodin	Sunspot, 4, 113	Solitary Dancer, 5, 114	12	1:54.03	98,610
2000	Profit Option, 5, 111	L. J. Meche	Good Night, 4, 114	Garbu, 6, 115	8	1:52.52	95,460
1999	Aboriginal Apex, 6, 115	L. J. Melancon	Chorwon, 6, 117	Dernier Croise (Fr), 4, 113	11	1:51.71	67,770
1998	Joyeux Danseur, 5, 118	R. Albarado	Chorwon, 5, 114	Boy Stuff, 4, 112	7	1:50.60	77,640
1997	Snake Eyes, 7, 117	R. Albarado	Scott's Scoundrel, 5, 113	Da Bull, 5, 114	8	1:52.65	91,440
1996	Born Wild, 4, 116	M. Walls	Kazabaiyn, 6, 113	Bene Erit, 4, 113	8	1:52.97	61,395
1995	Yukon Robbery, 6, 113	R. J. Faul	Dynaguard, 4, 108	Milt's Sovereign, 4, 113	6	1:51.50	61,185
1994	Yukon Robbery, 5, 113	R. J. Faul	Grand Hooley, 5, 114	Empire Pool (GB), 4, 116	9	1:50.27	61,635
1993	Yukon Robbery, 4, 115	R. J. Faul	Spending Record, 6, 114	Seattle Bound, 5, 113	6	1:50.60	46,440
1992	Rainbows for Life, 4, 120	S. P. Romero	City Ballet, 5, 113	†Palace Chill, 5, 113	10	1:53.00	46,680
1991	First Tea, 4, 113	K. Bourque	Noble Savage (Ire), 5, 114	Take a Flight, 6, 116	9	1:53.30	46,500
1990	Tower Above 'Em, 6, 112	S. P. Romero	Jack's Kingdom, 7, 113	Majesty's Imp, 4, 114	10	1:55.80	46,080
1989	Ingot's Ruler, 7, 116	R. D. Ardoin	Vaguely Crafty, 6, 113	Top Guest (Ire), 6, 115	10	1:51.20	17,640
1988	Top Guest (Ire), 5, 117	J. Samyn	Royal Treasurer, 5, 121	Grey Classic, 5, 119	5	1:54.20	40,125

Fair Grounds Budweiser Breeders' Cup H. 1988-'95. Fair Grounds Breeders' Cup H. 1996-2007. Held at Louisiana Downs 2006. 1 1/16 miles 2006. Dirt 1995. Three-year-olds and up 1988-'91, 1993, 1995-2000. †Denotes female.

Fair Grounds Oaks

Grade 2 in 2008. Fair Grounds, three-year-olds, fillies, 1 1/16 miles, dirt. Held March 8, 2008, with a gross value of $376,000. First held in 1966. First graded in 1982. Stakes record 1:42.20 (1997 Blushing K. D.).

Year	Winner	Jockey	Second	Third	Strs	Time	1st Purse
2008	Proud Spell, 3, 121	G. Saez	Indian Blessing, 3, 121	Acacia, 3, 121	4	1:44.01	$240,000
2007	Mistical Plan, 3, 121	C. S. Nakatani	Octave, 3, 121	Whatdreamsmadeof, 3, 121	8	1:44.02	240,000
2005	Summerly, 3, 121	J. D. Bailey	Carlea, 3, 121	Runway Model, 3, 121	6	1:43.79	180,000
2004	Ashado, 3, 121	C. H. Velasquez	Victory U. S. A., 3, 121	Shadow Cast, 3, 121	6	1:43.07	180,000
2003	Lady Tak, 3, 121	D. J. Meche	Atlantic Ocean, 3, 121	Belle of Perintown, 3, 121	6	1:44.36	210,000
2002	Take Charge Lady, 3, 121	A. J. D'Amico	Lake Lady, 3, 121	Chamrousse, 3, 121	8	1:43.30	210,000
2001	Real Cozzy, 3, 121	E. M. Martin Jr.	Mystic Lady, 3, 121	She's a Devil Due, 3, 121	6	1:44.58	210,000
2000	Shawnee Country, 3, 121	D. J. Meche	Eden Lodge, 3, 121	Zoftig, 3, 121	9	1:44.81	210,000
1999	Silverbulletday, 3, 121	G. L. Stevens	Runaway Venus, 3, 112	Brushed Halory, 3, 114	7	1:44.99	223,740
1998	Lu Ravi, 3, 112	W. Martinez	Well Chosen, 3, 121	Silent Eskimo, 3, 112	6	1:43.70	180,000

Year	Winner	Jockey	Second	Third	Strs	Time	1st Purse
1997	Blushing K. D., 3, 121	L. J. Meche	Tomisue's Delight, 3, 114	Cozy Blues, 3, 112	5	1:42.20	$105,000
1996	Bright Time, 3, 112	L. F. Diaz	Mackie, 3, 121	Proper Dance, 3, 114	6	1:45.98	94,530
1995	Brushing Gloom, 3, 112	J. Brown	Kuda, 3, 118	Legendary Priness, 3, 121	9	1:45.12	90,000
1994	Two Altazano, 3, 112	K. P. LeBlanc	Tricky Code, 3, 121	Minority Dater, 3, 112	6	1:42.50	93,840
1993	Silky Feather, 3, 112	E. J. Perrodin	She's a Little Shy, 3, 121	Sum Runner, 3, 121	7	1:44.60	64,080
1992	Prospectors Delite, 3, 118	P. Day	Glitzi Bj, 3, 118	Desert Radiance, 3, 118	7	1:44.20	63,990
1991	Rare Pick, 3, 112	P. A. Johnson	Nalees Pin, 3, 121	Lady Blockbuster, 3, 118	9	1:46.50	65,640
1990	Pampered Star, 3, 112	S. P. Romero	Windansea, 3, 118	Gayla's Pleasure, 3, 115	9	1:44.60	59,520
1989	Mistaurian, 3, 113	D. Valiente	Affirmed Classic, 3, 121	Exquisite Mistress, 3, 118	6	1:44.80	57,900
1988	Quite a Gem, 3, 115	E. J. Perrodin	False Glitter, 3, 118	Sable Decor, 3, 118	9	1:46.40	59,580
1987	Up the Apalachee, 3, 121	M. R. Torres	Cathy Quick, 3, 118	Out of the Bid, 3, 121	6	1:45.40	60,000
1986	Tiffany Lass, 3, 121	R. L. Frazier	Patricia J. K., 3, 121	Turn and Dance, 3, 112	6	1:45.00	97,400
1985	Marshua's Echelon, 3, 121	R. J. Franklin	Golden Silence, 3, 113	Little Biddy Comet, 3, 118	13	1:44.80	113,400
1984	My Darling One, 3, 112	C. J. McCarron	Texas Cowgirl Nite, 3, 118	Rays Joy, 3, 112	8	1:44.60	101,400
1983	Bright Crocus, 3, 121	S. Hawley	Miss Molly, 3, 118	Shamivor, 3, 115	6	1:45.80	66,100
1982	Before Dawn, 3, 121	J. Velasquez	Girlie, 3, 121	Linda North, 3, 118	7	1:45.40	66,400
1981	Truly Bound, 3, 121	W. Shoemaker	Lou's Dance, 3, 118	‡Sunwontshine, 3, 112	7	1:44.80	61,400
1980	Honest and True, 3, 118	A. Guajardo	Smart Angle, 3, 121	Lady Taurian Peace, 3, 118	8	1:44.40	33,875
1978	La Doree (Arg), 4, 108	B. Fann	Royal Graustark, 4, 114	Burn the Money, 4, 107	10	1:52.40	25,738
	Shadycroft Lady, 3, 109	R. Martinez Jr.	Miss Baja, 3, 117	Belle of Dodge Me, 4, 114	9	1:52.60	25,737
1977	Table the Rumor, 3, 112	W. Shoemaker	La Doree (Arg), 3, 112	Ivory Castle, 3, 118	9	1:52.40	57,800
	Quid Kit, 3, 115	A. J. Trosclair	Royal Graustark, 3, 112	Pay Dust, 3, 112	11	1:45.60	21,025
1976	Bronze Point, 3, 118	H. Arroyo	Little Broadway, 3, 118	Confort Zone, 3, 118	9	1:44.40	20,075
1975	Lucky Leslie, 3, 118	D. Brumfield	Regal Rumor, 3, 121	Decanter, 3, 118	6	1:46.60	19,650
1974	Bold Rosie, 3, 118	P. Rubbicco	Trade Me Later, 3, 112	Kaye's Commander, 3, 118	12	1:46.60	20,625
1973	Knitted Gloves, 3, 118	J. C. Espinoza	Fussy Girl, 3, 118	Westward, 3, 118	11	1:46.00	14,825

Formerly sponsored by the Coca-Cola Co. of Atlanta 1989-'90. Grade 3 1982-2000. Coca-Cola Fair Grounds Oaks 1989-'90. Not held 1979, 2006. 1 1/16 miles 1977-'78. Three- and four-year-olds 1978. Run in March and December 1977. Two divisions 1978. ‡Plain Speaking finished third, DQ to fourth, 1981. Equaled track record 1994.

Falls City Handicap

Grade 2 in 2008. Churchill Downs, three-year-olds and up, fillies and mares, 1 1/8 miles, dirt. Held November 22, 2007, with a gross value of $324,300. First held in 1875. First graded in 1973. Stakes record 1:48.85 (1999 Silent Eskimo).

Year	Winner	Jockey	Second	Third	Strs	Time	1st Purse
2007	Kettleoneup, 4, 118	C. H. Borel	High Heels, 3, 115	Panty Raid, 3, 120	6	1:50.28	$199,058
2006	Ermine, 3, 114	E. Castro	Joint Effort, 3, 118	Cursora (Arg), 4, 114	8	1:49.90	198,644
2005	Indian Vale, 3, 115	J. R. Velazquez	Pampered Princess, 5, 123	Miss Fortunate, 5, 115	10	1:50.25	209,994
2004	Halory Leigh, 4, 116	E. M. Martin Jr.	Susan's Angel, 3, 114	Miss Fortunate, 4, 113	7	1:51.81	201,624
2003	Lead Story, 4, 116	C. H. Borel	Mayo On the Side, 4, 114	Cloakof Vagueness, 3, 114	9	1:51.23	207,204
2002	Allamerican Bertie, 3, 117	P. Day	Take Charge Lady, 3, 122	Softly, 4, 116	6	1:49.60	167,400
2001	Forest Secrets, 3, 113	C. Perret	Printemps (Chi), 4, 117	Unbridled Elaine, 3, 121	7	1:49.49	169,570
2000	Bordelaise (Arg), 5, 117	P. Day	Spain, 3, 122	On a Soapbox, 4, 116	5	1:50.01	168,020
1999	Silent Eskimo, 4, 117	C. H. Borel	Let, 4, 116	Pleasant Temper, 5, 115	8	**1:48.85**	171,585
1998	Tomisue's Delight, 4, 121	S. J. Sellers	Top Secret, 5, 115	Silent Eskimo, 3, 113	8	1:51.05	171,740
1997	Feasibility Study, 5, 122	M. E. Smith	Omi, 4, 114	Naskra Colors, 5, 112	7	1:50.65	170,345
1996	Halo America, 6, 118	C. H. Borel	Bedroom Blues, 5, 115	Debit My Account, 4, 113	8	1:49.08	171,120
1995	Mariah's Storm, 4, 120	R. N. Lester	Alcovy, 5, 112	Heavenliness, 5, 112	7	1:51.37	143,390
1994	Alcovy, 4, 114	S. E. Miller	Pennyhill Park, 4, 115	Hey Hazel, 4, 114	7	1:51.16	141,440
1993	Gray Cashmere, 4, 120	P. Day	Avie's Shadow, 4, 110	Princess Polonia, 5, 112	7	1:50.96	142,090
1992	Bungalow, 5, 118	P. Day	Wilderness Song, 4, 123	Auto Dial, 4, 115	7	1:52.03	70,915
1991	Screen Prospect, 4, 117	S. J. Sellers	Fit for a Queen, 5, 124	Bungalow, 4, 112	11	1:51.23	73,580
1990	Screen Prospect, 3, 114	P. Day	Sleek Feet, 3, 110	Degenerate Gal, 5, 119	13	1:51.40	75,920
1989	Degenerate Gal, 4, 116	L. J. Melancon	Luthier's Launch, 3, 113	Blackened, 3, 112	9	1:52.60	72,410
1988	Top Corsage, 5, 121	D. Brumfield	Epitome, 3, 116	Lawyer Talk, 4, 111	14	1:51.86	76,895
1987	Royal Cielo, 4, 114	K. K. Allen	Firgie's Jule, 4, 115	Fantasy Lover, 4, 113	8	1:53.00	47,330
1986	Queen Alexandra, 4, 124	D. Brumfield	Kapalua Butterfly, 5, 113	Gerrie Singer, 5, 116	13	1:51.40	49,248
1985	Donut's Pride, 3, 112	L. J. Melancon	Playful Queen, 4, 114	My Inheritance, 3, 111	8	1:53.20	35,743
	Electric Fanny, 4, 115	J. C. Espinoza	Mrs. Revere, 4, 121	Chattahoochee, 3, 113	10	1:52.60	26,780
1984	Pretty Perfect, 4, 121	G. Gallitano	Electric Fanny, 3, 116	Queen of Song, 5, 122	12	1:50.80	37,115
1983	Narrate, 3, 117	M. S. Sellers	Queen of Song, 4, 116	Promising Native, 4, 116	9	1:51.60	36,335
1982	Mezimica, 4, 112	D. E. Foster	Charge My Account, 3, 111	Shade Miss, 3, 112	10	1:51.40	39,910
	What Glitter, 4, 114	D. Brumfield	Sprite Flight, 4, 114	Betty Money, 3, 118	11	1:52.80	36,823
1981	Safe Play, 3, 123	S. A. Spencer	Sweetest Chant, 3, 118	Friendly Frolic, 4, 112	13	1:46.20	37,993
1980	Sweet Audrey, 3, 113	C. R. Woods Jr.	Likely Exchange, 6, 123	Impetuous Gal, 5, 122	11	1:48.20	36,156
1979	Holy Mount, 3, 112	M. R. Morgan	Impetuous Gal, 4, 118	Cup of Honey, 3, 115	11	1:47.60	39,163
1978	Navajo Princess, 4, 123	C. Perret	Love to Tell, 3, 118	Likely Exchange, 4, 120	12	1:45.40	36,043
1977	Time for Pleasure, 3, 115	T. Barrow	Dear Irish, 3, 114	Famed Princess, 4, 115	13	1:46.20	22,084
1976	Hope of Glory, 4, 118	D. Brumfield	Hail to El, 4, 116	Flama Ardiente, 4, 117	12	1:48.20	21,938
1975	Flama Ardiente, 3, 119	B. Fann	Costly Dream, 4, 120	Go On Dreaming, 3, 116	11	1:38.20	18,623
1974	Susan's Girl, 5, 126	W. Gavidia	Crystal Stone, 4, 113	Enchanted Native, 3, 112	9	1:37.40	18,184
1973	Delta Empress, 3, 111	E. Fires	Pig Party, 4, 113	Fine Tuning, 3, 115	7	1:37.40	15,348
	Fairway Flyer, 4, 115	D. E. Whited	Nalees Folly, 4, 118	Knitted Gloves, 3, 113	11	1:37.20	15,185

Named for the early nickname of Louisville, "Falls City." Grade 3 1973-2001. Not held 1878-'81, 1885-'91, 1893-1909, 1928-

'40. 1 mile 1875-'55, 1892, 1941-'75. 1½ miles 1882-'83. 1 1/16 miles 1884, 1919, 1976-'81. 6 furlongs 1910, 1912-'18. Three-year-olds 1875-'77. Two-year-olds and up 1882-'92. Both sexes 1875-'77, 1882-'92, 1910-'26. Two divisions 1973, '82, '85.

Fantasy Stakes

Grade 2 in 2008. Oaklawn Park, three-year-olds, fillies, 1 1/16 miles, dirt. Held April 6, 2008, with a gross value of $237,500. First held in 1973. First graded in 1975. Stakes record 1:41.20 (1984 My Darling One).

Year	Winner	Jockey	Second	Third	Strs	Time	1st Purse
2008	Eight Belles, 3, 121	R. A. Dominguez	Alina, 3, 121	Pure Clan, 3, 121	4	1:43.06	$150,000
2007	High Heels, 3, 117	J. M. Johnson	Cotton Blossom, 3, 121	Cash Included, 3, 121	8	1:44.43	150,000
2006	Ready to Please, 3, 117	S. Elliott	Miss Norman, 3, 117	Brownie Points, 3, 121	8	1:45.63	150,000
2005	Round Pond, 3, 121	S. Elliott	Rugula, 3, 117	R Lady Joy, 3, 121	7	1:43.49	150,000
2004	House of Fortune, 3, 121	A. O. Solis	Island Sand, 3, 121	Stellar Jayne, 3, 121	11	1:42.62	120,000
2003	Ruby's Reception, 3, 121	T. J. Thompson	Harbor Blues, 3, 121	Go for Glamour, 3, 117	6	1:44.61	120,000
2002	See How She Runs, 3, 117	D. R. Pettinger	Lake Lady, 3, 121	Chamrousse, 3, 117	6	1:43.80	120,000
2001	Mystic Lady, 3, 121	E. Coa	Collect Call, 3, 121	Mysia Jo, 3, 117	10	1:43.32	120,000
2000	Classy Cara, 3, 121	I. Puglisi	Eden Lodge, 3, 117	Gold for My Gal, 3, 117	8	1:43.95	120,000
1999	Excellent Meeting, 3, 121	K. Desormeaux	The Happy Hopper, 3, 121	Dreams Gallore, 3, 121	6	1:42.73	150,000
1998	Silent Eskimo, 3, 117	C. Gonzalez	Misty Hour, 3, 121	Came Unwound, 3, 121	8	1:43.84	150,000
1997	Blushing K. D., 3, 121	L. J. Meche	Valid Bonnet, 3, 121	Ajina, 3, 121	5	1:42.60	150,000
1996	Escena, 3, 117	P. Day	Antespend, 3, 121	Ski Trail, 3, 117	7	1:43.93	150,000
1995	Cat's Cradle, 3, 121	C. W. Antley	Forever Cherokee, 3, 117	Humble Eight, 3, 121	8	1:44.29	150,000
1994	Two Altazano, 3, 121	K. P. LeBlanc	Slide Show, 3, 121	Flying in the Lane, 3, 121	11	1:43.64	150,000
1993	Aztec Hill, 3, 121	M. E. Smith	Adorydar, 3, 117	Stalcreek, 3, 117	7	1:44.33	150,000
1992	Race the Wild Wind, 3, 117	C. J. McCarron	Golden Treat, 3, 121	Now Dance, 3, 121	8	1:43.74	150,000
1991	Lite Light, 3, 121	C. S. Nakatani	Withallprobability, 3, 121	Nalees Pin, 3, 121	8	1:41.93	150,000
1990	Silvered, 3, 112	D. L. Howard	Lonely Girl, 3, 114	Fit to Scout, 3, 118	8	1:44.20	150,000
1989	Fantastic Look, 3, 113	C. J. McCarron	Imaginary Lady, 3, 121	Affirmed Classic, 3, 114	7	1:43.20	150,000
1988	Jeanne Jones, 3, 118	W. Shoemaker	Fara's Team, 3, 112	Costly Shoes, 3, 114	4	1:42.20	150,000
1987	‡Very Subtle, 3, 121	C. J. McCarron	Up the Apalachee, 3, 121	Hometown Queen, 3, 116	7	1:42.40	162,780
1986	Tiffany Lass, 3, 121	G. L. Stevens	Lotka, 3, 116	Turn and Dance, 3, 112	4	1:42.00	164,640
1985	Rascal Lass, 3, 118	R. Sibille	Denver Express, 3, 113	Little Biddy Comet, 3, 114	11	1:43.20	169,620
1984	My Darling One, 3, 121	C. J. McCarron	Althea, 3, 121	Personable Lady, 3, 118	6	**1:41.20**	160,440
1983	Brindy Brindy, 3, 115	K. Jones Jr.	Fifth Question, 3, 115	Choose a Partner, 3, 112	11	1:44.60	169,080
1982	Flying Partner, 3, 118	R. Sibille	Skillful Joy, 3, 121	Before Dawn, 3, 121	7	1:47.00	163,020
1981	Heavenly Cause, 3, 121	L. A. Pincay Jr.	Nell's Briquette, 3, 121	Wayward Lass, 3, 121	9	1:43.80	133,890
1980	Bold 'n Determined, 3, 121	E. Delahoussaye	Satin Ribera, 3, 115	Honest and True, 3, 118	7	1:45.20	101,940
1979	Davona Dale, 3, 121	J. Velasquez	Caline, 3, 121	Very Special Lady, 3, 110	7	1:44.40	101,610
1978	Equanimity, 3, 110	H. E. Moreno	Ba Ba Bee, 3, 115	Miss Baja, 3, 121	4	1:44.60	77,850
1977	Our Mims, 3, 112	D. Brumfield	Sweet Alliance, 3, 118	Meteor Dancer, 3, 110	15	1:45.00	83,970
1976	T. V. Vixen, 3, 121	B. Walt	Answer, 3, 121	All Rainbows, 3, 112	8	1:43.40	73,170
1975	Hoso, 3, 121	M. Solomone	Luxury, 3, 114	Dancers Countess, 3, 118	6	1:46.00	70,830
1974	Miss Musket, 3, 121	W. Shoemaker	Out to Lunch, 3, 115	Fairway Fable, 3, 118	12	1:44.80	79,740
1973	Knitted Gloves, 3, 121	J. C. Espinoza	Fussy Girl, 3, 121	Westward, 3, 118	14	1:42.60	36,960

The name was suggested to Charles Cella by Spencer Drayton, first head of the TRPB, while they were discussing the "fantasy" of creating a Racing Festival of the South; the Fantasy was the headline stakes of the first Racing Festival in 1974. Grade 1 1978-'89. 1 mile 70 yards 1973. ‡Up the Apalachee finished first, DQ to second, 1987.

Fayette Stakes

Grade 3 in 2008. Keeneland Race Course, three-year-olds and up, 1 1/8 miles, all weather. Held October 27, 2007, with a gross value of $150,000. First held in 1959. First graded in 1979. Stakes record 1:46.80 (1987 Good Command).

Year	Winner	Jockey	Second	Third	Strs	Time	1st Purse
2007	Go Between, 4, 121	M. Mena	Stream Cat, 4, 121	Kona Blend, 4, 119	9	1:47.97	$93,000
2006	Eccentric (GB), 5, 121	E. Castro	Ball Four, 5, 123	Good Reward, 5, 119	12	1:49.16	93,000
2005	Alumni Hall, 6, 121	C. H. Borel	On Thin Ice, 4, 119	M B Sea, 6, 119	9	1:51.37	93,000
2004	Midway Road, 4, 121	C. H. Borel	Total Impact (Chi), 6, 125	Alumni Hall, 5, 119	5	1:50.39	99,975
2003	M B Sea, 4, 119	C. Perret	Tenpins, 5, 121	dh-Changeintheweather, 4, 119 dh-Seattle Fitz (Arg), 4, 119	7	1:50.30	101,556
2002	Tenpins, 4, 123	C. Perret	X Country, 4, 119	Crafty Shaw, 4, 119	4	1:51.17	99,789
2001	Connected, 4, 119	M. St. Julien	Broken Vow, 4, 121	Outofthebox, 3, 122	9	1:50.05	103,509
2000	Jadada, 5, 118	S. J. Sellers	Mojave Moon, 4, 118	Get Away With It (Ire), 7, 118	5	1:54.92	133,176
1999	Social Charter, 4, 120	M. St. Julien	Master O Foxhounds, 4, 118	Early Warning, 4, 118	4	1:55.28	135,904
1998	Arch, 3, 123	S. J. Sellers	Touch Gold, 4, 115	Wild Tempest, 4, 115	4	1:53.87	98,801
1997	Whiskey Wisdom, 4, 115	W. Martinez	City by Night, 4, 123	Pyramid Peak, 5, 120	8	1:48.64	101,184
1996	Isitingood, 5, 120	D. R. Flores	Distorted Humor, 3, 114	Strawberry Wine, 4, 117	8	1:50.42	120,110
1995	Judge T C, 4, 112	J. M. Johnson	Powerful Punch, 6, 120	Sir Vixen, 7, 114	9	1:49.05	104,625
1994	Sunny Sunrise, 7, 120	J. D. Carle	Key Contender, 6, 117	Powerful Punch, 5, 117	7	1:50.18	67,766
1993	Grand Jewel, 3, 120	J. D. Bailey	Split Run, 5, 120	Secreto's Hideaway, 4, 114	8	1:46.87	68,634
1992	Barkerville, 4, 114	S. J. Sellers	Medium Cool, 4, 117	Majesterian, 4, 114	11	1:48.43	70,680
1991	Summer Squall, 4, 122	P. Day	Unbridled, 4, 122	Secret Hello, 4, 115	5	1:48.84	69,810
1990	Lac Ouimet, 7, 114	R. P. Romero	Din's Dancer, 5, 121	Secret Hello, 3, 116	6	1:47.20	70,233
1989	Drapeau Tricolore, 4, 114	J. E. Bruin	Air Worthy, 4, 116	Blue Buckaroo, 6, 118	8	1:48.20	71,695
1988	Homebuilder, 4, 121	D. Brumfield	Blue Buckaroo, 5, 120	Ile de Jinsky, 4, 112	4	1:51.20	68,315
1987	Good Command, 4, 118	D. Brumfield	Minneapple, 5, 120	Savings, 4, 115	12	**1:46.80**	73,921
1986	Harham's Sizzler, 7, 120	R. A. Meier	Derby Wish, 4, 119	Pirate's Skiff, 3, 112	5	1:49.20	34,792
1985	Wop Wop, 3, 112	D. E. Foster	Banner Bob, 3, 117	Exclusive Greer, 4, 114	10	1:51.40	36,530

Racing — Graded Stakes

Year	Winner	Jockey	Second	Third	Strs	Time	1st Purse
1984	Star Choice, 5, 112	J. McKnight	Explosive Wagon, 4, 117	Bright Baron, 4, 112	8	1:47.40	$47,492
1983	dh-Cad, 5, 116	D. Brumfield		Bold Style, 4, 120	5	1:48.80	22,663
	dh-Frost King, 5, 123	R. Platts					
1982	Rivalero, 6, 115	R. P. Romero	Cad, 4, 114	Recusant, 4, 120	7	1:50.40	35,563
	El Baba, 3, 118	D. Brumfield	Vodika Collins, 4, 120	Hechizado (Arg), 6, 115	7	1:50.20	38,813
1981	Ironworks, 3, 117	P. Day	Two's a Plenty, 4, 116	Sun Catcher, 4, 118	11	1:49.20	39,861
1980	Hurry Up Blue, 3, 112	G. Gallitano	Marcy Road, 3, 111	All the More, 7, 116	10	1:49.00	39,423
1979	Architect, 3, 117	S. A. Spencer	Coverack, 6, 121	Trimlea, 5, 120	8	1:49.60	35,669
1978	‡Silver Series, 4, 121	D. Brumfield	Buckfinder, 4, 121	Romeo, 5, 118	6	1:41.20	20,768
1977	Bob's Dusty, 3, 117	R. DePass	Man's Man, 3, 115	Packer Captain, 5, 118	11	1:42.80	18,395
1976	Silver Badge, 5, 111	G. Patterson	Easy Gallop, 3, 117	Topinabee, 5, 112	9	1:44.60	17,981
	Yamanin, 4, 114	G. Patterson	Run for Clem, 3, 111	Faneuil Boy, 5, 118	8	1:43.20	17,899
1975	Warbucks, 5, 120	J. Nichols	Hasty Flyer, 4, 119	Mr. Door, 4, 114	11	1:44.40	18,460
1974	Jesta Dream Away, 4, 115	A. Rini	Super Sail, 6, 121	Joyous Jester, 4, 112	9	1:41.60	18,119
1973	Chateauvira, 5, 112	G. Gallitano	Grocery List, 4, 116	O So Big, 4, 115	13	1:42.80	19,093

Named for Fayette County, Kentucky, where Keeneland is located. Grade 2 1987-'96. Fayette H. 1959-'91. Fayette Breeders' Cup S. 1999-2000. 1¹/₁₆ miles 1963-'78. 1³/₁₆ miles 1998-2000. Turf 1985. Dirt 1959-'84, 1986-2005. Two divisions 1976, '82. Dead heat for first 1983. Dead heat for third 2003. ‡Buckfinder finished first, DQ to second, 1978. Equaled track record 1993. Track record 1998, 2007.

Fifth Third Elkhorn Stakes

Grade 2 in 2008. Keeneland Race Course, four-year-olds and up, 1½ miles, turf. Held April 25, 2008, with a gross value of $200,000. First held in 1986. First graded in 1988. Stakes record 2:27.84 (1999 African Dancer).

Year	Winner	Jockey	Second	Third	Strs	Time	1st Purse
2008	Dancing Forever, 5, 118	R. R. Douglas	Drilling for Oil, 5, 120	Brass Hat, 7, 118	11	2:29.79	$124,000
2007	Ascertain (Ire), 6, 118	J. Theriot	Always First (GB), 6, 118	Drilling for Oil, 4, 118	12	2:30.40	124,000
2006	Pellegrino (Brz), 7, 118	S. Bridgmohan	Go Deputy, 6, 118	Silverfoot, 6, 118	11	2:29.84	124,000
2005	Macaw (Ire), 6, 118	J. Castellano	European (Ire), 5, 118	Rochester, 9, 118	12	2:32.62	124,000
2004	Epicentre, 5, 116	J. D. Bailey	Rochester, 8, 116	Art Variety (Brz), 6, 115	10	2:31.96	93,000
2003	Kim Loves Bucky, 6, 117	K. Desormeaux	Man From Wicklow, 6, 123	Williams News, 8, 116	10	2:29.39	93,000
2002	Kim Loves Bucky, 5, 116	J. F. Chavez	Rochester, 6, 116	Cetewayo, 8, 118	10	2:32.49	93,000
2001	Williams News, 6, 116	R. Albarado	Gritty Sandie, 5, 116	Craigsteel (GB), 6, 118	9	2:29.13	70,308
2000	Drama Critic, 4, 116	J. D. Bailey	Craigsteel (GB), 5, 116	Dixie's Crown, 4, 116	10	2:28.03	69,750
1999	African Dancer, 7, 114	J. D. Bailey	Magest, 4, 116	Chorwon, 6, 113	8	**2:27.84**	68,136
1998	African Dancer, 6, 114	J. D. Bailey	Chief Bearhart, 5, 122	Chorwon, 5, 114	5	2:31.71	66,712
1997	Chief Bearhart, 4, 114	J. A. Santos	Snake Eyes, 7, 113	Lassigny, 6, 122	8	2:28.43	68,324
1996	Vladivostok, 6, 118	P. Day	Penn Fifty Three, 4, 114	Party Season (GB), 5, 119	7	2:30.83	68,262
1995	Marvin's Faith (Ire), 4, 123	C. Perret	Hasten To Add, 5, 120	Opera Score, 4, 120	10	1:47.10	70,680
1994	Lure, 5, 123	M. E. Smith	Buckhar, 4, 120	Pride of Summer, 6, 120	5	1:53.76	66,526
1993	Coaxing Matt, 4, 118	P. Day	Cleone, 4, 113	Maxigroom, 5, 118	9	1:47.64	68,603
1992	Fourstars Allstar, 4, 113	J. D. Bailey	Slew the Slewor, 5, 120	Rainbows for Life, 4, 120	10	1:47.66	72,995
1991	Itsallgreektome, 4, 123	R. A. Baze	Pirate Army, 5, 113	Spark O'Dan, 6, 113	7	1:51.28	71,143
1990	Ten Keys, 5, 123	R. P. Romero	Yankee Affair, 8, 123	Maceo, 6, 118	8	1:51.80	71,468
1989	Exclusive Partner, 7, 120	F. Toro	Yankee Affair, 7, 120	Pappas Swing, 4, 120	7	1:50.40	54,958
1988	Yankee Affair, 6, 123	P. Day	Storm On the Loose, 5, 118	Blazing Bart, 4, 123	10	1:49.60	56,485
1987	Manila, 4, 117	J. Vasquez	Lieutenant's Lark, 5, 112	Royal Treasurer, 4, 112	7	1:48.40	35,019
1986	Lieutenant's Lark, 4, 113	F. Lovato Jr.	Leprechauns Wish, 4, 115	Majestic Jabot, 5, 115	10	1:54.60	36,351

Named for a large local creek, the Elkhorn, long used as a water source by Bluegrass-area farms. Sponsored by Fifth Third Bancorp of Cincinnati 2005-'08. Grade 3 1988-'89, 1996-2007. 1⅛ miles 1986-'95. Course record 1995, '99.

Firecracker Handicap

Grade 2 in 2008. Churchill Downs, three-year-olds and up, 1 mile, turf. Held June 30, 2007, with a gross value of $232,000. First held in 1983. First graded in 1995. Stakes record 1:33.78 (1995 Jaggery John).

Year	Winner	Jockey	Second	Third	Strs	Time	1st Purse
2007	Remarkable News (Ven), 5, 122	R. A. Dominguez	Brilliant, 4, 121	Outperformance, 4, 115	8	1:34.74	$122,387
2006	Miesque's Approval, 7, 120	E. Castro	Free Thinking, 4, 115	Therecomesatiger, 4, 116	7	1:34.52	170,605
2005	Kitten's Joy, 4, 124	E. S. Prado	Old Forester, 4, 115	America Alive, 4, 119	6	1:35.25	169,880
2004	Quantum Merit, 5, 117	S. J. Sellers	‡Perfect Soul (Ire), 6, 121	Senor Swinger, 4, 117	9	1:34.15	178,455
2003	Tap the Admiral, 5, 115	J. McKee	Freefourinternet, 5, 114	Package Store, 5, 114	9	1:35.48	178,870
2002	Good Journey, 6, 118	P. Day	Morluc, 6, 114	Even the Score, 4, 114	9	1:34.83	181,350
2001	Irish Prize, 5, 122	G. L. Stevens	‡Aly's Alley, 5, 117	Where's Taylor, 5, 114	7	1:34.68	175,770
2000	Conserve, 4, 116	S. J. Sellers	Riviera (Fr), 6, 115	King Slayer (GB), 5, 115	8	1:35.12	177,940
1999	Joe Who (Brz), 6, 113	R. Albarado	Middlesex Drive, 4, 115	Wild Event, 6, 121	9	1:36.78	132,680
1998	Claire's Honor, 4, 109	A. J. D'Amico	Soviet Line (Ire), 8, 115	Optic Nerve, 5, 113	9	1:35.93	177,630
1997	Soviet Line (Ire), 7, 114	P. Day	Volochine (Ire), 6, 115	Same Old Wish, 7, 118	10	1:37.60	126,077
1996	Rare Reason, 5, 115	P. A. Johnson	Artema (Ire), 5, 114	Wavy Run (Ire), 5, 116	9	1:33.81	131,950
1995	Jaggery John, 4, 113	D. Kutz	Rare Reason, 4, 115	Fly Cry, 4, 119	10	**1:33.78**	74,360
1994	First and Only, 7, 118	T. J. Hebert	†Weekend Madness (Ire), 4, 111	Avid Affection, 5, 112	8	1:35.33	73,580
1993	Cleone, 4, 115	C. Perret	Magesterial Cheer, 5, 113	Harlan, 4, 110	9	1:35.90	74,815
1985	Rapid Gray, 6, 122	L. J. Melancon	Silahis, 8, 116	Silver Wraith, 4, 110	5	1:21.20	35,263
1984	Turn and Cheer, 4, 113	P. A. Johnson	Coax Me Matt, 4, 112	Keep At It, 3, 118	7	1:25.60	35,912
1983	Shot n' Missed, 6, 121	L. Moyers	Dave's Friend, 8, 124	Rackensack, 5, 118	4	1:23.20	28,145

Traditionally held during the July 4 holiday. Grade 3 1995-'99. Firecracker Breeders' Cup H. 1996-2006. Not held 1986-

'92. 7 furlongs 1983-'85. Dirt 1983-'85. Course record 1995. ‡Where's Taylor finished second, DQ to third, 2001. ‡Senor Swinger finished second, DQ to third, 2004. †Denotes female.

First Flight Handicap

Grade 2 in 2008. Belmont Park, three-year-olds and up, fillies and mares, 7 furlongs, dirt. Held July 8, 2007, with a gross value of $147,000. First held in 1978. First graded in 1982. Stakes record 1:20.65 (1992 Shared Interest).

Year	Winner	Jockey	Second	Third	Strs	Time	1st Purse
2007	Ginger Punch, 4, 117	R. Bejarano	Sweet Fervor, 4, 116	Swap Fliparoo, 4, 115	5	1:22.64	$90,000
2006	Carmandia, 4, 114	C. P. DeCarlo	Win McCool, 3, 114	Swap Fliparoo, 3, 114	7	1:22.91	90,000
2005	Great Intentions, 3, 114	E. S. Prado	Habiboo, 4, 113	Smokey Glacken, 4, 114	8	1:23.98	90,000
2004	Bending Strings, 3, 116	S. Bridgmohan	Smokey Glacken, 3, 115	Passing Shot, 5, 118	6	1:22.13	90,000
2003	Randaroo, 3, 115	H. Castillo Jr.	Shine Again, 6, 121	Zawzooth, 4, 113	8	1:23.65	90,000
2002	Shine Again, 5, 117	J. Samyn	Redhead Riot, 3, 112	Raging Fever, 4, 119	5	1:23.75	90,000
2001	Shine Again, 4, 116	J. Samyn	Dream Supreme, 4, 121	Kalookan Queen, 5, 119	6	1:23.21	90,000
2000	Country Hideaway, 4, 117	J. L. Espinoza	Go to the Ink, 4, 113	Cat Cay, 3, 114	7	1:22.60	90,000
1999	Country Hideaway, 3, 114	H. Castillo Jr.	Harpia, 5, 117	Anklet, 5, 114	8	1:23.00	90,000
1998	Catinca, 3, 116	R. Migliore	Glitter Woman, 4, 121	Blue Begonia, 5, 115	7	1:22.14	82,260
1997	Dixie Flag, 3, 113	M. J. Luzzi	Silent City, 3, 113	Aldiza, 3, 116	4	1:22.84	64,800
1996	Thunder Achiever, 3, 112	R. G. Davis	Miss Golden Circle, 4, 117	Call Account, 4, 110	10	1:21.59	81,864
1995	Twist Afleet, 4, 121	G. L. Stevens	Igotrhythm, 3, 109	Lottsa Talc, 4, 116	5	1:22.95	66,780
1994	Twist Afleet, 3, 117	J. D. Bailey	Ann Dear, 4, 117	Incinerate, 4, 113	8	1:23.02	66,120
1993	Raise Heck, 5, 114	R. I. Velez	Regal Victress, 6, 113	Shared Interest, 5, 121	6	1:23.51	69,000
1992	Shared Interest, 4, 111	J. D. Bailey	Missy's Mirage, 4, 121	Nannerl, 5, 119	7	1:20.65	120,000
1991	Missy's Mirage, 3, 113	E. Maple	Makin Faces, 3, 112	Withallprobability, 3, 114	10	1:21.98	74,160
1990	Queena, 4, 113	J. D. Bailey	Quick Mischief, 4, 115	A Penny Is a Penny, 5, 122	5	1:22.40	51,480
1989	Grecian Flight, 5, 122	C. Perret	Feel the Beat, 4, 121	Dance Teacher, 4, 112	5	1:22.00	51,480
1988	Cagey Exuberance, 4, 119	J. Imparato	Nasty Affair, 4, 114	Intently, 5, 111	10	1:24.40	55,350
1987	Al's Helen, 4, 112	J. D. Bailey	Girl Powder, 4, 117	Willowy Mood, 5, 118	9	1:21.80	54,180
1986	Chaldea, 6, 115	J. Samyn	Le Slew, 5, 114	Gene's Lady, 5, 120	4	1:22.40	53,100
1985	Alabama Nana (Ire), 4, 121	J. Velasquez	Gene's Lady, 4, 115	Paradies (Arg), 4, 119	5	1:22.20	50,040
1984	Shortley, 4, 114	M. G. Pino	Quixotic Lady, 4, 116	Rarely Layte, 4, 108	7	1:22.60	42,060
1983	Pert, 4, 112	F. Lovato Jr.	Pretty Sensible, 3, 112	Quixotic Lady, 3, 121	8	1:25.20	34,620
1982	Number, 3, 112	E. Maple	Lady Dean, 4, 123	Privacy, 4, 118	11	1:22.80	34,500
1981	Island Charm, 4, 120	R. Migliore	Tax Holiday, 4, 116	Chain Bracelet, 4, 123	8	1:23.60	33,720
1980	Samarta Dancer, 4, 112	C. B. Asmussen	Jedina, 4, 115	Damask Fan, 3, 112	9	1:25.60	33,780
1979	Gladiolus, 5, 120	L. A. Pincay Jr.	Imarebel, 4, 117	Plankton, 3, 114	5	1:22.40	25,740
1978	What a Summer, 5, 126	J. Fell	Flying Above, 4, 120	Mrs. Warren, 4, 113	5	1:22.30	25,410

Named for C. V. Whitney's 1946 champion two-year-old filly and '46 Futurity S. winner First Flight (1944 f. by *Mahmoud). Grade 3 1982-'89. I Love New York First Flight H. 1995. Held at Aqueduct 1978-'89, 1991, 1993-'94, 1996-2000, 2002, '04, '06.

First Lady Handicap

Grade 3 in 2008. Gulfstream Park, four-year-olds and up, fillies and mares, 6 furlongs, dirt. Held January 13, 2008, with a gross value of $100,000. First held in 1981. First graded in 1993. Stakes record 1:08.98 (2006 Smokey Glacken).

Year	Winner	Jockey	Second	Third	Strs	Time	1st Purse
2008	Sugar Swirl, 5, 119	J. Castellano	Rgirldoesn'tbluff, 5, 117	Bereba, 5, 116	7	1:10.06	$60,000
2007	Any Limit, 4, 114	R. Bejarano	Contrast, 5, 116	Actslikealady, 4, 113	8	1:10.58	60,000
2006	Smokey Glacken, 5, 117	J. Castellano	Kuanyan, 6, 116	So Much More, 7, 113	8	1:08.98	60,000
2005	Savorthetime, 6, 116	J. R. Velazquez	Cologny, 5, 117	Ebony Breeze, 5, 116	7	1:09.21	60,000
2004	Harmony Lodge, 6, 119	R. Migliore	House Party, 4, 118	Mayo On the Side, 5, 115	9	1:09.64	60,000
2003	Harmony Lodge, 5, 113	J. R. Velazquez	Fly Me Crazy, 5, 114	Haunted Lass, 4, 114	6	1:10.31	60,000
2002	Raging Fever, 4, 118	J. R. Velazquez	Cat Cay, 5, 118	Mandy's Gold, 4, 116	7	1:10.36	60,000
2001	Another, 4, 113	E. S. Prado	Curious Treasures, 4, 114	Dynamite Diablo, 4, 115	11	1:10.41	60,000
2000	Hurricane Bertie, 5, 118	P. Day	Marley Vale, 4, 118	Cassidy, 5, 113	7	1:10.22	45,000
1999	Scotzanna, 7, 114	R. Migliore	U Can Do It, 6, 118	Foil, 4, 116	8	1:10.17	45,000
1998	U Can Do It, 5, 115	S. J. Sellers	Start At Once, 5, 113	Vivace, 5, 118	10	1:09.86	45,000
1997	Chip, 4, 113	J. Bravo	Phone the Doctor, 5, 116	Surprising Fact, 4, 113	10	1:09.76	45,000
1996	Chaposa Springs, 4, 122	J. D. Bailey	Phone the Doctor, 4, 117	Market Slide, 5, 113	9	1:10.23	45,000
1995	Recognizable, 4, 113	M. E. Smith	Insight to Cope, 5, 114	Maison de Reve, 4, 114	10	1:09.74	30,000
1994	Santa Catalina, 6, 114	J. D. Bailey	Insight to Cope, 4, 119	Capture the Crown, 5, 113	11	1:11.26	30,000
1993	Si Si Sezyou, 5, 112	R. Hernandez	Illeria, 6, 113	Jeano, 5, 114	11	1:10.06	30,000
1992	Withallprobability, 4, 118	C. Perret	Christina Czarina, 4, 114	Spirit of Fighter, 9, 114	14	1:11.14	30,000
1991	Spirit of Fighter, 8, 118	J. A. Velez Jr.	Mistaurian, 5, 115	Love's Exchange, 5, 128	9	1:11.70	30,000
1990	Sez Fourty, 4, 114	M. A. Gonzalez	Classic Value, 4, 118	Fit for a Queen, 4, 114	7	1:11.20	22,764
1989	Waggley, 6, 112	J. Samyn	Damality, 6, 113	My Peace, 4, 114	5	1:11.00	27,288
1988	Funistrada, 5, 120	W. A. Guerra	Easter Mary, 4, 114	Cadillacing, 4, 113	9	1:11.20	29,232
1987	One Fine Lady, 5, 114	R. Danjean	Fleur de Soleil, 4, 112	Sheer Ice, 5, 113	6	1:10.40	24,045
1986	Sugar's Image, 5, 115	J. A. Velez Jr.	Summer Mood, 5, 120	Mr. T's Tune, 5, 117	10	1:11.20	29,736
1985	Nany, 5, 120	G. St. Leon	Mickey's Echo, 6, 113	Birdie Belle, 4, 118	9	1:09.80	29,352
1983	Prime Prospect, 5, 118	D. MacBeth	Miss Hitch, 7, 114	Mrs. Roberts, 5, 113	16	1:10.80	24,282
1981	Island Charm, 4, 113	J. Velasquez	La Voyageuse, 6, 114	Lacey, 4, 114	11	1:11.20	22,556

First held in 1981 following a presidential election year and run in mid-January when presidential inaugurations take place, the race is named in honor of the first lady of the United States. First Lady Breeders' Cup H. 1990. Not held 1982 '84. Three-year-olds and up 1981-2006.

First Lady Stakes

Grade 1 in 2008. Keeneland Race Course, three-year-olds and up, fillies and mares, 1 mile, turf. Held October 6, 2007, with a gross value of $432,000. First held in 1998. First graded in 2000. Stakes record 1:34.14 (2006 Gorella [Fr]).

Year	Winner	Jockey	Second	Third	Strs	Time	1st Purse
2007	Vacare, 4, 121	C. S. Nakatani	Precious Kitten, 4, 125	Quite a Bride, 4, 121	9	1:35.85	$248,000
2006	Gorella (Fr), 4, 125	J. R. Leparoux	Karen's Caper, 4, 121	My Typhoon (Ire), 4, 123	8	1:34.14	248,000
2005	Intercontinental (GB), 5, 123	J. D. Bailey	Wend, 4, 123	Katdogawn (GB), 5, 123	9	1:37.40	248,000
2004	Stay Forever, 7, 121	E. Castro	Super Brand (SAf), 5, 119	Shaconage, 4, 121	9	1:57.08	310,000
2003	Bien Nicole, 5, 121	D. R. Pettinger	Approach (GB), 3, 116	New Economy, 5, 121	6	1:55.87	310,000
2002	Owsley, 4, 122	E. S. Prado	Snow Dance, 4, 120	Surya, 4, 118	6	1:56.72	337,590
2001	Spook Express (SAf), 7, 120	M. E. Smith	Solvig, 4, 118	Veil of Avalon, 4, 118	9	1:54.24	349,370
2000	Tout Charmant, 4, 117	C. J. McCarron	Perfect Sting, 4, 121	License Fee, 5, 119	7	1:54.74	343,480
1999	Happyanunoit (NZ), 4, 119	B. Blanc	Pleasant Temper, 5, 119	Fiji (GB), 5, 117	9	1:53.91	346,270
1998	Witchful Thinking, 4, 115	C. J. McCarron	Memories of Silver, 5, 120	Starry Dreamer, 4, 115	6	1:54.24	169,415

Formerly sponsored by Bill Casner's and Kenny Troutt's WinStar Farm of Versailles, Kentucky 2000-'05. Formerly sponsored by Vinery of Lexington 1998-'99. Grade 3 2000. Grade 2 2001-'07. Vinery First Lady S. 1998-'99. WinStar Galaxy S. 2000-'05. 1 1/16 miles 1998-2005.

Fitz Dixon Cotillion Handicap

Grade 2 in 2008. Philadelphia Park, three-year-olds, fillies, 1 1/16 miles, dirt. Held September 22, 2007, with a gross value of $750,000. First held in 1969. First graded in 1973. Stakes record 1:41.21 (2007 Bear Now).

Year	Winner	Jockey	Second	Third	Strs	Time	1st Purse
2007	Bear Now, 3, 119	J. Baird	Octave, 3, 123	Talkin About Love, 3, 118	7	1:41.21	$426,000
2006	India, 3, 118	J. Bravo	Amandatude, 3, 117	Baby Bird, 3, 113	5	1:43.26	300,000
2005	Nothing But Fun, 3, 115	R. Migliore	Yolanda B. Too, 3, 117	Shebelongstoyou, 3, 117	6	1:46.64	180,000
2004	Ashado, 3, 124	E. Coa	Ender's Sister, 3, 117	My Lordship, 3, 115	7	1:41.68	150,000
2003	Fast Cookie, 3, 116	N. Santagata	Ladyecho, 3, 116	Savedbythelight, 3, 117	5	1:45.83	150,000
2002	Smok'n Frolic, 3, 118	J. A. Velez Jr.	Pupil, 3, 114	Jilbab, 3, 120	9	1:44.27	150,000
2001	Mystic Lady, 3, 121	E. Coa	Zonk, 3, 117	Celtic Melody, 3, 115	8	1:43.86	150,000
2000	Jostle, 3, 124	M. E. Smith	Gold for My Gal, 3, 112	Prized Stamp, 3, 114	7	1:42.54	120,000
1999	Skipping Around, 3, 114	M. J. McCarthy	Strolling Belle, 3, 120	Waltz, 3, 114	10	1:43.45	120,000
1998	Lu Ravi, 3, 121	W. Martinez	Sister Act, 3, 115	Let, 3, 117	8	1:43.55	90,000
1997	Snit, 3, 114	R. E. Colton	Proud Run, 3, 116	Salt It, 3, 117	9	1:43.91	90,000
1996	Double Dee's, 3, 111	F. Leon	Ginny Lynn, 3, 121	Princess Eloise, 3, 113	5	1:44.69	90,000
1995	Clear Mandate, 3, 113	J. C. Ferrer	Blue Sky Princess, 3, 114	Country Cat, 3, 118	11	1:42.87	98,730
1994	Sovereign Kitty, 3, 118	W. H. McCauley	Cinnamon Sugar (Ire), 3, 120	Cavada, 3, 114	8	1:43.52	97,440
1993	Jacody, 3, 118	T. G. Turner	Aztec Hill, 3, 121	Cearas Dancer, 3, 109	6	1:43.22	95,520
1992	Star Minister, 3, 117	A. J. Seefeldt	Diamond Duo, 3, 121	Squirm, 3, 116	7	1:44.06	80,760
1990	Valay Maid, 3, 119	L. Saumell	Toffeefee, 3, 115	Trumpet's Blare, 3, 116	8	1:43.80	81,600
1989	Sharp Dance, 3, 115	K. Castaneda	Misty Ivor, 3, 113	Tactile, 3, 117	11	1:43.80	81,900
1988	Aquaba, 3, 115	J. Cruguet	Ice Tech, 3, 113	Mother of Eight, 3, 114	8	1:44.40	79,320
1987	‡Silent Turn, 3, 118	R. P. Romero	Sacahuista, 3, 119	Single Blade, 3, 117	8	1:42.80	65,280
1986	Toes Knows, 3, 119	D. Wright	Life At the Top, 3, 121	I'm Sweets, 3, 119	8	1:42.80	65,880
1985	Koluctoo's Jill, 3, 119	W. H. McCauley	Overwhelming, 3, 115	Tabayour, 3, 118	8	1:42.80	65,520
1984	Squan Song, 3, 122	R. Z. Hernandez	Given, 3, 122	You're Too Special, 3, 113	9	1:42.60	60,945
	Dowery, 3, 122	V. A. Bracciale Jr.	Duo Disco, 3, 122	Hot Milk, 3, 117	9	1:42.60	60,945
1983	Quixotic Lady, 3, 122	G. McCarron	Lady Hawthorn, 3, 117	Springtime Sharon, 3, 117	8	1:42.80	33,180
1982	Lady Eleanor, 3, 122	C. Perret	Smart Heiress, 3, 122	Glass House, 3, 117	12	1:45.00	34,800
1981	Truly Bound, 3, 121	R. J. Franklin	Pukka Princess, 3, 118	Debonair Dancer, 3, 118	8	1:42.80	33,810
1980	Sugar and Spice, 3, 116	G. Martens	Pepi Wiley, 3, 118	Nijit, 3, 116	8	1:45.00	34,800
1979	Alada, 3, 116	J. Fell	Too Many Sweets, 3, 116	Heavenly Ade, 3, 116	6	1:43.80	33,090
1978	Queen Lib, 3, 121	D. MacBeth	Silken Delight, 3, 116	Sharp Belle, 3, 117	11	1:43.20	28,620
1977	Suede Shoe, 3, 116	A. S. Black	Raise Old Glory, 3, 113	Bafflin Lil, 3, 116	11	1:42.60	27,930
1976	Revidere, 3, 118	J. Vasquez	Critical Miss, 3, 116	Hay Patcher, 3, 116	8	1:44.00	20,190
1975	My Juliet, 3, 116	D. Brumfield	Hot n Nasty, 3, 116	Gala Lil, 3, 118	7	1:43.60	20,160
1974	Honky Star, 3, 121	D. G. McHargue	Special Team, 3, 118	Kudara, 3, 121	4	1:44.00	32,910
1973	Lilac Hill, 3, 113	D. MacBeth	Ladies Agreement, 3, 114	Suzi Sunshine, 3, 114	10	1:43.60	34,590

Named in honor of Fitz Eugene Dixon Jr. (1923-2006), owner of Erdenheim Farms in Pennsylvania and a local Philadelphia sports legend; Dixon was heir to the Widener fortune. A cotillion is a traditional dance where debutantes are formally presented to society. Grade 1 1973-'74. Grade 3 1981-'88. Cotillion S. 1975-'84. Cotillion H. 1985-2005. Fitz Dixon Cotillion Breeders' Cup H. 2006. Held at Liberty Bell 1969-'74. Held at Keystone 1975-'84. Not held 1991. Two divisions 1984. ‡Sacahuista finished first, DQ to second, 1987.

Fleur de Lis Handicap

Grade 2 in 2008. Churchill Downs, three-year-olds and up, fillies and mares, 1 1/8 miles, dirt. Held June 16, 2007, with a gross value of $327,600. First held in 1975. First graded in 1988. Stakes record 1:48.26 (2000 Heritage of Gold).

Year	Winner	Jockey	Second	Third	Strs	Time	1st Purse
2007	Indian Vale, 5, 119	J. R. Velazquez	Asi Siempre, 5, 122	Kettleoneup, 4, 117	7	1:49.12	$199,052
2006	Happy Ticket, 5, 120	J. R. Leparoux	Oonagh Maccool (Ire), 4, 120	Character Builder, 4, 115	7	1:49.23	199,578
2005	Two Trail Sioux, 4, 114	P. Day	Storm's Darling, 4, 116	Rare Gift, 4, 115	7	1:48.53	204,600
2004	Adoration, 5, 122	V. Espinoza	Bare Necessities, 5, 120	La Reason, 4, 110	6	1:52.15	272,304
2003	You, 4, 119	J. D. Bailey	Printemps (Chi), 6, 114	Nonsuch Bay, 4, 114	6	1:49.12	203,298
2002	Spain, 5, 121	J. F. Chavez	With Ability, 4, 117	Dancethruthedawn, 4, 119	6	1:49.64	204,228

Year	Winner	Jockey	Second	Third	Strs	Time	1st Purse
2001	Saudi Poetry, 4, 114	V. Espinoza	Secret Status, 4, 119	Asher, 4, 112	8	1:49.27	$206,460
2000	Heritage of Gold, 5, 121	S. J. Sellers	Silverbulletday, 4, 119	Roza Robata, 5, 115	5	**1:48.26**	201,252
1999	Banshee Breeze, 4, 124	R. Albarado	Silent Eskimo, 4, 114	Meadow Vista, 4, 109	4	1:50.02	197,718
1998	Escena, 5, 123	S. J. Sellers	One Rich Lady, 4, 113	Tomisue's Delight, 4, 118	5	1:50.19	199,020
1997	Gold n Delicious, 4, 113	C. H. Borel	Effectiveness, 4, 111	Everhope, 4, 111	10	1:52.87	104,718
1996	Serena's Song, 4, 124	G. L. Stevens	Halo America, 6, 117	Alcovy, 6, 117	9	1:50.30	109,493
1995	Fit to Lead, 5, 117	S. J. Sellers	Pennyhill Park, 5, 118	Low Key Affair, 4, 112	7	1:51.59	107,055
1994	Trishyde, 5, 117	C. J. McCarron	Eskimo's Angel, 5, 115	Ma Guerre, 4, 109	8	1:51.34	107,315
1993	Quilma (Chi), 6, 117	R. P. Romero	Fappies Cosy Miss, 5, 110	Hitch, 4, 112	6	1:50.80	71,240
1992	Bungalow, 5, 114	F. C. Torres	Til Forbid, 4, 113	Beth Believes, 6, 112	12	1:50.87	74,815
1991	Maskra's Lady, 4, 111	J. M. Johnson	Fit for a Queen, 5, 116	Under Oath, 5, 113	10	1:50.46	73,515
1990	A Penny Is a Penny, 5, 120	A. T. Gryder	Stoneleigh's Hope, 5, 115	Lady Hoolihan, 4, 112	7	1:51.20	70,980
1989	Stoneleigh's Hope, 4, 112	J. Deegan	Way It Should Be, 5, 111	Lt. Lao, 5, 116	8	1:52.60	71,435
1988	Lt. Lao, 4, 116	D. Brumfield	Lawyer Talk, 4, 111	She's a Mystery, 5, 111	9	1:49.60	72,215
1987	Infinidad (Chi), 5, 118	M. Solomone	Marianna's Girl, 4, 117	Queen Alexandra, 5, 126	8	1:50.60	64,815
1986	Queen Alexandra, 4, 117	D. Brumfield	Tide, 4, 111	Zenobia Empress, 5, 119	11	1:49.20	66,083
1985	Straight Edition, 5, 113	C. R. Woods Jr.	Dusty Gloves, 4, 110	Del Dun Gee, 5, 110	8	1:50.80	36,108
1984	Heatherten, 5, 124	S. Maple	Satiety, 5, 110	Hotsy Totsy, 4, 112	5	1:51.40	35,233
1983	Try Something New, 4, 121	P. Day	Naskra Magic, 4, 116	Header Card, 4, 114	5	1:51.60	35,328
1982	Classic Ambition, 4, 112	W. Gavidia	Beyond Reproof, 4, 113	Mean Martha, 4, 117	10	1:44.80	36,855
1981	Forever Cordial, 4, 114	D. Haire	Salud, 4, 114	Passolyn, 4, 118	10	1:45.40	23,205
1980	Likely Exchange, 6, 121	M. S. Sellers	Salzburg, 5, 116	Smooth Bore, 4, 115	9	1:45.00	23,026
1979	Table the Rumor, 5, 118	D. E. Whited	Likely Exchange, 5, 123	Pretty Delight, 4, 116	8	1:45.20	22,864
1978	Likely Exchange, 4, 113	J. McKnight	Time for Pleasure, 4, 123	Bold Rendezvous, 3, 114	5	1:45.40	13,894
1977	Go On Dreaming, 5, 115	P. Nicolo	B. J. King, 5, 114	Kittyluck, 4, 117	7	1:43.80	14,381
1976	Pago Hop, 4, 116	H. Arroyo	Flama Ardiente, 4, 122	Precious Proof, 5, 113	6	1:38.40	14,056
1975	Bundler, 4, 120	J. Nichols	Jay Bar Pet, 4, 112	Tappahannock, 4, 116	7	1:39.40	14,511

Named for the fleur de lis ("lily" in French), symbol of the city of Louisville. Grade 3 1998-2001. 1 mile 1975-'76. 1 1/16 miles 1977-'82. Four-year-olds and up 1983-'89, 1987-'89.

Florida Derby

Grade 1 in 2008. Gulfstream Park, three-year-olds, 1 1/8 miles, dirt. Held March 29, 2008, with a gross value of $1,000,000. First held in 1952. First graded in 1973. Stakes record 1:46.80 (1957 Gen. Duke).

Year	Winner	Jockey	Second	Third	Strs	Time	1st Purse
2008	Big Brown, 3, 122	K. J. Desormeaux	Smooth Air, 3, 122	Tomcito, 3, 122	12	1:48.16	$600,000
2007	Scat Daddy, 3, 122	E. S. Prado	Notional, 3, 122	Chelokee, 3, 122	9	1:49.00	600,000
2006	Barbaro, 3, 122	E. S. Prado	Sharp Humor, 3, 122	Sunriver, 3, 122	11	1:49.01	600,000
2005	High Fly, 3, 122	J. D. Bailey	Noble Causeway, 3, 122	B. B. Best, 3, 122	9	1:49.43	600,000
2004	Friends Lake, 3, 122	R. Migliore	Value Plus, 3, 122	The Cliff's Edge, 3, 122	10	1:51.38	600,000
2003	Empire Maker, 3, 122	J. D. Bailey	Trust N Luck, 3, 122	Indy Dancer, 3, 122	7	1:49.05	600,000
2002	Harlan's Holiday, 3, 122	E. S. Prado	Blue Burner, 3, 122	Peekskill, 3, 122	11	1:48.80	600,000
2001	Monarchos, 3, 122	J. F. Chavez	Outofthebox, 3, 122	Invisible Ink, 3, 122	13	1:49.95	600,000
2000	Hal's Hope, 3, 122	R. I. Velez	High Yield, 3, 122	Tahkodha Hills, 3, 122	10	1:51.49	450,000
1999	Vicar, 3, 122	S. J. Sellers	Wondertross, 3, 122	Cat Thief, 3, 122	10	1:50.83	450,000
1998	‡Cape Town, 3, 122	S. J. Sellers	Lil's Lad, 3, 122	Halory Hunter, 3, 122	6	1:49.21	450,000
1997	Captain Bodgit, 3, 122	A. O. Solis	Pulpit, 3, 122	Frisk Me Now, 3, 122	8	1:50.60	300,000
1996	Unbridled's Song, 3, 122	M. E. Smith	Editor's Note, 3, 122	Skip Away, 3, 122	9	1:47.85	300,000
1995	Thunder Gulch, 3, 122	M. E. Smith	Suave Prospect, 3, 122	Mecke, 3, 122	10	1:49.70	300,000
1994	Holy Bull, 3, 122	M. E. Smith	Ride the Rails, 3, 122	Halo's Image, 3, 122	14	1:47.66	300,000
1993	Bull Inthe Heather, 3, 122	W. S. Ramos	Storm Tower, 3, 122	Wallenda, 3, 122	13	1:51.38	300,000
1992	Technology, 3, 122	J. D. Bailey	Dance Floor, 3, 122	Pistols and Roses, 3, 122	12	1:50.72	300,000
1991	Fly So Free, 3, 122	J. A. Santos	Strike the Gold, 3, 118	Hansel, 3, 122	10	1:50.44	300,000
1990	Unbridled, 3, 122	P. Day	Slavic, 3, 122	Run Turn, 3, 122	9	1:52.00	300,000
1989	Mercedes Won, 3, 122	E. Fires	Western Playboy, 3, 118	Big Stanley, 3, 122	11	1:49.60	300,000
1988	Brian's Time, 3, 118	R. P. Romero	Forty Niner, 3, 122	Notebook, 3, 122	10	1:49.80	300,000
1987	Cryptoclearance, 3, 122	J. A. Santos	No More Flowers, 3, 118	Talinum, 3, 122	9	1:49.60	300,000
1986	Snow Chief, 3, 122	A. O. Solis	Badger Land, 3, 122	Mogambo, 3, 122	16	1:51.80	300,000
1985	Proud Truth, 3, 122	J. Velasquez	Irish Sur, 3, 122	Do It Again Dan, 3, 122	11	1:50.00	180,000
1984	Swale, 3, 122	L. A. Pincay Jr.	Dr. Carter, 3, 122	Darn That Alarm, 3, 122	9	1:47.60	180,000
1983	Croeso, 3, 118	F. Olivares	Copelan, 3, 122	Law Talk, 3, 118	13	1:49.80	150,000
1982	Timely Writer, 3, 122	J. Fell	Star Gallant, 3, 122	Our Escapade, 3, 122	7	1:49.60	150,000
1981	Lord Avie, 3, 122	C. J. McCarron	Akureyri, 3, 122	Linnleur, 3, 118	11	1:50.40	147,388
1980	Plugged Nickle, 3, 122	B. Thornburg	Naked Sky, 3, 122	Lord Gallant, 3, 118	8	1:50.20	110,000
1979	Spectacular Bid, 3, 122	R. J. Franklin	Lot o' Gold, 3, 122	Fantasy 'n Reality, 3, 122	7	1:48.80	115,000
1978	Alydar, 3, 122	J. Velasquez	Believe It, 3, 122	Dr. Valeri, 3, 122	7	1:47.00	100,000
1977	Coined Silver, 3, 118	B. Thornburg	Nearly On Time, 3, 122	Fort Prevel, 3, 122	8	1:48.80	68,700
	Ruthie's Native, 3, 122	C. Perret	For The Moment, 3, 122	Sir Sir, 3, 122	10	1:50.20	69,900
1976	Honest Pleasure, 3, 122	B. Baeza	Great Contractor, 3, 122	Proud Birdie, 3, 122	6	1:47.80	91,440
1975	Prince Thou Art, 3, 118	B. Baeza	Sylvan Place, 3, 118	Foolish Pleasure, 3, 122	9	1:50.40	94,440
1974	Judger, 3, 118	L. A. Pincay Jr.	Cannonade, 3, 122	Buck's Bid, 3, 118	16	1:49.00	130,200
1973	Royal and Regal, 3, 122	W. Blum	Forego, 3, 118	Restless Jet, 3, 122	8	1:47.40	78,120

Honoring Gulfstream Park's home state, the race name first was used at Tampa in 1926. After a two-year hiatus, the race was run at Hialeah Park. In 1937, Hialeah's leading three-year-old race was renamed the Flamingo S. ‡Lil's Lad finished first, DQ to second, 1998. Two divisions 1977.

Flower Bowl Invitational Stakes

Grade 1 in 2008. Belmont Park, three-year-olds and up, fillies and mares, 1¼ miles, turf. Held September 29, 2007, with a gross value of $600,000. First held in 1978. First graded in 1980. Stakes record 1:59.05 (2007 Lahudood [GB]).

Year	Winner	Jockey	Second	Third	Strs	Time	1st Purse
2007	**Lahudood (GB)**, 4, 119	A. Garcia	Rosinka (Ire), 4, 119	Wait a While, 4, 121	9	**1:59.05**	$360,000
2006	**Honey Ryder**, 5, 121	J. R. Velazquez	Film Maker, 6, 119	Jade Queen, 3, 115	5	2:02.47	360,000
2005	**Riskaverse**, 6, 121	J. A. Santos	Wonder Again, 6, 121	Film Maker, 5, 119	9	2:00.27	450,000
2004	**Riskaverse**, 5, 118	C. H. Velasquez	Commercante (Fr), 4, 118	Moscow Burning, 4, 120	8	2:04.65	450,000
2003	**Dimitrova**, 3, 114	J. D. Bailey	Walzerkoenigin, 4, 120	Heat Haze (GB), 4, 123	7	2:02.74	450,000
2002	**Kazzia (Ger)**, 3, 118	J. F. Chavez	Turtle Bow (Fr), 3, 115	Mot Juste (GB), 4, 118	7	2:05.22	450,000
2001	**Lailani (GB)**, 3, 118	J. D. Bailey	England's Legend (Fr), 4, 123	Starine (Fr), 4, 120	6	2:01.88	450,000
2000	**Colstar**, 4, 116	J. Samyn	Snow Polina, 5, 121	Pico Teneriffe, 4, 115	5	2:01.78	450,000
1999	**Soaring Softly**, 4, 119	J. D. Bailey	Coretta (Ire), 5, 118	Mossflower, 5, 115	7	2:01.41	300,000
1998	**Auntie Mame**, 4, 121	J. R. Velazquez	B. A. Valentine, 5, 114	Bahr (GB), 3, 118	5	1:59.33	240,000
1997	**Yashmak**, 3, 114	C. S. Nakatani	Maxzene, 4, 123	Memories of Silver, 4, 123	8	1:59.73	240,000
1996	**Chelsey Flower**, 5, 115	R. G. Davis	Powder Bowl, 4, 116	Electric Society (Ire), 5, 118	10	2:05.96	210,000
1995	**Northern Emerald**, 5, 113	R. B. Perez	Danish (Ire), 4, 116	Duda, 4, 113	10	2:06.68	120,000
1994	**Dahlia's Dreamer**, 5, 112	J. F. Chavez	Alywow, 3, 114	Danish (Ire), 3, 113	12	2:05.52	120,000
1993	**Far Out Beast**, 6, 111	J. Samyn	Dahlia's Dreamer, 4, 110	Lady Blessington (Fr), 5, 118	10	2:03.88	90,000
1992	**Christiecat**, 5, 116	J. Samyn	Ratings, 4, 117	Plenty of Grace, 5, 115	9	2:01.06	120,000
1991	**Lady Shirl**, 4, 117	R. Migliore	Franc Argument, 5, 111	Christiecat, 4, 120	12	2:02.43	120,000
1990	**Laugh and Be Merry**, 5, 115	W. H. McCauley	Foresta, 4, 115	Gaily Gaily (Ire), 7, 117	13	2:00.20	78,840
1989	**River Memories**, 5, 112	P. Day	Capades, 3, 116	Miss Unnameable, 5, 116	11	2:06.80	74,880
1988	**Gaily Gaily (Ire)**, 5, 109	J. A. Krone	Love You by Heart, 3, 113	Princely Proof, 5, 116	12	2:02.80	76,800
1987	**Slew's Exceller**, 5, 113	J. A. Santos	Videogenic, 5, 118	Fiesta Gal, 3, 114	8	2:02.20	91,020
1986	**dh-Dismasted**, 4, 115	J. Samyn		Cope of Flowers, 4, 112	12	2:00.00	52,152
	dh-Scoot, 3, 106	W. Shoemaker					
1985	**Dawn's Curtsey**, 3, 111	E. Maple	Vers La Caisse, 4, 116	Agacerie, 4, 117	9	2:02.20	87,540
1984	**Rossard (Den)**, 4, 117	L. A. Pincay Jr.	Aspen Rose, 4, 115	Persian Tiara (Ire), 4, 116	9	2:03.40	72,840
1983	**First Approach**, 5, 117	J. Velasquez	If Winter Comes, 5, 113	Mintage (Fr), 4, 111	8	2:02.20	68,160
1982	**Trevita (Ire)**, 5, 117	R. Hernandez	Hunston (GB), 4, 108	Hush Dear, 4, 112	12	2:01.40	71,880
1981	**Rokeby Rose**, 4, 114	J. Fell	De La Rose, 3, 116	Euphrosyne, 5, 110	6	2:01.60	67,220
1980	**Just a Game (Ire)**, 4, 124	D. Brumfield	Hey Babe, 4, 114	Euphrosyne, 4, 112	11	2:00.80	68,640
1979	**Pearl Necklace**, 5, 125	W. Shoemaker	The Very One, 4, 112	Terpsichorist, 4, 118	8	2:02.20	68,160
1978	**Waya (Fr)**, 4, 120	A. T. Cordero Jr.	Magnificence, 4, 108	Leave Me Alone, 5, 108	7	2:00.60	32,490

Named for Brookmeade Stable's 1956 Ladies H. winner Flower Bowl (1952 f. by *Alibhai), dam of champion Bowl of Flowers and leading sires Graustark and His Majesty. Grade 2 1980-'81. Flower Bowl H. 1978-'93. Flower Bowl Invitational H. 1994-2000. Dirt 1987. Dead heat for first 1986.

Forego Stakes

Grade 1 in 2008. Saratoga Race Course, three-year-olds and up, 7 furlongs, dirt. Held September 1, 2007, with a gross value of $250,000. First held in 1980. First graded in 1983. Stakes record 1:21 (1988 Quick Call).

Year	Winner	Jockey	Second	Third	Strs	Time	1st Purse
2007	**Midnight Lute**, 4, 117	S. Bridgmohan	Benny the Bull, 4, 117	Attila's Storm, 5, 119	10	1:21.26	$150,000
2006	**Pomeroy**, 5, 117	J. R. Velazquez	War Front, 4, 121	Friendly Island, 5, 119	11	1:23.39	150,000
2005	**Mass Media**, 4, 117	J. Castellano	Battle Won, 5, 121	Silver Wagon, 4, 117	6	1:22.59	150,000
2004	**Midas Eyes**, 4, 117	E. S. Prado	Clock Stopper, 4, 114	Gygistar, 5, 114	9	1:22.2	150,000
2003	**Aldebaran**, 5, 123	J. D. Bailey	Najran, 4, 114	Gygistar, 4, 119	7	1:21.26	150,000
2002	**Orientate**, 4, 122	J. D. Bailey	Aldebaran, 4, 115	Multiple Choice, 4, 114	8	1:15.68	150,000
2001	**Delaware Township**, 5, 116	J. D. Bailey	Left Bank, 4, 115	Alannan, 5, 117	9	1:15.53	150,000
2000	**Shadow Caster**, 4, 113	J. F. Chavez	Intidab, 7, 118	Successful Appeal, 4, 119	10	1:15.00	150,000
1999	**Crafty Friend**, 6, 119	G. L. Stevens	Affirmed Success, 5, 119	Sir Bear, 6, 119	9	1:21.32	150,000
1998	**Affirmed Success**, 4, 115	J. F. Chavez	Receiver, 5, 114	Purple Passion, 4, 114	4	1:21.98	120,000
1997	**Score a Birdie**, 6, 113	W. H. McCauley	Victor Cooley, 4, 120	Royal Haven, 5, 120	8	1:22.47	120,000
1996	**Langfuhr**, 4, 110	J. F. Chavez	Top Account, 4, 115	Lite the Fuse, 5, 121	7	1:21.90	90,000
1995	**Not Surprising**, 5, 121	R. G. Davis	Our Emblem, 4, 113	Lite the Fuse, 4, 123	4	1:21.91	64,200
1994	**American Chance**, 5, 113	P. Day	Evil Bear, 4, 114	Go for Gin, 3, 117	7	1:22.74	66,000
1993	**Birdonthewire**, 4, 117	M. E. Smith	Harlan, 4, 110	Senor Speedy, 6, 117	9	1:21.88	73,080
1992	**Rubiano**, 5, 124	J. A. Krone	Drummond Lane, 5, 115	Diablo, 4, 112	8	1:22.54	70,080
1991	**Housebuster**, 4, 126	C. Perret	Senor Speedy, 4, 112	Clever Trevor, 5, 120	6	1:21.08	69,480
1990	**Lay Down**, 5, 117	C. W. Antley	Quick Call, 6, 120	Traskwood, 4, 117	6	1:22.80	51,840
1989	**Quick Call**, 5, 116	P. Day	Dancing Spree, 4, 117	Sewickley, 4, 119	5	1:21.80	67,920
1988	**Quick Call**, 4, 110	P. Day	Mawsuff (GB), 5, 110	High Brite, 4, 122	6	**1:21.00**	68,520
1987	**Groovy**, 4, 132	A. T. Cordero Jr.	Purple Mountain, 5, 113	Sun Master, 6, 118	6	1:21.80	81,060
1986	**Groovy**, 3, 118	J. A. Santos	Turkoman, 4, 124	Innamorato, 5, 110	8	1:21.20	83,820
1985	**Ziggy's Boy**, 3, 115	A. T. Cordero Jr.	Taylor's Special, 4, 124	Knight of Armor, 5, 112	5	1:21.20	66,510
1984	**Mugatea**, 4, 111	R. G. Davis	Eskimo, 4, 108	I Enclose, 4, 111	6	1:22.40	53,370
1983	**Maudlin**, 5, 119	A. T. Cordero Jr.	Danebo, 5, 118	Singh Tu, 4, 113	5	1:21.60	32,580
1982	**Engine One**, 4, 112	R. Hernandez	Rise Jim, 6, 121	Pass the Tab, 4, 120	5	1:21.20	33,360
1981	**Fappiano**, 4, 119	A. T. Cordero Jr.	Herb Water, 4, 108	Guilty Conscience, 5, 112	5	1:33.80	51,270
1980	**Tanthem**, 5, 114	J. Velasquez	Dr. Patches, 6, 114	Hold Your Tricks, 5, 116	7	1:35.00	51,030

Named for Mrs. Martha Gerry's Racing Hall of Fame member, 1974, '75, '76 Horse of the Year, and '74, '75, '76, '77

Racing — Graded Stakes 323

Woodward H. (G1) winner Forego (1970 g. by *Forli). Grade 3 1983. Grade 2 1984-2000. Forego H. 1980-2004. Held at Belmont Park 1980-'81. 1 mile 1980-'81. 6 furlongs 2000-'02.

Fort Marcy Handicap

Grade 3 in 2008. Aqueduct, three-year-olds and up, 1 1/16 miles, turf. Held April 27, 2008, with a gross value of $110,600. First held in 1975. First graded in 1980. Stakes record 1:40.88 (2000 Spindrift [Ire]).

Year	Winner	Jockey	Second	Third	Strs	Time	1st Purse
2008	**Silver Tree**, 8, 117	E. S. Prado	Operation Red Dawn, 6, 114	Twilight Meteor, 4, 116	7	1:42.07	$66,360
2007	**Woodlander**, 5, 114	A. Garcia	Golden Commander, 7, 116	Grand Couturier (GB), 4, 116	7	1:44.88	68,460
2006	**Foreverness**, 7, 115	E. Coa	Pa Pa Da, 5, 114	Sabre d'Argent, 6, 115	6	1:42.99	65,400
2005	**Better Talk Now**, 6, 123	R. A. Dominguez	Remind, 5, 117	Ecclesiastic, 4, 115	5	1:42.74	65,640
2004	**Chilly Rooster**, 4, 113	S. Uske	Union Place, 5, 113	Slew Valley, 7, 119	8	1:42.47	66,840
2003	**Saint Verre**, 5, 117	J. L. Espinoza	Windsor Castle, 5, 119	Judge's Case, 6, 115	8	1:33.77	70,500
2002	**Pyrus**, 4, 113	E. S. Prado	Proud Man, 4, 116	Capsized, 6, 113	8	1:44.53	67,260
2001	**Strategic Mission**, 6, 118	R. Migliore	Pine Dance, 4, 116	Legal Jousting (Ire), 4, 114	9	1:41.62	67,740
2000	**Spindrift (Ire)**, 5, 115	J. Samyn	Middlesex Drive, 5, 118	Wised Up, 5, 114	9	**1:40.88**	67,680
1999	**Wised Up**, 4, 112	M. J. Luzzi	N B Forrest, 7, 116	La-Faah (Ire), 4, 114	11	1:45.03	69,660
1998	**Subordination**, 4, 118	J. F. Chavez	Fortitude, 5, 116	Crimson Guard, 6, 110	6	1:35.24	67,620
1997	**Influent**, 6, 117	J. Samyn	Slicious (GB), 5, 115	Montjoy, 5, 117	8	1:47.59	67,140
1996	**Warning Glance**, 5, 119	M. E. Smith	Shahid (GB), 4, 115	Grand Continental, 5, 113	10	1:42.48	51,450
1995	**Fourstars Allstar**, 7, 118	J. A. Santos	Chief Master, 5, 112	A in Sociology, 5, 118	8	1:41.69	50,250
1994	**Adam Smith (GB)**, 6, 118	M. E. Smith	Halissee, 4, 117	Nijinsky's Gold, 5, 113	7	1:42.49	49,650
1993	**Adam Smith (GB)**, 5, 112	J. Samyn	Kiri's Clown, 4, 114	Casino Magistrate, 4, 113	11	1:42.30	55,260
1992	**Maxigroom**, 4, 117	J. A. Krone	Colchis Island (Ire), 7, 111	Buchman, 5, 111	6	1:42.66	53,460
1991	**Stage Colony**, 4, 115	C. Perret	Chenin Blanc, 5, 114	Scottish Monk, 8, 116	9	1:42.38	54,630
1990	**Crystal Moment**, 5, 113	S. N. Chavez	Impersonator, 5, 112	Wanderkin, 7, 117	7	1:43.40	53,010
1989	**Arlene's Valentine**, 4, 112	J. A. Krone	Fourstardave, 4, 113	Sunshine Forever, 4, 126	5	1:50.20	52,920
1988	**Equalize**, 6, 115	J. A. Santos	All Hands On Deck, 6, 109	Glaros (Fr), 6, 111	12	1:42.60	89,340
1987	**Dance of Life**, 4, 120	R. P. Romero	Regal Flier, 6, 113	Iroko (GB), 5, 113	7	1:45.00	84,240
	Glaros (Fr), 5, 112	E. Maple	Onyxly, 6, 113	Explosive Dancer, 5, 111	8	1:45.00	85,200
1986	**Onyxly**, 5, 117	J. A. Santos	Equalize, 4, 114	Lieutenant's Lark, 4, 117	9	1:42.20	55,890
1985	**Forzando (GB)**, 4, 120	J. Velasquez	Native Raid, 5, 115	Solidified, 4, 113	6	1:46.00	54,180
1984	**Hero's Honor**, 4, 115	J. D. Bailey	Super Sunrise (GB), 5, 126	Reinvested, 5, 113	9	1:43.60	54,270
1983	**John's Gold**, 4, 108	A. Graell	Acaroid, 5, 115	Beagle (Arg), 5, 105	8	1:47.40	36,600
1982	**Folge**, 4, 110	J. Velasquez	Johnny Dance, 4, 114	St. Brendan, 4, 116	12	1:42.80	36,060
1981	**Masked Marvel (Ire)**, 5, 112	R. I. Encinas	Blue Ensign, 4, 116	Freeo, 4, 113	8	1:44.80	33,330
	Key to Content, 4, 117	J. Fell	Ghazwan (Ire), 4, 114	Contare, 5, 107	7	1:46.00	33,060
1980	**Sten**, 5, 115	C. B. Asmussen	Native Courier, 5, 126	Told, 4, 113	10	1:44.00	35,460
1979	**Uncle Pokey (GB)**, 5, 113	J. Cruguet	Alias Smith, 6, 114	Proud Arion, 5, 111	7	1:45.60	32,550
1978	**True Colors**, 4, 114	E. Maple	Proud Arion, 4, 112	Cinteelo, 5, 119	5	1:42.80	25,410
	Tiller, 4, 112	J. Fell	Noble Dancer (GB), 6, 127	Arachnoid, 5, 111	5	1:41.80	25,410
1976	**Bold Sunrise**, 3, 109	R. W. Cox	Lean To, 3, 113	Scrutiny, 3, 112	10	1:37.60	19,500
1975	***Apollo Nine**, 8, 110	M. Venezia	Silver Badge, 4, 112	Bold Play, 5, 112	11	1:23.00	24,630
	Beau Buck, 5, 113	J. Cruguet	Ribot Grande, 5, 112	New Alibhai, 7, 112	8	1:22.40	24,510

Named for Rokeby Stable's Racing Hall of Fame member, 1970 Horse of the Year, and '70 Man o' War S. winner Fort Marcy (1964 g. by *Amerigo). Held at Belmont Park 1975, 1981, 1987-'88. Not held 1977. 7 furlongs 1975. 1 mile 1998, 2003. Dirt 1998, 2003. Originally scheduled on turf 2003. Two divisions 1975, '78, '81, '87. Nonwinners of a stakes 1975.

Forward Gal Stakes

Grade 2 in 2008. Gulfstream Park, three-year-olds, fillies, dirt. Held February 9, 2008, with a gross value of $150,000. First held in 1981. First graded in 1986. Stakes record 1:21.76 (1997 Glitter Woman).

Year	Winner	Jockey	Second	Third	Strs	Time	1st Purse
2008	**Bsharpsonata**, 3, 120	E. Camacho	Keep the Peace, 3, 116	Melissa Jo, 3, 117	7	1:23.09	$90,000
2007	**Forever Together**, 3, 118	E. Trujillo	Silver Knockers, 3, 116	You Asked, 3, 117	7	1:22.60	90,000
2006	**Miraculous Miss**, 3, 120	J. Rose	India, 3, 116	Misty Rosette, 3, 120	10	1:22.78	90,000
2005	**Letgomyecho**, 3, 115	J. Castellano	Little Money Down, 3, 115	Hot Storm, 3, 121	7	1:23.24	90,000
2004	**Madcap Escapade**, 3, 121	J. D. Bailey	La Reina, 3, 121	Frenchglen, 3, 115	5	1:22.97	90,000
2003	**Midnight Cry**, 3, 117	E. S. Prado	Final Round, 3, 117	Chimichurri, 3, 121	8	1:22.55	60,000
2002	**Take the Cake**, 3, 117	R. R. Douglas	A New Twist, 3, 121	Cherokee Girl, 3, 117	7	1:25.47	60,000
2001	**Gold Mover**, 3, 121	J. D. Bailey	Hazino, 3, 114	Thunder Bertie, 3, 118	5	1:22.43	60,000
2000	**Miss Inquisitive**, 3, 114	T. G. Turner	Swept Away, 3, 118	Regally Appealing, 3, 118	9	1:22.25	45,000
1999	**China Storm**, 3, 114	P. Day	Three Ring, 3, 121	Extended Applause, 3, 112	5	1:23.69	45,000
1998	**Uanme**, 3, 113	S. J. Sellers	Diamond On the Run, 3, 114	Holy Capote, 3, 112	7	1:24.56	45,000
1997	**Glitter Woman**, 3, 114	M. E. Smith	City Band, 3, 121	Southern Playgirl, 3, 112	6	**1:21.76**	45,000
1996	**Mindy Gayle**, 3, 112	J. A. Krone	Marfa's Finale, 3, 113	Supah Jen, 3, 114	7	1:24.54	45,000
1995	**Chaposa Springs**, 3, 114	H. Castillo Jr.	Culver City, 3, 113	Mackenzie Slew, 3, 114	5	1:24.18	44,580
1994	**Mynameispanama**, 3, 113	M. Castaneda	Frigid Coed, 3, 116	Wonderlan, 3, 114	9	1:22.97	45,960
1993	**Sum Runner**, 3, 118	R. P. Romero	Boots 'n Jackie, 3, 121	Lunar Spook, 3, 118	9	1:23.67	45,270
1992	**Spinning Round**, 3, 118	J. A. Santos	Patty's Princess, 3, 118	Super Doer, 3, 118	5	1:24.45	44,550
1991	**Withallprobability**, 3, 114	C. Perret	Private Treasure, 3, 118	Far Out Nurse, 3, 112	8	1:22.50	48,240
1990	**Charon**, 3, 112	E. Fires	Trumpet's Blare, 3, 121	De La Devil, 3, 121	8	1:24.80	36,180
1989	**Open Mind**, 3, 118	A. T. Cordero Jr.	Surging, 3, 114	Georgies Doctor, 3, 118	9	1:24.20	36,780
1988	**On to Royalty**, 3, 114	C. Perret	Social Pro, 3, 122	Most Likely, 3, 112	10	1:23.20	37,020
1987	**Added Elegance**, 3, 121	J. Vasquez	Beau Love Flowers, 3, 112	Easter Mary, 3, 112	11	1:24.60	37,380

Year	Winner	Jockey	Second	Third	Strs	Time	1st Purse
1986	Noranc, 3, 116	W. H. McCauley	Dancing Danzig, 3, 112	I'm Sweets, 3, 121	8	1:23.80	$36,000
1985	Lucy Manette, 3, 114	C. Perret	Grand Glory, 3, 112	Boldly Dared, 3, 112	13	1:23.40	39,690
1984	Miss Oceana, 3, 121	E. Maple	Katrinka, 3, 112	Scorched Panties, 3, 121	5	1:22.40	24,108
1983	Unaccompanied, 3, 114	R. Woodhouse	Lisa's Capital, 3, 114	Quixotic Lady, 3, 113	15	1:23.40	28,203
1982	Trove, 3, 116	L. Saumell	Here's to Peg, 3, 112	Wendy's Ten, 3, 113	8	1:22.80	17,828
	All Manners, 3, 116	O. J. Londono	Acharmer, 3, 114	Smart Heiress, 3, 112	9	1:23.00	17,978
1981	Dame Mysterieuse, 3, 118	J. Samyn	Heavenly Cause, 3, 121	Masters Dream, 3, 113	10	1:22.20	26,040

Named for Aisco Stable's 1970 Florida-bred champion two-year-old filly Forward Gal (1968 f. by Native Charger). Formerly sponsored by Robert and Janice McNair's Stonerside Stable of Paris, Kentucky 2004-'06. Grade 3 1986-'90, 1997-2003. Forward Gal Breeders' Cup S. 1991-'95. Forward Gal S. 1996-2003. Stonerside Forward Gal S. 2004-'06. Two divisions 1982.

Fountain of Youth Stakes

Grade 2 in 2008. Gulfstream Park, three-year-olds, 1 1/16 miles, dirt. Held February 24, 2008, with a gross value of $350,000. First held in 1945. First graded in 1973. Stakes record 1:49 (2006 Corinthian [DQ to third]).

Year	Winner	Jockey	Second	Third	Strs	Time	1st Purse
2008	Cool Coal Man, 3, 118	K. J. Desormeaux	Elysium Fields, 3, 116	Court Vision, 3, 122	12	1:50.07	$210,000
2007	Scat Daddy, 3, 120	J. R. Velazquez	Stormello, 3, 122	Nobiz Like Shobiz, 3, 122	9	1:49.11	210,000
2006	‡First Samurai, 3, 120	E. S. Prado	Flashy Bull, 3, 116	Corinthian, 3, 116	10	1:49.00	180,000
2005	High Fly, 3, 120	J. D. Bailey	Bandini, 3, 116	B. B. Best, 3, 120	9	1:49.70	180,000
2004	Read the Footnotes, 3, 122	J. D. Bailey	Second of June, 3, 120	Silver Wagon, 3, 120	8	1:42.71	150,000
2003	Trust N Luck, 3, 122	C. H. Velasquez	Supah Blitz, 3, 120	Midway Cat, 3, 116	8	1:43.33	120,000
2002	Booklet, 3, 122	J. F. Chavez	Harlan's Holiday, 3, 122	Blue Burner, 3, 116	8	1:44.49	120,000
2001	Songandaprayer, 3, 117	E. S. Prado	Outofthebox, 3, 114	City Zip, 3, 117	11	1:43.48	120,000
2000	High Yield, 3, 117	P. Day	Hal's Hope, 3, 117	Elite Mercedes, 3, 117	11	1:42.56	120,000
1999	Vicar, 3, 114	S. J. Sellers	Cat Thief, 3, 119	Certain, 3, 117	10	1:45.64	120,000
1998	Lil's Lad, 3, 112	J. D. Bailey	Coronado's Quest, 3, 119	Halory Hunter, 3, 112	4	1:42.63	120,000
1997	Pulpit, 3, 112	S. J. Sellers	Blazing Sword, 3, 117	Captain Bodgit, 3, 117	9	1:41.86	120,000
1996	Built for Pleasure, 3, 112	G. Boulanger	Unbridled's Song, 3, 119	Victory Speech, 3, 114	9	1:43.64	120,000
1995	Thunder Gulch, 3, 119	M. E. Smith	Suave Prospect, 3, 117	Jambalaya Jazz, 3, 119	12	1:43.21	120,000
1994	Dehere, 3, 119	C. Perret	Go for Gin, 3, 119	Ride the Rails, 3, 117	6	1:44.70	120,000
1993	Duc d'Sligovil, 3, 112	J. A. Krone	Bull Inthe Heather, 3, 113	Silver of Silver, 3, 122	9	1:45.16	113,094
	Storm Tower, 3, 113	R. Wilson	Great Navigator, 3, 117	Kissin Kris, 3, 117	9	1:44.98	113,094
1992	Dance Floor, 3, 122	C. W. Antley	‡Pistols and Roses, 3, 119	Tiger Tiger, 3, 117	11	1:45.32	150,258
1991	Fly So Free, 3, 122	J. A. Santos	Moment of True, 3, 117	Subordinated Debt, 3, 113	9	1:44.60	73,737
1990	Shot Gun Scott, 3, 122	D. Penna	Smelly, 3, 119	Unbridled, 3, 117	13	1:44.60	77,427
1989	Dixieland Brass, 3, 112	R. P. Romero	Mercedes Won, 3, 122	Triple Buck, 3, 117	13	1:44.60	78,000
1988	Forty Niner, 3, 122	E. Maple	Notebook, 3, 122	Buoy, 3, 119	9	1:43.20	98,991
1987	Bet Twice, 3, 122	C. Perret	No More Flowers, 3, 112	Gone West, 3, 114	9	1:43.40	100,482
1986	Ensign Rhythm, 3, 112	J. M. Pezua	Jig's Haven, 3, 113	Regal Dreamer, 3, 117	10	1:45.60	57,210
	My Prince Charming, 3, 112	J. A. Santos	Mykawa, 3, 117	Papal Power, 3, 122	10	1:45.00	78,060
1985	Proud Truth, 3, 112	J. Velasquez	Stephan's Odyssey, 3, 122	Do It Again Dan, 3, 112	14	1:43.60	106,860
1984	Darn That Alarm, 3, 112	M. Venezia	Counterfeit Money, 3, 112	Swale, 3, 122	8	1:43.60	73,200
1983	Highland Park, 3, 122	D. Brumfield	Thalassocrat, 3, 117	Chumming, 3, 117	9	1:44.60	45,338
	Copelan, 3, 122	L. A. Pincay Jr.	Current Hope, 3, 117	Blink, 3, 112	8	1:43.60	44,888
1982	Star Gallant, 3, 117	S. Hawley	Distinctive Pro, 3, 117	Cut Away, 3, 113	9	1:43.20	54,630
1981	Akureyri, 3, 119	E. Maple	Pleasant Colony, 3, 122	Lord Avie, 3, 122	9	1:44.40	47,697
1980	Naked Sky, 3, 112	J. D. Bailey	Joanie's Chief, 3, 122	Gold Stage, 3, 122	8	1:43.80	29,820
1979	Spectacular Bid, 3, 122	R. J. Franklin	Lot o' Gold, 3, 117	Bishop's Choice, 3, 122	6	1:41.20	35,880
1978	Sensitive Prince, 3, 114	M. Solomone	Believe It, 3, 122	Kissing U., 3, 113	11	1:41.00	22,170
1977	Ruthie's Native, 3, 122	C. Perret	‡Steve's Friend, 3, 112	Fort Prevel, 3, 117	15	1:42.00	26,010
1976	Sonkisser, 3, 117	B. Baeza	Proud Birdie, 3, 122	Archie Beamish, 3, 113	7	1:43.80	22,770
1975	Greek Answer, 3, 122	M. Solomone	Decipher, 3, 115	Gatch, 3, 116	8	1:42.80	22,650
1974	Green Gambados, 3, 112	C. Baltazar	Judger, 3, 115	Eric's Champ, 3, 112	15	1:42.40	46,440
1973	Shecky Greene, 3, 122	B. Baeza	Twice a Prince, 3, 117	My Gallant, 3, 112	6	1:43.80	22,590

Named for the spring that granted eternal youth, sought by Spanish explorer Ponce de Leon in Florida. Grade 3 1973-'81. Grade 1 1999-2003. Fountain of Youth H. 1947-'56, 1958. Not held 1946, '48, '52. 1 mile 70 yards 1945, '47. 6 furlongs 1947. 1 1/16 miles 1949-'51, 1953-2004. Two-year-olds 1945-'47. Two divisions 1983, '86, '93. Held in March and December 1947. ‡Fort Prevel finished second, DQ to third, 1977. ‡Careful Gesture finished second, DQ to fifth, 1992. ‡Corinthian finished first, DQ to third, 2006.

Fourstardave Handicap

Grade 2 in 2008. Saratoga Race Course, three-year-olds and up, 1 1/16 miles, turf. Held August 5, 2007, with a gross value of $150,000. First held in 1985. First graded in 1988. Stakes record 1:38.91 (1991 Fourstardave).

Year	Winner	Jockey	Second	Third	Strs	Time	1st Purse
2007	Silver Tree, 7, 118	K. J. Desormeaux	Drum Major, 5, 116	Host (Chi), 7, 118	7	1:41.88	$90,000
2006	Remarkable News (Ven), 4, 117	J. Castellano	Ashkal Way (Ire), 4, 116	Diamond Green (Fr), 4, 115	9	1:40.81	90,000
2005	Leroidesanimaux (Brz), 5, 122	J. R. Velazquez	Silver Tree, 5, 117	Steel Light, 4, 117	6	1:39.92	120,000
2004	Nothing to Lose, 4, 117	J. R. Velazquez	Silver Tree, 4, 117	Royal Regalia, 6, 114	10	1:39.57	120,000
2003	Trademark (SAf), 7, 118	R. Migliore	Quest Star, 4, 116	Tap the Admiral, 5, 117	11	1:39.29	120,000
2002	Capsized, 6, 115	J. A. Santos	Pure Prize, 4, 119	Pyrus, 4, 113	5	1:50.90	120,000

Racing — Graded Stakes 325

Year	Winner	Jockey	Second	Third	Strs	Time	1st Purse
2001	Dr. Kashnikow, 4, 113	J. R. Velazquez	Tubrok, 4, 113	Aly's Alley, 5, 117	12	1:39.30	$120,000
2000	Hap, 4, 118	J. D. Bailey	Altibr, 5, 115	Weatherbird, 5, 112	11	1:40.24	120,000
1999	Comic Strip, 4, 115	P. Day	Divide and Conquer, 5, 114	Bomfim, 6, 113	11	1:41.76	90,000
1998	Wild Event, 5, 116	M. Guidry	Bomfim, 5, 114	Rob 'n Gin, 4, 119	11	1:39.25	68,940
1997	Soviet Line (Ire), 7, 118	P. Day	Val's Prince, 5, 114	Outta My Way Man, 5, 114	7	1:39.99	67,500
1996	Da Hoss, 4, 113	J. R. Velazquez	Green Means Go, 4, 113	Rare Reason, 5, 118	13	1:40.54	71,100
1995	Pride of Summer, 7, 115	E. Maple	Fourstars Allstar, 7, 120	Jaggery John, 4, 120	8	1:40.85	69,240
1994	A in Sociology, 4, 115	J. Samyn	Namaqualand, 4, 113	Fourstars Allstar, 6, 120	9	1:41.23	68,340
1993	Lure, 4, 122	M. E. Smith	Fourstardave, 8, 122	Scott the Great, 7, 115	6	1:40.84	72,120
1992	Now Listen, 5, 119	J. R. Velazquez	Crackedbell, 7, 119	Cold Hoist, 4, 115	5	1:36.64	71,640
1991	Fourstardave, 6, 115	M. E. Smith	Who's to Pay, 5, 122	Kate's Valentine, 6, 117	7	1:38.91	71,640
1990	Fourstardave, 5, 115	M. E. Smith	Foreign Survivor, 5, 119	Wanderkin, 7, 119	8	1:41.20	57,150
1989	Steinlen (GB), 6, 122	A. T. Cordero Jr.	Expensive Decision, 3, 117	Sparkling Wit, 3, 110	8	1:41.00	53,955
	Highland Springs, 5, 122	E. S. Prado	Fourstardave, 4, 122	Soviet Lad, 4, 115	7	1:41.60	53,955
1988	San's the Shadow, 4, 115	A. T. Cordero Jr.	My Big Boy, 5, 117	Real Courage, 5, 115	10	1:40.00	56,340
1987	Persian Mews (Ire), 4, 115	J. A. Santos	Island Sun, 5, 115	Explosive Dancer, 5, 115	8	1:42.00	51,120
	Duluth, 5, 117	J. Cruguet	Mourjane (Ire), 7, 115	I'm a Banker, 5, 115	8	1:41.20	51,120
1986	Mourjane (Ire), 6, 119	J. A. Santos	Island Sun, 4, 117	Little Look, 5, 115	6	1:42.80	33,960
1985	Roving Minstrel, 4, 119	A. T. Cordero Jr.	Four Bases, 6, 115	Alev (GB), 6, 117	8	1:45.40	33,540

Named for Richard M. Bomze's local favorite and 1990, '91 Daryl's Joy S. (G3) winner Fourstardave (1985 g. by Compliance); Fourstardave won a race at Saratoga for eight consecutive years and is one of four horses buried on the Saratoga grounds. Formerly named for R. K. C. Goh's multiple SW *Daryl's Joy (1966 c. by Stunning). Grade 3 1988-'99, 2002. Daryl's Joy S. 1985-'93, 1995. Daryl's Joy H. 1994. Fourstardave S. 1996-'97. 1 1/16 miles 1985-'91, 1993-2001. 1 mile 1992. Dirt 1992, 2002. Originally scheduled on turf 2002. Two divisions 1987, '89.

Frances A. Genter Stakes

Grade 3 in 2008. Calder Race Course, three-year-olds, fillies, 7 1/2 furlongs, turf. Held December 29, 2007, with a gross value of $100,000. First held in 1993. First graded in 2005. Stakes record 1:27.07 (2005 Laurafina).

Year	Winner	Jockey	Second	Third	Strs	Time	1st Purse
2007	Rutherienne, 3, 121	R. R. Douglas	dh-Pretoria Light, 3, 118		11	1:28.16	$58,280
			dh-Sweet Ransom, 3, 116				
2006	Bayou's Lassie, 3, 121	E. Trujillo	J'ray, 3, 121	Amansara, 3, 116	11	1:29.37	60,000
2005	Laurafina, 3, 116	R. Bejarano	Champagne Ending, 3, 121	More Than Promised, 3, 121	12	1:27.07	60,000
2004	R Obsession, 3, 121	M. R. Cruz	Our Exploit, 3, 116	Marina de Chavon, 3, 118	12	1:28.05	60,000
2003	Changing World, 3, 118	J. Bravo	Campsie Fells (UAE), 3, 121	Formal Miss, 3, 121	12	1:27.67	60,000
2002	Cellars Shiraz, 3, 121	E. Coa	Madeira Mist (Ire), 3, 118	May Gator, 3, 116	12	1:29.45	60,000
2001	Amelia, 3, 121	J. Castellano	Sara's Success, 3, 121	Ing Ing (Fr), 3, 118	12	1:28.56	60,000
2000	Zeiting (Ire), 3, 114	R. R. Douglas	Jemima (GB), 3, 113	Golden Saint, 3, 114	11	1:30.08	45,000
1999	Seducer, 3, 114	J. A. Santos	Crystal Symphony, 3, 119	Talamanca, 3, 113	11	1:28.67	60,000
1998	Justenuffheart, 3, 119	E. Coa	Terreavigne, 3, 114	Robyns Tune, 3, 114	12	1:28.68	60,000
1997	Oh My Butterfly, 3, 114	A. R. Toribio	More Silver, 3, 114	Basse Besogne (Ire), 3, 115	12	1:28.40	60,000
1996	Voy Si No, 3, 113	E. O. Nunez	Courtlin, 3, 113	Victoria Regia (Ire), 3, 114	11	1:28.19	30,000
1995	Majestic Dy, 3, 114	A. Toribio	With a Princess, 3, 114	Reign Dance, 3, 113	10	1:27.90	32,550
1994	Clean Wager, 3, 113	A. Toribio	Sunset Gal, 3, 112	Notable Sword, 3, 114	6	1:39.92	19,710
1993	Putthepowdertoit, 3, 116	R. R. Douglas	Liberada, 3, 116	Tenacious Tiffany, 3, 114	12	1:28.64	20,970

Named for Frances A. Genter (1898-1992), Eclipse Award-winning Florida breeder and owner. Dead heat for second 2007.

Frank E. Kilroe Mile Handicap

Grade 1 in 2008. Santa Anita Park, four-year-olds and up, 1 mile, turf. Held March 1, 2008, with a gross value of $300,000. First held in 1955. First graded in 1973. Stakes record 1:31.89 (1997 Atticus).

Year	Winner	Jockey	Second	Third	Strs	Time	1st Purse
2008	Ever a Friend, 5, 113	T. Baze	Artiste Royal (Ire), 7, 118	War Monger, 4, 116	6	1:33.37	$180,000
2007	Kip Deville, 4, 115	R. Migliore	Bayeux, 6, 114	Silent Name (Jpn), 5, 119	12	1:33.88	180,000
2006	Milk It Mick (GB), 5, 116	K. Desormeaux	Aragorn (Ire), 4, 119	Chinese Dragon, 4, 116	13	1:34.49	180,000
2005	Leroidesanimaux (Brz), 5, 119	J. K. Court	Buckland Manor, 5, 116	Sweet Return (GB), 5, 117	9	1:33.89	180,000
2004	Sweet Return (GB), 4, 119	G. L. Stevens	Singletary, 4, 117	Inesperado (Fr), 5, 116	14	1:33.87	210,000
2003	Redattore (Brz), 8, 120	A. O. Solis	Good Journey, 7, 124	Decarchy, 6, 118	11	1:34.94	240,000
2002	Decarchy, 5, 119	K. Desormeaux	Sarafan, 5, 116	Designed for Luck, 5, 117	11	1:34.04	180,000
2001	Road to Slew, 6, 117	L. A. Pincay Jr.	Val Royal (Fr), 5, 117	dh-Exchange Rate, 4, 115	10	1:35.96	240,000
				dh-Hawksley Hill (Ire), 8, 118			
2000	Commitisize, 5, 112	V. Espinoza	Chullo (Arg), 6, 117	Sultry Substitute, 5, 114	6	1:36.61	120,000
1999	Lord Smith (GB), 4, 116	G. K. Gomez	Hawksley Hill (Ire), 6, 122	Ladies Din, 4, 120	6	1:34.53	90,000
1998	Hawksley Hill (Ire), 5, 115	P. Day	Via Lombardia (Fr), 4, 119	A Magicman (Fr), 6, 120	10	1:34.84	101,190
1997	Atticus, 5, 117	C. S. Nakatani	Pinfloran (Fr), 5, 115	Rainbow Blues (Ire), 4, 121	9	1:31.89	97,400
1996	Tychonic (GB), 6, 116	G. L. Stevens	Debutant Trick, 6, 117	Silver Wizard, 6, 117	8	1:35.52	99,400
1995	College Town, 4, 117	L. A. Pincay Jr.	Romarin (Brz), 5, 120	Finder's Fortune, 6, 113	5	1:40.62	63,800
1994	Megan's Interco, 5, 118	C. A. Black	Tinners Way, 4, 115	Ibero (Arg), 7, 118	7	1:33.86	64,400
1993	Super Cat (Arg), 7, 114	C. S. Nakatani	Luthier Enchanteur, 6, 116	The Name's Jimmy, 4, 115	12	1:34.19	70,800
1992	Fly Till Dawn, 6, 120	L. A. Pincay Jr.	Itsallgreektome, 5, 123	Qathif, 5, 115	11	1:34.69	100,200
1991	Madjaristan, 5, 115	E. Delahoussaye	Trebizond, 5, 116	Major Moment, 5, 114	13	1:33.30	105,400
1990	Prized, 4, 124	E. Delahoussaye	Happy Toss (Arg), 5, 115	On the Menu, 4, 112	9	1:34.40	67,000
1989	Bello Horizonte (Ire), 6, 116	E. Delahoussaye	Sarhoob, 4, 117	Patchy Groundfog, 6, 117	7	1:36.20	64,700
1988	Mohamed Abdu (Ire), 4, 118	E. Delahoussaye	The Medic, 4, 118	The Scout, 4, 118	10	1:37.00	95,300

Year	Winner	Jockey	Second	Third	Strs	Time	1st Purse
1987	Thrill Show, 4, 121	W. Shoemaker	Skywalker, 5, 123	Aventino (Ire), 4, 115	9	1:36.00	$92,150
1986	Strawberry Road (Aus), 7, 125	G. L. Stevens	Hail Bold King, 5, 116	Schiller, 4, 115	7	2:03.40	76,800
1985	Fatih, 5, 116	W. Shoemaker	Tsunami Slew, 4, 119	Swoon, 7, 113	8	1:59.60	64,300
1984	Sir Pele, 5, 114	R. Q. Meza	Lucence, 5, 117	Ginger Brink (Fr), 4, 117	6	2:01.20	49,850
1983	Manantial (Chi), 5, 115	K. D. Black	Bohemian Grove, 7, 115	Western, 5, 120	5	2:03.40	46,500
1982	Perrault (GB), 5, 124	L. A. Pincay Jr.	Silveyville, 4, 117	Le Duc de Bar, 5, 111	7	2:04.60	47,700
1981	Premier Ministre, 5, 117	L. A. Pincay Jr.	Galaxy Libra (Ire), 5, 119	Bold Tropic (SAf), 6, 126	7	2:02.60	38,350
1980	Henschel, 6, 114	W. Shoemaker	Silver Eagle (Ire), 6, 120	Balzac, 5, 112	11	1:58.80	40,900
1979	Fluorescent Light, 5, 121	L. A. Pincay Jr.	†Waya (Fr), 5, 123	As de Copas (Arg), 6, 118	9	2:03.60	39,650
1978	Exceller, 5, 126	W. Shoemaker	Soldier's Lark, 4, 113	Tacitus, 4, 115	6	2:01.20	31,750
1977	Caucasus, 5, 124	F. Toro	dh-Exact Duplicate, 5, 115		9	2:00.00	33,900
			dh-Victorian Prince, 7, 116				
1976	Ga Hai, 5, 115	F. Olivares	Riot in Paris, 5, 120	Copper Mel, 4, 117	10	2:00.40	34,050
1975	Ga Hai, 4, 114	J. Vasquez	Indefatigable, 5, 115	Gold Standard, 4, 111	8	2:07.00	32,800
1974	Court Ruling, 4, 114	B. Baeza	Scantling, 4, 116	Barrydown, 4, 116	8	2:01.40	32,800
1973	River Buoy, 8, 117	D. Pierce	Wing Out, 5, 116	*Mazus, 5, 121	9	2:02.80	20,875
	Kobuk King, 7, 116	J. Lambert	Triggairo, 4, 114	Presidial, 4, 116	8	2:02.80	20,475

Named in honor of James E. "Jimmy" Kilroe (1912-'96), longtime racing secretary and handicapper at Santa Anita Park. Formerly named for Arcadia, California, city in which Santa Anita Park is located. Formerly named for the El Camino Real, "the Royal Road" through the California frontier. Grade 3 1973-'83, 1990-'94, 2000. Camino Real H. 1955-'59. Arcadia H. 1960-2000. 1 1/4 miles 1955-'71, 1973-'86. About 1 1/4 miles 1972. Dirt 1975-'76, '78, '83, '95, 2000. Originally scheduled on turf 2000. Three-year-olds and up 1955-'61. Two divisions 1973. Dead heat for second 1977. Dead heat for third 2001. World record 1997. Course record 1997. †Denotes female.

Frank J. De Francis Memorial Dash Stakes

Grade 1 in 2008. Laurel Park, three-year-olds and up, 6 furlongs, dirt. Held November 24, 2007, with a gross value of $250,000. First held in 1990. First graded in 1992. Stakes record 1:07.95 (2000 Richter Scale).

Year	Winner	Jockey	Second	Third	Strs	Time	1st Purse
2007	Benny the Bull, 4, 118	E. S. Prado	Talent Search, 4, 118	†Miraculous Miss, 4, 115	8	1:09.86	$150,000
2006	Thor's Echo, 4, 122	C. S. Nakatani	Diabolical, 3, 116	Nightmare Affair, 5, 122	9	1:08.71	180,000
2005	I'm the Tiger, 5, 118	J. D. Bailey	Tiger Heart, 4, 118	Clever Electrician, 6, 118	14	1:09.06	180,000
2004	Wildcat Heir, 4, 119	S. Elliott	Midas Eyes, 4, 123	Clock Stopper, 4, 119	10	1:09.45	180,000
2003	A Huevo, 7, 119	R. A. Dominguez	Shake You Down, 5, 123	Gators N Bears, 3, 115	10	1:08.90	180,000
2002	D'wildcat, 4, 122	J. F. Chavez	Deer Run, 5, 118	Sassy Hound, 5, 118	8	1:10.81	180,000
2001	Delaware Township, 5, 125	J. D. Bailey	Early Flyer, 3, 115	†Xtra Heat, 3, 117	7	1:09.00	180,000
2000	Richter Scale, 6, 123	R. Migliore	Just Call Me Carl, 5, 119	Falkenburg, 5, 114	4	**1:07.95**	180,000
1999	Yes It's True, 3, 114	J. D. Bailey	Good and Tough, 4, 123	Storm Punch, 4, 114	6	1:08.67	180,000
1998	Kelly Kip, 4, 117	J. Samyn	Affirmed Success, 4, 114	Partner's Hero, 4, 114	8	1:08.50	180,000
1997	Smoke Glacken, 3, 113	C. Perret	Wise Dusty, 6, 112	†Capote Belle, 4, 110	7	1:09.40	180,000
1996	Lite the Fuse, 5, 117	J. A. Krone	Meadow Monster, 5, 119	Prospect Bay, 4, 114	7	1:08.81	180,000
1995	Lite the Fuse, 4, 119	J. A. Krone	Crafty Dude, 6, 117	Hot Jaws, 5, 119	7	1:08.89	180,000
1994	Cherokee Run, 4, 114	C. Perret	Boom Towner, 6, 119	Fu Man Slew, 3, 107	11	1:08.92	180,000
1993	Montbrook, 3, 112	C. J. Ladner III	Lion Cavern, 4, 117	Flaming Emperor, 7, 114	9	1:08.71	180,000
1992	Superstrike (GB), 3, 112	D. Sorenson	†Parisian Flight, 4, 114	King Corrie, 4, 117	12	1:10.90	180,000
1991	Housebuster, 4, 126	C. Perret	Clever Trevor, 5, 123	†Safely Kept, 5, 121	6	1:08.76	180,000
1990	Northern Wolf, 4, 120	M. J. Luzzi	Glitterman, 5, 124	Sewickley, 5, 126	7	1:09.00	210,000

Named in honor of Frank J. De Francis (1927-'89), president and chairman of Laurel Park and Pimlico Race Course. Grade 3 1992-'93. Grade 2 1994-'98. Held at Pimlico 1990, 2004. Track record 2000. †Denotes female.

Fred W. Hooper Handicap

Grade 3 in 2008. Calder Race Course, three-year-olds and up, 1 1/8 miles, dirt. Held December 15, 2007, with a gross value of $100,000. First held in 1938. First graded in 1992. Stakes record 1:46.60 (1960 On-and-On).

Year	Winner	Jockey	Second	Third	Strs	Time	1st Purse
2007	Electrify, 4, 122	E. Trujillo	Summer Book, 6, 116	Imawildandcrazyguy, 3, 115	12	1:52.56	$57,660
2006	Hesanoldsalt, 3, 113	R. Bejarano	Rehoboth, 3, 117	Dry Martini, 3, 113	11	1:51.87	60,000
2005	Andromeda's Hero, 3, 114	R. Bejarano	Seek Gold, 5, 114	Whos Crying Now, 5, 117	9	1:53.46	60,000
2004	Pies Prospect, 3, 114	E. S. Prado	Twilight Road, 7, 115	Hear No Evil, 4, 112	11	1:50.74	60,000
2003	Predawn Raid, 4, 112	J. F. Chavez	Best of the Rest, 8, 122	Deeliteful Guy, 4, 112	9	1:52.47	60,000
2002	The Judge Sez Who, 3, 116	C. H. Velasquez	Best of the Rest, 7, 121	Dancing Guy, 7, 112	8	1:50.53	60,000
2001	Kiss a Native, 4, 116	C. H. Velasquez	Hal's Hope, 4, 115	Groomstick Stock's, 5, 113	8	1:51.05	60,000
2000	American Halo, 4, 111	C. Hunt	General Grant, 3, 112	Sir Bear, 7, 118	8	1:51.68	60,000
1999	Dancing Guy, 4, 120	J. C. Ferrer	Wicapi, 7, 118	Loon, 4, 112	8	1:50.83	60,000
1998	Wicapi, 6, 113	J. Bravo	Smuggler's Prize, 4, 111	Best of the Rest, 3, 115	5	1:52.15	60,000
1997	Shrike, 4, 113	J. D. Bailey	Wicapi, 5, 112	Sir Bear, 4, 113	11	1:50.50	60,000
1996	Cimarron Secret, 5, 115	J. A. Velez Jr.	Laughing Dan, 3, 114	Wicapi, 4, 116	8	1:52.70	60,000
1995	Bound by Honor, 4, 112	J. A. Krone	Bay Street Star, 4, 113	Halo's Image, 4, 121	10	1:51.81	60,000
1994	Halo's Image, 3, 117	G. Boulanger	Fight for Love, 4, 119	Migrating Moon, 4, 122	7	1:51.44	60,000
	Take Me Out, 6, 115	M. E. Smith	Migrating Moon, 4, 119	Meena, 6, 114	11	1:51.80	60,000
1993	Barkerville, 5, 114	R. P. Romero	Pistols and Roses, 4, 114	Count the Time, 4, 117	7	1:52.47	45,000
1992	Classic Seven, 4, 110	C. E. Lopez Sr.	Honest Ensign, 4, 111	Le Merle Blanc, 4, 112	13	1:53.01	102,960
1990	Public Account, 5, 117	H. Castillo Jr.	Zalipour, 3, 114	Cefis, 5, 114	9	1:52.60	49,860
1989	Primal, 4, 119	J. A. Velez Jr.	Big Stanley, 3, 122	Falerno (Arg), 7, 111	10	1:51.90	66,960

Racing — Graded Stakes

Year	Winner	Jockey	Second	Third	Strs	Time	1st Purse
1988	Creme Fraiche, 6, 118	W. A. Guerra	Fast Forward, 4, 114	Primal, 3, 118	7	1:51.80	$65,940
	Creme Fraiche, 6, 118	A. T. Cordero Jr.	Cryptoclearance, 4, 122	All Sincerity, 6, 111	8	2:05.80	131,760
	Homebuilder, 4, 115	L. Saumell	All Sincerity, 6, 111	Silver Comet, 5, 116	8	1:53.20	93,000
1987	Arctic Honeymoon, 4, 114	C. Perret	Smile, 5, 122	Darn That Alarm, 6, 120	6	1:59.60	92,460
1986	Uptown Swell, 4, 117	W. A. Guerra	Ride the Skies, 5, 113	Act Upon, 4, 113	8	1:53.20	33,810
	Racing Star, 4, 115	E. Fires	Lyphard Line, 3, 114	Show Dancer, 4, 121	12	1:45.20	31,370

Named in honor of Fred W. Hooper (1989-2000), longtime Florida breeder. Formerly named for old Tropical Park, a Miami racetrack that closed in January 1972. Tropical H. 1938-'40, 1942-'58. Tropical Park H. 1941, 1959-'96. Held at Tropical Park 1938-'71. Not held 1943, '45, '48, '51, 1972-'85, '91. 1¹⁄₁₆ miles 1938-'41, 1946-'49, '87. 1¹⁄₄ miles 1988. Turf 1986. Three-year-olds 1944. Four-year-olds and up 1949, '92. Held in January and December 1986. Held in March (twice) and December 1988. Held in January and December 1994. Track record 1960.

Frizette Stakes

Grade 1 in 2008. Belmont Park, two-year-olds, fillies, 1 mile, dirt. Held October 6, 2007, with a gross value of $400,000. First held in 1945. First graded in 1973. Stakes record 1:35.40 (1967 Queen of the Stage; 1978 Golferette; 1990 Meadow Star).

Year	Winner	Jockey	Second	Third	Strs	Time	1st Purse
2007	Indian Blessing, 2, 120	G. K. Gomez	Backseat Rhythm, 2, 120	Sunday Holiday, 2, 120	9	1:37.64	$240,000
2006	Sutra, 2, 120	M. J. Luzzi	Enchanting Star, 2, 120	Lilly Carson, 2, 120	10	1:40.22	240,000
2005	Adieu, 2, 120	J. R. Velazquez	Along the Sea, 2, 120	Keeneland Kat, 2, 120	9	1:38.07	300,000
2004	Balletto (UAE), 2, 120	C. S. Nakatani	Ready's Gal, 2, 120	Sis City, 2, 120	8	1:43.52	300,000
2003	Society Selection, 2, 120	R. Ganpath	Victory U. S. A., 2, 120	Ashado, 2, 120	8	1:43.95	300,000
2002	Storm Flag Flying, 2, 120	J. R. Velazquez	Santa Catarina, 2, 120	Appleby Gardens, 2, 120	7	1:44.20	300,000
2001	You, 2, 120	E. S. Prado	Cashier's Dream, 2, 120	Riskaverse, 2, 120	5	1:43.94	300,000
2000	Raging Fever, 2, 120	J. D. Bailey	Out of Sync, 2, 120	Western Justice, 2, 120	10	1:43.57	300,000
1999	Surfside, 2, 119	P. Day	Darling My Darling, 2, 119	March Magic, 2, 119	5	1:43.18	240,000
1998	Confessional, 2, 119	J. D. Bailey	Things Change, 2, 119	Pico Teneriffe, 2, 119	5	1:42.88	240,000
1997	Silver Maiden, 2, 119	J. D. Bailey	Diamond On the Run, 2, 119	Brac Drifter, 2, 119	6	1:42.74	240,000
1996	Storm Song, 2, 119	C. Perret	Sharp Cat, 2, 119	Aldiza, 2, 119	7	1:42.47	240,000
1995	Golden Attraction, 2, 119	G. L. Stevens	My Flag, 2, 119	Flat Fleet Feet, 2, 119	5	1:42.95	150,000
1994	Flanders, 2, 119	P. Day	Change Fora Dollar, 2, 119	Pretty Discreet, 2, 119	4	1:43.94	150,000
1993	Heavenly Prize, 2, 119	M. E. Smith	Facts of Love, 2, 119	Footing, 2, 119	7	1:35.46	150,000
1992	Educated Risk, 2, 119	J. D. Bailey	Standard Equipment, 2, 119	Beal Street Blues, 2, 119	8	1:36.62	150,000
1991	Preach, 2, 119	J. A. Krone	Vivano, 2, 119	Anh Duong, 2, 119	12	1:37.20	150,000
1990	Meadow Star, 2, 119	J. A. Santos	Champagne Glow, 2, 119	Flawlessly, 2, 119	5	**1:35.40**	171,000
1989	Stella Madrid, 2, 119	A. T. Cordero Jr.	Go for Wand, 2, 119	Dance Colony, 2, 119	7	1:38.80	176,700
1988	Some Romance, 2, 119	L. A. Pincay Jr.	Open Mind, 2, 119	Ms. Gold Pole, 2, 119	7	1:36.80	209,520
1987	Classic Crown, 2, 119	A. T. Cordero Jr.	Tap Your Toes, 2, 119	Justsayno, 2, 119	9	1:37.20	215,640
1986	Personal Ensign, 2, 119	R. P. Romero	Collins, 2, 119	Flying Katuna, 2, 119	3	1:36.40	161,400
1985	Family Style, 2, 119	L. A. Pincay Jr.	Funistrada, 2, 119	Guadery, 2, 119	7	1:37.20	133,200
1984	Charleston Rag (Ire), 2, 119	D. MacBeth	Tiltalating, 2, 119	Mom's Command, 2, 119	6	1:39.00	130,860
1983	Miss Oceana, 2, 119	E. Maple	Life's Magic, 2, 119	Lucky Lucky Lucky, 2, 119	10	1:36.60	68,040
1982	Princess Rooney, 2, 119	J. Fell	Winning Tack, 2, 119	Weekend Surprise, 2, 119	13	1:39.00	70,080
1981	Proud Lou, 2, 119	D. Beckon	Mystical Mood, 2, 119	Chilling Thought, 2, 119	12	1:38.80	70,920
1980	Heavenly Cause, 2, 119	L. A. Pincay Jr.	Sweet Revenge, 2, 119	Prayers'n Promises, 2, 119	8	1:38.00	66,000
1979	Smart Angle, 2, 119	S. Maple	Royal Suite, 2, 119	Hardship, 2, 119	11	1:38.20	66,240
1978	Golferette, 2, 119	J. Fell	It's in the Air, 2, 119	Terlingua, 2, 119	7	**1:35.40**	63,780
1977	Lakeville Miss, 2, 119	R. Hernandez	Misgivings, 2, 119	Itsamaza, 2, 119	8	1:36.20	64,680
1976	Sensational, 2, 119	J. Velasquez	Northern Sea, 2, 119	Mrs. Warren, 2, 119	7	1:36.40	64,740
1975	Optimistic Gal, 2, 119	B. Baeza	Artfully, 2, 121	Picture Tube, 2, 121	12	1:36.80	69,360
1974	Molly Ballantine, 2, 121	L. A. Pincay Jr.	Copernica, 2, 121	Mystery Mood, 2, 121	6	1:37.00	67,140
1973	Bundler, 2, 121	J. Vasquez	Chris Evert, 2, 121	I'm a Pleasure, 2, 121	14	1:36.40	72,660

Named for James R. Keene's stakes winner and foundation mare Frizette (1905 f. by Hamburg). Held at Jamaica 1945-'58. Held at Aqueduct 1959-'61, 1963-'67. Not held 1949-'51. 6 furlongs 1945-'47, 1952-'53. 5 furlongs 1948. 1¹⁄₁₆ miles 1948, 1954-'58, 1994-2004.

Futurity Stakes

Grade 2 in 2008. Belmont Park, two-year-olds, 7 furlongs, dirt. Held September 15, 2007, with a gross value of $250,000. First held in 1888. First graded in 1973. Stakes record 1:21.60 (1977 Affirmed).

Year	Winner	Jockey	Second	Third	Strs	Time	1st Purse
2007	Tale of Ekati, 2, 120	E. Coa	Kodiak Kowboy, 2, 120	Mythical Pegasus, 2, 120	6	1:22.33	$150,000
2006	King of the Roxy, 2, 120	J. R. Velazquez	C P West, 2, 120	Kong's Revenge, 2, 120	6	1:24.09	150,000
2005	Private Vow, 2, 120	J. D. Bailey	Changing Weather, 2, 120	Dixiewink (GB), 2, 120	6	1:24.05	180,000
2004	Park Avenue Ball, 2, 120	J. Castellano	Wallstreet Scandal, 2, 120	Evil Minister, 2, 120	6	1:38.84	180,000
2003	Cuvee, 2, 120	J. D. Bailey	Value Plus, 2, 120	El Prado Rob, 2, 120	6	1:35.75	120,000
2002	Whywhywhy, 2, 120	E. S. Prado	Pretty Wild, 2, 120	Truckle Feature, 2, 120	7	1:36.33	120,000
2000	‡Burning Roma, 2, 122	R. Wilson	City Zip, 2, 122	Scorpion, 2, 122	6	1:37.90	120,000
1999	Bevo, 2, 122	J. Bravo	Greenwood Lake, 2, 122	More Than Ready, 2, 122	8	1:36.16	90,000
1998	Lemon Drop Kid, 2, 122	J. R. Velazquez	Yes It's True, 2, 122	Medievil Hero, 2, 122	5	1:37.50	90,000
1997	Grand Slam, 2, 122	G. L. Stevens	K. O. Punch, 2, 122	Devil's Pride, 2, 122	10	1:35.69	90,000
1996	Traitor, 2, 122	J. R. Velazquez	Night in Reno, 2, 122	Harley Tune, 2, 122	9	1:35.29	90,000
1995	Maria's Mon, 2, 122	R. G. Davis	Louis Quatorze, 2, 122	Honour and Glory, 2, 122	7	1:35.12	90,000
1994	Montreal Red, 2, 122	J. A. Santos	Northern Ensign, 2, 122	Wild Escapade, 2, 122	6	1:36.22	66,180
1993	Holy Bull, 2, 122	M. E. Smith	Dehere, 2, 122	Prenup, 2, 122	6	1:23.31	69,360

Year	Winner	Jockey	Second	Third	Strs	Time	1st Purse
1992	Strolling Along, 2, 122	C. W. Antley	Fight for Love, 2, 122	Caponostro, 2, 122	9	1:23.67	$72,120
1991	Agincourt, 2, 122	J. F. Chavez	Tri to Watch, 2, 122	Pine Bluff, 2, 122	7	1:23.89	73,140
1990	Eastern Echo, 2, 122	J. D. Bailey	Deposit Ticket, 2, 122	Groom's Reckoning, 2, 122	4	1:22.40	69,360
1989	Senor Pete, 2, 122	J. A. Santos	Adjudicating, 2, 122	Dawn Quixote, 2, 122	5	1:23.20	75,360
1988	Trapp Mountain, 2, 122	A. T. Cordero Jr.	Bio, 2, 122	Fast Play, 2, 122	5	1:23.80	74,280
1987	Forty Niner, 2, 122	E. Maple	Tsarbaby, 2, 122	Crusader Sword, 2, 122	5	1:22.60	80,100
1986	Gulch, 2, 122	A. T. Cordero Jr.	Demons Begone, 2, 122	Captain Valid, 2, 122	7	1:22.20	82,920
1985	Ogygian, 2, 122	W. A. Guerra	Groovy, 2, 122	dh-Mr. Classic, 2, 122	6	1:22.40	81,600
				dh-Sovereign Don, 2, 122			
1984	Spectacular Love, 2, 122	L. A. Pincay Jr.	Chief's Crown, 2, 122	Mugzy's Rullah, 2, 122	8	1:23.20	105,900
1983	Swale, 2, 122	E. Maple	Shuttle Jet, 2, 122	Hail Bold King, 2, 122	5	1:24.00	72,915
1982	Copelan, 2, 122	J. D. Bailey	Satan's Charger, 2, 122	Pax in Bello, 2, 122	6	1:24.20	97,110
1981	Irish Martini, 2, 122	J. Velasquez	Herschelwalker, 2, 122	Timely Writer, 2, 122	8	1:24.40	103,605
1980	Tap Shoes, 2, 122	R. Hernandez	Dash o' Pleasure, 2, 122	McCracken, 2, 122	6	1:23.80	85,605
1979	Rockhill Native, 2, 122	J. Oldham	Sportful, 2, 122	Gold Stage, 2, 122	8	1:22.00	90,150
1978	‡Crested Wave, 2, 122	J. Cruguet	dh-Picturesque, 2, 122		8	1:24.00	75,660
			dh-Strike Your Colors, 2, 122				
1977	Affirmed, 2, 122	S. Cauthen	Alydar, 2, 122	Nasty and Bold, 2, 122	5	**1:21.60**	63,570
1976	For The Moment, 2, 122	E. Maple	Banquet Table, 2, 122	Western Wind, 2, 122	10	1:23.20	67,353
1975	Soy Numero Uno, 2, 122	J. Vasquez	Jackknife, 2, 122	Beau Talent, 2, 122	7	1:17.80	66,408
1974	Just the Time, 2, 122	M. A. Castaneda	High Steel, 2, 122	Valid Appeal, 2, 122	12	1:16.40	66,801
1973	Wedge Shot, 2, 122	J. Vasquez	‡Protagonist, 2, 122	Judger, 2, 122	10	1:17.00	82,230

Named for the future nominations, before a foal was born, of early futurity races. Grade 1 1973-2003. Held at Sheepshead Bay 1888-1909. Held at Saratoga Race Course 1910, 1913-'14. Held at Aqueduct 1959-'60, 1963-'67. Not held 1911-'12. Not held due to World Trade Center attack 2001. 6 furlongs 1888-'91, 1902-'09. About 6 furlongs 1892-1901. 6½ furlongs 1910-'24, 1934-'75. About 7 furlongs 1925-'33. 7 furlongs 1976-'93. Colts and fillies 1944. Colts and geldings 1977. Dead heat for second 1978. Dead heat for third 1985. ‡Judger finished second, DQ to third, 1973. ‡Fuzzbuster finished first, DQ to fourth, 1978. ‡City Zip finished first, DQ to second, 2000.

Gallant Bloom Handicap

Grade 2 in 2008. Belmont Park, three-year-olds and up, fillies and mares, 6½ furlongs, dirt. Held September 22, 2007, with a gross value of $147,000. First held in 1992. First graded in 1997. Stakes record 1:15.60 (1998 Catinca).

Year	Winner	Jockey	Second	Third	Strs	Time	1st Purse
2007	Jazzy (Arg), 5, 115	G. K. Gomez	Cuaba, 4, 116	Pussycat Doll, 5, 119	5	1:16.71	$90,000
2006	Great Intentions, 4, 115	J. Castellano	Annika Lass, 5, 115	Getcozywithkaylee, 5, 115	5	1:16.13	90,000
2005	Umpateedle, 6, 116	A. T. Gryder	Smokey Glacken, 4, 116	Travelator, 5, 115	5	1:16.35	90,000
2004	Lady Tak, 4, 122	J. R. Velazquez	Molto Vita, 4, 115	Zawzooth, 5, 115	7	1:16.04	90,000
2003	Harmony Lodge, 5, 117	R. Migliore	House Party, 3, 116	Slews Final Answer, 4, 112	6	1:16.20	90,000
2002	Nasty Storm, 4, 114	J. A. Santos	Raging Fever, 4, 120	Shine Again, 5, 118	6	1:17.89	90,000
2001	Finder's Fee, 4, 113	J. R. Velazquez	Cedar Knolls, 4, 114	Gold Mover, 5, 115	4	1:17.60	79,928
2000	Dream Supreme, 3, 118	P. Day	Finder's Fee, 3, 116	Tropical Punch, 4, 114	5	1:15.86	64,380
1999	Positive Gal, 3, 116	J. D. Bailey	Flamingo Way, 5, 114	Torch, 6, 113	6	1:16.86	65,820
1998	Catinca, 3, 114	R. Migliore	Dixie Flag, 4, 117	Crab Grass, 4, 114	9	**1:15.60**	50,595
1997	Top Secret, 4, 120	J. R. Velazquez	Aldiza, 3, 116	Dixie Flag, 3, 114	7	1:16.00	49,260
1996	Miss Golden Circle, 4, 215	R. Migliore	J J'sdream, 3, 119	Nappelon, 4, 117	9	1:16.26	50,040
1995	Classy Mirage, 5, 123	J. D. Bailey	Dust Bucket, 4, 114	Fantastic Women, 3, 110	5	1:17.34	48,375
1994	Vivano, 5, 116	W. H. McCauley	Ann Dear, 4, 118	Strategic Reward, 5, 113	5	1:10.93	48,255
1992	Apelia, 3, 118	L. Attard	Preach, 3, 116	Fretina, 3, 116	8	1:08.97	32,400

Named for King Ranch's Racing Hall of Fame member and '69 Gazelle H. winner Gallant Bloom (1966 f. by *Gallant Man). Grade 3 1997-2000. Not held 1993. 6 furlongs 1994.

Gallorette Handicap

Grade 3 in 2008. Pimlico Race Course, three-year-olds and up, fillies and mares, 1 1/16 miles, turf. Held May 17, 2008, with a gross value of $100,000. First held in 1952. First graded in 1973. Stakes record 1:40.32 (2007 Precious Kitten).

Year	Winner	Jockey	Second	Third	Strs	Time	1st Purse
2008	Roshani, 5, 119	J. R. Velazquez	Lady Digby, 4, 116	Valbenny (Ire), 4, 121	5	1:49.08	$60,000
2007	Precious Kitten, 4, 122	R. Bejarano	A True Pussycat, 4, 116	Trick's Pic, 4, 114	8	**1:40.32**	60,000
2006	Ozone Bere (Fr), 4, 115	J. Castellano	Humoristic, 5, 115	Art Fan, 5, 114	13	1:42.08	60,000
2005	Film Maker, 5, 121	J. D. Bailey	Briviesca (GB), 4, 115	Humoristic, 4, 114	9	1:44.29	60,000
2004	Ocean Drive, 4, 116	J. D. Bailey	Film Maker, 4, 117	With Patience, 5, 112	8	1:45.65	60,000
2003	Carib Lady (Ire), 4, 116	P. A. Valenzuela	Affirmed Dancer, 4, 113	Lady of the Future, 5, 114	7	1:50.69	60,000
2002	Quidnaskra, 7, 116	C. J. McCarron	De Aar, 5, 111	Step With Style, 5, 115	7	1:46.73	60,000
2001	License Fee, 6, 118	P. Day	Starine, 5, 117	Crystal Sea, 4, 113	8	1:42.81	60,000
2000	Colstar, 4, 120	A. Delgado	Melody Queen (GB), 4, 122	Terreavigne, 5, 118	10	1:43.60	60,000
1999	Winfama, 6, 114	E. S. Prado	Pleasant Temper, 5, 119	Earth to Jackie, 5, 116	8	1:43.31	60,000
1998	Tresoriere, 4, 113	J. A. Santos	Bursting Forth, 4, 114	Starry Dreamer, 4, 114	7	1:45.35	60,000
1997	Palliser Bay, 5, 111	C. H. Marquez Jr.	Elusive, 5, 114	Sangria, 4, 117	8	1:43.81	60,000
1996	Aucilla, 5, 114	M. E. Smith	Julie's Brilliance, 4, 115	Brushing Gloom, 4, 114	7	1:44.96	60,000
1995	It's Personal, 5, 112	J. A. Krone	Churchbell Chimes, 4, 112	Open Toe, 5, 113	6	1:43.72	60,000
1994	Tribulation, 4, 117	J. Samyn	McKaymackenna, 5, 118	Fleet Broad, 4, 115	6	1:41.66	60,000
1993	You'd Be Surprised, 4, 113	J. D. Bailey	Captive Miss, 4, 117	Dior's Angel, 4, 112	12	1:43.54	60,000
1992	Brilliant Brass, 5, 113	E. S. Prado	Spanish Dior, 5, 112	Stem the Tide, 4, 112	8	1:44.81	60,000
1991	Miss Josh, 5, 121	E. S. Prado	Splendid Try, 5, 113	Highland Penny, 6, 115	6	1:41.91	60,000

Year	Winner	Jockey	Second	Third	Strs	Time	1st Purse
1990	Highland Penny, 5, 116	R. I. Rojas	Saphaedra, 6, 112	dh-Channel Three, 4, 112	8	1:42.40	$60,000
				dh-Double Bunctious, 6, 113			
1989	Dance Teacher, 4, 115	J. Samyn	Arcroyal, 5, 114	Fortunate Facts, 5, 118	9	1:44.00	60,000
1988	Just Class (Ire), 4, 115	C. Perret	Landaura, 4, 115	Hangin On a Star, 4, 119	8	1:42.80	54,145
1987	Scotch Heather, 5, 113	M. G. Pino	Catatonic, 5, 117	Foot Stone, 4, 113	6	1:44.40	54,600
1986	Natania, 4, 114	J. W. Edwards	Scotch Heather, 4, 115	Valid Doge, 5, 108	12	1:45.60	71,448
1985	La Reine Elaine, 4, 113	G. W. Hutton	Stufida (GB), 4, 115	Lady Emerald, 4, 107	12	1:41.60	58,013
1984	Kattegat's Pride, 5, 118	D. A. Miller Jr.	Amanti, 5, 114	Bright Choice, 5, 110	7	1:42.80	55,770
1983	Wedding Party, 4, 119	C. Perret	Sunny Sparkler, 4, 122	Bemissed, 3, 110	8	1:50.00	56,648
1982	Island Charm, 5, 117	N. Santagata	Lovely Lei, 4, 112	Vibro Vibes, 5, 115	10	1:46.40	57,168
1981	Exactly So (Ire), 4, 112	G. McCarron	Crimson April, 4, 110	Ernestine, 4, 111	8	1:47.20	55,998
1980	Jamila Kadir, 6, 109	M. G. Pino	The Very One, 5, 122	Wild Bidder, 4, 108	10	1:44.40	57,428
1979	Calderina (Ity), 4, 121	C. Perret	Dottie O., 5, 105	Warfever (Fr), 4, 116	10	1:44.80	56,875
1978	Huggle Duggle, 4, 113	B. Gonzalez	Council House, 4, 118	Nanticious (Ire), 4, 112	10	1:44.20	37,765
1977	Summertime Promise, 5, 121	L. Moyers	Summer Session, 4, 111	Siz Ziz Zit, 4, 112	9	1:43.60	37,050
1976	Redundancy, 5, 119	R. Broussard	Dos a Dos, 4, 113	Margravine, 4, 112	8	1:42.20	29,575
	*Deesse Du Val, 5, 119	C. H. Marquez	Summertime Promise, 4, 117	Jabot, 4, 114	9	1:42.20	29,835
1975	Gulls Cry, 4, 117	E. Maple	Sarah Percy, 7, 115	Twixt, 6, 127	10	1:46.20	37,960
1974	Serre Green, 6, 113	T. Lee	Unknown Heiress, 3, 103	Out Cold, 4, 112	14	1:44.60	22,295
1973	Deb Marion, 3, 107	A. Agnello	dh-Aglimmer, 4, 115		11	1:44.00	22,068
			dh-Groton Miss, 4, 115				

Named for Mrs. M. A. Moore's Racing Hall of Fame member, 1946 champion handicap female and '45 Pimlico Oaks winner Gallorette (1942 f. by *Challenger II). Gallorette S. 1952-'66. 1 1/8 miles 1952-'66. Dirt 1952-'72, 1979-'80, 1984, 1986-'87, 1995-'96. Two divisions 1976. Dead heat for second 1973. Dead heat for third 1990. Course record 2007.

Gamely Stakes

Grade 1 in 2008. Hollywood Park, three-year-olds and up, fillies and mares, 1 1/8 miles, turf. Held May 26, 2008, with a gross value of $283,000. First held in 1939. First graded in 1973. Stakes record 1:45.07 (1993 Toussaud).

Year	Winner	Jockey	Second	Third	Strs	Time	1st Purse
2008	Precious Kitten, 5, 123	R. Bejarano	Diamond Diva (GB), 4, 117	Rutherienne, 4, 123	5	1:45.23	$176,400
2007	Citronnade, 4, 119	D. R. Flores	Price Tag (GB), 4, 123	Vacare, 4, 123	6	1:45.73	224,280
2006	Shining Energy, 4, 118	V. Espinoza	Dancing Edie, 4, 116	Argentina (Ire), 4, 116	6	1:46.86	210,900
2005	Mea Domina, 4, 115	T. Baze	Solar Echo, 5, 116	Amorama (Fr), 4, 116	9	1:46.47	276,900
2004	Noches De Rosa (Chi), 6, 115	M. E. Smith	Megahertz (GB), 4, 122	Quero Quero, 4, 115	4	1:48.34	187,500
2003	Tates Creek, 5, 122	P. A. Valenzuela	Dublino, 4, 122	Megahertz (GB), 4, 118	6	1:46.97	263,400
2002	Astra, 6, 123	K. Desormeaux	Starine (Fr), 5, 122	Voodoo Dancer, 4, 119	6	1:46.93	300,000
2001	Happyanunoit (NZ), 6, 121	B. Blanc	Tranquility Lake, 6, 124	Beautiful Noise, 5, 116	7	1:47.34	115,710
2000	Astra, 4, 117	K. Desormeaux	Happyanunoit (NZ), 5, 121	Tout Charmant, 4, 119	5	1:45.81	157,170
1999	Tranquility Lake, 4, 119	E. Delahoussaye	Midnight Line, 4, 117	Green Jewel (GB), 5, 117	5	1:46.04	157,800
1998	Fiji (GB), 4, 123	K. Desormeaux	Kool Kat Katie (Ire), 4, 119	Squeak (Arg), 4, 116	6	1:47.40	158,880
1997	Donna Viola (GB), 5, 121	G. L. Stevens	Real Connection, 6, 115	Different (Arg), 5, 121	7	1:47.40	120,000
1996	Auriette (Ire), 4, 118	K. Desormeaux	Flagbird, 5, 119	Didina (GB), 4, 116	6	1:46.59	128,760
1995	Possibly Perfect, 5, 123	K. Desormeaux	Lady Affirmed, 4, 114	Don't Read My Lips, 4, 114	6	1:46.99	92,900
1994	Hollywood Wildcat, 4, 122	E. Delahoussaye	Mz. Zill Bear, 5, 114	Flawlessly, 6, 124	6	1:46.55	92,900
1993	Toussaud, 4, 116	K. Desormeaux	Gold Fleece, 5, 114	Bel's Starlet, 6, 116	9	1:45.07	97,700
1992	Metamorphose, 4, 114	G. L. Stevens	Guiza, 5, 113	Silvered, 5, 116	6	1:46.56	93,300
1991	Miss Josh, 5, 118	L. A. Pincay Jr.	Island Jamboree, 5, 116	Fire the Groom, 4, 120	11	1:47.50	68,000
1990	Double Wedge, 5, 112	R. G. Davis	Stylish Star, 4, 116	Beautiful Melody, 4, 115	6	1:47.80	62,700
1989	Fitzwilliam Place (Ire), 5, 119	C. A. Black	Claire Marine (Ire), 4, 117	Ravinella, 4, 116	7	1:47.80	63,400
1988	Pen Bal Lady (GB), 4, 120	E. Delahoussaye	Chapel of Dreams, 4, 117	Galunpe (Ire), 5, 120	3	1:47.00	72,800
1987	Northern Aspen, 5, 119	G. L. Stevens	Reloy, 4, 115	Frau Altiva (Arg), 5, 115	6	1:47.60	89,800
1986	La Koumia (Fr), 4, 118	R. Sibille	Estrapade, 6, 123	Tax Dodge, 5, 115	8	1:45.80	92,400
1985	Estrapade, 5, 124	C. J. McCarron	Johnica, 4, 115	Possible Mate, 4, 116	6	1:46.60	62,500
1984	Sabin, 4, 125	E. Maple	Triple Tipple, 5, 116	Fenny Rough (Ire), 4, 117	8	1:47.60	65,400
1983	Pride of Rosewood (NZ), 5, 115	E. Delahoussaye	Sangue (Ire), 5, 123	Mademoiselle Forli, 4, 119	6	1:48.80	64,800
1982	Ack's Secret, 6, 122	L. A. Pincay Jr.	Miss Huntington, 5, 117	Vocalist (GB), 4, 114	9	1:46.80	66,100
1981	Kilijaro (Ire), 5, 127	M. Castaneda	Princess Karenda, 4, 121	Wishing Well, 6, 122	6	1:48.20	62,900
1980	Wishing Well, 5, 119	F. Toro	Country Queen, 5, 123	Image of Reality, 4, 118	12	1:47.80	69,600
1979	Sisterhood, 4, 118	F. Toro	Country Queen, 4, 118	Camarado, 4, 117	11	1:47.80	50,450
1978	*Lucie Manet, 5, 119	D. G. McHargue	Sensational, 4, 120	*Glenaris, 4, 113	7	1:48.20	38,975
	*Star Ball, 6, 122	D. G. McHargue	Up to Juliet, 5, 114	Teisen Lap, 4, 116	7	1:48.80	38,975
1977	Hail Hilarious, 4, 123	D. Pierce	Cascapedia, 4, 118	Swingtime, 5, 119	6	1:49.60	31,250
1976	Katonka, 4, 121	L. A. Pincay Jr.	Fascinating Girl, 4, 117	*Tizna, 7, 126	5	1:50.40	30,750
1975	Susan's Girl, 6, 124	J. E. Tejeira	Bold Ballet, 4, 118	*Dulcia, 6, 121	6	1:48.00	25,200
1974	Sister Fleet, 4, 115	A. Pineda	*La Zanzara, 4, 121	*Tizna, 5, 122	7	1:47.40	25,550
1973	Bird Boots, 4, 115	E. Belmonte	Susan's Girl, 4, 130	Hill Circus, 5, 120	7	1:47.40	25,550

Named for William Haggin Perry's Racing Hall of Fame member, 1967 champion three-year-old filly, '68, '69 champion older female, and '68 Vanity H. winner Gamely (1964 f. by Bold Ruler). Formerly named for the city for Long Beach, California. Grade 2 1977-'82. Not graded 1976. Long Beach H. 1939-'75. Gamely H. 1976-'97. Gamely Breeders' Cup H. 1998-2005. Gamely Breeders' Cup S. 2006. Not held 1940-'67. 1 mile 1939, '69. 1 1/16 miles 1968, 1970-'72. Dirt 1939-'68, 1973. Both sexes 1968. Two divisions 1978.

Garden City Stakes

Grade 1 in 2008. Belmont Park, three-year-olds, fillies, 1 1/8 miles, turf. Held September 8, 2007, with a gross value of $219,800. First held in 1904. First graded in 1985. Stakes record 1:45.62 (2005 Luas Line [Ire]).

Year	Winner	Jockey	Second	Third	Strs	Time	1st Purse
2007	Alexander Tango (Ire), 3, 118	S. Bridgmohan	Bit of Whimsy, 3, 118	Sharp Susan, 3, 120	10	1:48.97	$120,000
2006	Magnificent Song, 3, 118	G. K. Gomez	Take the Ribbon, 3, 116	Jade Queen, 3, 116	11	1:48.48	150,000
2005	Luas Line (Ire), 3, 116	J. R. Velazquez	Asi Siempre, 3, 116	My Typhoon (Ire), 3, 116	4	1:45.62	180,000
2004	Lucifer's Stone, 3, 118	J. A. Santos	Barancella (Fr), 3, 116	Noahs Ark (Ire), 3, 116	7	1:48.88	180,000
2003	Indy Five Hundred, 3, 113	P. Day	Dimitrova, 3, 122	Campsie Fells (UAE), 3, 116	8	1:48.44	150,000
2002	Wonder Again, 3, 119	E. S. Prado	Riskaverse, 3, 119	Pertuisane (GB), 3, 115	10	1:47.33	150,000
2001	Voodoo Dancer, 3, 120	C. S. Nakatani	Shooting Party, 3, 113	Wander Mom, 3, 116	10	1:47.69	150,000
2000	Gaviola, 3, 123	J. D. Bailey	Flawly (GB), 3, 115	Millie's Quest, 3, 116	8	1:48.89	150,000
1999	Perfect Sting, 3, 120	P. Day	Nordican Inch (GB), 3, 116	Ronda (GB), 3, 121	12	1:49.41	129,900
1998	Pharatta (Ire), 3, 120	C. S. Nakatani	Tenski, 3, 122	Pratella, 3, 115	12	1:47.10	129,720
1997	Auntie Mame, 3, 122	J. D. Bailey	Parade Queen, 3, 115	Swearingen, 3, 117	9	1:48.49	128,040
1996	True Flare, 3, 121	G. L. Stevens	Henlopen, 3, 113	Zephyr, 3, 114	9	1:42.58	128,460
1995	Perfect Arc, 3, 123	J. R. Velazquez	Bail Out Becky, 3, 121	Christmas Gift, 3, 118	8	1:42.35	101,070
1994	Jade Flush, 3, 111	R. G. Davis	Lady Affirmed, 3, 117	Sexuality, 3, 117	8	1:46.79	67,140
1993	Sky Beauty, 3, 124	M. E. Smith	Fadetta, 3, 112	For all Seasons, 3, 114	6	1:35.76	68,400
1992	November Snow, 3, 124	C. W. Antley	Vivano, 3, 112	Easy Now, 3, 124	4	1:35.50	66,480
1991	Dazzle Me Jolie, 3, 115	J. A. Santos	Grand Girlfriend, 3, 112	Wide Country, 3, 124	9	1:35.61	72,000
1990	Aishah, 3, 115	J. A. Santos	Screen Prospect, 3, 115	Vitola (GB), 3, 112	11	1:35.40	57,690
1989	Highest Glory, 3, 115	J. A. Santos	Warfie, 3, 114	Tremolos, 3, 114	7	1:37.20	70,440
1988	Topicount, 3, 115	A. T. Cordero Jr.	Toll Fee, 3, 112	Fara's Team, 3, 115	5	1:38.00	82,260
1987	Personal Ensign, 3, 115	R. P. Romero	One From Heaven, 3, 118	Key Bid, 3, 118	9	1:36.60	82,140
1986	Life At the Top, 3, 118	C. J. McCarron	Lotka, 3, 118	Funistrada, 3, 115	6	1:34.40	51,210
1985	Kamikaze Rick, 3, 118	A. T. Cordero Jr.	Wising Up, 3, 115	Videogenic, 3, 116	5	1:36.00	50,490
1984	Given, 3, 118	M. J. Vigliotti	Maharadoon, 3, 112	Recharged, 3, 118	9	1:43.40	42,960
1983	Pretty Sensible, 3, 112	A. Smith Jr.	High Schemes, 3, 112	Lovin Touch, 3, 115	8	1:37.80	33,600
1982	Nafees, 3, 112	J. Velasquez	Middle Stage, 3, 112	Beau Cougar, 3, 112	7	1:38.40	33,120
1981	Banner Gala, 3, 113	A. T. Cordero Jr.	Expressive Dance, 3, 118	In True Form, 3, 118	9	1:33.60	33,900
1980	Mitey Lively, 3, 113	J. Velasquez	Rose of Morn, 3, 112	Paintbrush, 3, 112	6	1:36.40	33,480
1979	Danielle B., 3, 113	R. Hernandez	Distinct Honor, 3, 114	Seascape, 3, 118	10	1:45.40	33,000

Named for the community of Garden City, located in the heart of New York's Long Island. Formerly named for George D. Widener's 1949 Fashion S. winner Rare Perfume (1947 f. by Eight Thirty). Grade 3 1985-'86. Grade 2 1987-'98. Garden City S. 1904-'13. Garden City Selling S. 1915-'32. Rare Perfume S. 1979-'95. Rare Perfume Breeders' Cup H. 1996-'97. Garden City Breeders' Cup H. 1998-2003. Garden City Breeders' Cup S. 2004-'06. Not held 1908, 1910-'12, 1914, 1933-'78. 1 1/16 miles 1904-'79, 1994-'96. 1 mile 70 yards 1984. Dirt 1904-'93. Three-year-olds and up 1904-'32.

Gardenia Handicap

Grade 3 in 2008. Ellis Park, three-year-olds and up, fillies and mares, 1 mile, dirt. Held August 18, 2007, with a gross value of $150,000. First held in 1982. First graded in 1988. Stakes record 1:35.32 (2005 Dream of Summer).

Year	Winner	Jockey	Second	Third	Strs	Time	1st Purse
2007	Pleasant Hill, 4, 113	L. Melancon	High Heels, 4, 115	Brownie Points, 4, 118	11	1:38.85	$90,000
2006	Prospective Saint, 5, 119	E. Castro	Maggie Slew, 3, 112	Plaid, 5, 112	10	1:36.13	90,000
2005	Dream of Summer, 6, 122	C. S. Nakatani	Halory Leigh, 5, 119	Tempus Fugit, 5, 117	8	1:35.32	90,000
2004	Angela's Love, 4, 115	M. Guidry	Miss Fortunate, 4, 116	Bare Necessities, 5, 119	6	1:49.54	120,000
2003	Bare Necessities, 4, 119	R. R. Douglas	Desert Gold, 4, 114	So Much More, 4, 115	9	1:50.09	120,000
2002	Minister's Baby, 4, 117	C. Perret	Lakenheath, 4, 115	Softly, 4, 114	8	1:49.73	120,000
2001	Asher, 5, 116	M. Guidry	Zenith, 4, 112	Royal Fair, 5, 116	9	1:50.16	120,000
2000	Silent Eskimo, 5, 116	J. Lopez	Roza Robata, 5, 119	Tap to Music, 5, 120	7	1:50.56	120,000
1999	Lines of Beauty, 4, 112	F. Torres	Roza Robata, 4, 113	Castle Blaze, 6, 109	10	1:49.60	120,000
1998	Meter Maid, 4, 119	P. A. Johnson	Proper Banner, 4, 114	Three Fanfares, 5, 113	7	1:51.00	120,000
1997	Three Fanfares, 4, 113	F. A. Arguello Jr.	Gold n Delicious, 4, 119	Birr, 4, 116	7	1:49.00	120,000
1996	Country Cat, 4, 115	D. M. Barton	Bedroom Blues, 5, 111	Alcovy, 6, 116	8	1:49.60	120,000
1995	Laura's Pistolette, 4, 115	E. M. Martin Jr.	Sadie's Dream, 5, 112	Cat Appeal, 3, 116	9	1:50.80	120,000
1994	Alphabulous, 5, 112	O. Thorwarth	Added Asset, 4, 115	Hey Hazel, 4, 116	10	1:50.00	120,000
1993	Erica's Dream, 5, 114	W. Martinez	Fappies Cosy Miss, 5, 111	Hitch, 4, 114	8	1:49.80	120,000
1992	Bungalow, 5, 118	F. C. Torres	Forever Fond, 4, 113	Fappies Cosy Miss, 4, 112	11	1:48.60	120,000
1991	Summer Matinee, 4, 113	C. A. Black	Blissful Union, 4, 113	Beth Believes, 5, 113	11	1:50.50	90,000
1990	Evangelical, 4, 113	L. J. Melancon	Degenerate Gal, 5, 117	Anitas Surprise, 4, 113	10	1:49.80	90,000
1989	Lawyer Talk, 5, 114	M. E. Doser	Gallant Ryder, 4, 120	Miss Barbour, 4, 112	10	1:50.00	90,000
1988	Lt. Lao, 4, 123	D. Brumfield	Saucy Deb, 4, 118	Silk's Lady, 4, 112	12	1:47.60	90,000
1987	No Choice, 4, 113	C. R. Woods Jr.	Layovernite, 5, 117	Firgie's Jule, 4, 112	11	1:49.20	94,500
1986	Queen Alexandra, 4, 123	D. E. Foster	Fleet Secretariat, 5, 119	Sherizar, 5, 113	7	1:49.20	63,000
1985	Crimson Orchid, 3, 114	S. E. Miller	Electric Fanny, 4, 114	Dusty Gloves, 4, 116	14	1:49.80	41,535
1984	Rambling Rhythm, 3, 114	L. J. Martinez	Run Tulle Run, 5, 118	Queen of Song, 5, 122	8	1:50.20	39,325
1983	Migola, 3, 115	G. Patterson	Kitchen, 4, 117	Run Tulle Run, 4, 113	14	1:51.60	42,315
1982	Sweetest Chant, 4, 121	E. Fires	Muriesk, 3, 111	Run Tulle Run, 4, 118	11	1:49.80	43,778

Named for the flower used in the winner's garland. Formerly sponsored by the Coca-Cola Co. of Atlanta, Georgia 1985-'86. Formerly sponsored by Stroh's Brewery of Minneapolis, Minnesota 1982-'84. Stroh's H. 1982-'84. Coca-Cola Summer Festival H. 1985. Coca-Cola Centennial H. 1986. Gardenia S. 1990, 1997-'98. 1 1/8 miles 1982-2004.

Racing — Graded Stakes

Gazelle Stakes

Grade 1 in 2008. Belmont Park, three-year-olds, fillies, 1 1/8 miles, dirt. Held September 15, 2007, with a gross value of $245,000. First held in 1887. First graded in 1973. Stakes record 1:46.80 (1974 Maud Muller).

Year	Winner	Jockey	Second	Third	Strs	Time	1st Purse
2007	Lear's Princess, 3, 115	E. Coa	Rags to Riches, 3, 122	Tough Tiz's Sis, 3, 119	5	1:47.86	$150,000
2006	Pine Island, 3, 122	J. Castellano	Teammate, 3, 119	Last Romance, 3, 115	6	1:48.93	150,000
2005	In the Gold, 3, 117	G. L. Stevens	Leave Me Alone, 3, 119	Yolanda B. Too, 3, 115	5	1:49.75	150,000
2004	Stellar Jayne, 3, 122	R. Albarado	Daydreaming, 3, 115	He Loves Me, 3, 117	6	1:48.25	150,000
2003	Buy the Sport, 3, 113	P. Day	Lady Tak, 3, 119	Spoken Fur, 3, 121	8	1:48.57	150,000
2002	Imperial Gesture, 3, 117	J. A. Santos	Take Charge Lady, 3, 121	Bella Bellucci, 3, 118	7	1:47.12	150,000
2001	Exogenous, 3, 118	J. Castellano	Two Item Limit, 3, 118	Fleet Renee, 3, 122	8	1:47.68	150,000
2000	Critical Eye, 3, 115	M. E. Smith	Plenty of Light, 3, 115	Resort, 3, 116	8	1:48.40	120,000
1999	Silverbulletday, 3, 124	J. D. Bailey	Queen's Word, 3, 113	Awful Smart, 3, 115	6	1:47.71	120,000
1998	Tap to Music, 3, 112	P. Day	Keeper Hill, 3, 122	French Braids, 3, 115	7	1:49.72	120,000
1997	Royal Indy, 3, 113	P. Day	Starry Dreamer, 3, 114	Pearl City, 3, 117	7	1:49.11	120,000
1996	My Flag, 3, 121	J. D. Bailey	Escena, 3, 121	Top Secret, 3, 117	6	1:48.08	120,000
1995	Serena's Song, 3, 124	G. L. Stevens	Miss Golden Circle, 3, 113	Golden Bri, 3, 121	6	1:47.29	90,000
1994	Heavenly Prize, 3, 123	M. E. Smith	Cinnamon Sugar (Ire), 3, 118	Sovereign Kitty, 3, 118	5	1:47.20	90,000
1993	Dispute, 3, 120	J. D. Bailey	Silky Feather, 3, 117	In Her Glory, 3, 112	8	1:47.20	90,000
1992	Saratoga Dew, 3, 120	W. H. McCauley	Vivano, 3, 114	Tiney Toast, 3, 113	6	1:47.63	103,140
1991	Versailles Treaty, 3, 123	A. T. Cordero Jr.	Grand Girlfriend, 3, 115	Immerse, 3, 112	8	1:47.47	105,840
1990	Highland Talk, 3, 111	J. Samyn	Dance Colony, 3, 116	She Can, 3, 116	7	1:50.80	69,960
1989	Tactile, 3, 114	R. Migliore	Dream Deal, 3, 117	Fantastic Find, 3, 114	5	1:48.40	67,440
1988	Classic Crown, 3, 117	R. P. Romero	Willa On the Move, 3, 120	Make Change, 3, 118	6	1:49.80	69,360
1987	Single Blade, 3, 113	C. W. Antley	Without Feathers, 3, 121	Silent Turn, 3, 114	5	1:48.20	80,100
1986	Classy Cathy, 3, 121	E. Fires	Life At the Top, 3, 118	Dynamic Star, 3, 116	4	1:48.40	66,480
1985	Kamikaze Rick, 3, 113	A. T. Cordero Jr.	Overwhelming, 3, 112	Fran's Valentine, 3, 121	7	1:48.60	68,880
1984	Miss Oceana, 3, 121	E. Maple	Sintra, 3, 117	Life's Magic, 3, 122	5	1:47.60	66,840
1983	High Schemes, 3, 121	J. Samyn	Lass Trump, 3, 120	Lady Norcliffe, 3, 115	6	1:48.20	66,720
1982	Broom Dance, 3, 121	G. McCarron	Number, 3, 113	Mademoiselle Forli, 3, 114	7	1:47.60	33,360
1981	Discorama, 3, 117	R. Hernandez	Secrettame, 3, 114	Tina Tina Too, 3, 114	7	1:48.20	33,300
1980	Love Sign, 3, 121	R. Hernandez	Sugar and Spice, 3, 117	Kelley's Day, 3, 112	6	1:49.20	32,580
1979	Himalayan, 3, 113	E. Maple	Croquis, 3, 113	Fourdrinier, 3, 112	9	1:48.40	32,580
1978	Tempest Queen, 3, 117	J. Velasquez	Lulubo, 3, 116	Terpsichorist, 3, 113	5	1:49.80	31,710
1977	Pearl Necklace, 3, 111	S. Cauthen	Sensational, 3, 120	Road Princess, 3, 118	6	1:48.00	31,770
1976	Revidere, 3, 124	A. T. Cordero Jr.	Pacific Princess, 3, 112	Ancient Fables, 3, 112	5	1:47.80	31,950
1975	Land Girl, 3, 114	J. Vasquez	Hooray Hooray, 3, 108	Let Me Linger, 3, 119	8	1:49.40	33,690
1974	Maud Muller, 3, 120	A. T. Cordero Jr.	Raisela, 3, 115	Stage Door Betty, 3, 115	7	**1:46.80**	33,900
1973	Desert Vixen, 3, 126	J. Velasquez	Bag of Tunes, 3, 117	Poker Night, 3, 120	7	1:47.40	33,780

Named for the speedy hooved mammal, the gazelle. Grade 2 1973-'83. Gazelle H. 1922, 1956-2004. Held at Gravesend Park 1887-1909. Held at Aqueduct 1910-'55, 1960, 1963-'68. Not held 1911-'16, 1933-'35. 1 1/16 miles 1900-'58. 1 mile 1959-'60. Fillies and mares 1917-'20. Three-year-olds and up 1917-'20.

General George Handicap

Grade 2 in 2008. Laurel Park, three-year-olds and up, 7 furlongs, dirt. Held February 18, 2008, with a gross value of $246,750. First held in 1973. First graded in 1991. Stakes record 1:21.96 (1992 Senor Speedy).

Year	Winner	Jockey	Second	Third	Strs	Time	1st Purse
2008	Bustin Stones, 4, 115	R. A. Dominguez	Lord Snowdon, 5, 115	Premium Wine, 4, 113	7	1:24.47	$135,000
2007	Silver Wagon, 6, 120	E. S. Prado	Ah Day, 4, 117	Ryan's for Real, 4, 114	9	1:23.13	180,000
2005	Saratoga County, 4, 114	J. Castellano	Don Six, 5, 118	Gators N Bears, 5, 118	9	1:23.43	120,000
2004	Well Fancied, 6, 118	E. S. Prado	Unforgettable Max, 4, 114	Gators N Bears, 4, 116	9	1:22.49	120,000
2003	My Cousin Matt, 4, 113	R. A. Dominguez	Peeping Tom, 6, 114	Disturbingthepeace, 5, 118	11	1:22.12	120,000
2002	Wrangler, 4, 115	A. T. Gryder	Rusty Spur, 4, 111	Affirmed Success, 8, 121	8	1:22.53	120,000
2001	Peeping Tom, 4, 114	S. Bridgmohan	Delaware Township, 5, 120	Disco Rico, 4, 117	7	1:22.00	120,000
2000	Affirmed Success, 6, 121	J. F. Chavez	Young At Heart, 6, 114	Badge, 4, 114	9	1:22.02	120,000
1999	Esteemed Friend, 5, 116	M. J. Luzzi	Star of Valor, 6, 114	Purple Passion, 5, 117	9	1:22.54	150,000
1998	Royal Haven, 6, 122	R. Migliore	Purple Passion, 4, 116	Wire Me Collect, 5, 117	9	1:23.04	150,000
1997	Why Change, 4, 113	M. Guidry	Appealing Skier, 4, 118	Le Grande Pos, 6, 111	10	1:22.41	120,000
1996	Meadow Monster, 5, 120	R. Wilson	Splendid Sprinter, 4, 113	Cat Be Nimble, 4, 114	9	1:22.11	120,000
1995	Who Wouldn't, 6, 119	J. Rocco	Storm Tower, 5, 116	Powis Castle, 4, 118	8	1:22.08	120,000
1994	Blushing Julian, 4, 118	R. E. Colton	Chief Desire, 4, 123	Who Wouldn't, 5, 118	12	1:22.91	120,000
1993	Majesty's Turn, 4, 118	A. Delgado	Senor Speedy, 6, 118	Ameri Valay, 4, 123	7	1:22.66	120,000
1992	Senor Speedy, 5, 126	J. F. Chavez	Sunny Sunrise, 5, 123	Formal Dinner, 4, 123	12	**1:21.96**	120,000
1991	Star Touch (Fr), 5, 118	M. J. Luzzi	Profit Key, 4, 118	Fire Plug, 8, 118	11	1:22.90	120,000
1990	King's Nest, 5, 119	M. T. Hunter	Wind Splitter, 4, 117	Notation, 4, 119	12	1:22.00	120,000
1989	Little Bold John, 7, 122	D. A. Miller Jr.	Oraibi, 4, 119	Finder's Choice, 4, 117	13	1:22.00	120,000
1988	Private Terms, 3, 116	K. Desormeaux	Dynaformer, 3, 122	Delightful Doctor, 3, 122	13	1:38.80	74,328
1987	Templar Hill, 3, 116	G. W. Hutton	Hay Halo, 3, 122	Win Dusty Win, 3, 114	11	1:44.00	74,620
1986	Broad Brush, 3, 122	V. A. Bracciale Jr.	Fast Step, 3, 113	Swallow, 3, 116	7	1:45.00	54,373
	‡Lil Tyler, 3, 122	J. Nied Jr.	Fobby Forbes, 3, 116	Fork Union Cadet, 3, 110	6	1:45.60	53,723
1985	Roo Art, 3, 122	D. A. Miller Jr.	Joyfull John, 3, 112	I Am the Game, 3, 119	8	1:37.60	55,380
1984	‡Judge Mc Guire, 3, 122	C. H. Mendoza	American Artist, 3, 110	S. S. Hot Sauce, 3, 122	9	1:46.60	55,543
1981	Classic Go Go, 3, 122	B. Fann	Thirty Eight Paces, 3, 122	Aztec Crown, 3, 115	9	1:23.20	37,115

Year	Winner	Jockey	Second	Third	Strs	Time	1st Purse
1980	Galaxy Road, 3, 122	G. McCarron	Leader of the Pack, 3, 113	Ashanti Gold, 3, 110	7	1:24.60	$36,660
1978	Ten Ten, 3, 122	W. J. Passmore	Game Prince, 3, 113	Gala Forecast, 3, 113	8	1:45.80	18,200
1977	Do the Bump, 3, 122	C. J. McCarron	John U to Berry, 3, 115	Steel Bandit, 3, 113	6	1:47.20	17,778
1976	Princely Game, 3, 119	A. Agnello	On the Sly, 3, 110	Troll By, 3, 116	7	1:44.60	17,940
1975	Pendulum Sam, 3, 110	L. Gino	King of Fools, 3, 113	Broadway Reviewer, 3, 110	7	1:48.20	18,005
1974	Sharp Gary, 3, 122	C. Barrera	Jolly Johu, 3, 119	Ground Breaker, 3, 110	10	1:46.60	19,045
1973	Ecole Etage, 3, 113	G. Cusimano	Big Red L., 3, 113	Select Performance, 3, 110	9	1:44.60	18,265

Named for Gen. George Washington (1731-'99), first president of the United States. General George S. 1973-'94. General George Breeders' Cup H. 2007. Held at Bowie 1973-'84. Held at Pimlico 1986. Not held 1979, 1982-'83, 2006. 1 1/16 miles 1973-'78, 1984, 1986-'87. 1 mile 1985. Three-year-olds 1973-'88. Two divisions 1986. ‡American Artist finished first, DQ to second, 1984. ‡Fobby Forbes finished first, DQ to second, 1986 (2nd Div.).

Generous Stakes

Grade 3 in 2008. Hollywood Park, two-year-olds, 1 mile, turf. Held November 23, 2007, with a gross value of $111,800. First held in 1982. First graded in 1986. Stakes record 1:34.28 (2007 The Leopard).

Year	Winner	Jockey	Second	Third	Strs	Time	1st Purse
2007	The Leopard, 2, 117	G. K. Gomez	Indian Sun, 2, 117	Meer Kat (Ire), 2, 117	9	**1:34.28**	$71,800
2006	Warning Zone, 2, 119	C. S. Nakatani	Unusual Suspect, 2, 118	‡Man to Man, 2, 117	8	1:36.59	45,000
	Whatsthescript (Ire), 2, 117	I. D. Enriquez	Vauquelin (Ire), 2, 117	Sevengoldnmissiles, 2, 117	8	1:36.04	45,000
2004	Dubleo, 2, 121	C. S. Nakatani	Littlebitoflzip, 2, 116	Sunny Sky (Fr), 2, 116	12	1:37.21	60,000
2003	Castledale (Ire), 2, 116	J. A. Krone	Dealer Choice (Fr), 2, 116	Lucky Pulpit, 2, 116	12	1:35.43	60,000
2002	Peace Rules, 2, 118	V. Espinoza	Lismore Knight, 2, 121	Outta Here, 2, 115	9	1:35.49	120,000
2001	Mountain Rage, 2, 116	D. R. Flores	Miesque's Approval, 2, 121	National Park (GB), 2, 117	8	1:40.31	120,000
2000	Startac, 2, 118	A. O. Solis	Broadway Moon, 2, 116	Deeliteful Irving, 2, 119	9	1:34.76	120,000
1999	Jokerman, 2, 118	P. Day	Purely Cozzene, 2, 121	Kleofus, 2, 121	6	1:35.23	120,000
1998	Incurable Optimist, 2, 121	J. R. Velazquez	Company Approval, 2, 114	Brave Gun, 2, 117	8	1:37.72	150,000
1997	Mantles Star (GB), 2, 114	C. J. McCarron	F J's Pace, 2, 116	Commitisize, 2, 121	8	1:36.73	150,000
1996	Hello (Ire), 2, 114	C. J. McCarron	Steel Ruhlr, 2, 114	Divine Insight, 2, 114	12	1:34.77	150,000
1995	Old Chapel, 2, 121	G. L. Stevens	Ayrton S, 2, 116	Heza Gone West, 2, 117	10	1:35.11	137,500
1994	Native Regent, 2, 121	D. Penna	Dangerous Scenario, 2, 116	Claudius, 2, 121	9	1:37.15	137,500
1993	Delineator, 2, 118	R. A. Baze	Devon Port (Fr), 2, 116	Ferrara, 2, 114	8	1:34.73	137,500
1992	Earl of Barking (Ire), 2, 114	A. O. Solis	Devil's Rock, 2, 115	Corby, 2, 118	8	1:34.49	137,500
1991	Silver Ray, 2, 114	M. A. Pedroza	Thinkernot, 2, 115	African Colony, 2, 114	9	1:35.00	74,775
	Contested Bid, 2, 114	C. S. Nakatani	Turbulent Kris, 2, 114	Sevengreenpairs, 2, 114	9	1:34.41	71,575
1990	Satis (Fr), 2, 115	C. A. Black	What a Spell, 2, 114	Ev for Shir, 2, 114	12	1:35.20	67,800
1989	Single Dawn, 2, 114	A. O. Solis	Pleasant Tap, 2, 118	Doyouseewhatisee, 2, 120	12	1:35.60	69,600
1988	Music Merci, 2, 121	G. L. Stevens	Double Quick, 2, 121	Crown Collection, 2, 115	9	1:36.40	58,220
	Shipping Time, 2, 114	C. A. Black	Super May, 2, 115	Past Ages, 2, 116	7	1:37.20	58,220
1987	Purdue King, 2, 121	C. J. McCarron	Chinese Gold, 2, 121	Blade of the Ball, 2, 115	6	1:36.00	47,500
	White Mischief, 2, 115	J. A. Santos	King Alobar, 2, 115	Texas Typhoon, 2, 115	8	1:35.40	68,750
1986	Persevered, 2, 120	G. L. Stevens	Wilderness Bound, 2, 120	Quietly Bold, 2, 115	9	1:41.60	86,050
	†Sweettuc, 2, 113	G. L. Stevens	Savona Tower, 2, 116	Lord Duckworth, 2, 114	9	1:41.60	68,050
1985	Darby Fair, 2, 120	A. L. Castanon	Snow Chief, 2, 120	Acks Lika Ruler, 2, 114	6	1:37.00	119,400
1984	Overtrump, 2, 120	C. J. McCarron	Right Con, 2, 120	Herat, 2, 120	11	1:41.80	123,350
1983	Artichoke, 2, 120	W. Shoemaker	Nagurski, 2, 114	Fortune's Kingdom, 2, 115	8	1:38.40	50,100
	Precisionist, 2, 116	C. J. McCarron	Fali Time, 2, 120	Tights, 2, 115	9	1:37.60	50,100
1982	Fifth Division, 2, 117	L. A. Pincay Jr.	Dominating Dooley, 2, 114	Mezzo, 2, 116	12	1:35.60	33,450

Named for Fahd Salman's 1991 Irish Horse of the Year and dual European classic winner Generous (Ire) (1988 c. by Caerleon [Ire]). Formerly named for Mrs. Stephen C. Clark Jr.'s 1970 champion two-year-old male and '87 leading North American broodmare sire Hoist the Flag (1968 c. by Tom Rolfe). Grade 2 1988-'89. Hoist the Flag S. 1982-'92. Not held 2005. 1 1/16 miles 1984, '86. Dirt 1985, '88. Two divisions 1983, 1986-'88, 1991, 2006. ‡Private Wind finished third, DQ to seventh, 2006 (1st Div.). †Denotes female.

Glens Falls Handicap

Grade 3 in 2008. Saratoga Race Course, three-year-olds and up, fillies and mares, 1 3/8 miles, turf. Held September 3, 2007, with a gross value of $111,200. First held in 1996. First graded in 1999. Stakes record 2:12.81 (1999 Idle Rich).

Year	Winner	Jockey	Second	Third	Strs	Time	1st Purse
2007	Rosinka (Ire), 4, 119	J. Rose	Mauralakana (Fr), 4, 117	Pictavia (Ire), 5, 116	8	2:13.00	$66,720
2006	Noble Stella (Ger), 5, 118	M. E. Smith	Latice (Ire), 5, 116	Louve Royale (Ire), 5, 116	9	2:16.02	67,260
2005	Honey Ryder, 4, 120	J. R. Velazquez	Film Maker, 5, 122	Banyu Dewi (Ger), 6, 115	6	2:14.51	65,520
2004	Humaita (Ger), 4, 114	C. H. Velasquez	Where We Left Off (GB), 4, 116	Savedbythelight, 4, 115	8	2:15.25	66,240
	Arvada (GB), 4, 112	J. R. Velazquez	Spice Island, 5, 118	Film Maker, 4, 121	8	2:14.12	65,580
2003	Sixty Seconds (NZ), 5, 115	J. A. Santos	Primetimevalentine, 4, 113	Alternate, 4, 110	9	2:13.96	67,860
2002	Owsley, 4, 116	E. S. Prado	Mot Juste (GB), 4, 116	Sunstone (GB), 4, 114	10	2:15.99	68,100
2001	Irving's Baby, 4, 126	J. D. Bailey	New Assembly (Ire), 4, 113	Caveat's Shot, 6, 114	7	2:07.56	65,995
2000	I'm Indy Mood, 5, 116	H. Castillo Jr.	Idle Rich, 5, 114	Cybil, 4, 114	6	2:07.41	66,120
1999	Idle Rich, 4, 115	J. D. Bailey	Adrian, 5, 114	Bundling, 5, 114	7	**2:12.81**	65,760
1998	Auntie Mame, 4, 120	J. R. Velazquez	Yvecrique (Fr), 4, 115	Makethemostofit, 4, 111	6	2:13.15	66,000
1997	Shemozzle (Ire), 4, 115	J. D. Bailey	Picture Hat, 5, 113	Last Approach, 5, 113	5	2:12.89	64,740
1996	Ampulla, 5, 113	S. J. Sellers	Look Daggers, 4, 118	Electric Society (Ire), 5, 120	6	2:16.49	67,500

Named for Glens Falls, New York, a town about 15 miles north of Saratoga Springs. Glens Falls S. 1996-'97. 1 1/4 miles 2000-'01. Dirt 2000-'01. Originally scheduled on turf 2001. Two divisions 2004.

Go for Wand Handicap

Grade 1 in 2008. Saratoga Race Course, three-year-olds and up, fillies and mares, 1 1/8 miles, dirt. Held July 28, 2007, with a gross value of $250,000. First held in 1954. First graded in 1973. Stakes record 1:47.86 (2004 Azeri).

Year	Winner	Jockey	Second	Third	Strs	Time	1st Purse
2007	Ginger Punch, 4, 117	R. Bejarano	Miss Shop, 4, 115	Teammate, 4, 117	6	1:49.19	$150,000
2006	Spun Sugar, 4, 118	M. J. Luzzi	Balletto (UAE), 4, 115	Pool Land, 4, 117	6	1:49.93	150,000
2005	Ashado, 4, 121	J. R. Velazquez	Bending Strings, 4, 115	Andujar, 4, 118	5	1:50.30	150,000
2004	Azeri, 6, 120	P. Day	Sightseek, 5, 122	Storm Flag Flying, 4, 117	5	**1:47.86**	150,000
2003	Sightseek, 4, 121	J. D. Bailey	She's Got the Beat, 4, 112	Nonsuch Bay, 4, 113	6	1:50.92	150,000
2002	Dancethruthedawn, 4, 118	J. D. Bailey	Transcendental, 4, 113	Too Scarlet, 4, 112	7	1:50.21	150,000
2001	Serra Lake, 4, 113	E. S. Prado	Pompeii, 4, 114	March Magic, 4, 114	8	1:49.62	150,000
2000	Heritage of Gold, 5, 123	S. J. Sellers	Beautiful Pleasure, 5, 125	Roza Robata, 5, 114	5	1:49.84	150,000
1999	Banshee Breeze, 4, 124	J. D. Bailey	Beautiful Pleasure, 4, 113	Heritage of Gold, 4, 117	5	1:49.95	150,000
1998	Aldiza, 4, 114	M. E. Smith	Escena, 5, 124	Tomisue's Delight, 4, 116	7	1:49.88	150,000
1997	Hidden Lake, 4, 123	R. Migliore	Flat Fleet Feet, 4, 120	Clear Mandate, 5, 113	7	1:49.60	150,000
1996	Exotic Wood, 4, 115	C. J. McCarron	Shoop, 5, 118	Frolic, 4, 113	8	1:49.44	105,000
1995	Heavenly Prize, 4, 123	P. Day	Forcing Bid, 4, 108	Little Buckles, 4, 111	5	1:49.90	105,000
1994	Sky Beauty, 4, 123	M. E. Smith	Link River, 4, 123	Life Is Delicious, 4, 123	5	1:49.47	90,000
1993	Turnback the Alarm, 4, 123	C. W. Antley	Nannerl, 6, 116	November Snow, 4, 116	4	1:36.02	120,000
1992	Easy Now, 3, 111	J. D. Bailey	‡Train Robbery, 5, 118	Wide Country, 4, 116	5	1:36.13	120,000
1991	Queena, 5, 123	A. T. Cordero Jr.	Fit to Scout, 4, 123	Screen Prospect, 4, 116	6	1:34.89	120,000
1990	Go for Wand, 3, 118	R. P. Romero	Feel the Beat, 5, 123	Mistaurian, 4, 116	6	1:35.60	68,760
1989	Miss Brio (Chi), 5, 116	J. D. Bailey	Proper Evidence, 4, 116	Aptostar, 4, 123	5	1:35.60	67,080
1988	Personal Ensign, 4, 123	R. P. Romero	Winning Colors, 3, 118	Sham Say, 3, 115	4	1:34.20	67,080
1987	North Sider, 5, 123	A. T. Cordero Jr.	Wisla, 4, 111	Funistrada, 4, 116	7	1:35.00	85,500
1986	Lady's Secret, 4, 125	P. Day	Steal a Kiss, 3, 109	Endear, 4, 120	6	1:33.40	81,060
1985	Lady's Secret, 3, 111	J. Velasquez	Dowery, 4, 117	Mrs. Revere, 4, 117	8	1:34.80	85,020
1984	Miss Oceana, 3, 120	E. Maple	Paradies (Arg), 4, 114	Nany, 4, 120	6	1:35.20	70,560
1983	Ambassador of Luck, 4, 116	A. Graell	A Kiss for Luck, 4, 120	Am Capable, 3, 109	6	1:36.40	67,560
1982	Too Chic, 3, 110	R. Hernandez	Ambassador of Luck, 3, 111	Anti Lib, 4, 116	4	1:34.80	67,920
1981	Jameela, 5, 123	J. Vasquez	Love Sign, 4, 123	Island Charm, 4, 116	5	1:35.00	65,280
1980	Bold 'n Determined, 3, 122	E. Delahoussaye	Genuine Risk, 3, 118	Love Sign, 3, 120	5	1:35.40	49,140
1979	Blitey, 3, 112	A. T. Cordero Jr.	It's in the Air, 3, 122	Pearl Necklace, 5, 125	5	1:34.80	48,015
1978	Pearl Necklace, 4, 123	R. Hernandez	Ida Delia, 4, 113	Sensational, 4, 117	5	1:33.80	48,195
1977	What a Summer, 4, 126	J. Vasquez	Crab Grass, 5, 114	Harvest Girl, 3, 111	8	1:37.40	32,280
1976	Artfully, 3, 108	P. Day	Snooze, 4, 108	Land Girl, 4, 109	7	1:34.00	25,920
	Sugar Plum Time, 4, 111	J. Imparato	Pacific Princess, 3, 110	Fleet Victress, 4, 115	9	1:34.00	26,220
1975	Let Me Linger, 3, 117	L. A. Pincay Jr.	Honorable Miss, 5, 121	Susan's Girl, 6, 128	8	1:35.20	34,590
1974	‡Ponte Vecchio, 4, 118	J. Vasquez	Poker Night, 4, 116	Twixt, 5, 124	12	1:34.60	35,850
1973	Light Hearted, 4, 126	E. Nelson	Convenience, 5, 121	Krislin, 4, 111	6	1:34.80	17,040

Named for Christiana Stable's Racing Hall of Fame member, 1989 champion two-year-old filly, '90 champion three-year-old filly, and '90 Maskette S. (G1) winner Go for Wand (1987 f. by Deputy Minister). Go for Wand is buried in Saratoga's infield. Formerly named for James R. Keene's 1908 champion two-year-old filly and Futurity S. winner Maskette (1906 f. by Disguise). Maskette H. 1954-'78. Maskette S. 1979-'91. Go for Wand S. 1992-'97. Held at Belmont Park 1954-'58, 1961, 1969-'93. Held at Aqueduct 1959-'60, 1962-'68. 1 mile 1954-'93. Two divisions 1976. ‡Desert Vixen finished first, DQ to 12th for a positive drug test, 1974. ‡Nannerl finished second, DQ to 12th, 1992.

Golden Gate Fields Stakes

Grade 3 in 2008. Golden Gate Fields, three-year-olds and up, 1 3/8 miles, turf. Held May 31, 2008, with a gross value of $100,000. First held in 1947. First graded in 1975. Stakes record 2:13 (1984 John Henry).

Year	Winner	Jockey	Second	Third	Strs	Time	1st Purse
2008	Sudan (Ire), 5, 123	D. R. Flores	Fitz Flag (Arg), 8, 123	Uffizi, 5, 123	6	2:16.86	$60,000
2007	Fantastic Spain, 7, 122	C. P. Schvaneveldt	Notable Guest, 6, 122	Macduff (GB), 5, 122	8	2:17.64	118,900
2006	Cosmonaut, 4, 113	T. Farina	Adreamisborn, 7, 122	Cheroot, 5, 114	5	1:48.75	82,500
2005	Adreamisborn, 6, 117	R. A. Baze	Night Bokbel (Ire), 6, 116	Fantastic Spain, 5, 112	8	1:46.28	68,750
2004	Tronare (Chi), 6, 115	R. M. Gonzalez	Soud, 6, 118	Aly Bubba, 5, 116	9	1:48.48	41,250
2003	Ninebanks, 5, 116	R. J. Warren Jr.	Surprise Halo, 5, 115	Royal Gem, 4, 118	4	1:50.07	82,500
2002	No Slip (Fr), 4, 117	K. Desormeaux	Kerrygold (Fr), 6, 116	Sumitas (Ger), 6, 119	5	1:49.41	82,500
2001	Northern Quest (Fr), 6, 118	V. Espinoza	Eagleton, 5, 114	Entorchado (Ire), 4, 115	6	1:58.58	137,500
2000	Deploy Venture (GB), 4, 115	R. A. Baze	Single Empire (Ire), 6, 121	Bonapartiste (Fr), 6, 119	6	2:19.12	120,000
1999	Sayarshan (Fr), 4, 112	B. Blanc	Alvo Certo (Brz), 6, 117	Plicck (Fr), 5, 117	8	2:15.56	120,000
1998	Dushyantor, 5, 118	C. S. Nakatani	Eternity Range, 5, 114	Star Performance, 5, 116	6	2:15.26	150,000
1997	Irish Wings (Ire), 5, 114	D. Carr	Savinio, 5, 116	Mufattish, 4, 114	7	1:49.60	120,000
1996	Time Star, 5, 116	C. A. Black	Sand Reef (GB), 5, 116	Bon Point (GB), 6, 117	6	2:16.37	120,000
1995	Special Price, 6, 122	E. Delahoussaye	Bluegrass Prince (Ire), 4, 122	Sans Ecocide (GB), 4, 122	6	2:15.14	110,000
1994	Alex the Great (GB), 5, 118	P. A. Valenzuela	Fanmore, 6, 117	Emerald Jig, 5, 113	8	2:15.41	165,000
1993	Val des Bois (Fr), 7, 119	P. A. Valenzuela	Norwich (GB), 6, 116	Never Black, 6, 116	5	1:48.21	165,000
1992	Algenib (Arg), 6, 115	L. A. Pincay Jr.	Missionary Ridge (GB), 5, 114	Never Black, 5, 113	7	2:13.96	220,000
1991	Forty Niner Days, 4, 115	R. Q. Meza	Aksar, 4, 115	Missionary Ridge (GB), 4, 114	9	2:17.30	220,000
1990	†Petite Ile (Ire), 4, 113	C. A. Black	Valdali (Ire), 4, 114	Pleasant Variety, 6, 116	11	2:15.60	220,000
1989	Frankly Perfect, 4, 117	E. Delahoussaye	Pleasant Variety, 5, 114	†Brown Bess, 7, 114	7	2:15.00	165,000
1988	Great Communicator, 5, 120	R. Sibille	Putting (Fr), 5, 117	Rivlia, 6, 120	5	2:15.40	165,000
1987	Rivlia, 5, 116	C. J. McCarron	Air Display, 4, 115	Reco (Fr), 5, 113	8	2:14.20	165,000

Year	Winner	Jockey	Second	Third	Strs	Time	1st Purse
1986	dh-Le Solaret (Fr), 4, 113	M. Castaneda		Complice (Fr), 5, 115	5	2:16.40	$113,875
	dh-Val Danseur, 6, 117	G. L. Stevens					
1985	Fatih, 5, 119	T. Lipham	†Fact Finder, 6, 115	dh-Nak Ack, 4, 115	9	2:15.40	171,770
				dh-Semillero (Chi), 5, 115			
1984	John Henry, 9, 125	C. J. McCarron	Silveyville, 6, 117	Lucence, 5, 116	6	**2:13.00**	184,200
1983	Silveyville, 5, 115	D. Winick	Ask Me, 4, 115	Majesty's Prince, 4, 122	9	2:16.40	165,800
1982	Regal Bearing (GB), 6, 117	R. A. Baze	Visible Pole, 4, 110	Score Twenty Four, 5, 121	5	1:46.00	73,900
1981	Caterman (NZ), 5, 123	M. Castaneda	Opus Dei (Fr), 6, 121	His Honor, 6, 118	9	1:41.40	77,000
1980	Eagle Toast, 6, 113	P. A. Valenzuela	Daranstone, 5, 108	Saboulard (Fr), 5, 116	7	1:41.00	63,200
1979	As de Copas (Arg), 6, 120	H. E. Moreno	True Statement, 5, 121	Bywayofchicago, 5, 123	6	1:43.40	62,600
1978	Bad 'n Big, 4, 120	A. L. Diaz	Effervescing, 5, 123	Jumping Hill, 6, 124	9	1:44.80	65,500
1977	Announcer, 5, 115	M. Castaneda	The Fop, 4, 114	Sir Jason, 6, 116	14	1:40.40	71,700
1976	Pass the Glass, 5, 119	F. Olivares	Willie Pleasant, 5, 111	Barrydown, 6, 117	6	1:41.40	31,250
1975	Pass the Glass, 4, 115	F. Olivares	Confederate Yankee, 4, 116	Ga Hai, 4, 118	10	1:41.80	33,150
1974	Acclimatization, 6, 119	S. Valdez	*Yvetot, 6, 118	Wild World, 5, 111	9	2:27.80	46,350
1973	Wing Out, 5, 124	R. Schacht	Fair Test, 5, 116	*Yvetot, 5, 116	7	1:43.80	30,800

Formerly named for Stanford University, located in nearby Palo Alto, California 2005. Grade 2 1985-'96. Golden Gate H. 1947-2000. Golden Gate Breeders' Cup H. 2001-'04. Stanford Breeders' Cup H. 2005. Golden Gate Fields H. 2006. Golden Gate Fields Breeders' Cup S. 2007. Held at Bay Meadows 2005. 1¼ miles 1947-'50, 1952, 1955, 1959-'61. 1⅛ miles 1951, 1954, 1956-'58, 1965-'67, 1993, 1997, 2001-'04, 2006. 1³⁄₁₆ miles 1953. 1¹⁄₁₆ miles 1962-'64, 1968-'73, 1975-'82, 2005. 1½ miles 1974. Dirt 1947-'71, 1982, 2006. Originally scheduled on turf 2006. Four-year-olds and up 2006. Dead heat for third 1985. Dead heat for first 1986. Course record 1975. Equaled course record 1993. †Denotes female.

Golden Rod Stakes

Grade 2 in 2008. Churchill Downs, two-year-olds, fillies, 1¹⁄₁₆ miles, dirt. Held November 24, 2007, with a gross value of $276,500. First held in 1910. First graded in 1973. Stakes record 1:43.59 (2007 Pure Clan).

Year	Winner	Jockey	Second	Third	Strs	Time	1st Purse
2007	Pure Clan, 2, 119	J. R. Leparoux	C J's Leelee, 2, 119	Turn Away, 2, 119	8	**1:43.59**	$166,288
2006	Lady Joanne, 2, 119	J. McKee	Change Up, 2, 119	High Heels, 2, 119	9	1:44.12	133,684
2005	French Park, 2, 122	M. Guidry	She Says It Best, 2, 122	Lady Danza, 2, 118	8	1:47.26	137,764
2004	Runway Model, 2, 122	E. M. Martin Jr.	Kota, 2, 118	Summerly, 2, 116	6	1:45.97	133,548
2003	Be Gentle, 2, 122	J. McKee	Lotta Kim, 2, 116	Dynaville, 2, 116	11	1:45.91	142,600
2002	My Boston Gal, 2, 117	C. H. Borel	Holiday Lady, 2, 115	My Trusty Cat, 2, 115	7	1:45.00	136,152
2001	Belterra, 2, 117	J. K. Court	Take Charge Lady, 2, 122	Lotta Rhythm, 2, 122	5	1:43.82	133,424
2000	Miss Pickums, 2, 122	J. J. Vitek	Nasty Storm, 2, 113	My White Corvette, 2, 119	9	1:48.84	138,384
1999	Humble Clerk, 2, 119	J. K. Court	Cash Run, 2, 122	Secret Status, 2, 111	9	1:45.26	138,880
1998	Silverbulletday, 2, 122	G. L. Stevens	Here I Go, 2, 113	Lefty's Dollbaby, 2, 113	6	1:43.87	134,292
1997	Love Lock, 2, 119	R. Albarado	Barefoot Dyana, 2, 119	Grechelle, 2, 111	9	1:44.49	139,996
1996	City Band, 2, 122	S. J. Sellers	Glitter Woman, 2, 113	Water Street, 2, 122	10	1:46.82	139,996
1995	Gold Sunrise, 2, 113	W. Martinez	Birr, 2, 119	Solana, 2, 113	11	1:45.46	97,500
1994	Lilly Capote, 2, 113	D. M. Barton	Morris Code, 2, 113	Cat Appeal, 2, 119	8	1:46.66	97,500
1993	At the Half, 2, 122	P. Day	Spiritofpocahontas, 2, 115	Mystic Union, 2, 111	9	1:46.83	97,500
1992	Boots 'n Jackie, 2, 120	M. A. Lee	Mollie Creek, 2, 115	Dance Account, 2, 113	6	1:47.29	97,500
1991	Vivid Imagination, 2, 115	J. M. Johnson	Met Her Dream, 2, 113	Pennant Fever, 2, 113	8	1:46.38	97,500
1990	Fancy Ribbons, 2, 114	J. E. Bruin	Nice Assay, 2, 115	Til Forbid, 2, 113	8	1:45.40	97,500
1989	De La Devil, 2, 117	J. A. Krone	Crowned, 2, 120	Flew by Em, 2, 117	7	1:44.60	97,500
1988	Born Famous, 2, 120	E. Fires	Coax Chelsie, 2, 120	Darby Shuffle, 2, 120	6	1:48.20	97,500
1987	Darien Miss, 2, 118	P. A. Johnson	Tap Your Toes, 2, 118	Most Likely, 2, 118	7	1:48.20	83,814
1986	Stargrass, 2, 118	K. K. Allen	Zero Minus, 2, 121	Laserette, 2, 113	11	1:46.60	98,353
1985	Slippin n' Slyding, 2, 116	C. R. Woods Jr.	Turn and Dance, 2, 110	Bonded Miss, 2, 113	9	1:46.20	95,693
1984	Kamikaze Rick, 2, 116	R. Migliore	Boldly Dared, 2, 114	Gallant Libby, 2, 118	9	1:47.80	101,155
1983	Flippers, 2, 119	P. Day	Robin's Rob, 2, 116	Mallorca, 2, 116	11	1:47.60	86,153
1982	Weekend Surprise, 2, 119	P. Day	National Banner, 2, 116	Quarrel Over, 2, 116	6	1:47.00	77,701
1981	Betty Money, 2, 119	D. Brumfield	Hoist Emy's Flag, 2, 116	Subdeb, 2, 119	12	1:45.80	91,669
1980	Mamzelle, 2, 116	M. S. Sellers	Switch Point, 2, 116	Brent's Star, 2, 119	7	1:46.20	83,236
1979	Remote Ruler, 2, 116	S. Maple	Forever Cordial, 2, 116	Peachblow, 2, 116	10	1:25.00	43,095
1978	Angel Island, 2, 119	E. Delahoussaye	Safe, 2, 113	Too Many Sweets, 2, 119	8	1:24.20	36,325
1977	Bold Rendezvous, 2, 113	P. Nicolo	Rainy Princess, 2, 116	Silver Spook, 2, 113	10	1:27.00	46,449
1976	Bring Out the Band, 2, 114	D. Brumfield	Shady Lou, 2, 116	Ciao, 2, 113	10	1:25.20	38,688
1975	Old Goat, 2, 119	M. Hole	Confort Zone, 2, 113	Silent Bidder, 2, 114	7	1:24.80	37,941
1974	Mirthful Flirt, 2, 119	W. J. Passmore	Sun and Snow, 2, 119	Yale Coed, 2, 119	10	1:26.60	38,597
1973	Chris Evert, 2, 116	L. A. Pincay Jr.	Bundler, 2, 119	Kiss Me Darlin, 2, 116	13	1:25.20	38,200

Named for the state flower of Kentucky, the goldenrod. Grade 3 1973-'82, 1989-'99. Not graded 1983-'88. Not held 1928-'61. 6 furlongs 1910-'18. 1 mile 1919. 7 furlongs 1920-'27, 1962-'79.

Goodwood Stakes

Grade 1 in 2008. Oak Tree at Santa Anita, three-year-olds and up, 1⅛ miles, all weather. Held September 29, 2007, with a gross value of $520,000. First held in 1982. First graded in 1982. Stakes record 1:46.72 (1994 Bertrando).

Year	Winner	Jockey	Second	Third	Strs	Time	1st Purse
2007	Tiago, 3, 121	M. E. Smith	Awesome Gem, 4, 124	Big Booster, 6, 124	8	1:46.93	$300,000
2006	Lava Man, 5, 126	C. S. Nakatani	Brother Derek, 3, 116	Giacomo, 4, 118	7	1:48.15	300,000
2005	Rock Hard Ten, 4, 121	G. L. Stevens	Roman Ruler, 3, 114	Choctaw Nation, 5, 118	4	1:48.68	300,000

Year	Winner	Jockey	Second	Third	Strs	Time	1st Purse
2004	Lundy's Liability (Brz), 4, 118	D. R. Flores	Total Impact (Chi), 6, 119	Supah Blitz, 4, 117	5	1:48.39	$300,000
2003	Pleasantly Perfect, 5, 116	A. O. Solis	Fleetstreet Dancer, 5, 113	Star Cross (Arg), 6, 110	8	1:48.37	300,000
2002	Pleasantly Perfect, 4, 115	A. O. Solis	Momentum, 4, 119	Reba's Gold, 5, 116	9	1:46.80	300,000
2001	Freedom Crest, 5, 116	K. Desormeaux	Skimming, 5, 123	Tiznow, 4, 124	6	1:48.86	300,000
2000	Tiznow, 3, 116	C. J. McCarron	Captain Steve, 3, 117	Euchre, 4, 115	7	1:47.38	240,000
1999	Budroyale, 6, 119	G. K. Gomez	General Challenge, 3, 120	Old Trieste, 4, 120	6	1:48.31	300,000
1998	Silver Charm, 4, 124	G. L. Stevens	Free House, 4, 124	Score Quick, 6, 115	6	1:47.21	262,800
1997	Benchmark, 6, 118	E. Delahoussaye	Score Quick, 5, 114	Hesabull, 4, 117	5	1:47.60	158,700
1996	‡Savinio, 6, 117	C. S. Nakatani	Dare and Go, 5, 122	Alphabet Soup, 5, 120	4	1:47.88	189,300
1995	Soul of the Matter, 4, 121	K. Desormeaux	Tinners Way, 5, 121	Alphabet Soup, 4, 116	5	1:47.54	144,450
1994	Bertrando, 5, 120	G. L. Stevens	Dramatic Gold, 3, 115	Tossofthecoin, 4, 115	6	**1:46.72**	124,400
1993	Lottery Winner, 4, 115	K. Desormeaux	Region, 4, 116	Pleasant Tango, 3, 115	7	1:47.71	127,200
1992	Reign Road, 4, 116	K. Desormeaux	Sir Beaufort, 5, 116	Marquetry, 5, 120	6	1:48.36	125,200
1991	The Prime Minister, 4, 115	C. J. McCarron	Marquetry, 4, 119	Pleasant Tap, 4, 117	6	1:47.99	152,300
1990	Lively One, 5, 120	A. O. Solis	Miserden, 4, 112	Festin (Arg), 4, 116	7	1:48.00	126,800
1989	Present Value, 5, 119	E. Delahoussaye	Rahy, 4, 121	Happy Toss (Arg), 4, 116	8	1:47.20	128,800
1988	Cutlass Reality, 6, 124	G. L. Stevens	Lively One, 3, 116	Stylish Winner, 4, 113	8	1:47.20	130,400
1987	Ferdinand, 4, 127	W. Shoemaker	Candi's Gold, 3, 117	Skywalker, 5, 123	6	1:50.80	102,500
1986	Super Diamond, 6, 122	L. A. Pincay Jr.	Epidaurus, 4, 116	Prince Don B., 5, 115	8	1:41.20	65,500
1985	Lord At War (Arg), 5, 125	W. Shoemaker	Matafao, 4, 116	Last Command, 4, 115	6	1:50.20	62,800
1984	Lord At War (Arg), 4, 117	W. Shoemaker	Video Kid, 4, 118	Menswear, 6, 117	6	1:42.00	60,150
1983	Pettrax, 5, 117	K. D. Black	Konewah, 4, 115	Stancharry, 5, 117	6	1:42.60	46,650
1982	Cajun Prince, 5, 115	W. A. Guerra	Caterman (NZ), 6, 122	Rock Softly, 4, 116	6	1:40.20	46,600

Named for Goodwood Race Course in England, the Oak Tree Racing Association's sister track. Grade 3 1982, 1985-'89. Not graded 1983-'84. Grade 2 1990-2006. Goodwood H. 1982-'95. Goodwood Breeders' Cup H. 1996-2006. 1¹⁄₁₆ miles 1982-'84, 1986. Dirt 1982-2006. ‡Alphabet Soup finished first, DQ to third, 1996.

Gotham Stakes

Grade 3 in 2008. Aqueduct, three-year-olds, 1¹⁄₁₆ miles, dirt. Held March 8, 2008, with a gross value of $250,000. First held in 1953. First graded in 1973. Stakes record 1:43 (1959 Atoll).

Year	Winner	Jockey	Second	Third	Strs	Time	1st Purse
2008	Visionaire, 3, 116	J. Lezcano	Texas Wildcatter, 3, 116	Larrys Revenge, 3, 116	9	1:44.60	$150,000
2007	Cowtown Cat, 3, 116	R. A. Dominguez	Wafi City, 3, 116	Summer Doldrums, 3, 120	9	1:44.75	120,000
2006	Like Now, 3, 116	F. Jara	Keyed Entry, 3, 120	Sweetnorthernsaint, 3, 116	10	1:43.17	120,000
2005	Survivalist, 3, 116	R. Migliore	‡Galloping Grocer, 3, 120	Naughty New Yorker, 3, 116	9	1:35.61	90,000
2004	Saratoga County, 3, 116	J. Castellano	Pomeroy, 3, 116	Eddington, 3, 116	8	1:35.53	120,000
2003	Alysweep, 3, 120	R. Migliore	Grey Comet, 3, 120	Spite the Devil, 3, 116	9	1:40.60	120,000
2002	Mayakovsky, 3, 116	E. S. Prado	Saarland, 3, 120	Parade of Music, 3, 116	7	1:34.90	120,000
2001	Richly Blended, 3, 116	R. Wilson	Mr. John, 3, 116	Voodoo, 3, 116	9	1:35.14	120,000
2000	Red Bullet, 3, 113	A. O. Solis	Aptitude, 3, 113	Performing Magic, 3, 114	9	1:34.27	120,000
1999	Badge, 3, 120	S. Bridgmohan	Apremont, 3, 120	Robin Goodfellow, 3, 113	11	1:34.72	90,000
1998	Wasatch, 3, 117	J. D. Bailey	Dr J, 3, 119	Late Edition, 3, 114	10	1:36.56	90,000
1997	Smokin Mel, 3, 112	J. R. Velazquez	Ordway, 3, 122	Wild Wonder, 3, 119	11	1:34.38	120,000
1996	Romano Gucci, 3, 119	J. A. Krone	Tiger Talk, 3, 117	Feather Box, 3, 114	10	1:34.40	120,000
1995	Talkin Man, 3, 122	M. E. Smith	Da Hoss, 3, 117	Devious Course, 3, 117	11	1:36.82	150,000
1994	Irgun, 3, 114	J. D. Bailey	Bit of Puddin, 3, 116	Jesse F, 3, 114	12	1:36.27	150,000
1993	As Indicated, 3, 114	C. V. Bisono	Itaka, 3, 114	Strolling Along, 3, 121	8	1:36.24	120,000
1992	dh-Devil His Due, 3, 114	W. H. McCauley		Best Decorated, 3, 114	8	1:35.63	102,500
	dh-Lure, 3, 114	M. E. Smith					
1991	Kyle's Our Man, 3, 121	A. T. Cordero Jr.	King Mutesa, 3, 118	Another Review, 3, 118	8	1:34.69	150,000
1990	Thirty Six Red, 3, 114	M. E. Smith	Senor Pete, 3, 121	Burnt Hills, 3, 114	10	1:33.80	182,400
1989	Easy Goer, 3, 123	P. Day	Diamond Donnie, 3, 114	Expensive Decision, 3, 114	5	1:32.40	168,300
1988	Private Terms, 3, 126	C. W. Antley	Seeking the Gold, 3, 114	Perfect Spy, 3, 121	8	1:34.80	181,500
1987	Gone West, 3, 114	R. G. Davis	Shawklit Won, 3, 114	Gulch, 3, 123	9	1:34.60	190,200
1986	Mogambo, 3, 121	J. Vasquez	‡Tasso, 3, 123	Zabaleta, 3, 121	9	1:34.60	214,200
1985	Eternal Prince, 3, 114	R. Migliore	Pancho Villa, 3, 121	El Basco, 3, 114	7	1:34.40	147,840
1984	Bear Hunt, 3, 114	D. MacBeth	Lt. Flag, 3, 123	On the Sauce, 3, 114	5	1:40.40	136,440
1983	Assault Landing, 3, 114	V. A. Bracciale Jr.	Bounding Basque, 3, 123	Jacque's Tip, 3, 123	9	1:35.80	50,895
	Chas Conerly, 3, 123	J. Fell	Elegant Life, 3, 123	Law Talk, 3, 114	8	1:36.60	50,055
1982	Air Forbes Won, 3, 114	M. Venezia	Shimatoree, 3, 123	Big Brave Rock, 3, 114	8	1:35.60	50,760
1981	Proud Appeal, 3, 123	J. Fell	Cure the Blues, 3, 126	Noble Nashua, 3, 123	6	1:33.60	50,040
1980	Colonel Moran, 3, 123	J. Velasquez	Dunham's Gift, 3, 114	Bucksplasher, 3, 115	12	1:37.00	53,370
1979	General Assembly, 3, 123	J. Vasquez	Belle's Gold, 3, 123	Screen King, 3, 123	8	1:43.60	49,680
1978	Slap Jack, 3, 114	J. Velasquez	Quadratic, 3, 114	Shelter Half, 3, 121	9	1:38.60	33,210
1977	Cormorant, 3, 123	D. R. Wright	Fratello Ed, 3, 121	Papelote, 3, 114	9	1:43.60	32,850
1976	Zen, 3, 116	J. Vasquez	Cojak, 3, 124	Play the Red, 3, 114	10	1:35.60	34,740
1975	Laramie Trail, 3, 121	M. Venezia	Lefty, 3, 121	Kalong, 3, 116	5	1:38.00	27,180
	Singh, 3, 121	A. T. Cordero Jr.	Round Stake, 3, 116	Mr. Duds, 3, 116	8	1:37.00	27,630
1974	Rube the Great, 3, 119	M. A. Rivera	Hosiery, 3, 116	Cumulo Nimbus, 3, 116	8	1:35.20	27,420
	Stonewalk, 3, 116	M. A. Rivera	L'Amour Rullah, 3, 116	Wing South, 3, 119	9	1:36.00	27,570
1973	Secretariat, 3, 126	R. Turcotte	Champagne Charlie, 3, 117	Flush, 3, 117	6	1:33.40	33,330

Named for the unofficial nickname of New York City, "Gotham." Grade 2 1973-'97. Held at Jamaica 1953-'59. 1 mile 70 yards 1984, 2003. 1 mile 1960-'76, 1978, 1980-'83, 1985-2002, 2004-'05. Four-year-olds and up 1958. Two divisions

1974-'75, 1983. Dead heat for first 1992. ‡Groovy finished second, DQ to fifth, 1986. ‡Pavo finished second, DQ to fourth, 2005. Equaled track record 1973. Track record 1989.

Gravesend Handicap

Grade 3 in 2008. Aqueduct, three-year-olds and up, 6 furlongs, dirt. Held December 29, 2007, with a gross value of $105,100. First held in 1959. First graded in 1988. Stakes record 1:08.60 (1973 Petrograd).

Year	Winner	Jockey	Second	Third	Strs	Time	1st Purse
2007	City Attraction, 4, 115	M. J. Luzzi	Joey P., 5, 117	Debussy, 5, 113	5	1:11.97	$64,260
2006	Bishop Court Hill, 6, 117	J. R. Velazquez	Santana Strings, 4, 115	Will He Shine, 4, 115	9	1:09.23	66,360
2005	Banjo Picker, 5, 114	T. Hemmings	Pioneer Empire, 4, 114	Saay Mi Name, 5, 115	10	1:10.17	67,200
2004	Don Six, 4, 114	M. J. Luzzi	Mr. Whitestone, 4, 114	Papua, 5, 114	6	1:08.97	65,640
2003	Shake You Down, 5, 124	M. J. Luzzi	Way to the Top, 5, 114	Gators N Bears, 3, 115	7	1:09.55	65,400
2002	Multiple Choice, 4, 118	V. Carrero	Sing Me Back Home, 4, 114	Gold I. D., 3, 113	7	1:09.26	65,520
2001	Here's Zealous, 4, 114	E. S. Prado	Peeping Tom, 4, 120	Say Florida Sandy, 7, 120	6	1:10.37	64,740
2000	Say Florida Sandy, 6, 116	J. Bravo	Liberty Gold, 6, 115	Lake Pontchartrain, 5, 116	11	1:09.80	51,450
1999	Cowboy Cop, 5, 115	A. T. Gryder	Brushed On, 4, 112	Unreal Madness, 4, 116	9	1:09.41	50,370
1998	Say Florida Sandy, 4, 117	S. Bridgmohan	Esteemed Friend, 4, 114	Home On the Ridge, 4, 117	8	1:11.17	50,220
1997	dh-Royal Haven, 5, 122	R. Migliore		Laredo, 4, 115	7	1:10.08	32,670
	dh-Stalwart Member, 4, 118	A. T. Gryder					
1996	Victor Avenue, 3, 119	J. F. Chavez	Royal Haven, 4, 117	Stalwart Member, 3, 114	9	1:09.25	50,325
1995	Cold Execution, 4, 116	J. M. Pezua	Crafty Alfel, 7, 117	Golden Tent, 6, 114	10	1:09.50	50,820
1994	Mining Burrah, 4, 111	J. R. Velazquez	Golden Pro, 4, 115	Won Song, 4, 111	9	1:10.85	51,270
1993	Astudillo (Ire), 3, 108	F. A. Arguello Jr.	Fabersham, 5, 113	Ferociously, 3, 110	6	1:11.91	51,300
1992	Hidden Tomahawk, 4, 111	J. F. Chavez	Smart Alec, 4, 113	Miner's Dream, 5, 114	8	1:08.65	52,920
1991	Shuttleman, 5, 113	A. T. Cordero Jr.	Senor Speedy, 4, 120	Gallant Step, 4, 112	8	1:10.24	52,830
1990	Mr. Nasty, 3, 113	J. D. Bailey	Senor Speedy, 3, 114	Dargai, 4, 113	6	1:09.80	41,220
1989	Never Forgotten, 5, 117	A. Madrid Jr.	Proud and Valid, 4, 111	Garemma, 3, 113	5	1:12.60	40,980
1988	High Brite, 4, 122	A. T. Cordero Jr.	King's Swan, 8, 119	Matter of Honor, 3, 111	6	1:10.60	48,540
1987	Vinnie the Viper, 4, 116	J. A. Krone	King's Swan, 7, 122	Best by Test, 5, 117	6	1:09.60	54,360
1986	Comic Blush, 3, 106	A. Graell	King's Swan, 6, 122	Cutlass Reality, 4, 117	6	1:09.40	41,100
1985	Love That Mac, 3, 111	J. Velasquez	Raja's Shark, 4, 126	Aggressive Bid, 4, 110	6	1:11.00	40,860
1984	Elegant Life, 4, 115	J. Velasquez	Tarantara, 5, 120	Top Avenger, 6, 126	8	1:09.40	42,180
1983	Main Stem, 5, 109	V. Lopez	Havagreatdate, 5, 119	In From Dixie, 6, 113	10	1:14.00	34,440
1982	Chan Balum, 3, 108	J. Samyn	Maudlin, 4, 126	In From Dixie, 5, 120	9	1:11.20	34,320
1981	Lines of Power, 4, 116	D. MacBeth	Stiff Sentence, 4, 110	Bayou Black, 5, 115	6	1:09.60	32,760
1980	Clever Trick, 4, 117	J. Velasquez	Rise Jim, 4, 119	Dr. Blum, 3, 114	6	1:09.00	32,460
1979	Shelter Half, 4, 116	S. A. Boulmetis Jr.	Double Zeus, 4, 114	Tanthem, 4, 126	8	1:11.00	26,220
1978	Half High, 5, 113	A. Santiago	Intercontinent, 4, 114	dh-Bold and Stormy, 6, 107	6	1:09.60	25,755
				dh-Fratello Ed, 4, 119			
1977	Full Out, 4, 116	A. T. Cordero Jr.	Great Above, 5, 114	Jackson Square, 5, 114	7	1:10.20	22,065
1976	Christopher R., 5, 131	W. J. Passmore	Mac Corkle, 4, 115	Gallant Bob, 4, 128	8	1:09.80	26,940
1975	†Honorable Miss, 5, 123	J. Vasquez	Queen City Lad, 4, 111	Piamem, 5, 118	7	1:10.00	16,485
1974	Mr. Prospector, 4, 124	J. Vasquez	Infuriator, 4, 112	Lonetree, 4, 119	8	1:09.00	22,830
1973	Petrograd, 4, 120	A. T. Cordero Jr.	Full Pocket, 4, 120	Delta Oil, 4, 111	6	**1:08.60**	16,635

Named for old Gravesend Park, a racetrack located in the Coney Island section of Brooklyn, New York. Held at Jamaica 1959-'60. Held at Belmont Park 1974. 7 furlongs 1962. Dead heat for first 1978. Dead heat for first 1997. ‡Unreal Madness finished third, DQ to ninth, 1999. Equaled track record 1973, '92. †Denotes female.

Grey Goose Bewitch Stakes

Grade 3 in 2008. Keeneland Race Course, four-year-olds and up, fillies and mares, 1½ miles, turf. Held April 24, 2008, with a gross value of $150,000. First held in 1962. First graded in 1982. Stakes record 2:27.54 (1999 Bursting Forth).

Year	Winner	Jockey	Second	Third	Strs	Time	1st Purse
2008	Communique, 4, 118	G. K. Gomez	Tejida, 5, 118	Rising Cross (GB), 5, 118	10	2:28.91	$93,000
2007	Safari Queen (Arg), 5, 124	J. R. Velazquez	Barancella (Fr), 6, 118	Moon Berry (Brz), 6, 118	6	2:28.75	93,000
2006	Noble Stella (Ger), 5, 118	E. S. Prado	Louve Royale (Ire), 5, 118	Sweet Science, 5, 118	9	2:33.15	66,588
2005	Angara (GB), 4, 118	G. L. Stevens	Cape Town Lass, 4, 118	Strike Me Lucky, 4, 118	7	2:36.24	67,766
2004	Meridiana (Ger), 4, 118	E. S. Prado	Alternate, 5, 116	Binya (Ger), 5, 118	10	2:31.05	70,308
2003	Lilac Queen (Ger), 5, 116	J. D. Bailey	Beyond the Waves, 6, 116	San Dare, 5, 118	10	2:29.70	69,503
2002	Sweetest Thing, 4, 120	M. Guidry	Lapuma, 5, 116	Lady Upstage (Ire), 5, 116	9	2:31.97	68,634
2001	Keemoon (Fr), 5, 120	J. D. Bailey	Playact (Ire), 4, 116	Krisada, 5, 116	8	2:30.28	124,000
2000	The Seven Seas, 4, 116	A. O. Solis	Innuendo (Ire), 5, 116	Hollywood Baldcat, 5, 116	10	2:29.31	70,122
1999	Bursting Forth, 5, 114	J. F. Chavez	Moments of Magic, 4, 114	Pinafore Park, 4, 114	9	**2:27.54**	68,758
1998	Maxzene, 5, 113	J. A. Santos	Cuando, 4, 113	Gastronomical, 5, 113	8	2:30.50	69,626
1997	Cymbala (Fr), 4, 113	P. Day	Noble Cause, 4, 113	Last Approach, 5, 113	10	2:28.87	69,130
1996	Memories (Ire), 5, 117	S. J. Sellers	Future Act, 4, 117	Curtain Raiser, 4, 114	5	2:30.14	66,030
1995	Market Booster, 6, 119	P. Day	Memories (Ire), 4, 113	Abigailthewife, 6, 114	7	2:29.33	50,732
1994	Freewheel, 5, 114	P. Day	Key Chance, 5, 114	Amal Hayati, 4, 115	6	1:50.24	50,871
1993	Miss Lenora, 4, 112	J. A. Krone	Hero's Love, 5, 117	Radiant Ring, 5, 119	8	1:50.60	51,367
1992	La Gueriere, 4, 114	B. D. Peck	Indian Fashion, 5, 117	Plenty of Grace, 5, 112	10	1:48.37	54,438
1991	Miss Moskovia, 7, 112	P. Day	Cheerful Spree, 4, 117	The Caretaker (Ire), 4, 110	10	1:50.00	56,225
1990	Coolawin, 4, 122	J. D. Bailey	To the Lighthouse, 4, 114	Ann Alleged, 5, 112	7	1:49.20	54,048
1989	Gaily Gaily (Ire), 6, 122	J. A. Krone	Chez Chez Chez, 5, 114	Blossoming Beauty, 4, 113	6	1:50.00	53,853

Racing — Graded Stakes

Year	Winner	Jockey	Second	Third	Strs	Time	1st Purse
1988	Beauty Cream, 5, 121	P. Day	Native Mommy, 5, 121	Fraulein Lieber, 4, 113	9	1:51.60	$55,933
1987	Gerrie Singer, 6, 113	R. L. Frazier	Innsbruck (GB), 4, 110	Debutant Dancer, 5, 110	10	1:52.60	36,221
1986	Devalois (Fr), 4, 118	E. Maple	Debutant Dancer, 4, 113	Natural Approach, 5, 113	8	1:54.00	35,685
1985	Sintra, 4, 119	K. K. Allen	Electric Fanny, 4, 110	Switching Trick, 5, 110	7	1:43.60	43,964
1984	Heatherten, 5, 119	S. Maple	Any Spray, 4, 110	Marisma (Chi), 6, 119	10	1:45.80	36,628
1983	Try Something New, 4, 110	P. Day	Kattegat's Pride, 4, 119	Number, 4, 119	10	1:44.20	37,001
1982	Expressive Dance, 4, 116	D. Brumfield	Mean Martha, 4, 115	Really Royal, 4, 116	10	1:43.40	36,416
1981	Bold 'n Determined, 4, 121	E. Delahoussaye	Likely Exchange, 7, 113	Save Wild Life, 4, 110	5	1:43.80	38,236
1980	Jolie Dutch, 4, 113	R. P. Romero	Miss Baja, 5, 112	Mi Muchacha, 5, 113	9	1:43.00	29,039
1979	Miss Baja, 4, 119	E. Maple	Likely Exchange, 5, 110	Plains and Simple, 4, 113	7	1:43.00	23,286
1978	Twenty One Inch, 2, 119	E. Delahoussaye	All's Well, 2, 119	Satan's Pride, 2, 116	10	:52.60	11,846
1977	Crystalan, 2, 119	G. Patterson	No No-Nos, 2, 119	Surprise Trip, 2, 119	11	:53.00	11,947
1976	Olden, 2, 116	R. Breen	Bagiorix, 2, 116	Foreverness, 2, 119	6	:51.40	11,030
	Fun and Tears, 2, 119	L. J. Melancon	Miss Cigarette, 2, 119	Every Move, 2, 116	9	:51.40	11,291
1975	Pink Jade, 2, 119	E. Delahoussaye	Old Goat, 2, 119	T. V. Vixen, 2, 119	12	:51.60	12,139
1974	Secret's Out, 2, 119	D. Brumfield	Floral Princess, 2, 116	Ain't Easy, 2, 119	8	:51.60	11,727
	Dancing Home, 2, 116	A. Patterson	Semi Princess, 2, 119	Spark, 2, 116	9	:53.60	11,793
1973	Me and Connie, 2, 121	J. Nichols	Lady Bahia, 2, 115	Bundler, 2, 115	8	:52.40	12,604

Named for Calumet Farm's Racing Hall of Fame member, 1947 champion two-year-old filly, '49 champion older female, and '48 Ashland S. winner Bewitch (1945 f. by Bull Lea). Sponsored by Grey Goose Importing Co., Miami 2008. About 4 furlongs 1962-'64. 4½ furlongs 1965-'78. 1 1/16 miles 1979-'85. 1 1/8 miles 1986-'94. Dirt 1962-'85. Two-year-olds 1962-'78. Three-year-olds 1980-'85. Fillies 1962-'78. Two divisions 1974, 1976.

Gulfstream Park Handicap

Grade 2 in 2008. Gulfstream Park, four-year-olds and up, 1 3/16 miles, dirt. Held March 1, 2008, with a gross value of $343,000. First held in 1946. First graded in 1973. Stakes record 1:54.74 (2005 Eddington).

Year	Winner	Jockey	Second	Third	Strs	Time	1st Purse
2008	Sir Whimsey, 4, 117	E. S. Prado	Fairbanks, 5, 115	Kiss the Kid, 5, 115	5	1:56.96	$210,000
2007	Corinthian, 4, 117	J. Castellano	Hesanoldsalt, 4, 116	A. P. Arrow, 5, 116	6	1:55.06	210,000
2006	Harlington, 4, 114	J. R. Velazquez	Contante (Arg), 6, 113	It's No Joke, 4, 116	8	1:55.18	180,000
2005	Eddington, 4, 115	E. Coa	Pies Prospect, 4, 113	Zakocity, 4, 117	8	1:54.74	180,000
2004	Jackpot, 6, 113	J. Bravo	Newfoundland, 4, 116	The Lady's Groom, 4, 113	8	2:02.80	180,000
2003	Hero's Tribute, 5, 115	E. S. Prado	Aeneas, 4, 115	Puzzlement, 4, 114	8	2:04.24	180,000
2002	Hal's Hope, 5, 119	R. I. Velez	Mongoose, 4, 115	Sir Bear, 9, 117	5	2:02.91	180,000
2001	Sir Bear, 8, 116	E. Coa	Pleasant Breeze, 6, 115	Broken Vow, 4, 114	9	2:02.96	120,000
2000	Behrens, 6, 120	J. F. Chavez	Adonis, 4, 115	With Anticipation, 5, 113	6	2:01.79	210,000
1999	Behrens, 5, 114	J. F. Chavez	Archers Bay, 4, 114	Sir Bear, 6, 118	8	2:01.91	210,000
1998	Skip Away, 5, 127	J. D. Bailey	Unruled, 5, 112	Behrens, 4, 114	6	2:03.21	300,000
1997	Mt. Sassafras, 5, 113	J. D. Bailey	Skip Away, 4, 122	Tejano Run, 5, 114	6	2:02.39	300,000
1996	Wekiva Springs, 5, 117	J. D. Bailey	Star Standard, 4, 112	Powerful Punch, 7, 113	8	2:03.15	300,000
1995	Cigar, 5, 118	J. D. Bailey	Pride of Burkaan, 5, 114	Mahogany Hall, 4, 113	11	2:02.95	300,000
1994	Scuffleburg, 5, 113	C. Perret	Migrating Moon, 4, 114	Wallenda, 4, 117	10	2:00.46	180,000
1993	Devil His Due, 4, 113	W. H. McCauley	Offbeat, 4, 112	Pistols and Roses, 4, 114	9	2:01.33	300,000
1992	Sea Cadet, 4, 119	A. O. Solis	Strike the Gold, 4, 115	Sunny Sunrise, 5, 114	6	2:01.79	180,000
1991	Jolie's Halo, 4, 119	R. Platts	Primal, 6, 117	Chief Honcho, 4, 118	8	2:01.04	180,000
1990	Mi Selecto, 5, 114	J. D. Bailey	Tour d'Or, 8, 118	Lay Down, 6, 113	8	2:03.60	180,000
1989	Slew City Slew, 5, 117	A. T. Cordero Jr.	Bold Midway, 5, 113	Cryptoclearance, 4, 123	7	2:03.20	180,000
1988	Jade Hunter, 4, 113	J. D. Bailey	Cryptoclearance, 4, 122	Creme Fraiche, 6, 123	6	2:01.60	180,000
1987	Skip Trial, 5, 118	R. P. Romero	Creme Fraiche, 5, 120	Snow Chief, 4, 124	4	2:02.80	150,000
1986	Skip Trial, 4, 121	R. P. Romero	Proud Truth, 4, 123	Important Business, 4, 113	5	2:03.20	180,000
1985	Dr. Carter, 4, 119	J. Velasquez	Key to the Moon, 4, 120	Pine Circle, 4, 116	8	2:02.00	171,480
1984	Mat-Boy (Arg), 5, 118	J. Valdivieso	Lord Darnley, 6, 109	Courteous Majesty, 4, 114	7	1:59.00	86,700
1983	†Christmas Past, 4, 117	J. Velasquez	Crafty Prospector, 4, 115	Rivalero, 7, 120	12	2:02.60	111,630
1982	Lord Darnley, 4, 113	M. Russ	Joanie's Chief, 5, 113	Double Sonic, 4, 111	9	2:01.80	91,200
1981	Hurry Up Blue, 4, 119	C. C. Lopez	Yosi Boy, 5, 111	Imperial Dilemma, 4, 113	9	2:03.20	114,888
1980	Private Account, 4, 119	J. Fell	Lot o' Gold, 4, 120	Silent Cal, 5, 118	7	2:01.40	100,000
1979	Sensitive Prince, 4, 120	J. Vasquez	Jumping Hill, 7, 126	Silent Cal, 4, 119	7	1:59.20	100,000
1978	Bowl Game, 4, 112	J. Velasquez	True Statement, 4, 108	Silver Series, 4, 126	11	2:00.60	100,000
1977	Strike Me Lucky, 5, 109	J. D. Bailey	Legion, 7, 115	Yamanin, 5, 122	12	2:00.80	88,200
1976	Hail the Pirates, 6, 116	B. Baeza	Legion, 6, 113	Packer Captain, 4, 113	7	2:01.80	73,560
1975	Gold and Myrrh, 4, 114	W. Blum	Proud and Bold, 5, 120	Buffalo Lark, 5, 117	9	2:01.80	74,520
1974	Forego, 4, 127	H. Gustines	True Knight, 5, 123	Golden Don, 4, 118	6	1:59.80	72,360
1973	West Coast Scout, 5, 116	L. Adams	Super Sail, 5, 110	Freetex, 4, 113	10	2:01.00	80,880

Grade 1 1975-2002. Gulfstream H. 1946, '68. 1¼ miles 1946-2004. Three-year-olds and up 1947-2006. †Denotes female. Held as an allowance race 1949-'51.

Gulfstream Park Turf Stakes

Grade 1 in 2008. Gulfstream Park, four-year-olds and up, 1 3/8 miles, turf. Held February 23, 2008, with a gross value of $273,000. First held in 1986. First graded in 1990. Stakes record 2:10.73 (1999 Yagli).

Year	Winner	Jockey	Second	Third	Strs	Time	1st Purse
2008	Einstein (Brz), 6, 123	J. Lezcano	Dancing Forever, 5, 123	Stream of Gold (Ire), 7, 123	10	2:12.87	$150,000
2007	Jambalaya, 5, 123	J. Castellano	†Honey Ryder, 6, 118	Einstein (Brz), 5, 123	11	2:12.28	180,000
2006	Einstein (Brz), 4, 123	R. Bejarano	Go Deputy, 6, 123	Gun Salute, 4, 123	8	2:23.91	90,000

Racing — Graded Stakes

Year	Winner	Jockey	Second	Third	Strs	Time	1st Purse
2005	Prince Arch, 4, 119	B. Blanc	Gigli (Brz), 7, 114	Mustanfar, 4, 118	11	2:11.44	$150,000
2004	Hard Buck (Brz), 5, 117	E. S. Prado	Balto Star, 6, 122	Kicken Kris, 4, 118	8	2:11.56	90,000
2003	Man From Wicklow, 6, 119	J. D. Bailey	Just Listen, 7, 113	Sardaukar (GB), 7, 114	10	2:11.62	120,000
2002	Cetewayo, 8, 115	C. H. Velasquez	Band Is Passing, 6, 117	Profit Option, 7, 115	12	2:17.44	120,000
2001	Subtle Power (Ire), 4, 113	P. Day	Whata Brainstorm, 4, 113	Stokosky, 5, 114	9	2:13.50	60,000
2000	Royal Anthem, 5, 121	J. D. Bailey	Thesaurus, 6, 112	Band Is Passing, 4, 116	7	2:11.34	120,000
1999	Yagli, 6, 121	J. D. Bailey	Wild Event, 6, 117	Unite's Big Red, 5, 115	6	2:10.73	120,000
1998	Flag Down, 8, 120	J. A. Santos	Buck's Boy, 5, 115	Copy Editor, 6, 116	12	2:12.59	120,000
1997	Lassigny, 6, 116	J. D. Bailey	Flag Down, 7, 117	Awad, 7, 119	11	2:11.33	102,840
1996	Celtic Arms (Fr), 5, 114	M. E. Smith	Broadway Flyer, 5, 117	Flag Down, 6, 118	11	2:13.90	101,880
1995	Misil, 7, 119	J. A. Santos	Myrmidon, 4, 113	Star of Manila, 4, 118	11	2:12.41	94,200
1994	Strolling Along, 4, 117	J. D. Bailey	Conveyor, 6, 119	Awad, 4, 112	6	2:05.01	93,150
1993	Stagecraft (GB), 6, 115	J. D. Bailey	Social Retiree, 6, 116	Futurist, 5, 116	8	2:13.24	93,600
1992	†Passagere du Soir (GB), 5, 114	J. D. Bailey	Colchis Island (Ire), 7, 111	Crystal Moment, 7, 116	14	2:15.71	95,130
1991	Shy Tom, 5, 115	C. Perret	Dr. Root, 4, 112	Runaway Raja, 5, 112	13	2:14.70	94,800
1990	Youmadeyourpoint, 4, 112	D. Valiente	Blazing Bart, 6, 118	Iron Courage, 6, 116	10	1:39.60	94,560
1989	Equalize, 7, 124	J. A. Santos	Posen, 4, 115	Nisswa, 4, 111	11	1:41.00	93,210
1988	Salem Drive, 6, 116	G. St. Leon	Equalize, 6, 112	Kings River (Ire), 6, 113	14	1:40.60	94,530
1987	Bolshoi Boy, 4, 116	R. P. Romero	Arctic Honeymoon, 4, 114	Little Bold John, 5, 115	5	1:44.60	80,286
1986	Sondrio (Ire), 5, 113	J. A. Santos	Chief Run Run, 4, 113	Ends Well, 5, 115	10	1:40.60	80,772

Grade 3 1990-'91. Grade 2 1992-'98. Gulfstream Park Budweiser Breeders' Cup H. 1987-'95. Gulfstream Park Breeders' Cup H. 1996-2005. Gulfstream Park Breeders' Cup Turf S. 2006-'07. 1 1/16 miles 1986-'90. About 1 3/8 miles 1991. 1 1/4 miles 1994. 1 7/16 miles 2006. Dirt 1987, '94. Three-year-olds and up 1986-2006. Course record 1993, '99. Equaled course record 1997. Established course record 2006. †Denotes female.

Hal's Hope Handicap

Grade 3 in 2008. Gulfstream Park, four-year-olds and up, 1 mile, dirt. Held January 6, 2008, with a gross value of $100,000. First held in 1990. First graded in 1993. Stakes record 1:33.87 (2007 Chatain).

Year	Winner	Jockey	Second	Third	Strs	Time	1st Purse
2008	Chatain, 5, 118	C. H. Velasquez	Miner's Lamp, 5, 112	Actin Good, 4, 116	11	1:36.39	$60,000
2007	Chatain, 4, 115	C. H. Velasquez	Sir Greeley, 5, 118	Sweetnorthernsaint, 4, 120	10	1:33.87	60,000
2006	On Thin Ice, 5, 114	S. Bridgmohan	Network, 4, 113	Seek Gold, 6, 114	9	1:48.65	60,000
2005	Badge of Silver, 5, 115	J. D. Bailey	Dynever, 5, 117	Contante (Arg), 5, 114	12	1:48.57	60,000
2004	Puzzlement, 5, 116	J. F. Chavez	Bowman's Band, 6, 118	Stockholder, 4, 117	7	1:42.39	60,000
2003	Windsor Castle, 5, 115	E. Coa	Saint Verre, 5, 114	Najran, 4, 114	8	1:42.33	60,000
2002	Hal's Hope, 5, 112	R. I. Velez	American Halo, 6, 113	Windsor Castle, 4, 112	9	1:42.40	60,000
2000	Dancing Guy, 5, 120	J. D. Bailey	Yankee Victor, 4, 113	Midway Magistrate, 6, 117	8	1:44.40	45,000
1999	Jazz Club, 4, 114	P. Day	Rock and Roll, 4, 113	Hanarsam, 6, 113	7	1:42.76	45,000
1998	K. J.'s Appeal, 4, 114	J. R. Velazquez	Powerful Goer, 4, 112	Tour's Big Red, 5, 114	8	1:42.34	45,000
1997	Louis Quatorze, 4, 121	P. Day	Strawberry Wine, 5, 113	Exalto, 6, 108	5	1:43.43	45,000
1996	Geri, 4, 114	J. D. Bailey	Halo's Image, 5, 120	Second Childhood, 4, 113	6	1:41.49	45,000
1995	Warm Wayne, 4, 112	J. D. Bailey	Meadow Monster, 4, 113	Silent Lake, 5, 113	9	1:43.11	45,000
1994	Forever Whirl, 4, 113	W. H. McCauley	Northern Trend, 6, 113	Royal n Gold, 5, 113	10	1:41.81	45,000
1993	Classic Seven, 5, 116	C. E. Lopez Sr.	Devil On Ice, 4, 115	Keratoid, 4, 111	10	1:43.49	60,000
1992	Peanut Butter Onit, 6, 114	J. A. Santos	Sunny Sunrise, 5, 117	Honest Ensign, 4, 109	7	1:43.78	45,000
1991	New York Swell, 8, 111	J. O. Alferez	Rhythm, 4, 121	Mercedes Won, 5, 112	5	1:42.50	45,000
1990	Big Sal, 5, 119	E. Fires	Twice Too Many, 5, 117	Groomstick, 4, 119	6	1:24.80	20,340

Named for Harold Rose's 2000 Florida Derby (G1) and '02 Gulfstream Park H. (G1) winner Hal's Hope (1997 c. by Jolie's Halo). Formerly named for Brushwood Stable's 1986 Donn H. (G2) winner Creme Fraiche (1982 g. by Rich Cream). Creme Fraiche S. 1990. Creme Fraiche H. 1991-2002. Not held 2001. 7 furlongs 1990. 1 1/16 miles 1991-2004. 1 1/8 miles 2005-'06. Three-year-olds and up 1991-2006. Track record 2006-'07.

Hanshin Cup Handicap

Grade 3 in 2008. Arlington Park, three-year-olds and up, 1 mile, dirt. Held May 24, 2008, with a gross value of $100,000. First held in 1941. First graded in 1983. Stakes record 1:33.20 (1979 Bask).

Year	Winner	Jockey	Second	Third	Strs	Time	1st Purse
2008	Coragil Cat, 4, 115	D. Sanchez	Morada Key, 4, 116	Steve's Double, 4, 117	8	1:34.86	$58,200
2007	Spotsgone, 4, 116	E. Fires	Lewis Michael, 4, 118	Gouldings Green, 6, 120	10	1:33.72	57,000
2006	‡Gouldings Green, 5, 118	C. J. Lanerie	Fifteen Rounds, 6, 117	Three Hour Nap, 4, 117	5	1:34.05	60,000
2005	Lord of the Game, 4, 117	E. Razo Jr.	Gouldings Green, 4, 115	Nkosi Reigns, 4, 115	8	1:34.62	60,000
2004	Crafty Shaw, 6, 119	C. Perret	Apt to Be, 7, 119	Kodema, 5, 116	7	1:35.36	60,000
2003	Apt to Be, 6, 117	E. Razo Jr.	There's Zealous, 5, 116	San Pedro, 5, 116	7	1:34.00	60,000
2002	Bonapaw, 6, 121	G. Melancon	Slider, 4, 115	Discreet Hero, 4, 116	7	1:34.80	60,000
2001	Bright Valour, 5, 115	R. Albarado	Apt to Be, 4, 114	Castlewood, 4, 115	8	1:36.21	60,000
2000	‡Bright Valour, 4, 114	J. Campbell	Desert Demon, 4, 113	Battle Mountain, 6, 114	5	1:34.97	60,000
1997	Announce, 4, 116	C. C. Bourque	Victor Cooley, 4, 117	Hunk of Class, 4, 115	7	1:36.95	60,000
1996	Golden Gear, 5, 122	M. Guidry	Exclusive Garth, 4, 113	Prospect for Love, 4, 113	10	1:36.13	105,000
1995	Tarzans Blade, 4, 115	P. Day	Swank, 4, 114	Come On Flip, 4, 114	9	1:35.64	45,000
1994	Slerp, 5, 117	E. Fires	Seattle Morn, 4, 116	Dancing Jon, 6, 113	5	1:35.43	60,000
1993	Split Run, 5, 114	E. Fires	Gee Can He Dance, 4, 114	Danc'n Jake, 4, 114	11	1:34.46	60,000
1992	Katahaula County, 5, 114	C. C. Bourque	The Great Carl, 5, 111	Stalwars, 7, 116	9	1:37.27	45,000
1991	Bright Again, 4, 112	P. Day	Secret Hello, 4, 115	Irish Swap, 4, 112	5	1:35.39	45,000
1990	Black Tie Affair (Ire), 4, 119	J. Velasquez	Bio, 4, 112	New Plymouth, 7, 110	4	1:36.00	47,923

Racing — Graded Stakes

Year	Winner	Jockey	Second	Third	Strs	Time	1st Purse
1989	**Present Value**, 5, 114	F. Olivares	Paramount Jet, 4, 114	Sutter's Prospect, 4, 110	8	1:34.40	$50,310
1987	**Red Attack**, 5, 116	M. E. Smith	Taylor's Special, 6, 127	Come Summer, 5, 114	5	1:34.20	48,570
1986	**Smile**, 4, 121	J. Vasquez	Taylor's Special, 5, 124	Red Attack, 4, 114	7	1:34.00	69,180
1985	**Timeless Native**, 5, 122	J. E. Tejeira	Par Flite, 4, 115	Harham's Sizzler, 6, 115	7	1:33.80	49,275
1984	**Win Stat**, 7, 117	D. Pettinger	Le Cou Cou, 4, 116	Harham's Sizzler, 5, 111	8	1:37.80	49,860
1983	**‡Hale Herk**, 4, 113	R. D. Evans	Thumbsucker, 4, 116	Spoonful of Honey, 4, 115	14	1:36.00	52,560
1982	**Summer Advocate**, 5, 123	R. P. Romero	Prince Freddie, 6, 109	Fabulous Find, 4, 110	9	1:36.40	49,860
1981	**J. Burns**, 6, 115	J. D. Bailey	Summer Advocate, 4, 115	Brent's Trans Am, 4, 114	11	1:35.80	68,340
1980	**Prince Majestic**, 6, 113	G. Patterson	Sea Ride, 5, 114	Braze and Bold, 5, 118	12	1:39.20	69,300
1979	**Bask**, 5, 112	M. R. Morgan	Bold Standard, 5, 111	Hold Your Tricks, 4, 120	9	**1:33.20**	22,605
1976	**Visier**, 4, 120	R. Riera Jr.	Dare to Command, 4, 118	Auberge, 3, 112	7	1:47.00	31,650
1975	**Sr. Diplomat**, 4, 113	P. Day	Recaptured, 5, 109	Mike James, 5, 111	10	1:44.40	37,440
1974	**Our Pappa Joe**, 7, 114	R. Cox	Radnor, 4, 113	We're Ready Now, 4, 116	11	1:36.60	45,000
	Henry Tudor, 5, 121	R. Platts	Recaptured, 4, 108	Sharp Gary, 3, 118	10	1:36.00	45,000
1973	**Test Run**, 7, 112	J. Keene	Chateauvira, 5, 120	Fame and Power, 4, 120	12	1:38.20	21,037

Named in honor of the Japan Racing Association, which conducts a race at Hanshin Racecourse in honor of Arlington Park. Formerly named for C. V. Whitney's 1932, '33 Horse of the Year, '42 leading North American sire, and '32 Stars and Stripes H. winner Equipoise (1928 c. by Pennant). Equipoise Mile H. 1941-'97. Hanshin H. 2000. Held at Washington Park 1943-'45. Not held 1977-'78, 1988, 1998-'99. Dirt 1941-2006. Two divisions 1974. ‡Thumbsucker finished first, DQ to second, 1983. ‡Yankee Victor finished first, DQ to fifth for a positive drug test, 2000. ‡Fifteen Rounds finished first, DQ to second, 2006. Equaled track record 1974 (2nd Div.).

Harold C. Ramser Sr. Handicap

Grade 3 in 2008. Oak Tree at Santa Anita, three-year-olds, fillies, 1 mile, turf. Held October 14, 2007, with a gross value of $110,600. First held in 1981. First graded in 1989. Stakes record 1:32.87 (2003 Valentine Dancer).

Year	Winner	Jockey	Second	Third	Strs	Time	1st Purse
2007	**Gotta Have Her**, 3, 116	R. Migliore	Silky Smooth, 3, 119	Runway Rosie, 3, 114	9	1:34.16	$66,360
2006	**Illuminise (Ire)**, 3, 119	C. S. Nakatani	Diplomat Lady, 3, 119	Zoemeg, 3, 114	9	1:34.62	60,000
2005	**Louvain (Ire)**, 3, 119	T. Baze	Shining Energy, 3, 119	Thatswhatimean, 3, 116	10	1:35.14	60,000
2004	**Mea Domina**, 3, 116	G. L. Stevens	Penny's Fortune, 3, 116	Costume Designer, 3, 115	9	1:33.90	60,000
2003	**Valentine Dancer**, 3, 116	P. A. Valenzuela	Fencelineneighbor, 3, 118	Shezsospiritual, 3, 112	12	**1:32.87**	68,340
2002	**Sentimental Value**, 3, 115	V. Espinoza	Company B, 3, 116	Dancing (GB), 3, 116	8	1:33.98	50,580
	Kithira (GB), 3, 117	P. A. Valenzuela	Super High, 3, 120	Crousille (Fr), 3, 114	7	1:33.73	49,980
2001	**Cindy's Hero**, 3, 117	G. K. Gomez	Gabriellina Giof (GB), 3, 118	Walts Wharf, 3, 117	8	1:33.70	66,300
2000	**High Margin**, 3, 118	K. J. Desormeaux	Janet (GB), 3, 117	Fire Sale Queen, 3, 116	6	1:35.19	64,800
1999	**Olympic Charmer**, 3, 118	C. J. McCarron	Camargo (Ire), 3, 115	Bright Magic, 3, 116	10	1:34.30	67,080
1998	**Sapphire Ring (GB)**, 3, 118	G. L. Stevens	Diamond On the Run, 3, 119	Black Velvet (Fr), 3, 116	9	1:38.32	60,000
1995	**Ski Dancer**, 3, 117	K. J. Desormeaux	Radu Cool, 3, 114	Jewel Princess, 3, 117	10	1:36.78	62,200
1993	**Zoonaqua**, 3, 114	A. O. Solis	Mamselle Bebette, 3, 114	Icy Warning, 3, 118	8	1:34.42	51,550
1991	**Flawlessly**, 3, 123	C. J. McCarron	Gravieres (Fr), 3, 117	Zama Hummer, 3, 117	10	1:33.42	67,500
1989	**Present Value**, 5, 117	W. Shoemaker	Rahy, 4, 121	On the Line, 5, 124	5	1:40.60	61,600
1988	**Mi Preferido**, 3, 116	E. J. Delahoussaye	Conquering Hero, 5, 116	Redoble II (Uru), 4, 112	7	1:41.80	90,600
1987	**Super Diamond**, 7, 125	L. A. Pincay Jr.	Stop the Fighting (Ire), 4, 116	†Infinidad (Chi), 5, 116	5	1:40.80	61,500
1986	**Precisionist**, 5, 127	G. L. Stevens	Garthorn, 6, 124	Tasso, 3, 117	5	1:48.40	60,500
1985	**†Fran's Valentine**, 3, 115	P. A. Valenzuela	Artichoke, 4, 117	Last Command, 4, 116	6	1:41.80	61,550
1984	**Pettrax**, 6, 120	K. D. Black	American Standard, 4, 113	Lord At War (Arg), 4, 117	8	1:42.40	38,500
1983	**‡Pettrax**, 5, 117	K. D. Black	Water Bank, 4, 117	Match Winner (Fr), 4, 117	7	1:41.80	38,100
1981	**Shamgo**, 5, 118	L. A. Pincay Jr.	Major Sport, 4, 118	Love Is Blue, 4, 116	7	1:42.80	31,850

Named in memory of the former vice president of the Oak Tree Racing Association, and one of the original Oak Tree officers, Harold C. Ramser Sr. (1908-'89). Formerly named for Yankee Valor (1944 c. by Heelfly); Yankee Valor was a popular California-bred winner of several major Southern California stakes races. Not graded 1991-2007. Yankee Valor H. 1981-'88. Not held 1982, 1990, 1992, 1994, 1996-'97. 1 1/16 miles 1981-'85, 1987-'89. 1 1/8 miles 1986. Dirt 1981-'89. Three-year-olds and up 1981-'89. Both sexes 1981-'89. Two divisions 2002. ‡Water Bank finished first, DQ to second, 1983. †Denotes female.

Haskell Invitational Stakes

Grade 1 in 2008. Monmouth Park, three-year-olds, 1 1/8 miles, dirt. Held August 5, 2007, with a gross value of $1,060,000. First held in 1885. First graded in 1973. Stakes record 1:47 (1987 Bet Twice; 1976 Majestic Light).

Year	Winner	Jockey	Second	Third	Strs	Time	1st Purse
2007	**Any Given Saturday**, 3, 118	G. K. Gomez	Hard Spun, 3, 118	Curlin, 3, 122	7	1:48.35	$600,000
2006	**Bluegrass Cat**, 3, 118	J. R. Velazquez	Praying for Cash, 3, 118	Strong Contender, 3, 118	9	1:48.85	600,000
2005	**Roman Ruler**, 3, 118	J. D. Bailey	Sun King, 3, 119	Park Avenue Ball, 3, 118	7	1:49.88	600,000
2004	**Lion Heart**, 3, 121	J. Bravo	My Snookie's Boy, 3, 116	Pies Prospect, 3, 116	8	1:48.95	600,000
2003	**Peace Rules**, 3, 121	E. S. Prado	Sky Mesa, 3, 118	Funny Cide, 3, 123	7	1:49.32	600,000
2002	**War Emblem**, 3, 124	V. Espinoza	Magic Weisner, 3, 118	Like a Hero, 3, 117	5	1:48.21	600,000
2001	**Point Given**, 3, 124	G. L. Stevens	Touch Tone, 3, 115	Burning Roma, 3, 119	6	1:49.77	900,000
2000	**Dixie Union**, 3, 117	A. O. Solis	Captain Steve, 3, 118	Milwaukee Brew, 3, 117	9	1:50.00	600,000
1999	**Menifee**, 3, 124	P. Day	Cat Thief, 3, 123	Forestry, 3, 117	7	1:48.06	600,000
1998	**Coronado's Quest**, 3, 124	M. E. Smith	Victory Gallop, 3, 125	Grand Slam, 3, 118	6	1:48.60	600,000
1997	**Touch Gold**, 3, 125	C. J. McCarron	Anet, 3, 120	Free House, 3, 125	5	1:47.60	850,000
1996	**Skip Away**, 3, 124	J. A. Santos	Dr. Caton, 3, 115	Victory Speech, 3, 121	7	1:47.73	450,000
1995	**†Serena's Song**, 3, 118	G. L. Stevens	Pyramid Peak, 3, 120	Citadeed, 3, 118	11	1:48.94	300,000

Year	Winner	Jockey	Second	Third	Strs	Time	1st Purse
1994	Holy Bull, 3, 126	M. E. Smith	Meadow Flight, 3, 118	Concern, 3, 118	6	1:48.36	$300,000
1993	Kissin Kris, 3, 118	J. A. Santos	Storm Tower, 3, 119	Dry Bean, 3, 113	7	1:49.58	300,000
1992	Technology, 3, 120	J. D. Bailey	Nines Wild, 3, 112	Scudan, 3, 113	9	1:48.78	300,000
1991	Lost Mountain, 3, 118	C. Perret	Corporate Report, 3, 120	Hansel, 3, 126	5	1:48.06	300,000
1990	Restless Con, 3, 118	T. T. Doocy	Baron de Vaux, 3, 117	Rhythm, 3, 121	7	1:49.20	300,000
1989	King Glorious, 3, 123	C. J. McCarron	Music Merci, 3, 120	Shy Tom, 3, 116	10	1:49.80	300,000
1988	Forty Niner, 3, 126	L. A. Pincay Jr.	Seeking the Gold, 3, 125	Primal, 3, 117	5	1:47.60	300,000
1987	Bet Twice, 3, 126	C. Perret	Alysheba, 3, 126	Lost Code, 3, 124	5	**1:47.00**	300,000
1986	Wise Times, 3, 114	C. P. DeCarlo	Personal Flag, 3, 114	Danzig Connection, 3, 123	9	1:48.60	180,000
1985	Skip Trial, 3, 116	J. Samyn	Spend a Buck, 3, 127	Creme Fraiche, 3, 126	7	1:48.60	180,000
1984	Big Pistol, 3, 119	G. Patterson	Birdie's Legend, 3, 115	Locust Bayou, 3, 115	6	1:47.80	120,000
1983	Deputed Testamony, 3, 124	W. H. McCauley	Bet Big, 3, 116	Parfaitement, 3, 116	10	1:49.20	120,000
1982	Wavering Monarch, 3, 117	R. P. Romero	Aloma's Ruler, 3, 126	Lejoli, 3, 112	7	1:47.80	120,000
1981	Five Star Flight, 3, 119	C. Perret	Lord Avie, 3, 126	Ornery Odis, 3, 112	6	1:48.40	120,000
1980	Thanks to Tony, 3, 111	C. E. Lopez Sr.	Superbity, 3, 124	Amber Pass, 3, 121	8	1:49.40	90,000
1979	Coastal, 3, 127	R. Hernandez	Steady Growth, 3, 120	Worthy Piper, 3, 112	5	1:48.80	65,000
1978	Delta Flag, 3, 112	D. Nied	Dave's Friend, 3, 120	Special Honor, 3, 118	7	1:53.20	65,000
1977	Affiliate, 3, 117	M. A. Rivera	Don Sebastian, 3, 112	Iron Constitution, 3, 118	7	1:50.60	65,000
1976	Majestic Light, 3, 122	S. Hawley	Appassionato, 3, 113	Honest Pleasure, 3, 126	9	**1:47.00**	65,000
1975	Wajima, 3, 118	B. Baeza	Intrepid Hero, 3, 115	My Friend Gus, 3, 116	8	1:49.60	65,000
1974	Holding Pattern, 3, 117	M. Miceli	Little Current, 3, 127	Better Arbitor, 3, 119	10	1:49.80	65,000
1973	Our Native, 3, 123	M. A. Rivera	Annihilate 'em, 3, 118	Aljamin, 3, 118	8	1:48.60	65,000

Named for Amory L. Haskell (1894-1966), former president of Monmouth Park. Formerly sponsored by General Motors Corp. of Detroit 1996-'98. Choice S. 1885-'92, 1946-'67. Monmouth Invitational H. 1968-'80. Buick Haskell Invitational H. 1996-'98. Haskell Invitational H. 1981-2005. Not held 1893-1945. 1 1/2 miles 1885-'92. 1 1/4 miles 1946-'52. 1 1/16 miles 1958-'67. †Denotes female.

Hawthorne Derby

Grade 3 in 2008. Hawthorne Race Course, three-year-olds, 1 1/8 miles, turf. Held October 13, 2007, with a gross value of $250,000. First held in 1965. First graded in 1973. Stakes record 1:44.70 (1991 Rainbows for Life).

Year	Winner	Jockey	Second	Third	Strs	Time	1st Purse
2007	Bold Hawk, 3, 116	J. Samyn	Twilight Meteor, 3, 118	Western Prize, 3, 116	11	1:47.45	$141,000
2006	Best of Buddies, 3, 118	E. M. Martin Jr.	Crested (GB), 3, 116	Arbuckle Bandit, 3, 116	8	1:50.59	150,000
2005	Gun Salute, 3, 122	C. H. Velasquez	Cosmic Kris, 3, 116	Embossed (Ire), 3, 114	5	1:47.51	150,000
2004	Cool Conductor, 3, 115	J. A. Santos	Bankruptcy Court, 3, 115	Crown Prince, 3, 113	10	1:47.89	150,000
2003	False Promises, 3, 115	C. H. Marquez Jr.	Megoman, 3, 115	Beau Classic, 3, 113	11	1:48.48	150,000
2002	‡Scooter Roach, 3, 115	J. M. Campbell	Quest Star, 3, 115	Colorful Tour, 3, 117	7	1:58.88	150,000
2001	Kalu, 3, 119	J. A. Santos	Proud Man, 3, 119	Rahy's Secret, 3, 115	7	1:50.49	150,000
2000	dh-Hymn (Ire), 3, 115	L. A. Pincay Jr.		Lonely Place (Ire), 3, 113	10	1:53.79	100,000
	dh-Rumsonontheriver, 3, 115	A. J. Juarez Jr.					
1999	Minor Wisdom, 3, 115	R. Zimmerman	Air Rocket, 3, 119	Fred of Gold, 3, 113	12	1:49.06	150,000
1998	Stay Sound, 3, 115	A. J. D'Amico	El Mirasol, 3, 111	Yankee Brass, 3, 114	11	1:47.54	150,000
1997	River Squall, 3, 119	C. Perret	Honor Glide, 3, 122	Blazing Sword, 3, 115	6	1:48.20	120,000
1996	Jaunatxo, 3, 122	J. L. Diaz	Trail City, 3, 122	Canyon Run, 3, 122	11	1:47.18	120,000
1995	Cuzzin Jeb, 3, 117	C. C. Lopez	Hawk Attack, 3, 122	Seven n Seven, 3, 114	9	1:48.90	90,000
1994	Chrysalis House, 3, 115	M. Guidry	Unfinished Symph, 3, 122	Marvin's Faith (Ire), 3, 116	11	1:51.88	90,000
1993	Snake Eyes, 3, 122	G. K. Gomez	Lt. Pinkerton, 3, 117	Ft. Bent, 3, 115	12	1:50.28	90,000
1992	Bantan, 3, 115	C. C. Bourque	†Words of War, 3, 114	Gee Can He Dance, 3, 117	11	1:48.05	60,000
1991	Rainbows for Life, 3, 122	D. Penna	Drummer Boy, 3, 117	Kiltartan Cross, 3, 115	11	**1:44.70**	65,370
1990	Tutu Tobago, 3, 113	P. A. Johnson	Take That Step, 3, 122	Seti I., 3, 115	11	1:53.60	64,740
1989	Broto, 3, 115	S. J. Sellers	Joey Jr., 3, 117	Chenin Blanc, 3, 115	11	1:53.00	94,350
1988	Pappas Swing, 3, 119	E. S. Prado	Djedar, 3, 115	Foolish Intent, 3, 117	11	1:55.80	94,200
1987	Zaizoom, 3, 119	E. Fires	Sir Bask, 3, 114	Rio's Lark, 3, 116	7	2:09.80	89,280
1986	Autobot, 3, 120	E. Fires	Spellbound, 3, 117	Son of the Desert, 3, 115	11	2:00.40	96,360
1985	Derby Wish, 3, 123	R. P. Romero	Day Shift, 3, 115	Explosive Darling, 3, 123	8	2:00.20	64,320
1984	Pass the Line, 3, 117	C. H. Marquez	Mr. Japan, 3, 117	Bet Blind, 3, 115	12	1:57.60	66,750
1983	St. Forbes, 3, 117	E. Fires	His Flower, 3, 117	Saverton, 3, 117	14	1:44.40	67,200
1982	Drop Your Drawers, 3, 118	P. Day	Harham's Sizzler, 3, 118	Northern Majesty, 3, 118	9	1:42.80	64,830
1981	Jeremy Jet, 3, 112	C. H. Silva	Loose Thoughts, 3, 112	Recusant, 3, 112	14	1:45.60	67,200
1980	Jaklin Klugman, 3, 121	C. J. McCarron	Summer Advocate, 3, 115	Hurry Up Blue, 3, 121	7	1:40.80	64,440
1979	Architect, 3, 115	S. A. Spencer	Incredible Ease, 3, 112	Door King, 3, 112	9	1:44.60	48,360
1978	Sensitive Prince, 3, 118	J. Vasquez	Gordie H., 3, 112	Esops Foibles, 3, 124	8	1:39.60	73,680
1977	Silver Series, 3, 114	L. Snyder	Courtly Haste, 3, 114	Affiliate, 3, 112	14	1:41.20	100,860
1976	Wardlaw, 3, 117	J. E. Tejeira	Practitioner, 3, 114	Hurricane Ed, 3, 117	8	1:42.80	82,200
1975	Winter Fox, 3, 109	B. Fann	Intrepid Hero, 3, 115	American History, 3, 115	14	1:49.20	93,800
1974	Stonewalk, 3, 123	R. Turcotte	Tytus Casella, 3, 116	Mr. Door, 3, 114	10	1:40.60	63,150
1973	‡Golden Don, 3, 116	M. Manganello	Impecunious, 3, 123	Cades Cove, 3, 114	10	1:41.20	40,600

Hawthorne Diamond Jubilee H. 1965-'68. Hawthorne Derby H. 1969-'75. Held at Sportsman's Park 1979. 1 1/16 miles 1965-'74, 1976-'84. 1 3/16 miles 1985-'87. Dirt 1965-'83. Dead heat for first 2000. ‡Impecunious finished first, DQ to second, 1973. ‡Flying Dash (Ger) finished first, DQ to seventh for a positive drug test, 2002. †Denotes female.

Hawthorne Gold Cup Handicap

Grade 2 in 2008. Hawthorne Race Course, three-year-olds and up, 1¼ miles, dirt. Held September 29, 2007, with a gross value of $500,000. First held in 1928. First graded in 1973. Stakes record 1:58.80 (1970 Gladwin; 1974 Group Plan).

Year	Winner	Jockey	Second	Third	Strs	Time	1st Purse
2007	Student Council, 5, 119	R. Migliore	Jonesboro, 5, 116	A. P. Arrow, 5, 115	5	2:05.00	$300,000
2006	It's No Joke, 4, 118	E. Razo Jr.	A. P. Arrow, 4, 112	Kid Grindstone, 4, 115	7	2:03.89	300,000
2005	Super Frolic, 5, 118	V. Espinoza	Lord of the Game, 4, 117	Desert Boom, 5, 115	10	2:04.66	450,000
2004	Freefourinternet, 6, 112	G. Kuntzweiler	Perfect Drift, 5, 121	Sonic West, 5, 115	7	2:03.34	450,000
2003	Perfect Drift, 4, 122	P. Day	Tenpins, 5, 119	Aeneas, 4, 114	6	2:03.63	450,000
2002	Hail The Chief (GB), 5, 114	J. F. Chavez	Dollar Bill, 4, 114	Parade Leader, 5, 115	5	2:02.80	300,000
2001	Duckhorn, 4, 112	R. A. Meier	Lido Palace (Chi), 4, 114	Guided Tour, 5, 116	7	2:01.61	300,000
2000	Dust On the Bottle, 5, 112	T. T. Doocy	Guided Tour, 4, 113	Golden Missile, 5, 121	8	2:03.09	300,000
1999	Supreme Sound (GB), 5, 112	R. A. Meier	Golden Missile, 4, 115	Beboppin Baby, 6, 113	8	2:01.19	300,000
1998	Awesome Again, 4, 123	P. Day	Unruled, 5, 114	Muchacho Fino, 4, 118	8	2:02.71	240,000
1997	Buck's Boy, 4, 114	M. Guidry	Cairo Express, 5, 115	Beboppin Baby, 4, 115	7	2:00.54	180,000
1996	Come On Flip, 5, 113	C. A. Emigh	Michael's Star, 4, 114	Mt. Sassafras, 4, 120	10	2:03.40	180,000
1995	Yourmissinthepoint, 4, 113	M. Guidry	Basqueian, 4, 114	Sky Carr, 5, 112	9	2:01.00	150,000
1994	Recoup the Cash, 4, 117	J. L. Diaz	Run Softly, 3, 114	Kissin Kris, 4, 118	11	2:01.99	240,000
1993	Evanescent, 6, 115	A. T. Gryder	Marquetry, 6, 123	Valley Crossing, 5, 117	7	2:02.19	240,000
1992	Irish Swap, 5, 115	B. E. Poyadou	Sea Cadet, 4, 121	Evanescent, 5, 112	8	2:01.12	240,000
1991	Sunny Sunrise, 4, 114	C. W. Antley	Sports View, 4, 116	Discover, 3, 114	14	2:04.10	309,840
1990	Black Tie Affair (Ire), 4, 116	J. L. Diaz	Mi Selecto, 5, 115	Silver Tower, 3, 112	10	2:03.40	307,800
1989	Cryptoclearance, 5, 122	J. A. Santos	Proper Reality, 4, 120	Classic Account, 4, 112	7	2:00.40	305,730
1988	Cryptoclearance, 4, 117	J. A. Santos	Cutlass Reality, 6, 124	Nostalgia's Star, 6, 113	4	2:00.20	303,690
1987	Nostalgia's Star, 5, 117	F. Toro	Savings, 4, 114	Minneapple, 5, 117	9	2:02.00	277,440
1986	Ends Well, 5, 121	R. P. Romero	Harham's Sizzler, 7, 115	Inevitable Leader, 7, 113	6	2:00.60	182,340
1985	Garthorn, 5, 116	R. Q. Meza	Magic North, 3, 115	Leroy S., 4, 114	10	2:01.80	158,220
1984	Proof, 4, 118	E. Delahoussaye	Jack Slade, 4, 119	Bounding Basque, 4, 117	14	2:01.20	160,170
1983	Water Bank, 4, 114	C. Lamance	Cad, 5, 116	Gallant Gentleman, 4, 111	13	2:01.40	130,050
1982	Recusant, 4, 122	R. J. Hirdes Jr.	Harham's Sizzler, 3, 116	Irish Heart (Ire), 4, 115	12	2:01.80	98,760
1981	Spruce Bouquet, 4, 119	K. D. Clark	Lord Gallant, 4, 114	Bill Monroe, 3, 119	16	2:04.20	101,760
1980	Tunerup, 4, 125	J. Vasquez	Pole Position, 4, 120	The Trader Man, 4, 112	9	2:00.60	82,590
1979	Young Bob, 4, 114	R. L. Turcotte	All the More, 6, 113	Architect, 3, 121	7	1:51.00	62,460
1977	On the Sly, 4, 121	G. McCarron	Milwaukee Avenue, 4, 114	Romeo, 4, 111	8	2:01.60	75,072
1976	Almost Grown, 4, 110	M. R. Morgan	Teddy's Courage, 3, 113	Romeo, 3, 113	10	2:01.60	86,720
1975	Royal Glint, 5, 124	J. E. Tejeira	Buffalo Lark, 5, 123	Group Plan, 5, 126	5	2:02.20	74,480
1974	Group Plan, 4, 115	J. Velasquez	Buffalo Lark, 4, 117	Billy Come Lately, 4, 119	5	1:58.80	66,120
1973	Tri Jet, 4, 117	B. Baeza	Golden Don, 3, 113	Cloudy Dawn, 4, 114	9	2:01.40	75,720

Grade 3 1997-2000. Hawthorne Gold Cup S. 1928-'35. Budweiser-Hawthorne Gold Cup H. 1985-'86, 1988-'91. Hawthorne Budweiser Gold Cup H. 1987, '92. Not held 1934, 1936, 1940-'45, 1978. Held at Sportsman's Park 1979. 1⅛ miles 1979. Equaled track record 1974.

Hawthorne Handicap

Grade 3 in 2008. Hollywood Park, three-year-olds and up, fillies and mares, 1 1/16 miles. Held May 4, 2008, with a gross value of $108,500. First held in 1974. First graded in 1982. Stakes record 1:41.12 (1993 Freedom Cry).

Year	Winner	Jockey	Second	Third	Strs	Time	1st Purse
2008	Tough Tiz's Sis, 4, 121	A. T. Gryder	Santa Teresita, 4, 117	Dawn After Dawn, 4, 117	7	1:41.84	$65,100
2007	River Savage (Brz), 5, 114	O. A. Berrio	Cantabria (GB), 4, 116	Ballado's Thunder, 4, 116	5	1:44.08	64,380
2006	Star Parade (Arg), 7, 118	M. A. Pedroza	Hollywood Story, 5, 118	Healthy Addiction, 5, 120	5	1:42.26	60,000
2005	Hollywood Story, 4, 119	V. Espinoza	Siphon Honey, 6, 112	House of Fortune, 4, 117	7	1:42.42	64,980
2004	Summer Wind Dancer, 4, 116	V. Espinoza	Pesci, 4, 115	Miss Loren (Arg), 6, 116	7	1:41.56	65,160
2003	Keys to the Heart, 4, 115	J. Valdivia Jr.	Rhiana, 6, 116	‡Alexine (Arg), 7, 117	4	1:42.97	63,240
2002	Queen of Wilshire, 6, 115	P. A. Valenzuela	Alexine (Arg), 4, 119	Verruma (Brz), 4, 115	5	1:43.16	63,660
2001	Printemps (Chi), 4, 116	C. J. McCarron	Feverish, 6, 119	Brianda (Ire), 4, 109	4	1:43.21	90,060
2000	Ribolletta (Brz), 5, 117	C. J. McCarron	Excellent Meeting, 4, 122	Speaking of Time, 4, 115	5	1:42.33	90,000
1999	Victory Stripes (Arg), 5, 115	C. J. McCarron	Magical Allure, 4, 118	Housa Dancer (Fr), 6, 115	4	1:41.73	90,000
1998	I Ain't Bluffing, 4, 118	C. J. McCarron	Fun in Excess, 4, 116	Tomorrows Sunshine, 4, 115	5	1:41.49	63,720
1997	Twice the Vice, 4, 120	C. J. McCarron	Chile Chatte, 4, 115	Listening, 4, 117	7	1:42.72	64,860
1996	Borodislew, 6, 119	C. S. Nakatani	Jewel Princess, 4, 120	Urbane, 4, 118	5	1:41.28	64,200
1995	Paseana (Arg), 8, 122	C. J. McCarron	Pirate's Revenge, 4, 117	Top Rung, 4, 117	7	1:42.40	63,300
1994	Golden Klair (GB), 4, 118	K. Desormeaux	Likeable Style, 4, 119	Andestine, 4, 117	4	1:41.41	60,000
1993	Freedom Cry, 5, 117	A. O. Solis	Vieille Vigne (Fr), 6, 114	Miss High Blade, 5, 114	11	1:41.12	67,600
1992	Sacramentada (Chi), 6, 117	K. Desormeaux	Brought to Mind, 5, 120	Re Toss (Arg), 5, 116	5	1:43.04	61,600
1991	Brought to Mind, 4, 116	P. A. Valenzuela	Fantastic Look, 5, 117	Fit to Scout, 4, 118	6	1:41.50	62,300
1990	Bayakoa (Arg), 6, 125	L. A. Pincay Jr.	Stormy But Valid, 4, 119	Fantastic Look, 4, 115	6	1:34.00	61,400
1989	Bayakoa (Arg), 5, 122	L. A. Pincay Jr.	Goodbye Halo, 4, 123	Behind the Scenes, 5, 114	6	1:32.80	61,400
1988	Integra, 4, 118	G. L. Stevens	Invited Guest (Ire), 4, 118	Behind the Scenes, 4, 117	5	1:36.00	59,400
1987	Seldom Seen Sue, 4, 114	C. J. McCarron	Clabber Girl, 4, 116	Tiffany Lass, 4, 123	5	1:33.60	59,900
1986	Dontstop Themusic, 6, 121	L. A. Pincay Jr.	Till You, 5, 115	Fran's Valentine, 4, 122	7	1:35.40	46,950
1985	Adored, 5, 124	L. A. Pincay Jr.	Mitterand, 4, 122	Her Royalty, 4, 118	4	1:34.80	45,350
1984	Adored, 4, 117	F. Toro	Holiday Dancer, 4, 116	Princess Rooney, 4, 123	4	1:41.80	36,200
1983	Marisma (Chi), 5, 115	K. D. Black	Sierva (Arg), 5, 115	Matching, 5, 121	5	1:44.80	30,700

Racing — Graded Stakes

Year	Winner	Jockey	Second	Third	Strs	Time	1st Purse
1982	Weber City Miss, 5, 122	S. Hawley	Miss Huntington, 5, 117	Aduana, 5, 114	7	1:42.40	$31,750
1981	Save Wild Life, 4, 113	C. J. McCarron	Princess Karenda, 4, 122	Spiffy Laree, 5, 113	6	1:42.80	37,400
1980	Country Queen, 5, 122	L. A. Pincay Jr.	Devon Ditty (GB), 4, 117	Wishing Well, 5, 121	6	1:40.60	30,800
1979	Country Queen, 4, 118	L. A. Pincay Jr.	Grande Brisa, 5, 113	Sisterhood, 4, 120	9	1:41.20	26,600
1978	Sensational, 4, 119	L. A. Pincay Jr.	Up to Juliet, 5, 114	Grand Luxe, 4, 117	10	1:41.80	27,300
1977	Cascapedia, 4, 123	S. Hawley	*Bastonera II, 6, 124	*Star Ball, 5, 121	10	1:40.80	26,850
1976	Swingtime, 4, 118	W. Shoemaker	Call Me Prover, 4, 116	Tuscarora, 4, 113	5	1:41.80	19,150
	Mia Amore, 4, 116	F. Toro	*Bastonera II, 5, 118	Summertime Promise, 4, 119	7	1:41.80	19,950
1975	*Tizna, 6, 122	J. Lambert	Modus Vivendi, 4, 121	Lucky Spell, 4, 121	7	1:20.60	22,600
1974	Tallahto, 4, 119	L. A. Pincay Jr.	Sister Fleet, 4, 116	Lt.'s Joy, 4, 119	9	1:20.60	23,200

Named for the nearby town of Hawthorne, California. Grade 2 1983-2001. 7 furlongs 1974-'75. 1 mile 1985-'90. Turf 1976-'80. Dirt 1974-'75, 1981-2006. Two divisions 1976. ‡Se Me Acabo finished third, DQ to fourth, 2003.

Herecomesthebride Stakes

Grade 3 in 2008. Gulfstream Park, three-year-olds, fillies, 1 1/8 miles, turf. Held March 25, 2007, with a gross value of $107,000. First held in 1984. First graded in 1998. Stakes record 1:46.40 (1997 Auntie Mame).

Year	Winner	Jockey	Second	Third	Strs	Time	1st Purse
2007	Sharp Susan, 3, 118	C. H. Velasquez	Communique, 3, 118	Perfect Motion, 3, 118	8	1:47.90	$60,000
2006	Aunt Henny, 3, 118	J. Castellano	Diamond Spirit, 3, 118	Miss Shop, 3, 118	5	1:46.88	60,000
2005	Cape Hope, 3, 119	J. A. Santos	Dynamite Lass, 3, 117	Dansetta Light, 3, 121	8	1:48.28	60,000
2004	Lucifer's Stone, 3, 117	J. A. Santos	Dynamia, 3, 115	Honey Ryder, 3, 117	12	1:52.78	60,000
2003	Gal O Gal, 3, 117	C. P. DeCarlo	Formal Miss, 3, 117	Devil At the Wire, 3, 117	8	1:42.38	60,000
2002	Cellars Shiraz, 3, 117	C. H. Velasquez	August Storm, 3, 121	She's Vested, 3, 115	10	1:43.21	60,000
2001	Mystic Lady, 3, 116	J. D. Bailey	Open Minded, 3, 114	Ruff, 3, 118	7	1:46.73	60,000
2000	Gaviola, 3, 114	J. D. Bailey	Solvig, 3, 117	Are You Up, 3, 114	8	1:47.28	45,000
1999	Pico Teneriffe, 3, 118	J. D. Bailey	European Rose, 3, 112	Wild Heart Dancing, 3, 114	8	1:48.82	45,000
1998	Rashas Warning, 3, 118	M. E. Smith	Quick Lap, 3, 116	Runnaway Dream, 3, 116	7	1:51.44	45,000
1997	Auntie Mame, 3, 114	J. D. Bailey	Witchful Thinking, 3, 116	Classic Approval, 3, 114	7	1:46.40	45,000
1996	Lulu's Ransom, 3, 116	J. D. Bailey	Cymbala (Fr), 3, 114	Vashon, 3, 114	9	1:47.55	30,000
1995	Clever Thing, 3, 114	C. Perret	Transient Trend, 3, 114	Palliser Bay, 3, 114	6	1:53.06	30,000
1994	Cut the Charm, 3, 116	W. Ramos	Mynameispanama, 3, 113	Tambien Me Voy, 3, 113	11	1:43.72	30,000
1993	Sigrun, 3, 116	R. R. Douglas	So Say all of Us, 3, 112	Supah Gem, 3, 116	8	1:45.79	30,000
1992	Morriston Belle, 3, 118	D. Penna	Snazzle Dazzle, 3, 113	Miss Jealski, 3, 116	11	1:42.23	30,000
1989	Darby Shuffle, 3, 121	C. Perret	Seattle Meteor, 3, 121	Imago, 3, 112	8	1:42.80	36,510
1988	Topicount, 3, 112	J. Samyn	Aquaba, 3, 116	Above Special, 3, 113	15	1:43.20	40,350
1987	Sum, 3, 121	R. Woodhouse	Easter Mary, 3, 113	Dawandeh, 3, 116	8	1:43.20	25,410
1986	Judy's Red Shoes, 3, 114	G. St. Leon	Tea for Top, 3, 112	Minstress, 3, 121	8	1:43.00	35,790
1985	Debutant Dancer, 3, 113	G. Gallitano	One Fine Lady, 3, 118	Affirmance, 3, 118	11	1:42.80	38,640
1984	Delta Mary, 3, 112	F. A. Pennisi	Vast Domain, 3, 114	Ingot Way, 3, 114	10	1:42.00	14,955
	Oakbrook Lady, 3, 112	J. A. Velez Jr.	Illaka, 3, 112	Rain Devil, 3, 112	8	1:42.80	14,655

Named for Pelican Stable's and Mrs. Warren A. Croll Jr.'s 1977 Bonnie Miss S. winner Herecomesthebride (1974 f. by Al Hattab). Not held 1990-'91, 2008. 1 1/16 miles 1984-'89, 1992-'94, 2001-'03. About 1 1/8 miles 1998. Dirt 1993-'95, 2001. Two divisions 1984. Equaled course record 1997.

Hill 'n' Dale Cigar Mile Handicap

Grade 1 in 2008. Aqueduct, three-year-olds and up, 1 mile, dirt. Held November 24, 2007, with a gross value of $294,000. First held in 1988. First graded in 1990. Stakes record 1:32.46 (2006 Discreet Cat).

Year	Winner	Jockey	Second	Third	Strs	Time	1st Purse
2007	Daaher, 3, 114	M. J. Luzzi	Midnight Lute, 4, 123	Naughty New Yorker, 5, 114	5	1:33.79	$180,000
2006	Discreet Cat, 3, 124	G. K. Gomez	Badge of Silver, 6, 117	Silver Train, 4, 120	5	**1:32.46**	180,000
2005	Purge, 4, 115	G. K. Gomez	Mass Media, 4, 118	Gygistar, 6, 115	11	1:34.26	210,000
2004	Lion Tamer, 4, 115	J. A. Santos	Badge of Silver, 4, 115	Pico Central (Brz), 5, 123	8	1:33.46	210,000
2003	Congaree, 5, 124	J. D. Bailey	Midas Eyes, 3, 115	Toccet, 3, 115	7	1:34.30	210,000
2002	Congaree, 4, 119	J. D. Bailey	Aldebaran, 4, 116	Crafty C. T., 4, 117	8	1:33.11	210,000
2001	Left Bank, 4, 120	J. R. Velazquez	Graeme Hall, 3, 118	Red Bullet, 4, 118	9	1:33.35	210,000
2000	El Corredor, 3, 116	J. D. Bailey	Peeping Tom, 3, 111	Affirmed Success, 6, 120	11	1:34.68	210,000
1999	Affirmed Success, 5, 118	J. F. Chavez	Adonis, 3, 115	Honorifico (Arg), 5, 113	9	1:34.18	210,000
1998	Sir Bear, 5, 116	J. D. Bailey	Affirmed Success, 4, 119	Distorted Humor, 5, 116	8	1:34.05	180,000
1997	Devious Course, 5, 112	J. F. Chavez	Lucayan Prince, 4, 114	Basqueian, 6, 115	12	1:34.98	150,000
1996	Gold Fever, 3, 115	M. E. Smith	Diligence, 3, 114	Top Account, 4, 117	14	1:34.98	150,000
1995	Flying Chevron, 3, 112	R. G. Davis	Wekiva Springs, 4, 117	Dramatic Gold, 4, 120	13	1:34.57	150,000
1994	Cigar, 4, 111	J. D. Bailey	Devil His Due, 5, 124	Punch Line, 4, 112	12	1:36.10	150,000
1992	Ibero (Arg), 5, 117	L. A. Pincay Jr.	Irish Swap, 5, 116	Nines Wild, 3, 111	7	1:33.97	300,000
1991	Rubiano, 4, 116	J. A. Santos	Sultry Song, 3, 111	Diablo, 4, 112	15	1:33.68	300,000
1990	Quiet American, 4, 118	C. J. McCarron	Dancing Spree, 5, 119	Sewickley, 5, 124	12	1:32.80	382,800
1989	Dispersal, 3, 115	A. T. Cordero Jr.	Sewickley, 4, 120	Speedratic, 4, 117	7	1:32.80	348,600
1988	Forty Niner, 3, 121	W. I. Fox Jr.	Mawsuff (GB), 5, 115	Precisionist, 7, 124	6	1:34.00	340,200

Sponsored by John G. Sikura's Hill 'n' Dale Farms of Lexington, Kentucky 2005-'07. Named for Allen E. Paulson's 1995, '96 Horse of the Year, '94 NYRA Mile H. (G1) winner, and world's leading earner at his retirement, Cigar (1990 c. by Palace Music). Formerly named for the New York Racing Association 1988-'96. Not held 1993. NYRA Mile H. 1988-'96. Equaled track record 2006.

Hill Prince Stakes

Grade 3 in 2008. Belmont Park, three-year-olds, 1 mile, turf. Held June 6, 2008, with a gross value of $111,000. First held in 1975. First graded in 1981. Stakes record 1:33.45 (2007 Marcavelly).

Year	Winner	Jockey	Second	Third	Strs	Time	1st Purse
2008	Gio Ponti, 3, 120	G. K. Gomez	Prussian, 3, 120	Moral Compass, 3, 116	7	1:35.03	$66,600
2007	Marcavelly, 3, 120	E. S. Prado	Distorted Reality, 3, 116	Codeword (Ire), 3, 116	5	**1:33.45**	64,620
2006	Outperformance, 3, 120	J. Castellano	Spider Power (Ire), 3, 118	Carnera, 3, 116	10	1:36.74	69,240
2005	Rey de Cafe, 3, 123	J. Castellano	Prince Rahy, 3, 116	Classic Campaign, 3, 116	9	1:49.25	68,820
2004	Artie Schiller, 3, 120	R. Migliore	Timo, 3, 122	Big Booster, 3, 114	6	1:50.06	66,000
2003	Happy Trails, 3, 120	S. Bridgmohan	Traffic Chief, 3, 114	Chilly Rooster, 3, 114	6	1:50.13	67,860
2002	Van Minister, 3, 114	M. J. Luzzi	Miesque's Approval, 3, 120	Westcliffe, 3, 114	5	1:54.42	65,580
2001	Proud Man, 3, 122	R. R. Douglas	Package Store, 3, 114	Navesink, 3, 118	10	1:48.25	68,760
2000	Promontory Gold, 3, 119	E. S. Prado	Rob's Spirit, 3, 113	Avezzano (GB), 3, 115	7	1:49.15	66,540
1999	Time Off, 3, 113	J. Samyn	Hoyle, 3, 113	Lenny's Ransom, 3, 113	8	1:47.48	66,720
1998	Recommended List, 3, 119	J. F. Chavez	Daniel My Brother, 3, 119	Availability, 3, 119	5	1:49.28	67,800
1997	Subordination, 3, 113	J. R. Velazquez	Rob 'n Gin, 3, 119	Tekken (Ire), 3, 119	8	1:45.69	67,200
1996	Optic Nerve, 3, 114	J. A. Santos	Fortitude, 3, 117	Allied Forces, 3, 119	7	1:39.70	66,420
1995	Green Means Go, 3, 117	J. D. Bailey	Smells and Bells, 3, 114	Debonair Dan, 3, 119	10	1:40.33	68,160
1994	Pennine Ridge, 3, 112	J. D. Bailey	Check Ride, 3, 119	Add the Gold, 3, 114	9	1:39.87	50,925
1993	Halissee, 3, 121	J. A. Krone	Proud Shot, 3, 117	Logroller, 3, 114	5	1:40.91	52,020
1992	‡Free At Last, 3, 126	J. D. Bailey	Casino Magistrate, 3, 123	Kiri's Clown, 3, 114	8	1:41.05	53,190
1991	Young Daniel, 3, 114	A. T. Cordero Jr.	Share the Glory, 3, 119	Lech, 3, 114	13	1:39.87	58,050
1990	Solar Splendor, 3, 114	E. Maple	Divine Warning, 3, 119	Bismarck Hills, 3, 114	13	1:41.20	57,870
1989	Slew the Knight, 3, 121	C. W. Antley	Orange Sunshine, 3, 117	Expensive Decision, 3, 121	10	1:41.00	56,520
1988	Sunshine Forever, 3, 114	A. T. Cordero Jr.	Posen, 3, 121	Kris Green, 3, 114	7	1:41.20	85,620
1987	Forest Fair, 3, 119	J. A. Santos	Kindly Court, 3, 117	First Patriot, 3, 121	7	1:42.80	86,220
1986	Double Feint, 3, 121	J. A. Santos	Glow, 3, 121	Jack of Clubs, 3, 114	7	1:41.40	53,190
1985	Danger's Hour, 3, 119	D. MacBeth	Foundation Plan, 3, 119	Exclusive Partner, 3, 114	13	1:40.60	59,310
1984	A Gift, 3, 114	D. MacBeth	Is Your Pleasure, 3, 126	Jesse's Hope, 3, 117	7	1:48.40	43,680
1983	Domynsky (GB), 3, 114	J. D. Bailey	White Birch, 3, 114	Macho Duck, 3, 114	11	1:48.80	36,660
1982	Majesty's Prince, 3, 114	R. Hernandez	A Real Leader, 3, 114	†Honed Edge, 3, 109	8	1:43.40	33,180
	†Larida, 3, 112	E. Maple	Dew Line, 3, 117	John's Gold, 3, 114	8	1:42.60	33,180
1981	Summing, 3, 114	A. T. Cordero Jr.	Stage Door Key, 3, 114	Sportin' Life, 3, 114	10	1:42.40	35,700
1980	Ben Fab, 3, 126	J. Cruguet	Vatza, 3, 113	Don Daniello, 3, 117	8	1:43.40	34,800
1979	Bends Me Mind, 3, 114	J. Velasquez	Crown Thy Good, 3, 115	T. V. Series, 3, 110	11	1:46.00	34,470
1978	Darby Creek Road, 3, 121	A. T. Cordero Jr.	John Henry, 3, 111	Scythian Gold, 3, 111	9	1:35.20	22,605
1977	Forward Charger, 3, 115	J. Vasquez	Stir the Embers, 3, 112	Winter Wind, 3, 112	7	1:34.40	22,575
1976	Fifth Marine, 3, 126	R. Turcotte	Quick Card, 3, 120	Drover's Dawn, 3, 112	9	1:41.20	27,405
1975	‡Don Jack, 3, 110	G. Martens	Annie's Brat, 3, 115	Rapid Invader, 3, 113	7	2:23.20	34,650

Named for Christopher T. Chenery's Racing Hall of Fame member, 1950 Horse of the Year, and '50 Jockey Club Gold Cup winner Hill Prince (1947 c. by *Princequillo). Hill Prince H. 1975-'80. Held at Aqueduct 1979-'80, 1982. 1 3/8 miles 1975. 1 1/16 miles 1976, 1979-'86. 1 1/8 miles 1987-2005. Dirt 1998. Two divisions 1982. ‡Annie's Brat finished first, DQ to second, 1975. ‡Casino Magistrate finished first, DQ to second, 1992. Course record 1997. †Denotes female.

Hillsborough Stakes

Grade 3 in 2008. Tampa Bay Downs, four-year-olds and up, fillies and mares, 1 1/8 miles, turf. Held March 15, 2008, with a gross value of $175,000. First held in 1999. First graded in 2004. Stakes record 1:48.83 (2004 Coney Kitty [Ire]).

Year	Winner	Jockey	Second	Third	Strs	Time	1st Purse
2008	Dreaming of Anna, 4, 122	C. H. Velasquez	Lady Digby, 4, 117	Mary Louhana (GB), 5, 116	6	1:52.18	$105,000
2007	Cassydora (GB), 5, 122	J. R. Velazquez	My Typhoon (Ire), 5, 116	Masseuse, 5, 116	9	1:48.90	90,000
2006	Ready's Gal, 4, 116	J. R. Velazquez	Amorama (Fr), 5, 116	Marchonin, 4, 116	12	1:50.50	75,000
2005	Rizzi Girl, 7, 116	O. Castillo	Sister Star, 4, 116	Noisete, 5, 116	9	1:52.59	75,000
2004	Coney Kitty (Ire), 6, 116	J. A. Santos	Madeira Mist (Ire), 5, 122	Alternate, 5, 116	12	1:48.83	60,000
2003	Strait From Texas, 4, 116	J. L. Castanon	Dedication (Fr), 4, 118	Stylish, 5, 118	11	1:41.14	60,000
2002	Platinum Tiara, 4, 116	M. R. Cruz	Step With Style, 5, 116	Ioya Two, 7, 116	11	1:41.34	60,000
2001	Song for Annie, 5, 116	L. J. Melancon	Megans Bluff, 4, 116	Inside Affair, 6, 122	11	1:41.23	60,000
2000	St Clair Ridge (Ire), 4, 117	P. Day	Office Miss, 6, 122	Royal Bloomer, 5, 115	11	1:41.17	45,000
1999	Pleasant Temper, 5, 117	P. Day	Sandy Gator, 6, 115	Scatter Buy, 4, 115	10	1:42.62	34,800

Named for Hillsborough County, Florida; the city of Tampa is the county seat. Three-year-olds and up 1999-2001. 1 1/16 miles 1999-2003.

Hirsch Jacobs Stakes

Grade 3 in 2008. Pimlico Race Course, three-year-olds, 6 furlongs, dirt. Held May 17, 2008, with a gross value of $100,000. First held in 1975. First graded in 2006. Stakes record 1:09.10 (2008 Lantana Mob).

Year	Winner	Jockey	Second	Third	Strs	Time	1st Purse
2008	Lantana Mob, 3, 122	R. Albarado	Silver Edition, 3, 116	Force Freeze, 3, 116	8	**1:09.10**	$60,000
2007	Street Magician, 3, 122	R. Bejarano	Southwestern Heat, 3, 117	Hobbitontherocks, 3, 116	7	1:10.97	60,000
2006	Songster, 3, 116	E. S. Prado	Valid Brush, 3, 116	Urban Guy, 3, 120	6	1:09.72	60,000
2004	Abbondanza, 3, 115	R. A. Dominguez	Bwana Charlie, 3, 122	Penn Pacific, 3, 117	9	1:10.72	60,000
2003	Mt. Carson, 3, 122	R. A. Dominguez	Gators N Bears, 3, 117	Only the Best, 3, 122	6	1:10.85	60,000
2002	True Direction, 3, 117	R. A. Dominguez	Listen Here, 3, 122	It's a Monster, 3, 117	8	1:10.90	45,000
2001	City Zip, 3, 122	J. F. Chavez	Sea of Green, 3, 119	Stake Runner, 3, 119	7	1:10.20	45,000
2000	Max's Pal, 3, 119	R. Wilson	Ultimate Warrior, 3, 119	Stormin Oedy, 3, 119	8	1:10.32	45,000

344   Racing — Graded Stakes

Year	Winner	Jockey	Second	Third	Strs	Time	1st Purse
1999	**Erlton**, 3, 122	R. Wilson	Jeanies Rob, 3, 122	Jovial Brush, 3, 117	7	1:10.60	$45,000
1998	**Klabin's Gold**, 3, 115	R. Wilson	Carnivorous Habit, 3, 115	Greenspring Willy, 3, 122	7	1:11.51	32,760
1997	**Original Gray**, 3, 122	C. H. Marquez Jr.	American Champ, 3, 122	Stroke, 3, 122	9	1:10.85	33,585
1996	**Viv**, 3, 122	M. T. Johnston	Fort Dodge, 3, 122	Big Rut, 3, 115	6	1:12.11	32,805
1995	**Ft. Stockton**, 3, 115	J. D. Bailey	Splendid Sprinter, 3, 115	Sittin Cool, 3, 115	6	1:10.29	32,265
1994	**Foxie G**, 3, 114	E. S. Prado	Distinct Reality, 3, 114	Spartan's Hero, 3, 114	7	1:11.51	32,520
1993	**Montbrook**, 3, 114	M. J. Luzzi	Without Dissent, 3, 122	Mighty Game, 3, 114	7	1:12.10	32,490
1992	**Speakerphone**, 3, 114	C. J. Ladner III	Coin Collector, 3, 122	Golden Phase, 3, 122	7	1:10.52	26,160
1991	**Ameri Run**, 3, 119	G. W. Hutton	Exclusive Dove, 3, 114	Nasty Hero, 3, 122	6	1:10.86	25,860
1990	**Collegian**, 3, 117	H. Vega	Hit the Mahagoney, 3, 117	Bardland, 3, 114	5	1:10.20	26,115
1989	**Pulverizing**, 3, 122	A. T. Stacy	Jimmy Coggins, 3, 114	Midas, 3, 114	6	1:11.20	32,460
1988	**Finder's Choice**, 3, 122	J. A. Santos	†Smarter Than, 3, 117	Royal Highlander, 3, 110	4	1:12.20	27,820
1987	**Green Book**, 3, 122	G. W. Hutton	Judge's Dream, 3, 110	Silano, 3, 122	7	1:11.80	28,730
1986	**Super Delight**, 3, 122	J. Nied Jr.	Part Dutch, 3, 113	Fun Bunch, 3, 115	8	1:11.80	21,515
1985	**Beat Me Daddy**, 3, 122	V. A. Bracciale Jr.	Banjo Dancing, 3, 116	Urigo, 3, 119	7	1:11.80	21,775
1984	**Mickey Mall**, 3, 119	R. Wilson	Moschini, 3, 116	Bold Flunky, 3, 122	7	1:10.80	20,995
1983	**Emperial Age**, 3, 116	J. Nied Jr.	Unreal Zeal, 3, 116	Zeb's Hel Cat, 3, 116	5	1:10.80	20,963
1982	**Mortgage Man**, 3, 122	A. S. Black	Woody's Wish, 3, 116	St. Chrisbee, 3, 122	7	1:10.60	21,353
1981	**Century Prince**, 3, 122	V. A. Bracciale Jr.	J. D. Quill, 3, 116	Irish King, 3, 119	5	1:10.20	21,027
1980	**Amber Pass**, 3, 116	D. MacBeth	Pickett's Charge, 3, 116	Peace for Peace, 3, 119	8	1:10.80	21,418
1979	**Breezing On**, 3, 122	W. J. Passmore	Fearless McGuire, 3, 113	Our Gary, 3, 122	8	1:14.80	21,645
1978	**Shelter Half**, 3, 119	G. Lindberg	Star de Naskra, 3, 122	Game Prince, 3, 116	9	1:11.00	21,645
1977	**Iron Derby**, 3, 119	D. R. Wright	Jeff's Try, 3, 116	Tiny Monk, 3, 116	7	1:11.20	17,875
1976	**Zen**, 3, 116	J. Vasquez	Cojak, 3, 122	Greek Victor, 3, 113	4	1:11.40	17,518
1975	**Bombay Duck**, 3, 122	M. Aristone	Gallant Bob, 3, 122	Ben S., 3, 116	9	1:11.20	18,622

Named for Racing Hall of Fame trainer Hirsch Jacobs (1904-'70); Jacobs was also a leading breeder and owner. Not held 2005. †Denotes female.

Hollywood Derby

Grade 1 in 2008. Hollywood Park, three-year-olds, 1 1/4 miles, turf. Held November 25, 2007, with a gross value of $500,000. First held in 1938. First graded in 1973. Stakes record 1:59.35 (2006 Showing Up).

Year	Winner	Jockey	Second	Third	Strs	Time	1st Purse
2007	**Daytona (Ire)**, 3, 122	M. E. Smith	Medici Code (GB), 3, 122	Bold Hawk, 3, 122	10	1:59.75	$300,000
2006	**Showing Up**, 3, 122	C. H. Velasquez	Obrigado (Fr), 3, 122	Ivan Denisovich (Ire), 3, 122	10	**1:59.35**	300,000
2004	**Good Reward**, 3, 122	J. D. Bailey	Fast and Furious (Fr), 3, 122	Imperialism, 3, 122	13	2:01.53	300,000
2003	**Sweet Return (GB)**, 3, 122	J. A. Krone	Fairly Ransom, 3, 122	Kicken Kris, 3, 122	13	2:04.27	360,000
2002	**Johar**, 3, 122	A. O. Solis	Mananan McLir, 3, 122	Royal Gem, 3, 122	9	1:48.70	300,000
2001	**Denon**, 3, 122	C. J. McCarron	Sligo Bay (Ire), 3, 122	Aldebaran, 3, 122	12	1:49.22	300,000
2000	**‡Brahms**, 3, 122	P. Day	David Copperfield, 3, 122	Zentsov Street, 3, 122	12	1:46.73	300,000
1999	**Super Quercus (Fr)**, 3, 122	A. O. Solis	Manndar (Ire), 3, 122	Fighting Falcon, 3, 122	14	1:45.82	300,000
1998	**Vergennes**, 3, 122	J. R. Velazquez	Dixie Dot Com, 3, 122	Lone Bid (Fr), 3, 122	10	1:49.44	300,000
1997	**Subordination**, 3, 122	J. D. Bailey	Lasting Approval, 3, 122	Blazing Sword, 3, 122	13	1:50.00	300,000
1996	**Marlin**, 3, 122	J. R. Velazquez	Rainbow Blues (Ire), 3, 122	Devil's Cup, 3, 122	14	1:46.08	300,000
1995	**Labeeb (GB)**, 3, 122	E. Delahoussaye	Helmsman, 3, 122	Da Hoss, 3, 122	13	1:46.42	220,000
1994	**River Flyer**, 3, 122	C. W. Antley	Dare and Go, 3, 122	Fadeyev, 3, 122	13	1:47.48	220,000
1993	**Explosive Red**, 3, 122	C. S. Nakatani	Jeune Homme, 3, 122	Earl of Barking (Ire), 3, 122	14	1:46.88	220,000
1992	**Paradise Creek**, 3, 122	P. Day	Bien Bien, 3, 122	Kitwood, 3, 122	12	1:47.36	220,000
1991	**Eternity Star**, 3, 122	E. Delahoussaye	Native Boundary, 3, 122	Perfectly Proud, 3, 122	11	1:47.30	110,000
	Olympio, 3, 124	E. Delahoussaye	Bistro Garden, 3, 122	River Traffic, 3, 122	10	1:47.10	110,000
1990	**Itsallgreektome**, 3, 122	C. S. Nakatani	Septieme Ciel, 3, 122	Anshan (GB), 3, 122	12	1:46.60	110,000
1989	**Live the Dream**, 3, 122	A. O. Solis	Charlie Barley, 3, 122	River Master, 3, 122	13	1:47.00	110,000
1988	**Silver Circus**, 3, 122	G. L. Stevens	Raykour (Ire), 3, 122	Dr. Death, 3, 122	14	1:48.40	110,000
1987	**Political Ambition**, 3, 122	E. Delahoussaye	The Medic, 3, 122	Light Sabre, 3, 122	7	1:48.20	101,600
	Stately Don, 3, 122	J. Vasquez	Lockton (GB), 3, 122	Noble Minstrel, 3, 122	9	1:47.40	104,600
1986	**Thrill Show**, 3, 122	W. Shoemaker	Air Display, 3, 122	Bold Arrangement (GB), 3, 122	11	1:46.80	146,000
	Spellbound, 3, 122	R. Sibille	Double Feint, 3, 122	Bruiser (GB), 3, 122	12	1:46.80	147,500
1985	**Charming Duke (Fr)**, 3, 122	Y. Saint-Martin	Herat, 3, 122	†La Koumia (Fr), 3, 119	13	1:46.80	171,225
	Slew the Dragon, 3, 122	J. Velasquez	†Savannah Dancer, 3, 119	Catane, 3, 122	12	1:46.40	168,725
1984	**Procida**, 3, 122	C. B. Asmussen	Executive Pride (Ire), 3, 122	†Reine Mathilde, 3, 122	9	1:48.40	139,250
	Foscarini (Ire), 3, 122	D. G. McHargue	Roving Minstrel, 3, 122	Bean Bag, 3, 122	10	1:47.40	140,750
1983	**†Royal Heroine (Ire)**, 3, 119	F. Toro	Interco, 3, 122	Pac Mania, 3, 122	11	1:48.20	87,400
	Ginger Brink (Fr), 3, 122	F. Toro	Fifth Division, 3, 122	Hur Power, 3, 122	10	1:49.20	86,400
1982	**Racing Is Fun**, 3, 122	W. Shoemaker	Prince Spellbound, 3, 122	Uncle Jeff, 3, 122	7	1:47.80	67,150
	Victory Zone, 3, 122	E. Delahoussaye	The Hague, 3, 122	Ask Me, 3, 122	9	1:47.80	70,150
1981	**†De La Rose**, 3, 119	E. Maple	High Counsel, 3, 122	Lord Trendy (Ire), 3, 122	8	1:47.60	68,700
	Silveyville, 3, 122	D. Winick	French Sassafras (GB), 3, 122	Waterway Drive, 3, 122	8	1:48.20	68,700
1980	**Codex**, 3, 122	E. Delahoussaye	Rumbo, 3, 122	Cactus Road, 3, 122	11	1:47.80	195,250
1979	**Flying Paster**, 3, 122	D. Pierce	Switch Partners, 3, 122	Shamgo, 3, 122	7	1:47.60	166,750
1978	**Affirmed**, 3, 122	S. Cauthen	Think Snow, 3, 122	Radar Ahead, 3, 122	9	1:48.20	174,750
1977	**Steve's Friend**, 3, 122	R. Hernandez	Affiliate, 3, 122	*Habitony, 3, 122	8	1:47.80	140,000
1976	**Crystal Water**, 3, 122	W. Shoemaker	Life's Hope, 3, 122	Double Discount, 3, 122	11	1:48.40	152,750
1975	**Intrepid Hero**, 3, 126	D. Pierce	Terete, 3, 126	Sibirri, 3, 126	7	2:29.00	90,000

Year	Winner	Jockey	Second	Third	Strs	Time	1st Purse
1974	Agitate, 3, 126	W. Shoemaker	Stardust Mel, 3, 126	Top Crowd, 3, 126	9	2:28.20	$90,000
1973	*Amen II, 3, 126	E. Belmonte	Groshawk, 3, 126	Kirrary, 3, 126	11	2:27.80	90,000

Formerly sponsored by the Crown Royal Co. of Stamford, Connecticut 1995-'96. Formerly sponsored by Early Times Distillery Co. of Louisville 1998-2000. Westerner S. 1948-'58. Held at Santa Anita Park 1949. Not held 1942-'44, 2005. 1 1/8 miles 1945, 1950, 1976-2002. 1 1/2 miles 1973-'75. Dirt 1938-'72, 1976-'80. Two divisions 1981-'87, 1991. ‡Designed for Luck finished first, DQ to fifth, 2000. †Denotes female.

Hollywood Gold Cup Stakes

Grade 1 in 2008. Hollywood Park, three-year-olds and up, 1 1/4 miles, all weather. Held June 30, 2007, with a gross value of $750,000. First held in 1938. First graded in 1973. Stakes record 1:58.20 (1972 Quack).

Year	Winner	Jockey	Second	Third	Strs	Time	1st Purse
2007	Lava Man, 6, 124	C. S. Nakatani	A. P. Xcellent, 4, 116	Big Booster, 6, 113	9	2:03.21	$450,000
2006	Lava Man, 5, 124	C. S. Nakatani	Ace Blue (Brz), 6, 114	Super Frolic, 6, 116	5	2:01.16	450,000
2005	Lava Man, 4, 118	P. A. Valenzuela	Borrego, 4, 115	Congrats, 5, 117	9	1:59.63	450,000
2004	Total Impact (Chi), 6, 124	M. E. Smith	Olmodavor, 5, 124	Even the Score, 6, 124	7	2:00.72	450,000
2003	Congaree, 5, 124	J. D. Bailey	Harlan's Holiday, 4, 124	Kudos, 6, 124	7	2:00.48	450,000
2002	Sky Jack, 6, 124	L. A. Pincay Jr.	Momentum, 4, 124	Milwaukee Brew, 5, 124	6	2:01.73	450,000
2001	‡Aptitude, 4, 124	L. A. Pincay Jr.	Skimming, 5, 124	Futural, 5, 124	5	2:01.79	450,000
2000	Early Pioneer, 5, 124	V. Espinoza	General Challenge, 4, 124	David, 4, 124	9	2:01.40	600,000
1999	Real Quiet, 4, 124	J. D. Bailey	Budroyale, 6, 124	Malek (Chi), 6, 124	4	1:59.67	600,000
1998	Skip Away, 5, 124	J. D. Bailey	Puerto Madero (Chi), 4, 124	Gentlemen (Arg), 6, 124	8	2:00.16	600,000
1997	Gentlemen (Arg), 5, 124	G. L. Stevens	Siphon (Brz), 6, 124	Sandpit (Brz), 8, 124	6	1:59.26	600,000
1996	Siphon (Brz), 5, 117	D. R. Flores	Geri, 4, 118	Helmsman, 4, 120	8	2:00.50	600,000
1995	Cigar, 5, 124	J. D. Bailey	Tinners Way, 5, 118	Tossofthecoin, 5, 118	8	1:59.46	550,000
1994	Slew of Damascus, 6, 124	G. L. Stevens	Fanmore, 6, 116	Del Mar Dennis, 4, 116	5	2:00.76	412,500
1993	Best Pal, 5, 121	C. A. Black	Bertrando, 4, 118	Major Impact, 4, 114	10	2:00.17	412,500
1992	Sultry Song, 4, 113	J. D. Bailey	Marquetry, 5, 124	Another Review, 4, 120	6	2:00.23	550,000
1991	Marquetry, 4, 110	D. R. Flores	Farma Way, 4, 122	Itsallgreektome, 4, 119	9	1:59.50	550,000
1990	Criminal Type, 5, 121	J. A. Santos	Sunday Silence, 4, 126	Opening Verse, 4, 119	7	1:59.80	550,000
1989	Blushing John, 4, 122	P. Day	Sabona, 7, 116	Payant (Arg), 5, 116	7	2:00.40	275,000
1988	Cutlass Reality, 6, 116	G. L. Stevens	Alysheba, 4, 126	Ferdinand, 5, 125	6	1:59.40	275,000
1987	Ferdinand, 4, 124	W. Shoemaker	dh-Judge Angelucci, 4, 118 dh-Tasso, 4, 115		11	2:00.60	275,000
1986	Super Diamond, 6, 118	L. A. Pincay Jr.	Alphabatim, 5, 120	Precisionist, 5, 127	6	2:00.40	275,000
1985	Greinton (GB), 4, 120	L. A. Pincay Jr.	Precisionist, 4, 125	Kings Island (Ire), 4, 112	6	1:58.40	275,000
1984	Desert Wine, 4, 122	E. Delahoussaye	John Henry, 9, 125	Sari's Dreamer, 5, 114	8	2:00.40	275,000
1983	Island Whirl, 5, 120	E. Delahoussaye	Poley, 4, 116	Prince Spellbound, 4, 120	6	1:59.40	275,000
1982	Perrault (GB), 5, 127	L. A. Pincay Jr.	Erins Isle (Ire), 4, 118	It's the One, 4, 125	8	1:59.20	275,000
1981	‡Eleven Stitches, 4, 122	S. Hawley	Caterman (NZ), 5, 120	Super Moment, 4, 117	10	2:00.40	275,000
1980	Go West Young Man, 5, 116	E. Delahoussaye	Balzac, 5, 120	Caro Bambino (Ire), 5, 116	10	1:58.80	220,000
1979	Affirmed, 4, 132	L. A. Pincay Jr.	Sirlad (Ire), 5, 120	Text, 5, 119	10	1:58.40	275,000
1978	Exceller, 5, 128	W. Shoemaker	Text, 4, 118	Vigors, 5, 129	7	1:59.20	192,500
1977	Crystal Water, 4, 129	L. A. Pincay Jr.	†Cascapedia, 4, 116	Caucasus, 5, 124	12	2:00.00	210,000
1976	Pay Tribute, 4, 117	M. Castaneda	Avatar, 4, 123	Riot in Paris, 5, 123	8	1:58.40	150,000
1975	Ancient Title, 5, 125	L. A. Pincay Jr.	Big Band, 5, 115	*El Tarta, 5, 115	7	1:59.20	90,000
1974	Tree of Knowledge, 4, 115	W. Shoemaker	Ancient Title, 4, 125	War Heim, 7, 114	10	1:59.80	90,000
1973	Kennedy Road, 5, 126	W. Shoemaker	Quack, 4, 127	*Cougar II, 7, 128	6	1:59.40	90,000

Formerly sponsored by Sempra Energy of San Diego, California 2000. Hollywood Gold Cup H. 1938-'71, 1973, 1976-'96, 2005. Hollywood Gold Cup Invitational H. 1972, 1974-'75. Held at Santa Anita Park 1949. Not held 1942-'43. Dirt 1938-2006. Dead heat for second 1987. ‡Caterman (NZ) finished first, DQ to second, 1981. ‡Futural finished first, DQ to third, 2001. Track record 2007. †Denotes female.

Hollywood Juvenile Championship Stakes

Grade 3 in 2008. Hollywood Park, two-year-olds, 6 furlongs, all weather. Held July 4, 2007, with a gross value of $114,900. First held in 1938. First graded in 1973. Stakes record 1:08.60 (1974 Dimaggio).

Year	Winner	Jockey	Second	Third	Strs	Time	1st Purse
2007	Salute the Sarge, 2, 117	M. C. Baze	Leonides, 2, 117	Whatever Whenever, 2, 117	11	1:12.08	$68,940
2006	E Z Warrior, 2, 117	D. R. Flores	Great Hunter, 2, 119	Tom Rickey, 2, 115	9	1:09.96	60,000
2005	What a Song, 2, 117	V. Espinoza	Bashert, 2, 117	Stevie Wonderboy, 2, 115	5	1:09.55	62,750
2004	Chandtrue, 2, 120	V. Espinoza	Actxecutive, 2, 117	Commandant, 2, 115	4	1:10.88	63,840
2003	Perfect Moon, 2, 117	P. A. Valenzuela	Blairs Roarin Star, 2, 117	Ruler's Court, 2, 117	5	1:10.39	61,500
2002	Crowned Dancer, 2, 120	A. O. Solis	Outta Here, 2, 117	Chief Planner, 2, 117	7	1:10.10	64,980
2001	Came Home, 2, 117	C. J. McCarron	Metatron, 2, 117	A Major Pleasure, 2, 117	6	1:09.20	64,440
2000	Squirtle Squirt, 2, 120	L. A. Pincay Jr.	Legendary Weave, 2, 117	Drumcliff, 2, 117	5	1:09.58	63,540
1999	Dixie Union, 2, 117	A. O. Solis	Exchange Rate, 2, 117	High Yield, 2, 115	5	1:09.45	63,780
1998	Yes It's True, 2, 120	J. D. Bailey	O'Rey Fantasma, 2, 117	Worldly Manner, 2, 117	7	1:09.58	61,620
1997	K. O. Punch, 2, 120	A. O. Solis	Old Topper, 2, 117	Majorbigtimesheet, 2, 120	9	1:09.80	66,120
1996	Swiss Yodeler, 2, 120	A. O. Solis	Red, 2, 117	Vermilion, 2, 117	5	1:09.77	61,740
1995	Hennessy, 2, 117	G. L. Stevens	Reef Reef, 2, 117	Desert Native, 2, 117	6	1:09.85	57,400
1994	Mr Purple, 2, 117	C. J. McCarron	†Serena's Song, 2, 117	Cyrano, 2, 117	7	1:10.16	57,600
1993	Ramblin Guy, 2, 117	E. Delahoussaye	Swift Walker, 2, 117	Individual Style, 2, 117	8	1:10.09	57,600
1992	Altazarr, 2, 117	E. Delahoussaye	Tatum Canyon, 2, 117	Just Sid, 2, 117	6	1:10.01	58,700

Year	Winner	Jockey	Second	Third	Strs	Time	1st Purse
1991	Scherando, 2, 117	F. Mena	Prince Wild, 2, 117	Burnished Bronze, 2, 120	7	1:09.70	$56,400
1990	Deposit Ticket, 2, 117	G. L. Stevens	Avenue of Flags, 2, 117	Stone God, 2, 117	8	1:09.00	56,500
1989	Magical Mile, 2, 117	E. Delahoussaye	Forty Niner Days, 2, 117	Willing Worker, 2, 117	7	1:10.00	61,200
1988	King Glorious, 2, 120	C. J. McCarron	Bruho, 2, 117	Mountain Ghost, 2, 117	9	1:08.80	64,200
1987	Mi Preferido, 2, 117	A. O. Solis	Mixed Pleasure, 2, 120	Purdue King, 2, 117	8	1:10.00	75,900
1986	Captain Valid, 2, 117	C. J. McCarron	Qualify, 2, 117	Jazzing Around, 2, 117	12	1:11.60	73,600
1985	Hilco Scamper, 2, 120	G. L. Stevens	Little Red Cloud, 2, 117	Exuberant's Image, 2, 117	9	1:09.80	64,400
1984	Saratoga Six, 2, 117	A. T. Cordero Jr.	Ten Grand, 2, 117	Spectacular Love, 2, 117	11	1:10.20	90,500
1983	†Althea, 2, 117	L. A. Pincay Jr.	Rejected Suitor, 2, 117	Auto Commander, 2, 117	9	1:09.40	66,200
1982	Desert Wine, 2, 116	F. Olivares	Ft. Davis, 2, 117	Full Choke, 2, 120	6	1:09.60	57,900
1981	The Captain, 2, 117	L. A. Pincay Jr.	Remember John, 2, 115	Helen's Beau, 2, 120	12	1:10.40	64,000
1980	Loma Malad, 2, 122	L. A. Pincay Jr.	Motivity, 2, 122	Bold Ego, 2, 122	13	1:10.00	101,150
1979	Parsec, 2, 122	W. Shoemaker	Doonesbury, 2, 122	Encino, 2, 122	8	1:10.00	89,350
1978	†Terlingua, 2, 119	D. G. McHargue	Flying Paster, 2, 122	Exuberant, 2, 122	8	1:08.80	77,000
1977	Affirmed, 2, 122	L. A. Pincay Jr.	He's Dewan, 2, 122	Esops Foibles, 2, 122	8	1:09.20	60,975
	Noble Bronze, 2, 117	S. Hawley	Little Reb, 2, 122	Tally Ho the Fox, 2, 122	10	1:09.80	62,225
1976	Fleet Dragoon, 2, 122	F. Olivares	Grey Moon Runner, 2, 122	Red Sensation, 2, 117	13	1:09.60	103,250
1975	Restless Restless, 2, 122	S. Hawley	Imacornishprince, 2, 122	Telly's Pop, 2, 122	8	1:09.80	79,350
1974	Dimaggio, 2, 122	L. A. Pincay Jr.	The Bagel Prince, 2, 122	George Navonod, 2, 122	12	**1:08.60**	74,500
1973	Century's Envoy, 2, 122	J. Lambert	Such a Rush, 2, 122	Tinsley's Image, 2, 122	8	1:09.00	78,550

Grade 2 1973-'96. Starlet Sweepstakes 1938-'39. Starlet S. 1940-'58. Held at Santa Anita 1949. Not held 1942-'43. 5½ furlongs 1938. 7 furlongs 1944. 1¹⁄₁₆ miles 1950. Dirt 1938-2006. Two divisions 1977. †Denotes female.

Hollywood Oaks

Grade 2 in 2008. Hollywood Park, three-year-olds, fillies, 1¹⁄₁₆ miles, all weather. Held June 8, 2008, with a gross value of $157,600. First held in 1946. First graded in 1973. Stakes record 1:41.55 (2004 House of Fortune).

Year	Winner	Jockey	Second	Third	Strs	Time	1st Purse
2008	Lethal Heat, 3, 113	R. Bejarano	Smooth Performer, 3, 113	Tasha's Miracle, 3, 113	6	1:43.00	$94,560
2007	Tough Tiz's Sis, 3, 119	A. T. Gryder	Silver Swallow, 3, 115	High Cholesterol, 3, 113	5	1:43.30	63,840
2006	Hystericalady, 3, 119	P. A. Valenzuela	Squallacious, 3, 119	Downthedustyroad, 3, 114	7	1:43.08	95,040
2005	Brooke's Halo, 3, 113	V. Espinoza	Memorette, 3, 116	Cee's Irish, 3, 119	8	1:42.80	111,900
2004	House of Fortune, 3, 119	A. O. Solis	Elusive Diva, 3, 115	Hollywood Story, 3, 119	5	**1:41.55**	109,725
2003	Santa Catarina, 3, 116	G. L. Stevens	Buffythecenterfold, 3, 113	Princess V., 3, 113	5	1:41.62	127,320
2002	Adoration, 3, 115	G. K. Gomez	Sister Girl Blues, 3, 114	Saint Bernadette, 3, 115	7	1:43.73	160,080
2001	Affluent, 3, 116	E. Delahoussaye	Collect Call, 3, 115	Secret of Mecca, 3, 116	5	1:49.20	90,000
2000	Kumari Continent, 3, 117	K. Desormeaux	Queenie Belle, 3, 119	Saudi Poetry, 3, 115	5	1:49.13	90,000
1999	Smooth Player, 3, 117	E. Delahoussaye	Excellent Meeting, 3, 121	Nany's Sweep, 3, 116	5	1:48.17	90,000
1998	Manistique, 3, 115	G. L. Stevens	Sweet and Ready, 3, 119	Yolo Lady, 3, 116	5	1:48.40	120,000
1997	Sharp Cat, 3, 121	A. O. Solis	Freeport Flight, 3, 121	Really Happy, 3, 121	5	1:49.60	120,000
1996	Listening, 3, 121	C. J. McCarron	Antespend, 3, 121	Ocean View, 3, 121	4	1:48.70	110,640
1995	Sleep Easy, 3, 121	C. S. Nakatani	‡Bello Cielo, 3, 121	Carsona, 3, 121	5	1:50.24	122,400
1994	Lakeway, 3, 121	K. Desormeaux	Sardula, 3, 121	Fancy 'n Fabulous, 3, 121	4	1:46.93	120,000
1993	Hollywood Wildcat, 3, 121	E. Delahoussaye	Fit to Lead, 3, 121	Adorydar, 3, 121	9	1:48.48	130,400
1992	Pacific Squall, 3, 121	K. Desormeaux	Race the Wild Wind, 3, 121	Alysbelle, 3, 121	7	1:48.07	127,200
1991	Fowda, 3, 121	E. Delahoussaye	Grand Girlfriend, 3, 121	Masake, 3, 121	7	1:49.70	94,400
1990	Patches, 3, 121	G. L. Stevens	Jefforee, 3, 121	Pampered Star, 3, 121	8	1:49.80	96,100
1989	Gorgeous, 3, 121	E. Delahoussaye	Kelly, 3, 121	Lea Lucinda, 3, 121	6	1:47.80	92,700
1988	Pattern Step, 3, 121	C. J. McCarron	Super Avie, 3, 121	Comedy Court, 3, 121	7	1:48.60	94,700
1987	Perchance to Dream, 3, 121	R. Sibille	Sacahuista, 3, 121	Pen Bal Lady (GB), 3, 121	6	1:48.60	93,200
1986	Hidden Light, 3, 121	W. Shoemaker	An Empress, 3, 121	Family Style, 3, 121	4	1:47.80	116,600
1985	Fran's Valentine, 3, 121	C. J. McCarron	Magnificent Lindy, 3, 121	Deal Price, 3, 121	6	1:47.40	120,300
1984	Moment to Buy, 3, 121	T. M. Chapman	Mitterand, 3, 121	Lucky Lucky Lucky, 3, 121	9	1:49.20	97,150
1983	Heartlight No. One, 3, 121	L. A. Pincay Jr.	Preceptress, 3, 121	Ready for Luck, 3, 121	7	1:49.80	63,900
1982	Tango Dancer, 3, 121	L. A. Pincay Jr.	Faneuil Lass, 3, 121	Royal Donna, 3, 121	9	1:49.00	66,100
1981	Past Forgetting, 3, 121	C. J. McCarron	Balletomane, 3, 121	Glitter Hitter, 3, 121	7	1:50.00	64,100
1980	Princess Karenda, 3, 121	D. Pierce	Secretarial Queen, 3, 121	Disconiz, 3, 121	10	1:48.20	67,400
1979	Prize Spot, 3, 121	S. Hawley	It's in the Air, 3, 121	Variety Queen, 3, 124	7	1:48.20	63,300
1978	B. Thoughtful, 3, 121	D. Pierce	Country Queen, 3, 121	Grenzen, 3, 121	9	1:47.60	65,400
1977	*Glenaris, 3, 116	W. Shoemaker	One Sum, 3, 116	Taisez Vous, 3, 121	11	1:48.80	68,100
1976	Answer, 3, 121	D. G. McHargue	Franmari, 3, 116	I Going, 3, 115	9	1:48.40	49,200
1975	Nicosia, 3, 121	W. Shoemaker	Snap Apple, 3, 121	Mia Amore, 3, 112	9	1:48.40	49,450
1974	Miss Musket, 3, 124	L. A. Pincay Jr.	Lucky Spell, 3, 121	Modus Vivendi, 3, 112	8	1:47.80	49,550
1973	Sandy Blue, 3, 121	D. Pierce	Cellist, 3, 121	Jungle Princess, 3, 112	10	1:48.00	50,380

Grade 1 1976-'96. Hollywood Breeders' Cup Oaks 2002-'07. Held at Santa Anita Park 1949. 1 mile 1946, 1948-'50. 7 furlongs 1947. 1¹⁄₈ miles 1954-2001. Dirt 1938-2006. ‡Predicted Glory finished second, DQ to fifth, 1995.

Hollywood Prevue Stakes

Grade 3 in 2008. Hollywood Park, two-year-olds, 7 furlongs, all weather. Held November 22, 2007, with a gross value of $109,200. First held in 1981. First graded in 1985. Stakes record 1:20.63 (2003 Lion Heart).

Year	Winner	Jockey	Second	Third	Strs	Time	1st Purse
2007	Massive Drama, 2, 116	K. J. Desormeaux	Into Mischief, 2, 116	Meal Penalty, 2, 118	11	1:21.48	$69,200
2006	Belgravia, 2, 114	J. R. Leparoux	Dilemma, 2, 118	Notional, 2, 119	7	1:22.42	60,000

Year	Winner	Jockey	Second	Third	Strs	Time	1st Purse
2005	Your Tent Or Mine, 2, 118	P. A. Valenzuela	Da Stoops, 2, 114	The Pharaoh, 2, 114	5	1:21.12	$60,000
2004	Declan's Moon, 2, 122	V. Espinoza	Bushwacker, 2, 114	Seize the Day, 2, 117	8	1:21.74	60,000
2003	Lion Heart, 2, 114	M. E. Smith	Cooperation, 2, 116	Voladero, 2, 113	5	**1:20.63**	60,000
2002	Roll Hennessy Roll, 2, 119	A. O. Solis	Red Apache, 2, 115	Hell Cat, 2, 114	7	1:22.68	75,000
2001	Fonz's, 2, 117	L. A. Pincay Jr.	Popular, 2, 113	Labamta Babe, 2, 113	7	1:22.03	60,000
2000	Proud Tower, 2, 122	V. Espinoza	Chinook Cat, 2, 116	Yonaguska, 2, 122	8	1:23.01	60,000
1999	Grey Memo, 2, 115	M. S. Garcia	Magical Dragon, 2, 115	Cameron Pass, 2, 116	6	1:24.44	60,000
1998	Premier Property, 2, 119	D. R. Flores	Select Few, 2, 114	American Spirit, 2, 115	7	1:23.29	60,000
1997	Commitisize, 2, 113	D. R. Flores	Buttons N Moes, 2, 122	Search Me, 2, 117	6	1:21.64	60,000
1996	In Excessive Bull, 2, 115	C. S. Nakatani	Thisnearlywasmine, 2, 118	Constant Demand, 2, 116	5	1:21.54	61,020
1995	Cobra King, 2, 121	C. J. McCarron	Hennessy, 2, 121	Exetera, 2, 116	6	1:21.25	58,800
1994	Afternoon Deelites, 2, 115	K. Desormeaux	Valid Wager, 2, 114	Hunt for Missouri, 2, 114	4	1:20.98	57,500
1993	Individual Style, 2, 121	C. W. Antley	Egayant, 2, 117	Soul of the Matter, 2, 115	6	1:21.17	46,100
1992	Stuka, 2, 115	P. A. Valenzuela	Codified, 2, 114	Altazarr, 2, 121	8	1:21.94	62,350
1991	Star of the Crop, 2, 114	G. L. Stevens	Seahawk Gold, 2, 121	Salt Lake, 2, 121	5	1:22.30	57,700
1990	Olympio, 2, 116	E. Delahoussaye	Barrage, 2, 115	General Meeting, 2, 114	10	1:21.80	62,600
1989	Individualist, 2, 115	R. G. Davis	Top Cash, 2, 122	Tarascon, 2, 115	6	1:22.20	46,600
1988	King Glorious, 2, 122	C. J. McCarron	Past Ages, 2, 116	Shipping Time, 2, 115	7	1:21.20	47,150
1986	Exclusive Enough, 2, 112	W. Shoemaker	Perseveed, 2, 122	Gold On Green, 2, 116	8	1:23.00	45,900
1985	Judge Smells, 2, 117	C. J. McCarron	Raised On Stage, 2, 112	Old Bid, 2, 115	8	1:23.00	46,850
1984	First Norman, 2, 112	W. Shoemaker	Teddy Naturally, 2, 112	Dan's Diablo, 2, 122	6	1:22.20	63,700
1983	So Vague, 2, 115	P. J. Cooksey	Country Manor, 2, 115	French Legionaire, 2, 115	16	1:22.20	76,300
1982	Copelan, 2, 122	J. D. Bailey	R. Awacs, 2, 115	Desert Wine, 2, 122	8	1:21.40	62,450
1981	Sepulveda, 2, 112	C. J. McCarron	Gato Del Sol, 2, 122	Desert Envoy, 2, 112	6	1:22.00	44,625

Traditionally used as a prep race for the CashCall Futurity (G1). Formerly sponsored by Jack Daniel's Distillery of Lynchburg, Tennessee 2003. Hollywood Prevue Breeders' Cup S. 1990-'95. Not held 1987. Dirt 1981-'86, 1988-2005.

Hollywood Starlet Stakes

Grade 1 in 2008. Hollywood Park, two-year-olds, fillies, 1 1/16 miles, all weather. Held December 15, 2007, with a gross value of $425,500. First held in 1981. First graded in 1983. Stakes record 1:40.54 (2007 Country Star).

Year	Winner	Jockey	Second	Third	Strs	Time	1st Purse
2007	Country Star, 2, 120	R. Bejarano	Grace and Power, 2, 120	The Golden Noodle, 2, 120	9	**1:40.54**	$255,300
2006	Romance Is Diane, 2, 120	D. R. Flores	Quick Little Miss, 2, 120	Down, 2, 120	12	1:42.61	275,550
2005	Diplomat Lady, 2, 120	T. Baze	Balance, 2, 120	Sabatini, 2, 120	11	1:43.89	273,600
2004	Splendid Blended, 2, 120	K. Desormeaux	Sharp Lisa, 2, 120	Northern Mischief, 2, 120	7	1:41.82	233,400
2003	Hollywood Story, 2, 120	P. A. Valenzuela	Rahy Dolly, 2, 120	House of Fortune, 2, 120	6	1:42.87	209,700
2002	Elloluv, 2, 120	P. A. Valenzuela	Composure, 2, 120	Summer Wind Dancer, 2, 120	7	1:42.88	213,900
2001	Habibti, 2, 120	V. Espinoza	You, 2, 120	Tali'sluckybusride, 2, 120	5	1:43.12	214,800
2000	I Believe in You, 2, 120	A. O. Solis	Jetin Excess, 2, 120	Whoopddoo, 2, 120	6	1:43.57	205,050
1999	Surfside, 2, 120	P. Day	She's Classy, 2, 120	Abby Girl, 2, 120	5	1:43.51	228,150
1998	Excellent Meeting, 2, 120	K. Desormeaux	Lacquaria, 2, 120	Perfect Six, 2, 120	6	1:42.14	240,000
1997	Love Lock, 2, 120	K. Desormeaux	Career Collection, 2, 120	Snowberg, 2, 120	6	1:42.17	174,600
1996	Sharp Cat, 2, 120	C. S. Nakatani	City Band, 2, 120	High Heeled Hope, 2, 120	8	1:44.69	165,600
1995	Cara Rafaela, 2, 120	C. S. Nakatani	Advancing Star, 2, 120	Chile Chatte, 2, 120	5	1:43.10	137,500
1994	Serena's Song, 2, 120	C. S. Nakatani	Urbane, 2, 120	Ski Dancer, 2, 120	5	1:41.96	137,500
1993	Sardula, 2, 120	E. Delahoussaye	Princess Mitterand, 2, 120	Viz, 2, 120	5	1:42.34	139,095
1992	Creaking Board (GB), 2, 120	C. S. Nakatani	Passing Vice, 2, 120	Madame l'Enjoleur, 2, 120	9	1:43.73	137,500
1991	Magical Maiden, 2, 120	G. L. Stevens	Looie Capote, 2, 120	Soviet Sojourn, 2, 120	8	1:42.74	138,105
1990	Cuddles, 2, 120	G. L. Stevens	Lite Light, 2, 120	Garden Gal, 2, 120	10	1:36.20	247,500
1989	Cheval Volant, 2, 120	A. O. Solis	Annual Reunion, 2, 120	Special Happening, 2, 120	9	1:35.60	247,500
1988	Stocks Up, 2, 120	A. O. Solis	Fantastic Look, 2, 120	One of a Klein, 2, 120	8	1:35.00	292,325
1987	Goodbye Halo, 2, 120	J. Velasquez	Variety Baby, 2, 120	Jeanne Jones, 2, 120	7	1:36.20	274,505
1986	Very Subtle, 2, 120	P. A. Valenzuela	Sacahuista, 2, 120	Infringe, 2, 120	6	1:36.00	267,025
1985	I'm Splendid, 2, 120	C. J. McCarron	Trim Colony, 2, 120	Twilight Ridge, 2, 120	9	1:36.00	344,217
1984	Outstandingly, 2, 120	W. A. Guerra	Fran's Valentine, 2, 120	Wising Up, 2, 120	16	1:44.00	386,402
1983	Althea, 2, 120	L. A. Pincay Jr.	Life's Magic, 2, 120	Spring Loose, 2, 120	7	1:43.00	261,250
1982	Fabulous Notion, 2, 120	D. Pierce	O'Happy Day, 2, 120	Stephanie Bryn, 2, 120	9	1:42.40	271,618
1981	Skillful Joy, 2, 120	C. J. McCarron	Header Card, 2, 120	Flying Partner, 2, 120	8	1:43.20	221,238

Young actresses in old Hollywood were traditionally known as starlets before reaching full star status. 1 mile 1985-'90. Dirt 1981-2005.

Hollywood Turf Cup Stakes

Grade 1 in 2008. Hollywood Park, three-year-olds and up, 1 1/2 miles, turf. Held December 8, 2007, with a gross value of $250,000. First held in 1981. First graded in 1983. Stakes record 2:24.61 (2006 Boboman).

Year	Winner	Jockey	Second	Third	Strs	Time	1st Purse
2007	Sunriver, 4, 126	G. K. Gomez	Champs Elysees (GB), 4, 126	Spring House, 5, 126	7	2:27.07	$150,000
2006	Boboman, 5, 126	G. K. Gomez	Runaway Dancer, 7, 126	dh-Artiste Royal (Ire), 5, 126 dh-Meteor Storm (GB), 7, 126	8	**2:24.61**	150,000
2004	Pellegrino (Brz), 5, 126	G. L. Stevens	†Megahertz (GB), 5, 123	License To Run (Brz), 4, 126	9	2:29.73	150,000
2003	‡Continuously, 4, 126	A. O. Solis	Bowman Mill, 5, 126	Epicentre, 4, 126	7	2:29.01	150,000
2002	Sligo Bay (Ire), 4, 126	L. A. Pincay Jr.	Grammarian, 4, 126	Delta Form (Aus), 6, 126	11	2:27.22	150,000
2001	Super Quercus (Fr), 5, 126	A. O. Solis	Bonapartiste (Fr), 7, 126	Blazing Fury, 3, 122	9	2:29.86	150,000

Year	Winner	Jockey	Second	Third	Strs	Time	1st Purse
2000	Bienamado, 4, 126	C. J. McCarron	Northern Quest (Fr), 5, 126	Lazy Lode (Arg), 6, 126	8	2:25.98	$240,000
1999	Lazy Lode (Arg), 5, 126	L. A. Pincay Jr.	Public Purse, 5, 126	Single Empire (Ire), 5, 126	7	2:25.85	240,000
1998	Lazy Lode (Arg), 4, 126	C. S. Nakatani	Yagli, 5, 126	Ferrari (Ger), 4, 126	10	2:28.36	300,000
1997	River Bay, 4, 126	A. O. Solis	Awad, 7, 126	Flag Down, 7, 126	12	2:26.47	300,000
1996	Running Flame (Fr), 4, 126	C. J. McCarron	Marlin, 3, 122	Talloires, 6, 126	10	2:28.53	300,000
1995	Royal Chariot, 5, 126	A. O. Solis	Talloires, 5, 126	Earl of Barking (Ire), 5, 126	14	2:25.18	275,000
1994	Frenchpark (GB), 4, 126	C. A. Black	Dare and Go, 3, 122	Regency (GB), 4, 126	11	2:25.66	275,000
1993	Fraise, 5, 126	C. J. McCarron	Know Heights (Ire), 4, 126	Explosive Red, 3, 122	6	2:32.34	275,000
1992	‡Bien Bien, 3, 122	C. J. McCarron	Fraise, 4, 126	†Trishyde, 3, 119	6	2:31.28	275,000
1991	†Miss Alleged, 4, 123	C. J. McCarron	Itsallgreektome, 4, 126	Quest for Fame (GB), 4, 126	7	2:30.00	275,000
1990	Itsallgreektome, 3, 122	C. S. Nakatani	Mashkour, 7, 126	Live the Dream, 4, 126	14	2:24.80	275,000
1989	Frankly Perfect, 4, 126	C. J. McCarron	Yankee Affair, 7, 126	Pleasant Variety, 5, 126	10	2:26.60	275,000
1988	Great Communicator, 5, 126	R. Sibille	Putting (Fr), 5, 126	Nasr El Arab, 3, 122	10	2:34.40	275,000
1987	Vilzak, 4, 126	P. Day	Forlitano (Arg), 6, 126	Political Ambition, 3, 122	14	2:27.00	275,000
1986	Alphabatim, 5, 126	W. Shoemaker	Dahar, 5, 126	Theatrical (Ire), 4, 126	8	2:25.80	275,000
1985	Zoffany, 5, 126	E. Delahoussaye	Win, 5, 126	Vanlandingham, 4, 126	13	2:28.40	275,000
1984	Alphabatim, 3, 122	C. J. McCarron	Raami (GB), 3, 122	dh-Both Ends Burning, 4, 126 dh-Scrupules (Ire), 4, 126	6	2:15.80	275,000
1983	John Henry, 8, 126	C. J. McCarron	†Zalataia (Fr), 4, 123	Palikaraki (Fr), 5, 126	12	2:16.60	275,000
1982	Prince Spellbound, 3, 122	M. Castaneda	Majesty's Prince, 3, 122	Lithan, 4, 126	11	2:14.00	220,000
	The Hague, 3, 122	F. Toro	Caterman (NZ), 6, 126	It's the One, 4, 126	13	2:13.40	220,000
1981	Providential (Ire), 4, 126	A. Lequeux	†Queen to Conquer, 5, 123	Goldiko (Fr), 4, 126	10	2:26.80	325,500

Hollywood Turf Cup H. 1981-'85, 1988, 1990, 2003-'04. Hollywood Turf Cup Invitational H. 1986-'87. Not held 2005. 1 3/8 miles 1982-'84. Two divisions 1982. Dead heat for third 1984, 2006. ‡Fraise finished first, DQ to second, 1992. ‡Epicentre finished first, DQ to third, 2003. †Denotes female.

Hollywood Turf Express Handicap

Grade 3 in 2008. Hollywood Park, three-year-olds and up, 6 furlongs, turf. Held November 24, 2007, with a gross value of $150,000. First held in 1985. First graded in 1994. Stakes record 1:07 (1990 Answer Do).

Year	Winner	Jockey	Second	Third	Strs	Time	1st Purse
2007	Unusual Suspect, 3, 114	T. Baze	Bonfante, 6, 117	Desert Code, 3, 116	9	1:09.06	$90,000
2006	Jungle Prince, 5, 118	A. Delgadillo	In Summation, 3, 117	Moth Ball (GB), 4, 115	8	1:08.76	90,000
2004	Cajun Beat, 4, 122	R. A. Dominguez	Geronimo (Chi), 5, 117	Mighty Beau, 5, 117	9	1:02.08	90,000
2003	King Robyn, 3, 120	T. Baze	Geronimo (Chi), 4, 116	Golden Arrow, 4, 115	9	1:02.08	90,000
2002	Texas Glitter, 6, 119	J. R. Velazquez	Rocky Bar, 4, 114	Malabar Gold, 5, 118	5	1:01.52	120,000
2001	Swept Overboard, 4, 122	E. Delahoussaye	Speak in Passing, 4, 117	Blu Air Force (Ire), 4, 118	10	1:01.86	120,000
2000	El Cielo, 6, 122	C. S. Nakatani	Texas Glitter, 4, 117	Full Moon Madness, 5, 121	7	1:01.73	120,000
1999	Mr. Doubledown, 5, 115	V. Espinoza	Howbaddouwantit, 4, 120	Champ's Star, 4, 115	8	1:01.98	120,000
1998	Soldier Field, 3, 117	R. Wilson	Surachai, 5, 118	Bodyguard (GB), 3, 115	10	1:02.19	120,000
1997	†Advancing Star, 4, 119	K. Desormeaux	Latin Dancer, 3, 116	Surachai, 4, 117	9	1:02.68	120,000
1996	Sandtrap, 3, 114	A. O. Solis	Cyrano Storme (Ire), 6, 118	Suggest, 4, 114	8	1:01.46	120,000
1995	Cyrano Storme (Ire), 5, 116	R. R. Douglas	Lakota Brave, 6, 115	Pembroke, 5, 121	9	1:01.64	110,500
1994	Rotsaluck, 3, 118	F. H. Valenzuela	†Marina Park (GB), 4, 116	D'Hallevant, 4, 117	11	1:02.27	82,500
1993	Wild Harmony, 4, 117	C. J. McCarron	Robin des Pins, 5, 119	Monde Bleu (GB), 5, 119	8	1:01.88	110,000
1992	Answer Do, 6, 121	E. Delahoussaye	Repriced, 4, 118	Gundaghia, 5, 117	11	1:02.14	110,000
1991	Gundaghia, 4, 114	C. S. Nakatani	Club Champ, 3, 116	†Sun Brandy, 4, 115	9	1:01.40	61,875
	Answer Do, 5, 120	E. Delahoussaye	Apollo, 3, 115	Cardmania, 5, 116	8	1:01.40	61,875
1990	Answer Do, 4, 115	R. A. Baze	Waterscape, 4, 115	Yes I'm Blue, 4, 118	11	1:07.00	51,200
1989	Summer Sale, 3, 114	B. A. Hernandez	Ofanto, 5, 117	Oraibi, 4, 120	9	1:07.80	51,000
1988	On the Line, 4, 121	G. L. Stevens	Little Red Cloud, 5, 115	Faro, 6, 116	6	1:09.20	47,650
1987	Lord Ruckus, 4, 117	L. A. Pincay Jr.	Bundle of Iron, 5, 114	Faro, 5, 115	7	1:08.20	49,600
1986	Zany Tactics, 5, 117	J. L. Kaenel	Bolder Than Bold, 4, 115	Faro, 4, 113	5	1:07.40	46,100
1985	Temerity Prince, 5, 122	W. A. Ward	French Legionaire, 4, 113	Debonaire Junior, 4, 124	5	1:11.40	38,300

Hollywood Turf Sprint Championship 1985. Not held 2005. 5 1/2 furlongs 1991-2004. Dirt 1985, '88. Two divisions 1991. †Denotes female.

Holy Bull Stakes

Grade 3 in 2008. Gulfstream Park, three-year-olds, 1 1/16 miles, dirt. Held April 12, 2008, with a gross value of $150,000. First held in 1972. First graded in 1995. Stakes record 1:58.14 (2008 Hey Byrn).

Year	Winner	Jockey	Second	Third	Strs	Time	1st Purse
2008	Hey Byrn, 3, 118	C. C. Lopez	Dream Maestro, 3, 118	Famous Patriot, 3, 118	7	1:58.14	$90,000
2007	Nobiz Like Shobiz, 3, 120	C. H. Velasquez	Drums of Thunder, 3, 120	Scat Daddy, 3, 120	8	1:35.47	90,000
2006	Barbaro, 3, 122	E. S. Prado	Great Point, 3, 116	My Golden Song, 3, 116	12	1:49.31	90,000
2005	Closing Argument, 3, 120	C. H. Velasquez	Kansas City Boy, 3, 118	High Fly, 3, 122	8	1:50.14	90,000
2004	Second of June, 3, 122	C. H. Velasquez	Silver Wagon, 3, 120	Friends Lake, 3, 122	9	1:43.00	60,000
2003	Offlee Wild, 3, 116	M. Guidry	Powerful Touch, 3, 116	Bham, 3, 118	13	1:43.00	60,000
2002	Booklet, 3, 122	E. Coa	Harlan's Holiday, 3, 122	Thiscannonsloaded, 3, 116	7	1:46.16	60,000
2001	Radical Riley, 3, 119	E. O. Nunez	Buckle Down Ben, 3, 119	Cee Dee, 3, 117	8	1:46.06	60,000
2000	Hal's Hope, 3, 112	R. I. Velez	Personal First, 3, 117	Megacles, 3, 113	11	1:44.52	60,000
1999	Grits'n Hard Toast, 3, 114	R. G. Davis	Doneraile Court, 3, 119	Mountain Range, 3, 119	7	1:45.32	60,000
1998	Cape Town, 3, 119	J. D. Bailey	Comic Strip, 3, 114	Sweetsouthernsaint, 3, 119	7	1:44.15	60,000
1997	Arthur L., 3, 122	J. R. Velazquez	Acceptable, 3, 114	Captain Bodgit, 3, 119	9	1:42.93	60,000

Racing — Graded Stakes 349

Year	Winner	Jockey	Second	Third	Strs	Time	1st Purse
1996	Cobra King, 3, 117	C. J. McCarron	Editor's Note, 3, 119	Tilden, 3, 114	7	1:43.42	$45,000
1995	Suave Prospect, 3, 119	J. D. Bailey	Bullet Trained, 3, 114	Rush Dancer, 3, 112	8	1:44.03	45,000
1994	Go for Gin, 3, 119	J. D. Bailey	Halo's Image, 3, 114	Senor Conquistador, 3, 112	6	1:41.62	45,000
1993	Pride of Burkaan, 3, 112	J. D. Bailey	Kassec, 3, 112	Jetting Along, 3, 114	8	1:44.74	45,000
1992	Waki Warrior, 3, 114	E. Fires	Scream Machine, 3, 112	Careful Gesture, 3, 113	13	1:44.32	78,258
1991	Shoot to Kill, 3, 112	W. S. Ramos	Shotgun Harry J., 3, 114	Cahill Road, 3, 114	5	1:43.54	120,000
1990	Home At Last, 3, 118	J. D. Bailey	Run Turn, 3, 122	Sound of Cannons, 3, 118	12	1:53.20	140,160
1979	Northern Prospect, 3, 112	J. D. Bailey	Duke of Gansvoort, 3, 114	Coup de Chance, 3, 112	8	1:10.60	18,060
1977	Smashing Native, 3, 114	D. Brumfield	Cheeky Cheetah, 3, 113	Caribe Pirate, 3, 111	7	1:12.60	18,480
1974	Real Supreme, 3, 110	M. Miceli	Eric's Champ, 3, 113	Lord Rebeau, 3, 112	11	1:09.20	20,220

Named for Warren A. Croll Jr.'s Racing Hall of Fame member and 1994 Florida Derby (G1) winner Holy Bull (1991 c. by Great Above). Once named the Preview S., the race was considered a "preview" of or prep for the Florida Derby (G1). Preview S. 1972-'95. Not held 1973, 1975-'76, 1978, 1980-'89. 6 furlongs 1972-'79. 1 1/16 miles 1991-2004. 1 1/8 miles 1990, 2005-'06. 1 mile 2007.

Honeybee Stakes

Grade 3 in 2008. Oaklawn Park, three-year-olds, fillies, 1 1/16 miles, dirt. Held March 16, 2008, with a gross value of $100,000. First held in 1988. First graded in 1990. Stakes record 1:43 (1989 Imaginary Lady).

Year	Winner	Jockey	Second	Third	Strs	Time	1st Purse
2008	Eight Belles, 3, 119	R. A. Dominguez	Pure Clan, 3, 119	Kadira, 3, 117	6	1:43.91	$60,000
2007	Time's Mistress, 3, 117	J. Jacinto	High Heels, 3, 118	Grace Happens, 3, 115	9	1:45.49	60,000
2006	Ermine, 3, 116	C. H. Borel	Brownie Points, 3, 119	Morner, 3, 115	6	1:44.48	45,000
2005	Round Pond, 3, 114	S. Elliott	Rugula, 3, 115	Southern, 3, 117	6	1:45.16	45,000
2004	Yoursmineours, 3, 115	D. R. Pettinger	Stephan's Angel, 3, 115	Solitary Emerald, 3, 114	7	1:45.14	45,000
2003	My Trusty Cat, 3, 116	D. R. Pettinger	Ruby's Reception, 3, 114	Explosive Beauty, 3, 117	7	1:44.15	45,000
2002	Bedanken, 3, 114	D. R. Pettinger	Cozy Susie, 3, 116	Sarah Jade, 3, 115	6	1:46.41	45,000
2001	Xtreme Bid, 3, 116	D. C. Nuesch	My White Corvette, 3, 116	Pajamas, 3, 114	7	1:46.07	45,000
2000	Fiesty Countess, 3, 114	T. T. Doocy	Asher, 3, 114	Prairie Pioneer, 3, 113	7	1:44.76	45,000
1999	Dreams Gallore, 3, 114	G. Murphy	The Happy Hopper, 3, 116	Humble Retha, 3, 114	7	1:43.49	45,000
1998	Roza Robata, 3, 114	F. A. Arguello Jr.	Sweet and Ready, 3, 114	Bucquestor, 3, 114	9	1:45.95	45,000
1997	Valid Bonnet, 3, 118	T. T. Doocy	Alyssum, 3, 116	Hooten Annie, 3, 116	6	1:43.60	45,000
1996	Jetto, 3, 114	L. Melancon	Mama's Pro, 3, 118	Wise Action, 3, 114	7	1:46.32	45,000
1995	Humble Eight, 3, 112	D. Guillory	Lilly Capote, 3, 119	Traces of Gold, 3, 116	6	1:45.26	45,000
1994	Shadow Miss, 3, 112	W. Martinez	Slide Show, 3, 116	Accountinquestion, 3, 113	8	1:44.74	45,000
1993	Aztec Hill, 3, 122	A. T. Gryder	Avie's Shadow, 3, 116	Life Is Delicious, 3, 112	8	1:44.50	45,000
1992	Totemic, 3, 122	D. R. Miller	Take the Cure, 3, 113	Royal Amazon, 3, 116	5	1:43.29	45,000
1991	Be Cool, 3, 116	D. Guillory	Primarily Irish, 3, 112	Pink Tomato, 3, 116	9	1:44.90	45,000
1990	Train Robbery, 3, 122	P. Day	Silvered, 3, 112	Mercedes Miss, 3, 112	4	1:45.60	45,000
1989	Imaginary Lady, 3, 122	J. D. Bailey	Affirmed Classic, 3, 116	Midnight Stroll, 3, 112	9	**1:43.00**	45,000
1988	Lost Kitty, 3, 115	J. A. Santos	Epitome, 3, 115	Fara's Team, 3, 115	8	1:43.80	53,100

Many of Oaklawn Park's races are named for things associated with spring; honeybees are frequently seen in spring. Not graded 2003-'07.

Honey Fox Handicap

Grade 3 in 2008. Gulfstream Park, four-year-olds and up, fillies and mares, 1 1/16 miles, turf. Held March 4, 2007, with a gross value of $100,000. First held in 1985. First graded in 1994. Stakes record 1:38.31 (2006 Wend).

Year	Winner	Jockey	Second	Third	Strs	Time	1st Purse
2007	Wait a While, 4, 123	J. R. Velazquez	Precious Kitten, 4, 117	Chaibia (Ire), 4, 116	7	1:39.37	$60,000
2006	Wend, 5, 119	E. S. Prado	Brunilda (Arg), 6, 116	Honey Ryder, 5, 121	7	**1:38.31**	60,000
2005	Sand Springs, 5, 115	J. D. Bailey	Potra Fabulous (Arg), 6, 116	Shaconage, 5, 115	11	1:38.41	60,000
2004	Delmonico Cat, 5, 116	J. D. Bailey	Coney Kitty (Ire), 6, 115	Madeira Mist (Ire), 5, 117	10	1:41.30	60,000
2003	San Dare, 5, 115	M. Guidry	Calista (GB), 5, 118	Laurica, 6, 114	10	1:46.19	60,000
2002	Batique, 6, 117	J. F. Chavez	My Sweet Westly, 6, 115	Silver Bandana, 6, 114	8	1:49.32	60,000
2001	Spook Express (SAf), 7, 115	M. E. Smith	Please Sign In, 5, 116	Lady Dora, 4, 115	12	1:35.60	60,000
2000	Dominique's Joy, 5, 113	J. D. Bailey	Circus Charmer, 5, 114	Pico Teneriffe, 4, 117	7	1:39.91	45,000
1999	Colcon, 6, 119	J. D. Bailey	Lovers Knot (GB), 4, 115	Tampico, 6, 114	10	1:41.71	45,000
1998	Parade Queen, 4, 118	P. Day	Dispersion, 5, 113	Dance Clear (Ire), 5, 114	12	1:42.10	45,000
1997	Rare Blend, 4, 118	J. D. Bailey	Queen Tutta, 5, 114	Hurricane Viv, 4, 121	6	1:44.28	45,000
1996	Apolda, 5, 116	J. D. Bailey	Class Kris, 4, 116	Alice Springs, 6, 121	11	1:41.55	45,000
1995	Regal Joy, 4, 113	D. Penna	Sambacarioca, 6, 119	Sovereign Kitty, 4, 119	6	1:44.79	36,000
1994	Sambacarioca, 5, 121	J. D. Bailey	Tiney Toast, 5, 114	Marshua's River, 7, 114	6	1:43.41	36,000
1993	Hero's Love, 5, 113	E. Fires	Quilma (Chi), 6, 112	Lady Blessington (Fr), 5, 114	14	1:42.90	30,000
1992	Explosive Kate, 5, 113	D. Penna	Indian Fashion, 5, 114	Belleofbabsinstreet, 4, 111	14	1:43.37	30,000
1991	Vigorous Lady, 5, 116	M. A. Lee	Joyce Azalene, 4, 112	Stacie's Toy, 4, 115	8	1:40.30	30,000
1990	Fieldy (Ire), 7, 120	J. D. Bailey	Betty Lobelia, 5, 115	Leave It Be, 5, 117	12	1:37.60	30,000
1989	Vana Turns, 4, 113	R. P. Romero	For Kicks, 4, 112	Stolie, 4, 110	9	1:36.00	30,435
	Fieldy (Ire), 6, 114	C. Perret	Miss Unnameable, 5, 110	Aquaba, 4, 116	8	1:35.80	30,135
1988	Allegedum, 5, 112	A. T. Cordero Jr.	Autumn Glitter, 5, 117	Fama, 5, 111	11	1:35.20	31,515
	Shaughnessy Road, 4, 112	J. A. Velez Jr.	Rally for Justice (GB), 5, 112	Fieldy (Ire), 5, 118	10	1:36.00	31,215
1987	Small Virtue, 4, 114	J. Vasquez	Thirty Zip, 4, 113	Chaldea, 7, 118	10	1:37.00	27,915
	Top Socialite, 5, 119	C. Perret	Give a Toast, 4, 113	Judy's Red Shoes, 4, 116	9	1:37.40	27,615
1986	Gypsy Prayer, 5, 110	R. N. Lester	Four Flings, 5, 112	Isayso, 7, 120	7	1:21.00	29,985
	One Fine Lady, 4, 112	J. A. Velez Jr.	Shocker T., 4, 119	Donna's Dolly, 4, 113	5	1:22.00	29,685

Year	Winner	Jockey	Second	Third	Strs	Time	1st Purse
1985	**One Fine Lady**, 3, 116	V. H. Molina	Foxy Deen, 3, 116	Boldly Dared, 3, 114	9	1:34.60	$19,257
	Affirmative, 3, 116	E. Maple	Miss Delice, 3, 114	Deceit Dancer, 3, 116	11	1:35.60	19,617

Named for Dr. Jerome S. Torsney's 1981 Orchid H. (G2) winner Honey Fox (1977 f. by Minnesota Mac). Formerly named for NFL Hall of Fame quarterback Joe Namath. Joe Namath H. 1985-2000. Not held 2008. 1 mile 1985, 1987-'89, 2001. 7 furlongs 1986. About 1 mile 1990. 1 mile 70 yards 1991. Dirt 1986, 1991, 1994-'95, 1997. Three-year-olds 1985. Three-year-olds and up 1986-2006. Fillies 1985. Two divisions 1985-'89.

Honeymoon Handicap

Grade 2 in 2008. Hollywood Park, three-year-olds, fillies, 1 1/8 miles, turf. Held June 7, 2008, with a gross value of $173,250. First held in 1952. First graded in 1976. Stakes record 1:46.84 (2005 Three Degrees [Ire]).

Year	Winner	Jockey	Second	Third	Strs	Time	1st Purse
2008	**Misty Ocean**, 3, 118	J. Rosario	Bel Air Sizzle, 3, 120	Sweeter Still (Ire), 3, 121	6	1:47.56	$111,750
2007	**Valbenny (Ire)**, 3, 123	A. O. Solis	Super Freaky, 3, 120	Mystic Soul, 3, 117	7	1:48.17	82,650
2006	**Attima (GB)**, 3, 118	V. Espinoza	Foxysox (GB), 3, 122	Proxenia (GB), 3, 116	7	1:47.36	82,290
2005	**Three Degrees (Ire)**, 3, 117	G. L. Stevens	Thatswhatimean, 3, 116	Isla Cozzene, 3, 117	13	**1:46.84**	88,275
2004	**Lovely Rafaela**, 3, 114	V. Espinoza	Western Hemisphere, 3, 114	Sagitta Ra, 3, 116	8	1:49.96	113,355
2003	**Quero Quero**, 3, 113	T. Baze	Atlantic Ocean, 3, 121	Sharpbill (GB), 3, 113	10	1:49.34	130,170
2002	**Megahertz (GB)**, 3, 120	P. A. Valenzuela	Arabic Song (Ire), 3, 117	High Society (Ire), 3, 116	7	1:51.97	97,830
2001	**Innit (Ire)**, 3, 117	C. J. McCarron	Live Your Dreams, 3, 116	Beefeater Baby, 3, 115	9	2:01.28	120,000
2000	**Classy Cara**, 3, 122	I. Puglisi	Kumari Continent, 3, 119	Minor Details, 3, 117	9	1:48.05	90,000
1999	**Sweet Ludy (Ire)**, 3, 116	G. L. Stevens	Tout Charmant, 3, 118	Aviate, 3, 118	7	1:48.05	65,160
1998	**Country Garden (GB)**, 3, 120	K. Desormeaux	Janine Rose, 3, 113	Chenille (Ire), 3, 114	6	1:48.74	64,080
1997	**Famous Digger**, 3, 116	B. Blanc	Freeport Flight, 3, 115	Kentucky Kaper, 3, 117	8	1:47.68	65,460
1996	**Antespend**, 3, 122	C. W. Antley	Clamorosa, 3, 116	Najecam, 3, 113	9	1:47.50	82,410
1995	**Auriette (Ire)**, 3, 117	E. Delahoussaye	Artica, 3, 119	Top Shape (Fr), 3, 118	6	1:41.68	62,100
1994	**Work the Crowd**, 3, 117	C. J. McCarron	Malli Star, 3, 117	Fancy 'n Fabulous, 3, 118	8	1:39.68	64,700
1993	**Likeable Style**, 3, 122	E. Delahoussaye	Adorydar, 3, 114	Vinista, 3, 113	5	1:46.29	62,020
1992	**Pacific Squall**, 3, 115	K. Desormeaux	Miss Turkana, 3, 119	Morriston Belle, 3, 118	10	1:41.02	67,100
1991	**Masake**, 3, 115	M. A. Pedroza	Haunting, 3, 114	Now Showing, 3, 116	4	1:42.10	60,400
1990	**Materco**, 3, 117	E. Delahoussaye	Annual Reunion, 3, 119	Slew of Pearls, 3, 117	9	1:41.40	65,800
1989	**Hot Option**, 3, 116	E. Delahoussaye	Formidable Lady, 3, 118	Black Stockings, 3, 113	6	1:40.20	62,600
1988	**Do So**, 3, 118	A. O. Solis	Pattern Step, 3, 119	Jeanne Jones, 3, 120	5	1:41.80	75,400
1987	**Pen Bal Lady (GB)**, 3, 119	E. Delahoussaye	Some Sensation, 3, 117	Davie's Lamb, 3, 115	10	1:41.20	80,300
1986	**An Empress**, 3, 115	P. A. Valenzuela	Top Corsage, 3, 118	Miraculous, 3, 118	10	1:41.80	66,900
1985	**Sharp Ascent**, 3, 115	E. Delahoussaye	Rose Cream, 3, 117	Akamini (Fr), 3, 119	9	1:41.40	79,400
1984	**Vagabond Gal**, 3, 118	E. Delahoussaye	Heartlight, 3, 119	Allusion, 3, 115	8	1:41.40	65,100
1983	**Stage Door Canteen**, 3, 118	C. J. McCarron	Saucy Bobbie, 3, 117	Hot n Pearly, 3, 115	8	1:42.00	65,200
1982	**Castilla**, 3, 116	R. Sibille	Tango Dancer, 3, 117	Skillful Joy, 3, 121	5	1:40.60	61,400
1981	**Amber Ever**, 3, 114	C. J. McCarron	Verbalize, 3, 117	Bee a Scout, 3, 115	10	1:41.60	50,950
1980	**Lady Roberta**, 3, 116	S. Hawley	Finance Charge, 3, 112	Street Ballet, 3, 123	8	1:41.80	60,050
1979	**Variety Queen**, 3, 118	R. Rosales	Prize Spot, 3, 117	Whydidju, 3, 121	8	1:41.60	32,550
1978	**Country Queen**, 3, 114	M. Castaneda	Collect Call, 3, 116	Equanimity, 3, 121	11	1:43.20	33,700
1977	**Joyous Ways**, 3, 116	L. A. Pincay Jr.	Penny Pueblo, 3, 113	*Glenaris, 3, 119	8	1:43.00	26,150
1976	**Cascapedia**, 3, 121	W. Shoemaker	Go March, 3, 117	Dream of Spring, 3, 118	10	1:42.20	26,750
1975	**Katonka**, 3, 123	L. A. Pincay Jr.	Nicosia, 3, 125	Just a Kick, 3, 118	9	1:42.20	33,150
1974	**Bedknob**, 3, 115	A. Pineda	Bold Tullah, 3, 118	Bold Ballet, 3, 116	11	1:42.20	20,750
1973	**Meilleur**, 3, 118	D. Pierce	Sphere, 3, 118	Goddess Roman, 3, 116	8	1:42.40	20,350

Named for Louis B. Mayer's 1946 Hollywood Derby winner Honeymoon (1943 f. by *Beau Pere), once the leading California-bred distaff earner. Formerly named in honor of the nearby Pacific Ocean. Grade 3 1976-'80, 1983-'97. Sea Breeze S. 1952-'55. Honeymoon S. 1956-'74. Honeymoon H. 1975-2000. Honeymoon Breeders' Cup Invitational H. 2001. Honeymoon Breeders' Cup H. 2002-'07. 6 furlongs 1952-'53. 7 furlongs 1954. 1 mile 1955-'67, 1970. 1 1/16 miles 1968-'69, 1971-'95. 1 1/4 miles 2001. Dirt 1952-'72, 1993. Nonwinners of a race worth $12,500 to the winner 1973-'74.

Honorable Miss Handicap

Grade 2 in 2008. Saratoga Race Course, three-year-olds and up, fillies and mares, 6 furlongs, dirt. Held August 3, 2007, with a gross value of $147,000. First held in 1985. First graded in 1996. Stakes record 1:08.93 (2000 Bourbon Belle [2nd Div.]).

Year	Winner	Jockey	Second	Third	Strs	Time	1st Purse
2007	**Burmilla**, 4, 114	R. Bejarano	Indian Flare, 5, 117	G City Gal, 4, 116	5	1:09.51	$90,000
2006	**Stormy Kiss (Arg)**, 4, 114	J. Castellano	Malibu Mint, 5, 117	Miss Elsie, 5, 115	6	1:10.58	90,000
2005	**Forest Music**, 4, 114	J. R. Velazquez	Ebony Breeze, 5, 116	Bank Audit, 4, 120	8	1:10.06	90,000
2004	**My Trusty Cat**, 4, 115	P. Day	Ebony Breeze, 4, 115	Smok'n Frolic, 5, 116	7	1:10.37	90,000
2003	**Willa On the Move**, 4, 114	E. S. Prado	Shine Again, 6, 120	Smok'n Frolic, 4, 117	6	1:09.92	64,560
2002	**Mandy's Gold**, 4, 116	E. S. Prado	Shine Again, 5, 116	Dat You Miz Blue, 5, 114	8	1:09.24	65,100
2001	**My Big Bambu**, 4, 118	J. D. Bailey	Country Hideaway, 5, 118	Dat You Miz Blue, 4, 120	7	1:09.64	63,708
2000	**Debby d'Or**, 5, 114	S. J. Sellers	Tropical Punch, 4, 115	Katz Me If You Can, 3, 113	9	1:10.11	66,450
	Bourbon Belle, 5, 116	W. Martinez	Cassidy, 5, 114	Go to the Ink, 4, 114	8	**1:08.93**	65,850
1999	**Bourbon Belle**, 4, 116	P. A. Johnson	Gold Princess, 4, 116	License Fee, 4, 114	10	1:09.53	67,560
1998	**Furlough**, 4, 113	M. E. Smith	Angel's Tearlet, 5, 114	Dixie Flag, 4, 119	6	1:11.32	48,765
1997	**Dancin Renee**, 5, 116	R. Migliore	Ashboro, 4, 115	Vivace, 4, 113	6	1:09.16	48,465
1996	**Twist Afleet**, 5, 119	M. E. Smith	Broad Smile, 4, 116	In Conference, 4, 113	9	1:09.91	49,005
1995	**Low Key Affair**, 4, 120	P. Day	Classy Mirage, 5, 123	Twist Afleet, 4, 120	5	1:09.67	48,195

Racing — Graded Stakes   351

Year	Winner	Jockey	Second	Third	Strs	Time	1st Purse
1994	**Classy Mirage**, 4, 122	J. A. Krone	Spinning Round, 5, 119	For all Seasons, 4, 117	6	1:09.72	$48,675
1993	**Nannerl**, 6, 117	J. D. Bailey	Vivano, 4, 117	Via Dei Portici, 4, 117	6	1:15.19	29,040
1992	**Nice Assay**, 4, 115	C. J. McCarron	Madam Bear, 4, 119	Real Irish Hope, 5, 117	5	1:08.97	31,620
1987	**Funistrada**, 4, 122	R. G. Davis	Tricky Squaw, 4, 122	I'm Sweets, 4, 122	5	1:36.80	33,300
1986	**Wisla**, 3, 113	J. Vasquez	Cherry Jubilee, 4, 122	Dancing Danzig, 3, 113	6	1:36.40	32,940
1985	**Schematic**, 3, 114	R. G. Davis	Ripley, 5, 116	Tiltalating, 3, 114	7	1:10.20	51,570

Named for Pen-Y-Bryn Farm's 1975, '76 Fall Highweight H. (G2) winner Honorable Miss (1970 f. by Damascus). Grade 3 1996-2003. Honorable Miss S. 1992-'97. Not held 1988-'91. 6½ furlongs 1993. Two divisions 2000.

Hopeful Stakes

Grade 1 in 2008. Saratoga Race Course, two-year-olds, 7 furlongs, dirt. Held September 3, 2007, with a gross value of $237,500. First held in 1903. First graded in 1973. Stakes record 1:21.94 (2001 Came Home).

Year	Winner	Jockey	Second	Third	Strs	Time	1st Purse
2007	**Majestic Warrior**, 2, 120	G. K. Gomez	Ready's Image, 2, 120	Maimonides, 2, 120	4	1:23.04	$150,000
2006	**Circular Quay**, 2, 120	G. K. Gomez	Scat Daddy, 2, 120	Unbridled Express, 2, 120	5	1:23.00	150,000
2005	**First Samurai**, 2, 120	J. D. Bailey	Henny Hughes, 2, 120	Too Much Bling, 2, 120	5	1:23.25	150,000
2004	**Afleet Alex**, 2, 122	J. Rose	Devils Disciple, 2, 122	Flamenco, 2, 122	7	1:23.58	150,000
2003	**Silver Wagon**, 2, 122	J. D. Bailey	Chapel Royal, 2, 122	Notorious Rogue, 2, 122	7	1:23.47	120,000
2002	**Sky Mesa**, 2, 122	E. S. Prado	Pretty Wild, 2, 122	Zavata, 2, 122	6	1:23.08	120,000
2001	**Came Home**, 2, 122	C. J. McCarron	Mayakovsky, 2, 122	Thunder Days, 2, 122	7	**1:21.94**	120,000
2000	dh-**City Zip**, 2, 122	J. A. Santos	Mayakovsky, 2, 122	Macho Uno, 2, 122	11	1:24.52	80,000
	dh-**Yonaguska**, 2, 122	J. D. Bailey					
1999	**High Yield**, 2, 122	J. D. Bailey	Settlement, 2, 122	Exciting Story, 2, 122	9	1:22.85	120,000
1998	**Lucky Roberto**, 2, 122	R. G. Davis	Tactical Cat, 2, 122	Time Bandit, 2, 122	7	1:23.81	120,000
1997	**Favorite Trick**, 2, 122	P. Day	K. O. Punch, 2, 122	Jess M, 2, 122	7	1:23.87	120,000
1996	**Smoke Glacken**, 2, 122	C. Perret	Ordway, 2, 122	Gun Fight, 2, 122	8	1:23.63	120,000
1995	**Hennessy**, 2, 122	G. L. Stevens	Louis Quatorze, 2, 122	Maria's Mon, 2, 122	7	1:23.44	120,000
1994	**Wild Escapade**, 2, 122	J. F. Chavez	Montreal Red, 2, 122	Law of the Sea, 2, 122	6	1:23.24	120,000
1993	**Dehere**, 2, 122	C. J. McCarron	Slew Gin Fizz, 2, 122	Whitney Tower, 2, 122	7	1:15.97	120,000
1992	**Great Navigator**, 2, 122	A. T. Gryder	Strolling Along, 2, 122	England Expects, 2, 122	8	1:15.71	120,000
1991	**Salt Lake**, 2, 122	M. E. Smith	Slew's Ghost, 2, 122	Caller I. D., 2, 122	9	1:17.74	120,000
1990	**Deposit Ticket**, 2, 122	G. L. Stevens	Hansel, 2, 122	Link, 2, 122	6	1:16.20	139,680
1989	**Summer Squall**, 2, 122	P. Day	Sir Richard Lewis, 2, 122	Eternal Flight, 2, 122	8	1:16.80	140,400
1988	**Mercedes Won**, 2, 122	R. G. Davis	Fast Play, 2, 122	Leading Prospect, 2, 122	6	1:16.60	142,320
1987	**Crusader Sword**, 2, 122	R. P. Romero	Bill E. Shears, 2, 122	Success Express, 2, 122	5	1:18.60	104,580
1986	**Gulch**, 2, 122	A. T. Cordero Jr.	Persevered, 2, 122	Flying Granville, 2, 122	4	1:16.40	126,720
1985	**Papal Power**, 2, 122	D. MacBeth	Danny's Keys, 2, 122	Bullet Blade, 2, 122	10	1:18.40	103,320
1984	**Chief's Crown**, 2, 122	D. MacBeth	Tiffany Ice, 2, 122	Mugzy's Rullah, 2, 122	9	1:16.00	100,440
1983	**Capitol South**, 2, 122	J. D. Bailey	Don Rickles, 2, 122	Swale, 2, 122	13	1:17.40	72,720
1982	**Copelan**, 2, 122	J. D. Bailey	Victorious, 2, 122	Aloha Hawaii, 2, 122	9	1:16.60	69,000
1981	**Timely Writer**, 2, 122	R. Danjean	Out of Hock, 2, 122	Lejoli, 2, 122	8	1:16.20	51,390
1980	**Tap Shoes**, 2, 122	R. Hernandez	Lord Avie, 2, 122	Well Decorated, 2, 122	9	1:17.00	51,750
1979	‡**J. P. Brother**, 2, 122	J. Imparato	Gold Stage, 2, 122	Googolplex, 2, 122	12	1:16.20	50,490
1978	**General Assembly**, 2, 122	D. G. McHargue	Exuberant, 2, 122	Fuzzbuster, 2, 122	6	1:16.40	48,600
1977	**Affirmed**, 2, 122	S. Cauthen	Alydar, 2, 122	Regal and Royal, 2, 122	7	1:15.40	48,105
1976	**Banquet Table**, 2, 122	J. Cruguet	Turn of Coin, 2, 122	P. R. Man, 2, 122	13	1:16.20	51,345
1975	**Jackknife**, 2, 121	J. Cruguet	Ferrous, 2, 121	Whatsyourpleasure, 2, 121	9	1:16.60	41,625
	Eustace, 2, 121	J. Nichols	Iron Bit, 2, 121	Gentle King, 2, 121	9	1:16.40	41,850
1974	**The Bagel Prince**, 2, 121	A. T. Cordero Jr.	Knightly Sport, 2, 121	Cardinal George, 2, 121	7	1:16.80	40,995
	Foolish Pleasure, 2, 121	B. Baeza	Greek Answer, 2, 121	Our Talisman, 2, 121	8	1:16.60	41,445
1973	**Gusty O'Shay**, 2, 121	R. Kotenko	Take by Storm, 2, 121	Prince of Reason, 2, 121	7	1:16.40	50,400

As the first major two-year-old race longer than six furlongs, owners are "hopeful" their horses will be able to go a classic distance. Held at Belmont Park 1943-'45. Not held 1911-'12. 6 furlongs 1903-'09. 6½ furlongs 1910-'93. Two divisions 1974-'75. Dead heat for first 2000. ‡Rockhill Native finished first, DQ to sixth, 1979.

Humana Distaff Handicap

Grade 1 in 2008. Churchill Downs, four-year-olds and up, fillies and mares, 7 furlongs, dirt. Held May 3, 2008, with a gross value of $334,800. First held in 1987. First graded in 1990. Stakes record 1:20.70 (2001 Dream Supreme).

Year	Winner	Jockey	Second	Third	Strs	Time	1st Purse
2008	**Intangaroo**, 4, 124	A. Quinonez	Baroness Thatcher, 4, 118	Hystericalady, 5, 120	8	1:22.03	$201,351
2007	**Hystericalady**, 4, 118	R. Bejarano	Pussycat Doll, 5, 124	Carriage Trail, 4, 118	10	1:21.87	200,732
2006	**Pussycat Doll**, 4, 119	G. K. Gomez	Behaving Badly, 5, 122	Bending Strings, 5, 119	8	1:21.62	175,000
2005	**My Trusty Cat**, 5, 115	J. Castellano	Molto Vita, 5, 115	Puxa Saco, 5, 115	9	1:21.43	174,685
2004	**Mayo On the Side**, 5, 114	P. Day	Azeri, 6, 125	Randaroo, 4, 121	4	1:22.78	174,375
2003	**Sightseek**, 4, 116	J. D. Bailey	Gold Mover, 5, 119	Miss Lodi, 4, 114	8	1:22.12	137,888
2002	‡**Celtic Melody**, 4, 114	M. Guidry	Gold Mover, 4, 115	Hattiesburg, 4, 115	9	1:22.98	141,360
2001	**Dream Supreme**, 4, 120	P. Day	La Feminn, 5, 115	Nany's Sweep, 5, 117	5	**1:20.70**	102,300
2000	**Ruby Surprise**, 5, 114	J. C. Judice	Honest Lady, 4, 119	Cassidy, 5, 114	7	1:21.25	102,951
1999	**Zuppardo Ardo**, 5, 114	S. J. Sellers	French Braids, 4, 114	Prospector's Song, 4, 114	9	1:23.40	105,183
1998	**Colonial Minstrel**, 4, 115	J. R. Velazquez	Stop Traffic, 5, 117	Meter Maid, 4, 114	11	1:22.12	71,300
1997	**Capote Belle**, 4, 118	J. R. Velazquez	Hidden Lake, 4, 115	J J'sdream, 4, 117	8	1:22.38	70,060

Racing — Graded Stakes

Year	Winner	Jockey	Second	Third	Strs	Time	1st Purse
1996	In Conference, 4, 113	M. E. Smith	Supah Jess, 4, 113	Morris Code, 4, 116	8	1:23.30	$72,930
1995	Laura's Pistolette, 4, 114	C. S. Nakatani	Morning Meadow, 5, 113	Traverse City, 5, 114	10	1:22.24	74,425
1994	Roamin Rachel, 4, 118	M. E. Smith	Arches of Gold, 5, 121	Glory's Ghost, 4, 113	7	1:23.83	72,345
1993	Court Hostess, 5, 115	C. J. McCarron	Santa Catalina, 5, 115	Ifyoucouldseemenow, 5, 113	12	1:23.18	56,550
1992	Ifyoucouldseemenow, 4, 120	C. Perret	Madam Bear, 4, 114	Magal, 5, 113	10	1:22.22	56,599
1991	Illeria, 4, 112	P. Day	Nurse Dopey, 4, 117	Tipsy Girl, 5, 115	10	1:23.26	37,603
1990	Medicine Woman, 5, 114	P. Day	Lost Lode, 5, 114	Gallant Ryder, 5, 111	9	1:23.40	36,693
1989	Sunshine Always, 5, 113	P. Day	Littlebitapleasure, 7, 115	Lt. Lao, 5, 119	5	1:24.40	35,425
1988	Le l'Argent, 6, 119	P. Day	Lady Gretchen, 4, 113	Intently, 5, 117	7	1:22.80	36,270
1987	Lazer Show, 4, 120	P. Day	Weekend Delight, 5, 123	Ten Thousand Stars, 5, 118	7	1:22.80	26,442

Races for females are typically referred to as distaff races. Sponsored by Humana Inc., a major medical corporation headquartered in Louisville, 1995-2008. Formerly sponsored by Brown & Williamson Tobacco Corp., also headquartered in Louisville 1987-'94. Grade 3 1990-'98. Grade 2 1999-2001. Brown & Williamson S. 1987. Brown & Williamson H. 1988-'94. Humana Distaff H. 1995-2006. ‡Gold Mover finished first, DQ to second, 2002.

Hurricane Bertie Handicap

Grade 3 in 2008. Gulfstream Park, four-year-olds and up, fillies and mares, 7 furlongs, dirt. Held February 17, 2008, with a gross value of $101,500. First held in 2001. First graded in 2005. Stakes record 1:22.77 (2008 Sugar Swirl).

Year	Winner	Jockey	Second	Third	Strs	Time	1st Purse
2008	Sugar Swirl, 5, 121	J. Castellano	Change Up, 4, 118	Silver Knockers, 4, 116	6	**1:22.77**	$60,000
2007	Any Limit, 4, 116	R. Bejarano	My Lucky Free, 4, 115	Stolen Prayer, 4, 116	10	1:17.16	60,000
2006	Smokey Glacken, 5, 119	J. Castellano	Atlas Valley, 4, 116	Beautiful Bets, 6, 116	10	1:15.47	60,000
2005	Lilah, 8, 114	R. Maragh	Forty Moves, 4, 114	Molto Vita, 5, 118	6	1:15.45	60,000
2004	House Party, 4, 117	J. A. Santos	Mooji Moo, 5, 115	Zawzooth, 5, 113	10	1:15.55	60,000
2003	Gold Mover, 5, 117	E. S. Prado	Harmony Lodge, 5, 116	Belterra, 4, 116	5	1:15.83	60,000
2002	Gold Mover, 4, 116	E. Coa	Celtic Melody, 4, 114	Mandy's Gold, 4, 114	5	1:15.38	60,000
2001	Swept Away, 4, 121	E. S. Prado	Sahara Gold, 4, 115	Lily's Affair, 5, 115	10	1:09.85	48,720

Named for Richard, Bertram, and Elaine Klein's 2000 First Lady H. (G3) winner Hurricane Bertie (1995 f. by Storm Boot). Three-year-olds and up 2001-'06. 6 furlongs 2001. 6½ furlongs 2002-'07.

Hutcheson Stakes

Grade 2 in 2008. Gulfstream Park, three-year-olds, 7 furlongs, dirt. Held January 5, 2008, with a gross value of $150,000. First held in 1955. First graded in 1973. Stakes record 1:20.80 (1973 Shecky Greene).

Year	Winner	Jockey	Second	Third	Strs	Time	1st Purse
2008	Smooth Air, 3, 116	M. R. Cruz	Silver Edition, 3, 117	Halo Najib, 3, 117	8	1:23.21	$90,000
2007	King of the Roxy, 3, 120	E. S. Prado	Bold Start, 3, 116	Out of Gwedda, 3, 118	9	1:28.00	90,000
2006	Keyed Entry, 3, 116	J. R. Velazquez	First Samurai, 3, 122	Express News, 3, 118	7	1:27.12	90,000
2005	Proud Accolade, 3, 122	J. R. Velazquez	Park Avenue Ball, 3, 120	Vicarage, 3, 118	6	1:29.90	90,000
2004	Limehouse, 3, 122	J. R. Velazquez	Deputy Storm, 3, 118	Saratoga County, 3, 116	10	1:22.23	90,000
2003	Lion Tamer, 3, 118	M. E. Smith	Strength Within, 3, 116	Crafty Guy, 3, 122	6	1:22.60	90,000
2002	Showmeitall, 3, 118	J. F. Chavez	Monthir, 3, 116	Royal Lad, 3, 116	8	1:26.07	90,000
2001	Yonaguska, 3, 119	J. D. Bailey	City Zip, 3, 122	Sparkling Sabre, 3, 112	11	1:22.63	90,000
2000	dh-More Than Ready, 3, 122	J. R. Velazquez		American Bullet, 3, 114	8	1:21.76	60,000
	dh-Summer Note, 3, 113	S. J. Sellers					
1999	Bet Me Best, 3, 122	J. D. Bailey	Texas Glitter, 3, 119	Cat Thief, 3, 119	7	1:22.33	90,000
1998	Time Limit, 3, 119	J. D. Bailey	Coronado's Quest, 3, 122	Zippy Zeal, 3, 114	5	1:22.53	60,000
1997	Frisk Me Now, 3, 112	E. L. King Jr.	Confide, 3, 117	Crown Ambassador, 3, 117	8	1:22.51	60,000
1996	Appealing Skier, 3, 119	R. Wilson	Unbridled's Song, 3, 119	Gold Fever, 3, 117	7	1:24.72	45,000
1995	Valid Wager, 3, 119	M. A. Pedroza	Mr. Greeley, 3, 117	Don Juan A, 3, 119	7	1:23.51	45,000
1994	Holy Bull, 3, 122	M. E. Smith	Patton, 3, 113	You and I, 3, 119	7	1:21.23	45,000
1993	Hidden Trick, 3, 114	R. P. Romero	‡Great Navigator, 3, 119	Forever Whirl, 3, 113	9	1:23.61	54,108
1992	My Luck Runs North, 3, 113	R. D. Lopez	Sneaky Solicitor, 3, 117	Frosted Spy, 3, 117	9	1:24.95	55,008
1991	Fly So Free, 3, 122	J. A. Santos	To Freedom, 3, 119	Sunny and Pleasant, 3, 114	10	1:23.30	55,527
1990	Housebuster, 3, 119	R. P. Romero	Yonder, 3, 122	Stalker, 3, 119	11	1:24.40	56,787
1989	Dixieland Brass, 3, 114	R. P. Romero	Western Playboy, 3, 112	Tricky Creek, 3, 122	12	1:22.80	58,320
1988	Perfect Spy, 3, 114	J. Samyn	Forty Niner, 3, 122	Notebook, 3, 122	7	1:23.00	52,335
1987	Well Selected, 3, 113	J. Vasquez	Gone West, 3, 114	Faster Than Sound, 3, 119	8	1:23.00	53,376
1986	Papal Power, 3, 122	D. MacBeth	Raja's Revenge, 3, 122	Mr. Classic, 3, 112	10	1:23.80	55,440
1985	Banner Bob, 3, 119	K. K. Allen	‡Creme Fraiche, 3, 114	Do It Again Dan, 3, 114	12	1:21.60	45,720
1984	Swale, 3, 114	E. Maple	For Halo, 3, 114	Darn That Alarm, 3, 112	7	1:22.00	38,790
1983	Current Hope, 3, 114	A. O. Solis	Highland Park, 3, 122	Country Pine, 3, 114	13	1:22.20	39,330
1982	Distinctive Pro, 3, 117	J. Velasquez	Center Cut, 3, 114	Real Twister, 3, 114	6	1:22.40	34,650
1981	Lord Avie, 3, 122	C. J. McCarron	Spirited Boy, 3, 114	Linnleur, 3, 114	7	1:23.40	34,080
1980	Plugged Nickle, 3, 122	B. Thornburg	Execution's Reason, 3, 122	One Son, 3, 114	6	1:22.60	17,640
1979	Spectacular Bid, 3, 122	R. J. Franklin	Lot o' Gold, 3, 114	Northern Prospect, 3, 114	7	1:21.40	17,766
1978	Sensitive Prince, 3, 114	M. Solomone	Kissing U., 3, 114	Pipe Major, 3, 114	11	1:20.80	19,890
1977	Silver Series, 3, 112	L. Snyder	Medieval Man, 3, 114	One in a Million, 3, 113	9	1:22.80	20,610
1976	Sonkisser, 3, 116	B. Baeza	Gay Jitterbug, 3, 116	Star of the Sea, 3, 116	7	1:21.00	19,350
1975	Greek Answer, 3, 122	M. Castaneda	Fashion Sale, 3, 113	Rich Sun, 3, 112	8	1:21.60	20,370
1974	Frankie Adams, 3, 114	R. Turcotte	dh-Judger, 3, 110		13	1:22.40	31,845
			dh-Training Table, 3, 114				
1973	Shecky Greene, 3, 122	B. Baeza	Forego, 3, 116	Leo's Pisces, 3, 112	7	**1:20.80**	19,170

Named for labor leader William Levi Hutcheson (1874-1953), who served as a member of the Gulfstream Park Advi-

sory Board. Formerly sponsored by Danka Office Imaging Co. of St. Petersburg, Florida 1997. Not graded 1975-'81. Hutcheson H. 1955, '84. 6½ furlongs 1955-'60. 7½ furlongs 2005-'07. Dead heat for second 1974. Dead heat for first 2000. ‡Do It Again Dan finished second, DQ to third, 1985. ‡Demaloot Demashoot finished second, DQ to fourth, 1993. Equaled track record 1973. Track record 2006. Held as an allowance race 1954.

Illinois Derby

Grade 2 in 2008. Hawthorne Race Course, three-year-olds, 1⅛ miles, dirt. Held April 5, 2008, with a gross value of $500,000. First held in 1923. First graded in 1973. Stakes record 1:47.51 (1997 Wild Rush).

Year	Winner	Jockey	Second	Third	Strs	Time	1st Purse
2008	**Recapturetheglory**, 3, 122	E. T. Baird	Golden Spikes, 3, 122	Z Humor, 3, 122	7	1:49.01	$300,000
2007	**Cowtown Cat**, 3, 122	F. Jara	Reporting for Duty, 3, 122	Bold Start, 3, 122	9	1:51.21	300,000
2006	**Sweetnorthernsaint**, 3, 122	K. J. Desormeaux	Mister Triester, 3, 122	Cause to Believe, 3, 122	10	1:49.82	300,000
2005	**Greeley's Galaxy**, 3, 122	K. Desormeaux	Monarch Lane, 3, 122	Magna Graduate, 3, 122	8	1:49.62	300,000
2004	**Pollard's Vision**, 3, 114	E. Coa	Song of the Sword, 3, 116	Suave, 3, 114	11	1:50.80	300,000
2003	**Ten Most Wanted**, 3, 114	P. Day	Fund of Funds, 3, 114	Foufa's Warrior, 3, 118	10	1:51.47	300,000
2002	**War Emblem**, 3, 114	L. J. Sterling Jr.	Repent, 3, 124	Fonz's, 3, 117	9	1:49.92	300,000
2001	**Distilled**, 3, 114	M. E. Smith	Saint Damien, 3, 119	Dream Run, 3, 114	8	1:51.37	300,000
2000	**Performing Magic**, 3, 119	S. J. Sellers	Country Only, 3, 117	Country Coast, 3, 114	9	1:50.86	300,000
1999	**Vision and Verse**, 3, 114	H. Castillo Jr.	Prime Directive, 3, 117	Pineaff, 3, 122	10	1:48.47	300,000
1998	**Yarrow Brae**, 3, 114	W. Martinez	‡One Bold Stroke, 3, 117	Orville N Wilbur's, 3, 124	10	1:51.21	300,000
1997	**Wild Rush**, 3, 117	K. Desormeaux	Anet, 3, 124	Saratoga Sunrise, 3, 119	8	**1:47.51**	300,000
1996	**Natural Selection**, 3, 114	R. P. Romero	El Amante, 3, 124	Irish Conquest, 3, 114	13	1:48.60	300,000
1995	**Peaks and Valleys**, 3, 124	J. A. Krone	Da Hoss, 3, 117	Western Echo, 3, 117	13	1:48.99	300,000
1994	**Rustic Light**, 3, 117	E. Fires	Amathos, 3, 114	Seminole Wind, 3, 114	7	1:51.89	300,000
1993	**Antrim Rd.**, 3, 114	A. T. Gryder	Seattle Morn, 3, 114	Secret Negotiator, 3, 114	13	1:48.68	300,000
1992	**Dignitas**, 3, 117	J. D. Bailey	American Chance, 3, 112	Straight to Bed, 3, 114	13	1:49.09	320,100
1991	**Richman**, 3, 124	J. D. Bailey	Doc of the Day, 3, 119	Nowork all Play, 3, 114	14	1:49.36	319,200
1990	**Dotsero**, 3, 117	A. T. Gryder	Sound of Cannons, 3, 112	Hofre, 3, 112	9	1:50.60	190,290
1989	‡**Music Merci**, 3, 124	G. L. Stevens	Notation, 3, 119	Endow, 3, 124	7	1:50.20	310,140
1988	**Proper Reality**, 3, 124	J. D. Bailey	Jim's Orbit, 3, 122	Classic Account, 3, 112	6	1:50.20	321,000
1987	**Lost Code**, 3, 124	G. St. Leon	Blanco, 3, 119	Valid Prospect, 3, 112	7	1:49.60	188,130
1986	**Bolshoi Boy**, 3, 118	R. Migliore	Speedy Shannon, 3, 118	Blue Buckaroo, 3, 116	8	1:52.20	189,432
1985	**Important Business**, 3, 116	J. L. Diaz	Nostalgia's Star, 3, 122	Another Reef, 3, 124	13	1:51.60	192,786
1984	**Delta Trace**, 3, 124	K. K. Allen	Wind Flyer, 3, 122	Birdie's Legend, 3, 124	10	1:51.80	127,530
1983	**Gen'l Practitioner**, 3, 126	J. A. Santiago	Passing Base, 3, 114	Aztec Red, 3, 124	10	1:50.40	127,200
1982	**Star Gallant**, 3, 126	R. Sibille	Drop Your Drawers, 3, 122	Soy Emperor, 3, 119	8	1:52.60	126,420
1981	**Paristo**, 3, 126	D. C. Ashcroft	Pass the Tab, 3, 126	Bitterrook, 3, 114	13	1:49.60	93,300
1980	**Ray's Word**, 3, 124	R. DePass	Mighty Return, 3, 114	Stutz Blackhawk, 3, 121	11	1:52.00	92,970
1979	**Smarten**, 3, 124	S. Maple	Clever Trick, 3, 124	Julie's Dancer, 3, 116	6	1:49.40	91,710
1978	**Batonnier**, 3, 124	R. J. Hirdes Jr.	Raymond Earl, 3, 121	Silver Nitrate, 3, 124	12	1:51.60	62,820
1977	**Flag Officer**, 3, 124	L. Ahrens	Time Call, 3, 116	Cisk, 3, 116	11	1:52.20	62,955
1976	**Life's Hope**, 3, 124	S. Hawley	Wardlaw, 3, 124	New Collection, 3, 116	9	1:51.40	77,295
1975	**Colonel Power**, 3, 124	P. Rubbicco	Ruggles Ferry, 3, 124	Methdioxya, 3, 124	14	1:50.20	63,360
1974	**Sharp Gary**, 3, 124	G. J. Gallitano	Sr. Diplomat, 3, 114	Sports Editor, 3, 119	12	1:50.60	63,060
1973	**Big Whippendeal**, 3, 119	L. Adams	†What Will Be, 3, 121	Golden Don, 3, 126	9	1:50.20	43,491

Named for the home state of Hawthorne Race Course. Grade 3 1973-'87. Held at Sportsman's Park 1924-'32, 1939-'98, 2000-'02. Held at Aurora 1933-'38. Not held 1924-'32, 1939-'62, 1970-'71. 1¼ miles 1923. ‡Notation finished first, DQ to second, 1989. ‡Orville N Wilbur's finished second, DQ to third, 1998. Track record 1997. †Denotes female.

Indiana Derby

Grade 2 in 2008. Hoosier Park, three-year-olds, 1 1/16 miles, dirt. Held October 6, 2007, with a gross value of $510,600. First held in 1995. First graded in 2002. Stakes record 1:41.40 (1996 Canyon Run).

Year	Winner	Jockey	Second	Third	Strs	Time	1st Purse
2007	**Zanjero**, 3, 124	R. Albarado	Bwana Bull, 3, 124	Flashstorm, 3, 121	9	1:43.95	$294,360
2006	dh-**Cielo Gold**, 3, 124	B. Hernandez Jr.		Smokeyjonessutton, 3, 121	10	1:42.84	195,016
	dh-**Star Dabbler**, 3, 121	R. Migliore					
2005	**Don't Get Mad**, 3, 124	B. Blanc	Scrappy T, 3, 124	Thor's Echo, 3, 124	9	1:42.71	306,780
2004	**Brass Hat**, 3, 124	W. Martinez	Suave, 3, 124	Hasslefree, 3, 115	9	1:44.04	306,780
2003	**Excessivepleasure**, 3, 124	J. K. Court	Grand Hombre, 3, 124	Wando, 3, 124	8	1:43.48	247,080
2002	**Perfect Drift**, 3, 124	J. K. Court	Easyfromthegitgo, 3, 124	Premeditation, 3, 121	12	1:43.50	248,820
2001	**Orientate**, 3, 124	R. Albarado	Saratoga Games, 3, 121	Trion Georgia, 3, 124	11	1:42.22	188,460
2000	**Mister Deville**, 3, 119	L. S. Quinonez	Performing Magic, 3, 119	One Call Close, 3, 119	5	1:41.80	184,500
1999	**Forty One Carats**, 3, 115	J. F. Chavez	Zanetti, 3, 122	First American, 3, 122	12	1:42.24	187,290
1998	**One Bold Stroke**, 3, 122	R. Albarado	Dixie Dot Com, 3, 117	Da Devil, 3, 122	11	1:43.14	188,700
1997	**Dubai Dust**, 3, 113	S. P. LeJeune Jr.	Frisk Me Now, 3, 122	Tansit, 3, 119	8	1:44.00	127,440
1996	**Canyon Run**, 3, 115	F. C. Torres	Broadway Bit, 3, 113	Hunk of Class, 3, 117	10	**1:41.40**	64,560
1995	**Peruvian**, 3, 117	D. Kutz	I Still Believe, 3, 117	Mine Inspector, 3, 119	11	1:43.00	66,900

Hoosier Park is located in Anderson, Indiana. Grade 3 2002-'03. Dead heat for first 2006.

Indiana Oaks

Grade 2 in 2008. Hoosier Park, three-year-olds, fillies, 1 1/16 miles, dirt. Held October 5, 2007, with a gross value of $406,900. First held in 1995. First graded in 2001. Stakes record 1:42.40 (2000 Humble Clerk).

Year	Winner	Jockey	Second	Third	Strs	Time	1st Purse
2007	**Tessa Blue**, 3, 115	M. E. Smith	Boca Grande, 3, 121	Marietta, 3, 121	10	1:44.42	$232,140

Year	Winner	Jockey	Second	Third	Strs	Time	1st Purse
2006	**Baghdaria**, 3, 121	R. Bejarano	Cryptoquip, 3, 121	Southern Flu, 3, 118	8	1:43.64	$237,076
2005	**Flying Glitter**, 3, 121	R. Albarado	Eyes On Eddy, 3, 114	Miss Matched, 3, 121	6	1:44.10	243,060
2004	**Daydreaming**, 3, 118	J. R. Velazquez	Capeside Lady, 3, 121	Stellar Jayne, 3, 121	7	1:43.65	243,780
2003	**Awesome Humor**, 3, 116	R. Albarado	Cloakof Vagueness, 3, 114	Shot Gun Favorite, 3, 118	10	1:45.75	184,140
2002	**Bare Necessities**, 3, 118	J. Valdivia Jr.	Erica's Smile, 3, 121	Tarnished Lady, 3, 118	9	1:45.83	183,840
2001	**Scoop**, 3, 121	R. Albarado	Gold Huntress, 3, 115	Caressing, 3, 121	9	1:44.06	123,480
2000	**Humble Clerk**, 3, 114	L. J. Melancon	Megans Bluff, 3, 121	Miss Seffens, 3, 116	5	**1:42.40**	92,580
1999	**Brushed Halory**, 3, 121	E. M. Martin Jr.	The Happy Hopper, 3, 116	Chelsie's House, 3, 116	10	1:44.64	123,330
1998	**French Braids**, 3, 116	W. Martinez	Remember Ike, 3, 121	Barefoot Dyana, 3, 118	7	1:43.11	124,080
1997	**Cotton Carnival**, 3, 121	E. M. Martin Jr.	Sheepscot, 3, 116	Valid Bonnet, 3, 121	9	1:43.30	64,440
1996	**Princess Eloise**, 3, 118	S. T. Saito	Talking Tower, 3, 116	Shuffle Again, 3, 116	6	1:37.00	33,540
1995	**Niner's Home**, 3, 121	T. J. Hebert	Alltheway Bertie, 3, 118	Graceful Minister, 3, 114	6	1:37.00	24,480

Hoosier Park is located in Anderson, Indiana. Grade 3 2001-'07. Indiana Breeders' Cup Oaks 1998-2006. 1 mile 1995-'96.

Inglewood Handicap

Grade 3 in 2008. Hollywood Park, three-year-olds and up, 1¹⁄₁₆ miles, turf. Held May 3, 2008, with a gross value of $109,500. First held in 1938. First graded in 1973. Stakes record 1:38.45 (2004 Leroidesanimaux (Brz)).

Year	Winner	Jockey	Second	Third	Strs	Time	1st Purse
2008	**El Roblar**, 6, 118	V. Espinoza	Heroi Do Bafra (Brz), 6, 115	Uffizi, 5, 116	7	1:40.35	$65,700
2007	**After Market**, 4, 116	A. O. Solis	Red Fort (Ire), 7, 117	Willow O Wisp, 5, 117	6	1:39.63	64,920
2006	**Willow O Wisp**, 4, 117	V. Espinoza	Artiste Royal (Ire), 5, 116	New Export (Brz), 5, 116	7	1:39.05	60,000
2005	**King of Happiness**, 6, 117	P. A. Valenzuela	Red Fort (Ire), 5, 117	Just Wonder (GB), 5, 116	6	1:39.47	64,320
2004	**Leroidesanimaux (Brz)**, 4, 114	J. K. Court	Designed for Luck, 7, 118	Devious Boy (GB), 4, 115	9	**1:38.45**	66,540
2003	**Gondolieri (Chi)**, 4, 116	F. T. Alvarado	Truly a Judge, 5, 114	Freefourinternet, 5, 116	4	1:40.32	63,540
2002	**Night Patrol**, 6, 113	V. Espinoza	Redattore (Brz), 7, 120	Seinne (Chi), 5, 117	7	1:39.35	65,820
2001	**Fateful Dream**, 4, 114	D. R. Flores	National Anthem (GB), 5, 115	Casino King (Ire), 6, 115	5	1:41.65	64,260
2000	**Montemiro (Fr)**, 6, 113	V. Espinoza	Bonapartiste (Fr), 6, 118	Takarian (Ire), 5, 118	8	1:40.71	66,300
1999	**Brave Act (GB)**, 5, 120	G. F. Almeida	Lord Smith (GB), 4, 119	Expressionist, 4, 116	8	1:39.13	66,420
1998	**Fantastic Fellow**, 4, 118	C. S. Nakatani	Via Lombardia (Ire), 6, 116	Sharekann (Ire), 6, 113	6	1:38.77	64,740
1997	**El Angelo**, 5, 116	C. S. Nakatani	Irish Wings (Ire), 5, 114	Tychonic (GB), 7, 118	5	1:40.20	63,900
1996	**Fastness (Ire)**, 6, 122	C. S. Nakatani	Helmsman, 4, 120	Tychonic (GB), 6, 120	5	1:39.54	79,470
1995	**Blaze O'Brien**, 8, 116	C. A. Black	Savinio, 5, 118	Stoller, 4, 117	7	1:39.53	79,800
1994	**Gothland (Fr)**, 5, 117	C. S. Nakatani	Rapan Boy (Aus), 6, 117	Johann Quatz (Fr), 5, 117	4	1:39.60	60,700
1993	**The Tender Track**, 6, 116	E. Delahoussaye	Journalism, 5, 118	Johann Quatz (Fr), 4, 117	6	1:40.00	62,500
1992	**Golden Pheasant**, 6, 121	G. L. Stevens	Blaze O'Brien, 4, 118	Native Boundary, 4, 116	7	1:39.86	64,900
1991	**Tight Spot**, 6, 117	L. A. Pincay Jr.	Somethingdifferent, 4, 116	Razeen, 4, 114	6	1:40.30	63,900
1990	**Mohamed Abdu (Ire)**, 6, 117	G. L. Stevens	Peace, 5, 117	Classic Fame, 4, 117	8	1:39.40	64,800
1989	**Steinlen (GB)**, 6, 120	G. L. Stevens	Pasakos, 4, 115	Mi Preferido, 4, 117	7	1:39.60	63,400
1988	**Steinlen (GB)**, 5, 119	G. L. Stevens	Deputy Governor, 4, 120	†Galunpe (Ire), 5, 115	9	1:40.40	66,200
1987	**Le Belvedere**, 4, 113	W. Shoemaker	Sharrood, 4, 118	Barbery, 6, 114	8	1:40.40	65,100
1986	**Zoffany**, 6, 121	E. Delahoussaye	Palace Music, 5, 124	Truce Maker, 8, 112	6	1:45.60	63,000
1985	**Al Mamoon**, 4, 116	E. Delahoussaye	The Noble Player, 5, 118	Swoon, 7, 114	6	1:40.20	62,900
1984	**†Royal Heroine (Ire)**, 4, 116	F. Toro	Bel Bolide, 6, 120	Vin St Benet (GB), 5, 118	13	1:40.20	71,500
1983	**Bold Style**, 4, 115	P. Day	Noalto (GB), 5, 117	Western, 5, 116	8	1:41.40	65,400
1982	**Maipon (Chi)**, 5, 112	D. G. McHargue	Spence Bay (Ire), 7, 122	Wickerr, 7, 116	11	1:40.00	68,900
1981	**Bold Tropic (SAf)**, 6, 124	W. Shoemaker	The Bart, 5, 117	Adraan (GB), 4, 117	11	1:40.00	52,300
1980	**Red Crescent**, 4, 112	C. J. McCarron	Henschel, 6, 118	Numa Pompilius, 6, 115	8	1:40.80	31,300
1979	**Johnny's Image**, 4, 117	C. J. McCarron	Rich Cream, 4, 117	Smoggy (GB), 5, 112	8	1:40.80	26,875
	Star Spangled, 5, 119	L. A. Pincay Jr.	Bywayofchicago, 5, 122	As de Copas (Arg), 6, 121	6	1:40.00	25,875
1978	**Star Spangled**, 4, 114	A. T. Cordero Jr.	Bad 'n Big, 4, 122	No Turning, 5, 116	8	1:39.80	26,800
	Star of Erin (Ire), 4, 117	W. Shoemaker	Landscaper, 6, 113	Life's Hope, 5, 117	7	1:40.60	26,300
1977	**Today 'n Tomorrow**, 4, 117	S. Hawley	Anne's Pretender, 5, 122	Sir Jason, 6, 118	7	1:41.00	32,300
1976	**Riot in Paris**, 5, 117	J. Lambert	Absent Minded, 4, 114	Passionate Pirate, 5, 116	6	1:41.60	25,750
	King Pellinore, 4, 118	W. Shoemaker	Antique, 5, 114	Big Band, 6, 117	7	1:42.00	26,250
1975	***El Botija**, 5, 116	J. E. Tejeira	Kirrary, 5, 115	Against the Snow, 5, 117	8	1:41.60	25,475
	†Gay Style, 5, 120	W. Shoemaker	Out of the East, 5, 116	June's Love, 4, 116	10	1:41.40	26,475
1974	**Shirley's Champion**, 3, 118	H. Grant	Rocket Review, 3, 117	Such a Rush, 3, 121	9	1:14.80	20,100
1973	**Ancient Title**, 3, 122	F. Toro	Groshawk, 3, 122	Pontoise, 3, 114	8	1:21.00	32,550

Named for the city of Inglewood, California, location of Hollywood Park. Formerly sponsored by the Miller Brewing Co. of Milwaukee 1972. Grade 2 1973-'74, 1987-'94. Not graded 1975-'81, 2003. Inglewood Mile H. 1938-'39. Miller High Life Inglewood H. 1972. Held at Santa Anita Park 1949. Not held 1942-'44. 1 mile 1938-'39. 7 furlongs 1945-'47, 1973. 6 furlongs 1948. 1¹⁄₈ miles 1950, 1968-'72. 6½ furlongs 1974. Dirt 1983-'66, 1968-'74, 2003. Originally scheduled on turf 2003. Three-year-olds 1973-'74. Two divisions 1975-'76, 1978-'79. Course record 1998, 2004. †Denotes female.

Iowa Oaks

Grade 3 in 2008. Prairie Meadows, three-year-olds, fillies, 1¹⁄₁₆ miles, dirt. Held June 29, 2007, with a gross value of $200,000. First held in 1989. First graded in 2004. Stakes record 1:41.64 (2003 Wildwood Royal).

Year	Winner	Jockey	Second	Third	Strs	Time	1st Purse
2007	**Marietta**, 3, 115	R. Bejarano	Humble Janet, 3, 115	High Again, 3, 121	9	1:43.17	$120,000
2006	**Baghdaria**, 3, 121	R. Bejarano	Maggie Slew, 3, 115	Brownie Points, 3, 118	6	1:43.12	120,000
2005	**Whimsy**, 3, 116	C. H. Marquez Jr.	Cee's Irish, 3, 121	Mary Alex, 3, 113	5	1:43.60	75,000
2004	**He Loves Me**, 3, 118	J. Z. Santana	Prospective Saint, 3, 115	Home Court, 3, 115	8	1:42.80	75,000

Racing — Graded Stakes 355

Year	Winner	Jockey	Second	Third	Strs	Time	1st Purse
2003	Wildwood Royal, 3, 121	S. Danush	Golden Reputashn, 3, 112	Tulupai, 3, 112	8	1:41.64	$75,000
2002	Lost At Sea, 3, 115	T. J. Thompson	See How She Runs, 3, 121	Don't Ruffle Me, 3, 115	6	1:42.27	90,000
2001	Unbridled Elaine, 3, 115	P. Day	Supreme Song, 3, 115	Sharky's Review, 3, 118	6	1:43.88	90,000
2000	Trip, 3, 121	W. Martinez	Lady Melesi, 3, 118	Fiesty Countess, 3, 118	7	1:43.56	90,000
1999	Golden Temper, 3, 121	S. J. Sellers	Undermine, 3, 118	Sweeping Story, 3, 121	6	1:42.95	75,000
1998	Shardona, 3, 114	K. Shino	Danzig Foxxy Woman, 3, 118	Lady Tamworth, 3, 121	10	1:46.94	43,305
1997	Bon Ami, 3, 116	G. W. Corbett	Windy City Raja, 3, 114	Quick n Steady, 3, 121	9	1:44.73	37,317
1996	Vaguely Who, 3, 121	V. L. Warhol	Swiss Saphire, 3, 118	Dee's Anny, 3, 117	11	1:43.63	24,439
1995	Our Gaggy, 3, 118	D. R. Bickel	Don't Tary Stalker, 3, 121	Melinda Jo, 3, 114	6	1:41.80	17,184
1994	Punkerdoo, 3, 121	D. Schroeck	Maria Badria, 3, 118	Chateau Queen, 3, 114	7	1:44.00	9,555
1993	Medical History, 3, 114	V. L. Warhol	Millie's Key, 3, 118	Fashioncense, 3, 119	5	1:42.40	8,950
1992	Giggles Up, 3, 120	G. A. Schaefer	Chelle Rae, 3, 120	Cobilion, 3, 120	9	1:46.02	10,120
1991	Chocolate Tuesday, 3, 121	C. G. Lowrance	Proudest Royal, 3, 121	Amdors Love, 3, 115	7	1:43.10	8,266
1990	Sixmo, 3, 115	V. L. Warhol	Dance for the Gold, 3, 115	Pay Her in Gold, 3, 116	12	1:46.60	11,069
1989	Clickety Click, 3, 119	K. M. Murray	She's Due Black, 3, 117	Hurry Home, 3, 115	8	1:38.80	15,450

Prairie Meadows is located in Altoona, Iowa. Held at Canterbury Park 1992. 1 mile 1989. 1 mile 70 yards 1990-'98.

Iroquois Stakes

Grade 3 in 2008. Churchill Downs, two-year-olds, 1 mile, dirt. Held October 28, 2007, with a gross value of $171,150. First held in 1982. First graded in 1990. Stakes record 1:35.01 (2001 Harlan's Holiday).

Year	Winner	Jockey	Second	Third	Strs	Time	1st Purse
2007	Court Vision, 2, 117	J. R. Leparoux	Halo Najib, 2, 117	St. Joe, 2, 117	9	1:37.26	$101,872
2006	Tiz Wonderful, 2, 117	G. K. Gomez	What a Tale, 2, 117	Starbase, 2, 117	7	1:35.92	67,384
2005	Catcominatcha, 2, 116	R. Bejarano	High Cotton, 2, 118	Mondavi, 2, 118	13	1:36.38	72,354
2004	Straight Line, 2, 122	B. Blanc	Social Probation, 2, 120	Greater Good, 2, 122	7	1:36.62	67,952
2003	The Cliff's Edge, 2, 117	S. J. Sellers	Korbyn Gold, 2, 121	Grand Score, 2, 117	9	1:35.57	70,494
2002	Champali, 2, 118	P. Day	Alke, 2, 116	What a Bad Day, 2, 118	10	1:37.06	70,804
2001	Harlan's Holiday, 2, 121	A. J. D'Amico	Request for Parole, 2, 121	Gold Dollar, 2, 116	10	1:35.01	70,184
2000	Meetyouathebrig, 2, 118	G. L. Stevens	Hero's Tribute, 2, 114	Keats, 2, 112	13	1:35.24	77,066
1999	Mighty, 2, 112	M. St. Julien	Ifittobeitsuptome, 2, 113	Nature, 2, 114	7	1:35.88	68,758
1998	Exploit, 2, 115	C. J. McCarron	Crowning Storm, 2, 114	Olympic Journey, 2, 114	8	1:36.26	71,114
1997	Keene Dancer, 2, 121	P. Day	Yarrow Brae, 2, 113	Dawn Exodus, 2, 113	7	1:37.84	68,882
1996	Global View, 2, 112	K. Bourque	Partner's Hero, 2, 112	Haint, 2, 121	6	1:36.49	68,200
1995	Ide, 2, 121	C. Perret	El Amante, 2, 116	City by Night, 2, 114	8	1:36.89	73,645
1994	Peruvian, 2, 121	J. A. Santos	Our Gatsby, 2, 116	Super Jeblar, 2, 116	11	1:36.68	77,025
1993	Tarzans Blade, 2, 121	B. E. Bartram	Dove Hunt, 2, 121	Amathos, 2, 114	11	1:37.00	74,945
1992	Shoal Creek, 2, 114	B. E. Bartram	Saw Mill, 2, 116	Demaloot Demashoot, 2, 116	13	1:37.51	76,375
1991	Portroe, 2, 114	M. E. Smith	Walkie Talker, 2, 121	Richard of England, 2, 121	11	1:37.96	76,570
1990	Richman, 2, 121	P. Day	Speedy Cure, 2, 114	Honor Grades, 2, 116	8	1:36.60	36,628
1989	Insurrection, 2, 116	P. A. Johnson	Bite the Bullet, 2, 121	Silent Generation, 2, 116	10	1:36.80	37,375
1988	Dansil, 2, 118	L. A. Pincay Jr.	Western Playboy, 2, 114	Lorenzoni, 2, 116	9	1:38.20	36,498
1987	Buoy, 2, 116	K. K. Allen	Key Voyage, 2, 118	Delightful Doctor, 2, 116	12	1:37.80	32,285
1986	Icetrain, 2, 117	M. E. Smith	Grantley, 2, 117	Authentic Hero, 2, 117	12	1:40.20	34,263
1985	Tile, 2, 122	P. Day	Bachelor Beau, 2, 117	Dance to the Wire, 2, 117	11	1:37.20	36,062
1984	Banner Bob, 2, 117	K. K. Allen	Nordic Scandal, 2, 114	Tasheen, 2, 117	8	1:37.60	18,078
1983	Taylor's Special, 2, 117	D. Brumfield	Bello, 2, 119	At the Threshold, 2, 114	9	1:37.20	19,858
1982	Highland Park, 2, 122	D. Brumfield	Coax Me Matt, 2, 114	White Fig, 2, 117	8	1:38.20	19,907

Named for the Iroquois Park area of the city of Louisville. Colts and geldings 1982.

Jaipur Stakes

Grade 3 in 2008. Belmont Park, three-year-olds and up, 6 furlongs, turf. Held May 27, 2007, with a gross value of $113,800. First held in 1984. First graded in 1986. Stakes record 1:07.31 (2006 Around the Cape).

Year	Winner	Jockey	Second	Third	Strs	Time	1st Purse
2007	Ecclesiastic, 6, 118	J. Castellano	Salute the Count, 7, 120	Weigelia, 6, 120	9	1:07.64	$68,280
2006	Around the Cape, 4, 118	C. H. Velasquez	Bold Decision, 4, 118	Summer Service, 6, 120	7	1:07.31	66,900
2005	Ecclesiastic, 4, 118	C. H. Velasquez	Old Forester, 4, 124	Gulch Approval, 5, 120	7	1:20.71	66,960
2004	Multiple Choice, 6, 113	J. Castellano	†Dedication (Fr), 5, 114	Geronimo (Chi), 5, 118	8	1:22.32	67,320
2003	Garnered, 5, 116	V. Carrero	Speightstown, 5, 121	Whitewaterspritzer, 6, 115	5	1:23.49	67,260
2002	Shibboleth, 5, 121	J. D. Bailey	Malabar Gold, 5, 121	†Cozzy Corner, 4, 111	7	1:20.08	67,140
2001	Affirmed Success, 7, 123	J. D. Bailey	Texas Glitter, 5, 116	Bought in Dixie, 5, 114	3	1:21.69	66,475
2000	Gone Fishin, 4, 114	J. R. Velazquez	Weatherbird, 5, 113	French Envoy, 4, 113	12	1:21.73	52,290
1999	Notoriety, 6, 115	J. L. Espinoza	Optic Nerve, 6, 116	Cryptic Rascal, 4, 117	12	1:21.35	52,335
1998	Elusive Quality, 5, 115	J. D. Bailey	Bristling, 6, 111	Optic Nerve, 5, 115	11	1:20.99	51,750
1997	Atraf (GB), 4, 116	J. R. Velazquez	Mighty Forum (GB), 6, 115	Play Smart, 5, 112	4	1:23.64	49,635
1996	Grand Continental, 5, 114	R. Migliore	Inside the Beltway, 5, 115	Goldmine (Fr), 5, 111	10	1:23.78	51,720
1995	Inside the Beltway, 4, 114	J. F. Chavez	Gabr (GB), 5, 117	Golden Cloud, 7, 114	5	1:21.23	49,245
	Mighty Forum (GB), 4, 117	G. L. Stevens	Dominant Prospect, 5, 117	City Nights (Ire), 4, 114	9	1:21.12	49,995
1994	Nijinsky's Gold, 5, 114	J. A. Santos	Dominant Prospect, 4, 117	Home of the Free, 6, 122	7	1:20.06	34,905
	A in Sociology, 4, 119	E. Maple	Roman Envoy, 6, 114	Halissee, 4, 119	7	1:20.38	34,905
1993	Home of the Free, 5, 117	J. D. Bailey	Wind Symbol (GB), 4, 117	Fourstardave, 8, 117	8	1:20.69	55,080
1992	To Freedom, 4, 117	J. A. Krone	Fourstardave, 7, 122	Smart Alec, 4, 117	5	1:22.83	55,710
1991	Kanatiyr (Ire), 5, 117	J. D. Bailey	Senor Speedy, 4, 117	Fourstardave, 6, 122	9	1:23.96	54,630

Year	Winner	Jockey	Second	Third	Strs	Time	1st Purse
1990	**Fourstardave**, 5, 122	M. E. Smith	Harperstown, 4, 117	Wanderkin, 7, 119	9	1:21.00	$57,240
1989	**Harp Islet**, 4, 117	C. Perret	Fourstardave, 4, 119	†Down Again, 5, 114	10	1:27.00	57,150
1988	**Real Courage**, 5, 117	J. Vasquez	Tinchen's Prince, 5, 117	Spectacularphantom, 4, 117	14	1:22.00	60,570
1987	**Raja's Revenge**, 4, 117	M. Venezia	Trubulare, 4, 117	†Give a Toast, 4, 114	11	1:25.20	52,200
1986	**Red Wing Dream**, 5, 117	J. D. Bailey	Creme Fraiche, 4, 122	Roy, 3, 109	5	1:23.60	48,510
	Basket Weave, 5, 117	R. Migliore	Alev (GB), 7, 117	Judge Costa, 5, 117	4	1:22.80	48,330
1985	**Mt. Livermore**, 4, 119	J. Velasquez	Main Top, 6, 117	Cozzene, 5, 117	7	1:09.20	49,020
1984	**Cannon Shell**, 5, 115	D. J. Murphy	Chan Balum, 5, 115	Believe the Queen, 4, 115	12	1:09.20	35,280

Named for George D. Widener's 1962 champion three-year-old male and '62 Belmont S. winner Jaipur (1959 c. by *Nasrullah). Not graded 1990-'91, 2001, 2003. Jaipur H. 1996-2004, 2006. 7 furlongs 1986-2005. Dirt 1984-'86, 1992, 1997, 2001, 2003. Originally scheduled on turf 2001, '03. Two divisions 1986, 1994-'95. Course record 1993, '94 (1st Div.). †Denotes female.

Jamaica Handicap

Grade 2 in 2008. Belmont Park, three-year-olds, 1 1/8 miles, turf. Held October 6, 2007, with a gross value of $300,000. First held in 1929. First graded in 1978. Stakes record 1:45.50 (2004 Artie Schiller).

Year	Winner	Jockey	Second	Third	Strs	Time	1st Purse
2007	**Nobiz Like Shobiz**, 3, 121	J. Castellano	Red Giant, 3, 121	Pays to Dream, 3, 117	9	1:46.80	$180,000
2006	**Showing Up**, 3, 124	C. H. Velasquez	Outperformance, 3, 115	Spider Power (Ire), 3, 115	8	1:47.81	180,000
2005	**Watchmon**, 3, 118	J. Castellano	Crown Point, 3, 119	Woodlander, 3, 115	3	1:49.28	180,000
2004	**Artie Schiller**, 3, 123	R. Migliore	Rousing Victory, 3, 113	Icy Atlantic, 3, 120	6	**1:45.50**	120,000
2003	**Stroll**, 3, 121	J. D. Bailey	Kicken Kris, 3, 121	Joe Bear (Ire), 3, 117	7	1:46.02	120,000
2002	**Finality**, 3, 116	J. R. Velazquez	Union Place, 3, 115	Chiselling, 3, 121	9	1:46.66	120,000
2001	**Navesink**, 3, 118	E. S. Prado	Strategic Partner, 3, 118	Baptize, 3, 123	7	1:51.53	120,000
2000	**King Cugat**, 3, 123	J. D. Bailey	Mandarin Marsh, 3, 114	Parade Leader, 3, 115	8	1:49.63	120,000
1999	**Monarch's Maze**, 3, 117	J. Bravo	Killer Joe, 3, 112	Monkey Puzzle, 3, 118	8	1:51.66	90,000
1998	**Vergennes**, 3, 115	J. R. Velazquez	Tangazi, 3, 114	Middlesex Drive, 3, 114	10	1:50.42	90,000
1997	**Subordination**, 3, 120	J. F. Chavez	Premier Krischief, 3, 119	Skybound, 3, 121	12	1:49.00	90,000
1996	**Allied Forces**, 3, 119	R. Migliore	Cliptomania, 3, 116	Lite Approval, 3, 114	11	1:40.91	86,325
1994	**Pennine Ridge**, 3, 118	J. R. Velazquez	Holy Mountain, 3, 116	I'm Very Irish, 3, 113	7	1:35.13	66,540
1993	**Mi Cielo**, 3, 116	M. E. Smith	Prospector's Flag, 3, 113	Cherokee Run, 3, 120	8	1:35.20	70,440
1992	**West by West**, 3, 112	J. Samyn	Offbeat, 3, 110	Portroe, 3, 111	9	1:34.27	70,320
1991	**Sultry Song**, 3, 113	C. W. Antley	Honest Ensign, 3, 110	Take Me Out, 3, 116	7	1:34.44	70,320
1990	**Confidential Talk**, 3, 111	J. F. Chavez	Rubiano, 3, 112	Sunshine Jimmy, 3, 114	7	1:35.60	52,470
1989	**Domasca Dan**, 3, 116	S. Hawley	Garemma, 3, 114	Is It True, 3, 120	7	1:35.40	70,920
1988	**Ruhlmann**, 3, 113	G. L. Stevens	Teddy Drone, 3, 112	Din's Dancer, 3, 112	8	1:35.40	84,540
1987	**Stacked Pack**, 3, 110	R. P. Romero	Gulch, 3, 123	Homebuilder, 3, 112	8	1:34.80	67,770
1986	**Waquoit**, 3, 112	R. Migliore	Mogambo, 3, 119	‡Moment of Hope, 3, 110	8	1:34.20	53,280
1985	**Don's Choice**, 3, 114	D. MacBeth	I Enrich, 3, 110	Easton, 3, 109	6	1:36.00	53,010
1984	**Raja's Shark**, 3, 112	R. Migliore	Is Your Pleasure, 3, 116	Leroy S., 3, 117	6	1:36.60	52,560
1983	**Bounding Basque**, 3, 115	G. McCarron	A Phenomenon, 3, 120	Bet Big, 3, 115	8	1:34.00	51,480
1982	**John's Gold**, 3, 113	A. T. Cordero Jr.	Lord Lister, 3, 111	Estorill, 3, 114	5	1:37.00	33,180
1981	**Pass the Tab**, 3, 112	J. Velasquez	Spirited Boy, 3, 117	Counter Espionage, 3, 112	7	1:35.20	33,300
1980	**Far Out East**, 3, 113	C. B. Asmussen	Dunham's Gift, 3, 112	Settlement Day, 3, 111	12	1:34.00	35,100
1979	**Belle's Gold**, 3, 118	L. A. Pincay Jr.	Lean Lad, 3, 107	Gallant Best, 3, 113	10	1:33.60	33,180
1978	**Regal and Royal**, 3, 116	J. Fell	Squire Ambler, 3, 111	Roman Reasoning, 3, 112	8	1:35.00	32,460
1977	**Affiliate**, 3, 124	A. T. Cordero Jr.	Buckfinder, 3, 113	Proud Arion, 3, 115	12	1:35.20	33,660
1976	**Dance Spell**, 3, 119	R. Hernandez	Cojak, 3, 119	Quiet Little Table, 3, 119	8	1:34.00	33,330
1975	**Funalon**, 3, 113	V. A. Bracciale Jr.	Busy Saxon, 3, 114	Precious Elaine, 3, 113	10	1:35.80	34,140

Named for the Jamaica neighborhood of Queens, New York. Jamaica racetrack was located there until it closed in 1959. Grade 3 1978-'87, 2005. Jamaica Breeders' Cup H. 2006. Held at Jamaica 1929-'59. Held at Aqueduct 1960-'77, 1979-'81, 1987. Not held 1933-'35, 1955-'56, 1961-'74, 1995. 6 furlongs 1929-'53, 1957-'60. 1 mile 1975-'94. 1 1/16 miles 1996. Dirt 1929-'93, 2005. Originally scheduled on turf 2005. Three-year-olds and up 1929-'44, 1949-'54, 1960. Fillies 1975. ‡Midnight Call finished third, DQ to fourth, 1986.

Jefferson Cup Stakes

Grade 2 in 2008. Churchill Downs, three-year-olds, 1 1/8 miles, turf. Held June 16, 2007, with a gross value of $221,000. First held in 1977. First graded in 2001. Stakes record 1:47.27 (2000 King Cugat).

Year	Winner	Jockey	Second	Third	Strs	Time	1st Purse
2007	**Inca King**, 3, 117	S. Bridgmohan	Duveen, 3, 123	Jazz Quest, 3, 117	7	1:48.94	$134,280
2006	**Brilliant**, 3, 118	R. Albarado	Tahoe Warrior, 3, 116	Storm Treasure, 3, 116	6	1:48.47	134,547
2005	**Rush Bay**, 3, 116	R. Albarado	Big Prairie, 3, 116	Gun Salute, 3, 120	7	1:48.75	136,648
2004	**Prince Arch**, 3, 120	B. Blanc	Kitten's Joy, 3, 122	Cool Conductor, 3, 116	9	1:50.61	140,244
2003	**Senor Swinger**, 3, 120	R. Albarado	Remind, 3, 116	Rapid Proof, 3, 120	7	1:47.54	136,772
2002	**Orchard Park**, 3, 119	M. Guidry	Mr. Mellon, 3, 112	Quest Star, 3, 113	8	1:48.53	172,050
2001	**Indygo Shiner**, 3, 113	L. J. Meche	Strategic Partner, 3, 119	Fast City, 3, 114	9	1:48.81	175,150
2000	**King Cugat**, 3, 122	R. Albarado	Four On the Floor, 3, 122	Field Cat, 3, 122	10	**1:47.27**	177,940
1999	**Special Coach**, 3, 122	C. H. Velasquez	Silver Chadra, 3, 119	Air Rocket, 3, 122	12	1:49.82	180,110
1998	**Buff**, 3, 122	C. H. Borel	Keene Dancer, 3, 122	Ladies Din, 3, 122	7	1:50.80	175,770
1997	**Greed Is Good**, 3, 115	W. Martinez	Royal Strand (Ire), 3, 117	Crimson Classic, 3, 117	5	1:49.47	69,068
1996	**Unruled**, 3, 119	C. Perret	Broadway Beau, 3, 122	Trail City, 3, 122	7	1:50.07	54,210
1995	**Ago**, 3, 115	S. J. Sellers	Michael's Star, 3, 119	Lemon Drop, 3, 113	11	1:49.48	56,550

Racing — Graded Stakes 357

Year	Winner	Jockey	Second	Third	Strs	Time	1st Purse
1994	Milt's Overture, 3, 112	P. Day	Jaggery John, 3, 122	Camptown Dancer, 3, 117	6	1:48.21	$53,528
1993	Lt. Pinkerton, 3, 115	T. J. Hebert	Snake Eyes, 3, 119	Mi Cielo, 3, 117	6	1:48.27	35,555
1992	Senor Tomas, 3, 122	P. Day	Coaxing Matt, 3, 112	Black Question, 3, 122	7	1:49.80	35,945
1991	Hanging Curve, 3, 119	J. M. Johnson	Wall Street Dancer, 3, 119	Air Force, 3, 112	8	1:50.89	36,368
1990	Divine Warning, 3, 117	J. Deegan	Super Abound, 3, 115	Bioblast, 3, 110	8	1:52.20	36,238
1989	Shy Tom, 3, 120	E. Fires	Captain Savy, 3, 116	Ruszhinka, 3, 112	4	1:49.20	52,114
1988	Stop the Stage, 3, 115	M. McDowell	Cold Cathode, 3, 114	Bates Fay, 3, 115	9	1:51.60	62,310
1987	Fast Forward, 3, 120	R. L. Frazier	Unleavened, 3, 118	Gretna Green, 3, 112	5	1:50.00	63,109
1986	Buffalo Beau, 3, 110	J. McKnight	Clear Choice, 3, 124	Sumptious, 3, 113	7	1:52.80	53,040
1985	Avey's Brother, 3, 110	D. Montoya	La Marseillaise, 3, 110	Hollywood Hackett, 3, 113	10	1:50.00	50,420
1984	Coax Me Chad, 3, 119	W. H. McCauley	Fairly Straight, 3, 114	Last Command, 3, 110	7	1:50.60	48,958
1983	Pron Regard, 3, 116	C. R. Woods Jr.	Le Cou Cou, 3, 125	Whitesburg Lark, 3, 112	9	1:51.60	36,303
1982	Wavering Monarch, 3, 111	R. P. Romero	Forli's Jet, 3, 117	Noted, 3, 111	6	1:44.20	23,026
1981	Talent Town, 2, 122	B. Sayler	Helen's Tip, 2, 122	Ken's Revenge, 2, 122	11	1:05.40	19,858
1980	Golden Derby, 2, 125	J. C. Espinoza	†Plain Speaking, 2, 119	Bold Tyson, 2, 125	7	1:04.20	19,256
1979	Rockhill Native, 2, 122	J. Oldham	Earl of Odessa, 2, 122	Egg's Dynamite, 2, 122	9	1:05.20	19,581
1978	Future Hope, 2, 122	A. Rini	Backstabber, 2, 125	Amber White, 2, 117	6	1:05.20	14,073
1977	Old Jake, 2, 122	J. C. Espinoza	Bolero's Orphan, 2, 122	Set in My Ways, 2, 122	7	1:04.80	14,219

Named for Jefferson County, Kentucky, home of Churchill Downs. Grade 3 2001-'05. 5½ furlongs 1977-'81. 1¹⁄₁₆ miles 1982. Dirt 1977-'87. Two-year-olds 1977-'81. †Denotes female.

Jenny Wiley Stakes

Grade 2 in 2008. Keeneland Race Course, four-year-olds and up, fillies and mares, 1¹⁄₁₆ miles, turf. Held April 12, 2008, with a gross value of $200,000. First held in 1989. First graded in 1995. Stakes record 1:40.78 (1996 Apolda).

Year	Winner	Jockey	Second	Third	Strs	Time	1st Purse
2008	Rutherienne, 4, 119	G. K. Gomez	Stormy West, 4, 117	Lady of Venice (Fr), 5, 119	10	1:44.76	$124,000
2007	My Typhoon (Ire), 5, 119	E. Castro	Precious Kitten, 4, 123	Fantastic Shirl, 4, 117	6	1:43.37	124,000
2006	Wend, 5, 117	E. S. Prado	Asi Siempre, 4, 117	Mirabilis, 4, 118	8	1:41.34	124,000
2005	Intercontinental (GB), 5, 123	J. D. Bailey	Delta Princess, 6, 117	Sister Swank, 4, 117	7	1:41.89	124,000
2004	Intercontinental (GB), 4, 116	J. D. Bailey	Ocean Drive, 4, 116	Madeira Mist (Ire), 5, 118	7	1:41.41	68,386
2003	Sea of Showers, 4, 116	J. D. Bailey	Magic Mission (GB), 5, 116	Snow Dance, 5, 116	10	1:41.89	70,246
2002	Tates Creek, 4, 116	K. Desormeaux	Snow Dance, 4, 123	Step With Style, 5, 116	10	1:42.27	70,432
2001	Penny's Gold, 4, 116	J. A. Santos	License Fee, 6, 118	Solvig, 4, 117	9	1:40.93	70,618
2000	Astra, 4, 118	C. S. Nakatani	Pratella, 5, 118	Ronda (GB), 4, 116	8	1:42.48	69,688
1999	Pleasant Temper, 5, 117	J. D. Bailey	Mingling Glances, 5, 114	Red Cat, 4, 117	8	1:40.93	70,246
1998	Maxzene, 5, 114	J. A. Santos	Parade Queen, 4, 121	Rumpipumpy (GB), 5, 114	7	1:42.82	69,192
1997	Thrilling Day (GB), 4, 115	W. Martinez	Romy, 6, 121	Gastronomical, 4, 115	7	1:41.16	68,634
1996	Apolda, 5, 121	J. D. Bailey	Mediation (Ire), 4, 118	Luzette (Brz), 6, 121	9	**1:40.78**	69,006
1995	Romy, 4, 119	F. C. Torres	Weekend Madness (Ire), 5, 121	Bold Ruritana, 5, 121	9	1:43.32	52,173
1994	Misspitch, 4, 118	M. E. Smith	Park Dream (Ire), 5, 112	Sh Bang, 5, 118	10	1:43.83	34,658
1993	Lady Blessington (Fr), 5, 118	P. Day	Radiant Ring, 5, 118	Super Fan, 6, 118	6	1:42.59	34,844
1992	Indian Fashion, 5, 115	J. A. Santos	Spanish Parade, 4, 121	Radiant Ring, 4, 121	10	1:41.26	36,514
1991	Foresta, 5, 115	A. T. Cordero Jr.	Dance for Lucy, 5, 121	The Caretaker (Ire), 4, 115	10	1:43.88	37,115
1990	Regal Wonder, 6, 121	R. D. Lopez	Majestic Legend, 5, 121	Phoenix Sunshine, 5, 115	8	1:46.20	36,043
1989	Native Mommy, 6, 121	C. Perret	Blossoming Beauty, 4, 113	Here's Your Silver, 4, 115	8	1:43.60	35,864

Named for Eastern Kentucky heroine Jenny Wiley (1760-1831), a pioneer woman who was captured by Indians and escaped to return to her family. Grade 3 1995-2005. About 1¹⁄₁₆ miles 1991. All weather 2006. Originally scheduled on turf 2006. Course record 1992, '96.

Jerome Handicap

Grade 2 in 2008. Belmont Park, three-year-olds, 1 mile, dirt. Held October 7, 2007, with a gross value of $160,100. First held in 1866. First graded in 1973. Stakes record 1:33.20 (1981 Noble Nashua).

Year	Winner	Jockey	Second	Third	Strs	Time	1st Purse
2007	Daaher, 3, 115	M. J. Luzzi	Forefathers, 3, 115	Owners Manual, 3, 115	8	1:34.28	$96,060
2006	Discreet Cat, 3, 124	G. K. Gomez	Valid Notebook, 3, 114	Nar, 3, 116	5	1:36.46	95,280
2005	Silver Train, 3, 114	E. S. Prado	High Fly, 3, 120	Naughty New Yorker, 3, 115	6	1:34.24	90,000
2004	Teton Forest, 3, 116	S. Bridgmohan	Ice Wynnd Fire, 3, 116	Mahzouz, 3, 112	7	1:35.74	90,000
2003	During, 3, 118	J. A. Santos	Tafaseel, 3, 114	Pretty Wild, 3, 116	9	1:36.32	90,000
2002	Boston Common, 3, 118	J. F. Chavez	Vinemeister, 3, 115	No Parole, 3, 115	7	1:36.12	90,000
2001	Express Tour, 3, 115	J. R. Velazquez	Illusioned, 3, 117	Burning Roma, 3, 120	5	1:34.57	90,000
2000	Fusaichi Pegasus, 3, 124	K. Desormeaux	El Corredor, 3, 117	Albert the Great, 3, 120	6	1:34.07	90,000
1999	Doneraile Court, 3, 117	C. W. Antley	Vicar, 3, 120	Badger Gold, 3, 115	7	1:35.63	90,000
1998	Limit Out, 3, 117	J. Samyn	Grand Slam, 3, 120	Scatmandu, 3, 115	5	1:36.22	90,000
1997	Richter Scale, 3, 118	S. J. Sellers	Trafalger, 3, 117	Smokin Mel, 3, 115	8	1:35.88	90,000
1996	Why Change, 3, 112	C. C. Lopez	Distorted Humor, 3, 115	Diligence, 3, 117	10	1:34.22	90,000
1995	French Deputy, 3, 113	G. L. Stevens	Mr. Greeley, 3, 117	Top Account, 3, 115	6	1:33.53	120,000
1994	Prenup, 3, 113	J. D. Bailey	Ulises, 3, 112	End Sweep, 3, 118	6	1:34.59	120,000
1993	Schossberg, 3, 113	J. D. Bailey	Williamstown, 3, 118	Mi Cielo, 3, 116	5	1:35.53	120,000
1992	Furiously, 3, 113	J. D. Bailey	Colony Light, 3, 111	Dixie Brass, 3, 122	6	1:34.20	120,000
1991	Scan, 3, 117	J. A. Santos	Excellent Tipper, 3, 113	King Mutesa, 3, 113	8	1:34.09	120,000
1990	Housebuster, 3, 126	C. Perret	Citidancer, 3, 114	D'Parrot, 3, 112	5	1:34.00	102,060

Racing — Graded Stakes

Year	Winner	Jockey	Second	Third	Strs	Time	1st Purse
1989	De Roche, 3, 108	D. Carr	Fast Play, 3, 116	I'm Influential, 3, 111	5	1:34.40	$134,880
1988	Evening Kris, 3, 119	J. D. Bailey	dh-Din's Dancer, 3, 113		7	1:37.80	176,400
			dh-Parlay Me, 3, 113				
1987	Afleet, 3, 115	G. Stahlbaum	Stacked Pack, 3, 109	Templar Hill, 3, 117	9	1:33.80	107,640
1986	Ogygian, 3, 126	W. A. Guerra	Mogambo, 3, 119	Moment of Hope, 3, 111	5	1:34.00	127,620
1985	Creme Fraiche, 3, 124	E. Maple	Pancho Villa, 3, 119	El Basco, 3, 114	8	1:34.60	109,260
1984	Is Your Pleasure, 3, 114	D. MacBeth	Track Barron, 3, 124	Concorde Bound, 3, 115	9	1:35.20	109,080
1983	A Phenomenon, 3, 116	A. T. Cordero Jr.	Desert Wine, 3, 124	Copelan, 3, 118	8	1:35.00	104,940
1982	Fit to Fight, 3, 112	J. D. Bailey	John's Gold, 3, 115	Lord Lister, 3, 107	6	1:35.40	101,880
1981	Noble Nashua, 3, 120	C. B. Asmussen	Maudlin, 3, 112	Sing Sing, 3, 109	11	**1:33.20**	69,000
1980	Jaklin Klugman, 3, 122	C. J. McCarron	Fappiano, 3, 114	Plugged Nickle, 3, 124	6	1:34.20	67,320
1979	Czaravich, 3, 122	J. Cruguet	Valdez, 3, 122	Gallant Best, 3, 112	10	1:35.20	65,580
1978	Sensitive Prince, 3, 118	J. Vasquez	Darby Creek Road, 3, 122	Sorry Lookin, 3, 112	5	1:36.00	62,940
1977	‡Broadway Forli, 3, 111	P. Day	‡To the Quick, 3, 112	Affiliate, 3, 120	10	1:36.20	66,360
1976	Dance Spell, 3, 117	R. Hernandez	Soy Numero Uno, 3, 117	Clean Bill, 3, 112	10	1:35.00	66,600
1975	Guards Up, 3, 114	C. C. Lopez	Valid Appeal, 3, 119	Great Above, 3, 114	7	1:34.20	33,720
1974	Stonewalk, 3, 126	A. T. Cordero Jr.	Best of It, 3, 117	Heir to the Line, 3, 113	9	1:34.00	34,470
1973	Step Nicely, 3, 118	A. T. Cordero Jr.	Forego, 3, 124	Linda's Chief, 3, 126	10	1:34.00	34,800

Named for Leonard Jerome (1817-'91), builder of Jerome Park and president of Coney Island Jockey Club. Jerome was also the maternal grandfather of Sir Winston Churchill. Grade 1 1984-'94. Jerome S. 1866, 1872-'92. Champion S. 1867-'71. Jerome Breeders' Cup H. 2006. Held at Jerome Park 1866-'89. Held at Morris Park 1890-1904. Held at Aqueduct 1960, 1962-'67, 1972-'74. Not held 1910-'13. One mile heats 1866-'70. Two miles 1871-'77. 1¾ miles 1878-'89. 1⁵/₁₆ miles 1890-'91, 1903-'09. 1½ miles 1892. 1¼ miles 1893-'94, 1896, 1914. 1⅛ miles 1895. Dead heat for second 1988. ‡To the Quick finished first, DQ to second, 1977. ‡Affiliate finished second, DQ to third, 1977.

Jersey Shore Stakes

Grade 3 in 2008. Monmouth Park, three-year-olds, 6 furlongs, dirt. Held July 4, 2007, with a gross value of $150,000. First held in 1992. First graded in 1994. Stakes record 1:07.47 (2007 Idiot Proof).

Year	Winner	Jockey	Second	Third	Strs	Time	1st Purse
2007	Idiot Proof, 3, 119	R. Maragh	Spin Master, 3, 123	Principle Secret, 3, 119	7	**1:07.47**	$90,000
2006	Henny Hughes, 3, 119	J. Bravo	Saint Daimon, 3, 119	He's Got Grit, 3, 119	4	1:08.26	90,000
2005	Joey P., 3, 117	J. Bravo	Celtic Innis, 3, 122	Razor, 3, 122	5	1:08.30	75,000
2004	Pomeroy, 3, 113	J. Bravo	Gotaghostofachance, 3, 115	Midnight Express, 3, 113	5	1:09.07	60,000
2003	Gators N Bears, 3, 115	C. C. Lopez	Mt. Carson, 3, 122	Don Six, 3, 115	6	1:09.80	60,000
2002	Boston Common, 3, 117	E. M. Martin Jr.	Listen Here, 3, 117	It's a Monster, 3, 115	6	1:09.35	60,000
2001	City Zip, 3, 119	J. C. Ferrer	Sea of Green, 3, 117	Songandaprayer, 3, 122	5	1:09.02	60,000
2000	Disco Rico, 3, 115	J. Bravo	Max's Pal, 3, 122	Stormin Oedy, 3, 117	6	1:09.05	60,000
1999	Yes It's True, 3, 122	J. D. Bailey	Erlton, 3, 122	Flying Griffoni, 3, 112	4	1:08.59	60,000
1998	Good and Tough, 3, 117	W. H. McCauley	Klabin's Gold, 3, 117	El Mirasol, 3, 112	6	1:10.01	45,000
1997	Smoke Glacken, 3, 122	C. Perret	Partner's Hero, 3, 115	King Buck, 3, 115	4	1:08.53	45,000
1996	Swing and Miss, 3, 112	T. G. Turner	Seacliff, 3, 119	Dixie Connection, 3, 115	6	1:10.00	60,000
1995	Ft. Stockton, 3, 115	J. Bravo	Jealous Crusader, 3, 115	Gala Knockout, 3, 115	9	1:22.64	64,050
1994	End Sweep, 3, 115	M. E. Smith	Meadow Flight, 3, 122	Foxie G, 3, 115	5	1:21.20	63,450
1993	Montbrook, 3, 122	C. J. Ladner III	Evil Bear, 3, 114	Shu Fellow, 3, 114	7	1:21.04	63,420
1992	Surely Six, 3, 112	R. Wilson	Superstrike (GB), 3, 122	Salt Lake, 3, 119	4	1:21.94	64,230

Monmouth Park is located on the coast of New Jersey. Jersey Shore Budweiser Breeders' Cup S. 1992-'95. Jersey Shore Breeders' Cup S. 1996-2007. Held at Atlantic City 1992-'96. 7 furlongs 1992-'95. Track record 2007.

Jim Dandy Stakes

Grade 2 in 2008. Saratoga Race Course, three-year-olds, 1⅛ miles, dirt. Held July 29, 2007, with a gross value of $500,000. First held in 1964. First graded in 1973. Stakes record 1:47.26 (1996 Louis Quatorze).

Year	Winner	Jockey	Second	Third	Strs	Time	1st Purse
2007	Street Sense, 3, 123	C. H. Borel	C P West, 3, 115	Sightseeing, 3, 121	6	1:48.99	$300,000
2006	Bernardini, 3, 123	J. Castellano	Minister's Bid, 3, 115	Hemingway's Key, 3, 115	5	1:50.50	300,000
2005	Flower Alley, 3, 121	J. R. Velazquez	Reverberate, 3, 115	Andromeda's Hero, 3, 117	5	1:49.50	300,000
2004	Purge, 3, 121	J. R. Velazquez	The Cliff's Edge, 3, 123	‡Niigon, 3, 117	6	1:47.56	300,000
2003	Strong Hope, 3, 121	J. R. Velazquez	Empire Maker, 3, 123	Congrats, 3, 115	6	1:48.10	300,000
2002	Medaglia d'Oro, 3, 121	J. D. Bailey	‡Gold Dollar, 3, 115	Essence of Dubai, 3, 121	9	1:47.82	300,000
2001	Scorpion, 3, 114	J. D. Bailey	Free of Love, 3, 114	Congaree, 3, 123	6	1:48.90	360,000
2000	Graeme Hall, 3, 120	J. D. Bailey	Curule, 3, 114	Unshaded, 3, 120	7	1:48.95	240,000
1999	Ecton Park, 3, 116	A. O. Solis	Lemon Drop Kid, 3, 124	Badger Gold, 3, 114	7	1:49.52	180,000
1998	Favorite Trick, 3, 119	P. Day	Deputy Diamond, 3, 114	Raffie's Majesty, 3, 114	7	1:50.00	150,000
1997	Awesome Again, 3, 116	M. E. Smith	Glitman, 3, 114	Affirmed Success, 3, 114	9	1:51.00	150,000
1996	Louis Quatorze, 3, 124	P. Day	Will's Way, 3, 114	Secreto de Estado, 3, 114	8	**1:47.26**	90,000
1995	Composer, 3, 121	J. D. Bailey	Malthus, 3, 117	Pat n Jac, 3, 112	7	1:51.13	82,575
1994	Unaccounted For, 3, 112	J. A. Santos	Tabasco Cat, 3, 126	Ulises, 3, 114	5	1:49.69	80,820
1993	Miner's Mark, 3, 117	C. J. McCarron	Virginia Rapids, 3, 121	Colonial Affair, 3, 126	6	1:49.01	90,000
1992	Thunder Rumble, 3, 114	W. H. McCauley	Dixie Brass, 3, 126	Devil His Due, 3, 126	8	1:47.53	108,000
1991	Fly So Free, 3, 126	J. A. Santos	Upon My Soul, 3, 114	Strike the Gold, 3, 128	8	1:48.88	107,820
1990	Chief Honcho, 3, 114	M. E. Smith	Senator to Be, 3, 114	Paradise Found, 3, 114	4	1:51.60	67,680
1989	Is It True, 3, 121	J. A. Santos	Fast Play, 3, 114	Roi Danzig, 3, 126	7	1:48.40	99,180
1988	Brian's Time, 3, 126	A. T. Cordero Jr.	Evening Kris, 3, 121	Din's Dancer, 3, 114	10	1:48.20	109,980

Racing — Graded Stakes 359

Year	Winner	Jockey	Second	Third	Strs	Time	1st Purse
1987	Polish Navy, 3, 117	P. Day	Pledge Card, 3, 117	Cryptoclearance, 3, 126	7	1:48.40	$106,740
1986	Lac Ouimet, 3, 114	E. Maple	Moment of Hope, 3, 114	Wayar, 3, 114	5	1:48.00	69,360
1985	Stephan's Odyssey, 3, 123	L. A. Pincay Jr.	Don's Choice, 3, 114	Government Corner, 3, 121	9	1:48.80	73,080
1984	Carr de Naskra, 3, 114	E. Maple	Slew the Coup, 3, 114	Raja's Shark, 3, 114	10	1:47.40	75,720
1983	A Phenomenon, 3, 114	A. T. Cordero Jr.	Timeless Native, 3, 126	Head of the House, 3, 114	8	1:49.40	33,900
1982	Conquistador Cielo, 3, 128	E. Maple	Lejoli, 3, 114	No Home Run, 3, 114	4	1:48.60	32,700
1981	Willow Hour, 3, 117	E. Maple	Lemhi Gold, 3, 117	Silver Supreme, 3, 114	8	1:49.20	34,200
1980	Plugged Nickle, 3, 128	J. Fell	Current Legend, 3, 121	Herb Water, 3, 114	8	1:49.40	34,140
1979	Private Account, 3, 114	J. Fell	Instrument Landing, 3, 126	Pianist, 3, 114	4	1:48.40	25,500
1978	Affirmed, 3, 128	S. Cauthen	Sensitive Prince, 3, 119	Bound Green, 3, 114	5	1:47.80	22,155
1977	Music of Time, 3, 114	M. Venezia	Sanhedrin, 3, 114	Super Joy, 3, 114	10	1:50.40	22,830
1976	Father Hogan, 3, 114	M. Venezia	Dance Spell, 3, 121	El Portugues, 3, 114	10	1:48.80	22,410
1975	Forceten, 3, 126	D. Pierce	Prince Thou Art, 3, 123	Northerly, 3, 114	6	1:48.40	25,725
1974	Sea Songster, 3, 114	A. T. Cordero Jr.	‡Hatchet Man, 3, 120	Bobby Murcer, 3, 114	7	1:50.60	22,860
1973	Cheriepe, 3, 117	E. Belmonte	Arbees Boy, 3, 120	Bemo, 3, 123	9	1:50.20	17,310

Named for 100-to-1 1930 Travers S. winner Jim Dandy (1927 g. by Jim Gaffney), who upset heavily favored rivals Gallant Fox and Whichone. Grade 3 1973-'83. Grade 1 2001. 1 mile 1964-'70. 7 furlongs 1971. ‡T. V. Newscaster finished second, DQ to fourth, 1974. ‡Quest finished second, DQ to eighth, 2002. ‡Eddington finished third, DQ to fourth, 2004.

Jim Murray Memorial Handicap

Grade 2 in 2008. Hollywood Park, three-year-olds and up, 1½ miles, turf. Held May 10, 2008, with a gross value of $245,000. First held in 1990. First graded in 2005. Stakes record 2:25.31 (2003 Storming Home [GB]).

Year	Winner	Jockey	Second	Third	Strs	Time	1st Purse
2008	On the Acorn (GB), 7, 116	B. Blanc	Champs Elysees (GB), 5, 119	Sudan (Ire), 5, 116	4	2:27.36	$150,000
2007	On the Acorn (GB), 6, 116	V. Espinoza	Prospect Park (GB), 6, 119	Notable Guest, 6, 115	6	2:29.07	150,000
2006	Grey Swallow (Ire), 5, 121	A. O. Solis	Brecon Beacon (GB), 4, 118	Runaway Dancer, 7, 115	5	2:27.33	150,000
2005	Runaway Dancer, 6, 115	G. K. Gomez	Vangelis, 6, 117	Exterior, 4, 117	8	2:26.75	210,000
2004	Rhythm Mad (Fr), 4, 116	A. O. Solis	Continental Red, 8, 117	Gassan Royal, 4, 113	7	2:26.73	210,000
2003	Storming Home (GB), 5, 122	G. L. Stevens	Denon, 5, 122	Ballingarry (Ire), 4, 120	8	**2:25.31**	240,000
2002	Skipping (GB), 5, 116	K. Desormeaux	Startac, 4, 120	Our Main Man, 4, 114	7	2:26.23	46,485
2001	Kudos, 4, 116	E. Delahoussaye	Indigo Myth, 4, 115	Piranesi (Ire), 5, 113	4	2:26.74	45,900
2000	Bienamado, 4, 121	C. J. McCarron	Casino King (Ire), 5, 117	Adcat, 5, 116	8	1:58.93	47,070
1999	Lazy Lode (Arg), 5, 122	C. S. Nakatani	Musgrave, 4, 116	Astarabad, 5, 121	7	2:01.44	42,690
1998	Cote d'Azur (Ire), 4, 114	C. S. Nakatani	Belgravia (GB), 4, 113	Kaafih Homm (Ire), 7, 115	5	2:30.23	42,800
1997	Percutant (GB), 6, 120	G. L. Stevens	Seaborg (Arg), 6, 119	Big Sky Jim, 5, 116	7	2:26.10	43,800
1996	Polish Admiral (GB), 5, 117	B. Blanc	Big Sky Jim, 4, 116	Bedivere, 4, 115	6	2:26.13	40,500
1995	Jahafil (GB), 7, 117	C. J. McCarron	Talloires, 5, 119	Exalto, 4, 114	7	2:25.45	63,700
1994	Mashaallah, 6, 119	L. A. Pincay Jr.	Marfamatic, 5, 114	Samourzakan (Ire), 5, 116	4	2:25.37	46,600
1993	Toulon (GB), 5, 117	E. Delahoussaye	Beyton, 4, 118	Super Fleet, 4, 111	4	2:26.67	45,850
1992	Berillon (GB), 5, 115	C. S. Nakatani	Single Dawn, 5, 112	Carnival Baby, 4, 114	7	2:26.80	48,900
1991	Sahib's Light, 5, 116	G. L. Stevens	Black Monday (GB), 5, 114	Razeen, 4, 117	12	2:25.90	52,150
1990	Shotiche, 4, 114	C. A. Black	Record Boom, 4, 114	Kaboi, 4, 115	12	2:00.60	50,450

Named for Pulitzer Prize-winning Los Angeles Times sports columnist Jim Murray (1919-'98). Grade 3 2005.

Jockey Club Gold Cup Stakes

Grade 1 in 2008. Belmont Park, three-year-olds and up, 1¼ miles, dirt. Held September 30, 2007, with a gross value of $765,000. First held in 1919. First graded in 1973. Stakes record 1:58.89 (1997 Skip Away).

Year	Winner	Jockey	Second	Third	Strs	Time	1st Purse
2007	Curlin, 3, 122	R. Albarado	Lawyer Ron, 4, 126	Political Force, 4, 126	7	2:01.20	$450,000
2006	Bernardini, 3, 122	J. Castellano	Wanderin Boy, 5, 126	Andromeda's Hero, 4, 126	4	2:01.38	450,000
2005	Borrego, 4, 126	G. K. Gomez	Suave, 4, 126	Sun King, 3, 122	8	2:02.86	600,000
2004	Funny Cide, 4, 126	J. A. Santos	Newfoundland, 4, 126	The Cliff's Edge, 3, 122	7	2:02.44	600,000
2003	Mineshaft, 4, 126	R. Albarado	Quest, 4, 126	Evening Attire, 5, 126	5	2:00.25	600,000
2002	Evening Attire, 4, 126	S. Bridgmohan	Lido Palace (Chi), 5, 126	Harlan's Holiday, 3, 122	8	1:59.58	600,000
2001	Aptitude, 4, 126	J. D. Bailey	Generous Rosi (GB), 6, 126	Country Be Gold, 4, 126	7	2:01.49	600,000
2000	Albert the Great, 3, 122	J. F. Chavez	Gander, 4, 126	Vision and Verse, 4, 126	7	1:59.24	600,000
1999	River Keen (Ire), 7, 126	C. W. Antley	Behrens, 5, 126	Almutawakel (GB), 4, 126	8	2:01.40	600,000
1998	Wagon Limit, 4, 126	R. G. Davis	Gentlemen (Arg), 6, 126	Skip Away (GB), 6, 126	6	2:00.62	600,000
1997	Skip Away, 4, 126	J. D. Bailey	Instant Friendship, 4, 126	Wagon Limit, 3, 121	7	**1:58.89**	600,000
1996	Skip Away, 3, 121	S. J. Sellers	Cigar, 6, 126	Louis Quatorze, 3, 121	6	2:00.70	600,000
1995	Cigar, 5, 126	J. D. Bailey	Unaccounted For, 4, 126	Star Standard, 3, 121	7	2:01.29	450,000
1994	Colonial Affair, 4, 126	J. A. Santos	Devil His Due, 5, 126	Flag Down, 4, 126	8	2:02.19	450,000
1993	Miner's Mark, 3, 121	C. J. McCarron	Colonial Affair, 3, 121	Brunswick, 4, 126	7	2:02.79	510,000
1992	Pleasant Tap, 5, 126	G. L. Stevens	Strike the Gold, 4, 126	A.P. Indy, 3, 121	7	1:58.95	510,000
1991	Festin (Arg), 5, 126	E. Delahoussaye	Chief Honcho, 4, 126	Strike the Gold, 3, 121	8	2:02.20	510,000
1990	Flying Continental, 4, 126	C. A. Black	De Roche, 4, 126	Izvestia, 3, 121	6	2:00.60	503,100
1989	Easy Goer, 3, 121	P. Day	Cryptoclearance, 5, 126	Forever Silver, 4, 126	7	2:29.20	659,400
1988	Waquoit, 4, 126	J. A. Santos	Personal Flag, 5, 126	Easy N Dirty, 4, 126	7	2:28.60	637,800
1987	Creme Fraiche, 5, 126	L. A. Pincay Jr.	Java Gold, 3, 121	Easy N Dirty, 4, 126	6	2:30.80	650,400
1986	Creme Fraiche, 4, 126	R. P. Romero	Turkoman, 4, 126	Danzig Connection, 3, 121	6	2:28.00	510,300
1985	Vanlandingham, 4, 126	P. Day	Gate Dancer, 4, 126	Creme Fraiche, 3, 121	7	2:27.00	516,600
1984	Slew o' Gold, 4, 126	A. T. Cordero Jr.	Hail Bold King, 3, 126	Bounding Basque, 4, 126	5	2:28.80	1,350,400

Year	Winner	Jockey	Second	Third	Strs	Time	1st Purse
1983	Slew o' Gold, 3, 121	A. T. Cordero Jr.	Highland Blade, 5, 126	Bounding Basque, 3, 121	11	2:26.20	$342,000
1982	Lemhi Gold, 4, 126	C. J. McCarron	Silver Supreme, 4, 126	†Christmas Past, 3, 118	10	2:31.20	337,800
1981	John Henry, 6, 126	W. Shoemaker	Peat Moss, 6, 126	†Relaxing, 5, 123	11	2:28.40	340,800
1980	Temperence Hill, 3, 121	E. Maple	John Henry, 5, 126	Ivory Hunter, 6, 126	7	2:30.20	329,400
1979	Affirmed, 4, 126	L. A. Pincay Jr.	Spectacular Bid, 3, 121	Coastal, 3, 121	4	2:27.40	225,000
1978	Exceller, 5, 126	W. Shoemaker	Seattle Slew, 4, 126	Great Contractor, 5, 126	6	2:27.20	193,080
1977	On the Sly, 4, 126	G. McCarron	Great Contractor, 4, 126	Cox's Ridge, 3, 121	13	2:28.20	208,080
1976	Great Contractor, 3, 121	P. Day	Appassionato, 3, 121	†Revidere, 3, 118	10	2:28.80	201,360
1975	Group Plan, 5, 124	J. Velasquez	Wajima, 3, 119	Outdoors, 6, 124	4	3:23.20	95,850
1974	Forego, 4, 124	H. Gustines	*Copte, 4, 124	Group Plan, 4, 124	8	3:21.20	67,140
1973	Prove Out, 4, 124	J. Velasquez	Loud, 6, 124	Twice a Prince, 3, 119	6	3:20.00	66,060

Named for the Jockey Club, keeper of the *American Stud Book*, and registrar of North American Thoroughbreds. Jockey Club S. 1919-'20. Held at Aqueduct 1959-'61, 1963-'67, 1969-'74. 1½ miles 1919-'20, 1976-'89. 2 miles 1921-'75. Colts and fillies 1944. †Denotes female. Winner's purse includes $1-million bonus for winning the Woodward S. (G1), Marlboro Cup (G1), and Jockey Club Gold Cup (G1) 1984.

Joe Hirsch Turf Classic Invitational Stakes

Grade 1 in 2008. Belmont Park, three-year-olds and up, 1½ miles, turf. Held September 30, 2007, with a gross value of $612,000. First held in 1977. First graded in 1979. Stakes record 2:24.50 (1992 Sky Classic).

Year	Winner	Jockey	Second	Third	Strs	Time	1st Purse
2007	English Channel, 5, 126	J. R. Velazquez	Stream of Gold (Ire), 6, 126	Interpatation, 5, 126	7	2:25.73	$360,000
2006	English Channel, 4, 126	J. R. Velazquez	†Freedonia (GB), 4, 123	†Royal Highness (Ger), 4, 123	7	2:28.69	360,000
2005	Shakespeare, 4, 126	J. D. Bailey	English Channel, 3, 121	Ace (Ire), 4, 126	7	2:27.22	450,000
2004	Kitten's Joy, 3, 121	J. R. Velazquez	Magistretti, 4, 126	Tycoon (GB), 3, 121	7	2:29.97	450,000
2003	Sulamani (Ire), 4, 126	J. D. Bailey	Deeliteful Irving, 5, 126	Balto Star, 5, 126	7	2:27.51	450,000
2002	Denon, 4, 126	E. S. Prado	Blazing Fury, 4, 126	Delta Form (Aus), 6, 126	8	2:28.47	450,000
2001	Timboroa (GB), 5, 126	E. S. Prado	King Cugat, 4, 126	Ceteways, 7, 126	6	2:29.43	450,000
2000	John's Call, 9, 126	J. Samyn	Craigsteel (GB), 5, 126	†Ela Athena (GB), 4, 126	12	2:28.58	450,000
1999	Val's Prince, 7, 126	J. F. Chavez	Dream Well (Fr), 4, 126	Fahris (Ire), 5, 126	7	2:28.63	360,000
1998	Buck's Boy, 5, 126	S. J. Sellers	Cetewayo, 4, 126	Lazy Lode (Arg), 4, 126	6	2:33.25	300,000
1997	Val's Prince, 5, 126	M. E. Smith	Flag Down, 7, 126	Ops Smile, 5, 126	5	2:28.92	300,000
1996	Diplomatic Jet, 4, 126	J. F. Chavez	Awad, 6, 126	Marlin, 3, 121	10	2:27.51	300,000
1995	Turk Passer, 5, 126	J. R. Velazquez	Hernando (Fr), 5, 126	Celtic Arms (Fr), 4, 126	8	2:36.63	300,000
1994	Tikkanen, 3, 121	C. B. Asmussen	Vaudeville, 3, 121	†Yenda (GB), 3, 118	6	2:25.88	300,000
1993	Apple Tree (Fr), 4, 126	M. E. Smith	Solar Splendor, 6, 126	George Augustus, 5, 126	5	2:28.31	300,000
1992	Sky Classic, 5, 126	P. Day	Fraise, 4, 126	Solar Splendor, 5, 126	6	2:24.50	300,000
1991	Solar Splendor, 4, 126	W. H. McCauley	Dear Doctor (Fr), 4, 126	‡Fortune's Wheel (Ire), 3, 121	9	2:27.89	300,000
1990	Cacoethes, 4, 126	R. Cochrane	Alwuhush, 5, 126	With Approval, 4, 126	6	2:25.00	360,000
1989	Yankee Affair, 7, 126	J. A. Santos	El Senor, 5, 126	My Big Boy, 6, 126	7	2:27.20	392,550
1988	Sunshine Forever, 3, 121	A. T. Cordero Jr.	My Big Boy, 5, 126	Most Welcome (GB), 4, 126	9	2:33.80	360,000
1987	Theatrical (Ire), 5, 126	P. Day	†River Memories, 3, 116	Talakeno, 7, 126	6	2:29.20	360,000
1986	Manila, 3, 119	J. A. Santos	Damister, 4, 126	Danger's Hour, 4, 126	9	2:27.80	423,150
1985	Noble Fighter, 3, 119	A. Lequeux	Win, 5, 126	Strawberry Road (Aus), 6, 126	12	2:25.40	431,100
1984	John Henry, 9, 126	C. J. McCarron	Win, 4, 126	Majesty's Prince, 5, 126	6	2:25.20	375,150
1983	†All Along (Fr), 4, 123	W. R. Swinburn	Thunder Puddles, 4, 126	Erins Isle (Ire), 5, 126	10	2:34.00	351,420
1982	†April Run (Ire), 4, 123	C. B. Asmussen	Naskra's Breeze, 5, 126	Bottled Water, 7, 126	9	2:29.80	286,080
1981	†April Run (Ire), 3, 118	P. Paquet	Galaxy Libra (Ire), 5, 126	†The Very One, 6, 123	9	2:31.20	180,000
1980	†Anifa, 4, 123	A. Gilbert	Golden Act, 4, 126	John Henry, 5, 126	8	2:30.60	180,000
1979	Bowl Game, 5, 126	J. Velasquez	†Trillion, 5, 123	Native Courier, 4, 126	7	2:28.20	150,000
1978	†Waya (Fr), 4, 123	A. T. Cordero Jr.	Tiller, 4, 126	†Trillion, 4, 123	6	2:26.80	130,000
1977	Johnny D., 3, 122	S. Cauthen	Majestic Light, 4, 126	Crow (Fr), 4, 126	9	2:23.20	130,000

Named in honor of Joe Hirsch, retired executive columnist of the *Daily Racing Form* and dean of American Turf writers. Turf Classic Invitational S. 1977-2003. Held at Aqueduct 1977-'79, 1981-'83. ‡Spinning (Ire) finished third, DQ to fourth, 1991. Course record 1992. †Denotes female.

John B. Connally Turf Handicap

Grade 3 in 2008. Sam Houston Race Park, three-year-olds and up, 1⅛ miles, turf. Held April 5, 2008, with a gross value of $168,500. First held in 1995. First graded in 2006. Stakes record 1:47.65 (1999 Chorwon).

Year	Winner	Jockey	Second	Third	Strs	Time	1st Purse
2008	Scrappy Roo, 5, 115	P. M. Nolan	Going Ballistic, 4, 116	Eighteenthofmarch, 4, 114	8	1:51.65	$90,000
2007	Mending Fences, 5, 114	Q. Hamilton	Embossed (Ire), 5, 117	General Charley, 5, 114	7	1:52.34	128,400
2006	Fort Prado, 5, 120	R. Albarado	Dynareign, 6, 116	Dontbotherknocking, 8, 115	11	1:49.41	103,800
2005	Rapid Proof, 5, 118	B. Hernandez Jr.	Warleigh, 7, 117	Dynareign, 5, 114	8	1:51.31	129,600
2004	Warleigh, 6, 116	J. Beasley	Skate Away, 5, 117	Gentlemen J J, 4, 109	11	1:53.01	133,200
2003	Candid Glen, 5, 113	E. J. Perrodin	Red Mountain, 6, 113	Dynameaux, 5, 114	11	1:53.21	133,800
2002	Candid Glen, 4, 114	E. J. Perrodin	Nat's Big Party, 8, 114	El Gran Papa, 5, 116	10	1:50.38	133,200
2001	Candid Glen, 4, 114	E. J. Perrodin	Profit Option, 6, 114	Gold Nugget, 4, 114	9	1:50.51	131,400
2000	Rod and Staff, 7, 115	R. Albarado	Vilaxy, 5, 114	Tangazi, 5, 115	11	1:51.68	100,350
1999	Chorwon, 6, 117	C. H. Borel	El Angelo, 5, 117	Houston Slue, 4, 114	11	1:47.65	99,900
1998	Chorwon, 5, 115	G. Melancon	Western Trader, 7, 114	Top Seed, 4, 114	10	1:51.86	83,160
1997	Scott's Scoundrel, 5, 118	R. D. Ardoin	Western Trader, 6, 119	Volochine (Ire), 6, 121	10	1:53.60	75,000

Year	Winner	Jockey	Second	Third	Strs	Time	1st Purse
1996	Western Trader, 5, 115	C. Gonzalez	Jury Duty, 4, 114	Mine Inspector, 4, 113	12	1:52.30	$75,000
1995	Marastani, 5, 122	C. C. Bourque	Glaring, 5, 120	Artema (Ire), 4, 117	12	1:51.25	45,000

Named in honor of John B. Connally Jr. (1917-'93), governor of Texas, Sam Houston Race Park's home state, from 1963-'69; Connally was also U. S. Treasury Secretary from 1971-'72. John B. Connally Jr. Turf Cup H. 1995. John B. Connally Breeders' Cup Turf H. 1996-2007.

John C. Mabee Handicap

Grade 1 in 2008. Del Mar, three-year-olds and up, fillies and mares, 1 1/8 miles, turf. Held August 4, 2007, with a gross value of $400,000. First held in 1945. First graded in 1973. Stakes record 1:46.34 (2007 Precious Kitten).

Year	Winner	Jockey	Second	Third	Strs	Time	1st Purse
2007	Precious Kitten, 4, 119	R. Bejarano	Dancing Edie, 5, 119	Memorette, 5, 115	5	1:46.34	$240,000
2006	Dancing Edie, 4, 119	C. S. Nakatani	Moscow Burning, 6, 119	Island Fashion, 6, 116	7	1:48.26	240,000
2005	Amorama (Fr), 4, 115	M. A. Pedroza	Island Fashion, 5, 117	Intercontinental (GB), 5, 122	8	1:48.01	240,000
2004	Musical Chimes, 4, 116	K. Desormeaux	Moscow Burning, 4, 117	Notting Hill (Brz), 5, 113	6	1:47.09	240,000
2003	Megahertz (GB), 4, 116	A. O. Solis	dh-Dublino, 4, 121		5	1:49.09	240,000
			dh-Golden Apples (Ire), 5, 122				
			dh-Tates Creek, 5, 123				
2002	Affluent, 4, 118	E. Delahoussaye	Golden Apples (Ire), 4, 120	Janet (GB), 5, 118	7	1:48.37	240,000
2001	Janet (GB), 4, 116	D. R. Flores	Tranquility Lake, 6, 123	Minor Details, 4, 112	6	1:48.20	240,000
2000	Caffe Latte (Ire), 4, 117	B. Blanc	Tout Charmant, 4, 120	Alexine (Arg), 4, 115	7	1:47.16	240,000
1999	Tuzla (Fr), 5, 121	D. R. Flores	Happyanunoit (NZ), 4, 115	Spanish Fern, 4, 115	10	1:47.66	240,000
1998	See You Soon (Fr), 4, 114	C. S. Nakatani	Sonja's Faith (Ire), 4, 113	Fiji (GB), 4, 125	8	1:47.40	180,000
1997	Escena, 4, 115	P. Day	Real Connection, 6, 115	Different (Arg), 5, 121	7	1:49.80	180,000
1996	Matiara, 4, 118	C. S. Nakatani	Alpride (Ire), 5, 119	Pourquoi Pas (Ire), 4, 114	6	1:49.28	193,560
1995	Possibly Perfect, 5, 123	C. S. Nakatani	Morgana, 4, 115	Yearly Tour, 4, 116	7	1:49.98	180,600
1994	Flawlessly, 6, 124	C. J. McCarron	Hollywood Wildcat, 4, 124	Skimble, 5, 116	5	1:48.25	181,000
1993	Flawlessly, 5, 125	C. J. McCarron	Heart of Joy, 6, 114	Let's Elope (NZ), 6, 118	7	1:48.38	186,500
1992	Flawlessly, 4, 123	C. J. McCarron	Re Toss (Arg), 5, 115	Polemic, 4, 115	7	1:50.00	187,500
1991	Campagnarde (Arg), 4, 115	J. A. Garcia	Bequest, 5, 118	Somethingmerry, 4, 118	10	1:49.41	196,250
1990	Double Wedge, 5, 114	R. G. Davis	Reluctant Guest, 4, 117	Nikishka, 5, 116	8	1:49.00	158,000
1989	Brown Bess, 7, 117	J. L. Kaenel	Daring Doone (GB), 6, 117	Galunpe (Ire), 6, 118	7	1:48.40	157,750
1988	Annoconnor, 4, 116	C. A. Black	Chapel of Dreams, 4, 118	Short Sleeves (GB), 6, 121	10	1:48.40	134,000
1987	Short Sleeves (GB), 5, 118	E. Delahoussaye	Festivity, 4, 117	Auspiciante (Arg), 4, 120	9	1:50.20	97,900
1986	Auspiciante (Arg), 5, 114	G. L. Stevens	Justicara (Ire), 5, 116	Sauna (Aus), 5, 119	8	1:48.40	81,600
1985	Daily Busy (Fr), 4, 115	W. Shoemaker	Eastland, 4, 114	Envie de Rire (Fr), 4, 116	7	1:48.20	93,500
1984	Flag de Lune, 4, 115	F. Olivares	Royal Heroine (Ire), 4, 126	Salt Spring (Arg), 5, 115	9	1:48.40	97,200
1983	Sangue (Ire), 5, 123	W. Shoemaker	Castilla, 4, 121	First Advance, 4, 115	8	1:48.80	80,450
1982	Honey Fox, 5, 122	M. Castaneda	Sangue (Ire), 4, 112	French Charmer, 4, 115	10	1:48.80	83,900
1981	Queen to Conquer, 5, 120	M. Castaneda	Amber Ever, 3, 112	Track Robbery, 5, 123	10	1:48.80	84,000
1980	Queen to Conquer, 4, 115	W. Shoemaker	A Thousand Stars, 5, 118	Wishing Well, 5, 122	13	1:49.40	74,050
1979	Country Queen, 4, 121	L. A. Pincay Jr.	More So (Ire), 4, 119	Prize Spot, 3, 116	10	1:48.60	69,500
1978	Drama Critic, 4, 120	D. G. McHargue	Country Queen, 3, 113	B. Thoughtful, 3, 115	8	1:49.20	47,500
1977	Dancing Femme, 4, 122	D. G. McHargue	Up to Juliet, 4, 113	Swingtime, 5, 121	11	1:48.40	37,150
1976	Vagabonda, 5, 115	S. Hawley	*Stravina, 5, 115	Miss Tokyo, 4, 116	8	1:51.00	34,550
1975	*Dulcia, 6, 122	W. Shoemaker	*Tizna, 6, 123	Charger's Star, 5, 115	7	1:48.80	33,550
1974	*Tizna, 5, 120	W. Shoemaker	Modus Vivendi, 3, 118	*La Zanzara, 4, 122	11	1:49.20	29,800
1973	Minstrel Miss, 6, 122	D. Pierce	Le Cle, 4, 123	Pallisima, 4, 118	8	1:49.40	19,750

Named for John C. Mabee (1921-2002), owner of Golden Eagle Farm, located in Ramona, California, and longtime chairman of Del Mar Turf Club. Formerly named for the town of Ramona. Grade 3 1973-'79. Grade 2 1980-'83. Ramona H. 1945-2001. John C. Mabee Ramona H. 2002. Not held 1946-'58. 1 mile 1945. Dirt 1945-'69. Triple dead heat for second 2003.

John Deere Breeders' Cup Turf

Grade 1 in 2008. Monmouth Park, three-year-olds and up, 1 1/2 miles, turf. Held October 27, 2007, with a gross value of $2,748,000. First held in 1984. First graded in 1984. Stakes record 2:23.92 (1997 Chief Bearhart).

Year	Winner	Jockey	Second	Third	Strs	Time	1st Purse
2007	English Channel, 5, 126	J. R. Velazquez	Shamdinan (Fr), 3, 121	Red Rocks (Ire), 4, 126	8	2:36.96	$1,620,000
2006	Red Rocks (Ire), 3, 122	L. Dettori	Better Talk Now, 7, 126	English Channel, 4, 126	11	2:27.32	1,620,000
2005	Shirocco (Ger), 4, 126	C. Soumillon	Ace (Ire), 4, 126	Azamour (Ire), 4, 126	13	2:29.30	1,185,600
2004	Better Talk Now, 5, 126	R. A. Dominguez	Kitten's Joy, 3, 121	Powerscourt (GB), 4, 126	8	2:29.70	1,040,000
2003	dh-High Chaparral (Ire), 4, 126	M. J. Kinane	Falbrav (Ire), 5, 126		8	2:24.24	763,200
	dh-Johar, 4, 126	A. O. Solis					
2002	High Chaparral (Ire), 3, 121	M. J. Kinane	With Anticipation, 7, 126	Falcon Flight (Fr), 6, 126	8	2:30.14	1,258,400
2001	Fantastic Light, 5, 126	L. Dettori	Milan (GB), 3, 121	Timboroa (GB), 3, 121	11	2:24.36	1,112,800
2000	Kalanisi (Ire), 4, 126	J. P. Murtagh	Quiet Resolve, 5, 126	John's Call, 9, 126	13	2:26.96	1,289,600
1999	Daylami (Ire), 5, 126	L. Dettori	Royal Anthem, 4, 126	Buck's Boy, 6, 126	14	2:24.73	1,040,000
1998	Buck's Boy, 5, 126	S. J. Sellers	Yagli, 5, 126	Dushyantor, 5, 126	13	2:28.74	1,040,000
1997	Chief Bearhart, 4, 126	J. A. Santos	†Borgia (Ger), 3, 121	Flag Down, 7, 126	11	2:23.92	1,040,000
1996	Pilsudski (Ire), 4, 126	W. R. Swinburn	Singspiel (Ire), 4, 126	Swain (Ire), 4, 126	14	2:30.20	1,040,000
1995	Northern Spur (Ire), 4, 126	C. J. McCarron	Freedom Cry (GB), 4, 126	Carnegie (Ire), 4, 126	13	2:42.07	1,040,000
1994	Tikkanen, 3, 122	M. E. Smith	†Hatoof, 5, 126	Paradise Creek, 5, 126	14	2:26.50	1,040,000
1993	Kotashaan (Fr), 5, 126	K. Desormeaux	Bien Bien, 4, 126	Luazur (Fr), 4, 126	14	2:25.16	1,040,000
1992	Fraise, 4, 126	P. A. Valenzuela	Sky Classic, 5, 126	Quest for Fame (GB), 5, 126	10	2:24.08	1,040,000

Racing — Graded Stakes

Year	Winner	Jockey	Second	Third	Strs	Time	1st Purse
1991	†Miss Alleged, 4, 123	E. Legrix	Itsallgreektome, 4, 126	Quest for Fame (GB), 4, 126	13	2:30.95	$1,040,000
1990	In the Wings (GB), 4, 126	G. L. Stevens	With Approval, 4, 126	El Senor, 6, 126	11	2:29.60	900,000
1989	Prized, 3, 122	E. Delahoussaye	†Sierra Roberta (Fr), 3, 119	Star Lift (GB), 5, 126	14	2:28.00	900,000
1988	Great Communicator, 5, 126	R. Sibille	Sunshine Forever, 3, 122	†Indian Skimmer, 4, 123	10	2:35.20	900,000
1987	Theatrical (Ire), 5, 126	P. Day	Trempolino, 3, 122	Village Star (Fr), 4, 126	14	2:24.40	900,000
1986	Manila, 3, 122	J. A. Santos	Theatrical (Ire), 4, 126	†Estrapade, 6, 123	9	2:25.40	900,000
1985	†Pebbles (GB), 4, 123	P. Eddery	Strawberry Road (Aus), 6, 126	Mourjane (Ire), 5, 126	14	2:27.00	900,000
1984	Lashkari (GB), 3, 122	Y. Saint-Martin	†All Along (Fr), 5, 123	Raami (GB), 3, 122	11	2:25.20	900,000

Sponsored by John Deere & Co. of Moline, Illinois 2002-'07. Held at Hollywood Park 1984, '87, '97. Held at Aqueduct 1985. Held at Santa Anita Park 1986, '93, 2003. Held at Churchill Downs 1988, '91, '94, '98, 2000, '06. Held at Gulfstream Park 1989, '92, '99. Held at Belmont Park 1990, '95, 2001, '05. Held at Woodbine 1996. Held at Arlington Park 2002. Held at Lone Star Park 2004. Dead heat for first 2003. Course record 1992. †Denotes female.

Juddmonte Spinster Stakes

Grade 1 in 2008. Keeneland Race Course, three-year-olds and up, fillies and mares, 1 1/8 miles, all weather. Held October 7, 2007, with a gross value of $540,000. First held in 1956. First graded in 1973. Stakes record 1:47 (1990 Bayakoa [Arg]).

Year	Winner	Jockey	Second	Third	Strs	Time	1st Purse
2007	Panty Raid, 3, 120	G. K. Gomez	Lady Joanne, 3, 120	Teammate, 4, 123	11	1:51.30	$310,000
2006	Asi Siempre, 4, 123	J. R. Leparoux	Soul Search, 4, 123	Promenade Girl, 4, 123	9	1:51.97	310,000
2005	Pampered Princess, 5, 123	E. Castro	Pleasant Home, 4, 123	Capeside Lady, 4, 123	11	1:53.91	310,000
2004	Azeri, 6, 123	P. Day	Tamweel, 4, 123	Mayo On the Side, 5, 123	7	1:49.74	310,000
2003	Take Charge Lady, 4, 123	E. S. Prado	You, 4, 123	Miss Linda (Arg), 6, 123	6	1:49.57	310,000
2002	Take Charge Lady, 3, 120	E. S. Prado	You, 3, 120	Printemps (Chi), 5, 123	7	1:49.90	338,520
2001	Miss Linda (Arg), 4, 123	R. Migliore	Starrer, 3, 120	Printemps (Chi), 5, 123	10	1:49.79	348,440
2000	Plenty of Light, 3, 120	G. K. Gomez	Spain, 3, 120	Roza Robata, 5, 123	6	1:48.18	336,970
1999	Keeper Hill, 4, 123	K. Desormeaux	Banshee Breeze, 4, 123	A Lady From Dixie, 4, 123	9	1:47.19	344,410
1998	Banshee Breeze, 3, 119	R. Albarado	Runup the Colors, 4, 123	Aldiza, 4, 123	8	1:47.04	341,930
1997	Clear Mandate, 5, 123	P. Day	Feasibility Study, 5, 123	Naskra Colors, 5, 123	7	1:50.47	336,350
1996	Different (Arg), 4, 123	C. J. McCarron	Top Secret, 3, 119	Belle of Cozzene, 4, 123	6	1:49.74	336,040
1995	Inside Information, 4, 123	M. E. Smith	Jade Flush, 4, 123	Mariah's Storm, 4, 123	4	1:50.01	198,276
1994	Dispute, 4, 123	P. Day	Lets Be Alert, 3, 119	Miss Dominique, 5, 123	8	1:48.91	204,414
1993	Paseana (Arg), 6, 123	C. J. McCarron	Gray Cashmere, 4, 123	Jacody, 3, 119	9	1:48.46	205,902
1992	Fowda, 4, 123	P. A. Valenzuela	Paseana (Arg), 5, 123	Meadow Star, 4, 123	10	1:49.91	209,994
1991	Wilderness Song, 3, 119	P. Day	Screen Prospect, 4, 123	Til Forbid, 3, 119	14	1:49.69	226,980
1990	Bayakoa (Arg), 6, 123	L. A. Pincay Jr.	Gorgeous, 4, 123	Luthier's Launch, 4, 123	8	**1:47.00**	174,606
1989	Bayakoa (Arg), 5, 123	L. A. Pincay Jr.	Goodbye Halo, 4, 123	Sharp Dance, 3, 119	6	1:47.80	172,413
1988	Hail a Cab, 5, 123	J. Vasquez	Willa On the Move, 3, 119	Integra, 4, 123	5	1:51.00	171,600
1987	Sacahuista, 3, 119	R. P. Romero	Ms. Margi, 3, 119	Tall Poppy, 4, 123	13	1:48.60	148,395
1986	Top Corsage, 3, 119	S. Hawley	Endear, 4, 123	Life At the Top, 3, 119	8	1:48.20	142,610
1985	Dontstop Themusic, 5, 123	L. A. Pincay Jr.	Life's Magic, 4, 123	Dowery, 4, 123	11	1:50.40	110,419
1984	Princess Rooney, 4, 123	E. Delahoussaye	Lucky Lucky Lucky, 3, 119	Heatherten, 5, 123	9	1:50.40	123,840
1983	Try Something New, 4, 123	P. Day	Dance Number, 4, 123	Miss Huntington, 6, 123	9	1:49.80	107,689
1982	Track Robbery, 6, 123	P. A. Valenzuela	Blush With Pride, 3, 119	Our Darling, 3, 119	9	1:47.80	110,517
1981	Glorious Song, 5, 123	R. Platts	Truly Bound, 3, 119	Safe Play, 3, 119	7	1:49.20	106,567
1980	Bold 'n Determined, 3, 119	E. Delahoussaye	Love Sign, 3, 119	Likely Exchange, 6, 123	6	1:49.20	114,660
1979	Safe, 3, 119	E. Fires	Spark of Life, 4, 123	Miss Baja, 4, 123	11	1:49.20	79,852
1978	Tempest Queen, 3, 119	J. Velasquez	Northernette, 4, 123	Likely Exchange, 4, 123	10	1:49.00	72,865
1977	Cum Laude Laurie, 3, 119	A. T. Cordero Jr.	Mississippi Mud, 4, 123	Ivory Wand, 4, 123	10	1:48.40	54,974
1976	Optimistic Gal, 3, 119	C. Perret	Ivory Wand, 3, 119	Rocky Trip, 4, 123	8	1:51.60	53,008
1975	Susan's Girl, 6, 123	L. A. Pincay Jr.	Flama Ardiente, 3, 119	Costly Dream, 4, 123	7	1:49.80	37,830
1974	Summer Guest, 5, 123	D. Montoya	Desert Vixen, 4, 123	Coraggioso, 4, 123	5	1:48.40	36,953
1973	Susan's Girl, 4, 123	B. Baeza	Light Hearted, 4, 123	Coraggioso, 3, 119	6	1:48.80	38,090

A spinster is an unmarried woman beyond the traditional marriage age, hence an appropriate name for a race for females still racing in the fall. Sponsored by Khalid Abdullah's Juddmonte Farms, located in Lexington, Kentucky 2005-'07. Formerly sponsored by the Young family's Overbrook Farm, located in Lexington 2001-'04. Formerly sponsored by Robert N. Clay's Three Chimneys Farm, located in Midway, Kentucky 1996-2000. Spinster S. 1956-'95. Dirt 1956-2005. Three, four, and five-year-olds 1956-'63.

Just a Game Stakes

Grade 1 in 2008. Belmont Park, three-year-olds and up, fillies and mares, 1 mile, turf. Held June 7, 2008, with a gross value of $400,000. First held in 1992. First graded in 1997. Stakes record 1:32.53 (1995 Caress).

Year	Winner	Jockey	Second	Third	Strs	Time	1st Purse
2008	Ventura, 4, 120	G. K. Gomez	Lady of Venice (Fr), 5, 118	Forever Together, 4, 118	10	1:32.75	$240,000
2007	My Typhoon (Ire), 5, 118	E. Castro	Wait a While, 4, 118	Take the Ribbon, 4, 120	5	1:34.92	180,000
2006	Gorella (Fr), 4, 120	J. R. Leparoux	Pommes Frites, 4, 116	Ozone Bere (Fr), 4, 116	4	1:37.14	180,000
2005	Sand Springs, 5, 117	J. R. Velazquez	Intercontinental (GB), 5, 123	Wonder Again, 6, 121	9	1:33.05	180,000
2004	Intercontinental (GB), 4, 118	J. D. Bailey	Vanguardia (Arg), 4, 113	Etoile Montante, 4, 121	8	1:33.33	150,000
2003	Mariensky, 4, 116	J. A. Santos	Riskaverse, 4, 119	Wonder Again, 4, 119	8	1:43.28	128,700
2002	Babae (Chi), 6, 115	J. F. Chavez	Tates Creek, 4, 117	Stylish, 4, 115	8	1:34.57	67,920
2001	License Fee, 6, 118	P. Day	Shopping for Love, 4, 114	Veil of Avalon, 4, 115	11	1:32.62	114,780
2000	Perfect Sting, 4, 121	J. D. Bailey	Ronda (GB), 4, 116	Snow Polina, 5, 116	7	1:34.48	111,180

Racing — Graded Stakes 363

Year	Winner	Jockey	Second	Third	Strs	Time	1st Purse
1999	Cozy Blues, 5, 112	J. F. Chavez	U R Unforgetable, 5, 114	Mysterious Moll, 4, 115	7	1:33.33	$94,620
1998	Witchful Thinking, 4, 118	C. J. McCarron	Sopran Mariduff (GB), 4, 117	Dixie Ghost, 4, 111	9	1:33.45	95,745
1997	Memories of Silver, 4, 120	J. D. Bailey	Dynasty, 4, 113	Elusive, 5, 115	7	1:32.80	95,370
1996	‡Caress, 5, 117	R. G. Davis	Class Kris, 4, 122	Upper Noosh, 4, 112	7	1:33.30	94,890
1995	Caress, 4, 119	R. G. Davis	Coronation Cup, 4, 119	Grafin, 4, 117	5	**1:32.53**	49,320
1994	Elizabeth Bay, 4, 114	M. E. Smith	Tiffany's Taylor, 5, 117	Statuette, 4, 119	5	1:32.85	33,330
1992	Lady Lear, 5, 115	G. Brocklebank	Flaming Torch (Ire), 5, 119	Totemic, 3, 116	5	2:15.90	47,340

Named for Peter M. Brant's 1980 champion grass female and '80 Flower Bowl H. (G2) winner Just a Game (Ire) (1976 f. by Tarboosh). Formerly sponsored by Emirates Airline of Dubai, United Arab Emirates 2005. Grade 3 1997-2003. Grade 2 2004-'07. Just a Game S. 1992-'95. Just a Game Breeders' Cup H. 1996-2005. Just a Game H. 2006. Not held 1993. Equaled course record 1995. ‡Class Kris finished first, DQ to second, 1996.

Kelso Handicap

Grade 2 in 2008. Belmont Park, three-year-olds and up, 1 mile, turf. Held September 29, 2007, with a gross value of $249,200. First held in 1980. First graded in 1984. Stakes record 1:32.07 (2006 Ashkal Way [Ire]).

Year	Winner	Jockey	Second	Third	Strs	Time	1st Purse
2007	Trippi's Storm, 4, 115	J. Castellano	After Market, 4, 124	Palace Episode, 4, 116	10	1:32.36	$150,000
2006	Ashkal Way (Ire), 4, 118	M. J. Luzzi	Free Thinking, 5, 116	Art Master, 5, 117	7	**1:32.07**	150,000
2005	Funfair (GB), 6, 115	E. S. Prado	Artie Schiller, 4, 123	Keep The Faith (Aus), 5, 115	10	1:32.95	210,000
2004	Mr O'Brien (Ire), 5, 119	E. Coa	Millennium Dragon (GB), 5, 119	Gulch Approval, 4, 114	8	1:32.69	150,000
2003	Freefourinternet, 5, 113	J. L. Espinoza	Proud Man, 5, 114	Rouvres (Fr), 4, 115	10	1:34.73	210,000
2002	Green Fee, 6, 113	J. R. Velazquez	Forbidden Apple, 7, 121	Moon Solitaire (Ire), 5, 117	9	1:33.83	210,000
2001	Forbidden Apple, 6, 118	J. A. Santos	Sarafan, 4, 114	City Zip, 3, 112	9	1:36.77	150,000
2000	Forbidden Apple, 5, 116	J. Samyn	Affirmed Success, 6, 120	Johnny Dollar, 4, 113	9	1:34.39	150,000
1999	Middlesex Drive, 4, 117	S. J. Sellers	Divide and Conquer, 5, 114	Wised Up, 4, 113	10	1:35.45	150,000
1998	Dixie Bayou, 5, 112	J. F. Chavez	Sahm, 4, 115	Let Goodtimes Roll, 5, 112	6	1:36.21	150,000
1997	Lucky Coin, 4, 119	R. G. Davis	Hawksley Hill (Ire), 4, 115	†Colcon, 4, 112	12	1:33.72	120,000
1996	Same Old Wish, 6, 113	S. J. Sellers	Da Hoss, 4, 120	Volochine (Ire), 5, 116	10	1:34.42	105,000
1995	Mighty Forum (GB), 4, 115	E. Delahoussaye	Fastness (Ire), 5, 119	Dowty, 3, 112	14	1:39.58	120,000
1994	Nijinsky's Gold, 5, 114	J. A. Santos	Lure, 4, 128	A in Sociology, 4, 117	7	1:34.18	120,000
1993	Lure, 4, 125	M. E. Smith	Paradise Creek, 4, 120	Daarik (Ire), 6, 112	10	1:35.86	120,000
1992	Roman Envoy, 4, 117	C. Perret	Lure, 3, 111	Val des Bois (Fr), 6, 118	9	1:36.39	120,000
1991	Star of Cozzene, 3, 114	J. A. Santos	Known Ranger (GB), 5, 113	Fourstardave, 6, 117	6	1:33.37	69,720
1990	Expensive Decision, 4, 112	J. Samyn	Who's to Pay, 4, 115	Great Commotion, 4, 113	9	1:32.40	57,420
1989	I Rejoice, 6, 114	J. D. Bailey	Quick Call, 5, 113	Wanderkin, 6, 118	9	1:36.40	75,360
1988	San's the Shadow, 4, 116	C. W. Antley	Posen, 5, 117	Tinchen's Prince, 5, 114	7	1:42.00	72,240
1987	I'm a Banker, 5, 107	A. Graell	Tertiary Zone, 3, 113	Island Sun, 5, 112	11	2:10.80	76,920
1986	I'm a Banker, 4, 111	A. Graell	Duluth, 4, 113	Premier Mister (Mor), 6, 113	9	2:03.20	54,720
1985	Mourjane (Ire), 5, 114	R. Migliore	Cool, 4, 116	Palace Panther (Fr), 4, 116	9	2:02.00	70,560
1984	Who's for Dinner, 5, 115	W. A. Guerra	Pin Puller, 5, 112	Norwick, 5, 109	11	2:01.20	71,100
1982	Worthy Too, 4, 119	J. Samyn	Nice Pirate, 4, 112	Jadosa Toker, 5, 113	12	3:24.40	69,840
1981	Peat Moss, 6, 126	F. Lovato Jr.	Field Cat, 4, 114	Birthday List, 6, 114	8	3:20.80	66,240
1980	Peat Moss, 5, 108	F. Lovato Jr.	Ivory Hunter, 6, 114	Ring of Light, 5, 117	10	3:24.60	68,160

Named for Bohemia Stable's Racing Hall of Fame member, 1960, '61, '62, '63, '64 Horse of the Year, and '60, '61, '62, '63, '64 Jockey Club Gold Cup winner Kelso (1957 g. by Your Host); Kelso is the only five-time Horse of the Year. Grade 3 1984-'96. Kelso Breeders' Cup H. 2003-'06. Held at Aqueduct 1980-'82. Not held 1983. 2 miles 1980-'82. 1 1/4 miles 1984-'87. Dirt 1980-'82. †Denotes female.

Kenny Noe Jr. Handicap

Grade 3 in 2008. Calder Race Course, three-year-olds and up, 7 furlongs, dirt. Held December 15, 2007, with a gross value of $100,000. First held in 1975. First graded in 2006. Stakes record 1:22.62 (2004 Medallist).

Year	Winner	Jockey	Second	Third	Strs	Time	1st Purse
2007	Paradise Dancer, 7, 120	E. Trujillo	Finallymadeit, 3, 118	Finance Minister, 4, 115	10	1:23.46	$58,900
2006	Weigelia, 5, 117	E. Castro	Paradise Dancer, 6, 115	How's Your Halo, 3, 113	9	1:24.02	60,000
2005	Mister Fotis, 4, 114	J. F. Chavez	Storm Surge, 3, 113	Silver Wagon, 4, 118	7	1:22.97	60,000
2004	Medallist, 3, 114	J. A. Santos	Paradise Dancer, 3, 112	Hasty Kris, 7, 115	10	**1:22.62**	60,000
2003	Hasty Kris, 6, 116	R. R. Douglas	Wake At Noon, 6, 116	Tour of the Cat, 5, 119	10	1:23.82	60,000
2002	Built Up, 4, 114	E. Coa	Tour of the Cat, 4, 121	Sea of Tranquility, 6, 118	6	1:23.30	60,000
2001	Fappie's Notebook, 4, 117	J. F. Chavez	Kiss a Native, 4, 117	Dancing Guy, 6, 117	6	1:23.31	60,000
2000	Miners Gamble, 4, 114	E. O. Nunez	Alice's Notebook, 4, 114	Stormy Do, 7, 114	9	1:22.86	60,000
1999	Thrillin Discovery, 4, 112	J. Castellano	Mountain Top, 4, 115	Stormy Do, 6, 113	7	1:23.72	60,000
1998	Thrillin Discovery, 3, 114	J. Castellano	Flashing Tammany, 3, 115	Oro de Mexico, 4, 115	7	1:23.19	60,000
1997	Heckofaralph, 4, 116	J. A. Velez Jr.	Irish Conquest, 4, 113	Oro de Mexico, 3, 113	11	1:25.77	60,000
1996	Splendid Sprinter, 4, 115	J. R. Velazquez	Stormy Do, 3, 112	Ghostly Moves, 4, 114	10	1:23.45	60,000
1995	Hyroglyphic, 3, 113	W. H. McCauley	Excelerate, 3, 113	Ponche, 6, 120	10	1:23.53	60,000
1994	Birdonthewire, 5, 119	C. Perret	Fortunate Joe, 4, 116	Honest Colors, 3, 113	8	1:23.68	60,000
1993	Song of Ambition, 4, 118	R. D. Lopez	American Chance, 4, 114	Swedaus, 6, 115	11	1:23.58	30,000
1992	Poulain d'Or, 3, 116	M. A. Lee	Frozen Runway, 5, 115	Groomstick, 6, 116	8	1:23.68	30,000
	Drummond Lane, 5, 112	H. Castillo Jr.	Groomstick, 6, 114	Frozen Runway, 5, 114	8	1:23.08	49,710
1991	Groomstick, 5, 120	W. S. Ramos	Swedaus, 4, 110	Greg At Bat, 6, 113	6	1:23.50	32,250
1990	Groomstick, 4, 110	W. S. Ramos	Carborundum, 6, 118	The Red Rolls, 6, 113	9	1:24.00	50,475

Racing — Graded Stakes

Year	Winner	Jockey	Second	Third	Strs	Time	1st Purse
1988	Position Leader, 3, 117	D. Valiente	The Red Rolls, 4, 114	Above Normal, 3, 114	12	1:24.60	$52,620
	Princely Lad, 5, 115	L. Saumell	Hail the Ruckus, 5, 112	Baldski's Star, 4, 110	9	1:24.80	67,020
1986	Chief Steward, 5, 120	M. A. Lee	Play the King, 3, 114	Mugatea, 6, 117	8	1:25.80	31,080
1985	Show Dancer, 3, 114	G. St. Leon	Fortunate Prospect, 4, 119	Opening Lead, 5, 118	10	1:23.60	48,120
1984	Mo Exception, 3, 118	V. H. Molina	Jim Bracken, 3, 116	Brother Liam, 4, 118	8	1:24.60	37,695
	For Halo, 3, 118	B. Fann	Forbes' Best, 3, 113	Naskra Drummer, 4, 113	9	1:23.60	37,995
1983	Eminency, 5, 121	P. Day	My Mac, 3, 117	Command Attention, 5, 115	11	1:24.20	34,290
1982	Spirited Boy, 4, 114	M. Russ	In all Honesty, 3, 110	Moreton Bay, 3, 110	12	1:24.60	27,780
1981	‡Speedy Prospect, 4, 114	C. Astorga	Explosive Bid, 3, 115	Wooster Sq., 3, 113	8	1:11.60	22,935
1980	†Burn's Return, 4, 120	M. A. Rivera	Speedy Prospect, 3, 113	Southern General, 4, 112	8	1:11.00	16,515
1979	†Burn's Return, 3, 113	M. A. Rivera	Dargelo, 3, 112	Soldier Boy, 3, 115	13	1:38.20	17,250
1978	Robb's Charm, 3, 115	J. Giovanni	Reggie F., 3, 114	Fleet Gar, 3, 113	10	1:37.80	18,000
1977	Jonkiller, 3, 120	C. Astorga	Jachal II, 3, 118	Haverty, 3, 111	9	1:39.40	17,850
1976	Irish Captain, 3, 116	J. Salinas	‡Controller Ike, 3, 122	El Rosillo, 3, 119	8	1:40.20	17,400
1975	Bad Turn, 3, 115	M. Perna	Ameri Flyer, 3, 114	American Holme, 3, 114	10	1:39.60	18,000

Named in honor of Kenny Noe Jr. (1928-), former president and general manager of Calder from 1979-'90. Sunny Isles H. 1975-'93. Not held 1987, '89. 6 furlongs 1980-'81. 1 mile 1975-'79. Three-year-olds 1975-'79. Two divisions 1984. Held in March and December 1988. Held in April and December 1992. ‡El Rosillo finished second, DQ to third, 1976. ‡Explosive Bid finished first, DQ to second, 1981. †Denotes female.

Kent Stakes

Grade 3 in 2008. Delaware Park, three-year-olds, 1 1/8 miles, turf. Held September 1, 2007, with a gross value of $501,200. First held in 1937. First graded in 1973. Stakes record 1:47.32 (2005 Seeking Slew).

Year	Winner	Jockey	Second	Third	Strs	Time	1st Purse
2007	Nobiz Like Shobiz, 3, 120	J. Castellano	Twilight Meteor, 3, 116	Strike a Deal, 3, 116	9	1:49.60	$300,000
2006	Brilliant, 3, 120	M. Guidry	Carnera, 3, 116	Sea of Trees, 3, 116	10	1:56.63	300,000
2005	‡Seeking Slew, 3, 115	R. A. Dominguez	‡Chattahoochee War, 3, 119	Spring House, 3, 115	11	1:47.32	300,000
2004	Timo, 3, 117	R. Migliore	Icy Atlantic, 3, 117	Commendation, 3, 115	8	1:55.75	150,000
2003	Foufa's Warrior, 3, 115	R. A. Dominguez	Remind, 3, 115	Lismore Knight, 3, 119	7	1:47.44	150,000
2002	Miesque's Approval, 3, 115	J. D. Bailey	Regal Sanction, 3, 115	dh-Coco's Madness, 3, 115 dh-Quest Star, 3, 115	8	1:48.81	150,000
2001	Navesink, 3, 115	R. A. Dominguez	Bowman Mill, 3, 115	Harrisand (Fr), 3, 115	10	1:49.98	151,000
2000	Three Wonders, 3, 115	P. Day	Field Cat, 3, 117	Dawn of the Condor, 3, 115	8	1:48.95	150,000
1999	North East Bound, 3, 114	J. A. Velez Jr.	Courtside, 3, 113	Swamp, 3, 119	8	1:51.93	150,000
1998	Keene Dancer, 3, 115	P. Day	Red Reef, 3, 115	Danielle's Gray, 3, 117	11	1:50.65	120,000
1997	Royal Strand (Ire), 3, 122	P. Day	Subordination, 3, 122	Broad Choice, 3, 113	7	1:48.00	90,000
1996	Sir Cat, 3, 113	J. D. Bailey	Optic Nerve, 3, 122	Fortitude, 3, 116	5	1:52.93	60,000
1982	Cagey Cougar, 3, 114	V. A. Bracciale Jr.	King's Dusty, 3, 113	Big Shot (Fr), 3, 113	7	1:43.20	14,495
1979	T. V. Series, 3, 116	C. Barrera	Bear Arms, 3, 113	Buck's Chief, 3, 114	11	1:43.60	22,978
1976	Improve It, 3, 117	L. Saumell	Return of a Native, 3, 120	Impeccable, 3, 120	7	1:38.00	12,795
	*King Streaker, 3, 111	H. Pilar	Chati, 3, 117	Parade to Glory, 3, 111	7	1:38.40	12,795
1975	Talc, 3, 117	R. Broussard	King of Fools, 3, 117	Leader of the Band, 3, 111	10	1:39.20	15,503
	Grey Beret, 3, 120	J. Canessa	My Friend Gus, 3, 117	Too Easy, 3, 111	10	1:39.40	15,503
1974	Splitting Headache, 3, 120	R. Woodhouse	Malaga Bay, 3, 114	Clyde William, 3, 117	12	1:40.80	20,475
1973	Shane's Prince, 3, 117	E. Maple	*Amen II, 3, 117	My Darling Boy, 3, 117	12	1:37.60	21,352

Named for Kent County, Delaware. Kent H. 1937-'41. Kent Breeders' Cup S. 1996-2007. Not held 1943, 1977-'78, 1980-'81, 1983-'95. 1 1/16 miles 1937-'68, 1979, 1982. 1 mile 1969-'76. Dirt 1937-'68. Two divisions 1975-'76. Dead heat for third 2002. ‡Touched by Madness finished first, DQ to fourth, 2005. ‡Spring House finished second, DQ to third, 2005. Course record 1997, 2003, '05.

Kentucky Cup Classic Stakes

Grade 2 in 2008. Turfway Park, three-year-olds and up, 1 1/8 miles, all weather. Held September 29, 2007, with a gross value of $402,500. First held in 1994. First graded in 1996. Stakes record 1:47.43 (1996 Atticus).

Year	Winner	Jockey	Second	Third	Strs	Time	1st Purse
2007	Hard Spun, 3, 118	M. G. Pino	Street Sense, 3, 120	Stream Cat, 4, 118	4	1:48.48	$280,000
2006	Ball Four, 5, 118	W. Martinez	Perfect Drift, 7, 118	Good Reward, 5, 118	6	1:48.29	221,500
2005	Shaniko, 4, 118	R. Bejarano	Ball Four, 4, 118	Silver Axe, 8, 118	10	1:49.74	221,500
2004	Roses in May, 4, 118	J. R. Velazquez	Pie N Burger, 6, 117	Sonic West, 5, 113	6	1:49.13	221,500
2003	Perfect Drift, 4, 120	P. Day	Congaree, 5, 124	Crafty Shaw, 5, 115	5	1:50.43	221,500
2002	Pure Prize, 4, 115	M. E. Smith	Dollar Bill, 4, 117	Hero's Tribute, 4, 113	8	1:51.24	254,000
2001	Guided Tour, 5, 119	L. J. Melancon	Balto Star, 3, 114	A Fleets Dancer, 6, 115	6	1:47.90	254,000
2000	Captain Steve, 3, 115	S. J. Sellers	Golden Missile, 5, 121	Early Pioneer, 5, 120	6	1:49.95	314,500
1999	Da Devil, 4, 112	C. H. Borel	Social Charter, 4, 115	Cat Thief, 3, 117	6	1:50.54	314,500
1998	dh-Silver Charm, 4, 123	G. L. Stevens		Acceptable, 4, 117	5	1:47.48	143,500
	dh-Wild Rush, 4, 117	P. Day					
1997	Semoran, 4, 116	K. Desormeaux	Distorted Humor, 4, 116	Coup D' Argent, 5, 114	8	1:48.08	217,000
1996	Atticus, 4, 115	C. S. Nakatani	Judge T C, 5, 117	Isitingood, 5, 117	10	1:47.43	325,000
1995	Thunder Gulch, 3, 121	G. L. Stevens	Judge T C, 4, 112	Bound by Honor, 4, 113	6	1:49.42	260,000
1994	Tabasco Cat, 3, 120	P. Day	Mighty Avanti, 4, 115	Best Pal, 6, 115	6	1:50.32	260,000

Turfway Park is located in Florence, Kentucky. Grade 3 1996-'98. Kentucky Cup Classic H. 1994-2004. Dirt 1994-2005. Dead heat for first 1998. Track record 2006.

Kentucky Cup Distaff Stakes

Grade 3 in 2008. Turfway Park, three-year-olds and up, fillies and mares, 1 1/16 miles, all weather. Held September 29, 2007, with a gross value of $160,000. First held in 1986. First graded in 1990. Stakes record 1:41.67 (1995 Mariah's Storm).

Year	Winner	Jockey	Second	Third	Strs	Time	1st Purse
2007	Danzon, 4, 118	J. R. Leparoux	Delicate Dynamite, 4, 120	Kettleoneup, 4, 122	11	1:43.42	$104,780
2006	Beautiful Bets, 6, 116	W. Martinez	La Reason, 6, 120	Slew Peg, 3, 112	10	1:42.79	62,000
2005	Miss Fortunate, 5, 120	L. J. Melancon	Sheer Luck, 4, 118	Whoopi Cat, 4, 116	9	1:44.48	108,500
2004	Susan's Angel, 3, 116	R. Bejarano	Mayo On the Side, 5, 120	Angela's Love, 4, 122	6	1:44.21	108,500
2003	Smok'n Frolic, 4, 122	E. S. Prado	Awesome Humor, 3, 112	So Much More, 4, 118	9	1:44.98	108,500
2002	Trip, 5, 116	P. Day	Mystic Lady, 4, 118	Red n'Gold, 4, 118	9	1:43.01	125,500
2001	Trip, 4, 118	C. Perret	Precious Feather, 4, 114	Spain, 4, 122	7	1:42.47	125,500
2000	Spain, 3, 118	P. Day	Ruby Surprise, 5, 118	Undermine, 4, 118	9	1:44.85	156,500
1999	Ruby Surprise, 4, 118	W. Martinez	Let, 4, 118	French Braids, 4, 114	8	1:44.95	162,886
1998	Biding Time, 4, 117	C. S. Nakatani	Meter Maid, 4, 121	Dancing Gulch, 4, 119	7	1:43.13	162,266
1997	Feasibility Study, 5, 119	M. E. Smith	City Band, 3, 114	Gold n Delicious, 4, 121	5	1:42.50	161,522
1996	Golden Attraction, 3, 114	G. L. Stevens	Bedroom Blues, 5, 117	Betty Van, 4, 119	8	1:42.53	205,920
1995	Mariah's Storm, 4, 117	R. N. Lester	Serena's Song, 3, 119	Alcovy, 5, 117	5	1:41.67	116,415
1994	Pennyhill Park, 4, 123	C. J. McCarron	Roamin Rachel, 4, 118	Hey Hazel, 4, 123	10	1:44.20	118,073
1993	Gray Cashmere, 4, 117	D. Kutz	Deputation, 4, 120	November Snow, 4, 113	8	1:43.39	117,130
1992	Fit for a Queen, 6, 123	R. D. Lopez	Auto Dial, 4, 120	Hitch, 3, 112	9	1:43.30	117,975
1991	Fit for a Queen, 5, 123	R. D. Lopez	Til Forbid, 3, 118	Screen Prospect, 4, 114	8	1:43.22	117,358
1990	Barbarika, 5, 123	A. T. Gryder	Colonial Waters, 5, 114	Luthier's Launch, 4, 112	11	1:44.00	119,015
1989	Winning Colors, 4, 115	C. J. McCarron	Grecian Flight, 5, 123	Lawyer Talk, 5, 123	7	1:44.80	101,368
1988	Darien Miss, 3, 115	P. A. Johnson	Integra, 4, 123	Ms. Eloise, 5, 120	9	1:43.60	101,758
1987	In Neon, 5, 111	M. McDowell	Northern Maiden, 4, 122	Just Barely Able, 5, 113	7	1:45.20	50,180
1986	Gypsy Prayer, 5, 111	M. W. Bryan	Queen Alexandra, 4, 114	Donut's Break, 4, 111	10	1:43.20	19,180

Grade 2 1992–'98. Latonia Breeders' Cup S. 1986. Turfway-Budweiser Breeders' Cup S. 1987. Turfway Park Budweiser Breeders' Cup S. 1988. Turfway Budweiser Breeders' Cup H. 1989. Turfway Park Budweiser Breeders' Cup H. 1990. Turfway Budweiser Breeders' Cup S. 1991, 1993–'95. Turfway Breeders' Cup S. 1992, 1996-2006. Host track known as Latonia Race Course 1986. Dirt 1986-2005.

Kentucky Cup Juvenile Stakes

Grade 3 in 2008. Turfway Park, two-year-olds, 1 1/16 miles, all weather. Held September 29, 2007, with a gross value of $100,000. First held in 1986. First graded in 1989. Stakes record 1:42.89 (1996 Boston Harbor).

Year	Winner	Jockey	Second	Third	Strs	Time	1st Purse
2007	Texas Fever, 2, 114	J. R. Leparoux	Chitoz, 2, 114	Blackberry Road, 2, 116	10	1:44.95	$58,900
2006	U D Ghetto, 2, 116	M. E. Smith	Shermanesque, 2, 114	Son of the West, 2, 114	12	1:43.86	62,000
2005	Stream Cat, 2, 118	G. L. Stevens	Rungius, 2, 116	Cab, 2, 114	8	1:46.42	62,000
2004	Greater Good, 2, 118	J. McKee	Magna Graduate, 2, 114	Norainonthisparty, 2, 114	6	1:44.96	62,000
2003	‡Mr. Jester, 2, 118	R. Bejarano	The Cliff's Edge, 2, 114	Pomeroy, 2, 116	8	1:46.61	62,000
2002	Vindication, 2, 116	M. E. Smith	Private Gold, 2, 118	Tito's Beau, 2, 114	8	1:46.70	62,750
2001	Repent, 2, 114	A. J. D'Amico	French Assault, 2, 118	Gold Dollar, 2, 114	7	1:43.78	62,750
2000	Point Given, 2, 114	S. J. Sellers	Holiday Thunder, 2, 114	The Goo, 2, 116	11	1:47.01	62,600
1999	Millencolin, 2, 114	P. Day	Personal First, 2, 118	Deputy Warlock, 2, 118	10	1:47.02	62,600
1998	Aly's Alley, 2, 118	P. A. Johnson	Time Bandit, 2, 120	Mac's Rule, 2, 116	9	1:45.63	62,600
1997	Laydown, 2, 114	M. E. Smith	Time Limit, 2, 118	Da Devil, 2, 114	7	1:43.17	62,600
1996	Boston Harbor, 2, 120	D. M. Barton	Play Waki for Me, 2, 118	Dr. Spine, 2, 112	8	1:42.89	65,000
1995	Editor's Note, 2, 115	G. L. Stevens	Devil's Honor, 2, 118	Never to Squander, 2, 110	8	1:45.07	65,000
1994	Tejano Run, 2, 120	J. D. Bailey	Gold Miner, 2, 120	Bick, 2, 120	7	1:46.10	65,000
1993	Bibury Court, 2, 120	S. T. Saito	Moving Van, 2, 120	Durham, 2, 120	11	1:47.75	81,250
1992	Mountain Cat, 2, 120	C. R. Woods Jr.	Saw Mill, 2, 120	Shoal Creek, 2, 120	10	1:43.50	97,500
1991	Star Recruit, 2, 120	R. D. Lopez	Pick Up the Phone, 2, 120	Battenburg, 2, 120	9	1:45.68	97,500
1990	Fire in Ice, 2, 120	A. J. Garcia	Wall Street Dancer, 2, 120	Gold Shoulder, 2, 120	10	1:46.60	81,250
1989	Fighting Fantasy, 2, 120	D. W. Cox	Top Snob, 2, 120	Hardburly, 2, 120	9	1:48.40	81,250
1988	Light Crude, 2, 120	R. L. Frazier	Bravoure, 2, 120	Revive, 2, 120	8	1:44.80	81,250
1987	Jim's Orbit, 2, 120	P. Day	Kingpost, 2, 120	Delightful Doctor, 2, 120	11	1:37.80	81,250
1986	Rainbow East, 2, 120	O. B. Aviles	Alysheba, 2, 120	David L.'s Rib, 2, 120	11	1:37.20	78,500

Turfway Park is located in Florence, Kentucky. Formerly named for Dorothy and Pam Scharbauer's 1988 Horse of the Year Alysheba (1984 c. by Alydar); Alysheba placed second in the 1986 In Memoriam S. Formerly named for 1923 champion three-year-old male and '23 Latonia Championship S. winner In Memoriam (1920 c. by *McGee). Formerly sponsored by James McIngvale's Gallery Furniture Co. of Houston, Texas 1998. In Memoriam S. 1986–'88. Alysheba S. 1989–'93. 1 mile 1986–'87. Dirt 1986-2005. ‡Pomeroy finished first, DQ for bumping, 2003.

Kentucky Cup Sprint Stakes

Grade 3 in 2008. Turfway Park, three-year-olds and up, 6 furlongs, all weather. Held September 29, 2007, with a gross value of $100,000. First held in 1994. First graded in 1996. Stakes record 1:08.24 (1996 Appealing Skier).

Year	Winner	Jockey	Second	Third	Strs	Time	1st Purse
2007	Piratesonthelake, 3, 118	D. Sanchez	Base Commander, 3, 118	Stormin Baghdad, 3, 118	11	1:09.09	$58,280
2006	Reigning Court, 3, 118	C. J. Lanerie	Island Warrior, 3, 120	Hallowed Flag, 3, 118	12	1:09.13	62,000
2005	Estate Collection, 3, 116	P. A. Valenzuela	Humor At Last, 3, 116	Going Wild, 3, 119	7	1:09.75	62,000
2004	Level Playingfield, 3, 116	J. McKee	Cuvee, 3, 116	Swift Attraction, 3, 116	5	1:09.76	62,000
2003	Cajun Beat, 3, 122	C. H. Velasquez	Clock Stopper, 3, 116	Champali, 3, 122	11	1:09.54	62,000

Year	Winner	Jockey	Second	Third	Strs	Time	1st Purse
2002	Day Trader, 3, 118	P. Day	Premier Performer, 3, 114	Ecstatic, 3, 114	11	1:10.01	$94,500
2001	Snow Ridge, 3, 114	P. Day	City Zip, 3, 122	Dream Run, 3, 117	5	1:09.22	94,500
2000	Caller One, 3, 120	K. Desormeaux	Millencolin, 3, 116	Kings Command, 3, 116	6	1:09.46	93,750
1999	Successful Appeal, 3, 122	E. S. Prado	Five Star Day, 3, 114	American Spirit, 3, 118	6	1:09.42	74,400
1998	Reraise, 3, 116	C. S. Nakatani	Copelan Too, 3, 114	Mr Bert, 3, 114	7	1:08.50	93,900
1997	Partner's Hero, 3, 114	P. Day	Oro de Mexico, 3, 116	Prosong, 3, 114	6	1:09.02	74,400
1996	Appealing Skier, 3, 118	M. E. Smith	†Capote Belle, 3, 119	Delay of Game, 3, 114	9	**1:08.24**	97,500
1995	Lord Carson, 3, 116	M. E. Smith	Ft. Stockton, 3, 122	Evansville Slew, 3, 116	10	1:08.60	97,500
1994	End Sweep, 3, 120	C. J. McCarron	Exclusive Praline, 3, 122	Chimes Band, 3, 122	7	1:09.99	97,500

Turfway Park is located in Florence, Kentucky. Grade 2 1996-2001. Dirt 1994-2005. Equaled track record 1995. †Denotes female.

Kentucky Cup Turf Stakes

Grade 3 in 2008. Kentucky Downs, three-year-olds and up, 1½ miles, turf. Held September 22, 2007, with a gross value of $200,000. First held in 1998. First graded in 2001. Stakes record 2:26.98 (2007 General Jumbo [GB]).

Year	Winner	Jockey	Second	Third	Strs	Time	1st Purse
2007	General Jumbo (GB), 5, 116	J. Rose	Fri Guy, 4, 116	Golden Strategy, 4, 116	8	**2:26.98**	$123,628
2006	Embossed (Ire), 4, 116	L. Melancon	Lord Carmen, 5, 116	Rochester, 10, 116	8	2:36.92	124,000
2005	Silverfoot, 5, 120	R. Bejarano	Rochester, 9, 116	Gallo Del Bar (Chi), 5, 116	8	2:30.30	124,000
2004	Sabiango (Ger), 6, 119	B. Blanc	Rochester, 8, 117	Gottabeachboy, 4, 115	6	2:33.70	124,000
2003	‡Rochester, 7, 116	E. M. Martin Jr.	Quest Star, 4, 116	Art Variety (Brz), 6, 116	8	2:31.39	124,000
2002	Rochester, 6, 115	E. M. Martin Jr.	Nowrass (GB), 6, 112	Continental Red, 6, 117	11	2:38.28	186,000
2001	Chorwon, 8, 113	J. K. Court	The Knight Sky, 5, 114	Man From Wicklow, 4, 114	7	2:28.68	186,000
2000	Down the Aisle, 7, 117	R. Albarado	Crowd Pleaser, 5, 113	Royal Strand (Ire), 6, 115	8	2:27.70	186,000
1999	Fahris (Ire), 5, 116	S. J. Sellers	Yaqthan (Ire), 9, 116	Royal Strand (Ire), 5, 114	12	2:29.60	186,000
1998	Yaqthan (Ire), 8, 115	B. Peck	Perim (Fr), 5, 114	Chorwon, 5, 116	8	2:27.60	186,000

Kentucky Cup Turf H. 1998-2005. ‡Art Variety (Brz) finished first, DQ to third, 2003. Established course record 1998. Course record 2007.

Kentucky Derby Presented by Yum! Brands

Grade 1 in 2008. Churchill Downs, three-year-olds, 1¼ miles, dirt. Held May 3, 2008, with a gross value of $2,211,800. First held in 1875. First graded in 1973. Stakes record 1:59.40 (1973 Secretariat).

(See Triple Crown section for complete history of the Kentucky Derby)

Year	Winner	Jockey	Second	Third	Strs	Time	1st Purse
2008	Big Brown, 3, 126	K. J. Desormeaux	†Eight Belles, 3, 121	Denis of Cork, 3, 126	20	2:01.82	$1,451,800
2007	Street Sense, 3, 126	C. H. Borel	Hard Spun, 3, 126	Curlin, 3, 126	20	2:02.17	1,450,900
2006	Barbaro, 3, 126	E. S. Prado	Bluegrass Cat, 3, 126	Steppenwolfer, 3, 126	20	2:01.36	1,453,200
2005	Giacomo, 3, 126	M. E. Smith	Closing Argument, 3, 126	Afleet Alex, 3, 126	20	2:02.75	1,639,600
2004	Smarty Jones, 3, 126	S. Elliott	Lion Heart, 3, 126	Imperialism, 3, 126	18	2:04.06	884,800
2003	Funny Cide, 3, 126	J. A. Santos	Empire Maker, 3, 126	Peace Rules, 3, 126	16	2:01.19	800,200
2002	War Emblem, 3, 126	V. Espinoza	Proud Citizen, 3, 126	Perfect Drift, 3, 126	18	2:01.13	1,875,000
2001	Monarchos, 3, 126	J. F. Chavez	Invisible Ink, 3, 126	Congaree, 3, 126	17	1:59.97	812,000
2000	Fusaichi Pegasus, 3, 126	K. Desormeaux	Aptitude, 3, 126	Impeachment, 3, 126	19	2:01.12	1,038,400
1999	Charismatic, 3, 126	C. W. Antley	Menifee, 3, 126	Cat Thief, 3, 126	19	2:03.29	886,200
1998	Real Quiet, 3, 126	K. Desormeaux	Victory Gallop, 3, 126	Indian Charlie, 3, 126	15	2:02.38	700,000
1997	Silver Charm, 3, 126	G. L. Stevens	Captain Bodgit, 3, 126	Free House, 3, 126	13	2:02.44	700,000
1996	Grindstone, 3, 126	J. D. Bailey	Cavonnier, 3, 126	Prince of Thieves, 3, 126	19	2:01.06	869,800
1995	Thunder Gulch, 3, 126	G. L. Stevens	Tejano Run, 3, 126	Timber Country, 3, 126	19	2:01.27	707,400
1994	Go for Gin, 3, 126	C. J. McCarron	Strodes Creek, 3, 126	Blumin Affair, 3, 126	14	2:03.72	628,800
1993	Sea Hero, 3, 126	J. D. Bailey	Prairie Bayou, 3, 126	Wild Gale, 3, 126	19	2:02.42	735,900
1992	Lil E. Tee, 3, 126	P. Day	Casual Lies, 3, 126	Dance Floor, 3, 126	18	2:03.04	724,800
1991	Strike the Gold, 3, 126	C. W. Antley	Best Pal, 3, 126	Mane Minister, 3, 126	16	2:03.08	655,800
1990	Unbridled, 3, 126	C. Perret	Summer Squall, 3, 126	Pleasant Tap, 3, 126	15	2:02.00	581,000
1989	Sunday Silence, 3, 126	P. A. Valenzuela	Easy Goer, 3, 126	Awe Inspiring, 3, 126	15	2:05.00	574,200
1988	†Winning Colors, 3, 121	G. L. Stevens	Forty Niner, 3, 126	Risen Star, 3, 126	17	2:02.20	611,200
1987	Alysheba, 3, 126	C. J. McCarron	Bet Twice, 3, 126	Avies Copy, 3, 126	17	2:03.40	618,600
1986	Ferdinand, 3, 126	W. Shoemaker	Bold Arrangement (GB), 3, 126	Broad Brush, 3, 126	16	2:02.80	609,400
1985	Spend a Buck, 3, 126	A. T. Cordero Jr.	Stephan's Odyssey, 3, 126	Chief's Crown, 3, 126	13	2:00.20	406,800
1984	Swale, 3, 126	L. A. Pincay Jr.	Coax Me Chad, 3, 126	At the Threshold, 3, 126	20	2:02.40	537,400
1983	Sunny's Halo, 3, 126	E. Delahoussaye	Desert Wine, 3, 126	Caveat, 3, 126	20	2:02.20	426,000
1982	Gato Del Sol, 3, 126	E. Delahoussaye	Laser Light, 3, 126	Reinvented, 3, 126	19	2:02.40	428,850
1981	Pleasant Colony, 3, 126	J. Velasquez	Woodchopper, 3, 126	Partez, 3, 126	21	2:02.00	317,200
1980	‡Genuine Risk, 3, 121	J. Vasquez	Rumbo, 3, 126	Jaklin Klugman, 3, 126	13	2:02.00	250,550
1979	Spectacular Bid, 3, 126	R. J. Franklin	General Assembly, 3, 126	Golden Act, 3, 126	10	2:02.40	228,650
1978	Affirmed, 3, 126	S. Cauthen	Alydar, 3, 126	Believe It, 3, 126	11	2:01.20	186,900
1977	Seattle Slew, 3, 126	J. Cruguet	Run Dusty Run, 3, 126	Sanhedrin, 3, 126	15	2:02.20	214,700
1976	Bold Forbes, 3, 126	A. T. Cordero Jr.	Honest Pleasure, 3, 126	Elocutionist, 3, 126	9	2:01.60	165,200
1975	Foolish Pleasure, 3, 126	J. Vasquez	Avatar, 3, 126	Diabolo, 3, 126	15	2:02.00	209,600
1974	Cannonade, 3, 126	A. T. Cordero Jr.	Hudson County, 3, 126	Agitate, 3, 126	23	2:04.00	274,000
1973	Secretariat, 3, 126	R. Turcotte	Sham, 3, 126	Our Native, 3, 126	13	**1:59.40**	155,050

The Kentucky Derby was named for the Derby S. (Eng-G1) in England, commonly known as the Epsom Derby, its pred-

ecessor and model. Kentucky is the home state of Churchill Downs. Presented by Yum! Brands of Louisville 2006-'07. Kentucky Derby 1875-2005. 1½ miles 1875-'95. Track record 1973. †Denotes female. Winner's purse includes $1-million bonus for winning the Illinois Derby (G2) and the Kentucky Derby (G1) 2002. Winner's purse includes $5-million bonus from Oaklawn Park 2004.

Kentucky Jockey Club Stakes

Grade 2 in 2008. Churchill Downs, two-year-olds, 1 1/16 miles, dirt. Held November 24, 2007, with a gross value of $276,750. First held in 1920. First graded in 1973. Stakes record 1:42.84 (2006 Tiz Wonderful).

Year	Winner	Jockey	Second	Third	Strs	Time	1st Purse
2007	Anak Nakal, 2, 122	J. R. Leparoux	Blackberry Road, 2, 122	Racecar Rhapsody, 2, 122	7	1:43.16	$168,156
2006	Tiz Wonderful, 2, 122	J. R. Velazquez	Any Given Saturday, 2, 122	Dominican, 2, 122	9	1:42.84	133,208
2005	Private Vow, 2, 120	S. Bridgmohan	High Cotton, 2, 116	Hyte Regency, 2, 122	7	1:45.80	137,888
2004	Greater Good, 2, 122	J. McKee	Rush Bay, 2, 116	Wild Desert, 2, 118	9	1:45.14	138,384
2003	The Cliff's Edge, 2, 122	S. J. Sellers	Gran Prospect, 2, 116	Proper Prado, 2, 118	8	1:45.50	137,764
2002	Soto, 2, 117	L. J. Melancon	Ten Cents a Shine, 2, 115	Most Feared, 2, 122	12	1:44.67	143,344
2001	Repent, 2, 122	A. J. D'Amico	Request for Parole, 2, 117	High Star, 2, 115	6	1:44.42	134,540
2000	Dollar Bill, 2, 113	C. H. Borel	Holiday Thunder, 2, 113	Gift of the Eagle, 2, 113	6	1:47.18	135,656
1999	Captain Steve, 2, 122	R. Albarado	Mighty, 2, 122	Personal First, 2, 119	12	1:43.14	143,840
1998	Exploit, 2, 122	C. J. McCarron	Vicar, 2, 113	Grits'n Hard Toast, 2, 113	11	1:44.16	140,740
1997	Cape Town, 2, 113	W. Martinez	Time Limit, 2, 119	Real Quiet, 2, 116	11	1:43.97	142,228
1996	Concerto, 2, 119	C. H. Marquez Jr.	Celtic Warrior, 2, 113	Carmen's Baby, 2, 122	11	1:46.91	142,104
1995	Ide, 2, 122	C. Perret	Editor's Note, 2, 119	El Amante, 2, 113	5	1:44.31	97,500
1994	Jambalaya Jazz, 2, 113	S. Maple	You're the One, 2, 112	Peaks and Valleys, 2, 117	7	1:46.46	97,500
1993	War Deputy, 2, 112	G. K. Gomez	Tarzans Blade, 2, 122	Rustic Light, 2, 119	11	1:46.75	97,500
1992	Wild Gale, 2, 116	S. J. Sellers	Mi Cielo, 2, 116	Shoal Creek, 2, 121	11	1:45.64	105,918
1991	Dance Floor, 2, 121	C. W. Antley	Waki Warrior, 2, 116	Choctaw Ridge, 2, 116	10	1:45.21	104,891
1990	Richman, 2, 121	P. Day	Discover, 2, 116	Honor Grades, 2, 116	10	1:45.40	107,718
1989	Grand Canyon, 2, 121	A. T. Cordero Jr.	Insurrection, 2, 121	Dusty's Command, 2, 118	6	1:44.60	95,550
1988	Tricky Creek, 2, 118	L. J. Melancon	Western Playboy, 2, 116	Revive, 2, 118	10	1:45.40	106,083
1987	‡Notebook, 2, 122	J. A. Santos	Buoy, 2, 122	Hey Pat, 2, 119	6	1:47.40	74,701
1986	Mt. Pleasant, 2, 116	K. K. Allen	Mondulick, 2, 113	Funny Tunes, 2, 113	11	1:46.40	93,561
1985	Mustin Lake, 2, 116	P. Day	Bachelor Beau, 2, 116	Regal Dreamer, 2, 122	10	1:46.80	87,432
1984	Fuzzy, 2, 114	D. Brumfield	Banner Bob, 2, 119	Nordic Scandal, 2, 113	13	1:45.00	106,902
1983	Biloxi Indian, 2, 119	G. Patterson	Country Manor, 2, 119	Taylor's Special, 2, 119	7	1:46.20	71,721
1982	Highland Park, 2, 122	D. Brumfield	Coax Me Matt, 2, 116	Caveat, 2, 122	5	1:47.00	75,869
1981	El Baba, 2, 119	R. P. Romero	Crown the King, 2, 116	Talent Town, 2, 119	9	1:45.20	85,888
1980	Television Studio, 2, 119	D. Brumfield	Linnleur, 2, 119	Bear Creek Dam, 2, 116	8	1:47.00	73,226
1979	King Neptune, 2, 116	D. Brumfield	Royal Sporan, 2, 119	Silver Shears, 2, 116	7	1:37.80	37,001
1978	Lot o' Gold, 2, 119	R. DePass	Arctic Action, 2, 116	Uncle Fudge, 2, 119	12	1:37.80	37,645
1977	Going Investor, 2, 119	R. DePass	Jaycean, 2, 119	Silver Nitrate, 2, 116	7	1:38.20	36,121
1976	Run Dusty Run, 2, 122	D. G. McHargue	Get the Axe, 2, 116	Silver Series, 2, 116	8	1:37.20	34,831
1975	Play Boy, 2, 116	D. Brumfield	Khyber King, 2, 119	Please Find John, 2, 116	9	1:36.80	30,492
	Pastry, 2, 116	B. R. Feliciano	Bold Laddie, 2, 119	Bid to Fame, 2, 116	8	1:36.80	30,329
1974	Circle Home, 2, 116	M. Hole	Master Derby, 2, 122	Ruggles Ferry, 2, 116	9	1:36.00	36,748
1973	Cannonade, 2, 119	P. Anderson	Satan's Hills, 2, 116	Don't Be Late Jim, 2, 116	15	1:36.80	49,510

Kentucky is the home state of Churchill Downs. Formerly sponsored by Brown & Williamson Tobacco Corp. of Louisville 1987-'93, 1996-2000. Grade 3 1973-'82, 1984-'86, 1989-'97. Not graded 1983. Held at Old Latonia 1931-'33. Not held 1939-'45. 1 mile 1920-'79. Two divisions 1975. ‡Buoy finished first, DQ to second, 1987.

Kentucky Oaks

Grade 1 in 2008. Churchill Downs, three-year-olds, fillies, 1 1/8 miles, dirt. Held May 2, 2008, with a gross value of $581,650. First held in 1875. First graded in 1973. Stakes record 1:48.64 (2003 Bird Town).

Year	Winner	Jockey	Second	Third	Strs	Time	1st Purse
2008	Proud Spell, 3, 121	G. Saez	Little Belle, 3, 121	Pure Clan, 3, 121	10	1:50.01	$342,596
2007	Rags to Riches, 3, 121	G. K. Gomez	Octave, 3, 121	High Heels, 3, 121	14	1:49.99	332,428
2006	Lemons Forever, 3, 121	M. Guidry	Ermine, 3, 121	‡Wait a While, 3, 121	14	1:50.07	426,479
2005	Summerly, 3, 121	J. D. Bailey	In the Gold, 3, 121	Gallant Secret, 3, 121	7	1:50.23	343,728
2004	Ashado, 3, 121	J. R. Velazquez	Island Sand, 3, 121	Madcap Escapade, 3, 121	11	1:50.81	354,640
2003	Bird Town, 3, 121	E. S. Prado	Santa Catarina, 3, 121	Yell, 3, 121	12	1:48.64	355,756
2002	Farda Amiga, 3, 121	C. J. McCarron	Take Charge Lady, 3, 121	Habibti, 3, 121	9	1:50.41	348,502
2001	Flute, 3, 121	J. D. Bailey	Real Cozzy, 3, 121	Collect Call, 3, 121	13	1:48.85	377,704
2000	Secret Status, 3, 121	P. Day	Rings a Chime, 3, 121	Classy Cara, 3, 121	14	1:50.30	378,696
1999	Silverbulletday, 3, 121	G. L. Stevens	Dreams Gallore, 3, 121	Sweeping Story, 3, 121	7	1:49.92	341,620
1998	Keeper Hill, 3, 121	D. R. Flores	Banshee Breeze, 3, 121	Really Polish, 3, 121	13	1:52.06	375,410
1997	Blushing K. D., 3, 121	L. J. Meche	Tomisue's Delight, 3, 121	‡Storm Song, 3, 121	9	1:50.29	362,514
1996	Pike Place Dancer, 3, 121	C. S. Nakatani	Escena, 3, 121	Cara Rafaela, 3, 121	6	1:49.88	325,000
1995	Gal in a Ruckus, 3, 121	W. H. McCauley	Urbane, 3, 121	Sneaky Quiet, 3, 121	8	1:50.09	235,040
1994	Sardula, 3, 121	E. Delahoussaye	Lakeway, 3, 121	Dianes Halo, 3, 121	7	1:51.16	184,340
1993	Dispute, 3, 121	J. D. Bailey	Eliza, 3, 121	Quinpool, 3, 121	11	1:52.47	191,230
1992	Luv Me Luv Me Not, 3, 121	F. A. Arguello Jr.	Pleasant Stage, 3, 121	Prospectors Delite, 3, 121	6	1:51.41	182,455
1991	Lite Light, 3, 121	C. S. Nakatani	Withallprobability, 3, 121	Til Forbid, 3, 121	10	1:48.83	207,285

Year	Winner	Jockey	Second	Third	Strs	Time	1st Purse
1990	Seaside Attraction, 3, 121	C. J. McCarron	Go for Wand, 3, 121	Bright Candles, 3, 121	10	1:52.80	$156,910
1989	Open Mind, 3, 121	A. T. Cordero Jr.	Imaginary Lady, 3, 121	Blondeinamotel, 3, 121	5	1:50.60	150,540
1988	Goodbye Halo, 3, 121	P. Day	Jeanne Jones, 3, 121	Willa On the Move, 3, 121	10	1:50.40	156,715
1987	Buryyourbelief, 3, 121	J. A. Santos	Hometown Queen, 3, 121	Super Cook, 3, 121	8	1:50.40	155,415
1986	Tiffany Lass, 3, 121	G. L. Stevens	Life At the Top, 3, 121	Family Style, 3, 121	12	1:50.60	122,103
1985	Fran's Valentine, 3, 121	P. A. Valenzuela	Foxy Deen, 3, 121	Rascal Lass, 3, 121	9	1:50.00	118,365
1984	Lucky Lucky Lucky, 3, 121	A. T. Cordero Jr.	Miss Oceana, 3, 121	My Darling One, 3, 121	6	1:51.80	112,710
1983	Princess Rooney, 3, 121	J. Vasquez	Bright Crocus, 3, 121	Bemissed, 3, 121	7	1:50.80	116,968
1982	Blush With Pride, 3, 121	W. Shoemaker	Before Dawn, 3, 121	Flying Partner, 3, 121	7	1:50.20	126,133
1981	Heavenly Cause, 3, 121	L. A. Pincay Jr.	De La Rose, 3, 121	Wayward Lass, 3, 121	6	1:43.80	79,300
1980	Bold 'n Determined, 3, 121	E. Delahoussaye	Mitey Lively, 3, 121	Honest and True, 3, 121	8	1:44.80	83,915
1979	Davona Dale, 3, 121	J. Velasquez	Himalayan, 3, 121	Prize Spot, 3, 121	6	1:47.20	83,590
1978	White Star Line, 3, 121	E. Maple	Grenzen, 3, 121	Bold Rendezvous, 3, 121	11	1:45.20	60,889
1977	Sweet Alliance, 3, 121	C. J. McCarron	Our Mims, 3, 121	Mrs. Warren, 3, 121	12	1:43.60	60,889
1976	Optimistic Gal, 3, 121	B. Baeza	Confort Zone, 3, 121	Carmelita Gibbs, 3, 121	7	1:44.60	40,186
1975	Sun and Snow, 3, 121	G. Patterson	Funalon, 3, 121	Funny Cat, 3, 121	11	1:44.60	42,315
1974	Quaze Quilt, 3, 121	W. Gavidia	Special Team, 3, 121	Kaye's Commander, 3, 121	14	1:46.60	43,631
1973	Bag of Tunes, 3, 121	D. Gargan	La Prevoyante, 3, 121	Coraggioso, 3, 121	13	1:44.20	43,648

Named for the Oaks S. (Eng-G1), commonly known as the Epsom Oaks, its prototype in England. Kentucky is the home state of Churchill Downs. Grade 2 1973-'77. 1½ miles 1875-'90. 1¼ miles 1891-'95. 1¹/₁₆ miles 1896-1919, 1942-'81. ‡Sharp Cat finished third, DQ to eighth, 1997. ‡Bushfire finished third, DQ to sixth, 2006.

Kentucky Stakes

Grade 3 in 2008. Churchill Downs, two-year-olds, 5 furlongs, dirt. Held May 1, 2008, with a gross value of $163,000. First held in 1988. First graded in 1999. Stakes record :57.46 (2007 Rated Fiesty).

Year	Winner	Jockey	Second	Third	Strs	Time	1st Purse
2008	Run Away and Hide, 2, 120	R. Albarado	†Garden District, 2, 117	Dream of Kaylee, 2, 118	6	:57.56	$103,429
2007	†Rated Fiesty, 2, 117	S. Bridgmohan	†Yogi'ssplashofgold, 2, 117	Ready's Image, 2, 120	9	:57.46	110,255
2006	Datrick, 2, 117	S. Bridgmohan	†Pro Pink, 2, 114	Sentry, 2, 117	12	:58.37	109,852
2004	Lunarpal, 2, 121	S. J. Sellers	Consolidator, 2, 115	Smoke Warning, 2, 117	4	1:04.07	86,025
2003	Cuvee, 2, 117	L. J. Meche	First Money, 2, 117	Exploit Lad, 2, 117	6	1:04.45	109,554
2002	Posse, 2, 115	D. J. Meche	Del Diablo, 2, 115	Blackjack Boy, 2, 115	8	1:03.73	102,300
2001	Leelanau, 2, 115	J. K. Court	Gygistar, 2, 115	†Lakeside Cup, 2, 112	6	1:03.11	100,812
2000	†Gold Mover, 2, 113	C. Perret	City Zip, 2, 115	Unbridled Time, 2, 121	6	1:03.67	101,091
1999	†Chilukki, 2, 112	R. Albarado	Barrier, 2, 115	Sky Dweller, 2, 115	7	1:04.01	106,485
1998	Yes It's True, 2, 121	S. J. Sellers	Tactical Cat, 2, 115	Alannan, 2, 115	8	1:03.61	85,948
1997	Favorite Trick, 2, 121	P. Day	Jess M, 2, 115	†Cutie Luttie, 2, 112	8	1:04.80	68,882
1996	†Move, 2, 113	S. J. Sellers	Prairie Junction, 2, 115	†Live Your Best, 2, 112	7	1:05.74	71,175
1995	†Miraloma, 2, 112	D. M. Barton	Great Southern, 2, 114	A. V. Eight, 2, 112	9	1:04.04	68,933
1994	My My, 2, 116	S. J. Sellers	Wise Affair, 2, 116	Hyroglyphic, 2, 116	11	1:05.96	37,310
1993	†Astas Foxy Lady, 2, 118	T. J. Hebert	Dish It Out, 2, 116	Riverinn, 2, 116	9	1:05.51	68,738
1992	Tempered Halo, 2, 121	P. A. Johnson	‡Mountain Cat, 2, 116	†Secret Bundle, 2, 113	7	1:05.39	50,326
1991	Hippomenes, 2, 112	P. Day	Cold Gate, 2, 118	It's Chemistry, 2, 113	9	1:06.30	50,716
1990	To Freedom, 2, 118	J. C. Espinoza	St. Alegis, 2, 112	Maxwell Street, 2, 112	5	1:05.00	17,647
1989	Summer Squall, 2, 118	C. R. Woods Jr.	Dr. Bobby A., 2, 118	Wink Road, 2, 118	7	1:05.00	50,294
1988	†Island Escape, 2, 115	C. R. Woods Jr.	One That Got Away, 2, 121	Papa Leonard, 2, 114	7	1:04.60	50,456

Churchill Downs is located in Louisville, Kentucky. Kentucky Budweiser Breeders' Cup S. 1988-'91, 1993-'95. Kentucky Breeders' Cup S. 1992, 1996-2007. Not held 2005. 5½ furlongs 1988-2004. Track record 1998, 2001. ‡Exclusive Zone finished second, DQ to fourth, 1992. †Denotes female.

King's Bishop Stakes

Grade 1 in 2008. Saratoga Race Course, three-year-olds, 7 furlongs, dirt. Held August 25, 2007, with a gross value of $250,000. First held in 1984. First graded in 1987. Stakes record 1:20.99 (2004 Pomeroy).

Year	Winner	Jockey	Second	Third	Strs	Time	1st Purse
2007	Hard Spun, 3, 121	M. G. Pino	First Defence, 3, 119	E Z Warrior, 3, 119	11	1:22.34	$150,000
2006	Henny Hughes, 3, 121	J. R. Velazquez	Star Dabbler, 3, 117	Court Folly, 3, 121	9	1:21.96	150,000
2005	Lost in the Fog, 3, 123	R. A. Baze	Social Probation, 3, 117	Better Than Bonds, 3, 119	7	1:22.56	150,000
2004	Pomeroy, 3, 121	E. S. Prado	Weigelia, 3, 121	Ice Wynnd Fire, 3, 117	8	1:20.99	150,000
2003	Valid Video, 3, 121	J. Bravo	Great Notion, 3, 117	Ghostzapper, 3, 117	13	1:22.14	120,000
2002	Gygistar, 3, 124	J. R. Velazquez	Boston Common, 3, 121	Thunder Days, 3, 115	8	1:22.65	120,000
2001	Squirtle Squirt, 3, 121	J. D. Bailey	Illusioned, 3, 119	City Zip, 3, 124	8	1:21.97	120,000
2000	More Than Ready, 3, 124	P. Day	Valiant Halory, 3, 114	Millencolin, 3, 121	6	1:22.49	120,000
1999	Forestry, 3, 124	C. W. Antley	Five Star Day, 3, 115	Successful Appeal, 3, 124	12	1:21.00	120,000
1998	Secret Firm, 3, 121	E. S. Prado	Mint, 3, 121	Scatmandu, 3, 116	8	1:22.78	120,000
1997	Tale of the Cat, 3, 114	J. A. Krone	Oro de Mexico, 3, 116	Trafalger, 3, 121	6	1:21.71	90,000
1996	Honour and Glory, 3, 123	J. A. Santos	Elusive Quality, 3, 112	Distorted Humor, 3, 115	6	1:21.78	64,920
1995	Top Account, 3, 112	P. Day	Ft. Stockton, 3, 120	Excelerate, 3, 113	10	1:22.50	68,100
1994	Chimes Band, 3, 117	J. D. Bailey	End Sweep, 3, 122	Halo's Image, 3, 115	7	1:21.82	65,700
1993	Mi Cielo, 3, 115	M. E. Smith	Williamstown, 3, 122	Schossberg, 3, 115	11	1:21.73	74,280
1992	Salt Lake, 3, 117	M. E. Smith	Binalong, 3, 115	Agincourt, 3, 122	10	1:21.53	73,440
1991	Take Me Out, 3, 115	M. E. Smith	Joey the Student, 3, 115	To Freedom, 3, 119	10	1:21.73	74,400

Year	Winner	Jockey	Second	Third	Strs	Time	1st Purse
1990	Housebuster, 3, 122	C. Perret	Poppiano, 3, 115	Sunshine Jimmy, 3, 115	9	1:21.80	$54,090
1989	Houston, 3, 119	P. Day	Fast Play, 3, 117	Fierce Fighter, 3, 115	6	1:22.00	51,930
1988	King's Nest, 3, 115	C. J. McCarron	Tejano, 3, 117	Parlay Me, 3, 115	8	1:21.80	53,280
1987	Templar Hill, 3, 119	C. J. McCarron	Mister S. M., 3, 119	Homebuilder, 3, 115	8	1:23.00	51,660
1985	Pancho Villa, 3, 122	D. G. McHargue	El Basco, 3, 119	Cullendale, 3, 115	9	1:22.20	33,540
1984	Commemorate, 3, 119	F. Lovato Jr.	All Fired Up, 3, 122	Raja's Shark, 3, 115	8	1:22.60	33,900

Named for Bohemia Stable's 1973 Carter H. (G2) winner King's Bishop (1969 c. by Round Table). Grade 3 1987-'91. Grade 2 1992-'98. Not held 1986.

Knickerbocker Handicap

Grade 3 in 2008. Aqueduct, three-year-olds and up, 1 1/8 miles, turf. Held October 28, 2007, with a gross value of $112,900. First held in 1960. First graded in 1973. Stakes record 1:48.69 (1998 Sahm).

Year	Winner	Jockey	Second	Third	Strs	Time	1st Purse
2007	Fishy Advice, 5, 116	J. Castellano	Thorn Song, 4, 116	Operation Red Dawn, 5, 114	9	1:52.06	$67,740
2006	Drum Major, 4, 115	J. Bravo	Fishy Advice, 4, 117	Giant Wrecker, 4, 115	10	1:50.59	68,460
2005	Atlando (Ire), 4, 116	J. D. Bailey	Certifiably Crazy, 5, 115	Rousing Victory, 4, 115	10	1:50.93	90,000
2004	Host (Chi), 4, 115	C. P. DeCarlo	Evening Attire, 6, 114	Sailaway, 4, 113	9	1:49.95	90,000
2003	Better Talk Now, 4, 116	E. S. Prado	Del Mar Show, 6, 116	Millennium Dragon (GB), 4, 115	12	1:50.53	90,000
2002	Dawn of the Condor, 5, 114	J. F. Chavez	Serial Bride, 5, 114	Polish Miner, 5, 114	9	1:52.54	90,000
2001	Sumitas (Ger), 5, 115	E. S. Prado	Manndar (Ire), 5, 116	Crash Course, 5, 115	11	2:02.55	90,000
2000	Charge d'Affaires (GB), 5, 115	J. A. Santos	Devine Wind, 4, 116	Understood, 4, 111	7	1:49.01	90,000
1999	Charge d'Affaires (GB), 4, 114	J. A. Santos	Comic Strip, 4, 119	Nat's Big Party, 5, 113	7	1:49.06	66,480
1998	Sahm, 4, 116	J. R. Velazquez	Glok, 4, 113	Let Goodtimes Roll, 5, 112	8	**1:48.69**	67,440
1997	Sir Cat, 4, 115	M. E. Smith	Tamhid, 4, 114	Outta My Way Man, 5, 114	5	1:50.02	69,060
1996	Mr. Bluebird, 5, 113	M. E. Smith	Devil's Cup, 3, 107	Ops Smile, 4, 116	12	1:49.21	69,660
1995	Diplomatic Jet, 3, 113	M. E. Smith	Flag Down, 5, 114	Easy Miner, 4, 110	11	2:04.97	87,870
1994	Kiri's Clown, 5, 114	M. J. Luzzi	River Majesty, 5, 117	Red Earth, 3, 111	12	1:49.38	52,335
1993	River Majesty, 4, 115	M. E. Smith	Daarik (Ire), 6, 114	Home of the Free, 5, 118	6	1:54.54	52,920
1992	Binary Light, 3, 111	J. Cruguet	Share the Glory, 4, 110	Turkey Point, 7, 113	7	1:52.70	56,160
1991	Home of the Free, 3, 110	J. R. Velazquez	Turkey Point, 6, 114	Fourstars Allstar, 3, 113	7	1:48.73	56,070
1990	Who's to Pay, 4, 115	J. D. Bailey	Yankee Affair, 8, 120	Green Line Express, 4, 121	8	1:49.20	57,240
1989	Trans Banner, 4, 112	J. Samyn	Soviet Lad, 4, 112	Impersonator, 4, 114	12	1:53.60	58,770
1988	Jimmy's Bronco, 4, 112	J. Cruguet	Coeur de Lion (Fr), 4, 118	†Gai Minois (Fr), 6, 113	11	1:54.80	58,590
1987	Laser Lane, 4, 113	J. A. Santos	Yankee Affair, 5, 116	Wanderkin, 4, 112	12	1:51.60	73,260
1986	Duluth, 4, 113	J. Cruguet	Dance of Life, 3, 122	Broadway Tommy, 4, 109	8	2:20.80	55,710
1985	Putting Green, 5, 112	E. Maple	Domynsky (GB), 5, 113	Capricorn Son (Ire), 3, 109	7	2:23.80	54,405
	Rocamadour (Ire), 6, 109	J. Cruguet	‡Sondrio (Ire), 4, 115	He's Vivacious, 5, 110	7	2:23.80	54,405
1984	He's Vivacious, 4, 108	R. G. Davis	Nassipour, 4, 109	Lucky Scott (GB), 3, 107	12	2:26.00	46,440
1983	Four Bases, 4, 105	R. J. Thibeau Jr.	Moon Spirit, 3, 114	Ask Me, 4, 117	10	2:17.80	34,230
	Piling, 5, 114	E. Maple	Chem, 4, 116	Charging Through, 3, 110	8	2:19.00	34,470
1982	Half Iced, 3, 114	D. MacBeth	No Neck, 7, 109	Erin's Tiger, 4, 112	8	2:19.00	33,330
	†If Winter Comes, 4, 108	M. Venezia	Ten Below, 3, 113	Forkali, 4, 112	8	2:19.60	33,330
1981	†Euphrosyne, 5, 110	R. Migliore	Our Captain Willie, 3, 115	Naskra's Breeze, 4, 115	8	2:18.40	33,330
	Ghazwan (Ire), 4, 110	C. Hernandez	Wicked Will (GB), 3, 108	†Hunston (GB), 3, 107	7	2:20.60	33,540
1980	Foretake, 4, 112	J. Ruane	El Barril (Chi), 4, 113	Ministrel (Fr), 4, 109	9	2:22.20	33,450
	Lobsang (Ire), 4, 111	M. Venezia	Match the Hatch, 4, 115	King Crimson (Fr), 5, 111	7	2:23.60	33,450
1979	French Colonial, 4, 114	J. Vasquez	T. V. Series, 3, 113	Golden Reserve, 5, 112	12	2:21.40	35,880
1978	Fluorescent Light, 4, 115	J. Cruguet	Banquet Table, 4, 109	Scythian Gold, 3, 110	10	2:14.20	34,560
1977	Dance d'Espoir, 5, 112	J. Cruguet	Java Rajah, 4, 106	Diagrammatic, 4, 112	5	2:05.00	26,010
	Keep the Promise, 5, 112	J. Cruguet	Soldier's Lark, 5, 110	Star Spangled, 3, 114	8	2:04.40	26,460
1976	†Javamine, 3, 111	J. Velasquez	*Recupere, 6, 112	Banghi, 3, 118	9	2:20.60	26,400
	Oilfield, 3, 112	S. Hawley	Royal Mission, 3, 111	Trumpeter Swan, 5, 112	7	2:22.60	26,100
1975	Shady Character, 4, 113	A. T. Cordero Jr.	Blue Times, 4, 115	*Yvetot, 7, 113	8	2:16.20	33,900
1974	Shady Character, 3, 115	A. T. Cordero Jr.	John Drew, 3, 119	Crafty Khale, 5, 126	5	2:41.40	33,690
1973	Astray, 4, 112	C. Baltazar	Triangular, 6, 114	*Yvetot, 5, 112	11	2:39.80	34,710

Named for a Washington Irving fictional character, Diedrich Knickerbocker; in the 19th century, New Yorkers were often called "Knickerbockers." Grade 3 1973-'97. Held at Belmont 1962, '75, '95, 2001, '05. 1 5/8 miles 1960-'61, 1970-'74. 1 3/8 miles 1962, 1975-'76, 1978-'86. 1 3/16 miles 1963-'69. 1 1/4 miles 1977, '95, 2001. Dirt 1977, '92, '97. Two divisions 1976-'77, 1980-'83, 1985. ‡He's Vivacious finished second, DQ to third (2nd Div.). †Denotes female.

La Brea Stakes

Grade 1 in 2008. Santa Anita Park, three-year-olds, fillies, 7 furlongs, all weather. Held December 29, 2007, with a gross value of $250,000. First held in 1974. First graded in 1983. Stakes record 1:20.45 (1993 Mamselle Bebette).

Year	Winner	Jockey	Second	Third	Strs	Time	1st Purse
2007	Dearest Trickski, 3, 117	M. E. Smith	Unspoken Word, 3, 117	Glorified, 3, 116	11	1:21.09	$150,000
2006	Downthedustyroad, 3, 115	J. K. Court	Squallacious, 3, 116	Balance, 3, 123	9	1:21.40	150,000
2005	Pussycat Doll, 3, 119	G. K. Gomez	Leave Me Alone, 3, 123	Thrilling Victory, 3, 119	11	1:21.36	150,000
2004	Alphabet Kisses, 3, 117	M. E. Smith	Bending Strings, 3, 121	Elusive Diva, 3, 119	10	1:21.38	150,000
2003	Island Fashion, 3, 123	K. Desormeaux	Randaroo, 3, 119	Buffythecenterfold, 3, 119	10	1:21.79	150,000
2002	Got Koko, 3, 117	A. O. Solis	Spring Meadow, 3, 119	Erica's Smile, 3, 117	10	1:22.57	120,000
2001	Affluent, 3, 121	E. Delahoussaye	Royally Chosen, 3, 119	Love At Noon, 3, 117	12	1:21.29	120,000
2000	Spain, 3, 123	V. Espinoza	Cover Gal, 3, 119	Serenita (Arg), 3, 115	6	1:22.27	120,000

Year	Winner	Jockey	Second	Third	Strs	Time	1st Purse
1999	Hookedonthefeelin, 3, 119	D. R. Flores	Olympic Charmer, 3, 119	Kalookan Queen, 3, 119	8	1:21.84	$120,000
1998	Magical Allure, 3, 121	G. L. Stevens	Gourmet Girl, 3, 117	Tranquility Lake, 3, 116	7	1:22.06	120,000
1997	I Ain't Bluffing, 3, 119	E. Delahoussaye	Minister's Melody, 3, 119	Praviana (Chi), 3, 115	9	1:21.23	99,540
1996	Hidden Lake, 3, 115	C. J. McCarron	Belle's Flag, 3, 119	Tiffany Diamond, 3, 115	7	1:22.00	80,900
1995	Exotic Wood, 3, 119	C. J. McCarron	Evil's Pic, 3, 119	Jewel Princess, 3, 119	6	1:21.57	80,250
1994	Top Rung, 3, 115	G. L. Stevens	Klassy Kim, 3, 119	Twice the Vice, 3, 119	7	1:21.84	63,700
1993	Mamselle Bebette, 3, 115	C. S. Nakatani	Desert Stormer, 3, 116	Island Orchid, 3, 115	9	**1:20.45**	65,900
1992	Arches of Gold, 3, 115	E. Delahoussaye	Race the Wild Wind, 3, 121	Terre Haute, 3, 117	8	1:21.28	64,800
1991	D'Or Ruckus, 3, 115	C. J. McCarron	Good Potential, 3, 119	Garden Gal, 3, 117	6	1:22.05	48,800
	Teresa Mc, 3, 119	P. A. Valenzuela	Remarkably Easy, 3, 119	Suziqcute, 3, 119	6	1:23.05	48,800
1990	Brought to Mind, 3, 117	A. O. Solis	A Wild Ride, 3, 119	Mama Simba, 3, 114	8	1:21.60	65,000
	Akinemod, 4, 117	G. L. Stevens	Fantastic Look, 4, 122	Reluctant Guest, 4, 117	8	1:21.60	62,650
1989	Very Subtle, 4, 117	C. A. Black	T. V. of Crystal, 4, 117	Forewarning, 4, 117	6	1:21.60	49,050
1988	Very Subtle, 4, 124	P. A. Valenzuela	Saros Brig, 4, 114	Fold the Flag, 4, 117	6	1:21.20	60,300
1987	Family Style, 4, 122	G. L. Stevens	Sari's Heroine, 4, 119	Winter Treasure, 4, 117	6	1:22.60	46,700
1985	Savannah Slew, 3, 119	W. Shoemaker	Lady's Secret, 3, 124	Ambra Ridge, 3, 114	7	1:22.40	39,150
	Mitterand, 4, 117	E. Delahoussaye	Percipient, 4, 119	Lady Trilby, 4, 117	9	1:21.80	39,950
1983	Lovlier Linda, 3, 114	W. Shoemaker	Angel Savage (Mex), 3, 115	Fabulous Notion, 3, 124	9	1:22.20	40,700
1982	Beautiful Glass, 3, 114	C. J. McCarron	Skillful Joy, 3, 122	Header Card, 3, 119	11	1:21.00	42,450
	Nell's Briquette, 4, 122	C. J. McCarron	Bannockburn, 4, 115	Bee a Scout, 4, 117	8	1:25.80	40,150
1981	Dynanite, 4, 114	W. Shoemaker	Bold 'n Determined, 4, 125	Pachena, 4, 114	5	1:21.40	31,750
1980	Terlingua, 4, 121	D. G. McHargue	Glorious Song, 4, 116	Prize Spot, 4, 121	4	1:20.80	31,350
1979	Great Lady M., 4, 117	L. A. Pincay Jr.	dh-B. Thoughtful, 4, 121	Sound of Summer, 4, 121	11	1:22.60	35,850
			dh-Queen Yasna, 4, 114				
1978	Taisez Vous, 4, 121	D. Pierce	Ida Delia, 4, 114	Sound of Summer, 4, 121	7	1:22.80	26,700
1976	Kirby Lane, 3, 117	L. A. Pincay Jr.	Tregillick, 3, 116	Missing Marbles, 3, 116	9	1:45.20	23,750
1975	Featherfoot, 3, 114	W. Shoemaker	Banyan Road, 3, 120	Graham Heagney, 3, 114	5	1:43.20	13,025
	Big Destiny, 3, 114	S. Hawley	Bending Away, 3, 120	Mark's Place, 3, 120	6	1:42.80	13,325
	Bobby Murcer, 4, 120	E. Belmonte	Bold Clarion, 4, 120	Roger's Dandy, 4, 117	11	1:43.40	20,800
1974	Niner Power, 4, 117	S. Valdez	First Majesty, 4, 117	Handsome Native, 4, 117	10	1:43.80	20,350

Named for Rancho La Brea in Los Angeles County, California; brea means "tar." Grade 3 1983–'93. Grade 2 1994–'96. Not held 1977, '84, '86. 1¹/₁₆ miles 1974–'76. Dirt 1974–2006. Four-year-olds 1974, 1975 (January), 1978–'81, 1982 (January), 1985 (January), 1987–'89, 1990 (January). Both sexes 1974–'76. Two divisions 1975 (December), 1991. Held in January and December 1975, '82, '85, '90. Dead heat for second 1979. Nonwinners of a race worth $10,000 to the winner 1974. Nonwinners of a race worth $12,500 to the winner 1975. Nonwinners of a race worth $15,000 to the winner 1976.

La Canada Stakes

Grade 2 in 2008. Santa Anita Park, four-year-olds, fillies, 1¹/₈ miles, all weather. Held February 10, 2008, with a gross value of $200,000. First held in 1975. First graded in 1977. Stakes record 1:47.60 (1980 Glorious Song; 1982 Safe Play).

Year	Winner	Jockey	Second	Third	Strs	Time	1st Purse
2008	Dawn After Dawn, 4, 116	G. K. Gomez	Say You Will (Ire), 4, 116	Caressive, 4, 116	5	1:50.37	$120,000
2007	Balance, 4, 123	V. Espinoza	Bai and Bai, 4, 118	Les Ry Leigh, 4, 118	6	1:49.41	120,000
2006	Seafree, 4, 118	P. A. Valenzuela	Play Ballado, 4, 118	Sharp Lisa, 4, 120	5	1:50.04	120,000
2005	Tarlow, 4, 117	P. A. Valenzuela	Sweet Lips, 4, 121	A. P. Adventure, 4, 118	5	1:48.64	120,000
2004	Cat Fighter, 4, 115	A. O. Solis	Fencelineneighbor, 4, 116	Tangle (Ire), 4, 116	8	1:50.41	120,000
2003	Got Koko, 4, 121	A. O. Solis	Sightseek, 4, 118	Bella Bellucci, 4, 116	5	1:48.41	120,000
2002	Summer Colony, 4, 119	G. L. Stevens	Azeri, 4, 115	Ask Me No Secrets, 4, 115	6	1:49.26	120,000
2001	Spain, 4, 122	V. Espinoza	Chilukki, 4, 119	Letter of Intent, 4, 116	5	1:49.74	120,000
2000	Scholars Studio, 4, 116	C. S. Nakatani	Smooth Player, 4, 117	The Seven Seas, 4, 116	5	1:49.14	120,000
1999	Manistique, 4, 119	G. L. Stevens	Magical Allure, 4, 119	Gourmet Girl, 4, 117	7	1:48.81	120,000
1998	Fleet Lady, 4, 119	G. K. Gomez	Minister's Melody, 4, 117	I Ain't Bluffing, 4, 117	7	1:48.59	120,000
1997	Belle's Flag, 4, 115	C. S. Nakatani	Chile Chatte, 4, 115	Housa Dancer (Fr), 4, 115	8	1:48.26	133,200
1996	Jewel Princess, 4, 119	A. O. Solis	Dixie Pearl, 4, 116	Privity, 4, 117	6	1:49.42	129,900
1995	Dianes Halo, 4, 115	C. S. Nakatani	Twice the Vice, 4, 119	Klassy Kim, 4, 119	6	1:49.35	123,800
1994	Stalcreek, 4, 119	G. L. Stevens	Alyshena, 4, 115	Hollywood Wildcat, 4, 122	6	1:48.85	120,000
1993	Alysbelle, 4, 116	E. Delahoussaye	Pacific Squall, 4, 119	Interactive, 4, 117	9	1:49.85	130,850
1992	Exchange, 4, 119	L. A. Pincay Jr.	Winglet, 4, 117	Damewood, 4, 116	8	1:49.96	128,250
1991	Fit to Scout, 4, 120	J. A. Garcia	Vieille Vigne (Fr), 4, 116	A Wild Ride, 4, 121	7	1:48.50	126,700
1990	Gorgeous, 4, 121	E. Delahoussaye	Luthier's Launch, 4, 117	Kelly, 4, 116	5	1:50.00	122,000
1989	Goodbye Halo, 4, 126	P. Day	Seattle Smooth, 4, 117	Savannah's Honor, 4, 115	7	1:54.00	125,300
1988	Hollywood Glitter, 4, 117	L. A. Pincay Jr.	By Land by Sea, 4, 119	Very Subtle, 4, 126	7	1:49.20	94,200
1987	Family Style, 4, 122	G. L. Stevens	Winter Treasure, 4, 117	Sari's Heroine, 4, 121	6	1:49.60	94,800
1986	Lady's Secret, 4, 126	C. J. McCarron	Shywing, 4, 119	North Sider, 4, 118	6	1:49.60	120,200
1985	Mitterand, 4, 121	E. Delahoussaye	Percipient, 4, 117	Life's Magic, 4, 126	5	1:49.20	90,700
1984	Sweet Diane, 4, 120	R. Sibille	Weekend Surprise, 4, 115	Lovlier Linda, 4, 120	4	1:49.20	117,200
1983	Avigaition, 4, 117	E. Delahoussaye	Elusive, 4, 115	Etoile Du Matin, 4, 116	11	1:49.80	101,450
1982	Safe Play, 4, 119	D. Brumfield	Rainbow Connection, 4, 121	Native Plunder, 4, 117	11	**1:47.60**	100,800
1981	Summer Siren, 4, 117	M. Castaneda	Miss Huntington, 4, 119	Tobin's Rose, 4, 118	10	1:48.60	86,250
1980	Glorious Song, 4, 118	C. J. McCarron	Prize Spot, 4, 119	It's in the Air, 4, 125	7	**1:47.60**	80,350
1979	B. Thoughtful, 4, 119	D. Pierce	Petron's Love, 4, 117	Island Kiss, 4, 115	8	1:48.80	69,900

Racing — Graded Stakes 371

Year	Winner	Jockey	Second	Third	Strs	Time	1st Purse
1978	Taisez Vous, 4, 120	D. Pierce	Drama Critic, 4, 116	Table the Rumor, 4, 117	5	1:49.80	$65,000
1977	*Lucie Manet, 4, 115	W. Shoemaker	Hail Hilarious, 4, 121	Up to Juliet, 4, 115	7	1:48.20	68,300
1976	Raise Your Skirts, 4, 119	W. Shoemaker	Fascinating Girl, 4, 117	Our First Delight, 4, 117	8	1:48.40	50,150
1975	Chris Evert, 4, 128	J. Velasquez	Mercy Dee, 4, 116	Lucky Spell, 4, 119	7	1:41.60	35,400

Named for Rancho La Canada where the city of La Crescenta, California, is located; canada means "glen" or "dell."
Grade 1 1976-'89. 1 1/16 miles 1975. Dirt 1975-2007.

Lady's Secret Stakes

Grade 1 in 2008. Oak Tree at Santa Anita, three-year-olds and up, fillies and mares, 1 1/16 miles, all weather. Held October 7, 2007, with a gross value of $196,500. First held in 1993. First graded in 1995. Stakes record 1:40.61 (1994 Hollywood Wildcat).

Year	Winner	Jockey	Second	Third	Strs	Time	1st Purse
2007	Tough Tiz's Sis, 3, 121	V. Espinoza	Hystericalady, 4, 123	Bai and Bai, 4, 123	6	1:41.64	$105,000
2006	Healthy Addiction, 5, 120	V. Espinoza	Downthedustyroad, 3, 112	Hollywood Story, 5, 118	5	1:43.60	150,000
2005	Healthy Addiction, 4, 115	G. K. Gomez	Star Parade (Arg), 6, 114	Island Fashion, 5, 117	6	1:42.23	150,000
2004	Island Fashion, 4, 120	K. John	Miss Loren (Arg), 6, 116	Elloluv, 4, 118	7	1:43.43	150,000
2003	Got Koko, 4, 118	A. O. Solis	‡Azeri, 5, 128	Adoration, 4, 115	6	1:42.92	180,000
2002	Azeri, 4, 127	M. E. Smith	Starrer, 4, 115	Mystic Lady, 4, 116	7	1:41.10	130,500
2001	Queenie Belle, 4, 116	B. Blanc	Letter of Intent, 4, 116	Nany's Sweep, 5, 116	6	1:43.64	126,240
2000	Smooth Player, 4, 116	E. Delahoussaye	Speaking of Time, 4, 109	Bordelaise (Arg), 5, 116	6	1:42.27	126,360
1999	Manistique, 4, 123	C. S. Nakatani	Cookin Vickie, 4, 111	Kalosca (Fr), 5, 114	5	1:42.39	125,100
1998	Magical Allure, 3, 116	D. R. Flores	Victory Stripes (Arg), 4, 114	Housa Dancer (Fr), 5, 117	8	1:42.55	110,280
1997	Sharp Cat, 3, 117	A. O. Solis	Twice the Vice, 6, 122	Minister's Melody, 3, 115	5	1:41.40	109,400
1996	Top Rung, 5, 116	E. Fires	Jewel Princess, 4, 122	Sleep Easy, 4, 113	5	1:41.84	109,450
1995	Borodislew, 5, 120	G. L. Stevens	Top Rung, 4, 116	Golden Klair (GB), 5, 117	6	1:41.61	74,000
1994	Hollywood Wildcat, 4, 124	E. Delahoussaye	Exchange, 6, 121	Dancing Mirage, 3, 113	5	**1:40.61**	61,400
1993	Hollywood Wildcat, 3, 117	E. Delahoussaye	Re Toss (Arg), 6, 117	Wedding Ring (Ire), 4, 113	5	1:41.05	61,700

Named for Mr. and Mrs. Eugene V. Klein's 1986 Horse of the Year and '86 Breeders' Cup Distaff (G1) (at Santa Anita Park) winner Lady's Secret (1982 f. by Secretariat). Grade 3 1995. Grade 2 1996-2006. Lady's Secret H. 1993-'95. Lady's Secret Breeders' Cup H. 1996-2006. Dirt 1993-2006. ‡Elloluv finished second, DQ to fourth, 2003.

La Habra Stakes

Grade 3 in 2008. Santa Anita Park, three-year-olds, fillies, 6 1/2 furlongs, turf. Held February 2, 2008, with a gross value of $113,350. First held in 1973. First graded in 2008. Stakes record 1:12.66 (2007 Super Freaky).

Year	Winner	Jockey	Second	Third	Strs	Time	1st Purse
2008	Passion, 3, 118	R. Bejarano	Ariege, 3, 116	Sweet August Moon, 3, 116	9	1:13.52	$68,010
2007	Super Freaky, 3, 116	J. K. Court	‡Pay Wright, 3, 122	Seaside Affair, 3, 118	11	**1:12.66**	68,040
2006	Harriett Lane, 3, 118	K. J. Desormeaux	Bettarun Fast, 3, 116	Dance Daily, 3, 122	7	1:13.97	65,670
2005	Shining Energy, 3, 115	R. R. Douglas	Kohar, 3, 115	dh-Berbatim, 3, 116 dh-Royal Wave, 3, 117	9	1:13.61	66,840
2004	Very Vegas, 3, 118	M. Ruis	Aspen Gal, 3, 115	Fortunately (GB), 3, 114	9	1:13.99	66,810
2003	Luvah Girl (GB), 3, 116	M. E. Smith	Katdogawn (GB), 3, 114	Himalayan, 3, 116	8	1:14.03	66,480
2002	High Society (Ire), 3, 116	B. Blanc	Fun House, 3, 116	Ayzal (GB), 3, 116	11	1:12.96	67,890
2001	Serena's Tune, 3, 116	G. L. Stevens	Langoureuse, 3, 116	Innit (Ire), 3, 116	11	1:14.81	69,060
2000	Squall City, 3, 118	C. W. Antley	Classic Olympio, 3, 120	Minor Details, 3, 118	8	1:13.99	65,790
1999	Aviate, 3, 115	C. J. McCarron	Open Secret (Ire), 3, 115	Perfect Six, 3, 118	10	1:15.08	67,650
1998	Conectis (Ire), 3, 114	J. Valdivia Jr.	Loveontheroad, 3, 116	Miss Fleet Diablo, 3, 117	12	1:14.37	68,100
1997	Lavender, 3, 114	A. O. Solis	Wealthy, 3, 116	Granja Realeza, 3, 116	9	1:13.71	66,350
1996	To B. Super, 3, 114	C. S. Nakatani	Staffin (GB), 3, 114	Hear the Music (Ire), 3, 117	9	1:15.36	66,850
1995	Cat's Cradle, 3, 120	C. W. Antley	Christmas Gift, 3, 116	Kindred Soul, 3, 115	10	1:14.70	51,050
1994	Dezibelle's Star, 3, 116	G. L. Stevens	Sophisticatedcielo, 3, 116	Ballerina Gal, 3, 116	6	1:14.04	47,450
1993	Miss Timebank, 3, 115	K. J. Desormeaux	Voluptuous, 3, 114	Frans Lass, 3, 120	8	1:15.03	48,800
1992	Hopeful Amber, 3, 120	A. O. Solis	Peaceful Road, 3, 116	Wine 'n Music, 3, 120	9	1:13.59	49,750
1991	Nice Assay, 3, 118	D. R. Flores	Perky Slew, 3, 116	Officer Lea, 3, 114	9	1:17.30	50,350
1990	High Hatted, 3, 116 Somethingperfect, 3, 117	K. J. Desormeaux L. A. Pincay Jr.	Tasteful T. V., 3, 120 Brought to Mind, 3, 115	Devil's Orchid, 3, 116 Forest Fealty, 3, 116	6 11	1:14.40 1:14.00	39,100 42,700
1989	Stormy But Valid, 3, 116	G. L. Stevens	Hot Novel, 3, 120	No Torsion, 3, 116	7	1:14.80	47,850
1988	Bolchina, 3, 114 Sheesham, 3, 118	S. Hawley L. A. Pincay Jr.	Hasty Pasty, 3, 116 Super Avie, 3, 116	Valid Allure, 3, 114 Sadie B. Fast, 3, 116	8 7	1:15.20 1:15.60	37,312 37,312
1987	Devil's Bride, 3, 118	R. Q. Meza	Footy, 3, 116	Timely Reserve, 3, 118	8	1:16.00	39,150
1986	Hidden Light, 3, 114	W. Shoemaker	Sari's Heroine, 3, 120	Top Corsage, 3, 116	12	1:14.80	42,600
1985	Trunk, 3, 114	G. L. Stevens	Akameni (Fr), 3, 116	Azorrable, 3, 114	11	1:15.80	41,800
1984	Costly Array, 3, 114	J. Fell	Danzadar, 3, 114	I'm Really Smokin, 3, 114	12	1:16.40	42,800
1983	Little Hailey, 3, 114	W. Shoemaker	Hot n Pearly, 3, 117	Mazatleca (Mex), 3, 115	7	1:16.00	39,700
1982	Gladdie's Reb, 3, 114	W. A. Guerra	Jones Time Machine, 3, 117	Coffee Maid, 3, 114	8	1:18.00	40,000
1981	Glitter Hitter, 3, 115	E. Delahoussaye	Interview Time, 3, 114	Flying Baton, 3, 114	10	1:14.20	34,700
1980	Thundertee, 3, 114	D. G. McHargue	Street Ballet, 3, 120	Regal Ara, 3, 117	10	1:13.40	28,000
1979	Celine, 3, 116	L. A. Pincay Jr.	Billie Bets, 3, 117	Variety Queen, 3, 114	9	1:13.60	27,300
1978	Eximious, 3, 114	W. Shoemaker	Grenzen, 3, 120	Dallas Deb, 3, 117	7	1:16.20	26,500
1977	Reminiscing, 3, 117	L. A. Pincay Jr.	Drama Critic, 3, 114	*Glenaris, 3, 114	9	1:14.20	23,800
1976	Dancing Femme, 3, 114	W. Shoemaker	Cascapedia, 3, 115	Doc Shah's Siren, 3, 117	9	1:13.60	20,850
1974	June's Love, 3, 122	J. Tejeira	First Back, 3, 122	Miradero, 3, 122	3	1:09.60	18,350

Year	Winner	Jockey	Second	Third	Strs	Time	1st Purse
1973	Driftin' Along, 3, 119	F. Olivares	Tumble Lane, 3, 119	Chios, 3, 122	3	1:09.80	$13,465
	Crown the Prince, 3, 119	A. Pineda	Security Aim, 3, 122	*Mariache II, 3, 122	3	1:08.80	13,815

Named for an 1839 land grant, Rancho Canada de La Habra, located in present-day Orange County, California, and site of the modern city of La Habra. Not held 1975. 6 furlongs 1973-'74. Dirt 1973-'74, 1978, 1982-'83, 1991. Both sexes 1973-'74. Two divisions 1973, '88, '90. Dead heat for third 2005. ‡Macadamia finished second, DQ to sixth, 2007.

La Jolla Handicap

Grade 2 in 2008. Del Mar, three-year-olds, 1 1/16 miles, turf. Held August 11, 2007, with a gross value of $150,000. First held in 1937. First graded in 1973. Stakes record 1:40.39 (2003 Singletary).

Year	Winner	Jockey	Second	Third	Strs	Time	1st Purse
2007	‡Worldly (GB), 3, 121	M. C. Baze	Latin Rhythms, 3, 115	Ten a Penny, 3, 118	8	1:42.57	$90,000
2006	A. P. Warrior, 3, 120	D. R. Flores	Porto Santo (Fr), 3, 118	Get Funky, 3, 116	7	1:40.71	90,000
2005	Willow O Wisp, 3, 121	G. K. Gomez	Juliesugardaddy, 3, 119	El Roblar, 3, 120	7	1:41.45	90,000
2004	Blackdoun (Fr), 3, 120	C. S. Nakatani	Semi Lost, 3, 116	Bedmar (GB), 3, 113	7	1:41.03	90,000
2003	Singletary, 3, 118	P. A. Valenzuela	Devious Boy (GB), 3, 117	Senor Swinger, 3, 120	7	**1:40.39**	90,000
2002	Inesperado (Fr), 3, 118	E. Delahoussaye	Regiment, 3, 121	Mountain Rage, 3, 119	4	1:43.92	90,000
2001	Marine (GB), 3, 117	C. S. Nakatani	Romanceishope, 3, 118	Mister Approval, 3, 113	8	1:41.72	90,000
2000	Purely Cozzene, 3, 120	D. R. Flores	Duke of Green (GB), 3, 117	Sign of Hope (GB), 3, 115	9	1:41.50	90,000
1999	Eagleton, 3, 119	I. D. Enriquez	In Frank's Honor, 3, 117	Zanetti, 3, 117	9	1:41.89	90,000
1998	Ladies Din, 3, 120	G. L. Stevens	Success and Glory (Ire), 3, 116	Lucayan Indian (Ire), 3, 116	7	1:41.94	80,670
1997	Fantastic Fellow, 3, 118	A. O. Solis	Worldly Ways (GB), 3, 119	Falkenham (GB), 3, 115	7	1:43.43	85,450
1996	Ambivalent, 3, 116	R. R. Douglas	The Barking Shark, 3, 114	Caribbean Pirate, 3, 117	10	1:43.34	82,850
1995	Petionville, 3, 120	C. S. Nakatani	Private Interview, 3, 115	Beau Temps (GB), 3, 115	7	1:44.26	74,600
1994	Marvin's Faith (Ire), 3, 114	C. W. Antley	Unfinished Symph, 3, 120	Ocean Crest, 3, 114	7	1:42.38	62,800
1993	Manny's Prospect, 3, 115	C. J. McCarron	Golden Slewpy, 3, 116	Hawk Spell, 3, 116	9	1:42.12	64,700
1992	Blacksburg, 3, 119	K. Desormeaux	Free At Last, 3, 121	Fax News, 3, 114	9	1:41.60	64,700
1991	Track Monarch, 3, 116	P. A. Valenzuela	Soweto (Ire), 3, 116	Persianalli (Ire), 3, 115	6	1:41.91	61,400
1990	Tight Spot, 3, 118	E. Delahoussaye	Itsallgreektome, 3, 119	Music Prospector, 3, 118	6	1:41.80	62,100
1989	River Master, 3, 115	C. J. McCarron	Tokatee, 3, 113	Art Work, 3, 114	8	1:42.60	65,100
1988	Perfecting, 3, 116	G. L. Stevens	Roberto's Dancer, 3, 115	Prove Splendid, 3, 115	8	1:41.60	64,800
1987	The Medic, 3, 116	C. J. McCarron	Something Lucky, 3, 117	Savona Tower, 3, 117	11	1:42.20	66,250
1986	Vernon Castle, 3, 120	E. Delahoussaye	Tripoli Shores, 3, 117	Marvin's Policy, 3, 116	12	1:35.20	64,650
1985	Floating Reserve, 3, 117	P. A. Valenzuela	First Norman, 3, 116	Derby Dawning, 3, 119	9	1:34.60	62,750
1984	Tights, 3, 120	C. J. McCarron	Ocean View, 3, 113	Refueled (Ire), 3, 115	6	1:35.60	59,150
1983	Tanks Brigade, 3, 120	E. Delahoussaye	Dr. Daly, 3, 121	Pair of Aces, 3, 116	7	1:35.80	50,150
1982	Hugabay, 3, 115	K. D. Black	Bargain Balcony, 3, 118	The Captain, 3, 118	8	1:35.60	33,050
	Take the Floor, 3, 115	C. J. McCarron	Craelius, 3, 116	Sword Blade, 3, 115	8	1:35.80	33,050
1981	Minnesota Chief, 3, 122	C. J. McCarron	High Counsel, 3, 117	Stancharry, 3, 124	11	1:35.20	40,950
1980	Aristocratical, 3, 117	C. J. McCarron	Son of a Dodo, 3, 117	Exploded, 3, 117	9	1:36.20	32,850
1979	Relaunch, 3, 117	L. A. Pincay Jr.	Hyannis Port, 3, 122	Pole Position, 3, 124	7	1:35.40	25,600
1978	Singular, 3, 114	D. G. McHargue	Misrepresentation, 3, 119	Sea Ride, 3, 114	9	1:35.80	23,150
1977	Stone Point, 3, 114	M. Castaneda	Pay the Toll, 3, 114	Windy Dancer, 3, 114	9	1:35.80	18,850
1976	Today 'n Tomorrow, 3, 114	D. Pierce	Noble Envoy, 3, 114	Wood Green, 3, 115	8	1:35.20	19,400
1975	Larrikin, 3, 123	D. Pierce	Wood Carver, 3, 115	Sibirri, 3, 119	9	1:35.00	16,850
1974	Lightning Mandate, 3, 125	A. Pineda	Within Hail, 3, 120	Sea Aglo, 3, 113	6	1:34.40	15,800
1973	Groshawk, 3, 125	W. Shoemaker	Dancing Papa, 3, 115	Expression, 3, 123	6	1:34.20	16,300

Named for the resort community of La Jolla, California, located in the San Diego area. Grade 3 1973-2003. La Jolla Mile H. 1937-'65, 1982-'86. La Jolla Mile S. 1977-'81. Not held 1939, 1942-'44. 1 mile 1938-'86. Dirt 1937-'74. Three-year-olds and up 1937-'38, 1945-'46, 1949-'50. Two divisions 1982. Course record 1975. ‡Medici Code (GB) finished first, DQ to eighth, 2007.

Lake George Stakes

Grade 2 in 2008. Saratoga Race Course, three-year-olds, fillies, 1 1/16 miles, turf. Held July 27, 2008, with a gross value of $115,100. First held in 1996. First graded in 1998. Stakes record 1:40.11 (1999 Nani Rose).

Year	Winner	Jockey	Second	Third	Strs	Time	1st Purse
2007	Rutherienne, 3, 122	G. K. Gomez	Lady Attack, 3, 117	Sharp Susan, 3, 122	11	1:40.34	$69,060
2006	Magnificent Song, 3, 120	G. K. Gomez	Somethinaboutbetty, 3, 116	Quite a Bride, 3, 122	8	1:45.88	67,740
2005	Ready's Gal, 3, 116	J. R. Velazquez	Dream Lady, 3, 116	Who's Cozy, 3, 116	8	1:41.90	66,600
2004	Seducer's Song, 3, 115	J. D. Bailey	Venturi (GB), 3, 119	Fortunate Damsel, 3, 117	10	1:42.01	68,340
2003	Film Maker, 3, 115	E. S. Prado	Ocean Drive, 3, 119	Gal O Gal, 3, 122	11	1:41.80	68,700
2002	Nunatall (GB), 3, 115	J. F. Chavez	Guana (Fr), 3, 117	Mariensky, 3, 117	11	1:40.71	69,000
2001	Light Dancer, 3, 117	M. Guidry	Owsley, 3, 117	Cozzy Corner, 3, 115	9	1:41.06	67,050
	Voodoo Dancer, 3, 122	J. D. Bailey	Sadler's Sarah, 3, 117	O K to Dance, 3, 122	9	1:41.45	67,350
2000	Millie's Quest, 3, 114	J. R. Velazquez	Shopping for Love, 3, 117	Battenkill, 3, 114	9	1:44.52	70,080
1999	Nani Rose, 3, 122	S. J. Sellers	Perfect Sting, 3, 122	Intrigued, 3, 122	8	**1:40.11**	67,680
1998	Caveat Competor, 3, 116	J. R. Velazquez	Mysterious Moll, 3, 114	Recording, 3, 121	10	1:41.05	50,760
	Tenski, 3, 114	R. Migliore	Pratella, 3, 114	Camella, 3, 114	8	1:40.86	50,070
1997	Auntie Mame, 3, 121	J. D. Bailey	Crab Grass, 3, 114	Innovate, 3, 116	9	1:42.80	51,120
1996	Memories of Silver, 3, 112	J. D. Bailey	Clamorosa, 3, 118	Captive Number, 3, 113	10	1:42.98	33,780
	Dynasty, 3, 112	J. D. Bailey	River Antoine, 3, 113	Vashon, 3, 116	8	1:42.26	33,630

Named for a favorite summertime resort in upstate New York, just north of Saratoga Springs. Grade 3 1998-2006. Lake George H. 1999. Two divisions 1996, '98, 2001.

Lake Placid Stakes

Grade 2 in 2008. Saratoga Race Course, three-year-olds, fillies, 1 1/8 miles, turf. Held August 17, 2007, with a gross value of $150,000. First held in 1984. First graded in 1986. Stakes record 1:46.33 (1998 Tenski).

Year	Winner	Jockey	Second	Third	Strs	Time	1st Purse
2007	Sharp Susan, 3, 120	K. J. Desormeaux	New Edition, 3, 118	Lady Attack, 3, 117	8	1:46.69	$90,000
2006	Wait a While, 3, 120	G. K. Gomez	Lady of Venice (Fr), 3, 120	Dancing Band, 3, 116	5	1:46.59	90,000
2005	Naissance Royale (Ire), 3, 118	E. S. Prado	My Typhoon (Ire), 3, 118	Victory Lap, 3, 118	6	1:47.14	90,000
2004	Spotlight (GB), 3, 118	J. D. Bailey	Mambo Slew, 3, 120	Fortunate Damsel, 3, 116	7	1:50.54	90,000
2003	Sand Springs, 3, 121	M. Guidry	Indy Five Hundred, 3, 114	Film Maker, 3, 119	10	1:49.03	90,000
2002	Wonder Again, 3, 114	E. S. Prado	Riskaverse, 3, 120	Miss Marcia, 3, 114	9	1:49.24	90,000
2001	Snow Dance, 3, 116	R. Migliore	Wander Mom, 3, 116	Mystic Lady, 3, 117	12	1:47.42	90,000
2000	Gaviola, 3, 122	J. D. Bailey	Good Game, 3, 117	Millie's Quest, 3, 117	11	1:48.04	90,000
1999	Badouizm, 3, 113	R. G. Davis	Confessional, 3, 115	Emanating, 3, 115	8	1:46.44	90,000
1998	Tenski, 3, 119	R. Migliore	Naskra's de Light, 3, 117	Caveat Competor, 3, 118	12	1:46.33	90,000
1997	Witchful Thinking, 3, 123	S. J. Sellers	Miss Huff n' Puff, 3, 114	Majestic Sunlight, 3, 114	12	1:47.65	90,000
1996	Memories of Silver, 3, 115	J. D. Bailey	Unify, 3, 113	Henlopen, 3, 112	9	1:47.80	68,640
1995	Class Kris, 3, 112	P. Day	In a Daydream, 3, 112	Shocking Pleasure, 3, 113	9	1:40.90	67,380
	Bail Out Becky, 3, 115	S. J. Sellers	Fashion Star, 3, 112	Grand Charmer, 3, 120	9	1:41.87	67,680
1994	Alywow, 3, 121	M. E. Smith	Irish Forever, 3, 121	Knocknock, 3, 114	9	1:43.81	66,660
	Coronation Cup, 3, 114	J. D. Bailey	Stretch Drive, 3, 114	Golden Tajniak (Ire), 3, 118	7	1:43.88	65,760
1993	Amal Hayati, 3, 121	J. D. Bailey	Eloquent Silver, 3, 114	Irving's Girl, 3, 114	10	1:40.97	56,940
	Statuette, 3, 114	M. E. Smith	Icy Warning, 3, 114	Dispute, 3, 118	8	1:41.58	55,980
1992	Shannkara (Ire), 3, 114	M. E. Smith	Tiney Toast, 3, 116	Favored Lady, 3, 114	11	1:41.84	73,380
	Heed, 3, 114	M. E. Smith	Captive Miss, 3, 114	Mystic Hawk, 3, 114	10	1:40.98	72,420
1991	Jinski's World, 3, 121	J. A. Santos	Belleofbasinstreet, 3, 114	Verbasle, 3, 114	11	1:41.01	59,760
	Grab the Green, 3, 114	A. T. Cordero Jr.	Shareefa, 3, 121	Irish Linnet, 3, 114	11	1:40.20	59,280
1990	Jefforee, 3, 114	J. A. Santos	Toffeefee, 3, 114	Colonial Runner, 3, 114	9	1:49.00	60,030
1989	Capades, 3, 121	A. T. Cordero Jr.	To the Lighthouse, 3, 116	Vanities, 3, 114	8	1:41.00	55,620
1988	Betty Lobelia, 3, 116	J. A. Santos	Curlew, 3, 114	‡Costly Shoes, 3, 121	8	1:41.60	66,780
	Love You by Heart, 3, 114	R. P. Romero	Another Paddock, 3, 116	Flashy Runner, 3, 114	8	1:41.80	66,780
1987	Graceful Darby, 3, 116	J. D. Bailey	Spectacular Bev, 3, 114	Token Gift, 3, 114	7	1:41.40	50,760
1986	An Empress, 3, 121	J. A. Santos	Fama, 3, 116	Spring Innocence, 3, 114	11	1:42.00	52,200
1985	Videogenic, 3, 114	R. G. Davis	My Regrets (Ire), 3, 114	Forever Command, 3, 116	9	1:41.80	33,720
1984	Possible Mate, 3, 114	D. MacBeth	Proud Nova, 3, 114	Miss Audemar, 3, 114	6	1:50.00	26,070

Named for the popular Adirondack mountain resort that has hosted the Winter Olympics twice. Formerly named for Cragwood Stable's 1975 Schuylerville S. (G3) winner Nijana (1973 f. by Nijinsky II). Grade 3 1991-'98. Nijana S. 1984-'97. Lake Placid H. 1998-2005. 1 1/16 miles 1984-'89, 1991-'95. Dirt 1990. Two divisions 1988, 1991-'95. ‡Tunita finished third, DQ to fourth, 1988 (1st Div.).

Lane's End Breeders' Futurity

Grade 1 in 2008. Keeneland Race Course, two-year-olds, 1 1/16 miles, all weather. Held October 6, 2007, with a gross value of $560,000. First held in 1910. First graded in 1973. Stakes record 1:42.23 (1993 Polar Expedition).

Year	Winner	Jockey	Second	Third	Strs	Time	1st Purse
2007	Wicked Style, 2, 121	R. Albarado	Slew's Tiznow, 2, 121	Old Man Buck, 2, 121	12	1:45.21	$310,000
2006	Great Hunter, 2, 121	V. Espinoza	Circular Quay, 2, 121	Street Sense, 2, 121	8	1:44.09	310,000
2005	Dawn of War, 2, 121	J. Jacinto	Catcominatcha, 2, 121	Stream Cat, 2, 121	12	1:48.77	310,000
2004	Consolidator, 2, 121	R. Bejarano	Patriot Act, 2, 121	Diamond Isle, 2, 121	10	1:43.67	310,000
2003	Eurosilver, 2, 121	J. Castellano	Tiger Hunt, 2, 121	Limehouse, 2, 121	11	1:43.42	248,000
2002	Sky Mesa, 2, 121	E. S. Prado	Lone Star Sky, 2, 121	Truckle Feature, 2, 121	6	1:46.78	269,576
2001	Siphonic, 2, 121	C. J. McCarron	Harlan's Holiday, 2, 121	Metatron, 2, 121	11	1:43.79	281,728
2000	Arabian Light, 2, 121	S. J. Sellers	Dollar Bill, 2, 121	Holiday Thunder, 2, 121	10	1:43.18	279,744
1999	Captain Steve, 2, 121	G. K. Gomez	Graeme Hall, 2, 121	Millencolin, 2, 121	8	1:42.59	274,040
1998	Cat Thief, 2, 121	P. Day	Answer Lively, 2, 121	Yes It's True, 2, 121	8	1:44.17	272,552
1997	Favorite Trick, 2, 121	P. Day	Time Limit, 2, 121	Laydown, 2, 121	5	1:43.36	265,112
1996	Boston Harbor, 2, 121	J. D. Bailey	Blazing Sword, 2, 121	Haint, 2, 121	5	1:45.31	1,166,005
1995	Honour and Glory, 2, 121	P. Day	City by Night, 2, 121	Blushing Jim, 2, 121	10	1:43.33	139,252
1994	Tejano Run, 2, 121	J. D. Bailey	Cinch, 2, 121	Gold Miner, 2, 121	11	1:44.71	71,548
1993	Polar Expedition, 2, 121	C. C. Bourque	Goodbye Doeny, 2, 121	Solly's Honor, 2, 121	8	1:42.23	122,200
1992	Mountain Cat, 2, 121	P. Day	Living Vicariously, 2, 121	Boundlessly, 2, 121	4	1:45.42	1,122,200
1991	Dance Floor, 2, 121	C. R. Woods Jr.	Star Recruit, 2, 121	Count the Time, 2, 121	7	1:44.37	122,200
1990	Sir Bordeaux, 2, 121	W. S. Ramos	Wall Street Dancer, 2, 121	Fire in Ice, 2, 121	6	1:44.40	145,925
1989	Slavic, 2, 121	J. A. Santos	Top Snob, 2, 121	Harry, 2, 121	4	1:44.60	159,770
1988	Fast Play, 2, 121	A. T. Cordero Jr.	Lorenzoni, 2, 121	Bio, 2, 121	6	1:45.20	129,350
1987	Forty Niner, 2, 121	E. Maple	Hey Pat, 2, 121	Sea Trek, 2, 121	7	1:43.80	104,868
1986	Orono, 2, 121	S. Hawley	Alysheba, 2, 121	Pledge Card, 2, 121	10	1:45.20	116,711
1985	Tasso, 2, 121	L. A. Pincay Jr.	Regal Dreamer, 2, 121	Thundering Force, 2, 121	11	1:46.00	122,424
1984	Crater Fire, 2, 121	D. Montoya	Nickel Back, 2, 121	Cullendale, 2, 121	8	1:45.80	110,474
1983	Swale, 2, 121	E. Maple	Spender, 2, 121	Back Bay Barrister, 2, 121	8	1:44.00	108,631
1982	Highland Park, 2, 121	J. Lively	Caveat, 2, 121	Bright Baron, 2, 121	12	1:43.60	97,825
1981	D'Accord, 2, 121	D. G. McHargue	Lets Dont Fight, 2, 121	Shooting Duck, 2, 121	10	1:44.40	94,575
1980	Fairway Phantom, 2, 121	J. Lively	Total Pleasure, 2, 121	Quick Ice, 2, 121	7	1:28.80	94,575
1979	Gold Stage, 2, 121	D. Brumfield	Degenerate Jon, 2, 121	Tonka Wakhan, 2, 121	5	1:26.80	81,608

Year	Winner	Jockey	Second	Third	Strs	Time	1st Purse
1978	**Strike Your Colors**, 2, 122	E. Delahoussaye	Lot o' Gold, 2, 122	Uncle Fudge, 2, 122	13	1:26.20	$92,284
1977	**Gonquin**, 2, 122	F. Olivares	Sunny Songster, 2, 122	Jaycean, 2, 122	7	1:28.00	83,866
1976	**Run Dusty Run**, 2, 122	D. G. McHargue	Banquet Table, 2, 122	Get the Axe, 2, 122	10	1:27.40	84,695
1975	**Harbor Springs**, 2, 122	E. Maple	Best Bee, 2, 122	‡Scrutiny, 2, 122	10	1:27.00	82,046
1974	**Packer Captain**, 2, 122	D. Brumfield	Master Derby, 2, 122	Ruggles Ferry, 2, 122	11	1:25.80	53,277
1973	**Provante**, 2, 122	M. Manganello	Training Table, 2, 122	Wage Raise, 2, 122	10	1:27.20	48,327

Named in honor of Kentucky breeders. Sponsored by W. S. Farish's Lane's End, located near Versailles, Kentucky 1997-2007. Grade 3 1973-'75. Grade 2 1976-2003. Held at Kentucky Association 1910-'30. Held at Old Latonia 1931-'33. Held at Churchill Downs 1943-'45. Not held 1934-'37. 4 furlongs 1910-'11. 4½ furlongs 1912. 5 furlongs 1913-'16. About 6 furlongs 1917-'33. 6 furlongs 1938-'49. 7 furlongs 1950-'55. About 7 furlongs 1956-'80. Dirt 1910-2005. ‡Vuelo finished third, DQ to fourth, 1975. Winner's purse includes $1-million bonus from the Kentucky Thoroughbred Development Fund 1992, '96.

Lane's End Stakes

Grade 2 in 2008. Turfway Park, three-year-olds, 1⅛ miles, all weather. Held March 22, 2008, with a gross value of $500,000. First held in 1972. First graded in 1984. Stakes record Stakes record 1:46.70 (1991 Hansel).

Year	Winner	Jockey	Second	Third	Strs	Time	1st Purse
2008	**Adriano**, 3, 121	E. S. Prado	Halo Najib, 3, 121	Medjool, 3, 121	11	1:50.20	$291,400
2007	**Hard Spun**, 3, 121	M. G. Pino	Sedgefield, 3, 121	Joe Got Even, 3, 121	12	1:49.41	300,000
2006	**With a City**, 3, 121	B. Blanc	Seaside Retreat, 3, 121	Malameeze, 3, 121	12	1:51.11	300,000
2005	**Flower Alley**, 3, 121	J. F. Chavez	Wild Desert, 3, 121	Mr Sword, 3, 121	9	1:50.33	300,000
2004	**Sinister G**, 3, 121	P. R. Toscano	Tricky Taboo, 3, 121	Little Matth Man, 3, 121	11	1:50.71	300,000
2003	**New York Hero**, 3, 121	N. Arroyo Jr.	Eugene's Third Son, 3, 121	Champali, 3, 121	9	1:50.68	300,000
2002	**Perfect Drift**, 3, 121	E. Delahoussaye	Azillion (Ire), 3, 121	Request for Parole, 3, 121	8	1:48.83	300,000
2001	**Balto Star**, 3, 121	M. Guidry	Halo's Stride, 3, 121	Mongoose, 3, 121	9	1:47.23	360,000
2000	**Globalize**, 3, 121	F. C. Torres	Elite Mercedes, 3, 121	Rollin With Nolan, 3, 121	10	1:49.16	360,000
1999	**Stephen Got Even**, 3, 121	S. J. Sellers	K One King, 3, 121	Epic Honor, 3, 121	8	1:49.03	450,000
1998	**Event of the Year**, 3, 121	R. A. Baze	Yarrow Brae, 3, 121	Truluck, 3, 121	10	1:47.12	360,000
1997	**Concerto**, 3, 121	C. H. Marquez Jr.	Jack Flash, 3, 121	Shammy Davis, 3, 121	10	1:48.23	360,000
1996	**Roar**, 3, 121	M. E. Smith	Ensign Ray, 3, 121	Victory Speech, 3, 121	9	1:49.70	360,000
1995	**†Serena's Song**, 3, 116	C. S. Nakatani	Tejano Run, 3, 121	Mecke, 3, 121	8	1:49.65	360,000
1994	**Polar Expedition**, 3, 121	C. C. Bourque	Powis Castle, 3, 121	Chimes Band, 3, 121	11	1:49.03	360,000
1993	**Prairie Bayou**, 3, 121	C. J. McCarron	Proudest Romeo, 3, 121	Miner's Mark, 3, 121	9	1:50.97	360,000
1992	**Lil E. Tee**, 3, 121	P. Day	Vying Victor, 3, 121	Treekster, 3, 121	11	1:53.44	300,000
1991	**Hansel**, 3, 121	J. D. Bailey	Richman, 3, 121	Wilder Than Ever, 3, 121	11	**1:46.70**	300,000
1990	**Summer Squall**, 3, 121	P. Day	Bright Again, 3, 121	Yonder, 3, 121	10	1:49.40	300,000
1989	**Western Playboy**, 3, 121	P. Day	Feather Ridge, 3, 121	Mercedes Won, 3, 121	12	1:49.00	300,000
1988	**Kingpost**, 3, 121	E. J. Sipus Jr.	Stalwars, 3, 121	Brian's Time, 3, 121	11	1:50.80	300,000
1987	**J. T.'s Pet**, 3, 121	P. Day	Faster Than Sound, 3, 121	Homebuilder, 3, 121	12	1:42.80	300,000
1986	**Broad Brush**, 3, 121	V. A. Bracciale Jr.	Miracle Wood, 3, 121	Bachelor Beau, 3, 121	12	1:44.20	210,000
1985	**Banner Bob**, 3, 121	K. K. Allen	Image of Greatness, 3, 121	Roo Art, 3, 121	10	1:42.00	227,540
1984	**At the Threshold**, 3, 121	P. Day	Bold Southerner, 3, 121	The Wedding Guest, 3, 121	12	1:42.80	195,000
1983	**Marfa**, 3, 120	J. Velasquez	Noble Home, 3, 120	Hail to Rome, 3, 120	12	1:42.40	151,515
1982	**Good n' Dusty**, 3, 120	M. T. Moran	Fast Gold, 3, 120	Cupecoy's Joy, 3, 115	12	1:44.60	125,450
1981	**Mythical Ruler**, 3, 114	K. B. Wirth	Classic Go Go, 3, 122	Iron Gem, 3, 115	10	1:38.00	33,210
1980	**Major Run**, 3, 116	M. S. Sellers	Ray's Word, 3, 122	Misty Bell, 3, 113	8	1:37.60	18,740
	Spruce Needles, 3, 116	J. C. Espinoza	Avenger M., 3, 122	Summer Advocate, 3, 113	6	1:36.20	18,440
1979	**Lot o' Gold**, 3, 122	D. Brumfield	Julie's Dancer, 3, 113	Will Henry, 3, 113	8	1:37.60	29,030
1978	**Five Star General**, 3, 113	J. C. Espinoza	As in Elbow, 3, 113	Doc's Rock, 3, 119	9	1:37.80	12,900
	Raymond Earl, 3, 113	J. C. Espinoza	Washington County, 3, 119	Shake Rattl'n Fly, 3, 113	10	1:38.80	12,960
1977	**Smiley's Dream**, 3, 114	W. Destefano	Lighten the Load, 3, 111	Vestry's Best, 3, 111	8	1:39.40	12,788
	Bob's Dusty, 3, 122	J. C. Espinoza	A Letter to Harry, 3, 116	John Washington, 3, 116	7	1:38.80	12,817
1976	**Inca Roca**, 3, 122	W. Nemeti	Here Comes Jo, 3, 116	Brentwood Prince, 3, 116	8	1:37.40	18,780
1975	**Naughty Jake**, 3, 119	G. Vasquez	Promenade Left, 3, 114	Jim Dan Bob, 3, 112	8	1:40.00	15,840
	Ambassador's Image, 3, 122	E. Snell	Clarence Henry, 3, 116	Upper Need, 3, 116	8	1:38.40	15,870
1974	**King of Rome**, 3, 112	K. Wirth	Consigliori, 3, 112	Aroyoport, 3, 116	8	1:44.60	12,204
	Aglorite, 3, 119	J. Beech Jr.	Joint Agreement, 3, 116	Robard, 3, 112	8	1:45.40	12,236
1973	**Jacks Chevron**, 3, 117	B. Phelps	Trip Stop, 3, 116	Mr. Champ, 3, 116	9	1:42.00	9,785
	Bootlegger's Pet, 3, 116	M. Solomone	Out Ahead, 3, 117	Babingtons Image, 3, 113	8	1:41.00	9,720

Originally designed as a prep race that "spiraled up" to the Blue Grass S. (G1) and the Kentucky Derby Presented by Yum! Brands (G1). Sponsored by W. S. Farish's Lane's End, located near Versailles, Kentucky 2002-'08. Formerly sponsored by James B. Beam Distilling Co. of Clermont, Kentucky 1982-'98. Formerly sponsored by James McIngvale's Gallery Furniture Co. of Houston 1999. Spiral S. 1972-'81. Jim Beam Spiral S. 1982-'83. Jim Beam S. 1984-'98. Gallery Furniture.com S. 1999. Turfway Spiral S. 2000-'01. Lane's End Spiral S. 2002. Host track known as Latonia Race Course 1972-'85. 1 mile 1972-'81. 1 1/16 miles 1982-'87. Dirt 1972-2005. Two divisions 1973, 1977-'78, 1980. †Denotes female.

La Prevoyante Handicap

Grade 2 in 2008. Calder Race Course, three-year-olds and up, fillies and mares, 1½ miles, turf. Held December 15, 2007, with a gross value of $200,000. First held in 1976. First graded in 1982. Stakes record 2:25.20 (1988 Singular Bequest).

Year	Winner	Jockey	Second	Third	Strs	Time	1st Purse
2007	**Redaspen**, 5, 115	E. Castro	Green Girl (Fr), 5, 116	Dalvina (GB), 3, 117	11	2:26.63	$116,560
2006	**Safari Queen (Arg)**, 4, 113	J. R. Velazquez	Barancella (Fr), 5, 114	Private Betty, 3, 112	5	2:38.57	120,000

Racing — Graded Stakes 375

Year	Winner	Jockey	Second	Third	Strs	Time	1st Purse
2005	Film Maker, 5, 119	E. S. Prado	Kate Winslet, 4, 115	Noble Stella (Ger), 4, 114	12	2:27.75	$120,000
2004	Arvada (GB), 4, 117	E. S. Prado	Humaita (Ger), 4, 119	Honey Ryder, 3, 113	11	2:27.19	120,000
2003	Volga (Ire), 5, 119	R. Migliore	Lady Annaliese (NZ), 4, 116	Lost Appeal, 5, 115	11	2:26.13	120,000
2002	New Economy, 4, 113	R. Homeister Jr.	Jennasietta, 4, 112	Tweedside, 4, 114	12	2:28.55	120,000
2001	Krisada, 5, 115	P. Day	Sweetest Thing, 3, 115	Great Fever (Fr), 4, 113	10	2:26.63	90,000
2000	Prospectress, 5, 114	J. D. Bailey	Innuendo (Ire), 5, 114	Orange Sunset (Ire), 4, 114	10	2:26.97	90,000
1999	Coretta (Ire), 5, 120	J. A. Santos	Idle Rich, 4, 116	St. Bernadette (Per), 3, 114	8	2:27.27	90,000
1998	Coretta (Ire), 4, 117	J. A. Santos	Starry Dreamer, 4, 114	dh-Cuando, 4, 115	12	2:26.67	90,000
				dh-Tedarshana (GB), 4, 113			
1997	Last Approach, 5, 110	J. A. Krone	Flying Concert, 4, 118	Grey Way, 4, 110	6	2:39.13	90,000
1996	Ampulla, 5, 122	S. J. Sellers	Miss Caerleona (Fr), 4, 114	Electric Society (Ire), 5, 117	8	2:27.50	90,000
1995	Interim (GB), 4, 116	C. S. Nakatani	Northern Emerald, 5, 116	Caromana, 4, 114	10	2:26.38	90,000
1994	Abigailthewife, 5, 114	J. A. Santos	Trampoli, 5, 118	Market Booster, 5, 118	14	2:28.91	90,000
	Trampoli, 5, 120	M. E. Smith	Putthepowdertoit, 4, 115	Adoryphar, 5, 112	14	2:28.14	90,000
1993	Lemhi Go, 5, 112	M. A. Gonzalez	Indian Chris (Brz), 6, 112	Silvered, 6, 118	6	2:37.53	60,000
1992	Sardaniya (Ire), 4, 113	J. Cruguet	Flaming Torch (Ire), 5, 112	Expensiveness, 4, 111	9	2:29.62	90,000
1991	Rigamajig, 5, 114	J. F. Chavez	Roseate Tern (GB), 5, 117	Ahead (GB), 4, 112	11	2:26.10	60,000
1990	Yestday's Kisses, 4, 113	W. H. McCauley	Black Tulip (Fr), 5, 115	Coolawin, 4, 116	11	2:30.80	60,000
1989	Judy's Red Shoes, 6, 120	D. Valiente	Gaily Gaily (Ire), 6, 111	Beauty Cream, 6, 118	14	2:26.40	90,000
1988	Singular Bequest, 5, 115	E. Fires	Autumn Glitter, 5, 114	Green Oasis (Fr), 6, 114	9	**2:25.20**	120,000
1987	Lotka, 4, 121	E. Maple	Bonne Ile (GB), 6, 116	After Party, 5, 112	13	2:36.00	120,000
1986	Powder Break, 5, 116	J. A. Santos	Shocker T., 4, 119	Devalois (Fr), 4, 118	9	2:30.40	120,000
1985	Persian Tiara (Ire), 5, 120	J. Terry	Dictina (Fr), 4, 117	Silver in Flight, 5, 115	11	2:28.80	85,335
	Sabin, 5, 126	D. Brumfield	Key Dancer, 4, 118	Burst of Colors, 5, 117	11	2:27.40	72,285
1984	Bolt From the Blue, 4, 113	J. Samyn	Bezique (Ire), 7, 112	Gabfest, 5, 110	9	2:33.40	51,960
	Sabin, 4, 120	E. Maple	Grunip (GB), 5, 113	Pat's Joy, 6, 118	10	2:32.80	52,260
1983	London LII, 4, 117	A. Smith Jr.	Dana Calqui (Arg), 5, 114	Middle Stage, 4, 116	14	1:47.40	54,680
	Fact Finder, 4, 115	A. T. Cordero Jr.	Sunny Sparkler, 4, 122	Seaholme, 5, 112	11	1:48.00	53,780
	Canaille (Ire), 5, 118	A. T. Cordero Jr.	Castle Royale, 4, 115	Genuine Diamond, 4, 113	13	1:46.60	54,380
1982	Judgable Gypsy, 4, 114	J. O'Driscoll	Castle Royale, 4, 110	Imayrrahtoo, 5, 110	12	1:50.20	42,165
	Just a Game (Ire), 6, 123	A. T. Cordero Jr.	Sweetest Chant, 4, 115	Irish Joy, 4, 114	9	1:50.40	41,655
1981	Mairzy Doates, 5, 121	O. B. Aviles	Champagne Ginny, 4, 118	Knightly Noble, 4, 110	11	1:47.20	41,670
	Deuces Over Seven, 4, 114	G. Gallitano	Little Bonny (Ire), 4, 121	Quick as Lightning, 4, 119	8	1:48.00	40,950
1980	Impetuous Gal, 5, 113	E. Fires	Tangerine Doll, 4, 118	Highland Gypsy, 4, 116	5	1:52.20	23,775
	Jolie Dutch, 4, 116	B. Thornburg	Reina Del Rulo (Arg), 7, 114	Behave Taurian, 4, 108	6	1:54.60	23,925
1979	Unreality, 5, 119	J. D. Bailey	Excitable, 4, 117	Sans Arc, 5, 117	12	1:48.20	37,200
1978	Len's Determined, 4, 114	A. Smith Jr.	Regal Gal, 5, 120	Carolina Moon, 6, 114	11	1:48.40	37,200
1976	Forty Nine Sunsets, 3, 116	C. Marquez	Cycylya Zee, 3, 121	Satan's Cheer, 4, 116	14	1:46.00	27,510
	Redundancy, 5, 117	A. Haldar	Katonka, 4, 125	Yes Dear Maggy, 4, 121	12	1:41.60	26,040

Named for Jean-Louis Levesque's Racing Hall of Fame member La Prevoyante (1970 f. by Buckpasser). Grade 3 1982-'87. La Prevoyante Invitational H. 1986-'93. Not held 1977. 1 1/16 miles 1976. About 1 1/8 miles 1978-'79, 1981-'83. 1 1/8 miles 1980. About 1 1/2 miles 1992. Dirt 1980, '87, '90, '93, '97, 2006. Originally scheduled on turf 2006. Two divisions 1980-'82, 1984-'85. Three divisions 1983. Held in January and December 1994. Dead heat for third 1998.

Las Cienegas Handicap

Grade 3 in 2008. Santa Anita Park, four-year-olds and up, fillies and mares, about 6 1/2 furlongs, turf. Held April 13, 2008, with a gross value of $112,700. First held in 1974. First graded in 1992. Stakes record 1:11.66 (2005 Elusive Diva).

Year	Winner	Jockey	Second	Third	Strs	Time	1st Purse
2008	‡Lightmyfirebaby, 5, 116	A. O. Solis	Wake Up Maggie (Ire), 5, 119	Super Freaky, 4, 119	11	1:13.25	$67,620
2007	River's Prayer, 4, 117	C. L. Potts	Indian Flare, 5, 118	Strong Faith, 6, 113	7	1:12.99	65,220
2006	Cambiocorsa, 4, 120	J. K. Court	Lock And Key (Ire), 4, 119	Sandra's Rose, 4, 115	9	1:12.60	67,740
2005	Elusive Diva, 4, 117	P. A. Valenzuela	Quero Quero, 5, 116	Winendynme, 4, 116	9	**1:11.66**	66,660
2004	Etoile Montante, 4, 121	J. Santiago	Dedication (Fr), 5, 118	Any for Love (Arg), 6, 115	9	1:13.32	67,680
2003	Heat Haze (GB), 4, 114	J. Valdivia Jr.	Icantgoforthat, 4, 114	Paga (Arg), 6, 116	8	1:13.11	66,000
2002	Rolly Polly (Ire), 4, 119	K. Desormeaux	Penny Marie, 6, 119	Twin Set (Ger), 5, 116	7	1:12.59	65,100
2001	Go Go, 4, 118	E. Delahoussaye	Separata (Chi), 5, 118	Dianehill (Ire), 5, 116	8	1:13.54	65,700
2000	Evening Promise (GB), 4, 114	D. Sorenson	La Madame (Chi), 5, 116	Reciclada (Chi), 5, 113	9	1:13.66	63,840
1999	Desert Lady (Ire), 5, 118	C. S. Nakatani	Hula Queen, 5, 112	Bella Chiarra, 4, 115	7	1:13.15	65,640
1998	Dance Parade, 4, 119	K. Desormeaux	Advancing Star, 4, 121	Imroz, 4, 115	6	1:13.60	64,800
1997	Advancing Star, 4, 116	G. L. Stevens	Ski Dancer, 5, 118	Grab the Prize, 5, 116	6	1:12.50	96,550
1996	Ski Dancer, 4, 115	G. L. Stevens	Klassy Kim, 5, 117	Igotrhythm, 4, 117	6	1:14.59	64,300
1995	Marina Park (GB), 5, 119	A. O. Solis	Pirate's Revenge, 4, 115	Rabiadella, 4, 118	9	1:13.77	63,175
1994	Mamselle Bebette, 4, 120	C. J. McCarron	Cool Air, 4, 122	Bel's Starlet, 7, 122	6	1:13.05	45,975
1993	Glen Kate (Ire), 6, 121	C. A. Black	Heart of Joy, 6, 121	Worldly Possession, 5, 115	6	1:12.71	61,225
1992	Heart of Joy, 5, 123	C. J. McCarron	Sheltered View, 5, 118	Crystal Gazing, 4, 119	9	1:12.72	63,475
1991	Flower Girl (GB), 4, 116	E. Delahoussaye	Mahaska, 4, 117	Survive, 7, 117	8	1:13.30	49,650
1990	Stylish Star, 4, 117	C. J. McCarron	‡Hot Novel, 4, 118	Warning Zone, 5, 116	6	1:13.00	47,100
1989	Imperial Star (GB), 5, 115	R. G. Davis	Down Again, 5, 117	Serve n' Volley (GB), 5, 116	10	1:15.60	50,450
1988	Hairless Heiress, 5, 117	G. L. Stevens	Chick Or Two, 5, 115	Aromacor, 5, 113	12	1:15.00	52,050
1987	Lichi (Chi), 7, 115	G. Baze	An Empress, 4, 119	Aromacor, 4, 112	7	1:14.40	38,150
1986	Shywing, 4, 120	L. A. Pincay Jr.	Reigning Countess, 4, 118	Her Royalty, 5, 121	4	1:18.00	37,550
1985	Danzadar, 4, 114	D. A. Lozoya	Pampas (Ire), 5, 120	Natural Summit, 4, 116	5	1:14.00	37,250

Racing — Graded Stakes

Year	Winner	Jockey	Second	Third	Strs	Time	1st Purse
1984	Tangent (NZ), 4, 120	G. Barrera	Irish O'Brien, 6, 118	Frieda Frame, 6, 118	8	1:15.00	$39,600
1983	Faneuil Lass, 4, 120	L. A. Pincay Jr.	Queen of Song, 4, 115	Waving, 4, 117	9	1:17.40	41,200
1982	Excitable Lady, 4, 119	E. Delahoussaye	‡Peppy's Lucky Girl, 5, 117	Glitter Hitter, 4, 119	7	1:14.40	37,450
1981	Wishing Well, 6, 122	F. Toro	Back At Two, 4, 114	Peppy's Lucky Girl, 4, 113	9	1:13.40	34,250
1980	Great Lady M., 5, 116	P. A. Valenzuela	Wishing Well, 5, 120	Billie Bets, 4, 115	10	1:14.80	28,100
1979	Pressing Date, 5, 114	A. T. Cordero Jr.	Country Queen, 4, 121	Critic, 5, 114	8	1:16.40	27,550
1978	Drama Critic, 4, 119	D. G. McHargue	Perils of Pauline, 4, 118	Little Happiness, 4, 120	10	1:14.00	27,800
1977	Dancing Femme, 4, 117	W. Shoemaker	Winter Solstice, 5, 123	Katonka, 5, 120	4	1:13.60	24,600
1976	Life's Hope, 3, 116	L. A. Pincay Jr.	Sure Fire, 3, 119	Private Signal, 3, 114	7	1:09.40	20,100
1974	Woodland Pines, 5, 120	D. Pierce	Pataha Prince, 9, 122	dh-Pontoise, 4, 116	9	1:13.00	18,650
				dh-Single Agent, 6, 116			

Named for Rancho Las Cienegas in southwestern Los Angeles County, California; las cienegas means "the swamps." Las Cienegas S. 1976. Las Cienegas Breeders' Cup H. 1992-'95. Not held 1975. 6 furlongs 1976. 6½ furlongs 1979, 1982-'83, 1986. Dirt 1976, 1979, 1982-'83, 1986. Three-year-olds 1976. Both sexes 1974-'76. Dead heat for third 1974. ‡Queen of Cornwall finished second, DQ to sixth, 1982. ‡Stormy But Valid finished second, DQ to fifth, 1990. ‡Bahama Mama finished first, DQ to fourth, 2008.

Las Flores Handicap

Grade 3 in 2008. Santa Anita Park, four-year-olds and up, fillies and mares, 6½ furlongs, all weather. Held April 6, 2008, with a gross value of $150,000. First held in 1951. First graded in 1973. Stakes record 1:21.04 (2008 Tiz Elemental).

Year	Winner	Jockey	Second	Third	Strs	Time	1st Purse
2008	Tiz Elemental, 4, 120	V. Espinoza	Glorified, 4, 115	Intangaroo, 4, 116	6	**1:21.04**	$90,000
2007	Hello Lucky, 5, 114	M. C. Baze	Selvatica, 6, 117	Babe Hall, 4, 115	12	1:09.34	68,160
2006	Behaving Badly, 5, 120	V. Espinoza	Awesome Lady, 5, 114	Spirit to Spare, 5, 111	6	1:09.09	64,200
2005	Miss Terrible (Arg), 6, 116	A. O. Solis	Puxa Saco, 5, 115	Mazella, 4, 113	8	1:09.47	65,760
2004	Ema Bovary (Chi), 5, 121	R. M. Gonzalez	Buffythecenterfold, 4, 117	Coconut Girl, 5, 113	6	1:08.02	64,380
2003	Spring Meadow, 4, 117	C. S. Nakatani	Brisquette, 5, 116	dh-September Secret, 4, 116	7	1:10.20	81,300
				dh-Wild Tickle, 5, 117			
2002	Above Perfection, 4, 117	C. S. Nakatani	Kalookan Queen, 6, 122	Enchanted Woods, 5, 117	4	1:08.65	78,642
2001	Go Go, 4, 116	E. Delahoussaye	La Feminn, 5, 120	Cover Gal, 4, 119	6	1:08.83	80,400
2000	Show Me the Stage, 4, 118	K. Desormeaux	Theresa's Tizzy, 6, 117	Woodman's Dancer, 6, 115	5	1:08.54	79,440
1999	Enjoy the Moment, 4, 117	L. A. Pincay Jr.	Tomorrows Sunshine, 5, 114	Closed Escrow, 4, 116	5	1:08.55	78,720
1998	Funallover, 4, 114	A. O. Solis	Advancing Star, 5, 122	Zenda's Diablo, 4, 109	7	1:09.10	79,800
1997	Our Summer Bid, 5, 114	J. Silva	Track Gal, 6, 120	Advancing Star, 4, 116	6	1:09.15	80,100
1996	Igotrhythm, 4, 115	C. S. Nakatani	Miss L Attack, 6, 115	Little Blue Sheep, 4, 115	7	1:08.88	81,100
1995	Desert Stormer, 5, 117	K. Desormeaux	Velvet Tulip, 5, 114	Flying in the Lane, 4, 114	5	1:08.49	59,725
1994	Mamselle Bebette, 4, 118	C. S. Nakatani	Arches of Gold, 5, 120	Aspasante, 5, 114	7	1:08.32	47,475
1993	Bountiful Native, 5, 121	P. A. Valenzuela	Freedom Cry, 5, 119	Forest Fealty, 6, 112	6	1:09.42	60,325
1992	Forest Fealty, 5, 116	M. A. Pedroza	Middlefork Rapids, 4, 118	Phil's Illusion, 5, 113	9	1:08.87	49,350
1991	Classic Value, 5, 116	G. L. Stevens	Devil's Orchid, 4, 116	Hasty Pasty, 6, 116	6	1:10.30	60,325
1990	Stormy But Valid, 4, 117	E. Delahoussaye	Survive, 6, 117	Warning Zone, 5, 119	7	1:08.20	47,850
1989	Very Subtle, 5, 124	L. A. Pincay Jr.	Sadie B. Fast, 4, 113	Comical Cat, 4, 116	3	1:08.60	44,350
1987	Flying Julia, 4, 112	F. Olivares	Pine Tree Lane, 5, 122	Le l'Argent, 5, 119	9	1:10.20	48,850
	Pine Tree Lane, 5, 124	A. T. Cordero Jr.	Rangoon Ruby (Ire), 5, 117	Her Royalty, 6, 120	8	1:09.80	38,350
1986	Baroness Direct, 5, 120	E. Delahoussaye	Her Royalty, 5, 120	Aerturas (Fr), 5, 113	7	1:08.40	38,850
1985	Foggy Nation, 5, 117	L. A. Pincay Jr.	Lovlier Linda, 5, 124	Tangent (NZ), 5, 122	5	1:09.60	37,250
1984	Bara Lass, 5, 122	P. A. Valenzuela	Champagne Isle, 4, 116	Bally Knockan, 5, 114	9	1:09.40	40,100
1983	Matching, 5, 122	L. A. Pincay Jr.	Bara Lass, 4, 115	Past Forgetting, 5, 122	7	1:09.00	38,650
1982	Back At Two, 5, 117	C. J. McCarron	Abisinia (Ven), 5, 116	Excitable Lady, 4, 120	5	1:12.40	37,750
1981	Shine High, 5, 114	T. Lipham	Image of Reality, 5, 119	Parsley, 5, 117	7	1:08.60	32,600
1979	Terlingua, 3, 121	D. G. McHargue	Powder Room, 4, 113	Ideal Exchange, 3, 116	7	1:08.40	32,800
1978	Sweet Little Lady, 3, 117	D. G. McHargue	Grenzen, 3, 122	Great Lady M., 3, 114	8	1:09.00	33,200
1977	Winter Solstice, 5, 120	D. G. McHargue	Squander, 3, 114	Don's Music, 3, 115	6	1:11.80	26,100
	My Juliet, 5, 128	A. S. Black	Just a Kick, 5, 121	Juliana F., 4, 115	7	1:10.20	26,750
1976	Just a Kick, 4, 114	E. Munoz	Raise Your Skirts, 4, 121	Mismoyola, 6, 115	9	1:09.20	21,550
1975	Lucky Spell, 4, 120	J. E. Tejeira	‡*Tizna, 6, 123	Impressive Style, 6, 122	8	1:09.60	21,700
1973	Sandy Blue, 3, 120	D. Pierce	Market Again, 5, 122	Impressive Style, 4, 120	10	1:08.60	22,150

Named for the 1844 land grant of Rancho Las Flores, located in Tehama County, California; flores means "flowers." Not graded 1975-'84. Las Flores Breeders' Cup H. 1990-'95. Not held 1953, '69, '71, '74, '80, '88. Three-year-olds and up 1951-'52, 1956-'68, 1970, 1977 (December), 1978, 1987 (December). Two-year-olds and up 1972 (December), '73, '83. Held in January and December 1977, '87. Dead heat for third 2003. ‡Modus Vivendi finished second, DQ to fourth, 1975. 6 furlongs 1951-2007.

Las Palmas Handicap

Grade 2 in 2008. Oak Tree at Santa Anita, three-year-olds and up, fillies and mares, 1 mile, turf. Held November 4, 2007, with a gross value of $150,000. First held in 1969. First graded in 1973. Stakes record 1:33.33 (2006 Beautyandthebeast [GB]).

Year	Winner	Jockey	Second	Third	Strs	Time	1st Purse
2007	Naissance Royale (Ire), 5, 118	G. K. Gomez	Black Mamba (NZ), 4, 114	Meribel, 4, 119	10	1:34.14	$90,000
2006	Beautyandthebeast (GB), 4, 119	C. S. Nakatani	Clinet (Ire), 4, 116	Quemar (NZ), 4, 114	8	**1:33.33**	90,000
2005	Mea Domina, 4, 118	T. Baze	Elusive Diva, 4, 119	Star Parade (Arg), 6, 115	10	1:33.59	90,000
2004	Theater R. N., 4, 114	R. R. Douglas	Lots of Hope (Brz), 4, 117	Good Student (Arg), 4, 114	7	1:47.81	90,000

Racing — Graded Stakes

Year	Winner	Jockey	Second	Third	Strs	Time	1st Purse
2002	Tates Creek, 4, 120	J. D. Bailey	Voodoo Dancer, 4, 121	Magic Mission (GB), 4, 113	8	1:47.69	$120,000
2001	Golden Apples (Ire), 3, 115	G. K. Gomez	Dancingonice, 5, 113	Janet (GB), 4, 120	9	1:46.61	150,000
2000	Smooth Player, 4, 117	E. Delahoussaye	Beautiful Noise, 4, 115	Happyanunoit (NZ), 5, 121	10	1:46.99	105,000
1999	Sapphire Ring (GB), 4, 118	G. L. Stevens	Cyrillic, 4, 117	Country Garden (GB), 4, 113	11	1:48.20	150,000
1998	Sonja's Faith (Ire), 4, 115	E. Ramsammy	See You Soon (Fr), 4, 116	Idealistic Cause, 4, 113	6	1:48.92	90,000
1997	Real Connection, 6, 115	G. F. Almeida	Toda Una Dama (Arg), 4, 114	Luna Wells (Ire), 4, 119	9	1:47.60	75,000
1996	Wandesta (GB), 5, 120	C. S. Nakatani	Real Connection, 5, 113	Alpride (Ire), 5, 120	5	1:46.72	79,700
1995	Onceinabluemamoon, 4, 116	B. Blanc	Yearly Tour, 4, 117	Don't Read My Lips, 4, 117	9	1:50.34	76,400
1994	Aube Indienne (Fr), 4, 115	K. Desormeaux	Queens Court Queen, 5, 115	Skimble, 5, 116	5	1:49.62	61,300
1993	Miatuschka, 5, 114	C. A. Black	Skimble, 4, 115	Potridee (Arg), 4, 115	6	1:47.98	62,650
1992	Super Staff, 4, 116	K. Desormeaux	Flawlessly, 4, 124	Re Toss (Arg), 5, 115	7	1:46.89	77,550
1991	Kostroma (Ire), 5, 117	K. Desormeaux	Kikala (GB), 5, 113	Campagnarde (Arg), 4, 118	6	1:43.92	80,750
1990	Little Brianne, 5, 115	J. A. Garcia	Double Wedge, 5, 117	Reluctant Guest, 4, 121	5	1:46.80	93,200
1989	Nikishka, 4, 116	E. Delahoussaye	No Review, 4, 117	Agirlfromars, 3, 111	7	1:46.60	96,800
1988	Annoconnor, 4, 120	C. A. Black	No Review, 3, 114	Goodbye Halo, 3, 120	7	1:47.00	97,800
1987	Autumn Glitter, 4, 116	P. Day	Galunpe (Ire), 4, 119	Festivity, 4, 117	8	1:50.40	91,800
1986	Outstandingly, 4, 118	G. L. Stevens	Shywing, 4, 118	Justicara (Ire), 5, 118	6	1:47.60	63,400
1985	Estrapade, 5, 124	W. Shoemaker	L'Attrayante (Fr), 5, 118	Johnica, 4, 118	11	1:47.20	69,100
1984	Fenny Rough (Ire), 4, 118	K. D. Black	Comedy Act, 5, 117	Pride of Rosewood (NZ), 6, 115	8	1:47.40	78,800
1983	Castilla, 4, 121	C. J. McCarron	Night Fire, 4, 113	Berry Bush, 6, 117	7	1:49.20	64,300
1982	Berry Bush, 5, 115	M. Castaneda	Satin Ribera, 5, 115	Northern Fable, 4, 115	13	1:47.40	70,400
1981	Ack's Secret, 5, 119	D. G. McHargue	Queen to Conquer, 5, 123	Berry Bush, 4, 118	9	1:47.00	50,500
1980	Ack's Secret, 4, 114	P. A. Valenzuela	A Thousand Stars, 5, 119	Princess Toby, 5, 117	9	1:46.00	40,400
1979	High Pheasant, 4, 114	F. Olivares	Prize Spot, 3, 119	Axe Me Dear, 5, 114	7	1:54.00	39,700
1978	Grenzen, 3, 119	L. A. Pincay Jr.	Country Queen, 3, 119	Drama Critic, 4, 123	8	1:48.40	39,400
1977	Swingtime, 5, 119	F. Toro	Theia (Fr), 4, 113	Summertime Promise, 5, 118	6	1:47.20	25,650
1976	Vagabonda, 5, 118	O. Vergara	*Bastonera II, 5, 122	*Accra II, 4, 115	12	1:48.60	34,500
1975	Charger's Star, 5, 116	W. Shoemaker	*Tizna, 6, 126	Hinterland, 5, 116	8	1:47.20	26,000
1974	Lucky Spell, 3, 117	J. E. Tejeira	Bold Ballet, 3, 117	Fresh Pepper, 4, 112	10	1:47.40	26,750
1973	Minstrel Miss, 6, 123	D. Pierce	*Cruz de Roble, 6, 113	Veiled Desire, 4, 111	10	1:47.80	27,100

Named for Las Palmas (1929 f. by Bon Homme), winner of the first race run at Santa Anita Park on December 25, 1934. Grade 3 1973-'82. Not held 2003. 1 1/16 miles 1969, '82. 1 1/8 miles 1970-'81, 1983-2004. Dirt 1969, '79.

Las Virgenes Stakes

Grade 1 in 2008. Santa Anita Park, three-year-olds, fillies, 1 mile, all weather. Held February 9, 2008, with a gross value of $250,000. First held in 1983. First graded in 1985. Stakes record 1:35.14 (1994 Lakeway).

Year	Winner	Jockey	Second	Third	Strs	Time	1st Purse
2008	Golden Doc A, 3, 118	R. Bejarano	Lovely Isle, 3, 116	Tasha's Miracle, 3, 118	6	1:35.86	$150,000
2007	Rags to Riches, 3, 116	G. K. Gomez	Baroness Thatcher, 3, 116	Runway Rosie, 3, 120	8	1:37.85	150,000
2006	Balance, 3, 120	V. Espinoza	Wild Fit, 3, 120	Itty Bitty Pretty, 3, 120	7	1:36.54	150,000
2005	Sharp Lisa, 3, 119	C. S. Nakatani	Memorette, 3, 119	Charming Colleen, 3, 117	6	1:35.64	150,000
2004	A. P. Adventure, 3, 118	A. O. Solis	Hollywood Story, 3, 120	Friendly Michelle, 3, 118	8	1:36.50	150,000
2003	Composure, 3, 120	J. D. Bailey	Elloluv, 3, 122	Watching You, 3, 116	6	1:36.13	120,000
2002	You, 3, 122	J. D. Bailey	Habibti, 3, 122	Tali'sluckybusride, 3, 120	6	1:36.84	120,000
2001	Golden Ballet, 3, 122	C. J. McCarron	Two Item Limit, 3, 120	Affluent, 3, 114	7	1:36.89	120,000
2000	Surfside, 3, 122	P. Day	Spain, 3, 115	Rings a Chime, 3, 116	4	1:37.00	120,000
1999	Excellent Meeting, 3, 122	K. Desormeaux	Tout Charmant, 3, 116	Weekend Squall, 3, 115	5	1:35.35	120,000
1998	Keeper Hill, 3, 114	D. R. Flores	Star of Broadway, 3, 116	Occhi Verdi (Ire), 3, 116	9	1:36.94	120,000
1997	Sharp Cat, 3, 122	C. S. Nakatani	High Heeled Hope, 3, 118	Demon Acquire, 3, 116	8	1:35.52	98,800
1996	Antespend, 3, 120	C. W. Antley	Cara Rafaela, 3, 122	Hidden Lake, 3, 116	12	1:36.45	96,900
1995	Serena's Song, 3, 122	C. S. Nakatani	Cat's Cradle, 3, 118	Urbane, 3, 116	7	1:35.45	92,700
1994	Lakeway, 3, 117	K. Desormeaux	Fancy 'n Fabulous, 3, 114	Princess Mitterand, 3, 116	8	**1:35.14**	93,600
1993	Likeable Style, 3, 117	G. L. Stevens	Incindress, 3, 117	Blue Moonlight, 3, 119	6	1:36.67	91,000
1992	Magical Maiden, 3, 121	G. L. Stevens	Golden Treat, 3, 115	Red Bandana, 3, 115	10	1:36.23	96,800
1991	Lite Light, 3, 121	C. S. Nakatani	Garden Gal, 3, 121	Nice Assay, 3, 119	4	1:35.70	93,800
1990	Cheval Volant, 3, 123	A. O. Solis	Nasers Pride, 3, 119	Bright Candles, 3, 119	7	1:38.00	78,150
1989	Kool Arrival, 3, 121	L. A. Pincay Jr.	Some Romance, 3, 123	Fantastic Look, 3, 115	7	1:36.20	77,200
1988	Goodbye Halo, 3, 123	J. Velasquez	Winning Colors, 3, 119	Sadie B. Fast, 3, 115	5	1:36.80	74,750
1987	Timely Assertion, 3, 114	G. L. Stevens	Very Subtle, 3, 117	My Turbulent Beau, 3, 114	5	1:36.80	74,900
1986	Life At the Top, 3, 114	R. Q. Meza	Twilight Ridge, 3, 121	An Empress, 3, 117	7	1:36.20	77,050
1985	Fran's Valentine, 3, 117	P. A. Valenzuela	Rascal Lass, 3, 121	Wising Up, 3, 121	7	1:36.40	77,150
1984	Althea, 3, 124	L. A. Pincay Jr.	Vagabond Gal, 3, 117	My Darling One, 3, 114	6	1:37.00	50,500
1983	Saucy Bobbie, 3, 114	L. A. Pincay Jr.	A Lucky Sign, 3, 121	Little Hailey, 3, 114	9	1:36.20	50,100

Named for Rancho Las Virgenes, an 1837 land grant located in Los Angeles County, California. Grade 3 1985-'86. Grade 2 1987. Dirt 1983-2007.

La Troienne Stakes

Grade 3 in 2008. Churchill Downs, three-year-olds, fillies, 7 1/2 furlongs, dirt. Held May 3, 2008, with a gross value of $168,450. First held in 1956. First graded in 1998. Stakes record 1:28.18 (2006 Joint Effort).

Year	Winner	Jockey	Second	Third	Strs	Time	1st Purse
2008	Game Face, 3, 120	J. R. Velazquez	Keep the Peace, 3, 116	Tiz to Dream, 3, 116	7	1:28.44	$102,352

Year	Winner	Jockey	Second	Third	Strs	Time	1st Purse
2007	Silverinyourpocket, 3, 117	C. H. Borel	Suaveness, 3, 118	Upcoming Story, 3, 116	10	1:30.14	$107,703
2006	Joint Effort, 3, 122	E. S. Prado	Adieu, 3, 122	Smart N Pretty, 3, 117	9	1:28.18	71,186
2005	Seek a Star, 3, 116	J. F. Chavez	Cool Spell, 3, 116	Hot Storm, 3, 122	9	1:28.75	70,804
2004	Friendly Michelle, 3, 118	A. O. Solis	Ender's Sister, 3, 122	Bohemian Lady, 3, 122	7	1:28.26	69,564
2003	Final Round, 3, 116	J. D. Bailey	Lovely Sage, 3, 116	Fast Cookie, 3, 118	6	1:22.13	69,316
2002	Cashier's Dream, 3, 121	D. J. Meche	Shameful, 3, 113	Colonial Glitter, 3, 121	5	1:24.83	69,812
2001	Caressing, 3, 121	P. Day	Sweet Nanette, 3, 121	Golly Greeley, 3, 116	9	1:22.90	75,020
2000	Roxelana, 3, 116	L. J. Melancon	Magicalmysterycat, 3, 121	Watchfull, 3, 116	7	1:21.97	70,308
1999	Sapphire n' Silk, 3, 113	P. Day	English Bay, 3, 116	Grand Deed, 3, 121	6	1:23.85	69,936
1998	Sister Act, 3, 113	C. H. Borel	Bourbon Belle, 3, 118	Marie J, 3, 114	6	1:24.46	69,874
1997	Star of Goshen, 3, 115	A. O. Solis	Pearl City, 3, 115	Flying Lauren, 3, 116	8	1:22.75	70,370
1996	Rare Blend, 3, 121	P. Day	Ruby Baby, 3, 113	Prissy One, 3, 113	8	1:23.75	55,624
1995	Dixieland Gold, 3, 121	D. Penna	Daylight Ridge, 3, 113	Ivorilla, 3, 121	7	1:22.74	55,088
1994	Packet, 3, 113	J. M. Johnson	Golden Braids, 3, 113	Miss Ra He Ra, 3, 121	10	1:24.14	55,770
1993	Traverse City, 3, 116	J. A. Krone	Added Asset, 3, 113	Bellewood, 3, 113	10	1:24.38	38,025
1992	Bell Witch, 3, 111	J. A. Krone	Take the Cure, 3, 116	Meadow Storm, 3, 121	6	1:24.35	36,497
1991	Exclusive Bird, 3, 116	J. D. Bailey	Wilderness Song, 3, 121	Through Flight, 3, 121	8	1:23.64	36,953
1990	Screen Prospect, 3, 121	P. Day	Hard Freeze, 3, 116	Windansea, 3, 116	7	1:24.60	37,018
1989	Top of My Life, 3, 122	P. Day	Seaquay, 3, 122	Exquisite Mistress, 3, 122	7	1:23.80	36,595
1988	Gerri n Jo Go, 3, 122	P. Day	Raging Lady, 3, 114	Whitesburg Express, 3, 114	7	1:25.40	36,205
1987	Footy, 3, 122	C. J. McCarron	Sheena Native, 3, 117	Only a Glance, 3, 122	11	1:23.80	38,025
1986	Lazer Show, 3, 121	P. Day	Miss Bid, 3, 115	In Full View, 3, 121	6	1:23.60	24,817
1985	Magnificent Lindy, 3, 118	E. Delahoussaye	Turn to Wilma, 3, 115	Sewing Classic, 3, 115	8	1:23.40	21,824
1984	Sintra, 3, 115	K. K. Allen	Robin's Rob, 3, 121	Tah Dah, 3, 121	7	1:23.20	23,855
1983	How Clever, 3, 121	G. Gallitano	Super Belle, 3, 115	Weekend Surprise, 3, 121	8	1:25.40	24,245
1982	Betty Money, 3, 121	L. J. Melancon	Avadewan, 3, 112	All Sold Out, 3, 112	9	1:26.20	23,774
	Hoist Emy's Flag, 3, 118	P. Day	Plucky Hussy, 3, 121	Jay Birdie, 3, 115	8	1:26.20	23,579
1981	Heavenly Cause, 3, 121	P. Day	Fiddleatune, 3, 121	Roger's Turn, 3, 121	6	1:24.00	17,030
1980	Ribbon, 3, 121	R. D. Ardoin	Tilly's Curve, 3, 121	Noble Appeal, 3, 121	12	1:26.60	19,435
1979	Justa Reflection, 3, 118	A. L. Fernandez	Hand Creme, 3, 115	Disco Diane, 3, 115	11	1:25.80	17,680
1978	White Star Line, 3, 121	E. Maple	Unconscious Doll, 3, 121	Miss Mary Deb, 3, 121	4	1:25.20	13,520
1977	Sweet Alliance, 3, 121	C. J. McCarron	Like Ducks, 3, 121	La Lonja, 3, 118	10	1:25.20	14,300
1976	Moreland Hills, 3, 121	A. Rini	Thunder Lady, 3, 115	Three Colors, 3, 118	6	1:26.60	13,780
1975	High Estimate, 3, 121	E. Delahoussaye	Hoso, 3, 121	My Juliet, 3, 121	6	1:25.60	13,780
1974	‡Shantung Silk, 3, 121	A. T. Cordero Jr.	Clemanna, 3, 118	Irish Sonnet, 3, 118	11	1:25.40	14,430
1973	La Prevoyante, 3, 121	J. O. LeBlanc	Old Goldie, 3, 115	Coraggioso, 3, 118	8	1:23.80	14,040

Named for Idle Hour Stock Farm's great foundation mare *La Troienne (1926 f. by *Teddy). Formerly held as a prep race for the Kentucky Oaks (G1). Oaks Prep S. 1956-'66. 6 furlongs 1956-'60. 7 furlongs 1961-2003. Two divisions 1982. ‡Clemanna finished first, DQ to second, 1974.

Lazaro Barrera Memorial Stakes

Grade 3 in 2008. Hollywood Park, three-year-olds, 7 furlongs, all weather. Held May 18, 2008, with a gross value of $107,200. First held in 1953. First graded in 2001. Stakes record 1:20.42 (2001 Early Flyer).

Year	Winner	Jockey	Second	Third	Strs	Time	1st Purse
2008	Two Step Salsa, 3, 117	M. A. Pedroza	Afleet Ruler, 3, 115	Dixie Chatter, 3, 121	6	1:20.66	$64,320
2007	Time to Get Even, 3, 115	D. R. Flores	Principle Secret, 3, 123	Desert Code, 3, 123	8	1:21.91	65,820
2006	Northern Soldier, 3, 115	C. J. Rollins	Remembering Star, 3, 115	Arson Squad, 3, 120	7	1:22.46	90,000
2005	Storm Wolf, 3, 116	A. O. Solis	Dover Dere, 3, 115	Ransom Demanded, 3, 115	6	1:22.26	90,000
2004	Twice as Bad, 3, 116	A. O. Solis	Wimplestiltskin, 3, 116	Don'tsellmeshort, 3, 123	8	1:21.57	90,000
2003	Blazonry, 3, 115	M. E. Smith	Fly to the Wire, 3, 116	Jimmy O, 3, 115	9	1:22.19	90,000
2002	Captain Squire, 3, 123	C. J. Rollins	Fonz's, 3, 123	Kamsack, 3, 117	5	1:21.95	90,000
2001	Early Flyer, 3, 123	C. J. McCarron	Squirtle Squirt, 3, 123	Top Hit, 3, 118	7	1:20.42	65,160
2000	Caller One, 3, 122	C. S. Nakatani	Dixie Union, 3, 122	Swept Overboard, 3, 122	4	1:21.10	60,960
1999	Love That Red, 3, 122	G. K. Gomez	Apremont, 3, 118	O'Rey Fantasma, 3, 118	7	1:20.81	56,910
1998	Reraise, 3, 116	E. Delahoussaye	Souvenir Copy, 3, 122	Full Moon Madness, 3, 118	6	1:08.51	39,930
1996	Future Quest, 3, 122	K. Desormeaux	Slews Royal Son, 3, 119	Tiger Talk, 3, 120	7	1:15.17	35,100
1995	Flying Standby, 3, 115	C. W. Antley	Desert Pirate, 3, 119	Boundless Moment, 3, 116	6	1:09.09	40,200

Named for Racing Hall of Fame and Eclipse Award-winning trainer Lazaro S. Barrera (1924-'91), trainer of 1978 Triple Crown winner Affirmed. Formerly named for the city of Playa del Rey, California. Grade 2 2002-'06. Playa del Rey S. 1953-'54, 1995-'96, 1998. Not held 1955-'94, 1997. 6 furlongs 1954, '95, '98. 6½ furlongs 1996. Dirt 1953-2006.

Lecomte Stakes

Grade 3 in 2008. Fair Grounds, three-year-olds, 1 mile, dirt. Held January 12, 2008, with a gross value of $99,000. First held in 1943. First graded in 2003. Stakes record 1:37.60 (1993 Dixieland Heat).

Year	Winner	Jockey	Second	Third	Strs	Time	1st Purse
2008	Z Fortune, 3, 120	S. Bridgmohan	Blackberry Road, 3, 116	Mad Flatter, 3, 118	8	1:37.79	$60,000
2007	Hard Spun, 3, 122	M. G. Pino	Izzie's Halo, 3, 116	Teuflesberg, 3, 122	7	1:37.87	60,000
2005	Storm Surge, 3, 122	R. Albarado	Smooth Bid, 3, 122	Kansas City Boy, 3, 114	5	1:39.34	60,000
2004	Fire Slam, 3, 119	S. J. Sellers	Shadowland, 3, 118	Two Down Automatic, 3, 117	7	1:38.48	60,000

Racing — Graded Stakes

Year	Winner	Jockey	Second	Third	Strs	Time	1st Purse
2003	Saintly Look, 3, 122	S. J. Sellers	Call Me Lefty, 3, 122	Winning Fans, 3, 114	11	1:37.62	$60,000
2002	Easyfromthegitgo, 3, 114	D. J. Meche	Sky Terrace, 3, 119	It'sallinthechase, 3, 122	11	1:37.98	60,000
2001	Sam Lord's Castle, 3, 122	R. Albarado	Wild Hits, 3, 122	Mc Mahon, 3, 119	10	1:37.98	60,000
2000	Noble Ruler, 3, 114	L. J. Melancon	Mighty, 3, 122	Peninsula, 3, 114	10	1:39.11	60,000
1999	Some Actor, 3, 114	E. M. Martin Jr.	Desert Demon, 3, 114	Silver Chadra, 3, 114	14	1:38.59	60,000
1998	Western City, 3, 112	R. Albarado	Captain Maestri, 3, 116	Slick Report, 3, 112	6	1:37.84	60,000
1997	Cash Deposit, 3, 120	R. D. Ardoin	Stroke, 3, 114	Kalispell, 3, 113	5	1:37.97	36,000
1996	Boomerang, 3, 116	E. M. Martin Jr.	Commanders Palace, 3, 116	Playing to Win, 3, 115	8	1:39.49	25,845
1995	Moonlight Dancer, 3, 112	L. J. Melancon	Beavers Nose, 3, 114	Timeless Honor, 3, 120	8	1:40.13	25,725
1994	Fly Cry, 3, 119	R. D. Ardoin	Smilin Singin Sam, 3, 114	Sweet Wager, 3, 115	12	1:39.29	19,905
1993	Dixieland Heat, 3, 116	E. J. Perrodin	Apprentice, 3, 117	Masters Windfall, 3, 112	13	1:37.60	19,995
1992	Line In The Sand, 3, 112	S. P. Romero	Greinton's Dancer, 3, 113	Best Boy's Jade, 3, 116	7	1:39.80	19,215
1991	Big Courage, 3, 116	T. L. Fox	Near the Limit, 3, 118	Slick Groom, 3, 111	11	1:48.30	19,725
1990	Martha's Buck, 3, 113	B. J. Walker Jr.	Axe It, 3, 115	Arrowhead Al, 3, 112	7	1:47.00	16,050
1989	Majesty's Imp, 3, 116	S. R. Rydowski	Nooo Problema, 3, 119	Esker Island, 3, 113	10	1:45.60	16,455
1988	Pastourelles, 3, 113	B. J. Walker Jr.	Risen Star, 3, 122	Run Paul Run, 3, 114	7	1:46.60	16,275
1987	One Tough Cat, 3, 114	K. P. LeBlanc	Authentic Hero, 3, 118	French 'n Irish, 3, 113	8	1:48.20	17,250
1986	Timely Albert, 3, 109	P. Rubbicco	Irish Irish, 3, 114	New Plymouth, 3, 117	9	1:45.60	34,200
1985	Encolure, 3, 114	R. D. Ardoin	Northern Bid, 3, 119	Ten Times Ten, 3, 116	11	1:45.80	33,450
1984	Silent King, 3, 115	C. Mueller	Taylor's Special, 3, 122	Fairly Straight, 3, 115	8	1:45.20	24,150
1983	Explosive Wagon, 3, 116	C. Mueller	Found Pearl Harbor, 3, 116	Pronto Forli, 3, 120	11	1:45.00	26,900
1982	Linkage, 3, 120	G. P. Smith	Soy Emperor, 3, 113	Mid Yell, 3, 109	7	1:45.00	23,350
1981	Law Me, 3, 113	J. McKnight	Brazen Ruler, 3, 119	Corsicana, 3, 114	10	1:46.40	24,500
1980	Withholding, 3, 108	B. Fann	Brent's Trans Am, 3, 120	Bold Source, 3, 107	10	1:44.20	23,650
1979	Fuego Seguro, 3, 116	M. R. Morgan	Bo, 3, 114	Will Henry, 3, 116	12	1:46.60	21,175
1978	Dragon Tamer, 3, 118	R. Sibille	Batonnier, 3, 110	Traffic Warning, 3, 114	14	1:44.60	22,050
1977	Clev Er Tell, 3, 119	R. Broussard	A Letter to Harry, 3, 118	Sea Defier, 3, 110	8	1:44.80	16,725
1976	Tudor Tambourine, 3, 117	D. Copling	Glassy Dip, 3, 112	Go East Young Man, 3, 117	12	1:46.20	18,000
1975	Colonel Power, 3, 123	P. Rubbicco	Davey Dan, 3, 113	Rustic Ruler, 3, 113	13	1:40.60	18,625
1974	Crimson Ruler, 3, 119	K. LeBlanc	Don't Be Late Jim, 3, 116	Heavy Mayonnaise, 3, 120	11	1:43.80	17,650
1973	Vodika, 3, 119	T. Barrow	Navajo, 3, 120	Rocket Pocket, 3, 123	14	1:46.00	15,825

Named for Gen. T. J. Wells's Lecomte (1850 c. by Boston); Lecomte was the only horse to defeat Lexington, in a match race at Metairie Race Course near New Orleans. Not held 2006.

Lexus Raven Run Stakes

Grade 2 in 2008. Keeneland Race Course, three-year-olds, fillies, 7 furlongs, all weather. Held October 20, 2007, with a gross value of $300,000. First held in 1999. First graded in 2002. Stakes record 1:20.88 (2000 Darling My Darling).

Year	Winner	Jockey	Second	Third	Strs	Time	1st Purse
2007	Jibboom, 3, 117	R. Albarado	West Coast Swing, 3, 117	Mini Sermon, 3, 117	13	1:22.01	$186,000
2006	Leah's Secret, 3, 117	M. Guidry	Vestrey Lady, 3, 119	Ex Caelis, 3, 117	12	1:22.74	186,000
2005	For All We Know, 3, 116	S. Bridgmohan	Flying Glitter, 3, 118	Career Oriented, 3, 116	11	1:23.74	186,000
2004	Josh's Madelyn, 3, 118	J. Shepherd	Vision of Beauty, 3, 116	Feline Story, 3, 118	10	1:22.86	139,004
2003	Yell, 3, 123	P. Day	Ebony Breeze, 3, 123	Tina Bull, 3, 117	12	1:21.75	108,159
2002	Sightseek, 3, 117	J. D. Bailey	Miss Lodi, 3, 123	Respectful, 3, 117	12	1:23.98	106,578
2001	Nasty Storm, 3, 123	P. Day	Hattiesburg, 3, 123	Forest Secrets, 3, 123	7	1:23.30	68,138
2000	Darling My Darling, 3, 117	M. E. Smith	Surfside, 3, 123	Cat Cay, 3, 117	6	1:20.88	51,104
1999	Dreamy Maiden, 3, 117	P. Day	Golden Illusion, 3, 117	Cosmic Wing, 3, 117	6	1:22.64	37,076

Named for the Raven Run nature sanctuary located outside Lexington, Kentucky. Sponsored by the Lexus Division of Toyota Motor Manufacturing Co. of Georgetown, Kentucky 2005-'07. Grade 3 2002-'03. Dirt 1999-2005.

Locust Grove Handicap

Grade 3 in 2008. Churchill Downs, three-year-olds and up, fillies and mares, 1 1/8 miles, turf. Held July 8, 2007, with a gross value of $162,900. First held in 1982. First graded in 1998. Stakes record 1:46.75 (2004 Shaconage).

Year	Winner	Jockey	Second	Third	Strs	Time	1st Purse
2007	Mauralakana (Fr), 4, 118	J. R. Leparoux	Quiet Royal, 4, 115	Quite a Bride, 4, 123	6	1:47.99	$99,989
2006	Rich in Spirit, 4, 118	M. Guidry	Cape Hope, 4, 114	Pyrana, 4, 113	7	1:50.00	100,529
2005	Delta Princess, 6, 119	B. Blanc	Shaconage, 5, 116	Marwood, 5, 116	6	1:48.90	102,021
2004	Shaconage, 4, 116	B. Blanc	Halory Leigh, 4, 111	Sand Springs, 4, 119	6	1:46.75	102,765
2003	Ipi Tombe (Zim), 5, 123	P. Day	Kiss the Devil, 5, 116	Quick Tip, 5, 117	5	1:47.70	101,928
2002	Voodoo Dancer, 4, 120	J. A. Santos	Blue Moon (Fr), 5, 116	Solvig, 5, 116	9	1:46.91	104,718
2001	Colstar, 5, 121	J. K. Court	Solvig, 4, 115	Megans Bluff, 4, 119	11	1:48.79	107,136
2000	Colstar, 4, 121	A. Delgado	Pricearose, 4, 113	Histoire Sainte (Fr), 4, 113	6	1:47.44	102,300
1999	Shires Ende, 4, 117	W. Martinez	Formal Tango, 4, 116	Uanme, 4, 112	11	1:49.11	107,508
1998	Colcon, 5, 118	S. J. Sellers	Leo's Gypsy Dancer, 4, 113	Mingling Glances, 4, 112	6	1:48.53	103,974
1997	Romy, 6, 115	F. Torres	Yokama, 4, 112	Cymbala (Fr), 4, 116	6	1:48.89	68,634
1996	Bail Out Becky, 4, 121	C. Perret	Ms. Isadora, 4, 113	Memories (Ire), 5, 117	6	1:47.38	72,675
1995	Memories (Ire), 4, 114	S. J. Sellers	Market Booster, 6, 120	Thread, 4, 115	7	1:47.48	71,760
1994	Life Is Delicious, 4, 113	J. R. Martinez Jr.	Eurostorm, 4, 113	Obtain, 4, 112	4	1:53.87	70,850
1993	Lady Blessington (Fr), 5, 121	C. A. Black	Gone Seeking, 4, 109	Crusie, 4, 115	9	1:50.16	74,425
1992	Behaving Dancer, 5, 117	D. L. Howard	Firm Stance, 4, 118	Olden Rijn, 4, 112	10	1:47.27	74,750

Year	Winner	Jockey	Second	Third	Strs	Time	1st Purse
1991	Nice Serve, 4, 111	J. M. Johnson	Super Fan, 4, 118	Behaving Dancer, 4, 113	9	1:51.30	$73,840
1990	Dibs, 4, 111	A. T. Gryder	City Crowds (Ire), 4, 111	Phillipa Rush (NZ), 4, 116	6	1:50.60	71,435
1989	Jungle Gold, 4, 111	C. R. Woods Jr.	Here's Your Silver, 4, 116	Heretic, 4, 115	7	1:43.20	53,381
1988	Chez Chez Chez, 4, 111	J. J. Garcia	Lt. Lao, 4, 115	How I Wish, 4, 113	10	1:45.20	55,575
1987	Luckiest Girl, 4, 114	D. J. Soto	Slippin n' Slyding, 4, 111	Marianna's Girl, 4, 120	9	1:51.60	36,465
1986	Glorious View, 4, 113	C. R. Woods Jr.	Zenobia Empress, 5, 120	Tide, 4, 112	9	1:44.00	36,693
1985	Sintra, 4, 123	K. K. Allen	Sweet Missus, 5, 112	Switching Trick, 5, 112	6	1:43.40	21,076
1984	Heatherten, 5, 122	S. Maple	Mickey's Echo, 5, 110	Forest Maiden, 4, 113	6	1:43.00	26,462
1983	Try Something New, 4, 117	P. Day	Kitchen, 4, 114	Naskra Magic, 4, 117	6	1:45.20	23,156
1982	Excitable Lady, 4, 120	D. G. McHargue	Dawn's Beginning, 4, 111	Sweetest Fantasy, 4, 111	9	1:37.20	24,310

Named for the historic landmark Locust Grove, a house once owned by the brother-in-law and surveying partner of George Rogers Clark. Locust Grove S. 1982-'85, 1988. 1 mile 1988. 1 1/16 miles 1983-'86, 1988-'89. About 1 1/8 miles 1990. Dirt 1982-'86, 1994. Four-year-olds and up 1983-'89.

Lone Star Derby

Grade 3 in 2008. Lone Star Park, three-year-olds, 1 1/16 miles, dirt. Held May 10, 2008, with a gross value of $400,000. First held in 1997. First graded in 2002. Stakes record 1:40.88 (1997 Anet).

Year	Winner	Jockey	Second	Third	Strs	Time	1st Purse
2008	El Gato Malo, 3, 122	R. Bejarano	Leonides, 3, 122	Samba Rooster, 3, 122	13	1:43.04	$225,000
2007	Slew's Tizzy, 3, 122	R. Albarado	Moyer's Pond, 3, 122	dh-Forty Grams, 3, 122	10	1:45.49	165,000
				dh-Mr. Nightlinger, 3, 122			
2006	Wanna Runner, 3, 122	V. Espinoza	Wait in Line, 3, 122	Admiral's Arch, 3, 122	6	1:43.71	185,000
2005	Southern Africa, 3, 122	J. K. Court	Shamoan (Ire), 3, 122	Real Dandy, 3, 122	11	1:41.92	165,000
2004	Pollard's Vision, 3, 122	J. R. Velazquez	Cryptograph, 3, 122	Flamethrowintexan, 3, 122	12	1:42.10	150,000
2003	Dynever, 3, 122	E. S. Prado	Most Feared, 3, 122	Commander's Affair, 3, 122	12	1:50.43	277,500
2002	Wiseman's Ferry, 3, 122	J. F. Chavez	Tracemark, 3, 122	Peekskill, 3, 122	14	1:49.92	277,500
2001	Percy Hope, 3, 122	J. K. Court	Fifty Stars, 3, 122	Gift of the Eagle, 3, 122	8	1:50.27	292,500
2000	Tahkodha Hills, 3, 122	E. Coa	Jeblar Sez Who, 3, 122	Big Numbers, 3, 122	7	1:44.05	180,000
1999	T. B. Track Star, 3, 122	E. M. Martin Jr.	Desert Demon, 3, 122	Congratulate, 3, 122	11	1:42.92	165,000
1998	Smolderin Heart, 3, 122	T. T. Doocy	Shot of Gold, 3, 122	Troy's Play, 3, 122	8	1:46.29	145,000
1997	Anet, 3, 122	D. R. Flores	Frisk Me Now, 3, 122	Holzmeister, 3, 122	9	1:40.88	140,000

Formerly sponsored by John T. L. Jones III's and Bobby Trussell's Walmac Farm LLC of Lexington 2004-'06. The track and the race are named for Texas's (Lone Star Park's home state) nickname, the Lone Star State. Walmac Lone Star Derby 2004-'06. 1 1/16 miles 1997-2000. Dead heat for third 2007.

Lone Star Park Handicap

Grade 3 in 2008. Lone Star Park, three-year-olds and up, 1 1/16 miles, dirt. Held May 26, 2008, with a gross value of $400,000. First held in 1997. First graded in 2000. Stakes record 1:40.53 (2001 Dixie Dot Com).

Year	Winner	Jockey	Second	Third	Strs	Time	1st Purse
2008	Giant Gizmo, 4, 118	G. K. Gomez	Zanjero, 4, 118	Stella Mark, 4, 116	7	1:43.01	$240,000
2007	Bob and John, 4, 120	G. K. Gomez	Sweetnorthernsaint, 4, 120	Jonesboro, 5, 117	4	1:45.02	240,000
2006	Magnum (Arg), 5, 119	P. A. Valenzuela	Texcess, 4, 116	Real Dandy, 4, 116	10	1:42.88	240,000
2005	Supah Blitz, 5, 118	J. K. Court	Cryptograph, 4, 116	Absent Friend, 5, 115	10	1:41.90	180,000
2004	Yessirgeneralsir, 4, 114	O. Figueroa	Sonic West, 5, 117	Spanish Empire, 4, 117	6	1:41.29	180,000
2003	Pie N Burger, 5, 117	J. Theriot	dh-Bluesthestandard, 6, 120		8	1:42.03	180,000
			dh-Maysville Slew, 7, 114				
2002	Congaree, 4, 119	P. Day	Prince Iroquois, 5, 115	Mercenary, 4, 116	12	1:42.96	180,000
2001	Dixie Dot Com, 6, 118	D. R. Flores	Fan the Flame, 4, 113	Big Numbers, 4, 114	8	1:40.53	180,000
2000	Luftikus, 4, 114	D. R. Flores	Nite Dreamer, 5, 118	Sultry Substitute, 5, 114	11	1:40.87	180,000
1999	Mocha Express, 5, 116	M. St. Julien	Littlebitlively, 5, 118	Nite Dreamer, 4, 113	7	1:43.36	183,300
1998	Mocha Express, 4, 114	M. St. Julien	Prince of the Mt., 7, 114	Dickey Rickey, 5, 114	5	1:42.17	123,000
1997	Connecting Terms, 4, 112	L. J. Melancon	Humble Seven, 5, 112	Isitingood, 6, 122	7	1:41.97	120,000

The track and the race are named for Texas's (Lone Star Park's home state) nickname, the Lone Star State. Equaled track record 2000. Track record 2001. Dead heat for second 2003.

Longacres Mile Handicap

Grade 3 in 2008. Emerald Downs, three-year-olds and up, 1 mile, dirt. Held August 19, 2007, with a gross value of $391,250. First held in 1935. First graded in 1975. Stakes record 1:33 (2003 Sky Jack).

Year	Winner	Jockey	Second	Third	Strs	Time	1st Purse
2007	The Great Face, 5, 118	J. M. Gutierrez	Raise the Bluff, 4, 119	Wasserman, 5, 115	12	1:35.40	$220,000
2006	Flamethrowintexan, 5, 120	R. Frazier	Papi Chullo, 4, 117	Southern Africa, 4, 119	11	1:34.40	137,500
2005	No Giveaway, 4, 117	J. M. Gutierrez	Quiet Cash, 4, 117	Desert Boom, 5, 121	11	1:35.60	137,500
2004	Adreamisborn, 5, 116	R. A. Baze	Demon Warlock, 4, 114	Mr. Makah, 4, 112	12	1:34.80	137,500
2003	Sky Jack, 7, 123	R. A. Baze	Poker Brad, 5, 116	Lord Nelson, 6, 116	10	1:33.00	137,500
2002	Sabertooth, 4, 114	N. J. Chaves	Moonlight Meeting, 7, 119	San Nicolas, 4, 115	12	1:34.60	137,500
2001	Irisheyesareflying, 5, 117	I. Puglisi	Handy N Bold, 5, 119	Makors Mark, 4, 116	10	1:35.40	137,500
2000	Edneator, 4, 111	G. V. Mitchell	Big Ten (Chi), 5, 119	Crafty Boy, 5, 114	11	1:33.22	137,500
1999	Budroyale, 6, 119	G. K. Gomez	Mike K, 5, 117	Kid Katabatic, 6, 116	8	1:34.60	137,500
1998	Wild Wonder, 4, 121	E. Delahoussaye	Mocha Express, 4, 115	Hal's Pal (GB), 5, 117	9	1:33.20	110,000
1997	Kid Katabatic, 4, 113	C. Loseth	Hesabull, 4, 119	Liberty Road, 4, 114	7	1:34.20	110,000
1996	Isitingood, 5, 117	D. R. Flores	Cleante (Arg), 7, 121	Humpty's Hoedown, 6, 114	10	1:35.60	110,000

Year	Winner	Jockey	Second	Third	Strs	Time	1st Purse
1995	L. J. Express, 5, 119	M. Allen	Funboy, 4, 121	Secret Damascus, 5, 114	10	1:34.60	$50,350
1994	Want a Winner, 4, 119	V. Belvoir	Sneakin Jake, 7, 118	Forgotten Days, 8, 114	8	1:35.20	48,250
1993	Adventuresome Love, 7, 117	G. Baze	Sneakin Jake, 6, 118	For the Children, 3, 115	8	1:34.60	48,050
1992	Bolulight, 4, 121	R. D. Hansen	Ibero (Arg), 5, 122	Charmonnier, 4, 118	12	1:34.00	181,300
1991	Louis Cyphre (Ire), 5, 120	G. L. Stevens	Captain Condo, 9, 116	Ever Steady, 4, 113	11	1:36.10	178,500
1990	Snipledo, 5, 115	J. R. Corral	Adventuresome Love, 4, 114	dh-Captain Condo, 8, 116	14	1:35.60	187,700
				dh-Kent Green, 7, 112			
1989	Simply Majestic, 5, 122	R. D. Hansen	Crystal Run, 5, 114	Harmony Creek, 3, 113	9	1:34.20	154,000
1988	Simply Majestic, 4, 116	R. A. Baze	Kent Green, 5, 113	Chan's Dragon, 4, 113	9	1:33.80	147,800
1987	Judge Angelucci, 4, 121	G. Baze	Leading Hour, 4, 111	Slyly Gifted, 4, 117	8	1:34.20	150,000
1986	Skywalker, 4, 123	L. A. Pincay Jr.	Bedside Promise, 4, 120	Sir Macamillion, 7, 116	7	1:34.20	177,000
1985	Chum Salmon, 5, 122	G. Baze	Dear Rick, 4, 120	M. Double M., 4, 123	9	1:34.20	150,000
1984	Travelling Victor, 5, 123	C. Loseth	Night Mover, 4, 121	Iron Billy, 5, 114	10	1:34.80	115,000
1983	Chinook Pass, 4, 125	L. A. Pincay Jr.	Travelling Victor, 4, 118	Earthquack, 4, 119	14	1:35.60	115,000
1982	Pompeii Court, 5, 121	S. Hawley	Chinook Pass, 3, 113	Police Inspector, 5, 119	11	1:35.60	100,000
1981	Trooper Seven, 5, 126	G. Baze	Reb's Golden Ale, 6, 121	Loto Canada, 4, 117	13	1:35.40	100,650
1980	Trooper Seven, 4, 123	G. Baze	Island Sultan, 5, 125	Tilt the Balance, 5, 121	10	1:34.40	78,200
1979	Always Gallant, 5, 127	D. G. McHargue	Tilt the Balance, 4, 119	Bad 'n Big, 5, 127	13	1:33.80	79,500
1978	Bad 'n Big, 4, 128	W. Shoemaker	Smiley's Dream, 4, 118	Run'n Prince, 4, 111	8	1:34.00	75,000
1977	Theologist, 4, 118	B. B. Cooper	Ben Adhem, 6, 116	Detrimental, 6, 120	13	1:38.40	65,000
1976	Yu Wipi, 4, 123	S. Hawley	Holding Pattern, 5, 121	Ben Adhem, 4, 124	10	1:34.80	55,500
1975	Jim, 5, 118	A. Cuthbertson	Times Rush, 7, 121	Whoa Boy, 4, 116	12	1:37.00	39,500
1974	Times Rush, 6, 119	B. Frazier	Red Eye Express, 5, 123	Red Wind, 6, 120	13	1:35.20	38,400
1973	Silver Mallet, 5, 122	L. Pierce	Pataha Prince, 8, 118	Reluctant Lord, 4, 120	10	1:34.00	30,250

Named for Longacres Park in Renton, Washington; Longacres closed in 1992. Formerly named for Mt. Rainier, which is located in Washington State. Grade 2 1982-'89. Rainier Mile H. 1991. Budweiser Mile H. 1993. Emerald Budweiser Mile H. 1994-'95. Held at Longacres Park 1935-'92. Held at Yakima Meadows 1993-'95. Not held 1943. Four-year-olds and up 1970. Dead heat for third 1990. Established track record 1996. Track record 1998, 2003. Equaled track record 2000.

Long Island Handicap

Grade 3 in 2008. Aqueduct, three-year-olds and up, fillies and mares, 1½ miles, turf. Held November 11, 2007, with a gross value of $150,000. First held in 1956. First graded in 1973. Stakes record 2:29.04 (1992 Villandry).

Year	Winner	Jockey	Second	Third	Strs	Time	1st Purse
2007	Dalvina (GB), 3, 115	C. H. Velasquez	Barancella (Fr), 6, 119	My Rachel, 5, 115	8	2:34.35	$90,000
2006	Safari Queen (Arg), 4, 115	C. P. DeCarlo	Royal Highness (Ger), 4, 121	Reform Act, 3, 114	8	2:30.93	90,000
2005	Olaya, 3, 114	E. S. Prado	Spotlight (GB), 4, 116	Kate Winslet, 4, 115	7	2:30.28	90,000
2004	Eleusis, 3, 115	J. A. Santos	Literacy, 4, 114	Arvada (GB), 4, 117	7	2:31.51	90,000
2003	Spice Island, 4, 117	V. Carrero	Volga (Ire), 5, 120	Banyu Dewi (Ger), 4, 114	11	2:32.58	90,000
2002	Uriah (Ger), 3, 112	N. Arroyo Jr.	Sunstone (GB), 4, 114	Mot Juste (GB), 4, 119	11	2:42.48	90,000
2001	Queue, 4, 115	J. L. Espinoza	Sweetest Thing, 3, 115	Lady Dora, 4, 114	13	2:29.36	90,000
2000	Moonlady (Ger), 3, 114	C. P. DeCarlo	Playact (Ire), 4, 114	La Ville Rouge, 4, 118	11	2:17.94	90,000
1999	Midnight Line, 4, 120	J. D. Bailey	Win for Us (Ger), 3, 116	Horatia (Ire), 3, 112	10	2:29.67	90,000
1998	Coretta (Ire), 4, 114	J. A. Santos	Starry Dreamer, 4, 115	Dixie Ghost, 4, 114	11	2:29.73	60,000
	Yokama, 5, 120	J. D. Bailey	Moments of Magic, 3, 113	Bristol Channel (GB), 3, 114	11	2:31.03	60,000
1997	Sweetzie, 5, 115	J. F. Chavez	Sweet Sondra, 4, 114	Scenic Point, 4, 120	6	2:16.66	90,000
1996	Ampulla, 5, 121	S. J. Sellers	Wandering Star, 3, 118	Beyrouth, 4, 113	12	2:30.70	87,270
1995	Yenda (GB), 4, 114	C. S. Nakatani	Windsharp, 4, 111	Market Booster, 6, 118	10	2:37.15	86,400
1994	Market Booster, 5, 115	M. J. Luzzi	Tiffany's Taylor, 5, 114	Lady Affirmed, 3, 113	12	2:31.95	87,495
1993	Trampoli, 4, 119	M. E. Smith	Bright Generation (Ire), 3, 114	Northern Emerald, 3, 108	5	2:31.57	68,760
1992	Villandry, 4, 115	M. E. Smith	Ratings, 4, 115	Gina Romantica, 4, 113	8	**2:29.04**	71,160
1991	Shaima, 3, 115	L. Dettori	Highland Penny, 6, 116	Franc Argument, 5, 111	9	2:31.48	73,560
1990	Rigamajig, 4, 110	J. F. Chavez	Narwala (Ire), 4, 116	Roberto's Hope, 3, 112	10	2:29.60	72,120
	Peinture Bleue, 3, 115	J. A. Santos	Franc Argument, 4, 113	Roseate Tern (GB), 4, 119	10	2:29.80	72,600
1989	Warfie, 3, 111	W. H. McCauley	River Memories, 5, 113	Noble Links, 4, 111	6	2:14.40	72,480
1988	Dancing All Night, 4, 108	J. J. Vazquez	Casey (GB), 3, 113	Gaily Gaily (Ire), 5, 111	10	2:34.20	112,320
1987	Stardusk, 3, 109	J. Cruguet	Spruce Fir, 4, 121	Videogenic, 5, 118	13	2:30.40	115,740
1986	Dismasted, 4, 120	J. Samyn	Dawn's Curtsey, 4, 113	Anka Germania (Ire), 4, 114	13	2:30.40	115,560
1985	Videogenic, 4, 116	J. Cruguet	Duty Dance, 3, 114	Mariella, 3, 110	9	2:29.20	92,175
	Faburola (Fr), 4, 114	E. Legrix	Halloween Queen, 4, 107	Easy to Copy, 4, 114	9	2:29.40	105,675
1984	Heron Cove, 4, 114	J. Cruguet	Key Dancer, 3, 115	Secret Sharer, 4, 110	13	2:32.80	109,650
1983	Hush Dear, 5, 125	J. Samyn	Mintage (Fr), 4, 111	If Winter Comes, 5, 113	13	2:34.60	70,920
1982	Hush Dear, 4, 111	E. Beitia	Canaille (Ire), 4, 112	Mintage (Fr), 3, 111	14	2:31.40	71,160
1981	Euphrosyne, 5, 110	R. Migliore	Mairzy Doates, 5, 120	Noble Damsel, 3, 112	12	2:33.00	70,440
1980	The Very One, 5, 120	J. Velasquez	Relaxing, 4, 113	Proud Barbara, 3, 113	5	2:35.20	68,400
1979	Flitalong, 3, 107	R. I. Encinas	Terpsichorist, 4, 122	Catherine's Bet, 4, 114	10	2:31.40	52,245
1978	Terpsichorist, 3, 116	A. T. Cordero Jr.	Leave Me Alone, 5, 109	Proud Event, 4, 113	9	2:34.00	48,555
1977	Pearl Necklace, 3, 123	R. Hernandez	Javamine, 4, 121	Leave Me Alone, 4, 113	7	1:43.80	32,430
1976	Javamine, 3, 113	J. Velasquez	Nijana, 3, 115	Fun Forever, 3, 112	11	1:41.60	33,270
1975	Slip Screen, 3, 115	G. P. Intelisano Jr.	Fleet Victress, 3, 115	Jabot, 3, 115	6	1:42.80	33,930

Year	Winner	Jockey	Second	Third	Strs	Time	1st Purse
1974	D. O. Lady, 3, 115	M. A. Rivera	Speak Action, 3, 113	Gulls Cry, 3, 116	10	1:43.20	$28,080
	Lie Low, 3, 114	J. Velasquez	Victorian Queen, 3, 120	Markhimoff, 3, 115	10	1:42.00	28,080
1973	Tuerta, 3, 116	J. Vasquez	North of Venus, 3, 117	Spring in the Air, 3, 118	12	1:43.80	17,850

Named for the largest island in the continental United States, Long Island, New York; Aqueduct is located on Long Island. Grade 2 1981-'99, 2001-'06. Held at Jamaica 1956-'58. Held at Belmont Park 1960, 1962, 1968-'69, 1975-'76, 1990-'98, 1995. 1⅝ miles 1956-'58. 1³⁄₁₆ miles 1959, 1961, 1963-'67, 1970-'71. 1³⁄₈ miles 1960, 1962, 1968-'69, 2000. 1 mile 1972. 1¹⁄₁₆ miles 1973-'77. Dirt 1956-'58, 1961, 1972, 1989, 1997, 2000. Originally scheduled on turf 1975. Three-year-olds 1972-'76. Both sexes 1956-'71. Fillies 1972-'76. Two divisions 1959, 1962, 1966-'70, 1972, 1974, 1985, 1990, 1998.

Los Angeles Handicap

Grade 3 in 2008. Hollywood Park, three-year-olds and up, 6 furlongs, all weather. Held May 10, 2008, with a gross value of $110,500. First held in 1938. First graded in 1973. Stakes record 1:07.55 (2008 Street Boss).

Year	Winner	Jockey	Second	Third	Strs	Time	1st Purse
2008	Street Boss, 4, 116	D. R. Flores	Sailors Sunset, 5, 115	High Standards, 6, 114	9	**1:07.55**	$66,300
2007	Sailors Sunset, 4, 116	J. K. Court	Peace Chant, 4, 116	Northern Soldier, 4, 116	5	1:09.03	63,480
2006	Siren Lure, 5, 120	A. O. Solis	Areyoutalkintome, 5, 118	Prorunner, 4, 114	8	1:08.57	60,000
2005	Forest Grove, 4, 117	C. S. Nakatani	Areyoutalkintome, 4, 117	Woke Up Dreamin, 5, 115	6	1:08.57	90,000
2004	Pohave, 6, 114	J. K. Court	Marino Marini, 4, 119	Summer Service, 4, 117	9	1:08.12	90,000
2003	Hombre Rapido, 6, 116	J. Valdivia Jr.	Publication, 4, 116	Giovannetti, 4, 116	8	1:08.49	120,000
2002	Kona Gold, 8, 125	A. O. Solis	No Armistice, 5, 116	Komax, 4, 114	6	1:08.72	64,500
2001	Caller One, 4, 124	C. S. Nakatani	Stormy Jack, 4, 115	Rapidough, 6, 115	6	1:08.35	64,380
2000	Highland Gold, 5, 115	C. J. McCarron	Mellow Fellow, 5, 113	Your Halo, 5, 114	6	1:09.11	64,260
1999	Son of a Pistol, 7, 122	A. O. Solis	Men's Exclusive, 6, 118	Ray of Sunshine (Ire), 4, 118	4	1:08.17	63,300
1998	Gold Land, 7, 116	K. Desormeaux	Mr. Doubledown, 4, 119	The Exeter Man, 6, 114	7	1:08.06	64,800
1997	Men's Exclusive, 4, 117	L. A. Pincay Jr.	‡First Intent, 8, 117	Gold Land, 6, 115	7	1:08.80	80,970
1996	dh-Abaginone, 5, 119	G. L. Stevens		Score Quick, 4, 115	6	1:08.33	53,480
	dh-Paying Dues, 4, 115	C. W. Antley					
1995	Forest Gazelle, 4, 117	K. Desormeaux	Lucky Forever, 6, 114	Cardmania, 9, 119	10	1:07.90	83,650
1994	J. F. Williams, 5, 115	C. J. McCarron	Gundaghia, 7, 117	Thirty Slews, 7, 120	6	1:09.03	61,900
1993	Star of the Crop, 4, 119	G. L. Stevens	Fabulous Champ, 4, 115	Wild Harmony, 4, 116	7	1:08.78	63,300
1992	Cardmania, 6, 118	E. Delahoussaye	Gray Slewpy, 4, 119	Robyn Dancer, 5, 119	5	1:08.73	61,200
1991	Black Jack Road, 7, 117	R. A. Baze	Sunny Blossom, 6, 121	Tanker Port, 6, 116	6	1:09.10	62,000
1990	Timeless Answer, 4, 114	R. G. Davis	Prospectors Gamble, 5, 116	Sam Who, 5, 120	8	1:08.80	64,500
1989	Sam Who, 4, 118	L. A. Pincay Jr.	Prospectors Gamble, 4, 114	Mi Preferido, 4, 119	5	1:09.40	46,200
1988	Olympic Prospect, 4, 116	A. O. Solis	Happy in Space, 4, 113	Sylvan Express (Ire), 5, 119	7	1:08.80	47,700
1987	Bedside Promise, 5, 126	G. L. Stevens	Bolder Than Bold, 5, 117	Lincoln Park, 5, 115	5	1:08.40	46,200
1986	Rosie's K. T., 5, 116	P. A. Valenzuela	Mane Magic, 4, 116	Much Fine Gold, 5, 112	6	1:10.00	47,050
1985	Charging Falls, 4, 114	W. Shoemaker	Fifty Six Ina Row, 4, 117	Premiership, 5, 115	8	1:08.80	48,650
1984	Night Mover, 4, 118	E. Delahoussaye	Debonaire Junior, 3, 114	Croeso, 4, 117	6	1:08.40	47,150
1983	Mr. Prime Minister, 7, 115	M. A. Pedroza	Poley, 4, 118	Unreal Zeal, 3, 107	4	1:09.80	45,550
1982	Terresto's Singer, 5, 113	P. A. Valenzuela	Remember John, 3, 115	Petro D. Jay, 6, 116	7	1:09.20	47,800
1981	Doonesbury, 4, 121	S. Hawley	Reb's Golden Ale, 6, 115	Summer Time Guy, 5, 122	7	1:08.80	37,900
1980	Beau's Eagle, 4, 123	L. A. Pincay Jr.	Real Soul, 4, 116	Minstrel Grey, 6, 114	8	1:08.20	32,400
1979	Hawkin's Special, 4, 117	D. G. McHargue	White Rammer, 5, 117	Whatsyourpleasure, 6, 117	6	1:08.40	31,350
1978	J. O. Tobin, 4, 130	S. Cauthen	Maheras, 5, 125	Drapier (Arg), 6, 121	4	1:21.40	30,200
1977	Beat Inflation, 4, 120	D. G. McHargue	Full Out, 4, 117	Mark's Place, 5, 126	5	1:20.20	30,500
1976	Century's Envoy, 5, 123	S. Hawley	Home Jerome, 6, 116	Sporting Goods, 6, 120	7	1:20.80	31,950
1975	Big Band, 5, 117	L. A. Pincay Jr.	Century's Envoy, 4, 121	Shirley's Champion, 4, 120	8	1:20.60	32,300
1974	Ancient Title, 4, 126	L. A. Pincay Jr.	Woodland Pines, 5, 118	Soft Victory, 6, 118	8	1:20.40	32,200
1973	Soft Victory, 5, 118	D. Pierce	Crusading, 5, 124	†Convenience, 5, 117	7	1:21.00	31,850

Named for the city of Los Angeles. Formerly named for the Los Angeles Times, daily newspaper of Los Angeles. Grade 2 1973-'79. Los Angeles Times H. 2003-'05. Not held 1940-'54. 1¹⁄₁₆ miles 1938-'39. 7 furlongs 1957-'78. Dirt 1938-2006. Dead heat for first 1996. ‡Surachai finished second, DQ to sixth, 1997. Track record 1995, 2008. †Denotes female.

Louisiana Derby

Grade 2 in 2008. Fair Grounds, three-year-olds, 1¹⁄₁₆ miles, dirt. Held March 8, 2008, with a gross value of $600,000. First held in 1894. First graded in 1973. Stakes record 1:42.60 (1997 Crypto Star).

Year	Winner	Jockey	Second	Third	Strs	Time	1st Purse
2008	Pyro, 3, 122	S. Bridgmohan	My Pal Charlie, 3, 122	Yankee Bravo, 3, 122	9	1:44.44	$360,000
2007	Circular Quay, 3, 122	J. R. Velazquez	Ketchikan, 3, 122	Zanjero, 3, 122	8	1:43.01	360,000
2005	High Limit, 3, 122	R. A. Dominguez	Vicarage, 3, 122	Storm Surge, 3, 122	9	1:42.74	360,000
2004	Wimbledon, 3, 122	J. Santiago	Borrego, 3, 122	Pollard's Vision, 3, 122	11	1:42.71	360,000
2003	Peace Rules, 3, 122	E. S. Prado	‡Funny Cide, 3, 122	Lone Star Sky, 3, 122	10	1:42.67	450,000
2002	Repent, 3, 122	J. D. Bailey	Easyfromthegitgo, 3, 122	It'sallinthechase, 3, 122	7	1:43.86	450,000
2001	Fifty Stars, 3, 122	D. J. Meche	Millennium Wind, 3, 122	Hero's Tribute, 3, 122	8	1:44.78	450,000
2000	Mighty, 3, 122	S. J. Sellers	More Than Ready, 3, 122	Captain Steve, 3, 122	10	1:43.29	450,000
1999	Kimberlite Pipe, 3, 122	R. Albarado	Answer Lively, 3, 122	Ecton Park, 3, 122	8	1:43.56	384,000
1998	Comic Strip, 3, 122	S. J. Sellers	Nite Dreamer, 3, 122	Captain Maestri, 3, 122	10	1:43.36	300,000
1997	Crypto Star, 3, 118	P. Day	Stop Watch, 3, 118	Smoke Glacken, 3, 122	9	**1:42.60**	240,000
1996	Grindstone, 3, 118	J. D. Bailey	Zarb's Magic, 3, 122	Commanders Palace, 3, 118	8	1:42.79	222,000
1995	Petionville, 3, 118	C. W. Antley	In Character (GB), 3, 118	Moonlight Dancer, 3, 122	11	1:42.96	210,000
1994	Kandaly, 3, 118	C. Perret	Game Coin, 3, 118	Argolid, 3, 118	10	1:42.86	195,750

Racing — Graded Stakes

Year	Winner	Jockey	Second	Third	Strs	Time	1st Purse
1993	Dixieland Heat, 3, 117	R. P. Romero	Offshore Pirate, 3, 117	Tossofthecoin, 3, 115	13	1:44.80	$180,000
1992	‡Line In The Sand, 3, 117	P. Day	Hill Pass, 3, 117	Colony Light, 3, 112	9	1:43.40	120,000
1991	Richman, 3, 122	P. Day	Near the Limit, 3, 114	Far Out Wadleigh, 3, 122	11	1:44.50	120,000
1990	Heaven Again, 3, 113	C. S. Nakatani	Big E. Z., 3, 113	Very Formal, 3, 113	9	1:43.80	100,440
1989	Dispersal, 3, 118	J. A. Santos	Majesty's Imp, 3, 118	Dansil, 3, 123	9	1:43.80	100,560
1988	Risen Star, 3, 120	S. P. Romero	Word Pirate, 3, 118	Pastourelles, 3, 118	7	1:43.20	98,520
1987	J. T.'s Pet, 3, 115	P. Day	Authentic Hero, 3, 118	Plumcake, 3, 115	8	1:51.00	70,260
1986	Country Light, 3, 123	P. Day	Bolshoi Boy, 3, 118	Lightning Touch, 3, 118	13	1:50.40	112,000
1985	Violado, 3, 115	J. Vasquez	Creme Fraiche, 3, 120	Irish Fighter, 3, 113	11	1:50.20	112,000
1984	Taylor's Special, 3, 118	S. Maple	Silent King, 3, 120	Fight Over, 3, 123	7	1:49.60	112,000
1983	Balboa Native, 3, 118	J. Velasquez	Found Pearl Harbor, 3, 113	Slewpy, 3, 123	8	1:50.60	112,000
1982	El Baba, 3, 123	D. Brumfield	Linkage, 3, 120	Spoonful of Honey, 3, 113	8	1:50.60	112,000
1981	Woodchopper, 3, 113	J. Velasquez	A Run, 3, 123	Beau Rit, 3, 126	13	1:50.80	125,800
1980	Prince Valiant, 3, 115	M. A. Gonzalez	Native Uproar, 3, 118	Brent's Trans Am, 3, 123	10	1:50.40	97,150
1979	Golden Act, 3, 123	S. Hawley	Rivalero, 3, 115	Incredible Ease, 3, 120	9	1:51.20	100,750
1978	Esops Foibles, 3, 118	C. J. McCarron	Quadratic, 3, 123	Batonnier, 3, 120	10	1:50.80	79,750
1977	Clev Er Tell, 3, 120	R. Broussard	Run Dusty Run, 3, 123	A Letter to Harry, 3, 115	9	1:48.80	61,000
1976	Johnny Appleseed, 3, 118	M. Castaneda	Glassy Dip, 3, 113	Gay Jitterbug, 3, 118	15	1:49.80	61,000
1975	Master Derby, 3, 123	D. G. McHargue	Colonel Power, 3, 120	Honey Mark, 3, 118	11	1:49.60	61,000
1974	Sellout, 3, 118	M. A. Castaneda	Buck's Bid, 3, 115	Beau Groton, 3, 120	12	1:51.20	55,800
1973	Leo's Pisces, 3, 115	R. Breen	Navajo, 3, 120	Angle Light, 3, 118	11	1:51.60	50,000

Named in honor of Fair Grounds' home state. Grade 3 1985-'98. Held at Crescent City 1894-1908. Held at Jefferson Park 1920-'31. Not held 1895-'97, 1909-'19, 1921-'22, 1940-'42, 1945, 2006. 1 mile 1894. 1¹⁄₁₆ miles 1898-1987. ‡Colony Light finished first, DQ to third, 1992. ‡Kafwain finished second, DQ to tenth for a positive drug test, 2003.

Louisville Handicap

Grade 3 in 2008. Churchill Downs, three-year-olds and up, 1¹⁄₂ miles, turf. Held May 24, 2008, with a gross value of $170,100. First held in 1895. First graded in 2002. Stakes record 2:28.35 (2007 Drilling for Oil).

Year	Winner	Jockey	Second	Third	Strs	Time	1st Purse
2008	Lattice, 4, 116	R. Albarado	Transduction Gold, 5, 115	Birdbirdistheword, 4, 117	11	2:31.13	$99,134
2007	Drilling for Oil, 4, 116	K. J. Desormeaux	Always First (GB), 6, 118	Ramazutti, 5, 117	11	2:28.35	99,311
2006	Silverfoot, 6, 118	M. Guidry	Ramazutti, 4, 117	Quest Star, 7, 116	6	2:16.90	66,537
2005	Silverfoot, 5, 117	R. Albarado	Rochester, 9, 115	Epicentre, 6, 116	7	2:18.77	68,448
2004	Silverfoot, 4, 114	R. Albarado	Rochester, 8, 116	Ballingarry (Ire), 5, 120	9	2:17.63	69,688
2003	Kim Loves Bucky, 6, 117	S. J. Sellers	Rochester, 7, 117	Dr. Kashnikow, 6, 117	8	2:14.09	69,440
2002	‡dh-Classic Par, 4, 114	D. J. Meche	Red Mountain, 5, 114		9	2:15.82	47,355
	‡dh-Pisces, 5, 116	R. Albarado					
2001	With Anticipation, 6, 112	J. K. Court	Profit Option, 6, 112	Gritty Sandie, 5, 115	6	2:16.28	68,138
2000	Buff, 5, 113	F. C. Torres	Williams News, 5, 116	Royal Strand (Ire), 6, 115	11	2:14.31	71,734
1999	Chorwon, 6, 114	C. H. Borel	Buff, 4, 114	Keats and Yeats, 5, 110	6	2:14.15	69,812
1998	Chorwon, 5, 114	P. Day	African Dancer, 6, 117	Thesaurus, 4, 115	11	2:17.10	67,890
1997	Chorwon, 4, 113	C. H. Borel	Down the Aisle, 4, 111	Snake Eyes, 7, 116	5	2:19.45	67,952
1996	Nash Terrace (Ire), 4, 105	D. M. Barton	Vladivostok, 6, 117	Hawkeye Bay, 5, 110	6	2:18.82	71,760
1995	Lindon Lime, 5, 114	C. Perret	Caesour, 5, 116	Snake Eyes, 5, 116	8	1:48.12	72,800
1994	L'Hermine (GB), 5, 110	L. J. Melancon	Llandaff, 4, 116	Snake Eyes, 4, 118	5	1:48.36	70,525
1993	Stark South, 5, 116	R. P. Romero	Cleone, 4, 115	Coaxing Matt, 4, 116	5	1:48.88	71,955
1992	Lotus Pool, 5, 115	C. R. Woods Jr.	Buchman, 5, 114	Magesterial Cheer, 4, 111	8	1:47.69	74,230
1991	Chenin Blanc, 5, 118	J. A. Krone	Tees Prospect, 4, 109	Cameroon, 4, 113	8	1:52.21	55,120
	Allijeba, 5, 115	D. Kutz	Tutu Tobago, 4, 115	Alaqua, 5, 114	8	1:51.59	55,770
1990	Silver Medallion, 4, 114	P. A. Johnson	Spark O'Dan, 5, 113	Mr. Adorable, 4, 111	8	1:50.40	73,125
1989	El Clipper, 5, 113	L. J. Melancon	Set a Record, 5, 113	Pollenate (GB), 5, 113	10	1:50.00	55,478
1988	First Patriot, 4, 116	E. Fires	Rio's Lark, 4, 118	Uncle Cam, 4, 114	9	1:51.80	54,698
1987	Icy Groom, 4, 117	M. McDowell	Niccolo Polo, 4, 108	Blandford Park, 4, 117	9	1:37.80	36,595
1986	Ten Times Ten, 4, 114	K. K. Allen	Little Missouri, 4, 114	Fuzzy, 4, 112	11	1:43.60	25,402
1985	Big Pistol, 4, 114	P. Day	Hopeful Word, 4, 111	Big Mav, 7, 111	5	1:48.60	35,100
1984	Le Cou Cou, 4, 114	D. L. Howard	Big Mav, 6, 111	Jack Slade, 4, 117	5	1:50.80	34,872
1983	Big Mav, 5, 111	P. A. Johnson	Eminency, 5, 123	Diverse Dude, 5, 114	9	1:53.80	35,393
1982	Bobrobbery, 4, 114	R. P. Romero	Swinging Light, 4, 114	Boys Nite Out, 4, 111	7	1:51.40	38,968
1981	Dreadnought, 4, 115	T. Meyers	Oil City, 4, 115	Withholding, 4, 116	5	1:44.60	22,393
1980	Dr. Riddick, 6, 117	D. Brumfield	Incredible Ease, 4, 117	King Celebrity, 4, 113	7	1:44.00	20,703
1979	Hot Words, 4, 114	J. McKnight	Prince Majestic, 5, 124	Dr. Riddick, 5, 119	5	1:45.00	22,750
1978	It's Freezing, 6, 119	L. J. Melancon	To the Quick, 4, 119	Prince Majestic, 4, 120	6	1:45.40	14,105
1977	Amano, 4, 112	L. J. Melancon	‡Inca Roca, 4, 120	Buddy Larosa, 4, 116	8	1:43.80	14,381
1976	Ski Run, 4, 115	G. Patterson	Dragset, 5, 117	Yamanin, 4, 117	7	1:44.00	14,203
1975	Navajo, 5, 125	J. Nichols	Silver Badger, 5, 110	Vodika, 5, 115	8	1:43.20	14,463
1974	List, 6, 115	R. Breen	Royal Knight, 4, 122	Model Husband, 5, 116	12	1:44.40	15,129
1973	Knight Counter, 5, 122	D. Brumfield	‡List, 5, 121	Sipin Whiskey, 4, 110	9	1:43.00	14,771

Named for the city of Louisville, home of Churchill Downs. Formerly held as a "special" race; special races were traditionally "winner takes all." Churchill Downs Special 1946. Louisville S. 1982-'86. Not held 1897, 1900-'06, 1914-'37, 1939-'45, 1953-'56. 1¹⁄₁₆ miles 1895-'99, 1938, 1957-'81, 1986. 6 furlongs 1907-'13. 1¹⁄₈ miles 1946-'52, 1982-'85, 1988-'95. 1 mile 1987. 1³⁄₈ miles 1996-2006. Dirt 1895-1986. Four-year-olds and up 1986-'87. Two divisions 1991. Dead heat

for first 2002. ‡Sipin Whiskey finished second, DQ to third, 1973. ‡Buddy Larosa finished second, DQ to third, 1977. ‡Two Point Two Mill finished first, DQ to eighth, 2002.

Louisville Stakes

Grade 2 in 2008. Churchill Downs, three-year-olds and up, fillies and mares, 1¹/₁₆ miles, dirt. Held May 2, 2008, with a gross value of $268,200. First held in 1986. First graded in 1988. Stakes record 1:42.43 (2005 Shadow Cast).

Year	Winner	Jockey	Second	Third	Strs	Time	1st Purse
2008	Ginger Punch, 5, 124	R. Bejarano	Leah's Secret, 5, 118	Lear's Princess, 4, 122	5	1:43.08	$148,924
2007	Fiery Pursuit, 4, 118	C. H. Borel	Asi Siempre, 5, 122	Baghdaria, 4, 118	6	1:44.11	202,072
2006	Oonagh Maccool (Ire), 4, 117	R. Bejarano	La Reason, 6, 114	Gallant Secret, 4, 114	8	1:42.96	140,127
2005	Shadow Cast, 4, 116	R. Albarado	Island Sand, 4, 115	Storm's Darling, 4, 115	9	**1:42.43**	210,366
2004	Lead Story, 5, 116	C. H. Borel	Yell, 4, 114	Cat Fighter, 4, 116	6	1:44.37	202,740
2003	You, 4, 118	J. D. Bailey	Fly Borboleta, 4, 111	Seven Four Seven, 5, 113	5	1:43.21	201,810
2002	Spain, 5, 118	J. D. Bailey	Mystic Lady, 4, 118	De Bertie, 5, 115	6	1:43.93	207,204
2001	Saudi Poetry, 4, 112	V. Espinoza	Royal Fair, 5, 113	Dreams Gallore, 4, 112	8	1:42.53	172,980
2000	Heritage of Gold, 5, 119	S. J. Sellers	Roza Robata, 5, 112	Bella Chiarra, 5, 116	6	1:42.99	170,655
1999	Silent Eskimo, 4, 113	C. H. Borel	Lu Ravi, 4, 118	Leo's Gypsy Dancer, 5, 112	6	1:43.82	169,415
1998	Escena, 5, 119	J. D. Bailey	One Rich Lady, 4, 113	Three Fanfares, 5, 109	10	1:44.84	178,405
1997	Halo America, 7, 120	C. H. Borel	Escena, 4, 116	Rare Blend, 4, 116	7	1:42.78	138,012
1996	Jewel Princess, 4, 118	C. J. McCarron	Serena's Song, 4, 123	Naskra Colors, 4, 116	4	1:42.50	143,000
1995	Fit to Lead, 5, 113	K. Desormeaux	Jade Flush, 4, 115	Teewinot, 4, 109	9	1:43.46	138,125
1994	One Dreamer, 6, 115	G. L. Stevens	Kalita Melody (GB), 6, 117	Added Asset, 4, 114	7	1:43.73	136,630
1993	Quilma (Chi), 6, 113	J. A. Santos	Looie Capote, 4, 118	Hitch, 4, 113	12	1:44.61	37,570
1992	Fowda, 4, 117	P. A. Valenzuela	Dance Colony, 5, 114	Fit for a Queen, 6, 120	7	1:44.16	100,750
1991	Fit for a Queen, 5, 113	J. D. Bailey	Crowned, 4, 115	Topsa, 4, 109	8	1:43.13	101,530
1990	Connie's Gift, 4, 111	P. Day	Affirmed Classic, 4, 115	Barbarika, 5, 115	6	1:45.80	100,425
1989	Darien Miss, 4, 115	P. A. Johnson	Savannah's Honor, 4, 119	Miss Barbour, 4, 109	6	1:46.00	100,750
1988	By Land by Sea, 4, 124	F. Toro	Bound, 4, 115	Bestofbothworlds, 4, 115	5	1:43.20	100,198
1987	Queen Alexandra, 5, 117	D. Brumfield	Infinidad (Chi), 5, 116	I'm Sweets, 4, 116	6	1:42.80	100,295
1986	Hopeful Word, 5, 119	P. Day	Little Missouri, 4, 116	Czar Nijinsky, 4, 121	4	1:49.40	99,808

Named for the city of Louisville, home of Churchill Downs. Grade 3 1988-'89. Louisville Budweiser Breeders' Cup H. 1987-'95. Louisville Breeders' Cup H. 1996-2007. 1¹/₈ miles 1986. Both sexes 1986.

Mac Diarmida Handicap

Grade 2 in 2008. Gulfstream Park, four-year-olds and up, 1³/₈ miles, turf. Held March 16, 2008, with a gross value of $150,000. First held in 1995. First graded in 1997. Stakes record 2:10.87 (2008 Stream of Gold [Ire]).

Year	Winner	Jockey	Second	Third	Strs	Time	1st Purse
2008	Stream of Gold (Ire), 7, 117	E. Castro	True Cause, 5, 116	Cougar Bay (Ire), 5, 116	12	**2:10.87**	$90,000
2007	Ramazutti, 5, 115	J. R. Velazquez	Dreadnaught, 7, 116	Interpatation, 5, 115	12	2:11.86	90,000
2006	Hotstufanthensome, 6, 117	R. Maragh	Go Deputy, 6, 118	Honor in War, 7, 118	12	2:10.90	60,000
2005	Host, 5, 114	J. Castellano	Navesink River, 4, 112	Burning Sun, 6, 118	12	2:12.83	60,000
2004	Request for Parole, 5, 115	J. A. Santos	Slew Valley, 7, 117	Sir Brian's Sword, 6, 113	12	2:12.58	60,000
2003	Riddlesdown (Ire), 6, 113	R. I. Velez	Macaw (Ire), 4, 114	Just Listen, 7, 113	12	2:14.75	60,000
2002	Crash Course, 6, 114	J. D. Bailey	Unite's Big Red, 8, 112	Eltawaasul, 6, 113	12	2:16.27	60,000
2000	Unite's Big Red, 6, 113	J. F. Chavez	Thesaurus, 6, 112	Carpenter's Halo, 4, 113	8	2:12.14	60,000
1999	Panama City, 5, 114	J. D. Bailey	The Kaiser, 4, 113	Notoriety, 6, 111	5	2:20.65	60,000
1998	Copy Editor, 6, 114	J. D. Bailey	Inkatha (Fr), 4, 114	Lafitte the Pirate (GB), 5, 112	12	2:16.72	60,000
1997	Mecke, 5, 123	J. D. Bailey	Fabulous Frolic, 6, 112	Spicilege, 5, 113	4	2:05.80	45,000
1996	A Real Zipper, 3, 114	A. T. Gryder	Tour's Big Red, 3, 114	Shananie's Finale, 3, 114	12	1:42.66	30,000
1995	Kings Fiction, 3, 112	R. G. Davis	Ops Smile, 3, 113	Mecke, 3, 119	10	1:43.12	30,000

Named for Dr. Jerome M. Torsney's 1978 champion turf horse and '78 Golden Grass H. winner Mac Diarmida (1975 c. by Minnesota Mac). Grade 3 1997-2006. Mac Diarmida S. 1995-'96. Not held 2001. 1 mile 70 yards 1995. 1¹/₁₆ miles 1996. 1¹/₄ miles 1997. About 1³/₈ miles 1999. Dirt 1995, '97. Three-year-olds 1995-'96. Three-year-olds and up 1997-2006. Course record 2006. Course record 2008.

Madison Stakes — *See* Vinery Madison Stakes

Maker's Mark Mile Stakes

Grade 1 in 2008. Keeneland Race Course, four-year-olds and up, 1 mile, turf. Held April 11, 2008, with a gross value of $300,000. First held in 1989. First graded in 1991. Stakes record 1:33.54 (2004 Perfect Soul [Ire]).

Year	Winner	Jockey	Second	Third	Strs	Time	1st Purse
2008	Kip Deville, 5, 123	C. H. Velasquez	Einstein (Brz), 6, 123	Thorn Song, 5, 117	10	1:36.78	$186,000
2007	Kip Deville, 4, 123	E. S. Prado	Showing Up, 4, 123	Purim, 5, 117	8	1:35.51	155,000
2006	Miesque's Approval, 7, 117	E. Castro	Artie Schiller, 5, 123	Good Reward, 5, 117	6	1:34.06	155,000
2005	Artie Schiller, 4, 121	E. S. Prado	Gulch Approval, 5, 117	Good Reward, 4, 123	10	1:34.09	155,000
2004	Perfect Soul (Ire), 6, 116	E. S. Prado	Burning Roma, 6, 116	Royal Spy, 6, 116	10	**1:33.54**	124,000
2003	Royal Spy, 5, 118	R. Albarado	Miesque's Approval, 4, 118	Touch of the Blues (Fr), 6, 117	9	1:35.82	124,000
2002	Touch of the Blues (Fr), 5, 116	K. Desormeaux	Pisces, 5, 123	Boastful, 4, 116	13	1:35.02	124,000
2001	North East Bound, 5, 120	J. A. Velez Jr.	Brahms, 4, 123	Strategic Mission, 6, 116	8	1:34.44	140,492
2000	Conserve, 4, 116	S. J. Sellers	Marquette, 4, 120	Inkatha (Fr), 6, 116	9	1:35.08	105,927
1999	Soviet Line (Ire), 9, 115	J. R. Velazquez	Trail City, 6, 115	Rob 'n Gin, 5, 120	8	1:35.37	68,696
1998	Lasting Approval, 4, 122	R. Albarado	Soviet Line (Ire), 8, 113	Same Old Wish, 8, 122	10	1:35.57	70,060

Racing — Graded Stakes

Year	Winner	Jockey	Second	Third	Strs	Time	1st Purse
1997	Influent, 6, 116	J. Samyn	Chief Bearhart, 4, 114	Foolish Pole, 4, 113	9	1:34.59	$69,936
1996	Tejano Run, 4, 113	J. D. Bailey	Sandpit (Brz), 7, 116	Dove Hunt, 5, 116	10	1:35.03	70,618
1995	Dove Hunt, 4, 113	J. A. Santos	Road of War, 5, 114	Night Silence, 5, 116	10	1:35.95	53,196
1994	First and Only, 7, 116	T. J. Hebert	The Name's Jimmy, 5, 113	Pride of Summer, 6, 116	7	1:36.63	50,685
1993	Ganges, 5, 113	J. D. Bailey	Bidding Proud, 4, 119	Rocket Fuel, 6, 114	10	1:35.40	52,731
1992	Shudanz, 4, 114	C. Perret	To Freedom, 4, 113	Cudas, 4, 116	9	1:36.52	55,283
1991	Opening Verse, 5, 113	J. D. Bailey	Jalaajel, 7, 113	Buchman, 4, 113	8	1:36.17	53,138
1990	Charlie Barley, 4, 119	R. Platts	Known Ranger (GB), 4, 113	Careafolie (Ire), 5, 113	10	1:35.80	36,790
1989	Yankee Affair, 7, 119	R. P. Romero	Jalaajel, 5, 114	Pollenate (GB), 5, 114	10	1:43.60	36,693

Formerly named for Fort Harrod, located in present-day Harrodsburg, Kentucky, first permanent settlement west of the Allegheny Mountains. Sponsored by Maker's Mark Distillery of Loretto, Kentucky 1997-2008. Grade 3 1991-'99. Grade 2 2000-'07. Fort Harrod S. 1989-'96. About 1 1/16 miles 1989. Course record 2004.

Malibu Stakes

Grade 1 in 2008. Santa Anita Park, three-year-olds, 7 furlongs, all weather. Held December 26, 2007, with a gross value of $250,000. First held in 1952. First graded in 1973. Stakes record 1:20 (1980 Spectacular Bid).

Year	Winner	Jockey	Second	Third	Strs	Time	1st Purse
2007	Johnny Eves, 3, 117	D. R. Flores	Carrilero (Arg), 3, 117	Horse Greeley, 3, 115	14	1:21.08	$150,000
2006	Latent Heat, 3, 115	E. S. Prado	Spring At Last, 3, 119	Midnight Lute, 3, 119	12	1:21.39	150,000
2005	Proud Tower Too, 3, 119	D. Cohen	Attila's Storm, 3, 119	Thor's Echo, 3, 121	14	1:21.62	150,000
2004	Rock Hard Ten, 3, 121	G. L. Stevens	Lava Man, 3, 115	Harvard Avenue, 3, 115	10	1:21.89	150,000
2003	Southern Image, 3, 115	V. Espinoza	Marino Marini, 3, 115	Midas Eyes, 3, 119	12	1:22.65	150,000
2002	Debonair Joe, 3, 119	J. A. Krone	Total Limit, 3, 117	American System, 3, 117	11	1:22.40	120,000
2001	Mizzen Mast, 3, 117	K. Desormeaux	Giant Gentleman, 3, 115	I Love Silver, 3, 117	13	1:22.13	120,000
2000	Dixie Union, 3, 121	A. O. Solis	Caller One, 3, 119	Wooden Phone, 3, 116	6	1:21.62	120,000
1999	Love That Red, 3, 119	G. K. Gomez	Straight Man, 3, 118	Cat Thief, 3, 123	7	1:22.06	120,000
1998	Run Man Run, 3, 115	M. J. Luzzi	Artax, 3, 119	Event of the Year, 3, 121	10	1:21.51	120,000
1997	Lord Grillo (Arg), 3, 119	E. Delahoussaye	Silver Charm, 3, 123	Swiss Yodeler, 3, 115	9	1:21.46	120,000
1996	King of the Heap, 3, 116	K. Desormeaux	Hesabull, 3, 118	Northern Afleet, 3, 116	9	1:21.84	134,300
1995	Afternoon Deelites, 3, 120	K. Desormeaux	Score Quick, 3, 120	High Stakes Player, 3, 116	9	1:21.73	100,000
1994	Powis Castle, 3, 117	P. A. Valenzuela	Ferrara, 3, 116	Numerous, 3, 118	9	1:20.96	64,300
1993	Diazo, 3, 120	L. A. Pincay Jr.	Concept Win, 3, 116	Mister Jolie, 3, 116	8	1:21.17	64,700
1992	Star of the Crop, 3, 118	G. L. Stevens	The Wicked North, 3, 116	Bertrando, 3, 116	11	1:20.67	67,850
1991	Olympio, 3, 122	E. Delahoussaye	Charmonnier, 3, 120	Apollo, 3, 118	10	1:21.28	66,850
1990	Pleasant Tap, 3, 117	A. O. Solis	Bedeviled, 3, 120	Due to the King, 3, 117	10	1:21.60	67,600
1989	Music Merci, 3, 123	L. A. Pincay Jr.	Exemplary Leader, 3, 117	Doncareer, 3, 114	11	1:21.60	67,300
1988	Oraibi, 3, 117	L. A. Pincay Jr.	Perceive Arrogance, 3, 120	Speedratic, 3, 120	13	1:21.60	70,550
1987	On the Line, 3, 117	A. T. Cordero Jr.	Temperate Sil, 3, 126	Candi's Gold, 3, 123	9	1:21.00	66,550
1986	Ferdinand, 3, 123	W. Shoemaker	Snow Chief, 3, 126	Don B. Blue, 3, 114	12	1:21.60	72,300
1985	Banner Bob, 3, 123	G. Baze	Encolure, 3, 120	Carload, 3, 114	9	1:21.00	71,600
1984	Precisionist, 3, 126	C. J. McCarron	Bunker, 3, 117	Milord, 3, 115	9	1:21.40	66,700
	Glacial Stream, 4, 120	C. J. McCarron	Total Departure, 4, 120	Hula Blaze, 4, 117	8	1:22.20	43,150
	Pac Mania, 4, 115	P. A. Valenzuela	Retsina Run, 4, 114	Desert Wine, 4, 123	8	1:22.00	43,150
1983	Time to Explode, 4, 117	L. A. Pincay Jr.	Prince Spellbound, 4, 123	Wavering Monarch, 4, 123	8	1:21.00	52,550
1982	Island Whirl, 4, 123	L. A. Pincay Jr.	Shanekite, 4, 120	It's the One, 4, 120	8	1:26.00	64,000
1981	Doonesbury, 4, 117	S. Hawley	Roper, 4, 114	Unalakleet, 4, 114	9	1:20.40	44,100
	Raise a Man, 4, 120	L. A. Pincay Jr.	Just Right Mike, 4, 114	Aristocratical, 4, 117	9	1:20.40	44,400
1980	Spectacular Bid, 4, 126	W. Shoemaker	Flying Paster, 4, 123	Rosie's Seville, 4, 117	5	**1:20.00**	47,800
1979	Little Reb, 4, 120	F. Olivares	Radar Ahead, 4, 123	Affirmed, 4, 126	5	1:21.00	38,200
1978	J. O. Tobin, 4, 123	S. Cauthen	Bad 'n Big, 4, 120	Eagle Ki, 4, 114	9	1:23.00	35,050
1977	Cojak, 4, 117	W. Shoemaker	Double Discount, 4, 117	Little Riva, 4, 114	8	1:23.00	26,050
	Romantic Lead, 4, 114	W. Shoemaker	Maheras, 4, 120	Life's Hope, 4, 124	6	1:22.40	24,800
1976	Forceten, 4, 123	D. Pierce	Messenger of Song, 4, 120	†My Juliet, 4, 115	8	1:21.20	35,450
1975	Lightning Mandate, 4, 120	A. Pineda	Rocket Review, 4, 117	Century's Envoy, 4, 120	8	1:20.60	28,525
	Princely Native, 4, 117	B. Baeza	First Back, 4, 115	Holding Pattern, 4, 123	7	1:20.80	27,775
1974	Ancient Title, 4, 120	F. Toro	Linda's Chief, 4, 126	Dancing Papa, 4, 120	7	1:22.80	34,800
1973	Bicker, 4, 117	G. Brogan	Royal Owl, 4, 126	Tri Jet, 4, 117	13	1:21.40	39,300

Named for Topanga Malibu Sequit Rancho in Los Angeles County, California. Grade 2 1973-'94. Malibu Sequet S. 1952-'57. Not held 1959, '64, '67, '70. Dirt 1952-2006. Four-year-olds 1955 (January), 1960 (January), 1965, 1966 (January), 1968-'75, 1977-'83, 1984 (January). Four-year-olds and up 1976. Two divisions 1975, '77, '81, '84 (January). Held in January and December 1984. Equaled track record 1975. Track record 1980. †Denotes female.

Man o' War Stakes

Grade 1 in 2008. Belmont Park, three-year-olds and up, 1 3/8 miles, turf. Held September 8, 2007, with a gross value of $500,000. First held in 1959. First graded in 1973. Stakes record 2:11.65 (2005 Better Talk Now).

Year	Winner	Jockey	Second	Third	Strs	Time	1st Purse
2007	Doctor Dino (Fr), 5, 126	O. Peslier	Sunriver, 4, 126	Grand Couturier (GB), 4, 126	7	2:12.26	$300,000
2006	Cacique (Ire), 5, 126	E. S. Prado	Go Deputy, 6, 126	Showing Up, 3, 121	7	2:15.68	300,000
2005	Better Talk Now, 6, 126	R. A. Dominguez	King's Drama (Ire), 5, 126	Relaxed Gesture (Ire), 4, 126	11	**2:11.65**	300,000
2004	Magistretti, 4, 126	E. S. Prado	Epalo (Ger), 5, 126	King's Drama (Ire), 4, 126	8	2:14.65	300,000
2003	Lunar Sovereign, 4, 126	R. Migliore	Slew Valley, 6, 126	Denon, 5, 126	8	2:17.99	300,000

Racing — Graded Stakes

Year	Winner	Jockey	Second	Third	Strs	Time	1st Purse
2002	With Anticipation, 7, 126	P. Day	Balto Star, 4, 126	Man From Wicklow, 5, 126	8	2:15.05	$300,000
2001	With Anticipation, 6, 126	P. Day	Silvano (Ger), 5, 126	†Ela Athena (GB), 5, 123	8	2:15.11	300,000
2000	Fantastic Light, 4, 126	J. D. Bailey	†Ela Athena (GB), 4, 123	Drama Critic, 4, 126	8	2:17.44	300,000
1999	Val's Prince, 7, 126	J. F. Chavez	Single Empire (Ire), 5, 126	Federal Trial, 4, 126	7	2:16.69	300,000
1998	Daylami (Ire), 4, 126	J. D. Bailey	Buck's Boy, 5, 126	Indy Vidual, 4, 126	9	2:13.18	240,000
1997	Influent, 6, 126	J. D. Bailey	Val's Prince, 5, 126	Awad, 7, 126	10	2:11.69	240,000
1996	Diplomatic Jet, 4, 126	J. F. Chavez	Mecke, 4, 126	Marlin, 3, 120	8	2:14.37	240,000
1995	Millkom (GB), 4, 126	G. L. Stevens	Kaldounevees (Fr), 4, 126	Signal Tap, 4, 126	12	2:12.80	240,000
1994	Royal Mountain Inn, 5, 126	J. A. Krone	Flag Down, 4, 126	Fraise, 6, 126	9	2:11.75	240,000
1993	Star of Cozzene, 5, 126	J. A. Santos	Serrant, 5, 126	Dr. Kiernan, 4, 126	8	2:23.14	240,000
1992	Solar Splendor, 5, 126	W. H. McCauley	Dear Doctor (Fr), 5, 126	Spinning (Ire), 5, 126	8	2:12.45	240,000
1991	Solar Splendor, 4, 126	W. H. McCauley	Dear Doctor (Fr), 4, 126	Beau Sultan, 3, 120	9	2:12.01	240,000
1990	Defensive Play, 3, 126	P. Eddery	Shy Tom, 4, 126	†Ode, 4, 123	7	2:17.80	284,160
1989	Yankee Affair, 7, 126	J. A. Santos	My Big Boy, 6, 126	Alwuhush, 4, 126	8	2:20.80	282,240
1988	Sunshine Forever, 3, 120	A. T. Cordero Jr.	Pay the Butler, 4, 126	My Big Boy, 5, 126	9	2:14.40	357,600
1987	Theatrical (Ire), 4, 126	P. Day	Le Glorieux (GB), 3, 121	Midnight Cousins, 4, 126	8	2:14.40	351,000
1986	Dance of Life, 3, 121	P. Day	†Duty Dance, 4, 123	Pillaster, 3, 121	7	2:14.40	201,000
1985	Win, 5, 126	R. Migliore	Bob Back, 4, 126	Baillamont, 3, 121	8	2:15.40	183,600
1984	Majesty's Prince, 5, 126	V. A. Bracciale Jr.	Win, 4, 126	Cozzene, 4, 126	9	2:14.60	214,200
1983	Majesty's Prince, 4, 126	E. Maple	Erins Isle (Ire), 5, 126	L'Emigrant, 3, 121	11	2:23.60	176,700
1982	Naskra's Breeze, 5, 126	J. Samyn	Sprink, 4, 126	Thunder Puddles, 3, 121	9	2:13.00	103,860
1981	Galaxy Libra (Ire), 5, 126	W. Shoemaker	Match the Hatch, 5, 126	‡Great Neck, 5, 126	6	2:14.80	99,180
1980	French Colonial, 5, 126	J. Vasquez	†Just a Game (Ire), 4, 123	Golden Act, 4, 126	5	2:15.40	84,300
1979	Bowl Game, 5, 126	J. Velasquez	Native Courier, 4, 126	Czaravich, 3, 121	4	2:19.00	82,425
1978	†Waya (Fr), 4, 123	A. T. Cordero Jr.	Tiller, 4, 126	Mac Diarmida, 3, 121	5	2:16.20	79,725
1977	Majestic Light, 4, 126	S. Hawley	Exceller, 4, 126	Johnny D., 3, 121	11	2:27.60	67,860
1976	Effervescing, 3, 121	A. T. Cordero Jr.	Banghi, 3, 121	‡dh-Erwin Boy, 5, 126 ‡dh-Rouge Sang, 4, 126	13	2:31.20	67,500
1975	‡*Snow Knight, 4, 126	J. Velasquez	One On the Aisle, 3, 121	Drollery, 5, 126	8	2:29.20	68,400
1974	†Dahlia, 4, 123	R. Turcotte	Crafty Khale, 5, 126	London Company, 4, 126	13	2:26.60	71,700
1973	Secretariat, 3, 121	R. Turcotte	Tentam, 4, 126	Big Spruce, 4, 126	7	2:24.80	68,160

Named for Samuel D. Riddle's 1920 Horse of the Year, '20 Belmont S. winner, and '26 leading North American sire Man o' War (1917 c. by Fair Play). Man o' War H. 1959, '61. Held at Aqueduct 1959, 1961, 1963-'67, 1987. 1½ miles 1959-'60, 1962, 1968-'77. 1⅝ miles 1961, 1963-'67. Dead heat for third 1976. ‡One On the Aisle finished first, DQ to second, 1975. ‡Crackle finished third, DQ to fifth, 1976. ‡Native Courier finished third, DQ to fourth, 1981. Course record 1973. †Denotes female.

Maryland Lottery Pimlico Special Handicap

Grade 1 in 2008. Pimlico Race Course, four-year-olds and up, 1³/₁₆ miles, dirt. Held May 16, 2008, with a gross value of $250,000. First held in 1937. First graded in 1990. Stakes record 1:52.55 (1991 Farma Way).

Year	Winner	Jockey	Second	Third	Strs	Time	1st Purse
2008	Student Council, 6, 118	S. Bridgmohan	Gottcha Gold, 5, 118	Sir Whimsey, 4, 117	7	1:54.87	$150,000
2006	Invasor (Arg), 4, 116	R. A. Dominguez	Wanderin Boy, 5, 117	West Virginia, 5, 115	5	1:54.40	300,000
2005	Eddington, 4, 116	E. Coa	Pollard's Vision, 4, 117	Presidentialaffair, 6, 115	7	1:58.05	300,000
2004	Southern Image, 4, 120	V. Espinoza	Midway Road, 4, 116	Bowman's Band, 6, 114	6	1:55.89	300,000
2003	Mineshaft, 4, 121	R. Albarado	Western Pride, 5, 116	Judge's Case, 6, 113	9	1:56.16	400,000
2001	Include, 4, 114	J. D. Bailey	Albert the Great, 4, 121	Pleasant Breeze, 6, 114	6	1:55.61	450,000
2000	Golden Missile, 5, 116	K. Desormeaux	Pleasant Breeze, 5, 111	Lemon Drop Kid, 4, 120	8	1:54.65	450,000
1999	Real Quiet, 4, 120	G. L. Stevens	Free House, 5, 124	Fred Bear Claw, 5, 113	5	1:54.31	300,000
1998	Skip Away, 5, 128	J. D. Bailey	Precocity, 4, 115	Hot Brush, 4, 113	5	1:54.26	450,000
1997	Gentlemen (Arg), 5, 122	G. L. Stevens	Skip Away, 4, 119	Tejano Run, 5, 114	8	1:53.03	360,000
1996	Star Standard, 4, 111	P. Day	Key of Luck, 5, 120	Geri, 4, 118	4	1:54.46	360,000
Y1995	Cigar, 5, 122	J. D. Bailey	Devil His Due, 6, 126	Concern, 4, 121	6	1:53.72	360,000
1994	As Indicated, 4, 120	R. G. Davis	Devil His Due, 5, 121	Valley Crossing, 6, 113	6	1:55.08	360,000
1993	Devil His Due, 4, 120	W. H. McCauley	Valley Crossing, 5, 112	Pistols and Roses, 4, 114	5	1:55.53	510,000
1992	Strike the Gold, 4, 114	C. Perret	Fly So Free, 4, 116	Twilight Agenda, 6, 122	7	1:54.86	420,000
1991	Farma Way, 4, 119	G. L. Stevens	Summer Squall, 4, 120	Jolie's Halo, 4, 119	7	**1:52.55**	450,000
1990	Criminal Type, 5, 117	J. A. Santos	Ruhlmann, 5, 124	De Roche, 4, 114	10	1:53.20	600,000
1989	Blushing John, 4, 117	P. Day	Proper Reality, 4, 118	Granacus, 4, 113	12	1:53.20	450,000
1988	Bet Twice, 4, 124	C. Perret	Lost Code, 6, 126	Cryptoclearance, 4, 121	6	1:53.20	425,000

In the past, "special" races were "winner takes all" (the winner got all of the purse money). Sponsored by the Maryland State Lottery Agency of Baltimore 2008. Not held 1959-'87, 2002, 2007. Three-year-olds 1937, '54. Four-year-olds and up 1988-'97. Winner's share included mid-series bonus of $150,000 from ACRS 1993.

Maryland Sprint Handicap

Grade 3 in 2008. Pimlico Race Course, three-year-olds and up, 6 furlongs, dirt. Held May 17, 2008, with a gross value of $100,000. First held in 1987. First graded in 1994. Stakes record 1:09.07 (1996 Forest Wildcat).

Year	Winner	Jockey	Second	Third	Strs	Time	1st Purse
2008	Starforaday, 5, 115	E. S. Prado	Suave Jazz, 5, 115	Cognac Kisses, 5, 115	5	1:09.56	$60,000
2007	Diabolical, 4, 120	M. G. Pino	Talent Search, 4, 115	Semaphore Man, 5, 116	7	1:09.16	120,000
2006	Friendly Island, 5, 116	G. K. Gomez	Celtic Innis, 4, 111	Gaff, 4, 116	7	1:09.94	120,000

Racing — Graded Stakes 387

Year	Winner	Jockey	Second	Third	Strs	Time	1st Purse
2005	Willy o'the Valley, 4, 114	E. S. Prado	With Distinction, 4, 115	Take Achance On Me, 7, 114	8	1:09.95	$120,000
2004	Gators N Bears, 4, 117	C. C. Lopez	Highway Prospector, 7, 114	Sassy Hound, 7, 115	9	1:10.84	120,000
2003	Pioneer Boy, 5, 113	J. Rose	Sassy Hound, 6, 113	dh-Highway Prospector, 6, 115	7	1:10.35	60,000
				dh-Tasty Caberneigh, 5, 114			
2002	Snow Ridge, 4, 120	M. E. Smith	Smile My Lord, 4, 113	Clever Gem, 6, 116	7	1:10.06	120,000
2001	Disco Rico, 4, 118	H. Vega	Flame Thrower, 3, 114	Istintaj, 5, 116	6	1:10.40	120,000
2000	Dr. Max, 4, 113	S. J. Sellers	Moon Over Prospect, 4, 114	Crucible, 5, 113	7	1:10.91	60,000
1999	Yes It's True, 3, 113	J. D. Bailey	The Trader's Echo, 5, 109	Purple Passion, 5, 114	8	1:09.20	120,000
1998	Richter Scale, 4, 117	J. D. Bailey	Trafalger, 4, 113	Original Gray, 4, 112	7	1:09.45	120,000
1997	Cat Be Nimble, 5, 118	J. Rocco	Political Whit, 4, 116	Excelerate, 5, 112	7	1:10.12	127,560
1996	Forest Wildcat, 5, 109	J. Bravo	Kayrawan, 4, 113	Demaloot Demashoot, 6, 115	9	**1:09.07**	129,720
1995	Commanche Trail, 4, 113	M. E. Smith	Goldminer's Dream, 6, 116	Marry Me Do, 6, 114	6	1:09.35	92,850
1994	Secret Odds, 4, 119	E. S. Prado	Honor the Hero, 6, 117	Linear, 4, 119	10	1:10.38	93,615
1993	Senor Speedy, 6, 117	J. D. Bailey	He Is Risen, 5, 115	Who Wouldn't, 4, 113	7	1:09.69	93,390
1992	Potentiality, 6, 117	P. Day	Smart Alec, 4, 114	Boom Towner, 4, 117	9	1:10.25	93,300
1991	Jeweler's Choice, 6, 115	C. J. McCarron	Shuttleman, 5, 116	Hadif, 5, 118	5	1:10.38	92,610
1990	Norquestor, 4, 115	C. Perret	Kechi, 4, 115	Amerrico's Bullet, 4, 112	9	1:09.40	93,540
1989	King's Nest, 4, 120	J. Rocco	Silano, 5, 115	Regal Intention, 4, 119	6	1:09.60	92,760
1988	Fire Plug, 5, 116	J. F. Hampshire Jr.	Harriman, 4, 117	High Brite, 4, 121	6	1:10.60	35,620
1987	Purple Mountain, 5, 111	E. Ortiz Jr.	Little Bold John, 5, 120	Berngoo, 5, 106	6	1:24.40	100,100

Sponsored by Emirates Airline of Dubai, United Arab Emirates 2005-'07. Maryland Budweiser Breeders' Cup H. 1987-'95. Maryland Breeders' Cup H. 1996-2005. Emirates Airline Maryland Breeders' Cup Sprint H. 2006. Held at Laurel Park 1987. 7 furlongs 1987. Dead heat for third 2003.

Matchmaker Stakes — See Taylor Made Matchmaker Stakes

Matriarch Stakes

Grade 1 in 2008. Hollywood Park, three-year-olds and up, fillies and mares, 1 mile, turf. Held November 25, 2007, with a gross value of $500,000. First held in 1981. First graded in 1983. Stakes record 1:33.63 (2007 Precious Kitten).

Year	Winner	Jockey	Second	Third	Strs	Time	1st Purse
2007	**Precious Kitten**, 4, 123	R. Bejarano	Wait a While, 4, 123	Lady of Venice (Fr), 4, 123	6	**1:33.63**	$300,000
2006	Price Tag (GB), 4, 123	E. S. Prado	Three Degrees (Ire), 4, 123	Pommes Frites, 4, 123	14	1:34.70	300,000
2004	Intercontinental (GB), 4, 123	J. D. Bailey	Etoile Montante, 4, 123	Ticker Tape (GB), 3, 120	14	1:35.87	300,000
2003	Heat Haze (GB), 4, 123	J. R. Velazquez	Musical Chimes, 3, 120	Dedication (Fr), 4, 123	14	1:34.43	300,000
2002	Dress To Thrill (Ire), 3, 120	P. Smullen	Golden Apples (Ire), 4, 123	Magic Mission (GB), 4, 123	6	1:48.31	300,000
2001	Starine (Fr), 4, 123	J. R. Velazquez	Lethals Lady (GB), 4, 123	Golden Apples (Ire), 3, 120	12	1:50.16	300,000
2000	Tout Charmant, 4, 123	C. J. McCarron	Tranquility Lake, 5, 123	Happyanunoit (NZ), 5, 123	9	1:46.06	300,000
1999	Happyanunoit (NZ), 4, 123	B. Blanc	Tuzla (Fr), 5, 123	Spanish Fern, 4, 123	9	1:46.30	300,000
1998	Squeak (GB), 4, 123	A. O. Solis	Real Connection, 7, 123	Green Jewel (GB), 4, 123	8	2:05.08	420,000
1997	Ryafan, 3, 120	A. O. Solis	Maxzene, 4, 123	Yokama, 4, 120	8	2:05.80	420,000
1996	Wandesta (GB), 5, 123	C. S. Nakatani	Windsharp, 5, 123	Memories of Silver, 3, 120	12	2:00.14	420,000
1995	Duda, 4, 123	J. D. Bailey	Angel in My Heart (Fr), 3, 120	Wandesta (GB), 4, 123	14	2:00.37	385,000
1994	Exchange, 5, 123	L. A. Pincay Jr.	Aube Indienne (Fr), 4, 123	Wandesta (GB), 3, 120	8	1:49.42	220,000
1993	Flawlessly, 5, 123	C. J. McCarron	Toussaud, 4, 123	Skimble, 4, 123	7	1:46.78	220,000
1992	Flawlessly, 4, 123	C. J. McCarron	Super Staff, 4, 123	Kostroma (Ire), 6, 123	9	1:46.14	220,000
1991	Flawlessly, 3, 120	C. J. McCarron	Fire the Groom, 4, 123	Free At Last (GB), 4, 123	14	1:46.60	110,000
1990	Countus In, 5, 123	C. S. Nakatani	Taffeta and Tulle, 4, 123	Little Brianne, 5, 123	14	1:46.20	110,000
1989	Claire Marine (Ire), 4, 123	C. J. McCarron	General Charge (Ire), 3, 120	Royal Touch (Ire), 4, 123	7	1:47.40	110,000
1988	Nastique, 4, 123	W. Shoemaker	Annoconnor, 4, 123	White Mischief (GB), 4, 123	10	1:47.40	110,000
1987	Asteroid Field, 4, 123	A. T. Gryder	Nashmeel, 3, 120	Any Song (Ire), 4, 123	10	1:51.00	110,000
1986	Auspiciante (Arg), 5, 123	C. B. Asmussen	Aberuschka (Ire), 4, 123	Reloy, 3, 120	12	1:48.00	110,000
1985	Fact Finder, 6, 123	S. Hawley	Tamarinda (Fr), 4, 123	Possible Mate, 4, 123	10	1:48.20	137,000
1984	Royal Heroine (Ire), 4, 123	F. Toro	Reine Mathilde, 3, 123	Sabin, 4, 123	6	1:49.40	164,000
1983	Sangue (Ire), 5, 123	W. Shoemaker	Castilla, 4, 123	Geraldine's Store, 4, 123	10	1:49.40	110,000
1982	Pale Purple, 4, 123	R. Sibille	Berry Bush, 5, 123	Ticketed, 3, 123	9	1:48.60	104,600
	Castilla, 3, 120	R. Sibille	Sangue (Ire), 4, 123	Star Pastures (GB), 4, 123	9	1:47.40	104,600
1981	Kilijaro (Ire), 5, 123	L. A. Pincay Jr.	Glorious Song, 5, 123	Bersid, 3, 120	9	1:47.00	131,600

Older women are sometimes known as "matriarchs." Matriarch Invitational S. 1983-'87. Not held 2005. 1⅛ miles 1981-'94, 1999-2002. 1¼ miles 1995-'98. Two divisions 1982.

Matron Stakes

Grade 2 in 2008. Belmont Park, two-year-olds, fillies, 7 furlongs, dirt. Held September 15, 2007, with a gross value of $250,000. First held in 1892. First graded in 1973. Stakes record 1:22.80 (1977 Lakeville Miss; 1990 Meadow Star).

Year	Winner	Jockey	Second	Third	Strs	Time	1st Purse
2007	Proud Spell, 2, 119	G. Saez	Armonk, 2, 119	Dagger, 2, 119	7	1:24.20	$150,000
2006	Meadow Breeze, 2, 119	K. Desormeaux	dh-Featherbed, 2, 119		6	1:24.82	150,000
			dh-Octave, 2, 119				
2005	Folklore, 2, 119	E. S. Prado	Miss Norman, 2, 119	Along the Sea, 2, 119	7	1:23.70	180,000
2004	Sense of Style, 2, 119	E. S. Prado	Balletto (UAE), 2, 119	Play With Fire, 2, 119	6	1:37.67	180,000

Racing — Graded Stakes

Year	Winner	Jockey	Second	Third	Strs	Time	1st Purse
2003	Marylebone, 2, 119	E. S. Prado	Lokoya, 2, 119	Eye Dazzler, 2, 119	8	1:38.02	$120,000
2002	Storm Flag Flying, 2, 119	J. R. Velazquez	Wild Snitch, 2, 119	Fircroft, 2, 119	7	1:38.52	120,000
2000	Raging Fever, 2, 120	J. D. Bailey	Dancinginmydreams, 2, 120	Ilusoria, 2, 120	5	1:38.20	120,000
1999	Finder's Fee, 2, 119	H. Castillo Jr.	Darling My Darling, 2, 119	Circle of Life, 2, 119	7	1:36.68	90,000
1998	Oh What a Windfall, 2, 119	S. J. Sellers	Arrested Dreams, 2, 119	Marley Vale, 2, 119	6	1:39.29	90,000
1997	Beautiful Pleasure, 2, 119	J. D. Bailey	Diamond On the Run, 2, 119	Carrielle, 2, 119	11	1:35.71	90,000
1996	Sharp Cat, 2, 119	J. D. Bailey	Storm Song, 2, 119	Fabulously Fast, 2, 119	6	1:36.19	90,000
1995	Golden Attraction, 2, 119	G. L. Stevens	Cara Rafaela, 2, 119	My Flag, 2, 119	8	1:36.33	90,000
1994	‡Stormy Blues, 2, 119	J. A. Santos	Pretty Discreet, 2, 119	Phone Caller, 2, 119	6	1:35.16	64,740
1993	Strategic Maneuver, 2, 119	J. A. Santos	Astas Foxy Lady, 2, 119	Sovereign Kitty, 2, 119	8	1:23.84	70,680
1992	Sky Beauty, 2, 119	E. Maple	Educated Risk, 2, 119	Family Enterprize, 2, 119	9	1:23.32	72,480
1991	Anh Duong, 2, 119	A. T. Cordero Jr.	Miss Iron Smoke, 2, 119	Vivano, 2, 119	9	1:23.47	81,300
1990	Meadow Star, 2, 119	J. A. Santos	Verbasle, 2, 119	Clark Cottage, 2, 119	6	1:22.80	93,240
1989	Stella Madrid, 2, 119	A. T. Cordero Jr.	Golden Reef, 2, 119	Miss Cox's Hat, 2, 119	7	1:24.40	72,720
1988	Some Romance, 2, 119	G. L. Stevens	Seattle Meteor, 2, 119	Dreamy Mimi, 2, 119	3	1:24.80	68,580
1987	Over All, 2, 119	A. T. Cordero Jr.	Justsayno, 2, 119	Flashy Runner, 2, 119	6	1:24.80	82,140
1986	Tappiano, 2, 119	J. Cruguet	Sea Basque, 2, 119	Daytime Princess, 2, 119	5	1:23.40	72,000
1985	Musical Lark (Ire), 2, 119	D. MacBeth	Family Style, 2, 119	I'm Sweets, 2, 119	5	1:24.00	66,240
1984	Fiesta Lady, 2, 119	L. A. Pincay Jr.	Tiltalating, 2, 119	Contredance, 2, 119	4	1:24.80	57,060
1983	Lucky Lucky Lucky, 2, 119	A. T. Cordero Jr.	Miss Oceana, 2, 119	Buzz My Bell, 2, 119	9	1:23.60	76,590
1982	Wings of Jove, 2, 119	W. H. McCauley	Share the Fantasy, 2, 119	Weekend Surprise, 2, 119	5	1:24.00	72,600
1981	Before Dawn, 2, 119	J. Velasquez	Arabian Dancer, 2, 119	Mystical Mood, 2, 119	9	1:23.20	81,210
1980	Prayers'n Promises, 2, 119	A. T. Cordero Jr.	Heavenly Cause, 2, 119	Sweet Revenge, 2, 119	8	1:24.60	70,725
1979	Smart Angle, 2, 119	S. Maple	Royal Suite, 2, 119	Nuit d'Amour, 2, 119	6	1:23.80	69,075
1978	Fall Aspen, 2, 119	R. I. Velez	Fair Advantage, 2, 119	Island Kitty, 2, 119	4	1:23.80	58,980
1977	Lakeville Miss, 2, 119	R. Hernandez	Stub, 2, 119	Akita, 2, 119	10	1:22.80	49,335
1976	Mrs. Warren, 2, 119	E. Maple	Negotiator, 2, 119	Resolver, 2, 119	7	1:24.60	51,162
1975	Optimistic Gal, 2, 119	B. Baeza	Pacific Princess, 2, 119	Prowess, 2, 119	8	1:23.00	51,132
1974	Alpine Lass, 2, 119	A. T. Cordero Jr.	Copernica, 2, 119	Spring Is Here, 2, 119	13	1:23.00	52,674
1973	Talking Picture, 2, 119	R. Turcotte	Dancealot, 2, 119	Raisela, 2, 119	9	1:23.20	64,050

Grade 1 1973-2006. Held at Morris Park 1892-1904. Held at Pimlico 1910. Held at Aqueduct 1960, 1964-'68. Not held 1895-'98, 1911-'13, 1915-'22. Not held due to World Trade Center attack 2001. 6 furlongs 1892-1971. 1 mile 1994-2004. Colts and fillies 1892-1901. Colt and filly divisions 1902-'14. Dead heat for second 2006. ‡Flanders finished first, DQ to sixth, 1994.

Meadowlands Cup Stakes

Grade 2 in 2008. Meadowlands, three-year-olds and up, 1 1/8 miles, dirt. Held October 5, 2007, with a gross value of $499,000. First held in 1977. First graded in 1979. Stakes record 1:46.06 (1998 K. J.'s Appeal).

Year	Winner	Jockey	Second	Third	Strs	Time	1st Purse
2007	Diamond Stripes, 4, 119	C. H. Velasquez	Magna Graduate, 5, 123	Xchanger, 3, 120	7	1:48.36	$300,000
2006	Master Command, 4, 119	J. R. Velazquez	Wild Desert, 4, 119	Awesome Twist, 4, 119	7	1:46.21	300,000
2005	Tap Day, 4, 119	E. Coa	Alumni Hall, 6, 121	Purge, 4, 119	8	1:48.86	300,000
2004	Balto Star, 6, 123	J. R. Velazquez	Dynever, 4, 119	Gygistar, 5, 119	8	1:48.68	300,000
2003	Bowman's Band, 5, 119	R. A. Dominguez	Dynever, 3, 120	‡Volponi, 5, 123	6	1:46.84	240,000
2002	Burning Roma, 4, 115	E. Coa	Volponi, 4, 116	Windsor Castle, 4, 112	9	1:48.95	240,000
2001	Gander, 5, 114	J. R. Velazquez	Broken Vow, 4, 120	Include, 4, 121	5	1:47.11	300,000
2000	North East Bound, 4, 116	J. A. Velez Jr.	Lord Sterling, 4, 115	Where's Taylor, 4, 113	10	1:48.84	240,000
1999	Pleasant Breeze, 4, 110	J. F. Chavez	Jazz Club, 4, 118	Vision and Verse, 3, 112	8	1:47.17	300,000
1998	K. J.'s Appeal, 4, 112	J. R. Velazquez	Hal's Pal (GB), 5, 116	Sir Bear, 5, 119	8	1:46.06	300,000
1996	Dramatic Gold, 5, 119	K. Desormeaux	Formal Gold, 3, 117	Mt. Sassafras, 4, 114	11	1:48.02	450,000
1995	Peaks and Valleys, 3, 116	J. A. Krone	Poor But Honest, 5, 116	Concern, 4, 122	8	1:48.07	300,000
1994	Conveyor, 6, 113	M. E. Smith	Personal Merit, 3, 109	Bruce's Mill, 3, 114	11	1:47.96	300,000
1993	Marquetry, 6, 120	K. Desormeaux	Michelle Can Pass, 5, 110	Northern Trend, 5, 112	9	1:47.21	300,000
1992	Sea Cadet, 4, 120	A. O. Solis	Valley Crossing, 4, 111	American Chance, 3, 109	10	1:48.19	300,000
1991	Twilight Agenda, 5, 121	C. J. McCarron	Scan, 3, 116	Sea Cadet, 3, 115	9	1:46.63	300,000
1990	Great Normand, 5, 113	C. E. Lopez Sr.	Norquestor, 4, 116	Beau Genius, 5, 122	10	1:47.20	300,000
1989	Mi Selecto, 4, 115	J. A. Santos	Make the Most, 4, 110	dh-Master Speaker, 4, 114 dh-Slew City Slew, 5, 116	8	2:00.00	300,000
1988	Alysheba, 4, 127	C. J. McCarron	Slew City Slew, 4, 116	Pleasant Virginian, 4, 114	5	1:58.80	360,000
1987	Creme Fraiche, 5, 123	L. A. Pincay Jr.	Afleet, 3, 118	Cryptoclearance, 3, 120	7	2:01.80	300,000
1986	Broad Brush, 3, 117	A. T. Cordero Jr.	Skip Trial, 4, 122	Little Missouri, 4, 116	10	2:01.60	300,000
1985	Bounding Basque, 5, 113	R. G. Davis	Wild Again, 5, 120	Al Mamoon, 4, 115	11	2:00.40	300,000
1984	Wild Again, 4, 115	R. Migliore	Canadian Factor, 4, 114	Inevitable Leader, 5, 116	9	2:00.60	300,000
1983	Slewpy, 3, 116	A. T. Cordero Jr.	Deputy Minister, 4, 118	Water Bank, 4, 117	9	2:02.40	240,000
1982	Mehmet, 4, 118	E. Delahoussaye	Thirty Eight Paces, 4, 113	John Henry, 7, 129	9	2:01.40	240,000
1981	Princelet, 3, 110	W. Nemeti	Niteange, 7, 114	Peat Moss, 6, 121	14	2:02.40	202,080
1980	Tunerup, 4, 117	J. Vasquez	Dr. Patches, 6, 116	Dewan Keys, 5, 115	12	2:00.40	196,500
1979	Spectacular Bid, 3, 126	W. Shoemaker	Smarten, 3, 120	Valdez, 3, 121	5	2:01.20	234,650
1978	Dr. Patches, 4, 119	A. T. Cordero Jr.	Do Tell George, 5, 114	Niteange, 6, 119	7	2:01.60	104,878
1977	Pay Tribute, 5, 117	A. T. Cordero Jr.	Father Hogan, 4, 112	Super Boy, 4, 110	11	2:02.60	114,920

Formerly sponsored by General Motors Corp. of Detroit 1996. Grade 1 1983-'98. Meadowlands Cup H. 1977-'95, 1996-2002. Buick Meadowlands Cup H. 1996. Meadowlands Breeders' Cup S. 2003-'06. Not held 1997. 1 1/4 miles 1977-'89. Dead heat for third 1989. ‡Unforgettable Max finished third, DQ to fourth, 2003. Track record 1998.

Memorial Day Handicap

Not graded in 2008 (originally scheduled as a Grade 3, but was downgraded due to a purse reduction). Calder Race Course, three-year-olds and up, 1 1/16 miles, dirt. Held May 26, 2008, with a gross value of $36,000. First held in 1971. First graded in 2002. Stakes record 1:44.60 (1985 Rexson's Hope).

Year	Winner	Jockey	Second	Third	Strs	Time	1st Purse
2008	Finallymadeit, 4, 119	E. O. Nunez	Rehoboth, 5, 119	Voorhee's Ballad, 4, 119	6	1:47.10	$23,000
2007	Dry Martini, 4, 115	E. Trujillo	Rehoboth, 4, 115	Too Many Toyz, 4, 116	8	1:46.41	60,140
2006	Siphon City, 4, 115	E. Trujillo	Congrats, 6, 118	Bob's Proud Moment, 5, 115	7	1:45.87	60,000
2005	Twilight Road, 8, 119	P. Teator	Whos Crying Now, 5, 115	Hear No Evil, 5, 114	8	1:47.71	60,000
2004	Twilight Road, 7, 111	P. Teator	Hear No Evil, 4, 115	Gold Dollar, 5, 112	12	1:45.79	60,000
2003	Dancing Guy, 8, 113	R. I. Velez	Shotgun Fire, 5, 110	High Ideal, 5, 113	7	1:45.56	60,000
2002	Best of the Rest, 7, 123	C. H. Velasquez	High Ideal, 4, 112	Hal's Hope, 5, 117	4	1:44.75	60,000
2001	Hal's Hope, 4, 115	R. I. Velez	American Halo, 5, 115	Takhodha Hills, 4, 118	7	1:45.81	45,000
2000	Dancing Guy, 5, 121	J. C. Ferrer	Reporter, 5, 117	Groomstick Stock's, 4, 111	9	1:46.28	45,000
1999	Wicapi, 7, 116	E. Coa	Dancing Guy, 4, 114	Golf Game, 4, 112	8	1:46.79	45,000
1998	Born Mighty, 4, 114	J. A. Rivera II	Hard Rock Ridge, 5, 113	Auroral, 6, 114	7	1:40.96	30,000
1997	Vilhelm, 5, 114	J. C. Ferrer	‡Sir Bear, 4, 113	Donthelumbertrader, 4, 118	9	1:40.80	30,000
1996	Marcie's Ensign, 4, 115	E. Coa	Derivative, 5, 114	Halo Bird (Arg), 5, 110	9	1:50.02	30,000
1995	Mr. Light Tres (Arg), 6, 113	K. L. Chapman	Fabulous Frolic, 4, 112	Flying American, 6, 116	11	1:47.17	30,000
1994	Final Sunrise, 4, 113	P. A. Rodriguez	Crucial Trial, 4, 114	Bill Mooney, 4, 112	4	1:51.86	30,000
1993	Boots 'n Buck, 4, 116	M. Russ	Yankee Axe, 6, 113	Darian's Reason, 5, 113	10	1:53.82	30,000
1992	Jodi's Sweetie, 4, 114	J. C. Duarte Jr.	Scottish Ice, 4, 114	Bidding Proud, 3, 113	9	1:44.21	30,000
1991	S. W. Wildcard, 5, 116	P. A. Rodriguez	So Dashing, 5, 113	Bold Circle, 5, 114	9	1:46.92	34,110
1990	Primal, 5, 122	H. Castillo Jr.	Eagle Watch, 6, 116	Public Account, 5, 113	7	1:47.40	33,180
1989	Hooting Star, 4, 116	J. A. Velez Jr.	Val d'Enchere, 6, 116	Bright Balloon, 5, 111	8	1:41.00	33,330
1988	Billie Osage, 4, 116	G. St. Leon	Fabulous Devotion, 4, 110	Engrupido II (Uru), 6, 114	7	1:46.20	33,150
1985	Rexson's Hope, 4, 113	G. W. Bain	Brother Liam, 5, 121	Amerilad, 4, 115	10	**1:44.60**	33,660
1983	Bolivar (Chi), 6, 116	S. B. Soto	Dallas Express, 5, 114	Grey Adorn, 5, 115	11	1:46.00	23,700
1982	Two's a Plenty, 5, 122	A. Smith Jr.	Catch That Pass, 4, 114	Poking, 6, 117	5	1:45.40	19,470
1980	Poverty Boy, 5, 119	M. Fromin	J. Rodney G., 5, 115	Irish Swords, 4, 117	11	1:45.60	20,565
1979	Great Sound (Ire), 5, 115	W. A. Guerra	Raymond Earl, 4, 123	Prince Misko, 4, 116	9	1:45.40	20,835
1978	One Moment, 5, 114	J. Giovanni	Out Door Johnny, 4, 115	Haverty, 4, 112	8	1:52.20	21,240
1977	‡Lightning Thrust, 4, 121	G. St. Leon	Jatski, 3, 110	What a Threat, 5, 116	10	1:45.80	21,780
1976	Freepet, 6, 117	R. Broussard	Chilean Chief, 5, 119	Rastafarian, 7, 112	7	1:53.80	20,700
1975	Plagiarize, 4, 118	G. St. Leon	*Rimsky II, 4, 115	Trusted, 4, 115	7	1:45.80	13,800
1974	Snurb, 4, 121	G. St. Leon	Stairway to Stars, 5, 113	Somewhat Striking, 4, 116	8	1:46.20	14,040
1973	*Correntoso, 6, 116	R. Danjean	Great Divide, 5, 121	*Asher, 5, 104	9	1:47.80	10,620

Traditionally held during Memorial Day weekend. Not graded 2008. Memorial H. 1972. Empty Saddles H. 1975. Memorial Day H. 1971, 1973-'74, 1976-2007. Not held 1981, 1984, 1986-'87. 1 mile 1971. 1 1/8 miles 1976, 1978, 1993-'96. About 1 1/8 miles 1977, '92. Turf 1977, 1989, 1992, 1995, 1997-'98. ‡What a Threat finished second, DQ to third, 1977. ‡Donthelumbertrader finished second, DQ to third, 1997.

Mervin H. Muniz Jr. Memorial Handicap

Grade 2 in 2008. Fair Grounds, four-year-olds and up, about 1 1/8 miles, turf. Held March 8, 2008, with a gross value of $500,000. First held in 1992. First graded in 1996. Stakes record 1:48.29 (2004 Mystery Giver).

Year	Winner	Jockey	Second	Third	Strs	Time	1st Purse
2008	Proudinsky (Ger), 5, 118	G. K. Gomez	French Beret, 5, 115	Daytona (Ire), 4, 121	10	1:50.44	$300,000
2007	Einstein (Brz), 5, 119	R. Albarado	Cloudy's Knight, 7, 116	†Naissance Royale (Ire), 5, 114	11	1:49.57	300,000
2005	‡A to the Z, 5, 121	V. Espinoza	America Alive, 4, 116	Honor in War, 6, 117	11	1:50.99	300,000
2004	Mystery Giver, 6, 120	R. Albarado	Herculated, 4, 115	Skate Away, 5, 117	10	**1:48.29**	300,000
2003	Candid Glen, 6, 114	E. J. Perrodin	Rouvres (Fr), 4, 115	Freefourinternet, 5, 115	11	1:51.15	390,000
2002	Sarafan, 5, 114	C. S. Nakatani	Beat Hollow (GB), 5, 115	Even the Score, 4, 116	14	1:48.88	420,000
2001	Tijiyr (Ire), 5, 110	R. Albarado	Northcote Road, 6, 115	King Cugat, 4, 121	13	1:50.72	360,000
2000	Brave Act (GB), 6, 121	C. B. Asmussen	Where's Taylor, 4, 113	Chester House, 5, 114	13	1:48.98	360,000
1999	Lord Smith (GB), 4, 117	G. K. Gomez	Hawksley Hill (Ire), 6, 122	Chorwon, 6, 116	12	1:51.27	398,160
1998	Joyeux Danseur, 5, 121	R. Albarado	Martiniquais (Ire), 5, 118	Hollie's Chief, 7, 113	9	1:49.30	223,980
1997	Always a Classic, 4, 114	E. M. Martin Jr.	Rainbow Blues (Ire), 4, 120	Snake Eyes, 7, 118	7	1:54.83	131,970
1996	Kazabaiyn, 6, 113	K. Desormeaux	Party Season (GB), 5, 116	Coaxing Matt, 7, 112	10	1:50.80	93,195
1995	Earl of Barking (Ire), 5, 115	G. F. Almeida	Kazabaiyn, 5, 114	Coaxing Matt, 6, 113	10	1:52.01	93,375
1994	Snake Eyes, 4, 115	B. E. Bartram	Yukon Robbery, 5, 115	dh-Cozzene's Prince, 7, 122 dh-Dipotamos, 6, 115	8	1:49.41	76,305
	Pride of Summer, 6, 113	R. J. King Jr.	Alpine Choice, 6, 114	Empire Pool (GB), 4, 116	10	1:49.59	76,425
1993	Coaxing Matt, 4, 114	E. M. Martin Jr.	Dixie Poker Ace, 6, 120	Spending Record, 6, 114	12	1:50.80	47,010
1992	‡Slick Groom, 4, 112	K. P. LeBlanc	Little Bro Lantis, 4, 113	Brownsboro, 8, 117	10	1:52.60	31,590

Named for longtime Fair Grounds racing secretary Mervin H. Muniz Jr., who died in 2003. Formerly named for Hawksworth Farm's 1984 Louisiana H. winner Explosive Bid (1978 c. by Explodent). Grade 3 1996-2000. Explosive Bid S. 1992-'94. Explosive Bid H. 1995-2003. Mervin H. Muniz Jr. Memorial H. 2004-'07. Not held 2006. Two divisions 1994. Dead heat for third 1994 (2nd Div.). ‡City Ballet finished first, DQ to sixth, 1992. ‡Rapid Proof finished first, DQ to eleventh for a positive drug test, 2005. Course record 2004. †Denotes female.

Mervyn LeRoy Handicap

Grade 2 in 2008. Hollywood Park, three-year-olds and up, 1 1/16 miles, all weather. Held April 26, 2008, with a gross value of $150,000. First held in 1980. First graded in 1980. Stakes record 1:40.20 (1989 Ruhlmann).

Year	Winner	Jockey	Second	Third	Strs	Time	1st Purse
2008	Surf Cat, 6, 120	A. O. Solis	Desert Code, 4, 116	Global Hunter (Arg), 5, 115	8	1:41.13	$90,000

Year	Winner	Jockey	Second	Third	Strs	Time	1st Purse
2007	Molengao (Brz), 6, 118	V. Espinoza	Porto Santo (Fr), 4, 116	Buzzards Bay, 5, 120	8	1:42.86	$90,000
2006	Surf Cat, 4, 121	A. O. Solis	Spellbinder, 5, 116	Dixie Meister, 4, 115	5	1:40.65	90,000
2005	Ace Blue (Brz), 5, 119	D. R. Flores	Ender's Shadow, 5, 116	Borrego, 4, 119	7	1:41.45	90,000
2004	Even the Score, 6, 116	D. R. Flores	Ender's Shadow, 4, 113	Total Impact (Chi), 6, 116	8	1:40.81	90,000
2003	Total Impact (Chi), 5, 114	M. E. Smith	Fleetstreet Dancer, 5, 114	Piensa Sonando (Chi), 5, 115	8	1:40.88	90,000
2002	Sky Jack, 6, 117	L. A. Pincay Jr.	Bosque Redondo, 5, 117	Devine Wind, 6, 114	6	1:41.36	90,000
2001	Futural, 5, 117	C. J. McCarron	Skimming, 5, 119	Moonlight Charger, 6, 114	5	1:42.02	90,000
2000	Out of Mind (Brz), 5, 116	E. Delahoussaye	Early Pioneer, 5, 116	Skimming, 4, 111	7	1:41.82	90,000
1999	Budroyale, 6, 118	G. K. Gomez	Moore's Flat, 5, 107	Wild Wonder, 5, 120	6	1:42.12	90,000
1998	Wild Wonder, 4, 116	E. Delahoussaye	Budroyale, 5, 116	Flick (GB), 6, 117	7	1:40.92	64,320
1997	Hesabull, 4, 115	G. F. Almeida	Region, 8, 112	Kingdom Found, 7, 116	5	1:41.30	63,720
1996	Siphon (Brz), 5, 117	D. R. Flores	Del Mar Dennis, 6, 119	Dramatic Gold, 5, 117	4	1:40.44	61,500
1995	Tossofthecoin, 5, 118	C. S. Nakatani	Ferrara, 4, 114	Polar Route, 5, 116	8	1:40.70	64,640
1994	Del Mar Dennis, 4, 115	S. Gonzalez Jr.	Tinners Way, 4, 114	Hill Pass, 5, 115	6	1:40.48	93,300
1993	Marquetry, 6, 117	K. Desormeaux	Potrillon (Arg), 5, 117	Lottery Winner, 4, 115	6	1:49.10	92,800
1992	Another Review, 4, 116	K. Desormeaux	Sir Beaufort, 5, 116	Marquetry, 5, 119	5	1:41.38	87,900
1991	Louis Cyphre (Ire), 5, 114	J. A. Santos	Warcraft, 4, 115	Anshan (GB), 4, 116	6	1:40.90	110,600
1990	Super May, 4, 116	R. G. Davis	Charlatan (Chi), 5, 110	Lively One, 5, 122	12	1:40.80	121,600
1989	Ruhlmann, 4, 121	L. A. Pincay Jr.	Sabona, 7, 114	Perfec Travel, 7, 115	5	**1:40.20**	122,800
1988	Judge Angelucci, 5, 123	E. Delahoussaye	Simply Majestic, 4, 118	Mark Chip, 5, 117	8	1:40.80	129,600
1987	Zabaleta, 4, 117	L. A. Pincay Jr.	Nostalgia's Star, 5, 116	Sabona, 5, 114	7	1:34.80	127,000
1986	Skywalker, 4, 117	L. A. Pincay Jr.	Sabona, 4, 113	Al Mamoon, 5, 120	8	1:34.80	123,600
1985	Precisionist, 4, 126	C. J. McCarron	Greinton (GB), 4, 121	My Habitony, 5, 115	5	1:32.80	118,700
1984	Sari's Dreamer, 5, 112	R. Q. Meza	Fighting Fit, 5, 120	Ancestral (Ire), 4, 115	7	1:34.20	95,000
1983	Fighting Fit, 4, 115	W. Shoemaker	Island Whirl, 5, 122	Kangroo Court, 6, 116	7	1:35.80	63,600
1982	Mehmet, 4, 116	S. Hawley	A Run, 4, 112	Major Sport, 5, 112	6	1:34.60	63,100
1981	Eleven Stitches, 4, 115	S. Hawley	†Glorious Song, 5, 121	Summer Time Guy, 5, 114	8	1:36.40	97,100
1980	Spectacular Bid, 4, 132	W. Shoemaker	Peregrinator (Ire), 5, 119	Beau's Eagle, 4, 121	6	1:40.40	120,400

Named for Mervyn LeRoy (1900-'87), one of the organizers of Hollywood Park and its president until 1985; LeRoy was a leading Hollywood producer and director. Grade 1 1988-'91. 1 mile 1981-'87. 1 1/8 miles 1993. Dirt 1980-2006. †Denotes female.

Metropolitan Handicap

Grade 1 in 2008. Belmont Park, three-year-olds and up, 1 mile, dirt. Held May 26, 2008, with a gross value of $600,000. First held in 1891. First graded in 1973. Stakes record 1:32.81 (1996 Honour and Glory).

Year	Winner	Jockey	Second	Third	Strs	Time	1st Purse
2008	Divine Park, 4, 117	A. Garcia	Commentator, 7, 122	Lord Snowdon, 5, 116	9	1:36.91	$360,000
2007	Corinthian, 4, 117	K. J. Desormeaux	Political Force, 4, 116	Lawyer Ron, 4, 119	9	1:34.77	360,000
2006	Silver Train, 4, 119	E. S. Prado	Sun King, 4, 118	Mass Media, 5, 116	7	1:34.27	360,000
2005	Ghostzapper, 5, 123	J. Castellano	Silver Wagon, 4, 115	Sir Shackleton, 4, 116	6	1:33.29	450,000
2004	Pico Central (Brz), 5, 119	A. O. Solis	Bowman's Band, 6, 114	Strong Hope, 4, 119	5	1:35.47	450,000
2003	Aldebaran, 5, 119	J. D. Bailey	Saarland, 4, 114	Peeping Tom, 6, 114	8	1:34.15	450,000
2002	Swept Overboard, 5, 117	J. F. Chavez	Aldebaran, 4, 115	Crafty C. T., 4, 116	10	1:33.34	450,000
2001	Exciting Story, 4, 115	P. Husbands	Peeping Tom, 4, 119	Alannan, 5, 118	10	1:37.14	450,000
2000	Yankee Victor, 4, 117	H. Castillo Jr.	†Honest Lady, 4, 112	Sir Bear, 7, 117	8	1:34.64	450,000
1999	Sir Bear, 6, 117	J. R. Velazquez	Crafty Friend, 6, 114	Liberty Gold, 5, 114	8	1:34.55	300,000
1998	Wild Rush, 4, 119	J. D. Bailey	Banker's Gold, 4, 115	Accelerator, 4, 113	9	1:33.50	300,000
1997	Langfuhr, 5, 122	J. F. Chavez	Western Winter, 5, 115	Northern Afleet, 4, 117	10	1:33.11	240,000
1996	Honour and Glory, 3, 110	J. R. Velazquez	dh-Afternoon Deelites, 4, 123 dh-Lite the Fuse, 5, 122		9	**1:32.81**	240,000
1995	You and I, 4, 112	J. F. Chavez	Lite the Fuse, 4, 113	Our Emblem, 4, 114	9	1:34.63	300,000
1994	Holy Bull, 3, 112	M. E. Smith	Cherokee Run, 4, 118	Devil His Due, 5, 122	10	1:33.98	300,000
1993	Ibero (Arg), 6, 119	L. A. Pincay Jr.	Bertrando, 4, 121	Alydeed, 4, 124	9	1:34.29	300,000
1992	Dixie Brass, 3, 107	J. M. Pezua	Pleasant Tap, 5, 119	In Excess (Ire), 5, 121	11	1:33.68	300,000
1991	In Excess (Ire), 4, 117	P. A. Valenzuela	Rubiano, 4, 117	Gervazy, 4, 114	9	1:35.45	300,000
1990	Criminal Type, 5, 120	J. A. Santos	Housebuster, 3, 113	Easy Goer, 4, 127	9	1:34.40	357,000
1989	Proper Reality, 4, 117	J. D. Bailey	Seeking the Gold, 4, 126	Dancing Spree, 4, 113	8	1:34.00	353,400
1988	Gulch, 4, 125	J. A. Santos	Afleet, 4, 124	Stacked Pack, 4, 110	8	1:34.60	351,600
1987	Gulch, 3, 110	P. Day	King's Swan, 7, 121	Broad Brush, 4, 128	9	1:34.80	360,900
1986	Garthorn, 6, 124	R. Q. Meza	Love That Mac, 4, 117	†Lady's Secret, 4, 120	8	1:33.60	179,700
1985	Forzando (GB), 4, 118	D. MacBeth	Mo Exception, 4, 113	Track Barron, 4, 125	8	1:34.40	207,600
1984	Fit to Fight, 5, 124	J. D. Bailey	A Phenomenon, 4, 126	Moro, 5, 116	10	1:34.00	209,100
1983	Star Choice, 4, 113	J. Velasquez	Tough Critic, 4, 110	John's Gold, 4, 111	13	1:33.80	145,200
1982	Conquistador Cielo, 3, 111	E. Maple	Silver Buck, 4, 111	Star Gallant, 3, 111	14	1:33.00	91,800
1981	Fappiano, 4, 115	A. T. Cordero Jr.	Irish Tower, 4, 127	Amber Pass, 4, 115	7	1:33.80	85,650
1980	Czaravich, 4, 125	L. A. Pincay Jr.	State Dinner, 5, 117	Silent Cal, 5, 120	8	1:35.80	83,850
1979	State Dinner, 4, 115	J. C. McCarron	Dr. Patches, 5, 118	Sorry Lookin, 4, 113	9	1:34.00	64,980
1978	Cox's Ridge, 4, 130	E. Maple	Buckfinder, 4, 112	Quiet Little Table, 5, 118	9	1:34.60	66,180
1977	Forego, 7, 133	W. Shoemaker	Co Host, 5, 111	Full Out, 4, 115	12	1:34.80	68,640
1976	Forego, 6, 130	H. Gustines	Master Derby, 4, 126	Lord Rebeau, 5, 119	6	1:34.40	66,660
1975	Gold and Myrrh, 4, 121	W. Blum	Stop the Music, 5, 124	Forego, 5, 136	7	1:33.80	66,840

Year	Winner	Jockey	Second	Third	Strs	Time	1st Purse
1974	Arbees Boy, 4, 112	E. Maple	Forego, 4, 134	Timeless Moment, 4, 109	8	1:34.40	$67,200
1973	Tentam, 4, 116	J. Velasquez	Key to the Mint, 4, 127	King's Bishop, 4, 118	8	1:35.00	68,580

Held at Morris Park 1891-1904. Held at Aqueduct 1960-'67, 1969, 1975. Not held 1891, 1911-'12. 1 1/8 miles 1891-'96. Dead heat for second 1996. †Denotes female.

Miami Mile Handicap

Grade 3 in 2008. Calder Race Course, three-year-olds and up, 1 mile, turf. Held April 28, 2007, with a gross value of $105,000. First held in 1987. First graded in 1989. Stakes record 1:33.75 (2001 Mr. Livingston).

Year	Winner	Jockey	Second	Third	Strs	Time	1st Purse
2007	Jet Propulsion, 4, 114	E. O. Nunez	Giant Wrecker, 5, 116	Paradise Dancer, 7, 115	11	1:34.11	$45,000
2006	Gigawatt, 6, 114	C. Sutherland	dh-Old Forester, 5, 116		10	1:34.50	90,000
			dh-Spring House, 4, 116				
2005	Bob's Proud Moment, 4, 115	M. R. Cruz	Dancing Master (Ire), 7, 113	Southern Cal, 4, 119	9	1:38.18	45,000
2004	Twilight Road, 7, 114	P. Teator	Gold Dollar, 5, 114	Paradise Dancer, 4, 115	9	1:39.56	90,000
2003	Tour of the Cat, 5, 115	A. Cabassa Jr.	Last Stand, 4, 113	Lavender's Lad, 5, 114	10	1:38.65	90,000
2002	Band Is Passing, 6, 117	C. H. Velasquez	Pisces, 5, 116	Doowaley (Ire), 6, 113	8	1:37.78	90,000
2001	Mr. Livingston, 4, 115	A. Castellano Jr.	Honorable Pic, 4, 114	Pisces, 4, 112	8	**1:33.75**	90,000
2000	Band Is Passing, 4, 120	E. Coa	Hurrahy, 7, 115	Tiger Shark, 4, 112	9	1:37.28	90,000
1999	Sharp Appeal, 6, 114	J. Castellano	Shamrock City, 4, 114	Hurrahy, 6, 115	10	1:35.70	135,000
1998	Unite's Big Red, 4, 115	E. O. Nunez	Fig Fest, 5, 113	dh-Copy Editor, 6, 117	10	1:36.62	120,000
				dh-Ensign Ray, 5, 113			
1997	Vilhelm, 5, 114	J. C. Ferrer	Marcie's Ensign, 5, 114	Elite Jeblar, 7, 113	11	1:36.67	120,000
1996	Satellite Nealski, 3, 112	J. C. Ferrer	Marcie's Ensign, 4, 115	Copy Editor, 4, 117	10	1:47.63	95,805
1995	Elite Jeblar, 5, 113	E. Fires	Myrmidon, 4, 117	Fabulous Frolic, 4, 114	10	1:47.67	94,200
1994	The Vid, 4, 114	R. R. Douglas	Mr. Angel, 3, 114	Carterista, 5, 116	9	1:48.28	94,350
1993	Carterista, 4, 117	M. A. Lee	Wild Forest, 4, 112	Mr. Explosive, 5, 112	13	1:47.51	95,610
1992	Jodi's Sweetie, 4, 115	J. D. Bailey	‡Walkie Talker, 3, 114	‡Futurist, 4, 117	10	1:43.94	94,140
1991	Run Turn, 4, 111	G. St. Leon	Scottish Ice, 3, 118	Hidden Tomahawk, 3, 115	6	1:52.96	93,150
1990	Public Account, 5, 115	P. A. Rodriguez	Bold Circle, 4, 112	Primal, 5, 126	8	1:52.00	93,300
1989	Simply Majestic, 5, 117	H. Castillo Jr.	Maceo, 5, 113	Bold Circle, 3, 110	8	1:48.60	93,510
1988	Simply Majestic, 4, 117	J. D. Bailey	Val d'Enchere, 5, 116	Racing Star, 6, 115	8	1:43.60	93,900
1987	Blazing Bart, 3, 117	J. A. Santos	Silver Voice, 4, 115	New Colony, 4, 114	9	1:44.20	93,630

Named for the city of Miami, home site of Calder. Miami Budweiser Breeders' Cup H. 1987-'95. Miami Breeders' Cup H. 1996-'98. Miami Mile Breeders' Cup H. 1999-2007. About 1 1/8 miles 1987-'89, 1992-'93. 1 1/8 miles 1990-'91, 1994-'96. Dirt 1990-'91. Dead heat for third 1998. Dead heat for second 2006. ‡Say Dance finished third, DQ to fourth, 1992. ‡Futurist finished second, DQ to third, 1992.

Miesque Stakes

Grade 3 in 2008. Hollywood Park, two-year-olds, fillies, 1 mile, turf. Held November 24, 2007, with a gross value of $113,200. First held in 1990. First graded in 1995. Stakes record 1:34.30 (1995 Antespend).

Year	Winner	Jockey	Second	Third	Strs	Time	1st Purse
2007	Sea Chanter, 2, 122	M. E. Smith	Macellya (Fr), 2, 117	dh-Golden Doc A, 2, 117	11	1:35.84	$73,200
				dh-Set Play, 2, 119			
2006	Valbenny (Ire), 2, 117	A. O. Solis	Mystic Soul, 2, 115	Spenditallbaby, 2, 119	12	1:36.58	60,000
2004	Louvain (Ire), 2, 115	R. A. Dominguez	Royal Copenhagen (Fr), 2, 114	La Maitresse (Ire), 2, 114	8	1:37.19	45,000
	Paddy's Daisy, 2, 121	C. S. Nakatani	Conveyor's Angel, 2, 118	Kenza, 2, 116	8	1:36.92	45,000
2003	Mambo Slew, 2, 116	M. E. Smith	Ticker Tape (GB), 2, 116	Winendynme, 2, 116	11	1:36.17	60,000
2002	Atlantic Ocean, 2, 121	D. R. Flores	Tangle (Ire), 2, 114	Major Idea, 2, 116	8	1:34.63	120,000
2001	Forty On Line (GB), 2, 117	C. S. Nakatani	Riskaverse, 2, 121	Daisyago, 2, 118	10	1:36.38	120,000
2000	Fantastic Filly (Fr), 2, 116	G. K. Gomez	Smart Timing, 2, 115	Eminent, 2, 118	11	1:35.11	120,000
1999	Prairie Princess, 2, 116	A. O. Solis	She's Classy, 2, 118	Mary Kies, 2, 121	6	1:37.30	120,000
1998	Here's to You, 2, 116	E. Delahoussaye	Sweet Ludy (Ire), 2, 118	Nausicaa, 2, 116	7	1:36.57	120,000
1997	Star's Proud Penny, 2, 116	G. K. Gomez	Superlative, 2, 121	Ransom the Dreamer, 2, 121	9	1:37.42	120,000
1996	Ascutney, 2, 116	E. Delahoussaye	Wealthy, 2, 116	Clever Pilot, 2, 118	8	1:35.16	120,000
1995	Antespend, 2, 121	C. W. Antley	Wheatly Special, 2, 121	Platinum Blonde, 2, 121	10	**1:34.30**	110,000
1994	Bail Out Becky, 2, 121	K. Desormeaux	Miss Union Avenue, 2, 121	Makin Whopee (Fr), 2, 117	10	1:37.26	110,000
1993	Tricky Code, 2, 116	C. S. Nakatani	Irish Forever, 2, 121	Roget's Fact, 2, 116	6	1:35.15	137,500
1992	Creaking Board (GB), 2, 115	K. Desormeaux	Ask Anita, 2, 117	Zoonaqua, 2, 121	10	1:35.62	137,500
1991	More Than Willing, 2, 116	E. Delahoussaye	Stormagain, 2, 115	Looie Capote, 2, 114	8	1:35.51	61,875
	Hopeful Amber, 2, 114	D. R. Flores	Storm Ring, 2, 115	Crownette, 2, 114	8	1:36.72	61,875
1990	Dead Heat, 3, 114	J. A. Garcia	Bel's Starlet, 3, 114	Somethingmerry, 3, 114	7	1:41.00	35,650

Named for Flaxman Holding's Racing Hall of Fame member, English and French champion, 1987, '88 U. S. champion grass female, and '87 Breeders' Cup Mile (G1) (at Hollywood Park) winner Miesque (1984 f. by Nureyev). Not held 2005. 1 1/16 miles 1990. Three-year-olds 1990. Two divisions 1991, 2004. Dead heat for third 2007.

Milady Handicap

Grade 2 in 2008. Hollywood Park, three-year-olds and up, fillies and mares, 1 1/16 miles, all weather. Held May 31, 2008, with a gross value of $183,300. First held in 1952. First graded in 1973. Stakes record 1:40.20 (1980 Image of Reality).

Year	Winner	Jockey	Second	Third	Strs	Time	1st Purse
2008	Zenyatta, 4, 122	M. E. Smith	Santa Teresita, 4, 116	Kris' Sis, 5, 113	5	1:41.17	$110,580
2007	Nashoba's Key, 4, 115	J. Talamo	Hystericalady, 4, 121	Balance, 4, 123	6	1:42.16	111,660

Racing — Graded Stakes

Year	Winner	Jockey	Second	Third	Strs	Time	1st Purse
2006	Proposed, 4, 120	P. A. Valenzuela	Star Parade (Arg), 7, 120	Somethinaboutlaura, 4, 115	5	1:42.92	$110,400
2005	Andujar, 4, 117	C. S. Nakatani	Hollywood Story, 4, 121	Star Parade (Arg), 6, 115	7	1:41.59	127,290
2004	Star Parade (Arg), 5, 116	V. Espinoza	Quero Quero, 4, 115	Pesci, 4, 114	5	1:41.83	125,670
2003	Azeri, 5, 125	M. E. Smith	Enjoy, 4, 114	Tropical Blossom, 5, 111	6	1:41.87	127,080
2002	Azeri, 4, 122	M. E. Smith	Affluent, 4, 119	Collect Call, 4, 115	6	1:42.02	126,840
2001	Lazy Slusan, 6, 119	V. Espinoza	Lady Melesi, 4, 116	Feverish, 6, 118	6	1:42.25	157,980
2000	Riboletta (Brz), 5, 120	C. J. McCarron	Bordelaise (Arg), 5, 117	Excellent Meeting, 4, 121	6	1:42.01	112,860
1999	Gourmet Girl, 4, 115	E. Delahoussaye	Yolo Lady, 4, 115	Victory Stripes (Arg), 5, 117	5	1:40.97	112,440
1998	I Ain't Bluffing, 4, 120	C. J. McCarron	Fleet Lady, 4, 119	Real Connection, 7, 112	6	1:42.16	158,640
1997	Listening, 4, 116	A. O. Solis	Chile Chatte, 4, 114	Exotic Wood, 5, 118	5	1:41.20	95,220
1996	Twice the Vice, 5, 120	C. J. McCarron	Jewel Princess, 4, 120	Urbane, 4, 117	5	1:40.96	110,100
1995	Pirate's Revenge, 4, 116	C. W. Antley	Paseana (Arg), 8, 123	Private Persuasion, 4, 116	5	1:41.57	91,000
1994	Andestine, 4, 116	C. J. McCarron	Golden Klair (GB), 4, 119	Zarani Sidi Anna, 4, 116	7	1:41.40	94,900
1993	Paseana (Arg), 6, 125	C. J. McCarron	Bold Windy, 4, 114	Re Toss (Arg), 6, 116	7	1:41.67	94,500
1992	Paseana (Arg), 5, 125	C. J. McCarron	Re Toss (Arg), 5, 115	Fowda, 4, 119	7	1:41.46	94,200
1991	Brought to Mind, 4, 118	P. A. Valenzuela	Luna Elegante (Arg), 5, 114	Vieille Vigne (Fr), 4, 117	8	1:41.70	95,800
1990	Bayakoa (Arg), 6, 127	L. A. Pincay Jr.	Fantastic Look, 4, 113	Kelly, 4, 110	4	1:41.20	89,700
1989	Bayakoa (Arg), 5, 124	L. A. Pincay Jr.	Flying Julia, 6, 113	Carita Tostada (Chi), 5, 115	5	1:42.00	91,500
1988	By Land by Sea, 4, 124	F. Toro	Invited Guest (Ire), 4, 114	Integra, 4, 121	4	1:43.60	89,200
1987	Seldom Seen Sue, 4, 117	C. J. McCarron	Tiffany Lass, 4, 120	Frau Altiva (Arg), 5, 115	7	1:48.20	95,000
1986	Dontstop Themusic, 6, 122	D. G. McHargue	Magnificent Lindy, 4, 117	Truffles, 5, 110	7	1:48.80	63,500
1985	Adored, 5, 125	L. A. Pincay Jr.	Lovlier Linda, 5, 120	Mitterand, 4, 120	4	1:33.60	73,500
1984	Adored, 4, 119	L. A. Pincay Jr.	Princess Rooney, 4, 122	Lass Trump, 4, 117	7	1:41.00	63,800
1983	Marisma (Chi), 5, 118	K. D. Black	A Kiss for Luck, 4, 113	Sangue (Ire), 5, 123	7	1:42.20	63,100
1982	Cat Girl, 4, 114	C. J. McCarron	Track Robbery, 6, 124	Ack's Secret, 6, 123	6	1:41.60	62,500
1981	Save Wild Life, 4, 115	C. J. McCarron	Princess Karenda, 4, 120	Swift Bird, 4, 115	9	1:42.80	65,700
1980	Image of Reality, 4, 117	D. G. McHargue	It's in the Air, 4, 122	Fondre, 5, 113	6	1:40.20	36,050
1979	Innuendo, 5, 113	D. Pierce	It's in the Air, 3, 112	Country Queen, 4, 121	9	1:41.20	32,700
1978	Taisez Vous, 4, 127	D. Pierce	Drama Critic, 4, 118	Sensational, 4, 121	8	1:41.80	32,150
1977	Cascapedia, 4, 126	S. Hawley	Rocky Trip, 5, 115	Just a Kick, 5, 118	6	1:40.80	31,250
1976	*Bastonera II, 5, 117	L. A. Pincay Jr.	Swingtime, 4, 120	Just a Kick, 4, 121	6	1:42.00	31,600
1975	Modus Vivendi, 4, 121	D. Pierce	*Tizna, 6, 124	Mercy Dee, 4, 111	6	1:42.00	32,100
1974	Twixt, 5, 123	W. J. Passmore	Tallahto, 4, 121	*La Zanzara, 4, 121	10	1:41.00	33,900
1973	Minstrel Miss, 6, 118	D. Pierce	Susan's Girl, 4, 128	Pallisima, 4, 115	6	1:41.80	38,000

Grade 1 1973-2004. Milady H. 1952-'95. Milady Breeders' Cup H. 1996-2007. 7 furlongs 1952-'53. 1 mile 1954, 1958-'66, 1970-'72, 1985. 6 furlongs 1955-'57. 1¹/₈ miles 1986-'87. Dirt 1952-2006.

Mineshaft Handicap

Grade 3 in 2008. Fair Grounds, four-year-olds and up, 1¹/₁₆ miles, dirt. Held February 9, 2008, with a gross value of $147,000. First held in 1973. First graded in 2003. Stakes record 1:42.28 (2007 Master Command).

Year	Winner	Jockey	Second	Third	Strs	Time	1st Purse
2008	Grasshopper, 4, 117	R. Albarado	Silver Lord, 5, 116	Magna Graduate, 6, 118	7	1:43.46	$90,000
2007	Master Command, 5, 120	J. R. Velazquez	Patriot Act, 5, 115	Well Said, 4, 114	6	1:42.28	120,000
2005	Wanderin Boy, 4, 113	L. J. Melancon	Pollard's Vision, 4, 121	‡Gigawatt, 5, 115	9	1:43.08	60,000
2004	Olmodavor, 5, 121	C. J. Lanerie	Spanish Empire, 4, 118	Almuhathir, 6, 114	9	1:45.59	60,000
2003	Balto Star, 5, 118	E. M. Martin Jr.	Mineshaft, 4, 116	Bonapaw, 7, 115	8	1:43.74	75,000
2002	Valhol, 6, 115	R. Albarado	Parade Leader, 5, 115	Fight for Ally, 5, 113	10	1:42.94	75,000
2001	Include, 4, 112	L. J. Meche	Connected, 4, 112	Kombat Kat, 4, 113	8	1:44.01	75,000
2000	Take Note of Me, 6, 118	R. Albarado	Crimson Classic, 6, 114	Nite Dreamer, 5, 116	6	1:42.94	75,000
1999	Precocity, 5, 117	E. M. Martin Jr.	Prory, 7, 114	Take Note of Me, 5, 117	8	1:43.42	75,000
1998	Moonlight Dancer, 6, 114	C. C. Bourque	Precocity, 4, 117	Hot Brush, 4, 113	7	1:44.34	75,000
1997	Byars, 4, 115	C. C. Bourque	Bucks Nephew, 7, 117	Clash by Night, 4, 113	7	1:44.47	60,000
1996	Bucks Nephew, 6, 116	C. Perret	Prory, 4, 114	Vast Joy, 4, 114	9	1:43.40	38,025
1995	Adhocracy, 5, 112	L. J. Melancon	Dynamic Brush, 5, 111	Cool Quaker, 6, 113	7	1:43.10	31,530
1994	Cool Quaker, 5, 114	E. M. Martin Jr.	Dixie Poker Ace, 7, 121	Dixieland Heat, 4, 114	6	1:42.55	31,005
1993	West by West, 4, 117	J. Samyn	Place Dancer, 4, 112	Genuine Meaning, 6, 113	5	1:43.80	18,885
1992	Irish Swap, 5, 118	B. E. Poyadou	Jarraar, 5, 113	Wild and Tingley, 5, 113	6	1:43.00	18,975
1985	Rapid Gray, 6, 122	R. P. Romero	Hopeful Word, 4, 113	Silver Diplomat, 4, 118	8	1:43.00	19,250

Named for W. S. Farish's 2003 Horse of the Year and '03 New Orleans H. (G2) winner Mineshaft. Formerly named for Calumet Farm's 1941, '42 Horse of the Year, '41 Triple Crown winner, and '42 Louisiana H. winner Whirlaway (1938 c. by *Blenheim II). Whirlaway H. 1985, 1992, 1998-2004. Whirlaway S. 1993-'97. Not held 1978-'80, 1982-'84, 1986-'91, 2006. 1 mile 40 yards 1973-'81. ‡Alumni Hall finished third, DQ to ninth for a positive drug test, 2005. Overnight handicap 1973-'77, 1981.

Mint Julep Handicap — *See* Early Times Mint Julep Handicap

Miss Grillo Stakes

Grade 3 in 2008. Belmont Park, two-year-olds, 1¹/₁₆ miles, turf. Held September 30, 2007, with a gross value of $81,900. First held in 1980. First graded in 1982. Stakes record 1:40.49 (2007 Namaste's Wish).

Year	Winner	Jockey	Second	Third	Strs	Time	1st Purse
2007	Namaste's Wish, 2, 117	K. J. Desormeaux	Sea Chanter, 2, 117	Remarkable Remy, 2, 117	7	1:40.49	$49,140
2006	Chestoria, 2, 117	E. Coa	Mystic Soul, 2, 117	Christmas Kid, 2, 117	10	1:50.82	50,625
2005	Wait a While, 2, 117	J. D. Bailey	Swap Fliparoo, 2, 115	Interpretation, 2, 115	6	1:52.87	49,530

Year	Winner	Jockey	Second	Third	Strs	Time	1st Purse
2004	Melhor Ainda, 2, 117	J. A. Santos	Gemilli, 2, 117	Accretion, 2, 121	6	1:51.28	$49,320
2003	Please Take Me Out, 2, 117	A. T. Gryder	Bobbie Use, 2, 117	Lucifer's Stone, 2, 117	9	1:50.75	50,640
2002	Fircroft, 2, 115	J. Samyn	Marc's Rainbow, 2, 119	One and Twenty, 2, 121	6	1:49.79	50,400
2001	Riskaverse, 2, 118	R. G. Davis	Lujien Lujien, 2, 118	Kathy K D, 2, 118	12	1:51.61	52,020
2000	Ruff, 2, 116	J. R. Velazquez	Mystic Lady, 2, 116	Medicine Bow, 2, 114	8	1:49.79	66,780
1999	Wolf Alert, 2, 113	J. D. Bailey	Windsong, 2, 113	Cherry Flambe, 2, 113	8	1:54.01	66,600
1998	Belle Cherie, 2, 116	J. R. Velazquez	Seducer, 2, 116	Civilynn, 2, 112	8	1:49.79	65,460
1997	Compassionate, 2, 113	R. G. Davis	Mississippi Queen, 2, 114	Mysterious Moll, 2, 112	10	1:49.53	67,500
1996	Miss Huff n' Puff, 2, 114	R. Migliore	Reach the Top, 2, 114	Ascutney, 2, 116	10	1:53.13	68,700
1995	Mountain Affair, 2, 118	T. Kabel	Lulu's Ransom, 2, 114	Casanova Storm, 2, 114	9	1:41.47	68,040
1994	Upper Noosh, 2, 114	E. Maple	Another Legend, 2, 114	Lady She Is Too, 2, 114	12	1:53.91	69,360
1993	Chelsey Flower, 2, 114	J. Velasquez	Casa Eire, 2, 121	Betamillion Bock, 2, 114	5	1:47.10	48,975
1992	Missymooiloveyou, 2, 114	W. H. McCauley	Statuette, 2, 114	Port of Silver, 2, 118	10	1:45.21	74,520
1991	Good Mood, 2, 114	M. E. Smith	Point Spread, 2, 114	Gold of Autumn, 2, 114	11	1:42.57	74,400
1990	‡Purana, 2, 114	W. H. McCauley	Seewillo, 2, 114	Madam Sandie, 2, 116	14	1:42.76	78,720
1989	Savina, 2, 114	J. F. Belmonte	Rootentootenwooten, 2, 114	Slew of Pearls, 2, 121	10	1:51.40	55,980
1988	Memories, 2, 114	J. Cruguet	Shine Up, 2, 114	C. Sharp, 2, 114	11	1:56.20	79,320
	Darby's Daughter, 2, 121	C. H. Borel	Lyfestar, 2, 114	Le Famo, 2, 115	11	1:58.80	86,820
1987	Betty Lobelia, 2, 114	R. Hernandez	Dangerous Type, 2, 114	Last Cause, 2, 116	11	1:59.20	73,800
1986	Lovelier, 2, 116	A. T. Cordero Jr.	Nastique, 2, 114	Spectacular Bev, 2, 118	8	1:55.00	69,930
1985	Cadabra Abra, 2, 114	J. Velasquez	Roberto's Key, 2, 114	Fighter Fox, 2, 114	6	1:52.20	54,990
1984	Endear, 2, 116	G. McCarron	Double Smooth, 2, 114	Exclusive Story, 2, 118	6	1:55.40	52,650
1983	Heartlight, 2, 114	A. T. Cordero Jr.	Banquet Scene, 2, 114	Mile High Lady, 2, 114	9	1:55.00	51,930
1982	Bemissed, 2, 121	F. Lovato Jr.	Cryptic, 2, 121	Magnifique, 2, 114	8	2:04.80	33,780
1981	Baby Duck, 2, 114	G. McCarron	Maniches, 2, 121	Pamir, 2, 114	9	1:51.80	50,490
1980	Smilin' Sera, 2, 118	J. Samyn	De La Rose, 2, 121	Seaholme, 2, 118	8	1:51.40	33,000

Named for Mill River Stable's Argentinian champion three-year-old filly and 1946, '47 Diana H. winner Miss Grillo (1942 f. by Rolando). Grade 2 1988. Not graded 1996, 2001-'07. Held at Aqueduct 1980-'90, 1995, 1997, 2001-'02. 1 1/8 miles 1980-'90, 1997-2006. Dirt 1986, '96, 2005. Two divisions 1988. ‡Seewillo finished first, DQ to second, 1990.

Miss Preakness Stakes — *See* Adena Stallions' Miss Preakness Stakes

Modesty Handicap

Grade 3 in 2008. Arlington Park, three-year-olds and up, fillies and mares, 1 3/16 miles, turf. Held July 21, 2007, with a gross value of $150,000. First held in 1942. First graded in 1985. Stakes record 1:54.62 (2007 Bridge Game).

Year	Winner	Jockey	Second	Third	Strs	Time	1st Purse
2007	Bridge Game, 4, 116	J. Rose	Jennie R., 6, 115	Rich in Spirit, 5, 115	8	1:54.62	$87,500
2006	Chic Dancer, 5, 116	C. A. Emigh	Louve Royale (Ire), 5, 117	Minge Cove, 5, 113	10	1:57.48	90,000
2005	Noisette, 5, 116	C. H. Velasquez	Shaconage, 5, 117	Spring Season, 6, 113	11	1:57.30	90,000
2004	Bedanken, 6, 119	D. R. Pettinger	Aud, 4, 116	Shaconage, 4, 118	8	1:57.00	90,000
2003	Owsley, 5, 120	R. R. Douglas	Bien Nicole, 5, 119	Beret, 4, 115	7	1:55.06	90,000
2002	England's Legend (Fr), 5, 121	R. R. Douglas	Quick Tip, 4, 114	Innit (Ire), 4, 116	8	1:55.69	90,000
2001	Ioya Two, 6, 115	M. Guidry	Megans Bluff, 4, 118	Solvig, 4, 116	11	1:55.47	90,000
2000	Wade for Me, 5, 116	C. A. Emigh	Candleinthedark, 5, 113	Wild Heart Dancing, 4, 115	10	1:57.06	60,000
1997	War Thief, 5, 116	S. J. Sellers	My Secret (Jpn), 5, 114	Bog Wild, 4, 117	8	1:57.40	60,000
1996	Belle of Cozzene, 4, 114	D. R. Pettinger	Trick Attack, 5, 112	Naskra Colors, 4, 113	6	1:58.24	60,000
1994	‡Assert Oneself, 4, 115	F. H. Valenzuela	One Dreamer, 6, 117	Seventies, 4, 112	9	1:56.01	60,000
1993	Hero's Love, 5, 120	E. Fires	Villandry, 5, 114	Silvered, 6, 120	10	1:55.31	60,000
1992	Tango Charlie, 3, 114	A. G. Sorrows Jr.	Alcando (Ire), 6, 114	Hero's Love, 4, 117	13	1:58.79	45,000
1991	Lady Shirl, 4, 120	S. J. Sellers	Lyphover, 6, 114	Country Casual, 4, 114	10	1:56.53	45,000
1990	Gaily Gaily (Ire), 7, 114	M. E. Smith	Coolawin, 4, 123	Marsha's Dancer, 4, 114	11	1:55.40	51,405
1989	Gaily Gaily (Ire), 6, 123	J. A. Krone	Baba Cool (Ire), 4, 117	Coolawin, 3, 115	13	1:58.20	52,740
1987	Spruce Luck, 6, 114	D. Brumfield	Dancing On a Cloud, 4, 120	Autumn Glitter, 4, 114	9	1:51.60	34,080
1986	Zenobia Empress, 5, 118	E. Fires	Navarchus, 4, 112	Flying Girl (Fr), 4, 118	11	1:44.00	53,580
1985	Kapalua Butterfly, 4, 115	D. G. McHargue	Trinado, 4, 116	Another Penny, 4, 111	11	1:55.00	44,265
1984	Jay's Sue, 4, 115	P. Day	Dictina (Fr), 3, 109	Pretty Perfect, 4, 113	9	2:01.20	43,719
1983	Dana Calqui (Arg), 5, 114	F. Lovato Jr.	Unknown Lady, 4, 113	Sarah's a Beauty, 5, 115	12	2:01.40	34,470
1982	Office Wife, 5, 113	E. Fires	Sprite Flight, 4, 112	Touch of Glamour, 4, 117	9	1:58.20	33,750
1981	Innocent Victim, 3, 108	R. W. Cox	Passolyn, 4, 113	Touch of Glamour, 3, 112	13	1:59.00	35,040
1980	Allisons' Gal, 4, 112	M. R. Morgan	La Bonzo, 4, 112	Jolie Dutch, 4, 114	14	2:01.20	35,160

Named for Modesty (1881 f. by War Dance), first female winner of the American Derby. Modesty S. 1942-'50, 1991-'93. Held at Washington Park 1942-'45, 1958-'61. Held at Hawthorne 1985. Not held 1969-'79, 1988, 1995, 1998-'99. 1 mile 1942, 1944-'46, 1952, 1966. 7 furlongs 1943, 1963-'65. 6 furlongs 1947-'51, 1953-'54, 1959-'62. 1 1/16 miles 1955-'58, 1967-'68. 1 1/8 miles 1987. Dirt 1942-'54, 1959-'65, 1996. Three-year-olds 1942. ‡Aube Indienne (Fr) finished first, DQ to seventh, 1994.

Molly Pitcher Handicap

Grade 2 in 2008. Monmouth Park, three-year-olds and up, fillies and mares, 1 1/16 miles, dirt. Held August 25, 2007, with a gross value of $280,000. First held in 1946. First graded in 1973. Stakes record 1:41.20 (1983 Ambassador of Luck; 1986 Lady's Secret).

Year	Winner	Jockey	Second	Third	Strs	Time	1st Purse
2007	Hysterical Lady, 4, 119	E. Castro	Lexi Star, 5, 117	India, 4, 121	7	1:41.85	$180,000

Racing — Graded Stakes

Year	Winner	Jockey	Second	Third	Strs	Time	1st Purse
2006	Promenade Girl, 4, 117	J. Rose	Round Pond, 4, 121	La Reason, 6, 117	5	1:42.98	$180,000
2005	Capeside Lady, 4, 116	C. P. DeCarlo	Bending Strings, 4, 117	Emerald Earrings, 4, 114	7	1:41.49	180,000
2004	La Reason, 4, 111	C. C. Lopez	Yell, 4, 114	Bare Necessities, 5, 119	7	1:51.10	180,000
2003	Summer Colony, 5, 120	G. L. Stevens	She's Got the Beat, 4, 112	Call an Audible, 4, 110	4	1:51.83	180,000
2002	Atelier, 5, 115	E. Coa	Summer Colony, 4, 119	Spain, 5, 122	5	1:48.63	180,000
2001	March Magic, 4, 113	M. J. Luzzi	Vivid Sunset, 4, 112	Shine Again, 4, 113	7	1:43.79	180,000
2000	Lu Ravi, 5, 116	P. Day	Silverbulletday, 4, 118	Bella Chiarra, 5, 116	7	1:43.17	180,000
1999	Heritage of Gold, 4, 114	C. T. Lambert	Harpia, 5, 116	Tap to Music, 4, 116	6	1:41.76	180,000
1998	Relaxing Rhythm, 4, 116	P. Day	Minister's Melody, 4, 117	Glitter Woman, 4, 120	6	1:42.30	120,000
1997	Rare Blend, 4, 116	M. E. Smith	Top Secret, 4, 116	Chip, 4, 115	5	1:43.60	120,000
1996	Halo America, 6, 117	P. Day	Rogues Walk, 4, 116	Why Be Normal, 8, 112	6	1:41.75	120,000
1995	Inside Information, 4, 124	M. E. Smith	Jade Flush, 4, 115	Halo America, 5, 118	5	1:43.81	90,000
1994	Hey Hazel, 4, 114	R. C. Landry	Ann Dear, 4, 113	Future of Gold, 4, 110	6	1:46.41	120,000
1993	Wilderness Song, 5, 119	D. Clark	Quilma (Chi), 6, 117	Looie Capote, 4, 116	6	1:44.79	90,000
1992	Versailles Treaty, 4, 120	M. E. Smith	Quick Mischief, 6, 115	Cozzene's Wish, 5, 113	6	1:43.18	90,000
1991	Valay Maid, 4, 116	M. Castaneda	Train Robbery, 4, 112	Toffeefee, 4, 116	9	1:43.88	90,000
1990	A Penny Is a Penny, 5, 120	A. T. Gryder	Leave It Be, 5, 116	Bodacious Tatas, 5, 117	9	1:43.40	90,000
1989	Bodacious Tatas, 4, 111	R. Wilson	Make Change, 4, 112	Grecian Flight, 5, 122	5	1:42.40	90,000
1988	Personal Ensign, 4, 125	R. P. Romero	Grecian Flight, 4, 119	Le l'Argent, 6, 117	5	1:41.80	90,000
1987	Reel Easy, 4, 112	W. H. McCauley	Lady's Secret, 5, 125	Catatonic, 5, 117	8	1:42.00	99,300
1986	Lady's Secret, 4, 126	P. Day	Chaldea, 5, 117	Key Witness, 4, 112	8	1:41.20	95,610
1985	Sefa's Beauty, 6, 119	P. Day	Mitterand, 4, 119	Dowery, 4, 115	11	1:42.60	69,090
1984	Sultry Sun, 4, 116	M. Solomone	Quixotic Lady, 4, 118	Nany, 4, 114	10	1:41.60	68,640
1983	Ambassador of Luck, 4, 117	A. Graell	Kattegat's Pride, 4, 122	Dance Number, 4, 115	8	1:41.20	67,830
1982	Jameela, 6, 120	J. L. Kaenel	Pukka Princess, 4, 114	Prismatical, 4, 117	8	1:42.60	67,620
1981	Weber City Miss, 4, 119	R. Hernandez	Jameela, 5, 118	Wistful, 4, 121	6	1:44.00	49,455
1980	Plankton, 4, 120	V. A. Bracciale Jr.	Doing It My Way, 4, 114	Whose Bid, 4, 113	12	1:44.20	34,950
1979	Navajo Princess, 5, 120	C. Perret	Frosty Skater, 4, 121	Water Malone, 5, 116	8	1:43.40	36,335
1978	Creme Wave, 4, 114	D. MacBeth	Pearl Necklace, 4, 123	Flame Lily, 4, 110	8	1:45.20	36,530
1977	Dottie's Doll, 4, 113	C. Perret	Proud Delta, 5, 123	Mississippi Mud, 4, 115	11	1:41.80	37,180
1976	Garden Verse, 4, 112	F. Lovato Sr.	Spring Is Here, 4, 111	Vodka Time, 4, 112	8	1:46.00	36,433
1975	Honky Star, 4, 123	J. E. Tejeira	Twixt, 6, 126	Bundler, 4, 119	9	1:43.00	36,156
1974	Lady Love, 4, 117	M. Hole	Ponte Vecchio, 4, 116	Belle Marie, 4, 117	8	1:43.80	28,908
1973	Light Hearted, 4, 120	E. Nelson	Wanda, 4, 118	Alma North, 5, 121	7	1:41.40	28,259

Named for Molly Pitcher, famed for firing a cannon during the Battle of Monmouth, New Jersey, during the Revolutionary War. Molly Pitcher H. 1946–'95. Molly Pitcher Breeders' Cup H. 1996-2007. 1 1/8 miles 2002–'04.

Monmouth Oaks

Grade 3 in 2008. Monmouth Park, three-year-olds, fillies, 1 1/16 miles, dirt. Held August 12, 2007, with a gross value of $200,000. First held in 1871. First graded in 1973. Stakes record 1:41.92 (1997 Blushing K. D.).

Year	Winner	Jockey	Second	Third	Strs	Time	1st Purse
2007	Talkin About Love, 3, 118	S. Elliott	Scooter Girl, 3, 118	Lady Marlboro, 3, 118	6	1:43.78	$120,000
2006	Mo Cuishle, 3, 118	J. A. Santos	Gasia, 3, 120	Peak Maria's Way, 3, 118	6	1:43.16	120,000
2005	Flying Glitter, 3, 116	E. Trujillo	Shebelongstoyou, 3, 116	Toll Taker, 3, 119	7	1:44.60	120,000
2004	Capeside Lady, 3, 115	C. P. DeCarlo	Hopelessly Devoted, 3, 118	Habiboo, 3, 115	8	1:42.18	120,000
2002	Magic Storm, 3, 112	E. L. King Jr.	Alternate, 3, 114	Bronze Autumn, 3, 114	5	1:51.17	150,000
2001	Unbridled Elaine, 3, 121	E. Coa	Unrestrained, 3, 112	Indy Glory, 3, 114	7	1:51.02	150,000
2000	Spain, 3, 114	J. A. Velez Jr.	North Lake Jane, 3, 116	Prized Stamp, 3, 114	7	1:42.78	150,000
1999	Silverbulletday, 3, 121	J. D. Bailey	Boom Town Girl, 3, 121	Bag Lady Jane, 3, 116	4	1:43.03	150,000
1998	Kirby's Song, 3, 121	T. Kabel	Santaria, 3, 114	Brave Deed, 3, 112	6	1:43.31	120,000
1997	Blushing K. D., 3, 121	L. J. Meche	Holiday Ball, 3, 116	Snowy Apparition, 3, 121	7	1:41.92	120,000
1996	Top Secret, 3, 114	J. Bravo	Yanks Music, 3, 121	Mesabi Maiden, 3, 121	5	1:42.33	120,000
1995	Kathie's Colleen, 3, 112	J. McAleney	Gal in a Ruckus, 3, 121	Country Cat, 3, 121	5	1:51.50	90,000
1994	Two Altazoon, 3, 121	C. Perret	Stellarina, 3, 118	Cavada, 3, 121	5	1:52.19	90,000
1993	Jacody, 3, 121	T. G. Turner	Deputy Jane West, 3, 121	Sheila's Revenge, 3, 114	5	1:50.77	90,000
1992	Diamond Duo, 3, 121	T. G. Turner	dh-C. C.'s Sheet, 3, 114 dh-Secretly, 3, 112		8	1:51.40	90,000
1991	Fowda, 3, 121	R. Migliore	Shared Interest, 3, 114	Nalees Pin, 3, 116	8	1:50.48	90,000
1990	Pampered Star, 3, 121	J. C. Ferrer	Valay Maid, 3, 121	Jefforee, 3, 112	9	1:52.40	90,000
1989	Dream Deal, 3, 114	C. Perret	Some Romance, 3, 121	Top of My Life, 3, 121	8	1:49.20	69,000
1988	Maplejinsky, 3, 113	C. W. Antley	Make Change, 3, 114	Mother of Eight, 3, 114	6	1:53.60	102,000
1987	Without Feathers, 3, 116	C. W. Antley	Single Blade, 3, 121	Grecian Flight, 3, 121	8	1:48.00	66,240
1986	Fighter Fox, 3, 114	W. H. McCauley	Toes Knows, 3, 114	Dynamic Star, 3, 118	12	1:49.60	97,170
1985	Golden Horde, 3, 116	W. H. McCauley	Koluctoo's Jill, 3, 121	Tabayour, 3, 118	9	1:48.00	94,380
1984	Life's Magic, 3, 121	J. Velasquez	Flippers, 3, 118	Cassowary, 3, 112	10	1:50.00	94,050
1983	Quixotic Lady, 3, 116	E. Maple	Am Capable, 3, 114	Pop Rock, 3, 116	7	1:50.40	64,770
1982	Christmas Past, 3, 121	J. Vasquez	Milingo, 3, 119	Mademoiselle Forli, 3, 121	9	1:49.40	67,050
1981	Prismatical, 3, 117	D. Brumfield	Stunning Native, 3, 112	Privacy, 3, 117	7	1:49.80	49,500
1980	Rose of Morn, 3, 114	D. Brumfield	Weber City Miss, 3, 121	Sami Sutton, 3, 117	7	1:50.40	33,030
1979	Burn's Return, 3, 117	J. Vasquez	Heavenly Ade, 3, 114	Dominant Dream, 3, 114	8	1:48.80	35,718
1978	Sharp Belle, 3, 117	D. B. Thomas	Mucchina, 3, 119	Jevalin, 3, 114	8	1:52.40	35,783
1977	Small Raja, 3, 121	M. Solomone	Herecomesthebride, 3, 117	Suede Shoe, 3, 114	8	1:49.60	35,978

Racing — Graded Stakes 395

Year	Winner	Jockey	Second	Third	Strs	Time	1st Purse
1976	Revidere, 3, 121	J. Vasquez	Javamine, 3, 112	Quacker, 3, 114	8	1:50.60	$36,238
1975	Aunt Jin, 3, 119	C. H. Marquez	Let Me Linger, 3, 112	Sarsar, 3, 121	6	1:49.20	35,295
1974	Honky Star, 3, 117	W. Blum	Kudara, 3, 117	Raisela, 3, 117	14	1:49.40	38,642
1973	Desert Vixen, 3, 114	M. Hole	Ladies Agreement, 3, 111	Lady Love, 3, 111	11	1:49.00	37,473

Grade 1 1973-'79, 1985-'89. Grade 2 1980-'84, 1990-2004. Monmouth Breeders' Cup Oaks 1996-2007. Held at Jerome Park 1891. Not held 1878, 1894-1945, 2003. 1½ miles 1871-'77. 1¼ miles 1879-'93. 1⅛ miles 1953-'95, 2001-'03. Dead heat for second 1992.

Monrovia Handicap

Grade 3 in 2008. Santa Anita Park, four-year-olds and up, fillies and mares, about 6½ furlongs, turf. Held January 1, 2008, with a gross value of $110,400. First held in 1968. First graded in 1973. Stakes record 1:12.40 (1981 Kilijaro [Ire]).

Year	Winner	Jockey	Second	Third	Strs	Time	1st Purse
2008	Alexandra Rose (SAf), 6, 115	R. Bejarano	‡Good Mood (Ire), 4, 115	Audacious Chloe, 4, 117	8	1:12.86	$66,240
2007	Society Hostess, 5, 119	G. K. Gomez	Clinet (Ire), 5, 117	Kitty Hawk (GB), 4, 113	12	1:12.85	69,660
2005	Awesome Lady, 4, 119	T. Baze	Beneficial Bartok, 4, 118	Allswellthatnswell, 4, 116	9	1:16.77	67,560
2004	Resplendency, 3, 112	C. Fusilier	Puxa Saco, 4, 115	Market Garden, 4, 115	9	1:15.34	68,130
2003	Icantgoforthat, 4, 114	T. Baze	Polygreen (Fr), 4, 116	Spring Star (Fr), 4, 119	6	1:13.07	65,580
2002	Lil Sister Stich, 5, 117	L. A. Pincay Jr.	Pina Colada (Br), 3, 115	I'm the Business (NZ), 5, 116	12	1:13.81	68,820
2001	Paga (Arg), 4, 117	M. E. Smith	Twin Set (Ger), 4, 115	Impeachable, 4, 115	13	1:15.09	70,890
2000	Evening Promise (GB), 4, 120	K. Desormeaux	Squall Linda, 4, 113	New Heaven (Arg), 6, 119	12	1:12.62	68,640
1999	Show Me the Stage, 3, 117	K. Desormeaux	Chichim, 4, 118	Honest Lady, 3, 114	4	1:15.14	64,140
	Desert Lady (Ire), 4, 116	C. S. Nakatani	Sweet Mazarine (Ire), 5, 118	Supercilious, 6, 119	7	1:14.59	65,100
1998	Madame Pandit, 5, 118	E. Delahoussaye	Ski Dancer, 6, 115	Dixie Pearl, 6, 117	7	1:15.80	65,700
1997	Grab the Prize, 5, 116	A. O. Solis	Finite E. F., 4, 111	Evil's Pic, 5, 116	7	1:16.69	66,900
1996	Klassy Kim, 5, 116	G. F. Almeida	Ski Dancer, 4, 116	Baby Diamonds, 5, 114	8	1:14.48	65,650
1995	Rabiadella, 4, 117	P. A. Valenzuela	Dezibelle's Star, 4, 113	Las Meninas (Ire), 4, 120	5	1:14.92	47,450
1994	Mamselle Bebette, 4, 117	C. S. Nakatani	Shuggleswon, 4, 114	Kalita Melody (GB), 6, 117	6	1:15.35	49,650
1993	Glen Kate (Ire), 6, 118	C. A. Black	Bel's Starlet, 6, 122	Heart of Joy, 6, 121	7	1:12.89	48,650
1992	Middlefork Rapids, 4, 116	P. A. Valenzuela	Remarkably Easy, 4, 115	Crystal Gazing, 4, 121	11	1:12.55	51,150
1991	Wedding Bouquet (Ire), 4, 116	K. Desormeaux	Linda Card, 5, 118	Flower Girl (GB), 4, 116	11	1:13.90	51,875
1990	Down Again, 6, 117	C. A. Black	Sexy Slew, 4, 111	Hot Novel, 4, 116	9	1:13.00	50,200
1989	Daloma (Fr), 5, 117	F. H. Valenzuela	Valdemosa (Arg), 5, 116	Sadie B. Fast, 4, 116	8	1:16.20	49,550
1988	Aberuschka (Ire), 6, 121	G. L. Stevens	Pen Bal Lady (GB), 4, 118	Aromacor, 5, 114	10	1:14.60	50,050
1987	Sari's Heroine, 4, 117	P. A. Valenzuela	Lichi (Chi), 7, 116	Aberuschka (Ire), 5, 124	7	1:15.00	38,400
1986	Water Crystals, 5, 116	G. L. Stevens	Baroness Direct, 5, 120	Solva (GB), 5, 116	8	1:15.60	40,100
1985	Lina Cavalieri (GB), 5, 120	E. Delahoussaye	Air Distingue, 5, 117	Tangent (NZ), 5, 121	8	1:14.00	39,650
1984	Tangent (NZ), 4, 117	J. A. Garcia	Irish O'Brien, 6, 115	Frieda Frame, 6, 119	10	1:14.60	41,750
1983	Matching, 5, 123	R. Sibille	Irish O'Brien, 5, 115	Night Fire, 4, 115	9	1:13.20	40,640
1982	Cat Girl, 4, 117	C. J. McCarron	Excitable Lady, 4, 122	Chateau Dancer, 4, 117	10	1:14.60	41,250
1981	Kilijaro (Ire), 5, 127	M. Castaneda	Love You Dear, 5, 115	She Can't Miss, 4, 119	10	**1:12.40**	34,950
1980	Fondre, 5, 113	F. Olivares	Powder Room, 5, 117	Celine, 4, 118	8	1:15.20	27,500
1979	Camarado, 4, 119	W. Shoemaker	Pet Label, 6, 115	Sister Julie, 6, 115	11	1:15.40	22,900
	Palmistry, 4, 114	C. J. McCarron	Sing Back, 6, 113	Pressing Date, 5, 114	10	1:15.20	22,500
1978	Little Happiness, 4, 116	L. A. Pincay Jr.	Perils of Pauline, 4, 115	Harvest Girl, 4, 119	6	1:16.00	26,200
1977	Winter Solstice, 5, 119	M. S. Sellers	Nana Lee, 5, 116	Olive Wreath, 4, 113	9	1:13.60	27,600
1976	Winter Solstice, 4, 117	J. Lambert	Miss Tokyo, 4, 121	Exotic Age, 5, 115	7	1:17.60	20,300
1975	‡Special Goddess, 4, 119	S. Hawley	Charger's Star, 5, 115	Miss Musket, 4, 124	8	1:13.80	20,700
1974	Viva La Vivi, 4, 118	D. Pierce	Impressive Style, 5, 120	Charger's Star, 4, 113	9	1:15.00	17,800
1973	*Tizna, 4, 117	F. Toro	Generous Portion, 5, 120	‡Soul Mate, 4, 120	11	1:13.80	22,700

Named for railroad pioneer W. N. Monroe (1841-1935), founder of the city of Monrovia, California. Not graded 1975-'89, 2004-'05. Not held 2006. 6½ furlongs 1969-'70, 1976, 1978, 1980, 1989, 1994, 1997-'99. Dirt 1969-'70, 1976, 1978, 1980, 1989, 1994, 1997-'99, 2004-'05. Originally scheduled on turf 2004-'05. Three-year-olds and up 1999-'05. Two divisions 1979. Held in January and December 1999. ‡*Rich Return II finished third, DQ to fourth, 1973. ‡Viva La Vivi finished first, DQ to eighth, 1975. ‡Society Hostess finished second, DQ to fifth, 2008.

Morvich Handicap

Grade 3 in 2008. Oak Tree at Santa Anita, three-year-olds and up, about 6½ furlongs, turf. Held October 27, 2007, with a gross value of $110,000. First held in 1974. First graded in 1999. Stakes record 1:11.46 (2001 El Cielo).

Year	Winner	Jockey	Second	Third	Strs	Time	1st Purse
2007	Get Funky, 4, 118	M. Garcia	Relato Del Gato, 6, 118	Becrux (Ity), 5, 121	8	1:13.23	$66,000
2006	Moth Ball (GB), 4, 113	M. C. Baze	Apalachee Tiger, 4, 112	Osidy, 4, 118	9	1:11.61	60,000
2005	Geronimo (Chi), 6, 118	K. Desormeaux	King Robyn, 5, 118	Jungle Prince, 4, 114	6	1:12.10	60,000
2004	Leroidesanimaux (Brz), 4, 117	J. K. Court	De Valmont (Aus), 7, 115	Cayoke (Fr), 7, 116	6	1:11.76	60,000
2003	King Robyn, 3, 117	A. O. Solis	Medecis (GB), 4, 116	Geronimo (Chi), 4, 115	9	1:13.22	66,480
2002	Master Belt (NZ), 4, 114	T. Baze	I Love Silver, 4, 116	Kachamandi (Chi), 5, 117	10	1:12.26	67,020
2001	El Cielo, 7, 123	J. Valdivia Jr.	Speak in Passing, 4, 116	Islander, 6, 115	6	**1:11.46**	64,680
2000	El Cielo, 6, 119	J. Valdivia Jr.	Kahal (GB), 5, 116	Montemiro (Fr), 6, 116	10	1:12.00	67,020
1999	‡Riviera (Fr), 5, 118	B. Blanc	Kahal (GB), 5, 114	Howbaddouwantit, 4, 121	10	1:12.99	66,840
1998	Musafi, 4, 117	G. K. Gomez	Fabulous Guy (Ire), 4, 114	Expelled, 6, 119	8	1:14.54	60,000
1997	Reality Road, 5, 115	C. S. Nakatani	Latin Dancer, 6, 116	Torch Rouge (GB), 6, 115	7	1:13.60	60,000
1996	Comininalittlehot, 5, 117	K. Desormeaux	Wild Zone, 6, 116	Wavy Run (Ire), 5, 116	7	1:11.57	65,100
1995	Score Quick, 3, 113	G. F. Almeida	Dramatic Gold, 4, 120	Fu Man Slew, 4, 114	7	1:14.64	60,700

Racing — Graded Stakes

Year	Winner	Jockey	Second	Third	Strs	Time	1st Purse
1994	Rotsaluck, 3, 115	F. H. Valenzuela	D'Hallevant, 4, 118	Didyme, 4, 115	7	1:13.66	$47,925
1993	†Western Approach, 4, 125	K. Desormeaux	†Yousefia, 4, 116	Exemplary Leader, 7, 115	6	1:12.12	47,025
1992	Regal Groom, 5, 118	M. A. Pedroza	Bailarin, 5, 112	Repriced, 4, 118	4	1:16.88	45,150
1991	Waterscape, 5, 119	K. Desormeaux	Hollywood Reporter, 5, 113	Anjiz, 3, 115	6	1:11.95	47,250
1990	Yes I'm Blue, 4, 116	D. R. Flores	Waterscape, 4, 115	Oraibi, 5, 118	9	1:12.40	49,350
1989	Basic Rate, 4, 113	R. Q. Meza	Patchy Groundfog, 6, 118	Major Current, 5, 116	12	1:12.20	52,125
1988	Dr. Brent, 3, 115	F. Toro	†Serve n' Volley (GB), 4, 115	Caballo de Oro, 4, 114	12	1:15.80	51,350
1987	Sabona, 5, 117	C. J. McCarron	†Aberuschka (Ire), 5, 117	Deputy Governor, 3, 118	8	1:14.80	38,900
1986	River Drummer, 4, 121	G. L. Stevens	Prince Sky (Ire), 4, 118	Perfec Travel, 4, 116	11	1:13.80	69,700
1985	Dear Rick, 4, 118	C. J. McCarron	Champagne Bid, 6, 121	Hegemony (Ire), 4, 121	8	1:14.20	38,650
1984	Tsunami Slew, 3, 119	E. Delahoussaye	Night Mover, 4, 121	Debonaire Junior, 3, 120	8	1:14.00	39,000
1983	Kangroo Court, 6, 119	J. J. Steiner	Shanekite, 5, 120	Dave's Friend, 8, 121	7	1:16.00	38,350
1982	Shanekite, 4, 115	S. Hawley	Remember John, 3, 120	Smokite, 6, 117	7	1:12.80	37,050
1981	Forlion, 5, 116	M. Castaneda	Aristocratical, 4, 117	Syncopate, 6, 122	8	1:13.80	32,800
1980	To B. Or Not, 4, 118	M. Castaneda	Someonenoble, 5, 115	†Great Lady M., 5, 119	9	1:13.80	32,200
1979	Arachnoid, 6, 119	D. Pierce	He's Dewan, 4, 118	Bywayofchicago, 5, 120	6	1:12.60	25,150
1978	Impressive Luck, 5, 119	F. Toro	Bad 'n Big, 4, 126	Eagle in Flight, 7, 114	6	1:13.20	25,250
1977	Impressive Luck, 4, 118	F. Toro	Jumping Hill, 5, 120	Key Account, 5, 115	9	1:13.60	19,650
1976	Cherry River, 6, 120	L. A. Pincay Jr.	Mark's Place, 4, 119	Uniformity, 4, 117	10	1:13.40	20,400
1975	Century's Envoy, 4, 125	J. Lambert	Sir Jason, 4, 117	Cherry River, 5, 123	6	1:13.40	15,900
1974	Palladium, 5, 121	A. Pineda	Against the Snow, 4, 118	Soft Victory, 6, 119	8	1:16.20	15,800

Named for Benjamin Block's 1921 champion two-year-old male and '22 Kentucky Derby winner Morvich (1919 c. by Runnymede); Morvich was that race's first California-bred winner. 6½ furlongs 1983, '92, '95. Dirt 1983, '92, '95. Two-year-olds and up 1974-'92. ‡Kahal (GB) finished first, DQ to second, 1999. †Denotes female.

Mother Goose Stakes

Grade 1 in 2008. Belmont Park, three-year-olds, fillies, 1⅛ miles, dirt. Held June 30, 2007, with a gross value of $237,500. First held in 1957. First graded in 1973. Stakes record 1:46.58 (1994 Lakeway).

Year	Winner	Jockey	Second	Third	Strs	Time	1st Purse
2007	Octave, 3, 121	J. R. Velazquez	Lady Joanne, 3, 121	Boca Grande, 3, 121	4	1:47.19	$150,000
2006	Bushfire, 3, 121	E. S. Prado	Pine Island, 3, 121	Ready to Please, 3, 121	7	1:49.86	150,000
2005	Smuggler, 3, 121	E. S. Prado	Spun Sugar, 3, 121	Summerly, 3, 121	6	1:48.55	180,000
2004	Stellar Jayne, 3, 121	R. Albarado	Ashado, 3, 121	Island Sand, 3, 121	6	1:48.13	180,000
2003	Spoken Fur, 3, 121	J. D. Bailey	Yell, 3, 121	Final Round, 3, 121	6	1:50.41	180,000
2002	Nonsuch Bay, 3, 121	J. D. Bailey	Chamrousse, 3, 121	Seba (GB), 3, 121	4	1:49.09	150,000
2001	Fleet Renee, 3, 121	J. R. Velazquez	Real Cozzy, 3, 121	Exogenous, 3, 121	10	1:47.19	150,000
2000	Secret Status, 3, 121	P. Day	Jostle, 3, 121	Finder's Fee, 3, 121	7	1:48.03	150,000
1999	Dreams Gallore, 3, 121	R. Albarado	Oh What a Windfall, 3, 121	Better Than Honour, 3, 121	6	1:48.69	150,000
1998	Jersey Girl, 3, 121	M. E. Smith	Keeper Hill, 3, 121	Banshee Breeze, 3, 121	11	1:47.77	120,000
1997	Ajina, 3, 121	M. E. Smith	Sharp Cat, 3, 121	Tomisue's Delight, 3, 121	6	1:48.40	120,000
1996	Yanks Music, 3, 121	J. R. Velazquez	Escena, 3, 121	Cara Rafaela, 3, 121	7	1:47.90	120,000
1995	Serena's Song, 3, 121	G. L. Stevens	Golden Bri, 3, 121	Forested, 3, 121	6	1:50.37	120,000
1994	Lakeway, 3, 121	K. Desormeaux	Cinnamon Sugar (Ire), 3, 121	Inside Information, 3, 121	6	**1:46.58**	120,000
1993	Sky Beauty, 3, 121	M. E. Smith	Dispute, 3, 121	Silky Feather, 3, 121	4	1:49.69	120,000
1992	Turnback the Alarm, 3, 121	C. W. Antley	Easy Now, 3, 121	Queen of Triumph, 3, 121	7	1:48.80	120,000
1991	Meadow Star, 3, 121	J. D. Bailey	Lite Light, 3, 121	Nalees Pin, 3, 121	4	1:48.92	120,000
1990	Go for Wand, 3, 121	R. P. Romero	Charon, 3, 121	Stella Madrid, 3, 121	6	1:48.80	136,560
1989	Open Mind, 3, 121	A. T. Cordero Jr.	Gorgeous, 3, 121	Nite of Fun, 3, 121	5	1:47.40	136,320
1988	Goodbye Halo, 3, 121	J. Velasquez	Make Change, 3, 121	Aptostar, 3, 121	9	1:49.80	142,320
1987	Fiesta Gal, 3, 121	A. T. Cordero Jr.	Grecian Flight, 3, 121	Chic Shirine, 3, 121	12	1:50.20	150,240
1986	Life At the Top, 3, 121	J. A. Santos	Dynamic Star, 3, 121	Family Style, 3, 121	8	1:49.60	132,300
1985	Mom's Command, 3, 121	A. Fuller	Le l'Argent, 3, 121	Willowy Mood, 3, 121	11	1:49.60	109,860
1984	Life's Magic, 3, 121	J. Velasquez	Miss Oceana, 3, 121	Wild Applause, 3, 121	5	1:48.80	127,620
1983	Able Money, 3, 121	A. Graell	High Schemes, 3, 121	Far Flying, 3, 121	7	1:49.20	84,150
1982	Cupecoy's Joy, 3, 121	A. Santiago	Christmas Past, 3, 121	Blush With Pride, 3, 121	12	1:48.40	69,120
1981	Wayward Lass, 3, 121	C. B. Asmussen	Heavenly Cause, 3, 121	Banner Gala, 3, 121	8	1:48.80	66,720
1980	Sugar and Spice, 3, 121	J. Fell	Bold 'n Determined, 3, 121	Erin's Word, 3, 121	6	1:49.60	68,040
1979	Davona Dale, 3, 121	J. Velasquez	Eloquent, 3, 121	Plankton, 3, 121	6	1:48.80	63,960
1978	Caesar's Wish, 3, 121	D. R. Wright	Lakeville Miss, 3, 121	Tempest Queen, 3, 121	8	1:47.60	48,600
1977	Road Princess, 3, 121	J. Cruguet	Mrs. Warren, 3, 121	Cum Laude Laurie, 3, 121	16	1:48.80	51,480
1976	Girl in Love, 3, 121	J. Cruguet	Optimistic Gal, 3, 121	Ancient Fables, 3, 121	5	1:48.80	48,510
1975	Ruffian, 3, 121	J. Vasquez	Sweet Old Girl, 3, 121	Sun and Snow, 3, 121	7	1:47.80	50,220
1974	Chris Evert, 3, 121	J. Velasquez	Maud Muller, 3, 121	Quaze Quilt, 3, 121	14	1:48.60	53,775
1973	Windy's Daughter, 3, 121	E. Belmonte	Lady Love, 3, 121	North Broadway, 3, 121	10	1:48.40	52,965

Named for Harry Payne Whitney's consensus 1924 champion two-year-old filly and '24 Fashion S. winner Mother Goose (1922 f. by *Chicle). Held at Aqueduct 1963-'67, 1969, 1975. 1¹⁄₁₆ miles 1957-'58.

Mr. Prospector Handicap

Grade 3 in 2008. Gulfstream Park, four-year-olds and up, 6 furlongs, dirt. Held January 5, 2008, with a gross value of $100,000. First held in 1946. First graded in 1999. Stakes record 1:08.45 (1997 Punch Line).

Year	Winner	Jockey	Second	Third	Strs	Time	1st Purse
2008	Noonmark, 5, 117	R. R. Douglas	Mach Ride, 5, 117	Finallymadeit, 4, 115	8	1:09.72	$60,000

Racing — Graded Stakes

Year	Winner	Jockey	Second	Third	Strs	Time	1st Purse
2007	Kelly's Landing, 6, 118	E. S. Prado	High Finance, 4, 113	Mach Ride, 4, 114	6	1:08.84	$60,000
2006	Gaff, 4, 113	S. Bridgmohan	War Front, 4, 115	Friendly Island, 5, 116	8	1:08.50	60,000
2005	Saratoga County, 4, 112	J. Castellano	Limehouse, 4, 116	All Hail Stormy, 4, 113	10	1:08.99	60,000
2004	Cajun Beat, 4, 121	C. H. Velasquez	Gygistar, 5, 118	Deer Lake, 5, 115	6	1:09.06	60,000
2003	Baileys Edge, 6, 114	G. Boulanger	Friendly Frolic, 4, 114	Out of Fashion, 7, 115	6	1:09.95	60,000
2002	Hook and Ladder, 5, 116	J. R. Velazquez	Kipperscope, 5, 114	Red's Honor, 4, 114	8	1:09.69	60,000
2001	Istintaj, 5, 116	J. D. Bailey	Miners Gamble, 5, 115	Smokin Pete, 4, 115	13	1:09.63	60,000
2000	Mountain Top, 5, 115	J. A. Santos	Lifeisawhirl, 4, 112	Silver Season, 4, 115	6	1:10.80	45,000
1999	Cowboy Cop, 5, 114	P. Day	Good and Tough, 4, 115	Mint, 4, 115	6	1:09.65	45,000
1998	Rare Rock, 5, 116	P. Day	Heckofaralph, 5, 115	Banjo, 4, 114	8	1:08.67	45,000
1997	Punch Line, 7, 116	P. Day	Appealing Skier, 4, 119	Constant Escort, 5, 115	8	**1:08.45**	45,000
1996	Meadow Monster, 5, 114	R. Wilson	Lord Carson, 4, 119	Ponche, 7, 118	8	1:09.47	30,000
1995	Sweet Beast, 5, 118	M. E. Smith	Exclusive Praline, 4, 119	Distinct Reality, 4, 113	5	1:09.36	30,000
1994	Binalong, 5, 116	J. D. Bailey	I Can't Believe, 6, 113	Golden Pro, 4, 113	12	1:09.68	30,000
1993	Surely Six, 4, 113	R. Wilson	Groomstick, 7, 114	Poulain d'Or, 4, 117	9	1:21.85	30,000
1992	Take Me Out, 4, 115	J. D. Bailey	Gizmo's Fortune, 4, 111	Ocala Flame, 4, 113	10	1:23.75	30,000
1991	Stalker, 4, 114	C. Perret	Secret Hello, 4, 117	Shuttleman, 5, 114	11	1:22.50	30,000
1990	Beau Genius, 5, 117	W. Shoemaker	The Red Rolls, 6, 112	Norquestor, 4, 116	6	1:23.20	30,000
1989	Miami Slick, 4, 112	J. D. Bailey	Dancing Spree, 4, 115	The Red Rolls, 5, 112	6	1:09.20	34,200
1988	Jato D'Agua (Brz), 6, 110	W. A. Guerra	Banbury Cross, 5, 111	Our Happy Warrior, 4, 110	11	1:09.80	37,560
1987	Uncle Ho, 4, 111	J. A. Santos	Splendid Catch, 5, 113	Mugatea, 7, 114	7	1:22.60	27,984
1986	Fortunate Prospect, 5, 118	R. I. Velez	It's a Done Deal, 4, 113	Basket Weave, 5, 115	8	1:10.40	28,608
1985	For Halo, 4, 120	B. Fann	Northern Trader, 4, 115	Rupert's Wing, 4, 111	11	1:09.60	37,620
1984	D. White, 3, 112	A. O. Solis	Mo Exception, 3, 112	Reach for More, 3, 117	7	1:44.40	24,276
1983	Chan Balum, 4, 111	J. Samyn	Center Cut, 4, 118	Royal Hierarchy, 6, 114	10	1:10.00	25,683
1982	Noble Warrior, 6, 119	O. J. Londono	Morold (Fr), 7, 116	San Sal, 4, 110	9	2:27.20	18,585
1980	Archie Beamish, 7, 111	W. A. Guerra	Proud Manner, 6, 114	Foretake, 4, 115	10	2:27.20	14,970
1978	Practitioner, 5, 121	J. A. Santiago	Unilateral, 4, 110	Odd Man, 7, 113	8	3:18.20	14,520

Named for Aisco Stable's 1987, '88 leading North American sire and ten-time leading North American broodmare sire Mr. Prospector (1970 c. by Raise a Native), who set a six-furlong track record at Gulfstream Park in 1973. Formerly named for Hallandale, Florida, location of Gulfstream Park. Hallandale H. 1946-2000. Not held 1949, 1957-'77, 1979, 1981. 1 1/16 miles 1946, '84. 1 1/8 miles 1947-'56. About 2 miles 1978. 1 1/2 miles 1980, '82. 7 furlongs 1987, 1990-'93. Turf 1978-'82. Three-year-olds 1946, '84. Three-year-olds and up 1948-'83, 1985-2006. Track record 2006. Held as an allowance race 1950-'55.

Mrs. Revere Stakes

Grade 2 in 2008. Churchill Downs, three-year-olds, fillies, 1 1/16 miles, turf. Held November 10, 2007, with a gross value of $174,900. First held in 1991. First graded in 1995. Stakes record 1:42.86 (2001 Snow Dance).

Year	Winner	Jockey	Second	Third	Strs	Time	1st Purse
2007	Bit of Whimsy, 3, 123	J. Castellano	Ciao, 3, 117	Cat Charmer, 3, 117	11	1:43.16	$101,933
2006	Precious Kitten, 3, 117	R. Bejarano	J'ray, 3, 117	Quite a Bride, 3, 121	11	1:45.65	99,402
2005	My Typhoon (Ire), 3, 120	R. Albarado	Isla Cozzene, 3, 120	Silver Cup (Ire), 3, 120	7	1:43.36	103,509
2004	River Belle (GB), 3, 120	K. Fallon	Lenatareese, 3, 120	Cape Town Lass, 3, 114	10	1:44.59	106,113
2003	Hoh Buzzard (Ire), 3, 120	R. Fogelsonger	Aud, 3, 120	Gamble to Victory, 3, 116	12	1:45.01	108,903
2002	Caught in the Rain, 3, 119	E. L. King Jr.	Glia, 3, 115	Bedanken, 3, 122	11	1:46.25	107,694
2001	Snow Dance, 3, 122	C. Perret	Stylish, 3, 115	Cozy Island, 3, 111	9	**1:42.86**	106,950
2000	Megans Bluff, 3, 122	M. Guidry	Uncharted Haven (GB), 3, 119	Impending Bear, 3, 119	12	1:43.37	107,973
1999	Silver Comic, 3, 115	L. J. Melancon	St Clair Ridge (Ire), 3, 119	Circle of Gold (Ire), 3, 119	12	1:45.13	108,345
1998	Anguilla, 3, 119	P. Day	Darling Alice, 3, 119	White Beauty, 3, 119	11	1:45.67	107,601
1997	Parade Queen, 3, 122	P. Day	Mystery Code, 3, 117	Starry Dreamer, 3, 122	11	1:45.46	108,624
1996	Maxzene, 3, 117	J. A. Krone	Fasta, 3, 119	Turkappeal, 3, 119	12	1:43.78	72,354
1995	Petrouchka, 3, 122	D. Penna	Christmas Gift, 3, 122	Ms. Isadora, 3, 117	11	1:44.20	75,725
1994	Mariah's Storm, 3, 122	R. N. Lester	Avie's Fancy, 3, 119	Bear Truth, 3, 119	10	1:43.99	75,400
1993	Weekend Madness (Ire), 3, 117	C. R. Woods Jr.	Flower Circle, 3, 117	Amal Hayati, 3, 122	10	1:46.32	74,685
1992	McKaymackenna, 3, 119	J. Velasquez	Spinning Round, 3, 122	Aquilegia, 3, 117	10	1:45.04	56,209
1991	Spanish Parade, 3, 117	P. Day	Liz Cee, 3, 117	Savethelastdance, 3, 117	10	1:46.19	37,408

Named for Dr. Hiram Polk Jr.'s and Dr. David Richardson's 1984 Dogwood, Edgewood, and Regret S. winner Mrs. Revere (1981 f. by Silver Series). Grade 3 1995-'97.

My Charmer Handicap

Grade 3 in 2008. Calder Race Course, three-year-olds and up, fillies and mares, 1 1/8 miles, turf. Held December 1, 2007, with a gross value of $100,000. First held in 1984. First graded in 1998. Stakes record 1:45.40 (1988 Sunny Issues).

Year	Winner	Jockey	Second	Third	Strs	Time	1st Purse
2007	J'ray, 4, 120	M. R. Cruz	Bayou's Lassie, 4, 116	Redaspen, 5, 116	9	1:48.93	$59,520
2006	Amorama (Fr), 5, 117	M. R. Cruz	Bayou's Lassie, 3, 114	Rutledge Ballado, 4, 115	10	1:46.51	60,000
2005	Snowdrops (GB), 5, 115	B. Blanc	La Reina, 4, 116	Ticker Tape (GB), 4, 117	9	1:48.33	60,000
2004	Something Ventured, 5, 116	J. R. Velazquez	Snowdrops (GB), 4, 115	Changing World, 4, 117	12	1:46.79	60,000
2003	New Economy, 5, 115	R. Homeister Jr.	Something Ventured, 4, 116	Ivanavinalot, 3, 113	12	1:46.97	60,000
2002	Wander Mom, 4, 114	E. Coa	Strawberry Blonde (Ire), 4, 114	Babae (Chi), 6, 121	10	1:48.43	60,000
2001	Batique, 5, 116	J. F. Chavez	Please Sign In, 5, 114	Wander Mom, 3, 114	12	1:49.85	60,000

Year	Winner	Jockey	Second	Third	Strs	Time	1st Purse
2000	‡Wild Heart Dancing, 4, 116	J. F. Chavez	Megans Bluff, 3, 116	Orange Sunset (Ire), 4, 114	12	1:47.58	$60,000
1999	Crystal Symphony, 3, 114	C. H. Velasquez	Winfama, 6, 114	Khumba Mela (Ire), 4, 120	12	1:47.65	60,000
1998	Colcon, 5, 118	J. D. Bailey	Cuando, 4, 117	Winfama, 5, 117	12	1:50.51	60,000
1997	Overcharger, 5, 116	J. A. Rivera II	Dance Clear (Ire), 4, 113	Hero's Pride (Fr), 4, 116	12	1:48.18	60,000
1996	Romy, 5, 114	F. C. Torres	Delta Love, 3, 114	Ms. Mostly, 3, 115	7	1:47.33	60,000
1995	Danish (Ire), 4, 116	J. A. Santos	Cox Orange, 5, 119	Alice Springs, 5, 123	11	1:46.40	60,000
1994	Caress, 3, 114	R. G. Davis	Putthepowdertoit, 4, 114	Cox Orange, 4, 116	12	1:50.63	60,000
1993	Chickasha, 4, 115	R. D. Lopez	Marshua's River, 6, 113	Always Nettie, 4, 114	14	1:47.36	30,000
1992	Explosive Kate, 5, 118	D. Penna	Mia Bird Too, 3, 113	Kiwi Mint, 4, 114	9	1:46.58	30,000
	Julie La Rousse (Ire), 4, 120	J. D. Bailey	Marshua's River, 5, 114	Highland Crystal, 4, 115	10	1:45.78	30,000
	Lady Shirl, 5, 120	E. Fires	Ratings, 4, 115	Seaquay, 6, 111	11	1:44.74	51,150
1990	Primetime North, 3, 112	W. S. Ramos	Igmaar (Fr), 4, 112	Be Exclusive (Ire), 4, 113	11	1:45.60	27,825
1989	Princess Mora, 3, 111	M. A. Gonzalez	Coolawin, 3, 118	Yestday's Kisses, 3, 115	13	1:47.60	36,000
1988	Sunny Issues, 3, 109	W. A. Guerra	Beauty Cream, 5, 119	Miss Unnameable, 4, 112	10	**1:45.40**	28,830
	Judy's Red Shoes, 5, 117	D. Valiente	Orange Motiff, 3, 113	Chores At Dawn, 4, 113	13	1:45.60	29,130
	Princely Proof, 5, 113	R. Breen	Fraulein Lieber, 4, 112	Judy's Red Shoes, 5, 114	8	1:46.20	33,870
	Fama, 5, 111	J. M. Pezua	Singular Bequest, 5, 116	Ladanum, 4, 115	9	1:44.80	24,570
1986	Donna's Dolly, 4, 112	M. A. Lee	Fritzie Bey, 4, 113	Thirty Zip, 3, 117	6	1:55.00	31,010
1985	Powder Break, 4, 116	J. A. Santos	Duty Dance, 3, 117	Dictina (Fr), 4, 117	10	1:47.80	20,555
	Shocker T., 3, 119	G. St. Leon	Erin's Dunloe, 3, 109	Spruce Luck, 4, 112	12	1:48.80	20,675
1984	Our Reverie, 3, 114	G. St. Leon	Id Am Fac, 3, 114	Break In, 3, 114	13	1:47.20	13,927
	Burst of Colors, 4, 116	J. A. Santos	Ava Romance, 3, 111	Cosmic Sea Queen, 4, 115	13	1:47.60	13,928

Named for Ben S. Castleman's SW My Charmer (1969 f. by Poker), dam of 1977 Horse of the Year and '77 Triple Crown winner Seattle Slew. Not held 1987, '91. Two divisions 1984-'85, 1988 (March and December), 1992 (December). Held in March and December. Held in April and December 1992. About 1 1/8 miles 1984-'85, 1988-'93. Dirt 1986. ‡Megans Bluff finished first, DQ to second, 2000.

Nashua Stakes

Grade 3 in 2008. Aqueduct, two-year-olds, 1 mile, dirt. Held October 28, 2007, with a gross value of $105,800. First held in 1975. First graded in 1982. Stakes record 1:35.40 (1977 Quadratic).

Year	Winner	Jockey	Second	Third	Strs	Time	1st Purse
2007	Etched, 2, 116	A. Garcia	Anak Nakal, 2, 116	Anakim, 2, 116	5	1:36.96	$64,680
2006	Day Pass, 2, 116	F. Jara	Sightseeing, 2, 116	Xchanger, 2, 122	8	1:36.09	67,740
2005	Bluegrass Cat, 2, 116	J. R. Velazquez	Political Force, 2, 116	Diabolical, 2, 116	10	1:36.02	67,980
2004	Rockport Harbor, 2, 118	S. Elliott	Defer, 2, 116	Better Than Bonds, 2, 116	6	1:36.67	65,700
2003	Read the Footnotes, 2, 116	J. D. Bailey	Paddington, 2, 120	Who Is Chris G., 2, 116	9	1:36.48	67,860
2002	Added Edge, 2, 122	P. Husbands	Outer Reef, 2, 116	Boston Bull, 2, 122	7	1:36.77	65,820
2001	Listen Here, 2, 117	J. D. Bailey	Monthir, 2, 115	Thunder Days, 2, 115	6	1:37.61	65,580
2000	Ommadon, 2, 115	A. T. Gryder	Windsor Castle, 2, 117	Griffinite, 2, 115	10	1:36.74	67,920
1999	Mass Market, 2, 117	M. E. Smith	Polish Miner, 2, 114	Parade Leader, 2, 117	9	1:38.60	67,020
1998	Doneraile Court, 2, 115	J. D. Bailey	Successful Appeal, 2, 122	Exiled Groom, 2, 113	8	1:36.17	66,600
1997	Coronado's Quest, 2, 122	M. E. Smith	Not Tricky, 2, 117	Dice Dancer, 2, 119	5	1:37.06	65,100
1996	Jules, 2, 114	J. A. Santos	Shammy Davis, 2, 114	Sal's Driver, 2, 114	9	1:36.89	68,340
1994	Devious Course, 2, 114	F. T. Alvarado	Mighty Magee, 2, 112	Old Tascosa, 2, 122	7	1:37.50	65,580
1993	Popol's Gold, 2, 114	W. H. McCauley	Personal Merit, 2, 117	Sonny's Bruno, 2, 114	11	1:46.68	74,400
1992	Dalhart, 2, 114	M. E. Smith	Rohwer, 2, 114	Peace Baby, 2, 114	11	1:44.60	74,640
1991	Pine Bluff, 2, 124	C. Perret	Speakerphone, 2, 114	Best Decorated, 2, 114	11	1:46.14	75,960
1990	Kyle's Our Man, 2, 114	J. D. Bailey	Oregon, 2, 114	Vouch for Me, 2, 117	11	1:45.40	55,980
1989	Champagneforashley, 2, 119	J. Vasquez	Armed for Peace, 2, 114	Flathorn, 2, 114	4	1:45.20	66,480
1988	Traskwood, 2, 117	A. T. Cordero Jr.	Doc's Leader, 2, 119	Triple Buck, 2, 117	10	1:45.20	63,240
1987	Cougarized, 2, 117	J. A. Santos	Blew by Em, 2, 119	Chicot County, 2, 117	12	1:46.00	104,160
1986	Bold Summit, 2, 114	C. W. Antley	Drachma, 2, 114	Perdition's Son, 2, 114	8	1:45.00	72,360
1985	Raja's Revenge, 2, 117	R. G. Davis	Royal Doulton, 2, 117	Bordeaux Bob, 2, 114	12	1:44.40	56,610
1984	Stone White, 2, 119	R. G. Davis	Banner Bob, 2, 117	Old Main, 2, 114	12	1:38.20	71,550
1983	Don Rickles, 2, 114	A. T. Cordero Jr.	Arabian Gift, 2, 114	Raja's Shark, 2, 114	9	1:38.40	34,860
1982	I Enclose, 2, 114	R. Hernandez	Loose Cannon, 2, 114	Moment of Joy, 2, 114	11	1:37.60	35,460
1981	Our Escapade, 2, 114	D. MacBeth	John's Gold, 2, 114	Hostage, 2, 114	10	1:36.80	35,280
1980	‡A Run, 2, 114	C. J. McCarron	Copper Mine, 2, 114	Triocala, 2, 114	12	1:37.20	35,640
1979	Googolplex, 2, 117	L. A. Pincay Jr.	Thanks to Tony, 2, 114	Comptroller, 2, 114	8	1:36.40	32,550
1978	Instrument Landing, 2, 114	J. Fell	Miroman, 2, 114	Bold Ruckus, 2, 117	12	1:37.00	26,520
1977	Quadratic, 2, 119	E. Maple	No Sir, 2, 114	Quip, 2, 114	5	**1:35.40**	21,975
1976	Nearly On Time, 2, 114	J. Vasquez	Ruthie's Native, 2, 114	Upper Nile, 2, 114	5	1:35.60	22,005
1975	Lord Henribee, 2, 115	E. Maple	Cojak, 2, 120	Expletive Deleted, 2, 115	6	1:35.80	33,030

Named for Belair Stud's 1955 Horse of the Year and '55 Belmont S. winner Nashua (1952 c. by *Nasrullah). Grade 2 1986-'88. Held at Belmont 2001, '05. Not held 1995. 1 mile 70 yards 1985. 1 1/16 miles 1986-'93. ‡Willow Hour finished first, DQ to 12th, 1980.

Nassau County Stakes

Grade 3 in 2008. Belmont Park, three-year-olds, fillies, 7 furlongs, dirt. Held May 3, 2008, with a gross value of $208,400. First held in 1996. First graded in 1999. Stakes record 1:22.04 (2007 Dream Rush).

Year	Winner	Jockey	Second	Third	Strs	Time	1st Purse
2008	Zaftig, 3, 116	J. F. Chavez	Carolyn's Cat, 3, 122	J Z Warrior, 3, 116	7	1:22.74	$125,640

Year	Winner	Jockey	Second	Third	Strs	Time	1st Purse
2007	Dream Rush, 3, 122	E. Coa	Lady Marlboro, 3, 116	Changeisgonnacome, 3, 118	5	1:22.04	$123,960
2006	Hello Liberty, 3, 120	N. Arroyo Jr.	Win McCool, 3, 116	Swap Fliparoo, 3, 119	6	1:22.65	124,560
2005	Seeking the Ante, 3, 116	M. J. Luzzi	Slew Motion, 3, 116	Exit to Heaven, 3, 116	7	1:22.86	120,000
2004	Bending Strings, 3, 1-6	J. D. Bailey	Grey Traffic, 3, 116	A Lulu Ofa Menifee, 3, 116	6	1:22.70	120,000
2003	House Party, 3, 122	J. A. Santos	Cyber Secret, 3, 122	City Sister, 3, 116	4	1:23.28	120,000
2002	Nonsuch Bay, 3, 116	J. Castellano	Wopping, 3, 116	Wilzada, 3, 116	8	1:23.90	120,000
2001	Cat Chat, 3, 114	J. R. Velazquez	Xtra Heat, 3, 122	Shooting Party, 3, 114	6	1:23.02	90,000
2000	C'Est L' Amour, 3, 115	E. S. Prado	Tugger, 3, 114	Miss Inquistive, 3, 119	6	1:23.46	90,000
1999	Oh What a Windfall, 3, 118	M. E. Smith	Paved in Gold, 3, 118	Things Change, 3, 118	8	1:23.59	66,480
1998	Jersey Girl, 3, 121	M. E. Smith	Countess Diana, 3, 118	Foil, 3, 114	4	1:22.63	48,831
1997	Alyssum, 3, 116	J. A. Santos	Screamer, 3, 121	Sinclara, 3, 112	7	1:22.90	49,065
1996	Star de Lady Ann, 3, 114	J. F. Chavez	Stop Traffic, 3, 114	J J'sdream, 3, 121	8	1:22.19	49,590

Named for Nassau County, Long Island, New York, where Belmont Park is located. Grade 2 2000-'07. Nassau County Breeders' Cup S. 2002-'07.

National Museum of Racing Hall of Fame Stakes

Grade 2 in 2008. Saratoga Race Course, three-year-olds, 1 1/8 miles, turf. Held August 6, 2007, with a gross value of $158,000. First held in 1985. First graded in 1987. Stakes record 1:46.65 (1992 Paradise Creek).

Year	Winner	Jockey	Second	Third	Strs	Time	1st Purse
2007	Nobiz Like Shobiz, 3, 115	C. H. Velasquez	Marcavelly, 3, 122	Distorted Reality, 3, 119	6	1:49.29	$95,700
2006	After Market, 3, 122	C. H. Velasquez	Spider Power (Ire), 3, 117	Green Lemon, 3, 116	8	1:48.45	97,020
2005	T. D. Vance, 3, 119	T. Kabel	Silver Whistle, 3, 115	Crown Point, 3, 119	9	1:48.15	90,000
2004	Artie Schiller, 3, 122	R. Migliore	Mustanfar, 3, 122	Good Reward, 3, 115	8	1:47.71	90,000
2003	Stroll, 3, 117	J. D. Bailey	Urban King (Ire), 3, 115	Saint Stephen, 3, 115	11	1:49.34	90,000
2002	Quest Star, 3, 117	P. Day	Union Place, 3, 115	Patrol, 3, 120	5	1:49.66	90,000
2001	Baptize, 3, 122	J. D. Bailey	Strategic Partner, 3, 120	Saint Verre, 3, 113	7	1:47.94	90,000
2000	Turnofthecentury, 3, 118	A. T. Gryder	Aldo, 3, 114	Polish Miner, 3, 123	5	1:52.35	90,000
1999	Marquette, 3, 119	J. D. Bailey	Phi Beta Doc, 3, 118	Good Night, 3, 118	13	1:49.33	90,000
1998	Parade Ground, 3, 120	S. J. Sellers	Vergennes, 3, 115	Stay Sound, 3, 115	8	1:47.82	90,000
1997	Rob 'n Gin, 3, 120	J. D. Bailey	River Squall, 3, 114	Subordination, 3, 120	6	1:42.09	66,000
1996	Sir Cat, 3, 113	J. D. Bailey	Fortitude, 3, 113	Optic Nerve, 3, 120	9	1:40.46	68,340
1995	Flitch, 3, 113	M. E. Smith	Diplomatic Jet, 3, 120	Nostra, 3, 112	8	1:48.08	83,700
1994	Islefaxyou, 3, 113	E. Maple	Jaggery John, 3, 122	dh-Lahint, 3, 115 dh-Mr. Impatience, 3, 119	13	1:48.61	70,200
1993	A in Sociology, 3, 115	C. W. Antley	Strolling Along, 3, 117	Palashall, 3, 117	10	1:48.81	73,080
1992	Paradise Creek, 3, 115	M. E. Smith	Smiling and Dancin, 3, 119	Spectacular Tide, 3, 122	8	1:46.65	72,660
1991	Lech, 3, 122	A. T. Cordero Jr.	Sultry Song, 3, 117	Fourstars Allstar, 3, 122	10	1:49.02	73,920
1990	Social Retiree, 3, 115	M. E. Smith	Go Dutch, 3, 115	Divine Warning, 3, 119	7	1:48.20	54,720
1989	Orange Sunshine, 3, 117	J. Cruguet	Fast 'n' Gold, 3, 115	Expensive Decision, 3, 122	10	1:49.00	55,980
1988	Posen, 3, 122	J. D. Bailey	‡Blew by Em, 3, 119	Harp Islet, 3, 115	9	1:47.00	55,710
1987	Drachma, 3, 115	R. G. Davis	Crown the Leader, 3, 115	Major Beard, 3, 115	8	1:49.80	51,480
1986	Dance of Life, 3, 115	J. D. Bailey	Southjet, 3, 115	Dance Card Filled, 3, 115	6	1:52.20	49,860
1985	Duluth, 3, 115	J. Cruguet	Explosive Dancer, 3, 115	Equalize, 3, 122	8	1:47.60	51,570

Named for the National Museum of Racing and Hall of Fame located in Saratoga Springs, New York. Formerly named for Ralph Lowe's 1957 Travers S. winner *Gallant Man (1954 c. by *Migoli). Gallant Man S. 1985-'91. National Museum of Racing Hall of Fame H. 1998-2003. National Museum of Racing Hall of Fame Breeders' Cup S. 2006. 1 3/16 miles 1991. 1 1/16 miles 1996-'97. Dirt 2000. Three-year-olds and up 1991. Fillies and mares 1991. Dead heat for third 1994. ‡Fourstardave finished second, DQ to fourth, 1988.

Native Diver Handicap

Grade 3 in 2008. Hollywood Park, three-year-olds and up, 1 1/8 miles, all weather. Held December 8, 2007, with a gross value of $111,800. First held in 1979. First graded in 1979. Stakes record 1:45.35 (1996 Gentlemen [Arg]).

Year	Winner	Jockey	Second	Third	Strs	Time	1st Purse
2007	Heatseeker (Ire), 4, 1-5	M. C. Baze	Racketeer, 4, 114	Isipingo, 4, 116	10	1:47.23	$71,800
2006	Saint Stephen, 6, 114	G. K. Gomez	Southern Africa, 4, 114	Molengao (Brz), 5, 115	6	1:48.71	60,000
2005	Trotamondo (Chi), 4, 117	G. K. Gomez	Bully Hayes, 5, 116	Spellbinder, 4, 116	10	1:49.92	60,000
2004	Truly a Judge, 6, 115	M. A. Pedroza	Dynever, 4, 119	Calkins Road, 5, 116	8	1:47.06	60,000
2003	Olmodavor, 4, 117	A. O. Solis	Nose The Trade (GB), 5, 115	Chinkapin, 7, 118	5	1:49.16	60,000
2002	Piensa Sonando (Chi), 4, 117	L. A. Pincay Jr.	Fleetstreet Dancer, 4, 112	Nose The Trade (GB), 4, 116	8	1:48.43	60,000
2001	Momentum, 4, 117	C. S. Nakatani	Euchre, 5, 117	Last Parade (Arg), 5, 117	7	1:48.24	60,000
2000	Sky Jack, 4, 118	L. A. Pincay Jr.	Lethal Instrument, 4, 116	Grey Memo, 3, 116	8	1:46.81	60,000
1999	General Challenge, 3, 123	C. J. McCarron	Moore's Flat, 5, 117	Koslanin (Arg), 5, 113	6	1:49.07	60,000
1998	Puerto Madero (Chi), 4, 117	K. Desormeaux	Musical Gambler, 4, 117	River Keen (Ire), 6, 114	5	1:48.43	60,000
1997	Refinado Tom (Arg), 4, 119	G. L. Stevens	Steel Ruhlr, 3, 112	Boggle, 5, 114	8	1:47.84	60,000
1996	Gentlemen (Arg), 4, 121	G. L. Stevens	Dramatic Gold, 5, 122	Don't Blame Rio, 3, 113	5	1:45.35	63,840
1995	Alphabet Soup, 4, 117	C. W. Antley	El Florista (Arg), 5, 118	Regal Rowdy, 6, 116	5	1:47.03	61,400
1994	Best Pal, 6, 121	C. J. McCarron	Tossofthecoin, 4, 117	Royal Chariot, 4, 114	7	1:48.44	64,000
1993	Slew of Damascus, 5, 118	C. S. Nakatani	Lottery Winner, 4, 115	L'Express (Chi), 4, 115	7	1:47.46	63,300
1992	Sir Beaufort, 5, 119	C. J. McCarron	Memo (Chi), 5, 114	Berillon (GB), 5, 115	5	1:47.26	61,700
1991	Twilight Agenda, 5, 124	C. J. McCarron	Ibero (Arg), 4, 117	Cobra Classic, 4, 117	4	1:49.00	60,600
1990	Warcraft, 3, 117	C. J. McCarron	Pleasant Tap, 3, 115	Go and Go (Ire), 3, 115	7	1:47.40	63,500

400   Racing — Graded Stakes

Year	Winner	Jockey	Second	Third	Strs	Time	1st Purse
1989	Ruhlmann, 4, 121	C. J. McCarron	Lively One, 4, 122	Stylish Winner, 5, 116	7	1:48.00	$63,100
1988	Cutlass Reality, 6, 124	G. L. Stevens	Precisionist, 7, 123	Payant (Arg), 4, 116	7	1:48.60	63,700
1987	Epidaurus, 5, 116	P. A. Valenzuela	Midwest King, 4, 116	He's a Saros, 4, 116	8	1:47.60	91,200
1986	Hopeful Word, 5, 117	L. A. Pincay Jr.	Epidaurus, 4, 115	Nostalgia's Star, 4, 118	7	1:47.80	90,800
1985	Innamorato, 4, 107	S. Hawley	Beldale Lear, 4, 116	Lord At War (Arg), 5, 125	4	1:33.40	87,900
1984	Lord At War (Arg), 4, 120	W. Shoemaker	Fighting Fit, 5, 118	Video Kid, 4, 118	6	1:35.40	62,700
1983	Menswear, 5, 115	F. Toro	Fighting Fit, 4, 117	Major Sport, 6, 115	6	1:42.40	63,200
1982	Native Tactics, 4, 116	E. Delahoussaye	Belfort (Fr), 5, 116	Rock Softly, 4, 115	10	1:41.60	67,000
1981	Syncopate, 6, 117	C. J. McCarron	King Go Go, 6, 115	Wickerr, 6, 121	6	1:38.80	63,500
1980	Replant, 6, 111	W. Shoemaker	Relaunch, 4, 120	Flying Paster, 4, 124	6	1:34.20	63,000
1979	Life's Hope, 6, 117	L. A. Pincay Jr.	Hawkin's Special, 4, 117	White Rammer, 5, 116	6	1:35.00	31,500

Named for Mr. and Mrs. L. K. Shapiro's Racing Hall of Fame member, and 1965, '66, '67 Hollywood Gold Cup winner Native Diver (1959 g. by Imbros); Native Diver won 34 stakes, a tie with Exterminator for the most stakes wins in North American racing history. Grade 2 1979. 1 mile 1979-'81, 1984-'85. 1 1/16 miles 1982-'83. Dirt 1979-2005. Track record 2007.

NetJets Breeders' Cup Mile

Grade 1 in 2008. Monmouth Park, three-year-olds and up, 1 mile, turf. Held October 27, 2007, with a gross value of $2,409,080. First held in 1984. First graded in 1984. Stakes record 1:32.05 (2001 Val Royal [Fr]).

Year	Winner	Jockey	Second	Third	Strs	Time	1st Purse
2007	Kip Deville, 4, 126	C. H. Velasquez	Excellent Art (GB), 3, 122	Cosmonaut, 5, 126	13	1:39.78	$1,420,200
2006	Miesque's Approval, 7, 126	E. Castro	Aragorn (Ire), 4, 126	Badge of Silver, 6, 126	14	1:34.75	1,171,800
2005	Artie Schiller, 4, 126	G. K. Gomez	Leroidesanimaux (Brz), 5, 126	†Gorella (Fr), 3, 120	12	1:36.10	1,053,000
2004	Singletary, 4, 126	D. R. Flores	Antonius Pius, 3, 122	†Six Perfections (Fr), 4, 123	14	1:36.90	873,650
2003	†Six Perfections (Fr), 3, 119	J. D. Bailey	Touch of the Blues (Fr), 6, 126	Century City (Ire), 4, 126	13	1:33.86	780,000
2002	Domedriver (Ire), 4, 126	T. Thulliez	Rock of Gibraltar (Ire), 3, 122	Good Journey, 6, 126	14	1:36.92	556,400
2001	Val Royal (Fr), 5, 126	J. Valdivia Jr.	Forbidden Apple, 6, 126	Bach (Ire), 4, 126	12	**1:32.05**	592,800
2000	War Chant, 3, 123	G. L. Stevens	North East Bound, 4, 126	Dansili (Ib), 4, 126	14	1:34.67	608,400
1999	Silic (Fr), 4, 126	C. S. Nakatani	†Tuzla (Fr), 5, 123	Docksider, 4, 126	14	1:34.26	520,000
1998	Da Hoss, 6, 126	J. R. Velazquez	Hawksley Hill (Ire), 5, 126	Labeeb (GB), 6, 126	14	1:35.27	520,000
1997	Spinning World, 4, 126	C. B. Asmussen	Geri, 5, 126	Decorated Hero (GB), 5, 126	12	1:32.77	572,000
1996	Da Hoss, 4, 126	G. L. Stevens	Spinning World, 3, 122	Same Old Wish, 6, 126	14	1:35.80	520,000
1995	†Ridgewood Pearl (GB), 3, 119	J. P. Murtagh	Fastness (Ire), 5, 126	†Sayyedati (GB), 5, 123	13	1:43.65	520,000
1994	Barathea (Ire), 4, 126	L. Dettori	Johann Quatz (Fr), 5, 126	Unfinished Symph, 3, 123	14	1:34.50	520,000
1993	Lure, 4, 126	M. E. Smith	†Ski Paradise, 3, 120	Fourstars Allstar, 5, 126	13	1:33.58	520,000
1992	Lure, 3, 122	M. E. Smith	Paradise Creek, 3, 122	Brief Truce, 3, 126	14	1:32.90	520,000
1991	Opening Verse, 5, 126	P. A. Valenzuela	Val des Bois (Fr), 5, 126	Star of Cozzene, 3, 123	14	1:37.59	520,000
1990	Royal Academy, 3, 122	L. Piggott	Itsallgreektome, 3, 122	Priolo, 3, 122	13	1:35.20	450,000
1989	Steinlen (GB), 6, 126	J. A. Santos	Sabona, 7, 126	Most Welcome (GB), 6, 126	11	1:37.20	450,000
1988	†Miesque, 4, 123	F. Head	Steinlen (GB), 5, 126	Simply Majestic, 4, 126	12	1:38.60	450,000
1987	†Miesque, 3, 120	F. Head	Show Dancer, 5, 126	†Sonic Lady, 4, 123	14	1:32.80	450,000
1986	Last Tycoon (Ire), 3, 123	Y. Saint-Martin	Palace Music, 5, 126	Fred Astaire, 3, 126	14	1:35.00	450,000
1985	Cozzene, 5, 126	W. A. Guerra	‡Al Mamoon, 4, 126	Shadeed, 3, 126	14	1:35.00	450,000
1984	†Royal Heroine (Ire), 4, 123	F. Toro	Star Choice, 5, 126	Cozzene, 4, 126	10	1:32.60	450,000

Sponsored by NetJets Inc. of Woodbridge, New Jersey 2002-'07. Held at Hollywood Park 1984, '87, '97. Held at Aqueduct 1985. Held at Santa Anita Park 1986, '93, 2003. Held at Churchill Downs 1988, '91, '94, '98, 2000, '06. Held at Gulfstream Park 1989, '92, '99. Held at Belmont Park 1990, '95, 2001, '05. Held at Woodbine 1996. Held at Arlington Park 2002. Held at Lone Star Park 2004. ‡Palace Music finished second, DQ to ninth, 1985. Course record 1992, '94. †Denotes female.

New Orleans Handicap

Grade 2 in 2008. Fair Grounds, four-year-olds and up, 1 1/8 miles, dirt. Held March 8, 2008, with a gross value of $480,000. First held in 1918. First graded in 1973. Stakes record 1:48.13 (1998 Phantom On Tour).

Year	Winner	Jockey	Second	Third	Strs	Time	1st Purse
2008	Circular Quay, 4, 116	G. K. Gomez	Grasshopper, 4, 119	Reporting for Duty, 4, 115	6	1:49.80	$300,000
2007	Master Command, 5, 122	J. R. Velazquez	Patriot Act, 5, 115	Smokeyjonessutton, 4, 114	9	1:49.89	300,000
2006	Brass Hat, 5, 117	W. Martinez	Dixie Meister, 4, 113	Alumni Hall, 7, 116	8	1:51.35	261,360
2005	Badge of Silver, 5, 118	J. D. Bailey	Limehouse, 4, 115	Second of June, 4, 115	9	1:48.78	300,000
2004	Peace Rules, 4, 119	J. D. Bailey	Saint Liam, 4, 114	Funny Cide, 4, 118	8	1:48.61	300,000
2003	Mineshaft, 4, 115	R. Albarado	Olmodavor, 4, 117	Strive, 4, 114	11	1:48.92	300,000
2002	Parade Leader, 5, 115	C. J. Lanerie	Graeme Hall, 5, 116	Keats, 4, 113	9	1:54.45	300,000
2001	Include, 4, 114	J. D. Bailey	Nite Dreamer, 6, 112	Valhol, 5, 116	5	1:49.18	300,000
2000	Allen's Oop, 5, 112	W. Martinez	Take Note of Me, 6, 116	Ecton Park, 4, 117	8	1:48.80	300,000
1999	Precocity, 5, 117	E. M. Martin Jr.	Real Quiet, 4, 116	Allen's Oop, 4, 117	6	1:49.17	320,640
1998	Phantom On Tour, 4, 114	L. J. Melancon	Precocity, 4, 114	Lord Cromby (Ire), 4, 110	8	**1:48.13**	300,000
1997	Isitingood, 6, 121	D. R. Flores	Western Trader, 6, 114	Scott's Scoundrel, 5, 113	7	1:48.43	180,000
1996	Scott's Scoundrel, 4, 116	R. D. Ardoin	Knockadoon, 4, 113	Patio de Naranjos (Chi), 5, 114	9	1:49.97	162,540
1995	Concern, 4, 116	M. E. Smith	Fly Cry, 4, 118	Tossofthecoin, 5, 117	7	1:49.40	120,000
1994	Brother Brown, 4, 118	P. Day	Far Out Wadleigh, 6, 112	Eequalsmcsquared, 5, 116	10	1:48.83	120,000
1993	Latin American, 5, 112	G. K. Gomez	Delafield, 4, 115	West by West, 4, 119	12	1:49.20	90,000
1992	Jarraar, 5, 112	B. J. Walker Jr.	Irish Swap, 5, 120	Bayou Reality, 4, 113	8	1:48.80	60,000
1991	Silver Survivor, 5, 120	L. J. Melancon	El Zorzal (Arg), 5, 110	Sangria Time, 4, 115	9	1:50.60	60,000
1990	Festive, 5, 117	B. J. Walker Jr.	Majesty's Imp, 4, 116	De Roche, 4, 115	8	1:50.40	60,000
1989	Galba, 5, 115	A. L. Castanon	Honor Medal, 8, 123	Position Leader, 4, 116	9	1:51.20	60,000

Racing — Graded Stakes

Year	Winner	Jockey	Second	Third	Strs	Time	1st Purse
1988	Honor Medal, 7, 121	P. Day	New York Swell, 5, 114	Manzotti, 5, 115	12	1:50.00	$60,000
1987	Honor Medal, 6, 116	R. A. Baze	Dramatic Desire, 6, 117	Inevitable Leader, 8, 116	10	1:52.20	71,040
1986	Herat, 4, 116	R. Q. Meza	Hopeful Word, 5, 120	Kamakura (GB), 4, 108	11	2:01.80	112,000
1985	Westheimer, 4, 112	L. Snyder	Inevitable Leader, 6, 116	Vornorco, 4, 108	9	2:01.80	112,000
1984	Wild Again, 4, 112	P. Day	Explosive Bid, 6, 112	Crazy Moon, 4, 110	10	2:02.00	112,000
1983	Listcapade, 4, 112	E. J. Perrodin	Bold Style, 4, 113	Aspro, 5, 114	9	2:03.20	112,000
1982	It's the One, 4, 124	W. A. Guerra	Boys Nite Out, 4, 116	Aspro, 4, 113	11	2:01.80	112,000
1981	Sun Catcher, 4, 123	A. Guajardo	Prince Majestic, 7, 118	Yosi Boy, 5, 112	7	2:03.40	103,550
1980	Pool Court, 5, 111	R. D. Ardoin	Five Star General, 5, 112	Book of Kings, 6, 113	7	2:04.60	84,500
1979	A Letter to Harry, 5, 126	E. Delahoussaye	Prince Majestic, 5, 118	Johnny's Image, 4, 112	6	2:02.60	84,050
1978	Life's Hope, 5, 112	C. J. McCarron	Silver Series, 4, 125	Inca Roca, 5, 111	10	2:02.20	77,550
1977	Tudor Tambourine, 4, 112	A. J. Trosclair	Inca Roca, 4, 113	Soy Numero Uno, 4, 127	11	1:49.80	65,000
1976	Master Derby, 4, 127	D. G. McHargue	Hatchet Man, 5, 118	‡Promised City, 4, 116	9	1:50.00	61,000
1975	Lord Rebeau, 4, 116	C. H. Marquez	Warbucks, 5, 113	Diamond Black, 6, 110	16	1:50.60	61,000
1974	Smooth Dancer, 4, 116	L. Adams	*Trupan, 7, 108	Rastaferian, 5, 115	12	1:50.60	56,300
1973	Combat Ready, 4, 111	L. Moyers	Hustlin Greek, 4, 111	Guitar Player, 5, 114	9	1:51.00	50,000

Named for the city of New Orleans, home of Fair Grounds. Grade 3 1973-'80, 1990-2000. Held at Louisiana Downs 2006. Not held 1919-'23, 1941-'42, 1945. 1¹/₁₆ miles 1918, 1925-'31, 1933, 1936, 1938-'39, 1943-'53. 1 mile 1924, '35, '37. 1 mile 70 yards 1940. 1¹/₄ miles 1978-'86. Three-year-olds and up 1918-'36, 1939-'78. Three-year-olds 1937-'38. ‡*Zografos finished third, DQ to ninth, 1976. Track record 1997, '98. Equaled track record 1992, '94.

New York Stakes

Grade 2 in 2008. Belmont Park, three-year-olds and up, fillies and mares, 1¹/₄ miles, turf. Held June 23, 2007, with a gross value of $190,000. First held in 1940. First graded in 1977. Stakes record 1:58.40 (1990 Capades).

Year	Winner	Jockey	Second	Third	Strs	Time	1st Purse
2007	Makderah (Ire), 4, 116	A. Garcia	Masseuse, 5, 120	Hostess, 4, 116	6	2:00.07	$90,000
2006	Noble Stella (Ger), 5, 116	M. E. Smith	Angara (GB), 5, 118	Argentina (Ire), 4, 116	7	2:08.26	90,000
2005	Wend, 4, 116	J. D. Bailey	Wonder Again, 6, 120	Film Maker, 5, 121	6	2:02.23	150,000
2004	Wonder Again, 5, 115	E. S. Prado	Stay Forever, 7, 115	Spice Island, 5, 118	7	2:05.60	150,000
2003	Snow Dance, 5, 116	R. Migliore	Pertuisane (GB), 4, 115	Riskaverse, 4, 119	8	1:59.63	150,000
2002	Owsley, 4, 114	E. S. Prado	Volga (Ire), 4, 116	Janet (GB), 5, 119	7	1:59.81	150,000
2001	England's Legend (Fr), 4, 115	C. S. Nakatani	Gaviola, 4, 119	Spook Express (SAf), 7, 116	7	1:59.63	150,000
2000	Perfect Sting, 4, 122	J. D. Bailey	Snow Polina, 5, 116	Pico Teneriffe, 4, 115	8	2:05.36	150,000
1999	Soaring Softly, 4, 117	M. E. Smith	Tampico, 6, 116	Anguilla, 4, 119	6	2:02.25	150,000
1998	Auntie Mame, 4, 118	J. R. Velazquez	Tresoriere, 4, 115	Cuando, 4, 113	8	1:59.50	120,000
1997	Maxzene, 4, 120	M. E. Smith	Memories of Silver, 4, 122	Shemozzle (Ire), 4, 114	6	1:59.80	120,000
1996	Electric Society (Ire), 5, 115	J. F. Chavez	Danish (Ire), 5, 115	Chelsey Flower, 5, 116	7	2:03.79	90,000
1995	Irish Linnet, 7, 118	J. R. Velazquez	Danish (Ire), 4, 116	Market Booster, 6, 119	6	1:59.92	65,520
1994	You'd Be Surprised, 5, 118	J. D. Bailey	Dahlia's Dreamer, 5, 112	Aquilegia, 4, 115	6	1:59.69	65,340
1993	Aquilegia, 4, 114	J. A. Krone	Via Borghese, 4, 117	Ginny Dare, 4, 108	11	1:59.05	74,760
1992	Plenty of Grace, 5, 111	J. A. Krone	Dancing Devlette, 5, 111	Flaming Torch (Ire), 5, 115	9	2:00.74	72,720
1991	Foresta, 5, 121	A. T. Cordero Jr.	Crockadore, 4, 112	Flaming Torch (Ire), 4, 110	8	1:59.38	72,360
1990	Capades, 4, 115	A. T. Cordero Jr.	Laugh and Be Merry, 5, 114	Key Flyer, 4, 109	7	**1:58.40**	71,640
1989	Miss Unnameable, 5, 108	R. I. Rojas	‡Love You by Heart, 4, 119	Gaily Gaily (Ire), 6, 113	8	2:05.80	72,000
1988	Beauty Cream, 5, 119	P. Day	Antique Mystique, 4, 109	Key to the Bridge, 4, 114	8	2:03.00	70,200
1987	Anka Germania (Ire), 5, 117	C. Perret	Videogenic, 5, 117	Lead Kindly Light, 4, 109	7	2:01.00	83,580
1986	Possible Mate, 5, 123	J. Samyn	Lucky Touch, 4, 110	Perfect Point, 4, 113	5	2:02.40	51,750
1985	Powder Break, 4, 115	J. D. Bailey	Annie Edge (Ire), 5, 112	Pull the Wool, 5, 107	7	2:03.60	53,280
1984	Annie Edge (Ire), 4, 112	J. Velasquez	Thirty Flags, 4, 114	Geraldine's Store, 5, 121	11	2:02.20	58,950
1983	Sabin, 3, 111	E. Maple	If Winter Comes, 5, 113	Doodle, 4, 113	12	2:01.00	53,010
1982	Noble Damsel, 4, 114	J. Velasquez	Office Wife, 5, 113	Castle Royale, 4, 111	8	2:07.00	34,620
1981	Mairzy Doates, 5, 120	A. T. Cordero Jr.	Love Sign, 4, 114	Wayward Lassie, 4, 107	6	2:04.00	33,960
1980	Just a Game (Ire), 4, 121	D. Brumfield	Poppycock, 4, 112	Please Try Hard, 4, 113	6	2:00.40	33,720
1979	La Soufriere, 4, 111	J. Cruguet	Navajo Princess, 5, 118	Emerald Hill (Brz), 5, 120	8	1:41.20	33,600
1978	Pearl Necklace, 4, 122	R. Hernandez	Waya (Fr), 4, 116	Dottie's Doll, 5, 118	7	1:40.00	33,360
	Late Bloomer, 4, 115	J. Velasquez	Island Kiss, 3, 108	Fia, 4, 113	9	1:41.40	33,810
1977	Fleet Victress, 5, 115	R. Hernandez	Lady Singer (Ire), 4, 113	*Welsh Pearl, 5, 119	9	1:39.20	33,330
1976	Sugar Plum Time, 4, 113	A. T. Cordero Jr.	‡*Deesse Du Val, 5, 120	Dos a Dos, 4, 113	9	1:39.40	33,780

Named for New York City, home of Belmont Park. Grade 3 1977-'82. New York H. 1940-2005. New York Breeders' Cup H. 2006. Held at Aqueduct 1940-'60, 1963-'72. Not held 1957, 1973-'75. 2¹/₄ miles 1940-'50. 1¹/₈ miles 1951-'54, 1959-'60. 1³/₈ miles 1955-'58, 1961. 1³/₁₆ miles 1963, 1968-'71. 1¹/₁₆ miles 1965-'67, 1977-'79. 7 furlongs 1972. Dirt 1940-'54, 1972. Three-year-olds 1972. Both sexes 1940-'62. Fillies 1972. Two divisions 1978. ‡Carolerno finished second, DQ to ninth, 1976. ‡Laugh and Be Merry finished second, DQ to fourth, 1989.

Next Move Handicap

Grade 3 in 2008. Aqueduct, three-year-olds and up, fillies and mares, 1¹/₈ miles, dirt. Held March 29, 2008, with a gross value of $104,400. First held in 1975. First graded in 1977. Stakes record Stakes record 1:48.96 (1999 Diggins).

Year	Winner	Jockey	Second	Third	Strs	Time	1st Purse
2008	Wow Me Free, 4, 116	A. Garcia	Runway Rosie, 4, 116	Wild Hoots, 4, 116	5	1:50.86	$63,840
2007	Indian Vale, 5, 119	M. J. Luzzi	A True Pussycat, 4, 116	Daytime Promise, 4, 113	5	1:50.51	64,080
2006	Fleet Indian, 5, 115	J. A. Santos	Flaming Heart, 5, 115	No Sleep, 4, 115	4	1:49.32	63,720
2005	Daydreaming, 4, 119	E. S. Prado	Saintliness, 5, 117	Rare Gift, 4, 116	8	1:50.77	66,000

Racing — Graded Stakes

Year	Winner	Jockey	Second	Third	Strs	Time	1st Purse
2004	Smok'n Frolic, 5, 119	R. Migliore	Stake, 4, 112	U K Trick, 4, 110	7	1:51.55	$65,040
2003	Smok'n Frolic, 4, 120	J. R. Velazquez	Ellie's Moment, 5, 116	Pupil, 4, 113	6	1:49.11	64,800
2002	With Ability, 4, 113	J. Castellano	Irving's Baby, 5, 117	Diversa, 4, 113	7	1:49.88	65,160
2001	Atelier, 4, 117	E. S. Prado	Pompeii, 4, 117	Tax Affair, 4, 114	4	1:50.65	64,264
2000	Biogio's Rose, 6, 117	N. Arroyo Jr.	Up We Go, 4, 115	Perlinda (Arg), 5, 114	7	1:51.32	49,875
1999	Diggins, 5, 113	J. L. Espinoza	Biogio's Rose, 5, 116	Powerful Nation, 5, 114	7	**1:48.96**	48,915
1998	Panama Canal, 4, 117	S. Bridgmohan	Endowment, 4, 110	Dewars Rocks, 4, 116	8	1:51.37	49,455
1997	Full and Fancy, 5, 115	R. Migliore	Shoop, 6, 117	Prophet's Warning, 4, 117	8	1:51.12	49,500
1996	Madame Adolphe, 4, 110	F. Leon	Shoop, 5, 114	Lotta Dancing, 5, 122	7	1:51.39	49,080
1995	Restored Hope, 4, 118	M. J. Luzzi	Cherokee Wonder, 4, 114	Sterling Pound, 4, 114	6	1:52.26	48,975
1994	Groovy Feeling, 5, 123	M. J. Luzzi	Broad Gains, 4, 116	Megaroux, 4, 112	7	1:59.79	63,735
1993	Low Tolerance, 4, 114	M. E. Smith	Hilbys Brite Flite, 4, 112	Lady Lear, 6, 114	8	1:55.93	67,470
1992	Spy Leader Lady, 4, 112	M. E. Smith	Haunting, 4, 117	Grecian Pass, 5, 115	6	2:00.26	67,560
1991	Buy the Firm, 5, 119	W. H. McCauley	Overturned, 4, 111	Won Scent, 4, 112	6	1:56.57	65,850
1990	Bold Wench, 5, 117	J. Velasquez	Buy the Firm, 4, 112	Dactique, 4, 113	8	1:58.40	53,280
1989	Rose's Cantina, 5, 118	E. Maple	To the Hunt, 4, 111	No Butter, 5, 108	5	1:59.80	49,950
1988	Triple Wow, 5, 116	R. Migliore	With a Twist, 5, 112	Cuantalamera, 5, 104	5	1:57.60	66,120
1987	Tricky Squaw, 4, 110	C. W. Antley	Ms. Eloise, 4, 115	Videogenic, 5, 104	9	1:58.40	70,440
1986	Cherry Jubilee, 4, 110	C. H. Marquez Jr.	Madame Called, 4, 109	Lady On the Run, 4, 121	11	1:56.00	68,220
1985	Flip's Pleasure, 5, 112	J. Samyn	Sintrillium, 7, 121	Emphatic, 5, 104	7	1:58.20	52,380
1984	Adept, 5, 109	M. Venezia	Far Flying, 4, 120	Chieftan's Command, 5, 123	8	1:57.80	67,860
1983	Chieftan's Command, 4, 116	A. Smith Jr.	Noble Damsel, 5, 115	Pert, 4, 113	6	1:53.20	32,880
1982	Andover Way, 4, 122	J. Velasquez	Autumn Glory, 4, 111	Who's to Answer, 4, 109	8	1:50.20	50,940
1981	Plankton, 5, 123	R. Hernandez	Nalee's Fantasy, 4, 107	Ms. Balding, 5, 109	6	1:53.40	50,130
1980	Water Lily (Fr), 4, 113	M. Castaneda	Plankton, 4, 121	Propitiate, 5, 116	7	1:51.00	49,410
1979	One Sum, 5, 116	R. Hernandez	Kit's Double, 6, 111	Municipal Bond, 4, 111	7	1:53.00	48,105
1978	One Sum, 4, 121	R. Hernandez	Crab Grass, 6, 121	Sweet Bernice, 5, 114	10	1:52.80	48,690
1977	Forty Nine Sunsets, 4, 116	J. Vasquez	Double Quester, 4, 115	Shark's Jaws, 4, 116	11	1:51.00	48,915
1976	Yes Dear Maggy, 4, 119	R. Hernandez	Pass a Glance, 5, 115	Mary Queenofscots, 5, 119	8	1:49.40	48,360
1975	My Juliet, 3, 125	D. G. McHargue	Channelette, 3, 117	Spring Is Here, 3, 113	7	1:35.60	33,660

Named for Alfred G. Vanderbilt's 1950 champion three-year-old filly, '52 champion older female, and '50, '52 Beldame H. winner Next Move (1947 f. by Bull Lea). Next Move Breeders' Cup H. 1990-'95. 1 mile 1975. 1 1/16 miles 1984-'94. Three-year-olds 1975. Fillies 1975.

Noble Damsel Handicap

Grade 3 in 2008. Belmont Park, three-year-olds and up, fillies and mares, 1 mile, turf. Held September 15, 2007, with a gross value of $113,500. First held in 1985. First graded in 1988. Stakes record 1:32.79 (2002 Tates Creek).

Year	Winner	Jockey	Second	Third	Strs	Time	1st Purse
2007	Dance Away Capote, 5, 115	A. Garcia	Fantastic Shirl, 4, 116	Pommes Frites, 5, 117	10	1:34.82	$68,100
2006	Karen's Caper, 4, 116	E. S. Prado	Pommes Frites, 4, 118	Mauralakana (Fr), 3, 115	8	1:34.91	97,320
2005	Bright Abundance, 4, 115	R. Migliore	My Lordship, 4, 116	Asti (Ire), 4, 113	12	1:33.93	90,000
2004	Ocean Drive, 4, 120	J. R. Velazquez	High Court (Brz), 4, 115	Hour of Justice, 4, 116	9	1:34.71	90,000
2003	Wonder Again, 4, 117	E. S. Prado	Dancal (Ire), 5, 114	Something Ventured, 4, 115	11	1:33.07	90,000
2002	Tates Creek, 4, 119	J. D. Bailey	Amonita (GB), 4, 117	Dat You Miz Blue, 5, 114	8	**1:32.79**	68,640
2001	Tugger, 4, 119	J. D. Bailey	Shine Again, 4, 123	Tippity Witch, 4, 113	9	1:35.18	68,280
2000	Gino's Spirits (GB), 4, 114	E. S. Prado	La Ville Rouge, 4, 115	Solar Bound, 4, 114	8	1:36.61	66,720
1999	Khumba Mela (Ire), 4, 118	J. A. Santos	Uanme, 4, 114	Cyrillic, 4, 116	8	1:35.50	67,740
1998	Oh Nellie, 4, 113	J. R. Velazquez	Heaven's Command (GB), 4, 116	Irish Daisy, 5, 114	7	1:32.80	50,400
1997	Colcon, 4, 113	J. D. Bailey	Antespend, 4, 118	Tiffany's Taylor, 8, 113	11	1:32.80	69,360
1996	Perfect Arc, 4, 125	J. R. Velazquez	Fashion Star, 4, 112	Tough Broad, 4, 112	7	1:42.41	60,160
1995	Irish Linnet, 7, 121	J. R. Velazquez	Caress, 4, 120	Weekend Madness (Ire), 5, 120	7	1:40.67	60,048
1994	Irish Linnet, 6, 117	J. R. Velazquez	Statuette, 4, 113	Cox Orange, 4, 117	10	1:39.59	50,790
1993	McKaymackenna, 4, 120	C. W. Antley	La Piaf (Fr), 4, 116	Heed, 4, 116	10	1:43.74	55,620
1992	Miss Otis, 5, 115	A. Madrid Jr.	Big Big Affair, 5, 115	Tiney Toast, 3, 115	4	1:43.64	53,460
1991	Highland Penny, 6, 116	A. T. Cordero Jr.	Southern Tradition, 4, 116	Virgin Michael, 4, 116	8	1:40.20	50,850
1990	Christiecat, 3, 112	E. Maple	Aldbourne (Ire), 4, 120	To the Lighthouse, 4, 116	7	1:43.40	54,090
1989	Miss Unnameable, 5, 120	R. I. Rojas	High Browser, 4, 116	Highland Penny, 4, 116	9	1:40.60	55,080
1988	Glowing Honor, 3, 115	P. Day	Love You by Heart, 4, 115	Fieldy (Ire), 5, 116	8	1:42.00	55,350
1987	Fieldy (Ire), 4, 116	A. T. Cordero Jr.	Perfect Point, 5, 120	Bailrullah, 5, 123	9	1:43.40	34,500
1986	Slew's Exceller, 4, 115	J. Samyn	Tri Argo, 4, 115	Chinguetti (Fr), 4, 115	6	1:42.20	32,460
	Fama, 3, 113	R. P. Romero	Tax Dodge, 5, 119	Anka Germania (Ire), 4, 115	7	1:41.00	32,580
1985	Alabama Nana (Ire), 4, 115	P. A. Valenzuela	Paradies (Arg), 5, 115	Nany, 5, 115	8	1:35.20	34,800

Named for G. Watts Humphrey Jr.'s 1982 New York H. (G3) winner Noble Damsel (1978 f. by *Vaguely Noble). Leixable S. 1985-'88. Noble Damsel S. 1989-'93. Noble Damsel Breeders' Cup H. 2006. 1 1/16 miles 1988-'96. Dirt 1992, 2001. Two divisions 1986.

Norfolk Stakes

Grade 1 in 2008. Oak Tree at Santa Anita, two-year-olds, 1 1/16 miles, all weather. Held September 30, 2007, with a gross value of $250,000. First held in 1970. First graded in 1973. Stakes record 1:41.27 (2003 Ruler's Court).

Year	Winner	Jockey	Second	Third	Strs	Time	1st Purse
2007	Dixie Chatter, 2, 122	R. Migliore	Salute the Sarge, 2, 122	Shore Do, 2, 122	9	1:42.64	$150,000
2006	Stormello, 2, 122	K. Desormeaux	Principle Secret, 2, 122	Spot the Diplomat, 2, 122	9	1:43.10	150,000

Racing — Graded Stakes 403

Year	Winner	Jockey	Second	Third	Strs	Time	1st Purse
2005	Brother Derek, 2, 122	A. O. Solis	A. P. Warrior, 2, 122	Jealous Profit, 2, 122	8	1:44.38	$120,000
2004	Roman Ruler, 2, 120	C. S. Nakatani	Boston Glory, 2, 120	Littlebitofzip, 2, 120	4	1:44.27	120,000
2003	Ruler's Court, 2, 120	A. O. Solis	Capitano, 2, 120	Perfect Moon, 2, 120	9	**1:41.27**	150,000
2002	Kafwain, 2, 120	V. Espinoza	Bull Market, 2, 120	Listen Indy, 2, 120	7	1:42.75	120,000
2001	Essence of Dubai, 2, 118	A. O. Solis	Ibn Al Haitham (GB), 2, 118	‡Ecstatic, 2, 118	6	1:37.16	150,000
2000	Flame Thrower, 2, 118	V. Espinoza	Street Cry (Ire), 2, 118	Mr Freckles, 2, 118	8	1:34.86	120,000
1999	Dixie Union, 2, 118	A. O. Solis	Forest Camp, 2, 118	Anees, 2, 118	6	1:35.79	120,000
1998	Buck Trout, 2, 118	E. Delahoussaye	Eagleton, 2, 118	Daring General, 2, 118	9	1:37.55	120,000
1997	Souvenir Copy, 2, 118	G. L. Stevens	Old Trieste, 2, 118	Double Honor, 2, 118	7	1:36.00	120,000
1996	Free House, 2, 118	K. Desormeaux	Zippersup, 2, 118	Swiss Yodeler, 2, 118	7	1:43.54	120,000
1995	Future Quest, 2, 118	K. Desormeaux	Odyle, 2, 118	Exetera, 2, 118	7	1:43.31	120,000
1994	Supremo, 2, 118	G. L. Stevens	Desert Mirage, 2, 118	Strong Ally, 2, 118	9	1:43.48	120,000
1993	Shepherd's Field, 2, 118	C. J. McCarron	Ramblin Guy, 2, 118	Ferrara, 2, 118	7	1:43.11	120,000
1992	River Special, 2, 118	K. Desormeaux	Imperial Ridge, 2, 118	Devil Diamond, 2, 118	5	1:43.58	120,000
1991	Bertrando, 2, 118	A. O. Solis	Zurich, 2, 118	Bag, 2, 118	9	1:42.87	164,820
1990	Best Pal, 2, 118	P. A. Valenzuela	Pillaring, 2, 118	Formal Dinner, 2, 118	12	1:42.80	178,620
1989	Grand Canyon, 2, 118	C. J. McCarron	Single Dawn, 2, 118	Due to the King, 2, 118	7	1:43.20	166,440
1988	Hawkster, 2, 118	P. A. Valenzuela	Bold Bryn, 2, 118	Double Quick, 2, 118	9	1:43.40	187,740
1987	Saratoga Passage, 2, 118	J. J. Steiner	Purdue King, 2, 118	Bold Second, 2, 118	7	1:45.00	181,140
1986	Capote, 2, 118	L. A. Pincay Jr.	Gulch, 2, 118	Gold On Green, 2, 118	6	1:45.20	193,680
1985	Snow Chief, 2, 118	A. O. Solis	Lord Allison, 2, 118	Darby Fair, 2, 118	9	1:44.60	167,340
1984	Chief's Crown, 2, 118	D. MacBeth	Matthew T. Parker, 2, 118	Viva Maxi, 2, 118	6	1:42.40	201,960
1983	Fali Time, 2, 118	S. Hawley	†Life's Magic, 2, 117	Artichoke, 2, 118	10	1:44.20	168,930
1982	Roving Boy, 2, 118	E. Delahoussaye	Desert Wine, 2, 118	Aguila, 2, 118	9	1:41.60	181,110
1981	Stalwart, 2, 118	C. J. McCarron	Racing Is Fun, 2, 118	Gato Del Sol, 2, 118	9	1:42.20	140,790
1980	Sir Dancer, 2, 118	F. Olivares	Chiaroscuro, 2, 118	Partez, 2, 118	8	1:43.80	100,980
	High Counsel, 2, 118	L. M. Gilligan	Regalberto, 2, 118	Cogency, 2, 118	7	1:42.80	99,780
1979	The Carpenter, 2, 118	C. J. McCarron	Rumbo, 2, 118	Idyll, 2, 118	8	1:41.60	119,280
1978	Flying Paster, 2, 118	D. Pierce	Golden Act, 2, 118	Knights Choice, 2, 118	6	1:42.20	118,860
1977	Balzac, 2, 118	W. Shoemaker	Misrepresentation, 2, 118	Noble Bronze, 2, 118	10	1:45.40	157,230
1976	*Habitony, 2, 118	W. Shoemaker	Replant, 2, 118	Hey Hey J. P., 2, 118	11	1:42.00	79,290
1975	Telly's Pop, 2, 118	F. Mena	Imacornishprince, 2, 118	Thermal Energy, 2, 118	8	1:43.60	74,295
1974	George Navonod, 2, 118	D. Pierce	Diabolo, 2, 118	Fleet Velvet, 2, 118	7	1:42.20	77,370
1973	Money Lender, 2, 118	J. Lambert	Merry Fellow, 2, 118	Holding Pattern, 2, 118	7	1:42.60	58,050

Named for Theodore Winter's undefeated Norfolk (1861 b. by Lexington), member of the great "triumvirate" of Lexington sons, with Asteroid and Kentucky. Norfolk Breeders' Cup S. 2006. Grade 2 1973-'79, 1993-'95, 1997-2006. 1 mile 1997-2001. Dirt 1970-2006. Two divisions 1980. ‡Roman Dancer finished third, DQ to fourth, 2001. †Denotes female.

Northern Dancer Stakes

Grade 3 in 2008. Churchill Downs, three-year-olds, 1¹/₁₆ miles, dirt. Held June 16, 2007, with a gross value of $223,800. First held in 1998. First graded in 2004. Stakes record 1:42.46 (2005 Don't Get Mad; 2007 Chelokee).

Year	Winner	Jockey	Second	Third	Strs	Time	1st Purse
2007	Chelokee, 3, 120	R. A. Dominguez	Zanjero, 3, 116	Sam P., 3, 116	8	**1:42.46**	$135,525
2006	High Cotton, 3, 122	G. K. Gomez	Simon Pure, 3, 116	Sayhellotolarry, 3, 116	6	1:43.33	135,594
2005	Don't Get Mad, 3, 120	G. L. Stevens	Unbridled Energy, 3, 120	Real Dandy, 3, 116	6	**1:42.46**	134,788
2004	Suave, 3, 114	R. Bejarano	J Town, 3, 114	Ecclesiastic, 3, 114	12	1:44.50	144,088
2003	Champali, 3, 122	P. Day	Lone Star Sky, 3, 120	During, 3, 114	8	1:34.69	68,882
2002	Danthebluegrassman, 3, 119	J. D. Bailey	Stephentown, 3, 113	Sky Terrace, 3, 119	7	1:35.04	67,890

Named for E. P. Taylor's Racing Hall of Fame member and 1964 Kentucky Derby winner Northern Dancer (1961 c. by Nearctic). Northern Dancer Breeders' Cup S. 2005-'06. 1 mile 2002-'03. Run as an overnight handicap 1998-2001.

Oaklawn Handicap

Grade 2 in 2008. Oaklawn Park, four-year-olds and up, 1¹/₈ miles, dirt. Held April 5, 2008, with a gross value of $500,000. First held in 1946. First graded in 1973. Stakes record 1:46.60 (1987 Snow Chief).

Year	Winner	Jockey	Second	Third	Strs	Time	1st Purse
2008	Tiago, 4, 117	M. E. Smith	Heatseeker (Ire), 5, 119	Reporting for Duty, 4, 113	7	1:50.34	$300,000
2007	Lawyer Ron, 4, 120	E. S. Prado	Brother Bobby, 4, 116	Boboman, 6, 116	7	1:49.00	300,000
2006	Buzzards Bay, 4, 115	J. Valdivia Jr.	Magnum (Arg), 5, 115	Gouldings Green, 5, 116	8	1:48.22	300,000
2005	Grand Reward, 4, 112	J. McKee	Second of June, 4, 117	Eddington, 4, 117	5	1:49.54	300,000
2004	Peace Rules, 4, 120	J. D. Bailey	Ole Faunty, 5, 116	Saint Liam, 4, 114	6	1:48.26	300,000
2003	Medaglia d'Oro, 4, 122	J. D. Bailey	Slider, 5, 112	Kudos, 6, 117	5	1:47.66	300,000
2002	Kudos, 5, 117	E. Delahoussaye	Bowman's Band, 4, 114	Dollar Bill, 4, 114	8	1:48.34	300,000
2001	Traditionally, 4, 112	P. Day	Mr Ross, 6, 117	Wooden Phone, 4, 118	7	1:48.15	360,000
2000	K One King, 4, 113	C. H. Borel	Almutawakel (GB), 5, 117	Cat Thief, 4, 118	6	1:48.02	360,000
1999	Behrens, 5, 116	J. F. Chavez	Littlebitlively, 5, 112	Precocity, 5, 119	7	1:47.77	450,000
1998	Precocity, 4, 114	C. Gonzalez	Frisk Me Now, 4, 117	Phantom On Tour, 4, 117	7	1:48.28	450,000
1997	Atticus, 5, 114	S. J. Sellers	Isitingood, 6, 120	Tejano Run, 5, 115	8	1:48.20	450,000
1996	Geri, 4, 115	J. D. Bailey	Wekiva Springs, 5, 119	Scott's Scoundrel, 4, 113	7	1:47.52	450,000
1995	Cigar, 5, 120	J. D. Bailey	Silver Goblin, 4, 119	Concern, 4, 122	7	1:47.22	450,000
1994	The Wicked North, 5, 119	K. Desormeaux	Devil His Due, 5, 124	Brother Brown, 4, 116	7	1:47.86	450,000
1993	Jovial (GB), 6, 117	E. Delahoussaye	Lil E. Tee, 4, 123	Best Pal, 5, 123	10	1:48.63	450,000
1992	Best Pal, 4, 125	K. Desormeaux	Sea Cadet, 4, 120	Twilight Agenda, 6, 123	7	1:48.10	300,000

Racing — Graded Stakes

Year	Winner	Jockey	Second	Third	Strs	Time	1st Purse
1991	Festin (Arg), 5, 115	E. Delahoussaye	Primal, 6, 115	Jolie's Halo, 4, 120	8	1:48.71	$300,000
1990	Opening Verse, 4, 118	C. J. McCarron	De Roche, 4, 114	Silver Survivor, 4, 116	8	1:47.20	300,000
1989	Slew City Slew, 5, 118	A. T. Cordero Jr.	Stalwars, 4, 113	Homebuilder, 5, 115	8	1:49.00	240,000
1988	Lost Code, 4, 126	C. Perret	Cryptoclearance, 4, 122	Gulch, 4, 120	8	1:47.00	300,000
1987	Snow Chief, 4, 123	A. O. Solis	Red Attack, 5, 112	Vilzak, 4, 108	7	1:46.60	163,020
1986	Turkoman, 4, 123	C. J. McCarron	Gate Dancer, 5, 123	Red Attack, 4, 114	4	1:47.40	159,180
1985	Imp Society, 4, 125	P. Day	Strength in Unity, 4, 109	Pine Circle, 4, 118	11	1:48.40	168,540
1984	Wild Again, 4, 115	P. Day	Win Stat, 7, 114	Dew Line, 5, 118	14	1:46.80	173,940
1983	Bold Style, 4, 113	P. Day	Eminency, 5, 123	Listcapade, 4, 123	8	1:43.00	165,180
1982	Eminency, 4, 116	P. Day	Reef Searcher, 5, 117	Thirty Eight Paces, 4, 120	9	1:44.00	166,740
1981	Temperence Hill, 4, 126	E. Maple	Sun Catcher, 4, 123	Uncool, 6, 114	5	1:43.40	128,310
1980	Uncool, 5, 116	J. Velasquez	Hold Your Tricks, 5, 111	Braze and Bold, 5, 118	8	1:44.40	103,110
1979	San Juan Hill, 4, 114	D. Brumfield	Alydar, 4, 127	A Letter to Harry, 5, 125	7	1:43.60	101,730
1978	Cox's Ridge, 4, 128	E. Maple	Prince Majestic, 4, 115	All the More, 5, 120	11	1:43.20	80,190
1977	Soy Numero Uno, 4, 123	R. Broussard	Romeo, 4, 119	Dragset, 6, 114	13	1:42.40	80,610
1976	Master Derby, 4, 125	D. G. McHargue	Royal Glint, 6, 128	Dragset, 5, 113	6	1:41.60	70,890
1975	Warbucks, 5, 121	D. Gargan	Hey Rube, 5, 112	Eastern Pageant, 4, 115	10	1:42.80	37,380
1974	Royal Knight, 4, 123	I. Valenzuela	Crimson Falcon, 4, 122	Visualizer, 4, 121	11	1:43.40	38,070
1973	Prince Astro, 4, 116	D. W. Whited	Herbalist, 6, 116	Gage Line, 7, 118	8	1:43.60	34,470

Grade 3 1973-'76. Grade 1 1988-2002. Not held 1955-'62. 1 1/16 miles 1946-'83. Three-year-olds and up 1946-'76.

Oak Leaf Stakes

Grade 1 in 2008. Oak Tree at Santa Anita, two-year-olds, fillies, 1 1/16 miles, all weather. Held September 29, 2007, with a gross value of $244,000. First held in 1969. First graded in 1973. Stakes record 1:41.20 (1978 It's in the Air).

Year	Winner	Jockey	Second	Third	Strs	Time	1st Purse
2007	Cry and Catch Me, 2, 122	M. E. Smith	Izarra, 2, 122	Runforthemoneybaby, 2, 122	10	1:42.91	$150,000
2006	Cash Included, 2, 122	C. S. Nakatani	Point Ashley, 2, 122	Quick Little Miss, 2, 122	11	1:42.86	150,000
2005	Diamond Omi, 2, 122	D. R. Flores	Wild Fit, 2, 122	Golden Silk, 2, 122	7	1:45.57	120,000
2004	Sweet Catomine, 2, 119	C. S. Nakatani	Splendid Blended, 2, 119	Memorette, 2, 119	9	1:42.98	120,000
2003	Halfbridled, 2, 119	J. A. Krone	Tarlow, 2, 119	Hollywood Story, 2, 119	7	1:43.72	150,000
2002	Composure, 2, 119	M. E. Smith	Buffythecenterfold, 2, 119	Sea Jewel, 2, 119	7	1:42.65	120,000
2001	Tali'sluckybusride, 2, 117	J. Valdivia Jr.	Imperial Gesture, 2, 117	Ms Louisett, 2, 117	6	1:37.77	150,000
2000	Notable Career, 2, 118	D. R. Flores	Euro Empire, 2, 118	Cindy's Hero, 2, 118	7	1:36.34	120,000
1999	Chilukki, 2, 118	D. R. Flores	Abby Girl, 2, 118	Spain, 2, 118	5	1:36.12	120,000
1998	Excellent Meeting, 2, 115	K. Desormeaux	Antahkarana, 2, 115	Stylish Talent, 2, 115	7	1:37.71	120,000
1997	Vivid Angel, 2, 116	E. Delahoussaye	Love Lock, 2, 116	Balisian Beauty, 2, 115	9	1:37.33	120,000
1996	City Band, 2, 115	J. A. Garcia	Clever Pilot, 2, 115	Wealthy, 2, 115	8	1:44.57	120,000
1995	Tipically Irish, 2, 117	L. A. Pincay Jr.	Ocean View, 2, 115	Gastronomical, 2, 117	7	1:42.60	120,000
1994	Serena's Song, 2, 115	C. S. Nakatani	Call Now, 2, 115	Mama Mucci, 2, 115	8	1:41.83	120,000
1993	Phone Chatter, 2, 117	L. A. Pincay Jr.	Sardula, 2, 116	Tricky Code, 2, 115	6	1:41.78	120,000
1992	Zoonaqua, 2, 115	C. J. McCarron	Turkstand, 2, 115	Madame l'Enjoleur, 2, 115	10	1:43.91	120,000
1991	Pleasant Stage, 2, 116	E. Delahoussaye	Soviet Sojourn, 2, 116	La Spia, 2, 115	5	1:43.53	156,540
1990	Lite Light, 2, 115	R. A. Baze	Garden Gal, 2, 115	Beyond Perfection, 2, 115	4	1:42.80	148,320
1989	Dominant Dancer, 2, 116	E. Delahoussaye	Bel's Starlet, 2, 115	Materco, 2, 115	7	1:44.60	153,870
1988	One of a Klein, 2, 115	C. J. McCarron	Stocks Up, 2, 115	Lady Lister, 2, 115	7	1:44.00	168,090
1987	Dream Team, 2, 115	C. J. McCarron	Lost Kitty, 2, 117	Tomorrow's Child, 2, 115	6	1:44.40	158,910
1986	Sacahuista, 2, 115	C. J. McCarron	Silk's Lady, 2, 115	Delicate Vine, 2, 115	7	1:44.60	187,050
1985	Arewehavingfunyet, 2, 115	P. A. Valenzuela	Trim Colony, 2, 115	Laz's Joy, 2, 115	8	1:44.60	192,420
1984	Folk Art, 2, 117	L. A. Pincay, Jr.	Pirate's Glow, 2, 115	Wayward Pirate, 2, 115	6	1:42.60	186,540
1983	Life's Magic, 2, 115	C. J. McCarron	Althea, 2, 117	Percipient, 2, 115	9	1:44.40	164,310
1982	Landaluce, 2, 117	L. A. Pincay Jr.	Sophisticated Girl, 2, 115	Granja Reina, 2, 115	7	1:41.80	155,610
1981	Header Card, 2, 115	D. G. McHargue	A Kiss for Luck, 2, 117	Model Ten, 2, 115	9	1:43.00	144,390
1980	Astrious, 2, 115	T. Lipham	Irish Arrival, 2, 115	Bee a Scout, 2, 115	8	1:43.80	90,180
1979	Bold 'n Determined, 2, 115	A. T. Cordero Jr.	Hazel R., 2, 115	Arcades Ambo, 2, 115	8	1:42.60	82,440
1978	It's in the Air, 2, 115	E. Delahoussaye	Caline, 2, 115	Spiffy Laree, 2, 115	8	1:41.20	75,570
1977	B. Thoughtful, 2, 115	D. G. McHargue	Grenzen, 2, 115	High Pheasant, 2, 117	7	1:43.80	73,530
1976	Any Time Girl, 2, 115	R. Schacht	Lady T. V., 2, 115	*Glenaris, 2, 115	8	1:44.00	73,140
1975	Answer, 2, 115	M. Hole	Queen to Be, 2, 115	Awaken, 2, 115	12	1:44.20	84,720
1974	Cut Class, 2, 115	F. Toro	Double You Lou, 2, 115	Sweet Old Girl, 2, 115	13	1:42.80	84,300
1973	Divine Grace, 2, 115	S. Valdez	Chalk Face, 2, 115	Round Rose, 2, 115	6	1:43.60	59,940

Run at Santa Anita Park's fall Oak Tree Racing Association meet. Grade 2 1973-'79, 1990-'91, 2002-'05. Oak Leaf Breeders' Cup S. 2006. 1 mile 1997-2001. Dirt 1969-2006.

Oak Tree Derby

Grade 2 in 2008. Oak Tree at Santa Anita, three-year-olds, 1 1/8 miles, turf. Held October 13, 2007, with a gross value of $150,000. First held in 1969. First graded in 1974. Stakes record 1:45.80 (1989 Seven Rivers).

Year	Winner	Jockey	Second	Third	Strs	Time	1st Purse
2007	Daytona (Ire), 3, 118	M. E. Smith	Ten a Penny, 3, 118	Stoneside (Ire), 3, 118	10	1:46.40	$90,000
2006	Dark Islander (Ire), 3, 118	J. Valdivia Jr.	Obrigado (Fr), 3, 118	A. P. Warrior, 3, 120	6	1:46.21	90,000
2005	Aragorn (Ire), 3, 118	P. A. Valenzuela	Eastern Sand, 3, 118	Brecon Beacon (GB), 3, 118	7	1:46.48	90,000
2004	Greek Sun, 3, 118	E. S. Prado	Laura's Lucky Boy, 3, 118	Hendrix, 3, 118	9	1:48.08	90,000
2003	Devious Boy (GB), 3, 118	J. A. Krone	Sweet Return (GB), 3, 118	Urban King (Ire), 3, 118	5	1:48.82	90,000

Year	Winner	Jockey	Second	Third	Strs	Time	1st Purse
2002	Johar, 3, 118	A. O. Solis	Rock Opera, 3, 118	Mananan McLir, 3, 120	8	1:46.00	$90,000
2001	No Slip (Fr), 3, 118	K. Desormeaux	Sligo Bay (Ire), 3, 118	Romanceishope, 3, 122	9	1:46.56	90,000
2000	Sign of Hope (GB), 3, 118	A. O. Solis	David Copperfield, 3, 118	El Gran Papa, 3, 118	5	1:47.71	150,000
1999	Mula Gula, 3, 118	G. L. Stevens	Eagleton, 3, 118	Super Quercus (Fr), 3, 118	9	1:46.67	150,000
1998	Ladies Din, 3, 120	G. L. Stevens	Dr Fong, 3, 120	Bouccaneer (Fr), 3, 118	7	1:50.24	150,000
1997	Lasting Approval, 3, 118	A. O. Solis	Voyagers Quest, 3, 118	Early Colony, 3, 118	7	1:50.84	150,000
1996	Odyle, 3, 117	C. J. McCarron	Lago, 3, 115	Rainbow Blues (Ire), 3, 117	6	1:46.83	80,250
1995	Helmsman, 3, 115	C. J. McCarron	Virginia Carnival, 3, 118	Mr Purple, 3, 121	8	1:48.98	75,650
1994	Run Softly, 3, 117	L. A. Pincay Jr.	Alphabet Soup, 3, 114	Powis Castle, 3, 118	8	1:49.96	64,800
1993	Eastern Memories (Ire), 3, 113	J. D. Bailey	Cigar, 3, 117	Snake Eyes, 3, 120	9	1:48.03	66,800
1992	Blacksburg, 3, 118	A. O. Solis	Siberian Summer, 3, 117	Star Recruit, 3, 115	10	1:48.12	67,700
1991	General Meeting, 3, 116	K. Desormeaux	Dominion Gold (GB), 3, 115	Eternity Star, 3, 120	12	1:46.78	69,500
1990	In Excess (Ire), 3, 117	G. L. Stevens	Warcraft, 3, 118	Barton Dene (Ire), 3, 113	8	1:46.60	65,300
1989	Seven Rivers, 3, 115	R. G. Davis	Bruho, 3, 117	Raise a Stanza, 3, 121	9	**1:45.80**	66,100
1988	Coax Me Clyde, 3, 116	P. A. Valenzuela	Bel Air Dancer, 3, 117	Undercut, 3, 120	11	1:48.40	81,500
1987	The Medic, 3, 119	S. Hawley	Temperate Sil, 3, 122	Hot and Smoggy, 3, 115	9	1:47.80	63,800
1986	Air Display, 3, 114	G. L. Stevens	Armada (GB), 3, 117	Vernon Castle, 3, 124	9	1:48.00	64,700
1985	Justoneoftheboys, 3, 115	A. O. Solis	Floating Reserve, 3, 118	Schiller, 3, 113	8	1:47.60	65,000
1984	Tights, 3, 121	C. J. McCarron	Tsunami Slew, 3, 122	Blind Spot, 3, 115	8	1:46.60	65,500
1983	Mamaison, 3, 117	C. J. McCarron	Sunny's Halo, 3, 126	Fifth Division, 3, 118	6	1:49.80	63,900
1982	Lamerok, 3, 117	L. A. Pincay Jr.	Craelius, 3, 118	Sari's Dreamer, 3, 113	9	1:46.20	66,300
1981	dh-Seafood, 3, 118	M. Castaneda		High Counsel, 3, 117	11	1:49.00	33,350
	dh-Waterway Drive, 3, 120	J. D. Bailey					
1980	Pocketful in Vail, 3, 115	F. Toro	Son of a Dodo, 3, 118	Always Best, 3, 117	8	1:47.80	39,400
1979	Hyannis Port, 3, 118	W. Shoemaker	Red Crescent, 3, 115	Relaunch, 3, 126	7	1:47.60	32,300
1978	Wayside Station, 3, 117	L. A. Pincay Jr.	April Axe, 3, 120	John Henry, 3, 122	11	1:47.80	34,600
1977	Kulak, 3, 123	W. Shoemaker	Hill Fox, 3, 114	Kaskee, 3, 110	8	1:46.80	19,800
1976	Today 'n Tomorrow, 3, 121	L. A. Pincay Jr.	Pocket Park, 3, 115	Kings Cliffe, 3, 115	8	1:46.80	19,450
1975	Messenger of Song, 3, 119	J. Lambert	Larrikin, 3, 123	Forceten, 3, 125	6	1:46.80	25,450
1974	Within Hail, 3, 124	W. Shoemaker	Orders, 3, 117	Chief Pronto, 3, 113	11	1:48.40	27,250

Run at Santa Anita Park's fall Oak Tree Racing Association meet. Formerly named for Elias J. "Lucky" Baldwin's American Derby winner Volante, one of four horses whose gravesites were moved to the entrance of the paddock gardens at Santa Anita Park from their original location on Baldwin's ranch across the street from the present-day track. Grade 3 1974-'87, 1990-'95. Volante H. 1969-'76. Not held 1973. Dead heat for first 1981.

Oak Tree Mile Stakes

Grade 2 in 2008. Oak Tree at Santa Anita, three-year-olds and up, 1 mile, turf. Held October 7, 2007, with a gross value of $252,000. First held in 1986. First graded in 1989. Stakes record 1:32.44 (1996 Urgent Request [Ire]).

Year	Winner	Jockey	Second	Third	Strs	Time	1st Purse
2007	Out of Control (Brz), 4, 123	M. C. Baze	Zann, 4, 119	Courtnall, 6, 119	6	1:34.16	$150,000
2006	Aragorn (Ire), 4, 123	C. S. Nakatani	Courtnall, 5, 119	Lord Admiral, 5, 119	7	1:32.87	150,000
2005	Singletary, 5, 119	D. R. Flores	Designed for Luck, 8, 119	Buckland Manor, 5, 119	6	1:34.54	150,000
2004	†Musical Chimes, 4, 118	K. Desormeaux	Buckland Manor, 4, 119	Singletary, 4, 119	6	1:33.29	150,000
2003	Designed for Luck, 6, 119	P. A. Valenzuela	Sarafan, 6, 119	Century City (Ire), 4, 119	8	1:32.61	180,000
2002	Night Patrol, 6, 120	J. Valdivia Jr.	Kachamandi (Chi), 5, 119	Nicobar (GB), 5, 119	8	1:32.93	150,000
2001	Val Royal (Fr), 5, 119	J. Valdivia Jr.	Thady Quill, 4, 119	I've Decided, 4, 119	6	1:33.21	120,000
2000	War Chant, 3, 117	G. L. Stevens	Road to Slew, 5, 119	Sharan (GB), 5, 119	8	1:33.75	172,050
1999	Silic (Fr), 4, 121	C. S. Nakatani	Bouccaneer (Fr), 4, 119	Brave Act (GB), 5, 119	7	1:33.76	150,000
1998	Hawksley Hill (Ire), 5, 123	A. O. Solis	Mr Lightfoot (Ire), 4, 119	Magellan, 5, 119	5	1:36.72	166,200
1997	Fantastic Fellow, 3, 115	K. Desormeaux	Magellan, 4, 119	Taiki Blizzard, 6, 123	8	1:36.23	165,000
1996	Urgent Request (Ire), 6, 115	C. J. McCarron	Megan's Interco, 7, 119	Felon (Ire), 4, 116	6	**1:32.44**	110,250
1995	Ventiquattrofogli (Ire), 5, 116	G. F. Almeida	Megan's Interco, 6, 119	Debutant Trick, 5, 115	8	1:35.30	76,850
1994	Bon Point (GB), 4, 116	E. Delahoussaye	Journalism, 6, 120	Johann Quatz (Fr), 5, 119	5	1:33.86	62,050
1993	Johann Quatz (Fr), 4, 119	E. Delahoussaye	Myrakalu (Fr), 5, 114	The Tender Track, 6, 117	5	1:36.28	62,350
1992	Twilight Agenda, 6, 120	C. J. McCarron	Luthier Enchanteur, 5, 117	Bourgogne (GB), 4, 115	8	1:33.36	65,300
1991	Ibero (Arg), 4, 115	A. O. Solis	Val des Bois (Fr), 5, 118	Tokatee, 5, 116	9	1:33.77	67,000
1990	Notorious Pleasure, 4, 117	L. A. Pincay Jr.	Kanatiyr (Ire), 4, 114	Fly Till Dawn, 4, 116	11	1:33.00	68,700
1989	Political Ambition, 5, 122	E. Delahoussaye	Mister Wonderful (GB), 6, 118	Sabona, 7, 117	10	1:33.40	67,800
1988	Mohamed Abdu (Ire), 4, 120	G. L. Stevens	Mazilier, 4, 116	Deputy Governor, 5, 119	7	1:34.40	65,550
1987	Double Feint, 4, 117	F. Toro	Deputy Governor, 3, 118	Vilzak, 4, 115	10	1:37.00	64,810
1986	Palace Music, 5, 122	G. L. Stevens	‡Skywalker, 4, 122	Mangaki, 5, 116	6	1:35.00	59,350

Run at Santa Anita Park's fall Oak Tree Racing Association meet. Formerly named for Col. F. W. Koester, general manager of the California Thoroughbred Breeders' Association. Grade 3 1989, 1996-'99. Col. F. W. Koester H. 1986-'95. Col. F. W. Koester Breeders' Cup H. 1996. Oak Tree Breeders' Cup Mile H. 1997, 2000. Oak Tree Breeders' Cup Mile S. 1998-'99, 2001-'06. Course record 1996. ‡Mangaki finished second, DQ to third, 1986. †Denotes female.

Obeah Handicap

Grade 3 in 2008. Delaware Park, three-year-olds and up, fillies and mares, 1 1/8 miles, dirt. Held June 16, 2007, with a gross value of $101,800. First held in 1984. First graded in 2008. Stakes record 1:49.05 (2006 Fleet Indian).

Year	Winner	Jockey	Second	Third	Strs	Time	1st Purse
2007	Peak Maria's Way, 4, 119	J. Rocco	Unbridled Belle, 4, 117	Lila Paige, 6, 119	11	1:49.38	$60,000
2006	Fleet Indian, 5, 123	J. A. Santos	Friel's for Real, 6, 117	Take a Check, 4, 117	7	**1:49.05**	60,000

Year	Winner	Jockey	Second	Third	Strs	Time	1st Purse
2005	Isola Piu Bella (Chi), 5, 120	R. A. Dominguez	City Fire, 5, 116	Becky in Pink, 4, 115	5	1:53.68	$60,000
2004	Misty Sixes, 6, 117	M. G. Pino	Redoubled Miss, 5, 115	Nonsuch Bay, 5, 118	6	1:51.23	60,000
2003	Devon Rose, 4, 117	A. S. Black	Shiny Sheet, 5, 114	True Sensation, 4, 113	5	1:50.24	60,000
2002	Your Out, 4, 117	R. A. Dominguez	Quiet Lake, 4, 117	Shag, 6, 115	9	1:52.54	60,000
2001	Under the Rug, 6, 119	M. T. Johnston	Zenith, 4, 115	Irving's Baby, 4, 115	10	1:51.20	60,000
2000	Her Halo, 4, 119	M. J. McCarthy	Proud Owner, 5, 114	dh-Batuka, 4, 122	8	1:50.85	60,000
				dh-Saluteloot, 5, 116			
1999	Pocho's Dream Girl, 5, 113	J. L. Castanon	Timely Broad, 5, 116	Endowment, 5, 114	8	1:50.30	60,000
1998	Winter Melody, 5, 117	M. J. McCarthy	See Your Point, 6, 115	Tuxedo Junction, 5, 119	8	1:49.54	45,000
1997	Winter Melody, 4, 116	A. S. Black	Power Play, 5, 114	Ontherightwicket, 4, 115	8	1:50.80	30,000
1996	Scratch Paper, 4, 112	K. Whitley	Churchbell Chimes, 5, 119	Cavada, 5, 117	7	1:44.81	30,000
1995	Shananie's Beat, 4, 123	E. L. King Jr.	Easily Majestic, 3, 109	Mistress Fletcher, 3, 112	5	1:10.55	12,540
1984	Bishop's Fling, 5, 119	A. Delgado	Queen's Statue, 3, 106	Twin Cities, 4, 112	8	1:42.60	13,320

Named for Christiana Stable's 1969, '70 Delaware H. winner Obeah (1965 f. by Cyane). Obeah S. 1995-'96, 1998-2002. Not held 1985-'94. 1 1/16 miles 1984, '96. Furlongs 1995. Turf 1984. Dead heat for third 2000.

Oceanport Stakes

Grade 3 in 2008. Monmouth Park, three-year-olds and up, 1 1/16 miles, turf. Held August 5, 2007, with a gross value of $150,000. First held in 1947. First graded in 1973. Stakes record 1:38.99 (2007 Silent Roar).

Year	Winner	Jockey	Second	Third	Strs	Time	1st Purse
2007	Silent Roar, 4, 117	S. Elliott	Kiss the Kid, 4, 117	Kip Deville, 4, 123	8	1:38.99	$90,000
2006	Three Valleys, 5, 117	R. A. Dominguez	Hotstufanthensome, 6, 121	Rebel Rebel (Ire), 4, 121	10	1:40.06	90,000
2005	Ay Caramba (Brz), 5, 117	G. L. Stevens	Hotstufanthensome, 5, 118	Stormy Roman, 6, 116	9	1:42.53	90,000
2004	Gulch Approval, 4, 117	P. Day	Kathir, 7, 116	Stormy Roman, 5, 115	10	1:42.31	60,000
2003	Runspastum, 6, 113	J. Pimentel	Balto Star, 5, 119	Saint Verre, 5, 118	6	1:42.31	60,000
2002	Tempest Fugit, 5, 115	J. A. Velez Jr.	Runspastum, 5, 112	One Eyed Joker, 4, 114	3	1:42.72	60,000
2001	Key Lory, 7, 111	C. C. Lopez	North East Bound, 5, 121	Crash Course, 5, 115	13	1:40.39	60,000
2000	North East Bound, 4, 114	J. A. Velez Jr.	Rize, 4, 112	Selective, 7, 114	6	1:44.70	60,000
1999	Mi Narrow, 5, 113	J. Bravo	Hurrahy, 6, 114	Forbidden Apple, 4, 111	8	1:39.40	60,000
1998	Daylight Savings, 4, 115	H. Castillo Jr.	Mi Narrow, 4, 112	Rob 'n Gin, 4, 120	8	1:42.31	60,000
1997	Boyce, 6, 118	J. A. Krone	Foolish Pole, 4, 113	Jambalaya Jazz, 5, 116	7	1:40.20	60,000
1995	Boyce, 4, 114	A. S. Black	Myrmidon, 4, 117	Rocket City, 4, 112	9	1:40.91	45,000
1994	Nijinsky's Gold, 5, 120	R. G. Davis	Winnetou, 4, 116	Marco Bay, 4, 116	5	1:41.66	45,000
1993	Furiously, 4, 119	J. D. Bailey	Adam Smith (GB), 5, 120	Rocket Fuel, 6, 114	5	1:39.60	45,000
1992	Maxigroom, 4, 113	R. G. Davis	Rocket Fuel, 5, 112	Go Dutch, 5, 112	9	1:41.77	45,000
1991	Fiftysevenvette, 4, 113	J. C. Ferrer	Great Normand, 6, 118	Thunder Regent, 4, 112	6	1:44.94	45,000
1990	Bill E. Shears, 5, 118	R. Wilson	Pete the Chief, 4, 115	Timely Warning, 5, 113	9	1:42.80	53,910
1989	Yankee Affair, 7, 121	P. Day	River of Sin, 5, 116	Primino (Fr), 4, 110	7	1:43.40	51,870
1988	Feeling Gallant, 6, 119	C. W. Antley	Copper Cup, 5, 111	Sovereign Song, 6, 107	8	1:45.20	41,820
1987	Sovereign Song, 5, 106	J. A. Krone	Feeling Gallant, 5, 120	Spellbound, 4, 117	8	1:41.60	35,100
1986	Salem Drive, 4, 115	D. B. Thomas	Exclusive Partner, 4, 114	Pine Belt, 4, 113	10	1:42.60	34,650
1985	Cozzene, 5, 121	W. A. Guerra	Stay the Course, 4, 119	Roving Minstrel, 4, 118	9	1:42.40	34,470
1984	World Appeal, 4, 120	C. Perret	Rocca Reale, 5, 109	Castle Guard, 5, 120	8	1:42.80	34,950
1983	Fray Star (Arg), 5, 114	O. Vergara	Domynsky (GB), 3, 112	And More, 5, 117	12	1:43.40	35,190
1982	McCann, 4, 114	J. Fell	Sprink, 4, 108	Lord Carnavon, 4, 111	9	1:43.60	27,555
	Erin's Tiger, 4, 114	K. Skinner	Dom Menotti (Fr), 5, 111	War of Words, 5, 114	9	1:43.00	27,555
1981	Winds of Winter, 4, 113	G. McCarron	Foretake, 5, 116	No Bend, 4, 115	12	1:43.40	24,225
1980	North Course, 5, 114	B. Thornburg	Horatius, 5, 119	Lucy's Axe, 4, 116	11	1:44.00	24,210
1979	Revivalist, 5, 117	W. Nemeti	Horatius, 4, 117	Gristle, 4, 112	10	1:38.00	18,866
	Alias Smith, 6, 114	M. Solomone	Qui Native, 5, 114	Fed Funds, 5, 114	9	1:38.00	18,671
1978	Mr. Red Wing, 4, 110	W. H. McCauley	Chati, 5, 118	Dan Horn, 6, 116	15	1:43.20	23,514
1977	Quick Card, 4, 115	M. Solomone	Bemo, 7, 115	Star of the Sea, 4, 115	2	1:42.60	19,516
1976	Toujours Pret, 7, 114	J. W. Edwards	Hat Full, 5, 114	Our Hermis, 5, 113	10	1:43.00	15,072
	Break Up the Game, 5, 114	E. Delahoussaye	Expropriate, 6, 120	Leader of the Band, 4, 118	6	1:44.20	14,682
1975	R. Tom Can, 4, 115	D. Brumfield	Prod, 4, 117	Royal Glint, 5, 119	11	1:49.80	15,291
	Haraka, 5, 113	J. Velasquez	London Company, 5, 124	East Sea, 4, 115	9	1:49.80	15,096
1974	Mo Bay, 5, 118	W. Tichenor	Shane's Prince, 4, 118	Barbizon Streak, 6, 118	10	1:42.40	18,541
1973	Lexington Park, 6, 118	J. Imparato	Prince of Truth, 5, 116	Halo, 4, 117	9	1:45.20	15,056
	Dartsum, 4, 110	M. Cedeno	Dundee Marmalade, 5, 114	Return to Reality, 4, 111	8	1:46.20	14,893

Monmouth Park is located in Oceanport, New Jersey. Grade 3 1984-2001. Not graded 2002. Oceanport H. 1947-2004. Not held 1996. 6 furlongs 1947-'63. 5 furlongs 1964-'67. 1 mile 1968-'72, 1979. Dirt 1947-51, 1970, 1984, 1990-'91, 2000, 2002. Originally scheduled for turf 2002. Two divisions 1973, 1975-'76, 1979, 1982. Course record 1993, '99, 2007.

Ogden Phipps Handicap

Grade 1 in 2008. Belmont Park, three-year-olds and up, fillies and mares, 1 1/16 miles, dirt. Held June 16, 2007, with a gross value of $300,000. First held in 1961. First graded in 1973. Stakes record 1:39.90 (1998 Mossflower).

Year	Winner	Jockey	Second	Third	Strs	Time	1st Purse
2007	Take D' Tour, 6, 118	E. Coa	Ginger Punch, 4, 114	Promenade Girl, 5, 116	6	1:41.39	$180,000
2006	Take D' Tour, 5, 117	C. H. Velasquez	Nothing But Fun, 4, 116	Balletto (UAE), 4, 116	7	1:42.63	180,000
2005	Ashado, 4, 120	J. R. Velazquez	Society Selection, 4, 119	Bending Strings, 4, 115	5	1:41.02	180,000
2004	Sightseek, 5, 120	J. D. Bailey	Storm Flag Flying, 4, 117	Passing Shot, 5, 116	4	1:41.46	180,000

Year	Winner	Jockey	Second	Third	Strs	Time	1st Purse
2003	Sightseek, 4, 118	J. D. Bailey	Take Charge Lady, 4, 119	Mandy's Gold, 5, 118	5	1:40.89	$180,000
2002	Raging Fever, 4, 120	J. R. Velazquez	Transcendental, 4, 113	Two Item Limit, 4, 114	9	1:41.75	180,000
2001	Critical Eye, 4, 115	M. J. Luzzi	Jostle, 4, 117	Apple of Kent, 5, 117	7	1:42.18	150,000
2000	Beautiful Pleasure, 5, 124	J. F. Chavez	Pentatonic, 5, 112	Roza Robata, 5, 115	6	1:41.54	150,000
1999	Sister Act, 4, 117	P. Day	Beautiful Pleasure, 4, 112	Catinca, 4, 122	6	1:40.79	150,000
1998	Mossflower, 4, 114	R. G. Davis	Glitter Woman, 4, 120	Colonial Minstrel, 4, 118	6	**1:39.90**	150,000
1997	Hidden Lake, 4, 117	R. Migliore	Twice the Vice, 6, 121	Jewel Princess, 5, 124	9	1:40.87	150,000
1996	Serena's Song, 4, 125	J. D. Bailey	Shoop, 5, 115	Restored Hope, 5, 114	8	1:41.63	120,000
1995	Heavenly Prize, 4, 122	P. Day	Little Buckles, 4, 111	Sky Beauty, 5, 124	4	1:43.37	90,000
1994	Sky Beauty, 4, 128	M. E. Smith	You'd Be Surprised, 5, 118	Schway Baby Sway, 4, 109	5	1:47.48	90,000
1993	Turnback the Alarm, 4, 119	C. W. Antley	Deputation, 4, 117	You'd Be Surprised, 4, 112	6	1:48.14	90,000
1992	Missy's Mirage, 4, 118	E. Maple	Harbour Club, 5, 110	Versailles Treaty, 4, 119	6	1:47.03	120,000
1991	A Wild Ride, 4, 120	M. E. Smith	Fit to Scout, 4, 115	Buy the Firm, 5, 121	6	1:49.09	120,000
1990	Fantastic Find, 4, 113	C. Perret	Mistaurian, 4, 113	Dreamy Mimi, 4, 113	8	1:50.00	139,680
1989	Rose's Cantina, 5, 117	J. Cruguet	Make Change, 4, 111	Colonial Waters, 4, 114	6	1:48.60	135,120
1988	Personal Ensign, 4, 123	R. P. Romero	Hometown Queen, 4, 109	Clabber Girl, 5, 118	5	1:47.60	131,760
1987	Catatonic, 5, 116	D. A. Miller Jr.	Ms. Eloise, 4, 118	Steal a Kiss, 4, 111	7	1:50.00	137,520
1986	Endear, 4, 111	E. Maple	Lady's Secret, 4, 128	Ride Sally, 4, 124	5	1:48.60	97,650
1985	Heatherten, 6, 124	R. P. Romero	Life's Magic, 4, 122	Sefa's Beauty, 6, 120	6	1:48.80	84,300
1984	Heatherten, 5, 118	S. Maple	Quixotic Lady, 4, 118	Thirty Flags, 4, 114	10	1:49.20	92,400
1983	Number, 4, 117	E. Maple	Dance Number, 4, 114	Broom Dance, 4, 121	4	1:48.40	65,880
1982	Love Sign, 5, 123	R. Hernandez	Anti Lib, 4, 116	Jameela, 6, 122	4	1:48.00	65,280
1981	Wistful, 4, 119	D. Brumfield	Chain Bracelet, 4, 119	Love Sign, 4, 115	5	1:49.80	64,200
1980	Misty Gallore, 4, 125	D. MacBeth	Blitey, 4, 115	What'll I Do, 4, 110	6	1:48.60	32,760
1979	Pearl Necklace, 5, 122	J. Fell	Miss Baja, 4, 115	Sweet Woodruff, 4, 108	5	1:48.60	31,470
1978	Dottie's Doll, 5, 115	J. Vasquez	One Sum, 4, 123	Water Malone, 4, 119	6	1:47.60	32,040
1977	Pacific Princess, 4, 112	E. Maple	Mississippi Mud, 4, 114	Fleet Victress, 5, 113	10	1:49.20	32,700
1976	Proud Delta, 4, 124	J. Velasquez	Garden Verse, 4, 111	Let Me Linger, 4, 114	8	1:48.40	33,690
1975	Raisela, 4, 114	E. Maple	Pass a Glance, 4, 114	Sarsar, 3, 115	7	1:49.20	33,510
1974	Poker Night, 4, 114	J. Velazquez	Krislin, 5, 115	Fairway Flyer, 5, 117	8	1:48.60	33,330
1973	Light Hearted, 4, 123	E. Nelson	Inca Queen, 5, 116	Blessing Angelica, 5, 117	6	1:48.80	32,880

Named for Ogden Phipps (1908-2002), former chairman of the Jockey Club and New York Racing Association. Formerly named for Hempstead, New York, located in Nassau County, home of Belmont Park. Grade 2 1973-'83. Hempstead H. 1961-2001. Held at Aqueduct 1973-'74. Not held 1910-'60, 1962-'69. 6 furlongs 1970-'71. 1 1/2 miles 1961. 1 1/8 miles 1972-'94. Both sexes 1961.

Ohio Derby

Grade 2 in 2008. Thistledown, three-year-olds, 1 1/8 miles, dirt. Held May 31, 2008, with a gross value of $300,000. First held in 1876. First graded in 1973. Stakes record 1:47.40 (1979 Smarten).

Year	Winner	Jockey	Second	Third	Strs	Time	1st Purse
2008	Smooth Air, 3, 117	M. R. Cruz	Cherokee Artist, 3, 115	Z Fortune, 3, 117	8	1:50.26	$180,000
2007	Delightful Kiss, 3, 115	J. Sanchez	Moyer's Pond, 3, 115	Reporting for Duty, 3, 115	8	1:49.36	180,000
2006	Deputy Glitters, 3, 121	R. R. Douglas	High Cotton, 3, 121	Flashy Bull, 3, 113	6	1:50.32	210,000
2005	Palladio, 3, 115	R. A. Dos Ramos	Magna Graduate, 3, 117	It's Time to Smile, 3, 115	8	1:51.56	210,000
2004	Brass Hat, 3, 115	W. Martinez	Pollard's Vision, 3, 121	Trieste's Honor, 3, 115	9	1:49.50	210,000
2003	Wild and Wicked, 3, 114	S. J. Sellers	Hackendiffy, 3, 112	Midway Road, 3, 114	7	1:50.08	180,000
2002	Magic Weisner, 3, 116	R. Migliore	Wiseman's Ferry, 3, 120	The Judge Sez Who, 3, 114	4	1:49.28	195,000
2001	Western Pride, 3, 119	D. G. Whitney	Woodmoon, 3, 113	Macho Uno, 3, 119	6	1:48.66	180,000
2000	Milwaukee Brew, 3, 116	M. J. McCarthy	Brave Quest, 3, 113	Kiss a Native, 3, 116	10	1:50.58	180,000
1999	Stellar Brush, 3, 119	M. J. McCarthy	Ecton Park, 3, 116	Valhol, 3, 114	13	1:49.22	180,000
1998	Classic Cat, 3, 122	S. J. Sellers	One Bold Stroke, 3, 118	Hot Wells, 3, 118	10	1:49.92	180,000
1997	Frisk Me Now, 3, 122	E. L. King Jr.	Anet, 3, 122	Mr. Groush, 3, 118	7	1:48.28	180,000
1996	Skip Away, 3, 122	J. A. Santos	Victory Speech, 3, 118	Clash by Night, 3, 118	10	1:47.86	180,000
1995	Petionville, 3, 122	P. Day	Dazzling Falls, 3, 124	Is Sveikatas, 3, 116	6	1:48.93	180,000
1994	Exclusive Praline, 3, 118	W. Martinez	Concern, 3, 122	Smilin Singin Sam, 3, 122	8	1:48.54	180,000
1993	Forever Whirl, 3, 122	A. Toribio	Boundlessly, 3, 120	Mighty Avanti, 3, 114	10	1:49.44	180,000
1992	Majestic Sweep, 3, 117	E. Fires	Technology, 3, 126	Always Silver, 3, 117	8	1:50.07	180,000
1991	Private Man, 3, 114	J. R. Velazquez	Richman, 3, 126	Shudanz, 3, 114	9	1:50.30	180,000
1990	Private School, 3, 120	J. Vasquez	Restless Con, 3, 123	Real Cash, 3, 123	15	1:51.20	180,000
1989	King Glorious, 3, 120	C. J. McCarron	Roi Danzig, 3, 114	Caesar, 3, 114	10	1:50.40	180,000
1988	Jim's Orbit, 3, 123	S. P. Romero	Primal, 3, 114	Intensive Command, 3, 114	8	1:50.60	150,000
1987	Lost Code, 3, 126	G. St. Leon	Proudest Duke, 3, 117	Homebuilder, 3, 114	9	1:51.60	150,000
1986	Broad Brush, 3, 126	G. L. Stevens	Bolshoi Boy, 3, 123	Forty Kings, 3, 114	9	1:51.20	150,000
1985	Skip Trial, 3, 114	J. Samyn	Encolure, 3, 123	Jacque l'Heureux, 3, 114	8	1:49.00	120,000
1984	At the Threshold, 3, 123	G. Patterson	Biloxi Indian, 3, 114	Perfect Player, 3, 114	7	1:49.60	120,000
1983	Pax Nobiscum, 3, 120	R. Platts	Bet Big, 3, 114	Fightin Hill, 3, 114	9	1:50.20	90,000
1982	Spanish Drums, 3, 123	J. Vasquez	Air Forbes Won, 3, 126	Lejoli, 3, 114	9	1:49.60	90,000
1981	Pass the Tab, 3, 120	A. Graell	Paristo, 3, 123	Classic Go Go, 3, 123	9	1:49.20	90,000
1980	Stone Manor, 3, 123	P. Day	Colonel Moran, 3, 123	Hillbizon, 3, 114	13	1:52.00	90,000
1979	Smarten, 3, 124	S. Maple	Bold Ruckus, 3, 115	Picturesque, 3, 122	12	**1:47.40**	90,000
1978	Special Honor, 3, 115	R. Breen	Batonnier, 3, 122	Star de Naskra, 3, 120	10	1:47.80	90,000
1977	Silver Series, 3, 122	L. Snyder	Cormorant, 3, 122	Pruneplum, 3, 115	12	1:49.20	90,000

Year	Winner	Jockey	Second	Third	Strs	Time	1st Purse
1976	Return of a Native, 3, 115	G. Patterson	Cojak, 3, 122	Dream 'n Be Lucky, 3, 115	14	1:49.80	$75,000
1975	Brent's Prince, 3, 115	B. R. Feliciano	Sylvan Place, 3, 112	Canvasser, 3, 115	11	1:49.40	66,780
1974	Stonewalk, 3, 120	M. A. Rivera	Better Arbitor, 3, 122	Sharp Gary, 3, 122	9	1:53.20	63,000
1973	Our Native, 3, 122	A. Rini	Hearts of Lettuce, 3, 112	Arbees Boy, 3, 115	12	1:50.20	63,882

Thistledown is located in North Randall, Ohio. Held at Chester Park 1876-'83. Held at Maple Heights 1924-'26. Held at Bainbridge Park 1928-'35. Held at Cranwood Park 1952. Held at Randall Park 1961-'62. Not held 1884-1923, 1927, 1933-'34, 1936-'51. 1 1/2 miles 1876-'83. 1 1/16 miles 1960-'64.

Old Hat Stakes

Grade 2 in 2008. Gulfstream Park, three-year-olds, fillies, 6 1/2 furlongs, dirt. Held January 12, 2008, with a gross value of $100,000. First held in 1976. First graded in 2005. Stakes record 1:15.87 (2008 Game Face).

Year	Winner	Jockey	Second	Third	Strs	Time	1st Purse
2008	Game Face, 3, 115	J. R. Velazquez	Melissa Jo, 3, 117	Orinoquia, 3, 115	9	**1:15.87**	$60,000
2007	Dream Rush, 3, 119	R. Bejarano	You Asked, 3, 117	Dreaming of Anna, 3, 121	6	1:16.60	60,000
2006	Misty Rosette, 3, 115	S. O. Madrid	Swap Fliparoo, 3, 119	Smart N Pretty, 3, 115	6	1:16.03	60,000
2005	Maddalena, 3, 115	J. R. Velazquez	Alfonsina, 3, 119	Holy Trinity, 3, 115	7	1:16.31	60,000
2004	Madcap Escapade, 3, 115	R. R. Douglas	Sweet Vision, 3, 115	Smokey Glacken, 3, 119	9	1:08.85	60,000
2003	House Party, 3, 115	J. A. Santos	Chimicurri, 3, 119	Glorious Miss, 3, 119	5	1:10.81	60,000
2002	A New Twist, 3, 115	E. S. Prado	Forest Heiress, 3, 119	French Satin, 3, 115	7	1:10.61	60,000
2000	Swept Away, 3, 112	E. Coa	Petite Deputy, 3, 113	Sabre Dance, 3, 118	10	1:09.96	45,000
1999	Belle's Appeal, 3, 114	R. Migliore	Extended Applause, 3, 112	Preciosa V., 3, 112	7	1:11.59	45,000
1998	Evening Hush, 3, 114	R. G. Davis	Cotton House Bay, 3, 116	Argos Appeal, 3, 116	7	1:10.63	45,000
1997	Cupids Revenge, 3, 112	E. Coa	Supah Syble, 3, 112	Witchful Thinking, 3, 116	6	1:09.47	45,000
1996	J J'sdream, 3, 116	M. E. Smith	Mindy Gayle, 3, 112	Nic's Halo, 3, 113	8	1:10.60	30,000
1995	Bluff's Dividend, 3, 116	J. A. Santos	Mackenzie Slew, 3, 114	Twist a Lime, 3, 112	9	1:10.82	30,000
1994	Pagofire, 3, 112	J. D. Bailey	Deaf Power, 3, 116	Vivance, 3, 113	11	1:10.32	30,000
1993	Sum Runner, 3, 114	E. Fires	Best in Sale, 3, 114	Hidden Fire, 3, 114	9	1:10.25	30,000
1992	Super Doer, 3, 114	R. R. Douglas	Ravensmoor, 3, 114	Miss Valid Pache, 3, 116	7	1:10.99	30,000
1991	My Own True Love, 3, 114	H. Castillo Jr.	Flashing Eyes, 3, 116	Parisian Flight, 3, 114	7	1:10.30	30,000
1990	dh-Sun Luck, 3, 112	M. A. Gonzalez		Miss Cox's Hat, 3, 115	9	1:12.00	14,000
	dh-Traki Traki, 3, 114	E. Fires					
1989	Surging, 3, 114	C. Perret	Royal Snub, 3, 121	Coax Chelsie, 3, 110	6	1:10.40	27,528
1988	On to Royalty, 3, 113	J. Vasquez	Willing'n Waiting, 3, 114	Level, 3, 112	9	1:11.40	28,848
1987	Sheer Ice, 5, 113	R. Woodhouse	Grand Creation, 5, 110	One Fine Lady, 5, 115	7	1:23.80	20,862
1986	Noranc, 3, 117	W. H. McCauley	Spirit of Fighter, 3, 114	Bespeak, 3, 112	15	1:11.00	31,776
1985	Glorious Glory, 3, 112	B. Zoppo-Bundy	Sheer Ice, 3, 116	Golden Silence, 3, 112	14	1:11.60	31,752
1984	Flip for Luck, 4, 114	G. St. Leon	Pretty as Patty, 4, 115	Amber's Desire, 4, 113	11	1:23.40	13,572
1983	Unaccompanied, 3, 112	R. Woodhouse	Lisa's Capital, 3, 114	Masked Romance, 3, 112	11	1:10.80	22,518
1981	Dame Mysterieuse, 3, 118	E. Maple	Masters Dream, 3, 112	Irish Joy, 3, 112	9	1:10.20	21,906
1976	Anne Campbell, 3, 114	M. Solomone	Veroom Maid, 3, 114	Jet Set Jennifer, 3, 113	8	1:09.80	9,960

Named for Stanley Conrad's 1964, '65 champion older female and '63, '65 Suwannee River H. winner Old Hat (1959 f. by Boston Doge). Grade 3 2005-'07. Not held 1977-'80, 1982, 2001. Dead heat for first 1990.

Orchid Handicap

Grade 3 in 2008. Gulfstream Park, four-year-olds and up, fillies and mares, 1 1/2 miles, turf. Held March 30, 2008, with a gross value of $150,000. First held in 1954. First graded in 1973. Stakes record 2:23.07 (2006 Honey Ryder).

Year	Winner	Jockey	Second	Third	Strs	Time	1st Purse
2008	Hostess, 5, 116	J. R. Velazquez	Mauralakana (Fr), 5, 120	Herboriste (GB), 5, 117	8	2:25.83	$90,000
2007	Safari Queen (Arg), 5, 117	C. P. DeCarlo	Almonsoon, 4, 113	La Dolce Vita, 5, 114	7	2:25.17	90,000
2006	Honey Ryder, 5, 120	J. A. Santos	Olaya, 4, 118	Noble Stella (Ger), 5, 116	8	**2:23.07**	90,000
2005	Honey Ryder, 4, 116	J. R. Velazquez	Ellieonthemarch, 4, 114	Pretty Jane, 4, 114	7	2:27.15	90,000
2004	Meridiana (Ger), 4, 114	E. S. Prado	Savedbythelight, 4, 114	Miss Hellie, 5, 114	10	2:26.99	120,000
2003	Tweedside, 5, 116	R. R. Douglas	San Dare, 5, 119	Hi Tech Honeycomb, 4, 115	7	2:32.36	120,000
2002	Julie Jalouse, 4, 114	J. A. Santos	Sweetest Thing, 4, 115	Refugee, 4, 110	9	2:25.89	120,000
2001	Innuendo (Ire), 6, 116	J. D. Bailey	Windsong, 4, 113	Aiglonne, 4, 114	4	2:25.24	120,000
2000	Lisieux Rose (Ire), 5, 114	J. A. Santos	Champagne Royal, 6, 114	Fly for Avie, 5, 114	10	2:25.64	120,000
1999	Coretta (Ire), 5, 118	J. A. Santos	Delilah (Ire), 5, 117	Almost Skint (Ire), 5, 113	11	2:23.85	120,000
1998	Colonial Play, 4, 113	R. G. Davis	Almost Skint (Ire), 4, 114	Gastronomical, 5, 113	11	2:24.75	120,000
1997	Golden Pond (Ire), 4, 116	W. H. McCauley	Tocopilla (Arg), 7, 115	Miss Caerleona (Fr), 5, 114	11	2:26.80	120,000
1996	Memories (Ire), 5, 114	J. A. Santos	Caromana, 5, 114	Curtain Raiser, 4, 113	11	2:31.51	120,000
1995	Exchange, 7, 120	L. A. Pincay Jr.	Market Booster, 6, 116	Northern Emerald, 5, 115	10	2:29.02	120,000
1994	Trampoli, 5, 121	M. E. Smith	Good Morning Smile, 6, 110	Northern Emerald, 4, 113	7	2:25.42	120,000
1993	Fairy Garden, 5, 115	W. S. Ramos	Rougeur, 4, 115	Trampoli, 4, 113	14	2:25.79	120,000
1992	Crockadore, 5, 115	M. E. Smith	Indian Fashion, 5, 112	Sardaniya (Ire), 4, 114	10	2:28.32	120,000
1991	Star Standing, 4, 114	C. W. Antley	Coolawin, 5, 118	Peinture Bleue, 4, 119	9	2:25.02	120,000
1990	Coolawin, 4, 112	J. D. Bailey	Laugh and Be Merry, 5, 113	Gaily Gaily (Ire), 7, 121	10	2:24.20	120,000
1989	Gaily Gaily (Ire), 6, 110	J. A. Krone	Anka Germania (Ire), 7, 120	Laugh and Be Merry, 4, 110	13	2:26.80	120,000
1988	Beauty Cream, 5, 115	P. Day	Ladanum, 4, 112	Green Oasis (Fr), 6, 112	14	2:28.40	120,000
1987	Anka Germania (Ire), 5, 117	C. Perret	Singular Bequest, 4, 116	Ivor's Image, 4, 119	14	2:31.40	90,000
1986	Videogenic, 4, 121	R. G. Davis	Powder Break, 5, 118	Devalois (Fr), 4, 117	14	2:27.20	118,440
1985	Pretty Perfect, 5, 120	G. Gallitano	Early Lunch, 4, 113	Trinado, 4, 113	13	1:41.60	61,980
	Aspen Rose, 5, 116	J. Velasquez	Over Your Shoulder, 4, 113	Dictina (Fr), 4, 117	14	1:42.00	63,180
1984	Sabin, 4, 125	E. Maple	Jubilous, 4, 114	Sulemeif, 4, 115	7	1:41.40	70,680

Racing — Graded Stakes

Year	Winner	Jockey	Second	Third	Strs	Time	1st Purse
1983	**Sweetest Chant**, 5, 116	E. Fires	Betty Money, 4, 114	Norsan, 4, 115	8	1:43.60	$53,040
	Larida, 4, 118	E. Maple	Syrianna, 4, 116	Promising Native, 4, 115	8	1:44.80	53,640
1982	**Blush**, 4, 112	J. Vasquez	Pine Flower, 4, 114	Honey Fox, 5, 125	12	1:41.00	76,500
1981	**Honey Fox**, 4, 115	J. Vasquez	The Very One, 6, 125	Solo Haina, 5, 114	16	1:41.20	88,530
1980	**Just a Game (Ire)**, 4, 119	D. Brumfield	La Soufriere, 5, 115	La Rouquine (GB), 4, 114	10	1:40.40	80,340
1979	**Sans Arc**, 5, 116	E. Fires	‡Terpsichorist, 4, 122	Time for Pleasure, 5, 119	13	1:41.40	86,093
1978	**Time for Pleasure**, 4, 115	T. Barrow	Late Bloomer, 4, 113	Rich Soil, 4, 116	11	1:41.00	37,800
1977	**Copano**, 5, 122	M. Solomone	Jabot, 5, 117	Carolina Moon, 5, 114	13	1:41.40	43,500
1976	***Deesse Du Val**, 5, 116	C. H. Marquez	Redundancy, 5, 120	K D Princess, 5, 110	12	1:41.80	28,785
1975	***Protectora**, 6, 114	H. Gustines	Zippy Do, 6, 118	Lorraine Edna, 5, 116	7	1:41.20	26,100
1974	**Dogtooth Violet**, 4, 113	D. Brumfield	Dove Creek Lady, 4, 124	Shearwater, 5, 115	8	1:41.00	39,420
1973	**Deb Marion**, 3, 106	F. Iannelli	Tico's Donna, 5, 113	Barely Even, 4, 125	9	1:42.60	27,240

James Donn Sr., Gulfstream Park founder, was a world-renowned florist who developed a special breed of orchid in honor of his wife. Grade 2 1981-2005. Orchid S. 1954-'66. Not held 1955-'64. 6 furlongs 1954. 1¹⁄₁₆ miles 1965-'66, 1969-'85. 1 mile 1967-'68. About 1¹⁄₂ miles 1992. Dirt 1954-'66, 1983-'84, 2003. Originally scheduled at about 1¹⁄₂ miles on turf 2003. Three-year-olds 1954-'66. Three-year-olds and up 1967-2006. Two divisions 1983, 1985. ‡Time for Pleasure finished second, DQ to third, 1979. Course record 1992, 2006.

Ouija Board Distaff Handicap

Grade 3 in 2008. Lone Star Park, three-year-olds and up, fillies and mares, 1 mile, turf. Held May 26, 2008, with a gross value of $200,000. First held in 1999. First graded in 2003. Stakes record 1:35.82 (2008 Brownie Points).

Year	Winner	Jockey	Second	Third	Strs	Time	1st Purse
2008	**Brownie Points**, 5, 118	L. S. Quinonez	Tears I Cry, 4, 115	Costume (GB), 4, 119	11	**1:35.82**	$120,000
2007	**Lady of Venice (Fr)**, 4, 118	G. K. Gomez	Brownie Points, 4, 118	Rich Fantasy, 4, 117	8	1:38.32	120,000
2006	**Sweet Talker**, 4, 120	R. A. Dominguez	Joint Aspiration (GB), 4, 115	Stretching, 4, 116	10	1:38.66	120,000
2005	**Katdogawn (GB)**, 5, 120	J. D. Bailey	Valentine Dancer, 5, 120	Voz De Colegiala (Chi), 6, 115	11	1:39.53	120,000
2004	**Academic Angel**, 5, 117	S. J. Sellers	Janeian (NZ), 6, 119	Katdogawn (GB), 4, 120	12	1:35.98	120,000
2003	**Eagle Lake**, 5, 116	G. Melancon	Little Treasure (Fr), 4, 117	Magic Mission (GB), 5, 116	9	1:43.02	120,000
2002	**Queen of Wilshire**, 6, 117	D. R. Flores	Pleasant State, 7, 115	Blushing Bride (GB), 4, 115	12	1:38.96	120,000
2001	**Voladora**, 6, 114	M. C. Berry	Dyna Likes Bingo, 6, 109	Iftiraas (GB), 4, 118	10	1:42.23	120,000
2000	**Mumtaz (Fr)**, 4, 113	V. Espinoza	Evening Promise (GB), 4, 117	Really Polish, 5, 114	9	1:37.28	120,000
1999	**Heritage of Gold**, 4, 114	C. T. Lambert	Red Cat, 4, 116	Nalynn, 5, 114	10	1:37.75	90,000

Named for Lord Derby's 2004, '06 European Horse of the Year, '04, '06 champion turf female, and '04 (at Lone Star), '06 Breeders' Cup Filly and Mare Turf (G1) winner Ouija Board (GB) (2001 f. by Cape Cross [Ire]); Ouija Board is one of only two horses to win a Breeders' Cup race in non-consecutive years. Formerly sponsored by Bill Casner's and Kenny Troutt's WinStar Farm of Versailles, Kentucky 2000-'06. Formerly sponsored by Prestonwood Farm (predecessor of WinStar Farm) of Versailles 1999. Prestonwood H. 1999. WinStar Distaff H. 2000-'06.

Pacific Classic Stakes

Grade 1 in 2008. Del Mar, three-year-olds and up, 1¼ miles, all weather. Held August 19, 2007, with a gross value of $1,000,000. First held in 1991. First graded in 1993. Stakes record 1:59.11 (2003 Candy Ride [Arg]).

Year	Winner	Jockey	Second	Third	Strs	Time	1st Purse
2007	**Student Council**, 5, 124	R. Migliore	Awesome Gem, 4, 124	Hello Sunday (Fr), 4, 124	12	2:07.29	$600,000
2006	**Lava Man**, 5, 124	C. S. Nakatani	Good Reward, 5, 124	Super Frolic, 6, 124	8	2:01.62	600,000
2005	**Borrego**, 4, 124	G. K. Gomez	Perfect Drift, 6, 124	Lava Man, 4, 124	11	2:00.71	600,000
2004	**Pleasantly Perfect**, 6, 124	J. D. Bailey	Perfect Drift, 5, 124	Total Impact (Chi), 6, 124	8	2:01.17	600,000
2003	**Candy Ride (Arg)**, 4, 124	J. A. Krone	Medaglia d'Oro, 4, 124	Fleetstreet Dancer, 5, 124	4	**1:59.11**	600,000
2002	**Came Home**, 3, 117	M. E. Smith	Momentum, 4, 124	Milwaukee Brew, 5, 124	14	2:01.45	600,000
2001	**Skimming**, 5, 124	G. K. Gomez	Dixie Dot Com, 6, 124	Dig for It, 6, 124	6	1:59.96	600,000
2000	**Skimming**, 4, 124	G. K. Gomez	Tiznow, 3, 117	Ecton Park, 4, 124	7	2:01.22	600,000
1999	**General Challenge**, 3, 117	D. R. Flores	River Keen (Ire), 7, 124	Barter Town, 4, 124	8	2:00.57	700,000
1998	**Free House**, 4, 124	C. J. McCarron	Gentlemen (Arg), 6, 124	Pacificbounty, 4, 124	9	2:00.29	600,000
1997	**Gentlemen (Arg)**, 5, 124	G. L. Stevens	Siphon (Brz), 6, 124	Crafty Friend, 4, 124	5	2:00.56	600,000
1996	**Dare and Go**, 5, 124	A. O. Solis	Cigar, 6, 124	Siphon (Brz), 5, 124	6	1:59.85	600,000
1995	**Tinners Way**, 5, 124	E. Delahoussaye	Soul of the Matter, 4, 124	Blumin Affair, 4, 124	6	1:59.63	550,000
1994	**Tinners Way**, 4, 124	E. Delahoussaye	Best Pal, 6, 124	Dramatic Gold, 3, 117	9	1:59.43	550,000
1993	**Bertrando**, 4, 124	G. L. Stevens	Missionary Ridge (GB), 6, 124	Best Pal, 5, 124	7	1:59.55	550,000
1992	**Missionary Ridge (GB)**, 5, 124	K. Desormeaux	Defensive Play, 4, 124	Claret (Ire), 4, 124	7	2:00.87	550,000
1991	**Best Pal**, 3, 116	P. A. Valenzuela	Twilight Agenda, 5, 124	Unbridled, 4, 124	8	1:59.86	550,000

Named for the Pacific Ocean, where Del Mar's "turf meets the surf." Dirt 1991-2006. Track record 1993-'94, 2003.

Palm Beach Handicap — *See* Bulleit Bourbon Palm Beach Handicap

Palomar Handicap

Grade 2 in 2008. Del Mar, three-year-olds and up, fillies and mares, 1¹⁄₁₆ miles, turf. Held September 1, 2007, with a gross value of $222,000. First held in 1945. First graded in 1981. Stakes record 1:39.67 (2006 Mea Domina).

Year	Winner	Jockey	Second	Third	Strs	Time	1st Purse
2007	**Precious Kitten**, 4, 122	J. R. Leparoux	Black Mamba (NZ), 4, 112	Kris' Sis, 4, 115	9	1:40.42	$150,000
2006	**Mea Domina**, 5, 119	T. Baze	Three Degrees (Ire), 4, 116	Island Fashion, 6, 116	10	**1:39.67**	120,000
2005	**Intercontinental (GB)**, 5, 122	J. D. Bailey	Amorama (Fr), 4, 119	Ticker Tape (GB), 4, 118	5	1:39.84	120,000
2004	**Etoile Montante**, 4, 120	J. Valdivia Jr.	Katdogawn (GB), 4, 117	Tangle (Ire), 4, 117	7	1:40.59	120,000

Racing — Graded Stakes

Year	Winner	Jockey	Second	Third	Strs	Time	1st Purse
2003	Spring Star (Fr), 4, 116	A. O. Solis	Magic Mission (GB), 5, 117	Garden in the Rain (Fr), 6, 114	5	1:40.78	$120,000
2002	Voodoo Dancer, 4, 120	K. Desormeaux	I'm the Business (NZ), 5, 114	Skywriting, 4, 114	7	1:41.56	90,000
2001	Tranquility Lake, 6, 123	E. Delahoussaye	La Ronge, 4, 116	Al Desima (GB), 4, 113	6	1:41.94	90,000
2000	Tranquility Lake, 5, 121	E. Delahoussaye	Tout Charmant, 4, 121	Miss of Wales (Chi), 5, 114	7	1:41.01	82,170
1999	Happyanunoit (NZ), 4, 113	B. Blanc	Tuzla (Fr), 5, 123	Isle de France, 4, 118	6	1:41.28	80,520
1998	Tuzla (Fr), 4, 117	C. S. Nakatani	Ecoute, 5, 114	Call Me (GB), 5, 116	7	1:42.28	80,970
1997	Blushing Heiress, 5, 117	C. J. McCarron	Traces of Gold, 5, 115	Listening, 4, 120	6	1:43.32	83,200
1996	Yearly Tour, 5, 116	C. J. McCarron	Slewvera, 4, 115	Real Connection, 5, 114	8	1:42.56	81,350
1995	Morgana, 4, 118	G. L. Stevens	Yearly Tour, 4, 118	Lady Affirmed, 4, 117	7	1:42.41	74,450
1994	Shir Dar (Fr), 4, 114	C. S. Nakatani	Baby Diamonds, 3, 110	Prying (Arg), 6, 117	7	1:42.95	63,600
1993	Heart of Joy, 6, 119	D. R. Flores	Kalita Melody (GB), 5, 114	Amal Hayati, 3, 114	8	1:42.07	63,000
1992	Super Staff, 4, 114	C. J. McCarron	Odalea (Arg), 6, 114	Only Yours (GB), 4, 115	10	1:42.20	64,900
1991	Guiza, 4, 114	G. L. Stevens	Agirlfromars, 5, 114	Run to Jenny (Ire), 5, 113	8	1:42.11	49,300
	Somethingmerry, 4, 117	L. A. Pincay Jr.	Countus In, 6, 117	Sweet Roberta (Fr), 7, 115	7	1:41.84	48,800
1990	Jabalina Brown (Arg), 5, 112	J. A. Garcia	Stylish Star, 4, 116	Nikishka, 5, 117	8	1:42.60	64,200
1989	Claire Marine (Ire), 4, 122	R. G. Davis	Galunpe (Ire), 6, 118	Daring Doone (GB), 6, 118	8	1:43.20	64,800
1988	Chapel of Dreams, 4, 117	E. Delahoussaye	Short Sleeves (GB), 6, 121	Davie's Lamb, 4, 117	7	1:42.60	78,000
1987	Festivity, 4, 115	A. O. Solis	Adorable Micol, 4, 117	Secuencia (Chi), 5, 117	9	1:35.80	64,850
1986	Aberuschka (Ire), 4, 118	P. A. Valenzuela	Sauna (Aus), 5, 118	Fran's Valentine, 4, 119	9	1:34.40	62,750
1985	Capichi, 5, 116	R. A. Baze	L'Attrayante (Fr), 5, 119	Gala Event (Ire), 4, 115	8	1:35.20	50,150
1984	‡Moment to Buy, 3, 115	T. M. Chapman	L'Attrayante (Fr), 4, 120	Royal Heroine (Ire), 4, 125	8	1:35.20	50,550
1983	Triple Tipple, 4, 118	C. J. McCarron	Castilla, 4, 121	First Advance, 4, 115	10	1:35.60	52,050
1982	Northern Fable, 4, 114	S. Hawley	Sangue (Ire), 4, 114	Princess Gayle (Ire), 4, 116	8	1:35.20	33,500
	Star Pastures (GB), 4, 117	W. Shoemaker	Honey Fox, 5, 122	Cannon Boy, 5, 111	9	1:35.40	34,000
1981	Kilijaro (Ire), 5, 129	M. Castaneda	Lisawan, 4, 115	Satin Ribera, 4, 118	9	1:35.40	40,700
1980	A Thousand Stars, 5, 115	E. Delahoussaye	Wishing Well, 5, 121	Devon Ditty (GB), 4, 120	9	1:34.80	34,150
1979	More So (Ire), 4, 115	W. Shoemaker	Giggling Girl, 5, 119	Wishing Well, 4, 118	9	1:35.40	34,150
1978	Drama Critic, 4, 115	D. Pierce	Afifa, 4, 119	Fact (Arg), 5, 115	9	1:36.40	26,550
1977	Dancing Femme, 4, 120	D. Pierce	Swingtime, 5, 121	Dacani (Ire), 4, 115	12	1:35.60	17,250
1976	Just a Kick, 4, 120	L. A. Pincay Jr.	Our First Delight, 4, 114	Effusive, 5, 113	5	1:29.40	15,900
1975	Modus Vivendi, 4, 122	F. Toro	Move Abroad, 4, 113	*Tizna, 6, 124	10	1:28.80	14,100
1974	Sphere, 4, 114	S. Valdez	Lt.'s Joy, 4, 121	Modus Vivendi, 3, 122	9	1:28.40	14,050
1973	Meilleur, 3, 114	D. Pierce	Lady Debbie, 5, 116	Probation, 4, 113	9	1:28.80	10,775
	Belle Marie, 3, 114	W. Shoemaker	Best Go, 5, 115	Chargerette, 4, 116	5	1:28.80	9,975

Named for Palomar and Mt. Palomar, California, located near San Diego; Mt. Palomar was once the site of the world's largest telescope. Grade 3 1981-'84, 1997-2000. Palomar Breeders' Cup H. 2003-'06. 6 furlongs 1945-'69. 7½ furlongs 1970-'76. 1 mile 1977-'87. Dirt 1945-'69. Two divisions 1973, '82, '91. ‡Royal Heroine (Ire) finished first, DQ to third, 1984. Course record 2006.

Palos Verdes Handicap

Grade 2 in 2008. Santa Anita Park, four-year-olds and up, 6 furlongs, all weather. Held January 21, 2008, with a gross value of $150,000. First held in 1951. First graded in 1973. Stakes record 1:06.67 (2008 In Summation).

Year	Winner	Jockey	Second	Third	Strs	Time	1st Purse
2008	In Summation, 5, 122	R. Bejarano	Barbecue Eddie, 4, 116	Surf Cat, 6, 120	7	**1:06.67**	$90,000
2007	Friendly Island, 6, 118	G. K. Gomez	Harvard Avenue, 6, 118	Limited Creole, 4, 111	4	1:08.95	90,000
2006	Major Success, 5, 114	T. Baze	Jet West, 5, 118	Attila's Storm, 4, 119	7	1:09.23	90,000
2005	Saint Afleet, 4, 117	P. A. Valenzuela	Hombre Rapido, 8, 116	Bluesthestandard, 8, 116	8	1:09.15	90,000
2004	Bluesthestandard, 7, 117	M. E. Smith	Marino Marini, 4, 115	Our New Recruit, 5, 114	7	1:08.13	90,000
2003	Avanzado (Arg), 6, 116	T. Baze	Mellow Fellow, 8, 117	Disturbingthepeace, 5, 120	6	1:07.85	90,000
2002	Snow Ridge, 4, 116	M. E. Smith	Squirtle Squirt, 4, 122	Ceeband, 5, 117	7	1:07.70	90,000
2001	Men's Exclusive, 8, 116	L. A. Pincay Jr.	Big Jag, 8, 120	Freespool, 5, 116	6	1:08.33	120,000
2000	Kona Gold, 6, 121	A. O. Solis	Big Jag, 7, 121	Freespool, 4, 115	8	1:08.85	120,000
1999	Big Jag, 6, 116	J. Valdivia Jr.	Kona Gold, 5, 121	Swiss Yodeler, 5, 114	5	1:08.05	120,000
1998	Funontherun, 4, 113	G. F. Almeida	Red, 4, 116	Elmhurst, 8, 119	9	1:08.93	120,000
1997	High Stakes Player, 5, 118	C. S. Nakatani	Rotsaluck, 6, 114	Larry the Legend, 5, 116	7	1:08.44	131,600
1996	Lit de Justice, 6, 122	E. Delahoussaye	Siphon (Brz), 5, 119	Lakota Brave, 7, 115	8	1:08.88	135,100
1995	D'Hallevant, 5, 117	C. S. Nakatani	Cardmania, 9, 120	Subtle Trouble, 4, 115	10	1:08.44	94,400
1994	Concept Win, 4, 115	G. L. Stevens	J. F. Williams, 5, 117	Scherando, 5, 116	6	1:07.71	62,100
1993	Music Merci, 7, 114	D. R. Flores	Star of the Crop, 4, 119	Cardmania, 7, 117	9	1:08.82	63,700
1992	Individualist, 5, 117	L. A. Pincay Jr.	High Energy, 5, 114	Rushmore, 5, 114	9	1:08.66	65,600
1990	Frost Free, 5, 119	C. J. McCarron	Valiant Pete, 4, 117	Kipper Kelly, 3, 112	5	1:08.60	61,400
1989	Sunny Blossom, 4, 115	G. L. Stevens	Olympic Prospect, 5, 123	Sam Who, 4, 122	6	1:07.20	62,400
1988	On the Line, 4, 124	G. L. Stevens	Claim, 3, 118	Basic Rate, 3, 115	6	1:07.60	62,700
1987	High Brite, 3, 116	G. L. Stevens	Hilco Scamper, 4, 117	Zany Tactics, 6, 122	6	1:09.00	62,500
1986	Bedside Promise, 4, 123	G. L. Stevens	Bolder Than Bold, 4, 116	Rocky Marriage, 6, 115	6	1:08.40	60,000
1985	Phone Trick, 3, 117	L. A. Pincay Jr.	Five North, 4, 112	Debonaire Junior, 4, 123	6	1:08.00	50,150
1984	Debonaire Junior, 3, 120	C. J. McCarron	Charging Falls, 3, 112	Premiership, 4, 117	7	1:10.20	51,700
1983	Fighting Fit, 4, 122	E. Delahoussaye	Expressman, 3, 115	Gemini Dreamer, 3, 115	6	1:09.00	38,150
1982	Chinook Pass, 3, 120	L. A. Pincay Jr.	General Jimmy, 4, 113	Unpredictable, 3, 122	8	1:07.60	40,050
1981	I'm Smokin, 5, 119	P. A. Valenzuela	To B. Or Not, 5, 121	Solo Guy, 3, 119	7	1:08.00	39,200
1980	To B. Or Not, 4, 121	M. Castaneda	Unalakleet, 3, 115	Syncopate, 5, 123	9	1:08.20	34,000
1979	Beau's Eagle, 3, 122	S. Hawley	Always Gallant, 5, 124	‡Charley Sutton, 5, 115	7	1:10.00	32,750
1978	Little Reb, 3, 116	F. Olivares	Crash Program, 3, 112	Bad 'n Big, 4, 125	9	1:08.60	33,900
1977	Impressive Luck, 4, 119	S. Hawley	Maheras, 4, 120	Current Concept, 3, 117	6	1:10.40	26,000

Year	Winner	Jockey	Second	Third	Strs	Time	1st Purse
1976	Maheras, 3, 119	L. A. Pincay Jr.	Sure Fire, 3, 116	Ancient Title, 6, 126	13	1:08.60	$29,400
1975	Messenger of Song, 3, 125	J. Lambert	Willmar, 7, 115	Rise High, 5, 118	6	1:08.60	19,800
1974	Ancient Title, 4, 126	L. A. Pincay Jr.	Princely Native, 3, 116	King of the Blues, 5, 113	8	1:08.80	20,900
1973	Woodland Pines, 4, 115	D. Pierce	Tragic Isle, 4, 117	Ancient Title, 3, 122	8	1:09.00	20,800

Named for the 1824 California land grant named Los Palos Verdes Ranchos; palos verdes means "green trees." Grade 3 1973-'74, 1988-'97. Not held 1969-'70, 1991. Dirt 1951-2007. Three-year-olds and up 1951-'66, 1971 (January). Two-year-olds and up 1967-'68, 1971 (December) 1972-'89. ‡Grand Alliance finished third, DQ to fourth, 1979.

Pan American Handicap

Grade 3 in 2008. Gulfstream Park, four-year-olds and up, 1½ miles, turf. Held April 5, 2008, with a gross value of $150,000. First held in 1962. First graded in 1973. Stakes record 2:23.15 (1999 Unite's Big Red).

Year	Winner	Jockey	Second	Third	Strs	Time	1st Purse
2008	Presious Passion, 5, 117	A. Smith	Drilling for Oil, 5, 116	Interpatation, 6, 116	8	2:26.15	$90,000
2007	Jambalaya, 5, 120	J. Castellano	Hotstufanthensome, 7, 117	Fri Guy, 4, 114	11	2:24.98	90,000
2006	Silver Whistle, 4, 115	E. S. Prado	Ramazutti, 4, 113	Go Deputy, 6, 118	8	2:24.35	90,000
2005	Navesink River, 4, 114	J. R. Velazquez	Quest Star, 6, 114	Deputy Lad, 5, 115	8	2:25.95	90,000
2004	Quest Star, 5, 114	P. Day	Request for Parole, 5, 115	Megantic, 6, 112	7	2:26.46	120,000
2003	Quest Star, 4, 113	E. S. Prado	Man From Wicklow, 6, 122	Reduit (GB), 5, 114	9	2:28.45	120,000
2002	Deeliteful Irving, 4, 113	C. P. DeCarlo	Cetewayo, 8, 118	Mr. Livingston, 5, 114	9	2:24.14	120,000
2001	Whata Brainstorm, 4, 114	J. R. Velazquez	Subtle Power (Ire), 4, 115	Craigsteel (GB), 6, 114	7	2:23.75	150,000
2000	Buck's Boy, 7, 122	E. S. Prado	Thesaurus, 6, 113	‡Epistolaire (Ire), 5, 114	7	2:24.80	150,000
1999	Unite's Big Red, 5, 114	M. E. Smith	African Dancer, 7, 116	Panama City, 5, 116	7	**2:23.15**	150,000
1998	Buck's Boy, 5, 115	E. Fires	African Dancer, 6, 115	Royal Strand (Ire), 4, 114	9	2:23.43	150,000
1997	Flag Down, 7, 117	J. A. Santos	Lassigny, 6, 117	Awad, 7, 117	6	2:27.00	180,000
1996	Celtic Arms (Fr), 5, 115	M. E. Smith	Broadway Flyer, 5, 116	Flag Down, 6, 117	7	2:25.71	180,000
1995	Awad, 5, 114	E. Maple	Misil, 7, 120	Frenchpark (GB), 5, 117	9	2:29.44	180,000
1994	Fraise, 6, 124	M. E. Smith	Summer Ensign, 5, 113	†Fairy Garden, 6, 115	10	2:24.65	180,000
1993	Fraise, 5, 124	P. A. Valenzuela	Stagecraft (GB), 6, 117	Futurist, 5, 114	8	2:32.86	180,000
1992	Wall Street Dancer, 4, 114	J. Velasquez	†Passagere du Soir (GB), 5, 116	Missionary Ridge (GB), 5, 115	14	2:25.53	210,000
1991	Phantom Breeze (Ire), 5, 116	J. A. Krone	Dr. Root, 4, 114	Runaway Raja, 5, 111	11	2:29.55	180,000
1990	My Big Boy, 7, 112	H. Castillo Jr.	Marksmanship, 5, 113	Turfah, 7, 115	12	2:29.20	180,000
1989	Mi Selecto, 4, 114	J. A. Santos	Pay the Butler, 5, 121	Fabulous Indian, 4, 112	8	2:01.60	180,000
1988	†Carotene, 5, 115	D. J. Seymour	†Ladanum, 4, 110	Salem Drive, 6, 117	13	2:25.00	180,000
1987	Iroko (GB), 5, 112	E. Fires	Akabir, 6, 113	Glaros (Fr), 5, 112	7	2:26.40	150,000
1986	†Powder Break, 5, 112	S. B. Soto	Uptown Swell, 4, 116	Flying Pidgeon, 5, 118	11	2:25.00	180,000
1985	Selous Scout, 4, 112	R. Platts	Norclin, 5, 111	Nassipour, 5, 115	13	2:25.20	185,280
1984	Tonzarun, 6, 112	W. H. McCauley	Ayman, 4, 114	Nassipour, 4, 110	9	2:26.80	109,275
1983	Highland Blade, 5, 121	J. Vasquez	Tonzarun, 5, 117	Dhausli (Fr), 6, 113	10	2:29.20	80,225
	Field Cat, 6, 110	J. Samyn	Pin Puller, 4, 112	Santo's Joe, 6, 109	11	2:29.60	82,095
1982	Robsphere, 5, 117	J. Velasquez	Come Rain Or Shine, 5, 110	The Bart, 6, 126	16	2:26.00	102,150
1981	†Little Bonny (Ire), 4, 114	E. Maple	Lobsang (Ire), 5, 115	Buckpoint (Fr), 5, 124	12	2:32.40	121,030
1980	†Flitalong, 4, 110	R. I. Encinas	Morning Frolic, 5, 119	Novel Notion, 5, 117	12	2:28.40	100,000
1979	Noble Dancer (GB), 7, 129	J. Vasquez	Fleet Gar, 4, 116	†Warfever (Fr), 4, 113	9	2:25.20	100,000
1978	Bowl Game, 4, 117	J. Vasquez	That's a Nice, 4, 116	Court Open, 4, 112	10	2:30.20	100,000
1977	Gravelines (Fr), 5, 124	J. D. Bailey	Le Cypriote, 5, 110	Gay Jitterbug, 4, 124	9	2:24.80	80,400
1976	Improviser, 4, 114	J. Cruguet	Green Room, 6, 109	Pampered Jabneh, 6, 113	13	2:26.60	86,880
1975	Buffalo Lark, 5, 120	L. Snyder	London Company, 5, 123	Duke Tom, 5, 115	6	2:27.60	84,120
1974	London Company, 4, 119	A. T. Cordero Jr.	Outdoors, 5, 112	*Bush Fleet, 5, 113	12	2:26.40	84,720
1973	Lord Vancouver, 5, 112	W. Blum	Life Cycle, 4, 118	Windtex, 4, 116	11	2:26.60	83,520

Named in honor of the multicultural heritage of South Florida's residents. Formerly sponsored by the Bulleit Distilling Co. of Lawrenceburg, Kentucky 2007. Formerly sponsored by the Crown Royal Co. of Stamford, Connecticut 1996. Grade 1 1983-'89. Grade 2 1973-'82, 1990-2005. Pan American H. 1962-'95, 1997-2006. Crown Royal Pan American H. 1996. 1⅛ miles 1989. About 1½ miles 1993, 2003. Dirt 1962-'64, 1975, 1989. Three-year-olds and up 1962-2006. Two divisions 1983. ‡Beautiful Dancer finished third, DQ to sixth, 2000. Track record 1975. Course record 1999. †Denotes female.

Pat O'Brien Handicap

Grade 2 in 2008. Del Mar, three-year-olds and up, 7 furlongs, all weather. Held August 19, 2007, with a gross value of $300,000. First held in 1986. First graded in 1994. Stakes record 1:20.06 (1995 Lit de Justice).

Year	Winner	Jockey	Second	Third	Strs	Time	1st Purse
2007	Greg's Gold, 6, 117	V. Espinoza	Surf Cat, 5, 122	Soul City Slew, 4, 113	6	1:23.95	$180,000
2006	Siren Lure, 5, 122	A. O. Solis	Pure as Gold, 4, 116	Areyoutalkintome, 5, 114	7	1:21.89	180,000
2005	Imperialism, 4, 117	V. Espinoza	Gotaghostofachance, 4, 114	Taste of Paradise, 6, 115	8	1:21.70	180,000
2004	Kela, 6, 116	T. Baze	Domestic Dispute, 4, 116	Pico Central (Brz), 5, 122	5	1:21.17	120,000
2003	Disturbingthepeace, 5, 116	V. Espinoza	Rushin' to Altar, 4, 117	Full Moon Madness, 8, 119	10	1:21.53	90,000
2002	Disturbingthepeace, 4, 119	V. Espinoza	Hot Market, 4, 115	I Love Silver, 4, 117	5	1:21.89	90,000
2001	El Corredor, 4, 119	V. Espinoza	Swept Overboard, 4, 117	Ceeband, 4, 114	7	1:20.42	90,000
2000	Love That Red, 4, 118	C. S. Nakatani	Cliquot, 4, 117	Son of a Pistol, 8, 117	5	1:21.89	90,000
1999	Regal Thunder, 5, 116	C. W. Antley	Christmas Boy, 6, 118	Bet On Sunshine, 7, 116	9	1:21.13	90,000
1998	Old Topper, 3, 116	E. Delahoussaye	Son of a Pistol, 6, 123	Uncaged Fury, 7, 115	5	1:21.51	95,220
1997	Tres Paraiso, 5, 116	G. L. Stevens	High Stakes Player, 5, 119	Gold Land, 6, 114	7	1:21.45	68,200
1996	Alphabet Soup, 5, 118	C. W. Antley	Boundless Moment, 4, 116	Ice de Justice, 6, 123	8	1:20.79	65,450
1995	Lit de Justice, 5, 118	C. S. Nakatani	D'Hallevant, 5, 117	Pembroke, 5, 119	7	**1:20.06**	60,400

Year	Winner	Jockey	Second	Third	Strs	Time	1st Purse
1994	D'Hallevant, 4, 115	C. S. Nakatani	Minjinsky, 4, 115	J. F. Williams, 5, 117	5	1:20.25	$59,725
1993	Slerp, 4, 117	A. D. Lopez	Portoferraio (Arg), 5, 114	Cardmania, 7, 116	7	1:21.36	47,850
1992	Light of Morn, 6, 116	E. Delahoussaye	Three Peat, 3, 116	Slerp, 3, 114	12	1:20.65	66,025
1991	Bruho, 5, 118	C. S. Nakatani	Burn Annie, 6, 115	Due to the King, 4, 116	5	1:21.45	46,350
1990	Sensational Star, 6, 116	R. Q. Meza	Frost Free, 5, 116	Earn Your Stripes, 6, 116	9	1:20.60	49,275
1989	Olympic Native, 4, 116	R. G. Davis	On the Line, 5, 126	Sam Who, 4, 121	4	1:20.20	44,850
1988	Sebrof, 4, 116	G. L. Stevens	Synastry, 5, 116	Epidaurus, 6, 119	9	1:20.40	39,350
1987	Zany Tactics, 6, 123	J. L. Kaenel	Bold Smoocher, 5, 114	Bolder Than Bold, 5, 120	7	1:21.20	31,750
1986	Bold Brawley, 3, 115	P. A. Valenzuela	First Norman, 4, 115	American Legion, 6, 121	5	1:20.40	30,850

Named in honor of actor Pat O'Brien (1899-1983), co-founder with Bing Crosby of the Del Mar Turf Club. Grade 3 1994-'98. Pat O'Brien Breeders' Cup H. 1990-'95, 2004-'06. Dirt 1986-2006.

Pegasus Stakes

Grade 3 in 2008. Monmouth Park, three-year-olds, 1 1/8 miles, dirt. Held October 27, 2007, with a gross value of $250,000. First held in 1980. First graded in 1983. Stakes record 1:45.50 (1999 Forty One Carats).

Year	Winner	Jockey	Second	Third	Strs	Time	1st Purse
2007	Actin Good, 3, 119	C. H. Velasquez	Now a Victor, 3, 119	Slew's Tizzy, 3, 122	5	1:51.54	$150,000
2006	Diamond Stripes, 3, 118	E. S. Prado	On Board Again, 3, 118	Hesanoldsalt, 3, 118	8	1:47.30	150,000
2005	Magna Graduate, 3, 120	J. R. Velazquez	Crown Point, 3, 118	Network, 3, 120	8	1:47.47	150,000
2004	Pies Prospect, 3, 118	E. S. Prado	Eddington, 3, 118	Zakocity, 3, 118	8	1:48.57	180,000
2002	Regal Sanction, 3, 115	J. A. Santos	No Parole, 3, 117	This Guns for Hire, 3, 115	6	1:49.87	210,000
2001	Volponi, 3, 114	S. Bridgmohan	Burning Roma, 3, 119	Giant Gentleman, 3, 116	6	1:46.55	150,000
2000	Kiss a Native, 3, 119	M. K. Walls	Cool N Collective, 3, 115	Pine Dance, 3, 121	7	1:48.33	150,000
1999	Forty One Carats, 3, 120	J. F. Chavez	Unbridled Jet, 3, 116	Talk's Cheap, 3, 118	6	**1:45.50**	240,000
1998	Tomorrows Cat, 3, 113	J. Bravo	Limit Out, 3, 115	Comic Strip, 3, 119	6	1:46.95	300,000
1997	Behrens, 3, 117	J. D. Bailey	Anet, 3, 120	Frisk Me Now, 3, 119	4	1:46.61	600,000
1996	Allied Forces, 3, 116	R. Migliore	Lite Approval, 3, 112	Defacto, 3, 116	5	1:47.19	120,000
1995	Flying Chevron, 3, 112	R. G. Davis	Da Hoss, 3, 122	Ghostly Moves, 3, 113	4	1:40.27	120,000
1994	Brass Scale, 3, 114	E. S. Prado	Hello Chicago, 3, 114	Serious Spender, 3, 111	9	1:49.27	120,000
1993	Diazo, 3, 117	L. A. Pincay Jr.	Press Card, 3, 116	Schossberg, 3, 116	7	1:47.18	150,000
1992	Scuffleburg, 3, 111	J. A. Krone	Nines Wild, 3, 113	Agincourt, 3, 115	11	1:49.09	300,000
1991	Scan, 3, 119	J. A. Santos	Sea Cadet, 3, 119	Sultry Song, 3, 114	8	1:46.53	180,000
1990	Silver Ending, 3, 119	E. Delahoussaye	Music Prospector, 3, 116	Runaway Stream, 3, 113	12	1:47.20	180,000
1989	Norquestor, 3, 114	J. A. Krone	Rampart Road, 3, 113	Fast Play, 3, 116	12	1:49.60	180,000
1988	Brian's Time, 3, 121	A. T. Cordero Jr.	Festive, 3, 110	Congeleur, 3, 112	14	1:47.00	180,000
1987	Cryptoclearance, 3, 122	J. A. Santos	Lost Code, 3, 122	Templar Hill, 3, 118	8	1:48.60	180,000
1986	Danzig Connection, 3, 122	P. Day	Broad Brush, 3, 122	Ogygian, 3, 124	5	1:49.00	180,000
1985	Skip Trial, 3, 123	J. Samyn	Stephan's Odyssey, 3, 123	Violado, 3, 117	7	1:51.00	200,040
1984	Hail Bold King, 3, 115	J. Velasquez	Carr de Naskra, 3, 122	dh-Jyp, 3, 115	8	1:49.20	131,040
				dh-Morning Bob, 3, 119			
1983	World Appeal, 3, 114	A. Graell	Hyperborean, 3, 118	Bounding Basque, 3, 115	10	1:46.60	135,360
1982	Fast Gold, 3, 110	J. Samyn	Muttering, 3, 120	Exclusive One, 3, 119	8	1:49.00	131,150
1981	Summing, 3, 122	G. Martens	Johnny Dance, 3, 114	Maudlin, 3, 112	11	1:51.00	133,620
1980	Dr. Blum, 3, 115	R. Hernandez	Bill Wheeler, 3, 115	Peace for Peace, 3, 115	7	1:11.00	15,150

Named for the winged horse of Greek mythology. Formerly sponsored by the General Motors Corp. of Detroit, Michigan 1997-'98. Grade 1 1987-'93. Grade 2 1994-2002. Pegasus H. 1981-'95, 1997-2002. Pegasus Breeders' Cup H. 1996. Buick Pegasus H. 1997-'98. Held at The Meadowlands 1980-2006. Not held 2003. 6 furlongs 1980. 1 1/16 miles 1995-'96. Turf 1996. Dead heat for third 1984. Track record 1999.

Pennsylvania Derby

Grade 2 in 2008. Philadelphia Park, three-year-olds, 1 1/8 miles, dirt. Held September 3, 2007, with a gross value of $1,000,000. First held in 1979. First graded in 1981. Stakes record 1:47.60 (1989 Western Playboy).

Year	Winner	Jockey	Second	Third	Strs	Time	1st Purse
2007	Timber Reserve, 3, 114	J. Castellano	Xchanger, 3, 122	Zanjero, 3, 122	11	1:47.67	$544,000
2005	Sun King, 3, 122	R. Bejarano	Southern Africa, 3, 122	Smokescreen, 3, 114	14	1:49.43	397,500
2004	Love of Money, 3, 116	R. Albarado	Pollard's Vision, 3, 122	Swingforthefences, 3, 119	7	1:48.42	450,000
2003	Grand Hombre, 3, 114	J. Bravo	Gimmeawink, 3, 122	Ashmore, 3, 114	10	1:49.03	450,000
2002	Harlan's Holiday, 3, 122	E. S. Prado	Essence of Dubai, 3, 122	Make the Bend, 3, 119	5	1:51.10	300,000
2001	Macho Uno, 3, 116	G. L. Stevens	†Unbridled Elaine, 3, 119	Touch Tone, 3, 122	6	1:49.69	300,000
2000	Pine Dance, 3, 122	M. J. McCarthy	Mass Market, 3, 122	Cherokeeinthehills, 3, 114	10	1:49.03	180,000
1999	Smart Guy, 3, 119	R. E. Colton	Ghost Ring, 3, 114	Pineaff, 3, 122	10	1:49.40	180,000
1998	Rock and Roll, 3, 114	H. Castillo Jr.	Tomorrows Cat, 3, 114	Black Blade, 3, 119	11	1:47.69	150,000
1997	Frisk Me Now, 3, 122	E. L. King Jr.	Envy of the Crown, 3, 119	Christian Soldier, 3, 114	8	1:48.14	120,000
1996	Devil's Honor, 3, 122	A. S. Black	Formal Gold, 3, 117	Clash by Night, 3, 119	7	1:48.58	120,000
1995	Pineing Patty, 3, 122	L. J. Melancon	Royal Haven, 3, 117	Tenants Harbor, 3, 117	12	1:48.05	120,000
1994	Meadow Flight, 3, 122	J. Bravo	Red Tazz, 3, 117	Kandaly, 3, 122	9	1:49.08	120,000
1993	Wallenda, 3, 114	W. H. McCauley	Press Card, 3, 117	Saintly Prospector, 3, 122	9	1:49.33	120,000
1992	Thelactrusade, 3, 114	V. H. Molina	Ecstatic Ride, 3, 114	Nines Wild, 3, 117	10	1:49.47	90,000
1991	Valley Crossing, 3, 119	A. J. Seefeldt	Gala Spinaway, 3, 122	Riflery, 3, 117	5	1:50.10	90,000
1990	Summer Squall, 3, 122	P. Day	Challenge My Duty, 3, 122	Sports View, 3, 122	9	1:48.20	180,000
1989	Western Playboy, 3, 122	K. D. Clark	Roi Danzig, 3, 122	Tricky Creek, 3, 122	12	**1:47.60**	180,000
1988	Cefis, 3, 122	L. Saumell	Congeleur, 3, 119	Ballindaggin, 3, 122	10	1:49.60	180,000
1987	Afleet, 3, 122	G. Stahlbaum	Lost Code, 3, 122	Homebuilder, 3, 119	8	1:48.20	180,000

Racing — Graded Stakes

Year	Winner	Jockey	Second	Third	Strs	Time	1st Purse
1986	**Broad Brush**, 3, 122	A. T. Cordero Jr.	Sumptious, 3, 122	Glow, 3, 122	7	1:50.80	$180,000
1985	**Skip Trial**, 3, 122	J. Samyn	El Basco, 3, 122	Jacque l'Heureux, 3, 119	13	1:50.20	180,000
1984	**Morning Bob**, 3, 122	G. McCarron	At the Threshold, 3, 122	dh-Biloxi Indian, 3, 122	7	1:49.40	132,240
				dh-Raja's Shark, 3, 122			
1983	**Dixieland Band**, 3, 122	W. J. Passmore	Jacque's Tip, 3, 122	Intention, 3, 122	9	1:49.40	136,500
1982	**Spanish Drums**, 3, 122	J. Vasquez	Air Forbes Won, 3, 122	A Magic Spray, 3, 122	11	1:49.00	101,460
1981	**Summing**, 3, 122	G. Martens	Sportin' Life, 3, 122	Classic Go Go, 3, 122	9	1:49.00	100,380
1980	**Lively King**, 3, 122	C. J. Baker	Mutineer, 3, 122	Stutz Blackhawk, 3, 122	7	1:48.80	99,480
1979	**Smarten**, 3, 122	S. Maple	Incredible Ease, 3, 122	Incubator, 3, 122	6	1:49.20	68,880

Philadelphia Park is located in Bensalem, Pennsylvania. Grade 3 1981-'84, 1996-2003. Not held 2006. Dead heat for third 1984. †Denotes female.

Perryville Stakes

Grade 3 in 2008. Keeneland Race Course, three-year-olds, about 7 furlongs, all weather. Held October 13, 2007, with a gross value of $200,000. First held in 1999. First graded in 2005. Stakes record 1:24.38 (2006 Midnight Lute).

Year	Winner	Jockey	Second	Third	Strs	Time	1st Purse
2007	**Steve's Double**, 3, 117	J. Theriot	Les Grands Trois, 3, 117	Shrewd Operator, 3, 117	8	1:25.36	$124,000
2006	**Midnight Lute**, 3, 117	V. Espinoza	Lewis Michael, 3, 117	Court Folly, 3, 123	11	**1:24.38**	124,000
2005	**Vicarage**, 3, 120	J. R. Velazquez	Straight Line, 3, 123	Social Probation, 3, 117	8	1:26.06	124,000
2004	**Commentator**, 3, 117	R. Bejarano	Eurosilver, 3, 123	Weigelia, 3, 123	7	1:25.19	69,812
2003	**Clock Stopper**, 3, 117	R. Albarado	Ballado Chieftan, 3, 117	Champali, 3, 123	5	1:25.33	67,146
2002	**Najran**, 3, 118	P. Day	Flying Free, 3, 118	Premier Performer, 3, 118	9	1:26.00	52,127
2001	**Dream Run**, 3, 118	P. Day	Strawberry Affair, 3, 118	Solingen, 3, 117	5	1:27.25	50,360
2000	**Smokin Pete**, 3, 118	S. J. Sellers	Classic Appeal, 3, 120	Chervy, 3, 118	6	1:25.38	44,020
1999	**National Saint**, 3, 118	R. Albarado	Moon Over Prospect, 3, 118	Hidden City, 3, 120	6	1:25.21	36,674

Named for Perryville, Kentucky, where the largest Civil War battle in the state was fought on October 8, 1862. Dirt 1999-2005.

Personal Ensign Stakes

Grade 1 in 2008. Saratoga Race Course, three-year-olds and up, fillies and mares, 1¼ miles, dirt. Held August 24, 2007, with a gross value of $400,000. First held in 1948. First graded in 1973. Stakes record 2:02.07 (2005 Shadow Cast).

Year	Winner	Jockey	Second	Third	Strs	Time	1st Purse
2007	**Miss Shop**, 4, 118	J. Castellano	Unbridled Belle, 4, 118	Indian Vale, 5, 118	6	2:03.48	$240,000
2006	**Fleet Indian**, 5, 118	J. A. Santos	Balletto (UAE), 4, 116	Soul Search, 4, 116	5	2:03.87	240,000
2005	**Shadow Cast**, 4, 118	R. Albarado	Personal Legend, 5, 116	Two Trail Sioux, 4, 118	6	**2:02.07**	240,000
2004	**Storm Flag Flying**, 4, 116	J. R. Velazquez	Azeri, 6, 122	Nevermore, 4, 114	5	2:03.63	240,000
2003	**Passing Shot**, 4, 114	J. A. Santos	Wild Spirit (Chi), 4, 122	Miss Linda (Arg), 6, 114	5	2:03.33	240,000
2002	**Summer Colony**, 4, 120	J. R. Velazquez	Transcendental, 4, 114	Dancethruthedawn, 4, 120	6	2:03.15	240,000
2001	**Pompeii**, 4, 117	R. Migliore	Beautiful Pleasure, 6, 117	Irving's Baby, 4, 117	7	2:04.60	240,000
2000	**Beautiful Pleasure**, 5, 124	J. F. Chavez	‡Heritage of Gold, 5, 124	Pentatonic, 5, 113	5	2:03.77	240,000
1999	**Beautiful Pleasure**, 4, 113	J. F. Chavez	Banshee Breeze, 4, 124	Keeper Hill, 4, 118	6	2:02.57	240,000
1998	**Tomisue's Delight**, 4, 115	P. Day	Tuzia, 4, 114	One Rich Lady, 4, 114	8	2:04.08	240,000
1997	**Clear Mandate**, 5, 115	M. E. Smith	Shoop, 6, 111	Power Play, 5, 117	6	2:03.71	210,000
1996	**Urbane**, 4, 119	A. O. Solis	Shoop, 5, 114	Frolic, 4, 113	8	2:03.05	180,000
1995	**Heavenly Prize**, 4, 127	P. Day	Forcing Bid, 4, 108	Cinnamon Sugar (Ire), 4, 114	8	2:04.16	120,000
1994	**Link River**, 4, 114	J. A. Krone	You'd Be Surprised, 5, 120	Dispute, 4, 119	7	1:50.46	120,000
1993	**You'd Be Surprised**, 4, 115	J. D. Bailey	Avian Assembly, 4, 111	Gray Cashmere, 4, 114	8	1:48.59	90,000
1992	**Quick Mischief**, 6, 113	C. Perret	Versailles Treaty, 4, 122	Shared Interest, 4, 111	7	1:47.96	120,000
1991	**Fit to Scout**, 4, 114	C. W. Antley	Train Robbery, 4, 112	Her She Shawklit, 4, 111	7	1:50.30	120,000
1990	**Personal Business**, 4, 111	C. W. Antley	Buy the Firm, 4, 112	Lady Hoolihan, 4, 110	8	1:51.20	70,200
1989	**Colonial Waters**, 4, 116	A. T. Cordero Jr.	Topicount, 4, 116	Rose's Cantina, 5, 119	5	1:50.00	67,080
1988	**Rose's Cantina**, 4, 111	J. A. Santos	Ms. Eloise, 5, 115	Clabber Girl, 5, 120	4	1:49.80	67,080
1987	**Coup de Fusil**, 5, 116	A. T. Cordero Jr.	Clabber Girl, 4, 113	I'm Sweets, 4, 118	7	1:49.20	83,700
1986	**Shocker T.**, 4, 124	G. St. Leon	Bharal, 5, 113	Natania, 4, 115	5	1:50.00	66,840
1985	**Lady On the Run**, 3, 115	A. T. Cordero Jr.	Verbality, 4, 112	Halloween Queen, 4, 112	6	1:52.00	51,210
1984	**Solar Halo**, 4, 110	R. G. Davis	It's Fine, 4, 109	Quixotic Lady, 4, 115	8	1:49.20	53,640
1983	**Chieftan's Command**, 4, 117	A. T. Cordero Jr.	Adept, 4, 110	Sintrillium, 5, 116	7	1:51.60	34,440
1982	**Number**, 3, 114	E. Maple	Sintrillium, 4, 112	Norsan, 3, 112	5	1:51.40	32,340
1981	**Tina Tina Too**, 3, 114	D. MacBeth	Explorare, 4, 111	Office Wife, 4, 113	8	1:51.00	33,060
1980	**Relaxing**, 4, 118	J. Velasquez	Sugar and Spice, 3, 115	Plankton, 4, 121	8	1:49.20	33,540
1979	**Catherine's Bet**, 4, 113	D. Montoya	Water Malone, 5, 117	Miss Baja, 4, 114	7	1:50.20	32,340
1978	**Mrs. Warren**, 4, 113	J. Velasquez	Water Malone, 4, 114	One Sum, 4, 111	7	1:51.40	32,190
1977	**Water Malone**, 3, 121	J. Samyn	Northernette, 3, 120	Sweet Bernice, 4, 113	8	1:50.40	32,280
1976	**Sugar Plum Time**, 4, 113	A. T. Cordero Jr.	Ten Cents a Dance, 3, 110	Quacker, 3, 111	9	1:51.00	32,610
1975	**Lie Low**, 4, 115	J. Velasquez	Princesse Grey, 4, 114	Carolerno, 4, 112	12	2:15.20	35,910
1974	**Lie Low**, 4, 116	J. Velasquez	Aglimmer, 5, 116	D. O. Lady, 3, 115	4	1:49.00	27,840
	Twixt, 5, 121	W. J. Passmore	Garland of Roses, 5, 114	Fairway Flyer, 5, 124	10	1:49.80	28,290
1973	**Aglimmer**, 4, 115	M. Venezia	Garland of Roses, 4, 111	Cathy Baby, 4, 120	13	1:49.40	36,150

Named for Ogden Phipps's undefeated 1988 champion older female, '88 Whitney H. (G1) winner, and '96 Broodmare of the Year Personal Ensign (1984 f. by Private Account). Formerly named for John A. Morris (1892-1985), former president of the Thoroughbred Racing Association and Jamaica racetrack. Formerly named for James Ben Ali Haggin's multiple SW Firenze (1884 f. by Glenelg). Grade 2 1983-'86. Firenze H. 1948-'85. John A. Morris H. 1986-'97. Personal Ensign H. 1998-2005. Held at Jamaica 1948-'57. Held at Aqueduct 1958-'74, 1976-'85. Held at Belmont Park 1975.

1¹/₁₆ miles 1948-'51, 1958. 1¹/₈ miles 1952-'57, 1959, 1962-'74, 1976-'94. 1 mile 1960-'61. 1³/₈ miles 1975. Turf 1972-'75. Two divisions 1974. ‡Back in Shape finished second, DQ to fourth, 2000. Equaled track record 1980.

Peter Pan Stakes

Grade 2 in 2008. Belmont Park, three-year-olds, 1¹/₈ miles, dirt. Held May 10, 2008, with a gross value of $200,000. First held in 1940. First graded in 1978. Stakes record 1:46.35 (2005 Oratory).

Year	Winner	Jockey	Second	Third	Strs	Time	1st Purse
2008	Casino Drive, 3, 116	K. J. Desormeaux	Mint Lane, 3, 116	Ready's Echo, 3, 116	9	1:47.87	$120,000
2007	Sightseeing, 3, 116	E. S. Prado	Prom Shoes, 3, 116	Fearless Vision, 3, 116	6	1:48.89	120,000
2006	Sunriver, 3, 116	R. Bejarano	Lewis Michael, 3, 116	Strong Contender, 3, 116	9	1:49.39	120,000
2005	Oratory, 3, 116	J. D. Bailey	Reverberate, 3, 116	Golden Man, 3, 116	8	**1:46.35**	120,000
2004	Purge, 3, 115	J. R. Velazquez	Swingforthefences, 3, 115	Master David, 3, 115	10	1:47.98	120,000
2003	Go Rockin' Robin, 3, 117	S. Bridgmohan	Alysweep, 3, 123	Supervisor, 3, 115	6	1:48.47	120,000
2002	Sunday Break (Jpn), 3, 121	G. L. Stevens	Puzzlement, 3, 115	Deputy Dash, 3, 115	7	1:48.10	120,000
2001	Hero's Tribute, 3, 117	J. F. Chavez	E Dubai, 3, 123	Dayton Flyer, 3, 115	7	1:47.47	120,000
2000	Postponed, 3, 113	E. S. Prado	Unshaded, 3, 123	Globalize, 3, 123	9	1:49.71	120,000
1999	Best of Luck, 3, 113	J. Samyn	Treasure Island, 3, 114	Lemon Drop Kid, 3, 120	9	1:47.94	90,000
1998	Grand Slam, 3, 120	J. D. Bailey	Rubiyat, 3, 113	Parade Ground, 3, 120	7	1:49.14	90,000
1997	Banker's Gold, 3, 113	E. Maple	Zede, 3, 120	Prince Guistino, 3, 114	4	1:48.60	90,000
1996	Jamies First Punch, 3, 118	J. R. Velazquez	Unbridled's Song, 3, 123	Diligence, 3, 118	5	1:47.32	90,000
1995	Citadeed, 3, 112	E. Maple	Pat n Jac, 3, 113	Treasurer (GB), 3, 115	10	1:50.03	90,000
1994	Twining, 3, 122	J. A. Santos	Lahint, 3, 117	Gash, 3, 119	5	1:49.11	90,000
1993	Virginia Rapids, 3, 114	E. Maple	Colonial Affair, 3, 117	Itaka, 3, 114	6	1:48.48	90,000
1992	A.P. Indy, 3, 126	E. Delahoussaye	Colony Light, 3, 114	Berkley Fitz, 3, 114	7	1:47.49	106,380
1991	Lost Mountain, 3, 114	C. Perret	Man Alright, 3, 114	Scan, 3, 126	6	1:49.47	106,380
1990	Profit Key, 3, 117	J. A. Santos	Country Day, 3, 114	Paradise Found, 3, 114	8	1:47.20	106,560
1989	Imbibe, 3, 117	A. T. Cordero Jr.	Irish Actor, 3, 126	Pro Style, 3, 117	9	1:48.60	110,160
1988	Seeking the Gold, 3, 120	P. Day	Tejano, 3, 126	Gay Rights, 3, 117	7	1:47.60	140,880
1987	Leo Castelli, 3, 114	J. A. Santos	Gone West, 3, 126	Shawklit Won, 3, 114	9	1:48.00	132,360
1986	Danzig Connection, 3, 117	P. Day	Clear Choice, 3, 123	Parade Marshal, 3, 117	8	1:48.40	85,380
1985	Proud Truth, 3, 126	J. Velasquez	Cutlass Reality, 3, 114	Salem Drive, 3, 117	7	1:47.60	67,050
1984	Back Bay Barrister, 3, 117	D. MacBeth	Gallant Hour, 3, 114	Romantic Tradition, 3, 114	9	1:50.00	57,330
1983	Slew o' Gold, 3, 126	A. T. Cordero Jr.	I Enclose, 3, 123	Foyt, 3, 117	5	1:46.80	34,380
1982	Wolfie's Rascal, 3, 120	A. T. Cordero Jr.	John's Gold, 3, 114	Illuminate, 3, 117	6	1:48.80	34,020
1981	Tap Shoes, 3, 126	R. Hernandez	Willow Hour, 3, 117	West On Broad, 3, 120	7	1:48.40	34,080
1980	Comptroller, 3, 114	R. I. Encinas	Bar Dexter, 3, 117	Suzanne's Star, 3, 114	8	1:49.20	34,080
1979	Coastal, 3, 120	R. Hernandez	Lucy's Axe, 3, 123	Pianist, 3, 117	6	1:47.00	32,820
1978	Buckaroo, 3, 114	J. Velasquez	Darby Creek Road, 3, 117	Star de Naskra, 3, 123	8	1:48.00	32,520
1977	Spirit Level, 3, 114	A. Graell	Sanhedrin, 3, 114	Lynn Davis, 3, 114	9	1:49.20	32,910
1976	Sir Lister, 3, 114	J. Velasquez	‡Jamming, 3, 117	El Portugues, 3, 114	9	1:36.00	34,620
1975	Singh, 3, 114	E. Maple	Majestic One, 3, 114	Sir Paulus, 3, 115	8	1:35.20	33,420

Named for James R. Keene's champion and 1907 Belmont S. winner Peter Pan (1904 c. by Commando). Grade 3 1978-'82. Grade 1 1984-'86. Peter Pan H. 1940-'60. Held at Aqueduct 1940-'43, 1945-'49, 1952-'55, 1958-'60, 1975. Not held 1961-'74. 1 mile 1975-'76. Three-year-olds and up 1979. ‡El Portugues finished second, DQ to third, 1976.

Philip H. Iselin Stakes

Grade 3 in 2008. Monmouth Park, three-year-olds and up, 1¹/₈ miles, dirt. Held August 18, 2007, with a gross value of $300,000. First held in 1884. First graded in 1973. Stakes record 1:46.80 (1985 Spend a Buck; 1992 Jolie's Halo).

Year	Winner	Jockey	Second	Third	Strs	Time	1st Purse
2007	Gottcha Gold, 4, 121	C. C. Lopez	Brother Bobby, 4, 117	Indy Wind, 5, 117	8	1:48.36	$180,000
2006	Park Avenue Ball, 4, 119	C. P. DeCarlo	Survivalist, 4, 119	Master Command, 4, 121	8	1:49.73	165,000
2005	West Virginia, 4, 115	J. A. Velez Jr.	Zoffinger, 5, 114	Purge, 4, 118	8	1:50.83	90,000
2004	Ghostzapper, 4, 120	J. Castellano	Presidentialaffair, 5, 117	Zoffinger, 4, 115	4	1:47.66	120,000
2003	Tenpins, 5, 119	R. Albarado	Aeneas, 4, 114	Jersey Giant, 4, 115	9	1:50.35	120,000
2002	Cat's At Home, 5, 116	J. A. Velez Jr.	Bowman's Band, 4, 117	Runspastum, 5, 114	7	1:49.10	210,000
2001	Broken Vow, 4, 119	R. A. Dominguez	First Lieutenant, 4, 115	Sir Bear, 8, 117	5	1:49.55	210,000
2000	Rize, 4, 112	J. C. Ferrer	Sir Bear, 7, 118	Talk's Cheap, 4, 114	6	1:48.42	210,000
1999	Frisk Me Now, 5, 117	E. L. King Jr.	Call Me Mr. Vain, 5, 110	Black Cash, 4, 112	6	1:49.00	210,000
1998	Skip Away, 5, 131	J. D. Bailey	Stormin Fever, 4, 110	‡Devil's Fire, 6, 113	7	1:47.33	300,000
1997	Formal Gold, 4, 121	K. Desormeaux	Skip Away, 4, 124	Distorted Humor, 4, 115	4	1:40.20	250,000
1996	Smart Strike, 4, 115	C. Perret	Eltish, 4, 115	†Serena's Song, 4, 115	7	1:41.59	180,000
1995	Schossberg, 5, 118	D. Penna	Poor But Honest, 5, 115	Mickeray, 4, 114	10	1:49.22	180,000
1994	Taking Risks, 4, 115	M. T. Johnston	Valley Crossing, 6, 117	Proud Shot, 4, 112	9	1:48.33	150,000
1993	Valley Crossing, 5, 113	C. W. Antley	Devil His Due, 4, 123	Bertrando, 4, 119	8	1:47.40	150,000
1992	Jolie's Halo, 5, 116	E. S. Prado	Out of Place, 5, 113	Valley Crossing, 4, 111	11	**1:46.80**	300,000
1991	Black Tie Affair (Ire), 5, 119	P. Day	Farma Way, 4, 122	Chief Honcho, 4, 115	8	1:47.80	300,000
1990	Beau Genius, 5, 122	R. D. Lopez	Tricky Creek, 4, 112	De Roche, 4, 115	8	1:48.20	300,000
1989	Proper Reality, 4, 119	J. D. Bailey	Bill E. Shears, 4, 112	Mi Selecto, 4, 114	9	1:48.00	150,000
1988	Alysheba, 4, 124	C. J. McCarron	Bet Twice, 4, 123	Gulch, 4, 122	6	1:47.80	150,000
1987	Bordeaux Bob, 4, 115	C. W. Antley	Silver Comet, 4, 114	Lost Code, 4, 117	7	1:48.20	163,920
1986	Roo Art, 4, 117	W. Shoemaker	Precisionist, 5, 125	†Lady's Secret, 4, 120	5	1:48.80	188,280
1985	Spend a Buck, 3, 118	L. A. Pincay Jr.	Carr de Naskra, 4, 118	‡Valiant Lark, 5, 115	6	**1:46.80**	162,180
1984	Believe the Queen, 4, 120	D. A. Miller Jr.	World Appeal, 4, 121	Bet Big, 4, 117	9	1:48.20	194,040
1983	Bates Motel, 4, 124	T. Lipham	Island Whirl, 5, 124	Linkage, 4, 115	9	1:47.20	167,520

Racing — Graded Stakes

Year	Winner	Jockey	Second	Third	Strs	Time	1st Purse
1982	**Mehmet**, 4, 115	E. Delahoussaye	†Pukka Princess, 4, 108	Summer Advocate, 5, 117	13	1:48.20	$174,240
1981	**Amber Pass**, 4, 117	C. B. Asmussen	Joanie's Chief, 4, 108	Ring of Light, 6, 114	10	1:47.40	170,580
1980	**Spectacular Bid**, 4, 132	W. Shoemaker	†Glorious Song, 4, 117	The Cool Virginian, 4, 112	8	1:48.00	158,160
1979	‡**Text**, 5, 118	W. Shoemaker	Cox's Ridge, 5, 120	Silent Cal, 4, 115	6	1:47.60	70,948
1978	**Life's Hope**, 5, 115	C. Perret	Wise Philip, 5, 114	Father Hogan, 5, 115	7	2:03.20	72,183
1977	**Majestic Light**, 4, 124	S. Hawley	Capital Idea, 4, 108	Peppy Addy, 5, 116	6	2:00.40	71,143
1976	**Hatchet Man**, 5, 112	V. A. Bracciale Jr.	Intrepid Hero, 4, 119	Forego, 6, 136	8	2:00.60	71,793
1975	**Royal Glint**, 5, 121	C. Perret	Proper Bostonian, 5, 118	Stonewalk, 4, 121	6	2:00.60	70,948
1974	**True Knight**, 5, 124	M. A. Rivera	Ecole Etage, 4, 112	Hey Rube, 4, 111	9	2:02.00	72,215
1973	**West Coast Scout**, 5, 114	L. Adams	Tentam, 4, 118	Windtex, 4, 113	11	2:01.20	74,295

Named for Philip H. Iselin (1902-'76), president and chairman of the board of Monmouth Park (1966-'77). Formerly named for Amory L. Haskell (1894-1966), former president of Monmouth Park. Grade 1 1973-'96. Grade 2 1997-2002. Monmouth H. 1884-'93, 1946-'66, 1981-'85. Amory L. Haskell H. 1967-'80. Philip H. Iselin H. 1986-2002. Philip H. Iselin Breeders' Cup H. 2003-'07. Not held 1894-1945. 1½ miles 1884-'93. 1¼ miles 1956-'78. 1 1/16 miles 1996-'97. Two-year-olds and up 1884-'86. ‡Cox's Ridge finished first, DQ to second, 1979. ‡Rumptious finished third, DQ to sixth, 1985. ‡Testafly finished third, DQ to seventh for a positive drug test, 1998. Track record 1974. Equaled track record 1992. †Denotes female.

Phoenix Stakes

Grade 3 in 2008. Keeneland Race Course, three-year-olds and up, 6 furlongs, all weather. Held October 6, 2007, with a gross value of $203,000. First held in 1831. First graded in 2000. Stakes record 1:07.78 (1993 Anjiz).

Year	Winner	Jockey	Second	Third	Strs	Time	1st Purse
2007	**Off Duty**, 4, 118	L. Melancon	Rebellion (GB), 4, 118	Saint Anddan, 5, 122	10	1:10.17	$93,000
2006	**Kelly's Landing**, 5, 118	R. Bejarano	Areyoutalkintome, 5, 118	Level Playingfield, 5, 118	9	1:09.94	166,532
2005	**Elusive Jazz**, 4, 118	R. Albarado	Wild Tale, 4, 118	Premium Saltine, 6, 118	8	1:11.60	165,230
2004	**Champali**, 4, 122	R. Bejarano	Gold Storm, 4, 118	Clock Stopper, 4, 118	11	1:08.72	168,175
2003	**Najran**, 4, 122	J. Castellano	Ethan Man, 4, 118	Take Achance On Me, 5, 118	8	1:08.32	169,880
2002	†**Xtra Heat**, 4, 123	H. Vega	Day Trader, 3, 120	Touch Tone, 4, 118	5	1:10.13	155,000
2001	**Bet On Sunshine**, 9, 123	C. H. Borel	Robin de Nest, 4, 121	Erlton, 5, 119	6	1:09.65	166,470
2000	**Five Star Day**, 4, 119	G. K. Gomez	Istintaj, 4, 119	Bet On Sunshine, 8, 123	6	1:07.90	167,245
1999	**Richter Scale**, 5, 117	K. Desormeaux	Bet On Sunshine, 7, 117	Vicar, 3, 121	6	1:08.40	166,780
1998	**Partner's Hero**, 4, 117	C. H. Borel	Pyramid Peak, 6, 117	High Stakes Player, 6, 123	6	1:09.25	100,533
1997	**Bet On Sunshine**, 5, 123	F. Torres	Receiver, 4, 117	Valid Expectations, 4, 117	5	1:08.70	97,464
1996	**Forest Wildcat**, 5, 121	J. Bravo	Valid Expectations, 3, 119	Bet On Sunshine, 4, 115	10	1:09.57	101,246
1995	**Golden Gear**, 4, 124	C. Perret	Hello Paradise, 4, 115	Mississippi Chat, 3, 113	6	1:08.96	67,456
1994	**Lost Pan**, 4, 114	D. M. Barton	Pacific West, 4, 112	Fort Chaffee, 4, 116	5	1:09.45	33,728
1993	**Anjiz**, 5, 114	D. A. Miller Jr.	Gold Spring (Arg), 5, 124	Friendly Lover, 5, 121	6	**1:07.78**	50,251
1992	**British Banker**, 4, 114	D. Kutz	Megas Vukefalos, 4, 124	Binalong, 3, 113	6	1:09.20	49,693
1991	**Deposit Ticket**, 3, 114	P. Day	Tom Cobbley, 5, 114	Hammocker, 7, 113	6	1:10.38	51,838
1990	**Hadif**, 4, 120	D. Penna	Fighting Fantasy, 3, 115	Raise a Tradition, 4, 114	11	1:09.40	52,796
1989	**Momsfurrari**, 5, 114	M. E. Smith	Hammocker, 5, 114	Irish Open, 5, 118	9	1:10.60	36,319
1988	**Carload**, 6, 114	E. Fires	Conquer, 4, 117	Carborundum, 4, 117	8	1:09.80	45,275
1987	**Diapason**, 7, 112	P. A. Johnson	Hail the Ruckus, 4, 116	Dr. Koch, 5, 114	9	1:09.80	35,783
1986	**Lucky North**, 5, 115	P. Day	Clever Wake, 4, 114	Fortunate Prospect, 5, 121	5	1:11.00	34,613
1985	**Harry 'n Bill**, 5, 115	M. Russ	Irish Freeze, 4, 116	Diapason, 5, 113	9	1:09.60	35,913
1984	**Timeless Native**, 4, 121	D. Brumfield	Euathlos, 4, 116	Runderbar, 4, 112	10	1:10.80	36,286
1983	**Shot n' Missed**, 6, 115	L. Moyers	Gallant Gentleman, 4, 114	†Excitable Lady, 5, 115	6	1:09.00	35,214
1982	**Golden Derby**, 4, 115	J. C. Espinoza	Shot n' Missed, 5, 117	Aristocratical, 4, 119	13	1:10.00	40,853
1981	**Turbulence**, 5, 115	J. C. Espinoza	Final Tribute, 5, 114	It's a Rerun, 5, 114	9	1:09.45	35,783
	Zuppardo's Prince, 5, 116	J. C. Espinoza	Convenient, 5, 118	Done Well, 4, 116	8	1:09.40	38,870
1980	**Zuppardo's Prince**, 4, 116	J. C. Espinoza	Cregan's Cap, 5, 111	Cabrini Green, 5, 116	9	1:09.00	35,165
1979	**Shelter Half**, 4, 116	S. A. Boulmetis Jr.	Cabrini Green, 4, 118	Going Investor, 4, 115	9	1:09.20	29,494
1978	**Amadevil**, 4, 117	S. Maple	It's Freezing, 6, 121	See the U. S. A., 8, 118	11	1:09.40	22,539
1977	**It's Freezing**, 5, 118	E. Maple	Harbor Springs, 4, 118	Dixmart, 5, 113	13	1:09.60	19,143
1976	**Gallant Bob**, 4, 126	D. Brumfield	Real Value, 4, 120	Amerrico, 4, 115	6	1:08.40	18,736
1975	**Delta Oil**, 6, 118	R. Breen	Jazziness, 5, 117	Hasty Flyer, 4, 116	12	1:09.40	19,468
1974	**Penholder**, 5, 116	B. Thornburg	List, 6, 118	Grocery List, 5, 118	12	1:09.40	18,330
1973	**Honey Jay**, 5, 123	J. C. Espinoza	Three Martinis, 5, 116	Mighty Mackie, 4, 110	12	1:11.40	18,493

Named for the old Phoenix Hotel in Lexington, Kentucky; oldest recognized race in North America. The race has also been known as the Brennan, Chiles, Association, and Phoenix Hotel S. Not held 1898-1904, 1906-'10, 1914-'16, 1929, 1931-'36. Phoenix H. 1937-'80. Phoenix Breeders' Cup H. 1990. Phoenix Breeders' Cup S. 1991-'93, 1996-2006. Held at Kentucky Association 1831-1930. Held at Churchill Downs 1943-'45. Dirt 1831-2005. Two divisions 1981. Track record 1993. †Denotes female. Held as a heat race 1831-'77.

Pilgrim Stakes

Grade 3 in 2008. Belmont Park, two-year-olds, 1 1/16 miles, turf. Held September 29, 2007, with a gross value of $81,000. First held in 1979. First graded in 1982. Stakes record 1:41.39 (1991 Smiling and Dancin).

Year	Winner	Jockey	Second	Third	Strs	Time	1st Purse
2007	**The Leopard**, 2, 116	J. R. Velazquez	He Aint Easy, 2, 116	Grasberg, 2, 118	6	1:41.61	$48,600
2006	**Pickapocket**, 2, 122	E. Coa	Strike a Deal, 2, 118	Giant Chieftan, 2, 116	12	1:52.62	51,555
2005	**Fagan's Legacy**, 2, 116	J. Bravo	Church Service, 2, 116	Go Between, 2, 116	6	1:52.11	49,545
2004	**Crown Point**, 2, 118	J. L. Espinoza	Wallstreet Scandal, 2, 116	Drum Major, 2, 118	8	1:50.31	49,725
2003	**Timo**, 2, 116	J. R. Velazquez	Artie Schiller, 2, 120	Milestone Victory, 2, 118	7	1:57.46	49,515

Racing — Graded Stakes

Year	Winner	Jockey	Second	Third	Strs	Time	1st Purse
2002	One Colony, 2, 118	A. T. Gryder	Celtic Memories, 2, 118	Blakelock, 2, 116	5	1:51.00	$49,770
2001	Miesque's Approval, 2, 119	J. D. Bailey	Finality, 2, 117	Regal Sanction, 2, 115	9	1:50.80	50,085
2000	Volponi, 2, 115	J. R. Velazquez	Baptize, 2, 122	Strategic Partner, 2, 115	10	1:48.02	67,980
1999	Kachemak Bay, 2, 117	J. R. Velazquez	King Cugat, 2, 113	Aldo, 2, 117	7	1:54.67	66,960
1998	Incurable Optimist, 2, 117	J. R. Velazquez	In Frank's Honor, 2, 114	Senor Fizz, 2, 112	5	1:48.05	64,860
1997	Cryptic Rascal, 2, 113	M. E. Smith	Sheikh Rattle, 2, 112	Recommended List, 2, 122	12	1:50.83	69,420
1996	Accelerator, 2, 113	M. E. Smith	dh-Let's Go to Dodge, 2, 114 dh-Skippin Stoned, 2, 114		8	1:41.98	68,280
1995	Play It Again Stan, 2, 113	W. H. McCauley	Old Chapel, 2, 122	Optic Nerve, 2, 112	11	1:50.28	69,540
1994	Diplomatic Jet, 2, 117	J. D. Bailey	Houston Connection, 2, 115	Islamabad, 2, 115	5	1:46.67	49,245
1993	Dove Hunt, 2, 113	J. D. Bailey	Tomorrow's Comet, 2, 113	Dynamite Laugh, 2, 113	9	1:44.73	73,560
1992	Awad, 2, 113	J. A. Krone	Dr. Alfoos, 2, 113	Compadre, 2, 113	10	1:42.69	76,200
1991	Smiling and Dancin, 2, 114	R. Migliore	Stress Buster, 2, 115	Casino Magistrate, 2, 113	9	1:41.39	73,680
1990	Fourstars Allstar, 2, 115	M. E. Smith	Club Champ, 2, 113	Wild Dancer, 2, 113	8	1:51.60	54,000
1989	Super Mario, 2, 117	R. Migliore	Duke's Cup, 2, 119	Libor, 2, 113	11	1:56.00	76,080
1988	Tuneful Tip, 2, 117	C. Gambardella	Alydrome, 2, 113	Alabrio, 2, 113	12	1:59.00	79,320
1987	Blew by Em, 2, 115	C. W. Antley	Cefis, 2, 113	Smart Lad, 2, 113	8	1:53.60	69,210
1986	David's Bird, 2, 113	J. Samyn	Quietly Bold, 2, 113	Blue Finn, 2, 122	12	1:53.00	58,770
1985	Pillaster, 2, 113	A. T. Cordero Jr.	Canadian Winter, 2, 113	Loose, 2, 113	8	1:54.40	53,730
1984	Tent Up, 2, 115	V. A. Bracciale Jr.	Space Rider, 2, 113	Nordance, 2, 113	10	1:53.20	56,700
1983	Pied A'Tierre, 2, 115	L. Saumell	Judge Mc Guire, 2, 117	Golf Ace, 2, 113	6	1:51.40	32,820
	Vision, 2, 113	E. Maple	The Accomodator, 2, 113	Roving Minstrel, 2, 113	7	1:50.20	32,820
1982	Fortnightly, 2, 122	A. T. Cordero Jr.	Caveat, 2, 122	Dominating Dooley, 2, 113	8	1:57.60	51,480
1981	Gnome's Gold, 2, 122	J. Samyn	Thunder Puddles, 2, 113	Days Dawn, 2, 113	9	1:57.20	50,580
1980	Akureyri, 2, 115	E. Maple	Pleasant Colony, 2, 115	Jetzier, 2, 122	14	1:54.80	35,040
1979	Freeo, 2, 115	S. Maple	Current Winner, 2, 114	French Cut, 2, 117	7	1:53.00	25,710
	I Take All, 2, 115	A. T. Cordero Jr.	Prune Dew, 2, 114	Dressage, 2, 119	10	1:52.40	25,830

Named for Joseph E. Widener's 1919 Remsen H. winner Pilgrim (1917 g. by Garry Herrmann). Grade 2 1988-'89. Not graded 1996, 2001-'07. Held at Aqueduct 1979-'90, 1995, 1997, 2001-'02. 1 1/8 miles 1979-'90, 1997-2006. Dirt 1983, '96, 2005. Two divisions 1979, '83. Dead heat for second 1999.

Pin Oak Valley View Stakes

Grade 3 in 2008. Keeneland Race Course, three-year-olds, fillies, 1 1/16 miles, turf. Held October 19, 2007, with a gross value of $150,000. First held in 1991. First graded in 1999. Stakes record 1:41.51 (1992 Spinning Round).

Year	Winner	Jockey	Second	Third	Strs	Time	1st Purse
2007	Bel Air Beauty, 3, 117	M. Guidry	Bachata, 3, 119	Pitamakan, 3, 117	12	1:44.39	$93,000
2006	Meribel, 3, 117	G. K. Gomez	Precious Kitten, 3, 117	May Night, 3, 117	13	1:42.95	77,500
2005	Asi Siempre, 3, 120	G. L. Stevens	Dynamite Lass, 3, 116	Victory Lap, 3, 120	9	1:45.37	77,500
2004	Sister Swank, 3, 116	P. Day	Jinny's Gold, 3, 116	Shadow Cast, 3, 119	12	1:46.75	72,106
2003	Dyna Da Wyna, 3, 119	P. Day	Mexican Moonlight, 3, 116	Derrianne, 3, 123	10	1:43.54	69,998
2002	Bedanken, 3, 119	D. R. Pettinger	Mariensky, 3, 119	High Maintenance (GB), 3, 119	10	1:44.24	71,734
2001	dh-Chausson Poire, 3, 119	R. W. Woolsey		Quick Tip, 3, 123	10	1:42.93	46,576
	dh-Cozzy Corner, 3, 119	L. J. Meche					
2000	Good Game, 3, 119	P. Day	Impending Bear, 3, 119	Soccory, 3, 119	10	1:45.69	71,176
1999	Gimmeakissee, 3, 115	P. J. Cooksey	The Happy Hopper, 3, 119	Celestialbutterfly, 3, 119	9	1:42.05	70,122
1998	White Beauty, 3, 115	C. H. Borel	Shires Ende, 3, 117	Leaveemlaughing, 3, 117	8	1:43.09	56,591
1997	Mingling Glances, 3, 117	J. Bravo	Majestic Sunlight, 3, 113	Fluid Move, 3, 113	9	1:44.51	52,592
1996	Turkappeal, 3, 117	D. M. Barton	Inner Circle, 3, 113	Mariuka, 3, 117	9	1:46.10	52,126
1995	Country Cat, 3, 121	D. M. Barton	Appointed One, 3, 121	Petrouchka, 3, 121	10	1:44.88	51,150
1994	Pharma, 3, 121	C. W. Antley	Mariah's Storm, 3, 121	Thread, 3, 121	9	1:42.48	50,747
1993	Weekend Madness (Ire), 3, 121	C. R. Woods Jr.	Life Is Delicious, 3, 121	Augusta Springs, 3, 121	10	1:43.06	23,870
1992	Spinning Round, 3, 121	F. A. Arguello Jr.	Shes Just Super, 3, 121	Enticed, 3, 121	9	1:41.51	23,870
1991	La Gueriere, 3, 121	B. D. Peck	Dance O'My Life, 3, 121	Spanish Parade, 3, 121	9	1:43.49	29,250

Named for the Valley View ferry, Kentucky's oldest recorded commerical business. Sponsored by Pin Oak Stud of Versailles, Kentucky 2007. Valley View Breeders' Cup S. 1994-'95. All weather 2006. Originally scheduled on turf 2006. Dead heat for first 2001.

Pocahontas Stakes

Grade 3 in 2008. Churchill Downs, two-year-olds, fillies, 1 mile, dirt. Held October 28, 2007, with a gross value of $185,000. First held in 1969. First graded in 2005. Stakes record 1:34.82 (2000 Unbridled Elaine).

Year	Winner	Jockey	Second	Third	Strs	Time	1st Purse
2007	Pure Clan, 2, 119	J. R. Leparoux	Authenicat, 2, 121	Sky Mom, 2, 121	14	1:38.30	$104,774
2006	Change Up, 2, 121	G. K. Gomez	Mistical Plan, 2, 121	Lady Joanne, 2, 117	9	1:35.97	68,034
2005	French Park, 2, 118	M. Guidry	Trippi Street, 2, 118	Coolwind, 2, 118	12	1:37.19	74,772
2004	Punch Appeal, 2, 122	P. Day	Holy Trinity, 2, 118	Kota, 2, 122	7	1:37.77	67,890
2003	Stellar Jayne, 2, 119	C. H. Velasquez	Turn to Lass, 2, 119	Sister Star, 2, 117	9	1:38.97	69,626
2002	Belle of Perintown, 2, 116	M. Guidry	Star of Atticus, 2, 116	Souris, 2, 121	8	1:36.52	68,882
2001	Lotta Rhythm, 2, 116	M. St. Julien	Cunning Play, 2, 116	Joanies Bella, 2, 121	8	1:37.96	69,130
2000	Unbridled Elaine, 2, 113	S. J. Sellers	Ilusoria, 2, 117	Gold Mover, 2, 121	8	1:34.82	70,060
1999	Crown of Crimson, 2, 112	R. Albarado	Maddie's Promise, 2, 121	Dance for Dixie, 2, 114	8	1:37.81	69,812
1998	The Happy Hopper, 2, 121	W. Martinez	Tutorial, 2, 112	Gold From the West, 2, 112	9	1:37.73	70,556
1997	Mission Park, 2, 113	C. H. Borel	Rave, 2, 113	So Generous, 2, 112	10	1:38.55	70,432
1996	Water Street, 2, 112	C. Perret	Cotton Carnival, 2, 114	Private Pursuit, 2, 114	9	1:36.90	69,936

Year	Winner	Jockey	Second	Third	Strs	Time	1st Purse
1995	Birr, 2, 112	P. Day	Gold Sunrise, 2, 116	Classy 'n' Bold, 2, 114	8	1:36.84	$73,580
1994	Minister Wife, 2, 116	P. Day	Valor Lady, 2, 114	Musical Cat, 2, 114	6	1:38.64	73,385
1993	At the Half, 2, 121	S. J. Sellers	Footing, 2, 116	Mystic Union, 2, 112	12	1:38.13	75,660
1992	Coni Bug, 2, 121	S. J. Sellers	Sock City, 2, 121	Far Out Countess, 2, 114	8	1:37.85	54,698
1991	Fretina, 2, 116	J. E. Bruin	Pleasant Baby, 2, 116	Vivid Imagination, 2, 116	9	1:40.25	55,478
1990	Middlefork Rapids, 2, 116	R. M. Gonzalez	Dark Stage, 2, 116	Til Forbid, 2, 114	10	1:38.00	37,700
1989	Crowned, 2, 116	M. E. Smith	Charitable Gift, 2, 114	Truly My Style, 2, 114	6	1:39.80	36,010
1988	Solid Eight, 2, 121	R. P. Romero	Box Office Gold, 2, 114	Northern Wife, 2, 114	8	1:40.60	36,270
1987	Epitome, 2, 114	P. Day	Darien Miss, 2, 114	Cushion Cut, 2, 118	9	1:38.20	34,589
1986	Bestofbothworlds, 2, 112	P. J. Cooksey	Laserette, 2, 114	Combative, 2, 117	12	1:42.60	34,649
1985	Prime Union, 2, 119	D. E. Foster	Northern Maiden, 2, 112	Whirl Series, 2, 117	8	1:38.40	22,133
1984	Gallant Libby, 2, 119	P. Day	Off Shore Breeze, 2, 117	Gallants Gem, 2, 122	10	1:41.80	18,460
1983	Geevilla, 2, 114	P. Day	Robin's Rob, 2, 119	Sintra, 2, 114	11	1:40.20	18,403
	Flippers, 2, 117	P. Day	Shelbiana, 2, 114	Jay Paree, 2, 117	8	1:39.80	19,703
1982	Brindy Brindy, 2, 117	J. C. Espinoza	Roberto's Doll, 2, 119	Issues n' Answers, 2, 122	7	1:38.20	19,500
	Weekend Surprise, 2, 122	D. Brumfield	Decision, 2, 119	Quarrel Over, 2, 119	9	1:37.80	19,663
1981	Majestic Gold, 2, 118	J. C. Espinoza	I See Spring, 2, 112	Golden Try, 2, 112	15	1:26.80	20,768
	Taylor Park, 2, 121	J. McKnight	Ecoie d'Humanite, 2, 118	Dreamtide, 2, 112	14	1:26.40	20,605
1980	Kathy T., 2, 118	L. J. Melancon	Silver Doll, 2, 115	Fleet Pocket, 2, 114	10	1:27.60	18,476
	Masters Dream, 2, 118	G. Gallitano	Taralina, 2, 118	Singing Rockett, 2, 118	11	1:27.40	20,101
1979	Dancing Blade, 2, 121	A. S. Black	Champagne Ginny, 2, 115	Ribbon, 2, 115	13	1:26.80	17,258
1978	Starclock, 2, 121	R. DePass	Silver Oaks, 2, 114	Sensuous Sinnamon, 2, 115	9	1:25.40	14,820
	Safe, 2, 118	E. Fires	Sexy, 2, 115	Fair Advantage, 2, 121	10	1:25.60	14,983
1977	Rainy Princess, 2, 118	L. Snyder	Silver Spook, 2, 121	Irish Agate, 2, 118	8	1:25.20	14,909
	Plains and Simple, 2, 118	A. L. Fernandez	Salzburg, 2, 118	She's Debonair, 2, 112	9	1:26.20	14,909
1976	Ciao, 2, 121	W. Gavidia	Shady Lou, 2, 121	Every Move, 2, 112	9	1:27.40	14,812
	Sweet Alliance, 2, 115	C. J. McCarron	Pocket Princess, 2, 115	My Bold Beauty, 2, 118	8	1:25.60	14,649
1975	Alvarada, 2, 118	D. Brumfield	Confort Zone, 2, 121	Bells and Blades, 2, 121	11	1:27.60	15,941
1974	My Light, 2, 121	A. Hill	Channelette, 2, 115	Yale Coed, 2, 121	12	1:23.60	15,941
1973	Shoo Dear, 2, 121	D. Brumfield	Escrolla, 2, 118	Snow Peak, 2, 115	10	1:27.80	15,308
	Fairway Fable, 2, 118	D. E. Whited	Clemanna, 2, 121	Passing Look, 2, 118	9	1:26.00	15,308

Named for Pocahontas (1837 f. by *Glencoe), one of the great foundation mares of all time and ancestress of numerous American classic winners. Two divisions 1973, 1976-'78, 1980-'83. Nonwinners of a stakes worth $7,500 to the winner 1973. Nonwinners of a stakes 1975.

Poker Handicap

Grade 3 in 2008. Belmont Park, three-year-olds and up, 1 mile, turf. Held July 14, 2007, with a gross value of $112,600. First held in 1983. First graded in 1988. Stakes record 1:31.63 (1998 Elusive Quality).

Year	Winner	Jockey	Second	Third	Strs	Time	1st Purse
2007	Art Master, 6, 116	G. K. Gomez	Woodlander, 5, 114	Host (Chi), 7, 119	9	1:33.21	$67,560
2006	Rebel Rebel (Ire), 4, 116	E. S. Prado	Remarkable News (Ven), 4, 118	Vicarage, 4, 112	7	1:33.34	66,540
2005	Mr. Light (Arg), 6, 117	C. H. Velasquez	Willard Straight, 5, 115	Remind, 5, 117	7	1:32.18	67,080
2004	Christine's Outlaw, 4, 113	S. Bridgmohan	Millennium Dragon (GB), 5, 120	Silver Tree, 4, 117	9	1:32.46	67,560
2003	War Zone, 4, 117	J. Castellano	Trademark (SAf), 7, 117	Saint Verre, 5, 112	11	1:32.81	69,720
2002	Volponi, 4, 115	S. Bridgmohan	Saint Verre, 4, 112	Navesink, 4, 117	7	1:32.24	66,720
2001	Affirmed Success, 7, 121	J. D. Bailey	In Frank's Honor, 5, 114	Union One, 4, 114	6	1:34.60	66,240
2000	Affirmed Success, 6, 117	J. F. Chavez	Rabi (Ire), 5, 114	Weatherbird, 5, 113	10	1:34.06	68,280
1999	Rob 'n Gin, 5, 118	J. F. Chavez	Bomfim, 6, 115	Wised Up, 4, 115	9	1:32.81	69,120
1998	Elusive Quality, 5, 117	J. D. Bailey	Za-Im (GB), 4, 114	Fortitude, 5, 114	9	1:31.63	51,240
1997	Draw Shot, 4, 118	C. W. Antley	Val's Prince, 4, 114	Fortitude, 4, 112	10	1:33.08	51,345
1996	Smooth Runner, 5, 113	J. A. Krone	Mighty Forum (GB), 5, 116	Da Hoss, 4, 119	10	1:33.62	51,600
1995	†Caress, 4, 117	R. G. Davis	Fourstars Allstar, 7, 119	Pennine Ridge, 4, 119	9	1:34.20	51,030
1994	Dominant Prospect, 4, 114	J. F. Chavez	Fourstardave, 9, 114	Nijinsky's Gold, 5, 114	8	1:32.69	49,905
1993	Fourstardave, 8, 117	R. Migliore	Adam Smith (GB), 5, 122	Lech, 5, 117	7	1:33.02	53,190
1992	Scott the Great, 6, 117	J. Samyn	Kate's Valentine, 7, 117	Cigar Toss (Arg), 5, 117	8	1:33.27	54,810
1991	Who's to Pay, 5, 117	J. D. Bailey	Scott the Great, 5, 117	Senor Speedy, 4, 117	10	1:33.55	56,160
1990	Scottish Monk, 7, 117	A. T. Cordero Jr.	Quick Call, 6, 117	Yankee Affair, 8, 122	5	1:33.40	52,110
1989	Fourstardave, 4, 117	J. A. Santos	Feeling Gallant, 7, 117	Valid Fund, 4, 117	9	1:33.20	56,610
1988	Wanderkin, 5, 122	J. A. Santos	Kings River (Ire), 6, 122	dh-My Prince Charming, 5, 117	7	1:35.60	54,720
				dh-Silver Voice, 5, 117			
1987	Double Feint, 4, 117	J. A. Santos	Onyxly, 6, 117	Island Sun, 5, 117	8	1:35.20	34,320
1986	Island Sun, 4, 119	R. Migliore	Divulge, 4, 119	Equalize, 4, 119	10	2:02.40	33,300
1985	Mr. Chromacopy, 4, 119	C. Cruguet	Roving Minstrel, 4, 121	Regal Humor, 4, 119	6	1:42.40	33,420
1983	Freon, 6, 115	R. G. Davis	Nadasdy (Ire), 3, 113	Kentucky River, 5, 117	5	2:03.20	24,870

Named for Ogden Phipps's 1967 Bowling Green H. winner Poker (1963 c. by Round Table), broodmare sire of Seattle Slew and Silver Charm. Poker S. 1985-'95. Not held 1984. Dead heat for third 1988. Course record 1998. World record 1998. †Denotes female.

Potrero Grande Handicap

Grade 2 in 2008. Santa Anita Park, four-year-olds and up, 6½ furlongs, all weather. Held April 5, 2008, with a gross value of $200,000. First held in 1983. First graded in 1988. Stakes record 1:13.71 (1998 Son of a Pistol).

Year	Winner	Jockey	Second	Third	Strs	Time	1st Purse
2008	Greg's Gold, 7, 119	V. Espinoza	Surf Cat, 6, 120	El Roblar, 6, 118	6	1:14.62	$120,000

Year	Winner	Jockey	Second	Third	Strs	Time	1st Purse
2007	Smokey Stover, 4, 122	A. T. Gryder	Greg's Gold, 6, 118	Sailors Sunset, 4, 117	5	1:14.83	$120,000
2006	Surf Cat, 4, 119	A. O. Solis	Grinding It Out, 6, 116	Oceanus (Brz), 7, 114	5	1:15.00	60,000
2005	Harvard Avenue, 4, 115	G. K. Gomez	Rushin' to Altar, 6, 116	Roi Charmant, 4, 114	9	1:16.12	120,000
2004	McCann's Mojave, 4, 116	J. Valdivia Jr.	Unfurl the Flag, 4, 114	Bluesthestandard, 7, 118	5	1:15.60	66,840
2003	Bluesthestandard, 6, 115	M. E. Smith	Joey Franco, 4, 116	Kona Gold, 9, 121	7	1:14.86	72,000
2002	†Kalookan Queen, 6, 116	A. O. Solis	Ceeband, 5, 116	Elaborate, 7, 115	8	1:15.31	130,620
2001	Kona Gold, 7, 126	A. O. Solis	dh-Explicit, 4, 116 dh-Hollycombe, 7, 114		4	1:15.03	123,000
2000	Kona Gold, 6, 122	A. O. Solis	Old Topper, 5, 116	Your Halo, 5, 116	4	1:14.75	123,060
1999	Big Jag, 6, 119	J. Valdivia Jr.	‡Gold Land, 8, 117	Son of a Pistol, 7, 120	5	1:15.09	123,720
1998	Son of a Pistol, 6, 114	G. K. Gomez	White Bronco, 4, 114	Gold Land, 7, 115	9	**1:13.71**	66,420
1997	First Intent, 8, 114	R. R. Douglas	Hesabull, 4, 117	Northern Afleet, 4, 118	6	1:14.60	64,250
1996	Abaginone, 5, 115	G. L. Stevens	Dramatic Gold, 5, 117	Kingdom Found, 6, 118	6	1:14.59	124,400
1995	Lit de Justice, 5, 115	C. S. Nakatani	Cardmania, 9, 119	Phone Roberto, 6, 116	6	1:14.65	63,000
1994	Sir Hutch, 4, 117	P. A. Valenzuela	Concept Win, 4, 117	Furiously, 5, 117	5	1:14.48	61,100
1993	Gray Slewpy, 5, 118	K. Desormeaux	Cardmania, 7, 117	Star of the Crop, 4, 119	8	1:14.40	64,700
1992	Cardmania, 6, 117	E. Delahoussaye	Frost Free, 7, 117	Answer Do, 6, 123	4	1:17.16	60,200
1991	Jacodra, 4, 111	C. S. Nakatani	Answer Do, 5, 118	Bruho, 5, 117	6	1:15.10	62,300
1990	Olympic Prospect, 6, 121	P. A. Valenzuela	Raise a Stanza, 4, 118	Doncareer, 4, 114	4	1:14.20	60,400
1989	On the Line, 5, 125	G. L. Stevens	Ron Bon, 4, 116	Jamoke, 5, 114	10	1:14.00	66,500
1988	Gulch, 4, 117	E. Delahoussaye	†Very Subtle, 4, 120	Gallant Sailor, 5, 111	3	1:15.00	44,050
1987	Zabaleta, 4, 117	L. A. Pincay Jr.	Zany Tactics, 6, 120	Bedside Promise, 5, 125	4	1:15.00	44,850
1986	Halo Folks, 5, 124	C. J. McCarron	Bozina, 5, 111	American Legion, 6, 112	5	1:15.60	43,050
1985	Fifty Six Ina Row, 4, 117	L. A. Pincay Jr.	Hula Blaze, 5, 120	Coyotero, 7, 114	6	1:15.40	44,650
1984	Honeyland, 5, 117	W. Shoemaker	American Legion, 4, 113	Shecky Blue, 4, 116	9	1:15.40	40,450
1983	Chinook Pass, 4, 123	L. A. Pincay Jr.	Haughty But Nice, 5, 115	The Captain, 4, 114	5	1:14.60	37,050

Named for Potrero Grande Rancho, near present-day El Monte, California; potrero grande means "big pasture." Grade 3 1988–'96. Potrero Grande Breeders' Cup H. 1996-2007. Dirt 1983-2007. Dead heat for second 2001. ‡Early Pioneer finished second, DQ to fourth, 1999. Track record 1998. †Denotes female.

Prairie Meadows Cornhusker Handicap

Grade 2 in 2008. Prairie Meadows, three-year-olds and up, 1 1/8 miles, dirt. Held June 30, 2007, with a gross value of $300,000. First held in 1966. First graded in 1973. Stakes record 1:46.62 (1998 Beboppin Baby).

Year	Winner	Jockey	Second	Third	Strs	Time	1st Purse
2007	Dry Martini, 4, 115	E. Trujillo	Silent Pleasure, 4, 121	Patriot Act, 5, 116	9	1:48.41	$180,000
2006	Siphon City, 4, 115	E. Trujillo	Three Hour Nap, 4, 116	Gouldings Green, 5, 117	13	1:47.76	180,000
2005	Lord of the Game, 4, 117	E. Razo Jr.	Silver Axe, 8, 113	Mambo Train, 4, 115	8	1:49.94	180,000
2004	Roses in May, 4, 115	M. Guidry	Perfect Drift, 5, 119	Crafty Shaw, 6, 117	4	1:46.63	180,000
2003	Tenpins, 5, 118	R. Albarado	Bowman's Band, 5, 116	Woodmoon, 5, 118	6	1:48.39	210,000
2002	Mr. John, 4, 114	M. Guidry	Unshaded, 4, 115	Fajardo, 5, 113	10	1:47.97	240,000
2001	Euchre, 5, 116	G. K. Gomez	Dixie Dot Com, 6, 119	Sure Shot Biscuit, 5, 116	7	1:47.72	240,000
2000	Sir Bear, 7, 116	E. Coa	Skimming, 4, 111	Ecton Park, 4, 117	5	1:48.49	240,000
1999	Nite Dreamer, 4, 113	R. Albarado	Mocha Express, 4, 117	Worldly Ways (GB), 5, 116	7	1:48.85	231,000
1998	Beboppin Baby, 5, 114	J. Campbell	Acceptable, 4, 116	Pacificbounty, 4, 113	8	**1:46.62**	150,000
1997	Semoran, 4, 117	D. R. Flores	Mister Fire Eyes (Ire), 5, 115	Come On Flip, 6, 114	9	1:48.40	120,000
1995	Powerful Punch, 6, 115	C. C. Bourque	All Gone, 5, 115	Glaring, 5, 116	8	1:49.80	90,000
1994	Zeeruler, 6, 116	R. N. Lester	Powerful Punch, 5, 118	Dancing Jon, 6, 114	8	1:50.20	75,000
1993	Link, 5, 114	R. D. Ardoin	Rapid World, 5, 115	Flying Continental, 7, 117	9	1:50.40	75,000
1992	Irish Swap, 5, 117	B. E. Poyadou	Zeeruler, 4, 115	Stalwars, 7, 116	11	1:47.80	75,000
1991	Black Tie Affair (Ire), 5, 124	P. Day	Bedeviled, 4, 117	Whodam, 6, 113	4	1:48.70	75,000
1990	Dispersal, 4, 122	J. Velasquez	No More Cash, 4, 114	Protect Yourself, 8, 113	9	1:50.00	90,000
1989	Blue Buckaroo, 6, 115	S. J. Sellers	Henbane, 4, 117	Advancing Ensign, 4, 112	10	1:49.40	120,000
1988	Palace March (Ire), 4, 118	J. A. Krone	Outlaws Sham, 5, 114	Galba, 4, 117	8	1:49.00	120,000
1987	Bolshoi Boy, 4, 117	C. W. Antley	Forkintheroad, 5, 112	Honor Medal, 6, 119	10	1:48.40	120,000
1986	Gourami, 4, 116	T. T. Doocy	Honor Medal, 5, 114	Smile, 4, 120	7	1:49.40	150,000
1985	Gate Dancer, 4, 126	C. J. McCarron	Badwagon Harry, 6, 114	Eminency, 7, 119	8	1:48.60	100,800
1984	Timeless Native, 4, 122	D. Brumfield	‡Inevitable Leader, 5, 120	Wild Again, 4, 121	12	1:49.60	90,000
1983	Win Stat, 6, 111	D. Pettinger	†Bersid, 5, 116	Aspro, 5, 121	11	1:53.20	92,978
1982	Recusant, 4, 118	R. J. Hirdes Jr.	Plaza Starr, 4, 121	Vodika Collins, 4, 118	10	1:51.60	92,895
1981	Summer Advocate, 4, 118	K. Jones Jr.	Sun Catcher, 4, 121	Brent's Trans Am, 4, 116	11	1:48.20	93,143
1980	Hold Your Tricks, 5, 116	D. Pettinger	Overskate, 5, 126	Daring Damascus, 4, 117	10	1:49.20	88,688
1979	Star de Naskra, 4, 125	J. Fell	Prince Majestic, 5, 119	Quiet Jay, 4, 117	13	1:48.40	90,613
1978	True Statement, 4, 118	B. Fann	Big John Taylor, 5, 114	Giboulee, 4, 116	9	1:48.00	60,913
1977	Private Thoughts, 4, 118	R. R. Perez	Latimer, 5, 124	Dragset, 6, 113	8	1:48.00	62,782
1976	Dragset, 5, 112	S. Maple	Sharp Gary, 5, 113	Methdioxya, 4, 120	7	1:48.00	60,500
1975	Stonewalk, 4, 120	R. Turcotte	Sharp Gary, 4, 115	Rooter, 5, 114	14	1:48.40	59,290
1974	Blazing Gypsey, 5, 114	S. Burgos	Tom Tulle, 4, 121	Super Sail, 6, 117	14	1:49.60	57,963
1973	Joey Bob, 5, 118	L. Moyers	Haveago, 6, 121	Prince Astro, 4, 114	12	1:42.80	30,828

The Cornhusker Handicap was formerly held at Ak-Sar-Ben in Nebraska, the "Cornhusker State." Grade 3 1973-'77, 1990-2004. Cornhusker H. 1966-'72, 1985-'95. Ak-Sar-Ben Cornhusker H. 1973-'84. Prairie Meadows Cornhusker Breeders' Cup H. 1998-2006. Held at Ak-Sar-Ben 1966-'95. Not held 1996. 1 1/16 miles 1966-'73. ‡Pron Regard finished second, DQ to sixth, 1984. Track record 1998. †Denotes female.

Preakness Stakes

Grade 1 in 2008. Pimlico Race Course, three-year-olds, 1 3/16 miles, dirt. Held May 17, 2008, with a gross value of $1,000,000. First held in 1873. First graded in 1973. Stakes record 1:53.40 (1985 Tank's Prospect).

(See Triple Crown section for complete history of the Preakness Stakes)

Year	Winner	Jockey	Second	Third	Strs	Time	1st Purse
2008	**Big Brown**, 3, 126	K. J. Desormeaux	Macho Again, 3, 126	Icabad Crane, 3, 126	12	1:54.80	$600,000
2007	**Curlin**, 3, 126	R. Albarado	Street Sense, 3, 126	Hard Spun, 3, 126	9	1:53.46	600,000
2006	**Bernardini**, 3, 126	J. Castellano	Sweetnorthernsaint, 3, 126	Hemingway's Key, 3, 126	9	1:54.65	600,000
2005	**Afleet Alex**, 3, 126	J. Rose	Scrappy T, 3, 126	Giacomo, 3, 126	14	1:55.04	650,000
2004	**Smarty Jones**, 3, 126	S. Elliott	Rock Hard Ten, 3, 126	Eddington, 3, 126	10	1:55.59	650,000
2003	**Funny Cide**, 3, 126	J. A. Santos	Midway Road, 3, 126	Scrimshaw, 3, 126	10	1:55.61	650,000
2002	**War Emblem**, 3, 126	V. Espinoza	Magic Weisner, 3, 126	Proud Citizen, 3, 126	13	1:56.36	650,000
2001	**Point Given**, 3, 126	G. L. Stevens	A P Valentine, 3, 126	Congaree, 3, 126	11	1:55.51	650,000
2000	**Red Bullet**, 3, 126	J. D. Bailey	Fusaichi Pegasus, 3, 126	Impeachment, 3, 126	8	1:56.04	650,000
1999	**Charismatic**, 3, 126	C. W. Antley	Menifee, 3, 126	Badge, 3, 126	13	1:55.32	650,000
1998	**Real Quiet**, 3, 126	K. Desormeaux	Victory Gallop, 3, 126	Classic Cat, 3, 126	10	1:54.75	650,000
1997	**Silver Charm**, 3, 126	G. L. Stevens	Free House, 3, 126	Captain Bodgit, 3, 126	10	1:54.84	488,150
1996	**Louis Quatorze**, 3, 126	P. Day	Skip Away, 3, 126	Editor's Note, 3, 126	12	1:53.43	458,120
1995	**Timber Country**, 3, 126	P. Day	Oliver's Twist, 3, 126	Thunder Gulch, 3, 126	11	1:54.45	446,810
1994	**Tabasco Cat**, 3, 126	P. Day	Go for Gin, 3, 126	Concern, 3, 126	10	1:56.47	447,720
1993	**Prairie Bayou**, 3, 126	M. E. Smith	Cherokee Run, 3, 126	El Bakan, 3, 126	12	1:56.61	471,835
1992	**Pine Bluff**, 3, 126	C. J. McCarron	Alydeed, 3, 126	Casual Lies, 3, 126	14	1:55.60	484,120
1991	**Hansel**, 3, 126	J. D. Bailey	Corporate Report, 3, 126	Mane Minister, 3, 126	8	1:54.05	432,770
1990	**Summer Squall**, 3, 126	P. Day	Unbridled, 3, 126	Mister Frisky, 3, 126	9	1:53.60	445,900
1989	**Sunday Silence**, 3, 126	P. A. Valenzuela	Easy Goer, 3, 126	Rock Point, 3, 126	8	1:53.80	438,230
1988	**Risen Star**, 3, 126	E. Delahoussaye	Brian's Time, 3, 126	†Winning Colors, 3, 121	9	1:56.20	413,700
1987	**Alysheba**, 3, 126	C. J. McCarron	Bet Twice, 3, 126	Cryptoclearance, 3, 126	9	1:55.80	421,700
1986	**Snow Chief**, 3, 126	A. O. Solis	Ferdinand, 3, 126	Broad Brush, 3, 126	7	1:54.80	411,900
1985	**Tank's Prospect**, 3, 126	P. Day	Chief's Crown, 3, 126	Eternal Prince, 3, 126	11	**1:53.40**	423,200
1984	**Gate Dancer**, 3, 126	A. T. Cordero Jr.	Play On, 3, 126	Fight Over, 3, 126	10	1:53.60	243,600
1983	**Deputed Testamony**, 3, 126	D. A. Miller Jr.	Desert Wine, 3, 126	High Honors, 3, 126	12	1:55.40	251,200
1982	**Aloma's Ruler**, 3, 126	J. L. Kaenel	Linkage, 3, 126	Cut Away, 3, 126	7	1:55.40	209,900
1981	**Pleasant Colony**, 3, 126	J. Velasquez	Bold Ego, 3, 126	Paristo, 3, 126	13	1:54.60	200,800
1980	**Codex**, 3, 126	A. T. Cordero Jr.	†Genuine Risk, 3, 121	Colonel Moran, 3, 126	8	1:54.20	180,600
1979	**Spectacular Bid**, 3, 126	R. J. Franklin	Golden Act, 3, 126	Screen King, 3, 126	5	1:54.20	165,300
1978	**Affirmed**, 3, 126	S. Cauthen	Alydar, 3, 126	Believe It, 3, 126	7	1:54.40	136,200
1977	**Seattle Slew**, 3, 126	J. Cruguet	Iron Constitution, 3, 126	Run Dusty Run, 3, 126	9	1:54.40	138,600
1976	**Elocutionist**, 3, 126	J. Lively	Play the Red, 3, 126	Bold Forbes, 3, 126	6	1:55.00	129,700
1975	**Master Derby**, 3, 126	D. G. McHargue	Foolish Pleasure, 3, 126	Diabolo, 3, 126	10	1:56.40	158,100
1974	**Little Current**, 3, 126	M. A. Rivera	Neapolitan Way, 3, 126	Cannonade, 3, 126	13	1:54.60	156,500
1973	**Secretariat**, 3, 126	R. Turcotte	Sham, 3, 126	Our Native, 3, 126	6	1:54.40	129,900

Named for M. H. Sanford's Preakness (1867 c. by Lexington), first winner of the Dinner Party S. (now the Dixie S. [G2]) at Pimlico. Held at Morris Park, New York 1890. Held at Gravesend Park, New York 1894-1908. Not held 1891-'93. 1 1/2 miles 1894. 1 1/4 miles 1889. 1 1/16 miles 1894-1900, 1908. 1 mile 70 yards 1901-'07. 1 mile 1909-'10. 1 1/8 miles 1911-'24. ‡Dancer's Image finished third, DQ to eighth, 1968. †Denotes female. In 1973 *Daily Racing Form* reported the time as 1:53⅖, a track and stakes record; official time is recorded as 1:54⅖.

Princess Rooney Handicap

Grade 1 in 2008. Calder Race Course, three-year-olds and up, fillies and mares, 6 furlongs, dirt. Held July 7, 2007, with a gross value of $500,000. First held in 1985. First graded in 1999. Stakes record 1:09.93 (2005 Madcap Escapade).

Year	Winner	Jockey	Second	Third	Strs	Time	1st Purse
2007	**River's Prayer**, 4, 118	C. L. Potts	Shaggy Mane, 4, 118	G City Gal, 4, 114	13	1:10.66	$285,200
2006	**Malibu Mint**, 4, 116	J. Arce	Prospective Saint, 5, 116	Hot Storm, 4, 117	7	1:10.02	294,000
2005	**Madcap Escapade**, 4, 120	J. D. Bailey	Happy Ticket, 4, 117	Savorthetime, 6, 117	6	**1:09.93**	294,000
2004	**Ema Bovary (Chi)**, 5, 119	R. M. Gonzalez	Bear Fan, 5, 122	Lady Tak, 4, 119	6	1:10.81	294,000
2003	**Gold Mover**, 5, 118	J. D. Bailey	Vision in Flight, 4, 113	Harmony Lodge, 5, 116	8	1:11.31	294,000
2002	**Gold Mover**, 4, 115	J. D. Bailey	Xtra Heat, 4, 127	Fly Me Crazy, 4, 112	6	1:10.21	240,000
2001	**Dream Supreme**, 4, 122	P. Day	Hidden Assets, 4, 114	Sugar N Spice, 6, 114	9	1:10.48	240,000
2000	**Hurricane Bertie**, 5, 117	P. Day	Bourbon Belle, 5, 116	Cassidy, 5, 115	7	1:11.43	240,000
1999	**Princess Pietrina**, 5, 114	R. Homeister Jr.	Hurricane Bertie, 4, 118	U Can Do It, 6, 119	8	1:10.49	180,000
1998	**U Can Do It**, 5, 118	E. Coa	Closed Escrow, 5, 117	Colonial Minstrel, 4, 118	9	1:10.12	150,000
1997	**Vivace**, 4, 117	R. P. Romero	Ashboro, 4, 119	Special Request, 4, 115	9	1:10.94	150,000
1996	**Chaposa Springs**, 4, 126	L. A. Pincay Jr.	Reign Dance, 4, 113	Supah Jess, 4, 113	6	1:23.54	60,000
1995	**Miss Gibson County**, 4, 115	G. Boulanger	Goldarama, 5, 113	Sigrun, 5, 116	7	1:23.18	60,000
1994	**Roamin Rachel**, 4, 119	W. S. Ramos	Sigrun, 5, 113	Goldarama, 4, 110	10	1:24.01	60,000
1993	**Lady Sonata**, 4, 115	M. A. Lee	Fortune Forty Four, 4, 112	Treasured, 6, 112	5	1:23.00	30,000
1992	**Magal**, 5, 117	R. Hernandez	Fortune Forty Four, 4, 111	My Own True Love, 4, 116	8	1:23.60	30,000
1991	**Magal**, 4, 112	R. Hernandez	Joyce Azalene, 4, 110	Wekive Run, 3, 112	7	1:24.62	32,550
1990	**Sweet Proud Polly**, 3, 112	P. A. Rodriguez	Legend One, 4, 110	Love's Exchange, 4, 117	6	1:25.00	32,450
1989	**Ana T.**, 4, 113	R. N. Lester	‡Ells Once Again, 5, 111	My Sweet Replica, 5, 112	8	1:24.80	48,990
1988	**Spirit of Fighter**, 5, 121	O. J. Londono	Stanleys Run, 3, 111	Sheer Ice, 6, 117	7	1:24.60	32,550
1987	**Classy Tricks**, 4, 115	M. C. Suckie	Sheer Ice, 5, 117	Spirit of Fighter, 4, 123	5	1:25.00	32,040

Year	Winner	Jockey	Second	Third	Strs	Time	1st Purse
1986	Classy Tricks, 3, 112	R. N. Lester	Fleur de Soleil, 3, 113	Southern Velvet, 5, 113	6	1:25.00	$28,130
1985	Birdie Belle, 4, 121	J. A. Santiago	Private Secretary, 4, 119	T. V. Snow, 5, 118	8	1:24.40	33,240

Named for Paula J. Tucker's 1984 champion older female and '82 Melaleuca S. winner Princess Rooney (1980 f. by Verbatim). Grade 3 1999-2001. Grade 2 2002-'05. 7 furlongs 1985-'96. ‡Spirit of Fighter finished second, DQ to fifth, 1989.

Prioress Stakes

Grade 1 in 2008. Belmont Park, three-year-olds, fillies, 6 furlongs, dirt. Held July 7, 2007, with a gross value of $240,000. First held in 1948. First graded in 1973. Stakes record 1:08.26 (2001 Xtra Heat).

Year	Winner	Jockey	Second	Third	Strs	Time	1st Purse
2007	Dream Rush, 3, 122	E. Coa	Graeme Six, 3, 116	Silver Knockers, 3, 116	9	1:09.02	$150,000
2006	Wildcat Bettie B, 3, 120	M. G. Pino	Wild Gams, 3, 120	Livernore Valley, 3, 118	8	1:09.18	150,000
2005	Acey Deucey, 3, 119	D. Nelson	Maddalena, 3, 119	Sense of Style, 3, 121	7	1:10.37	150,000
2004	Friendly Michelle, 3, 119	C. S. Nakatani	Feline Story, 3, 121	Forest Music, 3, 119	9	1:09.09	150,000
2003	House Party, 3, 121	J. A. Santos	Chimichurri, 3, 119	Princess V., 3, 115	8	1:09.45	120,000
2002	Carson Hollow, 3, 114	J. R. Velazquez	Spring Meadow, 3, 121	Proper Gamble, 3, 121	7	1:08.79	120,000
2001	Xtra Heat, 3, 121	R. Wilson	Above Perfection, 3, 116	Harmony Lodge, 3, 116	7	**1:08.26**	120,000
2000	I'm Brassy, 3, 113	M. J. Luzzi	Dat You Miz Blue, 3, 114	Lucky Livi, 3, 121	9	1:09.53	90,000
1999	Sapphire n' Silk, 3, 121	P. Day	Marley Vale, 3, 112	Confessional, 3, 118	9	1:09.55	90,000
1998	Hurricane Bertie, 3, 121	P. Day	Catinca, 3, 114	Foil, 3, 114	11	1:08.85	68,220
1997	Pearl City, 3, 118	J. D. Bailey	Alyssum, 3, 121	Vegas Prospector, 3, 121	5	1:09.40	64,680
1996	Capote Belle, 3, 112	J. R. Velazquez	Flat Fleet Feet, 3, 118	Miss Maggie, 3, 116	10	1:08.81	67,200
1995	Scotzanna, 3, 121	R. Platts	Culver City, 3, 116	Miss Golden Circle, 3, 118	9	1:10.61	66,840
1994	Penny's Reshoot, 3, 116	J. R. Velazquez	Heavenly Prize, 3, 116	Beckys Shirt, 3, 114	6	1:09.07	64,500
1993	Classy Mirage, 3, 114	J. A. Krone	Missed the Storm, 3, 118	Educated Risk, 3, 118	5	1:08.89	67,680
1992	American Royale, 3, 118	J. A. Santos	Debra's Victory, 3, 121	Preach, 3, 118	6	1:09.36	68,280
1991	Zama Hummer, 3, 114	G. L. Stevens	Missy's Mirage, 3, 114	Devilish Touch, 3, 118	10	1:09.88	74,760
1990	Token Dance, 3, 114	E. Maple	Stella Madrid, 3, 121	Charging Fire, 3, 114	4	1:09.40	49,770
1989	Safely Kept, 3, 118	A. T. Cordero Jr.	Cojinx, 3, 114	The Way It's Binn, 3, 114	5	1:11.60	49,770
1988	Fara's Team, 3, 114	J. D. Bailey	Lake Valley, 3, 112	Raging Lady, 3, 114	6	1:10.20	65,700
1987	Firey Challenge, 3, 114	R. Migliore	Up the Apalachee, 3, 118	Monogram, 3, 114	12	1:10.60	69,300
1986	Religiosity, 3, 112	J. A. Santos	Fighter Fox, 3, 112	Trompbe de Naskra, 3, 114	8	1:11.00	54,450
1985	Clocks Secret, 3, 115	J. Nied Jr.	Lady's Secret, 3, 118	Ride Sally, 3, 112	8	1:10.20	53,010
1984	Proud Clarioness, 3, 115	J. Samyn	Dumdedumdedum, 3, 112	Suavite, 3, 112	6	1:10.40	41,400
1983	Able Money, 3, 112	A. Graell	Quixotic Lady, 3, 118	Captivating Grace, 3, 118	10	1:11.00	34,440
1982	Trove, 3, 118	M. Venezia	Larida, 3, 114	Dearly Too, 3, 112	8	1:10.00	34,380
1981	Tina Tina Too, 3, 118	C. B. Asmussen	Sweet Revenge, 3, 121	Ruler's Dancer, 3, 112	8	1:11.20	33,420
1980	Lien, 3, 115	E. Maple	Cybele, 3, 112	Nuit d'Amour, 3, 115	10	1:11.00	27,390
1979	Fall Aspen, 3, 121	R. I. Velez	Spanish Fake, 3, 118	Too Many Sweets, 3, 115	7	1:11.40	25,740
1978	Tempest Queen, 3, 118	J. Velasquez	Sweet Joyce, 3, 112	Silver Ice, 3, 115	5	1:11.40	25,320
1977	Ring O'Bells, 3, 116	A. T. Cordero Jr.	Road Princess, 3, 118	Pearl Necklace, 3, 116	10	1:10.40	22,410
1976	Dearly Precious, 3, 121	B. Baeza	Old Goat, 3, 118	Answer, 3, 118	4	1:09.80	22,110
1975	Sarsar, 3, 118	W. Shoemaker	Stulcer, 3, 114	Gallant Trial, 3, 114	7	1:10.80	17,070
1974	Clear Copy, 3, 115	D. Montoya	Heartful, 3, 118	Talking Picture, 3, 115	12	1:11.00	17,745
1973	Windy's Daughter, 3, 121	B. Baeza	Voler, 3, 115	Waltz Fan, 3, 115	10	1:10.20	17,355

Named for the first American Thoroughbred to ever win a race in England, Prioress (1853 f. by *Sovereign). Grade 3 1973-'74, 1985-'87. Not graded 1975-'84. Grade 2 1988-2000. Prioress Breeders' Cup S. 2006. Held at Jamaica 1948-'59. Held at Aqueduct 1960-'86.

Providencia Stakes

Grade 2 in 2008. Santa Anita Park, three-year-olds, fillies, 1 mile, turf. Held April 5, 2008, with a gross value of $150,000. First held in 1981. First graded in 2005. Stakes record 1:34.55 (2004 Ticker Tape [GB]).

Year	Winner	Jockey	Second	Third	Strs	Time	1st Purse
2008	Missit (Ire), 3, 115	V. Espinoza	Sweeter Still (Ire), 3, 119	Bel Air Sizzle, 3, 117	9	1:34.91	$90,000
2007	Super Freaky, 3, 117	J. K. Court	Passified (GB), 3, 119	Gotta Have Her, 3, 115	11	1:35.59	67,560
2006	Foxysox (GB), 3, 119	A. Bisono	Harriett Lane, 3, 119	Chosen Royalty, 3, 116	9	1:34.88	65,640
2005	Berbatim, 3, 116	A. O. Solis	Royal Copenhagen (Fr), 3, 117	Thatswhatimean, 3, 119	10	1:47.66	66,960
2004	Ticker Tape (GB), 3, 118	K. Desormeaux	Amorama (Fr), 3, 114	Winendynme, 3, 115	12	**1:34.55**	68,220
2003	Star Vega (GB), 3, 114	M. E. Smith	Makeup Artist, 3, 115	Shapes and Shadows, 3, 115	6	1:47.89	90,000
2002	Megahertz (GB), 3, 118	A. O. Solis	La Martina (GB), 3, 118	Ayzal (GB), 3, 114	7	1:47.34	48,690
2001	Dynamous, 3, 117	V. Espinoza	Heads Will Roll (GB), 3, 114	Little Firefly (Ire), 3, 116	7	1:50.13	49,875
2000	Kumari Continent, 3, 116	D. R. Flores	Minor Details, 3, 118	Velvet Morning, 3, 115	7	1:48.37	47,790
1999	Sweet Life, 3, 118	A. O. Solis	Lady At Peace, 3, 116	Smittenby (Ire), 3, 116	6	1:49.85	48,375
1998	Country Garden (GB), 3, 118	K. Desormeaux	Star's Proud Penny, 3, 120	Marie J, 3, 115	8	1:50.84	49,050
1997	Famous Digger, 3, 114	B. Blanc	Cerita, 3, 114	Clever Pilot, 3, 114	7	1:49.85	48,160
1996	Gastronomical, 3, 116	K. Desormeaux	Wish You, 3, 114	Staffin (GB), 3, 114	6	1:50.40	47,880
1995	Artica, 3, 117	L. A. Pincay Jr.	Kindred Soul, 3, 114	One Hot Mama, 3, 115	6	1:49.36	46,725
1994	Fancy 'n Fabulous, 3, 114	A. O. Solis	Rabiadella, 3, 117	Espadrille, 3, 117	7	1:47.40	47,700
1993	On the Catwalk (Ire), 3, 116	E. Delahoussaye	Amal Hayati, 3, 118	Voluptuous, 3, 114	6	1:50.35	46,650
1992	Miss Turkana, 3, 115	A. L. Castanon	Red Bandana, 3, 114	More Than Willing, 3, 117	7	1:47.32	47,475
1991	Fantastic Ways, 3, 115	C. J. McCarron	Island Shuffle, 3, 114	Saucy Lady B, 3, 115	7	1:49.50	49,425
1990	Materco, 3, 120	E. Delahoussaye	Somethingmerry, 3, 120	Nijinsky's Lover, 3, 120	9	1:47.40	48,900

Year	Winner	Jockey	Second	Third	Strs	Time	1st Purse
1989	Formidable Lady, 3, 117	G. L. Stevens	General Charge (Ire), 3, 117	Kelly, 3, 117	10	1:50.60	$49,350
1988	Pattern Step, 3, 120	C. J. McCarron	Do So, 3, 117	Twice Titled, 3, 117	8	1:48.00	48,000
1987	Some Sensation, 3, 117	L. A. Pincay Jr.	Davie's Lamb, 3, 113	Pink Slipper, 3, 113	7	1:48.20	37,950
1986	Miraculous, 3, 113	G. L. Stevens	Top Corsage, 3, 116	Roberto's Key, 3, 115	8	1:47.80	38,350
1985	Soft Dawn, 3, 113	W. Shoemaker	Rose Cream, 3, 114	Charming Susan, 3, 117	7	1:49.60	37,850
1984	Class Play, 3, 117	L. A. Pincay Jr.	Pronto Miss, 3, 115	Powder Break, 3, 113	7	1:50.20	37,850
1983	Spruce Song, 3, 115	S. Hawley	Yours Or Mine, 3, 114	Stage Door Canteen, 3, 115	10	1:47.40	39,850
1982	Phaedra, 3, 117	L. A. Pincay Jr.	Northern Style, 3, 115	Carry a Tune, 3, 115	10	1:47.00	39,800
1981	Flying Baton, 3, 113	T. Lipham	Ice Princess, 3, 115	Bee a Scout, 3, 115	11	1:47.60	34,050

Named for an 1843 California land grant, Rancho Providencia, located near present-day Burbank; providencia means "providence" or "foresight." Grade 3 2005-'07. 1 1/8 miles 1981-2003, 2005.

Pucker Up Stakes

Grade 3 in 2008. Arlington Park, three-year-olds, fillies, 1 1/8 miles, turf. Held September 8, 2007, with a gross value of $200,000. First held in 1961. First graded in 1973. Stakes record 1:47.58 (1991 Jinski's World).

Year	Winner	Jockey	Second	Third	Strs	Time	1st Purse
2007	Dreaming of Anna, 3, 122	E. T. Baird	Touch My Soul (Fr), 3, 118	Bel Air Beauty, 3, 118	12	1:48.20	$111,600
2006	Vacare, 3, 116	C. H. Marquez Jr.	Walklikeanegyptian (Ire), 3, 116	Ballet Pacifica, 3, 118	9	1:49.71	120,000
2005	Royal Copenhagen (Fr), 3, 116	S. Bridgmohan	Singhalese (GB), 3, 122	Isla Cozzene, 3, 116	11	1:48.76	120,000
2004	Ticker Tape (GB), 3, 122	K. Desormeaux	Spotlight (GB), 3, 122	Sister Swank, 3, 116	11	1:48.63	120,000
2003	Aud, 3, 118	B. D. Peck	Hail Hillary, 3, 116	Julie's Prize, 3, 120	12	1:49.16	105,000
2002	Little Treasure (Fr), 3, 122	R. R. Douglas	Cellars Shiraz, 3, 122	Kathy K D, 3, 116	11	1:49.92	90,000
2001	Snow Dance, 3, 122	C. Perret	Kiss the Devil, 3, 116	Twilite Tryst, 3, 116	12	1:47.93	90,000
2000	Solvig, 3, 117	P. Day	Zoftig, 3, 118	Impending Bear, 3, 118	6	1:52.40	90,000
1997	Witchful Thinking, 3, 121	G. K. Gomez	Swearingen, 3, 116	Cozy Blues, 3, 116	8	1:48.80	75,000
1996	Ms. Mostly, 3, 114	R. P. Romero	Mountain Affair, 3, 116	Clamorosa, 3, 121	9	1:51.18	90,000
1995	Grand Charmer, 3, 116	P. Day	Upper Noosh, 3, 116	Set Me Straight, 3, 114	8	1:49.59	60,000
1994	Work the Crowd, 3, 118	A. T. Gryder	Irish Forever, 3, 116	Looking for Heaven, 3, 116	14	1:49.32	60,000
1993	Amal Hayati, 3, 113	W. S. Ramos	Warside, 3, 113	Future Starlet, 3, 111	11	1:53.39	60,000
1992	Ziggy's Act, 3, 116	G. Boulanger	Bernique, 3, 111	Luv Me Luv Me Not, 3, 121	10	1:48.79	60,000
1991	Jinski's World, 3, 111	A. Madrid Jr.	Ms. Aerosmith, 3, 116	Radiant Ring, 3, 121	9	**1:47.58**	60,000
1990	Southern Tradition, 3, 116	E. Fires	Virgin Michael, 3, 116	Slew of Pearls, 3, 116	11	1:49.20	70,140
1989	Oczy Czarnie, 3, 112	C. A. Black	Adira, 3, 112	Vanities, 3, 115	9	1:55.00	67,680
1987	Sum, 3, 118	E. Fires	Spectacular Bev, 3, 118	Lucie's Bower, 3, 113	10	1:51.80	47,790
1986	Top Corsage, 3, 120	S. Hawley	Marianna's Girl, 3, 115	Innsbruck (GB), 3, 114	10	1:44.20	34,620
1985	Itsagem, 3, 118	K. K. Allen	Miss Ultimo, 3, 121	Tide, 3, 112	7	1:57.60	35,520
1984	Witwatersrand, 3, 112	E. Fires	Madam Flutterby, 3, 118	Mr. T.'s Tune, 3, 112	9	1:52.40	48,885
	Dictina (Fr), 3, 112	J. L. Diaz	Nettie Cometti, 3, 121	Princess Moran, 3, 116	7	1:51.40	48,285
1983	Decision, 3, 121	E. Fires	Narrate, 3, 118	Won'tyoucomehome, 3, 116	15	1:51.20	35,310
1982	Rose Bouquet, 3, 121	R. P. Romero	Stay a Leader, 3, 116	Smart Heiress, 3, 121	11	1:53.60	34,710
1981	Melanie Frances, 3, 116	R. Sibille	Safe Play, 3, 121	Touch of Glamour, 3, 116	9	1:51.80	33,660
1980	Ribbon, 3, 114	P. Day	Satin Ribera, 3, 121	Cannon Boy, 3, 113	14	1:52.20	35,250
1979	Allisons' Gal, 3, 112	M. R. Morgan	Safe, 3, 121	Cup of Honey, 3, 116	12	2:00.40	34,500
1978	Key to the Saga, 3, 119	J. Samyn	Pretty Delight, 3, 119	Xandu, 3, 122	13	1:51.40	34,650
1977	Rich Soil, 3, 122	M. A. Rivera	New Scent, 3, 114	Ivory Castle, 3, 122	12	1:50.40	34,530
1976	T. V. Vixen, 3, 122	M. Manganello	Three Colors, 3, 119	True Reality, 3, 113	8	1:48.40	36,600
1975	Kissapotamus, 3, 118	D. Stover	Miami Game, 3, 118	Be Victorious, 3, 113	11	1:45.60	21,400
1974	Tappahannock, 3, 113	W. Gavidia	Pot Roast Billie, 3, 112	Miss Indian Chief, 3, 115	13	1:47.60	22,350
1973	Eleven Pleasures, 3, 112	H. Arroyo	Princess Doubleday, 3, 121	Guided Missle, 3, 112	9	1:37.60	16,150

Named for Mrs. Ada L. Rice's 1957 champion older female and '57 Washington Park H. winner Pucker Up (1953 f. by Olympia). Not graded 1979. Grade 2 1996-'97. Pucker Up H. 1961, 1963-'73. Held at Hawthorne Race Course 1985. Not held 1988, 1998-'99. 1 mile 1961, 1966-'73. 1 1/16 miles 1962-'65, 1974-'75, 1986. 1 3/16 miles 1979. Dirt 1961-'74, 1976. Originally scheduled at 1 1/8 miles on turf 1973. Originally scheduled at 1 1/16 miles on turf 1974. Two divisions 1984.

Queen Elizabeth II Challenge Cup Stakes

Grade 1 in 2008. Keeneland Race Course, three-year-olds, fillies, 1 1/8 miles, turf. Held October 13, 2007, with a gross value of $500,000. First held in 1984. First graded in 1986. Stakes record 1:45.81 (1996 Memories of Silver).

Year	Winner	Jockey	Second	Third	Strs	Time	1st Purse
2007	Bit of Whimsy, 3, 121	J. Castellano	Dreaming of Anna, 3, 121	Coquerelle (Ire), 3, 121	9	1:48.73	$310,000
2006	Vacare, 3, 121	C. H. Marquez Jr.	Mauralakana (Fr), 3, 121	Quiet Royal, 3, 121	11	1:48.42	310,000
2005	Sweet Talker, 3, 121	R. Bejarano	Karen's Caper, 3, 121	Gorella (Fr), 3, 121	7	1:51.20	310,000
2004	Ticker Tape (GB), 3, 121	K. Desormeaux	Barancella (Fr), 3, 121	River Belle (GB), 3, 121	7	1:51.35	310,000
2003	Film Maker, 3, 121	E. S. Prado	Maiden Tower (GB), 3, 121	Casual Look, 3, 121	7	1:47.82	310,000
2002	Riskaverse, 3, 121	M. Guidry	Zenda (GB), 3, 121	Lush Soldier, 3, 121	9	1:49.84	310,000
2001	Affluent, 3, 121	E. Delahoussaye	Golden Apples (Ire), 3, 121	Snow Dance, 3, 121	10	1:50.03	310,000
2000	Collect the Cash, 3, 121	S. J. Sellers	Blue Moon, 3, 121	Theoretically, 3, 121	9	1:47.94	310,000
1999	Perfect Sting, 3, 121	P. Day	Tout Charmant, 3, 121	Wannabe Grand (Ire), 3, 121	9	1:50.66	310,000
1998	Tenski, 3, 121	R. Migliore	Shires Ende, 3, 121	Sierra Voyager, 3, 121	9	1:48.54	248,000
1997	Ryafan, 3, 121	A. O. Solis	Auntie Mame, 3, 121	Golden Arches (Fr), 3, 121	8	1:46.66	248,000
1996	Memories of Silver, 3, 121	R. G. Davis	Shake the Yoke (GB), 3, 121	Antespend, 3, 121	10	**1:45.81**	248,000
1995	Perfect Arc, 3, 121	J. R. Velazquez	Auriette (Ire), 3, 121	Country Cat, 3, 121	8	1:49.84	155,000
1994	Danish (Ire), 3, 121	J. A. Krone	Eternal Reve, 3, 121	Avie's Fancy, 3, 121	10	1:48.89	124,000

Year	Winner	Jockey	Second	Third	Strs	Time	1st Purse
1993	Tribulation, 3, 121	J. Samyn	Miami Sands (Ire), 3, 121	Possibly Perfect, 3, 121	9	1:53.62	$124,000
1992	Captive Miss, 3, 121	J. A. Krone	Suivi, 3, 121	Trampoli, 3, 121	10	1:48.66	124,000
1991	La Gueriere, 3, 121	B. D. Peck	Satin Flower, 3, 121	Radiant Ring, 3, 121	9	1:49.86	130,000
1990	Plenty of Grace, 3, 121	J. D. Bailey	Christiecat, 3, 121	My Girl Jeannie, 3, 121	10	1:51.40	65,000
1989	Coolawin, 3, 121	J. A. Velez Jr.	To the Lighthouse, 3, 121	Songlines, 3, 121	8	1:43.20	65,000
1988	Love You by Heart, 3, 121	R. P. Romero	Siggebo, 3, 121	Glowing Honor, 3, 121	8	1:44.80	65,000
1987	Graceful Darby, 3, 121	J. D. Bailey	Shot Gun Bonnie, 3, 121	Sum, 3, 121	10	1:47.20	65,000
1986	Lotka, 3, 121	W. A. Guerra	Minstress, 3, 121	Top Corsage, 3, 121	9	1:50.00	65,000
1985	Contredance, 3, 112	E. Maple	Debutant Dancer, 3, 115	Folk Art, 3, 120	10	1:47.00	55,608
1984	Sintra, 3, 112	K. K. Allen	Solar Halo, 3, 112	Mr. T.'s Tune, 3, 112	12	1:43.40	69,644

Named in honor of the 1984 visit of Queen Elizabeth II of England to Central Kentucky; she presented the first winner's trophy. Grade 3 1986-'87. Grade 2 1988-'90. 1¹/₁₆ miles 1987. Dirt 1984-'86.

Queens County Handicap

Grade 3 in 2008. Aqueduct, three-year-olds and up, 1⁹/₁₆ miles, dirt. Held December 8, 2007, with a gross value of $104,900. First held in 1902. First graded in 1973. Stakes record 1:54.40 (1972 Sunny and Mild).

Year	Winner	Jockey	Second	Third	Strs	Time	1st Purse
2007	Evening Attire, 9, 115	E. S. Prado	Barcola, 4, 116	Hunting, 4, 115	5	1:58.01	$64,140
2006	Magna Graduate, 4, 118	J. R. Velazquez	Papi Chullo, 4, 116	Smart Growth, 5, 115	6	1:55.19	64,620
2005	Philanthropist, 4, 115	E. Coa	West Virginia, 4, 115	We Can Seek (Chi), 4, 113	5	1:56.99	64,440
2004	Classic Endeavor, 6, 117	A. T. Gryder	Evening Attire, 6, 123	Colita, 4, 115	9	1:57.13	67,260
2003	Thunder Blitz, 5, 114	J. F. Chavez	Evening Attire, 5, 123	Seattle Fitz (Arg), 4, 115	6	1:55.90	64,980
2002	Snake Mountain, 4, 117	J. A. Santos	Docent, 4, 115	Cat's At Home, 5, 115	7	1:56.84	66,000
2001	Evening Attire, 3, 113	S. Bridgmohan	Balto Star, 3, 118	Top Official, 6, 113	8	1:55.08	67,140
2000	Boston Party, 4, 114	N. Arroyo Jr.	Talk's Cheap, 4, 115	Turnofthecentury, 3, 116	9	1:56.32	50,340
1999	Early Warning, 4, 116	J. F. Chavez	Doc Martin, 4, 112	Yankee Victor, 3, 114	7	1:55.03	49,230
1998	Fire King, 5, 113	F. Lovato Jr.	Las Vegas Ernie, 4, 112	Mr. Sinatra, 4, 119	7	1:56.88	49,140
1997	Mr. Sinatra, 3, 115	R. Migliore	Delay of Game, 4, 118	Draw, 4, 113	8	1:55.68	49,725
1996	Topsy Robsy, 4, 111	P. Keim-Bruno	More to Tell, 5, 114	Colonial Secretary, 4, 116	5	1:55.30	48,705
1995	Aztec Empire, 5, 113	J. Samyn	Mighty Magee, 3, 115	More to Tell, 4, 115	9	1:55.56	50,340
1994	Federal Funds, 5, 112	D. Carr	Jacksonport, 5, 110	Contract Court, 4, 116	8	1:56.42	49,665
1993	Repletion, 4, 111	M. E. Smith	Dibbs n' Dubbs, 5, 111	Primitive Hall, 4, 113	8	1:44.35	53,010
1992	Shots Are Ringing, 5, 117	J. R. Velazquez	A Call to Rise, 4, 111	Jacksonport, 5, 111	6	1:54.90	51,120
1991	Nome, 5, 112	E. Maple	Runaway Stream, 4, 116	Challenge My Duty, 4, 114	5	1:56.18	51,390
1990	Sports View, 3, 114	C. Perret	I'm Sky High, 4, 115	dh-Killer Diller, 3, 115	8	1:57.00	53,550
				dh-Lost Opportunity, 4, 112			
1989	Its Acedemic, 5, 115	J. D. Bailey	Homebuilder, 5, 113	Ole Atocha, 4, 113	7	1:58.00	52,290
1988	Lay Down, 4, 109	J. Samyn	Nostalgia's Star, 6, 113	Pleasant Virginian, 4, 113	6	1:57.20	64,980
1987	Personal Flag, 4, 116	R. P. Romero	Easy N Dirty, 4, 113	Gold Alert, 4, 114	5	1:59.00	64,170
1986	Pine Belt, 4, 111	E. Maple	Scrimshaw, 3, 108	Cost Conscious, 4, 111	6	1:57.20	55,260
1985	Late Act, 6, 118	E. Maple	Lightning Leap, 3, 110	Morning Bob, 4, 113	8	1:55.40	52,380
1984	Puntivo, 4, 114	R. G. Davis	High Honors, 4, 114	Moro, 5, 121	9	1:58.00	44,640
1983	Country Pine, 3, 118	J. D. Bailey	Count Normandy, 4, 108	Megaturn, 3, 113	8	1:58.00	33,240
1982	Bar Dexter, 5, 112	J. Fell	Castle Knight, 4, 111	Nice Pirate, 4, 110	5	1:58.20	32,880
1981	French Cut, 4, 112	D. MacBeth	Bar Dexter, 4, 110	Alla Breva, 4, 109	11	1:56.40	35,040
1980	Fool's Prayer, 5, 112	J. Velasquez	Ring of Light, 5, 115	Picturesque, 4, 114	7	1:56.00	33,360
1979	Dewan Keys, 4, 112	R. P. Romero	Mr. International, 6, 108	Gallant Best, 3, 116	8	1:56.80	32,940
1978	†Cum Laude Laurie, 4, 114	A. T. Cordero Jr.	Wise Philip, 5, 112	Do Tell George, 5, 112	8	1:55.80	32,580
1977	Cox's Ridge, 3, 126	E. Maple	Father Hogan, 4, 111	Popular Victory, 5, 115	7	1:55.80	32,670
1976	It's Freezing, 4, 113	J. Vasquez	Distant Land, 4, 111	Nalees Rialto, 4, 108	8	1:56.60	32,640
1975	Hail the Pirates, 5, 111	R. Turcotte	‡Sharp Gary, 4, 110	Herculean, 4, 111	10	1:55.60	34,560
1974	Free Hand, 4, 109	J. Amy	Arbees Boy, 4, 121	Group Plan, 4, 123	8	1:55.00	33,780
1973	True Knight, 4, 126	A. T. Cordero Jr.	Triangular, 6, 110	North Sea, 4, 117	12	1:55.00	35,070

Named for Queens County, New York, where Aqueduct is located. Grade 2 1973-'74. Not graded 1980. Held at Belmont Park 1946. Held at Jamaica 1956-'58. Not held 1909, 1911-'13. 1 mile 70 yards 1902-'03. 1 mile 1904-'39, 1959-'62. 1¹/₁₆ miles 1940-'58, 1993. 1¹/₈ miles 1963-'71. Dead heat for third 1990. ‡Festive Mood finished second, DQ to tenth, 1975. †Denotes female.

Railbird Stakes

Grade 3 in 2008. Hollywood Park, three-year-olds, fillies, 7 furlongs, all weather. Held May 11, 2008, with a gross value of $110,400. First held in 1963. First graded in 1973. Stakes record 1:20.60 (1979 Eloquent).

Year	Winner	Jockey	Second	Third	Strs	Time	1st Purse
2008	Million Dollar Run, 3, 115	J. Rosario	Tasha's Miracle, 3, 123	Lethal Heat, 3, 121	8	1:20.66	$66,240
2007	Ashley's Kitty, 3, 117	J. Talamo	Silver Swallow, 3, 117	Sindy With an S, 3, 117	9	1:22.80	66,600
2006	Bettarun Fast, 3, 120	A. T. Gryder	Mystery Girl, 3, 115	So Long Sonoma, 3, 118	9	1:23.29	60,000
2005	Short Route, 3, 118	P. A. Valenzuela	Inspiring, 3, 123	Off the Richter, 3, 115	8	1:22.99	65,820
2004	Elusive Diva, 3, 116	P. A. Valenzuela	M. A. Fox, 3, 116	Speedy Falcon, 3, 122	8	1:21.36	65,760
2003	Buffythecenterfold, 3, 123	V. Espinoza	Honest Answer, 3, 117	Dash for Money, 3, 115	6	1:22.54	64,320
2002	September Secret, 3, 118	P. A. Valenzuela	Affairs of State, 3, 118	Fun House, 3, 118	5	1:22.95	63,780
2001	Golden Ballet, 3, 123	C. J. McCarron	Starrer, 3, 115	Pretty 'n Smart, 3, 115	6	1:21.57	90,000
2000	‡Cover Gal, 3, 122	L. A. Pincay Jr.	Wired to Fly, 3, 122	Classic Olympio, 3, 122	5	1:22.57	90,000
1999	Olympic Charmer, 3, 115	C. J. McCarron	Dianehill (Ire), 3, 115	Fee Fi Foe, 3, 116	9	1:21.18	90,000

Racing — Graded Stakes 423

Year	Winner	Jockey	Second	Third	Strs	Time	1st Purse
1998	Brulay, 3, 115	G. L. Stevens	Gourmet Girl, 3, 119	Unreal Squeal, 3, 116	6	1:20.84	$64,260
1997	I Ain't Bluffing, 3, 118	E. Delahoussaye	Really Happy, 3, 121	Montecito, 3, 114	7	1:22.60	65,100
1996	Supercilious, 3, 121	C. S. Nakatani	Tiffany Diamond, 3, 118	Raw Gold, 3, 121	6	1:22.55	64,260
1995	Sleep Easy, 3, 113	C. S. Nakatani	Texinadress, 3, 118	Laguna Seca, 3, 115	8	1:22.42	64,600
1994	Sportful Snob, 3, 118	P. A. Valenzuela	Pirate's Revenge, 3, 121	Accountable Lady, 3, 116	5	1:21.94	61,400
1993	Afto, 3, 114	P. Atkinson	Fit to Lead, 3, 121	Nijivision, 3, 113	8	1:22.48	64,500
1992	She's Tops, 3, 114	K. Desormeaux	Race the Wild Wind, 3, 121	Magical Maiden, 3, 121	9	1:22.78	66,500
1991	Suziqcute, 3, 119	C. J. McCarron	Zama Hummer, 3, 117	Ifyoucouldseemenow, 3, 122	6	1:21.90	62,800
1990	Forest Fealty, 3, 114	J. A. Garcia	Patches, 3, 122	Golden Reef, 3, 122	8	1:21.60	48,950
1989	Imaginary Lady, 3, 122	G. L. Stevens	Kiwi, 3, 114	Stormy But Valid, 3, 122	7	1:21.40	47,800
1988	Sheesham, 3, 122	L. A. Pincay Jr.	Affordable Price, 3, 114	Super Avie, 3, 116	9	1:22.60	49,700
1987	Very Subtle, 3, 122	W. Shoemaker	Joey the Trip, 3, 117	Sacahuista, 3, 122	4	1:22.60	45,750
1986	Melair, 3, 114	P. A. Valenzuela	Comparability, 3, 119	Silent Arrival, 3, 122	7	1:22.40	48,600
1985	Reigning Countess, 3, 122	G. L. Stevens	Window Seat, 3, 122	Charming Susan, 3, 115	6	1:22.40	38,300
1984	Mitterand, 3, 115	E. Delahoussaye	Gene's Lady, 3, 122	Lucky Lucky Lucky, 3, 122	10	1:22.20	40,000
1983	Ski Goggle, 3, 122	C. J. McCarron	Madam Forbes, 3, 115	Gatita, 3, 117	9	1:23.40	33,150
1982	Faneuil Lass, 3, 117	T. Lipham	Jones Time Machine, 3, 119	Hasty Hannah, 3, 119	8	1:23.20	32,400
1981	Cherokee Frolic, 3, 119	G. Cohen	Strangeways, 3, 114	Terra Miss, 3, 115	8	1:22.20	32,400
1980	Cinegita, 3, 114	T. Lipham	Thundertee, 3, 122	Back At Two, 3, 119	6	1:20.80	31,450
1979	Eloquent, 3, 122	D. Pierce	Celine, 3, 122	Joy's Jewel, 3, 114	9	**1:20.60**	26,800
1978	Eximious, 3, 117	W. Shoemaker	B. Thoughtful, 3, 122	Joe's Bee, 3, 114	7	1:22.20	25,550
1977	Taisez Vous, 3, 115	F. Toro	Wavy Waves, 3, 122	Silent Wisdom, 3, 114	8	1:22.60	22,650
1976	Hail Hilarious, 3, 114	D. Pierce	Doc Shah's Siren, 3, 119	I Going, 3, 115	10	1:21.40	20,550
1975	Raise Your Skirts, 3, 118	W. Mahorney	Miss Tokyo, 3, 117	Fascinating Girl, 3, 119	7	1:20.80	19,350
1974	Modus Vivendi, 3, 121	D. Pierce	Fleet Peach, 3, 118	Fresno Star, 3, 118	9	1:21.60	19,800
1973	Sandy Blue, 3, 118	D. Pierce	Sphere, 3, 113	Goddess Roman, 3, 113	9	1:21.80	20,250

Named for racing fans who watch races from along the rail, known as "railbirds". Grade 2 1988, 1991-2001. Railbird H. 1963-'64. Dirt 1963-2006. Both sexes 1963. ‡Abby Girl finished first, DQ to fifth for a positive drug test, 2000.

Rampart Handicap

Grade 2 in 2008. Gulfstream Park, four-year-olds and up, fillies and mares, 1 1/8 miles, dirt. Held March 9, 2008, with a gross value of $200,000. First held in 1976. First graded in 1986. Stakes record 1:47.92 (2003 Allamerican Bertie).

Year	Winner	Jockey	Second	Third	Strs	Time	1st Purse
2008	Spring Waltz, 5, 118	J. Castellano	Tessa Blue, 4, 118	Golden Velvet, 5, 119	7	1:49.73	$120,000
2007	Miss Shop, 4, 116	R. Bejarano	Prop Me Up, 5, 113	Swap Fliparoo, 4, 117	6	1:49.42	120,000
2006	Oonagh Maccool (Ire), 4, 114	R. Bejarano	Sweet Symphony, 4, 119	Classy Charm, 4, 116	6	1:49.99	120,000
2005	D' Wildcat Speed, 5, 113	M. R. Cruz	Isola Piu Bella (Chi), 5, 118	Pampered Princess, 5, 116	5	1:48.92	120,000
2004	Sightseek, 5, 122	J. D. Bailey	Redoubled Miss, 5, 118	Lead Story, 5, 117	4	1:51.07	120,000
2003	Allamerican Bertie, 4, 122	J. R. Velazquez	Smok'n Frolic, 4, 118	Softly, 5, 115	6	**1:47.92**	120,000
2002	Forest Secrets, 4, 117	P. Day	Summer Colony, 4, 118	Happily Unbridled, 4, 114	8	1:49.83	120,000
2001	De Bertie, 4, 116	J. F. Chavez	Apple of Kent, 5, 114	Scratch Pad, 4, 115	7	1:50.48	120,000
2000	Bella Chiarra, 5, 116	S. J. Sellers	Lines of Beauty, 5, 114	Up We Go, 4, 113	8	1:43.27	120,000
1999	Banshee Breeze, 4, 122	J. D. Bailey	Glitter Woman, 5, 119	Timely Broad, 5, 114	5	1:42.83	120,000
1998	Dance for Thee, 4, 113	J. Bravo	Escena, 5, 119	Glitter Woman, 4, 121	6	1:44.73	120,000
1997	Chip, 4, 114	J. Bravo	Rare Blend, 4, 122	Hurricane Viv, 4, 116	9	1:42.51	120,000
1996	Investalot, 5, 114	S. J. Sellers	Queen Tutta, 4, 113	Alcovy, 6, 117	9	1:43.99	120,000
1995	Educated Risk, 5, 126	M. E. Smith	Recognizable, 4, 117	Jade Flush, 4, 113	5	1:43.09	120,000
1994	Nine Keys, 4, 113	M. E. Smith	Educated Risk, 4, 120	Traverse City, 4, 113	6	1:42.12	120,000
1993	Girl On a Mission, 4, 112	J. D. Bailey	‡Luv Me Luv Me Not, 4, 116	Haunting, 5, 114	8	1:45.47	120,000
1992	Fit for a Queen, 6, 119	J. D. Bailey	Firm Stance, 4, 111	Nannerl, 5, 113	12	1:43.66	120,000
1991	Charon, 4, 121	C. Perret	Wortheroatsingold, 4, 112	Train Robbery, 4, 113	8	1:43.10	120,000
1990	Barbarika, 5, 113	C. Perret	Fit for a Queen, 4, 112	Natala, 4, 112	11	1:44.20	120,000
1989	Colonial Waters, 4, 112	W. H. McCauley	Savannah's Honor, 4, 113	Haiati, 4, 112	12	1:44.80	120,000
1988	By Land by Sea, 4, 118	F. Toro	Queen Alexandra, 6, 120	Bound, 4, 113	10	1:43.80	120,000
1987	Life At the Top, 4, 122	R. P. Romero	I'm Sweets, 4, 119	Natania, 5, 113	7	1:44.00	97,440
1986	Endear, 4, 113	E. Maple	Isayso, 7, 118	Natania, 4, 112	11	1:45.80	103,080
1985	Isayso, 6, 113	E. Maple	Pretty Perfect, 5, 122	Basie, 4, 114	7	1:44.20	70,080
1984	Thightatab, 4, 118	C. Perret	National Banner, 4, 117	Vestris, 5, 117	10	1:43.80	36,870
1983	Flag Waver, 4, 108	A. O. Solis	Prime Prospect, 5, 118	Our Darling, 4, 112	13	1:44.00	57,960
1982	Sweetest Chant, 4, 117	E. Fires	Deby's Willing, 5, 115	Pretorienne (Fr), 6, 114	10	1:43.40	25,662
1981	Wistful, 4, 117	D. Brumfield	Lillian Russell, 4, 109	Deby's Willing, 4, 112	9	1:44.60	54,180
1976	Moon Glitter, 4, 110	E. Fires	Regal Quillo, 3, 112	K D Princess, 5, 111	8	1:22.20	9,960

Named for Mrs. H. Haggerty's 1948 Gulfstream Park H. winner Rampart (1942 f. by Trace Call); Rampart was the race's first female winner. Formerly sponsored by Johnnie Walker Scotch Whisky 1989-'90. Grade 3 1986-'87. Johnnie Walker Black Classic H. 1989-'90. Not held 1977-'80. 7 furlongs 1976. 1 1/16 miles 1981-2000. Three-year-olds and up 1976-2006. ‡Now Dance finished second, DQ to fifth, 1993.

Rancho Bernardo Handicap

Grade 3 in 2008. Del Mar, three-year-olds and up, fillies and mares, 6 1/2 furlongs, all weather. Held August 17, 2007, with a gross value of $200,000. First held in 1967. First graded in 1988. Stakes record 1:14.28 (1995 Track Gal).

Year	Winner	Jockey	Second	Third	Strs	Time	1st Purse
2007	River's Prayer, 4, 121	C. L. Potts	Strong Faith, 6, 115	Lady Gamer, 4, 116	5	1:17.85	$120,000

Year	Winner	Jockey	Second	Third	Strs	Time	1st Purse
2006	Behaving Badly, 5, 122	V. Espinoza	True and True, 3, 110	Allswellthatnswell, 5, 116	6	1:15.04	$120,000
2005	Behaving Badly, 4, 113	V. Espinoza	Freakin Streakin, 4, 117	Dee Dee's Diner, 5, 118	8	1:15.32	90,000
2004	Dream of Summer, 5, 118	M. E. Smith	Barbara Orr, 4, 113	Cyber Slew, 4, 117	7	1:15.15	90,000
2003	Secret Liaison, 5, 120	C. S. Nakatani	Lacie Girl, 4, 116	Spring Meadow, 4, 117	8	1:15.53	90,000
2002	Kalookan Queen, 6, 123	A. O. Solis	Warren's Whistle, 4, 116	Fancee Bargain, 6, 112	5	1:16.40	90,000
2001	Kalookan Queen, 5, 119	A. O. Solis	Go Go, 4, 125	Warren's Whistle, 3, 111	6	1:15.52	90,000
2000	Theresa's Tizzy, 6, 117	L. A. Pincay Jr.	Nany's Sweep, 4, 117	Hookedonthefeelin, 4, 119	6	1:16.23	90,000
1999	Enjoy the Moment, 4, 119	D. R. Flores	Snowberg, 4, 117	Stop Traffic, 6, 121	6	1:15.97	90,000
1998	Advancing Star, 5, 120	C. J. McCarron	Closed Escrow, 5, 115	Tiffany Diamond, 5, 116	6	1:14.64	64,140
1997	Track Gal, 6, 120	G. L. Stevens	Madame Pandit, 4, 118	Advancing Star, 4, 116	8	1:15.64	69,125
1996	Track Gal, 5, 122	C. J. McCarron	Tricky Code, 5, 116	Evil's Pic, 4, 117	5	1:14.64	63,550
1995	Track Gal, 4, 118	C. J. McCarron	Desert Stormer, 5, 119	Lakeway, 4, 122	5	**1:14.28**	58,650
1994	Desert Stormer, 4, 117	E. Delahoussaye	Magical Maiden, 5, 120	Booklore, 4, 117	9	1:14.81	62,800
1993	Knight Prospector, 4, 119	K. Desormeaux	Interactive, 4, 119	Bountiful Native, 5, 120	5	1:16.14	45,675
1992	Bountiful Native, 4, 117	P. A. Valenzuela	Devil's Orchid, 5, 120	She's Tops, 3, 114	9	1:15.30	63,400
1991	Cascading Gold, 5, 117	L. A. Pincay Jr.	Survive, 7, 120	Suziqcute, 3, 114	5	1:15.42	60,100
1990	Hot Novel, 4, 118	K. Desormeaux	Sexy Slew, 4, 116	Down Again, 6, 115	9	1:14.60	62,875
1989	Kool Arrival, 3, 117	L. A. Pincay Jr.	Super Avie, 4, 117	Survive, 5, 116	7	1:15.20	47,625
1988	Clabber Girl, 5, 120	L. A. Pincay Jr.	Queen Forbes, 4, 113	Behind the Scenes, 4, 117	8	1:14.60	38,750
1987	Julie the Flapper, 3, 114	C. J. McCarron	Clabber Girl, 4, 117	Sari's Heroine, 4, 119	10	1:15.00	33,200
1986	Bold n Special, 3, 115	C. J. McCarron	Rangoon Ruby (Ire), 4, 116	Eloquack, 4, 117	5	1:14.60	30,850
1985	Take My Picture, 3, 114	F. Olivares	Sales Bulletin, 4, 118	Mimi Baker, 4, 112	10	1:09.20	33,200
1984	Pleasure Cay, 4, 121	L. A. Pincay Jr.	Lovlier Linda, 4, 120	Pride of Rosewood (NZ), 6, 115	8	1:08.60	32,250
1983	Bara Lass, 4, 120	C. J. McCarron	Excitable Lady, 5, 124	Milingo, 4, 113	7	1:09.40	31,800
1982	Lucky Lady Ellen, 3, 117	L. A. Pincay Jr.	Glitter Hitter, 4, 118	Excitable Lady, 4, 125	7	1:08.60	31,850
1981	Forluvofiv, 4, 118	E. Delahoussaye	Untamed Spirit, 4, 122	Ack's Secret, 5, 118	9	1:09.40	31,400
1980	Great Lady M., 5, 121	L. A. Pincay Jr.	Sal's High, 4, 118	Western Hand, 3, 110	8	1:08.60	25,800
1979	Fantastic Girl, 3, 112	W. Shoemaker	Happy Holme, 5, 120	Delice, 4, 122	8	1:09.20	22,850
1978	Happy Holme, 4, 120	C. J. McCarron	Telferner, 4, 117	Dallas Deb, 3, 114	5	1:13.00	18,200
1977	Lullaby Song, 4, 120	L. A. Pincay Jr.	Miss Rising Market, 4, 113	Honeyhugger, 4, 117	7	1:09.00	16,550
1976	Mama Kali, 5, 117	L. A. Pincay Jr.	Mismoyola, 6, 119	Vol Au Vent, 4, 120	6	1:09.20	16,400
1975	Mama Kali, 4, 120	J. Lambert	Hooley Ruley, 5, 117	Modus Vivendi, 4, 124	7	1:08.40	17,050
1974	Impressive Style, 5, 120	R. Rosales	Fleet Peach, 3, 115	Lt.'s Joy, 4, 120	10	1:08.60	16,300
1973	Fairly Certain, 4, 121	S. Valdez	Tannyhill, 4, 117	Normandy Grey, 4, 115	8	1:42.80	10,400
	dh-D. B. Carm, 4, 119	F. Toro		Dr. Kerlan, 4, 118	5	1:43.20	6,400
	dh-Dollar Discount, 4, 119	S. Valdez					

Named for the city of Rancho Bernardo, California. Rancho Bernardo Breeders' Cup H. 1990-'95. Not held 1968-'72. 1 mile 1967. 1¹/₁₆ miles 1973. 6 furlongs 1974-'85. Dirt 1967, 1974-2006. Turf 1973. Both sexes 1967-'73. Two divisions 1973. Dead heat for first 1973 (2nd Div.). Nonwinners of a race worth $10,000 to the winner 1973.

Raven Run Stakes — *See* Lexus Raven Run Stakes

Razorback Handicap

Grade 3 in 2008. Oaklawn Park, four-year-olds and up, 1¹/₁₆ miles, dirt. Held March 8, 2008, with a gross value of $149,000. First held in 1976. First graded in 1978. Stakes record 1:40.40 (1988 Lost Code).

Year	Winner	Jockey	Second	Third	Strs	Time	1st Purse
2008	Jonesboro, 6, 117	C. H. Borel	Gouldings Green, 7, 118	Going Ballistic, 4, 115	6	1:44.21	$90,000
2007	Magna Graduate, 5, 118	J. R. Velazquez	Student Council, 5, 117	Jonesboro, 5, 119	8	1:44.17	90,000
2006	Purim, 4, 116	R. Albarado	Arch Hall, 5, 115	Thunder Mission, 4, 116	8	1:43.77	90,000
2005	Added Edge, 5, 115	L. S. Quinonez	Mauk Four, 5, 112	Absent Friend, 5, 115	10	1:43.88	75,000
2004	Sonic West, 5, 113	W. Martinez	Crafty Shaw, 6, 117	Pie N Burger, 6, 119	7	1:43.62	60,000
2003	Colorful Tour, 4, 118	L. S. Quinonez	Crafty Shaw, 5, 119	Windward Passage, 4, 118	7	1:43.53	60,000
2002	Mr Ross, 7, 120	D. R. Pettinger	Remington Rock, 8, 115	Big Numbers, 5, 116	8	1:44.13	60,000
2001	Mr Ross, 6, 119	D. R. Pettinger	Graeme Hall, 4, 120	Maysville Slew, 5, 117	9	1:42.60	75,000
2000	Well Noted, 5, 112	T. T. Doocy	Crimson Classic, 6, 115	Mr Ross, 5, 115	7	1:43.21	75,000
1999	Desert Air, 4, 113	C. J. Lanerie	Magnify, 6, 113	Black Tie Dinner, 6, 112	7	1:44.75	75,000
1998	Brush With Pride, 6, 115	T. T. Doocy	Littlebitlively, 4, 112	Krigeorj's Gold, 5, 115	7	1:43.55	75,000
1997	No Spend No Glow, 5, 115	R. N. Lester	Illesam, 5, 114	Come on Flip, 6, 115	8	1:43.20	90,000
1996	Juliannus, 7, 113	R. Albarado	Judge T C, 5, 122	Dazzling Falls, 4, 118	5	1:43.97	90,000
1995	Silver Goblin, 4, 124	D. W. Cordova	Joseph's Robe, 4, 111	Wooden Ticket, 5, 115	7	1:42.79	120,000
1994	Prize Fight, 5, 113	P. A. Johnson	Brother Brown, 4, 120	Country Store, 4, 113	8	1:43.70	90,000
1993	Lil E. Tee, 4, 123	P. Day	Zeeruler, 5, 115	Senor Tomas, 4, 114	7	1:41.55	90,000
1992	Tokatee, 6, 115	G. K. Gomez	On the Edge, 5, 112	Total Assets, 7, 110	9	1:42.87	90,000
1991	Bedeviled, 4, 115	D. L. Howard	Din's Dancer, 6, 117	Black Tie Affair (Ire), 5, 118	7	1:42.50	75,000
1990	Opening Verse, 4, 116	P. Day	Primal, 5, 121	Silver Survivor, 4, 118	7	1:41.40	90,000
1989	Blushing John, 4, 117	P. Day	Lyphard's Ridge, 6, 111	Proper Reality, 4, 123	5	1:43.00	60,000
1988	Lost Code, 4, 123	C. Perret	Red Attack, 6, 112	Demons Begone, 4, 121	7	**1:40.40**	73,500
1987	Bolshoi Boy, 4, 119	R. P. Romero	Lyphard's Ridge, 4, 110	Sun Master, 6, 119	7	1:40.80	86,520
1986	Red Attack, 4, 111	L. Snyder	Vanlandingham, 5, 125	Inevitable Leader, 7, 111	9	1:42.00	96,900
1985	Imp Society, 4, 126	P. Day	Introspective, 4, 113	Strength in Unity, 4, 109	10	1:42.60	97,740
1984	Dew Line, 5, 116	S. Maple	Passing Base, 4, 112	Win Stat, 7, 115	14	1:41.60	74,520
1983	Eminency, 5, 120	P. Day	Cassaleria, 4, 115	Bold Style, 4, 113	10	1:43.60	70,740

Year	Winner	Jockey	Second	Third	Strs	Time	1st Purse
1982	Eminency, 4, 111	P. Day	Reef Searcher, 5, 119	Tally Ho the Fox, 7, 115	15	1:45.20	$76,200
1981	Temperence Hill, 4, 124	E. Maple	Blue Ensign, 4, 113	Belle's Ruler, 6, 112	6	1:44.20	66,660
1980	All the More, 7, 114	L. Snyder	Prince Majestic, 6, 116	Breaker Breaker, 4, 117	11	1:45.40	56,400
1979	Cisk, 5, 120	G. Patterson	Droll's Reason, 4, 113	Prince Majestic, 5, 121	8	1:45.40	53,700
1978	Cox's Ridge, 4, 125	E. Maple	Dr. Riddick, 4, 116	Mark's Place, 6, 124	12	1:43.00	37,110
1977	Dragset, 6, 111	J. Kunitake	Romeo, 4, 120	Last Buzz, 4, 115	9	1:44.40	35,910
1976	Royal Glint, 6, 126	J. E. Tejeira	Marauding, 4, 115	Heaven Forbid, 5, 112	8	1:42.40	35,550

Named for the unofficial state animal and University of Arkansas mascot, the razorback pig. Grade 2 1985-'96. Razorback Breeders' Cup H. 2005-'06.

Rebel Stakes

Grade 2 in 2008. Oaklawn Park, three-year-olds, 1 1/16 miles, dirt. Held March 15, 2008, with a gross value of $300,000. First held in 1976. First graded in 1990. Stakes record 1:41 (1984 Vanlandingham).

Year	Winner	Jockey	Second	Third	Strs	Time	1st Purse
2008	Sierra Sunset, 3, 119	C. A. Emigh	King's Silver Son, 3, 115	Isabull, 3, 115	9	1:43.88	$180,000
2007	Curlin, 3, 117	R. Albarado	Officer Rocket (GB), 3, 119	Teuflesberg, 3, 122	9	1:44.70	180,000
2006	Lawyer Ron, 3, 122	J. McKee	Red Raymond, 3, 117	Steppenwolfer, 3, 118	10	1:44.09	180,000
2005	Greater Good, 3, 122	J. McKee	Rockport Harbor, 3, 118	Batson Challenge, 3, 117	6	1:44.92	150,000
2004	Smarty Jones, 3, 122	S. Elliott	Purge, 3, 117	Pro Prado, 3, 117	9	1:42.07	120,000
2003	Crowned King, 3, 115	C. R. Rennie	Great Notion, 3, 119	Comic Truth, 3, 117	7	1:44.00	75,000
2002	Windward Passage, 3, 116	D. J. Meche	Ocean Sound (Ire), 3, 114	Dusty Spike, 3, 114	8	1:45.06	60,000
2001	Crafty Shaw, 3, 113	J. M. Johnson	Arctic Boy, 3, 114	Strike It Smart, 3, 114	9	1:43.82	60,000
2000	Snuck In, 3, 119	C. B. Asmussen	Big Numbers, 3, 114	Fan the Flame, 3, 113	12	1:42.99	60,000
1999	Etbauer, 3, 112	M. E. Smith	Desert Demon, 3, 119	Kutsa, 3, 112	11	1:44.02	75,000
1998	Victory Gallop, 3, 119	E. Coa	Robinwould, 3, 114	Whataflashyactor, 3, 114	10	1:44.72	75,000
1997	Phantom On Tour, 3, 117	L. J. Melancon	Direct Hit, 3, 119	River Squall, 3, 117	12	1:42.80	75,000
1996	Ide, 3, 122	C. Perret	Blow Out, 3, 112	Bunker Hill Road, 3, 113	7	1:44.10	60,000
1995	Mystery Storm, 3, 122	C. Perret	Rich Man's Gold, 3, 112	Valid Advantage, 3, 113	7	1:44.41	75,000
1994	Judge T C, 3, 119	J. M. Johnson	Concern, 3, 112	Milt's Overture, 3, 114	11	1:44.14	75,000
1993	Dalhart, 3, 122	M. E. Smith	Foxtrail, 3, 122	Mi Cielo, 3, 114	8	1:42.31	75,000
1992	Pine Bluff, 3, 122	J. D. Bailey	Desert Force, 3, 117	Looks Like Money, 3, 113	7	1:42.83	75,000
1991	Quintana, 3, 112	D. Guillory	Corporate Report, 3, 114	Far Out Wadleigh, 3, 119	8	1:42.70	60,000
1990	Nuits St. Georges, 3, 114	J. E. Bruin	Maverick Miner, 3, 114	Tarascon, 3, 122	11	1:46.00	60,000
1989	Manastash Ridge, 3, 119	A. L. Castanon	Big Stanley, 3, 122	Double Quick, 3, 122	14	1:43.00	60,000
1988	Sea Trek, 3, 112	P. A. Johnson	Din's Dancer, 3, 114	Notebook, 3, 122	10	1:42.60	73,500
1987	Demons Begone, 3, 119	P. Day	Fast Forward, 3, 114	You're No Bargain, 3, 112	6	1:41.40	86,520
1986	Rare Brick, 3, 119	M. E. Smith	Clear Choice, 3, 112	The Flats, 3, 114	8	1:43.20	68,760
1985	Clever Allemont, 3, 119	P. Day	Bonham, 3, 113	Proper Native, 3, 114	7	1:44.40	95,100
1984	Vanlandingham, 3, 115	P. Day	Wind Flyer, 3, 118	Leavesumdouble, 3, 112	10	**1:41.00**	70,740
1983	Sunny's Halo, 3, 121	L. Snyder	Sligh Jet, 3, 117	Le Cou Cou, 3, 115	11	1:42.20	68,850
1982	Bold Style, 3, 116	L. Snyder	Majesty's Prince, 3, 115	Lost Creek, 3, 114	8	1:43.80	51,420
1981	Bold Ego, 3, 122	J. Lively	Catch That Pass, 3, 117	Chapel Creek, 3, 112	10	1:41.40	35,580
1980	Temperence Hill, 3, 114	D. Haire	Royal Sporan, 3, 114	Be a Prospect, 3, 123	15	1:42.80	38,430
1979	Lucy's Axe, 3, 121	E. Maple	Tunerup, 3, 115	Arctic Action, 3, 118	8	1:42.80	35,070
1978	Chop Chop Tomahawk, 3, 126	L. Snyder	Abidan, 3, 114	Forever Casting, 3, 124	10	1:42.40	36,150
1977	United Holme, 3, 120	J. E. Tejeira	J. J. Battle, 3, 124	Tinsley's Affair, 3, 115	12	1:42.20	36,810
1976	Riverside Sam, 3, 113	G. Patterson	Elocutionist, 3, 121	Klen Klitso, 3, 113	14	1:41.60	37,710

Named for the nickname of Southerners, "rebels"; the nickname is derived from the South's rebellion against the United States during the Civil War. Rebel H. 1976-'83. Grade 3 1990-2002, 2005-'06. Not graded 2003-'04.

Red Bank Stakes

Grade 3 in 2008. Monmouth Park, three-year-olds and up, 1 mile, turf. Held September 1, 2007, with a gross value of $150,000. First held in 1974. First graded in 1986. Stakes record 1:32.42 (2007 Icy Atlantic).

Year	Winner	Jockey	Second	Third	Strs	Time	1st Purse
2007	Icy Atlantic, 6, 121	J. Bravo	Touched by Madness, 5, 117	Baron Von Tap, 6, 117	7	**1:32.42**	$90,000
2006	Miesque's Approval, 7, 123	E. Castro	Hotstufanthensome, 6, 117	Senor Swinger, 6, 117	9	1:33.36	90,000
2005	American Freedom, 7, 115	J. A. Velez Jr.	Spruce Run, 7, 113	Royal Affirmed, 7, 112	8	1:43.12	90,000
2004	Burning Roma, 6, 120	J. L. Castanon	Remind, 4, 117	American Freedom, 6, 115	11	1:34.73	60,000
2003	Just Le Facts, 4, 111	J. Bravo	Saint Verre, 5, 118	Runspastum, 6, 114	9	1:37.73	20,000
2002	Key Lory, 6, 117	H. Vega	Sardaukar (GB), 6, 113	Spruce Run, 4, 113	8	1:35.92	60,000
2001	Pavillon (Brz), 7, 122	J. Bravo	Western Summer, 4, 114	Runspastum, 4, 114	10	1:36.38	90,000
2000	Mi Narrow, 6, 114	C. H. Velasquez	Deep Gold, 4, 114	Inkatha (Fr), 6, 117	9	1:34.84	90,000
1999	Inkatha (Fr), 5, 114	H. Castillo Jr.	Rob 'n Gin, 5, 119	Soviet Line (Ire), 9, 118	8	1:33.95	90,000
1998	Statesmanship, 4, 117	J. A. Santos	Rob 'n Gin, 4, 120	Bomfim, 5, 114	11	1:35.00	60,000
1997	Basqueian, 6, 118	R. Wilson	Wild Night Out, 5, 111	Jambalaya Jazz, 5, 117	6	1:35.20	60,000
1996	Joker, 4, 113	J. A. Velez Jr.	Rare Reason, 5, 118	Diplomatic Jet, 4, 116	9	1:35.90	60,000
1995	Dove Hunt, 4, 118	W. H. McCauley	Rare Reason, 4, 115	Winnetou, 5, 113	9	1:33.95	45,000
1994	Adam Smith (GB), 6, 120	J. A. Krone	Discernment, 5, 113	Fourstardave, 9, 118	7	1:34.43	45,000
1993	Adam Smith (GB), 5, 116	J. Samyn	Fourstars Allstar, 5, 116	Rinka Das, 5, 115	8	1:34.39	45,000
1992	Daarik (Ire), 5, 114	L. Saumell	Leger Cat (Arg), 6, 116	Kate's Valentine, 7, 114	5	1:34.07	45,000
1991	Double Booked, 6, 122	J. C. Ferrer	Great Normand, 6, 118	Now Listen, 4, 112	10	1:33.34	45,000

Racing — Graded Stakes

Year	Winner	Jockey	Second	Third	Strs	Time	1st Purse
1990	Norquestor, 4, 118	J. Samyn	Master Speaker, 5, 120	Grande Jette, 5, 111	5	1:36.00	$52,980
1989	Arlene's Valentine, 4, 115	J. C. Ferrer	Yankee Affair, 7, 121	Alwasmi, 5, 114	6	1:40.20	52,290
1988	Iron Courage, 4, 113	W. H. McCauley	Spellbound, 5, 112	Ioskeha, 5, 113	7	1:35.40	42,210
1987	Feeling Gallant, 5, 117	C. W. Antley	Hi Ideal, 5, 114	Racing Star, 5, 117	5	1:37.20	35,610
1986	†Mazatleca (Mex), 6, 112	C. W. Antley	Feeling Gallant, 4, 114	Hi Ideal, 4, 113	8	1:35.80	34,800
1985	Castelets, 6, 115	V. A. Bracciale Jr.	Evzone, 4, 117	Gothic Revival, 4, 112	8	1:37.00	27,885
	Ends Well, 4, 116	M. R. Morgan	Domynsky (GB), 5, 117	Bold Southerner, 4, 115	9	1:35.60	28,065
1984	Tough Mickey, 4, 118	K. Skinner	Fortnightly, 4, 117	Roman Bend, 4, 108	9	1:36.40	28,470
	Castle Guard, 5, 118	J. C. Ferrer	Super Sunrise (GB), 4, 123	Fray Star (Arg), 6, 117	10	1:35.80	28,530
1983	Sun and Shine (GB), 4, 115	J. Terry	St. Brendan, 5, 116	Mr. Dreamer, 6, 113	11	1:36.60	24,480
1982	Alhambra Joe, 5, 111	W. Nemeti	Pepper's Segundo, 5, 117	Timely Counsel, 4, 112	5	1:38.60	23,265
1981	Colonel Moran, 4, 116	G. W. Donahue	Dan Horn, 9, 115	Contare, 5, 108	12	1:35.20	24,570
1980	Horatius, 5, 117	D. MacBeth	Pipedreamer (GB), 5, 116	North Course, 5, 114	11	1:35.00	24,495
1979	Navajo Princess, 5, 122	J. Vasquez	La Soufriere, 4, 116	Sans Arc, 5, 115	10	1:43.20	22,441
1978	Love Jenny, 4, 108	M. A. Gomez	Table Hopper, 5, 111	Chanctonbury, 4, 114	5	1:46.20	28,308
1977	Playin' Footsie, 4, 110	R. D. Ardoin	Desiree, 4, 110	Artfully, 4, 112	10	1:44.40	29,510
1976	Collegiate, 4, 116	J. W. Edwards	Show Me How, 4, 110	Four Bells, 5, 114	11	1:40.20	25,919
1975	Kudara, 4, 118	D. MacBeth	Enchanted Native, 4, 111	Twixt, 6, 121	11	1:42.20	18,850
1974	‡Mystery Mood, 2, 115	J. E. Tejeira	Molly Ballantine, 2, 121	Lucky Leslie, 2, 117	11	1:45.20	18,672

Named for the town of Red Bank, New Jersey. Not graded 2003. Red Bank H. 1975-2005. 1¹/₁₆ miles 1974-'75, 1977-'79. 1 mile 70 yards 1976. Dirt 1974-'78, 1982, 1987, 1990, 1997, 2003. Originally scheduled on turf 2003. Two-year-olds 1974. Fillies and mares 1975-'79. Two divisions 1984-'85. ‡Molly Ballantine finished first, DQ to second, 1974. Course record 1999, 2007. †Denotes female.

Red Smith Handicap

Grade 2 in 2008. Aqueduct, three-year-olds and up, 1³/₈ miles, turf. Held November 10, 2007, with a gross value of $150,000. First held in 1960. First graded in 1973. Stakes record 2:20.53 (1994 Franchise Player).

Year	Winner	Jockey	Second	Third	Strs	Time	1st Purse
2007	Dave, 6, 114	J. Bravo	True Cause, 4, 115	Musketier (Ger), 5, 116	12	2:21.45	$90,000
2006	Naughty New Yorker, 4, 118	J. Samyn	Angliana, 4, 116	Crown Point, 4, 114	5	2:04.52	90,000
2005	King's Drama (Ire), 5, 122	E. S. Prado	Rousing Victory, 4, 114	Dreadnaught, 5, 117	8	2:15.37	90,000
2004	Dreadnaught, 4, 115	J. Samyn	Certifiably Crazy, 4, 112	Alost (Fr), 4, 116	10	2:18.87	90,000
2003	Balto Star, 5, 120	J. R. Velazquez	Macaw (Ire), 4, 118	Cetewayo, 9, 117	11	2:18.86	90,000
2002	Evening Attire, 4, 126	S. Bridgmohan	Fisher Pond, 3, 116	Pleasant Breeze, 7, 120	6	2:14.81	90,000
2001	Mr. Pleasentfar (Brz), 4, 115	J. A. Santos	Eltawaasul, 5, 114	Regal Dynasty, 5, 113	12	2:16.94	90,000
2000	Cetewayo, 6, 114	R. Migliore	Understood, 4, 113	Val's Prince, 8, 118	13	2:17.93	90,000
1999	Monarch's Maze, 3, 113	J. Bravo	Williams News, 4, 114	Gritty Sandie, 3, 114	14	2:14.44	90,000
1998	Musical Ghost, 6, 115	J. R. Velazquez	Rice, 6, 116	Plato's Love, 3, 109	12	2:15.53	90,000
1997	Instant Friendship, 4, 123	J. R. Velazquez	Demi's Bret, 4, 117	Trample, 3, 112	5	2:17.08	150,000
1996	Mr. Bluebird, 5, 116	M. E. Smith	Ops Smile, 4, 116	Raintrap (GB), 6, 117	13	2:15.35	87,750
1995	Flag Down, 5, 114	J. A. Santos	‡Party Season (GB), 4, 116	Proceeded, 4, 110	11	2:22.03	69,060
1994	Franchise Player, 5, 109	D. V. Beckner	Red Bishop, 6, 119	Same Old Wish, 4, 112	14	**2:20.53**	72,120
1993	Royal Mountain Inn, 4, 110	J. A. Krone	Spectacular Tide, 4, 113	Share the Glory, 5, 111	8	1:59.82	71,760
1992	Montserrat, 4, 118	J. A. Krone	Preferences, 3, 110	First Rate (Ire), 7, 111	7	2:00.32	70,920
1991	Who's to Pay, 5, 117	J. D. Bailey	Simili (Fr), 5, 114	Solar Splendor, 4, 114	8	1:58.18	71,160
1990	Yankee Affair, 8, 122	J. A. Santos	Hodges Bay, 5, 116	Phantom Breeze (Ire), 4, 116	7	2:00.20	70,560
1989	Rambo Dancer, 5, 113	J. A. Santos	El Senor, 5, 117	Salem Drive, 7, 116	8	2:01.00	72,360
1988	Pay the Butler, 4, 110	R. G. Davis	Equalize, 6, 116	Yankee Affair, 6, 120	15	2:01.40	118,620
1987	Theatrical (Ire), 5, 122	P. Day	Dance of Life, 4, 122	Equalize, 5, 112	11	2:00.80	116,460
1986	Divulge, 4, 116	J. Cruguet	Tri for Size, 5, 113	Island Sun, 4, 118	9	1:59.00	88,950
	Equalize, 4, 114	W. A. Guerra	Palace Panther (Ire), 5, 116	Entitled To, 4, 112	8	2:02.20	103,650
1985	Sharannpour (Ire), 5, 112	A. T. Cordero Jr.	Inevitable Leader, 6, 116	Cold Feet (Fr), 4, 110	13	2:04.20	114,600
1984	Hero's Honor, 4, 117	J. D. Bailey	Win, 4, 114	Eskimo, 4, 112	5	2:02.20	102,900
1983	Super Sunrise (GB), 4, 114	C. Perret	Mariacho (Ire), 5, 116	Field Cat, 6, 111	7	2:06.80	67,200
	Thunder Puddles, 4, 117	J. Samyn	John's Gold, 4, 112	Open Call, 5, 124	7	2:06.40	67,200
1982	Highland Blade, 4, 124	J. Vasquez	Dom Menotti (Fr), 5, 109	Open Call, 4, 125	8	2:06.40	69,000
1981	Match the Hatch, 5, 114	K. Skinner	Passing Zone, 4, 108	Great Neck, 5, 114	9	1:59.60	68,160
1980	Marquee Universal (Ire), 4, 121	H. Pilar	Match the Hatch, 4, 114	Lyphard's Wish (Fr), 4, 122	8	1:58.80	67,680
1978	Tiller, 4, 114	J. Fell	True Colors, 4, 116	Tacitus, 4, 113	8	2:00.20	33,960
1977	Clout, 5, 114	G. Martens	Chati, 4, 117	Gay Jitterbug, 4, 122	8	1:40.00	25,927
	Quick Card, 4, 112	A. T. Cordero Jr.	Bemo, 7, 115	Noble Dancer (GB), 5, 119	6	1:39.60	25,687
1976	Erwin Boy, 5, 116	R. Turcotte	Clout, 4, 117	Quick Card, 3, 110	10	2:01.20	28,110
1975	*Telefonico, 4, 120	C. Perret	Drollery, 5, 114	Barcas, 4, 114	9	2:03.00	17,400
1974	Take Off, 5, 117	R. Turcotte	Jogging, 7, 112	Red Reality, 8, 112	7	2:00.40	23,070
1973	Red Reality, 7, 122	J. Velasquez	Malwak, 5, 116	New Hope, 4, 113	5	2:13.20	16,890

Named in honor of Walter "Red" Smith (1905-'82), Pulitzer Prize-winning sports columnist. Formerly named for Edgemere, New York, a Queens neighborhood. Grade 3 1973-'80, 2002, 2006. Edgemere H. 1960-'73, 1976-'81. Edgemere S. 1974-'75. Held at Belmont Park 1960-'62, 1968-'78, 1980-'93. Not held 1979. 1³/₁₆ miles 1963-'67. 1¼ miles 1972-'76, 1978, 1980-'93, 2006. 1¹/₁₆ miles 1977. Dirt 1960-'64, 1984, 1997, 2002, 2006. Originally scheduled on turf 2002, '06. Two divisions 1977, '83, '86. ‡Boyce finished second, DQ to 11th, 1995. Track record 1940.

Regret Stakes

Grade 3 in 2008. Churchill Downs, three-year-olds, fillies, 1 1/8 miles, turf. Held June 16, 2007, with a gross value of $228,600. First held in 1970. First graded in 1999. Stakes record 1:47.31 (2006 Lady of Venice [Fr]).

Year	Winner	Jockey	Second	Third	Strs	Time	1st Purse
2007	**Good Mood (Ire)**, 3, 116	E. S. Prado	You Go West Girl, 3, 118	Dashes N Dots, 3, 116	10	1:47.57	$134,646
2006	**Lady of Venice (Fr)**, 3, 120	J. R. Leparoux	Magnificent Song, 3, 120	Precious Kitten, 3, 116	11	**1:47.31**	133,462
2005	**Rich in Spirit**, 3, 120	G. L. Stevens	Sweet Talker, 3, 120	Royal Bean, 3, 116	8	1:49.76	139,500
2004	**Sister Star**, 3, 116	B. Blanc	Western Ransom, 3, 120	Jinny's Gold, 3, 118	7	1:51.40	137,516
2003	**Sand Springs**, 3, 118	M. Guidry	Personal Legend, 3, 116	Achnasheen, 3, 116	12	1:48.78	143,220
2002	**Distant Valley (GB)**, 3, 119	J. D. Bailey	Peace River Lady, 3, 115	Stylelistick, 3, 122	9	1:42.71	104,811
2001	**Casual Feat**, 3, 115	L. J. Melancon	Amaretta, 3, 117	La Vida Loca (Ire), 3, 119	8	1:42.75	103,695
2000	**Solvig**, 3, 122	P. Day	Trip, 3, 117	Miss Chief, 3, 115	9	1:42.95	104,439
1999	**Nani Rose**, 3, 115	S. J. Sellers	Solar Bound, 3, 122	Suffragette, 3, 115	8	1:42.40	104,439
1998	**Formal Tango**, 3, 115	C. R. Woods Jr.	Adel, 3, 122	Pratella, 3, 112	10	1:48.73	105,927
1997	**Starry Dreamer**, 3, 122	W. Martinez	Cozy Blues, 3, 115	Swearingen, 3, 122	8	1:42.77	69,378
1996	**Daylight Come**, 3, 117	C. C. Bourque	Fleur de Nuit, 3, 112	Esquive (GB), 3, 115	9	1:45.72	55,526
1995	**Christmas Gift**, 3, 122	C. R. Woods Jr.	Bail Out Becky, 3, 122	Grand Charmer, 3, 117	7	1:45.00	54,210
1994	**Packet**, 3, 117	J. M. Johnson	Thread, 3, 122	Slew Kitty Slew, 3, 112	7	1:42.14	54,551
1993	**Lovat's Lady**, 3, 112	B. D. Peck	Warside, 3, 122	Mari's Key, 3, 112	8	1:42.95	36,595
1992	**Tiney Toast**, 3, 122	S. P. Payton	Shes Just Super, 3, 122	Riverjinsky, 3, 115	10	1:42.06	37,440
1991	**Maria Balastiere**, 3, 117	A. T. Gryder	Savethelastdance, 3, 119	Lady Be Great, 3, 119	7	1:44.40	35,718
1990	**Secret Advice**, 3, 119	B. E. Bartram	Super Fan, 3, 122	Screen Prospect, 3, 119	6	1:44.40	35,815
1989	**Justice Will Come**, 3, 119	S. H. Bass	Luthier's Launch, 3, 119	Motion in Limine, 3, 117	10	1:46.20	36,693
1988	**Lets Do Lunch**, 3, 114	K. K. Allen	Stolie, 3, 119	Lucky Lydia, 3, 117	8	1:45.60	44,208
1987	**Jonowo**, 3, 119	M. McDowell	Lt. Lao, 3, 122	Sum, 3, 119	10	1:39.20	37,115
1986	**Rosemont Risk**, 3, 114	P. Day	Prime Union, 3, 122	Hail a Cab, 3, 122	8	1:36.80	25,090
1985	**Weekend Delight**, 3, 122	J. McKnight	Gallants Gem, 3, 122	Turn to Wilma, 3, 117	6	1:35.60	21,028
1984	**Mrs. Revere**, 3, 111	L. J. Melancon	Dusty Gloves, 3, 119	Robin's Rob, 3, 122	6	1:36.60	21,873
1983	**Rosy Spectre**, 3, 112	J. McKnight	Princesse Rapide, 3, 119	Fiesty Belle, 3, 111	9	1:37.80	19,939
1982	**Amazing Love**, 3, 116	L. J. Melancon	Jay Birdie, 3, 113	Noon Balloon, 3, 116	7	1:37.00	19,289
	Sefa's Beauty, 3, 113	M. S. Sellers	Mystical Mood, 3, 116	Smooth Fleet, 3, 113	5	1:37.60	19,143
1981	**Contrefaire**, 3, 121	T. Barrow	Solo Disco, 3, 121	Sweet Granny, 3, 118	13	1:11.60	16,705
1980	**Forever Cordial**, 3, 118	R. DePass	Missile Masquerade, 3, 118	Sweetladyroll, 3, 118	10	1:12.00	15,996
	No No Nona, 3, 115	M. A. Holland	Cerada Ridge, 3, 121	Romper, 3, 121	7	1:12.00	15,575
1979	**Fearless Dame**, 3, 121	R. DePass	Im for Joy, 3, 121	Shawn's Gal, 3, 121	10	1:10.80	16,120
1978	**Unconscious Doll**, 3, 121	E. Delahoussaye	Swervy, 3, 118	White Song, 3, 121	11	1:10.60	14,853
1977	**‡Shady Lou**, 3, 121	E. Delahoussaye	Time for Pleasure, 3, 121	Welsung, 3, 121	8	1:10.60	14,528
1976	**Carmelita Gibbs**, 3, 121	R. Breen	Sunny Romance, 3, 118	Island Venture, 3, 121	9	1:12.80	14,504
	Confort Zone, 3, 121	J. C. Espinoza	Rough Girl, 3, 121	My Fair Maid, 3, 115	6	1:12.80	14,114
1975	**Red Cross**, 3, 121	D. Brumfield	Flama Ardiente, 3, 121	Jill the Terrible, 3, 121	10	1:09.60	15,243
1974	**Clemanna**, 3, 121	J. C. Espinoza	Sarah Babe, 3, 121	Quick Sea, 3, 121	9	1:11.20	14,763
	Mary Dugan, 3, 121	J. McKnight	Princess Teamiga, 3, 118	Miss Orevent, 3, 121	12	1:10.40	15,153
1973	**Juke Joint**, 3, 118	W. Soirez	La Gentillesse, 3, 118	Never Ask, 3, 121	12	1:11.80	15,535

Named for Harry Payne Whitney's 1915 champion three-year-old filly and '15 Kentucky Derby winner Regret (1912 f. by Broomstick); Regret was the first filly to win the Derby. 6 furlongs 1970-'81. 1 mile 1982-'87. 1 1/16 miles 1988-2002. Dirt 1970-'86. Two divisions 1974, '76, '80, '82. ‡Time for Pleasure finished first, DQ to second, 1977. Nonwinners of a stakes worth $7,500 to the winner 1973-'75.

Remsen Stakes

Grade 2 in 2008. Aqueduct, two-year-olds, 1 1/8 miles, dirt. Held November 24, 2007, with a gross value of $200,000. First held in 1904. First graded in 1973. Stakes record 1:47.80 (1977 Believe It).

Year	Winner	Jockey	Second	Third	Strs	Time	1st Purse
2007	**Court Vision**, 2, 122	E. Coa	Atoned, 2, 120	Trust N Dustan, 2, 116	6	1:52.48	$120,000
2006	**Nobiz Like Shobiz**, 2, 116	C. H. Velasquez	Zanjero, 2, 116	Kong the King, 2, 116	8	1:48.82	120,000
2005	**Bluegrass Cat**, 2, 120	J. R. Velazquez	Flashy Bull, 2, 116	Parkhimonbroadway, 2, 116	8	1:52.20	120,000
2004	**Rockport Harbor**, 2, 120	S. Elliott	Galloping Grocer, 2, 120	Killenaule, 2, 120	6	1:48.88	120,000
2003	**Read the Footnotes**, 2, 122	J. D. Bailey	Master David, 2, 116	West Virginia, 2, 116	11	1:50.62	120,000
2002	**Toccet**, 2, 122	J. F. Chavez	Bham, 2, 116	Empire Maker, 2, 116	8	1:50.80	120,000
2001	**Saarland**, 2, 116	J. R. Velazquez	Nokoma, 2, 116	Silent Fred, 2, 116	9	1:51.28	120,000
2000	**Windsor Castle**, 2, 116	R. G. Davis	Ommadon, 2, 122	Buckle Down Ben, 2, 122	8	1:51.92	120,000
1999	**Greenwood Lake**, 2, 122	J. Samyn	Un Fino Vino, 2, 113	Polish Miner, 2, 113	8	1:50.63	120,000
1998	**Comeonmom**, 2, 113	J. Bravo	Millions, 2, 122	Wondertross, 2, 113	9	1:49.84	120,000
1997	**Coronado's Quest**, 2, 122	M. E. Smith	Halory Hunter, 2, 115	Brooklyn Nick, 2, 115	7	1:52.27	120,000
1996	**The Silver Move**, 2, 114	R. Migliore	Jules, 2, 122	Accelerator, 2, 122	8	1:53.54	120,000
1995	**Tropicool**, 2, 112	J. F. Chavez	Skip Away, 2, 112	Crafty Friend, 2, 113	11	1:50.30	170,000
1994	**Thunder Gulch**, 2, 115	G. L. Stevens	Western Echo, 2, 119	Maggie Magee, 2, 114	10	1:53.80	120,000
1993	**Go for Gin**, 2, 117	J. D. Bailey	Arrovente, 2, 113	Linkatariat, 2, 113	7	1:52.79	120,000
1992	**Silver of Silver**, 2, 122	J. Vasquez	Dalhart, 2, 115	Wild Gale, 2, 115	11	1:50.25	120,000
1991	**Pine Bluff**, 2, 113	C. Perret	Offbeat, 2, 113	Cheap Shades, 2, 113	6	1:50.80	120,000
1990	**Scan**, 2, 119	J. D. Bailey	Subordinated Debt, 2, 115	Kyle's Our Man, 2, 113	8	1:52.40	106,560
1989	**Roanoke**, 2, 115	E. Maple	Roanoke, 2, 113	Armed for Peace, 2, 113	10	1:51.20	145,680
1988	**Fast Play**, 2, 122	A. T. Cordero Jr.	Fire Maker, 2, 115	Silver Sunsets, 2, 122	15	1:50.60	197,400
1987	**Batty**, 2, 113	J. A. Santos	Old Stories, 2, 115	Three Engines, 2, 113	8	1:52.40	176,400

Year	Winner	Jockey	Second	Third	Strs	Time	1st Purse
1986	Java Gold, 2, 113	P. Day	Talinum, 2, 115	Drachma, 2, 113	8	1:49.60	$172,680
1985	Pillaster, 2, 119	A. T. Cordero Jr.	Mr. Classic, 2, 113	Dance of Life, 2, 113	10	1:49.00	175,800
1984	‡Mighty Appealing, 2, 122	G. P. Smith	Hot Debate, 2, 117	Bolting Holme, 2, 115	11	1:53.20	178,680
1983	Dr. Carter, 2, 113	J. Velasquez	Secret Prince, 2, 117	Hail Bold King, 2, 113	8	1:49.00	134,700
1982	Pax in Bello, 2, 113	J. Fell	Chumming, 2, 115	Primitive Pleasure, 2, 113	11	1:50.20	141,300
1981	Laser Light, 2, 113	E. Maple	Real Twister, 2, 115	Wolfie's Rascal, 2, 113	11	1:50.80	103,500
1980	‡Pleasant Colony, 2, 116	V. A. Bracciale Jr.	Foolish Tanner, 2, 113	Akureyri, 2, 117	8	1:50.20	67,920
1979	Plugged Nickle, 2, 122	B. Thornburg	Googolplex, 2, 117	Proctor, 2, 113	8	1:50.40	64,560
1978	Instrument Landing, 2, 119	J. Fell	Lucy's Axe, 2, 117	Picturesque, 2, 117	9	1:50.20	48,375
1977	Believe It, 2, 122	E. Maple	Alydar, 2, 122	Quadratic, 2, 116	5	**1:47.80**	48,015
1976	Royal Ski, 2, 122	J. Kurtz	Nostalgia, 2, 122	Hey Hey J. P., 2, 116	9	1:50.40	49,545
1975	Hang Ten, 2, 116	L. A. Pincay Jr.	Dance Spell, 2, 113	Play the Red, 2, 113	12	1:49.20	52,290
1974	El Pitirre, 2, 112	M. Venezia	Bombay Duck, 2, 118	Circle Home, 2, 115	10	1:49.40	34,380
1973	Heavy Mayonnaise, 2, 112	C. Baltazar	Hegemony, 2, 112	Flip Sal, 2, 112	13	1:51.40	17,925

Named for Col. Joremus Remsen (1735-'90), leader of the Revolutionary forces at the battle of Long Island, New York. Grade 1 1981-'88. Remsen H. 1904-'53. Held at Jamaica 1904-'58. Not held 1908, 1910-'17, 1951. 5½ furlongs 1904-'09. 6 furlongs 1918-'45, 1949-'50. 1 1/16 miles 1946-'47, 1952-'58. 5 furlongs 1948. 1 mile 1959-'72. Colts 1954-'57. Colts and geldings 1958-'60. ‡Akureyri finished first, DQ to third, 1980. ‡Stone White finished first, DQ to 11th, 1984.

Richter Scale Sprint Championship Handicap

Grade 2 in 2008. Gulfstream Park, four-year-olds and up, 7 furlongs, dirt. Held March 8, 2008, with a gross value of $190,000. First held in 1972. First graded in 1996. Stakes record 1:21.15 (2003 Tour of the Cat).

Year	Winner	Jockey	Second	Third	Strs	Time	1st Purse
2008	Commentator, 7, 123	J. R. Velazquez	Rexson's Rose, 5, 116	Elite Squadron, 4, 117	6	1:23.23	$120,000
2007	Half Ours, 4, 117	J. R. Velazquez	Park Avenue Ball, 5, 119	Diabolical, 4, 118	10	1:22.21	135,000
2006	Mister Fotis, 5, 115	R. Bejarano	Sir Greeley, 4, 116	Universal Form, 5, 116	9	1:21.73	120,000
2005	Sir Shackleton, 4, 116	J. Castellano	Lion Tamer, 5, 119	Clock Stopper, 5, 117	6	1:21.64	120,000
2004	Lion Tamer, 4, 116	J. R. Velazquez	Coach Jimi Lee, 4, 115	Wacky for Love, 4, 114	7	1:21.52	120,000
2003	Tour of the Cat, 5, 116	A. Cabassa Jr.	Burning Roma, 5, 116	Highway Prospector, 6, 114	8	**1:21.15**	120,000
2002	Dream Run, 4, 113	P. Day	Binthebest, 5, 114	Burning Roma, 4, 118	8	1:22.30	120,000
2001	Hook and Ladder, 4, 115	R. Migliore	Trippi, 4, 120	Rollin With Nolan, 4, 116	6	1:21.85	120,000
2000	Richter Scale, 6, 118	R. Migliore	Forty One Carats, 4, 116	Kelly Kip, 6, 120	10	1:23.30	120,000
1999	Frisk Me Now, 5, 117	E. L. King Jr.	Young At Heart, 5, 113	Good and Tough, 4, 115	6	1:22.86	60,000
1998	Rare Rock, 5, 117	P. Day	Irish Conquest, 5, 114	Frisco View, 5, 118	7	1:22.00	120,000
1997	Frisco View, 4, 116	J. D. Bailey	El Amante, 4, 114	Templado (Ven), 4, 114	7	1:23.14	98,160
1996	Patton, 5, 113	R. G. Davis	Forty Won, 5, 115	Our Emblem, 5, 115	10	1:21.81	100,140
1995	Cherokee Run, 5, 122	M. E. Smith	Waldoboro, 4, 115	Evil Bear, 5, 116	6	1:21.70	60,000
1994	I Can't Believe, 6, 113	E. Maple	American Chance, 5, 114	British Banker, 6, 114	8	1:22.55	60,000
1993	Binalong, 4, 112	J. D. Bailey	Loach, 5, 114	Richman, 5, 113	6	1:22.35	60,000
1992	Groomstick, 6, 112	W. S. Ramos	Ocala Flame, 4, 115	Cold Digger, 5, 113	9	1:23.98	60,000
1991	Gervazy, 4, 115	W. S. Ramos	Shuttleman, 5, 114	Swedaus, 4, 110	7	1:21.46	60,000
1990	‡Dancing Spree, 5, 126	A. T. Cordero Jr.	Pentelicus, 6, 114	Shuttleman, 4, 111	7	1:10.00	30,000
1989	Claim, 4, 115	C. Perret	Position Leader, 4, 117	Prospector's Halo, 5, 115	7	1:23.40	41,904
1988	Royal Pennant, 5, 113	J. A. Santos	dh-Grantley, 4, 112		12	1:23.20	45,612
			dh-Real Forest, 5, 113				
1987	Dwight D., 5, 116	R. N. Lester	Splendid Catch, 5, 113	Uncle Ho, 4, 112	7	1:10.80	27,816
1986	Hot Cop, 4, 115	J. Samyn	Dwight D., 4, 114	Opening Lead, 6, 115	12	1:22.80	45,324
1985	Key to the Moon, 4, 122	R. Platts	For Halo, 4, 123	Northern Ocean, 5, 112	8	1:22.60	42,552
1984	Number One Special, 4, 116	E. Fires	Ward Off Trouble, 4, 116	El Perico, 4, 114	6	1:21.80	23,793
1983	Deputy Minister, 4, 122	D. MacBeth	Wipe 'em Out, 4, 109	Center Cut, 4, 118	12	1:22.80	38,040
1981	King's Fashion, 6, 120	J. Samyn	Jaklin Klugman, 4, 124	Joanie's Chief, 4, 108	7	1:22.60	34,920
1977	Yamanin, 5, 122	W. Gavidia	Full Out, 4, 119	Rexson, 4, 114	6	1:22.80	37,860
1974	Cheriepe, 4, 115	J. Velasquez	Shecky Greene, 4, 127	Gay Pierre, 5, 112	4	1:22.40	25,236

Named for Wafare Farm's and Richard S. and Nancy Kaster's 2000 Gulfstream Park Breeders' Cup Sprint Championship H. (G2) winner Richter Scale (1994 c. by *Habitony). Grade 3 1996-'98. Sprint Championship H. 1972, '74, '77, '81. Gulfstream Sprint Championship H. 1983-'90. Gulfstream Park Sprint Championship H. 1991-'93. Gulfstream Park Sprint H. 1994-'95. Gulfstream Park Breeders' Cup Sprint Championship H. 1996-2002. Richter Scale Breeders' Cup Sprint Championship S. 2003. Richter Scale Breeders' Cup Sprint Championship H. 2004-'06. Richter Scale Sprint Championship H. 2007. Not held 1973, 1975-'76, 1978-'80, 1982. 6 furlongs 1987, '90. Three-year-olds and up 1972-2006. Dead heat for second 1988. ‡Pentelicus finished first, DQ to second, 1990.

Risen Star Stakes

Grade 3 in 2008. Fair Grounds, three-year-olds, 1 1/16 miles, dirt. Held February 9, 2008, with a gross value of $300,000. First held in 1988. First graded in 2002. Stakes record 1:42.98 (1996 Zarb's Magic).

Year	Winner	Jockey	Second	Third	Strs	Time	1st Purse
2008	Pyro, 3, 116	S. Bridgmohan	Z Fortune, 3, 122	Visionaire, 3, 118	11	1:44.68	$180,000
2007	Notional, 3, 122	R. Albarado	Imawildandcrazyguy, 3, 116	Zanjero, 3, 120	12	1:44.18	180,000
2006	Lawyer Ron, 3, 118	R. McKee	Mark of Success, 3, 116	Hyte Regency, 3, 116	7	1:43.13	160,800
2005	Scipion, 3, 117	G. L. Stevens	Real Dandy, 3, 118	Storm Surge, 3, 122	11	1:44.54	90,000
2004	Gradepoint, 3, 116	R. Albarado	Mr. Jester, 3, 122	Nightlifeatbigblue, 3, 118	6	1:45.36	90,000
2003	Badge of Silver, 3, 116	R. Albarado	Lone Star Sky, 3, 122	Defrere's Vixen, 3, 114	12	1:42.99	90,000
2002	Repent, 3, 122	A. J. D'Amico	Bob's Image, 3, 115	Easyfromthegitgo, 3, 122	9	1:43.17	90,000
2001	Dollar Bill, 3, 122	C. J. McCarron	Gracie's Dancer, 3, 114	Rahy's Secret, 3, 122	10	1:43.45	75,000

Racing — Graded Stakes

Year	Winner	Jockey	Second	Third	Strs	Time	1st Purse
2000	Exchange Rate, 3, 119	C. S. Nakatani	Mighty, 3, 122	Ifitstobeitsuptome, 3, 114	8	1:44.25	$75,000
1999	Ecton Park, 3, 114	S. J. Sellers	Answer Lively, 3, 122	Kimberlite Pipe, 3, 122	12	1:44.83	75,000
1998	Comic Strip, 3, 119	S. J. Sellers	Captain Maestri, 3, 122	Time Limit, 3, 122	7	1:44.27	75,000
1997	Open Forum, 3, 117	D. M. Barton	Crypto Star, 3, 117	Cash Deposit, 3, 122	5	1:44.20	60,000
1996	Zarb's Magic, 3, 122	E. J. Perrodin	Imminent First, 3, 114	Palikar, 3, 122	9	**1:42.98**	37,950
1995	Knockadoon, 3, 114	W. Martinez	Key to Malagra, 3, 114	Scott's Scoundrel, 3, 122	9	1:45.44	31,882
	Beavers Nose, 3, 117	K. Bourque	Moonlight Dancer, 3, 122	Fuzzy Me, 3, 114	8	1:45.22	31,792
1994	Fly Cry, 3, 122	R. D. Ardoin	Smilin Singin Sam, 3, 122	Little Jazz Boy, 3, 122	7	1:43.02	31,155
1993	Dixieland Heat, 3, 119	R. P. Romero	O'Star, 3, 114	Gold Angle, 3, 114	7	1:43.20	16,080
	Dry Bean, 3, 117	A. T. Gryder	Apprentice, 3, 119	Grand Jewel, 3, 114	6	1:43.80	16,020
1992	Line In The Sand, 3, 119	S. P. Romero	Hill Pass, 3, 119	Sheik to Sheik, 3, 114	11	1:45.00	19,635
1991	Big Courage, 3, 119	T. L. Fox	Slick Groom, 3, 114	Denizen, 3, 115	8	1:46.70	19,230
1990	Genuine Meaning, 3, 122	J. Hirdes	Very Formal, 3, 114	Diamond Prospector, 3, 114	12	1:40.80	16,740
1989	Nooo Problema, 3, 117	S. P. Romero	Alota Strawberry, 3, 114	Majesty's Imp, 3, 119	8	1:42.40	13,163
	Dispersal, 3, 114	B. J. Walker Jr.	Island Alibi, 3, 114	Major Prospect, 3, 114	7	1:44.20	13,103
1988	Risen Star, 3, 120	S. P. Romero	Pastourelles, 3, 115	Jim's Orbit, 3, 122	12	1:40.00	13,890

Named for Lamarque Racing Stable's and Louie J. Roussel III's 1988 champion three-year-old male and '88 Louisiana Derby (G3) winner Risen Star (1985 c. by Secretariat). Originally designed as a prep for the Louisiana Derby (G2). Louisiana Derby Trial S. 1988. Held at Louisiana Downs 2006. 1 mile 40 yards 1988-'90. Two divisions 1989, '93, '95.

River City Handicap

Grade 3 in 2008. Churchill Downs, three-year-olds and up, 1 1/8 miles, turf. Held November 23, 2007, with a gross value of $227,400. First held in 1978. First graded in 1996. Stakes record 1:47.90 (2001 Dr. Kashnikow).

Year	Winner	Jockey	Second	Third	Strs	Time	1st Purse
2007	Thorn Song, 4, 116	K. J. Desormeaux	Cosmonaut, 5, 122	Gun Salute, 5, 115	10	1:51.37	$133,940
2006	Bayeux, 5, 112	J. R. Velazquez	Lord Admiral, 5, 115	Ballast (Ire), 5, 115	9	1:48.77	100,531
2005	America Alive, 4, 119	R. Albarado	G P Fleet, 5, 117	Shaniko, 4, 116	8	1:50.78	103,974
2004	G P Fleet, 4, 115	J. R. Martinez Jr.	Cloudy's Knight, 4, 115	Ay Caramba (Brz), 4, 115	12	1:51.26	108,066
2003	Hard Buck (Brz), 4, 118	B. Blanc	Warleigh, 5, 117	Rowans Park, 3, 114	10	1:51.60	107,136
2002	Dr. Kashnikow, 5, 116	R. Albarado	Foster's Landing, 4, 109	Roxinho (Brz), 4, 115	11	1:51.44	108,903
2001	Dr. Kashnikow, 4, 116	R. Albarado	Tijiyr (Ire), 5, 117	Strategic Mission, 6, 115	8	**1:47.90**	109,926
2000	Brahms, 3, 112	P. Day	Vergennes, 5, 115	Super Quercus (Fr), 4, 116	9	1:48.09	111,879
1999	Comic Strip, 4, 119	P. Day	Keats and Yeats, 5, 112	Aboriginal Apex, 6, 114	10	1:50.71	106,113
1998	Wild Event, 5, 116	S. J. Sellers	Buff, 3, 113	Florisell, 4, 114	13	1:49.18	116,436
1997	Same Old Wish, 7, 117	S. J. Sellers	Aboriginal Apex, 4, 113	Joyeux Danseur, 4, 114	9	1:50.90	106,578
1996	Same Old Wish, 6, 119	S. J. Sellers	Jet Freighter, 5, 113	Franchise Player, 7, 111	7	1:49.21	70,122
1995	Homing Pigeon, 5, 113	R. P. Romero	Hawk Attack, 5, 118	Dusty Asher, 5, 111	8	1:51.00	73,320
1994	Lindon Lime, 4, 113	S. J. Sellers	Torch Rouge (GB), 3, 114	Jaggery John, 3, 115	11	1:49.30	75,660
1993	Secreto's Hideaway, 4, 110	W. Martinez	Little Bro Lantis, 5, 115	Ganges, 5, 113	5	1:53.83	72,670
1992	Cozzene's Prince, 5, 117	D. Penna	Lotus Pool, 5, 118	Stagecraft (GB), 5, 114	8	1:49.31	73,060
1991	Spending Record, 4, 114	P. Day	Stage Colony, 4, 113	Silver Medallion, 5, 118	10	1:50.34	75,075
1990	Silver Medallion, 4, 118	C. Perret	Blair's Cove, 5, 114	Rushing Raj, 4, 114	10	1:50.80	56,550
1989	Spark O'Dan, 4, 113	J. M. Johnson	Exclusive Greer, 8, 115	Air Worthy, 4, 118	10	1:50.80	55,429
1988	Ile de Jinsky, 4, 113	E. J. Sipus Jr.	Stop the Stage, 4, 114	Herakles, 5, 117	7	1:53.20	44,618
1987	Kings River (Ire), 5, 114	M. E. Smith	Lord Grundy (Ire), 5, 119	Boulder Run, 4, 117	10	1:45.40	37,148
1986	Taylor's Special, 5, 123	P. Day	Doonesbear, 3, 116	Sumptious, 3, 121	8	1:36.20	30,007
1985	Banner Bob, 3, 118	K. K. Allen	Rapid Gray, 6, 123	Cullendale, 3, 116	6	1:36.60	29,348
1984	Eminency, 6, 115	P. Day	Thumbsucker, 5, 123	Bayou Hebert, 3, 116	8	1:38.40	18,103
1983	Northern Majesty, 4, 120	S. Maple	Shot n' Missed, 6, 123	Straight Flow, 5, 115	8	1:37.00	18,243
1982	Pleasing Times, 3, 110	P. Day	Hechizado (Arg), 6, 115	Rackensack, 4, 118	13	1:38.20	20,719
1981	Suliman, 4, 117	L. Snyder	Tiger Lure, 7, 121	Senate Chairman, 3, 113	12	1:10.60	20,199
1980	Tinsley's Hope, 6, 113	J. C. Espinoza	Go With the Times, 4, 122	Withholding, 3, 114	6	1:11.00	19,208
1979	Go With the Times, 3, 120	G. Gallitano	Cossett Charlie, 6, 112	Bask, 5, 117	7	1:10.20	19,435
1978	Inca Roca, 5, 118	J. C. Espinoza	Perplext, 4, 114	Raymond Earl, 3, 115	8	1:10.40	17,859

Named for one of the nicknames of Louisville: the "River City." River City S. 1983-'86. 6 furlongs 1978-'81. 1 mile 1982-'86. 1 1/16 miles 1987. Dirt 1978-'86, 1988, 1993.

Robert B. Lewis Stakes

Grade 2 in 2008. Santa Anita Park, three-year-olds, 1 1/16 miles, all weather. Held February 2, 2008, with a gross value of $200,000. First held in 1935. First graded in 1998. Stakes record 1:40.76 (2008 Crown of Thorns).

Year	Winner	Jockey	Second	Third	Strs	Time	1st Purse
2008	Crown of Thorns, 3, 115	V. Espinoza	Coast Guard, 3, 115	Reflect Times (Jpn), 3, 117	5	**1:40.76**	$120,000
2007	Great Hunter, 3, 119	C. S. Nakatani	Sam P., 3, 117	Saint Paul, 3, 116	9	1:42.89	120,000
2006	Brother Derek, 3, 122	A. O. Solis	Sacred Light, 3, 115	Latent Heat, 3, 118	8	1:41.96	120,000
2005	Declan's Moon, 3, 122	V. Espinoza	Going Wild, 3, 122	Spanish Chestnut, 3, 122	6	1:42.41	120,000
2004	St Averil, 3, 113	T. Baze	Lucky Pulpit, 3, 115	Master David, 3, 113	9	1:41.62	90,000
2003	Domestic Dispute, 3, 113	D. R. Flores	Our Bobby V., 3, 113	Scrimshaw, 3, 115	8	1:42.20	90,000
2002	Labamta Babe, 3, 113	K. Desormeaux	Siphonic, 3, 123	Cottonwood Cowboy, 3, 115	6	1:42.50	90,000
2001	Millennium Wind, 3, 114	C. J. McCarron	Palmeiro, 3, 117	Denied, 3, 116	6	1:42.60	64,620
2000	The Deputy (Ire), 3, 115	C. J. McCarron	High Yield, 3, 117	Captain Steve, 3, 123	6	1:43.04	64,380
1999	General Challenge, 3, 117	G. L. Stevens	Buck Trout, 3, 120	Brilliantly, 3, 115	5	1:42.93	63,900
1998	Artax, 3, 114	C. J. McCarron	Souvenir Copy, 3, 120	Allen's Oop, 3, 117	6	1:42.32	64,320
1997	Hello (Ire), 3, 120	C. J. McCarron	Bagshot, 3, 116	Carmen's Baby, 3, 120	8	1:42.60	65,950

Racing — Graded Stakes

Year	Winner	Jockey	Second	Third	Strs	Time	1st Purse
1996	Prince of Thieves, 3, 113	G. L. Stevens	Smithfield, 3, 116	Matty G, 3, 124	6	1:42.94	$64,250
1995	Larry the Legend, 3, 117	K. Desormeaux	In Character (GB), 3, 115	Awesome Thought, 3, 119	5	1:42.93	45,975
1994	Wekiva Springs, 3, 121	K. Desormeaux	Gracious Ghost, 3, 116	Dream Trapp, 3, 117	5	1:41.94	45,900
1993	Art of Living, 3, 115	G. L. Stevens	Tossofthecoin, 3, 115	Glowing Crown, 3, 115	5	1:43.48	45,900
1992	Vying Victor, 3, 115	C. A. Black	Turbulent Kris, 3, 114	Al Sabin, 3, 117	11	1:44.33	51,000
1991	Mane Minister, 3, 114	D. R. Flores	Conveyor, 3, 114	Famed Devil, 3, 114	8	1:42.70	48,375
1990	Music Prospector, 3, 114	F. Olivares	Senegalaise, 3, 114	Tsu's Dawning, 3, 120	6	1:43.60	46,950
1989	Flying Continental, 3, 117	L. A. Pincay Jr.	Very Personably, 3, 114	Morlando, 3, 114	9	1:43.60	48,750
1988	Lively One, 3, 120	W. Shoemaker	Stalwars, 3, 114	Havanaffair, 3, 114	9	1:43.40	48,650
1987	Stylish Winner, 3, 114	G. L. Stevens	Prince Sassafras, 3, 117	Barb's Relic, 3, 116	7	1:43.80	38,200
1986	Ferdinand, 3, 114	W. Shoemaker	Variety Road, 3, 114	Grand Allegiance, 3, 117	8	1:43.00	38,750
1985	Floating Reserve, 3, 117	L. A. Pincay Jr.	Brecons Charge, 3, 117	Bolder Than Bold, 3, 114	11	1:42.60	40,450
1984	Tights, 3, 120	R. Q. Meza	Prince True, 3, 117	Gate Dancer, 3, 120	10	1:43.60	40,150
1983	Fast Passage, 3, 116	E. Delahoussaye	Hyperborean, 3, 114	My Habitony, 3, 114	8	1:42.60	38,900
1982	Water Bank, 3, 115	D. G. McHargue	Bargain Balcony, 3, 117	Crystal Star, 3, 115	8	1:42.40	38,850
1981	‡Stancharry, 3, 117	L. A. Pincay Jr.	Minnesota Chief, 3, 117	Litigator, 3, 120	8	1:41.40	31,900
1980	Super Moment, 3, 115	D. Pierce	Executive Counsel, 3, 117	Decent Davey, 3, 120	7	1:44.40	20,075
	Rumbo, 3, 117	W. Shoemaker	Idyll, 3, 114	Bold 'n Rulling, 3, 117	6	1:44.60	19,675
1979	Pole Position, 3, 120	C. J. McCarron	Grand Alliance, 3, 114	Shamgo, 3, 116	8	1:42.00	26,100
1978	Johnny's Image, 3, 115	S. Hawley	Kamehameha, 3, 115	Go Forth, 3, 115	8	1:44.00	26,350
1977	Text, 3, 118	D. Pierce	Cuzwuzwrong, 3, 118	Nordic Prince, 3, 114	9	1:42.00	24,600
1976	An Act, 3, 118	L. A. Pincay Jr.	Life's Hope, 3, 118	First Return, 3, 118	8	1:42.00	20,800
1975	Kinalmeaky, 3, 118	W. Shoemaker	Rock of Ages, 3, 118	Looks Impressive, 3, 118	10	1:42.80	22,400
1974	Rube the Great, 3, 118	A. Santiago	Aloha Mood, 3, 118	L'Amour Rullah, 3, 118	10	1:43.00	18,700
1973	Sham, 3, 118	L. A. Pincay Jr.	Out of the East, 3, 118	Scantling, 3, 118	5	1:45.00	19,800

Named for Robert B. Lewis (1924-2006), Eclipse Award-winning Southern California owner of 1999 Horse of the Year Charismatic and '97 champion three-year-old male Silver Charm. Formerly sponsored by Rancho Santa Catalina Island, which occupied the entire island of Santa Catalina off the California coast. Grade 3 1998. Santa Catalina H. 1935, 1941-'63. Santa Catalina California-Bred Championship 1937-'39. Santa Catalina Nursery S. 1940. Santa Catalina S. 1964-2006. Not held 1936, 1942-'44. 1 mile 1935. 1 1/8 miles 1939, 1947-'52, 1954-'63. 3 furlongs 1940. 7 furlongs 1970. Dirt 1935-2007. Three-year-olds and up 1937-'38, 1941-'46, 1991. Two-year-olds 1940. Four-year-olds and up 1947-'63. Two divisions 1980. ‡Minnesota Chief finished first, DQ to second, 1981. California-foaled 1963. Nonwinners of a race worth $12,500 to the winner 1973-'75. Nonwinners of a race worth $25,000 to the winner 1990, '92. California-breds 1937-'39.

Robert F. Carey Memorial Handicap

Grade 3 in 2008. Hawthorne Race Course, three-year-olds and up, 1 mile, turf. Held September 29, 2007, with a gross value of $150,000. First held in 1983. First graded in 1986. Stakes record 1:33.40 (1998 Soviet Line [Ire]).

Year	Winner	Jockey	Second	Third	Strs	Time	1st Purse
2007	Classic Campaign, 5, 116	R. Migliore	Crested (GB), 4, 115	Gold Hornet, 6, 112	7	1:33.95	$88,200
2006	No Tolerance, 5, 115	J. M. Campbell	Rapid Proof, 6, 116	Come On Jazz, 5, 114	9	1:35.54	90,000
2005	Spruce Run, 7, 115	R. A. Stokes III	Fort Prado, 4, 121	Remind, 5, 118	9	1:39.97	90,000
2004	Scooter Roach, 5, 115	J. M. Campbell	Gin and Sin, 4, 116	Cloudy's Knight, 4, 116	9	1:34.51	90,000
2003	Mystery Giver, 5, 120	C. H. Marquez Jr.	Al's Dearly Bred, 6, 118	Major Rhythm, 4, 116	8	1:34.70	90,000
2002	Kimberlite Pipe, 6, 115	C. A. Emigh	Aslaaf, 4, 114	Major Omansky, 6, 115	10	1:35.94	90,000
2001	Galic Boy, 6, 115	R. Sibille	Where's Taylor, 5, 121	Good Journey, 5, 115	10	1:35.10	90,000
2000	Where's Taylor, 4, 117	C. J. Lanerie	Dernier Croise (Fr), 5, 113	Associate, 5, 115	11	1:36.31	90,000
1999	Ray's Approval, 6, 114	E. Fires	Stay Sound, 4, 115	Inkatha (Fr), 5, 115	9	1:37.01	90,000
1998	Soviet Line (Ire), 8, 115	S. J. Sellers	Fun to Run, 5, 110	Wild Event, 5, 115	10	1:33.40	90,000
1997	Trail City, 4, 119	J. D. Bailey	Power of Opinion, 4, 113	Da Bull, 5, 114	8	1:36.04	90,000
1996	Homing Pigeon, 6, 114	R. Albarado	Joker, 4, 115	Why Change, 3, 115	12	1:36.58	90,000
1995	Homing Pigeon, 5, 114	R. Albarado	Gilder, 4, 113	Rare Reason, 4, 119	9	1:38.09	60,000
1994	Recoup the Cash, 4, 119	J. L. Diaz	Road of War, 4, 115	Glenfiddich Lad, 5, 114	7	1:40.91	60,000
1993	High Habitation, 5, 114	G. C. Retana	Beau Fasa, 7, 114	Glenfiddich Lad, 4, 114	12	1:35.33	60,000
1992	Double Booked, 7, 115	J. C. Ferrer	Evanescent, 5, 113	That's Sunny, 7, 114	11	1:39.82	60,000
1991	Slew the Slewor, 4, 114	G. K. Gomez	Jalaajel, 7, 118	The Great Carl, 4, 118	9	1:38.72	96,090
1990	Allijeba, 4, 118	K. D. Clark	Wave Wise, 4, 114	Expensive Decision, 4, 118	9	1:39.20	86,070
1989	Iron Courage, 5, 121	R. R. Pena	Saint Oxford, 5, 112	Do Loop, 6, 109	10	1:47.00	94,080
1988	New Colony, 5, 114	R. R. Douglas	Rio's Lark, 4, 115	Bank Fast, 4, 111	9	1:47.60	93,900
1987	The Sassman, 4, 113	K. D. Clark	Zaizoom, 3, 115	Zuppardo's Love, 6, 111	6	2:05.40	89,130
1986	Pass the Line, 5, 117	J. L. Diaz	Explosive Darling, 4, 117	Salem Drive, 4, 116	8	2:01.00	94,500
1985	River Lord, 6, 111	R. A. Meier	Harham's Sizzler, 6, 118	Attaway to Go, 4, 111	4	2:06.20	63,370
1984	Ronbra, 4, 115	C. H. Marquez	Grazie, 4, 115	Bold Run (Fr), 5, 115	12	2:03.80	66,540
1983	Sir Pele, 4, 112	O. Vergara	John's Gold, 4, 120	Energetic King, 4, 111	7	1:55.00	64,800

Named for Robert F. Carey (1904-'80), managing director of Hawthorne Race Course (1947-'80). Formerly sponsored by United Airlines of Chicago 1995. Not graded 1990-'97. Robert F. Carey H. 1984-'85. 1 3/16 miles 1983. 1 1/4 miles 1984-'87. 1 1/8 miles 1988-'89. 1 mile 70 yards 1994. Dirt 1985, '94.

Robert G. Dick Memorial Handicap

Grade 3 in 2008. Delaware Park, three-year-olds and up, fillies and mares, 1 3/8 miles, turf. Held July 14, 2007, with a gross value of $257,300. First held in 1997. First graded in 2008. Stakes record 2:15.04 (2003 Alternate).

Year	Winner	Jockey	Second	Third	Strs	Time	1st Purse
2007	Rosinka (Ire), 4, 121	J. Rose	Royal Highness (Ger), 5, 121	Humoristic, 6, 117	6	2:16.56	$150,000

Racing — Graded Stakes   431

Year	Winner	Jockey	Second	Third	Strs	Time	1st Purse
2006	Honey Ryder, 5, 123	J. R. Velazquez	Olaya, 4, 117	Latice (Ire), 5, 117	7	2:20.81	$180,000
2005	Honey Ryder, 4, 120	E. S. Prado	Sweet Science, 4, 114	Natalie Beach (Arg), 5, 117	10	2:20.58	180,000
2004	Alternate, 5, 119	R. A. Dominguez	Lady of the Future, 6, 118	Primetimevalentine, 5, 114	10	2:20.07	90,000
2003	Alternate, 4, 115	O. Castillo	Spice Island, 4, 114	Lady of the Future, 5, 115	11	2:15.04	90,000
2002	New Economy, 4, 115	R. A. Dominguez	Rhum, 5, 117	Jennasietta, 4, 117	10	2:17.78	90,000
2001	Amourette, 5, 115	T. L. Dunkelberger	Aiglonne, 4, 115	Krisada, 5, 115	9	2:17.20	91,000
2000	Camella, 5, 117	A. T. Gryder	dh-Free Vacation, 4, 113 dh-Sharp Apple, 4, 115		10	2:17.75	90,000
1999	Bursting Forth, 5, 119	E. S. Prado	Maria's Tiara, 4, 113	Adrian, 5, 114	9	2:19.50	90,000
1998	Memories of Silver, 5, 115	P. Day	Champagne Royal, 4, 115	Fickle Fate, 4, 115	5	1:43.66	60,000
1997	Double Stake, 4, 113	J. Rocco	Winter Melody, 4, 118	Clarify, 4, 113	9	1:52.61	60,000

Named in memory of Robert G. Dick (1920-'97), a former member of the Delaware Racing Commission. Robert G. Dick Memorial S. 1997-'98. Robert G. Dick Memorial Breeders' Cup S. 1999-2002. Robert G. Dick Memorial Breeders' Cup H. 2003-'06. 1¹⁄₈ miles 1997. 1¹⁄₁₆ miles 1998. Dirt 1997. Dead heat for second 2000.

Ruffian Handicap

Grade 1 in 2008. Belmont Park, three-year-olds and up, fillies and mares, 1¹⁄₁₆ miles, dirt. Held September 8, 2007, with a gross value of $285,000. First held in 1976. First graded in 1976. Stakes record 1:40.25 (2007 Ginger Punch).

Year	Winner	Jockey	Second	Third	Strs	Time	1st Purse
2007	Ginger Punch, 4, 120	R. Bejarano	Miss Shop, 4, 118	Teammate, 4, 116	4	1:40.25	$180,000
2006	Pool Land, 4, 116	J. R. Velazquez	Take D' Tour, 5, 119	Miss Shop, 3, 113	5	1:41.81	180,000
2005	Stellar Jayne, 4, 119	J. D. Bailey	Society Selection, 4, 118	Halory Leigh, 5, 116	6	1:41.87	180,000
2004	Sightseek, 5, 122	J. R. Velazquez	Pocus Hocus, 6, 114	Miss Loren (Arg), 6, 117	5	1:41.51	180,000
2003	Wild Spirit (Chi), 4, 121	J. D. Bailey	You, 4, 118	Passing Shot, 4, 115	6	1:41.23	180,000
2002	Mandy's Gold, 4, 116	J. A. Santos	You, 3, 117	Shine Again, 5, 117	5	1:42.57	180,000
2000	Riboletta (Brz), 5, 125	C. J. McCarron	Gourmet Girl, 5, 114	Country Hideaway, 4, 114	7	1:40.35	150,000
1999	Catinca, 4, 119	J. D. Bailey	Furlough, 5, 116	Keeper Hill, 4, 118	5	1:41.94	150,000
1998	Sharp Cat, 4, 124	C. S. Nakatani	Furlough, 4, 115	Stop Traffic, 5, 119	8	1:42.48	150,000
1997	Tomisue's Delight, 3, 113	J. D. Bailey	Clear Mandate, 5, 119	Mil Kilates, 4, 114	9	1:44.43	150,000
1996	Yanks Music, 3, 116	J. R. Velazquez	Serena's Song, 4, 126	Head East, 4, 108	6	1:41.84	150,000
1995	Inside Information, 4, 125	M. E. Smith	Unlawful Behavior, 5, 110	Incinerate, 5, 112	6	1:40.98	120,000
1994	Sky Beauty, 4, 130	M. E. Smith	Dispute, 4, 117	Educated Risk, 4, 114	5	1:41.79	120,000
1993	Shared Interest, 5, 114	R. G. Davis	Dispute, 3, 115	Turnback the Alarm, 4, 123	5	1:41.92	120,000
1992	Versailles Treaty, 4, 120	M. E. Smith	Quick Mischief, 6, 116	Nannerl, 5, 119	6	1:41.41	120,000
1991	Queena, 5, 117	A. T. Cordero Jr.	Sharp Dance, 5, 114	Lady d'Accord, 4, 113	7	1:41.65	120,000
1990	Quick Mischief, 4, 111	R. I. Rojas	Personal Business, 4, 113	Mistaurian, 4, 115	9	1:42.80	144,480
1989	Bayakoa (Arg), 5, 125	L. A. Pincay Jr.	Colonial Waters, 4, 118	Open Mind, 3, 120	6	1:48.40	135,840
1988	Sham Say, 3, 113	J. Vasquez	Classic Crown, 3, 115	Make Change, 3, 114	11	1:48.00	146,400
1987	‡Coup de Fusil, 5, 117	A. T. Cordero Jr.	Clabber Girl, 4, 112	Sacahuista, 3, 114	12	1:48.60	149,760
1986	Lady's Secret, 4, 129	P. Day	Steal a Kiss, 3, 109	Endear, 4, 119	6	1:46.80	165,240
1985	Lady's Secret, 3, 116	J. Velasquez	Isayso, 6, 115	Sintrillium, 7, 118	6	1:47.40	128,880
1984	Heatherten, 5, 118	R. P. Romero	Miss Oceana, 3, 119	Adored, 4, 123	7	1:47.20	103,320
1983	Heartlight No. One, 3, 117	L. A. Pincay Jr.	Mochila, 4, 113	Try Something New, 4, 116	12	1:47.20	103,140
1982	Christmas Past, 3, 117	J. Vasquez	Mademoiselle Forli, 3, 112	Love Sign, 5, 123	8	1:48.60	100,080
1981	Relaxing, 5, 123	A. T. Cordero Jr.	Love Sign, 4, 120	Jameela, 5, 122	4	1:47.60	97,020
1980	Genuine Risk, 3, 118	J. Vasquez	Misty Gallore, 4, 124	It's in the Air, 4, 118	6	1:49.20	81,900
1979	It's in the Air, 3, 122	L. A. Pincay Jr.	Blitey, 3, 113	Waya (Fr), 5, 126	4	1:47.40	79,875
1978	Late Bloomer, 4, 122	J. Velasquez	Pearl Necklace, 4, 124	Tempest Queen, 3, 117	9	1:47.00	64,860
1977	Cum Laude Laurie, 3, 114	A. T. Cordero Jr.	Mississippi Mud, 4, 123	Cascapedia, 4, 128	12	1:52.20	66,480
1976	Revidere, 3, 118	J. Vasquez	*Bastonera II, 5, 123	Optimistic Gal, 3, 118	5	2:01.00	79,425

Named for Locust Hill Farm's 1974 champion two-year-old filly, '75 champion three-year-old filly, and '75 Filly Triple Crown winner Ruffian (1972 f. by Reviewer); Ruffian is buried in the Belmont infield. Ruffian S. 1976. Not held due to World Trade Center attack 2001. 1¹⁄₄ miles 1976. 1¹⁄₈ miles 1977-'89. ‡Sacahuista finished first, DQ to third, 1987.

Sabin Handicap

Grade 3 in 2008. Gulfstream Park, four-year-olds and up, fillies and mares, 1 mile, dirt. Held January 6, 2008, with a gross value of $98,000. First held in 1991. First graded in 1994. Stakes record 1:37.21 (2008 dh-Lady Marlboro/dh-Golden Velvet).

Year	Winner	Jockey	Second	Third	Strs	Time	1st Purse
2008	dh-Golden Velvet, 5, 116	E. Coa		Mini Sermon, 4, 118	5	1:37.21	$40,000
	dh-Lady Marlboro, 4, 116	J. Castellano					
2007	Swap Fliparoo, 4, 115	J. Castellano	Getcozywithkaylee, 6, 114	Classy Charm, 5, 116	8	1:37.73	90,000
2006	Taittinger Rose, 5, 115	E. S. Prado	Mocita, 4, 119	Darling Daughter, 5, 116	6	1:50.49	60,000
2005	Isola Piu Bella (Chi), 5, 116	J. R. Velazquez	Pampered Princess, 5, 117	Adobe Gold, 4, 116	5	1:50.68	60,000
2004	Roar Emotion, 4, 116	J. R. Velazquez	Nonsuch Bay, 5, 115	Lead Story, 5, 119	9	1:43.32	60,000
2003	Allamerican Bertie, 4, 120	J. D. Bailey	Small Promises, 5, 112	Redoubled Miss, 4, 114	11	1:42.49	60,000
2002	Miss Linda (Arg), 5, 119	R. Migliore	Forest Secrets, 4, 117	Tap Dance, 4, 115	12	1:42.61	60,000
2001	De Bertie, 4, 115	J. F. Chavez	Royal Fair, 5, 113	Frankly My Dear, 4, 116	8	1:44.74	60,000
2000	Brushed Halory, 4, 115	M. E. Smith	Roza Robata, 5, 115	Mop Squeezer, 4, 113	5	1:41.84	45,000
1999	Timely Broad, 5, 115	N. J. Pino	Highfalutin, 5, 116	Mudslinger, 4, 116	9	1:42.50	45,000
1998	Radiant Megan, 5, 113	J. A. Krone	Escena, 5, 119	Biding Time, 4, 116	7	1:41.25	45,000
1997	Rare Blend, 4, 120	J. D. Bailey	Golden Gale, 4, 113	Termly, 4, 112	7	1:41.28	45,000

Year	Winner	Jockey	Second	Third	Strs	Time	1st Purse
1996	Lindsay Frolic, 4, 117	P. Day	Investalot, 5, 114	Queen Tutta, 4, 113	8	1:43.70	$45,000
1995	Recognizable, 4, 115	M. E. Smith	Jade Flush, 4, 113	Sambacarioca, 6, 118	8	1:42.50	45,000
1994	Hunzinga, 5, 113	J. E. Felix	Nine Keys, 4, 114	Pleasant Jolie, 6, 112	9	1:39.57	45,000
1993	Now Dance, 4, 113	M. Guidry	Spinning Round, 4, 115	Luv Me Luv Me Not, 4, 117	10	1:41.68	30,000
1992	Lemhi Go, 4, 113	R. N. Lester	Trumpet's Blare, 5, 114	Tappanzee, 4, 114	8	1:44.79	45,000
1991	Fit for a Queen, 5, 114	J. D. Bailey	Trumpet's Blare, 4, 114	Express Star, 5, 116	9	1:42.50	46,020

Named for Henryk de Kwiatkowski's 1984 Orchid H. (G2) winner Sabin (1980 f. by Lyphard). Sabin Breeders' Cup H. 1991. 1 1/16 miles 1991-'92, 2001-'04. 1 mile 70 yards 1993-2000. 1 1/8 miles 2005-'06. Three-year-olds and up 1991-2006. Dead heat for first 2008.

Safely Kept Stakes

Grade 3 in 2008. Laurel Park, three-year-olds, fillies, 6 furlongs, dirt. Held October 6, 2007, with a gross value of $200,000. First held in 1986. First graded in 1990. Stakes record 1:09.21 (1999 Godmother).

Year	Winner	Jockey	Second	Third	Strs	Time	1st Purse
2007	Sindy With an S, 3, 116	J. Rose	Ticket to Seattle, 3, 116	Change Up, 3, 120	7	1:10.16	$120,000
2006	Wild Gams, 3, 122	R. Fogelsonger	Wildcat Bettie B, 3, 122	G City Gal, 3, 116	7	1:09.93	120,000
2005	Trickle of Gold, 3, 116	J. Rose	Maddalena, 3, 120	Partners Due, 3, 116	5	1:10.45	90,000
2004	Bending Strings, 3, 119	H. Karamanos	Smokey Glacken, 3, 119	Then She Laughs, 3, 117	6	1:10.11	90,000
2003	Randaroo, 3, 119	H. Castillo Jr.	Follow Me Home, 3, 117	Awesome Charm, 3, 115	8	1:10.54	90,000
2002	Miss Lodi, 3, 117	R. Fogelsonger	For Rubies, 3, 117	Wilzada, 3, 117	8	1:11.20	60,000
2000	Swept Away, 3, 122	J. Beasley	Another, 3, 119	Cat Cay, 3, 117	8	1:09.51	60,000
1999	Godmother, 3, 117	M. G. Pino	Superduper Miss, 3, 117	Rills, 3, 113	7	**1:09.21**	60,000
1998	Hair Spray, 3, 117	J. A. Velez Jr.	Expensive Issue, 3, 115	Ninth Inning, 3, 119	8	1:10.67	66,390
1997	Weather Vane, 3, 119	M. G. Pino	Vegas Prospector, 3, 117	Requesting More, 3, 115	7	1:10.21	64,800
1996	J J'sdream, 3, 122	M. G. Pino	Flat Fleet Feet, 3, 119	Rare Blend, 3, 122	5	1:09.45	60,000
1995	Broad Smile, 3, 117	J. Brown	Scotzanna, 3, 122	Shebatim's Trick, 3, 115	7	1:10.30	60,000
1994	Twist Afleet, 3, 117	D. Carr	Penny's Reshoot, 3, 117	Our Royal Blue, 3, 114	7	1:10.88	60,000
1993	Miss Indy Anna, 3, 113	D. B. Thomas	Ann Dear, 3, 113	Lily of the North, 3, 113	7	1:10.12	60,000
1992	Meafara, 3, 119	B. Swatuk	Squirm, 3, 122	Super Doer, 3, 122	6	1:10.55	60,000
1991	Missy's Mirage, 3, 119	W. H. McCauley	Withallprobability, 3, 122	Corporate Fund, 3, 114	5	1:10.53	60,000
1990	Voodoo Lily, 3, 117	K. Desormeaux	Miss Spentyouth, 3, 119	Catchamenot, 3, 114	8	1:10.60	60,000
1989	Safely Kept, 3, 122	C. Perret	Cojinx, 3, 119	Kathleen the Queen, 3, 117	5	1:11.20	60,000
1988	Clever Power, 3, 120	J. A. Krone	Lake Valley, 3, 120	Ready Jet Go, 3, 120	8	1:16.40	65,000
1987	Endless Surprise, 4, 118	K. Desormeaux	Bea Quality, 5, 120	Miracle Wood, 4, 111	7	1:17.40	28,340
1986	Debtor's Prison, 5, 108	D. Byrnes	Night Above, 4, 117	Bea Quality, 4, 114	6	1:11.40	28,178

Named for Jayeff "B" Stables's and Barry Weisbord's 1989 champion sprinter and '89 Columbia S. winner Safely Kept (1986 f. by Horatius). Formerly named for the nearby city of Columbia, Maryland. Columbia H. 1986-'87. Columbia S. 1988-'95. Safely Kept Breeders' Cup S. 2003-'07. Held at Laurel Park 1988, 1990, 1998-2000. Held at Colonial Downs 1997. Not held 2001. 6 1/2 furlongs 1988.

Salvator Mile Stakes

Grade 3 in 2008. Monmouth Park, three-year-olds and up, 1 mile, dirt. Held June 23, 2007, with a gross value of $150,000. First held in 1894. First graded in 1973. Stakes record 1:34.25 (2007 Gottcha Gold).

Year	Winner	Jockey	Second	Third	Strs	Time	1st Purse
2007	Gottcha Gold, 4, 117	C. C. Lopez	Lawyer Ron, 4, 121	Indy Wind, 5, 119	5	**1:34.25**	$90,000
2006	Flower Alley, 4, 117	J. R. Velazquez	Park Avenue Ball, 4, 119	Network, 4, 117	5	1:35.87	90,000
2005	Cherokee's Boy, 5, 117	A. T. Gryder	Aggadan, 6, 117	Gygistar, 6, 119	5	1:36.79	90,000
2004	Presidentialaffair, 5, 117	S. Elliott	Unforgettable Max, 4, 117	Roaring Fever, 4, 115	5	1:35.27	60,000
2003	Vinemeister, 4, 114	J. A. Velez Jr.	Jersey Giant, 4, 117	Highway Prospector, 6, 113	6	1:35.89	60,000
2002	‡Sea of Tranquility, 6, 120	J. C. Ferrer	Free of Love, 4, 117	First Lieutenant, 5, 114	8	1:36.12	60,000
2001	Sea of Tranquility, 5, 115	J. C. Ferrer	Knock Again, 4, 112	Hal's Hope, 4, 117	7	1:36.74	90,000
2000	Leave It to Beezer, 7, 120	R. E. Alvarado Jr.	Delaware Township, 4, 112	Prime Directive, 4, 114	5	1:37.29	90,000
1999	Truluck, 4, 117	J. Bravo	Rock and Roll, 4, 119	Siftaway, 4, 114	6	1:35.18	90,000
1998	El Amante, 5, 119	J. A. Krone	Stormin Fever, 4, 117	Gold Token, 5, 114	8	1:34.95	60,000
1997	Distorted Humor, 4, 114	J. A. Krone	Wild Deputy, 4, 114	Smooth the Loot, 4, 113	4	1:36.03	60,000
1996	Smart Strike, 4, 113	S. Hawley	Cozy Drive, 4, 113	November Sunset, 4, 115	10	1:36.28	60,000
1995	Schossberg, 5, 116	D. Penna	Cast Iron, 4, 110	Relentless Star, 5, 109	9	1:35.86	45,000
1994	Storm Tower, 4, 119	R. Wilson	Cold Digger, 7, 113	Koluctoo Jimmy Al, 4, 114	8	1:36.26	45,000
1993	Dusty Screen, 5, 117	E. King Jr.	Count New York, 4, 112	Root Boy, 5, 118	8	1:35.86	45,000
1992	Peanut Butter Onit, 6, 120	A. T. Gryder	Root Boy, 4, 114	He Is Risen, 4, 118	7	1:36.21	45,000
1991	Peanut Butter Onit, 5, 115	W. S. Ramos	Private School, 4, 114	Runaway Stream, 4, 116	8	1:34.46	45,000
1990	Shy Tom, 4, 115	J. A. Krone	Bill E. Shears, 5, 121	Pete the Chief, 4, 115	5	1:36.00	49,020
1989	Bill E. Shears, 4, 112	R. Hernandez	Festive, 4, 110	Mi Selecto, 4, 117	7	1:35.40	49,890
1988	Slew City Slew, 4, 116	M. Castaneda	Bet Twice, 4, 125	Matthews Keep, 4, 115	5	1:35.00	38,880
1987	Moment of Hope, 4, 118	M. Venezia	Owens Troupe, 4, 117	Entitled To, 5, 116	6	1:34.60	33,270
1986	Jyp, 5, 115	J. Rocco	Minneapple, 4, 119	Valiant Lark, 6, 117	5	1:35.80	33,300
1985	Valiant Lark, 5, 116	V. A. Bracciale Jr.	Pat's Addition, 5, 115	Rumptious, 5, 116	10	1:36.00	33,990
1984	Rumptious, 4, 115	W. H. McCauley	English Master, 4, 112	World Appeal, 4, 122	10	1:34.60	34,260
1983	Naughty Jimmy, 6, 114	L. Saumell	Castle Guard, 4, 115	Star Gallant, 4, 120	7	1:37.00	33,510
1982	Count His Fleet, 4, 116	W. Nemeti	Explosive Bid, 4, 117	Accipiter's Hope, 4, 116	12	1:35.40	35,070
1981	Colonel Moran, 4, 117	C. Perret	Sun Catcher, 4, 120	Pikotazo (Mex), 4, 117	12	1:35.60	35,190
1980	Convenient, 4, 114	V. A. Bracciale Jr.	Tunerup, 4, 113	Foretake, 4, 113	8	1:36.60	26,640

Year	Winner	Jockey	Second	Third	Strs	Time	1st Purse
1979	‡Revivalist, 5, 122	D. MacBeth	Horatius, 4, 120	Nice Catch, 5, 120	9	1:35.40	$25,578
1978	Do Tell George, 5, 113	B. Mize	Buckfinder, 4, 118	Get Permission, 5, 114	5	1:36.40	17,664
1977	Peppy Addy, 5, 120	B. Phelps	Resound, 5, 115	Break Up the Game, 6, 117	8	1:36.00	18,168
1976	Royal Glint, 6, 126	J. E. Tejeira	Talc, 4, 113	Peppy Addy, 4, 118	9	1:35.20	18,395
1975	Proper Bostonian, 5, 117	M. Miceli	Rastaferian, 6, 113	Orbit Round, 4, 110	8	1:36.20	14,576
	Mongongo, 6, 119	B. Thornburg	Good John, 5, 114	Silver Hope, 4, 116	8	1:36.20	14,576
1974	Okavango, 4, 112	W. Blum	Hey Rube, 4, 114	Escaped, 5, 123	9	1:35.80	18,265
1973	Prince of Truth, 5, 117	W. Blum	Windtex, 4, 116	New Alibhai, 5, 115	7	1:35.80	17,761

Named for James Ben Ali Haggin's 1890 Monmouth Cup winner Salvator (1886 c. by *Prince Charlie); in 1890 he set an American record for one mile at Monmouth Park that stood for 28 years. Salvator Mile H. 1894-1956, 1957-'96, 1998-2005. Two divisions 1975. ‡Nice Catch finished first, DQ to third, 1979. ‡First Lieutenant finished first, DQ to third, 2002.

San Antonio Handicap

Grade 2 in 2008. Santa Anita Park, four-year-olds and up, 1 1/8 miles, all weather. Held February 9, 2008, with a gross value of $250,000. First held in 1935. First graded in 1973. Stakes record 1:46.20 (1978 Vigors).

Year	Winner	Jockey	Second	Third	Strs	Time	1st Purse
2008	Well Armed, 5, 115	A. T. Gryder	Heatseeker (Ire), 5, 116	Awesome Gem, 5, 118	9	1:47.73	$150,000
2007	Molengao (Brz), 6, 115	G. K. Gomez	Ball Four, 6, 117	El Roblar, 5, 115	7	1:48.67	150,000
2006	Spellbinder, 5, 114	M. A. Pedroza	With Distinction, 5, 115	Wilko, 4, 116	8	1:48.84	150,000
2005	Lundy's Liability (Brz), 5, 119	D. R. Flores	Truly a Judge, 7, 118	Congrats, 5, 116	9	1:49.05	150,000
2004	Pleasantly Perfect, 6, 121	A. O. Solis	Star Cross (Arg), 7, 114	Fleetstreet Dancer, 6, 116	4	1:47.25	150,000
2003	Congaree, 5, 123	J. D. Bailey	Milwaukee Brew, 6, 120	Pleasantly Perfect, 5, 117	6	1:47.60	150,000
2002	Redattore (Brz), 7, 116	A. O. Solis	Euchre, 6, 119	Irisheyesareflying, 6, 117	7	1:48.66	150,000
2001	Guided Tour, 5, 115	L. J. Melancon	Lethal Instrument, 5, 116	Moonlight Charger, 6, 113	8	1:48.70	180,000
2000	Budroyale, 7, 121	G. K. Gomez	Cat Thief, 4, 120	Elaborate, 5, 116	5	1:48.70	180,000
1999	Free House, 5, 123	C. J. McCarron	Malek (Chi), 6, 119	Dramatic Gold, 8, 116	4	1:48.54	180,000
1998	Gentlemen (Arg), 6, 124	G. L. Stevens	Da Bull, 6, 115	Refinado Tom (Arg), 5, 120	5	1:47.60	180,000
1997	Gentlemen (Arg), 5, 122	G. L. Stevens	Alphabet Soup, 6, 122	Kingdom Found, 7, 116	5	1:47.38	180,300
1996	Alphabet Soup, 5, 119	C. W. Antley	Soul of the Matter, 5, 121	Dare and Go, 5, 119	5	1:49.96	184,900
1995	Best Pal, 7, 121	C. J. McCarron	Slew of Damascus, 7, 119	Tossofthecoin, 5, 117	10	1:47.43	148,500
1994	The Wicked North, 5, 116	K. Desormeaux	‡Region, 5, 117	Hill Pass, 5, 116	9	1:47.48	155,500
1993	Marquetry, 6, 117	E. Delahoussaye	Sir Beaufort, 6, 120	Reign Road, 5, 116	6	1:48.96	155,500
1992	Ibero (Arg), 5, 115	A. O. Solis	In Excess (Ire), 5, 123	Cobra Classic, 5, 114	8	1:47.05	189,750
1991	Farma Way, 4, 118	G. L. Stevens	Anshan (GB), 4, 116	dh-Festin (Arg), 5, 116	9	1:47.30	196,750
				dh-Louis Cyphre (Ire), 5, 111			
1990	Criminal Type, 5, 117	A. O. Solis	Stylish Winner, 6, 113	Ruhlmann, 5, 117	7	1:49.00	190,500
1989	Super Diamond, 9, 121	L. A. Pincay Jr.	Frankly Perfect, 4, 116	Cherokee Colony, 4, 120	7	1:48.80	159,600
1988	Judge Angelucci, 5, 122	E. Delahoussaye	Ferdinand, 5, 128	Crimson Slew, 4, 115	6	1:48.60	156,700
1987	Bedside Promise, 5, 117	G. L. Stevens	Hopeful Word, 6, 118	Bruiser (GB), 4, 114	9	1:47.20	129,600
1986	Hatim, 5, 117	L. A. Pincay Jr.	Right Con, 4, 117	Nostalgia's Star, 4, 118	8	1:47.40	128,700
1985	Lord At War (Arg), 5, 122	W. Shoemaker	Al Mamoon, 4, 114	Hail Bold King, 4, 122	7	1:48.20	125,200
1984	Poley, 5, 120	C. J. McCarron	Water Bank, 5, 117	Danebo, 5, 122	9	1:48.00	156,900
1983	Bates Motel, 4, 114	T. Lipham	Time to Explode, 4, 121	It's the One, 5, 124	10	1:47.00	132,300
1982	Score Twenty Four, 5, 115	P. A. Valenzuela	Super Moment, 5, 124	High Counsel, 4, 114	6	1:47.80	124,200
1981	Flying Paster, 5, 126	C. J. McCarron	‡Doonesbury, 4, 121	King Go Go, 6, 119	5	1:46.60	91,700
1980	Beau's Eagle, 4, 121	D. Pierce	Relaunch, 4, 117	Double Discount, 7, 114	6	1:48.40	79,650
1979	Tiller, 5, 121	A. T. Cordero Jr.	Painted Wagon, 6, 114	‡Life's Hope, 6, 120	6	1:47.00	65,800
1978	Vigors, 5, 121	D. G. McHargue	Ancient Title, 8, 120	Double Discount, 5, 116	7	**1:46.20**	67,100
1977	Ancient Title, 7, 119	S. Hawley	Double Discount, 4, 115	Properantes, 4, 114	10	1:47.60	72,500
1976	Lightning Mandate, 5, 118	A. T. Cordero Jr.	Dancing Papa, 6, 117	Messenger of Song, 4, 122	10	1:48.20	54,350
1975	Cheriepe, 5, 120	A. Santiago	First Back, 4, 117	Ancient Title, 5, 128	9	1:46.80	52,850
1974	Prince Dantan, 4, 116	L. A. Pincay Jr.	Forage, 5, 119	Dancing Papa, 4, 116	8	1:47.60	51,550
1973	Kennedy Road, 5, 119	D. Pierce	Crusading, 5, 117	Big Spruce, 4, 117	6	1:47.60	49,400

Named for seven California land grants, each of which was called Rancho San Antonio; two were in Los Angeles County, one is now Beverly Hills. Grade 1 1983-'89. San Antonio S. 1968-'82. Not held 1941-'45. 1 1/16 miles 1940. Dirt 1935-2007. Three-year-olds and up 1946, 1948, 1950-'52, 1956, 1958, 1960. Dead heat for third 1991. ‡Mr. Redoy finished third, DQ to sixth, 1979. ‡King Go Go finished second, DQ to third, 1981. ‡Hill Pass finished second, DQ to third, 1994. Equaled track record 1940.

San Carlos Handicap

Grade 2 in 2008. Santa Anita Park, four-year-olds and up, 7 furlongs, all weather. Held February 16, 2008, with a gross value of $150,000. First held in 1935. First graded in 1973. Stakes record 1:20.20 (1981 Flying Paster).

Year	Winner	Jockey	Second	Third	Strs	Time	1st Purse
2008	Surf Cat, 6, 118	A. O. Solis	Greg's Gold, 7, 119	Soul City Slew, 5, 113	7	1:21.62	$90,000
2007	Latent Heat, 4, 118	E. S. Prado	Proud Tower Too, 5, 120	Ramsgate, 4, 114	10	1:21.11	90,000
2006	Surf Cat, 4, 117	A. O. Solis	Major Success, 5, 118	Oceanus (Brz), 7, 114	8	1:22.09	90,000
2005	Hasty Kris, 8, 115	R. R. Douglas	Harvard Avenue, 4, 115	Perfect Moon, 4, 117	8	1:21.42	90,000
2004	Pico Central (Brz), 5, 118	D. R. Flores	Publication, 6, 118	Pohave, 6, 112	10	1:21.76	90,000
2003	Aldebaran, 5, 116	J. Valdivia Jr.	Crafty C. T., 5, 116	Grey Memo, 6, 116	6	1:21.53	120,000
2002	Snow Ridge, 4, 118	M. E. Smith	Alyzig, 5, 112	Grey Memo, 5, 114	6	1:22.02	90,000
2001	Kona Gold, 7, 125	A. O. Solis	Blade Prospector (Brz), 6, 113	Grey Memo, 4, 115	7	1:21.35	90,000

434 Racing — Graded Stakes

Year	Winner	Jockey	Second	Third	Strs	Time	1st Purse
2000	Son of a Pistol, 8, 117	G. K. Gomez	Kona Gold, 6, 122	Old Topper, 5, 116	6	1:22.11	$96,930
1999	Big Jag, 6, 118	J. Valdivia Jr.	Kona Gold, 5, 120	Dramatic Gold, 8, 117	5	1:21.18	90,000
1998	Reality Road, 6, 116	C. J. McCarron	Gold Land, 7, 116	Son of a Pistol, 6, 114	10	1:21.62	100,530
1997	Northern Afleet, 4, 117	C. J. McCarron	Hesabull, 4, 117	High Stakes Player, 5, 120	7	1:21.45	97,700
1996	Kingdom Found, 6, 116	C. J. McCarron	Lakota Brave, 7, 114	Lit de Justice, 6, 123	8	1:22.23	98,850
1995	Softshoe Sure Shot, 9, 113	A. O. Solis	Ferrara, 4, 115	Subtle Trouble, 4, 113	7	1:21.46	91,600
1994	Cardmania, 8, 122	E. Delahoussaye	The Wicked North, 5, 117	Portoferraio (Arg), 6, 115	7	1:21.23	63,900
1993	Sir Beaufort, 6, 120	C. J. McCarron	Cardmania, 7, 117	Excavate, 5, 114	6	1:22.22	62,900
1992	Answer Do, 6, 120	G. L. Stevens	Individualist, 5, 115	Media Plan, 4, 116	7	1:21.23	63,700
1991	Farma Way, 4, 115	G. L. Stevens	Yes I'm Blue, 5, 117	Tanker Port, 6, 117	7	1:21.50	63,500
1990	Raise a Stanza, 4, 117	R. A. Baze	Oraibi, 5, 119	Tanker Port, 5, 117	8	1:21.60	64,500
1989	Cherokee Colony, 4, 117	R. Q. Meza	On the Line, 5, 126	Happy in Space, 5, 116	6	1:20.60	62,800
1988	Epidaurus, 6, 117	P. A. Valenzuela	Super Diamond, 8, 125	Lord Ruckus, 5, 118	7	1:22.00	63,500
1987	Zany Tactics, 6, 118	J. L. Kaenel	Bolder Than Bold, 5, 116	Epidaurus, 5, 115	8	1:22.40	65,600
1986	Phone Trick, 4, 125	L. A. Pincay Jr.	Temerity Prince, 6, 122	My Habitony, 6, 117	6	1:20.80	78,200
1985	Debonaire Junior, 4, 125	C. J. McCarron	Tennessee Rite, 4, 112	Fifty Six Ina Row, 4, 116	6	1:21.60	64,300
1984	Danebo, 5, 117	L. A. Pincay Jr.	Pac Mania, 4, 118	Poley, 5, 119	7	1:21.00	54,900
1983	Kangroo Court, 6, 118	J. J. Steiner	Dave's Friend, 8, 117	Shanekite, 5, 118	8	1:21.00	49,550
1982	Solo Guy, 4, 118	W. Shoemaker	‡Smokite, 6, 116	King Go Go, 7, 119	8	1:20.80	60,700
1981	Flying Paster, 5, 124	C. J. McCarron	To B. Or Not, 5, 123	Double Discount, 8, 115	8	**1:20.20**	51,550
1980	Handsomeness, 4, 118	L. A. Pincay Jr.	Relaunch, 4, 121	Beau's Eagle, 4, 125	5	1:24.00	49,100
1979	O Big Al, 4, 120	D. G. McHargue	Maheras, 6, 122	Bad 'n Big, 5, 124	7	1:22.00	40,800
1978	Double Discount, 5, 117	F. Mena	Impressive Luck, 5, 120	Romantic Lead, 5, 117	6	1:22.00	32,650
1977	Uniformity, 5, 115	F. Toro	†My Juliet, 5, 123	Messenger of Song, 5, 122	7	1:21.80	34,050
1976	No Bias, 6, 120	L. A. Pincay Jr.	Century's Envoy, 5, 126	Bahia Key, 6, 120	5	1:21.80	32,200
1975	Ancient Title, 5, 128	L. A. Pincay Jr.	dh-Bahia Key, 5, 117	Against the Snow, 4, 112	12	1:21.20	37,750
			dh-Hudson County, 4, 116				
1974	Royal Owl, 5, 117	L. A. Pincay Jr.	Soft Victory, 6, 116	Against the Snow, 4, 112	9	1:23.40	35,600
1973	‡Crusading, 5, 119	F. Toro	Kennedy Road, 5, 117	*Figonero, 8, 114	8	1:20.80	33,850

Named for Rancho El Potrero de San Carlos in Monterey County, California. Grade 1 2001-'03. Not held 1942-'45, 1960. 1 1/16 miles 1935-'39. Dirt 1935-2007. Three-year-olds and up 1946, 1949-'52, 1954-'59. Dead heat for second 1975. ‡Kennedy Road finished first, DQ to second, 1973. ‡King Go Go finished second, DQ to third, 1982. †Denotes female.

San Clemente Handicap

Grade 2 in 2008. Del Mar, three-year-olds, fillies, 1 mile, turf. Held July 28, 2007, with a gross value of $150,000. First held in 1950. First graded in 1994. Stakes record 1:33.62 (2003 Katdogawn [GB]).

Year	Winner	Jockey	Second	Third	Strs	Time	1st Purse
2007	Passified (GB), 3, 119	M. E. Smith	Fleet Caroline, 3, 114	Spenditallbaby, 3, 118	10	1:34.15	$90,000
2006	Attima (GB), 3, 120	V. Espinoza	Sol Mi Fa (Ire), 3, 116	Soothsay (Ire), 3, 119	8	1:34.65	90,000
2005	Shining Energy, 3, 117	R. R. Douglas	dh-Memorette, 3, 119		10	1:34.25	90,000
			dh-Royal Copenhagen (Fr), 3, 117				
2004	Sweet Win, 3, 114	V. Espinoza	Miss Vegas (Ire), 3, 121	Victory U. S. A., 3, 119	5	1:34.11	90,000
2003	Katdogawn (GB), 3, 116	J. A. Krone	Atlantic Ocean, 3, 120	Buffythecenterfold, 3, 118	9	**1:33.62**	90,000
2002	Little Treasure (Fr), 3, 117	K. Desormeaux	Pina Colada (GB), 3, 115	Arabic Song (Ire), 3, 118	9	1:33.97	90,000
2001	Reine de Romance (Ire), 3, 116	E. Delahoussaye	Gabriellina Giof (GB), 3, 116	La Vida Loca (Ire), 3, 116	9	1:34.88	90,000
2000	Uncharted Haven (GB), 3, 116	A. O. Solis	Automated, 3, 117	Islay Mist (GB), 3, 118	10	1:35.13	90,000
1999	Sweet Ludy (Ire), 3, 118	C. S. Nakatani	Caffe Latte (Ire), 3, 115	Sweet Life, 3, 117	10	1:35.02	90,000
1998	Sicy d'Alsace (Fr), 3, 115	C. S. Nakatani	Miss Hot Salsa, 3, 117	Tranquility Lake, 3, 114	10	1:34.97	67,500
1997	Famous Digger, 3, 120	B. Blanc	Cozy Blues, 3, 116	Really Happy, 3, 119	10	1:36.00	71,725
1996	True Flare, 3, 116	C. S. Nakatani	Gastronomical, 3, 119	Najecam, 3, 114	10	1:35.59	67,200
1995	Jewel Princess, 3, 115	C. J. McCarron	Auriette (Ire), 3, 119	Scratch Paper, 3, 119	6	1:36.12	59,650
1994	Work the Crowd, 3, 120	C. J. McCarron	Pharma, 3, 116	Dancing Mirage, 3, 115	8	1:36.07	48,550
1993	Hollywood Wildcat, 3, 120	E. Delahoussaye	Miami Sands (Ire), 3, 116	Beal Street Blues, 3, 117	10	1:34.89	49,950
1992	Golden Treat, 3, 121	K. Desormeaux	Morriston Belle, 3, 118	Alysbelle, 3, 118	8	1:35.20	49,350
1991	Flawlessly, 3, 120	C. J. McCarron	Gold Fleece, 3, 114	Miss High Blade, 3, 117	9	1:34.88	64,600
1990	Nijinsky's Lover, 3, 118	G. L. Stevens	Bimbo (GB), 3, 113	Slew of Pearls, 3, 116	9	1:36.40	50,300
	Lonely Girl, 3, 116	P. A. Valenzuela	Bel's Starlet, 3, 114	Bidder Cream, 3, 113	9	1:36.20	50,300
1989	Darby's Daughter, 3, 120	G. L. Stevens	Sticky Wile, 3, 117	Bel Darling, 3, 116	9	1:36.60	66,000
1988	Do So, 3, 117	A. O. Solis	Affordable Price, 3, 115	Variety Baby, 3, 117	8	1:35.80	50,650
1987	Davie's Lamb, 3, 115	F. Toro	Develop, 3, 114	Wild Manor, 3, 116	7	1:42.80	25,500
	Future Bright, 3, 114	P. A. Valenzuela	Chapel of Dreams, 3, 114	Down Again, 3, 116	7	1:44.60	25,300
1986	Our Sweet Sham, 3, 114	S. B. Soto	Mille Et Une, 3, 115	T. V. Residual, 3, 115	10	1:43.20	33,450
1985	Mint Leaf, 3, 122	C. J. McCarron	Queen of Bronze, 3, 115	Stakes to Win, 3, 117	10	1:42.60	33,650
1984	Fashionably Late, 3, 117	C. J. McCarron	Auntie Betty, 3, 117	Patricia James, 3, 114	8	1:43.20	32,800
1983	Eastern Bettor, 3, 113	R. Q. Meza	Nice 'n Proper, 3, 117	Olympic Bronze, 3, 116	9	1:44.00	25,875
	Lituya Bay, 3, 121	L. A. Pincay Jr.	Corselette, 3, 116	Capitalization, 3, 115	8	1:43.80	25,375
1982	Northern Style, 3, 114	M. Castaneda	Mama Tia, 3, 116	Marl Lee Ann, 3, 115	7	1:43.40	32,200
1981	French Charmer, 3, 118	D. G. McHargue	Tap Dancer (Fr), 3, 117	I Got Speed, 3, 121	9	1:44.20	26,850
1980	Plenty O'Toole, 3, 116	T. Lipham	Potter, 3, 115	Swift Bird, 3, 113	10	1:44.20	27,050
1979	Ancient Art, 3, 121	F. Toro	Our Suiti Pie, 3, 116	Double Deceit, 3, 117	9	1:44.20	23,550
1978	Miss Magnetic, 3, 117	M. Castaneda	Secala, 3, 112	Agree, 3, 114	9	1:44.20	13,550
	Joe's Bee, 3, 120	L. A. Pincay Jr.	Fairy Dance, 3, 117	Carrie's Angel, 3, 115	7	1:44.40	13,150

Year	Winner	Jockey	Second	Third	Strs	Time	1st Purse
1977	Teisen Lap, 3, 113	D. G. McHargue	Goldfilled, 3, 112	Lullaby, 3, 120	8	1:44.80	$12,850
1976	Go March, 3, 114	D. Pierce	Granja Sueno, 3, 112	I Going, 3, 115	8	1:42.80	13,150
1975	Miss Francesca, 3, 113	D. G. McHargue	Summer Evening, 3, 115	Bradley's Pago, 3, 113	8	1:43.20	10,475
	‡Princess Papulee, 3, 121	F. Toro	Mia Amore, 3, 115	Miracolo, 3, 113	7	1:43.80	10,275
1974	Bold Ballet, 3, 121	F. Toro	Shah's Envoy, 3, 121	Sweet Ramblin Rose, 3, 116	9	1:44.00	13,350
1973	Button Top, 3, 112	S. Valdez	Merry Madeleine, 3, 120	Gourmet Lark, 3, 117	5	1:43.80	12,750

Named for San Clemente, California, located in Orange County. Grade 3 1994-'95. Not held 1951-'69. 1 1/16 miles 1950, 1970-'87. Dirt 1950. Two divisions 1975, '78, '83, '87, '90. Dead heat for second 2005. ‡Mia Amore finished first, DQ to second, 1975 (2nd Div.). Nonwinners of a race worth $10,000 to the winner 1973-'74. Nonwinners of a race worth $12,500 to the winner 1975.

San Diego Handicap

Grade 2 in 2008. Del Mar, three-year-olds and up, 1 1/16 miles, all weather. Held July 21, 2007, with a gross value of $300,000. First held in 1937. First graded in 1983. Stakes record 1:40 (1965 Native Diver).

Year	Winner	Jockey	Second	Third	Strs	Time	1st Purse
2007	Sun Boat (GB), 5, 114	M. C. Baze	Awesome Gem, 4, 117	Salty Humor, 5, 114	9	1:45.39	$180,000
2006	Giacomo, 4, 117	M. E. Smith	Preachinatthebar, 5, 117	‡Southern Africa, 4, 116	7	1:42.15	180,000
2005	Choctaw Nation, 5, 115	V. Espinoza	Ace Blue (Brz), 5, 117	Preachinatthebar, 4, 115	6	1:42.40	150,000
2004	Choctaw Nation, 4, 114	V. Espinoza	Pleasantly Perfect, 6, 124	During, 4, 118	7	1:42.32	150,000
2003	Taste of Paradise, 4, 113	V. Espinoza	Gondolieri (Chi), 4, 117	Reba's Gold, 6, 116	8	1:42.62	150,000
2002	Grey Memo, 5, 116	E. Delahoussaye	Euchre, 6, 116	Congaree, 4, 120	8	1:43.48	150,000
2001	Skimming, 5, 120	G. K. Gomez	Futural, 5, 120	Captain Steve, 4, 122	7	1:41.62	150,000
2000	Skimming, 4, 112	G. K. Gomez	Prime Timber, 4, 116	National Saint, 4, 117	7	1:41.06	150,000
1999	Mazel Trick, 4, 117	C. J. McCarron	River Keen (Ire), 7, 116	Tibado, 5, 116	4	1:40.68	150,000
1998	Mud Route, 4, 117	C. J. McCarron	Hal's Pal (GB), 5, 113	Benchmark, 7, 117	5	1:41.11	150,300
1997	Northern Afleet, 4, 118	C. J. McCarron	Benchmark, 6, 117	New Century, 5, 114	6	1:41.80	100,300
1996	Savinio, 6, 116	C. W. Antley	Misnomer, 4, 117	Nonproductiveasset, 6, 118	6	1:40.82	95,350
1995	Blumin Affair, 4, 116	C. J. McCarron	Rapan Boy (Aus), 7, 116	Luthier Fever, 4, 115	4	1:41.29	87,200
1994	Kingdom Found, 4, 116	C. J. McCarron	Tossofthecoin, 4, 117	Rapan Boy (Aus), 6, 115	4	1:41.21	75,850
1993	Fanatic Boy (Arg), 6, 115	C. J. McCarron	Memo (Chi), 6, 116	Missionary Ridge (GB), 6, 116	5	1:48.59	74,450
1992	Another Review, 4, 120	L. A. Pincay Jr.	Claret (Ire), 4, 116	Quintana, 4, 114	6	1:47.00	76,050
1991	Twilight Agenda, 5, 118	C. S. Nakatani	Roanoke, 4, 118	Louis Cyphre (Ire), 5, 118	7	1:47.65	90,950
1990	Quiet American, 4, 115	K. Desormeaux	†Bayakoa (Arg), 6, 122	Bosphorus (Arg), 5, 112	6	1:40.40	89,800
1989	Lively One, 4, 120	R. G. Davis	Mi Preferido, 4, 115	Hot Operator, 4, 114	5	1:40.80	76,200
1988	Cutlass Reality, 6, 123	G. L. Stevens	Simply Majestic, 4, 115	Nostalgia's Star, 6, 116	7	1:41.40	63,700
1987	Super Diamond, 7, 123	L. A. Pincay Jr.	Nostalgia's Star, 5, 116	Good Command, 4, 114	7	1:40.80	48,050
1986	Skywalker, 4, 121	L. A. Pincay Jr.	Nostalgia's Star, 4, 118	Epidaurus, 4, 113	13	1:40.80	65,350
1985	Super Diamond, 5, 118	R. Q. Meza	M. Double M., 4, 119	French Legionaire, 4, 115	7	1:41.40	48,550
1984	Ancestral (Ire), 4, 116	E. Delahoussaye	Retsina Run, 4, 117	Slew's Royalty, 4, 117	8	1:41.20	60,550
1983	Bates Motel, 4, 122	T. Lipham	The Wonder (Fr), 5, 123	Runaway Groom, 4, 117	7	1:41.00	47,650
1982	Wickerr, 7, 117	E. Delahoussaye	Cajun Prince, 5, 117	Drouilly (Fr), 6, 114	9	1:41.40	50,350
1981	Summer Time Guy, 5, 115	S. Hawley	Shamgo, 5, 117	Exploded, 4, 115	7	1:41.00	48,550
1980	Island Sultan, 5, 114	M. Castaneda	Summer Time Guy, 4, 116	Borzoi, 4, 120	6	1:41.80	38,000
1979	Always Gallant, 5, 118	D. G. McHargue	Bad 'n Big, 5, 120	Blondie's Dancer, 4, 117	6	1:41.00	33,050
1978	Vic's Magic, 5, 116	F. Toro	Mr. Redoy, 4, 119	Clout, 6, 117	6	1:40.20	25,300
1977	Mark's Place, 5, 124	W. Shoemaker	Austin Mittler, 5, 113	Confederate Yankee, 6, 114	5	1:40.60	18,450
1976	‡Good Report, 6, 116	L. A. Pincay Jr.	Austin Mittler, 4, 117	Holding Pattern, 5, 115	7	1:42.40	19,000
1975	Chesapeake, 6, 116	F. Olivares	Top Command, 4, 116	Against the Snow, 5, 123	6	1:40.60	16,800
1974	*Matun, 5, 121	W. Shoemaker	Chesapeake, 5, 113	Imaginative, 8, 115	4	1:41.00	16,150
1973	Kennedy Road, 5, 126	W. Shoemaker	Imaginative, 7, 117	New Prospect, 4, 120	5	1:41.40	15,700

Named for the city of San Diego, California; the track is located in the nearby town of Del Mar, which means "by the sea." Grade 3 1983-2000. Not held 1939-'40, 1942-'44. 6 furlongs 1937, 1945-'47. 1 mile 1941. 1 1/8 miles 1991-'93. Dirt 1937-2006. ‡Mark's Place finished first, DQ to seventh, 1976. ‡Papi Chullo finished third, DQ to seventh, 2006. †Denotes female.

Sands Point Stakes

Grade 2 in 2008. Belmont Park, three-year-olds, fillies, 1 1/8 miles, turf. Held May 31, 2008, with a gross value of $150,000. First held in 1995. First graded in 1999. Stakes record 1:46.65 (1997 Auntie Mame).

Year	Winner	Jockey	Second	Third	Strs	Time	1st Purse
2008	Raw Silk, 3, 117	A. Garcia	Life Is Sweet, 3, 117	I Lost My Choo, 3, 119	7	1:48.46	$90,000
2007	dh-Bit of Whimsy, 3, 115	E. S. Prado		Classic Neel, 3, 117	6	1:48.53	43,600
	dh-Rutherienne, 3, 121	G. K. Gomez					
2006	Wait a While, 3, 115	G. K. Gomez	Diamond Spirit, 3, 115	Hostess, 3, 115	4	1:49.25	65,520
2005	Melhor Ainda, 3, 123	J. R. Velazquez	Laurafina, 3, 115	My Typhoon (Ire), 3, 121	7	1:47.50	66,720
2004	Mambo Slew, 3, 122	E. S. Prado	Lucifer's Stone, 3, 122	Vous, 3, 119	10	1:47.24	68,880
2003	Savedbythelight, 3, 115	R. Migliore	Virgin Voyage, 3, 117	Little Bonnet, 3, 115	5	1:49.18	68,760
2002	Riskaverse, 3, 119	R. G. Davis	Cyclorama, 3, 115	She's Vested, 3, 115	11	1:51.63	69,660
2001	Tweedside, 3, 119	R. Migliore	Owsley, 3, 114	Platinum Tiara, 3, 122	4	1:50.43	66,674
2000	Dublino, 3, 121	J. D. Bailey	Shopping for Love, 3, 121	Millie's Quest, 3, 113	8	1:47.77	66,780
1999	Perfect Sting, 3, 118	P. Day	Pico Teneriffe, 3, 121	Illiquidity, 3, 113	6	1:46.99	65,160
1998	Recording, 3, 113	J. F. Chavez	Royal Ransom, 3, 114	Naskra's de Light, 3, 116	11	1:48.93	69,600
1997	Auntie Mame, 3, 121	J. D. Bailey	Hoochie Coochie, 3, 114	Sagasious, 3, 113	8	**1:46.65**	66,720

Year	Winner	Jockey	Second	Third	Strs	Time	1st Purse
1996	**Merit Wings**, 3, 120	R. G. Davis	Unify, 3, 113	Turkappeal, 3, 117	10	1:45.83	$51,885
1995	**Perfect Arc**, 3, 117	J. R. Velazquez	Miss Union Avenue, 3, 123	Transient Trend, 3, 110	5	1:43.14	49,395

Named for the community of Sands Point, New York, located on Long Island. Not graded 2001, '03. Grade 3 1998-2000, 2002, 2004-'07. Sands Point H. 1995-'98, 2000, 2003. 1 1/16 miles 1995-'96. Dirt 2001, '03, '06. Originally scheduled on turf 2001, '03, '06. Dead heat for first 2007.

San Felipe Stakes

Grade 2 in 2008. Santa Anita Park, three-year-olds, 1 1/16 miles, all weather. Held March 15, 2008, with a gross value of $200,000. First held in 1935. First graded in 1973. Stakes record 1:40.11 (2005 Consolidator).

Year	Winner	Jockey	Second	Third	Strs	Time	1st Purse
2008	**Georgie Boy**, 3, 117	M. C. Baze	Gayego, 3, 115	Bob Black Jack, 3, 117	9	1:42.35	$120,000
2007	**Cobalt Blue**, 3, 116	V. Espinoza	Air Commander, 3, 116	Level Red, 3, 116	5	1:42.46	150,000
2006	**A. P. Warrior**, 3, 116	C. S. Nakatani	Point Determined, 3, 116	Bob and John, 3, 122	9	1:42.40	150,000
2005	**Consolidator**, 3, 116	R. Bejarano	Giacomo, 3, 116	Don't Get Mad, 3, 116	8	**1:40.11**	150,000
2004	**Preachinatthebar**, 3, 116	J. Santiago	St Averil, 3, 122	Harvard Avenue, 3, 116	9	1:42.87	150,000
2003	**Buddy Gil**, 3, 119	G. L. Stevens	Atswhatimtalknbout, 3, 119	Brancusi, 3, 116	10	1:43.64	150,000
2002	**Medaglia d'Oro**, 3, 116	L. A. Pincay Jr.	U S S Tinosa, 3, 116	Siphonic, 3, 122	6	1:41.95	150,000
2001	**Point Given**, 3, 122	G. L. Stevens	I Love Silver, 3, 116	Jamaican Rum, 3, 119	8	1:41.94	150,000
2000	**Fusaichi Pegasus**, 3, 116	K. Desormeaux	The Deputy (Ire), 3, 122	Anees, 3, 119	7	1:42.66	150,000
1999	**Prime Timber**, 3, 116	D. R. Flores	Exploit, 3, 122	High Wire Act, 3, 116	7	1:42.16	150,000
1998	**Artax**, 3, 122	C. J. McCarron	Real Quiet, 3, 119	Prosperous Bid, 3, 116	5	1:41.73	150,000
1997	**Free House**, 3, 119	D. R. Flores	Silver Charm, 3, 122	King Crimson, 3, 116	9	1:42.49	152,400
1996	**Odyle**, 3, 116	C. S. Nakatani	Smithfield, 3, 116	Cavonnier, 3, 122	7	1:42.43	152,400
1995	**Afternoon Deelites**, 3, 119	K. Desormeaux	Timber Country, 3, 122	Lake George, 3, 116	4	1:42.11	117,200
1994	**Soul of the Matter**, 3, 116	K. Desormeaux	Brocco, 3, 119	Valiant Nature, 3, 119	5	1:44.68	118,500
1993	**Corby**, 3, 116	C. J. McCarron	Personal Hope, 3, 116	Devoted Brass, 3, 122	6	1:42.11	121,100
1992	**Bertrando**, 3, 122	A. O. Solis	Arp, 3, 116	Hickman Creek, 3, 116	6	1:42.76	120,800
1991	**Sea Cadet**, 3, 119	C. J. McCarron	Scan, 3, 119	Compelling Sound, 3, 116	8	1:41.90	124,220
1990	**Real Cash**, 3, 113	A. O. Solis	Warcraft, 3, 117	Music Prospector, 3, 117	12	1:42.00	102,600
1989	**Sunday Silence**, 3, 119	P. A. Valenzuela	Flying Continental, 3, 118	Music Merci, 3, 124	5	1:42.60	91,800
1988	**Mi Preferido**, 3, 119	C. J. McCarron	Purdue King, 3, 119	Tejano, 3, 122	8	1:42.20	96,300
1987	**Chart the Stars**, 3, 116	E. Delahoussaye	Alysheba, 3, 120	Temperate Sil, 3, 122	8	1:43.00	107,450
1986	**Variety Road**, 3, 120	C. J. McCarron	Big Play, 3, 114	Dancing Pirate, 3, 116	5	1:45.40	75,350
1985	**Image of Greatness**, 3, 120	L. A. Pincay Jr.	Skywalker, 3, 120	Nostalgia's Star, 3, 117	8	1:43.20	106,350
1984	**FaliTime**, 3, 122	S. Hawley	Gate Dancer, 3, 117	Commemorate, 3, 117	6	1:42.60	103,450
1983	**‡Desert Wine**, 3, 124	C. J. McCarron	Naevus, 3, 115	Fifth Division, 3, 120	8	1:41.60	62,950
1982	**Advance Man**, 3, 117	C. J. McCarron	Gato Del Sol, 3, 118	Cassaleria, 3, 123	7	1:42.20	77,550
1981	**Stancharry**, 3, 118	F. Toro	Splendid Spruce, 3, 116	Flying Nashua, 3, 121	12	1:42.00	69,900
1980	**Raise a Man**, 3, 119	W. Shoemaker	The Carpenter, 3, 123	Rumbo, 3, 119	7	1:41.60	64,300
1979	**Pole Position**, 3, 119	S. Hawley	Switch Partners, 3, 114	Flying Paster, 3, 127	7	1:41.20	48,500
1978	**Affirmed**, 3, 126	S. Cauthen	Chance Dancer, 3, 117	Tampoy, 3, 118	6	1:42.60	38,100
1977	**Smasher**, 3, 115	S. Hawley	*Habitony, 3, 122	Miami Sun, 3, 115	5	1:42.60	32,850
1976	**Crystal Water**, 3, 117	W. Shoemaker	Beau Talent, 3, 117	Double Discount, 3, 113	6	1:42.60	34,000
1975	**Fleet Velvet**, 3, 120	F. Toro	George Navonod, 3, 122	Diabolo, 3, 124	6	1:42.40	33,200
1974	**Aloha Mood**, 3, 118	D. Pierce	Money Lender, 3, 124	Triple Crown, 3, 124	10	1:42.40	43,700
1973	**Linda's Chief**, 3, 126	B. Baeza	Ancient Title, 3, 120	Out of the East, 3, 115	9	1:41.80	42,700

Named for the Rancho Valle de San Felipe located in present-day San Diego County, California. Grade 1 1984-'88. San Felipe H. 1935-'41, 1952-'90. Not held 1942-'44. 1 mile 1935-'36. 7 furlongs 1937, 1941, 1947-'51. 6 furlongs 1938-'40, 1945-'46. Dirt 1935-2007. Three-year-olds and up 1935-'40. Colts and geldings 1935-'51. ‡Naevus finished first, DQ to second, 1983.

San Fernando Stakes

Grade 2 in 2008. Santa Anita Park, four-year-olds, 1 1/16 miles, all weather. Held January 12, 2008, with a gross value of $200,000. First held in 1952. First graded in 1973. Stakes record 1:40.16 (2008 Air Commander).

Year	Winner	Jockey	Second	Third	Strs	Time	1st Purse
2008	**Air Commander**, 4, 116	A. T. Gryder	Johnny Eves, 4, 120	Tiago, 4, 122	11	**1:40.16**	$120,000
2007	**Awesome Gem**, 4, 116	T. Baze	Midnight Lute, 4, 118	Brother Derek, 4, 122	11	1:41.90	120,000
2006	**Unbridled Energy**, 4, 118	G. K. Gomez	Canteen, 4, 118	Greeley's Galaxy, 4, 120	9	1:43.28	120,000
2005	**Minister Eric**, 4, 116	R. R. Douglas	Mass Media, 4, 118	Skipaslew, 4, 116	9	1:42.14	120,000
2004	**During**, 4, 120	D. R. Flores	Toccet, 4, 116	Touch the Wire, 4, 117	10	1:41.63	134,280
2003	**Pass Rush**, 4, 116	C. S. Nakatani	Tracemark, 4, 116	Tizbud, 4, 116	8	1:42.37	131,760
2002	**Western Pride**, 4, 122	G. K. Gomez	Orientate, 4, 120	Fancy As, 4, 120	10	1:41.30	134,640
2001	**Tiznow**, 4, 122	C. J. McCarron	Walkslikeaduck, 4, 120	Wooden Phone, 4, 116	6	1:42.05	98,880
2000	**Saint's Honor**, 4, 117	K. Desormeaux	Cat Thief, 4, 122	Mr. Broad Blade, 4, 118	7	1:41.94	190,200
1999	**Dixie Dot Com**, 4, 116	D. R. Flores	Event of the Year, 4, 122	Old Topper, 4, 118	8	1:41.06	190,800
1998	**Silver Charm**, 4, 122	G. L. Stevens	Mud Route, 4, 116	Lord Grillo (Arg), 4, 120	4	1:41.94	125,520
1997	**Northern Afleet**, 4, 116	C. J. McCarron	Ambivalent, 4, 116	Ready to Order, 4, 116	9	1:48.59	194,000
1996	**Helmsman**, 4, 118	C. J. McCarron	Gold and Steel (Fr), 4, 120	The Key Rainbow (Ire), 4, 116	8	1:48.87	134,500
1995	**Wekiva Springs**, 4, 118	K. Desormeaux	Dramatic Gold, 4, 120	Dare and Go, 4, 116	7	1:48.59	126,800
1994	**Zignew**, 4, 118	C. J. McCarron	Nonproductiveasset, 4, 116	Pleasant Tango, 4, 116	12	1:47.87	135,400
1993	**Bertrando**, 4, 120	C. J. McCarron	Star Recruit, 4, 120	The Wicked North, 4, 116	8	1:51.22	127,800
1992	**Best Pal**, 4, 122	K. Desormeaux	Olympio, 4, 122	Dinard, 4, 120	9	1:48.25	130,000

Year	Winner	Jockey	Second	Third	Strs	Time	1st Purse
1991	In Excess (Ire), 4, 126	G. L. Stevens	Warcraft, 4, 120	Go and Go (Ire), 4, 123	9	1:46.70	$128,800
1990	Flying Continental, 4, 120	C. A. Black	Splurger, 4, 114	Secret Slew, 4, 114	8	1:47.20	128,600
1989	Mi Preferido, 4, 123	C. J. McCarron	Speedratic, 4, 120	Perceive Arrogance, 4, 120	12	1:47.40	138,200
1988	On the Line, 4, 120	J. A. Santos	Candi's Gold, 4, 123	Grand Vizier, 4, 114	5	1:49.00	122,400
1987	Variety Road, 4, 123	L. A. Pincay Jr.	Broad Brush, 4, 126	Snow Chief, 4, 126	8	1:49.00	96,300
1986	Right Con, 4, 117	R. Q. Meza	Nostalgia's Star, 4, 120	Fast Account, 4, 114	10	1:48.40	101,800
1985	Precisionist, 4, 126	C. J. McCarron	Greinton (GB), 4, 120	Gate Dancer, 4, 126	7	1:47.40	123,350
1984	Interco, 4, 123	P. A. Valenzuela	Desert Wine, 4, 123	Paris Prince, 4, 120	12	1:48.60	92,850
1983	Wavering Monarch, 4, 123	E. Delahoussaye	Water Bank, 4, 120	Prince Spellbound, 4, 126	9	1:50.00	88,400
1982	It's the One, 4, 120	W. A. Guerra	Princelet, 4, 120	Rock Softly, 4, 114	9	1:47.60	84,650
1981	Doonesbury, 4, 120	S. Hawley	Raise a Man, 4, 120	Idyll, 4, 117	11	1:47.00	74,300
1980	Spectacular Bid, 4, 126	W. Shoemaker	Flying Paster, 4, 126	Relaunch, 4, 120	4	1:48.00	63,300
1979	Radar Ahead, 4, 123	D. G. McHargue	Affirmed, 4, 126	Little Reb, 4, 120	8	1:48.00	69,200
1978	Text, 4, 120	F. Toro	J. O. Tobin, 4, 123	Centennial Pride, 4, 114	5	1:49.40	65,500
1977	Kirby Lane, 4, 120	L. A. Pincay Jr.	Double Discount, 4, 117	Rajab, 4, 114	10	1:47.60	39,000
	‡Pocket Park, 4, 114	S. Cauthen	Properantes, 4, 114	Crystal Water, 4, 123	9	1:48.60	38,500
1976	Messenger of Song, 4, 120	J. Lambert	Avatar, 4, 123	Larrikin, 4, 120	11	1:48.20	54,350
1975	Stardust Mel, 4, 120	W. Shoemaker	Century's Envoy, 4, 120	Princely Native, 4, 120	8	1:48.60	36,700
	First Back, 4, 114	J. Vasquez	Lightning Mandate, 4, 120	Confederate Yankee, 4, 117	9	1:48.60	37,700
1974	Ancient Title, 4, 120	L. A. Pincay Jr.	Linda's Chief, 4, 123	*Mariachie II, 4, 114	7	1:47.60	50,250
1973	Bicker, 4, 120	G. Brogan	Royal Owl, 4, 120	Commoner, 4, 114	14	1:48.20	58,350

Named for San Fernando, California, west of Santa Anita Park. Grade 1 1981-'89. San Fernando Breeders' Cup S. 1997-2007. Not held 1970. 1 1/8 miles 1960-'97. Dirt 1952-2007. Four-year-olds and up 1981. Two divisions 1975, '77. ‡Properantes finished first, DQ to second, 1977 (2nd Div.).

Sanford Stakes

Grade 2 in 2008. Saratoga Race Course, two-year-olds, 6 furlongs, dirt. Held July 26, 2007, with a gross value of $150,000. First held in 1913. First graded in 1973. Stakes record 1:09.32 (2004 Afleet Alex).

Year	Winner	Jockey	Second	Third	Strs	Time	1st Purse
2007	Ready's Image, 2, 121	J. R. Velazquez	Tale of Ekati, 2, 119	The Roundhouse, 2, 119	9	1:09.90	$90,000
2006	Scat Daddy, 2, 119	J. R. Velazquez	Teuflesberg, 2, 117	War Wolf, 2, 119	5	1:11.18	90,000
2004	Afleet Alex, 2, 120	J. Rose	Flamenco, 2, 122	Consolidator, 2, 118	11	**1:09.32**	90,000
2003	Chapel Royal, 2, 122	J. R. Velazquez	Blushing Indian, 2, 118	Flushing Meadows, 2, 118	7	1:10.74	90,000
2002	Whywhywhy, 2, 122	E. S. Prado	Wildcat Heir, 2, 118	Spite the Devil, 2, 118	9	1:10.40	90,000
2001	Buster's Daydream, 2, 122	J. R. Velazquez	Seeking the Money, 2, 117	Heavyweight Champ, 2, 117	6	1:10.55	64,680
2000	City Zip, 2, 119	J. A. Santos	Yonaguska, 2, 119	Scorpion, 2, 119	7	1:10.69	65,220
1999	More Than Ready, 2, 122	J. R. Velazquez	Mighty, 2, 114	Bulling, 2, 114	5	1:09.65	64,560
1998	Time Bandit, 2, 119	P. Day	Prime Directive, 2, 117	Texas Glitter, 2, 117	9	1:11.59	66,480
1997	Polished Brass, 2, 116	P. Day	Double Honor, 2, 116	Jigadee, 2, 116	7	1:10.23	65,520
1996	Kelly Kip, 2, 118	J. Samyn	Boston Harbor, 2, 118	Say Florida Sandy, 2, 115	6	1:10.31	66,840
1995	Maria's Mon, 2, 115	R. G. Davis	Seeker's Reward, 2, 115	Frozen Ice, 2, 112	11	1:10.80	68,340
1994	Montreal Red, 2, 115	J. A. Santos	Boone's Mill, 2, 115	De Niro, 2, 122	5	1:10.56	64,620
1993	Dehere, 2, 122	C. J. McCarron	Prenup, 2, 115	Distinct Reality, 2, 122	6	1:10.48	68,520
1992	Mountain Cat, 2, 119	P. Day	‡Satellite Signal, 2, 115	Rule Sixteen, 2, 122	10	1:10.62	73,440
1991	Caller I. D., 2, 122	J. D. Bailey	Pick Up the Phone, 2, 119	Money Run, 2, 115	6	1:10.92	69,000
1990	Formal Dinner, 2, 115	J. A. Santos	Beaudaspic, 2, 115	Link, 2, 117	10	1:10.20	55,260
1989	Bite the Bullet, 2, 115	J. A. Santos	Graf, 2, 115	For Really, 2, 113	9	1:09.80	54,720
1988	Mercedes Won, 2, 119	R. G. Davis	Leading Prospect, 2, 115	Fire Maker, 2, 115	11	1:10.00	55,440
1987	Forty Niner, 2, 115	E. Maple	Once Wild, 2, 115	Velvet Fog, 2, 115	6	1:10.00	65,340
1986	Persevered, 2, 115	A. T. Cordero Jr.	Perdition's Son, 2, 115	Bucks Best, 2, 115	5	1:10.60	51,120
1985	Sovereign Don, 2, 122	J. Velasquez	Roy, 2, 115	Cause for Pause, 2, 119	9	1:10.60	54,000
1984	Tiffany Ice, 2, 115	G. McCarron	Vindaloo, 2, 115	Fortunate Dancer, 2, 113	4	1:10.80	51,300
1983	Big Walt, 2, 115	J. Fell	Fill Ron's Pockets, 2, 122	Agile Jet, 2, 115	5	1:11.00	34,260
1982	Copelan, 2, 115	J. D. Bailey	Smart Style, 2, 115	Safe Ground, 2, 117	5	1:10.40	33,660
1981	Mayanesian, 2, 115	J. Vasquez	Shipping Magnate, 2, 115	Lejoli, 2, 115	10	1:11.20	35,280
1980	Tap Shoes, 2, 115	R. Hernandez	Triocala, 2, 115	Painted Shield, 2, 117	10	1:10.00	34,260
1979	I Speedup, 2, 122	J. Fell	Muckraker, 2, 115	My Pal Jeff, 2, 117	7	1:10.40	26,175
1978	Fuzzbuster, 2, 115	J. Velazquez	Make a Mess, 2, 115	Turnbuckle, 2, 115	6	1:10.80	22,230
1977	Affirmed, 2, 124	S. Cauthen	Tilt Up, 2, 122	Jet Diplomacy, 2, 124	6	1:09.60	22,290
1976	Turn of Coin, 2, 122	A. T. Cordero Jr.	Hey Hey J. P., 2, 115	Super Joy, 2, 115	7	1:10.20	22,395
1975	Turn to Turia, 2, 121	E. Maple	Iron Bit, 2, 121	Gentle King, 2, 121	5	1:10.80	22,575
1974	Ramahorn, 2, 121	C. Baltazar	Prop Man, 2, 121	Knightly Sport, 2, 121	8	1:11.00	17,205
1973	Az Igazi, 2, 121	M. Venezia	Prince of Reason, 2, 121	Totheend, 2, 121	6	1:10.60	16,680

Named for the Sanford family, owners of Hurricane Stud in Amsterdam, New York. Grade 3 1990-'98. Sanford Memorial S. 1913-'26. Held at Belmont Park 1943-'45. Not held 1961, 2005. 5 1/2 furlongs 1962-'68. ‡Thirty Two Slew finished second, DQ to fourth, 1992.

San Francisco Mile Stakes

Grade 2 in 2008. Golden Gate Fields, three-year-olds and up, 1 mile, turf. Held April 28, 2007, with a gross value of $300,000. First held in 1948. First graded in 1987. Stakes record 1:33.40 (1980 Don Alberto).

Year	Winner	Jockey	Second	Third	Strs	Time	1st Purse
2007	Chinese Dragon, 5, 123	M. E. Smith	Vega's Lord (Ger), 4, 123	Charmo (Fr), 6, 123	5	1:35.81	$165,000

Year	Winner	Jockey	Second	Third	Strs	Time	1st Purse
2006	**Charmo (Fr)**, 5, 122	M. A. Pedroza	Aragorn (Ire), 4, 122	Place Cowboy (Ire), 5, 122	8	1:34.28	$165,000
2005	**Castledale (Ire)**, 4, 118	R. R. Douglas	Adreamisborn, 6, 119	Aly Bubba, 6, 116	9	1:37.40	55,000
2004	**Singletary**, 4, 119	J. Valdivia Jr.	Captain Squire, 5, 116	Gold Ruckus, 6, 116	7	1:35.16	82,500
2003	**Ninebanks**, 5, 117	R. J. Warren Jr.	Nicobar (GB), 6, 116	National Anthem (GB), 7, 116	8	1:37.20	110,000
2002	**Suances (GB)**, 5, 116	D. R. Flores	Decarchy, 5, 121	The Tin Man, 4, 116	4	1:35.19	110,000
2001	**Redattore (Brz)**, 6, 115	J. P. Lumpkins	Hawksley Hill (Ire), 8, 119	Kerrygold (Fr), 5, 116	9	1:35.14	137,500
2000	**Ladies Din**, 5, 120	K. Desormeaux	Fighting Falcon, 4, 116	Self Feeder (Ire), 6, 116	10	1:35.46	150,000
1999	**†Tuzla (Fr)**, 5, 112	B. Blanc	Poteen, 5, 116	Rob 'n Gin, 5, 117	10	1:35.46	180,000
1998	**Hawksley Hill (Ire)**, 5, 119	G. L. Stevens	Fantastic Fellow, 4, 121	Uncaged Fury, 7, 117	6	1:34.33	120,000
1997	**Wavy Run (Ire)**, 6, 116	B. Blanc	Savinio, 7, 118	Romarin (Brz), 7, 118	7	1:37.11	120,000
1996	**Gold and Steel (Fr)**, 4, 114	A. O. Solis	Savinio, 6, 115	Debutant Trick, 6, 117	7	1:35.07	120,000
1995	**Unfinished Symph**, 4, 118	C. W. Antley	Vaudeville, 4, 119	Torch Rouge (GB), 4, 115	9	1:34.14	110,000
1994	**Gothland (Fr)**, 5, 115	C. S. Nakatani	Emerald Jig, 5, 113	The Tender Track, 7, 116	11	1:35.46	110,000
1993	**Norwich (GB)**, 6, 114	K. Desormeaux	Qathif, 6, 115	Luthier Enchanteur, 6, 117	8	1:35.57	137,500
1992	**Tight Spot**, 5, 125	L. A. Pincay Jr.	Notorious Pleasure, 6, 116	Forty Niner Days, 5, 116	9	1:35.57	110,000
1991	**Forty Niner Days**, 4, 112	T. T. Doocy	Exbourne, 5, 116	Blaze O'Brien, 4, 116	6	1:38.90	110,000
1990	**Colway Rally (GB)**, 6, 116	C. A. Black	River Master, 4, 115	Miswaki Tern, 5, 117	10	1:35.80	110,000
1989	**Patchy Groundfog**, 6, 116	F. Olivares	No Commitment, 4, 113	Mazilier, 5, 115	7	1:38.20	82,500
1988	**Ifrad**, 6, 115	T. M. Chapman	The Medic, 4, 118	Blanco, 4, 117	9	1:36.40	82,500
1987	**Dormello (Arg)**, 6, 113	A. L. Diaz	Air Display, 4, 116	Barbery, 6, 115	8	1:36.20	82,500
1986	**Hail Bold King**, 5, 117	M. Castaneda	Right Con, 4, 119	Lucky n Green (Ire), 4, 114	12	1:36.40	69,900
1985	**Truce Maker**, 7, 112	J. A. Garcia	†Larkin Cavalieri (GB), 5, 115	Baron O'Dublin, 5, 116	11	1:35.20	69,500
1984	**Drumalis (Ire)**, 4, 117	E. Delahoussaye	Silveyville, 6, 117	Ten Below, 5, 115	8	1:35.60	43,275
	Icehot, 4, 115	M. Castaneda	Major Sport, 7, 117	Otter Slide, 5, 114	8	1:35.40	34,275
1983	**King's County (Ire)**, 4, 112	E. Munoz	Police Inspector, 6, 118	Silveyville, 5, 121	12	1:37.60	48,950
1982	**Silveyville**, 4, 121	D. Winick	Visible Pole, 4, 110	A Sure Hit, 4, 113	10	1:36.80	51,050
1981	**Opus Dei (Fr)**, 6, 119	F. Olivares	Drouilly (Fr), 5, 116	His Honor, 6, 117	13	1:34.80	41,850
1980	**Don Alberto**, 5, 114	R. M. Gonzalez	Saboulard (Fr), 5, 116	Capt. Don, 5, 121	10	**1:33.40**	33,300
1979	**Struttin' George**, 5, 117	T. M. Chapman	Crafty Native, 6, 111	Foreign Power, 5, 115	8	1:37.40	32,950
1978	**Jumping Hill**, 6, 121	J. Lambert	Boy Tike, 5, 115	Dr. Henry K., 4, 109	6	1:38.40	32,500
1977	**Crafty Native**, 4, 112	M. James	Cojak, 4, 122	Money Lender, 6, 119	8	1:38.40	26,350
1976	**Whoa Boy**, 4, 113	G. Baze	Ocala Boy, 5, 113	Star of Kuwait, 7, 116	7	1:39.00	18,100
1975	**Visualizer**, 4, 114	F. Mena	Roka Zaca, 4, 117	*Larkal II, 6, 110	10	1:38.00	21,900
1974	**New Prospect**, 4, 118	J. Sellers	Masked, 4, 116	Rock Bath, 5, 113	6	1:43.20	22,150

Named for the city of San Francisco. Grade 3 1987-'93. San Francisco Mile H. 1948-'98. San Francisco Breeders' Cup Mile H. 1999-2005. San Francisco Breeders' Cup Mile S. 2006. Held at Bay Meadows 2001-'05. Not held 1960, '76, 2008. Dirt 1948-'65, 1974. Originally scheduled on turf 1974. Four-year-olds and up 1968, 2006. Two divisions 1984.
†Denotes female.

San Gabriel Handicap

Grade 2 in 2008. Santa Anita Park, three-year-olds and up, 1 1/8 miles, turf. Held December 30, 2007, with a gross value of $150,000. First held in 1935. First graded in 1973. Stakes record 1:46.20 (1989 Wretham [GB]).

Year	Winner	Jockey	Second	Third	Strs	Time	1st Purse
2007	**Daytona (Ire)**, 3, 117	M. E. Smith	Proudinsky (Ger), 4, 115	Medici Code (GB), 3, 116	6	1:47.57	$90,000
2006	**King's Drama (Ire)**, 6, 121	D. R. Flores	Railroad, 4, 115	Hendrix, 5, 119	8	1:48.53	90,000
	Badge of Silver, 6, 118	P. A. Valenzuela	Atlando (Ire), 5, 116	Toasted, 5, 117	9	1:50.02	90,000
2005	**Truly a Judge**, 7, 115	M. A. Pedroza	Star Cross (Arg), 8, 112	Continental Red, 9, 116	8	1:48.90	90,000
2003	**Redattore (Brz)**, 8, 122	A. O. Solis	Continental Red, 7, 116	Denied, 5, 116	9	1:48.17	90,000
2002	**Grammarian**, 4, 117	J. Valdivia Jr.	David Copperfield, 5, 117	Decarchy, 5, 119	9	1:48.12	90,000
2001	**Irish Prize**, 5, 121	G. L. Stevens	Sligo Bay (Ire), 3, 117	El Gran Papa, 4, 114	11	1:50.56	90,000
	Irish Prize, 5, 117	K. Desormeaux	Manndar (Ire), 5, 121	Here Comes Big C, 6, 110	8	1:47.88	90,000
2000	**Brave Act (GB)**, 6, 120	A. O. Solis	Native Desert, 7, 116	Manndar (Ire), 4, 116	6	1:49.25	97,470
1998	**Brave Act (GB)**, 4, 118	G. F. Almeida	Mash One (Chi), 4, 116	Fabulous Guy (Ire), 4, 113	6	1:46.78	90,000
1997	**Martiniquais (Ire)**, 4, 116	C. S. Nakatani	Bienvenido (Arg), 4, 115	Da Bull, 5, 115	8	1:48.42	99,180
	Rainbow Blues (Ire), 4, 119	G. L. Stevens	River Deep, 6, 116	Via Lombardia (Ire), 5, 116	7	1:46.89	81,500
1996	**Romarin (Brz)**, 6, 119	C. S. Nakatani	Virginia Carnival, 4, 116	Silver Wizard, 6, 117	8	1:49.69	82,050
1995	**Romarin (Brz)**, 5, 119	C. S. Nakatani	Inner City (Ire), 6, 117	Ianomami (Ire), 5, 116	6	1:49.36	62,900
1994	**Earl of Barking (Ire)**, 5, 118	C. J. McCarron	Fanmore, 6, 116	Navarone, 6, 119	8	1:48.64	65,300
1993	**Star of Cozzene**, 5, 118	G. L. Stevens	Bistro Garden, 5, 114	Leger Cat (Arg), 7, 115	9	1:48.33	66,100
1992	**Classic Fame**, 6, 118	E. Delahoussaye	Super May, 6, 114	Defensive Play, 5, 116	6	1:46.69	64,300
1990	**In Excess (Ire)**, 3, 117	G. L. Stevens	Rouvignac (Fr), 4, 113	Kanatiyr (Fr), 4, 115	11	1:47.20	68,100
1989	**Wretham (GB)**, 4, 117	L. A. Pincay Jr.	Patchy Groundfog, 6, 117	In Extremis, 4, 117	10	**1:46.20**	67,700
1988	**Conquering Hero**, 5, 115	G. L. Stevens	Hot and Smoggy, 4, 117	Ten Keys, 4, 116	9	1:50.60	66,500
	Simply Majestic, 4, 120	J. D. Bailey	Payant (Arg), 4, 118	Dr. Death, 3, 115	8	1:47.40	66,100
1987	**Nostalgia's Star**, 5, 118	L. A. Pincay Jr.	Inevitable Leader, 8, 112	Spellbound, 4, 116	5	1:51.20	61,550
1986	**Yashgan (GB)**, 5, 124	C. J. McCarron	Tights, 5, 118	Rivlia, 4, 116	8	1:49.60	51,800
1985	**Dahar**, 4, 120	F. Toro	Paris Prince, 5, 118	Massera (Chi), 7, 116	7	1:47.60	50,750
1984	**Prince Florimund (SAf)**, 6, 118	P. A. Valenzuela	Ten Below, 5, 113	Ginger Brink (Fr), 4, 118	8	1:48.20	40,425
	Beldale Lustre, 5, 118	L. A. Pincay Jr.	I'll See You (GB), 6, 112	Color Bearer, 6, 111	7	1:48.80	39,425
1983	**Greenwood Star (GB)**, 6, 119	D. Pierce	Tell Again, 5, 118	Western, 5, 115	12	1:47.20	51,450
1981	**The Bart**, 5, 125	E. Delahoussaye	Irish Heart (Ire), 3, 115	Forlion, 5, 114	7	1:48.00	48,050

Year	Winner	Jockey	Second	Third	Strs	Time	1st Purse
1980	Premier Ministre, 4, 113	L. A. Pincay Jr.	Galaxy Libra (Ire), 4, 117	Fast, 4, 118	7	1:48.20	$38,250
	John Henry, 5, 123	D. G. McHargue	Smasher, 6, 111	As de Copas (Arg), 7, 117	9	1:49.80	39,300
1979	Fluorescent Light, 5, 118	A. T. Cordero Jr.	As de Copas (Arg), 6, 118	Tiller, 5, 127	7	1:47.60	32,200
1978	Mr. Redoy, 4, 110	S. Hawley	Dr. Krohn, 5, 116	Papelote, 4, 113	9	1:48.40	33,100
1977	Riot in Paris, 6, 125	W. Shoemaker	Distant Land, 5, 115	Ribot Grande, 7, 113	7	1:50.00	34,000
1975	Zanthe, 6, 117	S. Hawley	Copper Mel, 3, 115	Riot in Paris, 4, 124	9	1:47.40	26,550
1974	Fair Test, 6, 113	A. Santiago	Indefatigable, 4, 118	Montmartre, 4, 118	6	1:50.60	25,750
1973	Astray, 4, 115	J. Vasquez	Golden Doc Ray, 3, 114	Kirrary, 3, 117	8	1:48.20	26,250
	Kentuckian, 4, 114	J. Lambert	Artaxerxes, 5, 113	Harkville, 5, 112	10	1:47.60	26,950

Named for the nearby city of San Gabriel, California; the city is named for a Spanish mission. Grade 3 1973-'93, 2005. Not held 1936, 1939-'44, 1947-'51, 1970, 1976, 1982, 1991, 1999, 2004. 3 furlongs 1935-'38. 6 furlongs 1945-'46. 7 furlongs 1952-'54. 1¼ miles 1955-'59. Dirt 1935-'54, 1965, 1972, 1974, 1977, 1987, 2005. Originally scheduled on turf 2005. Two-year-olds 1935-'38. Three-year-olds 1952-'54. Four-year-olds and up 1954-'73, 1978-'80, 1983-'88 (January), 1992-'97, 2000-'01 (January), 2005-'06 (January). Two divisions 1984. Held in January and December 1973, '80, '88, '97, 2001, '06.

San Gorgonio Handicap

Grade 2 in 2008. Santa Anita Park, four-year-olds and up, fillies and mares, 1⅛ miles, turf. Held January 14, 2008, with a gross value of $150,000. First held in 1968. First graded in 1983. Stakes record 1:46.40 (1983 Castilla).

Year	Winner	Jockey	Second	Third	Strs	Time	1st Purse
2008	Wait a While, 5, 121	G. K. Gomez	Lavender Sky, 4, 116	Sohgol (Ire), 6, 116	5	1:46.81	$90,000
2007	Citronnade, 4, 115	D. R. Flores	Rahys' Appeal, 5, 115	Three Degrees (Ire), 5, 117	7	1:46.80	90,000
2006	Silver Cup (Ire), 4, 114	V. Espinoza	Ticker Tape (GB), 5, 117	Royal Copenhagen (Fr), 4, 116	11	1:47.46	90,000
2005	Fencelineneighbor, 5, 115	L. H. Jauregui	Uraib (Ire), 5, 115	Dolly Wells (Arg), 5, 113	5	1:49.82	90,000
2004	Megahertz (GB), 5, 119	A. O. Solis	Garden in the Rain (Fr), 7, 116	Firth of Lorne (Ire), 5, 116	4	1:49.51	90,000
2003	Tates Creek, 5, 121	P. A. Valenzuela	Megahertz (GB), 4, 117	Double Cat, 5, 114	7	1:46.91	90,000
2002	Tout Charmant, 6, 120	C. J. McCarron	Janet (GB), 5, 119	Vencera (Fr), 5, 115	8	1:47.22	90,000
2001	Uncharted Haven (GB), 4, 115	A. O. Solis	Brianda (Ire), 4, 110	Beautiful Noise, 5, 116	12	1:50.02	90,000
2000	Lady At Peace, 4, 115	G. K. Gomez	Spanish Fern, 5, 119	Riboletta (Brz), 5, 116	5	1:48.75	90,000
1999	See You Soon (Fr), 5, 118	K. Desormeaux	Sonja's Faith (Ire), 5, 118	Verinha (Brz), 5, 115	6	1:49.14	90,000
1998	Golden Arches (Fr), 4, 120	C. J. McCarron	Ecoute, 5, 115	‡Real Connection, 7, 116	6	1:49.42	96,870
1997	Sixieme Sens, 5, 116	C. S. Nakatani	Alpride (Ire), 6, 120	Grafin, 6, 116	9	1:47.16	82,950
1996	Wandesta (GB), 5, 119	C. S. Nakatani	Matiara, 4, 118	Yearly Tour, 5, 117	6	1:49.13	80,550
1995	Queens Court Queen, 6, 117	C. S. Nakatani	Wende, 5, 116	Vinista, 5, 115	5	1:48.70	62,000
1994	Hero's Love, 6, 119	L. A. Pincay Jr.	Skimble, 5, 118	Miss Turkana, 5, 118	10	1:47.65	66,800
1993	Southern Truce, 5, 114	C. S. Nakatani	Laura Ly (Arg), 7, 114	Lite Light, 5, 115	5	1:51.28	67,100
1992	Paseana (Arg), 5, 118	C. J. McCarron	Laura Ly (Arg), 6, 112	Reluctant Guest, 6, 117	4	1:53.88	77,250
1991	Royal Touch (Ire), 6, 118	C. J. McCarron	Countus In, 6, 119	Marsha's Dancer, 5, 113	10	1:47.90	83,850
1990	Invited Guest (Ire), 6, 117	R. A. Baze	White Mischief (GB), 6, 115	Oeilladine (Fr), 4, 115	10	1:46.40	83,750
1989	No Review, 4, 117	R. Q. Meza	Annoconnor, 5, 122	White Mischief (GB), 5, 116	6	1:48.80	79,950
1988	Miss Alto, 5, 116	E. Delahoussaye	Top Corsage, 5, 119	My Virginia Reel, 6, 115	6	1:49.20	63,200
1987	Frau Altiva (Arg), 5, 117	L. A. Pincay Jr.	Auspiciante, 6, 122	Solva (GB), 6, 119	7	1:50.20	63,100
1986	Mountain Bear (GB), 5, 118	E. Delahoussaye	Royal Regatta (NZ), 7, 115	Justicara (Ire), 5, 117	11	1:48.40	67,150
1985	Fact Finder, 6, 118	F. Toro	Capichi, 5, 118	Comedy Act, 6, 119	7	1:48.20	62,500
1984	First Advance, 5, 115	M. Castaneda	Avigaition, 5, 120	L'Attrayante (Fr), 4, 121	11	1:48.80	53,950
1983	Castilla, 4, 122	C. J. McCarron	Star Pastures (GB), 5, 119	Cat Girl, 5, 115	7	1:46.40	50,800
1982	Track Robbery, 6, 123	E. Delahoussaye	Rainbow Connection, 4, 117	Targa, 5, 114	5	1:52.60	45,700
1981	Kilijaro (Ire), 5, 128	W. Shoemaker	Queen to Conquer, 5, 122	Refinish, 4, 117	4	1:49.20	36,300
1980	Miss Magnetic, 5, 111	L. E. Ortega	Maytide, 4, 117	Persona, 4, 113	9	1:50.00	39,700
1979	Via Maris (Fr), 4, 113	A. T. Cordero Jr.	Drama Critic, 5, 122	Donna Inez, 4, 114	10	1:52.60	33,550
1977	*Lucie Manet, 4, 121	W. Shoemaker	Theia (Fr), 4, 116	Claire Valentine (Ire), 4, 114	4	1:54.00	30,250
	*Merry Lady III, 5, 119	L. A. Pincay Jr.	Our First Delight, 5, 117	*Pacara, 5, 114	10	1:50.80	36,200
1976	*Tizna, 7, 132	F. Alvarez	Miss Tokyo, 4, 120	Charger's Star, 6, 121	8	1:47.20	25,800
1975	*Madison Palace, 7, 119	D. Pierce	Grotonian, 6, 115	At the Dance, 6, 115	9	1:48.40	21,400
1974	Margum, 5, 119	W. Shoemaker	Harbor Point, 6, 117	Expediter, 5, 115	10	1:50.60	22,550
1973	Extra Hand, 7, 118	L. A. Pincay Jr.	Timoteo, 5, 122	Dundee Marmalade, 5, 115	8	1:49.00	23,200

Named for San Gorgonio Mountain, highest mountain in Southern California. Grade 3 1983-'84, 2005. San Gorgonio Claiming S. 1969-'75. Not held 1970, '78. 6½ furlongs 1968. Dirt 1969-'71, 1973-'74, 1977-'80, 1982, 1988-'89, 1992-'93, 1995, 2005. Originally scheduled on turf 1973, 2005. Three-year-olds and up 1977. Both sexes 1968-'75. Held in January and December 1977. ‡Escabiosa (Arg) finished third, DQ to fourth, 1998.

San Juan Capistrano Invitational Handicap

Grade 2 in 2008. Santa Anita Park, four-year-olds and up, about 1¾ miles, turf. Held April 20, 2008, with a gross value of $250,000. First held in 1935. First graded in 1973. Stakes record 2:42.96 (2001 Bienamado).

Year	Winner	Jockey	Second	Third	Strs	Time	1st Purse
2008	Big Booster, 7, 114	R. Bejarano	Warning Zone, 4, 115	Porfido (Chi), 6, 115	7	2:45.50	$150,000
2007	On the Acorn (GB), 6, 114	V. Espinoza	Sweet Return (GB), 7, 117	Fitz Flag (Arg), 7, 113	7	2:48.02	150,000
2006	T. H. Approval, 5, 117	A. O. Solis	One Off (GB), 6, 114	Quinquin the King (Fr), 4, 118	12	2:45.29	150,000
2005	T. H. Approval, 4, 115	R. R. Douglas	Exterior, 4, 116	Fitz Flag (Arg), 5, 113	8	2:45.02	150,000
2004	Meteor Storm (GB), 5, 116	J. Valdivia Jr.	Rhythm Mad (Fr), 4, 115	Runaway Dancer, 5, 115	9	2:45.98	150,000

Year	Winner	Jockey	Second	Third	Strs	Time	1st Purse
2003	Passinetti, 7, 111	B. Blanc	All the Boys, 6, 115	Champion Lodge (Ire), 6, 117	9	2:46.97	$240,000
2002	Ringaskiddy, 6, 116	E. Delahoussaye	Staging Post, 4, 115	Continental Red, 6, 117	8	2:44.49	240,000
2001	Bienamado, 5, 122	C. J. McCarron	Persianlux (GB), 5, 114	Blueprint (Ire), 6, 116	11	**2:42.96**	240,000
2000	Sunshine Street, 5, 115	J. D. Bailey	Single Empire (Ire), 6, 118	Chelsea Barracks (GB), 4, 109	5	2:49.06	240,000
1999	Single Empire (Ire), 5, 118	K. Desormeaux	Le Paillard (Ire), 5, 115	Lucayan Indian (Ire), 4, 113	9	2:45.93	240,000
1998	Amerique, 4, 116	E. Delahoussaye	Star Performance, 5, 115	Kessem Power (NZ), 6, 116	10	2:47.08	240,000
1997	Marlin, 4, 119	E. Delahoussaye	dh-African Dancer, 5, 114 dh-Sunshack (GB), 6, 118		7	2:44.56	240,000
1996	Raintrap (GB), 6, 115	A. O. Solis	†Windsharp, 5, 116	Awad, 6, 120	7	2:48.40	240,000
1995	Red Bishop, 7, 119	M. E. Smith	Special Price, 6, 116	Liyoun (Ire), 7, 112	8	2:48.02	220,000
1994	Bien Bien, 5, 122	C. J. McCarron	Grand Flotilla, 7, 116	Alex the Great (GB), 5, 114	9	2:46.69	220,000
1993	Kotashaan (Fr), 5, 121	K. Desormeaux	Bien Bien, 4, 119	Fraise, 5, 123	5	2:45.00	220,000
1992	Fly Till Dawn, 6, 121	P. A. Valenzuela	†Miss Alleged, 5, 118	Wall Street Dancer, 4, 114	9	2:46.53	275,000
1991	Mashkour, 8, 115	C. J. McCarron	River Warden, 5, 115	Aksar, 4, 116	11	2:47.70	275,000
1990	Delegant, 6, 115	K. Desormeaux	Valdali (Ire), 4, 114	Hawkster, 4, 123	7	2:46.60	275,000
1989	Nasr El Arab, 4, 123	P. A. Valenzuela	Pleasant Variety, 5, 117	Academic (Ire), 4, 113	8	2:51.40	220,000
1988	Great Communicator, 5, 119	R. Sibille	Fiction, 4, 116	†Carotene, 5, 115	7	2:51.60	220,000
1987	Rosedale, 4, 117	L. A. Pincay Jr.	Wylfa (GB), 6, 115	Rivlia, 5, 115	6	2:49.00	220,000
1986	Dahar, 5, 124	A. O. Solis	†Mountain Bear (GB), 5, 118	Jupiter Island (GB), 7, 123	10	2:48.20	220,000
1985	Prince True, 4, 124	C. J. McCarron	†Estrapade, 5, 120	Swoon, 7, 117	7	2:26.40	180,000
1984	Load the Cannons, 4, 119	L. A. Pincay Jr.	Jenkins Ferry, 4, 114	Norwick, 5, 115	9	2:48.00	180,000
1983	Erins Isle (Ire), 5, 125	L. A. Pincay Jr.	Wolver Heights (Ire), 5, 118	Victory Zone, 4, 115	12	2:48.60	180,000
1982	Lemhi Gold, 4, 121	W. A. Guerra	Exploded, 5, 118	Perrault (GB), 5, 129	9	2:45.60	180,000
1981	Obraztsovy, 6, 121	P. A. Valenzuela	Exploded, 4, 115	Singularity, 4, 115	9	2:50.40	120,000
1980	John Henry, 5, 126	D. G. McHargue	Fiestero (Chi), 5, 114	†The Very One, 5, 113	11	2:46.80	120,000
1979	Tiller, 5, 126	A. T. Cordero Jr.	Exceller, 6, 127	Noble Dancer (GB), 7, 128	11	2:48.00	120,000
1978	Exceller, 5, 126	W. Shoemaker	Noble Dancer (GB), 6, 125	Xmas Box, 4, 115	11	2:51.00	120,000
1977	Properantes, 4, 120	D. G. McHargue	Top Crowd, 6, 118	Caucasus, 5, 128	8	2:47.60	85,000
1976	One On the Aisle, 4, 119	S. Hawley	*Elaborado, 5, 113	Top Crowd, 5, 121	10	2:50.00	75,000
1975	†*La Zanzara, 5, 114	D. Pierce	Astray, 6, 125	Stardust Mel, 4, 126	12	2:52.20	75,000
1974	Astray, 5, 126	J. Vasquez	*El Rey, 6, 113	Big Spruce, 5, 125	6	2:45.40	75,000
1973	Queen's Hustler, 4, 115	R. Rosales	Big Spruce, 4, 119	*Cougar II, 7, 127	7	2:46.40	75,000

Named for San Juan Capistrano, California, which took its name from the mission. San Juan Capistrano H. 1935-'64. Grade 1 1973-2003. Not held 1942-'44, 1947-'48. 1 1/8 miles 1935-'38. 1 1/2 miles 1939, 1941, 1945-'46, 1949, 1954. 1 1/16 miles 1940. 1 3/4 miles 1950-'53. Dirt 1935-'53. Three-year-olds and up 1935-'39, 1941-'67. Three-year-olds 1940. Dead heat for second 1997. Course record 1993, 2001. †Denotes female.

San Luis Obispo Handicap

Grade 2 in 2008. Santa Anita Park, four-year-olds and up, 1 1/2 miles, turf. Held February 23, 2008, with a gross value of $150,000. First held in 1952. First graded in 1973. Stakes record 2:23.80 (1974 Captain Cee Jay [1st Div.]).

Year	Winner	Jockey	Second	Third	Strs	Time	1st Purse
2008	Spring House, 6, 116	G. K. Gomez	Church Service, 5, 111	On the Acorn (GB), 7, 117	9	2:27.21	$90,000
2007	Obrigado (Fr), 4, 117	G. K. Gomez	‡On the Acorn (GB), 6, 112	One Off (GB), 7, 117	7	2:27.21	90,000
2006	Atlando (Ire), 5, 115	M. A. Pedroza	T. H. Approval, 5, 116	King's Drama (Ire), 6, 122	8	2:23.95	90,000
2005	License To Run (Brz), 5, 117	P. A. Valenzuela	Californian (GB), 5, 114	T. H. Approval, 4, 115	8	2:28.72	90,000
2004	Puerto Banus, 5, 115	V. Espinoza	Continuously, 5, 116	Continental Red, 8, 117	12	2:28.00	120,000
2003	The Tin Man, 5, 121	M. E. Smith	Special Matter, 5, 113	Harrisand (Fr), 5, 116	5	2:31.22	120,000
2002	Nazirali (Ire), 5, 112	B. Blanc	Continental Red, 6, 116	Bonapartiste (Fr), 8, 114	7	2:26.09	120,000
2001	Persianlux (GB), 5, 113	T. Baze	Devon Deputy, 5, 114	Falcon Flight (Fr), 5, 116	10	2:27.70	120,000
2000	Dark Moondancer (GB), 5, 120	C. J. McCarron	The Fly (GB), 6, 115	Casino King (Ire), 5, 116	5	2:39.61	120,000
1999	Kessem Power (NZ), 7, 115	G. L. Stevens	Brave Act (GB), 5, 121	Lazy Lode (Arg), 5, 120	7	2:28.02	120,000
1998	Bienvenido (Arg), 5, 115	C. J. McCarron	Prize Giving (GB), 5, 117	Callisthene (Fr), 6, 117	6	2:29.34	120,000
1997	Shanawi (Ire), 5, 111	B. Blanc	Rainbow Dancer (Fr), 6, 117	Bon Point (GB), 7, 117	7	2:24.51	132,100
1996	†Windsharp, 5, 115	E. Delahoussaye	†Wandesta (GB), 5, 114	Virginia Carnival, 4, 115	6	2:30.33	130,800
1995	Square Cut, 6, 114	C. W. Antley	Ianomami (Ire), 5, 115	River Rhythm, 8, 111	10	2:26.04	133,200
1994	Fanmore, 6, 116	K. Desormeaux	Bien Bien, 5, 124	Navire (Fr), 5, 114	9	2:27.03	131,400
1993	Kotashaan (Fr), 5, 114	K. Desormeaux	Carnival Baby, 5, 112	The Name's Jimmy, 4, 115	8	2:27.64	129,600
1992	Quest for Fame (GB), 5, 121	G. L. Stevens	Cool Gold Mood, 5, 114	†Miss Alleged, 5, 121	9	2:28.79	158,500
1991	Rial (Arg), 6, 118	J. Velasquez	Intelligently, 5, 113	Royal Reach, 5, 113	9	2:24.10	163,400
1990	Frankly Perfect, 5, 124	C. J. McCarron	Delegant, 6, 116	Just as Lucky, 5, 114	12	2:28.00	171,100
1989	Great Communicator, 6, 124	R. Sibille	Vallotton (Fr), 4, 117	Roberto's Dancer, 4, 114	5	2:30.20	122,800
1988	Great Communicator, 5, 117	R. Sibille	Trokhos, 5, 118	†Ivor's Image, 5, 114	10	2:27.60	133,800
1987	Louis Le Grand, 5, 118	W. Shoemaker	Zoffany, 7, 125	Schiller, 5, 115	8	2:28.40	96,050
1986	Talakeno, 6, 115	P. A. Valenzuela	Foscarini (Ire), 5, 117	Strawberry Road (Aus), 7, 126	12	2:33.20	123,750
1985	Western, 7, 114	G. L. Stevens	Scrupules (Fr), 5, 121	Strong Dollar (Ire), 5, 118	6	2:25.40	89,250
1984	Sir Pele, 5, 118	R. Q. Meza	Lucence, 5, 118	Debonair Herc, 4, 114	9	2:27.40	79,375
1983	Pelerin (Fr), 6, 116	W. Shoemaker	Western, 5, 118	Massera (Chi), 5, 118	10	2:24.60	67,200
1982	Regal Bearing (GB), 6, 114	J. J. Steiner	Le Duc de Bar, 5, 114	Goldiko, 5, 119	10	2:27.20	80,450
1981	John Henry, 6, 127	L. A. Pincay Jr.	Galaxy Libra (Ire), 5, 119	Zor, 8, 115	6	2:24.00	62,800
1980	Silver Eagle (Ire), 6, 120	W. Shoemaker	Balzac, 5, 123	Friuli (Arg), 7, 114	8	2:30.20	65,100

Year	Winner	Jockey	Second	Third	Strs	Time	1st Purse
1979	Fluorescent Light, 5, 124	L. A. Pincay Jr.	As de Copas (Arg), 6, 118	dh-Alpha Boy, 5, 112	8	2:28.20	$48,950
				dh-Nostalgia, 5, 112			
1978	Copper Mel, 6, 115	S. Hawley	Avodire, 5, 110	Tacitus, 4, 115	11	2:28.00	42,300
1977	*Royal Derby II, 8, 126	W. Shoemaker	Gallivantor, 5, 115	Anne's Pretender, 5, 123	10	2:24.80	41,700
1976	Announcer, 4, 118	F. Toro	Top Crowd, 5, 123	Zanthe, 7, 121	6	2:30.80	38,200
1975	*Madison Palace, 7, 120	L. A. Pincay Jr.	Toujours Pret, 6, 121	*Barclay Joy, 5, 118	8	2:30.20	40,100
1974	Captain Cee Jay, 4, 113	F. Alvarez	Court Ruling, 4, 112	*El Rey, 6, 112	8	**2:23.80**	28,150
	Astray, 5, 118	J. Vasquez	Scantling, 4, 112	Wichita Oil, 6, 115	8	2:24.40	28,150
1973	Queen's Hustler, 4, 112	R. Rosales	China Silk, 4, 115	River Buoy, 8, 117	9	2:27.20	40,800

Named for St. Louis of Toulouse, a Franciscan bishop and Catholic saint. Formerly named in honor of George Washington's birthday; the race was held on that holiday. Grade 3 1990-'91. Washington's Birthday H. 1952-'62. Not held 1963-'67. 7 furlongs 1952-'53. 1¼ miles 1954, '70. About 1½ miles 1968, '72. Dirt 1952-'53, 1973, 1980, 2005. Originally scheduled on turf 2005. Two divisions 1974. Dead heat for third 1979. ‡One Off (GB) finished second, DQ to third, 2007. Track record 1973. †Denotes female.

San Luis Rey Handicap

Grade 2 in 2008. Santa Anita Park, four-year-olds and up, 1½ miles, turf. Held March 22, 2008, with a gross value of $200,000. First held in 1952. First graded in 1973. Stakes record 2:23 (1970 Fiddle Isle; 1980 John Henry).

Year	Winner	Jockey	Second	Third	Strs	Time	1st Purse
2008	Boule d'Or (Ire), 7, 112	T. Baze	Porfido (Chi), 6, 115	Warning Zone, 4, 115	7	2:25.48	$120,000
2007	Fourty Niners Son, 6, 117	G. K. Gomez	Notable Guest, 6, 115	Prospect Park (GB), 6, 119	7	2:27.50	120,000
2006	King's Drama (Ire), 6, 121	J. K. Court	T. H. Approval, 5, 116	Wild Buddy, 7, 113	7	2:26.50	120,000
2005	Stanley Park, 5, 116	G. L. Stevens	Meteor Storm (GB), 6, 118	Epicentre, 6, 115	12	2:24.45	120,000
2004	Meteor Storm (GB), 5, 115	J. Valdivia Jr.	Labirinto, 6, 114	Gene de Campeao (Brz), 5, 114	10	2:26.03	120,000
2003	Champion Lodge (Ire), 6, 116	A. O. Solis	Special Matter, 5, 113	Adminniestrator, 6, 116	7	2:33.48	150,000
2002	Continental Red, 6, 116	P. A. Valenzuela	†Keemoon (Fr), 6, 115	Speedy Pick, 4, 112	8	2:26.81	150,000
2001	Blueprint (Ire), 6, 116	G. L. Stevens	Devon Deputy, 5, 114	Kerrygold (Fr), 5, 116	8	2:28.57	150,000
2000	Dark Moondancer (GB), 5, 122	C. J. McCarron	Single Empire (Ire), 6, 122	Bonapartiste (Fr), 6, 122	6	2:26.00	150,000
1999	Single Empire (Ire), 5, 122	K. Desormeaux	Kessem Power (NZ), 7, 122	Alvo Certo (Brz), 6, 122	7	2:27.97	150,000
1998	Kessem Power (NZ), 6, 122	L. Dettori	Storm Trooper, 5, 122	Star Performance, 5, 122	12	2:28.40	150,000
1997	Marlin, 4, 122	C. J. McCarron	Sunshack (GB), 6, 122	Peckinpah's Soul (Fr), 5, 122	10	2:28.14	166,600
1996	†Windsharp, 5, 117	E. Delahoussaye	†Wandesta (GB), 5, 117	Silver Wizard, 6, 122	7	2:27.91	161,900
1995	Sandpit (Brz), 6, 124	C. S. Nakatani	River Rhythm, 8, 124	Square Cut, 6, 124	7	2:27.15	155,000
1994	Bien Bien, 5, 124	C. J. McCarron	Navire (Fr), 5, 124	Grand Flotilla, 7, 124	5	2:26.65	149,500
1993	Kotashaan (Fr), 5, 124	K. Desormeaux	Bien Bien, 4, 124	Fast Cure, 4, 124	4	2:23.91	148,250
1992	Fly Till Dawn, 6, 124	L. A. Pincay Jr.	Provins, 4, 124	Quest for Fame (GB), 5, 124	6	2:27.26	179,000
1991	Pleasant Variety, 7, 126	G. L. Stevens	Royal Reach, 5, 126	Mashkour, 8, 126	10	2:24.50	188,250
1990	Prized, 4, 126	E. Delahoussaye	Hawkster, 4, 126	Frankly Perfect, 5, 126	6	2:25.20	180,000
1989	Frankly Perfect, 4, 126	E. Delahoussaye	Great Communicator, 6, 126	Payant (Arg), 5, 126	5	2:32.80	152,400
1988	Rivlia, 6, 126	C. J. McCarron	Great Communicator, 5, 126	Swink, 5, 126	7	2:27.20	158,400
1987	Zoffany, 7, 126	E. Delahoussaye	Louis Le Grand, 5, 126	Long Mick (Fr), 6, 126	5	2:25.20	121,200
1986	Dahar, 5, 126	A. O. Solis	Strawberry Road (Aus), 7, 126	Alphabatim, 5, 126	7	2:26.40	148,600
1985	Prince True, 4, 126	C. J. McCarron	Western, 7, 126	Dahar, 4, 126	6	2:25.40	147,300
1984	Interco, 4, 126	P. A. Valenzuela	Gato Del Sol, 5, 126	John Henry, 9, 126	10	2:26.80	127,200
1983	Erins Isle (Ire), 5, 126	L. A. Pincay Jr.	Prince Spellbound, 4, 126	Majesty's Prince, 4, 126	6	2:26.20	120,900
1982	Perrault (GB), 5, 126	L. A. Pincay Jr.	Exploded, 5, 126	John Henry, 7, 126	5	2:24.00	116,200
1981	John Henry, 6, 126	L. A. Pincay Jr.	Obraztsovy, 6, 126	Fiestero (Chi), 6, 126	6	2:25.20	93,900
1980	John Henry, 5, 126	D. G. McHargue	Relaunch, 4, 126	Silver Eagle (Ire), 6, 126	7	**2:23.00**	94,800
1979	Noble Dancer (GB), 7, 126	J. Vasquez	Tiller, 5, 126	Good Lord (NZ), 8, 126	7	2:34.60	95,300
1978	Noble Dancer (GB), 6, 126	S. Cauthen	Properantes, 5, 126	Text, 4, 126	7	2:24.00	64,400
1977	Caucasus, 5, 126	F. Toro	King Pellinore, 5, 126	Top Crowd, 6, 126	7	2:25.60	64,400
1976	Avatar, 4, 126	L. A. Pincay Jr.	‡Top Crowd, 5, 126	Top Command, 5, 126	7	2:24.00	64,300
1975	Trojan Bronze, 4, 126	J. E. Tejeira	Okavango, 5, 126	Montmartre, 6, 126	6	2:29.60	63,500
1974	Astray, 5, 126	J. Vasquez	Big Spruce, 5, 126	Quack, 4, 126	10	2:24.40	67,000
1973	Big Spruce, 4, 126	D. Pierce	*Cicero's Court, 4, 126	*Cougar II, 7, 126	10	2:27.60	66,800

Named for the San Luis Rey Mission; the California mission was named in honor of King and Catholic St. Louis IX of France. Grade 1 1973-'96. San Luis Rey S. 1952-'53, 1973-2000. 7 furlongs 1952. 6 furlongs 1953. 1 mile 1954. Dirt 1952-'54, 1962, 1975. Originally scheduled on turf 1975. Three-year-olds and up 1958-'59. ‡Ga Hai finished second, DQ to fourth, 1976. †Denotes female. California-breds 1952-'54.

San Marcos Stakes

Grade 2 in 2008. Santa Anita Park, four-year-olds and up, 1¼ miles, turf. Held January 19, 2008, with a gross value of $150,000. First held in 1952. First graded in 1973. Stakes record 1:57.92 (2003 Johar).

Year	Winner	Jockey	Second	Third	Strs	Time	1st Purse
2008	Champs Elysees (GB), 5, 115	G. K. Gomez	Rocket Legs, 4, 117	Obrigado (Fr), 5, 115	6	2:00.88	$90,000
2007	One Off (GB), 7, 115	B. Blanc	Notable Guest, 6, 115	Obrigado (Fr), 4, 119	5	2:01.48	90,000
2006	The Tin Man, 8, 115	V. Espinoza	Milk It Mick (GB), 5, 115	Whilly (Ire), 5, 119	11	1:58.39	90,000
2005	Whilly (Ire), 4, 117	F. F. Martinez	Puppeteer (GB), 5, 116	T. H. Approval, 4, 117	6	2:00.68	90,000
2004	Sweet Return (GB), 4, 121	G. L. Stevens	Nothing to Lose, 4, 116	Blue Steller (Ire), 6, 116	9	1:58.82	90,000
2003	Johar, 4, 120	A. O. Solis	The Tin Man, 5, 122	Grammarian, 5, 122	7	**1:57.92**	90,000

Year	Winner	Jockey	Second	Third	Strs	Time	1st Purse
2002	Irish Prize, 6, 122	G. L. Stevens	Continental Red, 6, 116	Cagney (Brz), 5, 119	6	2:01.27	$90,000
2001	Bienamado, 5, 122	C. J. McCarron	Kerrygold (Fr), 5, 116	Northern Quest (Fr), 6, 122	7	2:02.75	90,000
2000	Public Purse, 6, 119	A. O. Solis	Dark Moondancer (GB), 5, 120	The Fly (GB), 6, 114	7	1:59.58	98,280
1999	Brave Act (GB), 5, 120	G. F. Almeida	Ferrari (Ger), 5, 117	Native Desert, 6, 117	7	2:04.25	90,000
1998	Prize Giving (GB), 5, 114	A. O. Solis	Bienvenido (Arg), 5, 115	Martiniquais (Ire), 5, 118	6	2:04.41	97,380
1997	Sandpit (Brz), 8, 123	C. S. Nakatani	River Deep, 6, 116	‡Shanawi (Ire), 5, 112	8	2:00.61	99,000
1996	Urgent Request (Ire), 6, 115	C. W. Antley	Bon Point (GB), 6, 114	Virginia Carnival, 4, 116	6	2:02.26	97,000
1995	River Flyer, 4, 118	C. W. Antley	Silver Wizard, 5, 117	Savinio, 5, 116	7	2:05.61	92,200
1994	Bien Bien, 5, 122	L. A. Pincay Jr.	Explosive Red, 4, 116	Myrakalu (Fr), 6, 113	6	2:00.55	75,850
1993	Star of Cozzene, 5, 120	G. L. Stevens	Kotashaan (Fr), 5, 116	Carnival Baby, 5, 112	7	2:01.71	77,650
1992	Classic Fame, 6, 120	E. Delahoussaye	Fly Till Dawn, 6, 120	French Seventyfive, 5, 115	6	1:58.02	90,600
1991	Fly Till Dawn, 5, 120	L. A. Pincay Jr.	Vaguely Hidden, 6, 115	The Medic, 7, 115	8	1:58.70	97,350
1990	Putting (Fr), 7, 114	C. A. Black	Colway Rally (GB), 6, 115	Live the Dream, 4, 119	13	1:58.20	105,600
1989	Trokhos, 6, 117	L. A. Pincay Jr.	Vallotton (Fr), 4, 117	Roberto's Dancer, 4, 113	8	2:02.00	97,200
1988	Great Communicator, 5, 115	R. Sibille	Schiller, 6, 113	Bello Horizonte (Ire), 5, 113	10	2:02.60	100,400
1987	Zoffany, 7, 123	E. Delahoussaye	Louis Le Grand, 5, 117	Strawberry Road (Aus), 8, 122	8	2:00.80	64,100
1986	Silveyville, 8, 120	C. J. McCarron	Strawberry Road (Aus), 7, 125	Nasib (Ire), 4, 116	7	2:00.80	63,200
1985	Dahar, 4, 121	F. Toro	Scrupules (Ire), 5, 122	Alphabatim, 4, 124	6	2:01.20	61,900
1984	Lucence, 5, 114	P. A. Valenzuela	Ginger Brink (Fr), 4, 117	Sir Pele, 5, 114	11	2:01.80	54,200
1983	Western, 5, 116	C. J. McCarron	Handsome One, 5, 116	Tell Again, 5, 117	2	2:04.00	47,950
1982	Super Moment, 5, 125	L. A. Pincay Jr.	Forlion, 6, 114	Le Duc de Bar, 5, 111	5	2:00.60	45,900
1981	Galaxy Libra (Ire), 5, 116	A. T. Cordero Jr.	Bold Tropic (SAf), 6, 127	Mike Fogarty (Ire), 6, 115	9	2:00.20	40,300
1980	John Henry, 5, 124	D. G. McHargue	El Fantastico, 5, 113	Conmemorativo, 5, 110	5	2:01.60	37,350
1979	Tiller, 5, 126	A. T. Cordero Jr.	Palton (Chi), 6, 121	How Curious, 5, 112	6	1:58.80	37,700
1978	Vigors, 5, 121	D. G. McHargue	Pay Tribute, 6, 122	Jumping Hill, 6, 123	9	1:46.60	33,350
1977	*Royal Derby II, 8, 124	W. Shoemaker	Anne's Pretender, 5, 123	Teddy's Courage, 4, 116	10	1:58.20	34,150
1976	Announcer, 4, 115	F. Toro	Zanthe, 7, 122	Top Crowd, 5, 123	9	1:58.40	32,800
1975	Trojan Bronze, 4, 117	W. Shoemaker	Indefatigable, 5, 115	*El Botija, 5, 114	11	1:59.80	34,550
1974	Triangular, 7, 118	D. Pierce	Big Spruce, 5, 124	Kentuckian, 5, 118	9	2:04.80	33,000
1973	*Tuqui II, 6, 114	L. A. Pincay Jr.	*Soudard, 5, 115	Aggressively, 6, 114	9	2:02.20	27,000

Named for Rancho San Marcos, which was located in Santa Barbara County, California. Grade 3 1973-'92. San Marcos H. 1952-2000. Not held 1970. 1 mile 1952-'53. 1 1/8 miles 1978. Dirt 1952-'53, 1956, 1962, 1969, 1973, 1975, 1978-'83, 1996. Originally scheduled on turf 1973. Three-year-olds and up 1955-'59. ‡Marlin finished third, DQ to fifth, 1997.

San Pasqual Handicap

Grade 2 in 2008. Santa Anita Park, four-year-olds and up, 1 1/16 miles, all weather. Held January 12, 2008, with a gross value of $150,000. First held in 1935. First graded in 1973. Stakes record 1:39.58 (2008 Zappa).

Year	Winner	Jockey	Second	Third	Strs	Time	1st Purse
2008	Zappa, 6, 114	J. Rosario	Well Armed, 5, 114	Heatseeker (Ire), 5, 117	7	**1:39.58**	$90,000
2007	Dixie Meister, 5, 116	D. R. Flores	Armenian Summer, 5, 114	Preachinatthebar, 6, 116	7	1:43.18	90,000
2006	High Limit, 4, 118	P. A. Valenzuela	Buckland Manor, 6, 116	Spellbinder, 5, 115	7	1:43.64	90,000
2005	Congrats, 5, 114	T. Baze	Total Impact (Chi), 7, 120	Sigfreto, 5, 111	5	1:41.97	90,000
2004	Star Cross (Arg), 7, 113	V. Espinoza	Nose The Trade (GB), 6, 115	Olmodavor, 5, 118	7	1:42.22	90,000
2003	Congaree, 5, 121	J. D. Bailey	Kudos, 6, 119	Hot Market, 5, 116	7	1:41.04	90,000
2002	Wooden Phone, 5, 119	D. R. Flores	Euchre, 6, 120	Red Eye, 6, 112	7	1:41.83	120,000
2001	Freedom Crest, 5, 116	G. L. Stevens	Bosque Redondo, 4, 114	Sultry Substitute, 6, 114	8	1:41.94	120,000
2000	Dixie Dot Com, 5, 118	P. A. Valenzuela	Budroyale, 7, 122	Six Below, 5, 116	6	1:40.95	120,000
1999	Silver Charm, 5, 125	G. L. Stevens	Malek (Chi), 6, 119	Crafty Friend, 6, 118	5	1:41.80	120,000
1998	Hal's Pal (GB), 5, 113	B. Blanc	Malek (Chi), 5, 116	Flick (GB), 6, 116	9	1:41.89	120,000
1997	Kingdom Found, 7, 115	G. L. Stevens	Savinio, 7, 117	Eltish, 5, 113	4	1:40.74	122,200
1996	Alphabet Soup, 5, 118	C. W. Antley	Luthier Fever, 5, 115	Cezind, 6, 114	9	1:41.66	130,100
1995	Del Mar Dennis, 5, 118	A. O. Solis	Slew of Damascus, 7, 120	Tossofthecoin, 5, 116	6	1:41.23	116,100
1994	Hill Pass, 5, 113	C. J. McCarron	Best Pal, 6, 122	Lottery Winner, 5, 116	7	1:41.00	87,800
1993	Jovial (GB), 6, 115	M. Walls	‡Marquetry, 6, 118	Provins, 5, 115	7	1:41.94	91,400
1992	Twilight Agenda, 6, 125	K. Desormeaux	Ibero (Arg), 5, 116	Answer Do, 6, 118	5	1:42.32	89,000
1991	Farma Way, 4, 114	G. L. Stevens	Flying Continental, 5, 122	Stylish Stud, 5, 114	6	1:40.90	93,100
1990	Criminal Type, 5, 114	C. J. McCarron	Lively One, 5, 122	Present Value, 6, 121	8	1:42.40	96,300
1989	On the Line, 5, 123	G. L. Stevens	Mark Chip, 6, 114	Stylish Winner, 5, 113	6	1:41.00	93,300
1988	Super Diamond, 8, 125	L. A. Pincay Jr.	Judge Angelucci, 5, 122	He's a Saros, 5, 114	5	1:43.00	92,300
1987	Epidaurus, 5, 116	G. Baze	Ascension, 5, 114	Nostalgia's Star, 5, 120	7	1:42.40	90,800
1986	Precisionist, 5, 126	C. J. McCarron	Bare Minimum, 5, 116	My Mahitony, 6, 116	6	1:41.20	90,000
1985	Hula Blaze, 5, 115	P. A. Valenzuela	Video Kid, 5, 117	Tennessee Rite, 4, 112	11	1:42.00	95,300
1984	Danebo, 5, 120	L. A. Pincay Jr.	Water Bank, 5, 118	Honeyland, 5, 116	6	1:41.80	91,900
1983	Regal Falcon, 5, 115	E. Delahoussaye	Time to Explode, 4, 121	West On Broad, 5, 113	7	1:43.20	63,900
1982	Five Star Flight, 4, 120	L. A. Pincay Jr.	Tahitian King (Ire), 6, 122	King Go Go, 7, 119	8	1:40.80	65,000
1981	Flying Paster, 5, 127	C. J. McCarron	King Go Go, 6, 117	Fiestero (Chi), 6, 113	6	1:40.60	47,150
1980	Valdez, 4, 117	L. A. Pincay Jr.	Prenotion, 5, 117	Balzac, 5, 122	7	1:40.20	46,350
1979	Mr. Redoy, 5, 117	A. T. Cordero Jr.	Life's Hope, 6, 116	Big John Taylor, 5, 115	8	1:42.20	38,900
1978	Ancient Title, 8, 124	D. G. McHargue	Mark's Place, 6, 120	Double Discount, 5, 120	4	1:40.80	30,250
1977	Uniformity, 5, 117	F. Toro	Distant Land, 5, 116	*Pisistrato, 5, 117	8	1:41.00	35,500
1976	Lightning Mandate, 5, 118	S. Hawley	Guards Up, 4, 113	Ga Hai, 5, 116	5	1:48.40	32,250

Racing — Graded Stakes 443

Year	Winner	Jockey	Second	Third	Strs	Time	1st Purse
1975	Okavango, 5, 114	F. Toro	†Tallahto, 5, 118	Cheriepe, 5, 114	12	1:41.40	$38,400
1974	Tri Jet, 5, 121	W. Shoemaker	Forage, 5, 121	†Susan's Girl, 5, 119	10	1:41.40	36,550
1973	Single Agent, 5, 119	J. Lambert	Kennedy Road, 5, 119	Autobiography, 5, 125	6	1:41.80	33,850

Named for El Rancho San Pasqual, which encompassed almost all of what is now the Pasadena, California, area. Not held 1942-'44. 6 furlongs 1935-'36. 7 furlongs 1938. 1 1/8 miles 1939-'41. 1 1/4 miles 1955. Dirt 1935-2007. Three-year-olds 1935-'36. Three-year-olds and up 1937-'53, 1958. ‡Best Pal finished second, DQ to fifth, 1993. †Denotes female.

San Rafael Stakes

Grade 3 in 2008. Santa Anita Park, three-year-olds, 1 mile, all weather. Held January 12, 2008, with a gross value of $150,000. First held in 1975. First graded in 1983. Stakes record 1:33.37 (2008 El Gato Malo).

Year	Winner	Jockey	Second	Third	Strs	Time	1st Purse
2008	El Gato Malo, 3, 119	D. R. Flores	Indian Sun, 3, 116	Massive Drama, 3, 119	6	1:33.37	$90,000
2007	Notional, 3, 119	C. S. Nakatani	Tenfold, 3, 116	Grapelli, 3, 116	7	1:36.48	90,000
2006	Brother Derek, 3, 122	A. O. Solis	Stevie Wonderboy, 3, 122	Wanna Runner, 3, 116	4	1:36.11	90,000
2005	Spanish Chestnut, 3, 116	G. L. Stevens	Iced Out, 3, 115	Texcess, 3, 121	5	1:36.69	90,000
2004	Imperialism, 3, 118	V. Espinoza	Lion Heart, 3, 121	Consecrate, 3, 115	10	1:36.11	120,000
2003	Rojo Toro, 3, 115	J. D. Bailey	Spensive, 3, 118	Crowned Dancer, 3, 118	7	1:35.89	120,000
2002	Came Home, 3, 118	C. J. McCarron	Easy Grades, 3, 116	Werblin, 3, 115	7	1:36.24	120,000
2001	Crafty C. T., 3, 116	E. Delahoussaye	Palmeiro, 3, 117	Early Flyer, 3, 118	9	1:35.79	120,000
2000	War Chant, 3, 116	K. Desormeaux	Archer City Slew, 3, 118	Cocky, 3, 115	6	1:36.45	120,000
1999	Desert Hero, 3, 116	C. S. Nakatani	Prime Timber, 3, 115	Capsized, 3, 115	9	1:36.45	120,000
1998	Orville N Wilbur's, 3, 115	C. S. Nakatani	Souvenir Copy, 3, 121	Futuristic, 3, 115	6	1:35.96	120,000
1997	Funontherun, 3, 115	G. F. Almeida	Inexcessivelygood, 3, 116	Hello (Ire), 3, 121	10	1:36.01	121,800
1996	Honour and Glory, 3, 116	G. L. Stevens	Halo Sunshine, 3, 115	Matty G, 3, 121	8	1:36.45	122,000
1995	Larry the Legend, 3, 118	K. Desormeaux	Fandarel Dancer, 3, 118	Timber Country, 3, 121	5	1:37.61	88,600
1994	Tabasco Cat, 3, 121	P. Day	Powis Castle, 3, 115	Shepherd's Field, 3, 121	5	1:36.39	89,700
1993	Devoted Brass, 3, 115	K. Desormeaux	Union City, 3, 115	Stuka, 3, 118	6	1:35.13	90,000
1992	A.P. Indy, 3, 121	E. Delahoussaye	Treekster, 3, 116	Prince Wild, 3, 118	6	1:35.41	90,300
1991	Dinard, 3, 118	C. J. McCarron	Apollo, 3, 118	Best Pal, 3, 121	5	1:35.90	91,900
1990	Mister Frisky, 3, 115	G. L. Stevens	Tight Spot, 3, 115	Land Rush, 3, 115	7	1:36.60	80,300
1989	Music Merci, 3, 121	G. L. Stevens	Manastash Ridge, 3, 118	Past Ages, 3, 118	5	1:34.80	76,300
1988	What a Diplomat, 3, 115	G. L. Stevens	Flying Victor, 3, 121	Success Express, 3, 121	9	1:38.00	79,350
1987	Masterful Advocate, 3, 122	L. A. Pincay Jr.	Chart the Stars, 3, 116	Hot and Smoggy, 3, 116	7	1:35.80	90,500
1986	Variety Road, 3, 116	C. J. McCarron	Ferdinand, 3, 116	Jetting Home, 3, 116	9	1:35.60	68,300
1985	Smarten Up, 3, 122	R. Q. Meza	Fast Account, 3, 122	Stan's Bower, 3, 118	9	1:36.20	94,500
1984	Precisionist, 3, 120	C. J. McCarron	Fali Time, 3, 122	Commemorate, 3, 118	6	1:35.00	91,680
1983	Desert Wine, 3, 119	C. J. McCarron	Naevus, 3, 114	Balboa Native, 3, 116	7	1:35.60	65,900
1982	Prince Spellbound, 3, 119	M. Castaneda	Muttering, 3, 121	Unpredictable, 3, 119	9	1:34.40	68,200
1981	Johnlee n' Harold, 3, 119	M. Castaneda	Minnesota Chief, 3, 115	A Run, 3, 119	10	1:36.00	51,500
1978	Little Happiness, 4, 116	S. Cauthen	*Merry Lady III, 6, 114	Up to Juliet, 5, 118	7	1:35.40	16,975
1976	Vagabonda, 5, 116	W. Shoemaker	*Bastonera II, 5, 117	Mia Amore, 4, 117	9	1:48.20	16,825
1975	Donna B Quick, 4, 114	W. Shoemaker	In Prosperity, 5, 122	Take Powder, 5, 122	10	1:09.60	11,300

Named for Rancho San Rafael, a 1785 land grant where Burbank, Glendale, and Montrose, California, are now located. Grade 2 1984-'07. Not held 1977, 1979-'80. 6 furlongs 1975. 1 1/8 miles 1976. Dirt 1975, 1977-2007. Turf 1976. Four-year-olds and up 1975-'78. Fillies and mares 1975-'78.

San Simeon Handicap

Grade 3 in 2008. Santa Anita Park, four-year-olds and up, about 6 1/2 furlongs, turf. Held April 19, 2008, with a gross value of $112,400. First held in 1968. First graded in 1973. Stakes record 1:11.46 (2004 Glick).

Year	Winner	Jockey	Second	Third	Strs	Time	1st Purse
2008	Stoneside (Ire), 4, 115	M. A. Pedroza	Night Chapter (GB), 7, 116	Tenga Cat, 5, 114	11	1:12.54	$67,440
2007	Bonfante, 6, 117	A. T. Gryder	Battle Won, 7, 117	Siren Lure, 6, 121	4	1:14.59	63,360
2006	Pure as Gold, 4, 118	P. A. Valenzuela	Saint Buddy, 6, 114	Siren Lure, 5, 122	8	1:12.56	65,640
2005	Shadow of Illinois, 5, 116	M. Guidry	Geronimo (Chi), 6, 117	Golden Arrow, 6, 116	6	1:12.62	64,200
2004	Glick, 8, 117	A. O. Solis	Cayoke (Fr), 7, 116	Summer Service, 4, 117	6	1:11.46	64,380
2003	Speak in Passing, 6, 118	D. R. Flores	Spinelessjellyfish, 7, 115	Rocky Bar, 5, 116	8	1:12.87	82,500
2002	Malabar Gold, 5, 117	C. J. McCarron	Astonished (GB), 6, 117	Nuclear Debate, 7, 118	9	1:11.73	82,425
2001	Lake William, 5, 114	V. Espinoza	Macward, 5, 117	Touch of the Blues (Fr), 4, 116	6	1:12.34	80,175
2000	El Cielo, 6, 117	J. Valdivia Jr.	King Slayer (GB), 5, 116	Scooter Brown, 5, 117	6	1:12.66	79,440
1999	Naninja, 6, 115	C. J. McCarron	Expressionist, 6, 114	Indian Rocket (GB), 5, 119	7	1:13.32	65,220
1998	Labeeb (GB), 6, 120	K. Desormeaux	Surachai, 5, 118	Captain Collins (Ire), 4, 115	11	1:12.94	77,860
1997	Sandtrap, 4, 117	A. O. Solis	‡Daggett Peak, 6, 113	Tychonic (GB), 7, 120	6	1:12.50	96,850
1996	†Ski Dancer, 4, 114	G. L. Stevens	Daggett Peak, 5, 115	Boulderdash Bay, 6, 118	6	1:13.98	64,200
1995	Finder's Fortune, 6, 117	P. A. Valenzuela	Rotsaluck, 4, 117	Pembroke, 5, 117	7	1:13.65	64,550
1994	Rapan Boy (Aus), 6, 114	G. L. Stevens	The Berkeley Man, 4, 115	Artistic Reef (GB), 5, 119	7	1:13.16	63,100
1993	Exemplary Leader, 7, 113	M. A. Pedroza	Prince Ferdinand (GB), 4, 119	Wild Harmony, 4, 117	8	1:13.98	64,300
1992	†Heart of Joy, 5, 119	C. J. McCarron	Regal Groom, 5, 115	Time Gentlemen (GB), 4, 117	10	1:12.94	69,600
1991	Forest Glow, 4, 116	J. A. Garcia	Answer Do, 5, 119	‡Shirkee, 6, 117	9	1:12.50	63,900
1990	Coastal Voyage, 6, 118	A. O. Solis	Patchy Groundfog, 7, 117	Raise a Stanza, 4, 119	4	1:12.20	60,000
1989	Mazilier, 5, 116	P. A. Valenzuela	†Imperial Star (GB), 5, 112	Caballo de Oro, 5, 116	8	1:15.80	48,750

444 Racing — Graded Stakes

Year	Winner	Jockey	Second	Third	Strs	Time	1st Purse
1988	Caballo de Oro, 4, 112	R. Q. Meza	Gallant Sailor, 5, 112	Sylvan Express (Ire), 5, 121	5	1:15.40	$46,700
1987	Bolder Than Bold, 5, 117	G. Baze	Prince Bobby B., 4, 122	†Lichi (Chi), 7, 112	9	1:13.60	49,800
1986	Estate, 7, 114	A. L. Castanon	Will Dancer (Fr), 4, 118	Exclusive Partner, 4, 116	8	1:13.80	52,150
1985	Champagne Bid, 6, 121	R. Sibille	Forzando (GB), 4, 122	Smart and Sharp, 6, 118	8	1:13.00	52,150
1984	Champagne Bid, 5, 121	R. Sibille	Retsina Run, 4, 115	Famous Star (GB), 5, 115	9	1:14.40	53,350
1983	Chinook Pass, 4, 124	L. A. Pincay Jr.	Shanekite, 5, 118	Earthquack, 4, 121	7	1:15.40	39,100
1982	Shagbark, 7, 122	L. A. Pincay Jr.	Shanekite, 4, 118	Belfort (Fr), 5, 116	8	1:13.00	39,850
1981	Syncopate, 6, 119	D. Pierce	Parsec, 4, 116	Matsadoon's Honey, 4, 115	4	1:16.40	31,450
1980	Dragon Command (NZ), 6, 115	E. Delahoussaye	Numa Pompilius, 6, 115	Bywayofchicago, 6, 115	11	1:12.60	29,050
1979	Bywayofchicago, 5, 120	D. G. McHargue	Maheras, 6, 118	Whatsyourpleasure, 6, 117	9	1:21.80	33,850
1978	Maheras, 5, 122	L. A. Pincay Jr.	dh-Bad 'n Big, 4, 119 dh-Yu Wipi, 6, 114		6	1:22.80	25,650
1977	Mark's Place, 5, 122	S. Hawley	Maheras, 4, 124	Painted Wagon, 4, 114	7	1:21.00	26,250
1976	Pay Tribute, 4, 118	L. A. Pincay Jr.	Against the Snow, 6, 118	King Pellinore, 4, 122	6	1:35.20	25,650
1975	Century's Envoy, 4, 121	J. E. Tejeira	First Back, 4, 121	Rocket Review, 4, 120	5	1:22.40	19,700
1974	*Matun, 5, 118	S. Valdez	‡Selecting, 5, 115	Forage, 5, 123	8	1:21.20	21,200
1973	Soft Victory, 5, 115	D. Pierce	Selecting, 4, 115	dh-Andrew Feeney, 4, 116 dh-Goalie, 4, 113	12	1:21.40	23,050

Named for Rancho San Simeon, California, originally attached to the San Miguel Mission. Not graded 1975-'83. 7 furlongs 1968-'75, 1977-'79. 1 mile 1976. 6½ furlongs 1980-'85, 1987-'90, 2007. Dirt 1968-'79, 1981, 1983, 1988, 2007. Originally scheduled on turf 2007. Dead heat for third 1973. Dead heat for second 1978. ‡Forage finished second, DQ to third, 1974. ‡Coastal Voyage finished third, DQ to fourth, 1991. ‡Destiny's Venture finished second, DQ to fourth, 1997. Course record 2004. †Denotes female.

Santa Ana Handicap

Grade 2 in 2008. Santa Anita Park, four-year-olds and up, fillies and mares, 1⅛ miles, turf. Held March 23, 2008, with a gross value of $150,000. First held in 1968. First graded in 1981. Stakes record 1:46.21 (2007 Citronnade).

Year	Winner	Jockey	Second	Third	Strs	Time	1st Purse
2008	Costume (GB), 4, 115	G. K. Gomez	Immortelle (Brz), 5, 115	Lavender Sky, 4, 116	8	1:48.08	$90,000
2007	Citronnade, 4, 117	D. R. Flores	Conveyor's Angel, 5, 116	Memorette, 5, 117	7	1:46.21	90,000
2006	Silver Cup (Ire), 4, 118	V. Espinoza	Argentina (Ire), 4, 116	Beautyandthebeast (GB), 4, 116	8	1:48.13	90,000
2005	Megahertz (GB), 6, 122	A. O. Solis	Katdogwan (GB), 4, 117	Valentine Dancer, 5, 117	7	1:47.95	90,000
2004	‡Katdogwan (GB), 4, 117	M. E. Smith	Fun House, 5, 118	Arabic Song (Ire), 5, 117	7	1:47.36	90,000
2003	Noches De Rosa (Chi), 5, 115	M. E. Smith	Garden in the Rain (Fr), 6, 116	Megahertz (GB), 4, 117	8	1:48.31	90,000
2002	Golden Apples (Ire), 4, 119	G. K. Gomez	Starine (Fr), 5, 122	Astra, 6, 122	9	1:47.05	90,000
2001	Beautiful Noise, 5, 115	C. J. McCarron	High Walden, 4, 114	Matiere Grise (Fr), 4, 113	12	1:47.27	90,000
2000	Spanish Fern, 5, 119	V. Espinoza	Virginie (Brz), 6, 120	Country Garden (GB), 5, 116	7	1:49.30	97,830
1999	See You Soon (Fr), 5, 119	K. Desormeaux	Blending Element (Ire), 6, 116	La Madame (Chi), 4, 116	6	1:49.46	90,000
1998	Fiji (GB), 4, 115	K. Desormeaux	Shake the Yoke (GB), 5, 116	Golden Arches (Fr), 4, 120	6	1:49.85	96,480
1997	Windsharp, 6, 121	E. Delahoussaye	Wheatly Special, 4, 113	Donna Viola (GB), 5, 120	7	1:49.47	97,750
1996	Pharma, 5, 116	C. J. McCarron	Angel in My Heart (Fr), 4, 120	Matiara, 4, 120	5	1:49.14	95,050
1995	Wandesta (GB), 4, 115	C. S. Nakatani	Yearly Tour, 4, 116	Aube Indienne (Fr), 5, 117	7	1:50.18	90.700
1994	Possibly Perfect, 4, 119	K. Desormeaux	Hero's Love, 6, 120	‡Lady Blessington (Fr), 6, 120	5	1:51.05	91,000
1993	Exchange, 5, 120	L. A. Pincay Jr.	Party Cited, 4, 115	Villandry, 5, 116	6	1:46.23	89,700
1992	Gravieres (Fr), 4, 116	G. L. Stevens	Appealing Missy, 5, 117	Explosive Ele, 5, 115	8	1:47.75	94,900
1991	dh-Annual Reunion, 4, 116 dh-Noble and Nice, 5, 113	G. L. Stevens K. Desormeaux		Bequest, 5, 117	8	1:46.70	63,400
1990	Annoconnor, 6, 119	C. A. Black	Royal Touch (Ire), 5, 121	Brown Bess, 8, 123	7	1:47.40	94,540
1989	Maria Jesse (Fr), 4, 116	G. L. Stevens	Fieldy (Ire), 6, 117	Claire Marine (Ire), 4, 115	8	1:47.20	97,100
1988	‡Pen Bal Lady (GB), 4, 118	E. Delahoussaye	Fitzwilliam Place (Ire), 4, 119	Galunpe (Ire), 5, 119	10	1:47.20	94,900
1987	Reloy, 4, 116	W. Shoemaker	Northern Aspen, 5, 119	North Sider, 5, 120	7	1:48.00	91,300
1986	Videogenic, 4, 120	R. G. Davis	Capichi, 6, 118	Water Crystals, 5, 114	6	1:48.40	62,800
1985	Estrapade, 5, 123	F. Toro	Fact Finder, 6, 119	Air Distingue, 5, 116	10	1:47.00	67,100
1984	Avigaition, 4, 118	W. Shoemaker	Pride of Rosewood (NZ), 6, 116	L'Attrayante (Fr), 4, 122	9	1:48.40	93,600
1983	Happy Bride (Ire), 5, 116	C. J. McCarron	Avigaition, 4, 121	Miss Huntington, 6, 115	6	1:47.80	63,400
1982	Track Robbery, 6, 123	E. Delahoussaye	Manzanera (Arg), 6, 117	Ack's Secret, 6, 123	8	1:47.20	65,100
1981	Queen to Conquer, 5, 121	L. A. Pincay Jr.	Track Robbery, 5, 119	Ack's Secret, 5, 123	7	1:48.00	46,900
1980	The Very One, 5, 117	C. Cooke	Sisterhood, 5, 118	Mairzy Doates, 4, 116	8	1:48.40	37,300
1979	Waya (Fr), 5, 127	A. T. Cordero Jr.	Amazer, 4, 123	Shua, 4, 115	10	1:48.20	38,450
1978	Kittyluck, 5, 115	F. Toro	Innuendo, 4, 111	‡Belle o' Reason, 5, 120	9	1:53.00	26,750
1977	Up to Juliet, 4, 120	L. A. Pincay Jr.	Quintas Fannie, 4, 114	Belle o' Reason, 4, 115	11	1:48.20	27,550
1976	Sun Festival, 7, 116	D. Pierce	Quaze Quilt, 5, 122	Cut Class, 4, 117	9	1:48.40	25,450
1975	Move Abroad, 4, 115	S. Hawley	Joli Vert, 4, 114	Bold Ballet, 4, 122	7	1:51.40	19,500
1974	Belle Marie, 4, 118	W. Shoemaker	Grasping, 5, 114	Flying Fur, 5, 115	12	1:46.60	26,800
1973	Bird Boots, 4, 115	E. Belmonte	Best Go, 5, 119	Resolutely, 6, 115	9	1:47.00	15,600
	Minstrel Miss, 6, 119	D. Pierce	*Rich Return II, 6, 118	Hill Circus, 5, 124	8	1:46.80	15,300

Named for the Rancho Santa Ana, located in present-day Ventura County, California. Grade 3 1981. Grade 1 1984-'96. 1¹⁄₁₆ miles 1971. Dirt 1981-'83, 1986. Two divisions 1973. Dead heat for first 1991. ‡Ida Delia finished third, DQ to fifth, 1978. ‡Fitzwilliam Place (GB) finished first, DQ to second, 1988. ‡Waitryst (NZ) finished third, DQ to seventh, 1994. ‡Megahertz (GB) finished first, DQ to seventh, 2004. Nonwinners of a race worth $12,500 to the winner 1973.

Santa Anita Derby

Grade 1 in 2008. Santa Anita Park, three-year-olds, 1⅛ miles, all weather. Held April 5, 2008, with a gross value of $750,000. First held in 1935. First graded in 1973. Stakes record 1:47 (1965 Lucky Debonair; 1973 Sham; 1998 Indian Charlie).

Year	Winner	Jockey	Second	Third	Strs	Time	1st Purse
2008	Colonel John, 3, 122	C. S. Nakatani	Bob Black Jack, 3, 122	Coast Guard, 3, 122	11	1:48.16	$450,000
2007	Tiago, 3, 122	M. E. Smith	King of the Roxy, 3, 122	Sam P., 3, 122	10	1:49.51	450,000
2006	Brother Derek, 3, 122	A. O. Solis	Point Determined, 3, 122	A. P. Warrior, 3, 122	5	1:48.00	450,000
2005	Buzzards Bay, 3, 122	M. Guidry	General John B, 3, 122	Wilko, 3, 122	11	1:49.18	450,000
2004	Castledale (Ire), 3, 122	J. Valdivia Jr.	‡Imperialism, 3, 122	Rock Hard Ten, 3, 122	7	1:49.24	450,000
2003	Buddy Gil, 3, 122	G. L. Stevens	Indian Express, 3, 122	Kafwain, 3, 122	9	1:49.36	450,000
2002	Came Home, 3, 122	C. J. McCarron	Easy Grades, 3, 122	Lusty Latin, 3, 122	8	1:50.02	450,000
2001	Point Given, 3, 122	G. L. Stevens	Crafty C. T., 3, 122	I Love Silver, 3, 122	6	1:47.77	450,000
2000	The Deputy (Ire), 3, 120	C. J. McCarron	War Chant, 3, 120	Captain Steve, 3, 120	6	1:49.08	600,000
1999	General Challenge, 3, 120	A. L. Solis	Prime Timber, 3, 120	Desert Hero, 3, 120	8	1:48.92	450,000
1998	Indian Charlie, 3, 120	G. L. Stevens	Real Quiet, 3, 120	Artax, 3, 120	7	**1:47.00**	450,000
1997	Free House, 3, 120	K. Desormeaux	Silver Charm, 3, 120	Hello (Ire), 3, 120	10	1:47.60	450,000
1996	Cavonnier, 3, 120	C. J. McCarron	‡Honour and Glory, 3, 120	Corker, 3, 120	8	1:48.81	600,000
1995	Larry the Legend, 3, 122	G. L. Stevens	Afternoon Deelites, 3, 122	Jumron (GB), 3, 122	8	1:47.99	385,000
1994	Brocco, 3, 122	G. L. Stevens	Tabasco Cat, 3, 122	Strodes Creek, 3, 122	6	1:48.33	275,000
1993	Personal Hope, 3, 122	G. L. Stevens	Union City, 3, 122	†Eliza, 3, 117	7	1:49.03	275,000
1992	A.P. Indy, 3, 122	E. Delahoussaye	Bertrando, 3, 122	Casual Lies, 3, 122	7	1:49.25	275,000
1991	Dinard, 3, 122	C. J. McCarron	Best Pal, 3, 122	Sea Cadet, 3, 122	9	1:48.10	275,000
1990	Mister Frisky, 3, 122	G. L. Stevens	Video Ranger, 3, 122	Warcraft, 3, 122	8	1:49.00	275,000
1989	Sunday Silence, 3, 122	P. A. Valenzuela	Flying Continental, 3, 122	Music Merci, 3, 122	7	1:47.60	275,000
1988	†Winning Colors, 3, 117	G. L. Stevens	Lively One, 3, 122	Mi Preferido, 3, 122	9	1:47.80	275,000
1987	Temperate Sil, 3, 122	W. Shoemaker	Masterful Advocate, 3, 122	Something Lucky, 3, 122	6	1:49.00	278,250
1986	Snow Chief, 3, 122	A. O. Solis	Icy Groom, 3, 122	Ferdinand, 3, 122	7	1:48.60	275,000
1985	Skywalker, 3, 122	L. A. Pincay Jr.	Fast Account, 3, 122	Nostalgia's Star, 3, 122	9	1:48.40	219,500
1984	Mighty Adversary, 3, 120	E. Delahoussaye	Precisionist, 3, 122	Prince True, 3, 120	8	1:49.00	189,700
1983	Marfa, 3, 120	J. Velasquez	My Habitony, 3, 120	Naevus, 3, 120	10	1:49.40	198,000
1982	Muttering, 3, 120	L. A. Pincay Jr.	Prince Spellbound, 3, 120	Journey At Sea, 3, 120	9	1:47.60	188,800
1981	Splendid Spruce, 3, 120	D. G. McHargue	Johnlee n' Harold, 3, 120	Hoedown's Day, 3, 120	13	1:49.00	180,600
1980	Codex, 3, 120	P. A. Valenzuela	Rumbo, 3, 120	Bic's Gold, 3, 120	9	1:47.60	117,200
1979	Flying Paster, 3, 120	D. Pierce	Beau's Eagle, 3, 120	Switch Partners, 3, 120	10	1:48.00	124,900
1978	Affirmed, 3, 120	L. A. Pincay Jr.	Balzac, 3, 120	Think Snow, 3, 120	12	1:48.00	127,300
1977	*Habitony, 3, 120	W. Shoemaker	For The Moment, 3, 120	Steve's Friend, 3, 120	15	1:48.20	131,000
1976	An Act, 3, 120	L. A. Pincay Jr.	Double Discount, 3, 120	Life's Hope, 3, 120	9	1:48.00	97,700
1975	Avatar, 3, 120	J. E. Tejeira	Rock of Ages, 3, 120	Diabolo, 3, 120	8	1:47.60	82,900
1974	Destroyer, 3, 120	I. Valenzuela	Aloha Mood, 3, 120	Agitate, 3, 120	8	1:48.40	85,200
1973	Sham, 3, 120	L. A. Pincay Jr.	Linda's Chief, 3, 120	Out of the East, 3, 120	8	**1:47.00**	79,400

The race and the track are both named in honor of Rancho Santa Anita, the name of the land when it was purchased by E. J. "Lucky" Baldwin. Not held 1942-'44. 1¹⁄₁₆ miles 1935-'37. 1¼ miles 1947. Dirt 1935-2007. ‡Alyrob finished second, DQ to eighth, 1996. ‡Rock Hard Ten finished second, DQ to third, 2004. †Denotes female.

Santa Anita Handicap

Grade 1 in 2008. Santa Anita Park, four-year-olds and up, 1¼ miles, all weather. Held March 1, 2008, with a gross value of $1,000,000. First held in 1935. First graded in 1973. Stakes record 1:58.60 (1979 Affirmed).

Year	Winner	Jockey	Second	Third	Strs	Time	1st Purse
2008	Heatseeker (Ire), 5, 116	R. Bejarano	Go Between, 5, 118	Champs Elysees (GB), 5, 117	14	2:00.42	$600,000
2007	Lava Man, 6, 124	C. S. Nakatani	Molengao (Brz), 6, 116	Boboman, 6, 116	8	2:02.11	600,000
2006	Lava Man, 5, 120	C. S. Nakatani	Magnum (Arg), 5, 113	Wilko, 4, 115	9	2:00.57	600,000
2005	Rock Hard Ten, 4, 119	G. L. Stevens	Congrats, 5, 116	Borrego, 4, 115	11	2:01.20	600,000
2004	Southern Image, 4, 118	V. Espinoza	†Island Fashion, 4, 115	Saint Buddy, 4, 111	8	2:01.64	600,000
2003	Milwaukee Brew, 6, 119	E. S. Prado	Congaree, 5, 124	Kudos, 6, 117	6	1:59.80	600,000
2002	Milwaukee Brew, 5, 115	K. Desormeaux	Western Pride, 4, 116	Kudos, 5, 116	14	2:01.02	600,000
2001	Tiznow, 4, 122	C. J. McCarron	Wooden Phone, 4, 117	Tribunal, 4, 116	12	2:01.55	600,000
2000	General Challenge, 4, 121	C. S. Nakatani	Budroyale, 7, 122	Puerto Madero (Chi), 6, 118	8	2:01.49	600,000
1999	Free House, 5, 118	C. J. McCarron	Event of the Year, 4, 119	Silver Charm, 5, 124	6	2:00.67	600,000
1998	Malek (Chi), 5, 115	A. O. Solis	Bagshot, 4, 113	Don't Blame Rio, 5, 117	4	2:02.26	600,000
1997	Siphon (Brz), 6, 120	D. R. Flores	Sandpit (Brz), 8, 121	Gentlemen (Arg), 5, 123	11	2:00.23	600,000
1996	Mr Purple, 4, 116	E. Delahoussaye	Luthier Fever, 5, 114	Just Java, 5, 114	11	2:02.04	600,000
1995	Urgent Request (Ire), 5, 120	G. L. Stevens	Best Pal, 7, 122	Dare and Go, 4, 120	10	1:59.25	550,000
1994	‡Stuka, 4, 115	C. W. Antley	Bien Bien, 5, 120	Myrakalu (Fr), 6, 114	8	2:00.17	550,000
1993	Sir Beaufort, 6, 119	P. A. Valenzuela	Star Recruit, 4, 117	Major Impact, 4, 114	11	2:00.55	550,000
1992	Best Pal, 4, 124	K. Desormeaux	Twilight Agenda, 6, 124	Defensive Play, 5, 115	7	1:59.08	550,000
1991	Farma Way, 4, 120	G. L. Stevens	Festin (Arg), 5, 115	Pleasant Tap, 4, 115	10	2:00.30	550,000
1990	Ruhlmann, 5, 121	G. L. Stevens	Criminal Type, 5, 119	Flying Continental, 4, 121	10	2:01.20	550,000
1989	Martial Law, 4, 113	M. A. Pedroza	Triteamtri, 4, 116	Stylish Winner, 5, 113	11	1:58.80	550,000
1988	Alysheba, 4, 126	C. J. McCarron	Ferdinand, 5, 127	Super Diamond, 8, 124	4	1:59.80	550,000
1987	Broad Brush, 4, 122	A. T. Cordero Jr.	Ferdinand, 4, 125	Hopeful Word, 6, 117	9	2:00.60	550,000
1986	Greinton (GB), 5, 122	L. A. Pincay Jr.	Herat, 4, 112	Hatim, 5, 118	13	2:00.00	689,500
1985	Lord At War (Arg), 5, 125	W. Shoemaker	Greinton (GB), 4, 120	Gate Dancer, 4, 125	7	2:00.60	275,600

446 Racing — Graded Stakes

Year	Winner	Jockey	Second	Third	Strs	Time	1st Purse
1984	Interco, 4, 121	P. A. Valenzuela	Journey At Sea, 5, 117	Gato Del Sol, 5, 117	12	2:00.60	$298,650
1983	Bates Motel, 4, 118	T. Lipham	It's the One, 5, 123	Wavering Monarch, 4, 121	17	1:59.60	317,350
1982	‡John Henry, 7, 130	W. Shoemaker	Perrault (GB), 5, 126	It's the One, 4, 120	11	1:59.00	318,800
1981	John Henry, 6, 128	L. A. Pincay Jr.	King Go Go, 6, 117	Exploded, 4, 115	11	1:59.40	238,150
1980	Spectacular Bid, 4, 130	W. Shoemaker	Flying Paster, 4, 123	Beau's Eagle, 4, 122	5	2:00.60	190,000
1979	Affirmed, 4, 128	L. A. Pincay Jr.	Tiller, 5, 127	dh-Exceller, 6, 127	8	**1:58.60**	192,800
				dh-Painted Wagon, 6, 115			
1978	Vigors, 5, 127	D. G. McHargue	Mr. Redoy, 4, 120	Jumping Hill, 6, 115	10	2:01.20	180,000
1977	Crystal Water, 4, 122	L. A. Pincay Jr.	Faliraki (Ire), 4, 114	King Pellinore, 5, 130	13	1:59.20	173,550
1976	Royal Glint, 6, 124	J. E. Tejeira	Ancient Title, 6, 124	Lightning Mandate, 5, 120	15	2:00.40	155,900
1975	Stardust Mel, 4, 123	W. Shoemaker	Out of the East, 5, 112	Okavango, 5, 116	8	2:06.40	105,000
1974	Prince Dantan, 4, 119	R. Turcotte	Ancient Title, 4, 125	Big Spruce, 5, 117	11	2:03.60	105,000
1973	*Cougar II, 7, 126	L. A. Pincay Jr.	Kennedy Road, 5, 119	Cabin, 5, 110	10	2:00.00	105,000

The race and the track are both named in honor of Rancho Santa Anita, the name of the land when it was purchased by E. J. "Lucky" Baldwin. Not held 1942-'44. Dirt 1935-2007. Three-year-olds and up 1935-'68. Dead heat for third 1979. ‡Perrault (GB) finished first, DQ to second, 1982. ‡The Wicked North finished first, DQ to fourth, 1994. Track record 1940, 2008. †Denotes female.

Santa Anita Oaks

Grade 1 in 2008. Santa Anita Park, three-year-olds, fillies, 1 1/16 miles, all weather. Held March 8, 2008, with a gross value of $300,000. First held in 1935. First graded in 1973. Stakes record 1:41.20 (1980 Bold 'n Determined).

Year	Winner	Jockey	Second	Third	Strs	Time	1st Purse
2008	Ariege, 3, 122	C. S. Nakatani	Golden Doc A, 3, 122	Final Fling, 3, 122	9	1:42.73	$180,000
2007	Rags to Riches, 3, 122	G. K. Gomez	Silver Swallow, 3, 122	Cash Included, 3, 122	5	1:42.84	180,000
2006	Balance, 3, 122	V. Espinoza	Quiet Kim, 3, 122	Wild Fit, 3, 122	7	1:42.99	180,000
2005	Sweet Catomine, 3, 121	C. S. Nakatani	Memorette, 3, 121	She Sings, 3, 121	7	1:44.44	180,000
2004	Silent Sighs, 3, 117	D. R. Flores	Halfbridled, 3, 117	A. P. Adventure, 3, 117	7	1:42.84	180,000
2003	Composure, 3, 117	J. D. Bailey	Elloluv, 3, 117	Go for Glamour, 3, 117	5	1:43.34	180,000
2002	You, 3, 117	J. D. Bailey	Habibti, 3, 117	Ile de France, 3, 117	9	1:42.70	180,000
2001	Golden Ballet, 3, 117	C. J. McCarron	Flute, 3, 117	Affluent, 3, 117	8	1:41.83	180,000
2000	Surfside, 3, 117	P. Day	Kumari Continent, 3, 117	Classy Cara, 3, 117	5	1:44.03	180,000
1999	Excellent Meeting, 3, 117	K. Desormeaux	Tout Charmant, 3, 117	Gleefully, 3, 117	6	1:43.26	150,000
1998	Hedonist, 3, 117	K. Desormeaux	Keeper Hill, 3, 117	Nijinsky's Passion, 3, 117	7	1:44.14	150,000
1997	Sharp Cat, 3, 117	C. S. Nakatani	Queen of Money, 3, 117	Double Park (Fr), 3, 117	5	1:42.22	128,800
1996	Antespend, 3, 117	C. W. Antley	Cara Rafaela, 3, 117	Hidden Lake, 3, 117	5	1:43.04	128,800
1995	Serena's Song, 3, 117	C. S. Nakatani	Urbane, 3, 117	Mari's Sheba, 3, 117	5	1:42.71	121,600
1994	Lakeway, 3, 117	K. Desormeaux	Dianes Halo, 3, 117	Flying in the Lane, 3, 117	6	1:41.66	122,800
1993	Eliza, 3, 117	P. A. Valenzuela	Stalcreek, 3, 117	Dance for Vanny, 3, 117	8	1:42.97	129,200
1992	Golden Treat, 3, 117	K. Desormeaux	Magical Maiden, 3, 117	Queens Court Queen, 3, 117	8	1:43.20	129,300
1991	Lite Light, 3, 117	C. S. Nakatani	Garden Gal, 3, 117	Ifyoucouldseemenow, 3, 117	5	1:42.50	122,100
1990	Hail Atlantis, 3, 117	G. L. Stevens	Bright Candles, 3, 117	Fit to Scout, 3, 117	8	1:43.00	122,800
1989	Imaginary Lady, 3, 117	G. L. Stevens	Some Romance, 3, 117	Kool Arrival, 3, 117	7	1:43.40	125,400
1988	Winning Colors, 3, 117	G. L. Stevens	Jeanne Jones, 3, 117	Goodbye Halo, 3, 117	4	1:42.00	89,900
1987	Timely Assertion, 3, 117	G. L. Stevens	Buryyourbelief, 3, 117	Very Subtle, 3, 117	7	1:43.60	95,100
1986	Hidden Light, 3, 117	W. Shoemaker	Twilight Ridge, 3, 117	An Empress, 3, 117	6	1:42.40	120,200
1985	Fran's Valentine, 3, 117	P. A. Valenzuela	Rascal Lass, 3, 117	Wising Up, 3, 117	7	1:42.40	122,100
1984	Althea, 3, 117	L. A. Pincay Jr.	Personable Lady, 3, 115	Life's Magic, 3, 115	6	1:43.60	118,500
1983	Fabulous Notion, 3, 115	D. Pierce	Capichi, 3, 115	O'Happy Day, 3, 115	6	1:43.80	93,900
1982	Blush With Pride, 3, 115	W. Shoemaker	Skillful Joy, 3, 115	Carry a Tune, 3, 115	10	1:45.80	100,400
1981	Nell's Briquette, 3, 115	W. Shoemaker	Bee a Scout, 3, 115	Ice Princess, 3, 115	8	1:42.80	82,550
1980	Bold 'n Determined, 3, 115	E. Delahoussaye	Street Ballet, 3, 115	Table Hands, 3, 115	7	**1:41.20**	67,100
1979	Caline, 3, 115	W. Shoemaker	Terlingua, 3, 115	It's in the Air, 3, 115	8	1:41.60	69,000
1978	Grenzen, 3, 115	D. G. McHargue	Equanimity, 3, 115	Mashteen, 3, 115	7	1:43.80	47,800
1977	Sound of Summer, 3, 115	F. Toro	Wavy Waves, 3, 115	Lady T. V., 3, 115	9	1:42.20	33,200
1976	Girl in Love, 3, 115	F. Toro	I'm a Charmer, 3, 115	Queen to Be, 3, 115	8	1:43.20	32,700
1975	Sarsar, 3, 115	W. Shoemaker	Double You Lou, 3, 115	Fascinating Girl, 3, 115	8	1:42.80	33,100
1974	Miss Musket, 3, 115	W. Shoemaker	Out to Lunch, 3, 115	Special Team, 3, 115	7	1:47.00	32,800
1973	Belle Marie, 3, 115	L. A. Pincay Jr.	Tallahto, 3, 115	Waltz Fan, 3, 115	6	1:41.80	31,800

The race and the track are both named in honor of Rancho Santa Anita, the name of the land when it was purchased by E. J. "Lucky" Baldwin. Formerly named for the community of Santa Susana, California. Santa Susana S. 1951-'85. Grade 2 1973-'78. Not held 1936, 1942-'44, 1955. 3 furlongs 1935. 6 furlongs 1937-'38, 1946. 7 furlongs 1939-'45, 1947-'51, 1956. 1 mile 1954, '57. Dirt 1935-2007. Two-year-olds 1935.

Santa Barbara Handicap

Grade 2 in 2008. Santa Anita Park, four-year-olds and up, fillies and mares, 1 1/4 miles, turf. Held April 19, 2008, with a gross value of $200,000. First held in 1935. First graded in 1973. Stakes record 1:57.50 (1991 Bequest).

Year	Winner	Jockey	Second	Third	Strs	Time	1st Purse
2008	Foxysox (GB), 5, 116	V. Espinoza	Black Mamba (NZ), 5, 114	I Can See, 5, 113	7	2:00.45	$120,000
2007	Naughty Rafaela (Brz), 5, 115	D. R. Flores	Mabadi, 4, 115	Sweet Belle, 4, 113	7	1:48.12	120,000
2006	Sharp Lisa, 4, 118	C. S. Nakatani	Eternal Melody (NZ), 6, 114	Cissy (Arg), 6, 114	6	2:02.17	120,000
2005	Megahertz (GB), 6, 123	A. O. Solis	Nadeszhda (GB), 5, 114	Hoh Buzzard (Ire), 5, 117	7	1:59.76	120,000
2004	Megahertz (GB), 5, 121	A. O. Solis	Noches De Rosa (Chi), 6, 116	Mandela (Ger), 4, 111	5	2:00.71	120,000

Racing — Graded Stakes 447

Year	Winner	Jockey	Second	Third	Strs	Time	1st Purse
2003	Megahertz (GB), 4, 117	A. O. Solis	Trekking, 4, 111	Noches De Rosa (Chi), 5, 117	5	2:00.08	$150,000
2002	Astra, 6, 121	K. Desormeaux	Golden Apples (Ire), 4, 121	Polaire (Ire), 6, 115	6	2:01.48	150,000
2001	Astra, 5, 118	K. Desormeaux	Beautiful Noise, 5, 116	Uncharted Haven (GB), 4, 116	7	2:01.33	150,000
2000	Caffe Latte (Ire), 4, 116	C. S. Nakatani	Happyanunoit (NZ), 5, 121	Country Garden (GB), 5, 116	6	2:00.51	150,000
1999	Tranquility Lake, 4, 116	E. Delahoussaye	Virginie (Brz), 5, 118	Midnight Line, 4, 118	7	2:01.06	150,000
1998	Fiji (GB), 4, 119	K. Desormeaux	Pomona (GB), 5, 115	Ecoute, 5, 114	5	2:00.35	150,000
1997	Donna Viola (GB), 5, 120	G. L. Stevens	Fanjica (Ire), 5, 114	Windsharp, 6, 122	8	1:59.85	197,200
1996	Auriette (Ire), 4, 116	K. Desormeaux	Angel in My Heart (Fr), 4, 119	Wandesta (GB), 5, 121	5	2:02.10	190,900
1995	Wandesta (GB), 4, 118	C. S. Nakatani	Yearly Tour, 4, 116	Morgana, 4, 116	7	2:01.77	126,400
1994	Possibly Perfect, 4, 121	K. Desormeaux	Pracer, 4, 115	Waitryst (NZ), 5, 114	5	2:00.56	122,800
1993	Exchange, 5, 121	L. A. Pincay Jr.	Trishyde, 4, 120	Revasser, 4, 118	4	2:02.26	120,400
1992	Kostroma (Ire), 6, 121	K. Desormeaux	Miss Alleged, 5, 124	Free At Last (GB), 5, 117	6	1:59.63	152,760
1991	Bequest, 5, 117	E. Delahoussaye	Noble and Nice, 5, 114	Annual Reunion, 4, 117	6	1:57.50	126,400
1990	Brown Bess, 8, 123	J. L. Kaenel	Royal Touch (Ire), 5, 121	Double Wedge, 5, 111	5	1:58.40	122,000
1989	No Review, 4, 116	E. Delahoussaye	Galunpe (Ire), 6, 117	Annoconnor, 5, 121	8	2:02.60	128,800
1988	Pen Bal Lady (GB), 4, 119	E. Delahoussaye	Carotene, 5, 121	Galunpe (GB), 5, 119	8	1:59.60	95,800
1987	Reloy, 4, 120	W. Shoemaker	Northern Aspen, 5, 119	Ivor's Image, 4, 119	9	2:00.00	97,600
1986	Mountain Bear (GB), 5, 119	C. J. McCarron	Estrapade, 6, 124	Royal Regatta (NZ), 7, 116	8	2:01.00	119,300
1985	Fact Finder, 6, 118	G. L. Stevens	Love Smitten, 4, 117	Salt Spring (Arg), 6, 114	6	2:01.60	116,600
1984	Comedy Act, 5, 116	C. J. McCarron	L'Attrayante (Fr), 4, 122	Lido Isle, 4, 114	10	2:00.40	121,200
1983	Avigaition, 4, 121	E. Delahoussaye	Happy Bride (Ire), 5, 120	Comedy Act, 4, 116	8	1:59.80	78,650
1982	Ack's Secret, 6, 122	L. A. Pincay Jr.	Landresse (Fr), 4, 116	Plenty O'Toole, 5, 114	8	2:00.60	78,550
1981	The Very One, 6, 122	J. Velasquez	Mairzy Doates, 5, 117	Ack's Secret, 5, 121	9	2:01.20	65,900
1980	Sisterhood, 5, 114	L. A. Pincay Jr.	Petron's Love, 5, 114	Relaxing, 4, 118	10	2:00.40	67,600
1979	Waya (Fr), 5, 131	A. T. Cordero Jr.	Petron's Love, 4, 117	Island Kiss, 4, 111	8	2:01.00	49,350
1978	Kittyluck, 5, 116	L. A. Pincay Jr.	Countess Fager, 4, 117	Sensational, 4, 120	9	2:00.60	40,400
1977	Desiree, 4, 110	V. Centeno	Swingtime, 5, 120	Charger's Star, 7, 113	6	2:02.60	38,100
1976	*Stravina, 5, 109	W. Shoemaker	Katonka, 4, 122	*Tizna, 7, 127	7	1:59.60	38,600
1975	Gay Style, 5, 125	W. Shoemaker	Move Abroad, 4, 113	*La Zanzara, 5, 117	6	2:01.40	31,600
1974	Tallahto, 4, 118	L. A. Pincay Jr.	*La Zanzara, 4, 120	*Tizna, 5, 122	8	1:59.20	39,600
1973	Susan's Girl, 4, 129	L. A. Pincay Jr.	Veiled Desire, 4, 110	Gray Mirage, 4, 112	5	2:03.60	37,600

Named for Santa Barbara, California, where an 1841 tax was the first on racing wagers. Grade 1 1973-'95. Not held 1939-'40, 1942-'45, 1947-'51, 1959-'61. 3 furlongs 1935-'41. 7 furlongs 1946-'52. 6 furlongs 1953-'54, 1958. 1 1/16 miles 1955-'57. 1 1/8 miles 2007. About 1 1/4 miles 1968. Dirt 1935-'58, 1973, 1977, 1982. Originally scheduled on turf 1973. Two-year-olds 1937-'41. Three-year-olds 1952-'54. Three-year-olds and up 1955-'65. California-breds 1935-'54.

Santa Margarita Invitational Handicap

Grade 1 in 2008. Santa Anita Park, four-year-olds and up, fillies and mares, 1 1/8 miles, all weather. Held March 9, 2008, with a gross value of $300,000. First held in 1935. First graded in 1973. Stakes record 1:47 (1954 Cerise Reine; 1986 Lady's Secret).

Year	Winner	Jockey	Second	Third	Strs	Time	1st Purse
2008	Nashoba's Key, 5, 122	G. K. Gomez	Dawn After Dawn, 4, 116	Double Trouble (Brz), 5, 117	5	1:48.82	$180,000
2007	Balance, 4, 120	V. Espinoza	Ermine, 4, 115	River Savage (Brz), 5, 113	7	1:49.25	180,000
2006	Healthy Addiction, 5, 116	J. K. Court	Dream of Summer, 7, 120	Seafree, 4, 115	8	1:48.18	180,000
2005	Tarlow, 4, 117	P. A. Valenzuela	Dream of Summer, 6, 116	Miss Loren (Arg), 7, 118	9	1:49.41	180,000
2004	Adoration, 5, 118	M. E. Smith	Star Parade (Arg), 5, 115	Bare Necessities, 5, 118	8	1:48.85	180,000
2003	Starrer, 5, 121	P. A. Valenzuela	Sightseek, 4, 116	Bella Bellucci, 4, 116	5	1:48.20	180,000
2002	Azeri, 4, 115	M. E. Smith	Spain, 5, 118	Printemps (Chi), 5, 116	7	1:49.01	180,000
2001	Lazy Slusan, 6, 116	D. R. Flores	Spain, 4, 122	Critikola (Arg), 6, 116	7	1:48.59	180,000
2000	Riboletta (Brz), 5, 115	C. S. Nakatani	Bordelaise (Arg), 5, 114	Snowberg, 5, 114	5	1:50.40	180,000
1999	Manistique, 4, 122	G. L. Stevens	Magical Allure, 4, 118	India Divina (Chi), 5, 116	4	1:48.31	180,000
1998	Toda Una Dama (Arg), 5, 114	G. F. Almeida	Exotic Wood, 6, 123	Praviana (Chi), 4, 114	10	1:48.87	180,000
1997	Jewel Princess, 5, 125	C. S. Nakatani	Top Rung, 6, 116	Hidden Lake, 4, 114	6	1:49.30	180,000
1996	Twice the Vice, 5, 117	C. J. McCarron	Sleep Easy, 4, 115	Jewel Princess, 4, 119	8	1:49.53	180,000
1995	Queens Court Queen, 6, 120	C. S. Nakatani	Paseana (Arg), 8, 123	Klassy Kim, 4, 116	5	1:48.81	180,000
1994	Paseana (Arg), 7, 123	C. J. McCarron	Kalita Melody (GB), 6, 117	Stalcreek, 4, 119	9	1:49.12	180,000
1993	Southern Truce, 5, 115	C. S. Nakatani	Paseana (Arg), 6, 124	Guiza, 6, 114	9	1:49.46	180,000
1992	Paseana (Arg), 5, 122	C. J. McCarron	Laramie Moon (Arg), 5, 116	Colour Chart, 5, 118	8	1:47.48	180,000
1991	Little Brianne, 6, 119	J. A. Garcia	Bayakoa (Arg), 7, 126	A Wild Ride, 4, 119	7	1:48.50	180,000
1990	Bayakoa (Arg), 6, 127	C. J. McCarron	Gorgeous, 4, 125	Luthier's Launch, 4, 113	4	1:48.40	180,000
1989	Bayakoa (Arg), 5, 118	L. A. Pincay Jr.	Goodbye Halo, 4, 125	No Review, 4, 117	7	1:48.40	180,000
1988	Flying Julia, 5, 114	F. Olivares	Hollywood Glitter, 4, 118	Clabber Girl, 5, 117	10	1:50.40	180,000
1987	North Sider, 5, 117	A. T. Cordero Jr.	Winter Treasure, 4, 115	Frau Altiva (Arg), 5, 117	12	1:48.80	180,000
1986	Lady's Secret, 4, 125	J. Velasquez	Johnica, 5, 120	Dontstop Themusic, 6, 122	9	1:47.00	180,000
1985	Lovlier Linda, 5, 119	C. J. McCarron	Mitterand, 5, 123	Percipient, 4, 116	8	1:48.00	180,000
1984	Adored, 4, 114	F. Toro	High Haven, 5, 118	Weekend Surprise, 4, 114	11	1:48.60	150,000
1983	Marimbula (Chi), 5, 119	S. Hawley	Avigaition, 4, 120	Sintrillium, 5, 114	11	1:48.20	150,000
1982	Ack's Secret, 6, 118	L. A. Pincay Jr.	Track Robbery, 6, 124	Past Forgetting, 4, 122	10	1:47.60	150,000
1981	Princess Karenda, 4, 118	L. A. Pincay Jr.	Glorious Song, 5, 130	Ack's Secret, 5, 122	10	1:47.20	120,000
1980	Glorious Song, 4, 120	C. J. McCarron	The Very One, 5, 116	Kankam (Arg), 5, 125	11	1:48.40	82,500
1979	Sanedtki (Ire), 5, 124	W. Shoemaker	‡Surera (Arg), 6, 115	Ida Delia, 5, 117	11	1:47.80	75,000

Year	Winner	Jockey	Second	Third	Strs	Time	1st Purse
1978	Taisez Vous, 4, 120	D. Pierce	Sensational, 4, 118	*Merry Lady III, 6, 114	11	1:49.00	$60,000
1977	*Lucie Manet, 4, 119	D. G. McHargue	*Bastonera II, 6, 126	Hope of Glory, 5, 114	9	1:48.40	60,000
1976	Fascinating Girl, 4, 115	F. Toro	Summertime Promise, 4, 114	Charger's Star, 6, 114	8	1:49.40	60,000
1975	*Tizna, 6, 120	D. Pierce	Susan's Girl, 6, 123	Gay Style, 5, 125	12	1:48.60	60,000
1974	*Tizna, 5, 117	F. Toro	Penny Flight, 4, 113	Tallahto, 4, 119	12	1:50.80	60,000
1973	Susan's Girl, 4, 127	L. A. Pincay Jr.	Convenience, 5, 123	Minstrel Miss, 6, 115	8	1:47.80	60,000

Named for the 1841 California land grant Rancho Santa Margarita y Las Flores. Santa Margarita H. 1935-'67. Not held 1942-'44. 7 furlongs 1935-'36. 6 furlongs 1937. 1¹/₁₆ miles 1938-'48, 1953-'54. Dirt 1935-2007. Three-year-olds and up 1935-'40, 1945-'60. Both sexes 1935-'37. ‡Queen Yasna finished second, DQ to seventh, 1979.

Santa Maria Handicap

Grade 1 in 2008. Santa Anita Park, four-year-olds and up, fillies and mares, 1¹/₁₆ miles, all weather. Held February 9, 2008, with a gross value of $245,000. First held in 1934. First graded in 1973. Stakes record 1:40.95 (1998 Exotic Wood).

Year	Winner	Jockey	Second	Third	Strs	Time	1st Purse
2008	Double Trouble (Brz), 5, 115	R. Bejarano	Tough Tiz's Sis, 4, 119	Somethinaboutlaura, 6, 118	4	1:42.46	$150,000
2007	Sugar Shake, 4, 115	D. R. Flores	Ermine, 4, 115	Rahys' Appeal, 5, 115	8	1:43.89	150,000
2006	Star Parade (Arg), 7, 116	M. A. Pedroza	Proposed, 4, 118	Hollywood Story, 5, 117	7	1:42.31	150,000
2005	Miss Loren (Arg), 7, 117	J. Valdivia Jr.	Good Student (Arg), 5, 114	Hollywood Story, 4, 117	8	1:42.42	150,000
2004	Star Parade (Arg), 5, 114	V. Espinoza	Bare Necessities, 5, 118	La Tour (Chi), 5, 115	6	1:43.87	150,000
2003	Starrer, 5, 119	P. A. Valenzuela	You, 4, 118	Rhiana, 6, 112	5	1:42.75	120,000
2002	Favorite Funtime, 5, 116	G. L. Stevens	Verruma (Brz), 6, 114	Printemps (Chi), 5, 116	7	1:44.15	120,000
2001	Lovellon (Arg), 5, 116	G. L. Stevens	Feverish, 6, 119	Critikola (Arg), 6, 115	5	1:43.37	120,000
2000	Manistique, 5, 125	C. S. Nakatani	Snowberg, 5, 114	Gourmet Girl, 5, 116	5	1:42.60	120,000
1999	India Divina (Chi), 5, 114	G. K. Gomez	Victory Stripes (Arg), 5, 115	Belle's Flag, 6, 117	5	1:42.71	120,000
1998	Exotic Wood, 6, 121	C. J. McCarron	Toda Una Dama (Arg), 5, 115	Tuxedo Junction, 5, 115	4	**1:40.95**	120,000
1997	Jewel Princess, 5, 123	C. S. Nakatani	Cat's Cradle, 5, 118	Top Rung, 6, 117	7	1:41.72	97,900
1996	Serena's Song, 4, 124	G. L. Stevens	Twice the Vice, 5, 118	Real Connection, 5, 114	5	1:42.21	95,860
1995	Queens Court Queen, 6, 118	C. S. Nakatani	Paseana (Arg), 8, 123	Key Phrase, 4, 117	5	1:41.61	89,300
1994	Supah Gem, 4, 116	C. S. Nakatani	Paseana (Arg), 7, 124	Alysbelle, 5, 116	7	1:41.83	90,700
1993	Race the Wild Wind, 4, 117	K. Desormeaux	Paseana (Arg), 6, 126	Southern Truce, 5, 116	6	1:41.27	90,500
1992	Paseana (Arg), 5, 120	C. J. McCarron	Colour Chart, 5, 118	Campagnarde (Arg), 5, 117	5	1:41.94	89,100
1991	Little Brianne, 6, 117	J. A. Garcia	Luna Elegante (Arg), 5, 114	Somethingmerry, 4, 114	4	1:41.70	89,700
1990	Bayakoa (Arg), 6, 126	C. J. McCarron	Nikishka, 5, 117	Carita Tostada (Chi), 6, 112	4	1:43.00	90,200
1989	Miss Brio (Chi), 5, 119	E. Delahoussaye	Bayakoa (Arg), 5, 118	Annoconnor, 5, 122	7	1:41.00	79,000
1988	Mausie (Arg), 6, 114	G. L. Stevens	Miss Alto, 5, 118	Novel Sprite, 5, 115	7	1:43.60	63,800
1987	Fran's Valentine, 5, 121	P. A. Valenzuela	North Sider, 5, 118	Infinidad (Chi), 5, 113	8	1:42.60	91,700
1986	Love Smitten, 5, 120	C. J. McCarron	Johnica, 5, 121	North Sider, 4, 118	9	1:44.60	65,600
1985	Adored, 5, 124	L. A. Pincay Jr.	Dontstop Themusic, 5, 121	Lovlier Linda, 5, 122	5	1:42.40	88,800
1984	Marisma (Chi), 6, 117	L. A. Pincay Jr.	Brindy Brindy, 4, 118	Sierva (Arg), 6, 118	7	1:44.20	69,850
	High Haven, 5, 116	R. Sibille	Castilla, 5, 122	Avigaition, 5, 120	8	1:42.40	50,600
1983	Star Pastures (GB), 5, 119	W. Shoemaker	Sintrillium, 5, 116	Viga (Chi), 6, 112	7	1:42.60	49,650
	Sangue (Ire), 5, 124	L. A. Pincay Jr.	Cat Girl, 5, 115	Happy Bride (Ire), 5, 116	8	1:41.00	50,650
1982	Targa, 5, 114	F. Olivares	Jameela, 6, 121	Track Robbery, 6, 124	8	1:42.00	65,100
1981	Glorious Song, 5, 127	C. J. McCarron	Track Robbery, 5, 117	Miss Huntington, 4, 113	4	1:43.20	45,450
1980	Kankam (Arg), 5, 123	E. Delahoussaye	Flaming Leaves, 5, 123	Miss Magnetic, 5, 117	5	1:41.80	47,400
1979	Grenzen, 4, 124	L. A. Pincay Jr.	Ida Delia, 5, 118	Drama Critic, 5, 122	6	1:47.20	37,650
1978	Swingtime, 6, 122	F. Toro	Winter Solstice, 6, 124	Granja Sueno, 5, 113	6	1:41.40	37,500
1977	Hail Hilarious, 4, 122	D. Pierce	Swingtime, 5, 120	*Bastonera II, 6, 126	10	1:42.00	36,050
1976	Gay Style, 6, 127	D. Pierce	Raise Your Skirts, 4, 120	*Tizna, 7, 127	9	1:41.40	35,100
1975	Gay Style, 5, 122	W. Shoemaker	*Tizna, 6, 120	Susan's Girl, 6, 124	8	1:42.80	34,650
1974	Convenience, 6, 121	L. A. Pincay Jr.	*Tizna, 5, 117	Tallahto, 4, 119	8	1:42.80	34,750
1973	Susan's Girl, 4, 125	L. A. Pincay Jr.	Convenience, 5, 123	Hill Circus, 5, 119	6	1:42.00	32,900

Named for the city of Santa Maria, California, located in Santa Barbara county. Grade 2 1973-'89. Santa Maria S. 1934-'47. Not held 1937, 1942-'45, 1948-'51. 6 furlongs 1934-'60. 3 furlongs 1941. 1 mile 1946-'53. 7 furlongs 1954-'56. Dirt 1934-2007. Two-year-olds and up 1934-'35. Three-year-olds 1936-'40, 1946-'47. Two-year-olds 1941. Three-year-olds and up 1952-'59. Fillies 1936-'47. Two divisions 1983-'84. California-breds 1941.

Santa Monica Handicap

Grade 1 in 2008. Santa Anita Park, four-year-olds and up, fillies and mares, 7 furlongs, all weather. Held February 2, 2008, with a gross value of $250,000. First held in 1957. First graded in 1973. Stakes record 1:20.60 (1982 Past Forgetting).

Year	Winner	Jockey	Second	Third	Strs	Time	1st Purse
2008	Intangaroo, 4, 112	A. Quinonez	Society Hostess, 6, 117	Overly Tempting, 5, 114	5	1:20.71	$150,000
2007	Pussycat Doll, 5, 121	G. K. Gomez	Nossa Cancao (Brz), 7, 114	Secret Scheme, 4, 114	10	1:22.32	150,000
2006	Behaving Badly, 5, 115	V. Espinoza	Miss Terrible (Arg), 7, 117	Leave Me Alone, 4, 119	8	1:21.93	150,000
2005	Salt Champ (Arg), 5, 116	G. L. Stevens	Island Fashion, 5, 120	Resplendency, 4, 114	9	1:22.14	150,000
2004	Island Fashion, 4, 120	K. Desormeaux	Buffythecenterfold, 4, 114	Got Koko, 5, 119	6	1:21.37	150,000
2003	Affluent, 5, 119	A. O. Solis	Sightseek, 4, 115	Secret of Mecca, 5, 110	7	1:22.17	120,000
2002	Kalookan Queen, 6, 119	A. O. Solis	Leading Light, 7, 115	Spain, 5, 120	5	1:22.37	120,000
2001	Nany's Sweep, 5, 117	K. Desormeaux	Serenita (Arg), 4, 115	Surfside, 4, 121	7	1:22.50	120,000

Year	Winner	Jockey	Second	Third	Strs	Time	1st Purse
2000	Honest Lady, 4, 114	C. S. Nakatani	Kalookan Queen, 4, 116	Enjoy the Moment, 5, 118	9	1:21.45	$132,840
1999	Stop Traffic, 6, 120	C. A. Black	Belle's Flag, 6, 118	Closed Escrow, 6, 116	8	1:22.17	120,000
1998	Exotic Wood, 6, 121	C. J. McCarron	Madame Pandit, 5, 119	Advancing Star, 5, 121	8	1:21.07	120,000
1997	Toga Toga Toga, 5, 114	J. A. Garcia	Ski Dancer, 5, 117	Grab the Prize, 5, 116	6	1:23.27	96,750
1996	Serena's Song, 4, 123	G. L. Stevens	Exotic Wood, 4, 118	Klassy Kim, 5, 116	6	1:21.56	96,800
1995	Key Phrase, 4, 116	C. W. Antley	Flying in the Lane, 4, 114	Desert Stormer, 5, 117	9	1:22.82	93,100
1994	Southern Truce, 6, 116	G. L. Stevens	Arches of Gold, 5, 119	Mamselle Bebette, 4, 115	9	1:21.44	93,100
1993	Freedom Cry, 5, 114	A. O. Solis	Devil's Orchid, 6, 119	Mama Simba, 6, 114	7	1:21.78	91,200
1992	Laramie Moon (Arg), 5, 116	E. Delahoussaye	D'Or Ruckus, 4, 114	Ifyoucouldseemenow, 4, 118	10	1:22.66	94,700
1991	Devil's Orchid, 4, 116	R. A. Baze	‡Stormy But Valid, 5, 121	Classic Value, 5, 118	7	1:21.90	90,800
1990	Stormy But Valid, 4, 119	G. L. Stevens	Survive, 6, 118	Hot Novel, 4, 117	5	1:22.40	61,300
1989	Miss Brio (Chi), 5, 117	E. Delahoussaye	Valdemosa (Arg), 5, 116	Josette, 4, 115	8	1:21.60	64,800
1988	Pine Tree Lane, 6, 121	G. L. Stevens	Fairly Old, 5, 115	Le l'Argent, 6, 120	6	1:23.00	60,000
1987	Pine Tree Lane, 5, 125	A. T. Cordero Jr.	Balladry, 5, 116	Her Royalty, 6, 119	8	1:21.80	58,140
1986	Her Royalty, 5, 120	C. J. McCarron	North Sider, 4, 119	Take My Picture, 4, 117	8	1:21.60	51,300
1985	Lovlier Linda, 5, 123	W. Shoemaker	Dontstop Themusic, 5, 123	Foggy Nation, 5, 119	5	1:22.80	48,900
1984	Bara Lass, 5, 124	W. A. Guerra	Holiday Dancer, 4, 117	Bally Knockan, 5, 113	9	1:22.00	52,250
1983	Past Forgetting, 5, 123	C. J. McCarron	‡Sierva (Arg), 5, 119	Bara Lass, 4, 115	10	1:23.40	49,850
1982	Past Forgetting, 4, 122	W. Shoemaker	Nell's Briquette, 4, 117	In True Form, 4, 117	9	1:20.60	49,250
1981	Parsley, 5, 116	A. T. Cordero Jr.	Ack's Secret, 5, 125	Splendid Girl, 5, 118	7	1:23.40	40,050
1980	Flack Flack, 5, 117	W. Shoemaker	Shine High, 4, 115	Flaming Leaves, 5, 123	6	1:23.80	39,100
1979	Grenzen, 4, 122	L. A. Pincay Jr.	Dottie's Doll, 6, 116	Bidding Bold, 4, 116	8	1:21.60	40,600
1978	Winter Solstice, 6, 123	D. G. McHargue	Little Happiness, 4, 115	Splendid Size, 4, 117	7	1:21.20	27,200
1977	Hail Hilarious, 4, 119	D. Pierce	*Bastonera II, 6, 125	Modus Vivendi, 6, 121	8	1:22.60	28,150
1976	Gay Style, 6, 125	D. Pierce	Raise Your Skirts, 4, 123	*Tizna, 7, 129	6	1:22.00	26,650
1975	Sister Fleet, 5, 115	F. Toro	Susan's Girl, 6, 125	Modus Vivendi, 5, 123	13	1:21.40	31,250
1974	*Tizna, 5, 116	F. Toro	Susan's Girl, 5, 127	Impressive Style, 5, 118	7	1:24.00	28,050
1973	Chou Croute, 5, 128	J. L. Rotz	Generous Portion, 5, 114	Minstrel Miss, 6, 115	7	1:23.60	27,800

Named for the city of Santa Monica, California. Grade 2 1973-'83, 1988-'89. Grade 3 1984-'87. Not held 1970. Dirt 1957-2007. Three-year-olds and up 1957-'59. ‡Marimbula (Chi) finished second, DQ to sixth, 1983. ‡Classic Value finished second, DQ to third, 1991.

Santa Paula Stakes

Grade 3 in 2008. Santa Anita Park, three-year-olds, fillies, 6½ furlongs, all weather. Held March 30, 2008, with a gross value of $108,500. First held in 1968. First graded in 1973. 1:14.61 (2007 Magnificience).

Year	Winner	Jockey	Second	Third	Strs	Time	1st Purse
2008	Lethal Heat, 3, 118	G. Olguin	P. S. U. Grad, 3, 118	Highland Torree, 3, 119	7	1:14.91	$65,100
2007	Magnificience, 3, 116	A. O. Solis	Swiss Diva, 3, 118	Coco Belle, 3, 116	4	1:14.61	61,590
2006	Bettarun Fast, 3, 116	A. T. Gryder	El Mirage Queen, 3, 116	Acceleration, 3, 116	7	1:15.08	63,390
2005	No Bull Baby, 3, 118	V. Espinoza	Leave Me Alone, 3, 114	Inspiring, 3, 118	6	1:15.79	48,240
2004	Friendly Michelle, 3, 116	T. Baze	Lyin Goddess, 3, 116	Very Vegas, 3, 118	5	1:17.34	48,690
2003	Buffythecenterfold, 3, 121	V. Espinoza	Watching You, 3, 116	Tavy's Plan, 3, 114	6	1:16.56	47,655
2002	Bella Bellucci, 3, 118	M. E. Smith	Shameful, 3, 116	Spring Meadow, 3, 117	5	1:16.36	47,745
2001	Starrer, 3, 114	C. J. McCarron	Skywriting, 3, 117	Warren's Whistle, 3, 121	7	1:16.46	49,920
2000	Abby Girl, 3, 116	C. S. Nakatani	Mintly Fresh, 3, 114	Classic Olympio, 3, 118	5	1:15.47	47,700
1999	Perfect Six, 3, 116	D. R. Flores	Olympic Charmer, 3, 116	Kalookan Queen, 3, 116	4	1:15.41	47,295
1998	Loveontheroad, 3, 117	K. Desormeaux	Holy Nola, 3, 118	Tippytoe Cat, 3, 116	7	1:16.07	48,690
1997	Lavender, 3, 118	A. O. Solis	Silken Magic, 3, 117	Soiree, 3, 116	6	1:16.34	64,300
1996	Raw Gold, 3, 121	C. W. Antley	Sheza Valentine, 3, 114	Supercilious, 3, 116	5	1:15.63	64,200
1995	Made to Perfection, 3, 114	A. O. Solis	Embroidered, 3, 116	Comstock Queen, 3, 114	5	1:16.24	45,975
1994	Sardula, 3, 121	E. Delahoussaye	Ballerina Gal, 3, 117	Serena's World, 3, 117	5	1:15.02	61,000
1992	Peaceful Road, 3, 116	M. A. Pedroza	Jetinwith Kennedy, 3, 115	Wicked Wit, 3, 118	9	1:16.33	65,200
1974	Viva Lu Vivi, 4, 121	D. Pierce	Miss Rebound, 6, 113	Sister Fleet, 4, 116	3	1:24.00	21,300
1973	*Tizna, 4, 124	F. Toro	Minstrel Miss, 6, 121	Judith, 5, 109	3	1:21.60	19,100

Named for the Santa Paula y Saticoy Rancho, site of present-day Saticoy, California. Saticoy is the Chumash Indian name for a native village. Not graded 1992-2005. Santa Paula H. 1968-'74. Not held 1975-'91, 1993. 7 furlongs 1968-'74. Four-year-olds and up 1968-'74. Fillies and mares 1968-'74.

Santa Ynez Stakes

Grade 2 in 2008. Santa Anita Park, three-year-olds, fillies, 7 furlongs, all weather. Held January 13, 2008, with a gross value of $150,000. First held in 1952. First graded in 1973. Stakes record 1:19.89 (2008 Indian Blessing).

Year	Winner	Jockey	Second	Third	Strs	Time	1st Purse
2008	Indian Blessing, 3, 123	G. K. Gomez	Golden Doc A, 3, 123	Peisinoe, 3, 116	5	1:19.89	$90,000
2007	Jump On In, 3, 118	C. S. Nakatani	Quick Little Miss, 3, 120	Sekira, 3, 116	7	1:23.45	90,000
2006	Dance Daily, 3, 114	J. K. Court	Talullah Lula, 3, 115	Folklore, 3, 123	6	1:23.34	90,000
2005	Sharp Lisa, 3, 114	T. Baze	No Bull Baby, 3, 121	Hot Attraction, 3, 114	7	1:23.10	90,000
2004	Yearly Report, 3, 114	J. D. Bailey	House of Fortune, 3, 121	Papa to Kinzie, 3, 115	8	1:21.13	90,000
2003	Elloluv, 3, 121	P. A. Valenzuela	Watching You, 3, 116	Himalayan, 3, 116	5	1:23.03	90,000
2002	Dancing (GB), 3, 116	G. L. Stevens	Respectful, 3, 116	Lady George, 3, 123	8	1:23.07	90,000
2001	Golden Ballet, 3, 123	C. J. McCarron	Affluent, 3, 114	Warren's Whistle, 3, 116	9	1:22.30	90,000
2000	Penny Blues, 3, 118	E. Delahoussaye	Classic Olympio, 3, 121	Mean Imogene, 3, 117	5	1:23.38	63,600
1999	Honest Lady, 3, 115	K. Desormeaux	Rayelle, 3, 118	Controlled, 3, 123	4	1:21.67	63,240

Year	Winner	Jockey	Second	Third	Strs	Time	1st Purse
1998	Nijinsky's Passion, 3, 121	C. A. Black	Well Chosen, 3, 115	Vivid Angel, 3, 123	7	1:23.15	$64,980
1997	Queen of Money, 3, 116	D. R. Flores	Goodnight Irene, 3, 116	High Heeled Hope, 3, 121	8	1:22.55	65,650
1996	Raw Gold, 3, 121	C. W. Antley	Pareja, 3, 121	Hidden Lake, 3, 116	6	1:22.66	64,550
1995	Serena's Song, 3, 123	C. S. Nakatani	Cat's Cradle, 3, 121	Call Now, 3, 121	5	1:21.45	59,800
1994	Tricky Code, 3, 121	C. S. Nakatani	Fancy 'n Fabulous, 3, 114	Sophisticatedcielo, 3, 116	5	1:22.16	59,575
1993	Fit to Lead, 3, 116	C. S. Nakatani	Nijivision, 3, 114	Booklore, 3, 115	8	1:22.55	62,500
1992	Looie Capote, 3, 114	K. Desormeaux	Icy Eyes, 3, 118	Soviet Sojourn, 3, 121	7	1:23.42	61,450
1991	Brazen, 3, 121	C. J. McCarron	Fowda, 3, 116	Ifyoucouldseemenow, 3, 121	5	1:23.70	46,050
1990	Fit to Scout, 3, 118	C. J. McCarron	Bright Candles, 3, 114	Heaven for Bid, 3, 116	6	1:23.80	60,625
1989	Hot Novel, 3, 121	E. Delahoussaye	Fantastic Look, 3, 114	Agotaras, 3, 121	6	1:22.80	46,950
1988	Goodbye Halo, 3, 123	J. Velasquez	Bolchina, 3, 116	Floral Magic, 3, 114	8	1:23.40	47,900
1987	Very Subtle, 3, 122	W. Shoemaker	Chic Shirine, 3, 119	Young Flyer, 3, 122	5	1:22.60	46,200
1986	Sari's Heroine, 3, 119	A. O. Solis	An Empress, 3, 117	Life At the Top, 3, 115	8	1:23.40	52,000
1985	Wising Up, 3, 119	E. Delahoussaye	Rascal Lass, 3, 122	Reigning Countess, 3, 119	9	1:23.40	52,700
1984	Gene's Lady, 3, 117	L. A. Pincay Jr.	Kennedy Express, 3, 115	Natural Summit, 3, 117	9	1:23.80	41,600
	Boo La Boo, 3, 122	L. A. Pincay Jr.	Personable Lady, 3, 122	Costly Array, 3, 117	7	1:23.20	39,900
1983	A Lucky Sign, 3, 121	C. J. McCarron	Sophisticated Girl, 3, 116	Fabulous Notion, 3, 124	3	1:23.40	49,050
1982	Flying Partner, 3, 114	R. Sibille	Skillful Joy, 3, 124	Carry a Tune, 3, 114	8	1:22.80	49,300
1981	Past Forgetting, 3, 119	S. Hawley	Rosie Doon, 3, 119	Nell's Briquette, 3, 121	11	1:22.40	41,800
1980	Table Hands, 3, 117	W. Shoemaker	Street Ballet, 3, 119	Hazel R., 3, 119	7	1:22.40	38,700
1979	Terlingua, 3, 121	L. A. Pincay Jr.	Caline, 3, 119	It's in the Air, 3, 121	5	1:21.20	37,900
1978	Grenzen, 3, 119	D. G. McHargue	Extravagant, 3, 121	Happy Kin, 3, 114	9	1:22.20	27,600
1977	Wavy Waves, 3, 121	L. A. Pincay Jr.	Don's Music, 3, 119	Any Time Girl, 3, 121	11	1:22.80	29,550
1976	Daisy Do, 3, 114	S. Hawley	Girl in Love, 3, 115	Windy Welcome, 3, 117	6	1:22.40	20,300
1975	Raise Your Skirts, 3, 117	W. Mahorney	Fascinating Girl, 3, 115	Miss Francesca, 3, 117	13	1:22.40	23,350
1974	Modus Vivendi, 3, 119	D. Pierce	Donna Chere, 3, 114	Special Team, 3, 121	9	1:22.40	28,500
1973	Tallahto, 3, 117	J. E. Tejeira	Waltz Fan, 3, 117	Windy's Daughter, 3, 121	5	1:21.40	25,800

Named for the city of Santa Ynez, California, which takes its name from an 1804 mission. Grade 3 1975-'80, 1984-'98. Santa Ynez Breeders' Cup S. 1990-'95. Not held 1953. 6 furlongs 1952, 1956-'57. 6½ furlongs 1958-'66. Dirt 1952-2007. Two-year-olds 1952 (December). Two divisions 1984.

Santa Ysabel Stakes

Grade 3 in 2008. Santa Anita Park, three-year-olds, fillies, 1 1/16 miles, all weather. Held January 13, 2008, with a gross value of $108,900. First held in 1968. First graded in 1998. Stakes record 1:41.34 (1997 Sharp Cat).

Year	Winner	Jockey	Second	Third	Strs	Time	1st Purse
2008	Final Fling, 3, 114	J. Talamo	Grace Anatomy, 3, 114	Kazamira, 3, 115	6	1:41.96	$65,340
2007	Baroness Thatcher, 3, 114	G. K. Gomez	Runway Rosie, 3, 122	Mistical Plan, 3, 119	7	1:44.31	64,920
2006	Itty Bitty Pretty, 3, 118	P. A. Valenzuela	Sabatini, 3, 115	Horse B With You, 3, 118	6	1:44.60	65,520
2005	Sweet Catomine, 3, 124	D. R. Flores	Pussycat Doll, 3, 115	On London Time, 3, 115	3	1:43.77	64,800
2004	A. P. Adventure, 3, 115	A. O. Solis	Salty Romance, 3, 120	Wildwood Flower, 3, 115	6	1:44.27	64,080
2003	Atlantic Ocean, 3, 120	D. R. Flores	Sea Jewel, 3, 115	Summer Wind Dancer, 3, 120	6	1:43.25	66,540
2002	Bella Bella Bella, 3, 115	C. J. McCarron	Tamarack Bay, 3, 116	No Turbulence, 3, 116	4	1:44.14	64,550
2001	Collect Call, 3, 115	A. O. Solis	Irguns Angel, 3, 115	Eminent, 3, 115	7	1:44.69	65,580
2000	Surfside, 3, 123	P. Day	Rings a Chime, 3, 115	She's Classy, 3, 118	4	1:43.53	62,880
1999	Holywood Picture, 3, 115	O. Vergara	Exbourne Free, 3, 116	Gleefully, 3, 116	7	1:43.48	64,860
1998	‡Nonies Dancer Ali, 3, 114	G. K. Gomez	Mamaison Miss, 3, 116	Continental Lea, 3, 113	5	1:44.14	63,660
1997	Sharp Cat, 3, 120	C. S. Nakatani	Clever Pilot, 3, 115	Guthrie, 3, 116	6	1:41.34	64,300
1996	Antespend, 3, 120	C. W. Antley	Dancing Prism, 3, 114	Rumpipumpy (GB), 3, 116	8	1:43.87	64,950
1995	Ski Dancer, 3, 115	K. Desormeaux	Dixie Pearl, 3, 117	Wilga, 3, 115	4	1:44.24	45,750
1994	Princess Mitterand, 3, 119	C. J. McCarron	Dianes Halo, 3, 115	Jacodra's Devil, 3, 115	4	1:43.25	44,925
1993	Likeable Style, 3, 115	G. L. Stevens	Fit to Lead, 3, 117	Amandari, 3, 117	5	1:44.74	45,900
1992	Crownette, 3, 116	P. A. Valenzuela	Golden Treat, 3, 114	Looie Capote, 3, 114	9	1:44.33	48,975
1991	Nice Assay, 3, 117	L. A. Pincay Jr.	Assombrie, 3, 117	Ms. Aerosmith, 3, 115	9	1:43.70	49,275
1990	Bright Candles, 3, 114	G. L. Stevens	Heaven for Bid, 3, 117	Annual Reunion, 3, 117	7	1:45.60	47,175
1989	Gorgeous, 3, 116	E. Delahoussaye	My Glamorous One, 3, 117	April Mon, 3, 114	9	1:42.40	46,450
1988	Jeanne Jones, 3, 114	W. Shoemaker	Pattern Step, 3, 120	Affordable Price, 3, 116	8	1:43.60	48,100
1987	Perchance to Dream, 3, 117	R. Sibille	Buryyourbelief, 3, 117	My Turbulent Beau, 3, 114	7	1:43.40	37,900
1986	Trim Colony, 3, 117	G. L. Stevens	Fashion Book, 3, 115	Top Corsage, 3, 115	6	1:44.80	36,900
1985	Savannah Dancer, 3, 120	W. Shoemaker	Pink Sapphire, 3, 117	Ed's Bold Lady (Ire), 3, 117	6	1:44.20	37,350
1984	Sales Bulletin, 3, 115	C. J. McCarron	Spring Loose, 3, 115	Agitated Miss, 3, 115	7	1:44.20	39,300
1983	Ski Goggle, 3, 115	C. J. McCarron	Sophisticated Girl, 3, 116	Saucy Bobbie, 3, 115	7	1:41.60	38,100
1982	Avigaition, 3, 115	E. Delahoussaye	Blush With Pride, 3, 117	Carry a Tune, 3, 114	10	1:42.40	39,750
1981	Lovely Robbery, 3, 117	L. A. Pincay Jr.	Bee a Scout, 3, 117	Ice Princess, 3, 117	10	1:44.20	33,350
1980	Back At Two, 3, 117	F. Toro	Thundertree, 3, 117	Regretfully, 3, 114	4	1:45.20	24,250
1979	Maytide, 3, 114	A. T. Cordero Jr.	Smile On Me, 3, 117	Smaller Bicker, 3, 119	8	1:44.00	19,875
	Top Soil, 3, 115	D. Pierce	Reporting Act, 3, 119	To the Top, 3, 114	9	1:44.00	20,675
1978	Palmistry, 3, 115	W. Shoemaker	Equanimity, 3, 115	My Buck, 3, 115	8	1:44.40	26,050
1977	Geothermal, 3, 116	M. Castaneda	*Glenaris, 3, 117	Sound of Summer, 3, 116	8	1:43.00	23,550
1976	Flunsa, 3, 116	S. Hawley	Girl in Love, 3, 116	Go March, 3, 116	7	1:43.80	20,100
1975	Double You Lou, 3, 116	S. Hawley	Fascinating Girl, 3, 116	Miss Francesca, 3, 116	10	1:44.80	21,300
1974	Miss Musket, 3, 116	S. Hawley	Acknowledge Me, 3, 116	Lucky Spell, 3, 116	4	1:44.60	17,800
1973	Belle Marie, 3, 116	L. A. Pincay Jr.	Wind Gap, 3, 116	Flo's Pleasure, 3, 116	7	1:45.40	20,800

Named for two California land grants called Rancho Santa Ysabel, home of the Santa Ysabel mission. 7 furlongs 1970.

Racing — Graded Stakes 451

Dirt 1968-2007. Two divisions 1979. ‡Love Lock finished first, DQ to fifth for a positive drug test, 1998. Nonwinners of a race worth $12,500 to the winner 1973. Nonwinners of a race worth $25,000 to the winner 1992.

San Vicente Stakes

Grade 2 in 2008. Santa Anita Park, three-year-olds, 7 furlongs, all weather. Held February 10, 2008, with a gross value of $147,000. First held in 1935. First graded in 1973. Stakes record 1:20.01 (2008 Georgie Boy).

Year	Winner	Jockey	Second	Third	Strs	Time	1st Purse
2008	**Georgie Boy**, 3, 122	R. Bejarano	Into Mischief, 3, 119	Massive Drama, 3, 119	4	**1:20.01**	$90,000
2007	**Noble Court**, 3, 118	C. S. Nakatani	Law Breaker, 3, 115	Half Famous, 3, 118	5	1:23.12	90,000
2006	**Too Much Bling**, 3, 116	G. K. Gomez	Peace Chant, 3, 115	New Joysey Jeff, 3, 116	8	1:22.50	90,000
2005	**Fusaichi Rock Star**, 3, 116	D. R. Flores	Don't Get Mad, 3, 115	Kirkendahl, 3, 116	4	1:22.59	90,000
2004	**Imperialism**, 3, 116	V. Espinoza	Hosco, 3, 120	Consecrate, 3, 116	6	1:22.34	90,000
2003	**Kafwain**, 3, 123	V. Espinoza	Sum Trick, 3, 120	Southern Image, 3, 117	5	1:21.12	90,000
2002	**Came Home**, 3, 123	C. J. McCarron	Jack's Silver, 3, 116	Werblin, 3, 116	6	1:21.92	90,000
2001	**Early Flyer**, 3, 114	C. J. McCarron	Lasersport, 3, 120	D'wildcat, 3, 117	5	1:21.51	90,000
2000	**Archer City Slew**, 3, 117	K. Desormeaux	Joopy Doopy, 3, 116	Gibson County, 3, 120	6	1:22.18	90,000
1999	**Exploit**, 3, 123	C. J. McCarron	Aristotle, 3, 116	Yes It's True, 3, 123	3	1:22.00	90,000
1998	**Sea of Secrets**, 3, 116	K. Desormeaux	Late Edition, 3, 115	Pleasant Drive, 3, 116	5	1:22.00	64,080
1997	**Silver Charm**, 3, 120	C. J. McCarron	Free House, 3, 120	Funontherun, 3, 114	9	1:21.07	66,400
1996	**Afleetaffair**, 3, 116	C. S. Nakatani	Honour and Glory, 3, 123	Ready to Order, 3, 120	5	1:22.28	63,850
1995	**Afternoon Deelites**, 3, 120	K. Desormeaux	Mr Purple, 3, 116	Fandarel Dancer, 3, 117	5	1:21.35	59,725
1994	**Fly'n J. Bryan**, 3, 114	C. A. Black	Gracious Ghost, 3, 114	Cois Na Tine (Ire), 3, 116	6	1:22.32	60,700
1993	**Yappy**, 3, 116	P. A. Valenzuela	Denmars Dream, 3, 118	Devoted Brass, 3, 116	9	1:22.33	63,100
1992	**Mineral Wells**, 3, 116	P. A. Valenzuela	Star of the Crop, 3, 116	Prince Wild, 3, 118	7	1:21.28	61,450
1991	**Olympio**, 3, 120	E. Delahoussaye	Dinard, 3, 118	Scan, 3, 123	6	1:21.50	61,075
1990	**Mister Frisky**, 3, 118	G. L. Stevens	Tarascon, 3, 120	Top Cash, 3, 120	6	1:22.60	47,325
1989	**Gum**, 3, 117	L. A. Pincay Jr.	Yes I'm Blue, 3, 120	Roman Avie, 3, 114	7	1:22.40	47,600
1988	**Mi Preferido**, 3, 120	A. O. Solis	No Commitment, 3, 120	Success Express, 3, 123	5	1:22.60	45,900
1987	**Stylish Winner**, 3, 119	G. L. Stevens	Prince Sassafras, 3, 116	Mount Laguna, 3, 116	6	1:23.80	46,750
1986	**Grand Allegiance**, 3, 114	R. Hernandez	Royal Treasure, 3, 114	Dancing Pirate, 3, 119	7	1:23.20	51,050
1985	**The Rogers Four**, 3, 124	C. J. McCarron	Teddy Naturally, 3, 119	Michadilla, 3, 122	5	1:22.80	49,400
1984	**Fortunate Prospect**, 3, 119	D. Pierce	Precisionist, 3, 122	Tights, 3, 117	5	1:22.80	49,700
1983	**Shecky Blue**, 3, 114	S. Hawley	Full Choke, 3, 117	Naevus, 3, 115	7	1:22.40	48,200
1982	**Unpredictable**, 3, 114	E. Delahoussaye	Prince Spellbound, 3, 122	Sepulveda, 3, 119	10	1:21.20	50,700
1981	**Flying Nashua**, 3, 114	A. T. Cordero Jr.	Minnesota Chief, 3, 117	Torso, 3, 117	9	1:23.40	40,450
1980	**Raise a Man**, 3, 114	W. Shoemaker	Super Moment, 3, 114	Bold 'n Rulling, 3, 117	8	1:21.40	39,550
1979	**Flying Paster**, 3, 124	D. Pierce	Oats and Corn, 3, 119	Infusive, 3, 122	5	1:21.20	37,300
1978	**Chance Dancer**, 3, 122	R. Culberson	O Big Al, 3, 122	Reb's Golden Ale, 3, 114	6	1:22.00	25,600
1977	**Replant**, 3, 117	D. G. McHargue	Current Concept, 3, 122	Smasher, 3, 122	8	1:21.20	29,750
1976	**Thermal Energy**, 3, 117	W. Shoemaker	Stained Glass, 3, 122	Bold Forbes, 3, 119	7	1:21.80	20,200
1975	**Boomie S.**, 3, 114	S. Hawley	George Navonod, 3, 122	Udonegood, 3, 114	8	1:22.00	21,350
1974	**Triple Crown**, 3, 114	B. Baeza	El Espanoleto, 3, 114	Destroyer, 3, 114	8	1:22.60	28,000
1973	**Ancient Title**, 3, 122	F. Toro	Linda's Chief, 3, 122	Out of the East, 3, 114	9	1:21.20	28,150

Named for El Rancho San Vicente, California; early horse races were held there on a mesa. Grade 3 1973-'82, 1984-'97. San Vicente H. 1956-'66. San Vicente Breeders' Cup S. 1990-'95. Not held 1942-'44, 1949-'51, 1970. 6 furlongs 1935-'36, 1952-'54. 1 mile 1940-'46. 1 1/16 miles 1947-'48. Dirt 1935-2007. Three-year-olds and up 1935-'36. Colts and geldings 1935-'53.

Sapling Stakes

Grade 3 in 2008. Monmouth Park, two-year-olds, 6 furlongs, dirt. Held September 2, 2007, with a gross value of $150,000. First held in 1883. First graded in 1973. Stakes record 1:07.84 (1992 Gilded Time).

Year	Winner	Jockey	Second	Third	Strs	Time	1st Purse
2007	**Lantana Mob**, 2, 121	S. Elliott	Preachin Man, 2, 121	Z Humor, 2, 121	7	1:09.97	$90,000
2006	**Xchanger**, 2, 121	J. Bravo	Actin Good, 2, 121	Buffalo Man, 2, 121	7	1:10.68	90,000
2005	**He's Got Grit**, 2, 121	A. T. Gryder	Diabolical, 2, 121	Confront, 2, 121	6	1:09.69	90,000
2004	**Evil Minister**, 2, 120	J. Pimentel	Park Avenue Ball, 2, 120	Upscaled, 2, 120	8	1:11.21	60,000
2003	**Dashboard Drummer**, 2, 120	J. C. Ferrer	Deputy Storm, 2, 120	Charming Jim, 2, 120	7	1:10.84	60,000
2002	**Valid Video**, 2, 120	C. C. Lopez	Farno, 2, 120	Boston Park, 2, 120	8	1:09.88	60,000
2001	**Pure Precision**, 2, 120	E. Coa	Truman's Raider, 2, 120	Wild Navigator, 2, 120	8	1:10.82	90,000
2000	**Shooter**, 2, 119	J. Bravo	Snow Ridge, 2, 119	T P Louie, 2, 119	7	1:10.63	120,000
1999	**Dont Tell the Kids**, 2, 122	J. E. Tejeira	Outrigger, 2, 122	House Burner, 2, 122	6	1:10.18	120,000
1998	**Yes It's True**, 2, 122	S. J. Sellers	Erlton, 2, 122	Heroofthegame, 2, 122	7	1:10.09	120,000
1997	**Double Honor**, 2, 122	J. Bravo	Jigadee, 2, 122	E Z Line, 2, 122	8	1:09.75	120,000
1996	**Smoke Glacken**, 2, 122	C. Perret	Harley Tune, 2, 122	Country Rainbow, 2, 122	10	1:10.16	120,000
1995	**Hennessy**, 2, 122	D. M. Barton	Built for Pleasure, 2, 122	Cashier Coyote, 2, 122	7	1:10.84	120,000
1994	**Boone's Mill**, 2, 122	P. Day	Enlighten, 2, 122	Western Echo, 2, 122	6	1:10.46	120,000
1993	**Sacred Honour**, 2, 122	C. E. Lopez Sr.	Meadow Flight, 2, 122	Solly's Honor, 2, 117	7	1:11.19	120,000
1992	**Gilded Time**, 2, 122	C. J. McCarron	Wild Zone, 2, 122	Great Navigator, 2, 122	8	**1:07.84**	120,000
1991	**Big Sur**, 2, 122	R. Migliore	Never Wavering, 2, 122	Dr Fountainstein, 2, 122	8	1:10.92	120,000
1990	**Deposit Ticket**, 2, 122	G. L. Stevens	Alaskan Frost, 2, 122	Hansel, 2, 122	9	1:11.00	120,000
1989	**Carson City**, 2, 122	J. A. Krone	Mr. Nasty, 2, 122	Adjudicating, 2, 122	7	1:10.00	120,000
1988	**Bio**, 2, 122	P. A. Johnson	Truely Colorful, 2, 122	Light My Fuse, 2, 122	8	1:10.40	111,600

Year	Winner	Jockey	Second	Third	Strs	Time	1st Purse
1987	Tejano, 2, 122	J. Vasquez	Unzipped, 2, 122	Jim's Orbit, 2, 122	8	1:09.00	$111,600
1986	Bet Twice, 2, 122	C. W. Antley	Faster Than Sound, 2, 122	Homebuilder, 2, 122	5	1:10.20	120,000
1985	Hilco Scamper, 2, 122	G. L. Stevens	Danny's Keys, 2, 122	Mr. Spiffy, 2, 122	9	1:10.80	114,555
1984	Doubly Clear, 2, 122	J. R. Garcia	†Tiltalating, 2, 119	Do It Again Dan, 2, 122	10	1:10.40	120,150
1983	Smart n Slick, 2, 122	D. A. Miller Jr.	Tonto, 2, 122	Triple Sec, 2, 122	9	1:10.80	120,615
1982	O. K. by You, 2, 122	C. Perret	Willow Drive, 2, 122	Love to Laugh, 2, 122	8	1:10.80	82,032
1981	Out of Hock, 2, 122	D. Brumfield	T. Dykes, 2, 122	What a Wabbit, 2, 122	9	1:10.20	90,591
1980	Travelling Music, 2, 122	C. Perret	Lord Avie, 2, 122	Timeless Event, 2, 122	8	1:11.00	78,438
1979	Rockhill Native, 2, 122	J. Oldham	Antique Gold, 2, 122	Gold Stage, 2, 122	7	1:08.80	75,366
1978	Tim the Tiger, 2, 122	J. Fell	Groton High, 2, 122	Spartan Emperor, 2, 116	7	1:11.80	86,682
1977	Alydar, 2, 122	E. Maple	Noon Time Spender, 2, 122	Dominant Ruler, 2, 122	5	1:10.60	65,829
1976	Ali Oop, 2, 122	L. Saumell	Ahoy Mate, 2, 122	First Ambassador, 2, 122	10	1:09.80	84,636
1975	Full Out, 2, 122	B. Thornburg	Riverside Sam, 2, 116	Eustace, 2, 122	13	1:11.60	82,227
1974	Foolish Pleasure, 2, 122	J. Vasquez	The Bagel Prince, 2, 122	Bombay Duck, 2, 122	15	1:10.40	86,997
1973	Tisab, 2, 122	W. Blum	Wedge Shot, 2, 122	Go for Love, 2, 122	11	1:10.20	77,721

Young trees are referred to as saplings. Grade 1 1973-'83. Grade 2 1984-'96. Not held 1894-1945. 5½ furlongs 1893. Track record 1992. †Denotes female.

Saranac Stakes

Grade 3 in 2008. Saratoga Race Course, three-year-olds, 1 3/16 miles, turf. Held September 2, 2007, with a gross value of $115,000. First held in 1901. First graded in 1973. Stakes record 1:51.61 (1999 Phi Beta Doc).

Year	Winner	Jockey	Second	Third	Strs	Time	1st Purse
2007	Mission Approved, 3, 117	E. Coa	Distorted Reality, 3, 121	Pays to Dream, 3, 119	11	1:53.81	$69,000
2006	Rock Lobster, 3, 119	E. Coa	Devil's Preacher, 3, 117	Murch, 3, 117	9	1:57.36	68,340
2005	Jambalaya, 3, 121	J. C. Jones	Silver Whistle, 3, 115	Woodlander, 3, 121	9	1:54.20	67,140
2004	Prince Arch, 3, 123	J. Castellano	Mustanfar, 3, 121	Catch the Glory, 3, 115	6	1:53.89	64,920
2003	Shoal Water, 3, 116	J. R. Velazquez	Urban King (Ire), 3, 115	Sharp Impact, 3, 116	6	1:55.43	65,280
2002	Ibn Al Haitham (GB), 3, 114	R. Migliore	Finality, 3, 116	Irish Colonial, 3, 115	9	1:55.30	66,900
2001	Blazing Fury, 3, 113	J. Castellano	Fast City, 3, 114	Rapid Ryan, 3, 114	9	1:54.88	67,500
2000	Rob's Spirit, 3, 120	J. D. Bailey	Whata Brainstorm, 3, 117	Dawn of the Condor, 3, 117	9	1:55.47	68,280
1999	Phi Beta Doc, 3, 118	R. A. Dominguez	Monarch's Maze, 3, 114	Big Rascal, 3, 113	6	1:51.61	67,020
1998	Crowd Pleaser, 3, 115	J. Samyn	Parade Ground, 3, 122	Reformer Rally, 3, 115	7	1:53.42	66,060
1997	River Squall, 3, 114	C. Perret	Daylight Savings, 3, 114	Inkatha (Fr), 3, 114	10	1:52.82	68,460
1996	Harghar, 3, 113	P. Day	Sir Cat, 3, 123	Defacto, 3, 115	11	1:48.58	69,180
1995	Debonair Dan, 3, 112	J. F. Chavez	Crimson Guard, 3, 122	Treasurer (GB), 3, 117	7	1:33.65	50,400
1994	†Casa Eire, 3, 114	J. Bravo	Warn Me (GB), 3, 114	Presently, 3, 117	8	1:34.67	66,480
1993	Halissee, 3, 114	J. A. Krone	Forest Wind, 3, 117	Compadre, 3, 114	9	1:34.34	74,280
1992	Casino Magistrate, 3, 120	E. Maple	Restless Doctor, 3, 114	Smiling and Dancin, 3, 117	10	1:39.37	76,440
1991	Club Champ, 3, 114	A. T. Cordero Jr.	Share the Glory, 3, 117	Young Daniel, 3, 115	11	1:34.34	81,480
1990	Rouse the Louse, 3, 114	J. D. Bailey	†My Girl Jeannie, 3, 118	V. J.'s Honor, 3, 114	12	1:37.00	78,600
1989	Expensive Decision, 3, 114	J. Samyn	Ninety Years Young, 3, 114	Valid Ordinate, 3, 114	8	1:36.00	55,140
	Slew the Knight, 3, 114	J. Samyn	Verbatree, 3, 114	Luge (GB), 3, 123	8	1:36.00	55,620
1988	Posen, 3, 123	D. Brumfield	Sunshine Forever, 3, 114	Blew by Em, 3, 117	12	1:38.40	73,560
1987	Lights and Music, 3, 114	E. Maple	Forest Fair, 3, 114	First Patriot, 3, 117	10	1:34.80	73,560
1986	Glow, 3, 114	E. Maple	Manila, 3, 114	Pillaster, 3, 120	11	1:34.60	72,270
1985	Equalize, 3, 114	R. G. Davis	Verification, 3, 114	Danger's Hour, 3, 114	9	1:39.00	71,820
1984	Is Your Pleasure, 3, 114	A. T. Cordero Jr.	Onyxly, 3, 114	Loft, 3, 123	12	1:35.20	61,470
1983	†Sabin, 3, 113	E. Maple	Fortnightly, 3, 117	Domynsky (GB), 3, 123	10	1:39.60	36,600
1982	Prince Westport, 3, 114	J. D. Bailey	Four Bases, 3, 114	A Real Leader, 3, 114	8	1:39.00	35,040
1981	†De La Rose, 3, 112	E. Maple	Stage Door Key, 3, 114	Color Bearer, 3, 114	7	1:34.40	35,400
1980	Key to Content, 3, 114	G. Martens	Current Legend, 3, 114	Ben Fab, 3, 123	13	1:33.80	36,300
1979	Told, 3, 114	J. Cruguet	Crown Thy Good, 3, 114	Quiet Crossing, 3, 123	10	1:34.40	35,250
1978	Buckaroo, 3, 123	J. Velasquez	Junction, 3, 123	Quadratic, 3, 123	5	1:35.00	31,950
1977	Bailjumper, 3, 114	A. T. Cordero Jr.	Lynn Davis, 3, 114	Gift of Kings, 3, 114	9	1:35.20	32,910
1976	Dance Spell, 3, 114	A. T. Cordero Jr.	Zen, 3, 123	Quiet Little Table, 3, 114	6	1:34.20	33,030
1975	Bravest Roman, 3, 114	E. Maple	Wajima, 3, 114	Valid Appeal, 3, 114	9	1:34.80	34,380
1974	Accipiter, 3, 123	A. Santiago	Best of It, 3, 117	Hosiery, 3, 117	11	1:36.40	34,980
1973	Linda's Chief, 3, 126	B. Baeza	Step Nicely, 3, 123	Illbredstylish, 3, 117	4	1:35.40	33,150

Named for an Adirondack mountain village in Clinton County, New York. Grade 2 1973-'89. Saranac H. 1901-'70, 1998-2004. Held at Jamaica 1948-'56. Held at Aqueduct 1957-'61, 1963-'67, 1972-'74, 1976. Held at Belmont Park 1962, 1968-'71, 1975, 1977-'95. Not held 1911-'12, 1944, 1946-'47. 1 1/8 miles 1901-'08, 1996-'97. 1 mile 1909, 1913-'42, 1960-'95. 1 1/16 miles 1948-'59. Dirt 1901-'79. Two divisions 1989. †Denotes female. Held as an allowance race 1943, '45.

Saratoga Special Stakes

Grade 2 in 2008. Saratoga Race Course, two-year-olds, 6½ furlongs, dirt. Held August 16, 2007, with a gross value of $150,000. First held in 1901. First graded in 1973. Stakes record 1:15.95 (2007 Kodiak Kowboy).

Year	Winner	Jockey	Second	Third	Strs	Time	1st Purse
2007	Kodiak Kowboy, 2, 122	S. Bridgmohan	The Roundhouse, 2, 118	Riley Tucker, 2, 118	6	1:15.95	$90,000
2006	Chace City, 2, 122	E. S. Prado	King of the Roxy, 2, 118	Shermanesque, 2, 118	6	1:16.83	120,000
2005	Henny Hughes, 2, 121	G. L. Stevens	Master of Disaster, 2, 117	Union Course, 2, 117	6	1:10.38	90,000
2003	Cuvee, 2, 122	J. D. Bailey	Pomeroy, 2, 118	Limehouse, 2, 122	8	1:15.97	90,000
2002	Zavata, 2, 122	J. D. Bailey	Lone Star Sky, 2, 122	Spite the Devil, 2, 116	5	1:17.65	90,000

Racing — Graded Stakes 453

Year	Winner	Jockey	Second	Third	Strs	Time	1st Purse
2001	Jump Start, 2, 115	P. Day	Heavyweight Champ, 2, 115	Booklet, 2, 117	6	1:17.35	$90,000
2000	City Zip, 2, 122	J. A. Santos	Scorpion, 2, 114	Standard Speed, 2, 117	8	1:16.88	90,000
1999	Bevo, 2, 117	E. S. Prado	Afternoon Affair, 2, 114	Settlement, 2, 114	6	1:17.78	90,000
1998	Prime Directive, 2, 114	J. F. Chavez	Silk Broker, 2, 114	Tactical Cat, 2, 117	4	1:17.18	90,000
1997	Favorite Trick, 2, 122	P. Day	Case Dismissed, 2, 114	K. O. Punch, 2, 119	5	1:17.15	90,000
1996	All Chatter, 2, 113	J. F. Chavez	Gray Raider, 2, 114	Just a Cat, 2, 113	10	1:16.37	84,375
1995	Bright Launch, 2, 112	J. A. Santos	Devil's Honor, 2, 114	Severe Clear, 2, 113	8	1:17.98	66,540
1994	Montreal Red, 2, 122	J. A. Santos	Flitch, 2, 115	Law of the Sea, 2, 115	5	1:17.96	64,800
1993	Dehere, 2, 117	E. Maple	Slew Gin Fizz, 2, 117	Whitney Tower, 2, 117	9	1:09.92	71,760
1992	Tactical Advantage, 2, 117	J. A. Krone	Strolling Along, 2, 117	Mi Cielo, 2, 117	10	1:10.59	72,600
1991	Caller I. D., 2, 117	J. D. Bailey	Pick Up the Phone, 2, 122	Coin Collector, 2, 122	8	1:09.55	71,040
1990	To Freedom, 2, 124	A. T. Cordero Jr.	Fighting Affair, 2, 117	Eugene Eugene, 2, 117	6	1:11.40	52,740
1989	Summer Squall, 2, 124	P. Day	Dr. Bobby A., 2, 117	Graf, 2, 117	8	1:09.80	53,370
1988	Trapp Mountain, 2, 117	J. D. Bailey	Bio, 2, 122	Leading Prospect, 2, 117	7	1:10.80	66,240
1987	Crusader Sword, 2, 117	R. G. Davis	Tejano, 2, 117	Endurance, 2, 119	8	1:10.20	66,420
1986	Gulch, 2, 122	A. T. Cordero Jr.	Jazzing Around, 2, 117	Java Gold, 2, 117	10	1:10.00	54,990
1985	Sovereign Don, 2, 122	J. Velasquez	Hagley Mill, 2, 117	Bullet Blade, 2, 117	9	1:11.40	43,200
1984	Chief's Crown, 2, 117	D. MacBeth	Do It Again Dan, 2, 117	Sky Command, 2, 122	6	1:10.20	42,060
1983	Swale, 2, 117	E. Maple	Shuttle Jet, 2, 117	Big Walt, 2, 117	7	1:12.60	33,720
1982	Victorious, 2, 122	A. T. Cordero Jr.	Pappa Riccio, 2, 124	Safe Ground, 2, 119	7	1:10.60	33,960
1981	Conquistador Cielo, 2, 117	E. Maple	Herschelwalker, 2, 117	Timely Writer, 2, 122	10	1:10.60	33,900
1980	Well Decorated, 2, 117	M. Venezia	Tap Shoes, 2, 117	Motivity, 2, 119	10	1:10.20	34,320
1979	J. P. Brother, 2, 122	E. Maple	Native Moment, 2, 117	Muckraker, 2, 122	5	1:12.00	25,365
1978	General Assembly, 2, 117	D. G. McHargue	‡Turnbuckle, 2, 117	Make a Mess, 2, 117	8	1:09.00	22,350
1977	Darby Creek Road, 2, 117	A. T. Cordero Jr.	Jet Diplomacy, 2, 122	Quadratic, 2, 122	10	1:10.00	22,470
1976	Banquet Table, 2, 122	J. Vasquez	Turn of Coin, 2, 122	May I Rule, 2, 117	9	1:11.60	22,455
1975	Bold Forbes, 2, 120	J. Velasquez	Family Doctor, 2, 117	Gentle King, 2, 120	5	1:09.80	22,680
1974	Our Talisman, 2, 117	M. Venezia	Valid Appeal, 2, 117	Knightly Sport, 2, 120	10	1:10.40	17,430
1973	Az Igazi, 2, 117	M. Venezia	Gusty O'Shay, 2, 117	Lakeville, 2, 117	8	1:11.00	17,025

The race and the track are named for the town of Saratoga Springs, New York. In the past, "special" races were "winner take all." Saratoga Special Sweepstakes 1901-'58. Saratoga Special Breeders' Cup S. 2006. Held at Belmont Park 1943-'45. Not held 1911-'12, 2004. 5½ furlongs 1901-'05. 6 furlongs 1906-'10, 1913-'93, 2005. ‡Smarten finished second, DQ to eighth, 1978.

Schuylerville Stakes

Grade 3 in 2008. Saratoga Race Course, two-year-olds, fillies, 6 furlongs, dirt. Held July 25, 2007, with a gross value of $111,000. First held in 1918. First graded in 1973. Stakes record 1:09.80 (1974 Laughing Bridge [2nd Div.]; 1988 Wonders Delight).

Year	Winner	Jockey	Second	Third	Strs	Time	1st Purse
2007	Subtle Aly, 2, 119	E. S. Prado	I Promise, 2, 119	Blitzing, 2, 119	8	1:11.06	$66,600
2006	Cotton Blossom, 2, 119	J. R. Velazquez	Desire to Excel, 2, 121	Chief Officer, 2, 119	8	1:11.63	66,780
2004	Classic Elegance, 2, 122	P. Day	Angel Trumpet, 2, 118	Wild Chick, 2, 118	10	1:12.48	90,000
2003	Ashado, 2, 118	E. S. Prado	Maple Syrple, 2, 122	Hermione's Magic, 2, 118	7	1:12.22	90,000
2002	Freedom's Daughter, 2, 118	J. R. Velazquez	Miss Mary Apples, 2, 118	Mymich, 2, 116	7	1:12.14	90,000
2001	Touch Love, 2, 119	J. F. Chavez	Lakeside Cup, 2, 117	Lost Expectations, 2, 117	6	1:11.12	65,460
2000	Gold Mover, 2, 122	C. Perret	Seeking It All, 2, 114	Miss Doolittle, 2, 114	5	1:10.33	64,920
1999	Magicalmysterycat, 2, 122	P. Day	Circle of Life, 2, 114	Regally Appealing, 2, 114	7	1:10.91	65,700
1998	Call Me Up, 2, 117	J. F. Chavez	Brittons Hill, 2, 117	Fantasy Lake, 2, 117	8	1:12.89	66,060
1997	Countess Diana, 2, 116	S. J. Sellers	Love Lock, 2, 119	Sequence, 2, 116	6	1:10.39	64,800
1996	How About Now, 2, 115	R. Migliore	Exclusive Hold, 2, 115	City College, 2, 115	11	1:12.37	68,220
1995	Golden Attraction, 2, 121	D. M. Barton	Daylight Come, 2, 112	Western Dreamer, 2, 121	8	1:10.84	65,940
1994	Changing Ways, 2, 114	M. E. Smith	Unacceptable, 2, 119	Artic Experience, 2, 114	10	1:12.66	67,980
1993	Strategic Maneuver, 2, 114	J. A. Santos	Astas Foxy Lady, 2, 119	She Rides Tonite, 2, 114	11	1:11.15	73,560
1992	Distinct Habit, 2, 119	J. D. Bailey	Tourney, 2, 114	Lily La Belle, 2, 114	9	1:11.03	72,480
1991	Turnback the Alarm, 2, 114	D. Carr	Speed Dialer, 2, 119	Teddy's Top Ten, 2, 114	13	1:12.04	76,200
1990	Meadow Star, 2, 119	C. W. Antley	Garden Gal, 2, 119	Prayerful Miss, 2, 114	7	1:11.20	53,010
1989	Golden Reef, 2, 114	J. A. Santos	Lucy's Glory, 2, 119	Miss Cox's Hat, 2, 114	10	1:10.40	54,360
1988	Wonders Delight, 2, 114	J. A. Santos	Coax Chelsie, 2, 114	Attu, 2, 112	9	**1:09.80**	67,680
1987	Over All, 2, 119	A. T. Cordero Jr.	Joe's Tammie, 2, 119	Flashy Runner, 2, 119	6	1:10.60	68,850
1986	Sacahuista, 2, 114	C. J. McCarron	Our Little Margie, 2, 114	Collins, 2, 114	9	1:10.60	54,540
1985	I'm Splendid, 2, 114	A. T. Cordero Jr.	Musical Lark (Ire), 2, 114	Famous Speech, 2, 114	6	1:10.80	41,820
1984	Weekend Delight, 2, 119	C. R. Woods Jr.	Resembling, 2, 114	Winters' Love, 2, 114	8	1:11.60	42,840
1983	Bottle Top, 2, 114	D. Brumfield	Officer's Ball, 2, 114	Ark, 2, 114	7	1:11.20	34,020
1982	Weekend Surprise, 2, 114	E. Maple	Share the Fantasy, 2, 116	Flying Lassie, 2, 114	7	1:11.40	34,620
1981	Mystical Mood, 2, 114	J. Vasquez	Aga Pantha, 2, 114	Trove, 2, 116	8	1:11.80	34,320
1980	Sweet Revenge, 2, 114	J. Velasquez	Companionship, 2, 114	Heavenly Cause, 2, 114	11	1:11.40	34,980
1979	Damask Fan, 2, 116	E. Maple	Jet Rating, 2, 114	Lovin' Lass, 2, 112	7	1:10.20	25,860
1978	Palm Hut, 2, 121	R. I. Velez	Hermanville, 2, 114	Please Try Hard, 2, 114	7	1:10.80	22,215
1977	L'Alezane, 2, 121	R. Turcotte	Akita, 2, 121	Lakeville Miss, 2, 114	8	1:11.80	22,350
1976	Mrs. Warren, 2, 114	E. Maple	Tickle My Toes, 2, 116	Spy Flag, 2, 112	12	1:11.80	22,980
1975	Nijana, 2, 112	J. Velasquez	Future Tense, 2, 114	Crown Treasure, 2, 116	7	1:12.20	22,680

Year	Winner	Jockey	Second	Third	Strs	Time	1st Purse
1974	Our Dancing Girl, 2, 116	V. A. Bracciale Jr.	Secret's Out, 2, 119	But Exclusive, 2, 116	7	1:11.20	$16,575
	Laughing Bridge, 2, 117	B. Baeza	Molly Ballantine, 2, 116	Fair Wind, 2, 119	7	1:09.80	16,500
1973	Talking Picture, 2, 116	B. Baeza	Imajoy, 2, 116	Celestial Lights, 2, 119	10	1:10.80	17,760

Named for a town located 12 miles east of Saratoga Springs in upstate New York. Grade 2 1973-'74, 1987-2004. Held at Belmont Park 1943-'45. Held at Jamaica 1952. Not held 2005. 5½ furlongs 1918-'59, 1962-'68. Two divisions 1974.

Secretariat Stakes

Grade 1 in 2008. Arlington Park, three-year-olds, 1¼ miles, turf. Held August 11, 2007, with a gross value of $400,000. First held in 1974. First graded in 1975. Stakes record 1:59.65 (2004 Kitten's Joy).

Year	Winner	Jockey	Second	Third	Strs	Time	1st Purse
2007	Shamdinan (Fr), 3, 119	J. R. Leparoux	Red Giant, 3, 123	Going Ballistic, 3, 121	9	2:04.02	$225,600
2006	Showing Up, 3, 126	C. H. Velasquez	Ivan Denisovich (Ire), 3, 119	Primary, 3, 119	6	2:00.09	240,000
2005	Gun Salute, 3, 123	C. H. Velasquez	English Channel, 3, 126	Chattahoochee War, 3, 121	8	2:03.79	240,000
2004	Kitten's Joy, 3, 123	J. D. Bailey	Greek Sun, 3, 121	Moscow Ballet (Ire), 3, 119	7	1:59.65	240,000
2003	Kicken Kris, 3, 116	J. Castellano	Joe Bear (Ire), 3, 116	Lismore Knight, 3, 121	11	2:02.53	240,000
2002	Chiselling, 3, 121	K. Desormeaux	Jazz Beat (Ire), 3, 117	Extra Check, 3, 116	7	2:04.16	240,000
2001	Startac, 3, 121	A. O. Solis	Strut the Stage, 3, 123	Sharp Performance, 3, 121	11	2:04.91	240,000
2000	Ciro, 3, 120	M. J. Kinane	King Cugat, 3, 123	Guillamou City (Fr), 3, 117	8	2:01.64	240,000
1997	Honor Glide, 3, 123	G. K. Gomez	Casey Tibbs (Ire), 3, 116	Glok, 3, 114	9	2:02.74	240,000
1996	Marlin, 3, 114	S. J. Sellers	Trail City, 3, 126	Dancing Fred, 3, 114	10	2:01.09	300,000
1995	Hawk Attack, 3, 120	P. Day	Mecke, 3, 117	Petit Poucet (GB), 3, 116	10	2:00.17	240,000
1994	Vaudeville, 3, 123	G. L. Stevens	Dare and Go, 3, 114	Jaggery John, 3, 120	13	2:01.11	240,000
1993	Awad, 3, 120	J. Velasquez	Explosive Red, 3, 123	Brazany, 3, 114	14	2:08.74	240,000
1992	Ghazi, 3, 114	R. G. Davis	Paradise Creek, 3, 123	†Tango Charlie, 3, 117	10	2:01.18	180,000
1991	Jackie Wackie, 3, 123	P. Day	Olympio, 3, 126	Sultry Song, 3, 114	8	2:01.27	180,000
1990	Super Abound, 3, 114	R. P. Romero	Unbridled, 3, 126	†Super Fan, 3, 117	8	2:01.60	150,000
1989	Hawkster, 3, 123	P. A. Valenzuela	Chenin Blanc, 3, 114	Ninety Years Young, 3, 114	8	2:04.00	150,000
1987	Stately Don, 3, 113	J. Vasquez	The Medic, 3, 120	Zaizoom, 3, 120	11	2:04.60	103,590
1986	Southjet, 3, 113	J. A. Santos	Glow, 3, 120	Tripoli Shores, 3, 115	10	2:02.00	102,510
1985	Derby Wish, 3, 114	R. P. Romero	‡Day Shift, 3, 114	Duluth, 3, 123	12	2:01.00	146,880
1984	Vision, 3, 114	G. McCarron	Mr. Japan, 3, 114	Pine Circle, 3, 114	8	2:38.40	117,240
1983	Fortnightly, 3, 117	P. Day	Jack Slade, 3, 114	Reap, 3, 114	13	2:32.40	102,360
1982	Half Iced, 3, 114	D. MacBeth	Dew Line, 3, 114	Continuing, 3, 114	8	2:31.20	90,000
1981	Sing Sing, 3, 114	M. Venezia	Television Studio, 3, 117	Jungle Tough, 3, 114	11	2:53.60	96,240
1980	Spruce Needles, 3, 122	J. C. Espinoza	Proctor, 3, 120	The Messanger, 3, 123	6	2:40.80	99,960
1979	Golden Act, 3, 126	S. Hawley	Smarten, 3, 120	Flying Dad, 3, 120	6	2:32.80	91,080
1978	Mac Diarmida, 3, 120	J. Cruguet	April Axe, 3, 120	The Liberal Member, 3, 114	11	2:29.80	99,600
1977	Text, 3, 120	M. Castaneda	Run Dusty Run, 3, 126	Flag Officer, 3, 123	7	1:42.00	73,140
1976	Joachim, 3, 123	S. Maple	Romeo, 3, 112	L'Heureux, 3, 123	10	1:50.80	88,400
1975	Intrepid Hero, 3, 123	A. T. Cordero Jr.	Gab Bag, 3, 117	Larrikin, 3, 117	14	1:49.80	94,000
1974	Glossary, 3, 114	A. Santiago	Stonewalk, 3, 123	Talkative Turn, 3, 117	10	1:44.00	96,440

Named for Meadow Stable's Racing Hall of Fame member, 1972, '73 Horse of the Year, and '73 Triple Crown winner Secretariat (1970 c. by Bold Ruler); he made his first start after the Belmont S. (G1) in a stakes race at Arlington Park. Grade 2 1975-'83. Held at Hawthorne Race Course 1985. Not held 1988, 1998-'99. 1 1/16 miles 1974, '77. 1⅛ miles 1975-'76. 1½ miles 1978-'84. Dirt 1977. ‡Racing Star finished second, DQ to fourth, 1985. †Denotes female.

Senator Ken Maddy Handicap

Grade 3 in 2008. Oak Tree at Santa Anita, three-year-olds and up, fillies and mares, about 6½ furlongs, turf. Held September 26, 2007, with a gross value of $114,900. First held in 1969. First graded in 1973. Stakes record 1:11.56 (2005 Elusive Diva).

Year	Winner	Jockey	Second	Third	Strs	Time	1st Purse
2007	Dancing Edie, 5, 122	C. S. Nakatani	Lady Gamer, 4, 116	Strong Faith, 6, 116	11	1:13.30	$68,940
2006	Cambiocorsa, 4, 122	J. K. Court	Sandra's Rose, 4, 116	Bettarun Fast, 3, 115	11	1:12.02	60,000
2005	Elusive Diva, 4, 119	P. A. Valenzuela	Chasethegold, 5, 116	Abounding Truth, 5, 116	11	1:11.56	60,000
2004	Belleski, 5, 118	C. S. Nakatani	Intercontinental (GB), 4, 120	Acago, 4, 116	9	1:12.86	60,000
2003	Belleski, 4, 118	V. Espinoza	Buffythecenterfold, 3, 116	Icantgoforthat, 4, 115	10	1:12.37	67,200
2002	Rolly Polly (Ire), 4, 119	P. A. Valenzuela	I'm the Business (NZ), 5, 117	Nanogram, 5, 113	12	1:12.86	68,460
2001	A La Reine, 4, 115	A. O. Solis	Nanogram, 4, 111	Global, 4, 113	8	1:13.27	66,240
2000	Evening Promise (GB), 4, 118	K. Desormeaux	Strawberry Way, 5, 114	Southern House (Ire), 4, 114	10	1:13.05	67,020
1999	Hula Queen, 5, 116	A. O. Solis	Desert Lady (Ire), 4, 121	Ecudienne, 5, 117	11	1:13.05	67,740
1998	Dance Parade, 4, 120	K. Desormeaux	Advancing Star, 5, 121	Green Jewel (GB), 4, 116	8	1:13.87	60,000
1997	Madame Pandit, 4, 118	E. Delahoussaye	Advancing Star, 4, 120	Highest Dream (Ire), 4, 116	7	1:12.69	60,000
1996	Dixie Pearl, 4, 116	E. Delahoussaye	Ski Dancer, 4, 119	Cat's Cradle, 4, 118	9	1:12.33	66,400
1995	Denim Yenem, 3, 115	C. J. McCarron	Miss L Attack, 5, 116	Jacodra's Devil, 4, 116	7	1:14.92	60,400
1994	Starolamo, 5, 117	K. Desormeaux	Sophisticatedcielo, 3, 114	Beautiful Gem, 3, 115	6	1:16.07	47,475
1993	Toussaud, 4, 122	K. Desormeaux	Best Dress, 3, 113	Yousefia, 4, 116	6	1:14.32	46,950
1992	Bel's Starlet, 5, 120	K. Desormeaux	Glen Kate (Ire), 5, 117	Brisa de Mar, 4, 117	9	1:11.63	49,575
1991	Bel's Starlet, 4, 115	K. Desormeaux	Sun Brandy, 4, 117	Bright Asset, 5, 115	12	1:11.89	52,125
1990	Stylish Star, 4, 118	E. Delahoussaye	Tasteful T. V., 3, 115	Linda Card, 4, 113	11	1:12.00	51,525
1989	Warning Zone, 4, 119	R. Q. Meza	Down Again, 5, 119	Stormy But Valid, 3, 116	11	1:12.80	51,675

Racing — Graded Stakes

Year	Winner	Jockey	Second	Third	Strs	Time	1st Purse
1988	Jeanne Jones, 3, 118	A. T. Gryder	Native Paster, 4, 116	Serve n' Volley (GB), 4, 116	14	1:14.80	$53,100
1987	Aberuschka (Ire), 5, 120	P. A. Valenzuela	Luisant (Arg), 5, 118	Down Again, 3, 113	11	1:14.80	41,050
1986	Shywing, 4, 120	L. A. Pincay Jr.	Her Royalty, 5, 119	Water Crystals, 5, 119	9	1:14.80	31,075
	Lichi (Chi), 6, 115	G. Baze	Tax Dodge, 5, 119	Outstandingly, 4, 120	7	1:14.60	29,875
1985	Love Smitten, 4, 119	G. L. Stevens	Danzadar, 4, 116	Sales Bulletin, 4, 117	7	1:15.40	29,725
1984	Irish O'Brien, 6, 116	J. J. Steiner	Mel's Whisper, 4, 111	Foggy Nation, 4, 116	11	1:14.60	32,200
	Lina Cavalieri (GB), 4, 116	E. Delahoussaye	Betty Money, 5, 115	Percipient, 3, 116	8	1:14.40	30,400
1983	Matching, 5, 122	R. Sibille	Excitable Lady, 5, 123	Nan's Dancer, 4, 113	6	1:17.00	37,850
1982	Maple Tree, 4, 115	E. Delahoussaye	Northern Fable, 4, 116	A Kiss for Luck, 3, 115	7	1:15.60	30,650
	Jones Time Machine, 3, 117	L. A. Pincay Jr.	Rosy Cloud, 5, 115	Manzanera (Arg), 6, 117	9	1:16.00	31,950
1981	Kilijaro (Ire), 5, 130	L. A. Pincay Jr.	Ack's Secret, 5, 118	Miss Huntington, 4, 110	9	1:13.80	28,550
	Save Wild Life, 4, 121	M. Castaneda	Disconiz, 4, 115	I Got Speed, 3, 112	11	1:14.20	29,750
1980	Great Lady M., 5, 122	P. A. Valenzuela	Evycostling, 5, 115	Conveniently, 4, 117	11	1:13.60	29,400
1979	Palmistry, 4, 115	C. J. McCarron	Splendid Size, 5, 116	Terresto's Dream, 4, 113	10	1:12.80	22,325
	Wishing Well, 4, 117	F. Toro	Great Lady M., 4, 116	Habeebti (GB), 5, 115	8	1:12.60	21,425
1978	Happy Holme, 4, 118	C. J. McCarron	Stellar Envoy, 4, 114	Pet Label, 5, 116	10	1:14.20	22,300
	‡Country Queen, 3, 118	F. Toro	Sweet Little Lady, 3, 116	Rich Soil, 4, 119	9	1:14.20	21,900
1977	Dancing Femme, 4, 125	D. G. McHargue	Lullaby Song, 4, 117	Swingtime, 5, 121	12	1:13.20	22,250
1976	If You Prefer, 5, 118	L. A. Pincay Jr.	*Accra II, 4, 115	Vagabonda, 5, 121	7	1:13.00	15,750
	Dancing Liz, 4, 114	W. Shoemaker	Miss Tokyo, 4, 120	Lucky Spell, 5, 113	8	1:12.40	16,050
1975	*Tizna, 6, 125	D. Pierce	Mama Kali, 4, 121	Modus Vivendi, 4, 122	9	1:12.80	17,700
1974	Impressive Style, 5, 123	R. Rosales	Modus Vivendi, 3, 121	*Tizna, 5, 124	12	1:13.80	19,150
1973	*New Moon II, 6, 116	W. Shoemaker	Minstrel Miss, 6, 124	Meilleur, 3, 116	11	1:13.20	19,200

Named for California state Senator Kenneth L. Maddy (1935-2000), a longtime racing enthusiast. The race is held during the autumn Oak Tree Racing Association meet at Santa Anita Park. Autumn Days S. 1969. Autumn Days H. 1970-'98. 6½ furlongs 1983, '94. Dirt 1983, '94. Two-year-olds and up 1975, 1988-'89. Both sexes 1969-'70. Two divisions 1976, 1978-'79, 1981-'82, 1984, 1986. ‡Sweet Little Lady finished first, DQ to second, 1978 (2nd Div.).

Senorita Stakes

Grade 3 in 2008. Hollywood Park, three-year-olds, fillies, 1 mile, turf. Held May 10, 2008, with a gross value of $109,800. First held in 1968. First graded in 1990. Stakes record 1:33.66 (1992 Charm a Gendarme).

Year	Winner	Jockey	Second	Third	Strs	Time	1st Purse
2008	Sweeter Still (Ire), 3, 121	M. Garcia	Magical Fantasy, 3, 117	Bel Air Sizzle, 3, 123	8	1:35.63	$65,880
2007	Valbenny (Ire), 3, 121	A. O. Solis	Super Freaky, 3, 121	Passified (GB), 3, 121	8	1:34.47	66,960
2006	Foxysox (GB), 3, 121	A. Bisono	Arlene, 3, 119	Shermeen (Ire), 3, 116	5	1:35.28	60,000
2005	Virden, 3, 119	O. Figueroa	Three Degrees (Ire), 3, 116	Thatswhatimean, 3, 117	10	1:35.37	67,140
2004	Miss Vegas (Ire), 3, 115	A. O. Solis	Ticker Tape (GB), 3, 121	Amorama (Fr), 3, 116	7	1:34.25	65,340
2003	Makeup Artist, 3, 117	V. Espinoza	Rutters Renegade (Ire), 3, 117	Shapes and Shadows, 3, 117	7	1:36.54	68,100
2002	Adoration, 3, 117	G. K. Gomez	High Society (Ire), 3, 115	Nunatall (GB), 3, 115	6	1:34.91	64,380
2001	Fantastic Filly (Fr), 3, 123	G. K. Gomez	Innit (Ire), 3, 115	Blushing Bride (GB), 3, 115	8	1:35.13	65,680
2000	Islay Mist (GB), 3, 116	D. R. Flores	Fire Sale Queen, 3, 118	Miss Pixie, 3, 114	10	1:34.16	67,080
1999	Coracle, 3, 119	K. Desormeaux	Aviate, 3, 118	Dianehill (Ire), 3, 115	11	1:34.04	67,740
1998	Dancing Rhythm, 3, 117	K. Desormeaux	Phone Alex (Ire), 3, 117	Star's Proud Penny, 3, 122	7	1:35.39	64,860
1997	Kentucky Kaper, 3, 114	R. R. Douglas	Ascutney, 3, 120	Ava Knowsthecode, 3, 115	13	1:34.74	66,780
1996	To B. Super, 3, 118	C. W. Antley	Gastronomical, 3, 118	Ribot's Secret (Ire), 3, 116	13	1:34.36	68,940
1995	Top Shape (Fr), 3, 114	C. S. Nakatani	Artica, 3, 118	Auriette (Ire), 3, 116	10	1:34.79	63,900
1994	Rabiadella, 3, 118	L. A. Pincay Jr.	Magical Avie, 3, 116	Fancy 'n Fabulous, 3, 118	6	1:34.84	60,800
1993	Likeable Style, 3, 118	K. Desormeaux	Adorydar, 3, 113	Icy Warning, 3, 118	7	1:34.56	61,250
1992	Charm a Gendarme, 3, 116	R. Q. Meza	Moonlight Elegance, 3, 116	Morriston Belle, 3, 118	13	**1:33.66**	61,250
1991	Paula Revere, 3, 117	J. A. Santos	Shy Trick, 3, 114	Island Shuffle, 3, 119	7	1:35.50	61,850
1990	Brought to Mind, 3, 119	A. O. Solis	Tasteful T. V., 3, 119	She's a V. P., 3, 117	8	1:34.40	62,650
1989	Reluctant Guest, 3, 114	C. J. McCarron	Formidable Lady, 3, 119	General Charge (Ire), 3, 119	7	1:34.00	50,200
1988	Do So, 3, 117	A. O. Solis	Pattern Step, 3, 119	Sheesham, 3, 117	4	1:34.20	45,950
1987	Pen Bal Lady (GB), 3, 117	E. Delahoussaye	Sweettuc, 3, 119	Davie's Lamb, 3, 116	6	1:35.40	61,350
1986	Nature's Way, 3, 117	C. J. McCarron	An Empress, 3, 115	Miraculous, 3, 119	7	1:42.60	39,200
1985	Akamini (Fr), 3, 117	F. Toro	Charming Susan, 3, 115	Sharp Ascent, 3, 114	6	1:35.40	32,250
	Shywing, 3, 117	T. Lipham	Delaware Ginny, 3, 117	Savannah Dancer, 3, 119	8	1:35.60	33,450
1984	Heartlight, 3, 117	L. A. Pincay Jr.	Table Ten, 3, 115	Dear Carrie, 3, 115	6	1:35.60	38,900
1983	Stage Door Canteen, 3, 114	C. J. McCarron	I'm Prestigious, 3, 116	O'Happy Day, 3, 115	6	1:35.60	25,675
	Preceptress, 3, 115	M. Castaneda	Madam Forbes, 3, 114	Toga, 3, 116	6	1:36.60	25,675
1982	Skillful Joy, 3, 119	C. J. McCarron	Phaedra, 3, 122	Faneuil Lass, 3, 122	5	1:35.60	31,050
1981	Shimmy, 3, 114	P. A. Valenzuela	Queen of Prussia (Ire), 3, 121	Bee a Scout, 3, 114	6	1:36.20	37,450
1980	Ballare, 3, 117	C. J. McCarron	Street Ballet, 3, 119	Cinegita, 3, 114	5	1:35.00	31,600
1979	Variety Queen, 3, 117	R. Rosales	Top Soil, 3, 119	Whydidju, 3, 122	7	1:37.00	25,850
1978	Blue Blood, 3, 117	D. Pierce	Equanimity, 3, 122	Eximious, 3, 119	6	1:37.60	25,000
1977	*Glenaris, 3, 114	W. Shoemaker	Countess Fager, 3, 119	Shop Windows, 3, 114	7	1:36.00	19,300
1976	Now Pending, 3, 117	D. Pierce	Cascapedia, 3, 115	Queen to Be, 3, 119	11	1:35.80	20,650
1975	Raise Your Skirts, 3, 119	W. Mahorney	Fresno Flyer, 3, 117	Vol Au Vent, 3, 117	7	1:36.40	19,050
1973	Cellist, 3, 119	J. L. Rotz	Jungle Princess, 3, 120	Meilleur, 3, 119	10	1:42.20	20,250

Young, unmarried women are known as senoritas in Spanish. Senorita Breeders' Cup S. 1992-'95. Not held 1974. 1¹⁄₁₆ miles 1973, '86. Dirt 1973. Two divisions 1983, '85. Nonwinners of a race worth $10,000 to the winner 1973.

Shadwell Turf Mile Stakes

Grade 1 in 2008. Keeneland Race Course, three-year-olds and up, 1 mile, turf. Held October 6, 2007, with a gross value of $648,000. First held in 1986. First graded in 1988. Stakes record 1:33.72 (2000 Altibr).

Year	Winner	Jockey	Second	Third	Strs	Time	1st Purse
2007	**Purim**, 5, 126	J. Theriot	Cosmonaut, 5, 126	Shakis (Ire), 7, 126	9	1:35.56	$372,000
2006	**Aussie Rules**, 3, 123	G. K. Gomez	Remarkable News (Ven), 4, 126	Old Dodge (Brz), 5, 126	9	1:34.23	372,000
2005	**Host (Chi)**, 5, 126	R. Bejarano	Vanderlin (GB), 6, 126	Gulch Approval, 5, 126	10	1:37.67	372,000
2004	**Nothing to Lose**, 4, 126	R. Albarado	Honor in War, 5, 126	Silver Tree, 4, 126	9	1:35.55	372,000
2003	**Perfect Soul (Ire)**, 5, 126	E. S. Prado	Honor in War, 4, 126	Touch of the Blues (Fr), 6, 126	10	1:36.01	372,000
2002	**Landseer (GB)**, 3, 123	E. S. Prado	Touch of the Blues (Fr), 5, 126	Beat Hollow (GB), 5, 126	8	1:35.55	372,000
2001	**Hap**, 5, 126	J. D. Bailey	Where's Taylor, 5, 126	Aly's Alley, 5, 126	9	1:35.98	346,270
2000	**Altibr**, 5, 126	R. Migliore	Strategic Mission, 5, 126	Quiet Resolve, 5, 126	9	**1:33.72**	279,744
1999	**Kirkwall (GB)**, 5, 126	V. Espinoza	Delay of Game, 6, 126	Ladies Din, 4, 126	10	1:37.96	281,232
1998	**Favorite Trick**, 3, 123	P. Day	Soviet Line (Ire), 8, 126	Wild Event, 5, 126	5	1:35.00	168,795
1997	**Wild Event**, 4, 126	M. Guidry	Trail City, 4, 126	Soviet Line (Ire), 7, 126	10	1:34.66	134,075
1996	**Dumaani**, 5, 126	J. A. Krone	Desert Waves, 6, 126	Dove Hunt, 5, 126	10	1:35.68	133,843
1995	**Dumaani**, 4, 126	J. A. Krone	Holy Mountain, 4, 126	Mr Purple, 3, 123	10	1:38.78	116,514
1994	**†Weekend Madness (Ire)**, 4, 123	S. J. Sellers	†Words of War, 5, 123	Pennine Ridge, 3, 123	10	1:38.73	116,328
1993	**Coaxing Matt**, 4, 126	E. M. Martin Jr.	Adam Smith (GB), 5, 126	Mr. Light Tres (Arg), 4, 126	9	1:53.16	116,421
1992	**Lotus Pool**, 5, 126	C. R. Woods Jr.	Thunder Regent, 5, 126	Chenin Blanc, 6, 126	6	1:48.36	114,902
1991	**Itsallgreektome**, 4, 126	J. Velasquez	Opening Verse, 5, 126	Super Abound, 4, 126	6	1:48.42	119,600
1990	**Silver Medallion**, 4, 126	C. Perret	Shot Gun Scott, 3, 122	†Coolawin, 4, 123	6	1:52.20	121,973
1989	**Steinlen (GB)**, 6, 126	J. A. Santos	Crystal Moment, 4, 126	Posen, 4, 126	10	1:52.40	122,103
1988	**Niccolo Polo**, 5, 126	D. Brumfield	Pollenate (GB), 4, 126	Eve's Error (Ire), 5, 126	10	1:53.00	101,823
1987	**Storm On the Loose**, 4, 126	J. C. Espinoza	Uptown Swell, 5, 126	Vilzak, 4, 126	9	1:52.60	101,855
1986	**Leprechauns Wish**, 4, 126	J. D. Bailey	Ingot's Ruler, 4, 126	Wop Wop, 4, 126	7	1:51.80	100,848

Sponsored by Sheikh Hamdan bin Rashid al Maktoum's Shadwell Farm, located a short distance from Keeneland in Lexington. Grade 3 1991-'97. Grade 2 1998-2001. Keeneland Breeders' Cup S. 1991-'95. Keeneland Breeders' Cup Mile S. 1996-'98. Shadwell Keeneland Turf Mile S. 1999-2002. 1 1/16 miles 1991-'93. †Denotes female.

Shakertown Stakes

Grade 3 in 2008. Keeneland Race Course, three-year-olds and up, 5 1/2 furlongs, turf. Held April 13, 2008, with a gross value of $125,000. First held in 1995. First graded in 2003. Stakes record 1:01.78 (2004 Soaring Free).

Year	Winner	Jockey	Second	Third	Strs	Time	1st Purse
2008	**Mr. Nightlinger**, 4, 118	J. Theriot	Smart Enough, 5, 121	Fort Prado, 7, 118	11	1:03.84	$77,500
2007	**The Nth Degree**, 6, 118	E. Castro	Congo King, 4, 118	Sgt. Bert, 6, 118	8	1:03.94	68,324
2006	**Atticus Kristy**, 5, 119	G. K. Gomez	Around the Cape, 4, 119	Man Of Illusion (Aus), 5, 119	12	1:01.83	71,300
2005	**Soaring Free**, 6, 121	J. D. Bailey	Mighty Beau, 6, 121	Parker Run, 4, 119	11	1:02.22	70,246
2004	**Soaring Free**, 5, 120	S. J. Sellers	Chosen Chief, 5, 118	Banned in Boston, 4, 118	12	**1:01.78**	71,362
2003	**No Jacket Required**, 6, 118	B. Blanc	Testify, 6, 120	Abderian (Ire), 6, 120	10	1:03.25	70,494
2002	**Morluc**, 6, 118	R. Albarado	Mighty Beau, 3, 116	Grangeville, 7, 118	10	1:03.25	52,731
2001	**Airbourne Command**, 6, 118	J. F. Chavez	Final Row (GB), 4, 118	Grangeville, 6, 118	10	1:02.71	52,824
2000	**Bold Fact**, 5, 115	R. Migliore	Howbaddouwantit, 5, 118	Claire's Honor, 6, 115	10	1:02.61	46,800
1999	**Prankster**, 6, 115	S. J. Sellers	Tyaskin, 5, 120	Howbadouwantit, 4, 123	10	1:02.43	43,850
1998	**Sesaro**, 6, 123	S. J. Sellers	Brave Pancho, 4, 114	Claire's Honor, 4, 114	9	1:02.35	43,850
1997	**G H's Pleasure**, 5, 114	J. A. Santos	Louie the Lucky, 6, 114	Parklo, 5, 117	10	1:03.00	34,410
1995	**Cinch**, 3, 112	R. P. Romero	Hollywood Flash, 3, 115	Ikickedthehabit, 3, 112	4	1:47.69	38,168

Named for Shakertown, a Shaker village located at Pleasant Hill, Kentucky, near Harrodsburg. Formerly named for Robert E. Sangster's 1977 English Horse of the Year The Minstrel (1974 c. by Northern Dancer). The Minstrel S. 1995, '97. Not held 1996. Course record 1997, '98.

Sham Stakes

Grade 3 in 2008. Santa Anita Park, three-year-olds, 1 1/8 miles, all weather. Held March 1, 2008, with a gross value of $200,000. First held in 2001. First graded in 2006. Stakes record 1:48.39 (2003 Man Among Men).

Year	Winner	Jockey	Second	Third	Strs	Time	1st Purse
2008	**Colonel John**, 3, 118	G. K. Gomez	El Gato Malo, 3, 120	Victory Pete, 3, 116	5	1:50.15	$120,000
2007	**Ravel**, 3, 118	G. K. Gomez	Liquidity, 3, 119	Song of Navarone, 3, 118	7	1:48.91	60,900
2006	**Bob and John**, 3, 120	V. Espinoza	Hawkinsville, 3, 118	Sacred Light, 3, 118	5	1:49.15	61,500
2005	**Going Wild**, 3, 117	V. Espinoza	Papi Chullo, 3, 117	Giacomo, 3, 117	9	1:50.18	61,380
2004	**Master David**, 3, 116	A. O. Solis	Borrego, 3, 120	Preachinatthebar, 3, 116	7	1:49.20	48,840
2003	**Man Among Men**, 3, 120	A. O. Solis	Empire Maker, 3, 115	Spensive, 3, 120	7	**1:48.39**	48,600
2002	**U S S Tinosa**, 3, 120	K. Desormeaux	Puerto Banus, 3, 116	Hot Contest, 3, 115	6	1:49.11	47,190
2001	**Wild and Wise**, 3, 117	V. Espinoza	Swordfish, 3, 116	Special Times, 3, 116	6	1:50.51	60,750

Named for Sigmund Sommer's 1973 Santa Anita Derby (G1) winner Sham (1970 c. by Pretense). Dirt 2001-'07.

Sheepshead Bay Handicap

Grade 2 in 2008. Belmont Park, three-year-olds and up, fillies and mares, 1 3/8 miles, turf. Held May 24, 2008, with a gross value of $150,000. First held in 1959. First graded in 1973. Stakes record 2:11.57 (1997 Maxzene).

Year	Winner	Jockey	Second	Third	Strs	Time	1st Purse
2008	**Mauralakana (Fr)**, 5, 119	K. J. Desormeaux	Herboriste (GB), 5, 116	Hostess, 5, 117	8	2:14.69	$90,000
2007	**Honey Ryder**, 6, 123	G. K. Gomez	Safari Queen (Arg), 5, 119	Hostess, 4, 113	7	2:13.00	90,000
2006	**Honey Ryder**, 5, 121	G. K. Gomez	Noble Stella (Ger), 5, 116	Angara (GB), 5, 119	7	2:12.98	90,000

Year	Winner	Jockey	Second	Third	Strs	Time	1st Purse
2005	**Sauvage (Fr)**, 4, 115	J. Castellano	Angara (GB), 4, 118	Barancella (Fr), 4, 116	8	2:15.65	$90,000
2004	**Moscow Burning**, 4, 114	M. E. Smith	Spice Island, 5, 119	Meridiana (Ger), 4, 119	7	2:18.24	90,000
2003	**Mariensky**, 4, 114	J. R. Velazquez	Owsley, 5, 119	Silent Crystal, 4, 112	8	2:28.19	90,000
2002	**Tweedside**, 4, 114	J. R. Velazquez	Sweetest Thing, 4, 119	Golden Corona, 4, 114	10	2:13.63	90,000
2001	**Critical Eye**, 4, 122	M. J. Luzzi	Playact (Ire), 4, 115	Janet (GB), 4, 116	5	2:18.18	90,000
2000	**Lisieux Rose (Ire)**, 5, 116	J. A. Santos	Melody Queen (GB), 4, 113	La Ville Rouge, 4, 113	7	2:14.16	90,000
1999	**Soaring Softly**, 4, 114	M. E. Smith	Starry Dreamer, 5, 114	Pinafore Park, 4, 113	6	2:15.11	90,000
1998	**Maxzene**, 5, 121	J. A. Santos	Sweetzie, 6, 111	Colonial Play, 4, 115	6	2:14.17	90,000
1997	**Maxzene**, 4, 117	M. E. Smith	Fanjica (Ire), 5, 117	Future Act, 5, 112	8	**2:11.57**	90,000
1996	**Chelsey Flower**, 5, 114	R. G. Davis	Look Daggers, 4, 114	Transient Trend, 4, 113	10	2:12.64	67,320
1995	**Duda**, 4, 112	J. D. Bailey	Danish (Ire), 4, 116	Chelsey Flower, 4, 112	7	2:13.69	65,700
1994	**Market Booster**, 5, 114	J. A. Santos	Irish Linnet, 6, 115	Fairy Garden, 6, 120	9	2:11.69	66,960
1993	**Trampoli**, 4, 116	M. E. Smith	Aquilegia, 4, 116	Revasser, 4, 114	4	2:14.08	67,680
1992	**Ratings**, 4, 112	J. Cruguet	Ristna (GB), 4, 110	Dancing Devlette, 5, 113	12	2:15.14	75,000
1991	**Crockadore**, 4, 112	M. E. Smith	Rigamajig, 5, 114	Star Standing, 4, 114	8	2:14.95	71,760
1990	**Destiny Dance**, 4, 111	J. A. Santos	Key Flyer, 4, 108	Yestday's Kisses, 4, 112	5	2:19.20	55,080
1989	**Love You by Heart**, 4, 118	J. Cruguet	Nastique, 5, 117	Laugh and Be Merry, 4, 112	10	2:12.60	72,480
1988	**Nastique**, 4, 111	R. G. Davis	Princely Proof, 5, 115	Anka Germania (Ire), 6, 124	9	2:16.40	71,040
1987	**Steal a Kiss**, 4, 111	E. Maple	Videogenic, 5, 117	Graceful Darby, 3, 112	5	2:23.80	87,180
1986	**Possible Mate**, 5, 124	J. Samyn	Tremulous, 4, 112	Dawn's Curtsey, 4, 113	9	2:14.00	75,480
1985	**Persian Tiara (Ire)**, 5, 116	J. Velasquez	Key Dancer, 4, 118	Dictina (Fr), 4, 112	10	2:16.00	86,820
1984	**Sabin**, 4, 125	E. Maple	Thirty Flags, 4, 114	Double Jeux, 4, 111	9	2:12.80	71,880
1983	**Sabin**, 3, 112	E. Maple	First Approach, 5, 118	Mintage (Fr), 4, 114	9	2:13.80	67,920
1982	**Castle Royale**, 4, 110	J. J. Miranda	Trevita (Ire), 5, 118	So Pleasantly, 4, 113	8	2:13.00	66,060
	Dana Calqui (Arg), 4, 110	A. T. Cordero Jr.	If Winter Comes, 4, 110	Noble Damsel, 4, 115	7	2:14.20	66,060
1981	**Love Sign**, 4, 114	R. Hernandez	Rokeby Rose, 4, 115	Mairzy Doates, 5, 122	8	2:13.00	67,680
1980	**The Very One**, 5, 116	C. Cooke	Euphrosyne, 4, 114	Baby Sister, 5, 115	15	2:13.00	71,520
1979	**Terpsichorist**, 4, 117	E. Maple	Late Bloomer, 5, 123	Warfever (Fr), 4, 110	10	2:01.60	67,200
1978	**Late Bloomer**, 4, 118	J. Velasquez	Waya (Fr), 4, 115	Pearl Necklace, 4, 124	11	2:01.00	68,880
1977	**Glowing Tribute**, 4, 118	J. Velasquez	Fleet Victress, 5, 119	Dottie's Doll, 4, 116	7	1:59.60	65,700
1976	**Glowing Tribute**, 3, 110	P. Day	Bubbling, 4, 119	Carmelize, 4, 109	6	1:49.20	50,700
	Fleet Victress, 4, 115	P. Day	‡Redundancy, 5, 123	Summertime Promise, 4, 119	8	1:49.00	51,600
1975	**Gems and Roses**, 5, 112	M. Venezia	Hinterland, 5, 113	Carolerno, 4, 110	11	2:01.60	34,740
1974	**North Broadway**, 4, 116	A. T. Cordero Jr.	Lorraine Edna, 4, 117	Gnome Home, 4, 109	10	1:56.20	35,190
1973	**Shearwater**, 4, 112	A. T. Cordero Jr.	Inca Queen, 5, 118	Aglimmer, 4, 115	13	1:59.80	35,610

Named for the old Brooklyn, New York, racetrack Sheepshead Bay, which closed in 1911 with the ban of racing in New York and never reopened. Grade 3 1991-'94. Held at Jamaica 1959. Held at Aqueduct 1960-'74, 1976. 1 1/16 miles 1959, 1963-'64. 1 1/8 miles 1960-'61, 1976. 1 mile 1962. 1 3/16 miles 1965-'74. 1 1/4 miles 1975, 1977-'79. Dirt 1959, '62, '74, '90, 2001. Originally scheduled on turf 1990, 2001. Both sexes 1959-'61. Two divisions 1976, '82. ‡Summertime Promise finished second, DQ to third, 1976 (2nd Div.). Course record 1997.

Shirley Jones Handicap

Grade 2 in 2008. Gulfstream Park, four-year-olds and up, fillies and mares, 7 furlongs, dirt. Held March 29, 2008, with a gross value of $170,000. First held in 1976. First graded in 1988. Stakes record 1:21.42 (2004 Randaroo).

Year	Winner	Jockey	Second	Third	Strs	Time	1st Purse
2008	**Sugar Swirl**, 5, 124	J. Castellano	Baroness Thatcher, 4, 116	Shaggy Mane, 5, 117	6	1:22.57	$90,000
2007	**Sweet Fervor**, 4, 114	F. Jara	Any Limit, 4, 118	My Lucky Free, 4, 116	8	1:22.67	120,000
2006	**Splendid Blended**, 4, 117	M. R. Cruz	Beautiful Bets, 6, 116	Injustice, 5, 116	10	1:21.62	120,000
2005	**Madcap Escapade**, 4, 118	J. D. Bailey	Alix M, 5, 115	D'Wildcat Speed, 5, 114	7	1:22.06	90,000
2004	**Randaroo**, 4, 118	J. R. Velazquez	Harmony Lodge, 6, 121	Halory Leigh, 4, 114	8	**1:21.42**	60,000
2003	**Harmony Lodge**, 5, 114	J. R. Velazquez	Gold Mover, 5, 117	Nonsuch Bay, 4, 117	6	1:22.35	60,000
2002	**Cat Cay**, 5, 118	P. Day	Raging Fever, 4, 119	Vague Memory, 5, 112	7	1:22.31	60,000
2001	**Hidden Assets**, 4, 114	J. D. Bailey	Another, 4, 115	Dream Supreme, 4, 120	6	1:22.40	60,000
2000	**Marley Vale**, 4, 118	J. R. Velazquez	Cassidy, 5, 113	Class On Class, 5, 113	8	1:22.24	60,000
1999	**Harpia**, 5, 118	R. Migliore	Scotzanna, 7, 115	Memories of Gold, 4, 113	5	1:22.17	60,000
1998	**U Can Do It**, 5, 116	S. J. Sellers	Glitter Woman, 4, 123	Flashy n Smart, 5, 118	5	1:23.33	60,000
1997	**Chip**, 4, 114	J. Bravo	Steady Cat, 4, 113	Flat Fleet Feet, 4, 117	7	1:22.24	60,000
1996	**Dust Bucket**, 5, 112	R. G. Davis	Russian Flight (Ire), 4, 110	Culver City, 4, 115	5	1:25.97	60,000
1995	**Educated Risk**, 5, 125	M. E. Smith	Elizabeth Bay, 5, 115	Clever Act, 4, 114	5	1:22.94	60,000
1994	**Santa Catalina**, 6, 115	P. Day	Jeano, 6, 113	Traverse City, 4, 113	11	1:21.94	60,000
1993	**Jeano**, 5, 113	S. J. Sellers	Santa Catalina, 5, 115	Miss Jealski, 4, 111	13	1:23.56	39,060
1992	**Nannerl**, 5, 111	J. A. Krone	Withallprobability, 4, 120	Fit for a Queen, 6, 119	10	1:23.23	36,600
1991	**Love's Exchange**, 5, 126	H. Castillo Jr.	Peach of It, 5, 116	Tipsy Girl, 5, 114	8	1:23.00	35,820
1990	**Love's Exchange**, 4, 112	E. Fires	Fantastic Find, 4, 113	Fit for a Queen, 4, 112	9	1:23.60	36,720
1989	**Social Pro**, 4, 110	J. F. Chavez	Haiati, 4, 113	Costly Shoes, 4, 114	8	1:23.60	35,640
1988	**Tappiano**, 4, 115	J. Cruguet	Cadillacing, 4, 111	Bound, 4, 115	13	1:23.00	52,110
1987	**Life At the Top**, 4, 121	R. P. Romero	I'm Sweets, 4, 120	Jose's Bomb, 4, 112	8	1:22.80	35,640
1986	**Soli**, 4, 113	J. D. Bailey	Bessarabian, 4, 123	Nany, 6, 117	14	1:23.80	39,390
1985	**Mickey's Echo**, 6, 117	W. A. Guerra	Sugar's Image, 4, 117	Nany, 5, 122	10	1:23.60	37,110
1984	**Chic Belle**, 4, 114	C. Perret	Promising Native, 5, 114	First Flurry, 5, 115	9	1:22.40	25,578
1983	**Meringue Pie**, 5, 115	J. Velasquez	Cherokee Frolic, 5, 118	Mara Mia, 5, 109	8	1:24.20	24,717
	Secrettame, 5, 116	J. Vasquez	Prime Prospect, 5, 120	Miss Hitch, 7, 114	9	1:23.60	25,158
1982	**Bushmaid**, 4, 112	J. D. Bailey	Expressive Dance, 4, 124	Sweetest Chant, 4, 117	11	1:23.20	19,470

458   Racing — Graded Stakes

Year	Winner	Jockey	Second	Third	Strs	Time	1st Purse
1981	**Sober Jig**, 4, 112	J. P. Souter	‡Likely Exchange, 7, 116	Island Charm, 4, 115	12	1:23.20	$27,153
1979	**Candy Eclair**, 3, 122	A. S. Black	Davona Dale, 3, 122	Drop Me a Note, 3, 114	4	1:08.60	17,766
1976	**Regal Quillo**, 3, 114	C. Baltazar	Forty Nine Sunsets, 3, 112	Tristana, 3, 112	10	1:42.20	10,200

Named for James V. Tigani's SW Shirley Jones (1956 f. by Double Jay); Shirley Jones, the horse, was named for the actress. Grade 3 1988-2004. Shirley Jones S. 1976, '79. Shirley Jones Breeders' Cup H. 2006-'07. Not held 1977-'78, 1980. 1¹/₁₆ miles 1976. 6 furlongs 1979. Three-year-olds and up 1976-2006. Two divisions 1983. ‡Cherry Berry finished second, DQ to fourth, 1981.

Shoemaker Mile Stakes

Grade 1 in 2008. Hollywood Park, three-year-olds and up, 1 mile, turf. Held May 26, 2008, with a gross value of $310,500. First held in 1938. First graded in 1973. Stakes record 1:32.64 (1994 Megan's Interco).

Year	Winner	Jockey	Second	Third	Strs	Time	1st Purse
2008	**Daytona (Ire)**, 4, 124	A. O. Solis	Ever a Friend, 5, 124	Hyperbaric, 5, 124	7	1:33.44	$186,300
2007	**The Tin Man**, 9, 124	V. Espinoza	Get Funky, 4, 124	Willow O Wisp, 5, 124	10	1:34.34	238,920
2006	**Aragorn (Ire)**, 4, 124	C. S. Nakatani	Charmo (Fr), 5, 124	Silent Name (Jpn), 4, 124	6	1:32.95	204,600
2005	**Castledale (Ire)**, 4, 124	R. R. Douglas	King of Happiness, 6, 124	Fast and Furious (Fr), 4, 124	7	1:33.17	205,800
2004	**Designed for Luck**, 7, 124	P. A. Valenzuela	Singletary, 4, 124	Tsigane (Fr), 5, 124	8	1:32.81	282,000
2003	**Redattore (Brz)**, 8, 124	A. O. Solis	Special Ring, 6, 124	Touch of the Blues (Fr), 6, 124	9	1:33.37	225,000
2002	**Ladies Din**, 7, 124	P. A. Valenzuela	Redattore (Brz), 7, 124	Spinelessjellyfish, 6, 124	10	1:33.39	240,000
2001	**Irish Prize**, 5, 124	G. L. Stevens	Touch of the Blues (Fr), 4, 124	Brahms, 4, 124	9	1:33.68	285,000
2000	**Silic (Fr)**, 5, 124	C. S. Nakatani	Ladies Din, 5, 124	Sharan (GB), 5, 124	11	1:33.36	304,800
1999	**Silic (Fr)**, 4, 124	C. S. Nakatani	Ladies Din, 4, 124	Hawksley Hill (Ire), 6, 124	8	1:32.95	280,200
1998	**Labeeb (GB)**, 6, 124	K. Desormeaux	Fantastic Fellow, 4, 124	Hawksley Hill (Ire), 5, 124	7	1:33.29	319,200
1997	**Pinfloron (Fr)**, 5, 124	D. R. Flores	Surachai, 4, 124	Helmsman, 5, 124	14	1:34.40	353,400
1996	**Fastness (Ire)**, 6, 124	C. S. Nakatani	Romarin (Brz), 6, 124	Atticus, 4, 124	7	1:32.74	420,000
1995	**Unfinished Symph**, 4, 121	C. W. Antley	Rapan Boy (Aus), 7, 115	Journalism, 7, 117	9	:33.14	98,400
1994	**Megan's Interco**, 5, 119	C. A. Black	Furiously, 5, 116	Rapan Boy (Aus), 6, 115	6	**1:32.64**	63,200
1993	**Journalism**, 5, 114	A. O. Solis	Lomitas (GB), 5, 118	Brief Truce, 4, 122	7	1:32.89	63,800
1991	**Exbourne**, 5, 118	G. L. Stevens	Super May, 5, 117	Dansil, 5, 111	7	1:33.50	65,300
1990	**Shining Steel (GB)**, 4, 114	J. C. McCarron	Super May, 4, 117	Brave Capade, 5, 111	5	1:34.00	63,000
1989	**Peace**, 4, 115	W. Shoemaker	Steinlen (GB), 6, 121	Political Ambition, 5, 122	8	1:33.00	65,700
1988	**Steinlen (GB)**, 5, 119	G. L. Stevens	Siyah Kalem, 6, 115	Neshad, 4, 115	8	1:33.20	80,200
1987	**Clever Song**, 5, 119	F. Toro	Al Mamoon, 6, 122	Le Belvedere, 4, 114	5	1.41.20	61,900
1986	**Clever Song**, 4, 116	F. Toro	Poly Test (Fr), 6, 115	Both Ends Burning, 6, 124	7	1:38.80	49,400
1985	**dh-Capture Him**, 4, 120	C. J. McCarron	Val Danseur, 5, 113		8	1:33.40	26,500
	dh-Retsina Run, 5, 116	E. Delahoussaye					
	Native Charmer (GB), 4, 113	S. Hawley	Gato Del Sol, 6, 120	Both Ends Burning, 5, 123	8	1:33.60	41,000
1984	**Massera (Chi)**, 6, 115	E. Delahoussaye	Sari's Dreamer, 5, 112	Barberstown, 4, 129	7	1:34.20	33,350
	Drumalis (Ire), 4, 119	E. Delahoussaye	Bel Bolide, 6, 122	Hula Blaze, 4, 114	8	1:33.80	33,950
1980	**Peregrinator (Ire)**, 5, 119	C. J. McCarron	Dragon Command (NZ), 6, 117	Life's Hope, 7, 117	7	1:41.60	31,850
1979	**Farnesio (Arg)**, 5, 119	W. Shoemaker	Harry's Love, 4, 114	Star Spangled, 5, 124	5	1:41.60	31,100
1978	**J. O. Tobin**, 4, 125	S. Cauthen	Mr. Redoy, 4, 121	Miami Sun, 4, 115	5	1:41.40	30,600
1977	**Barrera**, 4, 119	L. A. Pincay Jr.	Beat Inflation, 4, 120	Maheras, 4, 124	5	1:07.40	24,650
1976	**Sporting Goods**, 6, 115	F. Toro	Century's Envoy, 5, 124	Money Lender, 5, 115	10	1:08.20	20,500
1975	**Rise High**, 5, 116	S. Hawley	‡Selecting, 6, 117	Money Lender, 4, 115	6	1:09.00	18,900
1974	**Beira**, 5, 115	W. Mahorney	Woodland Pines, 5, 119	Linda's Chief, 4, 124	8	1:07.80	19,700
1973	**Diplomatic Agent**, 5, 115	R. Rosales	Rough Night, 5, 111	Selecting, 4, 116	9	1:09.00	20,150

Named for Racing Hall of Fame jockey William Shoemaker (1931-2003), who retired as leading rider by number of wins. Formerly named in honor of Hollywood's film industry. Formerly sponsored by the Miller Brewing Co. of Milwaukee, Wisconsin 1971. Grade 3 1987-'89. Not graded 1975-'86. Grade 2 1990-'99. Hollywood Premiere H. 1938-'63. Premiere H. 1964-'70, 1972-'80, 1984-'89. Miller High Life Premiere H. 1971. Shoemaker H. 1990-'95. Shoemaker Breeders' Cup Mile S. 1996-2006. Held at Santa Anita Park 1949. Not held 1942-'43, 1948, 1981-'83, 1992. 6 furlongs 1938-'49, 1951-'77. 7 furlongs 1950. 1¹/₁₆ miles 1978-'80, 1986-'87. Dirt 1938-'80. Two-year-olds and up 1944. Two divisions 1984-'85. Dead heat for first 1985 (1st Div.). ‡Shirley's Champion finished second, DQ to fourth, 1975. Equaled track record 1940. Equaled course record 1993, '96. Course record 1994.

Shuvee Handicap

Grade 2 in 2008. Belmont Park, three-year-olds and up, fillies and mares, 1 mile, dirt. Held May 17, 2008, with a gross value of $150,000. First held in 1976. First graded in 1978. Stakes record 1:34.23 (2005 Society Selection).

Year	Winner	Jockey	Second	Third	Strs	Time	1st Purse
2008	**Cowgirls Don't Cry**, 4, 113	M. J. Luzzi	Rite Moment, 4, 119	Wow Me Free, 4, 117	6	1:37.31	$90,000
2007	**Teammate**, 4, 116	C. H. Velasquez	Sugar Shake, 4, 118	Rahys' Appeal, 5, 116	6	1:38.19	90,000
2006	**Take D'Tour**, 5, 115	C. H. Velasquez	Balletto (UAE), 4, 116	Smuggler, 4, 120	5	1:36.10	90,000
2005	**Society Selection**, 4, 118	E. Coa	Daydreaming, 4, 119	Bohemian Lady, 4, 114	5	**1:34.23**	120,000
2004	**Storm Flag Flying**, 4, 116	J. R. Velazquez	Passing Shot, 5, 117	Roar Emotion, 4, 119	6	1:36.10	120,000
2003	**Wild Spirit (Chi)**, 4, 115	J. Castellano	Smok'n Frolic, 4, 119	You, 4, 120	6	1:34.51	120,000
2002	**Shiny Band**, 4, 113	R. G. Davis	Raging Fever, 4, 121	Victory Ride, 4, 118	5	1:34.96	120,000
2001	**Apple of Kent**, 5, 114	R. Migliore	March Magic, 4, 113	Country Hideaway, 5, 118	5	1:35.13	120,000
2000	**Beautiful Pleasure**, 5, 122	J. F. Chavez	Biogio's Rose, 6, 115	Up We Go, 4, 114	5	1:35.65	120,000
1999	**Catinca**, 4, 113	R. Migliore	Sister Act, 4, 115	Tap to Music, 4, 115	6	1:34.38	90,000
1998	**Colonial Minstrel**, 4, 117	J. R. Velazquez	Dixie Flag, 4, 120	Hidden Reserve, 4, 113	5	1:36.20	90,000
1997	**Hidden Lake**, 4, 115	R. Migliore	Flat Fleet Feet, 4, 120	Escena, 4, 116	9	1:35.27	90,000

Year	Winner	Jockey	Second	Third	Strs	Time	1st Purse
1996	Clear Mandate, 4, 111	J. A. Krone	Smooth Charmer, 4, 111	Restored Hope, 5, 115	7	1:35.01	$90,000
1995	Inside Information, 4, 119	J. A. Santos	Sky Beauty, 5, 126	Restored Hope, 4, 115	4	1:35.10	80,220
1994	Sky Beauty, 4, 125	M. E. Smith	For all Seasons, 4, 113	Looie Capote, 5, 112	4	1:40.60	90,000
1993	Turnback the Alarm, 4, 117	C. W. Antley	Shared Interest, 5, 113	Vivano, 4, 112	9	1:43.11	90,000
1992	Missy's Mirage, 4, 116	E. Maple	Harbour Club, 5, 110	Versailles Treaty, 4, 119	6	1:40.74	102,960
1991	A Wild Ride, 4, 119	M. E. Smith	Buy the Firm, 5, 122	Degenerate Gal, 6, 117	6	1:42.52	103,140
1990	Tis Juliet, 4, 113	R. Migliore	Survive, 6, 119	Dreamy Mimi, 4, 114	7	1:43.00	102,780
1989	Banker's Lady, 4, 122	A. T. Cordero Jr.	Rose's Cantina, 5, 117	Grecian Flight, 5, 117	7	1:40.80	104,280
1988	Personal Ensign, 4, 121	R. P. Romero	Clabber Girl, 5, 118	Bishop's Delight, 5, 111	6	1:41.60	102,060
1987	Ms. Eloise, 4, 117	R. G. Davis	North Sider, 5, 120	Clemanna's Rose, 6, 114	10	1:41.80	107,820
1986	Lady's Secret, 4, 126	P. Day	Endear, 4, 115	Ride Sally, 4, 125	6	1:41.80	81,780
1985	Life's Magic, 4, 121	J. Velasquez	Heatherten, 6, 126	Some for All, 4, 109	7	1:42.40	83,820
1984	Queen of Song, 5, 117	S. Maple	Try Something New, 5, 121	Narrate, 4, 116	6	1:43.00	86,340
1983	Dance Number, 4, 113	A. T. Cordero Jr.	Number, 4, 117	May Day Eighty, 4, 116	4	1:40.40	49,500
1982	Anti Lib, 4, 119	J. Vasquez	Tina Tina Too, 4, 112	Funny Bone, 4, 108	7	1:41.60	33,420
1981	Chain Bracelet, 4, 117	R. Hernandez	Weber City Miss, 4, 118	Wistful, 4, 120	5	1:42.80	32,700
1980	Alada, 4, 115	J. Fell	Lady Lonsdale, 5, 115	Blitey, 4, 116	5	1:43.00	32,460
1979	Pearl Necklace, 5, 121	J. Fell	Tingle Stone, 4, 120	Kit's Double, 6, 109	8	1:41.40	32,280
1978	One Sum, 4, 121	R. Hernandez	Sparkling Topaz, 4, 107	Charming Story, 4, 113	5	1:44.00	31,830
1977	‡Mississippi Mud, 4, 113	J. Vasquez	Sweet Bernice, 4, 109	Secret Lanvin, 4, 111	10	1:43.60	32,760
1976	Proud Delta, 4, 122	J. Vasquez	Snooze, 4, 108	Let Me Linger, 4, 115	8	1:35.00	33,810

Named for Mrs. Whitney Stone's 1970, '71 champion older female and '69 Coaching Club American Oaks winner Shuvee (1966 f. by Nashua). Grade 1 1986-'96. 1¹⁄₁₆ miles 1977-'94. ‡Secret Lanvin finished first, DQ to third, 1977.

Silverbulletday Stakes

Grade 3 in 2008. Fair Grounds, three-year-olds, fillies, 1¹⁄₁₆ miles, dirt. Held February 9, 2008, with a gross value of $196,000. First held in 1982. First graded in 1999. Stakes record 1:42.09 (2002 Take Charge Lady).

Year	Winner	Jockey	Second	Third	Strs	Time	1st Purse
2008	Indian Blessing, 3, 122	G. K. Gomez	Proud Spell, 3, 122	Highest Class, 3, 116	7	1:43.75	$120,000
2007	Appealing Zophie, 3, 122	J. R. Velazquez	Total, 3, 122	Get Ready Bertie, 3, 122	9	1:44.13	120,000
2006	Baghdaria, 3, 116	M. C. Berry	French Park, 3, 122	Capozzene, 3, 116	7	1:46.07	161,520
2005	Summerly, 3, 118	D. J. Meche	Eyes On Eddy, 3, 112	Enduring Will, 3, 122	9	1:43.79	90,000
2004	Shadow Cast, 3, 116	R. Albarado	Quick Temper, 3, 113	Sister Swank, 3, 117	6	1:46.82	90,000
2003	Belle of Perintown, 3, 122	C. H. Borel	Afternoon Dreams, 3, 112	Rebridled Dreams, 3, 117	8	1:44.48	90,000
2002	Take Charge Lady, 3, 122	J. K. Court	Charmed Gift, 3, 119	Chamrousse, 3, 115	5	**1:42.09**	90,000
2001	Lakenheath, 3, 119	C. J. Lanerie	Morning Sun, 3, 112	Beloved by All, 3, 114	5	1:46.09	75,000
2000	Shawnee Country, 3, 122	D. J. Meche	Chilukki, 3, 122	Humble Clerk, 3, 122	9	1:45.11	75,000
1999	Silverbulletday, 3, 122	G. L. Stevens	Brushed Halory, 3, 114	On a Soapbox, 3, 119	8	1:44.36	75,000
1998	Cool Dixie, 3, 122	R. D. Ardoin	Lu Ravi, 3, 114	Silent Eskimo, 3, 112	9	1:43.38	75,000
1997	Blushing K. D., 3, 122	L. J. Meche	Tomisue's Delight, 3, 119	Morelia, 3, 122	6	1:42.48	60,000
1996	Up Dip, 3, 114	C. C. Bourque	Brush With Tequila, 3, 113	Not Likely, 3, 122	8	1:44.61	37,635
1995	Legendary Priness, 3, 113	C. A. Emigh	Broad Smile, 3, 122	Hero's Valor, 3, 114	9	1:44.42	25,875
1994	Playcaller, 3, 119	R. D. Ardoin	Two Altazano, 3, 112	Briar Road, 3, 112	7	1:44.31	31,095
1993	Bright Penny, 3, 114	R. D. Ardoin	She's a Little Shy, 3, 114	Wakerup, 3, 112	7	1:44.80	19,095
1992	Prospectors Delite, 3, 117	B. J. Walker Jr.	Royal Med, 3, 112	Glitzi Bj, 3, 119	7	1:43.80	19,020
1991	Nalees Pin, 3, 122	K. Bourque	Oxford Screen, 3, 112	Lady Blockbuster, 3, 119	6	1:46.50	19,065
1990	Windansea, 3, 112	R. P. Romero	Everlasting Lady, 3, 119	A Hula, 3, 114	11	1:46.40	16,560
1989	Exquisite Mistress, 3, 114	C. H. Borel	Jewel Bid, 3, 117	Lunar Princess, 3, 112	6	1:46.80	16,065
1988	False Glitter, 3, 114	S. P. Romero	Part Native, 3, 117	Quite a Gem, 3, 114	10	1:47.40	16,710
1987	Out of the Bid, 3, 112	K. Bourque	Trapped, 3, 115	Quick Closing, 3, 122	7	1:47.20	25,170
1986	Tiffany Lass, 3, 122	R. L. Frazier	Super Set, 3, 122	Port of Departure, 3, 117	10	1:46.00	25,200
1985	Marshua's Echelon, 3, 122	R. J. Franklin	Turn to Wilma, 3, 114	Not Again Debbie, 3, 114	8	1:45.20	19,150
1984	Texas Cowgirl Nite, 3, 122	K. Bourque	Only Bid, 3, 114	Runny Nose, 3, 114	8	1:42.00	18,950
1983	Duped, 3, 122	J. C. Espinoza	Shamivor, 3, 117	Juliet's Pet, 3, 117	5	1:43.00	14,100
1982	Linda North, 3, 122	R. J. Franklin	‡Mickey's Echo, 3, 117	Rose Bouquet, 3, 122	9	1:42.80	13,950

Named for Mike Pegram's 1998 champion two-year-old filly, '99 champion three-year-old filly, and '99 Davona Dale S. (G3) winner Silverbulletday (1996 f. by Silver Deputy). Formerly named for Calumet Farm's 1979 champion three-year-old filly and Filly Triple Crown winner Davona Dale (1976 f. by Best Turn). Grade 2 2003-'04. Davona Dale S. 1982-2000. Held at Louisiana Downs 2006. 1 mile 40 yards 1982-'84. ‡Avadewan finished second, DQ to fifth, 1982.

Sir Beaufort Stakes

Grade 3 in 2008. Santa Anita Park, three-year-olds, 1 mile, turf. Held December 26, 2007, with a gross value of $122,100. First held in 2000. First graded in 2006. Stakes record 1:34.34 (2005 Tedo [Ger] [2nd Div.]).

Year	Winner	Jockey	Second	Third	Strs	Time	1st Purse
2007	Monterey Jazz, 3, 118	D. R. Flores	Mr Napper Tandy (GB), 3, 118	Twilight Meteor, 3, 118	13	1:34.36	$73,260
2006	Kip Deville, 3, 122	R. Migliore	Awesome Gem, 3, 118	Zann, 3, 118	12	1:36.12	68,580
2005	Chinese Dragon, 3, 118	K. Desormeaux	Hockey the General, 3, 118	Becrux (Ity), 3, 118	8	1:35.09	50,700
	Tedo (Ger), 3, 122	C. S. Nakatani	Eastern Sand, 3, 122	Follow the Rainbow, 3, 122	10	**1:34.34**	51,960
2004	Whilly (Ire), 3, 118	F. F. Martinez	We All Love Aleyna, 3, 120	Cozy Guy, 3, 118	9	1:34.60	67,620
2003	Buckland Manor, 3, 120	C. S. Nakatani	Saint Buddy, 3, 116	Kewen, 3, 118	9	1:36.08	46,800
2002	Inesperado (Fr), 3, 122	P. A. Valenzuela	Music's Storm, 3, 120	Golden Arrow, 3, 118	8	1:35.82	46,020

Year	Winner	Jockey	Second	Third	Strs	Time	1st Purse
2001	Orientate, 3, 122	C. J. McCarron	Sigfreto, 3, 122	Blue Steller (Ire), 3, 122	10	1:36.39	$46,440
2000	Fateful Dream, 3, 118	K. Desormeaux	Designed for Luck, 3, 122	†Vencera (Fr), 3, 116	8	1:35.03	45,705

Named for Victoria Calantoni's 1993 Santa Anita H. (G1) winner Sir Beaufort (1987 c. by Pleasant Colony). Dirt 2003. Originally scheduled on turf 2003. Two divisions 2005. †Denotes female.

Sixty Sails Handicap

Grade 3 in 2008. Hawthorne Race Course, three-year-olds and up, fillies and mares, 1 1/8 miles, dirt. Held April 19, 2008, with a gross value of $200,000. First held in 1976. First graded in 1984. Stakes record 1:46.69 (1999 Crafty Oak).

Year	Winner	Jockey	Second	Third	Strs	Time	1st Purse
2008	Golden Velvet, 5, 118	E. Coa	Tessa Blue, 4, 119	Kathleens Reel, 4, 117	8	1:51.30	$116,400
2007	Kettleoneup, 4, 118	C. H. Borel	My Chickadee, 4, 112	Rolling Sea, 4, 116	5	1:50.89	150,000
2006	Fleet Indian, 5, 116	J. A. Santos	Silver Highlight, 4, 114	Platinum Ballet, 5, 115	8	1:49.37	150,000
2005	Isola Piu Bella (Chi), 5, 118	J. R. Velazquez	Rare Gift, 4, 115	Ghostly Gate, 4, 117	7	1:49.58	150,000
2004	Allspice, 4, 115	C. A. Emigh	Bare Necessities, 5, 122	Mavoreen, 4, 114	6	1:50.66	150,000
2003	Bare Necessities, 4, 118	R. R. Douglas	Jaramar Rain, 4, 114	Lakenheath, 5, 114	9	1:52.84	150,000
2002	With Ability, 4, 115	J. Castellano	Lakenheath, 4, 115	Katy Kat, 4, 116	7	1:51.37	180,000
2001	License Fee, 6, 116	L. J. Melancon	Lady Melesi, 4, 116	Megans Bluff, 4, 116	8	1:49.11	180,000
2000	Lu Ravi, 5, 116	P. Day	Tap to Music, 5, 120	Batuka, 4, 116	8	1:49.15	180,000
1999	Crafty Oak, 5, 114	R. Sibille	Highfalutin, 5, 115	Lines of Beauty, 4, 114	7	**1:46.69**	180,000
1998	Glitter Woman, 4, 118	G. L. Stevens	Top Secret, 5, 115	dh-Im Out First, 5, 112	7	1:50.49	180,000
				dh-Tuxedo Junction, 5, 115			
1997	Top Secret, 4, 115	C. Perret	Hurricane Viv, 4, 119	Gold n Delicious, 4, 114	9	1:49.71	180,000
1996	Alcovy, 6, 119	W. Martinez	Shoop, 5, 118	Lotta Dancing, 5, 120	13	1:50.70	180,000
1995	Eskimo's Angel, 6, 114	M. Guidry	Little Buckles, 4, 113	Norfolk Lavender, 4, 112	13	1:51.53	180,000
1994	Princess Polonia, 4, 113	W. S. Ramos	Eskimo's Angel, 5, 115	Joyous Melody, 4, 113	8	1:51.88	180,000
1993	Pleasant Baby, 4, 117	J. L. Diaz	Miss Jealski, 4, 113	Steff Graf (Brz), 5, 115	9	1:49.30	180,000
1992	Peach of It, 6, 114	E. T. Baird	Bungalow, 5, 115	Zend to Aiken, 4, 113	13	1:51.28	162,090
1991	Balotra, 4, 112	R. A. Meier	Charon, 4, 122	Beth Believes, 5, 113	8	1:50.98	157,860
1990	Leave It Be, 5, 119	H. A. Sanchez	Anitas Surprise, 4, 114	Degenerate Gal, 5, 116	8	1:53.40	156,510
1989	Valid Vixen, 4, 116	J. L. Diaz	Scorned Lass, 5, 115	Arcroyal, 5, 116	8	1:52.60	156,480
1988	Top Corsage, 5, 118	P. A. Valenzuela	Yukon Dolly, 4, 114	Inspiracion (Uru), 7, 110	6	1:52.00	125,010
1987	Queen Alexandra, 5, 123	D. Brumfield	My Gallant Duchess, 5, 116	Happy Hollow Miss, 4, 113	7	1:49.60	126,330
1986	Sefa's Beauty, 7, 124	R. P. Romero	Flying Heat, 4, 122	Farer Belle Lee, 7, 118	10	1:50.00	112,290
1985	Sefa's Beauty, 6, 124	P. Day	Farer Belle Lee, 6, 115	Princess Moran, 4, 113	12	1:52.60	113,580
1984	Queen of Song, 5, 122	R. J. Hirdes Jr.	Frosty Tail, 4, 120	Herb Wine, 5, 118	11	1:46.60	97,710
1983	Queen of Song, 4, 115	R. J. Hirdes Jr.	Bersid, 5, 121	Sefa's Beauty, 4, 120	9	1:43.80	96,630
1982	Targa, 5, 116	R. D. Evans	Really Royal, 4, 115	Knights Beauty, 5, 115	12	1:45.00	98,040
1981	Karla's Enough, 4, 120	E. Fires	Favorite Prospect, 4, 117	Romantic Mood, 4, 113	9	1:37.60	46,890
	Gold Treasure, 4, 118	J. L. Diaz	Sissy's Time, 4, 120	Satin Ribera, 4, 120	10	1:38.00	47,040
1980	Doing It My Way, 4, 115	R. J. Hirdes Jr.	Powerless, 4, 118	Cookie Puddin, 4, 116	8	1:40.20	40,335
	Conga Miss, 4, 118	G. Gallitano	Century Type, 6, 120	Royal Villa, 3, 115	7	1:40.20	40,215
1979	Strate Sunshine, 5, 113	R. Lindsay	Timeforaturn, 4, 114	Century Type, 5, 112	9	1:40.80	46,830
1978	Drop the Pigeon, 4, 118	J. L. Diaz	Evelyn's Time, 5, 113	Creation, 5, 119	11	1:39.40	16,320
1977	Kissapotamus, 5, 115	G. Baze	Kittyluck, 4, 116	Lady B. Gay, 4, 116	10	1:38.80	22,470
1976	Enchanted Native, 5, 115	L. Snyder	Honky Star, 5, 121	Regal Rumor, 4, 118	11	1:40.00	31,650

Named for John J. Petre's and Chris Vodanovich's 1974 Louis S. Meen Memorial H. winner Sixty Sails (1970 f. by Creme dela Creme). Held at Sportsman's Park 1976-'89, 2001-'02. 1 mile 1976-'81. 1 1/16 miles 1982-'84. Four-year-olds and up 1984-'87. Two divisions 1980-'81. Dead heat for third 1998. Track record 1993. Equaled track record 1999.

Skip Away Handicap

Grade 3 in 2008. Gulfstream Park, four-year-olds and up, 1 1/8 miles, dirt. Held March 15, 2008, with a gross value of $141,000. First held in 1987. First graded in 1992. Stakes record 1:48.10 (1991 Chief Honcho).

Year	Winner	Jockey	Second	Third	Strs	Time	1st Purse
2008	Gottcha Gold, 5, 118	C. C. Lopez	Mr. Umphrey, 6, 115	Hunting, 5, 117	8	1:51.31	$90,000
2007	A. P. Arrow, 5, 117	E. S. Prado	Rehoboth, 4, 115	Political Force, 4, 113	7	˜:49.70	60,000
2006	Bandini, 4, 117	J. R. Velazquez	We Can Seek (Chi), 5, 113	O'Connell's (Brz), 5, 116	8	1:49.11	60,000
2005	Eurosilver, 4, 113	J. Castellano	Twilight Road, 8, 114	Zakocity, 4, 117	10	1:49.29	60,000
2004	Newfoundland, 4, 116	J. R. Velazquez	Supah Blitz, 4, 114	Bowman's Band, 6, 117	10	1:43.26	60,000
2003	Best of the Rest, 8, 121	E. Coa	Consistency, 4, 114	Roger E, 4, 114	5	1:42.72	60,000
2002	Sir Bear, 9, 116	E. S. Prado	Red Bullet, 5, 118	Hal's Hope, 5, 114	8	1:43.98	60,000
2001	American Halo, 5, 114	R. G. Davis	Vision and Verse, 5, 118	Pleasant Breeze, 6, 118	10	1:42.31	60,000
2000	Horse Chestnut (SAf), 5, 117	M. E. Smith	Isaypete, 4, 116	Rock and Roll, 5, 120	6	1:42.78	60,000
1999	Sir Bear, 6, 119	J. D. Bailey	Behrens, 5, 113	Hanarsaan, 6, 110	8	1:43.66	60,000
1998	Sir Bear, 5, 112	E. M. Jurado	Black Forest, 4, 113	Kiridashi, 6, 116	7	1:43.27	60,000
1997	Crafty Friend, 4, 114	M. E. Smith	Diligence, 4, 116	Ghostly Moves, 5, 114	8	1:42.27	45,000
1996	Halo's Image, 5, 119	P. Day	Wekiva Springs, 5, 119	Flying Chevron, 4, 116	7	1:42.71	45,000
1995	Fight for Love, 5, 113	J. D. Bailey	‡Danville, 4, 113	Pride of Burkaan, 5, 113	7	1:43.98	45,000
1994	Devil His Due, 5, 121	M. E. Smith	Migrating Moon, 4, 116	Northern Trend, 6, 111	7	1:43.17	45,000
1993	Technology, 4, 118	J. D. Bailey	Barkerville, 5, 117	Bidding Proud, 4, 114	8	1:42.47	45,000
1992	Honest Ensign, 4, 109	J. Cruguet	Peanut Butter Onit, 6, 114	Strike the Gold, 4, 117	7	1:49.41	45,000
1991	Chief Honcho, 4, 116	M. E. Smith	No Marker, 7, 113	Barkada, 5, 114	8	**1:48.10**	45,000

Racing — Graded Stakes

Year	Winner	Jockey	Second	Third	Strs	Time	1st Purse
1990	Primal, 5, 120	E. Fires	Ole Atocha, 5, 113	Wonderloaf, 4, 113	10	1:43.40	$60,000
1987	Big Blowup, 3, 115	C. Baltazar	Micanopy Boy, 3, 113	Jim Bowie, 3, 113	6	1:44.40	34,290

Named for Carolyn Hine's Racing Hall of Fame member, 1998 Horse of the Year, and '98 Donn H. (G1) winner Skip Away (1993 c. by Skip Trial). Formerly named for Broward County, Florida, location of Gulfstream Park. Broward H. 1987-2000. Not held 1988-'89. 1 1/16 miles 1987, 1993-2004. Turf 1987. Three-year-olds 1987. Three-year-olds and up 1988-2006. ‡Northern Trend finished second, DQ to fifth, 1995.

Smile Sprint Handicap

Grade 2 in 2008. Calder Race Course, three-year-olds and up, 6 furlongs, dirt. Held July 7, 2007, with a gross value of $500,000. First held in 1958. First graded in 2003. Stakes record 1:08.95 (2000 Forty One Carats).

Year	Winner	Jockey	Second	Third	Strs	Time	1st Purse
2007	Mach Ride, 4, 116	E. Trujillo	Paradise Dancer, 7, 115	Smokey Stover, 4, 123	7	1:09.89	$303,800
2006	Nightmare Affair, 5, 115	J. Sanchez	Pomeroy, 5, 116	Weigelia, 5, 115	13	1:10.56	294,000
2005	Woke Up Dreamin, 5, 117	M. E. Smith	Toscani, 5, 113	Nightmare Affair, 4, 113	9	1:09.80	294,000
2004	Champali, 4, 117	J. D. Bailey	Clock Stopper, 4, 115	Built Up, 6, 114	10	1:10.14	294,000
2003	Shake Ya Down, 5, 119	M. J. Luzzi	Private Horde, 4, 113	My Cousin Matt, 4, 116	13	1:10.03	294,000
2002	Orientate, 4, 116	M. E. Smith	Echo Eddie, 5, 117	Crafty C. T., 4, 117	7	1:09.98	240,000
2001	Fappie's Notebook, 4, 116	J. F. Chavez	Thrillin Discovery, 6, 112	Salty Glance, 6, 115	12	1:09.89	120,000
2000	Forty One Carats, 4, 116	J. Castellano	Personal First, 3, 114	Alice's Notebook, 4, 111	7	**1:08.95**	180,000
1999	Silver Season, 3, 107	E. Coa	Son of a Pistol, 7, 119	My Jeff's Mombo, 5, 116	7	1:10.03	180,000
1998	Heckofaralph, 5, 115	W. Ramos	Thunder Breeze, 4, 113	Nicholas Ds, 4, 115	13	1:11.48	180,000
1997	†Vivace, 4, 114	R. P. Romero	Score a Birdie, 6, 113	Valid Expectations, 4, 117	9	1:10.65	150,000
1996	Constant Escort, 4, 114	E. O. Nunez	Honest Colors, 5, 114	Excelerate, 4, 113	10	1:21.82	60,000
1995	Request a Star, 4, 113	A. Toribio	Thats Our Buck, 5, 113	Halo's Image, 4, 118	11	1:23.69	60,000
1994	Exclusive Praline, 3, 117	W. S. Ramos	Migrating Moon, 4, 118	Fortunate Joe, 3, 114	10	1:22.29	60,000
1993	Song of Ambition, 4, 116	R. D. Lopez	Coolin It, 4, 113	Daniel's Boy, 5, 117	12	1:22.52	45,000
1992	My Luck Runs North, 3, 114	R. D. Lopez	Groomstick, 6, 119	Cigar Toss (Arg), 5, 112	9	1:17.57	45,000
1991	Greg At Bat, 6, 114	J. Vasquez	Sunny and Pleasant, 3, 113	Perfection, 4, 115	11	1:24.26	51,105
1990	Groomstick, 4, 113	P. A. Rodriguez	Country Isle, 3, 113	Medieval Victory, 5, 119	7	1:24.20	49,170
1989	Glitterman, 4, 119	W. A. Guerra	Doddle Bug Mel, 4, 112	Proud and Valid, 4, 112	7	1:10.40	32,970
1988	Position Leader, 3, 112	D. Valiente	Medieval Victory, 3, 112	Hooting Star, 3, 113	9	1:24.80	49,635
1987	Princely Lad, 4, 110	B. Green	Rilial, 6, 113	Ward Off Trouble, 7, 114	6	1:23.80	32,580
1986	Jeblar, 4, 123	J. A. Velez Jr.	Power Plan, 4, 116	Mugatea, 6, 115	9	1:24.80	32,790
1985	Opening Lead, 5, 117	J. M. Pezua	Rexson's Hope, 4, 121	King of Bridlewood, 5, 115	7	1:24.00	32,760
1984	I Really Will, 4, 120	G. St. Leon	Mo Exception, 3, 120	El Kaiser, 4, 112	11	1:12.00	33,840
1978	J. Burns, 3, 114	N. B. Navarro	Jungle Adam, 4, 113	Forward Charger, 4, 114	8	1:45.20	17,400
1977	Ilefetchit, 5, 115	M. A. Rivera	‡Super Boy, 4, 110	Coverack, 4, 121	9	1:44.60	17,700
1974	Canvasser, 2, 116	M. Solomone	Hunka Papa, 2, 120	What a Threat, 2, 112	12	1:47.60	14,880
1973	Tai G. T., 2, 117	R. Hernandez	Mr. Sad, 2, 118	Neapolitan Way, 2, 118	12	1:46.40	14,880

Named for Frances A. Genter's 1986 champion sprinter and '85 Carry Back S. winner Smile (1982 c. by In Reality); Smile is the broodmare sire of 2004 champion three-year-old male Smarty Jones. Formerly named for the city of Miami Beach. Grade 3 2003-'04. City of Miami Beach S. 1958-'62. City of Miami Beach H. 1963-'69, 1978. Miami Beach H. 1970-'77, 1984-'93. Miami Beach Sprint H. 1994-'98. Not held 1975-'76, 1979-'83. 7 furlongs 1985-'88, 1990-'91, 1993-'96. 1 1/16 miles 1958-'60. 6 1/2 furlongs 1992. Two divisions 1958, '61. ‡Coverack finished second, DQ to third, 1977. Track record 2000. †Denotes female.

Sorrento Stakes

Grade 3 in 2008. Del Mar, two-year-olds, fillies, 6 1/2 furlongs, all weather. Held August 8, 2007, with a gross value of $150,000. First held in 1967. First graded in 1986. Stakes record 1:15.26 (1995 Batroyale).

Year	Winner	Jockey	Second	Third	Strs	Time	1st Purse
2007	Tasha's Miracle, 2, 119	D. R. Flores	Set Play, 2, 119	Foxy Danseur, 2, 117	8	1:19.59	$90,000
2006	Untouched Talent, 2, 119	V. Espinoza	Outofthepast, 2, 119	Smart n'Quiet, 2, 119	7	1:18.20	90,000
2005	Bully Bones, 2, 119	R. R. Douglas	Acceleration, 2, 117	Slick Road, 2, 119	9	1:17.36	90,000
2004	Inspiring, 2, 118	D. R. Flores	Souvenir Gift, 2, 122	Hello Lucky, 2, 118	8	1:18.29	90,000
2003	Tizdubai, 2, 118	D. R. Flores	Dirty Diana, 2, 122	Solar Fire, 2, 118	8	1:17.15	90,000
2002	Buffythecenterfold, 2, 121	M. S. Garcia	Tricks Her, 2, 115	Indy Groove, 2, 117	8	1:17.39	90,000
2001	Tempera, 2, 117	D. R. Flores	Respectful, 2, 115	Roaring Blaze, 2, 117	8	1:16.13	90,000
2000	Give Praise, 2, 116	L. A. Pincay Jr.	Sea Reel, 2, 115	Fort Lauderdale, 2, 117	7	1:17.88	90,000
1999	Chilukki, 2, 121	D. R. Flores	November Slew, 2, 117	She's Classy, 2, 117	6	1:16.40	90,000
1998	Silverbulletday, 2, 121	G. L. Stevens	Excellent Meeting, 2, 117	Colorado Song, 2, 117	7	1:17.56	64,980
1997	Career Collection, 2, 121	C. S. Nakatani	Griselle, 2, 117	Bent Creek City, 2, 121	7	1:17.43	67,825
1996	Desert Digger, 2, 116	E. Delahoussaye	Silken Magic, 2, 117	Montecito, 2, 117	9	1:16.03	65,950
1995	Batroyale, 2, 119	G. L. Stevens	Cosmic Fire, 2, 117	Waycross, 2, 117	8	**1:15.26**	47,100
1994	How So Oiseau, 2, 117	P. A. Valenzuela	Ski Dancer, 2, 117	Serena's Song, 2, 121	8	1:15.89	47,100
1993	Phone Chatter, 2, 117	L. A. Pincay Jr.	Rhapsodic, 2, 121	Noassemblyrequired, 2, 117	6	1:16.23	45,900
1992	Zoonaqua, 2, 117	E. Delahoussaye	Eliza, 2, 117	Medici Bells, 2, 115	11	1:22.67	49,125
1991	Soviet Sojourn, 2, 121	C. S. Nakatani	La Spia, 2, 117	She's Tops, 2, 117	4	1:22.38	44,475
1990	Lite Light, 2, 115	R. A. Baze	Beyond Perfection, 2, 117	Dragonetta, 2, 117	8	1:22.00	47,100
1989	Cheval Volant, 2, 117	L. A. Pincay Jr.	Breezing Dixie, 2, 115	Dancing Jamie, 2, 115	6	1:23.80	46,575
1988	Stocks Up, 2, 117	G. L. Stevens	Approved to Fly, 2, 116	Lea Lucinda, 2, 117	8	1:23.40	49,100
1987	Hasty Pasty, 2, 117	L. A. Pincay Jr.	Lost Kitty, 2, 117	Torch the Track, 2, 117	8	1:23.00	37,200
1986	Brave Raj, 2, 117	P. A. Valenzuela	Breech, 2, 117	Footy, 2, 121	10	1:22.60	33,250
1985	Arewehavingfunyet, 2, 120	P. A. Valenzuela	Life At the Top, 2, 116	Python, 2, 117	11	1:37.00	34,250

Year	Winner	Jockey	Second	Third	Strs	Time	1st Purse
1984	**Wayward Pirate**, 2, 114	W. Shoemaker	Doon's Baby, 2, 120	Trunk, 2, 116	6	1:37.20	$31,350
1983	**Leading Ladybug**, 2, 115	P. A. Valenzuela	Bright Orphan, 2, 118	Lapidist, 2, 116	6	1:40.20	31,150
1982	**Time of Sale**, 2, 113	W. Shoemaker	Sharili Brown, 2, 117	Infantes, 2, 115	8	1:38.40	32,300
1981	**First Advance**, 2, 113	W. Shoemaker	Merry Sport, 2, 115	Skillful Joy, 2, 113	8	1:38.60	26,100
1980	**Native Fancy**, 2, 117	L. A. Pincay Jr.	Raja's Delight, 2, 115	Wedding Reception, 2, 114	8	1:38.80	22,950
1979	**Hazel R.**, 2, 117	C. J. McCarron	Arcades Ambo, 2, 113	Princess Karenda, 2, 114	6	1:35.80	19,100
1978	**Beauty Hour**, 2, 114	M. Castaneda	Hand Creme, 2, 117	Top Soil, 2, 114	8	1:37.00	19,150
1977	**My Little Maggie**, 2, 114	W. Shoemaker	Extravagant, 2, 114	Short Stanza, 2, 114	8	1:36.40	16,150
1976	**Telferner**, 2, 114	L. A. Pincay Jr.	Lullaby, 2, 117	Asterisca, 2, 114	9	1:36.60	16,150
1975	**Queen to Be**, 2, 113	D. G. McHargue	T. V. Terese, 2, 114	Pet Label, 2, 116	8	1:36.80	13,350
1974	**Spout**, 2, 115	A. Pineda	Just a Kick, 2, 115	Cut Class, 2, 113	11	1:36.80	14,000
1973	**Fleet Peach**, 2, 113	D. Pierce	Calaki, 2, 116	Poona's Double, 2, 116	5	1:09.20	12,600

Named for Sorrento, California, and the Sorrento Valley region. Grade 2 1994-2003. Not held 1968-'69. About 7½ furlongs 1967. 6 furlongs 1970-'73. 1 mile 1974-'85. 7 furlongs 1986-'92. Turf 1967. Dirt 1968-2006. Ncnwinners of a race worth $10,000 to the winner 1974-'75.

Southwest Stakes

Grade 3 in 2008. Oaklawn Park, three-year-olds, 1 mile, dirt. Held February 18, 2008, with a gross value of $250,000. First held in 1985. First graded in 1995. Stakes record 1:34.60 (1987 Demons Begone).

Year	Winner	Jockey	Second	Third	Strs	Time	1st Purse
2008	**Denis of Cork**, 3, 117	R. Albarado	Sierra Sunset, 3, 119	dh-Liberty Bull, 3, 119 dh-Sacred Journey, 3, 117	11	1:37.89	$150,000
2007	**Teuflesberg**, 3, 117	S. Elliott	Officer Rocket (GB), 3, 119	Forty Grams, 3, 118	9	1:38.20	150,000
2006	**Lawyer Ron**, 3, 122	J. McKee	Steppenwolfer, 3, 119	Red Raymond, 3, 117	10	1:40.00	150,000
2005	**Greater Good**, 3, 119	J. McKee	Munificence, 3, 117	Humor At Last, 3, 117	7	1:39.09	60,000
2004	**Smarty Jones**, 3, 122	S. Elliott	Two Down Automatic, 3, 112	Pro Prado, 3, 117	9	1:37.57	60,000
2003	**Great Notion**, 3, 112	T. J. Thompson	Alke, 3, 114	Comic Truth, 3, 119	7	1:38.96	45,000
2002	**Paloma Parilla**, 3, 115	J. Lopez	Cope With an Image, 3, 112	Windward Passage, 3, 116	8	1:41.70	45,000
	Private Emblem, 3, 117	D. J. Meche	Dusty Spike, 3, 115	Clergy, 3, 115	8	1:40.29	45,000
2001	**Son of Rocket**, 3, 117	T. J. Thompson	Arctic Boy, 3, 114	Crafty Shaw, 3, 115	8	1:38.34	45,000
2000	**Afternoon Affair**, 3, 115	J. C. Judice	Fan the Flame, 3, 112	Big Numbers, 3, 115	8	1:37.18	45,000
1999	**Jim'smrtee**, 3, 112	T. W. Hightower	Kutsa, 3, 112	King of Scat, 3, 117	9	1:39.52	45,000
1998	**Hot Wells**, 3, 115	C. H. Borel	Whataflashyactor, 3, 117	Slew the Mark, 3, 115	11	1:38.69	45,000
1997	**Smoke Glacken**, 3, 117	C. Perret	Phantom On Tour, 3, 122	Always My Place, 3, 113	8	1:38.73	60,000
1996	**Ide**, 3, 122	C. Perret	Calexus, 3, 115	Bunker Hill Road, 3, 115	9	1:37.61	60,000
1995	**Mystery Storm**, 3, 115	C. Gonzalez	Hyroglyphic, 3, 119	Jetbye, 3, 115	6	1:36.63	60,000
1994	**Southern Rhythm**, 3, 112	G. K. Gomez	Dish It Out, 3, 113	Polar Expedition, 3, 122	6	1:36.95	60,000
1993	**Foxtrail**, 3, 119	W. Martinez	Dalhart, 3, 122	Rule Sixteen, 3, 119	7	1:36.51	60,000
1992	**Big Sur**, 3, 119	D. Guillory	Pine Bluff, 3, 122	Lil E. Tee, 3, 115	6	1:36.68	60,000
1991	**Fenter**, 3, 117	D. L. Howard	Battle Creek, 3, 115	Ole Grumby, 3, 119	9	1:37.06	45,000
1990	**Tarascon**, 3, 119	L. Snyder	Dotsero, 3, 122	Adjudicating, 3, 122	5	1:35.80	35,040
1989	**Termez**, 3, 112	D. Kutz	Damian's Groom, 3, 112	Heathrow, 3, 113	11	1:37.80	37,800
1988	**Proper Reality**, 3, 113	J. D. Bailey	Longview Ashley, 3, 119	Morgan's Levee, 3, 119	8	1:36.80	36,420
1987	**Demons Begone**, 3, 117	P. Day	Wayne's Crane, 3, 119	Saved by Zero, 3, 112	8	**1:34.60**	39,840
1986	**Rare Brick**, 3, 119	M. E. Smith	Bachelor Beau, 3, 115	Swingin Sway, 3, 117	14	1:36.20	39,840
1985	**Clever Allemont**, 3, 115	P. Day	It's a Done Deal, 3, 117	Numchuek, 3, 112	11	1:37.60	37,980

Oaklawn's home state of Arkansas is considered part of the southwestern United States; also, the University of Arkansas was once a member of the now-defunct Southwest Conference. Not graded 2006-'07. Two divisions 2002. Dead heat for third 2008.

Spend a Buck Handicap

Grade 3 in 2008. Calder Race Course, three-year-olds and up, 1 1/16 miles, dirt. Held October 13, 2007, with a gross value of $100,000. First held in 1991. First graded in 2003. Stakes record 1:42.59 (2001 Best of the Rest).

Year	Winner	Jockey	Second	Third	Strs	Time	1st Purse
2007	**Yes He's the Man**, 4, 113	J. A. Garcia	Electrify, 4, 122	Summer Book, 6, 117	11	1:45.14	$58,280
2006	**Nkosi Reigns**, 5, 115	J. Sanchez	Big Lover, 3, 115	Rehoboth, 3, 116	8	1:45.40	60,000
2005	**Supervisor**, 5, 116	A. Toribio Jr.	B. B. Best, 3, 114	Apalachian Thunder, 5, 118	6	1:46.94	60,000
2004	**Built Up**, 6, 115	E. Coa	Super Frolic, 4, 117	Gold Dollar, 5, 115	11	1:45.86	60,000
2003	**Tour of the Cat**, 5, 116	A. Cabassa Jr.	Best of the Rest, 8, 122	Dancing Guy, 8, 116	8	1:46.30	60,000
2002	**Pay the Preacher**, 4, 114	C. H. Velasquez	Best of the Rest, 7, 121	Built Up, 4, 112	8	1:44.91	60,000
2001	**Best of the Rest**, 6, 116	E. Coa	Dancing Guy, 6, 117	Sir Bear, 8, 117	7	**1:42.59**	60,000
2000	**Groomstick Stock's**, 4, 111	R. Homeister Jr.	Reporter, 5, 113	Broadway Tune, 4, 113	8	1:44.82	60,000
1999	**Best of the Rest**, 4, 114	E. Coa	Dancing Guy, 4, 113	High Security (Ven), 4, 114	10	1:44.67	60,000
1998	**Unruled**, 5, 116	G. Boulanger	Sir Bear, 5, 124	Laughing Dan, 5, 113	6	1:45.68	60,000
1997	**Derivative**, 6, 116	J. C. Ferrer	Shan's Ready, 5, 114	Sur Irish's Secret, 4, 114	8	1:45.65	30,000
1996	**King Rex**, 4, 116	R. D. Lopez	Derivative, 5, 113	Leave'm Inthedark, 4, 114	8	1:52.92	48,945
1995	**Pride of Burkaan**, 5, 119	R. R. Douglas	Crafty Chris, 5, 114	Dauntless Gem, 5, 114	10	1:51.96	60,000
1994	**Daniel's Boy**, 6, 111	P. A. Rodriguez	It'sali'lknownfact, 4, 110	Aggressive Chief, 4, 115	8	1:52.68	60,000
1991	**Higgler**, 3, 112	D. Nied	Jodi's Sweetie, 3, 115	Treblestaff, 8, 115	8	1:48.38	50,505

Named for Hunter Farm's 1985 Horse of the Year Spend a Buck (1982 c. by Buckaroo); Spend a Buck broke his maiden at Calder. Spend a Buck Breeders' Cup H. 1996. Not held 1993. 1 1/8 miles 1994-'96. Three-year-olds 1991. Held as an overnight handicap 1992.

Spinaway Stakes

Grade 1 in 2008. Saratoga Race Course, two-year-olds, fillies, 7 furlongs, dirt. Held September 2, 2007, with a gross value of $250,000. First held in 1881. First graded in 1973. Stakes record 1:23.18 (1994 Flanders).

Year	Winner	Jockey	Second	Third	Strs	Time	1st Purse
2007	Irish Smoke, 2, 119	J. R. Leparoux	A to the Croft, 2, 119	Yonagucci, 2, 119	9	1:24.24	$150,000
2006	Appealing Zophie, 2, 119	S. Bridgmohan	Cotton Blossom, 2, 119	X Star, 2, 119	8	1:23.79	150,000
2005	Adieu, 2, 119	J. R. Velazquez	Folklore, 2, 119	Along the Sea, 2, 119	7	1:23.68	150,000
2004	Sense of Style, 2, 121	E. S. Prado	Miss Matched, 2, 121	Play With Fire, 2, 121	7	1:23.83	150,000
2003	Ashado, 2, 121	E. S. Prado	Be Gentle, 2, 121	Daydreaming, 2, 121	6	1:24.08	120,000
2002	Awesome Humor, 2, 121	P. Day	Forever Partners, 2, 121	Midnight Cry, 2, 121	12	1:24.36	120,000
2001	Cashier's Dream, 2, 121	D. J. Meche	Smok'n Frolic, 2, 121	Magic Storm, 2, 121	7	1:23.47	120,000
2000	Stormy Pick, 2, 121	J. C. Ferrer	Nasty Storm, 2, 121	Seeking It All, 2, 121	9	1:24.33	120,000
1999	Circle of Life, 2, 121	J. R. Velazquez	Surfside, 2, 121	Miss Wineshine, 2, 121	6	1:23.25	120,000
1998	Things Change, 2, 121	J. A. Santos	Extended Applause, 2, 121	Miss Jennifer Lynn, 2, 121	7	1:24.82	120,000
1997	Countess Diana, 2, 121	S. J. Sellers	Brac Drifter, 2, 121	Aunt Anne, 2, 121	5	1:24.17	120,000
1996	Oath, 2, 121	S. J. Sellers	Pearl City, 2, 121	Fabulously Fast, 2, 121	9	1:23.71	120,000
1995	Golden Attraction, 2, 121	G. L. Stevens	Flat Fleet Feet, 2, 121	Western Dreamer, 2, 121	8	1:23.85	120,000
1994	Flanders, 2, 119	P. Day	Sea Breezer, 2, 119	Stormy Blues, 2, 119	6	**1:23.18**	120,000
1993	Strategic Maneuver, 2, 119	J. A. Santos	Astas Foxy Lady, 2, 119	Delta Lady, 2, 119	9	1:10.34	120,000
1992	‡Family Enterprize, 2, 119	P. Day	Standard Equipment, 2, 119	‡Sky Beauty, 2, 119	5	1:09.82	120,000
1991	Miss Iron Smoke, 2, 119	M. A. Pedroza	Turnback the Alarm, 2, 119	Preach, 2, 119	10	1:10.68	120,000
1990	Meadow Star, 2, 119	J. A. Santos	Garden Gal, 2, 119	Good Potential, 2, 119	8	1:10.20	143,040
1989	Stella Madrid, 2, 119	A. T. Cordero Jr.	Golden Reef, 2, 119	Saratoga Sizzle, 2, 119	7	1:10.40	141,840
1988	Seattle Meteor, 2, 119	R. P. Romero	Love and Affection, 2, 119	Moonlight Martini, 2, 119	6	1:12.60	141,120
1987	Over All, 2, 119	A. T. Cordero Jr.	Bold Lady Anne, 2, 119	Flashy Runner, 2, 119	4	1:11.00	101,340
1986	Tappiano, 2, 119	J. Cruguet	Our Little Margie, 2, 119	Daytime Princess, 2, 119	4	1:11.40	130,680
1985	Family Style, 2, 119	D. MacBeth	Musical Lark (Ire), 2, 119	Nervous Baba, 2, 119	7	1:12.00	97,680
1984	Tiltalating, 2, 119	A. T. Cordero Jr.	Sociable Duck, 2, 119	Contredance, 2, 119	7	1:11.00	85,380
1983	Buzz My Bell, 2, 119	J. Velasquez	Demetria, 2, 119	Bottle Top, 2, 119	10	1:13.20	52,740
1982	Share the Fantasy, 2, 119	J. Fell	Singing Susan, 2, 119	Midnight Rapture, 2, 119	6	1:09.80	50,040
1981	Before Dawn, 2, 119	G. McCarron	Betty Money, 2, 119	Take Lady Anne, 2, 119	10	1:09.40	52,920
1980	Prayers'n Promises, 2, 119	A. T. Cordero Jr.	Fancy Naskra, 2, 119	Companionship, 2, 119	9	1:11.00	50,850
1979	Smart Angle, 2, 119	S. Maple	Jet Rating, 2, 119	Marathon Girl, 2, 119	6	1:10.60	48,510
1978	Palm Hut, 2, 119	R. I. Velez	Himalayan, 2, 119	Golferette, 2, 119	5	1:10.60	31,770
1977	Sherry Peppers, 2, 119	A. T. Cordero Jr.	Akita, 2, 119	Stub, 2, 119	8	1:10.80	32,340
1976	Mrs. Warren, 2, 119	E. Maple	Exerene, 2, 119	Sensational, 2, 119	10	1:10.40	33,060
1975	Dearly Precious, 2, 120	M. Hole	Optimistic Gal, 2, 120	Quintas Vicki, 2, 120	6	1:10.60	47,880
1974	Ruffian, 2, 120	V. A. Bracciale Jr.	Laughing Bridge, 2, 120	Scottish Melody, 2, 120	4	1:08.60	33,060
1973	Talking Picture, 2, 120	R. Turcotte	Special Team, 2, 120	Fun Flag, 2, 120	5	1:10.60	35,040

Named for 1880 consensus champion two-year-old filly Spinaway (1878 f. by *Leamington). Grade 2 2004-'05. Held at Belmont Park 1943-'45. Not held 1892-1900, 1911-'12. 5 furlongs 1881-'91. 5½ furlongs 1901-'22. 6 furlongs 1923-'93. ‡Sky Beauty finished first, DQ to third, 1992. ‡Try in the Sky finished third, DQ to fourth, 1992.

Spinster Stakes — *See* Juddmonte Spinster Stakes

Sport Page Handicap

Grade 3 in 2008. Aqueduct, three-year-olds and up, 7 furlongs, dirt. Held October 27, 2007, with a gross value of $142,500. First held in 1953. First graded in 1984. Stakes record 1:21.10 (2004 Mass Media).

Year	Winner	Jockey	Second	Third	Strs	Time	1st Purse
2007	Tasteyville, 4, 115	M. J. Luzzi	Sir Greeley, 5, 117	Council Member, 5, 117	4	1:21.38	$90,000
2006	Silver Wagon, 5, 116	J. Bravo	Sir Greeley, 4, 117	Afrashad, 4, 115	7	1:21.52	95,160
2005	Gotaghostofachance, 4, 118	J. K. Court	Captain Squire, 6, 121	Wild Tale, 4, 116	9	1:23.16	168,900
2004	Mass Media, 3, 113	J. Castellano	Lion Tamer, 4, 118	Gygistar, 5, 123	9	**1:21.10**	66,720
2003	Voodoo, 5, 114	J. F. Chavez	Bowman's Band, 5, 120	Highway Prospector, 6, 114	9	1:22.18	67,620
2002	Multiple Choice, 4, 113	V. Carrero	Bowman's Band, 4, 118	‡Gold I. D., 3, 112	8	1:23.28	66,840
2001	Yonaguska, 3, 116	C. J. McCarron	Silky Sweep, 5, 115	Big E E, 4, 114	6	1:15.54	65,640
2000	Stalwart Member, 7, 117	N. Arroyo Jr.	Istintaj, 4, 117	Mister Tricky (GB), 5, 112	6	1:21.97	48,690
1999	Scatmandu, 4, 115	A. T. Gryder	Aristotle, 3, 114	Watchman's Warning, 4, 112	8	1:22.68	50,250
1998	Stormin Fever, 4, 120	R. Migliore	Olympic Cat, 4, 113	Adverse, 4, 113	9	1:21.49	50,115
1997	Stalwart Member, 4, 114	A. T. Gryder	Basqueian, 6, 116	Why Change, 4, 115	10	1:22.15	68,640
1996	Valid Expectations, 3, 117	C. B. Asmussen	Diligence, 3, 116	Blissful State, 4, 117	8	1:21.80	68,040
1995	Siphon (Brz), 4, 117	K. Desormeaux	In Case, 5, 113	Ft. Stockton, 3, 111	13	1:22.08	71,460
1994	Man's Hero, 4, 111	M. J. Luzzi	Itaka, 4, 117	Storm Tower, 4, 118	10	1:22.10	51,045
1993	Boom Towner, 5, 117	F. Lovato Jr.	†Raise Heck, 5, 115	Fabersham, 5, 113	9	1:10.62	53,730
1992	R. D. Wild Whirl, 4, 114	R. G. Davis	Senor Speedy, 5, 122	Burn Fair, 5, 114	6	1:09.93	51,570
1991	Senor Speedy, 4, 119	J. F. Chavez	Shuttleman, 5, 113	Gallant Step, 4, 113	7	1:09.34	55,080
1990	Senor Speedy, 3, 113	A. Santiago	Brave Adventure, 4, 116	Dargai, 4, 115	7	1:10.00	53,190
1989	Garemma, 3, 111	J. F. Chavez	Proud and Valid, 4, 111	Born to Shop, 5, 117	6	1:10.20	51,120
1988	High Brite, 4, 120	A. T. Cordero Jr.	Proud and Valid, 3, 109	Matter of Honor, 3, 112	7	1:09.60	64,980
1987	Vinnie the Viper, 4, 115	J. A. Krone	King's Swan, 7, 123	Banker's Jet, 5, 118	10	1:10.40	67,500
1986	Best by Test, 4, 112	F. Lovato Jr.	King's Swan, 6, 118	Sun Master, 5, 117	7	1:08.80	66,870
1985	Raja's Shark, 4, 120	A. T. Cordero Jr.	Love That Mac, 3, 110	Whoop Up, 5, 115	7	1:09.60	51,120
1984	Tarantara, 5, 117	R. Migliore	Muskoka Wyck, 5, 114	New Connection, 3, 113	13	1:10.80	46,140
1983	Fast as the Breeze, 4, 110	M. Toro	Maudlin, 5, 120	Swelegant, 5, 117	8	1:10.60	33,180

Year	Winner	Jockey	Second	Third	Strs	Time	1st Purse
1982	Maudlin, 4, 115	J. D. Bailey	‡Top Avenger, 4, 115	Duke Mitchell, 3, 115	11	1:09.40	$34,200
1981	Well Decorated, 3, 117	R. Hernandez	Engine One, 3, 116	Guilty Conscience, 5, 126	6	1:10.60	32,760
1980	Dave's Friend, 5, 126	V. A. Bracciale Jr.	Tilt Up, 5, 114	Hawkin's Special, 5, 114	8	1:08.20	34,380
1979	Amadevil, 5, 113	W. H. McCauley	Tanthem, 4, 123	Dave's Friend, 4, 119	7	1:09.40	32,580
1978	Topsider, 4, 109	M. Venezia	†What a Summer, 5, 124	Affiliate, 4, 118	6	1:10.20	32,400
1977	Affiliate, 3, 124	A. T. Cordero Jr.	Intercontinent, 3, 112	Gitche Gumee, 5, 117	4	1:10.00	31,560
1976	Amerrico, 4, 111	S. Hawley	†Honorable Miss, 6, 115	Relent, 5, 113	9	1:09.80	32,610
1975	Lonetree, 5, 122	E. Maple	Petrograd, 6, 119	Piamem, 5, 114	8	1:09.40	26,805
1974	Startahemp, 4, 114	J. Velasquez	Nostrum, 3, 114	Frankie Adams, 3, 121	7	1:09.60	22,950
1973	Timeless Moment, 3, 116	B. Baeza	Tap the Tree, 4, 122	North Sea, 4, 124	5	1:09.20	16,350

Named for Royce Martin's 1948 East View S. winner Sport Page (1946 c. by Our Boots). Sport Page Breeders' Cup H. 2006. Held at Jamaica 1953-'58. Held at Belmont 1968, 1970-'71, 1995, 2001, 2003, 2005. 6 furongs 1953-'93. 6½ furlongs 2001. Two-year-olds and up 1953-'58. ‡King's Fashion finished second, DQ to fifth, 1982. ‡Sing Me Back Home finished third, DQ to eighth for a positive drug test, 2002. †Denotes female.

Stage Door Betty Handicap

Grade 3 in 2008. Calder Race Course, three-year-olds and up, fillies and mares, 1¹/₁₆ miles, dirt. Held December 29, 2007, with a gross value of $100,000. First held in 2001. First graded in 2006. Stakes record 1:44.08 (2002 Stormy Frolic).

Year	Winner	Jockey	Second	Third	Strs	Time	1st Purse
2007	Bayou's Lassie, 4, 117	E. Trujillo	Amazing Speed, 4, 121	Cindy's Mom, 4, 116	9	1:46.16	$59,520
2006	Take D'Tour, 5, 124	E. Coa	Tiger Belle, 4, 115	Running Lass, 3, 115	7	1:45.38	60,000
2005	Mocita, 3, 118	E. Castro	Special Report, 4, 116	Pitanga, 3, 119	9	1:48.56	60,000
	Personal Legend, 5, 116	J. D. Bailey	Pampered Princess, 4, 118	Shady Woman, 5, 115	7	1:45.12	60,000
2003	Redoubled Miss, 4, 116	E. Coa	Grab Bag, 4, 112	Pampered Princess, 3, 114	9	1:46.76	60,000
2002	Stormy Frolic, 3, 114	J. A. Santos	Small Promises, 4, 113	Redoubled Miss, 3, 114	7	**1:44.08**	60,000
2001	Extend, 3, 112	E. Coa	Happily Unbridled, 4, 114	Halo Reality, 3, 114	9	1:46.74	60,000

Named for Betty Sessa's 1973 Vizcaya S. winner Stage Door Betty (1971 f. by Stage Door Johnny); Stage Door Betty won three races as a two-year-old at Calder. Not held 2004. Held in January and February 2005.

Stars and Stripes Turf Handicap

Grade 3 in 2008. Arlington Park, three-year-olds and up, 1½ miles, turf. Held July 4, 2007, with a gross value of $200,000. First held in 1929. First graded in 1973. Stakes record 2:27.50 (2002 Cetewayo).

Year	Winner	Jockey	Second	Third	Strs	Time	1st Purse
2007	Always First (GB), 6, 117	R. Albarado	Cloudy's Knight, 7, 116	Stream Cat, 4, 116	7	2:31.87	$118,500
2006	Major Rhythm, 7, 116	E. Fires	Come On Jazz, 5, 112	Ascertain (Ire), 5, 115	8	2:29.93	120,000
2005	Revved Up, 7, 114	B. Blanc	Cloudy's Knight, 5, 117	Swagger Stick, 4, 115	8	2:28.29	120,000
2004	Ballingarry (Ire), 5, 120	R. R. Douglas	‡Grey Beard, 5, 117	Art Variety (Brz), 6, 116	8	2:36.30	120,000
2003	Ballingarry (Ire), 4, 121	R. R. Douglas	Dr. Brendler, 5, 118	Jack's Own Time, 4, 112	9	2:28.30	131,520
2002	Cetewayo, 8, 118	R. R. Douglas	Private Son, 4, 115	Pisces, 5, 117	9	**2:27.50**	137,475
2001	Falcon Flight (Fr), 5, 114	R. R. Douglas	Langston, 4, 114	Williams News, 6, 116	11	2:27.86	96,300
2000	Williams News, 5, 115	R. Albarado	Profit Option, 5, 110	Buff, 5, 114	12	2:31.22	148,425
1997	Lakeshore Road, 4, 114	C. H. Borel	Chief Bearhart, 4, 119	Awad, 7, 119	9	2:29.57	140,025
1996	Vladivostok, 6, 116	C. Perret	Raintrap (GB), 6, 118	Special Price, 7, 118	8	2:30.23	138,075
1995	Snake Eyes, 5, 116	R. Albarado	Coaxing Matt, 6, 115	Bucks Nephew, 5, 114	7	1:56.46	45,000
1994	Marastani, 4, 113	A. T. Gryder	‡Snake Eyes, 4, 117	The Vid, 4, 113	¹2	1:54.60	60,000
1993	Little Bro Lantis, 5, 114	C. C. Bourque	Stark South, 5, 119	Coaxing Matt, 4, 115	¹2	1:56.92	60,000
1992	Plate Dancer, 7, 114	E. Fires	Little Bro Lantis, 4, 114	Stark South, 4, 114	9	1:55.00	60,000
1991	Blair's Cove, 6, 115	G. K. Gomez	Opening Verse, 5, 118	Cameroon, 4, 112	9	1:55.95	60,000
1990	Mister Sicy (Fr), 4, 114	C. A. Black	Silver Medallion, 4, 115	Careafolie (Ire) 5, 113	12	1:54.40	69,900
1989	Salem Drive, 7, 116	P. Day	Green Barb, 4, 115	Delegant, 5, 115	10	1:55.20	69,660
1987	Sharrood, 4, 120	F. Toro	Explosive Darling, 5, 121	Santella Mac (Ire), 4, 115	11	1:56.20	52,080
1986	Explosive Darling, 4, 115	E. Fires	Clever Song, 4, 120	Forkintheroad, 4, 113	13	1:48.40	70,560
1985	Drumalis (Ire), 5, 118	P. Day	Best of Both, 5, 116	Lofty (Ire), 5, 117	13	1:42.20	91,920
1984	Tough Mickey, 4, 119	J. Samyn	Fortnightly, 4, 115	Jack Slade, 4, 113	15	1:41.40	80,460
1983	Rossi Gold, 7, 122	P. Day	Who's for Dinner, 4, 110	Lucence, 4, 115	7	1:48.80	70,860
1982	Rossi Gold, 6, 124	P. Day	Johnny Dance, 4, 115	Don Roberto, 5, 118	7	1:46.00	70,560
1981	‡dh-Ben Fab, 4, 122	G. Stahlbaum		Opus Dei (Fr), 6, 116	8	1:43.80	48,600
	‡dh-Rossi Gold, 5, 123	P. Day					
1980	Told, 4, 114	J. Samyn	Rossi Gold, 4, 111	Overskate, 5, 130	8	1:43.00	72,960
1979	Overskate, 4, 125	R. Platts	That's a Nice, 5, 119	Bold Standard, 5, 111	8	1:44.00	33,360
1978	Old Frankfort, 6, 112	R. Turcotte	Capt. Stevens, 8, 114	That's a Nice, 4, 122	10	1:50.20	34,380
1977	Quick Card, 4, 118	M. Solomon	dh-Emperor Rex, 6, 116		14	1:43.00	35,640
			dh-Proponent, 5, 116				
1976	Passionate Pirate, 5, 114	H. Arroyo	Improviser, 4, 122	*Zografos, 8, 115	11	1:43.00	39,500
1975	Buffalo Lark, 5, 121	L. Snyder	*Kuryakin, 5, 111	‡*Zografos, 7, 115	7	1:43.00	40,600
1974	*Zografos, 6, 113	W. Gavidia	Smooth Dancer, 4, 111	Fun Co K., 5, 109	10	1:50.80	45,600
1973	Triumphant, 4, 119	A. Rini	Super Sail, 5, 116	Vegas Vic, 5, 114	11	1:34.80	36,400

Traditionally held during the July 4 holiday, celebrating the birth of the United States and its flag, the "stars and stripes." Grade 2 1973-'89. Stars and Stripes H. 1929-'95. Stars and Stripes Breeders' Cup H. 2000. Stars and Stripes Breed-

ers' Cup Turf H. 1996-'97, 2001-'06. Held at Washington Park 1958-'59. Not held 1988, 1998-'99. 1 1/8 miles 1929-'41, 1943-'72, 1974-'75, 1986. 1 3/16 miles 1942, 1987-'95. 1 mile 1973. 1 1/16 miles 1976-'85. Dirt 1929-'49, 1956-'58, 1960-'64, 1968-'74. Originally scheduled at 1 1/16 miles on turf 1973. Originally scheduled at 1 1/8 miles on turf 1974. Three-year-olds 1958. Dead heat for second 1977. Dead heat for first 1981. ‡*Nevermore II finished third, DQ to seventh, 1975. ‡Key to Content finished first, DQ to fourth, 1981. ‡Kazabaiyn finished second, DQ to fifth, 1994. ‡Silverfoot finished second, DQ to fourth, 2004.

Stephen Foster Handicap

Grade 1 in 2008. Churchill Downs, three-year-olds and up, 1 1/8 miles, dirt. Held June 16, 2007, with a gross value of $829,500. First held in 1982. First graded in 1988. Stakes record 1:47.28 (1999 Victory Gallop).

Year	Winner	Jockey	Second	Third	Strs	Time	1st Purse
2007	Flashy Bull, 4, 117	R. Albarado	Magna Graduate, 5, 118	Diamond Stripes, 4, 116	8	1:48.63	$498,863
2006	Seek Gold, 6, 116	C. H. Borel	Perfect Drift, 7, 118	West Virginia, 5, 115	9	1:49.24	502,647
2005	Saint Liam, 5, 121	E. S. Prado	Eurosilver, 4, 113	Perfect Drift, 6, 117	8	1:47.52	513,360
2004	Colonial Colony, 6, 111	R. Bejarano	Southern Image, 4, 122	Perfect Drift, 5, 119	6	1:50.40	502,665
2003	Perfect Drift, 4, 115	P. Day	Mineshaft, 4, 123	Aldebaran, 5, 120	10	1:47.55	531,030
2002	Street Cry (Ire), 4, 120	J. D. Bailey	Dollar Bill, 4, 114	Tenpins, 4, 115	8	1:47.84	516,615
2001	Guided Tour, 5, 113	L. J. Melancon	Captain Steve, 4, 123	Brahms, 4, 114	8	1:47.74	515,220
2000	Golden Missile, 5, 118	K. Desormeaux	Ecton Park, 4, 114	Cat Thief, 4, 117	6	1:49.56	502,200
1999	Victory Gallop, 4, 120	J. D. Bailey	Nite Dreamer, 4, 110	Littlebitlively, 5, 115	7	**1:47.28**	512,895
1998	Awesome Again, 4, 113	P. Day	Silver Charm, 4, 127	Semoran, 5, 114	7	1:48.61	495,690
1997	City by Night, 4, 113	S. J. Sellers	Victor Cooley, 4, 115	Semoran, 4, 113	6	1:50.40	101,649
1996	Tenants Harbor, 4, 112	F. C. Torres	Pleasant Tango, 6, 113	Mt. Sassafras, 4, 115	8	1:49.94	107,933
1995	Recoup the Cash, 5, 119	A. T. Gryder	Tyus, 5, 114	Powerful Punch, 6, 114	9	1:49.39	109,298
1994	Recoup the Cash, 4, 112	J. L. Diaz	Taking Risks, 4, 113	Dignitas, 5, 113	7	1:49.46	106,275
1993	Root Boy, 5, 113	T. G. Turner	Discover, 5, 114	Flying Continental, 7, 117	11	1:50.80	74,100
1992	Discover, 4, 116	B. E. Bartram	Barkerville, 4, 113	Classic Seven, 4, 113	13	1:50.14	75,335
1991	Black Tie Affair (Ire), 5, 119	J. L. Diaz	Private School, 4, 114	Greydar, 4, 115	5	1:49.81	70,915
1990	No Marker, 6, 115	A. T. Gryder	Western Playboy, 4, 117	Lucky Peach, 5, 114	10	1:49.80	72,930
1989	Air Worthy, 4, 115	D. J. Soto	J. T's Pet, 5, 115	Present Value, 5, 114	9	1:49.60	73,255
1988	Honor Medal, 7, 123	L. E. Ortega	Outlaws Sham, 5, 115	Momsfurrari, 4, 109	10	1:50.60	82,655
1987	Red Attack, 5, 119	J. L. Kaenel	Sir Naskra, 5, 116	Blue Buckaroo, 4, 117	9	1:51.20	65,254
1986	Hopeful Word, 5, 123	K. K. Allen	Dramatic Desire, 5, 114	Ten Gold Pots, 5, 122	7	1:49.40	64,133
1985	Vanlandingham, 4, 121	P. Day	Manantial (Chi), 7, 112	Sovereign Exchange, 4, 113	7	1:48.80	35,263
1984	Mythical Ruler, 6, 117	J. McKnight	Fairly Straight, 3, 114	Le Cou Cou, 4, 121	5	1:49.60	34,808
1983	Vodika Collins, 5, 118	L. Moyers	Mythical Ruler, 5, 120	Northern Majesty, 4, 114	7	1:49.20	35,588
1982	Vodika Collins, 4, 116	T. Barrow	Mythical Ruler, 4, 113	Two's a Plenty, 5, 115	7	1:51.80	38,610

Named for composer Stephen Foster (1826-'64), who wrote Kentucky's state song, "My Old Kentucky Home." Grade 3 1988-'94. Grade 2 1995-2001. Four-year-olds and up 1983, 1985-'87. Track record 1999.

Stonerside Beaumont Stakes

Grade 2 in 2008. Keeneland Race Course, three-year-olds, fillies, about 7 furlongs, all weather. Held April 10, 2008, with a gross value of $250,000. First held in 1986. First graded in 1990. Stakes record 1:24.93 (2007 Street Sounds).

Year	Winner	Jockey	Second	Third	Strs	Time	1st Purse
2008	Ariege, 3, 123	G. K. Gomez	Golden Doc A, 3, 123	Passion, 3, 119	9	1:25.81	$155,000
2007	Street Sounds, 3, 119	E. S. Prado	Forever Together, 3, 121	Palace Pier, 3, 119	7	**1:24.93**	155,000
2006	Diplomat Lady, 3, 123	C. H. Velasquez	Lake Alice, 3, 117	Wildcat Bettie B, 3, 117	10	1:27.97	155,000
2005	In the Gold, 3, 117	R. Bejarano	Holy Trinity, 3, 117	Hot Storm, 3, 119	5	1:26.04	155,000
2004	Victory U. S. A., 3, 118	J. D. Bailey	Halfbridled, 3, 123	Wildwood Flower, 3, 118	8	1:27.06	155,000
2003	My Boston Gal, 3, 120	P. Day	Bird Town, 3, 118	Midnight Cry, 3, 118	9	1:26.87	155,000
2002	Proper Gamble, 3, 118	J. Castellano	Respectful, 3, 116	Vicki Vallencourt, 3, 118	7	1:28.79	155,000
2001	Xtra Heat, 3, 120	R. Wilson	Mountain Bird, 3, 116	Raging Fever, 3, 123	5	1:27.86	155,000
2000	Sahara Gold, 3, 123	J. D. Bailey	Swept Away, 3, 118	Darling My Darling, 3, 116	6	1:26.58	84,847
1999	Swingin On Ice, 3, 115	R. Albarado	Secret Hills, 3, 115	Appealing Phylly, 3, 123	7	1:25.61	83,917
1998	Star of Broadway, 3, 119	P. Day	Santaria, 3, 119	Bourbon Belle, 3, 119	12	1:26.67	91,140
1997	dh-Make Haste, 3, 112	P. Day		Move, 3, 121	7	1:28.08	57,042
	dh-Screamer, 3, 112	R. Albarado					
1996	Golden Gale, 3, 115	M. E. Smith	Birr, 3, 115	Bright Time, 3, 115	7	1:26.10	84,398
1995	Dixieland Gold, 3, 118	D. Penna	Niner's Home, 3, 113	Conquistadoress, 3, 118	10	1:27.42	69,874
1994	Her Temper, 3, 112	P. Day	Lotta Dancing, 3, 113	Term Limits, 3, 121	6	1:28.41	67,456
1993	Roamin Rachel, 3, 122	C. W. Antley	Added Asset, 3, 114	Fit to Lead, 3, 122	10	1:26.48	69,998
1992	Fluttery Danseur, 3, 122	S. J. Sellers	Miss Iron Smoke, 3, 119	Spinning Round, 3, 122	8	1:27.46	53,918
1991	Ifyoucouldseemenow, 3, 122	M. A. Pedroza	Versailles Treaty, 3, 114	Ever a Lady, 3, 114	6	1:27.01	54,275
1990	Go for Wand, 3, 122	R. P. Romero	Trumpet's Blare, 3, 119	Seaside Attraction, 3, 119	6	1:26.40	53,983
1989	Exquisite Mistress, 3, 117	D. Brumfield	Love's Exchange, 3, 114	Up, 3, 114	10	1:28.60	36,774
1988	On to Royalty, 3, 121	C. Perret	Plate Queen, 3, 121	Tilt My Halo, 3, 121	9	1:26.60	46,680
1987	Fold the Flag, 3, 113	S. Hawley	Bound, 3, 113	Arctic Cloud, 3, 118	6	1:28.20	43,428
1986	Classy Cathy, 3, 112	E. Fires	She's a Mystery, 3, 119	Close Tolerance, 3, 112	13	1:27.60	37,408

Named for Hal Price Headley's Beaumont Farm; Headley was one of Keeneland's founders and the track's first president. Sponsored by Robert and Janice McNair's Stonerside Stables of Paris, Kentucky 2000-'08. Grade 3 1990-'92. Beaumont S. 1986-'99. Dirt 1986-2006. Dead heat for first 1997.

Strub Stakes

Grade 2 in 2008. Santa Anita Park, four-year-olds, 1 1/8 miles, all weather. Held February 2, 2008, with a gross value of $300,000. First held in 1948. First graded in 1973. Stakes record 1:45.65 (2008 Monterey Jazz).

Year	Winner	Jockey	Second	Third	Strs	Time	1st Purse
2008	Monterey Jazz, 4, 121	D. R. Flores	Tiago, 4, 123	Monzante, 4, 117	8	1:45.65	$180,000
2007	Arson Squad, 4, 121	G. K. Gomez	Spring At Last, 4, 119	Brother Derek, 4, 123	6	1:48.65	180,000
2006	High Limit, 4, 121	P. A. Valenzuela	Top This and That, 4, 117	Giacomo, 4, 123	11	1:49.14	180,000
2005	Rock Hard Ten, 4, 121	G. L. Stevens	Imperialism, 4, 119	Love of Money, 4, 123	9	1:49.24	180,000
2004	Domestic Dispute, 4, 117	K. Desormeaux	During, 4, 121	Buckland Manor, 4, 117	11	1:49.08	180,000
2003	Medaglia d'Oro, 4, 123	J. D. Bailey	Olmodavor, 4, 117	Tracemark, 4, 117	6	1:48.04	240,000
2002	Mizzen Mast, 4, 121	K. Desormeaux	Giant Gentleman, 4, 117	Fancy As, 4, 119	11	1:47.25	240,000
2001	Wooden Phone, 4, 117	C. S. Nakatani	Tiznow, 4, 123	Jimmy Z, 4, 117	6	1:48.43	300,000
2000	General Challenge, 4, 123	C. S. Nakatani	Luftikus, 4, 117	Saint's Honor, 4, 121	4	1:48.81	300,000
1999	Event of the Year, 4, 119	C. S. Nakatani	Dr Fong, 4, 121	Hanuman Highway (Ire), 4, 117	7	1:47.65	300,000
1998	Silver Charm, 4, 123	G. L. Stevens	Mud Route, 4, 117	Bagshot, 4, 117	6	1:47.27	300,000
1997	Victory Speech, 4, 124	J. D. Bailey	The Barking Shark, 4, 118	Ambivalent, 4, 118	9	2:01.50	300,000
1996	Helmsman, 4, 122	C. J. McCarron	Afternoon Deelites, 4, 120	Mr Purple, 4, 118	9	2:02.76	300,000
1995	Dare and Go, 4, 118	A. O. Solis	Dramatic Gold, 4, 124	Wekiva Springs, 4, 122	5	2:00.15	275,000
1994	Diazo, 4, 120	L. A. Pincay Jr.	Nonproductiveasset, 4, 118	Stuka, 4, 118	11	2:00.33	275,000
1993	Siberian Summer, 4, 118	C. S. Nakatani	Bertrando, 4, 122	Major Impact, 4, 118	8	2:00.78	275,000
1992	Best Pal, 4, 124	K. Desormeaux	Dinard, 4, 120	Reign Road, 4, 118	8	1:59.95	275,000
1991	Defensive Play, 4, 122	J. A. Santos	My Boy Adam, 4, 117	In Excess (Ire), 4, 121	7	2:00.90	275,000
1990	Flying Continental, 4, 119	C. A. Black	Quiet American, 4, 114	Hawkster, 4, 126	10	2:01.40	275,000
1989	Nasr El Arab, 4, 123	P. A. Valenzuela	Perceive Arrogance, 4, 117	Silver Circus, 4, 120	7	2:02.20	275,000
1988	Alysheba, 4, 126	C. J. McCarron	Candi's Gold, 4, 117	On the Line, 4, 119	6	2:00.40	275,000
1987	Snow Chief, 4, 126	P. A. Valenzuela	Ferdinand, 4, 126	Broad Brush, 4, 126	8	2:00.00	291,750
1986	Nostalgia's Star, 4, 116	F. Toro	Roo Art, 4, 117	Fast Account, 4, 115	12	2:03.60	314,250
1985	Precisionist, 4, 125	C. J. McCarron	Greinton (GB), 4, 117	Gate Dancer, 4, 126	5	2:00.20	189,300
1984	Desert Wine, 4, 117	E. Delahoussaye	Load the Cannons, 4, 115	Silent Fox, 4, 114	11	2:02.20	221,400
1983	Swing Till Dawn, 4, 115	P. A. Valenzuela	Wavering Monarch, 4, 121	Water Bank, 4, 117	10	2:02.00	178,000
1982	It's the One, 4, 118	W. A. Guerra	Dorcaro (Fr), 4, 115	Rock Softly, 4, 115	8	2:00.40	172,700
1981	Super Moment, 4, 116	F. Toro	Exploded, 4, 116	Doonesbury, 4, 118	10	2:01.20	145,000
1980	Spectacular Bid, 4, 126	W. Shoemaker	Flying Paster, 4, 121	Valdez, 4, 121	4	1:57.80	124,500
1979	Affirmed, 4, 126	L. A. Pincay Jr.	Johnny's Image, 4, 115	Quip, 4, 115	9	2:01.00	142,500
1978	Mr. Redoy, 4, 116	D. G. McHargue	Text, 4, 121	J. O. Tobin, 4, 122	9	2:01.00	140,200
1977	Kirby Lane, 4, 118	S. Hawley	Properantes, 4, 114	Double Discount, 4, 115	14	2:00.40	90,900
1976	George Navonod, 4, 115	F. Toro	Larrikin, 4, 118	Dancing Gun, 4, 115	8	2:12.00	76,900
1975	Stardust Mel, 4, 120	W. Shoemaker	Confederate Yankee, 4, 116	Rube the Great, 4, 122	9	2:04.20	86,300
1974	Ancient Title, 4, 121	L. A. Pincay Jr.	Dancing Papa, 4, 116	Prince Dantan, 4, 115	9	2:00.80	85,200
1973	Royal Owl, 4, 116	J. Sellers	Big Spruce, 4, 117	New Prospect, 4, 117	10	2:04.00	82,800

Originally named for Charles H. Strub (1884-1958), founder of modern Santa Anita Park. Race name shortened in 1993 to also honor Robert P. Strub (1919-'93), his son and former track president. Formerly the Santa Anita Maturity; maturities are typically for four-year-old and older horses. Grade 1 1973-'97. Santa Anita Maturity 1948-'62. Charles H. Strub S. 1963-'93. 1 1/4 miles 1948-'69, 1971-'97. Dirt 1948-2007.

Stuyvesant Handicap

Grade 3 in 2008. Aqueduct, three-year-olds and up, 1 1/8 miles, dirt. Held November 17, 2007, with a gross value of $108,500. First held in 1916. First graded in 1973. Stakes record 1:47 (1973 Riva Ridge).

Year	Winner	Jockey	Second	Third	Strs	Time	1st Purse
2007	Hunting, 4, 113	A. Garcia	Utopia (Jpn), 7, 117	Evening Attire, 9, 115	6	1:48.08	$65,100
2006	Accountforthegold, 4, 114	M. J. Luzzi	Carminooch, 4, 115	Organizer, 4, 115	7	1:48.96	66,060
2005	Evening Attire, 7, 116	J. A. Santos	West Virginia, 4, 115	Aggadan, 6, 116	6	1:51.38	65,160
2004	Classic Endeavor, 6, 114	E. S. Prado	Colita, 4, 115	Snake Mountain, 6, 115	7	1:49.70	65,940
2003	Presidentialaffair, 4, 117	R. Migliore	Thunder Blitz, 5, 114	Gander, 7, 115	6	1:50.86	66,180
2002	Snake Mountain, 4, 114	J. A. Santos	Windsor Castle, 4, 115	Docent, 4, 115	10	1:50.56	68,040
2001	Graeme Hall, 4, 119	J. R. Velazquez	Country Be Gold, 4, 115	Cat's At Home, 4, 114	6	1:47.95	64,620
2000	Lager, 6, 116	H. Castillo Jr.	Top Official, 5, 113	Fire King, 7, 115	6	1:50.03	64,860
1999	Best of Luck, 3, 114	M. E. Smith	Wild Imagination, 5, 115	Durmiente (Chi), 5, 113	9	1:47.67	67,200
1998	Mr. Sinatra, 4, 115	A. T. Gryder	Rock and Roll, 3, 114	Accelerator, 4, 114	5	1:48.16	65,280
1997	Delay of Game, 4, 114	J. Samyn	Concerto, 3, 118	Mr. Sinatra, 3, 117	8	1:47.72	66,060
1996	Poor But Honest, 6, 116	J. F. Chavez	Flitch, 4, 115	Admiralty, 4, 117	8	1:49.44	66,480
1995	Silver Fox, 4, 113	M. E. Smith	Yourmissinthepoint, 4, 111	Earth Colony, 4, 114	7	1:48.03	68,940
1994	Wallenda, 4, 118	W. H. McCauley	Lost Soldier, 4, 109	Pistols and Roses, 5, 117	7	1:50.69	64,560
1993	Michelle Can Pass, 5, 115	J. R. Velazquez	Key Contender, 5, 115	Primitive Hall, 4, 113	8	1:51.07	70,200
1992	Shots Are Ringing, 5, 114	J. R. Velazquez	Key Contender, 4, 111	Timely Warning, 7, 115	7	1:49.36	69,120
1991	Montubio (Arg), 6, 110	J. M. Pezua	Mountain Lore, 4, 112	Timely Warning, 6, 114	7	1:48.30	72,480
1990	I'm Sky High, 4, 114	M. E. Smith	Silver Survivor, 4, 113	Lost Opportunity, 4, 117	7	1:48.20	71,760
1989	Its Acedemic, 5, 110	J. D. Bailey	Congeleur, 4, 115	Homebuilder, 5, 114	8	1:48.80	70,560
1988	Talinum, 4, 112	M. Castaneda	Nostalgia's Star, 6, 113	Pleasant Virginian, 4, 113	9	1:51.20	111,240
1987	Moment of Hope, 4, 118	M. Venezia	Wind Chill, 4, 110	I Rejoice, 4, 111	9	1:49.60	109,080
1986	Little Missouri, 4, 116	R. G. Davis	Waquoit, 3, 115	Let's Go Blue, 5, 118	10	1:50.00	125,280
1985	Garthorn, 5, 112	R. Q. Meza	Morning Bob, 4, 114	Waitlist, 6, 118	7	1:48.40	70,320

Racing — Graded Stakes

Year	Winner	Jockey	Second	Third	Strs	Time	1st Purse
1984	Valiant Lark, 4, 112	V. A. Bracciale Jr.	Puntivo, 4, 112	Bounding Basque, 4, 117	8	1:51.40	$70,080
1983	Fit to Fight, 4, 117	J. D. Bailey	Deputy Minister, 4, 119	Sing Sing, 5, 115	7	1:49.00	68,280
1982	Engine One, 4, 123	R. Hernandez	Bar Dexter, 5, 112	Fit to Fight, 3, 118	6	1:49.60	67,200
1981	Idyll, 4, 114	C. B. Asmussen	Spoils of War, 4, 113	Silver Buck, 3, 112	12	1:48.80	68,280
1980	Plugged Nickle, 3, 122	C. B. Asmussen	Dr. Patches, 6, 115	Ring of Light, 5, 116	10	1:50.20	68,880
1979	Music of Time, 5, 114	J. Fell	What a Gent, 5, 111	Dewan Keys, 4, 112	6	1:50.40	65,220
1978	Seattle Slew, 4, 134	A. T. Cordero Jr.	Jumping Hill, 6, 115	Wise Philip, 5, 113	5	1:47.40	62,310
1977	Cox's Ridge, 3, 124	E. Maple	Wise Philip, 4, 114	Gentle King, 4, 112	8	1:48.40	32,760
1976	Distant Land, 4, 111	H. Gustines	Blue Times, 5, 114	It's Freezing, 4, 115	9	1:49.00	32,610
1975	Festive Mood, 6, 115	H. Hinojosa	‡Step Nicely, 5, 124	Stonewalk, 4, 122	6	1:48.40	33,210
1974	Crafty Khale, 5, 121	J. Cruguet	Stop the Music, 4, 120	True Knight, 5, 121	10	1:48.00	34,890
1973	Riva Ridge, 4, 130	E. Maple	Forage, 4, 116	True Knight, 4, 122	9	**1:47.00**	34,470

Named for the Bedford-Stuyvesant neighborhood in the borough of Brooklyn, New York. Held at Jamaica 1916-'24, 1937-'39. Held at Belmont Park 1990, '95, 2001. Not held 1925-'36, 1940-'62. 6 furlongs 1916-'17. 1 mile 1919-'24, 1965-'72, 1988. Three-year-olds 1916-'24. ‡Herculean finished second, DQ to sixth, 1975. Track record 1973.

Suburban Handicap

Grade 1 in 2008. Belmont Park, three-year-olds and up, 1¼ miles, dirt. Held June 30, 2007, with a gross value of $400,000. First held in 1884. First graded in 1973. Stakes record 1:58.33 (1991 In Excess [Ire]).

Year	Winner	Jockey	Second	Third	Strs	Time	1st Purse
2007	Political Force, 4, 116	C. H. Velasquez	Fairbanks, 4, 116	Malibu Moonshine, 5, 114	6	2:00.50	$240,000
2006	Invasor (Arg), 4, 118	F. Jara	Wild Desert, 4, 116	Andromeda's Hero, 4, 115	7	2:01.23	240,000
2005	Offlee Wild, 5, 116	E. S. Prado	Tap Day, 4, 115	Pollard's Vision, 4, 118	8	2:00.50	300,000
2004	Peace Rules, 4, 120	J. D. Bailey	Newfoundland, 4, 114	Funny Cide, 4, 117	8	1:59.52	300,000
2003	Mineshaft, 4, 121	R. Albarado	Volponi, 5, 121	Dollar Bill, 5, 115	8	2:01.57	300,000
2002	E Dubai, 4, 116	J. R. Velazquez	Lido Palace (Chi), 5, 119	Macho Uno, 4, 119	7	2:00.95	300,000
2001	Albert the Great, 4, 123	J. F. Chavez	Lido Palace (Chi), 4, 115	Include, 4, 122	6	2:00.39	300,000
2000	Lemon Drop Kid, 4, 122	E. S. Prado	Behrens, 6, 122	Lager, 6, 113	6	1:58.97	300,000
1999	Behrens, 5, 121	J. F. Chavez	Catienus, 5, 113	Social Charter, 4, 113	8	2:01.06	240,000
1998	Frisk Me Now, 4, 118	E. L. King Jr.	Ordway, 4, 110	Sir Bear, 5, 117	8	2:00.45	210,000
1997	Skip Away, 4, 122	S. J. Sellers	Will's Way, 4, 116	Formal Gold, 4, 120	6	2:02.39	210,000
1996	Wekiva Springs, 5, 122	M. E. Smith	Mahogany Hall, 5, 114	L'Carriere, 5, 118	7	2:02.78	300,000
1995	Key Contender, 7, 115	J. D. Bailey	Kissin Kris, 5, 113	Federal Funds, 6, 107	10	2:02.30	210,000
1994	Devil His Due, 5, 124	M. E. Smith	Valley Crossing, 6, 113	Federal Funds, 5, 110	5	2:02.52	210,000
1993	Devil His Due, 4, 121	W. H. McCauley	Pure Rumor, 4, 110	West by West, 4, 116	8	2:01.25	180,000
1992	Pleasant Tap, 5, 119	E. Delahoussaye	Strike the Gold, 4, 119	Defensive Play, 5, 115	7	2:00.33	337,500
1991	In Excess (Ire), 4, 119	G. L. Stevens	Chief Honcho, 4, 115	Killer Diller, 4, 113	7	**1:58.33**	300,000
1990	Easy Goer, 4, 126	P. Day	De Roche, 4, 113	Montubio (Arg), 5, 113	7	2:00.00	239,400
1989	Dancing Spree, 4, 114	A. T. Cordero Jr.	Forever Silver, 4, 116	Easy N Dirty, 6, 114	12	2:02.40	258,720
1988	Personal Flag, 5, 117	P. Day	Waquoit, 5, 121	Bet Twice, 4, 126	4	2:01.40	228,060
1987	Broad Brush, 4, 126	A. T. Cordero Jr.	Set Style (Chi), 4, 112	Bordeaux Bob, 4, 112	5	2:03.00	232,260
1986	Roo Art, 4, 116	P. Day	Proud Truth, 4, 121	Creme Fraiche, 4, 121	6	2:01.20	197,700
1985	Vanlandingham, 4, 115	D. MacBeth	Carr de Naskra, 4, 120	Dramatic Desire, 4, 109	9	2:01.00	180,600
1984	Fit to Fight, 5, 126	J. D. Bailey	Canadian Factor, 4, 116	Wild Again, 4, 116	7	2:00.60	201,300
1983	Winter's Tale, 7, 120	J. Fell	Sing Sing, 5, 119	Highland Blade, 5, 119	8	2:01.60	168,600
1982	Silver Buck, 4, 111	D. MacBeth	It's the One, 4, 124	Aloma's Ruler, 3, 112	8	1:59.60	100,620
1981	Temperence Hill, 4, 127	D. MacBeth	Ring of Light, 6, 115	Highland Blade, 3, 113	8	2:02.00	100,620
1980	Winter's Tale, 4, 114	J. Fell	State Dinner, 5, 117	Czaravich, 4, 127	7	2:00.60	97,920
1979	State Dinner, 4, 118	J. Velasquez	Mister Brea (Arg), 5, 120	Alydar, 4, 126	5	2:01.60	79,125
1978	Upper Nile, 4, 113	J. Velasquez	Nearly On Time, 4, 109	Great Contractor, 5, 114	6	2:01.80	63,840
1977	Quiet Little Table, 4, 114	E. Maple	Forego, 7, 138	Nearly On Time, 3, 104	6	2:03.00	63,840
1976	Foolish Pleasure, 4, 125	E. Maple	Forego, 6, 134	Lord Rebeau, 5, 116	4	1:55.40	65,280
1975	Forego, 5, 134	H. Gustines	Arbees Boy, 5, 118	Loud, 8, 114	7	2:27.80	66,840
1974	True Knight, 5, 127	A. T. Cordero Jr.	Plunk, 4, 114	Forego, 4, 131	10	2:01.40	68,880
1973	Key to the Mint, 4, 126	J. Baeza	True Knight, 4, 118	Cloudy Dawn, 4, 113	6	2:00.80	65,700

Named after the City and Suburban Handicap in England, won by Parole, one of the first American horses to win a major English stakes race. Grade 2 1997-2002. Held at Sheepshead Bay 1884-1910. Held at Aqueduct 1961-'74, 1976. Not held 1911-'12, 1914. 1½ miles 1975. 1 3/16 miles 1976.

Sunset Handicap

Grade 2 in 2008. Hollywood Park, three-year-olds and up, 1½ miles, turf. Held July 15, 2007, with a gross value of $150,400. First held in 1938. First graded in 1973. Stakes record 2:23.55 (1996 Talloires).

Year	Winner	Jockey	Second	Third	Strs	Time	1st Purse
2007	Runaway Dancer, 8, 117	A. O. Solis	Fitz Flag (Arg), 7, 114	Spring House, 5, 116	6	2:27.68	$96,240
2006	T. H. Approval, 5, 118	A. O. Solis	Molengao (Brz), 5, 115	Wild Buddy, 7, 114	9	2:26.65	99,420
2005	Always First (GB), 4, 113	V. Espinoza	dh-Runaway Dancer, 6, 118 dh-T. H. Approval, 4, 116		8	2:27.00	99,180
2004	Star Over the Bay, 6, 113	T. Baze	Continuously, 5, 116	Leprechaun Kid, 5, 114	7	2:26.47	90,000
2003	Puerto Banus, 4, 112	V. Espinoza	Cagney (Brz), 6, 116	Continental Red, 7, 116	8	2:26.95	90,000
2002	Grammarian, 4, 112	B. Blanc	Continental Red, 6, 116	Lord Flasheart, 5, 115	7	2:26.59	150,000
2001	Blueprint (Ire), 6, 116	G. L. Stevens	Kudos, 4, 116	Northern Quest (Fr), 6, 116	5	2:26.16	120,000

Year	Winner	Jockey	Second	Third	Strs	Time	1st Purse
2000	Bienamado, 4, 122	C. J. McCarron	Deploy Venture (GB), 4, 115	Single Empire (Ire), 6, 120	5	2:25.06	$150,000
1999	Plicck (Ire), 4, 116	D. R. Flores	River Bay, 6, 121	Lazy Lode (Arg), 5, 120	8	2:26.97	150,000
1998	River Bay, 5, 121	A. O. Solis	Lazy Lode (Arg), 4, 115	Devonwood, 4, 114	6	2:27.40	210,000
1997	Marlin, 4, 120	D. R. Flores	Flyway (Fr), 4, 117	Percutant (GB), 6, 118	6	2:25.20	240,000
1996	Talloires, 6, 116	K. Desormeaux	Awad, 6, 117	Sandpit (Brz), 7, 125	7	**2:23.55**	420,000
1995	Sandpit (Brz), 6, 124	C. S. Nakatani	Special Price, 6, 122	Liyoun (Ire), 7, 115	5	2:25.50	464,700
1994	Grand Flotilla, 7, 119	G. L. Stevens	Semillon (GB), 4, 116	Emerald Jig, 5, 115	7	2:26.35	158,000
1993	Bien Bien, 4, 122	C. J. McCarron	Emerald Jig, 4, 114	Beyton, 4, 116	6	2:25.69	154,300
1992	Qathif, 5, 114	A. O. Solis	Seven Rivers, 6, 114	Stark South, 4, 116	4	2:26.72	153,600
1991	Black Monday (GB), 5, 112	C. S. Nakatani	Super May, 5, 117	Razeen, 4, 116	7	2:26.10	158,400
1990	†Petite Ile (Ire), 4, 115	C. A. Black	Live the Dream, 4, 116	Soft Machine, 5, 110	9	2:25.60	163,600
1989	Pranke (Arg), 5, 117	P. A. Valenzuela	Frankly Perfect, 4, 123	Pleasant Variety, 5, 117	7	2:28.00	157,200
1988	Roi Normand, 5, 114	F. Toro	Putting (Fr), 5, 117	Circus Prince, 5, 114	11	2:24.60	170,000
1987	Swink, 4, 112	W. Shoemaker	Forlitano (Arg), 6, 122	Rivlia, 5, 122	10	2:25.00	165,300
1986	Zoffany, 6, 122	E. Delahoussaye	Dahar, 5, 125	Flying Pidgeon, 5, 121	8	2:24.40	161,500
1985	Kings Island (Ire), 4, 116	F. Toro	Greinton (GB), 4, 122	Val Danseur, 5, 114	5	2:25.80	148,800
1984	John Henry, 9, 126	C. J. McCarron	Load the Cannons, 4, 118	Pair of Deuces, 6, 113	9	2:24.80	129,800
1983	Craelius, 4, 118	C. J. McCarron	Palikaraki (Fr), 5, 115	Decadrachm, 4, 115	12	2:26.40	137,600
1982	Erins Isle (Ire), 4, 118	A. T. Cordero Jr.	Don Roberto, 5, 117	Exploded, 5, 119	8	2:25.60	129,600
1981	Galaxy Libra (Ire), 5, 119	W. Shoemaker	Caterman (NZ), 5, 122	The Bart, 5, 117	11	2:25.80	136,050
1980	Inkerman, 5, 115	W. Shoemaker	Balzac, 5, 120	Obraztsovy, 5, 121	7	2:24.40	94,700
1979	Sirlad (Ire), 5, 122	D. G. McHargue	Ardiente, 4, 115	Inkerman, 4, 119	12	2:24.00	102,000
1978	Exceller, 5, 130	W. Shoemaker	Diagramatic, 5, 122	Effervescing, 5, 122	8	2:27.00	96,600
1977	Today 'n Tomorrow, 4, 116	W. Shoemaker	Hunza Dancer, 5, 122	Copper Mel, 5, 117	13	2:27.60	104,450
1976	Caucasus, 4, 121	F. Toro	King Pellinore, 4, 124	Riot in Paris, 5, 123	10	2:26.40	81,350
1975	*Barclay Joy, 5, 117	W. Shoemaker	Captain Cee Jay, 5, 118	Top Crowd, 4, 115	8	2:26.80	50,450
	*Cruiser II, 6, 114	F. Olivares	Pass the Glass, 4, 119	Kirrary, 5, 116	7	2:27.00	49,450
1974	*Greco II, 5, 113	W. Shoemaker	Big Whippendeal, 4, 120	Scantling, 4, 118	12	2:27.00	69,600
1973	*Cougar II, 7, 128	W. Shoemaker	Life Cycle, 4, 120	Rock Bath, 5, 114	7	2:26.00	80,100

The Sunset is traditionally one of the last races run at the Hollywood Park spring meeting. Formerly named for the Hawaiian word for "goodbye," aloha. Formerly sponsored by Caesars International's hotel, Caesars Palace 1995-'96. Grade 1 1973-'89. Aloha H. 1938-'39. Caesars Palace Turf Championship H. 1995-'96. Sunset Breeders' Cup H. 2005-'06. Held at Santa Anita Park 1949. Not held 1942-'45. 1 1/8 miles 1938, '50. 1 5/8 miles 1941-'49, 1952, 1955-'59, 1961-'66. 2 miles 1969-'72. Dirt 1938-'66. Two divisions 1975. Dead heat for second 2005. Course record 1996. †Denotes female.

Super Derby

Grade 2 in 2008. Louisiana Downs, three-year-olds, 1 1/8 miles, dirt. Held September 22, 2007, with a gross value of $515,000. First held in 1980. First graded in 1982. Stakes record 1:48.60 (2006 Strong Contender).

Year	Winner	Jockey	Second	Third	Strs	Time	1st Purse
2007	Going Ballistic, 3, 124	M. C. Berry	Grasshopper, 3, 124	Past the Point, 3, 124	9	1:50.32	$275,000
2006	Strong Contender, 3, 124	R. Albarado	Lawyer Ron, 3, 124	Louisborg, 3, 124	7	**1:48.60**	275,000
2005	The Daddy, 3, 124	P. Morales	A. P. Arrow, 3, 124	Nolan's Cat, 3, 124	10	2:03.15	450,000
2004	Fantasticat, 3, 124	G. Melancon	Borrego, 3, 124	Britt's Jules, 3, 124	9	1:45.40	300,000
2003	Ten Most Wanted, 3, 124	P. Day	Soto, 3, 124	Crowned King, 3, 124	6	1:50.77	300,000
2002	Essence of Dubai, 3, 124	J. F. Chavez	Walk in the Snow, 3, 124	A. P. Five Hundred, 3, 124	8	1:49.43	300,000
2001	Outofthebox, 3, 124	L. J. Meche	E Dubai, 3, 124	Quadrophonic Sound, 3, 124	9	2:06.20	300,000
2000	Tiznow, 3, 124	C. J. McCarron	Commendable, 3, 124	Mass Market, 3, 124	6	1:59.84	300,000
1999	Ecton Park, 3, 126	A. O. Solis	Menifee, 3, 126	Pineaff, 3, 126	8	2:00.59	300,000
1998	Arch, 3, 126	C. S. Nakatani	Classic Cat, 3, 126	Sir Tiff, 3, 126	7	2:01.51	300,000
1997	Deputy Commander, 3, 126	C. J. McCarron	Precocity, 3, 126	Blazing Sword, 3, 126	6	2:00.80	300,000
1996	Editor's Note, 3, 126	G. L. Stevens	The Barking Shark, 3, 126	Devil's Honor, 3, 126	11	2:02.37	450,000
1995	Mecke, 3, 126	J. D. Bailey	Pineing Patty, 3, 126	Scott's Scoundrel, 3, 126	12	2:00.34	450,000
1994	Soul of the Matter, 3, 126	K. Desormeaux	Concern, 3, 126	Bay Street Star, 3, 126	6	2:03.57	450,000
1993	Wallenda, 3, 126	W. H. McCauley	Saintly Prospector, 3, 126	Peteski, 3, 126	12	2:02.71	450,000
1992	Senor Tomas, 3, 126	A. T. Gryder	Count the Time, 3, 126	Orbit's Revenge, 3, 126	14	2:04.09	450,000
1991	Free Spirit's Joy, 3, 126	C. H. Borel	Olympio, 3, 126	Zeeruler, 3, 126	7	2:00.96	600,000
1990	Home At Last, 3, 126	J. D. Bailey	Unbridled, 3, 126	Cee's Tizzy, 3, 126	9	2:02.00	600,000
1989	Sunday Silence, 3, 126	P. A. Valenzuela	‡Awe Inspiring, 3, 126	Dispersal, 3, 126	8	2:03.20	600,000
1988	Seeking the Gold, 3, 126	P. Day	Happyasalark Tomas, 3, 126	Lively One, 3, 126	9	2:03.80	600,000
1987	Alysheba, 3, 126	C. J. McCarron	Candi's Gold, 3, 126	Parochial, 3, 126	8	2:03.20	600,000
1986	Wise Times, 3, 126	E. Maple	dh-Cheapskate, 3, 126		7	2:04.00	300,000
			dh-Southern Halo, 3, 126				
1985	Creme Fraiche, 3, 126	E. Maple	Encolure, 3, 126	Government Corner, 3, 126	8	2:02.80	300,000
1984	Gate Dancer, 3, 126	L. A. Pincay Jr.	Precisionist, 3, 126	Big Pistol, 3, 126	8	2:00.20	300,000
1983	Sunny's Halo, 3, 126	L. A. Pincay Jr.	Play Fellow, 3, 126	My Habitony, 3, 126	6	2:01.60	300,000
1982	Reinvested, 3, 126	J. Velasquez	El Baba, 3, 126	Drop Your Drawers, 3, 126	10	2:01.60	300,000
1981	Island Whirl, 3, 126	L. A. Pincay Jr.	Summing, 3, 126	Willow Hour, 3, 126	12	2:03.20	300,000
1980	Temperence Hill, 3, 126	E. Maple	First Albert, 3, 126	Cactus Road, 3, 126	8	2:06.60	300,000

Formerly sponsored by the Isle of Capri Casino in Bossier City, Louisiana, location of Louisiana Downs 1995-'96. Super Derby Invitational 1980-'86. Grade 1 1983-2001. Isle of Capri Casino Super Derby 1995-'96. 1 1/4 miles 1980-2001, 2005. Dead heat for second 1986. ‡Big Earl finished second, DQ to eighth, 1989.

Suwannee River Handicap

Grade 3 in 2008. Gulfstream Park, four-year-olds and up, fillies and mares, 1 1/8 miles, turf. Held February 3, 2008, with a gross value of $100,000. First held in 1947. First graded in 1973. Stakes record 1:46.40 (2005 Snowdrops [GB]).

Year	Winner	Jockey	Second	Third	Strs	Time	1st Purse
2008	‡La Dolce Vita, 6, 117	K. J. Desormeaux	J'ray, 5, 121	Waquoit's Love, 5, 118	11	1:46.64	$60,000
2007	Naissance Royale (Ire), 5, 119	E. S. Prado	J'ray, 4, 119	Potra Clasica (Arg), 6, 115	10	1:46.58	60,000
2006	Eyes On Eddy, 4, 114	R. Bejarano	Taittinger Rose, 5, 115	Marchonin, 4, 114	5	1:49.56	60,000
2005	Snowdrops (GB), 5, 116	E. S. Prado	Angela's Love, 5, 117	High Court (Brz), 5, 116	10	**1:46.40**	60,000
2004	Wishful Splendor, 5, 114	J. A. Santos	May Gator, 5, 113	Mymich, 4, 113	5	1:54.86	60,000
2003	Amonita (GB), 5, 117	J. Samyn	What a Price, 5, 114	Calista (GB), 5, 118	9	1:47.90	60,000
2002	Snow Dance, 4, 119	P. Day	Step With Style, 5, 114	Windsong, 5, 113	6	1:49.04	60,000
2001	Spook Express (SAf), 7, 116	M. E. Smith	Gaviola, 4, 120	Windsong, 4, 113	8	1:47.28	60,000
2000	Pico Teneriffe, 4, 115	J. F. Chavez	Dominique's Joy, 5, 114	Crystal Symphony, 4, 115	8	1:47.83	45,000
1999	Winfama, 6, 114	R. Migliore	Circus Charmer, 4, 113	Colcon, 6, 120	10	1:52.38	45,000
1998	Seebe, 4, 114	D. Rice	Colcon, 5, 115	Parade Queen, 4, 119	10	1:47.58	45,000
1997	Golden Pond (Ire), 4, 115	J. D. Bailey	Rumpipumpy (GB), 4, 114	Elusive, 5, 113	11	1:47.87	45,000
1996	Class Kris, 4, 116	P. Day	Apolda, 5, 118	Majestic Dy, 4, 113	5	1:49.17	45,000
1995	Cox Orange, 5, 116	J. D. Bailey	Irving's Girl, 5, 113	Alice Springs, 5, 120	7	1:47.43	45,000
1994	Marshua's River, 7, 114	J. A. Santos	Sheila's Revenge, 4, 118	Icy Warning, 4, 115	12	1:46.68	45,000
1993	Via Borghese, 4, 114	J. D. Bailey	Marshua's River, 6, 113	Blue Daisy, 5, 114	14	1:48.22	45,000
1992	Julie La Rousse (Ire), 4, 115	J. D. Bailey	Christiecat, 5, 117	Grab the Green, 4, 120	11	1:48.48	40,230
1991	Vigorous Lady, 5, 117	M. A. Lee	Yen for Gold, 5, 111	Premier Question, 4, 116	5	1:45.10	38,670
1990	Princess Mora, 4, 111	M. A. Gonzalez	Fieldy (Ire), 7, 121	Northling, 6, 113	12	1:41.20	38,970
1989	Love You by Heart, 4, 117	R. P. Romero	Native Mommy, 6, 118	Aquaba, 4, 115	10	1:41.60	37,275
	Fieldy (Ire), 6, 116	C. Perret	Summer Secretary, 4, 110	Chapel of Dreams, 5, 122	9	1:41.60	36,975
1988	Go Honey Go (Ire), 5, 110	J. M. Pezua	Princely Proof, 5, 115	Fieldy (Ire), 5, 119	11	1:41.80	38,490
	Anka Germania (Ire), 6, 122	C. Perret	Sum, 4, 114	Fama, 5, 112	12	1:41.80	39,090
1987	dh-Fama, 4, 114	R. P. Romero		Navarchus, 5, 114	8	1:44.20	17,810
	dh-Fieldy (Ire), 4, 114	C. Perret					
	Singular Bequest, 4, 114	E. Fires	Cadabra Abra, 4, 114	Duckweed, 5, 112	7	1:43.60	26,415
1986	Chesire Kitten, 4, 112	J. Samyn	Chaldea, 6, 111	Four Flings, 5, 113	10	1:44.60	30,990
	Videogenic, 4, 120	R. G. Davis	Contredance, 4, 117	Verbality, 4, 112	9	1:44.60	30,690
1985	Early Lunch, 4, 112	W. A. Guerra	Eva G., 5, 114	Maidenhead, 6, 111	11	1:35.60	28,521
	Sherizar, 4, 113	J. McKnight	Madam Flutterby, 4, 114	Melanie Frances, 7, 115	12	1:36.40	28,820
	Burst of Colors, 5, 117	J. A. Santos	Queen of Song, 6, 121	Silver in Flight, 5, 115	12	1:35.60	28,820
1984	Sulemeif, 4, 113	J. D. Bailey	Jubilous, 4, 115	Melanie Frances, 6, 113	13	1:36.80	39,330
1983	Norsan, 4, 113	J. D. Bailey	Dana Calqui (Arg), 5, 114	Colatina, 4, 111	12	1:38.20	28,890
	Syrianna, 4, 114	J. Vasquez	Meringue Pie, 5, 115	Plenty O'Toole, 6, 114	9	1:24.20	27,390
	Promising Native, 4, 113	D. MacBeth	Avowal, 4, 117	Our Darling, 4, 112	7	1:23.80	27,060
1982	Pine Flower, 4, 113	C. Perret	Sweetest Chant, 4, 116	Fair Davina (Ire), 6, 110	9	1:35.40	27,000
	Teacher's Pet (GB), 5, 114	C. H. Marquez	Shark Song (GB), 4, 114	Blush, 4, 113	9	1:35.20	27,300
1981	Honey Fox, 4, 111	J. Samyn	Racquette (Ire), 4, 115	Pompoes (Den), 4, 110	9	1:35.20	22,568
	Exactly So (Ire), 4, 109	J. Samyn	Draw In, 5, 114	Champagne Ginny, 4, 118	9	1:35.80	22,568
1980	Ouro Verde, 4, 112	R. I. Encinas	No Disgrace (Ire), 4, 110	Anna Yrrah D., 4, 112	10	1:37.20	18,870
	Just a Game (Ire), 4, 117	D. Brumfield	La Soufriere, 5, 113	La Voyageuse, 5, 120	10	1:35.20	18,870
1979	Navajo Princess, 5, 124	C. Perret	La Soufriere, 4, 119	Unreality, 5, 121	13	1:35.20	19,650
	Calderina (Ity), 4, 117	J. Fell	Terpsichorist, 4, 122	She Can Dance, 4, 113	11	1:36.20	19,200
1978	Len's Determined, 4, 119	J. Cruguet	What a Summer, 5, 122	Late Bloomer, 4, 113	9	1:35.60	19,260
1977	Bronze Point, 4, 120	H. Arroyo	Funny Peculiar, 5, 114	Collegiate, 5, 114	7	1:24.20	21,390
1976	Jabot, 4, 112	H. Gustines	Redundancy, 5, 119	*Deesse Du Val, 5, 117	14	1:34.60	21,330
1975	*Deesse Du Val, 4, 115	M. Hole	North of Venus, 5, 118	Lorraine Edna, 5, 118	11	1:35.40	20,400
1974	Dove Creek Lady, 4, 121	M. A. Rivera	North Broadway, 4, 120	North of Venus, 4, 119	12	1:36.40	21,960
1973	Ziba Blue, 6, 110	M. Miceli	Cathy Baby, 4, 113	dh-Barely Even, 4, 127	13	1:35.80	21,270
				dh-Tico's Donna, 5, 114			

Named for Stephen Foster's song "Old Folks at Home (Suwannee River)," Florida's state song. Not graded 1979-'81, 2004, 2006. Not held 1949. 7 furlongs 1947, 1961-'66, 1977, 1983 (two divisions). 6 furlongs 1948. 1 1/16 miles 1953-'60, 1967-'68, 1986-'91. 1 mile 1969-'76, 1978-'79, 1981-'82, 1983 (one division), 1984-'85. About 1 1/8 miles 1990. Dirt 1965-'66, 1977, 1983 (two divisions), 1986, 1991, 2004, 2006. Originally scheduled on turf 2004, '06. Three-year-olds and up 1947-'93, 1995-2006. Two divisions 1979-'82, 1986-'89. Three divisions 1983, '85. Dead heat for third 1973. Dead heat for first 1987 (1st Div.). ‡Green Girl (Fr) finished first, DQ to 11th on a hearing officer's decision, 2008. Equaled course record 1992. Held as an overnight handicap 1950-'52.

Swale Stakes

Grade 2 in 2008. Gulfstream Park, three-year-olds, 6 1/2 furlongs, dirt. Held February 2, 2008, with a gross value of $150,000. First held in 1985. First graded in 1990. Stakes record 1:15.63 (2008 Eaton's Gift).

Year	Winner	Jockey	Second	Third	Strs	Time	1st Purse
2008	Eaton's Gift, 3, 117	K. J. Desormeaux	Surrealdeal, 3, 116	Wincat, 3, 116	7	**1:15.63**	$90,000
2007	Adore the Gold, 3, 118	C. H. Velasquez	Forefathers, 3, 116	Cowtown Cat, 3, 116	7	1:15.86	90,000
2006	Sharp Humor, 3, 118	M. Guidry	Noonmark, 3, 116	Court Folly, 3, 116	11	1:22.14	90,000
2005	Lost in the Fog, 3, 120	R. A. Baze	Around the Cape, 3, 116	More Smoke, 3, 118	10	1:22.21	90,000
2004	Wynn Dot Comma, 3, 120	E. S. Prado	Eurosilver, 3, 120	Dashboard Drummer, 3, 120	5	1:22.87	90,000
2003	Midas Eyes, 3, 116	J. D. Bailey	Posse, 3, 120	Whywhywhy, 3, 122	8	1:21.06	90,000
2002	Ethan Man, 3, 116	P. Day	Listen Here, 3, 120	Governor Hickel, 3, 116	5	1:22.29	90,000

Racing — Graded Stakes

Year	Winner	Jockey	Second	Third	Strs	Time	1st Purse
2001	D'wildcat, 3, 116	C. S. Nakatani	Tarek, 3, 112	Yonaguska, 3, 122	6	1:22.25	$90,000
2000	Trippi, 3, 113	J. D. Bailey	Ultimate Warrior, 3, 117	Harlan Traveler, 3, 114	8	1:23.43	60,000
1999	Yes It's True, 3, 122	J. D. Bailey	Texas Glitter, 3, 117	Lucky Roberto, 3, 119	5	1:22.29	60,000
1998	Favorite Trick, 3, 122	P. Day	Good and Tough, 3, 114	Dice Dancer, 3, 113	9	1:22.86	60,000
1997	Confide, 3, 117	M. E. Smith	Country Rainbow, 3, 112	The Silver Move, 3, 119	9	1:23.35	45,000
1996	Roar, 3, 113	M. E. Smith	Gomtuu, 3, 119	Dixie Connection, 3, 112	6	1:22.46	45,000
1995	Mr. Greeley, 3, 114	J. A. Krone	Devious Course, 3, 119	Pyramid Peak, 3, 114	6	1:22.18	45,000
1994	Arrival Time, 3, 115	C. J. McCarron	Senor Conquistador, 3, 113	Meadow Monster, 3, 112	7	1:22.53	45,000
1993	Premier Explosion, 3, 114	D. Penna	Demaloot Demashoot, 3, 113	Cherokee Run, 3, 114	8	1:23.23	53,520
1992	D. J. Cat, 3, 114	J. D. Bailey	Binalong, 3, 114	Always Silver, 3, 112	10	1:23.39	71,250
1991	Chihuahua, 3, 112	J. O. Alferez	To Freedom, 3, 119	Greek Costume, 3, 114	7	1:23.47	51,060
1990	Housebuster, 3, 122	C. Perret	Summer Squall, 3, 122	Thirty Six Red, 3, 113	6	1:22.20	34,350
1989	Easy Goer, 3, 122	P. Day	Trion, 3, 112	Tricky Creek, 3, 122	6	1:22.20	34,290
1988	Seeking the Gold, 3, 114	R. P. Romero	Above Normal, 3, 114	Perfect Spy, 3, 122	7	1:21.60	35,100
1986	One Magic Moment, 3, 113	C. Perret	Admiral's Image, 3, 122	Two Punch, 3, 113	11	1:25.40	31,230
1985	Chief's Crown, 3, 122	D. MacBeth	Creme Fraiche, 3, 117	Cherokee Fast, 3, 113	9	1:22.40	30,792

Named for Claiborne Farm's 1984 champion three-year-old male and '84 Florida Derby (G1) winner Swale (1981 c. by Seattle Slew). Grade 3 1990-2004. Not held 1987. 7 furlongs 1985-2006.

Swaps Stakes

Grade 2 in 2008. Hollywood Park, three-year-olds, 1 1/8 miles, all weather. Held July 14, 2007, with a gross value of $368,250. First held in 1974. First graded in 1975. Stakes record 1:45.80 (1997 Free House).

Year	Winner	Jockey	Second	Third	Strs	Time	1st Purse
2007	Tiago, 3, 122	M. E. Smith	Albertus Maximus, 3, 114	Souvenir Slew, 3, 112	6	1:48.76	$220,950
2006	Arson Squad, 3, 116	A. O. Solis	Point Determined, 3, 118	A. P. Warrior, 3, 120	4	1:48.45	217,050
2005	Surf Cat, 3, 115	A. O. Solis	Dover Dere, 3, 117	Indian Ocean, 3, 118	6	1:48.07	192,600
2004	Rock Hard Ten, 3, 116	C. S. Nakatani	Suave, 3, 120	Boomzeeboom, 3, 118	6	1:47.47	252,780
2003	During, 3, 115	J. D. Bailey	Ten Most Wanted, 3, 122	dh-Eye of the Tiger, 3, 118 dh-Outta Here, 3, 120	6	1:49.38	240,000
2002	Came Home, 3, 122	M. E. Smith	Like a Hero, 3, 114	Fonz's, 3, 116	7	1:48.28	300,000
2001	Congaree, 3, 122	G. L. Stevens	Until Sundown, 3, 118	Jamaican Rum, 3, 118	6	1:48.61	300,000
2000	Captain Steve, 3, 120	C. S. Nakatani	Tiznow, 3, 118	Spacelink, 3, 118	6	1:48.01	300,000
1999	Cat Thief, 3, 120	P. Day	General Challenge, 3, 122	Walk That Walk, 3, 117	4	1:47.87	300,000
1998	Old Trieste, 3, 118	C. J. McCarron	Grand Slam, 3, 120	Old Topper, 3, 117	6	1:47.00	300,000
1997	Free House, 3, 122	K. Desormeaux	Deputy Commander, 3, 118	Wild Rush, 3, 122	6	1:45.80	300,000
1996	Victory Speech, 3, 118	J. D. Bailey	Prince of Thieves, 3, 118	Hesabull, 3, 118	5	1:48.28	300,000
1995	Thunder Gulch, 3, 126	G. L. Stevens	Da Hoss, 3, 118	Petionville, 3, 120	7	1:49.09	275,000
1994	Silver Music, 3, 119	C. W. Antley	Dramatic Gold, 3, 119	Valiant Nature, 3, 121	6	2:00.76	123,800
1993	Devoted Brass, 3, 123	L. A. Pincay Jr.	Future Storm, 3, 119	Codified, 3, 123	6	2:00.64	124,000
1992	Bien Bien, 3, 119	C. J. McCarron	Treekster, 3, 123	Sevengreenpairs, 3, 119	5	2:02.91	123,400
1991	Best Pal, 3, 116	P. A. Valenzuela	Corporate Report, 3, 114	Compelling Sound, 3, 123	4	2:00.70	120,000
1990	Jovial (GB), 3, 120	G. L. Stevens	Silver Ending, 3, 126	Stalwart Charger, 3, 126	4	2:01.20	120,000
1989	Prized, 3, 120	E. Delahoussaye	Sunday Silence, 3, 126	Endow, 3, 123	5	2:01.80	232,400
1988	Lively One, 3, 120	W. Shoemaker	Blade of the Ball, 3, 114	Iz a Saros, 3, 123	9	2:01.00	131,200
1987	Temperate Sil, 3, 123	W. Shoemaker	Candi's Gold, 3, 123	Pledge Card, 3, 115	6	2:02.20	124,400
1986	Clear Choice, 3, 120	C. J. McCarron	Southern Halo, 3, 114	Jota, 3, 116	9	2:03.60	137,000
1985	Padua, 3, 115	P. A. Valenzuela	Turkoman, 3, 115	Don't Say Halo, 3, 120	8	2:01.40	123,500
1984	Precisionist, 3, 123	C. J. McCarron	Prince True, 3, 120	Majestic Shore, 3, 114	7	1:59.80	121,300
1983	Hyperborean, 3, 115	F. Toro	My Habitony, 3, 120	Tanks Brigade, 3, 120	3	2:01.00	97,500
1982	Journey At Sea, 3, 120	C. J. McCarron	West Coast Native, 3, 114	Cassaleria, 3, 123	5	2:00.20	91,300
1981	Noble Nashua, 3, 123	L. A. Pincay Jr.	Dorcaro (Fr), 3, 115	Stancharry, 3, 123	7	2:01.20	127,000
1980	First Albert, 3, 123	F. Mena	Amber Pass, 3, 123	Mr. Mud, 3, 114	11	2:00.80	162,200
1979	Valdez, 3, 120	L. A. Pincay Jr.	Shamgo, 3, 114	Paint King, 3, 114	6	1:59.40	124,250
1978	Radar Ahead, 3, 120	D. G. McHargue	Batonnier, 3, 123	Poppy Popowich, 3, 115	10	2:00.00	133,300
1977	J. O. Tobin, 3, 120	W. Shoemaker	Affiliate, 3, 117	Text, 3, 120	7	1:58.60	194,900
1976	Majestic Light, 3, 114	S. Hawley	Crystal Water, 3, 123	Double Discount, 3, 115	9	1:59.20	98,200
1975	Forceten, 3, 120	D. Pierce	Sibirri, 3, 114	Diabolo, 3, 123	8	1:59.80	119,800
1974	Agitate, 3, 123	W. Shoemaker	Stardust Mel, 3, 120	Master Music, 3, 114	9	1:59.60	66,300

Named for Rex Ellsworth's Racing Hall of Fame member, 1956 Horse of the Year, and '56 Hollywood Gold Cup H. winner Swaps (1952 c. by *Khaled). Grade 1 1975-'88, 1999-2001. Swaps Breeders' Cup S. 2004-'07. 1 1/4 miles 1974-'94. Dirt 1974-2006. Dead heat for third 2003.

Sword Dancer Invitational Stakes

Grade 1 in 2008. Saratoga Race Course, three-year-olds and up, 1 1/2 miles, turf. Held August 11, 2007, with a gross value of $500,000. First held in 1975. First graded in 1981. Stakes record 2:23.20 (1997 Awad).

Year	Winner	Jockey	Second	Third	Strs	Time	1st Purse
2007	Grand Couturier (GB), 4, 117	C. H. Borel	English Channel, 5, 123	Trippi's Storm, 4, 116	8	2:26.59	$300,000
2006	Go Deputy, 6, 118	E. Coa	Silver Whistle, 4, 116	Grand Couturier (GB), 3, 115	8	2:26.78	300,000
2005	King's Drama (Ire), 5, 116	J. F. Chavez	Relaxed Gesture (Ire), 4, 116	Vangelis, 6, 118	8	2:27.38	300,000
2004	Better Talk Now, 5, 118	R. A. Dominguez	Request for Parole, 5, 123	Balto Star, 6, 120	6	2:28.49	300,000
2003	Whitmore's Conn, 5, 115	J. Samyn	Macaw (Ire), 4, 123	Slew Valley, 6, 114	11	2:28.14	300,000

Year	Winner	Jockey	Second	Third	Strs	Time	1st Purse
2002	With Anticipation, 7, 120	P. Day	Denon, 4, 118	Volponi, 4, 115	11	2:24.06	$300,000
2001	With Anticipation, 6, 114	P. Day	King Cugat, 4, 120	Slew Valley, 4, 114	9	2:26.41	300,000
2000	John's Call, 9, 114	J. Samyn	Aly's Alley, 4, 114	Single Empire (Ire), 6, 119	8	2:32.17	300,000
1999	Honor Glide, 5, 116	J. A. Santos	Val's Prince, 7, 115	Chorwon, 6, 114	7	2:28.23	240,000
1998	Cetewayo, 4, 115	J. R. Velazquez	Val's Prince, 6, 113	Dushyantor, 5, 119	6	2:29.56	180,000
1997	Awad, 7, 117	P. Day	Fahim (GB), 4, 110	Val's Prince, 5, 112	10	**2:23.20**	150,000
1996	Broadway Flyer, 5, 118	M. E. Smith	Kiri's Clown, 7, 113	Flag Down, 6, 119	9	2:32.08	150,000
1995	Kiri's Clown, 6, 114	M. J. Luzzi	Awad, 5, 121	King's Theatre (Ire), 4, 113	13	2:25.45	150,000
1994	Alex the Great (GB), 5, 118	P. A. Valenzuela	Kiri's Clown, 5, 112	L'Hermine (GB), 5, 112	10	2:28.66	150,000
1993	Spectacular Tide, 4, 112	J. A. Krone	Square Cut, 4, 112	Dr. Kiernan, 4, 117	9	2:30.39	120,000
1992	Fraise, 4, 113	J. D. Bailey	Wall Street Dancer, 4, 116	Montserrat, 4, 112	8	2:25.88	150,000
1991	Dr. Root, 4, 109	J. Samyn	Karmani, 6, 113	El Senor, 7, 116	7	2:25.43	150,000
1990	El Senor, 6, 119	A. T. Cordero Jr.	With Approval, 4, 124	Hodges Bay, 5, 114	7	2:28.00	140,400
1989	El Senor, 5, 118	W. H. McCauley	Nediym (Ire), 4, 113	My Big Boy, 6, 115	7	2:27.00	139,920
1988	†Anka Germania (Ire), 6, 117	C. Perret	Sunshine Forever, 3, 114	†Carotene, 5, 114	7	2:32.20	141,120
1987	‡Theatrical (Ire), 5, 124	P. Day	Dance of Life, 4, 122	Akabir, 6, 114	4	2:26.00	133,080
1986	Southern Sultan, 4, 109	R. G. Davis	Talakeno, 6, 114	Tri for Size, 5, 111	8	2:39.40	143,460
1985	Tri for Size, 4, 110	R. J. Thibeau Jr.	Talakeno, 5, 112	†Persian Tiara (Ire), 5, 113	9	2:33.20	151,320
1984	Majesty's Prince, 5, 124	E. Maple	Nassipour, 4, 109	Four Bases, 5, 112	11	2:31.00	176,820
1983	Majesty's Prince, 4, 120	E. Maple	‡Thunder Puddles, 4, 118	Erins Isle (Ire), 5, 128	9	2:34.40	141,600
1982	Lemhi Gold, 4, 126	C. J. McCarron	Erins Isle (Ire), 4, 126	Field Cat, 5, 126	5	2:26.00	99,000
1981	John Henry, 6, 126	W. Shoemaker	Passing Zone, 4, 126	Peat Moss, 6, 126	5	2:26.80	97,380
1980	Tiller, 6, 126	R. Hernandez	John Henry, 5, 126	Sten, 5, 126	4	2:25.20	96,660
1979	Darby Creek Road, 4, 119	A. T. Cordero Jr.	John Henry, 4, 119	Poison Ivory, 4, 119	8	1:41.60	34,320
1978	True Colors, 4, 114	M. Venezia	Bill Brill, 4, 107	Blue Baron, 4, 114	12	1:41.00	34,020
1977	Effervescing, 4, 117	A. T. Cordero Jr.	Gentle King, 4, 110	Cinteelo, 4, 116	9	1:39.60	33,690
1976	Arabian Law, 3, 112	J. Vasquez	Full Out, 3, 118	Half High, 3, 111	7	1:10.60	26,535
1975	Gallant Bob, 3, 126	G. Gallitano	Our Hero, 3, 113	Due Diligence, 3, 113	9	1:09.60	27,630

Named for Brookmeade Stable's 1959 Horse of the Year and '59 Jockey Club Gold Cup winner Sword Dancer (1956 c. by Sunglow). Grade 3 1981. Grade 2 1982-'83. Sword Dancer H. 1975-'78, 1983-'93. Sword Dancer S. 1979-'82. Sword Dancer Invitational H. 1994-2003. Held at Aqueduct 1975-'76. Held at Belmont Park 1977-'91. 6 furlongs 1975-'76. 1 1/16 miles 1977-'79. Dirt 1975-'76. Three-year-olds 1975-'76. ‡Hush Dear finished second, DQ to fourth, 1983. ‡Dance of Life finished first, DQ to second, 1987. †Denotes female.

Sycamore Stakes

Grade 3 in 2008. Keeneland Race Course, three-year-olds and up, 1 1/2 miles, turf. Held October 5, 2007, with a gross value of $137,500. First held in 1995. First graded in 2003. Stakes record 2:29.55 (2003 Sharbayan [Ire]).

Year	Winner	Jockey	Second	Third	Strs	Time	1st Purse
2007	Transduction Gold, 4, 120	J. Graham	Bee Charmer (Ire), 5, 120	Dreadnaught, 7, 120	10	2:31.96	$93,000
2006	Revved Up, 8, 122	G. K. Gomez	Rush Bay, 4, 125	Always First (GB), 5, 122	10	2:29.83	101,556
2005	Rochester, 9, 120	G. L. Stevens	Dreadnaught, 5, 122	Vangelis, 6, 122	8	2:34.30	99,882
2004	Mustanfar, 3, 118	J. A. Santos	Deputy Strike, 6, 120	Rochester, 8, 122	9	2:30.88	100,626
2003	Sharbayan (Ire), 5, 120	P. Day	Cetewayo, 9, 122	Deputy Strike, 5, 120	10	**2:29.55**	73,904
2002	Rochester, 6, 125	P. Day	Roxinho (Brz), 4, 120	Lord Flasheart, 5, 120	7	2:30.48	101,928
2001	Rochester, 5, 119	P. Day	Chorwon, 8, 125	Regal Dynasty, 5, 119	7	2:31.29	103,044
2000	Crowd Pleaser, 5, 118	C. H. Borel	Dixie's Crown, 4, 122	Kim Loves Bucky, 3, 114	7	2:44.00	44,439
1999	Royal Strand (Ire), 5, 117	P. Day	Arizona Storm, 4, 117	Magest, 4, 117	6	2:36.68	42,315
1998	Royal Strand (Ire), 4, 116	S. J. Sellers	Thesaurus, 4, 116	Lakeshore Road, 5, 116	5	2:41.93	33,015
1997	Gleaming Key, 5, 116	S. J. Sellers	Double Leaf (GB), 4, 116	Seattle Blossom, 4, 116	5	2:45.86	33,015
1996	Gleaming Key, 4, 114	R. Albarado	Nash Terrace (Ire), 4, 120	Hawkeye Bay, 5, 114	4	2:44.49	32,860
1995	Lindon Lime, 5, 123	C. Perret	Hyper Shu, 5, 114	Lordly Prospect, 6, 114	9	2:42.11	39,098

Named for the sycamore tree at the entrance to Keeneland's walking ring. Sycamore Breeders' Cup S. 2001-'06.

Tampa Bay Derby

Grade 3 in 2008. Tampa Bay Downs, three-year-olds, 1 1/16 miles, dirt. Held March 15, 2008, with a gross value of $300,000. First held in 1981. First graded in 1984. Stakes record 1:43.11 (2007 Street Sense).

Year	Winner	Jockey	Second	Third	Strs	Time	1st Purse
2008	Big Truck, 3, 116	E. Coa	Atoned, 3, 116	Dynamic Wayne, 3, 116	7	1:44.25	$180,000
2007	Street Sense, 3, 122	C. H. Borel	Any Given Saturday, 3, 120	Delightful Kiss, 3, 116	7	**1:43.11**	180,000
2006	Deputy Glitters, 3, 116	J. Lezcano	Bluegrass Cat, 3, 122	Winnies Tigger Too, 3, 116	9	1:44.26	150,000
2005	Sun King, 3, 118	E. S. Prado	Forever Wild, 3, 116	Global Trader, 3, 116	7	1:43.98	150,000
2004	Limehouse, 3, 118	P. Day	Mustanfar, 3, 116	Swingforthefences, 3, 116	8	1:43.99	150,000
2003	Region of Merit, 3, 120	E. Coa	Aristocat, 3, 118	Hear No Evil, 3, 123	8	1:44.61	150,000
2002	Equality, 3, 118	R. A. Dominguez	Tails of the Crypt, 3, 123	Political Attack, 3, 123	9	1:43.66	120,000
2001	Burning Roma, 3, 123	R. Migliore	American Prince, 3, 123	Paging, 3, 116	11	1:44.30	120,000
2000	Wheelaway, 3, 116	R. Migliore	Impeachment, 3, 116	Perfect Cat, 3, 116	10	1:43.90	90,000
1999	Pineaff, 3, 122	J. A. Santos	Menifee, 3, 120	Doneraile Court, 3, 122	6	1:45.33	90,000
1998	Parade Ground, 3, 118	P. Day	Middlesex Drive, 3, 118	Rock and Roll, 3, 116	8	1:44.20	90,000
1997	Zede, 3, 118	J. D. Bailey	Brisco Jack, 3, 116	Favorable Regard, 3, 118	12	1:44.80	90,000

Racing — Graded Stakes

Year	Winner	Jockey	Second	Third	Strs	Time	1st Purse
1996	Thundering Storm, 3, 118	J. A. Guerra	El Amante, 3, 118	Natural Selection, 3, 116	10	1:43.80	$90,000
1995	Gadzook, 3, 116	G. Boulanger	Composer, 3, 116	Bet Your Bucks, 3, 116	10	1:45.20	90,000
1994	Prix de Crouton, 3, 120	M. Walls	Able Buck, 3, 120	Parental Pressure, 3, 122	7	1:46.60	90,000
1993	Marco Bay, 3, 120	R. D. Allen Jr.	Thriller Chiller, 3, 116	Tunecke Charlie, 3, 118	12	1:44.40	90,000
1992	Careful Gesture, 3, 118	R. N. Lester	Chief Speaker, 3, 116	Clipper Won, 3, 116	12	1:45.93	120,000
1991	Speedy Cure, 3, 118	R. D. Lopez	Link, 3, 118	Shudanz, 3, 116	9	1:46.26	90,000
1990	Champagneforashley, 3, 122	J. Vasquez	Slew of Angels, 3, 120	Always Running, 3, 116	10	1:44.60	90,000
1989	Storm Predictions, 3, 120	S. Gaffalione	With Approval, 3, 120	Mercedes Won, 3, 122	11	1:43.80	90,000
1988	Cefis, 3, 116	E. Maple	Buck Forbes, 3, 118	Twice Too Many, 3, 118	9	1:44.40	90,000
1987	Phantom Jet, 3, 122	K. K. Allen	Homebuilder, 3, 116	You're No Bargain, 3, 116	10	1:43.80	90,000
1986	My Prince Charming, 3, 122	C. Perret	Lucky Rebeau, 3, 120	Major Moran, 3, 116	13	1:46.60	98,100
1985	Regal Remark, 3, 122	J. Fell	Verification, 3, 122	Sport Jet, 3, 118	14	1:46.80	95,400
1984	Bold Southerner, 3, 116	W. Crews	Rexson's Hope, 3, 122	Stickler, 3, 120	13	1:44.60	95,400
1983	Morganmorganmorgan, 3, 118	W. Rodriguez	Slew o' Gold, 3, 118	Quick Dip, 3, 118	14	1:47.20	60,000
1982	Reinvested, 3, 114	R. D. Luhr	Stage Reviewer, 3, 120	Real Twister, 3, 120	12	1:45.20	40,140
1981	Paristo, 3, 112	D. C. Ashcroft	Bravestofall, 3, 120	Darby Gillic, 3, 122	14	1:45.40	43,560

The race and the track are named for the city of Tampa, Florida, and the bay on which it is located. Formerly sponsored by the Anheuser-Busch Co. of St. Louis, Missouri 1981-'86. Not graded 1990-2001. Budweiser Tampa Bay Derby 1981-'86. Track record 2007.

Taylor Made Matchmaker Stakes

Grade 3 in 2008. Monmouth Park, three-year-olds and up, fillies and mares, 1 1/8 miles, turf. Held August 5, 2007, with a gross value of $150,000. First held in 1967. First graded in 1973. Stakes record 1:46.19 (2001 Batique).

Year	Winner	Jockey	Second	Third	Strs	Time	1st Purse
2007	Roshani, 4, 117	G. K. Gomez	Trick's Pic, 4, 117	Humoristic, 6, 117	8	1:47.55	$90,000
2006	Ready's Gal, 4, 117	J. R. Velazquez	Prop Me Up, 4, 117	Humoristic, 6, 117	8	1:48.77	90,000
2005	Love Match, 5, 116	J. Castellano	Cat Alert, 5, 118	Emerald Earrings, 4, 116	10	1:50.38	90,000
2004	Where We Left (GB), 4, 118	C. S. Nakatani	Mrs. M, 5, 118	Spin Control, 4, 116	9	1:48.80	60,000
2003	Volga (Ire), 5, 116	J. Bravo	Something Ventured, 4, 117	Cocktailsandreams, 6, 115	10	1:48.22	60,000
2002	Clearly a Queen, 5, 115	E. Coa	Siringas (Ire), 4, 116	Platinum Tiara, 4, 115	7	1:47.76	60,000
2001	Batique, 5, 117	J. C. Ferrer	Melody Queen (GB), 5, 114	Lucky Lune (Fr), 4, 114	8	1:46.19	60,000
2000	Horatia (Ire), 4, 114	J. A. Santos	Camella, 5, 120	Champagne Royal, 6, 114	11	1:47.52	60,000
1999	Natalie Too, 5, 116	J. Bravo	Saralea (Fr), 4, 116	U R Unforgetable, 5, 120	6	1:46.81	60,000
1998	Bursting Forth, 4, 116	M. E. Verge	French Buster, 4, 116	Gastronomical, 5, 113	9	1:48.46	60,000
1997	Fleur de Nuit, 4, 113	J. A. Krone	Flame Valley, 4, 113	Overcharger, 5, 113	7	1:48.97	60,000
1996	Powder Bowl, 4, 113	D. S. Rice	Class Kris, 4, 120	Turkish Tryst, 5, 114	6	1:54.71	60,000
1995	Avie's Fancy, 4, 113	W. H. McCauley	Plenty of Sugar, 4, 118	Northern Emerald, 5, 113	8	1:54.19	60,000
1994	Alice Springs, 4, 118	J. A. Krone	Hero's Love, 6, 118	Cox Orange, 4, 118	8	1:55.21	60,000
1993	Fairy Garden, 5, 120	M. E. Smith	Saratoga Source, 4, 118	Logan's Mist, 4, 118	8	1:57.81	60,000
1992	Radiant Ring, 4, 115	R. E. Colton	Highland Crystal, 4, 118	La Gueriere, 4, 118	8	1:55.92	60,000
1991	Miss Josh, 5, 123	L. A. Pincay Jr.	Whip Cream, 5, 113	Le Famo, 5, 113	7	1:54.18	90,000
1990	Capades, 4, 118	A. T. Cordero Jr.	Gaily Gaily (Ire), 7, 115	Summer Secretary, 5, 115	7	1:55.60	90,000
1989	Spruce Fir, 6, 113	D. B. Thomas	Ravinella, 4, 120	Native Mommy, 6, 120	8	1:53.40	90,000
1988	Magdelaine (NZ), 5, 120	E. Maple	Spruce Fir, 5, 115	Carotene, 5, 120	7	1:56.20	60,000
1987	Carotene, 4, 118	D. J. Seymour	Spruce Fir, 4, 123	Cadabra Abra, 4, 120	10	1:56.60	73,500
1986	Lake Country, 5, 118	V. A. Bracciale Jr.	Capo Di Monte (Ire), 4, 120	Top Socialite, 4, 120	11	1:54.60	60,000
1985	Key Dancer, 4, 118	J. D. Bailey	Forest Maiden, 5, 118	Dictina (Fr), 4, 115	7	2:02.40	30,000
1984	Sabin, 4, 123	E. Maple	Doblique, 5, 113	Virgin Bride, 4, 113	8	1:53.80	30,000
1983	Luminaire, 4, 113	B. Thornburg	Vestris, 4, 113	Lonely Balladier, 5, 113	8	1:56.80	25,000
1982	Hunston (GB), 4, 113	J. Samyn	Trevita (Ire), 5, 118	Kuja Happa, 4, 115	9	1:58.60	35,000
1981	Mairzy Doates, 5, 120	C. B. Asmussen	Honey Fox, 4, 120	Little Bonny (Ire), 4, 120	7	1:56.00	25,000
1980	Just a Game (Ire), 4, 120	D. Brumfield	La Soufriere, 5, 115	Record Acclaim, 4, 115	10	1:57.60	25,000
1979	Warfever (Fr), 4, 113	J. Samyn	Smooth Journey, 3, 106	La Soufriere, 4, 118	10	2:03.20	25,000
1978	Queen Lib, 3, 112	D. MacBeth	Debby's Turn, 4, 114	Dottie's Doll, 5, 117	8	1:56.40	25,000
1977	Mississippi Mud, 4, 119	J. E. Tejeira	Vodka Time, 5, 114	*Lucie Manet, 4, 124	8	1:54.20	30,000
1976	Dancers Countess, 4, 119	C. J. McCarron	Vodka Time, 4, 114	Garden Verse, 4, 119	8	1:56.00	20,000
1975	Susan's Girl, 6, 121	R. Broussard	Aunt Jin, 3, 114	Pink Tights, 4, 114	6	1:54.20	20,000
1974	Desert Vixen, 4, 123	L. A. Pincay Jr.	Coraggioso, 4, 115	Twixt, 4, 123	9	1:55.20	30,000
1973	Alma North, 5, 118	F. Lovato	Light Hearted, 4, 121	Susan's Girl, 4, 125	9	1:55.20	30,000

The first three finishers of this race are awarded future breeding seasons; named for "matchmaking" between stallions and mares. Sponsored by Taylor Made Farm of Nicholasville, Kentucky 2005-'07. Formerly sponsored by Vinery of Lexington 1996, 1998-2001. Formerly sponsored by Gainesway of Lexington 1997. Grade 1 1973-'79. Grade 2 1980-'96. Matchmaker S. 1967-2001. Matchmaker H. 2002-'04. Held at Atlantic City Race Course 1967-'96. 1 3/16 miles 1967-'96. Dirt 1967-'78, 1983. Track record 1975. Course record 2001.

Tempted Stakes

Grade 3 in 2008. Aqueduct, two-year-olds, fillies, 1 mile, dirt. Held October 28, 2007, with a gross value of $106,600. First held in 1975. First graded in 1980. Stakes record 1:35.40 (1975 Secret Lanvin).

Year	Winner	Jockey	Second	Third	Strs	Time	1st Purse
2007	Elusive Lady, 2, 115	E. Coa	Meriwether Jessica, 2, 115	Sunday Holiday, 2, 116	5	1:38.40	$65,160
2006	Successful Outlook, 2, 115	J. Bravo	Spectacular Malibu, 2, 121	Five Star Daydream, 2, 119	5	1:37.36	64,920

Year	Winner	Jockey	Second	Third	Strs	Time	1st Purse
2005	**Better Now**, 2, 115	J. Castellano	Capote's Crown, 2, 115	Wonder Lady Anne L, 2, 115	7	1:38.35	$66,000
2004	**Summer Raven**, 2, 115	S. Elliott	K. D.'s Shady Lady, 2, 115	Salute, 2, 115	5	1:36.09	63,960
2003	**La Reina**, 2, 115	J. R. Velazquez	Eye Dazzler, 2, 115	Sisti's Pride, 2, 115	8	1:36.15	66,420
2002	**Chimichurri**, 2, 119	J. R. Velazquez	Reheat, 2, 115	Bonay, 2, 115	8	1:37.52	66,240
2001	**Smok'n Frolic**, 2, 119	J. R. Velazquez	Saintly Action, 2, 115	Wopping, 2, 117	8	1:37.77	66,900
2000	**Two Item Limit**, 2, 117	R. Migliore	Celtic Melody, 2, 115	Twining Star, 2, 115	6	1:38.53	65,520
1999	**Shawnee Country**, 2, 116	J. F. Chavez	To Marquet, 2, 114	Marigalante, 2, 116	5	1:38.60	65,460
1998	**Oh What a Windfall**, 2, 121	J. D. Bailey	La Ville Rouge, 2, 114	Honour a Bull, 2, 114	8	1:39.84	66,120
1997	**Dancing With Ruth**, 2, 118	T. G. Turner	Soft Senorita, 2, 118	Aunt Anne, 2, 116	6	1:37.40	65,340
1996	**Ajina**, 2, 112	J. D. Bailey	Glitter Woman, 2, 114	Aldiza, 2, 114	7	1:36.59	66,240
1994	**Special Broad**, 2, 114	J. A. Krone	Carson Creek, 2, 114	Golden Bri, 2, 114	7	1:37.20	66,000
1993	**Sovereign Kitty**, 2, 112	J. R. Velazquez	Seeking the Circle, 2, 112	Her Temper, 2, 112	8	1:46.84	69,720
1992	**True Affair**, 2, 121	J. Bravo	Broad Gains, 2, 121	Touch of Love, 2, 114	6	1:47.48	68,520
1991	**Deputation**, 2, 114	D. W. Lidberg	Turnback the Alarm, 2, 121	Bless Our Home, 2, 114	9	1:46.74	72,600
1990	**Flawlessly**, 2, 121	J. D. Bailey	Debutant's Halo, 2, 121	Slept Thru It, 2, 114	12	1:46.60	56,250
1989	**Worth Avenue**, 2, 113	R. P. Romero	Crown Quest, 2, 119	Voodoo Lily, 2, 114	6	1:46.80	69,480
1988	**Box Office Gold**, 2, 116	J. A. Santos	Dreamy Mimi, 2, 116	Surging, 2, 116	5	1:46.20	57,600
1987	**Thirty Eight Go Go**, 2, 121	K. Desormeaux	Best Number, 2, 114	Dangerous Type, 2, 116	9	1:44.60	100,920
1986	**Silent Turn**, 2, 119	C. W. Antley	Grecian Flight, 2, 119	Chase the Dream, 2, 119	11	1:46.20	74,400
1985	**Cosmic Tiger**, 2, 121	E. Maple	Tracy's Espoir, 2, 114	Roses for Avie, 2, 114	10	1:46.80	68,580
1984	**Willowy Mood**, 2, 121	J. Velasquez	Koluctoo's Jill, 2, 114	Easy Step, 2, 116	12	1:46.20	57,330
1983	**Surely Georgie's**, 2, 113	R. Hernandez	Baroness Direct, 2, 114	Dumdedumdedum, 2, 114	8	1:39.60	34,320
1982	**Only Queens**, 2, 114	M. A. Rivera	Future Fun, 2, 113	Blue Garter, 2, 114	6	1:37.00	33,180
1981	**Choral Group**, 2, 121	J. Velasquez	Michelle Mon Amour, 2, 114	Middle Stage, 2, 113	7	1:38.00	33,000
1980	**Tina Tina Too**, 2, 114	C. B. Asmussen	Prayers'n Promises, 2, 121	Explosive Kingdom, 2, 114	6	1:38.40	32,580
1979	**Genuine Risk**, 2, 114	J. Vasquez	Street Ballet, 2, 117	Tell a Secret, 2, 114	9	1:36.00	33,060
1978	**Whisper Fleet**, 2, 119	A. T. Cordero Jr.	Run Cosmic Run, 2, 114	Distinct Honor, 2, 113	6	1:36.20	25,665
1977	**Caesar's Wish**, 2, 116	G. McCarron	Itsamaza, 2, 116	Lucinda Lea, 2, 114	13	1:36.20	22,635
1976	**Pearl Necklace**, 2, 114	A. T. Cordero Jr.	Our Mims, 2, 113	Road Princess, 2, 115	10	1:39.60	22,380
1975	**Secret Lanvin**, 2, 113	J. Cruguet	Free Journey, 2, 121	Imaflash, 2, 113	9	**1:35.40**	33,600

Named for Mrs. Philip duPont's 1959 champion older female and '59 Ladies H. winner Tempted (1955 f. by *Half Crown). Grade 2 1981-'82, 1988. Held at Belmont 2001, '05. Not held 1995. 1 1/16 miles 1984-'93.

Test Stakes — *See* Darley Test Stakes

Texas Mile Stakes

Grade 3 in 2008. Lone Star Park, three-year-olds and up, 1 mile, dirt. Held April 26, 2008, with a gross value of $300,000. First held in 1997. First graded in 1999. Stakes record 1:34.44 (1997 Isitingood).

Year	Winner	Jockey	Second	Third	Strs	Time	1st Purse
2008	**Monterey Jazz**, 4, 123	D. R. Flores	Zanjero, 4, 118	Beta Capo, 4, 118	6	1:35.25	$185,000
2007	**Silent Pleasure**, 4, 120	T. J. Hebert	Bob and John, 4, 118	Dreamsandvisions, 5, 118	6	1:35.39	185,000
2006	**Preachinatthebar**, 5, 120	J. K. Court	Stockholder, 6, 116	Texcess, 4, 116	11	1:36.81	165,000
2005	**High Strike Zone**, 5, 118	R. J. Faul	Supah Blitz, 5, 120	Twilight Road, 8, 118	8	1:35.34	185,000
2004	**Kela**, 6, 119	D. C. Nuesch	Supah Blitz, 4, 116	Yessirgeneralsir, 4, 114	8	1:35.64	175,000
2003	**Bluestebstandard**, 6, 120	M. A. Pedroza	Bonapaw, 7, 116	Compendium, 5, 116	9	1:35.68	170,000
2002	**Unrullah Bull**, 5, 116	A. J. Lovato	Reba's Gold, 5, 118	Compendium, 4, 116	9	1:37.78	170,000
2001	**Dixie Dot Com**, 6, 116	D. R. Flores	Mr Ross, 6, 120	Five Straight, 4, 115	7	1:34.72	180,000
2000	**Sir Bear**, 7, 116	E. Coa	Lexington Park, 4, 118	Luftikus, 4, 118	9	1:35.98	170,000
1999	**Littlebitlively**, 5, 116	C. Gonzalez	Real Quiet, 4, 113	Allen's Oop, 4, 113	8	1:35.65	145,000
1998	**Littlebitlively**, 4, 118	C. Gonzalez	Anet, 4, 116	Scott's Scoundrel, 6, 118	5	1:37.07	160,000
1997	**Isitingood**, 6, 123	D. R. Flores	Spiritbound, 5, 116	Skip Away, 4, 116	7	**1:34.44**	150,000

Texas is the home state of Lone Star Park.

The Very One Handicap

Grade 3 in 2008. Gulfstream Park, four-year-olds and up, fillies and mares, 1 1/8 miles, turf. Held March 8, 2008, with a gross value of $100,000. First held in 1987. First graded in 1996. Stakes record 1:49.94 (2008 Mauralakana [Fr]).

Year	Winner	Jockey	Second	Third	Strs	Time	1st Purse
2008	**Mauralakana (Fr)**, 5, 117	R. R. Douglas	Tejida, 5, 116	Herboriste (GB), 5, 115	9	**1:49.94**	$60,000
2007	**Royal Highness (Ger)**, 5, 120	E. S. Prado	Safari Queen (Arg), 5, 117	Barancella (Fr), 6, 117	9	2:12.63	60,000
2006	**Dynamite Lass**, 4, 114	R. Bejarano	Olaya, 5, 116	Noble Stella (Ger), 5, 116	10	2:18.81	60,000
2005	**Honey Ryder**, 4, 114	J. R. Velazquez	Briviesca (GB), 4, 114	Vous, 4, 113	10	2:11.71	60,000
2004	**Binya (Ger)**, 5, 114	J. R. Velazquez	Ocean Silk, 4, 115	Boana (Ger), 6, 114	12	2:19.65	60,000
2003	**San Dare**, 5, 116	M. Guidry	Tweedside, 5, 115	Hi Tech Honeycomb, 4, 113	12	2:13.76	60,000
2002	**Moon Queen (Ire)**, 4, 118	J. D. Bailey	Jennasietta, 4, 114	Sweetest Thing, 4, 115	6	2:18.38	60,000
2001	**Innuendo (Ire)**, 6, 115	J. D. Bailey	Lucky Lune (Fr), 4, 114	Silver Bandana, 5, 114	10	2:13.62	60,000
2000	**My Sweet Westly**, 4, 110	P. Day	I'm Indy Mood, 5, 114	Manoa, 5, 114	8	2:06.79	45,000
1999	**Delilah (Ire)**, 5, 116	J. D. Bailey	Starry Dreamer, 5, 114	Justenuffheart, 4, 113	8	2:13.45	45,000
1998	**Shemozzle (Ire)**, 5, 114	J. R. Velazquez	Turkappeal, 5, 116	Yokama, 5, 119	8	2:19.06	45,000
1997	**Tocopilla (Arg)**, 7, 114	B. D. Peck	Ampulla, 6, 123	Beyrouth, 5, 113	6	2:14.35	45,000
1996	**Electric Society (Ire)**, 5, 113	M. E. Smith	Northern Emerald, 6, 117	Chelsey Flower, 5, 114	13	2:15.23	30,000

Racing — Graded Stakes

Year	Winner	Jockey	Second	Third	Strs	Time	1st Purse
1995	P J Floral, 6, 113	S. J. Sellers	Trampoli, 6, 118	Memories (Ire), 4, 113	6	2:14.44	$30,000
1994	Russian Tango, 4, 112	J. D. Bailey	Maxamount, 6, 116	Camiunch, 5, 112	6	2:02.58	30,000
1993	Fairy Garden, 5, 113	W. S. Ramos	Trampoli, 4, 115	Tango Charlie, 4, 114	11	2:14.67	30,000
1992	Bungalow, 5, 112	S. J. Sellers	Raffinierte (Ire), 4, 110	Lover's Quest, 4, 109	7	2:05.79	30,000
1991	Rigamajig, 5, 116	R. P. Romero	Star Standing, 4, 114	Ahead (GB), 4, 112	11	2:15.10	30,000
1990	Storm of Glory, 6, 113	J. D. Bailey	Tukwila, 4, 110	Topicount, 5, 113	8	1:25.00	30,000
1987	First Prediction, 5, 114	J. M. Pezua	Thirty Zip, 4, 113	Lady of the North, 4, 110	11	1:35.20	37,620

Named for Mrs. Helen M. Polinger's 1981 Orchid H. (G2) winner The Very One (1975 f. by One for All). Not graded 2000. Not held 1988-'89. 1 mile 1987. 7 furlongs 1990. 1 1/4 miles 1992, '94, 2000. About 1 3/8 miles 1998, 2002. 1 7/16 miles 2006. 1 5/8 miles 1991, '93, 1995-'97, 1999-2001, 2003-'05. Dirt 1990, '92, '94, 2000. Three-year-olds and up 1987-1995, 1997-2006. Course record 2006.

Thoroughbred Club of America Stakes

Grade 3 in 2008. Keeneland Race Course, three-year-olds and up, fillies and mares, 6 furlongs, all weather. Held October 6, 2007, with a gross value of $300,000. First held in 1981. First graded in 1988. Stakes record 1:08.70 (1998 Bourbon Belle).

Year	Winner	Jockey	Second	Third	Strs	Time	1st Purse
2007	Wild Gams, 4, 118	R. Dominguez	Sugar Swirl, 4, 118	Baroness Thatcher, 3, 118	9	1:10.00	$186,000
2006	Malibu Mint, 4, 124	K. Kaenel	Hide and Chic, 4, 122	Hot Storm, 4, 120	8	1:08.71	186,000
2005	Reunited, 3, 116	R. Albarado	Miss Terrible (Arg), 6, 122	Savorthetime, 6, 118	10	1:11.59	186,000
2004	Molto Vita, 4, 122	R. Bejarano	My Trusty Cat, 4, 124	My Boston Gal, 4, 118	6	1:09.92	77,500
2003	Summer Mis, 4, 122	R. R. Douglas	Don't Countess Out, 4, 122	Born to Dance, 4, 122	10	1:09.77	77,500
2002	French Riviera, 3, 116	D. J. Meche	Don't Countess Out, 3, 120	Away, 5, 122	10	1:09.75	77,500
2001	Cat Cay, 4, 118	P. Day	Spanish Glitter, 3, 120	Another, 4, 124	7	1:09.24	67,580
2000	Katz Me If You Can, 3, 115	J. F. Chavez	Hurricane Bertie, 5, 123	My Alibi, 4, 117	6	1:09.42	67,394
1999	‡Cinemine, 4, 120	E. M. Martin Jr.	Bourbon Belle, 4, 122	Lucky Again, 3, 114	5	1:08.86	62,000
1998	Bourbon Belle, 3, 111	W. Martinez	J J'sdream, 5, 121	Meter Maid, 4, 121	8	**1:08.70**	62,000
1997	Sky Blue Pink, 3, 111	P. Day	Bluffing Girl, 3, 114	Mama's Pro, 4, 116	7	1:10.06	62,000
1996	Surprising Fact, 3, 110	P. Day	Morris Code, 4, 118	Mama's Pro, 3, 113	9	1:10.14	62,000
1995	Cat Appeal, 3, 116	D. M. Barton	Russian Flight (Ire), 3, 113	Traverse City, 5, 118	9	1:10.02	46,500
1994	Tenacious Tiffany, 4, 113	C. Perret	Roamin Rachel, 4, 120	Jeano, 6, 120	7	1:11.04	46,500
1993	Jeano, 5, 120	P. Day	Apelia, 4, 117	Fluttery Danseur, 4, 120	6	1:09.39	46,500
1992	Ifyoucouldseemenow, 4, 120	C. Perret	Harbour Club, 5, 117	Madam Bear, 4, 117	8	1:09.67	48,750
1991	Avie Jane, 7, 117	C. Perret	Amen, 4, 114	Hoga, 5, 114	6	1:10.24	48,750
1990	Safely Kept, 4, 123	C. Perret	Volterra, 5, 117	Medicine Woman, 5, 117	5	1:10.40	48,750
1989	Plate Queen, 4, 117	R. P. Romero	Degenerate Gal, 4, 114	Social Pro, 4, 123	8	1:11.20	48,750
1988	Tappiano, 4, 123	J. Vasquez	Bound, 4, 117	Pine Tree Lane, 6, 123	7	1:10.20	48,750
1987	‡There Are Rainbows, 7, 120	R. Fletcher	Weekend Delight, 5, 123	Ten Thousand Stars, 5, 120	7	1:11.00	32,500
1986	Zenobia Empress, 5, 117	E. Fires	Endear, 4, 120	Weekend Delight, 4, 123	11	1:11.80	32,500
1985	Boldara, 4, 114	P. Rubbicco	Shamrock Boat, 4, 114	Space Angel, 5, 120	8	1:10.80	32,500
1984	Bids and Blades, 3, 114	D. Brumfield	Lass Trump, 4, 123	Grecian Comedy, 4, 123	8	1:11.60	32,500
1983	Excitable Lady, 5, 111	P. Day	Wendy's Ten, 4, 114	A Status Symbol, 4, 111	4	1:09.80	31,250
1982	Excitable Lady, 4, 123	D. G. McHargue	Privacy, 4, 117	Arbutus Toehold, 4, 114	10	1:09.20	27,350
1981	Gold Treasure, 4, 113	M. S. Sellers	Sweet Revenge, 3, 109	Weber City Miss, 4, 114	8	1:10.20	21,250

Named for the Thoroughbred Club of America, whose headquarters is a short distance from Keeneland. Thoroughbred Club Dinner S. 1981-'82. Dirt 1981-2005. ‡Zigbelle finished first, DQ to fourth, 1987. ‡Bourbon Belle finished first, DQ to second, 1999.

Toboggan Handicap

Grade 3 in 2008. Aqueduct, three-year-olds and up, 6 furlongs, dirt. Held March 8, 2008, with a gross value of $106,200. First held in 1890. First graded in 1973. Stakes record 1:08.40 (1956 Nance's Lad).

Year	Winner	Jockey	Second	Third	Strs	Time	1st Purse
2008	Sir Greeley, 6, 116	E. Coa	Man of Danger, 6, 115	Ravalo, 4, 114	5	1:10.22	$64,920
2007	Attila's Storm, 5, 120	R. A. Dominguez	Wild Jam, 6, 114	Pavo, 5, 113	5	1:10.12	64,260
2006	Kazoo, 8, 116	R. Migliore	Bishop Court Hill, 6, 117	Wild Jam, 5, 115	6	1:09.22	64,440
2005	Primary Suspect, 4, 115	P. Fragoso	Shake You Down, 7, 122	Houston's Prayer, 5, 115	6	1:09.47	64,260
2004	Well Fancied, 6, 118	E. Coa	Gators N Bears, 4, 115	Don Six, 4, 113	10	1:22.06	67,320
2003	Affirmed Success, 9, 118	R. Migliore	Peeping Tom, 6, 117	Captain Red, 6, 115	6	1:09.09	65,460
2002	Affirmed Success, 8, 119	R. Migliore	Vodka, 5, 114	Multiple Choice, 4, 115	6	1:22.87	64,920
2001	Peeping Tom, 4, 118	S. Bridgmohan	Say Florida Sandy, 7, 117	Lake Pontchartrain, 6, 113	6	1:21.25	64,380
2000	Brutally Frank, 5, 117	S. Bridgmohan	Master O Foxhounds, 5, 114	Watchman's Warning, 5, 113	8	1:20.77	49,410
1999	Wouldn't We All, 5, 114	R. Migliore	Brushed On, 4, 115	Esteemed Friend, 5, 120	7	1:20.95	48,900
1998	Home On the Ridge, 4, 114	W. H. McCauley	Wire Me Collect, 5, 118	King Roller, 7, 116	7	1:23.01	49,650
1997	Royal Haven, 5, 115	R. Migliore	Jamies First Punch, 4, 115	Cold Execution, 6, 113	6	1:22.40	48,600
1996	Placid Fund, 4, 112	J. F. Chavez	Valid Wager, 4, 116	Pat n Jac, 4, 112	12	1:22.92	51,480
1995	Boom Towner, 7, 117	F. Lovato Jr.	Virginia Rapids, 5, 113	Won Song, 5, 112	6	1:23.77	49,080
1994	Blare of Trumpets, 5, 112	D. Carr	Preporant, 5, 117	Fabersham, 6, 115	6	1:09.70	49,200
1993	Argyle Lake, 7, 109	D. Carr	The Great M. B., 4, 111	Regal Conquest, 5, 110	12	1:10.11	55,530
1992	Boom Towner, 4, 115	D. Nelson	Real Minx, 5, 112	Gallant Step, 5, 114	8	1:10.03	52,740
1991	Bravely Bold, 5, 115	M. E. Smith	True and Blue, 6, 116	Proud and Valid, 6, 110	8	1:10.71	52,020
1990	Sunny Blossom, 5, 117	E. Maple	Diamond Donnie, 4, 111	Once Wild, 5, 123	6	1:09.60	51,300
1989	Lord of the Night, 6, 114	J. Velasquez	Teddy Drone, 4, 117	Vinnie the Viper, 6, 115	7	1:10.40	52,290

Racing — Graded Stakes 475

Year	Winner	Jockey	Second	Third	Strs	Time	1st Purse
1988	Afleet, 4, 123	G. Stahlbaum	Pinecutter, 4, 115	Vinnie the Viper, 5, 122	4	1:09.20	$66,480
1987	Play the King, 4, 112	R. Hernandez	Comic Blush, 4, 117	Best by Test, 5, 124	6	1:09.60	50,400
1986	Rexson's Bishop, 4, 114	R. R. Baez	Green Shekel, 4, 126	Cullendale, 4, 116	5	1:11.40	50,760
1985	Fighting Fit, 6, 123	R. Migliore	Entropy, 5, 123	Shadowmar, 6, 107	6	1:09.60	51,210
1984	Top Avenger, 6, 120	A. Graell	Main Stem, 6, 109	Elegant Life, 4, 116	9	1:10.40	43,080
1983	Mouse Corps, 5, 111	R. X. Alvarado Jr.	Top Avenger, 5, 123	Prince Valid, 4, 115	7	1:09.40	33,000
1982	Always Run Lucky, 4, 110	J. J. Miranda	Swelegant, 4, 113	In From Dixie, 5, 125	7	1:10.00	33,180
1981	Dr. Blum, 4, 123	R. Hernandez	Guilty Conscience, 5, 115	Dunham's Gift, 4, 118	4	1:11.20	32,340
1980	Tilt Up, 5, 116	J. Fell	Ardaluan (Ire), 4, 111	Double Zeus, 4, 123	5	1:11.00	33,660
1979	Vencedor, 5, 127	M. A. Rivera	Jet Diplomacy, 4, 113	Al Battah, 4, 125	8	1:10.00	32,280
1978	Barrera, 5, 126	R. Hernandez	Pumpkin Moonshine, 4, 106	Fratello Ed, 4, 121	5	1:08.80	31,890
1977	Great Above, 5, 112	S. Cauthen	Full Out, 4, 117	Patriot's Dream, 4, 126	9	1:09.40	32,490
1976	Due Diligence, 4, 111	J. Velasquez	*Pompini, 6, 113	Gallant Bob, 4, 129	11	1:10.20	34,740
1975	†Honorable Miss, 5, 117	J. Vasquez	Frankie Adams, 4, 116	Startahemp, 5, 121	6	1:09.00	16,350
1974	Mike John G., 4, 112	V. A. Bracciale Jr.	Tap the Tree, 5, 115	Delta Champ, 4, 113	6	1:08.60	16,575
1973	Tentam, 4, 122	J. Velasquez	Spanish Riddle, 4, 115	Tap the Tree, 4, 118	7	1:09.40	16,710

Originally the Toboggan Slide H., held on the downhill course at Old Morris Park in the Bronx, New York. Not graded 1975-'83, 1996-2002. Toboggan Slide H. 1890-'94. Held at Morris Park 1890-'94. Held at Belmont Park 1896-1961. Not held 1891, 1895, 1911-'12. 7 furlongs 1896-1909, 1995-2002, 2004. †Denotes female.

Tokyo City Handicap

Grade 3 in 2008. Santa Anita Park, four-year-olds and up, 1 1/2 miles, all weather. Held March 29, 2008, with a gross value of $108,200. First held in 1957. First graded in 1973. Stakes record 2:29 (2008 Niagara Causeway).

Year	Winner	Jockey	Second	Third	Strs	Time	1st Purse
2008	Niagara Causeway, 5, 115	J. K. Court	Church Service, 5, 114	Big Booster, 7, 116	7	**2:29.00**	$64,920
2007	Fairbanks, 4, 115	R. Migliore	Neko Bay, 4, 115	Racketeer, 4, 113	6	1:47.87	64,320
2006	Preachinatthebar, 5, 116	J. K. Court	Texcess, 4, 116	Melanyhasthepapers, 5, 116	9	1:48.14	66,360
2005	Supah Blitz, 5, 116	V. Espinoza	Outta Here, 5, 116	Ender's Shadow, 5, 114	5	1:48.90	63,060
2004	Dynever, 4, 117	C. S. Nakatani	Total Impact (Chi), 6, 116	Even the Score, 6, 116	7	1:48.07	66,360
2003	Western Pride, 5, 116	P. A. Valenzuela	Total Impact (Chi), 5, 113	Fleetstreet Dancer, 5, 113	8	1:48.56	90,000
2002	Bosque Redondo, 5, 114	C. J. McCarron	Mysterious Cat, 4, 111	Freedom Crest, 6, 116	6	1:49.11	90,000
2001	Futural, 5, 115	G. K. Gomez	Irisheyesareflying, 5, 117	Tribunal, 4, 117	5	1:47.87	90,000
2000	Early Pioneer, 5, 113	M. S. Garcia	David, 4, 113	General Challenge, 4, 123	5	1:49.08	95,490
1999	Classic Cat, 4, 122	G. L. Stevens	Budroyale, 6, 119	Klinsman (Ire), 5, 115	4	1:47.77	90,000
1998	Budroyale, 5, 112	M. S. Garcia	Don't Blame Rio, 5, 114	Bagshot, 4, 116	10	1:48.48	100,530
1997	Benchmark, 6, 114	C. J. McCarron	Kingdom Found, 7, 115	Private Song, 4, 112	7	1:48.26	97,650
1996	Del Mar Dennis, 6, 118	K. Desormeaux	Just Java, 5, 116	Regal Rowdy, 7, 115	6	1:48.37	96,650
1995	Del Mar Dennis, 5, 117	C. W. Antley	Wharf, 5, 113	Stoller, 4, 115	8	1:47.27	130,000
1994	Del Mar Dennis, 4, 112	S. Gonzalez Jr.	Hill Pass, 5, 115	Tinners Way, 4, 115	8	1:48.36	129,400
1993	Memo (Chi), 6, 114	P. Atkinson	Charmonnier, 5, 117	Marquetry, 6, 118	7	1:47.49	125,800
1992	Another Review, 4, 114	K. Desormeaux	Defensive Play, 5, 115	Loach, 4, 116	11	1:47.33	163,100
1991	Anshan (GB), 4, 115	C. S. Nakatani	Louis Cyphre (Ire), 5, 112	Pleasant Tap, 4, 116	9	1:47.10	158,900
1990	Ruhlmann, 5, 123	G. L. Stevens	Criminal Type, 5, 119	Stylish Winner, 6, 113	6	1:47.20	240,800
1989	Ruhlmann, 4, 119	L. A. Pincay Jr.	Lively One, 4, 120	Saratoga Passage, 4, 116	6	1:47.20	185,600
1988	Alysheba, 4, 127	C. J. McCarron	Ferdinand, 5, 127	Good Taste (Arg), 6, 113	5	1:47.20	350,000
1987	Judge Angelucci, 4, 115	W. Shoemaker	Iron Eyes, 4, 116	Grecian Wonder, 4, 113	8	1:48.40	129,400
1986	Precisionist, 5, 126	C. J. McCarron	Greinton (GB), 5, 126	Encolure, 4, 116	4	1:47.60	148,200
1985	Greinton (GB), 4, 120	L. A. Pincay Jr.	Precisionist, 4, 127	Al Mamoon, 4, 115	6	1:47.00	117,300
1984	Journey At Sea, 5, 120	W. A. Guerra	My Habitony, 4, 118	Fighting Fit, 5, 123	5	1:48.00	102,050
1983	The Wonder (Fr), 5, 122	W. Shoemaker	Konewah, 4, 112	Swing Till Dawn, 4, 119	6	1:49.20	62,500
1982	Super Moment, 5, 124	C. J. McCarron	Mehmet, 4, 116	It's the One, 4, 126	5	1:48.60	75,450
1981	Borzoi, 5, 118	W. Shoemaker	Shamgo, 5, 117	King Go Go, 6, 122	8	1:46.20	64,700
1980	Peregrinator (Ire), 5, 115	C. J. McCarron	Lunar Probe (NZ), 6, 116	Henschel, 6, 120	6	1:47.80	65,300
1979	Star Spangled, 5, 117	L. A. Pincay Jr.	Farnesio (Arg), 5, 118	State Dinner, 4, 118	6	**1:45.80**	46,900
1978	J. O. Tobin, 4, 123	S. Cauthen	Henschel, 4, 115	Riot in Paris, 7, 119	6	1:47.80	31,950
1977	Today 'n Tomorrow, 4, 112	S. Hawley	Exact Duplicate, 5, 115	Rajab, 4, 114	9	1:46.40	35,300
1976	Zanthe, 7, 118	S. Hawley	Riot in Paris, 5, 121	Mateor, 5, 114	6	**1:45.80**	34,300
1975	Royal Glint, 5, 120	W. Shoemaker	Against the Snow, 5, 115	June's Love, 4, 115	8	**1:45.80**	34,800
1974	Court Ruling, 4, 117	B. Baeza	Captain Cee Jay, 4, 119	Acclimatization, 6, 115	8	1:48.40	25,900
	Wichita Oil, 5, 116	L. A. Pincay Jr.	*Madison Palace, 6, 117	Woodland Pines, 5, 118	8	1:47.60	25,800
1973	Quack, 4, 125	D. Pierce	River Buoy, 8, 119	Curious Course, 4, 112	8	1:49.00	36,500

Named for Tokyo City Racecourse in Japan, one of Santa Anita's sister racetracks. Formerly named for Rancho San Bernardino, location of the present-day city of San Bernardino, California. San Bernardino H. 1957-2004. Grade 2 1973-'77, 1979-2000. Not graded 1978. 1 1/16 miles 1957-'66, 1974. 1 1/8 miles 1967-2007. Turf 1957-'72, 1974-'78. Dirt 1973, 1979-2007. Originally scheduled on turf 1973. Three-year-olds 1957. Three-year-olds and up 1958-'67. Two divisions 1974. Equaled course record 1975.

Tom Fool Handicap

Grade 2 in 2008. Belmont Park, three-year-olds and up, 7 furlongs, dirt. Held July 4, 2007, with a gross value of $197,500. First held in 1975. First graded in 1981. Stakes record 1:20.17 (2002 Left Bank).

Year	Winner	Jockey	Second	Third	Strs	Time	1st Purse
2007	High Finance, 4, 114	J. R. Velazquez	Awesome Twist, 5, 115	Commentator, 6, 119	6	1:21.81	$120,000

Racing — Graded Stakes

Year	Winner	Jockey	Second	Third	Strs	Time	1st Purse
2006	Silver Train, 4, 121	E. S. Prado	War Front, 4, 115	Big Apple Daddy, 4, 115	6	1:21.66	$90,000
2005	Smokume, 4, 115	C. Sutherland	Willy o'the Valley, 4, 115	Clever Electrician, 6, 114	6	1:21.92	90,000
2004	Ghostzapper, 4, 119	J. Castellano	Aggadan, 5, 114	Unforgettable Max, 4, 114	4	1:20.42	90,000
2003	Aldebaran, 5, 122	J. D. Bailey	Peeping Tom, 6, 117	State City, 4, 118	7	1:22.54	90,000
2002	Left Bank, 5, 121	J. R. Velazquez	Affirmed Success, 8, 120	Summer Note, 5, 113	6	**1:20.17**	90,000
2001	Exchange Rate, 4, 114	J. D. Bailey	Say Florida Sandy, 7, 117	Here's Zealous, 4, 112	5	1:21.24	90,000
2000	Trippi, 3, 112	J. D. Bailey	Cornish Snow, 7, 113	Sailor's Warning, 4, 111	6	1:21.69	90,000
1999	Crafty Friend, 6, 116	R. Migliore	Affirmed Success, 5, 119	Artax, 4, 117	5	1:20.62	90,000
1998	Banker's Gold, 4, 115	J. F. Chavez	Boundless Moment, 6, 115	Partner's Hero, 4, 114	6	1:21.04	90,000
1997	Diligence, 4, 116	J. A. Santos	Royal Haven, 5, 118	Elusive Quality, 4, 114	7	1:22.40	90,000
1996	Kayrawan, 4, 113	R. Migliore	Cold Execution, 5, 112	Lite the Fuse, 5, 122	5	1:22.95	64,860
1995	Lite the Fuse, 4, 117	J. A. Krone	Our Emblem, 4, 115	Evil Bear, 5, 118	6	1:21.72	65,220
1994	Virginia Rapids, 4, 124	J. Samyn	Cherokee Run, 4, 121	Boundary, 4, 113	5	1:22.27	64,380
1993	Birdonthewire, 4, 119	C. Perret	Fly So Free, 5, 119	Take Me Out, 5, 119	5	1:20.93	67,680
1992	Rubiano, 5, 126	J. A. Krone	Take Me Out, 4, 119	Arrowtown, 4, 119	8	1:21.70	70,920
1991	Mr. Nasty, 4, 119	A. T. Cordero Jr.	Rubiano, 4, 121	Senor Speedy, 4, 119	4	1:21.79	67,800
1990	Quick Call, 6, 119	J. F. Chavez	Sewickley, 5, 123	Traskwood, 4, 119	5	1:21.40	52,680
1989	Sewickley, 4, 119	R. P. Romero	Houston, 3, 114	Crusader Sword, 4, 119	6	1:24.00	67,920
1988	King's Swan, 8, 128	A. T. Cordero Jr.	Gulch, 4, 128	Abject, 4, 119	4	1:22.40	100,980
1987	Groovy, 4, 128	A. T. Cordero Jr.	Sun Master, 6, 121	Moment of Hope, 4, 119	5	1:22.40	81,900
1986	Groovy, 3, 112	J. A. Santos	Phone Trick, 4, 126	Basket Weave, 5, 119	5	1:21.60	80,460
1985	Track Barron, 4, 123	A. T. Cordero Jr.	Mt. Livermore, 4, 126	Cannon Shell, 6, 126	6	1:22.00	82,260
1984	Believe the Queen, 4, 126	J. Velasquez	A Phenomenon, 4, 119	Cannon Shell, 5, 121	6	1:22.40	70,680
1983	Deputy Minister, 4, 126	D. MacBeth	Fit to Fight, 4, 119	Maudlin, 5, 126	9	1:22.20	52,020
1982	Rise Jim, 6, 119	A. T. Cordero Jr.	Maudlin, 4, 119	And More, 4, 119	5	1:23.80	32,940
1981	Rise Jim, 5, 119	A. T. Cordero Jr.	Proud Appeal, 3, 121	Rivalero, 4, 119	6	1:21.20	32,820
1980	Plugged Nickle, 3, 121	J. Fell	Dr. Patches, 6, 119	Isella, 4, 119	6	1:22.20	33,060
1979	Cox's Ridge, 5, 119	E. Maple	Nice Catch, 5, 121	Tilt Up, 4, 119	5	1:22.20	25,500
1978	J. O. Tobin, 4, 129	J. Fell	White Rammer, 4, 119	It's Freezing, 6, 116	8	1:20.80	25,950
1977	Mexican General, 4, 115	C. Perret	Full Out, 4, 119	Sticky Situation, 4, 110	9	1:22.00	22,605
1976	El Pitirre, 4, 114	A. T. Cordero Jr.	Nalees Knight, 5, 110	†Honorable Miss, 6, 118	6	1:24.40	26,550
1975	Kinsman Hope, 5, 116	J. Ruane	Lonetree, 5, 125	Right Mind, 4, 113	9	1:21.40	26,925

Named for Greentree Stable's 1953 Horse of the Year and '53 Carter H. winner Tom Fool (1949 c. by Menow). Grade 3 1981. Tom Fool S. 1979-'95. Tom Fool Breeders' Cup H. 2007. Held at Aqueduct 1975-'76. †Denotes female.

Top Flight Handicap

Grade 2 in 2008. Aqueduct, three-year-olds and up, fillies and mares, 1 mile, dirt. Held November 23, 2007, with a gross value of $150,000. First held in 1940. First graded in 1973. Stakes record 1:34.96 (1994 Educated Risk).

Year	Winner	Jockey	Second	Third	Strs	Time	1st Purse
2007	Mini Sermon, 3, 116	E. Coa	Lady Marlboro, 3, 114	Golden Velvet, 4, 113	8	1:37.29	$90,000
2006	‡Malibu Mint, 4, 119	E. Coa	Rahys' Appeal, 4, 114	Miss Shop, 3, 115	6	1:36.15	90,000
2005	Stellar Jayne, 4, 123	J. D. Bailey	Bohemian Lady, 4, 115	Seeking the Ante, 3, 116	8	1:35.94	90,000
2004	Daydreaming, 3, 117	J. D. Bailey	Bending Strings, 3, 118	Roar Emotion, 4, 116	6	1:35.29	90,000
2003	Randaroo, 3, 116	H. Castillo Jr.	Beauty Halo (Arg), 4, 115	Pocus Hocus, 5, 116	12	1:36.49	90,000
2002	Sightseek, 3, 113	J. D. Bailey	Zonk, 4, 116	Nasty Storm, 4, 116	9	1:35.46	90,000
2001	Cat Cay, 4, 117	J. R. Velazquez	Tugger, 4, 116	Atelier, 4, 120	9	1:35.45	90,000
2000	Reciclada (Chi), 5, 116	J. D. Bailey	Country Hideaway, 4, 120	Critical Eye, 3, 120	8	1:35.54	90,000
1999	Belle Cherie, 3, 113	J. R. Velazquez	dh-Furlough, 5, 118 dh-Harpia, 5, 117		7	1:35.46	90,000
1998	Catinca, 3, 119	R. Migliore	Furlough, 4, 115	Glitter Woman, 4, 120	5	1:35.81	90,000
1997	Dixie Flag, 3, 117	M. J. Luzzi	Aldiza, 3, 114	Mil Kilates, 4, 117	9	1:35.34	90,000
1996	Flat Fleet Feet, 3, 116	M. E. Smith	Queen Tutta, 4, 118	Miss Golden Circle, 4, 116	9	1:37.00	90,000
1995	Twist Afleet, 4, 123	M. E. Smith	Chaposa Springs, 3, 118	Lotta Dancing, 4, 114	8	1:35.26	90,000
1994	Educated Risk, 4, 120	M. E. Smith	Triumph At Dawn, 4, 111	Imah, 4, 111	8	**1:34.96**	90,000
1993	You'd Be Surprised, 4, 112	J. D. Bailey	Looie Capote, 4, 115	Shared Interest, 5, 114	7	1:48.82	90,000
1992	Firm Stance, 4, 114	P. Day	Haunting, 4, 112	Lady d'Accord, 5, 117	14	1:50.55	120,000
1991	Buy the Firm, 5, 119	J. A. Krone	Colonial Waters, 6, 118	Sharp Dance, 5, 113	6	1:52.30	120,000
1990	Dreamy Mimi, 4, 111	J. D. Bailey	She Can, 3, 108	Survive, 6, 120	7	1:50.40	136,800
1989	Banker's Lady, 4, 121	A. T. Cordero Jr.	Colonial Waters, 4, 114	Aptostar, 4, 117	5	1:51.20	133,680
1988	Clabber Girl, 5, 117	J. A. Santos	Psyched, 5, 112	Cadillacing, 3, 113	9	1:49.40	141,840
1987	Ms. Eloise, 4, 116	R. G. Davis	Beth's Song, 5, 111	Clemanna's Rose, 6, 115	8	1:50.20	138,480
1986	Ride Sally, 4, 123	W. A. Guerra	Squan Song, 5, 124	Leecoo, 5, 107	6	1:49.20	148,140
1985	Flip's Pleasure, 5, 117	J. Samyn	Sintrillium, 7, 119	Some for All, 4, 110	5	1:51.00	101,160
1984	Sweet Missus, 4, 103	R. J. Thibeau Jr.	Lady Norcliffe, 4, 115	Adept, 5, 110	7	1:50.20	104,040
1983	Adept, 4, 109	K. L. Rogers	Broom Dance, 4, 122	Dance Number, 4, 115	6	1:50.40	65,160
1982	Andover Way, 4, 117	J. Velasquez	Anti Lib, 4, 113	Discorama, 4, 116	9	1:50.00	66,360
1981	Chain Bracelet, 4, 115	R. Hernandez	Lady Oakley (Ire), 4, 115	Weber City Miss, 4, 116	9	1:49.60	64,680
1980	Glorious Song, 4, 123	J. Velasquez	Misty Gallore, 4, 126	Blitey, 4, 117	7	1:49.60	66,360
1979	Waya (Fr), 5, 128	A. T. Cordero Jr.	Pearl Necklace, 5, 120	Island Kiss, 4, 112	6	1:49.40	64,680
1978	Northernette, 4, 121	J. Fell	One Sum, 4, 121	Dottie's Doll, 5, 116	8	1:49.40	48,330
1977	Shawi, 4, 111	M. Venezia	Proud Delta, 5, 124	Mississippi Mud, 4, 114	9	1:49.80	48,285

Racing — Graded Stakes   477

Year	Winner	Jockey	Second	Third	Strs	Time	1st Purse
1976	**Proud Delta**, 4, 120	J. Velasquez	Let Me Linger, 4, 116	Spring Is Here, 4, 108	7	1:49.00	$49,455
1975	**Twixt**, 6, 125	W. J. Passmore	Heloise, 4, 109	Something Super, 5, 116	8	1:50.60	33,240
1974	**Lady Love**, 4, 114	E. Maple	Krislin, 5, 111	Penny Flight, 4, 115	7	1:48.60	33,120
1973	**Poker Night**, 3, 110	R. Woodhouse	Summer Guest, 4, 123	Roba Bella, 4, 113	7	1:48.20	33,420

Named for C. V. Whitney's 1931 champion two-year-old filly, '32 champion three-year-old filly, and '32 Coaching Club American Oaks winner Top Flight (1929 f. by *Dis Donc). Formerly sponsored by Delta Airlines of Atlanta 1996-2000, 2003, 2005. Grade 1 1973-'96. Delta Top Flight H. 1996-2000, 2003. Held at Belmont Park 1940-'61, 1993. 1$^{1}/_{16}$ miles 1940-'60. 1$^{1}/_{8}$ miles 1961-'93. Four-year-olds and up 1988, '90. Dead heat for second 1999. ‡Rahys' Appeal finished first, DQ to second, 2006.

Toyota Blue Grass Stakes

Grade 1 in 2008. Keeneland Race Course, three-year-olds, 1$^{1}/_{8}$ miles, all weather. Held April 12, 2008, with a gross value of $750,000. First held in 1911. First graded in 1973. Stakes record 1:47.29 (1996 Skip Away).

Year	Winner	Jockey	Second	Third	Strs	Time	1st Purse
2008	**Monba**, 3, 123	E. S. Prado	Cowboy Cal, 3, 123	Kentucky Bear, 3, 123	12	1:49.71	$465,000
2007	**Dominican**, 3, 123	R. Bejarano	Street Sense, 3, 123	Zanjero, 3, 123	7	1:51.33	465,000
2006	**Sinister Minister**, 3, 123	G. K. Gomez	Storm Treasure, 3, 123	Strong Contender, 3, 123	9	1:48.85	465,000
2005	**Bandini**, 3, 123	J. R. Velazquez	High Limit, 3, 123	Closing Argument, 3, 123	7	1:50.16	465,000
2004	**The Cliff's Edge**, 3, 123	S. J. Sellers	Lion Heart, 3, 123	Limehouse, 3, 123	8	1:49.42	465,000
2003	**Peace Rules**, 3, 123	E. S. Prado	Brancusi, 3, 123	Offlee Wild, 3, 123	9	1:51.73	465,000
2002	**Harlan's Holiday**, 3, 123	E. S. Prado	Booklet, 3, 123	Ocean Sound (Ire), 3, 123	6	1:51.51	465,000
2001	**Millennium Wind**, 3, 123	L. A. Pincay Jr.	Songandaprayer, 3, 123	Dollar Bill, 3, 123	7	1:48.32	465,000
2000	**High Yield**, 3, 123	P. Day	More Than Ready, 3, 123	Wheelaway, 3, 123	8	1:48.79	465,000
1999	**Menifee**, 3, 123	P. Day	Cat Thief, 3, 123	Vicar, 3, 123	8	1:48.66	465,000
1998	**Halory Hunter**, 3, 123	G. L. Stevens	Lil's Lad, 3, 123	Cape Town, 3, 123	5	1:47.98	434,000
1997	**Pulpit**, 3, 121	S. J. Sellers	Acceptable, 3, 121	Stolen Gold, 3, 121	9	1:49.91	434,000
1996	**Skip Away**, 3, 121	S. J. Sellers	Louis Quatorze, 3, 121	Editor's Note, 3, 121	7	**1:47.29**	434,000
1995	**Wild Syn**, 3, 121	R. P. Romero	Suave Prospect, 3, 121	Tejano Run, 3, 121	7	1:49.31	310,000
1994	**Holy Bull**, 3, 121	M. E. Smith	Valiant Nature, 3, 121	Mahogany Hall, 3, 121	7	1:50.02	310,000
1993	**Prairie Bayou**, 3, 121	M. E. Smith	Wallenda, 3, 121	Dixieland Heat, 3, 121	9	1:49.62	310,000
1992	**Pistols and Roses**, 3, 121	J. Vasquez	Conte Di Savoya, 3, 121	Ecstatic Ride, 3, 121	11	1:49.19	325,000
1991	**Strike the Gold**, 3, 121	C. W. Antley	Fly So Free, 3, 121	Nowork all Play, 3, 121	6	1:48.44	260,520
1990	**Summer Squall**, 3, 121	P. Day	Land Rush, 3, 121	Unbridled, 3, 121	5	1:48.60	185,006
1989	**Western Playboy**, 3, 121	R. P. Romero	Dispersal, 3, 121	Tricky Creek, 3, 121	6	1:51.20	185,900
1988	**Granacus**, 3, 121	J. Vasquez	Intensive Command, 3, 121	Regal Classic, 3, 121	9	1:52.20	190,856
1987	‡**War**, 3, 121	W. H. McCauley	Leo Castelli, 3, 121	Alysheba, 3, 121	5	1:48.40	148,135
1986	**Bachelor Beau**, 3, 121	L. J. Melancon	Bolshoi Boy, 3, 121	Bold Arrangement (GB), 3, 121	11	1:51.20	171,290
1985	**Chief's Crown**, 3, 121	D. MacBeth	Floating Reserve, 3, 121	Banner Bob, 3, 121	4	1:47.60	127,740
1984	**Taylor's Special**, 3, 121	P. Day	Silent King, 3, 121	Charmed Rook, 3, 121	9	1:52.20	133,883
1983	**Play Fellow**, 3, 121	J. Cruguet	‡Desert Wine, 3, 121	Copelan, 3, 121	12	1:49.40	121,924
1982	**Linkage**, 3, 121	W. Shoemaker	Gato Del Sol, 3, 121	Wavering Monarch, 3, 121	9	1:48.00	127,774
1981	**Proud Appeal**, 3, 121	J. Fell	Law Me, 3, 121	Golden Derby, 3, 121	11	1:51.40	120,559
1980	**Rockhill Native**, 3, 121	J. Oldham	Super Moment, 3, 121	Gold Stage, 3, 121	9	1:50.00	84,208
1979	**Spectacular Bid**, 3, 121	R. J. Franklin	Lot o' Gold, 3, 121	Bishop's Choice, 3, 121	4	1:50.00	79,658
1978	**Alydar**, 3, 121	J. Velasquez	Raymond Earl, 3, 121	Go Forth, 3, 121	9	1:49.60	77,350
1977	**For The Moment**, 3, 121	A. T. Cordero Jr.	Run Dusty Run, 3, 121	Western Wind, 3, 121	11	1:50.20	77,578
1976	**Honest Pleasure**, 3, 121	B. Baeza	Certain Roman, 3, 121	Inca Roca, 3, 121	7	1:49.40	73,028
1975	**Master Derby**, 3, 121	D. G. McHargue	Honey Mark, 3, 117	Prince Thou Art, 3, 123	9	1:49.00	39,878
1974	**Judger**, 3, 123	L. A. Pincay Jr.	Big Latch, 3, 117	Gold and Myrrh, 3, 114	14	1:49.20	42,608
1973	**My Gallant**, 3, 117	A. T. Cordero Jr.	Our Native, 3, 123	dh-Impecunious, 3, 126 dh-Warbucks, 3, 117	9	1:49.60	37,765

Named for the Bluegrass region of Kentucky. Sponsored by Toyota Motor Manufacturing Co. of Georgetown, Kentucky 1996-2008. Grade 2 1990-'98. Held at Kentucky Association 1911-'36. Held at Churchill Downs 1943-'45. Not held 1915-'18, 1927-'36. 6 furlongs 1964. Dirt 1911-2006. Dead heat for third 1973. ‡Marfa finished second, DQ to fourth, 1983. ‡Alysheba finished first, DQ to third, 1987.

Transylvania Stakes — *See* Central Bank Transylvania Stakes

Travers Stakes

Grade 1 in 2008. Saratoga Race Course, three-year-olds, 1$^{1}/_{4}$ miles, dirt. Held August 25, 2007, with a gross value of $1,000,000. First held in 1864. First graded in 1973. Stakes record 2:00 (1979 General Assembly).

Year	Winner	Jockey	Second	Third	Strs	Time	1st Purse
2007	**Street Sense**, 3, 126	C. H. Borel	Grasshopper, 3, 126	Helsinki, 3, 126	7	2:02.69	$600,000
2006	**Bernardini**, 3, 126	J. Castellano	Bluegrass Cat, 3, 126	Dr. Pleasure, 3, 126	6	2:01.60	600,000
2005	**Flower Alley**, 3, 126	J. R. Velazquez	Bellamy Road, 3, 126	Roman Ruler, 3, 126	7	2:02.76	600,000
2004	**Birdstone**, 3, 126	E. S. Prado	The Cliff's Edge, 3, 126	Eddington, 3, 126	7	2:02.45	600,000
2003	**Ten Most Wanted**, 3, 126	P. Day	Peace Rules, 3, 126	Strong Hope, 3, 126	6	2:02.14	600,000
2002	**Medaglia d'Oro**, 3, 126	J. D. Bailey	Repent, 3, 126	Nothing Flat, 3, 126	9	2:02.53	600,000
2001	**Point Given**, 3, 126	G. L. Stevens	E Dubai, 3, 126	Dollar Bill, 3, 126	9	2:01.40	600,000
2000	**Unshaded**, 3, 126	S. J. Sellers	Albert the Great, 3, 126	Commendable, 3, 126	9	2:02.59	600,000
1999	**Lemon Drop Kid**, 3, 126	J. A. Santos	Vision and Verse, 3, 126	Menifee, 3, 126	8	2:02.19	600,000

Year	Winner	Jockey	Second	Third	Strs	Time	1st Purse
1998	Coronado's Quest, 3, 126	M. E. Smith	Victory Gallop, 3, 126	Raffie's Majesty, 3, 126	7	2:03.40	$450,000
1997	Deputy Commander, 3, 126	C. J. McCarron	Behrens, 3, 126	Awesome Again, 3, 126	8	2:04.08	450,000
1996	Will's Way, 3, 126	J. F. Chavez	Louis Quatorze, 3, 126	Skip Away, 3, 126	7	2:02.55	450,000
1995	Thunder Gulch, 3, 126	G. L. Stevens	Pyramid Peak, 3, 126	Malthus, 3, 126	7	2:03.70	450,000
1994	Holy Bull, 3, 126	M. E. Smith	Concern, 3, 126	Tabasco Cat, 3, 126	5	2:02.03	450,000
1993	Sea Hero, 3, 126	J. D. Bailey	Kissin Kris, 3, 126	Miner's Mark, 3, 126	11	2:01.95	600,000
1992	Thunder Rumble, 3, 126	W. H. McCauley	Devil His Due, 3, 126	Dance Floor, 3, 126	10	2:00.99	600,000
1991	Corporate Report, 3, 126	C. J. McCarron	Hansel, 3, 126	Fly So Free, 3, 126	6	2:01.20	600,000
1990	Rhythm, 3, 126	C. Perret	Shot Gun Scott, 3, 126	Sir Richard Lewis, 3, 126	13	2:02.60	707,100
1989	Easy Goer, 3, 126	P. Day	Clever Trevor, 3, 126	Shy Tom, 3, 126	6	2:00.80	653,100
1988	Forty Niner, 3, 126	C. J. McCarron	Seeking the Gold, 3, 126	Brian's Time, 3, 126	6	2:01.40	653,100
1987	Java Gold, 3, 126	P. Day	Cryptoclearance, 3, 126	Polish Navy, 3, 126	9	2:02.00	673,800
1986	Wise Times, 3, 126	J. D. Bailey	‡Danzig Connection, 3, 126	Personal Flag, 3, 126	7	2:03.40	203,700
1985	Chief's Crown, 3, 126	A. T. Cordero Jr.	Turkoman, 3, 126	Skip Trial, 3, 126	7	2:01.20	202,800
1984	Carr de Naskra, 3, 126	L. A. Pincay Jr.	Pine Circle, 3, 126	Morning Bob, 3, 126	9	2:02.60	211,500
1983	Play Fellow, 3, 126	P. Day	Slew o' Gold, 3, 126	Hyperborean, 3, 126	7	2:01.00	135,000
1982	Runaway Groom, 3, 126	J. Fell	Aloma's Ruler, 3, 126	Conquistador Cielo, 3, 126	5	2:02.60	132,900
1981	Willow Hour, 3, 126	E. Maple	Pleasant Colony, 3, 126	Lord Avie, 3, 126	10	2:03.80	135,600
1980	Temperence Hill, 3, 126	E. Maple	First Albert, 3, 126	Amber Pass, 3, 126	9	2:02.80	100,980
1979	General Assembly, 3, 126	J. Vasquez	Smarten, 3, 126	Private Account, 3, 126	7	**2:00.00**	80,850
1978	‡Alydar, 3, 126	J. Velasquez	Affirmed, 3, 126	Nasty and Bold, 3, 126	4	2:02.00	62,880
1977	‡Jatski, 3, 126	S. Maple	Run Dusty Run, 3, 126	Silver Series, 3, 126	14	2:01.60	68,160
1976	Honest Pleasure, 3, 126	C. Perret	Romeo, 3, 126	Dance Spell, 3, 126	8	2:00.00	65,040
1975	Wajima, 3, 126	B. Baeza	Media, 3, 126	Prince Thou Art, 3, 126	5	2:02.00	65,220
1974	Holding Pattern, 3, 121	M. Miceli	Little Current, 3, 126	†Chris Evert, 3, 121	11	2:05.20	69,660
1973	Annihilate 'em, 3, 120	R. Turcotte	Stop the Music, 3, 122	See the Jaguar, 3, 120	8	2:01.60	68,280

Named for the first president of Saratoga Race Course, William R. Travers; he won the inaugural running with Kentucky. Travers Midsummer Derby 1927-'32. Held at Belmont Park 1943-'45. Not held 1896, 1898, 1900, 1911-'12. 1¾ miles 1864-'89. 1½ miles 1890-'92. 1⅛ miles 1895, 1901-'03. ‡Run Dusty Run finished first, DQ to second, 1977. ‡Affirmed finished first, DQ to second, 1978. ‡Broad Brush finished second, DQ to fourth, 1986. †Denotes female.

Triple Bend Invitational Handicap

Grade 1 in 2008. Hollywood Park, three-year-olds and up, 7 furlongs, all weather. Held July 7, 2007, with a gross value of $300,000. First held in 1952. First graded in 1988. Stakes record 1:19.40 (1980 Rich Cream).

Year	Winner	Jockey	Second	Third	Strs	Time	1st Purse
2007	Bilo, 7, 114	J. Talamo	Surf Cat, 5, 123	Battle Won, 7, 116	7	1:21.65	$180,000
2006	Siren Lure, 5, 121	A. O. Solis	Battle Won, 6, 115	Unfurl the Flag, 6, 116	10	1:21.29	180,000
2005	Unfurl the Flag, 5, 117	C. S. Nakatani	dh-Bear in the Woods, 4, 112 dh-McCann's Mojave, 5, 117		13	1:20.95	210,000
2004	Pohave, 6, 116	V. Espinoza	Rojo Toro, 4, 115	Revello, 6, 110	13	1:21.06	180,000
2003	Joey Franco, 4, 118	P. A. Valenzuela	Publication, 4, 116	‡Primerica, 5, 113	9	1:21.56	180,000
2002	Disturbingthepeace, 4, 113	V. Espinoza	D'wildcat, 4, 115	Mellow Fellow, 7, 120	9	1:21.09	180,000
2001	Ceeband, 4, 110	M. S. Garcia	Squirtle Squirt, 3, 114	Elaborate, 6, 118	10	1:21.10	180,000
2000	Elaborate, 5, 114	V. Espinoza	Cliquot, 4, 116	Lexicon, 5, 117	10	1:21.19	180,000
1999	Mazel Trick, 4, 115	C. J. McCarron	Christmas Boy, 6, 111	Regal Thunder, 5, 115	8	1:19.97	180,000
1998	Son of a Pistol, 6, 118	A. O. Solis	The Exeter Man, 6, 114	Benchmark, 7, 118	11	1:20.81	120,000
1997	Score Quick, 5, 113	G. F. Almeida	Elmhurst, 7, 115	First Intent, 8, 116	11	1:21.00	100,980
1996	Letthebighossroll, 8, 116	C. J. McCarron	Score Quick, 4, 116	Comininalittlehot, 5, 116	7	1:21.43	125,460
1995	Concept Win, 5, 118	P. A. Valenzuela	Gold Land, 4, 116	Lucky Forever, 6, 119	6	1:21.09	63,100
1994	Memo (Chi), 7, 120	P. Atkinson	Minjinsky, 4, 115	Slerp, 5, 119	8	1:20.52	62,400
1993	Now Listen, 6, 116	K. Desormeaux	Cardmania, 7, 116	Star of the Crop, 4, 120	10	1:20.63	66,400
1992	Slew the Surgeon, 4, 111	M. G. Linares	Softshoe Sure Shot, 6, 114	Record Boom, 6, 112	8	1:21.44	64,600
1991	Robyn Dancer, 4, 118	L. A. Pincay Jr.	Bruho, 5, 117	Black Jack Road, 7, 118	6	1:21.00	62,700
1990	Prospectors Gamble, 5, 114	J. A. Garcia	Raise a Stanza, 4, 117	Hot Operator, 5, 113	8	1:21.40	64,200
1989	Sensational Star, 5, 114	R. Q. Meza	Oraibi, 4, 117	Hot Operator, 4, 113	9	1:21.40	49,600
1988	Perfec Travel, 6, 115	C. A. Black	Reconnoitering, 4, 115	Don's Irish Melody, 5, 115	9	1:22.20	49,600
1987	Bedside Promise, 5, 124	R. Q. Meza	Zabaleta, 4, 118	Bolder Than Bold, 5, 118	5	1:21.20	46,500
1986	Sabona, 4, 115	C. J. McCarron	Innamorato, 5, 113	Michadilla, 4, 115	8	1:21.00	47,150
1985	Fifty Six Ina Row, 4, 117	L. A. Pincay Jr.	Premiership, 5, 115	French Legionaire, 4, 117	5	1:20.80	38,500
1984	Debonaire Junior, 3, 114	C. J. McCarron	Croeso, 4, 116	Night Mover, 4, 120	7	1:21.20	37,980
1983	Regal Falcon, 5, 117	E. Delahoussaye	Island Whirl, 5, 123	Kangroo Court, 6, 118	5	1:23.40	30,700
1982	Never Tabled, 5, 112	C. J. McCarron	Shanekite, 4, 117	Pompeii Court, 5, 116	7	1:21.20	31,750
1981	Summer Time Guy, 5, 118	C. J. McCarron	Back'n Time, 4, 118	Life's Hope, 8, 115	6	1:20.20	37,400
1980	Rich Cream, 5, 118	W. Shoemaker	I'm Smokin, 4, 115	Dragon Command (NZ), 6, 126	10	**1:19.40**	32,250
1979	White Rammer, 5, 120	W. Shoemaker	Arachnoid, 6, 124	Bad 'n Big, 5, 122	5	1:20.20	24,650
1978	Drapier (Arg), 6, 120	F. Toro	Voy Por Uno (Mex), 5, 120	Prince of Saron, 5, 115	4	1:21.20	24,200
1977	Painted Wagon, 4, 115	C. Baltazar	Beat Inflation, 4, 122	L'Natural, 4, 115	7	1:21.00	25,750
1976	Home Jerome, 6, 115	M. Castaneda	Shirley's Champion, 5, 116	Money Lender, 5, 116	6	1:21.20	25,050
1975	Messenger of Song, 3, 115	J. Lambert	Century's Envoy, 4, 122	Chesapeake, 6, 115	7	1:20.60	26,650
1974	Woodland Pines, 5, 119	L. A. Pincay Jr.	Soft Victory, 6, 118	Finalista, 5, 123	8	1:20.60	19,800
1973	Briartic, 5, 122	W. Shoemaker	New Prospect, 4, 121	Silver Mallet, 5, 115	8	1:21.20	25,950

Named for Frank McMahon's 1972 Los Angeles H. winner Triple Bend (1968 c. by Never Bend). Formerly named for

Hollywood Park's nickname, "The Track of Lakes and Flowers". Grade 3 1988-'97. Grade 2 1998-2002. Lakes and Flowers H. 1952-'78. Triple Bend H. 1979-'95. Triple Bend Breeders' Cup H. 1996-'97. Triple Bend Breeders' Cup Invitational H. 1998-2004. 6 furlongs 1956-'72. Dirt 1952-2006. Equaled track record 1993. Track record 1994, '99. Dead heat for second 2005. ‡Bluesthestandard finished third, DQ to sixth, 2003.

Tropical Park Derby

Grade 3 in 2008. Calder Race Course, three-year-olds, 1 1/8 miles, turf. Held January 1, 2008, with a gross value of $100,000. First held in 1976. First graded in 1978. Stakes record 1:46.60 (1983 My Mac; 1985 Irish Sur; 2000 Go Lib Go).

Year	Winner	Jockey	Second	Third	Strs	Time	1st Purse
2008	Cowboy Cal, 3, 119	J. R. Velazquez	Why Tonto, 3, 117	Cannonball, 3, 119	12	1:46.95	$57,660
2007	Soldier's Dancer, 3, 119	C. H. Velasquez	Sedgefield, 3, 115	Storm in May, 3, 117	9	1:48.95	60,000
2006	Barbaro, 3, 119	E. S. Prado	Wise River, 3, 117	Lewis Michael, 3, 119	12	1:46.65	60,000
2005	Lord Robyn, 3, 119	E. Coa	Fire Path, 3, 114	Crown Point, 3, 119	12	1:47.18	60,000
2004	Kitten's Joy, 3, 119	J. D. Bailey	Broadway View, 3, 112	Soverign Honor, 3, 117	11	1:46.95	60,000
2003	Nothing to Lose, 3, 115	J. D. Bailey	Millennium Storm, 3, 119	Supah Blitz, 3, 115	12	1:50.45	60,000
2002	Political Attack, 3, 119	M. Guidry	The Judge Sez Who, 3, 115	Deeliteful Guy, 3, 114	8	1:51.71	60,000
2001	Proud Man, 3, 115	R. R. Douglas	Mr Notebook, 3, 119	Cee Dee, 3, 119	11	1:47.95	60,000
2000	Go Lib Go, 3, 119	J. A. Santos	Mr. Livingston, 3, 115	Granting, 3, 115	12	**1:46.60**	60,000
1999	Valid Reprized, 3, 115	J. Castellano	Mr. Roark, 3, 115	Wertz, 3, 119	12	1:53.58	60,000
1998	Draw Again, 3, 117	J. Bravo	Buddha's Delight, 3, 115	Daddy's Dream, 3, 117	11	1:51.28	60,000
1997	Arthur L., 3, 119	E. Coa	Unite's Big Red, 3, 117	Keep It Strait, 3, 117	12	1:46.93	60,000
1996	Ok by Me, 3, 117	J. D. Bailey	Darn That Erica, 3, 114	Tour's Big Red, 3, 117	12	1:47.25	60,000
1995	Mecke, 3, 117	H. Castillo Jr.	Val's Prince, 3, 112	Claudius, 3, 119	14	1:51.12	60,000
1994	Fabulous Frolic, 3, 112	J. Cruguet	Wake Up Alarm, 3, 117	Gator Back, 3, 119	14	1:46.99	60,000
1993	Summer Set, 3, 112	M. A. Gonzalez	Duc d'Sligovil, 3, 112	Silver of Silver, 3, 122	10	1:53.87	60,000
1992	Technology, 3, 119	J. D. Bailey	Majestic Sweep, 3, 114	Always Silver, 3, 114	10	1:53.01	134,160
1991	Jackie Wackie, 3, 119	H. Castillo Jr.	Gizmo's Fortune, 3, 119	Paulrus, 3, 114	13	1:51.90	69,120
1990	Run Turn, 3, 117	E. Fires	Country Day, 3, 112	Shot Gun Scott, 3, 119	8	1:52.40	66,420
1989	Big Stanley, 3, 114	J. Vasquez	Appealing Pleasure, 3, 114	Prized, 3, 114	8	1:52.40	100,170
1988	Digress, 3, 117	E. Maple	Intensive Command, 3, 117	Granacus, 3, 117	11	1:54.60	176,460
1987	Baldski's Star, 3, 117	C. Perret	Manhattan's Woody, 3, 112	Schism, 3, 117	13	1:54.80	139,920
1986	Strong Performance, 3, 117	J. Cruguet	Dr. Dan Eyes, 3, 114	Real Forest, 3, 117	12	1:54.40	143,760
1985	Irish Sur, 3, 117	J. A. Santos	Artillerist, 3, 121	Banner Bob, 3, 121	16	**1:46.60**	107,370
1984	Morning Bob, 3, 121	E. Maple	‡Don Rickles, 3, 121	Papa Koo, 3, 121	15	1:46.00	89,310
1983	My Mac, 3, 121	D. MacBeth	Caveat, 3, 121	Blink, 3, 121	14	**1:46.60**	100,350
1982	Victorian Line, 3, 121	A. Smith Jr.	North Cat, 3, 121	Sandy Bee's Baby, 3, 121	10	1:45.40	68,280
1981	Double Sonic, 3, 121	A. Smith Jr.	Akureyri, 3, 121	Might Be Home, 3, 121	14	1:46.40	70,740
1980	Superbity, 3, 121	J. Vasquez	Ray's Word, 3, 121	Irish Tower, 3, 121	11	1:45.60	69,660
1979	Bishop's Choice, 3, 111	D. MacBeth	Lot o' Gold, 3, 119	Smarten, 3, 121	12	1:44.20	74,400
1978	Dr. Valeri, 3, 116	R. Riera Jr.	Quadratic, 3, 119	Galimore, 3, 119	11	1:45.20	73,200
1977	Ruthie's Native, 3, 112	L. Saumell	Fort Prevel, 3, 121	Dreaming of Moe, 3, 112	12	1:44.00	55,800
1976	Star of the Sea, 3, 115	C. Perret	Controller Ike, 3, 114	Great Contractor, 3, 121	12	1:44.00	55,800

Named for the old Tropical Park racetrack in Miami, which closed in 1972. Grade 2 1983-'89. 1 1/16 miles 1976-'85. About 1 1/8 miles 1994. Dirt 1978-'93, 2002. ‡Rexson's Hope finished second, DQ to fifth, 1984.

Tropical Turf Handicap

Grade 3 in 2008. Calder Race Course, three-year-olds and up, 1 1/8 miles, turf. Held December 1, 2007, with a gross value of $100,000. First held in 1935. First graded in 1981. Stakes record 1:44.99 (1995 The Vid).

Year	Winner	Jockey	Second	Third	Strs	Time	1st Purse
2007	Ballast (Ire), 6, 116	K. J. Desormeaux	National Saint (SAf), 5, 114	Minister's Joy, 5, 116	10	1:48.54	$58,900
2006	Ballast (Ire), 5, 114	R. Bejarano	Bob's Proud Moment, 5, 116	Drum Major, 4, 116	9	1:47.54	60,000
2005	Silver Tree, 5, 116	J. D. Bailey	Demeteor, 6, 114	Settle Up, 5, 115	11	1:46.28	60,000
2004	Host (Chi), 4, 118	J. R. Velazquez	Silver Tree, 4, 118	Demeteor, 5, 114	12	1:45.74	60,000
2003	Political Attack, 4, 116	R. R. Douglas	Millennium Dragon (GB), 4, 116	Sforza (Fr), 4, 115	12	1:45.81	60,000
2002	Krieger, 4, 113	E. Coa	Stokosky, 6, 113	Serial Bride, 5, 114	12	1:47.02	60,000
2001	Band Is Passing, 5, 118	C. Gonzalez	Crash Course, 5, 116	Groomstick Stock's, 5, 114	12	1:46.90	60,000
2000	Stokosky, 4, 114	C. A. Hernandez	dh-Band Is Passing, 4, 119 dh-Special Coach, 4, 114		11	1:48.77	60,000
1999	Hibernian Rhapsody (Ire), 4, 114	R. R. Douglas	Garbu, 5, 117	Shamrock City, 4, 114	12	1:46.17	60,000
1998	Unite's Big Red, 4, 115	E. O. Nunez	N B Forrest, 6, 115	Glok, 4, 115	8	1:48.96	60,000
1997	Sir Cat, 4, 116	J. A. Rivera II	Foolish Pole, 4, 115	Written Approval, 5, 112	6	1:54.08	60,000
1996	Mecke, 4, 124	R. G. Davis	Satellite Nealski, 5, 113	Elite Jeblar, 6, 114	10	1:46.51	60,000
1995	The Vid, 5, 120	W. H. McCauley	Elite Jeblar, 5, 114	Scannapieco, 5, 113	12	**1:44.99**	60,000
1994	The Vid, 4, 116	R. R. Douglas	Country Coy, 4, 113	Gone for Real, 3, 113	12	1:49.06	60,000
1993	Carterista, 4, 121	W. S. Ramos	Rinka Das, 4, 113	Daarik (Ire), 6, 114	12	1:44.95	45,000
1992	Carterista, 3, 112	M. A. Lee	Rinka Das, 4, 114	Pidgeon's Promise, 3, 110	11	1:46.35	30,000
	Bidding Proud, 3, 115	J. A. Santos	Buckhar, 4, 118	Plate Dancer, 7, 116	7	1:46.22	30,000
1990	Stolen Rolls, 4, 112	P. A. Rodriguez	Gay's Best Boy, 3, 111	Seasabb, 5, 111	13	1:45.20	35,700
1989	Vaguely Double, 4, 118	W. A. Guerra	Mr. Adorable, 4, 113	Highland Springs, 5, 120	11	1:48.80	35,490
1988	Equalize, 4, 118	J. A. Santos	Val d'Enchere, 5, 118	Racing Star, 6, 114	10	1:45.00	35,010
1986	Arctic Honeymoon, 3, 111	R. N. Lester	Lover's Cross, 3, 121	Darn That Alarm, 5, 122	7	1:54.00	32,550
1985	Ban the Blues, 6, 114	G. St. Leon	Jim Bracken, 4, 112	Bold Southerner, 4, 112	11	1:53.20	34,140

Racing — Graded Stakes

Year	Winner	Jockey	Second	Third	Strs	Time	1st Purse
1984	Biloxi Indian, 3, 114	B. Fann	Key to the Moon, 3, 122	Di Roma Feast, 3, 114	7	1:54.00	$32,700
1983	‡Eminency, 5, 122	P. Day	World Appeal, 3, 118	Ready to Prove, 3, 110	13	1:51.20	34,770
1982	Rivalero, 6, 120	J. Vasquez	Current Blade, 4, 115	In all Honesty, 3, 110	9	1:53.60	33,270
1981	The Liberal Member, 6, 115	J. D. Bailey	Jayme G., 5, 116	Recusant, 3, 112	14	1:51.80	35,130
1980	Yosi Boy, 4, 111	A. Smith Jr.	Two's a Plenty, 3, 120	Von Clausewitz, 5, 119	8	1:51.80	33,180
1979	Lot o' Gold, 3, 123	D. Brumfield	King Celebrity, 3, 117	J. Rodney G., 4, 114	8	1:52.60	33,330
1975	Proud Birdie, 2, 117	J. Fieselman	Controller Ike, 2, 117	†Noble Royalty, 2, 115	13	1:47.00	18,900
1974	L. Grant Jr., 4, 121	J. Combest	Super Sail, 6, 118	El Tordillo, 4, 115	11	1:45.80	18,300
1973	Proud and Bold, 3, 121	R. Woodhouse	Outatholme, 4, 116	Seminole Joe, 5, 112	7	1:45.60	17,100

Named for the old Tropical Park racetrack in Miami, which closed in 1972. Formerly run on or about December 25. Christmas H. 1935-'71. Christmas Day H. 1972-'92. Held at Tropical Park 1935-'71. Not held 1939-'45, 1947, 1950-'51, 1976-'78, 1987, 1991. 1 mile 1935-'36. 6 furlongs 1949. 1 1/16 miles 1960-'75. 1 mile 70 yards 1971. About 1 1/8 miles 1988-'93, 2003. Dirt 1972-'86, 1997. Two-year-olds and up 1935-'36. Two-year-olds 1975. Two divisions 1964, '67, '69, '92. Dead heat for second 2000. ‡World Appeal finished first, DQ to second, 1983. †Denotes female.

True North Handicap

Grade 2 in 2008. Belmont Park, three-year-olds and up, 6 furlongs, dirt. Held June 7, 2008, with a gross value of $250,000. First held in 1979. First graded in 1983. Stakes record 1:07.80 (1987 Groovy).

Year	Winner	Jockey	Second	Third	Strs	Time	1st Purse
2008	Benny the Bull, 5, 123	E. S. Prado	Man of Danger, 6, 115	Abraaj, 5, 115	7	1:09.06	$150,000
2007	Will He Shine, 5, 116	E. S. Prado	Suave Jazz, 4, 115	Dashboard Drummer, 6, 116	8	1:08.70	120,000
2006	Anew, 5, 113	A. Garcia	Tiger, 5, 116	Spanish Chestnut, 4, 117	8	1:08.10	120,000
2005	Woke Up Dreamin, 5, 116	M. E. Smith	Voodoo, 7, 113	Mass Media, 4, 117	10	1:08.38	128,220
2004	Speightstown, 6, 119	J. R. Velazquez	Cat Genius, 4, 116	Pohave, 6, 117	9	1:08.04	126,840
2003	Shake You Down, 5, 118	M. J. Luzzi	Highway Prospector, 6, 115	Vodka, 6, 114	6	1:09.59	90,000
2002	Explicit, 5, 119	L. J. Meche	Entepreneur, 5, 115	Late Carson, 6, 114	7	1:09.98	150,000
2001	Say Florida Sandy, 7, 123	A. T. Gryder	Wake At Noon, 4, 117	Explicit, 4, 115	8	1:08.77	90,000
2000	Intidab, 7, 117	R. G. Davis	Brutally Frank, 6, 119	Oro de Mexico, 6, 113	7	1:10.22	90,000
1999	Kashatreya, 5, 110	J. Samyn	Artax, 4, 119	The Trader's Echo, 5, 111	9	1:09.63	90,000
1998	Richter Scale, 4, 119	J. D. Bailey	Trafalger, 4, 114	Kelly Kip, 4, 122	8	1:08.83	83,160
1997	Punch Line, 7, 122	R. G. Davis	Cold Execution, 6, 112	Jamies First Punch, 4, 116	7	1:08.96	66,180
1996	Not Surprising, 6, 121	R. G. Davis	Prospect Bay, 4, 113	Forest Wildcat, 5, 114	8	1:09.17	66,720
1995	Waldoboro, 4, 112	E. Maple	Corma Ray, 5, 111	Mining Burrah, 5, 117	8	1:09.62	66,300
1994	Friendly Lover, 6, 114	R. Wilson	Boundary, 4, 117	Birdonthewire, 5, 119	9	1:09.65	67,380
1993	Lion Cavern, 4, 116	J. A. Krone	Arrowtown, 5, 115	Codys Key, 4, 111	7	1:10.33	69,120
1992	Shining Bid, 4, 112	E. Maple	Arrowtown, 4, 113	To Freedom, 4, 117	9	1:08.28	71,880
1991	Diablo, 4, 112	J. A. Krone	Sunny Blossom, 6, 120	Bravely Bold, 5, 119	7	1:08.24	69,720
1990	Mr. Nickerson, 4, 119	C. W. Antley	Sewickley, 5, 117	Dancing Spree, 5, 123	4	1:10.40	51,360
1989	Dancing Spree, 4, 113	A. T. Cordero Jr.	Dr. Carrington, 4, 109	Pok Ta Pok, 4, 118	6	1:09.40	68,160
1988	High Brite, 4, 120	A. T. Cordero Jr.	Irish Open, 4, 115	King's Swan, 8, 122	6	1:10.00	81,300
1987	Groovy, 4, 123	A. T. Cordero Jr.	King's Swan, 7, 120	Sun Master, 6, 117	4	**1:07.80**	78,780
1986	Phone Trick, 4, 127	J. Velasquez	Love That Mac, 4, 117	Cullendale, 4, 111	5	1:09.00	66,480
1985	Cannon Shell, 6, 114	D. J. Murphy	Basket Weave, 4, 114	Mt. Livermore, 4, 126	6	1:10.80	52,200
1984	Believe the Queen, 4, 114	J. Velasquez	Muskoka Wyck, 5, 112	Cannon Shell, 5, 115	5	1:09.80	52,110
1983	†Gold Beauty, 4, 121	D. Brumfield	Singh Tu, 4, 111	Fit to Fight, 4, 113	6	1:10.40	50,760
1982	Shimatoree, 3, 117	M. G. Pino	Pass the Tab, 4, 121	Will of Iron, 4, 112	8	1:08.60	49,590
1981	Joanie's Chief, 4, 109	J. Samyn	Proud Appeal, 3, 117	Guilty Conscience, 5, 113	7	1:09.00	33,480
1980	Syncopate, 5, 120	L. A. Pincay Jr.	Isella, 5, 117	Double Zeus, 5, 116	9	1:09.20	33,000
1979	Moleolus, 4, 110	J. Samyn	Jet Diplomacy, 4, 118	Northern Prospect, 3, 116	7	1:10.40	25,335

Named for Derring Howe's 1945 Fall Highweight H. winner True North (1940 g. by Only One). Grade 3 1983-'84. True North Breeders' Cup H. 2003-'05. †Denotes female.

Turf Classic Invitational Stakes — See Joe Hirsch Turf Classic Invitational Stakes

Turf Classic Stakes — See Woodford Reserve Turf Classic Stakes

Turf Sprint Stakes — see Aegon Turf Sprint Stakes

Turfway Park Fall Championship Stakes

Grade 3 in 2008. Turfway Park, three-year-olds and up, 1 mile, all weather. Held September 8, 2007, with a gross value of $100,000. First held in 1919. First graded in 1997. Stakes record 1:36.89 (2003 Crafty Shaw).

Year	Winner	Jockey	Second	Third	Strs	Time	1st Purse
2007	Istan, 5, 120	L. Melancon	Spotsgone, 4, 122	Gouldings Green, 6, 122	6	1:38.81	$61,380
2006	Gouldings Green, 5, 122	C. J. Lanerie	It's No Joke, 4, 118	Alumni Hall, 7, 118	12	1:38.15	62,000
2005	Artemus Sunrise, 4, 116	J. L. Castanon	Mr. Krisley, 7, 115	Mighty Military, 4, 117	12	1:37.31	62,000
2004	Cappuchino, 5, 115	D. A. Sarvis	Crafty Shaw, 6, 122	Added Edge, 4, 119	7	1:37.19	62,000
2003	Crafty Shaw, 5, 117	C. Perret	Cat Tracker, 5, 117	Cappuchino, 4, 119	8	**1:36.89**	62,000
2002	Crafty Shaw, 4, 117	J. Lopez	Rock Slide, 4, 117	Deferred Comp, 4, 115	7	1:52.29	62,750
2001	Generous Rosi (GB), 6, 115	L. J. Meche	Storm Day, 4, 117	Jadada, 6, 117	6	1:49.83	46,500

Year	Winner	Jockey	Second	Third	Strs	Time	1st Purse
2000	Mount Lemon, 6, 117	R. Albarado	Unloosened, 5, 114	Phil the Grip, 6, 117	7	1:51.14	$62,600
1999	Phil the Grip, 5, 112	R. Albarado	Part the Waters, 5, 111	Metatonia, 4, 110	5	1:52.15	49,600
1998	Acceptable, 4, 116	C. Perret	Magnify, 5, 114	Muchacho Fino, 4, 112	6	1:51.95	62,600
1997	Tejano Run, 5, 122	W. Martinez	Short Stay, 5, 114	Thesaurus, 3, 112	7	1:49.44	46,950
1996	Strawberry Wine, 4, 114	B. D. Peck	Kiridashi, 4, 121	Prospect for Love, 4, 114	8	1:50.15	65,000
1995	Bound by Honor, 4, 113	R. P. Romero	Lord Gordon, 5, 113	Lordly Prospect, 6, 112	6	1:51.54	48,750
1994	Meena, 6, 114	W. Martinez	Powerful Punch, 5, 122	It'sali'lknownfact, 4, 111	4	1:52.92	27,284
1993	Powerful Punch, 4, 116	C. C. Bourque	Medium Cool, 5, 114	Benburb, 4, 121	7	1:50.51	41,048
1992	Flying Continental, 6, 122	J. Velasquez	Alyten, 4, 116	Regal Affair, 6, 113	5	1:48.67	27,511
1991	Allijeba, 5, 116	J. E. Bruin	D. C. Tenacious, 4, 113	Discover, 3, 116	9	1:49.63	41,421
1990	Aly Mar, 4, 112	D. Kutz	Cefis, 5, 120	Cantrell Road, 4, 116	7	1:49.20	34,531
1989	Currentsville Lane, 4, 112	J. Neagle	Air Worthy, 4, 121	Loyal Pal, 6, 118	8	1:51.60	28,031
1988	Mr. Odie, 4, 110	S. Neff	Boyish Charm, 5, 115	Government Corner, 6, 114	11	1:52.40	28,795
1987	Lord Glacier, 4, 114	M. Solomone	Aggies Best, 5, 117	Ten Times Ten, 5, 115	12	1:43.60	28,860
1986	Big Pistol, 5, 123	L. J. Melancon	Exit Five B., 5, 119	Something Cool, 4, 117	6	1:42.80	19,565
1985	Country Hick, 4, 113	J. C. Espinoza	Turn Here, 4, 114	McShane, 6, 117	10	1:43.00	20,215
1984	Immediate Reaction, 4, 118	M. McDowell	Fairly Straight, 3, 120	Never Company, 4, 113	9	1:43.80	18,541
1983	Cad, 5, 115	D. Brumfield	His Flower, 3, 113	Noted, 4, 112	9	1:44.00	18,444
1982	Leader Jet, 4, 117	C. R. Woods Jr.	Rock Steady, 3, 113	Diverse Dude, 4, 118	10	1:44.00	13,680
1981	Exterminate, 4, 114	D. E. Foster	Kentucky Scout, 4, 119	Withholding, 4, 120	9	1:44.40	13,080
1980	Silver Shears, 3, 110	R. R. Matias	Penalty Declined, 6, 119	One Lucky Devil, 6, 124	9	1:43.20	12,975
1979	†Lotta Honey, 4, 116	J. C. Espinoza	Penalty Declined, 5, 114	One Lucky Devil, 5, 114	12	1:42.40	18,005
1978	†Likely Exchange, 4, 114	M. S. Sellers	Pirogue, 4, 113	Mr. Pitty Pat, 5, 110	8	1:45.60	16,020
1977	Certain Roman, 4, 111	M. McDowell	*The Pepe, 5, 114	Payne Street, 4, 120	9	1:44.80	12,855
1976	Brustigart, 6, 113	A. F. Herrera	Faneuil Boy, 5, 118	Visier, 4, 120	12	1:45.40	13,155
1975	Eager Wish, 6, 119	C. Bramble	*Zografos, 7, 124	†Princess Jillo, 4, 106	6	1:44.40	12,765
1974	Bootlegger's Pet, 4, 116	G. Solomon	Lester's Jester, 5, 113	Babingtons Image, 4, 111	8	1:47.60	13,878
1973	Knight Counter, 5, 123	D. Brumfield	Divorce Trial, 4, 114	On the Money, 5, 116	10	1:46.80	9,962

Traditionally held during Turfway Park's fall meet. Latonia Championship S. 1919-'33, 1964-'86. Turfway Championship S. 1987-'90. Turfway Championship H. 1991-'95, 1997. Kentucky Cup Classic Preview H. 1996, 1998-'99. Turfway Park Fall Championship H. 2000. Held at Old Latonia 1919-'33. Host track known as Latonia Race Course 1964-'86. Not held 1934-'63, 1972. 1⅛ miles 1913-'18, 1934-'63, 1988-2002. 1¾ miles 1919-'33. 1 1/16 miles 1964-'87. Dirt 1919-'33, 1964-'71, 1973-2004. Three-year-olds 1919-'33. †Denotes female.

Turnback the Alarm Handicap

Grade 3 in 2008. Aqueduct, three-year-olds and up, fillies and mares, 1⅛ miles, dirt. Held November 4, 2007, with a gross value of $105,300. First held in 1995. First graded in 1999. Stakes record 1:48.89 (1995 Incinerate).

Year	Winner	Jockey	Second	Third	Strs	Time	1st Purse
2007	Sugar Shake, 4, 119	J. Castellano	Cindy's Mom, 4, 113	Victory Pool, 5, 115	6	1:50.02	$64,380
2006	Miss Shop, 3, 114	R. I. Rojas	Dina, 4, 112	Marimba Rhythm, 4, 115	6	1:50.93	64,680
2005	Indian Vale, 3, 112	J. R. Velazquez	Taittinger Rose, 4, 116	Asti (Ire), 4, 115	5	1:49.83	64,680
2004	Personal Legend, 4, 115	J. D. Bailey	Roar Emotion, 4, 117	Fast Cookie, 4, 114	6	1:51.27	66,420
2003	Pocus Hocus, 5, 114	J. A. Santos	Nonsuch Bay, 4, 115	Miss Linda (Arg), 6, 118	6	1:50.67	64,500
2002	Svea Dal, 5, 114	R. Migliore	Mystic Lady, 4, 119	Critical Eye, 5, 115	5	1:50.42	64,680
2001	Rochelle's Terms, 4, 113	R. G. Davis	Resort, 4, 113	Strolling Belle, 5, 118	6	1:51.19	65,100
2000	Atelier, 3, 113	E. S. Prado	Tap to Music, 5, 119	Pentatonic, 4, 115	10	1:48.95	67,920
1999	Belle Cherie, 3, 112	J. R. Velazquez	Brushed Halory, 3, 114	Sweet Misty, 5, 116	8	1:50.03	66,000
1998	Snit, 4, 117	J. R. Velazquez	Manoa, 3, 112	Shoop, 7, 114	8	1:51.30	49,740
1997	Mil Kilates, 4, 116	J. Bravo	Radiant Megan, 4, 110	Shoop, 6, 114	5	1:49.40	48,330
1996	Shoop, 5, 121	J. D. Bailey	Queen Tutta, 4, 116	Madame Adolphe, 4, 113	4	1:51.35	48,420
1995	Incinerate, 5, 115	F. Leon	Lotta Dancing, 4, 115	Pretty Discreet, 3, 110	7	**1:48.89**	49,005

Named for Valley View Farm's and Dr. Richard Coburn's 1992 Coaching Club American Oaks (G1) winner Turnback the Alarm (1989 f. by Darn That Alarm).

Tuzla Handicap

Grade 3 in 2008. Santa Anita Park, four-year-olds and up, fillies and mares, 1 mile, turf. Held January 19, 2008, with a gross value of $110,300. First held in 2004. First graded in 2008. Stakes record 1:34.40 (2004 Fudge Fatale).

Year	Winner	Jockey	Second	Third	Strs	Time	1st Purse
2008	Trick's Pic, 5, 115	V. Espinoza	I Can See, 5, 115	Good Mood (Ire), 4, 115	8	1:35.09	$66,180
2007	‡Singalong (GB), 5, 116	V. Espinoza	dh-Charm the Giant (Ire), 5, 116		9	1:35.56	48,240
			dh-Dream's (Chi), 6, 118				
2006	Ticker Tape (GB), 5, 121	K. J. Desormeaux	Movie Star (Brz), 5, 118	Cyber Slew, 6, 114	6	1:34.82	47,190
2005	Good Student (Arg), 5, 116	T. Baze	Belle Ange (Fr), 4, 116	Katdogawn (GB), 5, 120	7	1:37.38	47,610
2004	Fudge Fatale, 5, 116	J. Valdivia Jr.	Polygreen (Fr), 5, 117	Fun House, 5, 117	9	**1:34.40**	46,110

Named for Stoneside Stable's 1999 Buena Vista H. (G2) winner Tuzla (Fr) (1994 f. by Panoramic [GB]). Dead heat for second 2007. ‡Conveyor's Angel finished first, DQ to seventh, 2007.

TVG Breeders' Cup Sprint

Grade 1 in 2008. Monmouth Park, three-year-olds and up, 6 furlongs, dirt. Held October 27, 2007, with a gross value of $1,832,000. First held in 1984. First graded in 1984. Stakes record 1:07.77 (2000 Kona Gold).

Year	Winner	Jockey	Second	Third	Strs	Time	1st Purse
2007	Midnight Lute, 4, 126	G. K. Gomez	Idiot Proof, 3, 123	Talent Search, 4, 126	10	1:09.18	$1,080,000

Year	Winner	Jockey	Second	Third	Strs	Time	1st Purse
2006	Thor's Echo, 4, 126	C. S. Nakatani	Friendly Island, 5, 126	Nightmare Affair, 5, 126	14	1:08.80	$1,150,200
2005	Silver Train, 3, 124	E. S. Prado	Taste of Paradise, 6, 126	Lion Tamer, 5, 126	11	1:08.86	551,200
2004	Speightstown, 6, 126	J. R. Velazquez	Kela, 6, 126	My Cousin Matt, 5, 126	13	1:08.11	551,200
2003	Cajun Beat, 3, 123	C. H. Velasquez	Bluesthestandard, 6, 126	Shake You Down, 5, 126	13	1:07.95	613,600
2002	Orientate, 4, 126	J. D. Bailey	Thunderello, 3, 123	Crafty C. T., 4, 126	13	1:08.89	592,800
2001	Squirtle Squirt, 3, 124	J. D. Bailey	†Xtra Heat, 3, 121	Caller One, 4, 126	14	1:08.41	520,000
2000	Kona Gold, 6, 126	A. O. Solis	†Honest Lady, 4, 123	Bet On Sunshine, 8, 126	14	1:07.77	520,000
1999	Artax, 4, 126	J. F. Chavez	Kona Gold, 5, 126	Big Jag, 6, 126	14	1:07.89	624,000
1998	Reraise, 3, 124	C. S. Nakatani	Grand Slam, 3, 124	Kona Gold, 4, 126	14	1:09.07	572,000
1997	Elmhurst, 7, 126	C. S. Nakatani	Hesabull, 4, 126	Bet On Sunshine, 5, 126	14	1:08.01	613,600
1996	Lit de Justice, 6, 126	C. S. Nakatani	Paying Dues, 4, 126	Honour and Glory, 3, 123	13	1:08.60	520,000
1995	†Desert Stormer, 5, 123	K. Desormeaux	Mr. Greeley, 3, 123	Lit de Justice, 5, 126	13	1:09.14	520,000
1994	Cherokee Run, 4, 126	M. E. Smith	†Soviet Problem, 4, 123	Cardmania, 8, 126	14	1:09.54	520,000
1993	Cardmania, 7, 126	E. Delahoussaye	†Meafara, 4, 123	Gilded Time, 3, 124	14	1:08.76	520,000
1992	Thirty Slews, 5, 126	E. Delahoussaye	†Meafara, 3, 123	Rubiano, 5, 126	14	1:08.21	520,000
1991	Sheikh Albadou (GB), 3, 126	P. Eddery	Pleasant Tap, 4, 126	Robyn Dancer, 4, 126	11	1:09.36	520,000
1990	†Safely Kept, 4, 123	C. Perret	Dayjur, 3, 123	Black Tie Affair (Ire), 4, 126	14	1:09.60	450,000
1989	Dancing Spree, 4, 126	A. T. Cordero Jr.	†Safely Kept, 3, 121	Dispersal, 3, 124	13	1:09.00	450,000
1988	Gulch, 4, 126	A. T. Cordero Jr.	Play the King, 5, 126	Afleet, 4, 126	13	1:10.40	450,000
1987	†Very Subtle, 3, 121	P. A. Valenzuela	Groovy, 4, 126	Exclusive Enough, 3, 124	13	1:08.80	450,000
1986	Smile, 4, 126	J. Vasquez	†Pine Tree Lane, 4, 123	Bedside Promise, 4, 126	9	1:08.40	450,000
1985	Precisionist, 4, 126	C. J. McCarron	Smile, 3, 124	Mt. Livermore, 4, 126	14	1:08.40	450,000
1984	Eillo, 4, 126	C. Perret	Commemorate, 3, 124	Fighting Fit, 5, 126	11	1:10.20	450,000

Sponsored by TVG Network, 2005-'07. Formerly sponsored by NAPA Auto Parts of Atlanta, Georgia 2002. Formerly sponsored by Penske Auto Center 2001. Held at Hollywood Park 1984, '87, '97. Held at Aqueduct 1985. Held at Santa Anita Park 1986, '93, 2003. Held at Churchill Downs 1988, '91, '94, '98, 2000, '06. Held at Gulfstream Park 1989, '92, '99. Held at Belmont Park 1990, '95, 2001, '05. Held at Woodbine 1996. Held at Arlington Park 2002. Held at Lone Star Park 2004. Equaled track record 1996, 1999. Track record 2000. †Denotes female.

United Nations Stakes

Grade 1 in 2008. Monmouth Park, three-year-olds and up, 1 3/8 miles, turf. Held July 7, 2007, with a gross value of $742,500. First held in 1953. First graded in 1973. Stakes record 2:12.78 (2003 Balto Star).

Year	Winner	Jockey	Second	Third	Strs	Time	1st Purse
2007	English Channel, 5, 118	J. R. Velazquez	†Honey Ryder, 6, 115	Better Talk Now, 8, 122	5	2:12.89	$450,000
2006	English Channel, 4, 122	J. R. Velazquez	Cacique (Ire), 5, 122	Relaxed Gesture (Ire), 5, 118	7	2:13.24	450,000
2005	Better Talk Now, 6, 118	R. A. Dominguez	Silverfoot, 5, 118	Request for Parole, 6, 118	9	2:20.57	450,000
2004	Request for Parole, 5, 118	E. S. Prado	Mr O'Brien (Ire), 5, 120	Nothing to Lose, 4, 118	11	2:13.37	450,000
2003	Balto Star, 5, 117	J. A. Velez Jr.	The Tin Man, 5, 121	Lunar Sovereign, 4, 112	7	**2:12.78**	450,000
2002	With Anticipation, 7, 119	P. Day	Denon, 4, 118	Sarafan, 5, 117	7	2:12.81	300,000
2001	‡Senure, 5, 116	R. G. Davis	With Anticipation, 6, 113	Gritty Sandie, 5, 112	8	2:13.56	300,000
2000	Down the Aisle, 7, 114	R. G. Davis	Aly's Alley, 4, 111	Honor Glide, 6, 116	7	2:13.63	210,000
1999	Yagli, 6, 124	J. D. Bailey	Supreme Sound (GB), 5, 113	Amerique, 4, 115	6	2:16.02	150,000
1997	Influent, 6, 117	J. Samyn	Geri, 5, 113	Flag Down, 7, 118	4	1:53.72	240,000
1996	Sandpit (Brz), 7, 122	C. S. Nakatani	Diplomatic Jet, 4, 117	Northern Spur (Ire), 5, 122	8	1:55.71	300,000
1995	Sandpit (Brz), 6, 122	C. S. Nakatani	Celtic Arms (Fr), 4, 118	†Alice Springs, 5, 115	9	1:57.25	300,000
1994	Lure, 5, 123	M. E. Smith	Fourstars Allstar, 6, 117	Star of Cozzene, 6, 121	5	1:52.66	300,000
1993	Star of Cozzene, 5, 120	J. A. Santos	Lure, 4, 123	Finder's Choice, 8, 113	7	1:53.22	300,000
1992	Sky Classic, 5, 123	P. Day	Chenin Blanc, 6, 115	Lotus Pool, 5, 114	9	1:52.53	300,000
1991	Exbourne, 5, 117	C. J. McCarron	Forty Niner Days, 4, 116	Goofalik, 4, 114	7	1:52.75	300,000
1990	Steinlen (GB), 7, 124	J. A. Santos	†Capades, 4, 112	Alwuhush, 5, 121	8	1:52.00	300,000
1989	Yankee Affair, 7, 121	P. Day	Salem Drive, 7, 117	Simply Majestic, 5, 119	5	1:53.20	120,000
1988	Equalize, 6, 116	J. A. Santos	Wanderkin, 5, 117	Bet Twice, 4, 124	9	1:52.60	120,000
1987	Manila, 4, 124	J. Vasquez	Racing Star, 5, 115	Air Display, 4, 110	5	1:58.80	90,000
1986	Manila, 3, 114	J. A. Santos	Uptown Swell, 4, 116	Lieutenant's Lark, 4, 121	8	1:52.60	104,040
1985	Ends Well, 4, 114	M. R. Morgan	Who's for Dinner, 6, 116	Cool, 4, 110	11	1:54.60	107,820
1984	Hero's Honor, 4, 123	J. D. Bailey	Cozzene, 4, 114	Who's for Dinner, 5, 110	11	1:54.00	106,200
1983	Acaroid, 5, 113	A. T. Cordero Jr.	†Trevita (Ire), 6, 116	Majesty's Prince, 4, 120	13	1:53.40	90,000
1982	Naskra's Breeze, 5, 117	J. Samyn	Acaroid, 4, 113	Don Roberto, 5, 116	10	1:55.60	90,000
1981	Key to Content, 4, 121	G. Martens	Ben Fab, 4, 123	Quality T. V., 4, 110	9	1:52.80	82,500
1980	Lyphard's Wish (Fr), 4, 118	A. T. Cordero Jr.	Match the Hatch, 4, 115	Scythian Gold, 5, 111	9	1:53.80	82,500
1979	Noble Dancer (GB), 7, 125	J. Vasquez	Dom Alaric (Fr), 5, 120	Overskate, 4, 128	6	1:56.60	75,000
1978	Noble Dancer (GB), 6, 127	S. Cauthen	Upper Nile, 4, 118	Dan Horn, 6, 117	5	1:56.40	81,250
1977	Bemo, 7, 116	D. Brumfield	Quick Card, 4, 124	Alias Smith, 4, 112	5	1:54.00	65,000
1976	Intrepid Hero, 4, 125	S. Hawley	Improviser, 4, 116	Break Up the Game, 5, 120	8	1:53.40	65,000
1975	Royal Glint, 5, 120	J. E. Tejeira	Stonewalk, 4, 120	R. Tom Can, 4, 116	9	1:57.00	65,000
1974	Halo, 5, 118	J. Velasquez	London Company, 4, 123	Scantling, 4, 115	10	1:56.80	65,000
1973	Tentam, 4, 123	J. Velasquez	Star Envoy, 5, 115	Return to Reality, 4, 115	12	1:54.60	75,000

Named for the United Nations, headquartered in New York City. Formerly sponsored by Caesars Palace Hotel of Atlantic City, New Jersey 1990-'97. Grade 2 1990-'93. United Nations Invitational H. 1953-'81. Caesars International H. 1990-'97. United Nations H. 1953-'72, 1975-'89, 1999-2003. Held at Atlantic City 1953-'97. Not held 1998. 1 3/16 miles 1953-'67. Dirt 1969. ‡With Anticipation finished first, DQ to second, 2001. Equaled course record 1999. Course record 2000, '03, '06, '07. †Denotes female.

Racing — Graded Stakes 483

Vagrancy Handicap

Grade 2 in 2008. Belmont Park, three-year-olds and up, fillies and mares, 6½ furlongs, dirt. Held May 25, 2008, with a gross value of $147,000. First held in 1948. First graded in 1973. Stakes record 1:14.46 (2004 Bear Fan).

Year	Winner	Jockey	Second	Third	Strs	Time	1st Purse
2008	Looky Yonder, 4, 115	G. K. Gomez	Dream Rush, 4, 120	Baroness Thatcher, 4, 117	5	1:17.63	$90,000
2007	Indian Flare, 5, 116	J. Castellano	Oprah Winney, 4, 117	Any Limit, 4, 118	6	1:16.44	90,000
2006	Dubai Escapade, 4, 120	E. S. Prado	High Button Shoes, 4, 114	Magnolia Jackson, 4, 117	6	1:15.39	90,000
2005	Sensibly Chic, 5, 116	J. R. Velazquez	Bank Audit, 4, 120	Ender's Sister, 4, 116	9	1:16.31	90,000
2004	Bear Fan, 5, 121	J. R. Velazquez	Smok'n Frolic, 5, 117	Aspen Gal, 3, 109	9	**1:14.46**	90,000
2003	Shawklit Mint, 4, 115	R. Migliore	Shine Again, 6, 121	Gold Mover, 5, 118	3	1:15.38	90,000
2002	Xtra Heat, 4, 127	H. Vega	Gold Mover, 4, 115	Shine Again, 5, 117	5	1:16.44	90,000
2001	Dat You Miz Blue, 4, 116	J. R. Velazquez	Dream Supreme, 4, 122	Katz Me If You Can, 4, 115	5	1:15.32	64,080
2000	Country Hideaway, 4, 117	J. D. Bailey	Hurricane Bertie, 5, 118	Imperfect World, 4, 115	7	1:17.05	65,640
1999	‡Gold Princess, 4, 114	J. R. Velazquez	Hurricane Bertie, 4, 114	Delta Music, 4, 113	5	1:16.57	63,840
1998	Chip, 5, 115	J. Bravo	Furlough, 4, 114	Parlay, 4, 115	6	1:15.69	48,945
1997	Inquisitive Look, 4, 111	J. F. Chavez	Flat Fleet Feet, 4, 123	Mama Dean, 4, 114	6	1:22.07	64,800
1996	Twist Afleet, 5, 122	J. A. Krone	Smooth Charmer, 4, 111	Lottsa Talc, 6, 120	8	1:20.94	66,300
1995	Sky Beauty, 5, 125	M. E. Smith	Aly's Conquest, 4, 114	Through the Door, 5, 110	4	1:21.56	47,865
1994	Sky Beauty, 4, 122	M. E. Smith	For all Seasons, 4, 114	Pamzig, 4, 107	6	1:21.67	48,855
1993	Spinning Round, 4, 112	J. F. Chavez	Reach for Clever, 6, 114	Nannerl, 6, 118	8	1:24.52	52,740
1992	Nannerl, 5, 116	J. A. Santos	Serape, 4, 115	Makin Faces, 4, 112	6	1:22.55	51,210
1991	Queena, 5, 115	M. E. Smith	Missy's Mirage, 3, 109	Gottagetitdone, 6, 111	10	1:22.07	55,080
1990	Mistaurian, 4, 113	W. H. McCauley	Feel the Beat, 5, 118	Fantastic Find, 4, 116	5	1:25.20	50,040
1989	Aptostar, 4, 118	A. T. Cordero Jr.	Toll Fee, 4, 110	Lambros, 4, 109	7	1:22.80	51,570
1988	Grecian Flight, 4, 121	C. Perret	Nasty Affair, 4, 114	Tappiano, 4, 123	7	1:20.80	66,240
1987	North Sider, 5, 121	A. T. Cordero Jr.	Storm and Sunshine, 4, 117	Funistrada, 4, 114	6	1:24.20	64,440
1986	Le Slew, 5, 113	J. A. Santos	Clocks Secret, 4, 121	Willowy Mood, 4, 114	8	1:23.80	54,630
1985	Nany, 5, 121	J. Velasquez	Sugar's Image, 4, 120	Brindy Brindy, 5, 113	6	1:23.80	52,020
1984	Grateful Friend, 4, 114	A. T. Cordero Jr.	Pleasure Cay, 4, 114	Sweet Laughter, 7, 108	7	1:24.00	52,470
1983	Broom Dance, 4, 121	G. McCarron	Syrianna, 4, 114	Sprouted Rye, 6, 115	7	1:22.80	33,480
1982	Westport Native, 4, 115	J. Velasquez	Tell a Secret, 5, 115	Raise 'n Dance, 4, 113	6	1:22.60	32,580
1981	Island Charm, 4, 110	R. Migliore	Contrary Rose, 5, 114	The Wheel Turns, 4, 114	5	1:23.60	32,520
1980	Lady Lonsdale, 5, 114	L. Saumell	Peaceful Banner, 4, 108	Worthy Poise, 6, 112	6	1:24.40	32,700
1979	Frosty Skater, 4, 119	D. MacBeth	Hagany, 5, 114	Skipat, 5, 126	10	1:23.20	33,240
1978	Dainty Dotsie, 4, 124	B. Phelps	What a Summer, 5, 127	Navajo Princess, 4, 110	6	1:21.80	32,160
1977	Shy Dawn, 6, 119	A. T. Cordero Jr.	Reasonable Win, 5, 118	Secret Lanvin, 4, 111	5	1:23.80	31,590
1976	My Juliet, 4, 127	J. Velasquez	Shy Dawn, 5, 119	Kudara, 5, 116	5	1:22.00	32,790
1975	Honorable Miss, 5, 120	J. Vasquez	Viva La Vivi, 5, 126	Coraggioso, 5, 121	8	1:22.20	34,020
1974	Coraggioso, 4, 119	D. Brumfield	Ponte Vecchio, 4, 114	‡Lady Love, 4, 118	14	1:22.40	35,940
1973	Krislin, 4, 113	M. A. Castaneda	Numbered Account, 4, 120	Fairway Flyer, 4, 115	8	1:22.60	16,845

Named for Belair Stud's 1942 champion three-year-old filly, '42 champion handicap female, and '42 Beldame H. winner Vagrancy (1939 f. by *Sir Gallahad III). Held at Aqueduct 1948–'55, 1960, 1963–'67, 1975, 1977–'86, 1997. Not held 1949–'51. 1¹⁄₁₆ miles 1948–'52. 7 furlongs 1953–'97. ‡Wanda finished third, DQ to 14th, 1974. ‡Hurricane Bertie finished first, DQ to second, 1999.

Valley View Stakes — *See* Pin Oak Valley View Stakes

Vanity Invitational Handicap

Grade 1 in 2008. Hollywood Park, three-year-olds and up, fillies and mares, 1⅛ miles, all weather. Held July 7, 2007, with a gross value of $294,000. First held in 1940. First graded in 1973. Stakes record 1:46.20 (1984 Princess Rooney).

Year	Winner	Jockey	Second	Third	Strs	Time	1st Purse
2007	Nashoba's Key, 4, 118	J. Talamo	Balance, 4, 122	Hystericalady, 4, 120	4	1:48.83	$180,000
2006	Hollywood Story, 5, 118	D. R. Flores	Healthy Addiction, 5, 119	Sharp Lisa, 4, 119	6	1:48.25	180,000
2005	Splendid Blended, 3, 115	J. D. Bailey	Island Fashion, 5, 117	Andujar, 4, 121	8	1:49.33	180,000
2004	Victory Encounter, 4, 116	A. O. Solis	Adoration, 5, 122	Star Parade (Arg), 5, 117	4	1:48.28	150,000
2003	Azeri, 5, 127	M. E. Smith	Sister Girl Blues, 4, 111	Bare Necessities, 4, 118	7	1:48.40	150,000
2002	Azeri, 4, 125	M. E. Smith	Affluent, 4, 119	dh-Collect Call, 4, 115 dh-Starrer, 4, 117	5	1:48.88	150,000
2001	Gourmet Girl, 6, 119	G. L. Stevens	Lazy Slusan, 6, 122	Setareh, 4, 111	5	1:49.21	150,000
2000	Riboletta (Brz), 5, 123	C. J. McCarron	Speaking of Time, 4, 108	Excellent Meeting, 4, 120	6	1:48.54	180,000
1999	Manistique, 4, 122	C. J. McCarron	Yolo Lady, 4, 115	Bella Chiarra, 4, 116	6	1:48.06	240,000
1998	Escena, 5, 124	J. D. Bailey	Housa Dancer (Fr), 5, 115	Different (Arg), 6, 119	7	1:48.13	210,000
1997	Twice the Vice, 6, 121	K. Desormeaux	Real Connection, 6, 114	Jewel Princess, 5, 123	5	1:46.40	240,000
1996	Jewel Princess, 4, 120	C. S. Nakatani	Serena's Song, 4, 125	Top Rung, 5, 116	6	1:47.17	150,000
1995	Private Persuasion, 4, 114	G. L. Stevens	Top Rung, 4, 118	Wandesta (GB), 4, 119	7	1:48.30	165,000
1994	Potridee (Arg), 5, 114	A. O. Solis	Exchange, 6, 118	Golden Klair (GB), 4, 119	8	1:48.08	165,000
1993	Re Toss (Arg), 6, 116	E. Delahoussaye	Paseana (Arg), 6, 126	Guiza, 6, 114	8	1:47.92	165,000
1992	Paseana (Arg), 5, 127	C. J. McCarron	Fowda, 4, 118	Re Toss (Arg), 5, 115	6	1:48.00	165,000
1991	Brought to Mind, 4, 120	P. A. Valenzuela	Fit to Scout, 4, 115	Luna Elegante (Arg), 5, 114	6	1:48.50	110,000
1990	Gorgeous, 4, 124	E. Delahoussaye	Fantastic Look, 4, 112	Kelly, 4, 110	5	1:48.20	110,000

Year	Winner	Jockey	Second	Third	Strs	Time	1st Purse
1989	Bayakoa (Arg), 5, 125	L. A. Pincay Jr.	Flying Julia, 6, 112	Goodbye Halo, 4, 122	6	1:47.20	$110,000
1988	Annoconnor, 4, 114	C. A. Black	Pen Bal Lady (GB), 4, 119	Abloom (Arg), 4, 113	7	1:49.20	110,000
1987	Infinidad (Chi), 5, 113	C. A. Black	North Sider, 5, 121	Clabber Girl, 4, 115	7	2:00.60	110,000
1986	Magnificent Lindy, 4, 116	C. J. McCarron	Dontstop Themusic, 6, 124	Outstandingly, 4, 118	5	2:02.00	137,000
1985	Dontstop Themusic, 5, 118	A. T. Cordero Jr.	Salt Spring (Arg), 6, 114	Estrapade, 5, 119	7	1:47.80	110,000
1984	Princess Rooney, 4, 120	E. Delahoussaye	Adored, 4, 120	Salt Spring (Arg), 5, 113	7	**1:46.20**	150,500
1983	A Kiss for Luck, 4, 114	C. J. McCarron	Try Something New, 4, 118	Sangue (Ire), 5, 122	11	1:49.20	110,000
1982	Sangue (Ire), 4, 120	W. Shoemaker	Track Robbery, 6, 123	Cat Girl, 4, 117	7	1:48.00	110,000
1981	Track Robbery, 5, 120	P. A. Valenzuela	Princess Karenda, 4, 118	Save Wild Life, 4, 117	7	1:47.00	110,000
1980	It's in the Air, 4, 120	L. A. Pincay Jr.	Conveniently, 4, 111	Image of Reality, 4, 119	7	1:47.00	94,600
1979	It's in the Air, 3, 113	W. Shoemaker	Country Queen, 4, 121	Innuendo, 5, 116	8	1:47.40	77,950
1978	Afifa, 4, 113	W. Shoemaker	Drama Critic, 4, 117	Dottie's Doll, 5, 117	7	1:46.40	77,050
1977	Cascapedia, 4, 129	S. Hawley	*Bastonera II, 6, 122	Swingtime, 5, 117	9	1:47.60	65,500
1976	Miss Toshiba, 4, 120	F. Toro	*Bastonera II, 5, 121	Bold Baby, 4, 115	11	1:48.00	67,200
1975	*Dulcia, 6, 118	W. Shoemaker	Susan's Girl, 6, 123	*La Zanzara, 5, 120	11	1:47.40	67,500
1974	Tallahto, 4, 126	L. A. Pincay Jr.	*La Zanzara, 4, 120	Dogtooth Violet, 4, 118	10	1:47.00	66,500
1973	Convenience, 5, 121	J. L. Rotz	Minstrel Miss, 6, 121	Susan's Girl, 4, 127	8	1:47.80	64,500

Vanity H. 1945-'80, 1997, 1999-2004. Held at Santa Anita Park 1949. Not held 1942-'43. 1 mile 1940. 1¹/₁₆ miles 1941-'53. 1¹/₄ miles 1986-'87. Dirt 1940-2006. Dead heat for third 2002.

Vernon O. Underwood Stakes

Grade 3 in 2008. Hollywood Park, three-year-olds and up, 6 furlongs, all weather. Held December 2, 2007, with a gross value of $105,800. First held in 1981. First graded in 1984. Stakes record 1:07.79 (2006 Sailors Sunset).

Year	Winner	Jockey	Second	Third	Strs	Time	1st Purse
2007	Bushwacker, 5, 118	J. Talamo	In Summation, 4, 124	Greg's Gold, 6, 126	5	1:08.47	$65,800
2006	Sailors Sunset, 3, 118	J. K. Court	Siren Lure, 5, 126	Declan's Moon, 4, 122	5	**1:07.79**	60,000
2005	Bordonaro, 4, 120	P. A. Valenzuela	Turnbolt, 4, 120	Captain Squire, 6, 124	4	1:08.11	60,000
2004	Taste of Paradise, 5, 122	J. Valdivia Jr.	Watchem Smokey, 4, 116	My Master (Arg), 5, 116	7	1:08.04	60,000
2003	Watchem Smokey, 3, 112	J. A. Krone	Our New Recruit, 4, 114	Hasty Kris, 6, 116	6	1:08.93	60,000
2002	Debonair Joe, 3, 112	J. A. Krone	F J's Pace, 7, 116	American System, 3, 116	9	1:09.17	60,000
2001	Men's Exclusive, 8, 120	L. A. Pincay Jr.	Tavasco, 4, 114	Caller One, 4, 124	7	1:09.04	60,000
2000	Men's Exclusive, 7, 116	L. A. Pincay Jr.	Love All the Way, 5, 117	Lexicon, 5, 122	7	1:09.02	60,000
1999	Five Star Day, 3, 120	A. O. Solis	Your Halo, 4, 122	Son of a Pistol, 7, 122	5	1:09.91	60,000
1998	†Love That Jazz, 4, 117	K. Desormeaux	Peyrano (Arg), 6, 116	Swiss Yodeler, 4, 120	8	1:08.79	60,000
1997	Tower Full, 5, 118	C. S. Nakatani	Trafalger, 3, 118	Swiss Yodeler, 3, 114	4	1:08.17	60,000
1996	Paying Dues, 4, 124	P. Day	Men's Exclusive, 3, 114	Kern Ridge, 5, 114	7	1:08.24	64,860
1995	Powis Castle, 4, 114	G. L. Stevens	Lucky Forever, 6, 122	Plenty Zloty, 5, 116	8	1:08.40	62,300
1994	Wekiva Springs, 3, 118	K. Desormeaux	Cardmania, 8, 120	Gundaghia, 7, 120	9	1:08.37	63,750
1993	†Meafara, 4, 119	G. L. Stevens	†Arches of Gold, 4, 121	Davy Be Good, 5, 116	6	1:10.01	60,900
1992	Gundaghia, 5, 116	G. L. Stevens	Gray Slewpy, 4, 124	Cardmania, 6, 124	5	1:09.33	61,300
1991	Individualist, 4, 114	K. Desormeaux	Thirty Slews, 4, 117	Cardmania, 5, 124	8	1:08.86	64,500
1990	Frost Free, 5, 120	C. J. McCarron	Timebank, 3, 112	Sam Who, 5, 114	9	1:08.20	65,300
1989	Olympic Prospect, 5, 120	A. O. Solis	Sam Who, 4, 122	Order, 4, 122	4	1:08.80	60,200
1988	Gallant Sailor, 5, 116	F. Olivares	Reconnoitering, 4, 116	†Very Subtle, 4, 117	7	1:09.60	63,400
1987	Hilco Scamper, 4, 114	C. A. Black	Reconnoitering, 3, 112	Zabaleta, 4, 122	6	1:09.60	62,800
1986	Bedside Promise, 4, 122	G. L. Stevens	Bolder Than Bold, 4, 114	†Pine Tree Lane, 4, 117	10	1:08.80	127,200
	Nasib (Ire), 4, 116	E. Delahoussaye	Will Dancer (Fr), 4, 116	Barbery, 5, 115	8	1:40.40	66,900
1985	Pancho Villa, 3, 122	L. A. Pincay Jr.	Charging Falls, 4, 122	Temerity Prince, 5, 122	6	1:08.80	121,900
1984	Fifty Six Ina Row, 3, 112	S. Hawley	Debonair Junior, 3, 120	Charging Falls, 3, 112	11	1:09.40	91,975
	†Lovlier Linda, 4, 121	W. Shoemaker	Sonrie Jorge, 4, 116	Fali Time, 3, 122	9	1:10.00	89,475
1983	Fighting Fit, 4, 120	E. Delahoussaye	Expressman, 3, 112	†Matching, 5, 119	10	1:09.60	101,950
1982	Mad Key, 5, 116	E. Delahoussaye	Shanekite, 4, 120	Dave's Friend, 7, 114	9	1:08.20	70,600
	Unpredictable, 3, 120	K. D. Black	Remember John, 3, 120	Chinook Pass, 3, 112	8	1:08.60	69,100
1981	Shanekite, 3, 114	S. Hawley	Syncopate, 6, 122	Big Presentation, 5, 114	8	1:08.20	50,500
	Smokite, 5, 116	D. C. Hall	I'm Smokin, 5, 120	Stand Pat, 6, 114	8	1:08.60	50,500

Named for Vernon O. Underwood, chief executive officer and chairman of the board of Hollywood Park (1972-'85). National Sprint Championship S. 1981-'89. Vernon O. Underwood Breeders' Cup S. 1993-'95. Dirt 1981-2005. Two divisions 1981-'82, 1984, 1986. †Denotes female.

Victory Ride Stakes

Grade 3 in 2008. Saratoga Race Course, three-year-olds, fillies, 6 furlongs, dirt. Held August 25, 2007, with a gross value of $114,700. First held in 2003. First graded in 2006. Stakes record 1:09.62 (2003 Country Romance).

Year	Winner	Jockey	Second	Third	Strs	Time	1st Purse
2007	La Traviata, 3, 120	J. R. Leparoux	Half Time Crown, 3, 116	Appealing Zophie, 3, 123	10	1:09.78	$68,820
2006	Wildcat Bettie B, 3, 123	M. G. Pino	G City Gal, 3, 116	Khalila, 3, 116	8	1:10.81	66,420
2005	Nothing But Fun, 3, 116	R. Migliore	Maddalena, 3, 116	Reunited, 3, 118	6	1:09.86	48,900
2004	Smokey Glacken, 3, 120	J. Bravo	Grand Prayer, 3, 116	Feline Story, 3, 120	7	1:09.64	46,080
2003	Country Romance, 3, 116	J. F. Chavez	She's Zealous, 3, 114	Ebony Breeze, 3, 122	9	**1:09.62**	45,720

Named for G. Watts Humphrey Jr.'s 2001 Test S. (G1) winner Victory Ride (1998 f. by Seeking the Gold).

Vinery Madison Stakes

Grade 2 in 2008. Keeneland Race Course, four-year-olds and up, fillies and mares, 7 furlongs, all weather. Held April 9, 2008, with a gross value of $200,000. First held in 2002. First graded in 2005. Stakes record 1:22.06 (2008 Ventura).

Year	Winner	Jockey	Second	Third	Strs	Time	1st Purse
2008	**Ventura**, 4, 117	G. K. Gomez	Street Sounds, 4, 117	Dawn After Dawn, 4, 123	11	**1:22.06**	$124,000
2007	**Mary Delaney**, 4, 117	E. S. Prado	Ginger Punch, 4, 117	Leah's Secret, 4, 123	10	1:22.24	124,000
2006	**Dubai Escapade**, 4, 117	E. S. Prado	Josh's Madelyn, 5, 117	Ever Elusive, 4, 117	9	1:22.34	124,000
2005	**Madcap Escapade**, 4, 123	J. D. Bailey	My Trusty Cat, 5, 117	Molto Vita, 5, 119	7	1:23.33	124,000
2004	**Ema Bovary (Chi)**, 5, 120	R. M. Gonzalez	Harmony Lodge, 6, 123	Yell, 4, 116	6	1:23.41	108,500
2003	**A New Twist**, 4, 116	P. Day	Flaxen Flyer, 4, 116	Forest Secrets, 4, 116	4	1:24.32	84,863
2002	**Victory Ride**, 4, 116	E. S. Prado	Celtic Melody, 4, 116	Away, 5, 116	7	1:23.70	69,006

Named for Madison County, Kentucky. Sponsored by Vinery of Lexington 2004-'07. Grade 3 2005. Madison S. 2002-'03. About 7 furlongs 2002-'06. Dirt 2002-'06.

Violet Stakes

Grade 3 in 2008. Meadowlands, three-year-olds and up, fillies and mares, 1 1/16 miles, turf. Held September 28, 2007, with a gross value of $150,000. First held in 1977. First graded in 1983. Stakes record 1:39.60 (1989 Gather The Clan [Ire]).

Year	Winner	Jockey	Second	Third	Strs	Time	1st Purse
2007	**Humoristic**, 6, 117	R. Maragh	‡Roshani, 4, 121	Pommes Frites, 5, 119	5	1:41.23	$90,000
2006	**No Sleep**, 4, 121	M. J. Luzzi	Prop Me Up, 4, 117	Phyllis Sassy Girl, 4, 119	5	1:42.48	90,000
2005	**Humoristic**, 4, 117	H. Vega	Delta Princess, 6, 123	Brunilda (Arg), 5, 119	11	1:42.23	90,000
2004	**Changing World**, 4, 113	P. Fragoso	High Court (Brz), 4, 117	Ocean Drive, 4, 121	7	1:41.53	120,000
2003	**Dancal (Ire)**, 5, 116	J. Castellano	Madeira Mist (Ire), 4, 116	Something Ventured, 4, 116	8	1:43.69	90,000
2002	**Babae (Chi)**, 6, 119	J. F. Chavez	Platinum Tiara, 4, 115	Stylish, 4, 119	10	1:41.17	90,000
2001	**Clearly a Queen**, 4, 115	J. F. Chavez	Queue, 4, 115	Paga (Arg), 4, 117	12	1:43.56	90,000
2000	**Follow the Money**, 4, 116	C. J. McCarron	Melody Queen (GB), 4, 116	Fickle Friends, 4, 114	12	1:42.65	90,000
1999	**Tookin Down**, 4, 113	E. S. Prado	Proud Run, 5, 115	Darling Alice, 4, 113	7	1:42.39	90,000
1998	**Heaven's Command (GB)**, 4, 115	R. Migliore	Maxzene, 5, 123	Oh Nellie, 4, 116	7	1:40.71	60,000
1997	**Sangria**, 4, 114	R. Wilson	Fasta, 4, 11	Shemozzle (Ire), 4, 117	8	1:42.02	60,000
1996	**Plenty of Sugar**, 5, 117	R. E. Colton	Brushing Gloom, 4, 121	Hello Mom, 4, 115	6	1:48.62	60,000
1995	**Symphony Lady**, 5, 116	J. Bravo	Kira's Dancer, 6, 115	Irish Linnet, 7, 122	8	1:45.48	60,000
1994	**It's Personal**, 4, 111	J. R. Velazquez	Carezza, 5, 115	Artful Pleasure, 4, 109	11	1:42.61	45,000
1993	**Mz. Zill Bear**, 4, 113	E. S. Prado	Vivano, 4, 115	Topsa, 6, 113	4	1:44.55	45,000
1992	**Highland Crystal**, 4, 116	E. S. Prado	Irish Actress, 5, 116	Navarra, 4, 111	8	1:41.26	45,000
1991	**Southern Tradition**, 4, 116	J. A. Santos	Songlines, 5, 115	Memories of Pam, 4, 114	7	1:43.68	45,000
1990	**Miss Josh**, 4, 116	M. G. Pino	Summer Secretary, 5, 117	Leave It Be, 5, 118	13	1:40.00	54,750
1989	**Gather The Clan (Ire)**, 4, 117	C. Perret	Sweet Blow Pop, 5, 119	Summer Secretary, 4, 117	10	**1:39.60**	55,260
1988	**Just Class (Ire)**, 4, 117	C. W. Antley	Shadowfay, 5, 109	Flying Katuna, 4, 115	8	1:40.20	53,400
	Graceful Darby, 4, 115	R. P. Romero	Mystical Lass, 4, 112	Kim Kimmie, 5, 111	6	1:41.00	42,900
1987	**Videogenic**, 5, 118	J. Cruguet	Spruce Fir, 4, 119	Cadabra Abra, 4, 120	7	1:42.00	45,180
	Dismasted, 5, 118	J. Samyn	Small Virtue, 4, 118	Country Recital, 4, 113	6	1:41.60	44,790
1986	**Lake Country**, 5, 118	V. A. Bracciale Jr.	Duckweed, 4, 111	Anka Germania (Ire), 4, 114	8	1:41.20	68,310
1985	**Possible Mate**, 4, 119	J. Samyn	Eastern Dawn, 4, 112	Carlypha (Ire), 4, 116	9	1:42.20	52,665
	Vers La Caisse, 4, 116	R. Migliore	Cato Double, 5, 117	Forest Maiden, 5, 117	10	1:43.00	63,240
1984	**Rash But Royal**, 4, 114	J. L. Kaenel	High Schemes, 4, 115	Candlelight Affair, 3, 110	8	1:42.20	49,020
	Aspen Rose, 4, 114	J. Velasquez	It's Fine, 4, 112	If Winter Comes, 6, 113	4	1:42.00	49,020
1983	**Twosome**, 4, 113	J. D. Bailey	Princess Roberta, 5, 115	Svarga, 4, 112	8	1:41.20	26,535
	Geraldine's Store, 4, 117	J. Samyn	Maidenhead, 4, 110	Mistretta (Fr), 4, 116	7	1:40.60	26,355
1982	**Pat's Joy**, 4, 114	J. D. Bailey	Prismatical, 4, 115	Kuja Happa, 4, 113	9	1:42.20	26,670
	Dearly Too, 3, 114	J. Samyn	Tableaux, 4, 112	Dance Troupe, 5, 114	9	1:42.20	26,670
1981	**Honey Fox**, 4, 120	J. Samyn	Adlibber, 4, 117	Hemlock, 4, 116	11	1:41.40	33,690
1980	**Producer**, 4, 119	J. Fell	Champagne Burning, 3, 116	Cannon Boy, 3, 113	8	1:41.60	26,325
	The Very One, 5, 117	J. Velasquez	Hey Babe, 4, 115	Poppycock, 4, 113	7	1:42.40	26,145
1979	**Terpsichorist**, 4, 122	M. Venezia	Spark of Life, 4, 111	Sisterhood, 4, 117	11	1:43.20	36,010
1978	**Navajo Princess**, 4, 115	C. Perret	Pressing Date, 4, 114	Fun Forever, 5, 118	6	1:44.00	35,360
1977	**Lady Singer (Ire)**, 4, 113	A. T. Cordero Jr.	Sans Arc, 3, 111	Jolly Song, 5, 112	6	1:48.40	35,035

Named for New Jersey's state flower, the common violet. Formerly sponsored by the Sheraton Meadowlands in East Rutherford, New Jersey 1995. Not graded 2006. Sheraton Meadowlands Violet H. 1995. Violet H. 1977-'94, 1996-2005. Dirt 1977, '93, '99, 2006. Originally scheduled on turf 2006. Two divisions 1980, 1982-'85, 1987-'88. ‡Pommes Frites finished second, DQ to third, 2007.

Virginia Derby

Grade 2 in 2008. Colonial Downs, three-year-olds, 1 1/4 miles, turf. Held July 21, 2007, with a gross value of $1,000,000. First held in 1998. First graded in 2004. Stakes record 1:59.62 (2007 Red Giant).

Year	Winner	Jockey	Second	Third	Strs	Time	1st Purse
2007	**Red Giant**, 3, 116	H. Karamanos	Strike a Deal, 3, 116	Soldier's Dancer, 3, 118	10	**1:59.62**	$600,000
2006	**Go Between**, 3, 118	G. K. Gomez	Seaside Retreat, 3, 118	Spider Power (Ire), 3, 116	10	1:59.74	600,000
2005	**English Channel**, 3, 120	J. R. Velazquez	Chattahoochee War, 3, 120	Rebel Rebel (Ire), 3, 116	9	2:02.57	450,000
2004	**Kitten's Joy**, 3, 117	E. S. Prado	Artie Schiller, 3, 117	Prince Arch, 3, 119	8	2:01.22	300,000
2003	**Silver Tree**, 3, 115	E. S. Prado	Kicken Kris, 3, 115	King's Drama (Ire), 3, 115	8	2:01.11	300,000
2002	**Orchard Park**, 3, 119	E. S. Prado	Flying Dash (Ger), 3, 119	Touring England, 3, 115	6	2:03.10	300,000

Year	Winner	Jockey	Second	Third	Strs	Time	1st Purse
2001	**Potaro (Ire)**, 3, 115	B. E. Bartram	Bay Eagle, 3, 115	Confucius Say, 3, 115	9	2:02.17	$120,000
2000	**Lightning Paces**, 3, 115	G. W. Hutton	Sunspot, 3, 115	Blaze and Blues, 3, 115	10	2:02.18	120,000
1999	**Phi Beta Doc**, 3, 117	R. A. Dominguez	Passinetti, 3, 115	North East Bound, 3, 119	13	1:59.97	120,000
1998	**Crowd Pleaser**, 3, 115	J. Samyn	Distant Mirage (Ire), 3, 115	Errant Escort, 3, 115	10	2:00.28	150,000

Colonial Downs is located in New Kent, Virginia. Grade 3 2004-'05. Course record 2006, '07.

Virginia Oaks

Grade 3 in 2008. Colonial Downs, three-year-olds, fillies, 1 1/8 miles, turf. Held July 21, 2007, with a gross value of $210,000. First held in 2004. First graded in 2008. Stakes record 1:47.11 (2006 Aunt Henny).

Year	Winner	Jockey	Second	Third	Strs	Time	1st Purse
2007	**Dreaming of Anna**, 3, 122	E. T. Baird	New Edition, 3, 118	Christmas Kid, 3, 122	12	1:47.38	$120,000
2006	**Aunt Henny**, 3, 120	R. Bejarano	May Night, 3, 118	Art Show, 3, 118	10	**1:47.11**	120,000
2005	**My Typhoon (Ire)**, 3, 118	J. D. Bailey	Masseuse, 3, 116	Rich in Spirit, 3, 122	8	1:49.63	120,000
2004	**Art Fan**, 3, 115	R. Fogelsonger	Galloping Gal, 3, 119	Vous, 3, 119	6	1:50.41	120,000

Colonial Downs is located in Virginia.

Vosburgh Stakes

Grade 1 in 2008. Belmont Park, three-year-olds and up, 6 furlongs, dirt. Held September 30, 2007, with a gross value of $416,000. First held in 1940. First graded in 1973. Stakes record 1:08.13 (2006 Henny Hughes).

Year	Winner	Jockey	Second	Third	Strs	Time	1st Purse
2007	**Fabulous Strike**, 4, 124	R. A. Dominguez	Talent Search, 4, 124	Discreet Cat, 4, 124	8	1:09.22	$240,000
2006	**Henny Hughes**, 3, 122	J. R. Velazquez	War Front, 4, 124	Attila's Storm, 4, 124	5	**1:08.13**	240,000
2005	**Taste of Paradise**, 6, 124	G. K. Gomez	Tiger Heart, 4, 124	Lion Tamer, 5, 124	10	1:08.82	300,000
2004	**Pico Central (Brz)**, 5, 124	V. Espinoza	Voodoo, 6, 124	Speightstown, 6, 124	5	1:09.74	300,000
2003	**Ghostzapper**, 3, 123	J. Castellano	Aggadan, 4, 126	Posse, 3, 123	10	1:14.72	300,000
2002	**Bonapaw**, 6, 126	G. Melancon	Aldebaran, 4, 126	Voodoo, 4, 126	6	1:22.34	180,000
2001	**Left Bank**, 4, 126	J. R. Velazquez	Squirtle Squirt, 3, 123	Big E E, 4, 126	6	1:20.73	180,000
2000	**Trippi**, 3, 123	J. D. Bailey	More Than Ready, 3, 123	One Way Love, 5, 126	10	1:21.66	180,000
1999	**Artax**, 4, 126	J. F. Chavez	Stormin Fever, 5, 126	Mountain Top, 4, 126	8	1:21.65	150,000
1998	**Affirmed Success**, 4, 126	J. F. Chavez	Stormin Fever, 4, 126	Tale of the Cat, 4, 126	7	1:21.99	150,000
1997	**Victor Cooley**, 4, 126	J. F. Chavez	Score a Birdie, 6, 126	Tale of the Cat, 3, 122	12	1:22.05	150,000
1996	**Langfuhr**, 4, 126	J. F. Chavez	Honour and Glory, 3, 122	Lite the Fuse, 5, 126	8	1:21.25	120,000
1995	**Not Surprising**, 5, 126	R. G. Davis	You and I, 4, 126	Our Emblem, 4, 126	13	1:22.48	120,000
1994	**Harlan**, 5, 126	J. D. Bailey	American Chance, 5, 126	Cherokee Run, 4, 126	10	1:21.82	120,000
1993	**Birdonthewire**, 4, 126	M. E. Smith	Take Me Out, 5, 126	Lion Cavern, 4, 126	6	1:22.28	120,000
1992	**Rubiano**, 5, 126	J. A. Krone	Sheikh Albadou (GB), 4, 126	Salt Lake, 3, 123	8	1:22.80	120,000
1991	**Housebuster**, 4, 126	C. Perret	Senator to Be, 4, 126	Sunshine Jimmy, 4, 126	6	1:21.85	120,000
1990	**Sewickley**, 5, 126	A. T. Cordero Jr.	Sunshine Jimmy, 3, 122	Glitterman, 5, 126	9	1:21.00	142,080
1989	**Sewickley**, 4, 126	R. P. Romero	Once Wild, 4, 126	Mr. Nickerson, 3, 126	5	1:23.00	135,120
1988	**Mining**, 4, 126	R. P. Romero	Gulch, 4, 126	High Brite, 4, 126	4	1:22.40	133,920
1987	**Groovy**, 4, 126	A. T. Cordero Jr.	Moment of Hope, 4, 126	Sun Master, 6, 126	7	1:22.60	139,680
1986	**King's Swan**, 6, 126	J. A. Santos	Love That Mac, 4, 126	Cutlass Reality, 4, 126	8	1:21.80	141,840
1985	**Another Reef**, 3, 124	N. Santagata	Pancho Villa, 3, 124	Whoop Up, 5, 126	6	1:21.80	102,420
1984	**Track Barron**, 3, 123	A. T. Cordero Jr.	Timeless Native, 4, 126	Raja's Shark, 3, 123	9	1:22.00	109,800
1983	**A Phenomenon**, 3, 123	A. T. Cordero Jr.	Fit to Fight, 4, 126	Deputy Minister, 4, 126	8	1:21.00	69,000
1982	**Engine One**, 4, 126	R. Hernandez	‡‡Gold Beauty, 3, 120	Maudlin, 4, 126	6	1:23.80	65,760
1981	**Guilty Conscience**, 5, 126	C. B. Asmussen	Rise Jim, 5, 126	Well Decorated, 4, 123	7	1:21.00	67,920
1980	**Plugged Nickle**, 3, 123	C. B. Asmussen	Jaklin Klugman, 3, 123	Dave's Friend, 5, 126	9	1:21.40	67,440
1979	**General Assembly**, 3, 123	J. Vasquez	Dr. Patches, 5, 126	Syncopate, 4, 126	6	1:21.00	48,195
1978	**Dr. Patches**, 4, 117	A. T. Cordero Jr.	†What a Summer, 5, 124	Sorry Lookin, 3, 109	8	1:21.00	48,960
1977	**Affiliate**, 3, 114	C. Perret	Broadway Forli, 3, 118	Great Above, 5, 112	9	1:21.00	49,905
1976	**†My Juliet**, 4, 120	A. S. Black	‡It's Freezing, 4, 113	Bold Forbes, 3, 126	6	1:21.80	31,980
1975	**No Bias**, 5, 116	A. Santiago	Step Nicely, 5, 126	Lonetree, 5, 117	11	1:22.80	34,590
1974	**Forego**, 4, 131	H. Gustines	Stop the Music, 4, 118	Prince Dantan, 4, 119	12	1:21.60	35,550
1973	**Aljamin**, 3, 118	A. T. Cordero Jr.	Highbinder, 5, 115	Timeless Moment, 3, 112	8	1:21.20	33,660

Named for Walter S. Vosburgh (1855-1938), official handicapper for the Jockey Club and various racing associations. Grade 2 1973-'79. Vosburgh H. 1940-'78. Held at Aqueduct 1959, 1961-'74, 1976-'77, 1979-'83, 1985-'86. 7 furlongs 1940-2002. Two-year-olds and up 1940-'57. ‡Bold Forbes finished second, DQ to third, 1976. ‡Duke Mitchell finished second, DQ to fourth, 1982. †Denotes female.

Washington Park Handicap

Grade 3 in 2008. Arlington Park, three-year-olds and up, 1 3/16 miles, all weather. Held July 28, 2007, with a gross value of $300,000. First held in 1926. First graded in 1973. Stakes record 1:53.53 (2006 Suave).

Year	Winner	Jockey	Second	Third	Strs	Time	1st Purse
2007	**Lewis Michael**, 4, 118	E. T. Baird	Mustanfar, 6, 116	A. P. Arrow, 5, 117	7	1:55.17	$176,400
2006	**Suave**, 5, 118	C. H. Borel	Perfect Drift, 7, 119	Second of June, 5, 116	7	**1:53.53**	180,000
2005	**Perfect Drift**, 6, 120	M. Guidry	Mambo Train, 4, 115	Home of Stars, 5, 114	7	1:54.27	180,000
2004	**Eye of the Tiger**, 4, 116	E. Razo Jr.	Olmodavor, 5, 121	Congrats, 4, 116	5	1:56.87	210,000
2003	**Perfect Drift**, 4, 120	P. Day	Aeneas, 4, 115	Flatter, 4, 115	5	1:55.49	240,000
2002	**Tenpins**, 4, 116	R. Albarado	Generous Rosi (GB), 7, 115	Bonus Pack, 4, 115	5	1:55.07	240,000
2001	**Guided Tour**, 5, 116	L. J. Melancon	A Fleets Dancer, 6, 115	Duckhorn, 4, 114	5	2:00.76	240,000

Year	Winner	Jockey	Second	Third	Strs	Time	1st Purse
2000	Blazing Sword, 6, 113	J. A. Rivera II	Mula Gula, 4, 114	Nite Dreamer, 5, 116	8	1:50.59	$150,000
1997	Beboppin Baby, 4, 112	G. K. Gomez	City by Night, 4, 116	Stephanotis, 4, 118	5	1:49.00	90,000
1996	Polar Expedition, 5, 115	M. Guidry	Knockadoon, 4, 115	Tejano Run, 4, 117	8	1:49.97	120,000
1994	Brother Brown, 4, 117	P. Day	Eequalsmcsquared, 5, 113	Antrim Rd., 4, 113	11	1:49.77	120,000
1993	Powerful Punch, 4, 114	C. C. Bourque	Memo (Chi), 6, 115	Northern Trend, 5, 113	13	1:50.19	120,000
1992	Irish Swap, 5, 118	B. E. Poyadou	Clever Trevor, 6, 119	Barkerville, 4, 113	7	1:47.83	90,000
1991	Black Tie Affair (Ire), 5, 120	S. J. Sellers	Summer Squall, 4, 119	Secret Hello, 4, 114	4	1:49.45	150,000
1990	Lay Down, 6, 115	W. H. McCauley	Sir Wesley, 6, 112	Mercedes Won, 4, 112	6	1:48.40	64,680
1989	Blushing John, 4, 124	P. Day	Grantley, 5, 112	Paramount Jet, 4, 113	5	1:50.80	48,030
1987	Taylor's Special, 6, 118	J. Lively	Blue Buckaroo, 4, 120	Fuzzy, 5, 114	6	1:51.60	61,965
1985	Par Flite, 4, 112	E. Fires	Big Pistol, 4, 122	Timeless Native, 5, 122	6	1:47.60	78,300
1984	Thumbsucker, 5, 115	S. Maple	Timeless Native, 4, 122	Le Cou Cou, 4, 122	10	1:48.60	80,940
1983	Harham's Sizzler, 4, 112	J. L. Diaz	Listcapade, 4, 122	Stage Reviewer, 4, 112	9	1:49.80	67,620
1982	Summer Advocate, 5, 115	P. Day	Mythical Ruler, 4, 112	Law Me, 4, 112	6	1:49.80	64,920
1981	Rossi Gold, 5, 119	P. Day	John's Monster, 4, 112	Lord Gallant, 4, 114	7	1:48.60	81,870
1980	Spectacular Bid, 4, 130	W. Shoemaker	Hold Your Tricks, 5, 119	Architect, 4, 119	6	1:46.20	155,880
1979	That's a Nice, 5, 117	I. J. Jimenez	†Calderina (Ity), 4, 113	Me Good Man, 5, 112	10	1:50.00	52,320
1978	That's a Nice, 4, 116	D. Richard	Court Open, 4, 115	Improviser, 6, 117	9	1:50.60	53,160
1977	Majestic Light, 4, 120	M. Venezia	Fifth Marine, 4, 122	Improviser, 5, 122	10	1:48.00	54,180
1976	Double Edge Sword, 6, 116	V. A. Bracciale Jr.	*Zografos, 8, 113	Proponent, 4, 109	5	1:48.20	70,400
1975	Hasty Flyer, 4, 115	H. Arroyo	Group Plan, 5, 116	Yaki King, 4, 113	6	1:48.60	38,100
1974	Super Sail, 6, 118	W. Gavidia	Smooth Dancer, 4, 112	Jesta Dream Away, 4, 111	7	2:03.00	38,300
1973	Burning On, 5, 114	D. Richard	New Hope, 4, 113	Vegas Vic, 5, 109	7	2:02.20	32,800

Named for old Washington Park racetrack near Chicago. Grade 2 1982-2007. Washington H. 1964. Held at Washington Park 1926-'57. Not held 1928, '37, '86, '88, '95, 1998-'99. 1 1/4 miles 1926, 1935-'36, 1940-'50, 1973-'74, 2001. 6 furlongs 1927-'34, '38. 1 mile 1939, 1951-'58, 1960-'62, 1965-'72. 1 1/8 miles 1959, 1963-'64, 1975-2000. Dirt 1926-'76, 1980-2006. Turf 1977-'79. Track record 2005, '06. †Denotes female.

Westchester Handicap

Grade 3 in 2008. Belmont Park, three-year-olds and up, 1 mile, dirt. Held April 30, 2008, with a gross value of $109,100. First held in 1918. First graded in 1973. Stakes record 1:32.24 (2003 Najran [track record and equaled world record]).

Year	Winner	Jockey	Second	Third	Strs	Time	1st Purse
2008	Divine Park, 4, 115	A. Garcia	Grasshopper, 4, 119	Sightseeing, 4, 115	6	1:32.74	$65,460
2007	Utopia (Jpn), 7, 117	M. J. Luzzi	‡Sun King, 5, 119	Political Force, 4, 117	5	1:33.23	64,620
2006	Sir Greeley, 4, 117	E. Coa	Love of Money, 5, 117	Happy Hunting, 5, 116	6	1:33.69	65,280
2005	Gygistar, 6, 118	J. Castellano	Swingforthefences, 4, 115	Value Plus, 4, 117	7	1:33.50	65,700
2004	Gygistar, 5, 115	J. Bravo	Saarland, 5, 114	Black Silk (GB), 8, 113	7	1:35.89	65,700
2003	Najran, 4, 113	E. S. Prado	Saarland, 4, 114	Justification, 6, 113	7	**1:32.24**	65,820
2002	Free of Love, 4, 114	J. D. Bailey	Dayton Flyer, 4, 112	Country Be Gold, 5, 114	9	1:35.56	67,500
2001	Cat's At Home, 4, 114	F. Leon	Little Hans, 4, 113	Milwaukee Brew, 4, 117	6	1:33.60	64,920
2000	Yankee Victor, 4, 115	H. Castillo Jr.	Golden Missile, 5, 116	Watchman's Warning, 5, 113	7	1:34.37	66,000
1999	Mr. Sinatra, 5, 115	C. C. Lopez	Laredo, 6, 114	Brushing Up, 6, 113	4	1:35.04	64,202
1998	Wagon Limit, 4, 114	J. Samyn	Draw, 5, 113	Lucayan Prince, 5, 116	8	1:34.06	66,420
1997	Pacific Fleet, 5, 114	F. T. Alvarado	Circle of Light, 4, 110	Stalwart Member, 4, 114	7	1:33.80	65,940
1996	Valid Wager, 4, 115	J. M. Pezua	Pat n Jac, 4, 111	More to Tell, 5, 118	7	1:34.74	66,240
1995	Mr. Shawklit, 4, 112	M. J. Luzzi	Devil His Due, 6, 124	Our Emblem, 4, 112	6	1:34.66	65,760
1994	Virginia Rapids, 4, 116	J. Samyn	Colonial Affair, 4, 121	Cherokee Run, 4, 119	7	1:34.52	65,640
1993	Bill Of Rights, 4, 110	J. Samyn	Fly So Free, 5, 118	Loach, 5, 113	10	1:34.69	72,720
1992	Rubiano, 5, 117	J. A. Santos	Out of Place, 5, 115	Wild Away, 5, 111	6	1:34.83	68,880
1991	Rubiano, 4, 111	J. D. Bailey	Senor Speedy, 4, 113	Killer Diller, 4, 115	9	1:34.94	71,520
1990	Once Wild, 5, 121	A. T. Cordero Jr.	dh-Its Acedemic, 6, 116 dh-King's Swan, 10, 113		5	1:35.00	67,800
1989	Lord of the Night, 6, 115	J. Velasquez	Dancing Spree, 4, 112	Congeleur, 4, 112	8	1:35.60	71,040
1988	Faster Than Sound, 4, 113	J. A. Krone	Ron Stevens, 4, 111	King's Swan, 8, 133	9	1:34.40	108,000
1987	King's Swan, 7, 122	J. A. Santos	Cutlass Reality, 5, 114	Landing Plot, 4, 115	6	1:36.20	69,120
1986	Garthorn, 6, 120	R. Q. Meza	Ends Well, 5, 115	Grand Rivulet, 5, 110	11	1:33.80	75,240
1985	Verbarctic, 5, 114	G. McCarron	Moro, 6, 122	Fighting Fit, 6, 124	7	1:36.60	53,460
1984	Jacque's Tip, 4, 114	A. T. Cordero Jr.	Minstrel Glory, 4, 107	Havagreatdate, 6, 111	8	1:41.80	55,440
1983	Singh Tu, 4, 109	J. Samyn	Master Digby, 4, 114	Fabulous Find, 5, 114	10	1:35.20	33,780
1982	John Casey, 5, 114	J. Fell	Brasher Doubloon, 4, 111	Accipiter's Hope, 4, 120	9	1:38.00	33,090
	Fabulous Find, 4, 109	J. O. Cintron	In From Dixie, 5, 112	Princelet, 4, 126	7	1:38.00	33,330
1981	Dunham's Gift, 4, 115	M. Venezia	Ring of Light, 6, 114	Dr. Blum, 4, 124	6	1:35.00	33,000
1980	Nice Catch, 6, 120	J. Fell	Ardaluan (Ire), 4, 119	Lark Oscillation (Fr), 5, 115	8	1:36.80	34,020
1979	Vencedor, 5, 126	R. Hernandez	Don Aronow, 5, 108	Coverack, 6, 114	10	1:44.00	33,060
1978	Pumpkin Moonshine, 4, 105	D. A. Borden	Lynn Davis, 4, 115	Sharpstone, 4, 111	7	1:44.40	32,250
1977	Cinteelo, 4, 113	E. Maple	Turn and Count, 4, 124	Cojak, 4, 120	9	1:43.40	33,090
1976	Double Edge Sword, 6, 114	A. T. Cordero Jr.	Dr. Emil, 4, 116	Bold and Fancy, 5, 114	9	1:33.40	34,170
1975	Step Nicely, 5, 126	J. Velasquez	*Tambac, 5, 116	Onion, 6, 119	9	1:34.00	33,900
1974	Dundee Marmalade, 6, 113	M. Hole	Infuriator, 4, 113	Prove Out, 5, 126	6	1:36.00	32,940
1973	North Sea, 4, 117	R. C. Smith	Forage, 5, 116	†Summer Guest, 4, 118	9	1:33.60	33,990

Named for Westchester County, New York, located north of the Bronx. Formerly named in honor of the Allied victory in World War I and the signing of the Versailles Peace Treaty in 1919. Formerly named for Yorktown, New York, a com-

munity located in Westchester County. Grade 2 1973-'79. Yorktown H. 1918, 1920-'39. Victory H. 1919. Westchester S. 1953-'71. Held at Empire City 1918-'42. Held at Jamaica 1943-'59. Held at Aqueduct 1960-2001. Not held 1932-'33, 1954-'58. 1 1/8 miles 1918, 1922-'39, 1951-'53. 1 1/4 miles 1919-'21. 1 3/16 miles 1940-'50. 1 1/16 miles 1977-'79. 1 mile 70 yards 1984. Four-year-olds and up 1959-'71. Two divisions 1982. Dead heat for second 1990. ‡Political Force finished second, DQ to third, 2007. Track record 2003. Equaled world record 2003. †Denotes female.

West Virginia Derby

Grade 3 in 2008. Mountaineer Race Track and Gaming Resort, three-year-olds, 1 1/8 miles, dirt. Held August 4, 2007, with a gross value of $750,000. First held in 1958. First graded in 2002. Stakes record 1:46.29 (2003 Soto).

Year	Winner	Jockey	Second	Third	Strs	Time	1st Purse
2007	Zanjero, 3, 111	S. Bridgmohan	Bwana Bull, 3, 117	Moyer's Pond, 3, 116	8	1:53.04	$450,000
2006	Bright One, 3, 114	M. Guidry	Cielo Gold, 3, 111	More Than Regal, 3, 115	10	1:50.08	450,000
2005	Real Dandy, 3, 114	M. Guidry	Magna Graduate, 3, 113	Anthony J., 3, 115	11	1:50.29	450,000
2004	Sir Shackleton, 3, 117	R. Bejarano	Pollard's Vision, 3, 119	Britt's Jules, 3, 115	7	1:49.16	363,000
2003	Soto, 3, 111	R. A. Dominguez	Dynever, 3, 117	Colita, 3, 111	9	1:46.29	360,000
2002	Wiseman's Ferry, 3, 122	J. F. Chavez	The Judge Sez Who, 3, 115	Captain Squire, 3, 115	9	1:49.63	360,000
2001	Western Pride, 3, 117	D. G. Whitney	Saratoga Games, 3, 115	Thunder Blitz, 3, 119	9	1:47.20	300,000
2000	Mass Market, 3, 115	R. Wilson	Hal's Hope, 3, 122	Bet On Red, 3, 122	10	1:49.94	180,000
1999	Stellar Brush, 3, 122	J. V. Stokes	American Spirit, 3, 113	Harry's Halo, 3, 119	11	1:49.02	150,000
1998	Da Devil, 3, 113	J. K. Court	One Bold Stroke, 3, 122	Jess M, 3, 115	12	1:48.84	120,000
1990	Challenge My Duty, 3, 113	I. B. Ayarza	My Other Brother, 3, 115	Gay's Best Boy, 3, 115	8	1:49.60	60,000
1989	Doc's Leader, 3, 114	W. I. Fox Jr.	Halo Hansom, 3, 117	Downtown Davey, 3, 117	7	1:50.00	60,000
1988	Old Stories, 3, 114	R. Hernandez	Viva Deputy, 3, 117	Rising Colors, 3, 112	10	1:52.20	60,000
1981	Park's Policy, 3, 115	J. S. Lloyd	Diverse Dude, 3, 115	Iron Gem, 3, 115	9	1:49.60	22,750
	Johnny Dance, 3, 115	F. Lovato Jr.	Master Tommy, 3, 115	Amasham, 3, 115	8	1:47.80	22,750
1980	Summer Advocate, 3, 115	W. L. Floyd	Lucky Pluck, 3, 115	Foolish Move, 3, 115	11	1:50.80	32,500
1979	Architect, 3, 115	S. A. Spencer	Sir Prince P., 3, 115	Lt. Bert, 3, 115	11	1:51.00	32,500
1978	Beau Sham, 3, 115	P. Day	Silent Cal, 3, 115	Morning Frolic, 3, 115	9	1:48.60	32,500
1977	Best Person, 3, 115	V. A. Bracciale Jr.	Swoon Swept, 3, 115	A Letter to Harry, 3, 115	9	1:48.60	32,500
1976	Wardlaw, 3, 121	J. E. Tejeira	American Trader, 3, 115	Joachim, 3, 121	7	1:47.60	32,500
1975	At the Front, 3, 117	A. Santiago	My Friend Gus, 3, 117	Packer Captain, 3, 117	10	1:48.60	32,500
1974	Park Guard, 3, 124	B. M. Feliciano	Sea Songster, 3, 126	Sahib Nearco, 3, 124	11	1:47.40	32,500
1973	Blue Chip Dan, 3, 118	M. Solomone	Dr. Pantano, 3, 121	Double Edge Sword, 3, 124	8	1:49.20	20,930

Mountaineer Race Track is located in Chester, West Virginia. Held at Wheeling Downs 1958-'61. Held at Waterford Park 1963-'81. Not held 1960, '62, 1982-'87, 1991-'97. Two divisions 1981. Track record 2001, '03.

Whitney Handicap

Grade 1 in 2008. Saratoga Race Course, three-year-olds and up, 1 1/8 miles, dirt. Held July 28, 2007, with a gross value of $810,000. First held in 1928. First graded in 1973. Stakes record 1:46.64 (2007 Lawyer Ron).

Year	Winner	Jockey	Second	Third	Strs	Time	1st Purse
2007	Lawyer Ron, 4, 118	J. R. Velazquez	Wanderin Boy, 6, 117	Diamond Stripes, 4, 116	11	1:46.64	$450,000
2006	Invasor (Arg), 4, 120	F. Jara	Sun King, 4, 117	West Virginia, 5, 114	9	1:49.06	450,000
2005	Commentator, 4, 116	G. L. Stevens	Saint Liam, 5, 122	Sir Shackleton, 4, 115	8	1:48.33	450,000
2004	Roses in May, 4, 114	E. S. Prado	Perfect Drift, 5, 117	Bowman's Band, 6, 114	9	1:48.54	450,000
2003	Medaglia d'Oro, 4, 123	J. D. Bailey	Volponi, 5, 120	Evening Attire, 5, 118	7	1:47.69	450,000
2002	Left Bank, 5, 118	J. R. Velazquez	Street Cry (Ire), 4, 123	Lido Palace (Chi), 5, 119	6	1:47.04	450,000
2001	Lido Palace (Chi), 4, 115	J. D. Bailey	Albert the Great, 4, 124	Gander, 5, 113	7	1:47.94	540,000
2000	Lemon Drop Kid, 4, 123	E. S. Prado	Cat Thief, 4, 117	Behrens, 6, 122	6	1:48.30	680,000
1999	Victory Gallop, 4, 123	J. D. Bailey	Behrens, 5, 123	Catienus, 5, 113	8	1:48.66	360,000
1998	Awesome Again, 4, 117	P. Day	Tale of the Cat, 4, 114	Crypto Star, 4, 116	8	1:49.71	240,000
1997	Will's Way, 4, 117	J. D. Bailey	Formal Gold, 4, 120	Skip Away, 4, 125	6	1:48.37	210,000
1996	Mahogany Hall, 5, 113	J. A. Santos	†Serena's Song, 4, 116	Peaks and Valleys, 4, 121	9	1:48.65	210,000
1995	Unaccounted For, 4, 114	P. Day	L'Carriere, 4, 111	Silver Fox, 4, 112	9	1:49.29	210,000
1994	Colonial Affair, 4, 117	J. A. Santos	Devil His Due, 5, 125	West by West, 5, 113	7	1:48.61	210,000
1993	Brunswick, 4, 112	M. E. Smith	West by West, 4, 115	Devil His Due, 4, 122	7	1:47.41	150,000
1992	Sultry Song, 4, 115	J. D. Bailey	Out of Place, 5, 115	Chief Honcho, 5, 116	9	1:47.29	150,000
1991	In Excess (Ire), 4, 121	G. L. Stevens	Chief Honcho, 4, 115	Killer Diller, 4, 112	7	1:48.01	150,000
1990	Criminal Type, 5, 126	G. L. Stevens	Dancing Spree, 5, 121	Mi Selecto, 5, 117	6	1:48.60	140,640
1989	Easy Goer, 3, 119	P. Day	Forever Silver, 4, 120	Cryptoclearance, 5, 122	6	1:47.40	172,500
1988	†Personal Ensign, 4, 117	R. P. Romero	Gulch, 4, 124	King's Swan, 8, 123	3	1:47.80	162,300
1987	Java Gold, 3, 113	P. Day	Gulch, 3, 117	Broad Brush, 4, 127	7	1:48.40	173,100
1986	†Lady's Secret, 4, 119	P. Day	Ends Well, 5, 116	Fuzzy, 4, 110	7	1:49.80	202,500
1985	Track Barron, 4, 124	A. T. Cordero Jr.	Carr de Naskra, 4, 120	Vanlandingham, 4, 124	5	1:47.60	160,680
1984	Slew o' Gold, 4, 126	A. T. Cordero Jr.	Track Barron, 3, 117	Thumbsucker, 5, 115	3	1:48.60	165,744
1983	Island Whirl, 5, 123	E. Delahoussaye	Bold Style, 4, 114	Sunny's Halo, 3, 116	8	1:48.40	103,860
1982	Silver Buck, 4, 115	D. MacBeth	Winter's Tale, 6, 119	Tap Shoes, 4, 113	6	1:47.80	99,000
1981	Fio Rito, 6, 113	L. Hulet	Winter's Tale, 5, 121	Ring of Light, 6, 114	8	1:48.00	105,300
1980	State Dinner, 5, 120	R. Hernandez	Dr. Patches, 6, 114	Czaravich, 4, 123	7	1:47.60	99,540
1979	Star de Naskra, 4, 120	J. Fell	Cox's Ridge, 5, 117	The Liberal Member, 4, 120	6	1:47.60	65,040
1978	Alydar, 3, 123	J. Velazquez	Buckaroo, 3, 112	Father Hogan, 5, 114	9	1:47.40	49,545
1977	Nearly On Time, 3, 103	S. Cauthen	American History, 5, 112	Dancing Gun, 5, 112	7	1:49.40	49,545
1976	Dancing Gun, 4, 108	R. I. Velez	American History, 4, 109	Erwin Boy, 5, 116	7	1:50.00	48,825
1975	Ancient Title, 5, 128	S. Hawley	Group Plan, 5, 115	Arbees Boy, 5, 118	3	1:48.20	50,085

Year	Winner	Jockey	Second	Third	Strs	Time	1st Purse
1974	Tri Jet, 5, 123	L. A. Pincay Jr.	Infuriator, 4, 120	Stop the Music, 4, 120	6	1:47.00	$33,390
1973	Onion, 4, 119	J. Vasquez	Secretariat, 3, 119	Rule by Reason, 6, 119	5	1:49.20	32,310

Named for the Whitney family, one of the most influential families of 20th-century American racing. Grade 2 1973-'80. Whitney S. 1928-'53, 1955-'59, 1961-'65, 1967-'74, 1978-'80. Held at Belmont Park 1943-'45. 1¼ miles 1928-'54. Four-year-olds and up 1957-'69. Colts and fillies 1928-'40. Track record 2007. †Denotes female.

William Donald Schaefer Handicap

Grade 3 in 2008. Pimlico Race Course, three-year-olds and up, 1⅛ miles, dirt. Held May 19, 2007, with a gross value of $100,000. First held in 1994. First graded in 2001. Stakes record 1:47.86 (2007 Flashy Bull).

Year	Winner	Jockey	Second	Third	Strs	Time	1st Purse
2007	Flashy Bull, 4, 114	A. Garcia	Hesanoldsalt, 4, 117	Ryan's for Real, 4, 115	8	**1:47.86**	$60,000
2006	Master Command, 4, 115	G. K. Gomez	Andromeda's Hero, 4, 117	Funny Cide, 6, 117	8	1:49.42	60,000
2005	Zakocity, 4, 117	J. D. Bailey	Clays Awesome, 5, 114	Royal Assault, 4, 112	8	1:49.19	60,000
2004	Seattle Fitz (Arg), 5, 116	R. Migliore	The Lady's Groom, 4, 115	Roaring Fever, 4, 114	8	1:49.43	60,000
2003	Windsor Castle, 5, 117	J. A. Santos	Changeintheweather, 4, 113	Tempest Fugit, 6, 116	8	1:50.08	60,000
2002	Tenpins, 4, 114	R. Albarado	Bowman's Band, 4, 117	Tactical Side, 5, 113	7	1:50.20	60,000
2001	Perfect Cat, 4, 115	J. D. Bailey	Rize, 5, 115	Judge's Case, 4, 115	8	1:49.55	60,000
2000	Ecton Park, 4, 116	P. Day	The Groom Is Red, 4, 111	Crosspatch, 6, 116	4	1:49.21	60,000
1999	Perfect to a Tee, 7, 112	A. C. Cortez	Allen's Oop, 4, 113	Smile Again, 4, 114	7	1:49.20	60,000
1998	Acceptable, 4, 118	J. D. Bailey	Littlebitlively, 4, 118	Testafly, 4, 114	8	1:48.76	60,000
1997	Western Echo, 5, 116	E. S. Prado	Suave Prospect, 5, 114	Mary's Buckaroo, 6, 120	5	1:49.41	60,000
1996	Canaveral, 5, 114	S. J. Sellers	Michael's Star, 4, 114	Rugged Bugger, 5, 113	7	1:49.03	45,000
1995	Tidal Surge, 5, 112	J. D. Carle	Mary's Buckaroo, 4, 113	Ameri Valay, 6, 119	5	1:48.19	60,000
1994	Taking Risks, 4, 117	M. T. Johnston	Frottage, 5, 115	Super Memory, 4, 112	6	1:49.53	45,000

Named for William Donald Schaefer, governor of Maryland (1987-'95) and mayor of Baltimore (1971-'86). Not held 2008.

Will Rogers Stakes

Grade 3 in 2008. Hollywood Park, three-year-olds, 1 mile, turf. Held May 17, 2008, with a gross value of $106,800. First held in 1938. First graded in 1973. Stakes record 1:33.45 (2004 Laura's Lucky Boy).

Year	Winner	Jockey	Second	Third	Strs	Time	1st Purse
2008	Polonius, 3, 117	J. K. Court	Indian Sun, 3, 117	Ez Dreamer, 3, 119	5	1:34.95	$64,080
2007	Worldly (GB), 3, 119	V. Espinoza	Silent Soul, 3, 119	Mayor Bozarth, 3, 119	6	1:35.19	64,920
2006	Stratham (Ire), 3, 121	D. Cohen	New Joysey Jeff, 3, 116	Obrigado (Fr), 3, 119	7	1:34.19	60,000
2005	Osidy, 3, 116	A. O. Solis	Willow O Wisp, 3, 119	Eastern Sand, 3, 117	8	1:34.67	65,940
2004	Laura's Lucky Boy, 3, 119	P. A. Valenzuela	Toasted, 3, 121	Street Theatre, 3, 117	6	**1:33.45**	65,640
2003	Private Chef, 3, 115	V. Espinoza	Banshee King, 3, 115	Singletary, 3, 117	6	1:35.57	67,560
2002	Doc Holliday, 3, 116	D. R. Flores	Johar, 3, 119	Golden Arrow, 3, 115	5	1:34.64	63,900
2001	dh-Dr. Park, 3, 117	T. Baze		Learing At Kathy, 3, 116	8	1:35.10	43,920
	dh-Media Mogul (GB), 3, 116	A. O. Solis					
2000	Purely Cozzene, 3, 120	V. Espinoza	Duke of Green (GB), 3, 116	Silver Axe, 3, 115	8	1:34.67	66,000
1999	Eagleton, 3, 118	C. A. Black	Hidden Magic (GB), 3, 115	Mr. Reignmaker, 3, 115	11	1:34.38	67,800
1998	Magical (GB), 3, 117	R. R. Douglas	Commitisize, 3, 119	Son's Corona, 3, 114	8	1:33.98	65,820
1997	Brave Act (GB), 3, 117	C. J. McCarron	P. T. Indy, 3, 118	Without Doubt (Ire), 3, 116	12	1:34.01	68,520
1996	Let Bob Do It, 3, 118	K. Desormeaux	Nightcapper, 3, 114	Dr. Sardonica, 3, 116	10	1:34.05	67,140
1995	Via Lombardia (Ire), 3, 117	E. Delahoussaye	Mr Purple, 3, 119	Bee El Tee, 3, 117	9	1:34.15	63,650
1994	Unfinished Symph, 3, 116	G. Baze	Silver Music, 3, 118	Valiant Nature, 3, 122	8	1:40.60	64,400
1993	Future Storm, 3, 116	K. Desormeaux	Lykatill Hil, 3, 119	Earl of Barking (Ire), 3, 122	12	1:40.01	68,900
1992	The Name's Jimmy, 3, 116	D. Sorenson	Bold Assert, 3, 117	Prospect for Four, 3, 114	7	1:40.99	63,600
1991	Compelling Sound, 3, 119	P. A. Valenzuela	Stark South, 3, 116	Persianalli (Ire), 3, 117	9	1:40.70	66,100
1990	Itsallgreektome, 3, 114	C. S. Nakatani	Warcraft, 3, 120	Balla Cove (Ire), 3, 116	9	1:40.20	66,500
1989	Notorious Pleasure, 3, 117	L. A. Pincay Jr.	Advocate Training, 3, 115	First Play, 3, 116	10	1:40.20	66,900
1988	Word Pirate, 3, 119	E. Delahoussaye	Perfecting, 3, 115	Roberto's Dancer, 3, 116	9	1:40.20	50,400
1987	Something Lucky, 3, 117	L. A. Pincay Jr.	The Medic, 3, 115	Persevered, 3, 119	9	1:43.00	49,600
1986	‡Mazaad (Ire), 3, 120	W. Shoemaker	Autobot, 3, 115	He's a Saros, 3, 115	7	1:42.40	48,800
1985	Pine Belt, 3, 113	R. Q. Meza	Rich Earth, 3, 119	Academy Road, 3, 116	10	1:41.00	40,700
1984	Tsunami Slew, 3, 119	L. A. Pincay Jr.	Swinging Scobie (GB), 3, 115	Tights, 3, 122	6	1:39.80	37,550
1983	Barberstown, 3, 116	F. Toro	Lover Boy Leslie, 3, 117	Tanks Brigade, 3, 120	13	1:41.40	35,200
1982	Give Me Strength, 3, 116	J. Samyn	Ask Me, 3, 115	Accoustical, 3, 113	8	1:40.60	26,500
	Sword Blade, 3, 112	D. G. McHargue	Art Director, 3, 118	Lucky Ship, 3, 114	7	1:41.80	26,050
1981	Splendid Spruce, 3, 123	D. G. McHargue	Seafood, 3, 119	Surprise George, 3, 115	8	1:41.40	38,900
1980	Stiff Diamond, 3, 113	T. Lipham	Naked Sky, 3, 117	Big Doug, 3, 115	11	1:41.40	34,300
1979	Ibacado (Chi), 3, 118	D. G. McHargue	Beau's Eagle, 3, 121	David's Gotcha (Ire), 3, 111	8	1:40.80	32,550
1978	April Axe, 3, 115	C. J. McCarron	Poppy Popowich, 3, 115	He's Dewan, 3, 117	9	1:41.60	33,100
1977	Nordic Prince, 3, 117	S. Hawley	Sonny Collins, 3, 119	Bad 'n Big, 3, 123	10	1:41.40	33,950
1976	Madera Sun, 3, 116	L. A. Pincay Jr.	An Act, 3, 126	‡Today 'n Tomorrow, 3, 115	7	1:42.00	32,100
1975	Uniformity, 3, 115	W. Shoemaker	Dusty County, 3, 117	Exact Duplicate, 3, 115	8	1:42.00	32,150
1974	Stardust Mel, 3, 120	F. Toro	Agitate, 3, 122	El Seetu, 3, 114	8	1:40.80	32,800
1973	Groshawk, 3, 123	W. Shoemaker	Ancient Title, 3, 124	dh-Mug Punter, 3, 113	10	1:35.60	33,600
				dh-Out of the East, 3, 118			

Named for actor and American humorist Will Rogers (1879-1935); Rogers was killed in a plane crash in Alaska. Grade 2 1973-'82, 1988-'89. Will Rogers Memorial H. 1938-'40. Will Rogers H. 1941-'51, 1973-'94, 1996-2000. Will Rogers Breeders' Cup H. 1995. Held at Santa Anita Park 1949. Not held 1942-'43, 1950. 7 furlongs 1938-'44, 1946-'47. 6 fur-

longs 1948-'54. 1¹/₁₆ miles 1974-'94. Dirt 1938-'68. Three-year-olds and up 1938, '44. Colts and geldings 1953-'73. Two divisions 1982. Dead heat for third 1973. Dead heat for first 2001. ‡Sure Fire finished third, DQ to fourth, 1976. ‡Sovereign Don finished first, DQ to fifth, 1986.

Wilshire Handicap

Grade 3 in 2008. Hollywood Park, three-year-olds and up, fillies and mares, 1 mile, turf. Held April 23, 2008, with a gross value of $110,800. First held in 1953. First graded in 1975. Stakes record 1:33.14 (2006 Heavenly Ransom).

Year	Winner	Jockey	Second	Third	Strs	Time	1st Purse
2008	Diamond Diva (GB), 4, 117	D. R. Flores	Kris' Sis, 5, 115	La Tee, 4, 114	9	1:33.21	$66,480
2007	Charm the Giant (Ire), 5, 117	M. C. Baze	Sohgol (Ire), 5, 116	Ghurra, 5, 114	10	1:34.16	66,900
2006	Heavenly Ransom, 4, 116	J. K. Court	Ticker Tape (GB), 5, 119	Flip Flop (Fr), 5, 115	6	**1:33.14**	60,000
2005	Pickle (GB), 4, 114	J. K. Court	Makeup Artist, 5, 114	Amorama (Fr), 4, 117	8	1:33.85	65,760
2004	Spring Star (Fr), 5, 117	A. O. Solis	Quero Quero, 4, 115	Dublino, 5, 120	9	1:33.41	66,540
2003	Dublino, 4, 120	K. Desormeaux	Southern Oasis, 5, 116	Final Destination (NZ), 5, 118	9	1:33.62	66,600
2002	Eurolink Raindance (Ire), 5, 118	C. J. McCarron	Crazy Ensign (Arg), 6, 118	Impeachable, 5, 115	5	1:34.31	63,960
2001	Tranquility Lake, 6, 123	E. Delahoussaye	Dianehill (Ire), 5, 116	Out of Reach (GB), 4, 117	7	1:34.69	65,160
2000	Tout Charmant, 4, 121	C. J. McCarron	Penny Marie, 4, 117	Perfect Copy, 4, 117	6	1:33.86	64,740
1999	Sapphire Ring (GB), 4, 119	G. L. Stevens	Bella Chiarra, 4, 116	Green Jewel (GB), 5, 118	7	1:33.86	65,160
1998	Shake the Yoke (GB), 5, 118	E. Delahoussaye	Traces of Gold, 6, 116	Cozy Blues, 4, 115	9	1:34.10	66,240
1997	Blushing Heiress, 5, 115	C. J. McCarron	Real Connection, 6, 115	De Puntillas (GB), 5, 117	7	1:40.80	65,040
1996	Pharma, 5, 118	C. S. Nakatani	Didina (GB), 4, 116	Matiara, 4, 120	5	1:40.96	79,770
1995	Possibly Perfect, 5, 121	K. Desormeaux	Morgana, 4, 116	Aube Indienne (Fr), 5, 119	5	1:40.37	76,600
1994	Skimble, 5, 118	E. Delahoussaye	Bel's Starlet, 7, 117	Miami Sands (Ire), 4, 116	6	1:41.39	62,800
1993	Toussaud, 4, 116	K. Desormeaux	Visible Gold, 5, 117	Wedding Ring (Ire), 4, 115	7	1:40.14	63,500
1992	Kostroma (Ire), 6, 123	K. Desormeaux	Danzante, 4, 114	Appealing Missy, 5, 116	6	1:41.35	62,600
1991	Fire the Groom, 4, 118	G. L. Stevens	Odalea (Arg), 5, 115	Agirlfromars, 5, 114	6	1:40.10	63,000
1990	Reluctant Guest, 4, 114	R. G. Davis	Beautiful Melody, 4, 115	Estrella Fuega, 4, 114	6	1:39.40	62,400
1989	Claire Marine (Ire), 4, 117	C. J. McCarron	Fitzwilliam Place (Ire), 5, 119	Galunpe (Ire), 6, 119	6	1:39.00	62,700
1988	Chapel of Dreams, 4, 115	G. L. Stevens	Fitzwilliam Place (Ire), 5, 119	Invited Guest (Ire), 4, 116	8	1:39.40	64,700
1987	Galunpe (Ire), 4, 118	F. Toro	Top Socialite, 5, 119	Perfect Match (Fr), 5, 116	6	1:41.00	75,900
1986	Outstandingly, 4, 117	G. L. Stevens	La Koumia (Fr), 4, 118	Estrapade, 6, 124	5	1:41.60	75,600
1985	Johnica, 4, 114	C. J. McCarron	Tamarinda (Fr), 4, 119	Salt Spring (Arg), 6, 113	6	1:40.60	63,100
1984	Triple Tipple, 5, 114	L. A. Pincay Jr.	Comedy Act, 5, 121	Nan's Dancer, 5, 116	7	1:41.20	48,900
1983	Mademoiselle Forli, 4, 118	P. A. Valenzuela	Night Fire, 4, 117	Nan's Dancer, 4, 115	5	1:44.80	47,300
1982	Miss Huntington, 5, 115	P. A. Valenzuela	Mi Quimera (Arg), 5, 114	French Charmer, 4, 116	10	1:41.40	51,250
1981	Track Robbery, 5, 118	P. A. Valenzuela	Luth Music (Fr), 4, 115	Save Wild Life, 4, 116	6	1:40.60	47,550
1980	Wishing Well, 5, 120	F. Toro	Sisterhood, 5, 119	Love You Dear, 4, 113	9	1:41.60	38,500
1979	Country Queen, 4, 121	L. A. Pincay Jr.	Giggling Girl, 5, 116	Camarado, 4, 119	8	1:40.40	33,100
1978	*Lucie Manet, 5, 119	C. J. McCarron	Swingtime, 6, 118	Drama Critic, 4, 119	6	1:49.00	30,950
1977	Now Pending, 4, 114	R. Campas	Swingtime, 5, 118	Up to Juliet, 4, 116	10	1:48.80	33,550
1976	Miss Toshiba, 4, 117	F. Toro	Charger's Star, 5, 116	Swingtime, 4, 120	8	1:49.20	32,300
1975	*Tizna, 6, 123	J. Lambert	Susan's Girl, 6, 123	*Dulcia, 6, 120	10	1:48.60	33,300
1974	Tallahto, 4, 121	L. A. Pincay Jr.	Ready Wit, 4, 113	Dogtooth Violet, 4, 119	11	1:47.60	33,650
1973	Balcony's Babe, 5, 116	J. Lambert	Ground Song, 4, 118	Dating, 6, 111	8	1:48.60	17,250
	Convenience, 5, 124	J. L. Rotz	Pallisima, 4, 120	Veiled Desire, 4, 109	7	1:49.00	16,900

Named for Wilshire, a historic district of Los Angeles. Grade 2 1983-'97. Wilshire S. 1953, 1970-'72. Not held 1954-'62. 7 furlongs 1963-'69. 1¹/₈ miles 1970-'78. 1¹/₁₆ miles 1979-'97. Dirt 1953-'69, 1983. Three-year-olds 1953, '70. Four-year-olds and up 1971-'72. Fillies 1953, '70. Two divisions 1973. Nonwinners of a race worth $10,000 to the winner 1973.

Winning Colors Stakes

Grade 3 in 2008. Churchill Downs, three-year-olds and up, fillies and mares, 6 furlongs, dirt. Held May 26, 2008, with a gross value of $107,600. First held in 2004. First graded in 2007. Stakes record 1:08.68 (2007 Miss Macy Sue).

Year	Winner	Jockey	Second	Third	Strs	Time	1st Purse
2008	Graeme Six, 4, 118	J. R. Leparoux	Miss Macy Sue, 5, 122	Change Up, 4, 118	6	1:09.17	$66,045
2007	Miss Macy Sue, 4, 118	E. Razo Jr.	Cuaba, 4, 118	Morethanaprincess, 4, 118	8	**1:08.68**	66,217
2006	Ever Elusive, 4, 118	R. Bejarano	Malibu Mint, 4, 122	Ebony Breeze, 6, 122	8	1:09.14	66,275
2005	Molto Vita, 5, 123	R. Bejarano	Heavenly Humor, 4, 121	Born to Dance, 6, 121	5	1:09.50	66,464
2004	Lady Tak, 4, 122	S. J. Sellers	Put Me In, 4, 117	Ebony Breeze, 4, 116	7	1:08.87	67,332

Named for Eugene V. Klein's Racing Hall of Fame member, 1988 champion 3-year-old filly, and '88 Kentucky Derby (G1) winner Winning Colors (1985 f. by Caro [Ire]).

Withers Stakes

Grade 3 in 2008. Aqueduct, three-year-olds, 1 mile, dirt. Held April 26, 2008, with a gross value of $142,500. First held in 1874. First graded in 1973. Stakes record 1:32.79 (1993 Williamstown).

Year	Winner	Jockey	Second	Third	Strs	Time	1st Purse
2008	Harlem Rocker, 3, 116	E. Coa	J Be K, 3, 123	Double Or Nothing, 3, 118	4	1:34.50	$90,000
2007	Divine Park, 3, 118	A. Garcia	C P West, 3, 116	Frosty Secret, 3, 118	7	1:34.65	90,000
2006	Bernardini, 3, 116	J. Castellano	Doc Cheney, 3, 116	Luxemburg, 3, 116	4	1:35.07	90,000
2005	Scrappy T, 3, 120	N. Arroyo Jr.	Park Avenue Ball, 3, 120	War Plan, 3, 116	7	1:35.74	90,000
2004	Medallist, 3, 116	J. F. Chavez	Forest Danger, 3, 123	Two Down Automatic, 3, 120	5	1:34.49	90,000
2003	Spite the Devil, 3, 116	L. Chavez	Alysweep, 3, 123	Stanislavsky, 3, 116	7	1:35.89	90,000
2002	Fast Decision, 3, 116	J. A. Santos	Shah Jehan, 3, 118	Listen Here, 3, 120	5	1:36.41	90,000

Racing — Graded Stakes 491

Year	Winner	Jockey	Second	Third	Strs	Time	1st Purse
2001	Richly Blended, 3, 123	R. Wilson	Le Grande Danseur, 3, 120	Telescam, 3, 116	7	1:35.66	$90,000
2000	Big E E, 3, 116	H. Castillo Jr.	Precise End, 3, 123	Port Herman, 3, 116	8	1:35.69	90,000
1999	Successful Appeal, 3, 120	J. L. Espinoza	Best of Luck, 3, 116	Treasure Island, 3, 116	8	1:35.18	90,000
1998	Dice Dancer, 3, 123	J. F. Chavez	Rubiyat, 3, 123	Limit Out, 3, 123	7	1:34.48	90,000
1997	Statesmanship, 3, 123	W. H. McCauley	Cryp Too, 3, 123	Stormin Fever, 3, 123	7	1:35.30	67,140
1996	Appealing Skier, 3, 123	R. Wilson	Jamies First Punch, 3, 123	Roar, 3, 123	5	1:35.02	66,120
1995	Blu Tusmani, 3, 123	J. A. Santos	Pat n Jac, 3, 123	‡Slice of Reality, 3, 123	9	1:35.19	67,260
1994	Twining, 3, 123	J. A. Santos	Able Buck, 3, 123	Presently, 3, 123	8	1:34.75	67,140
1993	Williamstown, 3, 124	C. Perret	Virginia Rapids, 3, 124	Farmonthefreeway, 3, 124	12	**1:32.79**	76,800
1992	Dixie Brass, 3, 126	J. M. Pezua	Big Sur, 3, 126	Superstrike (GB), 3, 126	8	1:33.71	73,080
1991	Subordinated Debt, 3, 126	J. A. Krone	Scan, 3, 126	Kyle's Our Man, 3, 126	9	1:34.03	73,920
1990	Housebuster, 3, 126	C. Perret	Profit Key, 3, 126	Sunny Serve, 3, 126	6	1:34.80	71,040
1989	Fire Maker, 3, 126	J. D. Bailey	Imbibe, 3, 126	Manastash Ridge, 3, 126	8	1:36.40	73,800
1988	Once Wild, 3, 126	P. Day	Tejano, 3, 126	Perfect Spy, 3, 126	5	1:35.20	69,360
1987	Gone West, 3, 126	E. Maple	High Brite, 3, 126	Mister S. M., 3, 126	6	1:36.40	82,620
1986	Clear Choice, 3, 126	J. Velasquez	Tasso, 3, 126	Landing Plot, 3, 126	10	1:35.60	71,550
1985	El Basco, 3, 126	J. Vasquez	Another Reef, 3, 126	Concert, 3, 126	12	1:36.60	72,990
1984	Play On, 3, 126	J. Samyn	Morning Bob, 3, 126	Back Bay Barrister, 3, 126	10	1:36.40	69,750
1983	Country Pine, 3, 126	J. D. Bailey	I Enclose, 3, 126	Megaturn, 3, 126	10	1:35.60	52,380
1982	Aloma's Ruler, 3, 126	J. L. Kaenel	Spanish Drums, 3, 126	John's Gold, 3, 126	6	1:35.40	33,300
1981	Spirited Boy, 3, 126	A. T. Cordero Jr.	Willow Hour, 3, 126	A Run, 3, 126	7	1:36.80	33,600
1980	Colonel Moran, 3, 126	J. Velasquez	Temperence Hill, 3, 126	J. P. Brother, 3, 126	7	1:34.40	34,200
1979	Czaravich, 3, 126	J. Cruguet	Instrument Landing, 3, 126	Strike the Main, 3, 126	9	1:35.60	33,330
1978	Junction, 3, 126	M. Solomone	Star de Naskra, 3, 126	Buckaroo, 3, 126	8	1:36.80	32,520
1977	Iron Constitution, 3, 126	J. Velasquez	Cormorant, 3, 126	Affiliate, 3, 126	8	1:37.00	33,360
1976	Sonkisser, 3, 126	B. Baeza	El Portugues, 3, 126	Full Out, 3, 126	6	1:35.00	32,760
1975	†Sarsar, 3, 121	W. Shoemaker	Laramie Trail, 3, 126	Ramahorn, 3, 126	13	1:34.60	36,360
1974	Accipiter, 3, 126	A. Santiago	Best of It, 3, 126	Hosiery, 3, 126	12	1:35.60	36,240
1973	Linda's Chief, 3, 126	J. Velasquez	Stop the Music, 3, 126	Forego, 3, 126	8	1:34.80	33,120

Named for David Dunham Withers (1821-'72), a founder of Jerome Park and president of Monmouth Park. Grade 2 1973-'99. Held at Jerome Park 1874-'89. Held at Morris Park 1890-1904. Held at Belmont Park 1905-'55, 1957-'59, 1972-'74, 1976, 1981, 1984-'85, 1987-'96. Held at Jamaica 1956. Not held 1911-'12. 1 1/16 miles 1956. Colts and fillies 1944. ‡Northern Ensign finished third, DQ to ninth, 1995. Track record 1993. †Denotes female.

W. L. McKnight Handicap

Grade 2 in 2008. Calder Race Course, three-year-olds and up, 1 1/2 miles, turf. Held December 15, 2007, with a gross value of $200,000. First held in 1973. First graded in 1975. Stakes record 2:24.11 (1995 Flag Down).

Year	Winner	Jockey	Second	Third	Strs	Time	1st Purse
2007	Presious Passion, 4, 116	E. Trujillo	Stream of Gold (Ire), 6, 118	Kiss the Kid, 4, 114	12	2:26.13	$115,320
2006	Devil's Preacher, 5, 110	R. Bejarano	Bob's Proud Moment, 5, 115	Ramazutti, 4, 113	6	2:38.28	120,000
2005	Meteor Storm (GB), 6, 118	J. Castellano	Revved Up, 7, 117	Scooter Roach, 6, 114	12	2:25.91	120,000
2004	Dreadnaught, 4, 116	J. Samyn	Demeteor, 5, 112	Scooter Roach, 5, 115	12	2:26.60	120,000
2003	Balto Star, 5, 121	J. R. Velazquez	Continuously, 4, 116	Rowans Park, 3, 114	11	2:24.87	120,000
2002	Man From Wicklow, 5, 118	J. D. Bailey	Serial Bride, 5, 114	Rochester, 6, 117	12	2:28.05	120,000
2001	Profit Option, 6, 115	M. Guidry	Deeliteful Irving, 3, 113	Eltawaasul, 5, 114	12	2:27.95	90,000
2000	A Little Luck, 6, 114	M. E. Smith	Stokosky, 4, 113	Whata Brainstorm, 3, 113	12	2:29.01	90,000
1999	‡Wicapi, 7, 114	C. H. Velasquez	Special Coach, 3, 114	King's Jewel, 3, 112	12	2:26.28	90,000
1998	Wild Event, 5, 116	S. J. Sellers	N B Forrest, 6, 114	Glok, 4, 114	8	2:26.93	90,000
1997	Panama City, 5, 117	P. Day	Slicious (GB), 5, 114	Skillington, 4, 113	12	2:27.19	90,000
1996	Diplomatic Jet, 4, 123	J. F. Chavez	Marcie's Ensign, 4, 114	dh-Identity, 4, 114	12	2:24.20	90,000
				dh-Lassigny, 5, 116			
1995	Flag Down, 5, 116	J. A. Santos	Mecke, 3, 118	Green Means Go, 3, 115	12	**2:24.11**	90,000
1994	Star of Manila, 3, 116	C. Perret	Spectacular Tide, 5, 114	Kissin Kris, 4, 117	13	2:28.43	90,000
	Cobblestone Road, 5, 113	J. C. Ferrer	Daarik (Ire), 7, 113	Fraise, 6, 126	12	2:27.89	60,000
1993	Antartic Wings, 5, 113	R. R. Douglas	Cigar Toss (Arg), 6, 112	Luv U. Jodi, 6, 110	9	2:33.44	60,000
1992	Bye Union Ave., 6, 113	R. R. Douglas	†Crockadore, 5, 113	Skate On Thin Ice, 5, 111	9	2:27.23	60,000
1991	Stolen Rolls, 5, 115	P. A. Rodriguez	Runaway Raja, 5, 112	Gallant Mel, 6, 110	13	2:27.10	60,000
1990	Drum Taps, 4, 114	J. A. Santos	†Black Tulip (Fr), 5, 112	Turfah, 7, 115	12	2:29.80	60,000
1989	Mataji, 5, 113	D. Valiente	Mi Selecto, 4, 118	Creme Fraiche, 7, 118	13	2:25.60	90,000
1988	All Sincerity, 6, 111	C. Hernandez	Blazing Bart, 4, 118	Creme Fraiche, 6, 118	8	2:25.40	120,000
1987	Creme Fraiche, 5, 115	E. Maple	Flying Pidgeon, 6, 120	Akabir, 6, 113	10	2:27.00	120,000
1986	Flying Pidgeon, 5, 117	J. A. Santos	Creme Fraiche, 4, 115	Ameriland, 5, 112	7	2:39.60	120,000
1985	Jack Slade, 5, 120	G. Gallitano	Rake (Fr), 5, 116	Rilial, 4, 120	9	2:26.20	69,900
	Flying Pidgeon, 4, 114	J. A. Santos	Pass the Line, 4, 114	Selous Scout, 4, 110	10	2:25.80	70,800
1984	Open Call, 6, 120	J. Velasquez	Dom Cimarosa (Ire), 5, 114	Bold Frond, 5, 113	10	2:30.20	63,075
	Nijinsky's Secret, 6, 124	J. A. Velez Jr.	Dom Menotti (Fr), 7, 112	Four Stages, 5, 114	11	2:31.20	63,675
1983	Current Blade, 5, 114	J. D. Bailey	Half Iced, 4, 122	Leader Jet, 5, 115	12	2:29.20	70,020
1982	Ghazwan (Ire), 5, 114	C. Hernandez	Gleaming Channel, 4, 116	Beyond Recall, 5, 110	11	2:28.80	61,920
	Russian George (Fr), 6, 114	M. A. Rivera	†Euphrosyne, 6, 117	Nar, 7, 113	10	2:29.80	61,920
1981	El Barril (Chi), 5, 118	J. Vasquez	Lord Bawlmer, 5, 115	Lobsang (Ire), 5, 117	9	2:28.40	51,630
	Buckpoint (Fr), 5, 122	J. D. Bailey	Scythian Gold, 6, 116	Proud Manner, 7, 112	10	2:28.00	52,230
1980	Old Crony, 5, 117	D. Brumfield	Once Over Lightly, 7, 114	Houdini, 5, 125	11	1:48.40	35,565
	Drum's Captain (Ire), 5, 118	J. Fell	Lot o' Gold, 4, 125	Scythian Gold, 5, 116	9	1:48.00	34,875

Year	Winner	Jockey	Second	Third	Strs	Time	1st Purse
1979	Bob's Dusty, 5, 119	R. DePass	Prince Misko, 4, 116	Bridewell, 4, 112	12	1:48.00	$55,800
1978	Practitioner, 5, 118	J. S. Rodriguez	Fort Prevel, 4, 111	Bob's Dusty, 4, 118	12	1:48.80	56,250
1977	Hall of Reason, 4, 119	M. Solomone	Visier, 5, 120	Lightning Thrust, 4, 116	8	1:47.20	52,200
1976	Toonerville, 5, 119	G. St. Leon	Ameri Flyer, 4, 117	Emperor Rex, 5, 115	12	1:44.60	55,800
1975	Snurb, 5, 119	G. St. Leon	Buffalo Lark, 5, 121	Lord Rebeau, 4, 116	13	1:46.00	37,800
1974	Shane's Prince, 4, 116	E. Maple	Star Envoy, 6, 125	Return to Reality, 5, 119	9	1:46.00	35,700
1973	Getajetholme, 4, 121	J. Imparato	Daring Young Man, 4, 120	Outdoors, 4, 116	14	1:47.20	38,700

Named for William L. McKnight (1881-1978), co-founder of Calder Race Course and founder of Tartan Farms. Grade 3 1976-'81. W. L. McKnight Invitational H. 1986-'93. 1⅛ miles 1973-'75, 1977-'80. About 1⅛ miles 1976. Dirt 1993, 2006. Originally scheduled on turf 2006. Two divisions 1980-'82, 1984-'85. Held in January and December 1994. Dead heat for third 1996. ‡Just Listen finished first, DQ to ninth, 1999. Course record 1976. †Denotes female.

Woodford Reserve Bourbon Stakes

Grade 3 in 2008. Keeneland Race Course, two-year-olds, 1 1/16 miles, turf. Held October 7, 2007, with a gross value of $150,000. First held in 1991. First graded in 2008. Stakes record 1:42.42 (1999 Gateman [GB]).

Year	Winner	Jockey	Second	Third	Strs	Time	1st Purse
2007	Gio Ponti, 2, 117	R. A. Dominguez	Nownownow, 2, 121	Caberneigh, 2, 117	7	1:45.92	$93,000
2006	Twilight Meteor, 2, 116	J. R. Velazquez	Marcavelly, 2, 120	Admiral Bird, 2, 116	5	1:43.25	77,500
2005	Yankee Master, 2, 116	R. Bejarano	Wedding Singer, 2, 116	Desert Wheat, 2, 116	8	1:43.65	77,500
2004	Rey de Cafe, 2, 116	C. Perret	Dubleo, 2, 122	Ready Ruler, 2, 122	10	1:42.90	69,564
2003	Commendation, 2, 120	C. H. Velasquez	Oncearoundtwice, 2, 116	Grand Heritage, 2, 120	10	1:43.99	69,936
2002	Rapid Proof, 2, 116	C. H. Borel	Zydeco Affair, 2, 122	Collateral Damage, 2, 116	10	1:46.45	71,300
2001	Stage Call (Ire), 2, 116	M. Guidry	†Daisyago, 2, 115	Midwatch, 2, 116	8	1:45.85	69,316
2000	Overview, 2, 115	M. E. Smith	Mc Henry Co. Kid, 2, 115	Summarily, 2, 115	9	1:43.02	52,241
1999	Gateman (GB), 2, 115	P. Day	dh-Field Cat, 2, 119 dh-Pay Ransom, 2, 115	Air Rocket, 2, 113	8	**1:42.42**	41,230
1998	Pineaff, 2, 113	P. Day	Draupner, 2, 119	Air Rocket, 2, 113	9	1:44.63	44,377
	Bold Caleb, 2, 116	R. Albarado	Phi Beta Doc, 2, 113	Dawn Flies By, 2, 118	9	1:44.73	44,377
1997	Reformer Rally, 2, 116	C. Perret	Heartland Hope, 2, 113	Magest, 2, 113	8	1:46.91	44,780
1996	Thesaurus, 2, 112	C. Perret	Letterhead, 2, 112	Royal Strand (Ire), 2, 112	10	1:44.49	34,100
1995	Red Shadow, 2, 112	W. Martinez	Never to Squander, 2, 114	Officious, 2, 115	9	1:46.71	31,558
1994	Claudius, 2, 115	J. R. Velazquez	Hawk Attack, 2, 115	Dixie Dynasty, 2, 115	10	1:45.50	33,780
1993	Star of Manila, 2, 121	S. J. Sellers	Milt's Overture, 2, 115	Camptown Dancer, 2, 115	10	1:43.34	30,695
1992	The Real Vaslav, 2, 115	S. J. Sellers	Randi's Pleasure, 2, 116	Eight for Slew, 2, 112	10	1:46.01	28,420
1991	Stress Buster, 2, 112	P. Day	Rail, 2, 115	In My Footsteps, 2, 115	5	1:44.84	28,665

Sponsored by Woodford Reserve Distillery of Versailles, Kentucky 2006-'07. Formerly named for nearby Bourbon County, Kentucky. Formerly named for the Hunt-Morgan house, Hopemont, located in Lexington. Hopemont S. 1991-2002. Bourbon County S. 2003-'05. All weather 2006. Colts and geldings 1994-'95. Two divisions 1998. Dead heat for second 1999. †Denotes female.

Woodford Reserve Manhattan Handicap

Grade 1 in 2008. Belmont Park, three-year-olds and up, 1¼ miles, turf. Held June 7, 2008, with a gross value of $400,000. First held in 1896. First graded in 1973. Stakes record 1:57.79 (1994 Paradise Creek).

Year	Winner	Jockey	Second	Third	Strs	Time	1st Purse
2008	Dancing Forever, 5, 118	R. R. Douglas	Out of Control (Brz), 5, 117	Pays to Dream, 4, 116	12	1:59.62	$240,000
2007	Better Talk Now, 8, 120	R. A. Dominguez	English Channel, 5, 122	Shakis (Ire), 7, 116	8	2:02.39	240,000
2006	Cacique (Ire), 5, 120	E. S. Prado	Relaxed Gesture (Ire), 5, 119	Grey Swallow (Ire), 5, 122	7	2:04.10	240,000
2005	Good Reward, 4, 117	J. D. Bailey	Relaxed Gesture (Ire), 4, 116	Artie Schiller, 4, 122	11	2:00.69	240,000
2004	Meteor Storm (GB), 5, 118	J. Valdivia Jr.	Millennium Dragon (GB), 5, 116	Mr O'Brien (Ire), 5, 116	9	1:59.34	240,000
2003	Denon, 5, 122	J. D. Bailey	Requete (GB), 4, 116	Dr. Brendler, 5, 116	10	2:14.16	240,000
2002	Beat Hollow (GB), 5, 118	A. O. Solis	Forbidden Apple, 7, 118	Strut the Stage, 4, 117	8	2:01.29	240,000
2001	Forbidden Apple, 6, 117	C. S. Nakatani	King Cugat, 4, 120	Tijiyr (Ire), 5, 115	9	2:00.77	240,000
2000	Manndar (Ire), 4, 117	C. S. Nakatani	Boatman, 4, 113	Spindrift (Ire), 5, 116	9	1:59.61	240,000
1999	Yagli, 6, 122	J. D. Bailey	Federal Trial, 4, 116	Middlesex Drive, 4, 116	10	1:58.48	180,000
1998	Chief Bearhart, 5, 122	J. A. Santos	Devonwood, 4, 113	Buck's Boy, 5, 117	9	1:58.25	150,000
1997	Ops Smile, 5, 116	R. G. Davis	Flag Down, 7, 118	Always a Classic, 4, 121	8	1:59.08	120,000
1996	Diplomatic Jet, 4, 117	J. F. Chavez	Flag Down, 6, 118	Kiri's Clown, 7, 121	12	2:00.14	120,000
1995	Awad, 5, 121	E. Maple	Blues Traveller (Ire), 5, 119	Kiri's Clown, 6, 115	12	1:58.57	120,000
1994	Paradise Creek, 5, 124	P. Day	Solar Splendor, 7, 112	River Majesty, 5, 113	7	**1:57.79**	275,000
1993	Star of Cozzene, 5, 118	J. A. Santos	Lure, 4, 127	Solar Splendor, 6, 112	8	1:58.99	190,000
1992	Sky Classic, 5, 123	P. Day	Roman Envoy, 4, 111	Leger Cat (Arg), 6, 116	11	2:02.42	252,860
1991	Academy Award, 5, 117	A. Madrid Jr.	Three Coins Up, 3, 110	Tarsho (Ire), 5, 113	10	1:59.78	111,600
1990	Phantom Breeze (Ire), 4, 113	M. E. Smith	Green Barb, 5, 111	Milesius, 6, 116	8	2:02.60	52,110
1989	Milesius, 5, 115	R. Migliore	Salem Drive, 7, 115	My Big Boy, 6, 114	8	2:00.00	73,440
1988	Milesius, 4, 112	C. W. Antley	My Big Boy, 5, 114	Maceo, 4, 115	5	2:04.40	71,760
1987	Silver Voice, 4, 109	J. M. Pezua	Talakeno, 7, 118	Duluth, 5, 113	9	2:01.40	86,220
1986	Danger's Hour, 4, 117	J. D. Bailey	Premier Mister (Mor), 6, 111	Exclusive Partner, 4, 115	8	2:02.60	87,300
1985	Cool, 4, 117	J. Vasquez	Win, 5, 126	Sondrio (Ire), 4, 110	13	2:02.00	77,280
1984	Win, 4, 114	A. Graell	Fortnightly, 4, 112	Norwick, 5, 110	12	2:00.60	77,520
1983	Acaroid, 5, 114	A. T. Cordero Jr.	Craelius, 4, 120	Half Iced, 4, 119	12	2:00.00	72,240
1982	Sprink, 4, 113	J. J. Miranda	Naskra's Breeze, 5, 119	Native Courier, 7, 116	8	2:01.00	51,570

Racing — Graded Stakes   493

Year	Winner	Jockey	Second	Third	Strs	Time	1st Purse
1981	**Match the Hatch**, 5, 114	J. Samyn	†Mrs. Penny, 4, 117	Native Courier, 6, 115	8	2:03.00	$52,470
1980	**Morold (Fr)**, 5, 113	E. Maple	Match the Hatch, 4, 111	Foretake, 4, 113	13	2:00.20	53,910
1979	**Fluorescent Light**, 5, 121	J. Fell	Tiller, 5, 124	Native Courier, 4, 122	8	2:04.80	51,615
1978	**Fabulous Time**, 4, 112	A. T. Cordero Jr.	Bill Brill, 4, 109	Tiller, 4, 127	8	2:01.40	48,690
1977	**Gentle King**, 4, 111	S. Cauthen	Double Quill, 8, 105	Keep the Promise, 5, 112	6	2:28.40	32,220
	Gallivantor, 5, 112	S. Cauthen	Gallapiat, 4, 112	Togus, 4, 112	5	2:28.00	32,070
1976	**Caucasus**, 4, 120	F. Toro	Trumpeter Swan, 5, 113	*Kamaraan II, 5, 116	13	2:14.40	33,930
1975	**Salt Marsh**, 5, 115	E. Maple	Drollery, 5, 109	London Company, 5, 118	7	2:16.60	33,600
	***Snow Knight**, 4, 123	J. Velasquez	Shady Character, 4, 113	One On the Aisle, 3, 114	3	2:16.20	33,900
1974	**Golden Don**, 4, 119	J. Cruguet	Anono, 4, 112	R. Tom Can, 3, 114	10	2:19.80	35,970
1973	**London Company**, 3, 116	L. A. Pincay Jr.	Big Spruce, 4, 120 *	Triangular, 6, 110	13	2:15.60	36,120

Named for the borough of Manhattan, principal borough of New York City. Sponsored by Woodford Reserve Distillery of Versailles, Kentucky 2008. Formerly sponsored by Early Times Distillery Co. of Louisville 1991-'96. Grade 2 1973-'83, 1990-'93. Manhattan H. 1896-1990, 1997-2007. Early Times Manhattan H. 1991-'92. Early Times Manhattan S. 1993-'96. Held at Morris Park 1896-1904. Held at Aqueduct 1959, 1961, 1963-'67. Not held 1897, 1909-'13. 6 furlongs 1898-1908. 7 furlongs 1914-'15. 1 mile 1916-'32. 1¹/₂ miles 1933-'58, 1960, 1962-'64, 1968-'69, 1977. 1⁵/₈ miles 1959, 1965-'67. 1⁵/₁₆ miles 1961. 1³/₈ miles 1970-'76. Dirt 1896-1969, 1977, 1988. Two divisions 1975, '77. Course record 1994. †Denotes female.

Woodford Reserve Turf Classic Stakes

Grade 1 in 2008. Churchill Downs, three-year-olds and up, 1¹/₈ miles, turf. Held May 3, 2008, with a gross value of $548,300. First held in 1987. First graded in 1989. Stakes record 1:46.34 (1993 Lure).

Year	Winner	Jockey	Second	Third	Strs	Time	1st Purse
2008	**Einstein (Brz)**, 6, 124	R. Albarado	Out of Control (Brz), 5, 119	Artiste Royal (Ire), 7, 124	7	1:50.50	$333,149
2007	**Sky Conqueror**, 5, 119	J. Castellano	Brilliant, 4, 119	†Danzon, 4, 114	10	1:49.01	330,430
2006	**English Channel**, 4, 122	G. K. Gomez	Cacique (Ire), 5, 122	Milk It Mick (GB), 5, 126	10	1:47.15	267,937
2005	**America Alive**, 4, 117	R. Albarado	Meteor Storm (GB), 6, 119	Quest Star, 6, 115	10	1:47.34	291,648
2004	**Stroll**, 4, 121	J. D. Bailey	Sweet Return (GB), 4, 123	Mystery Giver, 6, 123	11	1:53.00	281,418
2003	**Honor in War**, 4, 116	D. R. Flores	Requete (GB), 4, 123	Patrol, 4, 114	8	1:46.67	276,086
2002	**Beat Hollow (GB)**, 5, 115	A. O. Solis	With Anticipation, 7, 123	Hap, 6, 123	10	1:47.35	280,550
2001	**White Heart (GB)**, 6, 116	G. L. Stevens	King Cugat, 4, 120	Brahms, 4, 123	8	1:48.75	216,938
2000	**Manndar (Ire)**, 4, 114	C. S. Nakatani	Falcon Flight (Fr), 4, 118	Yagli, 7, 120	8	1:47.91	217,310
1999	**Wild Event**, 6, 120	S. J. Sellers	Garbu, 5, 116	Hawksley Hill (Ire), 6, 120	7	1:47.25	206,646
1998	**Joyeux Danseur**, 5, 123	R. Albarado	Lasting Approval, 4, 120	Hawksley Hill (Ire), 5, 120	8	1:48.14	174,282
1997	**Always a Classic**, 4, 120	J. D. Bailey	Labeeb (GB), 5, 118	Down the Aisle, 4, 114	8	1:49.29	145,328
1996	**Mecke**, 4, 123	P. Day	Petit Poucet (GB), 4, 116	Winged Victory, 6, 116	11	1:49.48	165,230
1995	**Romarin (Brz)**, 6, 118	C. S. Nakatani	Blues Traveller (Ire), 5, 120	Hasten To Add, 5, 120	12	1:46.86	160,095
1994	**Paradise Creek**, 5, 118	P. Day	Lure, 5, 123	Yukon Robbery, 5, 116	7	1:48.34	152,068
1993	**Lure**, 4, 123	M. E. Smith	Star of Cozzene, 5, 118	Cleone, 4, 116	8	**1:46.34**	117,683
1992	**Cudas**, 4, 117	P. A. Valenzuela	Sky Classic, 5, 123	Fourstars Allstar, 4, 118	12	1:46.56	124,703
1991	**Opening Verse**, 5, 116	C. J. McCarron	Itsallgreektome, 4, 123	Pedro the Cool, 5, 112	11	1:47.22	125,060
1990	**Ten Keys**, 6, 120	K. Desormeaux	Yankee Affair, 8, 120	Stellar Rival, 7, 113	5	1:50.80	110,435
1989	**Equalize**, 7, 118	J. A. Santos	Yankee Affair, 7, 116	Gallant Mel, 4, 114	8	1:51.40	114,140
1988	**Yankee Affair**, 6, 118	P. Day	Yucca, 4, 112	First Patriot, 4, 112	10	1:50.00	121,225
1987	**Manila**, 4, 120	J. Vasquez	Vilzak, 4, 112	Lieutenant's Lark, 5, 120	4	1:48.80	110,045

Sponsored by Woodford Reserve Distillery of Versailles, Kentucky 2000-'07. Sponsored by Early Times Distillery of Louisville 1987-'99. Grade 3 1989-'93. Grade 2 1994-'95. Early Times Turf Classic S. 1987-'99. Four-year-olds and up 1987-'91. Course record 1992, '93. †Denotes female.

Wood Memorial Stakes

Grade 1 in 2008. Aqueduct, three-year-olds, 1¹/₈ miles, dirt. Held April 5, 2008, with a gross value of $750,000. First held in 1925. First graded in 1973. Stakes record 1:47.16 (2005 Bellamy Road).

Year	Winner	Jockey	Second	Third	Strs	Time	1st Purse
2008	**Tale of Ekati**, 3, 123	E. S. Prado	War Pass, 3, 123	Court Vision, 3, 123	9	1:52.35	$450,000
2007	**Nobiz Like Shobiz**, 3, 123	C. H. Velasquez	Sightseeing, 3, 123	Any Given Saturday, 3, 123	6	1:49.46	450,000
2006	**Bob and John**, 3, 123	G. K. Gomez	Jazil, 3, 123	Keyed Entry, 3, 123	9	1:51.54	450,000
2005	**Bellamy Road**, 3, 123	J. Castellano	Survivalist, 3, 123	Scrappy T, 3, 123	7	**1:47.16**	450,000
2004	**Tapit**, 3, 123	R. A. Dominguez	Master David, 3, 123	Eddington, 3, 123	11	1:49.70	450,000
2003	**Empire Maker**, 3, 123	J. D. Bailey	Funny Cide, 3, 123	Kissin Saint, 3, 123	8	1:48.70	450,000
2002	**Buddha**, 3, 123	P. Day	Medaglia d'Oro, 3, 123	Sunday Break (Jpn), 3, 123	8	1:48.61	450,000
2001	**Congaree**, 3, 123	V. Espinoza	Monarchos, 3, 123	Richly Blended, 3, 123	6	1:47.96	450,000
2000	**Fusaichi Pegasus**, 3, 123	K. Desormeaux	Red Bullet, 3, 123	Aptitude, 3, 123	12	1:47.92	450,000
1999	**Adonis**, 3, 123	J. F. Chavez	Best of Luck, 3, 123	Cliquot, 3, 123	11	1:47.71	360,000
1998	**Coronado's Quest**, 3, 123	R. G. Davis	Dice Dancer, 3, 123	Parade Ground, 3, 123	11	1:47.47	300,000
1997	**Captain Bodgit**, 3, 123	A. O. Solis	Accelerator, 3, 123	Smokin Mel, 3, 123	10	1:48.39	300,000
1996	**Unbridled's Song**, 3, 123	M. E. Smith	In Contention, 3, 123	Romano Gucci, 3, 123	6	1:49.80	300,000
1995	**Talkin Man**, 3, 123	S. J. Sellers	‡Is Sveikatas, 3, 123	Candy Cone, 3, 123	8	1:49.24	300,000
1994	**Irgun**, 3, 123	G. L. Stevens	Go for Gin, 3, 123	Shiprock, 3, 123	9	1:49.07	300,000
1993	**Koluctoo Jimmy Al**, 3, 116	P. Day	Too Wild, 3, 113	Bounding Daisy, 3, 116	8	1:48.91	49,140
	Storm Tower, 3, 126	R. Wilson	Tossofthecoin, 3, 126	Marked Tree, 3, 126	7	1:48.40	300,000
1992	**Devil His Due**, 3, 126	M. E. Smith	West by West, 3, 126	Rokeby (GB), 3, 126	12	1:49.32	300,000
	Al Sabin, 3, 117	K. Desormeaux	Justfortherecord, 3, 117	Jay Gee, 3, 117	8	1:49.24	49,086

Year	Winner	Jockey	Second	Third	Strs	Time	1st Purse
1991	Cahill Road, 3, 126	C. Perret	Lost Mountain, 3, 126	Happy Jazz Band, 3, 126	10	1:48.44	$300,000
1990	Thirty Six Red, 3, 126	M. E. Smith	Burnt Hills, 3, 126	Champagneforashley, 3, 126	10	1:50.40	362,400
1989	Easy Goer, 3, 126	P. Day	Rock Point, 3, 126	Triple Buck, 3, 126	6	1:50.60	340,800
1988	Private Terms, 3, 126	C. W. Antley	Seeking the Gold, 3, 126	Cherokee Colony, 3, 126	10	1:47.20	359,400
1987	Gulch, 3, 126	J. A. Santos	Gone West, 3, 126	Shawklit Won, 3, 126	8	1:49.00	354,300
1986	Broad Brush, 3, 126	V. A. Bracciale Jr.	Mogambo, 3, 126	Groovy, 3, 126	7	1:50.60	178,500
1985	Eternal Prince, 3, 126	R. Migliore	Proud Truth, 3, 126	Rhoman Rule, 3, 126	6	1:48.80	204,900
1984	Leroy S., 3, 126	J. Cruguet	Raja's Shark, 3, 126	Bear Hunt, 3, 126	7	1:51.40	207,000
1983	Bounding Basque, 3, 126	G. McCarron	Country Pine, 3, 126	Aztec Red, 3, 126	8	1:51.40	100,980
	Slew o' Gold, 3, 126	E. Maple	Parfaitement, 3, 126	High Honors, 3, 126	7	1:51.00	101,700
1982	Air Forbes Won, 3, 126	A. T. Cordero Jr.	Shimatoree, 3, 126	Laser Light, 3, 126	10	1:51.00	105,120
1981	Pleasant Colony, 3, 126	J. Fell	Highland Blade, 3, 126	Cure the Blues, 3, 126	6	1:49.60	98,280
1980	Plugged Nickle, 3, 126	B. Thornburg	Colonel Moran, 3, 126	†Genuine Risk, 3, 121	11	1:50.80	87,300
1979	Instrument Landing, 3, 126	A. T. Cordero Jr.	Screen King, 3, 126	Czaravich, 3, 126	10	1:49.20	85,650
1978	Believe It, 3, 126	E. Maple	Darby Creek Road, 3, 126	Track Reward, 3, 126	11	1:49.80	65,940
1977	Seattle Slew, 3, 126	J. Cruguet	Sanhedrin, 3, 126	Catalan, 3, 126	7	1:49.60	66,180
1976	Bold Forbes, 3, 126	A. T. Cordero Jr.	On the Sly, 3, 126	Sonkisser, 3, 126	7	1:47.40	67,560
1975	Foolish Pleasure, 3, 126	J. Vasquez	Bombay Duck, 3, 126	Media, 3, 126	15	1:48.80	72,840
1974	Flip Sal, 3, 126	A. T. Cordero Jr.	Triple Crown, 3, 126	Sharp Gary, 3, 126	11	1:51.40	69,360
	Rube the Great, 3, 126	M. A. Rivera	Friendly Bee, 3, 126	Hudson County, 3, 126	11	1:49.60	69,660
1973	Angle Light, 3, 126	J. Vasquez	Sham, 3, 126	Secretariat, 3, 126	8	1:49.80	68,940

Named for Eugene D. Wood (d. 1924), one of the founders of Jamaica racetrack. Grade 2 1995-2001. Wood S. 1925-'26. Wood Memorial Invitational S. 1984-'93. Held at Jamaica 1925-'59. 1 mile 70 yards 1925-'39. 1 1/16 miles 1940-'51. Two divisions 1974, 1983, 1992-'93. ‡Knockadoon finished second, DQ to eighth, 1995. †Denotes female.

Woodward Stakes

Grade 1 in 2008. Saratoga Race Course, three-year-olds and up, 1 1/8 miles, dirt. Held September 1, 2007, with a gross value of $500,000. First held in 1954. First graded in 1973. Stakes record 1:45.80 (1976 Forego; 1990 Dispersal).

Year	Winner	Jockey	Second	Third	Strs	Time	1st Purse
2007	Lawyer Ron, 4, 126	J. R. Velazquez	Sun King, 5, 126	Diamond Stripes, 4, 126	8	1:48.60	$300,000
2006	Premium Tap, 4, 126	K. Desormeaux	Second of June, 5, 126	Sun King, 4, 126	10	1:50.65	300,000
2005	Saint Liam, 5, 126	J. D. Bailey	Sir Shackleton, 4, 126	Commentator, 4, 126	5	1:49.07	300,000
2004	Ghostzapper, 4, 126	J. Castellano	Saint Liam, 4, 126	Bowman's Band, 6, 126	7	1:46.38	300,000
2003	Mineshaft, 4, 126	R. Albarado	Hold That Tiger, 3, 122	Puzzlement, 4, 126	5	1:46.21	300,000
2002	Lido Palace (Chi), 5, 126	J. F. Chavez	Gander, 6, 126	Express Tour, 4, 126	6	1:47.75	300,000
2001	Lido Palace (Chi), 4, 126	J. D. Bailey	Albert the Great, 4, 126	Tiznow, 4, 126	5	1:47.42	300,000
2000	Lemon Drop Kid, 4, 126	E. S. Prado	Behrens, 6, 126	Gander, 4, 126	5	1:50.53	300,000
1999	River Keen (Ire), 7, 126	C. W. Antley	Almutawakel (GB), 4, 126	Stephen Got Even, 3, 121	7	1:46.85	300,000
1998	Skip Away, 4, 126	J. D. Bailey	Gentlemen (Arg), 6, 126	Running Stag, 4, 126	5	1:47.80	300,000
1997	Formal Gold, 4, 126	K. Desormeaux	Skip Away, 4, 126	Will's Way, 4, 126	5	1:47.51	300,000
1996	Cigar, 6, 126	J. D. Bailey	L'Carriere, 5, 126	Golden Larch, 5, 126	7	1:47.06	300,000
1995	Cigar, 5, 126	J. D. Bailey	Star Standard, 3, 121	Golden Larch, 4, 126	6	1:47.07	300,000
1994	Holy Bull, 3, 121	M. E. Smith	Devil His Due, 5, 126	Colonial Affair, 4, 126	8	1:46.89	300,000
1993	Bertrando, 4, 126	G. L. Stevens	Devil His Due, 4, 126	Valley Crossing, 5, 126	6	1:47.00	525,000
1992	Sultry Song, 4, 126	J. D. Bailey	Pleasant Tap, 5, 126	Out of Place, 5, 126	4	1:47.05	300,000
1991	In Excess (Ire), 4, 126	G. L. Stevens	Farma Way, 4, 126	Festin (Arg), 5, 126	6	1:46.33	300,000
1990	Dispersal, 4, 123	C. W. Antley	Quiet Ameriican, 4, 117	Rhythm, 3, 120	8	**1:45.80**	354,000
1989	Easy Goer, 3, 122	P. Day	Its Acedemic, 5, 109	Forever Silver, 4, 119	5	2:01.00	485,400
1988	Alysheba, 4, 126	C. J. McCarron	Forty Niner, 3, 126	Waquoit, 5, 122	8	1:59.40	498,600
1987	Polish Navy, 3, 116	R. P. Romero	Gulch, 3, 118	Creme Fraiche, 5, 119	9	1:47.00	357,000
1986	Precisionist, 5, 126	C. J. McCarron	†Lady's Secret, 4, 121	Personal Flag, 3, 110	5	1:46.00	199,200
1985	Track Barron, 4, 123	A. T. Cordero Jr.	Vanlandingham, 4, 126	Chief's Crown, 3, 121	6	1:46.60	200,400
1984	Slew o' Gold, 4, 126	A. T. Cordero Jr.	Shifty Sheik, 5, 116	Bet Big, 4, 116	6	1:47.80	175,200
1983	Slew o' Gold, 3, 118	A. T. Cordero Jr.	Bates Motel, 4, 123	Sing Sing, 5, 119	10	1:46.60	138,900
1982	Island Whirl, 4, 123	A. T. Cordero Jr.	Silver Buck, 4, 126	Silver Supreme, 4, 126	7	1:46.80	136,500
1981	Pleasant Colony, 3, 123	A. T. Cordero Jr.	Amber Pass, 4, 126	Herb Water, 4, 116	9	1:47.20	137,400
1980	Spectacular Bid, 4, 126	W. Shoemaker			1	2:02.40	73,300
1979	Affirmed, 4, 126	L. A. Pincay Jr.	Coastal, 3, 120	Czaravich, 3, 120	5	2:01.60	114,600
1978	Seattle Slew, 4, 126	A. T. Cordero Jr.	Exceller, 5, 126	It's Freezing, 6, 126	3	2:00.00	97,800
1977	Forego, 7, 133	W. Shoemaker	Silver Series, 3, 114	Great Contractor, 4, 115	10	1:48.00	105,000
1976	Forego, 6, 135	W. Shoemaker	Dance Spell, 3, 115	dh-Honest Pleasure, 3, 121 dh-Stumping, 6, 109	10	**1:45.80**	103,920
1975	Forego, 5, 126	H. Gustines	Wajima, 3, 119	Group Plan, 5, 126	6	2:27.20	64,920
1974	Forego, 4, 126	H. Gustines	Arbees Boy, 4, 126	Group Plan, 4, 126	10	2:27.40	69,240
1973	Prove Out, 4, 126	J. Velasquez	Secretariat, 3, 119	*Cougar II, 7, 126	5	2:25.80	64,920

Named for William Woodward (1876-1953), chairman of the Jockey Club from 1930-'50; Woodward also owned Belair Stud. Woodward H. 1955, 1976-'77, 1988-'90. Held at Belmont 1954-'58, 1961, 1968-2005. Held at Aqueduct 1959-'60, 1962-'67. 1 mile 1954. 1 1/4 miles 1956-'71, 1978-'80, 1988-'89. 1 1/2 miles 1972-'75. Dead heat for third 1976. †Denotes female. Won in a walkover 1980.

Woody Stephens Stakes

Grade 2 in 2008. Belmont Park, three-year-olds, 7 furlongs, dirt. Held June 7, 2008, with a gross value of $250,000. First held in 1985. First graded in 1988. Stakes record 1:20.33 (1994 You and I).

Year	Winner	Jockey	Second	Third	Strs	Time	1st Purse
2008	J Be K, 3, 123	G. K. Gomez	Silver Edition, 3, 119	True Quality, 3, 117	9	1:21.85	$150,000
2007	Teuflesberg, 3, 123	R. Albarado	Most Distinguished, 3, 115	Stormello, 3, 121	8	1:21.49	150,000
2006	Songster, 3, 123	E. S. Prado	Too Much Bling, 3, 123	Noonmark, 3, 115	7	1:21.45	150,000
2005	Lost in the Fog, 3, 123	E. S. Prado	Egg Head, 3, 119	Middle Earth, 3, 116	8	1:21.54	90,000
2004	Fire Slam, 3, 123	P. Day	Teton Forest, 3, 115	Abbondanza, 3, 123	7	1:20.94	120,000
2003	Posse, 3, 123	C. J. Lanerie	Midas Eyes, 3, 123	Halo Homewrecker, 3, 123	8	1:22.03	120,000
2002	Gygistar, 3, 119	P. Day	Draw Play, 3, 115	True Direction, 3, 119	9	1:22.61	120,000
2001	Put It Back, 3, 120	N. A. Wynter	Flame Thrower, 3, 120	Touch Tone, 3, 123	6	1:21.76	90,000
2000	Trippi, 3, 123	J. D. Bailey	Bevo, 3, 120	Sun Cat, 3, 116	6	1:23.68	90,000
1999	Yes It's True, 3, 123	J. D. Bailey	Lion Hearted, 3, 114	Silver Season, 3, 113	8	1:22.35	90,000
1998	Coronado's Quest, 3, 123	M. E. Smith	Mellow Roll, 3, 113	Flashing Tammany, 3, 120	7	1:22.50	82,050
1997	Smoke Glacken, 3, 123	C. Perret	Trafalger, 3, 123	Wild Wonder, 3, 120	6	1:20.98	66,060
1996	Gold Fever, 3, 118	M. E. Smith	Gameel, 3, 114	Bright Launch, 3, 120	9	1:23.30	67,620
1995	Western Larla, 3, 119	G. L. Stevens	Mr. Greeley, 3, 122	Blu Tusmani, 3, 122	8	1:24.24	66,960
1994	You and I, 3, 122	C. J. McCarron	End Sweep, 3, 114	Slew Gin Fizz, 3, 122	9	**1:20.33**	67,080
1993	Montbrook, 3, 117	C. J. Ladner III	As Indicated, 3, 122	Forever Whirl, 3, 122	10	1:23.34	74,160
1992	Superstrike (GB), 3, 115	J. A. Santos	Three Peat, 3, 122	Windundermywings, 3, 115	7	1:22.41	70,560
1991	Fly So Free, 3, 122	J. D. Bailey	Formal Dinner, 3, 122	Dodge, 3, 122	11	1:23.13	74,040
1990	Adjudicating, 3, 122	J. Vasquez	Silent Generation, 3, 115	Bayou Blurr, 3, 115	7	1:23.80	68,040
1989	Is It True, 3, 122	C. W. Antley	Mr. Nickerson, 3, 115	Fierce Fighter, 3, 115	8	1:22.20	70,200
1988	Evening Kris, 3, 117	L. A. Pincay Jr.	Perfect Spy, 3, 122	King's Nest, 3, 115	7	1:22.80	69,120
1987	Jazzing Around, 3, 115	J. A. Santos	dh-High Brite, 3, 119 dh-Polish Navy, 3, 122		7	1:22.40	48,240
1986	Ogygian, 3, 122	W. A. Guerra	Wayar, 3, 115	Landing Plot, 3, 122	5	1:23.40	48,900
1985	Ziggy's Boy, 3, 115	A. T. Cordero Jr.	Tiffany Ice, 3, 122	Huddle Up, 3, 115	6	1:22.20	48,960

Named for Racing Hall of Fame trainer Woodford C. Stephens (1913-'98); Stephens-trained horses won the Belmont S. (G1) five consecutive years (1982-'86). Formerly named for Meadow Stable's 1971 champion two-year-old male, '73 champion older male, and '72 Belmont S. winner Riva Ridge (1969 c. by First Landing). Grade 3 1988-'97. Riva Ridge S. 1985-2002. Riva Ridge Breeders' Cup S. 2003-'05. Woody Stephens Breeders' Cup S. 2006. Dead heat for second 1987. Track record 1994.

Yellow Ribbon Stakes

Grade 1 in 2008. Oak Tree at Santa Anita, three-year-olds and up, fillies and mares, 1 1/4 miles, turf. Held September 29, 2007, with a gross value of $400,000. First held in 1977. First graded in 1979. Stakes record 1:57.60 (1989 Brown Bess).

Year	Winner	Jockey	Second	Third	Strs	Time	1st Purse
2007	Nashoba's Key, 4, 123	J. Talamo	Citronnade, 4, 123	Black Mamba (NZ), 4, 123	6	1:59.73	$240,000
2006	Wait a While, 3, 120	G. K. Gomez	Dancing Edie, 4, 123	Three Degrees (Ire), 4, 123	8	1:59.52	240,000
2005	Megahertz (GB), 6, 123	A. O. Solis	Flip Flop (Fr), 4, 123	Halo Ola (Arg), 5, 123	7	2:00.50	300,000
2004	Light Jig (GB), 4, 123	R. R. Douglas	Tangle (Ire), 4, 123	Katdogawn (GB), 4, 123	10	1:59.28	300,000
2003	Tates Creek, 5, 123	P. A. Valenzuela	Musical Chimes, 4, 118	Crazy Ensign (Arg), 7, 123	8	2:00.77	300,000
2002	Golden Apples (Ire), 4, 123	P. A. Valenzuela	Voodoo Dancer, 4, 123	Banks Hill (GB), 4, 123	6	1:59.52	300,000
2001	Janet (GB), 4, 123	D. R. Flores	Tranquility Lake, 6, 123	Al Desima (GB), 4, 123	8	1:58.64	300,000
2000	Tranquility Lake, 5, 123	E. Delahoussaye	Spanish Fern, 5, 123	Polaire (Ire), 4, 123	6	2:02.98	300,000
1999	Spanish Fern, 4, 123	C. J. McCarron	Caffe Latte (Ire), 3, 118	Shabby Chic, 3, 118	7	1:59.52	300,000
1998	Fiji (GB), 4, 123	K. Desormeaux	‡Sonja's Faith (Ire), 4, 122	Pomona (GB), 5, 122	10	2:05.23	300,000
1997	Ryafan, 3, 118	A. O. Solis	Fanjica (Ire), 5, 122	Memories of Silver, 4, 122	8	2:03.89	300,000
1996	Donna Viola (GB), 4, 122	G. L. Stevens	Real Connection, 5, 122	Dixie Pearl, 4, 122	8	2:00.62	360,000
1995	Alpride (Ire), 4, 122	C. J. McCarron	Angel in My Heart (Fr), 3, 118	Bold Ruritana, 5, 122	12	2:01.65	360,000
1994	Aube Indienne (Fr), 4, 122	K. Desormeaux	Fondly Remembered, 4, 122	Zoonaqua, 4, 122	11	2:02.32	240,000
1993	Possibly Perfect, 3, 118	C. S. Nakatani	Tribulation, 3, 118	Miatuschka, 5, 122	13	2:02.91	240,000
1992	Super Staff, 4, 123	K. Desormeaux	Flawlessly, 4, 123	Campagnarde (Arg), 5, 123	9	1:59.36	240,000
1991	Kostroma (Ire), 5, 123	K. Desormeaux	Flawlessly, 3, 119	Fire the Groom, 4, 123	13	2:01.01	240,000
1990	Plenty of Grace, 3, 119	W. H. McCauley	Petite Ile (Fr), 4, 122	Royal Touch (Ire), 5, 123	13	1:58.40	240,000
1989	Brown Bess, 7, 123	J. L. Kaenel	Darby's Daughter, 4, 119	Colorado Dancer (Ire), 3, 119	11	**1:57.60**	240,000
1988	Delighter, 3, 119	C. J. McCarron	Nastique, 4, 123	No Review, 3, 119	12	2:02.40	240,000
1987	Carotene, 4, 123	J. A. Santos	Nashmeel, 3, 119	Khariyda (Fr), 3, 119	12	2:03.80	240,000
1986	Bonne Ile (GB), 5, 123	F. Toro	Top Corsage, 3, 118	Carotene, 3, 118	12	2:01.40	240,000
1985	Estrapade, 5, 123	W. Shoemaker	Alydar's Best, 3, 118	La Koumia (Fr), 3, 118	11	2:00.40	240,000
1984	Sabin, 4, 123	E. Maple	Grise Mine (Fr), 3, 118	Estrapade, 4, 123	8	2:00.00	240,000
1983	Sangue (Ire), 5, 123	W. Shoemaker	L'Attrayante (Fr), 3, 119	Infinite, 3, 119	12	2:02.20	240,000
1982	‡Castilla, 3, 117	R. Sibille	Avigaition, 3, 119	Sangue (Ire), 4, 123	12	1:58.60	180,000
1981	Queen to Conquer, 5, 123	M. Castaneda	Star Pastures (GB), 3, 119	Ack's Secret, 5, 123	10	1:58.60	180,000
1980	Kilijaro (Ire), 4, 123	A. Lequeux	Ack's Secret, 4, 123	Queen to Conquer, 4, 123	10	1:59.20	120,000
1979	Country Queen, 4, 123	L. A. Pincay Jr.	Prize Spot, 3, 119	Giggling Girl, 5, 123	10	2:00.20	90,000
1978	Amazer, 3, 119	W. Shoemaker	Drama Critic, 4, 123	Surera (Arg), 5, 123	9	1:59.20	90,000
1977	*Star Ball, 5, 123	H. Grant	Swingtime, 5, 123	Theia (Fr), 4, 123	11	2:02.60	60,000

Named for the song "Tie a Yellow Ribbon," which refers to tying a ribbon around the "old oak tree." The Yellow Ribbon is run at the Oak Tree Racing Association meet. Yellow Ribbon Invitational S. 1979-'87, 1989-'94. ‡Avigaition finished first, DQ to second, 1982. ‡See You Soon (Fr) finished second, DQ to fourth, 1998.

Previously Graded Stakes

Race	Last Grade	Track	Year Last Graded	Race	Last Grade	Track	Year Last Graded
Affectionately H.	3	Aqueduct	2004	Donald P. Ross H.	3	Delaware Park	1981
Aksarben Oaks	3	Aksarben	1997	Dover S.	3	Delaware Park	1974
Alabama Derby	3	Lousiana Downs	1997	Dragoon S.	3	Liberty Bell	1974
Alibhai H.	3	Santa Anita Park	1985	El Camino Real S.	3	Bay Meadows	1984
Allegheny S.	3	Keystone	1977	El Dorado H.	3	Hollywood Park	1981
Anne Arundel S.	3	Pimlico	2004	Endurance S.	3	Meadowlands	1995
Anoakia S.	3	Santa Anita Park	1987	Essex H.	3	Oaklawn Park	2007
Aqueduct H.	3	Aqueduct	2007	Everglades S.	3	Hialeah	2001
Ark-La-Tex H.	3	Louisiana Downs	1999	Fair Grounds Classic	3	Fair Grounds	1987
Arlington Classic S.	3	Arlington Park	2007	Fairmount Derby	3	Fairmount Park	1995
Ascot H.	3	Bay Meadows	2002	Fall Highweight H.	3	Aqueduct	2004
Assault H.	3	Aqueduct	1997	Fashion S.	3	Belmont Park	1974
Astarita S.	3	Belmont Park	2005	Fastness H.	3	Hollywood Park	2001
Astoria Breeders' Cup S.	3	Belmont Park	1994	Federico Tesio S.	3	Pimlico	1997
Bahamas S.	3	Hialeah	1974	Fifth Season S.	3	Oaklawn Park	2006
Baltimore Breeders' Cup H.	3	Pimlico	2003	Finger Lakes Breeders' Cup S.	3	Finger Lakes	1999
Bay Meadows Breeders' Cup H.	3	Bay Meadows	2007	Flamingo S.	3	Hialeah	2001
Bay Meadows Derby	3	Bay Meadows	2006	Flash S.	3	Belmont	2005
Bay Meadows Oaks	3	Bay Meadows	1998	Flintlock S.	3	Keystone	1974
Bayou Breeders' Cup H.	3	Fair Grounds	2007	Flirtation S.	3	Pimlico	1974
Bel Air H.	3	Hollywood Park	2001	Floral Park H.	3	Belmont	2006
Belmont Breeders' Cup H.	2	Belmont Park	2005	Florida Turf Cup H.	3	Calder Race Course	1989
Benjamin Franklin H.	3	Garden State	1974	Forerunner S.	3	Keeneland	1998
Best Turn S.	3	Aqueduct	1996	Forest Hills H.	2	Belmont Park	2002
Betsy Ross H.	3	Garden State	1995	Ft. Lauderdale H.	3	Gulfstream Park	2002
Black Helen H.	2	Hialeah	2001	Gallant Fox H.	3	Aqueduct	2002
Board of Governors' H.	3	Aksarben	1993	Garden State Breeders' Cup H.	3	Garden State	1995
Boardwalk S.	3	Atlantic City	1975	Garden State S.	3	Garden State	1994
Bold Reason H.	3	Saratoga	1988	Genuine Risk Breeders' Cup H.	2	Belmont Park	2006
Bougainvillea H.	3	Hialeah	2001	Golden Gate Derby	3	Golden Gate Fields	2004
Brandywine Turf H.	3	Delaware Park	1973	Golden Harvest H.	3	Louisiana Downs	1993
Brighton Beach H.	3	Belmont Park	1983	Golden Poppy H.	3	Golden Gate Fields	1994
Brown Bess H.	3	Golden Gate Fields	2004	Gold Rush Futurity	3	Arapahoe Park	1984
Bryn Mawr S.	3	Keystone	1975	Governor S.	1	Belmont Park	1975
Budweiser H.	3	Fairmount Park	1989	Governor's Cup H.	3	Bowie	1985
Busher S.	3	Aqueduct	1998	Governor's Cup H.	3	Arlington Park	1974
Caballero H.	3	Hollywood Park	1978	Great American S.	3	Aqueduct	1974
Cabrillo H.	3	Del Mar	1990	Grey Lag H.	3	Aqueduct	1999
California Derby	3	Golden Gate Fields	1999	Haggin S.	3	Hollywood Park	1974
California Jockey Club H.	3	Bay Meadows	1996	Hall of Fame Breeders' Cup H.	3	Thistledown	2000
California Juvenile S.	3	Bay Meadows	2000	Hawthorne Breeders' Cup H.	3	Hawthorne	1993
Camden H.	3	Garden State	1974	Hawthorne Juvenile S.	3	Hawthorne	1982
Canterbury Oaks	3	Canterbury	1989	Heirloom H.	3	Liberty Bell	1974
Carousel H.	3	Laurel Park	1992	Heritage S.	2	Keystone	1978
Chaposa Springs H.	3	Calder Race Course	2004	Hessian H.	3	Keystone	1974
Cherry Hill Mile S.	3	Garden State	1996	Hialeah Turf Cup H.	2	Hialeah	2001
Chesapeake H.	3	Bowie	1975	Hibiscus H.	3	Hialeah	1973
Choice H.	3	Monmouth	1995	Hillsborough H.	3	Bay Meadows	2000
Chrysanthemum H.	3	Laurel Park	1989	Hobson H.	2	Keystone	1977
Coaltown Breeders' Cup H.	3	Aqueduct	1995	Hollywood Express H.	3	Hollywood Park	1974
Colin S.	3	Belmont Park	1994	Honey Bee H.	3	Meadowlands	2001
Colleen S.	3	Monmouth	1974	Indian Maid H.	3	Hawthorne	1978
Colonial H.	3	Garden State	1976	Interborough H.	3	Aqueduct	2000
Columbiana H.	3	Hialeah	1989	Island Whirl H.	3	Louisiana Downs	1989
Correction H.	3	Aqueduct	1982	Jasmine S.	3	Hialeah	1974
Countess Fager H.	3	Golden Gate Fields	1994	Jersey Belle H.	3	Garden State	1977
Cowdin S.	3	Belmont Park	2002	Jersey Derby	3	Monmouth Park	2004
Cradle S.	3	River Downs	2004	John B. Campbell H.	3	Pimlico	1999
Cygnet S.	3	Hollywood Park	1974	John Henry H.	2	Hollywood Park	1994
Dade Turf Classic	3	Calder Race Course	1975	Junior League S.	3	Hollywood Park	1974
De La Rose H.	3	Gulfstream Park	2002	Junior Miss S.	3	Del Mar	1992
Delaware Valley H.	3	Garden State	1974	Juvenile S.	3	Aksarben	1988
Derby Trial S.	3	Churchill Downs	2004	Kelly-Olympic H.	3	Atlantic City	1979
Desert Stormer H.	3	Hollywood Park	2005	Keystone H.	3	Liberty Bell	1974
Display H.	3	Aqueduct	1989	Kindergarten S.	3	Liberty Bell	1974
Donald LeVine Memorial H.	3	Philadelphia Park	2004	Lafayette S.	3	Keeneland	2005

Racing — Previously Graded Stakes

Race	Last Grade	Track	Year Last Graded
Ladies H.	3	Aqueduct	2004
Lady Canterbury H.	3	Canterbury	1991
Lakeside H.	2	Hollywood Park	1980
Lamplighter H.	3	Monmouth Park	1998
Laurance Armour H.	3	Arlington Park	1996
Laurel Dash S.	3	Laurel Park	2000
Laurel Futurity	3	Laurel Park	2004
Laurel Turf Cup S.	3	Laurel Park	2000
Lazaro S. Barrera H.	3	Hollywood Park	1998
Letellier Memorial H.	3	Fair Grounds	1974
Lexington S.	3	Belmont Park	2006
Linda Vista H.	3	Santa Anita Park	1996
Little Silver H.	3	Monmouth Park	1988
Longacres Derby	3	Longacres	1988
Long Branch Breeders' Cup S.	3	Monmouth Park	2006
Longfellow H.	3	Monmouth Park	1997
Long Look Breeders' Cup H.	3	Meadowlands	1997
Louisiana Downs H.	3	Louisiana Downs	1996
Louis R. Rowan H.	3	Santa Anita Park	1998
Magnolia S.	3	Oaklawn Park	1974
Margate H.	3	Atlantic City	1978
Maria H.	3	Garden State	1996
Marlboro Cup Invitational H.	1	Belmont Park	1987
Marylander H.	3	Pimlico	1981
Massachusetts H.	2	Suffolk Downs	2004
Mermaid S.	3	Atlantic City	1975
Michigan Mile and One-Eighth H.	2	Detroit	1993
Militia S.	3	Keystone	1975
Mimosa S.	3	Hialeah	1973
Minnesota Derby S.	2	Canterbury	1991
Minuteman H.	3	Keystone	1978
Miss America H.	3	Golden Gate Fields	1996
Miss Woodford S.	3	Monmouth Park	1974
Monmouth Park Breeders' Cup H.	3	Monmouth Park	1992
Morven S.	3	Meadowlands	1987
Nassau County H.	1	Belmont Park	1993
New Hampshire Sweepstakes H.	3	Rockingham	2002
New Hope S.	3	Keystone	1975
New Jersey Turf Classic S.	3	Meadowlands	1993
Norristown H.	3	Philadelphia Park	1993
Oil Capitol H.	3	Hawthorne	1975
Oklahoma Derby	3	Remington Park	2004
Omaha Gold Cup S.	3	Aksarben	1994
Open Fire S.	3	Delaware Park	1978
Pageant S.	3	Atlantic City	1975
Pasadena S.	3	Santa Anita Park	1974
Paterson H.	3	Meadowlands	1995
Patriot S.	3	Keystone	1978
Paumonck H.	3	Aqueduct	1978
Pebbles H.	3	Belmont Park	2004
Pennsylvania Governor's Cup H.	3	Penn National	1989
Philadelphia H.	3	Monmouth Park	1974
Phoenix Gold Cup S.	3	Turf Paradise	1997
Pimlico Oaks	3	Pimlico	1991
Pimlico S.	3	Pimlico	1974
Poinsettia S.	3	Hialeah	1989
Polynesian H.	3	Pimlico	1994
Post-Deb S.	2	Monmouth Park	1993
President's Cup S.	3	Aksarben	1988
Princess S.	2	Hollywood Park	2001
Princeton S.	3	Garden State	1974
Quaker H.	3	Liberty Bell	1974
Queen Charlotte H.	3	Monmouth Park	1992
Queen's H.	3	Aksarben	1993
Rare Treat H.	3	Aqueduct	2002
Reeve Schley Jr. S.	3	Monmouth Park	2001
Regret H.	3	Monmouth Park	1974
Riggs H.	3	Pimlico	1992
River Cities Breeders' Cup S.	3	Lousiana Downs	1998
Roamer H.	3	Aqueduct	1983
Rolling Green H.	3	Golden Gate Fields	1994
Roseben H.	3	Belmont Park	1995
Rosemont S.	2	Delaware Park	1976
Round Table S.	3	Arlington Park	2001
Royal Palm H.	3	Hialeah	1999
Rutgers H.	3	Meadowlands	1996
Ruthless S.	3	Aqueduct	1982
San Jacinto S.	2	Santa Anita Park	1977
San Miguel S.	3	Santa Anita Park	2004
Santa Anita Breeders' Cup H.	3	Santa Anita Park	1995
Saratoga Breeders' Cup H.	2	Saratoga	2005
Saul Silberman H.	3	Calder	1979
Schuylkill S.	3	Liberty Bell	1974
Sea O Erin H.	3	Arlington Park	1994
Seashore H.	3	Atlantic City	1973
Select H.	3	Monmouth Park	1974
Selima S.	3	Laurel	1999
Seminole H.	2	Hialeah Park	19889
Seneca H.	3	Saratoga	1997
Sentinel S.	3	Liberty Bell	1974
Sheridan S.	3	Arlington Park	1996
Sierra Madre H.	3	Santa Anita Park	1990
Sierra Nevada H.	3	Santa Anita Park	1985
Signature S.	3	Keystone	1976
Snow Goose H.	3	Laurel	1996
Sorority S.	3	Monmouth Park	2003
Spicy Living H.	3	Rockingham	1994
Spotlight Breeders' Cup H.	3	Hollywood Park	1994
Stymie H.	3	Aqueduct	2002
Suffolk Downs Sprint H.	3	Suffolk Downs	1988
Sunny Slope S.	3	Santa Anita	1984
Sunrise H.	3	Atlantic City	1973
Super Bowl S.	3	Gulfstream Park	1997
Susquehanna H.	3	Keystone	1978
Sussex Turf H.	3	Delaware Park	1975
Sweetest Chant S.	3	Gulfstream Park	2000
Swift S.	3	Aqueduct	1989
Swoon's Son H.	3	Arlington Park	1996
Tanforan H.	3	Golden Gate Fields	2002
Thanksgiving Day H.	3	Bay Meadows	1979
Thomas D. Nash Memorial H.	3	Sportsman's Park	1993
Tidal H.	2	Belmont Park	1993
Tremont S.	3	Belmont Park	2003
Trenton H.	3	Garden State	1994
Tyro S.	3	Monmouth Park	1974
Valley Forge H.	3	Garden State	1974
Valley Stream S.	3	Aqueduct	2005
Ventnor H.	3	Monmouth Park	1975
Villager S.	3	Keystone	1977
Vineland H.	3	Garden State	1996
Virginia Belle S.	3	Bowie	1974
Washington, D.C., International S.	1	Laurel Park	1994
Week of Fame Fortune H.	3	Fair Grounds	1990
What a Pleasure S.	3	Calder	2000
Whitemarsh H.	3	Keystone	1977
Widener H.	3	Hialeah	2001
William du Pont Jr. H.	3	Delaware Park	1981
William P. Kyne H.	3	Bay Meadows	1999
Windy City H.	3	Sportsman's Park	1973
Woodlawn S.	3	Pimlico	1988
World's Playground S.	3	Atlantic City	1979
Yerba Buena Breeders' Cup H.	3	Golden Gate Fields	2006
Young America Breeders' Cup S.	3	Meadowlands	1995
Youthful S.	3	Belmont Park	1974

2007 North American Stakes Races

Achievement S. (R), Woodbine, June 30, $142,277, 3yo, Canadian-bred, 6fAW, 1:10.49, LEGAL MOVE, Dancer's Bajan, Red Raffles, 9 started.

ACK ACK H. (G3), Churchill Downs, Nov. 3, $221,600, 3&up, 1m, 1:34.08, ISTAN, Sun King, Ryan's for Real, 8 started.

ACK ACK H. (G3), Hollywood Park, June 9, $109,700, 3&up, 7½fAW, 1:28.51, EL ROBLAR, Siren Lure, Publication, 8 started.

A. C. Kemp H., The Downs at Albuquerque, Sept. 29, $45,000, 2yo, 7f, 1:23.14, YONEGWA, Rocket Included, Golem, 6 started.

ACORN S. (G1), Belmont Park, June 9, $250,000, 3yo, f, 1m, 1:34.70, COTTON BLOSSOM, Dream Rush, Christmas Kid, 6 started.

ACTRA Alberta-Bred S. (R), Grand Prairie, Aug. 18, $9,227, 2yo, Alberta-bred, 5½f, 1:08, DEVONAIRE JOE, Chatahoochie, Alameda Slim, 4 started.

ACTRA S. (1st Div.) (R), Grand Prairie, Aug. 4, $9,198, 3&up, Alberta-bred, 6f, 1:12.60, MOHAWK CHIEF, Stormy Gamble, Dr. Mo, 5 started.

ACTRA S. (2nd Div.) (R), Grand Prairie, Aug. 4, $9,198, 3&up, f&m, Alberta-bred, 6f, 1:13.80, PIXIE A GO GO, Lucky No Two, Wild County, 5 started.

Ada L. Rice Illinois Owners' S. (R), Arlington Park, Sept. 15, $100,000, 3&up, f&m, Illinois-owned, 1 1/16mT, 1:41.32, LOVE HANDLES, Jennie R., Honour Colony, 5 started.

Ada S., Remington Park, Oct. 20, $50,000, 3&up, f&m, 6f, 1:10.08, VALID LIL, Lunarlady, Youaremysweetheart, 9 started.

Adena Springs Matchmaker Turf Sprint S., Remington Park, Aug. 4, $50,000, 3&up, f&m, 5fT, :55.49, TEMPTING DATE, Annie Savoy, Amarula, 8 started.

ADENA STALLIONS' MISS PREAKNESS S. (G3), Pimlico Race Course, May 18, $125,000, 3yo, f, 6f, 1:10.53, TIME'S MISTRESS, Silver Knockers, Richwoman, 7 started.

ADIRONDACK S. (G2), Saratoga Race Course, Aug. 15, $150,000, 2yo, f, 6½f, 1:17.51, MORE HAPPY, A to the Croft, Passion, 9 started.

Adoration H. (R), Del Mar, Aug. 30, $104,820, 3&up, f&m, non-winners of a stakes worth $50,000 at one mile or over since February 1, 1mAW, 1:39.64, FUN LOGIC, Dona Amelia (Chi), Screen Giant, 7 started.

AEGON TURF SPRINT S. (G3), Churchill Downs, May 4, $169,050, 3&up, 5fT, :56.84, GAFF, Ellwood and Jake, Congo King, 8 started.

Affectionately H., Aqueduct, Jan. 13, $70,590, 3&up, f&m, 1 1/16m, 1:44.35, GREAT INTENTIONS, Homerette, Victory Pool, 6 started.

AFFIRMED H. (G3), Hollywood Park, June 17, $106,600, 3yo, 1 1/16mAW, 1:44.21, DESERT CODE, Albertus Maximus, Cobalt Blue, 5 started.

Affirmed S. (R), Calder Race Course, Sept. 1, $150,000, 2yo, progeny of eligible Florida stallions, 7f, 1:24.17, WISE ANSWER, Hey Byrn, Dynhocracy, 8 started.

Aflac U. S. Championship Supreme Hurdle S. (R), Pine Mountain, Calloway Garden, Nov. 3, $100,000, 4&up, non-winners over hurdles since June 1, 2006, a2¼mT, 3:58.80, PLANETS ALIGNED, Lead Us Not, Dr. Bloomer, 6 started.

African Prince S. (R), Suffolk Downs, July 4, $45,000, 3yo, Massachusetts-bred, 6f, 1:12.27, KIMRIDGE, Disco Fox, Senor St. Pat, 8 started.

Agassiz S. (R), Assiniboia Downs, Aug. 19, $42,404, 3&up, Manitoba-bred, 1m, 1:40, BRINELLO, Resurgent, Gus Again, 7 started.

A GLEAM INVITATIONAL H. (G2), Hollywood Park, July 6, $150,000, 3&up, f&m, 7fAW, 1:21.93, SOMETHINABOUTLAURA, Strong Faith, Theverythoughtof U, 10 started.

Ahwatukee Express S., Turf Paradise, Oct. 6, $45,000, 3yo, f, 6f, 1:09.80, FAMOUS GAL, Against the Law, Wine Tasting Room, 8 started.

A. J. Foyt S. (R), Indiana Downs, July 3, $45,000, 3&up, Indiana-bred and/or -sired, 1m70y, 1:42.43, LIEPERS FORK, Play Smart, Heza Wild Guy, 11 started.

ALABAMA S. (G1), Saratoga Race Course, Aug. 18, $600,000, 3yo, f, 1¼m, 2:03.62, LADY JOANNE, Lear's Princess, Octave, 7 started.

Alameda County H., Pleasanton, July 4, $50,930, 3&up, f&m, 1 1/16m, 1:42.66, SNOWDROP, Bai and Bai, Gentle Charmer, 6 started.

Alamedan H., Pleasanton, July 8, $49,270, 3&up, 1 1/16m, 1:42.63, BOLD CHIEFTAIN, Desert Boom, He's the Rage, 4 started.

Albany S. (R), Saratoga Race Course, Aug. 22, $150,000, 3yo, New York-bred, 1⅛m, 1:51.23, STUNT MAN, Dr. V's Magic, Chief's Lake, 7 started.

Alberta-Bred S. #1 (R), Lethbridge, Sept. 16, $15,720, 2yo, Alberta-bred, 5f, 1:01.40, HESADEMON, Alameda Slim, Princess Loretta, 8 started.

Alberta-Bred S. #2 (R), Lethbridge, Sept. 16, $15,720, 3&up, f&m, Alberta-bred, a5½f, 1:07.80, TROMPETA, She's Twenty Below, Real Sterling, 8 started.

Alberta-Bred S. #3 (R), Lethbridge, Sept. 16, $15,429, 3yo, f, Alberta-bred, a6f, 1:10.20, KIT FOX, Desperate Dancer, Queen City Kitty, 6 started.

Alberta-Bred S. #4 (R), Lethbridge, Sept. 16, $15,429, 3&up, Alberta-bred, a6f, 1:10.20, STORMY GAMBLE, Remarkable Weekend, Apollo Twelve, 6 started.

Alberta-Bred S. #5 (R), Lethbridge, Sept. 16, $15,575, 3yo, Alberta-bred, a6f, 1:08.40, COOL SYNSATION, Runaway Carbs, Pull the Trigger, 7 started.

Alberta-Bred S. #6 (R), Lethbridge, Sept. 16, $20,427, 3&up, Alberta-bred, 1 1/16m, 1:46.60, DR. MO, Mr. Alybro, Deputy Fudge, 7 started.

Alberta Breeders' H. (R), Northlands Park, Sept. 29, $75,413, 3&up, Alberta-bred, 1 1/16m, 1:44, ARTHURLOOKSGOOD, Candid Remark, Beau Brass, 7 started.

Alberta Derby, Stampede Park, June 16, $117,013, 3yo, 1 1/16m, 1:46.40, AMAZIN BLUE, Footprint, Ookashada, 10 started.

Alberta Oaks (R), Northlands Park, Sept. 29, $50,275, 3yo, f, Alberta-bred, 1m, 1:38.40, BEAR NOBILITY, Pat of Gold, Minimus, 7 started.

Alberta Premier's Futurity (R), Northlands Park, Sept. 29, $50,275, 2yo, Alberta-bred, 1m, 1:39.60, JIM'S CHOICE, Ballintoy, Mandarin, 10 started.

Alberta Sales S. (R), Lethbridge, Sept. 2, $14,204, 3yo, c&g, Alberta-bred, a6f, 1:10.40, RUNAWAY CARBS, Pull the Trigger, Sir Devon, 6 started.

Alberta Sales S. (R), Lethbridge, Sept. 2, $14,204, 3yo, f, Alberta-bred, a6f, 1:11.20, KIT FOX, Four Buck Freda, Jett Es, 7 started.

Alberta Two-Year-Old Sales S., Lethbridge, Sept. 30, $16,289, 2yo, 5f, 1:00, HESADEMON, Alameda Slim, Koloa Victor, 8 started.

Albert Dominguez Memorial H. (R), Sunland Park, Jan. 7, $100,000, 3&up, New Mexico-bred, 1 1/16m, 1:44.61, SOME GHOST, El Minuto, Romeos Wilson, 11 started.

Albuquerque Derby, The Downs at Albuquerque, Sept. 16, $50,000, 3yo, 1 1/16m, 1:44.15, CRYPTS SEEKER, Preferred Yield, Devil Red, 5 started.

Alcatraz S., Golden Gate Fields, May 19, $75,000, 3yo, 1 1/16mT, 1:44.01, MR EDDIE BOY, Boxelder, Zoning In, 8 started.

Alex M. Robb H. (R), Aqueduct, Dec. 30, $83,375, 3&up, New York-bred, 1 1/16m, 1:44.32, NAUGHTY NEWYORKER, Shuffling Maddnes, Run Red Run, 9 started.

ALFRED G. VANDERBILT H. (G2), Saratoga Race Course, July 28, $260,000, 3&up, 6f, 1:08.67, DIABOLICAL, Attila's Storm, Simon Pure, 8 started.

Algoma S. (R), Woodbine, Sept. 3, $118,363, 3&up, f&m, Canadian-bred, 1 1/16mAW, 1:45.75, ARDEN BELLE, Dance to My Tune, Blonde Wisdom, 5 started.

Alice Rickey Frost Memorial Classic S., Rillito Park, March 4, $9,310, 3&up, 7f, 1:27.50, TOMMY T., Shoot Out, Dark Regent, 8 started.

ALLAIRE DUPONT BREEDERS' CUP DISTAFF S. (G2), Pimlico Race Course, May 18, $134,000, 3&up, f&m, 1 1/16m, 1:42.88, ROLLING SEA, Leah's Secret, Kettleoneup, 7 started.

ALL ALONG BREEDERS' CUP S. (G3), Colonial Downs, June 16, $197,000, 3&up, f&m, 1⅛mT, 1:49.62, SILVER CHARADES, Humoristic, Bridge Game, 11 started.

ALL AMERICAN S. (G3), Golden Gate Fields, Nov. 17, $150,000, 3&up, 1⅛mAW, 1:50.04, MCCANN'S MOJAVE, Putmeinyourwill, Hello Sunday (Fr), 9 started.

All Brandy S. (R), Laurel Park, Nov. 17, $50,000, 3&up, f&m, Maryland-bred, 1⅛mT, 1:53.75, DATTTS AWESOME, Dutch Girl, Ten Bolts, 7 started.

Allen Bogan Memorial S. (R), Lone Star Park, July 7, $50,000, 3&up, f&m, Texas-bred, 1m, 1:38.27, SWEET IDEA, Stage Stop, Olmosta, 7 started.

Allen's Landing S., Sam Houston Race Park, Jan. 6, $29,250, 4&up, f&m, 1 1/16mT, 1:47.74, FAIRWELL MADRID, Night Speeker, I. B.'s Halo, 8 started.

All Sold Out S. (R), Fairmount Park, July 31, $45,700, 2yo, f, Illinois-bred and/or -foaled, 6f, 1:13, SARAHLINDS SISTER, Lune Rouge, Marikitten, 6 started.

Alma North S. (R), Timonium, Sept. 1, $45,000, 3&up, f&m, Maryland-bred, a6½f, 1:17.69, SOMETHINABOUTBETTY, Hanalei Bay, Long Time Gone, 7 started.

Alphabet Soup H. (R), Philadelphia Park, Oct. 6, $60,000, 3&up,

Pennsylvania-bred, 1 1/16mT, 1:42.74, DIRGE, Serene Harbor, Sonvida Red, 10 started.

A. L. (Red) Erwin S. (R), Louisiana Downs, Sept. 1, $53,750, 3yo, Louisiana-bred, a1mT, 1:38.09, WILDRALLY, Hallway, Quite Sultry, 10 started.

Al Swihart Memorial S., Fonner Park, May 5, $25,625, 3&up, f&m, 6½f, 1:20.80, SALTY ATTRACTION, Up 'n Blumin, G G's Dolly, 5 started.

Althear Rieland S., Grants Pass, June 30, $3,631, 3&up, 6½f, 1:20.20, TOUCHDOWN U S C, Cat Robber, Zatara, 7 started.

Alydar S., Hollywood Park, May 26, $80,800, 3yo, 1 1/8mAW, 1:50.25, AWESOME GAMBLER, Cobalt Blue, Freesgood, 8 started.

Alysheba Breeders' Cup S., Lone Star Park, June 30, $100,000, 3yo, 1m, 1:38.79, FORTY GRAMS, Takedown, Strong City, 6 started.

ALYSHEBA S. (G3), Churchill Downs, May 4, $112,300, 3&up, 1 1/16m, 1:43.45, WANDERIN BOY, Half Ours, Student Council, 7 started.

Alysheba S., Meadowlands, Nov. 3, $58,200, 3&up, 1 1/16m, 1:41.21, INDY WIND, Sleek John, Angelic Aura, 4 started.

Alyssa H. (R), Beulah Park, May 5, $20,000, 3&up, f&m, starters at the Beulah Park 2007 winter-spring meet, 6f, 1:10.40, DONAMOUR, Jeansmiledonme, Parthenope, 7 started.

Alyssum S. (R), Belmont Park, June 15, $64,950, 4&up, f&m, nonwinners of an open stakes, 6½f, 1:15.73, SUGAR SWIRL, Veneti, Last Romance, 5 started.

Alywow S., Woodbine, June 10, $97,716, 3yo, f, 6½fT, 1:15.62, SILKY SMOOTH, Quiet Action, Whisper to Me, 14 started.

Amadevil S. (R), Columbus Races, Aug. 11, $15,750, 3&up, Nebraska-bred, 6f, 1:12.60, SKWHIRL, Track Hero, Bevys Dazzler, 7 started.

Ambassador of Luck H. (R), Philadelphia Park, July 28, $100,000, 3&up, f&m, Pennsylvania-bred, 6½f, 1:15.40, S W ALY'SVALENTINE, Hailie's Girl, Cantrel, 5 started.

Ambehaving S., Calder Race Course, Sept. 8, $50,000, 3&up, 1 1/16m, 1:46.07, ELECTRIFY, Finallymadeit, Pop Goes the Tiger, 7 started.

Amelia Peabody S. (R), Suffolk Downs, Nov. 7, $45,000, 2yo, f, Massachusetts-bred, 6f, 1:13.65, CONSIDERING, Innocent Kip, Conquer the Wind, 4 started.

American Beauty H., Santa Anita Park, April 6, $76,650, 4&up, f&m, 1mT, 1:35.25, QUEMAR (NZ), Big Promise, Shermeen (Ire), 5 started.

American Beauty S., Oaklawn Park, Jan. 20, $50,000, 4&up, f&m, 6f, 1:11.36, COUNTRY DIVA, Fast Deal, Tax Refund, 8 started.

AMERICAN DERBY (G2), Arlington Park, July 21, $250,000, 3yo, 1 3/16mT, 1:54.85, LATTICE, Going Ballistic, Eighteenthofmarch, 9 started.

American Dreamer S., Calder Race Course, Aug. 18, $50,000, 3yo, 1m, 1:40.01, ZOOBSTICK, Bar Harbor, Notice Me Now, 9 started.

AMERICAN INVITATIONAL H. (G2), Hollywood Park, June 30, $250,000, 3&up, 1 1/8mT, 1:46.89, OUT OF CONTROL (BRZ), The Tin Man, Fast and Furious (Fr), 6 started.

AMERICAN INVITATIONAL OAKS (G1), Hollywood Park, July 7, $750,000, 3&4yos, f, 1 1/4mT, 2:01.53, PANTY RAID, Valbenny (Ire), Anamato (Aus), 9 started.

AMSTERDAM S. (G2), Saratoga Race Course, July 30, $150,000, 3yo, 6½f, 1:15.97, MOST DISTINGUISHED, Americanus, Starbase, 9 started.

ANCIENT TITLE S. (G1), Oak Tree at Santa Anita, Oct. 7, $300,000, 3&up, 6fAW, 1:07.57, IDIOT PROOF, Greg's Gold, Barbecue Eddie, 5 started.

Anderson Fowler S., Monmouth Park, Aug. 18, $58,200, 3yo, 5½f (originally scheduled on the turf), 1:03.65, CHEROKEE COUNTRY, Heezafrequentflyer, Southwestern Heat, 4 started.

Angenora S. (R), Thistledown, April 21, $50,000, 3&up, f&m, Ohio-bred, 6f, 1:11.32, PAY THE MAN, Magg's Choice, Just Michel, 8 started.

Angie C. S., Emerald Downs, July 15, $45,000, 2yo, f, 6f, 1:09.60, SMARTY DEB, Made for Magic, Princess Hiawatha, 8 started.

Angi Go S., Les Bois Park, June 30, $13,915, 3yo, f, 7f, 1:29, MISS VOYAGER, Charlie'sblueangel, Mati's Firstoption, 6 started.

Anna M. Fisher Debutante S., Ellis Park, Aug. 18, $50,000, 2yo, f, 7f, 1:24.98, MISS RED DELICIOUS, Wonderful Luck, French Kiss, 7 started.

Ann Arbor S. (R), Great Lakes Downs, Aug. 18, $50,000, 3yo, f, Michigan-bred, 1m, 1:46.86, CANDY CANE, Desert Symphony, Lets Get Creative, 8 started.

Ann Owens Distaff H. (R), Turf Paradise, April 28, $45,000, 3&up, f&m, Arizona-bred, 6f, 1:08.84, LITE WRITE, Society Cat, Mobile, 5 started.

Anoakia S., Oak Tree at Santa Anita, Oct. 20, $98,220, 2yo, f, 6fAW, 1:08.70, GOLDEN DOC A, Foxy Danseur, Spring Awakening, 9 started.

Answer Do S., Turf Paradise, April 9, $25,100, 3&up, 5½f, 1:01.87, FAMILY GUY, Icy Tobin, Dinner Magic, 8 started.

Answer Do S., Turf Paradise, Dec. 18, $31,000, 3&up, 6f, 1:09.37, GOIN' DANCIN, Sax Notes, Bobadieu, 10 started.

Anthony Fair H. (1st Div.), Anthony Downs, July 22, $4,450, 3&up, a6½f, 1:20.51 (NTR), CRANE AWAY, Coffee Bubbles, C'Mon Kreed, 5 started.

Anthony Fair H. (2nd Div.), Anthony Downs, July 22, $4,000, 3&up, a6½f, 1:20.91, TOUGH JOE, Red Hot Fox, Valley Haze, 5 started.

Anthony Thoroughbred Futurity, Anthony Downs, July 22, $10,450, 2yo, 5f, 1:03.18, TWISTER IN OZ, Monarch's Shuffle, Mamasoverdrawn, 6 started.

Apache County Fair Thoroughbred Maiden S., Apache County Fair, Sept. 23, $4,640, 3&up, 5½f, 1:11.40, AGAINST THE CLOCK, Candice Girl, Storm Stroller, 7 started.

Appalachian S., Keeneland Race Course, April 22, $115,700, 3yo, f, 1mT, 1:36.39, AUDACIOUS CHLOE, Classic Neel, Red Birkin, 12 started.

Appealing Guy S. (R), Aqueduct, March 9, $67,500, 3yo, New York-bred, 6f, 1:10.10, LANDOFOPPORTUNITY, Golden Dreamer, Five Towns, 6 started.

APPLE BLOSSOM H. (G1), Oaklawn Park, April 7, $500,000, 4&up, f&m, 1 1/16m, 1:44.02, ERMINE, Take D'Tour, Round Pond, 8 started.

APPLETON H. (G3), Gulfstream Park, March 4, $125,000, 4&up, 1mT, 1:32.12, SILVERTREE, Steel Light, Old Dodge (Brz), 8 started.

Appleton Hurdle S., Far Hills, Oct. 20, $50,000, 4&up, a2 1/8mT, 4:15.40, PARTY AIRS, Preemptive Strike, Swimming River, 6 started.

A. P. Smithwick Memorial Steeplechase S., Saratoga Race Course, Aug. 9, $84,900, 4&up, a2 1/16mT, 3:45.56, MIXED UP, Preemptive Strike, Sweet Shani (NZ), 6 started.

AQUEDUCT H. (G3), Aqueduct, Jan. 20, $109,800, 3&up, 1 1/16m, 1:43.66, LIQUOR CABINET (IRE), Angliana, Naughty New Yorker, 7 started.

Arapahoe Park Classic S., Arapahoe Park, Aug. 5, $28,900, 3&up, 1 1/8m, 1:50.76, SAINT AUGUSTUS, Tanya's Beau, Cut of Music, 9 started.

Arapahoe Park Sprint H., Arapahoe Park, June 3, $27,200, 3&up, 6f, 1:09.44, ZAMNATION, Absolutely True, Artistic Moment, 6 started.

ARCADIA H. (G2), Santa Anita Park, April 7, $150,000, 4&up, 1mT, 1:35.18, ICY ATLANTIC, El Roblar, Willow O Wisp, 9 started.

Arctic Queen H. (R), Finger Lakes Gaming and Race Track, Aug. 4, $50,000, 3&up, f&m, New York-bred, 6f, 1:10.76, GOLD LIKE U, Coney Island Baby, Watral's Dahlia, 5 started.

ARISTIDES S. (G3), Churchill Downs, June 2, $159,600, 3&up, 6f, 1:07.64, FABULOUS STRIKE, Cougar Cat, Gaff, 5 started.

Arizona-Bred Thoroughbred S. (R), Flagstaff, July 4, $7,228, 3&up, Arizona-bred, 6½f, 1:20.80, RYAN'S PARTNER, Beau C Fuss, Maxnificent, 7 started.

Arizona Breeders' Derby (R), Turf Paradise, April 28, $67,250, 3yo, Arizona-bred, 1 1/16m, 1:46.01, COMBO ROYALE, Restart, Lowman, 9 started.

Arizona Breeders' Futurity (R), Turf Paradise, Dec. 1, $55,300, 2yo, f, Arizona-bred, 6f, 1:10.46, CAVE SPRINGS, Table Mesa, Rerunner, 12 started.

Arizona Breeders' Futurity (R), Turf Paradise, Dec. 1, $61,579, 2yo, Arizona-bred, 6f, 1:09.78, WHITE SPAR, Ez Dreamer, El Mirage, 11 started.

Arizona County Fair Distance Series Final S., Mohave County Fair, May 20, $3,420, 3&up, 1 1/8m, 1:50.80 (NTR), PARADISE TREASURES, Meeting Ended, Sir Jer Bear, 4 started.

Arizona County Fair Speed Series Final S., Mohave County Fair, May 20, $3,570, 3&up, 6f, 1:13.40, ICE FANTASY, From A to Z, C Bs Deposit, 5 started.

Arizona Juvenile Fillies S., Turf Paradise, Dec. 29, $45,000, 2yo, f, 6½f, 1:15.61, HIGH RESOLVE, Nook and Granny, Cave Springs, 9 started.

Arizona Oaks, Turf Paradise, Feb. 17, $75,000, 3yo, f, 1m, 1:37.54, STATEN ISLAND, Slew o' Platinum, Torrance, 10 started.

Arizona Stallion S. (R), Turf Paradise, April 7, $48,129, 3yo, progeny of eligible Arizona stallions, 7½fT, 1:31.34, SHIMMERING DUNES, Combo Royale, Classic Gold Rush, 10 started.

ARKANSAS DERBY (G2), Oaklawn Park, April 14, $1,000,000, 3yo, 1 1/8m, 1:50.09, CURLIN, Storm in May, Deadly Dealer, 9 started.

ARLINGTON CLASSIC S. (G3), Arlington Park, June 23, $150,000, 3yo, 1 1/16mT, 1:42.05, PLEASANT STRIKE, Lovango, Quasicobra, 9 started.

ARLINGTON H. (G3), Arlington Park, July 21, $200,000, 3&up, 1¼mT, 2:01.32, COSMONAUT, Revved Up, Go Between, 9 started.

ARLINGTON MATRON H. (G3), Arlington Park, Sept. 8, $150,000, 3&up, f&m, 1⅛mAW, 1:49.94, SOLO SURVIVOR, Ms. Lydonia, Round Heels (Ire), 6 started.

ARLINGTON MILLION S. (G1), Arlington Park, Aug. 11, $1,000,000, 3&up, 1¼mT, 2:04.76, JAMBALAYA, The Tin Man, Doctor Dino (Fr), 7 started.

ARLINGTON OAKS (G3), Arlington Park, Aug. 18, $100,000, 3yo, f, 1⅛mAW, 1:49.39, MARIETTA, Humble Janet, Marquee Delivery, 7 started.

Arlington Sprint H., Arlington Park, Aug. 25, $134,500, 3&up, 6fAW, 1:09.14, dh-IN SUMMATION, dh-PIRATESONTHELAKE, Off Duty, 6 started.

ARLINGTON-WASHINGTON FUTURITY (G3), Arlington Park, Sept. 1, $198,500, 2yo, 1mAW, 1:36.52, WICKED STYLE, Riley Tucker, Sebastian County, 7 started.

ARLINGTON-WASHINGTON LASSIE S. (G3), Arlington Park, Sept. 8, $150,000, 2yo, f, 1mAW, 1:37.08, DREAMING OF LIZ, Rasierra, Minewander, 11 started.

Artax H., Gulfstream Park, April 7, $100,000, 4&up, 7½f, 1:28.08, ISTAN, Paradise Dancer, B. B. Best, 6 started.

Arthur I. Appleton Juvenile Turf S. (R), Calder Race Course, Nov. 10, $100,000, 2yo, Florida-bred, 1 1/16mT, 1:42.46, DYNHOCRACY, Sr. Henry, Big Al, 10 started.

Arthur L. S., Calder Race Course, July 1, $45,000, 3&up, 1½m, 2:33.87, DELOSVIENTOS, Kristali, Joey Blueeyes, 8 started.

Art Smith Memorial S., Crooked River Roundup, July 14, $4,375, 3&up, a7f, 1:29.40, DERBY DAY HOPE, Gassan Royal, Zee Chalupa, 5 started.

Ascot Graduation S., Hastings Race Course, Oct. 28, $115,356, 2yo, 1 1/16m, 1:46.50, ROYAL HUDSON, Desert Alf, Star Prospector, 11 started.

ASHLAND S. (G1), Keeneland Race Course, April 7, $500,000, 3yo, f, 1 1/16mAW, 1:42.90, CHRISTMAS KID, Octave, Dawn After Dawn, 8 started.

Ashley T. Cole H. (R), Belmont Park, Sept. 16, $112,800, 3&up, New York-bred, 1⅛mT, 1:48.90, DAVE, Al Basha, Spurred, 10 started.

Aspen Cup H., Ruidoso Downs, June 23, $40,000, 3yo, f, 6f, 1:12.20, LAURAS LAST MUSIC, Silent Fusaichi, Alexsayso, 4 started.

Aspen H. (R), Arapahoe Park, June 18, $36,525, 3&up, c&g, Colorado-bred, 6f, 1:09.84, CUT OF MUSIC, Takeittothebank, Cajun Pepper, 6 started.

Aspirant S. (R), Finger Lakes Gaming and Race Track, Sept. 3, $138,225, 2yo, New York-bred, 6f, 1:10.09, LAW ENFORCEMENT, Spanky Fischbein, Piquante Cat, 10 started.

Assault S. (R), Lone Star Park, July 7, $75,000, 3&up, Texas-bred, 1 1/16m, 1:45.16, GOOSEY MOOSE, Upstream, Dreamsandvisions, 8 started.

Assiniboia Oaks, Assiniboia Downs, Aug. 6, $42,669, 3yo, f, 1m, 1:40, POLYNESIAN KITTY, Dance to My Tune, Bold Angel, 11 started.

Astoria S., Belmont Park, July 1, $109,300, 2yo, f, 5½f, 1:03.85, GLACKEN'S GAL, Dubit, My Mammy, 6 started.

ATBA Fall Sales S. (R), Turf Paradise, Oct. 20, $94,970, 2yo, f, consigned to the 2006 ATBA sale, 6f, 1:12.39, BJORKLUND, Unbidable, Benchmark's Bounty, 12 started.

ATBA Fall Sales S. (R), Turf Paradise, Oct. 20, $101,992, 2yo, c&g, consigned to the 2006 ATBA sale, 6f, 1:11.53, TIMEHASCOMETODAY, Stormy Highland, Rule by Force, 12 started.

ATBA Spring Sales S. (R), Turf Paradise, May 6, $69,886, 2yo, consigned to the 2006 ATBA fall sale, 5f, :56.53, MARK'S MY NAME, Rule by Force, Brietta, 12 started.

Atchison Topeka and Santa Fe H., The Woodlands, Oct. 13, $20,000, 3&up, 6f, 1:09.80, MANOVAN, Just Viareggio, Proper Carson, 8 started.

ATHENIA H. (G3), Belmont Park, Oct. 13, $109,100, 3&up, f&m, 1 1/16mT, 1:45.09, CRIMINOLOGIST, I'm in Love, Dance Away Capote, 6 started.

Attaway Darbonne Memorial Starter S. (R), Evangeline Downs, June 30, $44,550, 3&up, Louisiana-bred starters for a claiming price of $10,000 or less in 2006-'07, 5f, :58.14, BUILDAKISS, Buddys Rebel, Call Me Collect, 8 started.

Auburn S., Emerald Downs, May 13, $45,000, 3yo, c&g, 6f, 1:08, CALL ON CARSON, Immigration, Jamaica Bound, 6 started.

Audrey Skirball-Kenis S., Hollywood Park, Nov. 10, $68,650, 3yo, f, 1⅛mT, 1:48.56, HUCKING HOT (GB), Lavender Sky, Model, 6 started.

Audubon Oaks, Ellis Park, July 28, $50,000, 3yo, f, 1 1/16mT, 1:45.46, KATERBUG, Bel Air Beauty, Si Si Mon Amie, 12 started.

Au Revoir H., Sun Downs, May 6, $3,000, 3&up, 7f, 1:25 (NTR), CHUZZ, Billy Stark, Oregon Merlot, 7 started.

Autotote Derby, Lethbridge, Oct. 28, $27,645, 3yo, 1 1/16m, 1:50.40, LOTTA JAZZ, One O Nine N One, Anchorman, 8 started.

Autumn Leaves H., Bay Meadows Race Course, Oct. 6, $75,000, 3&up, f&m, 1 1/16mT, 1:42.15, PRIVATE BANKING (FR), North Beach, Round Trip Flight, 8 started.

Autumn Leaves S., Mountaineer Race Track and Gaming Resort, Oct. 16, $75,000, 3&up, f&m, 1 1/16m, 1:49.59, KETTLEONEUP, Plaid, Superb Ravi, 11 started.

AUTUMN S. (CAN-G3), Woodbine, Nov. 17, $155,282, 3&up, 1 1/16mAW, 1:42.22 (NTR), TRUE METROPOLITAN, Leonnatus Anteas, Gouldings Green, 8 started.

Aventura S., Gulfstream Park, March 31, $139,500, 3yo, 7f, 1:22.38, STREET MAGICIAN, Yesbyjimminy, Our Sacred Honor, 9 started.

Awad S., Arlington Park, May 28, $48,450, 3yo, 1mT, 1:37.52, TOM ARCHDEACON, Pirate Saint, Lovango, 11 started.

Awad S., Belmont Park, Oct. 18, $78,000, 3&up, 1⅜mT, 2:18.29, TRICKY CAUSEWAY, True Cause, Prince Rahy, 8 started.

AZALEA BREEDERS' CUP S. (G3), Calder Race Course, July 7, $291,750, 3yo, f, 6f, 1:10.40, SHEETS, Sindy With an S, Holly Torque Tango, 9 started.

Azalea S. (R), Delta Downs, March 16, $75,000, 4&up, f&m, Louisiana-bred non-winners of a stakes, 7f, 1:27.92, QUEEZEE DEEZEE, Tsarina, dh-Punchy Louise, dh-Golden Demand, 10 started.

AZERI BREEDERS' CUP S. (G3), Oaklawn Park, March 10, $175,000, 4&up, f&m, 1 1/16m, 1:44.37, INDIA, Kettleoneup, A True Pussycat, 6 started.

Aztec Oaks (R), SunRay Park, June 23, $62,000, 3yo, f, New Mexico-bred, 6½f, 1:17.40, GOOD LOOKER R F, Tricky Trish, Nimble Band, 10 started.

Babae S., Belmont Park, June 8, $69,000, 3yo, f, 7fT, 1:22.01, SILENCE DOGOOD, Enchantal, Dinner Break, 8 started.

Babst/Palacios Memorial H. (R), Beulah Park, May 5, $50,000, 3&up, Ohio-bred, 6f, 1:09.42, PFORPERFECTSPISTOL, Catlaunch, Cat Singer, 5 started.

Bachman S., Fonner Park, March 4, $10,825, 3yo, 4f, :46.80, MY SECRET STAR, Favorite Rookie, The Bunster, 6 started.

BALDWIN S. (G3), Santa Anita Park, March 10, $106,600, 3yo, a6½fT, 1:11.96, DESERT CODE, Bitter Bill, Vaunt (GB), 5 started.

BALLERINA BREEDERS' CUP S. (CAN-G3), Hastings Race Course, Oct. 13, $132,597, 3&up, f&m, 1⅛m, 1:50.64, MONASHEE, Lady Raj, Slewpast, 4 started.

BALLERINA S. (G1), Saratoga Race Course, Aug. 26, $250,000, 3&up, f&m, 7f, 1:22.78, MARYFIELD, Baroness Thatcher, Miraculous Miss, 9 started.

BALLSTON SPA H. (G2), Saratoga Race Course, Aug. 23, $200,000, 3&up, f&m, 1 1/16mT, 1:40, WAIT A WHILE, Vacare, Meribel, 7 started.

Baltimore City Turf Sprint S., Pimlico Race Course, May 19, $100,000, 3&up, 5fT, :55.90, HEROS REWARD, Bingobear, Mr Mutter, 9 started.

Band Is Passing S., Calder Race Course, June 17, $45,000, 3&up, 1 1/16m, 1:45.82, CHEIRON, Rehoboth, Teofilo (Per), 6 started.

Bangles and Beads S., Fairplex Park, Sept. 24, $61,750, 3&up, f&m, 6½f, 1:17.51, SELVATICA, Ashley's Kitty, Meetmeinthewoods, 5 started.

Banshee Breeze S. (R), Saratoga Race Course, July 30, $78,000, 3&up, f&m, non-winners of a graded stakes over one mile in 2007, 1⅛m, 1:50.07, LADY JOANNE, Altesse, Leo's Pegasus, 4 started.

Bara Lass S. (R), Sam Houston Race Park, Dec. 1, $50,000, 2yo, f, Texas-bred, 7f, 1:24.39, MS CLASSIC SENECA, Taptam, Valid Lilly, 12 started.

Barbados Ballade S. (R), Woodbine, June 23, $117,984, 3&up, f&m, Ontario-foaled, 6fAW, 1:09.31 (NTR), FINANCINGAVAILABLE, Executive Flight, Shot Gun Ela, 8 started.

BARBARA FRITCHIE BREEDERS' CUP H. (G2), Laurel Park, Feb. 17, $285,000, 3&up, f&m, 7f, 1:24.92, OPRAH WINNEY, Silmaril, Smart and Fancy, 8 started.

Barbara Shinpoch S., Emerald Downs, Sept. 2, $72,000, 2yo, f, 1m, 1:36.20, SMARTY DEB, Princess Hiawatha, Made for Magic, 7 started.

Barbaro S., Pimlico Race Course, May 19, $100,000, 3yo, 1 1/16m, 1:43.44, CHELOKEE, Silver Express, Zephyr Cat, 5 started.

BARBARO S. (G3), Delaware Park, July 15, $300,600, 3yo, 1 1/16m, 1:43.40, XCHANGER, King of the Roxy, Phone Home, 7 started.

Barb's Dancer S. (R), Calder Race Course, Aug. 4, $50,000, 3&up, f&m, non-winners of a stakes worth $35,000 since January 2, 7f, 1:24.25, A SEA TRIPPI, Annabill, Songofthesouth, 11 started.

Barksdale H., Louisiana Downs, June 23, $50,000, 3&up, 1mT, 1:40.59, MIDDLEWEIGHT, Ruckus, Erroneous I D, 9 started.

Barretts Debutante S. (R), Fairplex Park, Sept. 15, $126,350, 2yo, f, sold at a Barretts sale, 6½f, 1:18.52, P. S. U. GRAD, Ididntmeantoo, Salt Castle, 10 started.

Barretts Juvenile S. (R), Fairplex Park, Sept. 16, $148,250, 2yo, sold at a Barretts sale, 6½f, 1:18.97, NENE, Guns On the Table, Topper Shopper, 10 started.

Barretts S. (R), Hollywood Park, April 29, $72,800, 3&up, California-bred non-winners of $7,500 other than maiden, claiming, or starter or non-winners of two races, 7fAW, 1:23.94, SOCIAL CLIMBER, One On the House, Sixcess, 12 started.

BASHFORD MANOR S. (G3), Churchill Downs, July 7, $165,150, 2yo, 6f, 1:09.15, KODIAK KOWBOY, Dr. Nick, Crackalackin, 6 started.

Battlefield S., Monmouth Park, June 17, $70,000, 3&up, 1⅛mT, 1:46.08 (NCR), FISHY ADVICE, Shake the Bank, dh-Ballonenostrikes, dh-Silent Roar, 8 started.

Battler Star S. (R), Fair Grounds, March 3, $75,000, 3yo, f, Louisiana-bred, 6f, 1:11.59, PRINCESS DEELITE, Huckie, Sara Bon Adeau, 7 started.

Baxter S., Fonner Park, April 7, $16,400, 3yo, 6f, 1:14.20, MY SECRET STAR, Heso, The Ruzz, 9 started.

BAYAKOA H. (G2), Hollywood Park, Dec. 1, $150,000, 3&up, f&m, 1 1/16mAW, 1:40.90 (NTR), ROMANCE IS DIANE, Tough Tiz's Sis, Fonce De (Fr), 5 started.

Bayakoa S., Oaklawn Park, April 11, $100,000, 4&up, f&m, 1 1/16m, 1:45.32, GASIA, Brownie Points, Fiery Pursuit, 7 started.

BAY MEADOWS BREEDERS' CUP H. (G3), Bay Meadows Race Course, Sept. 22, $140,000, 3&up, a1⅛mT, 1:47.17, NOW VICTORY, Jack's Wild, Macduff (GB), 9 started.

Bay Meadows Breeders' Cup Oaks, Bay Meadows Race Course, April 14, $76,875, 3yo, f, 1 1/16m, 1:43.66, ROUND TRIP FLIGHT, Glorification, Eastlake Avenue, 4 started.

BAY MEADOWS BREEDERS' CUP SPRINT H. (G3), Bay Meadows Race Course, March 11, $95,625, 4&up, 6f, 1:08.40, SMOKEY STOVER, Britt's Jules, Areyoutalkintome, 4 started.

Bay Meadows Debutante S., Bay Meadows Race Course, Sept. 8, $69,100, 2yo, f, 6f, 1:10.41, INDYANNE, This Side Up, Lady Railrider, 6 started.

Bay Meadows Derby, Bay Meadows Race Course, Sept. 29, $75,000, 3yo, 1 1/16mT, 1:44.59, UNUSUAL SUSPECT, Ten a Penny, Zoning In, 5 started.

Bay Meadows Juvenile S., Bay Meadows Race Course, Sept. 15, $72,310, 2yo, 6f, 1:10.99, SIERRA SUNSET, Fort Funston, Thundering Justice, 4 started.

Bay Meadows Speed H., Bay Meadows Race Course, Oct. 20, $71,550, 3&up, 6f, 1:09.23, WIND WATER, Court the King, Tontine Too, 8 started.

BAYOU BREEDERS' CUP H. (G3), Fair Grounds, Feb. 24, $118,000, 4&up, f&m, a1⅛mT, 1:52.44, J'RAY, Scarlet Butterfly, Candy Ball, 9 started.

Bayou State S. (R), Delta Downs, March 16, $73,500, 4&up, Louisiana-bred non-winners of a stakes, 7f, 1:26.63, FASS FEAT, Magic Sunset, Dr. Schwartz, 7 started.

BAY SHORE S. (G3), Aqueduct, April 7, $150,000, 3yo, 7f, 1:22.99, BILL PLACE, Hobbitontherocks, Les Grands Trois, 6 started.

B. B. Sixty Rayburn S. (R), Evangeline Downs, June 30, $74,250, 3yo, Louisiana-bred, 1m, 1:40.71, PINECREST BOY, St. Zarb, Heelbolt, 8 started.

B Cup Classic S., Lethbridge, Oct. 13, $21,783, 3&up, 1⅛m, 1:53.40, LAFLEUR, Shouldbevictory, Dr. Mo, 5 started.

B Cup Filly and Mare S., Lethbridge, Oct. 13, $16,646, 3&up, f&m, 7f, 1:26.60, TAYLOR M, Color Me Iris, She's Twenty Below, 8 started.

B Cup S. #1, Lethbridge, Oct. 13, $16,337, 2yo, a6f, 1:12, STRONG ARM WILLIE, Cool Ventura, Alameda Slim, 6 started.

B Cup S. #2, Lethbridge, Oct. 13, $16,337, 3yo, a6f, 1:10.40, ONE O NINE N ONE, Cool Turando, Anchorman, 6 started.

B Cup S. #3, Lethbridge, Oct. 13, $16,491, 3&up, 7f, 1:24.80, IT'S NOT OVER YET, Pure, Mont Tendre, 6 started.

B Cup Sprint Fillies and Mares S., Lethbridge, Oct. 13, $16,337, 3&up, f&m, a5½f, 1:08.40, KAYLA M, Lot a Smoke, Trompeta, 5 started.

B Cup Sprint S., Lethbridge, Oct. 13, $16,646, 3&up, a5½f, 1:07.80, RANSOME ROAD, Cool Honor, Captain Mojo, 8 started.

B Cup Three-Year-Old Fillies S., Lethbridge, Oct. 13, $16,491, 3yo, f, a6f, 1:11.60, DESPERATE DANCER, Steve's Girl, D C Bobby Shocks, 6 started.

B Cup Two-Year-Old Fillies S., Lethbridge, Oct. 13, $16,491, 2yo, f, a6f, 1:12.80, SUDDEN N' SASSY, Lovely Laine, Princess Loretta, 7 started.

Beau Brummel S., Fairplex Park, Sept. 12, $64,675, 2yo, 6½f, 1:17.58, RUN BROTHER RON, Rivergrade Boy, Reel Prime, 9 started.

Beaufort S. (R), Northlands Park, Sept. 29, $50,275, 3yo, Alberta-bred, 1 1/16m, 1:44.80, HURRICANETIKI, Howsitgoinghotshot, Wood B Nice, 9 started.

BEAUGAY H. (G3), Aqueduct, April 28, $113,600, 3&up, f&m, 1 1/16mT, 1:47.43, MASSEUSE, Stormy Kiss (Arg), Finlandia, 7 started.

Beautiful Day S., Delaware Park, July 4, $58,850, 3yo, f, 6f, 1:08.91, INTENTIONAL FEVER, Allude, Broadway Baby, 6 started.

Beautiful Pleasure S., Belmont Park, Sept. 26, $74,250, 4&up, f&m, 1 1/16m, 1:42.62, POOL LAND, Altesse, Swap Fliparoo, 4 started.

Bedanken S., Fair Grounds, March 25, $98,000, 3yo, f, a1 1/16mT, 1:43.33, MOONEE PONDS, Mount Glitter, Swingit, 7 started.

BED O' ROSES BREEDERS' CUP H. (G2), Aqueduct, April 21, $153,900, 3&up, f&m, 7f, 1:22.98, CARMANDIA, Magnolia Jackson, Swap Fliparoo, 5 started.

BELDAME S. (G1), Belmont Park, Sept. 30, $612,000, 3&up, f&m, 1⅛m, 1:48.63, UNBRIDLED BELLE, Indian Vale, Ginger Punch, 7 started.

Belle Geste S. (R), Woodbine, Aug. 25, $71,660, 3&up, f&m, Ontario-bred, 7fT, 1:24.42, ESSENTIAL EDGE, Count to Three, Becky Sharp, 6 started.

Belle Mahone S., Woodbine, Aug. 19, $94,230, 3&up, f&m, 1 1/16mAW, 1:44.29, ARDEN BELLE, Roving Angel, Serenading, 5 started.

Belle Roberts S. (R), Emerald Downs, Sept. 16, $50,000, 3&up, f&m, Washington-bred, 1 1/16m, 1:41.20, HIT A STAR, Gemstone Rush, She's All Silk, 7 started.

BELMONT S. (G1), Belmont Park, June 9, $1,000,000, 3yo, 1½m, 2:28.74, RAGS TO RICHES, Curlin, Tiago, 7 started.

BEN ALI S. (G3), Keeneland Race Course, April 26, $150,000, 4&up, 1⅛mAW, 1:49.93, JADE'S REVENGE, Minister's Joy, Mustanfar, 11 started.

Bergen County S., Meadowlands, Sept. 8, $60,000, 3yo, 6f, 1:09.46, APPEALING SPRING, Forefathers, Leonardo, 5 started.

BERKELEY S. (G3), Golden Gate Fields, June 2, $100,000, 3&up, 1 1/16m, 1:43.46, MY CREED, Visa Parade (Arg), Desert Boom, 8 started.

BERNARD BARUCH H. (G2), Saratoga Race Course, Aug. 25, $200,000, 3&up, 1⅛mT, 1:45.33 (NCR), SHAKIS (IRE), Big Prairie, Drum Major, 10 started.

Bernie Dowd H. (R), Monmouth Park, June 17, $60,000, 3&up, New Jersey-bred, 1m70y, 1:42.27, FAGEDABOUDIT SAL, Meadow Blue, Calabria Bella, 8 started.

Bersid S., Turf Paradise, Oct. 28, $31,000, 3&up, f&m, 1m, 1:37.21, EVENING ESCORT, Along Came Jones, Star of Whitney, 8 started.

Bert Delany Memorial S., Grand Prairie, Aug. 19, $5,652, 3&up, 5½f, 1:07.20, GLENS FRIEND, Nattandyahoo, Wartock, 4 started.

Bertram F. Bongard S. (R), Belmont Park, Sept. 23, $104,300, 2yo, New York-bred, 7f, 1:23.64, BIG TRUCK, Spanky Fischbein, Dazzling Derek, 5 started.

Bessarabian S., Woodbine, Nov. 25, $155,112, 3&up, f&m, 7fAW, 1:21.50, MY LIST, Wild Gams, Roving Angel, 10 started.

BESSEMER TRUST BREEDERS' CUP JUVENILE (G1), Monmouth Park, Oct. 27, $1,832,000, 2yo, c&g, 1 1/16m, 1:42.76, WAR PASS, Pyro, Kodiak Kowboy, 11 started.

Best Of Ohio Distaff S. (R), Beulah Park, Oct. 6, $100,000, 3&up, f&m, Ohio-bred, 1⅛m, 1:50.32, CRYPTOQUIP, Bright Pyrite, Pay the Man, 8 started.

Best of Ohio Endurance S. (R), Beulah Park, Oct. 6, $100,000, 3&up, Ohio-bred, 1¼m, 2:05.22, SMARMY, Pyrite Personal, Catlaunch, 8 started.

Best of Ohio Juvenile S. (R), Beulah Park, Oct. 6, $75,000, 2yo, Ohio-bred, 1 1/16m, 1:47.28, O'RIAIN, Buzz Bunny, Pyrite Gem, 12 started.

Best of Ohio Sprint S. (R), Beulah Park, Oct. 6, $75,000, 3&up, Ohio-bred, 6f, 1:09.51, DOOZE, Ben's Reflection, Royal Nemesis, 11 started.

BEST PAL S. (G2), Del Mar, Aug. 12, $147,000, 2yo, 6½fAW, 1:19.43, SALUTE THE SARGE, Georgie Boy, Sky Cape, 4 started.

Bet On Sunshine S., Churchill Downs, Nov. 17, $62,720, 3&up, 6f, 1:08.82, JUNIOR COLLEGE, Santana Strings, Celluloid Hero, 7 started.

Better Bee S., Arlington Park, Aug. 4, $47,700, 3&up, 6fAW, 1:09.92, CITY NUMBER, Star by Design, High Expectations, 8 started.

Betty An Bull S., Turf Paradise, May 4, $25,200, 3&up, f&m, $4\frac{1}{2}$fT, :50.82, SHIMMERING HEAT, Blumin Beauty, Mirando, 10 started.

Betty's Hat S. (R), Penn National Race Course, Aug. 30, $46,650, 3&up, f&m, Pennsylvania-bred, 1mT, 1:35.68, ROYAL PLEASURE, Tuff Partners, Western Pleaser, 9 started.

BEVERLY D. S. (G1), Arlington Park, Aug. 11, $750,000, 3&up, f&m, $1\frac{3}{16}$mT, 1:56.68, ROYAL HIGHNESS (GER), Irridescence (SAf), Lady of Venice (Fr), 7 started.

BEVERLY HILLS H. (G2), Hollywood Park, July 1, $150,000, 3&up, f&m, $1\frac{1}{4}$mT, 2:01.47, CITRONNADE, Andrea (NZ), Naughty Rafaela (Brz), 5 started.

BEWITCH S. (G3), Keeneland Race Course, April 25, $150,000, 4&up, f&m, $1\frac{1}{2}$mT, 2:28.75, SAFARI QUEEN (ARG), Barancella (Fr), Moon Berry (Brz), 6 started.

Bienville S., Fair Grounds, March 10, $100,000, 4&up, f&m, a$5\frac{1}{2}$fT, 1:02.92, SMITTY'S SUNSHINE, Miss Penny Fortune, Somethinaboutbetty, 11 started.

Big Earl H. (R), Louisiana Downs, May 19, $42,300, 3&up, Louisiana-bred, $5\frac{1}{2}$f, 1:03.01, CORT'S P. B., Majestic Commander, Zarb's Dahar, 4 started.

Big Red Mile S. (R), Lincoln State Fair, May 28, $20,950, 3&up, Nebraska-bred, 1m, 1:42.20, BEVYS DAZZLER, Blumin Attitude, High Dice, 9 started.

Bill Callihan S., Columbus Races, Sept. 2, $10,591, 3&up, f&m, $6\frac{1}{2}$f, 1:20.20, C. R. CHARMER, My Hobby, Any Dream Will Do, 3 started.

Bill Thomas Memorial H., Sunland Park, March 17, $50,000, 3&up, $6\frac{1}{2}$f, 1:15.59, DUCKY DRAKE, Dangerous Devon, Diligent Prospect, 10 started.

Bill Wineberg S. (R), Portland Meadows, Nov. 4, $21,200, 2yo, c&g, Oregon-bred, 6f, 1:12.67, JIMMIE THE GROUCH, Delegocho, Works Lika Bullet, 8 started.

Billy Powell Claiming H. (R), The Downs at Albuquerque, Oct. 7, $16,100, 3&up, starters for a claiming price of $5,000, 6f, 1:09.82, BARRICADED, Bold Emancipator, Sumpter, 6 started.

BING CROSBY H. (G1), Del Mar, July 29, $300,000, 3&up, 6fAW, 1:11.06, IN SUMMATION, Greg's Gold, Bordonaro, 9 started.

Birdcatcher S., Northlands Park, Aug. 5, $79,649, 2yo, c&g, $6\frac{1}{2}$f, 1:19.60, JUST CALL ME DUKE, Brazen Son, Mr Muffin Man, 7 started.

Bird of Pay S., Northlands Park, Aug. 3, $56,246, 2yo, f, $6\frac{1}{2}$f, 1:19, LITTLEMISS ALLISON, Bears Artiste, Highly Explosive, 7 started.

Birdonthewire S., Calder Race Course, Oct. 13, $90,000, 2yo, $5\frac{1}{2}$f, 1:04.19 (NTR), CARSON'S LEGACY, Surrealdeal, Sr. Henry, 8 started.

Birdstone S., Belmont Park, June 9, $100,250, 4&up, $1\frac{1}{8}$m, 1:47.33, PAPI CHULLO, Hesanoldsalt, A. P. Arrow, 5 started.

Bison City S. (R), Woodbine, July 1, $234,625, 3yo, f, Canadian-bred, $1\frac{1}{16}$mAW, 1:44.01, SEALY HILL, Street Sounds, Quiet Jungle, 5 started.

Black Bart Starter H. (R), Turf Paradise, Dec. 14, $17,400, 3&up, starters for a claiming price of $12,500 or less in 2007, a$1\frac{1}{8}$mT, 1:51.58, POWER STROKIN, Prospect Green, We Brothers, 9 started.

BLACK-EYED SUSAN S. (G2), Pimlico Race Course, May 18, $250,000, 3yo, f, $1\frac{1}{8}$m, 1:50.07, PANTY RAID, Winning Point, Baroness Thatcher, 8 started.

Black Gold S., Fair Grounds, Jan. 27, $72,750, 3yo, $5\frac{1}{2}$f (originally scheduled on the turf), 1:05.86, PROBATION READY, Pete the Poet, Tainted Money, 6 started.

Black Mesa S. (R), Remington Park, Aug. 26, $50,000, 3&up, f&m, Oklahoma-bred, 6f, 1:10.38, NOT MUCH MONEY, Mystical Moonlight, Annieville, 8 started.

Black Mountain S., Turf Paradise, Oct. 27, $31,400, 3&up, 1m, 1:36.32, HIGHLAND GAMES, Skipaslew, Organ Pipe, 6 started.

Black Tie Affair H. (R), Arlington Park, July 7, $84,150, 3&up, Illinois-conceived and/or -foaled, $1\frac{1}{16}$mT, 1:42.69, FORT PRADO, Tenpointfive, Majestic Zeal, 8 started.

Blair's Cove S. (R), Canterbury Park, July 3, $45,000, 3&up, c&g, Minnesota-bred, a$1\frac{1}{16}$mT, 1:43.74, TORPEDO MAN, Sir Tricky, Chaska, 10 started.

Blazing Sword S., Calder Race Course, June 2, $45,000, 3&up, 1m, 1:38.95, PARADISE DANCER, Fancy Silver, Hal's Image, 8 started.

B L's Sweep S., Calder Race Course, June 16, $50,000, 2yo, $5\frac{1}{2}$f, 1:06.23, BROTHER JOEY, Casino Gambler, Viva La Slew, 6 started.

Blue Hen S., Delaware Park, Oct. 27, $100,000, 2yo, f, $1\frac{1}{16}$m, 1:48.83, SAKI TO ME, Dagger, Hidden Wish, 5 started.

Blue Jay Way S. (R), Oak Tree at Santa Anita, Sept. 30, $65,350, 3&up, non-winners of a stakes worth $55,000 since May 15 other than state-bred, a$6\frac{1}{2}$fT, 1:11.87, NIGHT CHAPTER (GB), Moth Ball (GB), Leonetti, 7 started.

Blue Mountain Juvenile S. (R), Penn National Race Course, Oct. 18, $46,900, 2yo, f, Pennsylvania-bred, 5f, :59.24, ESPINDOLA, Dead Flowers, Jakes Heart, 6 started.

Blue Norther S., Santa Anita Park, Dec. 30, $85,200, 2yo, f, 1mT, 1:35.95, GORGEOUS GOOSE, Golden Doc A, Ariege, 10 started.

Blue Sparkler S., Monmouth Park, July 8, $60,000, 3&up, f&m, 6f, 1:08.92, MY SISTER SUE, Livermore Valley, Solarana (Arg), 7 started.

Bob Beale Tulameen Cup S., Sunflower Downs, June 29, $6,608, 3&up, a7f, 1:25.36, FUNKY FRIENDS, Billy Stark, Alferrari, 8 started.

Bobbie Bricker Memorial S. (R), Thistledown, Nov. 3, $50,000, 3&up, f&m, Ohio-bred, $1\frac{1}{16}$m, 1:47.14, MONEY CARD, Sybles Angel, Montfort Lane, 12 started.

Bob Bryant S. (R), Prairie Meadows, May 26, $63,058, 3yo, f, Iowa-bred, 6f, 1:09.97, IRISH PARTY, Des Moines, Tejano's Oasis, 6 started.

Bob Harding S., Monmouth Park, July 14, $60,000, 3&up, 1mT, 1:33.16, BARON VON TAP, Presious Passion, Drum Major, 8 started.

Bob Johnson Memorial S., Lone Star Park, July 21, $50,000, 3&up, 1mT, 1:34.45, SING BABY SING, Waupaca, Almost Certain, 8 started.

Bob Umphrey Turf Sprint H., Calder Race Course, July 7, $100,000, 3&up, 5f (originally scheduled on the turf), :57.87, D'ARTAGNANS' SPIRIT, Lord Robyn, Bow Out, 8 started.

Bob Weems Memorial S., Turf Paradise, March 20, $25,200, 3&up, $1\frac{1}{8}$mT, 1:48.87, AZA, In Joe's Honor, Ozzy's Shame, 9 started.

Boeing H., Emerald Downs, July 28, $45,000, 3&up, f&m, $1\frac{1}{16}$m, 1:42, BEAULENA, Sudden Departure, She's All Silk, 5 started.

BOILING SPRINGS S. (G3), Monmouth Park, June 30, $150,000, 3yo, f, $1\frac{1}{16}$mT, 1:40.60, RUTHERIENNE, Sharp Susan, Red Birkin, 6 started.

Boise Derby, Les Bois Park, July 7, $7,100, 3yo, 1m, 1:40.95, BEAUCARDI, Storm Irritater, Senator Bowden, 10 started.

Bold Accent S., Fonner Park, Feb. 10, $10,500, 3&up, f&m, 4f, :46.40, NIKKI NINE, Carson's Rumor, Salty Attraction, 6 started.

Bold Ego H., Sunland Park, Dec. 30, $50,000, 3&up, f&m, $5\frac{1}{2}$f, 1:02.28 (NTR), GLEAMING ELEGANCE, Kranky Karol, Diamond Chimes, 7 started.

Bold Ruckus S. (R), Woodbine, June 13, $118,662, 3yo, Ontario-foaled, 6fT, 1:08.79, LEGAL MOVE, Catsimile, Fudgethebottomline, 9 started.

BOLD RULER H. (G3), Belmont Park, May 12, $105,400, 3&up, 6f, 1:08.80, SONGSTER, Dashboard Drummer, Dark Cheetah, 5 started.

Bold Venture S., Woodbine, July 22, $119,619, 3&up, $6\frac{1}{2}$fAW, 1:16.02, GANGSTER, Just Rushing, Museeb, 6 started.

Bonapaw S., Fair Grounds, Dec. 22, $100,000, 3&up, $5\frac{1}{2}$f (originally scheduled on the turf), 1:04.03, STORMIN BAGHDAD, Natural Speed, Going Wild, 10 started.

Bonnie Heath Turf Cup H. (R), Calder Race Course, Nov. 10, $150,000, 3&up, Florida-bred, $1\frac{1}{8}$mT, 1:48.03, REVVED UP, Soldier's Dancer, Go Directlyto Jail, 10 started.

BONNIE MISS S. (G2), Gulfstream Park, March 10, $150,000, 3yo, f, $1\frac{1}{8}$m, 1:50.87, HIGH AGAIN, Christmas Kid, Fee Fi Fo Fum, 8 started.

Boomer Starter S. (R), Yavapai Downs, Aug. 25, $8,200, 3&up, starters for a claiming price of $5,000 or less since 2006, 1m, 1:35.20, MISTER COSMI (GB), Chaseur, Takin Dead Aim, 8 started.

Borderland Derby, Sunland Park, Feb. 17, $100,000, 3yo, $1\frac{1}{16}$m, 1:44.64, TAKEDOWN, Jack Hes Tops, Game of Skill, 9 started.

Bosselman/Gus Fonner S., Fonner Park, April 28, $100,000, 3&up, $1\frac{1}{16}$m, 1:47.60, TAP DANCING MAUK, Motion Approved, Yourmoneysnogood, 7 started.

Bountiful Harvest S., Sam Houston Race Park, Nov. 24, $28,000, 2yo, 6f, 1:12.08, DEPUTY DANCE, Brendyn Jo, Lucky Ned Pepper, 6 started.

BOURBONETTE OAKS (G3), Turfway Park, March 24, $150,000, 3yo, f, 1mAW, 1:37.51, SEALY HILL, Panty Raid, Aspiring, 12 started.

Bouwerie S. (R), Belmont Park, May 6, $115,200, 3yo, f, New York-bred, 7f, 1:24.07, TALKING TREASURE, My Kitty, Pastel Gal, 9 started.

BOWLING GREEN H. (G2), Belmont Park, July 15, $150,000, 3&up, $1\frac{3}{8}$mT, 2:12.68, SUNRIVER, Trippi's Storm, Silver Whistle, 8 started.

Racing — 2007 Stakes Races

BOYD GAMING'S DELTA JACKPOT S. (G3), Delta Downs, Dec. 7, $1,000,000, 2yo, 1 1/16m, 1:45.43, dh-Z HUMOR, dh-TURF WAR, Golden Yank, 10 started.

Boyd Gaming's Delta Princess Powered by Youbet.com S., Delta Downs, Dec. 7, $300,000, 2yo, f, 1m, 1:40.21, BY THE LIGHT, Miss Missile, Lady On Holiday, 10 started.

Bradley Rollins S., Yavapai Downs, Aug. 12, $11,500, 3&up, f&m, 5 1/2f, 1:01.80, WILD ENGLISH ROSE, Lil Celeste, Along Came Jones, 6 started.

Brandywine S., Delaware Park, June 9, $100,600, 3&up, 1 1/16m, 1:41 56, BARCOLA, Better Than Bonds, Trapped Again, 7 started.

Brave Raj S., Calder Race Course, Sept. 22, $147,750, 2yo, f, 1m70y, 1:44 60, SILK RIDGE, Asi Asi, Calico Bay, 7 started.

Break Through S. (R), Aqueduct, March 23, $69,700, 4&up, f&m, non-winners of a graded stakes, 6f, 1:12.26, SMART AND FANCY, Livermore Valley, Yolanda B. Too, 6 started.

BREEDERS' CUP CLASSIC POWERED BY DODGE (G1), Monmouth Park, Oct. 27, $4,580,000, 3&up, 1 1/4m, 2:00.59, CURLIN, Harc Spun, Awesome Gem, 9 started.

Breeders' Cup Dirt Mile, Monmouth Park, Oct. 26, $916,000, 3&up, 1m70y, 1:39.06, CORINTHIAN, Gottcha Gold, Discreet Cat, 8 started.

Breeders' Cup Filly & Mare Sprint, Monmouth Park, Oct. 26, $1,030,500, 3&up, f&m, 6f, 1:09.85, MARYFIELD, Miraculous Miss, Miss Macy Sue, 10 started.

Breeders' Cup Grand National Hurdle S., Far Hills, Oct. 20, $263,000, 4&up, a2 5/8mT, 5:30.60, MCDYNAMO, Sweet Shani (NZ), Best Attack 9 started.

BREEDERS' CUP JUVENILE FILLIES (G1), Monmouth Park, Oct. 27, $1,832,000, 2yo, f, 1 1/16m, 1:44.73, INDIAN BLESSING, Proud Spell, Backseat Rhythm, 13 started.

Breeders' Cup Juvenile Turf, Monmouth Park, Oct. 26, $916,000, 2yo, 1mT, 1:40.48, NOWNOWNOW, Achill Island (Ire), Cannonball, 12 started.

Breeders' S. (R), Woodbine, Aug. 5, $475,617, 3yo, Canadian-bred, 1 1/2mT, 2:29.50, MARCHFIELD, Twilight Meteor, It's Like This, 9 started.

Breeders' Special Fillies S. (R), Lincoln State Fair, July 7, $20,600, 3yo, f, Nebraska-bred, 6f, 1:13.60, SHADE ON, Sweet Launce, Completely Chrome, 6 started.

Brian Barenscheer Juvenile S., Canterbury Park, July 21, $45,000, 2yo, 5 1/2f, 1:03.97, DEPUTY DANCE, Rumbling Cloud, Tovah, 8 started.

Brickyard S. (R), Hoosier Park, Oct. 21, $45,000, 3&up, Indiana-bred, 6f, 1:11.12, FATHER JOHN, Mr. Mink, Laz Has Risen, 9 started.

Brighouse Belles S., Hastings Race Course, May 6, $46,749, 3&up, f&m, 6 1/2f, 1:17.09, MONASHEE, Slewpast, Socorro County, 5 started.

BRITISH COLUMBIA BREEDERS' CUP DERBY (CAN-G3), Hastings Race Course, Sept. 23, $263,569, 3yo, 1 1/8m, 1:49.50, CELTIC DREAMIN, Gandolf, Sir Gallovic, 10 started.

BRITISH COLUMBIA BREEDERS' CUP OAKS (CAN-G3), Hastings Race Course, Sept. 22, $142,206, 3yo, f, 1 1/8m, 1:52.33, ALPINE GARDEN, Pat of Gold, Napa, 8 started.

British Columbia Cup Debutante S. (R), Hastings Race Course, Aug. 6, $50,966, 2yo, f, British Columbia-bred, 6 1/2f, 1:18.30, REMARKABLE MISS, Alpine Lass, My Special Angel, 5 started.

British Columbia Cup Distaff H. (R), Hastings Race Course, Aug. 6, $50,917, 3&up, f&m, British Columbia-bred, 1 1/8m, 1:49.93, STARLITE STRIKE, Real Candy, Lady Raj, 6 started.

British Columbia Cup Dogwood H. (R), Hastings Race Course, Aug. 6, $52,599, 3yo, f, British Columbia-bred, 1 1/16m, 1:45.65, SUVA, Napa, Deadly Zone, 7 started.

British Columbia Cup Nursery S. (R), Hastings Race Course, Aug. 6, $47,410, 2yo, c&g, British Columbia-bred, 6 1/2f, 1:18.29, STAR PROSPECTOR, Call Me Tomorrow, Surprisal, 8 started.

British Columbia Cup Sprint H. (R), Hastings Race Course, Aug. 6, $50,458, 3&up, British Columbia-bred, 6 1/2f, 1:16.10, B R REMARK, Stole Another, Victim of Love, 7 started.

British Columbia Cup Stellar's Jay H. (R), Hastings Race Course, Aug. 6, $52,267, 3yo, British Columbia-bred, 1 1/16m, 1:44.89, OOKASHADA, Bad Sneakers, Stephanson, 9 started.

British Columbia Lottery Corporate Mile S., Kamloops, Aug. 18, $10,271, 3&up, a1m, 1:37.63, DALTON GREEN, Lukin Awesome, Funky Friends, 7 started.

British Columbia Lottery S., Kin Park, July 29, $9,418, 3&up, a1 1/4m, 1:53.37, LORD FREDERICK, Crescent Remark, Funky Friends, 7 started.

BRITISH COLUMBIA PREMIER'S H. (CAN-G3), Hastings Race Course, Oct. 14, $103,742, 3&up, 1 3/8m, 2:15.89, SIR GALLOVIC, True Metropolitan, Newton John, 6 started.

Broadway H. (R), Aqueduct, March 4, $72,840, 3&up, f&m, New York-bred, 6f, 1:10.88, WAYTOTHELEFT, Great Lady K, Slew Motion, 10 started.

BROOKLYN H. (G2), Belmont Park, Sept. 22, $154,200, 3&up, 1 1/8m, 1:48.31, ANY GIVEN SATURDAY, Tasteyville, Helsinki, 5 started.

Brookmeade S. (R), Colonial Downs, June 30, $60,000, 3&up, f&m, Virginia-bred and/or -sired, 1 1/16m, 1:43.29, SWEEDOWNTHELANE, Changeisgonnacome, Point Missed, 6 started.

Brooks Fields S., Canterbury Park, June 9, $45,000, 3&up, a7 1/2fT, 1:29.58, GENERAL CHARLEY, Prospective Kiss, Load a Chronic, 9 started.

Brother Brown S., Remington Park, Aug. 5, $51,320, 3&up, 5fT, :55.47, MYSTERY CLASSIC, Daring Child, Express News, 7 started.

Bryan Station S., Keeneland Race Course, Oct. 14, $150,000, 3yo, 1mT, 1:35.88, INCA KING, Distorted Reality, Admiral Bird, 10 started.

B. Thoughtful S. (R), Hollywood Park, April 29, $150,000, 4&up, f&m, California-bred, 7fAW, 1:23.06, SOMETHINABOUTLAURA, Getback Time, Two Times Won, 8 started.

Buckland S., Colonial Downs, June 23, $60,000, 3&up, f&m, 5 1/2fT, 1:03.10, ROYAL REGAN, Chinchilla, Privately Approved, 8 started.

Buck's Boy H. (R), Hawthorne Race Course, Nov. 3, $88,725, 3&up, Illinois-conceived and/or-foaled, 1 1/16m, 1:44.77, HE'S HAMMERED, Stonehouse, Win Me Over, 8 started.

Buddy Diliberto Memorial H., Fair Grounds, Dec. 15, $60,000, 3&up, a1 1/16mT, 1:44.86, STERWINS, Optimer (Arg), Save Big Money, 9 started.

Budweiser Challenger S., Tampa Bay Downs, March 10, $65,000, 4&up, 1 1/16m, 1:43.64, ISTAN, Anglers Reef, Cherokee Prince, 8 started.

Budweiser Emerald H., Emerald Downs, June 17, $60,000, 3&up, 1m, 1:34.20, WESTSIDECLYDE, Poker Brad, Courting Seattle, 10 started.

Budweiser H., Sunland Park, Feb. 10, $50,000, 3&up, 5f, :56.55, ARTESIAN, Any Questions, Dangerous Devon, 8 started.

Budweiser Special H., The Downs at Albuquerque, Oct. 6, $65,000, 3&up, 6 1/2f, 1:15.33, ABSOLUTELY TRUE, Express News, Rollicking Caller, 8 started.

Budweiser-Tondi S., Fonner Park, March 24, $25,000, 3&up, 6f, 1:12.80, STORMY BUSINESS, Pager, Tonight Rainbow, 9 started.

BUENA VISTA H. (G2), Santa Anita Park, Feb. 19, $150,000, 4&up, f&m, 1mT, 1:35.77, CONVEYOR'S ANGEL, Singalong (GB), Attima (GB), 8 started.

Buffalo Bayou S., Sam Houston Race Park, Dec. 8, $28,500, 3&up, 1 1/16mT, 1:45.24, GOLD SOUND (FR), Silver Haze, Smooth Bid, 7 started.

Buffalo S. (R), Assiniboia Downs, Sept. 16, $43,668, 2yo, Manitoba-bred, 1m, 1:45.20, EIGHT BY TEN, Meow Wow, Bella Mariella, 10 started.

Buffalo Trace Franklin County S., Keeneland Race Course, Oct. 12, $114,900, 3&up, f&m, 5 1/2fT, 1:03.71, STYLISH WILDCAT, Taletobetold, Adore You, 12 started.

Bull Dog S., Fresno, Oct. 14, $63,700, 3&up, 1m, 1:35.72, PASS THE HEAT, Family Guy, Slow N Easy, 6 started.

BULLEIT BOURBON PAN AMERICAN H. (G3), Gulfstream Park, March 3, $150,000, 4&up, 1 1/2mT, 2:24.98, JAMBALAYA, Hotstufanthensome, Fri Guy, 11 started.

Bullet S. (R), Hollywood Park, May 18, $65,760, 4&up, non-winners of stakes worth $60,000 to the winner in 2006-'07, 6fT, 1:08.23, PARMAR DAY (AUS), Scottsbluff, Exceeding, 5 started.

Bull Page S. (R), Woodbine, Oct. 13, $129,671, 2yo, c&g, Ontario-foaled, 6fAW, 1:08.84, NOT BOURBON, Stuck in Traffic, Lady's First Cat, 9 started.

Bullys Futurity, Lethbridge, Oct. 27, $16,681, 2yo, a6f, 1:12, HESADEMON, Cool Ventura, Strong Arm Willie, 6 started.

Bungalow H. (R), Fairmount Park, July 31, $45,800, 3&up, f&m, Illinois-bred and/or-foaled, 1m70y, 1:45.20, STOP A TRAIN, Meho Rouge, Lampoon, 7 started.

Bunty Lawless S. (R), Woodbine, Sept. 23, $132,823, 3&up, Ontario-foaled, 1mT, 1:37.66, RAHY'S ATTORNEY, Archers Alyancer, Fudgethebottomline, 12 started.

Busanda S., Aqueduct, Jan. 14, $70,850, 3yo, f, 1m70y, 1:43.20, SAGAMOON, My Kitty, That Girl Is Mine, 8 started.

Busher S., Aqueduct, Feb. 25, $69,745, 3yo, f, 1 1/16m, 1:44.76, OLIVINE, Sagamoon, Bare Dancer, 6 started.

Bustles and Bows S., Fairplex Park, Sept. 13, $63,050, 2yo, f, 6 1/2f, 1:18.26, NO MEANS MAYBE, Lauren C, Harlan's Song, 6 started.

Caballos del Sol S., Turf Paradise, Nov. 3, $45,000, 3&up, 6f, 1:09.68, BOBADIEU, Nationhood, Prorunner, 7 started.
Cab Calloway S. (R), Saratoga Race Course, Aug. 8, $150,000, 3yo, progeny of eligible New York stallions, 1 1/16mT, 1:50.62, THUNDERESTIMATE, Logic Way, Stunt Man, 8 started.
Cactus Cup S., Turf Paradise, March 11, $45,000, 3yo, f, 6 1/2f, 1:15.50, FAMOUS GAL, Extraordinary Girl, Against the Law, 6 started.
Cactus Flower H., Turf Paradise, April 21, $40,500, 3&up, f&m, 6f, 1:09.04, SWEET AMBITION, Shesa Private I, Boy Toy, 3 started.
Cactus Wren H. (R), Turf Paradise, Dec. 22, $45,000, 3&up, Arizonabred, 6 1/2f, 1:16.39, KING JUSTIN, Kingsburg, Corporal Tillman, 8 started.
Cactus Wren H. (R), Turf Paradise, Jan. 1, $45,000, 4&up, Arizonabred, 6 1/2f, 1:15.95, MY CUPID, Komax, Kingsburg, 7 started.
Caesar Rodney S., Delaware Park, July 15, $200,600, 3&up, 1 1/16mT, 1:41.62, SILVER TREE, Ballast (Ire), Silent Roar, 7 started.
Cajun S. (R), Louisiana Downs, July 21, $98,000, 3&up, Louisianabred, 6f, 1:10.46, ZARB'S DAHAR, Fass Feat, Storm Heat, 7 started.
Calcasieu S. (R), Delta Downs, Nov. 17, $58,200, 2yo, Louisianabred, 5f, :59.75, LEE'S SPIRIT, Super Ride, Must Acquit, 6 started.
CALDER DERBY (G3), Calder Race Course, Oct. 13, $200,000, 3yo, 1 1/8mT, 1:52.21, SOLDIER'S DANCER, Imawildandcrazyguy, Fair Weather Stan, 11 started.
Calder Oaks, Calder Race Course, Oct. 13, $200,000, 3yo, f, 1 1/8mT, 1:53.10, COZZI CAPITAL, Snow Cone, Casa Mimaty, 7 started.
California Breeders' Champion S. (R), Santa Anita Park, Dec. 26, $138,375, 2yo, California-bred, 7fAW, 1:20.37, BOB BLACK JACK, Dirty Dish Mitch, Red Hot Flame, 9 started.
California Breeders' Champion S. (R), Santa Anita Park, Dec. 29, $139,500, 2yo, f, California-bred, 7fAW, 1:22.09, SPRING AWAKENING, Onebadkitty, Lovehi, 9 started.
California Cup Classic H. (R), Oak Tree at Santa Anita, Nov. 3, $250,000, 3&up, California-bred, 1 1/8mAW, 1:47.23, BOLD CHIEFTAIN, Celtic Dreamin, Seminole Native, 10 started.
California Cup Distaff H. (R), Oak Tree at Santa Anita, Nov. 3, $150,000, 3&up, f&m, California-bred, a6 1/2fT, 1:12.31, GENTLE CHARMER, Lady Gamer, Excessiveobsession, 10 started.
California Cup Distance H. (R), Oak Tree at Santa Anita, Nov. 3, $100,000, 3&up, f&m, California-bred, 1 1/4mT, 2:01.90, IMAGINE, Rockella, Easy Obsession, 9 started.
California Cup Juvenile Fillies S. (R), Oak Tree at Santa Anita, Nov. 3, $125,000, 2yo, f, California-bred, 1 1/16mAW, 1:42.15, RUNFORTHEMONEYBABY, Always in Style, Shes a Real Keeper, 8 started.
California Cup Juvenile S. (R), Oak Tree at Santa Anita, Nov. 3, $125,000, 2yo, c&g, California-bred, 1 1/16mAW, 1:41.65, SIERRA SUNSET, My Redeemer, Harlene, 13 started.
California Cup Matron H. (R), Oak Tree at Santa Anita, Nov. 3, $150,000, 3&up, f&m, California-bred, 1 1/16mAW, 1:40.38, ROMANCE IS DIANE, Bai and Bai, dh-Purrfectly Fitting, dh-Swiss Current, 8 started.
California Cup Mile H. (R), Oak Tree at Santa Anita, Nov. 3, $175,000, 3&up, California-bred, 1mT, 1:33.89, UNUSUAL SUSPECT, Epic Power, Swift Winds, 11 started.
California Cup Sprint H. (R), Oak Tree at Santa Anita, Nov. 3, $150,000, 3&up, California-bred, 6fAW, 1:07.87, BILO, Bonfante, Wind Water, 7 started.
California Cup Starter H. (R), Oak Tree at Santa Anita, Nov. 3, $51,200, 3&up, California-bred starters for a claiming price of $40,000 or less in 2007, 1 1/2mT, 2:28.06, LIL MITCH, Yodelen Dan, My Man Murf, 8 started.
California Cup Starter Sprint H. (R), Oak Tree at Santa Anita, Nov. 3, $50,800, 3&up, California-bred starters for a claiming price of $40,000 or less in 2007, 6fAW, 1:07.34, SWITZERLAND, Bestdressed, Lead Stealer, 9 started.
California Derby, Golden Gate Fields, Jan. 28, $150,000, 3yo, 1 1/16m, 1:44.70, BWANA BULL, Boutrous, Chief's Magic, 6 started.
California Dreamin' H. (R), Del Mar, Aug. 3, $136,200, 3&up, Californiabred, 1 1/8mT, 1:39.98, BOLD CHIEFTAIN, Epic Power, Lucky J. H., 8 started.
CALIFORNIAN S. (G2), Hollywood Park, June 2, $250,000, 3&up, 1 1/8mAW, 1:49.72, BUZZARDS BAY, Sun Boat (GB), A. P. Xcellent, 10 started.
California Oaks, Golden Gate Fields, Feb. 10, $97,500, 3yo, f, 1 1/16m, 1:45.90, EASTLAKE AVENUE, Glorification, Black Hills Goldie, 4 started.
California Thoroughbred Breeders' Association S. (R), Del Mar, July 20, $137,000, 2yo, f, California-bred, 5 1/2fAW, 1:05.79, TREADMILL, I Dig Her, Comical Vacation, 8 started.

California Turf Championship H. (R), Bay Meadows Race Course, Aug. 25, $100,000, 3&up, California-bred, 1mT, 1:37.32, JACK'S WILD, Epic Power, Now Victory, 6 started.
California Turf Sprint Championship H. (R), Bay Meadows Race Course, March 31, $100,000, 4&up, California-bred, 5fT, :57.30, BONFANTE, No Derby, Vaderator, 7 started.
Cal National Snow Chief S. (R), Hollywood Park, April 29, $250,000, 3yo, California-bred, 1 1/16mAW, 1:52.31, LEESIDER, C. T. Zee, Tap It Light, 7 started.
Camelia S. (R), Delta Downs, Jan. 13, $50,000, 4&up, f&m, Louisianabred, 7f, 1:26.60, RASPBERRY WINE, Calista Ridge, Carl's Frosty Girl, 9 started.
Canada Day S., Assiniboia Downs, July 1, $28,155, 3&up, f&m, 1m, 1:41.20, BESHAIRT, Empress Pegasus, Miss Lucky Lou, 6 started.
CANADIAN DERBY (CAN-G3), Northlands Park, Aug. 25, $285,120, 3yo, 1 3/8m, 2:19.60, FOOTPRINT, Gandolf, Ookashada, 7 started.
Canadian Juvenile S., Northlands Park, Sept. 3, $71,018, 2yo, 1m, 1:43, HOUSE MOUSE, Devonaire Joe, Mr Muffin Man, 7 started.
CANADIAN S. (CAN-G2), Woodbine, Sept. 16, $331,489, 3&up, f&m, a1 1/8mT, 1:45.62, ESSENTIAL EDGE, Sealy Hill, Meribel, 9 started.
CANADIAN TURF H. (G3), Gulfstream Park, Feb. 3, $100,000, 4&up, 1 1/16mT, 1:39.70, GIANT WRECKER, Host (Chi), Jambalaya, 7 started.
Candy Eclair S., Delaware Park, June 17, $60,450, 3&up, f&m, a5fT, :57.83, TRULY BLUSHED, Top Ten List, Coli Bear, 7 started.
Candy Eclair S., Monmouth Park, June 3, $60,000, 3&up, f&m, 5 1/2fT, 1:01.54, HADDIE BE GOOD, Spanish Lullaby, Mohegan Sky, 8 started.
Canterbury Park Lassie S., Canterbury Park, July 21, $45,000, 2yo, f, 5 1/2f, 1:04.58, HURRICANE BERNIE, Mizzcan'tbewrong, Carolina Mist, 11 started.
Capades S., Saratoga Race Course, Aug. 22, $82,250, 3&up, f&m, 5 1/2fT, 1:02.79, JAZZY (ARG), Stormy Kiss (Arg), Smart and Fancy, 9 started.
Cape Henlopen S., Delaware Park, Sept. 3, $62,000, 3&up, 1 1/2mT, 2:28.56, ALWAYS FIRST (GB), Dubai Cat, Bee Charmer (Ire), 9 started.
Capital Request S., Calder Race Course, Sept. 29, $50,000, 3&up, f&m, 7 1/2fT, 1:30.84, ANNABILL, Running Lass, Cozzi Capital, 11 started.
Capitol City Futurity, Lincoln State Fair, July 15, $30,475, 2yo, f, 1:15.20, TELLIN ON YOU, Craftmaster, Irish Haystack, 9 started.
Capitol Claiming S., Les Bois Park, July 7, $12,050, 3&up, 7f, 1:26.20, ON LEAVE, Sam the Man, Dothedevilin, 10 started.
Capote S., Aqueduct, Dec. 12, $76,750, 2yo, 6f, 1:10.66, GRAND MINSTREL, All Expenses Paid, Red Reef, 7 started.
Captain Condo S. (R), Emerald Downs, Sept. 16, $45,000, 2yo, c&g, Washington-bred, 6f, 1:08.40, MARGO'S GIFT, Arrow Junction, Special Negotiator, 7 started.
Captain My Captain H. (R), Philadelphia Park, July 28, $100,000, 3&up, Pennsylvania-sired, 6f, 1:08.81, SECRETINTELLIGENCE, Thaddeus, Power by Leigh, 8 started.
Captain Squire H., Hollywood Park, June 29, $89,950, 3yo, 6fT, 1:08.81, ZONING IN, Noble Court, Quintons Shocker, 5 started.
CARDINAL H. (G3), Churchill Downs, Nov. 17, $164,550, 3&up, f&m, 1 1/8mT, 1:51.06, CRIMINOLOGIST, Argentina (Ire), Nottawasaga, 8 started.
Caressing H., Churchill Downs, Nov. 24, $64,900, 2yo, f, 1mT, 1:39.96, ABSOLUTELY CINDY, Steady Patter, Mine Or Who's, 11 started.
Caress S., Belmont Park, May 25, $68,650, 3&up, f&m, 6f, 1:08.05, BRUSHED BAYOU, Green Amira (GB), Runaway Cat, 9 started.
CARF-CMC Starter Series S. (R), Ferndale, Aug. 19, $10,650, 3&up, starters for a claiming price of $4,000 or less in 2006-'07, 1 1/4m, 1:46.27, WISENHEIMER, Looks Lika Fish, Ready to Flirt, 5 started.
CARLETON F. BURKE H. (G3), Oak Tree at Santa Anita, Oct. 28, $111,300, 3&up, 1 1/2mT, 2:24.13, SPRING HOUSE, Isipingo, Runaway Dancer, 10 started.
Carl G. Rose Classic H. (R), Calder Race Course, Nov. 10, $200,000, 3&up, Florida-bred, 1 1/8m, 1:52.53, ELECTRIFY, Imawildandcrazyguy, Summer Book, 8 started.
Carolina First Carolina Cup Hurdle S. (R), Camden, March 31, $72,750, 4&up, non-winners over hurdles before March 1, 2006, a2 1/8mT, 4:03.80, ORISON, Rare Bush, dh-Sovereign Duty, dh-Gliding (NZ), 12 started.
Carol Wilson S., Grants Pass, July 4, $3,601, 3&up, f&m, 6 1/2f, 1:18.20, PEARLS 'N' SATIN, Charlee Chop Chop, In Love With Loot, 6 started.
Carotene S. (R), Woodbine, Oct. 6, $152,775, 3yo, f, Ontario-foaled,

Racing — 2007 Stakes Races 505

1¹⁄₁₆mT, 1:54.42, SANS SOUCI ISLAND, Dance to My Tune, Siwa, 5 started.
Carousel S., Oaklawn Park, March 31, $50,000, 4&up, f&m, 6f, 1:10.29, MISS MACY SUE, True Tails, Wildcat Bettie B, 7 started.
CARRY BACK S. (G2), Calder Race Course, July 7, $300,000, 3yo, 6f, 1:09.84, BLACK SEVENTEEN, Teuflesberg, Yesbyjimminy, 9 started.
CARTER H. (G1), Aqueduct, April 7, $300,000, 3&up, 7f, 1:21.46, SILVER WAGON, Diabolical, Ah Day, 6 started.
Carterista H., Calder Race Course, Sept. 3, $88,650, 3&up, 1¹⁄₁₆mT, 1:39.46, JET PROPULSION, Magic Mecke, Bob's Proud Moment, 4 started.
Carter McGregor Jr. Memorial S. (R), Lone Star Park, June 16, $50,000, 3&up, Texas-bred, 6f, 1:09.93, TOGA TOO, Lissa's Star, War Bridle, 9 started.
Casey Darnell Pony Express S. (R), The Downs at Albuquerque, Aug. 19, $59,750, 3&up, New Mexico-bred, 5¹⁄₂f, 1:03.35, GHOSTLY ILLUSION, Boom Boom, dh-Stately'n Nicer, dh-Bill's Demon, 7 started.
CASHCALL FUTURITY (G1), Hollywood Park, Dec. 22, $753,000, 2yo, 1¹⁄₁₆mAW, 1:40.82, INTO MISCHIEF, Colonel John, Massive Drama, 12 started.
CASHCALL MILE INVITATIONAL S. (G2), Hollywood Park, July 6, $1,000,000, 3&up, f&m, 1mT, 1:33.56, LADY OF VENICE (FR), Precious Kitten, Price Tag (GB), 9 started.
Cassidy S., Calder Race Course, Oct. 13, $90,000, 2yo, f, 5¹⁄₂f, 1:05.38 (NTR), AREALHOTLOVER, Permanent Makeup, Banga Ridge, 8 started.
Castle Guard H. (R), Meadowlands, Sept. 28, $55,000, 3&up, New Jersey-bred, 1m, 1:36.56, ROLLED UP, Fagedaboudit Sal, Who's the Cowboy, 7 started.
Catcharisingstar S., Calder Race Course, Sept. 1, $45,000, 2yo, f, 5fT, :56.53, EXCESSIVE HEAT, Satellite Phone, Ariel Bright, 9 started.
Cat's Cradle H. (R), Hollywood Park, Dec. 21, $107,200, 3&up, f&m, California-bred, 7¹⁄₂fAW, 1:28.15, CURIOUSLY SWEET, Kalookan Year, Fun Logic, 9 started.
Caught in the Rain H. (R), Philadelphia Park, June 2, $60,000, 3&up, f&m, Pennsylvania-bred, 1m70y, 1:42.14, RAGING RAPIDS, Hailie's Girl, dh-Queen's Request, dh-J. D. Safari, 6 started.
Cavonnier Juvenile S., Santa Rosa, Aug. 5, $61,210, 2yo, 5¹⁄₂f, 1:03.12, WHATEVER WHENEVER, Sierra Sunset, Sea Captain, 8 started.
Cavonnier S. (R), Oak Tree at Santa Anita, Oct. 8, $81,110, 2yo, California-bred, 7fAW, 1:22.40, NEVADA WORRIER, Comissioner Gordon, Suit Yourself, 8 started.
Centennial Oklahoma Derby, Remington Park, Oct. 21, $300,000, 3yo, 1¹⁄₈m, 1:49.74, GOING BALLISTIC, Reporting for Duty, Sumac, 11 started.
Centennial S., Remington Park, Dec. 1, $50,000, 2yo, c&g, 1mT, 1:38.68, RED BIRDS MAGICIAN, Pursue a Dream, Wild Posse, 10 started.
CENTRAL BANK TRANSYLVANIA S. (G3), Keeneland Race Course, April 6, $150,000, 3yo, 1mT, 1:36.98, MARCAVELLY, In Jest, Cobrador, 9 started.
Central Iowa S., Prairie Meadows, Sept. 8, $46,800, 3&up, f&m, 1¹⁄₁₆m, 1:42.12, ROLLING SEA, Thekatcamehome, Texas Rush, 4 started.
CERF H. (R), Del Mar, Sept. 5, $97,960, 3&up, f&m, non-winners of a stakes worth $50,000 over one mile since March 1, 6fAW, 1:11.75, THEVERYTHOUGHTOF U, Sindy With an S, Sophie's Trophy, 13 started.
Certified Thoroughbred Inaugural S. (R), North Dakota Horse Park, July 27, $12,600, 3&up, North Dakota-bred, 6f, 1:14.60, MADDIES BLUES, My Friend Frank, J Dam Strike, 6 started.
Certified Thoroughbred S. (R), North Dakota Horse Park, Aug. 5, $12,600, 4&up, North Dakota-bred, 1m, 1:43.60, HIGH CLASS LAD, Maddies Blues, Aferds Code Red, 6 started.
Chamisa H., The Downs at Albuquerque, Aug. 31, $45,000, 3&up, f&m, 6¹⁄₂f, 1:15.73, TEMPTING DATE, I'm N Clover, Ladysgothelooks, 9 started.
Champagneforashley S. (R), Aqueduct, Feb. 16, $66,509, 4&up, New York-bred, 1m70y, 1:41.55, SHUFFLING MADDNES, Carminooch, Go Fernando Go, 5 started.
Champagne Isle S., Turf Paradise, Dec. 4, $30,700, 3&up, f&m, a4¹⁄₂fT, 51.76, DAMARA, Light My Ducks, Blumin Beauty, 7 started.
CHAMPAGNE S. (G1), Belmont Park, Oct. 6, $416,000, 2yo, 1m, 1:36.12, WAR PASS, Pyro, Z Humor, 8 started.

Champali S., Calder Race Course, June 16, $50,000, 3&up, 6f, 1:10.16, MACH RIDE, How's Your Halo, Electrify, 6 started.
Chandler S., Turf Paradise, Nov. 10, $45,000, 3yo, f, 7¹⁄₂fT, 1:30.06, GLORIFICAMUS (IRE), Silk Degrees, Zaylaway, 8 started.
Chantilly S., Assiniboia Downs, June 10, $42,444, 3yo, f, 6f, 1:11.60, DES MOINES, Out for Glory, Primetime Cat, 7 started.
Chaposa Springs H., Calder Race Course, Dec. 29, $100,000, 3&up, f&m, 7f, 1:24.23, CHER AMI, Change Up, Running Lass, 7 started.
Chariot Chaser H., Northlands Park, July 6, $47,315, 3yo, f, 6¹⁄₂f, 1:18.40, TANIKA, Bank Deposit, Hail to Dawn, 8 started.
Charles Hesse Jersey Breeders' H. (R), Monmouth Park, Aug. 26, $135,000, 3&up, New Jersey-bred, 1¹⁄₁₆m, 1:42.53, CARROTS ONLY, Fagedaboudit Sal, Midnight Express, 8 started.
Charles Taylor Derby, The Downs at Albuquerque, Aug. 11, $50,000, 3yo, 1¹⁄₁₆m, 1:45.08, WESTERN PRIZE, Preferred Yield, Rival Islands, 6 started.
Charles Town Dash Invitational H., Charles Town Races, July 4, $100,000, 3&up, 7f, 1:24.20, CONFUCIUS SAY, P. Kerney, Donald's Pride, 6 started.
CHARLES WHITTINGHAM MEMORIAL H. (G1), Hollywood Park, June 9, $300,000, 3&up, 1¹⁄₄mT, 1:58.77, AFTER MARKET, Lava Man, Obrigado (Fr), 8 started.
Charlie Barley S., Woodbine, June 24, $96,108, 3yo, 1mT, 1:33.82, ICE BEAR, Payday Peril, Artie Hot, 12 started.
Charlie Iles Express H., The Downs at Albuquerque, Sept. 2, $45,000, 4&up, 6¹⁄₂f, 1:22.03, WHIRL, Orphan Brigade, Rollicking Caller, 9 started.
Chaves County S., Zia Park, Nov. 24, $66,375, 3&up, f&m, 1m, 1:41, BUDDHA LADY, Silent Fusaichi, Camelita, 7 started.
Chelsey Flower S. (R), Belmont Park, Oct. 14, $78,150, 3&up, f&m, non-winners of a stakes on the turf in 2007, 1¹⁄₁₆mT, 1:50.17, SHAPIRA (CHI), Calla Lily, Miracle Moment, 7 started.
Chenery S., Colonial Downs, July 29, $60,000, 3&up, 5¹⁄₂fT, 1:02.30, HIGH APPEAL, Big Wig, Run Jickster Run, 5 started.
Cherokee River Stables Turf Classic S. (R), Tampa Bay Downs, April 7, $85,000, 4&up, Florida-bred, a1¹⁄₁₆mT, 1:48.06, GO BETWEEN, Therecomesatiger, Art of Diplomacy, 6 started.
Cherokee Run H., Churchill Downs, Nov. 3, $115,300, 3&up, 5fT, :56.53, SMART ENOUGH, Chihulykee, Fort Prado, 9 started.
Chesapeake S., Colonial Downs, Aug. 4, $60,000, 3&up, 6f, 1:09.30, UNBRIDLED BEHAVIOR, Mister Supremo, Hi Time Scott, 5 started.
CHICAGO H. (G3), Arlington Park, June 16, $175,000, 3&up, f&m, 7fAW, 1:23.10, LADY BELSARA, Trendy Lady, Dimple Pinch, 10 started.
Chicagoland H. (R), Hawthorne Race Course, April 28, $87,866, 4&up, Illinois-conceived and/or -foaled, 6f, 1:10.62, HIGH EXPECTATIONS, Distorted Groom, Sub Futz Jr, 8 started.
Chick Lang Jr. Memorial S., Retama Park, Sept. 15, $45,000, 3yo, 7¹⁄₂fT, 1:29.11, GOLD WONDER, Man Named Sue, Slew by Slew, 11 started.
Chief Bearhart S., Woodbine, Oct. 27, $104,346, 3&up, 1¹⁄₄mT, 2:06.37, ECCENTRIC (GB), Royal Challenger, Skipped Bail, 9 started.
Chief Narbona S. (R), The Downs at Albuquerque, Aug. 19, $63,250, 3yo, f, New Mexico-bred, 6f, 1:11.24, SILVER EXPRESSION, Good Looker R F, Hit the Chime, 5 started.
Chieftan's Command S. (R), Aqueduct, April 25, $64,950, 4&up, f&m, non-winners of a graded stakes, 1¹⁄₈m, 1:51.41, MAIZELLE, Daytime Promise, Femmina, 5 started.
CHILUKKI S. (G2), Churchill Downs, Nov. 3, $221,000, 3&up, f&m, 1m, 1:36.02, ROLLING SEA, High Heels, My Chickadee, 8 started.
China Doll S., Santa Anita Park, March 3, $96,850, 3yo, f, 1mT, 1:34.88, PASSIFIED (GB), Hucking Hot (GB), Gotta Have Her, 11 started.
CHINESE CULTURAL CENTRE SEAGRAM CUP S. (CAN-G3), Woodbine, July 29, $141,270, 3&up, 1¹⁄₁₆mAW, 1:43.73, GOULDINGS GREEN, Palladio, Judiths Wild Rush, 5 started.
Chinook Pass Sprint S. (R), Emerald Downs, Sept. 16, $45,000, 3&up, Washington-bred, 6f, 1:07.60, CHICKASAW PARK, Fort Madison, Light My Ducks, 4 started.
Chippewa Downs Certified S. (R), Chippewa Downs, June 23, $4,200, 2yo, North Dakota-bred, 4¹⁄₂f, :57, R ROXY, Dakota's Punch, Sher Worthy, 7 started.
Chippewa Downs Open S., Chippewa Downs, June 16, $2,900, 2yo, 4¹⁄₂f, :59, MISS HONEY CALLING, Dakota's Punch, Sher Worthy, 7 started.
Chippewa Downs Open Thoroughbred S., Chippewa Downs, June 24, $3,800, 4&up, 1¹⁄₁₆m, 1:58.20, FABULOUS WULLY, Harbour Axe, Red Briar (Ire), 8 started.

Chippewa Downs Thoroughbred S. (R), Chippewa Downs, June 24, $4,175, 3&up, North Dakota-bred, 6½f, 1:24, AFERDS CODE RED, High Class Lad, Rough Knight, 7 started.

Choice S., Monmouth Park, July 8, $60,000, 3yo, 1⅛mT, 1:49.02, FRENCH VINTAGE, Chaluiwitcane, You're the Mon, 6 started.

Chou Croute Breeders' Cup H., Fair Grounds, Feb. 17, $57,000, 4&up, f&m, 1 1/16m, 1:44.90, DELICATE DYNAMITE, Eyes On Eddy, Culinary, 5 started.

Chris Christian S., Les Bois Park, June 9, $2,000, 2yo, c&g, 5f, :59.30, POKETFULOFFEATHERS, Snowbound Vicky, Adam Good Heart, 8 started.

Chris Christian S., Les Bois Park, June 9, $2,000, 2yo, f, 5f, :59, LADY RAILRIDER, Storm Seige, Brownstown Jazz, 8 started.

Chris Christian S., Les Bois Park, June 23, $22,000, 2yo, 5f, 1:01, STORM SEIGE, Adam Good Heart, Richest Wager, 9 started.

Chris Loseth H., Hastings Race Course, July 8, $51,969, 3yo, 1 1/16m, 1:45.06, OOKASHADA, Bad Sneakers, Long Journey, 7 started.

Chris Thomas Turf Classic S., Tampa Bay Downs, May 5, $75,000, 3&up, a1⅛mT, 1:49.53, THERECOMESATIGER, Revved Up, Puppeteer (GB), 8 started.

Christmas S., Mountaineer Race Track and Gaming Resort, Dec. 22, $75,000, 3&up, 6f, 1:11.19, RAVALO, Coach Jimi Lee, Cowboy Hardware, 5 started.

Christopher Elser Memorial S. (R), Philadelphia Park, Oct. 28, $50,198, 2yo, have spent 90 days in South Carolina and paid a nomination fee to the SCTOBA, 6½f, 1:17.89, IZZY SPEAKING, Salty Cheeks, City Chatter, 4 started.

Chuck N Luck S., Turf Paradise, Dec. 11, $31,000, 3yo, a1mT, 1:39.50, PREFERREDYIELD, Mr Charlypotatoes, Rockinstomper, 8 started.

Chuck N Luck S., Turf Paradise, Jan. 30, $25,200, 4&up, 1m, 1:36.32, TRAIL THIS, Ozzy's Shame, Hey Slick, 9 started.

Chuck Taliaferro Memorial S., Remington Park, Sept. 9, $50,000, 3&up, 6f, 1:09.74, MYSTERY CLASSIC, Wheaton Home, Gyrovagi, 9 started.

CHURCHILL DISTAFF TURF MILE S. (G3), Churchill Downs, May 5, $166,350, 3&up, f&m, 1mT, 1:36.89, TAKE THE RIBBON, Quite a Bride, Rich Fantasy, 5 started.

CHURCHILL DOWNS S. (G2), Churchill Downs, May 5, $277,750, 4&up, 7f, 1:22.31, SAINT ANDDAN, Ah Day, Will He Shine, 6 started.

CICADA S. (G3), Aqueduct, March 24, $109,600, 3yo, f, 6f, 1:10.43, CONTROL SYSTEM, Golden Dreamer, Special Dream, 7 started.

Cimarron S., Remington Park, Nov. 18, $50,000, 2yo, f, 7½fT, 1:30.17, SLICK KITTY, Carolina Mist, Ballistae, 12 started.

Cincinnatian S. (R), River Downs, July 1, $55,000, 3yo, f, Ohio-bred, 1 1/16m, 1:46.60, MINI MOM, Montfort Lane, Anne Rides Again, 6 started.

Cincinnati Trophy S., Turfway Park, Jan. 20, $50,000, 3yo, f, 6½fAW, 1:16.46, OVER THE EDGE, Miss A. Bomb, She's Impossible, 8 started.

Cinderella S., Hollywood Park, May 27, $77,775, 2yo, f, 5½fAW, 1:06.48, WONDERFUL LUCK, Another Aleyna, Affirmed Cat, 9 started.

Cinderella S. (R), Charles Town Races, Sept. 8, $46,100, 2yo, f, West Virginia-bred, 4½f, :53.43, dh-WE'RE IN THE MONEY, dh-CHEZ LANG, Color Parade, 6 started.

CINEMA BREEDERS' CUP H. (G3), Hollywood Park, June 23, $113,500, 3yo, 1⅛mT, 1:47.40, WORLDLY (GB), Golden Balls (Ire), Tycoon Doby, 5 started.

Cinnamon Girl S., Calder Race Course, Sept. 22, $45,000, 3&up, f&m, 1 1/16m, 1:47.27, AMAZING SPEED, Funny Annie, Wild Wedding, 6 started.

CITATION H. (G1), Hollywood Park, Nov. 23, $400,000, 3&up, 1 1/16mT, 1:39.72, LANG FIELD, Zann, Proudinsky (Ger), 9 started.

City Centre Bingo Early Bird H., Marquis Downs, July 21, $5,723, 3&up, 7f, 1:23.35 (NTR), STANDOFF, Bethune, Tough Topic, 8 started.

City Centre Bingo Sweepstakes H., Marquis Downs, Sept. 7, $5,701, 3&up, 1 1/16m, 1:45.47, STANDOFF, Whirly Weekend, Notafigment, 4 started.

City Centre Bingo Twin Charities H., Marquis Downs, Aug. 24, $5,686, 3&up, 1m, 1:40.37, STANDOFF, Beau Ring, Flying Russian, 6 started.

City of Anderson S. (R), Hoosier Park, Oct. 13, $45,000, 2yo, f, Indiana-bred, 5½f, 1:07.39, LIL MAI TAI, Hey There Cupcake, Larry's Love, 6 started.

City of Edmonton Distaff H., Northlands Park, Aug. 25, $95,040, 3&up, f&m, 1 1/16m, 1:45.20, MONASHEE, Culpeper Moon, Dixietwostepper, 6 started.

City of Hollywood S. (R), Gulfstream Park, March 1, $50,000, 4&up, f&m, non-winners of a stakes, 1⅛mT, 1:47.25, LA DOLCE VITA, Factual Contender, Mama I'm Home, 10 started.

City of Phoenix S., Turf Paradise, Oct. 27, $45,000, 3&up, f&m, 6f, 1:10.23, PINATA, Blumin Beauty, Beaulena, 8 started.

Claiming Crown Emerald S. (R), Ellis Park, Aug. 4, $97,000, 3&up, starters for a claiming price of $25,000 or less since August 1, 2006, 1 1/16mT, 1:40.23, ONE EYED JOKER, Habaneros, Great Bloom, 11 started.

Claiming Crown Express S. (R), Ellis Park, Aug. 4, $47,500, 3&up, starters for a claiming price of $7,500 or less since August 1, 2006, 6f, 1:10.17, GOLDEN HARE, Implicit, Cool Lover, 9 started.

Claiming Crown Glass Slipper S. (R), Ellis Park, Aug. 4, $72,000, 3&up, f&m, starters for a claiming price of $16,000 or less since August 1, 2006, 6f, 1:10.70, ADORE YOU, Mama's Temper, Sumneytown, 10 started.

Claiming Crown Iron Horse S. (R), Ellis Park, Aug. 4, $47,000, 3&up, starters for a claiming price of $7,500 or less since August 1, 2006, 1m, 1:36.65, BARGAINWITHTHDEVIL, Kenai River, Western Revenge, 8 started.

Claiming Crown Jewel S. (R), Ellis Park, Aug. 4, $144,000, 3&up, starters for a claiming price of $35,000 or less since August 1, 2006, 1⅛m, 1:50.83, MIAMI SUNRISE, Semi Lost, Kings Challenge, 10 started.

Claiming Crown Rapid Transit S. (R), Ellis Park, Aug. 4, $72,000, 3&up, starters for a claiming price of $16,000 or less since August 1, 2006, 6f, 1:10.72, NEVERBEENDANCIN', Lookinforthesecret, Korbyn Gold, 10 started.

Claiming Crown Tiara S. (R), Ellis Park, Aug. 4, $96,000, 3&up, f&m, starters for a claiming price of $25,000 or less since August 1, 2006, 1 1/16mT, 1:42.04, UNPLUGGED, Heathersdaddysbaby, Westward Miss, 10 started.

Claire Marine S., Arlington Park, Sept. 3, $48,150, 3&up, f&m, 1½mT, 2:30.52, AROSA (IRE), Indy Trouble, Yanquee Reign, 10 started.

Clarendon S. (R), Woodbine, July 7, $144,505, 2yo, Canadian-bred, 5½fAW, 1:06.14, DONERAILE GEM, Druids Mound, Baldassare, 9 started.

CLARK H. (G2), Churchill Downs, Nov. 23, $554,000, 3&up, 1⅛m, 1:48.66, A. P. ARROW, Brass Hat, Diamond Stripes, 9 started.

Classy Mirage S. (R), Saratoga Race Course, Aug. 27, $82,500, 3&up, f&m, non-winners of an open stakes in 2007, 6½f, 1:16.10, CHEROKEE JEWEL, Sugar Swirl, Rich Fantasy, 6 started.

Classy 'n Smart S. (R), Woodbine, Oct. 8, $127,720, 3&up, f&m, Ontario-foaled, 1 1/16mAW, 1:45.78, FINANCINGAVAILABLE, Executive Flight, Blonde Wisdom, 6 started.

CLEMENT L. HIRSCH H. (G2), Del Mar, Aug. 5, $294,000, 3&up, f&m, 1 1/16mAW, 1:48.29, NASHOBA'S KEY, Bai and Bai, Balance, 4 started.

CLEMENT L. HIRSCH MEMORIAL TURF CHAMPIONSHIP S. (G1), Oak Tree at Santa Anita, Oct. 6, $250,000, 3&up, 1¼mT, 1:59.89, ARTISTE ROYAL (IRE), The Tin Man, Isipingo, 7 started.

Cleveland Gold Cup S. (R), Thistledown, June 30, $100,000, 3yo, Ohio-bred, 1⅛m, 1:51.22, PYRITE PERSONAL, Pay the Man, Smarmy, 14 started.

Cleveland Kindergarten S. (R), Thistledown, Aug. 10, $50,000, 2yo, Ohio-bred, 6f, 1:12.60, PERFECTLY PLAYED, Buzz Bunny, Gold Rush Casey, 7 started.

Clever Trevor S., Remington Park, Sept. 3, $50,000, 2yo, 6f, 1:09.88, DILL OR NO DILL, Ling Ling Qi, Jeri Harper, 8 started.

CLIFF HANGER S. (G3), Meadowlands, Sept. 21, $150,000, 3&up, 1 1/16mT, 1:41.48, PRESIOUS PASSION, Touched by Madness, Carnera, 7 started.

Club House Special S., Columbus Races, Aug. 25, $11,100, 2yo, 6f, 1:16.80, SCOOTER BLUE, Craftmaster, City Slicker, 5 started.

COACHING CLUB AMERICAN OAKS (G1), Belmont Park, July 21, $300,000, 3yo, f, 1¼m, 2:02.17, OCTAVE, Lear's Princess, Folk, 7 started.

Coca-Cola Bassinet S., River Downs, Sept. 1, $100,000, 2yo, f, 6f, 1:13, KADIRA, Dreabons Legacy, Palanka City, 7 started.

C. O. "Ken" Kendrick Memorial S. (R), SunRay Park, June 30, $61,200, 2yo, f, New Mexico-bred, 4½f, :51.20, PREMEDITATED LEGS, Blooming Pleasure, Penny Dancer, 10 started.

Colin S., Woodbine, July 21, $120,001, 2yo, 6fAW, 1:11.05, BEAR HOLIDAY, Dancing Allstar, Mighty Vow, 7 started.

Colleen S., Monmouth Park, July 29, $58,800, 2yo, f, 5½f, 1:04.12, NEW YORK CITY GIRL, Expect the End, Dubit, 4 started.

Collegian S., Suffolk Downs, Sept. 22, $45,000, 3yo, 6f, 1:09.95, ON THE VINEYARD, Southern Rainbow, Bootleggin Gent, 10 started.

Colonel E. R. Bradley H., Fair Grounds, Jan. 13, $100,000, 4&up, a$1\frac{1}{16}$mT, 1:43.22, PURIM, Fort Prado, Cloudy's Knight, 12 started.

Colonel Power S., Fair Grounds, Jan. 13, $100,000, 4&up, 6f, 1:09.58, VENOMOUS, Clock Stopper, Meteor Impact, 9 started.

COLONIAL TURF CUP S. (G3), Colonial Downs, June 16, $750,000, 3yo, $1\frac{3}{16}$mT, 1:55.68, SUMMER DOLDRUMS, Strike a Deal, Souvenir Slew, 9 started.

Colorado-Bred Stallion S. (R), Arapahoe Park, July 30, $23,395, 3yo, f, Colorado-bred progeny of stallions standing in Colorado in 2003, 7f, 1:24.43, MEADOW DANCER, Ima Shy Girl, Cocktails for Cash, 6 started.

Colorado Breeders' Stallion S. (R), Arapahoe Park, July 8, $23,792, 3yo, c&g, Colorado-bred, 7f, 1:25.31, MENOKEN MOON, Such a Deal, Dynamite Charlie, 5 started.

Colorado Derby, Arapahoe Park, July 22, $28,350, 3yo, $1\frac{1}{16}$m, 1:45.55, FOLSUM, Preferred Yield, Hidden Van, 9 started.

Colts Neck H. (R), Monmouth Park, July 4, $60,000, 3&up, New Jersey-bred, 6f, 1:08.33 (NTR), JOEY P., Hey Chub, Who's the Cowboy, 5 started.

Columbia River S., Portland Meadows, Nov. 19, $21,550, 2yo, 6f, 1:10.94, DIXIELAND EASY, Sam Angelo, Snowbound Tiger, 7 started.

Columbus Breeders' Special S. (R), Columbus Races, Aug. 26, $13,100, 3yo, c&g, Nebraska-bred, $6\frac{1}{2}$f, 1:20.20, BEVYS BEST, Show My Dancer, Heso, 6 started.

Columbus Breeders' Special S. (R), Columbus Races, Aug. 26, $13,200, 3yo, f, Nebraska-bred, $6\frac{1}{2}$f, 1:22.60, PLAER'S TRUMP, Shade On, Phyllee Rae, 7 started.

Columbus Debutante S. (R), Columbus Races, Sept. 7, $13,100, 2yo, f, Nebraska-bred, 6f, 1:15.40, DEPUTY'S WHIRL, Molly Pontz, Sunday Dancer, 6 started.

Columbus Futurity (R), Columbus Races, Sept. 7, $12,691, 2yo, c&g, Nebraska-bred, 6f, 1:17.60, JADYNS JET, Case On Ice, Blumin Dakota, 4 started.

COMELY S. (G2), Aqueduct, April 14, $150,000, 3yo, f, 1m, 1:36.54, BOCA GRANDE, Winning Point, Perfect Forest, 8 started.

Come Summer S., Canterbury Park, July 3, $45,000, 3yo, a1mT, 1:37.79, CHIEF THIEF, Just a Nibble, Pirate Saint, 12 started.

COMMONWEALTH BREEDERS' CUP S. (G2), Keeneland Race Course, April 14, $400,000, 3&up, 7fAW, 1:21.26, SILENT NAME (JPN), Lewis Michael, Steel Light, 11 started.

Commonwealth Turf S., Churchill Downs, Nov. 11, $166,500, 3yo, $1\frac{1}{16}$mT, 1:43.17, INCA KING, Equitable, Slew's Tizzy, 7 started.

Concern H., Louisiana Downs, Aug. 18, $74,475, 3&up, $1\frac{1}{16}$mT, 1:44.03, STARSPANGLED GATOR, Electric Chant, Middleweight, 8 started.

Con Jackson Claiming H. (R), The Downs at Albuquerque, Sept. 23, $16,550, 3&up, starters for a claiming price of $5,000, $1\frac{13}{16}$m, 3:11.97, HOPE FOR PEACE, Chocolate Reef, Butte City, 10 started.

CONNAUGHT CUP S. (CAN-G3), Woodbine, May 27, $139,701, 4&up, $1\frac{1}{16}$mT, 1:45.05, ECCENTRIC (GB), As Expected, Shoal Water, 7 started.

Connie Ann S., Calder Race Course, Nov. 24, $35,000, 3&up, f&m, 7f, 1:24.44, RUNNING LASS, Amazing Speed, Forever Together, 7 started.

Conniver S. (R), Laurel Park, March 10, $75,000, 3&up, f&m, Maryland-bred, 7f, 1:25.13, SILMARIL, La Chica Rica, Scheing E Jet, 5 started.

Continental Mile S., Monmouth Park, Aug. 18, $63,600, 2yo, 1m (originally scheduled on the turf), 1:38.89, ATONED, Hop Skip and Away, Run Sully Run, 7 started.

Cool Air S., Calder Race Course, May 13, $50,000, 3&up, f&m, 5fT, :56.11, CHARLIE PAPA, El Bank Robber, Silversider, 7 started.

COOLMORE LEXINGTON S. (G2), Keeneland Race Course, April 21, $325,000, 3yo, $1\frac{1}{16}$mAW, 1:43.20, SLEW'S TIZZY, Starbase, Forty Grams, 9 started.

Copano S., Calder Race Course, Oct. 27, $50,000, 3&up, f&m, 1m, 1:38.79, ANNABILL, Running Lass, Leona's Knight, 8 started.

Copper Top Futurity (R), Sunland Park, April 28, $200,869, 2yo, New Mexico-bred, $4\frac{1}{2}$f, :51.80, THATS OUR FRED, Brax, Danseur First, 10 started.

Cormorant S. (R), Aqueduct, Nov. 11, $75,000, 3&up, c&g, progeny of eligible New York stallions, $1\frac{1}{16}$mT, 1:46.47, RED ZIPPER, Pa Pa Da, Theconfidenceman, 9 started.

Coronado's Quest S., Monmouth Park, June 24, $60,000, 3yo, 1m70y, 1:39.42, CABLE BOY, Saratoga Lulaby, Pink Viper, 5 started.

Coronation Futurity (R), Woodbine, Nov. 4, $268,028, 2yo, Canadian-bred, $1\frac{1}{8}$mAW, 1:53.40, KESAGAMI, Cool Gator, Deputiformer, 6 started.

Correction H., Aqueduct, Feb. 11, $68,575, 3&up, f&m, 6f, 1:10.18, MAGNOLIA JACKSON, Yolanda B. Too, Towering Escape, 5 started.

Cortan S. (R), Charles Town Races, June 9, $50,900, 3&up, c&g, most starts at Charles Town in last four starts, 7f, 1:26.32, DONALD'S PRIDE, Raggedy Andy, It'sallaboutyoulou, 5 started.

Corte Madera S., Golden Gate Fields, Dec. 8, $75,000, 2yo, f, 1mAW, 1:38.07, LA MINA, Christmas Ship, Ice Lady, 7 started.

Costy Caras Memorial S. (R), Charles Town Races, May 12, $51,100, 3&up, c&g, most starts at Charles Town in last four starts, $4\frac{1}{2}$f, :53.05, CALISTHENIC, General Tommy, Morning Out, 7 started.

Cotton Fitzsimmons Mile H., Turf Paradise, Jan. 6, $75,000, 4&up, 1mT, 1:36.11, NIGHT CHAPTER (GB), dh-True Dancer, dh-Wait in Line, 8 started.

Cougar II H. (R), Del Mar, Aug. 1, $88,935, 3&up, non-winners of a stakes of $50,000 at one mile or over in 2007, $1\frac{3}{8}$mT, 2:13.18, ATLANDO (IRE), Toasted, Bravo Maestro, 6 started.

Count Fleet S., Aqueduct, Jan. 6, $70,865, 3yo, 1m70y, 1:42.94, PINK VIPER, Johannesburg Star, Sir Whimsey, 6 started.

COUNT FLEET SPRINT H. (G3), Oaklawn Park, April 13, $150,000, 4&up, 6f, 1:09.11, BORDONARO, Semaphore Man, Off Duty, 6 started.

Count Lathum S., Northlands Park, Aug. 4, $71,115, 3yo, $1\frac{1}{16}$m, 1:43.20, FOOTPRINT, Greenwood Meadow, Codio, 10 started.

Country Road S. (R), Charles Town Races, May 19, $51,150, 3yo, f, most starts at Charles Town in last four starts, $4\frac{1}{2}$f, :52.98, SNOW WAY, She's a Smash, Bird of War, 7 started.

Cowboy Up H., Sun Downs, April 15, $3,000, 3&up, 4f, :46.80, HEIGHT OF SUMMER, Dance Thief, Zee Chalupa, 7 started.

Coyote H. (R), Turf Paradise, March 17, $45,000, 3&up, starters at the 2006-'07 Turf Paradise meet, $6\frac{1}{2}$f, 1:14.28, TRAIL THIS, Royal Place, Family Guy, 5 started.

Coyote Lakes S., Aqueduct, Dec. 5, $76,700, 3&up, $1\frac{1}{2}$m, 2:34.33, NITE LIGHT, Successful Affair, Malibu Moonshine, 6 started.

Cozy Lace S. (R), Presque Isle Downs, Sept. 21, $90,000, 3yo, f, Pennsylvania-bred, 6fAW, 1:10.11, LOOK DEEP, Miss Blue Tye Dye, Power Pack, 5 started.

Cozzene S., Meadowlands, Oct. 19, $58,200, 3&up, 1m70y, 1:38.20, KISS THE KID, Pass Play, Westmoreland, 4 started.

Crank It Up S., Monmouth Park, June 16, $60,000, 3yo, f, a$5\frac{1}{2}$fT, 1:02.39, SEA THE JOY, Changeisgonnacome, Ticket to Seattle, 9 started.

Cree Way Gas H., Marquis Downs, Sept. 8, $5,690, 3&up, f&m, $1\frac{1}{16}$m, 1:47.28, WISPERINGWHITELIES, Rembecca, Bermuda Belle, 9 started.

Creme de la Creme S. (R), Delta Downs, Nov. 17, $60,000, 2yo, f, Louisiana-bred, 5f, :59.52, SHAN JADE, Little Thorn, Swifty Victress, 9 started.

Crescent City Derby (R), Fair Grounds, March 25, $100,000, 3yo, Louisiana-bred, $1\frac{1}{16}$m, 1:45.01, ST. ZARB, Hallway, Power Surge, 8 started.

Crescent City Oaks (R), Fair Grounds, March 24, $100,000, 3yo, f, Louisiana-bred, $1\frac{1}{16}$m, 1:45.18, MI ISABELLA, Ms. Katherine B, Zarb's Ballerina, 8 started.

Criterium S., Calder Race Course, July 7, $100,000, 2yo, 6f, 1:12.14, BIG CITY MAN, Surrealdeal, Honey Honey Honey, 8 started.

Crockadore S. (R), Belmont Park, July 7, $78,500, 3yo, f, New York-bred, $1\frac{1}{16}$mT, 1:45.08, JUNKANOO PARTY, Storm Dixie, As Do I, 10 started.

Crowder's Cara Lyn S., Yavapai Downs, June 2, $11,400, 3&up, f&m, $4\frac{1}{2}$f, :50, SHIMMERING HEAT, Stacey's Tune, Desert Glory, 5 started.

CROWN ROYAL AMERICAN TURF S. (G3), Churchill Downs, May 4, $188,700, 3yo, $1\frac{1}{16}$mT, 1:44.03, DUVEEN, Whatsthescript (Ire), Jazz Quest, 10 started.

Crown Royal Hurdle S., Pine Mountain, Calloway Garden, Nov. 3, $50,000, 3&up, f&m, a$2\frac{1}{4}$mT, 3:54.40, LAIR, Imagina (Chi), Thrumcap, 9 started.

Crystal Water H. (R), Santa Anita Park, March 18, $110,400, 4&up, California-bred, 1mT, 1:34.84, JACK'S WILD, Scottsbluff, Super Strut, 9 started.

CTBA Breeders' Oaks (R), Arapahoe Park, July 15, $37,195, 3yo, f, Colorado-bred, 1m70y, 1:44.04, MEADOW DANCER, Ecstatic Twist, Candys Slew, 6 started.

CTBA Derby (R), Arapahoe Park, Aug. 6, $39,615, 3yo, Colorado-bred, $1\frac{1}{16}$m, 1:47.01, FOLSUM, Such a Deal, Menoken Moon, 7 started.

CTBA Futurity (R), Arapahoe Park, July 16, $43,215, 2yo, Colorado-bred, 6f, 1:10.01, RASMUSSEN, Big Mission, Major River, 9 started.

CTBA Lassie S. (R), Arapahoe Park, July 9, $40,768, 2yo, f, Colorado-

bred, 6f, 1:11.59, SLEW'S BET, Dazzling Blu Skies, Olivers Rivulet, 10 started.

CTBA Marian S. (R), Fairplex Park, Sept. 17, $63,700, 3yo, f, California-bred, 1 1/16m, 1:46.65, SWISS CURRENT, D Pirates Marker, Lt. Lorraine, 7 started.

CTHS Kamloops Summer Futurity, Kamloops, Aug. 18, $5,461, 2yo, a4 1/2f, :49.54, LITTLE COUNTY, Oldwhatshisname, Mr. Byamyle, 3 started.

CTHS Sales S. (R), Assiniboia Downs, Sept. 3, $28,407, 2yo, c&g, sold at a CTHS sale, 6f, 1:14, EIGHT BY TEN, Vinegar Jim, Dust de Gold, 7 started.

CTHS Sales S. (R), Assiniboia Downs, Sept. 3, $28,407, 2yo, f, sold at a CTHS sale, 6f, 1:14.20, BELLA MARIELLA, Still Flying, Meow Wow, 5 started.

CTHS Sales S. (R), Hastings Race Course, April 28, $48,546, 3yo, f, Canadian-bred sold at a CTHS sale, 6 1/2f, 1:18.22, SUVA, Napa, Chelsey's Image, 4 started.

CTHS Sales S. (R), Hastings Race Course, April 29, $49,907, 3yo, c&g, Canadian-bred sold at a CTHS sale, 6 1/2f, 1:18.39, STEPHANSON, Ookashada, Thesaratogaexpress, 5 started.

CTHS Sales S. (R), Hastings Race Course, Sept. 8, $63,237, 2yo, f, Canadian-bred sold at a CTHS sale, 6 1/2f, 1:17.63, DANCING ALL-STAR, Nite Time News, Wanna Be Silver, 6 started.

CTHS Sales S. (R), Hastings Race Course, Sept. 9, $63,114, 2yo, c&g, Canadian-bred sold at a CTHS sale, 6 1/2f, 1:18.48, STAR PROSPECTOR, Desert Alf, Surprisal, 6 started.

CTT and Thoroughbred Owners of California H., Del Mar, Aug. 24, $103,565, 3&up, f&m, 1 3/8mT, 2:13.18, IMAGINE, Nakaba (Brz), Galileo's Star (Ire), 5 started.

Cup and Saucer S. (R), Woodbine, Oct. 14, $260,163, 2yo, Canadian-bred, 1 1/16mT, 1:44.47, DEPUTIFORMER, Cryptonite Kid, Seattle Hill, 13 started.

Cupecoy's Joy S. (R), Belmont Park, June 3, $75,000, 3yo, f, progeny of eligible New York stallions, 1m, 1:37.94, LAURENTIDE ICE, Smokin Sarah, City in the Clouds, 6 started.

Curribot H., Sunland Park, Feb. 25, $50,000, 3&up, 1 1/16m, 1:43.58, REAL DANDY, Rollicking Caller, Keep On Punching, 8 started.

Currie Cup S., Sunflower Downs, June 29, $4,720, 3&up, a5 1/2f, 1:06.76, LUKIN AWESOME, Dance Composer, Dancewithbigred, 8 started.

C. W. Doc Pardee Starter S. (R), Turf Paradise, April 28, $17,500, 3&up, f&m, Arizona-bred starters for a claiming price of $8,000 or less since October 5, 2006, 1m, 1:37.27, LADY CHADERLY, Dancing Fruition, Lil Blue Sky, 8 started.

Cyclones H. (R), Prairie Meadows, June 16, $70,000, 3&up, c&g, Iowa-bred, 1 1/16m, 1:43.71, SUR SANDPIT, Crimson King Cat, Diginandrun, 8 started.

Cypress S. (R), Delta Downs, Jan. 13, $48,000, 4&up, Louisiana-bred, 7f, 1:25.79, CORT'S P.B., Tensas Phone Call, Zarb's Dahar, 5 started.

Czaria H., Sunland Park, April 29, $50,000, 3&up, f&m, 6f, 1:09.63, TEMPTING DATE, White She Devil, Skirt Alert, 7 started.

DAHLIA H. (G2), Hollywood Park, Dec. 16, $150,000, 3&up, f&m, 1 1/4mT, 1:41.49, CITRONNADE, Black Mamba (NZ), Lavender Sky, 9 started.

Dahlia S., Laurel Park, April 14, $60,000, 3&up, f&m, 1mT, 1:36.14, HIGH MOMENT, Grigorieva (Ire), Redaspen, 9 started.

Da Hoss S., Colonial Downs, July 7, $60,000, 3&up, 1mT, 1:35.05, PASS PLAY, Midwatch, Ra Der Dean, 9 started.

Daily Courier Inaugural S., Grants Pass, June 16, $3,900, 3&up, 5 1/2f, 1:06.60, ROMAN GOVERNOR, Royal Ray, Santiago Express, 8 started.

Daisycutter H., Del Mar, July 26, $94,615, 3&up, f&m, 5fT, :55.92, RED DIADEM (GB), Stylish Wildcat, Silly Little Mama, 8 started.

Daisy Mae S. (R), Charles Town Races, Nov. 17, $46,100, 3&up, f&m, West Virginia-bred, 1 1/8m, 1:55.14, JULIE B, Try to Remember, Castina, 7 started.

Dale Irion Memorial Starter H. (R), Turf Paradise, Jan. 13, $12,800, 4&up, starters for a claiming price of $10,000 or less in 2006-'07, a1 1/16mT, 1:49.91 (NCR), BUZZ THE TOWER, Mighty Bodacious, Gold Bankers Gold, 7 started.

Dale Wood H., Ruidoso Downs, Sept. 3, $40,000, 2yo, 6f, 1:10.80, RUN LIKE FIRE, Brax, Unbridled F Five, 3 started.

DALLAS TURF CUP H. (G3), Lone Star Park, May 28, $200,000, 3&up, 1 1/8mT, 1:52.68, EMBOSSED (IRE), Crested (GB), Waupaca, 7 started.

Damon Runyon S. (R), Aqueduct, Dec. 9, $78,950, 2yo, New York-bred, 1 1/16m, 1:46.07, GIANT MOON, Spanky Fischbein, Alexandros, 8 started.

DANCE SMARTLY S. (CAN-G2), Woodbine, July 22, $290,845, 3&up, f&m, a1 1/4mT, 1:45.55, MASSEUSE, May Night, Elle Runaway, 6 started.

Dancin At the Wire S., Turf Paradise, Feb. 3, $25,000, 3yo, f, 6f, 1:09.60, AGAINST THE LAW, Famous Gal, Texas Bobbi R., 7 started.

Dancin At the Wire S., Turf Paradise, Dec. 30, $32,000, 3yo, f, 1m, 1:37.04, COASTAL SKIMMING, Buddha Lady, Wine Tasting Room, 5 started.

Dancing Count S., Laurel Park, Jan. 1, $63,200, 3yo, 5 1/2f, 1:06.21, HEART THROBBIN', Place Your Bet, Crafty Bear, 6 started.

Dancin Renee S. (R), Saratoga Race Course, July 26, $82,750, 3&up, f&m, New York-bred, 6 1/2f, 1:17.32, PRECISE LADY, Stolen Star, Lovely Dream, 7 started.

Daniel Van Clief S. (R), Colonial Downs, July 1, $60,000, 3&up, Virginia-bred and/or -sired, 1 1/16mT, 1:43.61, KONA BLEND, Love Conquers, Mount Weather, 7 started.

Danzig S. (R), Penn National Race Course, May 10, $45,700, 3yo, c&g, Pennsylvania-bred, 6f, 1:11.54, BET A BUCK, White Russian, Chase for the Gold, 6 started.

Darby's Daughter S. (R), Retama Park, Oct. 13, $125,000, 2yo, f, progeny of eligible Texas stallions, 6f, 1:11.29, VALID LILLY, Formal Flyer, My Abbie, 12 started.

DARLEY ALCIBIADES S. (G1), Keeneland Race Course, Oct. 5, $500,000, 2yo, f, 1 1/16mAW, 1:45.85, COUNTRY STAR, A to the Croft, Grace Anatomy, 10 started.

DARLEY TEST S. (G1), Saratoga Race Course, Aug. 4, $250,000, 3yo, f, 7f, 1:22.42, DREAM RUSH, Boca Grande, Baroness Thatcher, 12 started.

Daryl Wells Sr. Memorial S. (R), Fort Erie, July 15, $47,685, 3&up, Canadian-bred, 5fT, :57.04, MARCO BE GOOD, Golden Ice, Vintage Year, 9 started.

Dashing Beauty S., Delaware Park, May 30, $58,550, 3&up, f&m, 6f, 1:10.43, WILDCAT BETTIE B, Casanova Story, Coli Bear, 5 started.

Dating Game S., Lethbridge, Oct. 27, $16,837, 3&up, f&m, 7f, 1:28.20, WINSOME WITCH, Avenue of Silver, She's Twenty Below, 7 started.

Dat You Miz Blue S. (R), Aqueduct, Feb. 11, $66,750, 3yo, f, New York-bred non-winners of a stakes, 6f, 1:11.90, BECKY'S FLUTE, Cordilleran Ice, Love Cove, 7 started.

Dave's Friend S., Laurel Park, Oct. 27, $51,500, 3&up, 5 1/2f, 1:03.64, CRAFTY SCHEMER, Secretintelligence, Dale's Prospect, 7 started.

David L. "Zeke" Ferguson Memorial Hurdle S., Colonial Downs, July 15, $50,000, 3&up, a2 1/4mT, 4:01.63, MONEYTRAIN (GER), Class Vantage, Charlie Whiskey, 7 started.

DAVONA DALE S. (G2), Gulfstream Park, Feb. 10, $150,000, 3yo, f, 1m, 1:37.34, CHRISTMAS KID, High Again, Lisa M, 8 started.

Daylight Sprint Thoroughbred S., Sunland Park, March 31, $50,000, 3yo, 6f, 1:09.63, FOLSUM, Sir Five Star, Game of Skill, 9 started.

Daytona H., Santa Anita Park, Feb. 17, $80,000, 4&up, a6 1/2fT, 1:12.57, NIGHT CHAPTER (GB), Roi Charmant, Terrific Storm, 7 started.

Dayton Andrews Dodge Sophomore Turf S. (R), Tampa Bay Downs, April 7, $85,000, 3yo, Florida-bred, 1 1/16mT, 1:42.71, SOLDIER'S DANCER, A Bit of Madness, Fair Weather Stan, 10 started.

Dean Kutz Memorial S. (R), North Dakota Horse Park, Sept. 2, $21,100, 3&up, North Dakota-bred, 1m, 1:41.60, MADDIES BLUES, Tiger Jet, High Class Lad, 5 started.

Dean Kutz S., Canterbury Park, Aug. 11, $45,000, 3&up, f&m, 6f, 1:09.86, DIMPLE PINCH, Salty Attraction, A G's Dolly, 5 started.

Dearly Precious S., Aqueduct, Feb. 17, $69,875, 3yo, f, 6f, 1:11.36, SPECIAL DREAM, Aspiring, Luxury Class, 6 started.

Dearly Precious S., Monmouth Park, June 30, $60,000, 3yo, f, 6f, 1:08.96, ASTOR PARK, Princess Janie, Bianco, 5 started.

Debutante S., Assiniboia Downs, Aug. 6, $42,669, 2yo, f, 5 1/2f, 1:06, MISS MISSILE, Rasierra, Sophisticated Sis, 7 started.

DEBUTANTE S. (G3), Churchill Downs, July 7, $111,000, 2yo, f, 6f, 1:09.27, RATED FIESTY, Dreabons Legacy, American County, 8 started.

Decathlon S., Monmouth Park, May 12, $60,000, 3&up, 5 1/2f, 1:01.91 (NTR), JOEY P., Slam Bammy, Who's the Cowboy, 5 started.

Decoration Day H., Mountaineer Race Track and Gaming Resort, May 28, $75,000, 3&up, f&m, 1mT, 1:34.29, BOLD PASSAGE, Afleet Angel, Water Gap, 11 started.

De La Rose S. (R), Saratoga Race Course, Aug. 1, $83,500, 4&up, f&m, non-winners of a stakes on the turf in 2007, 1mT, 1:34.33, FANTASTIC SHIRL, Amansara, A True Pussycat, 10 started.

Delaware Certified Distaff S. (R), Delaware Park, Sept. 15, $75,300, 3&up, f&m, Delaware-certified, 6f, 1:10.15, ADORABLE JANE, Carolina Fuego, Kittery Point, 6 started.

Delaware Certified S. (R), Delaware Park, Sept. 15, $75,000, 3&up, Delaware-certified, 6f, 1:10.31, SECRETINTELLIGENCE, Cayman Condo, Just Don, 5 started.

DELAWARE H. (G2), Delaware Park, July 15, $1,000,900, 3&up, f&m, 1¼m, 2:01.16, UNBRIDLED BELLE, Lila Paige, Promenade Girl, 8 started.

DELAWARE OAKS (G2), Delaware Park, July 14, $505,600, 3yo, f, 1 1/16m, 1:42.39, MOON CATCHER, Winning Point, Cotton Blossom, 7 started.

Del Mar Debutante S., Del Mar, Sept. 3, $250,000, 2yo, f, 7fAW, 1:26.79, SET PLAY, Spring Awakening, Izarra, 12 started.

DEL MAR DERBY (G2), Del Mar, Sept. 2, $400,000, 3yo, 1⅛mT, 1:47.10, MEDICI CODE (GB), Augment, Worldly (GB), 10 started.

DEL MAR FUTURITY (G1), Del Mar, Sept. 5, $250,000, 2yo, 7fAW, 1:25.34, GEORGIE BOY, Salute the Sarge, Drill Down, 13 started.

DEL MAR H. (G2), Del Mar, Aug. 26, $250,000, 3&up, 1⅜mT, 2:13.01, AFTER MARKET, Runaway Dancer, Spring House, 7 started.

DEL MAR MILE H. (G2), Del Mar, Aug. 19, $314,000, 3&up, 1mT, 1:32.59, CROSSING THE LINE (NZ), Becrux (Ity), Isipingo, 9 started.

DEL MAR OAKS (G1), Del Mar, Aug. 18, $400,000, 3yo, f, 1⅛mT, 1:46.79, RUTHERIENNE, Valbenny (Ire), Super Freaky, 10 started.

Delta Colleen H., Hastings Race Course, Sept. 22, $51,047, 3&up, f&m, 1 1/16m, 1:45.61, MONASHEE, Lady Raj, Slewpast, 7 started.

Delta Express S., Delta Downs, March 2, $49,500, 4&up, 5f, :57.99, CHIEF WHAT IT IS, Shark, Danieltown, 8 started.

Delta Mile S., Delta Downs, March 2, $73,500, 4&up, 1m, 1:38.59, SILENT PLEASURE, Dreamsandvisions, Middleweight, 7 started.

DEMOISELLE S. (G2), Aqueduct, Nov. 24, $200,000, 2yo, f, 1⅛m, 1:51.61, MUSHKA, Elusive Lady, Melissa Jo, 7 started.

Denise Rhudy Memorial S., Delaware Park, June 30, $75,600, 3yo, f, 1 1/16mT, 1:44.67, NEW EDITION, Miss Tizzynow, Prom Party, 7 started.

Deputed Testamony S. (R), Laurel Park, Sept. 15, $50,000, 3yo, Maryland-bred, 1m, 1:35.23, DIGGER, Roaring Lion, P V Lightening, 8 started.

DEPUTY MINISTER H. (G3), Gulfstream Park, Feb. 3, $100,000, 4&up, 6½f, 1:15.72, KEYED ENTRY, Sir Greeley, Nar, 5 started.

Deputy Minister S. (R), Woodbine, July 18, $119,800, 3yo, Ontario-foaled, 7fAW, 1:23.94, DANCER'S BAJAN, Fudgethebottomline, Red Raffles, 4 started.

Derby Trial S., Assiniboia Downs, July 15, $42,917, 3yo, 1 1/16m, 1:46, RAGE TILL DAWN, Country Humor, Western Deed, 9 started.

Derby Trial S., Churchill Downs, April 28, $117,800, 3yo, 7½f, 1:29.28, FLYING FIRST CLASS, U D Ghetto, Bold Start, 11 started.

Derby Trial S., Fairplex Park, Sept. 7, $64,350, 3yo, 1 1/16m, 1:44.34, MY MAN MURF, Roman Commander, Mr. Nightlinger, 8 started.

Desert Rose H., Ruidoso Downs, Aug. 12, $40,000, 3&up, f&m, 6f, 1:12.60, HAILEY'S GONE WEST, I'm N Clover, Political Web, 7 started.

Desert Sky H. (R), Turf Paradise, May 5, $45,000, 3&up, f&m, starters at the Turf Paradise 2006-'07 meet, 1mT, 1:37.47, STAR OF WHITNEY, Evening Escort, Sweet Ambition, 10 started.

Desert Stormer H., Hollywood Park, May 19, $76,775, 3&up, f&m, 6fAW, 1:09.58, SELVATICA, Bully Bones, Nossa Cancao (Brz), 7 started.

Desert Vixen S. (R), Calder Race Course, Aug. 11, $100,000, 2yo, f, progeny of eligible Florida stallions, 6f, 1:13.64, SILK RIDGE, Calico Bay, Bond Princess, 8 started.

Dessie and Fern Sawyer Futurity (R), The Downs at Albuquerque, Sept. 23, $71,775, 2yo, f, New Mexico-bred, 6f, 1:12.01, FRITZIE'S CHIME, Blooming Pleasure, Sweetghostrun, 10 started.

Destiny Dance S., Belmont Park, May 3, $67,000, 4&up, f&m, 1¼mT, 2:03.64, FACTUAL CONTENDER, Hostess, Pictavia (Ire), 8 started.

Devil's Honor H. (R), Philadelphia Park, July 28, $100,000, 3&up, Pennsylvania-bred, 6f, 1:09.15, BANJO PICKER, Chase the Line, Shouldabeenaclown, 6 started.

DIANA S. (G1), Saratoga Race Course, July 28, $520,000, 3&up, f&m, 1⅛mT, 1:46.47, MYTYPHOON (IRE), Argentina (Ire), Makderah (Ire), 8 started.

Diane Kem H., Portland Meadows, Nov. 11, $22,150, 3&up, f&m, 6f, 1:12.49, BELLAMENTE, Blanding, Berry Viva, 9 started.

Diane Kem S. (R), Emerald Downs, Sept. 16, $45,000, 2yo, f, Washington-bred, 6f, 1:09.40, NO CONSTRAINTS, Ica's Rockette, Classic Rox, 8 started.

Dine' S. (R), SunRay Park, June 30, $61,000, 3yo, c&g, New Mexico-bred, 6½f, 1:17.80, SCOOBA DE, Run Riley Run, Ky's Quest, 10 started.

Dinner Diamond S. (R), Saratoga Race Course, July 27, $83,500, 3&up, f&m, New York-bred, 1mT, 1:35.15, REWRITE, Half Heaven, Iron Goddess, 10 started.

Dipsea Trail S., Golden Gate Fields, May 26, $50,625, 3yo, f, 6f, 1:09.67, INTO REALITY, Hot Spell, Dixie Crisp, 5 started.

DISCOVERY H. (G3), Aqueduct, Nov. 24, $109,900, 3yo, 1⅛m, 1:50.15, NOW A VICTOR, Shopton Lane, Dr. V's Magic, 7 started.

Display S., Woodbine, Nov. 24, $128,334, 2yo, 1 1/16mAW, 1:45.20, DISCREET COMMANDER, Briarwood Circle, Mighty Vow, 10 started.

DISTAFF BREEDERS' CUP H. (G2), Aqueduct, March 24, $158,000, 3&up, f&m, 6f, 1:09.73, MARYFIELD, Candy Box, Oprah Winney, 7 started.

Distaff S. (R), Assiniboia Downs, Aug. 18, $42,404, 3&up, f&m, Manitoba-bred, 1m, 1:42.40, THUNDER SKY, Hurri Coin, Shooting Astra, 6 started.

Distaff Turf Sprint Championship H., Calder Race Course, Aug. 11, $250,000, 3&up, f&m, 5fT, :56.23, FLYING CIRCLE, Unbridled Sidney, Smitty's Sunshine, 10 started.

Distaff Turf Sprint H., Calder Race Course, July 7, $100,000, 3&up, f&m, 5f (originally scheduled on the turf), :58.54, SMITTY'S SUNSHINE, Flying Circle, Shesgoldincolor, 6 started.

Dixie Belle S., Oaklawn Park, Jan. 27, $50,000, 3yo, f, 6f, 1:11.63, DEVIL HOUSE, Cat On a Cloud, Time's Mistress, 8 started.

Dixieland S., Oaklawn Park, Jan. 19, $50,000, 3yo, 5½f, 1:04.50, IRISH DREAMER, First Regent, Sir Five Star, 11 started.

Dixie Poker Ace S. (R), Fair Grounds, March 3, $75,000, 4&up, Louisiana-bred, a1mT, 1:40.65, DESERT WHEAT, Perfect Harmony, Diggy Fresh, 9 started.

DIXIE S. (G2), Pimlico Race Course, May 19, $250,000, 3&up, 1⅛mT, 1:46.36, REMARKABLE NEWS (VEN), Cosmonaut, Outperformance, 11 started.

DOGWOOD S. (G3), Churchill Downs, June 2, $167,550, 3yo, f, 1m, 1:35.35, LADY JOANNE, High Again, Upcoming Story, 8 started.

DOMINION DAY S. (CAN-G3), Woodbine, July 1, $188,075, 3&up, 1¼mAW, 2:04.20 (NTR), TRUE METROPOLITAN, Mustanfar, Palladio, 6 started.

Don Bernhardt S., Ellis Park, July 21, $50,000, 3&up, 6½f, 1:15.43, OFF DUTY, Funky Pirate, Junior College, 8 started.

Don Ciccio S., Hawthorne Race Course, Oct. 8, $46,750, 3&up, 5½fT, 1:02.06 (NCR), ALONE AT LAST, Mighty Rule, America West, 7 started.

Don Fleming H., Northlands Park, July 28, $70,635, 3&up, 1 1/16m, 1:44.20, TEST BOY, Trick of the North, Pickinontheolbanjo, 8 started.

Don Juan de Onate S. (R), The Downs at Albuquerque, Aug. 19, $63,250, 3yo, New Mexico-bred, 6f, 1:11.48, IRISH GLASS, Colorofrun, Bandontheloose, 5 started.

Donna Freyer S. (R), Philadelphia Park, Oct. 28, $52,550, 2yo, f, have spent 90 days in South Carolina and paid a nomination fee to the SCTOBA, 6½f, 1:18.92, VAIN VIXEN, Lads Starlit, Hard Rockin, 6 started.

Donna Jensen H., Portland Meadows, Feb. 25, $22,150, 4&up, f&m, 1 1/16m, 1:48.82, MY EMY MY AMY, Chancy Chancy, Quatorze, 10 started.

Donna Reed S. (R), Prairie Meadows, Aug. 25, $80,600, 4&up, f&m, Iowa-bred, 1m70y, 1:41.22, CAMELA CARSON, Thekatcamehome, Elite Lady, 8 started.

DONN H. (G1), Gulfstream Park, Feb. 3, $500,000, 4&up, 1⅛m, 1:48.43, INVASOR (ARG), Hesanoldsalt, A. P. Arrow, 8 started.

Donnie Wilhite Memorial S., Louisiana Downs, Aug. 18, $75,000, 2yo, f, 1mT, 1:39.86, TIMELY REFLECTION, Vengeful Shadow, American Prize, 9 started.

Don Rickles S., Aqueduct, Dec. 14, $76,500, 3yo, 1m70y, 1:41.48, STUNT MAN, Sir Whimsey, Pink Viper, 6 started.

Donthelumbertrader S., Calder Race Course, July 14, $50,000, 3yo, 7½fT, 1:30.03, FAIR WEATHER STAN, Fearless Eagle, Villainage, 9 started.

Don Valliere Memorial Cup S. (R), Fort Erie, Aug. 12, $23,733, 3&up, two or more starts at Fort Erie in 2007, 6f, 1:11.55, CHARLIE O, Faygo Dancing Home, Fleet Storm, 11 started.

Doris Grundy Memorial S., Yavapai Downs, Aug. 5, $15,000, 3yo, f, 6f, 1:11.20, WINE TASTING ROOM, Jeri G, Shaealltheway, 8 started.

Double Delta S., Arlington Park, June 2, $47,400, 3yo, f, 1mT, 1:37.96, DREAMING OF ANNA, Nice Inheritance, Lemonlime, 6 started.

DOUBLEDOGDARE S. (G3), Keeneland Race Course, April 18, $108,600, 4&up, f&m, 1 1/16mAW, 1:46.40, ASI SIEMPRE, Pyramid Love, Warrior Girl, 5 started.

Dover S., Delaware Park, Oct. 20, $101,650, 2yo, 1 1/16m, 1:44.84, CAVE'S VALLEY, Atoned, Cudjo, 5 started.
Dowd Mile S., Fonner Park, April 14, $30,000, 3&up, 1m, 1:39.20, YOURMONEYSNOGOOD, Stormy Business, Holy City, 8 started.
Dowling S. (R), Great Lakes Downs, Aug. 21, $50,000, 3yo, c&g, Michigan-bred, 1m, 1:42.26, ALL I CAN GET, Lite Legacy, Scarlet Fact, 7 started.
Dr. A. B. Leggio Memorial S., Fair Grounds, Jan. 13, $100,000, 4&up, f&m, a5 1/2 fT, 1:03.17, SMITTY'S SUNSHINE, Follow the Lite, No Fair, 10 started.
Dream Supreme H., Churchill Downs, Nov. 23, $57,590, 3&up, f&m, 6f, 1:09.51, PRETTY JENNY, Change Up, Generosity, 8 started.
Dream Supreme S., Belmont Park, Sept. 16, $76,500, 3yo, f, 6f, 1:10.83, MISS TIZZY, Quota, Control System, 6 started.
Dr. Ernest Benner S. (R), Charles Town Races, Sept. 29, $51,550, 2yo, West Virginia-bred nominated to the West Virginia Breeders' Classic, 6 1/2 f, 1:20.35, POW WOW POWER, Homer Dane, Milwaukee Fun, 10 started.
Dr. Fager S., Arlington Park, June 30, $46,800, 3&up, 1 1/8 mAW, 1:51.04, THRONG, Demeteor, Restless Mon, 6 started.
Dr. Fager S. (R), Calder Race Course, Aug. 11, $100,000, 2yo, progeny of eligible Florida stallions, 6f, 1:12.46, BIG CITY MAN, Wise Answer, Smooth Air, 11 started.
Dr. James Penny Memorial H., Philadelphia Park, July 4, $100,000, 3&up, f&m, 1 1/16 mT, 1:42.87, HIGH MOMENT, J'ray, Meribel, 7 started.
Dr. O. G. Fischer Memorial H., SunRay Park, June 16, $50,000, 3&up, f&m, 7f, 1:23, MOLLY'S PRIDE, Water Park, A Bit of Pressure, 9 started.
Dr. T. F. Classen Memorial S. (R), Thistledown, May 26, $50,000, 3&up, f&m, Ohio-bred, 6f, 1:11.38, MAGG'S CHOICE, Double Diva, Money Card, 9 started.
Drumtop S., Belmont Park, July 22, $75,950, 4&up, f&m, 1 3/8 mT, 2:14.15, PICTAVIA (IRE), Greenery, Bea Plus, 5 started.
D.S. "Shine" Young Memorial Futurity (R), Evangeline Downs, June 30, $130,025, 2yo, f, Louisiana-bred, 5f, :59.96, SWIFTY VICTRESS, Hisse, Iknowuthinkimsexy, 11 started.
D.S. "Shine" Young Memorial Futurity (R), Evangeline Downs, June 30, $131,125, 2yo, c&g, Louisiana-bred, 5f, :59.59, HONOUR THY LOVER, Jumpin for Jason, Must Acquit, 10 started.
DTHA Owners' Day H. (R), Delaware Park, Sept. 8, $100,300, 3&up, starters at Delaware Park in 2007, 1 1/16 mT, 1:48.92, AWFULLY SMART, Better Than Bonds, Easy Red, 6 started.
Duchess H., Marquis Downs, June 9, $5,654, 3yo, f, 6f, 1:15.28, SPANISH LACE, Buddha Bondurant, Stay and Play, 8 started.
Duchess of York S., Stampede Park, June 9, $65,600, 3&up, f&m, 1 1/16 mT, 1:44.40, SHE'S ITALIAN, Braetta, Selita's Dream, 8 started.
Duchess S., Woodbine, Aug. 11, $151,223, 3yo, f, 7fAW, 1:22.15, BEAR NOW, Speak Wisely, Lyrically, 7 started.
Duda S. (R), Belmont Park, July 7, $77,000, 4&up, f&m, non-winners of a stakes on the turf, 1 1/16 mT, 1:43.98, DANCE AWAY CAPOTE, Fantastic Shirl, Hopes and Dreams, 8 started.
Duncan F. Kenner S., Fair Grounds, March 24, $138,000, 3&up, 6f, 1:09.34, SAINT ANDDAN, Venomous, Smoke Mountain, 9 started.
Duncan Hopeful S., Greenlee County Fair, March 17, $8,183, 3&up, 5 1/2 f, 1:06.20, SINGING MEMO, Staffhouse Road, Bobjinski, 7 started.
DURHAM CUP S. (CAN-G3), Woodbine, Oct. 13, $154,947, 3&up, 1 1/8 mAW, 1:49.55 (NTR), LEONNATUS ANTEAS, Eccentric (GB), Arch Hall, 7 started.
Dust Commander S., Turfway Park, Feb. 17, $50,000, 4&up, 1mAW, 1:38.68, RECOGNITION, Esprit Du Roi (Chi), King of Speed, 9 started.
Dwight D. Patterson H. (R), Turf Paradise, April 28, $45,000, 3&up, Arizona-bred, 1 1/8 mT, 1:43.28, NO REVERSE, Mydak, Hey Slick, 8 started.
DWYER S. (G2), Belmont Park, July 4, $147,000, 3yo, 1 1/8 mT, 1:40.69, ANY GIVEN SATURDAY, Nobiz Like Shobiz, Sightseeing, 5 started.
Dynamic Lisa S. (R), Belmont Park, Sept. 29, $78,250, 3&up, f&m, New York-bred, 1mT, 1:33.39, FACTUAL CONTENDER, Rewrite, Half Heaven, 9 started.
Early's Farm and Garden H., Marquis Downs, June 23, $5,609, 3&up, 6f, 1:12.89, TOUGH TOPIC, Sand Rush, Double Bid, 9 started.
EARLY TIMES MINT JULEP H. (G3), Churchill Downs, June 16, $164,100, 3&up, f&m, 1 1/16 mT, 1:40.70 (NCR), QUITE A BRIDE, Magnificent Song, Danzon, 8 started.
East View S. (R), Aqueduct, Dec. 2, $83,375, 2yo, f, New York-bred, 1 1/16 mT, 1:47.36, SHERINE, Meriwether Jessica, The Material Girl, 8 started.

EATONTOWN S. (G3), Monmouth Park, June 16, $150,000, 3&up, f&m, 1 1/16 mT, 1:39.48 (NCR), KAREN'S CAPER, Redaspen, Roshani, 7 started.
Eatontown Staybridge Suites S., Monmouth Park, Aug. 4, $60,000, 3yo, f, 1 1/16 mT, 1:42.73, SOCIAL QUEEN, My Golden Quest, Limoncella, 7 started.
Eavesdrop S. (R), Philadelphia Park, Dec. 1, $75,000, 2yo, f, Pennsylvania-bred, 6f, 1:12.82, BARBAZILLA, Willow Grove, Driven by Winning, 7 started.
E. B. Johnston S., Fairplex Park, Sept. 9, $63,700, 3&up, f&m, 1 1/16 m, 1:45.34, VELVET MOONLITE, Quiet Kim, Debie Ginsburg, 7 started.
ECLIPSE S. (CAN-G3), Woodbine, May 21, $138,404, 4&up, 1 1/16 mAW, 1:43.07 (NTR), PALLADIO, Judiths Wild Rush, True Metropolitan, 7 started.
Eddie Logan S., Santa Anita Park, Dec. 29, $79,850, 2yo, 1mT, 1:37.64, YANKEE BRAVO, Sky Cape, Nistle's Crunch, 8 started.
EDDIE READ H. (G1), Del Mar, July 22, $400,000, 3&up, 1 1/8 mT, 1:47.36, AFTER MARKET, Out of Control (Brz), Rob Roy, 5 started.
Eddy County S., Zia Park, Nov. 23, $67,110, 2yo, 1m, 1:42.20, PONI COLADA, Star Defender, Rapper S S, 6 started.
Edgewood S., Churchill Downs, May 4, $171,150, 3yo, f, 1 1/16 mT, 1:43.99, SWINGIT, Luna Dorada, Good Mood (Ire), 8 started.
Edmonton Juvenile S., Northlands Park, July 11, $47,550, 2yo, c&g, 6f, 1:13.80, BRAZEN SON, Run Linkage Run, Rods Choice, 7 started.
Edward J. DeBartolo Sr. Memorial Breeders' Cup H., Remington Park, Sept. 3, $144,500, 3&up, 1 1/8 mT, 1:48.51, BREGO, Almost Certain, Smooth Bid, 11 started.
Eight Thirty S., Delaware Park, May 26, $61,050, 3&up, 1 1/8 mT, 1:48.40, WOOD BE WILLING, Tune of the Spirit, Salinja, 6 started.
Eillo S., Calder Race Course, Aug. 12, $50,000, 3yo, 6f, 1:10.57, YESBYJIMMINY, Finallymadeit, Dream of Angels, 5 started.
Eillo S., Meadowlands, Oct. 5, $76,700, 3&up, 6f, 1:09.15, JOEY P., Bound Notebook, Roman Candles, 6 started.
El Cajon S. (1st Div.), Del Mar, Aug. 31, $112,650, 3yo, 1mAW, 1:40.06, RUSH WITH THUNDER, Frank the Barber, I'm All Out, 9 started.
El Cajon S. (2nd Div.), Del Mar, Aug. 31, $111,400, 3yo, 1mAW, 1:39.14, LATIN RHYTHMS, Bad Boy, Daytona (Ire), 8 started.
EL CAMINO REAL DERBY (G3), Bay Meadows Race Course, March 10, $200,000, 3yo, 1 1/16 mT, 1:43.22, BWANA BULL, Freesgood, Zoning In, 7 started.
EL CONEJO H. (G3), Santa Anita Park, Jan. 1, $110,900, 4&up, 5 1/2 f, 1:02.68, HARVARD AVENUE, Areyoutalkintome, Proud Tower Too, 9 started.
Eleanor M. Casey Memorial S. (R), Charles Town Races, Dec. 22, $46,200, 2yo, f, West Virginia-bred, 6 1/2 f, 1:20.01, SHESDEBONAIRNESS, Veiled Reference, We're in the Money, 9 started.
EL ENCINO S. (G2), Santa Anita Park, Jan. 14, $150,000, 4yo, f, 1 1/16 m, 1:43.70, SUGAR SHAKE, Kris' Sis, Wonder Lady Anne L, 6 started.
E. L. Gaylord Memorial S. (R), Remington Park, Oct. 20, $48,500, 3yo, f, 6 1/2 f, 1:16.66, ALINA, Madonna Mia, O. K. Krystal, 5 started.
Elge Rasberry S. (R), Louisiana Downs, Aug. 31, $57,250, 3yo, f, Louisiana-bred, a1mT, 1:36.63, TENSAS YUCATAN, Ahead of Her Time, Louisiana Song, 8 started.
Elgin S. (R), Woodbine, Sept. 3, $119,120, 3&up, c&g, Canadian-bred, 1 1/16 mAW, 1:43.94, STONETOWN, Ever So Free, Head Chopper, 7 started.
Elko Thoroughbred Derby, Elko County Fair, Sept. 2, $21,100, 3yo, 7f, 1:27, DANCE WITH DANGER, Beaucardi, Slewpy G. D., 8 started.
Elko Thoroughbred Futurity, Elko County Fair, Sept. 3, $31,525, 2yo, 5 1/2 f, 1:08.20, NO DIRECTION HOME, Cattle Call, Bash the Gold, 8 started.
Elko Thoroughbred S. #1, Elko County Fair, Aug. 26, $5,792, 3&up, 1 1/16 m, 1:48.80 (NTR), CUT CLASS, Tizwar, Booker Time, 7 started.
Elko Thoroughbred S. #2, Elko County Fair, Aug. 26, $6,035, 3&up, 5 1/2 f, 1:08.80, ANTING ANTING, Primecat, Rodeo Champ, 8 started.
Elko Thoroughbred S. #3, Elko County Fair, Sept. 2, $8,584, 3&up, 7f, 1:25.80, COLDWATER, Jumpingjupiter, Rodeo Champ, 9 started.
Elko Thoroughbred S. #4, Elko County Fair, Sept. 3, $4,882, 3&up, f&m, 7f, 1:28, DERBY CAT, Loris Spirit Gazer, Gig's Star, 7 started.
Elkwood S., Monmouth Park, May 26, $60,000, 3&up, f, 1mT, 1:33.99, HOST (CHI), Bestowed, Ballonenostrikes, 7 started.
Ellis Park Breeders' Cup Turf S., Ellis Park, Aug. 25, $100,000, 3&up, f&m, 1 1/16 mT, 1:41.76, QUITE A BRIDE, Quiet Royal, Rich in Spirit, 7 started.
Elmer Heubeck Distaff H. (R), Calder Race Course, Nov. 10, $200,000,

3&up, f&m, Florida-bred, 1 1/16m, 1:47.09, ANNABILL, Bayou's Lassie, Peach Flambe, 9 started.

El Paso Times H., Sunland Park, Jan. 28, $50,000, 3yo, f, 6 1/2f, 1:18.57, STEALTH CAT, Berriestoheaven, Top Solitaire, 10 started.

Ema Bovary S., Calder Race Course, June 10, $50,000, 3&up, f&m, 6f, 1:10.82, STOLEN PRAYER, Running Lass, Send Me an Angel, 8 started.

Emerald Distaff H., Emerald Downs, Aug. 19, $100,000, 3&up, f&m, 1 1/4m, 1:48.60, GEMSTONE RUSH, Fortunate Event, Beaulena, 6 started.

Emerald Downs Breeders' Cup Derby, Emerald Downs, Sept. 3, $97,500, 3yo, 1 1/8m, 1:47.20, MULCAHY, Jamaica Bound, Song of Pirates, 6 started.

Emerald Downs H., Hastings Race Course, May 20, $51,152, 3yo, f, 6 1/2f, 1:19.25, NAPA, Restless Lady, Suva, 6 started.

Emergency Nurse S., Calder Race Course, May 6, $45,000, 3&up, f&m, 1m, 1:46.88, POTRA CLASICA (ARG), Saffronista, Cat Can Do, 7 started.

EMIRATES AIRLINE BREEDERS' CUP DISTAFF (G1), Monmouth Park, Oct. 27, $2,070,160, 3&up, f&m, 1 1/8m, 1:50.11, GINGER PUNCH, Hystericalady, Octave, 12 started.

EMIRATES AIRLINE BREEDERS' CUP FILLY & MARE TURF (G1), Monmouth Park, Oct. 27, $1,951,080, 3&up, f&m, 1 3/8mT, 2:22.75, LAHUDOOD (GB), Honey Ryder, Passage of Time (GB), 11 started.

EMIRATES AIRLINE MARYLAND SPRINT H. (G3), Pimlico Race Course, May 19, $198,500, 3&up, 6f, 1:09.16, DIABOLICAL, Talent Search, Semaphore Man, 7 started.

Empire Classic H. (R), Belmont Park, Oct. 28, $250,000, 3&up, New York-bred, 1 1/8m, 1:48.70, DR. V'S MAGIC, Who What Win, Run Red Run, 9 started.

Endeavour S., Tampa Bay Downs, Feb. 17, $108,750, 4&up, f&m, 1 1/16mT, 1:43.05, CASSYDORA (GB), Bright Abundance, Warrior Girl, 10 started.

ENDINE S. (G3), Delaware Park, Sept. 8, $200,600, 3&up, f&m, 6f, 1:09.52, SILMARIL, Ticket to Seattle, Sugar Swirl, 7 started.

Endowing Starter H. (R), Yavapai Downs, July 14, $9,500, 3&up, starters for a claiming price of $8,000 or less since July 10, 2006, 1 1/8m, 1:48.80 (NTR), TAKIN DEAD AIM, Mister Cosmi (GB), Chaseur, 7 started.

Epitome Breeders' Cup S., Monmouth Park, Oct. 26, $250,000, 2yo, f, 1mT, 1:39.21, SEA CHANTER, Annie Skates, Grace and Power, 10 started.

E. P. TAYLOR S. (CAN-G1), Woodbine, Oct. 21, $1,052,484, 3&up, f&m, 1 1/4mT, 2:00.68 (NCR), MRS. LINDSAY, Sealy Hill, Barancella (Fr), 10 started.

Ernie Samuel Memorial S. (R), Fort Erie, July 15, $47,685, 3&up, f&m, Canadian-bred, 5fT, :57.33, BOSSKIRI, Flashy Pink, Timely Matter, 8 started.

Esplanade S., Fair Grounds, Dec. 22, $99,000, 3&up, f&m, 5 1/2f, 1:04.62, TRES DREAM, Chatham, Valid Lil, 8 started.

ESSEX H. (G3), Oaklawn Park, Feb. 10, $100,000, 4&up, 1 1/16m, 1:44.20, JONESBORO, Red Raymond, More Than Regal, 9 started.

Eternal Search S. (R), Woodbine, Aug. 29, $118,101, 3yo, f, Ontario-foaled, 1 1/16mAW, 1:45.28, YOU WILL LOVE ME, Quite a Knightmare, Dash It Darling, 7 started.

E. T. Springer S. (R), The Downs at Albuquerque, Sept. 8, $50,000, 3&up, New Mexico-bred, 7f, 1:22.77, TANYA'S BEAU, Romeos Wilson, Boom Boom, 8 started.

Evangeline Mile H., Evangeline Downs, Aug. 11, $200,000, 1m, 1:36.51 (NTR), COSTA RISING, Super Frolic, Watchem Smokey, 9 started.

Evan Shipman H. (R), Belmont Park, July 22, $107,400, 3&up, New York-bred, 1 1/8m, 1:41.54, SHUFFLING MADDNES, Accountforthegold, Organizer, 6 started.

Evanston Speed H., Wyoming Downs, July 22, $3,625, 3&up, 4 1/2f, :51 (NTR), RESTRICTIONS APPLY, Primecat, World Escapade, 6 started.

Everett Nevin Alameda County Futurity (R), Pleasanton, July 1, $53,160, 2yo, California-bred, 5f, :57.34, RUN BROTHER RON, Younique Cat, Deputy Bertrando, 7 started.

Evil Bear S., Belmont Park, June 28, $65,950, 4&up, f&m, 6fT, 1:11.16, LEMON DROP GAL, Somethinaboutbetty, Brushed Bayou, 5 started.

Excelsior Breeders' Cup H., Aqueduct, April 7, $209,100, 3&up, 1 1/8m, 1:48.10, MAGNA GRADUATE, Naughty New Yorker, Accountforthegold, 6 started.

Excess Energy S., Turf Paradise, April 2, $25,000, 3&up, f&m, 6f, 1:08.84, BLUMIN BEAUTY, Shesa Private I, Shimmering Sunset, 7 started.

Excess Energy S., Turf Paradise, Nov. 20, $31,500, 3&up, f&m, 6f, 1:09.37, BLUMIN BEAUTY, Wild English Rose, Famous Gal, 6 started.

Fabersham S. (R), Aqueduct, Jan. 12, $65,150, 3yo, New York-bred, 6f, 1:10.68, SMASH 'EM SAMMY, Landofopportunity, Gonzo Bonzo Beans, 5 started.

Fain Road S., Yavapai Downs, Sept. 4, $11,500, 4 1/2f, :49.60, RUN NICHOLAS RUN, Win to Win, Mining Gold, 6 started.

Fairfax S., Golden Gate Fields, Feb. 3, $58,800, 4&up, 6f, 1:08.71, VADERATOR, Britt's Jules, Trickey Trevor, 5 started.

FAIR GROUNDS BREEDERS' CUP H. (G3), Fair Grounds, Feb. 10, $198,500, 4&up, a1 1/8mT, 1:49.48, CLOUDY'S KNIGHT, Devilment, Storm Treasure, 9 started.

FAIR GROUNDS OAKS (G2), Fair Grounds, March 10, $396,000, 3yo, f, 1 1/16m, 1:44.02, MISTICAL PLAN, Octave, Whatdreamsrmadeof, 8 started.

Fair Queen H., The Downs at Albuquerque, Sept. 14, $50,000, 3yo, f, 6 1/2f, 1:15.31, LAURAS LAST MUSIC, Buddha Lady, Seattle Rascal, 7 started.

Fairway Flyer S., Belmont Park, Sept. 23, $76,500, 3&up, f&m, 1 3/8mT, 2:14.27, BARANCELLA (FR), Jade Queen, Nunnery, 6 started.

Fairway Fun S., Turfway Park, March 31, $50,000, 4&up, f&m, 1 1/16mAW, 1:45.16, HALF HEAVEN, Sassy Skipper, My Chickadee, 11 started.

Fall Classic Distaff H. (R), Northlands Park, Sept. 29, $75,413, 3&up, f&m, Alberta-bred, 1 1/16m, 1:44.60, SHE'S ITALIAN, Banjo Babe, Speedy Gone Sally, 8 started.

Fall Highweight H., Aqueduct, Nov. 22, $109,200, 3&up, 6f, 1:09.90, GRAND CHAMPION, Joey P., City Attraction, 7 started.

Fall S., Mountaineer Race Track and Gaming Resort, Oct. 2, $75,000, 3&up, 1 1/4m, 1:51.46, M B SEA, Tepexpan, Come On Chas, 8 started.

Falls Amiss H. (R), Horsemen's Park, July 20, $28,850, 4&up, f&m, Nebraska-bred, 1m, 1:41, C. R. CHARMER, My Hobby, Scat's Princess, 7 started.

FALLS CITY H. (G2), Churchill Downs, Nov. 22, $324,300, 3&up, f&m, 1 1/8m, 1:50.28, KETTLEONEUP, High Heels, Panty Raid, 6 started.

Fall Sprint S., Lethbridge, Sept. 3, $15,056, 3&up, a5 1/2f, 1:06.60, LAFLEUR, Ransome Road, Goodbye Earl, 5 started.

Fanfreluche S. (R), Woodbine, Oct. 27, $156,311, 2yo, f, Ontario-bred, 6fAW, 1:09.62, SHILLA, Kid Sparkle, Dawn Raid, 6 started.

Fantango Lady S. (R), Horsemen's Park, July 19, $30,000, 3yo, f, Nebraska-bred, 1m, 1:42.60, PLAER'S TRUMP, Phyllee Rae, Yolly's Charm, 8 started.

Fantasia S. (R), Louisiana Downs, May 12, $49,500, 3yo, f, Louisiana-bred, 6f, 1:11.40, AHEAD OF HER TIME, Finally Alone, Anything But Quiet, 8 started.

FANTASY S. (G2), Oaklawn Park, April 6, $250,000, 3yo, f, 1 1/16m, 1:44.43, HIGH HEELS, Cotton Blossom, Cash Included, 8 started.

Fantasy S., Hastings Race Course, Oct. 27, $113,509, 2yo, f, 1 1/16m, 1:45.91, DANCING ALLSTAR, Remarkable Miss, Infinite Wealth, 5 started.

Farer Belle Lee H. (R), Great Lakes Downs, Sept. 1, $50,000, 3&up, f&m, Michigan-bred, 1 1/8m, 1:51.41, SILENT SUNSET, Nell's Enjoyment, Half a Glance, 9 started.

Fargo Open Thoroughbred Derby, North Dakota Horse Park, Aug. 26, $12,800, 3yo, 1m, 1:43, POLYNESIAN KITTY, Gratuity, Fancy N Quick, 6 started.

Fargo Thoroughbred S., North Dakota Horse Park, July 27, $6,000, 3&up, 6f, 1:14.20, dh-MEAN U GENE, dh-WALTER, Country Warrior, 7 started.

Fargo Thoroughbred S., North Dakota Horse Park, Sept. 3, $8,800, 4&up, 1m, 1:40.40, CANTERBURY GOLD, Strike the Moment, Fabulous Wully, 6 started.

Fargo Thoroughbred S. (R), North Dakota Horse Park, July 29, $20,758, 2&up, North Dakota-bred, 6f, 1:18, GIVEM HELL HARLEY, R Roxy, Miss Honey Calling, 6 started.

Farm Family Insurance Vincent Moscarelli Memorial Breeders' Classic S. (R), Charles Town Races, Oct. 20, $90,000, 2yo, West Virginia-bred, 6 1/2f, 1:20.47, LORD OF DANCE, Pow Wow Power, Medfordexpress, 10 started.

Fasig-Tipton Turf Dash S., Calder Race Course, Sept. 1, $55,000, 2yo, 5fT, :56.45, ULTIMATE AUTHORITY, Heaven's Awesome, Parisian Friend, 9 started.

Favorite Trick Breeders' Cup S., Monmouth Park, Oct. 26, $250,000, 2yo, 6f, 1:10.19, MARGO'S GIFT, Jazz Nation, Lantana Mob, 10 started.

FAYETTE S. (G3), Keeneland Race Course, Oct. 27, $150,000, 3&up, 1 1/8mAW, 1:47.97 (NTR), GO BETWEEN, Stream Cat, Kona Blend, 9 started.

Federal Way H., Emerald Downs, June 2, $53,775, 3yo, f, 6 1/2f, 1:15.20, SHAMPOO, Zaylaway, Skewing, 10 started.

Federico Tesio S., Pimlico Race Course, April 21, $100,000, 3yo, 1 1/8m, 1:49.98, XCHANGER, Pink Viper, Zephyr Cat, 6 started.

Fern Sawyer H., Ruidoso Downs, July 1, $40,000, 3&up, f&m, 7 1/2f, 1:32.60, SHESA PRIVATE I, I'm N Clover, Hailey's Gone West, 6 started.

Fiesta Mile S. (R), Retama Park, Oct. 13, $45,000, 3&up, f&m, Texas-bred, 1mT, 1:35.51, DURRYMANE, Jenz Benz, Boundus, 12 started.

Fifth Avenue S. (R), Aqueduct, Nov. 11, $100,000, 2yo, f, progeny of eligible New York stallions, 6f, 1:11.14, CANADIAN BALLET, Sweet Bama Breeze, Noble Fire, 8 started.

FIFTH SEASON S. (G3), Oaklawn Park, April 12, $100,000, 4&up, 1 1/16m, 1:42.95, SILENT PLEASURE, Kid Grindstone, Like an Eagle, 8 started.

FIFTH THIRD ELKHORN S. (G3), Keeneland Race Course, April 27, $200,000, 4&up, 1 1/2mT, 2:30.40, ASCERTAIN (IRE), Always First (GB), Drilling for Oil, 12 started.

Find H. (R), Laurel Park, Nov. 10; $50,000, 3&up, Maryland-bred, 1 1/8mT, 1:49.92, HEADSANDTALES, Foufa's Warrior, Easy Red, 8 started.

Finger Lakes Juvenile Fillies S., Finger Lakes Gaming and Race Track, Oct. 13, $50,000, 2yo, f, 6f, 1:12.64, SAY TOBA SANDY, Jovanna, Wise Choice, 9 started.

Finger Lakes Juvenile S., Finger Lakes Gaming and Race Track, Nov. 3, $50,000, 2yo, 6f, 1:11.25, TIN CUP CHALICE, Say Toba Sandy, Scary Trip, 8 started.

FIRECRACKER H. (G2), Churchill Downs, June 30, $232,000, 3&up, 1mT, 1:34.74, REMARKABLE NEWS (VEN), Brilliant, Outperformance, 8 started.

Firecracker S., Mountaineer Race Track and Gaming Resort, July 3, $75,000, 3&up, f&m, 1mT, 1:35.88, WATER GAP, Beautiful Venue, Sassy Skipper, 7 started.

Fire Plug S., Laurel Park, Jan. 20, $74,400, 4&up, 6f, 1:10.30, AH DAY, Crafty Schemer, Gold Cluster, 8 started.

First Approach S. (R), Presque Isle Downs, Sept. 21, $90,000, 3&up, f&m, Pennsylvania-bred, 1 1/16mAW, 1:46.33, WHO'S HAPPY, Raging Rapids, She's Fancy Free, 5 started.

First Episode S. (R), Suffolk Downs, Aug. 5, $44,100, 3&up, f&m, Massachusetts-bred, 1m70y, 1:44.46, ASK QUEENIE, Flirt for Fame, Southoftheborder, 5 started.

FIRST FLIGHT H. (G2), Belmont Park, July 8, $147,000, 3&up, f&m, 7f, 1:22.64, GINGER PUNCH, Sweet Fervor, Swap Fliparoo, 5 started.

First Lady H., Ruidoso Downs, June 16, $40,000, 3&up, f&m, 6f, 1:10.80, HAILEY'S GONE WEST, Shesa Private I, I'm N Clover, 8 started.

FIRST LADY H. (G3), Gulfstream Park, Jan. 20, $100,000, 4&up, f&m, 6f, 1:10.58, ANY LIMIT, Contrast, Actslikealady, 8 started.

FIRST LADY S. (G2), Keeneland Race Course, Oct. 6, $432,000, 3&up, f&m, 1mT, 1:35.85, VACARE, Precious Kitten, Quite a Bride, 9 started.

Fit for a Queen S., Arlington Park, May 19, $47,550, 3&up, f&m, 6 1/2fAW, 1:16.48, BLUESBDANCING, Pretty Jenny, Lady Belsara, 8 started.

FITZ DIXON COTILLION H. (G2), Philadelphia Park, Sept. 22, $750,000, 3yo, f, 1 1/16m, 1:41.21, BEAR NOW, Octave, Talkin About Love, 7 started.

Fitz Dixon Jr. Memorial Juvenile S., Presque Isle Downs, Sept. 29, $100,000, 2yo, 6 1/2fAW, 1:17.67, SOK SOK, Dixie Mon, Little Nick, 8 started.

Flame Thrower S. (R), Hollywood Park, June 17, $71,750, 3&up, non-winners of $60,000 since March 1, 2007, 6fT, 1:08.47, SCOTTSBLUFF, One Union, Northern Soldier, 5 started.

Flaming Page S., Woodbine, Sept. 23, $101,119, 3&up, f&m, 1 1/2mT, 2:28.91, THE NIAGARA QUEEN, Sant Elena (GB), Sheer Enchantment, 8 started.

Flat Fleet Feet S., Aqueduct, Dec. 14, $78,150, 3yo, f, 1m70y, 1:43.67, DINNER BREAK, Runway Rosie, Bitter Lemon, 7 started.

Flatterer Hurdle H. (R), Philadelphia Park, July 28, $72,750, 3&up, Pennsylvania-bred, a2 1/16mT, 3:42.32, JOHN LAW, Dark Equation, Sparkled, 7 started.

Flawlessly S., Hollywood Park, July 6, $107,500, 3yo, f, 1mT, 1:35.71, PASSIFIED (GB), Diva's Seastar, Spenditallbaby, 6 started.

Fleet Indian S. (R), Saratoga Race Course, Aug. 1, $81,750, 3&up, f&m, New York-bred, 1 1/8m, 1:51.32, LAUREN'S TIZZY, Shady Lane, Mama Theresa, 7 started.

Fleet Treat S. (R), Del Mar, July 22, $111,500, 3yo, f, California-bred, 7fAW, 1:25.32, SPENDITALLBABY, Swiss Diva, Romance Is Diane, 10 started.

FLEUR DE LIS H. (G2), Churchill Downs, June 16, $327,600, 3&up, f&m, 1 1/8m, 1:49.12, INDIAN VALE, Asi Siempre, Kettleoneup, 7 started.

Floor Show S., Delaware Park, June 19, $59,450, 3yo, 1 1/16m, 1:43.10, LONGLEY, Point Blake, Silver Express, 7 started.

Floral Park S. (R), Belmont Park, Sept. 27, $77,000, 3&up, f&m, New York-bred, 7f, 1:22.67, ICE COOL KITTY, Stolen Star, Scatkey, 8 started.

Florence Henderson S. (R), Indiana Downs, July 2, $45,000, 3&up, f&m, Indiana-bred and/or -sired, a1mT, 1:37.46 (NCR), PRINCESS COMPOSER, Easy Tee, Amature's Prize, 12 started.

Florida Breeders' Distaff S., Ocala Training Center, Feb. 12, $45,000, 3&up, f&m, 1 1/16m, 1:46.20, TOP NOTCH LADY, Running Lass, Nijinsky Bullet, 6 started.

FLORIDA DERBY (G1), Gulfstream Park, March 31, $1,000,000, 3yo, 1 1/8m, 1:49, SCAT DADDY, Notional, Chelokee, 9 started.

Florida Oaks, Tampa Bay Downs, March 17, $200,000, 3yo, f, 1 1/16m, 1:45.06, COTTON BLOSSOM, Suaveness, Maria's Kitty, 8 started.

Florida Thoroughbred Charities S. (R), Ocala Training Center, Feb. 12, $45,000, 3&up, progeny of stallion seasons donated to the 2003 Florida Thoroughbred Charities live auction, 5f, :57.60, FAR WEST, Put Back the Shu, Song Song Blue, 5 started.

FLOWER BOWL INVITATIONAL S. (G1), Belmont Park, Sept. 29, $600,000, 3&up, f&m, 1 1/4mT, 1:59.05, LAHUDOOD (GB), Rosinka (Ire), Wait a While, 9 started.

Flower Girl H. (R), Santa Anita Park, March 3, $94,450, 4&up, f&m, non-winners of a graded stakes in 2006-'07, a6 1/2fT, 1:12.28, INDIAN FLARE, Forest Code, Mighty Clever, 7 started.

Fonner Park Special S. (R), Fonner Park, April 21, $30,700, 3yo, c&g, Nebraska-bred, 6f, 1:14.80, HESO, Buffalo Road, Bevys Best, 7 started.

Fonner Park Special S. (R), Fonner Park, April 21, $30,800, 3yo, f, Nebraska-bred, 6f, 1:16.40, PLAER'S TRUMP, Shade On, Dazzling Seville, 8 started.

Foolish Pleasure S., Calder Race Course, Sept. 22, $120,000, 2yo, 1m70y, 1:45.04, WISE ANSWER, Sr. Henry, Hypocrite, 10 started.

Fool the Experts S., Turf Paradise, Dec. 4, $31,000, 2yo, 6 1/2f, 1:17.51, REMEMBER BOFFI, Rule by Force, Dixieland Easy, 7 started.

Foothill S., Fairplex Park, Sept. 10, $64,350, 3yo, 6 1/2f, 1:18.09, PRIME RULER, I'm All Out, Lit'sgoodlookngray, 8 started.

Ford Express S., Lone Star Park, May 19, $50,000, 3&up, 6f, 1:10.78, SMOKE MOUNTAIN, Wheaton Home, Orphan Brigade, 8 started.

FOREGO H. (G1), Saratoga Race Course, Sept. 1, $250,000, 3&up, 7f, 1:21.06, MIDNIGHT LUTE, Benny the Bull, Attila's Storm, 10 started.

Forego S., Turfway Park, Jan. 27, $50,000, 4&up, 6 1/2fAW, 1:16.87, BUDDY GOT EVEN, Outrageouslyfunny, Will He Shine, 8 started.

Forerunner S., Keeneland Race Course, April 19, $112,100, 3yo, 1 1/8mT, 1:50.16, MOUDEZ (IRE), Bullara, Trimaran, 8 started.

Foresta S. (R), Belmont Park, June 9, $83,500, 4&up, f&m, non-winners of a stakes on the turf, 1 1/16mT, 1:41.97, MERIBEL, I'm in Love, Calla Lily, 10 started.

Formal Gold S., Meadowlands, Sept. 15, $65,000, 3&up, 1 1/16m, 1:42.62, FIVE STEPS, Indian War Dance, Sleek John, 5 started.

Formula Powell Maturity, Grand Prairie, Aug. 5, $4,891, 4yo, 7f, 1:26.20, IT'S NOT OVER YET, Vying Gold, Selling Point, 5 started.

Forrest White S. (1st Div.), Stockton, June 24, $49,968, 3yo, 5 1/2f, 1:03.16, DOUBLE ACTION, Super Image, Corredor Del Oro, 6 started.

Forrest White S. (2nd Div.), Stockton, June 24, $52,667, 3yo, 5 1/2f, 1:03.61, ANOTHER KRIS, Something Sonic, Acquire the Fire, 6 started.

Fort Bend County S. (R), Sam Houston Race Park, March 31, $45,000, 3yo, Texas-bred, 7f, 1:24.58, I SPY WOLFIE, Filet Gumbo, Barnett Shale, 9 started.

Fort Erie Slots Cup S. (R), Fort Erie, July 1, $23,463, 3&up, f&m, starters at Fort Erie three times or more in 2007, 1 1/16m, 1:46.31, SPEEDSTORM, Marden Hill, Chan Ja Bang, 7 started.

Fortin H., Fair Grounds, March 17, $72,000, 4&up, f&m, 1m, 1:38.42, ROLLING SEA, Morlana, Space Cruise, 5 started.

FORT MARCY H. (G3), Aqueduct, April 29, $114,100, 3&up, 1 1/16mT, 1:44.88, WOODLANDER, Golden Commander, Grand Couturier (GB), 7 started.

Forty Niner S., Golden Gate Fields, Dec. 26, $75,000, 3&up, 1 1/16mAW, 1:42.15, NOW VICTORY, McCann's Mojave, Siren Lure, 8 started.

FORWARD GAL S. (G2), Gulfstream Park, March 10, $150,000, 3yo,

f, 7f, 1:22.60, FOREVER TOGETHER, Silver Knockers, You Asked, 7 started.

Forward Pass S., Arlington Park, Aug. 11, $48,000, 3yo, 7fAW, 1:21.02 (NTR), LOVANGO, Morada Key, Front Court, 10 started.

Foster City H., Bay Meadows Race Course, Feb. 24, $60,125, 4&up, f&m, 1m, 1:34.93, SOMETHINABOUTLAURA, Gins Majesty, Make a Pass, 7 started.

Founders' Cup Hurdle S., Little Everglades, March 11, $38,800, 4&up, a2⅛mT, 3:38.20, RIDDLE, Chivite (Ire), Toughkenamon, 6 started.

FOUNTAIN OF YOUTH S. (G2), Gulfstream Park, March 3, $350,000, 3yo, 1⅛m, 1:49.11, SCAT DADDY, Stormello, Nobiz Like Shobiz, 9 started.

FOURSTARDAVE H. (G2), Saratoga Race Course, Aug. 5, $150,000, 3&up, 1¹⁄₁₆mT, 1:41.88, SILVER TREE, Drum Major, Host (Chi), 7 started.

Foxbrook Supreme Hurdle S. (R), Far Hills, Oct. 20, $100,000, 4&up, non-winners over hurdles prior to June 1, 2006, a2½mT, 5:13.40 (NCR), GLIDING (NZ), Sovereign Duty, Planets Aligned, 6 started.

Fox Sports Network H., Emerald Downs, May 28, $45,000, 3&up, 6½f, 1:13.40, WESTSIDECLYDE, The Great Face, Norm's Nephew, 9 started.

Foxy J. G. S. (R), Philadelphia Park, June 23, $60,000, 3yo, f, Pennsylvania-bred, 1m70y, 1:43.29, WHO'S HAPPY, Holy Christmas, Syd N Carly's Rose, 7 started.

FRANCES A. GENTER S. (G3), Calder Race Course, Dec. 29, $100,000, 3yo, f, 7½fT, 1:28.16, RUTHERIENNE, dh-Pretoria Light, dh-Sweet Ransom, 11 started.

Frances Genter S. (R), Canterbury Park, July 7, $45,000, 3yo, f, Minnesota-bred, 6f, 1:09.94, RUN WITH JOY, Thanks for the Tip, Cant Catch Judy, 12 started.

Frances Slocum S. (R), Hoosier Park, Nov. 17, $45,000, 3&up, f&m, Indiana-bred, 1¹⁄₁₆m, 1:47.37, EASY TEE, Princess Composer, Amature's Prize, 11 started.

Francis "Jock" LaBelle Memorial S., Delaware Park, May 5, $75,000, 3yo, 6f, 1:09.53, WEST COAST FLIER, Cherokee Country, Bill Place, 5 started.

Frank A. "Buddy" Abadie Memorial S. (R), Evangeline Downs, June 30, $75,000, 3yo, f, Louisiana-bred, 1m, 1:39.59, AHEAD OF HER TIME, Many Moons, Prestons Star, 10 started.

Frank Arnason Sire S. (R), Assiniboia Downs, July 22, $28,617, 2yo, Manitoba-bred, 5f, 1:01.40, GEM DROP, Meow Wow, Bella Mariella, 11 started.

FRANK E. KILROE MILE H. (G1), Santa Anita Park, March 3, $300,000, 4&up, 1mT, 1:33.88, KIP DEVILLE, Bayeux, Silent Name (Jpn), 12 started.

Frank Gall Memorial H. (R), Charles Town Races, Aug. 25, $46,150, 3&up, West Virginia-bred, 7f, 1:25.83, DONALD'S PRIDE, Raggedy Andy, Rhythmic Moves, 7 started.

FRANK J. DE FRANCIS MEMORIAL DASH S. (G1), Laurel Park, Nov. 24, $250,000, 3&up, 6f, 1:09.86, BENNY THE BULL, Talent Search, Miraculous Miss, 8 started.

Franklin S., Kentucky Downs, Sept. 22, $50,000, 3&up, 1mT, 1:36.84, ART MODERNE, dh-Terrific Storm, dh-Salinja, 8 started.

Fran's Valentine S. (R), Hollywood Park, April 29, $150,000, 4&up, f&m, California-bred, 1¹⁄₁₆mT, 1:40.21, NASHOBA'S KEY, Dancing General, Memorette, 8 started.

Fred "Cappy" Capossela S., Aqueduct, Feb. 19, $70,070, 3yo, 6f, 1:10.75, WOLLASTON BAY, Bill Place, Landofopportunity, 6 started.

Fred Drysdale Memorial S., Grand Prairie, Aug. 18, $6,738, 3&up, f&m, 6½f, 1:22, REAL STERLING, Kinda Sassy, Way to Special, 4 started.

FRED W. HOOPER H. (G3), Calder Race Course, Dec. 15, $100,000, 3&up, 1⅛m, 1:52.56, ELECTRIFY, Summer Book, Imawildandcrazyguy, 12 started.

Freedom of the City S., Northlands Park, Sept. 2, $47,345, 2yo, f, 1m, 1:40.60, LITTLEMISS ALLISON, Bears Artiste, Testy Hussy, 6 started.

Free Press S., Assiniboia Downs, June 17, $42,125, 3&up, 6f, 1:11.40, ILLUSIVE FORCE, Lite Brigade, Elite Mercedes, 8 started.

Free Spirits H., Ruidoso Downs, June 24, $40,000, 3&up, 6f, 1:12, DANGEROUS DEVON, Tough Pilgrim, Pistol Creek, 7 started.

Free Spirit's Joy S. (R), Louisiana Downs, May 12, $48,500, 3yo, Louisiana-bred, 6f, 1:10.14, ST. ZARB, Ceasers March, Zarb's Bully, 7 started.

Fresa Louisiana-Bred Starter S. (R), Louisiana Downs, May 11, $39,200, 3&up, f&m, Louisiana-bred starters for a claiming price of $16,000 or less in 2006-'07, 1m70y, 1:42.38, MADISON'S MUSIC, Toolights Ruckus, Winsky, 7 started.

Friendly Lover H. (R), Monmouth Park, Aug. 26, $110,000, 3&up, New Jersey-bred, 6f, 1:09.74, JOEY P., Charley's Diamond, Karakorum Tuxedo, 7 started.

Frisk Me Now S., Monmouth Park, May 28, $65,000, 3&up, 1m70y, 1:39.54, INDY WIND, Gottcha Gold, Accountforthegold, 7 started.

FRIZETTE S. (G1), Belmont Park, Oct. 6, $400,000, 2yo, f, 1m, 1:37.64, INDIAN BLESSING, Backseat Rhythm, Sunday Holiday, 9 started.

Frontier H. (R), Great Lakes Downs, Sept. 4, $50,000, 3&up, Michigan-bred, 1⅛m, 1:56, ROCKEM SOCKEM, Demagoguery, Its His Time, 7 started.

Front Range S., Arapahoe Park, July 4, $27,400, 3&up, 7f, 1:23.23, ABSOLUTELY TRUE, Cut of Music, Nick Missed, 6 started.

Frost King S. (R), Woodbine, Nov. 14, $132,436, 2yo, Ontario-foaled, 7fAW, 1:23.09, STUCK IN TRAFFIC, Grazettes Landing, Lady's First Cat, 10 started.

Ft. Lauderdale S., Gulfstream Park, Jan. 6, $75,000, 4&up, 1¹⁄₁₆mT, 1:40.19, CLASSIC CAMPAIGN, Dreadnaught, Saint Stephen, 11 started.

Furlough S. (R), Aqueduct, April 19, $65,950, 4&up, f&m, non-winners of a graded stakes in 2006-'07, 6f, 1:09.98, SMART AND FANCY, Grecian Lover, Last Romance, 5 started.

Furl Sail H., Fair Grounds, Dec. 29, $60,000, 3&up, f&m, a1¹⁄₁₆mT, 1:45.27, SWINGIT, My Three Sisters, Shytoe Lafeet, 14 started.

Fury S. (R), Woodbine, May 6, $135,435, 3yo, f, Ontario-bred, 7fAW, 1:24.59, SASKAWEA, Quiet Action, Palace Pier, 5 started.

FUTURITY S. (G2), Belmont Park, Sept. 15, $250,000, 2yo, 7f, 1:22.33, TALE OF EKATI, Kodiak Kowboy, Mythical Pegasus, 6 started.

Ga Hai H. (R), Philadelphia Park, July 28, $100,000, 3&up, f&m, progeny of stallions standing in Pennsylvania, 6f, 1:09.88, SHE'S FANCY FREE, Miss Blue Tye Dye, Speechifying, 9 started.

Gaily Gaily S., Aqueduct, Nov. 18, $78,500, 3&up, f&m, 1mT, 1:39.07, REWRITE, Trouble Maker, Now More Than Ever, 10 started.

Gaily Gaily S., Gulfstream Park, Feb. 25, $76,500, 3yo, f, 1¹⁄₁₆mT, 1:41.71, AUDACIOUS CHLOE, Dreaming of Anna, Communique, 8 started.

GALLANT BLOOM H. (G2), Belmont Park, Sept. 22, $147,000, 3&up, f&m, 6½f, 1:16.71, JAZZY (ARG), Cuaba, Pussycat Doll, 5 started.

Gallant Bob H., Philadelphia Park, Sept. 29, $250,000, 3yo, 6f, 1:09.93, PREMIUM WINE, Double Action, Jacob's Run, 7 started.

Gallant Fox H., Aqueduct, Dec. 29, $80,700, 3&up, 1⅝m, 2:47.45, NITE LIGHT, Successful Affair, Malibu Moonshine, 6 started.

GALLORETTE H. (G3), Pimlico Race Course, May 19, $100,000, 3&up, f&m, 1¹⁄₁₆mT, 1:40.32 (NCR), PRECIOUS KITTEN, A True Pussycat, Trick's Pic, 8 started.

Game Cup S. (R), Fort Erie, Oct. 28, $25,982, 2yo, c&g, starters for a claiming price of $5,000 or less in 2006-'07 and have started at Fort Erie three times in 2007, 6f, 1:12.42, WAY TO DOUGH BOY, Belfast Dancer, While the Catsaway, 7 started.

GAMELY S. (G1), Hollywood Park, May 28, $367,800, 3&up, f&m, 1⅛mT, 1:45.73, CITRONNADE, Price Tag (GB), Vacare, 6 started.

Gander S. (R), Belmont Park, June 24, $69,500, 4&up, New York-bred, 1¹⁄₁₆m, 1:40.53, ACCOUNTFORTHEGOLD, Organizer, Building New Era, 6 started.

GARDEN CITY S. (G1), Belmont Park, Sept. 8, $219,800, 3yo, f, 1⅛mT, 1:48.97, ALEXANDER TANGO (IRE), Bit of Whimsy, Sharp Susan, 10 started.

GARDENIA H. (G3), Ellis Park, Aug. 18, $150,000, 3&up, f&m, 1m, 1:38.85, PLEASANT HILL, High Heels, Brownie Points, 11 started.

Garden State H. (R), Monmouth Park, Oct. 25, $75,000, 3&up, New Jersey-bred, 1m70y, 1:41.58, FRANK THE BARBER, Fagedaboudit Sal, Bonding, 8 started.

Garland of Roses H., Aqueduct, Dec. 1, $81,700, 3&up, f&m, 6f, 1:10.50, CONTROL SYSTEM, More Angels, Oprah Winney, 6 started.

Gasparilla S., Tampa Bay Downs, Jan. 20, $60,000, 3yo, f, 7f, 1:24.03, SUAVENESS, Foret, Pretoria Light, 9 started.

Gateway to Glory S., Fairplex Park, Sept. 20, $64,350, 2yo, 1¹⁄₁₆m, 1:45.83, MY REDEEMER, One Only, Bean Who, 8 started.

GAZELLE S. (G1), Belmont Park, Sept. 15, $245,000, 3yo, f, 1⅛m, 1:47.86, LEAR'S PRINCESS, Rags to Riches, Tough Tiz's Sis, 5 started.

GCFA Texas-Bred S. (R), Gillespie County Fairgrounds, Aug. 26, $18,200, 3&up, Texas-bred, 7f, 1:25.63, GENERAL NAEVUS, Guacamole, Aggies Rule, 10 started.

Geisha H. (R), Laurel Park, Dec. 8, $60,000, 3&up, f&m, Maryland-bred, 1⅛m, 1:53.90, LEXI STAR, Katie's Love, Scheing E Jet, 5 started.

Gene Francis and Associates H., Anthony Downs, July 21, $4,000,

3&up, 1 1/16m, 1:51.64 (NTR), DEVIL'S BANDIT, Coffee Bubbles, Lite Source, 5 started.

Gene Norman Memorial Starter S. (R), Evangeline Downs, June 30, $45,000, 3&up, f&m, Louisiana-bred starters for a claiming price of $10,000 or less in 2006-'07, 5f, :59.16, KOOKIE STORM, Shugafoot, Derbytown, 9 started.

General Douglas MacArthur H. (R), Belmont Park, Sept. 7, $108,800, 3&up, New York-bred, 1m, 1:34.26, NAUGHTY NEW YORKER, Shuffling Maddnes, Who What Win, 6 started.

GENERAL GEORGE BREEDERS' CUP H. (G2), Laurel Park, Feb. 19, $285,000, 3&up, 7f, 1:23.13, SILVER WAGON, Ah Day, Ryan's for Real, 9 started.

Generous Portion S. (R), Del Mar, Aug. 29, $108,800, 2yo, f, California-bred, 6fAW, 1:12.98, GOLDEN DOC A, Champagne Miss, Proud Garrison, 8 started.

GENEROUS S. (G3), Hollywood Park, Nov. 23, $111,800, 2yo, 1mT, 1:34.28, THE LEOPARD, Indian Sun, Meer Kat (Ire), 9 started.

Genesee Valley Breeders' H. (R), Finger Lakes Gaming and Race Track, Sept. 15, $50,000, 3&up, New York-bred, 1 1/16m, 1:46.36, MT. MAJESTY, Rises the Phoenix, Clery's Contender, 6 started.

Genesee Valley Hunt Cup Timber S., Genesee Valley, Oct. 13, $19,500, 4&up, a3 1/2mT, 8:01, MILES AHEAD, Stars Out Tonight (Ire), Earmark, 6 started.

Genesis S., Delta Downs, Jan. 26, $48,000, 3yo, f, 6 1/2f, 1:21.34, MAGNETIC MISS, Wrenice, Speedy Diva, 5 started.

Gentilly S. (R), Fair Grounds, Jan. 20, $75,000, 3yo, Louisiana-bred, 1 1/16m (originally scheduled on the turf), 1:47.60, POWER SURGE, Hallway, Forgotten Prince, 5 started.

George Lewis Memorial S. (R), Thistledown, July 14, $50,000, 3&up, Ohio-bred, 1 1/8m, 1:50.86, ACTS LIKE A KING, Catlaunch, Head to Toe, 12 started.

George Maloof Futurity (R), The Downs at Albuquerque, Sept. 23, $64,395, 2yo, c&g, New Mexico-bred, 6f, 1:12.24, BRAVO SAPELLO, Jack's Band, Abo Seamore, 8 started.

George Rosenberger Memorial S. (R), Delaware Park, Sept. 8, $101,500, 3&up, f&m, starters at Delaware Park in 2007 excluding stakes, 1 1/16mT, 1:41.67, I'M IN LOVE, Debbie Sue, Shytoe Lafeet, 10 started.

George Royal S., Hastings Race Course, May 5, $46,750, 3&up, 6 1/2f, 1:16.49, TRUE METROPOLITAN, Forceful Intention, Spaghetti Mouse, 8 started.

George W. Barker H. (R), Finger Lakes Gaming and Race Track, May 28, $50,000, 3&up, New York-bred, 6f, 1:09.71, JOHNIE BYE NIGHT, Mr. Bourbon Street, You Willgo Broke, 6 started.

Georgia Cup Hurdle S., Atlanta, April 14, $69,750, 4&up, a2mT, 3:45.80, SEAFARING MAN, Bow Strada (GB), The Looper, 5 started.

Gerry Howard Inaugural H., Yavapai Downs, May 26, $21,000, 3&up, 6f, 1:09.40, MOORES BRIDGE, Sax Notes, Lydia's Legacy, 8 started.

Gerry Howard Memorial S., Turf Paradise, April 29, $22,410, 3&up, 6f, 1:07.97, BUMP, Family Guy, Broke to Fight, 3 started.

Get Lucky S. (R), Aqueduct, Jan. 4, $67,900, 4yo, f, non-winners of a graded stakes in 2006, 1m, 1:37.52, A TRUE PUSSYCAT, Motel Dancing, Love Locket, 6 started.

Ghost and Goblins S., Delaware Park, Oct. 31, $56,260, 3yo, f, 1m70y, 1:42.13, LEMON DROP MOM, Buy the Barrel, Grand in Grey, 4 started.

Giant's Causeway S., Keeneland Race Course, April 21, $115,000, 3&up, f&m, 5 1/2fT, 1:02.73, FOREST CODE, Haddie Be Good, South Necking (Arg), 6 started.

Ginger Welch H., Les Bois Park, July 14, $6,350, 3&up, f&m, 7f, 1:27.02, CANDY GO, Derby Cat, Social Order, 8 started.

Gin Talking S. (R), Laurel Park, Sept. 29, $45,000, 2yo, f, Maryland-bred, 6fT, 1:08.94, HARTIGAN, Kosmo's Buddy, My Dance Partner, 8 started.

Glacial Princess S. (R), Beulah Park, Nov. 10, $50,000, 2yo, f, Ohio-bred, 1m, 1:44.56, SARASPONDA, Storm by You, Polly Pepperstone, 6 started.

Gladstone Hurdle S., Far Hills, Oct. 20, $48,500, 3yo, a2 1/8mT, 4:33.60, C R'S DEPUTY, Nat Grew, Be Certain, 5 started.

Glendale H., Turf Paradise, Jan. 6, $50,000, 4&up, f&m, 1 1/16mT, 1:41.86, GRAT, Jubilee, Bend, 10 started.

GLENS FALLS H. (G3), Saratoga Race Course, Sept. 3, $111,200, 3&up, f&m, 1 3/8mT, 2:13, ROSINKA (IRE), Mauralakana (Fr), Pictavia (Ire), 8 started.

Glorious Song S., Woodbine, Nov. 18, $137,515, 2yo, f, 7fAW, 1:22.75, INITIATION, Victory Romance, Shilla, 6 started.

Glow S. (R), Saratoga Race Course, Aug. 4, $82,250, 3yo, non-winners of an open stakes on the turf in 2007, 1mT, 1:35.71, PAYS TO DREAM, Teuflesberg, Biggerbadderbetter, 9 started.

G Malleah H., Turf Paradise, Feb. 3, $45,000, 4&up, 6f, 1:08.06, SNOWBOUND HALO, Diligent Prospect, Prorunner, 6 started.

Goddess S., Delta Downs, March 31, $97,000, 4&up, f&m, 1 1/16m, 1:44.78, DELICATE DYNAMITE, Plaid, Game for More, 6 started.

GO FOR WAND H. (G1), Saratoga Race Course, July 28, $250,000, 3&up, f&m, 1 1/8m, 1:49.19, GINGER PUNCH, Miss Shop, Teammate, 6 started.

Go for Wand S., Delaware Park, Sept. 1, $100,900, 3yo, f, 1 1/16m, 1:44.13, LEMON DROP MOM, Coy Coyote, Paying Off, 8 started.

Gold Breeders' Cup S., Assiniboia Downs, Sept. 23, $69,444, 3&up, 1 1/8m, 1:51.80, TEJANO TROUBLE, Car Keys, Brinello, 10 started.

Gold Cup S. (R), Delta Downs, Nov. 17, $97,000, 3&up, Louisiana-bred, 1 1/8m, 1:44.96, COSTA RISING, Southern Invasion, Magic Sunset, 6 started.

Golden Bear S., Golden Gate Fields, May 6, $53,625, 3yo, 6f, 1:09.17, DOUBLE ACTION, Super Image, Mr. Negotiator, 5 started.

Golden Boy S., Assiniboia Downs, June 2, $42,404, 3yo, 6f, 1:11.60, COUNTRY HUMOR, Western Deed, Holy Smoke Ya, 11 started.

Golden Circle S., Prairie Meadows, April 21, $53,000, 3yo, 6f, 1:09.41, BIGLIE SMALLWORLD, Crimson King Cat, Sir Five Star, 6 started.

GOLDEN GATE FIELDS BREEDERS' CUP S. (G3), Golden Gate Fields, May 28, $191,400, 3&up, 1 3/8mT, 2:17.64, FANTASTIC SPAIN, Notable Guest, Macduff (GB), 8 started.

Golden Gull "Chris Brown Memorial" S. (R), Charles Town Races, Sept. 29, $50,800, 2yo, f, West Virginia-bred nominated to the West Virginia Breeders' Classic, 4 1/2f, :52.88, WE'RE IN THE MONEY, Touch of Class, Color Parade, 5 started.

Golden Poppy S., Golden Gate Fields, May 12, $75,000, 3yo, f, 1 1/16mT, 1:43.15, MYSTIC SOUL, Rockella, Round Trip Flight, 7 started.

GOLDEN ROD S. (G2), Churchill Downs, Nov. 24, $276,500, 2yo, f, 1 1/16m, 1:43.59, PURE CLAN, C J's Leelee, Turn Away, 8 started.

Golden Sylvia H., Mountaineer Race Track and Gaming Resort, June 19, $75,000, 3&up, f&m, 1m, 1:38.60, BALLAD OF BERTIE, Stormy Amber, Julie Truly, 9 started.

Gold Finch H., Monmouth Park, July 19, $60,000, 3&up, f&m, New Jersey-bred, 6f, 1:08.53, PURE DISCO, Jenny Bean Girl, Solar Powered, 6 started.

Goldfinch S., Prairie Meadows, April 20, $59,000, 3yo, f, 6f, 1:10.04, IRISH PARTY, Sea the Joy, Smart Wildcat, 9 started.

Gold Rush Futurity, Arapahoe Park, Aug. 12, $43,680, 2yo, f, 1:09.42, BIG MISSION, Kepthecabin, Golem, 7 started.

Gold Rush S., Golden Gate Fields, Dec. 15, $75,000, 2yo, 1mAW, 1:37.62, EL GATO MALO, Bert's Law, Many Rivers, 8 started.

Gold Strike S. (R), Marquis Downs, Aug. 3, $9,493, 2yo, f, Saskatchewan-sired and/or -bred, 6f, 1:17.25, FIESTY CHEETAH, Strawberry Sheen, Ocean Bird, 8 started.

GOODWOOD S. (G1), Oak Tree at Santa Anita, Sept. 29, $520,000, 3&up, 1 1/8mAW, 1:46.93, TIAGO, Awesome Gem, Big Booster, 8 started.

GOTHAM S. (G3), Aqueduct, March 10, $200,000, 3yo, 1 1/16m, 1:44.75, COWTOWN CAT, Wafi City, Summer Doldrums, 9 started.

Go to Will S., Calder Race Course, Oct. 20, $45,000, 3&up, 7f, 1:23.36, PARADISE DANCER, Finallymadeit, Storm in May, 6 started.

Gottstein Futurity, Emerald Downs, Sept. 29, $90,000, 2yo, 1 1/16m, 1:42.40, SMARTY DEB, Gallon, Margo's Gift, 9 started.

Governor's Buckeye Cup S. (R), Thistledown, Sept. 3, $75,000, 3&up, Ohio-bred, 1 1/4m, 2:04.40, CATLAUNCH, Pyrite Personal, What the Devil, 8 started.

Governor's Cup H., Fairplex Park, Sept. 23, $75,000, 3&up, 6 1/2f, 1:16.85, WIND WATER, Ten Downing Street (Ire), The Pharaoh, 10 started.

Governor's Cup S., Remington Park, Dec. 1, $75,000, 3&up, 1 1/16m, 1:44.22, BETA CAPO, Sing Baby Sing, Greeley's Conquest, 5 started.

Governor's H., Ellis Park, Aug. 11, $50,000, 3&up, f&m, 1m, 1:35.68, ISTAN, Spellbinder, Red Raymond, 10 started.

Governor's H., Emerald Downs, July 29, $45,000, 3&up, 6 1/2f, 1:14.20, WASSERMAN, Norm's Nephew, Diligent Prospect, 7 started.

Governor's Lady H. (R), Hawthorne Race Course, April 28, $93,760, 4&up, f&m, Illinois-conceived and/or -foaled, 6f, 1:11.28, TROUT RIVER RED, Precious Zeal, Denoun N Deverb, 7 started.

Governor's S. (R), Indiana Downs, June 5, $45,000, 3yo, Indiana-bred and/or -sired, 7 1/2f, 1:31.72, WAVE LAND GROOVY, Father John, Need Money Dad, 10 started.

Governor's S., Zia Park, Oct. 28, $60,400, 2yo, 6f, 1:10.60, YONEGWA, T. J.'s Posse, Possetothemax, 6 started.

Governor's Speed H., Portland Meadows, Feb. 5, $20,550, 4&up,

6f, 1:13.26, CRIMSON DESIGN, Raggidy Rowe, Lethal Grande, 4 started.

Gowell S., Turfway Park, Dec. 22, $50,000, 2yo, f, 6fAW, 1:09.68, KADIRA, Birdgirl, Absolutely Cindy, 11 started.

Graceful Klinchit H., Marquis Downs, Aug. 25, $5,702, 3&up, f&m, 1m, 1:41.39, ON MANOEUVRES, Wisperingwhitelies, Rembecca, 7 started.

Graduation S. (R), Del Mar, July 25, $140,050, 2yo, California-bred, 5½fAW, 1:06.67, GEORGIE BOY, My Redeemer, Mix, 11 started.

Grand Canyon H., Churchill Downs, Nov. 24, $66,000, 2yo, 1¹⁄₁₆mT, 1:45.84, OLD MAN BUCK, Why Tonto, Seaspeak, 8 started.

Grande Prairie Derby, Grand Prairie, Aug. 17, $14,205, 3yo, 1m, 1:41.60, SIR DEVON, One O Nine N One, Desperate Dancer, 5 started.

Grand National Timber S., Grand National, April 21, $35,000, 5&up, a3¼mT, 6:07, BUBBLE ECONOMY, Make Your Own, Patriot's Path, 10 started.

Grand Prairie Turf Challenge S., Lone Star Park, April 28, $60,000, 3yo, 1mT, 1:35.74, BETA CAPO, Western Prize, Going Ballistic, 7 started.

Grand Slam S., Belmont Park, Oct. 21, $74,750, 2yo, 6f, 1:09.56, SMOKE'N COAL, Rollers, High Appeal, 5 started.

Grants Pass Thoroughbred H. (1st Div.), Grants Pass, July 8, $2,938, 3&up, 4½f, :51.80, PEARLS 'N' SATIN, Sowhatsyourpoint, Rosie Quatorze, 6 started.

Grants Pass Thoroughbred H. (2nd Div.), Grants Pass, July 8, $2,938, 3&up, 4½f, :52.20, LIGHTS OUT TONEY, Mago, Yodelew, 6 started.

Grants Pass Thoroughbred S., Grants Pass, July 8, $4,371, 3&up, 1¹⁄₁₆m, 1:47.80, TOUCHDOWN U S C, Okefenokee Slew, Oregon Miracle, 5 started.

Grasmick S., Fonner Park, Feb. 17, $10,550, 3&up, 4f, :45.60, TONIGHT RAINBOW, Classy Sheikh, Chasin the Wind, 5 started.

GRAVESEND H. (G3), Aqueduct, Dec. 29, $105,100, 3&up, 6f, 1:11.97, CITY ATTRACTION, Joey P., Debussy, 5 started.

Gray Pride Starter S. (R), Calder Race Course, July 28, $50,000, 3&up, gray or roan in color and starters for a claiming price of $25,000 or less in 2007 or eligible for a race other than maiden, claiming, or starter as of May 1, 2007, 1m70y, 1:44.08, ZOOBSTICK, Psychic Star, Minidrop, 7 started.

Gray's Lake S. (R), Prairie Meadows, May 28, $62,767, 3yo, c&g, Iowa-bred, 6f, 1:09.85, CRIMSON KING CAT, Red Hot N Gold, Tomcat Row, 6 started.

Great Falls S., Meadowlands, Oct. 13, $56,815, 3yo, 5fT, :57.21, NATURAL SPEED, Call Me Clash, Bythebeautifulsea, 7 started.

Great Falls Thoroughbred Inaugural S., Great Falls, July 14, $2,900, 3&up, 7f, 1:26.40, SHOULDBEVICTORY, Double Credit, Roberta's Matt, 5 started.

Great Falls Thoroughbred Inaugural S., Great Falls, July 14, $3,000, 3&up, a5¼f, 1:04.40, GOODBYE EARL, Slewthedude, My Irish Prince, 6 started.

Great Lady M. S., Hollywood Park, June 14, $97,375, 3&up, f&m, 6fT, 1:08.21, RIVER'S PRAYER, Valid's Valid, Silly Little Mama, 5 started.

Great White Way S. (R), Aqueduct, Nov. 11, $98,000, 2yo, c&g, progeny of eligible New York stallions, 6f, 1:10.16, SPANKY FISCHBEIN, Piquante Cat, Fort Drum, 5 started.

Green Carpet S. (R), River Downs, June 2, $50,000, 3yo, Ohio-bred, 1¹⁄₁₆mT, 1:42.40, PYRITE PERSONAL, Play the Hero, Smarty O, 12 started.

Green Flash H., Del Mar, Aug. 15, $95,760, 3&up, 5fT, :55.71, BARBER, Scottsbluff, Indian Breeze, 8 started.

Green Oaks S., Delta Downs, March 31, $98,000, 3yo, f, 1m, 1:40.24, ALBA DABAS SECRET, Magnetic Miss, Acrosstheborder, 7 started.

GREY BREEDERS' CUP S. (CAN-G3), Woodbine, Oct. 8, $252,740, 2yo, 1¹⁄₁₆mAW, 1:46.59, GLOBETROTTER, Cool Gator, Saada, 6 started.

Grindstone S., Fair Grounds, March 24, $98,000, 3yo, a1¹⁄₁₆mT, 1:44.51, JAZZ QUEST, Mayor Bozarth, Poschner, 7 started.

Groovy S. (R), Sam Houston Race Park, Dec. 1, $50,000, 2yo, Texas-bred, 7f, 1:24.54, CROOK'S BODGIT, Ferdinand's Flyer, Authentic Jones, 12 started.

GTOBA Debutante S. (R), Calder Race Course, Dec. 2, $75,000, 2yo, f, progeny of stallion seasons donated to the 2007 GTOBA stallion auction, 1¹⁄₁₆mT, 1:44.71, ROBBIE'S GAL, Nicole's Song, Okefenokee, 11 started.

GTOBA Juvenile Filly Turf Dash S. (R), Calder Race Course, Aug. 4, $75,000, 2yo, f, progeny of GTOBA nominated stallions, 5fT, :56.78, EXCESSIVE HEAT, Arealhotlover, Delayed Start, 12 started.

Gulf Coast Classic S., Delta Downs, March 31, $97,000, 4&up, 1¹⁄₁₆m, 1:44.07, SILENT PLEASURE, High Strike Zone, More Than Regal, 6 started.

GULFSTREAM PARK BREEDERS' CUP TURF S. (G1), Gulfstream Park, Feb. 24, $289,000, 4&up, 1⅜mT, 2:12.28, JAMBALAYA, Honey Ryder, Einstein (Brz), 11 started.

GULFSTREAM PARK H. (G2), Gulfstream Park, March 3, $350,000, 4&up, 1³⁄₁₆m, 1:55.06, CORINTHIAN, Hesanoldsalt, A. P. Arrow, 6 started.

Gus Grissom S. (R), Hoosier Park, Oct. 6, $45,000, 3&up, Indiana-bred and/or -sired, 1¹⁄₁₆m, 1:46.43, FATHER JOHN, Laz Has Risen, Liepers Fork, 10 started.

Hallandale Beach S., Gulfstream Park, Feb. 24, $77,250, 3yo, 1¹⁄₁₆mT, 1:40.76, TWILIGHT METEOR, Sedgefield, Le Dauphin, 12 started.

Hall of Fame S., Columbus Races, Aug. 4, $11,025, 3yo, 6f, 1:12.60, BEVYS BEST, My Secret Star, Recast, 6 started.

Hallowed Dreams S., Evangeline Downs, April 14, $50,000, 3yo, f, 5½f, 1:04.79, ALBA DABAS SECRET, Coach Mike, Inomuff, 9 started.

Hallowed Dreams S., Louisiana Downs, July 14, $115,000, 3&up, f&m, 6f, 1:12.56, RUBY'S GRAND SLAM, Star of Idabel, Cintarosa, 5 started.

HAL'S HOPE H. (G3), Gulfstream Park, Jan. 6, $100,000, 4&up, 1m, 1:33.87 (NTR), CHATAIN, Sir Greeley, Sweetnorthernsaint, 10 started.

Halton S. (R), Woodbine, Sept. 3, $119,878, 3&up, Canadian-bred, 1mT, 1:34.96, MY IMPERIAL DANCER, Full of Run, Sextet, 9 started.

Hancock County H., Mountaineer Race Track and Gaming Resort, May 15, $75,000, 3&up, f&m, 5f, :58.59, HIGH HERITAGE, Country Diva, Rupert's Prospect, 8 started.

Hank Mills Sr. H., Turf Paradise, Dec. 8, $45,000, 3&up, 1m, 1:37.67, HIGHLAND GAMES, Nationhood, Skipaslew, 6 started.

Hansel S., Turfway Park, March 24, $50,000, 3yo, 6fAW, 1:10.66, AWESOME HERO, Mr. Goodkat, Weather Warning, 9 started.

HANSHIN CUP H. (G3), Arlington Park, May 26, $100,000, 3&up, 1mAW, 1:33.72, SPOTSGONE, Lewis Michael, Gouldings Green, 10 started.

Happy Ticket S., Louisiana Downs, Sept. 22, $200,000, 2yo, f, 1¹⁄₁₆mT, 1:43.22, ZEE ZEE, Cato Major, Sammy Van Ammy, 9 started.

Happy Ticket S. (R), Fair Grounds, March 3, $75,000, 3yo, f, Louisiana-bred, 6f, 1:11.59, PRINCESS DEELITE, Huckie, Sara Bon Adeau, 7 started.

Harlequin S. (R), Marquis Downs, Aug. 4, $9,482, 2yo, c&g, Saskatchewan-sired and/or -bred, 6f, 1:15.28, BRILLIANT ACTION, Action Five, Y. C. Rail, 8 started.

Harmony Lodge S., Calder Race Course, May 12, $50,000, 3yo, f, 6½f, 1:19.16, CHER AMI, Adhrhythm, Sweet Exchange, 5 started.

Harold C. Ramser Sr. H., Oak Tree at Santa Anita, Oct. 14, $110,600, 3yo, f, 1mT, 1:34.16, GOTTA HAVE HER, Silky Smooth, Runway Rosie, 9 started.

Harold V. Goodman Memorial S. (R), Lone Star Park, July 7, $50,000, 3yo, Texas-bred, 6½f, 1:16.73, AUSTIN LIGHTS, Datrick, Be a Resident, 7 started.

Harper County H., Anthony Downs, July 15, $4,480, 3&up, a5f, 1:03.14, FOREIGN PENNANT, C'Mon Kreed, D D Dot Comm, 6 started.

Harrison E. Johnson Memorial H., Laurel Park, March 17, $63,000, 3&up, 1⅛m, 1:51.37, SWEETNORTHERNSAINT, Capac, Future Fantasy, 5 started.

Harry F. Brubaker H. (R), Del Mar, Aug. 16, $89,955, 3&up, nonwinners of a stakes worth $50,000 at one mile or over since March 1, 1¹⁄₁₆mT, 1:40.43, MASTERPIECE (ARG), Warrior Song, Chattahoochee War, 6 started.

Harry Henson S., Hollywood Park, April 27, $76,450, 3&up, 6fT, 1:08.60, HURRY HOME WARREN, Vaunt (GB), Candy's Bro, 5 started.

Harry Jeffrey S., Assiniboia Downs, Aug. 26, $28,512, 3yo, 1⅛m, 1:56.20, BARAK, Druid's Lodge, Mancini's Man, 7 started.

Harry W. Henson Breeders' Cup H., Sunland Park, March 18, $144,750, 3&up, f&m, 1m, 1:37.37, EYES ON EDDY, Jubilee, Kranky Karol, 8 started.

Harvest Futurity, Fresno, Oct. 12, $52,975, 2yo, 6f, 1:09.50, VADHEIM, Sky Cape, Orientate Me, 9 started.

Harvest H., The Downs at Albuquerque, Sept. 1, $45,000, 3yo, 5½f, 1:03.23, SUMFUN, Datrick, Smokem Slew, 4 started.

Harvey Arneault Memorial Breeders' Cup S., Mountaineer Race Track and Gaming Resort, Aug. 4, $123,950, 3&up, 6f, 1:11.71, COWBOY HARDWARE, Bairds Village, Forest Park, 7 started.

HASKELL INVITATIONAL S. (G1), Monmouth Park, Aug. 5, $1,060,000, 3yo, 1⅛m, 1:48.35, ANY GIVEN SATURDAY, Hard Spun, Curlin, 7 started.

Hasta La Vista H., Turf Paradise, May 6, $50,000, 3&up, 1 ⅞mT, 3:15.36, KEY OF SOLOMON (IRE), In Joe's Honor, Sleepless Joy, 10 started.

Hastings Park H., Emerald Downs, May 20, $45,000, 3&up, f&m, 6f, 1:09.40, DINNER AT ARLENE'S, Kissntheboysgoodby, Golden Pine, 9 started.

Hatoof S., Arlington Park, Aug. 19, $47,900, 3yo, f, 1¹⁄₁₆mAW (originally scheduled on the turf), 1:41.49, PITAMAKAN, You Go West Girl, Call the Kitty, 7 started.

Hawkeyes H. (R), Prairie Meadows, June 23, $68,600, 3&up, f&m, Iowa-bred, 1¹⁄₁₆m, 1:43.76, CAMELA CARSON, Thekatcamehome, Elite Lady, 5 started.

HAWTHORNE DERBY (G3), Hawthorne Race Course, Oct. 13, $250,000, 3yo, 1⅛mT, 1:47.45, BOLD HAWK, Twilight Meteor, Western Prize, 11 started.

HAWTHORNE GOLD CUP H. (G2), Hawthorne Race Course, Sept. 29, $500,000, 3&up, 1¼m, 2:05, STUDENT COUNCIL, Jonesboro, A. P. Arrow, 5 started.

HAWTHORNE H. (G3), Hollywood Park, May 6, $107,300, 3&up, f&m, 1¹⁄₁₆mAW, 1:44.08, RIVER SAVAGE (BRZ), Cantabria (GB), Ballado's Thunder, 6 started.

HBPA and WVRC S. (R), Charles Town Races, Aug. 5, $51,400, 3&up, most starts at Charles Town in last four starts, 1⅛m, 1:51.94, FIVE STEPS, Jenkin Jones, Donald's Pride, 9 started.

HBPA City of Charles Town H. (R), Charles Town Races, Oct. 19, $51,200, 3&up, West Virginia-bred, 4½f, :50.94, OUTCASHEM, Sir Five Star, Jose, 5 started.

HBPA City of Ranson H., Charles Town Races, Oct. 19, $51,400, 3&up, f&m, 7f, 1:26.17, COYA, Casse, Sacred Feather, 8 started.

HBPA Dash S. (R), Charles Town Races, Aug. 5, $51,200, 3&up, most starts at Charles Town in last four starts, 4½f, :51.47, BETTIN ON M J, Jose, Cat Genius, 7 started.

HBPA Governor's Cup H., Charles Town Races, Oct. 19, $51,200, 3&up, 1⅛m, 1:53.55, JENKIN JONES, Donald's Pride, Taming the Tiger, 6 started.

HBPA H., Ellis Park, July 14, $50,000, 3&up, f&m, 1mT, 1:36.39, HONEY ROSE (ARG), Barbette, Tiz Nik, 9 started.

HBPA Horsemen's S. (R), Charles Town Races, Aug. 5, $51,100, 3&up, f&m, most starts at Charles Town in last four starts, 4½f, :52.34, LOVE TO PLUNGE, Ghost Canyon, Monster Image, 7 started.

HBPA S., Presque Isle Downs, Sept. 29, $100,000, 3&up, f&m, 1m70yAW, 1:42.12, RASTA FARIAN, Victory Pool, Plaid, 7 started.

HBPA Vernon Cup S., Kin Park, July 15, $6,581, 3&up, a7f, 1:24.42, FUNKY FRIENDS, Zoolu Nights, Fisherman's Friend, 5 started.

HBPA West Virginia S. (R), Charles Town Races, Aug. 5, $50,850, 3&up, f&m, most starts at Charles Town in last four starts, 7f, 1:24.79, RUPERT'S PROSPECT, Hanalei Bay, Homesteader, 5 started.

Heavenly Prize S. (R), Saratoga Race Course, Aug. 24, $78,000, 3&up, f&m, non-winners of an open stakes since February 1, 2007, 1⅛m, 1:51.39, ALTESSE, A True Pussycat, Soul Search, 4 started.

Heckofaralph S., Calder Race Course, June 10, $50,000, 3&up, 5fT, :56.33, NACASCOLO, Lord Robyn, Dead Red, 10 started.

Heed S. (R), Saratoga Race Course, Aug. 10, $87,000, 3yo, f, non-winners of a stakes on the turf in 2007, 7f, 1:24.02, DORM FEVER, Le Chateau, Intentional Fever, 8 started.

Helen Anthony Memorial S., Yavapai Downs, June 4, $11,600, 3yo, f, 6f, 1:10.40, WINE TASTING ROOM, Scatienus, Citypro, 6 started.

HENDRIE S. (CAN-G3), Woodbine, May 13, $167,862, 4&up, f&m, 6½fAW, 1:16.20, STRIKE SOFTLY, Mary Delaney, Bosskiri, 8 started.

Henry P. Mercer Memorial S. (R), Charles Town Races, Sept. 8, $45,950, 2yo, c&g, West Virginia-bred, 4½f, :52.65, LORD OF DANCE, Pow Wow Power, Gliding Robb, 6 started.

Henry S. Clark S., Pimlico Race Course, April 28, $75,000, 3&up, 1mT, 1:37.36, STAY CLOSE (GB), Midwatch, Broadway Producer, 8 started.

Herald Gold Plate S., Stampede Park, June 10, $73,333, 3&up, 1¹⁄₁₆m, 1:43.60, TEAGUES FIGHT, Test Boy, Candid Remark, 6 started.

HERECOMESTHEBRIDE S. (G3), Gulfstream Park, March 25, $107,000, 3yo, f, 1⅛mT, 1:47.90, SHARP SUSAN, Communique, Perfect Motion, 8 started.

Hermosa Beach H., Hollywood Park, Dec. 5, $69,250, 3&up, f&m, 1½mT, 2:26.52, SOHGOL (IRE), Forest Melody, Wingspan, 7 started.

Hidden Light S. (R), Oak Tree at Santa Anita, Oct. 26, $65,340, 2yo, f, non-winners of a stakes at one mile or over, 1mT, 1:37, LA MINA, Ididntmeantoo, Set of Wings, 8 started.

High Yield S. (R), Philadelphia Park, Sept. 29, $60,000, 2yo, c&g, Pennsylvania-bred, 5½f, 1:05.04, SUPERFECTA, Terriffico, Body Rock, 7 started.

HILL 'N' DALE CIGAR MILE H. (G1), Aqueduct, Nov. 24, $294,000, 3&up, 1m, 1:33.79, DAAHER, Midnight Lute, Naughty New Yorker, 5 started.

Hill 'n' Dale S., Woodbine, June 16, $94,359, 3&up, f&m, 1¹⁄₁₆mAW, 1:43.78, BEAR NOW, Like a Gem, Top Notch Lady, 7 started.

HILL PRINCE S. (G3), Belmont Park, June 8, $105,700, 3yo, 1mT, 1:33.45, MARCAVELLY, Distorted Reality, Codeword (Ire), 5 started.

Hillsborough H., Bay Meadows Race Course, March 24, $54,425, 4&up, f&m, 1¹⁄₁₆mT, 1:45.60, CHARM THE GIANT (IRE), Strong Faith, Somethinaboutlaura, 6 started.

HILLSBOROUGH S. (G3), Tampa Bay Downs, March 17, $150,000, 4&up, f&m, a1⅛mT, 1:48.90, CASSYDORA (GB), My Typhoon (Ire), Masseuse, 9 started.

Hillsdale S. (R), Hoosier Park, Oct. 14, $45,000, 2yo, c&g, Indiana-bred, 5½f, 1:06.29, MADE YOUR MOVES, Sea of Steven, Moonshine Still, 8 started.

Hilltop S., Pimlico Race Course, May 12, $60,000, 3yo, f, 1mT, 1:36.66, STREET SOUNDS, Ethan's Car, Cabbage Key, 6 started.

Hilton Garden Inn Sprint S., Tampa Bay Downs, April 7, $50,000, 4&up, 6f, 1:10.61, ROMAN CANDLES, Lookinforthesecret, Weigelia, 7 started.

HIRSCH JACOBS S. (G3), Pimlico Race Course, May 19, $100,000, 3yo, 6f, 1:10.97, STREET MAGICIAN, Southwestern Heat, Hobbitontherocks, 7 started.

Hockessin S., Delaware Park, Oct. 6, $58,650, 3&up, 6f, 1:10.06, SPOOKY MULDER, Secretintelligence, Banjo Picker, 4 started.

Hoist Her Flag S., Canterbury Park, June 2, $45,000, 3&up, f&m, 6f, 1:10.73, KATY SMILES, Genuine True, Shimmering Sunset, 8 started.

Holiday Cheer S., Turfway Park, Dec. 29, $50,000, 3&up, 6fAW, 1:09.83, JUNIOR COLLEGE, Three Twenty Three, Storm Marcopolo (Arg), 9 started.

Holiday Inaugural S., Turfway Park, Dec. 1, $50,000, 3&up, f&m, 6fAW, 1:09.77, FAST DEAL, Lady Belsara, Mary Delaney, 10 started.

Holiday Inn Fort Erie Cup S., Fort Erie, July 8, $23,830, 3&up, 1¹⁄₁₆m, 1:44.86, FREZACON, Benz Boy, Smiling Jordan, 5 started.

Hollie Hughes H. (R), Aqueduct, Feb. 18, $72,425, 3&up, New York-bred, 6f, 1:11.64, INTROSPECT, Ferocious Won, Scary Bob, 8 started.

Holly S., Meadowlands, Sept. 29, $55,000, 2yo, f, 1m70yT, 1:41.77, GRACE AND POWER, Sales Tax, Return to Paradise, 5 started.

HOLLYWOOD BREEDERS' CUP OAKS (G2), Hollywood Park, June 10, $126,400, 3yo, f, 1¹⁄₁₆mAW, 1:43.30, TOUGH TIZ'S SIS, Silver Swallow, High Cholesterol, 5 started.

HOLLYWOOD DERBY (G1), Hollywood Park, Nov. 25, $500,000, 3yo, 1¼mT, 1:59.75, DAYTONA (IRE), Medici Code (GB), Bold Hawk, 10 started.

HOLLYWOOD GOLD CUP S. (G1), Hollywood Park, June 30, $750,000, 3&up, 1¼mAW, 2:03.21 (NTR), LAVA MAN, A. P. Xcellent, Big Booster, 9 started.

HOLLYWOOD JUVENILE CHAMPIONSHIP S. (G3), Hollywood Park, July 4, $114,900, 2yo, 6fAW, 1:12.08, SALUTE THE SARGE, Leonides, Whatever Whenever, 11 started.

HOLLYWOOD PREVUE S. (G3), Hollywood Park, Nov. 22, $109,200, 2yo, 7fAW, 1:21.48, MASSIVE DRAMA, Into Mischief, Meal Penalty, 11 started.

HOLLYWOOD STARLET S. (G1), Hollywood Park, Dec. 15, $425,500, 2yo, f, 1¹⁄₁₆mAW, 1:40.54 (NTR), COUNTRY STAR, Grace and Power, The Golden Noodle, 9 started.

HOLLYWOOD TURF CUP S. (G1), Hollywood Park, Dec. 8, $250,000, 3&up, 1½mT, 2:27.07, SUNRIVER, Champs Elysees (GB), Spring House, 7 started.

HOLLYWOOD TURF EXPRESS H. (G3), Hollywood Park, Nov. 24, $150,000, 3&up, 6fT, 1:09.06, UNUSUAL SUSPECT, Bonfante, Desert Code, 9 started.

Hollywood Wildcat Breeders' Cup H., Calder Race Course, April 28, $126,750, 3&up, f&m, 1¹⁄₁₆mT, 1:40.76, LA DOLCE VITA, Potra Clasica (Arg), Silversider, 7 started.

HOLY BULL S. (G3), Gulfstream Park, Feb. 3, $150,000, 3yo, 1m, 1:35.47, NOBIZ LIKE SHOBIZ, Drums of Thunder, Scat Daddy, 8 started.

Honest Lady H., Hollywood Park, July 2, $78,450, 3yo, f, 6½fAW, 1:16, DESIRE TO EXCEL, Glorified, Coco Belle, 6 started.

Honey Bee H., Meadowlands, Oct. 5, $60,000, 3&up, f&m, 1m70y, 1:40.26, EXCHANGING FIRE, A True Pussycat, Leap in the Sun, 5 started.

Honeybee S., Oaklawn Park, March 16, $100,000, 3yo, f, 1 1/16m, 1:45.49, TIME'S MISTRESS, High Heels, Grace Happens, 9 started.

HONEY FOX H. (G3), Gulfstream Park, March 4, $100,000, 4&up, f&m, 1 1/16mT, 1:39.37, WAIT A WHILE, Precious Kitten, Chaibia (Ire), 7 started.

Honey Jay S. (R), Thistledown, Sept. 15, $50,000, 3&up, Ohio-bred, 6f, 1:10.94, DOOZE, Tri Uimet, Forest Picnic, 8 started.

Honey Mark S., Hawthorne Race Course, March 24, $47,700, 4&up, 1 1/16m, 1:45.63, AWESOMEWITHBROADS, Holy City, Air Academy, 6 started.

HONEYMOON BREEDERS' CUP H. (G2), Hollywood Park, June 9, $154,750, 3yo, f, 1 1/8mT, 1:48.17, VALBENNY (IRE), Super Freaky, Mystic Soul, 7 started.

Hong Kong Jockey Club H., Hastings Race Course, Sept. 1, $48,411, 3yo, f, 1 1/16m, 1:45.32, ALPINE GARDEN, Pat of Gold, Napa, 6 started.

HONORABLE MISS H. (G2), Saratoga Race Course, Aug. 3, $147,000, 3&up, f&m, 6f, 1:09.51, BURMILLA, Indian Flare, G City Gal, 5 started.

Honor Grades S., Arlington Park, Sept. 9, $48,250, 3yo, 1 1/16mT, 1:41.89, VOY POR UNO MAS, Gentleman Chester, Demarcation, 9 started.

Honor the Hero Turf Express S., Canterbury Park, May 28, $45,000, 3&up, 5fT, :56.06, LOOKINFORTHESECRET, Smoke Smoke Smoke, Slick Carson, 8 started.

Hoofprint on My Heart H., Stampede Park, May 26, $46,320, 3yo, 1m, 1:38.40, CHIEF'S MAGIC, Bling, Footprint, 5 started.

Hooting Star H., Calder Race Course, Oct. 6, $50,000, 3&up, 5f, :57.75, FINALLYMADEIT, Bow Out, Tale of a Monster, 5 started.

Hoover S. (R), River Downs, July 22, $50,000, 2yo, Ohio-bred, 5 1/2f, 1:06, COLD TRIAL, O'Riain, Gold Rush Casey, 6 started.

HOPEFUL S. (G1), Saratoga Race Course, Sept. 3, $237,500, 2yo, 7f, 1:23.04, MAJESTIC WARRIOR, Ready's Image, Maimonides, 4 started.

Horatius S., Laurel Park, March 3, $74,600, 3yo, 6f, 1:10.49, CALL ME CLASH, Casey Doon, Heart Throbbin', 6 started.

Horizon Heritage S. (R), Marquis Downs, Sept. 1, $9,469, 4&up, f&m, Saskatchewan-bred, 1m, 1:41.47, ALLOURWISHES, Shadazzle, Royal Rouge, 9 started.

Horizon S. (R), River Downs, Aug. 4, $55,000, 3yo, Ohio-bred, 1 1/16mT, 1:45.60, MINI MOM, Play the Hero, Smarmy, 12 started.

Hot Springs S., Oaklawn Park, March 24, $50,000, 4&up, 6f, 1:10.05, JUNIOR COLLEGE, Semaphore Man, Four Sevens, 6 started.

Howard H. Noonan S. (R), Beulah Park, April 14, $50,000, 3yo, Ohio-bred, 6f, 1:10.64, POLITE LIL SIR, Pyrite Personal, Matcher, 9 started.

Hudson H. (R), Belmont Park, Oct. 20, $125,000, 3&up, New York-bred, 6f, 1:09.41, FEROCIOUS FIRES, Stormin Normandy, I'm a Numbers Guy, 9 started.

Hula Chief S., Hawthorne Race Course, March 17, $48,150, 4&up, 6f, 1:11.20, CATALISSA, Star by Design, High Expectations, 7 started.

HUMANA DISTAFF S. (G1), Churchill Downs, May 5, $340,800, 4&up, f&m, 7f, 1:21.87, HYSTERICALADY, Pussycat Doll, Carriage Trail, 10 started.

Humphrey S. Finney S. (R), Laurel Park, Aug. 18, $50,000, 3yo, Maryland-bred, 1 1/16mT, 1:47.12, PV LIGHTENING, Encaustic, Tiger Rag, 9 started.

HURRICANE BERTIE H. (G3), Gulfstream Park, Feb. 17, $108,500, 4&up, f&m, 6 1/2f, 1:17.16, ANY LIMIT, My Lucky Free, Stolen Prayer, 10 started.

Hush Dear S., Saratoga Race Course, July 26, $82,450, 3&up, f&m, 5 1/2fT, 1:02.02, TRULY BLUSHED, Serena's Cat, Taletobetold, 9 started.

HUTCHESON S. (G2), Gulfstream Park, March 3, $150,000, 3yo, 7 1/2f, 1:28, KING OF THE ROXY, Bold Start, Out of Gwedda, 9 started.

Hyali Talk S., Turf Paradise, May 1, $25,100, 3&up, 1m, 1:35.18, PRORUNNER, Ozzy's Shame, Conditional, 8 started.

Icecapade S., Monmouth Park, Sept. 1, $103,000, 3&up, 6f, 1:08.82, SMOKEY STOVER, Park Avenue Ball, Cougar Cat, 4 started.

Idaho Cup Claiming S. (R), Les Bois Park, Aug. 4, $15,515, 3&up, Idaho-bred starters for a claiming price of $4,000 or less, 7f, 1:24.70, MOAB Reno Bound, More Thunder, 8 started.

Idaho Cup Classic S. (R), Les Bois Park, Aug. 4, $35,000, 4&up, Idaho-bred, 1m, 1:38.13, SILENT SNOW, Lookn East, Spud Man, 10 started.

Idaho Cup Derby (R), Les Bois Park, Aug. 4, $35,000, 3&up, Idaho-bred, 1m, 1:38.61, CRYPTS SEEKER, Mr Madraar, Birthday Boy, 7 started.

Idaho Cup Distaff Derby (R), Les Bois Park, Aug. 4, $35,000, 3yo, Idaho-bred, 1m, 1:41.32, CHARLIE'SBLUEANGEL, I'll Never Be King, Sheza Redneck, 5 started.

Idaho Cup Distaff Maturity (R), Les Bois Park, Aug. 4, $35,000, 3&up, Idaho-bred, 1m, 1:40.28, PETITE MOTION, Gig's Star, Spicey N Hot, 6 started.

Idaho Cup Juvenile Championship S. (R), Les Bois Park, Aug. 4, $55,000, 2yo, Idaho-bred, 5f, :58.09, JOE'S CANNON, Cattle Call, Interest Earnings, 10 started.

Idaho Cup Sprint S. (R), Les Bois Park, Aug. 4, $20,425, 3&up, Idaho-bred, 5f, :57.66, DUN RINGILL, Northern Buck, Jazzing Jack, 8 started.

Illini Princess H. (R), Hawthorne Race Course, Nov. 3, $91,275, 3&up, f&m, Illinois-conceived and/or -foaled, 1 1/16mT, 1:45.83, LAMPOON, Stop a Train, Boudoir, 10 started.

ILLINOIS DERBY (G2), Hawthorne Race Course, April 7, $500,000, 3yo, 1 1/8m, 1:51.21, COWTOWN CAT, Reporting for Duty, Bold Start, 9 started.

Illinois Thoroughbred Breeders' and Owners' Foundation Sales Graduate S. (R), Hawthorne Race Course, April 12, $45,000, 3yo, c&g, consigned to the ITBOF two-year-olds in training sale, 6 1/2f, 1:19.03, HE'S HOT SAUCE, Sweet Baby Ray, T J Charge, 10 started.

Illinois Thoroughbred Breeders' and Owners' Foundation Sales Graduate S. (R), Hawthorne Race Course, April 12, $45,000, 3yo, f, consigned to the ITBOF two-year-olds in training sale, 6 1/2f, 1:20.67, TINSEL TIME, Tootie's Gal, Aly's Sweet Sheba, 11 started.

Impressive Luck H., Santa Anita Park, Dec. 31, $84,500, 3&up, a6 1/2fT, 1:12.83, EVER A FRIEND, Bonfante, Night Chapter (GB), 7 started.

Impressive Luck H., Santa Anita Park, Jan. 10, $77,500, 4&up, a6 1/2fT, 1:13.13, FAST PARADE, Cat and a Half, Scheffer, 6 started.

I'm Smokin S. (R), Del Mar, Sept. 3, $113,400, 2yo, California-bred, 6fAW, 1:13.76, TOPPER SHOPPER, Raise the River, My Redeemer, 10 started.

Inaugural H., Les Bois Park, May 5, $7,000, 3&up, 6 1/2f, 1:19.10, KID ROYAL, Height of Summer, Robs Coin, 9 started.

Inaugural H., Portland Meadows, Oct. 7, $21,900, 3&up, 6f, 1:11.10, ROCKINSTOMPER, Gold Lad, Lethal Grande, 7 started.

Inaugural H., SunRay Park, May 5, $32,800, 3&up, 6 1/2f, 1:17.40, JAMMIN GEARS, Excessive Contact, Western Act, 7 started.

Inaugural H., Wyoming Downs, June 30, $4,000, 3&up, 6f, 1:10.70, RODEO CHAMP, Restrictions Apply, Cut Class, 8 started.

Inaugural S., Columbus Races, July 27, $10,725, 3yo, f, 6f, 1:15.60, THE JOKE IS ON YOU, Completely Chrome, Jackie's Charm, 6 started.

Inaugural S., Evangeline Downs, April 7, $48,500, 3yo, f, 6f, 1:11.92, PROBATION READY, Heelbolt, Trippi Toes, 6 started.

Inaugural S., Presque Isle Downs, Sept. 1, $100,000, 3yo, f, 6fAW, 1:11.34, MISS A. BOMB, Tres Dream, Unforgotten, 8 started.

Inaugural S., Tampa Bay Downs, Dec. 29, $65,000, 2yo, 6f, 1:11.85, HONEY HONEY HONEY, Run Sully Run, Surrealdeal, 13 started.

Incredible Revenge S., Monmouth Park, July 21, $60,000, 3&up, f&m, 5 1/2fT, 1:02.86, SEND ME AN ANGEL, Jazzy (Arg), Top Ten List, 6 started.

Independence Day S., Mountaineer Race Track and Gaming Resort, July 3, $75,000, 3&up, 1mT, 1:35.33, CHEROKEE PRINCE, Load a Chronic, Cat Shaker, 10 started.

INDIANA DERBY (G2), Hoosier Park, Oct. 6, $510,600, 3yo, 1 1/16m, 1:43.95, ZANJERO, Bwana Bull, Flashstorm, 9 started.

Indiana First Lady S. (R), Indiana Downs, June 4, $45,000, 3yo, f, Indiana-bred and/or -sired, 7 1/2fT, 1:32.73, AMATURE'S PRIZE, My Gal Lexie, She's a Red Devil, 10 started.

Indiana Futurity (R), Hoosier Park, Nov. 10, $45,000, 2yo, Indiana-bred, 6f, 1:14.39, MIDDLE LINEBACKER, Chow Wagon, Hopeheruns, 8 started.

INDIANA OAKS (G3), Hoosier Park, Oct. 5, $406,900, 3yo, f, 1 1/16m, 1:44.42, TESSA BLUE, Boca Grande, Marietta, 10 started.

Indiana Stallion S. (R), Hoosier Park, Nov. 23, $45,000, 2yo, f, Indiana-bred and/or -sired, 6f, 1:15.15, CLASSIC RAMONA, Dr. Powers, Rachel Wiggles, 6 started.

Indiana Stallion S. (R), Hoosier Park, Nov. 24, $45,000, 2yo, Indiana-bred and/or -sired, 6f, 1:13.65, OUR LUCKY SOX, Jacks Are Lucky, Honky Tonk Gold, 9 started.

Indian Maid H., Hawthorne Race Course, Sept. 29, $120,850, 3&up,

f&m, 1 1/16mT, 1:40.46 (NCR), JENNIE R., Barbette, Glitter Star, 11 started.
INGLEWOOD H. (G3), Hollywood Park, April 28, $108,200, 3&up, 1 1/16mT, 1:39.63, AFTER MARKET, Red Fort (Ire), Willow O Wisp, 6 started.
Ingrid Knotts S. (R), Arapahoe Park, June 4, $35,650, 3&up, f&m, Colorado-bred, 6f, 1:10.11, VANNACIDE, Ladysgotthelooks, My Prized Lady, 7 started.
In Reality S. (R), Calder Race Course, Oct. 13, $400,000, 2yo, progeny of eligible Florida stallions, 1 1/16m, 1:45.51, WISE ANSWER, Cigar Man, Check It Twice, 8 started.
Inside Information Breeders' Cup S., Monmouth Park, Oct. 26, $250,000, 3yo, f, 1 1/16m, 1:41.74, TESSA BLUE, Lost Etiquette, Talkin About Love, 5 started.
Inside the Belt Way S., Belmont Park, July 8, $77,000, 3yo, 6fT, 1:09.07, ENGLISH COLONY (GB), Quietly Mine, Out of Gwedda, 8 started.
Instant Racing Breeders' Cup S., Oaklawn Park, April 14, $95,000, 3yo, f, 1m, 1:38.88, CREAM ONLY, Nice Inheritance, Chatham, 9 started.
Interborough H., Aqueduct, Jan. 1, $70,590, 3&up, f&m, 6f, 1:09.51, OPRAH WINNEY, Smart and Fancy, Magnolia Jackson, 7 started.
Intercontinental H., Hollywood Park, Nov. 28, $68,775, 3&up, f&m, 1mT, 1:34.56, CHARM THE GIANT (IRE), I Can See, Double Trouble (Brz), 8 started.
International Gold Cup Timber S., Great Meadows, Oct. 20, $48,500, 4&up, a3 1/2mT, 7:01.80 (NCR), SEEYOUATTHEEVENT, Woodmont, Shady Valley, 6 started.
Iowa Breeders' Derby (R), Prairie Meadows, Aug. 25, $73,566, 3yo, c&g, Iowa-bred, 1 1/16m, 1:43.68, RED HOT N GOLD, Ghazi Up, Joggins, 7 started.
Iowa Breeders' Oaks (R), Prairie Meadows, Aug. 25, $73,058, 3yo, f, Iowa-bred, 1m70y, 1:41.99, TEJANO'S OASIS, Irish Party, Money Tak, 6 started.
Iowa Classic Sprint S. (R), Prairie Meadows, Aug. 25, $51,842, 3&up, Iowa-bred, 6f, 1:08.97, WILD L, Dazzling Man, Will E Scat, 5 started.
Iowa Cradle S. (R), Prairie Meadows, Aug. 25, $72,150, 2yo, c&g, Iowa-bred, 6f, 1:09.26, MAYA'S STORM, Kate's Main Man, Abidon, 8 started.
Iowa Derby, Prairie Meadows, June 29, $250,000, 3yo, 1 1/16m, 1:42.05, DELIGHTFUL KISS, Flashstorm, Going Ballistic, 11 started.
Iowa Distaff Breeders' Cup S., Prairie Meadows, June 30, $125,000, 3&up, f&m, 1 1/16m, 1:43.84, BROWNIE POINTS, Plaid, Dynabin, 6 started.
IOWA OAKS (G3), Prairie Meadows, June 29, $200,000, 3yo, f, 1 1/16m, 1:43.17, MARIETTA, Humble Janet, High Again, 9 started.
Iowa Sorority S. (R), Prairie Meadows, Aug. 25, $71,466, 2yo, f, Iowa-bred, 6f, 1:10.64, JUDY FAYE, Sweet Bonnie, Bitsy's Blessing, 7 started.
Iowa Sprint H., Prairie Meadows, June 30, $125,000, 3&up, 6f, 1:08.48, BENNY THE BULL, Cougar Cat, Kingsfield, 9 started.
Iowa Stallion Auction S. (R), Prairie Meadows, July 21, $77,920, 3yo, progeny of eligible Iowa stallions, 1m70y, 1:41.67, GHAZI UP, Nitak, Timelysupreme, 5 started.
Iowa Stallion Futurity (R), Prairie Meadows, Aug. 11, $88,889, 2yo, progeny of eligible Iowa stallions, 6f, 1:10.99, BRAVO CYCLONE, Abidon, Judy Faye, 8 started.
Iowa State Fair S., Prairie Meadows, Aug. 18, $45,000, 3&up, f&m, 6f, 1:08.46, SPLENDID IN SPRING, Another Audible, Katy Smiles, 6 started.
Irish Actress S. (R), Saratoga Race Course, Sept. 2, $82,700, 3yo, f, New York-bred, 1mT, 1:35.42, JESSE'S JUSTICE, Tishmeister, dh-Jocassee, dh-Acquired Cat, 10 started.
Irish Day H., Emerald Downs, June 24, $45,000, 3yo, f, 1m, 1:37, SHAMPOO, Zaylaway, Firetrail, 8 started.
Irish O'Brien S. (R), Santa Anita Park, March 17, $133,750, 4&up, f&m, California-bred, a6 1/2fT, 1:12.66, RIVER'S PRAYER, Bachelorette One, Gn. Group Meeting, 6 started.
Irish Sonnet S., Delaware Park, Sept. 22, $56,260, 2yo, f, 1m, 1:39.16, BSHARPSONATA, Erin's Golden Star, Unbridled Rhapsody, 4 started.
Iroquois H. (R), Belmont Park, Oct. 20, $125,000, 3&up, f&m, New York-bred, 7f, 1:24.04, KARAKORUM STARLET, Mama Theresa, Ice Cool Kitty, 10 started.
Iroquois Hurdle S., Percy Warner, May 12, $150,000, 4&up, a3mT, 5:50.40, GOOD NIGHT SHIRT, Sur La Tete, Chivite (Ire), 10 started.
IROQUOIS S. (G3), Churchill Downs, Oct. 28, $171,150, 2yo, 1m, 1:37.26, COURT VISION, Halo Najib, St. Joe, 9 started.

Irving Distaff S., Lone Star Park, April 28, $60,000, 3&up, f&m, 7 1/2f, 1:29.45, CAROLINA SKY, My Three Sisters, Not in My House, 11 started.
Isaac Murphy H. (R), Arlington Park, July 7, $83,750, 3&up, f&m, Illinois-conceived and/or -foaled, 6fAW, 1:10.91, MODJADJI, Pretty Jenny, Bluesbdancing, 7 started.
Isadorable S. (R), Suffolk Downs, June 9, $44,100, 3&up, f&m, Massachusetts-bred, 6f, 1:11.87, ASK QUEENIE, Flirt for Fame, Lily's Goldmine, 5 started.
Island Fashion S., Sunland Park, Feb. 18, $50,000, 3yo, f, 1m, 1:38.11, NICE INHERITANCE, Berriestoheaven, Stealth Cat, 7 started.
ITA Sophomore Distaff S., Les Bois Park, June 2, $10,945, 3yo, 6 1/2f, 1:21.30, BRISABYOU, Miss Voyager, Get It Done, 5 started.
ITA Sophomore S., Les Bois Park, June 2, $11,125, 3yo, 6 1/2f, 1:21.40, BONK, Mr Madraar, Sheriff Tillet, 6 started.
ITBOA Sales Futurity (R), Prairie Meadows, July 14, $67,593, 2yo, graduates of the 2006 ITBOA two-year-olds-in-training sale, 5 1/2f, 1:05.99, MAYA'S STORM, Better Make Money, Frozen Angel, 12 started.
Jack Betta Be Rite S. (R), Finger Lakes Gaming and Race Track, Aug. 25, $50,000, 3&up, f&m, New York-bred, 1 1/16m, 1:48.04, FLY TO ME, Watral's Dahlia, Hoosick Falls, 8 started.
Jack Diamond Futurity (R), Hastings Race Course, Oct. 8, $108,735, 2yo, c&g, Canadian-bred, 6 1/2f, 1:18.63, DESERT ALF, Cabron, Surprisal, 9 started.
Jack Dudley Sprint H. (R), Calder Race Course, Nov. 10, $150,000, 3&up, Florida-bred, 6f, 1:11.08, FINALLYMADEIT, Storm in May, Blue Pepsi Lodge, 6 started.
Jack Goodman S., Oak Tree at Santa Anita, Oct. 21, $94,675, 2yo, 6fAW, 1:08.42, WISE MANDATE, Guns On the Table, Remember Boffi, 8 started.
Jack Hardy S., Assiniboia Downs, Sept. 1, $28,407, 3yo, f, 1 1/16m, 1:47.40, SPILLWAY, Polynesian Kitty, Talkin Money Honey, 7 started.
Jackie Wackie S., Calder Race Course, Oct. 20, $43,650, 3&up, 1 1/16m, 1:46.39, GOLDEN STRATEGY, Golden Flame, Teddy Ballgame, 4 started.
Jack Price Juvenile S. (R), Calder Race Course, Nov. 10, $150,000, 2yo, Florida-bred, 7f, 1:24.32, HE'S EZE, Smooth Air, Wise Answer, 6 started.
Jack Shoemaker Memorial S., Rillito Park, Feb. 25, $3,508, 3&up, f&m, 5 1/2f, 1:05.50, MSRIOBOUND, Answer Cats Line, Lady's Royal Slew, 8 started.
Jacques Cartier S., Woodbine, April 14, $110,993, 4&up, 6fAW, 1:09.68, STRADIVINSKY, Judiths Wild Rush, Are You Serious, 8 started.
JAIPUR S. (G3), Belmont Park, May 27, $113,800, 3&up, 6fT, 1:07.64, ECCLESIASTIC, Salute the Count, Weigelia, 9 started.
JAMAICA H. (G2), Belmont Park, Oct. 6, $300,000, 3yo, 1 1/8mT, 1:46.80, NOBIZ LIKE SHOBIZ, Red Giant, Pays to Dream, 9 started.
James B. Moseley Sprint H., Suffolk Downs, Sept. 12, $100,000, 3&up, 6f, 1:09.05, AFRASHAD, Council Member, Roman Candles, 6 started.
James C. Ellis Juvenile S., Ellis Park, Aug. 18, $50,000, 2yo, 7f, 1:26.78, YONEGAWA, Pulaski Runner, D. C. Eight, 7 started.
Jamestown S. (R), Colonial Downs, July 7, $60,000, 2yo, Virginia-bred/and or -sired, 6f, 1:10.52, T. J.'S POSSE, Pillow Pal, Social Quest, 8 started.
Jammed Lovely S. (R), Woodbine, Nov. 11, $160,378, 3yo, f, Ontario-bred, 7fAW, 1:23.27, DANCE TO MY TUNE, Glitter Rox, You Will Love Me, 8 started.
Jane Driggers Debutante S. (R), Portland Meadows, Dec. 9, $10,650, 2yo, f, Oregon-bred, 6f, 1:12.68, OCHOCO FLAME, Tequila Tipsy, Baby Sunshine, 5 started.
Janet Wineberg S. (R), Portland Meadows, Nov. 4, $21,200, 2yo, f, Oregon-bred, 6f, 1:12.30, JIMBOS FIRE ANT, Lady's Purse, Ochoco Flame, 7 started.
J. Archie Sebastien Memorial S. (R), Evangeline Downs, June 30, $97,000, 4&up, f&m, Louisiana-bred, 1m70y, 1:42.46, MADISON'S MUSIC, Punchy Louise, Raspberry Wine, 6 started.
Jean Lafitte S., Delta Downs, Nov. 9, $150,000, 2yo, 1m, 1:40.29, GOLDEN YANK, Gangbuster, Take the Money, 9 started.
JEFFERSON CUP S. (G2), Churchill Downs, June 16, $221,000, 3yo, 1 1/8mT, 1:48.94, INCA KING, Duveen, Jazz Quest, 7 started.
JEH Stallion Station S. (R), Lone Star Park, April 21, $50,000, 3&up, f&m, Texas-bred, 6 1/2f, 1:16.20, OLMOSTA, Sweet Idea, Annie Savoy, 6 started.
Jena Jena S. (R), Saratoga Race Course, Aug. 27, $82,500, 2yo, f, New York-bred, 6f, 1:11.52, EXPECT THE END, Myakka, Crazy Catlady, 6 started.

Jennings H. (R), Laurel Park, Dec. 1, $60,000, 3&up, Maryland-bred, 1 1/16m, 1:51.49, DIGGER, Evil Storm, Forty Crowns, 7 started.
JENNY WILEY S. (G3), Keeneland Race Course, April 14, $200,000, 4&up, f&m, 1 1/16mAW (originally scheduled on the turf), 1:43.37, MY TYPHOON (IRE), Precious Kitten, Fantastic Shirl, 6 started.
JEROME H. (G2), Belmont Park, Oct. 7, $160,100, 3yo, 1m, 1:34.28, DAAHER, Forefathers, Owners Manual, 8 started.
Jersey Derby, Monmouth Park, Aug. 5, $100,000, 3yo, 1 1/16mT, 1:41.64, BUDDY'S HUMOR, Chaluiwitcane, French Vintage, 7 started.
Jersey Girl H. (R), Monmouth Park, Aug. 26, $110,000, 3&up, f&m, New Jersey-bred, 1 1/16m, 1:44.77, JENNY BEAN GIRL, Jersey Gia, Solar Powered, 7 started.
Jersey Lilly S., Sam Houston Race Park, April 7, $50,000, 4&up, f&m, 1 1/16mT, 1:45.64, FAIRWELL MADRID, La Raine of Terror, Wild Encounter, 12 started.
JERSEY SHORE BREEDERS' CUP S. (G3), Monmouth Park, July 4, $150,000, 3yo, 6f, 1:07.47 (NTR), IDIOT PROOF, Spin Master, Principle Secret, 7 started.
Jersey Village S. (R), Sam Houston Race Park, Feb. 10, $45,000, 4&up, f&m, Texas-bred, 1 1/16m, 1:46.64, WILD ENCOUNTER, Sweet Idea, La Raine of Terror, 9 started.
Jim Coleman Province H., Hastings Race Course, May 21, $50,836, 3yo, 6 1/2f, 1:18.06, OOKASHADA, Thesaratogaexpress, Stephanson, 5 started.
JIM DANDY S. (G2), Saratoga Race Course, July 29, $500,000, 3yo, 1 1/8m, 1:48.99, STREET SENSE, C P West, Sightseeing, 6 started.
Jim Edgar Illinois Futurity (R), Hawthorne Race Course, Dec. 15, $114,700, 2yo, c&g, Illinois-conceived and/or -foaled, 1 1/16m, 1:47.77, INSTILL, River Bear, Best Buddy, 10 started.
Jim McKay Sprint S., Pimlico Race Course, April 21, $77,800, 3&up, 6f, 1:09.43, LATENT SEARCH, Euro Code, Celtic Innis, 7 started.
JIM MURRAY MEMORIAL H. (G2), Hollywood Park, May 12, $250,000, 3&up, 1 1/2mT, 2:29.07, ON THE ACORN (GB), Prospect Park (GB), Notable Guest, 6 started.
Jimmy Winkfield S., Aqueduct, Jan. 15, $62,082, 3yo, 6f, 1:10.44, BILL PLACE, Wollaston Bay, B. B. Mancini, 3 started.
Jim Rasmussen Memorial S., Prairie Meadows, June 2, $50,000, 3&up, 1 1/16m, 1:42.37, PATRIOT ACT, Wayzata Bay, Spellbinder, 7 started.
Jim Smith Ribbons and Lace H., Sun Downs, May 5, $3,050, 3&up, f&m, 6f, 1:15.40, SCHU TRUE SLEEPER, Ireza, Charlee Chop Chop, 4 started.
Jim's Orbit S., Sam Houston Race Park, Feb. 17, $125,000, 3yo, c&g, nominated and eligible for the Texas Stallion Stakes Series, 1m, 1:40.56, BANQUO, Daddy Warbucks, Power Surge, 11 started.
Jiva Coolit S. (R), Charles Town Races, May 26, $51,000, 3yo, c&g, most starts at Charles Town in last four starts, 4 1/2f, :52.77, HEEZAFREQUENTFLYER, No Lac O Zip, Georgenator, 6 started.
J J'sdream S., Calder Race Course, July 7, $100,000, 2yo, f, 6f, 1:13.02, YONAGUCCI, Britten's Beauty, Arealhotlover, 9 started.
Joanne Dye S. (R), Turf Paradise, April 28, $45,000, 3yo, f, Arizona-bred, 6 1/2f, 1:15.01, STATEN ISLAND, Texas Bobbi R., Baby Swiss, 7 started.
JOCKEY CLUB GOLD CUP S. (G1), Belmont Park, Sept. 30, $765,000, 3&up, 1 1/4m, 2:01.20, CURLIN, Lawyer Ron, Political Force, 7 started.
JOE HIRSCH TURF CLASSIC INVITATIONAL S. (G1), Belmont Park, Sept. 30, $612,000, 3&up, 1 1/2mT, 2:25.73, ENGLISH CHANNEL, Stream of Gold (Ire), Interpatation, 7 started.
Joe O'Farrell Juvenile Fillies S. (R), Calder Race Course, Nov. 10, $150,000, 2yo, f, Florida-bred, 7f, 1:25.52, HIGH RESOLVE, Paint Me Red, Silk Ridge, 7 started.
John and Kitty Fletcher S. (R), Emerald Downs, Sept. 16, $45,000, 3yo, f, Washington-bred, 1m, 1:35.20, FIRETRAIL, Gadget Queen, Carrie's Choice, 8 started.
John Battaglia Memorial S., Turfway Park, March 3, $100,000, 3yo, 1 1/16mAW, 1:45.42, CATMAN RUNNING, Joe Got Even, Cobrador, 11 started.
John B. Campbell H., Laurel Park, Feb. 17, $83,000, 3&up, 1 1/8m, 1:53.74, FUTURE FANTASY, Bay Bank President, 8 started.
John B. Connally Breeders' Cup Turf H., Sam Houston Race Course, April 7, $201,000, 3&up, 1 3/8mT, 1:52.34, MENDING FENCES, Embossed (Ire), General Charley, 7 started.
John Bullit S., Canterbury Park, Aug. 4, $45,000, 3&up, 1 1/16mT, 1:44.25, PROSPECTIVE KISS, On Safari, Honour Colony, 5 started.
JOHN C. MABEE H. (G1), Del Mar, Aug. 4, $400,000, 3&up, f&m, 1 1/8mT, 1:46.34, PRECIOUS KITTEN, Dancing Edie, Memorette, 5 started.

JOHN DEERE BREEDERS' CUP TURF (G1), Monmouth Park, Oct. 27, $2,748,000, 3&up, 1 1/2mT, 2:36.96, ENGLISH CHANNEL, Shamdinan (Fr), Red Rocks (Ire), 8 started.
John D. Marsh S. (R), Colonial Downs, Aug. 5, $60,000, 3&4yos, Virginia-bred, 1 1/16mT, 1:41.03, KONA BLEND, Wye, Cryptogram, 8 started.
John D. Schapiro Memorial Breeders' Cup H., Laurel Park, Sept. 22, $100,000, 3&up, 1 3/8mT, 1:46.41 (NCR), STAY CLOSE (GB), Jungle Fighter, Bastille, 8 started.
John Franks Juvenile Fillies Turf S. (R), Calder Race Course, Nov. 10, $100,000, 2yo, f, Florida-bred, 1 1/16mT, 1:43.27, WISE COOKIE, Robbie's Gal, Awesome Dreamer, 8 started.
John Franks Memorial S. (R), Evangeline Downs, Aug. 3, $100,000, 2yo, f, passed through the ring at the Evangeline Downs March sale, 5 1/2f, 1:07.16, SWIFTY VICTRESS, Iknowuthinkimsexy, Sefapiano Rules, 11 started.
John Franks Memorial S. (R), Evangeline Downs, Aug. 4, $100,000, 2yo, passed through the ring at the Evangeline Downs March sale, 5 1/2f, 1:07.42, DELTA VIXEN, Big Erl, Delta Angel, 9 started.
John Franks Memorial S. (R), Louisiana Downs, May 12, $50,000, 3&up, Louisiana-bred, 1mT, 1:38.71, WILLIST, Diggy Fresh, Chip Hunter, 9 started.
John Henry S., Arlington Park, Sept. 16, $47,550, 3&up, 1 1/16mT, 1:41.32, PURIM, Prospective Kiss, Rey Del Sol, 8 started.
John Henry S., Evangeline Downs, April 21, $49,000, 3&up, 1m, 1:37.81, HIGH STRIKE ZONE, Recognition, More Than Regal, 7 started.
John Henry H., Meadowlands, Oct. 5, $60,000, 3&up, 1 3/8mT, 2:14.24, DUBAI CAT, Phil the Power, French Vintage, 9 started.
Johnie L. Jamison H. (R), Sunland Park, Dec. 16, $125,000, 3&up, New Mexico-bred, 6 1/2f, 1:16.76, ROMEOS WILSON, Some Ghost, Z Z Dome, 12 started.
John J. Reilly H. (R), Monmouth Park, May 26, $60,000, 3&up, New Jersey-bred, 6f, 1:08.78, HEY CHUB, Who's the Cowboy, Trueamericanspirit, 5 started.
John Kirby S. (R), Suffolk Downs, Oct. 6, $45,000, 3yo, Massachusetts-bred, 1m, 1:41.82, FIFTY SEVEN G, Sundance Richie, Invite Disco Cindo, 8 started.
John Longden "6000" H., Hastings Race Course, May 27, $50,242, 3&up, 1 1/4mT, 1:43.77, FORCEFUL INTENTION, Spaghetti Mouse, Alexandersrun, 8 started.
John McSorley S., Monmouth Park, July 15, $58,200, 3&up, a5 1/2fT, 1:01.69, JOHN'S PIC, Diamond Wildcat, War's Prospect, 4 started.
John Morrissey S., Saratoga Race Course, Aug. 2, $79,650, 3&up, New York-bred non-winners of a graded stakes in 2007, 6 1/2f, 1:16.01, GOLD AND ROSES, Executive Search, Coined for Success, 5 started.
John Patrick H., Northlands Park, July 15, $47,685, 3&up, f&m, 1m, 1:37.80, BANJO BABE, She's Italian, Selita's Dream, 9 started.
John's Call S. (R), Saratoga Race Course, Aug. 19, $82,450, 4&up, non-winners of a graded stakes in 2007, 1 3/8mT, 2:42.67, REVVED UP, General Jumbo (GB), Bailador (Ire), 8 started.
John Wayne S. (R), Prairie Meadows, May 19, $65,000, 4&up, c&g, Iowa-bred, 1m, 1:36.10, WILD K, Roarofvictory, Dazzling Man, 7 started.
John W. Galbreath Memorial S. (R), Beulah Park, Oct. 6, $75,000, 2yo, f, Ohio-bred, 1 1/16m, 1:48.38, SARASPONDA, Pyriteville, Pyrite Marci, 10 started.
John W. Rooney Memorial S. (R), Delaware Park, June 2, $100,300, 3&up, f&m, 1 3/8mT, 1:48.48, ROSINKA (IRE), Palmilla, Omeya (Chi), 6 started.
Jonathan Kiser Novice S. (R), Saratoga Race Course, Aug. 2, $70,000, 4&up, non-winners over hurdles prior to January 1, 2007, a2 1/16mT, 3:48.16, RUM SQUALL, Baby League, Prep School, 9 started.
Joseph A. Gimma S. (R), Belmont Park, Sept. 23, $108,500, 2yo, f, New York-bred, 7f, 1:24.31, EXPECT THE END, Meriwether Jessica, Beam of Love, 8 started.
Joseph T. Grace H., Santa Rosa, Aug. 4, $50,930, 3&up, 1 1/16mT, 1:42.06, NOW VICTORY, Eager Pharisien, Saratoga's Magic, 6 started.
Jostle S., Philadelphia Park, June 16, $97,000, 3yo, f, 6 1/2f, 1:15.08, AKRONISM, Cantrel, Richwoman, 4 started.
Journal H., Northlands Park, June 23, $46,745, 3&up, 6 1/2f, 1:18, SUMMER SENSATION, Plagiarist, Tiger Energy, 8 started.
JPMorgan Chase Jessamine S., Keeneland Race Course, Oct. 11,

$150,000, 2yo, f, 1 1/16mT, 1:45.34, WIND IN MY WINGS, Lickety Lemon, Jolie Visage, 9 started.

J. R. Straus Memorial S., Retama Park, Sept. 29, $45,000, 3&up, 6f, 1:08.84, MYSTERY CLASSIC, Nuttyboom, War Bridle, 5 started.

Juan Gonzalez Memorial S., Pleasanton, June 30, $53,017, 2yo, f, 5f, :58.01, CARBELLA, Livia La Vida Loca, Sassy Blend, 6 started.

JUDDMONTE SPINSTER S. (G1), Keeneland Race Course, Oct. 7, $540,000, 3&up, f&m, 1⅛mAW, 1:51.30, PANTY RAID, Lady Joanne, Teammate, 11 started.

Judy's Red Shoes S., Calder Race Course, Sept. 22, $100,000, 3yo, f, 1 1/16mT, 1:43.13, SNOW CONE, Arch Nemesis, Sweet Exchange, 12 started.

Junior Champion S., Monmouth Park, Aug. 19, $63,420, 2yo, f, 1mT, 1:36.90, SALES TAX, Sammy Van Ammy, Sumwhrovrtherainbw, 10 started.

Junius Delahoussaye Memorial Sprint S. (R), Evangeline Downs, June 30, $100,000, 3&up, Louisiana-bred, 5½f, 1:04.41, CORT'S P. B., Magic Sunset, Fass Feat, 9 started.

JUST A GAME S. (G2), Belmont Park, June 9, $294,000, 3&up, f&m, 1mT, 1:34.92, MY TYPHOON (IRE), Wait a While, Take the Ribbon, 5 started.

Justakiss S., Delaware Park, Oct. 13, $58,350, 3&up, f&m, 1 1/16m, 1:44.22, PEAK MARIA'S WAY, Lemon Drop Mom, Bondage, 5 started.

Just Smashing S., Monmouth Park, May 20, $60,000, 3yo, f, 6f, 1:09.57, PRINCESS JANIE, Suzy Smart, Deep Dish Wildcat, 8 started.

J. William (Bill) Petro Memorial S. (R), Thistledown, June 23, $50,000, 3&up, f&m, Ohio-bred, 1 1/16m, 1:46.56, CASEY'S JET, Magg's Choice, Money Card, 12 started.

J. W. Sifton S. (R), Assiniboia Downs, Sept. 15, $43,668, 3yo, Manitoba-bred, 1⅛m, 1:56.40, COMMAND THUNDER, Roman Dodger, Super Duper Me, 7 started.

Kachina H., Turf Paradise, Jan. 27, $45,000, 4&up, f&m, 1m, 1:37.56, QUEEN RAZYANA, Molly's Pride, Jubilee, 7 started.

Kaiser S., Calder Race Course, Dec. 16, $50,000, 3&up, 5f, 57.64, BLUE PEPSI LODGE, Winnies Tigger Too, World War, 9 started.

Kan of Spots Louisiana-Bred Starter S. (R), Louisiana Downs, May 11, $33,950, 3&up, Louisiana-bred starters for a claming price of $7,500 or less in 2006-'07, 6f, 1:11.54, WHO'S ZARY NOW, Buildakiss, Skymeister, 6 started.

Kansas-Bred H. (R), Anthony Downs, July 21, $8,000, 3&up, Kansas-bred, a5f, 1:01.76, D D DOT COMM, Missy Can Do, Rapid Baby, 6 started.

Kansas Oaks, The Woodlands, Oct. 21, $20,000, 3yo, f, 1m70y, 1:44.60, CELERITAS, Grammy Girl, Occupational, 7 started.

Kansas Thoroughbred Association Derby (R), The Woodlands, Oct. 6, $18,000, 3yo, c&g, progeny of eligible Kansas stallions, 1m70y, 1:46.20, ADMIRAL CLIFF, U S S Indy, Give Me Time, 6 started.

Kansas Thoroughbred Association Futurity (R), The Woodlands, Oct. 8, $20,000, 2yo, f, progeny of eligible Kansas stallions, 5½f, 1:07.80, MISS MARY'S MUSIC, Victory's Beech, Just Plain Blue, 7 started.

Kansas Thoroughbred Association Futurity (R), The Woodlands, Oct. 9, $20,000, 2yo, c&g, progeny of eligible Kansas stallions, 5½f, 1:05.80, DEE INDY GO, City Slicker, Covenant, 8 started.

Kansas Thoroughbred Association Oaks (R), The Woodlands, Oct. 7, $11,200, 3yo, f, progeny of eligible Kansas stallions, 1m70y, 1:45.80, CREEK WOMAN, Baba's Choice, Gettinoneforandy, 6 started.

Karl Boyes Memorial Northwestern Pennsylvania S., Presque Isle Downs, Sept. 15, $175,000, 3&up, 5½fAW, 1:02.51, INDIAN CHANT, Santana Strings, Connections, 8 started.

Kathryn's Doll S., Turf Paradise, March 9, $25,000, 3&up, f&m, a4½fT, 52.30, BLUMIN BEAUTY, Sweet Kendall Jo, Mirando, 7 started.

KELSO H. (G2), Belmont Park, Sept. 29, $249,200, 3&up, 1mT, 1:32.36, TRIPPI'S STORM, After Market, Palace Episode, 10 started.

Kelso S., Delaware Park, Sept. 29, $100,300, 3&up, 1 3/16m, 1:56.56, BARCOLA, Taming the Tiger, Smart Growth, 6 started.

KENNEDY ROAD S. (CAN-G3), Woodbine, Nov. 18, $130,840, 3&up, 6fAW, 1:08.78, CONNECTIONS, Ballado Dancer, Just Rushing, 11 started.

KENNY NOE JR. H. (G3), Calder Race Course, Dec. 15, $100,000, 3&up, 7f, 1:23.46, PARADISE DANCER, Finallymadeit, Finance Minister, 10 started.

Kenny Schoepf S. (R), Canterbury Park, Sept. 2, $30,000, 3&up, Minnesota-bred, 6f, 1:09.46, MACK'S MONARCH, Rock' N Fire, Sir Tricky, 9 started.

Kenora S. (R), Woodbine, Sept. 3, $119,499, 3&up, Canadian-bred, 6fAW, 1:09.34, LAKE SECRET, Dancer's Bajan, Crease Infraction, 8 started.

Ken Pearson Memorial H., Stampede Park, May 21, $45,890, 3&up, f&m, 1m, 1:39.40, BRAETTA, Mia Cat Dancer, Banjo Babe, 9 started.

KENT BREEDERS' CUP S. (G3), Delaware Park, Sept. 1, $501,200, 3yo, 1⅛mT, 1:49.60, NOBIZ LIKE SHOBIZ, Twilight Meteor, Strike a Deal, 9 started.

KENTUCKY BREEDERS' CUP S. (G3), Churchill Downs, May 3, $183,150, 2yo, 5f, :57.46, RATED FIESTY, Yogi'ssplashofgold, Ready's Image, 9 started.

KENTUCKY CUP CLASSIC S. (G2), Turfway Park, Sept. 29, $402,500, 3&up, 1⅛mAW, 1:48.48, HARD SPUN, Street Sense, Stream Cat, 4 started.

KENTUCKY CUP DISTAFF S. (G3), Turfway Park, Sept. 29, $160,000, 3&up, f&m, 1 1/16mAW, 1:43.42, DANZON, Delicate Dynamite, Ketleoneup, 11 started.

Kentucky Cup Juvenile Fillies S., Turfway Park, Sept. 29, $100,000, 2yo, f, 1mAW, 1:38.11, SKY MOM, Mims Eppi, Kadira, 11 started.

KENTUCKY CUP JUVENILE S. (G3), Turfway Park, Sept. 29, $100,000, 2yo, 1 1/16mAW, 1:44.95, TEXAS FEVER, Chitoz, Blackberry Road, 10 started.

Kentucky Cup Ladies Turf S., Kentucky Downs, Sept. 22, $100,000, 3&up, f&m, 1mT, 1:37.42, QUIET ROYAL, Rich Fantasy, Camela Carson, 11 started.

KENTUCKY CUP SPRINT S. (G3), Turfway Park, Sept. 29, $100,000, 3yo, 6fAW, 1:09.09, PIRATESONTHELAKE, Base Commander, Stormin Baghdad, 11 started.

Kentucky Cup Turf Dash S., Kentucky Downs, Sept. 22, $100,000, 3&up, 6fT, 1:09.25 (NCR), HOLD THE SALT, Shark, Ecclesiastic, 8 started.

KENTUCKY CUP TURF S. (G3), Kentucky Downs, Sept. 22, $200,000, 3&up, 1½mT, 2:26.98 (NCR), GENERAL JUMBO (GB), Fri Guy, Golden Strategy, 8 started.

KENTUCKY DERBY PRESENTED BY YUM! BRANDS (G1), Churchill Downs, May 5, $2,210,000, 3yo, 1¼m, 2:02.17, STREET SENSE, Hard Spun, Curlin, 20 started.

KENTUCKY JOCKEY CLUB S. (G2), Churchill Downs, Nov. 24, $276,750, 2yo, 1 1/16m, 1:43.16, ANAK NAKAL, Blackberry Road, Racecar Rhapsody, 7 started.

KENTUCKY OAKS (G1), Churchill Downs, May 4, $589,200, 3yo, f, 1⅛m, 1:49.99, RAGS TO RICHES, Octave, High Heels, 14 started.

Kimscountrydiamond S., Calder Race Course, May 20, $50,000, 3&up, f&m, 6½f, 1:18.07, STOLEN PRAYER, Iztla, Running Lass, 7 started.

Kindergarten Consolation S., Portland Meadows, May 5, $10,600, 2yo, 5f, 1:01.40, EVEN STEPHAN, Rogerbur, Skamania, 5 started.

Kindergarten S., Portland Meadows, May 5, $22,400, 2yo, 5f, 1:00.78, LADY'S PURSE, Works Lika Bullet, Tommy Desert, 9 started.

Kingarvie S. (R), Woodbine, Dec. 1, $126,463, 2yo, Ontario-foaled, 1 1/16mAW, 1:46.44, DELAFORCE, Lady's First Cat, Promising Dancer, 5 started.

King Bold Reality S., Meadowlands, Sept. 3, $55,000, 3&up, 5fT, :54.73 (NCR), REMAIN SILENT, Silver Timber, Wild Babe, 8 started.

King Cotton S., Oaklawn Park, Feb. 9, $50,000, 4&up, 6f, 1:10.11, SEMAPHORE MAN, Level Playingfield, Rodeo's Castle, 9 started.

King County H., Emerald Downs, July 4, $45,000, 3&up, f&m, 1m, 1:34.20, SUDDEN DEPARTURE, She's All Silk, Beaulena, 9 started.

King Cugat S., Belmont Park, Oct. 21, $79,200, 2yo, 1mT, 1:36.92, CANNONBALL, Sundaysunday, Moral Compass, 12 started.

KING EDWARD BREEDERS' CUP S. (CAN-G2), Woodbine, July 2, $225,991, 3&up, 1⅛mT, 1:46.83, ECCENTRIC (GB), Sky Conqueror, Jambalaya, 7 started.

King George's Wrong Way Starter S. (R), Calder Race Course, July 28, $45,000, 3&up, starters for a claiming price of $16,000 or less in 2007, 1¼m (originally scheduled clockwise on the turf), 2:06.69, KRISTALI, Starlight Serenade, Mean Kisser, 9 started.

KING'S BISHOP S. (G1), Saratoga Race Course, Aug. 25, $250,000, 3yo, 7f, 1:22.34, HARD SPUN, First Defence, E Z Warrior, 11 started.

Kings Point H. (R), Aqueduct, April 29, $68,550, 3&up, New York-bred, 1⅛m, 1:48.41, ACCOUNTFORTHEGOLD, Who What Win, Funny Cide, 5 started.

Kingston H. (R), Belmont Park, May 13, $113,100, 3&up, New York-bred, 1⅛mT, 1:49.37, RED ZIPPER, Golden Commander, Dave, 9 started.

Kitten's Joy S., Colonial Downs, July 21, $60,000, 3&up, 1 1/16mT, 1:41.80, JUNGLE FIGHTER, Karelian, Logaritimo (Arg), 9 started.

KLAQ H., Sunland Park, Dec. 15, $50,000, 3&up, 5½f, 1:03.64, DUCKY DRAKE, Dragooner, Absolutely True, 11 started.

Klassy Briefcase S., Monmouth Park, July 1, $63,600, 3&up, f&m, 5½fT, 1:02.61, SERENA'S CAT, Pure Disco, Cherokee Jewel, 5 started.

KNICKERBOCKER H. (G3), Aqueduct, Oct. 28, $112,900, 3&up, 1⅛mT, 1:52.06, FISHY ADVICE, Thorn Song, Operation Red Dawn, 9 started.

Knights Choice S. (R), Emerald Downs, Aug. 11, $45,000, 2yo, f, progeny of eligible Washington stallions standing in 2004, 6½f, 1:17.40, NO CONSTRAINTS, Russian, Silky Sally, 7 started.

Knoll Lake S. (R), Turf Paradise, Nov. 19, $30,600, 3&up, f&m, Arizona-bred, 6½f, 1:17.28, BEACON FALLS, Pop the Latch, Stacey's Tune, 6 started.

Korbel H. (R), Hollywood Park, June 30, $76,525, 3&up, California-bred, 1mT, 1:35.20, EPIC POWER, Now Victory, Exceeding, 5 started.

Kudzu Juvenile S. (R), Fair Grounds, Dec. 13, $45,000, 2yo, Alabama-bred, 6f, 1:11.17, ROYAL DIANA, Ikan, Q Up, 11 started.

Ky Alta H., Northlands Park, July 14, $71,528, 3yo, 1m, 1:36.40, FOOTPRINT, Sin Toro, Bling, 8 started.

Labatt Cup S. (R), Fort Erie, Sept. 3, $23,673, 3&up, f&m, three or more starts at Fort Erie in 2007, a1 1/16mT, 1:45.99, LADYINBLUE, Intothewilderness, Princess Avalon, 10 started.

Labatt Woodbine Oaks (R), Woodbine, June 10, $473,486, 3yo, f, Canadian-bred, 1⅛mAW, 1:50.68, SEALY HILL, Saskawea, Street Sounds, 10 started.

Labeeb S. (R), Woodbine, Oct. 28, $106,009, 3&up, Ontario-bred, 1mT, 1:38.05, AWESOME ACTION, Just Rushing, Bear's Kid, 10 started.

Labor Day S., Columbus Races, Sept. 3, $10,750, 3&up, 6½f, 1:20.60, FIRST CLASS BRASS, Skwhirl, Power Sweep Left, 5 started.

Labor Day S., Mountaineer Race Track and Gaming Resort, Sept. 3, $75,000, 3&up, 1m70yT, 1:40.67, MUQBIL, Come On Chas, Guardianofthenorth, 8 started.

LA BREA S. (G1), Santa Anita Park, Dec. 29, $250,000, 3yo, f, 7fAW, 1:21.09, DEARESTTRICKSKI, Unspoken Word, Glorified, 11 started.

LA CANADA S. (G2), Santa Anita Park, Feb. 11, $200,000, 4yo, f, 1⅛m, 1:49.41, BALANCE, Bai and Bai, Les Ry Leigh, 6 started.

La Coneja H. (R), Sunland Park, Dec. 22, $125,000, 3yo, f, New Mexico-bred, 5½f, 1:03.90, GOOD LOOKER R F, Shezapirate, Lady Lance, 6 started.

Ladies H., Aqueduct, Dec. 15, $79,550, 3&up, f&m, 1¼m, 2:04.63, WOW ME FREE, Cryptoquip, Borrowing Base, 6 started.

Ladnesian S., Hastings Race Course, July 15, $52,568, 2yo, 6½f, 1:18.62, CALL ME TOMORROW, Remarkable Miss, Cabron, 7 started.

Lady Angela S. (R), Woodbine, May 26, $117,282, 3yo, f, Ontario-foaled, 7fAW, 1:24.50, YOU WILL LOVE ME, Bellicose Belle, Boldly Seductive, 9 started.

Lady Canterbury Breeders' Cup S., Canterbury Park, July 14, $100,000, 3&up, f&m, a1mT, 1:35.85, HONOUR COLONY, On Safari, Best Mom, 9 started.

Lady Charles Town S. (R), Charles Town Races, June 16, $51,200, 3yo, f, most starts at Charles Town in last four starts, 7f, 1:27.75, SUGARBUZZ, Swampoodle, Snow Way, 7 started.

Lady D'Accord S. (R), Saratoga Race Course, Aug. 9, $82,750, 3yo, f, New York-bred, 7f, 1:22.54, TALKING TREASURE, Cammy's Choice, Smokin Sarah, 7 started.

Lady Finger S. (R), Finger Lakes Gaming and Race Track, Sept. 3, $137,825, 2yo, f, New York-bred, 6f, 1:11.10, BY THE LIGHT, Canadian Ballet, Beam of Love, 7 started.

Lady Hallie S. (R), Hawthorne Race Course, April 28, $88,950, 3yo, f, Illinois-conceived and/or -foaled, 6f, 1:11.59, SECRET KIN, Magnetic Miss, Copper State, 8 started.

Lady Luck Starter S. (R), Calder Race Course, July 28, $45,000, 3&up, f&m, starters for a claiming price of $16,000 or less in 2007, 7f, 1:25.46, IMELDA OH, Lauraelises Sister, Steady Slew, 7 started.

Lady On the Run S., Aqueduct, Jan. 31, $66,500, 4&up, f&m, 1m70y, 1:44.34, A TRUE PUSSYCAT, Freedom Ridge, Daytime Promise, 6 started.

Lady Razorback Futurity (R), Louisiana Downs, Oct. 6, $45,000, 2yo, f, Arkansas-bred, 6f, 1:13.67, TRICKY ETBAUER, Stormy Rumor, Gone Dixie, 9 started.

Lady Slipper S. (R), Canterbury Park, May 19, $45,000, 3&up, f&m, Minnesota-bred, 6f, 1:09.97, SENTIMENTAL CHARM, Jills Classy, Blumin Beauty, 9 started.

Lady Sonata S., Calder Race Course, Oct. 14, $50,000, 3yo, f, 6f, 1:09.94, CHER AMI, Pretoria Light, Banda Victoria, 7 started.

LADY'S SECRET S. (G1), Oak Tree at Santa Anita, Oct. 7, $196,500, 3&up, f&m, 1 1/16mAW, 1:41.64, TOUGH TIZ'S SIS, Hystericalady, Bai and Bai, 6 started.

Lady's Secret S., Monmouth Park, Aug. 5, $100,000, 3&up, f&m, 1 1/16m, 1:44.95, PROP ME UP, Tap Gold, Victory Pool, 7 started.

Lady's Secret S., Remington Park, Nov. 18, $52,450, 3&up, f&m, 1m, 1:38.63, D FINE OKIE, Dynabin, Critikal Reason, 7 started.

Lady Tak S., Aqueduct, Nov. 10, $78,750, 3yo, f, 6f, 1:10.76, YOUR FLAME IN ME, Frisk Her, Half Time Crown, 7 started.

Lafayette S., Keeneland Race Course, April 7, $114,200, 3yo, 7fAW, 1:21.05 (NTR), CARNACKS CHOICE, Call Me Clash, Ollie Jet, 11 started.

Lafayette S., Evangeline Downs, Sept. 3, $125,000, 2yo, 6f, 1:11.51, MIKIMOTO'S MOJO, Mr Bubba, Possetothemax, 10 started.

La Fiesta H., The Downs at Albuquerque, Aug. 12, $45,000, 3yo, f, 5½f, 1:02.68, LAURAS LAST MUSIC, Lady Lance, Seattle Rascal, 11 started.

La Habra S., Santa Anita Park, March 4, $113,400, 3yo, f, a6½fT, 1:12.66, SUPER FREAKY, Pay Wright, Seaside Affair, 11 started.

LA JOLLA H. (G2), Del Mar, Aug. 11, $150,000, 3yo, 1 1/16mT, 1:42.57, WORLDLY (GB), Latin Rhythms, Ten a Penny, 8 started.

LAKE GEORGE S. (G3), Saratoga Race Course, July 27, $115,100, 3yo, f, 1 1/16mT, 1:40.34, RUTHERIENNE, Lady Attack, Sharp Susan, 11 started.

Lakeland Heritage S. (R), Marquis Downs, Aug. 31, $10,117, 4&up, c&g, Saskatchewan-bred, 1m, 1:41.48, ROYAL RUST, Beau Ring, Stop the Act, 8 started.

LAKE PLACID S. (G2), Saratoga Race Course, Aug. 17, $150,000, 3yo, f, 1⅛mT, 1:46.69, SHARP SUSAN, New Edition, Lady Attack, 8 started.

Lake Tahoe Starter H. (R), Oak Tree at Santa Anita, Oct. 20, $26,500, 3&up, starters for a claiming price of $16,000 or less in 2006-'07, 1mT, 1:34.98, PRINCE OF GOLD, Dixie Banker, Driven by Excess, 9 started.

Lakeway S., Retama Park, Sept. 8, $45,000, 3yo, f, 6f, 1:09.70, WRENICE, Tear Jerker, Lunarlady, 8 started.

La Lorgnette S., Woodbine, Sept. 22, $160,772, 3yo, f, 1 1/16mAW, 1:45.71, DANCE TO MY TUNE, Serenading, Lyrically, 6 started.

Lamplighter S., Monmouth Park, May 28, $60,000, 3yo, 1 1/16mT, 1:41.15, TOP CROSS, Chaluiwitcane, Encaustic, 8 started.

Landaluce S., Hollywood Park, June 30, $111,000, 2yo, f, 6fAW, 1:11.49, THE GOLDEN NOODLE, Treadmill, Set Play, 9 started.

L and D Farm Turf Distaff S. (R), Tampa Bay Downs, April 7, $85,000, 4&up, f&m, Florida-bred, 1 1/16mT, 1:42.30, QUITE A BRIDE, Prop Me Up, A Different Tune, 11 started.

Land of Enchantment H. (R), Ruidoso Downs, July 29, $45,000, 3&up, New Mexico-bred, 7½f, 1:32.80, FULLOFENERGY, Doubletree Express, Dear Bull, 10 started.

Land of Jazz S., Ferndale, Aug. 17, $7,232, 3&up, 7f, 1:27.90, RIVERRUNS THRUIT, Draw Off, Tormento de Oro, 5 started.

Land of Lincoln S. (R), Hawthorne Race Course, April 28, $80,400, 3yo, Illinois-conceived and/or -foaled, 6f, 1:10.37, CARUSO, Stonehouse, Icandazzle, 4 started.

LANE'S END BREEDERS' FUTURITY (G1), Keeneland Race Course, Oct. 6, $560,000, 2yo, 1 1/16mAW, 1:45.21, WICKED STYLE, Slew's Tiznow, Old Man Buck, 12 started.

LANE'S END S. (G2), Turfway Park, March 24, $500,000, 3yo, 1⅛mAW, 1:49.41, HARD SPUN, Sedgefield, Joe Got Even, 12 started.

Lansing S. (R), Great Lakes Downs, June 12, $50,000, 3yo, c&g, Michigan-bred, 6f, 1:15.87, BORN TO TANGO, Oberalp, Al's Best Man, 10 started.

La Paz S., Turf Paradise, Dec. 7, $30,800, 2yo, f, 6½f, 1:17.22, HARLAN'S SONG, Pure and Simple, Kooky Kelly, 8 started.

LA PREVOYANTE H. (G2), Calder Race Course, Dec. 15, $200,000, 3&up, f&m, 1½mT, 2:26.63, REDASPEN, Green Girl (Fr), Dalvina (GB), 11 started.

La Prevoyante S. (R), Woodbine, Sept. 15, $122,464, 3yo, f, Ontario-foaled, 1mT, 1:36.17, SIWA, Galipette, You Will Love Me, 8 started.

La Puente S., Santa Anita Park, April 14, $108,300, 3yo, 1mT, 1:34.61, GOLDEN BALLS (IRE), Desert Code, Vauquelin (Ire), 7 started.

Larkspur H. (R), Great Lakes Downs, June 16, $50,000, 3&up, f&m, Michigan-bred, 6f, 1:15.61, CHAREDI'S PEAK, Nell's Enjoyment, Sure Silver, 10 started.

Larry R. Riviello President's Cup S., Philadelphia Park, Sept. 15, $200,000, 3&up, a1⅛mT, 1:51.45, INTERPATATION, Giant Wrecker, Ballonenostrikes, 9 started.

LAS CIENEGAS H. (G3), Santa Anita Park, April 15, $108,700, 4&up, f&m, a6½fT, 1:12.99, RIVER'S PRAYER, Indian Flare, Strong Faith, 7 started.

La Senora H. (R), Sunland Park, Jan. 20, $125,000, 3yo, f, New Mexico-bred, 6f, 1:14.29, SILVER EXPRESSION, Wild Ms. Pinke, La Mora Bonita, 11 started.

LAS FLORES H. (G3), Santa Anita Park, Feb. 24, $113,600, 4&up, f&m, 6f, 1:09.34, HELLO LUCKY, Selvatica, Babe Hall, 12 started.

Las Madrinas H., Fairplex Park, Sept. 21, $99,000, 3&up, f&m, 1 1/16m, 1:44.38, BAI AND BAI, Sweet Belle, Logan Avenue Linda, 8 started.

LAS PALMAS H. (G2), Oak Tree at Santa Anita, Nov. 4, $150,000, 3&up, f&m, 1mT, 1:34.14, NAISSANCE ROYALE (IRE), Black Mamba (NZ), Meribel, 10 started.

Lassie S., Hastings Race Course, Aug. 25, $52,242, 2yo, f, 6 1/2f, 1:18.72, ROSADA, Chianti Dancer, Sophisticated Sis, 7 started.

Lassie S., Portland Meadows, Nov. 18, $21,550, 2yo, f, 6f, 1:11.78, LADY'S PURSE, Jimbos Fire Ant, Blue Sky Holiday, 7 started.

Last Chance Derby, Turf Paradise, Dec. 31, $31,600, 3yo, 1 1/16m, 1:43.56, MR CHARLYPOTATOES, Canard, Organ Pipe, 11 started.

Last Dance S. (R), Suffolk Downs, Aug. 4, $45,000, 3&up, Massachusetts-bred, 1m70y, 1:45.75, GORGEOUS SILK, Petesamassbred, Senor St. Pat, 6 started.

Last Don B. S. (R), Turf Paradise, Oct. 26, $30,700, 3&up, Arizona-bred, 6f, 1:09.82, BLACKBIRD, Mr. Mayer, Corporal Tillman, 7 started.

LAS VIRGENES S. (G1), Santa Anita Park, Feb. 10, $250,000, 3yo, f, 1m, 1:37.85, RAGS TO RICHES, Baroness Thatcher, Runway Rosie, 8 started.

LA TROIENNE S. (G3), Churchill Downs, May 5, $182,850, 3yo, f, 7 1/2f, 1:30.14, SILVERINYOURPOCKET, Suaveness, Upcoming Story, 10 started.

Laurel Futurity, Laurel Park, Nov. 24, $105,000, 2yo, 1 1/16mT, 1:42.80, COWBOY CAL, Casanova Jack, Titan of Industry, 13 started.

Laurel Lane S. (R), Louisiana Downs, July 21, $99,000, 2yo, f, Louisiana-bred, 6f, 1:12.56, HISSE, Rich and Famous, T C's Charmer, 8 started.

La Verendrye S., Assiniboia Downs, June 3, $42,404, 3&up, f&m, 6f, 1:12, DOCTOR JANE, Beshairt, Pretty Beaucat, 10 started.

La Zanzara H., Santa Anita Park, Feb. 1, $77,300, 4&up, f&m, 1 1/4mT, 2:02.38, SOLVA (GB), Lasika (GB), Naughty Rafaela (Brz), 7 started.

LAZARO BARRERA MEMORIAL S. (G3), Hollywood Park, May 20, $109,700, 3yo, 7fAW, 1:21.91, TIME TO GET EVEN, Principle Secret, Desert Code, 8 started.

Lea County Sprint S., Zia Park, Nov. 4, $58,500, 3yo, 6f, 1:09.80, SUMFUN, Datrick, Hunters Wine, 3 started.

Le Bois Thoroughbred H., Les Bois Park, May 19, $6,950, 3&up, 7f, 1:24.10, SOCIAL ORDER, Petite Motion, Truly Jest, 6 started.

LECOMTE S. (G3), Fair Grounds, Jan. 13, $98,000, 3yo, 1m, 1:37.87, HARD SPUN, Izzie's Halo, Teuflesberg, 7 started.

Lemhi Go S., Calder Race Course, Dec. 30, $45,000, 3&up, f&m, 7 1/2fT, 1:28.26, GIFT OF SONG, Le Cordon Bleu, Shapira (Chi), 10 started.

Lemon Drop Kid S. (R), Saratoga Race Course, Aug. 5, $82,000, 3yo, non-winners of a stakes over one mile in 2007, 1 1/8m, 1:50.67, LOOSE LEAF, Past the Point, Believeinmenow, 8 started.

Leonard Madden and Leland Meier Memorial S., Turf Paradise, April 22, $25,000, 3yo, a7 1/2fT, 1:30.56, MR CHARLYPOTATOES, Hidden Point, Red Line, 9 started.

Leon Reed Memorial H. (R), Finger Lakes Gaming and Race Track, Aug. 12, $50,000, 3&up, New York-bred, 6f, 1:10.36, SCARY BOB, Pinky Freud, Long Lost Pal, 4 started.

Les Bois Maiden Derby, Les Bois Park, June 9, $21,800, 3yo, 6 1/2f, 1:20.10, BEAUCARDI, Walnut Avenue, Senator Bowden, 9 started.

Les Bois Park Thoroughbred S., Les Bois Park, Aug. 3, $4,200, 3&up, f&m, 7f, 1:25.46, CHARGING, Wild Vegas, Yougottabe the One, 7 started.

Les Mackin S., Yavapai Downs, June 19, $15,000, 3&up, 1m, 1:35.40, POWER STROKIN, Lydia's Legacy, Western Act, 8 started.

Les Mademoiselle Don Harmon Memorial S., Ferndale, Aug. 18, $10,440, 3&up, f&m, 1 1/16m, 1:48.82, ICE FANTASY, Dancin Gypsy, Bold Mystique, 5 started.

Letellier Memorial S., Fair Grounds, Dec. 22, $100,000, 2yo, f, 6f, 1:10.79, BLITZING, Syriana's Song, La Wildcat, 11 started.

Letellier Memorial S., Fair Grounds, Jan. 1, $75,000, 3yo, f, 6f, 1:10.05, TOTAL, Pro Pink, Cat On a Cloud, 9 started.

Lethal Grande Oregon Sprint Championship S. (R), Portland Meadows, Dec. 9, $10,875, 3&up, Oregon-bred, 6f, 1:11.28, HUNT FOR GLORY, Brave Hearted, Seattle Sailor Boy, 6 started.

Lethbridge Fillies and Mares Spring S., Lethbridge, June 10, $15,280, 3&up, f&m, 5 1/2f, 1:08.60, TROMPETA, Bushmill Girl, Color Me Iris, 8 started.

Lethbridge Fillies Oaks, Lethbridge, Sept. 30, $16,289, 3yo, f, a6f, 1:10.20, METIGOSHE, Desperate Dancer, Queen City Kitty, 8 started.

Lethbridge Filly and Mare S., Lethbridge, June 24, $15,145, 3&up, f&m, 7f, 1:25.40, COLOR ME IRIS, Lot a Smoke, Feudal Lady, 8 started.

Lethbridge Filly and Mare S., Lethbridge, Sept. 1, $15,340, 3&up, f&m, a6f, 1:10.60, TROMPETA, Color Me Iris, Avenue of Silver, 8 started.

Lethbridge Open S., Lethbridge, June 23, $15,145, 3&up, 7f, 1:24, LAFLEUR, Pure, Dr. Mo, 9 started.

Lethbridge Open S., Lethbridge, Sept. 1, $15,340, 3&up, 7f, 1:24.80, DR. MO, Little Abner, Stormy Gamble, 8 started.

Lethbridge Open S., Lethbridge, Sept. 29, $18,501, 3&up, 1 1/16m, 1:47.20, LAFLEUR, Shouldbevictory, Sefapianos Way, 7 started.

Lethbridge Starter Allowance S. #1, Lethbridge, Sept. 23, $8,293, 3&up, 1 1/16m, 1:53, CHIEF JOSEPH, A. K. A. Sparky, Tulsa Stateofmind, 7 started.

Lethbridge Starter Allowance S. #2, Lethbridge, Sept. 23, $8,293, 3&up, 1 1/16m, 1:52.80, TATA PANTOJA, Larry the Longshot, George's Stick, 7 started.

Lethbridge Starter Allowance S. #3, Lethbridge, Oct. 21, $8,490, 3&up, 1 3/16m, 2:03.20, CHIEF JOSEPH, Pakawalup, Larry the Longshot, 6 started.

Lethbridge Three-Year-Old Fillies S., Lethbridge, June 30, $15,204, 3yo, f, a6f, 1:10, DESPERATE DANCER, Blue Banjo, Speedy Two Socks, 7 started.

Lethbridge Three-Year-Old Fillies S., Lethbridge, Oct. 27, $16,681, 3yo, f, 7f, 1:28.20, DESPERATE DANCER, Queen City Kitty, Metigoshe, 7 started.

Lethbridge Three-Year-Old Fillies S., Lethbridge, Sept. 30, $16,138, 3yo, 7f, 1:25, ONE O NINE N ONE, Anchorman, Cool Turando, 7 started.

Lethbridge Three-Year-Old S., Lethbridge, June 30, $15,204, 3yo, a6f, 1:09.40, ONE O NINE N ONE, Anchorman, Runaway Carbs, 8 started.

Lexington S., Belmont Park, July 8, $106,000, 3yo, 1 1/8mT, 1:48.45, DISTORTED REALITY, Buddy's Humor, Perusal, 5 started.

LEXUS RAVEN RUN S. (G2), Keeneland Race Course, Oct. 20, $300,000, 3yo, f, 7fAW, 1:22.01, JIBBOOM, West Coast Swing, Mini Sermon, 13 started.

Liberada S., Calder Race Course, June 24, $45,000, 3&up, f&m, 1 1/16mT, 1:46.29, FUNNY ANNIE, Potra Clasica (Arg), El Bank Robber, 10 started.

LIEUTENANT GOVERNORS' H. (CAN-G3), Hastings Race Course, July 1, $101,218, 3&up, 1 1/8m, 1:49.61, SPAGHETTI MOUSE, Timeless Passion, Forceful Intention, 8 started.

Life's Magic S., Belmont Park, Oct. 12, $78,000, 3yo, f, 7f, 1:22.01, LADY MARLBORO, Dorm Fever, Ruban Bleu, 8 started.

Light Hearted S., Delaware Park, July 15, $101,800, 3&up, f&m, 5fT, :56.08, SMART AND FANCY, Truly Blushed, Spanish Lullaby, 11 started.

Lighthouse S., Monmouth Park, July 7, $60,000, 3&up, f&m, 1mT, 1:33.82, POMMES FRITES, Beat the Band, A Different Tune, 7 started.

Lightning City S., Tampa Bay Downs, Dec. 8, $65,000, 3&up, f&m, 5fT, :56.61, ROYAL REGAN, Bucky's Prayer, Message of a Myth, 10 started.

Lightning City S., Tampa Bay Downs, May 5, $65,000, 3&up, f&m, 5fT, :55.50, BUCKY'S PRAYER, Zooming By, Mohegan Sky, 6 started.

Lightning Jet H.(R), Hawthorne Race Course, Nov. 3, $87,900, 3&up, Illinois-conceived and/or -foaled, 6f, 1:09.58, MIGHTY RULE, Shrewd Operator, High Expectations, 6 started.

Lights and Music S., Belmont Park, Sept. 9, $76,700, 3yo, 7fT, 1:20.13, ENGLISH COLONY (GB), Quietly Mine, Perfect Casting, 6 started.

Likely Exchange S., Turfway Park, Feb. 10, $50,000, 4&up, f&m, 1mAW, 1:39.86, ELLA BELLE. Half Heaven, Daring Julie, 10 started.

Lil Abner S. (R), Charles Town Races, Nov. 24, $46,050, 3&up, c&g, West Virginia-bred, 1 1/8m, 1:54.95, DONALD'S PRIDE, Eastern Delite, Double Tollgate, 7 started.

Lilac H., Stampede Park, May 27, $46,320, 3yo, f, 1m, 1:38.40, TANIKA, Pleasant Bear, Running Apache, 8 started.

Lil E Tee H. (R), Presque Isle Downs, Sept. 21, $90,000, 3yo, c&g, Pennsylvania-bred, 6fAW, *:09.84, WHISTLE PIG, Diplomatic Charm, Call Me Dude, 5 started.

Lincoln Heritage H. (R), Arlington Park, July 7, $83,950, 3&up, f&m, Illinois-conceived and/or -foaled, 1 1/16mT, 1:44.03, ROYAL LEAH, Lampoon, Now, 8 started.

Lincoln H. (R), Ruidoso Downs, July 29, $45,000, 3&up, f&m, New Mexico-bred, 6f, 1:11.40, PEPPERS PRIDE, Theregoesdancer, Hang Glide, 7 started.

Lincroft H. (R), Monmouth Park, Aug. 5, $65,000, 3&up, New Jersey-bred, 1m70y, 1:41.22, FAGEDABOUDIT SAL, Carrots Only, Rolled Up, 9 started.

Lindsay Frolic S., Calder Race Course, Sept. 1, $55,000, 2yo, f, 1m, 1:42.71, ASI ASI, Awesome Dreamer, Tidal Dance, 8 started.
Lineage S. (R), The Downs at Albuquerque, Aug. 19, $56,250, 3&up, New Mexico-bred, 1 1/16m, 1:44.11, MIDNITE PROSPECTOR, Romeos Wilson, Fullofenergy, 6 started.
Little Ones S. (R), Great Lakes Downs, Aug. 28, $50,000, 2yo, c&g, Michigan-bred, 6f, 1:15.18, HOT CHILI, Native Britches, Berry's Pride, 9 started.
Little Silver S., Monmouth Park, June 9, $60,000, 3yo, f, 1 1/16mT, 1:40.27 (NCR), AUDACIOUS CHLOE, Cabbage Key, Wine Diva, 8 started.
LOCUST GROVE H. (G3), Churchill Downs, July 8, $162,900, 3&up, f&m, 1 1/8mT, 1:47.99, MAURALAKANA (FR), Quiet Royal, Quite a Bride, 6 started.
Lola Bella S., Calder Race Course, Jan. 2, $40,000, 4&up, 5f, :57.94, STEEL THE GLORY, British Attitude, Lord Robyn, 8 started.
Lonesome Glory Hurdle S., Belmont Park, Sept. 22, $168,400, 4&up, a2 1/2mT, 4:42.45, GOOD NIGHT SHIRT, Orison, Preemptive Strike, 9 started.
LONE STAR DERBY (G3), Lone Star Park, May 12, $300,000, 3yo, 1 1/16m, 1:45.49, SLEW'S TIZZY, Moyer's Pond, dh-Forty Grams, dh-Mr. Nightlinger, 10 started.
Lone Star Oaks, Lone Star Park, June 30, $50,000, 3yo, f, 1 1/16mT, 1:44.62, ALICE BELLE, Katys Gold Touch, Kid Majic, 9 started.
LONE STAR PARK H. (G3), Lone Star Park, May 28, $388,000, 3&up, 1 1/16m, 1:45.02, BOB AND JOHN, Sweetnorthernsaint, Jonesboro, 4 started.
Lone Star Park Turf Sprint H., Lone Star Park, July 4, $50,000, 3&up, 5f (originally scheduled on the turf), :56.73, MYSTERY CLASSIC, Orphan Brigade, Toga Too, 7 started.
LONGACRES MILE H. (G3), Emerald Downs, Aug. 19, $391,250, 3&up, 1m, 1:35.40, THE GREAT FACE, Raise the Bluff, Wasserman, 12 started.
Long Branch Breeders' Cup S., Monmouth Park, July 14, $150,000, 3yo, 1 1/16m, 1:42.30, FIRST DEFENCE, Get Serious, Saratoga Lulaby, 6 started.
Longfellow S., Monmouth Park, June 9, $65,000, 3&up, 6f, 1:09.30, WILDEYED DREAMER, Wild Jam, Kazoo, 5 started.
LONG ISLAND H. (G3), Aqueduct, Nov. 11, $150,000, 3&up, f&m, 1 1/2mT, 2:34.35, DALVINA (GB), Barancella (Fr), My Rachel, 8 started.
Long Look S., Meadowlands, Sept. 15, $58,200, 3&up, f&m, 1 1/8m, 1:49.49, PROP ME UP, Tap Gold, Peak Maria's Way, 4 started.
Longshots OTB Cup S. (R), Fort Erie, Oct. 21, $25,885, 2yo, f, starters for a claiming price of $5,000 or less in 2006-'07 and have started at Fort Erie three times in 2007, 6f, 1:12.37, JAN'S TROPHY, Gold Abby, Flawless Case, 8 started.
Lookout S. (R), Delta Downs, Dec. 28, $54,500, 3&up, non-winners of a stakes, 1m, 1:40.62, COZY TIME, Thunder Mission, Double Again, 9 started.
Lord Juban S., Calder Race Course, June 23, $50,000, 3yo, 1 1/16mT, 1:45.15, FEARLESS EAGLE, Sparkling Notion, Unbridled Music, 10 started.
LOS ANGELES H. (G3), Hollywood Park, May 12, $105,800, 3&up, 6fAW, 1:09.03, SAILORS SUNSET, Peace Chant, Northern Soldier, 9 started.
Lost Code S., Hawthorne Race Course, April 7, $47,925, 3yo, 6f, 1:10.98, CARUSO, Thatsalottabull, Piratesonthelake, 6 started.
Lost in the Fog Juvenile S., Turf Paradise, Dec. 29, $50,000, 2yo, 6 1/2f, 1:15.24, EL MIRAGE, White Spar, Ez Dreamer, 8 started.
Lost in the Fog S., Golden Gate Fields, June 10, $55,550, 2yo, 5f, :57.70, IMAGINARY SAILOR, Deputy Bertrando, Younique Cat, 6 started.
Louise Kimball S. (R), Suffolk Downs, Sept. 15, $45,000, 3yo, f, Massachusetts-bred, 1m, 1:41.40, LILY'S GOLDMINE, Classy Baby Jane, Halo It's Me, 6 started.
Louisiana Breeders' Cup H., Fair Grounds, Jan. 6, $75,000, 3&up, 1 1/8m, 1:45.10, SANDBURR, Jonesboro, Patriot Act, 6 started.
Louisiana Breeders' Derby (R), Louisiana Downs, July 21, $100,000, 3yo, Louisiana-bred, 1 1/16m, 1:46.07, ST. ZARB, Hallway, Grim Hooligan, 10 started.
Louisiana Breeders' Oaks (R), Louisiana Downs, July 21, $99,000, 3yo, f, Louisiana-bred, 1 1/16m, 1:44.27, AHEAD OF HER TIME, Tensas Yucatan, Zarb's Ballerina, 8 started.
Louisiana Champions Day Classic S. (R), Fair Grounds, Dec. 8, $150,000, 3&up, Louisiana-bred, 1 1/8m, 1:50.76, COSTA RISING, Hallway, Lash, 5 started.
Louisiana Champions Day Juvenile S. (R), Fair Grounds, Dec. 8, $100,000, 2yo, Louisiana-bred, 6f, 1:11.18, STAR GUITAR, Cubera, Pantara Phantom, 14 started.
Louisiana Champions Day Ladies S. (R), Fair Grounds, Dec. 8, $100,000, 3&up, f&m, Louisiana-bred, 1 1/16m, 1:44.77, AHEAD OF HER TIME, Tensas Yucatan, Tar Pot, 7 started.
Louisiana Champions Day Ladies Sprint S. (R), Fair Grounds, Dec. 8, $100,000, 3&up, f&m, Louisiana-bred, 6f, 1:10.67, CARL'S FROSTY GIRL, Calmed, Ida Maria, 10 started.
Louisiana Champions Day Lassie S. (R), Fair Grounds, Dec. 8, $100,000, 2yo, f, Louisiana-bred, 6f, 1:11.63, SUPERIOR STORM, Hisse, Claudia Bertha, 13 started.
Louisiana Champions Day Sprint S. (R), Fair Grounds, Dec. 8, $100,000, 3&up, Louisiana-bred, 6f, 1:10.62, FASS FEAT, Tortuga Straits, Magic Sunset, 14 started.
Louisiana Champions Day Starter H. (R), Fair Grounds, Dec. 8, $50,000, 3&up, Louisiana-bred starters for a claiming price of $20,000 or less in 2007, 1 1/16m, 1:46.10, Z STORM, Autobeacat, Zarb's Music Man, 11 started.
Louisiana Champions Day Turf S. (R), Fair Grounds, Dec. 8, $100,000, 3&up, Louisiana-bred, a1 1/16mT, 1:44.18, WILLIST, Wildrally, Desert Wheat, 7 started.
LOUISIANA DERBY (G2), Fair Grounds, March 10, $594,000, 3yo, 1 1/16m, 1:43.01, CIRCULAR QUAY, Ketchikan, Zanjero, 8 started.
Louisiana Futurity (R), Fair Grounds, Dec. 31, $106,135, 2yo, Louisiana-bred, 6f, 1:11.70, CUBERA, Doble Quebrado, Cush, 7 started.
Louisiana Futurity (R), Fair Grounds, Dec. 31, $112,935, 2yo, f, Louisiana-bred, 6f, 1:11.67, VERY SEXCESSFUL, T C's Charmer, Sax Appeal, 13 started.
Louisiana Lagniappe Classic S. (R), Fair Grounds, March 24, $100,000, 4&up, Louisiana-bred, 1 1/16m, 1:44.51, PERFECT HARMONY, Liquid Silver, Nowandforevermore, 8 started.
Louisiana Lagniappe Ladies Sprint S. (R), Fair Grounds, March 25, $100,000, 4&up, f&m, Louisiana-bred, 5 1/2f, 1:04.47, LEESA LEE, Ida Maria, Indigo Girl, 9 started.
Louisiana Lagniappe Sprint S. (R), Fair Grounds, March 25, $100,000, 4&up, Louisiana-bred, 5 1/2f, 1:02.65 (NTR), CORT'S P.B., Brother Bean, Sparkling Jack, 5 started.
Louisiana Premier Night Bon Temps Starter S. (R), Delta Downs, Feb. 3, $44,550, 4&up, f&m, Louisiana-bred starters for a claiming price of $7,500 or less in 2006-'07, 5f, 1:00.12, SHUGAFOOT, Graduate Course, Bucktown Belle, 8 started.
Louisiana Premier Night Championship S. (R), Delta Downs, Feb. 3, $194,000, 4&up, Louisiana-bred, 1 1/16m, 1:45.09, COSTA RISING, Mean Butterbean, Diggy Fresh, 6 started.
Louisiana Premier Night Distaff S. (R), Delta Downs, Feb. 3, $147,000, 4&up, f&m, Louisiana-bred, 1m, 1:41.71, RASPBERRY WINE, Carl's Frosty Girl, Calista Ridge, 7 started.
Louisiana Premier Night Gentlemen Starter S. (R), Delta Downs, Feb. 3, $55,000, 4&up, Louisiana-bred starters for a claiming price of $15,000 or less in 2006-'07, 1 1/16m, 1:46.53, Z STORM, Prince Slew, Boo Boo, 9 started.
Louisiana Premier Night Ladies Starter S. (R), Delta Downs, Feb. 3, $45,450, 4&up, f&m, Louisiana-bred starters for a claiming price of $15,000 or less in 2006-'07, 1m, 1:40.38, MADISON'S MUSIC, Golden Demand, Little Dirty Herty, 8 started.
Louisiana Premier Night Matron S. (R), Delta Downs, Feb. 3, $98,000, 4&up, f&m, Louisiana-bred, 5f, :59.59, INDIGO GIRL, Sammie Sam, My American Lady, 7 started.
Louisiana Premier Night Prince S. (R), Delta Downs, Feb. 3, $125,000, 3yo, Louisiana-bred, 7f, 1:28.02, TORTUGA STRAITS, Forgotten Prince, Timely Sweep, 10 started.
Louisiana Premier Night Ragin Cajun Starter S. (R), Delta Downs, Feb. 3, $45,000, 4&up, Louisiana-bred starters for a claiming price of $7,500 or less in 2006-'07, 5f, 1:00.62, CONSTANT COMMOTION, Uncle Clip, Cro Dome, 9 started.
Louisiana Premier Night Sprint S. (R), Delta Downs, Feb. 3, $100,000, 4&up, Louisiana-bred, 5f, :58.44, BROTHER BEAN, Kim's Gem, Cort's P.B., 9 started.
Louisiana Premier Night Starlet S. (R), Delta Downs, Feb. 3, $125,000, 3yo, f, Louisiana-bred, 7f, 1:27.74, MY FRIEND BELE, Tensas Yucatan, Huckie, 10 started.
LOUISVILLE BREEDERS' CUP S. (G2), Churchill Downs, May 4, $328,200, 3&up, f&m, 1 1/16m, 1:44.11, FIERY PURSUIT, Asi Siempre, Baghdaria, 9 started.
LOUISVILLE H. (G3), Churchill Downs, May 26, $170,400, 3&up, 1 1/2mT, 2:28.35, DRILLING FOR OIL, Always First (GB), Ramazutti, 11 started.
Love Addiction S., Yavapai Downs, June 18, $11,700, 3&up, f&m, 1m, 1:36.80, SUMMER LAKE, Mobile, Woman of Choice, 6 started.
Luck Be a Lady H., Bay Meadows Race Course, Oct. 13, $71,910,

3&up, f&m, 6f, 1:09.28, SOMETHINABOUTLAURA, Victorina, Truly Quiet, 5 started.
Luck of the Irish H., Bay Meadows Race Course, March 18, $50,625, 4&up, 1 1/16mT, 1:44.63, DEALER CHOICE (FR), Salty Humor, dh-True Dancer, dh-Courtly Jazz, 5 started.
Luke Gibson Memorial S., Sunflower Downs, June 29, $5,664, 3&up, f&m, a5 1/2f, 1:05.88, MARQUETRY ROSE, Sindi's Success, Feu Kan Promise, 7 started.
LuLu's Ransom S., Calder Race Course, May 20, $50,000, 3yo, f, 1m, 1:40.97, DANTRELLE LIGHT, Sweet Exchange, Trippin Star, 7 started.
Lure S., Gulfstream Park, April 1, $75,000, 4&up, 1 1/16mT, 1:40.36, ASHKAL WAY (IRE), Classic Campaign, Electric Light, 5 started.
Luther Burbank H., Santa Rosa, July 28, $56,985, 3&up, f&m, 1 1/16mT, 1:45.14, SHERMEEN (IRE), Gentle Charmer, Round Trip Flight, 5 started.
Lyman Sprint H. (R), Philadelphia Park, May 5, $60,000, 3&up, c&g, Pennsylvania-bred, 6f, 1:09.70, POWER BY LEIGH, Banjo Picker, Songofthesailor, 6 started.
Lyrique S., Louisiana Downs, Aug. 18, $75,450, 3yo, f, 1 1/16mT, 1:43.96, WHISPER TO ME, Blue Angel, Wine Diva, 11 started.
M2 Technology La Senorita S., Retama Park, Oct. 27, $100,000, 2yo, f, 1mT, 1:35.42, HARTFELT, Wasted Tears, Timely Reflection, 12 started.
MAC DIARMIDA H. (G2), Gulfstream Park, Jan. 28, $150,000, 4&up, 1 3/8mT, 2:11.86, RAMAZUTTI, Dreadnaught, Interpatation, 12 started.
Mackinac H. (R), Great Lakes Downs, Sept. 11, $50,000, 3yo, c&g, Michigan-bred, 1 1/16m, 1:50, ALL I CAN GET, My First Buck, Scarlet Fact, 7 started.
Mac's Sparkler S., Belmont Park, May 20, $65,200, 4&up, f&m, 6f, 1:09.65, MAY DAY VOW, Magnolia Jackson, Wild Gams, 5 started.
Mademoiselle S., Delta Downs, March 2, $49,000, 4&up, f&m, 5f, :58.83, INDIGO GIRL, Ocean Current, Deep Woods, 7 started.
Mademoiselle S., Northlands Park, Aug. 10, $47,330, 3&up, f&m, 1 1/16m, 1:44, MONASHEE, She's Italian, Dixietwostepper, 7 started.
Magali Farms S. (R), Hollywood Park, April 29, $61,600, 3&up, f&m, California-bred maidens, 6 1/2fAW, 1:16.26, RARE EXCHANGE, Alpine Jewel, D Pirates Marker, 9 started.
Magic City Classic S. (R), Turfway Park, Nov. 25, $55,000, 3&up, Alabama-bred, 1mAW, 1:40.32, ACK MAGICAL, Seducing Mr. G, Chief Tudor, 12 started.
Magna Distaff S., Gulfstream Park, April 1, $75,000, 4&up, f&m, 1 1/16mT, 1:40.23, VACARE, Aunt Henny, Pictavia (Ire), 8 started.
Magnolia S. (R), Delta Downs, Nov. 17, $73,500, 4&up, f&m, Louisiana-bred, 1m, 1:41.08, ZARB'S BALLERINA, Carl's Frosty Girl, Doeny Ghost, 7 started.
Maid of the Mist S. (R), Belmont Park, Oct. 20, $100,000, 2yo, f, New York-bred, 1m, 1:38.01, EXPECT THE END, Meriwether Jessica, Sibley, 7 started.
Major Moran S., Calder Race Course, Aug. 26, $50,000, 3&up, 6f, 1:10.33, FINALLYMADEIT, Dream of Angels, Yes He's the Man, 5 started.
MAKER'S MARK MILE S. (G2), Keeneland Race Course, April 13, $250,000, 4&up, 1mT, 1:35.51, KIP DEVILLE, Showing Up, Purim, 8 started.
MALIBU S. (G1), Santa Anita Park, Dec. 26, $250,000, 3yo, 7fAW, 1:21.08, JOHNNY EVES, Carrilero (Arg), Horse Greeley, 14 started.
Mamie Eisenhower S. (R), Prairie Meadows, May 12, $65,000, 4&up, f&m, Iowa-bred, 6f, 1:10.08, SEEKINGTHEREINBOW, Camela Carson, Dixie Kate, 6 started.
Mamzelle S., Churchill Downs, May 3, $111,100, 3&up, f&m, 5fT, :56.92, SMITTY'S SUNSHINE, Fan Time, Flying Circle, 8 started.
Manatee S., Tampa Bay Downs, Feb. 3, $60,000, 4&up, f&m, 7f, 1:25.43, SUMMER CRUISE, Gadolinium, Zooming By, 10 started.
Manhattan Beach S., Hollywood Park, June 2, $83,125, 3yo, f, 6fT, 1:08.49, SINDY WITH AN S, You Are the Answer, Desire to Excel, 8 started.
MANHATTAN H. (G1), Belmont Park, June 9, $400,000, 3&up, 1 1/4mT, 2:02.39, BETTER TALK NOW, English Channel, Shakis (Ire), 8 started.
Manhattan S. (R), The Woodlands, Sept. 30, $20,000, 3&up, f&m, Kansas-bred, 6f, 1:11, SUMMER RECITAL, Lady Legend, Miss Turnpiker, 8 started.
Manitoba Lotteries Derby, Assiniboia Downs, Aug. 6, $94,820, 3yo, 1 1/16m, 1:52, WEATHER WARNING, Rage Till Dawn, Great Discovery, 12 started.
Manitoba Maturity (R), Assiniboia Downs, July 7, $42,894, 4yo, Manitoba-bred, 1 1/16m, 1:49, CALLIE'S WISDOM, Hurri Coin, Win by a Margin, 10 started.

Manitoba S. (R), Assiniboia Downs, June 23, $28,047, 3yo, Manitoba-bred, 1m, 1:39.80, SIR OFFICER, Gold Chester, Jimmijazz, 5 started.
Manor Downs Distance Cup S. (R), Manor Downs, April 1, $45,000, 3&up, Texas-bred, 1 1/4m, 1:44.80, MOON KID, Bid From Bourtai, Olmos Creek, 9 started.
Manor Downs Thoroughbred Futurity, Manor Downs, April 22, $45,000, 2yo, 4 1/2f, :52.69, RUSTED STEEL, Almendrado, Bg Hi Hi Is Ben, 10 started.
MAN O'WAR S. (G1), Belmont Park, Sept. 8, $500,000, 3&up, 1 3/8mT, 2:12.26, DOCTOR DINO (FR), Sunriver, Grand Couturier (GB), 7 started.
Maple Leaf S., Woodbine, Nov. 10, $219,565, 3&up, f&m, 1 1/8mAW, 2:03.51 (NTR), LIKE A GEM, I'm in Love, Tell It as It Is, 10 started.
Marathon Series Final S., Turf Paradise, Feb. 24, $23,600, 4&up, 1 5/8m, 2:46.63, LAST OUTPOST, Fiesty, Hai Ichiban, 9 started.
Marcellus Frost Hurdle S., Percy Warner, May 12, $50,000, 4&up, a2mT, 3:54.40, PARADISE'S BOSS, Preemptive Strike, Moneytrain (Ger), 8 started.
Mardi Gras S., Fair Grounds, Feb. 26, $74,250, 3yo, a7 1/2fT, 1:33.15, CORRUPT, Royal War Academy, Awesome Hero, 8 started.
Marfa S., Turfway Park, Sept. 15, $65,250, 3&up, 6 1/2fAW, 1:16.82, OFF DUTY, Reigning Court, Cowboy Hardware, 7 started.
Margaret Currey Henley Sport of Queens Hurdle S., Percy Warner, May 12, $50,000, 4&up, f&m, a2 1/4mT, 4:25, ORCHID PRINCESS, Feeling So Pretty, Footlights, 12 started.
Mariah's Storm S., Churchill Downs, Nov. 18, $111,100, 3&up, f&m, 5fT, :57.43, FLYING CIRCLE, Taletobetold, Smitty's Sunshine, 9 started.
Maria's Mon S., Aqueduct, Nov. 14, $76,950, 3yo, 6f, 1:09.52, ROI MAUDIT, Leonardo, I Ain't No Saint, 7 started.
Marie G. Krantz Memorial H., Fair Grounds, March 25, $97,000, 4&up, a1 1/4mT, 1:43.33, J'RAY, Bridge Game, My Three Sisters, 6 started.
Marie P. DeBartolo Oaks, Louisiana Downs, Sept. 22, $216,000, 3yo, f, 1 1/16mT, 1:41.78, TENSAS YUCATAN, Ahead of Her Time, Blue Angel, 9 started.
Marigold S., Kamloops, June 2, $4,994, 3&up, f&m, 6 1/2f, 1:21.76, REGAL PROMISE, Who Let the Katout, Mahonia, 5 started.
MARINE S. (CAN-G3), Woodbine, May 19, $138,771, 3yo, 1 1/16mAW, 1:46.47, SAHARA HEAT, Approval Rating, Angel of the House, 8 started.
Marion du Pont Scott Colonial Cup Hurdle S., Camden, Nov. 18, $150,000, 4&up, a2 3/4mT, 5:19.20, GOOD NIGHT SHIRT, Three Carat, Sovereign Duty, 8 started.
Marking Time S. (R), Belmont Park, June 22, $65,950, 3yo, f, non-winners of a graded stakes in 2007, 1m, 1:34.84, MINI SERMON, Lady Marlboro, Officer in Pursuit, 5 started.
Marquis Downs Sales S. (R), Marquis Downs, July 14, $4,769, 3yo, passed through the ring at a CTHS sale, 7f, 1:24.44 (NTR), MISCHEVIOUSFIGHTER, Cole Bay, Britt of Seattle, 6 started.
Marshua S., Laurel Park, Jan. 6, $74,600, 3yo, f, 5 1/2f, 1:06.01, LAILA'S PUNCH, Luxury Class, Deep Dish Wildcat, 7 started.
Marshua's River S., Gulfstream Park, Jan. 13, $75,000, 4&up, f&m, 1 1/16mT, 1:39.77, BRIGHT ABUNDANCE, Naissance Royale (Ire), Calla Lily, 10 started.
Martanza S., Sam Houston Race Park, Dec. 1, $75,000, 3&up, f&m, Texas-bred, 1m, 1:39.04, HOLLYE LYNNE, Sweet Idea, Magic Money Meg, 7 started.
Martha Washington S., Oaklawn Park, Feb. 18, $50,000, 3yo, f, 1m, 1:38.13, DEVIL HOUSE, Spartan Queen, Time's Mistress, 9 started.
Mary Goldblatt S. (R), Portland Meadows, March 17, $10,350, 3yo, f, Oregon-bred, 1m, 1:41.65, BAGELS BABY, Silver Patrona, Precious Prospect, 4 started.
Maryland Hunt Cup Timber S., Glyndon, April 28, $69,750, 5&up, a4mT, 9:36.80, THE BRUCE (NZ), dh-Bug River, dh-Lear Charm, 7 started.
Maryland Juvenile Championship S. (R), Laurel Park, Dec. 29, $50,000, 2yo, Maryland-bred, 1m, 1:39.20, APPLE SPECIAL, Malibu Kid, Regal Solo, 8 started.
Maryland Juvenile Filly Championship S. (R), Laurel Park, Dec. 22, $50,000, 2yo, f, Maryland-bred, 1m, 1:40.16, ASK THE MOON, Hartigan, Kosmo's Buddy, 8 started.
Maryland Million Classic S. (R), Laurel Park, Oct. 13, $285,000, 3&up, progeny of sires eligible for the Maryland Million program, 1 3/16m, 1:58.19, EVIL STORM, Five Steps, Diamond David, 8 started.
Maryland Million Distaff H. (R), Laurel Park, Oct. 13, $142,500, 3&up, f&m, progeny of sires eligible for the Maryland Million program, 7f, 1:24, AKRONISM, Silmaril, For Kisses, 8 started.

Maryland Million Distaff Starter H. (R), Laurel Park, Oct. 13, $47,500, 3&up, f&m, progeny of sires eligible for the Maryland Million program which have started for a claiming price of $15,000 or less since October 14, 2006, 1m, 1:40.02, SWEAR TO IT, Met a Miner, Gussie's Secret, 12 started.

Maryland Million Ladies S. (R), Laurel Park, Oct. 13, $190,000, 3&up, f&m, progeny of sires eligible for the Maryland Million program, 1⅛mT, 1:47.26 (NCR), MADDY'S HEART, Beau's Trip, Lexi Star, 8 started.

Maryland Million Lassie S. (R), Laurel Park, Oct. 13, $142,500, 2yo, f, progeny of sires eligible for the Maryland Million program, 7f, 1:26.11, LOVE FOR NOT, All Attitude, Kosmo's Buddy, 9 started.

Maryland Million Nursery S. (R), Laurel Park, Oct. 13, $142,500, 2yo, progeny of sires eligible for the Maryland Million program, 7f, 1:25.79, REGAL SOLO, Smooth It Over, Izzy Speaking, 8 started.

Maryland Million Oaks (R), Laurel Park, Oct. 13, $142,500, 3yo, f, progeny of sires eligible for the Maryland Million program, 1m, 1:37.47, MOON CATCHER, Paying Off, Loveyasister, 7 started.

Maryland Million Sprint H. (R), Laurel Park, Oct. 13, $142,500, 3&up, progeny of sires eligible for the Maryland Million program, 6f, 1:10.27, GRAND CHAMPION, Lemons of Love, Cayman Condo, 7 started.

Maryland Million Sprint Starter H. (R), Laurel Park, Oct. 13, $28,500, 3&up, progeny of sires eligible for the Maryland Million program who have started for a claiming price of $7,500 or less since October 14, 2006, 6f, 1:11.02, BE OH BE, All Star Prospect, Season Ticket, 11 started.

Maryland Million Starter H. (R), Laurel Park, Nov. 24, $50,000, 3&up, Maryland-bred starters for a claiming price of $10,000 or less since November 25, 2006, 1m, 1:39.63, FIRE HERO, Oorah, Irish Colony, 7 started.

Maryland Million Starter H. (R), Laurel Park, Oct. 13, $47,500, 3&up, progeny of sires eligible for the Maryland Million program which have started for a claiming price of $15,000 or less since October 14, 2006, 1⅛m, 1:52.37, OFF THE GLASS, Joel's Touch, Fire Hero, 11 started.

Maryland Million Turf S. (R), Laurel Park, Oct. 13, $190,000, 3&up, progeny of sires eligible for the Maryland Million program, 1⅛mT, 1:46.03, FORTY CROWNS, Dr Rico, Broadway Producer, 13 started.

Maryland Million Turf Sprint H. (R), Laurel Park, Oct. 13, $95,000, 3&up, progeny of sires eligible for the Maryland Million program, 5½fT, 1:01.62 (NCR), HAPPY SURPRISE, Whata Monster, Mr Mutter, 7 started.

Maryland My Maryland S., Calder Race Course, May 19, $45,000, 3&up, 1 3/16m, 2:00.05, TACIT AGREEMENT, A. J. Melini, Maraquero, 5 started.

Maryland Racing Media H., Laurel Park, Feb. 24, $86,400, 3&up, f&m, 1⅛m, 1:51.27, LEXI STAR, It's True Love, Raging Rapids, 7 started.

Maryland Stallion Station S. (R), Pimlico Race Course, April 21, $75,750, 3yo, Maryland-bred and/or Maryland Million-nominated, 6f, 1:11.51, HEARTTHROBBIN', Hobbitontherocks, Call Me Clash, 4 started.

Mason Houghland Memorial Timber S., Percy Warner, May 12, $75,000, 4&up, a3mT, 6:33.80, IRISH PRINCE (NZ), Woodmont, Sharp Face, 10 started.

Massachusetts H., Suffolk Downs, Sept. 22, $500,000, 3&up, 1⅛m, 1:49.72, BRASS HAT, Fairbanks, Dr. Pleasure, 7 started.

Master Dad Starter H. (R), Turf Paradise, Feb. 13, $7,824, 4&up, starters for a claming price of $15,000 or less in 2006-'07, 6½f, 1:15.61, SPORTS TOUR, Skyline Trail, Fierce Cat, 4 started.

Mataji S., Calder Race Course, June 9, $43,650, 3&up, 1¼m, 2:06.49, TACIT AGREEMENT, Foreign Ruckus, Bucharest, 4 started.

Matchmaker S. (R), Lincoln State Fair, June 16, $20,800, 3&up, f&m, Nebraska-bred, 1m, 1:40.60, C. R. CHARMER, Scat's Princess, Whispering Hope, 7 started.

MATRIARCH S. (G1), Hollywood Park, Nov. 25, $500,000, 3&up, f&m, 1mT, 1:33.63, PRECIOUS KITTEN, Wait a While, Lady of Venice (Fr), 6 started.

Matron Breeders' Cup S., Assiniboia Downs, Sept. 22, $69,944, 3&up, f&m, 1⅛m, 1:53.60, POLYNESIAN KITTY, Spillway, Selita's Dream, 8 started.

Matron H., Evangeline Downs, Sept. 1, $96,000, 3&up, f&m, 1m, 1:38.27, MADISON'S MUSIC, Plaid, Delicate Dynamite, 5 started.

MATRON S. (G2), Belmont Park, Sept. 15, $250,000, 2yo, f, 7f, 1:24.20, PROUD SPELL, Armonk, Dagger, 7 started.

Matt Winn S., Churchill Downs, May 19, $108,500, 3yo, 6f, 1:08.30, SPIN MASTER, Demarcation, Run Alex Run, 6 started.

Maxxam Gold Cup H., Sam Houston Race Park, Jan. 27, $100,000, 4&up, 1⅛m, 1:51.89, STUDENT COUNCIL, Mr. Pursuit, Goosey Moose, 10 started.

MAZARINE BREEDERS' CUP S. (CAN-G3), Woodbine, Sept. 29, $248,358, 2yo, f, 1 1/16mAW, 1:46.49, OFFICER CHERRIE, Victory Romance, Born to Be, 5 started.

McAlester Casino S., Blue Ribbon Downs, Nov. 11, $15,550, 3&up, f&m, 5½f, 1:04.19, COME ON HELEN, Lucky Cutie, Roarin Heart, 8 started.

McFadden Memorial S. (R), Portland Meadows, March 26, $11,800, 3yo, c&g, Oregon-bred, 1 1/16m, 1:49.63, HE'SABIGTALKER, Red E to Go, La Ultima Cisco, 6 started.

MEADOWLANDS CUP S. (G2), Meadowlands, Oct. 5, $499,000, 3&up, 1⅛m, 1:48.36, DIAMOND STRIPES, Magna Graduate, Xchanger, 7 started.

Meafara S., Hawthorne Race Course, April 7, $47,700, 3yo, f, 6f, 1:12.62, ORANGE CRUSH, Rich N Clever, Missing Treasure, 6 started.

Mecke H., Calder Race Course, July 4, $100,000, 3&up, 1⅛m (originally scheduled on the turf), 1:51.49, ELECTRIFY, Cheiron, Golden Strategy, 9 started.

Melair S. (R), Hollywood Park, April 29, $200,000, 3yo, f, California-bred, 1 1/16mAW, 1:45.51, TIZ ELEMENTAL, Curiously Sweet, You Are the Answer, 10 started.

Mellow Roll S. (R), Aqueduct, Dec. 1, $80,000, 3&up, New York-bred, 1m70y, 1:42.16, WHO WHAT WIN, Run Red Run, Lord Langfuhr, 8 started.

Mel's Hope S., Calder Race Course, Dec. 9, $45,000, 3yo, 1 1/16mT, 1:41.88, MYSTERIOUS PEINTRE (FR), French Vintage, Fair Weather Stan, 10 started.

Melville Cup S., Melville District Agripar, Aug. 12, $1,661, 3&up, a1m, 1:46, SAND RUSH, Tough Topic, By Jasper, 5 started.

MEMORIAL DAY H. (G3), Calder Race Course, May 28, $100,000, 3&up, 1 1/16m, 1:46.41, DRY MARTINI, Rehoboth, Too Many Toyz, 8 started.

Memorial Day H., Mountaineer Race Track and Gaming Resort, May 28, $75,000, 3&up, 1mT, 1:34.11, PUPPETEER (GB), Muqbil, Otis Ridge, 10 started.

Merrillville S. (R), Hoosier Park, Oct. 20, $45,000, 3&up, f&m, Indiana-bred, 6f, 1:11.96, BASIN BANANNIE, Linda's Lace, Princess Composer, 9 started.

Merry Colleen S., Hawthorne Race Course, March 25, $47,700, 4&up, f&m, 1 1/16m, 1:47.86, TURBULENT THINKING, Coolwind, For Gillian, 6 started.

MERVIN H. MUNIZ JR. MEMORIAL H. (G2), Fair Grounds, March 10, $500,000, 4&up, a1⅛mT, 1:49.57, EINSTEIN (BRZ), Cloudy's Knight, Naissance Royale (Ire), 11 started.

Mervin Muniz Memorial Starter S. (R), Evangeline Downs, June 30, $45,000, 3&up, Louisiana-bred starters for a claiming price of $10,000 or less in 2006-'07, 1m70y, 1:44.51, TIGER MONARCH, I Nv Slew, Z Storm, 9 started.

MERVYN LEROY H. (G2), Hollywood Park, May 5, $150,000, 3&up, 1 1/16mAW, 1:42.86, MOLENGAO (BRZ), Porto Santo (Fr), Buzzards Bay, 8 started.

Mesa H., Turf Paradise, Dec. 15, $45,000, 3&up, f&m, 6½f, 1:15.88, BULLY BONES, Wild English Rose, Evening Escort, 7 started.

Methuselah Starter S. (R), Calder Race Course, July 28, $50,000, 5&up, starters for a claiming price of $16,000 or less in 2007 or eligible for a race other than maiden, claiming, or starter on May 1, 2007, 7f, 1:23.09, FIREBROOK, D. L. Renzo, Stormy Roman, 7 started.

METROPOLITAN H. (G1), Belmont Park, May 28, $600,000, 3&up, 1m, 1:34.77, CORINTHIAN, Political Force, Lawyer Ron, 9 started.

MIAMI MILE BREEDERS' CUP H. (G3), Calder Race Course, April 28, $105,000, 3&up, 1mT, 1:34.11, JET PROPULSION, Giant Wrecker, Paradise Dancer, 11 started.

Michael F. Rowland Memorial H. (R), Thistledown, June 1, $50,000, 3&up, Ohio-bred, 6f, 1:11.10, CATLAUNCH, Go Johnny Go, Alias's N Alibi's, 6 started.

Michael G. Schaefer Mile S., Hoosier Park, Oct. 6, $104,050, 3&up, 1m, 1:37.40, CASINO EVIL, Simon Pure, Unbridled Behavior, 9 started.

Michael G. Walsh Novice S. (R), Saratoga Race Course, Aug. 23, $67,900, 4&up, non-winners over hurdles prior to January 1, 2007, a2⅜mT, 4:40.78, PLANETS ALIGNED, Rum Squall, Gigger, 7 started.

Michigan Breeders' H. (R), Great Lakes Downs, July 24, $50,000, 3&up, Michigan-bred, 1 1/16m, 1:49.54, ROCKEM SOCKEM, Dorthys Champ, Demagoguery, 8 started.

Michigan Futurity (1st Div.) (R), Great Lakes Downs, Oct. 30, $50,000, 2yo, c&g, Michigan-bred, 7f, 1:30.37, BERRY'S PRIDE, Kick the Breeze, Bipolar Express, 7 started.

Racing — 2007 Stakes Races

Michigan Futurity (2nd Div.) (R), Great Lakes Downs, Oct. 30, $50,000, 2yo, c&g, Michigan-bred, 7f, 1:31.22, WITH WINGS, Dance in the Sea, Hot Chili, 7 started.

Michigan Juvenile Fillies S. (1st Div.) (R), Great Lakes Downs, Oct. 29, $50,000, 2yo, f, Michigan-bred, 7f, 1:32.24, CHERIES CHALLENGE, dh-Tillie the Hunn, dh-Run West, 7 started.

Michigan Juvenile Fillies S. (2nd Div.) (R), Great Lakes Downs, Oct. 29, $50,000, 2yo, f, Michigan-bred, 7f, 1:30.32, IRISH DATE, Clever Idea, Dancing Till Dawn, 7 started.

Michigan Oaks (R), Great Lakes Downs, Sept. 8, $50,000, 3yo, f, Michigan-bred, 1 1/16m, 1:53.57, VALLEY LOOT, Aultimate Reign, Seductiveenjoyment, 7 started.

Michigan Sire S. (R), Great Lakes Downs, Oct. 6, $124,633, 2yo, f, eligible for the Michigan sire stakes program, 6f, 1:14.35, EQUALITYSDEBUTANTE, Cheries Challenge, Shez Got Sisu, 9 started.

Michigan Sire S. (R), Great Lakes Downs, Oct. 6, $124,733, 4&up, f&m, eligible for the Michigan sire stakes program, 1 1/8m, 1:55.80, NELL'S ENJOYMENT, Half a Glance, Silent Sunset, 10 started.

Michigan Sire S. (R), Great Lakes Downs, Oct. 6, $124,833, 3yo, f, eligible for the Michigan sire stakes program, 1 1/16m, 1:49.90, VALLEY LOOT, Lets Get Creative, Seductiveenjoyment, 10 started.

Michigan Sire S. (R), Great Lakes Downs, Oct. 6, $125,033, 4&up, c&g, eligible for the Michigan sire stakes program, 1 1/8m, 1:54.78, MEADOW VESPERS, Rockem Sockem, Demagoguery, 10 started.

Michigan Sire S. (R), Great Lakes Downs, Oct. 6, $125,233, 2yo, c&g, eligible for the Michigan sire stakes program, 6f, 1:14.70, HOT CHILI, Native Britches, Bipolar Express, 9 started.

Michigan Sire S. (R), Great Lakes Downs, Oct. 6, $125,233, 3yo, c&g, eligible for the Michigan sire stakes program, 1 1/16m, 1:49.33, J. P'S BIG BOY, Scarlet Fact, My First Buck, 10 started.

Middleground Breeders' Cup S., Lone Star Park, July 29, $55,000, 2yo, c&g, 6f, 1:10.38, GOLD COYOTE, South Branch Storm, Possetothemax, 8 started.

MIESQUE S. (G3), Hollywood Park, Nov. 24, $113,200, 2yo, f, 1mT, 1:35.84, SEA CHANTER, Macellyra (Fr), dh-Set Play, dh-Golden Doc A, 11 started.

Mike Anderson Memorial Cup S. (R), Fort Erie, Aug. 6, $23,705, 3&up, f&m, starters for a claiming price of $10,000 or less in 2006-'07 and have started at Fort Erie three times in '07, 6f, 1:12.26, CUT THE MUSTARD, Streetwise, Blue Ridge Linda, 10 started.

Mike Lee S. (R), Belmont Park, June 24, $107,700, 3yo, New York-bred, 7f, 1:23.14, CHIEF'S LAKE, Stunt Man, Dr. V's Magic, 6 started.

MILADY BREEDERS' CUP H. (G2), Hollywood Park, June 3, $186,100, 3&up, f&m, 1 1/16mAW, 1:42.16, NASHOBA'S KEY, Hystericalady, Balance, 6 started.

Mile Hi H., Yavapai Downs, Aug. 26, $21,000, 3&up, 1 1/8m, 1:44.60, BIG ARCHIE, Hollywood Payday, Cat of Fifty Seven, 8 started.

Miles City Thoroughbred Maiden S., Cow Capital Turf Club, May 19, $3,000, 3&up, 5 1/2f, 1:12.20, SNOOKINS, Mill Valley Babe, Here Comes Rewards, 5 started.

Millard Harrell Memorial S. (R), Charles Town Races, Sept. 21, $51,050, 3yo, West Virginia-bred nominated to the West Virginia Breeders' Classic, 7f, 1:26.01, GOLD STANDARD, Fancy Dan, Blues in the Night, 8 started.

Millarville Derby, Millarville Race Society, July 1, $14,078, 3&up, 1 1/8m, 2:08.60, TATA PANTOJA, Simmering, Pakawalup, 6 started.

Miller Lite Cradle S., River Downs, Sept. 3, $200,000, 2yo, 1 1/16mT, 1:42.40, OLD MAN BUCK, Cherokee Triangle, Caberneigh, 10 started.

Milwaukee Avenue H. (R), Hawthorne Race Course, April 28, $102,375, 3&up, Illinois-conceived and/or -foaled, 1 1/16m, 1:44.36, WIGGINS, Air Academy, Infectious Spirit, 7 started.

Minaret S., Tampa Bay Downs, Jan. 6, $60,000, 4&up, f&m, 6f, 1:11.06, SUMMER CRUISE, Rgirldoesn'tbluff, Taylor Madison, 10 started.

MINESHAFT H. (G3), Fair Grounds, Feb. 10, $194,000, 4&up, 1 1/8m, 1:42.28, MASTER COMMAND, Patriot Act, Well Said, 6 started.

Minneapolis S., Canterbury Park, Sept. 3, $45,000, 3&up, 1m70y, 1:40.34, WAYZATA BAY, Tepexpan, Kingsfield, 9 started.

Minnesota Classic Championship S. (R), Canterbury Park, Aug. 19, $45,000, 3&up, Minnesota-bred, 1 1/16m, 1:45.50, TRICKYVILLE DEW, Rock' N Fire, Mack's Monarch, 8 started.

Minnesota Derby (R), Canterbury Park, July 28, $60,000, 3yo, c&g, Minnesota-bred, 1m70y, 1:42.57, PALM READER, Sul Lago, Jagan, 12 started.

Minnesota Distaff Classic Championship S. (R), Canterbury Park, Aug. 19, $45,000, 3&up, f&m, Minnesota-bred, 1 1/16m, 1:46.61, GLITTER STAR, Ma Home Cat, Heavens Work, 8 started.

Minnesota Distaff Sprint Championship S. (R), Canterbury Park, Aug. 19, $45,000, 3&up, f&m, Minnesota-bred, 6f, 1:12.24, SENTIMENTAL CHARM, Speed Wagon, Cant Catch Judy, 7 started.

Minnesota HBPA Mile S., Canterbury Park, June 16, $45,000, 3&up, f&m, 1mT, 1:35.91, TENS HOLY SPIRIT, On Safari, Kindling, 9 started.

Minnesota HBPA Sprint S., Canterbury Park, June 30, $45,000, 3&up, 6f, 1:08.92, LOOKINFORTHESECRET, Seneca Summer, Careless Navigator, 5 started.

Minnesota Oaks (R), Canterbury Park, July 28, $60,000, 3yo, f, Minnesota-bred, 1m70y, 1:43.49, RUN WITH JOY, Sucara, Seasahm, 10 started.

Minnesota Sprint Championship (R), Canterbury Park, Aug. 19, $45,000, 3&up, Minnesota-bred, 6f, 1:10.58, CARELESS NAVIGATOR, Vazandar, Sir Tricky, 9 started.

Minnesota Turf Championship S. (R), Canterbury Park, Aug. 19, $45,000, 3&up, Minnesota-bred, 1m (originally scheduled on the turf), 1:38.59, SMITHTOWN BAY, Chaska, Torpedo Man, 9 started.

Minstrel S., Louisiana Downs, July 14, $48,000, 2yo, 5f (originally scheduled on the turf), :59.37, PREACHIN MAN, Mr Bubba, Galiano, 5 started.

Minute Star Starter S. (R), Yavapai Downs, July 7, $6,700, 3&up, f&m, starters for a claiming price of $4,000 or less since July 7, 2006, 5 1/2f, 1:02.80, LIL CELESTE, Incredible You, Way Up There, 6 started.

Miracle Wood S., Laurel Park, Feb. 3, $50,900, 3yo, 1m, 1:38.55, CRAFTY BEAR, Saratoga Lulaby, Place Your Bet, 4 started.

Miss America S., Golden Gate Fields, Nov. 11, $73,500, 3&up, f&m, 1 1/8mAW, 1:52.03, NORTH BEACH, Round Trip Flight, Grat, 4 started.

Miss Gibson County S., Turf Paradise, Nov. 12, $30,700, 2yo, f, 6f, 1:09.74, LA MISMA, Respecttheofficer, Benchmark's Bounty, 7 started.

Miss Grillo S., Belmont Park, Sept. 30, $81,900, 2yo, f, 1 1/16mT, 1:40.49, NAMASTE'S WISH, Sea Chanter, Remarkable Remy, 7 started.

Miss Indiana S. (R), Hoosier Park, Nov. 9, $45,000, 2yo, f, Indiana-bred, 6f, 1:14.69, LIL MAI TAI, Ring Ring Ring, Rachel Wiggles, 8 started.

Miss Kansas City S., The Woodlands, Oct. 20, $20,000, 3&up, f&m, 1 1/16m, 1:47.60, ON SAFARI, Sinister Sister, Joyce G, 6 started.

Miss Liberty S., Monmouth Park, July 6, $65,000, 3&up, f&m, 1m70y, 1:39.95, INDIA, Altesse, Victory Pool, 5 started.

Miss Ohio S. (R), Thistledown, Aug. 25, $50,000, 2yo, f, Ohio-bred, 6f, 1:12.34, PYRITEVILLE, Nakagawa, Pyrite Gem, 9 started.

Miss Power Puff S., Hawthorne Race Course, Nov. 17, $47,750, 2yo, f, 6f, 1:12.10, LA WILDCAT, Bamboo, Capricious, 7 started.

Miss Woodford S., Monmouth Park, Oct. 27, $200,000, 3yo, f, 1 1/16m, 1:09.15, COCO BELLE, Intentional Fever, Control System, 12 started.

Mister Diz S. (R), Laurel Park, Sept. 8, $50,000, 3&up, Maryland-bred, 5 1/2fT, 1:01.05 (NCR), TOMMIE'S STAR, Hands On, Whata Monster, 7 started.

Mister Gus S., Arlington Park, June 3, $46,650, 3&up, 1mT, 1:37.88, TIGANELLO (GER), Rapid Proof, Come On Jazz, 5 started.

Mo Bay S., Delaware Park, July 7, $60,100, 3&up, a5fT, :56.72, HESA BIG STAR, Mr Mutter, Sandys Gold, 7 started.

Moccasin S., Hollywood Park, Nov. 11, $108,100, 2yo, f, 7fAW, 1:21.38, SPRING AWAKENING, Sindy Jacobson, The Golden Noodle, 7 started.

MODESTY H. (G3), Arlington Park, July 21, $150,000, 3&up, f&m, 1 3/16mT, 1:54.62, BRIDGE GAME, Jennie R., Rich in Spirit, 8 started.

Mohawk H. (R), Belmont Park, Oct. 20, $150,000, 3&up, New York-bred, 1 1/8mT, 1:53.73, AL BASHA, Spurred, Gimme Credit, 9 started.

Molly Brown S., Arapahoe Park, June 17, $27,200, 3&up, f&m, 6f, 1:09.81, LADYSGOTTHELOOKS, Vannacide, Patches of Speed, 6 started.

MOLLY PITCHER BREEDERS' CUP H. (G2), Monmouth Park, Aug. 25, $280,000, 3&up, f&m, 1 1/16m, 1:41.85, HYSTERICALADY, Lexi Star, India, 7 started.

Mongo Queen S., Monmouth Park, Aug. 29, $75,000, 3yo, f, 6f, 1:09.34, PRINCESS JANIE, Astor Park, Bianco, 6 started.

Monmouth Beach S., Monmouth Park, May 19, $60,000, 3&up, f&m, 1m, 1:36.31, MAIZELLE, Prop Me Up, Promenade Girl, 7 started.
MONMOUTH BREEDERS' CUP OAKS (G3), Monmouth Park, Aug. 12, $200,000, 3yo, f, 1¹⁄₁₆m, 1:43.78, TALKIN ABOUT LOVE, Scooter Girl, Lady Marlboro, 6 started.
Monmouth University S., Monmouth Park, Oct. 25, $109,300, 3&up, 5½f (originally scheduled on the turf), 1:03.87, FOREST PARK, Joey P., Charley's Diamond, 7 started.
MONROVIA H. (G3), Santa Anita Park, Jan. 1, $116,100, 4&up, f&m, a6½fT, 1:12.85, SOCIETY HOSTESS, Clinet (Ire), Kitty Hawk (GB), 12 started.
Montauk H. (R), Aqueduct, Nov. 25, $84,325, 3&up, f&m, New York-bred, 1¹⁄₈m, 1:53.53, ICE COOL KITTY, Scatkey, Borrowing Base, 9 started.
Montclair State University S., Meadowlands, Nov. 10, $69,000, 3&up, f&m, 6f, 1:09.97, PURE DISCO, Lakes Tune, Solarana (Arg), 4 started.
Monterey H., Bay Meadows Race Course, April 21, $52,300, 4&up, f&m, 5fT, :56.72, STYLISH WILDCAT, Vaca City Flyer, Calamity Girl, 7 started.
Moonbeam H. (R), Great Lakes Downs, July 21, $50,000, 3&up, f&m, Michigan-bred, 1m, 1:44.32, HALF A GLANCE, Silent Sunset, Deb's Favoite Gift, 9 started.
More Than Ready S., Belmont Park, Sept. 12, $75,250, 3yo, 1m, 1:35, STUNT MAN, Tiz Wonderful, Flashstorm, 4 started.
MORVICH H. (G3), Oak Tree at Santa Anita, Oct. 27, $110,000, 3&up, a6½fT, 1:13.23, GET FUNKY, Relato Del Gato, Becrux (Ity), 8 started.
MOTHER GOOSE S. (G1), Belmont Park, June 30, $237,500, 3yo, f, 1¹⁄₈m, 1:47.19, OCTAVE, Lady Joanne, Boca Grande, 4 started.
Motivo S., Yavapai Downs, June 2, $11,400, 3&up, 4½f, :49 (NTR), KING JUSTIN, Girvan, Mining Gold, 5 started.
Mountaineer Juvenile Fillies S., Mountaineer Race Track and Gaming Resort, Aug. 4, $85,000, 2yo, f, 6f, 1:12.78, ELOCUTION, La Wildcat, Hurricane Bernie, 9 started.
Mountaineer Juvenile S., Mountaineer Race Track and Gaming Resort, Aug. 4, $85,000, 2yo, 6f, 1:12.54, CRACKALACKIN, Preachin Man, Robbing the Bank, 10 started.
Mountaineer Mile H., Mountaineer Race Track and Gaming Resort, Nov. 10, $125,000, 3&up, 1m, 1:41.50, BERNIE BLUE, M B Sea, Real Dandy, 5 started.
Mountain State S., Mountaineer Race Track and Gaming Resort, July 3, $75,000, 3&up, 5½f, 1:04.32, BERNIE BLUE, Cognac Kisses, Lucky Express, 7 started.
Mountain Valley S., Oaklawn Park, Feb. 24, $50,000, 3yo, 6f, 1:11.69, SIR FIVE STAR, Irish Dreamer, The Hitman, 6 started.
Mount Elbert S. (R), Arapahoe Park, July 23, $35,150, 3&up, c&g, Colorado-bred, 1¹⁄₁₆m, 1:45.79, CUT OF MUSIC, Haxtun's Hustler, One Pit Wonder, 5 started.
Mount Royal H., Stampede Park, May 6, $47,854, 3yo, f, 6f, 1:10, CALENDAR GIRL, Tanika, Iron Resolve, 8 started.
Mount Vernon H. (R), Belmont Park, June 10, $109,800, 3&up, f&m, New York-bred, 1¹⁄₁₆mT, 1:48.66, FACTUAL CONTENDER, Half Heaven, Latitude Forty, 6 started.
M. R. Jenkins Memorial H., Stampede Park, April 29, $44,805, 4&up, f&m, 6f, 1:10.60, SHE'S ITALIAN, Pretty Beaucat, Banjo Babe, 10 started.
MR. PROSPECTOR H. (G3), Gulfstream Park, Jan. 6, $100,000, 4&up, 6f, 1:08.84, KELLY'S LANDING, High Finance, Mach Ride, 6 started.
Mr. Prospector S., Monmouth Park, July 7, $65,000, 3&up, 6f, 1:08.52, HERECOMESHOLLYWOOD, Suave Jazz, War Tempo, 6 started.
Mrs. Penny S. (R), Philadelphia Park, July 28, $100,000, 3&up, f&m, Pennsylvania-bred, 1¹⁄₁₆mT, 1:43.04, REDASPEN, Royal Pleasure, Jet Away Jane, 10 started.
MRS. REVERE S. (G2), Churchill Downs, Nov. 10, $174,900, 3yo, f, 1¹⁄₁₆mT, 1:43.16, BIT OF WHIMSY, Ciao, Cat Charmer, 11 started.
Ms Brookski S., Calder Race Course, July 8, $50,000, 3&up, f&m, 1m, 1:40.30, MIA'S REFLECTION, Running Lass, Kicks, 7 started.
Ms., Portland Meadows, Jan. 28, $20,524, 3yo, f, 6f, 1:15.28, SILVER PATRONA, Little Cascadian, Bagels Baby, 4 started.
MTA Stallion Auction Laddie S. (R), Canterbury Park, Sept. 1, $45,000, 3&up, progeny of stallion seasons sold at the MTA auction, 6½f, 1:16.66, GHAZI UP, Bee O Bee Bob, Dakota Hills, 8 started.
MTA Stallion Auction Lassie S. (R), Canterbury Park, Sept. 1, $45,000, 3yo, f, progeny of stallion seasons sold at the MTA auction, 6½f, 1:16.18, THANKS FOR THE TIP, Beyond the Reach, Cant Catch Judy, 8 started.

Mt. Cristo Rey H. (R), Sunland Park, April 8, $100,000, 3&up, New Mexico-bred, 4½f, :50.44, HECAMEFROMACLAIM, Gulchrunssweet, Values of the Hunt, 10 started.
Mt. Hood S., Portland Meadows, Oct. 29, $21,950, 3yo, 1m70y, 1:44.52, ROCKINSTOMPER, Mystic Wood, Millers Charm, 8 started.
Mt. Rainier H., Emerald Downs, July 29, $68,125, 3&up, 1¹⁄₈m, 1:47.40, THE GREAT FACE, Don'twritemeoff, Schoolin You, 10 started.
Mt. Sassafras S. (R), Woodbine, Nov. 7, $76,388, 3&up, Ontario-foaled, 7fAW, 1:22.63, SAIL FROM SEATTLE, Dancer's Bajan, Just Rushing, 4 started.
Muckleshoot Tribal Classic S. (R), Emerald Downs, Sept. 16, $50,000, 3&up, Washington-bred, 1¹⁄₁₆m, 1:41.80, EXCLUSIVE EAGLE, Norm's Nephew, Wasserman, 6 started.
Muir Woods S., Golden Gate Fields, Jan. 6, $59,175, 4&up, f&m, 1¹⁄₁₆m, 1:42.71, BAI AND BAI, Victorina, Codi Dee, 6 started.
Murmur Farm Starter H. (R), Pimlico Race Course, May 19, $50,000, 3&up, Maryland Million-nominated starters for a claiming price of $16,000 or less since May 20, 2006, 1¹⁄₁₆m, 1:45.43, FIRE HERO, Ensee, Boogyman, 11 started.
Muscogee Nation S. (R), Fair Meadows at Tulsa, June 30, $45,000, 3&up, f&m, Oklahoma-bred, 5½f, 1:05.80, ZIPPIE OKIE, Red Mint Julep, Shari Bank, 10 started.
Muskoka S. (R), Woodbine, Sept. 3, $120,635, 2yo, f, Canadian-bred, 7fAW, 1:23.94, SIMPLE SISTER, Six Pack Sammy, Executrix, 11 started.
MY CHARMER H. (G3), Calder Race Course, Dec. 1, $100,000, 3&up, f&m, 1¹⁄₈mT, 1:48.93, J'RAY, Bayou's Lassie, Redaspen, 9 started.
My Charmer S., Turfway Park, Dec. 8, $50,000, 3&up, f&m, 1¹⁄₁₆mAW, 1:43.34, HALF HEAVEN, Marquee Delivery, April Frost, 10 started.
My Dandy Texas Stallion S. (R), Retama Park, Oct. 13, $125,000, 2yo, c&g, progeny of eligible Texas stallions, 6f, 1:10.77, FERDINAND'S FLYER, Namesake, Stormy Wedding, 11 started.
My Dear Girl S. (R), Calder Race Course, Oct. 13, $400,000, 2yo, f, progeny of stallions standing in Florida, 1¹⁄₁₆m, 1:48.49, CALICO BAY, Silk Ridge, Awesome Dreamer, 9 started.
My Dear S., Woodbine, July 2, $119,847, 2yo, f, 5fAW, :57.53, DANCING ALLSTAR, Sky Mom, Sarcasm, 8 started.
My Frenchman S., Monmouth Park, Aug. 11, $58,200, 3&up, 5½f (originally scheduled on the turf), 1:03.04, SAFE PLAY, John's Pic, River City Rebel, 3 started.
My Juliet S., Philadelphia Park, Sept. 29, $260,000, 3&up, f&m, 6f, 1:09.96, SPEECHIFYING, Miraculous Miss, S W Aly'svalentine, 6 started.
My Lady's Manor Timber S., Monkton, April 14, $30,000, 5&up, a3mT, 6:26.75, FAPPA FIRE, Bubble Economy, Mr Bombastic (Ger), 9 started.
My Old Kentucky Home S., Calder Race Course, May 5, $45,000, 3&up, 1¹⁄₄m, 2:07.47, TACIT AGREEMENT, A. J. Melini, Texas Red, 7 started.
Mystery Jet S. (R), Suffolk Downs, June 23, $44,100, 3yo, f, Massachusetts-bred, 6f, 1:15.01, LILY'S GOLDMINE, Mary Ann's Jet, Bright Tomorrows, 5 started.
My Trusty Cat S., Delta Downs, Nov. 9, $100,000, 2yo, f, 7f, 1:27.07, MISS MISSILE, Diamondaire, Madonna Mia, 9 started.
Naked Greed S., Calder Race Course, April 29, $43,650, 3yo, 6f, 1:12.10, DOUBLE COLICO, Pop Goes the Tiger, James Wilfred, 4 started.
Nancy's Glitter H., Calder Race Course, July 21, $90,000, 3&up, f&m, 1¹⁄₁₆m, 1:46.70, CAT CAN DO, Mia's Reflection, Gadolinium, 9 started.
Nandi S. (R), Woodbine, Aug. 4, $120,042, 2yo, f, Ontario-foaled, 6fAW, 1:12.31, EXECUTRIX, Dancing Doris, Do It Anyway, 9 started.
Nany S. (R), Belmont Park, July 14, $74,750, 3yo, f, non-winners of an open stakes in 2007, 7f, 1:23.36, OFFICER IN PURSUIT, Street Sass, Debbie Got Even, 5 started.
NASHUA S. (G3), Aqueduct, Oct. 28, $105,800, 2yo, 1m, 1:36.96, ETCHED, Anak Nakal, Anakim, 5 started.
Naskra's Breeze S. (R), Belmont Park, July 12, $77,750, 4&up, New York-bred, 1¹⁄₁₆mT, 1:43.99, FOREVERNESS, Dave, Sabellina, 7 started.
NASSAU COUNTY BREEDERS' CUP S. (G2), Belmont Park, May 5, $196,600, 3yo, f, 7f, 1:22.04, DREAM RUSH, Lady Marlboro, Changeisgonnacome, 5 started.
NASSAU S. (CAN-G2), Woodbine, June 2, $317,273, 3&up, f&m, 1¹⁄₈mT, 1:39.90, STRIKE SOFTLY, May Night, Essential Edge, 8 started.
NATALMA S. (Can-G3), Woodbine, Sept. 9, $153,625, 2yo, f, 1mT, 1:36.12, CLEARLY FOXY, Nite in Rome, Lickety Lemon, 10 started.
NATC Futurity (R), Meadowlands, Sept. 29, $194,000, 2yo, f, cata-

loged during 2007 and paid '07 advertising fund fee, 6f, 1:09.02, PHANTOM INCOME, New York City Girl, La Wildcat, 7 started.

NATC Futurity (R), Meadowlands, Sept. 29, $198,000, 2yo, c&g, cataloged during 2007 and paid '07 advertising fund fee, 6f, 1:09.80, PREACHIN MAN, Cobra Strike, Indy Joe, 9 started.

National Hunt Cup Hurdle S. (R), Malvern, May 19, $75,000, 4&up, non-winners over hurdles prior to March 1, 2006, a2⅜mT, 4:36.20 (NCR), BEST ATTACK, Orison, Orsay, 7 started.

NATIONAL JOCKEY CLUB H. (G3), Hawthorne Race Course, April 21, $250,000, 3&up, 1⅛m, 1:49.47, MASTER COMMAND, Sweetnorthernsaint, Le Jester, 4 started.

NATIONAL MUSEUM OF RACING HALL OF FAME S. (G2), Saratoga Race Course, Aug. 6, $158,000, 3yo, 1⅛mT, 1:49.29, NOBIZ LIKE SHOBIZ, Marcavelly, Distorted Reality, 6 started.

National Sporting Library Chronicle Cup Timber S., Middleburg, Oct. 6, $32,550, 4&up, a3mT, 7:08.80, FIELDS OF OMAGH, Noble Bob, Navesink View, 4 started.

National Treasure S., Aqueduct, March 25, $66,750, 3yo, f, 1m70y, 1:43.85, OFFICER IN PURSUIT, Greenstreet, Sister Desiree, 7 started.

Native Dancer S., Arlington Park, June 24, $47,300, 3yo, 1$\frac{1}{16}$mAW, 1:43.81, SNOWBLIND FRIEND, Galloping Home, Harrow Land, 6 started.

Native Dancer S., Laurel Park, Jan. 13, $62,200, 4&up, 1m, 1:36.43, JUDITHS WILD RUSH, Your Bluffing, Easy Red, 9 started.

NATIVE DIVER H. (G3), Hollywood Park, Dec. 8, $111,800, 3&up, 1⅛mAW, 1:47.23 (NTR), HEATSEEKER (IRE), Racketeer, Isipingo, 10 started.

Navajo Princess S., Meadowlands, Sept. 8, $60,000, 3&up, f&m, 1mT, 1:35.52, BEAUTIFUL DANIELE, Naissance Royale (Ire), Rasta Farian, 6 started.

NEARCTIC S. (CAN-G2), Woodbine, Oct. 21, $518,942, 3&up, 6fT, 1:08.04, HEROS REWARD, Quietly Mine, Smart Enough, 8 started.

Need for Speed S., Evangeline Downs, June 2, $49,000, 3&up, 5f, :57.43, JIMMY'S BOY, Heza Hot Cat, Sabio, 7 started.

Needles S., Calder Race Course, Sept. 22, $100,000, 3yo, 1$\frac{1}{16}$mT, 1:43.03, FAIR WEATHER STAN, Fearless Eagle, Imawildandcrazyguy, 12 started.

Nellie Morse S., Laurel Park, Jan. 27, $91,400, 4&up, f&m, 1m, 1:38.75, LEXI STAR, It's True Love, Yolanda B. Too, 8 started.

Nepal H. (R), Philadelphia Park, July 28, $100,000, 3&up, progeny of eligible Pennsylvania stallions, 1$\frac{1}{16}$mT, 1:42.94, HISSOUTHERNMAJESTY, R. Earl, Inapinch, 10 started.

NETJETS BREEDERS' CUP MILE (G1), Monmouth Park, Oct. 27, $2,409,080, 3&up, 1mT, 1:39.78, KIP DEVILLE, Excellent Art (GB), Cosmonaut, 13 started.

Nevill/Kyocera S., Lone Star Park, June 23, $50,000, 3&up, f&m, 5fT, :57, INDIAN BREEZE, Seneca Song, Most Beautiful, 8 started.

New Braunfels S., Retama Park, Oct. 6, $45,000, 3&up, f&m, 6f, 1:09.85, VALID LIL, Fresa Margarita, Gleaming Elegance, 7 started.

New Jersey Futurity (R), Meadowlands, Nov. 9, $53,121, 2yo, f, New Jersey-bred, 6f, 1:09.74, LOVE FOR NOT, Sister Shockey, Sammy Van Ammy, 6 started.

New Jersey Futurity (R), Meadowlands, Nov. 9, $57,333, 2yo, c&g, New Jersey-bred, 6f, 1:10.97, ROUGH ROAD AHEAD, Hop Skip and Away, Primal Impact, 6 started.

New Jersey Hunt Cup S., Far Hills, Oct. 20, $44,000, 4&up, a3¼mT, 7:39.40, IRISH PRINCE (NZ), Hot Springs, Erin Go Bragh (NZ), 5 started.

New Mexico Breeders' Association H. (R), SunRay Park, May 20, $80,200, 3&up, New Mexico-bred, 1m, 1:37.60, MIDNITE PROSPECTOR, Captain Cooper, Boom Boom, 7 started.

New Mexico Breeders' Derby (R), Sunland Park, March 18, $100,000, 3yo, New Mexico-bred, 1m, 1:41.04, GENES BOY, Z Z Dome, Shaken the Cage, 12 started.

New Mexico Cup Championship Fillies and Mares S. (R), Zia Park, Nov. 11, $182,460, 3&up, f&m, New Mexico-bred, 6f, 1:10.60, PEPPERS PRIDE, Hang Glide, Let the Musicbegin, 10 started.

New Mexico Cup Championship Fillies S. (R), Zia Park, Nov. 11, $151,460, 3yo, f, New Mexico-bred, 6f, 1:10.40, GOOD LOOKER R F, Shezapirate, Silver Expression, 10 started.

New Mexico Cup Classic Championship Colts and Geldings S. (R), Zia Park, Nov. 11, $153,890, 3yo, c&g, New Mexico-bred, 6f, 1:11.20, Z Z DOME, Blazing Rockstar, Key's Band, 12 started.

New Mexico Cup Classic Championship Sprint S. (R), Zia Park, Nov. 11, $183,175, 3&up, New Mexico-bred, 6f, 1:11, HIGHLAND'S BEST, Rocky Gulch, Alex's Ragtimeband, 11 started.

New Mexico Cup Classic Championship S. (R), Zia Park, Nov. 11, $190,245, 3&up, New Mexico-bred, 1m, 1:38.20, SOME GHOST, Spelling Bee Jones, Romeos Wilson, 9 started.

New Mexico Cup Classic Juvenile Colt and Geldings S. (R), Zia Park, Nov. 11, $153,891, 2yo, New Mexico-bred, 6f, 1:10.60, RUN LIKE FIRE, Our Choice, Playingwithchimes, 12 started.

New Mexico Cup Classic Juvenile Fillies S. (R), Zia Park, Nov. 11, $153,890, 2yo, f, New Mexico-bred, 6f, 1:10.20, ETOILE DE DOME, One Bad Ghost, Red Peaches, 12 started.

New Mexico Distaff H. (R), SunRay Park, May 12, $79,600, 3&up, f&m, New Mexico-bred, 6½f, 1:17.40, PEPPERS PRIDE, Skirt Alert, La Mamie, 7 started.

New Mexico State Fair H., The Downs at Albuquerque, Sept. 23, $75,000, 3&up, 1⅛m, 1:51.73, ROLLICKING CALLER, Don't Strike Out, A Gallant Discover, 8 started.

New Mexico State Fair Thoroughbred Breeders' Derby (R), The Downs at Albuquerque, Sept. 22, $50,000, 3yo, New Mexico-bred, 1$\frac{1}{16}$m, 1:49.05, IRISH GLASS, I B Six, She's Long Gone, 6 started.

New Mexico State Racing Commission H. (R), Sunland Park, Dec. 16, $125,000, 3&up, f&m, New Mexico-bred, 6f, 1:10.24, PEPPERS PRIDE, Hollywood Gone, Hang Glide, 6 started.

New Mexico State University H. (R), Sunland Park, March 3, $125,000, 4&up, New Mexico-bred, 1m, 1:37.28, ROCKY GULCH, Some Ghost, Fullofenergy, 12 started.

NEW ORLEANS H. (G2), Fair Grounds, March 10, $485,000, 4&up, 1⅛m, 1:49.89, MASTER COMMAND, Patriot Act, Smokeyjonessutton, 6 started.

New Providence S. (R), Woodbine, May 12, $114,186, 3&up, Ontario-foaled, 6fAW, 1:11.10, DAVE THE KNAVE, Marco Be Good, Bold Thing, 10 started.

New Westminster H., Hastings Race Course, Aug. 26, $52,536, 2yo, 6½f, 1:18.09, STAR PROSPECTOR, Call Me Tomorrow, Freequartersmine, 8 started.

New Year's Eve S., Mountaineer Race Track and Gaming Resort, Dec. 30, $75,000, 3&up, f&m, 6f, 1:10.37, COUNTRY DIVA, La Chica Rica, Roving Angel, 12 started.

New York Breeders' Futurity (R), Finger Lakes Gaming and Race Track, Oct. 6, $269,200, 2yo, New York-bred, 6f, 1:10.35, BY THE LIGHT, Law Enforcement, Canadian Ballet, 7 started.

New York Derby (R), Finger Lakes Gaming and Race Track, July 14, $163,000, 3yo, New York-bred, 1$\frac{1}{16}$m, 1:44.54, CHIEF'S LAKE, Berry Bound, Stunt Man, 9 started.

New York New York S. (R), Calder Race Course, June 9, $50,000, 3&up, non-winners of two races other than maiden, claiming, or starter as of April 20, 2007 or $25,000 claiming or starters for $16,000 or less in 2006-'07, 1½m, 2:36.25, FAMOUS FROLIC, Mean Kisser, Kristali, 8 started.

New York Oaks (R), Finger Lakes Gaming and Race Track, Sept. 2, $75,000, 3yo, f, New York-bred, 1$\frac{1}{16}$m, 1:44.09, TALKING TREASURE, My Kitty, Laurentide Ice, 5 started.

NEW YORK S. (G2), Belmont Park, June 23, $190,000, 3&up, f&m, 1¼mT, 2:00.07, MAKDERAH (IRE), Masseuse, Hostess, 6 started.

New York Turf Writers' Cup Steeplechase H., Saratoga Race Course, Aug. 30, $160,800, 4&up, a2⅝mT, 4:33.01, FOOTLIGHTS, Underbidder, The Looper, 8 started.

NEXT MOVE H. (G3), Aqueduct, March 31, $104,800, 3&up, f&m, 1⅛m, 1:50.51, INDIAN VALE, A True Pussycat, Daytime Promise, 5 started.

Niagara S. (R), Finger Lakes Gaming and Race Track, July 14, $50,000, 3yo, f, New York-bred, 6f, 1:10.94, COOL PARADIGM, Talking Treasure, Klassic Kayla, 4 started.

Nick Shuk Memorial S., Delaware Park, Aug. 4, $75,900, 3yo, 1$\frac{1}{16}$mT, 1:42.89, STARVINSKY, Dinner in Odem, Discreet Charmer, 8 started.

Nicole's Dream S., Arlington Park, Aug. 11, $47,750, 3&up, f&m, 5½fT, 1:04.50, TAX REFUND, Bluesbdancing, Ready to Talk, 8 started.

NIJINSKY S. (CAN-G2), Woodbine, Aug. 26, $285,880, 3&up, 1½mT, 2:31.25, LAST ANSWER, Cloudy's Knight, Sky Conqueror, 7 started.

NOBLE DAMSEL H. (G3), Belmont Park, Sept. 15, $113,500, 3&up, f&m, 1mT, 1:34.82, DANCE AWAY CAPOTE, Fantastic Shirl, Pommes Frites, 10 started.

Noble Robyn S., Calder Race Course, July 21, $50,000, 3yo, f, 1$\frac{1}{16}$mT, 1:41.83, MARISTA, Sweet Exchange, Cozzi Capital, 5 started.

Noel Laing Hurdle S., Montpelier, Nov. 3, $35,000, 4&up, a2½mT, 5:12.80, MON VILLEZ (FR), Gliding (NZ), Preemptive Strike, 8 started.

No Le Hace S., Retama Park, Nov. 17, $45,000, 3&up, 7½fT, 1:28.95, MAN NAMED SUE, Smooth Bid, Goosey Moose, 9 started.

NORFOLK S. (G1), Oak Tree at Santa Anita, Sept. 30, $250,000, 2yo,

1¹⁄₁₆mAW, 1:42.64, DIXIE CHATTER, Salute the Sarge, Shore Do, 9 started.
Norgor Derby, Ruidoso Downs, May 27, $40,000, 3yo, 6f, 1:10.40, HUNTERS WINE, Where's the Dough, Topper Power, 8 started.
Norman Hall S. (R) Suffolk Downs, Nov. 10, $45,000, 2yo, Massachusetts-bred, 6f, 1:14.37, SULTAN'S PRINCE, For Charlie G, Merrimack Pat, 7 started.
Northbound Pride S., Canterbury Park, June 23, $45,000, 3yo, f, a1mT, 1:36.66, LEMONLIME, Angel Smoke, Demon's Storm, 8 started.
North Dakota-Bred Thoroughbred Derby (R), North Dakota Horse Park, Sept. 3, $19,623, 3yo, North Dakota-bred, 1m, 1:43.40, AFERDS CODE RED, Tater Patch, Sunny Daze, 5 started.
North Dakota Derby (R), Assiniboia Downs, July 1, $15,500, 3yo, North Dakota-bred, 1m, 1:44.20, AFERDS CODE RED, Kravin a Win, Key Motion, 10 started.
North Dakota Futurity (R), Assiniboia Downs, Sept. 2, $16,476, 2yo, North Dakota-bred, 6f, 1:15.80, GIVEM HELL HARLEY, Beaver Lakes Best, Lil Bit of Freedom, 4 started.
North Dakota Stallion S. (R), Assiniboia Downs, July 28, $16,482, 3yo, eligible through the North Dakota Thoroughbred Association, 1m, 1:42.20, SUPER DUPER ME, Key Motion, Smart Miss, 10 started.
North Dakota Thoroughbred Futurity, North Dakota Horse Park, Aug. 25, $8,148, 2yo, 6f, 1:17, STORMY MARKET, Wizard of Ghaz, On to Khatef, 4 started.
North Dakota Thoroughbred S. (R), North Dakota Horse Park, Aug. 19, $12,600, 3&up, North Dakota-bred, 1¹⁄₁₆m, 1:50, TIGER JET, Maddies Blues, High Class Lad, 5 started.
NORTHERN DANCER BREEDERS' CUP TURF S. (CAN-G2), Woodbine, July 22, $666,013, 3&up, 1½mT, 2:27.45, SKY CONQUEROR, Marsh Side, Jambalaya, 8 started.
NORTHERN DANCER S. (G3), Churchill Downs, June 16, $223,800, 3yo, 1¹⁄₁₆m, 1:42.46, CHELOKEE, Zanjero, Sam P, 8 started.
Northern Dancer S. (R), Laurel Park, Nov. 3, $50,000, 3yo, Marylandbred, 1¹⁄₁₆m, 1:50.81, DIGGER, P V Lightening, Silent Assassin, 5 started.
Northern Fling H. Philadelphia Park, July 28, $100,000, 3&up, f&m, progeny of eligible Pennsylvania stallions, 1¹⁄₁₆m, 1:43.91, RAGING RAPIDS, Who's Happy, J. D. Safari, 6 started.
Northern Lights Debutante S. (R), Canterbury Park, Aug. 19, $55,000, 2yo, f, Minnesota-bred, 6f, 1:11.37, A. J. BAKES, Marina Nolan, Pretty as a Smile, 8 started.
Northern Lights Futurity (R), Canterbury Park, Aug. 19, $55,000, 2yo, Minnesota-bred, 6f, 1:13.45, WILD SHIFTER, B. B. Hill, Dazling Danni, 10 started.
Northern Spur Breeders' Cup S., Oaklawn Park, April 14, $99,250, 3yo, 1m, 1:38.82, TAKEDOWN, Harrow Land, Speedway, 8 started.
Northlands Oaks, Northlands Park, July 21, $95,390, 3yo, f, 1¹⁄₁₆m, 1:43.40 TANIKA, Calendar Girl, Zaylaway, 5 started.
Northlands Park Three-Year-Old Filly Sales S. (R), Northlands Park, Sept. 7, $46,555, 3yo, f, Canadian-bred sold at a CTHS sale, 1m, 1:42, MINIMUS, Bear Nobility, Apilonia, 5 started.
Northlands Park Three-Year-Old Sales S. (R), Northlands Park, Sept. 9, $46,467, 3yo, c&g, Canadian-bred sold at a CTHS sale, 1m, 1:39.60, KADENCE, Howsitgoinghotshot, Hurricane Tiki, 6 started.
Northlands Park Two-Year-Old Filly Sales S. (R), Northlands Park, Aug. 18, $55,407, 2yo, f, Canadian-bred sold at the CTHS sale, 6½f, 1:19.20, VICTORY ROMANCE, Bears Artiste, Heidi's Rosette, 6 started.
Northlands Park Two-Year-Old Sales S. (R), Northlands Park, Aug. 18, $55,407, 2yo, c&g, Canadian-bred sold at the CTHS sale, 6½f, 1:18, BRAZEN SON, Mandarin, I'm the Guy, 7 started.
Northview Stallion Station S. (R), Pimlico Race Course, April 21, $88,000, 3&up, f&m, Maryland-bred and/or Maryland Millionnominated, 1¹⁄₁₆m, 1:43.96, MY GIRLIE, Silmaril, Take a Check, 5 started.
Notoriety S., Belmont Park, June 17, $70,200, 4&up, 7fT, 1:20.71, GIMME CREDIT, First Word, Defer, 8 started.
No Winking S., Calder Race Course, June 16, $45,000, 3&up, f&m, 5f, :58.76, SHESGOLDINCOLOR, Flying Circle, True and True, 7 started.
NTRA S. (R), Hollywood Park, April 29, $63,600, 3&up, Californiabred maidens, 6½fAW, 1:17.73, SCANDALOUS, Vice Admiral, Abandoneer, 14 started.
Oak Hall S., Evangeline Downs, July 21, $48,500, 3&up, 7f, 1:23.90, HE'S ROYAL DEE, Watchem Smokey, Marion's Man, 6 started.
Oakland S., Golden Gate Fields, April 29, $51,775, 3&up, 6f, 1:08.96, TRICKEY TREVOR, The Pharaoh, Court's in Session, 8 started.

OAKLAWN H. (G2), Oaklawn Park, April 7, $500,000, 4&up, 1¹⁄₁₆m, 1:49, LAWYER RON, Brother Bobby, Boboman, 7 started.
OAK LEAF S. (G1), Oak Tree at Santa Anita, Sept. 29, $244,000, 2yo, f, 1¹⁄₁₆mAW, 1:42.91, CRY AND CATCH ME, Izarra, Runforthemoneybaby, 10 started.
OAK TREE DERBY (G2), Oak Tree at Santa Anita, Oct. 13, $150,000, 3yo, 1¹⁄₈mT, 1:46.40, DAYTONA (IRE), Ten a Penny, Stoneside (Ire), 10 started.
OAK TREE MILE S. (G2), Oak Tree at Santa Anita, Oct. 7, $252,000, 3&up, 1mT, 1:34.16, OUT OF CONTROL (BRZ), Zann, Courtnall, 6 started.
Obeah H., Delaware Park, June 16, $101,800, 3&up, f&m, 1⅛m, 1:49.38, PEAK MARIA'S WAY, Unbridled Belle, Lila Paige, 11 started.
Ocala Breeders' Sales Championship S. (R), Ocala Training Center, Feb. 12, $100,000, 3yo, c&g, sold at an OBS sale, 1¹⁄₁₆m, 1:44.20, BUFFALO MAN, No Reply, Green Vegas, 10 started.
Ocala Breeders' Sales Championship S. (R), Ocala Training Center, Feb. 12, $100,000, 3yo, f, sold at an OBS sale, 1¹⁄₁₆m, 1:46.20, DINNER BREAK, Maria's Kitty, Synergy, 11 started.
Ocala Breeders' Sales Sophomore S., Tampa Bay Downs, April 7, $50,000, 3yo, 7f, 1:25.07, WHISKEY LIT, Steelix, Chief Thief, 9 started.
Ocala Breeders' Sales Sprint S. (R), Ocala Training Center, Feb. 12, $50,000, 3yo, c&g, sold at an OBS sale, 6f, 1:10.20, JODI'S STAR, Frosty Secret, B. B. Mancini, 10 started.
Ocala Breeders' Sales Sprint S. (R), Ocala Training Center, Feb. 12, $50,000, 3yo, f, sold at an OBS sale, 6f, 1:10.40, FOREVER TOGETHER, Taletobetold, Lia's Luck, 8 started.
Ocean Bay S., Turf Paradise, Dec. 10, $31,000, 3&up, f&m, a1¹⁄₁₆mT, 1:45.51, STAR OF WHITNEY, Along Came Jones, Colominas, 8 started.
Ocean Bay S., Turf Paradise, March 19, $25,100, 3&up, f&m, 1mT, 1:36.12, KISSNTHEBOYSGOODBY, Woman of Choice, Society Cat, 9 started.
OCEANPORT S. (G3), Monmouth Park, Aug. 5, $150,000, 3&up, 1¹⁄₁₆mT, 1:38.99 (NCR), SILENT ROAR, Kiss the Kid, Kip Deville, 8 started.
Oceanside S. (1st Div.) (R), Del Mar, July 18, $84,200, 3yo, nonwinners of a race worth $50,000 to the winner in 2007, 1mT, 1:35.51, TEN A PENNY, Unusual Suspect, Bernasconi, 6 started.
Oceanside S. (2nd Div.) (R), Del Mar, July 18, $88,300, 3yo, nonwinners of a race worth $50,000 to the winner in 2007, 1mT, 1:35.45, KNOCKOUT ARTIST, Medici Code (GB), Tycoon Doby, 10 started.
Oceanside S. (3rd Div.) (R), Del Mar, July 18, $87,300, 3yo, nonwinners of a race worth $50,000 to the winner in 2007, 1mT, 1:36.78, VAUQUELIN (IRE), Yario (Ire), Teeman, 9 started.
Office Miss S. (R), Belmont Park, Oct. 20, $78,000, 3yo, f, New Yorkbred, 1mT, 1:39.79, CUTE COGNAC, Them There Eyes, Western Sweep, 12 started.
Ogataul S. (R), Fonner Park, March 10, $25,900, 3&up, Nebraskabred, 6f, 1:13.80, MY HALO, Track Hero, Bevys Dazzler, 9 started.
OGDEN PHIPPS H. (G1), Belmont Park, June 16, $300,000, 3&up, f&m, 1¹⁄₁₆m, 1:41.39, TAKE D' TOUR, Ginger Punch, Promenade Girl, 6 started.
Oygigian S. (R), Belmont Park, May 16, $66,500, 3yo, non-winners of a graded stakes, 6½f, 1:15.67, SPORTSTOWN, Cherokee Country, Silver Source, 6 started.
OHIO DERBY (G2), Thistledown, June 2, $300,000, 3yo, 1¹⁄₈m, 1:49.36, DELIGHTFUL KISS, Moyer's Pond, Reporting for Duty, 8 started.
Ohio Freshman S. (R), Beulah Park, Oct. 27, $50,000, 2yo, Ohiobred, 1m, 1:42.05, O'RIAIN, Type A Personality, Buzz Bunny, 8 started.
Ohio Valley H., Mountaineer Race Track and Gaming Resort, May 29, $75,000, 3&up, f&m, 6f, 1:11.37, TROUT RIVER RED, Dixie's Jubilee, A Little Wild, 7 started.
Oh Say S., Delaware Park, July 28, $56,822, 3yo, 6f, 1:08.93, CHEROKEE COUNTRY, Southwestern Heat, Vista Moon, 4 started.
Oklahoma Classics Day Classic S. (R), Remington Park, Sept. 29, $100,000, 3&up, Oklahoma-bred, 1¹⁄₁₆m, 1:43.93, D FINE OKIE, Aisle Two, Zee Oh Six, 6 started.
Oklahoma Classics Day Distaff S. (R), Remington Park, Sept. 29, $60,000, 3&up, f&m, Oklahoma-bred, 1m70y, 1:42.45, MIDSUMMER MAGIC, Alidoon, Mystical Moonlight, 5 started.
Oklahoma Classics Day Filly and Mare Turf S. (R), Remington Park, Sept. 29, $60,000, 3&up, f&m, Oklahoma-bred, 7½fT, 1:31.95, ROSEMAUI, Beata, Asari, 5 started.
Oklahoma Classics Day Filly Sprint S. (R), Remington Park, Sept.

29, $60,000, 3&up, f&m, Oklahoma-bred, 6½f, 1:17.29, ANNIEVILLE, Carsoncityprospect, Zippie Okie, 6 started.
Oklahoma Classics Day Juvenile S. (R), Remington Park, Sept. 29, $50,000, 2yo, c&g, Oklahoma-bred, 6f, 1:11.19, PICASO, Noggin, Cryptographer, 8 started.
Oklahoma Classics Day Lassie S. (R), Remington Park, Sept. 29, $50,000, 2yo, f, Oklahoma-bred, 6f, 1:11.27, NAKALI, Approved Bluff, Tellmewhat, 7 started.
Oklahoma Classics Day Sprint S. (R), Remington Park, Sept. 29, $60,000, 3&up, Oklahoma-bred, 6f, 1:09.42, GARBU ROAD, Marq French, Explosive Okie, 8 started.
Oklahoma Classics Day Turf S. (R), Remington Park, Sept. 29, $60,000, 3&up, Oklahoma-bred, 1mT, 1:37.71, NOTABLE OKIE, Some Quick, Artic Heat, 11 started.
Old Dutch H., Marquis Downs, July 20, $5,749, 3&up, f&m, 7f, 1:25.76, ELLA MARIA, Sweep the Place, Picture the Answer, 5 started.
OLD HAT S. (G3), Gulfstream Park, Feb. 10, $101,500, 3yo, f, 6½f, 1:16.60, DREAM RUSH, You Asked, Dreaming of Anna, 6 started.
Old Nelson H., Colonial Downs, June 16, $45,000, 3&up, 1¹⁄₁₆mT, 1:43.14, JUNGLE FIGHTER, Bastille, Logaritimo (Arg), 12 started.
Oliver S., Calder Race Course, Sept. 23, $45,000, 3&up, 1¼m, 2:06.81, KRISTALI, Supervisor, Bob's Proud Moment, 6 started.
Oliver's Twist S. (R), Laurel Park, Sept. 29, $45,000, 2yo, Maryland-bred, 6fT, 1:08.76, CASANOVA JACK, Ovechkin, Jo's Mojo, 6 started.
Omaha S., Horsemen's Park, July 22, $52,500, 3&up, 1m, 1:37.60, TEPEXPAN, First Class Brass, Bye Bye Beylen, 10 started.
Omnibus S., Monmouth Park, Aug. 25, $70,000, 3&up, f&m, 1⅜mT, 2:13.35, ERES MAGICA (CHI), Greenery, Anura (Ire), 8 started.
Ontario Colleen S., Woodbine, Sept. 1, $121,771, 3yo, f, 1mT, 1:34.71, SPEAK WISELY, Sprung, Audacious Chloe, 14 started.
Ontario County S. (R), Finger Lakes Gaming and Race Track, July 22, $50,000, 3yo, New York-bred, 6f, 1:10.28, GRAND REFER, Indian Camp, Smash 'Em Sammy, 6 started.
Ontario Damsel S. (R), Woodbine, July 8, $143,743, 3yo, f, Ontario-bred, 6½fT, 1:18.40, QUIET ACTION, You Will Love Me, Banker's Street, 7 started.
Ontario Debutante S., Woodbine, Aug. 18, $123,347, 2yo, f, 6fAW, 1:10.45, OFFICER CHERRIE, Dancing Allstar, Simple Sister, 6 started.
Ontario Derby, Woodbine, Sept. 30, $152,032, 3yo, 1⅛mAW, 1:51.19, ARTIE HOT, Alezzandro, Mike Fox, 8 started.
Ontario Fashion S., Woodbine, Nov. 3, $186,250, 3&up, f&m, 6fAW, 1:08.56 (NTR), FINANCINGAVAILABLE, Count to Three, Lyrically, 10 started.
Ontario Jockey Club S. (R), Woodbine, July 21, $73,450, 3&up, Canadian-bred, 7fT, 1:20.47, AWESOME ACTION, Sterwins, Le Cinquieme Essai, 10 started.
Ontario Lassie S. (R), Woodbine, Dec. 5, $149,720, 2yo, f, Canadian-bred, 1¹⁄₁₆mAW, 1:46.19, KRZ EXEC, Tip Toe Annie, Salomea, 9 started.
Ontario Matron S., Woodbine, July 22, $132,020, 3&up, f&m, 1¹⁄₁₆mAW, 1:44.22, SHE'S INDY MONEY, Arden Belle, Be Envied, 6 started.
On Trust H. (R), Hollywood Park, Dec. 22, $107,800, 3&up, California-bred, 7½fAW, 1:26.78 (NTR), GREG'S GOLD, Big Bad Leroybrown, Add Heat, 6 started.
Opening Verse H., Churchill Downs, June 2, $105,245, 3&up, 1¹⁄₁₆mT, 1:43.64, THERECOMESATIGER, Icy Atlantic, Go Between, 4 started.
Open Mind H. (R), Monmouth Park, May 27, $60,000, 3&up, f&m, New Jersey-bred, 6f, 1:09.10, JERSEY GIA, Pure Disco, Midnight Mile, 7 started.
Open Mind S., Belmont Park, Oct. 21, $77,700, 2yo, f, 6f, 1:11.16, PORTE BONHEUR, Freakstein, Yogi'ssplashofgold, 6 started.
Open Mind S., Churchill Downs, May 12, $114,700, 3yo, f, 5fT, :57.26, TALETOBETOLD, Simply Divine, Miss A. Bomb, 11 started.
ORCHID H. (G3), Gulfstream Park, March 31, $150,000, 4&up, f&m, 1½mT, 2:25.17, SAFARI QUEEN (ARG), Almonsoon, La Dolce Vita, 7 started.
Oregon Derby, Portland Meadows, May 5, $21,300, 3yo, 1⅛m, 1:54.37, OCHOCO SALMON, Lil Bit Ruff, Eduardo, 6 started.
Oregon Distaff Starter H. (R), Portland Meadows, Dec. 9, $9,250, 3&up, f&m, Oregon-bred starters for a claiming price of $6,250 or less in 2007, 6f, 1:12.84, LIL'S SASSY PATTY, Delecana, Yougottabe the One, 10 started.
Oregon Hers S. (R), Portland Meadows, Dec. 9, $10,850, 3yo, f, Oregon-bred, 1m, 1:41.05, LITTLE CASCADIAN, Ochoco Salmon, Midways Icksnay, 6 started.
Oregon His S. (R), Portland Meadows, Dec. 9, $11,000, 3yo, c&g, Oregon-bred, 1¹⁄₁₆m, 1:46.11, BAQUERO RULER, Red E to Go, Jack Ryan, 7 started.
Oregon Oaks, Portland Meadows, April 2, $21,850, 3yo, f, 1¹⁄₁₆m, 1:48.16, OCHOCO SALMON, Lemony Sweet, Silver Patrona, 8 started.
Orphan Kist S. (R), Fonner Park, March 3, $25,600, 3&up, f&m, Nebraska-bred, 6f, 1:13, LOVESABLUMIN, Scat's Princess, Sweetime First, 6 started.
Osage Hills S. (R), Remington Park, Oct. 28, $50,000, 3&up, Oklahoma-bred, 5fT, :57.16, MARQ FRENCH, Daring Child, Laidbacklynny, 6 started.
Osunitas H. (R), Del Mar, July 21, $90,715, 3&up, f&m, non-winners of a stakes of $50,000 at one mile or over in 2007, 1¹⁄₁₆mT, 1:41.75, KRIS' SIS, Private Banking (Fr), Double Trouble (Brz), 8 started.
OS West Oregon Futurity (R), Portland Meadows, Dec. 9, $42,000, 2yo, Oregon-bred, 1m, 1:42.69, JIMBOS FIRE ANT, Lady's Purse, Delegocho, 8 started.
OTBA Stallion S. (R), Portland Meadows, Feb. 5, $16,450, 3yo, Oregon-bred, 6f, 1:14.61, I'M ZEE ONE, Baba Balou, Red E to Go, 7 started.
OTOBA Sales S. (R), Portland Meadows, Oct. 21, $12,650, 2yo, passed through the OTOBA sales ring, 6f, 1:12.52, SNOWBOUND TIGER, Rogerbur, Delegocho, 8 started.
OUIJA BOARD DISTAFF H. (G3), Lone Star Park, May 28, $200,000, 3&up, f&m, 1mT, 1:38.32, LADY OF VENICE (FR), Brownie Points, Rich Fantasy, 8 started.
Our Dear Peggy S., Calder Race Course, Dec. 26, $45,000, 3&up, 1⅛mT, 1:47.74, DANCING FOREVER, dh-Croton Road, dh-Terrific Storm, 7 started.
Overskate S. (R), Woodbine, Sept. 19, $123,288, 3&up, Ontario-foaled, 7fAW, 1:23.21, DANCER'S BAJAN, Main Executive, Cool Selection, 5 started.
PACIFIC CLASSIC S. (G1), Del Mar, Aug. 19, $1,000,000, 3&up, 1¼mAW, 2:07.29, STUDENT COUNCIL, Awesome Gem, Hello Sunday (Fr), 12 started.
Pacific Heights S. (R), Golden Gate Fields, Dec. 1, $75,000, 3&up, f&m, California-bred, 1¹⁄₁₆mAW, 1:44.93, SOMETHINABOUTLAURA, Swiss Current, Eastlake Avenue, 6 started.
Pago Hop S., Fair Grounds, Nov. 24, $60,000, 3yo, f, a1mT, 1:38.68, AUTOBAHN GIRL, Our Dancing Babe, Beautiful Venue, 12 started.
PALM BEACH S. (G3), Gulfstream Park, March 24, $115,500, 3yo, 1⅛mT, 1:47.48, DUVEEN, Soldier's Dancer, Storm in May, 7 started.
Palo Alto H., Bay Meadows Race Course, Sept. 3, $75,000, 3yo, f, 7½fT, 1:31.50, ROCKELLA, Macadamia, Forest Huntress, 8 started.
PALOMAR H. (G2), Del Mar, Sept. 1, $222,000, 3&up, f&m, 1¹⁄₁₆mT, 1:40.42, PRECIOUS KITTEN, Black Mamba (NZ), Kris' Sis, 9 started.
PALOS VERDES H. (G2), Santa Anita Park, Jan. 20, $147,000, 4&up, 6f, 1:08.95, FRIENDLY ISLAND, Harvard Avenue, Limited Creole, 4 started.
Palo Verde S., Turf Paradise, March 4, $45,000, 3yo, 6½f, 1:15.15, CAPT. JOE BLOW, In to the West, Top Emblem, 8 started.
Panhandle H., Mountaineer Race Track and Gaming Resort, May 5, $75,000, 3&up, 5f, :57.18, FABULOUS STRIKE, Smoke Mountain, Bernie Blue, 4 started.
Panthers S., Prairie Meadows, June 9, $54,000, 3yo, f, 1m, 1:39.31, GIRLS PEARLS, Irish Party, Comarillo, 9 started.
Pan Zareta Breeders' Cup S., Fair Grounds, Feb. 3, $74,250, 4&up, f&m, 6f, 1:10.83, MYKINDASAINT, Vote Early, Annika Lass, 8 started.
Paradise Valley S., Turf Paradise, Nov. 17, $45,000, 3yo, 7½fT, 1:29.36, MILLER'S TURBO, Song of Pirates, Mr Charlypotatoes, 10 started.
Par Four S., Delaware Park, Aug. 18, $64,816, 2yo, 6f, 1:12.15, JET RUN, Haddenfield, Scary Trip, 6 started.
Park Avenue S. (R), Aqueduct, April 22, $100,000, 3yo, f, progeny of eligible New York stallions, 7f, 1:22.56, MIGHTY EROS, City in the Clouds, Margies Smile, 6 started.
Parkland Heritage S. (R), Marquis Downs, Aug. 18, $18,846, 3yo, f, Saskatchewan-bred, 1m, 1:42.65, DOROTHY HAZEL, Stay and Play, Exit Stage North, 9 started.
Pasadena S., Santa Anita Park, March 16, $81,400, 3yo, 1mT, 1:33.88, WHATSTHESCRIPT (IRE), Silent Soul, Blues Street, 11 started.
Pasco S., Tampa Bay Downs, Jan. 27, $75,000, 3yo, 7f, 1:24.31, BARKLEY SOUND, Steelix, Dippi Trippi, 10 started.
Paseana H., Santa Anita Park, Jan. 12, $79,100, 4&up, f&m, 1¹⁄₁₆m, 1:43.66, RIVER SAVAGE (BRZ), Notre Dame (Brz), Dona Amelia (Chi), 7 started.

Passing Mood S. (R), Woodbine, July 25, $121,992, 3yo, f, Ontario-foaled, 7fT, 1:23.03, YOU WILL LOVE ME, Birsay, Quite a Knightmare, 9 started.

Pass the Line S., Calder Race Course, Nov. 25, $35,000, 3&up, 1m, 1:39.68, FINANCE MINISTER, Rexson's Rose, Bob's Proud Moment, 7 started.

Pat Johnson Memorial Starter H. (R), Turf Paradise, Jan. 14, $12,800, 4&up, f&m, starters for a claiming price of $10,000 or less in 2006-'07, a1mT, 1:37.53, BE MY FRIEND, V'ville Lady, Estrelita D' Cielo, 8 started.

PAT O'BRIEN H. (G2), Del Mar, Aug. 19, $300,000, 3&up, 7fAW, 1:23.95, GREG'S GOLD, Surf Cat, Soul City Slew, 6 started.

Patrick Wood S. (R), Great Lakes Downs, Sept. 18, $50,000, 2yo, c&g, Michigan-bred, 6f, 1:16.40, HOT CHILI, Berry's Pride, Curpico, 9 started.

PATTISON CANADIAN INTERNATIONAL S. (CAN-G1), Woodbine, Oct. 21, $2,073,699, 3&up, 1½mT, 2:27.71, CLOUDY'S KNIGHT, Ask (GB), Quijano (Ger), 12 started.

Pat Whitworth Illinois Debutante S. (R), Hawthorne Race Course, Dec. 8, $110,025, 2yo, f, Illinois-conceived and/or -foaled, 1$^1/_{16}$m, 1:47.14, LINK TO MY HEART, Apple Martini, Carbella, 11 started.

Paul Cacci-Eel River Starter Sprint S. (R), Ferndale, Aug. 12, $7,185, 3&up, starters for a claiming price of $12,500 or less in 2007, 5f, :59.67, WESTERN BOOT, Rockin' Rizzi, Bears Mo Red, 5 started.

Paumonok H., Aqueduct, Jan. 27, $67,925, 3&up, 6f, 1:09.20, BISHOP COURT HILL, Attila's Storm, Super Fuse, 5 started.

Peach Blossom S., Delaware Park, May 19, $75,300, 3yo, f, 6f, 1:09.81, TICKET TO SEATTLE, Miss Tizzy, Paying Off, 6 started.

Peach of It H. (R), Hawthorne Race Course, April 28, $105,900, 3&up, f&m, Illinois-conceived and/or -foaled, 1$^1/_{16}$m, 1:45.94, TUFFTED, Dyna Slam, Stop a Train, 9 started.

Peapack Hurdle S., Far Hills, Oct. 20, $50,000, 3&up, f&m, a2⅛mT, 4:15.40, IMAGINA (CHI), Slew's Peak, Lair, 8 started.

Pearl Necklace S. (R), Pimlico Race Course, June 2, $75,000, 3yo, f, Maryland-bred, 1$^1/_{16}$mT, 1:44.20, MARIAS GOLDEN ROSE, Ziggly, Gentlemen's Locket, 6 started.

Pebbles S., Belmont Park, Oct. 8, $111,000, 3yo, f, 1mT, 1:34.85, CAT CHARMER, Queen Joanne, New Edition, 7 started.

PEGASUS S. (G3), Monmouth Park, Oct. 27, $250,000, 3yo, 1⅛m, 1:51.54, ACTIN GOOD, Now a Victor, Slew's Tizzy, 5 started.

Pelican S., Tampa Bay Downs, Jan. 13, $60,000, 4&up, 6f, 1:09.88, ROMAN CANDLES, Wonone, D'artagnans'spirit, 12 started.

PENNSYLVANIA DERBY (G2), Philadelphia Park, Sept. 3, $1,000,000, 3yo, 1⅛m, 1:47.67, TIMBER RESERVE, Xchanger, Zanjero, 11 started.

Pennsylvania Governor's Cup H., Penn National Race Course, Aug. 9, $50,000, 3&up, 5f, :57.46, MR MUTTER, Procreate, Sandys Gold, 5 started.

Pennsylvania Hunt Cup Timber S., Unionville, Nov. 4, $23,400, 5&up, a4mT, 8:56.60, EARMARK, Shady Valley, Patriot's Path, 5 started.

Pennsylvania Nursery S. (R), Philadelphia Park, Nov. 24, $101,400, 2yo, Pennsylvania-bred, 7f, 1:23.59, NOTGIVINMYLOVEAWAY, Sweet Sugar, Double Down Vinman, 12 started.

Penny Ridge S., Stampede Park, June 17, $70,208, 3yo, f, 1m, 1:39.80, FOREST HUNTRESS, Tanika, Calendar Girl, 9 started.

Peppy Addy S. (R), Philadelphia Park, June 9, $60,000, 3yo, c&g, Pennsylvania-bred, 1m70y, 1:42.28, MR. BOXCAR, My Three Boys, Louie's Terra, 5 started.

Pepsi-Cola H., Emerald Downs, June 3, $50,738, 3yo, c&g, 6½f, 1:15, CALL ON CARSON, Immigration, Wild Cycle, 6 started.

Pepsi-Cola H. (R), Sunland Park, Jan. 27, $125,000, 3yo, New Mexico-bred, 6f, 1:12.97, Z Z DOME, Shaken the Cage, Colorofrun, 8 started.

Pepsi S., Fonner Park, March 17, $15,675, 3yo, f, 6f, 1:15.80, JACKIE'S CHARM, Sunbeach, Ebony Evening, 8 started.

Perfect Arc S. (R), Aqueduct, Nov. 11, $75,000, 3&up, f&m, progeny of eligible New York stallions, 1$^1/_{16}$mT, 1:45.71, FACTUAL CONTENDER, Higher Incentive, Artistic Express, 8 started.

Perfect Sting S. (R), Saratoga Race Course, Aug. 29, $81,700, 4&up, f&m, non-winners of a stakes on the turf in 2007, 1⅛mT, 1:45.61 (NCR), CRIMINOLOGIST, Amansara, Mo Cuishle, 6 started.

Permian Basin S., Zia Park, Oct. 21, $60,400, 2yo, f, 6f, 1:12.40, CITI GIRLFRIEND, Dubit, Sweet Roseman, 6 started.

PERRYVILLE S. (G3), Keeneland Race Course, Oct. 13, $200,000, 3yo, a7fAW, 1:25.36, STEVE'S DOUBLE, Les Grands Trois, Shrewd Operator, 8 started.

Personal Bid S. (R), Aqueduct, Dec. 2, $78,000, 3yo, f, New York-bred, 6f, 1:13.04, LIGHT TACTIC, Brown Eyed Belle, Sunset Cocktail, 8 started.

PERSONAL ENSIGN S. (G1), Saratoga Race Course, Aug. 24, $400,000, 3&up, f&m, 1¼m, 2:03.48, MISS SHOP, Unbridled Belle, Indian Vale, 6 started.

Pete Axthelm S., Calder Race Course, Dec. 29, $100,000, 3yo, 7½fT, 1:27.22, FEARLESS EAGLE, Buffalo Man, Mysterious Peintre (Fr), 12 started.

Pete Condellone Memorial H. (R), Fairmount Park, July 31, $45,700, 3yo, c&g, Illinois-bred and/or -foaled, 6f, 1:11, HE'S HOT SAUCE, Caruso, Gotem Cart, 6 started.

PETER PAN S. (G2), Belmont Park, May 20, $200,000, 3yo, 1⅛m, 1:48.89, SIGHTSEEING, Prom Shoes, Fearless Vision, 6 started.

Peter Redekop British Columbia Cup Classic H. (R), Hastings Race Course, Aug. 6, $101,552, 3&up, British Columbia-bred, 1⅛m, 1:50.05, SHACANE, Timeless Passion, Act of God, 7 started.

Pete Selin Memorial Happy Minute S., Rillito Park, March 4, $6,210, 3&up, f&m, 5½f, 1:06.40, ICE FANTASY, Soha What, Answer Cats Line, 8 started.

Petro D. Jay S., Turf Paradise, Nov. 25, $31,000, 3&up, a4½fT, :50.39, BOBADIEU, Mr. Ching, King Justin, 7 started.

Petro West S., Grand Prairie, Aug. 11, $8,630, 3&up, 6½f, 1:18.80, TA KEEL, Vying Gold, Stormy Gamble, 5 started.

P. G. Johnson S. (R), Meadowlands, Oct. 20, $55,000, 3yo, f, non-winners of a stakes, 5fT, :57.74, ANOFFICERANDALADY, Featherbed, Ahvee's Destiny, 9 started.

Phil D. Shepherd S., Fairplex Park, Sept. 8, $63,050, 3&up, 1$^1/_{16}$m, 1:45.21, BRAVO MAESTRO, Black Spot, Sensational Score, 6 started.

PHILIP H. ISELIN BREEDERS' CUP H. (G3), Monmouth Park, Aug. 18, $300,000, 3&up, 1⅛m, 1:48.36, GOTTCHA GOLD, Brother Bobby, Indy Wind, 8 started.

Phoenix Gold Cup H., Turf Paradise, Feb. 24, $100,000, 4&up, 6f, 1:07.68, RELATO DEL GATO, Sailors Sunset, Family Guy, 10 started.

Phoenix S., Meadowlands, Sept. 22, $55,000, 3&up, f&m, 5fT, :55.31, LAKES TUNE, Beau Dare, Weeks, 5 started.

PHOENIX S. (G3), Keeneland Race Course, Oct. 6, $203,000, 3&up, 6fAW, 1:10.17, OFF DUTY, Rebellion (GB), Saint Anddan, 10 started.

Pierces Homeremedy Starter S., Yavapai Downs, Aug. 26, $7,400, 3&up, 5f, :55.60, RUN NICHOLAS RUN, Swiss Bounty, Wasatch Flyer, 5 started.

Pierre LeBlanc Memorial Ladies Sprint S. (R), Evangeline Downs, June 30, $100,000, 3&up, f&m, Louisiana-bred, 5½f, 1:04.96, LEESA LEE, Indigo Girl, Cutie Sabrina, 9 started.

Pilgrim S., Belmont Park, Sept. 29, $81,000, 2yo, 1$^1/_{16}$mT, 1:41.61, THE LEOPARD, He Aint Easy, Grasberg, 6 started.

Pine Tree Lane S. (R), Oak Tree at Santa Anita, Oct. 20, $57,300, 3&up, f&m, non-winners of a stakes worth $60,000 since June 15 other than state-bred, 6½fAW, 1:14.07, THEVERYTHOUGHTOF U, Ashley's Kitty, Selvatica, 6 started.

Pinjara S. (R), Oak Tree at Santa Anita, Oct. 26, $63,200, 2yo, non-winners of a stakes at one mile or over, 1mT, 1:36.70, YES IT'S A CAT, Sky Cape, Dixie Mon, 7 started.

Pin Oak Stud USA S., Lone Star Park, May 28, $100,000, 3yo, 1$^1/_{16}$mT, 1:45.29, GOING BALLISTIC, Later Gater, Beta Capo, 8 started.

PIN OAK VALLEY VIEW S. (G3), Keeneland Race Course, Oct. 19, $150,000, 3yo, f, 1$^1/_{16}$mT, 1:44.39, BEL AIR BEAUTY, Bachata, Pitamakan, 12 started.

Pio Pico S. (R), Fairplex Park, Sept. 14, $59,150, 3&up, f&m, California-bred, 6½f, 1:18.26, KALOOKAN DANCER, Vaca City Flyer, Camelita, 5 started.

Pippin S., Oaklawn Park, Feb. 17, $50,000, 4&up, f&m, 1$^1/_{16}$m, 1:44.57, PLAID, Kettleoneup, Angel Flying, 7 started.

Pirate's Bounty H. (R), Del Mar, Sept. 5, $90,890, 3&up, non-winners of a stakes of $50,000 since March 1, 6fAW, 1:12.04, DOUBLE ACTION, Relato Del Gato, Fly Dorcego (Brz), 6 started.

Pistol Packer H. (R), Philadelphia Park, May 12, $60,000, 3&up, f&m, Pennsylvania-bred, 6f, 1:10.51, S W ALY'SVALENTINE, Jet Away Jane, Hailie's Girl, 5 started.

Plate Trial S. (R), Woodbine, June 3, $142,476, 3yo, Canadian-bred, 1⅛mAW, 1:50.77, JIGGS COZ, Marchfield, Alezzandro, 8 started.

Playa del Rey S., Hollywood Park, Dec. 9, $83,985, 3&up, f&m, 6fAW, 1:08.99, LADY GAMER, You Are the Answer, Selvatica, 5 started.

PLAY THE KING S. (CAN-G2), Woodbine, Aug. 25, $191,220, 3&up, 7fT, 1:26.28, LE CINQUIEME ESSAI, Just Rushing, Awesome Action, 8 started.

Pleasant Colony S., Aqueduct, April 7, $78,700, 4&up, 1¾m, 2:57.54, MALIBU MOONSHINE, Monopoly Pricing, Successful Affair, 6 started.

Pleasant Temper S., Kentucky Downs, Sept. 15, $45,000, 3&up, f&m, 1mT, 1:36.59, PUT AWAY THE HALO, St. Hildegard, Moon Berry (Brz), 11 started.

Plymouth S. (R), Great Lakes Downs, July 14, $50,000, 3yo, f, Michigan-bred, 7f, 1:28.87, VALLEY LOOT, Desert Symphony, Tropic Rose, 9 started.

POCAHONTAS S. (G3), Churchill Downs, Oct. 28, $185,700, 2yo, f, 1m, 1:38.30, PURE CLAN, Authenicat, Sky Mom, 14 started.

POKER H. (G3), Belmont Park, July 14, $112,600, 3&up, 1mT, 1:33.21, ART MASTER, Woodlander, Host (Chi), 9 started.

Pola Benoit Memorial S. (R), Evangeline Downs, June 30, $99,000, 4&up, Louisiana-bred, 1 1/16m, 1:46, GRAND MINIT, Diggy Fresh, Costa Rising, 8 started.

Politely S., Monmouth Park, May 27, $60,000, 3&up, f&m, 1mT, 1:34.24, REDASPEN, A Different Tune, Somethinaboutbetty, 9 started.

Pollyanna Pixie S. (R), Fairmount Park, July 31, $46,000, 3yo, f, Illinois-bred and/or -foaled, 6f, 1:11, SEA BUTTON, Magnetic Miss, Frances Cat, 6 started.

Polly's Jet S., Delaware Park, May 12, $60,050, 3yo, f, 1 1/16m, 1:44.14, GREENSTREET, Bees, Perfect Forest, 7 started.

Pomona Derby, Fairplex Park, Sept. 22, $99,000, 3yo, a1 1/8m, 1:53.07, FRANK THE BARBER, Big Bad Leroybrown, Mr. Nightlinger, 8 started.

Ponca City S., Remington Park, Aug. 3, $50,000, 3yo, f, 6f, 1:08.43, TRES DREAM, Gallant Dreamer, Irish Party, 11 started.

Ponche H., Calder Race Course, April 28, $100,000, 3&up, 6f, 1:11.09, WEIGELIA, Gower, Finallymadeit, 12 started.

Portland Meadows Invitational H., Portland Meadows, Jan. 7, $8,100, 3yo, f, 1:12.74, BAGELS BABY, Danjuria, Little Cascadian, 5 started.

Portland Meadows Invitational H., Portland Meadows, Jan. 21, $8,050, 4&up, 5f, :58.61, LETHAL GRANDE, Crimson Design, Knightsbridge Road, 5 started.

Portland Meadows Invitational H., Portland Meadows, March 19, $8,150, 4&up, 1 1/16m, 1:46.26, BRAVE HEARTED, My Friend Dave, J D's Date, 4 started.

Portland Meadows Invitational H., Portland Meadows, Nov. 5, $9,214, 3&up, 1m, 1:38.92, BRAVE HEARTED, Flaming Bullet, Gold Lad, 5 started.

Portland Meadows Invitational H., Portland Meadows, Nov. 26, $9,700, 3&up, 1m70y, 1:43.98, GOLD LAD, Brave Hearted, Flaming Bullet, 9 started.

Portland Meadows Invitational H., Portland Meadows, Oct. 14, $9,500, 3&up, f&m, 5 1/2f, 1:05.88, LADY YODELER, Texas Bobbi R., Musical Wine, 5 started.

Portland Meadows Mile H., Portland Meadows, Feb. 25, $27,400, 3&up, 1m, 1:40.19, DERBY RIDER (ARG), Lethal Grande, Brave Hearted, 9 started.

Possibly Perfect S., Arlington Park, June 23, $48,000, 3&up, f&m, 1 1/16mT, 1:48.09, JENNIE R., Chic Dancer, Arosa (Ire), 9 started.

Post Deb S., Monmouth Park, June 22, $60,000, 3yo, f, 5 1/2f, 1:01.98, LA TRAVIATA, Sea the Joy, Change Up, 5 started.

Potomac S. (R), Charles Town Races, July 7, $46,350, 3yo, West Virginia-bred, 4 1/2f, :53.01, LOVE TO PLUNGE, Zacky's Go Go, Winagain Finnegan, 9 started.

POTRERO GRANDE BREEDERS' CUP H. (G2), Santa Anita Park, April 7, $192,000, 4&up, 6 1/2f, 1:14.83, SMOKEY STOVER, Greg's Gold, Sailors Sunset, 5 started.

Power by Far H. (R), Philadelphia Park, Sept. 8, $60,000, 3&up, Pennsylvania-bred, 6f, 1:08.74, BANJO PICKER, Obi Wan, Power by Leigh, 7 started.

Powerless H. (R), Hawthorne Race Course, Nov. 3, $105,375, 3&up, f&m, Illinois-conceived and/or -foaled, 6f, 1:10.68, DENOUN N DEVERB, Modjadji, Pretty Jenny, 9 started.

Powhatan S. (R), Charles Town Races, Sept. 16, $45,900, 3&up, c&g, West Virginia-bred, 4 1/2f, :51.76, MISSACITY LUKE, Earth Power, Fax Amatic, 7 started.

Prairie Bayou S., Turfway Park, Dec. 15, $50,000, 3&up, 1 1/16mAW, 1:50.84, KETTLE HILL, Drilling for Oil, Sea of Trees, 8 started.

Prairie Gold Juvenile S., Prairie Meadows, July 2, $50,000, 2yo, 5f, :57.33, POSSETOTHEMAX, Robbing the Bank, Alex's Tomcat, 9 started.

Prairie Gold Lassie S., Prairie Meadows, July 2, $50,000, 2yo, f, 5f, :57.71, AMAZING TALE, A. J. Bakes, Rasierra, 7 started.

Prairie Lily Sales S. (R), Marquis Downs, Sept. 1, $23,673, 2yo, passed through the ring at the 2006 Prairie Lily sale, 6 1/2f, 1:21.75, Y. C. RAIL, Gigs, Up Tempo, 6 started.

PRAIRIE MEADOWS CORNHUSKER H. (G2), Prairie Meadows, June 30, $300,000, 3&up, 1 1/8m, 1:48.41, DRY MARTINI, Silent Pleasure, Patriot Act, 9 started.

Prairie Meadows Debutante S., Prairie Meadows, Sept. 8, $47,025 2yo, f, 6f, 1:10.70, BATHED IN BLUE, Big Lou, Judy Faye, 7 started.

Prairie Meadows Derby, Prairie Meadows, Sept. 15, $81,750, 3yo, 1 1/16m, 1:42.48, JAMES THE GREATER, Red Hot N Gold, Western Prize, 6 started.

Prairie Meadows Freshman S., Prairie Meadows, Sept. 8, $52,088, 2yo, 6f, 1:09.21, WEST COAST COACH, Maya's Storm, Kate's Main Man, 8 started.

Prairie Meadows H., Prairie Meadows, July 28, $78,375, 3&up, 1 1/16f, 1:43.03, WAYZATA BAY, Real Dandy, Sur Sandpit, 7 started.

Prairie Meadows Oaks, Prairie Meadows, Sept. 15, $75,000, 3yo, f, 1 1/16m, 1:41.19, WEST COAST SWING, Tessa Blue, Celeritas, 8 started.

Prairie Meadows Sprint S., Prairie Meadows, Aug. 4, $75,000, 3&up, 6f, 1:08.08, INDIAN CHANT, Piratesonthelake, Markum, 6 started.

Prairie Meats H., Marquis Downs, Aug. 31, $5,668, 3yo, f, 1m, 1:42.48, DANCIN' SAMI, Lady Richter, Chain of Events, 5 started.

Prairie Mile S., Prairie Meadows, June 9, $50,000, 3yo, 1m, 1:38.03, GREELEY'S CONQUEST, Who Let the Cat In, Sumac, 8 started.

Prairie Rose S., Prairie Meadows, April 28, $50,000, 3&up, f&m, 6f, 1:09.56, MISS MACY SUE, Flashy Lady, Shimmering Sunset, 6 started.

PREAKNESS S. (G1), Pimlico Race Course, May 19, $1,000,000, 3yo, 1 3/16m, 1:53.46, CURLIN, Street Sense, Hard Spun, 9 started.

Premier Breeders' Cup H., Zia Park, Sept. 23, $151,030, 3&up, 6f, 1:09.20, WHIRL, Orphan Brigade, Tontine Too, 8 started.

Premiere S. (R), Lone Star Park, April 12, $50,000, 3&up, Texas-bred, 1m, 1:36.95, SANDBURR, Goosey Moose, Agrivating General, 6 started.

Premio Esmeralda S., Emerald Downs, July 21, $45,000, 2yo, c&g, 6f, 1:09.20, MARGO'S GIFT, Gallon, Courageous Son, 6 started.

Presidential Affair H. (R), Presque Isle Downs, Sept. 21, $90,000, 3&up, Pennsylvania-bred, 6 1/2fAW, 1:17.58, OBI WAN, Thaddeus, Makin Peace, 4 started.

President's Cup S., Lincoln State Fair, June 17, $15,000, 3&up, 6f, 1:11.60, ANOTHER AUDIBLE, First Class Brass, No Term Limit, 5 started.

President's Day H., Bay Meadows Race Course, Feb. 19, $53,975, 4&up, 1 1/16m, 1:41.70, MY CREED, Passive Income, A Gallant Discover, 6 started.

President's H., Stampede Park, May 5, $45,145, 3yo, c&g, 6f, 1:12.60, CHIEF'S MAGIC, Footprint, Sin Toro, 10 started.

Presque Isle Downs Masters S., Presque Isle Downs, Sept. 15, $400,000, 3&up, f&m, 6fAW, 1:08.21, MISS MACY SUE, Wild Gams, Smart and Fancy, 8 started.

Presque Isle Mile S., Presque Isle Downs, Sept. 15, $175,000, 3&up, 1mAW, 1:38.14, INDEPENDENT GEORGE, Bestowed, Real Dandy, 7 started.

Preview S., Portland Meadows, April 16, $21,700, 3yo, 1 1/16m, 1:49.50, OCHOCO SALMON, He'sabigtalker, Red E to Go, 8 started.

Prime Rewards S. (R), Delta Downs, Dec. 28, $55,000, 3&up, f&m, non-winners of a stakes, 1m, 1:40.13, KATHLEENS REEL, Jersey Bond, Beat the Band, 9 started.

Primonetta S., Laurel Park, April 7, $63,600, 3&up, f&m, 6f, 1:10.71, MY SISTER SUE, Homesteader, Coli Bear, 6 started.

Prince of Wales S. (R), Fort Erie, July 15, $476,850, 3yo, Canadian-bred, 1 3/16m, 1:55.04, ALEZZANDRO, Jiggs Coz, Daaher, 6 started.

Princess Elaine S. (R), Canterbury Park, July 3, $45,000, 3&up, f&m, Minnesota-bred, a1 1/16mT, 1:45, MA HOME CAT, Nishani, Blumin Beauty, 7 started.

Princess Elizabeth S. (R), Woodbine, Oct. 20, $258,850, 2yo, f, Canadian-bred, 1 1/16mAW, 1:47.10, MRS. BEGAN, Victory Romance, Reverently, 5 started.

Princess Margaret S., Northlands Park, July 13, $47,820, 2yo, f, 6f, 1:11.80, LITTLEMISS ALLISON, Highly Explosive, I Lost My Halo, 7 started.

Princess of Palms H. (R), Turf Paradise, Feb. 10, $45,000, 4&up, f&m, starters at the 2006-'07 Turf Paradise meet, 6f, 1:08.50, VICTORINA, Katy Smiles, Mirando, 5 started.

PRINCESS ROONEY H. (G1), Calder Race Course, July 7, $500,000, 3&up, f&m, 6f, 1:10.66, RIVER'S PRAYER, Shaggy Mane, G City Gal, 13 started.

Princess S., Lincoln State Fair, May 13, $15,500, 3yo, f, 6f, 1:14.20, PLAER'S TRUMP, Dazzling Seville, I Talk, 5 started.

Princess S., Louisiana Downs, July 14, $49,000, 2yo, f, 5f (originally

scheduled on the turf), :59.19, SHEDOESROCK, American Prize, Top Story, 7 started.

Princeton S., Meadowlands, Sept. 14, $60,000, 3yo, 1⅜mT, 2:18.91, MISSION APPROVED, Phil the Power, French Vintage, 8 started.

PRIORESS S. (G1), Belmont Park, July 7, $240,000, 3yo, f, 6f, 1:09.02, DREAM RUSH, Graeme Six, Silver Knockers, 9 started.

Private Terms S., Laurel Park, March 24, $72,000, 3yo, 1m, 1:37.97, ETUDE, Saratoga Lulaby, Not for Money, 9 started.

Prom S., Meadowlands, Oct. 19, $60,000, 2yo, f, 6f, 1:09.99, D J LIGHTNING, How Bout Tonight, Sumptuous, 5 started.

Pro Or Con H. (R), Santa Anita Park, April 8, $107,200, 4&up, f&m, California-bred, 1mT, 1:37.16, DANCING GENERAL, Two Times Won, Del Mar Ticket, 6 started.

Proud Appeal S., Aqueduct, Jan. 28, $65,950, 4&up, 1¼m, 2:03.87, CARMINOOCH, Successful Affair, Tall Story, 5 started.

Proud Puppy H., Finger Lakes Gaming and Race Track, Oct. 6, $50,000, 3&up, f&m, 6f, 1:10.54, HOOSICK FALLS, Fly to Me, Baby Gray, 8 started.

Providencia S., Santa Anita Park, April 7, $112,600, 3yo, f, 1mT, 1:35.59, SUPER FREAKY, Passified (GB), Gotta Have Her, 11 started.

PUCKER UP S. (G3), Arlington Park, Sept. 8, $200,000, 3yo, f, 1⅛mT, 1:48.20, DREAMING OF ANNA, Touch My Soul (Fr), Bel Air Beauty, 12 started.

Punch Line S. (R), Colonial Downs, July 22, $60,000, 3&up, Virginia-bred and/or -sired, 5fT, :56.67, SANDYS GOLD, Power Jeans, Swayin, 9 started.

Purple Violet S. (R), Arlington Park, July 7, $84,800, 3yo, f, Illinois-conceived and/or -foaled, 1mAW, 1:37.49, MAGNETIC MISS, Secret Kin, Lil Cora Tee, 8 started.

Puss n Boots Cup S. (R), Fort Erie, Sept. 3, $23,673, 3&up, three or more starts at Fort Erie in 2007, a1 1/16mT, 1:45.78, SILVER STRIP, Faygo Dancing Home, Slice of Glory, 9 started.

Queen City Oaks (R), River Downs, July 21, $100,000, 3yo, f, Ohio-bred, 1⅛m, 1:52.40, PAY THE MAN, Magg's Choice, Cryptohio, 10 started.

QUEEN ELIZABETH II CHALLENGE CUP S. (G1), Keeneland Race Course, Oct. 13, $500,000, 3yo, f, 1⅛mT, 1:48.73, BIT OF WHIMSY, Dreaming of Anna, Coquerelle (Ire), 9 started.

Queen of the Green H., Turf Paradise, Nov. 17, $45,000, 3&up, f&m, 1mT, 1:36.79, STAR OF WHITNEY, Along Came Jones, Beaulena, 7 started.

Queen S., Turfway Park, March 24, $50,000, 4&up, f&m, 6fAW, 1:09.28, MARY DELANEY, Hot Storm, New Dimension, 10 started.

QUEENS COUNTY H. (G3), Aqueduct, Dec. 8, $104,900, 3&up, 1 3/16m, 1:58.01, EVENING ATTIRE, Barcola, Hunting, 5 started.

Queen's Plate S. (R), Woodbine, June 24, $936,022, 3yo, Canadian-bred, 1¼mAW, 2:05.45, MIKE FOX, Alezzandro, Jiggs Coz, 8 started.

Queenston S. (R), Woodbine, May 5, $136,518, 3yo, Ontario-bred, 7fAW, 1:24.42, JIGGS COZ, Markdale, Dancer's Bajan, 8 started.

Quick Card S., Delaware Park, April 30, $57,800, 3&up, 1m, 1:36.17, BETTER THAN BONDS, Tartlet, Donald's Pride, 4 started.

Quicken Tree S. (R), Hollywood Park, May 25, $76,375, 4&up, California-bred, 1½mT, 2:25.53, RUNNING FREE, Ring of Friendship, Super Strut, 5 started.

Radar Love S., Calder Race Course, Nov. 24, $35,000, 3&up, 6½f, 1:17.21, FINALLYMADEIT, D'artagnans'spirit, Winnies Tigger Too, 5 started.

Radnor Hunt Cup Timber S., Malvern, May 19, $40,000, 4&up, a3¼mT, 6:41.20, SEEYOUATTHEEVENT, Mr Bombastic (Ger), Move West, 8 started.

RAILBIRD S. (G3), Hollywood Park, May 13, $111,000, 3yo, f, 7fAW, 1:22.80, ASHLEY'S KITTY, Silver Swallow, Sindy With an S, 9 started.

Rainbow Connection S. (R), Fort Erie, Aug. 19, $117,788, 3&up, f&m, Ontario-foaled, 5fT, :57.83, FLASHY PINK, Timely Matter, Shot Gun Ela, 8 started.

Rainbow Miss S. (R), Oaklawn Park, March 30, $50,000, 3yo, f, Arkansas-bred, 6f, 1:12.39, RITA KATRINA, Ile St Jaycee, Abby the Great, 8 started.

Rainbow S. (R), Oaklawn Park, April 1, $50,000, 3yo, c&g, Arkansas-bred, 6f, 1:12.46, ELITE ETBAUER, Cinnamonsluckypic, Eagle Town, 6 started.

Raise Heck S., Aqueduct, Dec. 7, $77,500, 3yo, f, 6f, 1:10.19, FRISK HER, Your Flame in Me, Golden Dawn, 6 started.

Ralph Hayes S. (R), Prairie Meadows, Aug. 25, $82,300, 4&up, c&g, Iowa-bred, 1 1/16m, 1:43.64, WON WON WONDER WHY, Mingo Mohawk, Gilded Leader, 10 started.

Ralph M. Hinds Invitational H., Fairplex Park, Sept. 23, $121,250, 3&up, a1⅛m, 1:51.31, PLUG ME IN, Courtly Jazz, Raise the Bluff, 6 started.

RAMPART H. (G2), Gulfstream Park, March 11, $200,000, 4&up, f&m, 1⅛m, 1:49.42, MISS SHOP, Prop Me Up, Swap Fliparoo, 6 started.

RANCHO BERNARDO H. (G3), Del Mar, Aug. 17, $200,000, 3&up, f&m, 6½fAW, 1:17.85, RIVER'S PRAYER, Strong Faith, Lady Gamer, 5 started.

Randy Bailey Memorial S., Blue Ribbon Downs, Aug. 12, $15,800, 3&up, 4f, :44.58 (NTR), GARBU'S TAB, G. T. Crusader, Gold Brick (Jpn), 10 started.

Rare Treat H., Aqueduct, Feb. 24, $70,175, 3&up, f&m, 1⅛m, 1:51.33, DINA, Daytime Promise, A Bit of Pressure, 6 started.

Rattlesnake S., Turf Paradise, Jan. 26, $45,000, 3yo, 1m, 1:36.12, TIE ROD, Mr Charlypotatoes, In to the West, 9 started.

Ravolia S., Calder Race Course, Sept. 2, $50,000, 3yo, f, 1mT, 1:35.10, SWEET EXCHANGE, Snow Cone, Cozzi Capital, 12 started.

Raymond G. Woolfe Memorial Hurdle S., Camden, Nov. 18, $25,000, 3&up, a2mT, 4:16.80, BE CERTAIN, C R's Deputy, Multie Colored, 7 started.

Razorback Futurity (R), Louisiana Downs, Oct. 6, $45,000, 2yo, c&g, Arkansas-bred, 6f, 1:12.23, JERI HARPER, Humble Cat, Brother Norm, 12 started.

RAZORBACK H. (G3), Oaklawn Park, March 9, $150,000, 4&up, 1 1/16m, 1:44.17, MAGNA GRADUATE, Student Council, Jonesboro, 8 started.

R. C. Anderson S. (R), Assiniboia Downs, July 21, $42,926, 3yo, f, Manitoba-bred, 1m, 1:43.80, SHOOTING ASTRA, Smart Miss, Easters Lily, 8 started.

Ready Jet Go S., Meadowlands, Sept. 3, $63,600, 3&up, f&m, 6f, 1:08.14, GENEROSITY, Pure Disco, Livermore Valley, 6 started.

Real Good Deal S. (R), Del Mar, Aug. 10, $107,200, 3yo, California-bred, 7fAW, 1:23.53, BIG BAD LEROYBROWN, Zoning In, Idiot Proof, 6 started.

Real Quiet S., Hollywood Park, Nov. 18, $105,900, 2yo, 1 1/16mAW, 1:42.92, COLONEL JOHN, Overextended, Cafe Tortoni, 7 started.

Reappeal S., Calder Race Course, May 12, $50,000, 3&up, 5fT, :55.10, LORD ROBYN, Not Acclaim, Nacascolo, 9 started.

REBEL S. (G3), Oaklawn Park, March 17, $300,000, 3yo, 1 1/16m, 1:44.70, CURLIN, Officer Rocket (GB), Teuflesberg, 9 started.

RED BANK S. (G3), Monmouth Park, Sept. 1, $150,000, 3&up, 1mT, 1:32.42 (NCR), ICY ATLANTIC, Touched by Madness, Baron Von Tap, 7 started.

Red Camelia H. (R), Fair Grounds, March 24, $100,000, 4&up, f&m, Louisiana-bred, a1 1/16mT, 1:44.12, RASPBERRY WINE, Autobesarah, Intractabie, 11 started.

Red Cross S., Meadowlands, Nov. 9, $60,000, 3&up, f&m, 1 1/16m, 1:43.18, PROP ME UP, Lexi Star, Lucky Revival, 5 started.

Red Diamond Express H. (R), Northlands Park, Sept. 29, $50,275, 3&up, Alberta-bred, 6½f, 1:16.60, COOL SYNSATION, Mocha John, Fly Esteem, 7 started.

Red Earth Derby (R), Remington Park, Aug. 26, $50,000, 3yo, Oklahoma-bred, 7½fT, 1:30.10, CLASSIC ACTRESS, Garbu's Son, Some Quick, 7 started.

Red Hedeman Mile H. (R), Sunland Park, Dec. 29, $125,000, 2yo, New Mexico-bred, 1m, 1:37.92, OUR CHOICE, Etoile de Dome, Top Set, 10 started.

Red Legend S. (R), Charles Town Races, June 23, $51,050, 3yo, c&g, most starts at Charles Town in last four starts, 7f, 1:28.61, HEEZAFREQUENTFLYER, Another Vow, Norjac, 7 started.

Redondo Beach S. (R), Hollywood Park, June 9, $95,575, 3&up, f&m, non-winners of a Grade 1 or 2 stakes in 2006 or a stakes at one mile or over, 1mT, 1:34.66, SOMETHINABOUTLAURA, Dancing Edie, Arm Candy (Ire), 8 started.

RED SMITH H. (G2), Aqueduct, Nov. 10, $150,000, 3&up, 1⅜mT, 2:21.45, DAVE, True Cause, Musketier (Ger), 12 started.

Regaey Island S., Ellis Park, Aug. 18, $50,000, 3yo, 1 1/16mT, 1:40.59, REVIVAL RIDGE, Voy Por Uno Mas, Self Made Man, 11 started.

Regal Gal S., Calder Race Course, Aug. 25, $50,000, 3yo, f, 1m, 1:39.44, SCOOTER GIRL, Langworthy, Pretoria Light, 6 started.

Regal Rumor S., Hawthorne Race Course, March 10, $48,375, 4&up, f&m, 6f, 1:11.84, BLUESBDANCING, Modjadji, Trout River Red, 7 started.

REGRET S. (G3), Churchill Downs, June 16, $228,600, 3yo, f, 1⅛mT, 1:47.57, GOOD MOOD (IRE), You Go West Girl, Dashes N Dots, 10 started.

Regret S., Monmouth Park, Aug. 5, $100,000, 3&up, f&m, 6f, 1:09.35, OPRAH WINNEY, Sweet Fervor, Cherokee Jewel, 7 started.

Racing — 2007 Stakes Races

Regret S. (R), Great Lakes Downs, June 9, $50,000, 3yo, f, Michigan-bred, 6f, 1:14.88, VALLEY LOOT, Tropic Rose, Desert Symphony, 7 started.
Reluctant Guest S., Arlington Park, June 2, $47,400, 3&up, f&m, 1mT, 1:36.36, QUIET ROYAL, Chic Dancer, Black Java, 7 started.
Remington Green S., Remington Park, Oct. 21, $100,000, 3&up, 1 1/16mT, 1:43.52, ASCERTAIN (IRE), Red Rock Creek, Smooth Bid, 11 started.
Remington MEC Mile S., Remington Park, Oct. 21, $100,000, 2yo, 1m, 1:38.40, GOLDEN YANK, Seeking the Lead, Jeri Harper, 12 started.
Remington Park Oaks, Remington Park, Oct. 20, $76,470, 3yo, f, 1mT, 1:38.31, ALICE BELLE, Midsummer Magic, Aidan's Bella, 12 started.
Remington Park Sprint Championship S., Remington Park, Oct. 21, $75,000, 3&up, 7f, 1:22.48, SING BABY SING, Greeley's Conquest, Nuttyboom, 11 started.
REMSEN S. (G2), Aqueduct, Nov. 24, $200,000, 2yo, 1 1/8m, 1:52.48, COURT VISION, Atoned, Trust N Dustan, 6 started.
Restoration S., Monmouth Park, June 17, $60,000, 3yo, 1mT, 1:34.82, RED GIANT, Chaluiwitcane, Encaustic, 6 started.
Revidere S., Monmouth Park, Oct. 25, $115,000, 3&up, f&m, 1 1/16m (originally scheduled on the turf), 1:43.68, PURE DISCO, Delicate Dynamite, Jenny Bean Girl, 6 started.
Richard King S. (R), Sam Houston Race Park, Dec. 1, $50,000, 3&up, Texas-bred, 1 1/8mT, 1:53.28, ALLEGED HUG, Northern Scene, Spiffy Agenda, 8 started.
Richland Hills Farm S., Lone Star Park, April 28, $50,000, 3yo, f, 6f, 1:09.24, WRENICE, Richwoman, She's Outrageous, 6 started.
Richmond Derby Trial H., Hastings Race Course, Sept. 2, $48,185, 3yo, 1 1/16m, 1:43.23, SIR GALLOVIC, Long Journey, Bad Sneakers, 7 started.
Richmond Runner S. (R), Belmont Park, May 28, $65,350, 4&up, New York-bred, 6 1/2f, 1:15.69, COMMENTATOR, Executive Search, Starcastic, 5 started.
Richmond S. (R), Hoosier Park, Nov. 5, $45,000, 3&up, f&m, Indiana-bred and/or -sired, 1 1/16m, 1:49.12, BASIN BANANNIE, Burke's Sister, Brean Can, 8 started.
RICHTER SCALE SPRINT CHAMPIONSHIP H. (G2), Gulfstream Park, March 3, $225,000, 4&up, 7f, 1:22.21, HALF OURS, Park Avenue Ball, Diabolical, 10 started.
Ricks Memorial S., Remington Park, Sept. 3, $51,320, 3&up, f&m, 1m, 1:36.73, MY THREE SISTERS, D Fine Okie, Honor the Flag, 9 started.
Riley Allison Futurity, Sunland Park, Dec. 30, $105,950, 2yo, 6 1/2f, 1:15.81, RAPPER S S, Yonegwa, Capetown Royal, 7 started.
Rio Grande Senor Futurity (R), Ruidoso Downs, July 29, $108,041, 2yo, c&g, New Mexico-bred, 5 1/2f, 1:06.80, BRAX, Playingwithchimes, Booger Boo, 10 started.
Rio Grande Senorita Futurity (R), Ruidoso Downs, July 29, $122,641, 2yo, f, New Mexico-bred, 5 1/2f, 1:06.40, POCKETFULLACHIME, Blooming Pleasure, One Bad Ghost, 9 started.
Rise Jim S. (R), Suffolk Downs, June 10, $45,000, 3&up, Massachusetts-bred, 6f, 1:11.63, SENOR ST. PAT, Petesamassbred, Fifty Seven G, 9 started.
RISEN STAR S. (G3), Fair Grounds, Feb. 10, $300,000, 3yo, 1 1/16m, 1:44.18, NOTIONAL, Imawildandcrazyguy, Zanjero, 12 started.
Riverblack Starter H. (R), Portland Meadows, May 5, $6,425, 4&up, starters for a claiming price of $4,000 or less since October 7, 2006, 1 1/4m, 2:10.25, KINGJAMES DELIVERS, Truth Buster, Macarthur Landing, 6 started.
River Cities S., Louisiana Downs, June 23, $50,000, 3&up, f&m, 1mT, 1:38.65, D FINE OKIE, Comalagold, Boundus, 10 started.
RIVER CITY H. (G3), Churchill Downs, Nov. 23, $227,400, 3&up, 1 1/8mT, 1:51.37, THORN SONG, Cosmonaut, Gun Salute, 10 started.
River Memories S., Woodbine, Oct. 27, $108,503, 3&up, f&m, 1mT, 1:38.58, LIKE A GEM, Bankin On Candy, Nottawasaga, 16 started.
R. J. Speers S., Assiniboia Downs, Sept. 2, $28,407, 3&up, 1 1/16m, 1:46.20, CAR KEYS, Arthurlooksgood, Illusive Force, 8 started.
Road Runner H. (R), Ruidoso Downs, July 29, $45,000, 3yo, New Mexico-bred, 5 1/2f, 1:05.80, CATABOLIZE, Key's Band, Run Riley Run, 12 started.
ROBERT B. LEWIS S. (G2), Santa Anita Park, March 3, $200,000, 3yo, 1 1/16m, 1:42.89, GREAT HUNTER, Sam P., Saint Paul, 9 started.
ROBERT F. CAREY MEMORIAL H. (G3), Hawthorne Race Course, Sept. 29, $150,000, 3&up, 1mT, 1:33.95, CLASSIC CAMPAIGN, Crested (GB), Gold Hornet, 7 started.
Robert G. Dick Memorial Breeders' Cup H., Delaware Park, July 14, $257,300, 3&up, f&m, 1 3/8mT, 2:16.56, ROSINKA (IRE), Royal Highness (Ger), Humoristic, 6 started.
Robert G. Leavitt Memorial S. (R), Charles Town Races, Aug. 11, $46,450, 3yo, West Virginia-bred, 7f, 1:27.35, BLUES IN THE NIGHT, Western Skyline, Eagle Speed, 9 started.
Robert Kerlan Memorial H., Hollywood Park, July 15, $94,000, 3&up, 6fT, 1:07.54, SCOTTSBLUFF, Bonfante, Quintons Shocker, 5 started.
Robert R. Hilton Memorial S. (R), Charles Town Races, Sept. 22, $51,500, 3&up, West Virginia-bred nominated to the West Virginia Breeders' Classic, 7f, 1:26.60, THREE'S A CROWD, Hello Out There, Eastern Delite, 9 started.
Robert W. Camac Memorial S. (R), Philadelphia Park, July 28, $100,000, 3&up, Pennsylvania-bred, 5fT, :57.21, REMAIN SILENT, Byandlarge, Makin Peace, 9 started.
Rocket Man S., Calder Race Course, July 28, $50,000, 3&up, 2f, :21.15, CALLER ONE, Rain Song, Bow Out, 8 started.
Rockin' River Stallion S. (R), Prairie Meadows, Aug. 4, $30,000, 3yo, progeny of Rockin' River Ranch, 6f, 1:11.38, CANT CATCH JUDY, Lee's Line, Premium Option, 7 started.
Roger Van Hoozer Memorial S. (R), Charles Town Races, Sept. 22, $50,800, 3&up, f&m, West Virginia-bred nominated to the West Virginia Breeders' Classic, 7f, 1:26.15, JULIE B, Shesagrumptoo, Carnival Chrome, 7 started.
Ron Dwyer Memorial S., Yavapai Downs, June 5, $11,400, 3yo, 6f, 1:09.20, CORREDOR DEL ORO, Yes Talk to Me, Snowbound Warrior, 6 started.
Rood and Riddle Dowager S., Keeneland Race Course, Oct. 21, $150,000, 3&up, f&m, 1 1/2mT, 2:31.15, OMEYA (CHI), Eres Magica (CHI), Jade Queen, 9 started.
Rose DeBartolo Memorial S. (R), Thistledown, Sept. 1, $75,000, 3&up, f&m, Ohio-bred, 1 1/4m, 1:50.88, PAY THE MAN, Cryptoquip, Bright Pyrite, 11 started.
Rossi Gold S., Arlington Park, Sept. 3, $47,300, 3&up, 1 3/16mT, 1:55.16, DEMETEOR, Go Between, Come On Jazz, 7 started.
Round Table H., Hollywood Park, June 16, $78,375, 3&up, 1 3/4mT, 2:54.75, STORMIN AWAY, Spring House, Runaway Dancer, 9 started.
Round Table S., Arlington Park, July 14, $100,000, 3yo, 1 1/16mAW, 1:49.75, PAVAROTTI, Time Squared, Dominican, 6 started.
Route 66 S. (R), Fair Meadows at Tulsa, July 14, $47,500, 3&up, Oklahoma-bred, 6 1/2f, 1:18.80, EVENING REWARD, Okie Time, Reality Mountain, 10 started.
Royal Chase for the Sport of Kings Hurdle S., Keeneland Race Course, April 20, $159,125, 4&up, a2 1/2mT, 4:42.95, MIXED UP, Good Night Shirt, Paradise's Boss, 11 started.
Royal North S. (R), Beulah Park, March 31, $50,000, 3yo, f, Ohio-bred, 6f, 1:10.68, MAGG'S CHOICE, Cruise Liner, Laird's Prize, 11 started.
Royal North S., Woodbine, Aug. 6, $160,531, 3&up, f&m, 6fT, 1:09.17, VESTREY LADY, Financingavailable, Becky Sharp, 7 started.
R. R. M. Carpenter Jr. Memorial H., Delaware Park, July 14, $97,000, 3&up, 1 1/16m, 1:41.88, BARCOLA, Better Than Bonds, Awfully Smart, 4 started.
Ruby Rubles S. (R), Aqueduct, March 29, $64,950, 3yo, f, New York-bred non-winners of a stakes, 6f, 1:13.52, MARGIES SMILE, Sunset Cocktail, Pasqualina, 11 started.
RUFFIAN H. (G1), Belmont Park, Sept. 8, $285,000, 3&up, f&m, 1 1/16m, 1:40.25, GINGER PUNCH, Miss Shop, Teammate, 4 started.
Ruffian S., Arapahoe Park, July 1, $28,650, 3yo, f, 7f, 1:23.88, LOVE THIS STAR, Meadow Dancer, Grammy Girl, 9 started.
Ruff/Kirchberg Memorial H. (R), Beulah Park, Nov. 17, $50,000, 3&up, Ohio-bred, 1 1/8m, 1:51.78, CATLAUNCH, Acts Like a King, Smarmy, 9 started.
Ruidoso Thoroughbred Championship S., Ruidoso Downs, Sept. 3, $50,000, 3&up, 1 1/16m, 1:45, PISTOL CREEK, Homemaker, Dear Bull, 10 started.
Ruidoso Thoroughbred Derby, Ruidoso Downs, Sept. 2, $50,000, 3yo, 1 1/16m, 1:45.20, WESTERN PRIZE, Folsum, One Tough Hombre, 10 started.
Ruidoso Thoroughbred Sale Futurity (R), Ruidoso Downs, June 16, $102,731, 2yo, New Mexico-bred, 5f, :58.40, PLAYINGWITHCHIMES, Grizzly Band, Arctic Storm Cloud, 10 started.
Ruling Angel S., Woodbine, Oct. 24, $105,580, 3yo, f, 6 1/2fAW, 1:15.52 (NTR), SASKAWEA, My List, Prophetically, 10 started.
Rumson S., Monmouth Park, June 10, $60,000, 3yo, 6f, 1:09.33, CHEROKEE COUNTRY, West Coast Flier, Southwestern Heat, 6 started.
Runaway Marcie S., Calder Race Course, Nov. 3, $50,000, 3yo, f, 1m, 1:39.43, CHER AMI, Pretoria Light, Suaveness, 7 started.

Racing — 2007 Stakes Races

Runza S., Fonner Park, April 7, $17,100, 3&up, f&m, 6f, 1:14.20, UP 'N BLUMIN, Salty Attraction, Butter Crunch, 3 started.

Rushaway S., Turfway Park, March 24, $100,000, 3yo, 1 1/16mAW, 1:43.50, DOMINICAN, Trust Your Luck, Reata's Rocket, 9 started.

Russell L. Reineman Illinois Owners' S. (R), Arlington Park, May 5, $100,000, 3&up, Illinois-owned, 1 1/16mT, 1:44.12, FORT PRADO, Toasted, Lord Carmen, 6 started.

Russian Rhythm H. (R), Philadelphia Park, June 16, $60,000, 3&up, f&m, Pennsylvania-bred, 5fT, :58.77, JET AWAY JANE, Miss Blue Tye Dye, Manukai, 10 started.

Rustic Ruler S., Hawthorne Race Course, Oct. 13, $46,500, 3&up, 6f, 1:09.61, STAR BY DESIGN, Celluloid Hero, High Expectations, 6 started.

Rutgers University S., Monmouth Park, Oct. 24, $100,000, 3yo, 1 1/16mT, 1:41.82, WAR MONGER, Pleasant Strike, Bujagali, 10 started.

Ruth C. Funkhouser S. (R), Charles Town Races, Sept. 28, $51,200, 3yo, f, West Virginia-bred nominated to the West Virginia Breeders' Classic, 7f, 1:26.98, B'S WILD RUSH, Sassy Sheri, Jip's Girl, 9 started.

Ruthless S., Aqueduct, Jan. 7, $67,965, 3yo, f, 6f, 1:10.26, GOLDEN DREAMER, Special Dream, Small Lies, 5 started.

SABIN H. (G3), Gulfstream Park, Feb. 17, $140,000, 4&up, f&m, 1m, 1:37.73, SWAP FLIPAROO, Getcozywithkaylee, Classy Charm, 8 started.

Sadie Diamond Futurity (R), Hastings Race Course, Oct. 7, $109,450, 2yo, f, Canadian-bred, 6 1/2f, 1:15.78, DANCING ALLSTAR, My Special Angel, Remarkable Miss, 7 started.

Sadie Hawkins S. (R), Charles Town Races, Aug. 18, $46,100, 3&up, f&m, West Virginia-bred, 7f, 1:26.83, CARNIVAL CHROME, Cedar Run's Emblem, Alaska Ash, 7 started.

SAFELY KEPT BREEDERS' CUP S. (G3), Laurel Park, Oct. 6, $200,000, 3yo, f, 6f, 1:10.16, SINDY WITH AN S, Ticket to Seattle, Change Up, 7 started.

Safely Kept S., Arlington Park, Sept. 13, $47,700, 3&up, f&m, 6fAW, 1:10.20, EXCELLERANT, Shriek, Modjadji, 9 started.

Sagebrush Downs Sprint S., Kamloops, May 26, $5,095, 3&up, 6 1/2f, 1:21.95, LOOKING AFTER BIZ, Favour for Joey, Dollarwatchcrossing, 10 started.

Saguaro S., Turf Paradise, Oct. 13, $45,000, 3yo, 6f, 1:08.99, CORREDOR DEL ORO, Song of Pirates, Snowbound Warrior, 7 started.

Sail On By S., Turf Paradise, Nov. 17, $31,100, 2yo, 5 1/2f, 1:03.30, RULE BY FORCE, Nordic Wind, Polish Pete, 5 started.

Salem County S., Meadowlands, Oct. 12, $58,200, 3yo, f, 1m70y, 1:40.84, LOST ETIQUETTE, Who's Happy, Bold Assurance, 4 started.

SALVATOR MILE S. (G3), Monmouth Park, June 23, $150,000, 3&up, 1m, 1:34.25, GOTTCHA GOLD, Lawyer Ron, Indy Wind, 5 started.

Sambacarioca S., Calder Race Course, Aug. 25, $50,000, 3&up, f&m, 1 1/16m, 1:47.55, CAT CAN DO, Saffronista, Funny Annie, 8 started.

Sam F. Davis S., Tampa Bay Downs, Feb. 17, $146,000, 3yo, 1 1/16m, 1:44.27, ANY GIVEN SATURDAY, All I Can Get, James Wilfred, 7 started.

Sam Houston Distaff H., Sam Houston Race Park, Jan. 27, $50,000, 4&up, f&m, 1 1/16m, 1:45.57, CHRISTMAS LILY, Plaid, I. B.'s Halo, 8 started.

Sam Houston Oaks, Sam Houston Race Park, March 10, $45,000, 3yo, f, 1m, 1:39.80, BOLD ANGEL, Hart's Sunset, Spartan Queen, 9 started.

Sam Houston Turf Sprint Cup S., Sam Houston Race Park, April 7, $50,000, 4&up, 5fT, :58.17, CAT GENIUS, Chief What It Is, Orphan Brigade, 8 started.

Sam J. Whiting Memorial S., Pleasanton, July 7, $50,930, 3&up, 6f, 1:09.79, TRICKEY TREVOR, Barber, The Pharaoh, 6 started.

Sam's Town S., Delta Downs, Dec. 7, $72,750, 3&up, 7f, 1:25.40, JONESBORO, Thunder Mission, Watchem Smokey, 6 started.

SAN ANTONIO H. (G2), Santa Anita Park, Feb. 4, $250,000, 4&up, 1 1/8m, 1:48.67, MOLENGAO (BRZ), Ball Four, El Roblar, 7 started.

SAN CARLOS H. (G2), Santa Anita Park, Feb. 17, $150,000, 4&up, 7f, 1:21.11, LATENT HEAT, Proud Tower Too, Ramsgate, 10 started.

SAN CLEMENTE H. (G2), Del Mar, July 28, $150,000, 3yo, f, 1mT, 1:34.16, PASSIFIED (GB), Fleet Caroline, Spenditallbaby, 10 started.

Sandia Sprint H., The Downs at Albuquerque, Sept. 15, $50,000, 3&up, 5f, :56.53, ABSOLUTELY TRUE, Tough Pilgrim, Artesian, 7 started.

SAN DIEGO H. (G2), Del Mar, July 21, $300,000, 3&up, 1 1/16mAW, 1:45.39, SUN BOAT (GB), Awesome Gem, Salty Humor, 9 started.

Sandpiper S., Tampa Bay Downs, Dec. 29, $65,000, 2yo, f, 6f, 1:11.37, UNFOLDING WISH, Bear Lahaina, Awesome Chic, 10 started.

Sandra Hall Grand Canyon H. (R), Turf Paradise, April 28, $50,000, 3&up, Arizona-bred, 6f, 1:09.22, MOORES BRIDGE, Desert Prospector, Corporal Tillman, 9 started.

SANDS POINT S. (G3), Belmont Park, June 2, $109,000, 3yo, f, 1 1/16mT, 1:48.53, dh-RUTHERIENNE, dh-BIT OF WHIMSY, Classic Neel, 6 started.

SAN FELIPE S. (G2), Santa Anita Park, March 17, $250,000, 3yo, 1 1/16m, 1:42.46, COBALT BLUE, Air Commander, Level Red, 5 started.

SAN FERNANDO BREEDERS' CUP S. (G2), Santa Anita Park, Jan. 13, $200,000, 4yo, 1 1/16m, 1:41.90, AWESOME GEM, Midnight Lute, Brother Derek, 11 started.

SANFORD S. (G2), Saratoga Race Course, July 26, $150,000, 2yo, 6f, 1:09.90, READY'S IMAGE, Tale of Ekati, The Roundhouse, 9 started.

SAN FRANCISCO MILE S. (G2), Golden Gate Fields, April 28, $300,000, 3&up, 1mT, 1:35.81, CHINESE DRAGON, Vega's Lord (Ger), Charmo (Fr), 5 started.

SAN GABRIEL H. (G2), Santa Anita Park, Dec. 30, $150,000, 3&up, 1 1/16mT, 1:47.57, DAYTONA (IRE), Proudinsky (Ger), Medici Code (GB), 6 started.

SAN GORGONIO H. (G2), Santa Anita Park, Jan. 7, $150,000, 4&up, f&m, 1 1/8mT, 1:46.80, CITRONNADE, Rahys' Appeal, Three Degrees (Ire), 7 started.

San Jacinto S. (R), Sam Houston Race Park, Dec. 1, $50,000, 3&up, f&m, Texas-bred, 1 1/16mT, 1:45.80, JENZ BENZ, Funny Tune, Senora Tormenta, 10 started.

SAN JUAN CAPISTRANO INVITATIONAL H. (G2), Santa Anita Park, April 22, $250,000, 4&up, a1 3/4mT, 2:48.02, ON THE ACORN (GB), Sweet Return (GB), Fitz Flag (Arg), 7 started.

San Juan County Commissioners H., SunRay Park, July 15, $75,000, 3&up, 1 1/8m, 1:53.20, THUNDER BELLE, A Gallant Discover, Rollicking Caller, 8 started.

SAN LUIS OBISPO H. (G2), Santa Anita Park, Feb. 25, $150,000, 4&up, 1 1/2mT, 2:27.21, OBRIGADO (FR), On the Acorn (GB), One Off (GB), 7 started.

SAN LUIS REY H. (G2), Santa Anita Park, March 24, $200,000, 4&up, 1 1/2mT, 2:27.50, FOURTY NINERS SON, Notable Guest, Prospect Park (GB), 7 started.

SAN MARCOS S. (G2), Santa Anita Park, Jan. 21, $150,000, 4&up, 1 1/4mT, 2:01.48, ONE OFF (GB), Notable Guest, Obrigado (Fr), 8 started.

San Miguel S., Santa Anita Park, Jan. 7, $80,000, 3yo, 6f, 1:08.82, E Z WARRIOR, Hurry Up Austin, Noble Court, 6 started.

SAN PASQUAL H. (G2), Santa Anita Park, Jan. 6, $150,000, 4&up, 1 1/16m, 1:43.18, DIXIE MEISTER, Armenian Summer, Preachinatthebar, 7 started.

San Pedro S., Santa Anita Park, April 8, $83,250, 3yo, 6 1/2f, 1:15.38, TRY TO FLY, Principle Secret, Street Lights, 9 started.

SAN RAFAEL S. (G2), Santa Anita Park, Jan. 13, $150,000, 3yo, 1m, 1:36.48, NOTIONAL, Tenfold, Grapelli, 7 started.

SAN SIMEON S. (G3), Santa Anita Park, April 21, $103,488, 4&up, 6 1/2f (originally scheduled on the turf), 1:14.59, BONFANTE, Battle Won, Siren Lure, 4 started.

SANTA ANA H. (G2), Santa Anita Park, March 25, $150,000, 4&up, f&m, 1 1/4mT, 1:46.21, CITRONNADE, Conveyor's Angel, Memorette, 7 started.

SANTA ANITA DERBY (G1), Santa Anita Park, April 7, $750,000, 3yo, 1 1/8m, 1:49.51, TIAGO, King of the Roxy, Sam P., 10 started.

SANTA ANITA H. (G1), Santa Anita Park, March 3, $1,000,000, 4&up, 1 1/4m, 2:02.11, LAVA MAN, Molengao (Brz), Boboman, 8 started.

SANTA ANITA OAKS (G1), Santa Anita Park, March 11, $300,000, 3yo, f, 1 1/16m, 1:42.84, RAGS TO RICHES, Silver Swallow, Cash Included, 5 started.

SANTA BARBARA H. (G2), Santa Anita Park, April 21, $200,000, 4&up, f&m, 1 3/8mT, 1:48.12, NAUGHTY RAFAELA (BRZ), Mabadi, Sweet Belle, 7 started.

Santa Lucia H. (R), Santa Anita Park, April 14, $79,550, 4&up, f&m, non-winners of a stakes at one mile or over in 2007, 1 1/16m, 1:42.41, BALLADO'S THUNDER, Freakin Streakin, Kris' Sis, 8 started.

SANTA MARGARITA INVITATIONAL H. (G1), Santa Anita Park, March 10, $300,000, 4&up, f&m, 1 1/8m, 1:49.25, BALANCE, Ermine, River Savage (Brz), 7 started.

SANTA MARIA H. (G1), Santa Anita Park, Feb. 10, $250,000, 4&up, f&m, 1 1/16m, 1:43.89, SUGAR SHAKE, Ermine, Rahys' Appeal, 8 started.

SANTA MONICA H. (G1), Santa Anita Park, Jan. 28, $250,000, 4&up,

f&m, 7f, 1:22.32, PUSSYCAT DOLL, Nossa Cancao (Brz), Secret Scheme, 10 started.

Santana Mile H., Santa Anita Park, March 11, $78,650, 4&up, 1m, 1:35.65, RAISE THE BLUFF, C'Mon Tiger, Yes He's a Pistol, 6 started.

SANTA PAULA S. (G3), Santa Anita Park, April 1, $100,597, 3yo, f, 6½f, 1:14.61, MAGNIFICIENCE, Swiss Diva, Coco Belle, 4 started.

Santa Teresa H., Sunland Park, Feb. 24, $50,000, 3&up, f&m, 6½f, 1:17.01, KRANKY KAROL, Handlewoman, Water Park, 10 started.

SANTA YNEZ S. (G2), Santa Anita Park, Jan. 15, $150,000, 3yo, f, 7f, 1:23.45, JUMP ON IN, Quick Little Miss, Sekira, 7 started.

SANTA YSABEL S. (G3), Santa Anita Park, Jan. 6, $108,200, 3yo, f, 1¹⁄₁₆m, 1:44.31, BARONESS THATCHER, Runway Rosie, Mistical Plan, 7 started.

SAN VICENTE S. (G2), Santa Anita Park, Feb. 11, $150,000, 3yo, 7f, 1:23.12, NOBLE COURT, Law Breaker, Half Famous, 5 started.

SAPLING S. (G3), Monmouth Park, Sept. 2, $150,000, 2yo, 6f, 1:09.97, LANTANA MOB, Preachin Man, Z Humor, 7 started.

Sarah Lane's Oates S. (R), Fair Grounds, Feb. 17, $75,000, 3yo, f, Louisiana-bred, a1mT, 1:39.39, MI ISABELLA, Perfectforthepart, Huckie, 10 started.

SARANAC S. (G3), Saratoga Race Course, Sept. 2, $115,000, 3yo, 1³⁄₁₆mT, 1:53.81, MISSION APPROVED, Distorted Reality, Pays to Dream, 11 started.

Sara's Success S., Calder Race Course, May 26, $50,000, 3&up, f&m, 1m, 1:41.06, CAT CAN DO, Silversider, A Sea Trippi, 7 started.

Saratoga Dew S. (R), Saratoga Race Course, Aug. 27, $81,500, 3&up, f&m, New York-bred, 1⅛m, 1:51.10, ICE COOL KITTY, Borrowing Base, Stolen Star, 6 started.

SARATOGA SPECIAL S. (G2), Saratoga Race Course, Aug. 16, $150,000, 2yo, 6½f, 1:15.95, KODIAK KOWBOY, The Roundhouse, Riley Tucker, 6 started.

Saratoga Sunrise S. (R), Saratoga Race Course, Aug. 11, $80,900, 3&up, New York-bred, 1⅛m, 1:49.34, NAUGHTY NEW YORKER, Building New Era, Lord Langfuhr, 6 started.

Saskatchewan Derby, Marquis Downs, Sept. 8, $14,225, 3yo, 1¹⁄₁₆m, 1:46.35, SIN TORO, Mischeviousfighter, Icicle Nose, 5 started.

Saskatoon H., Marquis Downs, June 30, $5,631, 3yo, 6f, 1:14.38, MISCHEVIOUSFIGHTER, Cole Bay, Mr. Malice, 7 started.

Sausalito S., Golden Gate Fields, Nov. 23, $75,000, 3&up, 6fAW, 1:08.32, TRIBESMAN, Barber, Big Bad Leroybrown, 8 started.

Say Florida Sandy S. (R), Belmont Park, June 30, $66,500, 4&up, New York-bred, 6f, 1:09.28, BIG APPLE DADDY, Gold and Roses, Yankee Mon, 6 started.

Saylorville S., Prairie Meadows, June 29, $100,000, 3&up, f&m, 6f, 1:08.66, MISS MACY SUE, Ready to Please, Country Diva, 6 started.

Scarlet and Gray H. (R), Beulah Park, Oct. 20, $50,000, 3&up, f&m, Ohio-bred, 6f, 1:12.44, BRIGHT PYRITE, Casey's Jet, Misty Tab, 14 started.

Schenectady H. (R), Belmont Park, Sept. 9, $104,700, 3&up, f&m, New York-bred, 6f, 1:09.60, OPRAH WINNEY, Scatkey, Karakorum Starlet, 5 started.

SCHUYLERVILLE S. (G3), Saratoga Race Course, July 25, $111,000, 2yo, f, 6f, 1:11.06, SUBTLE ALY, I Promise, Blitzing, 8 started.

Scoot S., Aqueduct, Nov. 9, $78,500, 3yo, f, 1mT, 1:37.50, THEM THERE EYES, Unspoken Word, Maddy's Heart, 10 started.

Scottsdale H., Turf Paradise, March 31, $45,000, 3yo, f, 1mT, 1:36.15, MARKET DAY (GB), Cool All Over, Point Me the Way, 5 started.

SCOTTS HIGHLANDER S. (CAN-G3), Woodbine, June 24, $188,102, 3&up, 6fT, 1:08.53, SMART ENOUGH, Heros Reward, Stradivinsky, 8 started.

Screenland S. (R), Belmont Park, May 9, $66,750, 3yo, New York-bred, 6½f, 1:15.50, BUSTIN STONES, Indian Camp, Chief's Lake, 7 started.

Seabiscuit H., Bay Meadows Race Course, Nov. 3, $61,830, 3&up, 1¹⁄₁₆mT, 1:43.71, PUTMEINYOURWILL, Heroi Do Bafra (Brz), Mulcahy, 9 started.

Seacliff S., Calder Race Course, Sept. 1, $55,000, 2yo, 1m, 1:42.08, HONEY HONEY HONEY, Ed the Boxer, Hypocrite, 8 started.

Sea O Erin Mile H., Arlington Park, Aug. 11, $148,500, 3&up, a1mT, 1:38.10, SPOTSGONE, Galantas, Load a Chronic, 8 started.

Seattle H., Emerald Downs, May 6, $45,000, 3&up, 6f, 1:08.40, STARBIRD ROAD, Wasserman, Westsideclyde, 9 started.

Seattle Slew H., Emerald Downs, Aug. 5, $60,300, 3yo, c&g, 1¹⁄₁₆m, 1:41.20, MULCAHY, Wild Cycle, Call On Carson, 7 started.

SEAWAY S. (CAN-G3), Woodbine, Sept. 8, $159,789, 3&up, f&m, 7fAW, 1:22.54, SHE'S INDY MONEY, Financingavailable, Count to Three, 5 started.

SECRETARIAT S. (G1), Arlington Park, Aug. 11, $400,000, 3yo, 1¼mT, 2:04.02, SHAMDINAN (FR), Red Giant, Going Ballistic, 9 started.

Seeking the Gold S., Louisiana Downs, June 23, $49,000, 3yo, 1mT, 1:39.31, CAJUN CONQUEST, Slew by Slew, Forty Acres, 7 started.

Select S., Monmouth Park, Oct. 27, $200,000, 3yo, 6f, 1:10.54, COBALT BLUE, E Z Warrior, Appealing Spring, 9 started.

SELENE S. (CAN-G3), Woodbine, May 20, $241,198, 3yo, f, 1¹⁄₁₆mAW, 1:43.73 (NTR), BEAR NOW, Saskawea, Marietta, 12 started.

Selima S., Laurel Park, Nov. 24, $100,000, 2yo, f, 1¹⁄₁₆mT, 1:43.66, BSHARPSONATA, Grace and Power, Fareena, 12 started.

Selma S. (R), Retama Park, Oct. 13, $45,000, 3yo, f, Texas-bred, 5fT, :55.64, TEMPERAMENTAL MISS, Touchofreality, Calirose, 10 started.

Senate Appointee H., Hastings Race Course, May 26, $48,250, 3&up, f&m, 6½f, 1:16.61, MONASHEE, Starlite Strike, Slewpast, 6 started.

SENATOR KEN MADDY H. (G3), Oak Tree at Santa Anita, Sept. 26, $114,900, 3&up, f&m, a6½fT, 1:13.30, DANCING EDIE, Lady Gamer, Strong Faith, 11 started.

SENORITA S. (G3), Hollywood Park, May 12, $111,600, 3yo, f, 1mT, 1:34.47, VALBENNY (IRE), Super Freaky, Passified (GB), 8 started.

Sensational Star H. (R), Santa Anita Park, Feb. 18, $134,375, 4&up, California-bred, a6½fT, 1:13, BEDLAM BERTIE, Areyoutalkintome, Red Warrior, 6 started.

Serena's Song S., Monmouth Park, July 21, $60,000, 3yo, f, 1m70y, 1:40.22, EXCHANGING FIRE, Ethan's Car, Lady Marlboro, 8 started.

Seton Hall University S., Meadowlands, Oct. 6, $73,590, 3&up, f&m, 6f, 1:09.51, PURE DISCO, dh-Summer Sting, dh-Solarana (Arg), 5 started.

Seven Stars S. (R), Louisiana Downs, May 12, $48,500, 3&up, f&m, Louisiana-bred, 1¹⁄₁₆mT, 1:46.35, RASPBERRY WINE, Equestrian Girls, Intractabie, 6 started.

SHADWELL TURF MILE S. (G1), Keeneland Race Course, Oct. 6, $648,000, 3&up, 1mT, 1:35.56, PURIM, Cosmonaut, Shakis (Ire), 9 started.

Shady Well S. (R), Woodbine, July 15, $143,436, 2yo, f, Ontario-bred, 5½fAW, 1:04.09 (NTR), ALVENA, Executrix, Mrs. Began, 6 started.

SHAKERTOWN S. (G3), Keeneland Race Course, April 15, $110,200, 3&up, 5½fT, 1:03.94, THE NTH DEGREE, Congo King, Sgt. Bert, 8 started.

Shakopee S., Canterbury Park, Sept. 3, $45,000, 3&up, f&m, 1m70y, 1:41.25, GLITTER STAR, Dynabin, Tens Holy Spirit, 6 started.

SHAM S. (G3), Santa Anita Park, Feb. 3, $101,500, 3yo, 1⅛m, 1:48.91, RAVEL, Liquidity, Song of Navarone, 7 started.

Sharp Cat S., Hollywood Park, Nov. 17, $107,100, 2yo, f, 1¹⁄₁₆mAW, 1:43.06, FOXY DANSEUR, Champagne Eyes, Czechers, 5 started.

Shecky Greene S., Arlington Park, May 4, $47,100, 3yo, 6f-AW, 1:10.91, PIRATE SAINT, Front Court, Thatsalottabull, 7 started.

SHEEPSHEAD BAY H. (G2), Belmont Park, May 26, $150,000, 3&up, f&m, 1⅜mT, 2:13, HONEY RYDER, Safari Queen (Arg), Hostess, 7 started.

Shelby County S. (R), Indiana Downs, May 18, $45,000, 3&up, f&m, Indiana-bred, 6f, 1:10.99, LADY BLUE SKY, Iron Girl, Basin Banannie, 12 started.

Shepperton S. (R), Woodbine, Aug. 5, $119,663, 3&up, Ontario-foaled, 6½fAW, 1:16.77, MAIN EXECUTIVE, Cool Selection, Marco Be Good, 8 started.

She Rides Tonite S. (R), Belmont Park, June 23, $66,750, 3yo, f, New York-bred non-winners of a stakes in 2007, 6f, 1:09.71, STREET SASS, Cammy's Choice, Nordberg, 7 started.

Sherpa Guide S. (R), Belmont Park, Sept. 26, $76,500, 3&up, New York-bred, 1¹⁄₁₆m, 1:43.20, WHO WHAT WIN, French Transition, Building New Era, 6 started.

Shine Again S. (R), Pimlico Race Course, May 26, $50,000, 3&up, f&m, Maryland-bred non-winners of a stakes, 1¹⁄₁₆m, 1:45.51, KATIE'S LOVE, Hanalei Bay, Take a Check, 6 started.

SHIRLEY JONES BREEDERS' CUP H. (G2), Gulfstream Park, March 17, $200,000, 4&up, f&m, 7f, 1:22.67, SWEET FERVOR, Any Limit, My Lucky Free, 8 started.

Shiskabob S. (R), Louisiana Downs, July 21, $100,000, 3&up, Louisiana-bred, 1¹⁄₁₆m, 1:43.92, DESERT WHEAT, Lee's Say So, Rock 'n Rail, 9 started.

Shocker T. H., Calder Race Course, Oct. 13, $100,000, 3&up, f&m, 1¹⁄₁₆m, 1:47.11, AMAZING SPEED, Gadolinium, Saffronista, 10 started.

SHOEMAKER MILE S. (G1), Hollywood Park, May 28, $370,200, 3&up, 1mT, 1:34.34, THE TIN MAN, Get Funky, Willow O Wisp, 10 started.

Shortgrass Heritage S. (R), Marquis Downs, Aug. 18, $18,846, 3yo,

c&g, Saskatchewan-bred, 1m, 1:43.48, MISCHEVIOUSFIGHTER, Exit Stage West, Double Beam, 6 started.

Shorty's Star Starter S., Yavapai Downs, May 30, $8,700, 3&up, 1$\frac{1}{16}$m, 1:45.80, CHASEUR, Devil Cop, Spider Armstrong, 9 started.

Shot of Gold S., Canterbury Park, May 5, $45,000, 3&up, 5½f, 1:03.23, SENECA SUMMER, Vazandar, Smoke Smoke Smoke, 7 started.

Showtime Deb S. (R), Hawthorne Race Course, Nov. 3, $110,125, 2yo, f, Illinois-conceived and/or -foaled, 6f, 1:12.32, CARTS ITALIAN ROSE, My Facts, Carbella, 7 started.

SHUVEE H. (G2), Belmont Park, May 19, $150,000, 3&up, f&m, 1m, 1:38.19, TEAMMATE, Sugar Shake, Rahys' Appeal, 6 started.

Shy Riannon S., Turf Paradise, Jan. 30, $25,200, 4&up, f&m, 5½f, 1:02.65, MIRANDO, Kissntheboysgoodby, Shimmering Heat, 7 started.

Sickle's Image S. (R), Great Lakes Downs, Sept. 15, $50,000, 2yo, f, Michigan-bred, 6f, 1:16.65, CLEVER IDEA, Equalitysdebutante, Cheries Challenge, 7 started.

Sierra Starlet H. (R), Ruidoso Downs, July 29, $45,000, 3yo, f, New Mexico-bred, 5½f, 1:03, SILVER EXPRESSION, Shezapirate, La Mora Bonita, 10 started.

SILVERBULLETDAY S. (G3), Fair Grounds, Feb. 10, $200,000, 3yo, f, 1$\frac{1}{16}$m, 1:44.13, APPEALING ZOPHIE, Total, Get Ready Bertie, 9 started.

Silver Cup Futurity, Arapahoe Park, July 23, $19,710, 2yo, f, 5½f, 1:04.89, SEATTLE SHEBA, Dazzling Blu Skies, Pray for Cash, 5 started.

Silver Cup Futurity, Arapahoe Park, July 30, $21,020, 2yo, c&g, 5½f, 1:05.28, ASPEN MIST, Sunny Serenade, Radar Rated, 8 started.

Silver Deputy S., Woodbine, Aug. 25, $95,420, 2yo, 6½fAW, 1:17.32, BEAR HOLIDAY, Stuck in Traffic, Doneraile Gold, 6 started.

Silver Goblin S. (R), Remington Park, Aug. 19, $50,000, 3&up, Oklahoma-bred, 6½f, 1:16.46, MARQ FRENCH, Evening Reward, Tonight Rainbow, 6 started.

Silver Spur Breeders' Cup S., Lone Star Park, July 28, $67,250, 2yo, f, 6f, 1:11.29, AMERICAN PRIZE, Valid Lilly, Dill Or No Dill, 9 started.

Silvey's Image S., Turf Paradise, April 15, $24,800, 3yo, 4½fT, :50.84, QUINTON'S FLEET, Actually, Capt. Joe Blow, 5 started.

Simcoe S. (R), Woodbine, Sept. 3, $121,393, 2yo, c&g, Canadian-bred, 7fAW, 1:23.39, DON'S FOLLY, Drunken Love, Seattle Hill, 13 started.

Similkameen Cup S., Sunflower Downs, June 29, $10,006, 3&up, a1$\frac{1}{16}$m, 1:46.07 (NTR), CRESCENT REMARK, Lethal Grande, Regal Promise, 6 started.

Singspiel S., Woodbine, June 24, $94,986, 3&up, 1½mT, 2:27.79, PELLEGRINO (BRZ), Royal Challenger, French Beret, 9 started.

Sir Barton S. (R), Woodbine, Dec. 8, $126,340, 3&up, Ontario-foaled, 1$\frac{1}{16}$mAW, 1:42.85, EXECUTIVE CHOICE, Archers Alyancer, Dancer's Bajan, 10 started.

SIR BEAUFORT S. (G3), Santa Anita Park, Dec. 26, $122,100, 3yo, 1mT, 1:34.36, MONTEREY JAZZ, Mr Napper Tandy (GB), Twilight Meteor, 13 started.

Sir Winston Churchill H., Hastings Race Course, Sept. 23, $50,575, 3&up, 1⅛m, 1:49.90, TRUE METROPOLITAN, Winter Warning, Shacane, 6 started.

Sissy Woolums Memorial S. (R), Colonial Downs, Aug. 3, $40,000, 3&up, f&m, Virginia-bred and/or -sired, North Carolina-bred and/or -sired, South Carolina-bred and/or -sired, and progeny of stallions donated to the 2006 Mid-South Stallion Season Auction, 5½fT, 1:02.28, ANDREA'S PIC, Je Suis Prest, Meadow Phone Home, 9 started.

SIXTY SAILS H. (G3), Hawthorne Race Course, April 21, $250,000, 3&up, f&m, 1⅛m, 1:50.89, KETTLEONEUP, My Chickadee, Rolling Sea, 5 started.

Skipat S., Pimlico Race Course, June 9, $88,200, 3&up, f&m, 6f, 1:10.89, SILMARIL, My Sister Sue, Homesteader, 5 started.

SKIP AWAY H. (G3), Gulfstream Park, March 31, $114,500, 4&up, 1⅛m, 1:49.70, A. P. ARROW, Rehoboth, Political Force, 7 started.

Skip Away S., Monmouth Park, July 28, $70,000, 3&up, 1$\frac{1}{16}$m, 1:41.33, INDY WIND, Touched by Madness, Too Many Toyz, 6 started.

Ski Roundtop Timber S., Shawan Downs, Sept. 29, $26,500, 4&up, a3mT, 6:06 (NCR), IRISH PRINCE (NZ), Bubble Economy, Seeyouattheevent, 8 started.

Skunktail S. (R), Horsemen's Park, July 22, $28,800, 3yo, c&g, Nebraska-bred, 1m, 1:39, JAMES THE GREATER, Heso, Show My Dancer, 7 started.

SKY CLASSIC S. (CAN-G2), Woodbine, Sept. 23, $301,758, 3&up, 1⅜mT, 2:14.10, CLOUDY'S KNIGHT, Sterwins, Windward Islands, 10 started.

Skyy El Joven S., Retama Park, Oct. 27, $100,000, 2yo, c&g, 1mT, 1:35.97, ROYAL NIGHT, Twentieth Century, Letmeby, 9 started.

Sleepy Hollow S. (R), Belmont Park, Oct. 20, $100,000, 2yo, New York-bred, 1m, 1:38.46, GIANT MOON, Coastal Drive, Big Truck, 7 started.

Slipton Fell H., Mountaineer Race Track and Gaming Resort, June 9, $75,000, 3&up, 1m70y, 1:42.52, BERNIE BLUE, M B Sea, Mr. Pursuit, 6 started.

Smart Angle S., Aqueduct, Nov. 11, $77,700, 3&up, f&m, 6f, 1:09.72, MORE ANGELS, Karakorum Starlet, Swap Fliparoo, 6 started.

Smart Halo S., Laurel Park, March 31, $86,400, 3yo, f, 6f, 1:12.39, LAILA'S PUNCH, Paying Off, Now It Begins, 7 started.

Smarty Jones Classic S. (R), Philadelphia Park, July 28, $125,000, 3&up, Pennsylvania-bred, 1$\frac{1}{16}$m, 1:42.10, DELAWARE RIVER, Putonyerdancinshuz, Serene Harbor, 7 started.

SMILE SPRINT H. (G2), Calder Race Course, July 7, $500,000, 3&up, 6f, 1:09.89, MACH RIDE, Paradise Dancer, Smokey Stover, 7 started.

Sneakbox S., Monmouth Park, June 23, $60,000, 3&up, 5½fT, 1:01.85 (NCR), IN SUMMATION, Mr. Silver, Vicarage, 8 started.

Solana Beach H. (R), Del Mar, Aug. 25, $133,900, 3&up, f&m, California-bred, 1mT, 1:34.28, BAI AND BAI, Spenditallbaby, Gentle Charmer, 6 started.

Somerset Medical Center Hurdle S. (R), Meadowlands, Sept. 21, $75,000, 4&up, non-winners over hurdles prior to June 1, 2006, a2½mT, 4:28.31, DIVINE FORTUNE, Planets Aligned, Dark Equation, 7 started.

Somethingroyal S. (R), Colonial Downs, July 14, $60,000, 3&up, f&m, Virginia-bred/and or -sired, 5½fT, 1:03.19, ANDREA'S PIC, Meadow Phone Home, Leaves of Autumn, 7 started.

Sonic Gray S., Calder Race Course, Dec. 8, $45,000, 3&up, f&m, 1$\frac{1}{16}$m, 1:45.88, AMAZING SPEED, Cat Can Do, Running Lass, 7 started.

Sonny Hine S., Laurel Park, Oct. 20, $50,000, 3yo, 6f, 1:11.36, SOUTHWESTERN HEAT, Jacob's Run, Norjac, 8 started.

Sonoma H., Northlands Park, Aug. 11, $94,930, 3yo, f, 1$\frac{1}{16}$m, 1:44.80, ALPINE GARDEN, Tanika, Beau Spirit, 6 started.

Sophomore Sprint Championship S., Mountaineer Race Track and Gaming Resort, Nov. 20, $75,000, 3yo, 6f, 1:10.60, RAVALO, Piratesonthelake, Bawdens, 9 started.

Sorority S., Monmouth Park, Sept. 2, $120,000, 2yo, f, 6f, 1:11.72, A LITTLE GEM, Bold Child, Reata's Quik Punch, 7 started.

SORRENTO S. (G3), Del Mar, Aug. 8, $150,000, 2yo, f, 6½fAW, 1:19.59, TASHA'S MIRACLE, Set Play, Foxy Danseur, 8 started.

Southern Bank and Trust Imperial Cup Hurdle S., Aiken, March 24, $40,000, 4&up, a2¼mT, 4:19.20 (NCR), PARADISE'S BOSS, Niello, River Bed, 6 started.

Southern Belle S., Grants Pass, June 23, $3,332, 3&up, f&m, 5½f, 1:06.60, TRULY JEST, Rosie Quatorze, In Love With Loot, 7 started.

South Mississippi Owners' and Breeders' S. (R), Fair Grounds, Feb. 2, $40,000, 3yo, Mississippi-owned, 6f, 1:13.55, IDE'S CHILD, Richters Star, Bobo Is Loose, 10 started.

South Ocean S. (R), Woodbine, Nov. 7, $137,820, 2yo, f, Ontario-foaled, 1$\frac{1}{16}$mAW, 1:46.52, KRZ EXEC, Lady d'Wildcat, Short Shorts, 10 started.

Southwest S., Oaklawn Park, Feb. 19, $250,000, 3yo, 1m, 1:38.20, TEUFLESBERG, Officer Rocket (GB), Forty Grams, 9 started.

Spangled Jimmy H., Northlands Park, July 7, $47,660, 3&up, 1m, 1:37.60, TEAGUES FIGHT, Trick of the North, Test Boy, 9 started.

Spartan S. (R), Great Lakes Downs, July 17, $50,000, 3yo, c&g, Michigan-bred, 7f, 1:28.28, ALL I CAN GET, Candid Image, Born to Tango, 8 started.

Spectacular Bid S., Gulfstream Park, Jan. 7, $77,750, 3yo, 6f, 1:09.60, BUFFALO MAN, Out of Gwedda, Green Vegas, 7 started.

Spectacular Bid S. (R), Belmont Park, June 3, $75,000, 3yo, c&g, progeny of eligible New York stallions, 1m, 1:36.53, DR. V'S MAGIC, Stunt Man, Good Prospect, 8 started.

Speed S., Lincoln State Fair, May 19, $15,000, 3&up, 4½f, :51.20, ANOTHER AUDIBLE, Country Warrior, First Class Brass, 9 started.

Speed to Spare S., Northlands Park, Sept. 8, $94,830, 3&up, 1⅜m, 2:17, TRUE METROPOLITAN, Test Boy, Trick of the North, 5 started.

SPEND A BUCK H. (G3), Calder Race Course, Oct. 13, $100,000, 3&up, 1$\frac{1}{16}$m, 1:45.14, YES HE'S THE MAN, Electrify, Summer Book, 11 started.

Spend a Buck S., Monmouth Park, June 2, $58,200, 3yo, 1m, 1:35.84, NERVE, Saratoga Lulaby, Whiskey Lit, 4 started.

Spicy H. (R), Arapahoe Park, Aug. 12, $35,532, 3&up, f&m, Colorado-bred, 1$\frac{1}{16}$m, 1:44.87, VANNACIDE, Ladysgotthelooks, Oliver the Moon, 5 started.

SPINAWAY S. (G1), Saratoga Race Course, Sept. 2, $250,000, 2yo, f, 7f, 1:24.24, IRISH SMOKE, A to the Croft, Yonagucci, 9 started.

Spirit of Texas S. (R), Sam Houston Race Park, Dec. 1, $50,000, 3&up, Texas-bred, 6f, 1:09.55, MYSTERY CLASSIC, Rain On Monday, Snuck By, 6 started.

Sport of Queens Filly and Mare Hurdle S., Camden, Nov. 18, $25,000, 3&up, f&m, a2¼mT, 4:23.20, SLEW'S PEAK, Lair, Feeling So Pretty, 8 started.

SPORT PAGE H. (G3), Aqueduct, Oct. 27, $142,500, 3&up, 7f, 1:21.38, TASTEYVILLE, Sir Greeley, Council Member, 4 started.

Sportsman's Paradise S., Delta Downs, March 31, $99,000, 3yo, 1m, 1:39.19, BETA CAPO, Wannabeinclued, Mr. Unstoppable, 8 started.

Spring Fever S., Oaklawn Park, March 3, $50,000, 4&up, f&m, 5½f, 1:04.94, TRUE TAILS, Miss Elsie, Hot Storm, 6 started.

Springfield S. (R), Arlington Park, July 7, $88,300, 3yo, Illinois-conceived and/or -foaled, 1mAW, 1:37.63, GENTLEMAN CHESTER, Wayoff, Stonehouse, 12 started.

Spring Sprint S., Lethbridge, June 3, $15,265, 3&up, 5½f, 1:05.60 (NTR), LAFLEUR, Height of Summer, Dr. Mo, 7 started.

Spring S. (R), Sam Houston Race Park, March 17, $45,000, 4&up, Texas-bred, 7f, 1:23.84, DREAMSANDVISIONS, Goosey Moose, Snuck By, 9 started.

Spruce Fir H. (R), Monmouth Park, June 27, $60,000, 3&up, f&m, New Jersey-bred, 1m70y, 1:41.83, JENNY BEAN GIRL, Murphy Style, I'mtoogoodtobetrue, 6 started.

Spruce Knob S. (R), Charles Town Races, July 21, $45,900, 3yo, f, West Virginia-bred starters with most starts at Charles Town in last four starts, 4½f, :52.17, LOVE TO PLUNGE, Oak Hill Princess, Makin Copy, 5 started.

Squan Song S. (R), Laurel Park, Dec. 15, $45,000, 3&up, f&m, Maryland-bred non-winners of a stakes, 7f, 1:26.75, FOR KISSES, Now It Begins, Take a Check, 10 started.

STAGE DOOR BETTY H. (G3), Calder Race Course, Dec. 29, $100,000, 3&up, f&m, 1¹⁄₁₆m, 1:46.16, BAYOU'S LASSIE, Amazing Speed, Cindy's Mom, 9 started.

Stage View S. (R), Belmont Park, June 27, $69,750, 3&up, f&m, New York-bred, 7fT, 1:20.90, IRON GODDESS, Mohegan Sky, Rewrite, 11 started.

Stampede Park Sales H. (R), Stampede Park, April 14, $42,215, 4&up, sold at the CTHS sale, 6f, 1:10, TEAGUES FIGHT, Wye Red, Mocha John, 5 started.

Stampede Park Sales H. (R), Stampede Park, April 14, $43,095, 4&up, f&m, sold at the CTHS sale, 6f, 1:10.80, CERTAINLY REGAL, Pretty Beaucat, To Dream Again, 7 started.

Stampede Park Sprint Championship H., Stampede Park, April 28, $44,805, 4&up, 6f, 1:10.20, PLAGIARIST, Churchbridge, Vested in Slew, 9 started.

Stanton S., Delaware Park, July 21, $59,850, 3yo, 1¹⁄₁₆mT, 1:42.96, DIAMOND FEVER, Wheels Up At Noon, Dinner in Odem, 7 started.

Stardust S. (R), Louisiana Downs, July 21, $100,000, 2yo, Louisiana-bred, 6f, 1:11.31, PANTARA PHANTOM, Smith B Quick, West Coast Time, 10 started.

Star of Texas S. (R), Sam Houston Race Park, Dec. 1, $100,000, 3&up, Texas-bred, 1¹⁄₁₆m, 1:44.53, SANDBURR, Moon Kid, Goosey Moose, 6 started.

STARS AND STRIPES TURF H. (G3), Arlington Park, July 4, $200,000, 3&up, 1½mT, 2:31.87, ALWAYS FIRST (GB), Cloudy's Knight, Stream Cat, 7 started.

Star Shoot S., Woodbine, April 22, $112,079, 3yo, f, 6fAW, 1:10.97, NATIVE LEGEND, Silky Smooth, Bear Now, 9 started.

State Fair Board S. (1st Div.), Lincoln State Fair, July 4, $18,200, 3&up, 1m70y, 1:42, FIRST CLASS BRASS, High Dice, Mike's Pet, 6 started.

State Fair Board S. (2nd Div.), Lincoln State Fair, July 4, $18,988, 3&up, 1m70y, 1:41.40, BEVYS DAZZLER, Blumin Attitude, Nine K Enigma, 7 started.

State Fair Breeders' Special S. (R), Lincoln State Fair, June 15, $20,600, 3yo, Nebraska-bred, 1m, 1:40.40, HESO, Dice, Hamtaro, 6 started.

State Fair Futurity (R), Lincoln State Fair, July 1, $20,650, 2yo, Nebraska-bred, 4½f, :51.80, ITTAKESTWOBABY, Tellin On You, Tammy, 6 started.

Staten Island S. (R), Aqueduct, Nov. 11, $75,000, 3&up, f&m, progeny of eligible New York stallions, 7f, 1:23.14, TAMBERINO, Duchess of Rokeby, Cammy's Choice, 9 started.

Statue of Liberty S. (R), Saratoga Race Course, Aug. 9, $150,000, 3yo, f, progeny of eligible New York stallions, 1⅛mT, 1:50.16, TISH-MEISTER, Don't Mind Me, Western Sweep, 6 started.

Steady Growth S. (R), Woodbine, June 9, $118,655, 3&up, Ontario-foaled, 1¹⁄₁₆mAW, 1:43.68, EXECUTIVE CHOICE, Bold Finish, Soul Rebel, 7 started.

Steal a Kiss S. (R), Belmont Park, May 17, $70,150, 4&up, f&m, non-winners of a graded stakes on the turf in 2006-'07, 1¹⁄₁₆mT, 1:42.73, MERIBEL, Fantastic Shirl, Jade Queen, 5 started.

Steinlen S., Belmont Park, Sept. 13, $76,500, 4&up, 7fT, 1:22.51, REBELLION (GB), Giant Basil, River City Rebel, 6 started.

STEPHEN FOSTER H. (G1), Churchill Downs, June 16, $829,500, 3&up, 1⅛m, 1:48.63, FLASHY BULL, Magna Graduate, Diamond Stripes, 8 started.

St. Georges S., Delaware Park, May 28, $61,895, 3yo, f, 1¹⁄₁₆mT, 1:43.31, MISS TIZZYNOW, New Edition, Eurydice, 7 started.

Stinson Beach S., Golden Gate Fields, Jan. 1, $50,275, 3yo, 6f, 1:09.23, VICARINO, Candy's Bro, Double Action, 4 started.

Stonehedge Farm South Sophomore Fillies S. (R), Tampa Bay Downs, April 7, $85,000, 3yo, f, Florida-bred, 7f, 1:25.71, TRAINEE, Suaveness, Saint Barbara, 11 started.

STONERSIDE BEAUMONT S. (G2), Keeneland Race Course, April 12, $250,000, 3yo, f, a7fAW, 1:24.93, STREET SOUNDS, Forever Together, Palace Pier, 7 started.

Stonerside S., Lone Star Park, May 28, $100,000, 3yo, f, 7f, 1:24.55, ATLANTA HIGHWAY, Gallant Dreamer, She's Outrageous, 8 started.

Stonewall Stallions Georgia Oaks (R), Calder Race Course, May 5, $75,000, 3yo, f, progeny of GTOBA nominated stallions, 1¹⁄₁₆mT, 1:41.12, WINE DIVA, Snow Cone, Dantrelle Light, 11 started.

Storm Flag Flying S., Belmont Park, Oct. 19, $75,750, 4&up, f&m, 7f, 1:24.01, PUSSYCAT DOLL, Great Intentions, Swap Fliparoo, 5 started.

Stormy Frolic S., Calder Race Course, Nov. 18, $35,000, 3yo, f, 1¹⁄₁₆m, 1:47.76, SUAVENESS, Casa Mimaty, Sweet Exchange, 5 started.

Stormy Krissy S., Aqueduct, Feb. 22, $66,750, 4&up, f&m, 6f, 1:11.45, CANDY BOX, Livermore Valley, Secret Brook, 7 started.

Straight Deal S., Belmont Park, May 23, $69,700, 3yo, 1mT, 1:34.74, STRIKE A DEAL, Summer Doldrums, Twilight Meteor, 6 started.

Strate Sunshine S., Hawthorne Race Course, Oct. 10, $47,750, 3&up, f&m, 6f, 1:10.29, PRETTY JENNY, Ally's Little Sis, Denoun N Deverb, 7 started.

Strawberry Morn H., Hastings Race Course, June 23, $48,889, 3&up, f&m, 1¹⁄₁₆m, 1:44.61, MONASHEE, Starlite Strike, Avenging Kat, 5 started.

Strong Ruler S. (R), Emerald Downs, Aug. 12, $45,000, 2yo, c&g, progeny of eligible Washington stallions standing in 2004, 6½f, 1:16, MARGO'S GIFT, Courageous Son, Arrow Junction, 7 started.

STRUB S. (G2), Santa Anita Park, Feb. 3, $300,000, 4yo, 1⅛m, 1:48.65, ARSON SQUAD, Spring At Last, Brother Derek, 6 started.

Sturgeon River S. (R), Northlands Park, Sept. 29, $50,275, 2yo, f, Alberta-bred, 1m, 1:41.40, BEARS ARTISTE, Spicy Candy, Call Me Cory, 6 started.

STUYVESANT H. (G3), Aqueduct, Nov. 17, $108,500, 3&up, 1⅛m, 1:48.08, HUNTING, Utopia (Jpn), Evening Attire, 6 started.

Stymie H., Aqueduct, March 3, $72,605, 3&up, 1⅛m, 1:49.57, EVENING ATTIRE, Malibu Moonshine, Angliana, 9 started.

Stymie S., Delaware Park, Nov. 4, $56,066, 3&up, 1⅛m, 1:50.56, AW-FULLY SMART, Better Than Bonds, Smart Growth, 4 started.

SUBURBAN H. (G1), Belmont Park, June 30, $400,000, 3&up, 1¼m, 2:00.50, POLITICAL FORCE, Fairbanks, Malibu Moonshine, 6 started.

Sugar Bowl S., Fair Grounds, Dec. 22, $99,000, 2yo, 6f, 1:09.44, SOK SOK, Liberty Bull, Ben and the Twin, 8 started.

Sugar N Spice S., Calder Race Course, Oct. 21, $45,000, 3&up, f&m, 6½f, 1:18.05, RGIRLDOESN'TBLUFF, Bereba, Shadow Belle, 6 started.

Sugar Plum Time S., Belmont Park, May 12, $68,750, 3yo, f, 1¹⁄₁₆mT, 1:43.04, RUTHERIENNE, Silence Dogood, Olivine, 7 started.

Summer Finale S., Mountaineer Race Track and Gaming Resort, Sept. 3, $75,000, 3&up, f&m, 1m70yT, 1:40.22, BAVARIAN BELLE, Water Gap, Dancing Band, 8 started.

SUMMER S. (CAN-G3), Woodbine, Sept. 16, $244,153, 2yo, 1mT, 1:35.26, PRUSSIAN, Briarwood Circle, Your Round, 9 started.

Summertime Promise S., Hawthorne Race Course, Oct. 21, $47,000, 3&up, f&m, 1¹⁄₁₆mT, 1:41.81, JENNIE R., Glitter Star, Classical Ryder, 4 started.

Sumter S., Calder Race Course, May 5, $50,000, 3&up, 1¹⁄₁₆m, 1:46.16, TOO MANY TOYZ, Electric Light, Big Lover, 9 started.

Sun City H., Turf Paradise, Feb. 24, $50,000, 4&up, f&m, 1mT, 1:36.40, HOMEMAKER, Shadowy Waters, Haka Girl, 8 started.

Suncoast S., Tampa Bay Downs, Feb. 17, $75,000, 3yo, f, a1m, 1:38.39, AUTOBAHN GIRL, Trainee, Saint Barbara, 9 started.
Sunday Silence S., Louisiana Downs, Sept. 22, $198,000, 2yo, 1⅟₁₆mT, 1:42.28, CHEROKEE TRIANGLE, Gangbuster, Moody Jones, 8 started.
Sun Devil S., Turf Paradise, Jan. 20, $45,000, 3yo, f, 1m, 1:44.29, SLEW O' PLATINUM, Staten Island, Wavy Lass, 6 started.
Sun Downs Thoroughbred H., Sun Downs, April 15, $3,200, 3&up, f&m, 4f, :46.80, SCHU TRUE SLEEPER, Buffyslew, Charlee Chop Chop, 6 started.
Sunflower S. (R), The Woodlands, Sept. 29, $20,000, 3&up, c&g, Kansas-bred, 6f, 1:10, MANOVAN, Nick Missed, Donnie O, 5 started.
Sunland Park H., Sunland Park, April 21, $100,000, 3&up, 1⅛m, 1:50.50, DON'T STRIKE OUT, Keep On Punching, Rollicking Caller, 8 started.
Sun Life H., Marquis Downs, June 22, $5,584, 3&up, f&m, 6f, 1:12.49, ELLA MARIA, Target's Answer, Devdrudan, 9 started.
Sunny Issues S., Calder Race Course, Dec. 8, $50,000, 3yo, f, 1mT, 1:35.41, PRETORIA LIGHT, Snow Cone, Cher Ami, 10 started.
Sunny's Halo S., Louisiana Downs, Aug. 18, $72,825, 2yo, 1mT, 1:39.16, JUSTACLOWN, Canny, Pantara Phantom, 5 started.
Sun Power S. (R), Hawthorne Race Course, Nov. 3, $100,300, 2yo, c&g, Illinois-conceived and/or -foaled, 6f, 1:11.83, DAKOTA REBEL, River Bear, Billys Bar Buddy, 11 started.
SunRay Park and Casino H., SunRay Park, June 3, $40,000, 3yo, 1m, 1:37.60, CRYPTS SEEKER, Mr Charlypotatoes, Sharan's Pride, 7 started.
Sunset Gun S. (R), Suffolk Downs, Sept. 3, $45,000, 3&up, f&m, Massachusetts-bred, a1⅟₁₆mT, 1:49.42, ASK QUEENIE, Southoftheborder, Auntie Millie, 6 started.
SUNSET H. (G2), Hollywood Park, July 15, $150,400, 3&up, 1½mT, 2:27.68, RUNAWAY DANCER, Fitz Flag (Arg), Spring House, 6 started.
Sunshine Millions Classic S. (R), Gulfstream Park, Jan. 27, $1,000,000, 4&up, California- or Florida-bred, 1⅛m, 1:49.89, MCCANN'S MOJAVE, Summer Book, Silver Wagon, 12 started.
Sunshine Millions Dash S. (R), Gulfstream Park, Jan. 27, $250,000, 3yo, California- or Florida-bred, 6f, 1:10.22, STORM IN MAY, Idiot Proof, Texas Voyager, 14 started.
Sunshine Millions Distaff S. (R), Santa Anita Park, Jan. 27, $500,000, 4&up, f&m, California- or Florida-bred, 1⅟₁₆m, 1:43.36, JOINT EFFORT, Take D' Tour, Getback Time, 12 started.
Sunshine Millions Filly and Mare Sprint S. (R), Gulfstream Park, Jan. 27, $300,000, 4&up, f&m, California- or Florida-bred, 6f, 1:09.31, SHAGGY MANE, Swap Fliparoo, Hot Storm, 13 started.
Sunshine Millions Filly and Mare Turf S. (R), Gulfstream Park, Jan. 27, $500,000, 4&up, f&m, California- or Florida-bred, 1⅛mT, 1:46.69, MISS SHOP, Memorette, Charmsil, 12 started.
Sunshine Millions Oaks (R), Santa Anita Park, Jan. 27, $250,000, 3yo, f, California- or Florida-bred, 6f, 1:10.50, MISTICAL PLAN, Tiz Elemental, Double Major, 12 started.
Sunshine Millions Padua Stables Sprint S. (R), Santa Anita Park, Jan. 27, $300,000, 4&up, California- or Florida-bred, 6f, 1:08.03, SMOKEY STOVER, Proud Tower Too, Bordonaro, 8 started.
Sunshine Millions San Manuel Indian Bingo and Casino Turf S. (R), Santa Anita Park, Jan. 27, $500,000, 4&up, California- or Florida-bred, 1⅛mT, 1:47.60, LAVA MAN, Icy Atlantic, Go Between, 10 started.
Sun Sprint Championship H., Northlands Park, Aug. 6, $47,410, 3&up, 6½f, 1:17.80, LAKETON, Rindanica, Plagiarist, 7 started.
Super Bowl Party Starter H., Santa Anita Park, Feb. 4, $45,950, 4&up, f&m, 1⅛mT, 1:49.94, CHRISTMAS STOCKING, Strong Faith, Brag (Ire), 6 started.
SUPER DERBY (G2), Louisiana Downs, Sept. 22, $515,000, 3yo, 1⅛m, 1:50.32, GOING BALLISTIC, Grasshopper, Past the Point, 9 started.
Super Derby Prelude S., Louisiana Downs, Aug. 18, $100,000, 3yo, 1⅟₁₆m, 1:44.92, FORTY ACRES, Beta Capo, Strong City, 12 started.
Supernaturel H., Hastings Race Course, July 7, $51,132, 3yo, f, 1⅟₁₆m, 1:45.10, NAPA, Calendar Girl, Loving Laur, 8 started.
Super S., Tampa Bay Downs, Feb. 10, $75,000, 4&up, 7f, 1:23.62, D'ARTAGNANS'SPIRIT, Weigelia, Above the Wind, 13 started.
Susan B. Anthony H. (R), Finger Lakes Gaming and Race Track, June 17, $50,000, 3&up, f&m, New York-bred, 6f, 1:11.07, HOOSICK FALLS, Waytotheleft, Her Royal Nibs, 9 started.
Susan's Girl Breeders' Cup S., Delaware Park, June 16, $185,600, 3yo, f, 1⅟₁₆m, 1:42.90, MOON CATCHER, Winning Point, Greenstreet, 7 started.
Susan's Girl S. (R), Calder Race Course, Sept. 1, $150,000, 2yo, f, progeny of eligible Florida stallions, 7f, 1:24.61, SILK RIDGE, Calico Bay, Bond Princess, 9 started.
Sussex S., Delaware Park, June 23, $100,300, 3&up, 1⅟₁₆mT, 1:42.35, TUNE OF THE SPIRIT, Dreadnaught, Giant Wrecker, 6 started.
SUWANNEE RIVER H. (G3), Gulfstream Park, Feb. 3, $100,000, 4&up, f&m, 1⅛mT, 1:46.58, NAISSANCE ROYALE (IRE), J'ray, Potra Clasica (Arg), 10 started.
SWALE S. (G2), Gulfstream Park, Feb. 3, $150,000, 3yo, 6½f, 1:15.86, ADORE THE GOLD, Forefathers, Cowtown Cat, 7 started.
SWAPS BREEDERS' CUP S. (G2), Hollywood Park, July 14, $368,250, 3yo, 1⅛mAW, 1:48.76, TIAGO, Albertus Maximus, Souvenir Slew, 6 started.
Sweepida S., Stockton, June 23, $49,638, 3yo, f, 5½f, 1:04.74, BUTTERS, Cosmopolitan Lady (GB), Hammett Star, 10 started.
Sweet and Sassy S., Delaware Park, April 28, $75,600, 3&up, f&m, 6f, 1:10.11, TRAVEL PLANS, Amandatude, Summer Cruise, 7 started.
Sweet Briar Too S., Woodbine, July 1, $94,225, 3&up, f&m, 7fAW, 1:23.55, ARDEN BELLE, Vestrey Lady, Saoirse Cat, 6 started.
Sweetest Chant S., Arlington Park, July 28, $47,450, 3yo, f, 1⅟₁₆mAW, 1:42.94, MINI SERMON, Marquee Delivery, dh-Early Vintage, dh-Aspiring, 7 started.
Sweetheart S., Delta Downs, March 2, $75,000, 4&up, f&m, 1m, 1:39.50, BAGHDARIA, Superb Ravi, No Sleep, 10 started.
Sweettrickydancer S., Calder Race Course, July 7, $45,000, 3yo, f, 1m, 1:39.90, CASA MIMATY, Suaveness, Dantrelle Light, 8 started.
Swept Away S., Calder Race Course, June 16, $50,000, 3yo, f, 6f, 1:11.02, CHER AMI, Banda Victoria, Appealing Runner, 6 started.
Swift S., Turf Paradise, Jan. 6, $45,000, 4&up, 5½f, 1:02.23, FAMILY GUY, Pure American, Bay Town Boy, 10 started.
Swinging Mood S., Belmont Park, Oct. 21, $79,950, 2yo, f, 1mT, 1:38.32, REMARKABLE REMY, Return to Paradise, Lucky Copy, 7 started.
Swingtime S. (R), Oak Tree at Santa Anita, Oct. 8, $71,950, 3&up, f&m, non-winners of a stakes worth $50,000 at one mile or over other than state-bred, 1mT, 1:35.08, SWEET BELLE, Trick's Pic, Shermeen (Ire), 9 started.
SWORD DANCER INVITATIONAL S. (G1), Saratoga Race Course, Aug. 11, $500,000, 3&up, 1½mT, 2:26.59, GRAND COUTURIER (GB), English Channel, Trippi's Storm, 8 started.
S. W. Randall Plate H., Hastings Race Course, Sept. 3, $48,523, 3&up, 1⅛m, 1:50.61, WINTER WARNING, Shacane, Act of God, 7 started.
Swynford S., Woodbine, Sept. 15, $121,300, 2yo, 7fAW, 1:23.02, TURF WAR, Storm Code, Soca Tempo, 5 started.
SYCAMORE S. (G3), Keeneland Race Course, Oct. 5, $137,500, 3&up, 1½mT, 2:31.96, TRANSDUCTION GOLD, Bee Charmer (Ire), Dreadnaught, 10 started.
Sydney Gendelman Memorial H. (R), River Downs, June 16, $50,000, 3&up, Ohio-bred, 1⅟₁₆mT, 1:41.40, THE POTTERS HAND, Catlaunch, Acts Like a King, 12 started.
Sydney Valentini H. (R), Sunland Park, March 24, $100,000, 3&up, f&m, New Mexico-bred, 1m, 1:38.42, PEPPERS PRIDE, La Mamie, Skirt Alert, 7 started.
Tacoma H., Emerald Downs, July 1, $45,000, 3yo, c&g, 1m, 1:35.20, WILD CYCLE, Call On Carson, Mulcahy, 6 started.
Tah Dah S. (R), River Downs, July 29, $50,000, 2yo, f, Ohio-bred, 5½f, 1:05.60, READY TO ROCK, Got Bling, Title Princess, 8 started.
Taking Risks S. (R), Timonium, Sept. 3, $45,000, 3&up, Maryland-bred, a6½f, 1:16.87, P. KERNEY, Two Terms, Love's Strong Hart, 6 started.
TAMPA BAY DERBY (G3), Tampa Bay Downs, March 17, $300,000, 3yo, 1⅟₁₆m, 1:43.11 (NTR), STREET SENSE, Any Given Saturday, Delightful Kiss, 7 started.
Tampa Bay S., Tampa Bay Downs, Feb. 24, $150,000, 4&up, 1⅟₁₆mT, 1:41.24, HOTSTUFANTHENSOME, Classic Campaign, Defer, 8 started.
Tanforan S., Golden Gate Fields, Nov. 10, $75,000, 3&up, 1⅜mT, 2:21.06, TISSY FIT, Zappa, Porfido (Chi), 6 started.
TAYLOR MADE MATCHMAKER S. (G3), Monmouth Park, Aug. 5, $150,000, 3&up, f&m, 1⅛mT, 1:47.55, ROSHANI, Trick's Pic, Humoristic, 8 started.
Taylor's Special H., Fair Grounds, Feb. 10, $98,000, 4&up, a5½fT, 1:03.12, GAFF, Wrzeszcz, Santana Strings, 7 started.
Teddy Drone S., Monmouth Park, Aug. 8, $100,000, 3&up, 6f, 1:08.99, TALENT SEARCH, Suave Jazz, Who's the Cowboy, 5 started.
Teeworth Plate H., Stampede Park, May 19, $45,890, 3&up, 1m, 1:35.80 (ETR), TEST BOY, Teagues Fight, Fly Esteem, 10 started.

Racing — 2007 Stakes Races

Tejano Run S., Turfway Park, March 17, $50,000, 4&up, 1 1/16mAW, 1:50.11, JADE'S REVENGE, Sidcup, Dynareign, 11 started.
Tellike S., Evangeline Downs, May 19, $48,000, 3&up, f&m, 6f, 1:09.17, INDIGO GIRL, Olmosta, Ada's Dream, 5 started.
Tempe H., Turf Paradise, March 24, $45,000, 3yo, a1mT, 1:36.20, PART TIMER (IRE), Organ Pipe, Capt. Joe Blow, 8 started.
Temperence Hill S., Louisiana Downs, June 23, $48,500, 3&up, 6f, 1:10.31, VENOMOUS, Wheaton Home, Express News, 6 started.
Temple Gwathmey Hurdle S. (R), Middleburg, April 21, $75,000, 4&up, non-winners over hurdles prior to March 1, 2006, a2 1/4mT, 4:34.20, GLIDING (NZ), Rare Bush, Best Attack, 8 started.
TEMPTED S. (G3), Aqueduct, Oct. 28, $106,600, 2yo, f, 1m, 1:38.40, ELUSIVE LADY, Meriwether Jessica, Sunday Holiday, 5 started.
Temptress S. (R), Great Lakes Downs, Aug. 25, $50,000, 2yo, f, Michigan-bred, 6f, 1:15.37, EQUALITYSDEBUTANTE, Exit Sixty, Irish Date, 9 started.
Tenacious H., Fair Grounds, Dec. 1, $58,800, 3&up, 1 1/16m, 1:44.74, STEVE'S DOUBLE, Crossword, Catmantoo, 7 started.
Ten Thousand Lakes S. (R), Canterbury Park, May 19, $45,000, 3&up, c&g, Minnesota-bred, 6f, 1:09.10, SIR TRICKY, Careless Navigator, Vazandar, 8 started.
Testum S., Les Bois Park, June 29, $12,453, 3yo, 7f, 1:27.98, WALNUT AVENUE, Mr Madraar, Sheriff Tillet, 5 started.
Texans S., Sam Houston Race Park, Feb. 3, $25,000, 4&up, f&m, 5fT, :59.05, AIRIZON, Special Hunter, Inspired Dancer, 11 started.
Texas Heritage S., Sam Houston Race Park, March 3, $45,000, 3yo, 1m, 1:39.78, SPEEDWAY, I Spy Wolfie, Makeithapencaptain, 9 started.
Texas Horse Racing Hall of Fame S. (R), Retama Park, Oct. 13, $100,000, 3&up, Texas-bred, 1 1/16mT, 1:40.65 (NCR), GENERAL CHARLEY, Bullet Crane, Goosey Moose, 10 started.
TEXAS MILE S. (G3), Lone Star Park, April 28, $300,000, 3&up, 1m, 1:35.39, SILENT PLEASURE, Bob and John, Dreamsandvisions, 6 started.
Texas Stallion S. (R), Lone Star Park, July 7, $125,000, 2yo, c&g, progeny of eligible Texas stallions, 5 1/2f, 1:03.04, GOLD COYOTE, Spark Plug, Stormy Date, 8 started.
Texas Stallion S. (R), Lone Star Park, July 7, $125,000, 2yo, f, progeny of eligible Texas stallions, 5 1/2f, 1:04.76, VALID LILLY, Classie Baloo, Fiesty Lula, 7 started.
Texas Stallion S. (R), Lone Star Park, May 12, $125,000, 3yo, c&g, progeny of eligible Texas stallions, 1 1/16m, 1:47, SPOONERISM, Austin Lights, Power Surge, 12 started.
Texas Stallion S. (R), Lone Star Park, May 12, $125,000, 3yo, f, progeny of eligible Texas stallions, 1 1/16m, 1:48.06, LILLY LADUE, Stage Stop, Real Soup, 7 started.
Texas Thoroughbred Breeders'S. (R), Gillespie County Fairgrounds, July 21, $13,000, 3&up, Texas-bred, 6f, 1:13.05 (NTR), AGGIES RULE, Mach Twee, Appealing Air, 10 started.
Tex's Zing H. (R), Fairmount Park, July 31, $45,800, 3&up, Illinois-bred and/or -foaled, 1m70y, 1:44.40, OUST, Barely Union Scale, Holy City, 8 started.
Thanksgiving H., Fair Grounds, Nov. 22, $60,000, 3&up, 6f, 1:09.26, STORMIN BAGHDAD, Going Wild, Thunder Mission, 9 started.
THE VERY ONE H. (G3), Gulfstream Park, Feb. 25, $100,000, 4&up, f&m, 1 3/8mT, 2:12.63, ROYAL HIGHNESS (GER), Safari Queen (Arg), Barancella (Fr), 9 started.
The Very One S., Pimlico Race Course, May 18, $75,000, 3&up, f&m, 5fT, :55.77, UNBRIDLED SIDNEY, Wild Berry, Keep On Talking, 8 started.
The Vid S., Calder Race Course, Aug. 12, $45,000, 3&up, 1 1/16mT, 1:39.82, CROTON ROAD, Jet Propulsion, Magic Mecke, 7 started.
Thomas Edison S., Meadowlands, Oct. 6, $56,815, 3&up, 5fT, :55.52, SMART ENOUGH, Man of Danger, John's Pic, 6 started.
Thomas F. Moran S. (R), Suffolk Downs, Aug. 18, $45,000, 3&up, Massachusetts-bred, a1 1/16mT, 1:48.32, ASK QUEENIE, Disco Fox, Silent Scamper, 11 started.
THOROUGHBRED CLUB OF AMERICA S. (G3), Keeneland Race Course, Oct. 6, $300,000, 3&up, f&m, 6fAW, 1:10, WILD GAMS, Sugar Swirl, Baroness Thatcher, 9 started.
Three Phase S., Turf Paradise, May 4, $24,900, 3yo, 6f, 1:09.05, CAPT. JOE BLOW, In to the West, Quinton's Fleet, 6 started.
Three Ring S., Calder Race Course, Dec. 1, $100,000, 2yo, f, 1 1/16m, 1:48.06, INDY'S ALEXANDRA, Awesome Dreamer, Paint Me Red, 5 started.
Thunder Road H., Santa Anita Park, Feb. 3, $80,050, 4&up, 1mT, 1:35.47, SWEET RETURN (GB), Bayeux, Boule d'Or (Ire), 8 started.
Thunder Rumble S. (R), Aqueduct, Nov. 11, $75,000, 3&up, c&g,

progeny of eligible New York stallions, 7f, 1:22.41, STUNT MAN, Gold and Roses, Smash 'Em Sammy, 6 started.
Tiburon H., Golden Gate Fields, Jan. 13, $50,650, 3yo, f, 6f, 1:09.34, GLORIFICATION, Storming Starlet, Quite a Rush, 6 started.
Ticonderoga H. (R), Belmont Park, Oct. 20, $150,000, 3&up, f&m, New York-bred, 1 1/16mT, 1:53.59, REWRITE, Factual Contender, Latitude Forty, 10 started.
Tiffany Lass S., Fair Grounds, Jan. 13, $100,000, 3yo, f, 1m, 1:39.52, GET READY BERTIE, Dawn After Dawn, Stage Stop, 10 started.
Tillamook Thoroughbred Derby, Tillamook County Fair, Aug. 9, $3,500, 3yo, a5f, 1:05.40, LYRLYRPANTSONFIRE, Champ's Houdini, Sassy Minstrel, 6 started.
Tillamook Thoroughbred S., Tillamook County Fair, Aug. 11, $5,000, 3&up, a5f, 1:03, MOUNTAIN MUSTANG, Larron, Our Last Hero, 6 started.
Timber Music S., Hastings Race Course, July 14, $51,138, 2yo, f, 6 1/2f, 1:17.78, ALPINE LASS, Archery, Dancing Melody, 6 started.
Timeless Native S., Arlington Park, May 5, $47,550, 3&up, 1mAW, 1:36.73, BUDDY GOT EVEN, Throng, Sadler's Trick, 6 started.
Times Square S. (R), Aqueduct, April 22, $100,000, 3yo, c&g, progeny of eligible New York stallions, 7f, 1 22.33, BUSTIN STONES, Smash 'Em Sammy, Market Psychology, 7 started.
Tippett S., Colonial Downs, July 28, $60 000, 2yo, f, 5 1/2fT, 1:02.22, SALES TAX, My Little Josie, Valin Time, 9 started.
Tiznow Breeders' Cup H., Louisiana Downs, July 14, $119,000, 3&up, 1 1/16mT, 1:45.97, SILENT PLEASURE, Super Frolic, Cozy Time, 5 started.
Tiznow S. (R), Hollywood Park, April 29, $150,000, 4&up, California-bred, 7 1/2fAW, 1:28.90, GREG'S GOLD, He's the Rage, Bilo, 8 started.
TOBOGGAN H. (G3), Aqueduct, March 10, $105,100, 3&up, 6f, 1:10.02, ATTILA'S STORM, Wild Jam, Pavo, 6 started.
TOKYO CITY H. (G3), Santa Anita Park, March 31, $107,200, 4&up, 1 1/16m, 1:47.87, FAIRBANKS, Neko Bay, Racketeer, 6 started.
Tomball S. (R), Sam Houston Race Park, Feb. 24, $45,000, 3&up, Texas-bred, 1 1/16mT, 1:43.94, GENERAL CHARLEY, Goosey Moose, Northern Scene, 7 started.
Tom Bane Starter S. (R), Turf Paradise April 28, $17,500, 3&up, Arizona-bred starters for a claiming price of $8,000 or less since October 5, 2006, 6f, 1:08.56, KING HUNTER, Pepper Dan, Max's Ace, 9 started.
Tomboy S. (R), River Downs, May 19, $50,000, 3yo, f, Ohio-bred, 1 1/16mT, 1:43.20, MINI MOM, Littlebitabling, Spirit of Fire, 10 started.
TOM FOOL BREEDERS' CUP H. (G2), Belmont Park, July 4, $197,500, 3&up, 7f, 1:21.81, HIGH FINANCE, Awesome Twist, Commentator, 6 started.
Tom Ridge Labor Day S., Presque Isle Downs, Sept. 3, $100,000, 3yo, 6fAW, 1:10.69, ELITE SQUADRON, Cherokee Country, Front Court, 8 started.
To Much Coffee S. (R), Hoosier Park, Nov. 18, $45,000, 3&up, Indiana-bred, 1 1/16m, 1:45.33, SAHMMY DAVIS JR, Squeaky Rich, Need Money Dad, 10 started.
Tony Gatto Dream Big S., Atlantic City Race Course, May 3, $50,000, 3&up, 5fT, :56.09, SANDYS GOLD, Southern Missile, Midnight Express, 10 started.
Tony Sanchez Memorial Mile S., Manor Downs, April 21, $45,000, 3&up, 1m, 1:37.91, BEGBORROWANDDEAL, Play the Chime, Unbridled Thunder, 10 started.
TOP FLIGHT H. (G2), Aqueduct, Nov. 23, $150,000, 3&up, f&m, 1m, 1:37.29, MINI SERMON, Lady Marlboro, Golden Velvet, 8 started.
Toronto Cup S., Woodbine, July 14, $144,581, 3yo, 1 1/16mT, 1:49.58, WINDWARD ISLANDS, Angel of the House, Skip Code, 9 started.
Torrey Pines S., Del Mar, Sept. 2, $140,650, 3yo, f, 1mAW, 1:41.04, SEASIDE AFFAIR, Romance Is Diane, Silver Swallow, 11 started.
Totah Futurity (R), SunRay Park, June 30, $62,200, 2yo, c&g, New Mexico-bred, 4 1/2f, :51.20, RUN LIKE FIRE, D Mexico, Brax, 8 started.
Touch of Love S. (R), Belmont Park, June 1, $66,750, 3yo, f, New York-bred, 6f, 1:10.85, SILVERCUP BABY, Western Sweep, Nordberg, 7 started.
TOYOTA BLUE GRASS S. (G1), Keeneland Race Course, April 14, $750,000, 3yo, 1 1/8mAW, 1:51.33, DOMINICAN, Street Sense, Zanjero, 7 started.
TRAVERS S. (G1), Saratoga Race Course, Aug. 25, $1,000,000, 3yo, 1 1/4m, 2:02.69, STREET SENSE, Grasshopper, Helsinki, 7 started.
Treasure Chest S., Delta Downs, Dec. 7, $72,750, 3&up, f&m, 7f, 1:26.40, COOLWIND, Game for More, Kathleens Reel, 6 started.
Treasure Town S., Turf Paradise, April 11, $25,200, 3&up, f&m, 7 1/2fT, 1:30.48, EVENING ESCORT, Parioli's Legacy, Woman of Choice, 8 started.

Treasure Town S., Turf Paradise, Dec. 7, $31,000, 3yo, f, a1mT, 1:39.20, WINE TASTING ROOM, Zaylaway, Glorificamus (Ire), 8 started.

Tremont S., Belmont Park, July 1, $110,600, 2yo, 5½f, 1:02.86, READY'S IMAGE, Izzy Speaking, Twenty Eight Hours, 8 started.

Trenton S., Monmouth Park, Aug. 12, $60,000, 3yo, f, a5½fT, 1:01.97, MARINA BALLERINA, Sea the Joy, Big Cat Walks Late, 8 started.

Tribute to Newt Starter S. (R), Yavapai Downs, Aug. 11, $7,800, 3&up, starters for a claiming price of $5,000 or less in 2007, 6f, 1:07.80 (NTR), RUN NICHOLAS RUN, Devil Cop, Swiss Bounty, 5 started.

TRIPLE BEND INVITATIONAL H. (G1), Hollywood Park, July 7, $300,000, 3&up, 7fAW, 1:21.65, BILO, Surf Cat, Battle Won, 7 started.

Triple Sec S., Delta Downs, Jan. 26, $48,500, 3yo, 6½f, 1:21.26, DADDY WARBUCKS, Who Let the Cat In, Fortune's Praise, 6 started.

Tri-State Futurity (R), Charles Town Races, Nov. 10, $72,212, 2yo, c&g, Maryland-, Virginia-, or West Virginia-bred, 7f, 1:26.63, GHOSTLY THUNDER, Milwaukee Fun, King of Windsor, 7 started.

Tri-State Futurity (R), Charles Town Races, Nov. 10, $72,212, 2yo, f, Maryland-, Virginia-, or West Virginia-bred, 7f, 1:28.23, SAXET HEIGHTS, We're in the Money, Color Parade, 7 started.

Tri-State H., Ellis Park, Sept. 1, $50,000, 3&up, 1¹⁄₁₆mT, 1:40.35, OBI WAN KENOBI, Cat Shaker, Cat and a Half, 7 started.

Trooper Seven S. (R), Emerald Downs, Sept. 16, $45,000, 3yo, c&g, Washington-bred, 1m, 1:35.60, MULCAHY, Wild Cycle, Ogieogilthorpe, 7 started.

TROPICAL PARK DERBY (G3), Calder Race Course, Jan. 1, $100,000, 3yo, 1⅛mT, 1:48.95, SOLDIER'S DANCER, Sedgefield, Storm in May, 9 started.

Tropical Park Oaks, Calder Race Course, Jan. 1, $100,000, 3yo, f, 1¹⁄₁₆mT, 1:43.19, CHRISTMAS KID, Perfect Motion, Lisa M, 12 started.

TROPICAL TURF H. (G3), Calder Race Course, Dec. 1, $100,000, 3&up, 1⅛mT, 1:48.54, BALLAST (IRE), National Captain (SAf), Minister's Joy, 10 started.

Troy Our Boy S. (R), Fairmount Park, July 31, $45,800, 2yo, c&g, Illinois-bred and/or -foaled, 6f, 1:13.60, RIVER BEAR, Just Luke, Wheres Denton, 7 started.

Troy S., Saratoga Race Course, Aug. 13, $81,700, 4&up, 5½fT, 1:03.15, T. D. VANCE, Mr. Silver, Midwatch, 6 started.

True Affair S., Aqueduct, April 11, $64,950, 3yo, f, 6f, 1:10.20, CASH'S GIRL, Half Time Crown, Lady Marlboro, 5 started.

TRUE NORTH H. (G2), Belmont Park, June 9, $200,000, 3&up, 6f, 1:08.70, WILL HE SHINE, Suave Jazz, Dashboard Drummer, 8 started.

Truly Bound H., Fair Grounds, Jan. 20, $74,250, 4&up, f&m, 1¹⁄₁₆m, 1:46.44, DELICATE DYNAMITE, Eyes On Eddy, Dash of Humor, 8 started.

TTA Sales Futurity (R), Lone Star Park, June 9, $93,530, 2yo, f, sold at a TTA sale, 5f, :58.35, MAILEYS CAT, Valid Lilly, Shedoesrock, 10 started.

TTA Sales Futurity (R), Lone Star Park, June 9, $95,130, 2yo, c&g, sold at a TTA sale, 5f, :57.93, NAMESAKE, Kinetic Motion, Stormy Date, 10 started.

Turf Amazon H., Philadelphia Park, May 28, $100,000, 3&up, f&m, 5fT, :57, SMART AND FANCY, Cajun Mistress, Truly Blushed, 8 started.

Turf Dash S., Tampa Bay Downs, March 17, $75,000, 3&up, 5fT, :56.51, LOOKINFORTHESECRET, Mr. Silver, The Nth Degree, 10 started.

Turf Distance Series Final S., Turf Paradise, April 17, $35,300, 3&up, 1⅜mT, 2:17.25, WE BROTHERS, Power Strokin, Nicol n' Dime Me, 12 started.

Turf Marathon H., Calder Race Course, July 28, $50,000, 3&up, 2m (originally scheduled on the turf), 3:32.34, GOLDEN STRATEGY, Legacy Reserve, Supervisor, 6 started.

Turf Monster H., Philadelphia Park, Sept. 3, $200,000, 3&up, 5fT, :55.53 (NCR), SMART ENOUGH, Heros Reward, Gaff, 10 started.

Turf Paradise Derby, Turf Paradise, Feb. 17, $100,000, 3yo, 1¹⁄₁₆m, 1:43.91, TIE ROD, Gregorian Bay, In to the West, 9 started.

Turf Paradise H., Turf Paradise, Feb. 24, $75,000, 4&up, 1¹⁄₁₆mT, 1:42.03, CAPITANO, Cervelo, Night Dash, 9 started.

Turf Sprint Championship H., Calder Race Course, Aug. 11, $250,000, 3&up, 5fT, :55.76, DEAD RED, Mach Ride, Lord Robyn, 9 started.

TURFWAY PARK FALL CHAMPIONSHIP S. (G3), Turfway Park, Sept. 8, $100,000, 3&up, 1mAW, 1:38.81, ISTAN, Spotsgone, Gouldings Green, 6 started.

Turfway Prevue S., Turfway Park, Jan. 6, $50,000, 3yo, 6½fAW, 1:15.82, CARNACKS CHOICE, Joe Got Even, Cajun Mon, 7 started.

TURNBACK THE ALARM H. (G3), Aqueduct, Nov. 4, $105,300, 3&up, f&m, 1⅛m, 1:50.02, SUGAR SHAKE, Cindy's Mom, Victory Pool, 6 started.

Turn Capp S. (R), Charles Town Races, June 2, $51,200, 3&up, f&m, most starts at Charles Town in last four starts, 7f, 1:26.89, THE HOLY ONE, Unlawful Spirit, Julie B, 8 started.

Tuzla H., Santa Anita Park, Jan. 24, $80,400, 4&up, f&m, 1mT, 1:35.56, SINGALONG (GB), dh-Charm the Giant (Ire), dh-Dream's (Chi), 9 started.

Tuzla S. (R), Hollywood Park, May 11, $72,280, 4&up, f&m, non-winners of a stakes worth $60,000 to the winner since August 1, 2006, 6fT, 1:09, VALID'S VALID, Stylish Wildcat, No Lullaby, 6 started.

TVG BREEDERS' CUP SPRINT (G1), Monmouth Park, Oct. 27, $1,832,000, 3&up, 6f, 1:09.18, MIDNIGHT LUTE, Idiot Proof, Talent Search, 10 started.

TVG Khaled S. (R), Hollywood Park, April 29, $150,000, 4&up, California-bred, 1⅛mT, 1:47.40, EPIC POWER, Running Free, Jack's Wild, 9 started.

Tweedside S., Belmont Park, July 1, $67,200, 3yo, f, 1¹⁄₁₆mT, 1:41.97, LEAR'S PRINCESS, Christies Treasure, Unspoken Word, 8 started.

Twin Lights S., Monmouth Park, Sept. 2, $80,000, 3yo, f, 1⅛mT, 1:47.33, BACHATA, Dattts Awesome, Miss Tizzynow, 9 started.

Twixt S. (R), Laurel Park, Aug. 11, $50,000, 3yo, f, Maryland-bred, 1m, 1:41.08, PAYING OFF, Welcome Inn, Ethan's Car, 8 started.

Two Altazano S. (R), Sam Houston Race Park, Feb. 17, $125,000, 3yo, f, nominated and eligible for the Texas Stallion Stakes Series, 1m, 1:39.48, WRENICE, Stage Stop, Lilly Ladue, 11 started.

Tyro S., Monmouth Park, July 28, $60,000, 2yo, 5½f, 1:03.83, LANTANA MOB, Spanky Fischbein, Run Sully Run, 7 started.

U Can Do It H., Calder Race Course, Sept. 15, $100,000, 3&up, f&m, 6½f, 1:17.25, RGIRLDOESN'TBLUFF, Stolen Prayer, Annabill, 7 started.

Unbridled Breeders' Cup H., Louisiana Downs, Sept. 22, $195,000, 3&up, 1¹⁄₁₆mT, 1:40.64, GO BETWEEN, Erroneous I D, Corey County, 7 started.

Unbridled S., Calder Race Course, April 28, $100,000, 3yo, 1¹⁄₁₆m, 1:47.31, HAL'S MY HOPE, Rogers, Green Vegas, 5 started.

Union Avenue S. (R), Saratoga Race Course, Aug. 20, $81,650, 3&up, f&m, New York-bred non-winners of a graded stakes in 2007, 6f, 1:10.95, KARAKORUM STARLET, Scatkey, Precise Lady, 5 started.

UNITED NATIONS S. (G1), Monmouth Park, July 7, $742,500, 3&up, 1⅜mT, 2:12.89 (NCR), ENGLISH CHANNEL, Honey Ryder, Better Talk Now, 5 started.

University of New Mexico H. (R), The Downs at Albuquerque, Oct. 7, $50,000, 3&up, New Mexico-bred, 1m, 1:36.84, TANYA'S BEAU, Romeos Wilson, Boom Boom, 7 started.

U. S. Bank S., Emerald Downs, May 12, $45,000, 3yo, f, 6f, 1:08.40, SHAMPOO, On Duty, Wings of Justice, 9 started.

Vacaville H., Solano County Fair, July 14, $59,100, 3&up, f&m, 6f, 1:08.30, VICTORINA, Vaca City Flyer, Denaesalildevil, 5 started.

VAGRANCY H. (G2), Belmont Park, June 17, $150,000, 3&up, f&m, 6½f, 1:16.44, INDIAN FLARE, Oprah Winney, Any Limit, 6 started.

Valdale S., Turfway Park, Feb. 24, $50,000, 3yo, f, 1mAW, 1:38.98, OUR DANCING BABE, Bavarian Belle, Miss A. Bomb, 11 started.

Valedictory S., Woodbine, Dec. 9, $125,545, 3&up, 1¾mAW, 3:01.08, TORQUAY, Tap Show, Encinas (Ger), 8 started.

Valentine Memorial Sport of Queen's Hurdle S., Fair Hill, May 26, $26,400, 4&up, f&m, a2¼mT, 4:45.40, IMAGINA (CHI), Gold Mitten, Mary Cat, 3 started.

Valid Expectations S., Lone Star Park, May 28, $100,000, 3&up, f&m, 6f, 1:12, CINTAROSA, Moroccan Rose, Yo Fanci, 6 started.

Valid Leader S., Turf Paradise, Feb. 25, $25,000, 4&up, f&m, 6½f, 1:15.62, EVENING ESCORT, Kissntheboysgoodby, Spice Thief, 6 started.

Valid Leader S., Turf Paradise, Oct. 9, $30,900, 3&up, f&m, 7½fT, 1:28.69, STAR OF WHITNEY, Evening Escort, Couragious Sam, 8 started.

Valid Video S., Calder Race Course, June 17, $50,000, 3yo, 6f, 1:10.92, FINALLYMADEIT, Yesbyjimminy, Frosty Secret, 7 started.

Valkyr S. (R), Hollywood Park, June 24, $76,450, 3&up, f&m, California-bred, 6fAW, 1:09.86, LADY GAMER, Getback Time, Vaca City Flyer, 5 started.

Valor Farm S. (R), Lone Star Park, July 7, $50,000, 3yo, f, Texas-bred, 6f, 1:11.23, MONEYINMYWRANGLERS, Foolish Girl, Dawali, 5 started.

Valor Lady S., Belmont Park, Sept. 20, $77,000, 4&up, f&m, 6fT,

1:08.18, ASTRONOMIA (NZ), Stormy Kiss (Arg), Somethinabout-betty, 8 started.

Van Berg Derby, Columbus Races, Aug. 18, $10,725, 3yo, 1m70y, 1:44.40, MY SECRET STAR, The Ruzz, Ordville, 6 started.

Vandal S. (R), Woodbine, Aug. 12, $144,294, 2yo, Canadian-bred, 6fAW, 1:10.01, STUCK IN TRAFFIC, Don's Folly, Not Bourbon, 10 started.

VANITY INVITATIONAL H. (G1), Hollywood Park, July 7, $294,000, 3&up, f&m, 1⅛mAW, 1:48.83, NASHOBA'S KEY, Balance, Hystericalady, 4 started.

Vector Communications Last Chance S., Grand Prairie, Aug. 19, $5,484, 3&up, 6f, 1:14.20, LARRY THE LONGSHOT, Domesticdisturbanz, Ezee Target, 5 started.

VERNON O. UNDERWOOD S. (G3), Hollywood Park, Dec. 2, $105,800, 3&up, 6fAW, 1:08.47, BUSHWACKER, In Summation, Greg's Gold, 5 started.

Very Subtle S., Churchill Downs, Nov. 4, $110,900, 3&up, f&m, 6f, 1:09.90, SUGAR SWIRL, Generosity, Country Diva, 8 started.

Veterans S., Zia Park, Nov. 10, $63,370, 3&up, 1¹⁄₁₆m, 1:45.60, ROLLICKING CALLER, dh-War Bridle, dh-Guiding Hand, 9 started.

Vice Regent S. (R), Woodbine, Sept. 2, $118,363, 3yo, Ontario-foaled, 1mT, 1:36.20, RAHY'S ATTORNEY, Red Raffles, Orna, 5 started.

Victoriana S. (R), Woodbine, Aug. 19, $117,788, 3&up, f&m, Ontario-foaled, 1¹⁄₁₆mT, 1:41.26, FINANCINGAVAILABLE, Executive Flight, London Snow, 5 started.

Victorian Queen S. (R), Woodbine, Oct. 3, $126,503, 2yo, f, Ontario-foaled, 6fAW, 1:09.81, AUTHENICAT, D'wild Lady, Lady d'Wildcat, 8 started.

Victoria Park S., Woodbine, June 10, $118,655, 3yo, 1⅛mAW, 1:50.89, APPROVAL RATING, Skip Code, Angel of the House, 7 started.

Victoria S. (R), Louisiana Downs, July 21, $98,000, 3&up, f&m, Louisiana-bred, 6f, 1:10.54, IDA MARIA, Leesa Lee, Sammie Sam, 7 started.

Victoria S., Woodbine, June 17, $118,885, 2yo, 5fAW, :59.44, KODIAK KOWBOY, Lacadena, Yes It's Bull, 10 started.

Victor S. Myers Jr. S. (R), Canterbury Park, July 7, $45,000, 3yo, Minnesota-bred, 6f, 1:09.84, SUL LAGO, Ghazi's Big Easy, Banker's D Light, 6 started.

VICTORY RIDE S. (G3), Saratoga Race Course, Aug. 25, $114,700, 3yo, f, 6f, 1:09.78, LA TRAVIATA, Half Time Crown, Appealing Zophie, 10 started.

Viejas Casino H., Del Mar, Aug. 19, $89,275, 3yo, f, 1mT, 1:34.60, SILKY SMOOTH, Honored Gold, Nootka Island, 6 started.

VIGIL S. (CAN-G3), Woodbine, April 28, $134,773, 4&up, 7fAW, 1:23.87, JUST RUSHING, Are You Serious, Judiths Wild Rush, 6 started.

Vilaxy Louisiana-Bred Starter S. (R), Louisiana Downs, May 12, $39,200, 3&up, Louisiana-bred starters for a claming price of $16,000 or less in 2006-'07, 1¹⁄₁₆m, 1:44.43, LASH, Tiger Monarch, Setemup Joe, 7 started.

Vincent A. Moscarelli Memorial S., Delaware Park, Nov. 3, $100,300, 3&up, 6f, 1:11.24, SUAVE JAZZ, Banjo Picker, Bound Notebook, 6 started.

VINERY MADISON S. (G2), Keeneland Race Course, April 11, $200,000, 4&up, f&m, 7fAW, 1:22.24, MARY DELANEY, Ginger Punch, Leah's Secret, 10 started.

VIOLET S. (G3), Meadowlands, Sept. 28, $150,000, 3&up, f&m, 1¹⁄₁₆mT, 1:41.23, HUMORISTIC, Roshani, Pommes Frites, 5 started.

VIRGINIA DERBY (G2), Colonial Downs, July 21, $1,000,000, 3yo, 1¼mT, 1:59.62 (NCR), RED GIANT, Strike a Deal, Soldier's Dancer, 10 started.

Virginia Gold Cup Timber S., Great Meadows, May 5, $100,000, 5&up, a4mT, 8:24.60, SALMO, Mr Bombastic (Ger), Ghost Valley, 12 started.

Virginia Oaks, Colonial Downs, July 21, $210,000, 3yo, f, 1⅛mT, 1:47.38, DREAMING OF ANNA, New Edition, Christmas Kid, 12 started.

Vivacious H. (R), River Downs, Aug. 11, $50,000, 3&up, f&m, Ohio-bred, 1¹⁄₁₆m, 1:43.80, WAR CHARM, Mini Mom, Misty Tab, 9 started.

Volponi S., Aqueduct, Nov. 7, $78,250, 3yo, 1mT, 1:36.63, SLEEPING INDIAN, Starvinsky, Adagio (GB), 9 started.

VOSBURGH S. (G1), Belmont Park, Sept. 30, $416,000, 3&up, 6f, 1:09.22, FABULOUS STRIKE, Talent Search, Discreet Cat, 8 started.

Wade Snapp Memorial H., Les Bois Park, Aug. 3, $5,100, 3&up, 7f, 1:24.94, INVADER'S JUSTICE, Cold Water, Kingjames Delivers, 8 started.

Wadsworth Memorial H. (R), Finger Lakes Gaming and Race Track, July 4, $100,000, 3&up, New York-bred, 1⅛m, 1:51.77, FUNNY CIDE, Johnie Bye Night, Tiger Speech, 8 started.

Wagon Limit S., Belmont Park, May 18, $67,750, 4&up, 1½m, 2:31.29, RISING MOON, Malibu Moonshine, Funny Cide, 7 started.

Walking in Da Sun S., Delaware Park, Sept. 5, $60,250, 3yo, f, 5fT, :56.29, INTENTIONAL FEVER, Ms. Sabbatical, Impossible Tune, 7 started.

Walmac Farm Matchmaker S. (R), Louisiana Downs, July 21, $100,000, 3&up, f&m, Louisiana-bred, 1¹⁄₁₆mT, 1:44.41, RASPBERRY WINE, Tortuga Flats, Royal Madame, 9 started.

Walter R. Cluer Memorial S., Turf Paradise, Oct. 5, $45,000, 3&up, 7½fT, 1:29.77, ORGAN PIPE, Skipaslew, Preferred Yield, 10 started.

Waquoit S., Suffolk Downs, Sept. 22, $45,000, 3&up, 1m70y, 1:42.96, REPRIZED STRIKE, De Roode, Joma, 9 started.

War Chant S., Hollywood Park, Nov. 7, $69,750, 3yo, 1mT, 1:33.75, WARNING ZONE, Bad Boy, Barbecue Eddie, 9 started.

War Chant S. (R), Oak Tree at Santa Anita, Oct. 13, $67,150, 3&up, non-winners of a stakes worth $50,000 at one mile or over since April 1 other than state-bred, 1mT, 1:35.29, STORMIN AWAY, Storm Military (Arg), Lang Field, 9 started.

War Emblem S., Hawthorne Race Course, March 18, $47,250, 3yo, 1¹⁄₁₆m, 1:46.15, QUITE ACCEPTABLE, Galloping Home, Slam My Heart, 5 started.

Warren's Thoroughbreds S. (R), Hollywood Park, April 29, $72,800, 3&up, f&m, California-bred non-winners of $3,000 other than maiden, claiming, or starter, 7fAW, 1:24.63, SILVER Z, Cathrine's Hope, Sunday Dress, 12 started.

Washington Oaks, Emerald Downs, Aug. 18, $93,125, 3yo, f, 1⅛m, 1:49.80, RIVOLTELLA, Firetrail, Eclatante, 10 started.

WASHINGTON PARK H. (G2), Arlington Park, July 28, $300,000, 3&up, 1³⁄₁₆mAW, 1:55.17, LEWIS MICHAEL, Mustanfar, A. P. Arrow, 7 started.

Washington's Lottery H., Emerald Downs, July 22, $61,650, 3yo, f, 1¹⁄₁₆m, 1:41, SHAMPOO, Firetrail, Just Get'er Done, 7 started.

Washington State Legislators H., Emerald Downs, June 10, $45,000, 3&up, f&m, 6½f, 1:15.80, SHE'S ALL SILK, Sudden Departure, Kissntheboysgoodby, 11 started.

Washington Thoroughbred Breeders' Association Lads S., Emerald Downs, Sept. 1, $49,500, 2yo, c&g, 1m, 1:37.20, GALLON, Cafe Tortoni, Ice Cube, 6 started.

Watchman's Warning S. (R), Penn National Race Course, July 5, $45,700, 3&up, Pennsylvania-bred, 1¹⁄₁₆m, 1:43.20, DELAWARE RIVER, R. Earl, Grey Dorian, 6 started.

Waterford Park H., Mountaineer Race Track and Gaming Resort, May 19, $75,000, 3&up, 6f, 1:10.22, COACH JIMI LEE, Bernie Blue, Cognac Kisses, 6 started.

Watson MacManus Memorial S. (R), Retama Park, Oct. 13, $45,000, 3yo, Texas-bred, 5fT, :56.14, DATRICK, Shake a Lake, Eye Wonder, 10 started.

Waya S. (R), Saratoga Race Course, Aug. 10, $84,050, 4&up, f&m, non-winners of a graded stakes on the turf in 2007, 1³⁄₁₆m (originally scheduled on the turf), 1:59.89, NUNNERY, Warrior Girl, Daytime Promise, 5 started.

Wayward Lass S., Tampa Bay Downs March 3, $60,000, 4&up, f&m, 1¹⁄₁₆m, 1:45.23, FUNNY ANNIE, Potra Clasica (Arg), Gadolinium, 10 started.

WEBN S., Turfway Park, Feb. 10, $50,000, 3yo, 1mAW, 1:39.73, JOE GOT EVEN, Cobrador, Eighteenthofmarch, 11 started.

Weekend Delight S., Turfway Park, Sept. 22, $71,250, 3&up, f&m, 6fAW, 1:10.42 (NTR), EXCITING JUSTICE, Marina Ballerina, Over the Edge, 9 started.

Weekend Madness S. (R), Saratoga Race Course, Sept. 3, $83,750, 3yo, f, non-winners of a stakes on the turf, 1¹⁄₁₆mT, 1:40.08, CLASSIC NEEL, Unspoken Word, Lady Digby, 11 started.

Weekend Surprise S. (R), Saratoga Race Course, Aug. 6, $82,750, 3yo, f, non-winners of a stakes in 2007, 6f, 1:10.76, FEATHERBED, Allude, Dicey Girl, 7 started.

Wende S., Turf Paradise, April 21, $24,900, 3yo, f, a7½fT, 1:30.71, BOOTLEG ANNIE, Wine Tasting Room, Potentilla, 7 started.

Wendy Walker S. (R), Belmont Park, June 2, $67,750, 4&up, f&m, New York-bred, 1m, 1:35.98, ICE COOL KITTY, Stolen Star, Shady Lane, 7 started.

WESTCHESTER H. (G3), Belmont Park, May 2, $105,700, 3&up, 1m, 1:33.23, UTOPIA (JPN), Sun King, Political Force, 5 started.

Western Canada H., Northlands Park, July 1, $46,925, 3yo, 6½f, 1:18.20, SIN TORO, Footprint, Bling, 9 started.

Westerner S., Northlands Park, Aug. 19, $47,115, 3&up, 1¹⁄₁₆m, 1:42.80, TRUE METROPOLITAN, Teagues Fight, Tejano Trouble, 6 started.

Western Heritage S. (R), Marquis Downs, Aug. 18, $18,846, 2yo, c&g, Saskatchewan-bred, 6f, 1:17.25, BRILLIANT ACTION, Gigs, You've Got Corona, 8 started.

West Long Branch S., Monmouth Park, June 10, $65,000, 3&up, f&m, 6f, 1:09.47, SWEET FERVOR, Solarana (Arg), Suzzane (Arg), 7 started.

West Mesa H., The Downs at Albuquerque, Sept. 21, $45,000, 3&up, f&m, 7f, 1:27.07, LIL E ROSE, Bold Cara, Ladysgotthelooks, 5 started.

West Point H. (R), Saratoga Race Course, Aug. 12, $110,300, 3&up, New York-bred, 1⅛mT, 1:47.77, CLASSIC PACK, Red Zipper, Foreverness, 8 started.

West Virginia Breeders' Classic S. (R), Charles Town Races, Oct. 20, $450,000, 3&up, West Virginia-bred, 1⅛m, 1:54.05, EASTERN DELITE, Confucius Say, Double Tollgate, 10 started.

WEST VIRGINIA DERBY (G3), Mountaineer Race Track and Gaming Resort, Aug. 4, $750,000, 3yo, 1⅛m, 1:53.04, ZANJERO, Bwana Bull, Moyer's Pond, 8 started.

West Virginia Distaff S. (R), Charles Town Races, May 5, $51,400, 3&up, f&m, most starts at Charles Town in last four starts, 4½f, :52.93, UNLAWFUL SPIRIT, Kickstand Kelli, Rain Song, 8 started.

West Virginia Division of Tourism Breeders' Classic S. (R), Charles Town Races, Oct. 20, $90,000, 3yo, f, West Virginia-bred, 7f, 1:26.46, B'S WILD RUSH, Glorious Appearing, Jip's Girl, 10 started.

West Virginia Futurity (R), Charles Town Races, Dec. 1, $68,800, 2yo, West Virginia-bred, 7f, 1:28.80, GHOSTLY THUNDER, Brother Bryant, Love to Sing, 8 started.

West Virginia Governor's S., Mountaineer Race Track and Gaming Resort, Aug. 4, $125,000, 3&up, 1 1/16m, 1:46.96, M B SEA, Mr. Pursuit, Come On Chas, 7 started.

West Virginia House of Delegates Speaker's Cup S., Mountaineer Race Track and Gaming Resort, Aug. 4, $85,000, 3&up, 1m70yT, 1:38.24, BUCKEYE BUDDY, Guardianofthenorth, Dynareign, 9 started.

West Virginia Jefferson County Chamber of Commerce Dash for Cash Breeders' Classic S. (R), Charles Town Races, Oct. 20, $90,000, 3&up, West Virginia-bred, 4½f, :52.17, MISSACITY LUKE, Not for Sam, Proper Jazz, 9 started.

West Virginia Jefferson Security Bank Cavada Breeders' Classic S. (R), Charles Town Races, Oct. 20, $315,000, 3&up, f&m, West Virginia-bred, 7f, 1:26.12, CARNIVAL CHROME, Julie B, Shesagrumptoo, 10 started.

West Virginia Legislature Chairman's Cup S., Mountaineer Race Track and Gaming Resort, Aug. 4, $85,000, 3&up, 4½f, :52.40, BERNIE BLUE, He's Got Grit, Lucky Express, 8 started.

West Virginia Lottery Breeders' Classic S. (R), Charles Town Races, Oct. 20, $90,000, 3yo, West Virginia-bred, 7f, 1:26.89, GOLD STANDARD, Blues in the Night, Peaceful Bliss, 10 started.

West Virginia "Onion Juice" Breeders' Classic S. (R), Charles Town Races, Oct. 20, $90,000, 3&up, c&g, West Virginia-bred, 7f, 1:26.44, HELLO OUT THERE, Pagan Moon, Raggedy Andy, 10 started.

West Virginia Secretary of State S., Mountaineer Race Track and Gaming Resort, Aug. 4, $85,000, 3&up, f&m, 6f, 1:11.89, COUNTRY DIVA, Excellerant, Quelle Surprise, 7 started.

West Virginia Senate President's Breeders' Cup S., Mountaineer Race Track and Gaming Resort, Aug. 4, $119,000, 3&up, f&m, 1m70yT, 1:38.14 (NCR), BEAUTIFUL VENUE, Afleet Angel, Water Gap, 6 started.

West Virginia Triple Crown Nutrition Breeders' Classic S. (R), Charles Town Races, Oct. 20, $90,000, 2yo, f, West Virginia-bred, 4½f, :53.09, WE'RE IN THE MONEY, Burnwell Princess, Color Parade, 10 started.

West Wood Fibre S., Kamloops, May 12, $3,884, 3&up, a4½f, :50.77, CHIEF SWAN, Top Victory, Here's Your Ticket, 7 started.

What a Pleasure S., Calder Race Course, Dec. 1, $100,000, 2yo, 1 1/16m, 1:46.19, CHECK IT TWICE, Coal Play, Honey Honey Honey, 5 started.

What a Summer S., Laurel Park, Jan. 20, $96,400, 4&up, f&m, 6f, 1:11.11, SILMARIL, Scheing E Jet, La Chica Rica, 5 started.

Wheat City S., Assiniboia Downs, Aug. 6, $42,669, 3&up, 1m, 1:38.60, ARTHURLOOKSGOOD, Otis Ridge, Coast Line, 8 started.

WHIMSICAL S. (CAN-G3), Woodbine, April 15, $137,026, 4&up, f&m, 6fAW, 1:12.27, SEDUCTIVELY, Hide and Chic, Summer Girlfriend, 7 started.

Whimsical S. (R), Pimlico Race Course, May 18, $84,750, 3&up, f&m, non-winners of an open stakes in 2006-'07, 6f, 1:10.99, LA CHICA RICA, Homesteader, Waytotheleft, 4 started.

Whippleton S., Calder Race Course, Sept. 23, $50,000, 3&up, 6f, 1:09.46, FINALLYMADEIT, Yesbyjimminy, How's Your Halo, 6 started.

Whirlaway S., Aqueduct, Feb. 10, $70,070, 3yo, 1 1/16m, 1:42.23, SUMMER DOLDRUMS, Sir Whimsey, Sports Town, 6 started.

Whirling Ash S., Delaware Park, Sept. 17, $60,100, 2yo, 1m, 1:39.38, CAVE'S VALLEY, Atoned, Cudjo, 5 started.

White Clay Creek S., Delaware Park, Aug. 25, $57,950, 2yo, f, 6f, 1:09.15, PROUD SPELL, Extra Sexy Psychic, Tusculum Rd, 5 started.

White Oak H. (R), Arlington Park, July 7, $82,550, 3&up, Illinois-conceived and/or -foaled, 6fAW, 1:10.84, HIGH EXPECTATIONS, Caruso, Last Gran Standing, 7 started.

White Pine Racing Derby, White Pine County Horse Races, Aug. 19, $5,350, 3yo, 5½f, 1:09.40, BIRTHDAY BOY, Apollo's Double, Celestial View, 7 started.

White Pine Racing Thoroughbred Futurity, White Pine County Horse Races, Aug. 18, $3,900, 2yo, 5½f, 1:12.40, CANDICE THUNDER, Snowbound Reigns, Fifty Six Paydays, 6 started.

WHITNEY H. (G1), Saratoga Race Course, July 28, $810,000, 3&up, 1⅛m, 1:46.64 (NTR), LAWYER RON, Wanderin Boy, Diamond Stripes, 11 started.

Who Doctor Who H. (R), Horsemen's Park, July 21, $28,850, 4&up, Nebraska-bred, 1m, 1:39.80, BLUMIN ATTITUDE, Skwhirl, Did, 7 started.

Wickerr H. (R), Del Mar, July 27, $90,385, 3&up, non-winners of a stakes for $50,000 other than state-bred at one mile or over since May 1, 1mT, 1:33.04, BECRUX (ITY), Zann, Lang Field, 7 started.

Wide Country S., Laurel Park, Feb. 10, $60,400, 3yo, f, 1m, 1:40.08, BARE DANCER, Laila's Punch, Wow Me Free, 9 started.

Wild Again S., Aqueduct, Nov. 1, $78,700, 3yo, 1m, 1:34.41, C P WEST, Buffalo Man, Giant Deputy, 6 started.

Wild Applause S., Belmont Park, Sept. 19, $78,950, 3yo, f, 7fT, 1:22.04, UNSPOKEN WORD, Stormy West, Sweet Ransom, 11 started.

Wildcat H., Turf Paradise, April 14, $45,000, 3&up, 1⅜mT, 2:18.34, GERIRIG, In Joe's Honor, Mighty Bodacious, 9 started.

Wild Rose H., Northlands Park, June 30, $70,388, 3&up, f&m, 6½f, 1:18, MONTERO, Dixietwostepper, She's Italian, 9 started.

Wild Rose S., Prairie Meadows, June 2, $54,688, 3&up, f&m, 1 1/16m, 1:44.66, PLAID, Elite Lady, Turbulent Thinking, 6 started.

Willard L. Proctor Memorial S., Hollywood Park, May 27, $82,825, 2yo, 5½fAW, 1:05.71, THOROUGHLY, Run Brother Ron, Bold Trust, 8 started.

WILLIAM DONALD SCHAEFER H. (G3), Pimlico Race Course, May 19, $100,000, 3&up, 1⅛m, 1:47.86, FLASHY BULL, Hesanoldsalt, Ryan's for Real, 8 started.

William Henry Harrison S. (R), Indiana Downs, May 19, $45,000, 3&up, Indiana-bred, 6f, 1:09.97, LIEPERS FORK, Father John, Ambassador Jack, 11 started.

William Livingston S., Meadowlands, Nov. 3, $60,000, 3&up, 6f, 1:08.58, CHATAIN, Mr. Umphrey, Divisa, 7 started.

Willow Lake H., Yavapai Downs, July 23, $15,000, 3&up, f&m, 1m, 1:39, NIGHT POWER, Lil Celeste, Island Hopping, 6 started.

WILL ROGERS S. (G3), Hollywood Park, May 19, $108,200, 3yo, 1mT, 1:35.19, WORLDLY (GB), Silent Soul, Mayor Bozarth, 6 started.

Willy Fiddle S., Les Bois Park, July 21, $13,848, 3&up, 7½f, 1:31.93, SILENT SNOW, Dangerously Dunn, Lookn East, 9 started.

Willy Wank H. (R), Presque Isle Downs, Sept. 21, $90,000, 3&up, Pennsylvania-bred, 1⅛mAW, 1:53.43, GREY DORIAN, Serene Harbor, Captain Ernie, 6 started.

WILSHIRE H. (G3), Hollywood Park, April 25, $111,500, 3&up, f&m, 1mT, 1:34.16, CHARM THE GIANT (IRE), Sohgol (Ire), Ghurra, 10 started.

Windy Sands H., Del Mar, Sept. 3, $89,190, 3&up, 1mAW, 1:40, WANNA RUNNER, Heatseeker (Ire), Plug Me In, 6 started.

Wine Country Juvenile Filly S., Santa Rosa, July 21, $60,035, 2yo, f, 5½f, 1:03.78, CARBELLA, Shes a Lucky Wager, Kooky Kelly, 9 started.

WINNING COLORS S. (G3), Churchill Downs, May 28, $110,100, 3&up, f&m, 6f, 1:08.68, MISS MACY SUE, Cuaba, Morethanaprincess, 8 started.

Winning Colors S., Les Bois Park, June 22, $14,793, 3&up, f&m, 7f, 1:27, DERBY CAT, Spicey N Hot, Petite Motion, 9 started.

Winnipeg Futurity, Assiniboia Downs, Sept. 23, $44,964, 2yo, 1m, 1:40.40, MIKAYLA'S BABY, Air Pegasus, Cherokee Wild, 7 started.

Winnipeg Sun S., Assiniboia Downs, Aug. 5, $42,669, 3&up, f&m, 1 1/16m, 1:46.20, CULPEPER MOON, Daisy Mountain, Julie Truly, 9 started.

Winsham Lad H., Sunland Park, Jan. 13, $50,000, 3&up, 1m, 1:38.45, GUIDING HAND, Real Dandy, Takin Issue, 11 started.
WinStar Derby, Sunland Park, March 18, $591,000, 3yo, 1¹⁄₁₆m, 1:49.53, SONG OF NAVARONE, Solemn Promise, Forty Grams, 7 started.
WinStar Sunland Park Oaks, Sunland Park, March 18, $200,000, 3yo, f, 1¹⁄₁₆m, 1:45.18, TOUGH TIZ'S SIS, Swiss Current, Purely Surprized, 9 started.
Wintergreen S., Turfway Park, March 10, $50,000, 4&up, f&m, 1mAW, 1:37.91, HALF HEAVEN, Hayden Valley, Ella Belle, 12 started.
Winter Melody S., Delaware Park, May 14, $57,950, 3&up, f&m, 1¹⁄₁₆T, 1:43.88, IT'S TRUE LOVE, Daytime Promise, Les Ry Leigh, 5 started.
Wishing Well H., Santa Anita Park, Jan. 28, $81,100, 4&up, f&m, a6½fT, 1:12.62, ATTIMA (GB), Somethinaboutbetty, Wild Storm (Chi), 10 started.
Wishing Well S., Turfway Park, Jan. 13, $50,000, 4&up, f&m, 6fAW, 1:09.37, MARY DELANEY, Mocha Queen, Asyouwish, 11 started.
Witches Brew S., Meadowlands, Oct. 31, $55,000, 3&up, f&m, 5fT, :57.01, WEEKS, Beau Dare, Robin des Tune, 9 started.
With Anticipation S., Saratoga Race Course, Aug. 31, $83,250, 2yo, 1¹⁄₁₆mT, 1:41.26, NOWNOWNOW, Zee Zee, Sherine, 9 started.
With Approval S. (R), Woodbine, Aug. 12, $71,577, 3&up, Canadian-bred, 1¹⁄₈mT, 1:47.98, STERWINS, The Niagara Queen, French Beret, 6 started.
WITHERS S. (G3), Aqueduct, April 28, $150,000, 3yo, 1m, 1:34.65, DIVINE PARK, C P West, Frosty Secret, 7 started.
Without Feathers S., Monmouth Park, June 23, $60,000, 3yo, f, 1m, 1:35.05, EXCHANGING FIRE, Coy Coyote, Ethan's Car, 7 started.
W. L. MCKNIGHT H. (G2), Calder Race Course, Dec. 15, $200,000, 3&up, 1½mT, 2:26.13, PRESIOUS PASSION, Stream of Gold (Ire), Kiss the Kid, 12 started.
W. Meredith Bailes Memorial S. (R), Colonial Downs, July 8, $54,600, 3&up, Virginia-bred and/or -sired, 1m, 1:36.17, PARK AVENUE PRINCE, In the Nick, Catenare, 4 started.
Wolf Hill S., Monmouth Park, June 2, $60,000, 3&up, 5½fT, 1:00.81 (NCR), SMART ENOUGH, Mr. Silver, Bingobear, 8 started.
Wolverine S. (R), Great Lakes Downs, June 19, $50,000, 3&up, Michigan-bred, 6f, 1:13.70, WEATHERSTORM, Demagoguery, Its His Time, 7 started.
Wonders Delight S. (R), Penn National Race Course, May 17, $45,650, 3yo, f, Pennsylvania-bred, 6f, 1:09.20, CANTREL, Blitzensfoxyvixsin, All Night Special, 6 started.
WonderWhere S. (R), Woodbine, July 28, $236,957, 3yo, f, Canadian-bred, 1¹⁄₈mT, 2:02.17, SEALY HILL, Saskawea, Street Sounds, 9 started.
WOODBINE MILE S. (CAN-G1), Woodbine, Sept. 16, $973,893, 3&up, 1mT, 1:33.58, SHAKESPEARE, Kip Deville, Galantas, 14 started.
Woodchopper H., Fair Grounds, Dec. 24, $58,200, 3yo, a1mT, 1:38.48, INCA KING, Jazz Quest, Tactical Weapon, 6 started.
Wooden Star S., Hawthorne Race Course, Nov. 18, $48,000, 3&up, f&m, 5fT, :56.23, BYENNE, Summer Recital, Miss Greenley, 12 started.
Woodford Reserve Bourbon S., Keeneland Race Course, Oct. 7, $150,000, 2yo, 1¹⁄₁₆mT, 1:45.92, GIO PONTI, Nownownow, Caberneigh, 7 started.
WOODFORD RESERVE TURF CLASSIC S. (G1), Churchill Downs, May 5, $561,000, 3&up, 1¹⁄₈mT, 1:49.01, SKY CONQUEROR, Brilliant, Danzon, 10 started.
Woodford S., Keeneland Race Course, Oct. 18, $112,600, 3&up, 5½fT, 1:03.20, FORT PRADO, T. D. Vance, Atticus Kristy, 10 started.
Woodland Heritage S. (R), Marquis Downs, Aug. 18, $18,846, 2yo, f, Saskatchewan-bred, 6f, 1:15.75, TIME TO DANZE, Kellys Signal, Whiz Girl, 9 started.
Woodlands Derby, The Woodlands, Oct. 14, $20,000, 3yo, 1¹⁄₁₆m, 1:45.60, NAVY WINGS, Glory to Spare, I Spy Wolfie, 5 started.
Woodlands Juvenile S., The Woodlands, Oct. 27, $20,000, 2yo, 6f, 1:12.20, MONOJET, Kepthecabin, Get Even Stephen, 10 started.
Woodlands S., The Woodlands, Oct. 27, $20,000, 3&up, 1¹⁄₁₆m, 1:44.60, MANOVAN, Oust, Indian Moonshine, 8 started.
Woodlawn S., Pimlico Race Course, May 5, $60,000, 3yo, 1mT, 1:37.56, REBEL YELLER, Encaustic, Brahms Melody, 9 started.
WOOD MEMORIAL S. (G1), Aqueduct, April 7, $750,000, 3yo, 1¹⁄₈m, 1:49.46, NOBIZ LIKE SHOBIZ, Sightseeing, Any Given Saturday, 6 started.
Woodstock S., Woodbine, April 21, $111,017, 3yo, 6fAW, 1:09.68, LIKE MOM LIKE SONS, Dancer's Bajan, Forbidden Bear, 6 started.

WOODWARD S. (G1), Saratoga Race Course, Sept. 1, $500,000, 3&up, 1¹⁄₈m, 1:48.60, LAWYER RON, Sun King, Diamond Stripes, 8 started.
WOODY STEPHENS S. (G2), Belmont Park, June 9, $247,166, 3yo, 7f, 1:21.49, TEUFLESBERG, Most Distinguished, Stormello, 8 started.
Work the Crowd H. (R), Golden Gate Fields, May 13, $75,000, 3&up, f&m, California-bred, 1¹⁄₁₆mT, 1:43.50, SOMETHINABOUT-LAURA, Gentle Charmer, Awesome Beginning, 6 started.
World Appeal S., Meadowlands, Sept. 28, $55,000, 2yo, 1m70yT, 1:40.26, WHY TONTO, Piquante Cat, Hugo, 6 started.
Xtra Heat H., Belmont Park, Oct. 14, $105,700, 3&up, f&m, 6fT, 1:08.65, GENUINE DEVOTION (IRE), Trouble Maker, Stormy Kiss (Arg), 5 started.
Xtra Heat S., Aqueduct, Dec. 6, $77,750, 2yo, f, 6f, 1:11.47, THROBBIN' HEART, Dill Or No Dill, D J Lightning, 7 started.
Xtra Heat S., Delaware Park, Aug. 11. $60,200, 3&up, f&m, 6f, 1:10.36, WILDCAT BETTIE B, Coli Bear, Cajun Mistress, 6 started.
Xtra Heat S., Pimlico Race Course, April 28, $62,200, 3yo, f, 5¹⁄₂f, 1:04.75, YOUR FLAME IN ME, Paying Off, Earlybird Road, 4 started.
Yaddo H. (R), Saratoga Race Course, Aug. 18, $112,600, 3&up, f&m, New York-bred, 1¹⁄₁₆mT, 1:47.84, LATITUDE FORTY, Factual Contender, Symphony of Psalms, 10 started.
Yank's Music S. (R), Belmont Park, May 23, $66,700, 4&up, f&m, non-winners of a graded stakes in 2006-'07, 1¹⁄₁₆m, 1:42.27, DANCE AWAY CAPOTE, Altesse, Sugar Swir, 6 started.
Yavapai Classic H., Yavapai Downs, June 3, $15,000, 3&up, f&m, 6f, 1:09.40, WILD ENGLISH ROSE, Summer Lake, Continentalmeeting, 8 started.
Yavapai County Arizona Breeders' Futurity (R), Yavapai Downs, June 24, $35,215, 2yo, Arizona-bred, 5f, :58.60, MY ROYAL GIRL, Stormy Highland, Retrack, 10 started.
Yavapai Downs Derby, Yavapai Downs, Aug. 18, $21,000, 3yo, 1¹⁄₁₆m, 1:43.80, PARTY WITH TODD, Snowbound Warrior, Preferred Yield, 10 started.
Yavapai Downs Futurity, Yavapai Downs, Sept. 3, $46,450, 2yo, 6f, 1:09.60, RULE BY FORCE, Stormy Highland, Midnight Wish, 11 started.
Yavapai Downs H., Yavapai Downs, July 10, $15,000, 3&up, 5¹⁄₂f, 1:01.80, KING JUSTIN, Yes Talk to Me, Lydia's Legacy, 5 started.
YELLOW RIBBON S. (G1), Oak Tree at Santa Anita, Sept. 29, $400,000, 3&up, f&m, 1¹⁄₄mT, 1:59.73, NASHOBA'S KEY, Citronnade, Black Mamba (NZ), 9 started.
Yellow Rose S. (R), Sam Houston Race Park, Dec. 1, $50,000, 3&up, f&m, Texas-bred, 6f, 1:10.18, ANNIE SAVOY, Stealth Cat, Moneyinmywranglers, 9 started.
Yellowstone Downs Thoroughbred Derby, Yellowstone Downs, Sept. 16, $4,300, 3yo, 1f, 1:30.20, D C BOBBY SHOCKS, Ourticketohome, C B Spicy Duck, 5 started.
Yellowstone Downs Thoroughbred Futurity, Yellowstone Downs, Sept. 16, $10,485, 2yo, 5¹⁄₄f, 1:06.40, REMEMBER FREEDOM, Adam Good Heart, C C Bound, 8 started.
Yerba Buena S., Golden Gate Fields, June 9, $75,000, 3&up, f&m, 1³⁄₈mT, 2:17.87, MABADI, Veyana (Fr), Christmas Stocking, 6 started.
Your Ladyship S. (R), Arlington Park, June 17, $46,650, 3&up, f&m, Illinois-conceived and/or -foaled, 7fAW, 1:24.41, STORM ROLLING IN, Dyna Slam, Magnetic Miss, 5 started.
Zadracarta S. (R), Woodbine, June 17, $70,582, 3&up, f&m, Canadian-bred, 6fT, 1:08.87, SIWA, Becky Sharp, Arden Belle, 6 started.
Zany Tactics S., Turf Paradise, May 6. $25,000, 3yo, 6f, 1:08.69, SHIMMERING DUNES, Yes Talk to Me, Call Me Mr. Cash, 7 started.
Zen S. (R), Arlington Park, June 15, $46,950, 3&up, Illinois-bred, 7fAW, 1:23.97, HIGH EXPECTATIONS, Last Gran Standing, Caruso, 11 started.
Zia Park Derby, Zia Park, Dec. 8, $106,600, 3yo, 1¹⁄₁₆m, 1:45.40, REPORTING FOR DUTY, Devil Red Forty Acres, 6 started.
Zia Park Distaff S., Zia Park, Oct. 7, $59 400, 3&up, f&m, 6f, 1:08.80, KIN TO A KITTY, I'm N Clover, Mykindasaint, 4 started.
Zia Park Distance Championship H., Zia Park, Dec. 9, $186,960, 3&up, 1¹⁄₂m, 1:51 (NTR), TAP DANCING MAUK, Red Rock Creek, Guiding Hand, 10 started.
Zia Park Express S., Zia Park, Nov. 25, $60,500, 2yo, 6¹⁄₂f, 1:18.40, DUCKY DRAKE, Dragooner, Mint Fly, 4 started.
Zip Pocket S., Turf Paradise, Oct. 16, $30,700, 3&up, 5¹⁄₂f, 1:02.49, NATIONHOOD, Run Nicholas Run, Prorunner, 7 started.
Zydeco S., Delta Downs, Oct. 19, $55,000, 3&up, 5f, :57.24 (NTR), ALL WIRED UP, Captain Buddy, High Strike Zone, 10 started.

Oldest Stakes Races

Although horse racing in North America dates from the Colonial period, stakes races did not become popular until the mid-1800s.

The oldest continually run stakes in North America—meaning the race has been run every year since its inception—is the Queen's Plate Stakes at Woodbine. First run in 1860, the race was named for Queen Victoria, then in the 23rd year of her 64-year reign, and was for horses of all ages foaled in the province of Ontario. The winner of that first Queen's Plate was Don Juan, a five-year-old Sir Tatton Sykes gelding. (Another Queen's Plate, restricted to horses foaled in Quebec, dated from 1836 and was discontinued after World War II.) From 1902 through '51, the race was known as the King's Plate, for a succession of English male monarchs.

North America's oldest stakes race still in existence is the Phoenix Breeders' Cup Stakes (G3), first run in 1831 at the Kentucky Association track in Lexington. Known at various times as the Phoenix Hotel S., Phoenix S., Brennan S., Chiles S., Association S., and the Phoenix H., the race was discontinued in 1930. It was revived with the first spring race meeting of Keeneland Race Course in 1937.

Oldest Continuously Run Stakes

Race	Track	First Running	First Winner
Queen's Plate S.	Woodbine	1860	Don Juan
Kentucky Derby	Churchill	1875	Aristides
Kentucky Oaks	Churchill	1875	Vinaigrette
Clark H.	Churchill	1875	Voltigeur
Bashford Manor S.	Churchill	1902	Von Rouse
Fall Highweight H.	Aqueduct	1914	Comely
Coaching Club American Oaks	Belmont	1917	Wistful
Jockey Club Gold Cup S.	Belmont	1919	Purchase
Wood Memorial S.	Aqueduct	1925	Backbone
Whitney H.	Saratoga	1928	Black Maria
Canadian Derby	Northlands	1930	Jack Whittier

Oldest Stakes Races

Race	Track	First Running	First Winner
PHOENIX BREEDERS' CUP S.	**Keeneland**	**1831**	**McDonough**

1831-'77, held as a heat race; 1898-1904,1906-'10, 1914-'16, 1929, 1931-'36, not held; before 1937, held at the Kentucky Association track; 1943-'45, held at Churchill Downs; 1972, 1981, held in two divisions; before 1989, held during the spring meeting; inaugurated in 1831 as the Phoenix Hotel S.; has also been held as Brennan S., Chiles S., Phoenix S., Association S., and Phoenix H.

QUEEN'S PLATE S. — Woodbine — 1860 — Don Juan

Before 1887, held at $1\frac{1}{2}$ miles; 1924-'56, held at $1\frac{1}{8}$ miles; before 1938, for three-year-olds and up; 1938, for three- and four-year-olds; 1902-'51, held as the King's Plate; before 1956, held at Old Woodbine; before 1959, for three-year-olds bred and owned in Canada

TRAVERS S. — Saratoga — 1864 — Kentucky

1943-'45, held at Belmont Park; 1896, 1898-1900, 1911-'12, not held; before 1890, held at $1\frac{3}{4}$ miles; 1890-'92, held at $1\frac{1}{2}$ miles; 1895, 1901-'03, held at $1\frac{1}{8}$ miles; 1927-'32, held as the Travers Midsummer Derby

JEROME H. — Belmont — 1866 — Watson

1866-'89, held at Jerome Park; 1890-1905, held at Morris Park; 1960, 1962-'67, held at Aqueduct; 1910-'13, not held; 1866-'70, held in two divisions; 1871-'77, held at two miles; 1878-'89, held at $1\frac{3}{4}$ miles; 1890-'91, 1903, held at $1\frac{5}{16}$ miles; 1892, held at $1\frac{1}{2}$ miles; 1893-'94, 1896-1909, held at $1\frac{1}{4}$ miles; 1895, held at $1\frac{1}{8}$ miles

BELMONT S. — Belmont — 1867 — Ruthless

1867-'89, held at Jerome Park; 1890-1904, held at Morris Park; 1963-'67, held at Aqueduct; 1911-'12, not held; 1867-'73, held at $1\frac{5}{8}$ miles; 1890-'92, 1895, 1904-'05, held at $1\frac{1}{4}$ miles; 1893-'94, held at $1\frac{1}{8}$ miles; 1896-1903, 1906-'25, held at $1\frac{3}{8}$ miles; 1895, 1913, held as a handicap stakes

CHAMPAGNE S. — Belmont — 1867 — Sarah B.

Before 1890, held at Jerome Park; 1890-1905, held at Morris Park; 1959, 1963-'67, 1984, held at Aqueduct; 1910-'13, 1956, not held; 1871-'80, held at six furlongs; 1891-1904, held at seven furlongs; 1905-'32, about seven furlongs; 1933-'39, held at $6\frac{1}{2}$ furlongs; 1940-'83, 1985-'93, held at one mile; 1984, held at $1\frac{1}{8}$ miles; 1973, held in two divisions

LADIES H. — Aqueduct — 1868 — Bonnie Braes

Before 1913, for three-year-old fillies; 1913-'39, two-year-olds and up; before 1890, held at Jerome Park; 1890-1904, held at Morris Park; 1950-'58, 1960, held at Belmont Park; 1895, 1911-'12, not held; before 1874, held at $1\frac{5}{8}$ miles; 1889, 1892, held at $1\frac{1}{8}$ miles; 1890-'91, held at 1,400 yards; 1893-'94, held at $1\frac{1}{16}$ miles; 1896-1939, held at one mile; 1961-'62, held at $1\frac{5}{16}$ miles; 1874-'85, 1940-'58, 1960, 1963-'64, held at $1\frac{1}{2}$ miles

DIXIE S. — Pimlico — 1870 — Preakness

1870, held as Dinner Party S.; 1871, held as Reunion S.; 1903-'04, held at Benning, Washington, D.C., at $1\frac{3}{4}$ miles for three-year-olds; 1870-'88, held at two miles for three-year-olds; 1924-'52, held at $1\frac{3}{16}$ miles; 1960-'87, 1989-'90, held at $1\frac{1}{2}$ miles; 1955-'59, held at $1\frac{3}{8}$ miles; 1988, held at $1\frac{5}{8}$ miles; before 1955, 1988, held on dirt; 1889-1901, 1905-'23, not held; 1965-'78, held in two divisions

MONMOUTH OAKS — Monmouth — 1871 — Salina

1871-'77, held at $1\frac{1}{2}$ miles; 1879-'93, held at $1\frac{1}{4}$ miles; 1946-'52, 1996-2001, held at $1\frac{1}{16}$ miles; 1953-'95, held at $1\frac{1}{8}$ miles; 1891, held at Jerome Park; 1878, 1894-1945, 2003, not held; 1976, held as Monmouth Bicentennial Oaks

ALABAMA S. — Saratoga — 1872 — Woodbine

1943-'45, held at Belmont Park; 1893-'96, 1898-1900, 1911-'12, not held; before 1901, 1904, 1906-'16, held at $1\frac{1}{8}$ miles; 1901-'03, held at $1\frac{1}{16}$ miles; 1903, held on turf; 1905, held at $1\frac{5}{16}$ miles

CALIFORNIA DERBY — Golden Gate Fields — 1873 — Camilla Urso

1897-1909, held at $1\frac{1}{4}$ miles; 1923, held at $1\frac{1}{2}$ miles; 1936-'48, 1976-'81, held at $1\frac{1}{16}$ miles; 1874, 1891-'96, 1900, 1911-'22, 1924-'34, 1939-'40, 1942-'43, 1945, 1947, 1949-'53, 1957, 2005, not held; 1873-1959, 1962, held at Tanforan; 1963, 2001-'04, held at Bay Meadows

PREAKNESS S. — Pimlico — 1873 — Survivor

Before 1894, held at $1\frac{1}{2}$ miles; 1889, held at $1\frac{1}{4}$ miles; 1894-1900, 1908, held at $1\frac{1}{16}$ miles; 1901-'07, held at one mile and 70 yards; 1909-'10, held at one mile; 1911-'24, held at $1\frac{1}{8}$ miles; 1891-'93, not held; 1890, for three-year-olds and up; 1890, held at Morris Park, New York; 1894-1908, held at Gravesend, New York; 1918, held in two divisions

Leading North American-Raced Horses of 2007

Leading North American-Raced Horses by 2007 Earnings

Name, YOB Sex	Starts	Wins	Earnings
Curlin, 2004 c.	9	6	$5,102,800
Dylan Thomas (Ire), 2003 h.	11	5	4,116,100
Invasor (Arg), 2002 h.	2	2	3,900,000
Street Sense, 2004 c.	8	4	3,205,000
English Channel, 2002 h.	7	4	2,640,000
Doctor Dino (Fr), 2002 h.	6	3	2,579,991
Hard Spun, 2004 c.	10	4	2,572,500
Kip Deville, 2003 h.	7	3	1,965,780
Ginger Punch, 2003 m.	8	5	1,827,060
Cloudy's Knight, 2000 g.	9	3	1,762,868
Quijano, 2002 c.	11	6	1,721,296
Lahudood (GB), 2003 m.	5	3	1,560,500
Lava Man, 2001 g.	8	3	1,410,000
War Pass, 2005 c.	4	4	1,397,400
Robe Decollete, 2004 f.	7	2	1,376,264
Midnight Lute, 2003 h.	6	4	1,368,000
Indian Blessing, 2005 f.	3	3	1,357,200
Rags to Riches, 2004 f.	6	5	1,340,028
Lawyer Ron, 2003 h.	8	4	1,320,000
Nobiz Like Shobiz, 2004 c.	10	5	1,318,330
Kelly's Landing, 2001 g.	4	2	1,313,000
Tiago, 2004 c.	8	4	1,234,750
Corinthian, 2003 h.	7	4	1,174,173
Mrs. Lindsay, 2004 f.	6	4	1,170,915
Oracle West, 2001 g.	7	0	1,126,272
Shamdinan (Fr), 2004 c.	8	2	1,120,298
Unbridled Belle, 2003 m.	5	2	1,116,500
Precious Kitten, 2003 m.	9	4	1,090,000
Excellent Art (GB), 2004 c.	7	1	1,065,583
Zanjero, 2004 c.	8	2	1,060,977
Octave, 2004 f.	8	2	1,050,234
Student Council, 2002 h.	9	4	1,041,755
Awesome Gem, 2003 g.	9	2	1,032,400
Panty Raid, 2004 f.	8	4	1,024,180
Dia de la Novia (Jpn), 2002 m.	8	2	1,010,057
Any Given Saturday, 2004 c.	8	4	994,320
Hystericalady, 2003 m.	8	3	984,438
Jambalaya, 2002 g.	6	3	979,421
Nashoba's Key, 2003 m.	8	7	972,090
Sealy Hill, 2004 f.	8	4	958,389
Koiuta (Jpn), 2003 m.	8	1	918,688
Maryfield, 2001 m.	8	3	896,330
Red Giant, 2004 c.	8	4	846,720
Lady of Venice (Fr), 2003 m.	6	3	835,272
Sky Conqueror, 2002 h.	7	2	827,043
Scat Daddy, 2004 c.	4	3	826,500
Lady Joanne, 2004 f.	7	4	808,993
Idiot Proof, 2004 c.	8	4	803,136
Miss Shop, 2003 m.	10	3	787,408
Bear Now, 2004 f.	8	4	747,517

Name, YOB Sex	Starts	Earnings	Average Earnings
Friendly Island, 2001 h.	2	$ 490,000	$245,000
Ginger Punch, 2003 m.	8	1,827,060	228,383
Midnight Lute, 2003 h.	6	1,368,000	228,000
Rags to Riches, 2004 f.	6	1,340,028	223,338
Unbridled Belle, 2003 m.	5	1,116,500	223,300
Scat Daddy, 2004 c.	4	826,500	206,625
Robe Decollete, 2004 f.	7	1,376,264	196,609
Cloudy's Knight, 2000 g.	9	1,762,868	195,874
Mrs. Lindsay, 2004 f.	6	1,170,915	195,153
Country Star, 2005 f.	3	575,900	191,967
Ask, 2003 h.	3	556,546	185,515
Lava Man, 2001 g.	8	1,410,000	176,250
Corinthian, 2003 h.	7	1,174,173	167,739
Lawyer Ron, 2003 h.	8	1,320,000	165,000
Jambalaya, 2002 g.	6	979,421	163,237
Oracle West, 2001 g.	7	1,126,272	160,896
Quijano, 2002 c.	11	1,721,296	156,481
Song of Navarone, 2004 c.	2	312,180	156,090
Tiago, 2004 c.	8	1,234,750	154,344
Notional, 2004 c.	3	460,000	153,333
Strike Softly, 2003 m.	2	305,775	152,888
Excellent Art (GB), 2004 c.	7	1,065,583	152,226
Proud Spell, 2005 f.	4	608,770	152,193
Into Mischief, 2005 c.	3	448,800	149,600
Bob and John, 2003 h.	2	295,000	147,500
Spring At Last, 2003 h.	5	722,000	144,400
Shamdinan (Fr), 2004 c.	8	1,120,298	140,037
Lady of Venice (Fr), 2003 m.	6	835,272	139,212
The Tin Man, 1998 g.	4	536,920	134,230
Zanjero, 2004 c.	8	1,060,977	132,622
Nobiz Like Shobiz, 2004 c.	10	1,318,330	131,833
Octave, 2004 f.	8	1,050,234	131,279
Pyro, 2005 c.	4	516,718	129,180
Panty Raid, 2004 f.	8	1,024,180	128,023
Dia de la Novia (Jpn), 2002 m.	8	1,010,057	126,257

Leading North American-Raced Horses by Average Earnings per Start in 2007

Name, YOB Sex	Starts	Earnings	Average Earnings
Invasor (Arg), 2002 h.	2	$3,900,000	$1,950,000
Curlin, 2004 c.	9	5,102,800	566,978
Indian Blessing, 2005 f.	3	1,357,200	452,400
Doctor Dino (Fr), 2002 h.	6	2,579,991	429,999
Street Sense, 2004 c.	8	3,205,000	400,625
English Channel, 2002 h.	7	2,640,000	377,143
Dylan Thomas (Ire), 2003 h.	11	4,116,100	374,191
War Pass, 2005 c.	4	1,397,400	349,350
Kelly's Landing, 2001 g.	4	1,313,000	328,250
Shakespeare, 2001 h.	2	629,640	314,820
Lahudood (GB), 2003 m.	5	1,560,500	312,100
Timber Reserve, 2004 c.	2	577,600	288,800
Kip Deville, 2003 h.	7	1,965,780	280,826
Joint Effort, 2003 m.	1	275,000	275,000
Hard Spun, 2004 c.	10	2,572,500	257,250

International Leading Earners of 2007, Excluding North America

Name, YOB Sex	Countries Raced	Wins	Earnings
Admire Moon, 2003 c.	HK, Jpn, UAE	4	$7,397,076
Subscribe, 2000 c.	HK, UAE	3	5,489,953
Comic Strip, 2002 g.	HK	3	5,241,821
Dylan Thomas (Ire), 2003 h.	Eng, Fr, HK, Ire	5	4,041,100
Ramonti, 2002 h.	Eng, Fr, HK	5	4,037,246
Daiwa Scarlet, 2004 f.	Jpn	4	3,985,857
Meisho Samson, 2003 c.	Jpn	3	3,894,358
Vermilion, 2002 c.	Jpn, UAE	4	3,609,013
Invasor (Arg), 2002 h.	UAE	1	3,600,000
Good Ba Ba, 2002 g.	HK, Jpn	7	3,433,325
Floral Pegasus, 2002 c.	HK	5	3,128,809
Vodka, 2004 f.	Jpn	3	2,980,561
Efficient, 2003 g.	Aus	1	2,884,003
Daiwa Major, 2001 c.	Jpn, UAE	2	2,825,606
Matsurida Gogh, 2003 c.	Jpn	3	2,810,329
Jumbo Star, 2003 g.	HK	8	2,635,123
Pop Rock, 2001 c.	Jpn, UAE	1	2,569,270
Izzat, 2002 g.	HK	3	2,477,008
Asakusa Kings, 2004 c.	Jpn	2	2,459,944
Authorized, 2004 c.	Eng, Fr	3	2,365,763
Suzuka Phoenix, 2002 c.	Jpn	3	2,242,095
Doctor Dino (Fr), 2002 h.	Eng, Fr, HK	2	2,180,471
El Segundo, 2001 g.	Aus	4	2,168,806
Haradasun, 2003 c.	Aus	4	1,888,993
Master O'Reilly, 2002 g.	Aus	5	1,741,894
Forensics, 2004 f.	Aus	3	1,714,179
Genius And Evil, 2001 g.	HK	2	1,707,830
Blue Concorde, 2000 c.	Jpn	2	1,693,107
Sunrise Bacchus, 2002 c.	Jpn	1	1,625,032
Sans Adieu, 2002 f.	Jpn	3	1,604,557
Gold Edition, 2003 f.	Aus	7	1,575,984
Soldier of Fortune, 2004 c.	Eng, Fr, Ire	4	1,570,120
Youmzain, 2003 h.	Eng, Fr, Ger, Ire, UAE	0	1,565,735

Racing — 2007 Leading North American-Raced Horses

Name, YOB Sex	Countries Raced	Wins	Earnings
Meisho Tokon, 2002 c.	Jpn	3	$1,543,178
Lawman, 2004 c.	Fr	3	1,538,005
Super Hornet, 2003 c.	Jpn	4	1,528,831
Miss Andretti, 2001 f.	Aus, Eng, HK	6	1,526,943
Able One, 2002 g.	HK, Jpn	3	1,525,543
Asiatic Boy, 2003 c.	Eng, UAE	4	1,518,803
Quijano, 2002 c.	Fr, Ger, HK, UAE	6	1,493,508
Roc de Cambes, 2004 c.	Jpn	4	1,485,570
Joyful Winner, 2000 g.	HK, Jpn	2	1,417,937
Luck Money, 2005 c.	Eng, Ire	2	1,408,391
Victory, 2004 c.	Jpn	2	1,398,976
Darjina, 2004 f.	Eng, Fr, HK	4	1,398,706
Agnes Ark, 2003 c.	Jpn	2	1,398,225
Peeping Fawn, 2004 f.	Eng, Ire	5	1,388,309
Creachadoir, 2004 c.	Eng, Fr, HK, Ire	3	1,383,617
Admire Aura, 2004 c.	Jpn	2	1,369,521
Lush Lashes, 2005 f.	Ire	1	1,367,771

Most Starts in North America in 2007

Starts	Name, YOB Sex	Wins	Earnings
29	I'm an Evil One, 2002 m.	0	$ 9,839
28	Electric Lake, 2003 m.	0	12,425
	Not Ready Yet, 2003 h.	0	3,324
27	Kingjames Delivers, 2003 g.	3	15,199
26	Canavati, 2001 g.	1	9,630
	Karin's Girl, 2001 m.	3	38,730
	Meeting Ended, 2002 g.	0	6,118
	Rio Ruckus, 2001 g.	1	11,285
25	Boula Boula, 2001 m.	1	10,311
	Go Geta Job, 2002 g.	1	8,961
	Prize Money, 2003 g.	3	13,806
	Thegreyofthegoose, 2004 f.	0	15,847
	Weedle, 2000 g.	0	16,385
24	Alondra C, 2003 m.	0	4,734
	Blaine's Storm, 2001 h.	2	16,727
	Dalewoods Promise, 2001 g.	1	15,109
	Divine Dancer, 2001 g.	4	22,825
	Fairly Liberal, 2003 g.	2	8,741
	Fella, 2003 g.	1	13,009
	First Count, 2002 g.	1	11,573
	Happy Bert, 2002 h.	2	32,148
	Juranees, 2002 g.	1	14,835
	Kriss Is School, 2000 g.	2	17,155
	Let Me Be Frank, 2002 g.	5	34,110
	Minardi Gras, 2004 f.	0	13,854
	Moracruz, 2004 f.	0	11,488
	Mr. Maybee Slew, 2003 g.	0	10,378
	Out of Answers, 2002 g.	2	20,963
	Primary Purpose, 2001 g.	2	17,166
	Real Monarch, 2000 g.	0	11,819
	Shoot the Alarm, 2003 g.	6	15,677
	Speed and Heart, 2002 g.	1	22,610
	Super Annie, 2003 m.	2	29,496
	Treasure's Joy, 2004 c.	0	10,121

Most Wins in North America in 2007

Wins	Name, YOB Sex	Starts	Earnings
14	Golden Hare, 1999 g.	17	$150,144
11	Fortunate Trail, 2001 g.	17	119,240
	Princess Composer, 2002 m.	17	102,475
10	Mi Preferido, 2001 h.	14	61,130
	Raving Rocket, 2002 g.	14	63,166
9	Batavia Light, 2003 m.	11	160,730
	Lightning Al Boy, 2002 g.	21	50,535
	Soft Day, 2003 m.	18	65,044
8	Bachatera, 2004 f.	15	79,707
	Bettin On M J, 2002 g.	12	152,647
	Bootleg Annie, 2004 f.	13	118,910
	Brilliant Mrs. W, 2004 f.	17	70,270
	Carol's Concert, 2004 g.	19	47,975
	Dearest Trickski, 2004 f.	12	280,500
	Defensora, 2005 f.	8	240,202
	Eastern Wind, 2002 g.	16	35,760
	Finallymadeit, 2004 c.	19	362,450
	Humble Chris, 2001 g.	12	95,149

Wins	Name, YOB Sex	Starts	Earnings
8	Ice Fantasy, 2002 m.	12	$ 34,347
	It's Not Over Yet, 2003 g.	10	42,964
	La Bomba, 2004 f.	15	109,110
	Lady Blue Sky, 2002 m.	8	101,232
	La Greca, 2003 m.	16	42,689
	Lookinforthesecret, 2002 h.	13	192,580
	Mindy's Peak, 2003 g.	17	102,630
	President's Intern, 2003 m.	14	54,658
	Run Nicholas Run, 2002 g.	11	44,606
	Shes Appealing, 2003 m.	9	83,420
	Sir Pyy, 2002 g.	17	51,291
	Spades Prospect, 2002 g.	15	32,247
	Unbridled Sunshine, 2002 m.	15	114,585

Most Graded Stakes Wins in North America in 2007

Name, YOB Sex	GSWs	Graded Stakes Earnings
Citronnade, 2003 m.	5	$ 701,405
Curlin, 2004 c.	5	5,080,000
Nobiz Like Shobiz, 2004 c.	5	1,318,330
Rutherienne, 2004 f.	5	501,940
After Market, 2003 h.	4	684,920
Dream Rush, 2004 f.	4	533,960
Ginger Punch, 2003 m.	4	1,800,400
Hard Spun, 2004 c.	4	2,560,000
Nashoba's Key, 2003 m.	4	820,290
Precious Kitten, 2003 m.	4	1,090,000
Rags to Riches, 2004 f.	4	1,312,428
Street Sense, 2004 c.	4	3,205,000
Any Given Saturday, 2004 c.	3	919,320
Bit of Whimsy, 2004 f.	3	505,533
Cloudy's Knight, 2000 g.	3	1,752,868
Daytona (Ire), 2004 g.	3	480,000
English Channel, 2002 h.	3	2,610,000
Jambalaya, 2002 g.	3	979,421
Kip Deville, 2003 h.	3	1,965,780
Lawyer Ron, 2003 h.	3	1,290,000
Master Command, 2002 h.	3	598,170
My Typhoon (Ire), 2002 m.	3	639,000
Panty Raid, 2004 f.	3	990,105
River's Prayer, 2003 m.	3	470,420
Sugar Shake, 2003 m.	3	382,380
Tiago, 2004 c.	3	1,205,950
Worldly (GB), 2004 g.	3	266,820

Most Grade 1 Stakes Wins in North America in 2007

Name, YOB Sex	Grade 1 Stakes Wins	Grade 1 Stakes Earnings
Citronnade, 2003 m.	5	$ 701,405
Curlin, 2004 c.	5	5,080,000
Nobiz Like Shobiz, 2004 c.	5	1,318,330
Rutherienne, 2004 f.	5	501,940
After Market, 2003 h.	4	684,920
Dream Rush, 2004 f.	4	533,960
Ginger Punch, 2003 m.	4	1,800,400
Hard Spun, 2004 c.	4	2,560,000
Nashoba's Key, 2003 m.	4	820,290
Precious Kitten, 2003 m.	4	1,090,000
Rags to Riches, 2004 f.	4	1,312,428
Street Sense, 2004 c.	4	3,205,000
Any Given Saturday, 2004 c.	3	919,320
Bit of Whimsy, 2004 f.	3	505,533
Cloudy's Knight, 2000 g.	3	1,752,868
Daytona (Ire), 2004 g.	3	480,000
English Channel, 2002 h.	3	2,610,000
Jambalaya, 2002 g.	3	979,421
Kip Deville, 2003 h.	3	1,965,780
Lawyer Ron, 2003 h.	3	1,290,000
Master Command, 2002 h.	3	598,170
My Typhoon (Ire), 2002 m.	3	639,000
Panty Raid, 2004 f.	3	990,105
River's Prayer, 2003 m.	3	470,420
Sugar Shake, 2003 m.	3	382,380
Tiago, 2004 c.	3	1,205,950
Worldly (GB), 2004 g.	3	266,820

Fastest Times of 2007

Dirt

Dist.	Time	Winner, Age	Track	Date	Cond.
$1\frac{1}{2}$f	:17.18	Raulin, 2	Hipodromo Camarero	March 30	my
2f	:20.78	Sea of Pleasure, 2	Santa Anita Park	March 29	ft
$2\frac{1}{2}$f	:32.80	Buz the Party, 2	Chippewa Downs	June 10	ft
3f	:32.08	Talkin Fine, 6	Remington Park	Aug. 3	ft
$3\frac{1}{2}$f	:39.48	Cabron, 2	Hastings Race Course	June 9	sy
4f	:44.00	Chacho, 4	Apache County Fair	Sept. 16	ft
$4\frac{1}{2}$f	:49.00	King Justin, 6	Yavapai Downs	June 2	ft
5f	:55.60	Run Nicholas Run, 5	Yavapai Downs	Aug. 26	ft
$5\frac{1}{2}$f	1:02.60	Harbour Axe, 6	Yellowstone Downs	Sept. 15	ft
$5\frac{1}{2}$f	1:01.20	The Great Face, 5	Emerald Downs	April 20	ft
6f	1:07.47	Idiot Proof, 3	Monmouth Park	July 4	ft
$6\frac{1}{2}$f	1:13.40	Westsideclyde, 5	Emerald Downs	May 28	ft
7f	1:20.96	First Defence, 3	Belmont Park	May 26	ft
$7\frac{1}{2}$f	1:27.85	Deadly Dealer, 3	Gulfstream Park	March 3	ft
1m	1:33.23	Utopia (Jpn), 7	Belmont Park	May 2	ft
1m 40Y	1:39.56	Piety, 5	Fair Grounds	Jan. 13	ft
1m 70Y	1:38.20	Kiss the Kid, 4	Meadowlands	Oct. 19	sy
$1\frac{1}{16}$m	1:39.89	Papi Chullo, 5	Belmont Park	May 4	ft
$1\frac{1}{8}$m	1:46.64	Lawyer Ron, 4	Saratoga Race Course	July 28	ft
$1\frac{3}{16}$m	1:53.46	Curlin, 3	Pimlico Race Course	May 19	ft
$1\frac{1}{4}$m	2:00.50	Political Force, 4	Belmont Park	June 30	ft
$1\frac{5}{16}$m	2:12.59	Red Rock Creek, 6	Lone Star Park	July 6	gd
$1\frac{3}{8}$m	2:15.89	Sir Gallovic, 3	Hastings Race Course	Oct. 14	ft
$1\frac{1}{2}$m	2:28.74	Rags to Riches, 3	Belmont Park	June 9	ft
$1\frac{5}{8}$m	2:46.39	Lettherebejustice, 6	Fort Erie	Oct. 7	ft
$1\frac{3}{4}$m	2:57.54	Malibu Moonshine, 5	Aqueduct	April 7	ft
$1\frac{13}{16}$m	3:11.97	Hope for Peace, 5	The Downs at Albuquerque	Sept. 23	ft
2m	3:27.91	Touchdown Peyton, 3	Saratoga Race Course	Aug. 18	ft
2m 70Y	3:33.75	Dancer's Legacy, 3	Fort Erie	Oct. 30	ft
$2\frac{1}{16}$m	3:36.37	Agent Danseur, 6	Canterbury Park	July 22	ft
$2\frac{1}{8}$m	3:44.57	Afternoon Express, 5	Hastings Race Course	Nov. 3	sy
$2\frac{1}{4}$m	4:02.28	Sir Dorset, 12	Ellis Park	Sept. 3	ft

All Weather

Dist.	Time	Winner, Age	Track	Date	Cond.
2f	:21.99	Bella Nevada, 2	Woodbine	May 19	ft
$4\frac{1}{2}$f	:48.87	One Hot Wish, 2	Keeneland Race Course	April 12	ft
5f	:56.51	Smack Daddy, 3	Arlington Park	Aug. 19	ft
$5\frac{1}{2}$f	1:02.09	Gray Black N White, 6	Hollywood Park	Dec. 5	ft
6f	1:07.34	Switzerland, 4	Oak Tree at Santa Anita	Nov. 3	ft
$6\frac{1}{2}$f	1:13.79	Banner Lodge, 3	Hollywood Park	Dec. 16	ft
7f	1:20.37	Bob Black Jack, 2	Santa Anita Park	Dec. 26	ft
$7\frac{1}{2}$f	1:26.78	Greg's Gold, 6	Hollywood Park	Dec. 22	ft
1m	1:33.72	Spotsgone, 4	Arlington Park	May 26	ft
1m 70Y	1:41.79	Miner's Claim, 2	Woodbine	Nov. 2	ft
$1\frac{1}{16}$m	1:40.38	Romance Is Diane, 3	Oak Tree at Santa Anita	Nov. 3	ft
$1\frac{1}{8}$m	1:46.93	Tiago, 3	Oak Tree at Santa Anita	Sept. 29	ft
$1\frac{3}{16}$m	1:55.17	Lewis Michael, 4	Arlington Park	July 28	ft
$1\frac{1}{4}$m	2:01.79	Rocket Legs, 3	Hollywood Park	Dec. 7	ft
$1\frac{1}{2}$m	2:30.71	Pellegrino (Brz), 8	Woodbine	Nov. 16	ft
$1\frac{5}{8}$m	2:47.89	Jive, 4	Keeneland Race Course	Oct. 24	ft
$1\frac{3}{4}$m	3:01.08	Torquay, 5	Woodbine	Dec. 9	ft
$1\frac{7}{8}$m	3:13.79	Benz Boy, 6	Woodbine	Dec. 9	ft

Turf

Dist.	Time	Winner, Age	Track	Date	Cond.
4f	:43.87	Classy Cade, 6	Lone Star Park	April 21	fm
$4\frac{1}{2}$f	:49.88	Blackjack Boy, 7	Turf Paradise	March 4	fm
5f	:54.41	Lifestyle, 7	Gulfstream Park	March 2	fm
$5\frac{1}{2}$f	1:00.81	Smart Enough, 4	Monmouth Park	June 2	fm
6f	1:07.43	Silver Timber, 4	Belmont Park	July 22	fm
$6\frac{1}{2}$f	1:14.42	Ju Ju Beast, 5	Woodbine	May 30	fm
7f	1:20.13	English Colony (GB), 3	Belmont Park	Sept. 9	fm
$7\frac{1}{2}$f	1:27.22	Fearless Eagle, 3	Calder Race Course	Dec. 29	fm
1m	1:32.12	Silver Tree, 7	Gulfstream Park	March 4	fm
1m 70Y	1:38.07	Inside Lane, 6	Penn National Race Course	July 31	fm
$1\frac{1}{16}$m	1:38.99	Silent Roar, 4	Monmouth Park	Aug. 5	fm
$1\frac{1}{8}$m	1:44.51	English Channel, 5	Gulfstream Park	Feb. 22	fm
$1\frac{3}{16}$m	1:53.70	Prom Party, 3	Saratoga Race Course	Aug. 29	fm
$1\frac{1}{4}$m	1:58.77	After Market, 4	Hollywood Park	June 9	fm
$1\frac{3}{8}$m	2:11.86	Ramazutti, 5	Gulfstream Park	Jan. 28	fm
$1\frac{1}{2}$m	2:24.13	Spring House, 5	Oak Tree at Santa Anita	Oct. 28	fm
$1\frac{9}{16}$m	2:40.39	A to Z, 5	Hawthorne Race Course	Nov. 17	fm
$1\frac{5}{8}$m	2:42.67	Revved Up, 9	Saratoga Race Course	Aug. 19	fm
$1\frac{3}{4}$m	2:54.75	Stormin Away, 5	Hollywood Park	June 16	fm
$1\frac{13}{16}$m	3:07.61	Aleric, 5	Remington Park	Dec. 1	fm

Dist.	Time	Winner, Age	Track	Date	Cond.
1⅞m	3:14.00	Pirate's Bid, 5	River Downs	Sept. 3	fm
2m	3:39.40	King Hoss, 5	Shawan Downs	Sept. 29	fm
2 1/16m	3:43.55	Footlights, 7	Saratoga Race Course	July 26	fm
2⅛m	3:36.60	Summersville, 9	Little Everglades	March 11	fm
2¼m	3:54.40	Lair, 5	Pine Mountain, Calloway Garden	Nov. 3	fm
2⅜m	4:19.92	Divine Fortune, 4	Saratoga Race Course	Aug. 16	fm
2½m	4:28.31	Divine Fortune, 4	Meadowlands	Sept. 21	fm
2⅝m	5:10.20	Bon Fleur, 7	Middleburg	April 21	gd
2¾m	5:19.20	Good Night Shirt, 6	Camden	Nov. 18	fm
3m	5:43.80	Praise the Prince (NZ), 12	Foxfield	April 28	fm
3⅛m	5:47.60	Underbidder, 6	Pine Mountain, Calloway Garden	Nov. 3	fm
3¼m	6:07.00	Bubble Economy, 8	Grand National	April 21	fm
3½m	6:56.80	Bubble Economy, 8	Camden	Nov. 18	fm
4m	8:24.60	Salmo, 11	Great Meadows	May 5	gd

North American Records

Dirt

Dist.	Time	Winner, Age Sex	Track	Date
2f	:20.71	Pensglitter, 7 h.	Penn National Race Course	10/9/2004
2½f	:26⅕	Nice Choice, 7 m.	Nuevo Laredo	9/25/1983
3f	:31.01	Eclat, 5 g.	Remington Park	11/28/2005
3½f	:38.00	Primero Del Anno, 5 g.	Flagstaff	7/4/1998
4f	:43.10	Slewofrainbows, 7 g.	Mohave County Fair	5/23/1999
4½f	:49.00	Motivo, 5 g.	Yavapai Downs	9/9/2006
		King Justin, 6 g.	Yavapai Downs	6/2/2007
5f	:55⅕	Chinook Pass, 3 c.	Longacres	9/17/1982
5½f	1:01.10	Plenty Zloty, 5 g.	Turf Paradise	4/18/1998
6f	1:06.60	G Malleah, 4 g.	Turf Paradise	4/8/1995
6¼f	1:15⅘	Montanic, 4 g.	Washington Park	7/20/1901
6½f	1:13.00	Sabertooth, 7 g.	Emerald Downs	5/22/2005
7f	1:19⅖	Rich Cream, 5 h.	Hollywood Park	5/28/1980
		Time to Explode, 3 c.	Hollywood Park	6/26/1982
7½f	1:26.26	Awesome Daze, 5 g.	Hollywood Park	11/23/1997
1m	1:32⅕	Dr. Fager, 4 c.	Arlington Park	8/24/1968
	1:32.24	Najran, 4 c.	Belmont Park	5/7/2003
1m 20y	1:39.00	Froglegs, 4 c.	Churchill Downs	5/13/1913
1m 40Y	1:38⅕	Zaffarancho (Arg), 5 h.	Rockingham	6/19/1987
1m 70Y	1:37.90	Schedule (GB), 3 f.	The Meadowlands	10/15/2004
		With Probability, 4 c.	The Meadowlands	10/28/2005
1m 100y	1:43⅘	Old Honesty, 3 c.	Empire City	8/20/1907
1 1/16m	1:38⅖	Hoedown's Day, 5 h.	Bay Meadows Race Course	10/23/1983
1⅛m	1:45.00	Simply Majestic, 4 c.	Golden Gate Fields	4/2/1988
1 3/16m	1:52⅖	Riva Ridge, 4 c.	Aqueduct	7/4/1973
	1:52.40	Farma Way, 4, c.	Pimlico	5/11/1991
1¼m	1:57⅘	Spectacular Bid, 4 c.	Santa Anita Park	2/3/1980
1 5/16m	2:07.32	Gold Star Deputy, 5 g.	Aqueduct	4/10/1999
1⅜m	2:12.31	Demi's Bret, 4 g.	Aqueduct	10/26/1997
1 7/16m	2:23.00	Who's In Command, 5 h.	Hastings Park	8/10/1987
1½m	2:24.00	Secretariat, 3 c.	Belmont Park	6/9/1973
1 9/16m	2:35.77	Well Lit, 5 g.	Sportsman's Park	4/25/1992
1⅝m	2:38⅕	Swaps, 4 c.	Hollywood Park	7/25/1956
1¾m	2:50⅗	Paper Junction, 4 c.	Lincoln State Fair	11/10/1985
1⅞m	3:11.56	Asserche, 6 g.	Laurel Park	3/20/1994
2m	3:19.20	Kelso, 7 g.	Aqueduct	10/31/1964
2¼m	3:47.00	Fenelon, 4 c.	Belmont Park	10/4/1941
2½m	4:14⅗	*Miss Grillo, 6 m.	Pimlico Race Course	11/12/1948

All Weather

Dist.	Time	Winner, Age Sex	Track	Date
2f	:21.99	Bella Nevada, 2 f.	Woodbine	5/19/2007
4½f	:48.87	One Hot Wish, 2 f.	Keeneland Race Course	4/12/2007
5f	:56.51	Smack Daddy, 3 g.	Arlington Park	8/19/2007
5½f	1:02.09	Gray Black N White, 6 g.	Hollywood Park	12/5/2007
6f	1:07.34	Switzerland, 4 g.	Oak Tree at Santa Anita	11/3/2007
6½f	1:13.79	Banner Lodge, 3 c.	Hollywood Park	12/16/2007
7f	1:20.37	Bob Black Jack, 2 c.	Santa Anita Park	12/26/2007
7½f	1:26.78	Greg's Gold, 6 g.	Hollywood Park	12/22/2007
1m	1:33.72	Spotsgone, 4 c.	Arlington Park	5/26/2007
1m 70Y	1:41.79	Miner's Claim, 2 c.	Woodbine	11/2/2007
1 1/16m	1:40.38	Romance Is Diane, 3 f.	Oak Tree at Santa Anita	11/3/2007
1⅛m	1:46.93	Tiago, 3 c.	Oak Tree at Santa Anita	9/29/2007
1 3/16m	1:55.17	Lewis Michael, 4 c.	Arlington Park	7/28/2007
1¼m	2:01.79	Rocket Legs, 3 c.	Hollywood Park	12/7/2007
1½m	2:30.71	Pellegrino (Brz), 8 h.	Woodbine	11/16/2007
1⅝m	2:47.89	Jive, 4 f.	Keeneland Race Course	10/24/2007
1¾m	2:58.27	Marsh Side, 3 c.	Woodbine	12/10/2006
1⅞m	3:13.79	Benz Boy, 6 g.	Woodbine	12/9/2007

Turf

Dist.	Time	Winner, Age Sex	Track	Date
4f	:43.87	Classy Cade, 6 g.	Lone Star Park	4/21/2007
4½f	:49.26	Dan's Groovy, 7 g.	Turf Paradise	4/13/2003
5f	:53.79	Procreate, 7 g.	Gulfstream park	4/9/2005
5½f	1:00.26	Scottsbluff, 4 g.	Hollywood Park	5/15/2006
6f	1:06.82	Keep The Faith (Aus), 5 h.	Belmont Park	7/24/2005
6½f	1:13.97	My Luck Strike, 6 g.	Woodbine	8/7/2005
7f	1:19.38	Soaring Free, 5 g.	Woodbine	7/24/2004
7½f	1:26.54	Court Lark, 6 g.	Calder Race Course	7/16/1994
1m	1:31.41	Mr. Light (Arg), 6 h.	Gulfstream Park	1/3/2005
1m 40Y	1:38.08	Castaneto (Arg), 7 g.	Atlantic City	6/28/1991
1m 70Y	1:37.20	Aborigine, 6 h.	Penn National	8/20/1978
1¹⁄₁₆m	1:38.00	Told, 4 c.	Penn National	9/14/1980
1⅛m	1:43.92	Kostroma (Ire), 5 m.	Santa Anita Park	10/20/1991
1³⁄₁₆m	1:51⅖	Toonerville, 4 g.	Hialeah Park	2/7/1976
1¼m	1:57⅖	Double Discount, 4 c.	Santa Anita Park	10/9/1977
1⁵⁄₁₆m	2:06.00	Ruff Mack, 5 m.	Mountaineer Race Track	8/25/1962
1⅜m	2:10⅕	With Approval, 4 c.	Belmont Park	6/17/1990
1⁷⁄₁₆m	2:17.64	Giant Hope, 4 c.	Gulfstream Park	3/12/2006
1½m	2:22⅘	Hawkster, 3 c.	Santa Anita Park	10/14/1989
1⁹⁄₁₆m	2:40.26	To the Floor, 7 g.	Fair Grounds	3/29/1999
1⅝m	2:37.00	Tom Swift, 5 h.	Saratoga Race Course	8/23/1978
1¾m	2:53.35	Inaugural Address, 6 g.	Mountaineer Race Track	8/15/2005
1⅞m	3:08.23	Code's Best, 6 g.	Mountaineer Race Track	9/4/2000
2m	3:18.00	*Petrone, 5 h.	Hollywood Park	7/23/1969
2¼m	3:48⅖	Buteo, 6 g.	River Downs	9/3/1990

Progression of Fastest Times on Dirt

Six Furlongs

Time	Horse	YOB Sex, Sire	Date	Track	Weight
1:06.60	G Malleah	1991 g., Fool the Experts	4/8/1995	Turf Paradise	120
1:06⅘	Zany Tactics	1981 g., Zanthe	3/8/1987	Turf Paradise	126
1:07⅕	Petro D. Jay	1976 h., *Grey Tudor	5/9/1982	Turf Paradise	120
1:07⅕	Grey Papa	1967 g., Grey Eagle	9/4/1972	Longacres	116
1:07⅖	Vale of Tears	1963 h., *Royal Vale	6/7/1969	Ak-Sar-Ben	120
1:07⅖	Zip Pocket	1964 c., Nantallah	12/4/1966	Turf Paradise	126
1:07⅘	Admirably	1962 f., *Oceanus II	4/7/1965	Golden Gate Fields	118
1:07⅘	Crazy Kid	1958 c., Krakatao	8/18/1962	Del Mar	118
1:08	*Dumpty Humpty	1953 c., Stalino	11/2/1957	Golden Gate Fields	115
1:08⅕	Bolero	1946 c., Eight Thirty	5/27/1950	Golden Gate Fields	122
1:08⅖	*Fair Truckle	1943 c., Fair Trial	10/4/1947	Golden Gate Fields	119
1:09⅕	Polynesian	1942 c., Unbreakable	9/16/1946	Atlantic City	126
1:09⅕	*Mafosta	1942 c., Fair Trial	7/14/1946	Longacres	116
1:09⅕	Clang	1932 g., Stimulus	10/12/1935	Coney Island (Oh.)	110
1:09⅗	Iron Mask	1908 g., Disguise	1/4/1914	Juarex (Mex)	115
1:10⅘	Orb	1911 c., Luck and Charity	12/9/1913	Juarez (Mex)	90
1:10⅘	Leochares	1910 g., Broomstick	10/3/1913	Douglas Park	109
1:10⅘	Iron Mask	1908 g., Disguise	9/23/1913	Douglas Park	127
1:11	Priscillian	1905 g., Hastings	6/19/1911	Hamilton (Can)	113
1:11	Prince Ahmed	1904 h., King Hanover	7/29/1909	Empire City	117
1:11	Chapultepec	1905 c., *Gerolstein	12/28/1908	Santa Anita (old)	112
1:11⅗	Col. Bob	1905 c., Cesarion	12/27/1907	Santa Anita (old)	92
1:11⅗	Roseben	1901 g., *Ben Strome	10/6/1905	Belmont Park (old)	147
1:11⅘	Ivan the Terrible	1902 c., *Pirate of Penzance	10/27/1904	Worth (Il.)	92
1:11⅘	Dick Welles	1900 c., King Eric	6/30/1903	Washington Park	109
1:12	*Lux Casta	1899 f., Donovan	7/23/1902	Brighton Beach	111
1:12	Bummer II	1896 c., Register	10/17/1900	Kinloch (Mo.)	80
1:12⅕	*Voter	1894 h., Friar's Balsam	7/6/1900	Brighton Beach	123
1:12¼	Mary Black	1895 f., *Islington	7/16/1898	Washington Park	93
1:12¼	Flora Louise	1895 f., *Florist	9/30/1897	Harlem (Il.)	88
1:12¼	O'Connell	1890 g., Harry O' Fallon	7/18/1895	Oakley (Oh.)	121
1:13	Tom Hood	1884 c., Virgil	9/19/1888	Churchill Downs	115
1:13	Force	1878 h., West Roxbury	9/24/1883	Churchill Downs	121
1:14	Monarch	1879 h., Monarchist	8/22/1882	Saratoga	91
1:14	Knight Templar	1877 g., Fellowcraft	9/18/1880	Gravesend	77
1:14	Barrett	1878 c., *Bonnie Scotland	8/14/1880	Monmouth Park	110
1:15	First Chance	1871 g., Baywood	10/17/1876	Philadelphia	110
1:15½	Bill Bruce	1872 c., Enquirer	5/12/1876	Lexington (Ky.)	108
1:15¾	Madge	1871 f., *Australian	8/21/1874	Saratoga	87
1:16	Alarm	1869 c., *Eclipse	7/15/1872	Saratoga	90
1:16¾	Tom Bowling	1870 c., Lexington	8/6/1872	Long Branch (N.J.)	100

Seven Furlongs

Time	Horse	YOB Sex, Sire	Date	Track	Weight
1:19⅖	Time to Explode	1979 h., Explodent	6/26/1982	Hollywood Park	117
1:19⅖	Rich Cream	1975 h., Creme dela Creme	5/28/1980	Hollywood Park	118
1:19⅘	Triple Bend	1968 h., Never Bend	5/6/1972	Hollywood Park	123
1:20	Native Diver	1959 g., Imbros	5/22/1965	Hollywood Park	126
1:20	El Drag	1951 h., *Khaled	5/21/1955	Hollywood Park	115

Time	Horse	YOB Sex, Sire	Date	Track	Weight
1:20⅗	Imbros	1950 h., Polynesian	1/2/1954	Santa Anita Park	118
1:21	Bolero	1946 h., Eight Thirty	1/1/1951	Santa Anita Park	121
1:21⅖	Ky. Colonel	1946 h., Balladier	8/10/1949	Washington Park	116
1:21⅘	Buzfuz	1942 g., Zacaweista	6/20/1947	Hollywood Park	120
1:21⅘	Honeymoon	1943 m., *Beau Pere	6/3/1947	Hollywood Park	114
1:22	High Resolve	1941 g., Zacaweista	10/17/1945	Hollywood Park	126
1:22	Clang	1932 g., Stimulus	7/19/1935	Arlington Park	105
1:22	Roseben	1901 g., *Ben Strome	10/16/1906	Belmont Park	126
1:25	The Musketeer	1898 h., *Masetto	8/18/1902	Saratoga	108
1:25⅖	Clifford	1890 h., Bramble	8/29/1894	Sheepshead Bay	127
1:26⅖	Britannic	1884 h., Plevna	9/5/1889	Sheepshead Bay	110
1:27¼	Kingston	1884 h., Spendthrift	9/1/1887	Sheepshead Bay	118
1:28½	Joe Murray	1879 h., Rebel	7/17/1884	Chicago	117
1:28¾	Little Phil	1878 h., Enquirer	7/3/1882	Monmouth Park	111
1:30	Brambaletta	1878 m., *Bonnie Scotland	9/24/1881	Brighton Beach	92
1:30	Reporter	1877 g., King Ernest	8/13/1881	Brighton Beach	95

One Mile

Time	Horse	YOB Sex, Sire	Date	Track	Weight
1:32.24	Najran	1999 c., Runaway Groom	5/7/2003	Belmont Park	113
1:32⅕	Dr. Fager	1964 c., Rough'n Tumble	8/24/1968	Arlington Park	134
1:32⅗	Buckpasser	1963 c., Tom Fool	6/25/1966	Arlington Park	125
1:33⅕	Hedevar	1962 c., Count of Honor	6/18/1966	Arlington Park	116
1:33⅕	Pia Star	1961 c., Olympia	6/19/1965	Arlington Park	112
1:33⅕	Intentionally	1956 c., Intent	6/27/1959	Washington Park	121
1:33⅕	Swaps	1952 c., *Khaled	6/9/1956	Hollywood Park	128
1:33⅗	Citation	1945 h., Bull Lea	6/3/1950	Golden Gate Fields	128
1:34	Coaltown	1945 c., Bull Lea	8/20/1949	Washington Park	130
1:34⅖	Prevaricator	1943 g., Omaha	10/2/1948	Golden Gate Fields	118
1:34⅖	Equipoise	1928 c., Pennant	6/30/1932	Arlington Park	128
1:34⅘	Roamer	1911 g., Knight Errant	8/21/1918	Saratoga	110
1:36⅕	*Sun Briar	1915 c., Sundridge	8/6/1918	Saratoga	113
1:36¼	Amalfi	1908 g., The Scribe	9/3/1914	Syracuse (N.Y.)	107
1:36⅘	Christophine	1911 f., Plaudit	3/11/1914	Juarez (Mex)	102
1:37	Bonne Chance	1909 g., Orsini	1/18/1914	Juarez (Mex)	98
1:37⅕	Vested Rights	1910 g., Abe Frank	12/25/1913	Juarez (Mex)	105
1:37⅕	Manasseh	1909 f., *Star Shoot	12/12/1913	Juarez (Mex)	93
1:37⅕	Centre Shot	1905 f., *Sain	12/22/1908	Santa Anita (old)	105
1:37⅖	Kiamesha	1902 f., *Esher	10/9/1905	Belmont Park	104
1:37⅖	Dick Welles	1900 c., King Eric	8/14/1903	Harlem (Il.)	112
1:37⅗	Alan-a-Dale	1899 c., Halma	7/1/1903	Washington Park	110
1:37⅘	Brigadier	1897 g., *Rayon d'Or	6/22/1901	Sheepshead Bay	112
1:38	Orimar	1894 h., Sir Dixon	7/21/1900	Washington Park	109
1:38	*Voter	1894 h., Friar's Balsam	7/17/1900	Brighton Beach	122
1:38¾	Libertine	1891 c., Leonatus	10/24/1894	Harlem (Il.)	90
1:39	Arab	1886 g., *Dalnacardoch	6/11/1894	Morris Park	93
1:39¼	Chorister	1890 c., Falsetto	6/1/1893	Morris Park	112
1:39½	Racine	1887 c., Bishop	6/28/1890	Washington Park	107
1:39¾*	Ten Broeck	1872 h., *Phaeton	5/24/1877	Churchill Downs	110
1:41¼	Kadi	1870 g., Lexington	9/2/1875	Hartford (Ct.)	90
1:41⅗	Searcher	1872 c., Enquirer	5/13/1875	Lexington (Ky.)	90
1:42½*	Grey Planet	1869 h., Planet	8/13/1874	Saratoga	110
1:42¾	Springbok	1870 c., *Australian	6/25/1874	Utica (N.Y.)	108
1:42¾	Alarm	1869 c., *Eclipse	7/17/1872	Saratoga	90
1:43½	Herzog	1866 c., Vandal	5/25/1869	Cincinnati	—

*Against time

1⅛ Miles

Time	Horse	YOB Sex, Sire	Date	Track	Weight
1:45	Simply Majestic	1984 h., Majestic Light	4/2/1988	Golden Gate Fields	114
1:45⅖	Secretariat	1970 h., Bold Ruler	9/15/1973	Belmont Park	124
1:46⅕	Canonero II	1968 h., *Pretendre	9/20/1972	Belmont Park	110
1:46⅕	*Figonero	1965 h., Idle Hour	9/1/1969	Del Mar	124
1:46⅖	Ole Bob Bowers	1963 h., Prince Blessed	10/12/1968	Bay Meadows Race Course	114
1:46⅖	Quicken Tree	1963 g., Royal Orbit	9/2/1968	Del Mar	120
1:46⅖	*Colorado King	1959 h., *Grand Rapids II	7/4/1964	Hollywood Park	119
1:46⅖	Bug Brush	1955 m., *Nasrullah	2/14/1959	Santa Anita Park	113
1:46⅘	Round Table	1954 h., *Princequillo	2/25/1958	Santa Anita Park	130
1:46⅘	Gen. Duke	1954 h., Bull Lea	3/30/1957	Gulfstream Park	122
1:46⅘	Swaps	1952 h., *Khaled	7/4/1956	Hollywood Park	130
1:46⅘	Alidon	1951 g., *Alibhai	7/4/1955	Hollywood Park	116
1:46⅘	*Noor	1945 h., *Nasrullah	6/17/1950	Golden Gate Fields	123
1:47⅗	Coaltown	1945 h., Bull Lea	2/14/1949	Hialeah Park	114
1:47⅗	*Shannon II	1941 h., Midstream	10/9/1948	Golden Gate Fields	124
1:47⅗	Indian Broom	1933 h., Brooms	4/11/1936	Tanforan	94
1:48⅕	Discovery	1931 h., Display	6/22/1935	Aqueduct	123
1:48⅖	Blessed Event	1930 g., Happy Argo	3/10/1934	Hialeah Park	111
1:48⅖	Hot Toddy	1926 g., Ed Crump	9/13/1929	Belmont Park	110
1:48⅗	Peanuts	1922 h., *Ambassador IV	9/18/1926	Aqueduct	114
1:48⅘	Chilhowee	1921 h., Ballot	10/14/1924	Latonia	115

Time	Horse	YOB Sex, Sire	Date	Track	Weight
1:49	Grey Lag	1918 h., *Star Shoot	7/7/1921	Aqueduct	123
1:49	*Goaler	1916 h., Duke Michael	6/10/1921	Belmont Park	94
1:49⅕	Man o' War	1917 h., Fair Play	7/10/1920	Aqueduct	126
1:49⅖	Boots	1911 g., *Hessian	7/7/1917	Aqueduct	127
1:49⅖	Borrow	1908 g., Hamburg	6/25/1917	Aqueduct	117
1:49⅗	Roamer	1911 g., Knight Errant	10/10/1914	Laurel Park	124
1:50	Vox Populi	1904 h., *Voter	12/19/1908	Santa Anita (old)	110
1:50⅗	Charles Edward	1904 h., *Golden Garter	7/10/1907	Brighton Beach	126
1:51	Bonnibert	1898 h., *Albert	7/30/1902	Brighton Beach	120
1:51⅕	Roehampton	1898 h., *Bathampton	7/26/1901	Brighton Beach	94
1:51⅕	Watercure	1897 g., *Watercress	6/18/1900	Brighton Beach	100
1:51½	Tristan	1885 h., *Glenelg	6/2/1891	Morris Park	114
1:53	Terra Cotta	1884 h., Harry o' Fallon	6/23/1888	Sheepshead Bay	124
1:53¼	Grover Cleveland	1883 h., Monday	10/12/1887	Los Angeles	118
1:53¼	Spalding	1882 g., *Billet	7/1/1886	Washington Park	97
1:53¼	Rosalie	1877 m., *Leamington	8/13/1881	Brighton Beach	80
1:54	Bob Woolley	1872 h., *Leamington	9/6/1875	Lexington	90
1:56	Fadladeen	1867 h., War Dance	8/19/1874	Saratoga	101
1:56	Picolo	1871 h., Concord	8/15/1874	Saratoga	83
1:56½	Fanny Ludlow	1865 m., *Eclipse	8/10/1869	Saratoga	105

1¼ Miles

Time	Horse	YOB Sex, Sire	Date	Track	Weight
1:57⅘	Spectacular Bid	1976 c., Bold Bidder	2/3/1980	Santa Anita	126
1:58⅕	Quack	1969 c., T. V. Lark	7/15/1972	Hollywood Park	115
1:58⅕	*Noor	1945 h., *Nasrullah	6/24/1950	Golden Gate Fields	127
1:59⅘	Coaltown	1945 c., Bull Lea	3/19/1949	Gulfstream Park	128
1:59⅘	*Shannon II	1941 h., Midstream	10/23/1948	Golden Gate Fields	124
2:00	Cover Up	1943 c., *Alibhai	7/26/1947	Hollywood Park	117
2:00	Whisk Broom II	1907 h., Broomstick	6/28/1913	Belmont Park (old)	139
2:02⅘	Olambala	1906 c., *Ornus	7/2/1910	Sheepshead Bay	122
2:02⅘	Broomstick	1901 c., Ben Brush	7/9/1904	Brighton Park	104
2:03⅕	Waterboy	1899 h., *Watercress	7/1/1903	Brighton Park	124
2:03¾*	Banquet	1887 g., *Rayon d'Or	7/17/1890	Monmouth Park (old)	108
2:05	Salvator	1886 c., *Prince Charlie	6/25/1890	Sheepshead Bay	122
2:06½	Kingston	1884 h., Spendthrift	9/24/1889	Brooklyn	122
2:07	Dry Monopole	1883 c., Glenelg	5/14/1887	Brooklyn	106
2:07½	La Sylphide	1882 f., Fellowcraft	10/22/1886	Lexington (Ky.)	98
2:07½	Binette	1881 m., Billet	7/12/1886	Washington Park	101
2:07¾	Getaway	1878 c., Enquirer	8/4/1881	Saratoga	100
2:08	Mendelssohn	1877 c., Buckden	5/10/1880	Lexington (Ky.)	95
2:08½	Charles Gorham	1874 g., Blarneystone	5/18/1877	Lexington (Ky.)	87
2:08¾	Grinstead	1871 c., Gilroy	7/24/1875	Saratoga	108
2:09½	Frogtown	1868 c., *Bonnie Scotland	5/14/1872	Lexington (Ky.)	104
2:10	R. B. Conolly	1864 h., Lexington	7/20/1870	Saratoga	111

*Straight course

All-Time Leading North American-Raced Earners

Horse, YOB Sex, Sire	Years Raced	Starts	Wins	Stakes Wins	Earnings
Cigar, 1990 h., by Palace Music	4	33	19	15	$9,999,815
Skip Away, 1993 h., by Skip Trial	4	38	18	16	9,616,360
Curlin, 2004 c., by Smart Strike	2	11	8	6	8,807,800
Fantastic Light, 1996 h., by Rahy	4	25	12	10	8,486,957
Invasor (Arg), 2002 h., by Candy Stripes	4	12	11	10	7,804,070
Pleasantly Perfect, 1998 h., by Pleasant Colony	4	18	9	6	7,789,880
Smarty Jones, 2001 h., by Elusive Quality	2	9	8	7	7,613,155
Silver Charm, 1994 h., by Silver Buck	4	24	12	11	6,944,369
Captain Steve, 1997 h., by Fly So Free	3	25	9	8	6,828,356
Alysheba, 1984 h., by Alydar	3	26	11	10	6,679,242
Dylan Thomas (Ire), 2003 c., by Danehill	3	20	10	8	6,620,852
John Henry, 1975 g., by Ole Bob Bowers	8	83	39	30	6,591,860
Tiznow, 1997 h., by Cee's Tizzy	2	15	8	7	6,427,830
Ouija Board (GB), 2001 m., by Cape Cross (Ire)	4	22	10	9	6,312,552
Singspiel (Ire), 1992 h., by In the Wings (GB)	4	20	9	8	5,952,825
Falbrav (Ire), 1998 h., by Fairy King	4	26	13	8	5,825,517
Medaglia d'Oro, 1999 h., by El Prado (Ire)	4	17	8	7	5,754,720
Best Pal, 1988 g., by *Habitony	7	47	18	17	5,668,245
Taiki Blizzard, 1991 h., by Seattle Slew	4	23	6	3	5,523,549
Roses in May, 2000 h., by Devil His Due	3	13	8	4	5,490,187
Dance in the Mood (Jpn), 2001 m., by Sunday Silence	4	25	6	4	5,456,107
High Chaparral (Ire), 1999 h., by Sadler's Wells	3	13	10	9	5,331,231
English Channel, 2002 h., by Smart Strike	4	23	13	10	5,319,028
Sulamani (Ire), 1999 h., by Hernando (Fr)	3	17	9	8	5,252,368
Lava Man, 2001 g., by Slew City Slew	5	43	17	13	$5,214,706
Street Cry (Ire), 1998 h., by Machiavellian	3	12	5	3	5,150,837
Jim and Tonic (Fr), 1994 g., by Double Bed (Fr)	7	39	13	9	4,975,807
Sunday Silence, 1986 h., by Halo	3	14	9	7	4,968,554
Easy Goer, 1986 h., by Alydar	3	20	14	12	4,873,770
Perfect Drift, 1999 g., by Dynaformer	7	46	11	8	4,680,691
Daylami (Ire), 1994 h., by Doyoun	4	21	11	8	4,614,762
Behrens, 1994 h., by Pleasant Colony	4	27	9	7	4,563,500
Unbridled, 1987 h., by Fappiano	3	24	8	5	4,489,475
Saint Liam, 2000 h., by Saint Ballado	3	20	9	5	4,456,995
Street Sense, 2004 c., by Street Cry (Ire)	2	13	6	5	4,383,200
Awesome Again, 1994 h., by Deputy Minister	2	12	9	7	4,374,590
Moon Ballad (Ire), 1999 h., by Singspiel (Ire)	3	14	5	4	4,364,791
Spend a Buck, 1982 h., by Buckaroo	2	15	10	7	4,220,689
David Junior, 2002 h., by Pleasant Tap	3	13	7	6	4,116,358
Pilsudski (Ire), 1992 h., by Polish Precedent	4	22	10	8	4,080,297
Azeri, 1998 m., by Jade Hunter	4	24	17	14	4,079,820
Better Talk Now, 1999 g., by Talkin Man	7	41	14	10	4,052,788
Collier Hill (GB), 1998 g., by Dr Devious (Ire)	5	44	15	7	4,048,951
Creme Fraiche, 1982 g., by Rich Cream	6	64	17	14	4,024,727
Seeking the Pearl, 1994 m., by Seeking the Gold	4	21	8	7	4,021,716
Point Given, 1998 h., by Thunder Gulch	2	13	9	8	3,968,500
Cat Thief, 1996 h., by Storm Cat	3	30	4	3	3,951,012
Ashado, 2001 m., by Saint Ballado	3	21	12	11	3,931,440
Devil His Due, 1989 h., by Devil's Bag	4	41	11	9	3,920,405

Horse, YOB Sex, Sire	Years Raced	Starts	Wins	Stakes Wins	Earnings
Sandpit (Brz), 1989 h., by Baynoun (Ire)	7	40	14	12	$3,812,597
Swain (Ire), 1992 h., by Nashwan	4	22	10	8	3,797,566
Ferdinand, 1983 h., by Nijinsky II	4	29	8	7	3,777,978
The Tin Man, 1998 g., by Affirmed	7	31	13	8	3,663,780
Almutawakel (GB), 1995 h., by Machiavellian	4	19	4	2	3,643,021
Harlan's Holiday, 1999 h., by Harlan	3	22	9	8	3,632,664
Gentlemen (Arg), 1992 h., by Robin des Bois	5	24	13	11	3,608,558
Spain, 1997 m., by Thunder Gulch	4	35	9	7	3,540,542
Slew o' Gold, 1980 h., by Seattle Slew	3	21	12	8	3,533,534
Funny Cide, 2000 g., by Distorted Humor	6	38	11	9	3,529,412
Victory Gallop, 1995 h., by Cryptoclearance	3	17	9	7	3,505,895
War Emblem, 1999 h., by Our Emblem	2	13	7	4	3,491,000
Precisionist, 1981 h., by Crozier	5	46	20	17	3,485,398
Strike the Gold, 1988 h., by Alydar	4	31	6	4	3,457,026
Ghostzapper, 2000 h., by Awesome Again	4	11	9	6	3,446,120
Lando (Ger), 1990 h., by Acatenango	4	24	10	8	3,438,727
Paradise Creek, 1989 h., by Irish River (Fr)	4	25	14	10	3,401,416
Snow Chief, 1983 h., by Reflected Glory	3	24	13	12	3,383,210
Chief Bearhart, 1993 h., by Chief's Crown	4	26	12	9	3,381,557
Cryptoclearance, 1984 h., by Fappiano	4	44	12	9	3,376,327
Black Tie Affair (Ire), 1986 h., by Miswaki	4	45	18	13	3,370,694
Agnes World, 1995 h., by Danzig	4	20	8	5	3,365,680
Sky Classic, 1987 h., by Nijinsky II	4	29	15	13	3,320,398
Paseana (Arg), 1987 m., by Ahmad	6	36	19	17	3,317,427
Bet Twice, 1984 h., by Sportin' Life	3	26	10	7	3,308,599
Steinlen (GB), 1983 h., by Habitat	5	45	20	16	3,297,169
Serena's Song, 1992 m., by Rahy	3	38	18	17	3,283,388
Real Quiet, 1995 h., by Quiet American	3	20	6	5	3,271,802
Awad, 1990 h., by Caveat	7	70	14	11	3,270,131
Congaree, 1998 h., by Arazi	5	25	12	10	3,267,490
Dance Smartly, 1988 m., by Danzig	3	17	12	10	3,263,835
Paolini (Ger), 1997 h., by Lando (Ger)	6	28	5	4	3,253,469
Sakhee, 1997 h., by Bahri	4	14	8	5	3,253,253
Caller One, 1997 g., by Phone Trick	8	29	11	9	3,249,429
Lemon Drop Kid, 1996 h., by Kingmambo	3	24	10	7	3,245,370
Volponi, 1998 h., by Cryptoclearance	4	31	7	4	3,187,232
Bertrando, 1989 h., by Skywalker	5	24	9	8	3,185,610
Free House, 1994 h., by Smokester	4	22	9	8	3,178,971
Montjeu (Ire), 1996 h., by Sadler's Wells	3	16	11	10	3,178,177
Siphon (Brz), 1991 h., by Itajara	5	25	12	9	3,136,428
Gulch, 1984 h., by Mr. Prospector	3	32	13	11	3,095,521
Silverbulletday, 1996 m., by Silver Deputy	3	23	15	14	3,093,207
Peace Rules, 2000 h., by Jules	3	19	9	8	3,084,278
Concern, 1991 h., by Broad Brush	3	30	7	4	3,079,350
Giant's Causeway, 1997 h., by Storm Cat	2	13	9	8	3,078,989
Bernardini, 2003 h., by A.P. Indy	1	8	6	5	3,060,480
Lady's Secret, 1982 m., by Secretariat	4	45	25	22	3,021,325
Albert the Great, 1997 h., by Go for Gin	4	22	8	5	3,012,490
Alphabet Soup, 1991 h., by Cozzene	4	24	10	7	2,990,270
A.P. Indy, 1989 r., by Seattle Slew	2	11	8	6	2,979,815
Escena, 1993 m., by Strawberry Road (Aus)	4	29	11	7	2,962,639
Theatrical (Ire), 1982 h., by Nureyev	4	22	10	8	2,940,036
Hansel, 1988 h., by Woodman	2	14	7	6	2,936,586
Sea Hero, 1990 h., by Polish Navy	3	24	6	3	2,929,869
Great Communicator, 1983 g., by Key to the Kingdom	6	56	14	9	2,922,615
Thunder Gulch, 1992 h., by Gulch	2	16	9	8	2,915,086
Farma Way, 1987 h., by Marfa	3	23	8	6	2,897,175
Milwaukee Brew, 1997 h., by Wild Again	4	24	8	5	2,879,612
General Challenge, 1996 g., by General Meeting	4	21	9	8	2,877,178
With Approval, 1986 h., by Caro (Ire)	3	23	13	9	2,863,540
Bayakoa (Arg), 1984 m., by Consultant's Bid	6	39	21	17	2,861,701
Rough Habit (NZ), 1986 g., by Roughcast	7	66	28	21	2,861,579
Marquetry, 1987 h., by Conquistador Cielo	5	36	10	7	2,857,886
Budroyale, 1993 g., by Cee's Tizzy	7	52	17	7	2,840,810
Kotashaan (Fr), 1988 h., by Darshaan	4	22	10	8	2,812,114
Lawyer Ron, 2003 h., by Langfuhr	3	26	12	9	2,790,008
Banshee Breeze, 1995 m., by Unbridled	3	18	10	8	2,784,798
Honey Ryder, 2001 m., by Lasting Approval	5	33	13	11	2,784,160
Spectacular Bid, 1976 h., by Bold Bidder	3	30	26	23	2,781,608
Afleet Alex, 2002 h., by Northern Afleet	2	12	8	6	2,765,800
Symboli Rudolf (Jpn), 1981 h., by Partholon	4	16	13	10	2,764,980
Buck's Boy, 1993 g., by Bucksplasher	5	30	16	9	2,750,148
Evening Attire, 1998 g., by Black Tie Affair (Ire)	8	63	14	10	2,749,894
Beautiful Pleasure, 1995 m., by Maudlin	5	25	10	7	2,734,078
Forty Niner, 1985 h., by Mr. Prospector	2	19	11	9	2,726,000
Pleasant Tap, 1987 h., by Pleasant Colony	4	32	9	6	2,721,169

Progression of Leading Earner

North America

Because of the paucity and unreliability of published records of Thoroughbred racing before the Civil War, the earliest leading North American earner whose record can be reliably verified is the great American Eclipse, who became an American popular hero in the 1820s. More than 20 years later, the baton was handed to the giant filly Peytona, who collected the largest purse on the continent to date, $41,000, for her victory in the Peyton Stakes at Nashville, Tennessee, in 1843. Her owner promptly changed her name from the unwieldy Glumdalclitch and named her after her most famous win.

The pace of change on the leading earner list has quickened since antebellum days. Perhaps the most exciting exchange occurred in 1947, when Racing Hall of Fame members Assault, Armed, and Stymie batted Whirlaway's previous record around like a badminton shuttlecock. Stymie's durability finally outlasted the other two, and he ended his career with earnings of $918,485. Citation, who became the leading earner in 1950, moved the mark above $1-million the following year.

The great two-year-old and epochal sire Domino held the torch for the longest period, 27 years, from 1893 until supplanted by Man o' War in 1920. Assault and Stymie each held the title for the shortest period, seven days, during their duel in 1947. The only stallion to sire two leading North American money earners is Bull Lea. Peytona and Miss Woodford are the only females to hold the title.

International racing has always complicated the issue. Parole's record earnings include about $20,000 earned on his sojourn in England in 1879-'80. Cigar's earnings similarly include the $2.4-million earned in his Dubai World Cup victory.

Chronology of Leading American Money Winners

1823—American Eclipse, 1814 ch. h., Duroc—Millers Damsel, by Messenger. 8-8-0-0, **$56,700.**

1845—Peytona, 1839 ch. f., *Glencoe—Giantess, by *Leviathan. 8-6-1-0, **$62,400.**

1861—Planet, 1855 ch. h., Revenue—Nina, by Boston. 31-27-4-0, **$69,700.**

1881—Hindoo, 1878 b. h., Virgil—Florence, by Lexington. 35-30-3-2, **$71,875.**

1881—Parole, 1873 br. h., *Leamington—Maiden, by Lexington. 129-59-22-16, **$82,816.**

1885—Miss Woodford, 1880 br. f., *Billet—Fancy Jane, by Neil Robinson. 48-37-7-2, **$118,270.**

1889—Hanover, 1884 ch. h., Hindoo—Bourbon Belle, by Bonnie Scotland. 50-32-14-2, **$118,887.**

1892—Kingston, 1884 dk. b. or br. h., Spendthrift—*Kapanga, by Victorious. 138-89-33-12, **$138,917.**

1893—Domino, 1891 br. h., Himyar—Mannie Gray, by Enquirer. 25-19-3-1, **$193,550.**

1920—Man o' War, 1917 ch. h., Fair Play—Mahubah, by *Rock Sand. 21-20-1-0, **$249,465.**

- **1923—Zev**, 1920 dk. b. or br. h., The Finn—Miss Kearney, by *Planudes. 43-23-8-5, **$313,639.**
- **1930—Gallant Fox**, 1927 b. h., *Sir Gallahad III—Marguerite, by Celt. 17-11-3-2, **$328,165.**
- **1931—Sun Beau**, 1925 b. h., *Sun Briar—Beautiful Lady, by Fair Play. 74-33-12-10, **$376,744.**
- **1940—Seabiscuit**, 1933 b. h., Hard Tack—Swing On, by Whisk Broom II. 89-33-15-13, **$437,730.**
- **1942—Whirlaway**, 1938 ch. h., *Blenheim II—Dustwhirl, by Sweep. 60-32-15-9, **$561,161.**
- **1947 (June 21)—Assault**, 1943 ch. h., Bold Venture—Igual, by Equipoise. 42-18-6-7, **$576,670.**
- **1947 (July 5)—Stymie**, 1941 ch. h., Equestrian—Stop Watch, by On Watch. 131-35-33-28, **$595,510.**
- **1947 (July 12)—Assault, $613,370 (career $675,470).**
- **1947 (July 19)—Stymie, $678,510.**
- **1947 (October 9)—Armed**, 1941 dk. b. or br. g., Bull Lea—Armful, by Chance Shot. 81-41-20-10, **$761,500 (career $817,475).**
- **1947 (October 25)—Stymie $816,060 (career $918,485).**
- **1950—Citation**, 1945 b. h., Bull Lea—*Hydroplane II, by Hyperion. 45-32-10-2, **$1,085,760.**
- **1956—Nashua**, 1952 b. h., *Nasrullah—Segula, by Johnstown. 30-22-4-1, **$1,288,565.**
- **1958—RoundTable**, 1954 b. h., *Princequillo—*Knight's Daughter, by Sir Cosmo. 66-43-8-5, **$1,749,869.**
- **1965—Kelso**, 1957 dk. b. or br. g., Your Host—Maid of Flight, by Count Fleet. 63-39-12-2, **$1,977,896.**
- **1979—Affirmed**, 1975 ch. h., Exclusive Native—Won't Tell You, by Crafty Admiral. 29-22-5-1, **$2,393,818.**
- **1980—Spectacular Bid**, 1976 gr. h., Bold Bidder—Spectacular, by Promised Land. 30-26-2-1, **$2,781,608.**
- **1981—John Henry**, 1975 b. g., Ole Bob Bowers—Once Double, by Double Jay. 83-39-15-9, **$6,591,860.**
- **1988—Alysheba**, 1984 b. h., Aydar—Bel Sheba, by Lt. Stevens. 26-11-8-2, **$6,679,242.**
- **1996—Cigar**, 1990 b. h., Palace Music—Solar Slew, by Seattle Slew. 33-19-4-5, **$9,999,815.**

International

In the 20th century, America became so accustomed to being the home of the world's leading money-winning racehorse that it did not even notice when Japanese-bred and -trained Oguri Cap soared past American leader Alysheba in 1990.

Since organized Thoroughbred racing originated in England in the early 18th century, it is obvious the earliest leading earners must have resided there as well. Determining the first world's richest Thoroughbred is all but impossible because early records are nonexistent or unclear on purse awards.

English record-keepers recorded that in 1889 Donovan broke the record previously held by the French-bred Gladiateur. In turn, Gladiateur had broken the previous record of England's The Flying Dutchman.

The earliest horse who can reliably be accorded the palm of world's leading earner is the undefeated Highflyer, who was foaled in 1774. Based on the exchange rate of $5 to £1 that prevailed in the 19th century (America was still a British colony in 1774), Highflyer earned the equivalent of $38,395 by winning all 12 of his races.

By that standard, American Eclipse surpassed Highflyer, but 1830 Epsom Derby winner *Priam earned more money by the same exchange rate. The title remained in Europe until 1923, when Zev's victory over *Papyrus propelled him past Isinglass, who remained England's leading earner for more than 60 years.

Zev began a 67-year reign for American horses at the same time the American economy began to dominate the world. Only the huge increases in Japanese purses beginning in the 1980s changed that equation. As shown by the accompanying list of the world's current leading earners, the earnings of T.M.Opera O far exceed any American horse.

Chronology of Leading International Money Winners

- **1780—Highflyer**, 1774 b. h., Herod—Rachel, by Blank. 12-12-0-0, **$38,395.**
- **1823—American Eclipse**, 1814 ch. h., Duroc—Miller's Damsel, by *Messenger. 8-8-0-0, **$56,700.**
- **1830—*Priam**, 1827 br. h., Emilius—Cressida, by Whiskey. 16-14-1-1, **$65,100.**
- **1850—The Flying Dutchman**, 1846 b. h., Bay Middleton—Barbelle, by Sandbeck. 15-14-1-0, **$93,900.**
- **1865—Gladiateur**, 1862 b. h., Monarque—Miss Gladiator, by Gladiator. 19-16-0-1, **$236,537.**
- **1889—Donovan**, 1886 b. h., Galopin—Mowerina, by The Scottish Chief. 21-18-2-1, **$275,775.**
- **1895—Isinglass**, 1890 b. h., Isonomy—Dead Lock, by Wenlock. 12-11-1-0, **$287,275.**
- **1923—Zev**, 1920 dk. b. or br. h., The Finn—Miss Kearney, by *Planudes. 43-23-8-5, **$313,639.**
- **1930—Gallant Fox**, 1927 b. h., *Sir Gallahad III—Marguerite, by Celt. 17-11-3-2, **$328,165.**
- **1931—Sun Beau**, 1925 b. h., *Sun Briar—Beautiful Lady, by Fair Play. 74-33-12-10, **$376,744.**
- **1940—Seabiscuit**, 1933 b. h., Hard Tack—Swing On, by Whisk Broom II. 89-33-15-13, **$437,730.**
- **1942—Whirlaway**, 1938 ch. h., *Blenheim II—Dustwhirl, by Sweep. 60-32-15-9, **$561,161.**
- **1947 (June 21)—Assault**, 1943 ch. h., Bold Venture—Igual, by Equipoise. 42-18-6-7, **$576,670.**
- **1947 (July 5)—Stymie**, 1941 ch. h., Equestrian—Stop Watch, by On Watch. 131-35-33-28, **$595,510.**
- **1947 (July 12)—Assault, $613,370 (career $675,470).**
- **1947 (July 19)—Stymie, $678,510.**
- **1947 (October 9)—Armed**, 1941 dk. b. or br. g., Bull Lea—Armful, by Chance Shot. 81-41-20-10, **$761,500 (career $817,475).**
- **1947 (October 25)—Stymie $816,060 (career $918,485).**
- **1950—Citation**, 1945 b. h., Bull Lea—*Hydroplane II, by Hyperion. 45-32-10-2, **$1,085,760.**
- **1956—Nashua**, 1952 b. h., *Nasrullah—Segula, by Johnstown. 30-22-4-1, **$1,288,565.**
- **1958—RoundTable**, 1954 b. h., *Princequillo—*Knight's Daughter, by Sir Cosmo. 66-43-8-5, **$1,749,869.**
- **1965—Kelso**, 1957 dk. b. or br. g., Your Host—Maid of Flight, by Count Fleet. 63-39-12-2, **$1,977,896.**
- **1979—Affirmed**, 1975 ch. h., Exclusive Native—Won't

Tell You, by Crafty Admiral. 29-22-5-1, **$2,393,818.**
1980—**Spectacular Bid**, 1976 gr. h., Bold Bidder—Spectacular, by Promised Land. 30-26-2-1, **$2,781,608.**
1981—**John Henry**, 1975 b. g., Ole Bob Bowers—Once Double, by Double Jay. 83-39-15-9, **$6,591,860.**
1988—**Alysheba**, 1984 b. h., Alydar—Bel Sheba, by Lt. Stevens. 26-11-8-2, **$6,679,242.**
1990—**Oguri Cap**, 1985 gr. h., Dancing Cap—White Narubi, by *Silver Shark. 32-22-6-1, **$6,919,201.**

1993—**Mejiro McQueen**, 1987 gr. h., Mejiro Titan—Mejiro Aurola, by Remand. 14-9-3-0, **$7,618,803.**
1995—**Narita Brian**, 1991 dk b. or br. h., Brian's Time—Pacificus, by Northern Dancer. 21-12-3-1, **$9,296,552.**
1996—**Cigar**, 1990 b. h., Palace Music—Solar Slew, by Seattle Slew. 33-19-4-5, **$9,999,815.**
2000—**T.M.Opera O**, 1996 ch. h., Opera House (GB)—Once Wed, by Blushing Groom (Fr). 26-14-6-3, **$16,200,337.**

World's Leading Earners
Through June 29, 2008

Rank	Horse	YOB, Color, Sex, Pedigree	Country	Earnings (in Dollars)
1.	T.M.Opera O	1996 ch. h., Opera House (GB)—Once Wed, by Blushing Groom (Fr)	Jpn	$16,200,337
2.	Deep Impact	2002 b. h., Sunday Silence—Wind in Her Hair (Ire), by Alzao	Jpn	12,825,285
3.	Makybe Diva	1999 b. m., Desert King—Tugela, by Riverman	Aus	10,767,186
4.	Zenno Rob Roy	2000 dk. b. or br. h., Sunday Silence—Roamin Rachel, by Mining	Jpn	10,483,242
5.	Admire Moon	2003 b. h., End Sweep—My Katies, by Sunday Silence	Jpn	10,219,948
6.	Cigar	1990 b. h., Palace Music—Solar Slew, by Seattle Slew	USA	9,999,815
7.	Skip Away	1993 gr. h., Skip Trial—Ingot Way, by Diplomat Way	USA	9,616,360
8.	Tap Dance City	1997 b. h., Pleasant Tap—All Dance, by Northern Dancer	Jpn	9,586,479
9.	Curlin	2004 ch. c., Smart Strike—Sherriff's Deputy, by Deputy Minister	USA	9,396,800
10.	Special Week	1995 dk. b. or br. h., Sunday Silence—Campaign Girl, by Maruzensky	Jpn	9,346,435
11.	Narita Brian	1991 dk. b. or br. h., Brian's Time—Pacificus, by Northern Dancer	Jpn	9,296,552
12.	Meisho Samson	2003 b. h., Opera House (GB)—My Vivien, by Dancing Brave	Jpn	9,283,218
13.	Daiwa Major	2001 dk. h., Sunday Silence—Scarlet Bouquet, by Northern Taste	Jpn	9,208,471
14.	Time Paradox	1998 ch. h., Brian's Time—Jolie Zaza, by Alzao	Jpn	8,820,070
15.	Stay Gold	1994 dk. b. or br. h., Sunday Silence—Golden Sash, by Dictus	Jpn	8,682,142
16.	Vengeance of Rain	2000 b. g., Zabeel—Danelagh, by Danehill	HK	8,557,899
17.	Fantastic Light	1996 b. h., Rahy—Jood, by Nijinsky II	GB	8,486,957
18.	Symboli Kris S	1999 dk. b. or br. h., Kris S.—Tee Kay, by Gold Meridian	Jpn	8,401,282
19.	Narita Top Road	1996 ch. h., Soccer Boy—Floral Magic, by Affirmed	Jpn	8,389,594
20.	Hokuto Vega	1990 b. m., Nagurski—Takeno Falcon, by Philip of Spain	Jpn	8,300,301
21.	Agnes Digital	1997 ch. h., Crafty Prospector—Chancey Squaw, by Chief's Crown	Jpn	8,095,160
22.	Meisho Doto	1996 b. h., Bigstone (Ire)—Princess Reema, by Affirmed	Jpn	8,088,202
23.	Heart's Cry	2001 b. h., Sunday Silence—Irish Dance, by Tony Bin	Jpn	8,054,175
24.	Invasor (Arg)	2002 dk. b. or br. h., Candy Stripes—Quendom, by Interprete	USA	7,804,070
25.	Pleasantly Perfect	1998 b. h., Pleasant Colony—Regal State, by Affirmed	USA	7,789,880
26.	Admire Don	1999 b. h., Timber Country—Vega, by Tony Bin	Jpn	7,712,841
27.	Bullish Luck	1999 b. g., Royal Academy—Wild Vintage, by Alysheba	HK	7,643,033
28.	Mejiro Mc Queen	1987 gr. h., Mejiro Titan—Mejiro Aurola, by Remand	Jpn	7,618,803
29.	Smarty Jones	2001 ch. h., Elusive Quality—I'll Get Along, by Smile	USA	7,613,155
30.	Biwa Hayahide	1990 gr. h., Sharrood—Pacificus, by Northern Dancer	Jpn	7,555,480
31.	Blue Concorde	2000 b. h., Fusaichi Concorde—Ebisu Family, by Brian's Time	Jpn	7,530,552
32.	Mayano Top Gun	1992 b. h., Brian's Time—Alp Me Please, by Blushing Groom (Fr)	Jpn	7,463,557
33.	Eishin Preston	1997 dk. b. or br. h., Green Dancer—Warranty Applied, by Monteverdi (Ire)	Jpn	7,408,086
34.	Hishi Amazon	1991 dk. b. or br. m., Theatrical (Ire)—Katies (Ire), by Nonoalco	Jpn	6,981,102
35.	Silver Charm	1994 gr. h., Silver Buck—Bonnie's Poker, by Poker	USA	6,944,369
36.	Oguri Cap	1985 gr. h., Dancing Cap—White Narubi, by *Silver Shark	Jpn	6,940,077
37.	Mejiro Bright	1994 b. h., Mejiro Ryan—Reru du Temps, by Maruzensky	Jpn	6,848,423
38.	Air Groove	1993 b. m., Tony Bin—Dyna Carle, by Northern Taste	Jpn	6,832,242
39.	Captain Steve	1997 ch. h., Fly So Free—Sparkling Delite, by Vice Regent	USA	6,828,356
40.	Alysheba	1984 b. h., Alydar—Bel Sheba, by Lt. Stevens	USA	6,679,242
41.	Vermilion	2002 dk. b. or br. h., El Condor Pasa—Scarlet Lady, by Sunday Silence	Jpn	6,638,142
42.	Sweep Tosho	2001 b. m., End Sweep—Tabatha Tosho, by Dancing Brave	Jpn	6,631,021
43.	Sunline	1995 b. m., Desert Sun (GB)—Songline, by Western Symphony	Aus	6,625,105
44.	Dylan Thomas (Ire)	2003 b. h., Danehill—Lagrion, by Diesis (GB)	Ire	6,620,852
45.	John Henry	1975 b. g., Ole Bob Bowers—Once Double, by Double Jay	USA	6,591,860
46.	Silent Witness	1999 b. g., El Moxie—Jade Tiara, by Bureaucracy	HK	6,556,477
47.	Tiznow	1997 ch. h., Cee's Tizzy—Cee's Song, by Seattle Song	USA	6,427,830
48.	Ouija Board	2001 b. m., Cape Cross (Ire)—Selection Board, by Welsh Pageant	GB	6,312,552
49.	Wing Arrow	1995 b. h., Assatis—Sanyo Arrow, by Mr C B	Jpn	6,273,733
50.	Mejiro Dober	1994 b. m., Mejiro Ryan—Mejiro Beauty, by Partholon	Jpn	6,240,681

Leading North American Earners by Year
North American Racing Only

Year	Horse, YOB Sex, Pedigree	Earnings
2007	Curlin, 2004 c., Smart Strike—Sherriff's Deputy, by Deputy Minister	$5,102,800
2006	Invasor (Arg), 2002 c., Candy Stripes—=Quendom (Arg), by =Interprete (Arg)	3,690,000
2005	Saint Liam, 2000 h., Saint Ballado—Quiet Dance, by Quiet American	3,696,960
2004	Smarty Jones, 2001 c., Elusive Quality—I'll Get Along, by Smile	7,563,535
2003	Pleasantly Perfect, 1998 h., Pleasant Colony—Regal State, by Affirmed	2,470,000
2002	War Emblem, 1999 c., Our Emblem—Sweetest Lady, by Lord At War (Arg)	3,455,000
2001	Point Given, 1998 c., Thunder Gulch—Turko's Turn, by Turkoman	3,350,000
2000	Tiznow, 1997 c., Cee's Tizzy—Cee's Song, by Seattle Song	3,445,950
1999	Cat Thief, 1996 c., Storm Cat—Train Robbery, by Alydar	3,020,500
1998	Awesome Again, 1994 c., Deputy Minister—Primal Force, by Blushing Groom (Fr)	3,845,990
1997	Skip Away, 1993 c., Skip Trial—Ingot Way, by Diplomat Way	4,089,000
1996	Skip Away, 1993 c., Skip Trial—Ingot Way, by Diplomat Way	2,699,280
1995	Cigar, 1990 h., Palace Music—Solar Slew, by Seattle Slew	4,819,800
1994	Concern, 1991 c., Broad Brush—Fara's Team, by Tunerup	2,541,670
1993	Sea Hero, 1990 c., Polish Navy—Glowing Tribute, by Graustark	2,484,190
1992	A.P. Indy, 1989 c., Seattle Slew—Weekend Surprise, by Secretariat	2,622,560
1991	Dance Smartly, 1988 f., Danzig—Classy 'n Smart, by Smarten	2,876,821
1990	Unbridled, 1987 c., Fappiano—Gana Facil, by *Le Fabuleux	3,718,149
1989	Sunday Silence, 1986 c., Halo—Wishing Well, by Understanding	4,578,454
1988	Alysheba, 1984 c., Alydar—Bel Sheba, by Lt. Stevens	3,808,600
1987	Alysheba, 1984 c., Alydar—Bel Sheba, by Lt. Stevens	2,511,156
1986	Snow Chief, 1983 c., Reflected Glory—Miss Snowflake, by *Snow Sporting	1,875,200
1985	Spend a Buck, 1982 c., Buckaroo—Belle de Jour, by Speak John	3,552,704
1984	Slew o' Gold, 1980 c., Seattle Slew—Alluvial, by Buckpasser	2,627,944
1983	Sunny's Halo, 1980 c., Halo—Mostly Sunny, by Sunny	1,011,962
1982	Perrault (GB), 1977 h., Djakao—Innocent Air, by *Court Martial	1,197,400
1981	John Henry, 1975 g., Ole Bob Bowers—Once Double, by Double Jay	1,798,030
1980	Temperence Hill, 1977 c., Stop the Music—Sister Shannon, by Etonian	1,130,452
1979	Spectacular Bid, 1976 c., Bold Bidder—Spectacular, by Promised Land	1,279,334
1978	Affirmed, 1975 c., Exclusive Native—Won't Tell You, by Crafty Admiral	901,541
1977	Seattle Slew, 1974 c., Bold Reasoning—My Charmer, by Poker	641,370
1976	Forego, 1970 g., *Forli—Lady Golconda, by Hasty Road	491,701
1975	Foolish Pleasure, 1972 c., What a Pleasure—Fool-Me-Not, by Tom Fool	716,278
1974	Chris Evert, 1971 f., Swoon's Son—Miss Carmie, by T. V. Lark	551,063
1973	Secretariat, 1970 c., Bold Ruler—Somethingroyal, by *Princequillo	860,404
1972	Droll Role, 1968 c., Tom Rolfe—*Pradella, by Precipic	471,633
1971	Riva Ridge, 1969 c., First Landing—Iberia, by *Heliopolis	503,263
1970	Personality, 1967 c., Hail to Reason—Affectionately, by Swaps	444,049
1969	Arts and Letters, 1966 c., *Ribot—All Beautiful, by Battlefield	555,604
1968	Forward Pass, 1965 c., On-and-On—Princess Turia, by *Heliopolis	546,674
1967	Damascus, 1964 c., Sword Dancer—Kerala, by *My Babu	817,941
1966	Buckpasser, 1963 c., Tom Fool—Busanda, by War Admiral	669,078
1965	Buckpasser, 1963 c., Tom Fool—Busanda, by War Admiral	568,096
1964	Gun Bow, 1960 c., Gun Shot—Ribbons and Bows, by War Admiral	580,100
1963	Candy Spots, 1960 c., *Nigromante—Candy Dish, by *Khaled	604,481
1962	Never Bend, 1960 c., *Nasrullah—Lalun, by *Djeddah	402,969
1961	Carry Back, 1958 c., Saggy—Joppy, by Star Blen	565,349
1960	Bally Ache, 1957 c., *Ballydam—Celestial Blue, by Supremus	455,045
1959	Sword Dancer, 1956 c., Sunglow—Highland Fling, by By Jimminy	537,004
1958	Round Table, 1954 c., *Princequillo—*Knight's Daughter, by Sir Cosmo	662,780
1957	Round Table, 1954 c., *Princequillo—*Knight's Daughter, by Sir Cosmo	600,383
1956	Needles, 1953 c., Ponder—Noodle Soup, by Jack High	440,850
1955	Nashua, 1952 c., *Nasrullah—Segula, by Johnstown	752,550
1954	Determine, 1951 c., *Alibhai—Koubis, by *Mahmoud	328,700
1953	Native Dancer, 1950 c., Polynesian—Geisha, by Discovery	513,425
1952	Crafty Admiral, 1948 c., Fighting Fox—Admiral's Lady, by War Admiral	277,225
1951	Counterpoint, 1948 c., Count Fleet—Jabot, by *Sickle	250,525
1950	*Noor, 1945 h., *Nasrullah—Queen of Baghdad, by *Bahram	346,940
1949	Ponder, 1946 c., Pensive—Miss Rushin, by *Blenheim II	321,825
1948	Citation, 1945 c., Bull Lea—*Hydroplane II, by Hyperion	709,470
1947	Armed, 1941 g., Bull Lea—Armful, by Chance Shot	376,325
1946	Assault, 1943 c., Bold Venture—Igual, by Equipoise	424,195
1945	Busher, 1942 f., War Admiral—Baby League, by Bubbling Over	273,735
1944	Pavot, 1942 c., Case Ace—Coquelicot, by Man o' War	179,040
1943	Count Fleet, 1940 c., Reigh Count—Quickly, by Haste	174,055
1942	Shut Out, 1939 c., Equipoise—Goose Egg, by *Chicle	238,972
1941	Whirlaway, 1938 c., *Blenheim II—Dustwhirl, by Sweep	272,386
1940	Bimelech, 1937 c., Black Toney—*La Troienne, by *Teddy	110,005
1939	Challedon, 1936 c., *Challenger II—Laura Gal, by *Sir Gallahad III	184,535
1938	Stagehand, 1935 c., *Sickle—Stagecraft, by Fair Play	189,710
1937	Seabiscuit, 1933 c., Hard Tack—Swing On, by Whisk Broom II	168,580
1936	Granville, 1933 c., Gallant Fox—Gravita, by *Sarmatian	110,295
1935	Omaha, 1932 c., Gallant Fox—Flambino, by *Wrack	142,255
1934	Cavalcade, 1931 c., *Lancegaye—*Hastily, by Hurry On	111,235
1933	Singing Wood, 1931 c., *Royal Minstrel—Glade, by Touch Me Not	88,050
1932	Gusto, 1929 c., American Flag—Daylight Again, by *Star Shoot	145,940
1931	Top Flight, 1929 f., *Dis Donc—Flyatit, by Peter Pan	219,000
1930	Gallant Fox, 1927 c., *Sir Gallahad III—Marguerite, by Celt	308,275

Leading Earners in North America
North American Racing Only Through 2007

Horse, YOB Sex, Sire	Wins	Stakes Wins	Earnings
Skip Away, 1993 h., by Skip Trial	18	16	$9,616,360
Smarty Jones, 2001 h., by Elusive Quality	8	7	7,613,155
Cigar, 1990 h., by Palace Music	18	14	7,599,815
Alysheba, 1984 h., by Alydar	11	10	6,679,242
John Henry, 1975 g., by Ole Bob Bowers	39	30	6,591,860
Tiznow, 1997 h., by Cee's Tizzy	8	7	6,427,830
Best Pal, 1988 g., by *Habitony	18	17	5,668,245
English Channel, 2002 h., by Smart Strike	13	10	5,319,028
Lava Man, 2001 g., by Slew City Slew	17	13	5,214,706
Curlin, 2004 c., by Smart Strike	6	5	5,102,800
Sunday Silence, 1986 h., by Halo	9	7	4,968,554
Easy Goer, 1986 h., by Alydar	14	12	4,873,770
Perfect Drift, 1999 g., by Dynaformer	11	8	4,680,691
Medaglia d'Oro, 1999 h., by El Prado (Ire)	8	7	4,554,720
Unbridled, 1987 h., by Fappiano	8	5	4,489,475
Saint Liam, 2000 h., by Saint Ballado	9	5	4,456,995
Silver Charm, 1994 h., by Silver Buck	11	10	4,444,369
Street Sense, 2004 c., by Street Cry (Ire)	6	5	4,383,200
Awesome Again, 1994 h., by Deputy Minister	9	7	4,374,590
Spend a Buck, 1982 h., by Buckaroo	10	7	4,220,689
Pleasantly Perfect, 1998 h., by Pleasant Colony	8	5	4,189,880
Azeri, 1998 m., by Jade Hunter	17	14	4,079,820
Better Talk Now, 1999 g., by Talkin Man	14	10	4,052,788
Creme Fraiche, 1982 g., by Rich Cream	17	14	4,024,727
Invasor (Arg), 2002 h., by Candy Stripes	5	5	3,990,000
Point Given, 1998 h., by Thunder Gulch	9	8	3,968,500
Cat Thief, 1996 h., by Storm Cat	4	3	3,951,012
Ashado, 2001 m., by Saint Ballado	12	11	3,931,440
Devil His Due, 1989 h., by Devil's Bag	11	9	3,920,405
Ferdinand, 1983 h., by Nijinsky II	8	7	3,777,978
Spain, 1997 m., by Thunder Gulch	9	7	3,540,542
Slew o' Gold, 1980 h., by Seattle Slew	12	8	3,533,534
Funny Cide, 2000 g., by Distorted Humor	11	9	3,529,412
War Emblem, 1999 h., by Our Emblem	7	4	3,491,000
Precisionist, 1981 h., by Crozier	20	17	3,485,398
Strike the Gold, 1988 h., by Alydar	6	4	3,457,026
Ghostzapper, 2000 h., by Awesome Again	9	6	3,446,120
Snow Chief, 1983 h., by Reflected Glory	13	12	3,383,210
Cryptoclearance, 1984 h., by Fappiano	12	9	3,376,327
Gentlemen (Arg), 1992 h., by Robin des Bois	9	8	3,374,890
Black Tie Affair (Ire), 1986 h., by Miswaki	18	13	3,370,694
Sky Classic, 1987 h., by Nijinsky II	15	13	3,320,398
Bet Twice, 1984 h., by Sportin' Life	10	7	3,308,599
Serena's Song, 1992 m., by Rahy	18	17	3,283,388
Real Quiet, 1995 h., by Quiet American	6	5	3,271,802
Congaree, 1998 h., by Arazi	12	10	3,267,490
Dance Smartly, 1988 m., by Danzig	12	10	3,263,835
Lemon Drop Kid, 1996 h., by Kingmambo	10	7	3,245,370
Behrens, 1994 h., by Pleasant Colony	9	7	3,243,500
Steinlen (GB), 1983 h., by Habitat	16	14	3,229,752
Captain Steve, 1997 h., by Fly So Free	8	7	3,228,356
Chief Bearhart, 1993 h., by Chief's Crown	12	9	3,219,017
Volponi, 1998 h., by Cryptoclearance	7	4	3,187,232
Bertrando, 1989 h., by Skywalker	9	8	3,185,610
Free House, 1994 h., by Smokester	9	8	3,178,971
Sandpit (Brz), 1989 h., by Baynoun (Ire)	9	8	3,147,973
Paseana (Arg), 1987 m., by Ahmad	14	14	3,111,292
Gulch, 1984 h., by Mr. Prospector	13	11	3,095,521
Silverbulletday, 1996 m., by Silver Deputy	15	14	3,093,207
Peace Rules, 2000 h., by Jules	9	8	3,084,278
Concern, 1991 h., by Broad Brush	7	4	3,079,350
Bernardini, 2003 h., by A.P. Indy	6	5	3,060,480
Lady's Secret, 1982 m., by Secretariat	25	22	3,021,325
Albert the Great, 1997 h., by Go for Gin	8	5	3,012,490
Victory Gallop, 1995 h., by Cryptoclearance	9	7	3,005,895

Leading Female Earners in North America

Horse, YOB Sex, Sire	Wins	Stakes Wins	Earnings
Azeri, 1998 m., by Jade Hunter	17	14	$4,079,820
Ashado, 2001 m., by Saint Ballado	12	11	3,931,440
Spain, 1997 m., Thunder Gulch	9	7	3,540,542
Serena's Song, 1992 m., Rahy	18	17	3,283,388
Dance Smartly, 1988 m., Danzig	12	10	3,263,835
Paseana (Arg), 1987 m., Ahmad	14	14	3,111,292
Silverbulletday, 1996 m., Silver Deputy	15	14	3,093,207
Lady's Secret, 1982 m., Secretariat	25	22	3,021,325
Escena, 1993 m., Strawberry Road (Aus)	11	7	2,962,639
Bayakoa (Arg), 1984 m., Consultant's Bid	18	16	2,785,259
Banshee Breeze, 1995 m., Unbridled	10	8	2,784,798
Honey Ryder, 2001 m., Lasting Approval	13	11	2,784,160
Beautiful Pleasure, 1995 m., Maudlin	10	7	2,734,078
Flawlessly, 1988 m., Affirmed	16	15	2,572,536
Take Charge Lady, 1999 m., Dehere	11	9	2,480,377
Sightseek, 1999 m., Distant View	12	10	2,445,216
Heritage of Gold, 1995 m., Gold Legend	16	11	2,381,762
Life's Magic, 1981 m., Cox's Ridge	8	7	2,255,218
Megahertz (GB), 1999 m., Pivotal	13	13	2,237,160
Film Maker, 2000 m., Dynaformer	8	6	2,203,730
Perfect Sting, 1996 m., Red Ransom	14	11	2,202,042
Safely Kept, 1986 m., Horatius	24	22	2,194,206
Xtra Heat, 1998 m., Dixieland Heat	26	25	2,189,635
Riskaverse, 1999 m., Dynaformer	9	6	2,182,429
Ouija Board (GB), 2001 m., Cape Cross (Ire)	2	2	2,133,200
You, 1999 m., You and I	9	8	2,101,353
Adoration, 1999 m., Honor Grades	8	7	2,051,160
Island Fashion, 2000 m., Petionville	6	6	2,037,970
Sharp Cat, 1994 m., Storm Cat	15	14	2,032,575
Round Pond, 2002 m., Awesome Again	7	5	1,998,700
Society Selection, 2001 m., Coronado's Quest	6	5	1,984,200
Storm Flag Flying, 2000 m., Storm Cat	7	5	1,951,828
Jewel Princess, 1992 m., Key to the Mint	13	10	1,904,060
Ginger Punch, 2003 m., Awesome Again	7	4	1,901,679
Intercontinental (GB), 2000 m., Danehill	9	8	1,863,586
Surfside, 1997 m., Seattle Slew	8	6	1,852,987
Open Mind, 1986 m., Deputy Minister	12	11	1,844,372
Estrapade, 1980 m., *Vaguely Noble	8	7	1,834,600
Heavenly Prize, 1991 m., Seeking the Gold	9	8	1,825,940
Lu Ravi, 1995 m., A.P. Indy	11	8	1,819,781
Tout Charmant, 1996 m., Slewvescent	9	7	1,781,879
Unbridled Elaine, 1998 m., Unbridled's Song	6	4	1,770,740
Wait a While, 2003 m., Maria's Mon	9	8	1,729,917
Goodbye Halo, 1985 m., Halo	11	10	1,706,702
Fleet Indian, 2001 m., Indian Charlie	13	7	1,704,513
Happy Ticket, 2001 m., Anet	12	10	1,688,838
Personal Ensign, 1984 m., Private Account	13	10	1,679,880
Tranquility Lake, 1995 m., Rahy	11	9	1,662,390
Keeper Hill, 1995 m., Deputy Minister	4	3	1,661,281
Octave, 2004 f., Unbridled's Song	4	3	1,660,934
Dreaming of Anna, 2004 f., Rahy	7	6	1,658,172
Golden Apples (Ire), 1998 m., Pivotal	5	5	1,652,346
Inside Information, 1991 m., Private Account	14	14	1,641,860
Dancethruthedawn, 1998 m., Mr. Prospector	7	5	1,609,643
Very Subtle, 1984 m., Hoist the Silver	12	10	1,608,360

North American Leaders by Graded Stakes Earnings
North American Racing Only Through 2007

Horse, YOB Sex, Sire	Years Raced	Graded Stakes Wins	Graded Stakes Earnings
Skip Away, 1993 h., by Skip Trial	4	16	$9,548,100
Smarty Jones, 2001 h., by Elusive Quality	2	7	7,334,820
Alysheba, 1984 h., by Alydar	3	10	6,616,417
Tiznow, 1997 h., by Cee's Tizzy	3	7	6,382,830
Cigar, 1990 h., by Palace Music	4	11	5,695,000
Curlin, 2004 c., by Smart Strike	1	5	5,080,000
John Henry, 1975 g., by Ole Bob Bowers	8	25	4,953,417
Sunday Silence, 1986 h., by Halo	3	7	4,929,254
English Channel, 2002 h., by Smart Strike	4	7	4,806,437
Easy Goer, 1986 h., by Alydar	4	7	4,775,280
Best Pal, 1988 g., by *Habitony	7	12	4,713,795
Medaglia d'Oro, 1999 h., by El Prado (Ire)	4	7	4,535,000
Perfect Drift, 1999 g., by Dynaformer	7	7	4,465,635
Silver Charm, 1994 h., by Silver Buck	4	10	4,416,416
Street Sense, 2004 c., by Street Cry (Ire)	2	5	4,357,000
Saint Liam, 2000 h., by Saint Ballado	3	5	4,292,920
Unbridled, 1987 h., by Fappiano	3	3	4,105,529
Pleasantly Perfect, 1998 h., by Pleasant Colony	4	5	4,070,000

Racing — Earnings Leaders

Horse, YOB Sex, Sire	Years Raced	Graded Stakes Wins	Graded Stakes Earnings
Awesome Again, 1994 h., by Deputy Minister	2	6	$4,065,590
Lava Man, 2001 g., by Slew City Slew	5	9	4,041,667
Azeri, 1998 m., by Jade Hunter	4	14	3,999,420
Invasor (Arg), 2002 h., by Candy Stripes	2	5	3,990,000
Point Given, 1998 h., by Thunder Gulch	2	8	3,930,900
Cat Thief, 1996 h., by Storm Cat	3	3	3,909,952
Ashado, 2001 m., by Saint Ballado	3	11	3,905,640
Devil His Due, 1989 h., by Devil's Bag	4	9	3,895,265
Better Talk Now, 1999 g., by Talkin Man	7	9	3,880,443
Spend a Buck, 1982 h., by Buckaroo	2	4	3,809,004
Creme Fraiche, 1982 h., by Rich Cream	6	11	3,689,091
Ferdinand, 1983 h., by Nijinsky II	4	5	3,619,978
Spain, 1997 m., by Thunder Gulch	4	7	3,490,307
Slew o' Gold, 1980 h., by Seattle Slew	3	8	3,454,694
War Emblem, 1999 h., by Our Emblem	2	4	3,425,000
Strike the Gold, 1988 h., by Alydar	4	4	3,391,210
Ghostzapper, 2000 h., by Awesome Again	4	6	3,362,000
Gentlemen (Arg), 1992 h., by Robin des Bois	3	8	3,324,140
Serena's Song, 1992 m., by Rahy	3	17	3,260,353
Funny Cide, 2000 g., by Distorted Humor	6	5	3,227,873
Behrens, 1994 h., by Pleasant Colony	4	7	3,204,500
Real Quiet, 1995 h., by Quiet American	3	5	3,195,740
Lemon Drop Kid, 1996 h., by Kingmambo	3	7	3,168,900
Cryptoclearance, 1984 h., by Fappiano	4	8	3,162,157
Snow Chief, 1983 h., by Reflected Glory	3	9	3,162,110
Free House, 1994 h., by Smokester	4	8	3,153,021
Precisionist, 1981 h., by Crozier	5	13	3,136,608
Black Tie Affair (Ire), 1986 h., by Miswaki	4	11	3,132,547
Bertrando, 1989 h., by Skywalker	5	7	3,131,320
Paseana (Arg), 1987 m., by Ahmad	5	14	3,074,292
Sandpit (Brz), 1989 h., by Baynoun (Ire)	4	7	3,066,480
Captain Steve, 1997 h., by Fly So Free	3	6	3,050,756
Gulch, 1984 h., by Mr. Prospector	3	11	3,049,671
Volponi, 1998 h., by Cryptoclearance	4	4	3,042,852
Bernardini, 2003 h., by A.P. Indy	1	5	3,040,000
Concern, 1991 h., by Broad Brush	3	4	3,004,530

North American Leaders by Grade 1 Earnings
North American Racing Only Through 2007

Horse, YOB Sex, Sire	Years Raced	Grade 1 Stakes Wins	Grade 1 Stakes Earnings
Skip Away, 1993 h., by Skip Trial	4	10	$7,310,920
Smarty Jones, 2001 h., by Elusive Quality	2	2	6,734,800
Alysheba, 1984 h., by Alydar	3	9	6,230,506
Tiznow, 1997 h., by Cee's Tizzy	2	4	5,815,400
Cigar, 1990 h., by Palace Music	4	11	5,660,000
Sunday Silence, 1986 h., by Halo	3	6	4,757,454
Easy Goer, 1986 h., by Alydar	3	9	4,606,980
English Channel, 2002 h., by Smart Strike	4	6	4,356,337
Curlin, 2004 c., by Smart Strike	1	3	4,300,000
John Henry, 1975 g., by Ole Bob Bowers	8	16	4,125,680
Unbridled, 1987 h., by Fappiano	3	3	4,039,360
Invasor (Arg), 2002 h., by Candy Stripes	2	5	3,990,000
Best Pal, 1988 g., by *Habitony	7	6	3,841,870
Saint Liam, 2000 h., by Saint Ballado	3	4	3,796,960
Street Sense, 2004 c., by Street Cry (Ire)	2	3	3,785,000
Point Given, 1998 h., by Thunder Gulch	2	6	3,718,300
Lava Man, 2001 g., by Slew City Slew	5	7	3,586,667
Medaglia d'Oro, 1999 h., by El Prado (Ire)	4	3	3,545,000
Devil His Due, 1989 h., by Devil's Bag	4	5	3,466,000
Slew o' Gold, 1980 h., by Seattle Slew	3	7	3,420,314
Azeri, 1998 m., by Jade Hunter	4	11	3,408,920
Cat Thief, 1996 h., by Storm Cat	3	2	3,366,500
Ashado, 2001 m., by Saint Ballado	3	7	3,335,640
Ferdinand, 1983 h., by Nijinsky II	4	3	3,326,678
Better Talk Now, 1999 g., by Talkin Man	7	5	3,284,647
Pleasantly Perfect, 1998 h., by Pleasant Colony	4	3	3,240,000
Ghostzapper, 2000 h., by Awesome Again	4	4	3,152,000
War Emblem, 1999 h., by Our Emblem	2	3	3,125,000
Awesome Again, 1994 h., by Deputy Minister	2	2	2,999,900
Real Quiet, 1995 h., by Quiet American	3	5	2,920,920
Creme Fraiche, 1982 g., by Rich Cream	6	7	2,897,068
Strike the Gold, 1988 h., by Alydar	4	2	2,800,876

Horse, YOB Sex, Sire	Years Raced	Grade 1 Stakes Wins	Grade 1 Stakes Earnings
Paseana (Arg), 1987 m., by Ahmad	5	10	$2,753,942
A.P. Indy, 1989 r., by Seattle Slew	2	4	2,725,660
Theatrical (Ire), 1982 h., by Nureyev	3	6	2,724,040
Silver Charm, 1994 h., by Silver Buck	4	2	2,716,350
Gulch, 1984 h., by Mr. Prospector	3	7	2,683,496
Bernardini, 2003 h., by A.P. Indy	1	3	2,650,000
Sea Hero, 1990 h., by Polish Navy	3	3	2,635,900
Lemon Drop Kid, 1996 h., by Kingmambo	3	5	2,630,900
Gentlemen (Arg), 1992 h., by Robin des Bois	3	3	2,610,000
Bet Twice, 1984 h., by Sportin' Life	3	4	2,573,337
Funny Cide, 2000 g., by Distorted Humor	6	3	2,568,534
Bertrando, 1989 h., by Skywalker	5	3	2,554,820
Fantastic Light, 1996 h., by Rahy	2	2	2,507,400
Spain, 1997 m., by Thunder Gulch	4	2	2,499,900
Beautiful Pleasure, 1995 m., by Maudlin	5	6	2,467,500
Volponi, 1998 h., by Cryptoclearance	4	1	2,406,000
Sandpit (Brz), 1989 h., by Baynoun (Ire)	4	5	2,396,000
Concern, 1991 h., by Broad Brush	3	2	2,375,780
Bayakoa (Arg), 1984 m., by Consultant's Bid	4	12	2,345,509
Farma Way, 1987 h., by Marfa	3	2	2,340,000
Perfect Drift, 1999 g., by Dynaformer	7	1	2,321,663
Chief Bearhart, 1993 h., by Chief's Crown	4	3	2,321,000
Cryptoclearance, 1984 h., by Fappiano	4	3	2,317,732
Lady's Secret, 1982 m., by Secretariat	4	11	2,314,731
Banshee Breeze, 1995 m., by Unbridled	3	5	2,311,680

North American Leading Males by Turf Earnings
North American Racing Only Through 2007

Horse, YOB Sex, Sire	Years Raced	Turf Wins	Turf Earnings
English Channel, 2002 h., by Smart Strike	4	13	$5,319,028
John Henry, 1975 g., by Ole Bob Bowers	8	30	5,269,212
Better Talk Now, 1999 g., by Talkin Man	7	14	4,036,428
Steinlen (GB), 1983 h., by Habitat	4	16	3,229,752
Sky Classic, 1987 h., by Nijinsky II	4	13	3,176,638
Chief Bearhart, 1993 h., by Chief's Crown	4	11	3,164,509
Great Communicator, 1983 g., by Key to the Kingdom	6	13	2,908,485
Awad, 1990 h., by Caveat	7	13	2,871,645
Theatrical (Ire), 1982 h., by Nureyev	3	7	2,840,500
Sandpit (Brz), 1989 h., by Baynoun (Ire)	4	9	2,752,973
Manila, 1983 h., by Lyphard	3	11	2,676,299
Paradise Creek, 1989 h., by Irish River (Fr)	4	14	2,675,514
The Tin Man, 1998 g., by Affirmed	7	13	2,663,780
Miesque's Approval, 1999 h., by Miesque's Son	7	12	2,648,879
Fraise, 1988 h., by Strawberry Road (Aus)	4	10	2,613,105
Fantastic Light, 1996 h., by Rahy	2	2	2,507,400
Buck's Boy, 1993 g., by Bucksplasher	5	10	2,493,520
Kip Deville, 2003 h., by Kipling	3	7	2,393,660
Lure, 1989 h., by Danzig	4	11	2,348,839
Quiet Resolve, 1995 g., by Affirmed	5	10	2,346,768
With Anticipation, 1995 g., by Relaunch	8	7	2,332,512
Daylami (Ire), 1994 h., by Doyoun	2	2	2,280,000
Marlin, 1993 h., by Sword Dance (Ire)	3	8	2,262,255
With Approval, 1986 h., by Caro (Ire)	3	7	2,254,760
Yankee Affair, 1982 h., by Northern Fling	5	18	2,204,524
Sunshine Forever, 1985 h., by Roberto	3	8	2,083,700
Cloudy's Knight, 2000 g., by Lord Avie	5	10	2,070,503
Artie Schiller, 2001 h., by El Prado (Ire)	4	10	2,067,705
Kitten's Joy, 2001 h., by El Prado (Ire)	3	9	2,065,241
High Chaparral (Ire), 1999 h., by Sadler's Wells	2	2	2,021,600
Kotashaan (Fr), 1988 h., by Darshaan	2	7	2,017,050
Star of Cozzene, 1988 h., by Cozzene	5	11	2,015,039
Sulamani (Ire), 1999 h., by Hernando (Fr)	2	3	2,013,600
Bien Bien, 1989 h., by Manila	3	8	1,998,725
Majesty's Prince, 1979 h., by His Majesty	4	9	1,942,922
Red Rocks (Ire), 2003 h., by Galileo (Ire)	2	1	1,920,000
Soaring Free, 1999 g., by Smart Strike	5	11	1,916,789
Ladies Din, 1995 g., by Din's Dancer	6	11	1,894,710
Itsallgreektome, 1987 g., by Sovereign Dancer	5	7	1,821,893
Sweet Return (GB), 2000 h., by Elmaamul	5	7	1,778,706
El Senor, 1984 h., by Valdez	5	12	1,767,245
Singletary, 2000 h., by Sultry Song	4	8	1,753,192
Good Journey, 1996 h., by Nureyev	4	7	1,722,965

Racing — Earnings Leaders

Horse, YOB Sex, Sire	Years Raced	Turf Wins	Turf Earnings
Sky Conqueror, 2002 h., by Sky Classic	3	7	$1,719,099
Yagli, 1993 h., by Jade Hunter	5	10	1,702,121
Leroidesanimaux (Brz), 2000 h., by Candy Stripes	2	8	1,650,900
Denon, 1998 h., by Pleasant Colony	4	4	1,647,269
Val's Prince, 1992 g., by Eternal Prince	7	10	1,585,940
Sarafan, 1997 g., by Lear Fan	6	6	1,582,673
Jambalaya, 2002 g., by Langfuhr	4	8	1,581,298
Strut the Stage, 1998 h., by Theatrical (Ire)	6	10	1,568,555
Da Hoss, 1992 g., by Gone West	4	8	1,559,780

North American Leading Females by Turf Earnings
North American Racing Only Through 2007

Horse, YOB Sex, Sire	Years Raced	Turf Wins	Turf Earnings
Honey Ryder, 2001 m., by Lasting Approval	5	13	$2,784,160
Flawlessly, 1988 m., by Affirmed	5	14	2,459,250
Megahertz (GB), 1999 m., by Pivotal	4	13	2,237,160
Film Maker, 2000 m., by Dynaformer	5	8	2,201,090
Perfect Sting, 1996 m., by Red Ransom	4	13	2,163,673
Ouija Board (GB), 2001 m., by Cape Cross (Ire)	3	2	2,133,200
Riskaverse, 1999 m., by Dynaformer	5	8	2,096,299
Intercontinental (GB), 2000 m., by Danehill	2	9	1,863,586
Estrapade, 1980 m., by *Vaguely Noble	3	8	1,789,600
Golden Apples (Ire), 1998 m., by Pivotal	3	5	1,652,346
Tout Charmant, 1996 m., by Slewvescent	5	7	1,607,219
Lahudood (GB), 2003 m., by Singspiel (Ire)	1	3	1,560,500
Starine (Fr), 1997 m., by Mendocino	2	4	1,560,189
Miss Alleged, 1987 m., by Alleged	2	2	1,532,500
Happyanunoit (NZ), 1995 m., by Yachtie	3	6	1,481,892
Tates Creek, 1998 m., by Rahy	3	11	1,470,834
Memories of Silver, 1993 m., by Silver Hawk	3	9	1,435,140
Wonder Again, 1999 m., by Silver Hawk	4	7	1,434,762
Voodoo Dancer, 1998 m., by Kingmambo	4	11	1,427,952
Tranquility Lake, 1995 m., by Rahy	4	9	1,420,770
Moscow Burning, 2000 m., by Moscow Ballet	4	9	1,404,075
Astra, 1996 m., by Theatrical (Ire)	4	11	1,378,424
Possibly Perfect, 1990 m., by Northern Baby	3	11	1,367,050
Ticker Tape (GB), 2001 m., by Royal Applause (GB)	4	6	1,364,045
All Along (Fr), 1979 m., by Targowice	2	3	1,337,146
Precious Kitten, 2003 m., by Catienus	2	6	1,323,068
Wait a While, 2003 m., by Maria's Mon	3	6	1,318,600
Sand Springs, 2000 m., by Dynaformer	4	9	1,270,058
Tuzla (Fr), 1994 m., by Panoramic (GB)	4	11	1,266,079
Carotene, 1983 m., by Great Nephew	4	10	1,242,126
Brown Bess, 1982 m., by *Petrone	6	13	1,224,265
Gorella (Fr), 2002 m., by Grape Tree Road (GB)	2	4	1,196,388
Soaring Softly, 1995 m., by Kris S.	3	7	1,193,450
Irish Linnet, 1988 m., by Seattle Song	6	18	1,191,980
Windsharp, 1991 m., by Lear Fan	3	6	1,191,600
Fieldy (Ire), 1983 m., by Northfields	4	18	1,182,530
Wandesta (GB), 1991 m., by Nashwan	3	6	1,170,650
My Typhoon (Ire), 2002 m., by Giant's Causeway	4	8	1,144,361
Heat Haze (GB), 1999 m., by Green Desert	2	5	1,135,660
Arravale, 2003 m., by Arch	3	5	1,111,236
Royal Heroine (Ire), 1980 m., by Lypheor (GB)	2	5	1,110,900
Bold Ruritana, 1990 m., by Bold Ruckus	6	14	1,102,790
Kostroma (Ire), 1986 m., by Caerleon	3	7	1,093,275
Lady of Venice (Fr), 2003 m., by Loup Solitaire	2	5	1,081,376
Banks Hill (GB), 1998 m., by Danehill	2	1	1,068,800
Maxzene, 1993 m., by Cozzene	3	11	1,067,587
Volga (Ire), 1998 m., by Caerleon	3	4	1,067,320
Angara (GB), 2001 m., by Alzao	2	4	1,064,213
Colstar, 1996 m., by Opening Verse	4	11	1,053,056

Leading Two-Year-Old Males by North American Earnings
North American Racing Only Through 2007

Horse, YOB Sex, Sire	Starts	Wins	Stakes Wins	Earnings
Boston Harbor, 1994 c., by Capote	7	6	5	$1,928,605
Mountain Cat, 1990 c., by Storm Cat	8	6	4	1,460,627
War Pass, 2005 c., by Cherokee Run	4	4	2	1,397,400
Favorite Trick, 1995 c., by Phone Trick	8	8	7	1,231,998

Horse, YOB Sex, Sire	Starts	Wins	Stakes Wins	Earnings
Street Sense, 2004 c., by Street Cry (Ire)	5	2	1	$1,178,200
Tejano, 1985 c., by Caro (Ire)	10	5	4	1,177,189
Stevie Wonderboy, 2003 c., by Stephen Got Even	5	3	2	1,028,940
Best Pal, 1988 g., by *Habitony	8	6	5	1,026,195
Grand Canyon, 1987 c., by Fappiano	8	4	3	1,019,540
Snow Chief, 1983 c., by Reflected Glory	9	5	4	935,740
Timber Country, 1992 c., by Woodman	7	4	3	928,590
Chief's Crown, 1982 c., by Danzig	9	6	5	920,890
Fly So Free, 1988 c., by Time for a Change	6	4	2	872,580
Gilded Time, 1990 c., by Timeless Moment	4	4	3	855,980
Wilko, 2002 c., by Awesome Again	2	1	1	833,580
Action This Day, 2001 c., by Kris S.	3	2	1	817,200
Regal Classic, 1985 c., by Vice Regent	8	4	3	812,500
Roving Boy, 1980 c., by Olden Times	7	5	4	800,425
Circular Quay, 2004 c., by Thunder Gulch	5	3	2	781,434
Macho Uno, 1998 c., by Holy Bull	4	3	2	768,803
Tasso, 1983 c., by Fappiano	7	5	3	761,534
Toccet, 2000 c., by Awesome Again	8	6	4	755,610
Fali Time, 1981 c., by Faliraki (Ire)	7	3	2	748,829
Captain Steve, 1997 c., by Fly So Free	8	4	3	744,880
Officer, 1999 c., by Bertrando	8	5	4	740,010
Success Express, 1985 c., by Hold Your Peace	8	4	3	737,207
Mr. Jester, 2001 c., by Silver Deputy	6	4	3	730,800
Texcess, 2002 g., by In Excess (Ire)	4	3	2	725,427
Siphonic, 1999 c., by Siphon (Brz)	4	3	3	703,978
Birdbirdistheword, 2004 c., by Pure Prize	5	3	2	702,100
Easy Goer, 1986 c., by Alydar	6	4	2	697,500
Answer Lively, 1996 c., by Lively One	7	4	2	695,296
Bet Twice, 1984 c., by Sportin' Life	7	5	3	690,565
First Samurai, 2003 c., by Giant's Causeway	5	4	2	682,575
Vindication, 2000 c., by Seattle Slew	4	4	2	680,950
Afleet Alex, 2002 c., by Northern Afleet	6	4	4	680,800
Spend a Buck, 1982 c., by Buckaroo	8	5	2	667,985
River Special, 1990 c., by Riverman	6	3	3	663,900
Capote, 1984 c., by Seattle Slew	4	3	2	654,680
Brocco, 1991 c., by Kris S.	4	3	1	653,550
Stephan's Odyssey, 1982 c., by Danzig	6	3	3	651,100
King Glorious, 1986 c., by Naevus	5	5	4	646,100
Henny Hughes, 2003 c., by Hennessy	6	3	3	644,820
Nownownow, 2005 c., by Whywhywhy	6	2	2	641,950
Forty Niner, 1985 c., by Mr. Prospector	6	5	4	634,908
Great Hunter, 2004 c., by Aptitude	7	2	2	630,000
Point Given, 1998 c., by Thunder Gulch	6	3	2	618,500
Swiss Yodeler, 1994 c., by Eastern Echo	9	6	5	617,200
Rhythm, 1987 c., by Mr. Prospector	5	3	1	612,920
Anees, 1997 c., by Unbridled	8	4	2	609,200
Music Merci, 1986 g., by Stop the Music	9	5	3	607,220
Is It True, 1986 c., by Raja Baba	6	2	1	605,342
Dehere, 1991 c., by Deputy Minister	7	5	4	595,912
Hennessy, 1993 c., by Storm Cat	9	4	3	580,400
Bertrando, 1989 c., by Skywalker	4	3	3	570,865
Buckpasser, 1963 c., by Tom Fool	11	9	6	568,096
Unbridled's Song, 1993 c., by Unbridled	3	2	1	568,000
Storm Cat, 1983 c., by Storm Bird	6	4	3	557,080

Leading Two-Year-Old Females by North American Earnings
North American Racing Only Through 2007

Horse, YOB Sex, Sire	Starts	Wins	Stakes Wins	Earnings
Indian Blessing, 2005 f., by Indian Charlie	3	3	2	$1,357,200
Dreaming of Anna, 2004 f., by Rahy	4	4	3	1,266,240
Silverbulletday, 1996 f., by Silver Deputy	7	6	5	1,114,110
Countess Diana, 1995 f., by Deerhound	6	5	4	1,019,785
Meadow Star, 1988 f., by Meadowlake	7	7	6	992,250
Storm Flag Flying, 2000 f., by Storm Cat	4	4	3	967,000
Brave Raj, 1984 f., by Rajab	9	6	5	933,650
Folklore, 2003 f., by Tiznow	4	3	2	927,500
Storm Song, 1994 f., by Summer Squall	7	4	3	898,205
Outstandingly, 1982 f., by Exclusive Native	6	3	2	867,872
Halfbridled, 2001 f., by Unbridled	4	4	3	849,400
Eliza, 1990 f., by Mt. Livermore	5	4	1	808,000
Family Style, 1983 f., by State Dinner	10	4	3	805,809
Flanders, 1992 f., by Seeking the Gold	5	4	3	805,000

Horse, YOB Sex, Sire	Starts	Wins	Stakes Wins	Earnings
Sweet Catomine, 2002 f., by Storm Cat	4	3	3	$799,800
Excellent Meeting, 1996 f., by General Meeting	8	4	3	773,824
Chilukki, 1997 f., by Cherokee Run	7	6	5	762,723
Phone Chatter, 1991 f., by Phone Trick	6	4	3	753,500
Open Mind, 1986 f., by Deputy Minister	6	4	3	724,064
Althea, 1981 f., by Alydar	9	5	4	692,625
Caressing, 1998 f., by Honour and Glory	5	3	2	690,642
Pleasant Stage, 1989 f., by Pleasant Colony	4	2	2	687,240
Surfside, 1997 f., by Seattle Slew	6	4	2	677,350
Golden Attraction, 1993 f., by Mr. Prospector	8	6	5	675,588
Tempera, 1999 f., by A.P. Indy	5	3	2	670,240
Cash Run, 1997 f., by Seeking the Gold	6	3	1	653,352
Twilight Ridge, 1983 f., by Cox's Ridge	5	3	2	617,808
My Flag, 1993 f., by Easy Goer	6	2	1	614,614
Balletto (UAE), 2002 f., by Timber Country	5	3	1	614,000
Ashado, 2001 f., by Saint Ballado	6	4	3	610,800
Octave, 2004 f., by Unbridled's Song	5	2	1	610,700
Proud Spell, 2005 f., by Proud Citizen	4	3	2	608,770
Raging Fever, 1998 f., by Storm Cat	6	5	4	598,500
Serena's Song, 1992 f., by Rahy	10	4	3	597,335
Runway Model, 2002 f., by Petionville	10	4	3	580,598
Boots 'n Jackie, 1990 f., by Major Moran	12	4	3	579,820
Country Star, 2005 f., by Empire Maker	3	2	2	575,900
Tappiano, 1984 f., by Fappiano	5	4	3	572,820
Sacahuista, 1984 f., by Raja Baba	9	4	3	564,965
I'm Splendid, 1983 f., by Our Native	7	4	3	560,857
Adieu, 2003 f., by El Corredor	6	4	3	554,470
Go for Wand, 1987 f., by Deputy Minister	4	3	1	548,390
Cara Rafaela, 1993 f., by Quiet American	9	3	2	546,962
You, 1999 f., by You and I	6	3	2	540,440
Life's Magic, 1981 f., by Cox's Ridge	7	2	1	537,259
Epitome, 1985 f., by Summing	8	3	2	534,805
Sardula, 1991 f., by Storm Cat	5	3	2	532,545
Be Gentle, 2001 f., by Tale of the Cat	7	4	3	523,078
Stella Madrid, 1987 f., by Alydar	7	4	3	519,096
Sharp Cat, 1994 f., by Storm Cat	7	4	2	505,950
Lost Kitty, 1988 f., by Magesterial	11	4	3	499,038
Aclassysassylassy, 2002 f., by Wild Event	7	5	4	498,800
She's a Devil Due, 1998 f., by Devil His Due	5	4	2	495,320
Love Lock, 1995 f., by Silver Ghost	9	4	3	483,122
Career Collection, 1995 f., by General Meeting	8	4	3	482,005
Arewehavingfunyet, 1983 f., by Sham	9	5	4	475,730
Nancy's Glitter, 1995 f., by Glitterman	8	5	4	464,460
Lea Lucinda, 1986 f., by Secreto	9	3	2	459,962
Three Ring, 1996 f., by Notebook	5	3	3	458,440
Private Treasure, 1988 f., by Explodent	8	3	2	457,242
Tiltalating, 1982 f., by Tilt Up	10	4	3	454,944
By the Light, 2005 f., by Malibu Moon	4	4	3	451,815

Horse, YOB Sex, Sire	Starts	Wins	Stakes Wins	Earnings
Alysheba, 1984 h., by Alydar	10	3	3	$2,511,156
Izvestia, 1987 h., by Icecapade	11	8	8	2,486,667
Sea Hero, 1990 h., by Polish Navy	9	2	2	2,484,190
Flower Alley, 2002 h., by Distorted Humor	9	4	3	2,435,200
Medaglia d'Oro, 1999 h., by El Prado (Ire)	9	4	3	2,250,600
Barbaro, 2003 c., by Dynaformer	5	4	4	2,233,200
Tabasco Cat, 1991 h., by Storm Cat	12	5	5	2,154,334
Seeking the Gold, 1985 h., by Mr. Prospector	12	6	4	2,145,620
Holy Bull, 1991 h., by Great Above	10	8	8	2,095,000
Forty Niner, 1985 h., by Mr. Prospector	13	6	5	2,091,092
Afleet Alex, 2002 h., by Northern Afleet	6	4	4	2,085,000
Sunshine Forever, 1985 h., by Roberto	12	8	5	2,032,636
Wando, 2000 h., by Langfuhr	8	5	5	2,017,323
Charismatic, 1996 h., by Summer Squall	10	4	3	2,007,404
Fusaichi Pegasus, 1997 h., by Mr. Prospector	8	6	4	1,987,800
Victory Gallop, 1995 h., by Cryptoclearance	8	3	3	1,981,720
Pine Bluff, 1989 h., by Danzig	6	3	3	1,970,896
Funny Cide, 2000 g., by Distorted Humor	8	2	2	1,963,200
Risen Star, 1985 h., by Secretariat	8	5	5	1,958,368
Empire Maker, 2000 h., by Unbridled	6	3	3	1,936,200
Proud Truth, 1982 h., by Graustark	11	7	5	1,926,327
Bet Twice, 1984 h., by Sportin' Life	9	3	3	1,922,642
Prized, 1986 h., by Kris S.	7	4	4	1,888,705
Captain Steve, 1997 h., by Fly So Free	11	3	3	1,382,276
Snow Chief, 1983 h., by Reflected Glory	9	6	6	1,375,200
Louis Quatorze, 1993 h., by Sovereign Dancer	12	4	2	1,354,908
Peace Rules, 2000 h., by Jules	7	3	3	1,350,000
Deputy Commander, 1994 h., by Deputy Minister	10	4	3	1,849,440
Giacomo, 2002 h., by Holy Bull	6	1	1	1,846,876
Manila, 1983 h., by Lyphard	10	8	6	1,814,729
Real Quiet, 1995 h., by Quiet American	6	2	2	1,788,800
With Approval, 1986 h., by Caro (Ire)	10	6	5	1,772,150
Coronado's Quest, 1995 h., by Forty Niner	11	5	5	1,739,950
Monarchos, 1998 h., by Maria's Mon	7	4	2	1,711,600
Menifee, 1996 h., by Harlan	9	3	2	1,695,400
General Challenge, 1996 g., by General Meeting	11	6	6	1,658,100
Silver Charm, 1994 h., by Silver Buck	7	3	3	1,638,750
Kitten's Joy, 2001 h., by El Prado (Ire)	8	6	6	1,625,796
Came Home, 1999 h., by Gone West	8	6	6	1,624,500
Java Gold, 1984 h., by Key to the Mint	8	6	6	1,621,300
Red Rocks (Ire), 2003 h., by Galileo (Ire)	1	1	1	1,620,000
Showing Up, 2003 h., by Strategic Mission	9	7	5	1,610,500
Harlan's Holiday, 1999 h., by Harlan	10	3	3	1,606,000
Bluegrass Cat, 2003 h., by Storm Cat	7	2	2	1,547,500
Ten Most Wanted, 2000 h., by Deputy Commander	10	4	3	1,544,860
Touch Gold, 1994 h., by Deputy Minister	7	4	3	1,522,313

Leading Three-Year-Old Males by North American Earnings in Single Season

North American Racing Only Through 2007

Horse, YOB Sex, Sire	Starts	Wins	Stakes Wins	Earnings
Smarty Jones, 2001 h., by Elusive Quality	7	6	6	$7,563,535
Curlin, 2004 c., by Smart Strike	9	6	5	5,102,800
Sunday Silence, 1986 h., by Halo	9	7	6	4,578,454
Easy Goer, 1986 h., by Alydar	11	8	8	3,837,150
Unbridled, 1987 h., by Fappiano	11	4	3	3,718,149
Spend a Buck, 1982 h., by Buckaroo	7	5	5	3,552,704
War Emblem, 1999 h., by Our Emblem	10	5	4	3,455,000
Tiznow, 1997 h., by Cee's Tizzy	9	5	4	3,445,950
Point Given, 1998 h., by Thunder Gulch	7	6	6	3,350,000
Street Sense, 2004 c., by Street Cry (Ire)	8	4	4	3,205,000
Bernardini, 2003 h., by A.P. Indy	8	6	5	3,060,480
Cat Thief, 1996 h., by Storm Cat	13	2	2	3,020,500
Skip Away, 1993 h., by Skip Trial	12	6	6	2,699,280
Thunder Gulch, 1992 h., by Gulch	10	7	7	2,644,080
A.P. Indy, 1989 h., by Seattle Slew	7	5	5	2,622,560
Hard Spun, 2004 c., by Danzig	10	4	4	2,572,500
Hansel, 1988 h., by Woodman	9	4	4	2,565,680
Concern, 1991 h., by Broad Brush	14	3	2	2,541,670

Leading Three-Year-Old Females by North American Earnings in Single Season

North American Racing Only Through 2007

Horse, YOB Sex, Sire	Starts	Wins	Stakes Wins	Earnings
Dance Smartly, 1988 m., by Danzig	8	8	8	$2,876,821
Ashado, 2001 m., by Saint Ballado	8	5	5	2,259,640
Spain, 1997 m., by Thunder Gulch	13	5	4	1,979,500
Silverbulletday, 1996 m., by Silver Deputy	11	8	8	1,707,640
Unbridled Elaine, 1998 m., by Unbridled's Song	8	4	3	1,663,175
Serena's Song, 1992 m., by Rahy	13	9	9	1,524,920
Banshee Breeze, 1995 m., by Unbridled	10	4	4	1,425,980
Take Charge Lady, 1999 m., by Dehere	10	6	6	1,388,635
Winning Colors, 1985 m., by Caro (Ire)	10	4	4	1,347,746
Rags to Riches, 2004 f., by A.P. Indy	6	5	4	1,340,028
Farda Amiga, 1999 m., by Broad Brush	6	3	2	1,248,902
Wait a While, 2003 m., by Maria's Mon	9	5	5	1,226,637
Ticker Tape (GB), 2001 f., by Royal Applause (GB)	10	5	5	1,159,075
Surfside, 1997 m., by Seattle Slew	7	4	4	1,147,637
Open Mind, 1986 m., by Deputy Minister	11	8	8	1,120,308
Island Fashion, 2000 m., by Petionville	10	4	4	1,112,970
Flute, 1998 m., by Seattle Slew	7	4	2	1,094,104

Horse, YOB Sex, Sire	Starts	Wins	Stakes Wins	Earnings
Octave, 2004 f., by Unbridled's Song	8	2	2	$1,050,234
Dancethruthedawn, 1998 m., by Mr. Prospector	6	3	2	1,045,039
Panty Raid, 2004 f., by Include	8	4	3	1,024,180
Xtra Heat, 1998 m., by Dixieland Heat	13	9	9	1,012,040
Lady's Secret, 1982 m., by Secretariat	17	10	10	994,349
Stellar Jayne, 2001 m., by Wild Rush	13	3	3	992,169
Ajina, 1994 m., by Strawberry Road (Aus)	9	3	3	979,175
Elloluv, 2000 m., by Gilded Time	8	2	2	978,775
Jostle, 1997 m., by Brocco	9	4	4	975,570
Arravale, 2003 m., by Arch	5	3	3	971,160
Ryafan, 1994 m., by Lear Fan	3	3	3	968,000
Sealy Hill, 2004 f., by Point Given	8	4	4	958,389
Dimitrova, 2000 m., by Swain (Ire)	4	2	2	950,000
Keeper Hill, 1995 m., by Deputy Minister	8	3	2	949,410
Very Subtle, 1984 m., by Hoist the Silver	12	6	6	947,135
My Flag, 1993 m., by Easy Goer	10	4	4	933,043
Society Selection, 2001 m., by Coronado's Quest	9	3	3	929,700
Sharp Cat, 1994 m., by Storm Cat	11	7	7	911,300
Exogenous, 1998 m., by Unbridled	7	4	2	901,500
Hollywood Wildcat, 1990 m., by Kris S.	9	5	5	893,330
You, 1999 m., by You and I	9	4	4	883,805
Life's Magic, 1981 m., by Cox's Ridge	12	4	4	873,956
Imperial Gesture, 1999 m., by Langfuhr	5	3	2	873,600
Blushing K. D., 1994 m., by Blushing John	8	6	6	845,040
Secret Status, 1997 m., by A.P. Indy	9	5	3	842,796
Go for Wand, 1987 m., by Deputy Minister	9	7	7	824,948
Life At the Top, 1983 m., by Seattle Slew	18	6	5	821,349
Bird Town, 2000 m., by Cape Town	8	3	3	815,976
Lady Joanne, 2004 f., by Orientate	7	4	3	808,993
Lite Light, 1988 m., by Majestic Light	9	5	5	804,685
Goodbye Halo, 1985 m., by Halo	11	5	5	789,117
Yearly Report, 2001 m., by General Meeting	7	5	5	787,500
Summerly, 2002 m., by Summer Squall	7	4	3	786,728
Six Perfections (Fr) 2000 m., by Celtic Swing	1	1	1	780,000
Mystic Lady, 1998 m., by Thunder Gulch	11	6	6	775,000
Bushfire, 2003 m., by Louis Quatorze	9	5	4	761,659
Yanks Music, 1993 m., by Air Forbes Won	7	5	4	751,000
Dispute, 1990 m., by Danzig	11	6	4	750,226
Bear Now, 2004 f., by Tiznow	8	4	4	747,517
Ouija Board (GB), 2001 m., by Cape Cross (Ire)	1	1	1	733,200
Affluent, 1998 m., by Affirmed	10	4	3	725,200
Sacahuista, 1984 m., by Raja Baba	9	2	2	724,857
Banks Hill (GB), 1998 m., by Danehill	1	1	1	722,800

Horse, YOB Sex, Sire	Age	Starts	Wins	Stakes Wins	Earnings
Criminal Type, 1985 h., by Alydar	5	11	7	6	$2,270,290
Theatrical (Ire), 1982 h., by Nureyev	5	9	7	7	2,235,500
Bertrando, 1989 h., by Skywalker	4	9	3	3	2,217,800
Mineshaft, 1999 h., by A.P. Indy	4	9	7	7	2,209,686
Ferdinand, 1983 h., by Nijinsky II	4	10	4	4	2,185,150
Gentlemen (Arg), 1992 h., by Robin des Bois	5	6	4	4	2,125,300
Fantastic Light, 1996 h., by Rahy	5	1	1	1	2,112,800
Wild Again, 1980 h., by Icecapade	4	16	6	4	2,054,409
Daylami (Ire), 1994 h., by Doyoun	5	1	1	1	2,040,000
Great Communicator, 1983 g., by Key to the Kingdom	5	11	6	6	2,017,950
Chief Bearhart, 1993 h., by Chief's Crown	4	7	5	5	2,011,259
Festin (Arg), 1986 h., by Mat-Boy (Arg)	5	11	3	3	2,003,250
Medaglia d'Oro, 1999 h., by El Prado (Ire)	4	5	3	3	1,990,000
Kotashaan (Fr), 1988 h., by Darshaan	5	9	6	6	1,984,100
Kip Deville, 2003 h., by Kipling	4	7	3	3	1,965,780
Pleasant Tap, 1987 h., by Pleasant Colony	5	10	4	4	1,959,914
Devil His Due, 1989 h., by Devil's Bag	4	11	4	4	1,939,120
Paradise Creek, 1989 h., by Irish River (Fr)	5	10	8	8	1,920,872
Strike the Gold, 1988 h., by Alydar	4	13	2	2	1,920,176
Miesque's Approval, 1999 h., by Miesque's Son	7	7	5	5	1,906,405
Buck's Boy, 1993 g., by Bucksplasher	5	10	6	6	1,874,020
Skywalker, 1982 h., by Relaunch	4	9	4	4	1,811,400
John Henry, 1975 g., by Ole Bob Bowers	6	10	8	8	1,798,030
Cloudy's Knight, 2000 g., by Lord Avie	7	9	3	3	1,762,868
Albert the Great, 1997 h., by Go for Gin	4	9	3	3	1,740,000
Budroyale, 1993 g., by Cee's Tizzy	6	11	4	4	1,735,640
Sky Classic, 1987 h., by Nijinsky II	5	9	5	5	1,735,482
Behrens, 1994 h., by Pleasant Colony	5	9	4	4	1,735,000
Roses in May, 2000 h., by Devil His Due	4	6	5	3	1,723,277
Lemon Drop Kid, 1996 h., by Kingmambo	4	9	5	4	1,673,900
Best Pal, 1988 g., by *Habitony	4	5	4	4	1,672,000
Star of Cozzene, 1988 h., by Cozzene	5	11	6	6	1,620,744
Southern Image, 2000 h., by Halo's Image	4	4	3	3	1,612,150
Congaree, 1998 h., by Arazi	5	9	5	5	1,608,000
Milwaukee Brew, 1997 h., by Wild Again	5	7	2	2	1,590,000
Twilight Agenda, 1986 h., by Devil's Bag	5	11	6	5	1,563,600
Arcangues, 1988 h., by Sagace (Fr)	5	1	1	1	1,560,000
Borrego, 2001 h., by El Prado (Ire)	4	8	3	2	1,536,600
Fraise, 1988 h., by Strawberry Road (Aus)	4	10	5	2	1,534,720
Turkoman, 1982 h., by Alydar	4	8	4	4	1,531,664
Marlin, 1993 h., by Sword Dance (Ire)	4	10	4	4	1,521,600
Steinlen (GB), 1983 h., by Habitat	6	11	7	4	1,521,378
English Channel, 2002 h., by Smart Strike	4	7	4	4	1,507,937
With Anticipation, 1995 g., by Relaunch	7	8	3	3	1,507,700
Perfect Drift, 1999 g., by Dynaformer	4	8	5	4	1,505,388

Leading Males Four or Older by North American Earnings in Single Season

North American Racing Only Through 2007

Horse, YOB Sex, Sire	Age	Starts	Wins	Stakes Wins	Earnings
Cigar, 1990 h., by Palace Music	5	10	10	9	$4,819,800
Skip Away, 1993 h., by Skip Trial	4	11	4	4	4,089,000
Awesome Again, 1994 h., by Deputy Minister	4	6	6	5	3,845,990
Alysheba, 1984 h., by Alydar	4	9	7	7	3,808,600
Saint Liam, 2000 h., by Saint Ballado	5	6	4	4	3,696,960
Invasor (Arg), 2002 h., by Candy Stripes	4	4	4	4	3,690,000
Tiznow, 1997 h., by Cee's Tizzy	4	6	3	3	2,981,880
Lava Man, 2001 g., by Slew City Slew	5	8	7	7	2,770,000
Skip Away, 1993 h., by Skip Trial	5	9	7	7	2,740,000
English Channel, 2002 h., by Smart Strike	5	6	4	3	2,640,000
Slew o' Gold, 1980 h., by Seattle Slew	4	6	5	4	2,627,944
Farma Way, 1987 h., by Marfa	4	11	5	5	2,598,350
Ghostzapper, 2000 h., by Awesome Again	4	4	4	4	2,590,000
Alphabet Soup, 1991 h., by Cozzene	5	7	4	4	2,536,450
Cigar, 1990 h., by Palace Music	6	7	4	4	2,510,000
Black Tie Affair (Ire), 1986 h., by Miswaki	5	10	8	7	2,483,540
Pleasantly Perfect, 1998 h., by Pleasant Colony	5	4	2	2	2,470,000
Volponi, 1958 h., by Cryptoclearance	4	8	3	2	2,389,200
John Henry, 1975 g., by Ole Bob Bowers	9	9	6	6	2,336,650
Silver Charm, 1994 h., by Silver Buck	4	8	5	5	2,296,506

Leading Females Four and Older by North American Earnings in a Single Season

North American Racing Only Through 2007

Horse, YOB Sex, Sire	Age	Starts	Wins	Stakes Wins	Earnings
Azeri, 1998 m., by Jade Hunter	4	9	8	7	$2,181,540
Escena, 1993 m., by Strawberry Road (Aus)	5	9	5	5	2,032,425
Lady's Secret, 1982 m., by Secretariat	4	15	10	10	1,871,053
Ginger Punch, 2003 m., by Awesome Again	4	8	5	4	1,827,060
Beautiful Pleasure, 1995 m., by Maudlin	4	7	4	3	1,716,404
Lahudood (GB), 2003 m., by Singspiel (Ire)	4	5	3	2	1,560,500
Paseana (Arg), 1987 m., by Ahmad	5	9	7	7	1,518,290
Fleet Indian, 2001 m., by Indian Charlie	5	7	6	6	1,473,720
Round Pond, 2002 m., by Awesome Again	4	5	3	2	1,469,400
Bayakoa (Arg), 1984 m., by Consultant's Bid	5	11	9	8	1,406,403
Riboletta (Brz), 1995 m., by Roi Normand	5	11	7	7	1,384,860
Perfect Sting, 1996 m., by Red Ransom	4	6	5	5	1,367,000
Banshee Breeze, 1995 m., by Unbridled	4	7	4	4	1,358,818
Miss Alleged, 1987 m., by Alleged	4	8	3	2	1,345,000
Heritage of Gold, 1995 m., by Gold Legend	5	8	5	5	1,332,282
Pleasant Home, 2001 m., by seeking the Gold	4	8	4	4	1,316,420
Intercontinental (GB), 2000 m., by Danehill	5	7	5	5	1,271,200
Bayakoa (Arg), 1984 m., by Consultant's Bid	6	10	7	7	1,234,406
Personal Ensign, 1984 m., by Private Account	4	7	7	7	1,202,640

Racing — Winningest Horse

Horse, YOB Sex, Sire	Age	Starts	Stakes Wins	Wins	Earnings
Soaring Softly, 1995 m., by Kris S.	4	8	7	5	$1,193,450
Ouija Board (GB), 2001 m., by Cape Cross (Ire)	5	1	1	1	1,188,000
Estrapade, 1980 m., by *Vaguely Noble	6	9	3	3	1,184,800
Sightseek, 1999 m., by Distant View	4	8	4	4	1,171,888
Serena's Song, 1992 m., by Rahy	4	15	5	5	1,161,133
Adoration, 1999 m., by Honor Grades	4	5	2	2	1,160,750
Inside Information, 1991 m., by Private Account	4	8	7	6	1,160,408
Jewel Princess, 1992 m., by Key to the Mint	4	9	5	5	1,150,800
Unbridled Belle, 2003 m., by Broken Vow	4	5	2	2	1,116,500
Golden Apples (Ire), 1998 m., by Pivotal	4	7	3	3	1,111,680
Heat Haze (GB), 1999 m., by Green Desert	4	7	4	4	1,101,460
Precious Kitten, 2003 m., by Catienus	4	9	4	4	1,090,000
Tout Charmant, 1996 m., by Slewvescent	4	7	3	3	1,089,044
Ashado, 2001 m., by Saint Ballado	4	7	3	3	1,061,000
Azeri, 1998 m., by Jade Hunter	6	8	3	3	1,035,000
Royal Heroine (Ire), 1980 m., by Lypheor (GB)	4	8	4	4	1,023,500
Sightseek, 1999 m., by Distant View	5	7	4	4	1,011,350
Summer Colony, 1998 m., by Summer Squall	4	8	4	4	992,500
Honey Ryder, 2001 m., by Lasting Approval	5	7	4	4	988,500
Hystericalady, 2003 m., by Distorted Humor	4	8	3	2	984,438
Nashoba's Key, 2003 m., by Silver Hawk	4	8	7	5	972,090
Storm Flag Flying, 2000 m., by Storm Cat	4	8	3	2	963,248
Safely Kept, 1986 m., by Horatius	4	10	8	7	959,280
Paseana (Arg), 1987 m., by Ahmad	6	8	3	3	950,402
Manistique, 1995 m., by Unbridled	4	9	6	6	935,100
Gorella (Fr), 2002 m., by Grape Tree Road (GB)	4	6	4	3	923,638
Lu Ravi, 1995 m., by A.P. Indy	5	8	3	3	918,200
Honey Ryder, 2001 m., by Lasting Approval	4	7	5	5	910,980
Happy Ticket, 2001 m., by Anet	5	7	2	2	906,578
Pebbles (GB), 1981 m., by Sharpen Up (GB)	4	1	1	1	900,000
Maryfield, 2001 m., by Elusive Quality	6	8	3	3	896,330
Heavenly Prize, 1991 m., by Seeking the Gold	4	7	4	4	895,900
Tuzla (Fr), 1994 m., by Panoramic (GB)	5	8	4	4	889,080
Flawlessly, 1988 m., by Affirmed	5	5	4	4	886,700
Spook Express (SAf), 1994 m., by Comic Blush	7	8	3	3	866,870
Happyanunoit (NZ), 1995 m., by Yachtie	4	8	4	3	862,792

Winningest Horses of All Time
North American Racing Only
Through 2007

Horse, YOB Sex, Sire	Starts	Wins	Earnings
Kingston, 1884 h., by Spendthrift	138	89	$140,195
Bankrupt, 1883 g., by Spendthrift	348	86	41,260
King Crab, 1885 g., by Kingfisher	310	85	55,682
Little Minch, 1880 h., by Glenelg	222	85	58,225
Hiblaze, 1935 h., by Blazes	406	79	32,647
Tippity Witchet, 1915 g., by Broomstick	265	78	88,241
Pan Zareta, 1910 m., by Abe Frank	151	76	39,082
Badge, 1885 h., by *Ill-Used	167	70	73,253
Raceland, 1885 g., by *Billet	130	70	116,391
W. B. Gates, 1896, g., by Prince Royal	297	70	26,541
Geraldine, 1885 m., by Grinstead	185	69	43,020
Care Free, 1918 g., by Colin	227	67	59,873
Welsh Lad, 1934 g., by Prince of Wales	329	67	25,317
Shot One, 1941 g., by Shoeless Joe	360	65	29,982
Perhaps, 1918, g., by Luke McLuke	350	64	38,865
Sweepstakes, 1920, g., by Sweep	220	63	50,054
Worthowning, 1935 g., by *Longworth	339	63	41,830
Back Bay, 1908 g., by Rubicon	289	62	40,377
Banquet, 1887 g., by *Rayon d'Or	166	62	118,872
Ed R., 1948 g., by Donnay	248	62	63,552
Imp, 1894 m., by *Wagner	171	62	70,069
Leochares, 1910 g., by Broomstick	175	62	68,867
Seth's Hope, 1924 h., by Seth	327	62	74,341
Vantime, 1939 g., by Playtime	295	62	46,290
Brandon Prince, 1929 h., by *Axenstein	280	61	47,287
Irene's Bob, 1929 h., by The Turk	237	61	58,010
Kenilworth, 1898 h., by *Sir Modred	163	61	28,255
Molasses Bill, 1933 g., by *Challenger II	262	61	50,699

Horse, YOB Sex, Sire	Starts	Wins	Earnings
Mucho Gusto, 1932 h., by Marvin May	217	61	$101,880
Shuchor, 1936 g., by Haste	261	61	33,607
Vantryst, 1936 h., by Tryster	334	61	31,971
Frank Fogarty, 1918 g., by Wrack	270	60	47,651
George de Mar, 1922 h., by *Colonel Vennie	333	60	69,091
Indiantown, 1930 h., by Trojan	224	60	55,455
Lewis A. D., 1947 h., by Galway	212	60	65,482
Merrick, 1903 g., by *Golden Garter	189	60	25,718
Noah's Pride, 1929 g., by Noah	317	60	41,507
Parole, 1873 g., by Leamington	127	59	82,111
Pearl Jennings, 1879 m., by Lelaps	163	59	55,332
Strathmeath, 1888 g., by Strathmore	133	59	114,958
Charlie Boy, 1955 h., by Graphic	241	58	207,642
Dr. Hickman, 1917 g., by Tony Bonero	166	58	54,136
Flag Bearer, 1926 h., by *Porte Drapeau	222	58	37,683
Golden Arrow, 1961 h., by Fort Salonga	176	58	167,264
Matinee Idol, 1915 g., by *All Gold	290	58	52,484
Top o' the Morning, 1912 h., by Peep o'Day	217	58	48,120
Columcille, 1948 h., by Alaking	182	57	89,665
El Puma, 1929 h., by *Spanish Prince II	242	57	44,807
End of Street, 1963 h., by Bunty's Flight	202	57	67,686
Bulwark, 1933 h., by *Bull Dog	252	56	65,125
Donald MacDonald, 1906, g., by Sombrero	146	56	36,980
Jack Atkin, 1904 h., by *Sain	131	56	84,450
Thistle Belle, 1906, m., by *Knight of the Thistle	272	56	16,675
Matchup, 1936 h., by Misstep	229	55	58,528
Tommy Whelan, 1936 g., by Enoch	233	55	33,279
Vote Boy, 1932 g., by Torchilla	304	55	39,240
Argos, 1937 g., by *Happy Argo	215	54	37,507
Bad News, 1900, g., by Flying Dutchman	186	54	46,889
Bee Golly, 1942 m., by Bee Line	183	53	54,544
Crying for More, 1965 h., by I'm For More	192	53	183,685
Door Prize, 1952 g., by Eight Thirty	131	53	109,920
Enfield, 1906 h., by *Star Shoot	180	53	18,998
Hamburger Jim, 1928 h., by Whiskaway	212	53	24,383
Onus, 1933 g., by Jack High	344	53	32,039
Post War Style, 1941 m., by Burgoo King	179	53	52,600
Agrarian-U, 1942 g., by Agrarian	236	52	199,345
Aliviso, 1932 h., by *Hand Grenade	193	52	41,898
Billy Brier, 1953 g., by Bunty Lawless	231	52	83,168
Cloudy Weather, 1934 g., by Mud	294	52	53,487
Fleet Argo, 1947 g., by *Happy Argo	243	52	149,000
Float Away, 1936 g., by Whiskaway	265	52	61,365
High Private, 1906 g., by *Oddfellow	129	52	50,182
My Blaze, 1930 h., by Big Blaze	338	52	32,707
Old Kickapoo, 1924 h., by Runnymede	217	52	35,827
Port Conway Lane, 1969 h., by Bold Commander	242	52	431,593
Roseben, 1901 g., by Ben Strome	111	52	75,310
Air Patrol, 1941 h., by Sun Teddy	146	51	63,100
Blenweed, 1938 g., by *Blenheim II	202	51	105,415
Commendable, 1935 g., by Insco	163	51	30,583
Dr. Johnson, 1940 h., by *Boswell	256	51	54,422
Estin, 1923 g., by Westy Hogan	205	51	46,901
Gay Parisian, 1924 g., by *Parisian Diamond	209	51	49,197
Sagely, 1970 h., by Sage and Sand	124	51	116,196
Small Change, 1930 h., by Aromatic	200	51	18,495
Talked About, 1934 h., by The Porter	235	51	49,447

Most Wins by Decade by Year of Birth
North American Racing Only
1931-1940

Horse, YOB Sex, Sire	Yrs. Raced	Starts	Wins	Earnings
Hiblaze, 1935 h., by Blazes	14	406	79	$32,647
Welsh Lad, 1934 g., by Prince of Wales	13	329	67	25,317
Worthowning, 1935 g., by *Longworth	14	339	63	41,830
Vantime, 1939 g., by Playtime	13	295	62	46,290
Molasses Bill, 1933 g., by *Challenger II	13	262	61	50,699
Mucho Gusto, 1932 h., by Marvin May	9	217	61	101,880
Shuchor, 1936 g., by Haste	13	261	61	33,607
Vantryst, 1936 h., by Tryster	13	334	61	31,971
Bulwark, 1933 h., by *Bull Dog	14	252	56	65,125
Matchup, 1936 h., by Misstep	12	229	55	58,528

Racing — Most Consecutive Victories

1941-1950

Horse, YOB Sex, Sire	Yrs. Raced	Starts	Wins	Earnings
Shot One, 1941 g., by Shoeless Joe	13	360	65	$29,982
Ed R., 1948 g., by Donnay	14	248	62	63,552
Lewis A. D., 1947 h., by Galway	12	212	60	65,482
Columcille, 1948 h., by Alaking	11	182	57	89,665
Bee Golly, 1942 m., by Bee Line	11	183	53	54,544
Post War Style, 1941 m., by Burgoo King	10	179	53	52,600
Agrarian-U, 1942 g., by Agrarian	12	236	52	199,345
Fleet Argc, 1947 g., by *Happy Argo	12	243	52	149,000
Air Patrol, 1941 h., by Sun Teddy	10	146	51	163,100
Brownskin, 1946 h., by Martinus	10	224	50	77,913

1951-1960

Horse, YOB Sex, Sire	Yrs. Raced	Starts	Wins	Earnings
Charlie Boy, 1955 h., by Graphic	11	241	58	$207,642
Door Prize, 1952 g., by Eight Thirty	10	131	53	109,920
Billy Brier, 1953 g., by Bunty Lawless	12	231	52	83,168
Go Lite, 1960 h., by Go Lightly	11	211	50	96,938
Imahead, 1955 h., by *Beau Gem	13	246	49	69,884
Apple, 1958 g., by *Ambiorix	15	195	48	102,385
Bill Pac, 1951 h., by Billings	10	272	48	73,374
Annette G., 1951 m., by Holdall	10	237	47	68,932
Aquanotte, 1960 h., by Decathlon	10	142	47	80,603
Grand Wizard, 1956 g., by Poised	13	220	47	222,312

1961-1970

Horse, YOB Sex, Sire	Yrs. Raced	Starts	Wins	Earnings
Golden Arrow, 1961 h., by Fort Salonga	16	176	58	$167,264
End of Street, 1963 h., by Bunty's Flight	11	202	57	67,686
Crying for More, 1965 h., by I'm For More	11	192	53	183,685
Port Conway Lane, 1969 h., by Bold Commander	13	242	52	431,593
Sagely, 1970 h., by Sage and Sand	14	124	51	116,196
Big Devil, 1963 h., by Call Over	12	237	50	222,715
Frosty Admiral, 1961 h., by Ace Admiral	9	151	50	166,305
Bayou Teche, 1961 g., by Bryan G.	12	281	48	107,577
Flyingphere, 1961 g., by Mr. Hemisphere	14	213	48	85,683
Saturnina, 1967 m., by *Ballydonnell	5	107	47	392,195

1971-1980

Horse, YOB Sex, Sire	Yrs. Raced	Starts	Wins	Earnings
Time to Bid, 1975 h., by Jig Time	12	179	50	$241,247
Dot the T., 1972 h., by *Notable II	12	261	48	227,033
Dobi's Knight, 1971 g., by Dobi Deenar	12	219	45	178,996
Guy, 1974 h., by Golden Ruler	11	161	45	281,085
Chrystal Gail, 1973 m., by Special Dunce	11	137	43	154,910
Flying Hitch, 1972 h., by Double Hitch	8	125	43	124,352
Kintla's Folly, 1972 g., by Run Like Mad	10	130	43	397,761
Norman Pensive, 1974 h., by Skookum	11	161	43	169,947
Missouri Brave, 1972 h., by *Indian Chief II	13	137	42	116,717
Moxeytown, 1977 h., by L'Aiglon	10	116	41	216,652

1981-1990

Horse, YOB Sex, Sire	Yrs. Raced	Starts	Wins	Earnings
Win Man, 1985 g., by Con Man	9	178	48	$416,316
Jilsie's Gigalo, 1984 g., by Gallant Knave	11	136	45	315,456
Boca Ratony, 1988 g., by Boca Rio	12	139	41	133,715
Best Boy's Jade, 1989 g., by Raja's Best Boy	12	175	40	223,983
Last Don B., 1987 g., by Don B.	9	104	40	471,461
Noble But Nasty, 1981 g., by Nasty and Bold	11	200	40	325,588
Sawmill Run, 1988 g., by It's Freezing	12	160	40	253,744
Inspector Mcomaw, 1987 g., by Entropy	10	179	38	269,052
Little Bold John, 1982 g., by John Alden	9	105	38	1,956,406
The Hive Five, 1983 g., by Raja Baba	10	159	38	178,907

1991-2000

Horse, YOB Sex, Sire	Yrs. Raced	Starts	Wins	Earnings
Bandit Bomber, 1991 h., by Prosperous	5	49	39	$471,445
Shotgun Pro, 1993 g., by Shot Gun Scott	9	137	39	250,862
Oh So Fabulous, 1992 g., by Singular	10	125	38	286,339
Secret Service Man, 1992 g., by Shot Gun Scott	9	132	37	364,263
Lightning Al, 1993 h., by Fortunate Prospect	7	63	36	680,146
J V Bennett, 1993 g., by Key to the Mint	11	109	35	438,431
Maybe Jack, 1993 g., by Classic Account	10	122	35	534,715
Cumberland Gap, 1992 g., by Allen's Prospect	12	156	34	323,345
Say Florida Sandy, 1994 h., by Personal Flag	8	98	33	2,085,408
King Kenny Roberts, 1991 g., by Slew Machine	9	107	32	166,306

2001-2007

Horse, YOB Sex, Sire	Yrs. Raced	Starts	Wins	Earnings
Ask Queenie, 2001 m., by Key Contender	5	42	22	$558,705
Catlaunch, 2001 g., by Noble Cat	5	55	20	430,418
Outcashem, 2001 g., by Mazel Trick	5	35	19	532,671
Thisonesforsam, 2001 g., by Safely's Mark	4	47	19	241,075
Code of Justice, 2001 m., by Double Honor	4	44	18	300,673
Demus, 2001 m., by Suave Prospect	5	51	18	178,966
Fortunate Trail, 2001 g., by Fortunate Prospect	4	55	18	253,240
Parthenope, 2001 m., by K. O. Punch	5	59	18	151,660
Rocky Gulch, 2001 g., by Dry Gulch	5	38	18	1,151,725
Shouldbevictory, 2001 g., by Victory Speech	5	44	18	114,041

Most Consecutive Victories

Camarero, an unfamiliar name to almost all racing fans, holds the record for the most consecutive victories by a Thoroughbred. His 56 straight wins were not registered in the sport's sometimes murky and poorly documented distant past, however. He raced in the 1950s, going undefeated until his 57th career start. All of his races were in Puerto Rico and were against other Puerto Rican-bred horses. Camarero broke the win mark set by undefeated Kincsem, a Hungarian-bred mare who raced in the late 19th century. Boston made the list of most consecutive wins twice, with 19 wins from 1839-'42 and 17 straight wins from 1836-'38.

Citation and Cigar share the modern North American record for most consecutive victories, 16, along with Louisiana-bred mare Hallowed Dreams, who won many of her races against overmatched state-breds. Citation and Cigar competed at the highest level of the sport in North America while compiling their win skeins.

Cons. Wins	Horse	YOB	Where Raced
56	Camarero	1951	Puerto Rico
54	Kincsem	1874	Europe, England
39	Galgo Jr.	1928	Puerto Rico
23	Leviathan	1793	United States
22	Miss Petty	1981	Australia
	Pooker T.	1957	Puerto Rico
21	Bond's First Consul	1798	United States
	Lottery	1803	United States
	Meteor	1783	England
	Picnic in the Park	1979	Australia
20	Fashion	1837	United States
	Filch	1773	Ireland
	Kentucky	1861	United States
19	Boston	1833	United States
	Skiff	1821	Scotland
18	Hindoo	1878	United States
	Karayel	1970	Turkey
17	Alice Hawthorn	1838	England
	Beeswing	1835	United States
	Boston	1833	United States
	Careless	1751	England
	Dudley	1914	England
	Gradisco	1957	Venezuela
	Hanover	1884	United States
	Harkaway	1834	Ireland
	Mainbrace	1947	New Zealand
	Silent Witness	1999	Hong Kong
	Sir Ken	1947	England
16	Cigar	1990	United States
	Citation	1945	United States
	Hallowed Dreams	1997	United States
	Luke Blackburn	1877	United States
	Master Bagot	1787	Ireland
	Minimo	1968	Turkey
	Miss Woodford	1880	United States
	Mister Frisky	1987	Puerto Rico, U.S.
	*Ormonde	1883	England
	Prestige	1903	France

Cons. Wins	Horse	YOB	Where Raced
16	*Ribot	1952	Europe, England
	The Bard	1883	England
15	Bayardo	1906	England
	*Bernborough	1939	Australia
	Brigadier Gerard	1968	England
	Buckpasser	1963	United States
	Carbine	1885	New Zealand, Australia
	Colin	1905	United States
	Macon	1922	Argentina
	Pretty Polly	1901	England, France
	Rattler	1816	United States
	Squanderer	1973	India
	Thebais	1878	England
	Vander Pool	1928	United States
14	Friponnier	1864	England
	Harry Bassett	1868	United States
	Lucifer	1813	Scotland
	Man o' War	1917	United States
	Nearco	1935	Europe
	Peppers Pride	2003	United States
	*Phar Lap	1926	New Zealand, Australia, Mexico
	*Prince Charlie	1869	England
	Springfield	1873	England
13	Dungannon	1780	England
	Effie Deans	1815	England
	Grano de Oro	1937	Ireland, Venezuela
	Hippolitus	1767	Ireland
	Kingston	1884	United States
	Limerick	1923	New Zealand, Australia
	Morello	1890	United States
	Personal Ensign	1984	United States
	Phenomenom	1780	England
	Planet	1855	United States
	Polar Star	1904	England
	Rockingham	1781	England
	Sweet Wall	1925	Ireland
	The Flying Dutchman	1846	England
	Timoleon	1814	United States
	Tremont	1884	United States
	Weimar	1968	Italy

Leading Unbeaten Racehorses

A rare breed indeed is the racehorse that completes its career without a defeat on its record. No modern horse can ever expect to equal the record of Kincsem, who went unbeaten in 54 starts over five racing seasons in Hungary. Although her pedigree was largely English, she was bred in Hungary; her name derives from the Magyar "kincs," which means treasure or jewel. The word itself means "my treasure," and she indeed was a jewel.

Following are some of the best-known horses who have retired unbeaten after careers at the top levels of their divisions. Eclipse's record, in particular, is worth noting because 18th-century records are unreliable. He is attributed in various sources with anywhere from ten to 18 victories. In this listing, he is assigned the highest number, and the one fact for certain is that he never was beaten.

Wins, Horse, YOB Sex, Pedigree
54 **Kincsem,** 1874 m., Cambuscan—Waternymph, by Cotswold
18 **Eclipse,** 1764 h., Marske—Spiletta, by Regulus
16 ***Ormonde,** 1883 h., Bend Or—Lily Agnes, by Macaroni
 ***Ribot,** 1952 h., Tenerani—Romanella, by El Greco
15 **Colin,** 1905 h., Commando—*Pastorella, by Springfield
14 **Nearco,** 1935 h., Pharos—Nogara, by Havresac II
13 **Personal Ensign,** 1984 m., Private Account—Grecian Banner, by Hoist the Flag
 Tremont, 1884 h., Virgil—Ann Fief, by Alarm
12 **Asteroid,** 1861 h., by Lexington—Nebula, by *Glencoe
 Barcaldine, 1878 h., Solon—Ballyroe, by Belladrum
 Crucifix, 1837 m., *Priam—Octaviana, by Octavian
9 ***Bahram,** 1932 h., Blandforc—Friar's Daughter, by Friar Marcus
 St. Simon, 1881 h., Galopin—St. Angela, by King Tom
8 **American Eclipse,** 1814 h., Duroc—Millers Damsel, by *Messenger
 Caracalla, 1942 h., Tourbillon—Astronomie, by Asterus
 Rare Brick, 1983 h., Rare Performer—Windy Brick, by Mr. Brick
 Sensation, 1877 h., *Leamington—Susan Beane, by Lexington
7 **El Rio Rey,** 1887 h., Norfolk—Mar an, by Malcolm
 Flying Childers, 1715 h., Darley Arabian—Betty Leedes, by Careless
 Regulus, 1739 h., Godolphin Arabian—Grey Robinson, by Bald Galloway
 The Tetrarch, 1911 h., Roi Herode—Vahren, by Bona Vista
6 **Candy Ride (Arg),** 1999 h., Ride the Rails—Candy Girl, by Candy Stripes
5 **Ajax,** 1901 h., Flying Fox—Amie, by Clamart
 Bay Middleton, 1833 h., Sultan—Cobweb, by Phantom
 Landaluce, 1980 f., Seattle Slew—Strip Poker, by Bold Bidder
 Norfolk, 1861 h., Lexington—Novice, by *Glencoe
4 **Cactus Ridge,** 2001 h., Hennessy—Double Park (Fr), by Lycius
 Golden Fleece, 1979 h., Nijinsky II—Exotic Treat, by *Vaguely Noble
 Kneller, 1985 h., Lomond—Fruition, by Rheingold
 Lammtarra, 1992 h., Nijinsky II—Snow Bride, by Blushing Groom (Fr)
 Raise a Native, 1961 h., Native Dancer—Raise You, by Case Ace
 Vindication, 2000 h., Seattle Slew—Strawberry Reason, by Strawberry Road (Aus)

Leading Winners of Million-Dollar Races in North America

Horse, YOB Sex	Starts in $1-M Races	Wins in $1-M Races	Earnings in $1-M Races
Skip Away, 1993 h.	8	5	$4,798,000
Lava Man, 2001 g.	8	4	2,476,667
Point Given, 1998 h.	5	4	2,750,000
Afleet Alex, 2002 h.	5	3	2,350,000
Cigar, 1990 h.	6	3	3,740,000
Curlin, 2004 c.	6	3	4,450,000
Easy Goer, 1986 h.	4	3	2,401,020
Funny Cide, 2000 g.	7	3	2,360,200
Lemon Drop Kid, 1996 h.	8	3	2,035,400
Smarty Jones, 2001 h.	4	3	2,334,800
Street Sense, 2004 h.	5	3	3,585,000
Tiznow, 1997 h.	4	3	5,360,400
Alysheba, 1984 h.	5	2	2,557,916
A.P. Indy, 1989 h.	3	2	2,048,880
Barbaro, 2003 c.	3	2	2,053,200
Bernardini, 2003 h.	3	2	2,200,000
Bertrando, 1989 h.	6	2	1,675,000
Best Pal, 1988 g.	11	2	2,237,000
Birdstone, 2001 h.	4	2	1,200,000
Borrego, 2001 h.	7	2	1,520,000
Charismatic, 1996 h.	3	2	1,646,200
Chief Bearhart, 1993 h.	6	2	2,162,000
Criminal Type, 1985 h.	3	2	1,350,000
Dance Smartly, 1988 m.	2	2	1,782,140
Empire Maker, 2000 h.	3	2	1,370,000
Free House, 1994 h.	4	2	1,385,000
General Challenge, 1996 g.	6	2	1,560,000
Gentlemen (Arg), 1992 h.	7	2	1,840,000
Go Between, 2003 h.	4	2	1,460,000
High Chaparral (Ire), 1999 h.	2	2	2,021,600
Izvestia, 1987 h.	5	2	1,813,600
John Henry, 1975 g.	2	2	1,200,000
Manila, 1983 h.	2	2	1,500,000
Milwaukee Brew, 1997 h.	7	2	1,900,000
Monarchos, 1998 h.	4	2	1,522,000
Ouija Board (GB), 2001 m.	2	2	1,921,200

Horse, YOB Sex	Starts in $1-M Races	Wins in $1-M Races	Earnings in $1-M Races
Pleasantly Perfect, 1998 h.	5	2	$3,240,000
Prized, 1986 h.	5	2	1,565,940
Real Quiet, 1995 h.	3	2	1,550,000
Siphon (Brz), 1991 h.	6	2	1,780,000
Skimming, 1996 h.	3	2	1,200,000
Snow Chief, 1983 h.	3	2	1,214,600
Southern Image, 2000 h.	2	2	1,150,000
Sulamani (Ire), 1999 h.	3	2	1,563,600
Sunday Silence, 1986 h.	4	2	3,301,624
Tinners Way, 1990 h.	7	2	1,330,000
War Emblem, 1999 h.	5	2	2,525,000

Leading Winners of Grade 1 Races in North America

Horse, YOB Sex	Wins	G1 SWs	SWs	Earnings
John Henry, g. 1975	39	16	30	$6,591,860
Affirmed, h. 1975	22	14	19	2,393,818
Forego, g. 1970	34	14	24	1,938,957
Spectacular Bid, h. 1976	26	13	23	2,781,608
Bayakoa (Arg), m. 1984	18	12	16	2,785,259
Azeri, m. 1998	17	11	14	4,079,820
Cigar, h. 1990	18	11	14	7,599,815
Lady's Secret, m. 1982	25	11	22	3,021,325
Serena's Song, m. 1992	18	11	17	3,283,388
Paseana (Arg), m. 1987	14	10	14	3,111,292
Skip Away, h. 1993	18	10	16	9,616,360
Alysheba, h. 1984	11	9	10	6,679,242
Easy Goer, h. 1986	14	9	12	4,873,770
Flawlessly, m. 1988	16	9	15	2,572,536
Sky Beauty, m. 1990	15	9	13	1,336,000
Chief's Crown, c. 1982	12	8	10	2,191,168
Heavenly Prize, m. 1991	9	8	8	1,825,940
Personal Ensign, m. 1984	13	8	10	1,679,880
Seattle Slew, h. 1974	14	8	9	1,208,726
Susan's Girl, m. 1969	29	8	24	1,251,668
Ashado, m. 2001	12	7	11	3,931,440
Creme Fraiche, g. 1982	17	7	14	4,024,727
Exceller, h. 1973	8	7	8	1,125,772
Foolish Pleasure, h. 1972	16	7	12	1,216,705
Go for Wand, f. 1987	10	7	8	1,373,338
Goodbye Halo, m. 1985	11	7	10	1,706,702
Gulch, h. 1984	13	7	11	3,095,521
Honest Pleasure, h. 1973	12	7	9	839,997
Lava Man, g. 2001	17	7	13	5,214,706
Open Mind, m. 1986	12	7	11	1,844,372
Sharp Cat, m. 1994	15	7	14	2,032,575
Sightseek, m. 1999	12	7	10	2,445,216
Slew o' Gold, h. 1980	12	7	8	3,533,534
Alydar, h. 1975	14	6	11	957,195
Beautiful Pleasure, m. 1995	10	6	7	2,734,078
Best Pal, g. 1988	18	6	17	5,668,245
Bold 'n Determined, m. 1977	16	6	11	949,599
Desert Vixen, m. 1970	13	6	9	421,538
English Channel, h. 2002	13	6	10	5,319,028
Holy Bull, h. 1991	13	6	11	2,481,760
Inside Information, m. 1991	14	6	9	1,641,806
Meadow Star, m. 1988	11	6	10	1,445,740
Miss Oceana, m. 1981	11	6	9	1,010,385
Optimistic Gal, m. 1973	13	6	10	686,861
Point Given, h. 1998	9	6	8	3,968,500
Possibly Perfect, m. 1990	11	6	8	1,367,050
Precisionist, h. 1981	20	6	17	3,485,398
Snow Chief, h. 1983	13	6	12	3,383,210
Sunday Silence, h. 1986	9	6	7	4,968,554
Theatrical (Ire), h. 1982	7	6	6	2,840,500

Leading Winners of Graded Stakes in North America

Horse, YOB Sex	Wins	Graded SWs	SWs	Earnings
John Henry, g. 1975	39	25	30	$6,591,860
Forego, g. 1970	34	23	24	$1,938,957
Spectacular Bid, h. 1976	26	21	23	2,781,608
Affirmed, h. 1975	22	18	19	2,393,818
Ancient Title, h. 1970	24	17	20	1,252,791
Serena's Song, m. 1992	18	17	17	3,283,388
Skip Away, h. 1993	18	16	16	9,616,360
Bayakoa (Arg), m. 1984	18	15	16	2,785,259
Lady's Secret, m. 1982	25	15	22	3,021,325
Azeri, m. 1998	17	14	14	4,079,820
Paseana (Arg), m. 1987	14	14	14	3,111,292
Flawlessly, m. 1988	16	13	15	2,572,536
Precisionist, h. 1981	20	13	17	3,485,398
Silverbulletday, m. 1996	15	13	14	3,093,207
Sky Beauty, m. 1990	15	13	13	1,336,000
Best Pal, g. 1988	18	12	17	5,668,245
Sabin, m. 1980	18	12	14	1,098,341
Safely Kept, m. 1986	24	12	22	2,194,206
Sharp Cat, m. 1994	15	12	14	2,032,575
Steinlen (GB), h. 1983	16	12	14	3,229,752
Susan's Girl, m. 1969	29	12	24	1,251,668
Ashado, m. 2001	12	11	11	3,931,440
Black Tie Affair (Ire), h. 1986	18	11	13	3,370,694
Cigar, h. 1990	18	11	14	7,599,815
Creme Fraiche, g. 1982	17	11	14	4,024,727
Foolish Pleasure, h. 1972	16	11	12	1,216,705
Gulch, h. 1984	13	11	11	3,095,521
Housebuster, h. 1987	15	11	14	1,229,696
Royal Glint, h. 1970	21	11	15	1,004,816
Xtra Heat, m. 1998	26	11	25	2,189,635
Alysheba, h. 1984	11	10	10	6,679,242
Congaree, h. 1998	12	10	10	3,267,490
Easy Goer, h. 1986	14	10	12	4,873,770
Goodbye Halo, m. 1985	11	10	10	1,706,702
King's Swan, g. 1980	31	10	12	1,924,845
Kona Gold, g. 1994	14	10	11	2,293,384
Lure, h. 1989	14	10	10	2,515,289
Optimistic Gal, m. 1973	13	10	10	686,861
Personal Ensign, m. 1984	13	10	10	1,679,880
Sightseek, m. 1999	12	10	10	2,445,216
Silver Charm, h. 1994	11	10	10	4,444,369
Sir Bear, g. 1993	19	10	11	2,538,422

Leading Winners of Stakes Races in North America

Horse, YOB Sex	Wins	Graded SWs	SWs	Earnings
Exterminator, g. 1915	50	0	34	$221,227
Native Diver, g. 1959	37	0	34	1,026,500
Miss Woodford, m. 1880	37	0	33	118,270
Firenze, m. 1884	47	0	32	112,471
Round Table, h. 1954	43	0	32	1,749,869
Kelso, g. 1957	39	0	31	1,977,896
Kingston, h. 1884	89	0	31	140,195
John Henry, g. 1975	39	25	30	6,591,860
Hanover, h. 1884	32	0	27	118,887
Roamer, g. 1911	39	0	27	98,828
Seabiscuit, h. 1933	33	0	27	437,730
Who Doctor Who, g. 1983	33	1	26	813,870
Hindoo, h. 1878	30	0	25	71,875
Little Bold John, g. 1982	38	5	25	1,956,406
Stymie, h. 1941	35	0	25	918,485
Xtra Heat, m. 1998	26	11	25	2,189,635
Equipoise, h. 1928	29	0	24	338,610
Forego, g. 1970	34	23	24	1,938,957
Susan's Girl, m. 1969	29	12	24	1,251,668
Whirlaway, h. 1938	32	0	24	561,161
Citation, h. 1945	32	0	23	1,085,760
Spectacular Bid, h. 1976	26	21	23	2,781,608
Curribot, h. 1977	37	0	22	491,527
Discovery, h. 1931	27	0	22	195,287
Lady's Secret, m. 1982	25	15	22	3,021,325
Royal Harmony, h. 1964	38	0	22	587,164

Horse, YOB Sex	Wins	Graded SWs	SWs	Earnings
Safely Kept, m. 1986	24	12	22	$2,194,206
Swoon's Son, h. 1953	30	0	22	970,605
Armed, g. 1941	41	0	21	817,475
Buckpasser, h. 1963	25	0	21	1,462,014
Frost King, h. 1978	26	2	21	1,033,260
Rosy Way, g. 1989	28	0	21	97,389
Amadevil, h. 1974	33	0	20	653,534
Ancient Title, g. 1970	24	17	20	1,252,791
Chilcoton Blaze, h. 1980	31	0	20	490,862
Hidden Treasure, h. 1957	24	0	20	187,734
Judy's Red Shoes, m. 1983	25	1	20	1,085,668
Sarazen, g. 1921	27	0	20	225,000
Affirmed, h. 1975	22	18	19	2,393,818
Alsab, h. 1939	25	0	19	350,015
Ben Brush, h. 1893	25	0	19	65,217
Decathlon, h. 1953	25	0	19	269,530
Delta Colleen, m. 1985	23	0	19	810,798
Man o' War, h. 1917	20	0	19	249,465
Nashua, h. 1952	22	0	19	1,288,565
Police Inspector, h. 1977	25	1	19	713,707
Rapido Dom, h. 1978	25	0	19	466,974
Say Florida Sandy, h. 1994	33	5	19	2,085,408
Scott's Scoundrel, h. 1992	22	2	19	1,270,052
Spirit of Fighter, h. 1983	33	0	19	847,454
Affectionately, m. 1960	28	0	18	546,659
Arctic Laur, h. 1988	21	0	18	634,809
Cicada, m. 1959	23	0	18	783,674
Copper Case, g. 1977	33	0	18	365,374
Devil Diver, h. 1939	22	0	18	261,064
Dixie Poker Ace, g. 1987	27	0	18	850,126
Energetic King, h. 1979	35	0	18	765,776
Fantango Lady, m. 1994	22	0	18	279,295
Grey Lag, h. 1918	25	0	18	136,715
In Rem, g. 1975	21	0	18	307,742
Lafleur, h. 1999	23	0	18	129,589
Orphan Kist, h. 1984	28	0	18	631,997
Overskate, h. 1975	24	3	18	791,634
Parole, g. 1873	59	0	18	82,111
Polynesian, h. 1942	27	0	18	310,410
Timely Ruckus, g. 1993	25	0	18	618,004
Tom Fool, h. 1949	21	0	18	570,165
Twixt, m. 1969	26	7	18	619,141
Victorian Era, h. 1962	23	0	18	198,410
Best Pal, g. 1988	18	12	17	5,668,245
Bewitch, m. 1945	20	0	17	462,605
Bold Ruler, h. 1954	23	0	17	764,204
Cagey Exuberance, m. 1984	18	3	17	765,017
Challedon, h. 1936	20	0	17	334,660
Coaltown, h. 1945	23	0	17	415,675
Damascus, h. 1964	21	0	17	1,176,781
Dance Trainer, g. 1983	27	0	17	276,262
Dave's Friend, g. 1975	35	2	17	1,079,915
Foncier, h. 1976	29	0	17	323,515
Full Pocket, h. 1969	27	1	17	424,031
Gallant Bob, g. 1972	23	2	17	489,992
Glacial Princess, m. 1981	27	0	17	542,792
Hallowed Dreams, m. 1997	25	0	17	740,144
Henry of Navarre, h. 1891	29	0	17	68,985
Imp, m. 1894	62	0	17	70,119
Isadorable, m. 1983	19	0	17	415,018
Leaping Plum, g. 1991	29	0	17	371,584
My Juliet, m. 1972	24	6	17	548,859
Native Dancer, h. 1950	21	0	17	785,240
Precisionist, h. 1981	20	13	17	3,485,398
Secret Romeo, h. 1998	23	0	17	865,790
Sefa's Beauty, m. 1979	25	5	17	1,171,628
Serena's Song, m. 1992	18	17	17	3,283,388
Special Intent, h. 1981	30	0	17	438,558
Spicy, m. 1955	33	0	17	135,233
Sun Beau, h. 1925	33	0	17	376,744
Tosmah, m. 1961	23	0	17	612,588

Most Stakes Wins by Decade by Year of Birth

1931-1940

Horse, YOB Sex, Sire	Yrs. Raced	Starts	Wins	Stk. Wins	Earnings
Seabiscuit, 1933 h., by Hard Tack	6	89	33	27	$437,730
Whirlaway, 1938 h., by *Blenheim II	4	60	32	24	561,161
Discovery, 1931 h., by Display	4	63	27	22	195,287
Alsab, 1939 h., by Good Goods	4	51	25	19	350,015
Devil Diver, 1939 h., by *St. Germans	5	47	22	18	261,064
Challedon, 1936 h., by *Challenger II	5	44	20	17	334,660
War Admiral, 1934 h., by Man o' War	4	26	21	15	273,240
Eight Thirty, 1936 h., by Pilate	4	27	16	13	155,475
Marriage, 1936 h., by *Strolling Player	8	99	35	11	216,090
Parasang, 1937 h., by Halcyon	10	134	29	11	102,627

1941-1950

Horse, YOB Sex, Sire	Yrs. Raced	Starts	Wins	Stk. Wins	Earnings
Stymie, 1941 h., by Equestrian	7	131	35	25	$918,485
Citation, 1945 h., by Bull Lea	4	45	32	23	1,085,760
Armed, 1941 g., by Bull Lea	7	81	41	21	817,475
Polynesian, 1942 h., by Unbreakable	4	58	27	18	310,410
Bewitch, 1945 m., by Bull Lea	5	55	20	17	462,605
Native Dancer, 1950 h., by Polynesian	3	22	21	17	785,240
Coaltown, 1945 h., by Bull Lea	4	39	23	17	415,675
Delegate, 1944 g., by Maeda	9	134	31	16	277,530
My Request, 1945 h., by Requested	4	52	22	16	385,495

1951-1960

Horse, YOB Sex, Sire	Yrs. Raced	Starts	Wins	Stk. Wins	Earnings
Native Diver, 1959 h., by Imbros	7	81	37	34	$1,026,500
Round Table, 1954 h., by *Princequillo	4	66	43	32	1,749,869
Kelso, 1957 g., by Your Host	8	63	39	31	1,977,896
Swoon's Son, 1953 h., by The Doge	4	51	30	22	970,605
Hidden Treasure, 1957 h., by Dark Star	5	65	24	20	187,734
Decathlon, 1953 h., by Olympia	3	42	25	19	269,530
Nashua, 1952 h., by *Nasrullah	3	30	22	19	1,288,565
Affectionately, 1960 m., by Swaps	4	52	28	18	546,659
Cicada, 1959 m., by Bryan G.	4	42	23	18	783,674
Bold Ruler, 1954 h., by *Nasrullah	3	33	23	17	764,204

1961-1970

Horse, YOB Sex, Sire	Yrs. Raced	Starts	Wins	Stk. Wins	Earnings
Forego, 1970 g., by *Forli	6	57	34	24	$1,938,957
Susan's Girl, 1969 m., by Quadrangle	5	63	29	24	1,251,668
Royal Harmony, 1964 h., by Royal Note	6	105	38	22	587,164
Buckpasser, 1963 h., by Tom Fool	3	31	25	21	1,462,014
Ancient Title, 1970 g., by Gummo	7	57	24	20	1,252,791
Twixt, 1969 m., by Restless Native	4	70	26	18	619,141
Victorian Era, 1962 h., by Victoria Park	4	48	23	18	198,410
Damascus, 1964 h., by Sword Dancer	3	32	21	17	1,176,781
Full Pocket, 1969 h., by Olden Times	4	47	27	17	424,031

1971-1980

Horse, YOB Sex, Sire	Yrs. Raced	Starts	Wins	Stk. Wins	Earnings
John Henry, 1975 g., by Ole Bob Bowers	8	83	39	30	$6,591,860
Spectacular Bid, 1976 h., by Bold Bidder	3	30	26	23	2,781,608
Curribot, 1977 g., by Little Current	12	139	37	22	491,527
Frost King, 1978 h., by Ruritania	4	55	27	21	1,196,954
Amadevil, 1974 h., by Jungle Savage	7	93	33	20	653,534
Chilcoton Blaze, 1980 h., by Victorian Host	10	83	31	20	490,862
Affirmed, 1975 h., by Exclusive Native	3	29	22	19	2,393,818
Police Inspector, 1977 h., by Police Car	6	71	25	19	713,707
Rapido Dom, 1978 h., by Sir Dom	8	105	25	19	466,974

1981-1990

Horse, YOB Sex, Sire	Yrs. Raced	Starts	Wins	Stk. Wins	Earnings
Who Doctor Who, 1983 g., by Doctor Stat	8	64	33	26	$313,870
Little Bold John, 1982 g., by John Alden	9	105	38	25	1,956,406
Lady's Secret, 1982 m., by Secretariat	4	45	25	22	3,021,325
Safely Kept, 1986 m., by Horatius	4	31	24	22	2,194,206
Rosy Way, 1989 g., by Lord Avie	8	51	28	21	97,389
Judy's Red Shoes, 1983 m., by Hold Your Tricks	6	83	25	20	1,085,668
Delta Colleen, 1985 m., by Golden Reserve	7	71	23	19	810,798

Racing — Leading Stakes Winners

Horse, YOB Sex, Sire	Yrs. Raced	Starts	Wins	Stk. Wins	Earnings
Spirit of Fighter, 1983 m., by Gallant Knave	8	72	33	19	$847,454
Arctic Laur, 1988 h., by Son of Briartic	7	60	21	18	634,809
Dixie Poker Ace, 1987 g., by Patriotically	8	86	27	18	850,126

1991-2000

Horse, YOB Sex, Sire	Yrs. Raced	Starts	Wins	Stk. Wins	Earnings
Xtra Heat, 1998 m., by Dixieland Heat	4	35	26	25	$2,389,635
Say Florida Sandy, 1994 h., by Personal Flag	8	98	33	19	2,085,408
Scott's Scoundrel, 1992 h., by L'Enjoleur	6	50	22	19	1,270,052
Fantango Lady, 1994 m., by Lytrump	5	55	22	18	279,295
Lafleur, 1999 h., by Tamourad	5	32	23	18	129,589
Timely Ruckus, 1993 g., by Bold Executive	8	68	25	18	618,004
Hallowed Dreams, 1997 m., by Malagra	4	30	25	17	740,144
Leaping Plum, 1991 g., by Lightning Leap	12	66	29	17	371,584
Secret Romeo, 1998 h., by Service Stripe	5	55	22	17	865,790
Serena's Song, 1992 m., by Rahy	3	38	18	17	3,283,388

2001-2007

Horse, YOB Sex, Sire	Yrs. Raced	Starts	Wins	Stk. Wins	Earnings
Ask Queenie, 2001 m., by Key Contender	5	42	22	15	$558,705
Rocky Gulch, 2001 g., by Dry Gulch	5	38	18	14	1,151,725
Lava Man, 2001 g., by Slew City Slew	5	43	17	13	5,214,706
Monashee, 2002 m., by Wolf Power (SAf)	4	23	17	13	645,555
Somethinaboutlaura, 2002 m., by Dance Floor	4	30	17	13	1,008,865
True Metropolitan, 2002 g., by Proud and True	4	33	16	13	853,688
Muir Beach, 2001 m., by Skip Away	5	39	15	12	488,044
Ashado, 2001 m., by Saint Ballado	3	21	12	11	3,931,440
Fort Prado, 2001 h., by El Prado (Ire)	5	38	16	11	968,551
Honey Ryder, 2001 m., by Lasting Approval	5	33	13	11	2,784,160
Rockem Sockem, 2001 g., by Ulises	5	34	12	11	526,244

North American Leading Runners by Most Stakes Placings

Horse, YOB Sex	Wins	Stakes Wins	Stakes Placings	Earnings
Find, 1950 g.	22	13	38	$803,615
Stymie, 1941 h.	35	25	38	918,485
Pampas Host, 1972 h.	19	13	32	310,922
Major Presto, 1963 g.	24	12	30	125,694
Tick Tock, 1953 g.	20	10	30	386,951
Alerted, 1948 h.	20	12	29	440,485
Orphan Kist, 1984 m.	28	18	28	631,997
Talent Show, 1955 g.	16	7	28	507,038
Exterminator, 1915 g.	50	34	27	252,596
Gene's Lady, 1981 m.	14	10	27	946,190
Royal Harmony, 1964 h.	38	22	27	587,164
Ruhe, 1948 g.	11	6	27	294,490
Gallorette, 1942 m.	21	13	26	445,535
Love Your Host, 1966 h.	22	16	26	160,683
*Grey Monarch, 1955 h.	13	7	25	216,146
Creme Fraiche, 1982 h.	17	14	25	4,024,727
Delegate, 1944 g.	31	15	25	277,530
Delta Colleen, 1985 m.	23	19	25	810,798
Military Hawk, 1987 g.	18	12	25	686,128
Nostalgia's Star, 1982 h.	9	7	25	2,154,827
Special Intent, 1981 m.	30	17	25	438,558
Strangleknot, 1949 g.	25	9	25	289,190
Fiftieth Star, 1972 h.	19	6	24	167,035
High Dice, 1995 g.	21	16	24	350,590
Armed, 1941 g.	41	19	23	817,475
Double B Express, 1975 g.	31	13	23	246,013
Eddie Schmidt, 1953 h.	20	12	23	526,292
Fourstardave, 1985 g.	21	13	23	1,636,737
In the Curl, 1984 m.	26	10	23	749,891
Ky Alta, 1977 h.	14	9	23	313,865
On Trust, 1944 h.	23	11	23	554,145
Straight Deal, 1962 m.	21	13	23	733,020
Arctic Laur, 1988 h.	21	18	22	634,809
Buzfuz, 1942 h.	35	11	22	286,740
Chompion, 1965 h.	14	10	22	604,401
Foncier, 1976 h.	29	17	22	323,515
Homebuilder, 1984 h.	11	8	22	$1,172,153
Honor Medal, 1981 h.	19	9	22	1,347,073
Judy's Red Shoes, 1983 m.	25	20	22	1,085,668
Lucky Salvation, 1980 h.	22	5	22	467,891
Ruler's Whirl, 1966 h.	27	8	22	116,354
Say Florida Sandy, 1994 h.	33	19	22	2,085,408
Sir Bear, 1993 g.	19	11	22	2,538,422
Susan's Girl, 1969 m.	29	24	22	1,251,668
Adventuresome Love, 1986 h.	16	9	21	436,244
Bye and Near, 1963 h.	21	10	21	202,040
Charlie Chalmers, 1985 g.	9	6	21	378,715
Dixie Poker Ace, 1987 g.	27	18	21	850,126
First Fiddle, 1939 h.	23	10	21	398,610
Fort Marcy, 1964 g.	21	16	21	1,109,791
Kent Green, 1983 g.	13	8	21	395,469
King's Swan, 1980 h.	31	12	21	1,924,845
Pongo Boy, 1992 g.	22	12	21	776,184

North American Leading Runners by Most Stakes Placings Without a Stakes Win

Horse, YOB Sex, Sire	Years Raced	Starts	Wins	Stakes Plcgs	Earnings
Guadalcanal, 1958 h., by Citation	8	91	7	13	$243,337
Stunning Native, 1978 m., by Our Native	3	35	3	13	155,312
Grand Galop, 1962 g., by Victoria Park	7	119	20	12	115,744
Take a Check, 2002 m., by Touch Gold	4	39	5	12	418,520
Big Numbers, 1997 h., by Numerous	6	54	5	11	342,904
Blue Trumpeter, 1949 h., by Thumbs Up	6	106	15	11	120,912
Gat's Girl, 1975 m., by Lurullah	5	70	6	11	119,242
Milk Wood (GB), 1995 g., by Zafonic	6	45	7	11	298,966
Mistress Fletcher, 1992 m., by Sovereign Don	6	71	9	11	260,638
Aces Court, 1981 m., by Know Your Aces	6	75	8	10	112,740
Autobesarah, 1998 m., by Autocracy	8	76	7	10	395,960
Behind the Scenes, 1984 h., by Hurry Up Blue	4	41	7	10	331,095
Dance Play, 1988 m., by Sovereign Dancer	3	42	4	10	168,431
Distinctive Moon, 1979 m., by Distinctive	3	36	4	10	124,086
Golden Arrow, 1999 h., by Rahy	6	40	7	10	459,718
Hold the Reins, 1977 h., by Northern Fling	10	186	18	10	175,528
Ladies Agreement, 1970 m., by Royal Union	5	68	14	10	295,193
Little Buckles, 1991 m., by Buckley Boy	5	43	9	10	466,755
Lonny's Secret, 1966 h., by Terrang	4	38	6	10	107,542
Lotta Tike, 1974 m., by Skin Head	5	58	10	10	91,760
March of Kings, 1993 g., by River of Kings (Ire)	9	95	17	10	497,643
Patti L., 1987 m., by Lyphard's Wish (Fr)	5	55	9	10	211,995
Phyxius, 1999 m., by Broad Brush	3	32	3	10	220,146
Rule by Reason, 1967 h., by Hail to Reason	5	91	15	10	263,547
Sharetheime, 1998 g., by Local Time	7	66	8	10	232,348
Sweets, 1985 g., by Mr. Redoy	8	85	8	10	196,524
Vaunted Vamp, 1992 m., by Racing Star	6	78	21	10	419,641
*Elegant Heir, 1965 h., by Pharamond	5	93	23	9	163,435
A Call to Rise, 1988 g., by Poles Apart	8	124	18	9	600,441
Beth Believes, 1986 m., by Believe It	5	44	10	9	357,936
Cup o' Shine, 1977 m., by Raise a Cup	4	77	9	9	95,556
Dance Card Filled, 1983 h., by Dance Bid	5	71	10	9	398,706
Dewans Mischief, 1984 m., by Dewan	4	55	18	9	256,399
Dusty Heather, 1996 m., by M. Double M.	4	42	5	9	464,887
Fappies Cosy Miss, 1988 m., by Fappiano	3	35	4	9	304,885
Habby's Stuff, 1995 m., by Habitonia	6	68	7	9	212,343
Intensitivo, 1996 m., by *Sensitivo	9	143	25	9	292,535
Iron Becky, 1977 m., by Iron Anthony	4	61	6	9	85,781
Judy's Joe, 1964 h., by *Ben Lomond	5	78	10	9	34,102
Lenny the Lender, 1996 g., by Lac Ouimet	9	62	7	9	523,495
Naskra Colors, 1992 m., by Star de Naskra	5	39	6	9	411,437
Paladin Power, 1998 g., by Blush Rambler	8	77	3	9	122,550
Princess Tiree, 1989 m., by Main Debut	6	59	10	9	87,601
River Bank Kid, 1989 m., by Eskimo	5	40	6	9	142,865
Runaway Magic, 1997 m., by Runaway Groom	3	18	3	9	131,025
Sensitive Music, 1969 h., by *Sensitivo	5	68	10	9	159,111
Sentosa, 1991 g., by Northern Supremo	12	93	13	9	54,879
She's Content, 1983 m., by Restivo	4	45	9	9	225,501
Shed Some Light, 1992 g., by Homebuilder	9	105	20	9	569,638
Shuttered, 1993 m., by Wild Again	4	26	7	9	226,918
Todd's Orphan, 1966 m., by Ambehaving	6	86	6	9	60,809
Treachery, 1960 m., by Promised Land	5	105	11	9	182,071
Wait in Line, 2003 h., by Line In The Sand	3	36	5	9	362,810
Whiz Along, 1985 h., by Cormorant	6	80	9	9	581,115

Losingest Horses of All Time
(Without a Win)

Dona Chepa, a Puerto Rican-bred mare, established a record for futility in 2007 when she raised her record to 129 starts without a victory, a modern record. Racing in her native jurisdiction, she managed only one second and two third-place finishes by the end of her seventh racing season.

The Stag Dinner mare supplanted Thrust, a Bold Salute gelding who had very little thrust and lost 105 races before being retired in 1956. Zippy Chippy, a foal of 1991, was notable for how long he raced without a victory. He raced for his 11th season in 2004, a longer career than any other horse with more than 58 defeats. He was retired at the end of that year after 100 consecutive losses. Following is a list of the sport's leading losers from 1930 through early 2008.

Losses	Horse, YOB	Years Raced	Earnings
129	Dona Chepa, 1998	7	$13,225
105	Thrust, 1950	5	8,180
100	Dona Fana, 1998	7	7,613
	Zippy Chippy, 1991	11	30,834
92	Star Time, 1943	5	7,215
91	Lil Red Rendezvous, 1999	6	26,290
89	Good Get, 1940	5	2,805
86	Fagrace, 1943	5	6,200
85	Maker of Trouble, 1922	4	565
84	Western Holiday, 1929	5	620
83	City Limit, 1934	5	1,105
82	Giant's Heel, 1943	6	1,560
	Master Mark, 1941	6	290
81	Jibberty Bell, 1955	4	4,802
79	Arvella, 1957	4	2,531
	Omashane, 1942	5	1,475
77	Fred Whitham, 1925	7	1,100
	Space, 1942	5	3,070
76	Diamond Kind, 2001	5	21,888
	Prima Whisk, 1936	4	670
	Punk, 1997	9	52,729
	Sure Its Legal, 1988	5	9,772
75	War Bull, 1980	4	10,568
74	Four Acres, 2001	5	13,568
73	*Cafre II, 1951	7	2,339
	Gray Leaves, 1961	4	1,424
	Judgaville, 1981	3	12,965
72	Lattanzio, 1991	5	19,163
	Winnie's Pride, 1988	6	6,790
71	Lady Jule, 1925	3	1,095
	Ninon, 1923	3	1,360
	Roman Sandal, 1924	4	990
	Stark Mad, 1946	4	2,950
70	Red Alley Cat, 1990	6	7,610
69	Buddugie, 1920	4	1,865
	Tuff Nuggets, 1980	4	8,120
68	Buck Flares, 1955	4	6,100
	Lucky Change, 1941	4	3,930
	Right Chief, 1961	4	3,689
67	Bengal Dancer, 1954	4	5,240
	Jimmy What, 1987	6	14,036
	Tchadar, 1924	6	480
66	Dominate'em, 1978	4	5,860
	Doug's Dame, 1965	4	3,558
	Filly Gumbo, 1970	3	4,667
	Really Rushing, 1995	5	17,184
	Rosette, 1926	4	243
	Unclebuck, 1939	7	730
65	Alpha's Star, 1990	6	12,530
	Amarushka, 1981	5	24,336
	Brill Lon, 1956	4	1,420
	Flashy Lark, 1981	5	14,510
	Goodyear, 1927	5	20
	Icy Ethel, 1948	5	3,215
	Jacinto's Arky, 1980	4	4,536
	Petulant, 1928	4	690
	Sam's Tip, 1975	4	14,344
	Tarbucket, 1932	3	945
64	Able Archer, 1957	3	1,847
	Clay K., 1965	6	2,570
	Dawn's Debbie, 1982	3	7,292
	Gosport, 1936	5	465
	Junior T., 1948	4	1,160
	Pacific Star, 1946	7	1,000
	Truckin, 1936	5	865
63	Bell's Luck, 1961	4	867
	Castle Rock, 1927	4	625
	Double Our Flag, 1994	5	22,175
	Dusky Boy, 1928	5	1,310
	Mail Plane, 1948	3	1,805
	Performance Critic, 1996	4	16,475
	Ruby's Crystal, 1980	4	5,575
	Sweet Bernice, 1935	8	995

Leading Horses of All Time By Starts

Horse, YOB Sex, Sire	Years Raced	Starts	Wins	2nd	3rd	Stakes Wins	Earnings
Hiblaze, 1935 h., by Blazes	14	406	79	73	52	0	$32,647
*Galley Sweep, 1933 g., by Aga Khan	14	399	19	34	46	0	10,677
Shot One, 1941 g., by Shoeless Joe	13	360	65	65	68	0	29,982
Perhaps, 1918 g., by Luke McLuke	10	350	64	46	46	0	38,865
Bankrupt, 1883 g., by Spendthrift	12	348	86	52	47	0	41,260
Onus, 1933 g., by Jack High	15	344	53	58	63	0	32,039
Worthowning, 1935 g., by *Longworth	14	339	63	62	64	0	41,830
My Blaze, 1930 h., by Big Blaze	11	338	52	35	51	1	32,707
Agreed, 1950 g., by Revoked	14	338	39	50	49	0	68,004
Marabou, 1925 h., by *Hourless	10	337	41	61	44	0	27,458
Vantryst, 1936 h., by Tryster	13	334	61	78	48	0	31,971
George de Mar, 1922 h., by *Colonel Vennie	13	333	60	54	64	0	69,091
Welsh Lad, 1934 g., by Prince of Wales	13	329	67	54	49	0	25,317
Buffoon, 1937 h., by St. Brideaux	10	329	37	36	45	0	11,538
Seth's Hope, 1924 g., by Seth	11	327	62	51	50	0	74,341
Panjab, 1937 g., by *Kiev	11	327	21	32	44	0	17,929
Copin, 1937 h., by Mate	13	323	42	40	53	0	27,926
Commission, 1935 h., by Banstar	13	319	41	36	39	0	25,626
Higher Bracket, 1936 h., by *Rolls Royce	11	318	37	50	51	0	15,661
Golden Sweep, 1923 h., by Flittergold	10	318	46	47	58	0	32,285
Noah's Pride, 1929 g., by Noah	12	317	60	50	61	1	41,507
Champ Sorter, 1952 h., by Four Freedoms	12	315	35	43	51	0	62,747

Racing — Most Starts

Horse, YOB Sex, Sire	Years Raced	Starts	Wins	2nd	3rd	Stakes Wins	Earnings
Bee's Little Man, 1961 h., by *Iceberg II	12	315	42	32	31	0	$108,675
Appease Not, 1946 g., by King Cole	13	314	42	44	46	0	122,802
Easiest Way, 1931 g., by *Waygood	11	311	27	38	44	0	24,375
Mister Snow Man, 1959 g., by *Iceberg II	14	310	43	37	36	0	104,074
Shannon's Hope, 1956 h., by *Shannon II	12	309	29	36	43	0	39,848
Port o' Play, 1926 h., by The Porter	9	308	44	47	34	1	39,234
Behavin Jerry, 1964 h., by Ambehaving	14	307	38	25	48	0	72,259
Star Soldier, 1934 g., by Son o' Battle	11	305	37	22	50	0	8,307
Vote Boy, 1932 g., by Torchilla	11	304	55	37	48	1	39,240
It's No Use, 1950 h., by *Basileus II	11	304	25	40	52	0	68,326
Dr. Jillson, 1930 h., by *Kiev	12	304	27	42	37	0	12,522
Mr. Minx, 1952 h., by *Mafosta	12	302	36	48	34	0	87,072
Chronology, 1935 g., by *Donnacona	13	302	44	41	46	0	14,632
Call Mac, 1965 g., by Loukenmac	13	301	13	61	58	0	82,664
Bull Market, 1932 g., by Happy Time	14	301	28	49	39	0	19,275

Most Starts by Decade by Year of Birth

1931-1940

Horse, YOB Sex, Sire	Yrs. Raced	Starts	Wins	Earnings
Hiblaze, 1935 h., by Blazes	14	406	79	$32,647
Onus, 1933 g., by Jack High	15	344	53	32,039
Worthowning, 1935 g., by *Longworth	14	339	63	41,830
Vantryst, 1936 h., by Tryster	13	334	61	31,971
Buffoon, 1937 h., by St. Brideaux	10	329	37	11,538
Welsh Lad, 1934 g., by Prince of Wales	13	329	67	25,317
Panjab, 1937 g., by *Kiev	11	327	21	17,929
Copin, 1937 h., by Mate	13	323	42	27,926
Commission, 1935 h., by Banstar	13	319	41	25,626

1941-1950

Horse, YOB Sex, Sire	Yrs. Raced	Starts	Wins	Earnings
Shot One, 1941 g., by Shoeless Joe	13	360	65	$29,982
Agreed, 1950 g., by Revoked	14	338	39	68,004
Appease Not, 1946 g., by King Cole	13	314	42	122,802
It's No Use, 1950 h., by *Basileus II	11	304	25	68,326
Bobs Ace, 1947 g., by War Jeep	10	286	31	56,957
Eagle Speed, 1946 g., by Sun Again	12	284	40	66,337
Shadow Shot, 1944 h., by Chance Shot	11	279	35	68,585
Royal Bones, 1947 g., by Mr. Bones	8	274	33	70,670
Quatrefoil, 1945 h., by *Quatre Bras II	10	273	18	46,994
Bee Lee Tee, 1947 h., by Roy T.	12	270	47	104,805

1951-1960

Horse, YOB Sex, Sire	Yrs. Raced	Starts	Wins	Earnings
Champ Sorter, 1952 h., by Four Freedoms	12	315	35	$62,747
Mister Snow Man, 1959 g., by *Iceberg II	14	310	43	104,074
Shannon's Hope, 1956 h., by *Shannon II	12	309	29	39,848
Mr. Minx, 1952 h., by *Mafosta	12	302	36	87,072
Ole Sarge, 1956 g., by Carrara Marble	12	296	24	36,373
Easy Knight, 1955 g., by Easy Mon	12	294	22	48,099
Asking, 1952 h., by Pry	12	287	27	46,442
Black Jet, 1957 h., by Lord Boswell	12	281	21	51,077
Knight-King, 1957 g., by Tuscany	12	277	26	79,141
Bell's Range, 1954 g., by Ramillies	13	274	41	65,100

1961-1970

Horse, YOB Sex, Sire	Yrs. Raced	Starts	Wins	Earnings
Bee's Little Man, 1961 h., by *Iceberg II	12	315	42	$108,675
Behavin Jerry, 1964 h., by Ambehaving	14	307	38	72,259
Call Mac, 1965 g., by Loukenmac	13	301	13	82,664
Royal Doctor, 1961 g., by *Royal Vale	12	286	21	50,793
Bayou Teche, 1961 g., by Bryan G.	12	281	48	107,577
Dandier, 1961 h., by Mohammedan	11	278	31	74,523
Pin Pan Dan, 1966 h., by Pan Dancer	12	278	33	86,330
Wild Wink, 1969 h., by Quickasawink	13	275	40	129,004
Bucket O'Suds, 1965 h., by Rattle Dancer	13	273	38	158,017
Candy Top, 1964 h., by Top Double	10	273	35	94,990

1971-1980

Horse, YOB Sex, Sire	Yrs. Raced	Starts	Wins	Earnings
Dot the T., 1972 h., by *Notable II	12	261	48	$227,033
Legrand, 1974 h., by Delta Judge	11	255	13	$104,322
Mr. Turnabout, 1971 h., by Reverse	11	252	25	89,061
Magic Flash, 1971 g., by *Babieca II	10	250	22	63,175
Catch Poppy, 1973 h., by Poppy Jay	12	246	30	122,346
Arrowsmith, 1976 h., by Briartic	12	243	20	166,106
One Purpose, 1978 g., by Sinister Purpose	13	242	13	145,894
Dan Dan, 1975 g., by Tumiga	11	238	29	171,438
Troy Knight, 1973 h., by Nashwood	12	235	38	143,287
Uhrich Enzurich, 1972 g., by *Semillant	13	234	21	60,247

1981-1990

Horse, YOB Sex, Sire	Yrs. Raced	Starts	Wins	Earnings
Z. Z. Quickfoot, 1982 g., by Master Derby	12	266	27	$122,752
Sharon Caper, 1983 g., by Cartesian	13	244	33	109,685
Passive Loser, 1987 m., by Highland Blade	13	225	22	121,356
Side Winding, 1985 g., by Shananie	12	218	26	121,648
Our Legal Eagle, 1990 g., by Exuberant	13	217	10	100,892
Valley Cat, 1985 g., by Valdez	14	216	29	123,612
Wicked Wike, 1982 g., by Olden Times	11	212	11	318,561
Callisto, 1987 g., by Nasty and Bold	11	210	28	329,002
Playing Politics, 1982 g., by In Reality	15	203	25	187,639
Noble But Nasty, 1981 g., by Nasty and Bold	11	200	40	325,588

1991-2000

Horse, YOB Sex, Sire	Yrs. Raced	Starts	Wins	Earnings
Smart And Regal, 1991 g., by Regal Classic	11	188	21	$148,253
Talc of Dreams, 1992 g., by Talc	11	172	11	110,421
He Makes Cents, 1992 g., by Narcotics Squad	9	171	7	99,747
Cumberland Gap, 1992 g., by Allen's Prospect	13	161	34	324,378
Motion to Suppress, 1992 g., by Timeless Native	12	161	20	164,156
Mr. Butterscotch, 1992 g., by Compliance	10	161	12	116,614
Lindapinda, 1992 m., by Unite	7	158	14	104,473
Acting Tips, 1995 g., by Noactor	10	157	14	136,221
Burnt Mill Road, 1994 g., by Wayne's Crane	12	157	30	341,141
Desiard, 1993 g., by Nalees Man	11	155	21	200,635
Francis Albert, 1992 g., by Cross Canal	11	155	27	267,055

2001-2007

Horse, YOB Sex, Sire	Yrs. Raced	Starts	Wins	Earnings
Storming On By, 2001 g., by Stormy Atlantic	5	94	4	$45,551
Dodi N Me, 2001 m., by Thats Our Buck	5	88	3	60,835
Hold Hard, 2001 g., by Halory Hunter	5	85	13	167,581
Dalewoods Promise, 2001 g., by World Stage (Ire)	4	83	4	60,706
Dble Diamond Norma, 2001 m., by Name for Norm	5	79	12	48,000
Actcelerate, 2001 g., by Noactor	5	78	7	84,276
Dandy Belle, 2001 m., by Boone's Mill	5	78	7	125,544
Let Me Be Frank, 2002 g., by Awad	4	78	10	100,842
Red Streak, 2001 g., by Gold Case	5	78	4	66,565
Satin Song, 2001 m., by Lit de Justice	5	78	11	109,882

All-Time Leading Earners by Deflated Dollars

Comparing horses of different eras is always an entertaining exercise. Was Secretariat a better racehorse than Citation? That question will never be answered definitively because they never met on the track, so comparing horses of one era to another is subjective.

Earnings are one measure of performance, though that yardstick also has its drawbacks because the purses of yesteryear do not compare with the purses of today. There is a way to use earnings as a measure of productivity, however, by deflating the earnings; that is, adjusting earnings to account for the effects of inflation.

In the tables presented on this page and the following two pages are deflated earnings of the all-time leaders in Thoroughbred racing since 1929. Considered for inclusion on the list is any horse that started at least once in North America. Horses that raced at least once in North America and also raced overseas have all their earnings included, all being converted to United States dollars and then deflated by racing year.

The all-time leading money winner adjusted for inflation is two-time Horse of the Year John Henry, who raced 83 times from 1977 through '84. The durable gelding won the first $1-million Thoroughbred race in the U.S., the 1981 Arlington Million Stakes (G1), and his career ended the year in which the Breeders' Cup was inaugurated. Second on the list is two-time Horse of the Year Cigar, the all-time leading earner in North America in current dollars.

The deflator used to convert all earnings is the Gross Domestic Product implicit price deflator published by the U.S. Bureau of Economic Analysis.

On the first two pages are the all-time leaders by deflated dollars regardless of sex. On the third page is a list of the all-time leading female earners by deflated dollars. Statistics are through December 31, 2007.

All-Time Leading Earners by Deflated Dollars

Horse, YOB Sex, Sire	Yrs. Raced	Starts	1st	2nd	3rd	Nominal Earnings	Deflated Earnings
John Henry, 1975 g., by Ole Bob Bowers	8	83	39	15	9	$6,591,860	$12,892,342
Cigar, 1990 h., by Palace Music	4	33	19	4	5	9,999,815	12,883,842
Skip Away, 1993 h., by Skip Trial	4	38	18	10	6	9,316,360	12,084,046
Kelso, 1957 g., by Your Host	8	63	39	12	2	1,977,896	10,950,777
Alysheba, 1984 h., by Alydar	3	26	11	8	2	6,579,242	10,730,982
Round Table, 1954 h., by *Princequillo	4	66	43	8	5	1,749,869	10,291,741
Fantastic Light, 1996 h., by Rahy	4	25	12	5	3	8,486,957	10,063,577
Silver Charm, 1994 h., by Silver Buck	4	24	12	7	2	6,944,369	8,635,589
Pleasantly Perfect, 1998 h., by Pleasant Colony	4	18	9	3	2	7,789,880	8,622,532
Smarty Jones, 2001 h., by Elusive Quality	2	9	8	1	0	7,613,155	8,327,686
Nashua, 1952 h., by *Nasrullah	3	30	22	4	1	1,288,565	8,175,845
Captain Steve, 1997 h., by Fly So Free	3	25	9	3	7	6,828,356	8,073,396
Citation, 1945 h., by Bull Lea	4	45	32	10	2	1,085,760	7,910,075
Invasor (Arg), 2002 h., by Candy Stripes	4	12	11	0	0	7,804,070	7,906,587
Best Pal, 1988 g., by *Habitony	7	47	18	11	4	5,668,245	7,871,748
Stymie, 1941 h., by Equestrian	7	131	35	33	28	918,485	7,781,237
Tiznow, 1997 h., by Cee's Tizzy	2	15	8	4	2	6,427,830	7,608,838
Buckpasser, 1963 h., by Tom Fool	3	31	25	4	1	1,462,014	7,598,009
Sunday Silence, 1986 h., by Halo	3	14	9	5	0	4,968,554	7,549,589
Singspiel (Ire), 1992 h., by In the Wings (GB)	4	20	9	8	0	5,952,825	7,536,240
Easy Goer, 1986 h., by Alydar	3	20	14	5	1	4,873,770	7,445,778
Spend a Buck, 1982 h., by Buckaroo	2	15	10	3	2	4,220,689	7,230,400
Taiki Blizzard, 1991 h., by Seattle Slew	4	23	6	8	2	5,523,549	7,034,948
Carry Back, 1958 h., by Saggy	4	62	21	11	11	1,241,165	6,955,174
Creme Fraiche, 1982 g., by Rich Cream	6	64	17	12	13	4,024,727	6,710,627
Armed, 1941 g., by Bull Lea	7	81	41	20	10	817,475	6,709,259
Dylan Thomas (Ire), 2003 h., by Danehill	4	20	10	4	1	6,620,852	6,684,578
Ouija Board (GB), 2001 m., by Cape Cross (Ire)	4	22	10	3	5	6,298,163	6,640,718
Spectacular Bid, 1976 h., by Bold Bidder	3	30	26	2	1	2,781,608	6,570,842
Unbridled, 1987 h., by Fappiano	3	24	8	6	6	4,489,475	6,565,344
Medaglia d'Oro, 1999 h., by El Prado (Ire)	4	17	8	7	0	5,754,720	6,480,104
Slew o' Gold, 1980 h., by Seattle Slew	3	21	12	5	1	3,533,534	6,312,169
Whirlaway, 1938 h., by *Blenheim II	4	60	32	15	9	561,161	6,301,744
Ferdinand, 1983 h., by Nijinsky II	4	29	8	9	6	3,777,978	6,212,014
Forego, 1970 g., by *Forli	6	57	34	9	7	1,938,957	6,196,436
Affirmed, 1975 h., by Exclusive Native	3	29	22	5	1	2,393,818	6,094,108
High Chaparral (Ire), 1999 h., by Sadler's Wells	3	13	10	1	2	5,331,231	6,086,167
Jim and Tonic (Fr), 1994 g., by Double Bed (Fr)	7	39	13	13	4	4,975,807	5,973,775
Street Cry (Ire), 1998 h., by Machiavellian	3	12	5	6	1	5,150,837	5,940,234
Swoon's Son, 1953 h., by The Doge	4	51	30	10	3	970,605	5,930,415
Precisionist, 1981 h., by Crozier	5	46	20	10	4	3,485,398	5,922,404
Roses in May, 2000 h., by Devil His Due	3	13	8	4	0	5,490,187	5,878,778

Racing — Leading Earners

Horse, YOB Sex, Sire	Yrs. Raced	Starts	1st	2nd	3rd	Nominal Earnings	Deflated Earnings
Damascus, 1964 h., by Sword Dancer	3	32	21	7	3	$1,176,781	$5,829,923
Dance in the Mood (Jpn), 2001 m., by Sunday Silence	4	25	6	6	1	5,456,107	5,811,827
Snow Chief, 1983 h., by Reflected Glory	3	24	13	3	5	3,383,210	5,691,656
Daylami (Ire), 1994 h., by Doyoun	4	21	11	3	4	4,614,762	5,670,092
Assault, 1943 h., by Bold Venture	6	42	18	6	7	675,470	5,580,095
Behrens, 1994 h., by Pleasant Colony	4	27	9	8	3	4,563,500	5,565,419
Awesome Again, 1994 h., by Deputy Minister	2	12	9	0	2	4,374,590	5,433,972
English Channel, 2002 h., by Smart Strike	4	23	13	4	1	5,319,028	5,429,343
Bet Twice, 1984 h., by Sportin' Life	3	26	10	6	4	3,308,599	5,402,810
Native Diver, 1959 h., by Imbros	7	81	37	7	12	1,026,500	5,396,626
Lava Man, 2001 g., by Slew City Slew	5	43	17	8	3	5,214,706	5,359,615
Cryptoclearance, 1984 h., by Fappiano	4	44	12	10	7	3,376,327	5,354,014
Swaps, 1952 h., by *Khaled	3	25	19	2	2	848,900	5,334,977
Seabiscuit, 1933 h., by Hard Tack	6	89	33	15	13	437,730	5,297,146
Devil His Due, 1989 h., by Devil's Bag	4	41	11	12	3	3,920,405	5,289,598
Dahlia, 1970 m., by *Vaguely Noble	5	48	15	3	7	1,489,105	5,178,304
Native Dancer, 1950 h., by Polynesian	3	22	21	1	0	785,240	5,167,152
Pilsudski (Ire), 1992 h., by Polish Precedent	4	22	10	6	2	4,080,297	5,156,540
Perfect Drift, 1999 g., by Dynaformer	7	46	11	14	6	4,680,691	5,140,116
T. V. Lark, 1957 h., by *Indian Hemp	4	72	19	13	6	902,194	5,119,692
Lady's Secret, 1982 m., by Secretariat	4	45	25	9	3	3,021,325	5,117,013
Fort Marcy, 1964 g., by *Amerigo	6	75	21	18	14	1,109,791	5,108,158
Curlin, 2004 c., by Smart Strike	1	9	6	1	2	5,102,800	5,102,800
Roman Brother, 1961 g., by Third Brother	4	42	16	10	5	943,473	5,093,738
Secretariat, 1970 h., by Bold Ruler	2	21	16	3	1	1,316,808	5,043,643
Seeking the Pearl, 1994 m., by Seeking the Gold	4	21	8	2	3	4,021,716	5,026,806
Steinlen (GB), 1983 h., by Habitat	5	45	20	10	7	3,297,169	5,026,342
Gulch, 1984 h., by Mr. Prospector	3	32	13	8	4	3,095,521	5,007,226
Trinycarol (Ven), 1979 m., by Velvet Cap	4	29	18	3	1	2,644,392	4,995,767
Dr. Fager, 1964 h., by Rough'n Tumble	3	22	18	2	1	1,002,642	4,956,107
Find, 1950 g., by Discovery	8	110	22	27	27	803,615	4,930,796
Sandpit (Brz), 1989 h., by Baynoun (Ire)	7	40	14	11	6	3,812,597	4,899,172
Theatrical (Ire), 1982 h., by Nureyev	4	22	10	4	2	2,940,036	4,841,328
Black Tie Affair (Ire), 1986 h., by Miswaki	4	45	18	9	6	3,370,694	4,835,699
Strike the Gold, 1988 h., by Alydar	4	31	6	8	5	3,457,026	4,834,242
Symboli Rudolf (Jpn), 1981 h., by Partholon	4	16	13	1	1	2,764,980	4,832,703
Cat Thief, 1996 h., by Storm Cat	3	30	4	9	8	3,951,012	4,826,057
Sword Dancer, 1956 h., by Sunglow	3	39	15	7	4	829,610	4,770,343
Swain (Ire), 1992 h., by Nashwan	4	22	10	4	6	3,797,566	4,762,390
Saint Liam, 2000 h., by Saint Ballado	3	20	9	6	1	4,456,995	4,750,912
Sky Classic, 1987 h., by Nijinsky II	4	29	15	6	1	3,320,398	4,698,076
Sulamani (Ire), 1999 h., by Hernando (Fr)	2	11	5	2	1	4,215,365	4,691,022
*Cougar II, 1966 h., by Tale of Two Cities	6	50	20	7	17	1,172,625	4,684,087
Point Given, 1998 h., by Thunder Gulch	2	13	9	3	0	3,968,500	4,655,339
Dance Smartly, 1988 m., by Danzig	3	17	12	2	3	3,263,835	4,630,005
Great Communicator, 1983 h., by Key to the Kingdom	6	56	14	10	7	2,922,615	4,610,768
Azeri, 1998 m., by Jade Hunter	4	24	17	4	0	4,079,820	4,610,723
Susan's Girl, 1969 m., by Quadrangle	5	63	29	14	11	1,251,668	4,600,052
Bold Ruler, 1954 h., by *Nasrullah	3	33	23	4	2	764,204	4,563,571
Exceller, 1973 h., by *Vaguely Noble	5	33	15	5	6	1,674,587	4,555,147
Paradise Creek, 1989 h., by Irish River (Fr)	4	25	14	7	1	3,401,416	4,552,091
Paseana (Arg), 1987 m., by Ahmad	6	36	19	10	2	3,317,427	4,545,074
Gentlemen (Arg), 1992 h., by Robin des Bois	5	24	13	4	2	3,608,538	4,533,199
Lando (Ger), 1990 h., by Acatenango	4	24	10	3	1	3,438,727	4,530,361
Candy Spots, 1960 h., by *Nigromante	3	22	12	5	1	824,718	4,525,923
First Landing, 1956 h., by *Turn-to	3	37	19	9	2	779,577	4,501,512
Mongo, 1959 h., by *Royal Charger	4	46	22	10	4	820,766	4,493,712
Moon Ballad (Ire), 1999 h., by Singspiel (Ire)	3	14	5	3	1	4,364,791	4,909,139
Manila, 1983 h., by Lyphard	3	18	12	5	0	2,692,799	4,484,519
Allez France, 1970 m., by *Sea-Bird	4	21	13	3	1	1,262,801	4,466,815
Almutawakel (GB), 1995 h., by Machiavellian	4	19	4	4	1	3,643,021	4,453,263
Riva Ridge, 1969 h., by First Landing	3	30	17	3	1	1,111,497	4,451,609
Crimson Satan, 1959 h., by Spy Song	4	58	18	9	9	796,077	4,416,035
Street Sense, 2004 h., by Street Cry (Ire)	2	13	6	4	2	4,383,200	4,414,604
Broad Brush, 1983 h., by Ack Ack	3	27	14	5	5	2,656,793	4,410,216
Cicada, 1959 m., by Bryan G.	4	42	23	8	6	783,674	4,371,441
Gate Dancer, 1981 h., by Sovereign Dancer	4	28	7	8	7	2,501,705	4,354,017
Bertrando, 1989 h., by Skywalker	5	24	9	6	2	3,185,610	4,352,413
Forty Niner, 1985 h., by Mr. Prospector	2	19	11	5	0	2,726,000	4,344,128
Bally Ache, 1957 h., by *Ballydam	2	31	16	9	4	758,522	4,338,336
Victory Gallop, 1995 h., by Cryptoclearance	3	17	9	5	1	3,505,895	4,326,038
With Approval, 1986 h., by Caro (Ire)	3	23	13	5	1	2,863,540	4,305,987

Female All-Time Leading Earners by Deflated Dollars

Horse, YOB Sex, Sire	Yrs. Raced	Starts	1st	2nd	3rd	Nominal Earnings	Deflated Earnings
Ouija Board (GB), 2001 m., by Cape Cross (Ire)	4	22	10	3	5	$6,312,552	$6,640,718
Dance in the Mood (Jpn), 2001 m., by Sunday Silence	4	25	6	6	1	5,456,107	5,811,827
Dahlia, 1970 m., by *Vaguely Noble	5	48	15	3	7	1,489,105	5,178,304
Lady's Secret, 1982 m., by Secretariat	4	45	25	9	3	3,021,325	5,117,013
Seeking the Pearl, 1994 m., by Seeking the Gold	4	21	8	2	3	4,021,716	5,026,806
Trinycarol (Ven), 1979 m., by Velvet Cap	4	29	18	3	1	2,644,392	4,995,767
Dance Smartly, 1988 m., by Danzig	3	17	12	2	3	3,263,835	4,630,005
Azeri, 1998 m., by Jade Hunter	4	24	17	4	0	4,079,820	4,610,723
Susan's Girl, 1969 m., by Quadrangle	5	63	29	14	11	1,251,668	4,600,052
Paseana (Arg), 1987 m., by Ahmad	6	36	19	10	2	3,317,427	4,545,074
Allez France, 1970 m., by *Sea-Bird	4	21	13	3	1	1,262,801	4,466,815
Cicada, 1959 m., by Bryan G.	4	42	23	8	6	783,674	4,371,441
Bayakoa (Arg), 1984 m., by Consultant's Bid	6	39	21	9	0	2,861,701	4,295,653
Ashado, 2001 m., by Saint Ballado	3	21	12	4	3	3,931,440	4,281,901
Serena's Song, 1992 m., by Rahy	3	38	18	11	3	3,283,388	4,253,946
Spain, 1997 m., by Thunder Gulch	4	35	9	9	7	3,540,542	4,190,242
Shuvee, 1966 m., by Nashua	4	44	16	10	6	890,445	4,003,593
Life's Magic, 1981 m., by Cox's Ridge	3	32	8	11	6	2,255,218	3,980,629
All Along (Fr), 1979 m., by Targowice	4	21	9	4	2	2,125,809	3,888,048
Triptych, 1982 m., by Riverman	5	41	14	5	11	2,318,946	3,821,729
Silverbulletday, 1996 m., by Silver Deputy	3	23	15	3	1	3,093,207	3,795,042
Straight Deal, 1962 m., by Hail to Reason	6	99	21	21	9	733,020	3,731,515
Gallorette, 1942 m., by *Challenger II	5	72	21	20	13	445,535	3,725,959
Escena, 1993 m., by Strawberry Road (Aus)	4	29	11	9	3	2,962,639	3,659,868
Let's Elope (NZ), 1987 m., by Nassipour	5	26	11	0	5	2,528,902	3,572,451
Flawlessly, 1988 m., by Affirmed	5	28	16	4	3	2,572,536	3,545,156
Banshee Breeze, 1995 m., by Unbridled	3	18	10	5	2	2,784,798	3,430,513
Bewitch, 1945 m., by Bull Lea	5	55	20	10	11	462,605	3,426,233
Miesque, 1984 m., by Nureyev	3	16	12	3	1	2,070,163	3,350,464
Beautiful Pleasure, 1995 m., by Maudlin	5	25	10	5	2	2,734,078	3,325,146
Estrapade, 1980 m., by *Vaguely Noble	4	30	12	5	5	1,937,142	3,293,721
Top Flight, 1929 m., by *Dis Donc	2	16	12	0	0	275,900	3,281,659
Tosmah, 1961 m., by Tim Tam	4	39	23	6	2	612,588	3,281,637
Safely Kept, 1986 m., by Horatius	4	31	24	2	3	2,194,206	3,245,958
Busher, 1942 m., by War Admiral	3	21	15	3	1	334,035	3,215,973
Honeymoon, 1943 m., by *Beau Pere	6	78	20	14	9	387,760	3,164,454
Old Hat, 1959 m., by Boston Doge	6	80	35	18	9	556,401	2,983,368
Affectionately, 1960 m., by Swaps	4	52	28	8	6	546,659	2,971,136
Honey Ryder, 2001 m., by Lasting Approval	5	33	13	4	8	2,784,160	2,879,214
Heritage of Gold, 1995 m., by Gold Legend	4	28	16	2	4	2,381,762	2,872,357
Open Mind, 1986 m., by Deputy Minister	3	19	12	2	2	1,844,372	2,851,465
Take Charge Lady, 1999 m., by Dehere	3	22	11	7	0	2,480,377	2,839,299
Next Move, 1947 m., by Bull Lea	4	46	17	11	3	398,550	2,838,351
Xtra Heat, 1998 m., by Dixieland Heat	4	35	26	5	2	2,389,635	2,774,159
Sickle's Image, 1948 m., by Sickletoy	5	73	27	13	16	413,275	2,767,984
Gamely, 1964 m., by Bold Ruler	3	41	16	9	6	574,961	2,746,402
Cesario (Jpn), 2002 m., by Special Week	2	6	5	1	0	2,578,568	2,730,863
Sightseek, 1999 m., by Distant View	3	20	12	5	0	2,445,216	2,725,023
Bed o' Roses, 1947 m., by Rosemont	4	46	18	8	6	383,925	2,724,191
Politely, 1963 m., by *Amerigo	4	49	21	9	5	552,972	2,714,832
Goodbye Halo, 1985 m., by Halo	3	24	11	5	4	1,706,702	2,693,630
Personal Ensign, 1984 m., by Private Account	3	13	13	0	0	1,679,880	2,689,476
Perfect Sting, 1996 m., by Red Ransom	4	21	14	3	0	2,202,042	2,652,020
Very Subtle, 1984 m., by Hoist the Silver	4	29	12	6	4	1,608,360	2,620,985
Family Style, 1983 m., by State Dinner	3	35	10	8	7	1,537,118	2,596,747
Sharp Cat, 1994 m., by Storm Cat	3	22	15	3	0	2,032,575	2,551,477
Convenience, 1968 m., by Fleet Nasrullah	4	35	15	9	4	648,933	2,529,406
Megahertz (GB), 1999 m., by Pivotal	5	34	14	6	5	2,261,594	2,497,859
Hatoof, 1989 m., by Irish River (Fr)	4	21	9	4	1	1,841,070	2,493,153
Miss Alleged, 1987 m., by Alleged	3	15	5	4	3	1,757,342	2,492,651
Gallant Bloom, 1966 m., by *Gallant Man	3	22	16	1	1	535,739	2,485,118
Numbered Account, 1969 m., by Buckpasser	3	22	14	3	2	607,048	2,480,020
Trillion, 1974 m., by Hail to Reason	3	32	9	14	3	957,413	2,459,929
Pebbles (GB), 1981 m., by Sharpen Up (GB)	3	15	8	4	0	1,419,632	2,452,846
Outstandingly, 1982 m., by Exclusive Native	4	28	10	4	5	1,412,206	2,451,053
The Very One, 1975 m., by One for All	5	71	22	12	9	1,104,623	2,450,250
User Friendly (GB), 1989 m., by Slip Anchor	3	16	8	1	2	1,764,938	2,432,430
Princess Rooney, 1980 m., by Verbatim	3	21	17	2	1	1,343,339	2,424,904
Jewel Princess, 1992 m., by Key to the Mint	4	29	13	4	7	1,904,060	2,424,236
Riskaverse, 1999 m., by Dynaformer	5	32	9	6	4	2,182,429	2,421,767

Leading Earners by Foal Crop

YOB	MALE, Sex, Sire	Yrs. Raced	Strts	Wins	Stk. Wins	Earnings	FEMALE, Sex, Sire	Yrs. Raced	Strts	Wins	Stk. Wins	Earnings
2005	War Pass, c., Cherokee Run	1	4	4	2	$1,397,400	Indian Blessing, f., Indian Charlie	1	3	3	2	$1,357,200
2004	Curlin, c., Smart Strike	1	9	6	5	5,102,800	Octave, f., Unbridled's Song	2	13	4	3	1,660,934
2003	Bernardini, h., A.P. Indy	1	8	6	5	3,060,480	Ginger Punch, m., Awesome Again	2	14	7	4	1,901,679
2002	English Channel, h., Smart Strike	4	23	13	10	5,319,028	Round Pond, m., Awesome Again	3	13	7	5	1,998,700
2001	Smarty Jones, h., Elusive Quality	2	9	8	7	7,613,155	Ashado, m., Saint Ballado	3	21	12	11	3,931,440
2000	Roses in May, h., Devil His Due	3	13	8	4	5,490,187	Film Maker, m., Dynaformer	5	27	8	6	2,203,730
1999	Medaglia d'Oro, h., El Prado (Ire)	4	17	8	7	5,754,720	Take Charge Lady, m., Dehere	3	22	11	9	2,480,377
1998	Pleasantly Perfect, h., Pleasant Colony	4	18	9	6	7,789,880	Azeri, m., Jade Hunter	4	24	17	14	4,079,820
1997	Captain Steve, h., Fly So Free	3	25	9	8	6,828,356	Spain, m., Thunder Gulch	4	35	9	7	3,540,542
1996	Fantastic Light, h., Rahy	4	25	12	10	8,486,957	Silverbulletday, m., Silver Deputy	3	23	15	14	3,093,207
1995	Victory Gallop, h., Cryptoclearance	3	17	9	7	3,505,895	Banshee Breeze, m., Unbridled	3	18	10	8	2,784,798
1994	Silver Charm, h., Silver Buck	4	24	12	11	6,944,369	Seeking the Pearl, m., Seeking the Gold	4	21	8	7	4,021,716
1993	Skip Away, h., Skip Trial	4	38	18	16	9,616,360	Escena, m., Strawberry Road (Aus)	4	29	11	7	2,962,639
1992	Thunder Gulch, h., Gulch	2	16	9	8	2,915,086	Serena's Song, m., Rahy	3	38	18	17	3,283,388
1991	Taiki Blizzard, h., Seattle Slew	4	23	6	3	5,523,549	Heavenly Prize, m., Seeking the Gold	4	18	9	8	1,825,940
1990	Cigar, h., Palace Music	4	33	19	15	9,999,815	Ski Paradise, m., Lyphard	3	20	6	5	1,470,588
1989	Devil His Due, h., Devil's Bag	4	41	11	9	3,920,405	Hatoof, m., Irish River (Fr)	4	21	9	8	1,841,070
1988	Best Pal, g., *Habitony	7	47	18	17	5,668,245	Dance Smartly, m., Danzig	3	17	12	10	3,263,835
1987	Unbridled, h., Fappiano	3	24	8	5	4,489,475	Miss Alleged, m., Alleged	3	15	5	4	1,757,342
1986	Sunday Silence, h., Halo	3	14	9	7	4,968,554	Safely Kept, m., Horatius	4	31	24	22	2,194,206
1985	Forty Niner, h., Mr. Prospector	2	19	11	9	2,726,000	Goodbye Halo, m., Halo	3	24	11	10	1,706,702
1984	Alysheba, h., Alydar	3	26	11	10	6,679,242	Miesque, m., Nureyev	3	16	12	11	2,070,163
1983	Ferdinand, h., Nijinsky II	4	29	8	7	3,777,978	Family Style, m., State Dinner	3	35	10	9	1,537,118
1982	Spend a Buck, h., Buckaroo	2	15	10	7	4,220,689	Lady's Secret, m., Secretariat	4	45	25	22	3,021,325
1981	Precisionist, h., Crozier	5	46	20	17	3,485,398	Life's Magic, m., Cox's Ridge	4	32	8	7	2,255,218
1980	Silver o' Gold, h., Seattle Slew	3	21	12	8	3,533,534	Estrapade, m., *Vaguely Noble	4	30	12	10	1,937,142
1979	Majesty's Prince, h., His Majesty	4	43	12	9	2,077,796	Sefa's Beauty, m., Lt. Stevens	5	52	25	17	1,171,628
1978	Silveryville, h., *Petrone	8	56	19	14	1,282,880	Sintrillium, m., Sinister Purpose	5	46	14	9	743,602
1977	Temperence Hill, h., Stop the Music	3	31	11	9	1,567,650	Bold 'n Determined, m., Bold and Brave	3	20	16	11	949,599
1976	Spectacular Bid, h., Bold Bidder	3	30	26	23	2,781,608	Track Robbery, m., No Robbery	6	59	22	13	1,098,527
1975	John Henry, g., Ole Bob Bowers	8	83	39	30	6,591,860	The Very One, m., One for All	5	71	22	13	1,104,623
1974	Seattle Slew, h., Bold Reasoning	3	17	14	9	1,208,726	Trillion, m., Hail to Reason	3	32	9	8	957,413
1973	Exceller, h., *Vaguely Noble	5	33	15	13	1,674,587	Optimistic Gal, m., Sir Ivor	2	21	13	10	686,861
1972	Foolish Pleasure, h., What a Pleasure	3	26	16	12	1,216,705	Ivanjica, m., Sir Ivor	3	15	6	5	626,682
1971	Sharp Gary, g., Carry Back	7	115	16	13	535,198	Chris Evert, m., Swoon's Son	3	15	10	7	679,475
1970	Forego, g., *Forli	6	57	34	24	1,938,957	Dahlia, m., *Vaguely Noble	5	48	15	14	1,489,105
1969	Riva Ridge, h., First Landing	3	30	17	13	1,111,497	Susan's Girl, m., Quadrangle	5	63	29	24	1,251,668
1968	Run the Gantlet, h., Tom Rolfe	3	21	9	7	559,079	Convenience, m., Fleet Nasrullah	4	35	15	8	648,933
1967	Loud, h., *Herbager	7	88	12	3	527,779	Saturnina, m., *Ballydonnell	5	107	47	8	392,195
1966	Ack Ack, h., Battle Joined	4	27	19	16	636,641	Shuvee, m., Nashua	4	44	16	15	890,445
1965	Nodouble, h., *Noholme II	4	42	13	9	846,749	Gay Matelda, m., Sir Gaylord	3	37	9	5	409,945
1964	Damascus, h., Sword Dancer	3	32	21	17	1,176,781	Gamely, m., Bold Ruler	3	41	16	13	574,961
1963	Buckpasser, h., Tom Fool	3	31	25	21	1,462,014	Politely, m., *Amerigo	4	49	21	13	552,972
1962	Tom Rolfe, h., *Ribot	3	32	16	9	671,297	Straight Deal, m., Hail to Reason	6	99	21	13	733,020
1961	Roman Brother, g., Third Brother	4	42	16	10	943,473	Tosmah, m., Tim Tam	4	39	23	16	612,588
1960	Candy Spots, h., *Nigromante	3	22	12	9	824,718	Affectionately, m., *Swaps	4	52	28	18	546,659
1959	Native Diver, h., Imbros	7	81	37	33	1,026,500	Cicada, m., Bryan G.	4	42	23	18	783,674
1958	Carry Back, h., Saggy	4	62	21	14	1,241,165	Bowl of Flowers, m., Sailor	2	16	10	6	398,504
1957	Kelso, h., Your Host	8	63	39	31	1,977,896	Airmans Guide, m., One Count	3	20	13	8	315,673
1956	Sword Dancer, h., Sunglow	3	39	15	10	829,610	Royal Native, m., *Royal Charger	4	49	18	11	422,769
1955	Bald Eagle, h., *Nasrullah	4	29	12	12	692,946	Idun, m., *Royal Charger	3	30	17	9	392,490
1954	Round Table, h., *Princequillo	4	66	43	31	1,749,869	Endine, m., *Rico Monte	3	45	10	4	306,547
1953	Swoon's Son, h., The Doge	4	51	30	22	970,605	Dotted Line, m., *Princequillo	5	67	11	5	324,159
1952	Nashua, h., *Nasrullah	3	30	22	19	1,288,565	High Voltage, m., *Ambiorix	3	45	13	10	362,240
1951	Determine, h., *Alibhai	3	44	18	10	573,360	Queen Hopeful, m., Roman	5	65	18	10	365,044
1950	Find, g., Discovery	8	110	22	13	803,615	Grecian Queen, m., *Heliopolis	4	53	12	9	323,575
1949	Mark-Ye-Well, h., Bull Lea	4	40	14	11	581,910	Real Delight, m., Bull Lea	2	15	12	10	261,822
1948	Crafty Admiral, h., Fighting Fox	4	39	18	12	499,200	Sickle's Image, m., Sickletoy	5	73	27	10	413,275
1947	Oil Capitol, h., *Mahmoud	5	80	19	14	580,756	Next Move, m., Bull Lea	4	46	17	12	398,550
1946	Ponder, h., Pensive	4	41	14	11	541,275	Two Lea, m., Bull Lea	4	26	15	9	309,250
1945	Citation, h., Bull Lea	4	45	32	22	1,085,760	Bewitch, m., Bull Lea	5	55	20	15	462,605
1944	On Trust, h., *Alibhai	7	88	31	17	554,145	But Why Not, m., Blue Larkspur	4	46	12	8	295,101
1943	Assault, h., Bold Venture	6	42	18	15	675,470	Honeymoon, m., *Beau Pere	6	78	14	13	387,760
1942	Pavot, h., Case Ace	4	32	14	12	373,365	Gallorette, m., *Challenger II	5	72	21	13	445,535
1941	Stymie, h., Equestrian	7	131	35	25	918,485	Twilight Tear, m., Bull Lea	3	24	18	10	202,165
1940	Count Fleet, h., Reigh Count	2	21	16	9	250,300	Happy Issue, m., Bow to Me	9	157	19	5	225,424
1939	First Fiddle, h., *Royal Minstrel	6	95	23	10	398,610	Vagrancy, m., *Sir Gallahad III	3	42	15	9	102,480
1938	Whirlaway, h., *Blenheim II	4	60	32	22	561,161	Moon Maiden, m., *Challenger II	6	109	19	1	76,780
1937	Billy Kelly, h., Black Toney	3	15	11	8	248,745	Fairy Chant, m., Chance Shot	3	42	10	7	81,985
1936	Challedon, h., *Challenger II	5	44	20	17	334,660	Loveday, m., Petee-Wrack	6	85	17	5	56,225
1935	Stagehand, h., *Sickle	3	25	9	6	200,110	Jacola, m., *Jacopo	3	25	11	4	70,060
1934	War Admiral, h., Man o' War	4	26	21	14	273,240	Dawn Play, m., Clock Tower	2	14	4	3	50,800
1933	Seabiscuit, h., Hard Tack	6	89	33	26	437,730	Columbiana, m., Petee-Wrack	4	28	11	1	60,925
1932	Rosemont, h., The Porter	4	23	7	5	168,750	Esposa, m., Espino	7	96	19	15	132,055
1931	Top Row, h., Peanuts	5	42	14	11	213,870	Mata Hari, m., Peter Hastings	2	16	7	5	66,699

All-Time Leading Earners by State Where Bred 1954-2007

Alabama

MALE, YOB, Sire	Yrs Raced	Strts	Wins	SWs	Earnings	FEMALE, YOB, Sire	Yrs Raced	Strts	Wins	SWs	Earnings
Winonly, 1957 h., Olympia	5	64	21	11	$326,264	Comalagold, 2000 m., Royal Empire	6	48	10	4	$311,680
Lombardi Time, 1987 g., Lombardi	6	68	25	5	270,933	My Portrait, 1958 m., Olympia	5	94	17	3	261,275
Chief Tudor, 1997 g., Chief Persuasion	9	77	15	4	259,715	Blacksher, 1995 m., Reack Boldly	9	100	20	0	173,144
Alpena Magic, 1990 g., L'Enjoleur	14	154	16	0	206,482	Rocky Turn, 1995 m., Rocky Mountain	6	62	10	0	158,335
Sky Gem, 1960 h., *Quibu	4	63	12	0	197,573	Vicki's Ryde, 1987 m., Society Max	7	81	24	1	130,758
Alagon, 1989 g., Rajab	6	80	10	3	169,353	Fancy Empire, 2001 m., Royal Empire	4	28	5	1	128,679
He's a Duster, 1991 g., Stark Duster	10	112	11	0	146,364	Teacher's Art, 1964 m., *Quibu	3	15	5	2	121,494
Ezgo, 1954 g., Olympia	6	72	12	4	135,731	Georges Cherub, 1985 m., If This Be So	5	76	11	0	101,905
King Oasis, 1974 h., Island Kingdom	8	102	32	6	134,508	Darling's Bid, 1993 m., Prospector's Bid	4	37	7	0	101,141
Knight Tres, 1994 g., Knight of Old	8	107	16	0	130,693	Jem Klip, 1988 m., Luck's Reality	8	102	12	0	81,835

Alaska

MALE, YOB, Sire	Yrs Raced	Strts	Wins	SWs	Earnings	FEMALE, YOB, Sire	Yrs Raced	Strts	Wins	SWs	Earnings
Austin Texas, 1988 g., Tom Tulle	7	76	9	0	$27,778	Ice Blue Moon, 1979 m., *Hard Water	4	60	4	0	$15,146
Cope Stetic, 1983 h., Romeo	3	36	3	0	9,157	Murph's Pet, 1979 m., J. R.'s Pet	3	21	2	0	7,911
Whistling Johnny, 1975 h., Whistling Kettle	2	15	1	0	3,202	Princess Will Win, 1988 m., Will Win	2	6	1	0	2,970

Arizona

MALE, YOB, Sire	Yrs Raced	Strts	Wins	SWs	Earnings	FEMALE, YOB, Sire	Yrs Raced	Strts	Wins	SWs	Earnings
Coyote Lakes, 1994 g., Society Max	8	63	20	5	$728,337	Monrow, 1996 m., Fool the Experts	5	43	17	3	$297,344
First Intent, 1989 g., Prima Voce	7	63	12	2	524,357	Knoll Lake, 1998 m., Benton Creek	6	26	12	9	270,155
Komax, 1998 g., Society Max	7	54	21	7	489,785	Nervous John, 1976 m., Nervous Energy	4	44	14	11	257,686
Last Don B., 1987 g., Don B.	9	104	40	15	471,461	To the Post, 1989 m., Bold Ego	4	22	11	7	241,912
Faro, 1982 h., Crafty Drone	7	59	20	6	460,103	Bueno, 1992 m., Society Max	6	49	14	9	233,130
G Malleah, 1991 g., Fool the Experts	10	61	17	13	439,613	Left the Latch, 1991 m., Society Max	4	40	16	5	207,848
Peaked, 1985 h., Drone	6	43	16	11	398,338	Reatta Pass, 1999 m., Benton Creek	6	46	14	1	188,685
Tropic Ruler, 1979 g., Key Rulla	4	21	11	4	395,898	Carte Madera, 1999 m., Society Max	5	35	8	0	180,835
Radar Ahead, 1975 h., *Repicado II	5	17	9	4	390,125	The Lord's Tune, 1997 m., Relaunch a Tune	3	26	12	0	176,305
Hyder, 1997 g., Calumar	7	58	13	0	354,318	Hugafool, 1994 m., Fool the Experts	5	29	9	4	175,653

Arkansas

MALE, YOB, Sire	Yrs Raced	Strts	Wins	SWs	Earnings	FEMALE, YOB, Sire	Yrs Raced	Strts	Wins	SWs	Earnings
Nodouble, 1965 h., *Noholme II	4	42	13	9	$846,749	Humble Clerk, 1997 m., Humble Eleven	3	17	6	4	$503,545
Beau's Town, 1998 g., Beau Genius	5	23	13	9	697,850	Ruddy Eagle, 1990 m., Beau's Leader	6	82	15	5	468,680
Dust On the Bottle, 1995 h., Temperence Hill	7	81	11	4	683,312	Nurse Dopey, 1987 m., Dr. Blum	4	32	16	11	456,362
Never Forgotten, 1984 g., Bold L. B.	8	119	15	6	499,606	Stoney Jody, 1994 m., Silver Survivor	3	39	14	1	384,813
E J Harley, 1992 g., Beat Inflation	10	54	17	4	456,915	Biolage, 1989 m., Hurricane Ed	7	122	12	1	294,983
Lanyons Star, 1988 g., Suzanne's Star	10	127	21	4	450,915	Downthedustyroad, 2003 m., Storm and a Half	2	12	4	1	289,908
Temperence Time, 1996 g., Temperence Hill	6	39	10	6	436,860	Jay's Sue, 1979 m., Jahan	5	51	18	5	282,560
Dirty Mike, 1995 g., Temperence Hill	9	93	18	2	431,063	Humble Eight, 1992 m., Seattle Battle	4	34	6	4	278,450
Be a Agent, 1984 h., Be a Prospect	7	81	16	0	355,362	Tsu Tsu Won, 1993 m., Air Forbes Won	10	117	18	0	270,878
Up Limit, 1978 g., Decimator	7	68	23	4	353,216	Cato Double, 1980 m., Nodouble	4	56	10	3	265,869

California

MALE, YOB, Sire	Yrs Raced	Strts	Wins	SWs	Earnings	FEMALE, YOB, Sire	Yrs Raced	Strts	Wins	SWs	Earnings
Tiznow, 1997 h., Cee's Tizzy	2	15	8	7	$6,427,830	Moscow Burning, 2000 m., Moscow Ballet	4	33	11	6	$1,417,800
Best Pal, 1988 g., *Habitony	7	47	18	17	5,668,245	Fran's Valentine, 1982 m., Saros (GB)	4	34	13	12	1,375,465
Lava Man, 2001 g., Slew City Slew	5	43	17	13	5,214,706	Brown Bess, 1982 m., *Petrone	6	36	16	11	1,300,920
Snow Chief, 1983 h., Reflected Glory	3	24	13	12	3,383,210	Gourmet Girl, 1995 m., Cee's Tizzy	5	33	9	6	1,255,373
Bertrando, 1989 h., Skywalker	5	24	9	8	3,185,610	Dream of Summer, 1999 m., Siberian Summer	4	20	10	6	1,191,150
Free House, 1994 h., Smokester	4	22	9	8	3,178,971	Lazy Slusan, 1995 m., Slewvescent	5	47	12	10	1,150,450
General Challenge, 1996 g., General Meeting	4	21	9	8	2,877,178	Valentine Dancer, 2000 m., In Excess (Ire)	4	29	8	5	1,144,126
Budroyale, 1993 g., Cee's Tizzy	7	52	17	7	2,840,815	Somethinaboutlaura, 2002 m., Dance Floor	5	30	17	13	1,008,865
Thor's Echo, 2002 g., Swiss Yodeler	4	18	5	4	2,372,990	House of Fortune, 2001 m., Free House	4	22	8	7	989,185
Nostalgia's Star, 1982 h., Nostalgia	5	59	9	7	2,154,827	Nashoba's Key, 2003 m., Silver Hawk	2	8	7	5	972,090

Colorado

MALE, YOB, Sire	Yrs Raced	Strts	Wins	SWs	Earnings	FEMALE, YOB, Sire	Yrs Raced	Strts	Wins	SWs	Earnings
To Erin, 1976 h., Epic Journey	7	104	28	9	$392,707	Prairie Maiden, 1993 m., Badger Land	4	30	10	5	$294,754
Rusty Canyon, 1975 h., Sound Off	9	94	16	5	372,935	Bar Bailey, 2000 m., Bates Motel	4	26	10	0	87,582
Personal Beau, 1996 g., Personal Flag	8	50	17	10	336,213	She's Finding Time, 1999 m., Ragtime Rascal	5	33	13	6	85,072
Lewistown, 1992 g., Strike Gold	10	64	21	0	308,547	Ladysgotthelooks, 2001 m., Seattle Sleet	5	25	9	5	76,576
Cut of Music, 2000 g., Coverallbases	6	78	15	9	298,015	Vannacide, 2001 m., Slewacide	5	29	11	6	65,218
Moro Grande, 1995 g., Fuzzy	8	43	7	5	247,119	Defrere's Vixen, 2000 g., Defrere	5	40	6	0	242,120	Kranky Karol, 2001 m., Pioneering	6	30	7	1	64,181

Racing — Leading Earners by State Where Bred

MALE, YOB, Sire	Yrs Raced	Strts	Wins	SWs	Earnings	FEMALE, YOB, Sire	Yrs Raced	Strts	Wins	SWs	Earnings
Cocoa Latte, 2001 g., Demidoff	4	29	13	8	$224,709	Windic, 1975 m., Dancing Dervish	5	55	9	1	$144,097
The Nth Degree, 2001 g., Distorted Humor	5	29	5	2	217,597	Jennaly, 1995 m., Alydarmer	5	48	9	3	135,263
High Rover, 1965 g., Star Rover	10	110	33	10	215,701	Gentle Gil, 1981 m., Gilligan	5	53	14	2	134,828
						Broncomania, 1977 m., Marv 'n Jeff	7	58	19	7	130,418

Connecticut

MALE, YOB, Sire	Yrs Raced	Strts	Wins	SWs	Earnings	FEMALE, YOB, Sire	Yrs Raced	Strts	Wins	SWs	Earnings
Nantucketeer, 1998 h., Departing Prints	6	48	12	0	$198,849	Skipat, 1974 m., Jungle Cove	5	45	26	14	$614,215
Fast Smile, 1970 h., Fast Gun	6	105	32	1	142,795	Leave No Prints, 1995 m., Departing Prints	5	53	18	1	232,377
Belle's Brat, 1974 h., Precision	8	173	27	0	131,872	Onyx Fox, 1974 m., Mr. Hasty	7	105	20	0	109,451
Reserve Native, 1974 h., Native Admiral	9	146	21	0	114,496	Poker's Thunder, 1992 m., Honest Turn	6	92	17	0	108,877
Lonesome Dawn, 1994 g., Fly Till Dawn	5	43	5	0	114,235	Pation, 1977 m., Patrician	7	96	17	0	91,313
President Jim, 1960 g., *Good Shot	7	84	20	1	101,722	Naskrahoney, 1974 m., Naskra	4	38	6	1	83,201
More Coins, 1960 g., Royal Visitor	9	193	23	0	92,858	Diplomatic King, 1984 m., Diplomatic Note	3	40	12	0	75,429
Chapel Creek, 1978 h., Our Native	3	28	4	0	84,456	Good Jane, 1961 m., *Good Shot	4	45	9	1	70,563
Peace Isle, 1956 g., *Good Shot	7	117	19	0	65,579	Lady Petee, 1983 m., Hairy Business	7	63	10	0	69,977
Gisele's Banker, 1969 h., My Banker	11	115	25	0	64,499	Clown's Gal, 1977 m., The Clown	5	88	10	0	66,893

Delaware

MALE, YOB, Sire	Yrs Raced	Strts	Wins	SWs	Earnings	FEMALE, YOB, Sire	Yrs Raced	Strts	Wins	SWs	Earnings
Baitman, 1961 g., Assemblyman	8	113	27	3	$298,198	Pokey Lady, 1984 m., Georgeandthedragon	5	74	20	0	$155,275
Golden Immigrant, 1981 g., Medaille d'Or	5	47	6	0	161,380	Wing Flutter, 1969 m., Sunrise Flight	6	86	13	0	90,894
Whale, 1969 g., Impressive	10	123	18	0	119,663	Shoe Off, 1972 m., Rambunctious	4	64	10	0	76,316
Proudest Doon, 1982 h., Matsadoon	3	11	4	2	104,620	Wild Beat, 1979 m., Iron Ruler	2	7	4	0	52,980
Space to Kevin, 1984 h., Travelling Music	5	78	9	0	96,530	Appear, 1969 m., Loom	3	39	7	0	47,689
Great Depths, 1962 h., *King of the Tudors	7	125	15	1	96,521	Double Hold, 1981 m., Hold Your Peace	4	28	4	0	41,915
Brixton Road, 1963 h., Great Captain	8	133	13	0	58,472	Foamy, 1954 m., Tide Rips	7	133	21	0	36,233
Parish Judge, 1968 g., Delta Judge	4	85	16	0	52,301	Tacky Lady, 1973 m., Nail	3	50	5	0	35,834
Devilfish, 1953 g., Greek Song	7	109	12	0	50,237	Wedge, 1969 m., Fulcrum	3	60	12	0	32,172
Frank's Ace, 1973 h., Rock Talk	5	78	5	0	49,600	Oh She May, 1979 m., Oceans Reward	5	64	7	0	25,555

Florida

MALE, YOB, Sire	Yrs Raced	Strts	Wins	SWs	Earnings	FEMALE, YOB, Sire	Yrs Raced	Strts	Wins	SWs	Earnings
Skip Away, 1993 h., Skip Trial	4	38	18	16	$9,616,360	Beautiful Pleasure, 1995 m., Maudlin	5	25	10	7	$2,734,078
Silver Charm, 1994 h., Silver Buck	4	24	12	11	6,944,369	Jewel Princess, 1992 m., Key to the Mint	4	29	13	10	1,904,060
Unbridled, 1987 h., Fappiano	3	24	8	5	4,489,475	Ginger Punch, 2003 m., Awesome Again	2	14	7	4	1,901,679
David Junior, 2002 h., Pleasant Tap	3	4	2	1	3,519,420	Smok'n Frolic, 1999 m., Smoke Glacken	4	33	9	8	1,534,720
Precisionist, 1981 h., Crozier	5	46	20	17	3,485,398	Halo America, 1990 m., Waquoit	5	40	15	9	1,460,992
Peace Rules, 2000 h., Jules	3	19	9	8	3,084,278	Meadow Star, 1988 m., Meadowlake	3	20	11	10	1,445,740
Afleet Alex, 2002 h., Northern Afleet	2	12	8	6	2,765,800	Hollywood Wildcat, 1990 m., Kris S.	4	21	9	11	1,432,160
Miesque's Approval, 1999 h., Miesque's Son	7	41	12	9	2,648,879	Tappiano, 1984 m., Fappiano	4	34	17	4	1,305,522
Sir Bear, 1993 g., Sir Leon	8	71	19	11	2,538,422	One Dreamer, 1988 m., Relaunch	4	25	12	7	1,266,067
Gate Dancer, 1981 h., Sovereign Dancer	4	28	7	4	2,501,705	Glitter Woman, 1994 m., Glitterman	4	23	10	5	1,256,805

Georgia

MALE, YOB, Sire	Yrs Raced	Strts	Wins	SWs	Earnings	FEMALE, YOB, Sire	Yrs Raced	Strts	Wins	SWs	Earnings
Bluesthestandard, 1997 g., American Standard	6	47	19	3	$1,041,618	Vivace, 1993 m., Shot Gun Scott	5	40	20	15	$1,037,671
Maybe Jack, 1993 g., Classic Account	10	122	35	1	534,715	Ayrial Delight, 1992 m., Quick Dip	6	63	18	6	458,992
Southern Slew, 1986 g., Slew Machine	6	41	13	0	207,610	Miss Hamma, 1999 m., Roaring Camp	5	32	10	4	301,295
Fortunate Lance, 1988 g., Fortunate Prospect	6	53	11	0	186,499	Bobbyrea, 1994 m., Classic Account	4	39	13	0	262,106
More Tell, 1996 g., Reach for More	8	59	15	0	161,641	Tia's Orphan Annie, 1995 m., Prospector's Halo	8	93	12	0	163,910
Rise Higher, 1991 g., Reach for More	10	119	20	0	156,289	Rose Darling, 1996 m., Roaring Camp	6	77	11	0	158,800
My Mac Flashys, 1986 g., Flashy Mac	4	28	8	1	139,195	Prime to Go, 1991 m., Classic Go Go	7	72	19	0	142,223
Jeshurun, 1986 h., First Sea Lord	7	73	14	0	115,333	Sarcasm, 1987 m., Noon Time Spender	8	87	11	0	136,154
Reach for Ameri, 1996 g., Reach for More	7	64	9	1	109,786	Rabs Lil Brit Brit, 1991 m., Classic Account	5	47	7	0	123,044
Finally Class, 1985 h., Finally Gotcha	6	41	8	1	102,808	Paddy's Princess, 1975 m., Irish Dude	5	64	8	0	120,750

Hawaii

MALE, YOB, Sire	Yrs Raced	Strts	Wins	SWs	Earnings	FEMALE, YOB, Sire	Yrs Raced	Strts	Wins	SWs	Earnings
Hawaii Boy, 1970 g., Kaaba	7	87	17	0	$46,817	Mapu, 1964 m., Hauli	5	99	9	0	$19,078
Kaniala, 1957 h., Bel Canto	10	142	22	0	36,912	Punahou, 1961 m., Skip Khal	7	93	2	0	4,641
Molokai, 1962 h., Skip Khal	11	143	23	0	34,343	Lace Lady, 1973 m., Braefox	2	11	0	0	3,200
Hey Sam, 1961 h., Hauli	5	53	6	0	31,622	Webb's Brunette, 1965 m., Star Hug	3	23	3	0	2,920
Alakahi, 1963 g., Bel Canto	6	98	10	0	27,845	Iwaiha, 1962 m., Hauli	4	26	3	0	2,048
Hoanani, 1958 g., Alicane	9	129	19	0	27,817	Waipio, 1962 m., Skip Khal	3	32	1	0	1,060
Manakuke, 1955 h., Alicane	8	136	15	0	22,810	Sushila, 1962 m., Hauli	2	11	0	0	905
Kawela, 1963 h., Skip Khal	7	89	11	0	20,175	Kauhiwai, 1963 m., Bel Canto	1	12	0	0	737
Pua Nalu, 1969 h., Kaaba	2	32	5	0	17,495	Go Margo, 1959 m., Bel Canto	1	13	0	0	630
Lukanela, 1955 g., Alicane	3	48	7	0	14,544	Bel Senora, 1967 m., Hauli	3	21	1	0	498

Racing — Leading Earners by State Where Bred

Idaho

MALE, YOB, Sire	Yrs Raced	Strts	Wins	SWs	Earnings
Gratteau, 1995 g., Synastry	8	50	14	4	$366,644
L'Effaceur, 1997 g., Jestic	6	30	10	1	324,064
Lookn East, 1998 g., Eastern Echo	6	50	11	4	304,768
Northern Provider, 1982 g., Staff Writer	7	51	8	2	231,619
Mining for Fun, 1998 g., L. B. Jaklin	7	72	7	0	214,339
San Diego Pete, 1995 g., Santiago Peak	7	63	16	4	199,210
Bojima's Majesty, 1990 g., Bojima	6	84	20	1	189,143
Curt's First Bid, 1999 g., Digression	6	43	11	0	177,036
Schuyler Road, 1992 g., Synastry	9	75	14	1	173,399
Hooten Harry, 1992 g., Unable	6	64	13	0	171,367

FEMALE, YOB, Sire	Yrs Raced	Strts	Wins	SWs	Earnings
Angi Go, 1990 m., Idaho's Majesty	5	36	15	8	$437,493
Lookn Mighty Fine, 1997 m., Peterhof	6	54	12	2	300,851
Lethal Leta, 1991 m., Synastry	5	32	12	8	300,602
Just Lookn, 1994 m., Synastry	2	18	8	4	213,675
Princess in Charge, 1991 m., Prince Card	5	46	7	0	193,105
Thou Shalt Not Lie, 1990 m., El Baba	4	39	8	1	183,687
Printasity, 1983 m., Growler	8	81	20	0	170,279
Thrill After Dark, 2000 m., Lyphaness	6	27	11	5	168,032
Riband, 1996 m., Lord of the Apes	6	50	11	0	166,671
Ladys Lil Cruiser, 1992 m., Key to the Carr	5	50	11	1	161,975

Illinois

MALE, YOB, Sire	Yrs Raced	Strts	Wins	SWs	Earnings
Buck's Boy, 1993 g., Bucksplasher	5	30	16	9	$2,750,148
Polar Expedition, 1991 g., Kodiack	7	49	20	14	1,491,071
Mystery Giver, 1998 g., Dynaformer	6	43	13	8	1,244,715
Western Playboy, 1986 h., Play Fellow	5	45	8	4	1,128,449
Fort Prado, 2001 h., El Prado (Ire)	6	38	16	11	968,551
Wiggins, 2000 g., Cartwright	6	39	16	9	892,800
Bucks Nephew, 1995 g., Bucksplasher	5	45	15	8	853,618
Harham's Sizzler, 1979 h., Good Behaving	7	73	24	14	843,406
Beboppin Baby, 1993 g., Hatchet Man	8	64	13	3	842,540
Scooter Roach, 1999 g., Mi Cielo	7	67	12	4	813,719

FEMALE, YOB, Sire	Yrs Raced	Strts	Wins	SWs	Earnings
Two Item Limit, 1998 m., Twining	3	28	7	4	$1,060,585
Lady Shirl, 1987 m., That's a Nice	6	41	18	10	951,523
Bungalow, 1987 m., Lord Avie	3	42	17	9	850,141
Peach of It, 1986 m., Navajo	5	53	15	9	625,721
Rolling Sea, 2003 m., Sefapiano	3	24	10	6	573,165
Summer Mis, 1999 m., Summer Squall	4	23	11	6	542,662
Your Ladyship, 1990 m., Moment of Hope	5	47	17	6	539,328
Darley Dancer, 1988 m., Play Fellow	6	48	17	5	516,098
Valid Vixen, 1985 m., Valid Appeal	4	27	10	6	492,655
Faccia Bella, 1996 m., Dixie Brass	7	57	8	4	488,442

Indiana

MALE, YOB, Sire	Yrs Raced	Strts	Wins	SWs	Earnings
Hillsdale, 1955 h., Take Away	3	41	23	14	$646,935
Pass Rush, 1999 h., Crown Ambassador	6	40	7	4	594,603
Fight for Ally, 1997 g., Fit to Fight	7	32	12	6	546,559
Navajo, 1970 h., *Grey Dawn II	5	48	22	6	351,982
Red's Honor, 1998 h., Glitterman	6	37	12	4	332,830
Edgerrin, 2001 g., Category Five	5	54	12	3	324,250
Mr. Mink, 2000 g., Gold Case	6	35	19	7	319,050
Vic's Rebel, 1994 g., Lac Ouimet	5	34	11	4	304,682
Pelican Beach, 1998 g., Air Forbes Won	4	34	17	1	277,817
Joanies No Phony, 1997 g., Buckhar	8	89	16	1	264,937

FEMALE, YOB, Sire	Yrs Raced	Strts	Wins	SWs	Earnings
Honky Star, 1971 m., Bupers	4	39	18	10	$353,012
Lady Blue Sky, 2002 m., Bidding Proud	4	32	17	3	279,567
Marciann, 1997 m., Speedy Cure	5	29	11	5	278,806
Ellens Lucky Star, 1999 m., Crown Ambassador	4	26	10	7	249,155
Senorita Ziggy, 1998 m., Senor Speedy	5	28	9	4	226,080
Maggie Slew, 2003 m., Seattle Slew	3	19	4	0	203,237
Maggie's Dream, 1998 m., Philadreamt	7	43	9	3	183,341
Lighting Bopers, 1996 m., Cape Storm	3	8	5	4	178,455
Lil E Rose, 2002 m., Lil E. Tee	4	34	9	1	162,949
Amanda's Crown, 1999 m., Crown Ambassador	3	21	5	3	161,152

Iowa

MALE, YOB, Sire	Yrs Raced	Strts	Wins	SWs	Earnings
Sure Shot Biscuit, 1996 g., Miracle Heights	6	54	23	13	$1,025,480
Take Me Up, 1998 g., Take Me Out	7	55	13	5	531,540
Cowboy Stuff, 1999 h., Evansville Slew	5	25	11	4	428,280
Country Warrior, 1999 g., Ghazi	7	66	17	0	370,455
Le Numerous, 1998 g., Numerous	8	80	13	1	362,117
Sur Sandpit, 2000 g., Sandpit (Brz)	7	51	13	2	342,954
Mingo Mohawk, 2002 g., Mercedes Won	4	34	8	3	327,067
Plum Sober, 2001 g., Blumin Affair	5	47	9	1	314,189
Cmego, 2000 g., Gold Case	5	58	11	0	299,656
Wild Wild West, 2001 g., Slewacide	6	33	9	2	298,830

FEMALE, YOB, Sire	Yrs Raced	Strts	Wins	SWs	Earnings
Sharky's Review, 1998 m., Sharkey	4	36	15	10	$685,425
Nut N Better, 1997 m., Miracle Heights	4	28	14	9	572,828
Lady Tamworth, 1995 m., No Louder	6	68	15	3	567,058
Switch Lanes, 1999 m., Deerhound	5	45	12	4	450,926
Camela Carson, 2002 m., Lord Carson	5	29	10	2	345,483
Vaguely Who, 1993 m., Hittias (GB)	6	48	12	5	333,745
Sumthintotalkabout, 1997 m., Kyle's Our Man	4	25	9	2	313,928
Danzig Foxxy Woman, 1995 m., Dr. Danzig	4	28	6	4	268,707
Sound of Gold, 1998 m., Mutakddim	5	40	13	4	263,243
Gamblers Passion, 2000 m., Prospectors Gamble	4	36	11	3	267,067

Kansas

MALE, YOB, Sire	Yrs Raced	Strts	Wins	SWs	Earnings
I Dancer, 1995 g., I Enclose	7	68	15	1	$270,862
Gay Revoke, 1958 h., Blue Gay	9	128	27	5	251,251
Kangaroo King, 1993 g., Tarsal	6	53	14	0	211,719
Polar Barron, 1996 g., Track Barron	9	66	15	3	182,633
Cheryl's Gazelle, 1995 g., Discover	7	70	11	0	179,306
Morning Merry, 2000 g., Scarlet 'n Gray	6	29	7	3	171,530
Scarlet Lad, 1998 g., Big Splash	7	72	11	3	170,772
Raise a Booger, 1999 g., Gold Ruler	8	93	15	5	170,473
Rio Gambler, 1990 g., Boca Rio	8	92	17	2	168,904
Jim Dunham, 1991 g., Dunham's Gift	11	109	17	2	168,455

FEMALE, YOB, Sire	Yrs Raced	Strts	Wins	SWs	Earnings
Sunnie Do It, 1994 m., Do It Again Dan	8	83	16	9	$315,722
Queena Corrina, 1999 m., Here We Come	5	31	10	0	267,770
Tiney Toast, 1989 m., Blue Jester	4	28	6	3	217,614
Bonnie J., 2000 m., Arab Speaker	4	35	7	0	165,965
Shero, 1993 m., Glorious Flag	6	63	9	0	164,203
Swinging Janie Gal, 1997 m., A. M. Swinger	6	36	5	0	157,815
Discreetly Irish, 1998 m., Big Splash	7	74	11	4	145,637
Amberaja, 1985 m., Kibe	7	90	23	6	141,868
Missy Can Do, 2000 m., Gold Ruler	6	42	15	8	141,465
Lady Take the Gold, 1989 m., Gold Ruler	8	16	17	0	137,492

Kentucky

MALE, YOB, Sire	Yrs Raced	Strts	Wins	SWs	Earnings
Fantastic Light, 1996 h., Rahy	4	25	12	10	$8,486,957

FEMALE, YOB, Sire	Yrs Raced	Strts	Wins	SWs	Earnings
Azeri, 1998 m., Jade Hunter	4	24	17	14	$4,079,820

Racing — Leading Earners by State Where Bred

MALE, YOB, Sire	Yrs Raced	Strts	Wins	SWs	Earnings	FEMALE, YOB, Sire	Yrs Raced	Strts	Wins	SWs	Earnings
Pleasantly Perfect, 1998 h., Pleasant Colony	4	18	9	6	$7,789,880	Ashado, 2001 m., Saint Ballado	3	21	12	11	$3,931,440
Captain Steve, 1997 h., Fly So Free	3	25	9	8	6,828,356	Spain, 1997 m., Thunder Gulch	4	35	9	7	3,540,542
Alysheba, 1984 h., Alydar	3	26	11	10	6,679,242	Serena's Song, 1992 m., Rahy	3	38	18	17	3,283,388
John Henry, 1975 g., Ole Bob Bowers	8	83	39	30	6,591,860	Silverbulletday, 1996 m., Silver Deputy	3	23	15	14	3,093,207
Medaglia d'Oro, 1999 h., El Prado (Ire)	4	17	8	7	5,754,720	Escena, 1993 m., Strawberry Road (Aus)	4	29	11	7	2,962,639
Taiki Blizzard, 1991 h., Seattle Slew	4	23	6	3	5,523,549	Banshee Breeze, 1995 m., Unbridled	3	18	10	8	2,784,798
Roses in May, 2000 h., Devil His Due	3	13	8	4	5,490,187	Honey Ryder, 2001 m., Lasting Approval	5	33	13	11	2,784,160
English Channel, 2002 h., Smart Strike	4	23	13	10	5,319,028	Flawlessly, 1988 m., Affirmed	5	28	16	15	2,572,536
Curlin, 2004 c., Smart Strike	1	9	6	5	5,102,800	Take Charge Lady, 1999 m., Dehere	3	22	11	9	2,480,377

Louisiana

MALE, YOB, Sire	Yrs Raced	Strts	Wins	SWs	Earnings	FEMALE, YOB, Sire	Yrs Raced	Strts	Wins	SWs	Earnings
Scott's Scoundrel, 1992 h., L'Enjoleur	6	50	22	19	$1,270,052	Happy Ticket, 2001 m., Anet	3	20	12	10	$1,688,544
Zarb's Magic, 1993 g., Zarbyev	8	69	23	5	893,946	Sarah Lane's Oates, 1994 m., Sunshine Forever	7	77	21	15	888,296
King Roller, 1991 g., Silent King	9	107	21	5	883,588	Fit to Scout, 1987 m., Fit to Fight	3	30	8	6	767,600
Costa Rising, 2003 h., Royal Strand (Ire)	3	22	14	10	861,366	Hallowed Dreams, 1997 m., Malagra	4	30	25	17	740,144
Dixie Poker Ace, 1987 g., Patriotically	8	86	27	18	850,126	Eskimo's Angel, 1989 m., Eskimo	5	39	11	8	701,539
Free Spirit's Joy, 1988 h., Joey Bob	5	32	8	5	841,277	Zuppardo Ardo, 1994 m., Zuppardo's Prince	5	39	14	10	667,886
Walk in the Snow, 1999 g., In a Walk	7	56	16	6	728,821	Destiny Calls, 2000 m., With Approval	4	27	14	6	644,220
Zarb's Luck, 1997 g., Zarbyev	9	61	12	6	647,744	Leslie's Love, 1997 m., Combat Ready	6	56	22	6	642,484
Oak Hall, 1996 g., Olympio	7	43	18	9	635,067	Hope List, 1990 m., List	6	81	20	7	601,475
Nijinsky's Gold, 1989 g., Lot o' Gold	7	45	10	7	622,160	Up the Apalachee, 1984 m., Apalachee	3	28	14	8	595,935

Maine

MALE, YOB, Sire	Yrs Raced	Strts	Wins	SWs	Earnings	FEMALE, YOB, Sire	Yrs Raced	Strts	Wins	SWs	Earnings
Seboomook, 1976 h., Sunny South	7	96	22	0	$124,837	North of Boston, 1972 m., Midland Man	4	25	4	0	$40,693
My Secret Love, 1965 g., Busy Harvest	10	172	24	0	69,853	Louisa Midland, 1975 m., George Lewis	3	20	5	0	40,149
Sokokis, 1971 h., Midland Man	2	32	5	0	54,232	Amblast, 1973 m., Blasting Charge	4	36	6	0	31,632
Atafu, 1966 h., Atoll	3	128	14	0	38,230	Limington, 1969 m., Black Mountain	2	24	4	1	25,854
Mr. Kippers, 1967 h., Hallursan	3	43	14	0	35,397	Favorite Act, 1959 m., Activate	6	100	14	0	25,075
Hyperides, 1969 h., Midland Man	9	107	16	0	28,147	Irish Dotty, 1959 m., Activate	6	108	16	0	20,665
Blue Katahdin, 1970 g., Black Mountain	7	115	13	0	25,534	Carrabasset, 1977 m., George Lewis	2	18	1	0	13,180
Mr. Jazzman, 1967 h., Midland Man	5	59	12	0	25,090	Lilac Ribbons, 1971 m., Cap Size	2	11	2	0	10,721
Hacienda Imperal, 1962 h., Activate	7	112	13	0	17,394	Hacienda Gal, 1967 m., Busy Harvest	4	74	5	0	9,198
Beau Harvest, 1968 h., Busy Harvest	4	71	8	0	15,044	Jet's Tru Dan, 1978 m., Danaus	3	34	2	0	8,875

Maryland

MALE, YOB, Sire	Yrs Raced	Strts	Wins	SWs	Earnings	FEMALE, YOB, Sire	Yrs Raced	Strts	Wins	SWs	Earnings
Cigar, 1990 h., Palace Music	4	33	19	15	$9,999,815	Safely Kept, 1986 m., Horatius	4	31	24	22	$2,194,206
Awad, 1990 h., Caveat	7	70	14	11	3,270,131	Shine Again, 1997 m., Wild Again	5	34	14	7	1,271,840
Concern, 1991 h., Broad Brush	3	30	7	4	3,079,350	Jameela, 1976 m., Rambunctious	4	58	27	16	1,038,704
Broad Brush, 1983 h., Ack Ack	3	27	14	12	2,656,793	Urbane, 1992 m., Citidancer	3	18	8	7	1,018,568
Little Bold John, 1982 g., John Alden	9	105	38	25	1,956,406	Silmaril, 2001 m., Diamond	6	35	15	11	984,973
Include, 1997 h., Broad Brush	4	20	10	7	1,659,560	Squan Song, 1981 m., Exceller	5	36	18	14	898,444
Valley Crossing, 1988 h., Private Account	5	48	8	4	1,616,490	Thirty Eight Go Go, 1985 m., Thirty Eight Paces	5	46	10	8	871,229
Our New Recruit, 1999 h., Alphabet Soup	3	19	6	2	1,470,915	Wide Country, 1988 m., Magesterial	3	26	12	11	819,728
Ten Keys, 1984 h., Sir Ivor Again	5	54	21	16	1,209,211	Brilliant Brass, 1987 m., Marine Brass	4	27	16	9	767,051
Cherokee's Boy, 2000 h., Citidancer	5	48	19	14	1,177,946	In the Curl, 1984 m., Shelter Half	8	85	26	10	749,891

Massachusetts

MALE, YOB, Sire	Yrs Raced	Strts	Wins	SWs	Earnings	FEMALE, YOB, Sire	Yrs Raced	Strts	Wins	SWs	Earnings
Rise Jim, 1976 h., Jim J.	5	52	27	12	$528,789	Ask Queenie, 2001 m., Key Contender	5	42	25	17	$558,705
Jini's Jet, 1998 g., A. P Jet	6	57	22	11	427,380	Isadorable, 1983 m., Moleolus	4	39	19	17	415,018
Garemma, 1986 g., Shananie	5	43	16	1	395,583	Big Miss, 1996 m., Chief Honcho	5	76	16	5	357,834
Mr. Meso, 2000 g., Mesopotamia	6	48	17	4	349,286	Sunlit Ridge, 1998 m., Sundance Ridge	6	64	16	10	347,780
Stylish Sultan, 1999 h., Sundance Ridge	7	48	17	10	341,401	Flirt for Fame, 2003 m., Freud	3	25	8	5	242,770
Galloping Gael, 1994 h., Lost Code	6	50	9	3	297,317	Land Ahoy, 1993 m., Oh Say	7	74	14	7	242,765
Second Episode, 1992 h., Potentiate	7	68	17	13	274,277	Lt'l Miss D. S., 1990 m., Hiromi the Great	4	54	12	7	220,064
Papa Ho Ho, 1993 g., On to Glory	8	87	18	6	265,882	African Princess, 1999 m., Sundance Ridge	5	45	7	7	211,400
Tonights the Night, 1978 h., Great Mystery	8	115	13	8	258,532	Potential Fire, 1991 m., Potentiate	6	46	10	5	202,938
Josiah W., 1977 h., Heat of Battle	7	104	18	7	193,244	Weepecket, 1997 m., Mr. Sparkles	6	56	8	3	184,775

Michigan

MALE, YOB, Sire	Yrs Raced	Strts	Wins	SWs	Earnings	FEMALE, YOB, Sire	Yrs Raced	Strts	Wins	SWs	Earnings
Tenpins, 1998 h., Smart Strike	4	17	9	5	$1,133,449	Peppen, 1994 m., Pep Up	4	37	15	11	$623,417
Secret Romeo, 1998 h., Service Stripe	5	55	23	17	865,790	Karate Miss, 1995 m., Chicanery Slew	4	38	17	14	602,465
Pongo Boy, 1992 g., Matchlite	9	87	22	12	776,184	Born to Dance, 1997 m., Service Stripe	6	38	11	9	577,519
Badwagon Harry, 1979 h., Ole Bob Bowers	9	121	19	10	742,412	Sefas Rose, 1997 m., Sefapiano	5	32	13	7	488,815
						Cashier's Dream, 1999 m., Service Stripe	2	7	5	3	423,042
Xclusive Imp, 1994 g., Majesty's Imp	8	87	12	9	584,130	Agiftfrom Bertie, 1993 m., Monetary Gift	4	38	10	9	408,378

Racing — Leading Earners by State Where Bred

MALE, YOB, Sire	Yrs Raced	Strts	Wins	SWs	Earnings	FEMALE, YOB, Sire	Yrs Raced	Strts	Wins	SWs	Earnings
Rockem Sockem, 2001 g., Ulises	5	34	12	11	$526,244	Sweetwater Promise, 1999 m., Service Stripe	6	42	10	5	$376,439
Thumbsucker, 1979 h., Great Sun	4	31	16	10	525,553	Farer Belle Lee, 1979 m., Seafarer	5	62	17	9	334,700
Above the Wind, 1997 g., Island Whirl	8	68	21	11	521,239	My Show, 1986 m., Tilt Up	6	77	19	6	331,408
Wind Chill, 1983 h., It's Freezing	7	73	15	6	502,492	North Rustim, 1978 m., Northern Native	5	61	19	15	328,002
That Gift, 1997 g., Monetary Gift	9	74	20	6	485,869						

Minnesota

MALE, YOB, Sire	Yrs Raced	Strts	Wins	SWs	Earnings	FEMALE, YOB, Sire	Yrs Raced	Strts	Wins	SWs	Earnings
Blair's Cove, 1985 h., Bucksplasher	6	58	17	10	$533,528	Courtly Kathy, 1991 m., Lost Code	8	89	18	4	$277,950
Wally's Choice, 2001 g., Quick Cut	4	28	13	9	428,590	Fortunate Faith, 1990 m., Fortunate Prospect	3	14	5	1	251,635
Super Abound, 1987 h., Superbity	4	36	6	2	398,418	Glitter Star, 2002 m., Glitterman	4	29	8	6	246,889
Cocoboy, 1988 g., Cozzene	13	196	30	1	371,567	Princess Elaine, 1985 m., Providential (Ire)	4	27	9	6	232,254
Crocrock, 1997 g., North Prospect	7	42	16	9	359,977	Northbound Pride, 1986 m., Proud Pocket	5	38	11	4	213,983
Timeless Prince, 1987 g., Prince Forli	7	69	16	6	326,977	Sentimental Charm, 2003 m., Silver Charm	3	17	7	5	213,185
It's Truly Obvious, 1992 g., Mufti	8	96	20	2	325,204	Samdanya, 1995 m., Northern Prospect	4	27	9	6	192,747
Ashar, 1995 g., Bucksplasher	8	53	9	5	274,654	Plana Dance, 1993 m., Northern Flagship	5	26	11	5	171,216
Bleu Victoriate, 1996 g., Victoriate	6	43	11	5	262,154	Shabana, 1991 m., Nasty and Bold	5	48	10	2	169,412
Buchman, 1987 h., Bucksplasher	3	32	8	1	254,929	Wishek's Kid, 1989 m., Pappa Riccio	7	67	18	3	167,359

Mississippi

MALE, YOB, Sire	Yrs Raced	Strts	Wins	SWs	Earnings	FEMALE, YOB, Sire	Yrs Raced	Strts	Wins	SWs	Earnings
Smalltown Slew, 2001 g., Evansville Slew	5	43	8	3	$320,033	Real Irish Hope, 1987 m., Tilt Up	5	49	15	3	$433,190
American Cowboy, 1994 g., Gold Crest	5	56	9	1	174,867	Blushing Sugarplum, 2003 m., Blushing Star	2	12	4	0	71,310
Lotsa Honey, 1981 h., Turn and Count	5	20	4	0	122,125	Miss Needlework, 1970 m., Needles	5	65	11	0	71,053
Dollars and Sense, 1991 g., Dollar Away	11	139	17	0	113,800	Miss Corinne, 1976 m., Grand Premiere	5	75	7	0	64,907
Go Star Buster, 2000 g., Blushing Star	6	42	5	1	113,050	Cocoa Baker, 1994 m., Jobaker	4	33	10	0	62,478
Nick's Palace, 1988 g., Palace Music	7	97	9	0	112,299	Pass the Money, 1987 m., Pass the Tab	5	57	10	0	59,178
Ruben Wizznat, 1986 h., North Rock	6	111	19	0	110,753	Ceasars Pleaser, 2003 m., Golden Omen	3	19	4	0	54,280
Pajima, 1985 h., Wajima	4	47	8	0	98,061	Proclaiming, 1973 m., Full Value	5	89	17	0	51,700
Jobaker, 1981 h., Heir to the Line	3	15	7	3	85,119	Claire's Secret, 1991 m., Happy Hooligan	5	37	3	0	40,590
Question of Gold, 1994 g., Gold Angle	9	82	7	0	83,589	Sweet Debbie, 2000 m., Sekari (GB)	4	26	3	0	34,050

Missouri

MALE, YOB, Sire	Yrs Raced	Strts	Wins	SWs	Earnings	FEMALE, YOB, Sire	Yrs Raced	Strts	Wins	SWs	Earnings
Carjack, 1981 h., Cojak	5	72	20	0	$469,181	Peaceful River, 1979 m., Peaceful Tom	5	72	14	4	$250,990
Fort Metfield, 1994 g., Metfield	10	107	23	0	441,847	Redoy's Drive, 1994 m., Mr. Redoy	6	51	11	0	224,534
Page Two, 1994 g., Victorious	11	122	20	0	264,413	Arctic Quest, 1995 m., Yukon	4	53	8	0	146,511
Missouri Ace, 1985 g., Taxachusetts	7	48	12	3	244,152	My Sister Kate, 1993 m., Haileys Tropic	6	56	17	0	146,489
Campinout, 1999 g., Victorious	6	68	14	0	218,115	Simply So, 1988 m., Gold Ruler	6	48	8	1	136,634
Mr. Springfield, 1989 g., Taxachusetts	11	107	24	0	216,230	Shared Reflections, 1986 m., Pursuit	6	67	12	1	114,601
Pilot Knob, 1965 h., Gun Shot	10	164	37	1	186,139	Caban Monere, 1992 m., Indian Detail	6	56	12	0	112,861
Hold Me Together, 1994 g., Comet Kat	9	109	19	0	168,611	Shergars Best, 1989 m., Shergar's Best (Ire)	7	90	20	0	107,596
Minor Flaw, 1986 h., Rolfson	6	47	6	3	154,418	Trip the Load, 1989 m., Positiveness	7	89	19	0	106,466
Uncle Zip, 1967 h., Bergamot	9	151	38	0	149,950	Silly Girl, 1998 m., Mandamus	5	53	10	0	104,330

Montana

MALE, YOB, Sire	Yrs Raced	Strts	Wins	SWs	Earnings	FEMALE, YOB, Sire	Yrs Raced	Strts	Wins	SWs	Earnings
Payday Mackee, 1990 g., Black Mackee	9	79	17	5	$214,668	Hallelujah Angel, 1991 m., Dance Centre	6	55	12	1	$197,496
River Lord, 1979 h., Eastern Lord	8	96	15	2	204,451	Mickey's Hot Stuff, 1995 m., Mickey Le Mousse	6	65	10	2	174,667
Dublin's Woodwin, 1999 g., Black Mackee	7	56	13	0	166,960	The Golden Noodle, 2005 f., D'wildcat	1	6	1	1	144,380
Toseek, 1993 g., Cave Creek	7	96	17	2	149,793	Hatti, 1985 m., One More Slew	3	38	6	2	139,545
Big Sky Rusher, 1994 g., Cave Creek	6	49	9	3	131,714	Montani, 1988 m., Kotani	8	92	20	0	121,780
Sonabove, 1992 g., Son of Briartic	8	79	11	0	117,204	Breath of Dawn, 1993 m., Black Mackee	7	75	13	0	121,437
Kelsos Kin, 1968 h., Scotsmans Bond	11	152	20	2	104,952	Jocko Miss, 1997 m., Black Mackee	4	37	10	0	102,217
Blazing Zulu, 1980 h., Zulu Tom	7	73	12	0	96,855	Belle of Nassau, 1993 m., Nassau Square	6	53	14	0	101,728
No Name Trail, 1991 g., Mr. Badger	8	56	15	2	92,558	Mission Gem, 1976 m., Prince Alert	4	35	11	1	101,223
Flying Whitesocks, 1990 g., Blushing Guest	9	93	18	0	91,914	Dancing River, 1975 m., Marketable	5	74	17	0	99,812

Nebraska

MALE, YOB, Sire	Yrs Raced	Strts	Wins	SWs	Earnings	FEMALE, YOB, Sire	Yrs Raced	Strts	Wins	SWs	Earnings
Dazzling Falls, 1992 h., Taylor's Falls	3	20	9	7	$904,622	Orphan Kist, 1984 m., Fort Prevel	8	100	28	18	$631,997
Who Doctor Who, 1983 h., Doctor Stat	8	64	33	26	813,870	Falls Amiss, 1986 m., Taylor's Falls	4	29	15	9	312,301
Amadevil, 1974 h., Jungle Savage	7	93	33	20	653,534	G. U. Dreamer, 1985 m., Tarsal	4	39	14	4	289,219
Darla's Charge, 1987 g., Ragtime Band	10	141	30	0	447,766	Fantango Lady, 1994 m., Lytrump	5	55	22	18	279,295
Roman Zipper, 1972 h., Zip Line	9	128	31	13	392,782	Clever Kat, 1986 m., Comet Kat	6	59	23	9	260,170
Skunktail, 1989 g., Music Prince	11	103	20	12	380,075	Oglala Sue, 1998 m., Verzy	4	29	8	3	235,232
Plaza Star, 1978 h., Lt. Stevens	9	108	20	7	361,742	Face the Verdict, 1979 m., Executioner	5	66	10	1	228,799

Racing — Leading Earners by State Where Bred

MALE, YOB, Sire	Yrs Raced	Strts	Wins	SWs	Earnings	FEMALE, YOB, Sire	Yrs Raced	Strts	Wins	SWs	Earnings
High Dice, 1995 g., Lytrump	10	81	21	16	$350,590	St. Patty Day, 1982 m., Majestic Red	8	67	24	3	$202,610
Irish Villon, 1990 g., Verzy	7	66	17	11	311,016	Robbers Doll, 1982 m., No Robbery	7	85	13	4	199,635
Wandarous, 1984 g., Replant	10	103	23	9	302,051	Nasty and Brave, 1994 m., Nasty and Bold	8	80	19	0	192,516

Nevada

MALE, YOB, Sire	Yrs Raced	Strts	Wins	SWs	Earnings	FEMALE, YOB, Sire	Yrs Raced	Strts	Wins	SWs	Earnings
Y Flash, 1960 h., Flash o' Night	2	28	6	3	$226,631	Wood and Wine, 1975 m., Fleet Allied	5	54	18	4	$261,174
Times Rush, 1968 h., Indian Rush	6	75	15	7	215,332	High Estimate, 1972 m., Windy Sands	5	45	16	5	164,749
Port of the Sea, 1971 h., Port Wine	7	61	13	3	113,649	Nevada Bond, 1955 m., Bymeabond	4	40	6	1	49,250
Washoe Lea, 1977 h., Double Lea	8	58	17	0	101,979	Petrones Own, 1972 m., *Petrone	4	38	8	1	45,219
Arvoicsal, 1996 g., King Alobar	5	61	8	0	90,431	Snow Spirit, 1985 m., Feather Dollar	2	18	1	0	44,110
Noti, 1960 h., Leisure Time	1	12	3	2	89,150	Bingo Bets, 1981 m., Art's Classy Jet	5	44	10	3	39,529
Import Wine, 1975 h., Port Wine	7	68	9	0	82,928	Ingrid H., 1969 m., Mr. Busher	3	54	5	0	38,027
First Estimate, 1969 h., Windy Sands	4	47	9	0	71,337	Orbit Rose, 1995 m., Pencil Point (Ire)	2	16	6	0	34,792
Crow Creek, 1968 g., *Rapido	6	63	17	0	62,170	Dharita, 1960 m., Dharan	8	143	23	0	32,631
Pee Jay Kit, 1970 g., Nevada P. J.	5	39	11	0	61,853	Fun Finder, 1978 m., Pleasure Seeker	2	11	4	0	32,555

New Hampshire

MALE, YOB, Sire	Yrs Raced	Strts	Wins	SWs	Earnings	FEMALE, YOB, Sire	Yrs Raced	Strts	Wins	SWs	Earnings
Road to Rock, 1963 g., Ross Sea	9	187	36	2	$248,113	Lite Ft., 1981 m., Last Dance	6	71	15	0	$137,000
Trim Clipper, 1963 g., *Pallestrelli	11	127	21	0	72,419	A Wish for Abby, 1993 m., Maudlin's Pleasure	6	40	9	0	40,644
Mystic Clown, 1972 h., The Clown	6	23	11	0	56,230	Frost Heaves, 1979 m., Buck Run	6	67	6	0	36,896
Easter Gloves, 1958 h., Golden Gloves	9	197	24	0	55,786	Toy Party, 1962 m., Pan	11	199	22	0	34,665
Ruff Enuff, 1971 h., *Arrebato II	7	90	18	0	51,737	Sunapee, 1990 m., Iron Brigade	5	57	8	0	32,478
Sailing Chance, 1960 h., Sailed Away	7	81	14	1	48,133	Pilot Fish, 1985 m., Star Spruce	4	44	1	0	26,885
Buttonwood Star, 1990 g., Rock Dance	6	72	3	0	43,455	Polly Pierce, 1980 m., Bert B. Don	4	44	5	0	25,627
Alybull, 1997 g., Alyfoe	3	16	4	0	41,944	Arpey, 1956 m., *River War	2	20	6	1	25,160
Tallymead Pip, 1964 h., Pan	5	76	13	0	41,351	Quick Glory, 1965 m., *Reprimand II	6	84	10	0	25,155
Life's Adventure, 1993 g., Lifer	4	66	8	0	41,221	Pandora Dee, 1962 m., Pan	6	105	13	0	17,695

New Jersey

MALE, YOB, Sire	Yrs Raced	Strts	Wins	SWs	Earnings	FEMALE, YOB, Sire	Yrs Raced	Strts	Wins	SWs	Earnings
Friendly Lover, 1988 h., Cutlass	7	66	22	12	$1,247,670	Open Mind, 1986 m., Deputy Minister	3	19	12	11	$1,844,372
Zoffany, 1980 h., Our Native	6	36	15	11	1,225,569	Missy's Mirage, 1988 m., Stop the Music	4	28	14	9	838,894
Park Avenue Ball, 2002 h., Citidancer	4	25	7	6	1,049,360	Classy Mirage, 1990 m., Storm Bird	3	25	13	7	716,712
Sewickley, 1985 h., Star de Naskra	4	32	11	5	1,017,517	Wild Gams, 2003 m., Forest Wildcat	3	18	7	5	708,486
Dance Floor, 1989 h., Star de Naskra	2	16	4	3	863,299	Spruce Fir, 1983 m., Big Spruce	5	40	16	12	698,703
Gators N Bears, 2000 h., Stormy Atlantic	4	32	10	6	804,393	Private Treasure, 1988 m., Explodent	2	19	5	4	603,189
Sea of Tranquility, 1996 h., Heff	8	76	23	13	784,902	Jersey Girl, 1995 m., Belong to Me	2	11	9	7	571,136
Frugal Doc, 1987 g., Baederwood	9	113	29	4	782,547	Just Smashing, 1982 m., Explodent	5	61	25	8	532,383
Joey P., 2002 g., Close Up	4	27	13	9	701,918	Pure Disco, 2003 m., Disco Rico	3	24	9	6	472,460
Who's the Cowboy, 2002 g., Intensity	4	31	11	6	662,367	Smart N Classy, 2000 m., Smart Strike	4	37	7	2	464,409

New Mexico

MALE, YOB, Sire	Yrs Raced	Strts	Wins	SWs	Earnings	FEMALE, YOB, Sire	Yrs Raced	Strts	Wins	SWs	Earnings
Rocky Gulch, 2001 g., Dry Gulch	5	38	18	14	$1,151,725	Peppers Pride, 2003 m., Desert God	3	14	14	10	$756,665
Ciento, 1998 h., Prospector Jones	7	40	20	14	806,564	Shemoveslikeaghost, 2000 m., Ghostly Moves	5	23	13	9	582,486
Romeos Wilson, 1998 g., Jack Wilson	8	65	15	5	638,779	Latenite Special, 2001 m., Super Special	4	24	13	8	464,709
Ninety Nine Jack, 1999 g., Jack Wilson	4	46	17	9	547,698	Yulla Yulla, 1995 m., Look See	5	27	21	14	443,022
Some Ghost, 2001 g., Ghostly Moves	6	31	10	4	532,389	Skirt Alert, 2002 m., Prospector Jones	3	17	10	5	441,251
Run Johnny, 1992 g., Johnny Blade	7	52	14	6	518,790	Hollywood Gone, 2002 m., Gone Hollywood	4	23	8	3	385,331
Bold Ego, 1978 h., Bold Tactics	3	35	15	5	511,648	Frosty Tail, 1980 m., It's Freezing	3	28	11	3	361,078
Gulchrunssweet, 2000 g., Dry Gulch	6	41	11	4	485,324	Espeedytoo, 1999 m., Ghost Ranch	3	24	10	6	340,564
Runmore Mema, 1997 h., Jack Wilson	8	60	14	5	450,819	Fearless Ego, 1985 m., Bold Ego	4	43	16	6	325,377
Star Smasher, 1999 h., Full Choke	3	24	12	10	437,992	Hat Creek, 2001 m., Prospector Jones	3	23	6	1	285,127

New York

MALE, YOB, Sire	Yrs Raced	Strts	Wins	SWs	Earnings	FEMALE, YOB, Sire	Yrs Raced	Strts	Wins	SWs	Earnings
Funny Cide, 2000 g., Distorted Humor	6	38	11	9	$3,529,412	Fleet Indian, 2001 m., Indian Charlie	3	19	13	7	$1,704,513
Say Florida Sandy, 1994 h., Personal Flag	8	98	33	19	2,085,408	Grecian Flight, 1984 m., Cormorant	5	40	21	14	1,320,215
Gander, 1996 g., Cormorant	7	60	15	6	1,824,011	Fit for a Queen, 1986 m., Fit to Fight	7	51	13	8	1,226,429
L'Carriere, 1991 g., Carr de Naskra	3	23	8	2	1,726,175	Irish Linnet, 1988 m., Seattle Song	6	62	19	13	1,220,180
Fourstardave, 1985 g., Compliance	9	100	21	13	1,636,737	Lottsa Talc, 1990 m., Talc	6	65	21	16	1,206,248
Fourstars Allstar, 1988 h., Compliance	6	59	14	9	1,596,760	Critical Eye, 1997 m., Dynaformer	3	38	14	5	1,060,984
Win, 1980 g., Barochois	5	44	14	7	1,408,980	Capades, 1986 m., Overskate	3	27	11	8	1,051,006
Friendly Island, 2001 h., Crafty Friend	4	19	8	4	1,369,714	Queen Alexandra, 1982 m., Determined King	5	46	19	14	1,034,144
Victory Speech, 1993 h., Deputy Minister	3	27	9	5	1,289,020	Capeside Lady, 2001 m., Cape Town	4	21	8	7	809,540
Thunder Rumble, 1989 h., Thunder Puddles	3	19	8	6	1,047,552	Dat You Miz Blue, 1997 m., Cure the Blues	4	33	14	7	806,291

North Carolina

MALE, YOB, Sire	Yrs Raced	Strts	Wins	SWs	Earnings	FEMALE, YOB, Sire	Yrs Raced	Strts	Wins	SWs	Earnings
Bold Circle, 1986 h., Circle Home	4	55	11	3	$372,488	Top Socialite, 1982 m., Topsider	5	34	10	7	$521,944
G H's Pleasure, 1992 g., Foolish Pleasure	7	52	9	3	356,293	Amanti, 1979 m., Anticipating	5	53	15	4	306,981
Triangular, 1967 g., Blue Prince	8	72	15	3	240,059	See Your Point, 1992 m., Rock Point	3	37	12	3	283,985
Insideangle, 1992 h., Allen's Prospect	4	60	10	0	233,738	Family Effort, 1991 m., Goldlust	5	69	13	0	252,855
Moment of Triumph, 1984 h., Timeless Moment	5	50	17	1	230,427	Hadee Mae, 1991 m., Goldlust	3	37	9	2	178,294
Dump Truck, 1973 h., Four Strings	10	188	31	0	211,930	Flashy Concorde, 1988 m., Super Concorde	4	59	19	0	176,032
R.T. Rise n Shine, 1984 g., Secretary of War	8	132	18	0	186,887	Clever Tune, 1992 m., Tricky Tab	7	96	15	0	149,597
We're Just Bluff, 1987 g., Fairway Phantom	8	86	15	0	180,435	One More Sue, 1990 m., One More Slew	6	91	16	0	148,091
Ben Ali's Rullah, 1989 h., Clever Trick	4	58	9	0	175,365	Lark's Impression, 1998 m., Above Normal	3	34	9	0	141,133
Gold Candy Too, 1990 g., Goldlust	4	38	11	1	172,550	Flying Hope, 1982 m., Inverness Drive	7	85	9	0	139,808

North Dakota

MALE, YOB, Sire	Yrs Raced	Strts	Wins	SWs	Earnings	FEMALE, YOB, Sire	Yrs Raced	Strts	Wins	SWs	Earnings
Dakota Prospect, 1997 g., Slewdledo	5	52	8	1	$131,159	Hoist Her Flag, 1982 m., Aferd	5	43	19	11	$290,849
Northern Ace, 1998 g., Northern Prospect	7	57	15	1	129,909	Creel Ribot, 1979 m., Domian	7	86	19	0	93,175
Bold Aferd, 1994 g., Aferd	5	29	6	5	107,388	Patty Kim, 1989 m., Aferd	4	23	6	4	87,944
Maddies Blues, 2000 g., Aferd	5	32	11	9	100,570	Strike an Image, 2001 m., Patriot Strike	5	37	5	3	86,831
Stilaferd, 1994 g., Aferd	9	63	9	2	96,994	Can I Lead, 1986 m., Lead Astray	8	98	23	0	60,700
Breaker Breaker, 1997 h., Power Break	3	16	4	3	91,322	Penny Bolinas, 1976 m., Bolinas Intent	6	80	11	0	49,862
Suntana, 2000 g., Sun Man	5	33	8	4	88,430	Music Time, 1993 m., Ragtime Reign	7	56	8	1	44,651
Leeaferd, 1995 g., Aferd	10	91	9	0	74,719	Milk N Cookies, 1996 m., Continental Morn	6	53	6	0	41,745
Hub Cap, 1981 h., Aferd	6	50	16	4	70,597	Sheza Broad, 1989 m., Au Point	5	46	15	0	40,637
Dakota Dixie, 2001 g., Dixieland Heat	4	29	4	1	59,048	Quillos Bolinas, 1978 m., Bolinas Intent	6	91	11	0	36,785

Ohio

MALE, YOB, Sire	Yrs Raced	Strts	Wins	SWs	Earnings	FEMALE, YOB, Sire	Yrs Raced	Strts	Wins	SWs	Earnings
Harlan's Holiday, 1999 h., Harlan	3	22	9	8	$3,632,664	Tougaloo, 1983 m., Lot o' Gold	5	33	13	11	$583,030
Phantom On Tour, 1994 h., Tour d'Or	4	20	7	6	724,605	Ashwood C C, 1998 m., Cryptoclearance	6	52	17	7	581,329
Kingpost, 1985 g., Stalwart	2	20	3	1	598,966	Lady Cherie, 1997 m., Al Sabin	5	39	17	13	552,095
One Bold Stroke, 1995 h., Broad Brush	3	16	5	4	595,662	Glacial Princess, 1981 m., Brent's Prince	4	52	27	17	542,792
Royal Harmony, 1964 h., Royal Note	6	105	38	22	587,164	Sadie's Dream, 1990 m., Rare Performer	5	37	10	6	488,529
Stormy Deep, 1987 g., Diamond Shoal (GB)	5	53	17	8	565,672	Just Michel, 2000 m., Pacific Waves	5	48	19	10	419,323
King of the Roxy, 2004 c., Littleexpectations	3	10	3	2	527,234	Cut the Cuteness, 1992 m., Cut Throat (GB)	5	38	13	12	411,459
Too Much Bling, 2003 h., Rubiano	2	11	5	4	509,674	Extended Applause, 1996 m., Exbourne	4	23	4	1	408,520
Majestic Dinner, 1997 g., Formal Dinner	8	54	19	7	497,374	Safe Play, 1978 m., Sham	3	27	11	7	393,085
Devil Time, 1997 g., Devil His Due	7	48	14	9	490,351	Crypto's Redjet, 1992 m., Cryptoclearance	5	39	17	8	364,640

Oklahoma

MALE, YOB, Sire	Yrs Raced	Strts	Wins	SWs	Earnings	FEMALE, YOB, Sire	Yrs Raced	Strts	Wins	SWs	Earnings
Kip Deville, 2003 h., Kipling	3	21	9	7	$2,434,422	Lady's Secret, 1982 m., Secretariat	4	45	25	22	$3,021,325
Clever Trevor, 1986 g., Slewacide	5	30	15	9	1,388,841	Voladora, 1995 m., Hickory Ridge	4	53	20	10	548,622
Mr Ross, 1995 g., Slewacide	6	44	18	14	1,091,046	Belle of Cozzene, 1992 m., Cozzene	4	22	9	7	522,455
Silver Goblin, 1991 g., Silver Ghost	6	26	16	11	1,083,895	D Fine Okie, 2002 m., Burbank	4	34	14	7	470,607
Brother Brown, 1990 g., Eminency	3	20	14	8	791,448	Slide Show, 1991 m., Slewacide	4	25	12	8	347,917
Mighty Beau, 1999 g., Rainbow Prospect	7	66	11	2	614,210	Fullasatick, 1993 m., Derby Wish	5	43	9	3	289,611
That Tat, 1998 g., Faltaat	7	59	17	8	602,430	Mean Martha, 1978 m., Menocal	4	40	8	3	276,985
Darrell Darrell, 1987 g., Boca Rio	7	53	23	13	591,646	Caznire, 1989 m., Bold Ego	5	30	14	8	271,582
Brush With Pride, 1992 g., Broad Brush	5	35	14	9	548,615	Southern Etiquette, 1988 m., Slewacide	4	27	10	6	259,459
Perfec Travel, 1982 g., Inverness Drive	8	52	14	10	514,747	Muhammad's Baby, 1986 m., Ask Muhammad	6	76	15	6	257,186

Oregon

MALE, YOB, Sire	Yrs Raced	Strts	Wins	SWs	Earnings	FEMALE, YOB, Sire	Yrs Raced	Strts	Wins	SWs	Earnings
Lethal Grande, 1999 g., Corslew	7	80	26	6	$409,788	Revillew Slew, 1996 m., Can't Be Slew	6	46	13	3	$383,824
Polynesian Flyer, 1982 h., Flying Lark	5	54	14	11	346,525	Moonlit Maddie, 1998 m., Abstract	5	38	12	6	207,358
Eternal Secrecy, 1997 g., Black Tie Affair (Ire)	9	69	16	1	256,479	La Famille, 1981 m., Bob Mathias	8	80	14	0	193,105
Lark's Legacy, 1981 g., Flying Lark	8	104	24	4	240,199	Valeri's Delight, 1984 m., Dr. Valeri	4	28	10	1	181,415
Annie's Turn, 1977 h., Joyous Turn	6	64	16	4	203,516	Solda Holme, 1986 m., Jeff's Companion	7	47	21	2	163,977
Weinhard, 1996 g., Falstaff	5	69	4	0	202,688	Cruisin' Two Su, 1983 m., Dr. Valeri	4	30	10	2	155,380
Family Fox, 1979 h., Bob Mathias	6	95	17	0	196,973	So Happy Together, 2001 m., Corslew	5	39	7	1	149,302
Strong Award, 1965 h., Strong Ruler	11	118	29	3	189,361	Solamente Un Vez, 1983 m., Relaunch	3	17	6	3	126,470
Supreme Lark, 1977 h., Flying Lark	8	112	24	5	186,799	Just Out Run, 1988 m., Just the Time	6	64	11	4	125,976
Praise Jay, 1964 h., Jaybil	5	54	12	6	186,578	Swoon's Bid, 1990 m., Swoon	7	81	14	0	116,999

Pennsylvania

MALE, YOB, Sire	Yrs Raced	Strts	Wins	SWs	Earnings	FEMALE, YOB, Sire	Yrs Raced	Strts	Wins	SWs	Earnings
Smarty Jones, 2001 h., Elusive Quality	2	9	8	7	$7,613,155	Go for Wand, 1987 f., Deputy Minister	2	13	10	8	$1,373,338
Alphabet Soup, 1991 h., Cozzene	4	24	10	7	2,990,270	Mrs. Lindsay, 2004 f., Theatrical (Ire)	2	6	4	3	1,170,915

Racing — Leading Earners by State Where Bred

MALE, YOB, Sire	Yrs Raced	Strts	Wins	SWs	Earnings	FEMALE, YOB, Sire	Yrs Raced	Strts	Wins	SWs	Earnings
Hard Spun, 2004 c., Danzig	2	13	7	6	$2,673,470	Bessarabian, 1982 m., Vice Regent	3	37	18	14	$1,032,640
With Anticipation, 1995 g., Relaunch	8	48	15	8	2,660,543	Alice Springs, 1990 m., Val de l'Orne (Fr)	5	26	9	5	768,889
Yankee Affair, 1982 h., Northern Fling	5	55	22	15	2,282,156	Mrs. Penny, 1977 m., Great Nephew	3	22	6	6	689,609
Tikkanen, 1991 h., Cozzene	3	17	4	3	1,599,335	Classy Cathy, 1983 m., Private Account	3	15	7	4	537,970
Lil E. Tee, 1989 h., At the Threshold	3	13	7	3	1,437,506	Contredance, 1982 m., Danzig	3	21	8	5	492,700
Rochester, 1996 g., Green Dancer	9	51	11	6	1,211,266	Ambassador of Luck, 1979 m., What Luck	4	23	14	9	489,583
High Yield, 1997 h., Storm Cat	2	14	4	3	1,170,196	Wonders Delight, 1986 m., Icecapade	3	36	9	4	481,521
Master Command, 2002 h., A.P. Indy	3	17	8	5	1,137,188	My Pal Lana, 2000 m., Kris S.	4	25	6	2	465,538

Rhode Island

MALE, YOB, Sire	Yrs Raced	Strts	Wins	SWs	Earnings	FEMALE, YOB, Sire	Yrs Raced	Strts	Wins	SWs	Earnings
Beau Britches, 1975 h., Oxford Accent	6	89	8	2	$121,145	Good Musical, 1977 m., Rock Talk	3	45	12	0	$155,580
Gulio Cesere, 1956 h., Mel Hash	4	59	16	2	106,308	Dandy Blitzen, 1955 m., Bull Dandy	4	48	14	4	131,499
Troll By, 1973 h., Military Plume	4	28	10	3	89,914	Venomous, 1953 m., Mel Hash	4	32	15	4	107,932
Tullo, 1956 h., Bull Dandy	9	202	23	1	81,680	Dandy Princess, 1958 m., Bull Dandy	4	58	15	0	80,533
New 'tricia, 1966 h., New Rullah	9	128	22	0	68,489	Musical Sadie, 1967 m., *Good Shot	6	90	16	0	51,094
Rival Hunter, 1978 h., Oxford Accent	8	123	12	0	53,358	Farrago, 1977 m., Oxford Accent	3	22	5	0	47,153
Melpet, Jr., 1954 g., Bull Dandy	4	66	13	0	53,325	Helipat, 1954 m., Bull Dandy	5	84	6	1	45,871
Bandito Billy, 1978 h., Banderilla	5	69	14	0	51,127	Distinctive Lady, 1970 m., Times Roman	4	36	8	0	44,410
David's Success, 1957 h., Bull Dandy	8	120	19	0	49,686	Sword of Mine, 1960 m., Swift Sword	7	161	25	0	33,545
Boy Brigand, 1959 h., Bull Dandy	8	145	19	0	48,451	Nile Melody, 1957 m., Mel Hash	5	49	10	0	32,331

South Carolina

MALE, YOB, Sire	Yrs Raced	Strts	Wins	SWs	Earnings	FEMALE, YOB, Sire	Yrs Raced	Strts	Wins	SWs	Earnings
Big Rut, 1993 g., Kokand	9	91	22	7	$570,488	Double Stake, 1993 m., Kokand	4	37	11	4	$343,480
Normandy Beach, 1996 g., Sewickley	9	108	21	1	481,074	Running Cousin, 1978 m., Double Hitch	5	86	22	8	291,440
American Prince, 1998 g., Miner	8	72	10	1	431,786	Has Beauty, 1991 m., Kokand	10	106	25	0	232,156
Intelligent Male, 2000 g., Ride the Storm	6	56	8	2	337,479	Frills and Ribbons, 1978 m., Double Hitch	5	77	15	1	199,354
Kiss and Run, 1998 h., Double Hitch	8	144	40	7	295,681	Sea Trip, 1981 m., Sea Songster	5	76	12	2	194,479
Double Quill, 1969 h., Double Hitch	8	152	30	3	283,890	Frezil, 1978 m., Double Hitch	7	88	17	1	189,019
Roman Report, 1983 g., Greatest Roman	7	94	23	0	256,369	Raise a Prince, 1988 m., Raise a Bid	5	54	13	2	188,653
Race 'N Brace, 1984 h., Hard Crush	5	63	19	2	242,459	Crushem, 1979 m., Hard Crush	4	62	12	1	178,283
Fooler, 2000 g., Kokand	7	63	16	0	235,820	Miss Hitch, 1976 m., Double Hitch	6	54	13	3	174,470
Niner's Echo, 1998 g., Signal	8	60	9	0	233,132	Winter's Work, 1989 m., Cool Corn	6	90	22	0	162,781

South Dakota

MALE, YOB, Sire	Yrs Raced	Strts	Wins	SWs	Earnings	FEMALE, YOB, Sire	Yrs Raced	Strts	Wins	SWs	Earnings
Little Bro Lantis, 1988 g., Lost Atlantis	9	120	23	8	$719,866	Reen Aferd, 1985 m., Aferd	6	78	13	1	$96,107
Win Stat, 1977 h., Doctor Stat	8	84	22	6	438,378	Ferns Image, 1986 m., Aferd	8	75	15	0	82,242
Disarco's Rib, 1980 h., Libra's Rib	5	40	10	1	125,558	Pro Raja, 1970 m., Semi-pro	4	46	15	7	74,510
Atlantis Blend, 1989 g., Lost Atlantis	10	68	17	6	117,680	Rajaja, 1978 m., Jacinto	2	29	6	1	70,330
Right Key, 1971 h., Key Issue	8	97	12	1	108,279	Hi-Mini, 1969 m., Hi-Hasty	3	41	7	1	60,463
Streaking On, 1975 h., Hi-Hasty	11	123	26	3	93,788	Palacity Jet, 1971 m., Jet Man	4	44	15	5	60,289
Shekmatyar, 1980 h., Bon Mot (Fr)	3	50	12	0	92,340	Rio Nite, 1981 m., Aferd	5	41	12	1	57,685
Officer's Call, 1971 g., Jet Man	5	53	13	3	88,543	Dakota Diamond, 1977 m., Four Way Split	5	62	12	1	51,053
John Jet, 1966 h., Jet Man	10	131	29	5	86,827	Beturio, 1979 m., *Centurio	5	62	10	0	47,893
Rosedale Boy, 1971 h., Hi-Hasty	6	90	16	2	74,790	Beautitious, 1978 m., Restitious	5	51	8	3	44,077

Tennessee

MALE, YOB, Sire	Yrs Raced	Strts	Wins	SWs	Earnings	FEMALE, YOB, Sire	Yrs Raced	Strts	Wins	SWs	Earnings
Slew of Damascus, 1988 g., Slewacide	7	48	16	12	$1,420,350	Fancy Naskra, 1978 m., Naskra	5	26	8	2	$291,769
Startahemp, 1970 g., Hempen	8	72	25	1	282,153	Tanya's Tuition, 1987 m., D'Accord	5	25	8	3	246,225
Approved by Dylan, 2002 h., With Approval	3	29	9	0	250,937	Tipper Time, 1992 m., Forward	6	78	13	1	171,282
Shot n' Missed, 1977 h., Naskra	3	29	12	3	228,711	Tourforsure, 1969 m., Above the Law	4	76	16	0	160,379
Act It Out, 1979 h., An Act	5	41	11	0	211,983	Alda's Will, 1993 m., Gallapiat	5	71	13	1	143,172
Bold Ruddy, 1972 h., Captain Cee Jay	8	75	10	2	206,886	Southern Sweet, 1998 m., Tethra	5	29	5	0	142,642
Jay Bar Toughie, 1980 h., Full Pocket	10	126	26	0	205,232	Jay Bar Pet, 1971 m., Bold and Brave	4	65	11	0	132,240
Temperence Week, 1984 g., Temperence Hill	7	117	15	0	185,026	Dark Contessa, 2002 m., Expanding Man	4	20	6	0	126,850
Hold the Beans, 1977 h., Northern Fling	10	186	18	0	175,528	Valieo, 2001 m., Evansville Slew	3	26	4	0	120,550
Charlie Jr., 1966 h., Charlevoix	9	144	25	1	159,262	Cellar's Best, 1985 m., Band Practice	5	59	10	1	112,800

Texas

MALE, YOB, Sire	Yrs Raced	Strts	Wins	SWs	Earnings	FEMALE, YOB, Sire	Yrs Raced	Strts	Wins	SWs	Earnings
Groovy, 1983 h., Norcliffe	3	26	12	12	$1,346,956	Got Koko, 1999 m., Signal Tap	3	15	7	5	$960,946
Mocha Express, 1994 h., Java Gold	4	34	16	10	960,216	Two Altazano, 1991 m., Manzotti	3	20	9	6	709,725
Feeling Gallant, 1982 h., Gallant Gambler	6	86	19	10	846,145	Traces of Gold, 1992 m., Strike Gold	5	48	12	10	664,672
Top Avenger, 1978 h., Staunch Avenger	6	57	23	11	721,237	Bara Lass, 1979 m., Barachois	4	60	17	5	542,362
Dixie Meister, 2002 g., Holzmeister	4	23	5	4	651,210	Take My Picture, 1992 m., Tyrant	3	28	13	7	541,273
Gold Nugget, 1995 g., Gold Legend	7	46	14	6	633,821	Eagle Lake, 1998 m., Desert Royalty	4	43	13	6	477,877
Jim's Orbit, 1985 h., Orbit Dancer	2	19	5	3	600,720	Grab the Green, 1988 m., Cozzene	4	26	9	6	454,023
Lights On Broadway, 1997 g., Majestic Light	8	78	15	6	571,789	Darby's Daughter, 1986 m., Darby Creek Road	3	15	5	4	435,104
Appealing Breeze, 1987 h., Breezing On	2	14	9	8	553,327	Sweet Misty, 1994 m., Lucky So n' So	4	45	15	8	422,005
Rare Cure, 1998 g., Rare Brick	7	66	12	7	515,590	Mastery's Gamble, 1992 m., Mastery	7	55	16	7	406,943

Utah

MALE, YOB, Sire	Yrs Raced	Strts	Wins	SWs	Earnings	FEMALE, YOB, Sire	Yrs Raced	Strts	Wins	SWs	Earnings
Pharaoh's Heart, 1990 g., Persevered	7	67	10	2	$340,470	Jones Time Machine, 1979 m., Current Concept	3	26	13	7	$329,500
R Friar Tuck, 1991 g., Religiously	4	24	4	1	236,641	Let's Get Raced, 1980 m., Joduke	5	67	14	0	137,664
Indian Express, 2000 h., Indian Charlie	4	7	3	0	174,628	Ancient River, 1983 m., Upper Nile	6	47	14	3	134,964
Charley Mc, 1993 g., High Counsel	5	25	5	2	141,813	Lovehermadly, 1997 m., Regal Groom	8	69	13	0	130,548
Pierces Homeremedy, 1988 g., Humbaba	11	102	27	3	128,693	Seasons Promise, 2000 m., Four Seasons (GB)	4	39	5	0	97,342
Raise a Kitten, 1985 h., Humbaba	7	78	16	2	119,102	Lady Supreme, 1996 m., Four Seasons (GB)	4	58	6	0	80,311
Ten Forty Easy, 2000 g., Tinners Way	6	40	9	0	109,542	Miss Table Talk, 1994 m., Never Tabled	5	64	8	0	71,950
Chory Four, 1999 g., Four Seasons (GB)	6	73	7	0	106,926	Synaster Angel, 1993 m., Synastry	4	29	3	0	69,495
Steeleon Season, 1999 g., Four Seasons (GB)	6	60	7	0	104,261	Bay Heart, 1973 m., *Epicuro	4	35	6	0	53,655
Nintyfiver, 1995 g., Navegante (Chi)	10	118	19	0	98,630	Tomencino, 1999 m., H E R E S Tommy	7	24	4	0	51,122

Vermont

MALE, YOB, Sire	Yrs Raced	Strts	Wins	SWs	Earnings	FEMALE, YOB, Sire	Yrs Raced	Strts	Wins	SWs	Earnings
Peter Orbit, 1971 h., Big Pete	8	90	17	0	$43,953	Snowshoes, 1961 m., *North Carolina	9	107	16	0	$29,685
Tong, 1974 h., The Hammer	9	25	4	0	31,910	Fling of Joy, 1969 m., Ribot's Fling	5	56	16	0	28,006
Persian Potentate, 1967 g., Bold Commander	5	83	7	0	30,933	English Gin, 1966 m., *Very English	6	53	9	0	17,627
Tropic Fling, 1972 h., Ribot's Fling	5	76	8	0	30,216	Frozen North, 1960 m., *North Carolina	4	64	7	0	17,007
Rambling Ribot, 1970 h., Ribot's Fling	7	89	11	0	29,646	Night of Dreams, 1970 m., Ribot's Fling	5	94	5	0	15,880
Mr. Kish, 1962 h., Auditing	7	94	7	0	28,695	Clever Mary, 1959 m., *North Carolina	2	20	5	0	13,660
Far West, 1975 h., Bold Legend	6	58	9	0	23,452	Sweet Snowdrop, 1963 m., *Reprimand II	3	19	4	0	13,410
Pocantico, 1998 g., Slew the Knight	2	9	3	0	23,430	Its Pouring, 1967 m., Rainy Lake	3	21	8	0	12,670
Fez, 1958 h., *Hafiz	6	52	14	0	23,040	George's Parlay, 1966 m., Canadian Flyer	6	98	5	0	11,046
Obligated Time, 1997 g., Obligato	2	13	1	0	22,954	Miss Sensation, 1969 m., Motivation	5	58	5	0	8,741

Virginia

MALE, YOB, Sire	Yrs Raced	Strts	Wins	SWs	Earnings	FEMALE, YOB, Sire	Yrs Raced	Strts	Wins	SWs	Earnings
Paradise Creek, 1989 h., Irish River (Fr)	4	25	14	10	$3,401,416	Seeking the Pearl, 1994 m., Seeking the Gold	4	21	8	7	$4,021,716
Hansel, 1988 h., Woodman	2	14	7	6	2,936,586	Sabin, 1980 m., Lyphard	4	25	18	14	1,398,341
Sea Hero, 1990 h., Polish Navy	3	24	6	3	2,929,869	Mandy's Gold, 1998 m., Gilded Time	4	24	11	7	1,081,744
Pleasant Tap, 1987 h., Pleasant Colony	4	32	9	6	2,721,169	Miss Oceana, 1981 m., Alydar	2	19	11	9	1,010,385
Majesty's Prince, 1979 h., His Majesty	4	43	12	9	2,077,796	Love Sign, 1977 m., Spanish Riddle	4	39	16	10	934,827
Java Gold, 1984 h., Key to the Mint	2	15	9	5	1,908,832	Shuvee, 1966 m., Nashua	4	44	16	15	890,445
Simply Majestic, 1984 h., Majestic Light	4	44	18	14	1,667,713	Possible Mate, 1981 m., King's Bishop	3	29	14	9	675,999
Colonial Affair, 1990 h., Pleasant Colony	3	20	7	4	1,635,228	Dismasted, 1982 m., Restless Native	3	36	14	6	629,803
Secretariat, 1970 h., Bold Ruler	2	21	16	14	1,316,808	Zoonaqua, 1990 m., Silver Hawk	6	28	5	4	611,225
Chief Honcho, 1987 h., Chief's Crown	5	34	10	4	1,265,719	Topicount, 1985 m., Private Account	4	43	9	5	607,618

Washington

MALE, YOB, Sire	Yrs Raced	Strts	Wins	SWs	Earnings	FEMALE, YOB, Sire	Yrs Raced	Strts	Wins	SWs	Earnings
Saratoga Passage, 1985 g., Pirateer	4	22	6	4	$800,212	Peterhof's Patea, 1988 m., Peterhof	5	52	16	14	$623,367
Military Hawk, 1987 g., Colonel Stevens	9	86	18	12	686,128	Rings a Chime, 1997 m., Metfield	2	13	4	2	606,315
Captain Condo, 1982 g., Captain Courageous	8	70	30	16	511,695	Run Away Stevie, 1989 m., Table Run	6	40	12	9	468,267
Chinook Pass, 1979 h., Native Born	3	25	16	11	480,073	Cadette Stevens, 1988 m., Colonel Stevens	4	30	11	10	453,539
Funboy, 1991 h., Gumboy	5	49	13	11	478,180	Belle of Rainier, 1979 m., Windy Tide	4	43	17	14	424,526
Pure as Gold, 2002 g., Stolen Gold	2	19	7	2	476,444	Classy Cara, 1997 m., General Meeting	2	10	4	3	405,847
Fast Parade, 2003 g., Delineator	3	11	6	5	475,013	Jazznwithwindy, 1994 m., Jazzing Around	7	71	18	0	391,739
Refried Dreams, 1993 g., Lac Ouimet	5	51	15	0	453,570	Delicate Vine, 1984 m., Knights Choice	1	5	4	3	390,370
Sneakin Jake, 1987 g., Table Run	8	76	16	12	439,590	Bonne Nuite, 1989 m., Knights Choice	5	65	16	7	376,161
Moscow M D, 1989 g., Moscow Ballet	8	69	16	0	435,843	Firesweeper, 1983 m., Drum Fire	4	34	13	13	363,394

West Virginia

MALE, YOB, Sire	Yrs Raced	Strts	Wins	SWs	Earnings	FEMALE, YOB, Sire	Yrs Raced	Strts	Wins	SWs	Earnings
Soul of the Matter, 1991 h., Private Terms	4	16	7	4	$2,302,818	Julie B, 2003 m., Eastover Court	3	18	10	6	$479,352
Afternoon Deelites, 1992 h., Private Terms	3	12	7	6	1,061,193	Evil's Pic, 1992 m., Piccolino	5	31	10	7	437,877
Speed Whiz, 2001 g., Weshaam	5	39	7	2	613,444	Carnival Chrome, 2002 m., Carnivalay	3	12	8	5	395,638
Confucius Say, 1998 g., Eastover Court	3	23	12	7	527,897	Original Gold, 2000 m., Slavic	4	17	7	3	372,649
Donald's Pride, 2000 g., Deputed Testamony	6	41	13	8	463,899	Alaska Ash, 2001 m., Weshaam	4	35	6	1	294,255
Not for Sam, 1998 g., Not For Love	8	50	14	4	428,126	Shes a Caper Too, 1993 m., Feel the Power	6	78	12	1	291,089
Rebellious Dreamer, 1996 h., My Boy Adam	5	53	10	6	407,918	Fancy Buckles, 2000 m., My Boy Adam	3	17	9	4	278,188
Ardent Arab, 1992 g., Weshaam	9	77	24	2	407,475	Mongo Queen, 1976 m., Mongo	3	40	8	2	277,837
A Huevo, 1996 g., Cool Joe	4	12	6	2	389,750	Sweet Annuity, 1997 m., Oh Say	5	37	9	5	260,052
Slew's Smile, 1997 g., Native Slew	8	80	13	0	345,786	Longfield Star, 1996 m., Allen's Prospect	5	41	8	3	254,077

Wisconsin

MALE, YOB, Sire	Yrs Raced	Strts	Wins	SWs	Earnings	FEMALE, YOB, Sire	Yrs Raced	Strts	Wins	SWs	Earnings
R's Star, 2003 g., Hacker	3	21	3	0	$80,930	Solaratee, 2001 m., Armed Truce	4	42	4	0	$47,430
Awtair, 2000 g., Armed Truce	5	44	8	0	80,244	Cheetah Chick, 1977 m., Captain Seaweed	5	36	10	0	43,882

Racing — Leading 2007 Earners by State Where Bred

MALE, YOB, Sire	Yrs Raced	Strts	Wins	SWs	Earnings	FEMALE, YOB, Sire	Yrs Raced	Strts	Wins	SWs	Earnings
Chad's Boy, 1965 h., Disdainful	9	106	31	1	$73,871	Theresadon, 1974 m., Ocala Kid	9	116	18	0	$38,689
Hope to Sea, 1986 g., Captain Seaweed	8	86	7	0	73,400	Jami Pari, 1996 m., Bold James	8	101	6	0	37,741
Sekao, 1974 h., Oakesun	7	77	10	0	65,124	Autumn Eagle, 1993 m., Curfew	6	50	6	0	32,745
Home Swiftly, 1975 h., Swift Pursuit	7	99	18	0	63,251	Weeds for Jennifer, 1978 m.,					
Island Command, 1975 h.,						Captain Seaweed	3	44	9	0	28,134
Command Decision	3	32	6	0	61,459	Connie's Fashion, 1980 m., Best Award	5	76	8	0	27,105
Hard Liquor, 1972 g., Nahr Love	9	140	25	0	53,125	Polynesian Lady, 1963 m., Tropic King	6	81	16	0	27,060
Racers Dream, 1984 h., Captain Seaweed	7	92	13	0	51,583	Pamela Jean, 1977 m., Captain Seaweed	6	71	8	0	24,200
Model Ribot, 1973 h., Model Fool	3	52	15	0	49,360	Balmay, 1968 m., Jomay	10	101	12	0	21,316

Wyoming

MALE, YOB, Sire	Yrs Raced	Strts	Wins	SWs	Earnings	FEMALE, YOB, Sire	Yrs Raced	Strts	Wins	SWs	Earnings
Peter Glory, 1956 h., New World	12	197	35	0	$81,319	Zip Pouch, 1990 m., Destroyer (SAf)	4	16	7	2	$48,981
Pappa Jeff, 1987 g., Pappagallo (Fr)	5	65	10	0	59,298	Vicsrose, 1972 m., Emma's Orphan	4	31	11	1	47,475
Toe to Toe, 1973 h., *Leandro	6	75	21	0	52,394	Sterling Memory, 1989 m., Hoist the Silver	3	24	6	0	36,517
Chalkland, 1987 g., Chalk Hill	6	54	9	0	46,911	Trivia, 1994 m., Mr. Prosperous	4	31	7	0	27,953
Monolo, 1979 h., *Rugger	4	38	9	3	46,701	Sage Princess, 1964 m., Georgian Prinz	9	145	13	0	26,133
Mail Messenger, 1967 h., Bright Liberty	7	117	23	0	42,364	Skitab, 1979 h., Hattab's Best	5	75	12	0	26,033
Khal Bell, 1962 h., Bright Liberty	6	80	11	0	41,970	Western Action, 1986 m., Ryan's Island	4	52	6	0	25,646
Living Pleasure, 1977 h., Joy of Living	8	59	7	1	40,722	Puddin Proof, 1978 m., Proper Proof	3	52	2	0	24,798
Supper Sport, 1974 h., Cokoking	7	107	14	0	39,045	Abiquiu Red, 1970 m., Polo Bell	4	83	10	0	24,481
Devil's Holiday, 1963 h., Georgian Prinz	7	70	25	1	37,289	Quality Time, 1992 m., Lightning Leap	4	35	2	0	23,048

Leading 2007 Earners by State Where Bred

State	MALE, YOB Sex, Sire	Strts	Wns	SWns	Earnings	FEMALE, YOB Sex, Sire	Strts	Wns	SWns	Earnings
Alabama	Chief Tudor, 1997 g., Chief Persuasion	13	4	0	$47,065	Comalagold, 2000 m., Royal Empire	10	1	0	$48,051
Arizona	Komax, 1998 g., Society Max	11	5	0	110,140	Staten Island, 2004 f., In Excess (Ire)	4	2	2	83,700
Arkansas	Forty Acres, 2004 g., West Acre	10	3	1	137,620	Humble Janet, 2004 f., Humble Eleven	10	3	0	143,527
California	Lava Man, 2001 g., Slew City Slew	8	3	3	1,410,000	Nashoba's Key, 2003 m., Silver Hawk	8	7	5	972,090
Colorado	Folsum, 2004 g., Twining	8	4	3	92,891	Kranky Karol, 2001 m., Pioneering	9	2	1	82,380
Connecticut	Heart Broken, 2004 g., Lear Fan	10	0	0	4,415	Sabael, 2005 f., Hook and Ladder	2	0	0	2,280
Florida	Going Ballistic, 2004 c., Lite the Fuse	11	3	0	690,140	Ginger Punch, 2003 m., Awesome Again	8	5	4	1,827,060
Georgia	Jag Man, 2001 g., Roaring Camp	4	1	0	24,300	Kickstand Kelli, 2003 m., Kelly Kip	4	2	0	46,793
Idaho	Crypts Seeker, 2004 g., Suave Prospect	11	4	3	94,884	Petite Motion, 2001 m., T. U. Slew	9	4	1	53,129
Illinois	Fort Prado, 2001 h., El Prado (Ire)	10	4	3	264,421	Rolling Sea, 2003 m., Sefapiano	10	6	4	361,081
Indiana	Father John, 2004 c., Crown Ambassador	7	3	2	83,400	Princess Composer, 2002 m., Composer	17	11	1	102,475
Iowa	Ghazi Up, 2004 g., Ghazi	7	3	2	140,290	Camela Carson, 2002 m., Lord Carson	6	3	2	128,720
Kansas	Manovan, 2003 g., Grand On Dave	7	3	3	40,777	Summer Recital, 2004 f., Exetera	11	3	1	72,040
Kentucky	Curlin, 2004 c., Smart Strike	9	6	5	5,102,800	Robe Decollete, 2004 f., Cozzene	7	2	1	1,376,264
Louisiana	Costa Rising, 2003 h., Royal Strand (Ire)	7	5	4	436,420	Raspberry Wine, 2002 m., Change Takes Time	9	5	5	299,560
Maryland	Heros Reward, 2002 g., Partner's Hero	10	5	2	515,826	Moon Catcher, 2004 f., Malibu Moon	11	6	3	663,450
Massachusetts	Mr. Meso, 2000 g., Mesopotamia	10	4	0	104,426	Ask Queenie, 2001 m., Key Contender	10	6	4	146,195
Michigan	Hot Chili, 2005 c., Daylight Savings	6	4	3	152,680	Valley Loot, 2004 f., Demaloot Demashoot	6	5	4	170,000
Minnesota	Sul Lago, 2004 g., Include	9	2	1	75,050	Run With Joy, 2004 f., Ghazi	5	3	2	84,027
Mississippi	Smalltown Slew, 2001 g., Evansville Slew	11	0	0	38,411	Ceasars Pleaser, 2003 m., Golden Omen	9	3	0	31,120
Missouri	Campinout, 1999 g., Victorious	10	3	0	44,640	Samba G, 2004 f., Liginsky	13	2	0	57,617
Montana	Lord's View, 2003 g., Global View	8	1	0	46,000	The Golden Noodle, 2005 f., D'wildcat	6	1	1	144,380
Nebraska	James the Greater, 2004 g., Temujin	7	3	2	83,670	Plaer's Trump, 2004 f., Shawkiit Player	5	4	4	53,488
Nevada	King's Option, 2001 g., Jestic	12	2	0	4,422	Hyatopthehills, 2002 m., Presidents Summit	5	1	0	6,248
New Jersey	Joey P., 2002 g., Close Up	12	4	4	282,119	Talkin About Love, 2004 f., Not For Love	7	5	1	375,875
New Mexico	Some Ghost, 2001 g., Ghostly Moves	8	3	2	262,051	Peppers Pride, 2003 m., Desert God	7	7	5	364,560
New York	Friendly Island, 2001 h., Crafty Friend	2	1	1	490,000	By the Light, 2005 f., Malibu Moon	4	4	3	451,815
North Carolina	Carolina Power, 2004 g., One More Power	7	1	0	29,590	Steady Slew, 2004 f., Mongoose	12	0	0	36,800
North Dakota	Maddies Blues, 2000 g., Aferd	4	2	2	25,260	Miss Free House, 2004 f., Free House	12	1	0	18,311
Ohio	King of the Roxy, 2004 h., Littleexpectations	5	1	1	300,834	Pay the Man, 2004 f., Bernstein	10	4	3	180,660
Oklahoma	Kip Deville, 2003 h., Kipling	7	3	3	1,965,780	D Fine Okie, 2002 m., Burbank	10	4	3	183,242
Oregon	Lethal Grande, 1999 g., Corslew	13	5	0	57,447	Ochoco Salmon, 2004 f., Ochoco	11	5	3	47,443
Pennsylvania	Hard Spun, 2004 c., Danzig	10	4	3	2,572,500	Mrs. Lindsay, 2004 f., Theatrical (Ire)	8	3	3	1,170,915
South Carolina	Taber's Tiger, 2002 g., Play Both Ends	7	3	0	46,800	Icy One O Four, 2004 f., Valiant Lark	6	0	0	23,320
South Dakota	Talkin to Myself, 2004 g., Crowning Season (GB)	4	1	0	4,941	Hat Trick, 2003 m., Crowning Season (GB)	6	4	0	21,168
Tennessee	Crimson Slasher, 2001 g., Dusty Screen	14	3	0	39,211	Dark Contessa, 2002 m., Expanding Man	8	3	0	67,650
Texas	General Charley, 2002 g., Truluck	10	4	3	162,645	Valid Lilly, 2005 f., Valid Expectations	7	4	2	213,406
Utah	Olympic Stride, 2002 g., Rhythm	8	3	0	14,377	Miss Fintry, 2003 m., Relagate	13	2	0	72,040
Virginia	Pleasant Strike, 2004 c., Smart Strike	9	3	1	178,300	Christmas Kid, 2004 f., Lemon Drop Kid	7	3	3	554,500
Washington	The Great Face, 2002 g., Cahill Road	7	4	2	292,875	Gemstone Rush, 2004 m., Wild Rush	9	3	1	121,575
West Virginia	Eastern Delite, 2003 g., Eastover Court	7	3	1	276,895	Carnival Chrome, 2002 m., Carnivalay	4	2	2	196,948
Wisconsin	Snow Country Cat, 2000 g., Quick Cut	17	1	0	9,687	Solaratee, 2001 m., Armed Truce	14	1	0	9,525
Wyoming	Bh Whada Challenge, 1998 g., Joy Challenge	3	2	0	3,340					

Leading 2007 Earners by Province Where Bred

Province	MALE, YOB Sex, Sire	Strts	Wns	SWns	Earnings	FEMALE, YOB Sex, Sire	Strts	Wns	SWns	Earnings
Alberta	Teagues Fight, 2003 g., Devonwood	6	3	3	$123,697	Victory Romance, 2005 f., Slew City Slew	6	1	1	$169,641
British Columbia	Ookashada, 2004 g., Millennium Allstar	9	3	3	159,692	Dancing Allstar, 2005 f., Millennium Allstar	7	5	4	299,428
Manitoba	Albarino, 2001 g., Langfurr	11	3	0	103,028	La Wildcat, 2005 f., Forest Wildcat	9	2	1	92,110
Ontario	Jambalaya, 2002 g., Langfurr	6	3	0	979,421	Sealy Hill, 2004 f., Point Given	8	4	4	958,389
Quebec	Chest of Silver, 2004 g., Silver Deputy	14	1	0	64,419	Hot Nopell, 2004 f., Salt Lake	3	2	0	43,550
Saskatchewan	Mischeviousfighter, 2004 g., Rosetti	8	3	3	22,958	Fleet Foot Fran, 2004 f., A Fleets Dancer	11	1	0	27,268

Performance Rates for 2007

Performance Rates are an objective measurement of racetrack performance developed by the Jockey Club Information Systems. Performance Rates were first published in *The Thoroughbred Record* in the 1960s. Performance Rates assign a rate to horses based on beaten lengths—who beat whom and by how much—with some adjustments made to standardize beaten distances to account for horses that were not pressed or were eased in large fields. Races in which individual horses did not finish are not counted for those horses.

Time is not a factor in Performance Rates, which are based on every start by every horse in North America in 2007. Performance Rates are expressed in lengths around a theoretical mean of zero. The average performances of the best horses in a given year are generally about 30 lengths better than an average performance of the average horse.

Two-Year-Old Males

Rank	Horse	Starts	Rating
1.	War Pass	4	33.99
2.	Pyro	4	30.22
3.	Check It Twice	5	24.27
4.	Wise Answer	7	23.65
5.	Tale of Ekati	4	23.57
6.	Roman Emperor	3	23.08
7.	Majestic Warrior	3	23.07
8.	Z Humor	5	23.05
9.	Golden Yank	4	22.32
10.	Big Truck	4	22.23
11.	Slew's Tiznow	3	21.83
12.	Fidelio	3	21.68
13.	Tend	3	21.46
14.	Halo Najib	3	20.98
15.	Sok Sok	6	20.90
16.	Monba	3	20.67
17.	Hedgefund Investor	3	20.57
18.	Ready's Image	6	20.52
19.	Red Reef	3	20.29
20.	Cool Coal Man	5	20.23
21.	Massive Drama	3	20.19
22.	Elysium Fields	3	20.08
23.	Texas Wildcatter	3	19.92
24.	Mad Flatter	3	19.75
25.	Big City Man	4	19.74
26.	Riley Tucker	3	19.69
27.	Kodiak Kowboy	7	19.55
28.	Lantana Mob	7	19.52
29.	The Roundhouse	4	19.51
30.	Hey Byrn	4	19.51
31.	Cigar Man	5	19.43
32.	Smooth Air	4	19.42
33.	Ferdinand's Flyer	3	19.32
34.	Law Enforcement	3	19.31
35.	Giant Moon	3	19.24
36.	Into Mischief	3	19.20
37.	Racecar Rhapsody	4	19.14
38.	Coal Play	3	19.10
39.	Court Vision	4	19.07
40.	Smoke'n Coal	3	18.92
41.	Rollers	3	18.88
42.	Old Man Buck	7	18.86
43.	Sir Dave	3	18.83
44.	Grand Minstrel	5	18.77
45.	Ready Set	5	18.75
46.	Cave's Valley	4	18.71
47.	Crackalackin	3	18.71
48.	El Mirage	4	18.66
49.	West Coast Coach	3	18.62
50.	Rasmussen	4	18.60

Two-Year-Old Fillies

Rank	Horse	Starts	Rating
1.	Indian Blessing	3	36.64
2.	Mushka	3	27.57
3.	Proud Spell	4	26.90
4.	Backseat Rhythm	3	26.59
5.	Country Star	3	24.55
6.	Rated Fiesty	3	24.25
7.	Smarty Deb	5	24.07
8.	Sunday Holiday	5	23.93
9.	Melissa Jo	3	23.57
10.	Elusive Lady	4	22.31
11.	High Resolve	4	22.29
12.	Game Face	3	21.98
13.	Tasha's Miracle	5	21.94
14.	Indy's Alexandra	3	21.46
15.	By the Light	4	21.02
16.	Tequilas Dayjur	3	20.99
17.	Ask the Moon	6	20.58
18.	Armonk	5	20.54
19.	Pure Clan	4	20.43
20.	Sweetness 'n Light	3	20.29
21.	Initiation	3	20.20
22.	Calico Bay	6	20.11
23.	Littlemiss Allison	4	20.10
24.	Unfolding Wish	3	19.91
25.	A to the Croft	5	19.86
26.	Made for Magic	3	19.84
27.	Throbbin' Heart	4	19.71
28.	Veiled Reference	3	19.59
29.	Meriwether Jessica	5	19.59
30.	Tazarine	5	19.41
31.	Morakami	4	19.22
32.	Syriana's Song	7	18.93
33.	Anachini	4	18.89
34.	Blitzing	5	18.85
35.	Clearly Foxy	3	18.80
36.	Yogi'ssplashofgold	3	18.77
37.	C J's Leelee	5	18.38
38.	American County	9	18.34
39.	Kadira	7	18.24
40.	Silk Ridge	10	18.02
41.	More Happy	3	17.78
42.	Carolyn's Cat	3	17.72
43.	D J Lightning	3	17.70
44.	Izarra	4	17.68
45.	A Little Gem	5	17.64
46.	Bond Princess	5	17.64
47.	Fareena	3	17.57
48.	Miss Stonestreet	4	17.55
49.	Dagger	6	17.50
50.	Latest Scoop	5	17.46

Three-Year-Old Males

Rank	Horse	Starts	Rating
1.	Curlin	9	33.04
2.	Street Sense	8	30.86
3.	Hard Spun	10	30.40
4.	Any Given Saturday	8	25.44
5.	Zanjero	8	25.03
6.	Chelokee	5	24.92
7.	King of the Roxy	5	24.37
8.	Ketchikan	3	24.21
9.	Circular Quay	5	24.02
10.	Tiago	8	23.87
11.	Notional	3	23.83
12.	Stormin Normandy	4	23.61
13.	Reporting for Duty	8	23.36
14.	Sam P.	7	23.14
15.	First Defence	4	23.11
16.	Grasshopper	5	22.64
17.	Nobiz Like Shobiz	10	22.41
18.	Fearless Vision	6	22.24
19.	Sightseeing	8	22.12
20.	C P West	7	21.66
21.	For You Reppo	6	21.66
22.	Nite Light	7	21.63
23.	Most Distinguished	10	21.47
24.	Shopton Lane	5	21.46
25.	Daaher	7	21.39
26.	Liquidity	4	21.19
27.	Joe Got Even	5	21.00
28.	Delightful Kiss	9	20.99
29.	Winstrella	6	20.98
30.	Imawildandcrazyguy	12	20.69
31.	Sports Town	3	20.38
32.	Codio	4	20.24
33.	Now a Victor	4	20.22
34.	Going Ballistic	11	20.21
35.	Sacrifice Bunt	8	20.14
36.	Street Magician	6	20.03
37.	Dominican	5	20.02
38.	Teuflesberg	9	19.96
39.	Teide	3	19.96
40.	Jiggs Ccz	4	19.95
41.	Merchart Marine	3	19.82
42.	Pavarott	6	19.80
43.	Marcavelly	4	19.73
44.	Past the Point	5	19.57
45.	Summer Doldrums	9	19.55
46.	Strike a Deal	5	19.54
47.	True Competitor	7	19.46
48.	Ravel	3	19.33
49.	Shamdinan (Fr)	4	19.32
50.	Moyer's Pond	7	19.32

Three-Year-Old Fillies

Rank	Horse	Starts	Rating
1.	Octave	8	31.11
2.	Rags to Riches	6	30.11
3.	Lady Joanne	7	28.48
4.	Ahead of Her Time	6	27.61
5.	Dream Rush	7	25.24
6.	West Coast Swing	4	24.86
7.	Winning Point	7	23.83
8.	La Traviata	4	23.81
9.	Mistical Plan	5	23.58
10.	Lear's Princess	7	23.18
11.	Tessa Blue	10	23.08
12.	Whatdreamsrmadeof	3	23.07
13.	High Heels	11	22.98
14.	Tough Tiz's Sis	10	22.97
15.	Cotton Blossom	6	22.93
16.	Panty Raid	8	22.70
17.	Mini Sermon	9	22.52
18.	Boca Grande	8	22.40
19.	Cantre	6	22.39
20.	Staten Island	4	22.25
21.	Bear Now	8	21.78
22.	Moonee Ponds	5	21.73
23.	Silvercup Baby	3	21.69
24.	Dreaming of Anna	7	21.61
25.	Belleplaine	3	21.49
26.	Pastel Gal	4	21.49
27.	Cash Included	4	21.31
28.	Partida	4	21.26
29.	You Go West Girl	7	21.20

Racing — Performance Rates

Rank	Horse	Starts	Rating
30.	Christmas Kid	7	21.03
31.	Stage Luck	3	21.03
32.	Perfect Forest	5	21.02
33.	Baroness Thatcher	10	20.84
34.	Talkin About Love	7	20.83
35.	Marietta	8	20.82
36.	Sarah's Prize	4	20.82
37.	Dawn After Dawn	8	20.77
38.	Marquee Delivery	10	20.52
39.	Secret Kin	4	20.32
40.	Jibboom	4	20.32
41.	Say You Will (Ire)	5	20.29
42.	Control System	6	20.25
43.	Silver Knockers	8	20.08
44.	Upcoming Story	4	19.85
45.	Sealy Hill	8	19.84
46.	Moon Catcher	11	19.82
47.	Dani Tom Boy	3	19.75
48.	Mi Isabella	7	19.66
49.	A Wonder She Is	3	19.59
50.	Lady Marlboro	10	19.55

Males, Four-Year-Olds and Older

Rank	Horse	Starts	Rating
1.	Lawyer Ron	8	26.89
2.	Costa Rising	7	26.37
3.	Corinthian	7	25.33
4.	Master Command	5	24.57
5.	English Channel	6	24.42
6.	Rising Moon	3	24.31
7.	Political Force	8	24.03
8.	Midnight Lute	3	23.62
9.	Tacit Agreement	4	23.33
10.	Half Ours	4	23.31
11.	Silver Wagon	4	23.15
12.	Successful Affair	6	23.04
13.	Humble Chris	12	23.02
14.	Silent Pleasure	8	23.00
15.	Dry Martini	6	22.90
16.	Wanderin Boy	5	22.89
17.	Flashy Bull	6	22.85
18.	Sweetnorthernsaint	6	22.56
19.	Tall Story	6	22.43
20.	Hesanoldsalt	8	22.04
21.	Always First (GB)	5	21.94
22.	Paradise Dancer	7	21.86
23.	Fairbanks	7	21.83
24.	Diamond Stripes	7	21.78
25.	Accountforthegold	5	21.75
26.	Monopoly Pricing	4	21.69
27.	Sun King	6	21.36
28.	Awesome Gem	9	21.34
29.	Brilliant Son	3	21.28
30.	Gottcha Gold	7	21.27
31.	Student Council	8	21.05
32.	Minister's Bid	3	20.85
33.	Latent Heat	3	20.82
34.	Diabolical	4	20.79
35.	Grand Couturier (GB)	5	20.78
36.	A. P. Arrow	8	20.68
37.	Tasteyville	10	20.45
38.	Brother Bobby	8	20.45
39.	Cosmonaut	8	20.41
40.	Fabulous Strike	4	20.40
41.	Brass Hat	6	20.37
42.	Lewis Michael	7	20.07
43.	Nolan's Cat	3	20.01
44.	Drilling for Oil	7	19.84
45.	Malibu Moonshine	12	19.83
46.	Five Steps	4	19.79
47.	Catlaunch	10	19.73
48.	Evening Attire	12	19.72
49.	Extreme Supreme	4	19.71
50.	Stream Cat	6	19.63

Females, Four-Year-Olds and Older

Rank	Horse	Starts	Rating
1.	Unbridled Belle	5	29.58
2.	Ginger Punch	8	27.80
3.	Hystericalady	8	24.79
4.	Indian Vale	7	24.28
5.	Kettleoneup	10	24.05
6.	The Holy One	3	24.01
7.	Take D' Tour	4	23.58
8.	India	4	22.88
9.	Lahudood (GB)	5	22.50
10.	Barancella (Fr)	5	21.64
11.	Altesse	8	21.57
12.	Cassydora (GB)	3	21.47
13.	Plaid	10	21.46
14.	Balance	7	21.04
15.	Royal Highness (Ger)	5	20.96
16.	Promenade Girl	5	20.71
17.	Nashoba's Key	8	20.70
18.	Miss Macy Sue	7	20.48
19.	Quite a Bride	6	20.21
20.	Lexi Star	10	20.04
21.	Miraculous Miss	6	20.00
22.	Miss Shop	10	19.91
23.	Vacare	4	19.90
24.	Grain of Truth (GB)	3	19.81
25.	Citronnade	7	19.75
26.	Charlotte's Di	5	19.73
27.	Wingspan	5	19.65
28.	Cryptoquip	7	19.62
29.	Any Limit	5	19.60
30.	Silk Queen	6	19.54
31.	Asi Siempre	5	19.46
32.	Screen Giant	3	19.44
33.	Wait a While	6	19.41
34.	Maizelle	4	19.39
35.	Sweet Fervor	6	19.32
36.	Rolling Sea	10	19.30
37.	Pictavia (Ire)	4	19.18
38.	Oprah Winney	8	19.15
39.	Rosinka (Ire)	7	19.11
40.	A True Pussycat	9	19.09
41.	Burmilla	3	19.04
42.	Lady of Venice (Fr)	6	19.03
43.	Makderah (Ire)	5	19.01
44.	Honey Ryder	5	18.92
45.	Pleasant Hill	5	18.88
46.	Baghdaria	4	18.82
47.	Jennie R.	7	18.77
48.	Ermine	6	18.71
49.	Bright Abundance	3	18.57
50.	J'ray	7	18.51
	Green Girl (Fr)	4	18.51

Sprint Males, Three-Year-Olds and Older

Rank	Horse	Starts	Rating
1.	Midnight Lute	3	25.63
2.	Teuflesberg	3	24.77
3.	Stormin Normandy	3	23.61
4.	First Defence	3	23.42
5.	Confucius Say	3	22.40
6.	Bold Start	3	20.93
7.	Diabolical	4	20.79
8.	Paradise Dancer	5	20.60
9.	Fabulous Strike	4	20.40
10.	Most Distinguished	4	20.30
11.	Street Magician	5	19.72
12.	Mach Ride	8	19.26
13.	Shone	4	19.25
14.	Talent Search	8	19.20
15.	Euroears	3	19.18
16.	Benny the Bull	8	19.15
17.	Commentator	8	18.98
18.	Ah Day	4	18.80
19.	Bustin Stones	3	18.77
20.	What a Tale	3	18.69
21.	Sing Baby Sing	8	18.64
22.	Barkley Sound	3	18.62

Rank	Horse	Starts	Rating
23.	Black Seventeen	4	18.54
24.	Idiot Proof	8	18.53
25.	Crimson King Cat	5	18.45
26.	Shrewd Operator	4	18.44
27.	Try to Fly	3	18.42
28.	Myoldmansam	5	18.36
29.	Bill Place	6	18.29
30.	Tortuga Straits	3	18.26
31.	All Wired Up	4	18.19
32.	Serious Fever	3	18.18
33.	Yesbyjimminy	6	18.06
34.	Catlaunch	4	17.92
35.	Rondo	4	17.87
36.	Semaphore Man	4	17.81
37.	Prom Shoes	4	17.77
38.	Park Avenue Ball	5	17.68
39.	Base Commander	4	17.66
40.	Going Wild	3	17.60
41.	Silver Source	7	17.59
42.	Killing Me	3	17.56
43.	St. Zarb	4	17.53
44.	Fass Feat	7	17.38
45.	Stradivinsky	3	17.37
46.	Premium Wine	9	17.28
47.	Frosty Secret	6	17.24
48.	Mucho Margaritas	3	17.21
49.	Junior College	6	17.17
50.	Sumfun	6	17.13

Sprint Females, Three-Year-Olds and Older

Rank	Horse	Starts	Rating
1.	Dream Rush	6	24.36
2.	La Traviata	4	23.81
3.	West Coast Swing	3	23.30
4.	Cantrel	6	22.39
5.	Looky Yonder	3	22.11
6.	Secret Kin	3	21.61
7.	Mini Sermon	3	21.45
8.	Boca Grande	3	20.86
9.	Baroness Thatcher	5	20.75
10.	Miss Macy Sue	7	20.48
11.	Silver Knockers	7	20.27
12.	Control System	6	20.25
13.	Appealing Zophie	3	20.00
14.	Miraculous Miss	6	20.00
15.	Upcoming Story	3	19.99
16.	Partida	5	19.83
17.	Dani Tom Boy	3	19.75
18.	Julie B	4	19.65
19.	Any Limit	5	19.60
20.	Silk Queen	6	19.54
21.	Your Flame in Me	4	19.52
22.	Quota	4	19.36
23.	Sugar Swirl	5	19.34
24.	Jibboom	3	19.33
25.	Ghost Dancing	3	19.33
26.	Sweet Fervor	3	19.32
27.	Cash's Girl	6	19.32
28.	Oprah Winney	8	19.15
29.	Gem Sleuth	8	19.06
30.	Burmilla	3	19.04
31.	Glorified	4	18.73
32.	Marquee Delivery	4	18.73
33.	Extra Classy	3	18.72
34.	Sheets	8	18.61
35.	Somethinaboutlaura	3	18.61
36.	Featherbed	5	18.49
37.	Carnival Chrome	3	18.43
38.	Sindy With an S	9	18.38
39.	Forever Together	5	18.35
40.	Look Deep	6	18.24
41.	Lady Marlboro	6	18.24
42.	Silver Swallow	3	18.10
43.	Ticket to Seattle	7	18.09
44.	Silmaril	7	18.08
45.	Graeme Six	8	18.04
46.	Change Up	4	18.00

Racing — Performance Rates, 1997-2007

Rank	Horse	Starts	Rating
47.	Early Vintage	4	17.99
48.	Akronism	7	17.90
49.	Beau Dare	4	17.90
50.	Maryfield	8	17.89

Turf Males, Three-Year-Olds and Older

Rank	Horse	Starts	Rating
1.	English Channel	6	24.42
2.	Always First (GB)	5	21.94
3.	Sunriver	6	21.49
4.	Grand Couturier (GB)	5	20.78
5.	Cosmonaut	8	20.41
6.	Trippi's Storm	9	19.94
7.	Marcavelly	4	19.73
8.	Dave	8	19.60
9.	Nobiz Like Shobiz	5	19.55
10.	Strike a Deal	5	19.54
11.	Drilling for Oil	6	19.52
12.	Cloudy's Knight	9	19.51
13.	Better Talk Now	4	19.41
14.	Shamdinan (Fr)	4	19.32
15.	Tenpointfive	3	19.07
16.	Red Giant	7	18.98
17.	Galantas	4	18.95
18.	Shakis (Ire)	5	18.83
19.	Remarkable News (Ven)	6	18.73
20.	Stream of Gold (Ire)	4	18.54
21.	Summer Doldrums	5	18.54
22.	Inca King	8	18.32
23.	Dirge	5	18.26
24.	Classic Pack	4	18.26
25.	Red Zipper	6	18.17
26.	Hotstufanthensome	4	18.08
27.	Lovango	3	18.06
28.	Twilight Meteor	7	18.06
29.	Jambalaya	6	18.02
30.	Thorn Song	6	18.01
31.	Silver Tree	7	17.99
32.	Eccentric (GB)	3	17.98
33.	Distorted Reality	9	17.97
34.	Drum Major	3	17.88
35.	Rahystrada	3	17.81
36.	Sky Conqueror	7	17.78
37.	Fishy Advice	5	17.74
38.	Trimaran	5	17.73
39.	Croton Road	4	17.70
40.	Going Ballistic	4	17.48
41.	Angelouie	3	17.46
42.	Operation Red Dawn	4	17.40
43.	Mending Fences	3	17.38
44.	Kip Deville	6	17.30
45.	Lattice	6	17.29
46.	Jazz Quest	10	17.28
47.	Proudinsky (Ger)	3	17.26
48.	Soldier's Dancer	11	17.25
49.	Pleasant Strike	8	17.23
50.	Einstein (Brz)	4	17.22

Turf Females, Three-Year-Olds and Older

Rank	Horse	Starts	Rating
1.	Lahudood (GB)	5	22.50
2.	Tensas Yucatan	3	21.80
3.	Barancella (Fr)	5	21.64
4.	Cassydora (GB)	3	21.47
5.	Dreaming of Anna	5	21.04
6.	Royal Highness (Ger)	5	20.96
7.	Lady Attack	4	20.82
8.	Wait a While	5	20.47
9.	You Go West Girl	4	20.23
10.	Quite a Bride	6	20.21
11.	Nashoba's Key	5	20.11
12.	Vacare	4	19.90
13.	Moonee Ponds	3	19.79
14.	Wingspan	4	19.76
15.	Citronnade	7	19.75
16.	Rosinka (Ire)	6	19.56
17.	Bit of Whimsy	7	19.48
18.	Bel Air Beauty	4	19.31
19.	Christmas Kid	3	19.24
20.	Palmilla	4	19.19
21.	Pictavia (Ire)	4	19.18
22.	Lady of Venice (Fr)	6	19.03
23.	Makderah (Ire)	5	19.01
24.	New Edition	7	13.95
25.	Sealy Hill	3	13.94
26.	Honey Ryder	5	13.92
27.	Costume (GB)	3	18.80
28.	Rutherienne	8	18.78
29.	Jennie R.	7	18.77
30.	Classic Neel	7	18.67
31.	Touch My Soul (Fr)	3	18.65
32.	Sharp Susan	8	18.65
33.	Green Girl (Fr)	4	18.51
34.	J'ray	7	18.51
35.	Fantastic Shirl	9	18.41
36.	Queen Joanne	4	18.38
37.	Safari Queen (Arg)	7	18.37
38.	Clifton Bay	4	18.32
39.	Dance Away Capote	5	18.30
40.	Valbenny (Ire)	6	18.29
41.	Precious Kitten	8	18.22
42.	Criminologist	9	18.21
43.	Cat Charmer	5	18.19
44.	Price Tag (GB)	3	18.15
45.	Factual Contender	8	18.13
46.	Love Handles	6	18.10
47.	Quiet Act on	3	18.07
48.	Kiss With a Twist	6	17.97
49.	Unspoken Word	8	17.96
50.	Bridge Game	5	17.94

Top Performance Rates, 1997-2007

Two-Year-Old Males

Year	Horse	Starts	Rating
2007	War Pass	4	**33.99**
2006	Nobiz Like Shobiz	3	31.84
2005	Henny Hughes	6	25.28
2004	Afleet Alex	6	26.28
2003	Tiger Hunt	4	24.53
2002	Funny Cide	3	26.40
2001	Harlan's Holiday	6	26.27
2000	Macho Uno	4	26.12
1999	Chief Seattle	4	29.94
1998	Johnny Dollar	3	27.45
1997	Lil's Lad	3	32.24

Two-Year-Old Fillies

Year	Horse	Starts	Rating
2007	Indian Blessing	3	**36.64**
2006	Successful Outlook	3	29.27
2005	French Park	3	26.06
2004	Splendid Blended	4	22.86
2003	Class Above	3	26.78
2002	Storm Flag Flying	4	31.50
2001	You	6	27.21
2000	Raging Fever	6	29.16
1999	Surfside	5	30.86
1998	Three Rings	4	30.36
1997	Countess Diana	6	29.21

Three-Year-Old Males

Year	Horse	Starts	Rating
2007	Curlin	9	33.04
2006	Achilles of Troy	3	33.58
2005	Bellamy Road	4	**38.60**
2004	Smarty Jones	7	35.30
2003	Empire Maker	6	32.55
2002	Medaglia d'Oro	9	32.25
2001	Monarchos	7	31.75
2000	Fusaichi Pegasus	8	28.99
1999	K One King	4	30.23
1998	Indian Charlie	4	32.86
1997	Captain Bodgit	6	32.06

Three-Year-Old Fillies

Year	Horse	Starts	Rating
2007	Octave	8	31.11
2006	Pine Island	6	31.33
2005	Nature's Dowry	3	**35.32**
2004	Ashado	8	30.55
2003	Buy the Sport	3	29.02
2002	Take Charge Lady	10	29.16
2001	Victory Ride	4	33.94
2000	Golden Sunray	3	28.48
1999	Silverbulletday	11	30.20
1998	Banshee Breeze	10	32.38
1997	Mossflower	3	31.62

Males, Four-Year-Olds and Older

Year	Horse	Starts	Rating
2007	Lawyer Ron	8	26.89
2006	Invasor (Arg)	4	29.74
2005	Saint Liam	6	32.05
2004	Ghostzapper	4	**33.90**
2003	Seattle Fitz (Arg)	8	24.82
2002	Wild Years	4	28.12
2001	Aptitude	5	29.52
2000	Lemon Drop Kid	9	23.52
1999	Victory Gallop	3	30.25
1998	Skip Away	9	30.17
1997	Will's Way	5	33.14

Females, Four-Year-Olds and Older

Year	Horse	Starts	Rating
2007	Unbridled Belle	5	29.58
2006	Fleet Indian	6	30.95
2005	Stellar Jayne	4	26.49
2004	Misty Sixes	8	23.65
2003	Wild Spirit (Chi)	4	29.32
2002	Dancethruthedawn	6	27.81
2001	License Fee	5	23.05
2000	Beautiful Pleasure	7	24.16
1999	Sister Act	5	30.01
1998	Sharp Cat	4	**35.78**
1997	Twice the Vice	4	24.59

Sprint Males, Three-Year-Olds and Older

Year	Horse	Starts	Rating
2007	Midnight Lute	3	25.63
2006	Protagonus	3	24.84
2005	Lost in the Fog	9	24.18
2004	Pomeroy	3	27.01
2003	Midas Eyes	4	26.48
2002	Gygistar	4	**27.78**
2001	D'wildcat	3	22.11
2000	Caller One	7	23.95
1999	Successful Appeal	4	23.93
1998	Affirmed Success	7	24.73
1997	Smoke Glacken	5	24.18

Sprint Females, Three-Year-Olds and Older			Turf Males, Three-Year-Olds and Older			Turf Females, Three-Year-Olds and Older		
Year	Horse	Starts Rating	Year	Horse	Starts Rating	Year	Horse	Starts Rating
2007	Dream Rush	6 24.36	2007	English Channel	6 24.42	2007	Lahodood (GB)	5 22.50
2006	Wildcat Bettie B	7 24.06	2006	Showing Up	5 24.42	2006	Wait a While	4 24.63
2005	Aspen Tree	6 27.01	2005	English Channel	8 24.14	2005	Melhor Ainda	5 22.01
2004	Madcap Escapade	3 26.56	2004	Kitten's Joy	7 22.73	2004	River Belle (GB)	4 22.35
2003	Bird Town	3 29.83	2003	Stroll	6 22.27	2003	Baie (Fr)	3 22.28
2002	Nonsuch Bay	3 26.24	2002	Nowrass (GB)	5 21.20	2002	Bedanken	4 22.55
2001	Victory Ride	3 **34.26**	2001	Hap	6 21.11	2001	License Fee	4 21.87
2000	Golden Surany	3 28.48	2000	Ciro	3 23.53	2000	Silent Emotion	4 21.79
1999	Country Hideaway	5 23.75	1999	Buck's Boy	3 **27.02**	1999	Nani Rose	4 **26.86**
1998	Santaria	4 27.32	1998	Buck's Boy	9 26.51	1998	Tenski	7 24.86
1997	I Ain't Bluffing	3 25.35	1997	Chief Bearhart	7 25.84	1997	Maxzene	3 24.06

Highest performance rates earned in bold type.

Experimental Free Handicap

The Experimental Free Handicap, published annually by the Jockey Club, is based on a hypothetical 1 1/16-mile race for two-year-olds on dirt. Walter S. Vosburgh, the legendary Jockey Club handicapper, compiled the first Experimental Free Handicap in 1933. He placed Sanford Stakes winner First Minstrel atop his list at 126 pounds, although the filly Mata Hari at 122 pounds effectively was the highweight when considering the five-pound sex allowance then in effect. The 126-pound high weight became the standard impost for a champion of average accomplishment.

Vosburgh, who had been the racing secretary at New York tracks since 1894, retired in 1934, and no Experimental Free Handicap was prepared for that year. John B. Campbell assumed the task in 1935 and continued to compile the list until his death in '54.

Campbell, also racing secretary at the New York tracks, wrote in a 1943 letter that his Experimental Free Handicap was intended primarily as a forecast of how the horses would perform as three-year-olds. The Experimental, he wrote, "is based mainly upon my opinion of what the two-year-olds will accomplish as three-year-olds and at distances of a mile and a furlong or greater."

Following Campbell's death, Frank E. "Jimmy" Kilroe assigned the weights through 1960. Thomas Trotter, who compiled the list through 1972, followed him.

Starting in 1969, at the behest of the Jockey Club, the thrust of the Experimental was changed from a prediction of future performance to a measure of accomplishment during the two-year-old season exclusively.

Kenneth Noe Jr. prepared the Experimental Free Handicap from 1972 through '75, and Trotter resumed the task in '76. Beginning in 1979, a committee of three racing secretaries was chosen to establish the Experimental weights. In 1985, for the first time, separate lists were compiled for males and fillies. The 2007 Experimental Free Handicap was prepared by P. J. Campo of the New York Racing Association, Ben Huffman of Keeneland Race Course, and Tom Robbins of Del Mar.

The highest Experimental weight ever assigned was 132 pounds to Count Fleet in 1942; the following year, he won the Triple Crown.

Past Experimental Free Handicap Highweights

Year	Male	Female	Year	Male	Female
2007	War Pass (127)	Indian Blessing (123)	1986	Capote (126)	Brave Raj (123)
2006	Street Sense (127)	Dreaming of Anna (123)	1985†	Ogygian (126)	I'm Splendid (123)
2005	Stevie Wonderboy (126)	Folklore (123)		Tasso (126)	
2004	Declan's Moon (126) Wilko (126)	Sweet Catomine (124)	1984	Chief's Crown (126)	Outstandingly (118)
			1983	Devil's Bag (128)	Miss Oceana (120)
2003	Action This Day (126) Cuvee (126) Ruler's Court (126)	Halfbridled (124)	1982	Copelan (126) Roving Boy (126)	Landaluce (121) Princess Rooney (121)
			1981	Deputy Minister (126) Timely Writer (126)	Before Dawn (120)
2002	Vindication (126)	Storm Flag Flying (123)			
2001	Johannesburg (126)	Tempera (123)	1980	Lord Avie (126)	Heavenly Cause (120)
2000	Macho Uno (126)	Caressing (123)	1979	Rockhill Native (126)	Smart Angle (120)
1999	Anees (126)	Cash Run (123) Chilukki (123) Surfside (123)	1978	Spectacular Bid (126)	Candy Eclair (119) It's in the Air (119)
			1977	Affirmed (126)	Lakeville Miss (119)
1998	Answer Lively (126)	Silverbulletday (123)	1976	Seattle Slew (126)	Sensational (119)
1997	Favorite Trick (128)	Countess Diana (125)	1975	Honest Pleasure (126)	Dearly Precious (119) Optimistic Gal (119)
1996	Boston Harbor (126)	Storm Song (124)			
1995	Maria's Mon (126) Unbridled's Song (126)	My Flag (123)	1974	Foolish Pleasure (127)	Ruffian (122)
			1973	Protagonist (126)	Talking Picture (121)
1994	Timber Country (126)	Flanders (124)	1972	Secretariat (129)	La Prevoyante (121)
1993	Brocco (126) Dehere (126)	Phone Chatter (123)	1971	Riva Ridge (126)	Numbered Account (119)
			1970	Hoist the Flag (126)	Forward Gal (118)
1992	Gilded Time (126)	Eliza (123)	1969	Silent Screen (128)	Fast Attack (116)
1991	Arazi (130)	Pleasant Stage (123)	1968	Top Knight (126)	Gallant Bloom (118) Process Shot (118)
1990	Fly So Free (126)	Meadow Star (123)			
1989	Rhythm (126)	Go for Wand (123)	1967	Vitriolic (126)	Queen of the Stage (117)
1988	Easy Goer (126)	Open Mind (123)	1966	Successor (126)	Regal Gleam (116)
1987	Forty Niner (126)	Epitome (123) Over All (123)	1965	Buckpasser (126)	Moccasin (120)

Racing — Experimental Free Handicap

Year	Male	Female
1964	Bold Lad (130)	Queen Empress (118)
1963	Raise a Native (126)	Castle Forbes (115)
		Tosmah (115)
1962	Never Bend (126)	Affectionately (115)
		Smart Deb (115)
1961	Crimson Satan (126)	Cicada (118)
1960	Hail to Reason (126)	Bowl of Flowers (120)
1959	Warfare (126)	My Dear Girl (117)
1958	First Landing (126)	Quill (117)
1957	Jewel's Reward (126)	Idun (120)
1956	Barbizon (126)	Alanesian (117)
1955	Career Boy (126)	Doubledogdare (116)
		Nasrina (116)
1954	Summer Tan (128)	HIgh Voltage (117)
1953	Porterhouse (126)	Evening Out (118)
	*Turn-to (126)	
1952	Native Dancer (130)	Bubbley (116)
		Sweet Patootie (116)
1951	Tom Fool (126)	Rose Jet (115)
1950	Uncle Miltie (126)	Aunt Jinny (115)
		How (115)
1949	Middleground (126)	Bed o' Roses (119)

Year	Male	Female
1948	Blue Peter (126)	Myrtle Charm (121)
1947	Citation (126)	Bewitch (121)
1946	Cosmic Bomb (126)	First Flight (126)
	Double Jay (126)	
1945	Lord Boswell (128)	Beaugay (121)
1944	Free for All (126)	Busher (119)
	Pavot (126)	
1943	Pukka Gin (126)	Durazna (121)
		Miss Keeneland (121)
1942	Count Fleet (132)	Askmenow (119)
		Good Morning (119)
1941	Alsab (130)	Chiquita Mia (115)
		Ficklebush (115)
1940	Whirlaway (126)	Level Best (121)
1939	Bimelech (130)	Now What (119)
1938	El Chico (126)	Inscoelda (116)
1937	Menow (126)	Jacola (116)
1936	Brooklyn (126)	Rifted Clouds (115)
1935	Red Rain (126)	Forever Yours (116)
1933	First Minstrel (126)	Mata Hari (122)

†Starting in 1985, fillies were weighted separately.
No weights assigned in 1934.

2007 Experimental Free Handicap Colts and Geldings

Wt.	Horse, Color, Pedigree	Sts	1st	2nd	3rd	Earnings
127	War Pass, dk. b. or br., by Cherokee Run—Vue, by Mr. Prospector	4	4	0	0	$1,397,400
120	Dixie Chatter, b., by Dixie Union—Mini Chat, by Deputy Minister	4	2	0	0	191,400
	Into Mischief, b., by Harlan's Holiday—Leslie's Lady, by Tricky Creek	3	2	1	0	448,800
	Pyro, dk. b. or br., by Pulpit—Wild Vision, by Wild Again	4	1	2	2	516,718
119	Court Vision, dk. b. or br., by Gulch—Weekend Storm, by Storm Bird	4	3	1	0	257,542
	Georgie Boy, b., by Tribal Rule—Ippodamia, by Peterhof	5	2	2	1	286,806
	Wicked Style, ch., by Macho Uno—Deviletta, by Trempolino	4	3	0	0	445,000
118	Kodiak Kowboy, b., by Posse—Kokadrie, by Coronado's Quest	7	4	1	1	544,825
	Majestic Warrior, b., by A.P. Indy—Dream Supreme, by Seeking the Gold	3	2	0	0	195,200
	Salute the Sarge, b., by Forest Wildcat—Dixie Ghost, by Silver Ghost	6	3	2	0	286,540
	Tale of Ekati, b., by Tale of the Cat—Silence Beauty (Jpn), by Sunday Silence	4	2	1	0	313,200
116	Colonel John, b., by Tiznow—Sweet Damsel, by Turkoman	4	2	2	0	255,300
115	Etched, ch., by Forestry—Unbridled Elaine, by Unbridled's Song	2	2	0	0	95,880
	Massive Drama, dk. b. or br., by Kafwain—Peyvon, by Slewacide	3	2	0	1	199,200
	Nownownow, b., by Whywhywhy—Here and Now (Fr), by Exit to Nowhere	6	2	3	0	641,950
114	Achill Island (Ire), dk. b. or br., by Sadler's Wells—Prawn Cocktail, by Artichoke	5	1	4	0	288,488
	Z Humor, b., by Distorted Humor—Offtheoldblock, by A.P. Indy	5	2	0	2	543,700
113	Anak Nakal, dk. b. or br., by Victory Gallop—Misk, by Quiet American	3	2	1	0	220,916
	Atoned, dk. b. or br., by Repent—Amidst, by Icecapade	7	2	4	0	136,757
	Monba, gr. or ro., by Maria's Mon—Hamba, by Easy Goer	3	2	0	0	112,534
	Ready's Image, dk. b. or br., by More Than Ready—Clever Phrase, by Clever Trick	6	3	1	1	259,422
	The Leopard, dk. b. or br., by Storm Cat—Moon Safari, by Mr. Prospector	6	3	1	0	173,700
112	Drill Down, dk. b. or br., by El Corredor—Who's Sorry Now, by Ogygian	3	1	0	2	69,000
	Slew's Tiznow, b., by Tiznow—Hepatica, by Slewpy	3	1	1	0	140,300
	Turf War, dk. b. or br., by Dixie Union—Grass Skirt, by Mr. Prospector	5	3	1	0	518,548
111	Beresford, b., by Touch Gold—Naughty n Haughty, by Crafty Prospector	5	1	0	0	49,800
	Blackberry Road, dk. b. or br., by Gone West—Strawberry Reason, by Strawberry Road (Aus)	6	1	1	2	108,235
	Cannonball, dk. b. or br., by Catienus—No Deadline, by Skywalker	5	2	0	1	177,580
	Golden Yank, b., by Yankee Gentleman—Golden Charm, by Strike the Gold	4	3	0	0	264,832
	Lantana Mob, b., by Posse—Lantana, by Copelan	7	3	1	1	219,048
	Mythical Pegasus, dk. b. or br., by Fusaichi Pegasus—Lilly Capote, by Capote	6	1	1	1	80,260
	Old Man Buck, ch., by Hold That Tiger—Victorian Woman, by Jeblar	7	3	0	2	228,312
	Paint, ch., by Include—Pat Copelan, by Copelan	2	1	0	0	49,700
	Racecar Rhapsody, b., by Tale of the Cat—Reflect the Music, by A.P. Indy	4	1	1	1	108,391
	Shore Do, ch., by Include—Dynashore, by Dynaformer	5	1	0	1	66,780
110	Riley Tucker, b., by Harlan's Holiday—My Sweet Country, by Bold Ruckus	3	1	1	1	85,600
	Strike the Deal, ch., by Van Nistelrooy—Countess Gold, by Mt. Livermore	8	2	2	1	267,665
	Texas Fever, b., by Victory Gallop—Fortyniner Fever, by Forty Niner	5	2	0	1	80,460
	Wise Answer, b., by Wised Up—All the Answers, by Colony Light	7	4	2	1	458,300
109	Check It Twice, b., by Repent—Christmas List, by Out of Place	5	3	1	1	144,500
	Chitoz, b., by Forest Wildcat—Wichitoz, by Affirmed	5	2	1	0	75,513
	Cowboy Cal, dk. b. or br., by Giant's Causeway—Texas Tammy, by Seeking the Gold	3	2	0	0	92,048
	El Gato Malo, dk. b. or br., by El Corredor—One Bad Cat, by Mountain Cat	2	2	0	0	70,200
	Indian Sun, b., by Indian Charlie—Unequivocal, by Alleged	4	1	2	0	84,400
	Leonides, b., by Richter Scale—North East Belle, by Beau Genius	3	1	1	0	65,580
	Margo's Gift, dk. b. or br., by Polish Gift—Burgundy Jones, by Knights Choice	7	5	0	1	243,714
	Sok Sok, ch., by Trippi—Vaca Sagrada, by Great Above	6	3	1	0	179,043
108	Halo Najib, ch., by Halo's Image—Najibe's Wish, by Sword Dance (Ire)	3	1	1	0	66,416
	Maimonides, b., by Vindication—Silvery Swan, by Silver Deputy	2	1	0	0	62,200
	Real Appeal, gr. or ro., by Successful Appeal—Formal Process, by Diablo	5	1	0	1	47,482
	Sebastian County, ch., by Hennessy—Double Park (Fr), by Lycius	3	2	0	1	56,770
	Sundaysunday, ch., by Sunday Break (Jpn)—Moi Moi, by St. Jovite	3	1	1	0	49,500

Wt.	Horse, Color, Pedigree	Sts	1st	2nd	3rd	Earnings
107	Cave's Valley, dk. b. or br., by Stephen Got Even—Kamaal, by Irgun	4	3	0	0	$142,210
	Gio Ponti, b., by Tale of the Cat—Chipeta Springs, by Alydar	3	2	0	0	124,200
	Sky Cape, ch., by Najran—Skyscape, by Marquetry	8	1	3	1	84,180
106	Big City Man, ch., by Northern Afleet—Mini Appeal, by Valid Appeal	4	3	1	0	143,540
	Cherokee Triangle, b., by Cherokee Run—Brief Bliss, by Navarone	6	2	1	1	175,125
	Overextended, gr. or ro., by Monarchos—Way of Life, by Gulch	9	1	2	1	86,160
	Smoke'n Coal, gr. or ro., by Smoke Glacken—Cherokyfrolicflash, by Green Dancer	3	2	0	0	85,950
	The Roundhouse, ch., by Fusaichi Pegasus—Circle of Life, by Belong to Me	4	1	1	1	76,600
105	Adriano, ch., by A.P. Indy—Gold Canyon, by Mr. Prospector	4	1	1	0	78,400
	Meal Penalty, gr. or ro., by Tale of the Cat—Unbridled Beauty, by Unbridled's Song	4	2	0	1	64,922
	Royal Night, ch., by Luhuk—Three Cat Nite, by It's Freezing	2	2	0	0	70,200
	Yankee Bravo, dk. b. or br., by Yankee Gentleman—Vickey Jane, by Royal Academy	2	2	0	0	52,049
104	Coal Play, b., by Mineshaft—Wiscasset, by Kris S.	3	1	1	0	52,147
	Gallon, dk. b. or br., by Victory Gallop—Bellehop, by Hennessy	6	2	3	0	82,165
	Grand Minstrel, gr. or ro., by Grand Slam—Colonial Minstrel, by Pleasant Colony	5	2	1	2	101,350
	St. Joe, ch., by Trippi—Load Up, by Dove Hunt	4	1	1	1	54,130
	Your Round, b., by Distorted Humor—Another Round, by Affirmed	5	1	0	2	51,811
103	Arakim, ch., by Giant's Causeway—Fleeting Fable, by Afleet	5	1	1	1	64,158
	Bcb Black Jack, dk. b. or br., by Stormy Jack—Molly's Prospector, by Native Prospector	4	2	1	0	131,425
	Crackalackin, dk. b. or br., by Tiger Ridge—Artic Experience, by Slewpy	3	2	0	1	82,229
	Justaclown, dk. b. or br., by Valid Expectations—Smokin N Jokin, by Metfield	3	2	1	0	64,200
	Meer Kat (Ire), b., by Red Ransom—Bush Cat, by Kingmambo	6	1	2	2	26,353
	Moral Compass, b., by Grand Slam—Affair With Aflair, by Well Decorated	5	1	2	1	63,180
	Pantara Phantom, dk. b. or br., by Stormy Atlantic—Jerold's Sister, by Zuppardo's Prince	5	2	0	2	103,093
	Thoroughly, dk. b. or br., by Full Mandate—King's Pact, by Slewacide	2	2	0	0	58,725
	Trust N Dustan, ch., by Trust N Luck—Lorraine, by Western Playboy	6	2	0	1	67,972
	Wise Mandate, b., by Perfect Mandate—Baroness V Ullmann, by Bold Badgett	8	2	1	0	108,060
102	Big Truck, b., by Hook and Ladder—Just a Ginny, by Go for Gin	4	2	0	1	117,380
	Caberneigh, dk. b. or br., by E Dubai—Smashing Halo, by Halo	7	1	2	2	65,025
	Carson's Legacy, b., by Carson City—Sue's Prospect, by Pass the Line	5	2	0	0	46,430
	Dixie Mon, b., by Maria's Mon—Sea Jamie Win, by Dixieland Band	5	1	1	2	64,248
101	Betatron, b., by Tale of the Cat—Adversity, by Seeking the Gold	5	2	0	0	80,782
	Canny, b., by Seeking the Gold—Cunning, by Lord At War (Arg)	4	1	1	1	34,750
	Dr. Nick, b., by Authenticate—La Riviera, by Affirmed	2	1	1	0	57,127
	Nistle's Crunch, b., by Van Nistelrooy—Sam Eye Am, by Island Whirl	4	1	0	2	47,322
	Preachin Man, dk. b. or br., by Songandaprayer—Sweet Cameron, by Devil's Bag	7	3	2	0	229,614
	Rapper S S, gr. or ro., by Monarchos—What'salltheruckas, by Bold Ruckus	5	3	1	1	101,865
	Rebounded, b., by Boundary—Merry Joyce, by Royal Academy	6	1	0	1	52,032
	Rollers, dk. b. or br., by Stormy Atlantic—Elise', by Distinctive Pro	3	1	1	0	54,850
	Spinning Sound (Ire), ch., by Spinning World—Beryl, by Bering (GB)	4	1	0	0	12,945
	Yonegwa, b., by Kafwain—Newmar, by Salt Lake	8	4	2	1	161,392
100	Cafe Tortoni, ch., by Katahaula County—Trillia, by Regal Classic	6	2	1	0	52,795
	He Aint Easy, dk. b. or br., by Louis Quatorze—Boca Juniors, by Peteski	7	1	2	0	58,918
	Horse Doctor, b., by Horse Chestnut (SAf)—Dr. Redoutable, by Storm Cat	6	1	2	0	33,700
	Izzy Speaking, b., by Partner's Hero—Moonshine Run, by Go for Gin	6	3	2	3	117,270
	Jazz Nation, b., by City Zip—Jazz Star, by Dixieland Band	3	1	2	0	99,418
	Law Enforcement, b., by Posse—Zambezi Belle, by Lord At War (Arg)	4	2	1	0	179,375
	Mikimoto's Mojo, ch., by Hold That Tiger—Munch N Grass, by Pleasant Colony	5	2	0	0	108,000
	Run Brother Ron, ch., by Perfect Mandate—Aloha Mangos, by Bold Badgett	7	3	1	0	102,007
	Snug, b., by Swamp—Tulia, by West by West	5	2	1	0	49,600
	T. J.'s Posse, b., by Posse—T. J.'s Turn, by Meadowlake	5	2	1	0	73,888
	Twentieth Century, gr. or ro., by Cactus Ridge—Lil'mary, by Known Fact	5	0	4	0	31,670
	Whatever Whenever, ch., by Delaware Township—Casino Bound, by Langfuhr	6	2	0	1	72,848

2007 Experimental Free Handicap Fillies

Wt.	Horse, Color, Pedigree	Sts	1st	2nd	3rd	Earnings
123	Indian Blessing, dk. b. or br., by Indian Charlie—Shameful, by Flying Chevron	3	3	0	0	$1,357,200
121	Country Star, dk. b. or br., by Empire Maker—Rings a Chime, by Metfield	3	2	1	0	575,900
119	Proud Spell, b., by Proud Citizen—Pacific Spell, by Langfuhr	4	3	1	0	608,770
118	Cry and Catch Me, dk. b. or br., by Street Cry (Ire)—Please Sign In, by Doc's Leader	3	2	1	0	191,000
117	Backseat Rhythm, b., by El Corredor—Kiss a Miss, by Kissin Kris	5	1	1	1	316,760
	Pure Clan, ch., by Pure Prize—Gather The Clan (Ire), by General Assembly	4	4	0	0	316,209
116	Irish Smoke, gr. or ro., by Smoke Glacken—Added Time, by Gilded Time	4	2	0	0	187,200
	Izarra, b., by Distorted Humor—Arlucea, by Broad Brush	4	1	0	1	111,800
	Mushka, b. or br., by Empire Maker—Sluice, by Seeking the Gold	3	2	0	1	157,100
114	Grace and Power, dk. b. or br., by More Than Ready—Lady in Power, by Defensive Play	5	2	2	1	189,600
	Sea Chanter, b., by War Chant—Smooth Charmer, by Easy Goer	6	3	1	0	271,477
	Set Play, ch., by Van Nistelrooy—Boldy's Reflection, by Bold Ruckus	8	2	1	2	255,450
113	A to the Croft, ch., by Menifee—Heart Warmer, by Devil's Bag	5	1	3	0	210,018
	Elusive Lady, gr. or ro., by Van Nistelrooy—Song of Royalty, by Unbridled's Song	4	2	1	0	136,538
	Runforthemoneybaby, ch., by Unusual Heat—Andover the Money, by Dynaformer	6	2	1	2	160,144
112	By the Light, b., by Malibu Moon—Dixie Tempo, by Major Impact	4	4	0	0	451,815
	More Happy, dk. b. or br., by Vindication—Apelia, by Cool Victor	3	2	0	0	129,300
	Rated Fiesty, b. or ro., by Exchange Rate—Fiesty Countess, by Count the Time	3	3	0	0	204,291
111	C J's Leelee, gr. or ro., by Mizzen Mast—Fight to Love, by Fit to Fight	5	2	1	0	120,023
	Dreaming of Liz, gr. or ro., by El Prado (Ire)—Silver Maiden, by Silver Buck	5	2	0	0	105,880
	Grace Anatomy, b., by Aldebaran—Propriety, by Storm Cat	5	1	0	2	97,160

Racing — Experimental Free Handicap

Wt.	Horse, Color, Pedigree	Sts	1st	2nd	3rd	Earnings
111	Subtle Aly, ch., by French Envoy—Aly Sweet, by Alydar	2	2	0	0	$ 91,028
	Tasha's Miracle, b., by Harlan's Holiday—Ms. Cuvee Napa, by Relaunch	5	2	1	0	233,800
110	Annie Skates, ch., by Mr. Greeley—Vivalita, by Deputy Minister	4	1	2	1	76,637
	Authenicat, ch., by D'wildcat—Authenic Deed, by Alydeed	6	3	2	0	190,216
	Bsharpsonata, b., by Pulpit—Apasionata Sonata, by Affirmed	6	3	0	0	135,750
	Gentle Audrey, b., by Elusive Quality—Fatat Alarab, by Capote	3	1	0	1	53,160
	Spring Awakening, b., by In Excess (Ire)—Catchofthecentury, by Carson City	6	3	1	2	251,662
	The Golden Noodle, ch., by D'wildcat—Golden Genie, by Beau Genius	6	1	1	3	144,380
	Turn Away, b., by Empire Maker—Averti, by Known Fact	2	1	0	1	56,832
109	Blitzing, b., by Montbrook—We Are Strike Ng, by Twilight Agenda	5	3	0	1	122,322
	I Promise, b., by Hook and Ladder—Affirm Promise, by Affirmed	3	1	1	0	47,550
	Indy's Alexandra, dk. b. or br., by Flatter—Hey Ghaz, by Ghazi	3	3	0	0	88,100
	Initiation, ch., by Deputy Minister—Proposal, by Mt. Livermore	3	2	0	0	117,985
108	Foxy Danseur, b., by Mr. Greeley—Ravish Me, by Wild Again	8	2	2	1	146,814
	Passion, dk. b. or br., by Came Home—Rajmata, by Known Fact	3	1	0	1	33,050
	Sky Mom, b., by Maria's Mon—Swiftly Classic, by Sky Classic	8	3	2	1	174,841
	Smarty Deb, ch., by Smart Strike—Taste the Passion, by Wild Again	5	4	0	0	171,055
107	Macellya (Fr), ch., by Testa Rossa—Macellum, by Machiavellian	3	1	1	1	51,316
	Rasierra, b., by Kafwain—Sierras Kiara, by Moscow Ballet	5	1	2	1	57,184
	Sunday Holiday, dk. b. or br., by Sunday Break (Jpn)—Militant Maid, by Metfield	5	1	1	2	98,356
106	Glacken's Gal, b., by Smoke Glacken—Lady Diplomat, by Silver Deputy	2	2	0	0	90,180
	Golden Doc A, ch., by Unusual Heat—Penpont (NZ), by Crested Wave	8	2	1	1	165,356
	Gorgeous Goose, gr. or ro., by Mongoose—Gorgeous Me, by Big Spruce	4	2	0	0	75,620
	Namaste's Wish, b., by Pulpit—Copelan's Bid Gal, by Copelan	5	2	0	0	97,288
	Saki to Me, dk. b. or br., by Fusaichi Pegasus—Buy the Cat, by Storm Cat	3	3	0	0	114,000
	Silk Ridge, b., by Eltish—Whisper of Silk, by Birdonthewire	10	4	2	1	369,240
105	Fareena, b., by Point Given—La Feria, by Elocutionist	3	2	0	1	39,500
	Wonderful Luck, ch., by Trust N Luck—No Small Wonder, by Capote	6	2	1	0	98,846
	Zee Zee, gr. or ro., by Exchange Rate—Emblem of Hope, by Dynaformer	4	2	1	0	174,450
104	A Little Gem, dk. b. or br., by Yonaguska—Dignified Diva, by Meadowlake	5	2	0	1	111,525
	Hartfelt, dk. b. or br., by Kafwain—Silver Trainor, by Silver Hawk	2	2	0	0	70,200
	Honest to Betsy, dk. b. or br., by Yonaguska—Hard Freeze, by It's Freezing	6	1	2	0	61,020
	Kadira, b., by Kafwain—Raw Gold, by Rahy	7	3	1	1	136,525
	La Mina, b., by Mineshaft—El Laoob, by Red Ransom	9	3	3	0	147,601
	Mims Eppi, gr. or ro., by Cactus Ridge—Mim's Bid, by Spectacular Bid	5	1	3	0	55,694
	Miss Missile, b., by Golden Missile—Whistling Bullet, by Silver Deputy	11	5	1	0	189,188
	Morakami, dk. b. or br., by Fusaichi Pegasus—Astrid, by Concern	4	1	0	0	72,746
	Throbbin' Heart, gr. or ro., by Smoke Glacken—Countless Affairs, by Storm Cat	4	2	2	0	99,450
103	American Prize, ch., by Pure Prize—Stars n' Bars, by Dixieland Band	5	2	1	1	84,300
	Melissa Jo, ch., by Fusaichi Pegasus—Takeaway, by Fly So Free	3	1	1	1	61,600
	Minewander, ch., by Mineshaft—Wander Storm, by Storm Bird	7	1	1	2	48,430
	Porte Bonheur, b., by Hennessy—Sous Entendu, by Shadeed	4	2	0	0	81,956
	Sherine, dk. b. or br., by Precise End—Willa Dear, by Red Ransom	6	3	0	2	129,007
	Sindy Jacobson, dk. b. or br., by More Than Ready—Behaving, by Rubiano	3	2	1	0	48,800
	Six Pack Sammy, b., by Yonaguska—Sara Six Pack, by Saratoga Six	4	1	1	0	72,335
	Wasted Tears, b., by Najran—Wishes and Roses, by Greinton (GB)	2	1	1	0	30,200
	Wind in My Wings, b., by Sligo Bay (Ire)—Sly Butterfly, by Pulpit	5	2	0	0	133,308
102	According to Plan, ch., by Out of Place—Waiting, by Affirmed	4	1	1	0	45,808
	Arealhotlover, b., by Untuttable—Hot Rod Helen, by Regal Search	7	2	2	1	105,500
	Armonk, gr. or ro., by Mizzen Mast—Flaming Satan, by Java Gold	5	1	1	2	112,600
	Awesome Dreamer, dk. b. or br., by West Acre—Beauchamp Point, by Glitterman	8	1	4	3	115,560
	Calico Bay, b., by Three Wonders—Countrywishingwell, by Country Pine	6	2	2	1	331,300
	Dagger, b., by Tactical Cat—Pat Hand, by Cape Town	6	1	2	1	89,800
	Lickety Lemon, b., by Lemon Drop Kid—Tustarta, by Trempolino	4	2	1	1	124,956
	Meriwether Jessica, ch., by Freud—Chunter's Joy, by Northern Jove	5	1	4	0	107,695
	Remarkable Remy, gr. or ro., by Hennessy—Most Remarkable, by Marquetry	5	2	0	1	97,627
	Timely Reflection, b., by Yankee Victor—Elmswood, by Woodman	4	2	0	1	75,000
	Yonagucci, b., by Yonaguska—Designer Label, by Pentelicus	8	2	0	1	112,545
101	Dreabons Legacy, b., by Proud Citizen—Kelly Amber, by Highland Park	6	1	2	0	73,570
	Dubit, ch., by E Dubai—Ucandoittoo, by Honour and Glory	5	1	3	1	82,366
	Jolie Visage, ch., by Broken Vow—Making Faces, by Lyphard	4	1	0	1	31,800
	Return to Paradise, dk. b. or br., by El Prado (Ire)—Winner's Edge, by Seeking the Gold	5	1	1	2	53,250
	Sunday Geisha, dk. b. or br., by Sunday Break (Jpn)—Above the Table, by Never Tabled	5	1	1	0	48,240
	Treadmill, b., by E Dubai—Lady Lang, by Langfuhr	5	2	1	0	132,000
	Vengeful Shadow, b., by Shadow Caster—Vengeful Val, by Tennessee Rite	7	1	1	3	35,265
100	American County, b., by Gibson County—Young American, by Pentelicus	9	2	3	3	103,799
	Ariege, dk. b. or br., by Doneraile Court—Kostroma (Ire), by Caerleon	4	1	0	1	28,158
	Bold Child, dk. b. or br., by Flatter—Protect the Child, by Housebuster	2	1	1	0	45,600
	Cato Major, dk. b. or br., by E Dubai—Love to Fight, by Fit to Fight	4	1	1	0	80,000
	Champagne Eyes, b., by Flatter—Corking, by Sensitive Prince	4	1	1	0	66,922
	D J Lightning, dk. b. or br., by Doneraile Court—Cozy Lady, by Grindstone	3	2	0	1	68,375
	Dill or No Dill, dk. b. or br., by Evansville Slew—Sapphire Halo, by Southern Halo	5	2	1	1	66,900
	Elocution, ch., by Mutakddim—Imaginary Number, by Hero's Honor	6	2	0	1	97,600
	Love Buzz, gr. or ro., by Silver Charm—Open Story, by Open Forum	12	1	1	0	69,134
	Lucky Copy, ch., by Unbridled's Song—Perfect Copy, by Deputy Minister	4	1	0	2	47,255
	Palanka City, ch., by Carson City—Indian Sunset, by Storm Bird	5	2	1	1	48,900
	Sammy Van Ammy, dk. b. or br., by Van Nistelrooy—Sammy Ammy, by Henbane	6	1	2	2	76,393
	Yasinisi (Ire), dk. b. or br., by Kalanisi (Ire)—Yazmin (Ire), by Green Desert	4	1	0	0	14,250

American Match Races

Match races, a prominent part of American Thoroughbred racing through the mid-1970s, slowed to a trickle after Ruffian's fatal showdown with Foolish Pleasure at Belmont Park on July 6, 1975. Of all the match races in North America during the 20th century, very few were contested after the undefeated filly shattered her right front ankle and was euthanized the next day. Only nine of those 13 were in the United States, and none of them commanded the national attention given the Ruffian–Foolish Pleasure match and such earlier match races as Seabiscuit–War Admiral and Nashua–Swaps.

Match races in America were mostly winner take all and trace back to the early 1820s, when American Eclipse engaged in and won two matches. Similarly, the great sire Lexington won twice in head-to-head competition in the 1850s. Since Domino defeated Clifford by three-quarters of a length in a one-mile match race at Sheepshead Bay Racetrack in New York on September 6, 1894, 15 match races have contained at least one starter who was recognized officially or unofficially as a champion. (*Daily Racing Form* first designated champions in 1936.) Thirteen of the 15 races offered wagering, and favorites lost nine of them. None was more noteworthy than War Admiral's loss to Seabiscuit in 1938, and none was more one-sided than Miss Musket's 50-length loss to Chris Evert on July 20, 1974, at Hollywood Park.

To appreciate America's greatest match races, it is necessary to understand the hype and expectations heading into them. For more than a year, racing fans had clamored for a match-up of Seabiscuit and War Admiral, the two dominant horses of the late 1930s. When the two finally met, they were the only entrants in the 1³⁄₁₆-mile Pimlico Special Stakes on November 1, 1938. A record crowd of 40,000 turned out to see Seabiscuit, a five-year-old grandson of Man o' War, take on War Admiral, a four-year-old son of Man o' War who had won the 1937 Triple Crown and 16 of 17 starts prior to the match.

Seabiscuit, breaking from the second post position, was sent off at 2.20-to-1 under George Woolf; War Admiral, thought to be the quicker from the gate, was 0.25-to-1 under Charley Kurtsinger. War Admiral was expected to lead at the start, but Seabiscuit outbroke him. Seabiscuit had been on the lead in just one of his previous 13 starts.

War Admiral made several moves at his opponent and once drew within a nose, but Seabiscuit had plenty left and won by four lengths in track-record time of 1:56.60.

Nearly 17 years later, Kentucky Derby winner Swaps went off as the 3-to-10 favorite against Preakness and Belmont Stakes winner Nashua in the $100,000 Washington Park Match Race at 1¼ miles on August 31, 1955. Swaps was undefeated as a three-year-old and owner-breeder Rex Ellsworth had returned him to California after he defeated Nashua by 1½ lengths in the 1955 Derby. Nashua's only loss in 11 starts had been in the Derby. Swaps was the favorite under Bill Shoemaker, while Nashua was 6-to-5 with Eddie Arcaro. Nashua won by 6½ lengths, leading from start to finish.

The race that effectively ended top-level match races pitted Foolish Pleasure, 1975 Kentucky Derby winner, against undefeated Ruffian, a three-year-old filly who never had been headed in ten career starts, all against other fillies. Jacinto Vasquez was the regular rider of both horses and chose to ride Frank Whiteley-trained Ruffian in the nationally televised race. Ruffian went off at 0.40-to-1; Foolish Pleasure was 0.90-to-1.

Ruffian broke from the rail and narrowly led Foolish Pleasure through a blazing first quarter-mile in :22⅕ on Belmont's deep 1¼-mile chute. Shortly after they entered the main track, however, Ruffian broke down and swerved to the outside. Foolish Pleasure finished the race under Braulio Baeza. Ruffian fought her handlers when coming out of anesthesia after surgery, reinjured her leg, and was euthanized early on July 7. Match races since then never have been the same.—*Bill Heller*

Match Races, 1868 to Present

Winner, Age, Sex	Loser, Age, Sex	Race	Date	Track	Distance	Time
Rosy Way, 10, g.	Howthewestwaswon, 6, g.	Match Race	July 21, 1999	Les Bois Park	6½f	1:19.20
Maybe Jack, 4, g.	Pro On Ice, 7, g.	Match Race	December 14, 1997	Suffolk Downs	1m	1:45.29
Isthataclaimgirl, 4, f.	Calico Rose, 5, m.	Match Race	June 24, 1996	Prairie Meadows	6f	1:13.03
Busy Banana, 4, c.	Richard of England, 7, g.	Match Race	March 23, 1996	Santa Anita	1¹⁄₁₆m	1:45.08
Soviet Problem, 4, f.	Mamselle Bebette, 4, f.	Match Race	August 21, 1994	Del Mar	5fT	:56.58
Soviet Problem, 4, f.	Lazor, 4, g.	Match Race	May 12, 1994	Golden Gate Fields	6f	1:08.55
Slash Adder, 5, h.	Win Your Heart, 4, f.	Match Race	September 18, 1988	Les Bois Park	4½f	:51.40
Who Doctor Who, 5, g.	Explosive Girl, 4, f.	Match Race	July 23, 1988	Ak-Sar-Ben	1m 70y	1:42.00
Keen Traveler, 3, f.	Graphic Miss, 3, f.	Match Race	June 7, 1981	Centennial	5f	:57.80
Foolish Pleasure, 3, c.	Ruffian, 3, f.	Great Match Race	July 6, 1975	Belmont Park	1¼m	2:02.80
Chris Evert, 3, f.	Miss Musket, 3, f.	Hollywood Special S.	July 20, 1974	Hollywood Park	1¼m	2:02.00
Ponderosa Jane, 5, m.	Distant U, 6, m.	Exhibition Race	October 10, 1973	Calder Race Course	6f	1:13.40
Jovial John, 4, g.	Blunt Man, 9, h.	Match Race	November 16, 1972	Cahokia Downs	5f	1:00.80
Convenience, 4, f.	Typecast, 6, m.	Match Race	June 17, 1972	Hollywood Park	1⅛m	1:47.60
Princess Khal, 4, f.	Off to Market, 5, m.	Match Race	August 16, 1970	Centennial	1m 70y	1:41.60
Emerald Chief, 4, c.	High Nail, 6, h.	Match Race	November 15, 1969	Shenandoah Downs	3½f	:40.00
Mr. Longwait, 6, h.	Sunday Cruz, 5, m.	Exhibition Race	March 22, 1969	Thistledown	1m	1:44.20
Christopher G., 3, c.	Moroni Joe, 6, h.	Match Race	August 27, 1967	Prescott Downs	5½f	1:06.40
Permano, 4, c.	Frannie, 5, m.	Match Race	September 7, 1966	Exhibition Park	6½f	1:17.00
Nasharco, 4, c.	Nancycee, 4, f.	Match Race	April 10, 1966	Turf Paradise	5½f	1:10.20
Nancycee, 4, f.	Nasharco, 4, c.	Match Race	March 20, 1966	Turf Paradise	5f	:56.20
Wandering Boy, 6, h.	Mr. McCoy, 5, h.	Match Race	April 11, 1965	Turf Paradise	2f	:21.40
Over Current, 5, h.	Golden Briar, 5, h.	Match Race	June 27, 1964	Exhibition Park	6f	1:11.60
Try It, 8, h.	Spinney, 10, g.	Match Race	April 14, 1963	Turf Paradise	1½m	2:30.40
Short Nail, 2, c.	Florida Cracker, 2, c.	Match Race	December 4, 1962	Garden State	6f	1:13.40
Cesca, 2, f.	Aim n Fire, 2, c.	Match Race	July 7, 1962	Woodbine	5½f	1:04.60
Wichita Maid, 4, f.	Gilhooley, 5, m.	Australian Welcome Inv. Match Race	August 19, 1961	Centennial	5½f	1:04.40
Routeen, 2, f	Modest Step, 2, f.	Latonia Match Race	October 1, 1960	Latonia	6f	1:13.60
Matisse, 4, g.	Tondi, 4, c.	Match Race	September 24, 1960	Albuquerque	5½f	1:03.00

Winner, Age, Sex	Loser, Age, Sex	Race	Date	Track	Distance	Time
Roman Colonel, 4, c.	Benedicto, 5, g.	Special Match Race	June 11, 1960	Detroit Race Course	6f	1:10.40
Lori Lynn, 4, f.	*Salmon Peter, 9, g.	Inv. Match Race	August 22, 1959	Centennial	1¼m	2:05.00
Wildoath, 3, c.	War Marshal, 4, c.	Special Match Race	October 12, 1957	Fresno	1 1/16m	1:43.60
Noorahge, 4, c.	Early Bull, 7, h.	Dapper Dan Match Race	September 14, 1957	Wheeling Downs	6½f	1:24.00
Queen Doris, 3, f.	Molly Darling, 4, f.	Inv. Match Race	July 28, 1956	Centennial	5½f	1:05.60
Nashua, 3, c.	Swaps, 3, c.	Washington Park Match Race	August 31, 1955	Washington Park	1¼m	2:04.20
Virginia Fair, 2, f.	Virden, 2, f.	Inv. Match Race	August 15, 1952	Edmonton	abt 5f	1:00.40
Capot, 3, c.	Coaltown, 4, c.	Pimlico Special	October 28, 1949	Pimlico	1 3/16m	1:56.80
Armed, 6, g.	Assault, 4, c.	The Special	September 27, 1947	Belmont Park	1¼m	2:02.80
Dinner Party, 6, g.	Float Me, 5, g.	New England Championship	November 23, 1946	Rockingham Park	1⅛m	1:57.60
Here's How, 2, f.	Lady Gunner, 2, f.	Match Race	September 15, 1945	Narragansett	6f	1:12.80
Busher, 3, f.	Durazna, 4, f.	Match Race	August 29, 1945	Washington Park	1m	1:37.80
Alsab, 3, c.	Whirlaway, 4, c.	Narragansett Championship	September 19, 1942	Narragansett	1 3/16m	1:56.40
Lavengro, 7, g.	*Sir Winsome, 4, c.	Pacific Coast Sprint Champ.	August 16, 1942	Longacres	6f	1:10.00
Wise Moss, 3, f.	Sweet Willow, 4, f.	New Hampshire Special	November 22, 1941	Rockingham	6f	1:11.20
Alsab, 2, c.	Requested, 2, c.	Match Race	September 23, 1941	Belmont Park	6½f	1:16.00
Soup and Fish, 4, c.	Betty Main, 3, f.	Match Race	September 20, 1941	Beulah Park	1m	1:37.80
Unerring, 3, f.	Flying Lill, 3, f.	Match Race	August 31, 1939	Washington Park	1m	1:37.80
Seabiscuit, 5, h.	War Admiral, 4, c.	Pimlico Special	November 1, 1938	Pimlico	1 3/16m	1:56.60
Seabiscuit, 5, h.	*Ligaroti, 6, h.	Special Stake Race	August 12, 1938	Del Mar	1⅛m	1:49.00
Rough Time, 3, c.	Appealing, 4, c.	Match Race	August 14, 1937	Suffolk Downs	6f	1:10.40
Myrtlewood, 4, f.	Miss Merriment, 5, m.	Special Sweepstakes	October 24, 1936	Keeneland	6f	1:11.80
Clang, 3, g.	Myrtlewood, 3, f.	Match Race	October 12, 1935	Coney Island	6f	1:09.20
Myrtlewood, 3, f.	Clang, 3, g.	Match Race	September 25, 1935	Hawthorne	6f	1:10.80
*Winooka, 5, c.	Onrush, 3, g.	International Match Race	September 16, 1933	Longacres	6f	1:14.00
Zev, 3, c.	In Memoriam, 4, c.	Match Race	November 17, 1923	Churchill Downs	1¼m	2:06.60
Sarazen, 2, g.	Happy Thoughts, 2, f.	Laurel Special	October 26, 1923	Laurel Park	6f	1:14.00
Zev, 3, c.	*Papyrus, 3, c.	International Race	October 20, 1923	Belmont Park	1½m	2:35.40
Man o' War, 3, c.	Sir Barton, 4, c.	Kenilworth Park Gold Cup	October 12, 1920	Kenilworth	1¼m	2:03.00
*Hourless, 3, c.	*Omar Khayyam, 3, c.	American Champion S.	October 18, 1917	Laurel Park	1¼m	2:02.00
Novelty, 2, c.	Textile, 2, c.	Two-Year-Old Special	August 17, 1910	Saratoga	6f	1:13.20
Dick Welles, 3, c.	Grand Opera, 4, c.	Special Race	August 14, 1903	Harlem	1m	1:37.40
Ethelbert, 4, c.	Jean Beraud, 4, c.	Special Sweepstakes	June 2, 1900	Gravesend	1¼m	2:08.20
Admiration, 3, f.	May Hempstead, 3, f.	Match Race	July 1, 1899	Coney Island	1m	1:40.20
Cleophas, 2, f.	Suisun, 2, f.	Match Race	May 14, 1896	Churchill Downs	5f	1:01.00
dh-Domino, 3, c.	dh-Henry of Navarre, 3, c.	The Third Special	September 15, 1894	Brooklyn	1⅛m	1:55.50
dh-Domino, 2, c.	dh-Dobbins, 2, c.	Match Race	August 31, 1893	Coney Island	abt 6f	1:12.60
Kingston, 7, h.	Van Buren, 3, c.	Match Race	August 31, 1891	Garfield Park	1 1/16m	1:50.75
Longstreet, 5, h.	Tenny, 5, h.	Match Race	August 1, 1891	Morris Park	1¼m	2:07.50
Salvator, 4, c.	Tenny, 4, c.	Match Race	June 25, 1890	Sheepshead Bay	1¼m	2:05.00
Troubadour, 4, c.	Miss Woodford, 5, m.	Special Race	June 29, 1886	Coney Island	1¼m	2:08.75
Miss Woodford, 5, m.	Freeland, 6, g.	Match Race	August 20, 1885	Monmouth Park	1¼m	2:09.50
General Harding, 4, c.	Shelby Barnes, 5, g.	Match Race	June 19, 1885	Brighton Beach	7f	1:38.00
Miss Woodford, 4, f.	Drake Carter, 4, g.	Match Race	September 18, 1884	Sheepshead Bay	2½m	4:28.75
Wallflower, 4, g.	Eulogy, 3, f.	Match Race	August 2, 1884	Saratoga	1m	1:46.00
East Lynne, 2, f.	Cricket, 2, f.	Match Race	July 24, 1884	Monmouth Park	6f	1:18.50
Corsair, 4, g.	Hospodar, 5, h.	Match Race	July 8, 1882	Monmouth Park	1m	1:46.75
Crickmore, 3, g.	Hindoo, 3, c.	Brighton Beach Purse	September 17, 1881	Sheepshead Bay	1½m	2:36.25
Hiawassa, 2, f.	Memento, 2, f.	Match Race	August 20, 1881	Monmouth Park	6f	1:16.50
Eole, 3, c.	Getaway, 3, c.	Match Race	August 12, 1881	Saratoga	1⅝m	2:52.25
Onondaga, 2, c.	Sachem, 2, c.	Match Race	June 25, 1881	Sheepshead Bay	6f	1:15.50
Geranium, 3, f.	Marathon, 3, g.	Match Race	June 23, 1881	Sheepshead Bay	1m	1:45.00
Marathon, 3, g.	Geranium, 3, f.	Match Race	June 4, 1881	Jerome Park	1m	1:53.00
Luke Blackburn, 3, c.	Uncas, 4, c.	Match Race	September 14, 1880	Gravesend Park	1½m	2:42.50
Spartan, 3, c.	Bramble, 3, c.	Match Race	July 6, 1878	Monmouth Park	1¼m	2:16.00
Ten Broeck, 6, h.	Mollie McCarthy, 5, m.	Match Race	July 4, 1878	Louisville	4m	heats
Mollie McCarthy, 5, m.	Jake, 5, h.	Match Race	March 2, 1878	Sacramento	2m	heats
Jake, 4, c.	Madge Duke, 3, f.	Match Race	November 29, 1877	San Francisco	2m	heats
Rappahannock, 4, c.	Kilburn, 6, g.	Match Race	October 26, 1877	Pimlico	2m	heats
Bazil, 3, g.	Cloverbrook, 3, c.	Match Race	June 18, 1877	Jerome Park	1¼m	2:12.75
Shirley, 3, g.	Resolute, 6, h.	Match Race	October 28, 1876	Pimlico	2m	3:44.50
Shylock, 5, h.	Vaultress, 3, f.	Match Race	July 18, 1874	Monmouth Park	2m	3:46.50
Joe Daniels, 4, c.	Nell Flaherty, 6, m.	Match Race	December 25, 1873	San Francisco	1½m	2:46.00
Girl of the Period, 4, f.	Ophelia, 4, f.	Match Race	October 4, 1873	Jerome Park	4f	heats
Shylock, 4, c.	M. A. B., 4, f.	Match Race	October 4, 1873	Jerome Park	1½m	heats
Survivor, 3, c.	Aerolite, 3, c.	Match Race	July 21, 1873	Monmouth Park	1m	1:46.00
Thad Stevens, 8, h.	Ben Wade, 4, c.	Match Race	June 28, 1873	Oakland	2m	heats
Nell Flaherty, 6, m.	Abi, 4, f.	Match Race	June 28, 1873	Oakland	1m	heats
Thad Stevens, 8, h.	Nettie Brown, 5, m.	Match Race	March 1, 1873	San Francisco	1m	heats
Alarm, 2, c.	Inverary, 2, f.	Match Race	August 16, 1871	Saratoga	1m	1:47.50
Virgil, 6, h.	Chalmette, 6, h.	Match Race	May 20, 1871	New Orleans	2m	heats
Nannie McNairy, 7, m.	Sarah McDonald, 4, f.	Match Race	December 4, 1869	New Orleans	6f	1:20.00
Finesse, 2, f.	Intrigue, 2, f.	Match Race	October 6, 1869	Jerome Park	1m	1:52.25
Intrigue, 2, f.	El Dorado, 2, c.	Match Race	June 6, 1869	Jerome Park	6f	1:25.75
Glenelg, 3, c.	Rapture, 3, f.	Match Race	June 3, 1869	Jerome Park	1m	1:49.25
Miss Alice, 2, f.	c. by Censor, 2	Match Race	June 3, 1869	Jerome Park	1m	1:54.25
Nannie McNairy, 6, m.	Lewis E. Smith, 5, h.	Match Race	April 8, 1869	New Orleans	4f	:49.75
Nannie McNairy, 5, m.	Le Noir, 6, m.	Match Race	December 7, 1868	New Orleans	4f	:54.50
Maid of Honor, 4, f.	Trovatore, 5, m.	Match Race	November 7, 1868	Jerome Park	1m	1:51.25

Notable Walkovers Since 1930

Walkovers are rare in Thoroughbred racing if only because competition is at the heart of the sport. The most recent walkover occurred in 1997 when Sharp Cat's two opponents, Alzora and Toda Una Dama (Arg) were scratched from the Bayakoa Handicap (G2) after December rains turned Hollywood Park's track muddy. Prior to that, champion Spectacular Bid walked over when Winter's Tale, Temperence Hill, and Dr. Patches were scratched from the 1980 Woodward Stakes (G1).

In consecutive years, Calumet Farm champions Coaltown and Citation walked over in Maryland races. Coaltown was unopposed in the 1949 Edward Burke Handicap at Havre de Grace, and Citation had no opponents entered against him in the 1948 Pimlico Special.

Although walkovers usually involve only one horse, two horses with the same owner may walk over if they are entered in a race and no horses oppose them. Here are several of the most important walkovers since 1930.

Walkovers, 1940 to Present

Horse, Age, Sex	Race (Grade)	Date	Track	Distance	Time
Sharp Cat, 3, f.	Bayakoa H. (G2)	December 7, 1997	Hollywood Park	1 1/16m	1:42.68
Spectacular Bid, 4, c.	Woodward S. (G1)	September 20, 1980	Belmont Park	1 1/4m	2:02.40
Coaltown, 4, c.	Edward Burke H.	April 23, 1949	Havre De Grace	1 1/8m	1:52.20
Citation, 3, c.	Pimlico Special	October 29, 1948	Pimlico	1 3/16m	1:59.80
Casa Camara, 2, f.	Diamond Ring S.	October 26, 1946	Long Branch	1m 70y	1:49.40
Stymie, 5, h.	Saratoga Cup	August 31, 1946	Saratoga Race Course	1 3/4m	3:07.40
Whirlaway, 4, c.	Pimlico Special	October 28, 1942	Pimlico	1 3/16m	2:05.40

Scale of Weights

The scale of weights provides a guideline to the weights that horses carry at different ages and over different distances. As in many standards in Thoroughbred racing, the current scale of weights evolved over time.

The earliest Thoroughbred races in the 17th century were run at catch weights—whatever the rider, usually the owner, weighed. As racing became more sophisticated, various methods were tried to make contests more fair as well as more competitive, including assigning different weights according to the height of the horse, known as "give-and-take" weights.

That concept eventually evolved into assigning different weights to horses of differing perceived abilities. The first recorded handicap race was the Subscription Handicap Plate at Newmarket in 1785.

In 1740, the English Parliament established minimum weights for horses of different ages. Those weights were not meant to be assigned to horses of different ages in the same race, however.

In the mid-19th century, Admiral Henry Rous, British racing's de facto dictator, applied and expanded the concept to horses of different ages in the same race. Rous published the world's first weight-for-age scale in his 1850 book *On the Laws and Practice of Horse Racing*. Rous's scale also recognized that Thoroughbreds mature steadily from ages two through four; he assigned different weights at different distances for every month of the year.

All subsequent scales essentially have been refinements of Rous's work. The scale of weights listed below is the official scale used by American racing secretaries.

Distance and Age	Jan.	Feb.	Mar.	Apr.	May	June	July	Aug.	Sept.	Oct.	Nov.	Dec.
Half mile												
2 years	x	x	x	x	x	x	x	105	108	111	114	114
3 years	117	117	119	119	121	123	125	126	127	128	129	129
4 years	130	130	130	130	130	130	130	130	130	130	130	130
5 years & up	130	130	130	130	130	130	130	130	130	130	130	130
6 furlongs												
2 years	x	x	x	x	x	x	x	102	105	108	111	111
3 years	114	114	117	117	119	121	123	125	126	127	128	128
4 years	129	129	130	130	130	130	130	130	130	130	130	130
5 years & up	130	130	130	130	130	130	130	130	130	130	130	130
1 mile												
2 years	x	x	x	x	x	x	x	x	96	99	102	102
3 years	107	107	111	111	113	115	117	119	121	122	123	123
4 years	127	127	128	128	128	126	126	126	126	126	126	126
5 years & up	128	128	128	128	127	126	126	126	126	126	126	126
1 1/4 miles												
2 years	x	x	x	x	x	x	x	x	x	x	x	x
3 years	101	101	107	107	111	113	116	118	120	121	122	122
4 years	125	125	127	127	127	126	126	126	126	126	126	126
5 years & up	127	127	127	127	127	126	126	126	126	126	126	126
1 1/2 miles												
2 years	x	x	x	x	x	x	x	x	x	x	x	x
3 years	98	98	104	104	108	111	114	117	119	121	122	122
4 years	124	124	126	126	126	126	126	126	126	126	126	126
5 years & up	126	126	126	126	126	126	126	126	126	126	126	126
2 miles												
3 years	96	96	102	102	106	109	112	114	117	119	120	120
4 years	124	124	126	126	126	126	125	125	125	124	124	124
5 years & up	126	126	126	126	126	126	125	125	125	124	124	124

(a) In races of intermediate lengths, the weights for the shorter distance are carried.
(b) In races exclusively for three-year-olds or four-year-olds, the weight is 126 lbs., and in races exclusively for two-year-olds, it is 122 lbs.
(c) In all races except handicaps and races where the conditions expressly state to the contrary, the scale of weights is less, by the following: for two-year-old fillies, 3 lbs.; for three-year-old and up fillies and mares, 5 lbs. before September 1, and 3 lbs. thereafter.
(d) In all handicaps that close more than 72 hours prior to the race the top weight shall not be less than 126 lbs., except in handicaps for fillies and mares, the top weight shall not be less than 126 lbs. less the sex allowance at the time of the race.

Oldest Male Grade 1 Stakes Winners Since 1976

Age	Horse, YOB Sex, Sire	Year Race(s)
9	John Henry, 1975 g., by Ole Bob Bowers	1984 Budweiser Million, Hollywood Inv. H., Sunset H., Turf Classic
	John's Call, 1991 g., by Lord At War (Arg)	2000 Sword Dancer Inv. H., Turf Classic Inv. S.
	Super Diamond, 1980 h., by Pass the Glass	1989 San Antonio H.
	The Tin Man, 1998 g., by Affirmed	2007 Shoemaker Mile S.
8	Affirmed Success, 1994 g., by Affirmed	2002 Carter H.
	Better Talk Now, 1999 g., by Talkin Man	2007 Manhattan H.
	Cetewayo, 1994 h., by His Majesty	2002 Gulfstream Park Breeders' Cup H.
	Collier Hill (Ire), 1998 g., by Dr Devious (Ire)	2006 Pattison Canadian International S.
	John Henry, 1975 g., by Ole Bob Bowers	1983 Hollywood Turf Cup
	Mashkour, 1983 h., by Irish River (Fr)	1991 San Juan Capistrano Inv. H.
	Redattore (Brz), 1995 h., by Roi Normand	2003 Shoemaker Breeders' Cup Mile S.
	Sir Bear, 1993 g., by Sir Leon	2001 Gulfstream Park H.
	The Tin Man, 1998 g., by Affirmed	2006 Arlington Million S., Clement L. Hirsch Memorial Turf Championsh p S.
7	A Huevo, 1996 g., by Cool Joe	2003 Frank J. De Francis Memorial Dash S.
	Ancient Title, 1970 h., by Gummo	1977 San Antonio S.
	Awad, 1990 h., by Caveat	1997 Sword Dancer Inv. H.
	Bemo, 1970 g., by Maribeau	1977 United Nations H.
	Bilo, 2000 g., by Bertrando	2007 Triple Bend Inv. H.
	Cardmania, 1986 g., by Cox's Ridge	1993 Breeders' Cup Sprint
	Cloudy's Knight, 2000 g., by Lord Avie	2007 Pattison Canadian International S.
	Designed for Luck, 1997 g., by Rahy	2004 Shoemaker Breeders' Cup Mile S.
	Down the Aisle, 1993 h., by Runaway Groom	2000 United Nations H.
	Elmhurst, 1990 g., by Wild Again	1997 Breeders' Cup Sprint
	Forego, 1970 g., by *Forli	1977 Metropolitan H., Woodward H.
	Grand Flotilla, 1987 h., by Caro (Ire)	1994 Hollywood Turf H.
	John Henry, 1975 g., by Ole Bob Bowers	1982 Oak Tree Inv. H., Santa Anita H.
	Jumping Hill, 1972 h., by Hillary	1979 Widener H.
	Key Contender, 1988 h., by Fit to Fight	1995 Suburban H.
	Kona Gold, 1994 g., by Java Gold	2001 San Carlos H.
	Ladies Din, 1995 g., by Din's Dancer	2002 Shoemaker Breeders' Cup Mile S.
	Miesque's Approval, 1999 h., by Miesque's Son	2006 NetJets Breeders' Cup Mile
	Noble Dancer (GB), 1972 h., by Prince de Galles	1979 San Luis Rey S., United Nations H.
	Passinetti, 1996 g., by Slew o' Gold	2003 San Juan Capistrano Inv. H.
	Pleasant Variety, 1984 h., by Pleasant Colony	1991 San Luis Rey S.
	Red Bishop, 1988 h., by Silver Hawk	1995 San Juan Capistrano Inv. H.
	River Keen (Ire), 1992 h., by Keen	1999 Jockey Club Gold Cup, Woodward S.
	Sabona, 1982 h., by Exclusive Native	1989 Californian S.
	Sandpit (Brz), 1989 h., by Baynoun (Ire)	1996 Caesars International H., Hollywood Turf H
	Sarrera, 2000 g., by Quest for Fame (GB)	
	Special Ring, 1997 g., by Nureyev	2004 Eddie Read H.
	Steinlen (GB), 1983 h., by Habitat	1990 Hollywood Turf H.
	Val's Prince, 1992 g., by Eternal Prince	1999 Man o' War S., Turf Classic Inv. S.
	Winter's Tale, 1976 g., by Arts and Letters	1983 Suburban H.
	With Anticipation, 1995 g., by Relaunch	2002 Man o' War S., Sword Dancer H., United Nations H.
	Yankee Affair, 1982 h., by Northern Fling	1989 Man o' War S., Turf Classic, United Nations H.
	Zoffany, 1980 h., by Our Native	1987 San Luis Rey S.

Oldest Female Grade 1 Stakes Winners Since 1976

Age	Horse, YOB Sex, Sire	Year Race(s)
8	Brown Bess, 1982 m., by *Petrone	1990 Santa Barbara H.
7	Brown Bess, 1982 m., by *Petrone	1989 Ramona H., Yellow Ribbon Inv. S.
	Halo America, 1990 m., by Waquoit	1997 Apple Blossom H.
	Miss Loren (Arg), 1998 m., by Numerous	2005 Santa Maria H.
	Paseana (Arg), 1987 m., by Ahmad	1994 Santa Margarita Inv. H.
	Star Parade (Arg), 1999 m., by Parade Marshal	2006 Santa Maria H.
6	Ack's Secret, 1976 m., by Ack Ack	1982 Santa Barbara H., Santa Margarita Inv. H.
	Anka Germania (Ire) 1982 m., by Malinowski	1988 Sword Dancer H.
	Annoconnor, 1984 m., by Nureyev	1990 Santa Ana H.
	Astra, 1996 m., by Theatrical (Ire)	2002 Beverly Hills H., Gamely Breeders' Cup H
	Azeri, 1998 m., by Jade Hunter	2004 Apple Blossom H., Go for Wand H., Overbrook Spinster S.
	Bayakoa (Arg), 1984 m., by Consultant's Bid	1990 Breeders' Cup Distaff, Milady H., Santa Margarita H., Santa Maria H., Spinster S.
	Dahlia, 1970 m., by *Vaguely Noble	1976 Hollywood Inv. H.
	Dream of Summer, 1999 m., by Siberian Summer	2005 Apple Blossom H.
	Estrapade, 1980 m., by *Vaguely Noble	1986 Budweiser-Arlington Million, Oak Tree Inv. S.
	Exchange, 1988 m., by Explodent	1994 Matriarch S.
	Exotic Wood, 1992 m., by Rahy	1998 Santa Maria H., Santa Monica H.
	Fact Finder, 1979 m., by Staff Writer	1985 Matriarch Inv. S., Santa Barbara H.
	Far Out Beast, 1987 m., by Far Out East	1993 Flower Bowl H.
	Flawlessly, 1988 m., by Affirmed	1994 Ramona H.
	Gourmet Girl, 1995 m., by Cee's Tizzy	2001 Apple Blossom H., Vanity H.
	Happyanunoit (NZ), 1995 m., by Yachtie	2001 Gamely Breeders' Cup H.
	Heatherten, 1979 m., by Forceten	1985 Hempstead H.
	Jameela, 1976 m., by Rambunctious	1982 Delaware H.
	Kalookan Queen, 1996 m., by Lost Code	2002 Ancient Title Breeders' Cup H., Santa Monica H.
	Kostroma (Ire), 1986 m., by Caerleon	1992 Beverly D. S., Santa Barbara H.
	Lazy Slusan, 1995 m., by Slewvescent	2001 Milady Breeders' Cup H., Santa Margarita Inv. H.
	Little Brianne, 1985 m., by Coastal	1991 Santa Margarita Inv. H., Santa Maria H.
	Maryfield, 2001 m., by Elusive Quality	2007 Ballerina S.

Racing — Oldest Stakes Winners

Age	Horse, YOB Sex, Sire	Year Race(s)
6	Megahertz (GB), 1999 m., by Pivotal	2005 Yellow Ribbon S.
	Miss Huntington, 1977 m., by Torsion	1983 Apple Blossom H.
	Noches De Rosa (Chi), 1998 m., by Stagecraft (GB)	2004 Gamely Breeders' Cup H.
	One Dreamer, 1988 m., by Relaunch	1994 Breeders' Cup Distaff
	Paseana (Arg), 1987 m., by Ahmad	1993 Apple Blossom H., Milady H., Spinster S.
	Queens Court Queen, 1989 m., by Lyphard	1995 Santa Margarita Inv. H., Santa Maria H.
	Quick Mischief, 1986 m., by Distinctive Pro	1992 John A. Morris H.
	Re Toss (Arg), 1987 m., by Egg Toss	1993 Vanity H.
	Riskaverse, 1999 m., by Dynaformer	2005 Flower Bowl Inv. S.
	Sefa's Beauty, 1979 m., by Lt. Stevens	1985 Apple Blossom H.
	Southern Truce, 1988 m., by Truce Maker	1994 Santa Monica H.
	Stop Traffic, 1993 m., by Cure the Blues	1999 Santa Monica H.
	Take D' Tour, 2001 m., by Tour d'Or	2007 Ogden Phipps H.
	The Very One, 1975 m., by One for All	1981 Santa Barbara H.
	Track Robbery, 1976 m., by No Robbery	1982 Apple Blossom H., Spinster S.
	Twice the Vice, 1991 m., by Vice Regent	1997 Vanity H.
	Windsharp, 1991 m., by Lear Fan	1997 Beverly Hills H.

Oldest Male Graded Stakes Winners Since 1976

Age	Horse, YOB Sex, Sire	Year Race(s)
9	Affirmed Success, 1994 g., by Affirmed	2003 Toboggan H. (G3)
	Bet On Sunshine, 1992 g., by Bet Big	2001 Aristides H. (G3), Phoenix Breeders' Cup S. (G3)
	Desert Waves, 1990 g., by Alysheba	1999 King Edward Breeders' Cup H. (Can-G2)
	Evening Attire, 1998 g., by Black Tie Affair (Ire)	2007 Queens County H. (G3)
	John Henry, 1975 g., by Ole Bob Bowers	1984 Budweiser Million (G1), Hollywood Inv. H. (G1), Sunset H. (G1), Turf Classic (G1), Golden Gate H. (G3)
	John's Call, 1991 g., by Lord At War (Arg)	2000 Sword Dancer Inv. H. (G1), Turf Classic Inv. S. (G1)
	Kona Gold, 1994 g., by Java Gold	2003 El Conejo H. (G3)
	Parose, 1994 g., by Parlay Me	2003 Durham Cup H. (Can-G3)
	Rochester, 1996 g., by Green Dancer	2005 Sycamore Breeders' Cup S. (G3)
	Sir Bear, 1993 g., by Sir Leon	2002 Skip Away H. (G3)
	Softshoe Sure Shot, 1986 g., by Bolger	1995 San Carlos H. (G2)
	Soviet Line (Ire), 1990 g., by Soviet Star	1999 Maker's Mark Mile S. (G3)
	Sunny Sunrise, 1987 g., by Sunny's Halo	1996 John B. Campbell H. (G3)
	Super Diamond, 1980 h., by Pass the Glass	1989 San Antonio H. (G1)
	The Tin Man, 1998 g., by Affirmed	2007 Shoemaker Mile S. (G1)
8	Affirmed Success, 1994 g., by Affirmed	2002 Carter H. (G1)
	Ancient Title, 1970 g., by Gummo	1978 San Pasqual H. (G2)
	Best of the Rest, 1995 h., by Skip Trial	2003 Skip Away H. (G3)
	Bet On Sunshine, 1992 g., by Bet Big	2000 Aristides H. (G3)
	Better Talk Now, 1999 g., by Talkin Man	2007 Manhattan H. (G1)
	Blaze O'Brien, 1987 g., by Interco	1995 Inglewood H. (G3)
	Cardmania, 1986 g., by Cox's Ridge	1994 San Carlos H. (G2)
	Cetewayo, 1994 h., by His Majesty	2002 Gulfstream Park Breeders' Cup H. (G1), Stars and Stripes Breeders' Cup Turf H. (G3)
	Chorwon, 1993 g., by Cozzene	2001 Kentucky Cup Turf H. (G3)
	Collier Hill (Ire), 1998 g., by Dr Devious (Ire)	2006 Pattison Canadian International S. (Can-G1)
	Country Be Gold, 1997 h., by Summer Squall	2005 Aqueduct H. (G3)
	Coyote Lakes, 1994 g., by Society Max	2002 Gallant Fox H. (G3)
	Dancing Guy, 1995 g., by Robyn Dancer	2003 Memorial Day H. (G3)
	Deputy Inxs, 1991 g., by Silver Deputy	1999 Durham Cup H. (Can-G3), Vigil H. (Can-G3)
	First Intent, 1989 g., by Prima Voce	1997 Potrero Grande Breeders' Cup H. (G2), Bing Crosby Breeders' Cup H. (G3)
	Flag Down, 1990 h., by Deputy Minister	1998 Gulfstream Park Breeders' Cup H. (G2)
	Forlitano (Arg), 1981 h., by Good Manners	1989 Bougainvillea H. (G3)
	Fourstardave, 1985 g., by Compliance	1993 Poker S. (G3)
	Friendly Lover, 1988 h., by Cutlass	1996 Philadelphia Park Breeders' Cup H. (G3)
	Glick, 1996 h., by Theatrical (Ire)	2004 San Simeon H. (G3)
	Hasty Kris, 1997 g., by Kissin Kris	2005 San Carlos H. (G2)
	Inevitable Leader, 1979 h., by Mr. Leader	1987 Ark-La-Tex H. (G3)
	John Henry, 1975 g., by Ole Bob Bowers	1983 Hollywood Turf Cup (G1), American H. (G2)
	John's Call, 1991 g., by Lord At War (Arg)	1999 Laurel Turf Cup S. (G3)
	Jurys Out, 1999 g., by Faltaat	
	Kazoo, 1998 h., by Tabasco Cat	2006 Toboggan H. (G3)
	Key Lory, 1994 h., by Key to the Mint	2002 Red Bank H. (G3)
	King's Swan, 1980 g., by King's Bishop	1988 Bold Ruler S. (G2), Tom Fool S. (G2), Assault H. (G3), Grey Lag H. (G3), Stymie H. (G3)
	Kona Gold, 1994 g., by Java Gold	2002 Los Angeles H. (G3)
	Le Cinquieme Essai, 1999 g., by Fastness (Ire)	2007 Play the King S. (Can-G2)
	Letthebighossroll, 1988 g., by Flying Paster	1996 Triple Bend Breeders' Cup H. (G3)
	Mashkour, 1983 h., by Irish River (Fr)	1991 San Juan Capistrano Inv. H. (G2)
	Men's Exclusive, 1993 g., by Exclusive Ribot	2001 Palos Verdes H. (G2), Vernon O. Underwood S. (G3)
	P Day, 1995 g., by Private Terms	2003 Baltimore Breeders' Cup H. (G3)
	Parose, 1994 g., by Parlay Me	2002 Woodbine Slots Cup H. (Can-G3)
	Punch Line, 1990 g., by Two Punch	1998 Fall Highweight H. (G2), Forest Hills H. (G2)
	Redattore (Brz), 1995 h., by Roi Normand	2003 Shoemaker Breeders' Cup Mile S. (G1), Citation H. (G2), Frank E. Kilroe Mile H. (G2), San Gabriel H. (G3)
	Revved Up, 1998 g., by Sultry Song	2006 Sycamore Breeders' Cup S. (G3)
	*Royal Derby II, 1969 h., by Bally Royal	1977 San Luis Obispo H. (G3)
	Runaway Dancer, 1999 g., by Runaway Groom	2007 Sunset H. (G2)
	Sandpit (Brz), 1989 h., by Baynoun (Ire)	1997 San Marcos H. (G2)
	Silveyville, 1978 h., by *Petrone	1986 San Marcos H. (G3)

Racing — Oldest Stakes Winners

Oldest Stakes Winners

Age	Horse, YOB Sex, Sire	Year Race(s)
8	Sir Bear, 1993 g., by Sir Leon	2001 Gulfstream Park H. (G1)
	Son of a Pistol, 1992 g., by Big Pistol	2000 San Carlos H. (G2)
	Soviet Line (Ire), 1990 g., by Soviet Star	1998 Robert F. Carey Memorial H. (G3)
	Stalwars, 1985 h., by Stalwart	1993 National Jockey Club H. (G3)
	Super Diamond, 1980 h., by Pass the Glass	1988 San Pasqual H. (G2)
	The Tin Man, 1998 g., by Affirmed	2006 Arlington Million S. (G1), Clement L. Hirsch Memorial Turf Championship S. (G1), American Inv. H. (G2), San Marcos S. (G2)
	Truce Maker, 1978 h., by Ack Ack	1986 Tanforan H. (G3)
	Twilight Road, 1997 g., by Cahill Road	2005 Memorial Day H. (G3)
	Variety Road, 1983 h., by Kennedy Road	1991 William P. Kyne H. (G3)
	Yankee Affair, 1982 h., by Northern Fling	1990 Red Smith H. (G2)

Oldest Female Graded Stakes Winners Since 1976

Age	Horse, YOB Sex, Sire	Year Race(s)
8	Brown Bess, 1982 m., by *Petrone	1990 Santa Barbara H. (G1)
	Lilah, 1997 m., by Defrere	2005 Hurricane Bertie H. (G3)
	Paseana (Arg), 1987 m., by Ahmad	1995 Hawthorne H. (G2)
	Ribella, 1999 m., by Revoque	2007 Anadolu, Ismet Inonu
7	Avie Jane, 1984 m., by Lord Avie	1991 Thoroughbred Club of America S. (G3)
	Brown Bess, 1982 m., by *Petrone	1989 Ramona H. (G1), Yellow Ribbon Inv. S. (G1), California Jockey Club H. (G3), Countess Fager H. (G3), Yerba Buena H. (G3)
	Exchange, 1988 m., by Explodent	1995 Orchid H. (G2)
	Fieldy (Ire), 1983 m., by Northfields	1990 Beaugay H. (G3), Lady Canterbury H. (G3)
	Gaily Gaily (Ire), 1983 m., by Cure the Blues	1990 Modesty H. (G3)
	Halo America, 1990 m., by Waquoit	1997 Apple Blossom H. (G1), Louisville Breeders' Cup H. (G2)
	Irish Linnet, 1988 m., by Seattle Song	1995 New York H. (G2), Noble Damsel H. (G3)
	Marshua's River, 1987 m., by Riverman	1994 Buckram Oak H. (G3), Suwannee River H. (G3)
	Miss Loren (Arg), 1998 m., by Numerous	2005 Santa Maria H. (G1)
	Miss Unnameable, 1984 m., by Great Neck	1991 Bewitch S. (G3)
	Paseana (Arg), 1987 m., by Ahmad	1994 Santa Margarita Inv. H. (G1), Chula Vista H. (G2)
	Quidnaskra, 1995 m., by Halo	2002 Gallorette H. (G3)
	Rizzi Girl, 1998 m., by Rizzi	2005 Hillsborough S. (G3)
	Scotzanna, 1992 m., by Silver Deputy	1999 First Lady H. (G3)
	Sefa's Beauty, 1979 m., by Lt. Stevens	1986 Sixty Sails H. (G3)
	Sintrillium, 1978 m., by Sinister Purpose	1985 Affectionately H. (G3)
	Skipat, 1974 m., by Jungle Cove	1981 Barbara Fritchie H. (G3)
	Spook Express (SAf), 1994 m., by Comic Blush	2001 WinStar Galaxy S. (G2), Honey Fox H. (G3), Suwannee River H. (G3)
	Star Parade (Arg), 1999 m., by Parade Marshal	2006 Santa Maria H. (G1), Hawthorne H. (G3)
	Stay Forever, 1997 m., by Stack	2004 WinStar Galaxy S. (G2), Mint Julep H. (G3)
	Survive, 1984 m., by Pass the Glass	1991 A Gleam H. (G2)
	Tocopilla (Arg), 1990 m., by El Basco	1997 The Very One H. (G3)

Oldest Male Stakes Winners Since 1976

Age	Horse, YOB Sex, Sire	Year Race(s)
12	Bold Sundance, 1989 g., by Bold Ryan	2001 Gene Francis & Associates S.
	Island Day Break, 1985 g., by Time to Explode	1997 Claiming Series #2 H., Cowboy Bar Claiming H., OMO Construction H.
	Leaping Plum, 1991 g., by Lightning Leap	2003 Grasmick H.
	Lost Again, 1994 g., by Lost Code	2006 Starter Allowance S.
	Mayruncouldfly, 1974 h., by Cheapers' David	1986 Rocking Chair Inv. H.
	Proven Cure, 1994 g., by Cure the Blues	2006 Littlebitlively S.
11	Antiash, 1978 h., by Anticipating	1989 Memorial Day H.
	Bad Toda Bone, 1992 g., by Taj Alriyadh	2003 Keddie's Track & Western Wear S.
	Brush Count, 1968 h., by Fleet Burn	1979 Governor's H.
	Curribot, 1977 g., by Little Current	1988 Albuquerque H., Sunland Park H.
	Dobi Pay, 1971 h., by Dobi Deenar	1982 Buck Buchanan Memorial H.
	Full Moon Madness, 1995 g., by Half a Year	2006 Blaze O'Brien S.
	High Dice, 1995 g., by Lytrump	2006 Who Doctor Who H.
	Lost Again, 1994 g., by Lost Code	2005 Canada Day S., Millarville Derby
	Major Zee, 1993 g., by Dayjur	2004 Parnitha S.
	Prexy Machree, 1970 h., by Prexy	1981 Vernon Sayler Memorial S.
	Proven Cure, 1994 g., by Cure the Blues	2005 Brother Brown S., Sam Houston Turf Sprint Cup S.
	Sir Echo, 1991 g., by Herat	2002 Yankee Affair S.
	Spend, 1985 g., by Draconic	1996 Pinon H.

Oldest Female Stakes Winners Since 1976

Age	Horse, YOB Sex, Sire	Year Race(s)
10	Alex Marie, 1992 m., by Trooper Seven	2002 Buttons and Bows S.
	Be My Friend, 1997 m., by Lytrump	2007 Pat Johnson Memorial Starter H.
	Chrystal Gail, 1973 m., by Special Dunce	1983 Carlton Cup, Dale Buick H.
	Favorite Pleasure, 1966 m., by *Favorite Prince	1976 Vicki Merrill H.
	Judge Smiles, 1991 m., by Judge Smells	2001 Matron H.
	Physical Law, 1982 m., by Wardlaw	1992 Merrimack Valley H.
9	All That Glitters, 1994 m., by Goldlust	2003 Buckland S., Somethingroyal S.
	Astral Moon, 1973 m., by *The Knack II	1982 Anniversary S.
	Crystal Cinders, 1994 m., by Incinderator	2003 Ralph Taylor/Vance Davenport Memorial S.
	Due to Win, 1995 m., by Lac Ouimet	2004 Cornucopia H., Fleur de Lis S., Matron H.
	Ghetto Doll, 1976 m., by Dendron	1985 Red Camelia H.
	Judge Smiles, 1991 m., by Judge Smells	2000 Matron H.
	Just Like Mama, 1975 m., by *Tenerosa	1984 Ladies H.
	Okie Miss, 1989 m., by Competitiveness	1998 Interior Royal Bank Futurity

Racing — Oldest Stakes Winners

Age	Horse, YOB Sex, Sire	Year Race(s)
9	Orientalspringhope, 1996 m., by Raj Waki	2005 Golden Horseshoe Cup S.
	Petrina Above, 1995 m., by Great Above	2004 Barb's Dancer S., U Can Do It H.
	Run Around Sue, 1995 m., by Coach George	2004 Falls Amiss H.
	Sea Kindly, 1973 m., by Night Invader	1982 Bed of Roses S.
	St. Patty Day, 1982 m., by Majestic Red	1991 South Sioux City H.
	Sum Day Flowers, 1981 m., by Jenny's Boy	1990 Raton Mile H.
	Swinglisa, 1996 m., by Nickel Slot	2005 Pat Hosie Memorial S.
	Wychnor (NZ), 1985 m., by Truly Vain	1994 Toolie's Country H.

Oldest Male Winners Since 1976

Age	Horse, YOB Sex, Sire	Track	Date	Race Condition
17	Behavin Jerry, 1964 h., Ambehaving	Com	9/7/1981	$1,500 clm
	Golden Arrow, 1961 h., Fort Salonga	GBF	9/25/1978	1,500 clm
16	Double Express, 1980 g., Viking Ruler	GF	7/6/1996	1,600 clm
	Maxwell G., 1961 h., Author	TuP	1/22/1977	2,000 clm
	Playing Politics, 1982 g., In Reality	Suf	1/4/1998	4,000 clm
	Silver Fir, 1963 h., Swoon's Son	FL	10/24/1979	2,000 clm
	Stonehenge, 1960 h., Call Over	Com	8/13/1976	1,500 clm
15	Beaver Cat, 1962 g., Brown Beaver	Bil	9/10/1977	1,000 clm
	Best Beau, 1962 h., Beauguerre	Poc	5/27/1977	1,500 clm
	Double Express, 1980 g., Viking Ruler	MeP	8/19/1995	1,600 clm
	Dr. Hecker, 1967 g., Clem Pac	MF	8/23/1982	1,500 clm
	Flyingphere, 1961 g., Mr. Hemisphere	FL	11/21/1976	1,500 clm
	Golden Arrow, 1961 h., Fort Salonga	LD	6/28/1976	2,000 clm
	Jymfyg, 1965 h., Beau Max	FL	10/28/1980	2,000 clm
	Lexington Park, 1967 g., Quadrangle	Com	5/22/1982	2,000 clm
	Lindsey-Jan, 1965 h., *Silver King II	GBF	7/23/1980	2,000 clm
	Maxwell G., 1961 h., Author	Haw	5/6/1976	4,000 clm
	Mi Prime Time, 1987 h., Lost Atlantis	BCF	5/25/2002	2,500 clm
	Mayruncouldfly, 1974 h., Cheapers' David	SJD	8/5/1989	2,000 clm
	Montana Winds, 1967 h., Windy Sands	Com	7/24/1982	2,000 clm
	Nellies Joy, 1977 g., Immediate Joy	MeP	8/16/1992	1,250 clm
	Northern Broadway, 1988 g., Northern Magus	Beu	4/3/2003	3,500 clm
	Playing Politics, 1982 g., In Reality	Suf	4/23/1997	4,000 clm
	Royal Rouser, 1968 g., Speed Rouser	Bil	8/18/1983	1,600 clm
	Sagely, 1970 h., Sage and Sand	FL	5/12/1985	3,500 clm
	Sailawayin, 1967 g., Bal Harbour	FP	9/18/1982	2,500 clm
	Satans Story, 1968 h., Crimson Satan	MF	8/24/1983	2,000 clm
	Sharon Caper, 1983 g., Cartesian	Nmp	9/6/1998	4,000 clm
	Silver Fir, 1963 h., Swoon's Son	FL	10/28/1978	1,500 clm
	Snappy Nashville, 1974 h., Nashville	YM	2/17/1979	1,600 clm

Oldest Female Winners Since 1976

Age	Horse, YOB Sex, Sire	Track	Date	Race Condition
14	Gloriella, 1964 m., *Nathoo	GBF	9/18/1978	$1,500 clm
13	Bewitching Eyes, 1994 m., Big Mukora	Mnr	3/5/2006	5,000 clm
	Carla Sparkles, 1993 m., Mr. Sparkles	RD	7/28/2006	4,000 clm
	Double the Count, 1980 m., Gala Double	BGD	10/27/1993	3,200 clm
	Fuzzy White, 1964 m., Roman Line	FD	1/28/1977	2,000 clm
	Gather Round, 1963 m., Blenban	GBF	9/22/1976	1,500 clm
	Gloriella, 1964 m., *Nathoo	MF	8/25/1977	1,500 clm
	Jackie H., 1965 m., Greek Star	Nar	8/3/1978	1,500 clm
	Johns Sis, 1965 m., Be Joyful	Bil	10/1/1978	1,000 clm
	Mabel My Love, 1970 m., *Puerto Madero	GBF	9/20/1983	2,000 clm
	Passive Loss, 1987 m., Highland Blade	Suf	5/21/2000	4,000 clm
	Vain Lass, 1964 m., *Newbus	LaD	1/29/1977	2,500 clm
12	Brandy Star, 1968 m., *Northern Star	CT	8/17/1980	1,600 clm
	Carla Sparkles, 1993 m., Mr. Sparkles	MNR	5/24/2005	5,000 clm
	Chotin, 1967 m., *Belliqueux	GBF	9/12/1979	1,500 clm
	College Fiddler, 1966 m., College Boy	PJ	8/19/1978	1,250 clm
	Culottes, 1965 m., *Khaled	Boi	5/25/1977	700 alw
	Doge Hill, 1967 m., Boston Doge	Nmp	9/2/1979	1,500 clm
	Everfast, 1966 m., Gordian Knot	GBF	10/2/1978	1,500 clm
	Favorite Pleasure, 1966 m., *Favorite Prince	AsD	6/11/1978	2,000 clm
	Flash Thru, 1967 m., Nir Thru	MD	8/1/1979	2,200 str
	Gambolak, 1964 m., Sid's Gambol	Nmp	9/2/1976	1,500 clm
	Gene's Hobby, 1974 m., Fincastle	MD	9/13/1986	1,500 clm
	Gloriella, 1964 m., *Nathoo	BD	9/24/1976	1,500 clm
	Johns Sis, 1965 m., Be Joyful	Reg	9/13/1977	1,500 clm
	Lindarella, 1966 m., *Bel Canto II	EIP	7/28/1978	2,500 clm
	Mabel My Love, 1970 m., *Puerto Madero	MF	8/20/1982	1,500 clm
	Mama Doc, 1964 m., Double Brandy	CT	3/27/1976	1,500 clm
	My Encore, 1964 m., Encore Fer	GM	7/5/1976	1,500 clm
	Old Toy, 1975 m., Obsolete	ErD	5/16/1987	2,500 clm
	Platters Honey, 1965 m., Platter	FL	6/25/1977	1,500 clm
	Polyego, 1965 m., Egotistical	FL	3/19/1977	1,500 clm
	Rainbow Gold, 1966 m., *Mont d'Or	MF	8/25/1978	1,500 clm
	Serenity Empress, 1986 m., Klassy Charger	FE	8/17/1998	5,000 clm
	Shore to Shore, 1987 m., Proctor	EIP	7/1/1999	4,000 clm

Racing — Oldest Stakes Winners

Age	Horse, YOB Sex, Sire	Track	Date	Race Condition
12	Sis Jane, 1966 m., Hay Hook	RD	6/25/1978	$2,500 clm
	Texas Toy, 1969 m., Green Hornet	RD	5/30/1981	$2,500 clm
	Troublesome Sal, 1964 m., War Trouble	EIP	8/20/1976	$2,000 clm

Oldest Winners of 2007 (Most Recent Win Listed)

Age	Horse, YOB Sex, Sire	Track	Date	Race Condition
13	Admiral Roxbury, 1994 g., Roxbury Park	MD	July 27	$2,000 clm
	Alaskan Lights, 1994 g., Alaskan Frost	LnN	May 12	2,500 clm
	Brave Miner, 1994 g., Mining	InD	June 15	4,000 clm
	Burnt Mill Road, 1994 g., Wayne's Crane	Mnr	May 29	5,000 clm
	King Diablo, 1994 g., Diablo	AnF	July 21	2,500 clm
	On Liberty, 1994 g., Mt. Livermore	CT	June 30	4,000 clm
	Page Two, 1994 g., Victorious	FP	May 1	3,200 clm
12	Candle Snuffer, 1995 g., Java Gold	BCF	May 28	1,500 clm
	Ditch Digger (Arg), 1995 g., Hidden Prize	WRD	April 21	3,500 clm
	Dream Counter, 1995 g., Geiger Counter	Suf	Oct. 2	10,000 clm
	Esther Egg, 1995 g., Secret Hello	InD	May 22	4,000 clm
	Full Moon Madness, 1995 g., Half a Year	GG	May 6	12,500 clm
	Fuzzy Eagle, 1995 h., Fuzzy	ArP	July 23	3,200 clm
	Go Not Whoa, 1995 g., Tilt Up	RD	July 29	4,000 clm
	Gretchen's Star, 1995 g., Mr. Leader	EIP	Aug. 18	Opt clm
	Gun Barrel, 1995 g., El Prado (Ire)	Pen	Sept. 6	3,500 clm
	Highland Leader, 1995 g., Mr. Leader	NP	July 7	22,000 clm
	Mighty Wind, 1995 g., Monde Bleu (GB)	Beu	Jan. 31	3,500 clm
	Mr Ammo, 1995 g., Groshawk	ArP	June 9	3,200 clm
	Mr. Insanity, 1995 g., Present Value	FP	Aug. 7	3,200 clm
	Riker, 1995 g., Marine Brass	Fon	April 14	2,500 clm
	Rim Dancer, 1995 g., Three Martinis	AsD	July 20	4,500 clm
	Rudirudy, 1995 g., Jolie's Halo	Cnl	June 24	16,000 clm
	Shady Remark, 1995 g., Regal Remark	StP	April 18	7,500 clm
	Shamrocks Fibber, 1995 g., Shamrock Ridge	Beu	March 26	3,500 clm
	Sir Dorset, 1995 g., Vicksburg	Mnr	Nov. 18	25,000 alw
	Stage Door Jade, 1995 g., Regal Remark	Lbg	Sept. 9	5,300 alw
	Vancouver Vice, 1995 g., Vice Regent	MD	Aug. 24	2,000 clm

Oldest Winners 1987-2007 (Most Recent Win Listed)

Year	Age	Name, YOB Sex, Sire	Track	Date	Race Condition
2007	13	Admiral Robbery, 1994 g., Roxbury Park	MD	July 27	$2,000 clm
		Alaskan Lights, 1994 g., Alaskan Frost	LnN	May 12	2,500 clm
		Brave Miner, 1994 g., Mining	InD	June 15	4,000 clm
		Burnt Mill Road, 1994 g., Wayne's Crane	Mnr	May 29	5,000 clm
		King Diablo, 1994 g., Diablo	AnF	July 21	2,500 clm
		On Liberty, 1994 g., Mt. Livermore	CT	June 30	4,000 clm
		Page Two, 1994 g., Victorious	FP	May 1	3,200 clm
2006	14	Hermosilla, 1992 g., Afleet	Tet	Sept. 17	2,000 clm
2005	13	Band Performance, 1992 g., Rare Brick	Pen	March 10	2,500 clm
		Cumberland Gap, 1992 g., Allen's Propsect	Tdn	Sept. 26	7,500 clm
		D J's Jubilee, 1922 g., Mister Modesty	Tdn	July 10	3,500 clm
		Hermosilla, 1992 g., Afleet	Elk	Sept. 4	2,500 clm
		Luckiestofthelucky, 1992 g., Something Lucky	Fon	April 10	2,500 clm
		The Issue Is Power, 1992 g., Wolf Power (SAf)	CT	March 31	3,000 clm
2004	14	Alpena Magic, 1990 g., L'Enjoleur	InD	May 27	4,000 clm
2003	15	Northern Broadway, 1988 g., Northern Magus	Beu	April 3	3,500 clm
2002	15	Mi Prime Time, 1987 h., Lost Atlantis	BCF	May 25	2,500 clm
2001	14	Mi Prime Time, 1987 h., Lost Atlantis	BCF	May 12	2,000 clm
2000	14	Son Coming, 1986 g., Son of Briartic	NP	Sept. 3	3,000 clm
1999	14	Blade of the Ball, 1985 g., Highland Blade	FP	April 24	3,000 clm
		Classic Jewel, 1985 g., Far Out East	FE	Aug. 10	4,000 clm
		Valley Cat, 1985 g., Valdez	FL	May 25	3,000 clm
1998	16	Playing Politics, 1982 g., In Reality	Suf	Jan. 4	4,000 clm
1997	15	Playing Politics, 1982 g., In Reality	Suf	April 23	4,000 clm
1996	16	Double Express, 1980 g., Viking Ruler	GF	July 6	1,600 clm
1995	15	Double Express, 1980 g., Viking Ruler	MeP	Aug. 19	1,600 clm
1994	14	Double Express, 1980 g., Viking Ruler	MeP	Sept. 18	1,600 clm
1993	13	Credentialed, 1980 h., Zanthe	Beu	Jan. 24	3,250 clm
		Double Express, 1980 g., Viking Ruler	MeP	Sept. 18	1,600 clm
		Double the Count, 1980 m., Gala Double	BGD	Oct. 27	3,200 clm
		Master Navajo, 1980 g., Navajo	Alb	April 16	2,500 clm
		Titan Ribot, 1980 h., Exclusive Ribot	Pha	Jan. 22	4,000 clm
1992	15	Nellies Joy, 1977 g., Immediate Joy	MeP	Aug. 16	1,250 clm
1991	17	Norman Prince, 1974 h., Skookum	Mil	June 30	1,500 clm
1990	16	Norman Prince, 1974 h., Skookum	GPR	July 22	N/A
1989	15	Mayruncouldfly, 1974 h., Cheapers' David	SJD	Aug. 5	2,000 clm
		Norman Prince, 1974 h., Skookum	Mil	July 1	N/A
1988	14	Mayruncouldfly, 1974 h., Cheapers' David	SJD	May 29	1,500 clm
		Norman Prince, 1974 h., Skookum	GPR	July 25	N/A
1987	13	Mayruncouldfly, 1974 h., Cheapers' David	SJD	Aug. 22	2,500 clm
		Eight Dominoes, 1974 h., Dominar	RD	May 4	3,000 clm
		Lancer's Pride, 1974 g., Protanto	Mnr	Oct. 12	1,500 clm

The Claiming Game

Claiming races are the heart of almost every racing meet in America. In 2006, nearly two-thirds of all races (65.6%) were either straight claiming or maiden claiming. The horses that populate those races are an eclectic band of warriors whose common bond is their owners' willingness to lose them for a specified price as soon as the race is over.

The claimers are typified by such horses as Creme de La Fete, a chestnut gelding who went to post with a price on his head in all but 20 of his 151 career starts in the late 1970s and early '80s. His claiming prices ranged from $7,000 to $72,500.

Creme de La Fete was so well known that he was saluted in a ceremony at Aqueduct. The National Horsemen's Benevolent and Protective Association annually selects a claimer of the year, and the Claiming Crown held each summer has given more attention to the sport's foot soldiers.

But publicity for claimers is rare, accorded usually to horses that were claimed early in their careers and developed into champions, as Stymie did in the 1940s. Or, the attention goes to horses that ran in claiming races but were not taken, such as two-time Horse of the Year John Henry or 1999 Horse of the Year Charismatic.

Most claimers toil in anonymity, week after week, start after start, battling their infirmities as much as the competition. Most males are geldings and race well past their prime.

Claiming races have been a part of Thoroughbred racing for more than three centuries, though they began in England in a much different fashion and were called selling races.

In a story in the January 1972 issue of *The Thoroughbred of California*, Barry H. Irwin uncovered the original set of horse racing rules used in England in 1698, '99, and 1700 for races "at Thettford in the Countys of Norfolke and Suffolke" for the last Friday in September of each year. Eight noblemen and 11 commoners wrote 15 conditions for the races. One was that every owner would sell every horse entered for "Thirty Guineys" and that the "Contributors present shall throw dice" and that "the Purchaser will be he who throwes most at three."

More than 300 years later, if more than one claim is entered on a particular horse, the winner is determined by lot by the stewards. Getting to that point took several revisions once racing became established in the United States.

According to the English Jockey Club's 1828 *Racing Calendar*, the owner of the second-place finisher in a selling race was entitled to purchase the winner for a specified sum. That rule was modified to allow all losing owners in a race to buy the winner, with the option to purchase determined by the order of finish. If the owner of the second-place horse did not want the winner, the option to buy passed to the third-place finisher.

In the early 1900s, Canadian racetracks introduced the concept of sealed bids for the winner being submitted within 15 minutes after the race. A similar rule was approved by the Kentucky Association on September 1, 1916, and used at the 1917 spring race meeting in Lexington. On opening day that spring, April 28, the Kentucky Association approved a Claiming Race Rule that allowed all horses in a claiming race to be purchased, and it set down the chilling reality for the person making a claim. The purchaser would become the owner of the horse "whether he be alive or dead, sound or unsound, or injured during the race or after it." To this day, the claim takes effect as soon as the starting gate opens. If a claimed horse dies during the race, the person who claimed it must not only buy the horse but also pay to remove the horse from the track and pay its burial fees.

Claiming races were well received and soon spread to East Coast tracks in the 1920s. However, selling races remained a part of the Jockey Club's rules of racing to the 1950s. By the 1940s, the selling race had become a variation of a claiming race in which only the winner was auctioned off for at least the offering price. All other horses in the race were eligible to be claimed for the stated claiming price.

Claiming rules today vary modestly from one racing jurisdiction to another, but two basic concepts apply in almost all of them. First, any licensed trainer or owner who has had at least one starter at a race meeting may claim any horse at that meeting, although an owner or trainer who lost the last horse of his stable on a claim at the previous meeting is eligible to make a claim. Second, for a period of 30 days, the horse must race for at least 25% more than the price for which it was claimed. For example, a horse claimed for $10,000 cannot start in a claiming race for less than $12,500 for 30 days. Under those restrictions, the horse is frequently referred to as being "in jail," ostensibly because the new owner does not have the freedom to place him at any claiming price. Some racing jurisdictions have experimented with eliminating jail time. In addition, the claimed horse cannot be sold privately to another party in the 30-day period, and the horse cannot race at another track until the end of the race meet at which it was claimed.

For every claimer, there is a claiming trainer, and, like their horses, some have risen to prominence. Hirsch Jacobs, who led the nation in victories 11 times between 1933 and '44, may have been the first great claiming trainer. Jacobs claimed Stymie from a maiden claimer for $1,500 on June 8, 1943, and Stymie rewarded him by winning more than $900,000.

On the West Coast, one of the most prominent

claiming trainers was R. H. "Red" McDaniel, who led the nation in victories from 1950 through '54. In 1955, McDaniel saddled a winner at Golden Gate Fields and a few minutes later jumped to his death from the San Francisco Bay Bridge.

Claimers have been an integral part of the success of father-son Racing Hall of Fame members Marion and Jack Van Berg. Jack Van Berg led the nation's trainers in victories nine times, including a still-record 496 wins in 1976.

Frank "Pancho" Martin won 11 New York training titles, the first in 1971 and then ten straight from '73 through '82. The Cuban-born Martin explained his training philosophy in a 1972 magazine article: "The most important thing to remember is to treat your cheapest horse as good as your best," Martin said. "Give a claimer the same care you give a stakes horse, and he'll win for you in his own class. If you improve a horse, move him up in company, but never ask him to do the impossible."

Three of Martin's greatest claimers were Manassa Mauler, a $12,800 claim who won the 1959 Wood Memorial Stakes and earned $359,171; Autobiography, a $29,000 claim who won the '72 Jockey Club Gold Cup over Key to the Mint and Riva Ridge; and *Big Shot II, a $25,000 claim who won a $100,000 stakes, the '71 Century Handicap.

Though Bobby Frankel shifted his base of operations to California in 1972, he had considerable success with claimers in his six New York seasons before heading west. In that period, Frankel developed claimers Barometer, Baitman, and Pataha Prince into stakes winners. Barometer, claimed for $15,000, won the 1970 Suburban Handicap and earned $174,584. Baitman, who was seven years old when Frankel claimed him for $15,000, earned more than $150,000 after the claim. In California, Frankel claimed Wickerr for $50,000 and then won the 1981 and '82 Eddie Read Handicaps (G1) with him. Wickerr also won the 1981 Del Mar Handicap (G2).

West Virginia-based Dale Baird led the nation's trainers in victories 15 times from 1971 through '99, almost exclusively with claimers. He was displaced as America's top trainer by victories in 2000 and '01 by Scott Lake, who also was the leader by wins in 2003 and '06. Steve Asmussen was the leader by wins in 2002, '04, and '05.

Sixty-one years after Hirsch Jacobs haltered Stymie for $1,500, Lava Man was taken for $50,000 from a Del Mar race with the intention of running the gelding in the Pomona Derby and California Cup races. He finished third in the Pomona Derby, but by that time he had won the Derby Trial Stakes at Fairplex and subsequently won the California Cup Classic Handicap. Those victories were only the beginning for the California-bred by Slew City Slew. At four in 2005, he won the Hollywood Gold Cup Handicap (G1) and repeated the following year. In 2006, he swept all the major California races for older horses, taking the Santa Anita Handicap (G1) and the Pacific Classic Stakes (G1) as well as the Hollywood Gold Cup. He scored repeat victories in the 2007 Santa Anita Handicap and Gold Cup and raised his career earnings above $5.2-million.

North American Claiming Races in 2007

Riding the crest of a significant increase in North American purses in 2007, claiming purses soared to a record, obliterating a mark set in 2004. Claiming purses across the continent surged to $462.6-million, up 5.2% from $439.6-million in 2006 and 3.5% above the '04 mark of $446.8-million. Total purses for all races were up the identical 5.2% in 2007 from a year earlier.

Proportionally, claiming races maintained their 37% share of all North American purses, although that share of the overall racing pie was by no means a record. The claimers' cut of purses was as high as 38% in 2002. Still, the claimers had what must be regarded as a banner year. Although the number of claiming races declined to 37,150 from 37,208 the year before, nonclaiming races had an even larger decline, thus claiming races filled 66.1% of all races, up from 65.6% in 2006.

With fewer races and a significantly larger pool of purse money, the average purse per claiming race zoomed to a record $12,451, a 5.4% increase from 2006. Also climbing into record territory was the average claiming price, which was $13,910. Fewer owners and trainers went to the claims box (14,396 claims in 2007 compared with 15,439 a year earlier), and the aggregate value of those claims totaled $200.2-million, down from $207.7-million a year earlier.

Claiming Races in North America, 1997-2007

Year	Number of Races	Percent of Races	Total Claiming Purses	Percent of Purses	Average Purse	Number of Claims	Value of All Claims	Average Claim Price
2007	37,150	66.1%	$462,560,424	37.0%	$12,451	14,396	$200,244,900	$13,910
2006	37,208	65.6%	439,619,708	37.0%	11,815	15,439	207,652,325	13,450
2005	37,793	66.0%	426,168,889	37.1%	11,276	15,381	200,467,775	13,303
2004	39,010	66.5%	446,836,040	37.9%	11,454	16,307	209,586,963	12,853
2003	39,111	66.5%	436,172,397	37.8%	11,152	14,777	202,646,625	13,714
2002	39,351	65.9%	444,901,718	38.0%	11,306	15,912	207,807,725	13,060
2001	39,655	65.5%	428,916,774	37.4%	10,816	14,974	200,883,275	13,415

Racing — Claiming Races

Year	Number of Races	Percent of Races	Total Claiming Purses	Percent of Purses	Average Purse	Number of Claims	Value of All Claims	Average Claim Price
2000	39,103	64.5%	$393,469,977	36.0%	$10,062	14,682	$202,498,225	$13,792
1999	39,420	65.6%	367,718,557	36.5%	9,328	13,909	177,754,863	12,780
1998	40,194	65.7%	354,541,816	36.6%	8,821	12,466	150,608,500	12,080
1997	42,368	66.7%	327,460,399	36.8%	7,729	11,703	136,154,325	11,634

Claims by Category at United States Tracks in 2007

Claiming Price Range	No. of Starts	No. Claims	% of Claimed	% of All of Claims	Total Value of Claims	Average Claim Price
$1,000 to $2,499	2,309	95	4.1%	0.7%	$ 185,100	$ 1,948
$2,500 to $4,999	64,360	1,825	2.8%	13.5%	6,621,350	3,628
$5,000 to $7,499	68,440	2,941	4.3%	21.8%	15,600,250	5,304
$7,500 to $9,999	28,780	1,412	4.9%	10.5%	10,838,000	7,676
$10,000 to $14,999	48,381	2,609	5.4%	19.3%	29,095,500	11,152
$15,000 to $19,999	22,495	1,508	6.7%	11.2%	23,881,000	15,836
$20,000 to $29,999	27,365	1,562	5.7%	11.6%	36,861,000	23,599
$30,000 to $39,999	13,239	768	5.8%	5.7%	24,660,000	32,109
$40,000 to $49,999	5,316	287	5.4%	2.1%	11,570,000	40,314
$50,000 to $74,999	5,493	427	7.8%	3.2%	22,555,000	52,822
$75,000 and up	934	50	5.4%	0.4%	4,015,000	80,300
TOTALS	**287,112**	**13,484**	**4.7%**	**100.0%**	**$185,882,200**	**$13,785**

Claims by Category at Canadian Tracks in 2007

Claiming Price Range	No. of Starts	No. Claims	% of Claimed	% of All of Claims	Total Value of Claims	Average Claim Price
$1,000 to $2,499	416	5	1.2%	0.5%	$ 10,000	$ 2,000
$2,500 to $4,999	4,456	110	2.5%	12.1%	412,200	3,747
$5,000 to $7,499	6,561	129	2.0%	14.1%	708,000	5,488
$7,500 to $9,999	3,953	102	2.6%	11.2%	833,000	8,167
$10,000 to $14,999	3,970	169	4.3%	18.5%	1,878,000	11,112
$15,000 to $19,999	2,696	106	3.9%	11.6%	1,741,500	16,429
$20,000 to $29,999	2,940	167	5.7%	18.3%	3,724,500	22,302
$30,000 to $39,999	1,490	57	3.8%	6.3%	1,825,500	32,026
$40,000 to $49,999	887	34	3.8%	3.7%	1,382,500	40,662
$50,000 to $74,999	727	31	4.3%	3.4%	1,690,000	54,516
$75,000 and up	104	2	1.9%	0.2%	157,500	78,750
TOTALS	**28,200**	**912**	**3.2%**	**100.0%**	**$14,362,700**	**$15,749**

United States Claiming Activity by State and Track in 2007

	Horses Claimed	No. of Total Value of Claims	Avg. Price of Claim		Horses Claimed	No. of Total Value of Claims	Avg. Price of Claim
Arizona				**Colorado**			
Cochise County Fair	1	$1,500	$1,500	Arapahoe Park	11	$43,200	$3,927
Flagstaff	2	4,000	2,000	**Total Colorado**	**11**	**$43,200**	**$3,927**
Graham County Fair	3	3,750	1,250	**Delaware**			
Greenlee County Fair	2	4,250	2,125	Delaware Park	300	$4,266,500	$14,222
Rillito Park	2	3,500	1,750	**Total Delaware**	**300**	**$4,266,500**	**$14,222**
Turf Paradise	438	2,804,250	6,402	**Florida**			
Yavapai Downs	37	116,700	3,154	Calder Race Course	355	$5,885,250	$16,578
Total Arizona	**485**	**$2,937,950**	**$6,058**	Gulfstream Park	471	12,432,500	26,396
Arkansas				Tampa Bay Downs	328	3,750,500	11,434
Oaklawn Park	211	$3,306,500	$15,671	**Total Florida**	**1,154**	**$22,068,250**	**$19,123**
Total Arkansas	**211**	**$3,306,500**	**$15,671**	**Idaho**			
California				Les Bois Park	31	$96,150	$3,102
Bay Meadows Fair	26	$258,200	$9,931	**Total Idaho**	**31**	**$96,150**	**$3,102**
Bay Meadows Race Course	317	3,871,000	12,211	**Illinois**			
Del Mar	299	8,894,500	29,747	Arlington Park	415	$6,568,500	$15,828
Fairplex Park	51	648,000	12,706	Fairmount Park	57	284,050	4,983
Ferndale	7	28,200	4,029	Hawthorne Race Course	404	4,778,500	11,828
Fresno	5	26,400	5,280	**Total Illinois**	**876**	**$11,631,050**	**$13,277**
Golden Gate Fields	317	3,924,250	12,379	**Indiana**			
Hollywood Park	344	10,026,500	29,147	Hoosier Park	70	$333,000	$4,757
Los Alamitos Race Course	284	842,500	2,967	Indiana Downs	63	336,250	5,337
Oak Tree at Santa Anita	98	2,608,500	26,617	**Total Indiana**	**133**	**$669,250**	**$5,032**
Pleasanton	44	477,300	10,848	**Iowa**			
Santa Anita Park	329	9,331,500	28,363	Prairie Meadows	153	$1,496,000	$9,778
Santa Rosa	42	347,500	8,274	**Total Iowa**	**153**	**$1,496,000**	**$9,778**
Solano County Fair	13	71,850	5,527				
Stockton	20	120,850	6,043				
Total California	**2,196**	**$41,477,050**	**$18,888**				

	No. of Horses Claimed	Total Value of Claims	Avg. Price of Claim
Kansas			
Eureka Downs	3	$10,500	$3,500
The Woodlands	10	38,500	3,850
Total Kansas	**13**	**$49,000**	**$3,769**
Kentucky			
Churchill Downs	502	$10,382,500	$20,682
Ellis Park	91	811,500	8,918
Keeneland Race Course	169	4,296,000	25,420
Kentucky Downs	1	10,000	10,000
Turfway Park	267	2,747,000	10,288
Total Kentucky	**1,030**	**$18,247,000**	**$17,716**
Louisiana			
Delta Downs	259	$1,984,000	$7,660
Evangeline Downs	325	2,328,000	7,163
Fair Grounds Race Course	531	7,844,750	14,774
Louisiana Downs	181	1,857,500	10,262
Total Louisiana	**1,296**	**$14,014,250**	**$10,813**
Maryland			
Laurel Park	475	$6,624,000	$13,945
Pimlico Race Course	112	1,576,000	14,071
Timonium	6	71,000	11,833
Total Maryland	**593**	**$8,271,000**	**$13,948**
Massachusetts			
Suffolk Downs	128	$893,250	$6,979
Total Massachusetts	**128**	**$893,250**	**$6,979**
Michigan			
Great Lakes Downs	22	$171,500	$7,795
Mt. Pleasant Meadows	1	2,500	2,500
Total Michigan	**23**	**$174,000**	**$7,565**
Minnesota			
Canterbury Park	100	$994,000	$9,940
Total Minnesota	**100**	**$994,000**	**$9,940**
Montana			
Yellowstone Downs	1	$1,600	$1,600
Total Montana	**1**	**$1,600**	**$1,600**
Nebraska			
Columbus Races	11	$45,000	$4,091
Fonner Park	31	120,000	3,871
Horsemen's Atokad Downs	4	14,500	3,625
Horsemen's Park	6	25,500	4,250
Lincoln State Fair	35	130,000	3,714
Total Nebraska	**87**	**$335,000**	**$3,851**
Nevada			
Elko County Fair	6	$14,000	$2,333
Total Nevada	**6**	**$14,000**	**$2,333**
New Jersey			
Meadowlands	116	$1,724,500	$14,866
Monmouth Park	320	5,303,500	16,573
Total New Jersey	**436**	**$7,028,000**	**$16,119**
New Mexico			
Ruidoso Downs	17	$103,000	$6,059
Sunland Park	197	1,998,250	10,143
SunRay Park	20	119,500	5,975
The Downs at Albuquerque	16	145,500	9,094
Zia Park	48	364,750	7,599
Total New Mexico	**298**	**$2,731,000**	**$9,164**
New York			
Aqueduct	302	$7,393,500	$24,482
Belmont Park	203	6,280,000	30,936
Finger Lakes Gaming and Race Track	162	984,500	6,077
Saratoga Race Course	123	4,310,000	35,041
Total New York	**790**	**$18,968,000**	**$24,010**
North Carolina			
Stoneybrook at Five Points	1	$10,000	$10,000
Total North Carolina	**1**	**$10,000**	**$10,000**
Ohio			
Beulah Park	40	$180,000	$4,500
River Downs	56	302,000	5,393
Thistledown	68	312,750	4,599
Total Ohio	**164**	**$794,750**	**$4,846**
Oklahoma			
Blue Ribbon Downs	2	$7,000	$3,500
Fair Meadows at Tulsa	13	67,000	5,154
Remington Park	173	1,531,000	8,850
Will Rogers Downs	19	93,500	4,921
Total Oklahoma	**207**	**$1,698,500**	**$8,205**
Oregon			
Grants Pass	4	$10,000	$2,500
Portland Meadows	99	342,700	3,462
Total Oregon	**103**	**$352,700**	**$3,424**
Pennsylvania			
Malvern	1	$30,000	$30,000
Penn National Race Course	219	1,135,750	5,186
Philadelphia Park	762	8,251,500	10,829
Presque Isle Downs	99	1,356,500	13,702
Total Pennsylvania	**1,081**	**$10,773,750**	**$9,966**
Texas			
Gillespie County Fairgrounds	2	$7,500	$3,750
Lone Star Park	195	2,024,000	10,379
Retama Park	23	194,500	8,457
Sam Houston Race Park	48	410,000	8,542
Total Texas	**268**	**$2,636,000**	**$9,836**
Virginia			
Colonial Downs	37	$456,000	$12,324
Total Virginia	**37**	**$456,000**	**$12,324**
Washington			
Emerald Downs	191	$2,066,500	$10,819
Total Washington	**191**	**$2,066,500**	**$10,819**
West Virginia			
Charles Town Races	637	$4,347,500	$6,825
Mountaineer Race Track and Gaming Resort	444	3,034,500	6,834
Total West Virginia	**1,081**	**$7,382,000**	**$6,829**

Canadian Claiming Activity by Province and Track in 2007

	No. of Horses Claimed	Total Value of Claims	Avg. Price of Claim
Alberta			
Lethbridge	17	$54,600	$3,212
Northlands Park	116	1,614,000	13,914
Stampede Park	84	1,177,000	14,012
Total Alberta	**217**	**$2,845,600**	**$13,113**
British Columbia			
Hastings Race Course	121	$1,567,500	$12,955
Total British Columbia	**121**	**$1,567,500**	**$12,955**
Manitoba			
Assiniboia Downs	84	$481,500	$5,732
Total Manitoba	**84**	**$481,500**	**$5,732**
Ontario			
Fort Erie	105	$577,500	$5,500
Woodbine	367	8,839,000	24,084
Total Ontario	**472**	**$9,416,500**	**$19,950**
Saskatchewan			
Marquis Downs	18	$51,600	$2,867
Total Saskatchewan	**18**	**$51,600**	**$2,867**

Horses With Highest Earnings After First Claim in 2007

Horse, YOB Sex, Sire	Claiming Price	Wins After Claim	Earnings After Claim
Stunt Man, 2004 g., by Western Expression	$25,000	5	$335,381
Celtic Dreamin, 2004 g., by Game Plan	40,000	4	321,463
Lila Paige, 2001 m., by Cryptoclearance	50,000	2	283,800
Sun Boat (GB), 2002 g., by Machiavellian	50,000	2	271,600
Dearest Trickski, 2004 f., by Proudest Romeo	12,500	7	269,680
Curiously Sweet, 2004 f., by Mud Route	40,000	4	207,160
Big Booster, 2001 g., by Accelerator	50,000	1	205,260
Exchanging Fire, 2004 f., by Exchange Rate	50,000	5	203,615
Sweet Belle, 2003 m., by Deputy Commander	40,000	3	202,485
Expect the End, 2005 f., by Precise End	30,000	3	192,600
Artie Hot, 2004 g., by Black Minnaloushe	30,000	3	185,985
Lookinforthesecret, 2002 h., by Cimarron Secret	12,500	7	184,140
More Angels, 2003 m., by Slew of Angels	32,000	4	183,740
Unspoken Word, 2004 f., by Catienus	75,000	2	182,778
Miami Sunrise, 2002 g., by Wheaton	10,000	4	179,130
Adore You, 2002 m., by Tactical Cat	12,500	5	176,268
Whistle Pig, 2004 g., by Patton	10,000	4	170,508
Unplugged, 2002 m., by Untuttable	8,000	6	168,430
Wind Water, 2002 g., by Bold Badgett	62,500	3	168,068
Whirl, 2003 g., by Unbridled's Song	15,000	4	162,315
Debussy, 2002 g., by Concerto	16,000	5	157,937
Bentrovhto, 2004 c., by Montbrook	16,000	6	157,035
Zappa, 2002 g., by Afternoon Deelites	25,000	6	156,180
Lord Snowdon, 2003 g., by Seeking the Gold	75,000	4	153,650
Rush With Thunder, 2004 g., by Tribal Rule	20,000	3	143,950
Fete, 2003 g., by Horse Chestnut (SAf)	62,500	4	136,130
Truly Blushed, 2003 m., by Yes It's True	50,000	2	132,892
Midnite Prospector, 2001 g., by Corwyn Bay (Ire)	15,000	4	131,943
Holy Nova, 2004 f., by Pure Prize	40,000	5	131,296

Leading Earners After First Claim, 1991-2007

Horse, YOB Sex, Sire	Initial Claim Price	Date of Claim	Starts After Claim	Wins After Claim	Earnings After Claim
Lava Man, 2001 g., by Slew City Slew	$50,000	8/13/2004	30	14	$5,116,103
Budroyale, 1993 g., by Cee's Tizzy	32,000	12/9/1995	51	17	2,837,610
Ladies Din, 1995 g., by Din's Dancer	32,000	7/30/1997	35	11	1,956,854
Native Desert, 1993 g., by Desert Classic	32,000	10/10/1996	72	20	1,815,827
Say Florida Sandy, 1994 h., by Personal Flag	70,000	9/14/1997	83	27	1,774,748
Peeping Tom, 1997 g., by Eagle Eyed	40,000	3/24/2000	53	13	1,415,127
Moscow Burning, 2000 m., by Moscow Ballet	25,000	8/7/2003	29	8	1,386,815
River Keen (Ire), 1992 h., by Keen	100,000	12/4/1998	16	3	1,338,880
One for Rose, 1999 m., by Tejano Run	40,000	10/4/2002	26	14	1,296,943
Shake You Down, 1998 g., by Montbrook	65,000	3/12/2003	39	15	1,258,094
Full Moon Madness, 1995 g., by Half a Year	32,000	6/25/1997	70	19	1,252,498
Maryfield, 2001 m., by Elusive Quality	50,000	1/16/2006	17	6	1,213,349
Lazy Slusan, 1995 m., by Slewvescent	20,000	10/22/1997	44	11	1,142,196
Recoup the Cash, 1990 g., by Copelan	15,000	6/3/1993	67	22	1,090,713
Parose, 1994 g., by Parlay Me	15,000	7/22/1998	89	20	1,084,593
License Fee, 1995 m., by Black Tie Affair (Ire)	75,000	9/2/1998	32	11	1,084,276
Early Pioneer, 1995 g., by Rahy	62,500	10/25/1998	21	6	1,068,815
Bluesthestandard, 1997 g., by American Standard	22,500	4/25/2001	46	18	1,032,018
Mr. Epperson, 1995 g., by Cabrini Green	50,000	7/10/1998	67	15	1,029,820
Tour of the Cat, 1998 g., by Tour d'Or	25,000	11/11/2000	62	15	1,025,626
Areyoutalkintome, 2001 g., by Smokester	32,000	12/20/2003	48	9	970,777
Designed for Luck, 1997 g., by Rahy	62,500	12/17/1999	26	9	959,260
Elated Guy, 1989 g., by Brave Shot (GB)	40,000	8/22/1991	63	9	941,904
One Way Love, 1995 h., by Regal Classic	50,000	11/1/1997	37	14	937,095
Pie N Burger, 1998 g., by Twining	62,500	9/13/2000	42	14	920,533
Dancing Guy, 1995 g., by Robyn Dancer	18,000	11/25/1997	89	20	912,953
Shoop, 1991 m., by Double Sonic	25,000	8/26/1995	70	11	911,515
Classic Endeavor, 1998 h., by Silver Buck	75,000	9/2/2000	59	16	853,693
Royal Haven, 1992 g., by Hail Emperor	75,000	8/6/1995	37	16	847,161
Beboppin Baby, 1993 g., by Hatchet Man	32,000	7/13/1996	62	12	830,990
Judge T C, 1991 h., by Judge Smells	30,000	6/11/1993	27	11	825,960
Siren Lure, 2001 g., by Joyeux Danseur	50,000	2/16/2005	23	10	813,534
Arromanches, 1993 h., by Relaunch	12,500	6/24/1996	75	30	800,224

Horse, YOB Sex, Sire	Initial Claim Price	Date of Claim	Starts After Claim	Wins After Claim	Earnings After Claim
My Cousin Matt, 1999 g., by Matty G	$85,000	9/25/2002	38	7	$842,795
Flamethrowintexan, 2001 g., by Way West (Fr)	40,000	12/11/2003	26	14	792,242
Chris's Bad Boy, 1997 g., by Marquetry	10,000	11/13/2001	41	18	783,455
Sis City, 2002 m., by Slew City Slew	50,000	8/5/2004	12	4	775,784
Spooky Mulder, 1998 g., by Brunswick	25,000	10/10/2003	53	21	767,068
Adminniestrator, 1997 g., by Incinderator	32,000	3/31/2000	40	9	761,716
Truly a Judge, 1998 g., by Judge T C	50,000	3/7/2001	49	12	757,192
Presidentialaffair, 1999 g., by Not For Love	20,000	6/28/2003	22	9	732,778
Coyote Lakes, 1994 g., by Society Max	12,500	10/26/1996	59	19	724,337

Horses With Most Wins After First Claim in 2007

Horse, YOB Sex, Sire	Claiming Price	Wins After Claim	Earnings After Claim
Fortunate Trail, 2001 g., by Fortunate Prospect	$16,000	11	$112,640
Raving Rocket, 2002 g., by Lil's Lad	4,000	10	59,026
Princess Composer, 2002 m., by Composer	5,000	9	95,035
Dearest Trickski, 2004 f., by Proudest Romeo	12,500	7	269,680
Lookinforthesecret, 2002 h., by Cimarron Secret	12,500	7	184,140
Bootleg Annie, 2004 f., by Go for Gin	5,000	7	112,535
Unbridled Sunshine, 2002 m., by Untuttable	10,000	7	100,085
Humble Chris, 2001 g., by Forever Dancer	5,000	7	88,549
La Bomba, 2004 f., by Menifee	30,000	7	85,105
President's Intern, 2003 m., by Impeachment	7,500	7	46,678
Rock the Stone, 1999 g., by Prospect Bay	3,000	7	27,758
Unplugged, 2002 m., by Untuttable	8,000	6	168,430
Bentrovhto, 2004 c., by Montbrook	16,000	6	157,035
Zappa, 2002 g., by Afternoon Deelites	25,000	6	156,180
Echo Quest, 2003 g., by Western Echo	6,500	6	88,320
Top of the Heap, 2002 g., by Peaks and Valleys	6,250	6	84,080
Grady O, 2003 g., by Proper Reality	12,500	6	81,415
Supahbuckdance, 2004 g., by Robyn Dancer	16,000	6	81,202
Assets of Gold, 2000 m., by Gold Alert	16,000	6	79,103
Visionary, 2002 g., by Silver Ghost	7,500	6	77,940
Hollye Lynne, 2004 f., by Uncle Abbie	10,000	6	77,844
De Roode, 2003 h., by Dixieland Band	10,000	6	70,200
Altar Offering, 2002 g., by Just a Cat	4,000	6	70,070
I'm No Cheerleader, 2003 m., by Crafty Prospector	25,000	6	68,255
Bump, 2001 g., by Eastern Echo	12,500	6	66,542
Oorah, 2004 g., by Perfecting	10,000	6	66,320
Wallace Station, 2002 g., by Capote	20,000	6	61,715
Uncoil, 2001 g., by Proud and True	6,000	6	49,170
Brandi's Starlite, 2003 m., by Brandon's Starlite	12,500	6	48,882
Huntin Gene, 2002 g., by Langfuhr	50,000	6	46,220
Burning Blur, 2003 g., by Renteria	6,250	6	44,440
Satin Sun, 2002 g., by Gilded Time	5,000	6	41,835
Unreal General, 1999 h., by Unreal Zeal	5,000	6	38,740
Archee More, 2002 g., by Archers Bay	4,000	6	36,245
Eastern Wind, 2002 g., by Cold n Calculating	2,500	6	28,755
Southall, 2002 h., by Moro Oro	4,000	6	24,542
Wegota Cisco, 2001 g., by Cisco Road	2,500	6	19,630

Horses With Most Wins After First Claim, 1991-2007

Horse, YOB Sex, Sire	Initial Claim Price	Date of Claim	Starts After Claim	Wins After Claim	Earnings After Claim
Sawmill Run, 1988 g., by It's Freezing	$4,000	6/28/1992	125	35	$224,514
Mankato, 1988 g., by Meadowlake	15,000	3/17/1992	145	34	330,856
Maybe Jack, 1993 g., by Classic Account	15,000	4/18/1997	107	33	512,395
Oh So Fabulous, 1992 g., by Singular	6,250	2/21/1997	97	33	229,402
It's the Wind, 1989 g., by Contare	5,000	3/1/1992	123	32	202,300
J V Bennett, 1993 g., by Key to the Mint	32,000	6/20/1996	99	32	384,370
Meine Empress, 1989 m., by Rex Imperator	14,000	9/12/1992	75	32	145,190
The Mighty Zip, 1988 g., by Fire Dancer	5,000	10/5/1992	121	32	223,453
Adorable Racer, 1992 g., by Two's a Plenty	3,500	2/13/1996	103	30	333,622
Arromanches, 1993 h., by Relaunch	12,500	6/24/1996	75	30	800,224
Belle's Ruckus, 1985 g., by Bold Ruckus	5,000	7/11/1992	106	30	156,856
Out for Gold, 1990 g., by Gold Crest	35,000	1/6/1993	179	30	284,711
Sgt. Ivor, 1990 g., by Ivor Street	5,000	1/28/1994	157	30	165,012

Horse, YOB Sex, Sire	Initial Claim Price	Date of Claim	Starts After Claim	Wins After Claim	Earnings After Claim
Tate Express, 1992 g., by Naevus	$12,500	12/29/1995	137	30	$236,159
Bell Buzzer, 1990 g., by Sauce Boat	4,000	11/17/1994	101	29	111,630
Cope With Peace, 1988 h., by Copelan	10,000	2/20/1992	109	29	182,749
Mahrally, 1991 g., by Ballydoyle	6,250	8/1/1994	142	29	146,535
Secret Service Man, 1992 g., by Shot Gun Scott	18,000	8/2/1996	98	29	290,043
Boca Ratony, 1988 g., by Boca Rio	14,000	7/31/1993	103	28	75,934
Cumberland Gap, 1992 g., by Allen's Prospect	14,500	3/4/1996	137	28	250,005
Fearless Peer, 1994 g., by Overpeer	5,000	8/1/1998	95	28	244,032
Gold Digs, 1987 g., by Regal and Royal	4,000	4/5/1992	103	28	150,206
Spacemaker, 1988 g., by Sunny Clime	5,000	10/11/1992	83	28	148,711
Victory Tower, 1990 g., by Singular	10,000	8/20/1993	152	28	151,654
Exuberant's Tip, 1990 g., by Exuberant	30,000	6/26/1992	87	27	116,315
Fit for Royalty, 1988 g., by Fighting Fit	9,000	4/9/1993	135	27	206,439
Northern Broadway, 1988 g., by Northern Magus	5,000	5/10/1992	160	27	108,542
Rosy Way, 1989 g., by Lord Avie	20,000	8/22/1993	46	27	88,779
Say Florida Sandy, 1994 h., by Personal Flag	70,000	9/14/1997	85	27	1,774,748
Scent a Grade, 1992 g., by Foolish Pleasure	5,000	7/20/1995	86	27	172,910
Win Man, 1985 g., by Con Man	8,250	2/23/1992	66	27	262,792

Horses With Most Claiming Wins in 2007

Horse, YOB Sex, Sire	Starts	Claiming Wins	Claiming Earnings
Eastern Wind, 2002 g., by Cold n Calculating	16	8	$35,760
Bettin On M J, 2002 g., by Quaker Ridge	12	7	119,447
Chardonnay Wine, 2003 m., by Desert Wine	14	7	15,932
I'm No Cheerleader, 2003 m., by Crafty Prospector	13	7	79,015
Leave It to Cleve, 2004 g., by Jazz Club	14	7	97,870
Mindy's Peak, 2003 g., by Pyramid Peak	17	7	91,960
Pop the Latch, 2001 m., by Swiss Yodeler	19	7	51,382
President's Intern, 2003 m., by Impeachment	14	7	43,798
Rock the Stone, 1999 g., by Prospect Bay	15	7	27,998
Shes Appealing, 2003 m., by B L's Appeal	9	7	66,620
Soft Day, 2003 m., by Dayjur	18	7	52,008
Spades Prospect, 2002 g., by Prospect Bay	15	7	25,667
Unbridled Sunshine, 2002 m., by Untuttable	15	7	96,985
Uncle Toodie, 2002 g., by Devious Course	18	7	70,525
Westside Lady, 2002 m., by Meadow Monster	14	7	83,870

Horses With Most Claiming Wins, 1991-2007

No. Claiming Wins	Horse, YOB Sex, Sire	Claiming Starts	Claiming Earnings	Total Earnings
36	Boca Ratony, 1988 g., by Boca Rio	117	$107,020	$123,587
34	Best Boy's Jade, 1989 g., by Raja's Best Boy	134	170,982	223,983
32	Mankato, 1988 g., by Meadowlake	139	299,146	381,821
	Spacemaker, 1988 g., by Sunny Clime	91	145,020	174,097
31	Sawmill Run, 1988 g., by It's Freezing	123	195,437	251,404
	Smart Graustark, 1990 h., by Special Graustark	94	51,057	52,487
30	Dundee Maverick, 1989 g., by Implore	110	112,638	125,220
	Gold Digs, 1987 g., by Regal and Royal	107	151,805	182,566
	Halo Round My Head, 1988 m., by Gregorian	97	112,852	130,383
29	Thar He Blows, 1988 g., by Dewan Keys	143	75,020	80,867
	The Mighty Zip, 1988 g., by Fire Dancer	114	183,953	265,341
28	Inspector Moomaw, 1987 g., by Entropy	128	184,689	207,948
	It's the Wind, 1989 g., by Contare	102	163,627	207,100
	Northern Broadway, 1988 g., by Northern Magus	163	119,212	127,096
	Sgt. Ivor, 1990 g., by Ivor Street	151	143,856	173,316
	Son Coming, 1986 g., by Son of Briartic	130	128,806	136,579
	Two the Twist, 1987 g., by Two's a Plenty	141	292,975	496,488
	Wilowy's Image, 1989 m., by Mongo's Image	70	130,208	154,698
27	Bon to Run, 1992 g., by Search for Gold	130	119,427	132,833
	Burnt Mill Road, 1994 g., by Wayne's Crane	132	306,104	341,141
	Elegant Bo, 1987 g., by Swelegant	121	153,132	199,284
	J V Bennett, 1993 g., by Key to the Mint	69	296,731	438,431
	Monsignor K., 1987 g., by Gala Harry	158	130,434	138,286
	Oh So Fabulous, 1992 g., by Singular	88	173,081	286,339
	Out for Gold, 1990 g., by Gold Crest	169	253,929	313,896
	Primetime Pirate, 1991 g., by Word Pirate	114	65,705	71,368
	Regal Peace, 1988 m., by Peace for Peace	112	113,460	115,383
	Sheila K., 1988 m., by Family Doctor	127	117,413	117,833

Horses Claimed Most Times, 1991-2007

No. Times Claimed	Horse, YOB Sex, Sire	Aggregate Claim Price	Average Claim Price	Starts	Wins	Earnings
24	Friday's a Comin', 1998 g., by Wheaton	$250,000	$10,417	76	16	$304,777
22	Sound System, 1993 g., by Waquoit	170,000	7,727	105	28	306,101
21	T. V. Secretary, 1998 m., by Wheaton	189,000	9,000	86	16	222,679
20	Above the Crowd, 1993 g., by Housebuster	541,500	27,075	88	24	461,886
	Game Skipper, 1992 g., by Skip Trial	165,000	8,250	128	19	237,043
	Tour of the Rose, 1997 m., by Tour d'Or	130,500	6,525	74	20	273,810
19	Devil's Mark, 1998 g., by Miner's Mark	235,750	12,408	96	19	259,295
	North Salem, 1994 h., by Badger Land	243,500	12,816	106	17	297,236
18	Brisa, 1995 m., by Prince of Fame	84,500	$4,694	99	10	149,426
	Erhard, 1996 g., by Gallant Prospector	157,000	8,722	75	13	111,011
	Nauset Flash, 1987 g., by Parfaitement	204,000	11,333	164	20	299,579
	Out for Gold, 1990 g., by Gold Crest	171,500	9,528	187	33	313,896
	Red Hot Secret, 2000 g., by Mr. Greeley	115,250	6,403	40	11	186,674
	Sharp n Strong, 1992 m., by Stalwart	226,000	12,556	86	14	290,071
	Storm's Secret, 1998 m., by Storm Creek	106,000	5,889	71	17	197,216
	Tenfortynine, 1998 g., by Ide	92,000	5,111	60	12	163,366
17	Casanova Slammer, 2000 g., by Grand Slam	325,500	19,147	63	10	200,964
	Ding Dang Outlaw, 1999 g., by Bag	81,500	4,794	90	12	173,135
	Euroclydon, 1995 g., by Momsfurrari	235,000	13,824	97	17	343,928
	Fancy M. D., 1999 g., by Glitterman	156,500	9,206	57	16	180,076
	Halos Wonder, 1993 m., by Hay Halo	109,750	6,456	77	18	140,509
	Imua Keoki, 1991 g., by Qui Native	178,500	10,500	86	17	201,224
	Lord Burleigh, 1999 g., by Langfuhr	171,250	10,074	66	14	245,802
	Palace Heroine, 1996 m., by Fort Chaffee	94,000	5,529	77	10	173,574
	Retail Sales, 1995 m., by Tour d'Or	171,500	10,088	96	19	205,712
	Rich Coins, 1998 h., by Rizzi	335,500	19,735	72	12	315,111
	Shot On Stage, 1991 g., by Gold Stage	154,000	9,059	129	12	184,274
	Takeitlikeaman, 1991 g., by Exuberant	148,000	8,706	111	14	291,699
	Wings of Jones, 1996 g., by Seneca Jones	146,000	8,588	102	19	361,682

Horses Claimed Most Times in 2007

No. Times Claimed	Horse, YOB Sex, Sire	Average Claim Price	Tracks Where Claimed	2007 Race Record
8	Medicine Eyes, 2001 g., by Hold for Gold	$16,000	AP, Haw	12-3-2-1, $57,906
	The Midnight Skier, 2001 g., by Appealing Skier	19,750	Aqu, Med, Mth, Pha	13-3-3-4, $76,660
	Uncle Divsie, 2001 g., by Souvenir Copy	13,188	Del, Med	12-2-2-4, $47,560
7	Brandi's Starlite, 2003 m., by Brandon's Starlite	8,357	LA, SA	12-6-2-2, $50,922
	Danish Dancer (Arg) 1999 g., by Lode	17,071	FG, LS, RP	14-4-3-1, $61,346
	Desert Sea, 2003 h., by Seacliff	28,000	CD, Dmr, FG, GG, Hol	12-3-2-0, $85,040
	Lethal Weapon (Arg), 1998 g., by Southern Halo	7,857	Aqu, Mnr, Mth	12-5-1-4, $51,175
	Sir Jackie, 2002 g., by Sweetsouthernsaint	27,929	Aqu, Bel, GP, Sar	13-3-4-2, $87,655
	Tee El, 2001 g., by Lac Ouimet	7,143	FG, LaD	13-2-5-1, $50,075
	Your Quote, 2003 m., by Belong to Me	16,857	Dmr, Hol, OSA, SA	13-3-1-1, $41,180
6	Bridge too Far, 2003 g., by Tychonic (GB)	8,500	BM, GG, Hol, LA	13-1-3-3, $21,562
	Burly Man, 2002 g., by Friendly Lover	13,333	Del, Lrl, Pim	8-2-2-1, $38,170
	Chameleon, 2000 g., by El Prado (Ire)	18,000	CD, FG, Med, OP	15-3-2-2, $55,044
	Coping, 1999 g., by Ide	12,167	CD, FG, Kee	15-4-0-6, $54,470
	Dancin Dusty, 2001 g., by Dusty Screen	10,083	CT, GP, Med, Mth	15-6-2-1, $78,425
	Every Three Days, 2003 g., by Valid Expectations	7,917	DeD, LaD, LS	9-3-2-0, $21,595
	First Command, 2003 g., by Deputy Commander	6,917	AP, CD, FG, Haw	14-2-4-1, $28,280
	Forli's Con Man, 2001 g., by Conveyor	16,000	Lrl, Med, Mth	16-2-4-2, $53,300
	Gambler's Prize, 2002 g., by Wild Gambler	13,500	CD, Haw, Med, Mth, Pha	15-5-5-2, $95,950
	Gentlemen's Club, 2000 g., by Gentlemen (Arg)	14,167	Cby, FG, Fon, Haw	16-2-4-3, $38,240
	Grady O, 2003 g., by Proper Reality	12,583	AP, CD, Haw, OP	13-6-2-0, $83,915
	Island Sky, 2003 g., by Island Whirl	13,333	Crc, GP	14-3-4-1, $48,485
	Jaygar Dancer, 2001 g., by Crimcino	13,667	AP, Haw	12-3-2-1, $55,842
	Keep It, 2003 g., by Put It Back	9,167	Cby, RP, Tam	15-3-4-2, $29,043
	Mazel Dancer, 2001 m., by Mazel Trick	5,000	Mnr, OP	6-0-2-1, $6,775
	Ocean Forest, 2003 h., by Forest Camp	27,333	Aqu, Bel	18-2-2-5, $76,670
	Savannahs Boy, 2003 g., by Our Boy Harvey	4,000	BM, GG, LA	13-2-3-3, $22,282
	Second Collection, 1999 g., by Evening Kris	7,917	Med, Mth, Tam	14-4-1-3, $49,510
	Seven Talents, 2000 g., by Louis Quatorze	10,833	Del, Lrl	15-4-4-1, $64,447
	Skipaslew, 2001 g., by Skip Away	18,583	Dmr, Fpx, Hol, OSA, SA	25-5-0-0, $50,080
	Stilts, 2003 g., by Appealing Skier	5,792	CT, Pha	16-3-6-1, $75,782
	Swiss Reserve, 2003 g., by Swiss Yodeler	10,042	CD, FG, Kee, LS, PID	17-4-1-2, $48,509

Racing — Claiming Races

No. Times Claimed	Horse, YOB Sex, Sire	Average Claim Price	Tracks Where Claimed	2007 Race Record
6	Unplugged, 2002 m., by Untuttable	$12,333	Del, GP, Pha	16-6-5-1, $172,830
	Unreal General, 1999 h., by Unreal Zeal	6,917	Cby, Haw, Tam	15-6-2-1, $39,852
	Westside Lady, 2002 m., by Meadow Monster	7,917	Del, Lrl	14-7-3-1, $83,870

Horses Claimed Most Consecutive Times, 1991-2007

Horse, YOB Sex, Sire	Cons. Claims	Initial Claim Price	Date	Wins During Claim Period	Earnings During Claim Period
I Wood Be a Winner, 1995 g., by Knight Skiing	9	$20,000	1/17/2000	4	$77,320
Opus Won, 1997 h., by Fit to Fight	9	3,500	10/29/2003	1	19,733
Red Hot Secret, 2000 g., by Mr. Greeley	9	7,500	10/23/2004	4	53,470
Adjustable Note, 1993 g., by Native Prospector	8	5,000	10/3/1998	0	5,740
Busher's Chad, 2000 g., by Fortunate Prospect	8	10,000	5/28/2005	3	27,900
Millennium Song, 1998 h., by Maudlin	8	10,000	3/11/2005	1	20,670
Professor Jones, 2000 g., by Prospector Jones	8	7,500	12/13/2005	3	30,524
Blazing Wind, 1997 g., by Zero for Conduct	7	4,000	11/30/2002	1	15,580
Bold Trick, 2000 g., by Phone Trick	7	7,500	8/4/2005	1	17,310
Dirty Harryette, 1999 m., by Unaccounted For	7	10,000	12/20/2003	2	45,845
Magicleigh, 1999 m., by Magic Prospect	7	3,500	7/21/2004	1	16,250
Mapeb, 1997 h., by Wallenda	7	3,000	9/29/2002	2	17,280
Mr. Sundancer, 1995 g., by Allen's Prospect	7	4,000	5/24/2002	3	22,904
Personal Stash, 1998 g., by Air Forbes Won	7	4,000	12/30/2003	1	18,192
Rally Mode, 1999 g., by Hasty Spirit	7	5,000	12/21/2003	1	16,826
Sabalucious, 2000 g., by Northern Afleet	7	12,500	8/5/2005	2	18,425
Short Fuse, 1998 g., by Lite the Fuse	7	5,000	6/5/2005	2	32,200
Silver Mystery, 1994 m., by Norquestor	7	16,000	2/21/1999	4	50,780
Takeitlikeaman, 1991 g., by Exuberant	7	10,000	9/29/2000	2	29,640
Tender Hearted, 1995 m., by Bello	7	18,000	11/28/1999	1	34,152
Uncle Divsie, 2001 g., by Souvenir Copy	7	12,500	6/19/2007	2	40,240
Well Travelled, 1999 h., by Fortunate Prospect	7	3,500	3/16/2003	2	17,655

Horses Claimed Most Consecutive Times in 2007

Cons. Claims	Horse, YOB Sex, Sire	Starts	Wins	Earnings
7	Uncle Divsie, 2001 g., by Souvenir Copy	12	2	$47,560
6	Island Sky, 2003 g., by Island Whirl	14	3	48,485
	Lethal Weapon (Arg), 1998 g., by Southern Halo	12	5	51,175
	Mazel Dancer, 2001 m., by Mazel Trick	6	0	6,775
5	Breezing Home, 2002 m., by Free House	7	2	17,217
	Get Wild, 2002 g., by Forest Wildcat	14	1	20,035
	No More Politics, 2002 g., by More Than Ready	5	0	7,740
	Randleston Rosa, 2002 m., by Sword Dance (Ire)	13	4	25,940
	Skipaslew, 2001 g., by Skip Away	13	2	50,080
	Velvet Hope, 2002 m., by Pine Bluff	10	3	45,450
4	Afleet Buck, 1999 g., by Bucksplasher	14	3	57,460
	Aledo Magic, 2002 m., by Magic Cat	15	1	27,386
	Bertrandos Freedom, 2003 g., by Bertrando	7	2	11,346
	Camptown King, 2002 g., by Prospect Bay	11	2	43,760
	Careless Candidate, 2001 g., by Deputy Commander	6	0	12,620
	Clerpark, 2001 g., by Deputy Minister	13	3	53,735
	Desert Sea, 2003 h., by Seacliff	12	3	85,040
	Every Three Days, 2003 g., by Valid Expectations	9	3	21,595
	Forli's Con Man, 2001 g., by Conveyor	16	2	53,300
	General Naevus, 2002 g., by Naevus	20	6	62,704
	Gotta Ballado, 1998 g., by Saint Ballado	8	1	10,908
	Haley's Buddy, 2000 g., by Editor's Note	10	1	8,610
	Isnt It Rich, 2002 g., by Accelerator	7	1	11,345
	Keep It, 2003 g., by Put It Back	15	3	29,043
	Kid Rigo, 1998 g., by Summer Squall	12	4	45,229
	Las Vegas Lucky, 2004 c., by Swiss Yodeler	12	4	55,720
	Lil Hanna, 2001 m., by Lil Honcho	9	4	27,465
	Markofexcess, 2002 g., by Indian Charlie	13	3	35,434
	Muni High Yield, 2003 g., by High Yield	4	1	7,420
	Nerinx, 2002 g., by Sahm	8	2	72,520
	Norway House, 2001 g., by Exploit	10	3	48,180
	Paradise Peak, 2001 g., by Scatmandu	15	3	57,390
	Peace Accord, 2004 g., by Bertrando	9	1	39,800
	Pegasus Prospector, 2004 f., by Deputy Cat	12	5	54,360
	Second Collection, 1999 g., by Evening Kris	14	4	49,510

Cons. Claims	Horse, YOB Sex, Sire	Starts	Wins	Earnings
4	Secure Line, 2001 g., by Phone Trick	8	3	$59,025
	Shakesperean Story, 2001 g., by Proudest Romeo	12	4	40,155
	Shoot the Alarm, 2003 g., by Bagshot	24	6	15,677
	Sir Gallant, 2002 g., by Mutakddim	16	2	57,370
	Smile Away, 2000 g., by Irish Open	8	2	43,300
	Sweet Hello, 2001 m., by Semoran	14	1	19,137
	The Midnight Skier, 2001 g., by Appealing Skier	13	3	76,660
	Vancouver, 2001 h., by Gone West	17	2	31,645
	Westside Lady, 2002 m., by Meadow Monster	14	7	83,870
	What's Your Point, 2002 m., by Wheaton	12	3	107,700
	Wild Roll, 2003 g., by Wild Wonder	14	5	36,404
	Zappa, 2002 g., by Afternoon Deelites	13	6	165,930
	Zona De Impacto (Chi), 1999 g., by Stagecraft (GB)	6	3	14,630

Claiming Crown

The Claiming Crown, started in 1999 by the Thoroughbred Owners and Breeders Association and the National Horsemen's Benevolent and Protective Association, is promoted as a championship event for the sport's hard-working claimers, and it certainly offers generous purses, a total of $600,000 spread over seven races. The event has been described as the "granddaddy of all starter allowances," which are races limited to horses that have started for a specific claiming price or less within a specified period of time. To be eligible for the Claiming Crown races, the horse must have made at least one start at the stated claiming price or lower within the prior year. The claiming prices range from $7,500 or less for the $50,000 Claiming Crown Iron Horse and Express to $35,000 or less for the $150,000 Claiming Crown Jewel. All races are for horses three years old and up, with weight allowances made to three-year-olds and females.

Owners must nominate their horses to the Claiming Crown program for $100 by April 25 or $500 by June 13, with a race specified by the latter date. Supplemental entries, at 5% of the purse, are permitted until July 18. Pre-entries are made ten days before the races, and entries are taken three days in advance of the event. A maximum of 14 horses can start in each race; if more than 14 horses are entered for a race, winners of official preview races will be given preference to start, as will the two highest-ranked horses based at the host track in each category. The remainder of the field will be selected according to a points system based on finish position and quality of races. For instance, a winner of a graded stakes race will receive 12 points, and the third finisher in a claimer or starter race with a price below that of the Claiming Crown contest will receive one point. Pre-entry, entry, and starting fees range from $1,000 for the Iron Horse to $3,000 for the Jewel.

The Claiming Crown has been held each year at Canterbury Park near Minneapolis with the exception of 2002, when the races were held at Philadelphia Park, and '07, when the Claiming Crown was held on August 4 at Ellis Park in Henderson, Kentucky.

Claiming Crown Emerald S.

Ellis Park, three-year-olds and up, starters for a claiming price of $25,000 or less, 1 1/16 miles, turf. Held August 4, 2007, with a gross value of $97,000. First held in 2000. Stakes record 1:40.23 (2007 One Eyed Joker).

Year	Winner	Jockey	Second	Third	Strs	Time	1st Purse
2007	**One Eyed Joker**, 9, 120	M. Mena	Habaneros, 8	Great Bloom, 9	11	**1:40.23**	$55,000
2006	**Al's Dearly Bred**, 9, 118	D. Bell	Nooligan, 5	Bodgiteer, 6	11	1:42.58	55,000
2005	**Mr. Mabee**, 4, 120	D. Bell	Sigfreto, 7	Rockhurst, 6	12	1:41.77	68,750
2004	**Stage Player**, 5, 124	T. A. Baze	Bristolville, 8	He Flies, 6	14	1:42.20	68,750
2003	**Image**, 5, 124	J. A. Krone	W. W. Robin de Hood, 5	Mega Gift, 6	10	1:42.12	68,750
2002	**Nowrass (GB)**, 6, 122	J. Valdivia Jr.	Grade One, 6	Taylorman (NZ), 7	9	1:46.66	68,750
2001	**Al's Dearly Bred**, 4, 120	S. Martinez	Metatonia, 6	Concielo, 5	11	1:42.22	68,750
2000	**P. D. Lucky**, 5, 124	R. Perez	Felite Patet, 6	G. R. Rabbit, 7	8	1:41.66	55,000.

Sponsored by the *Daily Racing Form* 2001. Held at Canterbury Park 2000-'01, 2003-'06. Held at Philadelphia Park 2002.

Claiming Crown Express S.

Ellis Park, three-year-olds and up, starters for a claiming price of $7,500 or less, 6 furlongs, dirt. Held August 4, 2007, with a gross value of $47,500. First held in 1999. Stakes record 1:08.04 (2005 Onlynurimagination).

Year	Winner	Jockey	Second	Third	Strs	Time	1st Purse
2007	**Golden Hare**, 8, 124	C. Lanerie	Implicit, 7	Cool Lover, 3	9	1:10.17	$27,500
2006	**Castello d'Oro**, 4, 124	H. Vanek	Texmckay, 5	Cicero Grimes, 7	11	1:10.12	27,500
2005	**Onlynurimagination**, 6, 124	B. Walker Jr.	Cicero Grimes, 6	Landler, 6	7	**1:08.04**	27,500
2004	**Chisholm**, 7, 124	J. Campbell	Settheehook, 5	Devil's Con, 5	8	1:10.10	27,500
2003	**Landler**, 4, 122	R. Fogelsonger	Pelican Peach, 5	Spooky Mulder, 5	10	1:09.65	27,500
2002	**Talknow**, 5, 124	E. Trujillo	Danny E, 4	Wise Sweep, 6	8	1:09.29	27,500
2001	**The Maccabee**, 5, 122	J. Flores	Lord of Time, 4	Hot Affair, 5	10	1:09.68	27,500
2000	**Spit Polish**, 8, 122	J. Flores	Modesto, 5	Citizen's Arrest, 5	10	1:10.74	27,500
1999	**Pioneer Spirit**, 5, 120	W. Martinez	Satchmo, 5	Exclusive Example, 5	10	1:10.45	33,000

Sponsored by Winticket.com 2001. Held at Canterbury Park 1999-2001, 2003-'06. Held at Philadelphia Park 2002. Track record 2005.

Claiming Crown Glass Slipper S.

Ellis Park, three-year-olds and up, fillies and mares, starters for a claiming price of $16,000 or less, 6 furlongs, dirt. Held August 4, 2007, with a gross value of $72,000. First held in 1999. Stakes record 1:09.93 (2006 Funny Woman).

Year	Winner	Jockey	Second	Third	Strs	Time	1st Purse
2007	Adore You, 5, 122	P. Nolan	Mama's Temper, 4	Sumneytown, 4	10	1:10.70	$41,250
2006	Funny Woman, 6, 124	N. Goodwin	Da Svedonya, 6	Wine and Spirits, 5	6	**1:09.93**	41,250
2005	Ells Editor, 4, 118	S. Stevens	I Will Survive, 6	Peekaboo Cat, 4	10	1:16.31	41,250
2004	Banished Lover, 6, 124	T. Clifton	Moving Fever, 4	Flaming Night, 5	8	1:17.29	41,250
2003	Mum's Gold, 4, 124	N. Santagata	Margarita's Garden, 4	Sentimentalromance, 7	9	1:16.82	41,500
2002	Won Moro, 5, 122	G. Melancon	Dandy Dulce, 4	Playmera, 5	9	1:17.01	41,500
2001	French Teacher, 5, 120	M. Johnston	Beauty's Due, 4	Lost Judgement, 5	13	1:16.68	41,250
2000	A Lot of Mary, 5, 124	J. Flores	Pretty Lilly, 5	Cinderella Island, 7	10	1:16.75	33,000
1999	You're a Lady, 5, 124	W. Martinez	Castle Blaze, 6	Dazzling Danielle, 6	8	1:44.33	41,250

Held at Canterbury Park 1999-2001, 2003-'06. Held at Philadelphia Park 2002. 1 1/16 miles 1999. 6 1/2 furlongs 2000-'05.

Claiming Crown Iron Horse S.

Ellis Park, three-year-olds and up, starters for a claiming price of $7,500 or less, 1 mile, dirt. Held August 4, 2007, with a gross value of $47,000. First held in 1999. Stakes record 1:36.65 (2007 Bargainwiththdevil).

Year	Winner	Jockey	Second	Third	Strs	Time	1st Purse
2007	Bargainwiththdevil, 5, 120	M. Mena	Kenai River, 6	Western Revenge, 7	8	**1:36.65**	$27,500
2006	Distinct Vision, 6, 122	J. Flores	Wheaty, 5	Harry Got Happy, 6	10	1:44.66	27,500
2005	My Extolled Honor, 7, 122	H. Castillo Jr.	King of Chicago, 5	Sacsahuaman (Chi), 7	12	1:43.91	27,500
2004	Superman Can, 4, 122	S. Stevens	Rough Draft, 7	Gram's Folly, 6	11	1:44.26	27,500
2003	Ghoastly Prize, 5, 120	B. Walker Jr.	Entrepreneurship, 6	Shut Out Time, 7	12	1:44.99	27,500
2002	Ruskin, 9, 120	J. Flores	Regal Tour, 4	Entrepreneurship, 5	7	1:45.37	27,500
2001	Secret Squall, 6, 122	L. Quinonez	Home a Winner, 7	Gothard, 4	13	1:45.75	27,500
2000	Gingerboy, 6, 122	M. Guidry	Irish Bacon, 7	Your Draw, 5	9	1:43.45	27,500
1999	A Point Well Made, 6, 120	D. Bell	Higher Desire, 7	Unruly Zeal, 7	9	1:45.65	27,500

Sponsored by Vetrap 2001. Held at Canterbury Park 1999-2001, 2003-'06. Held at Philadelphia Park 2002. 1 1/16 miles 1999-2005.

Claiming Crown Jewel S.

Ellis Park, three-year-olds and up, starters for a claiming price of $35,000 or less, 1 1/16 miles, dirt. Held August 4, 2007, with a gross value of $144,000. First held in 1999. Stakes record 1:43.37 (2006 Me My Mine).

Year	Winner	Jockey	Second	Third	Strs	Time	1st Purse
2007	Miami Sunrise, 5, 124	M. Mena	Semi Lost, 6	Kings Challenge, 4	10	1:50.83	$82,500
2006	Me My Mine, 6, 122	R. Gonzalez	Sinners N Saints, 5	Sandburr, 7	6	**1:43.37**	82,500
2005	Desert Boom, 5, 124	R. Gonzalez	Lord of the Game, 4	Habaneros, 6	6	1:47.32	82,500
2004	Intelligent Male, 4, 120	E. M. Martin Jr.	Musique Toujours, 4	Rize, 8	11	1:49.62	82,500
2003	Daunting, 5, 122	J. A. Krone	Freeze Alert, 6	Patton's Victory, 5	8	1:49.17	82,500
2002	Truly a Judge, 4, 122	J. Valdivia Jr.	Quiet Mike, 5	Prince Iroquois, 5	9	1:50.39	85,500
2001	Sing Because, 8, 124	J. Valdivia Jr.	Halo Kris, 4	Banner Salute, 4	8	1:50.74	82,500
2000	B Flat Major, 5, 126	R. Madrigal Jr.	Shot of Gold, 5	Snohomish Loot, 5	7	1:49.72	68,750
1999	One Brick Shy, 4, 120	E. M. Martin Jr.	Honest Venture, 6	Captain Ripperton, 4	14	1:50.79	82,500

Held at Canterbury Park 1999-2001, 2003-'06. Held at Philadelphia Park 2002. 1 1/8 miles 1999-2005.

Claiming Crown Rapid Transit S.

Ellis Park, three-year-olds and up, starters for a claiming price of $16,000 or less, 6 furlongs, dirt. Held August 4, 2007, with a gross value of $72,000. First held in 1999. Stakes record 1:08.74 (2006 Crafty Schemer).

Year	Winner	Jockey	Second	Third	Strs	Time	1st Purse
2007	Neverbeendancin', 4, 124	B. Hernandez Jr.	Lookinforthesecret, 5	Korbyn Gold, 6	10	1:10.72	$41,250
2006	Crafty Schemer, 7, 124	R. Fogelsonger	Seneca Summer, 5	Iron Rogue, 5	7	**1:08.74**	41,250
2005	Procreate, 7, 124	H. Castillo Jr.	The Student (Arg), 6	Crafty Player, 4	7	1:14.54	55,000
2004	Heroic Sight, 6, 124	T. Glasser	Quote Me Later, 4	Satan's Code, 6	8	1:15.56	55,000
2003	Pioneer Boy, 5, 124	R. Wilson	Debonair Joe, 6	Bensalem, 6	10	1:15.47	55,000
2002	Risen Warrior, 6, 124	S. Elliott	Yavapai, 6	Largenadincharge, 6	9	1:16.10	55,000
2001	Sassy Hound, 4, 124	M. Johnston	Crowns Runner, 8	Exert, 4	13	1:16.18	55,000
2000	Teddy Boy, 5, 122	M. Guidry	Bion, 6	Taylor's Day, 6	9	1:16.90	41,250
1999	Aplomado, 6, 120	L. A. Pincay Jr.	Emperor Tigere, 5	Oto No Icy, 5	12	1:16.27	55,000

Held at Canterbury Park 1999-2001, 2003-'06. Held at Philadelphia Park 2002. 6 1/2 furlongs 1999-2005.

Claiming Crown Tiara S.

Ellis Park, three-year-olds and up, fillies and mares, starters for a claiming price of $25,000 or less, 1 1/16 miles, turf. Held August 4, 2007, with a gross value of $96,000. First held in 1999. Stakes record 1:42.04 (2007 Unplugged).

Year	Winner	Jockey	Second	Third	Strs	Time	1st Purse
2007	Unplugged, 5, 124	C. Lanerie	Heathersdaddysbaby, 4	Westward Miss, 6	10	**1:42.04**	$55,000
2006	Tens Holy Spirit, 4, 124	P. Nolan	Spy Aly, 4	Moorebella, 5	8	1:42.84	55,000
2005	Inhonorofjohnnie, 4, 122	M. Ziegler	O. K. Corral, 5	Secret Lies, 3	7	1:43.51	55,000
2000	Look to the Day, 6, 118	P. Nolan	Vengeful Val, 7	Pine Baroness, 4	10	1:42.14	55,000
1999	Taffy, 4, 120	T. T. Doocy	Partial Prift, 4	Frosty Peace, 4	14	1:17.37	68,750

Held at Canterbury Park 1999-2000, 2005-'06. Not held 2001-'04. 6 1/2 furlongs 1999. Dirt 1999.

Some of the Best Claimers

Following are some of the most prominent horses who either were claimed prior to outstanding careers on the racetrack or at stud or started in claiming races but went unclaimed:

ASPIDISTRA—1954 b. m., Better Self—Tilly Rose, by Bull Brier. 14-2-2-2, $5,115. Bred by King Ranch, Aspidistra was purchased by William L. McKnight's Minnesota Mining & Manufacturing Co. employees as a 70th birthday gift in 1957. Aspidistra, named for a hardy house plant, then was in the midst of a nondescript racing career that did not improve after her purchase. For McKnight, she raced for a $6,500 claiming tag. Retired after one racing season at age three, she became the foundation of McKnight's Tartan Farms in Florida, producing 1968 Horse of the Year Dr. Fager and champion sprinter Ta Wee.

BOOM TOWNER—1988 b. g., Obligato—Perfect Profile, by Stop the Music. 82-29-16-14, $962,391. Boom Towner began his eight-year career in a $5,000 maiden claimer at Rockingham Park, winning by 10¾ lengths. He won the 1992 Toboggan Handicap (G3) and was claimed the following year for $50,000 by trainer Mike Hushion for Barry Schwartz. In Hushion's care, Boom Towner won the 1993 Boojum (G3) and Sport Page (G3) Handicaps, both at Aqueduct. He won the Toboggan again in 1995.

BROWN BESS—1982 dk. b. or br. m., *Petrone—Chickadee, by Windy Sands. 36-16-8-6, $1,300,920. Brown Bess's owner-breeder, Calbourne Farm, put her at risk only once, for $50,000 in a Bay Meadows Race Course claimer on September 28, 1986. It was her first start on grass, and she finished second by a nose. Brown Bess would thrive on the grass, winning the 1989 Yellow Ribbon Invitational Stakes (G1) and the Ramona Handicap (G1) on her way to an Eclipse Award as champion turf female.

BUDROYALE—1993 b. g., Cee's Tizzy—Cee's Song, by Seattle Song. 52-17-12-2, $2,840,810. First-time starter Budroyale was taken for $32,000 by trainer Dan Hendricks from breeder/co-owner Cecilia Straub-Rubens on December 9, 1995, at Hollywood Park. Budroyale was subsequently claimed for $40,000 by trainer Nick Canani on August 17, 1997, and for $50,000 by trainer Ted West for Jeffrey Sengara on February 15, 1998. He won the 1998 San Bernardino Handicap (G2) and in '99 scored victories in the Goodwood Breeders' Cup Handicap (G2), the Mervyn LeRoy Handicap (G2), and the Longacres Mile Handicap (G3). He was second five times, including the Breeders' Cup Classic (G1). In 2000, Budroyale won the San Antonio Handicap (G2) the same year his full brother Tiznow won the first of his two Breeders' Cup Classics.

CHARISMATIC—1996 ch. h., Summer Squall—Bail Babe, by Drone. 17-5-2-4, $2,038,064. Charismatic won only one of his first 13 starts and only raced four more times in his career. Trained by D. Wayne Lukas and owned by Robert and Beverly Lewis, Charismatic was placed first in a $62,500 claimer at Santa Anita Park on February 11, 1999. After finishing second in the El Camino Real Derby (G3) at Bay Meadows Race Course, Charismatic was a soundly beaten fourth in the Santa Anita Derby (G1). He subsequently won the Coolmore Lexington Stakes (G2), the Kentucky Derby (G1), and the Preakness Stakes (G1) before finishing third in the Belmont Stakes (G1), in which he sustained two fractures of his right foreleg. He was voted 1999 champion three-year-old male and Horse of the Year.

CREME DE LA FETE—1976 ch. g., Creme Dela Creme—Bridge Day, by *Tudor Minstrel. 151-40-27-16, $460,350. After winning his career debut by a nose as a two-year-old at Keeneland Race Course in 1978, Creme de La Fete finished fifth of six in the Bashford Manor Stakes at Churchill Downs. Unlike many two-year-olds that fade from the racing scene, Creme de La Fete would make 149 more starts. His two best years were in 1981, when he won 12 of 26 starts and $123,180, and in '83, when he won nine of 30 starts and earned $127,240.

DEPUTED TESTAMONY—1980 b. h., Traffic Cop—Proof Requested, by Prove It. 20-11-3-0, $674,329. Owned by Francis Sears and trained by J. William Boniface, Deputed Testamony was not competitive in his first start, finishing sixth by 12¾ lengths in a $25,000 maiden claimer at Bowie Race Course on September 21, 1982. In his next start, the colt won a $22,500 maiden claimer at Keystone Race Track, and Boniface put him at risk once more, in a $40,000 open claimer at the Meadowlands. Deputed Testamony won by three lengths and was not claimed. The following year, he won the Preakness Stakes (G1) and Monmouth Park's Haskell Invitational Handicap (G1). He won his 1984 starts, including a track-record effort in the City of Baltimore Handicap, before retiring to stud at Boniface's Bonita Farm, his birthplace.

GAIL'S BRUSH—1991 b. m., Broad Brush—Parade of Roses, by Blues Parade. 39-11-5-4, $250,701. Claimed by John E. Salzman Jr. on November 25, 1995, for $25,000, Gail's Brush made only two starts for the Maryland trainer before she was picked up by owner-trainer Edwin T. Broome from a $40,000 claimer on grass at Gulfstream Park in early 1996. Gail's Brush, whose performance had improved dramatically when switched to grass, made only six starts for Broome, but they included consecutive victories in the 1996 Eatontown Handicap (G3), Columbiana Handicap, Politely Stakes, and Rumson Stakes.

JEWEL PRINCESS—1992 b. m., Key to the Mint—Jewell Ridge, by Melyno (Ire). 29-13-4-7, $1,904,060. An Eclipse Award winner as outstand-

ing older female after winning the 1996 Breeders' Cup Distaff (G1), Jewel Princess began her career with a third-place finish in a $20,000 maiden claimer at Calder Race Course on October 27, 1994. She won her next start in a $30,000 maiden claimer and never looked back. In the care of Wally Dollase, Jewel Princess won the 1996 Vanity Invitational Handicap (G1) in addition to the Distaff, and in '97 she won the Santa Maria (G1) and Santa Margarita Invitational (G1) Handicaps. At the 2000 Keeneland November breeding stock sale, she was sold for $4.9-million to Coolmore Stud principal owner John Magnier.

JOHN HENRY—1975 b. g., Old Bob Bowers—Once Double, by Double Jay. 83-39-15-9, $6,591,860. John Henry raced five times in claiming races in 1978 but was not claimed. Purchased privately for $27,500 by Sam Rubin in 1978, he made his final claiming start for Sam and Dorothy Rubin's Dotsam Stable at $35,000 on June 28, 1978, at Belmont Park and won by 14 lengths. Trained by Robert Donato, Victor "Lefty" Nickerson, and Ron McAnally, he was Horse of the Year in 1981 and '84 as well as a four-time champion turf male and once champion older male. He retired as the richest North American Thoroughbred of all time.

KING COMMANDER—1949 dk. b. or br. g., Brown King—Guinea Egg, by *Cohort. 67-17-15-6, $100,295. King Commander made 27 of his first 31 starts in claimers although he was claimed only once, for $5,000 at Aqueduct in 1952. Converted to steeplechasing after winning three of 32 starts on the flat, King Commander won 14 of 35 starts over fences and was voted champion steeplechase horse in 1954.

KING'S SWAN—1980 b. h., King's Bishop—Royal Cygnet, by *Sea-Bird. 107-31-19-18, $1,924,845. King's Swan already had won 11 of 44 starts and $212,350 when he was claimed in 1985 for $80,000 by trainer Richard Dutrow. The following year, King's Swan won eight of 15 starts, including the Vosburgh Stakes (G1) and Boojum Handicap (G3), and earned $451,207. At seven, he won three Grade 3 stakes in 12 starts and earned $477,218. He was even better at eight, winning five graded stakes, including the Bold Ruler (G2) and Tom Fool (G2) Stakes in 14 starts and banking $539,681.

KOBUK KING—1966 dk. b. or br. h., One-Eyed King—Winby, by Crafty Admiral. 68-12-10-11, $173,921. After showing considerable promise as a two-year-old in 1968, winning three of 13 starts and finishing second in the El Camino Stakes at Bay Meadows Race Course, Kobuk King went zero-for-three as a three-year-old and zero-for-19 at four. Claimed for $15,000 in 1971, Kobuk King found himself and scored consecutive victories in the Cabrillo Handicap at Del Mar, the Tanforan Handicap at Bay Meadows, and Santa Anita Park's Carleton F. Burke Invitational Handicap for co-owners Allegre Stable and Ron McAnally, who trained the horse.

LADY MARYLAND—1934 gr. m., Sir Greysteel—Palestra, by *Prince Palatine. 82-18-14-14, $31,067. The 1939 champion handicap mare, Lady Maryland made 19 of her 82 starts in claimers and was taken for $2,500 in her 28th career start by B. B. Archer. Her final start in a claimer was as a four-year-old for $4,500 at Havre de Grace. She was not claimed and quickly improved in her five-year-old season, winning the Carroll and Ritchie Handicaps at Pimlico Race Course.

LAKEVILLE MISS—1975 dk. b. or br. m., Rainy Lake—Hew, by Blue Prince. 14-7-4-1, $371,582. While Affirmed and Alydar slugged it out for two-year-old male honors in 1977, the juvenile filly championship was taken by the strapping Lakeville Miss, who possessed a blue-collar pedigree and started her career as a $25,000 maiden claimer for owner-breeder Randolph Weinsier. She won a 5½ furlong claiming race at Belmont Park by four lengths on June 30 and never started again for a claiming tag. Trained by Jose Martin, Lakeville Miss won the Matron (G1) and Frizette (G1) Stakes at Belmont and the Selima Stakes (G1) at Laurel Race Course. She concluded her career with a four-length win in the 1978 Coaching Club American Oaks (G1).

LAVA MAN—2001 dk. b. or br. g., Slew City Slew—Li'l Ms. Leonard, by Nostalgia's Star. 45-17-8-5, $5,268,706. Lava Man by no means a cheap claim. Trainer Doug O'Neill haltered the California-bred as a three-year-old for $50,000 out of a Del Mar grass race on August 13, 2004. To that point in his career, Lava Man had won three races in Northern California. Switched to dirt, Lava Man won the Derby Trial Stakes at Fairplex Park but did not win again until he went on a tear the following spring, when he won the 2005 Californian Stakes (G2) and the Hollywood Gold Cup Handicap (G1). In 2006, Lava Man became the first horse to win the Santa Anita Handicap (G1), Hollywood Gold Cup, and Pacific Classic Stakes (G1) in the same season. In 2007, he became the third horse to win back-to-back editions of the Santa Anita Handicap and the second to win the Hollywood Gold Cup three times.

LEAVE IT TO BEEZER—1993 b. g., Henbane—Blue Shocker, by Copelan. 75-22-11-13, $587,086. Although he had lost ten straight races, six-year-old Leave It to Beezer was claimed for $32,000 by trainer Scott Lake for Leo Gaspari Racing Stable on December 22, 1999. His third-place finish that day extended his losing streak to 11. Lake backed off on the gelding's training regimen, and Leave It to Beezer responded by winning nine of 15 starts, including the Salvator Mile Handicap (G3) at Monmouth Park and the Baltimore Breeders' Cup Handicap (G3) at Pimlico on the way to earning $350,830 in 2000.

McKAYMACKENNA—1989 b. m., Ends Well—Amuse, by Secretariat. 38-15-6-2, $581,322. R Kay Stable claimed McKaymackenna for $35,000 from a Belmont Park race in which she was beaten by more than 35 lengths. Sloppy tracks like the one

she encountered at Belmont on May 16, 1992, were not to her liking; turf racing was her game. After trainer Gary Sciacca claimed her, she won seven grass stakes, including the 1993 Beaugay Handicap (G3) and Noble Damsel Stakes (G3).

MIESQUE'S APPROVAL—1999 b. h., Miesque's Son—Win Approval, by With Approval. 41-12-10-5, $2,648,879. Bred and owned by Live Oak Stud, trained by Bill Mott and Marty Wolfson. At the end of 2005, Miesque's Approval was nearing the conclusion of his New York racing career and twice finished off the board in two claiming races, the first for a $100,000 tag and the second for $50,000. Calder Race Course-based trainer Marty Wolfson approached Live Oak Stud owner Charlotte Weber about buying the horse as a stallion prospect, but Weber retained ownership and sent him to Wolfson to train for the 2006 season. The result was a year in which Miesque's Approval won the NetJets Breeders' Cup Mile (G1), was voted an Eclipse Award as champion turf male, and earned more than $1.9-million in a carefully orchestrated campaign.

PARKA—1958 br. g., *Arctic Prince—Manchon, by *Blenheim II. 93-27-14-18, $446,236. Bred by Marion duPont Scott and unraced at two, Parka was claimed for $10,000 in his 11th career start by Warren A. "Jimmy" Croll Jr. for client Rachel Carpenter. Parka won that Atlantic City Race Course race by a head, and Croll entered him in a $13,000 claimer 15 days later. He won that race by eight lengths and never raced in a claimer again. He was 1965 champion grass horse off victories in the Bougainvillea Handicap at Hialeah Park, the Kelly-Olympic and United Nations Handicaps at Atlantic City, and Aqueduct's Long Island Handicap in his final career start.

PEAT MOSS—1975 b. g., *Herbager—Moss, by Round Table. 55-15-7-9, $635,517. A little more than one year after winning a $10,000 claimer, Claiborne Farm-bred Peat Moss came within a head of upsetting John Henry in the 1981 Jockey Club Gold Cup (G1). Owned and trained by Murray Garren, Peat Moss loved to go a distance, winning the 1980 Display Handicap (G3) at 2¼ miles and the 1980 and '81 Kelso Handicap at two miles.

PORT CONWAY LANE—1969 gr. h., Bold Commander—*Grey Taffety, by Grey Sovereign. 242-52-39-36, $431,593. Port Conway Lane spent most of his lengthy career in claimers, although he started his career in allowance and stakes races, including a second-place finish in the 1971 Marlboro Nursery Stakes. He won Pimlico Race Course's City of Baltimore Handicap twice, in 1974 and '75, as well as Bowie Race Course's '74 Bowie Handicap and '75 Terrapin Handicap. By the end of 1976, however, he was racing principally in claimers and continued to do so through '83.

*PRINCEQUILLO—1940 b. h., by Prince Rose—*Cosquilla, by *Papyrus. 33-12-5-7, $96,550. Exported from England in 1941, *Princequillo was offered for a $2,500 claiming price by owner Anthony Pelleteri on August 20, 1942. Taking him for Boone Hall Stable was Horatio Luro, who would develop *Princequillo into a multiple stakes winner during World War II. At Claiborne Farm, he proved to be an outstanding stallion, leading the general sire list in 1957 and '58 and topping the broodmare sire list eight times in North America and once in England.

SEABISCUIT—1933 b. h., Hard Tack—Swing On, by Whisk Broom II. 89-33-15-13, $437,730. Long before he became a top handicap horse, Seabiscuit lost the first 14 races of his career, including three defeats in $2,500 claimers and a loss in a $4,000 claimer at Havre de Grace in April 1935. Nobody took him, and later Wheatley Stable sold him to Charles Howard. Under the care of Racing Hall of Fame trainer Tom Smith, Seabiscuit went on to spectacular success, including a seven-stakes win streak in 1937, when he was champion handicap horse. The following year, he was voted Horse of the Year and handicap champion.

STYMIE—1941 ch. h., Equestrian—Stop Watch, by On Watch. 131-35-33-28, $918,485. Taken in his third lifetime start for $1,500 by Hirsch Jacobs, Stymie became the richest Thoroughbred of all time by his retirement in 1949, a record that only lasted until Citation moved past him in 1950. In his prime from ages four through seven, he won 28 of 69 starts, including the Saratoga Cup Stakes and the Gallant Fox, Metropolitan, Grey Lag, Aqueduct, and Sussex Handicaps twice each.

TIMELY WRITER—1979 b., c., Staff Writer—Timely Roman, by Sette Bello. 15-9-1-2, $605,491. A $13,000 yearling purchase owned by Peter and Francis Martin and trained by Dominic Imprescia, Timely Writer made his debut with an eight-length victory in a $30,000 maiden claimer at Monmouth Park. He subsequently won Saratoga Race Course's Hopeful Stakes (G1) and the Champagne Stakes (G1) at Belmont Park, earning him co-highweight with Eclipse Award champion Deputy Minister on the 1981 Experimental Free Handicap. At three, he won the Flamingo Stakes (G1) and Florida Derby (G1), but surgery for an intestinal blockage knocked him out of the Triple Crown races. He returned in the fall but sustained a fatal breakdown in the Jockey Club Gold Cup (G1).

VIDEOGENIC—1982 b. m., Caucasus—Video Babe, by T.V. Commercial. 73-20-9-10, $1,154,360. Trainer Gasper Moschera convinced owner Albert Davis to claim Videogenic for $100,000 on May 24, 1985. She was not much to look at, but she could run, winning 11 stakes races after the claim, including the 1985 Ladies Handicap (G1) at Aqueduct and the 1986 Santa Ana Handicap (G1) at Santa Anita Park. She won more than $1-million for Davis on the racetrack and was sold as a broodmare prospect for $625,000 at the 1988 Keeneland November breeding stock sale.

RACETRACKS
Racetracks of North America
Arizona

Apache County Fair
Location: 825 W. 4th St. N., Box 357, Saint Johns, Az. 85936-0357
Phone: (928) 337-4469
Fax: (928) 337-3857
Year Founded: 1954
Abbreviation: SJ

Ownership
Apache County

Officers
President: Monty Long
General Manager: Herman Mineer
Racing Secretary: Jim Collins
Director of Mutuels: Pam Long
Track Announcer: Jim Collins
Track Photographer: Double B Photo

Racing Dates
2007: September 15-September 23, 4 days
2008: September 14-September 22, 4 days

Attendance
Average Daily Recent Meeting: 388, 2007
Total Attendance Recent Meeting: 1,554, 2007

Handle
Average On-Track Recent Meeting: $11,651, 2007
Total On-Track Recent Meeting: $46,604, 2007

Leaders
Recent Meeting, Leading Jockey: Terry Lee Gard, 3, 2007; Daniel W. Gutierrez, 2, 2007; Ashton Dale, 2, 2007; Anna M. Barrio, 2, 2007
Recent Meeting, Leading Trainer: Clyde W. England, 2, 2007

Fastest Times of 2007 (Dirt)
4 furlongs: Chacho, 4, :44, September 16, 2007
5½ furlongs: He's Bold, 5, 1:08.20, September 15, 2007
6 furlongs: Pick Me Buzz, 8, 1:13, September 15, 2007
7 furlongs: Magic Jake, 7, 1:26.60, September 22, 2007

Cochise County Fair
Location: 3677 N. Leslie Canyon Rd., Douglas, Az. 85607-6304
Phone: (520) 364-3819
Fax: (520) 364-1175
E-Mail: cochisefair@questoffice.net
Year Founded: 1924
Abbreviation: DG

Ownership
Cochise County Fair Association

Officers
Chairman: Bob Ford
President: Nick Forsythe
General Manager: Karen Strongin
Director of Racing: Geoffrey E. Gonsher
Racing Secretary: Doreen Rawls
Treasurer: Dennis McAvoy
Director of Mutuels: Jerry Doolittle
Vice President and Director of Publicity: Howard Henderson
Track Announcer: Jim Collins
Track Photographer: Double B Photography
Assistant Racing Secretary: Dodie Rawls
Horsemen's Bookkeeper: Connie Haggard

Racing Dates
2007: April 14-April 22, 4 days
2008: April 12-April 20, 4 days

Attendance
Average Daily Recent Meeting: 2,625, 2007
Total Attendance Recent Meeting: 8,250, 2007

Handle
Average On-Track Recent Meeting: $29,969, 2007
Total On-Track Recent Meeting: $119,876, 2007

Leaders
Recent Meeting, Leading Jockey: Fernando Manuel Gamez, 2, 2007; Steven Michael Karr, 2, 2007
Recent Meeting, Leading Trainer: 11 tied with 1, 2007

Fastest Times of 2007 (Dirt)
a3 furlongs: Flying Bill, 4, :38.20, April 22, 2007; Ice Fantasy, 5, :38.20, April 22, 2007
5½ furlongs: Town Gambler, 10, 1:06.40, April 15, 2007
6 furlongs: Cash in the Bank, 5, 1:14.60, April 22, 2007
6½ furlongs: Sweetvriana, 5, 1:21.80, April 22, 2007
7 furlongs: Chehalis, 9, 1:28.40, April 14, 2007
1 mile 70 yds: Shoot Out, 5, 1:45.80, April 22, 2007

Coconino County Fair
Location: HC 39 Box 3A, Flagstaff, Az. 86001
Phone: (928) 679-8000
Fax: (928) 774-2572
Website: www.coconino.az.gov/parks.aspx
E-Mail: cnemeth@cococonino.az.us
Year Founded: 1955
Abbreviation: Flg
Acreage: 411
Number of Stalls: 320
Seating Capacity: 3,500

Ownership
Coconino County Parks and Recreation

Officers
Director of Racing: Todd Graeff
Racing Secretary: Jim Collins
Director of Operations: Cynthia Nemeth
Director of Marketing: Regina Szal
Director of Mutuels: Jerry Doolittle
Track Announcer: Jim Collins
Track Photographer: Double B Photography
Track Superintendent: William Flick

Racing Dates
2007: June 30-July 5, 4 days
2008: July 4-July 7, 4 days

Track Layout
Main Circumference: 5 furlongs
Main Width: 75 Feet

Attendance
Average Daily Recent Meeting: 3,000, 2007
Total Attendance Recent Meeting: 12,000, 2007

Handle
Average All-Sources Recent Meeting: $432,277, 2007
Total All-Sources Recent Meeting: $2,593,660, 2007
Highest Single-Day Record Recent Meeting: $638,487, June 30, 2007

Fastest Times of 2007 (Dirt)
a3 furlongs: Stranger Among Us, 7, :40, July 4, 2007
5½ furlongs: Swiss Bounty, 6, 1:08.80, July 3, 2007

6 furlongs: Pick Me Buzz, 8, 1:15, July 4, 2007
6½ furlongs: Ryan's Partner, 9, 1:20.80, July 4, 2007
7 furlongs: Tricky Noble, 6, 1:28.60, July 4, 2007
1 mile: Bold General, 5, 1:45.40, June 30, 2007

Gila County Fair

Location: P.O. Box 2193, Globe, Az. 85502-2193
Phone: (928) 425-3809
Website: www.gilafair.net
E-Mail: dananddebg@cableone.net
Abbreviation: GCF

Officers
Chairman: Debbie Guthrey
Director of Publicity: Tamara Seymour

Attendance
Average Daily Recent Meeting: 413, 2007
Total Attendance Recent Meeting: 1,652, 2007

Handle
Average On-Track Recent Meeting: $18,910, 2007
Total On-Track Recent Meeting: $75,642, 2007

Racing Dates
2007: September 29-October 7, 4 days
2008: September 27-October 5, 4 days

Leaders
Recent Meeting, Leading Jockey: Terry Lee Gard, 2, 2007; Steven Michael Karr, 2, 2007; Anna M. Barrio, 2, 2007
Recent Meeting, Leading Trainer: Laurie Jones, 2, 2007

Fastest Times of 2007 (Dirt)
3 furlongs: Bright Jewell, 4, :36, September 30, 2007
5 furlongs: Great Quest, 8, :59.40, October 6, 2007
5½ furlongs: Great Quest, 8, 1:06.20, September 30, 2007
7 furlongs: Magic Jake, 7, 1:29.40, October 7, 2007

Graham County Fair

Location: 527 E. Armory Rd., Safford, Az. 85546-2231
Phone: (928) 428-7180
Fax: (928) 348-0023
E-Mail: cfaunce@graham.az.gov
Year Founded: 1965
Abbreviation: Saf
Acreage: 220

Officers
President: Phil Curtis
General Manager and Director of Racing: Casey Faunce
Racing Secretary: Jim Collins
Secretary: Jessie Hines
Director of Operations: Larry Jensen
Director of Mutuels: Jerome Doolittle
Vice President: Jon Haralson
Horsemen's Liaison: Robert Pledge
Stewards: Robert Clink, Roy Snedigar, Violet Smith
Track Announcer: Red Davis
Track Photographer: Double D
Track Superintendent: Jim Gutierrez

Racing Dates
2007: March 24-April 1, 4 days
2008: March 29-April 6, 4 days

Attendance
Average Daily Recent Meeting: 1,475, 2007
Total Attendance Recent Meeting: 5,900, 2007

Handle
Average On-Track Recent Meeting: $35,377, 2007
Total On-Track Recent Meeting: $141,509, 2007

Leaders
Recent Meeting, Leading Jockey: Ivan Ortiz Jr., 2, 2007; Don Lee French, 2, 2007; Terry Lee Gard, 2, 2007; Jess Chance, 2, 2007; David Reyes-Frisby, 4, 2008
Recent Meeting, Leading Trainer: Laurie Jones, 2, 2008

Track Records, Main Dirt
4 furlongs: Red Spark, :44.60, March 25, 2006
6 furlongs: Tooties Teddy, 1:12.40, March 31, 2002
7 furlongs: Mr. Machine, 1:26, March 26, 2006
1 mile: Paradise Treasures, 1:40.80, April 1, 2007
1¹/₁₆ miles: Cop Out, 1:46.60, March 31, 2001
Other: 3 furlongs, Aledo Cougar, :33.20, April 2, 2006

Fastest Times of 2007 (Dirt)
4 furlongs: Mytee N Blue, 6, :45.20, April 1, 2007
6 furlongs: Sweetvriana, 5, 1:16.20, March 24, 2007
6½ furlongs: Nopaynenogain, 8, 1:26, March 24, 2007
7 furlongs: Chopin's First, 7, 1:29.40. April 1, 2007
1 mile: Paradise Treasures, 5, 1:40.80, April 1, 2007

Greenelee County Fair

Location: 1248 Fairgrounds Rd., P.O. Box 292, Duncan, Az. 85534-0123
Phone: (928) 359-2032
Fax: (928) 359-2721
Website: www.co.greenlee.az.us
E-Mail: fairnracing@co.greenlee.az.us
Abbreviation: Dun

Ownership
Greenlee County

Officers
Chairman: Mike Looby
Director of Racing: Karla Ellis
Racing Secretary: James Collins
Director of Mutuels: Jerry Doolittle
Track Announcer: James Collins
Track Photographer: Double B Photography
Assistant Racing Secretary: Dodie Rawls
Horsemen's Bookkeeper: Connie Haggard

Racing Dates
2007: March 10-March 18, 4 days
2008: March 8-March 16, 4 days
2009: March 14-22, 4 days

Attendance
Average Daily Recent Meeting: 512, 2007
Total Attendance Recent Meeting: 2,048, 2007

Handle
Average On-Track Recent Meeting: $26,177, 2007
Total On-Track Recent Meeting: $104,710, 2007

Leaders
Recent Meeting, Leading Jockey: Steven Michael Karr, 3, 2007; Kelly L. Edge, 2, 2008; Terry Lee Gard, 2, 2008; Daniel W. Gutierrez, 2, 2008; David Reyes-Frisby, 2, 2008; Elliot Bachicha Jr., 2008
Recent Meeting, Leading Trainer: Monique Collins, 3, 2007; Matthew F. Lorefice, 2, 2008

Fastest Times of 2007 (Dirt)
5 furlongs: Flying Bill, 4, 1:00, March 17, 2007
5½ furlongs: Iplanonbeboppin, 6, 1:05.20, March 17, 2007
a6 furlongs: Go Wild Willie, 5, 1:12.20, March 17, 2007
7 furlongs: Pantages, 7, 1:26.60, March 18, 2007

Mohave County Fair

Location: 2600 Fairgrounds Blvd., Kingman, Az. 86401-4169
Phone: (928) 753-2636
Fax: (928) 753-8383

Website: www.mcfafairgrounds.org
E-Mail: racing@mcfafairgrounds.org
Abbreviation: MoF
Acreage: 63
Number of Stalls: 225
Seating Capacity: 1,000

Racing Dates
2007: May 12-May 20, 4 days
2008: May 10-May 18, 4 days

Attendance
Average Daily Recent Meeting: 775, 2007
Total Attendance Recent Meeting: 3,100, 2007

Handle
Average On-Track Recent Meeting: $31,323, 2007
Total On-Track Recent Meeting: $125,293, 2007

Leaders
Recent Meeting, Leading Jockey: Sherry Kirk, 3, 2007; Stacey Zavela, 4, 2008
Recent Meeting, Leading Trainer: Terry S. Roberts, 2, 2007; Frank K. Lykins, 2, 2007; Keith E. Craigmyle, 2, 2008; Caesar J. Lopez, 2, 2008; Juan Pablo Silva, 2, 2008

Track Records, Main Dirt
4 furlongs: Slewofrainbows, :43.10, May 23, 1999
5½ furlongs: Arizona Centre, 1:05.10, May 23, 1999
6 furlongs: Stan an a Half, 1:11.30, May 22, 1999
7 furlongs: Nintyfiver, 1:23.60, May 20, 2001

Fastest Times of 2007 (Dirt)
4 furlongs: Bright Creek, 4, :44.80, May 19, 2007
5½ furlongs: Natural Cat, 7, 1:06.60, May 19, 2007
6 furlongs: Ice Fantasy, 5, 1:13.40, May 20, 2007
6½ furlongs: Cabreo, 10, 1:20.40, May 20, 2007
7 furlongs: Jewels of Dumaani, 4, 1:28.80, May 13, 2007
1 1/16 miles: Paradise Treasures, 5, 1:50.80, May 20, 2007

Rillito Park

Location: 4502 N. 1st Ave., P.O. Box 65132, Tucson, Az. 85728
Phone: (520) 293-5011
Fax: (520) 887-6726
E-Mail: pawhite10@yahoo.com
Year Founded: 1946
Dates of Inaugural Meeting: November 1, 1953
Abbreviation: Ril
Number of Stalls: 500
Seating Capacity: 2,500

Ownership
Pima County

Officers
Chairman: Steve Brody
President: Patricia White
General Manager and Director of Racing: Patricia White
Racing Secretary: Jim Collins
Secretary/Treasurer: Patricia White
Director of Operations and Mutuels: Timothy Kelly
Director of Marketing and Publicity: Jim Collins
Vice President: Patricia Shirley
Horsemen's Liaison: Patricia Shirley
Track Announcer: Jim Collins
Track Photographer: Coady Photography
Track Superintendent: John King
Horsemen's Bookkeeper: Susan Rich
Security: Lisa Pina

Racing Dates
2007: February 10-March 4, 8 days
2008: February 2-February 24, 8 days
2009: January 17-February 22, 8 days

Track Layout
Main Circumference: 5 furlongs
Main Track Chute: 550 yards and 4 furlongs
Main Width: 80 feet
Main Length of Stretch: 660 feet

Attendance
Average Daily Recent Meeting: 4,508, 2007; 5,525, 2008
Total Attendance Recent Meeting: 39,491, 2007; 44,203, 2008
Lowest Single-Day Record: 1,770, February 3, 2008
Highest Single-Day Recent Meeting: 9,312, February 24, 2008
Highest Single-Day Record: 9,312, February 24, 2008
Record Daily Average Single Meeting: 5,525, 2008
Highest Single-Meeting Record: 44,203, 2008

Handle
Average On-Track Recent Meeting: $114,448, 2007; $94,771, 2008
Total On-Track Recent Meeting: $915,587, 2007; $758,166, 2008
Highest Single-Day On-Track Record Recent Meeting: $140,672, February 24, 2008
Average All-Sources Recent Meeting: $94,771, 2008
Total All-Sources Recent Meeting: $758,166, 2008
Highest Single-Day All-Sources Recent Meeting: $140,672, 2008

Leaders
Recent Meeting, Leading Jockey: David Reyes-Frisby, 6, 2008;
Recent Meeting, Leading Trainer: Eddie Tellez, 6, 2008
Recent Meeting, Leading Horse: Blood Red Bay, 2, 2008; Charming Fellow, 2, 2008

Notable Events
Rillito Park Weiner Cup

Track Records, Main Dirt
4 furlongs: Blushing God, :44.40, February 3, 2001
5½ furlongs: Cornino Bay, 1:04.60, February 4, 2001
6 furlongs: Turf's Bounty, 1:10 1/5, November 25, 1989
6½ furlongs: Club Champ, 1:15.80, February 18, 1996
7 furlongs: Stalk the Table, 1:22.60, January 29, 1994
Other: 3 furlongs, Alice Be Gay, :36, March 2, 1974; 3½ furlongs, Slow Dancing, :40 3/5, March 22, 1981; a6 furlongs, Loomis Trail, 1:20, February 15, 2000

Fastest Times of 2007 (Dirt)
4 furlongs: Soha What, 5, :44.92, February 24, 2007
5½ furlongs: Gold Fevers Gift, 9, 1:05.10, February 18, 2007
6 furlongs: Let George Do It, 9, 1:10.60, February 10, 2007
6½ furlongs: Tribellistic, 7, 1:28, February 17, 2007
7 furlongs: Pantages, 7, 1:23.40, February 11, 2007
1 7/16 miles: Mangazo (Arg), 8, 1:46.04, February 24, 2007

Santa Cruz County Fair

Location: 3142 S. Highway 83, P.O. Box 85, Sonoita, Az. 85637-0085
Phone: (520) 455-5553
Fax: (520) 455-5330
Website: www.sonoitafairgrounds.com
E-Mail: info@sonoitafairgrounds.com
Abbreviation: Son
Acreage: 36.5
Number of Stalls: 180
Seating Capacity: 2,200

Officers
Chairman: Burton S. Kruglick
President: John Titus
General Manager: Tina Letarte
Director of Racing: Geoffrey Gonsher
Racing Secretary: James Collins
Secretary: Charlie Hadden
Treasurer: Tom Boisvert
Director of Mutuels: Jerry Doolittle
Vice President: Ray Schock
Director of Publicity: Scott McDaniel
Track Announcer: James Collins
Track Photographer: Double B Photography
Track Superintendent: Harold Hager

Racing Dates
2007: April 28-May 6, 4 days
2008: April 26-May 4, 4 days

Track Layout
Main Circumference: 4 furlongs

Attendance
Average Daily Recent Meeting: 2,800, 2007
Total Attendance Recent Meeting: 11,200, 2007

Handle
Average On-Track Recent Meeting: $47,605, 2007
Total On-Track Recent Meeting: $190,421, 2007

Leaders
Recent Meeting, Leading Jockey: Fernando Manuel Gamez, 2, 2007; Don Lee French, 2, 2007; Michael Alan Cazares, 2, 2007; Terry Lee Gard, 4, 2008
Recent Meeting, Leading Trainer: Ronald Magrady, 2, 2007; Gary Duke, 2, 2007; Ceasar J. Lopez, 2, 2007; 10 tied with 1, 2008

Fastest Times of 2007 (Dirt)
5 furlongs: Natural Cat, 7, :59.20, April 29, 2007
5½ furlongs: Down by the Sea, 6, 1:05.80, May 5, 2007
6 furlongs: Summer Ivey, 6, 1:12, May 5, 2007
7 furlongs: Rubiano's Flag, 7, 1:27.40, April 28, 2007
1¹/₁₆ miles: Shoot Out, 5, 1:50.40, May 5, 2007

Turf Paradise

A Phoenix tradition for nearly a half-century, Turf Paradise has survived several ownership changes and the dramatic reshaping of Thoroughbred racing to remain a vital part of the winter racing scene. Turf Paradise was the vision of businessman Walter Cluer, who purchased 1,400 acres of desert land in 1954 and transformed it into a racetrack, which opened its doors on January 7, 1956. Cluer owned the track until 1980. The track's next two owners, Herb Owens and Robert Walker, added a turf course and off-track betting, respectively. Hollywood Park purchased the track in 1994 and weathered an influx of Native American casino gambling in Arizona before selling the track to Phoenix developer Jerry Simms in June 2000. In November 2002, Arizona voters rejected slot machines at the state's racetracks and approved more machines at Native American casinos.

Location: 1501 W. Bell Rd., Phoenix, Az. 85023-3431
Phone: (602) 942-1101
Fax: (602) 942-8659
Website: www.turfparadise.com
E-Mail: tp@turfparadise.net
Year Founded: 1955
Dates of Inaugural Meeting: January 7, 1956
Abbreviation: TuP
Acreage: 1,400
Number of Stalls: 2,050
Seating Capacity: 7,500

Ownership
Jerry Simms

Officers
General Manager: Eugene Joyce
Director of Racing and Racing Secretary: Shawn Swartz
Director of Finance: Jesse Gerdus
Director of Marketing and Publicity: Vincent Francia
Director of Mutuels: Frank Abbate
Vice President: Dave Johnson
Group Sales: Jennifer Hanblin, Michelle Andersen
Simulcast Coordinator: Stephanie Paredez

Horsemen's Liaison: Bucky Huff
Steward: Hank Mills
Track Announcer: Luke Kruytbosch
Track Photographer: Coady Photography
Track Superintendent: Dan Lenz
Security: Del Blodin

Racing Dates
2007: October 6, 2006-May 6, 2007, 152 days
2008: October 5, 2007-May 4, 2008, 156 days
2009: October 3, 2008-May 3, 2009

Track Layout
Main Circumference: 1 mile
Main Track Chute: 3 furlongs and 6½ furlongs
Main Width: Homestretch: 80 feet; Backstretch: 70 feet; Turns: 100 feet
Main Length of Stretch: 990 feet
Main Turf Circumference: 7 furlongs
Main Turf Chute: 1 furlong
Main Turf Width: 73 feet

Attendance
Average Daily Recent Meeting: 2,057, 2007/2008
Highest Single-Day Record: 16,000 est., March 18, 1984
Total Attendance Recent Meeting: 314,907, 2007/2008

Handle
Average All-Sources Recent Meeting: $1,462,998, 2007/2008
Average On-Track Recent Meeting: $88,361, 2007/2008
Total All-Sources Recent Meeting: $223,838,869, 2007/2008
Total On-Track Recent Meeting: $13,519,329, 2007/2008

Mutuel Records
Highest Win: $287.60, Gaye Rest, May 23, 1974
Highest Exacta: $17,092.20, May 8, 1988
Highest Trifecta: $42,774, October 18, 1987
Highest Daily Double: $5,355, April 24, 1985
Highest Pick Six: $137,372, March 3, 1986

Leaders
Career, Leading Jockey by Titles: Sam Powell, 16
Career, Leading Owner by Titles: Dennis Weir, 10
Career, Leading Trainer by Titles: Richard Hazelton, 27
Recent Meeting, Leading Jockey: Seth B. Martinez, 144, 2007/2008
Recent Meeting, Leading Trainer: Keith Bennett, 87, 2007/2008
Recent Meeting, Leading Horse: Cleard For Action, 6, 2007/2008; Your Highness Leia, 6, 2007/2008

Records
Single-Day Jockey Wins: Marty Wentz, 7; Ray York, 7
Single Meeting, Leading Jockey by Wins: Pat Steinberg, 225
Single Meeting, Leading Trainer by Wins: Bart Hone, 88

Principal Races
Cotton Fitzsimmons Mile, Turf Paradise Derby, Phoenix Gold Cup H., Arizona Oaks, Turf Paradise H.

Track Records, Main Dirt
4 furlongs: Beau Madison, :45, March 30, 1957
4½ furlongs: Iron Halo (Arg), :50, March 7, 2006
5 furlongs: Zip Pocket, :55⅖, April 22, 1967
5½ furlongs: Plenty Zloty, 1:01.10, April 18, 1995
6 furlongs: G Malleah, 1:06.60, April 8, 1995
6½ furlongs: G Malleah, 1:13.80, December 3, 1994
7 furlongs: Free Duty, 1:26⅕, January 23, 1985
1 mile: Mr. Pappion, 1:33.20, January 30, 1993
1¹/₁₆ miles: Down the Isle, 1:39⅕, February 11, 1987
1⅛ miles: Our Forbes, 1:47.60, November 29, 1996
1³/₁₆ miles: Erin Glen, 1:55⅗, January 15, 1967
1¼ miles: Truly a Pleasure, 2:01.40, March 26, 1995
1⅜ miles: Bloom n Character, 2:15⅖, April 12, 1980
1½ miles: Spinney, 2:29⅖, April 30, 1961
1⅝ miles: Masked Rider, 2:44.40, February 10, 2002
1¾ miles: Arsenal, 2:55⅖, February 7, 1971
2 miles: Vermejo, 3:24, April 20, 1969
Other: 2 furlongs, Wandering Boy, :21⅕, December 5, 1965; 3 furlongs, Never Shamed, :31.60, April 1, 1996

Track Records, Main Turf
4½ furlongs: Dan's Groovy, :49.26, April 13, 2003
5 furlongs: Honor the Hero, :56.20, February 5, 1995; Amersham, :56.29, February 2, 2002
7 furlongs: Lord Pleasant, 1:22.80, October 12, 1992
7½ furlongs: Briartic Gold, 1:28.18, April 13, 2003
1 mile: Prose (Ire), 1:34.83, March 27, 2001
1 1/16 miles: Caesour, 1:40.40, February 5, 1995
1 1/8 miles: Narghile, 1:48, February 1, 1987
1 3/8 miles: Free Corona, 2:15.17, April 27, 2003
1½ miles: Senator McGuire, 2:29 3/5, May 22, 1988
Other: a5 furlongs, J. Zac, :57.80, February 18, 1990; a7 furlongs, Faro, 1:25 1/5, November 23, 1986; a7½ furlongs, Alottadar, 1:29.26, March 9, 2007; a1 mile, Global Trader, 1:35.31, November 24, 2007; a1 1/16 miles, Lion Trouble, 1:42.20, March 12, 2007; a1 1/8 miles, Morning Watch, 1:49.65, March 30, 2007; a1 3/8 miles, Doctor Trotter, 2:16.80, April 18, 1998; a1½ miles, Estonia, 2:34, April 5, 1997; a1 7/8 miles, Amapour, 3:15 1/5, May 18, 1986; 1 7/8 miles, Shadows Fall, 3:09 2/5, May 17, 1987

Fastest Times of 2007 (Dirt)
2 furlongs: Emanation, 2, :21.52, April 2, 2007
4½ furlongs: King Justin, 6, :50.13, March 18, 2007
5 furlongs: Girvan, 4, :56, February 24, 2007
5½ furlongs: Family Guy, 5, 1:01.87, April 9, 2007
6 furlongs: Relato Del Gato, 6, 1:07.68, February 24, 2007
6½ furlongs: Trail This, 4, 1:14.28, March 17, 2007
1 mile: Prorunner, 5, 1:35.18, May 1, 2007
1 1/16 miles: Big Archie, 4, 1:43.55, May 6, 2007
1 1/8 miles: Last Outpost, 5, 1:50.74, January 17, 2007
1 ¼ miles: Nicol n' Dime Me, 10, 2:04.23, February 4, 2007
1 5/8 miles: Last Outpost, 5, 2:46.63, February 24, 2007

Fastest Times of 2007 (Turf)
4½ furlongs: Blackjack Boy, 7, :49.88, March 4, 2007
a4½ furlongs: Pepper Dan, 6, :49.55, March 16, 2007
7½ furlongs: Star of Whitney, 4, 1:28.69, October 9, 2007
a7½ furlongs: Alottadar, 6, 1:29.26, March 9, 2007
1 mile: Aza, 6, 1:35.61, March 2, 2007
a1 mile: Global Trader, 5, 1:35.31, November 24, 2007
1 1/16 miles: Grat, 5, 1:41.86, January 6, 2007
a1 1/16 miles: Lion Trouble, 5, 1:42.20, March 12, 2007
1 1/8 miles: Aza, 6, 1:48.87, March 20, 2007
a1 1/8 miles: Morning Watch, 7, 1:49.65, March 30, 2007
1 3/8 miles: We Brothers, 5, 2:17.25, April 17, 2007
1 7/8 miles: Key of Solomon (Ire), 5, 3:15.36, May 6, 2007

Yavapai Downs

The story of Yavapai Downs actually involves two tracks. Located in Arizona's Prescott Valley region, Yavapai opened its doors in 2001, replacing Prescott Downs, a half-mile oval that had been in operation since 1913. While Prescott was known for its rustic atmosphere and occasionally wild bullring racing, Yavapai quickly established a reputation as a more refined track, with modern amenities and a one-mile oval. The $23-million facility was completed in 13 months, almost one year ahead of schedule, allowing it to open in May 2001. The physical plant features a three-story clubhouse and grandstand with Arizona's Mingus Mountains as a backdrop. The backstretch offers stabling for 1,200 horses. During its first six meets, average purses exceeded $30,000 per day. Prescott, Arizona's summer racing home for the better part of nine decades, was the site of Racing Hall of Fame jockey Pat Day's first victory.

Location: 10501 Highway 89A, P.O. Box 26557, Prescott Valley, Az. 86312-6557
Phone: (928) 775-8000
Fax: (928) 445-0408
Website: www.yavapaidownsatpv.com
E-Mail: info@yavapaidownsatpv.com
Year Founded: 2001
Dates of Inaugural Meeting: May 26, 2001
Abbreviation: Yav
Acreage: 200
Number of Stalls: 1,300
Seating Capacity: 5,000

Ownership
Yavapai County Fair Association

Officers
President: Tom Oppelt
General Manager: James Grundy
Director of Racing and Racing Secretary: John Everly
Secretary: James Pickering
Treasurer: Phil Bybee
Director of Finance: Sharon Fischer
Director of Marketing and Sales: James Grundy
Director of Mutuels: Randy Fozzard
Vice President: Kathleen Findlayson
Director of Simulcasting: Don Rogers
Track Announcer: Greg "Boomer" Wry
Track Photographer: Coady Photography
Track Superintendent: Bubba French

Racing Dates
2007: May 26-September 4, 60 days
2008: May 24-September 2, 55 days
2009: May 23-September 4, 60 days

Track Layout
Main Circumference: 1 mile
Main Track Chute: 2 furlongs and 6 furlongs
Main Width: 75 feet
Main Length of Stretch: 1,020 feet

Attendance
Average Daily Recent Meeting: 2,303, 2007
Total Attendance Recent Meeting: 221,161, 2007
Highest Single-Day Recent Meeting: 8,298 on June 9, 2007

Handle
Average All-Sources Recent Meeting: $313,790, 2007
Total All-Sources Recent Meeting: $18,827,415

Leaders
Recent Meeting, Leading Jockey: Vince Guerra, 92, 2007
Recent Meeting, Leading Trainer: Raul Hernandez, 30, 2007
Recent Meeting, Leading Horse: Pistoli, 4, 2007

Principal Races
Gerry Howard Inaugural H., Yavapai Downs Thoroughbred Derby, Mile-Hi H., Yavapai County Arizona Breeders' Futurity, Yavapai Downs Thoroughbred Futurity

Track Records, Main Dirt
4½ furlongs: Motivo, :49, September 5, 2006; King Justin, :49, June 2, 2007
5 furlongs: Run Nicholas Run, 5, :55.60, August 26, 2007
5½ furlongs: Twin Sparks, 1:01.60, August 15, 2005
6 furlongs: Run Nicholas Run, 5, 1:07.80, August 11, 2007
1 mile: Suspicious Minds, 1:35, June 21, 2005
1 1/16 miles: Gusto Forzado, 1:42.63, June 24, 2002
1 1/8 miles: Takin Dead Aim, 4, 1:48.80, July 14, 2007
1 ¼ miles: Cajun Bound, 2:03.20, August 18, 2003

Fastest Times of 2007 (Dirt)
4½ furlongs: King Justin, 6, :49, June 2, 2007
5 furlongs: Run Nicholas Run, 5, :55.60, August 26, 2007
5½ furlongs: King Justin, 6, 1:01.80, July 10, 2007; Wild English Rose, 4, 1:01.80, August 12, 2007
6 furlongs: Run Nicholas Run, 5, 1:07.80, August 11, 2007
1 mile: Mister Cosmi (GB), 8, 1:35.20, August 25, 2007
1 1/16 miles: Party With Todd, 3, 1:43.80, August 18, 2007
1 1/8 miles: Takin Dead Aim, 4, 1:48.80, July 14, 2007

# Arkansas

Oaklawn Park

Arkansas's leading tourist attraction is Oaklawn Park in the resort community of Hot Springs. The track first opened in 1905 but closed two years later due to political problems in the state. The track reopened in 1916 under the ownership of Louis Cella, whose great-nephew, Charles Cella, is the track's current president and board chairman. Oaklawn, which offers live racing from January to mid-April, attracts runners from across the United States for its Racing Festival of the South. The festival features at least one stakes race each day on the final eight days of the meet, ending with the $1-milion Arkansas Derby (G2), which was first run in 1936. Other major races include the Apple Blossom Handicap (G1) for fillies and mares and the $500,000-guaranteed Oaklawn Handicap (G2) for older horses. In 2004, Oaklawn Park and the Cella family received the Eclipse Award of Merit for their contributions to racing.

Location: 2705 Central Ave., Hot Springs, Ar. 71901-7515
Phone: (501) 623-4411, (800) 625-5296
Website: www.oaklawn.com
E-Mail: winning@oaklawn.com
Year Founded: 1904
Dates of Inaugural Meeting: February 24, 1905
Abbreviation: OP
Acreage: 120
Number of Stalls: 1,600
Seating Capacity: 26,200

Officers
Chairman and President: Charles J. Cella
General Manager: R. Eric Jackson
Racing Secretary: Patrick J. Pope
Treasurer: William L. Cravens
Director of Operations: John Hopkins
Director of Marketing: Kim Baron
Director of Mutuels and Simulcasting: Bobby Geiger
Director of Publicity: Terry Wallace
Horsemen's Liaison: Deborah Keene
Stewards: Johnnie Johnson, Larry Snyder, Gary Wilfert
Track Announcer: Terry Wallace
Track Photographer: Coady Photography
Track Superintendent: Steve Breckling

Racing Dates
2007: January 19-April 14, 52 days
2008: January 18-April 12, 56 days
2009: January 16-April 11, 54 days

Track Layout
Main Circumference: 1 mile
Main Track Chute: 6 furlongs
Main Width: Straightaways: 70 feet; Turns: 80 feet
Main Length of Stretch: 1,155 feet

Attendance
Average Daily Recent Meeting: 11,890, 2007
Highest Single-Day Record: 72,464, April 15, 2006
Record Daily Average Single Meeting: 23,271, 1983
Highest Single-Meeting Record: 1,419,650, 1984
Total Attendance Recent Meeting: 618,284, 2007
Highest Single-Day Recent Meeting: 57,937, April 14, 2007

Handle
Average All-Sources Recent Meeting: $3,718, 588, 2007
Average On-Track Recent Meeting: $1,264,971, 2007
Single-Day All-Sources Handle: $15,133,537, April 15, 2000
Total All-Sources Recent Meeting: $193,366,592, 2007
Total On-Track Recent Meeting: $65,778,477, 2007
Highest Single-Day Record Recent Meeting: $11,746,167, April 14, 2007

Record Average All-Sources Single Meeting: $5,189,245, 2002
Record Total All-Sources Single Meeting: $280,341,701, 2005

Mutuel Records
Highest Win: $350.80; Phaltup, March 7, 1950
Highest Exacta: $3,915.20, April 8, 1994
Highest Trifecta: $17,925.40, March 19, 2005
Highest Daily Double: $6,902, March 30, 1971
Highest Pick Three: $36,686.80, February 17, 1996
Highest Pick Six: $818,693.40, February 15, 1995

Leaders
Career, Leading Jockey by Titles: Pat Day, 12
Career, Leading Trainer by Titles: Henry Forest, 11
Recent Meeting, Leading Jockey: Luis S. Quinonez, 52, 2007; Eusebio Razo Jr., 49, 2008
Recent Meeting, Leading Owner: Kalarikkal K. and Vilasini D. Jayaraman, 17, 2007; Jan Haynes, 17, 2008
Recent Meeting, Leading Trainer: Steven M. Asmussen, 36, 2007; Steven M. Asmussen, 33, 2008
Recent Meeting, Leading Horse: Humble Chris, 4, 2007; Bold Fury, 4, 2008

Records
Single-Day Jockey Wins: Larry Snyder, 6, April 1, 1969; Pat Day, 6, February 17, 1986; Pat Day, 6, March 11, 1993; Pat Day, 6, February 20, 1995
Single Meeting, Leading Jockey by Wins: Pat Day, 137, 1986
Single Meeting, Leading Trainer by Wins: Cole Norman, 62, 2005

Principal Races
Apple Blossom H. (G1), Arkansas Derby (G2), Rebel S. (G2), Azeri Breeders' Cup S. (G3), Count Fleet Sprint H. (G3), Southwest Stakes (G3), Honeybee Stakes (G3).

Track Records, Main Dirt
4 furlongs: Crimson Saint, :44$^{1}/_{5}$, April 1, 1971
4$^{1}/_{2}$ furlongs: Montague, :53, March 29, 1937
5 furlongs: Miss Brendy, :57$^{3}/_{5}$, February 22, 1966
5$^{1}/_{2}$ furlongs: Sis Pleasure Fager, 1:02$^{3}/_{5}$, February 15, 1984
6 furlongs: Karen's Tom, 1:07$^{4}/_{5}$, April 16, 1990
1 mile: Whitebrush, 1:34$^{2}/_{5}$, March 10, 1984
1 mile 70 yds: Win Stat, 1:38$^{2}/_{5}$, March 7, 1984
1$^{1}/_{16}$ miles: Heatherten, 1:40$^{1}/_{5}$, April 18, 1984; Hang On Slewpy, 1:40$^{1}/_{5}$, April 20, 1991
1$^{1}/_{8}$ miles: Snow Chief, 1:46$^{3}/_{5}$, April 17, 1987
1$^{3}/_{16}$ miles: Brassy, 1:57$^{2}/_{5}$, March 29, 1952
1$^{1}/_{4}$ miles: Out of Fire, 2:04, March 31, 1937
1$^{3}/_{8}$ miles: Dapper, 2:31$^{3}/_{5}$, March 30, 1957
1$^{1}/_{2}$ miles: Dapper, 2:31$^{3}/_{5}$, March 30, 1957
1$^{3}/_{4}$ miles: Flag Carrier, 2:58, April 13, 1987
Other: 3 furlongs, Gay Whip, :33$^{2}/_{5}$, March 7, 1967; Hempen's Song, :33$^{3}/_{5}$, February 16, 1971; 2m 70 yds, Turntable, 3:34, March 27, 1942

Fastest Times of 2007 (Dirt)
5$^{1}/_{2}$ furlongs: Gleaming Elegance, 4, 1:03.90, March 29, 2007
6 furlongs: Bordonaro, 6, 1:09.11, April 13, 2007
1 mile: Copy My Notes, 5, 1:37.80, April 13, 2007
1$^{1}/_{16}$ miles: Silent Pleasure, 4, 1:42.95, April 12, 2007
1$^{1}/_{8}$ miles: Lawyer Ron, 4, 1:49, April 7, 2007
1$^{3}/_{16}$ miles: Humble Chris, 6, 2:00.29, March 24, 2007
1$^{1}/_{4}$ miles: Humble Chris, 6, 3:03.21, April 14, 2007

California

Bay Meadows Fair

Location: 2600 South Delaware St., P.O. Box 1027, San Mateo, Ca. 94403-1902
Phone: (650) 574-7223
Fax: (650) 574-3985
Website: www.sanmateocountyfair.com
E-Mail: info@smeventcenter.com
Abbreviation: BMF
Number of Stalls: 900
Seating Capacity: 20,000

Ownership
San Mateo County Fair

Officers
President: Jack Olsen
General Manager and Director of Racing: Chris Carpenter
Racing Secretary: Tom Doutrich
Secretary/Treasurer: Melanie Hildebrand
Director of Mutuels: Bryan Wayte
Director of Publicity: Tom Ferrall
Director of Simulcasting: Kay Webb
Assistant Racing Secretary: C. Gregory Brent Jr.

Racing Dates
2007: August 8-August 19, 11 days
2008: August 6-August 17, 12 days

Track Layout
Main Circumference: 1 mile
Main Track Chute: 6 furlongs and 1¼ miles
Main Width: Homestretch: 85 feet; Backstretch: 75 feet
Main Length of Stretch: 990 feet
Main Turf Circumference: 7 furlongs, 32 feet
Main Turf Width: 75 feet

Attendance
Average Daily Recent Meeting: 2,016, 2007
Total Attendance Recent Meeting: 22,181, 2007

Handle
Average All-Sources Recent Meeting: $1,290,438, 2007
Average On-Track Recent Meeting: $166,475, 2007
Total All-Sources Recent Meeting: $14,194,822, 2007
Total On-Track Recent Meeting: $1,831,231, 2007

Leaders
Recent Meeting, Leading Jockey: Russell A. Baze, 15, 2007
Recent Meeting, Leading Trainer: Art Sherman, 11, 2007

Fastest Times of 2007 (Dirt)
5 furlongs: Aeblus, 5, :57.73, August 13, 2007
5½ furlongs: Denaesalildevil, 5, 1:03.33, August 8, 2007
6 furlongs: Bedford Falls, 4, 1:09.50, August 10, 2007
1 mile: Pat's Boy, 5, 1:37.70, August 10, 2007
1 1/16 miles: Slow N Easy, 6, 1:43.16, August 10, 2007

Fastest Times of 2007 (Turf)
7½ furlongs: Top Leese, 4, 1:30.19, August 17, 2007
1 mile: Wild Promises, 3, 1:36.59, August 16, 2007
1 1/16 miles: Higher Love, 4, 1:45.20, August 11, 2007

Bay Meadows Race Course

Located 20 miles south of San Francisco in San Mateo, Bay Meadows Race Course was founded in 1934 by the innovative William P. Kyne, who helped to bring about the legalization of pari-mutuel wagering in California that year. At Bay Meadows, Kyne introduced the totalizator system, photo-finish camera, and the still-popular daily double wager. Bay Meadows also was the site of the first all-enclosed starting gate in America in 1939 and, on October 27, 1945, the destination point of the first equine air passenger when El Lobo, a Thoroughbred, was flown from Los Angeles to an airstrip adjacent to Bay Meadows. Bay Meadows was the only California racetrack allowed to operate during World War II as Kyne pledged all profits to various war relief projects. In 1951, Coaltown captured the Children's Hospital Handicap, another charity fund-raiser. Bay Meadows introduced the El Camino Real Derby (G3) in 1982 as a prep for the Kentucky Derby (G1), and 17 years later Charismatic finished second by a head in the race (to Cliquot) before winning the Derby and Preakness Stakes (G1). Magna Entertainment Corp. leased the track from 2001 through '04, and Bay Meadows Land Co., which owns the property, resumed operation of the facility in '05. Jockey Russell Baze broke Laffit Pincay Jr.'s record for career wins when he registered his 9,531st victory, riding Butterfly Belle at Bay Meadows on December 1, 2006. After 74 years, racing came to end at Bay Meadows in 2008. The racetrack is scheduled to be torn down following the August 6-17 San Mateo County Fair Meet so that a housing and commercial development can be built on the grounds.

Location: 2600 S. Delaware St., P.O. Box 5050, San Mateo, Ca. 94402
Phone: (650) 574-7223
Fax: (925) 803-8168
Website: www.baymeadows.com
E-Mail: info@baymeadows.com
Year Founded: 1934
Dates of Inaugural Meeting: November 3, 1934
Abbreviation: BM
Acreage: 90
Number of Stalls: 900
Seating Capacity: 20,000

Ownership
Bay Meadows Land Co.

Officers
President: F. Jack Liebau
General Managers: Bernie Thurman, Mike Ziegler
Director of Racing and Racing Secretary: Tom Doutrich
Treasurer: Barbara Helm
Director of Mutuels: Bryan Wayte
Vice Presidents: Dyan Grealish, Mike Scalzo
Director of Publicity: Tom Ferrall
Director of Simulcasting: Kay Webb
Track Announcer: Michael Wrona
Track Photographer: William Vassar
Track Superintendent: Robert Turman
Assistant Racing Secretaries: Linda Anderson, C. Gregory Brent Jr.
Security: Michael Scalzo
Promotions and Events: Robin McHargue

Racing Dates
2007: February 14-April 22, 48 days; August 22-November 4, 56 days
2008: February 4-May 11, 70 days

Track Layout
Main Circumference: 1 mile
Main Track Chute: 6 furlongs and 1¼ miles
Main Width: Homestretch: 85 feet; Backstretch: 75 feet
Main Length of Stretch: 990 feet
Main Turf Circumference: 7 furlongs, 32 feet
Main Turf Width: 75 feet

Attendance
Average Daily Recent Meeting: 6,373, Spring 2007; 6,139, Fall 2007
Highest Single-Day Record: 29,300, April 17, 1948
Total Attendance Recent Meeting: 305,882, Spring 2007; 319,202, Fall 2007

Handle
Average On-Track Recent Meeting: $661,229, Spring 2007; $599,528 Fall 2007
Single-Day All-Sources Handle: $8,660,396, November 6, 1999
Total On-Track Recent Meeting: $31,739,002, Spring 2007; $31,175,463, Fall 2007

Mutuel Records
Highest Win: $599.80
Highest Exacta: $2,108
Highest Daily Double: $5,231
Highest Pick Six: $1,132,466
Highest Other Exotics: $1,298.80, Quinella; $347,970.40, Pick Nine

Leaders

Career, Leading Jockey by Titles: Russell Baze, 40
Career, Leading Trainer by Titles: Jerry Hollendorfer, 37
Recent Meeting, Leading Jockey: Russell Baze, 81, Spring 2007; Russell Baze, 79, Fall 2007; Russell Baze, 130, Spring 2008
Recent Meeting, Leading Trainer: Jerry Hollendorfer, 44, Spring 2007; Jerry Hollendorfer, 47, Fall 2007; Jerry Hollendorfer, 55, Spring 2008
Single-Day Jockey Wins: John Adams, 6, April 7, 1938; John Longden, 6, November 22, 1947; Bill Shoemaker, 6, October 13, 1950; William Harmatz, 6, September 23, 1954; Ralph Neves, 6, October 24, 1961; Russell Baze, 6, September 1, 1984; Russell Baze, 6,

Principal Races

El Camino Real Derby (G2), Bay Meadows Breeders' Cup Sprint H. (G3), Bay Meadows Breeders' Cup Oaks, California Turf Sprint H.

Track Records, Main Dirt

4 furlongs: Ima Dear, :46$^2/_5$, April 2, 1935
4$^1/_2$ furlongs: Metatron, :50.59, May 24, 2001
5 furlongs: Rockin' Rizzi, :55.95, December 18, 2006
5$^1/_2$ furlongs: Rio Oro, 1:01.69, October 7, 2001
6 furlongs: Black Jack Road, 1:07$^1/_5$, October 28, 1990
7$^1/_2$ furlongs: Lookabout, 1:30$^2/_5$, November 26, 1936
1 mile: Aristocratical, 1:33$^3/_5$, September 10, 1983
1 mile 70 yds: Redress, 1:41$^3/_5$, December 10, 1934
1$^1/_{16}$ miles: Hoedown's Day, 1:38$^2/_5$, October 23, 1983
1$^1/_8$ miles: Super Moment, 1:46$^1/_5$, December 13, 1980
1$^3/_{16}$ miles: Force of Reason, 1:52$^4/_5$, November 5, 1983
1$^1/_4$ miles: Ask Father, 2:00$^2/_5$, September 28, 1968
1$^1/_2$ miles: Cattle Creek, 2:27$^3/_5$, December 12, 1979
1$^5/_8$ miles: Rag King, 2:43$^1/_5$, December 15, 1990
1$^3/_4$ miles: Tornillo, 2:57$^3/_5$, November 21, 1936
Other: 2 furlongs, Lady Las Vegas, :21, March 20, 1997; 2 furlongs, Royalette, :21.11, April 12, 2002; 3$^1/_2$ furlongs, Harrogate, :40$^4/_5$, March 16, 1935

Track Records, Main Turf

4$^1/_2$ furlongs: Santano, :50.38, May 17, 2001
5 furlongs: Excessive Barb, :56.32, May 30, 2004
7 furlongs: First Flyer, 1:24.35, September 25, 1997
7$^1/_2$ furlongs: Hegemony (Ire), 1:28$^4/_5$, October 12, 1985
1 mile: Position's Best, 1:34$^3/_5$, September 6, 1987; Staff Rider, 1:34.68, August 28, 1993
1$^1/_{16}$ miles: Dreamer, 1:40.21, August 17, 1997
1$^1/_8$ miles: Ocean Queen, 1:47.80, October 12, 1996
1$^3/_8$ miles: Peu a Peu, 2:16.39, May 18, 2002
1$^1/_2$ miles: Swiss Conviction, 2:31.46, October 12, 1998
2 miles: Lighting Star, 3:28.39, March 23, 1997
Other: a1$^1/_8$ miles, Mula Gula, 1:45.34, September 25, 1999; a1$^3/_8$ miles, Handsome Weed, 2:17.10, October 24, 1991

Fastest Times of 2007 (Dirt)

2 furlongs: Sassy Blend, 2, :21.96, April 12, 2007
5 furlongs: T. J.'s Express, 4, :56.97, October 12, 2007
5$^1/_2$ furlongs: Thoughtuknew, 5, 1:02.16, October 12, 2007
6 furlongs: Colonel Courtney, 7, 1:08.40, February 22, 2007; Smokey Stover, 4, 1:08.40, March 11, 2007
1 mile: Hystericalady, 4, 1:33.95, April 5, 2007
1$^1/_{16}$ miles: My Creed, 6, 1:41.70, February 19, 2007
1$^1/_8$ miles: Soccer Dan, 6, 1:50.36, October 31, 2007
1$^1/_4$ miles: Walter Ringer, 6, 2:02.83, February 19, 2007

Fastest Times of 2007 (Turf)

5 furlongs: Pragmatico (Arg), 9, :56.59, October 24, 2007
7$^1/_2$ furlongs: Vote, 5, 1:29.57, September 26, 2007
1 mile: Cover Magic, 3, 1:36.14, October 31, 2007
1$^1/_{16}$ miles: Putmeinyourwill, 4, 1:42.14, October 6, 2007
a1$^1/_8$ miles: Now Victory, 6, 1:47.17, September 22, 2007
1$^3/_8$ miles: Earnest Storm, 9, 2:19.25, September 20, 2007

Del Mar

Known as the track "where the surf meets the turf," Del Mar is renowned for its laid-back atmosphere and rich purses. The Del Mar style is a legacy of the film stars who helped build it, principally Bing Crosby and Pat O'Brien. But the track's beginnings were rocky. In the mid-1930s, the 22nd District Agricultural Association began to build a fairgrounds with a one-mile racetrack and grandstand north of San Diego, and Crosby formed the Del Mar Turf Club to lease the facility for ten years. But the agricultural district soon ran out of money, and Crosby and O'Brien borrowed almost $600,000 to complete the project. The track opened on July 3, 1937, with Crosby greeting the first patron through the turnstiles. The following year, the crooner wrote "Where the Surf Meets the Turf" and sang it on opening day; it still is played every day at the track. Del Mar was closed during World War II, serving as a Marine training center and an assembly center for B-17 wing ribs. It reopened in 1945, and the lease was extended through '59. In 1970, a group of prominent California owners and breeders formed the Del Mar Thoroughbred Club and leased the facility for 20 years. The lease was extended for another 20 years in 1990. A rebuilt Del Mar grandstand and clubhouse costing $80-million were completed in 1993, two years after the first running of the track's now-signature event, the Pacific Classic Stakes (G1). The track installed a Polytrack synthetic racing surface in 2007.

Location: 2260 Jimmy Durante Blvd , P.O. Box 700, Del Mar, Ca. 92014
Phone: (858) 755-1141
Fax: (858) 792-4269
Website: *www.delmarracing.com*
E-Mail: info@dmtc.com
Year Founded: 1937
Dates of Inaugural Meeting: July 3-July 31, 1937
Abbreviation: Dmr
Acreage: 350
Number of Stalls: 2,100
Seating Capacity: 14,304

Ownership

Del Mar Thoroughbred Club

Officers

Chief Executive Officer: Joseph W. Harper
Chairman: Robert S. Strauss
President and General Manager: Joseph W. Harper
Director of Racing and Racing Secretary: Thomas S. Robbins
Director of Operations: Tim Read
Director of Finance: Michael R. Ernst
Director of Mutuels: William D. Navarro
Vice Presidents: Craig Dado, Michael Ernst, Craig R. Fravel, Thomas Robbins, Josh Rubinstein
Director of Media: Mac McBride
Director of Group Sales/Retail Operations: Jacquelyn King
Director of Simulcasting: Paul Porter
Horsemen's Liaison: Lisa Iaria
Track Announcer: Trevor Denman
Track Photographer: Benoit & Associates
Track Superintendent: Steve Wood
Director of Security: Bill Sullivan
Assistant Racing Secretaries: Rick Hammerle, Zachary Soto
Clerk of the Course: Melanie Stubblefield

Racing Dates

2007: July 18-September 5, 43 days
2008: July 16-September 3, 43 days

Track Layout

Main Circumference: 1 mile (Polytrack)
Main Track Chutes: 7 furlongs and 1$^1/_4$ miles
Main Width: 80 feet
Main Length of Stretch: 919 feet
Turf Course Circumference: 7 furlongs
Turf Course Chute: 1$^1/_8$ miles diagonal

Main Turf Course Width: 63 feet
Main Turf Course Length of Stretch: 761 feet
Training Track: 4 furlongs

Attendance

Average Daily Recent Meeting: 16,719, 2007
Highest Single-Day Record: 44,181, August 10, 1996
Record Daily Average Single Meeting: 19,776, 1985
Highest Single-Meeting Record: 846,495, 1987
Total Attendance Recent Meeting: 718,923, 2007

Handle

Average All-Sources Recent Meeting: $13,985,027, 2007
Average On-Track Recent Meeting: $2,437,225, 2007
Record Daily Average Single Meeting: $3,861,247, 1987
Single-Day On-Track Handle: $5,657,840, August 15, 1987
Single-Day All-Sources Handle: $24,667,351, August 19, 2007
Total All-Sources Recent Meeting: $601,356,177, 2007
Total On-Track Recent Meeting: $104,800,659, 2007
Total All-Sources Single Meeting: $608,916,117, 2005
Average All-Sources Single Meeting: $14,143,449, 2005
Highest Single-Day Record Recent Meeting: $24,667,351, August 19, 2007
Total Single Meeting: $166,033,640, 1987

Mutuel Records

Highest Win: $263.40, Cipria, September 1, 1955
Highest Exacta: $2,383, August 7, 1987
Highest Trifecta: $13,405.50, July 28, 1997
Highest Daily Double: $7,720, August 27, 2004
Highest Pick Three: $20,080.30, August 20, 2000
Highest Pick Six: $2,100,017, August 1, 2004
Highest Other Exotics: $133,013.40, Superfecta, September 6, 1998; $43,602.40, Place Pick All, September 8, 2002
Highest Quinella: $1,374, July 28, 1997
Highest Pick Four: $85,945.80, July 22, 2007

Leaders

Career, Leading Jockey by Titles: William Shoemaker, 7
Career, Leading Owner by Titles: Golden Eagle Farm, 6
Career, Leading Trainer by Titles: Farrell W. Jones, 11
Career, Leading Jockey by Stakes Wins: Chris McCarron, 134
Career, Leading Trainer by Stakes Wins: Bob Baffert, 78
Career, Leading Jockey by Wins: Laffit Pincay Jr., 1,011
Career, Leading Trainer by Wins: Ron McAnally, 428
Recent Meeting, Leading Jockey: Michael Baze, 50, 2007
Recent Meeting, Leading Owner: Ron Valenta (La Canada Stable), 6, 2007
Recent Meeting, Leading Trainer: Doug F. O'Neill, 23, 2007

Records

Single-Day Jockey Wins: Victor Espinoza, 7, September 4, 2006
Single-Day Trainer Wins: R. H. "Red" McDaniel, 4, September 4, 1954; R. H. "Red" McDaniel, 4, September 6, 1954; Farrell W. Jones, 4, August 13, 1963; Ron McAnally, 4, August 20, 1989; Jack Van Berg, 4, August 3, 1995
Single Meeting, Leading Jockey by Wins: William Shoemaker, 94, 1954
Single Meeting, Leading Trainer by Wins: R. H. "Red" McDaniel, 47, 1954
Single Meeting, Leading Trainer by Stakes Wins: Bob Baffert, 13, 2000
Single Meeting, Leading Jockey by Stakes Wins: Laffit Pincay Jr., 12, 1976; Chris McCarron, 12, 1995; Gary Stevens, 12, 1997; Corey Nakatani, 12, 1998

Principal Races

Pacific Classic S. (G1), Del Mar Oaks (G1), Eddie Read H. (G1), John C. Mabee H. (G1), Bing Crosby H. (G1), Del Mar Debutante S. (G1)

Track Records, Main Dirt

5 furlongs: Soldier Girl, :56$\frac{2}{5}$, August 13, 1964; Bro Lo, :56.46, July 20, 2005
5$\frac{1}{2}$ furlongs: Ack Ack, 1:02$\frac{1}{5}$, September 12, 1970; Lakeside Trail, 1:02$\frac{1}{5}$, August 18, 1974; Little Mustard, 1:02$\frac{1}{5}$, September 5, 1974; King's Sea Rullah, 1:02$\frac{1}{5}$, August 12, 1977; World Pleasure, 1:02$\frac{1}{5}$, August 24, 1977; Brainstorming, 1:02$\frac{1}{5}$, August 28, 1991; Captain Squire, 1:02.26, August 24, 2005
6 furlongs: King of Cricket, 1:07$\frac{3}{5}$, August 22, 1973
6$\frac{1}{2}$ furlongs: Native Paster, 1:13$\frac{3}{5}$, September 4, 1988
7 furlongs: Solar Launch, 1:20, August 10, 1990; Lit de Justice, 1:20, August 19, 1995
1 mile: Precisionist, 1:33$\frac{1}{5}$, August 1, 1988
1$\frac{1}{16}$ miles: Windy Sands, 1:40, August 4, 1962; Native Diver, 1:40, August 7, 1965; Matching, 1:40, August 18, 1982
1$\frac{1}{8}$ miles: Latin Touch, 1:46, September 1, 1979
1$\frac{3}{16}$ miles: Four By Five, 1:56$\frac{2}{5}$, August 16, 1954
1$\frac{1}{4}$ miles: Candy Ride (Arg), 1:59.11, August 24, 2003
1$\frac{1}{2}$ miles: Spring Boy, 2:29$\frac{2}{5}$, August 16, 1958
1$\frac{5}{8}$ miles: Ormolu, 2:45, August 24, 1957
1$\frac{3}{4}$ miles: Lurline B., 2:57$\frac{2}{5}$, August 26, 1949
2 miles: Pilot Anne, 3:24$\frac{1}{5}$, September 2, 1949
Other: a1$\frac{3}{16}$ miles, Ancient Title, 1:55$\frac{2}{5}$, September 5, 1977

Track Records, Main Turf

5 furlongs: Fast Parade, :54.75, August 16, 2006
7$\frac{1}{2}$ furlongs: Syncopate, 1:27$\frac{4}{5}$, August 24, 1981
1 mile: Three Valleys, 1:32.21, September 4, 2005
1$\frac{1}{16}$ miles: Mea Domina, 1:39.67, September 2, 2006
1$\frac{1}{8}$ miles: Aragorn (Ire), 1:44.79, July 23, 2006
1$\frac{3}{8}$ miles: Laura's Lucky Boy, 2:12.06, August 3, 2005
Other: a7$\frac{1}{2}$ furlongs, Buck Price, 1:27$\frac{2}{5}$, September 8, 1975

Fastest Times of 2007 (All Weather)

5$\frac{1}{2}$ furlongs: Spring Awakening, 2, 1:04.76, July 23, 2007
6 furlongs: In Summation, 4, 1:11.06, July 29, 2007
6$\frac{1}{2}$ furlongs: Look Deep, 3, 1:17.65, August 25, 2007
7 furlongs: Big Bad Leroybrown, 3, 1:23.53, August 10, 2007
1 mile: Latin Rhythms, 3, 1:39.14, August 31, 2007
1$\frac{1}{16}$ miles: Sun Boat (GB), 5, 1:45.39, July 21, 2007
1$\frac{1}{8}$ miles: T. H. Praise, 4, 1:54.86, August 25, 2007
1$\frac{1}{4}$ miles: Student Council, 5, 2:07.29, August 19, 2007

Fastest Times of 2007 (Turf)

5 furlongs: Leonetti, 5, :54.95, August 8, 2007
1 mile: Crossing The Line (NZ), 5, 1:32.59, August 19, 2007
1$\frac{1}{16}$ miles: Bold Chieftain, 4, 1:39.98, August 3, 2007
1$\frac{1}{8}$ miles: Precious Kitten, 4, 1:46.34, August 4, 2007
1$\frac{3}{8}$ miles: After Market, 4, 2:13.01, August 26, 2007

Fairplex Park

For more than 80 years, the Los Angeles County Fair Association has offered racing at Fairplex Park. In recent decades, the fair meeting has given the major Southern California circuit a welcome break between the Del Mar and Oak Tree at Santa Anita meets in September. The inaugural Los Angeles County Fair was conducted in 1922, a five-day meet over a half-mile track. By the mid-1930s, after pari-mutuel wagering had been legalized in California, the fair was extended to a 17-day meeting. With minor changes over the years, the meet has remained essentially the same. The Barretts Ltd. sales pavilion is located adjacent to the track.

Location: 1101 W. McKinley Ave., P.O. Box 2250, Pomona, Ca. 91768-1639
Phone: (909) 865-4630
Fax: (909) 865-3602
Website: *www.fairplex.com*
E-Mail: info@fairplex.com
Year Founded: 1922
Abbreviation: Fpx
Acreage: 543
Number of Stalls: 1,500
Seating Capacity: 10,000

Officers

Chairman: Richard P. Crean
President and Chief Executive Officer: James E. Henwood
Director of Racing: Paul Ryneveld
Racing Secretary: Richard Wheeler
Director of Mutuels: William D. Navarro
Vice President and Chief Financial Officer: Michael Seder

Communications and Public Relations Manager: Wendy Talarico
Stewards: Paul Nicolo, Kim Sawyer, Thomas Ward
Track Announcer: Trevor Denman
Track Photographer: Benoit & Asssociates
Track Superintendent: Steve Wood
Assistant Racing Secretary: Zachary Soto
Clerk of the Course: Lisa Jones

Racing Dates
2007: September 7-September 24, 16 days
2008: September 5-September 22, 16 days

Track Layout
Main Circumference: 5 furlongs
Main Track Chute: 4 furlongs and 1 1/8 miles
Main Width: 75 feet
Main Length of Stretch: 660 feet

Attendance
Average Daily Recent Meeting: 5,632, 2007
Highest Single-Day Record: 28,300, September 25, 1948
Highest Single-Meeting Record: 337,491, 1998
Record Daily Average Single Meeting: 18,750, 1998
Total Attendance Recent Meeting: 90,114, 2007
Highest Single-Day Recent Meeting: 18,333, September 15, 2007

Handle
Average All-Sources Recent Meeting: $4,674,072, 2007
Average On-Track Recent Meeting: $548,246, 2007
Single-Day On-Track Handle: $4,112,091, September 27, 1987
Single-Day All-Sources Handle: $10,390,081, September 20, 2006
Total All-Sources Recent Meeting: $74,785,157, 2007
Total On-Track Recent Meeting: $8,771,936, 2007

Mutuel Records
Highest Win: $182.20, Uncle Fox, September 21, 1976
Highest Exacta: $5,645, September 13, 1986
Highest Trifecta: $29,278.80, September 30, 1996
Highest Daily Double: $7,740.00 (Bar JF Geneo to What a Performance, 5-3, September 10, 2006)
Highest Pick Six: $416,435.20 (1 ticket, 1-3-8-9-6-5, September 29, 2002, 11th race)
Highest Other Exotics: $80.20, Place, September 12, 1999; $51.40, September 18, 1933; $53,130, Superfecta, September 18, 2004; $155,602.50, Daily Triple, October 1, 1993

Leaders
Career, Leading Jockey by Stakes Wins: David Flores, 58
Career, Leading Trainer by Stakes Wins: Mel Stute, 44
Career, Leading Jockey by Wins: Martin A. Pedroza, 519
Career, Leading Trainer by Wins: Melvin F. Stute, 186
Recent Meeting, Leading Jockey: Martin Pedroza, 35, 2007
Recent Meeting, Leading Trainer: Doug O'Neill, 12, 2007
Recent Meeting, Leading Owner: Dave Wood, 6, 2007
Recent Meeting, Leading Horse: Threeatonce, 2, 2007

Records
Single-Day Jockey Wins: David Flores, 6, September 20, 1992; David Flores, 6, September 30, 1992
Single-Day Trainer Wins: Gordon Campbell, 4, September 30, 1967; Jerry Fanning, 4, September 24, 1984
Single Meeting, Leading Jockey by Wins: Martin Pedroza, 51, 2004
Single Meeting, Leading Trainer by Wins: Jeff Mullins, 17, 2006

Principal Races
Barretts Juvenile, Barretts Debutante, Ralph M. Hinds Pomona Invitational H., Las Madrinas H., Pomona Derby

Track Records, Main Dirt
4 furlongs: Nashua's Asset, :45.55, September 15, 2002
6 furlongs: Ultimate Summer, 1:08.62, September 26, 2005
6 1/2 furlongs: Jungle Prince, 1:15.18, September 25, 2005
7 furlongs: Irish Honor, 1:22.25, September 25, 2005
1 1/16 miles: Monte Parnes (Arg), 1:41 3/5, September 29, 1990
1 3/8 miles: Mummy's Pleasure, 2:15, September 28, 1986
Other: a1 1/8 miles, Dachi's Folly, 1:48 2/5, September 29, 1990

Fastest Times of 2007 (Dirt)
a4 furlongs: My Master (Arg), 8, :45.56, September 16, 2007
6 furlongs: Ten Downing Street (Ire), 4, 1:11.04, September 9, 2007
6 1/2 furlongs: Monterey Jazz, 3, 1:16.63, September 21, 2007
7 furlongs: Slew Man Slew, 3, 1:24.45, September 19, 2007
1 1/16 miles: My Man Murf, 3, 1:44.34, September 7, 2007
a1 1/8 miles: Plug Me In, 4, 1:51.31, September 23, 2007
1 3/8 miles: Zappa, 5, 2:19.04, September 23, 2007

Ferndale

Location: 1250 Fifth St., P.O. Box 637, Ferndale, Ca. 95536-9712
Phone: (707) 786-9511
Fax: (707) 786-9450
Website: www.humboldtcountyfair.org
E-Mail: humcofair@frontiernet.net
Year Founded: 1896
Abbreviation: Fer
Number of Stalls: 258 permanent, 200 portable
Seating Capacity: 1,800

Ownership
County of Humboldt

Officers
President: Irv Parlato
General Manager and Director of Racing: Stuart Titus
Racing Secretary: Ella Robinson
Director of Mutuels: Dominick DePrenzio
Vice President: Bill Branstetter
Track Announcer: Frank Mirahmadi
Assistant Racing Secretary: Lisa Jones

Racing Dates
2007: August 9-August 19, 10 days
2008: August 7-August 17, 10 days

Track Layout
Main Circumference: 4 furlongs
Main Track Chute: 5 furlongs and 7 furlongs
Main Length of Stretch: 530 feet

Attendance
Average Daily Recent Meeting: 2,296, 2007
Total Attendance Recent Meeting: 22,968, 2007

Handle
Average On-Track Recent Meeting: $78,550, 2007
Average All-Sources Recent Meeting: $266,187, 2007
Total All-Sources Recent Meeting: $2,661,877, 2007
Total On-Track Recent Meeting: $785,505, 2007

Leaders
Recent Meeting, Leading Jockey: Otto Arriaga, 13, 2007
Recent Meeting, Leading Trainer: Karen Haverty, 8, 2007

Principal Races
Les Mademoiselle S.

Fastest Times of 2007 (Dirt)
5 furlongs: Miss Feather River, 8, :58.39, August 15, 2007
6 1/2 furlongs: Riverruns Thruit, 6, 1:18.93, August 11, 2007
7 furlongs: Louisiana Lawyer, 5, 1:23.98, August 19, 2007
1 1/16 miles: Wisenheimer, 7, 1:46.27, August 19, 2007
1 5/8 miles: Raise A Tune (Ire), 5, 2:47.15, August 19, 2007

Fresno

Location: 1121 S. Chance Ave., Fresno, Ca. 93702-3707
Phone: (559) 650-3247
Fax: (559) 650-3226
Website: www.fresnofair.com
E-Mail: dwhite@fresnofair.com
Year Founded: 1883
Dates of Inaugural Meeting: September 1935

Abbreviation: Fno
Number of Stalls: 634 permanent, 200 portable
Seating Capacity: 8,000

Ownership
State of California

Officers
Chief Executive Officer: John C. Alkire
Chairman: Ardie Der Manouel
President: Debbie Jacobsen
General Manager: John Alkire
Director of Racing: Dan White
Racing Secretary: Tom Doutrich
Director of Operations: Larry Swartzlander
Director of Marketing and Publicity: Debbie Nalchajian-Cohen
Director of Mutuels: Richard Horner
Director of Simulcasting: Kay Webb
Track Announcer: Frank Mirahmadi
Track Photographer: Photos by Frank
Track Superintendent: Chuck George
Assistant Racing Secretary: Ella Robinson
Clerk of the Course: Dawn Schmid

Racing Dates
2007: October 3-October 14, 11 days
2008: October 1-October 13, 11 days

Track Layout
Main Circumference: 1 mile
Main Track Chute: 2 furlongs and 6 furlongs
Main Length of Stretch: 979 feet

Attendance
Average Daily Recent Meeting: 7,863, 2007
Total Attendance Recent Meeting: 86,498, 2007

Handle
Average All-Sources Recent Meeting: $754,427, 2007
Average On-Track Recent Meeting: $288,110, 2007
Total All-Sources Recent Meeting: $8,298,703, 2007
Total On-Track Recent Meeting: $3,169,220, 2007

Leaders
Recent Meeting, Leading Jockey: Ricky Frazier, 20, 2007
Recent Meeting, Leading Trainer: John F. Martin, 15, 2007
Recent Meeting, Leading Horse: R Lucky Affair, 2, 2007; Sunny Wager, 2, 2007; FJ's Appeal, 2, 2007; Southside Johnny B, 2, 2007, Kings Whisper, 2, 2007

Principal Races
Bulldog S., Harvest Futurity

Track Records, Main Dirt
4 furlongs: Nellie's Girl, :44^{4}/$_{5}$, October 7, 1978; King Stephen, :44^{4}/$_{5}$, October 7, 1978
4½ furlongs: Janus Escrow Alina, :51.64, October 14, 2006
5 furlongs: Big Volume, :55^{2}/$_{5}$, November 15, 1977
5½ furlongs: Knight in Savannah, 1:01^{3}/$_{5}$, November 13, 1990
6 furlongs: Vicarino, 1:07.34, October 13, 2006
1 mile: The Ayes Have It, 1:33^{4}/$_{5}$, November 11, 1986
1^{1}/$_{16}$ miles: Dimaggio, 1:39^{1}/$_{5}$, October 16, 1976
1^{1}/$_{8}$ miles: Minutes Away, 1:46^{2}/$_{5}$, November 20, 1985
1¼ miles: Capt. Quicksilver, 1:59^{4}/$_{5}$, October 18, 1992
1½ miles: El Maduro, 2:30^{2}/$_{5}$, September 17, 1980
2 miles: Nina's Flag, 3:29^{2}/$_{5}$, October 9, 1954
Other: a6 furlongs, Tia Ping, 1:10^{1}/$_{5}$, October 11, 1963; 1^{1}/$_{16}$ miles, Bull Patch, 2:56, October 5, 1954

Fastest Times of 2007 (Dirt)
5 furlongs: Whiskey Lullaby, 3, :57.42, October 3, 2007
5½ furlongs: R Lucky Affair, 5, 1:03.37, October 5, 2007
6 furlongs: Rae's Totts, 7, 1:09, October 6, 2007
1 mile: Pass the Heat, 4, 1:35.72, October 14, 2007

Golden Gate Fields

On April 29, 1949, a 19-year-old apprentice jockey from Texas named Bill Shoemaker rode Shafter V. to victory in the second race at Golden Gate Fields in Albany, California. That win marked the first of a then-record 8,833 career victories for Shoemaker, a Racing Hall of Fame jockey. Several famous horses also have raced at the San Francisco-area track. Citation, the 1948 Triple Crown winner, defeated champion handicap horse *Noor in the '50 Golden Gate Mile Handicap, setting a world record for one mile in the process. Silky Sullivan captured his first stakes victory in the 1957 Golden Gate Futurity and went on to win 12 of 27 career starts and earned more than $150,000. In February 1941, entrepreneur Edward "Slip" Madigan opened the track, then known as the Albany Turf Club. The track closed after its first five days of racing due to flooding from heavy rains. During World War II, the United States Navy used Golden Gate as a landing base for amphibious craft. Racing resumed in 1947 after the water problem was solved, and in '71 the track added a turf course. In 1989, Ladbroke Group purchased Golden Gate for $41-million. As it wound down its North American racing operations, Ladbroke sold the facility to Magna Entertainment Corp. in 1999.

Location: 1100 Eastshore Hwy., Albany, Ca. 94710
Phone: (510) 559-7300
Fax: (510) 559-7467
Website: www.goldengatefields.com
E-Mail: questions@goldengatefields.com
Year Founded: 1941
Dates of Inaugural Meeting: February 1, 1941, 5 Days
Abbreviation: GG
Acreage: 225
Number of Stalls: 1,420
Seating Capacity: 14,750

Ownership
Magna Entertainment Corp.

Officers
Chairman: Frank Stronach
Director of Racing and Racing Secretary: Sean Greely
Secretary: William G. Ford
Treasurer: Blake S. Tohana
Director of Mutuels: Bryan Wayte
Vice President: Calvin Rainey
Director of Publicity: Tom Ferrall
Director of Sales, Promotions, and Events: Jerry Aldoroty
Director of Simulcasting: Aaron Vercruysse
Stewards: Dennis Nevin, John Herbuveaux, Darrel McHargue
Track Announcer: Michael Wrona
Track Photographer: William Vassar
Track Superintendent: Juan Meza
Security: T. W. Johnson

Racing Dates
2007: December 26, 2006-February 11, 2007, 31 days; April 25-June 10, 35 days; November 7-February 3, 2008, 62 days
2008: May 14-June 22, 30 days; September 17-December 21, 67 days

Track Layout
Main Circumference: 1 mile
Main Width: Homestretch: 78 feet; Backstretch: 75 feet
Main Length of Stretch: 1,000 feet
Main Turf Circumference: nine-tenths of a mile
Main Turf Chute: three-sixteenths of a mile
Main Turf Width: 65 feet

Attendance
Average Daily Recent Meeting: 6,331, 2006/2007; 7,049, Spring 2007
Highest Single-Day Record: 34,967, May 5, 1990
Total Attendance Recent Meeting: 196,258, 2006/2007; 246,717, Spring 2007

Handle
Average All-Sources Recent Meeting: $4,362,030, 2006/2007; $4,572,028, Spring 2007
Average On-Track Recent Meeting: $606,892, 2006/2007; $630,280, Spring 2007
Single-Day All-Sources Handle: $6,638,222, January 31, 2004
Total All-Sources Recent Meeting: $135,222,922, 2006/2007; $160,020,990, Spring 2007
Total On-Track Recent Meeting: $18,813,662, 2006/2007; $22,059,817, Spring 2007

Mutuel Records
Highest Win: $322.60, Pasadena Slim, October 28, 1957
Highest Exacta: $2,270.20, January 18, 1997
Highest Trifecta: $38,689.20, January 18, 1997
Highest Daily Double: $8,711.40, November 16, 1960
Highest Pick Three: $18,851, December 13, 1998
Highest Pick Six: $1,074,405.80, May 23, 1990
Highest Other Exotics: $63,954, Superfecta, March 2, 2002

Leaders
Career, Leading Jockey by Titles: Russell Baze, 32
Career, Leading Trainer by Titles: Jerry Hollendorfer, 32
Recent Meeting, Leading Jockey: Russell A. Baze, 108, 2007/2008
Recent Meeting, Leading Trainer: Jerry Hollendorfer, 50, 2007/2008

Records
Single-Day Jockey Wins: Russell Baze, 7, April 16, 1992
Single-Day Trainer Wins: Walter Greenman, 5, November 25, 1970; Ace Gibson, 5, February 24, 1971; Jerry Hollendorfer, 5, May 1, 1996; Jerry Hollendorfer, 5, January 23, 1997
Single Meeting, Leading Jockey by Wins: Russell Baze, 178, 1992
Single Meeting, Leading Trainer by Wins: Jerry Hollendorfer, 89, 1990

Principal Races
San Francisco Breeders' Cup Mile S. (G2), All American H. (G3), Golden Gate Fields H. (G3), Yerba Buena Breeders' Cup H. (G3)

Notable Events
Crab and wine festival for charity, Beer Fest for charity

Track Records, Main Dirt
4 furlongs: Carbella, :45.01, April 28, 2007
4½ furlongs: Victory Found, :50.30, April 30, 1992
5 furlongs: Thoughtuknew, :55.43, September 17, 2006
5½ furlongs: Proudest Hour, 1:02, May 30, 1986
6 furlongs: Lost in the Fog, 1:07.32, May 14, 2005
1 mile: Caros Love, 1:33, February 13, 1988
1 1/16 miles: Restless Con, 1:39.50, June 24, 1991
1 1/8 miles: Simply Majestic, 1:45, April 2, 1988
1 3/16 miles: Fleet Bird, 1:52 1/5, October 24, 1953
1 1/4 miles: *Noor, 1:58 1/5, June 24, 1950
1 3/8 miles: Forin Sea, 2:18 1/5, October 3, 1959
1 1/2 miles: Bo Donna, 2:29 1/5, June 8, 1979
1 3/4 miles: Sirmark, 2:57 1/5, October 16, 1948
2 miles: Mantourist, 3:25 1/5, October 23, 1948
Other: 2 furlongs, The Money Doctor, :21 4/5, February 21, 1975

Track Records, Main Turf
4½ furlongs: Bonne Nuite, :50.58, May 22, 1994
5 furlongs: Vaca City Flyer, :55.25, April 23, 2006
7½ furlongs: Struttin' George, 1:28, May 5, 1979; His Honor, 1:28, April 25, 1981; Clever Song, 1:28, May 25, 1986
1 mile: Don Alberto, 1:33 2/5, March 22, 1980
1 1/16 miles: Announcer, 1:40 2/5, April 16, 1977
1 1/8 miles: Blues Traveller (Ire), 1:47.71, May 14, 1994
1 3/8 miles: John Henry, 2:13, May 6, 1984
1 1/2 miles: Silveyville, 2:27 3/5, June 10, 1984; Kings Island (Ire), 2:27 2/5, June 9, 1985; Val Danseur, 2:27 1/5, June 8, 1986
2 miles: Never-Rust, 3:25 3/5, June 26, 1988
Other: 1 7/8 miles, Paired and Painted, 3:12 1/5, June 28, 1987; 2 3/8 miles, Situada (Chi), 4:10 4/5, June 25, 1990

Fastest Times of 2007 (All Weather)
5 furlongs: Hot Flame, 3, :56.68, November 22, 2007
5½ furlongs: Richest Wager, 2, 1:03.23, December 28, 2007
6 furlongs: Tribesman, 3, 1:08.32, November 23, 2007
1 mile: Cowboy Cruisser, 5, 1:36.20, December 22, 2007
1 1/16 miles: Now Victory, 6, 1:42.15, December 26, 2007
1 1/8 miles: McCann's Mojave, 7, 1:50.04, November 17, 2007

Fastest Times of 2007 (Dirt)
4 furlongs: Carbella, 2, :45.01, April 28, 2007
4½ furlongs: Sierra Sunset, 2, :51.43, May 31, 2007
5 furlongs: Quick Song, 4, :56.46, May 20, 2007
5½ furlongs: Mystic Wood, 3, 1:03, January 19, 2007
6 furlongs: Smokey Stover, 4, 1:08.11, January 7, 2007
1 mile: Bobby Dazzler, 7, 1:35.86, April 27, 2007; Sidepocket Cat, 3, 1:35.86, November 23, 2007
1 1/16 miles: Bai and Bai, 4, 1:42.71, January 6, 2007
1 1/8 miles: Irish Opinion, 10, 1:51.21, January 4, 2007

Fastest Times of 2007 (Turf)
5 furlongs: Monterey Jazz, 3, :56.48, June 9, 2007
1 mile: Now Victory, 6, 1:35.25, November 28, 2007
1 1/16 miles: Exclamation, 6, 1:43.11, May 16, 2007
1 3/8 miles: Fantastic Spain, 7, 2:17.64, May 28, 2007

Hollywood Park

Hollywood Park sprung to life in 1938 when the Hollywood Turf Club was formed with Warner Brothers executive Jack L. Warner as its chairman. Several Hollywood power brokers, including actors (Ralph Bellamy), singers (Bing Crosby), and studio executives (Walt Disney, Darryl Zanuck), were among the original shareholders. Not everything has had a Hollywood ending at the track, however. A fire in 1949 destroyed the club's physical plant and forced racing over to Santa Anita Park for one year. The track reopened in time for a typical Hollywood finish when Citation won the 1951 Hollywood Gold Cup and became racing's first equine millionaire in the process. Hollywood again was the backdrop of history 28 years later when Affirmed won the Hollywood Gold Cup (G1) to break racing's $2-million barrier. In 1983, John Henry became the first $4-million earner when he won the Hollywood Turf Cup (G1). The first Breeders' Cup championship day was staged at Hollywood in 1984. The event returned in 1987 and again in '97. Hollywood has not been immune from controversy. An expensive rebuilding of the track—including an extension of the track to 1 1/8 miles and construction of a new clubhouse structure, the Pavilion of the Stars—preceded the first Breeders' Cup, and fans resented the move of the finish line toward the new facility. A bitter fight for control of the track raged in the late 1980s and early '90s, and the struggle was resolved in February '91 when R. D. Hubbard wrested control from longtime executive Marjorie Lindheimer Everett in a proxy fight. Hubbard immediately launched a multimillion-dollar renovation program that spruced up the track and transformed the clubhouse pavilion into a card-club casino. As a part of that project, the finish line was returned to its original location. In 1999, Churchill Downs Inc. bought Hollywood Park (excluding the card club) for $140-million. On December 10, 1999, Laffit Pincay Jr. became the winningest rider in racing history with a triumph at Hollywood, surpassing the record of 8,833 wins of Bill Shoemaker. Churchill sold Hollywood to the Bay Meadows Land Co. for $257.5-million in 2005, and a Cushion Track synthetic surface was installed in '06.

Location: 1050 South Prairie Ave., P.O. Box 369, Inglewood, Ca. 90306-0369
Phone: (310) 419-1500

Racetracks — California

Fax: (310) 672-4664
Website: www.hollywoodpark.com
E-Mail: customerservice@hollywoodpark.com
Year Founded: 1938
Dates of Inaugural Meeting: June 10, 1938
Abbreviation: Hol
Acreage: 240
Number of Stalls: 1,958
Seating Capacity: 35,000

Ownership
Bay Meadows Land Co.

Officers
President: F. Jack Liebau
General Manager: Eual G. Wyatt Jr.
Director of Racing and Racing Secretary: Martin Panza
Vice Presidents: Eual G. Wyatt Jr., Michael Ziegler, Martin Panza
Director of Publicity: Michael P. Mooney
Horsemen's Liaison: Diana Hudak
Track Announcer: Vic Stauffer
Track Photographer: Benoit & Associates
Horsemen's Bookkeeper: Susan Winter

Racing Dates
2007: April 25-July 15, 59 days; November 7-December 16, 31 days
2008: April 23-July 13, 60 days; October 29-December 21, 40 days

Track Layout
Main Circumference: 1 1/8 miles
Main Track Chute: 7 1/2 furlongs
Main Width: Homestretch: 92 feet; Backstretch: 82 feet
Main Length of Stretch: 990 feet
Main Turf Circumference: 1 mile and 165 feet
Main Turf Width: 64 feet
Main Turf Length of Stretch: 990 feet
Training Track: 4 furlongs

Attendance
Average Daily Recent Meeting: 6,443, Spring-Summer 2007; 4,944, Fall 2007
Highest Single-Day Record: 80,348, May 4, 1980
Highest Single-Meeting Record: 2,398,528, Spring-Summer 1980
Record Daily Average Single Meeting: 34,516, 1965
Total On-Track Attendance Recent Meeting: 405,922, Spring-Summer 2007; 158,218, Fall 2007

Handle
Average All-Sources Recent Meeting: $11,966,243, Spring-Summer 2007; $10,960,416, Fall 2007
Average On-Track Recent Meeting: $1,697,597, Spring-Summer 2007; $1,348,663, Fall 2007
Record Daily Average Single Meeting: $11,966,243, 2007
Single-Day All-Sources Handle: $67,096,242, November 8, 1997
Total All-Sources Recent Meeting: $755,763,334, Spring-Summer 2007; $350,733,340, Fall 2007
Total On-Track Recent Meeting: $106,948,664, Spring-Summer 2007; $43,157,247, Fall 2007
Largest Single-Day All-Sources Recent Meeting: $29,298,014, Spring-Summer, May 5, 2007; $18,510,491, Fall, December 22, 2007
Largest Single-Day On-Track Recent Meeting: $4,991,298, May 5, 2007; $2,509,860, December 22, 2007

Mutuel Records
Highest Win: $361.80, Family Flair, June 29, 1989
Highest Exacta: $6,989.40, May 11, 1991
Highest Trifecta: $35,563.10, May 1, 2007
Highest Daily Double: $6,141.60, July 10, 1962
Highest Pick Three: $137,200.20, December 17, 1993
Highest Pick Six: $1,540,401.60, June 2, 2006
Highest Other Exotics: $148, Place, June 5, 1956; $87.20, Show, May 13, 1989; $215,845.40, Superfecta, April 28, 2006; $54,276.80, Place Pick All, July 4, 2001
Highest Pick Four: $355,727.10, April 27, 2007
Highest Stakes Win: $180.60, Perizade, July 1, 1961
Highest Quinella: $2,014, May 5, 2007

Leaders
Career, Leading Jockey by Titles: William Shoemaker, 18
Career, Leading Owner by Titles: Juddmonte Farms, 10
Career, Leading Trainer by Titles: Robert Frankel, 13
Career, Leading Jockey by Stakes Wins: Laffit A. Pincay Jr., 288
Career, Leading Trainer by Stakes Wins: Charles Whittingham, 222
Career, Leading Jockey by Wins: Laffit A. Pincay Jr., 3,049
Career, Leading Trainer by Wins: Robert Frankel, 936
Career, Leading Horse by Stakes Wins: Native Diver, 10
Recent Meeting, Leading Jockey: Michael Baze, 73, Spring-Summer 2007; Garrett K. Gomez, 35, Fall 2007
Recent Meeting, Leading Owner: Jay Em Ess Stable, Robert D. Bone, 10, Spring-Summer 2007; Gary and Cecil Barber, 8, Fall 2007
Recent Meeting, Leading Trainer: Jeff Mullins, Doug O'Neill 26, Spring-Summer 2007; John Sadler, 21, Fall 2007

Records
Single-Day Jockey Wins: William Shoemaker, 6, June 20, 1953; Laffit A. Pincay Jr., 6, April 27, 1968; William Shoemaker, 6, June 24, 1970; Kent J. Desormeaux, 6, July 3, 1992
Single-Day Owner Wins: Robert D. Bone, 4, November 16, 2005
Single-Day Trainer Wins: Allen Drumheller Sr., 5, July 4, 1955
Single Meeting, Leading Jockey by Wins: Laffit A. Pincay Jr., 148, 1974
Single Meeting, Leading Owner by Wins: Marion R. Frankel, 55, 1972
Single Meeting, Leading Trainer by Wins: Robert Frankel, 60, 1972
Single Meeting, Leading Trainer by Stakes Wins: Charles Whittingham, 14, 1971
Single Meeting, Leading Jockey by Stakes Wins: William Shoemaker, 18, 1971
Single Meeting, Leading Horse by Stakes Wins: Honeymoon, 5, 1946; A Gleam, 5, 1952; Swaps, 5, 1956; Round Table, 5, 1957; Hillsdale, 5, 1959; Turkish Trousers, 5, 1971
Single Meeting, Leading Horse by Wins: Flying Jean, 6, 1940; Kay Diane, 6, 1941; Security Check, 6, 1968

Principal Races
Fall: Hollywood Derby (G1), Matriarch S. (G1), Citation H. (G1), Hollywood Turf Cup H. (G1), CashCall Futurity (G1), Hollywood Starlet S. (G1)
Spring-Summer: Hollywood Gold Cup H. (G1), American Oaks Invitational (G1), CashCall Mile (G2), Shoemaker Mile S. (G1), Charles Whittingham Memorial H. (G1), Gamely Breeders' Cup H. (G1), Triple Bend Invitational H. (G1), Vanity Invitational H. (G1)

Notable Events
Gold Rush in April, Turf Festival on Thanksgiving weekend

Track Records, Main All Weather
5 furlongs: Bye Sweetie, :57.91, June 29, 2007
5 1/2 furlongs: Gray Black N White, 1:02.09, December 5, 2007
6 furlongs: Sailors Sunset, 1:07.79, December 2, 2006
6 1/2 furlongs: Banner Lodge, 1:13.79, December 16, 2007
7 furlongs: Soul City Slew, 1:20.50, December 8, 2007
7 1/2 furlongs: Greg's Gold, 1:26.78, December 22, 2007
1 1/16 miles: Country Star, 1:40.54, December 15, 2007
1 1/8 miles: Heatseeker (Ire), 1:47.23, December 8, 2007

Track Records, Main Turf
5 furlongs: Simply Because, :55.61, July 3, 2006
5 1/2 furlongs: Scottsbluff, 1:00.26, May 15, 2006
6 furlongs: Answer Do, 1:07.65, December 15, 1990
1 mile: Megan's Interco, 1:32.64, May 22, 1994
1 1/16 miles: Leroidesanimaux (Brz), 1:38.45, May 1, 2004
1 1/8 miles: Lava Man, 1:44.26, April 30, 2006
1 3/16 miles: Kudos, 1:51.99, April 25, 2001
1 1/4 miles: Bien Bien, 1:57.75, May 31, 1993
1 1/2 miles: Talloires, 2:23.55, July 21, 1996
Other: a 1 1/8 miles, Zoffany, 1:44 4/5, November 16, 1985; a 1 3/4 miles, Big Warning, 2:50 3/5, December 22, 1990

Fastest Times of 2007 (All Weather)
4 1/2 furlongs: Nook and Granny, 2, :51.61, May 17, 2007
5 furlongs: Bye Sweetie, 4, :57.91, June 29, 2007

5½ furlongs: Gray Black N White, 6, 1:02.09, December 5, 2007
6 furlongs: High Standards, 5, 1:08.12, December 21, 2007
6½ furlongs: Banner Lodge, 3, 1:13.79, December 16, 2007
7 furlongs: Soul City Slew, 4, 1:20.50, December 8, 2007
7½ furlongs: Greg's Gold, 6, 1:26.78, December 22, 2007
1¹/₁₆ miles: Country Star, 2, 1:40.54, December 15, 2007
1⅛ miles: Heatseeker (Ire), 4, 1:47.23, December 8, 2007
1¼ miles: Rocket Legs, 3, 2:01.79, December 7, 2007

Fastest Times of 2007 (Turf)
6 furlongs: Scottsbluff, 5, 1:07.54, July 15, 2007
1 mile: Monterey Jazz, 3, 1:32.86, November 10, 2007
1¹/₁₆ miles: Wild Promises, 3, 1:39.58, November 8, 2007
1⅛ miles: Citronnade, 4, 1:45.73, May 28, 2007
1¼ miles: After Market, 4, 1:58.77, June 9, 2007
1½ miles: Running Free, 6, 2:25.53, May 25, 2007
1¾ miles: Stormin Away, 5, 2:54.75, June 16, 2007

Los Alamitos Race Course

Thoroughbreds have competed at Los Alamitos Race Course in Cypress, California, since 1994, when the track received permission to begin offering races for the breed. Los Alamitos primarily had been known as a Quarter Horse track since 1947, when non-pari-mutuel racing debuted at the track built by Frank Vessels on his ranch. In 1951, Los Alamitos received approval to begin holding pari-mutuel racing. After Vessels's death in 1963, his son Frank Vessels Jr. took over operation of the track, which five years later began offering night racing. After Vessels Jr.'s death in 1974, his wife, Millie, assumed the track's presidency and became one of the first women to hold a leadership position in Thoroughbred racing. In 1984, Los Alamitos was sold to Hollywood Park and entered a period of decline. Five years later, businessmen and harness-racing enthusiasts Lloyd Arnold and Chris Bardis bought the facility. Edward C. Allred, a physician and the all-time leading breeder of Quarter Horses by earnings, then purchased a majority interest in Los Alamitos and today is sole owner of the track, which also offers Paint, Appaloosa, and Arabian racing.

Location: 4961 Katella Ave., Los Alamitos, Ca. 90720-2721
Phone: (714) 820-2800
Fax: (714) 820-2689
Website: www.losalamitos.com
E-Mail: larace@losalamitos.com
Year Founded: 1946
Dates of Inaugural Meeting: December 4, 1951
Abbreviation: LA
Number of Stalls: 1,400
Seating Capacity: 10,000

Ownership
Edward C. Allred

Officers
Chief Executive Officer, Chairman, and President: Edward C. Allred
General Manager: Edward C. Allred
Director of Racing and Racing Secretary: Ronald Church
Secretary: G. Michael Lyon
Assistant General Manager: Michael Monji
Controller: Bob Snyder
Director of Operations: Howard Knuchell
Director of Finance: Robert M. Passero
Director of Marketing and Publicity: Orlando Gutierrez
Director of Mutuels: Robert DiGiovanni
Vice President: John T. Seibly
Director of Simulcasting: Melodie Knuchell
Horsemen's Liaison: Charla Dreyer

Stewards: Albert Christiansen, Martin Hamilton, Randy Winick
Track Announcer: Ed Burgart
Track Photographer: Scott Martinez
Track Superintendent: Rick Hughes
Assistant Racing Secretary: Edward Reese
Group Sales: Vicki Cuthbertson
Security: Rick Castaneda

Racing Dates
2007: December 28, 2006-December 16, 2007, 200 days
2008: December 28, 2007-December 21, 2008, 205 days

Track Layout
Main Circumference: 5 furlongs
Main Track Chute: 550 yards and 4½ furlongs
Main Width: Homestretch: 100 feet; Backstretch: 90 feet
Main Length of Stretch: 558 feet

Attendance
Average Daily Recent Meeting: 1,201, 2007
Highest Single-Day Record: 19,970, May 6, 1983
Highest Single-Meeting Record: 1,046,158, 1994
Record Daily Average Single Meeting: 9,492, 1970
Total Attendance Recent Meeting: 246,205, 2007

Handle
Average All-Sources Recent Meeting: $1,380,776, 2007
Average On-Track Recent Meeting: $224,587, 2007
Record Daily Average Single Meeting: $1,281,868, 2004
Single-Day All-Sources Handle: $2,379,112, November 1, 2003
Total All-Sources Recent Meeting: $278,916,838, 2007
Total On-Track Recent Meeting: $45,366,574, 2007
Record Total All-Sources Single Meeting: $278,916,838, 2007

Mutuel Records
Highest Exacta: $8,650.30, August 30, 1996
Highest Trifecta: $27,386.10, July 27, 1996
Highest Daily Double: $2,107.90, June 12, 1997
Highest Pick Three: $12,017.60, August 21, 1991
Highest Other Exotics: $21,198, Superfecta, July 12, 1997

Leaders
Career, Leading Jockey by Titles: Alex Bautista, 3
Career, Leading Trainer by Titles: Charles S. Treece, 9
Recent Meeting, Leading Jockey: Cesar De Alba, 76, 2007
Recent Meeting, Leading Trainer: Keith Craigmyle, 59, 2007
Recent Meeting, Leading Owner: David and Susan Cook, 16, 2007

Principal Races
Los Alamitos Million Futurity, Golden State Million, Ed Burke Million Futurity, Champion of Champions

Interesting Facts
Achievements/Milestones: Los Alamitos is the home of the richest horse race of any breed in California—the $1.3-million Los Alamitos Million.

Notable Events
California Breeders Champions Night, Wiener Dog Nationals

Track Records, Main Dirt
4½ furlongs: Valiant Pete, :49⅕, August 11, 1990

Fastest Times of 2007 (Dirt)
4 furlongs: Millistocks Jumpin, 5, :44.71, October 13, 2007
4½ furlongs: Excessatory, 4, :49.73, January 6, 2007

Oak Tree Racing Association at Santa Anita

In 1968, Southern California horsemen Clement Hirsch, Jack K. Robbins, and Louis R. Rowan approached Santa Anita Park President Robert P. Strub with a proposal for a brief, high-quality fall meeting at the Arcadia track. Except for the brief Fairplex Park meet, the Southern California racing calendar was empty between

the close of Del Mar in September and the opening of Santa Anita's winter-spring meet each December 26. (Hollywood Park then had only a spring-summer meet.) Strub initially resisted, but Santa Anita officials finally agreed to try a fall meet under the auspices of the Oak Tree Racing Association, headed by Hirsch, in October 1969. In case the idea flopped, Oak Tree's directors had to guarantee the first day's purses. The initial 20-day fall meet was a success, and Oak Tree has become an important part of the racing scene in Southern California and nationally. Oak Tree secured rights to stage the third Breeders' Cup championship day in 1986, and the event attracted an on-track crowd of 69,155, the largest crowd to that time. Oak Tree hosted the championship day in 1993 and 2003 and will be the site for the event in '08 and '09, marking the first time a venue has conducted the series in consecutive years. In addition, Oak Tree's stakes serve as leading prep races for the Breeders' Cup championship events. Hirsch died in 2000 and was succeeded as Oak Tree president by Robbins.

Location: 285 W. Huntington Dr., Arcadia, Ca. 91007-3439
Phone: (626) 574-6345
Fax: (626) 447-2940
Website: *www.oaktreeracing.com*
E-Mail: info@oaktreeracing.com
Year Founded: 1968
Dates of Inaugural Meeting: October 7, 1969
Abbreviation: OSA

Ownership

Oak Tree Racing Association

Officers

President: Jack K. Robbins
General Manager: George Haines II
Director of Racing: Michael J. Harlow
Racing Secretary: Rick Hammerle
Secretary: Thomas R. Capehart
Director of Operations: Richard Price
Director of Marketing: Allen Gutterman
Director of Mutuels: Randy Hartzell
Vice President: Sherwood C. Chillingworth
Director of Publicity: Michael Willman
Director of Simulcasting: Aaron Vercruysse
Horsemen's Liaison: Nancy Wallen
Stewards: John Herbuveaux, George Slender, Tom Ward
Track Announcer: Trevor Denman
Track Photographer: Benoit & Associates
Track Superintendent: Steve Wood
Security: Dick Honaker
Assistant Racing Secretary: Richard D. Wheeler
Clerk of the Course: Melanie Stubblefield

Racing Dates

2007: September 26-November 4, 31 days
2008: September 24-October 26, 26 days

Attendance

Average Daily Recent Meeting: 8,194, 2007
Total Attendance Recent Meeting: 254,018, 2007
Total Highest Single-Day Record: 69,155, November 1, 1986
Highest Single-Meeting Record: 858,652, 1985
Record Daily Average Single Meeting: 28,822, 1982

Handle

Average On Track Recent Meeting: $1,259,838, 2007
Average All-Souces Recent Meeting: $8,116,245, 2007
Total On-Track Recent Meeting: $39,048,838, 2007
Total All-Sources Recent Meeting: $251,603,606, 2007
Record Daily Average Single Meeting: $5,607,928, 1986
Single-Day On-Track Handle: $17,171,128, October 25, 2003
Single-Day All-Sources Handle: $120,788,128, October 25, 2003
Record Average All-Sources Single Meeting: $10,647,918, 2002
Record Total Single Meeting: $169,252,456, 1987
Record Total All-Sources Single Meeting: $327,591,053, 1998

Mutuel Records

Highest Win: $269.20, Arcangues, November 6, 1993
Highest Exacta: $3,022.20, September 26, 2001
Highest Trifecta: $52,892.50, September 26, 2001
Highest Daily Double: $5,000, October 13, 1990
Highest Pick Three: $174,331.80, October 18, 1991
Highest Pick Six: $1,010,221.20, October 19, 1994
Highest Other Exotics: $98.20, Place, October 12, 1990; $42.60, Show, October 4, 1985; $91,543.90, Superfecta, November 6, 2003; $57,062.50, Place Pick All, November 11, 1995
Highest Pick Four: $58,803.30, September 26, 2001
Highest Quinella: $1,949.60, September 26, 2001

Leaders

Career, Leading Jockey by Titles: Laffit Pincay Jr., 6
Career, Leading Owner by Titles: Elmendorf, 3; Juddmonte Farms, 3
Career, Leading Trainer by Titles: Robert Frankel, 6
Career, Leading Jockey by Stakes Wins: Chris McCarron, 74
Career, Leading Trainer by Stakes Wins: Charles Whittingham, 68
Career, Leading Jockey by Wins: Laffit Pincay Jr., 671
Career, Leading Trainer by Wins: Robert Frankel, 257
Recent Meeting, Leading Jockey: Tyler Baze, 29, 2007
Recent Meeting, Leading Owner: La Canada Stables, 5, 2007; Barber & Barber, 5, 2007
Recent Meeting, Leading Trainer: Jeff Mullins, 13, 2007; Doug F. O'Neill, 13, 2007

Records

Single-Day Jockey Wins: Steve Valdez, 6, October 15, 1973; Darrel McHargue, 6, October 25, 1979; Patrick Valenzuela, 6, October 21, 1988; Martin Pedroza, 6, October 31, 1992

Principal Races

Yellow Ribbon S. (G1), Clement L. Hirsch Memorial Turf Championship S. (G1), Ancient Title Breeders' Cup S. (G1), Oak Tree Breeders' Cup Mile S. (G2), Goodwood Breeders' Cup H. (G2)

Notable Events

California Cup

Track Records, Main Dirt

5 furlongs: Zero Henry, :57.78, October 23, 1996
5$\frac{1}{2}$ furlongs: Davy Be Good, 1:02.17, November 14, 1993
6 furlongs: Beira, 1:07$\frac{4}{5}$, October 13, 1974; Grenzen, 1:07$\frac{4}{5}$, October 7, 1978; Hawkin's Special, 1:07$\frac{4}{5}$, October 27, 1978; Bordonaro, 1:07.93, October 7, 2006
6$\frac{1}{2}$ furlongs: Enjoy the Moment, 1:14.15, October 8, 1998
7 furlongs: Ancient Title, 1:20$\frac{4}{5}$, October 18, 1972
1 mile: Salud y Pesetas, 1:33$\frac{4}{5}$, October 7, 1987
1$\frac{1}{16}$ miles: Cajun Prince, 1:40$\frac{1}{5}$, October 9, 1982
1$\frac{1}{8}$ miles: My Sonny Boy, 1:46, November 3, 1990
1$\frac{1}{4}$ miles: King Pellinore, 2:00, November 6, 1976
1$\frac{1}{2}$ miles: Whisk Spree, 2:29.17, October 16, 1993

Track Records, Main Turf

1 mile: Urgent Request (Ire), 1:32.44, October 5, 1996
1$\frac{1}{8}$ miles: Kostroma (Ire), 1:43.92, October 20, 1991
1$\frac{1}{4}$ miles: Double Discount, 1:57$\frac{2}{5}$, October 9, 1977
1$\frac{1}{2}$ miles: Hawkster, 2:22$\frac{4}{5}$, October 14, 1989
Other: a6$\frac{1}{2}$ furlongs, El Cielo, 1:11.46, November 3, 2001

Fastest Times of 2007 (All Weather)

5$\frac{1}{2}$ furlongs: Smokin Forest, 5, 1:02.31, October 25, 2007
6 furlongs: Switzerland, 4, 1:07.34, November 3, 2007
6$\frac{1}{2}$ furlongs: Theverythoughtof U, 4, 1:14.07, October 20, 2007
7 furlongs: Heatseeker (Ire), 4, 1:20.90, October 8, 2007
1 mile: Gregorian Bay, 3, 1:34.60, October 21, 2007
1$\frac{1}{16}$ miles: Romance Is Diane, 3, 1:40.38, November 3, 2007
1$\frac{1}{8}$ miles: Tiago, 3, 1:46.93, September 29, 2007
1$\frac{1}{4}$ miles: Add Heat, 4, 2:02.14, October 18, 2007

Fastest Times of 2007 (Turf)

a6$\frac{1}{2}$ furlongs: T'aint War Sir, 3, 1:11.56, October 19, 2007
1 mile: Unusual Suspect, 3, 1:33.89, November 3, 2007

1 1/8 miles: Daytona (Ire), 3, 1:46.40, October 13, 2007
1 1/4 miles: Nashoba's Key, 4, 1:59.73, September 29, 2007
1 1/2 miles: Spring House, 5, 2:24.13, October 28, 2007

5 furlongs: Bear Creek, 2, :56.88, June 28, 2007
5 1/2 furlongs: Ooh Yeah, 3, 1:02.44, July 8, 2007
6 furlongs: Fete, 4, 1:09.08, July 4, 2007
1 mile 70 yds: Designer Breed, 4, 1:40.10, July 6, 2007
1 1/16 miles: Bold Chieftain, 4, 1:42.63, July 8, 2007

Pleasanton

Location: 4501 Pleasanton Ave., Pleasanton, Ca. 94566
Phone: (925) 426-7600
Fax: (925) 426-7599
Website: www.alamedacountyfair.com
E-Mail: info@alamedacountyfair.com
Year Founded: 1939
Dates of Inaugural Meeting: August 10, 1939
Abbreviation: Pln
Number of Stalls: 700
Seating Capacity: 6,608

Officers
Chief Executive Officer: Rick K. Pickering
Chairmen: Ario Ysit, Tony Macchiano
President: Anthony Varni
General Manager and Director of Racing: Rick K. Pickering
Racing Secretary: Tom Doutrich
Treasurer: Randy Magee
Director of Mutuels: Bryan Wayte
Director of Operations: Jeanne Wasserman
Director of Simulcasting: Kay Webb
Track Announcer: Frank Mirahmadi
Track Photographer: Vassar Photography
Track Superintendent: Jim Burns

Racing Dates
2007: June 27-July 8, 11 days
2008: June 25-July 6, 11 days

Track Layout
Main Circumference: 1 mile
Main Track Chute: 2 furlongs and 6 furlongs
Main Width: 60 feet
Main Length of Stretch: 1,085 feet

Attendance
Average Daily Recent Meeting: 4,442, 2007
Total Attendance Recent Meeting: 48,870, 2007
Highest Single-Day Recent Meeting: 7,226, July 1, 2007

Handle
Average All-Sources Recent Meeting: $1,836,539, 2007
Average On-Track Recent Meeting: $330,446, 2007
Single-Day On-Track Handle: $908,604, July 6, 2003
Single-Day All-Sources Handle: $4,586,825, July 3, 2004
Total All-Sources Recent Meeting: $20,201,932, 2007
Total On-Track Recent Meeting: $3,634,916, 2007
Largest Single-Day All-Sources Recent Meeting: $3,143,423, July 1, 2007
Largest Single-Day On-Track Recent Meeting: $836,167, June 30, 2007

Leaders
Recent Meeting, Leading Jockey: Russell A. Baze, 15, 2007
Recent Meeting, Leading Trainer: Jerry Hollendofer, 8, 2007
Recent Meeting, Leading Horse: Kiki's Dance, 2, 2007

Principal Races
Juan Gonzalez Memorial S., Everett Nevin Alameda County Futurity, Sam J. Whiting Memorial H., Alameda County Fillies and Mares H., Alamedan H.

Track Records, Main Dirt
4 1/2 furlongs: All Pro, :50.45, July 4, 2006
5 furlongs: A. V. Flynn, :55.92, June 28, 2006
5 1/2 furlongs: Boundary Ridge, 1:02, June 29, 1993
6 furlongs: Stone Rain, 1:08.17, July 8, 2006
1 mile 70 yds: Call It, 1:38.01, July 5, 2003
1 1/16 miles: Aunt Sophie, 1:40.34, July 5, 2003

Fastest Times of 2007 (Dirt)
4 1/2 furlongs: Western Boot, 9, :51.28, July 8, 2007

Sacramento

Location: 1600 Exposition Blvd., Sacramento, Ca. 95815-5104
Phone: (916) 263-3279
Fax: (916) 263-3198
Website: www.bigfun.org
E-Mail: horseracing@calexpo.com
Year Founded: 1968
Abbreviation: Sac
Number of Stalls: 1,024
Seating Capacity: 6,000

Ownership
State of California

Officers
Chairman: Marko Mlikotin
General Manager: Norbert Bartosik
Director of Racing: David Elliott
Racing Secretary: Tom Doutrich
Director of Operations: Kate Snider
Director of Marketing/Publicity: Erica Manuel
Director of Mutuels: Bill Cain
Stewards: Grant Baker, Will Meyers, Thomas Ward
Track Announcer: Vic Stauffer
Track Photographer: Vassar Photography
Track Superintendent: Steve Wood

Racing Dates
2008: August 20-September 1, 11 days

Track Layout
Main Circumference: 1 mile
Main Track Chute: 6 furlongs and 1 1/4 miles
Main Width: 80 feet
Main Length of Stretch: 990 feet

Attendance
Highest Single-Day Record: 18,722, September 1, 1975

Handle
Single-Day All-Sources Handle: $4,223,537, August 23, 2003

Notable Events
Dachshund Derby

Interesting Facts
In 2008, Thoroughbred racing returns to Sacramento for the first time since '04. The track also offers year-round Standardbred racing.

Santa Anita Park

With the San Bernardino Mountains as a backdrop, an undulating downhill turf course, and an abundance of quality racing, Santa Anita Park symbolizes racing's possibilities. On a big race day, with a sizable crowd in the stands and quality Thoroughbreds on the track, the Arcadia track is one of the world's finest facilities. The story of Santa Anita is told in two parts. The first part is the original track, the dream of early 20th-century California entrepreneur E. J. "Lucky" Baldwin. Opened in 1907, the track gave Los Angeles racing fans a tantalizing glimpse of racing as an opulent spectacle. But Baldwin's death two years later and the lack of legal pari-mutuel wagering in California postponed the Santa Anita dream until the 1930s. When pari-mutuel wager-

ing was legalized in 1933, the Los Angeles Turf Club was organized under the leadership of Dr. Charles H. Strub, and it built a $1-million facility near the site of Baldwin's track. Opened in 1934, the track's inaugural 1934-'35 racing season featured two races that immediately had an impact on the national racing calendar, the Santa Anita Handicap and the Santa Anita Derby. Now Grade 1 races, they continue to have an important place on the spring schedule. With a $100,000 purse for its inaugural running, the Big 'Cap immediately became one of America's best-known races. The race and its $1-million purse today draw some of the best handicap runners from around North America. The Santa Anita Derby is one of the top Kentucky Derby (G1) prep races and has been utilized by recent Kentucky Derby winners Silver Charm, Real Quiet, and Charismatic. Legendary jockey Bill Shoemaker rode in his final race at Santa Anita in February 1990. The track hosts the important Oak Tree Racing Association meet each fall. Magna Entertainment Corp. purchased the track in December 1998 for $126-million.

Location: 285 W. Huntington Dr., Arcadia, Ca. 91007-3439
Phone: (626) 574-7223
Fax: (626) 574-6682
Website: www.santaanita.com
E-Mail: comments@santaanita.com
Year Founded: 1934
Dates of Inaugural Meeting: December 25, 1934
Abbreviation: SA
Acreage: 320
Number of Stalls: 2,000
Seating Capacity: 26,000

Ownership
Magna Entertainment Corp.

Officers
Chairman: Tom Hodgson
President and Chief Executive Officer: Ron Charles
General Manager: George Haines
Director of Racing: Michael J. Harlow
Racing Secretary: Rick Hammerle
Assistant Racing Secretary: Richard D. Wheeler
Secretary: Gary M. Cohn
Treasurer: Barbara Helm
Director of Operations: Richard Price
Director of Finance: Douglas R. Tatters
Director of Marketing: Stuart A. Zanville
Director of Mutuels: Randy Hartzell
Vice Presidents: Frank DeMarco Jr., Allen Gutterman, George Haines, Gina Lavo
Director of Publicity: Mike Willman
Director of Sales: Dyan Grealish
Director of Simulcasting: Aaron Vercruysse
Track Announcer: Trevor Denman
Track Photographer: Benoit & Associates
Track Superintendent: Steve Wood
Security: Dick Honaker

Racing Dates
2006: December 26, 2005-April 23, 2006, 86 days
2007: December 26, 2006-April 22, 2007, 85 days
2008: December 26, 2007-April 20, 2008, 86 days

Track Layout
Main Circumference: 1 mile
Main Track Chute: 7 furlongs and 1 1/4 miles
Main Width: Homestretch: 85 feet; Backstretch: 80 feet
Main Length of Stretch: 990 feet
Main Turf Circumference: 7 furlongs
Main Turf Chute: a 6 1/2 furlongs or a 1 3/4 miles

Attendance
Average Daily Recent Meeting: 1,921, 2005/2006
Highest Single-Day Record: 85,527, March 3, 1985
Highest Single-Meet Record: 2,936,086, 1983/1984
Record Daily Average Single Meeting: 35,247, 1946/1947
Total Attendance Recent Meeting: 165,166, 2005/2006

Handle
Average All-Sources Recent Meeting: $8,003,466, 2005/2006
Average On-Track Recent Meeting: $2,245,925, 2005/2006
Record Daily Average Single Meeting: $6,176,295, 1986/1987
Single-Day All-Sources Handle: $25,282,789, April 8, 2000
Total All-Sources Recent Meeting: $688,298,084, 2005/2006
Total On-Track Recent Meeting: $193,149,553, 2005/2006

Mutuel Records
Highest Win: $673.40, Playmay, February 4, 1938
Highest Exacta: $1,502.50, February 15, 2002
Lowest Exacta: $1.60, April 1, 2001
Highest Trifecta: $21,771.80, February 6, 1999
Lowest Trifecta: $2.90, December 29, 2004
Highest Daily Double: $4,330, January 31, 2001
Lowest Daily Double: $4.40, March 29, 1996; $4.40, April 5, 2002
Highest Pick Three: $73,527.30, February 16, 1997
Lowest Pick Three: $2, March 9, 1997
Highest Pick Six: $1,567,984.60, March 3, 2004
Lowest Pick Six: $106.20, March 16, 1986
Highest Other Exotics: $148, Place, February 4, 1938; $104.60, Show, February 4, 1938; $187,651.20, Superfecta, February 21, 1999; $47,393.10, Place Pick All, March 7, 1998
Lowest Other Exotics: $8.70, Superfecta, February 12, 2005; $23.90, Place Pick All, February 11, 2005
Highest Pick Four: $124,199.10, December 27, 2003
Lowest Pick Four: $31.10, March 4, 2001
Highest Quinella: $1,482.80, February 3, 2000
Lowest Quinella: $2.20, March 8, 2003; $2.20, April 13, 2003
Highest Stakes Win: $55.60, Debonair Joe, December 26, 2002

Principal Races
Santa Anita H. (G1), Santa Anita Derby (G1), Santa Anita Oaks (G1), Santa Margarita Invitational H. (G1), Frank E. Kilroe Mile H. (G1)

Notable Events
Sunshine Millions

Track Records, Main Dirt
4 furlongs: Valiant Pete, :44 1/5, April 20, 1991
4 1/2 furlongs: Willy Float, :51 2/5, March 23, 1972
5 furlongs: Zero Henry, :57.78, October 23, 1996
5 1/2 furlongs: Kona Gold, 1:01.74, January 3, 1999
6 furlongs: Sunny Blossom, 1:07 1/5, December 30, 1989
6 1/2 furlongs: Son of a Pistol, 1:13.71, April 4, 1998
7 furlongs: Spectacular Bid, 1:20, January 5, 1980
1 mile: Ruhlmann, 1:33 3/5, March 5, 1989
1 1/16 miles: Efervescente (Arg), 1:39.18, January 6, 1993
1 1/8 miles: Star Spangled, 1:45 3/5, March 24, 1979
1 1/4 miles: Spectacular Bid, 1:57 4/5, February 3, 1980
1 3/8 miles: Be Faithful, 2:15 1/5, February 9, 1946
1 1/2 miles: Queen's Hustler, 2:27 1/5, February 19, 1973
1 5/8 miles: Ace Admiral, 2:39 4/5, July 23, 1949
1 3/4 miles: *Noor, 2:52 2/5, March 4, 1950
2 miles: Durango, 3:26 1/5, February 2, 1935; Fuego, 3:26 1/5, June 30, 1945; Jimmy John, 3:26 1/5, April 4, 1964
Other: 2 furlongs, Sea of Pleasure, :20.78, March 29, 2007; 3 furlongs, King Rhymer, :32, February 27, 1947; 2 1/4 miles, English Harry, 3:55 3/5, February 16, 1940; 2 1/2 miles, Big Ed, 4:22, February 23, 1940; 3 miles, English Harry, 5:20 1/5, March 1, 1940

Track Records, Main Turf
1 mile: Atticus, 1:31.89, March 1, 1997
1 1/8 miles: Kostroma (Ire), 1:43.92, October 20, 1991
1 1/4 miles: Double Discount, 1:57 2/5, October 9, 1977; Bequest, 1:57.50, March 31, 1991
1 1/2 miles: Hawkster, 2:22 4/5, October 14, 1989
Other: a 6 1/2 furlongs, Lennyfromalibu, 1:11.13, January 22, 2004; a 1 1/2 miles, *Practicante, 2:26 2/5, February 21, 1972; a 1 3/4 miles, Bienamado, 2:42.96, April 14, 2001

Fastest Times of 2007 (All Weather)
5½ furlongs: Sweet August Moon, 2, 1:02.32, December 26, 2007
6 furlongs: Home of the Bold, 3, 1:08.35, December 26, 2007
6½ furlongs: Trail Mix, 6, 1:14.63, December 29, 2007
7 furlongs: Bob Black Jack, 2, 1:20.37, December 26, 2007
1 mile: Giant Gizmo, 3, 1:34.59, December 30, 2007; Whatsthescript (Ire), 3, 1:34.59, March 16, 2007
1 1/16 miles: Champagne Eyes, 2, 1:42.20, December 31, 2007

Fastest Times of 2007 (Dirt)
2 furlongs: Sea of Pleasure, 2, :20.78, March 29, 2007
5½ furlongs: Texas Voyager, 3, 1:02.64, January 13, 2007
6 furlongs: Smokey Stover, 4, 1:08.03, January 27, 2007
6½ furlongs: Bonfante, 6, 1:14.59, April 21, 2007
7 furlongs: Latent Heat, 4, 1:21.11, February 17, 2007
1 mile: Double Galore, 4, 1:35.64, March 29, 2007
1 1/16 miles: Awesome Gem, 4, 1:41.90, January 13, 2007
1 1/8 miles: Fairbanks, 4, 1:47.87, March 31, 2007
1 1/4 miles: Lava Man, 6, 2:02.11, March 3, 2007

Fastest Times of 2007 (Turf)
a6½ furlongs: Soul City Slew, 4, 1:11.22, February 16, 2007
1 mile: Kip Deville, 4, 1:33.88, March 3, 2007
1 1/8 miles: Lang Field, 4, 1:46.08, April 13, 2007
1 1/4 miles: Ring of Friendship, 7, 1:59.41, April 18, 2007
1 1/2 miles: On the Acorn (GB), 6, 2:26.30, February 8, 2007
a1 3/4 miles: On the Acorn (GB), 6, 2:48.02, April 22, 2007

Santa Rosa
Location: 1350 Bennett Valley Rd., Santa Rosa, Ca. 95402
Phone: (707) 545-4200
Fax: (707) 573-9342
Website: www.sonomacountyfair.com
E-Mail: info@sonomacountyfair.com
Year Founded: 1936
Dates of Inaugural Meeting: October 8, 1936
Abbreviation: SR
Number of Stalls: 1,022

Officers
Chairman: Steve Butler
President: Tom Nunes
Director of Racing: Jim Moore
Racing Secretary: C. Gregory Brent Jr.
Director of Mutuels: Bryan Wayte
Track Announcer: Vic Stauffer
Assistant Racing Secretary: Linda Anderson

Racing Dates
2007: July 18-August 6, 18 days
2008: July 23-August 4, 12 days

Track Layout
Main Circumference: 1 mile
Main Track Chute: 6 furlongs and 1 1/4 miles
Main Length of Stretch: 1,145.8 feet
Main Turf Circumference: 7 furlongs
Main Turf Width: 60 feet

Attendance
Average Daily Recent Meeting: 3,693, 2007
Total Attendance Recent Meeting: 66,478, 2007

Handle
Average On-Track Recent Meeting: $244,817, 2007
Average All-Sources Recent Meeting: $1,816,216, 2007
Single-Day All-Sources Handle: $4,128,001, August 2, 2003
Total On-Track Recent Meeting: $4,406,717, 2007
Total All-Sources Recent Meeting: $32,691,904, 2007

Leaders
Recent Meeting, Leading Jockey: Russell A. Baze, 30, 2007
Recent Meeting, Leading Trainer: John F. Martin, 12, 2007
Recent Meeting, Leading Horse: What's That Sound, 2, 2007; Star Meteor, 2, 2007; Mom's Trippin, 2, 2007; Tribal Trouble, 2, 2007

Principal Races
Joseph T. Grace H., Luther Burbank H., Ernest Finley H., Cavonnier Juvenile S.

Fastest Times of 2007 (Dirt)
4½ furlongs: Wage a Kiss, 3, :50.76, July 29, 2007
5 furlongs: Star Meteor, 4, :57.12, July 23, 2007
5½ furlongs: Tribal Trouble, 3, 1:02.05, August 5, 2007
6 furlongs: I'm a Soft Touch, 3, 1:08.79, July 28, 2007
1 mile: Bariloche, 5, 1:35.87, July 18, 2007
1 1/16 miles: Dino and Tony, 3, 1:46.50, July 28, 2007

Fastest Times of 2007 (Turf)
5 furlongs: Buddy's Mandate, 3, :57.29, August 3, 2007
1 mile: Motel Staff, 10, 1:37.65, August 5, 2007
1 1/16 miles: Now Victory, 6, 1:42.06, August 4, 2007

Stockton
Location: 1658 S. Airport Way, Stockton, Ca. 95206
Phone: (209) 466-5041
Fax: (209) 466-5739
Website: www.sanjoaquinfair.com
E-Mail: fun@sanjoaquinfair.com
Year Founded: 1933
Dates of Inaugural Meeting: August 1934
Abbreviation: Stk
Number of Stalls: 800
Seating Capacity: 5,660

Officers
Chief Executive Officer: Forrest J. White
President: Arthur Perry
Vice President: Dr. Thomas Streeter
Racing Secretary: Robert Moreno
Director of Racing: Forrest J. White
Director of Mutuels: Annette Snezek
Track Announcer: Frank Mirahmadi
Track Photographer: Photos by Frank

Racing Dates
2007: June 14-June 24, 9 days
2008: September 3-September 14, 9 days

Track Layout
Main Circumference: 1 mile
Main Track Chute: 6 furlongs and 1 1/4 miles
Main Width: 80 feet
Main Length of Stretch: 1,003 feet

Attendance
Average Daily Recent Meeting: 4,490, 2007
Total Attendance Recent Meeting: 40,414, 2007

Handle
Average On-Track Recent Meeting: $166,728, 2007
Average All-Sources Recent Meeting: $1,422,964, 2007
Total On-Track Recent Meeting: $1,500,552, 2007
Total All-Sources Recent Meeting: $12,806,682, 2007

Leaders
Recent Meeting, Leading Jockey: Carlos Ignacio Silva, 11, 2007
Recent Meeting, Leading Trainer: John F. Martin, 10, 2007

Track Records, Main Dirt
5 furlongs: Shining Prince, :55.80, June 26, 1994
5½ furlongs: Colonel Courtney, 1:02.03, June 16, 2005
6 furlongs: Lynn's Notebook, 1:07.80, June 25, 1995
1 mile: Flying Cuantal, 1:33.40, June 15, 1997
1 1/16 miles: Athenia Green (GB), 1:40.40, June 28, 1992
1 1/8 miles: Episodic, 1:49.20, June 27, 1993
1 1/4 miles: Ali Kato, 2:01 3/5, August 17, 1986

Fastest Times of 2007 (Dirt)
4½ furlongs: R Lucky Affair, 5, :52.42, June 23, 2007
5 furlongs: Romantic Wager, 4, :58.19, June 14, 2007

$5\frac{1}{2}$ furlongs: Double Action, 3, 1:03.16, June 24, 2007
6 furlongs: Quick Song, 4, 1:10.37, June 17, 2007
1 mile: Welfare Cadillac, 4, 1:37.65, June 21, 2007

Vallejo

Location: 900 Fairgrounds Dr., Vallejo, Ca. 94589
Phone: (707) 551-2066
Fax: (707) 554-8045
Website: *www.scfair.com*
E-Mail: pskelton@scfair.org
Year Founded: 1950
Dates of Inaugural Meeting: June 16, 1951
Abbreviation: Sol
Number of Stalls: 864
Seating Capacity: 6,500

Ownership

County of Solano

Officers

Chairman: Raymond Simonds
President: William Luiz
General Manager and Director of Racing: Joe Barkett
Racing Secretary: C. Gregory Brent Jr.
Assistant Racing Secretary: Linda Anderson
Director of Operations: Stephen Hales
Director of Mutuels: Richard Horner
Vice President: Donald Heinitz
Track Announcer: Frank Mirahmadi
Track Photographer: Photos by Frank
Track Superintendent: Trackmasters Inc.
Promotions/Events: Emanuel Lorenzana
Security: Mark Coffman

Racing Dates

2007: July 11-July 15, 5 days
2008: July 9-July 20, 10 days

Track Layout

Main Circumference: 7 furlongs
Main Track Chute: 6 furlongs
Main Length of Stretch: 1,085 feet

Attendance

Average Daily Recent Meeting: 936, 2007
Total Attendance Recent Meeting: 4,681, 2007
Highest Single-Day Record: 18,127, June 14, 1980

Handle

Average All-Sources Recent Meeting: $1,536,327, 2007
Average On-Track Recent Meeting: $128,930, 2007
Total All-Sources Recent Meeting: $7,681,637, 2007
Total On-Track Recent Meeting: $644,654, 2007

Leaders

Recent Meeting, Leading Jockey: Luis V. Martinez, 20, 2006
Recent Meeting, Leading Trainer: Art Sherman, 8, 2006

Principal Races

Solano County Juvenile Filly S., Vacaville H., Fairfield S.

Track Records, Main Dirt

$4\frac{1}{2}$ furlongs: Notorious One, :51.26, July 25, 2005
5 furlongs: One Bad Shark, :56.60, July 14, 2002
$5\frac{1}{2}$ furlongs: Ridgewood High, 1:02$\frac{1}{5}$, July 18, 1982
6 furlongs: Salta's Pride, 1:07.80, July 13, 1996
1 mile: Kamalii King, 1:34$\frac{4}{5}$, July 18, 1982
$1\frac{1}{16}$ miles: Hoedown's Day, 1:39$\frac{4}{5}$, July 24, 1983
$1\frac{1}{8}$ miles: Baffi's Eagle, 1:48$\frac{2}{5}$, July 17, 1984
$1\frac{1}{4}$ miles: Super Sonet, 2:03$\frac{2}{5}$, June 20, 1974
$1\frac{3}{8}$ miles: Rain Storm, 2:15$\frac{4}{5}$, June 22, 1973
$1\frac{1}{2}$ miles: Always King, 2:32$\frac{3}{5}$, June 24, 1978

Fastest Times of 2007 (Dirt)

5 furlongs: Ice Fantasy, 5, :57.29, July 15, 2007
$5\frac{1}{2}$ furlongs: Yudaman Man, 4, 1:02.83, July 14, 2007
6 furlongs: Victorina, 4, 1:08.30, July 14, 2007
1 mile: Goinwest, 4, 1:36.02, July 15, 2007

Colorado

Arapahoe Park

One of racing's quiet survivors, Denver-area Arapahoe Park has survived a disastrous launch, increased gambling competition, and disputes with horsemen to remain a summer racing fixture in the Rocky Mountains region. The track opened in the mid-1980s, replacing longtime Denver track Centennial Park. But its location southeast of Denver was far from any interstate highways; interest in the track was negligible, and it was closed for several years after its opening. The track reopened in the early 1990s but has struggled to develop a fan base amid competition from a state lottery and Native American casinos, which were legalized in the state in the early '90s. A dispute between the track's former owner, Wembley USA, and horsemen over racing dates nearly forced the cancellation of the 2000 race meet. Arapahoe and other Wembley properties were sold to BLB Investors for $455-million in 2005.

Location: 26000 E. Quincy Ave., Aurora, Co. 80016-2026
Phone: (303) 690-2400
Fax: (303) 690-6730
Website: *www.mihiracing.com*
Dates of Inaugural Meeting: May 24, 1984
Abbreviation: Arp
Acreage: 297
Number of Stalls: 1,400
Seating Capacity: 7,500

Ownership

BLB Investors

Officers

General Manager: Bruce Seymore
Director of Racing: Bill Powers
Racing Secretary: Stuart Slagle
Track Announcer: Sean Beirne
Track Superintendent: William Byers

Racing Dates

2007: May 26-August 13, 36 days
2008: May 24-August 10, 36 days

Track Layout

Main Circumference: 1 mile
Main Track Chute: 6 furlongs, 7 furlongs, and $1\frac{5}{16}$ miles
Main Width: 90 feet
Main Length of Stretch: 1,029 feet

Attendance

Average Daily Recent Meeting: 1,945, 2007
Total Attendance Recent Meeting: 68,082, 2007

Handle

Average All-Sources Recent Meeting: $207,471, 2007
Single-Day All-Sources Handle: $463,432, July 30, 2007
Total All-Sources Recent Meeting: $4,234,777, 2007
Single Day All-Sources Recent Meeting: $463,432, July 30, 2007

Leaders

Recent Meeting, Leading Jockey: Travis Wales, 65, 2007
Recent Meeting, Leading Owner: Harry L. Veruchi, 28, 2007
Recent Meeting, Leading Trainer: Jon Arnett, 61. 2007
Recent Meeting, Leading Horse: Shazooms Doll, 4, 2007

Records

Single-Day Trainer Wins: Jon G. Arnett, 5, June 19, 2006

Principal Races

Gold Rush Futurity, Colorado Derby, Inaugural S., Arapahoe Park Sprint H., Molly Brown H.

Track Records, Main Dirt
4 furlongs: Et Tu Brutus, :44.60, July 26, 2004
4½ furlongs: V G's Catch, :50.40, June 23, 2002; Hugs Legacy, :50.40, July 19, 2004
5 furlongs: Nycity, :56, July 13, 2002
5½ furlongs: Choppers Passion, 1:02.20, June 22, 2001; Ribot Line, 1:02.20, June 30, 2002
6 furlongs: Absolutely True, 1:08.20, July 11, 2004
6½ furlongs: Pray for Booger, 1:18.60, August 25, 1995
7 furlongs: Daring Pegasus, 1:21, July 4, 2003
1 mile: Honor Bright, 1:35.20, August 7, 1993
1 mile 70 yds: Naskra's Advocate, 1:38.20, July 23, 1993
1¹/₁₆ miles: Run At Night, 1:42.40, August 14, 2004
1⅛ miles: Maysville Slew, 1:49, September 1, 2002
1¼ miles: Builder's Boy, 2:05.40, June 26, 1992
1½ miles: Calgary Classic, 2:33.20, July 24, 1993
1¾ miles: Read My Mind, 3:02, July 9, 1992
2 miles: Little Reeves, 3:28.40, August 27, 1994

Fastest Times of 2007 (Dirt)
4 furlongs: Heavens Gold, 2, :45.42, June 11, 2007
4½ furlongs: Invincible Sun, 5, :52.11, July 1, 2007
5 furlongs: Swinger Prospect, 5, :57.22, August 5, 2007
5½ furlongs: Absolutely True, 7, 1:02.51, June 23, 2007
6 furlongs: Brahms Haze, 4, 1:09.35, July 16, 2007
7 furlongs: Derouin, 3, 1:22.86, July 30, 2007
1 mile: Folsum, 3, 1:37.72, July 7, 2007
1 mile 70 yds: Meadow Dancer, 3, 1:44.04, July 15, 2007
1¹/₁₆ miles: Vannacide, 6, 1:44.87, August 12, 2007
1⅛ miles: Saint Augustus, 4, 1:50.76, August 5, 2007
1½ miles: Bossa Rio, 6, 2:35.85, August 12, 2007

Delaware

Delaware Park

Competition from racetracks in neighboring Pennsylvania, Maryland and New Jersey forced the closure of historic Delaware Park in Stanton in September 1982. In late 1983, Maryland developer William Rickman Sr. acquired Delaware Park in partnership with Maryland horseman William Christmas, and the track ran abbreviated meets in the spring and fall of '84. Rickman's son, William Rickman Jr., managed track operations and in 1994 helped to secure state approval for installing slot machines at the track. Delaware's slots facility opened in December 1995, and revenues from the slots have more than tripled purses. The Wilmington-area track was designed by banker and horseman William duPont Jr. and became a haven for summer racing fans throughout the Mid-Atlantic region. The track's richest race, the Delaware Handicap (G2), debuted in 1937 as the New Castle Handicap and has been won by some of the sport's leading fillies and mares.

Location: 777 Delaware Park Blvd., Wilmington, De. 19804
Phone: (302) 994-2521
Fax: (302) 994-3567
Website: www.delawarepark.com
E-Mail: programs@delawarepark.com
Year Founded: 1937
Abbreviation: Del

Ownership
Delaware Racing Association

Officers
President and Chief Executive Officer: William Rickman Jr.
Chief Operating Officer: William Fasy
General Manager: Andrew Gentile
Senior Vice Presidents: Christer Farr, Nancy Myshko, Greg Petkiewicz, Joseph Rudisill, Ray Spera
Vice President of Finance: Kevin DeLucia
Vice President of Marketing: Andy Gomeringer
Vice President of Purchasing: Austin Fiore
Vice President of Slots: Terry Smith
Racing Secretary: Ismael Trejo
Assistant Racing Secretary: Margie Stallings
Track Superintendent: Ken Brown
Executive Director of Marketing: Pam Cunningham
Executive Director of Mutuels: Scott Loomis
Executive Director of Security: Kathy Harer
Stewards: Fritz Burkhardt, Jack Houghton Jr., Dennis Lima
Track Announcer: John Curran
Track Photographer: Hoofprints Inc.
Horsemen's Liaison: Ismael Trejo
Horsemen's Bookkeeper: Cindy Houghton

Racing Dates
2007: April 28-November 4, 137 days
2008: April 19-November 11, 136 days

Track Layout
Main Circumference: 1 mile
Main Track Chute: 6 furlongs and 1¼ miles
Main Width: 100 feet
Main Length of Stretch: 995 feet
Main Turf Circumference: 7 furlongs

Handle
Average All-Sources Recent Meeting: $1,576,146
Average On-Track Recent Meeting: $106,811
Total All-Sources Recent Meeting: $212,779,754
Total On-Track Recent Meeting: $14,419,478
Highest Single-Day Record Recent Meeting: $4,981,402, July 15, 2007

Mutuel Records
Highest Win: $403.20, Gerabon, June 16, 1949
Lowest Win: $2.10, Spectacular Bid, August 26, 1979
Highest Exacta: $4,565.60, July 21, 1972
Lowest Exacta: $3.80, August 7, 1977; $3.80, August 26, 1979
Highest Trifecta: $50,870.80, May 25, 1974
Highest Daily Double: $5,507.80, July 4, 1941
Lowest Daily Double: $6.40, June 11, 1976
Highest Other Exotics: $699,100, Twin-Trifecta, June 13, 1986
Highest Quinella: $623.40, June 13, 1968
Lowest Quinella: $5.40, July 1, 1968

Leaders
Recent Meeting, Leading Jockey: Jeremy Rose, 155, 2007
Recent Meeting, Leading Owner: Bill Waldron, 27, 2007
Recent Meeting, Leading Trainer: Scott A. Lake, 97, 2007
Recent Meeting, Leading Horse: Ordained, Fryvolous, Awfully Smart, Charming Image, Our Machine, 5, 2007

Records
Single-Day Jockey Wins: Eldon Nelson, 6, June 20, 1958; George Cusimano, 6, July 16, 1968; Greg McCarron, 6, July 6, 1974; Jimmy Edwards, 6, May 28, 1984; Michael McCarthy, 6, November 2, 1997; Michael McCarthy, 6, May 24, 1998
Single Meeting, Leading Jockey by Wins: Ramon Dominguez, 254,, 2003
Single Meeting, Leading Trainer by Wins: Scott A. Lake, 126, 2005
Single Meeting, Leading Horse by Wins: Fionnghal, 10, 1987

Principal Races
Delaware H. (G2), Delaware Oaks (G2), Kent Breeders' Cup S. (G3), Barbaro S. (G3), Endine H. (G3), Robert G. Dick Memorial (G3), Obeah (G3).

Track Records, Main Dirt
4½ furlongs: Erlton, :51.80, May 5, 1998
5 furlongs: Milky Way Gal, :56.20, July 29, 1989
5½ furlongs: Trickle of Gold, 1:02.68, May 6, 2006
6 furlongs: Pisgah, 1:07.92, April 25, 2006
1 mile: Ashlar, 1:35.20, June 25, 1960
1 mile 70 yds: Distinct Vision, 1:39 20, August 25, 2003
1¹/₁₆ miles: Lies of Omission, 1:41.20, July 4, 1998
1⅛ miles: Victoria Park, 1:47.40, June 18, 1960
1³/₁₆ miles: Trapped Again, 1:55.41, October 1, 2005

Racetracks — Florida 633

1¼ miles: Coup de Fusil, 1:59.80, July 25, 1987
1½ miles: Bam, 2:31, June 26, 1948
1⅝ miles: Flying Restina Run, 2:45.40, September 4, 2000
1¾ miles: Cer Vantes, 2:56.40, June 27, 1951
2 miles: Dixies Act, 3:29.40, August 10, 1975
Other: 2 furlongs, Glitter River, :21.60, September 5, 2000; 2m 70 yds, Wolfe Tone, 3:34, November 7, 1993; 2¼ miles, Sanguine Sword, 3:58.60, July 2, 1986

Track Records, Main Turf
5 furlongs: Beer Stien, :55.84, June 29, 2005
1 mile: Galantas, 1:34.69, July 16, 2007
1 1/16 miles: Charablanc, 1:40.20, July 20, 1963
1⅛ miles: Seeking Slew, 1:47.32, June 25, 2005
1⅜ miles: Cool Prince, 2:12.40, July 3, 1965
1½ miles: Revved Up, 2:26.46, July 20, 2003
2 miles: Verdance, 3:24.40, September 21, 1986
Other: 1⅞ miles, El Moro, 3:11.80, July 22, 1963; 2⅜ miles, Lively London, 4:09, July 25, 1986; 2⅞ miles, Call Louis, 5:08.20, August 24, 1986

Fastest Times of 2007 (Dirt)
2 furlongs: Pure and Simple, 2, :22.18, May 27, 2007
4½ furlongs: Nordic Wind, 2, :51.86, May 26, 2007
5 furlongs: Carsoncityrose, 3, :57.36, August 21, 2007
5½ furlongs: Equity, 3, 1:03.45, July 28, 2007
6 furlongs: Fleet Valid, 4, 1:08.48, April 28, 2007
1 mile: Better Than Bonds, 5, 1:36.17, April 30, 2007
1 mile 70 yds: Belongs to Joe, 4, 1:39.72, April 29, 2007
1 1/16 miles: Barcola, 4, 1:41.56, June 9, 2007
1⅛ miles: Awfully Smart, 4, 1:48.92, September 8, 2007
1 3/16 miles: Barcola, 4, 1:56.56, September 29, 2007
1¼ miles: Unbridled Belle, 4, 2:01.16, July 15, 2007

Fastest Times of 2007 (Turf)
5 furlongs: Smart and Fancy, 4, :56.08, July 15, 2007
a5 furlongs: Hesa Big Star, 5, :56.72, July 7, 2007
1 mile: Galantas, 4, 1:34.69, July 16, 2007
a1 mile: Placia, 2, 1:39.24, September 17, 2007
1 1/16 miles: Pass Play, 6, 1:41.13, September 9, 2007
a1 1/16 miles: Sword of Dubai, 4, 1:43.26, September 16, 2007
1⅛ miles: Galantas, 4, 1:47.67, June 3, 2007
a1⅛ miles: Lights Out Angel, 4, 1:50.33, May 12, 2007
1⅜ miles: Rosinka (Ire), 4, 2:16.56, July 14, 2007
1½ miles: Always First (GB), 6, 2:28.56, September 3, 2007

Florida

Calder Race Course

Calder Race Course, which offers racing from late April through early January, is located in Miami next to Pro Player Stadium, home of the National Football League's Miami Dolphins. Built by real estate businessman Stephen A. Calder, the track was granted summer racing dates for 1970. Because the track was under construction, those dates were run at Tropical Park. Calder officially opened on May 6, 1971, debuting an all-weather synthetic track surface designed by 3M that remained in place until 1992. In 1972, Tropical Park closed and began holding its meet at Calder; the last several weeks of each year's season are known as the Tropical Park meet. From 1980-'84, Calder underwent $10.5-million in improvements. In 1988, Thoroughbred owner-breeder Bertram R. Firestone bought Calder. Three years later, Kawasaki Leasing Inc. assumed control of the track. The track underwent a $1-million renovation of its first floor, and in 1995 it added full-card simulcasting. In 1999, Churchill Downs Inc. bought Calder for approximately $86-million. Today, Calder features three racing events: the Florida Stallion Stakes, a series of races for offspring of Florida stallions; Festival of the Sun, a $1.6-million day of racing highlighted by the finals of the Florida Stallion Stakes series; and Summit of Speed, sprint stakes races with combined purses totaling $2-million in 2007. Two Calder stakes, the Smile Sprint and Princess Rooney, were added to the 2008 Breeders' Cup Challenge series.

Location: 21001 N.W. 27th Ave., Miami Gardens, Fl. 33056
Phone: (305) 625-1311
Fax: (305) 620-2569
Website: www.calderracecourse.com
E-Mail: blanco@calderracecourse.com
Year Founded: 1971
Dates of Inaugural Meeting: May 6, 1971
Abbreviation: Crc
Acreage: 220
Number of Stalls: 1,850
Seating Capacity: 15,585

Ownership
Churchill Downs Inc.

Officers
Chairman: Carl F. Pollard
General Manager: Michael Abes
Racing Secretary: Michael Anifantis
Secretary: Rebecca C. Reed
Treasurer: Michael Abes
Vice Presidents: Michael Abes, Michael Cronin
Director of Admissions: Bill Keers
Director of Marketing: Michael Cronin
Director of Mutuels: Edward Mackie Sr.
Director of Publicity: Michele Blanco
Director of Simulcasting: Diane Stoess
Horsemen's Liaison: Janet Kownacke
Stewards: Chip Spencer, Jeffrey Noe
Track Announcer: Bobby Neuman
Track Photographer: Jim Lisa
Track Superintendent: Steve Cross
Security: Tony Otero

Racing Dates
2007: April 25-October 14, 112 days
2008: April 21-October 19, 116 days

Track Layout
Main Circumference: 1 mile
Main Track Chute: 7 furlongs and 1¼ miles
Main Width: Homestretch: 80 feet; Backstretch: 75 feet
Main Length of Stretch: 990 feet
Main Turf Circumference: 7 furlongs
Main Turf Chute: 1⅛ miles
Main Turf Width: 67 feet
Main Turf Length of Stretch: 986 feet

Attendance
Highest Single-Day Record: 23,103, May 4, 1985
Record Daily Average Single Meeting: 9,401, 1976
Highest Single-Meeting Record: 1,113,017, 1975
Lowest Single Meeting Record: 461,715, 2006

Handle
Record Daily Average Single Meeting: $1,206,739, 1986
Single-Day On-Track Handle: $2,954,162, May 7, 1988
Single-Day All-Sources Handle: $10,843,994, July 10, 2004
Record Total All-Sources Single Meeting: $452,787,811, 2002
Record Average All-Sources Single Meeting: $3,537,405, 2002
Record Total Single Meeting: $152,326,480, 1990

Mutuel Records
Highest Win: $345.40, Lou Glory, September 12, 1991
Lowest Win: $2.10, Isle O'Style, June 12, 1974; $2.10, June 16, 2001
Highest Exacta: $31,133.20, November 3, 1972
Lowest Exacta: $3.40, August 16, 1989
Highest Trifecta: $58,432.40, October 25, 1986
Lowest Trifecta: $6.60, July 10, 2006
Highest Daily Double: $2,671, July 2, 1976
Lowest Daily Double: $3.20, September 16, 1992

Highest Pick Three: $39,548.80, April 26, 2004
Lowest Pick Three: $9, September 12, 2000
Highest Other Exotics: $74,622, Superfecta, October 26, 1996; $222, Place, October 17, 1975; $97.80, Show, December 31, 2004
Lowest Other Exotics: $12.60, Superfecta, July 10, 2006
Highest Pick Four: $10,846.70, April 26, 2004
Lowest Pick Four: $59.10, October 12, 2002

Leaders

Career, Leading Jockey by Titles: Eibar Coa, 4
Career, Leading Trainer by Titles: William P. White, 9
Career, Leading Jockey by Stakes Wins: Gene St. Leon, 73
Career, Leading Trainer by Stakes Wins: Frank Gomez, 95
Career, Leading Jockey by Wins: Gene St. Leon, 1,310
Career, Leading Trainer by Wins: Emanuel Tortora, 1,048
Career, Leading Horse by Stakes Wins: Spirit of Fighter, 17
Recent Meeting, Leading Jockey: Elvis Trujillo, 160, 2007
Recent Meeting, Leading Owner: Richard N. Averill, 18, 2007
Recent Meeting, Leading Trainer: Kirk Ziade, 53, 2007
Recent Meeting, Leading Horse: Fortunate Trail, 7, 2007

Records

Single-Day Jockey Wins: Eddie Castro, 9, June 4, 2005
Single-Day Trainer Wins: Arnold N. Winick, 5, September 16, 1972; Stanley Hough, 5, May 12, 1977
Single Meeting, Leading Jockey by Wins: Eddie Castro, 218, 2005
Single Meeting, Leading Trainer by Wins: Stanley Hough, 110, 1977
Single Meeting, Leading Trainer by Stakes Wins: Frank Gomez, 10, 1979
Single Meeting, Leading Jockey by Stakes Wins: Jose Velez Jr., 14, 1986

Principal Races

Princess Rooney H. (G1), Smile Sprint H. (G2), Carry Back S. (G2), Azalea Breeders' Cup S. (G3), Calder Derby (G3)

Notable Events

Summit of Speed, Festival of the Sun, Juvenile Showcase

Track Records, Main Dirt

4 furlongs: Diamond Studs, :46.21, July 14, 2001
$4^1/_2$ furlongs: Gold Phantom, :51.86, September 16, 2001
5 furlongs: Honest, :57.61, July 1, 1996
$5^1/_2$ furlongs: Bernard's Candy, 1:04.39, August 9, 2002
6 furlongs: Forty One Carats, 1:08.95, October 7, 2000
$6^1/_2$ furlongs: Tour of the Cat, 1:15.99, August 17, 2002
7 furlongs: Constant Escort, 1:21.82, September 28, 1996
1 mile: High Ideal, 1:36.25, September 15, 2001
1 mile 70 yds: Halo's Image, 1:41.78, October 31, 1995
$1^1/_{16}$ miles: Castlebrook, 1:42.55, September 15, 2001
$1^1/_8$ miles: Jumping Hill, 1:50, December 30, 1978
$1^3/_{16}$ miles: Arctic Honeymoon, $1{:}59^3/_5$, January 3, 1987
$1^1/_4$ miles: Wicapi, 2:05.08, June 24, 1996
$1^1/_2$ miles: Lead'm Home, $2{:}32^3/_5$, December 31, 1977
$1^5/_8$ miles: Timberlea Tune, $2{:}50^1/_5$, October 16, 1971
$1^3/_4$ miles: *Detective II, $3{:}03^1/_5$, October 23, 1971
2 miles: *Detective II, $3{:}30^1/_5$, November 11, 1971
Other: 2 furlongs, Baby Shark, :20.81, July 13, 2002

Track Records, Main Turf

5 furlongs: Whenthedoveflies, :54.78, May 23, 2004
7 furlongs: Carterista, 1:22.36, June 19, 1993
$7^1/_2$ furlongs: Court Lark, 1:26.54, July 16, 1994
1 mile: Mr. Explosive, $1{:}33^3/_5$, October 17, 1992; Dillonmyboy, 1:33.66, October 30, 2000
$1^1/_{16}$ miles: He's Crafty, 1:39.27, December 28, 2004
$1^1/_8$ miles: The Vid, 1:44.99, November 25, 1995
$1^3/_8$ miles: King's Design, 2:13.18, July 23, 1999
$1^1/_2$ miles: Flag Down, 2:24.11, December 16, 1995
2 miles: Skate On Thin Ice, 3:21.89, January 2, 1996

Fastest Times of 2007 (Dirt)

2 furlongs: Caller One, 10, :21.15, July 28, 2007
$4^1/_2$ furlongs: Wise Answer, 2, :52.56, June 9, 2007
7 furlongs: Firebrook, 5, 1:23.09, July 28, 2007
1 mile: Annabill, 4, 1:38.79, October 27, 2007; Minidrop, 4, 1:38.79, December 9, 2007
$1^1/_{16}$ miles: B. B. Best, 5, 1:44.20, August 24, 2007
$1^1/_8$ miles: Electrify, 4, 1:51.49, July 4, 2007
$1^3/_{16}$ miles: Tacit Agreement, 6, 2:00.05, May 19, 2007
$1^1/_4$ miles: Tacit Agreement, 6, 2:06.49, June 9, 2007
$1^1/_2$ miles: Delosvientos, 4, 2:33.87, July 1, 2007
2 miles: Golden Strategy, 4, 3:32.34, July 28, 2007

Fastest Times of 2007 (Turf)

5 furlongs: Lord Robyn, 5, :55.10, May 12, 2007
$7^1/_2$ furlongs: Fearless Eagle, 3, 1:27.22, December 29, 2007
1 mile: Tastefully Smart, 3, 1:33.93, December 28, 2007
$1^1/_{16}$ miles: Jet Propulsion, 4, 1:39.46, September 3, 2007
$1^1/_8$ miles: Quistopher, 4, 1:47.57, December 30, 2007
$1^1/_2$ miles: Presious Passion, 4, 2:26.[illegible]3, December 15, 2007

Gulfstream Park

Since the 1940s, Gulfstream Park, located north of Miami in Hallandale, Florida, has been a favorite winter destination for horsemen and annually offers high-quality winter racing. Gulfstream opened in February 1939 but went bankrupt and closed after four days of racing. In 1944, James Donn Sr., who owned a local floral shop and was a creditor of the track, reopened Gulfstream. In 1952, the Florida Derby (now a Grade 1 race) debuted and became a major stop on the road to the Kentucky Derby (G1). Eleven winners of the race, including Northern Dancer, Unbridled, Thunder Gulch, Monarchos, and Big Brown, went on to win the Kentucky Derby. Gulfstream in 1989 held the first of the track's three Breeders' Cup championship days. In 1999, Frank Stronach-led Magna Entertainment Corp. purchased Gulfstream for $95-million. In 2003, Magna opened Palm Meadows Training Center, a 304-acre training facility located near Boynton Beach, approximately 35 miles north of the track. Voters in Broward County, where Gulfstream is located, authorized slot machines at the track in 2005, and the track opened its slots casino in '06.

Location: 901 S. Federal Hwy., Hallandale Beach, Fl. 33009-7199
Phone: (954) 454-7000, (800) 771-TURF
Fax: (954) 457-6422
Website: *www.gulfstreampark.com*
E-Mail: mchung@gulfstreampark.com
Year Founded: 1939
Dates of Inaugural Meeting: February 1-February 4, 1939
Abbreviation: GP
Seating Capacity: 4,150

Ownership

Magna Entertainment Corp.

Officers

Chairman: Frank Stronach
President and General Manager: Bill Murphy
Racing Operations Manager: Bernie Hettel
Director of Racing: Bill Couch
Vice President of Operations: Dennis Testa
Director of Media Relations: Mike Mullaney
Track Announcer: Larry Collmus
Track Photographers: Adam Coglianese, Bob Coglianese
Track Superintendent: John Grillon (main track); Doug Kickbush (turf)
Director of Admissions: Marlon Chung
Director of Finance: Joe Wolff
Director of Mutuels: Edward Mackie
Horsemen's Liaison: Raina Chingos-Gunderson
Stewards: Chip Spencer, Jeffrey Noe, Kevin Scheen

Racing Dates

2007: January 3-April 22, 88 days
2008: January 3-April 20, 89 days

Track Layout
Main Circumference: 1 1/8 miles
Turf Circumference: 7 furlongs
Turf Width: 170 feet
Training Track: Palm Meadows

Attendance
Highest Single-Day Record: 33,864, March 4, 1989; 51,342, November 4, 1989 (Breeders' Cup day)
Highest Single-Meeting Record: 1,096,404, 1991

Handle
Daily Average Single Meeting: $2,121,121, 1998
Single-Day On-Track Handle: $7,993,485, March 12, 1994; $15,377,709, November 6, 1999 (Breeders' Cup Day)
Single-Day All-Sources Handle: $24,482,519, March 11, 2001
Average All-Sources Single Meeting: $9,475,530, 1998
Total Single Meeting: $149,984,344, 2002
Total All-Sources Single Meeting: $825,343,874, 2003

Leaders
Career, Leading Jockey by Titles: Walter Blum, 4; Jorge Chavez, 4
Career, Leading Trainer by Titles: Arnold Winick, 12
Career, Leading Jockey by Stakes Wins: Jerry Bailey, 147
Recent Meeting, Leading Jockey: Eibar Coa, 76, 2008
Recent Meeting, Leading Owner: Frank Calabrese, 23, 2008
Recent Meeting, Leading Trainer: Todd Pletcher, 26, 2008
Recent Meeting, Leading Horse: Stratostar, 4, 2008; One Dreamy Cat, 4, 2008

Records
Single-Day Jockey Wins: Jerry Bailey, 7, March 11, 1995
Single Meeting, Leading Jockey by Wins: Julio Pezua, 97, 1987; Wigberto Ramos, 97, 1991; Jerry Bailey, 97, 1996
Single Meeting, Leading Trainer by Wins: Mark Shuman, 87, 2003
Single Meeting, Leading Horse by Wins: Shir-Tee, 5, 1971

Principal Races
Florida Derby (G1), Donn H. (G1), Gulfstream Park Breeders' Cup Turf S. (G1), Gulfstream Park H. (G2), Fountain of Youth S. (G2)

Interesting Facts
Trivia: Bill Shoemaker rode the last winner of his career (Beau Genius) in the 1990 Hallandale Handicap. Turf course opened in 1959.

Notable Events
Sunshine Millions

Track Records, Main Dirt
5 1/2 furlongs: Shane Jules, 1:03.03, March 19, 2006
6 furlongs: Tiger, 1:08.46, February 16, 2006
6 1/2 furlongs: Forest Danger, 1:14.44, February 14, 2005
7 furlongs: Exclusive Quality, 1:21.11, March 4, 2006
7 1/2 furlongs: Keyed Entry, 1:27.12, February 4, 2006
1 mile: Chatain, 1:33.87, January 6, 2007
1 1/8 miles: Brass Hat, 1:47.79, February 4, 2006
1 3/16 miles: Eddington, 1:54.74, March 5, 2005
Other: 1 7/16 miles, Watchmon, 2:25.80, April 8, 2005

Track Records, Main Turf
5 furlongs: Procreate, :53.79, April 9, 2005
7 1/2 furlongs: Paula Smith, 1:27.72, January 13, 2005
1 mile: Mr. Light (Arg), 1:31.41, January 3, 2005
1 1/16 miles: Congleve, 1:38.17, January 20, 2006
1 1/8 miles: English Channel, 1:44.51, February 22, 2007
1 3/8 miles: Prince Arch, 2:11.44, March 6, 2005
1 1/2 miles: Honey Ryder, 2:23.07, April 1, 2006
Other: 1 7/16 miles, Giant Hope, 2:17.64, March 12, 2006

Fastest Times of 2007 (Dirt)
5 furlongs: Romanscoliseum, 4, :56.88, March 23, 2007
5 1/2 furlongs: Disco's Son, 4, 1:03.12, April 8, 2007
6 furlongs: Disco's Son, 4, 1:08.60, March 9, 2007
6 1/2 furlongs: Rondo, 4, 1:15.40, April 18, 2007
7 furlongs: Half Ours, 4, 1:22.21, March 3, 2007
7 1/2 furlongs: Deadly Dealer, 3, 1:27.85, March 3, 2007
1 mile: Chatain, 4, 1:33.87, January 6, 2007
1 1/8 miles: Corinthian, 4, 1:48.04, February 8, 2007
1 3/16 miles: Corinthian, 4, 1:55.06, March 3, 2007

Fastest Times of 2007 (Turf)
5 furlongs: Lifestyle, 7, :54.41, March 2, 2007
1 mile: Silver Tree, 7, 1:32.12, March 4, 2007
1 1/16 miles: Heat of the Night (SAf), 5, 1:39.27, January 14, 2007
1 1/8 miles: English Channel, 5, 1:44.51, February 22, 2007
1 3/8 miles: Ramazutti, 5, 2:11.86, January 28, 2007
1 1/2 miles: Jambalaya, 5, 2:24.98, March 31, 2007

Ocala Training Center
Location: 1701 S.W. 60th Ave., P.O. Box 99, Ocala, Fl. 34478
Phone: (352) 237-2154
Fax: (352) 237-3566
Website: www.obssales.com
E-Mail: obs@obssales.com
Abbreviation: OTC

Officers
General Manager: Tom Ventura
Director of Racing: Bob Gulick
Racing Secretary: Rick Coyne
Director of Auctions: Tom Ventura
Director of Publicity: Jay Friedman
Stewards: Charles Camac, Tommy Trotter, Bobby Wingo
Track Announcer: Bobby Neuman
Track Photographer: Jim Lisa
Track Superintendent: John Barbazon

Racing Dates
2007: February 12, 1 day
2008: February 11, 1 day

Leaders
Recent Meeting, Leading Jockey: Elvis Trujillo, 1, 2008; Eddie Castro, 1, 2008; Edgar Prado, 1, 2008; Manoel Cruz, 1, 2008; Kent Desormeaux, 1, 2008
Recent Meeting, Leading Trainer: Jose Pinchin, 1, 2008; Stephen DiMauro, 1, 2008; Cody Autrey, 1, 2008; William Kaplan, 1, 2008; Dale Romans, 1, 2008

Records
Single-Day Jockey Wins: Jorge Chavez, 3, 2000; Jorge Chavez, 3, 2001; Edgar Prado, 3, 2003; Jose Lezcano, 3, 2006
Single-Day Trainer Wins: Ben Perkins, 2, 1994; Manuel J. Azpurua, 2, 1996; Kenneth Wirth, 2, 1996; Dan Hurtak, 2, 1997; Kirk Ziadie, 2, 2006
Single Meeting, Leading Jockey by Wins: Jorge Chavez, 3, 2000; Jorge Chavez, 3, 2001; Edgar Prado, 3, 2003; Jose Lezcano, 3, 2006
Single Meeting, Leading Trainer by Wins: Ben Perkins, 2, 1994; Manuel J. Azpurua, 2, 1996; Kenneth Wirth, 2, 1996; Dan Hurtak, 2, 1997; Kirk Ziadie, 2, 2006

Track Records, Main Dirt
5 furlongs: Hana Highway, :56.40, March 17, 2003
6 furlongs: Lucky Livi, 1:09, March 20, 2000
1 1/16 miles: The Name's Bond, 1:44.20, March 17, 2003; Doc's Doll, 1:44.20, March 15, 2004; Humorously, 1:44.20, March 15, 2004

Fastest Times of 2007 (Dirt)
5 furlongs: Far West, 4, :57.60, February 12, 2007
6 furlongs: Jodi's Star, 3, 1:10.20, February 12, 2007
1 1/16 miles: Buffalo Man, 3, 1:44.40, February 12, 2007

Tampa Bay Downs

Tampa Bay Downs, the only Thoroughbred track on Florida's Gulf Coast, opened on February 18, 1926, as Tampa Downs. The initial 39-day meet was orchestrated by Harvey Mayers, a businessman from Ohio, and Churchill Downs executive Col. Matt J. Winn. Renamed Sunshine Park in 1947, it became known as the "Santa Anita of the South" in the '50s, a nickname provided by legendary sportswriters Grantland Rice, Red Smith, and Arthur Daley, who frequented the track while covering baseball spring training. Following the sale of the track, its name was changed to Florida Downs in 1965

and to Tampa Bay Downs in '80. On February 12, 1981, jockey Julie Krone scored the first victory of her Racing Hall of Fame career on Lord Farkle. Tampa Bay Downs was sold again in 1986 and has since added a picnic area, year-round simulcasting, a seven-furlong turf course, a luxurious Sports Gallery featuring an extensive video racing library, an updated grandstand with private work stations, central air conditioning, and a renovated deli, bar, and pizza area. In 2004, the track opened a card room. Though a Grade 3 stakes, the Tampa Bay Derby attracted the last two years' champion two-year-old male as Street Sense (in 2007) and War Pass (in '08) both competed in the race.

Location: 11225 Racetrack Rd., P.O. Box 2007, Oldsmar, Fl. 34677-7007
Phone: (813) 855-4401, (866) 823-6967
Fax: (813) 261-1832
Website: *www.tampabaydowns.com*
E-Mail: customerservice@tampabaydowns.com
Year Founded: 1926
Dates of Inaugural Meeting: February 18, 1926
Abbreviation: Tam
Acreage: 450
Number of Stalls: 1,462
Seating Capacity: 6,000

Ownership
Stella Thayer and Howell Ferguson

Officers
President: Stella F. Thayer
Vice President and General Manager: Peter N. Berube
Director of Racing and Racing Secretary: Allison De Luca
Secretary: Howell Ferguson
Treasurer: Stella F. Thayer
Vice President of Operations: Bob Cassanese
Vice President of Finance: Greg Gelyon
Vice President of Marketing and Publicity: Margo Flynn
Stewards: Robert Clark, Dennis Lima, Charles Miranda
Track Announcer: Richard Grunder
Track Photographer: Tom Cooley
Track Superintendent: Tom McLaughlin
Clerk of the Course: Judy Clark
Assistant Racing Secretary: Stanley Shina
Horsemen's Bookkeeper: Nerissa Steward

Racing Dates
2007: December 9, 2006-May 6, 2007, 94 days
2008: December 8, 2007-May 4, 2008, 94 days

Track Layout
Main Circumference: 1 mile
Main Track Chute: 3 furlongs and 7 furlongs
Main Width: 75 feet
Main Length of Stretch: 976 feet
Main Turf Circumference: 7 furlongs
Main Turf Chute: quarter-mile
Main Turf Width: 80 feet

Attendance
Average Daily Recent Meeting: 3,398, 2007/2008
Highest Single-Day Record: 12,746, March 15, 2008
Highest Single-Meeting Record: 457,414, 1988/1989
Total Attendance Recent Meeting: 319,408, 2007/2008
Highest Single-Day Recent Meeting: 12,746, March 15, 2008

Handle
Average All-Sources Recent Meeting: $4,084,508, 2007/2008
Average On-Track Recent Meeting: $283,900, 2007/2008
Single-Day All-Sources Handle: $10,916,634, March 17, 2007
Total All-Sources Recent Meeting: $383,943,754, 2007/2008
Total On-Track Recent Meeting: $26,686,586, 2007/2008
Record Total All-Sources Single Meeting: $385,787,682, 2006/2007
Record Average All-Sources Single Meeting: $4,104,124, 2006/2007
Highest Single-Day Record Recent Meeting: $10,282,952, March 15, 2008

Mutuel Records
Highest Win: $249, March 23, 1988
Highest Trifecta: $50,617, January 26 1999
Highest Daily Double: $3,320, January 17, 1950
Highest Pick Three: $12,913.40, January 9, 2001
Highest Other Exotics: $9,754, Perfecta, February 8, 1973; $34,632.80, Superfecta, March 18, 2006
Highest Quinella: $5,067.60, February 21, 1995

Leaders
Career, Leading Jockey by Titles: William Henry, 4
Career, Leading Trainer by Titles: Don R. Rice, 8
Career, Leading Jockey by Stakes Wins: William Henry, 22
Career, Leading Owner by Stakes Wins: Harold Queen, 6
Career, Leading Trainer by Stakes Wins: Don R. Rice, 11
Recent Meeting, Leading Jockey: Daniel Centeno, 144, 2007/2008
Recent Meeting, Leading Owner: Balkrisna Sukharan, 19, 2007/2008
Recent Meeting, Leading Trainer: Jamie Ness, 68, 2007/2008
Recent Meeting, Leading Horse: Lookinforthesecret, 5, 2007/2008; Awesome Attitude, 5, 2007/2008

Records
Single-Day Jockey Wins: Richard DePass, 7, March 15, 1980
Single-Day Owner Wins: Christos Gatis, 3, April 10, 2001
Single-Day Trainer Wins: Kathleen O'Connell, 4, February 23, 2003
Single Meeting, Leading Jockey by Wins: Daniel Centeno, 144, 2007/2008
Single Meeting, Leading Trainer by Wins: Jamie Ness, 68, 2007/2008

Principal Races
Tampa Bay Derby (G3), Hillsborough S. (G3), Florida Oaks, Sam F. Davis S.

Interesting Facts
Previous Names and Dates: Tampa Downs (1926-'46), Sunshine Park (1947-'64), Florida Downs (1965-'79)

Notable Events
Florida Cup Day, Festival Day, Festival Preview Day

Track Records, Main Dirt
4 furlongs: Camp Izard, :46.80, May 1, 1993
$4^1/_2$ furlongs: Geronimo J., :$52^4/_5$, March 16, 1984
5 furlongs: Arion Fair, :$57^1/_5$, March 20, 1982; We Can Do, :57.26, March 22, 2005
$5^1/_2$ furlongs: Schmoopy, 1:03.55, March 17, 2000
6 furlongs: Bootlegger's Pet, 1:09, January 26, 1974
$6^1/_2$ furlongs: Tytus, 1:16.20, December 27, 2007
7 furlongs: Sir Shackleton, 1:22.28, February 11, 2006
$7^1/_2$ furlongs: Secret Romeo, 1:22.52, January 22, 2002
1 mile: Double Prince, 1:$42^3/_5$, February 8, 1966; Rianan, 1:$42^3/_5$, February 11, 1966
1 mile 40 yds: Mistum, 1:$41^1/_5$, March 21, 1981
1 mile 70 yds: Deep Thought, 1:$41^4/_5$, January 21, 1956
$1^1/_{16}$ miles: Street Sense, 1:43.11, March 17, 2007
$1^1/_8$ miles: Las Olas, 1:$48^2/_5$, November 21, 1968
$1^3/_{16}$ miles: Warning Flag, 1:$59^3/_5$, January 25, 1986
$1^1/_4$ miles: Finale Puer, 2:$07^2/_5$, March 7, 1959
$1^3/_8$ miles: Banshee Brad, 2:20.30, March 26, 2005
$1^1/_2$ miles: Royal Jacopo, 2.33, March 12, 1955
$1^5/_8$ miles: Most Valiant, 2:48.20, March 29, 1997
$1^3/_4$ miles: Our Day, 3:$00^2/_5$, March 20, 1957
2 miles: Boss Man Jarett, 3:30.30, April 24, 1999
Other: 2 furlongs, Silver Dollar Boy, :$21^4/_5$, January 18, 1990; 3 furlongs, Hot Star, :$33^2/_5$, February 14, 1980; 3 furlongs, Wynn Dot Comma, :33.40, April 21, 2003; a1 mile, Prosico, 1:37.47, March 24, 2007; $1^7/_8$ miles, Best Hearted, 3:$18^3/_5$, March 22, 1986; 2m 70 yds, Turkey Foot Road, 3:$39^4/_5$, March 22, 1969; $2^1/_{16}$ miles, Mystic Fox, 3:$37^3/_5$, March 27, 1988

Track Records, Main Turf
5 furlongs: Atticus Kristy, :55.02, February 21, 2006
1 mile: Lucky J J, 1:33.79, February 12, 2000
$1^1/_{16}$ miles: Legs Galore, 1:39.65, February 20, 1999
$1^1/_8$ miles: Lilys Cousin, 1:46.34, May 6, 2000
$1^3/_8$ miles: Fun n' Gun, 2:24.06, March 30, 2002

Other: a5 furlongs, Charlie Papa, :56.04, April 21, 2007; a1 mile, Headline, 1:36.80, April 5, 2005; a1¹/₁₆ miles, Ben's Quixote, 1:41.23, December 28, 1999; a1¹/₈ miles, Go Between, 1:48.06, April 7, 2007; a1¹/₂ miles, Top Senor, 2:31.60, February 26, 2002; a2¹/₁₆ miles, Red Classic, 3:43.82, March 4, 2000

Fastest Times of 2007 (Dirt)
5 furlongs: Xep for Elmer, 4, :57.37, April 14, 2007
5¹/₂ furlongs: El Vaquero, 4, 1:05.84, April 22, 2007
6 furlongs: Roman Candles, 5, 1:09.88, January 13, 2007
6¹/₂ furlongs: Tytus, 3, 1:16.20, December 27, 2007
7 furlongs: Storm Thief, 5, 1:23.20, January 14, 2007
a1 mile: Prosico, 4, 1:37.47, March 24, 2007
1¹/₁₆ miles: Street Sense, 3, 1:43.11, March 17, 2007
1¹/₈ miles: Twisting Road, 4, 1:51.38, December 28, 2007

Fastest Times of 2007 (Turf)
5 furlongs: Bucky's Prayer, 5, :55.50, May 5, 2007
a5 furlongs: Charlie Papa, 6, :56.04, April 21, 2007
1 mile: Can't Spell, 5, 1:35.80, May 6, 2007
a1 mile: Aunt Jean, 4, 1:37.12, April 3, 2007
1¹/₁₆ miles: Hotstufanthensome, 7, 1:41.24, February 24, 2007
a1¹/₁₆ miles: Grato Recuerdo (Chi), 7, 1:45.31, March 10, 2007
a1¹/₈ miles: Go Between, 4, 1:48.06, April 7, 2007
a1³/₈ miles: Puppeteer (GB), 7, 2:20.82, March 24, 2007

Tropical Park

Tropical Park no longer has a physical presence but remains alive as the late fall-early winter meeting at Calder Race Course in northwest Miami. The Tropical Park meet at Calder Race Course runs from late October until the first days of January, which approximates the traditional Tropical Park spot in the South Florida rotation. Starting in the late 1940s, Tropical operated from late November until mid-January. Tropical Park first was located at a greyhound track and opened as a Thoroughbred track on December 26, 1931, in Coral Gables, a suburb southwest of Miami. The track was sold in 1941 and went through two ownership changes in the early '50s. Tropical was host for the first Calder meeting in 1970 and for that season used an experimental, synthetic Tartan track, developed by Minnesota Mining and Manufacturing Co., inside the main, one-mile oval. Calder's investors, including 3M Chairman William L. McKnight, bought out Tropical with the intention of moving its dates to the new track. Tropical closed on January 15, 1972, and was transformed into a municipal park. Several of Calder's graded stakes races are held during the Tropical Park meeting. Tropical Park still maintains separate meet records from Calder for leading jockey, trainer, and other categories, although track records are the same for both.

Location: 21001 N. W. 27th Ave., Miami Gardens, Fl. 33056
Phone: (305) 625-1311
Fax: (305) 620-2569
Website: www.calderracecourse.com
E-Mail: blanco@calderracecourse.com
Year Founded: 1972
Abbreviation: Crc
Number of Stalls: 1,850
Seating Capacity: 15,585

Ownership
Churchill Downs Inc.

Officers
Chairman: Carl F. Pollard
General Manager: Michael Abes
Racing Secretary: Michael Anifantis
Secretary: Rebecca C. Reed
Treasurer: Michael Abes

Director of Marketing: Michael Cronin
Director of Mutuels: Edward Mackie Sr.
Vice Presidents: Michael Abes, Michael Cronin
Director of Publicity: Michele Blanco
Director of Simulcasting: Diane Stoess
Horsemen's Liaison: Janet Kownacke
Stewards: Chip Spencer, Jeffrey Noe
Track Announcer: Bobby Neuman
Track Photographer: Jim Lisa
Track Superintendent: Steve Cross
Security: Tony Otero

Racing Dates
2007: October 15, 2007-January 2, 2008, 60 days
2008: October 20, 2008-January 2, 2009, 55 days

Track Layout
Main Circumference: 1 mile
Main Track Chute: 7 furlongs and 1¼ miles
Main Width: Homestretch: 80 feet; Backstretch: 75 feet
Main Length of Stretch: 990 feet
Main Turf Circumference: 7 furlongs
Main Turf Chute: 1⅛ miles
Main Turf Width: 67 feet
Main Turf Length of Stretch: 986 feet

Attendance
Highest Single-Day Record: 17,671, January 14, 1978
Highest Single-Meeting Record: 514,496, 1979/1980
Record Daily Average Single Meeting: 10,324, 1975/1976
Lowest Single Meeting Record: 226,709, 2005/2006

Handle
Record Daily Average Single Meeting: $1,475,680, 1988
Single-Day On-Track Handle: $2,793,767, January 7, 1989
Single-Day All-Sources Handle: $9,461,604, December 29, 2001
Record Total Single Meeting: $73,784,024, 1988
Record Total All-Sources Single Meeting: $240,373,189, 2004/2005
Highest Single-Day Record Recent Meeting: $7,695,401, December 30, 2006

Mutuel Records
Highest Win: $447.40, December 23, 1986
Lowest Win: $2.20, December 18, 1972
Highest Exacta: $10,837.20, December 18, 1988
Lowest Exacta: $4.80, December 18, 1972
Highest Trifecta: $63,599, November 13, 2005
Lowest Trifecta: $8.20, November 6, 2006
Highest Daily Double: $7,907.80, December 14, 1973
Lowest Daily Double: $6.40, April 18, 1992
Highest Pick Three: $28,275, December 21, 1993
Lowest Pick Three: $15.80, December 17, 1988
Highest Other Exotics: $68,684.20, Superfecta, November 16, 1996; $97.80, Show, December 31, 2004
Lowest Other Exotics: $16.80, Superfecta, November 6, 2006
Lowest Pick Four: $52.50, November 16, 2002
Highest Pick Four: $77,762.40, December 30, 2000

Leaders
Career, Leading Jockey by Titles: Jacinto Vasquez, 5
Career, Leading Trainer by Titles: Stanley Hough, 5; William P. White, 5
Career, Leading Jockey by Stakes Wins: Eibar Coa, 28
Career, Leading Trainer by Stakes Wins: Martin D. Wolfson, 22
Career, Leading Jockey by Wins: Eibar Coa, 552
Career, Leading Trainer by Wins: Emanuel Tortora, 404
Career, Leading Horse by Stakes Wins: Spirit of Fighter, 17
Recent Meeting, Leading Jockey: Manoel R. Cruz, 104, 2007/2008
Recent Meeting, Leading Owner: Richard Averill, 18, 2007/2008
Recent Meeting, Leading Trainer: Kirk Ziadie, 29, 2007/2008
Recent Meeting, Leading Horse: Blue Pepsi Lodge, 4, 2007/2008; Fortunate Trail, 4, 2007/2008

Records
Single-Day Jockey Wins: Jacinto Vasquez, 6, December 22, 1990; Rene Douglas, 6, December 8, 1993; Javier Castellano, 6, December 31, 2000; Eddie Castro, 6, October 17, 2005; Manoel Cruz, 6, November 27, 2005
Single Meeting, Leading Jockey by Wins: Jermaine V. Bridgmohan, 110, 2006/2007

Single Meeting, Leading Trainer by Wins: Stanley Hough, 35, 1978/1979; John Tammaro, 35, 1988
Single Meeting, Leading Trainer by Stakes Wins: George Gianos, 7, 1988/1989
Single Meeting, Leading Jockey by Stakes Wins: Douglas Valiente, 8, 1988/1989; Heberto Castillo Jr., 8, 1990/1991

Principal Races
La Prevoyante H. (G2), W. L. McKnight H. (G2), Tropical Park Derby (G3), Frances A. Genter S. (G3), Fred W. Hooper H. (G3)

Notable Events
Florida Million, Grand Slam I, II, and III

Track Records, Main Dirt
4 furlongs: Diamond Studs, :46.21, July 14, 2001
4½ furlongs: Gold Phantom, :51.86, September 16, 2001
5 furlongs: Honest, :57.61, July 1, 1996
5½ furlongs: Bernard's Candy, 1:04.39, August 9, 2002
6 furlongs: Forty One Carats, 1:08.95, October 7, 2000
6½ furlongs: Tour of the Cat, 1:15.99, August 17, 2002
7 furlongs: Constant Escort, 1:21.82, September 28, 1996
1 mile: High Ideal, 1:36.25, September 15, 2001
1 mile 70 yds: Halo's Image, 1:41.78, October 31, 1995
1¹/₁₆ miles: Castlebrook, 1:42.55, September 15, 2001
1⅛ miles: Jumping Hill, 1:50, December 30, 1978
1³/₁₆ miles: Arctic Honeymoon, 1:59³/₅, January 3, 1987
1¼ miles: Wicapi, 2:05.08, June 24, 1996
1½ miles: Lead'm Home, 2:32³/₅, December 31, 1977
1⅝ miles: Timberlea Tune, 2:50¹/₅, October 16, 1971
1¾ miles: *Detective II, 3:03¹/₅, October 23, 1971
2 miles: *Detective II, 3:30¹/₅, November 11, 1971
Other: 2 furlongs, Baby Shark, :20.81, July 13, 2002

Track Records, Main Turf
5 furlongs: Whenthedoveflies, :54.78, May 23, 2004
7 furlongs: Carterista, 1:22.36, June 19, 1993
7½ furlongs: Court Lark, 1:26.54, July 16, 1994
1 mile: Mr. Explosive, 1:33³/₅, October 17, 1992; Dillonmyboy, 1:33.66, October 30, 2000
1¹/₁₆ miles: He's Crafty, 1:39.27, December 28, 2004
1⅛ miles: The Vid, 1:44.99, November 25, 1995
1⅜ miles: King's Design, 2:13.18, July 23, 1999
1½ miles: Flag Down, 2:24.11, December 16, 1995
2 miles: Skate On Thin Ice, 3:21.89, January 2, 1996

Fastest Times of 2007 (Dirt)
2 furlongs: Caller One, 10, :21.15, July 28, 2007
4½ furlongs: Wise Answer, 2, :52.56, June 9, 2007
7 furlongs: Firebrook, 5, 1:23.09, July 28, 2007
1 mile: Annabill, 4, 1:38.79, October 27, 2007; Minidrop, 4, 1:38.79, December 9, 2007
1¹/₁₆ miles: B. B. Best, 5, 1:44.24, August 24, 2007
1⅛ miles: Electrify, 4, 1:51.49, July 4, 2007
1³/₁₆ miles: Tacit Agreement, 6, 2:00.05, May 19, 2007
1¼ miles: Tacit Agreement, 6, 2:06.49, June 9, 2007
1½ miles: Delosvientos, 4, 2:33.87, July 1, 2007
2 miles: Golden Strategy, 4, 3:32.34, July 28, 2007

Fastest Times of 2007 (Turf)
5 furlongs: Lord Robyn, 5, :55.10, May 12, 2007
7½ furlongs: Fearless Eagle, 3, 1:27.22, December 29, 2007
1 mile: Tastefully Smart, 3, 1:33.93, December 28, 2007
1¹/₁₆ miles: Jet Propulsion, 4, 1:39.46, September 3, 2007
1⅛ miles: Quistopher, 4, 1:47.57, December 30, 2007
1½ miles: Presious Passion, 4, 2:26.13, December 15, 2007

Idaho

Eastern Idaho State Fair
Location: P.O. Box 250, Blackfoot, Id. 83221-0350
Phone: (208) 785-2480
Fax: (208) 782-2483
Website: *www.funatthefair.com*
E-Mail: thefair@funatthefair.com
Abbreviation: BKF

Officers
General Manager: Doris Wallace
Track Superintendent: Trina Fackrell
Stewards: Richard Cade, Melvin Warr, David Wheeler

Racing Dates
2007: September 3-September 8, 4 days
2008: September 1-September 6, 4 days

Handle
Average On-Track Recent Meeting: $20,000, 2007
Total On-Track Recent Meeting: $80 000, 2007

Jerome Racing
Location: 200 N. Fir St., P.O. Box 414, Jerome, Id. 83338
Phone: (208) 324-7209
Website: *www.jeromecountyfair.com*
E-Mail: jerome@fair.myrf.net
Abbreviation: Jrm

Officers
General Manager: Kathleen Dietrick
Director of Racing: Bob Humphrey
Stewards: Richard Cade, Melvin Warr, David Wheeler

Racing Dates
2007: June 16-June 24, 3 days
2008: June 14-June 22, 3 days

Handle
Average On-Track Recent Meeting: $1,500, 2007
Total On-Track Recent Meeting, $4,500, 2007

Fastest Times of 2007 (Dirt)
5 furlongs: File Corrupted, 10, 1:03.40, June 16, 2007

Les Bois Park

Located in Boise on the Western Idaho Fairgrounds, Les Bois Park is one of the largest racetracks in the Northwest and annually holds the Idaho Cup for statebred Thoroughbreds, Quarter Horses, Paints, and Appaloosas. Seven Thoroughbred stakes with a combined value of nearly $200,000 are included in the series. Les Bois, which is French for "the woods," opened in May 1970, six years old after pari-mutuel wagering was legalized in Idaho. The track had difficult times in the late 1980s, when a downturn in horse racing caused the track owners, the Ada County Commission, to put the Les Bois lease up for auction. A group of horsemen led by veterinarian Chris Christian won the lease for $100 per month and successfully lobbied for full-card simulcasting, which turned the track around and allowed it to increase its purses. In April 2002, the track was leased to former professional basketball player Arnell Jones and his wife, Lanae, but their Lariat Productions failed to make required payments to Ada County in 2005. Capitol Racing of California was awarded the lease and conducted subsequent meets. The track features Thoroughbreds, Quarter Horses, Appaloosas, and Paints racing from early May to mid-August. Les Bois was the launching pad for Racing Hall of Fame jockey Gary Stevens, who scored his first career victory at the track aboard Little Star in 1979.

Location: 5610 N. Glenwood St., P.O. Box 140099, Boise, Id. 83714-1338
Phone: (208) 321-0222
Fax: (208) 321-4820
Website: *www.lesboisracing.com*

E-Mail: alanhorowitz@sprintmail.com
Year Founded: 1970
Dates of Inaugural Meeting: May 15, 1970
Abbreviation: Boi

Ownership
Steve Bieri

Officers
President: Steve Bieri
General Manager: Alan Horowitz
Racing Secretary: Fred Davis
Director of Operations: Matt Heggli
Director of Marketing and Publicity: Melinda Nothern
Director of Mutuels: Souix Wieckowicz
Vice President: Barbara Bieri
Stewards: Roger White, Terry Crystal, Doug Standlee
Track Announcer: Fred Davis
Track Photographer: Linda Bernsten
Track Superintendent: Chris Gianinni

Racing Dates
2007: May 4-August 11, 46 days
2008: May 2-August 16, 46 days

Track Layout
Main Circumference: 6 furlongs
Main Track Chute: 5 furlongs and 1 mile
Main Width: 80 feet
Main Length of Stretch: 660 feet

Attendance
Average Daily Recent Meeting: 1,924, 2007
Total Attendance Recent Meeting: 88,504, 2007

Handle
Average On-Track Recent Meeting: $46,198, 2007
Total On-Track Recent Meeting: $2,125,108, 2007

Leaders
Recent Meeting, Leading Jockey: Brian Long, 82, 2007
Recent Meeting, Leading Trainer: Farrell Christoffersen, 19, 2007
Recent Meeting, Leading Horse: Red Limo, 3, 2007

Principal Races
Idaho Cup Juvenile Championship S., Idaho Cup Classic S., Idaho Cup Derby, Idaho Cup Distaff Derby

Notable Events
Memorial Day Tribute to Veterans, Idaho Cup Day

Fastest Times of 2007 (Dirt)
4 furlongs: Van Lion, 4, :46, May 8, 2007
4½ furlongs: Red Limo, 6, :50.40, May 28, 2007
5 furlongs: Red Limo, 6, :56.40, May 15, 2007
6½ furlongs: Kid Royal, 6, 1:18.20, May 25, 2007
7 furlongs: Social Order, 4, 1:24.20, May 19, 2007
7½ furlongs: Silent Snow, 6, 1:31.93, July 21, 2007
1 mile: Silent Snow, 6, 1:38.13, August 4, 2007

Oneida County Fair

Location: P.O. Box 13, Malad, Id. 83252-0013
Phone: (208) 766-4607
Fax: (208) 766-4707
Abbreviation: One
Acreage: 30
Number of Stalls: 93
Seating Capacity: 1,000

Officers
President: John Paskett
Stewards: Richard Cade, Melvin Warr, David Wheeler

Racing Dates
2007: August 4-August 12, 4 days
2008: August 2-August 10, 4 days

Track Layout
Main Circumference: 4 furlongs
Main Width: 60 feet
Main Length of Stretch: 300 yds

Fastest Times of 2007 (Dirt)
5 furlongs: Mr. Will, 8, 1:03.80, August 11, 2007

Pocatello Downs

Location: 10560 Fairgrounds Rd., P.O. Box 0248, Pocatello, Id. 83204
Phone: (208) 238-1721
Abbreviation: PoD

Officers
General Manager: Treena Caverhill
Racing Secretary: Roger Hanson
Stewards: Richard Cade, Melvin Warr, David Wheeler

Racing Dates
2007: May 12-June 3, 8 days
2008: May 10-June 1, 9 days

Attendance
Average Daily Recent Meeting: 650, 2007
Total Attendance Recent Meeting: 5,200, 2007

Handle
Average On-Track Recent Meeting: $8,000, 2007
Total On-Track Recent Meeting: $64,000, 2007

Rupert Downs

Location: P.O. Box 153, Rupert, Id. 83350
Phone: (208) 436-1104
E-Mail: rupertdowns@yahoo.com
Abbreviation: Rup

Officers
Director of Operations: Becky Grant
Racing Secretary: Foster Crane
Stewards: Richard Cade, Melvin Warr, David Wheeler

Racing Dates
2007: June 30-July 8, 5 days
2008: July 4-July 13, 5 days
2009: July 3-July 12, 5 days

Attendance
Average Daily Recent Meeting: 350, 2007
Total Attendance Recent Meeting: 1,750, 2007

Handle
Average On-Track Recent Meeting: $2,500, 2007
Total On-Track Recent Meeting: $12,500, 2007

Illinois

Arlington Park

Arlington Park first opened on October 13, 1927, and has been home to many firsts in Thoroughbred racing. Located northwest of Chicago in Arlington Heights, the track became the first in Illinois to offer turf races in 1934. In 1966, Laffit Pincay Jr. recorded his first United States victory there on his way to a place in the Racing Hall of Fame and a record 9,530 victories. In 1981, Arlington became the world's first track to host a $1-million race for Thoroughbreds when it inaugurated the Arlington Million Stakes (G1). The first run-

ning was won by John Henry, who returned to win the race in 1984. Today, the Million is part of Arlington's International Festival of Racing, which also includes the Beverly D. (G1) and Secretariat (G1) Stakes. On July 31, 1985, fire destroyed Arlington's clubhouse, causing the track to shift most of its remaining races to Hawthorne Race Course. The exception was the Million, which was held on August 25 at Arlington, and more than 35,000 fans watched the race from tents and temporary facilities during what would be dubbed the "Miracle Million." Those efforts led to Arlington becoming the first racetrack to earn an Eclipse Award. Arlington was rebuilt lavishly by Chicago-area industrialist Richard Duchossois, who closed the track for two seasons—1998 and '99—due to unfavorable economic and regulatory conditions. Arlington reopened in 2000 and the Arlington Million was resumed. Also in 2000, Churchill Downs Inc. purchased the track and assumed about $80-million in loans, while Duchossois received close to 4-million shares of Churchill common stock. Arlington installed a Polytrack surface in 2007 at a cost of $11-million.

Location: 2200 W. Euclid Ave., Arlington Heights, Il. 60006
Phone: (847) 385-7500
Fax: (847) 385-7251
Website: www.arlingtonpark.com
E-Mail: track@arlingtonpark.com
Year Founded: 1926
Dates of Inaugural Meeting: October 13, 1927
Abbreviation: AP
Number of Stalls: 2,140
Seating Capacity: 35,000

Ownership
Churchill Downs Inc.

Officers
Chairman: Richard L. Duchossois
President: Roy A. Arnold
Senior Vice President of Racing: William A. Thayer Jr.
Vice President of Racing and Racing Secretary: Kevin Greely
Assistant Racing Secretary: Christian A. Polzin
Admissions Manager: Bill Adams
Senior Manager of Communications: David Zenner
Director of Administration: Dan Peters
Director of Mutuels: Jack Lisowski
Director of Sales: Jennifer Welding
Director of Security: Christopher Martin
Stewards: Eddie Arroyo, Joseph K. Lindeman, Steve Morgan, Peter Kosiba Jr.
Track Announcer: John G. Dooley
Track Superintendent: Javier Barajas

Racing Dates
2007: May 4-September 16, 94 days
2008: May 2-September 21, 96 days

Track Layout
Main Circumference: 1 1/8 miles (alternate finish line at sixteenth pole for 1 1/16-mile races)
Main Track Chute: 6 1/2 furlongs, 7 furlongs, 7 1/2 furlongs, and 1 mile
Main Width: 92 feet
Main Length of Stretch: 1,028 feet
Main Turf Circumference: 1 mile
Main Turf Width: 150 feet
Main Turf Length of Stretch: 1,020 feet
Training Track: a5 furlongs

Attendance
Average Daily Recent Meeting: 8,341, 2007
Highest Single-Day Record: 50,638, July 4, 1938
Total Attendance Recent Meeting: 784,117, 2007

Handle
Average All-Sources Recent Meeting: $952,319, 2007
Average On-Track Recent Meeting: $589,861, 2007
Single-Day On-Track Handle: $13,568,209, October 26, 2002
Single-Day All-Sources Handle: $116,059,574, October 26, 2002
Total All-Sources Recent Meeting: $89,518,062, 2007
Total On-Track Recent Meeting: $54,600,942, 2007

Mutuel Records
Highest Win: $382, Ivalinda, August 12 1963
Highest Exacta: $6267, August 7, 1991
Highest Trifecta: $58,116.20, September 14, 2001
Highest Daily Double: $3,835.20, July 5, 1939
Highest Pick Three: $21,775.40, June 11, 1990
Highest Pick Six: $269,253.60, September 25, 1984
Highest Other Exotics: $52,686, Superfecta, August 13, 1995; $2,701, Quinella, September 3, 2000; $16,349.30, Pick 5, October 26, 2002

Leaders
Career, Leading Jockey by Titles: Earlie Fires, 6
Career, Leading Owner by Titles: Calumet Farm, 9
Career, Leading Trainer by Titles: Richard P. Hazelton, 8; William Hal Bishop, 8
Career, Leading Jockey by Stakes Wins: Earlie Fires, 105
Career, Leading Owner by Stakes Wins: Calumet Farm, 57
Career, Leading Trainer by Stakes Wins: Harry Trotsek, 44
Career, Leading Jockey by Wins: Earlie Fires, 2,851
Career, Leading Trainer by Wins: Richard P. Hazelton, 1,167
Recent Meeting, Leading Jockey: Rene Douglas, 129, 2007
Recent Meeting, Leading Owner: Frank C. Calabrese, 74, 2007
Recent Meeting, Leading Trainer: Wayne M. Catalano, 74, 2007
Recent Meeting, Leading Horse: First Movement, Dancy's Angel & Salt Syn, 4, 2007

Records
Single-Day Jockey Wins: Pat Day, 8, September 13, 1989
Single Meeting, Leading Jockey by Wins: Shane Sellers, 219, 1991
Single Meeting, Leading Owner by Wins: Frank C. Calabrese, 74, 2007
Single Meeting, Leading Trainer by Wins: Wayne M. Catalano, 74, 2007

Principal Races
Arlington Million S. (G1), Beverly D. S (G1), Secretariat S. (G1), Washington Park H. (G3), American Derby (G2)

Interesting Facts
Trivia: June 24, 2003, jockey Rene Douglas won seven races, including first five on the card, from nine mounts.
Previous Name: Arlington International Racecourse
Achievements/Milestones: July 13, 1985, destroyed by fire. June 28, 1989, track reopened. June 16, 2003, third consecutive year with highest Father's Day attendance in U.S. of 26,101.

Notable Events
International Festival of Racing (Arlington Million Day)

Track Records, Main Dirt
4 1/2 furlongs: Wheat Penny, :51.64, June 8, 2000; Bold America, :51.64, June 28, 2002
5 furlongs: Staunch Avenger, :57 1/5, June 29, 1970; Heisanative, :57 1/5, June 12, 1971; Shecky Greene, :57 1/5, June 15, 1972; Zarb's Magic, :57.31, September 7, 2002
5 1/2 furlongs: Lil Tree, 1:02.47, September 11, 2006
6 furlongs: Taylor's Special, 1:08, August 22, 1986
6 1/2 furlongs: Pentelicus, 1:14 1/5, July 14, 1990
7 furlongs: Tumiga, 1:20 2/5, July 13, 1968
7 1/2 furlongs: Without a Doubt, 1:28.15, June 21, 2006
1 mile: Dr. Fager, 1:32 1/5, August 24, 1968
1 mile 70 yds: Geo. Groom, 1:42 1/5, October 25, 1927
1 1/16 miles: Kindly Manner, 1:41 2/5, August 22, 1977; Mojave, 1:41 2/5, June 30, 1981
1 1/8 miles: Spectacular Bid, 1:46 1/5, July 19, 1980
1 3/8 miles: Suave, 1:53.53, July 29, 2006
1 1/4 miles: Private Thoughts, 1:59 2/5, August 20, 1977
1 3/8 miles: Playdale, 2:15 2/5, July 19, 1932

$1\frac{1}{2}$ miles: El Misterio, 2:28$\frac{1}{5}$, September 5, 1960
$1\frac{5}{8}$ miles: Fool's Robbery, 2:45$\frac{3}{5}$, July 5, 1973
$1\frac{3}{4}$ miles: *Deux-Moulins, 2:59$\frac{2}{5}$, July 14, 1955
2 miles: Swede Of Norfolk, 3:26$\frac{2}{5}$, August 15, 1970
Other: a$1\frac{1}{16}$ miles, Ashleigh's Jet, 1:44.10, June 14, 2001; $1\frac{5}{16}$ miles, Rush Home, 2:10, August 7, 1971; $1\frac{5}{16}$ miles, Evanescent, 2:10, July 18, 1993; $2\frac{1}{4}$ miles, *Djem, 4:05$\frac{3}{5}$, July 30, 1953

Track Records, Main Turf

5 furlongs: Nicole's Dream, :55.90, July 16, 2006
$5\frac{1}{2}$ furlongs: Cat On a Cloud, 1:02.18, September 3, 2007
1 mile: Gee Can He Dance, 1:34.50, September 4, 1995
1 mile 70yds: Pass the Brandy, 1:38$\frac{4}{5}$, July 25, 1970
$1\frac{1}{16}$ miles: Zeeruler, 1:41, September 7, 1992
$1\frac{1}{8}$ miles: Mr. Leader, 1:47$\frac{2}{5}$, July 4, 1970; Jinski's World, 1:47$\frac{2}{5}$, July 6, 1991; World Class Splash, 1:47.40, July 11, 1992
$1\frac{3}{16}$ miles: Reluctant Guest, 1:53$\frac{1}{5}$, September 1, 1990
$1\frac{1}{4}$ miles: Awad, 1:58.69, August 27, 1995
$1\frac{1}{2}$ miles: Cetewayo, 2:27.50, July 6, 2002
$1\frac{5}{8}$ miles: Coincident, 2:45, July 26, 1951
$1\frac{3}{4}$ miles: *Pennsburg, 3:02$\frac{3}{5}$, July 5, 1941
2 miles: Penaway, 3:25$\frac{2}{5}$, July 24, 1953
Other: a5 furlongs, Nicole's Dream, :56.38, September 18, 2003; a$5\frac{1}{2}$ furlongs, Loco Kid, 1:01$\frac{3}{5}$, May 28, 1969; a6 furlongs, Mr. Sam A., 1:05$\frac{4}{5}$, July 12, 1966; a1 mile, Omaggio, 1:34.50, July 26, 2006; a1 mile 70yds, Elegant Heir, 1:41$\frac{2}{5}$, August 11, 1970; a$1\frac{1}{16}$ miles, Top Floor, 1:40$\frac{2}{5}$, June 18, 1969; a$1\frac{1}{16}$ miles, Crafty Bee, 1:40$\frac{2}{5}$, June 21, 1969; a$1\frac{1}{8}$ miles, Lotus Pool, 1:47.22, August 1, 1991; a$1\frac{3}{16}$ miles, Duckaroo, 1:57.51, June 10, 1992; a$1\frac{3}{16}$ miles, Quintillion, 1:57.51, August 20, 1990; a$1\frac{1}{2}$ miles, Noble Savage, 2:22$\frac{1}{5}$, July 20, 1991; a$1\frac{5}{8}$ miles, Roman Leader, 2:51, August 19, 1972; $2\frac{1}{16}$ miles, *Deux-Moulins, 3:30$\frac{4}{5}$, July 28, 1955; $2\frac{1}{8}$ miles, English Harry, 3:45, July 30, 1941

Fastest Times of 2007 (All Weather)

$4\frac{1}{2}$ furlongs: Possetothemax, 2, :51.71, June 2, 2007
5 furlongs: Smack Daddy, 3, :56.51, August 19, 2007
$5\frac{1}{2}$ furlongs: Officer Frank, 2, 1:03.10, September 16, 2007
6 furlongs: Chihulykee, 3, 1:08.84, September 16, 2007
$6\frac{1}{2}$ furlongs: Kemp, 6, 1:15.07, August 23, 2007
7 furlongs: Lovango, 3, 1:21.02, August 11, 2007
$7\frac{1}{2}$ furlongs: Coolwind, 4, 1:30.97, July 27, 2007
1 mile: Spotsgone, 4, 1:33.72, May 26, 2007
$1\frac{1}{16}$ miles: Pitamakan, 3, 1:41.49, August 19, 2007
$1\frac{1}{8}$ miles: On Safari, 4, 1:49.30, August 25, 2007
$1\frac{3}{16}$ miles: Lewis Michael, 4, 1:55.17, July 28, 2007
$1\frac{1}{4}$ miles: Heckofanactofollow, 7, 2:07.51, August 3, 2007

Fastest Times of 2007 (Turf)

5 furlongs: Fort Prado, 6, :56.52, September 16, 2007
a5 furlongs: Ocean Current, 4, :56.43, July 12, 2007
$5\frac{1}{2}$ furlongs: Cat On a Cloud, 3, 1:02.18, September 3, 2007
a$5\frac{1}{2}$ furlongs: McMurphy, 5, 1:02.34, September 2, 2007
1 mile: Starlet Sky, 5, 1:36.04, September 16, 2007
a1 mile: Giant Shift, 5, 1:35.48, September 3, 2007
$1\frac{1}{16}$ miles: Love Handles, 4, 1:41.32, September 15, 2007; Purim, 5, 1:41.32, September 16, 2007
a$1\frac{1}{16}$ miles: Flying Zombo, 3, 1:41.71, September 3, 2007
$1\frac{1}{8}$ miles: Jennie R., 6, 1:48.09, June 23, 2007
a$1\frac{1}{8}$ miles: Tenpointfive, 5, 1:49.98, June 16, 2007
$1\frac{3}{16}$ miles: Bridge Game, 4, 1:54.62, July 21, 2007
a$1\frac{3}{16}$ miles: Yanquee Reign, 5, 1:58.68, June 8, 2007
$1\frac{1}{4}$ miles: Cosmonaut, 5, 2:01.32, July 21, 2007
$1\frac{1}{2}$ miles: Arosa (Ire), 4, 2:30.52, September 3, 2007

Fairmount Park

Fairmount Park, located in Collinsville, about 30 minutes east of St. Louis, opened on September 26, 1925. The track was built to resemble a small Churchill Downs by Col. E. R. Bradley, who owned four Kentucky Derby winners, and Col. Matt Winn, who made the Kentucky Derby at Churchill a sporting institution. In 1947, Fairmount became the first one-mile oval racetrack in the world to provide lighting for night Thoroughbred racing. Fairmount's most famous horseman is jockey Dave Gall, who retired in 1999 with 7,396 wins, placing him among Thoroughbred racing's winningest jockeys. Fairmount was purchased by Fairmount Park Inc. from Ogden Services Corp. for $15.5-million in 2000.

Location: 9301 Collinsville Rd., Collinsville, Il. 62234-1729
Phone: (618) 345-4300
Fax: (618) 344-8218
Website: *www.fairmountpark.com*
E-Mail: fmtpark@fairmountpark.com
Year Founded: 1924
Dates of Inaugural Meeting: September 26, 1925
Abbreviation: FP
Acreage: 190
Number of Stalls: 1,000
Seating Capacity: 5,500

Ownership

Fairmount Park Inc.

Officers

President and General Manager: Brian F. Zander
Vice President: Joe Ruppert
Director of Racing and Racing Secretary: Bobby Pace
Assistant Racing Secretary: Darrel Cassity
Treasurer and Director of Operations: Joe Ruppert
Director of Admissions: Gregory G. Graves
Director of Marketing: Gregg Smith
Director of Publicity: Jon Sloane
Director of Mutuels and Simulcasting: Gregory G. Graves
Horsemen's Liaison: Lanny Brooks
Stewards: Jeffrey Bowen, David A. Smith, Roger Duff
Track Announcer: John Scully
Track Photographer: Jim Ainsley
Track Superintendent: Gale Franklin
Security: Steve Chambliss
Horsemen's Bookkeeper: Barbara Randazzo

Racing Dates

2007: March 6-September 29, 89 days
2008: April 18-September 1, 60 days

Track Layout

Main Circumference: 1 mile
Main Track Chute: 6 furlongs and $1\frac{1}{4}$ miles
Main Width: Homestretch: 80 feet; Backstretch: 70 feet
Main Length of Stretch: 1,050 feet

Attendance

Highest Single-Day Record: 13,898, September 7, 1953
Average Daily Recent Meeting: 2,355, 2007
Total Attendance Recent Meeting: 209,624, 2007

Handle

Total All-Sources Recent Meeting: $16,128,619, 2007
Average All-Sources Recent Meeting: $181,220, 2007
Total On-Track Recent Meeting: $11,437,020, 2007
Average On-Track Recent Meeting: $128,505, 2007
Single-Day All-Sources Handle: $1,380,880, May 5, 1990

Principal Races

All Sold Out S., Troy Our Boy S., Pollyanna Pixie S., Pete Condellone S., Bungalow H., Tex's Zing H.

Interesting Facts

Previous Name: Cahokia Downs

Notable Events

Party at the Park, Ultra Thursdays

Track Records, Main Dirt

4 furlongs: Aledo, :45.60, June 2, 1994; Nextquestor, :45.60, March 25, 2005
$4\frac{1}{2}$ furlongs: Vague Promise, :51$\frac{3}{5}$, May 19, 1978
5 furlongs: Slight in the Rear, :56$\frac{4}{5}$, July 25, 1989
$5\frac{1}{2}$ furlongs: Sarof Jr., 1:03$\frac{2}{5}$, June 5, 1980
6 furlongs: Ye Country, 1:08$\frac{3}{5}$, November 26, 1977

1 mile: Dusty Appeal, 1:37.40, June 20, 1992
1 mile 70 yds: Dusty Appeal, 1:39$\frac{4}{5}$, July 30, 1989
$1\frac{1}{16}$ miles: Lt. Lao, 1:40$\frac{4}{5}$, July 22, 1989
$1\frac{1}{8}$ miles: Andover Man, 1:47$\frac{3}{5}$, August 26, 1989
$1\frac{1}{4}$ miles: Leaddrop, 2:03, July 22, 1989
$1\frac{1}{2}$ miles: *Firth of Tay, 2:33, September 21, 1927
$1\frac{5}{8}$ miles: Monthazar, 2:48, November 3, 1973
$1\frac{3}{4}$ miles: Lightin Bill, 3:02$\frac{4}{5}$, October 14, 1939
2 miles: East Royalty, 3:32.60, December 1, 1991
Other: 2 furlongs, Don Manuel, :20.80, March 17, 2006; Penn Pacific, :20.80, September 26, 2006; 2m 70 yds, King Boogie, 3:33$\frac{3}{5}$, September 1, 1984; $2\frac{1}{16}$ miles, Tim Trefle, 3:38$\frac{4}{5}$, September 10, 1983; $2\frac{1}{8}$ miles, Lucrest, 3:46$\frac{1}{5}$, September 24, 1983; $2\frac{1}{4}$ miles, Baye Dawn, 4:00, October 8, 1983; $2\frac{1}{2}$ miles, Cat Walk, 4:29, October 22, 1983

Fastest Times of 2007 (Dirt)

2 furlongs: Penn Pacific, 6, :21.40, March 9, 2007
$4\frac{1}{2}$ furlongs: Chipotle, 6, :51.80, March 6, 2007
5 furlongs: Living a Dream, 10, :58.20, March 20, 2007; Shamuuu, 6, :58.20, March 30, 2007
$5\frac{1}{2}$ furlongs: Chipotle, 6, 1:04.20, March 20, 2007
6 furlongs: Mr. Mink, 7, 1:10.40, September 8, 2007; Peace and Joy, 8, 1:10.40, April 7, 2007; Stalwart Memory, 6, 1:10.40, April 6, 2007; Stop the Race, 5, 1:10.40, May 22, 2007
1 mile: Guccione, 4, 1:38.20, June 2, 2007
1 mile 70yds: Archee More, 5, 1:43, May 11, 2007
$1\frac{1}{16}$ miles: Never Was, 4, 1:45.40, September 22, 2007
$1\frac{1}{2}$ miles: Mount Tora Bora, 7, 2:37.80, September 25, 2007

Hawthorne Race Course

For nearly 100 years, members of the Carey family have overseen Hawthorne Race Course in the near Chicago suburb of Stickney. In 1909, Thomas Carey bought the track from horseman and noted gambler Ed Corrigan, who had opened the track in 1891. Under Corrigan's ownership, Hawthorne closed when the state Senate banned racing in Chicago in 1905, and new owner Carey attempted over the next several years to revive racing. He finally succeeded in 1922. In 1928, the track's most notable race, the Hawthorne Gold Cup (G2), debuted. Among the winners of the Hawthorne Gold Cup are five-time Horse of the Year Kelso, 1968 Horse of the Year Dr. Fager, and '91 Horse of the Year Black Tie Affair (Ire). In 1977, a fire destroyed Hawthorne's grandstand, and the remainder of its meet was held at Sportsman's Park, located a block away. Racing returned to the track in 1980 when a new grandstand was built. Over the years, Hawthorne also has conducted harness racing. In late 2002, Hawthorne merged with Sportsman's Park, with Thomas F. Carey III becoming president of the new entity, Hawthorne National. Sportsman's Park was sold for development and its racing dates and major races are now run at Hawthorne.

Location: 3501 S. Laramie Ave., Cicero, Il. 60804-4503
Phone: (708) 780-3700
Fax: (708) 780-3753
Website: *www.hawthorneracecourse.com*
E-Mail: jim@hawthorneracecourse.com
Year Founded: 1890
Dates of Inaugural Meeting: May 20, 1891
Abbreviation: Haw
Acreage: 119
Number of Stalls: 2,400
Seating Capacity: 18,000

Officers

President and General Manager: Tim Carey
Racing Secretary: Gary M. Duch
Assistant Racing Secretary: Christian Polzin
Secretary: Debbie Lindsay
Director of Operations: Jim Miller
Director of Admissions: Mike Harris
Director of Communications: Mitch Demick
Director of Marketing: Dakota Schultz
Director of Mutuels: John Demy
Director of Sales: Pam Dorr
Director of Simulcasting: John Walsh
Horsemen's Liaison: Tim Becker
Stewards: Eddie Arroyo, Joseph K. Lindeman, Steve Morgan
Track Announcer: Peter Galassi
Track Photographer: Four Footed Fotos
Track Superintendent: Gregorio Cardenas
Security: Dennis Taylor

Racing Dates

2007: February 23-April 29, 45 days; September 21-December 30, 73 days
2008: January 2-January 13, 10 days; March 7-April 28, 38 days; September 26-December 31, 66 days

Track Layout

Main Circumference: 1 mile
Main Track Chute: $6\frac{1}{2}$ furlongs
Main Width: 75 feet
Main Length of Stretch: 1,320 feet
Main Turf Circumference: 7 furlongs 148 feet

Attendance

Highest Single-Day Record: 37,792, September 6, 1937
Average Daily Recent Meeting: 1,446, January and Spring 2008
Total Attendance Recent Meeting: 69,440, January and Spring 2008

Handle

Average All-Sources Recent Meeting: \$2,291,470, January and Spring 2008
Average On-Track Recent Meeting: \$-34,500, January and Spring 2008
Single-Day All-Sources Handle: \$10,300,640, May 5, 2001
Total All-Sources Recent Meeting: 109,990,560, January and Spring 2008
Total On-Track Recent Meeting: \$6,456,000, January and Spring 2008
Record Average All-Sources Single Meeting: \$3,575,861, 1996

Leaders

Recent Meeting, Leading Jockey: Tim Thorton, 92, 2007/2008; Tim Thorton 61, Spring 2008
Recent Meeting, Leading Owner: Frank C. Calabrese, 26, 2007/2008; Eagle Valley Farm, 10, Spring 2008
Recent Meeting, Leading Trainer: Frank Kirby, 39, 2007/2008; Frank Kirby, 25, Spring 2008
Recent Meeting, Leading Horse: Queen Meave, 3, Spring 2008; Best Buddy, 3, Spring 2008

Records

Single-Day Jockey Wins: Johnny Heckman, 7, October 1, 1956
Single-Day Trainer Wins: Mike Reavis, 5, November 2, 2002
Single Meeting, Leading Jockey by Wins: Mark Guidry, 137, 1995
Single Meeting, Leading Trainer by Wins: Richard Hazelton, 48, 1976

Principal Races

Hawthorne Gold Cup H. (G2), Illinois Derby (G2), National Jockey Club H. (G3), Sixty Sails H. (G3), Hawthorne Derby (G3)

Interesting Facts

Trivia: First major United States track to use an electric timer (1931). Track announcer Phil Georgeff entered the *Guiness Book of World Records* when he called his 85,000th race on August 13, 1988.

Track Records, Main Dirt

$4\frac{1}{2}$ furlongs: Joanies Bella, :51.80, May 28, 2001
5 furlongs: De La Concorde, :57, November 11, 1992

$5\frac{1}{2}$ furlongs: Marluel's Troy, 1:02$\frac{2}{5}$, November 2, 1976
6 furlongs: Satan's Poppy, 1:08$\frac{1}{5}$, October 21, 1978
$6\frac{1}{2}$ furlongs: Dee Lance, 1:14$\frac{2}{5}$, August 27, 1988
1 mile: Actuary, 1:37$\frac{1}{5}$, July 17, 1923; Hopeless, 1:37$\frac{1}{5}$, August 29, 1925
1 mile 70 yds: Soldat Bleu, 1:39$\frac{1}{5}$, July 27, 1988
$1\frac{1}{16}$ miles: Sensitive Prince, 1:39$\frac{3}{5}$, September 23, 1978
$1\frac{1}{8}$ miles: *Zografos, 1:46$\frac{3}{5}$, October 9, 1974
$1\frac{3}{16}$ miles: Lindy's Lad, 1:59$\frac{2}{5}$, November 12, 1980; Steal the Account, 1:59.40, August 28, 1999
$1\frac{1}{4}$ miles: Gladwin, 1:58$\frac{4}{5}$, October 1, 1970; Group Plan, 1:58$\frac{4}{5}$, October 19, 1974
$1\frac{1}{2}$ miles: David II, 2:29$\frac{3}{5}$, October 1, 1969
$1\frac{5}{8}$ miles: Viale (Uru), 2:47.02, December 10, 2000
$1\frac{3}{4}$ miles: America Fore, 3:02$\frac{1}{5}$, October 2, 1943
Other: 2 furlongs, Minty Flavors, :20.88, May 14, 1999; 2m 70yds, Sun 'N Shine, 3:30$\frac{2}{5}$, October 19, 1974; $2\frac{1}{16}$ miles, Revoque, 3:35$\frac{2}{5}$, October 5, 1963; $2\frac{1}{8}$ miles, Hallandale, 3:41$\frac{4}{5}$, October 12, 1963

Track Records, Main Turf

5 furlongs: Sulemark, :56, October 25, 1992
7 furlongs: Glassy Dip, 1:22$\frac{3}{5}$, May 30, 1977
$7\frac{1}{2}$ furlongs: Joey Jr., 1:27$\frac{1}{5}$, November 5, 1989
1 mile: Soviet Line (Ire), 1:33.40, July 25, 1998
$1\frac{1}{16}$ miles: Jennie R., 1:40.46, September 29, 2007
$1\frac{1}{8}$ miles: Rainbows for Life, 1:44$\frac{3}{5}$, October 13, 1991
$1\frac{3}{16}$ miles: Royal Glint, 1:54$\frac{2}{5}$, September 28, 1974; Sari's Baba, 1:54$\frac{2}{5}$, September 24, 1985
$1\frac{1}{4}$ miles: Pass the Line, 2:00$\frac{2}{5}$, August 10, 1985
$1\frac{3}{8}$ miles: Shayzari (Ire), 2:15$\frac{1}{5}$, September 3, 1988
$1\frac{1}{2}$ miles: Lord Comet, 2:26.87, October 27, 1999
$1\frac{3}{4}$ miles: Neverest, 2:58$\frac{4}{5}$, August 31, 1973

Fastest Times of 2007 (Dirt)

$4\frac{1}{2}$ furlongs: Pixie, 2, :53.80, April 23, 2007
5 furlongs: Icandazzle, 3, :58.55, March 18, 2007; Spanning, 5, :58.55, April 26, 2007
$5\frac{1}{2}$ furlongs: He's Hot Sauce, 3, 1:05.07, March 24, 2007
6 furlongs: Worththebother, 4, 1:08.65, December 26, 2007
$6\frac{1}{2}$ furlongs: Deputy Too, 3, 1:15.98, December 14, 2007
1 mile 70 yds: Le Jester, 7, 1:39.54, March 3, 2007
$1\frac{1}{16}$ miles: Very Capo (Arg), 5, 1:42.69, December 26, 2007
$1\frac{1}{8}$ miles: Master Command, 5, 1:49.47, April 21, 2007
$1\frac{1}{4}$ miles: Slewey Armstrong, 5, 2:03.91, December 8, 2007

Fastest Times of 2007 (Turf)

5 furlongs: Byenne, 3, :56.23, November 18, 2007
$5\frac{1}{2}$ furlongs: Alone At Last, 6, 1:02.06, October 8, 2007
1 mile: Classic Campaign, 5, 1:33.95, September 29, 2007
$1\frac{1}{16}$ miles: Jennie R., 6, 1:40.46, September 29, 2007
$1\frac{1}{8}$ miles: War Club, 4, 1:47.27, October 26, 2007
$1\frac{1}{2}$ miles: Very Capo (Arg), 5, 2:31.37, October 12, 2007
$1\frac{9}{16}$ miles: A to Z, 5, 2:40.39, November 17, 2007

Indiana

Hoosier Park

In 1989, Indiana approved pari-mutuel wagering, and the state's first pari-mutuel racetrack, Hoosier Park, opened its inaugural season of Standardbred racing in '94. Thoroughbred racing debuted at Hoosier in 1995. Located northeast of Indianapolis in Anderson, the $10-million track was developed by majority owner Churchill Downs Inc. as the company's first racing interest outside Kentucky. Hoosier annually holds a Thoroughbred meet. For 2004, Hoosier hosted two graded stakes, the $500,000 Indiana Derby (G2) and the $350,000 Indiana Breeders' Cup Oaks (G3). A competitor, Indiana Downs, opened on April 1, 2003, only 40 miles from its facility. Churchill Downs Inc. sold its interest in Hoosier in 2007. A 92,000-square-foot racino with 2,000 slot machines opened in 2008.

Location: 4500 Dan Patch Circle, Anderson, In. 46013-3165
Phone: (765) 642-7223, (800) 526-7223
Fax: (765) 644-0467
Website: *www.hoosierpark.com*
E-Mail: info@hoosierpark.com
Year Founded: 1994
Dates of Inaugural Meeting: September 1-October 28, 1995
Abbreviation: Hoo
Acreage: 129
Number of Stalls: 1,032
Seating Capacity: 2,477

Ownership

Centaur Inc.

Officers

Chairman and CEO: Roderick J. Ratcliff
Executive Vice President/Chief Financial Officer: Kurt Wilson
Managing Director of Racing: Jeffrey M. Smith
President: John J. McLaughlin
General Manager of Racing: Richard B. Moore
General Manager of Casino: Jim Brown
Director of Racing/Racing Secretary: Raymond "Butch" Cook
Director of Facility Operations: Clint McKenzie
Public Relations Director: Tammy Knox
Director of Marketing: Jahnae Erpenbach
Director of Mutuels: Terri Douglas
Horsemen's Liaison: Gayle Christman
Stewards: Tim Day, Gary I. Wilfert, Jean Chalk
Track Announcer: Steve Cross
Track Photographer: Linscott Photography
Track Superintendent: Gary Wolff

Racing Dates

2007: September 1-November 24, 61 days
2008: August 29-November 23, 63 days

Track Layout

Main Circumference: 7 furlongs
Main Track Chute: 6 furlongs
Main Width: 90 feet
Main Length of Stretch: 1,255 feet

Attendance

Average Daily Recent Meeting: 930, 2007
Highest Single-Day Record: 10,827, October 7, 2000
Highest Single-Meeting Record: 95,468, 1995
Record Daily Average Single Meeting: 2,273, 1995
Total Attendance Recent Meeting: 66,326, 2007
Lowest Single Meeting Record: 56,345, 2004

Handle

Average All-Sources Recent Meeting: $1,192,047, 2007
Average On-Track Recent Meeting: $43,064, 2007
Record Daily Average Single Meeting: $153,786, 1995
Single-Day All-Sources Handle: $3,083,764, November 23, 2005
Total All-Sources Recent Meeting: $72,714,857, 2007
Total On-Track Recent Meeting: $2,626,890, 2007
Highest Single-Day On-Track Recent Meeting: $233,842, October 5, 2007
Highest Single-Day All-Sources Recent Meeting: $1,884,990, October 5, 2007
Record Total All-Sources Single Meeting: $106,034,147, 2006
Record Total Single Meeting: $6,459,004, 1995

Mutuel Records

Highest Win: $291.40, Mi Serenade, October 19, 2001
Highest Exacta: $3,212.60, September 10, 2000
Highest Trifecta: $34,077.20, November 22, 2002
Highest Daily Double: $5,986.40, October 17, 2002
Highest Pick Three: $8,952, November 22, 2002
Highest Other Exotics: $107.60, Place, October 7, 1996; $36.60, Show, November 19, 2003; $128,485.60, Superfecta, September 14, 2005; $4,270.95, 50 Cent Trifecta, September 4, 2005; $6,424.28, 10 Cent Superfecta, September 14, 2005
Highest Pick Four: $10,405.80, November 2, 2005

Leaders
Career, Leading Jockey by Titles: Jon Court, 3
Career, Leading Owner by Titles: Louis O'Brien, 5
Career, Leading Trainer by Titles: Ralph Martinez, 5
Career, Leading Jockey by Stakes Wins: Jon Court, 14
Career, Leading Owner by Stakes Wins: McKee Stables, 9
Career, Leading Trainer by Stakes Wins: Dale Romans, 18
Career, Leading Jockey by Wins: Terry J. Thompson, 500
Career, Leading Owner by Wins: Louis O'Brien, 269
Career, Leading Trainer by Wins: Ralph Martinez, 269
Recent Meeting, Leading Jockey: Orlando Mojica, 91, 2007
Recent Meeting, Leading Owner: Louis O'Brien, 41, 2007
Recent Meeting, Leading Trainer: Ralph Martinez, 41, 2007
Recent Meeting, Leading Horse: Satin Sun, 5, 2007

Records
Single-Day Jockey Wins: Terry J. Thompson, 7, November 18, 2001
Single-Day Owner Wins: Louis O'Brien, 4, October 21, 2004
Single-Day Trainer Wins: Ralph Martinez, 4, October 21, 2004
Single Meeting, Leading Jockey by Wins: Terry Thompson, 122, 2001
Single Meeting, Leading Owner by Wins: Louis O'Brien, 66, 2003
Single Meeting, Leading Trainer by Wins: Ralph Martinez, 66, 2003
Single Meeting, Leading Horse by Wins: Green Appeal, 5, 1997; Satin Sun, 5, 2007

Principal Races
Indiana Derby (G2), Indiana Breeders' Cup Oaks (G3), Michael G. Schaefer Mile S.

Notable Events
Indiana Derby Gala, Ladies' Night

Track Records, Main Dirt
5 furlongs: Win Again, :57.30, October 12, 2007
5½ furlongs: Moro Oro, 1:02.20, September 20, 1996; Chukker Creek, 1:02.20, November 24, 1996
6 furlongs: Moro Oro, 1:07.40, November 16, 1996
1 mile: Vic's Rebel, 1:33.99, October 13, 1998
1 1/16 miles: Alydar's Rib, 1:41, November 1, 1996
1 1/8 miles: Stay Forever Young, 1:51.86, October 12, 2005
1 3/16 miles: Mount Tora Bora, 2:22, October 29, 2005
1½ miles: Got Brass, 2:36.88, October 30, 2004
1 5/8 miles: Open Space, 2:41.20, November 16, 1996
Other: 1 5/16 miles, Our Forbes, 2:39.20, November 7, 1997; 1 7/8 miles, Raw New, 3:16.20, December 1, 2000

Fastest Times of 2007 (Dirt)
5 furlongs: Win Again, 5, :57.30, October 12, 2007
5½ furlongs: Raving Rocket, 5, 1:03.96, October 28, 2007
6 furlongs: Raving Rocket, 5, 1:10.78, November 11, 2007
1 mile: Casino Evil, 4, 1:37.40, October 6, 2007
1 1/16 miles: Zanjero, 3, 1:43.95, October 6, 2007
1 3/8 miles: Royal Medal, 6, 2:25.77, November 17, 2007

Indiana Downs

Located in Shelbyville, about 40 miles southeast of Indianapolis, Indiana Downs held its inaugural Thoroughbred meet in 2003. Construction of the $35-million track was opposed by Hoosier Park, but the red-and-white grandstand facility opened on schedule for its inaugural 2002 Standardbred meet. Owned by Oliver Racing and LHT Capital, the track opened its first off-track betting facility in February 2003 in Evansville, near Churchill-owned Ellis Park, and in '04 opened an OTB facility across the Ohio River from Louisville, home of Churchill Downs. Beginning in 2003, Indiana Downs and Hoosier split the state subsidy generated by a tax on riverboat admissions. Indiana Downs received approval from the state in 2007 to add 2,000 slot machines. A temporary casino opened in 2008.

Location: 4200 N. Michigan Rd., Shelbyville, In. 46176-8515
Phone: (317) 421-0000, (866) 478-7223
Fax: (317) 421-0100
Website: www.indianadowns.com
E-Mail: info@indianadowns.com
Year Founded: 2002
Dates of Inaugural Meeting: April 11-May 26, 2003
Abbreviation: InD
Acreage: 152

Ownership
Oliver Racing; LHT Capital

Officers
Chairman: Ross Mangano
General Manager: Jonathan Schuster
Assistant General Manager/Marketing Director: John Droghei Jr.
Director of Racing/Racing Secretary: Raymond "Butch" Cook
Director of Operations: Jamie Dean
Director of Mutuels: Nathan Runnebohm
Director of Simulcasting: Joe Melek
Track Announcer: John Bothe
Track Photographer: Coady Photography
Security: Michael Shaw

Racing Dates
2007: April 27-July 3, 48 days
2008: April 25-July 8, 54 days

Track Layout
Main Circumference: 1 mile
Main Turf Circumference: 7 furlongs

Handle
Average All-Sources Recent Meeting: $982,293, 2007
Average On-Track Recent Meeting: $51,363, 2007
Total All-Sources Recent Meeting: S47,150,081, 2007
Total On-Track Recent Meeting: $2,465,419, 2007

Leaders
Recent Meeting, Leading Jockey: Victor Lebron, 61, 2007
Recent Meeting, Leading Trainer: Ralph Martinez, 31, 2007

Principal Races
Shelby County S., William Henry Harrison S., Indiana First Lady S., Governor's S., Florence Henderson S., A. J. Foyt S.

Track Records, Main Dirt
5 furlongs: Cinnapie, :57, May 13, 2005
5½ furlongs: Speak of Kings, 1:03.16, May 17, 2005
6 furlongs: Call Roy, 1:09.38, May 18, 2005
1 mile: Longbranch Saloon, 1:36.61, June 23, 2006
1 mile 70 yds: K K Avey, 1:41.56, May 7, 2003
1 1/16 miles: Brass Punch, 1:42.70, May 30, 2005
1 1/8 miles: A Secret Scoop, 1:50.62, May 15, 2003

Track Records, Main Turf
5 furlongs: Don Manuel, :55.79, May 29, 2006
7½ furlongs: Awkward Moment, 1:28.15, June 16, 2007
1 mile: Hold the Salt, 1:35.31, June 16, 2007
1 1/16 miles: Mining for Silver, 1:41.13, May 7, 2007

Fastest Times of 2007 (Dirt)
4½ furlongs: Coping With David, 6, :51.10, June 2, 2007
5 furlongs: Indy Energy, 8, :57.63, June 5, 2007
5½ furlongs: General Purpose, 4, 1:03.58, April 27, 2007
6 furlongs: One Happy Cat, 3, 1:09.85, June 23, 2007
1 mile: Road Town, 7, 1:39.15, May 4, 2007
1 mile 70 yds: Liepers Fork, 6, 1:42.43, July 3, 2007
1¼ miles: Stormy Jim, 5, 2:07.21, July 3, 2007

Fastest Times of 2007 (Turf)
5 furlongs: Jp'shanna, 5, :56.47, June 2, 2007
7½ furlongs: Awkward Moment, 3, 1:28.15, June 16, 2007
a7½ furlongs: Craig's Tyler, 5, 1:27.56, May 7, 2007
1 mile: Hold the Salt, 5, 1:35.31, June 16, 2007
a1 mile: Princess Composer, 5, 1:37.46, July 2, 2007
1 1/16 miles: Mining for Silver, 6, 1:41.13, May 7, 2007

Iowa

Prairie Meadows Racetrack

The Thoroughbred industry in Iowa received a boost when Prairie Meadows Racetrack in Altoona, not far from Des Moines, opened in 1989. But financial difficulties forced the track to file for bankruptcy in 1991 and to close for live racing in '92. The following year, Prairie Meadows became the property of Polk County, which today leases the facility to the not-for-profit Racing Association of Central Iowa. The track's future was secured in 1995 when slot machines were installed, with a portion of revenues significantly increasing race purses. Today, Prairie Meadows's live racing schedule begins with a Thoroughbred meet that is followed by a mixed meet for Thoroughbreds and Quarter Horses, and concludes with a Standardbred racing season. One of the track's most popular events is the Iowa Classic, a ten-race event for state-bred Thoroughbreds and Quarter Horses. Table games supplemented the slot machines in 2005.

Location: 1 Prairie Meadows Dr., P.O. Box 1000, Altoona, Ia. 50009-0901
Phone: (515) 967-1000, (800) 325-9015
Fax: (515) 967-1344
Website: www.prairiemeadows.com
E-Mail:
Year Founded: 1984
Dates of Inaugural Meeting: March 1-15, 1989
Abbreviation: PrM
Acreage: 233.44
Number of Stalls: 1,400
Seating Capacity: 8,392

Ownership
Prairie Meadows Racetrack and Casino Inc.

Officers
President and Chief Executive Officer: Gary Palmer
Chairman: Jack Bishop
Vice President of Finance: Ann Long-Richards
Vice President of Operations: Ann Atkin
Director of Racing: Derron D. Heldt
Racing Secretary: Daniel J. Doocy
Assistant Racing Secretary: Chad Keller
Secretary: Michael Galloway
Director of Marketing: Jeff Nelson
Director of Publicity: Mary Lou Coady
Director of Simulcasting: Mark Loewe
Mutuels Manager: Aric Rasmussen
Horsemen's Liaison: Chuck Schott
Stewards: Ralph D'Amico, Gerald Hobby, Jim Smith
Track Announcer: Jim McAulay
Track Photographer: Jack Coady Jr.
Track Superintendent: Lamont Marks
Horsemen's Bookkeeper: Tami Burns

Racing Dates
2007: April 20-July 4, 46 days; July 10-September 15, 40 days
2008: April 18-July 5, 47 days; July 11-September 20, 41 days

Track Layout
Main Circumference: 1 mile
Main Track Chute: 2 furlongs and 6 furlongs
Main Width: Homestretch: 90 feet; Backstretch: 60 feet
Main Length of Stretch: 1,033 feet
Training Track: 5 furlongs

Handle
Average All-Sources Recent Meeting: $652,158, Spring 2007; $356,692, Summer 2007
Average On-Track Recent Meeting: $68,182, Spring 2007; $35,233, Summer 2007
Single-Day On-Track Handle: $488,070, May 5, 1990
Total All-Sources Recent Meeting: $29,999,257, Spring 2007; $14,267,671, Summer 2007
Total On-Track Recent Meeting: $3,136,377, Spring 2007; $1,409,337, Summer 2007
Highest Single-Day Record Recent Meeting: $1,255,415, Spring 2007; $796,780, Summer 2007

Mutuel Records
Highest Exacta: $2,424.20, May 19, 1997
Lowest Exacta: $3.60, July 28, 1994
Highest Trifecta: $35,761.40, August 31, 2002
Lowest Trifecta: $7.80, July 22, 2000
Highest Daily Double: $2,216, September 24, 1998
Lowest Daily Double: $3.00, August 28, 2004

Leaders
Career, Leading Jockey by Titles: Glenn W. Corbett, 6
Career, Leading Owner by Titles: River Ridge Ranch, 7
Career, Leading Trainer by Titles: Dick R. Clark, 20
Career, Leading Jockey by Stakes Wins: Glenn W. Corbett, 39
Career, Leading Owner by Stakes Wins: River Ridge Ranch, 24
Career, Leading Trainer by Stakes Wins: Dick R. Clark, 39
Career, Leading Jockey by Wins: Terry J. Thompson, 363
Career, Leading Owner by Wins: Maggi Moss, 321
Career, Leading Trainer by Wins: Dick R. Clark, 764
Recent Meeting, Leading Jockey: Terry Thompson, 61, Spring 2007; Alex Birzer, 43, Summer 2007
Recent Meeting, Leading Owner: Maggi Moss, 38, Spring 2007; River Ridge Ranch LC, 14, Summer 2007
Recent Meeting, Leading Trainer: Dick Clark, 51, Spring 2007; Dick Clark, 31, Summer 2007
Recent Meeting, Leading Horse: Hello Mo, 4, Spring 2007; Count On Bill, 3, Summer 2007

Records
Single-Day Jockey Wins: Terry J. Thompson, 6, May 20, 2002
Single Meeting, Leading Jockey by Wins: Terry J. Thompson, 94, Spring 2002
Single Meeting, Leading Owner by Wins: Maggi Moss, 77, 2006
Single Meeting, Leading Trainer by Wins: Suzanne Evans, 66, 1991

Principal Races
Prairie Meadows Cornhusker Breeders' Cup H. (G2), Iowa Oaks (G3), Iowa Derby, Iowa Sprint H., Iowa Distaff Breeders' Cup S.

Track Records, Main Dirt
4 furlongs: Straight Fever, :46.20, July 16, 1993
4$\frac{1}{2}$ furlongs: Southern Alert, :51.24, May 7, 2002
5 furlongs: Dayjob, :56, May 1, 1999
5$\frac{1}{2}$ furlongs: Leaping Plum, 1:02.50, August 5, 1997
6 furlongs: Coach Jimi Lee, 1:07.85, July 4, 2004
1 mile: Tartine, 1:35, August 11, 1998
1 mile 70 yds: Northwest Hill, 1:39.69, July 4, 2003
1$\frac{1}{16}$ miles: Excessivepleasure, 1:40.82, July 5, 2003
1$\frac{1}{8}$ miles: Beboppin Baby, 1:46.62, July 4, 1998
1$\frac{1}{4}$ miles: Famous Event, 2:02.60, June 23, 1995
1$\frac{1}{2}$ miles: Famous Event, 2:32, July 9, 1995
1$\frac{5}{8}$ miles: Sir Star, 2:44$\frac{3}{5}$, May 12, 1989
2 miles: Gritti Marco, 3:26, July 28, 1995
Other: 2 furlongs, Seadrift, :21, July 4, 2007

Fastest Times of 2007 (Dirt)
2 furlongs: Seadrift, 4, :21, July 4, 2007
4$\frac{1}{2}$ furlongs: Hateful, 2, :51.83, June 25, 2007
5 furlongs: Lookinforthesecret, 5, :56.63, May 11, 2007
5$\frac{1}{2}$ furlongs: Lake Kiowa, 6, 1:02.98, May 5, 2007
6 furlongs: Indian Chant, 4, 1:08.08, August 4, 2007
1 mile: Count On Bill, 5, 1:36.95, September 4, 2007
1 mile 70 yds: Sur Sandpit, 7, 1:40.76, September 1, 2007
1$\frac{1}{16}$ miles: West Coast Swing, 3, 1:41.19, September 15, 2007
1$\frac{1}{8}$ miles: Dry Martini, 4, 1:48.41, June 30, 2007
2 miles: Won Won Wonder Why, 6, 3:29.71, September 15, 2007

Kansas

Anthony Downs

Location: 521 East Sherman, P.O. Box 444, Anthony, Ks. 67003-0444
Phone: (620) 842-3796
Fax: (620) 842-3797
Website: www.anthonydownsraces.com
Year Founded: 1904
Abbreviation: AnF

Ownership
Anthony Fair Association

Officers
Chairman and President: Dan Bird
Director of Racing and Racing Secretary: Norris E. Gwin
Secretary: Vicki Knapic
Treasurer: Mel Kitts
Director of Mutuels: Connie Shellhammer
Vice President: Allen Thomas
Track Announcer: Jerry McNamar
Track Photographer: Gene Wilson and Associates
Security: John Blevins

Racing Dates
2007: July 13-July 22, 6 days
2008: July 11-13, 18-20, 6 days

Track Layout
Main Circumference: 4 furlongs

Attendance
Average Daily Recent Meeting: 516, 2007
Total Attendance Recent Meeting: 3,100, 2007

Handle
Average On-Track Recent Meeting: $19,066, 2007
Total On-Track Recent Meeting: $114,400, 2007
Highest Single-Day Record Recent Meeting: $30,300, July 22, 2007

Leaders
Recent Meeting, Leading Jockey: Zevi Ashlock, 12, 2007
Recent Meeting, Leading Trainer: Joe Thomas, 14, 2007
Recent Meeting, Leading Owner: Dan Block, 4, 2007

Principal Races
Anthony Downs Derby, , Harper County H., Anthony Fair H., Gene Francis and Associates S., Kansas Bred H.

Notable Events
Kansas City BBQ Society Contest

Fastest Times of 2007 (Dirt)
a4½ furlongs: Apealing Craft, 4, :56.30, July 22, 2007
5 furlongs: Tough Joe, 6, 1:00.79, July 15, 2007
a5 furlongs: D D Dot Comm, 10, 1:01.76, July 21, 2007
6½ furlongs: Honour and Fame, 9, 1:24.17, July 15, 2007
a6½ furlongs: Crane Away, 8, 1:20.51, July 22, 2007
1 1/16 miles: Devil's Bandit, 9, 1:51.64, July 21, 2007
a1 1/16 miles: Coffee Bubbles, 10, 1:52.37, July 14, 2007

Eureka Downs

Eureka Downs, located 60 miles east of Wichita, runs a mixed horse meet on weekends and holidays from the first week of May through July 4. The five-furlong track, which dates to 1872, raced Standardbreds in the late 1940s and was the site of Kansas's first pari-mutuel race for Thoroughbreds on September 3, 1988. The track closed in 1991 and reopened in '93 with the Greenwood County Fair Association and the Kansas Quarter Horse Racing Association co-licensed as operators. Eureka Downs races Thoroughbreds, Quarter Horses, Appaloosas, Paints, and mules. Non-betting mule contests began in the late 1990s and proved so popular that they were added to the pari-mutuel menu.

Location: 210 N. Jefferson St., P.O. Box 228, Eureka, Ks. 67045
Phone: (620) 583-5528
Fax: (620) 583-5381
Website: www.eurekadowns.com
E-Mail: info@eurekadowns.com
Year Founded: 1993
Abbreviation: Eur

Officers
General Manager: Lee Smith

Racing Dates
2007: May 5-July 4, 13 days
2008: May 31-July 4, 6 days

Track Layout
Main Circumference: 5 furlongs

Leaders
Recent Meeting, Leading Jockey: Brant McGhee, 5, 2007; Floyd Wethey Jr., 5, 2007
Recent Meeting, Leading Trainer: Joe Frederick Thomas Sr., 7, 2008
Recent Meeting, Leading Horse: Broken Time, 3, 2007

Fastest Times of 2007 (Dirt)
4 furlongs: True Luck, 6, :46.90, May 26, 2007
6 furlongs: Lode a Trouble, 7, 1:15.01, June 9, 2007
7 furlongs: Coffee Bubbles, 10, 1:29.71, June 23, 2007

The Woodlands

Opened in September 1989 for greyhound racing, the Woodlands began Thoroughbred racing on May 24, 1990. The track, located in the northwest corner of Kansas City, offers a 26-day mixed horse racing meet for Thoroughbreds and Quarter Horses in October and year-round greyhound racing on a separate track. The three types of racing have been conducted concurrently since 1990. The Woodlands set a single-day attendance record of 22,015 in its first year of Thoroughbred operation with a wallet giveaway. The track's then-parent company filed for bankruptcy protection from its creditors in 1996. The track was sold in 1998 to William M. Grace, principal owner of the St. Jo Frontier Casino in St. Joseph, Missouri. Voters in Wyandotte County overwhelmingly approved a measure in June 2007 that gave Woodlands the right to add slot machines.

Location: 9700 Leavenworth Rd., Kansas City, Ks. 66109-3551
Phone: (913) 299-9797, (800) 695-7223
Fax: (913) 299-9804
Website: www.woodlandskc.com
E-Mail: info@woodlandskc.com
Year Founded: 1989
Dates of Inaugural Meeting: May 24, 1990
Abbreviation: Wds
Acreage: 400
Number of Stalls: 1,250
Seating Capacity: 4,250

Ownership
Kansas Racing

Officers
President: Howard Grace
Vice President: Bruce Schmitter
General Manager: Jayme LaRocca
Director of Racing: Doug Schoepf

Racing Secretary: Larry Seckington
Secretary/Treasurer: Bruce Schmitter
Director of Operations and Simulcasting: Kevin King
Director of Finance: Wendy Malotte
Director of Marketing: Denise Souza
Director of Mutuels: Debbie Frost
Guest Services Supervisor: Amy Estes
Track Announcer: Keith Nelson
Track Photographer: Gene Wilson and Associates
Track Superintendent: Steve Bialek
Horsemen's Bookkeeper: Judy Laster
Security: Robert Fritz

Racing Dates
2007: September 24-November 4, 30 days
2008: September 20-October 25, 25 days

Track Layout
Main Circumference: 1 mile
Main Track Chute: 6 furlongs
Main Length of Stretch: 1,030 feet

Attendance
Highest Single-Day Record: 22,015, July 22, 1990
Average Daily Recent Meeting: 1,235, 2007
Total Attendance Recent Meeting: 30,870, 2007
Highest Single-Day Recent Meeting: 4,197, October 27, 2007

Handle
Total All-Sources Recent Meeting: $6,296,366, 2007
Average All-Sources Recent Meeting: $251,855
Total On-Track Recent Meeting: $1,253,741, 2007
Average On-Track Recent Meeting: $50,150, 2007
Largest Single-Day All-Sources Recent Meeting: $532,034, October 1, 2007
Largest Single-Day On-Track Recent Meeting: $106,800, October 27, 2007

Leaders
Recent Meeting, Leading Jockey: Alex Birzer, 42, 2007
Recent Meeting, Leading Trainer: Kenneth Gleason, 10, 2007

Principal Races
Woodlands Derby, Manhattan S., Sunflower S., Kansas Oaks, Woodlands S.

Track Records, Main Dirt
4 furlongs: King of Diamonds, :45.80, October 10, 2001
4½ furlongs: Lanyons Star, :51$^{2}/_{5}$, June 29, 1990
5 furlongs: Jungle Merit, :57.40, October 29, 1993
5½ furlongs: Axe Age, 1:03.20, August 15, 1993
6 furlongs: Great Immunity, 1:08.50, June 30, 1991
1 mile: French Fritter, 1:36, June 1, 1991
1 mile 70 yds: Holly's Wind, 1:40$^{3}/_{5}$, June 24, 1990
1$^{1}/_{16}$ miles: Axle Lode, 1:42.80, September 22, 1996
1⅛ miles: Model Age, 1:49$^{4}/_{5}$, July 18, 1990
1$^{3}/_{16}$ miles: Old Man's Delite, 1:58, October 21, 2003
1¼ miles: Midway Mail, 2:03.20, September 10, 1993
1½ miles: He's a Valentine, 2:33.20, October 14, 1994
1¾ miles: E K Power, 3:01.80, October 27, 2007

Fastest Times of 2007 (Dirt)
5 furlongs: Powder River Cat, 5, :58.20, October 3, 2007
5½ furlongs: Treasured Friend, 6, 1:04, September 23, 2007
6 furlongs: Another Audible, 4, 1:09.20, September 24, 2007
1 mile: Twisted Justice, 4, 1:39.80, October 27, 2007
1 mile 70 yds: Count On Bill, 5, 1:42.40, October 1, 2007
1$^{1}/_{16}$ miles: Manovan, 4, 1:44.60, October 27, 2007
1¾ miles: E K Power, 5, 3:01.80, October 27, 2007

Kentucky

Churchill Downs

Churchill Downs in Louisville is arguably the world's best-known racetrack, and its premier event, the Kentucky Derby (G1), is widely recognized as the sport's best-known race. First staged in 1875, the Derby is one of America's oldest continually run races and annually attracts an on-track throng exceeding 140,000, the nation's largest crowd for a Thoroughbred race, as well as worldwide television audience in the millions. The Derby has been held at Churchill since the track opened on its current site in 1875. Col. M. Lewis Clark Jr., the track's founder, built the first grandstand on land he secured from uncles John and Henry Churchill. Churchill Downs had financial problems for the first 28 years of its existence, forcing its sale by Clark and subsequent owners until Col. Matt Winn and partners bought the track in 1902. The track, whose famous twin spires date from 1895, today is owned by Churchill Downs Inc., which also owns Arlington Park near Chicago, Calder Race Course in Miami, and Fair Grounds in New Orleans. Churchill has hosted five runnings of the Breeders' Cup, beginning in 1988 and most recently in 2000. In 2005, Churchill completed a $121-million renovation project, including a $95-million rebuilding of the track's clubhouse. It was announced in 2008 that the ashes of Barbaro, the ill-fated winner of the '06 Kentucky Derby, would be buried at Churchill Downs, making him the first horse interred at the racetrack.

Location: 700 Central Ave., Louisville, Ky. 40208-1200
Phone: (502) 636-4400, (800) 28-DERBY
Fax: (502) 636-4430
Website: www.churchilldowns.com
E-Mail: customerservice@kyderby.com
Year Founded: 1874
Dates of Inaugural Meeting: May 17, 1875
Abbreviation: CD
Acreage: 147
Number of Stalls: 1,404
Seating Capacity: 51,851

Ownership
Churchill Downs Inc.

Officers
Chairman: Carl F. Pollard
Chief Executive Officer: Robert L. Evans
President: Steve Sexton
General Manager: Jim Gates
Assistant General Manager and Vice President of Guest Services: Tom Schneider
Senior Vice President of Racing: Donnie Richardson
Racing Secretary: Ben Huffman
Vice President of Operations: David Sweazy
Vice President of Finance: Scott Graff
Vice President of Communications: Julie Koenig Loignon
Vice Presidents: John Asher, Scott Graff, Julie Koenig Loignon, Raymond Lehr Jr., Donnie Richardson, Thomas Schneider, David Sweazy
Senior Director of Sponsorship Sales: Tricia Amburgey
Senior Director of Marketing: Brent Alexander
Director of Guest Services: Kaelyn Hardy
Director of Premium Seating and Membership Services: Lee Ann Shellman
Director of Group Marketing and Sales: Catherine Delaney
Director of Mutuels: Rick Smith
Director of Security: Charles Stallworth
Horsemen's Liaison: Julian "Buck" Wheat
Stewards: Brooks A. Becraft III, Richard S. Leigh, John Veitch
Track Announcer: Luke Kruytbosch
Track Photographer: Reed Palmer
Track Superintendent: Raymond Lehr Jr.

Racing Dates
2007: April 28-July 8, 52 days; October 28-November 24, 21 days
2008: April 26-July 6, 52 days; October 26-November 29, 26 days

Track Layout

Main Circumference: 1 mile
Main Track Chute: $1\frac{1}{4}$ miles
Main Width: Homestretch: 80 feet; Backstretch: 79 feet
Main Length of Stretch: 1,234.5 feet
Main Turf Circumference: 7 furlongs
Main Turf Width: 80 feet

Attendance

Highest Single-Day Record: 163,628, May 4, 1974; 80,452, November 7, 1998
Highest Single-Meeting Record: 811,446, Spring 1988; 337,977, Fall 1988
Record Daily Average Single Meeting: 20,066, Spring 1944; 14,082, Fall 1988
Highest Single-Day Recent Meeting: 157,770, May 3, 2008

Handle

Record Daily Average Single Meeting: \$2,077,364, Spring 1998; \$1,945,058, Fall 1988
Single-Day On-Track Handle: \$24,477,883, May 6, 2006; \$18,259,971, November 4, 2006
Single-Day All-Sources Handle: \$175,129,090, May 6, 2006; \$140,332,198, November 4, 2006
Record Total Single Meeting: \$102,302,494, Spring 2000; \$46,945,394, Fall 1988
Highest Single-Day All-Sources Recent Meeting: \$164,688,176, May 3, 2008
Highest Single Day On Track Recent Meeting: \$24,275,864, May 3, 2008

Mutuel Records

Highest Win: \$495.60, Gold and Rubies, November 21, 1978
Highest Exacta: \$9,814.80, May 7, 2005
Highest Trifecta: \$133,134.80, May 7, 2005
Highest Daily Double: \$6,818.20, October 29, 1984
Highest Pick Three: \$114,156, November 4, 2000
Highest Pick Six: \$1,168,136, June 25, 2003
Highest Other Exotics: \$864,253, Superfecta, May 7, 2005
Highest Pick Four: \$164,168, May 7, 2005

Leaders

Career, Leading Jockey by Titles: Pat Day, 34
Career, Leading Owner by Titles: Kenneth and Sarah Ramsey, 12
Career, Leading Trainer by Titles: D. Wayne Lukas, 11
Career, Leading Jockey by Stakes Wins: Pat Day, 155
Career, Leading Owner by Stakes Wins: Calumet Farm, 32
Career, Leading Trainer by Stakes Wins: William I. Mott, 73
Career, Leading Jockey by Wins: Pat Day, 2,481
Career, Leading Trainer by Wins: William I. Mott, 599
2007 Leading Jockey: Julien Leparoux, 69, Spring 2007; Julien Leparoux, 27, Fall 2007
2007 Leading Owners: Maggi Moss, 18, Spring 2007; Kenneth and Sarah Ramsey, 7, Fall 2007
2007 Leading Trainer: Steve Asmussen, 46, Spring 2007; Steve Asmussen, 14, Fall 2007

Records

Single-Day Jockey Wins: Pat Day, 7, June 20, 1984
Single Meeting, Leading Jockey by Wins: Pat Day, 169, Spring 1983; Pat Day, 55, Fall 1985
Single Meeting, Leading Trainer by Wins: William I. Mott, 54, Spring 1984; Dale Romans, 20, Fall, 2003

Principal Races

Fall Meeting: Clark H. (G2), Falls City H. (G2), Kentucky Jockey Club S. (G2), Golden Rod S. (G2), Chilukki S. (G2)
Spring Meeting: Kentucky Derby (G1), Kentucky Oaks (G1), Woodford Reserve Turf Classic S. (G1), Humana Distaff H. (G1), Stephen Foster H. (G1)

Notable Events

Spring Meeting: Kentucky Derby, Festival in the Field, Brew and Barbecue Fest
Fall Meeting: Churchill Downs Chili Cook-Off

Track Records, Main Dirt

4 furlongs: Fair Phantom, :$46\frac{3}{5}$, May 7, 1921; Casey :$46\frac{3}{5}$, May 9, 1921; Miss Joy, :$46\frac{3}{5}$, May 10, 1921
$4\frac{1}{2}$ furlongs: Subtle Aly, :50.48, June 23, 2007
5 furlongs: Wildcat Shoes, :56.49, May 20, 2005
$5\frac{1}{2}$ furlongs: Cashier's Dream, 1:02.52, July 7, 2001
6 furlongs: Indian Chant, 1:07.55, July 8, 2007
$6\frac{1}{2}$ furlongs: Love At Noon, 1:14.34, May 5, 2001
7 furlongs: Alannan, 1:20.50, May 5, 2001
$7\frac{1}{2}$ furlongs: Greater Good, 1:27.97, July 3, 2006
1 mile: Chilukki, 1:33.57, November 4, 2000
1 mile 70 yds: The Porter, 1:$41\frac{3}{5}$, May 30, 1919
$1\frac{1}{16}$ miles: Brass Hat, 1:41.27, July 8 2007
$1\frac{1}{8}$ miles: Victory Gallop, 1:47.28, June 12, 1999
$1\frac{3}{16}$ miles: Bonnie Andrew, 1:$58\frac{3}{5}$, November 14, 1942
$1\frac{1}{4}$ miles: Secretariat, 1:$59\frac{2}{5}$, May 5, 1973
$1\frac{3}{8}$ miles: Elliott, 2:$20\frac{3}{5}$, October 15, 1906
$1\frac{1}{2}$ miles: A Storm Is Brewing, 2:32.02, June 17, 2001
$1\frac{5}{8}$ miles: Tupolev (Arg), 2:$49\frac{2}{5}$, July 23, 1983
$1\frac{3}{4}$ miles: Caslon Bold, 2:59.64, July 4, 1995
2 miles: Libertarian, 3:22.26, November 28, 1998
Other: 1 mile 20 yds, Frog Legs, 1:39, May 13, 1913; 1 mile 50 yds, Hodge, 1:$41\frac{4}{5}$, October 4, 1916; 1 mile 100 yds, The Caxton, 1:$49\frac{1}{5}$, May 16, 1902; $2\frac{1}{16}$ miles, Hi Neighbor, 3:$40\frac{4}{5}$, November 11, 1949; $2\frac{1}{4}$ miles, Raincoat, 3:53, October 7, 1915; 3 miles, Ten Broeck, 5:$26\frac{1}{2}$, September 3, 1876; 4 miles, Sotemia, 7:$10\frac{4}{5}$, October 7, 1912

Track Records, Main Turf

5 furlongs: Unbridled Sidney, :55.54, July 9, 2005
1 mile: Jaggery John, 1:33.78, July 4, 1995
$1\frac{1}{16}$ miles: Quite a Bride, 1:40.70, June 16, 2007
$1\frac{1}{8}$ miles: Lure, 1:46.34, April 30, 1993
$1\frac{3}{8}$ miles: Snake Eyes, 2:13, May 22, 1997
$1\frac{1}{2}$ miles: Tikkanen, 2:26.50, November 5, 1994

Fastest Times of 2007 (Dirt)

$4\frac{1}{2}$ furlongs: Subtle Aly, 2, :50.48, June 23, 2007
5 furlongs: Sok Sok, 2, :57.08, June 16, 2007
$5\frac{1}{2}$ furlongs: La Traviata, 3, 1:02.86, June 8, 2007
6 furlongs: Indian Chant, 4, 1:07.55, July 8, 2007
$6\frac{1}{2}$ furlongs: Communicated, 3, 1:15.56, July 8, 2007
7 furlongs: Ghosttrapper, 4, 1:21.54, May 28, 2007
$7\frac{1}{2}$ furlongs: Flying First Class, 3, 1:29.28, April 28, 2007
1 mile: Wiggins, 7, 1:33.91, May 27, 2007
$1\frac{1}{16}$ miles: Brass Hat, 6, 1:41.27, July 8, 2007
$1\frac{1}{8}$ miles: Flashy Bull, 4, 1:48.63, June 16, 2007
$1\frac{1}{4}$ miles: Street Sense, 3, 2:02.17, May 5, 2007

Fastest Times of 2007 (Turf)

5 furlongs: Smart Enough, 4, :56.53, November 4, 2007
1 mile: Remarkable News (Ven), 5, 1:34.74, June 30, 2007
$1\frac{1}{16}$ miles: Quite a Bride, 4, 1:40.70, June 16, 2007
$1\frac{1}{8}$ miles: Good Mood (Ire), 3, 1:47.57, June 16, 2007
$1\frac{3}{8}$ miles: Broganville, 3, 2:18.41, June 7, 2007
$1\frac{1}{2}$ miles: Drilling for Oil, 4, 2:28.35, May 26, 2007

Ellis Park

Ellis Park near Henderson holds the distinction of being the only racetrack where soybeans are grown in the infield. Built in 1922 and designed after Saratoga Race Course, the track located on an island in the Ohio River near Evansville, Indiana, was originally named Dade Park and intended for Standardbred racing. Within one month of its opening, the track replaced Standardbred racing with Thoroughbred racing. Dade Park was plagued with financial problems and, in 1923 and '24, the only racing held was for race cards on Labor Day weekend. In 1924, James C. Ellis, who owned construction and oil enterprises, purchased the track for \$35,100 and reopened it for Thoroughbred racing in 1925. In 1954, two years before Ellis's death, the track's name was changed to James C. Ellis Park. In 1998, Churchill Downs Inc. purchased Ellis for \$22-million and sold it in 2006 to Kentucky businessman and horse owner Ron

Geary for an undisclosed price that yielded an $8-million tax benefit for Churchill. Ellis's richest race each year is the $200,000 Gardenia Handicap (G3) for fillies and mares. The 2007 Claiming Crown series was held at Ellis Park, generating a record all-sources handle of $4.9-million for the seven stakes. The Claiming Crown was scheduled to return to Canterbury Park in 2008.

Location: 3300 US Hwy. 41 N., P.O. Box 33, Henderson, Ky. 42419
Phone: (812) 425-1456; (800) 333-8110
Fax: (812) 425-0146
Website: www.ellisparkracing.com
Year Founded: 1922 (as Dade Park)
Dates of Inaugural Meeting: November 8, 1922
Abbreviation: EIP
Acreage: 210
Number of Stalls: 1,142
Seating Capacity: 7,750

Ownership
Ron Geary

Officers
President/General Manager: Ron Geary
Executive Vice President/CFO: Greg Hardt
Director of Development: Mark Geary
Racing Secretary/Director of Racing: Dan Bork
Director of Operations/Simulcasting: Robert Jackson
Director of Finance: Rhonda Thompson
Vice President of Marketing: Bonnie Schnautz
Track Announcer: Luke Kruytbosch
Track Photographer: Reed Palmer
Track Superintendent: Glenn Thompson
Horsemen's Bookkeeper: Lana Murphy

Racing Dates
2007: July 4-September 3, 46 days
2008: July 4-September 1, 44 days

Track Layout
Main Circumference: 1 1/8 miles
Main Track Chute: 7 furlongs and 1 mile
Main Width: Homestretch: 100 feet; Backstretch: 85 feet
Main Length of Stretch: 1,175 feet
Main Turf Circumference: 1 mile

Attendance
Average Daily Recent Meeting: 3,045
Highest Single-Day Record: 15,500 est., September 4, 1967
Total Attendance Recent Meeting: 141,000
Highest Single-Day Recent Meeting: 7,100 July 4, 2007

Handle
Average All-Sources Recent Meeting: $2,194,590
Average On-Track Recent Meeting: $318,088
Highest Single-Day Record On-Track Recent Meeting: $898,483, August 4, 2007
Highest Single-Day Record All-Sources Recent Meeting: $5,153,613, August 4, 2007
Total All-Sources Recent Meeting: $100,951,116
Total On-Track Recent Meeting: $14,632,037

Leaders
Career, Leading Jockey by Titles: Leroy Tauzin, 7
Career, Leading Owner by Titles: George "Hoolie" Hudson, 5
Career, Leading Trainer by Titles: Bernard S. Flint, 11
Recent Meeting, Leading Jockey: Orlando Mojica, 59, 2007
Recent Meeting, Leading Owner: Louis D. O'Brien, 22, 2007
Recent Meeting, Leading Trainer: Ralph Martinez, 22, 2007
Recent Meeting, Leading Horse: Greenstandingseam, 3, 2007; Annie Dugan, 3, 2007

Records
Single-Day Trainer Wins: Wayne Bearden, 5, August 7, 1997
Single Meeting, Leading Jockey by Wins: Mike McDowell, 89, 1986
Single Meeting, Leading Owner by Wins: Tom Dorris, 20, 1978
Single Meeting, Leading Trainer by Wins: Angel Montano, 34, 1976

Principal Races
Gardenia H. (G3), Ellis Park Breeders' Cup Turf S., HBPA H., Don Bernhardt S., Regaey Island S.

Interesting Facts
Previous Name: Dade Park

Notable Events
Family Day, Year-Round Simulcasting

Track Records, Main Dirt
5 furlongs: Hoho Tow, :56.46, July 19, 2006
5 1/2 furlongs: Flank Drive, 1:03.36, July 19, 2006
6 furlongs: Davids Expectation, 1:08.96, July 23, 2006
6 1/2 furlongs: Junior College, 1:14.56, July 29, 2006
7 furlongs: Josh's Madelyn, 1:21.37, September 5, 2004
1 mile: Still Waving, 1:34 3/5, August 13, 1988
1 1/16 miles: Lt. Lao, 1:47 3/5, August 27, 1988
1 1/4 miles: Won Du Loup, 2:03, September 4, 1988
1 3/8 miles: Ramona Jay, 2:23, August 24, 1985
1 1/2 miles: Unaccountable, 2:29 3/5, July 23, 1988
1 5/8 miles: Sir Lightning, 2:45 4/5, August 9, 1992
1 3/4 miles: Bondi, 3:00, August 27, 1966
2 miles: Classic Deal, 3:25 1/5, August 21, 1988
Other: 2 1/4 miles, Bondi, 3:54, September 5, 1966

Track Records, Main Turf
5 1/2 furlongs: Bettybird, 1:00.52, August 21, 2002
1 mile: Slewper Imp, 1:32 1/5, July 16, 1995; Suffragette, 1:32 3/5, July 24, 1999
1 1/16 miles: Onthedeanslist, 1:39.11, September 5, 2005
1 1/8 miles: Yaqthan (Ire), 1:44 3/5, September 2, 1996
1 1/4 miles: Ye Slew, 1:59 3/5, August 6, 1994
1 1/2 miles: Our Forbes, 2:25 2/5, August 10, 1994
2 miles: Irish Harbour, 3:20 1/5, September 2, 1996

Fastest Times of 2007 (Dirt)
5 furlongs: Greenstandingseam, 6, :58.04, July 12, 2007
5 1/2 furlongs: Pennyroyal, 6, 1:03.54, July 4, 2007
6 furlongs: Dick G, 4, 1:09.86, July 7, 2007
6 1/2 furlongs: Off Duty, 4, 1:15.43, July 21, 2007
7 furlongs: Art and Soul, 3, 1:22.85, July 14, 2007
1 mile: Istan, 5, 1:35.68, August 11, 2007
1 1/16 miles: Miami Sunrise, 5, 1:50.83, August 4, 2007
1 1/2 miles: Humble Chris, 6, 2:40.35, August 12, 2007
2 1/4 miles: Sir Dorset, 12, 4:02.28, September 3, 2007

Fastest Times of 2007 (Turf)
5 1/2 furlongs: Actual, 5, 1:01.46, July 22, 2007
1 mile: Gretchen's Star, 12, 1:34.22, August 18, 2007
1 1/16 miles: One Eyed Joker, 9, 1:40.23, August 4, 2007
1 1/4 miles: Serac, 3, 2:06.22, July 8, 2007
1 1/2 miles: Dan McGrew, 3, 2:27.79, August 3, 2007

Keeneland Race Course

Some tracks offer nothing more than an endless procession of live and simulcast races. But a few American tracks offer a sense of history and a state of mind. Keeneland Race Course falls into the latter category. Since its opening meet in October 1936, the Lexington track has developed a unique identity. The stately facility offers two short, marquee meetings—including races such as the Blue Grass Stakes (G1) in the spring and the Spinster Stakes (G1) in the fall—in an attractive setting. Profits from Keeneland's lucrative sales arm help to finance purses and make them among the highest in the country. The Keeneland Association was incorporated in 1935 and purchased 147.5 acres of land, including an ornate training track, from J. O. "Jack" Keene, to build the facility. Lexington, bereft of racing after the Kentucky Association track closed earlier in the 1930s, quickly embraced the new facility, and more than 25,000 people attended the inaugural

nine-day meeting. Crowds in excess of 25,000 on a single day are common at Keeneland, whose meets attract a wide range of spectators, including veteran racegoers, local business executives, socialites, breeders, and college students. In 2006, Keeneland installed a Polytrack racing surface.

Location: 4201 Versailles Rd., P.O. Box 1690, Lexington, Ky. 40588-1690
Phone: (859) 254-3412, (800) 456-3412
Fax: (859) 255-2484
Website: www.keeneland.com
E-Mail: webmaster@keeneland.com
Year Founded: 1935
Dates of Inaugural Meeting: October 15-24, 1936
Abbreviation: Kee
Acreage: 997
Number of Stalls: 1,951
Seating Capacity: 8,535

Ownership
Keeneland Association Inc.

Officers
Chief Executive Officer and President: Nick Nicholson
Vice President: Harvie B. Wilkinson
Director of Racing: W. B. Rogers Beasley
Racing Secretary: Ben Huffman
Assistant Racing Secretary: Daniel Bork
Secretary: J. David Smith
Treasurer: Jessica A. Green
Director of Communications: R. James Williams
Director of Mutuels: Robert A. Butcher
Director of Sales: Geoffrey G. Russell
Market Development Administrator: Fran Taylor
Stewards: Ronald L. Herbstreit, R. Spencer Leigh III, John Veitch
Track Announcer: Kurt Becker
Track Photographer: Patrick Lang
Track Superintendent: Mike Young
Security: Ed Blaser
Horsemen's Bookkeeper: Pam Barker

Racing Dates
2007: April 6-April 27, 15 days; October 5-October 27, 17 days
2008: April 4-April 26, 16 days; October 3-October 25, 17 days

Track Layout
Main Circumference: 1 1/16 miles
Main Track Chute: 4 1/2 furlongs and 7 furlongs
Main Width: 75-80 feet
Main Length of Stretch: 1,236 ft.
Main Turf Circumference: 7 1/2 furlongs
Main Turf Width: 70 feet at finish line; 58 feet at mile pole
Main Turf Length of Stretch: 1,190 ft.
Training Track: 5 furlongs

Attendance
Average Daily Recent Meeting: 14,091, Fall 2007; 15,225, Spring 2008
Highest Single-Day Record: 33,821, April 21, 2007; 28,880, Fall 2006
Highest Single-Meeting Record: 244,145, Spring 2006; 239,296, Fall 2007
Record Daily Average Single Meeting: 16,276, Spring 2006; 14,177, Fall 1992
Total Attendance Recent Meeting: 239,296, Fall 2007; 243,606, Spring 2008
Lowest Single-Day Record: 1,294, October 16, 1936
Highest Single-Day Recent Meeting: 24,480, October 6, 2007; 26,072, April 19, 2008

Handle
Average All-Sources Recent Meeting: $8,224,519, Fall 2007; $9,406,093, Spring 2008
Average On-Track Recent Meeting: $1,222,983, Fall 2007; $1,333,106, Spring 2008
Record Daily Average Single Meeting: $1,558,917, Spring 1988; $1,379,295, Fall 1987

Single-Day On-Track Handle: $3,599,547, April 16, 2005
Single-Day All-Sources Handle: $19,246,840, April 14, 2007
Total All-Sources Recent Meeting: $139,816,831, Fall 2007; $150,497,482, Spring 2007
Total On-Track Recent Meeting: $20,790,718, Fall 2007; $21,329,702 Spring 2008
Highest Single-Day Record Recent Meeting: $14,135,204, October 16, 2007; $18,738,582, April 12, 2008

Mutuel Records
Highest Win: $255.40, Rip Dabbs, October 8, 1988
Lowest Win: $2.10, Spectacular Bid, April 26, 1979
Highest Exacta: $5,200.40, October 27, 1993
Lowest Exacta: $3.60, April 13, 1988
Highest Trifecta: $37,832, October 28, 1995
Lowest Trifecta: $7.80, April 3, 2004
Highest Daily Double: $5,796.40, April 19, 1961
Lowest Daily Double: $4.60, October 12, 1983
Highest Pick Three: $49,628.60, April 6, 1997
Lowest Pick Three: $8.80, April 21, 1990
Highest Pick Six: $160,628.90, October 16, 2003
Lowest Pick Six: $74.80, October 9, 1991
Highest Other Exotics: Pick Five, $7,172.30, October 18, 2001; Superfecta, $120,550, October 24, 2001
Lowest Other Exotics: Pick Five, $375.80, October 12, 2001; Superfecta, $43, April 21, 2004
Lowest Quinella: $2.60, October 5, 2003
Highest Stakes Win: $222.60, Foxy Dean, October 13, 1984, Alcibiades S.
Highest Quinella: $1,535.40, October 8, 2004
Highest Pick Four: $78,634.80, October 24, 2007
Lowest Pick Four: $21.50, April 19, 2001
Highest Super High Five: $23,126.30 April 12, 2008

Leaders
Career, Leading Jockey by Titles: Pat Day, 22
Career, Leading Owner by Titles: T. A. and J. E. Grissom, 14
Career, Leading Trainer by Titles: D. Wayne Lukas, 16
Career, Leading Jockey by Stakes Wins: Pat Day, 95
Career, Leading Owner by Stakes Wins: Claiborne Farm, 26
Career, Leading Trainer by Stakes Wins: D. Wayne Lukas, 50
Career, Leading Jockey by Wins: Pat Day, 918
Career, Leading Owner by Wins: William S. Farish, 183
Career, Leading Trainer by Wins: D. Wayne Lukas, 271
Recent Meeting, Leading Jockey: Rafael Bejarano, 21, Fall 2007; Kent Desormeaux, 22, Spring 2008;
Recent Meeting, Leading Owner: Kenneth L. and Sarah K. Ramsey, 6, Fall 2007; Overbrook Farm, 6, Fall 2007; G. Watts Humphrey Jr., 4, Spring 2008; Overbrook Farm, 4, Spring 2008
Recent Meeting, Leading Trainer: William I. Mott, 9, Fall 2007; Todd Pletcher, 14, Spring 2008
Recent Meeting, Leading Horse: Communique, 2, Spring 2008; Xela, 2, Spring 2008; Lil Tree, 2, Spring 2008; Party Crasher, 2, Spring 2008

Records
Single-Day Jockey Wins: Randy Romero, 6, April 7, 1990; Craig Perret, 6, April 18, 1990
Single-Day Trainer Wins: William I. Mott, 4, April 9, 1995; Todd A. Pletcher, 4, April 19, 2008
Single Meeting, Leading Jockey by Wins: Randy Romero, 32; Spring 1990; Pat Day, 45, Fall 1991
Single Meeting, Leading Owner by Wins: Calumet Farm, 12, Spring 1941; Mr. and Mrs. Robert F. Roberts, 12, Fall 1968
Single Meeting, Leading Trainer by Wins: Todd A. Pletcher, 16, Spring 2005; D. Wayne Lukas, 22, Fall 1989

Principal Races
Fall: Shadwell Turf Mile S. (G1), Lane's End Breeders' Futurity (G1), Juddmonte Spinster S. (G1), Queen Elizabeth II Challenge Cup S. (G1), Darley Alcibiades S. (G2)
Spring: Blue Grass S. (G1), Ashland S. (G1), Maker's Mark Mile S. (G1), Commonwealth Breeders' Cup S. (G2), Coolmore Lexington S. (G2), Stonerside Beaumont S. (G2).

Track Records, Main All Weather
4 1/2 furlongs: One Hot Wish, :48.87, April 12, 2007
6 furlongs: He Loves Me Not, 1:08.30 April 12, 2007
6 1/2 furlongs: Lady Belsara, 1:14.41, April 19, 2007

7 furlongs: Carnacks Choice, 1:21.05, April 7, 2007
1 1/16 miles: Sadler's Trick, 1:41.70, October 20, 2006
1 1/8 miles: Go Between, 1:47.97, October 27, 2006
1 3/16 miles: Save Big Money, 1:56.09, April 15, 2007
1 1/4 miles: Skip Irish, 2:05.02, October 11, 2006
Other: 7 furlongs 184 feet, Midnight Lute, 1:24.38, October 13, 2006

Track Records, Main Turf
5 1/2 furlongs: Sgt. Bert, 1:01.67, October 8, 2006
1 mile: Perfect Soul (Ire), 1:33.54, April 9, 2004
1 1/16 miles: Quiet Resolve, 1:40.30, April 27, 2000
1 1/8 miles: Memories of Silver, 1:45.81, October 5, 1996
1 3/16 miles: Happyanunoit (NZ), 1:53.91, October 15, 1999
1 1/2 miles: Bursting Forth, 2:27.54, April 22, 1999
1 5/8 miles: Royal Strand (Ire), 2:38.68, October 24, 1999

Fastest Times of 2007 (All Weather)
4 1/2 furlongs: One Hot Wish, 2, :48.87, April 12, 2007
5 1/2 furlongs: Delta Storm, 6, 1:03.66, October 18, 2007
6 furlongs: He Loves Me Not, 4, 1:08.30, April 12, 2007
6 1/2 furlongs: Lady Belsara, 4, 1:14.41, April 19, 2007
7 furlongs: Carnacks Choice, 3, 1:21.05, April 7, 2007
a7 furlongs: Street Sounds, 3, 1:24.93, April 12, 2007
1 1/16 miles: Rathor (Ire), 5, 1:41.94, April 6, 2007
1 1/8 miles: Go Between, 4, 1:47.97, October 27, 2007
1 3/16 miles: Save Big Money, 4, 1:56.09, April 15, 2007
1 1/4 miles: Raisedtobeahawk, 6, 2:06.08, April 6, 2007
1 5/8 miles: Jive, 4, 2:47.89, October 24, 2007

Fastest Times of 2007 (Turf)
5 1/2 furlongs: Forest Code, 4, 1:02.73, April 21, 2007
1 mile: His Holiness, 4, 1:35.03, April 25, 2007
1 1/16 miles: Cosmonaut, 5, 1:41.15, April 21, 2007
1 1/8 miles: Bit of Whimsy, 3, 1:48.73, October 13, 2007
1 1/2 miles: Safari Queen (Arg), 5, 2:28.75, April 25, 2007
a2 1/2 miles: Mixed Up, 8, 4:42.95, April 20, 2007

Kentucky Downs

Straddling the Kentucky-Tennessee state border adjacent to Interstate 65, Kentucky Downs has enjoyed a short, colorful history. Opened in 1990 as Dueling Grounds Race Course—the track site was reputed to be the scene of several 19th-century duels—the turf-only racecourse was conceived as a simulcasting facility with one day of live steeplechase racing a year. But ownership controversies dogged the facility until the late 1990s, when businessman Brad Kelley, Turfway Park, and Churchill Downs purchased the facility. An investor group that included well-respected racetrack operator Corey Johnsen purchased the facility in 2007. Track officials have found ways to make Kentucky Downs's turf-only status pay off. The track now offers a series of turf stakes on the flat to coincide partly with the Kentucky Cup series of dirt-only races at Turfway in Florence, Kentucky.

Location: 5629 Nashville Rd., P.O. Box 405, Franklin, Ky. 42134
Phone: (270) 586-7778
Fax: (270) 586-8080
Website: www.kentuckydowns.com
Dates of Inaugural Meeting: April 22, 1990
Abbreviation: KD

Ownership
Corey Johnsen, Ray Reid, Churchill Downs Inc., Turfway Park, and Kelley Farms

Officers
President: Corey Johnsen
General Manager: Jon Goodman II
Director of Racing and Racing Secretary: Richard S. Leigh
Assistant Racing Secretary: Brook Hawkins

Director of Simulcasting: Mary Troilo
Directors of Mutuels: Jo Ann Yates, Bob Weatherspoon
Track Announcer: Luke Kruytbosch
Track Photographer: Jeff Zamaiko
Track Superintendent: Tommy Sullivan

Racing Dates
2007: September 15-September 25, 6 days
2008: September 13-September 23, 6 days

Track Layout
Main Turf Circumference: 1 3/8 miles

Handle
Total All Sources Handle Recent Meeting: $9,618,211, 2007
Average All Sources Handle Recent Meeting: $1,603,035, 2007
Total On-Track Handle Recent Meeting: $444,602, 2007
Average On-Track Handle Recent Meeting: $74,100, 2007
Largest One-Day All Sources Recent Meeting: $255,313, September 22, 2007
Largest One-Day On-Track Recent Meeting: $92,495, September 22, 2007

Leaders
Career, Leading Jockey by Titles: Jon Court, 2
Recent Meeting, Leading Jockey: Larry Sterling Jr., 10, 2007
Recent Meeting, Leading Trainer: D. Michael Smithwick, 6, 2007

Records
Single Meeting, Leading Jockey by Wins: Jon Court, 7, 1999

Principal Races
Kentucky Cup Turf H. (G3), Kentucky Cup Turf Dash S., Kentucky Cup Ladies Turf S., Yaqthan S.

Interesting Facts
Previous Names and Dates: Dueling Grounds (1990-'96)

Track Records, Main Turf
6 furlongs: Hold the Salt, 1:09.25, September 22, 2007
7 furlongs: Bastille, 1:22.68, September 20, 2005
1 mile: Rob 'n Gin, 1:35, September 19, 1998
1 1/2 miles: General Jumbo (GB), 2:26.98, September 22, 2007

Fastest Times of 2007 (Turf)
6 furlongs: Hold the Salt, 5, 1:09.25, September 22, 2007
7 furlongs: Jenna Lu Hu, 3, 1:23.23, September 18, 2007
1 mile: Put Away the Halo, 4, 1:36.59, September 15, 2007
1 1/2 miles: General Jumbo (GB), 5, 2:26.98, September 22, 2007

Turfway Park

Turfway Park is the Northern Kentucky successor to Old Latonia, a track that opened in the Latonia section of Covington in 1883 and shut down in 1939. In the late 1950s, an investor group built a new Latonia Race Course in Florence, approximately ten miles from the former site, and it opened on August 27, 1959. On April 9, 1986, Nashville real estate developer Jerry Carroll and partners bought Latonia for $13.5-million and renamed it Turfway Park. Carroll undertook an extensive renovation program and raised the purse of the track's spring race for three-year-old Triple Crown prospects, the Jim Beam Stakes (G2), to $500,000 in 1987. The race's purse would peak at $750,000 when it lost its initial sponsor and became the Galleryfurniture.com Stakes for 1999 only. In 2002, the race became the Lane's End Spiral Stakes, and in '03 it was renamed the Lane's End Stakes. During Carroll's tenure, Turfway was a leader in offering intertrack wagering in Kentucky (1988) and in promoting legislation for full-card simulcasting in '94. Also in 1994, Turfway launched its Kentucky Cup Day of Champions, a September event featuring five stakes races. Carroll and partners sold

the track to a partnership led by the Keeneland Association for $37-million on January 15, 1999. For its 2005 fall meeting, Turfway renovated its track by putting in Polytrack, becoming the first track in North America to install the synthetic surface as its main track.

Location: 7500 Turfway Rd., P.O. Box 8, Florence, Ky. 41022
Phone: (859) 371-0200, (800) 733-0200
Fax: (859) 647-4730
Website: *www.turfway.com*
E-Mail: info@turfway.com
Year Founded: 1959 as Latonia Race Track; 1986 as Turfway Park
Dates of Inaugural Meeting: August 27, 1959 (Latonia Race Track); April 9, 1986 (Turfway Park)
Abbreviation: TP
Acreage: 197
Number of Stalls: 1,000

Ownership

Keeneland Association and Harrah's Entertainment

Officers

Chief Executive Officer and President: Robert N. Elliston
Director of Racing and Racing Secretary: Richard S. Leigh
Assistant Racing Secretary: Tyler B. Picklesimer
Treasurer: Clifford Reed
Director of Operations: Daniel "Chip" Bach
Director of Marketing: Jack Gordon
Director of Mutuels: Kenny Kramer
Vice President: Clifford Reed
Director of Publicity: Sherry Pinson
Director of Simulcasting: Mary Troilo
Stewards: Brooks A. Becraft III, Ronald Herbstreit, John Veitch
Track Announcer: Mike Battaglia
Track Photographer: Patrick Lang
Track Superintendent: Jeff Chapman
Horsemen's Bookkeeper: Terry Moore

Racing Dates

2007: January 1-April 5, 60 days; September 5-October 4, 22 days; November 25-December 31, 27 days
2008: January 1-April 3, 67 days; September 3-October 2, 22 days; November 30-December 31, 22 days

Track Layout

Main Circumference: 1 mile
Main Track Chute: 6½ furlongs and 1¼ miles
Main Width: Homestretch: 90 feet; Backstretch: 50 feet
Main Length of Stretch: 970 feet

Attendance

Average Daily Recent Meeting: 2,208 est., Fall 2007; 1,199 est., 2007 Holiday; 1,803 est., 2008 Winter-Spring
Highest Single-Day Record: 23,815, March 24, 2007
Highest Single-Meeting Record: 354,867, Spring 1988
Record Daily Average Single Meeting: 5,377, Spring 1988
Total Attendance Recent Meeting: 48,575 est., Fall 2007; 32,361 est., Holiday 2007; 111,815 est., Winter-Spring 2008

Handle

Average All-Sources Recent Meeting: $2,425,646, Fall 2007; $2,728,053, Holiday 2007; $2,430,203, Winter-Spring 2008
Average On-Track Recent Meeting: $146,933, Fall 2007; $127,620, Holiday 2007; $127,523, Winter-Spring 2008
Total All-Sources Recent Meeting: $53,395,447, Fall 2007; $73,712,679, Holiday 2007; $150,672,555, Winter-Spring 2008

Mutuel Records

Highest Win: $267.60, Ante a Gold Penny, January 21, 1999
Highest Exacta: $6,777.20, January 29, 1988
Lowest Exacta: $3.20, September 26, 1998
Highest Trifecta: $50,847.40, February 21, 1996
Lowest Trifecta: $5.20, September 26, 1998
Highest Daily Double: $4,575.80, December 12, 1986
Lowest Daily Double: $5, September 24, 1994
Highest Pick Three: $12,376.20, December 16, 1993
Lowest Pick Three: $8.60, March 3, 2005
Highest Pick Six: $1,474,380, March 23, 1988
Highest Other Exotics: $106,848.20, Superfecta, March 20, 2004
Highest Pick Four: $40,027.20, March 26, 2005

Leaders

Career, Leading Jockey by Titles: Willie Martinez, 9
Career, Leading Trainer by Titles: Bernard S. Flint, 20
Career, Leading Jockey by Stakes Wins: Pat Day, 37
Career, Leading Trainer by Stakes Wins: D. Wayne Lukas, 36
Recent Meeting, Leading Jockey: Dylan Williams, 27, Fall 2007; John McKee, 28, Holiday 2007; Victor Lebron, 79, Winter-Spring 2008
Recent Meeting, Leading Owner: David Englund and James Wright (partnership), 5, Fall 2007; Ken and Sarah Ramsey, 2007 Holiday 2007; Ken and Sarah Ramsey, 12, Winter-Spring 2008
Recent Meeting, Leading Trainer: Eddie Kenneally, 7, Fall 2007; Michael Maker, 12, Holiday 2007; Michael Maker, 22, Winter-Spring 2008

Records

Single-Day Jockey Wins: Rafael Bejarano, 7, March 12, 2004
Single-Day Trainer Wins: Bernard S. Flint, 4; George Isaacs, 4; D. Wayne Lukas, 4; Harry Trotsek, 4; V. R. Wright, 4
Single Meeting, Leading Jockey by Wins: Julien R. Leparoux, 167, Winter-Spring 2006; Julien R. Leparoux, 38, Fall 2006; Rafael Bejarano, 46, Holiday 2003
Single Meeting, Leading Trainer by Wins: Bernard S. Flint, 44, Winter-Spring 2003; D. Wayne Lukas, 24, Fall 1995; D. Wayne Lukas, 21, Holiday 1995

Principal Races

Winter-Spring: Lane's End S. (G2), Bourbonette Breeders' Cup S., John Battaglia Memorial S., Rushaway S.
Fall: Kentucky Cup Classic H. (G2), Kentucky Cup Juvenile S. (G3), Kentucky Cup Sprint S. (G3), Turfway Breeders' Cup S. (G3), Turfway Park Fall Championship S. (G3), Kentucky Cup Juvenile Fillies S.

Interesting Facts

Previous Names and Dates: Latonia Race Track (1959-'86)
Achievements/Milestones: Became the first track in North America to install Polytrack as a racing surface. Polytrack opened for training on August 3, 2005, and racing commenced on the surface on September 7, 2005.

Notable Events

Kentucky Cup Day of Champions

Track Records, Main All Weather

5 furlongs: Skiptothegoodpart, :57.23, September 29, 2006
5½ furlongs: First At Summer, 1:03.34, December 9, 2007
6 furlongs: Malibu Mint, 1:08.40, September 23, 2006; Straight Line, 1:08.40, December 30, 2006
6½ furlongs: Cielo Song, 1:15.35, December 16, 2006
1 mile: Forth and Forever, 1:35.61, December 15, 2006
1¹⁄₁₆ miles: Miss Wellspring, 1:42.52, December 23, 2006
1⅛ miles: Ball Four, 1:48.29, September 30, 2006
1¼ miles: Swerve, 2:05.75, December 29, 2006
1⅝ miles: Anthem Hill, 2:53.59, April 5, 2006

Fastest Times of 2007 (All Weather)

5 furlongs: Jump for Joyeux, 7, :57.62, March 24, 2007
5½ furlongs: First At Summer, 3, 1:03.34, December 9, 2007
6 furlongs: Hoho Tow, 6, 1:08.53, January 14, 2007
6½ furlongs: Buddy Got Even, 5, 1:15.77, January 4, 2007
1 mile: Starspangled Gator, 4, 1:36.33, January 14, 2007
1¹⁄₁₆ miles: Purely Wild, 4, 1:43.27, December 13, 2007
1⅛ miles: Hard Spun, 3, 1:48.48, September 29, 2007
1¼ miles: Blackpool, 4, 2:06.35, December 26, 2007
1½ miles: Pirate's Bid, 5, 2:34.66, September 30, 2007

Louisiana

Delta Downs

Lee Berwick, a prominent Quarter Horse breeder and owner and a former president of the American

Quarter Horse Association, opened the first Delta Downs as a non-pari-mutuel match track on his farm at St. Joseph, Louisiana, on the banks of the Mississippi River. He moved the operation to Vinton, Louisiana, two hours northeast of Houston, Texas, and opened Delta Downs in 1973. Berwick served as track president until 1997, when his daughter, Kathryn, succeeded him in the position. In 1999, the Berwicks sold Delta Downs for more than $10-million to Shaun Scott and Jinho Cho, who began renovating the facility in hopes of installing slot machines. In 2001, the track was again sold for $125-million to Las Vegas-based Boyd Gaming Corp., which owns casinos in Louisiana, Nevada, Illinois, and Mississippi. In October 2001, Boyd received approval from the Louisiana Gaming Control Board to operate 1,700 slot machines. Delta Downs offers racing for Thoroughbreds, Quarter Horses, and Paints. The slots have resulted in sizable increases in Thoroughbred purses. The track sustained considerable damage from Hurricane Rita in 2005. The track did not reopen until November 2006.

Location: 2717 Delta Downs Dr., Vinton, La. 70668-6025
Phone: (337) 589-7441, (800) 589-7441
Fax: (337) 589-9195
Website: www.deltadowns.com
E-Mail: racefans@boydgaming.com
Year Founded: 1973
Abbreviation: DeD
Acreage: 240
Number of Stalls: 1,200
Seating Capacity: 3,400

Ownership
Boyd Gaming Corp.

Officers
Chairman: William S. Boyd
Chief Executive Officer: Keith Smith
Vice President: Jack Bernsmeier
General Manager: Jack Bernsmeier
Director of Racing: Chris Warren
Racing Secretary: Trent McIntosh
Director of Finance: Steve Meier
Director of Marketing: Adrian King
Director of Mutuels: Sylvia Rentz
Director of Publicity: Don Stevens
Director of Simulcasting: Chris Warren
Horsemen's Liaison: Trent McIntosh
Stewards: Duane Domingue, Sam Lato, Joel McCullar
Track Announcer: Don Stevens
Track Photographer: Jeff Coady
Track Superintendent: Darald Wilfer

Racing Dates
2007: November 1, 2006-March 31, 2007, 88 days
2008: October 19, 2007-March 29, 2008, 93 days
2009: October 29, 2008-March 28, 2009, 88 days

Track Layout
Main Circumference: 6 furlongs
Main Track Chute: 5 furlongs and 1 1/16 miles
Main Width: Homestretch: 80 feet; Backstretch and Turns: 70 feet
Main Length of Stretch: 660 feet

Handle
Average All-Sources Recent Meeting: $1,378,614, 2007/2008
Average On-Track Recent Meeting: $38,291, 2007/2008
Total All-Sources Recent Meeting: $128,211,071, 2007/2008
Total On-Track Recent Meeting: $3,561,029, 2007/2008
Highest Single-Day Record Recent Meeting: $2,458,316, December 7, 2007

Leaders
Recent Meeting, Leading Jockey: Gerard Melancon, 146, 2007/2008
Recent Meeting, Leading Owner: K.A.T. Racing Stables, 25, 2007/2008
Recent Meeting, Leading Trainer: Keith L. Bourgeois, 88, 2007/2008
Recent Meeting, Leading Horse: Kiss Meacham 4, Roar On Tour 4, Suicide Romance 4, Toolengthsoflite 4, Bandido 4, Fly By Moonlight 4, 2007/2008

Records
Single Meeting, Leading Jockey by Wins: Gerard Melancon, 146, 2007/2008
Single Meeting, Leading Owner by Wins: K.A.T. Racing Stables, 25, 2007/2008
Single Meeting, Leading Trainer by Wins: Keith L. Bourgeois, 88, 2007/2008

Principal Races
Delta Jackpot S. (G3), Delta Princess S. (G3), Gulf Coast Classic S., Goddess S., Gold Cup S.

Interesting Facts
Trivia: Three alligators live in the infield.

Notable Events
Louisiana Premier Night

Track Records, Main Dirt
4 furlongs: Rock Afire, :46 1/5, December 10, 1994
4 1/2 furlongs: Raisable Adversary, :51, February 15, 1992
5 furlongs: All Wired Up, :57.24, October 19, 2007
6 1/2 furlongs: Chief Okie Dokie, 1:18.76, February 8, 2002
7 furlongs: No Its Not, 1:24.31, January 24, 2003
7 1/2 furlongs: Junior Gent, 1:33 1/5, March 14, 1974
1 mile: Freon Flier, 1:37.52, March 10, 2002
1 mile 70 yds: Thriller, 1:42 2/5, September 27, 1973
1 1/16 miles: Norms Promise, 1:43 1/5, March 23, 1975
1 1/8 miles: Lucky Silence, 1:55 2/5, February 18, 1994
1 3/16 miles: Ponderosa Lark, 2:03 3/5, October 31, 1975
1 1/4 miles: Shy Bull, 2:10 1/5, November 3, 1974
1 3/8 miles: Surrogate's Irish, 2:23.52, March 22, 2003
1 1/2 miles: Art Work, 2:41 1/5, January 11, 1974
2 miles: Can 'em, 3:43 4/5, December 10, 1988
Other: 2 1/2 furlongs, Mrs. Deville, :27, February 19, 1976; 2 1/2 furlongs, Cajun Two Step, :27, February 10, 1985; 1 5/16 miles, Gentleman Mike, 2:17 3/5, December 1, 1974; 1 9/16 miles, Golden Foil, 2:46.86, March 27, 2004

Fastest Times of 2007 (Dirt)
4 1/2 furlongs: Hollywood Road, 4, :52.79, March 28, 2007
5 furlongs: All Wired Up, 5, :57.24, October 19, 2007
6 1/2 furlongs: Unofficial, 4, 1:19.82, March 30, 2007
7 furlongs: Jonesboro, 5, 1:25.40, December 7, 2007
7 1/2 furlongs: Sly Devil, 4, 1:36.73, January 13, 2007
1 mile: Silent Pleasure, 4, 1:38.59, March 2, 2007
1 mile 70 yds: Rakatack, 5, 1:48.80, February 23, 2007
1 1/16 miles: Silent Pleasure, 4, 1:44.07, March 31, 2007
1 1/4 miles: Wandaland's Turk, 8, 2:11.40, February 21, 2007
1 3/8 miles: Sharp Lad, 7, 2:24.80, December 27, 2007

Evangeline Downs

Located in Louisiana's colorful Cajun country, Evangeline Downs is known as the cradle of jockeys. Racing Hall of Fame members Eddie Delahoussaye and Kent Desormeaux as well as leading jockeys Shane Sellers and Mark Guidry all won their first races at the track. Several nationally known horses also have competed at Evangeline. In 1977, a two-year-old named John Henry won two of three starts at Evangeline and scored his first stakes win in the Lafayette Futurity. From that beginning, John Henry went on to earn more than $6.5-million and was voted Horse of the Year in 1981 and '84. In 1999 and 2000, Louisiana-bred Hallowed Dreams won 16 consecutive races, including six at Evangeline. The track, which offers some

Quarter Horse racing, conducts live racing from mid-April to early September. In 2005, the track moved to Opelousas to take advantage of a state law that permits slot machines at racetracks if authorized by local parishes. The new track has a grandstand that seats nearly 6,000 fans, a one-mile dirt oval, and a turf course inside the main track.

Location: 2235 Creswell Ln. Ext., Opelousas, La. 70570
Phone: (337) 594-3000, (866) 472-2466
Fax: (337) 594-3166
Website: www.evangelinedowns.com
E-Mail: generalmanager@evangelinedowns.com
Year Founded: 1966
Dates of Inaugural Meeting: April 28, 1966
Abbreviation: EvD
Acreage: 750
Number of Stalls: 1,000

Ownership
Peninsula Gaming

Officers
Chief Executive Officer: M. Brent Stevens
President: Michael S. Luzich
General Manager: Michael Howard
Director of Racing: Steve Darbonne
Racing Secretary: Jason M. Boulet
Track Announcer: John McGary
Director of Operations: Chuck Oswald
Director of Finance: Lynnette Bailey
Director of Marketing: Ashby Pettigrew
Director of Mutuels: Rachel Conway
Horsemen's Liaison: Dayne Dugas
Track Photographer: S.C.I. Photography
Security: Clinton James

Racing Dates
2007: April 4-September 3, 89 days
2008: Dates, April 9-September 1, 85 days

Track Layout
Main Circumference: 1 mile, field capacity 14 horses
Main Track Chute: 7 furlongs
Main Turf Circumference: 7 furlongs (Turf course scheduled to be completed July 2008)

Attendance
Highest Single-Day Record: 8,218, July 4, 1975

Handle
Average All-Sources Recent Meeting: $1,695,089, 2007
Single-Day All-Sources Recent Handle: $2,218,014, June 30, 2007
Total All-Sources Recent Meeting: $149,162,803, 2007
Average On-Track Recent Meeting: $69,278, 2007
Single-Day On-Track Recent Meeting: $209,723 June 30, 2007
Total On-Track Recent Meeting: $6,168,301, 2007

Mutuel Records
Highest Win: $412.20, Princely Greek, April 26, 1987
Highest Exacta: $24,213.90, August 1, 1982
Highest Trifecta: $37,995, August 23, 1997

Leaders
Career, Leading Trainer by Titles: Don Cormier Sr., 8
Recent Meeting, Leading Jockey: Curt Bourque, 93, 2007
Recent Meeting, Leading Trainer: Keith Bourgeois, 76, 2007
Recent Meeting, Leading Owner: K. A. T. Stable, 23, 2007
Recent Meeting, Leading Horse: Catquit, 4, 2007

Records
Single-Day Jockey Wins: Gerard Melancon, 6, 1984; Shane Sellers, 6, 1985; James Avant, 6, 1988; Curt Bourque, 6, 1989; Curt Bourque, 6, 1991; James Avant, 6, 1995; Kirk LeBlanc, 6, 1995
Single Meeting, Leading Jockey by Wins: Randy P. Romero, 140, 1978; Curt C. Bourque, 140, 1990
Single Meeting, Leading Trainer by Wins: Don Cormier Sr., 91, 1996

Principal Races
D. S. "Shine" Young Memorial Futurity, Evangeline Mile H., John Franks Memorial Sales S., Lafayette S.

Notable Events
Louisiana Legends Night

Track Records, Main Dirt
4½ furlongs: Mr. Rocket Man, :51.53, May 9, 2007
5 furlongs: Gold Storm, :56.94, June 3, 2006
5½ furlongs: Kim's Gem, 1:03.04, April 16, 2005
6 furlongs: High Strike Zone, 1:08.97, March 1, 2006
7 furlongs: Marion's Man, 1:22.43, May 4, 2007
1 mile: Clinch, 1:36.52, May 23, 2007
1 mile 70 yds: Rocket Strike, 1:42.18, May 3, 2007
1 1/16 miles: Drill Hall, 1:44.24, March 4, 2006

Fastest Times of 2007 (Dirt)
4 furlongs: Stellar Sergeant, 2, :47.42, May 2, 2007
4½ furlongs: Mr. Rocket Man, 8, :51.53, May 9, 2007
5 furlongs: I Forty Nine, 4, :57.18, May 25, 2007
5½ furlongs: Mr. Barracuda, 5, 1:03.38, May 25, 2007
6 furlongs: Indigo Girl, 5, 1:09.17, May 19, 2007
6½ furlongs: King of Mardi Gras, 6, 1 16.36, June 1, 2007
7 furlongs: Marion's Man, 7, 1:22.43, May 4, 2007
1 mile: Costa Rising, 4, 1:36.51, August 11, 2007
1 mile 70 yds: Rocket Strike, 3, 1:42.18, May 3, 2007
1 1/16 miles: Grand Minit, 4, 1:46, June 30, 2007

Fair Grounds

Thoroughbred racing has been conducted at the site of Fair Grounds in New Orleans with few interruptions since 1853, when a racetrack named Union Course held its first Thoroughbred meeting. The track, which has been called Fair Grounds since the 1860s, served as a military camp during the Civil and Spanish-American Wars. At times, changing political climates have halted racing, and devastating fires destroyed the facility in 1919 and '93. Fair Grounds survived, and some of the sport's most famous racehorses have run there. Legendary distaffer Pan Zareta died of pneumonia at Fair Grounds in 1918 and was buried at the track. Kentucky Derby winner Black Gold, winner of the Louisiana Derby at Fair Grounds in 1924, was fatally injured in the Salome Handicap in '28 and was buried in the track's infield. Other noted horses who have raced at Fair Grounds include 1941 Triple Crown winner Whirlaway, winner of the inaugural Louisiana Handicap in '42; multiple Fair Grounds stakes winner Master Derby, who captured the '75 Preakness Stakes (G1); and Silverbulletday, who won two Fair Grounds stakes during her '99 championship season. The Krantz family bought the facility in 1990 and rebuilt the track after the '93 fire. A $34.5-million grandstand and clubhouse opened on November 27, 1997. The track filed for bankruptcy in 2003 after a ruinous, $89.9-million court judgment to horsemen involving video-poker revenue, and it was sold in '04 for $47-million to Churchill Downs Inc. The track sustained damage from Hurricane Katrina in 2005 and ran an abbreviated 2005-'06 meet at Louisiana Downs. Slot machines arrived in 2007, and a permanent slots facility was to open in time for the 2008-'09 meet.

Location: 1751 Gentilly Blvd., New Orleans, La. 70119-2133
Phone: (504) 944-5515
Fax: (504) 944-2511
Website: www.fairgroundsracecourse.com
E-Mail: webmaster@fgno.com
Year Founded: 1872

Racetracks — Louisiana

Dates of Inaugural Meeting: April 13, 1872
Abbreviation: FG
Acreage: 145
Number of Stalls: 1,950
Seating Capacity: 6,500

Ownership
Churchill Downs Inc.

Officers
President: Randall E. Soth
Vice President and General Manager of OTBs/Slot Operations: Austin Miller
Assistant General Manager: Ed Fenasci
Director of Racing: Sam Abbey
Director of Marketing: Mark Conner
Director of OTB Operations: Leslie Hepting
Director of Facilities, Safety, and Security: David B. Martin
Director of Publicity and Simulcasting: Lenny Vangilder
Assistant Racing Secretary: David M. Heitzmann
Horsemen's Liaison: Brook Hawkins
Track Announcer: John G. Dooley
Track Photographer: Louis Hodges Jr.
Track Superintendent: Javier Barajas

Racing Dates
2007: November 23, 2006-March 25, 2007, 81 days
2008: November 22, 2007-March 23, 2008, 81 days
2009: November 14, 2008-March 29, 2009, 87 days

Track Layout
Main Circumference: 1 mile
Main Width: Homestretch: 75 feet; Backstretch: 70 feet
Main Length of Stretch: 1,346 feet
Main Turf Circumference: 7 furlongs

Attendance
Highest Single-Day Record: 23,662, November 27, 1969

Handle
Average All-Sources Recent Meeting: $4,361,099, 2007/2008
Average On-Track Recent Meeting: $225,048, 2007/2008
Single-Day On-Track Handle: $2,696,741, March 28, 1982
Single-Day All-Sources Handle: $12,962,024, March 8, 2008
Highest Single-Day All-Sources Handle Recent Meeting: $12,962,024, March 8, 2008
Record Single-Day On-Track Handle: $2,696,741, March 28, 1982

Mutuel Records
Highest Win: $500.60, Grey Hip, March 16, 1933
Lowest Win: $2.20, Shoot From the Hip, March 20, 2004
Highest Exacta: $25,257, February 8, 1971
Lowest Exacta: $2.20, January 3, 2002
Highest Daily Double: $2,917, January 5, 1971
Lowest Daily Double: $4.80, December 14, 2002
Highest Pick Three: $23,731.40, December 26, 1999
Lowest Pick Three: $12.60, December 23, 2000
Highest Pick Six: $108,848.20, March 9, 1999
Highest Other Exotics: $133,156.40, Superfecta, January 13, 2001; $673,602, Twin Trifecta, March 2, 1988
Lowest Other Exotics: $28.20 Superfecta, December 1, 2001

Leaders
Career, Leading Jockey by Titles: Robby Albarado, 6; Ronald Ardoin, 6
Career, Leading Trainer by Titles: Jack Van Berg, 10
Recent Meeting, Leading Jockey: Jamie Theriot, 94, 2007/2008
Recent Meeting, Leading Owner: Heflin and Driver Racing, 36, 2007/2008
Recent Meeting, Leading Trainer: Steven M. Asmussen, 86, 2007/2008

Records
Single-Day Jockey Wins: James P. Bowlds, 6, March 11, 1965; E. J. Perrodin, 6, November 18, 1979; Randy Romero, 6, February 8, 1984; V. L. "Billy" Smith, 6, March 15, 1990; Shane Romero, 6, February 10, 1991; Shane Romero, 6, February 24, 1991; Eddie Martin Jr., 6, January 18, 2004; Robby Albarado, March 11, 2004; Shaun Bridgmohan, 6, December 22, 2007
Single-Day Trainer Wins: Steven M. Asmussen, 6, December 22, 2007

Single Meeting, Leading Jockey by Wins: Randy Romero, 181, 1983/1984
Single Meeting, Leading Trainer by Wins: Jack Van Berg, 92, 1973/1974
Single Meeting, Leading Trainer by Stakes Wins: Steven M. Asmussen, 16, 2007/2008
Single Meeting, Leading Jockey by Stakes Wins: Robby Albarado, 13, 2003/2004 and 2004/2005
Single Meeting, Leading Horse by Wins: High Authority, 8, 1957/1958; Mickey C., 8, 1969/1970

Principal Races
Louisiana Derby (G2), New Orleans H. (G2), Mervin H. Muniz Jr. Memorial H. (G2), Fair Grounds Oaks (G2), Risen Star S. (G3)

Interesting Facts
Previous Names and Dates: Union Race Course (1853-'57)

Notable Events
Louisiana Champions Day, "Road to the Derby" Kickoff Day, Louisiana Derby Day

Track Records, Main Dirt
4 furlongs: Blue Carbon, :46^1/$_5$, March 18, 1967
4^1/$_2$ furlongs: Debs Mini Bars, :52^1/$_5$, March 8, 1971
5 furlongs: Posse, :57.35, February 10, 2003
5^1/$_2$ furlongs: Cort's P. B., 1:02.65, March 25, 2007
6 furlongs: Mountain General, 1:08.03, November 28, 2002
7 furlongs: For Fair, 1:24^2/$_5$, February 8, 1915
7^1/$_2$ furlongs: Begue, 1:33^3/$_4$, March 30, 1896
1 mile: Kitwe, 1:35.94, March 26, 1998
1 mile 40 yds: Total Rage, 1:38.52, March 23, 1997
1 mile 70 yds: Zevson, 1:41, November 26, 1936
1^1/$_{16}$ miles: Pie in Your Eye, 1:42.02, March 19, 1994
1^1/$_8$ miles: Phantom On Tour, 1:48.13, March 8, 1998
1^3/$_{16}$ miles: Half Magic, 1:56^1/$_5$, March 21, 1977
1^1/$_4$ miles: It's the One, 2:01^4/$_5$, March 21, 1982; Westheimer, 2:01^4/$_5$, March 24, 1985; Herat, 2:01^4/$_5$, March 16, 1986
1^3/$_8$ miles: Carroll Road, 2:18^1/$_5$, January 30, 1965; Tahuna, 2:18^1/$_5$, March 6, 1965
1^1/$_2$ miles: Tahuna, 2:32^2/$_5$, March 13, 1965
1^5/$_8$ miles: Major Mansir, 2:49^3/$_5$, January 4, 1904; From Afar, 2:49^3/$_5$, February 27, 1954
1^3/$_4$ miles: Aladdin Prince, 3:01^2/$_5$, April 5, 1981
2 miles: Bolster, 3:28^1/$_5$, February 7, 1920
Other: 2 furlongs, Baloma, :21^1/$_5$, January 26, 1952; 2 furlongs, Baloma, :21^1/$_5$, February 14, 1952; a2^1/$_2$ furlongs, Errand's Idol, :26, February 26, 1957; 3 furlongs, Henry's Baby, :33^3/$_5$, February 15, 1971; 3 furlongs, It's the Law, :33^3/$_5$, February 18, 1976; 3^1/$_2$ furlongs, Silver Finn, :41, February 24, 1925; 1 mile 20 yds, Lucky R., 1:40^3/$_5$, January 11, 1916; 1 mile 20 yds, Grumpy, 1:40^3/$_5$, February 5, 1916; 1^5/$_{16}$ miles, Retintin, 2:42^4/$_5$, March 28, 1970; 1^7/$_8$ miles, Julius Caesar, 3:19, February 27, 1900; 2m 70yds, Omar, 3:39^1/$_5$, March 3, 1940; 2^1/$_{16}$ miles, Quib's Bally, 3:47^1/$_5$, March 6, 1948; 2^1/$_4$ miles, Marvin Neal, 3:56, February 23, 1907; 3 miles, Colonist, 5:35, February 17, 1906; 4 miles, Major Mansir, 8:04^3/$_5$, March 21, 1903

Track Records, Main Turf
5^1/$_2$ furlongs: My Lord, 1:02.90, March 27, 2004
7^1/$_2$ furlongs: Northcote Road, 1:29.26, March 7, 2000
1 mile: Great Bloom, 1:35.57, March 20, 2004
1^1/$_{16}$ miles: Dixie Poker Ace, 1:42, January 8, 1994
1^1/$_8$ miles: Mystery Giver, 1:48.29, March 21, 2004
1^3/$_8$ miles: Present the Colors, 2:17^1/$_5$, April 4, 1982
1^1/$_2$ miles: Palace Panther (Ire), 2:32, April 6, 1986
Other: 1^5/$_{16}$ miles, To the Floor, 2:40.26, March 29, 1999

Fastest Times of 2007 (Dirt)
5^1/$_2$ furlongs: Cort's P. B., 7, 1:02.65, March 25, 2007
6 furlongs: First Word, 5, 1:09.23, March 1, 2007
1 mile: Honest Man, 3, 1:37.19, December 7, 2007
1 mile 40 yds: Piety, 5, 1:39.56, January 13, 2007
1^1/$_{16}$ miles: Master Command, 5, 1:42.28, February 10, 2007
1^1/$_8$ miles: Master Command, 5, 1:49.89, March 10, 2007

Fastest Times of 2007 (Turf)
a5^1/$_2$ furlongs: Smitty's Sunshine, 4, 1:02.92, March 10, 2007
a7^1/$_2$ furlongs: Rich Fantasy, 4, 1:31.18, March 23, 2007

a1 mile: Jazz Quest, 3, 1:37.98, January 15, 2007
a1 1/8 miles: Cloudy's Knight, 7, 1:49.48, February 10, 2007
a1 1/16 miles: Purim, 5, 1:43.22, January 13, 2007

Louisiana Downs

Louisiana Downs, located near Shreveport in Bossier City, opened in 1974. Built by the late shopping-center developer Edward DeBartolo Sr., the track introduced the Super Derby (now a Grade 2 race) in 1980, and since then the fall race has attracted leading three-year-olds. The first running was won by Temperence Hill, winner of that year's Belmont Stakes (G1). Two three-year-olds—Sunday Silence in 1989 and Tiznow in 2000—used the Super Derby as a steppingstone to victory in the Breeders' Cup Classic (G1) and Horse of the Year honors in their respective years. DeBartolo's racetrack holdings were sold following his death, and Louisiana Downs was acquired by his son-in-law, John York II. In November 2001, a group of investors headed by Shreveport lawyer Jim Davis announced plans to buy Louisiana Downs. In 2002, Harrah's Entertainment Corp. acquired approximately 95% of Louisiana Downs and opened a casino with 905 slot machines in 2003. By 2005, the renamed Harrah's Louisiana Downs had more than 1,400 machines. Harrah's valued the purchase, including renovations, at $183.4-million.

Location: 8000 E. Texas St., Bossier City, La. 71111-7016
Phone: (318) 742-5555, (800) 551-2361
Fax: (318) 741-2591
Website: www.ladowns.com
Year Founded: 1974
Dates of Inaugural Meeting: October 30, 1974-January 26, 1975
Abbreviation: LaD
Acreage: 350
Number of Stalls: 1,360
Seating Capacity: 17,240

Ownership
Harrah's Entertainment

Officers
General Manager: Geno Iafrate
Racing Secretary: Doug Bredar
Vice President of Operations: Brooks Robinson
Vice President of Racing: Mark Midland
Director of Mutuels: Holly Romain
Director of Simulcasting: Dick Pollock
Track Announcer: Travis Stone
Track Photographer: Reed Palmer
Track Superintendent: Brian Jabelemann

Racing Dates
2007: May 4-October 20, 92 days
2008: May 17-October 18, 85 days

Track Layout
Main Circumference: 1 mile
Main Track Chute: 1 1/4 miles
Main Track Chute: 7 furlongs
Main Width: 80 feet
Main Length of Stretch: 1,010 feet
Main Turf Circumference: 7 furlongs, 50 feet
Main Turf Width: 70 feet
Main Turf Length of Stretch: 940 feet

Attendance
Highest Single-Day Record: 26,513, May 26, 1986

Handle
Single-Day All-Sources Handle: $7,300,000, September 23, 2006

Mutuel Records
Highest Win: $249, B.J.'s Spruce, June 21, 1996
Lowest Win: $2.20, Appealing Breeze, 1989; $2.20, Richman, 1990; $2.20, Morning Meadow, 1993; $2.20, Runaway Venus, 1999; $2.20, Smart Ring, 1999
Highest Exacta: $2,780.80, May 1, 1994
Lowest Trifecta: $18.90, August 19, 1994
Highest Daily Double: $5,556.20, October 14, 1976
Highest Pick Three: $37,286.20, June 6, 1992
Lowest Pick Three: $11.80, September 12, 1994
Highest Pick Six: $555,287, May 25, 1991
Highest Other Exotics: $52,017.60, Superfecta, June 2, 1996

Leaders
Career, Leading Jockey by Titles: Ronald Ardoin, 6; Larry Snyder, 6
Career, Leading Owner by Titles: John Franks, 18
Career, Leading Trainer by Titles: Frank Brothers, 7
Career, Leading Jockey by Stakes Wins: Ronald Ardoin, 155
Career, Leading Owner by Stakes Wins: John Franks, 144
Career, Leading Trainer by Stakes Wins: Frank Brothers, 124
Career, Leading Jockey by Wins: Ronald Ardoin, 2,787
Career, Leading Trainer by Wins: C. W. Walker, 820
Recent Meeting, Leading Jockey: John Jacinto, 109, 2007
Recent Meeting, Leading Trainer: Jorge Lara, 56, 2007
Recent Meeting, Leading Owner: Jan Haynes, 39, 2007
Recent Meeting, Leading Horse: Tortuga Flats, 5, 2007

Records
Single-Day Jockey Wins: Ricky Frazier, 7, October 27, 1984
Single-Day Trainer Wins: Jack Van Berg, 5, December 5, 1976; Frank Brothers, 5, May 16, 1982; Frank Brothers, 5, September 3, 1984
Single Meeting, Leading Jockey by Wins: Ronald Ardoin, 198, 1993
Single Meeting, Leading Owner by Wins: John Franks, 65, 1983
Single Meeting, Leading Trainer by Wins: Frank Brothers, 99, 1987

Principal Races
Super Derby (G2), Sunday Silence S., Happy Ticket S., Unbridled Breeders' Cup S., Tiznow S., World Series of Poker S.

Track Records, Main Dirt
4 1/2 furlongs: Sondor, :51 3/5, May 16, 1984
5 furlongs: Oh Mar, :57.21, September 25, 2000
5 1/2 furlongs: Fighting K, 1:02.84, September 11, 1993
6 furlongs: Tangent, 1:08 1/5, April 28, 1984
6 1/2 furlongs: Prince of the Mt., 1:14.98, May 23, 1996
7 furlongs: Carrysport, 1:21 3/5, July 4, 1984; Skin Flint, 1:21.79, July 16, 2005
1 mile 70 yds: Country Jim, 1:39 2/5, July 4, 1982
1 1/16 miles: Nelson, 1:41.44, August 15, 1993
1 1/8 miles: Mocha Express, 1:48.14, July 24, 1999
1 3/16 miles: Jungle Pocket, 1:57 2/5, August 15, 1984
1 1/4 miles: Tiznow, 1:59.84, September 30, 2000
1 1/2 miles: Frankie's Pal, 2:31 4/5, September 3, 1990
1 5/8 miles: Frankie's Pal, 2:58 4/5, October 14, 1990
2 miles: Vain Lass, 3:35 1/5, November 16, 1975
Other: 1 13/16 miles, Stage Door Joey, 3:09.91, September 20, 1992

Track Records, Main Turf
5 furlongs: Mo Dinero, :55.40, September 26, 1999
7 1/2 furlongs: Our Love, 1:27.96, August 14, 2005
1 mile: Cherokee Circle, 1:34 1/5, July 24, 1983
1 1/16 miles: Erroneous I D, 1:40.17, September 2, 2006
1 1/4 miles: Middleweight, 2:02.76, September 4, 2005
1 3/8 miles: Semillero (Chi), 2:13 1/5, October 21, 1985

Fastest Times of 2007 (Dirt)
4 1/2 furlongs: Mr Bubba, 2, :52.82, June 29, 2007; Top Story, 2, :52.82, June 2, 2007
5 furlongs: Star of Idabel, 5, :57.48, May 17, 2007
5 1/2 furlongs: Cort's P. B., 7, 1:03.01, May 19, 2007
6 furlongs: Heelbolt, 3, 1:10.06, September 27, 2007
6 1/2 furlongs: Don's Boy, 3, 1:16.16, May 26, 2007
7 furlongs: St. Zarb, 3, 1:22.24, June 1, 2007
1 mile 70 yds: Forty Acres, 3, 1:41.26, July 26, 2007

1 1/16 **miles:** Ahead of Her Time, 3, 1:44.27, July 21, 2007
1 1/8 **miles:** Going Ballistic, 3, 1:50.32, September 22, 2007
1 1/4 **miles:** Meisque Party, 4, 2:04.92, September 21, 2007
1 1/2 **miles:** Son of Pistol (Arg), 8, 2:36.85, October 11, 2007

Fastest Times of 2007 (Turf)
a5 **furlongs:** Zarb's Dahar, 7, :56.88, September 8, 2007
7 1/2 **furlongs:** Meisque Party, 4, 1:29.81, October 13, 2007
a7 1/2 **furlongs:** Southern Invasion, 4, 1:29.97, October 6, 2007
1 **mile:** Candy Ball, 5, 1:36.61, October 20, 2007
a1 **mile:** Tortuga Flats, 4, 1:36.48, September 1, 2007
a1 1/4 **miles:** Meisque Party, 4, 2:05.84, August 12, 2007
1 1/16 **miles:** Go Between, 4, 1:40.64, September 22, 2007
a1 1/16 **miles:** Z Storm, 5, 1:43.08, October 4, 2007

Maryland

Laurel Park

Located in Laurel, midway between Baltimore and Washington, D.C., Laurel Park became a part of the Magna Entertainment Corp. family when the company headed by Frank Stronach bought a majority interest in the Maryland Jockey Club in 2002. Racing began at Laurel in 1911, and, three years later, New York City grocery entrepreneur James Butler acquired the track and hired Col. Matt Winn as the track's general manager. In 1947, the Maryland Jockey Club bought the track from Butler's estate, but the state's racing commission refused to permit Pimlico Race Course's dates to be moved to Laurel. Baltimore industrialist Morris Schapiro purchased the track in 1950 and put his youngest son, John D. Schapiro, in charge. Two years later, Laurel debuted the Washington, D.C., International, a turf stakes that was the first North American race to become a major annual target of European horses. Among the winners of the race was Racing Hall of Fame member Kelso in 1964. (The race was suspended after the 1994 running.) In 1984, Schapiro sold Laurel to a group of investors headed by Frank De Francis. In late 1986, De Francis and partners bought Pimlico, thus consolidating ownership of Maryland's major tracks. De Francis died in 1989 and was succeeded as president by his son, Joe. Magna Entertainment Corp. bought a majority interest in the tracks in 2002 and bought out the De Francis family in '07.

Location: P.O. Box 130, Laurel, Md. 20725-0130
Phone: (301) 725-0400
Fax: (301) 725-4561
Website: www.laurelpark.com
E-Mail: info@marylandracing.com
Year Founded: 1911
Dates of Inaugural Meeting: October 2, 1911
Abbreviation: Lrl
Acreage: 360
Number of Stalls: 880
Seating Capacity: 5,185

Ownership
Magna Entertainment Corp.

Officers
Chairman: Frank Stronach
President and Chief Operating Officer: Tom Chuckas
Chief Financial Officer: Douglas Illig
Senior Vice President and Associate General Manager: Dwayne Yuzik
Vice President of Security: Willie Coleman
Vice President of Marketing: Carrie Everly
Vice President of Communications: Mike Gathagan
Vice President of Facilities and Surfaces: Glen Kozak
Vice President of Wagering and Simulcast Operations: Dennis Smoter
Racing Secretary: Georganne Hale
Assistant Racing Secretaries: Clayton Beck, Jillian Sofarelli
Stakes Coordinator: Coley Blind
Horsemen's Bookkeeper: Kathryn Size
Director of Horsemen's Relations: Phoebe Hayes
Director of Guest Services: Scott Lishia
Track Announcer: Dave Rodman
Track Photographer: Jimmy McCue
Track Superintendent: David Whitman
Turf Superintendent: Robbie Mitten
Stewards: John Burke, Phil Grove, William Passmore

Racing Dates
2007: January 1-April 15, 75 days; August 10-August 23, 10 days; September 5-December 29, 68 days
2008: January 1-April 13, 60 days; August 8-August 23, 10 days; September 3-December 31, 68 days

Track Layout
Main Circumference: 1 mile and 600 feet
Main Track Chute: 7 1/2 furlongs
Main Width: 95 feet
Main Length of Stretch: First finish line: 1,089 feet; Second finish line: 1,419 feet
Main Turf Circumference: 7 furlongs
Main Turf Width: 142 feet
Main Turf Length of Stretch: 1,089 feet

Attendance
Average Daily Recent Meeting: 3,925, Winter 2007; 3,163, Summer 2007; 3,367, Fall 2007
Total Daily Recent Meeting: 294,375, Winter 2007; 31, 630, Summer 2007; 228,956, Fall 2007
Highest Single-Day Record: 40,276, November 11, 1958

Handle
Average All-Sources Recent Meeting: $2,805,776, Winter 2007; $1,119,384, Summer 2007; $2,159,563, Fall 2007
Total All-Sources Recent Meeting: $210,433,200, Winter 2007; $11,193,840, Summer 2007; $146,850,284, Fall 2007
Average On-Track Recent Meeting: $249,238, Winter 2007; $213,473, Summer 2007; $248,158, Fall 2007
Total On-Track Recent Meeting: $18,692,850, Winter 2007; $2,134,730, Summer 2007; $16,874,744, Fall 2007
Highest Single-Day On-Track Record Recent Meeting: $7,814,959, October 13, 2007

Leaders
Career, Leading Jockey by Titles: Edgar Prado, 10
Career, Leading Trainer by Titles: King Leatherbury, 26
Recent Meeting, Leading Jockey: Jeremy Rose, 75, Winter 2007; Luis Garcia, 11, Summer 2007; Horacio Karamanos, 55, Fall 2007; A.R. Napravnik, Winter 2008
Recent Meeting, Leading Owner: Robert Cole, 17, Winter 2007; Michael Gill, 4, Summer 2007; Robert Cole, 12, Fall 2007
Recent Meeting, Leading Trainer: Scott Lake, 49, Winter 2007; Dale Capuano, Hamilton Smith, and Gammy Vazquez, 4, Summer 2007; Scott A. Lake, 44, Fall 2007; Scott A. Lake, 51, Winter 2008

Records
Single-Day Jockey Wins: Chuck Baltazar, 7, December 15, 1969; Horacio Karamanos, 7, October 26, 2002
Single Meeting, Leading Jockey by Wins: Kent Desormeaux, 243, Winter 1988/1989
Single Meeting, Leading Trainer by Wins: King Leatherbury, 86, Winter 1993/1994 and Winter 1995

Principal Races
Frank J. De Francis Memorial Dash S. (G1), Barbara Fritchie H. (G2), General George H. (G2), Laurel Futurity, Selima S.

Notable Events
Maryland Million Day, SprintFest Weekend, Laurel Community Day

Track Records, Main Dirt
4 1/2 **furlongs:** Weighmaster, :52 2/5, April 13, 1964

5 furlongs: Dave's Friend, :57, November 21, 1980
5½ furlongs: Diamond's in Style, 1:02.42, September 8, 2006
6 furlongs: Richter Scale, 1:07.95, July 15, 2000
6½ furlongs: Ebonizer, 1:15²/₅, November 23, 1990
7 furlongs: Tappiano, 1:21²/₅, February 12, 1989; Nimble, 1:21.50, June 26, 1999
7½ furlongs: Tidal Surge, 1:29.52, March 12, 1994
1 mile: Skipper's Friend, 1:34²/₅, December 6, 1980
1¹/₁₆ miles: Willard Scott, 1:41⁴/₅, November 16, 1985; Carney's Prospect, 1:41.95, August 19, 2000
1⅛ miles: Excellent Tipper, 1:47.64, July 5, 1992
1³/₁₆ miles: Testing, 1:54.51, October 21, 2000
1¼ miles: Richie the Coach, 1:59.96, November 23, 1996
1⅜ miles: Amber Wave, 2:17⁴/₅, November 28, 1968
1¾ miles: Asserche, 2:58.51, February 13, 1994
Other: 1¹/₁₆ miles-chute, Spectacular Bid, 1:41³/₅, October 28, 1978

Track Records, Main Turf
5 furlongs: Cyberflash, :54.82, August 20, 2006
5½ furlongs: Tommie's Star, 1:01.05, September 8, 2007
1 mile: Sweet Talker, 1:34.17, April 15, 2006
1¹/₁₆ miles: Headsandtales, 1:39.98, September 6, 2007
1⅛ miles: Battle Chant, 1:46, September 17, 2005

Fastest Times of 2007 (Dirt)
5 furlongs: Carl's Smart, 6, :58.06, March 25, 2007
5½ furlongs: Southwestern Heat, 3, 1:03.36, April 11, 2007
6 furlongs: Kelp, 6, 1:09.47, January 12, 2007
7 furlongs: Silver Wagon, 6, 1:23.13, February 19, 2007
1 mile: Digger, 3, 1:35.23, September 15, 2007
1⅛ miles: Digger, 3, 1:50.81, November 3, 2007; My Dream (Brz), 6, 1:50.81, March 3, 2007
1³/₁₆ miles: Evil Storm, 6, 1:58.19, October 13, 2007

Fastest Times of 2007 (Turf)
5 furlongs: Ready to Blaze, 4, :55.60, April 5, 2007
5½ furlongs: Tommie's Star, 4, 1:01.05, September 8, 2007
6 furlongs: Chasin Tiger, 5, 1:07.91, September 27, 2007
1 mile: Wooden Stone, 8, 1:34.27, August 15, 2007
1¹/₁₆ miles: Headsandtales, 4, 1:39.98, September 6, 2007
1⅛ miles: Forty Crowns, 4, 1:46.03, October 13, 2007

Pimlico Race Course

The first horse to win a stakes race at Baltimore's Pimlico Race Course during the track's inaugural season in 1870 is the namesake of one of the world's most famous horse races. Preakness, a colt by legendary 19th-century sire Lexington, won the Dinner Party Stakes that year, and in 1873 the Preakness Stakes (now a Grade 1 race) made its debut. The race was not run in 1891, '92, or '93, and then it was held in New York for 15 years before it was returned to Pimlico in 1909. The Preakness now is the middle jewel of the Triple Crown and is run on the third Saturday in May. The day before the Preakness, Pimlico runs the race's three-year-old filly counterpart, the Black-Eyed Susan Stakes (G2). Another of the track's most famous races is the Pimlico Special Handicap (G1), which in 1938 captured the attention of the nation when Seabiscuit defeated War Admiral in a two-horse race. Magna Entertainment Corp. purchased majority ownership of Pimlico and Laurel Park near Washington, D.C., for $50.6-million in 2002, and bought the remaining interest in '07. Pimlico long has been called "Old Hilltop," a nickname that dates from the era when a small rise in the infield was a favorite gathering place for trainers and racing fans. The hill was removed in 1938, but the nickname remained.

Location: 5201 Park Heights Ave., Baltimore, Md. 21215-5117
Phone: (410) 542-9400
Fax: (410) 542-1221
Website: www.pimlico.com
E-Mail: info@marylandracing.com
Year Founded: 1743 (Maryland Jockey Club)
Dates of Inaugural Meeting: October 25, 1870
Abbreviation: Pim
Acreage: 140
Number of Stalls: 500
Seating Capacity: 14,852

Ownership
Magna Entertainment Corp.

Officers
Chairman: Frank Stronach
President and Chief Operating Officer: Tom Chuckas
Chief Financial Officer: Douglas Illig
Senior Vice President and Associate General Manager: Dwayne Yuzik
Vice President of Security: Willie Ccleman
Vice President of Marketing: Carrie Everly
Vice President of Communications: Mike Gathagan
Vice President of Facilities and Surfaces: Glen Kozak
Vice President of Wagering and Simulcast Operations: Dennis Smoter
Racing Secretary: Georganne Hale
Assistant Racing Secretaries: Clayton Beck, Jillian Sofarelli
Stakes Coordinator: Coley Blind
Horsemen's Bookkeeper: Kathryn Size
Director of Horsemen's Relations: Phoebe Hayes
Director of Guest Services: Scott Lishia
Track Announcer: Dave Rodman
Track Photographer: Jim McCue
Track Superintendent: Jamie Richardson
Turf Superintendent: Robbie Mitten
Stewards: John Burke, Phil Grove, William Passmore

Racing Dates
2007: April 19-June 9, 31 days
2008: April 17-June 7, 31 days

Track Layout
Main Circumference: 1 mile
Main Track Chute: 6 furlongs and 1¼ miles
Main Width: 70 feet
Main Length of Stretch: 1,152 feet
Main Turf Circumference: 7 furlongs

Attendance
Average Daily Recent Meeting: 8,251, 2007
Highest Single-Day Record: 121,263, May 19, 2007
Total Attendance Recent Meeting: 255,804, 2007
Highest Single-Day Recent Meeting: 121,263, May 19, 2007; 112,222, May 17, 2008

Handle
Single-Day On-Track Handle: $11,084,415, May 21, 2005
Single-Day All-Sources Handle: $91,028,704, May 21, 2005
Total All-Sources Recent Meeting: $236,905,825, 2007
Total On-Track Recent Meeting: $19,108,805, 2007
Highest Single-Day Record Recent Meeting: $87,194,161, May 19, 2007; $73,457,510, 2008

Mutuel Records
Highest Win: $574, Cadeaux, May 7, 1913
Lowest Win: $2.10, War Admiral, November 3, 1937
Highest Exacta: $5,223.60, May 27, 1989
Lowest Exacta: $2.60, March 28, 1981
Highest Trifecta: $73,278, March 15, 1982
Highest Daily Double: $11,271.20, April 27, 2006
Highest Pick Six: $294,169, March 8, 1986
Highest Other Exotics: $414,243.90, Twin Trifecta, April 4, 1991
Highest Pick Four: $36,227.50, May 16, 2001

Leaders
Career, Leading Jockey by Titles: Edgar Prado, 14
Career, Leading Trainer by Titles: King Leatherbury, 26
Recent Meeting, Leading Jockey: Luis Garcia, 37, 2007

Recent Meeting, Leading Owner: Circle Z Stables, 5, 2007
Recent Meeting, Leading Trainer: Scott Lake, 17, 2007
Recent Meeting, Leading Horse: 10 tied with 2, 2007

Records
Single-Day Jockey Wins: Paul Nicol Jr., 7, June 8, 1983
Single Meeting, Leading Jockey by Wins: Kent Desormeaux, 184, Spring 1989
Single Meeting, Leading Trainer by Wins: King Leatherbury, 100, 1976

Principal Races
Preakness S. (G1), Pimlico Special H. (G1), Black-Eyed Susan S. (G2), Dixie S. (G2), Allaire duPont Breeders' Cup Distaff S. (G2)

Track Records, Main Dirt
4 furlongs: Gavotte, :47$^{2}/_{5}$, May 4, 1925
4$^{1}/_{2}$ furlongs: Countess Diana, :51.50, June 6, 1997
5 furlongs: Kingmaker, :56.46, September 27, 2003
5$^{1}/_{2}$ furlongs: Higher Strata, 1:02.46, July 29, 1995
6 furlongs: Northern Wolf, 1:09, August 18, 1990; Forest Wildcat, 1:09.07, May 18, 1996; Xtra Heat, 1:09.07, August 18, 2001
7 furlongs: Zeus, 1:26, May 3, 1921
1 mile: June Grass, 1:37$^{3}/_{5}$, May 2, 1923
1 mile 70 yds: Sabotage, 1:41$^{2}/_{5}$, December 17, 1958
1$^{1}/_{16}$ miles: Deputed Testamony, 1:40$^{4}/_{5}$, May 19, 1984; Poor But Honest, 1:40.83, September 9, 1995
1$^{1}/_{8}$ miles: Private Terms, 1:47$^{1}/_{5}$, May 27, 1989
1$^{3}/_{16}$ miles: Farma Way, 1:52.55, May 11, 1991
1$^{1}/_{4}$ miles: Manzotti, 2:01$^{4}/_{5}$, March 19, 1988
1$^{3}/_{8}$ miles: Narwhal, 2:16$^{2}/_{5}$, December 16, 1962
1$^{1}/_{2}$ miles: War Trophy, 2:29$^{2}/_{5}$, November 8, 1948
1$^{5}/_{8}$ miles: Market Wise, 2:43$^{1}/_{5}$, November 13, 1941
1$^{3}/_{4}$ miles: Blue Hills, 2:55$^{2}/_{5}$, October 25, 1949
2 miles: Everett, 3:25$^{3}/_{5}$, October 31, 1920
Other: a6 furlongs, Dagger Counter, 1:11$^{2}/_{5}$, January 2, 1968; 1$^{11}/_{16}$ miles, Post Morton, 2:57$^{4}/_{5}$, December 7, 1957; 2m 70 yds, Filisteo, 3:30$^{4}/_{5}$, October 31, 1941; 2$^{1}/_{16}$ miles, Beau Diable, 3:35$^{3}/_{5}$, December 10, 1960; 2$^{1}/_{4}$ miles, Edith Cavell, 3:52$^{1}/_{5}$, November 13, 1926; 2$^{1}/_{2}$ miles, Miss Grillo, 4:14$^{3}/_{5}$, November 12, 1948

Track Records, Main Turf
5 furlongs: Smart Enough, :55.73, May 26, 2006
7 furlongs: Lofty Peak, 1:23$^{1}/_{5}$, May 14, 1956
1 mile: North East Bound, 1:33.42, May 7, 2000
1$^{1}/_{16}$ miles: Precious Kitten, 1:40.32, May 19, 2007
1$^{1}/_{8}$ miles: Mr. O'Brien, 1:46.34, May 15, 2004
1$^{3}/_{16}$ miles: Bayard Park, 2:01, May 7, 1966
1$^{3}/_{8}$ miles: Dunsinyne, 2:13.74, June 22, 1997
1$^{1}/_{2}$ miles: Fort Marcy, 2:27$^{2}/_{5}$, May 9, 1970
Other: 1$^{7}/_{8}$ miles, Brightly, 3:17, December 1, 1955

Fastest Times of 2007 (Dirt)
4$^{1}/_{2}$ furlongs: Fast Talking, 2, :53.95, June 1, 2007
5 furlongs: Dixie Tea Party, 5, :59.42, April 19, 2007
5$^{1}/_{2}$ furlongs: Visionary, 5, 1:03.44, April 19, 2007
6 furlongs: Diabolical, 4, 1:09.16, May 19, 2007
1$^{1}/_{16}$ miles: Rolling Sea, 4, 1:42.88, May 18, 2007
1$^{1}/_{8}$ miles: Flashy Bull, 4, 1:47.86, May 19, 2007
1$^{3}/_{16}$ miles: Curlin, 3, 1:53.46, May 19, 2007

Fastest Times of 2007 (Turf)
5 furlongs: Unbridled Sidney, 6, :55.77, May 18, 2007
1 mile: Accountant's Dream, 6, 1:35.12, May 18, 2007
1$^{1}/_{16}$ miles: Precious Kitten, 4, 1:40.32, May 19, 2007
1$^{1}/_{8}$ miles: Remarkable News (Ven), 5, 1:46.36, May 19, 2007

Timonium

Although Timonium's annual live meeting, run in conjunction with the Maryland State Fair, lasts only a few days through Labor Day, it attracts more than a half-million fans each year to the community located near Baltimore's northern border. In 2001, Timonium lost two dates of its usual ten dates because of insufficient purses but still had a successful meet. In 2002 and '03, the track again ran eight dates. In the early 1980s, it raced as many as 42 days, but its season was sharply reduced in 1985 when Maryland's mile tracks began running year-round. Timonium, which struggled in the early 1990s until the addition of simulcasting both into and out of the track, is operated by the not-for-profit Maryland State Fair and Agricultural Society Inc., which directs all profits to the fair, 4-H Club awards, and improvements. Racing at Timonium began in September 1887. Its five-furlong track has a four-furlong chute and a 6½-furlong chute.

Location: 2200 York Rd., P.O. Box 188, Timonium, Md. 21094
Phone: (410) 252-0200
Fax: (410) 561-5610
Website: www.marylandstatefair.com
E-Mail: msfair@msn.com
Year Founded: 1878
Dates of Inaugural Meeting: September 1878
Abbreviation: Tim
Acreage: 100
Number of Stalls: 600
Seating Capacity: 4,850

Ownership
Maryland State Fair and Agricultural Society Inc.

Officers
Chairman: F. Grove Miller
President and General Manager: Howard M. (Max) Mosner
Racing Secretary: Georganne Hale
Treasurer: John H. Mosner Jr.
Director of Mutuels: Richard Insley
Director of Publicity: Rich Paul
Stewards: John J. Burke III, Philip E. Grove, William J. Passmore
Track Announcer: Dave Rodman
Track Photographer: Jim McCue
Track Superintendent: Don Denmyer

Racing Dates
2007: August 24-September 3, 10 days
2008: August 22-September 1, 7 days

Track Layout
Main Circumference: 5 furlongs
Main Track Chute: 4 furlongs and 6$^{1}/_{2}$ furlongs
Main Width: 70 feet
Main Length of Stretch: 700 feet

Attendance
Highest Single-Day Record: 17,306, September 4, 1967

Leaders
Recent Meeting, Leading Jockey: J. D. Acosta, 13, 2007
Recent Meeting, Leading Trainer: Benjamin M. Feliciano Jr., 4, 2007; Dale Capuano, 4, 2007
Recent Meeting, Leading Horse: Snow Eagle, 2, 2007

Principal Races
Alma North S., Taking Risks S.

Interesting Facts
Achievements/Milestones: Trainer King T. Leatherbury won his 6,000th race on August 23, 2003, at Timonium.

Fastest Times of 2007 (Dirt)
4 furlongs: Queen Hypolita, 5, :45.36, August 24, 2007
6$^{1}/_{2}$ furlongs: Cranberry Covet, 4, 1:19.65, August 25, 2007
a6$^{1}/_{2}$ furlongs: Skeleton Crew, 4, 1:16.68, August 31, 2007
1 mile: Mr. Conover, 4, 1:40.27, September 3, 2007
1$^{1}/_{16}$ miles: Lord Catticus, 3, 1:50.19, August 25, 2007

Massachusetts

Suffolk Downs

Built in just 62 days for $2-million by the Eastern Racing Association, Suffolk Downs opened before an estimated crowd of 35,000 in East Boston on July 10, 1935, as the nation's only racetrack with a concrete grandstand. Just one month later, 52,726 fans set a Suffolk attendance record that still stands. Suffolk's signature race, the Massachusetts Handicap (G2), was inaugurated in 1935, and it has been won by such champions as Seabiscuit in '37 and two-time MassCap winners Cigar and Skip Away in the '90s. To conserve purse money for a longer meet, the MassCap was canceled in 2003, '05, and '06. Legendary promoter Bill Veeck carded chariot races, livestock giveaways, and mock Indian battles in the infield during his tenure there in 1969 and '70. He also successfully sued the state to allow children to attend the races. Following a two-year shutdown in 1990 and '91, James B. Moseley's and John Hall's Sterling Suffolk Racecourse Ltd. leased the track and Thoroughbred racing returned to Boston. In 1997, Suffolk Racecourse LLC bought Suffolk for $40-million. Developer Richard Fields purchased controlling interest in the track in 2007.

Location: 111 Waldemar Ave., East Boston, Ma. 02128-1035
Phone: (617) 567-3900
Fax: (617) 561-5100
Website: www.suffolkdowns.com
E-Mail: publicity@suffolkdowns.com
Year Founded: 1935
Dates of Inaugural Meeting: July 10-August 10, 1935, 28 days
Abbreviation: Suf
Acreage: 163
Number of Stalls: 1,380
Seating Capacity: 8,000

Ownership
Sterling Suffolk Racecourse LLC

Officers
Chairman: William Mulrow
President: John L. Hall II
Secretary: Charles A. Baker III
Chief Operating Officer: Chip Tuttle
Chief Financial Officer: John Rizzo
Vice President of Operations and Assistant General Manager: Joe Fatalo
Vice President of Racing: Samuel Elliott
Vice President of Marketing and Communications: Christian Teja
Senior Director of Operations: L. J. Pambianchi Jr.
Racing Secretary: Tom Creel
Controller: Mary Walukiewicz
Director of Mutuels: James R. Alcott
Director of Group Sales: Dominic Terlizzi
Stewards: Edward Cantlon Jr., Susan Walsh, John Morrissey
Track Announcers: Larry Collmus, T. D. Thornton
Track Photographer: Chip Bott
Track Superintendent: Steve Pini

Racing Dates
2007: May 5-November 10, 100 days
2008: May 3-November 8, 103 days

Track Layout
Main Circumference: 1 mile
Main Track Chute: 6 furlongs and 1 1/4 miles
Main Width: Homestretch: 90 feet; Backstretch: 70 feet
Main Length of Stretch: 1,030 feet
Main Turf Circumference: a7 furlongs
Main Turf Width: 65 to 70 feet
Main Turf Length of Stretch: 1,030 leet

Attendance
Average Daily Recent Meeting: 3,288, 2007
Highest Single-Day Record: 52,726, August 10, 1935
Record Daily Average Single Meeting: 18,388, 1945
Total Attendance Recent Meeting: 328,778, 2007

Handle
Average All-Sources Recent Meeting: $903,834, 2007
Average On-Track Recent Meeting: S122,702, 2007
Record Daily Average Single Meeting: $1,164,240, 1946
Single-Day On-Track Handle: $2,175 836, May 30, 1960
Single-Day All-Sources Handle: $5,867,414, May 31, 1997
Total All-Sources Recent Meeting: $90,383,438, 2007
Total On-Track Recent Meeting: $12,270,152, 2007
Highest Single-Day Record Recent Meeting: 3,137,927, September 22, 2007
Highest Single-Day On-Track Recent Meeting: $826,415, September 22, 2007

Mutuel Records
Highest Win: $445, Sue Harper, June 14, 1940
Highest Exacta: $9,923,80, January 13, 1985
Highest Trifecta: $51,778, January 13, 1985
Lowest Trifecta: $7.00, September 5, 2005
Highest Daily Double: $16,515, May 25, 1979
Lowest Daily Double: $3.40, June 6, 2007
Highest Pick Three: $10,515.40, December 26, 1992
Lowest Pick Three: $9.80, May 12, 2007
Highest Pick Six: $25,399, November 28, 1982
Highest Other Exotics: $9,923.80, Perfecta, January 13, 1985; $23,079.40, Superfecta, March 27, 1996
Lowest Other Exotics: $2.60, Perfecta, October 7, 2002

Leaders
Recent Meeting, Leading Jockey: Tammi Piermarini, 100, 2007
Recent Meeting, Leading Owner: Aurora Springs Stable, 38, 2007
Recent Meeting, Leading Trainer: John Rigattieri, 64, 2007
Recent Meeting, Leading Horse: De Roode, 6, 2007; Ask Queenie, 6, 2007; Brilliant Mrs. W, 6, 2007; President's Intern, 6, 2007

Records
Single-Day Jockey Wins: Leroy Moyers, 7, July 4, 1967
Single Meeting, Leading Jockey by Wins: S. Elliott, 381, 1989
Single Meeting, Leading Trainer by Wins: W. W. Perry, 140, 1989

Principal Races
Massachusetts H.

Notable Events
Hot Dog Safari (a fund-raiser for the Joey Fund/Cystic Fibrosis Foundation); Walk For Autism

Track Records, Main Dirt
4 furlongs: Crimson Streak, :45 1/5, April 6, 1970
4 1/2 furlongs: Lovely Gypsy, :51 1/5, May 7, 1965; Happy Voter, :51 1/5, May 16, 1966
5 furlongs: Rene Depot, :57 2/5, June 25, 1972
5 1/2 furlongs: Dennisport, 1:04.09, September 17, 2007
6 furlongs: Canal, 1:08 1/5, May 16, 1966
1 mile: Back Bay Brave, 1:35 1/5, July 12, 1986
1 mile 70 yds: Half Breed, 1:40, May 23, 1964; Half an Hour, 1:40.10, January 22, 1997
1 1/16 miles: Talent Show, 1:41 4/5, May 12, 1962; Bear the Palm, 1:41 4/5, July 3, 1977
1 1/8 miles: Skip Away, 1:47.27, May 30, 1998
1 3/16 miles: Shut Out, 1:55 2/5, July 4, 1942
1 1/4 miles: Helioscope, 2:01, May 19, 1955
1 1/2 miles: Connie Rab, 2:30 3/5, May 15, 1954
1 5/8 miles: Count Fire, 2:45 2/5, June 23, 1962
1 3/4 miles: Toulouse, 2:58 2/5, June 16, 1956

2 miles: Hutch, 3:35$^2/_5$, August 1, 1950
Other: 2 furlongs, Adriano's Girl, :21.94, June 4, 1997; 2m 70 yds, On the Square, 3:39$^4/_5$, April 16, 1973; 2$^1/_{16}$ miles, Bold Fencer, 3:35$^4/_5$, April 18, 1983; 2$^1/_4$ miles, Fundy Bay, 3:54$^1/_5$, December 9, 1973

Track Records, Main Turf

a5 furlongs: Bishop Ridley, :57$^1/_5$, July 19, 1987; Concorde Cal, :57.33, October 30, 1994
a7$^1/_2$ furlongs: Times Ahead, 1:32$^2/_5$, September 3, 1988
a1 mile: Diablo Reigns, 1:39.35, September 15, 2003
a1 mile 70yds: Alphabetical, 1:42.07, June 30, 2004
a1$^1/_{16}$ miles: Landing Court, 1:44.91, October 26, 1994
a1$^3/_8$ miles: Chompion, 2:20$^4/_5$, July 18, 1970 (Dead Heat); *Gaybrook Swan, 2:20$^4/_5$, July 18, 1970 (Dead Heat)
a1$^1/_2$ miles: *Akbar Khan, 2:30$^3/_5$, June 17, 1957
a1$^{15}/_{16}$ miles: Jamf, 3:11$^1/_5$, July 4, 1975
a2 miles: Jean-Pierre, 3:19$^1/_5$, June 28, 1969

Fastest Times of 2007 (Dirt)

4 furlongs: Johns Grooms, 2, :46.95, August 8, 2007
5 furlongs: Regent Executive, 6, :58.19, August 8, 2007
5$^1/_2$ furlongs: Dennisport, 6, 1:04.09, September 17, 2007
6 furlongs: Afrashad, 5, 1:09.05, September 22, 2007
1 mile: Disco Fox, 3, 1:38.10, August 8, 2007
1 mile 70 yds: Let Me Be Frank, 5, 1:42.66, September 18, 2007
1$^1/_{16}$ miles: Reason's Rapture, 6, 1:49.05, September 11, 2007
1$^1/_8$ miles: Brass Hat, 6, 1:49.72, September 22, 2007
1$^1/_4$ miles: Theatrical Talent, 4, 2:07.81, September 24, 2007

Fastest Times of 2007 (Turf)

a5 furlongs: Canyon's Way, 8, :58.28, July 14, 2007
a7$^1/_2$ furlongs: Mommyums, 5, 1:34.39, June 27, 2007
a1 mile: Sand Slider, 6, 1:40.85, June 13, 2007
a1 mile 70 yds: British Event, 5, 1:43.77, June 20, 2007
a1$^1/_{16}$ miles: Lucky Leo, 6, 1:48.03, September 22, 2007

Michigan

Great Lakes Downs

Great Lakes Downs was born in 1999 out of the necessity to preserve live racing in Michigan following the shuttering of Ladbroke-owned Detroit Race Course. Located at the site of a former Standardbred track in Muskegon, Great Lakes Downs came together quickly as a group of horse owners and racing enthusiasts raised the capital to renovate the facility and prepare for racing. After an understated first meeting in 1999, the track gained national attention in the winter of 2000 when Frank Stronach-led Magna Entertainment Corp., in the midst of a track-buying spree, added Great Lakes Downs to its holdings. In early 2003, Magna reported that Great Lakes was losing money and wrote down the book value of the track. Magna received preliminary local approval to build a new track near Detroit and racing ended at Great Lakes Downs after the 2007 season.

Location: 4800 S. Harvey St., Muskegon, Mi. 49444-9762
Phone: (231) 799-2400, (877) 800-4616
Fax: (231) 798-3120
Website: *www.greatlakesdowns.com*
E-Mail: glweb@greatlakesdowns.com
Year Founded: 1984
Dates of Inaugural Meeting: May 25, 1989 (Standardbred); April 23, 1999 (Thoroughbred)
Abbreviation: GLD
Acreage: 85
Number of Stalls: 800
Seating Capacity: 3,200

Mt. Pleasant Meadows

Location: 500 N. Mission Rd., P.O. Box 220, Mount Pleasant, Mi. 48858-4600
Phone: (989) 772-2725
Fax: (989) 773-7616
Website: *www.mpmhorseracing.com*
E-Mail: mpm989@hotmail.com
Year Founded: 1985
Dates of Inaugural Meeting: June 21, 1985
Abbreviation: MPM
Number of Stalls: 300
Seating Capacity: 3,400

Ownership

Walter Bay

Officers

President: Walter Bay

Racing Dates

2007: May 5-September 23, 35 days
2008: May 3-September 28, 57 days

Track Layout

Main Circumference: 4 furlongs
Main Width: 60 feet

Attendance

Highest Single-Day Record: 1,027, May 17, 1986

Handle

Average On-Track Recent Meeting: $4,709, 2007
Average All-Sources Recent Meeting: $70,087, 2007
Single-Day All-Sources Handle: $61,463, October 1, 1989
Total On-Track Recent Meeting: $164,847, 2007
Total All-Sources Recent Meeting: $2,453,061, 2007

Track Records, Main Dirt

4 furlongs: Bad Boy Eric, :48.35, August 25, 2001
4$^1/_2$ furlongs: Wildcat Express, :52.35, May 21, 2000
5 furlongs: My Friend Charlie, :59.30, June 29, 1991
5$^1/_2$ furlongs: Comedy Routine, 1:05.40, July 31, 1994
6 furlongs: My Friend Charlie, 1:14.30, July 28, 1991

Fastest Times of 2007 (Dirt)

2 furlongs: Flame of Justice, 5, :22.58, June 17, 2007; Wrench, 4, :22.58, July 7, 2007
4$^1/_2$ furlongs: Super Mood, 7, :54.30, September 15, 2007
5 furlongs: Bold Prospect, 8, 1:01.20, September 2, 2007
5$^1/_2$ furlongs: Waterbury, 6, 1:07, June 16, 2007
6 furlongs: Cache Monster, 6, 1:15.30, September 22, 2007

Pinnacle Race Course

After the 2007 closure of Magna-owned Great Lakes Downs left Michigan without a Thoroughbred racetrack, banker and Thoroughbred owner-breeder Jerry Campbell's Post It Stables was awarded a track license in March 2008. Construction on the southern Detroit site began later that month. Because of schedule restraints and the necessity for racing to continue in Michigan uninterrupted, the track conducted its inaugural meet while the grounds were still under construction, utilizing temporary grandstands similar to those used for the 2007 Breeders' Cup World Championships at Monmouth Park. The project was to be completed by the 2009 meet, with plans to prepare a seven-furlong turf course for '10. The opening of Pinnacle marked the return of Thoroughbred racing to the Detroit area after the closing of Detroit Race Course in 1998.

Location: 1800 Vining Rd., New Boston, Mi. 48164
Phone: (734) 753-2000

Website: www.pinnacleracecourse.com
E-Mail: aplever@pinnacleracecourse.com
Year Founded: 2008
Date of Inaugural Meet: July 18, 2008
Abbreviation: PRC
Acreage: 320
Number of Stalls: 580
Seating Capacity: 1,480

Ownership
Post It Stables

Officers
Chairperson and Chief Executive Officer: Felicia Campbell
President: Michael McInerney
Secretary and Treasurer: Jerry Campbell
Senior Adviser: Lonny Powell
General Manager: Allan Plever
Vice President of Sales and Marketing: Russ Gregory
Racing Secretary: Denver Beckner
Track Superintendent: John Pollert

Racing Dates
2008: July 18-November 2, 63 days

Track Layout
Main Circumference: One Mile
Main Track Chute: 2 furlongs and 7 furlongs
Main Width: 80 feet
Main Length of Stretch: 900 feet

Minnesota

Canterbury Park

Canterbury Park is located in Shakopee, southwest of Minneapolis and St. Paul. When the track first opened in 1985, three years after Minnesota legalized pari-mutuel wagering, it was known as Canterbury Downs, and its ownership group included the Santa Anita Operating Co. In 1990, the track was purchased by Ladbroke Racing Corp., but, due to declining business, closed in '92. One year later, Irwin Jacobs, a Twin Cities financier, purchased the track and sold it to businessman and breeder Curtis Sampson, Sampson's son Randy, and partner Dale Schenian. Four months later, the owners held an initial public offering of the newly created Canterbury Park Holding Corp. The track, which reopened in 1995 as Canterbury Park, offers Thoroughbred racing and some Quarter Horse racing during its live racing season, which runs from mid-May through early September. In 1999, Canterbury held the first running of the Claiming Crown series, which quickly became recognized as a major sporting event in Minnesota, and has been held at the Shakopee track every year but two. The Canterbury Card Club opened in 2000 at the track, and its gaming revenues supplement race purses.

Location: 1100 Canterbury Rd., Shakopee, Mn. 55379-1867
Phone: (952) 445-7223, (800) 340-6361
Fax: (952) 496-4676
Website: www.canterburypark.com
E-Mail: cbypark@canterburypark.com
Year Founded: 1985
Dates of Inaugural Meeting: June 26, 1985
Abbreviation: Cby
Acreage: 355
Number of Stalls: 1,620
Seating Capacity: 22,830

Ownership
Canterbury Park Holding Corp.

Officers
Chief Executive Officer: Randall D. Sampson
Chairman: Curtis A. Sampson
Vice Chairman: Dale H. Schenian
President: Randall D. Sampson
Director of Racing and Racing Secretary: Douglas Schoepf
Assistant Racing Secretary: John Simon
Secretary: Michelle Simon
Vice President of Finance: David Hansen
Vice President of Marketing: John Harty
Director of Mutuels: Linda Arnoldi
Director of Publicity: Jeff Maday
Director of Simulcasting: Eric Halstrom
Horsemen's Liaison: Mary Green
Stewards: Noble Hay, Hank Mills, David Moore
Track Announcer: Paul Allen
Track Photographer: Beth Rutzebeck
Track Superintendent: Moe Nye
Security: Sean Corrigan
Clerk of the Course: Peggy Davis
Horsemen's Bookkeeper: Terri Hoffrogge

Racing Dates
2007: May 5-September 3, 68 days
2008: May 3-September 1, 67 days

Track Layout
Main Circumference: 1 mile
Main Track Chute: $3^1/_2$ furlongs, $6^1/_2$ furlongs, and $1^1/_4$ miles
Main Turf Circumference: 7 furlongs
Main Turf Chute: $1^1/_{16}$ miles

Attendance
Average Daily Recent Meeting: 5,476, 2007
Highest Single-Day Record: 27,439, April 24, 1987
Highest Single-Meet Record: 1,392,940, 1986
Record Daily Average Single Meeting: 13,163, 1985
Total Attendance Recent Meeting: 372,358, 2007

Handle
Average All-Sources Recent Meeting: $513,933, 2007
Single-Day On-Track Handle: $999,719, August 6, 2000
Single-Day All-Sources Handle: $4,025,716, July 17, 2004
Total All-Sources Recent Meeting: $34,947,440, 2007
Highest Single-Day Record Recent Meeting: $1,113,194, July 3, 2007
Record Average All-Sources Single Meeting: $1,014,588, 1985

Leaders
Career, Leading Jockey by Titles: Luis Quinonez, 5
Career, Leading Owner by Titles: Stephen Herold, 2; Steve Richardson, 2; Curtis Sampson, 2; Valene Farm, 2
Career, Leading Trainer by Titles: Pat Cuccurullo, 3; Doug Oliver, 3; Mac Robertson, 3; David Van Winkle, 3
Career, Leading Jockey by Wins: Scott Stevens, 801
Career, Leading Trainer by Wins: Bernell Rhone, 459
Recent Meeting, Leading Jockey: Derek Bell, 81, 2007
Recent Meeting, Leading Trainer: Mac Robertson, 65, 2007

Records
Single Meet, Leading Jockey by Wins: Dean Kutz, 158, 1987
Single Meet, Leading Trainer by Wins: Pat Cuccurullo, 91, 1990

Principal Races
Lady Canterbury Breeders' Cup S., Minnesota Oaks, Minnesota Derby

Interesting Facts
Previous Names and Dates: Canterbury Downs (1985-'94)

Notable Events
Claiming Crown

Track Records, Main Dirt
$4^1/_2$ furlongs: Cold N Tricky, :51.15, July 22, 2007
5 furlongs: Tonight Rainbow, :57.11, May 31, 2004
$5^1/_2$ furlongs: Nickel Slot, 1:02$^1/_5$, May 17, 1989

6 furlongs: Onlynurimagination, 1:08.04, July 16, 2005
6½ furlongs: Don's Irish Melody, 1:14, June 12, 1988
1 mile: Minneapple, 1:35⅘, September 27, 1987
1 mile 70 yds: Come Summer, 1:40⅕, August 18, 1985; J. P. Jet, 1:40.26, August 3, 2002
1¹⁄₁₆ miles: Wally's Choice, 1:41.74, August 22, 2004
1⅛ miles: Olympio, 1:46.47, July 7, 1991
1¼ miles: John Bullit, 2:04⅗, July 25, 1986
1½ miles: Loustros (GB), 2:32⅗, August 28, 1987
1¾ miles: Luciole (Arg), 2:59⅘, October 12, 1985
2 miles: My Tulles Free, 3:25⅗, September 1, 1986
Other: a3 furlongs, In Moderation, :39.11, May 26, 1997; 3½ furlongs, Bye for Now, :40, June 30, 1985

Track Records, Main Turf

5 furlongs: Rockhurst, :56.01, May 30, 2005
7½ furlongs: Honor the Hero, 1:28, June 18, 1995
1 mile: Go Go Jack, 1:33.40, June 3, 1995
1 mile 70yds: Numchuek, 1:39⅕, July 6, 1988
1¹⁄₁₆ miles: Little Bro Lantis, 1:40.20 June 17, 1995
1⅛ miles: Fluffkins, 1:44, July 22, 1995
1⅜ miles: Treizieme, 2:12⅗, August 3, 1986
Other: a7½ furlongs, Kiltartan Cross, 1:27.82, August 11, 1991; a1 mile, Kiltartan Cross, 1:33.44, July 10, 1991; a1 mile 70yds, Tainer's Toy, 1:39.30, August 10, 1991; a1¹⁄₁₆ miles, Diplomat's Reward, 1:41.34, July 17, 1999; a1⅜ miles, Earnest Storm 2:14.25, July 3, 2005; 1⅞ miles, John Bullit, 3:11⅖, September 26, 1987; a1⅞ miles, Mark of Strength, 3:11.53, September 12, 1992

Fastest Times of 2007 (Dirt)

3½ furlongs: Zuella, 2, :40.17, May 28, 2007
4½ furlongs: Cold N Tricky, 5, :51.15, July 22, 2007
5 furlongs: Mizzcan'tbewrong, 2, :58.83, July 7, 2007
5½ furlongs: Devil Not Me, 4, 1:03.06, May 6, 2007
6 furlongs: Careless Navigator, 5, 1:08.73, June 9, 2007
6½ furlongs: Bay of Love, 8, 1:15.59, May 13, 2007
1 mile: Royalnregal Dreams, 4, 1:37.03, May 19, 2007
1 mile 70 yds: Wayzata Bay, 5, 1:40.34, September 3, 2007
1¹⁄₁₆ miles: Castor Troy (Ire), 7, 1:44.60, July 22, 2007
1¼ miles: Rajendra, 4, 2:08, August 11, 2007
2¹⁄₁₆ miles: Agent Danseur, 6, 3:36.37, July 22, 2007

Fastest Times of 2007 (Turf)

5 furlongs: Lookinforthesecret, 5, :56.06, May 28, 2007
a5 furlongs: Did, 4, :57.71, June 30, 2007
7½ furlongs: Prospective Kiss, 6, 1:29.75, May 26, 2007
a7½ furlongs: Chasm (GB), 5, 1:29.04, July 7, 2007
1 mile: Tens Holy Spirit, 5, 1:35.91, June 16, 2007
a1 mile: Honour Colony, 5, 1:35.85, July 14, 2007
1¹⁄₁₆ miles: Prospect Green, 9, 1:43.45, July 22, 2007
a1¹⁄₁₆ miles: Sir Swervalot, 5, 1:41.44, June 2, 2007

Montana

Great Falls

Location: 400 3rd St. N.W., P.O. Box 1888, Great Falls, Mt. 59403
Phone: (406) 727-8900
Fax: (406) 452-8955
Website: *www.montanastatefair.com*
E-Mail: info@mtexpopark.com
Abbreviation: GF

Ownership

Cascade County

Officers

General Manager and Director of Racing: Bill Ogg
Director of Operations: John Scott
Director of Finance: Lois Thomas
Director of Marketing: Lori Cox
Track Superintendent: Joe McCracken
Promotions/Events: Amy Robbins

Racing Dates

2007: July 14-July 29, 6 days
2008: July 12-July 27, 7 days

Track Layout

Main Circumference: 4 furlongs
Main Track Chute: 5 furlongs and 7 furlongs
Main Width: 60 feet
Main Length of Stretch: 410.1 feet

Leaders

Recent Meeting, Leading Jockey: Fernando Manuel Gamez, 11, 2007
Recent Meeting, Leading Trainer: Doug Johnson, 8, 2007
Recent Meeting, Leading Horse: Brit, 2, 2007; B. S. Smoked Duck, 2, 2007; Exciting Trick, 2, 2007; Lucky Tiger, 2, 2007; Shouldbevictory, 2, 2007; Strategic Storm, 2, 2007

Fastest Times of 2007 (Dirt)

5 furlongs: Skip's Star, 8, 1:01.40, July 14, 2007
a5¼ furlongs: Fruit Rapport, 10, 1:04, July 22, 2007
7 furlongs: Prince Rick, 5, 1:26, July 29, 2007; Tomufta, 8, 1:26, July 28, 2007
1 mile 70 yds: Shouldbevictory, 6, 1:45.40, July 29, 2007

Yellowstone Downs

Location: P.O. Box 1138, Billings, Mt. 59103-1138
Phone: (406) 869-5251
Fax: (406) 869-5253
Website: *www.yellowstonedowns.com*
E-Mail: racing@yellowstonedowns.com
Abbreviation: YD

Racing Dates

2007: August 17-September 16, 10 days
2008: August 15-September 14, 10 days

Leaders

Recent Meeting, Leading Jockey: Fernando Manuel Gamez, 10, 2007
Recent Meeting, Leading Trainer: Doug Johnson, 11, 2007
Recent Meeting, Leading Horse: B. S. Smoked Duck, 2, 2007; D C Bobby Shocks, 2, 2007; Magic Copy, 2, 2007; Northern Dandy, 2, 2007; Salt Lake Utah, 2, 2007; Shouldbevictory, 2, 2007; Specialize, 2, 2007

Principal Races

Yellowstone Futurity, Yellowstone Derby

Fastest Times of 2007 (Dirt)

5¼ furlongs: Harbour Axe, 6, 1:02.60, September 15, 2007
7 furlongs: Veloso, 4, 1:26.60, August 25, 2007
1 mile 70 yds: Prince Rick, 5, 1:46.80, September 2, 2007

Nebraska

Columbus Races

Opened in the 1950, Columbus Races in Columbus, 90 miles northwest of Lincoln, is operated on the Platte County Agricultural Society Fairgrounds. It was at Columbus that Racing Hall of Fame trainer Marion H. Van Berg and his son, Jack, also a Hall of Fame member, began their careers. The elder Van Berg operated a sales barn, offering hogs, cattle, and horses, in addition to running his stable. Columbus usually conducts a 24-day summer meet from late July through mid-September, racing on Fridays, Saturdays, and Sundays. Extensive simulcasting is also offered. The

five-furlong oval has a 6½-furlong chute. A record crowd of 8,856 attended on September 3, 1973. The record handle of $719,725 was set exactly 11 years later.

Location: 822 15th St., Columbus, Ne. 68601-5370
Phone: (402) 564-0133
Fax: (402) 564-0990
Website: *www.agpark.com*
Year Founded: 1941
Dates of Inaugural Meeting: July 1942
Abbreviation: Cls
Acreage: 160
Number of Stalls: 900
Seating Capacity: 4,000

Officers

Chairman: Lynn Anderson
General Manager: Gary Bock
Director of Racing and Racing Secretary: Dennis Kochevar
Secretary/Treasurer: Gary Kruse
Director of Operations and Simulcasting: Gary Bock
Director of Mutuels: Leon Ebel
Vice President: Eldon Engel
Director of Publicity: Gary Bock
Track Announcer: Keith Nelson
Track Photographer: Coady Photography
Track Superintendent: Bill Lusche

Racing Dates

2007: July 27-September 9, 23 days
2008: July 24-September 1, 24 days

Track Layout

Main Circumference: 5 furlongs
Main Track Chute: 6½ furlongs
Main Width: 75 feet
Main Length of Stretch: 720 feet

Attendance

Highest Single-Day Record: 8,856, September 3, 1973

Handle

Single-Day On-Track Handle: $719,725, September 3, 1984

Leaders

Recent Meeting, Leading Jockey: Yuri Yaranga, 35, 2007
Recent Meeting, Leading Trainer: David C. Anderson, 23, 2007
Recent Meeting, Leading Horse: 20 tied with 2, 2007

Principal Races

Columbus Breeders' Special H., Columbus Futurity, Columbus Debutante S.

Notable Events

Super Saver Sunday, Let the Bets Roll Saturdays

Track Records, Main Dirt

4 furlongs: Kips Flyer, :39.80, August 11, 2000
5$\frac{1}{2}$ furlongs: Foreign Flag, 1:05$\frac{1}{5}$, September 30, 1978
6 furlongs: Eve's Choice, 1:10$\frac{2}{5}$, August 27, 1994
6$\frac{1}{2}$ furlongs: Jae Ranch, 1:17, August 12, 1984
1 mile 70 yds: Ilatan, 1:41$\frac{3}{5}$, September 9, 1984
1$\frac{1}{16}$ miles: Foreign Intent, 1:44$\frac{2}{5}$, September 21, 1974
1$\frac{3}{8}$ miles: In Doc's Honor, 2:18$\frac{2}{5}$, September 3, 1994
2 miles: Blazing Don, 3:36$\frac{3}{5}$, September 26, 1982
Other: 3$\frac{1}{2}$ furlongs, Timetoprofit, :39.60, August 24, 2002; 1$\frac{5}{16}$ miles, Too Little Man, 2:19$\frac{1}{5}$, September 6, 1969; 1$\frac{7}{16}$ miles, Skeeter Do, 2:27$\frac{4}{5}$, September 12, 1994

Fastest Times of 2007 (Dirt)

3$\frac{1}{2}$ furlongs: Annadacious, 2, :42, August 19, 2007; Molly Pontz, 2, :42, August 3, 2007
6 furlongs: Bevys Best, 3, 1:12.60, August 4, 2007; Skwhirl, 4, 1:12.60, August 11, 2007
6$\frac{1}{2}$ furlongs: Grand Cherokee, 3, 1:19, August 5, 2007
1 mile 70 yds: My Secret Star, 3, 1:44.40, August 18, 2007
1$\frac{1}{16}$ miles: Indigo Rd, 4, 1:49.40, August 19, 2007
1$\frac{3}{8}$ miles: Will Rein, 5, 2:26.40, September 8, 2007

Fonner Park

The closing of Omaha's Ak-Sar-Ben racecourse in 1995 dealt a serious blow to Nebraska racing. But Fonner Park in Grand Island has been one of the tracks to keep the flame flickering in the Cornhusker State with its down-home brand of racing. The 280-acre facility staged its first race meet in 1954. Fonner Park is operated by a not-for-profit organization, with the track's profits going to charitable and community activities in the Grand Island region. With the advent of telephone-account wagering in Nebraska in October 2001, Fonner officials sought to reach more of the state's bettors. The five-furlong facility has never been known as a racing mecca, but some interesting horses have competed at Fonner. One of them is sprinter Leaping Plum, who in 2001 won his seventh consecutive renewal of the opening-week Grasmick Handicap. The gelding also won the Coca-Cola Sprint Handicap four consecutive times (1995-'98).

Location: 700 E. Stolley Park Rd., P.O. Box 490, Grand Island, Ne. 68802
Phone: (308) 382-4515
Fax: (308) 384-2753
Website: *www.fonnerpark.com*
E-Mail: fonnerpark@aol.com
Year Founded: 1951
Dates of Inaugural Meeting: April 29, 1954
Abbreviation: Fon
Acreage: 240
Number of Stalls: 1,300
Seating Capacity: 5,766

Officers

Chief Executive Officer and General Manager: Hugh M. Miner Jr.
President: Doyle Hulme
Vice Presidents: Barry Sandstrom, Jim Cannon, Larry Toner
Director of Racing and Racing Secretary: Douglas Schoepf
Assistant Racing Secretary: Wayne I. Anderson
Secretary: Roger Luebbe
Treasurer: Bill Westering
Director of Operations: Bruce A. Swihart
Director of Marketing: Linda Wilhelmy
Director of Mutuels: William McConnell
Director of Simulcasting: Todd W. Otto
Track Announcer: Steve Anderson
Track Photographer: Jim Linscott Photography
Track Superintendent: Rick L. Danburg
Horsemen's Bookkeeper: Carolyn Legenza

Racing Dates

2007: February 9-May 5, 38 days
2008: February 15-May 3, 35 days

Track Layout

Main Circumference: 5 furlongs
Main Track Chute: 4 furlongs and 6$\frac{1}{2}$ furlongs
Main Width: 70 feet
Main Length of Stretch: 700 feet

Attendance

Highest Single-Day Record: 10,930, March 17, 1990

Handle

Single-Day All-Sources Handle: $1,285,011, April 28, 1990

Mutuel Records

Highest Win: $520.40, Black Ticket, March 10, 1977
Lowest Win: $2.20, Ben's Whiz, March 30, 1974; $2.20, Real Style, March 30, 1974; $2.20, I'ma Game Master, April 29, 1995
Highest Exacta: $5,421, March 28, 1994
Lowest Exacta: $4, May 6, 2000
Highest Trifecta: $26,474.40, March 30, 1990

Lowest Trifecta: $14.60, March 15, 1998
Highest Daily Double: $5,451.20, March 18, 1977
Lowest Daily Double: $5, March 10, 1994; $5, April 21, 1995
Highest Pick Three: $13,800.80, February 27, 1988
Lowest Pick Three: $3.20, March 18, 2000
Highest Other Exotics: $17,526.60, Superfecta, March 23, 2001
Lowest Other Exotics: $271.40, Superfecta, March 4, 2001

Leaders

Recent Meeting, Leading Jockey: Yuri Yaranga, 58, 2008
Recent Meeting, Leading Trainer: David C. Anderson, 43, 2008
Recent Meeting, Leading Horse: One Zee Rebound, 4, 2008

Records

Single-Day Jockey Wins: Ken Shino, 8, April 2, 2000
Single-Day Trainer Wins: Tim Gleason, 5, February 18, 1989; Marvin Johnson, 5, February 26, 2000; Marvin Johnson, 5, April 2, 2000
Single Meeting, Leading Jockey by Wins: Perry Compton, 85, 2000
Single Meeting, Leading Trainer by Wins: M. A. Johnson, 50, 2000

Principal Races

Bosselman/Gus Fonner S.

Track Records, Main Dirt

4 furlongs: Leaping Plum, :44.20, February 17, 1996
$5^1/_2$ furlongs: Little L. M., 1:$04^2/_5$, April 12, 1975
6 furlongs: Orphan Kist, 1:10, April 8, 1989
$6^1/_2$ furlongs: Majority of One, 1:17, March 18, 1989
1 mile: Brian's Star, 1:$36^3/_5$, April 9, 1986; High On Laraka, 1:$36^3/_5$, April 19, 1986
1 mile 70 yds: Shamtastic, 1:40, April 26, 1986; Advice, 1:40, April 25, 1987
$1^1/_{16}$ miles: Sahara King, 1:43, April 27, 1996
$1^1/_8$ miles: Potro, 1:51.40, April 25, 1993
$1^3/_8$ miles: Meat Loaf, 2:$22^2/_5$, April 29, 1970
Other: $1^7/_{16}$ miles, Wenga, 2:$30^2/_5$, May 1, 1968

Fastest Times of 2007 (Dirt)

4 furlongs: Another Audible, 4, :44.80, February 9, 2007
6 furlongs: Rolls of Money, 5, 1:12.40, February 17, 2007
$6^1/_2$ furlongs: Lucky Feather, 5, 1:20.20, April 22, 2007
1 mile: Yourmoneysnogood, 4, 1:39.20, April 14, 2007
1 mile 70 yds: Latest Edition, 6, 1:46.20, April 21, 2007
$1^1/_{16}$ miles: Tap Dancing Mauk, 6, 1:47.60, April 28, 2007
$1^1/_8$ miles: Olympic Junction, 7, 1:56.20, May 5, 2007

Horsemen's Atokad Downs

Live Thoroughbred racing in Nebraska did not die when Omaha's Ak-Sar-Ben closed in 1995 after 74 years. Ak-Sar-Ben, which was torn down in 1997, is Nebraska spelled backward. Atokad is Dakota spelled backward, and the track is located in Dakota County, in the state's northwest corner near the South Dakota border. The five-furlong track in South Sioux City opened on September 20, 1956. Atokad conducted a late-summer meeting in most years, though it did not race from 1998 through 2000. A single-day meet was resurrected in 2001 by Robert E. Lee, president of the Nebraska Horsemen's Benevolent and Protective Association, and three days of racing were scheduled for mid-September 2007. A record crowd of 6,200 attended on October 18, 1958. The record handle of $483,486 was set on November 9, 1980.

Location: 1524 Atokad Dr., P.O. Box 796, South Sioux City, Ne. 68776
Phone: (402) 494-5722
Fax: (402) 241-0410
Year Founded: 1951
Dates of Inaugural Meeting: September 20, 1956
Abbreviation: Ato
Acreage: 50
Number of Stalls: 850
Seating Capacity: 3,112

Ownership

Nebraska HBPA

Officers

President: William Vannoy
Vice President: Gene McCloud
General Manager: Fred Stinger
Treasurer: Patricia Shefland
Director of Operations: Linda Wunderlin
Director of Marketing and Publicity: Linda Wunderlin
Track Announcer: Richard Grunder
Track Photographer: Jim Linscott Photography
Track Superintendent: Tim Hurd
Security: Titan Security Inc.
Horsemen's Bookkeeper: Carolyn Lezenza

Racing Dates

2007: September 14-September 16, 3 days
2008: September 5-September 7, 3 days

Track Layout

Main Circumference: 5 furlongs
Main Track Chute: $6^1/_2$ furlongs and $1^1/_8$ miles
Main Width: 68 feet
Main Length of Stretch: 660 feet

Handle

Single-Day All-Sources Handle: $483,486, November 9, 1980
Total On-Track Recent Meeting: $126,295, 2007
Average On-Track Recent Meeting: $42,098, 2007

Leaders

Recent Meeting, Leading Jockey: Dennis Michael Collins, 6, 2007
Recent Meeting, Leading Trainer: Daniel Coughlin, 4, 2007

Track Records, Main Dirt

4 furlongs: Shining Sea, :44.40, June 28, 1992
$5^1/_2$ furlongs: Slipped in Space, 1:$05^1/_5$, October 24, 1976
6 furlongs: Many Ministers, 1:11.20, September 14, 2007
$6^1/_2$ furlongs: Spanish Key, 1:$16^2/_5$, October 24, 1970
1 mile: Quilla Sue, 1:38, October 30, 1973
1 mile 70 yds: No Mystery, 1:$42^1/_5$, November 5, 1976
$1^1/_{16}$ miles: Great Commander, 1:$43^3/_5$, November 3, 1973
$1^1/_8$ miles: Reason to Explode, 1:50.20, July 13, 1991
$1^3/_8$ miles: Barker's Tip, 2:20, October 17, 1964
2 miles: Navy Grey, 3:$30^1/_5$, October 30, 1962; Middle Road, 3:$30^1/_5$, November 21, 1976
Other: a4 furlongs, Classy Fleet, :$43^4/_5$, November 19, 1977; a$6^1/_2$ furlongs, Hot Jelly Jam, 7, 1:14.60, September 14, 2007; $1^7/_{16}$ miles, Echo Bar, 2:28, October 30, 1968; a$1^7/_{16}$ miles, Duke of Badgerland, 2:29.60, November 6, 1996

Fastest Times of 2007 (Dirt)

6 furlongs: Many Ministers, 9, 1:11.20, September 14, 2007
a$6^1/_2$ furlongs: Hot Jelly Jam, 7, 1:14.60, September 14, 2007
1 mile: Booming Along, 5, 1:39.20, September 16, 2007
1 mile 70 yds: Nine K Enigma, 6, 1:43, September 15, 2007
$1^1/_{16}$ miles: Okie Thunder, 7, 1:46.40, September 15, 2007

Horsemen's Park

Boasting a simulcasting facility that offers wagering on 18 to 21 racetracks daily, Horsemen's Park opened on January 3, 1998, for simulcasting in Omaha, four miles south of the former Ak-Sar-Ben site. Two live races were held each day on two consecutive days in July 1998 by the Nebraska Horsemen's Benevolent and Protective Association, which owns and operates the track. The meet was expanded to four days in 2003, with $500,000 now offered in purses each year. The

track is a five-furlong oval. The simulcasting facility offers seating for 3,000 and contains 675 closed-circuit monitors.

Location: 6303 Q St., Omaha, Ne. 68117-1696
Phone: (402) 731-2900
Fax: (402) 731-5122
Website: www.horsemenspark.com
Year Founded: 1998
Dates of Inaugural Meeting: July 1998
Abbreviation: HPO
Seating Capacity: 3,000

Ownership
Nebraska HBPA

Officers
President: William Vannoy
General Manager: Gregory C. Hosch
Racing Secretary: Wayne Anderson
Treasurer: Patricia Shefland
Director of Marketing and Publicity: Gary Java
Director of Simulcasting: Patricia Shefland
Directors of Mutuels: Mary Palais, Mary Snelling
Track Superintendent: Tim Hurd

Racing Dates
2007: July 19-July 22, 4 days
2008: July 17-July 20, 4 days

Track Layout
Main Circumference: 5 furlongs
Main Width: 65 feet
Main Length of Stretch: 680 feet

Attendance
Average Daily Recent Meeting: 12,000
Total Attendance Recent Meeting: 48,000
Highest Single-Day Recent Meeting: 17,000, July 21, 2007

Handle
Total All-Sources Recent Meeting: $799,408, 2007
Average All-Sources Recent Meeting: $199,852, 2007
Total On-Track Recent Meeting: $669,032, 2007
Average On-Track Recent Meeting: $167,258, 2007
Largest Single-Day All-Sources Recent Meeting: $227,816, July 21, 2007
Largest Single-Day On-Track Recent Meeting: $187,763, July 21, 2007
Largest Record Single-Day All-Sources: $228,296, July 23, 2007
Largest Record Single-Day On-Track: $187,763, July 21, 2007

Fastest Times of 2007 (Dirt)
6 furlongs: Rare Crystal, 4, 1:11.60, July 21, 2007
1 mile: Tepexpan, 5, 1:37.60, July 22, 2007
1 3/8 miles: Will Rein, 5, 2:22.40, July 20, 2007

State Fair Park

Location: P.O. Box 81223, Lincoln, Ne. 68501
Phone: (402) 474-5371
Fax: (402) 473-4114
Website: www.statefair.org
E-Mail: mnewlin@statefair.org
Abbreviation: Lnn
Number of Stalls: 1,200
Seating Capacity: 5,800

Ownership
Nebraska State Fair Board

Officers
Director of Racing Operations: Mike Newlin
Secretary: Sherri Johnson
Director of Marketing and Publicity: Christine Rasmussen
Director of Mutuels: Mindy Franzen

Track Superintendent: Scott Yound
Security: Judd Bietz
Promotions/Events: Julie Burton

Racing Dates
2007: May 11-July 15, 37 days
2008: May 9-July 13, 37 days

Track Layout
Main Circumference: 5 furlongs
Main Track Chute: 4 1/2 furlongs
Main Length of Stretch: 480 feet

Attendance
Average Daily Recent Meeting: 2,000, 2007
Total Attendance Recent Meeting: 73,000, 2007

Handle
Single-Day On-Track Recent Meeting: $321,000, May 5, 2007

Leaders
Recent Meeting, Leading Jockey: Dennis Collins, 74, 2007
Recent Meeting, Leading Trainer: David Anderson, 33, 2007

Records
Single-Day Jockey Wins: Robert Dean Williams, 8, September 29, 1984

Principal Races
Capitol City Futurity, Big Red Mile S., State Fair Breeders' Special S., Matchmaker S., State Fair Futurity

Interesting Facts
Trivia: Triple dead heat for win on October 23, 1981; at the time one of only 17 such instances since 1940 and the only one ever in Nebraska. On July 18, 1999, a national record for a place pay-off was set at $493.

Track Records, Main Dirt
4 1/2 furlongs: Leaping Plum, :50, September 17, 1995
6 furlongs: Up 'n Blumin, 1:09.80, June 3, 2006
1 mile: Sensitive Ghost, 1:36, July 14, 2002
1 mile 70 yds: High Dice, 1:39.40, June 24, 2001

Fastest Times of 2007 (Dirt)
4 furlongs: City Slicker, 2, :47, June 24, 2007
4 1/2 furlongs: I'm Real, 7, :50.20, July 4, 2007
6 furlongs: Another Audible, 4, 1:11.60, June 17, 2007; Red Hot Fever, 4, 1:11.60, May 12, 2007; Toubeeb, 6, 1:11.60, July 6, 2007
1 mile: Chasin the Wind, 5, 1:38.60, June 22, 2007
1 mile 70 yds: Bevys Dazzler, 4, 1:41.40, July 4, 2007
1 1/16 miles: Palladian, 5, 1:47.40, June 29, 2007

Nevada

Elko County Fair

Location: P.O. Box 2067, Elko, Nv. 89803
Phone: (775) 738-3616
Fax: (775) 778-3468
Website: www.elkocountyfair.com
E-Mail: elkocountyfair@hotmail.com
Abbreviation: Elk

Officers
Racing Secretary: Fred Davis
Secretary/Treasurer: Jennifer "J. J." Roemmich
Director of Mutuels: Debbie Russell
Stewards: Carl Pacini, Doug Ray, Stu Wilson
Track Announcer: Ron Anderson
Track Superintendent: Travis Rutherford
Horsemen's Bookkeepers: Carla Gilligan, Linda McDermott

Racing Dates
2007: August 24-September 3, 6 days
2008: August 22-September 1, 7 days

Attendance

Average Daily Recent Meeting: 3,000, 2007
Total Attendance Recent Meeting: 21,000, 2007

Leaders

Recent Meeting, Leading Jockey: Brian Long, 9, 2007; Robert Boyce, 9, 2006
Recent Meeting, Leading Trainer: Karen Haverty, 8, 2007
Recent Meeting, Leading Horse: No Direction Home, 2, 2007; Dance With Danger, 2, 2007; Moab, 2, 2007; Weavemesomefreedom, 2, 2007; Truckin' Along, 2, 2007; Rob's Babe, 2, 2007

Principal Races

Elko County Thoroughbred Futurity, Elko County Thoroughbred Derby

Fastest Times of 2007 (Dirt)

$3\frac{1}{2}$ furlongs: T. C. Express, 3, :42, August 31, 2007
$5\frac{1}{2}$ furlongs: Big Scale, 6, 1:07.60, September 3, 2007; Gina Lolo, 4, 1:07.60, September 2, 2007
6 furlongs: Truckin' Along, 6, 1:13.40, September 2, 2007
$6\frac{1}{2}$ furlongs: Find My Halter, 8, 1:19.80, September 3, 2007
7 furlongs: Wide Out, 8, 1:25.60, August 26, 2007
1 mile: Dothedevilin, 8, 1:42.40, September 3, 2007
$1\frac{1}{16}$ miles: Cut Class, 8, 1:48.80, August 26, 2007
$1\frac{5}{16}$ miles: Moab, 6, 2:18.80, September 3, 2007

New Jersey

Atlantic City Race Course

When Atlantic City Race Course opened on July 22, 1946, its roster of stockholders read more like the A-list from a Hollywood party than investors in a racetrack in McKee City, 13 miles from the Jersey Shore resort. Bob Hope, Frank Sinatra, Harry James, Xavier Cugat, and Sammy Kaye were among the initial shareholders. John B. Kelly Sr., an Olympic gold-medal rower, brick magnate, and father of the late Princess Grace of Monaco, was Atlantic City's first president. Kelly was succeeded in 1960 by radio and television pioneer Leon Levy, whose son Robert succeeded him. An innovator who arranged the nation's first full-card simulcast from Meadowlands racetrack in September 1983, the younger Levy also raced 1987 Belmont Stakes (G1) winner Bet Twice and champion sprinter Housebuster. Crowds of more than 30,000 turned out to see such races as the United Nations Handicap, first run in 1953, and such outstanding horses as Dr. Fager, Round Table, and Mongo. The disruption of the New Jersey circuit with the 1977 Garden State Park fire and the opening of Atlantic City's first casinos the following year hurt the track's business and led to a gradual reduction in its schedule. Atlantic City conducted a six-day, all-turf meet in 1999 and 2000, and it raced ten days in '01 to qualify for year-round, full-card simulcasting. Atlantic City was sold to Greenwood Racing for $13-million in August 2001, and a rebuilding of the track was announced in '07. Atlantic City now runs a brief, all-turf meet each year.

Location: 4501 Black Horse Pike, Mays Landing, N.J. 08330-3142
Phone: (609) 645-5200
Fax: (609) 645-8309
Website: *www.acracecourse.com*
E-Mail: mbugdon@phillypark.net
Year Founded: 1944
Dates of Inaugural Meeting: July 22, 1946
Abbreviation: Atl
Acreage: 255
Number of Stalls: 1,602
Seating Capacity: 16,000

Ownership

Greenwood Racing Inc.

Officers

Chief Executive Officer: Bill Hogwood
Chief Operating Officer: Joe Wilson
Chief Financial Officer: Tony Ricci
President: Maureen G. Bugdon
Director of Racing: Sal Sinatra
Director of Grounds and Facilities: Bill Gatto
Director of Operations: Mary Jo Couts
Racebook General Manager: Jim Miller
Track Announcer: Keith Jones
Track Photographer: John Pantalone

Racing Dates

2008: April 23-May 2, 6 days

Track Layout

Main Circumference: $1\frac{1}{8}$ miles
Main Track Chute: 7 furlongs
Main Width: 100 feet
Main Length of Stretch: 947.29 feet
Main Turf Circumference: 1 mile
Main Turf Width: 100 feet

Attendance

Average Daily Recent Meeting: 4,610, 2007
Total Attendance Recent Meeting: 18,442
Highest Single Day Recent Meeting: 5,842, May 3, 2007
Highest Single-Day Record: 33,404, September 7, 1953
Record Daily Average Single Meeting: 17,468, 1957

Handle

Highest On-Track Single-Meeting Record: $91,255,066, 1968

Leaders

Recent Meeting, Leading Jockey: Victor H. Molina, 4, 2007
Recent Meeting, Leading Trainer: Michael V. Pino, 2, 2007; Alan S. Seewald, 2, 2007; Herald O. Whylie, 2, 2007

Track Records, Main Dirt

$4\frac{1}{2}$ furlongs: Jo Jo's Sparkle, :51$\frac{2}{5}$, June 22, 1988
5 furlongs: Dark Tzarina, :56$\frac{2}{5}$, July 16, 1988
$5\frac{1}{2}$ furlongs: Aeronotic, 1:02$\frac{3}{5}$, July 4, 1986
6 furlongs: Margerine, 1:08$\frac{1}{5}$, August 27, 1988
$6\frac{1}{2}$ furlongs: Zartarian, 1:15.80, June 26, 1994
7 furlongs: Mexican General, 1:20$\frac{2}{5}$, July 4, 1977
$1\frac{1}{16}$ miles: Prince of Truth, 1:41, June 28, 1975
$1\frac{1}{8}$ miles: World Appeal, 1:46$\frac{3}{5}$, July 16, 1983
$1\frac{3}{16}$ miles: Mississippi Mud, 1:54$\frac{1}{5}$, August 6, 1977
$1\frac{1}{4}$ miles: Greek Ship, 2:01$\frac{4}{5}$, September 29, 1951
$1\frac{3}{4}$ miles: Abdallati, 3:06$\frac{2}{5}$, November 22, 1973

Track Records, Main Turf

5 furlongs: Sandys Gold, :56.09, May 3, 2007
$5\frac{1}{2}$ furlongs: Legal Justice, 1:01$\frac{4}{5}$, July 12, 1989
1 mile: Canal, 1:34$\frac{1}{5}$, August 19, 1967
1 mile 40 yds: Castaneto (Arg), 1:38, June 28, 1991
$1\frac{1}{16}$ miles: Road At Sea, 1:41$\frac{1}{5}$, September 23, 1967; Chiati, 1:41$\frac{1}{5}$, July 6, 1979
$1\frac{1}{8}$ miles: Marco Bay, 1:46.80, June 10, 1994
$1\frac{3}{16}$ miles: Steinlen, 1:52, July 21, 1990
$1\frac{1}{2}$ miles: Advocator, 2:27$\frac{1}{5}$, September 21, 1968
Other: a5 furlongs, Bald Smile, :57.20, August 8, 1996; a$5\frac{1}{2}$ furlongs, Mr. Mink, 1:02$\frac{3}{5}$, September 8, 1967; a1 mile, Silvino, 1:36$\frac{4}{5}$, June 8, 1988; a1 mile 40yds, First Grade Reader, 1:40.80, June 7, 1991; a$1\frac{1}{16}$ miles, Home Front, 1:43$\frac{2}{5}$, June 12, 1976; a $1\frac{1}{8}$ miles, Emptor, 1:49.80, June 9, 1993; a$1\frac{3}{16}$ miles, Grey Lord II, 1:56$\frac{3}{5}$, September 30, 1969; a$1\frac{1}{2}$ miles, Northern Nights, 2:31.80, July 10, 1996; a$1\frac{11}{16}$ miles, Misty Model, 3:08$\frac{3}{5}$, August 19, 1977; a2 miles, Pier, 3:35$\frac{4}{5}$, September 2, 1977; a$2\frac{1}{16}$ miles, Bangguster, 3:45.80, July 6, 1995; $2\frac{1}{16}$ miles, Sticktoitive, 3:42.80, August 25, 1993

Fastest Times of 2007 (Turf)
5 furlongs: Sandys Gold, 5, :56.09, May 3, 2007
5½ furlongs: Proud Comic, 5, 1:03.31, May 3, 2007
1 mile: Perfect Arrival, 6, 1:37.58, May 2, 2007
1¹/₁₆ miles: Pass Play, 6, 1:42.85, May 3, 2007

Monmouth Park

The first Monmouth Park opened in July 1870 and was located three miles from Long Branch, New Jersey. The track's early years included performances by some of the era's most famous horses, including Longfellow and Miss Woodford, the latter the first racehorse to earn $100,000. However, Monmouth fell victim to changing times, and it closed in 1893 after New Jersey outlawed wagering. Fifty years later, pari-mutuel wagering was legalized, and a group of investors led by Amory L. Haskell built a new Monmouth in 1946 at its current location in Oceanport. Since then, the track known for its easygoing, seaside ambiance has been a popular destination for some of the sport's leading Thoroughbreds. The track's richest race is the Haskell Invitational Handicap (G1), a $1-million race for three-year-olds and the first major East Coast event after the Triple Crown races. Monmouth also features the United Nations Handicap (G1), which formerly was run at Atlantic City Race Course. The Philip H. Iselin Stakes (G3), named in honor of a former Monmouth president, formerly was known as the Monmouth Handicap, which was inaugurated in 1884. Monmouth was host to the Breeders' Cup World Championships in 2007 as the series expanded to a two-day format for the first time. Despite a deluge of rain, attendance for the two days was 69,584 with total wagering of more than $142-million.

Location: 175 Oceanport Ave., P.O. Box MP, Oceanport, N.J. 07757
Phone: (732) 222-5100
Fax: (732) 571-1534
Website: www.monmouthpark.com
E-Mail: mpinfo@njsea.com
Year Founded: Original: 1870; Current Track: 1946
Dates of Inaugural Meeting: July 30, 1870
Abbreviation: Mth
Acreage: 500
Number of Stalls: 1,600
Seating Capacity: 18,000

Ownership
New Jersey Sports and Exposition Authority

Officers
Chairman: Carl Goldberg
President and Chief Executive Officer: Dennis R. Robinson
General Manager: Robert J. Kulina
Racing Secretary: Michael P. Dempsey
Director of Operations: Horace Smith
Director of Admissions: Jeff Lowich
Director of Finance: James Jemas
Director of Marketing: Peter Verdee
Director of Publicity: John F. Heims
Director of Simulcasting: Sam McKee
Horsemen's Liaison: Mary Beth Yates
Stewards: Jimmy Edwards, Harvey I. Wardell Jr., Stephen Pagano
Track Announcer: Larry Collmus
Track Photographer: Equi-Photo Inc.
Security: William Kudlacik

Racing Dates
2007: May 12-September 2, 75 days; October 24-October 27, 4 days (Breeders' Cup)
2008: May 9-September 28, 99 days

Track Layout
Main Circumference: 1 mile
Main Track Chute: 6 furlongs and 1¼ miles
Main Width: Homestretch: 100 feet; Backstretch: 90 feet
Main Length of Stretch: 990 feet
Main Turf Circumference: 7 furlongs
Main Turf Chute: 5 furlongs, 5½ furlongs, ⁷/₁₆ miles, and 1⅛ miles
Main Turf Width: 90 feet, Chutes 100 feet

Attendance
Average Daily Recent Meeting: 8,97*, 2007; 20,490, Breeders' Cup 2007
Highest Single-Day Record: 53,638, August 3, 2003
Record Daily Average Single Meeting: 20,907, 1957
Highest Single-Meeting Record: 1,150,658, 1981
Total Attendance Recent Meeting: 672,790, 2007; 81,960, Breeders' Cup 2007

Handle
Average All-Sources Recent Meeting: $3,629,975, 2007; $37,088,788, Breeders' Cup 2007
Average On-Track Recent Meeting: $1,244,828, 2007; $4,676,960, Breeders' Cup 2007
Record Daily Average Single Meeting: $4,676,960, Breeders' Cup 2007
Single-Day All-Sources Handle: $112,446,442, October 27, 2007
Total All-Sources Recent Meeting: $272,248,145, 2007. $148,355,155, Breeders' Cup 2007
Total On-Track Recent Meeting: $93,562,145, 2007; $18,707,843, Breeders' Cup 2007
Record Average All-Sources Single Meeting: $37,088,788, Breeders' Cup 2007
Record Total All-Sources Single Meeting: $364,595,940, 2004
Record Total Single Meeting: $155,837,768, 1981

Mutuel Records
Highest Win: $229.20, July 15, 1951
Lowest Win: $2.10, Skip Away, August 30, 1998; $2.10, Silverbulletday, July 10, 1999; $2.10, Crafty Brutus, June 24, 2006
Highest Trifecta: $62,172, June 15, 1978
Lowest Trifecta: $6, August 16, 2006
Highest Daily Double: $3,962.50, July 19, 1952
Lowest Daily Double: $2.80, June 3, 1995
Highest Other Exotics: $92.60, Place, July 15, 1951; $79.60, Show, July 28, 2001

Leaders
Career, Leading Jockey by Titles: Joe Bravo, 13
Career, Leading Trainer by Titles: Budd Lepman, 5; John H. Forbes, 5; Juan Serey, 5
Recent Meeting, Leading Jockey: Joe Bravo, 110, 2007
Recent Meeting, Leading Trainer: Todd Pletcher, 33, 2007
Recent Meeting, Leading Horse: Talkin About Love, 5, 2007
Recent Meeting, Leading Owner: Peter Kazamias, 13, 2007

Records
Single-Day Jockey Wins: Walter Blum, 6, June 9, 1961; Chris Antley, 6, July 30, 1984; Julie Krone, 6, August 19, 1987; Joe Bravo, 6, August 31, 1994; Joe Bravo, 6, May 18, 2002; Joe Bravo, 6, September 18, 2005; Joe Bravo, 6, September 4, 2006
Single-Day Trainer Wins: J. Willard Thompson, 4, September 8, 1975; Robert Klesaris, 4, July 10, 1987; John H. Forbes, 4, August 28, 1989
Single Meeting, Leading Jockey by Wins: Chris Antley, 171, 1984
Single Meeting, Leading Trainer by Wins: John Tammaro III, 55, 1974; J. Willard Thompson, 55, 1975

Principal Races
Haskell Invitational H. (G1), United Nations S. (G1), Molly Pitcher Breeders' Cup H. (G2), Monmouth Breeders' Cup Oaks (G3), Philip H. Iselin S. (G3)

Interesting Facts
Achievements/Milestones: The 53,638 in attendance for the August 3, 2003, Haskell Invitational H. was the largest crowd ever for a horse race in New Jersey.

Track Records, Main Dirt
5 furlongs: L. B. On Tour, :56.16, August 21, 1999
5½ furlongs: Joey P., 1:01.91, May 12, 2007

6 furlongs: Idiot Proof, 1:07.47, July 4, 2007
1 mile: Forty Niner, 1:33$\frac{4}{5}$, July 16, 1988
1 mile 70 yds: Cable Boy, 1:38.78, May 26, 2007
$1\frac{1}{16}$ miles: Formal Gold, 1:40.20, August 23, 1997
$1\frac{1}{8}$ miles: Spend a Buck, 1:46$\frac{4}{5}$, August 17, 1985; Jolie's Halo, 1:46.80, August 8, 1992
$1\frac{3}{16}$ miles: Okamsel, 1:59$\frac{3}{5}$, June 20, 1951
$1\frac{1}{4}$ miles: Carry Back, 2:00$\frac{2}{5}$, July 14, 1962; Majestic Light, 2:00$\frac{2}{5}$, August 30, 1977
$1\frac{1}{2}$ miles: Malibu Moonshine, 2:31.54, June 10, 2006
$1\frac{3}{4}$ miles: *Halconero, 3:04$\frac{1}{5}$, August 5, 1950

Track Records, Main Turf

5 furlongs: Terrific Challenge, :54.67, July 16, 2006
$5\frac{1}{2}$ furlongs: Smart Enough, 1:00.81, June 2, 2007
1 mile: Icy Atlantic, 1:32.42, September 1, 2007
$1\frac{1}{16}$ miles: Mi Narrow, 1:39.40, July 11, 1999
$1\frac{1}{8}$ miles: Fishy Advice, 1:46.08, June 17, 2007
$1\frac{3}{8}$ miles: Balto Star, 2:12.78, July 5, 2003
Other: a$5\frac{1}{2}$ furlongs, Terrific Challenge, 1:01, September 10, 2006; $1\frac{1}{16}$ miles-chute, Three Valleys, 1:40.06, August 6, 2006

Fastest Times of 2007 (Dirt)

5 furlongs: Gambler's Prize, 5, :56.52, July 12, 2007
$5\frac{1}{2}$ furlongs: Joey P., 5, 1:01.91, May 12, 2007
6 furlongs: Idiot Proof, 3, 1:07.47, July 4, 2007
1 mile: Gottcha Gold, 4, 1:34.25, June 23, 2007
1 mile 70 yds: Cable Boy, 3, 1:38.78, May 26, 2007
$1\frac{1}{16}$ miles: Piety, 5, 1:41.32, July 1, 2007
$1\frac{1}{8}$ miles: Any Given Saturday, 3, 1:48.35, August 5, 2007
$1\frac{1}{4}$ miles: Curlin, 3, 2:00.59, October 27, 2007

Fastest Times of 2007 (Turf)

5 furlongs: Lakes Tune, 5, :54.73, August 17, 2007
$5\frac{1}{2}$ furlongs: Smart Enough, 4, 1:00.81, June 2, 2007
a$5\frac{1}{2}$ furlongs: John's Pic, 4, 1:01.69, July 15, 2007
1 mile: Icy Atlantic, 6, 1:32.42, September 1, 2007
$1\frac{1}{16}$ miles: Silent Roar, 4, 1:38.99, August 5, 2007
$1\frac{1}{8}$ miles: Fishy Advice, 5, 1:46.08, June 17, 2007
$1\frac{3}{8}$ miles: English Channel, 5, 2:12.89, July 7, 2007
a$1\frac{3}{8}$ miles: Eres Magica (Chi), 4, 2:13.35, August 25, 2007
$1\frac{1}{2}$ miles: English Channel, 5, 2:36.96, October 27, 2007

The Meadowlands

The Meadowlands racetrack, located on former marshland in East Rutherford, has been the economic engine of the Meadowlands Sports Complex. Built by the New Jersey Sports and Exposition Authority for \$340-million, the complex includes the Izod Center, home of basketball's New Jersey Nets, and Giants Stadium, where the New York Giants and Jets play football. The Meadowlands, which held its first Thoroughbred meet in September 1977, has been host to several memorable events in racing history. In 1978, Dr. Patches upset Seattle Slew in the Paterson Handicap. John Henry, once the sport's all-time leading earner, closed his career with a stunning, come-from-behind victory in the Ballantine's Scotch Classic Handicap in 1984. Four years later, Alysheba set a $1\frac{1}{4}$-mile track record when he captured the Meadowlands Cup Handicap (G1) during his Horse of the Year campaign. Meadowlands, whose world-renowned Standardbred meet runs from December through August, conducts Thoroughbred racing in the fall.

Location: 50 Route 120, East Rutherford, N.J. 07073-2131
Phone: (201) 843-2446
Fax: (201) 460-4042
Website: *www.meadowlandsracetrack.com*
E-Mail: asilver@njsea.com
Year Founded: 1976
Dates of Inaugural Meeting: September 6, 1977
Abbreviation: Med
Acreage: 220
Number of Stalls: 1,760
Seating Capacity: 4,587

Ownership

New Jersey Sports and Exposition Authority

Officers

Chairman: Carl J. Goldberg
Chief Executive Officer: Dennis Robinson
Senior Vice Presidents: Dennis O. Dowd, Lennon Register
Racing Secretary: Michael P. Dempsey
Vice President of Finance: James Jemas
Vice President of Event Marketing: Pete Verdee
Vice President of Security, Parking, and Traffic: Pat Aramini
Assistant Vice President of Racing Development and Distribution: Alex Dadoyan
Assistant Vice President of Operations: Marcello Esposito
Assistant Vice President of Wagering and Guest Services: Vernard Bennett
Assistant Racing Secretary: John Perlow
Director of Wagering Services: Robert Halpin
Director of Simulcasting and Television Production: Sam McKee
Director of Admissions: Marianne Rotella
Horsemen's Liaison: Marybeth DiAngelo
Stewards: James Edwards, Stephan Pagano, Harvey I. Wardell Jr.
Track Announcers: Dave Johnson, Sam McKee, Ken Warkentin
Track Photographer: Equi-Photo Inc.

Racing Dates

2007: September 3-November 10, 41 days
2008: September 9-November 15, 42 days

Track Layout

Main Circumference: 1 mile
Main Track Chute: 6 furlongs and $1\frac{1}{4}$ miles
Main Width: Homestretch: 90 feet; Backstretch: 80 feet
Main Length of Stretch: 990 feet
Main Turf Circumference: 7 furlongs

Attendance

Average Daily Recent Meeting: 3,137
Highest Single-Day Record: 41,155, September 4, 1979
Highest Single-Meeting Record: 1,772,209, 1977
Record Daily Average Single Meeting: 17,901, 1977
Total Attendance Recent Meeting: 128,627
Lowest Single-Meeting Record: 108,841, 2006

Handle

Average All-Sources Recent Meeting: \$1,466,524, 2007
Average On-Track Recent Meeting: \$252,066, 2007
Record Daily Average Single Meeting: \$2,085,003, 1982
Single-Day All-Sources Handle: \$5,025,645, October 14, 1994
Total All-Sources Recent Meeting: \$60,127,478, 2007
Total On-Track Recent Meeting: \$10,334,689, 2007
Record Average All-Sources Single Meeting: \$2,619,909, 1994

Mutuel Records

Highest Win: \$354.80, Great Normand, 1990
Lowest Win: \$2.20, Spectacular Bid, 1979

Leaders

Career, Leading Jockey by Titles: Joe Bravo, 9
Career, Leading Trainer by Titles: John H. Forbes, 7
Career, Leading Jockey by Stakes Wins: Nick Santagata, 31
Career, Leading Trainer by Stakes Wins: Philip G. Johnson, 29
Career, Leading Jockey by Wins: Nick Santagata, 991
Career, Leading Trainer by Wins: John H. Forbes, 601
Recent Meeting, Leading Jockey: Eddie Castro, 40, 2007
Recent Meeting, Leading Trainer: Bruce Levine, 19, 2007
Recent Meeting, Leading Horse: Dancin Dusty, 4, 2007

Records

Single-Day Jockey Wins: Julie Krone, 6, September 16, 1989
Single-Day Trainer Wins: John H. Forbes, 4, November 8, 1978
Single Meeting, Leading Jockey by Wins: Joe Bravo, 142, 1994
Single Meeting, Leading Owner by Wins: William C. Martucci, 34, 1990

Single Meeting, Leading Trainer by Wins: John H. Forbes, 47, 1982; Joseph Pierce Jr., 47, 1982; John H. Forbes, 47, 1990
Single Meeting, Leading Trainer by Stakes Wins: Ben W. Perkins Sr., 7, 1995
Single Meeting, Leading Jockey by Stakes Wins: Joe Bravo, 11, 1995
Single Meeting, Leading Horse by Wins: Holme Lane, 7, 1985; Crijinsky, 7, 1995
Single Meeting, Leading Owner by Stakes Wins: New Farm, 7, 1995

Principal Races
Meadowlands Cup H. (G2), Pegasus S. (G3), Cliff Hanger S. (G3), Violet S. (G3)

Track Records, Main Dirt
5 furlongs: Platinum Perfect, :55.45, October 29, 2005
5½ furlongs: Red Hot Spot, 1:02.33, October 14, 2003
6 furlongs: He's So Chic, 1:07.61, October 31, 2007
1 mile: Astrologist, 1:34.16, November 8, 2005
1 mile 70 yds: With Probability, 1:37.90, October 28, 2005
1 1/16 miles: Black Forest, 1:40.39, September 26, 1998
1 1/8 miles: Forty One Carats, 1:45.50, October 29, 1999
1 3/16 miles: Key Lory, 1:53.88, November 20, 1999
1 1/4 miles: Alysheba, 1:58 4/5, October 14, 1988

Track Records, Main Turf
5 furlongs: Remain Silent, :54.73, September 3, 2007
1 mile: Beckon the King, 1:33.88, October 19, 2001
1 mile 70 yds: My Lordship, 1:37.44, June 19, 2006
1 1/16 miles: Wanderkin, 1:39 2/5, September 30, 1988
1 3/8 miles: Rice, 2:12.02, September 25, 1998
Other: a5 furlongs, Tangier Sound, :59.05, November 4, 2002; a1 mile, Onasilverplatter, 1:38.96, October 23, 2002; a1 mile 70yds, Pyrite Search, 1:44.01, October 24, 2002

Fastest Times of 2007 (Dirt)
5 furlongs: Tricky Lak, 3, :57.35, October 10, 2007
5½ furlongs: Boss Zach, 4, 1:02.43, September 26, 2007
6 furlongs: He's So Chic, 3, 1:07.61, October 31, 2007
1 mile: Shopton Lane, 3, 1:35, October 5, 2007
1 mile 70 yds: Kiss the Kid, 4, 1:38.20, October 19, 2007
1 1/16 miles: Indy Wind, 5, 1:41.21, November 3, 2007
1 1/8 miles: Diamond Stripes, 4, 1:48.36, October 5, 2007

Fastest Times of 2007 (Turf)
5 furlongs: Remain Silent, 4, :54.73, September 3, 2007
1 mile: Jersey Kid, 5, 1:34.77, September 18, 2007
1 mile 70 yds: Discreet Charmer, 3, 1:38.34, October 2, 2007
1 1/16 miles: Revival, 5, 1:40.37, September 3, 2007
1 3/8 miles: Dubai Cat, 8, 2:14.24, October 5, 2007
1½ miles: Divine Fortune, 4, 4:28.31, September 21, 2007

New Mexico

Ruidoso Downs

Located 7,000 feet above sea level in the pine-covered mountains of southeastern New Mexico, Ruidoso Downs long has been a popular destination for Southwestern horsemen and racing fans seeking to escape the summer heat. Since 1959, the track has held Quarter Horse racing's richest and most famous event, the All American Futurity, which in '78 became the world's first $1-million horse race. Leading trainers such as D. Wayne Lukas and Bob Baffert raced Quarter Horses at Ruidoso before switching to Thoroughbred racing. Thoroughbred racing also is a fixture at Ruidoso, where purses have increased due to revenues from the Billy the Kid Casino, which opened at the track in 1999 and contains more than 300 video slot machines. Ruidoso has a unique track configuration for the two breeds that compete at the track. A separate straightaway for Quarter Horses is located on the outside of the seven-furlong Thoroughbred oval.

Location: 1461 Highway 70 W., P.O. Box 449, Ruidoso Downs, N.M. 88346-0449
Phone: (505) 378-4431
Fax: (505) 378-4631
Website: www.raceruidoso.com
E-Mail: info@raceruidoso.com
Year Founded: 1946
Dates of Inaugural Meeting: July 1, 1947
Abbreviation: Rui
Number of Stalls: 2,000
Seating Capacity: 7,000

Ownership
R. D. Hubbard

Officers
Chairman: R. D. Hubbard
President: Ann McGovern
Vice President: Edward Burger
General Manager: Ann McGovern
Director of Racing: Ryan Sherman
Racing Secretary: Maureen Murphy
Assistant Racing Secretary: Roddy Taylor
Secretary/Treasurer: Edward Burger
Director of Operations: Neal Mullarky
Director of Marketing: Jodi Jablonski
Director of Mutuels: Deano McTeigue
Director of Simulcasting: Kristian Lovelace
Horsemen's Liaison: Vicki McCabe
Stewards: Kenny Hart, Ed L'Eyuer, Pat Mackie
Track Announcer: Robert Fox
Track Photographer: Bill Pitt
Track Superintendent: Terry Brown
Horsemen's Bookkeeper: Shirley Hart
Security: Roy George

Racing Dates
2007: May 25-September 3, 60 days
2008: May 23-September 1, 60 days

Track Layout
Main Circumference: 7 furlongs
Main Track Chute: 6 furlongs and 1 1/8 miles
Main Width: 75 feet
Main Length of Stretch: 656 feet

Attendance
Average Daily Recent Meeting: 4,034, 2007
Highest Single-Day Record: 18,254 September 3, 2002
Total Attendance Recent Meeting: 242,028, 2007

Handle
Average All-Sources Recent Meeting: $314,245, 2007
Average On-Track Recent Meeting: $225,027, 2007
Total All-Sources Recent Meeting: $18,854,742, 2007
Total On-Track Recent Meeting: $10,491,755, 2007
Highest Single-Day Record Recent Meeting: $1,537,401, September 3, 2007

Leaders
Recent Meeting, Leading Jockey: Joe Martinez, 35, 2007
Recent Meeting, Leading Trainer: Cliff Lambert, 16, 2007
Recent Meeting, Leading Owner: Cliff Lambert, 10, 2007

Principal Races
Ruidoso Thoroughbred Derby, Ruidoso Thoroughbred Championship H., Ruidoso Mile H., Norgor Derby, First Lady H.

Track Records, Main Dirt
4½ furlongs: Professor Jones, :51.60, July 15, 2005
5 furlongs: Twilight Diamond, :56.60, July 17, 2004
5½ furlongs: Rocky Gulch, 1:02.80, August 1, 2004
6 furlongs: Jack Wilson, 1:08.80, August 16, 1992; Ninety Nine Jack, 1:08.80, July 18, 2004

$6\frac{1}{2}$ furlongs: Mr. Tattoo, 1:17$\frac{3}{5}$, July 4, 1973
7 furlongs: Fill Mackis Cup, 1:24$\frac{2}{5}$, July 15, 1984
$7\frac{1}{2}$ furlongs: Caliban, 1:29.40, July 19, 2003
1 mile: Set Records, 1:37, July 28, 1995; Strong Arm Robbery, 1:37, September 1, 2001
1 mile 70 yds: Brogander, 1:45$\frac{1}{5}$, January 1, 1954
$1\frac{1}{16}$ miles: Lucky Bluff, 1:43.40, September 2, 2001
$1\frac{1}{8}$ miles: Brownburough, 1:51$\frac{2}{5}$, June 28, 1964
$1\frac{1}{4}$ miles: Pentelipiano, 2:07.60, September 1, 2003
$1\frac{3}{8}$ miles: Start Jumpin, 2:24$\frac{1}{5}$, August 18, 1990
$1\frac{1}{2}$ miles: Decidedly Henry C., 2:37, August 19, 1989
$1\frac{5}{8}$ miles: More Than Glory, 2:52$\frac{4}{5}$, August 15, 1992
Other: $2\frac{1}{2}$ furlongs, Crafty Number, :27.80, August 18, 2001

Fastest Times of 2007 (Dirt)

5 furlongs: Honoring, 5, :57.60, August 9, 2007
$5\frac{1}{2}$ furlongs: Silver Expression, 3, 1:03, July 29, 2007
6 furlongs: Hunters Wine, 3, 1:10.40, May 27, 2007; Movin' Music, 3, 1:10.40, September 1, 2007
$7\frac{1}{2}$ furlongs: Shesa Private I, 5, 1:32.60, July 1, 2007
1 mile: Castelli Magic, 4, 1:40.80, June 14, 2007; Continuum, 7, 1:40.80, August 5, 2007
$1\frac{1}{16}$ miles: Pistol Creek, 4, 1:45, September 3, 2007

Sunland Park

Opened in 1959, Sunland Park was built just across the state line from El Paso, Texas, in New Mexico, which unlike its neighbor allowed pari-mutuel wagering. Sunland launched the career of several notable horsemen and horses. Jerry Bailey, one of Thoroughbred racing's all-time leading riders, began his career at the track in 1974. Bold Ego, who won Sunland's Riley Allison Futurity in 1980, captured the '81 Arkansas Derby (G1) and ran second in the Preakness Stakes (G1). In the mid-1990s, the track nearly closed because of competition from Native American casinos and pari-mutuel racing in Texas and Oklahoma. New Mexico horsemen and racetracks successfully lobbied for legalizing slot machines at tracks, and Sunland's casino opened in February 1999. With a portion of casino revenues earmarked to purses, the quality of racing improved significantly.

Location: 1200 Futurity Dr., Sunland Park, N.M. 88063-9057
Phone: (575) 874-5200
Fax: (575) 589-1518
Website: *www.sunland-park.com*
E-Mail: sunlandinfo@sunland-park.com
Year Founded: 1959
Dates of Inaugural Meeting: October 9, 1959
Abbreviation: Sun
Number of Stalls: 1,600
Seating Capacity: 5,710

Ownership

Stan E. Fulton

Officers

General Manager: Harold Payne
Director of Racing: Dustin A. Dix
Racing Secretary: Norm Amundson
Director of Marketing: Heath Battles
Director of Mutuels: Steve Fedunak
Director of Publicity: Eric Alwan
Director of Simulcasting: Steve Pedigo
Stewards: Robert Allison, Kenny Hart, Ed L'Ecuyer, Pat Mackey
Track Announcer: Robert Geller
Track Photographer: Coady Photography
Track Superintendent: Bob Patty
Horsemen's Bookkeeper: Shirley Hart
Security: Jessie Olivas

Racing Dates

2007: December 15, 2006-April 29, 2007, 79 days
2008: December 15, 2007-April 22, 2008, 77 days
2009: December 16, 2008-April 21, 2009, 77 days

Track Layout

Main Circumference: 1 mile
Main Track Chute: $6\frac{1}{2}$ furlongs and $1\frac{1}{4}$ miles
Main Width: 80 feet
Main Length of Stretch: 990 feet

Attendance

Average Daily Recent Meeting: 3,672, 2007/2008
Total Attendance Recent Meeting: 282,803, 2007/2008

Handle

Average All-Sources Recent Meeting: $813,083 2007/2008
Average On-Track Recent Meeting: $103,776.53 2007/2008
Single-Day Record All-Sources Handle: $2,194,229, February 3, 2004
Total All-Sources Recent Meeting: $62,607,430.04, 2007/2008
Total On-Track Recent Meeting: $7,990,792.80, 2007/2008
Highest Single-Day All-Sources Recent Meeting: $1,851,766, March 16, 2008

Leaders

Career, Leading Jockey by Titles: Bobby Harmon, 8
Career, Leading Trainer by Titles: Bob E. Arnett, 12
Recent Meeting, Leading Jockey: Ken S. Tohill, 72, 2007/2008
Recent Meeting, Leading Owner: Blackhawk Stable, 18, 2007/2008
Recent Meeting, Leading Trainer: Chris A. Hartman, 44, 2006/2008
Recent Meeting, Leading Horse: Fearless Anthony, 4, 2007/2008; Bossy Bush, 4, 2007/2008

Principal Races

WinStar Derby, WinStar Sunland Park Oaks, Copper Top Futurity, Harry W. Henson H., Sunland Park H.

Interesting Facts

Achievements/Milestones: Casino opened February 2, 1999.

Track Records, Main Dirt

4 furlongs: Tamran's Jet, :44$\frac{4}{5}$, March 22, 1968; Western Hand, :44$\frac{4}{5}$, April 7, 1979
$4\frac{1}{2}$ furlongs: Gulchrunssweet, :49.83, March 26, 2006
5 furlongs: Jimmy Jones, :55.90, February 7, 2004
$5\frac{1}{2}$ furlongs: Gleaming Elegance, 1:02.28, December 30, 2007
6 furlongs: Yet Anothernatalie, 1:08.24, December 11, 2004
$6\frac{1}{2}$ furlongs: Bang, 1:14.29, March 6, 2004
1 mile: Mr. Trieste, 1:35.38, December 7, 2004
$1\frac{1}{16}$ miles: Butte City, 1:41.92, December 12, 2004
$1\frac{1}{8}$ miles: Winsham Lad, 1:48$\frac{1}{5}$, January 8, 1961; Prenupcial, 1:48$\frac{1}{5}$, April 28, 1962
$1\frac{3}{16}$ miles: Mickey J., 1:58$\frac{1}{5}$, November 14, 1970
$1\frac{1}{4}$ miles: Curribot, 2:01$\frac{2}{5}$, May 6, 1984
$1\frac{3}{8}$ miles: Hot Deck, 2:19$\frac{2}{5}$, January 10, 1970
$1\frac{1}{2}$ miles: Houston Blaze, 2:33$\frac{1}{5}$, May 3, 1964
$1\frac{5}{8}$ miles: Rush Line, 2:47$\frac{3}{5}$, April 6, 1969
Other: 2 furlongs, Becky's Star, :21$\frac{1}{5}$, February 12, 1968; 3 furlongs, Sarah Dier, :33$\frac{3}{5}$, March 31, 1962

Fastest Times of 2007 (Dirt)

2 furlongs: Brax, 2, :22.72, March 9, 2007
$4\frac{1}{2}$ furlongs: Hecamefromaclaim, 6, :50.44, April 8, 2007
5 furlongs: Dreaming of Roses, 7, :56.22, April 22, 2007
$5\frac{1}{2}$ furlongs: Gleaming Elegance, 4, 1:02.28, December 30, 2007
6 furlongs: Jammin Gears, 5, 1:09.11, February 17, 2007
$6\frac{1}{2}$ furlongs: Boom Boom, 5, 1:14.79, April 14, 2007
1 mile: El Minuto, 5, 1:36.68, March 27, 2007
$1\frac{1}{16}$ miles: Guiding Hand, 4, 1:42.28, April 3, 2007
$1\frac{1}{8}$ miles: Song of Navarone, 3, 1:49.53, March 18, 2007
$1\frac{1}{4}$ miles: Sharm, 6, 2:05.35, April 29, 2007

SunRay Park

SunRay Park in Farmington, New Mexico, is located in an area called the Four Corners region, where north-

western New Mexico, northeastern Arizona, southeastern Utah, and southwestern Colorado meet. The racetrack, which offers Thoroughbred and Quarter Horse racing, originally was known as San Juan Downs; it was built by San Juan County at the county fairgrounds and opened in 1984. Declining business forced the track to close after its 1993 season. SunRay Gaming of New Mexico LLC secured a ten-year option to operate the track, which was renamed SunRay Park and reopened in October 1999. SunRay Gaming's interest in reviving horse racing at the facility largely was based on its ability to operate a casino with slot machines. A portion of revenues from the slots enhances race purses. Multiple stakes winner Peppers Pride equaled a modern North American record at SunRay by earning her 16th consecutive win when she captured the $75,000 Russell and Hellen Foutz Distaff Handicap on April 26, 2008.

Location: 39 Rd. 5568, Farmington, N.M. 87401-1466
Phone: (505) 566-1200
Fax: (505) 326-4292
Website: www.sunraygaming.com
E-Mail: racing@sunraygaming.com
Year Founded: 1984 as San Juan Downs; 1999 as SunRay Park
Abbreviation: SRP
Number of Stalls: 1,098
Seating Capacity: 3,000

Ownership
SunRay Gaming of New Mexico

Officers
Chief Executive Officer: Byron Campbell
Chief Operating Officer: Brad Boehm
Director of Racing: Lonnie S. Barber Jr.
Racing Secretary: Sean Winsor
Assistant Racing Secretary: Gordon Graham
Director of Mutuels and Simulcasting: Natalie Swisher
Stewards: Bob Allison, Wayne Epsteen, Ed L'Ecquyer
Track Announcer: Eric Alwan
Track Photographer: Coady Photography
Track Superintendent: Bob Patty
Security: Leonard Demoney
Horsemen's Bookkeeper: Robin Miller

Racing Dates
2007: May 3-July 15, 44 days
2008: April 18-June 29, 44 days

Attendance
Average Daily Recent Meeting: 1,594, 2007
Total Attendance Recent Meeting: 70,100, 2007
Highest Single-Day Recent Meeting: 4,225, May 5, 2007

Handle
Total All-Sources Recent Meeting: $2,929,008, 2007
Average All-Sources Recent Meeting: $66,568, 2007
Total On-Track Recent Meeting: $1,303,910, 2007
Average On-Track Recent Meeting: $29,634, 2007
Largest Single-Day All-Sources Recent Meeting: $114,309, May 10, 2007
Largest Single-Day On-Track Recent Meeting: $49,573, July 15, 2007

Leaders
Recent Meeting, Leading Jockey: Alfredo Juarez Jr., 45, 2007
Recent Meeting, Leading Trainer: Ramon O. Gonzalez, 23, 2007
Recent Meeting, Leading Owner: Maria Gonzalez, 20, 2007
Recent Meeting, Leading Horse: Mr Frenchman, 3, 2007; A Long Goodbye, 3, 2007; Dreaming Of Roses, 3, 2007

Principal Races
San Juan County Commissioners H., Russell and Hellen Foutz Distaff H., Jack Cole H., New Mexico Breeders' Association H., Aztec Oaks, Dine' S., Totah Thoroughbred S., C.O. Ken Kendricks Memorial S.

Track Records, Main Dirt
4 furlongs: Absolutely True, :44.60, November 16, 2003
4½ furlongs: Sky Diver, :49.80, October 10, 2003
6 furlongs: Unbridled Set, 1:11.40, October 11, 1999
6½ furlongs: Herecomesthemannow, 1:15.60, September 22, 2003
7 furlongs: Oh Gracie, 1:22.60, September 25, 2000
7½ furlongs: Dalt's Kingpin, 1:28.60, November 17, 2003
1 mile: Ben Told, 1:35.60, October 15, 2000
1⅛ miles: Line Guage, 1:48.80, November 21, 1999

Fastest Times of 2007 (Dirt)
4½ furlongs: Dangerous Devon, 5, :50.40, June 7, 2007; Dreaming of Roses, 7, :50.40, June 23, 2007; Sealed With a Kiss, 8, :50.40, July 1, 2007
6½ furlongs: Rollicking Caller, 6, 1:16, June 10, 2007
7 furlongs: Molly's Pride, 4, 1:23, June 16, 2007
7½ furlongs: A Few Good Friends, 5, 1:30, June 7, 2007
1 mile: Sharm, 6, 1:36, June 7, 2007
1⅛ miles: Thunder Belle, 5, 1:53.20, July 15, 2007

The Downs at Albuquerque

The Downs at Albuquerque, located on the New Mexico State Fairgrounds in Albuquerque, features Thoroughbred and Quarter Horse racing in late summer and during the 17-day New Mexico State Fair in September. The fair dates from 1881, while its race meeting, which opened in October 1938, is the oldest in New Mexico. The New Mexico State Fair Futurity for Quarter Horses debuted in 1946 and is the oldest continuously run stakes race for the breed. One notable Thoroughbred horseman who competed at Albuquerque early in his career was jockey Mike Smith, a New Mexico native who became a Racing Hall of Fame member in 2003. In 1990, the track debuted The Lineage, a day of racing exclusively for state-bred Thoroughbreds and Quarter Horses. Its slots casino opened in 1999, and the track was to move to Moriarty in 2010.

Location: 201 California St. N.E., Albuquerque, N.M. 87108-1802
Phone: (505) 266-5555
Fax: (505) 268-1970
Website: www.abqdowns.com
E-Mail: bethmk@abqdowns.com
Year Founded: 1938
Dates of Inaugural Meeting: October 1938
Abbreviation: Alb
Number of Stalls: 1,700

Officers
President: Paul Blanchard
Vice President: John Turner
General Manager: Don Cook
Racing Secretary: Stewart Slagle
Treasurer: Bill Windham
Director of Operations: Beth McKinney
Director of Marketing: Michael Lazarus
Director of Mutuels: Barbra Hewson
Director of Simulcasting: Beth McKinney
Track Superintendent: Tony Martinez

Racing Dates
2007: August 10-September 3, 17 days; September 7-September 23, 17 days; September 26-October 7, 10 days
2008: August 16-September 4, 11 days; September 5-September 21, 17 days; September 24-November 16, 32 days

Track Layout

Main Circumference: 1 mile
Main Track Chute: 2 furlongs and 7 furlongs
Main Width: 90 feet
Main Length of Stretch: 1,114 feet

Attendance

Highest Single-Day Record: 13,979, September 16, 1990
Average Daily Recent Meeting: 2,500, 2007
Total Attendance Recent Meeting: 150,000, 2007

Handle

Average All-Sources Recent Meeting: $127,458, 2007
Average On-Track Recent Meeting: $67,566, 2007
Total All-Sources Recent Meeting: $8,254,824, 2007
Total On-Track Recent Meeting: $4,391, 804
Highest Single-Day On-Track Recent Meeting: $193,854
Highest Single-Day All-Sources Recent Meeting: $295,568

Leaders

Recent Meeting, Leading Jockey: Miguel Perez, 40, 2007
Recent Meeting, Leading Owner: Marie Gonzalez, 16, 2007
Recent Meeting, Leading Trainer: Ramon Gonzalez, 27, 2007

Track Records, Main Dirt

4 furlongs: Key Sunday, :44.53, September 16, 2007
$4\frac{1}{2}$ furlongs: Silver Matt, :51.22, June 17, 2000
5 furlongs: Scout Revolt, :56.35, December 12, 1998
$5\frac{1}{2}$ furlongs: Yulla Yulla, 1:01.68, September 23, 2000
6 furlongs: Streak of Royalty, 1:08.43, April 23, 2005
$6\frac{1}{2}$ furlongs: Ben Told, 1:14.59, May 10, 2002
7 furlongs: Mighty Classy, 1:21, September 18, 1989; Star Smasher, 1:21.01, June 9, 2002
1 mile: Lester's Boy, 1:35.74, April 27, 2002
1 mile 70 yds: Fire Knight, 1:41$\frac{3}{5}$, September 26, 1959
$1\frac{1}{16}$ miles: Ciento, 1:40.60, September 22, 2001
$1\frac{1}{8}$ miles: Brew, 1:48.47, June 3, 2001
$1\frac{3}{16}$ miles: Savage Wind, 2:05$\frac{4}{5}$, September 23, 1981
$1\frac{1}{4}$ miles: Luedke, 2:03.69, April 14, 1996
$1\frac{1}{2}$ miles: Luedke, 2:33.73, September 25, 1994
$1\frac{5}{8}$ miles: Vikings Shield, 2:43$\frac{2}{5}$, April 17, 1988
$1\frac{3}{4}$ miles: Prince De-Or, 2:59$\frac{1}{5}$, September 25, 1966
2 miles: Betty Falcon, 3:28$\frac{3}{5}$ October 7, 1956
Other: $1\frac{13}{16}$ miles, Vermejo, 3:05$\frac{2}{5}$, September 27, 1970

Fastest Times of 2007 (Dirt)

4 furlongs: Key Sunday, 6, :44.53, September 16, 2007
$4\frac{1}{2}$ furlongs: Aint He a Bull, 4, :51.51, October 4, 2007
5 furlongs: Absolutely True, 7, :56.53, September 15, 2007
$5\frac{1}{2}$ furlongs: Lauras Last Music, 3, 1:02.68, August 12, 2007
6 furlongs: Paltu, 4, 1:09.58, August 26, 2007
$6\frac{1}{2}$ furlongs: Whirl, 4, 1:15, September 2, 2007
7 furlongs: Con Say One, 5, 1:22.18, September 19, 2007
1 mile: Tanya's Beau, 5, 1:36.84, October 7, 2007
$1\frac{1}{16}$ miles: Midnite Prospector, 6, 1:44.11, August 19, 2007
$1\frac{1}{8}$ miles: Rollicking Caller, 6, 1:51.73, September 23, 2007
$1\frac{1}{4}$ miles: Taziano, 5, 2:06.12, October 6, 2007
$1\frac{1}{2}$ miles: Butte City, 8, 2:35.60, September 3, 2007
$1\frac{13}{16}$ miles: Hope for Peace, 5, 3:11.97, September 23, 2007

Zia Park

The fifth and newest track in New Mexico, Zia Park is located in Hobbs near the Texas border. Opened in September 2005, the track stages both Thoroughbred and Quarter Horse racing. The complex also includes the Black Gold Casino, a simulcast pavilion, several restaurants, and a hotel. The track presents New Mexico Cup day, with seven stakes races for New Mexico-bred Thoroughbreds and four stakes races for state-bred Quarter Horses. The track is named for the cross-like symbol on the state's flag. Developed by R. D. Hubbard and partners, the track was sold for $200-million to Penn National Gaming Inc. in 2007.

Location: 3901 W. Millen Dr., Hobbs, N.M. 88240
Phone: (505) 492-7000, (888) 942-7275
Website: *www.blackgoldcasino.net*
E-Mail: info@blackgoldcasino.net
Dates of Inaugural Meeting: September 23-December 4, 2005
Abbreviation: Zia
Acreage: 320
Number of Stalls: 1650

Ownership

Penn National Gaming Inc.

Officers

President: Tim Wilmott
General Manager: Bill Hayles
Assistant General Manager: Rick Baugh
Director of Operations: Martha Rivera
Director of Finance: Rhonda Hasse
Director of Marketing: Mike McCarthy
Director of Mutuels: Dino McTeigue
Track Photographer: Bill Pitt
Security: Oscar Renteria

Racing Dates

2007: September 22-December 11, 48 days
2008: September 13-December 9, 53 days

Attendance

Average Daily Recent Meeting: 3197, 2007
Total Attendance Recent Meeting: 140,694, 2007
Highest Single-Day Recent Meeting: 5,064, 2007, November 11, 2007
Highest Single-Day Record: 5,064, 2007, November 11, 2007

Handle

Total All-Sources Recent Meeting: $26,642,834, 2007
Average All-Sources Recent Meeting: $605,518, 2007
Total On-Track Recent Meeting: $8,334,750, 2007
Average On-Track Recent Meeting: $189,426, 2007
Largest Single-Day All-Sources Recent Meeting: $1,121,231, December 7, 2007
Largest Single-Day On-Track Recent Meeting: $175,575, November 11, 2007

Mutuel Records

Highest Win: $141.00, October 23, 2007
Highest Exacta: $4,362.80, October 23, 2007
Highest Trifecta: $12,380.20, October 23, 2007

Leaders

Recent Meeting, Leading Jockey: Ken Tohill, 37, 2007
Recent Meeting, Leading Trainer: Joel Marr , 20, 2007
Recent Meeting, Leading Owner: H. Armando Orozco, 6, 2007

Notable Events

New Mexico Cup Day

Track Records, Main Dirt

$4\frac{1}{2}$ furlongs: Clever Assault, :52.80, December 2, 2005
5 furlongs: Orphan Brigade, :56.60, October 31, 2005; Thyer's (Brz), :56.60, November 18, 2005
$5\frac{1}{2}$ furlongs: Jilted Heart, 1:02.60, October 1, 2005
6 furlongs: Ashby Hill, 1:08.60, October 22, 2005
$6\frac{1}{2}$ furlongs: Jungle Prince, 1:15, December 4, 2005
1 mile: Mr. Trieste, 1:36.60, October 22, 2005
$1\frac{1}{16}$ miles: Mr. Trieste, 1:43, November 12, 2005
$1\frac{1}{8}$ miles: Tap Dancing Mauk, 1:55.20, December 10, 2006
$1\frac{1}{2}$ miles: Billy Bird, 2:35.20, December 4, 2005

Fastest Times of 2007 (Dirt)

5 furlongs: Day of the Derby, 4, :57, October 9, 2007
$5\frac{1}{2}$ furlongs: Distinct Prospect, 6, 1:03, October 9, 2007
6 furlongs: Honoring, 5, 1:08.80, September 29, 2007; Kin to a Kitty, 4, 1:08.80, October 7, 2007
$6\frac{1}{2}$ furlongs: Conceptual, 5, 1:17, October 16, 2007; Stone Canyon, 7, 1:17, October 2, 2007; Sulphur Water, 4, 1:17, November 19, 2007
1 mile: Thumb Wrestler, 5, 1:37.20, October 7, 2007
$1\frac{1}{16}$ miles: Mr. Pursuit, 4, 1:43.40, November 20, 2007
$1\frac{1}{8}$ miles: Tap Dancing Mauk, 6, 1:51, December 9, 2007

New York

Aqueduct

Occupying roughly half of the New York Racing Association's year-round schedule, the track known as the Big A offers racing in winter, spring, and fall. Aqueduct opened as a six-furlong track in New York's Queens Borough on September 27, 1894. Site of the only triple dead heat in a stakes race—Brownie, Bossuet, and Wait a Bit hit the wire together in the Carter Handicap on June 10, 1944—Aqueduct was torn down in '56 and completely rebuilt over three years. For four years, from 1964 through '67, Aqueduct played host to the Belmont Stakes while Belmont Park was rebuilt. An all-time record crowd of 73,435 watched Gun Bow win the Metropolitan Handicap on Memorial Day, May 31, 1965. In 1975, the one-mile inner dirt track was completed, allowing racing throughout the winter. Six years later, Aqueduct opened Equestris, a 300-foot-long, $7-million facility for 1,600 diners. A $3-million renovation in 1985 prior to its only Breeders' Cup championship day expanded Aqueduct's paddock and grandstand. The spring meet's principal race is the Wood Memorial Stakes (G1), a Kentucky Derby (G1) prep, and the Cigar Mile Handicap (G1) is one of its fall features. The New York Legislature in 2001 authorized video lottery terminals for the track, but political intrigue during the administration of Governor George Pataki effectively blocked their installation. After a long and tumultuous bidding process, NYRA retained its franchise to conduct racing at Aqueduct, Belmont Park, and Saratoga Race Course. The deal, reached in February 2008, was part of a 190-page racing bill that awarded NYRA a 25-year contract and gave the state ownership of the land on which the three tracks are housed.

Location: 110-00 Rockaway Blvd., P.O. Box 90, Jamaica, N.Y. 11417
Phone: (718) 641-4700
Fax: (718) 322-3814
Website: www.nyra.com
E-Mail: nyra@nyrainc.com
Year Founded: 1894
Dates of Inaugural Meeting: September 27, 1894
Abbreviation: Aqu
Capsule Description: The Big A
Acreage: 192
Number of Stalls: 547
Seating Capacity: 17,000

Ownership
New York Racing Association Inc.

Officers
Chairman: C. Steven Duncker
Vice Chairmen: Michael J. DelGiudice, James P. Heffernan, Stuart Subotnick
President and Chief Executive Officer: Charles E. Hayward
Executive Vice President and Chief Operating Officer: Harold G. Handel
Senior Vice President and General Counsel: Patrick L. Kehoe
Senior Vice President of Sales and Market Development: Gavin Landry
Senior Vice President and Chief Administrative Officer: John Ryan
Senior Vice President of Human Resources and Labor Relations: David A. Smukler
Vice President and Chief Financial Officer: Irene M. Posio
Vice President and Chief Information Officer: Tom Thill
Vice President of Pari-Mutuel Operations: Patrick Mahony
Vice President of Security: Kenneth T. Cook
Vice President of Facilities: John Tierney
Vice President and Director of Racing: Paul J. Campo
Vice President and Director of Simulcast Sales and Content Acquisition: Elizabeth Bracken
Director of Admissions and Parking: Jerry A. Davis Jr.
Director of Communications and Media Relations: John Lee
Director of Horsemen's Services: Carmen Barrera
Director of Marketing: Neema Ghazi
Director of Racing Surfaces: John Passero
OTB Relations: Robert Palumbo
Stable/Security Supervisor: Rick Wickman
Stewards: Braulio Baeza Jr., Carmine Donofrio, Dr. W. Theodore Hill, Stephen Lewandowski
Track Announcer: Tom Durkin, John Imbriale
Track Photographers: Adam Coglianese, Bob Coglianese

Racing Dates
2007: January 1-April 29, 76 days; October 24-December 30, 45 days
2008: January 1-April 27, 83 days; October 29-December 31, 39 days

Track Layout
Main Circumference: 1 1/8 miles
Main Track Chute: 1 mile
Main Width: 100 feet
Main Length of Stretch: 1,155.6 feet
Main Turf Circumference: 7 furlongs
Main Turf Chute: 1 1/8 miles
Inner Circumference: 1 mile

Attendance
Average Daily Recent Meeting: 2,460, Winter-Spring 2007; 2,619, Fall 2007
Highest Single-Day Record: 73,435, May 31, 1965
Total Attendance Recent Meeting: 204,232, Winter-Spring 2007; 117,882, Fall 2007

Handle
Average All-Sources Recent Meeting: $7,957,599, Winter-Spring 2007; $8,258,519 Fall 2007
Average On-Track Recent Meeting: $614,520 Winter-Spring 2007; $655,526 Fall 2007
Single-Day Record On-Track Handle: $8,171,520, November 2, 1985
Total All-Sources Recent Meeting: $596,819,923, Winter-Spring 2007; $338,599,297, Fall 2007
Total On-Track Recent Meeting: $46,088,996, Winter-Spring 2007; $26,876,579, Fall 2007
Highest Single-Day Record Recent Meeting: $17,780,232, April 7, 2007 (Winter-Spring); $12,400,114 November 10, 2007 (Fall)

Mutuel Records
Highest Win: $434, Markobob, September 3, 1943
Highest Pick Six: $1,120,287, January 17, 2004

Leaders
Recent Meeting, Leading Jockey: Eibar Coa, 102, Inner Track 2006/2007; Ramon Dominguez, 24, Spring 2007; Javier Castellano, 19, Fall 2007
Recent Meeting, Leading Trainer: Gary Contessa, 72, Inner Track 2006-2007; Richard Dutrow Jr., 16, Spring 2007; Richard Dutrow Jr., 10, Fall 2007
Recent Meeting, Leading Owner: Winning Move Stable, 38, Winter-Spring 2006/2007; Winning Move Stable, 18, Fall 2007
Single-Day Jockey Wins: Michael Venezia, 6, December 7, 1964; Rudy L. Turcotte, 6, December 2, 1969; Angel Cordero Jr., 6, March 12, 1975; Ron Turcotte, 6, March 5, 1976; Steve Cauthen, 6, January 22, 1977; Steve Cauthen, 6, April 7, 1977; Steve Cauthen, 6, November 29, 1977; Mike Smith, 6, January 13, 1992; Mike Smith, 6, January 30, 1992; Jorge Chavez, 6, February 18, 1996; Shaun Bridgmohan, 6, February 15, 1998

Principal Races
Wood Memorial S. (G1), Carter H. (G1), Cigar Mile H. (G1), Demoiselle S. (G2), Remsen S. (G2)

Notable Events
First East Coast track to host Breeders' Cup in 1985.

Track Records, Main Dirt

4 1/2 furlongs: About to Burst, :51 3/5, April 26, 1984
5 furlongs: Bazaar Change, :57, June 6, 1963
5 1/2 furlongs: Raise a Native, 1:02 3/5, July 17, 1963
6 furlongs: Kelly Kip, 1:07.54, April 10, 1999
6 1/2 furlongs: Coronado's Quest, 1:14.35, October 26, 1997
7 furlongs: Artax, 1:20.04, May 2, 1999
7 1/2 furlongs: Imafavoritetrick, 1:28.54, November 27, 2004
1 mile: Easy Goer, 1:32 2/5, April 8, 1989; Discreet Cat, 1:32.46, November 25, 2006
1 1/16 miles: McDee, 1:39.45, November 13, 1993
1 1/8 miles: Riva Ridge, 1:47, October 15, 1973
1 3/16 miles: Riva Ridge, 1:52 2/5, July 4, 1973
1 1/4 miles: Damascus, 1:59 1/5, July 20, 1968
1 3/8 miles: Demi's Bret, 2:12.31, October 26, 1997
1 1/2 miles: Going Abroad, 2:26 1/5, October 12, 1964
1 5/8 miles: Sharp Gray, 2:40 2/5, December 13, 1975
1 3/4 miles: Malmo, 2:53.73, March 30, 1996
2 miles: Kelso, 3:19 1/5, October 31, 1964
Other: 1 5/16 miles, Gold Star Deputy, 2:07.32, April 10, 1999; 1 7/8 miles, Erin Bright, 3:12 4/5, April 18, 1985; 2 1/4 miles, Paraje, 3:47 4/5, December 15, 1973

Track Records, Main Turf

1 mile: Possible Mate, 1:34 3/5, November 1, 1985; Tax Dodge, 1:34 3/5, November 1, 1985 (Dead Heat)
1 1/16 miles: Spindrift (Ire), 1:40.88, May 6, 2000
1 1/8 miles: Slew the Dragon, 1:47, November 3, 1985
1 3/8 miles: Fluorescent Light, 2:14 1/5, November 7, 1978
1 1/2 miles: Pebbles (GB), 2:27, November 2, 1985
2 miles: Putting Green, 3:30 2/5, November 23, 1984

Track Records, Inner Dirt

4 furlongs: Native Moment, :53 2/5, April 2, 1979
4 1/2 furlongs: Call Me Up, :52.29, April 16, 1998
5 1/2 furlongs: Melodeeman, 1:03.94, January 20, 2006
6 furlongs: Captain Red, 1:07.93, February 26, 2003
1 mile: Tejano Couture, 1:35.79, March 9, 2000
1 mile 70yds: Carry My Colors, 1:38.92, February 5, 2000
1 1/16 miles: Autoroute, 1:41, December 19, 1992
1 1/8 miles: Conveyor, 1:47.33, March 6, 1993
1 3/16 miles: Victoriously, 1:54.42, January 25, 1998
1 1/4 miles: Transient Trend, 2:01.53, December 21, 1995
1 1/2 miles: Piling, 2:29 3/5, March 13, 1983
1 5/8 miles: Relaxing, 2:42 2/5, December 13, 1980
1 3/4 miles: Sophie's Friend, 2:56.73, February 10, 1996
2 miles: Charlie Coast, 3:24 4/5, February 21, 1979
Other: 2 1/16 miles, Rollix, 3:38 4/5, February 3, 1983; 2 1/8 miles, Peat Moss 3:40 3/5, January 31, 1981; 2 1/4 miles, Field Cat, 3:51 4/5, December 31, 1981

Fastest Times of 2007 (Dirt)

5 1/2 furlongs: Carolyn's Cat, 2, 1:03.75, November 18, 2007; Trading Pro, 4, 1:03.75, January 27, 2007
6 furlongs: Man of Danger, 5, 1:09.05, December 28, 2007; Pavo, 5, 1:09.05, April 5, 2007
6 1/2 furlongs: Karakorum Tuxedo, 6, 1:15.68, April 18, 2007
7 furlongs: Tasteyville, 4, 1:21.38, October 27, 2007
7 1/2 furlongs: Market Psychology, 3, 1:28.83, April 7, 2007
1 mile: Daaher, 3, 1:33.79, November 24, 2007; Epigrammatic, 4, 1:33.79, March 1, 2007
1 mile 70 yds: Ricardo A, 8, 1:40.59, March 4, 2007
1 1/16 miles: Summer Doldrums, 3, 1:42.23, February 10, 2007
1 1/8 miles: Evening Attire, 9, 1:49.57, March 3, 2007; Hunting, 4, 1:49.57, November 17, 2007
1 3/16 miles: Evening Attire, 9, 1:58.01, December 8, 2007
1 1/4 miles: Carminooch, 5, 2:03.87, January 28, 2007
1 1/2 miles: Nite Light, 3, 2:34.33, December 5, 2007
1 5/8 miles: Nite Light, 3, 2:47.45, December 29, 2007
1 3/4 miles: Malibu Moonshine, 5, 2:57.54, April 7, 2007

Fastest Times of 2007 (Turf)

1 mile: Sleeping Indian, 3, 1:36.63, November 7, 2007
a1 mile: Raynicks Fan, 3, 1:41, December 1, 2007
1 1/16 miles: Kenta Kun, 6, 1:43.04, November 4, 2007
a1 1/16 miles: Dancing Tin Man, 4, 1:49.60, December 1, 2007
1 1/8 miles: Hangingbyathread, 3, 1:50.49, April 26, 2007
1 3/8 miles: Banrock, 4, 2:20.52, November 24, 2007
1 1/2 miles: Dalvina (GB), 3, 2:34.35, November 11, 2007

Belmont Park

With a 1 1/2-mile oval, Belmont Park on Long Island is the largest racetrack in North America, and its huge grandstand has a 90,000-person capacity. Originally built for $2.5-million and opened on May 4, 1905, Belmont is host to the third leg of the Triple Crown, the Belmont Stakes (G1), which was named for German-born financier August Belmont I. The first Belmont Stakes was run in 1867 at Jerome Park and was moved to Morris Park in 1890. Within a few years of Belmont's opening, anti-gambling legislation shut the track in 1911 and '12. The track reopened in 1913, and the grandstand was rebuilt in 1920, raising seating capacity to 17,500. In 1963, deterioration of the grandstand forced a five-year closure while the current facility was constructed for $30.7-million. In those years, the Belmont and most of the track's races and dates were run at Aqueduct. Belmont has played host to four runnings of the Breeders' Cup World Thoroughbred Championships, in 1990, '95, 2001, and '05. The 2001 running of the championship event marked the first international sporting event to be held in the New York City area following the September 11, 2001, terrorist attack on the World Trade Center.

Location: 2150 Hempstead Pike, Elmont, N.Y. 11003-1551
Phone: (516) 488-6000
Fax: (516) 352-0919
Website: *www.nyra.com*
E-Mail: nyra@nyrainc.com
Year Founded: 1902
Dates of Inaugural Meeting: May 4, 1905
Abbreviation: Bel
Acreage: 430
Number of Stalls: 2,200
Seating Capacity: 32,941

Ownership

New York Racing Association Inc.

Officers

Chairman: C. Steven Duncker
Vice Chairmen: Michael J. DelGiudice, James P. Heffernan, Stuart Subotnick
President and Chief Executive Officer: Charles E. Hayward
Executive Vice President and Chief Operating Officer: Harold G. Handel
Senior Vice President and General Counsel: Patrick L. Kehoe
Senior Vice President of Sales and Market Development: Gavin Landry
Senior Vice President and Chief Administrative Officer: John Ryan
Senior Vice President of Human Resources and Labor Relations: David Smukler
Vice President and Chief Financial Officer: Irene M. Posio
Vice President and Chief Information Officer: Tom Thill
Vice President of Pari-Mutuel Operations: Patrick Mahony
Vice President of Security: Kenneth T. Cook
Vice President of Facilities: John Tierney
Vice President and Director of Racing: Paul J. Campo
Vice President and Director of Simulcast Sales and Content Acquisition: Elizabeth Bracken
Director of Admissions and Parking: Jerry A. Davis Jr.
Director of Communications and Media Relations: John Lee
Director of Horsemen's Services: Carmen Barrera
Director of Marketing: Neema Ghazi
Director of Racing Surfaces: John Passero
OTB Relations: Robert Palumbo
Stable/Security Supervisor: Rick Wickman
Stewards: Braulio Baeza Jr., Carmine Donofrio, Dr. W. Theodore Hill, Stephen Lewandowski

Track Announcers: Tom Durkin, John Imbriale
Track Photographers: Adam Coglianese, Bob Coglianese

Racing Dates
2007: May 2-July 21, 59 days; September 7-October 21, 33 days
2008: April 30-July 20, 59 days; September 5-October 26, 38 days

Track Layout
Main Circumference: 1 1/2 miles
Main Length of Stretch: 1,097 feet
Main Turf Circumference: 1 5/16 miles
Main Turf Chute: 1 mile and 1 1/16 miles
Inner Turf Circumference: 1 3/16 miles, 103 feet
Inner Turf Chute: 1 1/16 miles
Training Track: 1 mile

Attendance
Average Daily Recent Meeting: 6,341, Spring-Summer 2007; 5,001, Fall 2007
Highest Single-Day Record: 120,139, June 5, 2004
Total Attendance Recent Meeting: 380,495, Spring-Summer 2007; 165,045, Fall 2007
Highest Single-Day Recent Meeting: 46,870, June 9, 2007 Spring-Summer

Handle
Average All-Sources Recent Meeting: $11,467,265, Spring-Summer 2007; $10,497,676, Fall 2007
Average On-Track Recent Meeting: $1,164,721, Spring-Summer 2007; $1,038,796, Fall 2007
Single-Day On-Track Handle: $14,461,402, June 5, 2004 Spring-Summer; $14,695,958, October 29, 2005 Fall
Single-Day All-Sources Handle: $114,887,594, June 5, 2004 Spring-Summer; $122,106,154, October 29, 2005 Fall
Total All-Sources Recent Meeting: $676,568,657, Spring-Summer 2007; $338,599,297, Fall 2007
Total On-Track Recent Meeting: $68,718,518, Spring-Summer 2007; $26,876,579, Fall 2007
Highest Single-Day Record Recent Meeting: $75,587,892, June 9, 2007 Spring-Summer; $17,292,385, September 15, 2007 (Fall)

Mutuel Records
Highest Exacta: $5,454, June 1, 1985
Highest Quinella: $1,244.20, June 1, 1985
Highest Pick Four: $215,730.50, June 4, 2002

Leaders
Recent Meeting, Leading Jockey: Eibar Coa, 72, Spring-Summer 2007; Eibar Coa, 49, Fall 2007
Recent Meeting, Leading Owner: Winning Move Stable, 29, Spring-Summer 2007; Winning Move Stable, 17, Fall 2007
Recent Meeting, Leading Trainer: Gary Contessa, 39, Spring-Summer 2007; Gary Contessa, 23, Fall 2007

Records
Single-Day Jockey Wins: Jorge Velasquez, 6, July 9, 1981
Single Meeting, Leading Trainer by Wins: Todd Pletcher, 40, Spring-Summer 2003

Principal Races
Spring-Summer: Belmont S. (G1), Metropolitan H. (G1), Manhattan H. (G1), Suburban H. (G1), Coaching Club American Oaks (G1)
Fall: Jockey Club Gold Cup S. (G1), Flower Bowl Invitational S. (G1), Joe Hirsch Turf Classic Invitational S. (G1), Beldame S. (G1)

Track Records, Main Dirt
5 furlongs: Kelly Kip, :55.75, June 21, 1996
5 1/2 furlongs: Mike's Classic, 1:02.26, June 20, 2004
6 furlongs: Artax, 1:07.66, October 16, 1999
6 1/2 furlongs: Bear Fan, 1:14.46, June 5, 2004
7 furlongs: Left Bank, 1:20.17, July 4, 2002
7 1/2 furlongs: Centerpart, 1:27.44, September 24, 2001
1 mile: Najran, 1:32.24, May 7, 2003
1 1/16 miles: Rock and Roll, 1:39.51, June 13, 1998
1 1/8 miles: Secretariat, 1:45 2/5, September 15, 1973
1 3/16 miles: Lueders, 1:56, June 24, 1982
1 1/4 miles: In Excess (Ire), 1:58 1/5, July 4, 1991
1 3/8 miles: Victoriously, 2:14.72, October 16, 1997
1 1/2 miles: Secretariat, 2:24, June 9, 1973

Track Records, Main Turf
6 furlongs: Keep The Faith (Aus), 1:06.82, July 24, 2005
7 furlongs: Officialpermission, 1:19.88, July 23, 2000
1 mile: Elusive Quality, 1:31.63, July 4, 1998
1 1/16 miles: Fortitude, 1:38.53, September 6, 1997
1 3/8 miles: Influent, 2:11.06, July 13, 1997
1 1/2 miles: Fantastic Light, 2:24.36, October 27, 2001
2 miles: King's General (GB), 3:20 2/5, July 4, 1983

Track Records, Inner Turf
6 furlongs: Titian Time, 1:09.90, September 25, 2005
1 1/16 miles: Roman Envoy, 1:39.38, May 23, 1992
1 1/8 miles: Shakespeare, 1:45.06, September 11, 2005
1 1/4 miles: Paradise Creek, 1:57.79, June 11, 1994
1 3/8 miles: With Approval, 2:10 1/5, June 17, 1990

Fastest Times of 2007 (Dirt)
5 furlongs: Fed Watcher, 2, :56.10, June 30, 2007
5 1/2 furlongs: Law Enforcement, 2, 1:02.53, July 20, 2007
6 furlongs: Callmetony, 6, 1:08.21, May 25, 2007; Silver Timber, 4, 1:08.21, July 22, 2007
6 1/2 furlongs: Posted, 4, 1:15.17, July 14, 2007
7 furlongs: First Defence, 3, 1:20.96, May 26, 2007
7 1/2 furlongs: Lady Byar, 5, 1:31.29, June 15, 2007
1 mile: Utopia (Jpn), 7, 1:33.23, May 2, 2007
1 1/16 miles: Papi Chullo, 5, 1:39.89, May 4, 2007; War Monger, 3, 1:39.89, June 24, 2007
1 1/8 miles: Octave, 3, 1:47.19, June 30, 2007
1 1/4 miles: Political Force, 4, 2:00.50, June 30, 2007; Sunriver, 4, 2:00.50, July 15, 2007
1 1/2 miles: Rags to Riches, 3, 2:28.74, June 9, 2007

Fastest Times of 2007 (Turf)
6 furlongs: Count On Pal, 4, 1:08.08, May 26, 2007
7 furlongs: English Colony (GB), 3, 1:20.13, September 9, 2007
1 mile: Trippi's Storm, 4, 1:32.36, September 29, 2007
1 1/16 miles: Lear's Princess, 3, 1:41.17, May 24, 2007
1 1/8 miles: Nobiz Like Shobiz, 3, 1:46.80, October 6, 2007
1 1/4 miles: Lahudood (GB), 4, 1:59.05, September 29, 2007
1 3/8 miles: Doctor Dino (Fr), 5, 2:12.26, September 8, 2007
1 1/2 miles: English Channel, 5, 2:25.73, September 30, 2007
1 1/2 miles: Good Night Shirt, 6, 4:42.45, September 22, 2007

Finger Lakes Gaming and Race Track

In Native American lore, the Finger Lakes region of upstate New York was created when the Great Spirit placed his hand down on the land to create the series of long, thin lakes. Finger Lakes, which is located 20 miles from Rochester in Farmington, opened May 23, 1962, and offers racing from mid-April to early December. Owned by Finger Lakes Racing Association Inc., a subsidiary of Delaware North Companies, the track has featured Eclipse Award-winning sprinters Not Surprising, Groovy, and Safely Kept. Fio Rito shipped out of the western New York track to win the 1981 Whitney Handicap (G1) at Saratoga Race Course. In 2001, Shesastonecoldfox became the first horse based at Finger Lakes to compete in the Breeders' Cup World Championships. The New York Derby, which has been held at Finger Lakes since 1969, annually is the track's richest race. Video lottery terminals began operation at the track in February 2004. Funny Cide, winner of the 2003 Kentucky Derby (G1) and Preakness Stakes (G1), made the final start of his

career at Finger Lakes, winning the Wadsworth Memorial Handicap on July 4, 2007.

Location: 5857 Route 96, P.O. Box 25250, Farmington, N.Y. 14425-0250
Phone: (585) 924-3232
Fax: (585) 924-3967
Website: www.fingerlakesracetrack.com
Year Founded: 1962
Dates of Inaugural Meeting: May 23, 1962
Abbreviation: FL
Acreage: 450
Number of Stalls: 1,214
Seating Capacity: 6,000

Ownership
Delaware North Companies

Officers
President and General Manager: Christian Riegle
Director of Racing: Patrick Placito
Racing Secretary: Joe Colasacco
Assistant Racing Secretary: Carl Anderson
Senior Director of Marketing and Gaming: Steve Martin
Director of Finance: Vieden Zahariev
Director of Marketing: Brian Moore
Director of Mutuels: David Bridger
Director of Simulcasting: Patrick Placito
Horsemen's Liaison: Kim DeLong
Stewards: Rick Coyne
Track Announcer: Tony Calo
Track Photographer: Tom Cooley
Track Superintendent: Rick Brongo
Security: Al D'Agostino

Racing Dates
2007: April 14-December 1, 160 days
2008: April 19-December 6, 160 days

Track Layout
Main Circumference: 1 mile
Main Track Chute: 6 furlongs and 1 1/4 miles
Main Width: 85 feet
Main Length of Stretch: 960 feet

Attendance
Average Daily Recent Meeting: 1,467, 2007
Total Attendance Recent Meeting: 231,722, 2007
Highest Single-Day Recent Meeting: 11,429, July 4, 2007
Highest Single-Day Record: 15,344, September 3, 1962
Highest Single-Meeting Record: 698,113, 1974
Record Daily Average Single Meeting: 5,032, 1962
Lowest Single Meeting Record: 190,353, 2003

Handle
Total All-Sources Recent Meeting: $148,717,080, 2007
Average All-Sources Recent Meeting: $941,247, 2007
Total On-Track Recent Meeting: $11,738,299
Average On-Track Recent Meeting: $74,293, 2007
Largest Single-Day All-Sources Recent Meeting: $1,963,628, July 27. 2007
Largest Single-Day On-Track Recent Meeting: $333,413, July 4, 2007
Record Daily Average Single Meeting: $348,608, 1982
Single-Day On-Track Handle: $765,580, September 24, 1978
Single-Day All-Sources Handle: $2,549,108, October 3, 1989

Mutuel Records
Highest Pick Six: $161,490, June 21, 2001

Leaders
Career, Leading Jockey by Titles: Kevin Whitley, 9
Career, Leading Trainer by Titles: Michael S. Ferraro, 18
Recent Meeting, Leading Jockey: John Davila Jr., 158, 2007
Recent Meeting, Leading Trainer: Chris Englehart, 117, 2007
Recent Meeting, Leading Owner: My Purple Haze Stable, 41, 2007
Recent Meeting, Leading Horse: Sweet Lorena, 7, 2007

Single-Day Jockey Wins: John Davila Jr., 6, November 21, 2006; Robert Messina, 6, November 23, 2001; John Grabowski, 6, 2000; Carlos Dominguez, 6, 1995; Leslie Hulet, 6, 1995; Kevin Whitley, 6, 1989 and 1992; Roger Cox, 6, 1971
Single Meeting, Leading Jockey by Wins: John Grabowski, 233, 2000
Single Meeting, Leading Trainer by Wins: Chris J. Englehart, 141, 2006

Principal Races
New York Derby, New York Breeders' Futurity, Lady Finger S., Aspirant S., New York Oaks

Notable Events
$10.5-million gaming floor with 1,010 video lottery terminals opened in 2004.

Track Records, Main Dirt
4 1/2 furlongs: Top End, :50.60, April 8, 1998
5 furlongs: Wonderous Wise, :57 1/5, April 11, 1989; Bobby's Code, :57.20, April 8, 1998
5 1/2 furlongs: Hilary Star, 1:02 4/5, April 16, 1989; With It, 1:02.80, June 12, 1994; What a Rollick, 1:02.80, December 12, 1994
6 furlongs: Kelly Kip, 1:08.20, June 20, 1998
1 mile: Transact, 1:36.20, August 29, 1994; Fling n Roll, 1:36.20, November 29, 1995
1 mile 70 yds: Neverabettercity, 1:38.99, November 24, 2007
1 1/16 miles: Strider's Ormsby, 1:42.85, December 3, 2005
1 1/8 miles: Copper Mount, 1:48.80, August 27, 1994
1 3/16 miles: North Warning, 1:58.40, July 10, 1994
1 1/4 miles: Caramba, 2:05 1/5, July 11, 1987
1 1/2 miles: Brave Beast, 2:33.70, September 22, 1991
1 5/8 miles: North Warning, 2:46.60, September 4, 1994
Other: 2 furlongs, Broadway Blondie, :21.80, April 3, 1998

Fastest Times of 2007 (Dirt)
4 1/2 furlongs: Tale of Wonder, 5, :52.15, April 24, 2007
5 furlongs: Strong Case, 4, :57.64, May 25, 2007
5 1/2 furlongs: Toot Ta Roo, 4, 1:03.20, November 24, 2007
6 furlongs: A Very Young Jet, 5, 1:09.54, November 13, 2007
1 mile 40 yds: Maastricht, 6, 1:41.93, September 18, 2007
1 mile 70 yds: Neverabettercity, 3, 1:38.99, November 24, 2007
1 1/16 miles: Goldispretty, 3, 1:43.88, November 24, 2007
1 1/8 miles: Funny Cide, 7, 1:51.77, July 4, 2007
1 3/16 miles: J's Real Badge, 4, 2:02.28, July 30, 2007

Saratoga Race Course

An American landmark and one of the world's leading sports venues, Saratoga Race Course operates six weeks each year and draws huge crowds to the foothills of the Adirondack Mountains in historic Saratoga Springs, approximately 25 miles north of Albany. Saratoga set records for total attendance, average attendance, and single-day attendance in 2003. Opened August 2, 1864, Saratoga is the oldest existing track in America. Major renovations of the facility occurred in 1902, '28, '40, '65, '85, and 2000, when $8-million was spent to remodel the track's three main entrances, construct state-of-the-art jockeys' quarters, and restore an elegant 19th-century fountain in front of the clubhouse gate. Known as the "graveyard of champions," Saratoga has been host to many of Thoroughbred racing's greatest upsets, none more notable than Man o' War's only career loss to Upset in the 1919 Sanford Stakes. Other noteworthy upsets were Gallant Fox's loss in the 1930 Travers Stakes to 100-to-1 longshot Jim Dandy; Onion's shocking victory over Secretariat in the '73 Whitney Handicap (G2); and Runaway Groom's '82 Travers Stakes (G1) upset of Conquistador Cielo. Racing at Saratoga is enhanced annually by the Hall of Fame inductions at the National Mu-

seum of Racing, Fasig-Tipton's yearling sale, and the Jockey Club Round Table Conference.

Location: 267 Union Ave., Saratoga Springs, N.Y. 12866-0564
Phone: (518) 584-6200
Fax: (518) 587-4646
Website: www.nyra.com
E-Mail: nyra@nyrainc.com
Year Founded: 1863
Dates of Inaugural Meeting: August 3-6, 1863
Abbreviation: Sar
Acreage: 350
Number of Stalls: 1,830
Seating Capacity: 18,000

Ownership
New York Racing Association Inc.

Officers
Chairman: C. Steven Duncker
Vice Chairmen: Michael J. DelGiudice, James P. Heffernan, Stuart Subotnick
President and Chief Executive Officer: Charles E. Hayward
Executive Vice President and Chief Operating Officer: Harold G. Handel
Senior Vice President and General Counsel: Patrick L. Kehoe
Senior Vice President of Sales and Market Development: Gavin Landry
Senior Vice President and Chief Administrative Officer: John Ryan
Senior Vice President of Human Resources and Labor Relations: David Smukler
Vice President and Chief Financial Officer: Irene M. Posio
Vice President and Chief Information Officer: Tom Thill
Vice President of Pari-Mutuel Operations: Patrick Mahony
Vice President of Security: Kenneth T. Cook
Vice President of Facilities: John Tierney
Vice President and Director of Racing: Paul J. Campo
Vice President and Director of Simulcast Sales and Content Acquisition: Elizabeth Bracken
Director of Communications and Media Relations: John Lee
Director of Horsemen's Services: Carmen Barrera
Director of Marketing: Neema Ghazi
Director of Racing Surfaces: John Passero
OTB Relations: Robert Palumbo
Stable/Security Supervisor: Rick Wickman
Stewards: Braulio Baeza Jr., Carmine Donofrio, Dr. W. Theodore Hill, Stephen Lewandowski
Track Announcer: Tom Durkin, John Imbriale
Track Photographers: Adam Coglianese, Bob Coglianese

Racing Dates
2007: July 25-September 3, 36 days
2008: July 23-September 1, 36 days

Track Layout
Main Circumference: 1 1/8 miles
Main Track Chute: 7 furlongs
Main Width: 100 feet
Main Length of Stretch: 1,144 feet
Main Turf Circumference: 1 mile
Main Turf Length of Stretch: 1,144 feet
Inner Turf Circumference: 7 furlongs
Inner Turf Length of Stretch: 1,164 feet
Training Track: 1 mile

Attendance
Average Daily Recent Meeting: 26,627, 2007
Highest Single-Day Record: 71,337, August 17, 2003
Record Daily Average Single Meeting: 29,147, 2003
Highest Single-Meeting Record: 1,049,309, 2003
Total Attendance Recent Meeting: 958,574, 2007

Handle
Average All-Sources Recent Meeting: $16,184,892, 2007
Average On-Track Recent Meeting: $3,739,077, 2007
Record Daily Average Single Meeting: $3,742,773, 1993
Single-Day Record On-Track Handle: $9,390,934, August 23, 2003
Total All-Sources Recent Meeting: $582,656,103, 2007
Total On-Track Recent Meeting: $134,606,756, 2007
Record Total Single Meeting: $134,606,756, 2007

Mutuel Records
Highest Trifecta: $63,624, August 22, 1974
Highest Daily Double: $4,313.90, August 27, 1945

Leaders
Career, Leading Jockey by Titles: Angel Cordero Jr., 14
Career, Leading Trainer by Titles: William I. Mott, 9
Recent Meeting, Leading Jockey: Cornelio Velasquez, 44, 2007
Recent Meeting, Leading Trainer: William I. Mott, 27, 2007
Recent Meeting, Leading Owner: Zayat Stables, 18, 2007
Recent Meeting, Leading Horse: 20 tied with 2, 2007

Records
Single-Day Jockey Wins: John Velazquez, 6, September 3, 2001
Single Meeting, Leading Jockey by Wins: John Velazquez, 65, 2004
Single Meeting, Leading Trainer by Wins: Todd Pletcher, 35, 2003; Todd Pletcher, 35, 2004

Principal Races
Travers S. (G1), Whitney H. (G1), Alabama S. (G1), Sword Dancer Invitational H. (G1), Diana S. (G1), Woodward S. (G1), Personal Ensign S. (G1)

Track Records, Main Dirt
5 furlongs: Fabulous Force, :56.71, August 18, 1993
5 1/2 furlongs: J Be K, 1:03.13, August 29, 2007
6 furlongs: Spanish Riddle, 1:08, August 18, 1972; Speightstown, 1:08.04, August 14, 2004
6 1/2 furlongs: Topsider, 1:14 2/5, August 1, 1979
7 furlongs: Darby Creek Road, 1:20 2/5, August 8, 1978
1 mile: Key Contender, 1:34.72, August 9, 1992
1 1/16 miles: Lawyer Ron, 1:46.64, July 28, 2007; Shakis (Ire), 1:46.64, August 25, 2007
1 3/16 miles: Winter's Tale, 1:54 3/5, August 21, 1982
1 1/4 miles: General Assembly, 2:00, August 18, 1979
1 5/8 miles: Green Highlander, 2:43.57, August 15, 1991
2 miles: James Boswell, 3:26, August 11, 1983

Track Records, Main Turf
5 1/2 furlongs: Second in Command, 1:01.11, August 14, 2006
1 1/16 miles: Fourstardave, 1:38.91, July 29, 1991
1 1/8 miles: Tentam, 1:45 2/5, August 10, 1973; Waya (Fr), 1:45 2/5, August 21, 1978
1 3/16 miles: Phi Beta Doc, 1:51.61, September 1, 1999
1 5/8 miles: Tom Swift, 2:37, August 23, 1978
Other: 2 1/16 miles, Popular Victory, 3:31 2/5, August 23, 1979

Track Records, Inner Turf
1 mile: L'Oiseau d'Argent, 1:33.42, August 5, 2004
1 1/16 miles: Leroideanimaux, 1:39.92, August 27, 2005
1 1/8 miles: Amarettitorun, 1:46.22, July 26, 1997
1 3/8 miles: Babinda (GB), 2:12, July 26, 1997
1 1/2 miles: Awad, 2:23.20, August 9, 1997

Fastest Times of 2007 (Dirt)
5 furlongs: Syriana's Song, 2, :57.48, August 22, 2007
5 1/2 furlongs: J Be K, 2, 1:03.13, August 29, 2007
6 furlongs: Diabolical, 4, 1:08.67, July 28, 2007
6 1/2 furlongs: Lord Snowdon, 4, 1:15.23, July 25, 2007
7 furlongs: Midnight Lute, 4, 1:21.06, September 1, 2007; Wait a While, 4, 1:21.06, August 23, 2007
1 1/16 miles: Lawyer Ron, 4, 1:46.64, July 28, 2007; Shakis (Ire), 7, 1:46.64, August 25, 2007
1 3/16 miles: Nunnery, 4, 1:59.89, August 10, 2007
1 1/4 miles: Street Sense, 3, 2:02.69, August 25, 2007
2 miles: Touchdown Peyton, 3, 3:27.91, August 18, 2007

Fastest Times of 2007 (Turf)
5 1/2 furlongs: Beau Dare, 4, 1:01.47, August 31, 2007
1 mile: Shakespeare, 6, 1:34.14, July 26, 2007
1 1/16 miles: Classic Neel, 3, 1:40.08, September 3, 2007
1 1/8 miles: Criminologist, 4, 1:45.61, August 29, 2007
1 3/16 miles: Prom Party, 3, 1:53.70, August 29, 2007
1 3/8 miles: Rosinka (Ire), 4, 2:13, September 3, 2007

1½ miles: Grand Couturier (GB), 4, 2:26.59, August 11, 2007
1⅝ miles: Revved Up, 9, 2:42.67, August 19, 2007
2¹/₁₆ miles: Footlights, 7, 3:43.55, July 26, 2007
2⅜ miles: Divine Fortune, 4, 4:19.92, August 16, 2007

North Dakota

North Dakota Horse Park

Location: 5180 19th Ave. N., P.O. Box 1917, Fargo, N.D. 58107-1917
Phone: (701) 277-8027
Website: www.northdakotahorsepark.org
E-Mail: info@hrnd.org
Abbreviation: Far
Acreage: 113
Number of Stalls: 400

Officers
President and Chairman: Dr. James Tilton
Vice President: Ryan Roshau
General Manager: Heather Benson
Director of Racing: Leslie A. Schmidt
Director of Marketing: June Renvall
Racing Secretary: James Collins
Secretary: Carolyn Goerger
Treasurer: Buel Sonderland
Stewards: Sam Lato
Track Announcer: Bubby Haar
Track Superintendent: Glen Thompson

Racing Dates
2007: July 26-September 3, 20 days
2008: August 1-September 1, 16 days

Track Layout
Main Circumference: 6½ furlongs
Main Track Chute: 2 furlongs and 6 furlongs
Main Width: 80 feet

Leaders
Recent Meeting, Leading Jockey: Jake Olesiak, 24, 2007
Recent Meeting, Leading Trainer: Dave Bernhardt, 12, 2007
Recent Meeting, Leading Horse: 13 tied with 2, 2007

Principal Races
North Dakota-bred Derby, North Dakota-bred Futurity, Dean Kutz Memorial S., North Dakota-bred Inaugural S., North Dakota-bred HRND S.

Fastest Times of 2007 (Dirt)
4 furlongs: Nicandro, 5, :47.40, August 31, 2007
4½ furlongs: Flyin Sky High, 4, :54.40, August 31, 2007
5 furlongs: Award Winning Team, 7, 1:00.60, August 31, 2007
5½ furlongs: Mean U Gene, 6, 1:07, August 31, 2007
6 furlongs: Tactical Delight, 7, 1:13.60, August 19, 2007
7 furlongs: Tactical Delight, 7, 1:28.20, September 1, 2007
1 mile: Canterbury Gold, 5, 1:40.40, September 3, 2007
1¹/₁₆ miles: Tiger Jet, 4, 1:50, August 19, 2007

Ohio

Beulah Park

Ohio's oldest racetrack, Beulah Park is located in Grove City, south of Columbus. Operating since 1923, the track offered a spring meet that once was a popular stopping point for horses in transit from Florida to New York. Beulah was started by successful paving contractor Robert J. Dienst. After Dienst's death, ownership of the track passed to his son, Robert Y. Dienst. In 1983, the younger Dienst sold Beulah, which passed through a succession of owners and was known as Darby Downs from 1983 to '86. Current owner Charles Ruma restored the track's original name in 1986. Under Ruma's leadership, Beulah was the first Ohio track to offer simulcasting, phone wagering, and Internet wagering through its www.winticket.com website, the online portal of AmericaTab, which was principally owned by Beulah and River Downs until its purchase by Churchill Downs Inc. in 2007. Along with Thistledown and River Downs, Beulah shares host duties for the annual Best of Ohio day, which offers five stakes races for Ohio-breds.

Location: 3811 Southwest Blvd., P.O. Box 850, Grove City, Oh. 43123-0850
Phone: (614) 871-9600
Fax: (614) 871-0433
Website: www.beulahpark.com
E-Mail: mikeweiss@beulahpark.com
Year Founded: 1923
Dates of Inaugural Meeting: April 21, 1923
Abbreviation: Beu
Number of Stalls: 1,200
Seating Capacity: 7,200

Ownership
Charles Ruma

Officers
President: Charles J. Ruma
Vice President and General Manager: Michael Weiss
Director of Racing: Ed Vomacka
Director of Operations and Mutuels: Holly Freking
Director of Finance: Jim McKinney
Director of Marketing and Publicity: Jessica Hamlin
Director of Simulcasting: Gina Schmidt
Horsemen's Liaison: Joe DeLuca
Stewards: James Beck, Joe DeLuca
Track Announcer: Bill Downes
Track Photographer: Harry Kaplan
Track Superintendent: Ernest Ratcliff

Racing Dates
2007: January 6-May 5, 77 days; October 8-December 21, 49 days
2008: January 7-May 3, 78 days; October 14-December 20, 51 days

Track Layout
Main Circumference: 1 mile
Main Track Chute: 6 furlongs and 1¼ miles
Main Width: 78 feet
Main Length of Stretch: 1,100 feet
Main Turf Circumference: 6 furlongs, less 223 feet

Handle
Total On-Track Recent Meeting: $7,417,144, Winter-Spring and Fall 2007
Average On-Track Recent Meeting: $57,946, Winter-Spring and Fall 2007
Record Total All-Sources Single Meeting: $112,983,481, Winter-Spring 2006
Record Average All-Sources Single Meeting: $1,506,446, Winter-Spring 2006

Leaders
Recent Meeting, Leading Jockey: Edgar Paucar, 123, Winter-Spring 2008
Recent Meeting, Leading Trainer: Charles Lawson, 39, Winter-Spring 2008
Recent Meeting, Leading Horse: Mystery Novel, 4, Winter-Spring 2008; Blazing Forest, 4, Winter-Spring 2008

Principal Races
Royal North S., Howard B. Noonan S., Babst/Palacios Memorial H., Ohio Freshman S., Glacial Princess S.

Notable Events
Best of Ohio Day

Track Records, Main Dirt

4 furlongs: Float Away, :46²/₅, May 12, 1938
4½ furlongs: Last Rebel, :50.96, April 18, 2003
5 furlongs: Love Pappa Mucci, :56.75, February 11, 1994
5½ furlongs: Long Star, 1:02.33, January 26, 2007
6 furlongs: Whatta Brave, 1:08.50, October 29, 2000
1 mile: Appygolucky, 1:35.47, January 17, 2003
1 mile 70 yds: King's Wailea, 1:40.15, November 19, 1993
1¹/₁₆ miles: Din's Dancer, 1:40⁴/₅, November 3, 1990
1⅛ miles: Lord Try On, 1:48.96, September 26, 1992
1³/₁₆ miles: World of Magic, 1:55, September 21, 1991
1¼ miles: On the Scent, 2:00.22, October 19, 1991
1½ miles: Doctor's Romance, 2:29.50, March 26, 1994
1⅝ miles: Big Beans, 2:46, October 5, 1957
1¾ miles: Dot Your Eye, 2:57³/₅, October 20, 1971
2 miles: Littlemagbrother, 3:25.69, December 20, 2005
Other: 2 furlongs, Go Chop, :21³/₅, May 7, 1989; 2 miles 70 yds, Benomen, 3:29.81, November 20, 1993; 2¹/₁₆ miles, She Looks Great, 3:41²/₅, November 28, 1983; 2⅛ miles, Second City, 3:48⁴/₅, November 25, 1984; 2¼ miles, Hallay's Pride, 3:48.90, May 4, 1991

Track Records, Main Turf

1 mile: Gaelic Cross, 1:35²/₅, September 23, 1987
1 mile 70yds: Twin To Win, 1:41, October 24, 1986
1⅜ miles: Syncospin, 2:12³/₅, September 25, 1987
1⅝ miles: Nigilik, 2:48¹/₅, October 24, 1986
Other: a6 furlongs, Brent's Gail, 1:07, September 1, 1986; a1 mile, Khal Me Sir, 1:38.60, October 4, 1992; a1 mile 70yds, Nail's McNally, 1:40²/₅, October 1, 1988; a1⅜ miles, Spend Ten, 2:12⁴/₅, October 8, 1988; a2 miles, Persian Jig, 3:23²/₅, May 17, 1987

Fastest Times of 2007 (Dirt)

4½ furlongs: One Way Out, 5, :52.44, March 14, 2007
5 furlongs: Unwavering Flight, 6, :57.18, January 30, 2007
5½ furlongs: Long Star, 8, 1:02.33, January 26, 2007
6 furlongs: Sarotess, 7, 1:09.39, January 29, 2007
1 mile: Turncoat Jim, 8, 1:36.28, February 9, 2007
1 mile 70 yds: Tambos Sword Dance, 6, 1:42.02, January 26, 2007
1¹/₁₆ miles: Plenty of Jacks, 7, 1:45.21, February 7, 2007
1⅛ miles: Cryptoquip, 4, 1:50.32, October 6, 2007
1¼ miles: Hoofin' It, 5, 2:03.60, February 9, 2007
1½ miles: Argentia Bay, 5, 2:37.97, February 26, 2007
1¾ miles: Learbo, 5, 3:04.40, March 19, 2007
2 miles: Mount Tora Bora, 7, 3:36.64, December 22, 2007
2¼ miles: Honor Prayer, 6, 4:06.34, May 5, 2007

River Downs

With the Ohio River serving as an attractive and sometimes destructive backdrop, River Downs has been part of the southern Ohio racing scene for more than 75 years. The track at Cincinnati's eastern edge opened in July 1925 as Coney Island racetrack. A crowd of 10,000 packed the facility for opening day, according to River Downs historians, and the track was off to a fast start. But the floods of 1937 put a temporary stop to that. The track was rebuilt following the flood and reopened as River Downs. Sixty years later, the track again endured major Ohio River flooding, but once more the track was cleaned up and reopened. The track's grandstand had undergone an extensive renovation in the 1980s. River Downs offers a pair of quality two-year-old stakes every year in the Cradle and the Bassinet (for fillies). The 1984 Cradle was won by Spend a Buck, who the next year won the Kentucky Derby (G1). River Downs was one of the first tracks at which Racing Hall of Fame jockey Steve Cauthen competed. In a 2007 promotion, Cincinnati Bengals wide receiver Chad Johnson beat a Thoroughbred, Restore the Roar, in a one-furlong race on River Down's turf course. Johnson was given a 100-yard head start in "The Man versus Beast" match race. Bengals receiver Cris Collinsworth lost to a Thoroughbred in a similar race in 1993. River Downs was also the site of jockey Perry Ouzts's 5,000th career victory on August 21, 2007.

Location: 6301 Kellogg Ave., P.O. Box 30286, Cincinnati, Oh. 45230-0826
Phone: (513) 232-8000
Fax: (513) 232-1412
Website: *www.riverdowns.com*
E-Mail: info@riverdowns.com
Year Founded: 1925
Dates of Inaugural Meeting: July 6, 1925
Abbreviation: RD
Number of Stalls: 1,350
Seating Capacity: 9,350

Ownership

Dr. J. David Rutherford Partnership

Officers

Chairman: J. David Rutherford
President and General Manager: Jack Hanessian
Vice President: Martin J. Stringer
Director of Racing and Racing Secretary: Ed Vomacka
Director of Operations: Kathy Ewing
Director of Communications/Publicity: John Engelhardt
Director of Marketing: Ed Meyer
Director of Mutuels: Larry Alexander
Director of Simulcasting: Vincent Cyster
Assistant Racing Secretary: Tim Richardson
Stewards: Mike Manganello, Vince Clark, Herb Clark
Track Superintendent: Jim Cornett
Horsemen's Bookkeeper: Terry Moore
Track Announcer: Keith Aiello
Track Photographer: Patrick Lang

Racing Dates

2007: April 6-September 3, 105 days
2008: April 11-September 1, 103 days

Track Layout

Main Circumference: 1 mile
Main Track Chute: 6 furlongs and 1¼ miles
Main Width: 80 feet
Main Length of Stretch: 1,117 feet
Main Turf Circumference: 7 furlongs

Handle

Average On-Track Recent Meeting: \$132,778, 2007
Total On-Track Recent Meeting: \$14,340,087, 2007
Single-Day On-Track Recent Meeting: \$470,427, September 2, 2007
Single-Day All-Sources Recent Meeting: \$1,710, 054, May 22, 2007
Average All-Sources Recent Meeting: \$765,018, 2007
Total On-Track Recent Meeting: \$80,326,946, 2007

Leaders

Recent Meeting, Leading Jockey: Edgar Paucar, 52, 2007
Recent Meeting, Leading Trainer: William Doug Cowans, 13, 2007
Career, Leading Jockey by Stakes Wins: Eugene Sipus Jr., 25; Sebastian Madrid, 25
Career, Leading Owner by Stakes Wins: Woodburn Farm, 16
Career, Leading Trainer by Stakes Wins: James E. Morgan, 52

Records

Single Meeting, Leading Jockey by Wins: Dean Sarvis, 83, 2004

Principal Races

Cradle S., Bassinet S.

Interesting Facts

Previous Names and Dates: Coney Island (1925-'37)

Track Records, Main Dirt

4½ furlongs: One Bad Dude, :52.20, July 9, 2004
5 furlongs: Banker's Forbes, :57.60, June 7, 1994

5 1/2 furlongs: Tazua, 1:03, August 1, 1964
6 furlongs: Francine M., 1:08 3/5, July 4, 1969
1 mile: Dondougold, 1:36 1/5, July 25, 1970; Alladin Rib, 1:36 1/5, August 8, 1988
1 mile 70 yds: South Dakota, 1:40, August 4, 1945
1 1/16 miles: Ingenero White, 1:41 4/5, July 5, 1969; Irish Dude, 1:41 4/5, July 5, 1969
1 1/8 miles: Brown Sugar, 1:49, September 2, 1925
1 1/4 miles: Crusader, 2:02, July 24, 1926
1 1/2 miles: South Dakota, 2:30 3/5, July 1, 1950
1 5/8 miles: Sada, 2:45 3/5, Ocotber 13, 1934
1 3/4 miles: Brigler, 2:59 3/5, October 19, 1940
2 miles: South Dakota, 3:21 2/5, July 8, 1950
Other: 1 11/16 miles, Distribute, 2:51 3/5, September 7, 1940; 1 7/8 miles, Shot Bills, 3:26 3/5, August 19, 1979; 2 miles 70 yds, Omar, 3:33 3/5, September 2, 1940; 2 1/4 miles, Almac, 3:54, October 31, 1936; 2 1/2 miles, Here Come Midge, 4:30 4/5, June 17, 1972; 3 miles 70 yds, Gloria Dream, 5:32 2/5, August 9, 1972

Track Records, Main Turf
4 1/2 furlongs: Adena, :50 4/5, April 26, 1977
5 furlongs: Long Star, :55.80, May 22, 2007
7 1/2 furlongs: Stormy Deep, 1:28 2/5, August 15, 1990
1 mile: Bad News Blues, 1:34.20, July 23, 1994
1 1/16 miles: Franchise Player, 1:40.60, June 12, 1994
1 3/8 miles: Hi Rise, 2:15.60, August 15, 2000
1 1/2 miles: Rebel Thunder, 2:28, June 28, 1996
Other: 1 7/16 miles, Dina's Pl'ymate, 2:25, August 30, 1969; 1 7/8 miles, Big Bettor, 3:10 1/5, May 31, 1986; 2 1/4 miles, Buteo, 3:48 2/5, September 3, 1990

Fastest Times of 2007 (Dirt)
4 1/2 furlongs: Mighty Big Man, 2, :54.20, May 1, 2007
5 furlongs: Never Forget, 3, :58.60, May 26, 2007
5 1/2 furlongs: Jp'shanna, 5, 1:04.60, July 7, 2007
6 furlongs: Catlaunch, 6, 1:10.20, April 21, 2007
1 mile: What the Devil, 5, 1:38.80, July 7, 2007
1 mile 70 yds: R P's Command, 3, 1:44.20, June 8, 2007
1 1/16 miles: Mini Mom, 3, 1:46.60, July 1, 2007
1 1/8 miles: Pay the Man, 3, 1:52.40, July 21, 2007
1 1/4 miles: Howard's Creek, 5, 2:05.60, July 8, 2007
1 5/8 miles: Archie B, 6, 2:51.40, August 5, 2007

Fastest Times of 2007 (Turf)
5 furlongs: Long Star, 8, :55.80, May 22, 2007
7 1/2 furlongs: Pyrite Personal, 3, 1:29, May 20, 2007
1 mile: Big Blue Slew, 5, 1:36, May 29, 2007
1 1/16 miles: The Potters Hand, 7, 1:41.40, June 16, 2007
1 1/2 miles: Timber Knot, 5, 2:31.20, July 22, 2007
1 7/8 miles: Pirate's Bid, 5, 3:14, September 3, 2007

Thistledown

Thistledown in suburban Cleveland is the home of Ohio's most important race, the Ohio Derby (G2). Opened on July 20, 1925, Thistledown was owned and operated by the DeBartolo family from 1959 through '99, when the track was purchased by Magna Entertainment Corp. Thistledown has inside its grandstand an interactive Starting Gate educational museum, which features exhibits, weekly handicapping seminars, and information on racing in Ohio. In 2000, the track reconfigured the outdoor paddock area, adding more than 9,000 square feet and such amenities as picnic tables, television monitors, and mutuel windows. The North Randall track typically races from April through late fall. A referendum that would have allowed alternative initiatives at Thistledown was defeated in November 2006.

Location: 21501 Emery Rd., North Randall, Oh. 44128-4513
Phone: (216) 662-8600, (800) 289-9956
Fax: (216) 662-5339

Website: www.thistledown.com
E-Mail: info@thistledown.com
Year Founded: 1924
Dates of Inaugural Meeting: July 20, 1925
Abbreviation: Tdn
Acreage: 128
Number of Stalls: 1,528
Seating Capacity: 5,878

Ownership
Magna Entertainment Corp.

Officers
Chairman: Frank Stronach
General Manager: Brent Reitz
Director of Racing: L. William Couch
Racing Secretary: Patrick Ellsworth
Controller: Rita Seuffert
Director of Operations: David Ellsworth
Director of Marketing: Heather McColloch
Director of Mutuels: Robert Hickey
Director of Publicity: Bob Roberts
Director of Simulcasting: Greg Davis
Steward: Philip T. Gore
Track Announcer: Matt Hook
Track Photographer: Jeff Zamaiko
Track Superintendent: John Banno
Horsemen's Bookkeeper: Frank Koch
Security: Arthur Pierre

Racing Dates
2007: April 12-November 19, 136 days
2008: May 1-October 25, 122 days

Track Layout
Main Circumference: 1 mile
Main Track Chute: 6 furlongs and 1 1/4 miles
Main Width: Homestretch: 95 feet; Backstretch: 75 feet
Main Length of Stretch: 978 feet

Attendance
Highest Single-Day Record: 19,411, June 18, 1978
Record Daily Average Single Meeting: 7,049, 1954
Highest Single-Meeting Record: 986,095, 1979

Handle
Total All-Sources Recent Meeting: $175,938,781, 2007
Average All-Sources Recent Meeting: $484,680, 2007

Mutuel Records
Highest Win: $500.20, Nobody's Secret, November 22, 1995
Highest Daily Double: $4,553.40, June 8, 1967
Highest Pick Six: $89,306.20, November 29, 1985

Leaders
Career, Leading Jockey by Titles: Michael Rowland, 29
Career, Leading Trainer by Titles: Gary Johnson, 24
Recent Meeting, Leading Jockey: Scott Spieth, 106, 2007
Recent Meeting, Leading Trainer: Jeff Radosevich, 94, 2007
Recent Meeting, Leading Owner: Bridgett Sipp, 45, 2007
Recent Meeting, Leading Horse: P.P.'s to Follow, 5, 2007

Records
Single-Day Jockey Wins: Buddy Haas, 6, August 28, 1933; John Adams, 6, September 2, 1942; Danny Weiler, 6, August 12, 1961; Anthony Rini, 6, June 12, 1970; Antonio Graell, 6, February 21, 1976; Benny Feliciano, 6, June 18, 1978; Antonio Graell, 6, November 14, 1980; Tom Ford, 6, December 13, 1982; Brian Mills, 6, August 28, 1983; Michael Rowland, 6, March 29, 1991; Michael Rowland, 6, October 19, 1999
Single-Day Trainer Wins: Gary Johnson, 6, November 27, 1999
Single Meeting, Leading Jockey by Wins: Antonio Graell, 338, 1976
Single Meeting, Leading Trainer by Wins: Jeffrey A. Radosevich, 119, 2005

Principal Races
Ohio Derby (G2), Cleveland Gold Cup S., Rose DeBartolo Memorial S., Governor's Buckeye Cup S.

Track Records, Main Dirt

4 furlongs: Ifufeelfroggyleap, :45.30, October 8, 2004
$4\frac{1}{2}$ furlongs: Onion Roll, :51.57, November 20, 1992
5 furlongs: Jet Bupers, :$57\frac{2}{5}$, June 4, 1978; Great Allegiance, :57.56, May 18, 1997
$5\frac{1}{2}$ furlongs: Down Thepike Mike, 1:03.20, August 10, 1998
6 furlongs: Fancy Threat, 1:$08\frac{2}{5}$, November 21, 1987
1 mile: Setting Limits, 1:$35\frac{3}{5}$, November 17, 1989
1 mile 40 yds: Ifthisbe Britches, 1:$38\frac{3}{5}$, December 8, 1989; North Island, 1:$38\frac{3}{5}$, December 9, 1989
1 mile 70 yds: Wisdom Seeker, 1:40.92, July 22, 1995
$1\frac{1}{16}$ miles: Entitled to Star, 1:41.32, November 25, 1995
$1\frac{1}{8}$ miles: Smarten, 1:$47\frac{2}{5}$, June 17, 1979
$1\frac{3}{16}$ miles: Smoke Screen, 1:$55\frac{3}{5}$, July 17, 1954
$1\frac{1}{4}$ miles: Pert Near, 2:03, December 1, 1979
$1\frac{1}{2}$ miles: Martha's Wave, 2:$31\frac{4}{5}$, June 18, 1955
$1\frac{5}{8}$ miles: Alsang, 2:46, August 8, 1936
$1\frac{3}{4}$ miles: Mala Kee, 2:$57\frac{3}{5}$, July 19, 1957
2 miles: Likely Advice, 3:27, December 15, 1980
Other: 2 furlongs, Onion Roll, :20.95, September 27, 1993; 5 furlongs, 580 feet, Wishing, 1:03, July 13, 1940; $1\frac{9}{16}$ miles, Military Girl, 2:$44\frac{1}{5}$, June 13, 1942; a$1\frac{11}{16}$ miles, Military Girl, 2:49, August 17, 1940; 2m 40 yds, Winning Mark, 3:$29\frac{2}{5}$, July 20, 1940; 2m 70 yds, Lonely Cloud, 3:$41\frac{3}{5}$, May 13, 1990; $2\frac{1}{16}$ miles, Bunker, 3:$32\frac{4}{5}$, July 13, 1955; $2\frac{1}{8}$ miles, Lonely Cloud, 3:52.65, July 3, 1992; $2\frac{3}{16}$ miles, Current Data, 3:$54\frac{3}{5}$, December 5, 1981; $2\frac{1}{4}$ miles, Son Richard, 3:$54\frac{3}{5}$, August 27, 1938; $2\frac{11}{16}$ miles, Bea Beauty, 4:$47\frac{4}{5}$, September 8, 1973; 3m 40 yds, Bea Beauty, 5:$31\frac{4}{5}$, September 22, 1973; $3\frac{5}{8}$ miles, Eastern Promise, 6:$49\frac{3}{5}$, October 6, 1973

Fastest Times of 2007 (Dirt)

2 furlongs: Hunterpunter, 3, :21.56, October 15, 2007
4 furlongs: Chicken Soup Kid, 7, :45.80, April 28, 2007
$4\frac{1}{2}$ furlongs: Eye Need a Drink, 3, :53.72, October 6, 2007
5 furlongs: Benjamin Baby, 5, :58.40, August 3, 2007
$5\frac{1}{2}$ furlongs: Little Nicky Regs, 6, 1:04.50, August 27, 2007
6 furlongs: Trophy Road, 3, 1:09.66, November 19, 2007
1 mile: Kannapolis, 6, 1:39.10, April 20, 2007
1 mile 40 yds: Rhodesleadtoheaven, 4, 1:42.44, May 31, 2007
1 mile 70 yds: Pyrite Springs, 5, 1:43.09, June 28, 2007
$1\frac{1}{16}$ miles: Pay the Man, 3, 1:45.24, June 9, 2007
$1\frac{1}{8}$ miles: Delightful Kiss, 3, 1:49.36, June 2, 2007
$1\frac{3}{16}$ miles: Grades Gold, 7, 2:01.45, June 23, 2007
$1\frac{1}{4}$ miles: Catlaunch, 6, 2:04.40, September 3, 2007
$1\frac{1}{2}$ miles: Honor Prayer, 6, 2:37.70, August 17, 2007

Oklahoma

Blue Ribbon Downs

Blue Ribbon Downs, located near Sallisaw, was developed by Blue Ribbon Ranch owner Bill Hedge on ranch property. It first offered racing in 1960 as a non-pari-mutuel racetrack, with all business operations based in Hedge's house. In 1973, Hedge sold the track to a group of investors. A decade later, Blue Ribbon was the first track to offer pari-mutuel racing in Oklahoma, but fire destroyed its grandstand two weeks before the 1983 meet was to open. Within one week, a new grandstand was erected. The track's richest Thoroughbred race is the Oklahoma-bred Thoroughbred Futurity for two-year-olds. The track conducts Thoroughbred, Quarter Horse, Appaloosa, and Paint racing from mid-February to early December. In 2004, the Oklahoma Legislature approved electronic gaming and non-house card games for Blue Ribbon and two other state tracks.

Location: 3700 W. Cherokee, P.O. Box 489, Sallisaw, Ok. 74955
Phone: (918) 775-7771
Fax: (918) 775-5805
Website: *www.blueribbondowns.net*
E-Mail: brd@blueribbondowns.net
Year Founded: 1960
Abbreviation: BRD
Acreage: 165
Number of Stalls: 1,064 Stalls
Seating Capacity: 3,500

Ownership

Backstretch LLC

Officers

President: Janie Dillard
Vice President: James Dry
General Manager: Blaine Story
Director of Racing and Racing Secretary: James Parsley
Treasurer: De Ellis
Director of Marketing: Bonnie Cusimano
Director of Mutuels: Rebeka Swain
Director of Publicity: Judy Allen
Director of Simulcasting: Charlie Bowen
Track Photographer: Gene Wilson and Associates
Track Superintendent: Clifford Frank
Security: Kevin Philpot
Horsemen's Bookkeeper: Jinx Blades

Racing Dates

2007: March 2-March 17, 3 days; August 3-December 2, 67 days
2008: March 1-March 15, 3 days; August 1-November 30, 67 days

Track Layout

Main Circumference: 7 furlongs, 30 yards
Main Track Chute: 6 furlongs and $1\frac{1}{8}$ miles
Main Width: 72 feet
Main Length of Stretch: 845 feet

Attendance

Highest Single-Day Record: 10,169, August 30, 1984

Handle

Average All-Sources Recent Meeting: $66,409, Fall 2007
Average On-Track Recent Meeting: $13,801, Fall 2007
Total All-Sources Recent Meeting: $5,352,244, Fall 2007
Total On-Track Recent Meeting: $952,292, Fall 2007

Leaders

Recent Meeting, Leading Jockey: Aldaberto Candanosa, 68, Fall 2007
Recent Meeting, Leading Trainer: Luis Villafranco, 57, Fall 2007
Recent Meeting, Leading Owner: Henry J. Smith, 16, Fall 2007

Track Records, Main Dirt

4 furlongs: Iwontbeback, :44.35, July 3, 1995
$4\frac{1}{2}$ furlongs: Rebel's Jon, :50.35, June 29, 1996
5 furlongs: Pow Wow Al, :56.45, May 27, 1996
$5\frac{1}{2}$ furlongs: Rebel's Jon, 1:02, October 1, 1995
6 furlongs: Rebel's Jon, 1:08.45, July 9, 1995
7 furlongs: Prententious Chief, 1:23, September 10, 1995
$7\frac{1}{2}$ furlongs: Karate Kick, 1:29.35, September 17, 1994
1 mile: Staged Attraction, 1:36.15, June 10, 1989
$1\frac{1}{16}$ miles: Just Ask Rudy, 1:43.15, April 6, 1996
$1\frac{1}{8}$ miles: Long On Rowdy, 1:49.35, July 17, 1994
$1\frac{1}{4}$ miles: Dare More, 2:03.35, August 28, 1994
$1\frac{3}{8}$ miles: Say It All, 2:17.15, October 1, 1995
$1\frac{1}{2}$ miles: Mr. Sanhedrin, 2:32.35, November 14, 1993
$1\frac{5}{8}$ miles: Sharp's Caliber, 2:47.15, December 11, 1994

Fastest Times of 2007 (Dirt)

4 furlongs: Garbu's Tab, 4, :44.58, August 12, 2007
$4\frac{1}{2}$ furlongs: Tethras Lil Mimi, 4, :51.23, September 23, 2007
5 furlongs: Blazin Brinlea, 5, :56.92, October 12, 2007
$5\frac{1}{2}$ furlongs: Come On Helen, 5, 1:02.61, October 26, 2007
6 furlongs: Gentlemen's Gun, 4, 1:09, December 8, 2007
7 furlongs: Photo Baba, 7, 1:24.05, September 2, 2007

7½ furlongs: Wood Tak, 4, 1:30.99, November 23, 2007
1 mile: Sheik of Wagoner, 6, 1:36.88, August 24, 2007

Fair Meadows at Tulsa

Offering nighttime Thoroughbred, Quarter Horse, Paint, and Appaloosa racing on its five-furlong oval, Fair Meadows at Tulsa is one of the entertainment facilities located at Expo Square, which hosts the Tulsa State Fair and some 400 other events each year. Fair Meadows, which has been conducting live racing since 1989, is located on a former auto-racing oval and is next to the stadium of the Tulsa Drillers, a minor-league baseball team affiliated with the Colorado Rockies. During racing season, a giant net between the stadium and Fair Meadows keeps foul balls from landing on the track's final turn. Expo Square includes an amusement park, water park, and hotel, and Fair Meadows offers a state-of-the-art simulcasting facility that operates year-round.

Location: 4705 E. 21st St., P.O. Box 4735, Tulsa, Ok. 74159
Phone: (918) 743-7223
Fax: (918) 743-8053
Website: www.fairmeadows.com
E-Mail: racing@fairmeadows.com
Abbreviation: FMT

Officers
General Manager and Director of Racing: Ron Shotts
Director of Operations: Don Paul Allison
Director of Marketing and Publicity: Richard Linihan
Director of Mutuels: Don Fontenot
Director of Simulcasting: Kevin Jones
Horsemen's Liaison: Troy Herron
Track Photographer: Gene Wilson and Associates
Track Superintendent: Don Paul Allison

Racing Dates
2007: May 22-July 28, 34 days
2008: May 20-July 26, 34 days

Track Layout
Main Circumference: 5 furlongs
Main Track Chute: 4 furlongs and 6½ furlongs

Attendance
Average Daily Recent Meeting: 776, 2007
Total Attendance Recent Meeting: 26,387, 2007

Handle
Total All-Sources Recent Meeting: $4,613,088, 2007
Average All-Sources Recent Meeting: $135,679, 2007
Total On-Track Recent Meeting: $1,946,196, 2007
Average On-Track Recent Meeting: $57,241, 2007

Leaders
Recent Meeting, Leading Jockey: Curtis Kimes, 35, 2007
Recent Meeting, Leading Trainer: Luis Villafranco, 22, 2007

Principal Races
Tulsa Dash S., Boomer S., Route 66 S., Muscogee (Creek) Nation S.

Track Records, Main Dirt
4 furlongs: Rachelsarompin, :44, June 24, 2006
5½ furlongs: Double Jack, 1:03.80, August 1, 2001
6 furlongs: Herecomesthemann, 1:10.60, June 11, 2005
6½ furlongs: Tic Tic, 1:16.60, July 10, 1998
1 mile: Yours Forever, 1:36.80, July 27, 2006
1¹⁄₁₆ miles: Stop the Bluffing, 1:45.60, May 29, 2003
1⅛ miles: Demascus Slew, 1:51.80, May 30, 1998
1⅜ miles: Second Avie, 2:20, August 5, 1995
1⅝ miles: Phantom Cottage, 2:51.80, August 1, 1992

Fastest Times of 2007 (Dirt)
4 furlongs: Catconquersall, 5, :45, June 9, 2007; Dr. Ginny, 4, :45, June 7, 2007; Fashionable Steve, 7, :45, June 23, 2007; Shadow's Image, 8, :45, June 15, 2007, Stars and Glitter, 5, :45, June 24, 2007; Talkin Fine, 6, :45, June 8, 2007
5½ furlongs: Farlo, 7, 1:04.60, June 7, 2007
6 furlongs: Roarin Heart, 3, 1:12.20, July 1, 2007; Second Sighting, 4, 1:12.20, July 20, 2007; Stan's Friend, 5, 1:12.20, July 12, 2007
6½ furlongs: Just Plain Bill, 7, 1:17.60, June 23, 2007
1 mile: Flim Flam Man, 4, 1:39.40, June 7, 2007

Remington Park

Built by the late Edward J. DeBartolo, Remington Park opened its gates on September 1, 1988, and was purchased by Magna Entertainment Corp. in October 1999 after average daily attendance had plummeted from a high of 11,263 in 1989 to 2,517 in '98. The track began a new era in 2001 with the addition of lights, thus allowing night racing. Thoroughbreds race during a summer-fall meet from mid-August to December, and Quarter Horses are featured in a spring meet. The track's feature Thoroughbred race is the Oklahoma Derby, which was to be run for the 20th time in 2008. Customers have multiple choices for settings, including the Players Sports Bar, the Silks Restaurant, the Eclipse Restaurant, and luxurious private suites. Slot machines began operation at Remington in November 2005. Afternoon racing returned to the track in 2007, marking the first daytime card since '04.

Location: One Remington Place, Oklahoma City, Ok. 73111-7101
Phone: (405) 424-1000, (866) 456-9880
Fax: (405) 425-3221
Website: www.remingtonpark.com
E-Mail: contact@remingtonpark.com
Year Founded: 1988
Dates of Inaugural Meeting: September 1, 1988
Abbreviation: RP
Acreage: 370
Number of Stalls: 1,312

Ownership
Magna Entertainment Corp.

Officers
Interim Chief Executive Officer: Frank Stronach
Chairman: Frank Stronach
Chief Operating Officer: Ron Charles
Executive Vice President of Racing: Scott Borgemenke
Executive Vice President and Chief Financial Officer: Blake Tohana
Vice President and General Manager: Scott Wells
Senior Vice Presidents of Operations: Brant Latta, James Bromby
Secretary: William G. Ford
Racing Secretary: Fred Hutton
Assistant Racing Secretary: Faye Crane
Director of Communications: Dale Day
Director of Marketing: Sharon Lair
Director of Mutuels: Carrie Stallbories
Stewards: Mike Corey, Norma Calhoun, David Southard, David Moore
Track Announcer: Dale Day
Track Photographer: Dustin Orona
Track Superintendent: Bobby Blackburn
Horsemen's Bookkeeper: Patsy Bessonett
Security: Herbert Billiot

Racing Dates
2007: August 2-December 1, 69 days
2008: August 21-December 14, 67 days

Racetracks — Oklahoma

Track Layout
Main Circumference: 1 mile
Main Track Chute: 7 furlongs
Main Track Chute: 1⅜ miles
Main Width: 100 feet
Main Length of Stretch: 990 feet
Main Turf Circumference: 7 furlongs
Main Turf Chute: 1⅛ miles
Main Turf Width: 80 feet
Main Turf Length of Stretch: 990 feet

Attendance
Average Daily Recent Meeting: 5,828, 2007
Highest Single-Day Record: 26,411, February 29, 1992
Record Daily Average Single Meeting: 11,128, 1988
Total Attendance Recent Meeting: 402,109

Handle
Average All-Sources Recent Meeting: $659,021, 2007
Average On-Track Recent Meeting: $78,371, 2007
Record Daily Average Single Meeting: $1,310,542, 1990
Single-Day On-Track Handle: $2,808,243, February 24, 1990
Total All-Sources Recent Meeting: $45,472,465, 2007
Total On-Track Recent Meeting: $5,407,587, 2007
Highest Single-Day Record Recent Meeting: $193,494, October 21, 2007
Highest Single-Day All-Sources Recent Meeting: $1,149,665, October 21, 2007

Mutuel Records
Highest Win: $254.20, Cherokee County, October 28, 2001
Highest Exacta: $5,495.80, December 3, 1988
Highest Trifecta: $58,662.40, February 24, 1995
Highest Daily Double: $3,980.80, November 11, 2007
Highest Pick Three: $18,057.60, November 13, 1994
Highest Other Exotics: $38,968.80, Superfecta, December 1, 1996
Highest 10-cent Superfecta: $14,412.05, October 20, 2006
Highest Pick Six: $1,070,482.50, February 24, 1990

Leaders
Career, Leading Jockey by Titles: M. Clifton Berry 12
Career, Leading Trainer by Titles: Donnie K. Von Hemel, 12
Career, Leading Jockey by Stakes Wins: Donald R. Pettinger, 126
Career, Leading Owner by Stakes Wins: Barbara and John Smicklas, 26
Career, Leading Trainer by Stakes Wins: Donnie K. Von Hemel, 143
Career, Leading Jockey by Wins: M. Clifton Berry, 1,608
Career, Leading Horse by Stakes Wins: Highland Ice, 9; Darrell Darrell, 9
Recent Meeting, Leading Jockey: M. Clifton Berry, 87, 2007
Recent Meeting, Leading Owner: Gary Owens, 12, 2007; Heflin Driver Racing LLC, 12, 2007
Recent Meeting, Leading Trainer: Steve Asmussen, 48, 2007
Recent Meeting, Leading Horse: Ilikewhatiamdoing, 4, 2007; Snuck By, 4, 2007; Hollye Lynne, 4, 2007

Records
Single-Day Jockey Wins: Timothy T. Doocy, 6, December 5, 1993; M. Clifton Berry, 6, September 30, 2001; M. Clifton Berry, 6, October 24, 2003; M. Clifton Berry, 6, August 5, 2005
Single-Day Trainer Wins: Wade White, 5, November 17, 1993
Single Meeting, Leading Jockey by Wins: Timothy T. Doocy, 127, 1997
Single Meeting, Leading Owner by Wins: Gary Owens, 36, 2005
Single Meeting, Leading Trainer by Wins: Joseph Petalino, 69, 1998

Principal Races
Oklahoma Derby, Edward J. DeBartolo Sr. Memorial H., Oklahoma Classics Day Classic S., Remington Park Oaks, Remington Green S., Remington MEC Mile S.

Notable Events
Oklahoma Classics Day

Track Records, Main Dirt
4½ furlongs: Payday Two, :52.20, February 26, 2000
5 furlongs: Sweepingly, :55.70, August 25, 2006
5½ furlongs: Run Johnny, 1:02, September 26, 1997
6 furlongs: Smoke of Ages, 1:08, September 29, 1991
6½ furlongs: Kangaroo King, 1:14.40, July 26, 1997
7 furlongs: Golden Gear, 1:20.40, March 18, 1995
1 mile: White Wheels, 1:35.40, August 17, 1997
1 mile 70 yds: Marked Tree, 1:39.60, March 13, 1993
1 1/16 miles: Valid Bonnet, 1:41.20, July 26, 1997
1⅛ miles: Classic Cat, 1:48, August 30, 1998
1 3/16 miles: Wild Rush, 1:53.60, August 10, 1997
1¼ miles: Double Platinum, 2:03.40, October 10, 1999
1⅜ miles: Wild and Comfy, 2:17.96, October 18, 2002
1½ miles: Bid the Zeal, 2:31.40, October 24, 1998
2 miles: Saavedra, 3:25⅕, December 10, 1989
Other: 3 furlongs, Eclat, :31.01, November 28, 2005

Track Records, Main Turf
5 furlongs: Calling Randy, :55.14, September 27, 2005
7½ furlongs: Foreign Justice, 1:27.46, August 27, 2004
1 mile: No More Hard Times, 1:33.80, September 20, 1992
1 1/16 miles: Burbank, 1:39.20, August 30, 1997
1⅛ miles: Major Rhythm, 1:46.22, September 6, 2004
1⅜ miles: Vergennes, 2:13, September 3, 2000
1½ miles: Cumulus, 2:38.38, November 8, 2004
2 miles: Big Notice, 3:29, November 20, 1993
Other: 1 13/16 miles, Aleric, 3:07.61, December 1, 2007

Fastest Times of 2007 (Dirt)
3 furlongs: Talkin Fine, 6, :32.08, August 3, 2007
5 furlongs: Snuck By, 4, :57.31, August 24, 2007
5½ furlongs: Snuck By, 4, 1:02.92, November 11, 2007
6 furlongs: Euroears, 3, 1:08.39, August 2, 2007
6½ furlongs: Visions in Color, 3, 1:16.26, August 30, 2007
7 furlongs: Markofexcess, 5, 1:22.22, August 2, 2007
1 mile: Toocooltobeforgotn, 4, 1:37.56, August 16, 2007
1 mile 70 yds: Jonesboro, 2, 1:40.87, September 8, 2007
1 1/16 miles: D Fine Okie, 5, 1:43.93, September 29, 2007
1⅛ miles: Going Ballistic, 3, 1:49.74, October 21, 2007

Fastest Times of 2007 (Turf)
5 furlongs: Rock Chalk, 4, :55.22, August 12, 2007
7½ furlongs: Miswaki's Best, 5, 1:29.10, August 2, 2007
1 mile: My Three Sisters, 5, 1:34.75, August 11, 2007
1 1/16 miles: Cry Havoc, 4, 1:41.78, November 16, 2007
1⅛ miles: Brego, 5, 1:48.51, September 3, 2007
1⅜ miles: Little Wagon, 4, 2:18.44, October 28, 2007
1 13/16 miles: Aleric, 5, 3:07.61, December 1, 2007

Will Rogers Downs

Will Rogers Downs is located on 210 acres just east of Claremore and approximately 25 miles from downtown Tulsa. No racing was conducted from 2001 through '05, but live racing resumed in '06 after Oklahoma approved gaming at Will Rogers and two other state tracks in '04 and the facility was purchased by the Cherokee Nation, which announced a $2-million renovation. The track is home to rodeos as well as Will Rogers County Jamborees every other Saturday night, presenting a family-oriented country show and concert.

Location: 20900 S. 4200 Rd., Claremore, Ok. 74019
Phone: (918) 283-8800
Website: www.cherokeecasino.com
Abbreviation: WRD
Number of Stalls: 600
Seating Capacity: 5,000

Ownership
Cherokee Nation Enterprise

Racetracks — Oregon

Officers
Chief Executive Officer: David Stewart
General Manager: Mark Enterline
Director of Racing and Racing Secretary: Kelly G. Cathey
Director of Mutuels: Coralee Farley
Director of Simulcasting: Kelly G. Cathey
Stewards: Tom Clark, Bill Brown, and Bill McNutt
Track Announcer: Jesse Ullery
Track Photographer: Coady Photography
Track Superintendent: Richard "Moe" Nye
Horsemen's Bookkeeper: Georgia Shipley

Racing Dates
2007: February 24-May 28, 42 days
2008: February 23-May 27, 44 days

Track Layout
Main Circumference: 1 mile
Main Track Chute: 6 furlongs
Main Length of Stretch: 872.76 feet
Training Track: 4 furlongs

Attendance
Highest Single-Day Recent Meeting: 4,500, May 3, 2007

Handle
Total All-Sources Recent Meeting: $6,602,598, 2007
Average All-Sources Recent Meeting: $169,297, 2007
Total On-Track Recent Meeting: $5,108,005, 2007
Average On-Track Recent Meeting: $130,974, 2007
Largest Single-Day All-Sources Recent Meeting: $544,569, April 8, 2007
Largest Single-Day On-Track Recent Meeting: $532,190, April 8, 2007

Leaders
Recent Meeting, Leading Jockey: Nena Matz, 65, 2007
Recent Meeting, Leading Trainer: Joe Lucas, 19, 2007; Kenneth Nolen, 19, 2007
Recent Meeting, Leading Horse: Dragooner, 4, 2007

Fastest Times of 2007 (Dirt)
4½ furlongs: Tabacco Roots, 7, :52.40, May 28, 2007
5 furlongs: Dragooner, 5, :56.60, May 28, 2007; Magdelena May, 6, :56.60, May 19, 2007
5½ furlongs: Come On Herb, 4, 1:04, May 20, 2007; Denia's Chief, 4, 1:04, May 21, 2007; Kisses for Nicki, 4, 1:04, April 30, 2007; Pistol's Rumor, 4, 1:04, May 19, 2007
6 furlongs: Green's Fair, 5, 1:08.40, May 20, 2007
1 mile: Attigo, 4, 1:36.20, May 19, 2007; Bubba's Quest, 6, 1:36.20, May 21, 2007
1 mile 70 yds: Costume Girl, 3, 1:44.20, May 26, 2007
1¹⁄₁₆ miles: Garbu's Son, 3, 1:44.20, May 26, 2007
1³⁄₁₆ miles: El Rojo Grande, 5, 1:59.80, May 28, 2007

Oregon

Eastern Oregon Livestock Show

Location: P.O. Box 4092, Union, Or. 97883-1052
Website: www.easternoregonlivestockshow.com

Officers
Director: Ron Droke
Mutuels Manager: Nate Jacobs
Assistant Racing Secretary: Gracie Tarter

Racing Dates
2007: June 8-June 10, 3 days
2008: June 6-June 8, 3 days

Handle
Average On-Track Recent Meeting: $15,623, 2007
Total On-Track Recent Meeting: $46,871, 2007

Leaders
Recent Meeting, Leading Jockey: Nikeela Renae Black, 5, 2007
Recent Meeting, Leading Trainer: Donald David Young, 3, 2007

Fastest Times of 2007 (Dirt)
5 furlongs: More Heart, 7, 1:00.20, June 9, 2007
5½ furlongs: David Strike Back, 7, 1:05, June 9, 2007; Joy's Toy, 10, 1:05, June 9, 2007
a5½ furlongs: Roman Governor, 6, 1:03.60, June 8, 2007
6½ furlongs: Messageforthegroom, 5, 1:27.60, June 9, 2007
a6½ furlongs: Scaffolds Legacy, 9, 1:28.20, June 8, 2007

Grants Pass

Location: 1451 Fairgrounds Rd., P.O. Box 672, Grants Pass, Or. 97528
Phone: (541) 476-3215
Fax: (541) 476-1027
Website: www.jocofair.com
E-Mail: jackie2@jocofair.com
Abbreviation: GrP

Officers
General Manager: Jackie McBee
Director of Racing: Al Westoff
Racing Secretary: Dan Bryson
Director of Marketing and Publicity: Gary Davison
Track Superintendent: Carl Stallings

Racing Dates
2007: June 16-July 8, 9 days
2008: June 14-July 6, 9 days

Attendance
Average Daily Recent Meeting: 1,428, 2007
Total Attendance Recent Meeting: 12,858, 2007

Handle
Total On-Track Recent Meeting: $471,092, 2007
Average On-Track Recent Meeting: $52,343, 2007

Leaders
Recent Meeting, Leading Jockey: Nikeela Renae Black, 13, 2007
Recent Meeting, Leading Trainer: Karen Haverty, 17, 2007
Recent Meeting, Leading Horse: Long Route Home, 3, 2007

Fastest Times of 2007 (Dirt)
4½ furlongs: Pearls 'n' Satin, 6, :51.80, July 8, 2007
5 furlongs: La Ultima Cisco, 3, :59.80, July 7, 2007
5½ furlongs: Lights Out Toney, 6, 1:05.60, July 1, 2007; Mountain Mustang, 6, 1:05.60, July 4, 2007
6½ furlongs: Pearls 'n' Satin, 6, 1:18.20, July 4, 2007
1¹⁄₁₆ miles: Touchdown U S C, 6, 1:47.80, July 8, 2007

Portland Meadows

Founded by Bay Meadows Race Course builder William Kyne, Portland Meadows has a rich history dating to September 14, 1946, when a crowd of 10,000 watched the nation's first evening Thoroughbred racing card. General Electric Co., which devised the lighting system, boasted at the time: "This system, the first of its kind, has enough power to light a four-lane super highway from Portland to Salem (a distance of more than 40 miles)." But Portland Meadows officials were powerless to fight the Vanport flood, which in 1948 forced cancellation of the track's season after just 13 cards and caused $250,000 in damage. The track was hit again in the early-morning hours of April 25, 1970, when a fire razed the grandstand. Portland Meadows was rebuilt, opening its 1971 season before a record crowd of 12,635. Portland Meadows served as an early proving ground for Racing Hall of Fame jockey Gary

Stevens, who won two riding titles there in the early 1980s. New Portland Meadows Inc. operated the track from 1991 until it leased the track to Magna Entertainment Corp. in mid-2001. In 2002, Magna purchased the long-term operating rights to Portland Meadows.

Location: 1001 N. Schmeer Rd., Portland, Or. 97217-7505
Phone: (503) 285-9144
Fax: (503) 286-9763
Website: www.portlandmeadows.com
E-Mail: info@portlandmeadows.com
Year Founded: 1945
Dates of Inaugural Meeting: September 14, 1946
Abbreviation: PM
Acreage: 100+
Number of Stalls: 850
Seating Capacity: 4,450

Ownership
Magna Entertainment Corp.

Officers
General Manager: William Alempijevic
Assistant General Manager and Director of Racing: Jerry Kohls
Racing Secretary: Jerry Kohls
Controller: Vestal Monroe
Facility Manager: Mark Folkman
Mutuel Manager: Keith Jones
Stable Area Manager: Ken Twiggs
Simulcast Contact: William Alempijevic
Track Announcer: Jason Beem
Track Photographer: Reed Palmer
Horsemen's Bookkeeper: Nichelle Milner

Racing Dates
2007: October 8, 2006-May 5, 2007, 73 days
2008: October 7, 2007-March 11, 2008, 61 days

Track Layout
Main Circumference: 1 mile
Main Track Chute: 6 furlongs and $1^1/_4$ miles
Main Length of Stretch: 990 feet

Attendance
Average Daily Recent Meeting: 460, 2007/2008
Highest Single-Day Record: 12,635, February 6, 1971
Total Attendance Recent Meeting: 35,000, 2007/2008

Handle
Average All-Sources Recent Meeting: $531,880, 2007/2008
Average On-Track Recent Meeting: $26,208, 2007/2008
Total All-Sources Recent Meeting: $32,444,670, 2007/2008
Total On-Track Recent Meeting: $1,598,709, 2007/2008
Highest Single-Day Record Recent Meeting: $63,449, March 10, 2008
Highest Single-Day All-Sources Recent Meeting: $1,114,528, December 18, 2007

Mutuel Records
Highest Win: $254.20, Cherokee County, October 28, 2001
Highest Exacta: $5,495.80, December 3, 1988
Highest Trifecta: $58,662.40, February 24, 1995
Highest Daily Double: $2,969.60, September 2, 2000
Highest Pick Three: $18,057.60, November 13, 1994
Highest Other Exotics: $38,968.80, Superfecta, December 1, 1996

Leaders
Recent Meeting, Leading Jockey: Joe A. Crispin, 156, 2007/2008
Recent Meeting, Leading Trainer: Jim Fergason, 60, 2007/2008
Recent Meeting, Leading Horse: Always Gold, 5, 2007/2008; Billeys Easter Dash, 5, 2007/2008; Rock The Stone, 5, 2007/2008; Cryptic Mem, 5, 2007/2008

Records
Single-Day Jockey Wins: Joe A. Crispin, 7, December 4, 1998; Joe A. Crispin, 7, November 28, 2006
Single Meeting, Leading Jockey by Wins: Joe A. Crispin, 190, 2006/2007

Principal Races
Portland Meadows Mile, Oregon Derby, Oregon Oaks, Donna Jensen Handicap, OS West Oregon Futurity

Track Records, Main Dirt
4 furlongs: Wayne S., :47, May 22, 1947
$4^1/_2$ furlongs: Star Expresso, :51.80, April 3, 1999
5 furlongs: Pajone's Hostess, :58, January 6, 1977
$5^1/_2$ furlongs: My Runaway, $1:02^4/_5$, January 6, 1977
6 furlongs: Lethal Grande, 1:09.01, March 30, 2003
1 mile: Star of Kuwait, $1:36^1/_5$, May 11, 1975
1 mile 70 yds: Beau Julian, $1:41^1/_5$, May 14, 1979
$1^1/_{16}$ miles: Me Brave, $1:43^1/_5$, May 5, 1969
$1^1/_8$ miles: Hannibal Khal, $1:48^4/_5$, December 30, 1978
$1^3/_{16}$ miles: Kitsap Kid, $1:58^2/_5$, April 27, 1968
$1^1/_4$ miles: True Enough, 2:03.20, April 9, 1994
$1^1/_2$ miles: Martins Lemon, 2:32, May 13, 1973
$1^3/_4$ miles: Moribana, $2:58^3/_5$, May 27, 1972
2 miles: Martins Lemon, $3:27^3/_5$, May 20, 1973
Other: 2 furlongs, Annie N Will, :21.69, April 15, 2000

Fastest Times of 2007 (Dirt)
$4^1/_2$ furlongs: Retirees Three, 7, :52.82, November 20, 2007
5 furlongs: Top O the Moon, 3, :58.30, November 11, 2007
$5^1/_2$ furlongs: Free Cocktails, 6, 1:04.93, October 16, 2007
6 furlongs: Mystic Wood, 3, 1:10.18, November 6, 2007
1 mile: Jack Ryan, 3, 1:38.86, November 18, 2007
1 mile 70 yds: Hunt for Glory, 6, 1:43.25, January 8, 2007
$1^1/_{16}$ miles: Baquero Ruler, 3, 1:46.11, December 9, 2007
$1^1/_8$ miles: Ochoco Salmon, 3, 1:54.37, May 5, 2007
$1^1/_4$ miles: Kingjames Delivers, 4, 2:10.25, May 5, 2007

Tillamook County Fair

Location: 4603 E. Third St., P.O. Box 455, Tillamook, Or. 97141-2943
Phone: (503) 842-2272
Fax: (503) 842-3314
Website: www.tillamookfair.com
E-Mail: tillamookfair@wcn.net
Year Founded: 1891
Abbreviation: Til

Ownership
Tillamook County

Officers
President: Jack DeSwart
Vice President: Mel Tupper
General Manager: Jerry Underwood
Racing Secretary: Nichelle Milner
Treasurer: Jerry Underwood
Director of Racing: Mel Tupper
Director of Marketing and Publicity: Jerry Underwood
Director of Mutuels: Jim Goff
Horsemen's Liaison: Lonnie Craig
Stewards: Mark Howard
Track Announcer: Dean Mazucca
Track Photographer: Roger Nielson
Track Superintendent: Mel Tupper

Racing Dates
2007: August 9-August 11, 3 days
2008: August 7-August 9, 3 days

Track Layout
Main Circumference: 4 furlongs

Attendance
Average Daily Recent Meeting: 1,500 est., 2007
Total Attendance Recent Meeting: 4,500 est., 2007

Handle
Average On-Track Recent Meeting: $42,706, 2007
Director of Operations: Jerry Underwood
Total On-Track Recent Meeting: $128,120, 2007

Fastest Times of 2007 (Dirt)
a5 furlongs: Mountain Mustang, 6, 1:03, August 11, 2007
a1 1/16 miles: Don Fernando (Mex), 7, 2:02.80, August 10, 2007

Pennsylvania

Penn National Race Course

Built by a group of Central Pennsylvania investors, Penn National Race Course is located 13 miles from the state capital, Harrisburg. It staged its first race meeting on August 30, 1972. The following year, Penn National bought the racing license of defunct Pitt Park and began an essentially year-round racing schedule. In 1978, Penn National built the state's first turf course. Led by principal owner Peter D. Carlino, Penn National has been an innovator in Pennsylvania's racing industry. Carlino, a Philadelphia-area businessman, bought one of the track's operating licenses in 1974 and the other in '83. With legalization of telephone betting in 1982, Penn National began the commonwealth's first account-wagering system, and the following year it began the first cable-television broadcast of its races. Following legislative approval of off-track wagering in 1989, Penn National built and operated six facilities in Central Pennsylvania. In 1994, the track's parent company, Penn National Gaming Inc., held an initial public stock offering. With those proceeds and subsequent stock issues, Penn National has financed the acquisitions of Charles Town Races, a Thoroughbred track in West Virginia, and Pocono Downs, a Standardbred track near Wilkes-Barre, Pennsylvania, as well as casino properties. Pocono Downs was sold in 2005 after Penn National Gaming received legislative approval for slot machines at its namesake track. The flagship Grantville facility was torn down in 2006 and replaced with a casino-racetrack that houses 2,020 slot machines.

Location: 777 Hollywood Boulevard, P.O. Box 32, Grantville, Pa. 17028-0032
Phone: (717) 469-2211
Fax: (717) 469-2910
Website: www.pnrc.com
E-Mail: fred.lipkin@pngaming.com
Year Founded: 1972
Dates of Inaugural Meeting: August 30-December 31, 1972
Abbreviation: Pen
Acreage: 600
Number of Stalls: 1,200
Seating Capacity: 9,570

Ownership
Penn National Gaming Inc.

Officers
Chairman and President: Peter M. Carlino
Vice President and General Manager: J. Gary Luderitz
Director of Racing and Operations: Rob Marella
Racing Secretary: Paul N. Jenkins
Assistant Racing Secretary: William H. Bell
Director of Marketing and Publicity: Frederick D. Lipkin
Director of Mutuels: Carole Kneasel
Director of Simulcasting: David Koepp
Stewards: Scott Campbell, Thomas L. Crouse, Rodney P. Peters
Track Announcer: John Bogar
Track Photographer: Gill's Positive Images
Track Superintendent: Jake Leitzel
Security: Karl Ikerman
Horsemen's Bookkeeper: Sherlene Servideo

Racing Dates
2007: January 2-December 21, 214 days
2008: January 12-December 31, 204 days

Track Layout
Main Circumference: 1 mile
Main Track Chute: 6 furlongs and 1 1/4 miles
Main Length of Stretch: 990 feet
Main Turf Circumference: 7 furlongs

Attendance
Highest Single-Day Record: 15,442, August 2, 1980

Handle
Average All-Sources Recent Meeting: $900,922, 2007
Average On-Track Recent Meeting: $23,558, 2007
Single-Day All-Sources Handle: $2,173,921, December 26, 1998
Total All-Sources Recent Meeting: $159,463,164, 2007
Total On-Track Recent Meeting: $4,169,736, 2007

Mutuel Records
Highest Win: $343.40, Busy Lady, December 20, 1977
Highest Exacta: $8,430, April 13, 1988
Highest Trifecta: $42,886.50, May 27, 1980
Lowest Daily Double: $27,985.80, July 11, 1975
Highest Other Exotics: $543,014, Twin Trifecta, June 14, 1988

Leaders
Recent Meeting, Leading Jockey: Thomas Clifton, 160, 2007
Recent Meeting, Leading Trainer: Murray L. Rojas, 114, 2007
Recent Meeting, Leading Horse: Favorite Knocker, 7, 2007

Principal Races
Pennsylvania Governor's Cup H., Blue Mountain Juvenile S., Danzig S., Wonders Delight S., Capital City H.

Track Records, Main Dirt
4 furlongs: Gross, :46 1/5, April 13, 1973
4 1/2 furlongs: Glacken, :50.56, September 20, 2007
5 furlongs: On the Phone, :56.60, July 13, 1996
5 1/2 furlongs: Cortan, 1:03 1/5, May 29, 1978; Flaming Emperor, 1:03.20, June 26, 1994; Hunter's Ridge, 1:03.20, May 1, 1996
6 furlongs: Jiva Coolit, 1:08 4/5, May 22, 1977; Dainty Dotsie, 1:08 4/5, August 13, 1977; Who's Bluffing, 1:08.77, May 30, 2006
1 mile: Vambourine, 1:36 1/5, June 12, 1977; Agate Bay, 1:36 1/5, March 22, 1981
1 mile 70 yds: Wee Thunder, 1:39.60, July 13, 1996
1 1/16 miles: A Letter to Harry, 1:41 1/5, September 10, 1978
1 1/8 miles: Collection Agent, 1:49 1/5, August 22, 1987
1 3/16 miles: Bar Tab, 1:55 2/5, October 14, 1972
1 1/4 miles: Adda Nickell, 2:03 3/5, October 30, 1976
1 1/2 miles: Holly Holme, 2:31 3/5, September 29, 1973
1 5/8 miles: New Episode, 2:48.15, May 18, 2001
1 3/4 miles: Chasqui, 3:00, June 21, 1980
2 miles: Finny Flyer, 3:28, May 25, 1974
Other: 2 furlongs, Pensglitter, :20.71, October 9, 2004

Track Records, Main Turf
5 furlongs: Bop, :54.61, August 3, 2002
1 mile: The Very One, 1:33 1/5, July 15, 1979
1 mile 70yds: Aborigine, 1:37 1/5, August 20, 1978
1 1/16 miles: Told, 1:38, September 14, 1980
1 1/2 miles: Coalitioncandidate, 2:27, May 27, 1991
Other: a5 furlongs, Threewitt, :56.28, July 14, 2005; a1 mile, Major Blast, 1:36.64, July 26, 2006; a1 mile 70yds, Jrsoutofcontrol, 1:40.22, July 13, 2005; a1 1/16 miles, Professor Biggs, 1:41.72, May 25, 2007

Fastest Times of 2007 (Dirt)
4 1/2 furlongs: Glacken, 7, :50.56, September 20, 2007
5 furlongs: Diamond Pretty, 4, :57.18, August 24, 2007
5 1/2 furlongs: Brendan Mac, 7, 1:03.44, May 11, 2007
6 furlongs: Cantrel, 3, 1:09.20, May 17, 2007
1 mile: Halo Heaven, 7, 1:37.50, April 4, 2007
1 mile 70 yds: Inside Lane, 6, 1:42.11, September 11, 2007
1 1/16 miles: Igor, 6, 1:43.19, May 9, 2007

1¹⁄₈ miles: Gandalf the Grey, 6, 1:51.59, August 8, 2007
1¹⁄₄ miles: Igor, 6, 2:04.52, April 26, 2007

Fastest Times of 2007 (Turf)
5 furlongs: Dream Counter, 12, :56.08, August 2, 2007
a5 furlongs: Dream Counter, 12, :56.72, May 23, 2007
1 mile: Irish Diva, 5, 1:35.63, September 4, 2007
a1 mile: Pure Jazz, 6, 1:37.47, May 22, 2007
1 mile 70 yds: Inside Lane, 6, 1:38.07, July 31, 2007
a1 mile 70 yds: Yankee Pal, 5, 1:41.37, May 18, 2007
1¹⁄₁₆ miles: Golden Sheriff, 8, 1:39.53, June 7, 2007
a1¹⁄₁₆ miles: Professor Biggs, 6, 1:41.72, May 25, 2007

Philadelphia Park

Built reluctantly and inexpensively in the early 1970s, the track now known as Philadelphia Park has had a difficult history, but it has emerged as a leader in providing fan amenities and phone wagering in its region. When racing first arrived in Pennsylvania in the late 1960s, both Thoroughbred and Standardbred racing were conducted at Liberty Bell Park in Philadelphia's Northeast section. But with regional lawmakers insisting on a separate Thoroughbred facility, Keystone Race Track was built for $20-million approximately one mile north of Liberty Bell in Bensalem Township, across the city border in Bucks County. It opened in November 1974 with two ownership groups, which often feuded. Keystone inaugurated the track's signature race, the Pennsylvania Derby (G3), in 1979, and phone betting was authorized in '82. In 1984, Robert Brennan-controlled International Thoroughbred Breeders Inc. bought Keystone for $37.5-million to avoid competition for its Garden State Park, which opened in April '85 and closed in 2001. Brennan's company renamed the track Philadelphia Park and spent several million dollars renovating the grandstand and the racing surface, including the addition of a turf course. Financially failing International Thoroughbred Breeders sold the track to Greenwood Racing, headed by British bookmaking executives Robert Green and William Hogwood, for $67-million in 1990, the year in which the track opened the first of its five off-track betting facilities. In 2006, the track's owners completed an extensive renovation of the plant to accommodate slot machines, which began operation in December of that year. Ground was broken in March 2008 for a stand-alone casino adjacent to the track. Plans call for the slot machines to be moved to that facility by late 2009, allowing Philadelphia Park to be retrofitted from a racino back into a racetrack facility by the first quarter of '10.

Location: 3001 Street Rd., P.O. Box 1000, Bensalem, Pa. 19020-8512
Phone: (215) 639-9000
Fax: (215) 639-8330
Website: www.philadelphiapark.com
E-Mail: kjones@philadelphiapark.com
Year Founded: 1974
Dates of Inaugural Meeting: November 4, 1974
Abbreviation: Pha
Acreage: 417
Number of Stalls: 1,600
Seating Capacity: 8,700

Ownership
Greenwood Racing

Officers
Chairman and President: Robert W. Green
Chief Operating Officer: Joe Wilson
Director of Racing and Racing Secretary: Salvatore Sinatra
Vice Presidents: Len Carey, Andrew J. Green
Treasurer: Matt Hayes
Director of Finance: Anthony D. Ricci
Director of Mutuels: William Barnes
Director of Publicity: Keith Jones
Director of Simulcasting: Merce Duffy
Assistant Racing Secretary: Nicholas P. Black
Stewards: Samuel A. Boulmetis Jr., Jonathan S. Gerweck, John P. Hicks
Track Announcer: Keith Jones
Track Photographer: Equi-Photo Inc.
Track Superintendent: David Ziegler
Clerk of the Course: Sandra Ricciardi

Racing Dates
2007: January 2-December 30, 207 days
2008: January 1-December 30, 221 days

Track Layout
Main Circumference: 1 mile
Main Track Chute: 7 furlongs and 1¹⁄₄ miles
Main Width: 80 feet
Main Length of Stretch: 974 feet
Main Turf Circumference: 7 furlongs
Main Turf Chute: 1¹⁄₈ miles

Attendance
Highest Single-Day Record: 28,692, May 30, 1983

Handle
Total All-Sources Recent Meeting: $310,690,858, 2007
Average All-Sources Recent Meeting: $1,530,496, 2007
Total On-Track Recent Meeting: $22,778,495, 2007
Average On-Track Recent Meeting: $112,209, 2007
Largest Single-Day All-Sources Recent Meeting: $6,823,063, May 5, 2007
Largest Single-Day On-Track Recent Meeting: $1,677,954, May 5, 2007

Mutuel Records
Highest Win: $588.80, Oak Tree, February 17, 1982
Highest Exacta: $6,792.60, November 18, 1976
Highest Trifecta: $55,608.90, November 1, 1976
Highest Daily Double: $2,943.40, December 13, 1976

Leaders
Career, Leading Jockey by Titles: Rick Wilson, 9
Career, Leading Trainer by Titles: Scott A. Lake, 7
Career, Leading Jockey by Stakes Wins: Rick Wilson, 75
Career, Leading Trainer by Stakes Wins: Dennis Heimer, 56
Recent Meeting, Leading Jockey: Harry Vega, 183, 2007
Recent Meeting, Leading Trainer: Jayne Vaders, 117, 2007
Recent Meeting, Leading Owner: Plumstead Stables, 66, 2007
Recent Meeting, Leading Horse: I'm No Cheerleader, 7, 2007

Records
Single Meeting, Leading Jockey by Wins: Frankie Pennington, 260, 2006
Single Meeting, Leading Trainer by Wins: David R. Vance, 172, 1976

Principal Races
Pennsylvania Derby (G2), Fitz Dixon Cotillion H. (G2), Gallant Bob H., Turf Monster H., My Juliet S., Greenwood Cup, PTHA President's Cup

Notable Events
President's Day

Interesting Facts
Previous Names and Dates: Liberty Bell Park Race Track (1969-'74); Keystone Race Track (1974-'84)

Track Records, Main Dirt
4 furlongs: Heres a Tip, :45, June 11, 1982
4¹⁄₂ furlongs: Distinctive Hat, :51.48, May 2, 1994; Annakova, :51.48, January 1, 2006

5 furlongs: My Favorite Grub, :56, September 7, 1998
5$\frac{1}{2}$ furlongs: Outcashem, 1:02.63, April 11, 2006
6 furlongs: Iron Punch, 1:07.89, July 29, 2000
6$\frac{1}{2}$ furlongs: Tricky Mister, 1:14.40, June 21, 1998
7 furlongs: Flaming Bridle, 1:20.61, September 28, 1999
1 mile: Regal Count, 1:34$\frac{4}{5}$, December 5, 1985
1 mile 70 yds: Tragedy, 1:38.70, December 12, 1995
1$\frac{1}{16}$ miles: Cool Spring Park, 1:40$\frac{4}{5}$, November 4, 1974
1$\frac{1}{8}$ miles: Selari Spirit, 1:47, November 30, 1974
1$\frac{3}{16}$ miles: Southern Shade, 1:56$\frac{2}{5}$, October 20, 1984
1$\frac{1}{4}$ miles: It's Always Archie, 2:02, November 23, 1974
1$\frac{1}{2}$ miles: Laugh a Minute, 2:31, January 4, 1992
1$\frac{5}{8}$ miles: River Wolf, 2:46$\frac{2}{5}$, October 13, 1990
1$\frac{3}{4}$ miles: Johnny's Silencer, 2:57$\frac{4}{5}$, December 17, 1988
2 miles: Perfect to a Tee, 3:25.87, September 2, 1996
Other: 2 furlongs, Queen Millie, :21.32, January 30, 1994; 1$\frac{9}{16}$ miles, Laugh a Minute, 2:40.85, January 18, 1992; 1$\frac{11}{16}$ miles, Laugh a Minute, 2:53.20, December 21, 1991; 1$\frac{13}{16}$ miles, Fire North, 3:04.80, March 14, 1992; 1$\frac{7}{8}$ miles, Haberdasher, 3:13$\frac{3}{5}$, October 17, 1987; 2$\frac{1}{8}$ miles, Heavy Medal Man, 3:39.59, April 25, 1992; 2$\frac{1}{4}$ miles, Transfer Ticket, 3:56, December 31, 1988; 2$\frac{1}{2}$ miles, Half Chance, 4:24.15, May 25, 1992

Track Records, Main Turf

5 furlongs: Max West, :55.91, October 2, 2005
7$\frac{1}{2}$ furlongs: Lucky Dreamer, 1:30.30, October 7, 2007
1 mile: Lake Cecebe, 1:35$\frac{3}{5}$, June 28, 1986
1 mile 70yds: Rolfe's Ruby, 1:39$\frac{2}{5}$, June 21, 1986; Marlish, 1:39$\frac{2}{5}$, August 13, 1986
1$\frac{1}{16}$ miles: Whatever For, 1:40$\frac{2}{5}$, June 22, 1986
1$\frac{1}{8}$ miles: Whatever For, 1:46$\frac{1}{5}$, September 1, 1986
1$\frac{3}{8}$ miles: Juanca (Arg), 2:16$\frac{2}{5}$, September 1, 1986
1$\frac{1}{2}$ miles: Lord Zada, 2:28.38, June 10, 2000
2 miles: Chippenham Park, 3:28$\frac{4}{5}$, September 1, 1990
Other: a5 furlongs, Sport d'Hiver, :56.61, August 26, 2001; a7$\frac{1}{2}$ furlongs, Tia's Miss 1:32.55, September 25, 2005; a1 mile, Auction Watch, 1:37.30, July 17, 2007; a1 mile 70yds, Vin Rouge, 1:41.38, July 17, 1994; a1$\frac{1}{16}$ miles, Mount Bleu, 1:43.26, October 4, 1994; a1$\frac{1}{8}$ miles, Brenton Reef, 1:50$\frac{1}{5}$, August 6, 1989; a1$\frac{3}{8}$ miles, Bostic Hill, 2:20.49, September 29, 2001; a1$\frac{1}{2}$ miles, Mort the Sport, 2:31, August 22, 1989; a2 miles, Proctor's Image, 3:27$\frac{2}{5}$, October 15, 1988

Fastest Times of 2007 (Dirt)

4$\frac{1}{2}$ furlongs: Hold On Smokey, 2, :52.16, July 7, 2007
5 furlongs: Blue's Nugget, 4, :57.30, January 2, 2007
5$\frac{1}{2}$ furlongs: Jacob's Run, 3, 1:02.72, September 8, 2007
6 furlongs: Cognac Kisses, 4, 1:08.28, December 30, 2007
6$\frac{1}{2}$ furlongs: Akronism, 3, 1:15.08, June 16, 2007
7 furlongs: Marital Asset, 4, 1:21.40, October 9, 2007
1 mile: Again and Again, 4, 1:36.17, February 26, 2007
1 mile 70 yds: Wild Hoots, 3, 1:40.12, December 28, 2007
1$\frac{1}{16}$ miles: Bear Now, 3, 1:41.21, September 22, 2007
1$\frac{1}{8}$ miles: Timber Reserve, 3, 1:47.67, September 3, 2007
1$\frac{1}{4}$ miles: Seize, 5, 2:06.09, July 29, 2007

Fastest Times of 2007 (Turf)

5 furlongs: Smart Enough, 4, :55.53, September 3, 2007
a5 furlongs: Makin Peace, 5, :56.55, July 7, 2007
7$\frac{1}{2}$ furlongs: Lucky Dreamer, 5, 1:30.30, October 7, 2007
a7$\frac{1}{2}$ furlongs: Knight in Flight, 5, 1:31.95, July 9, 2007
1 mile: Key Event, 5, 1:35.24, July 2, 2007
a1 mile: Auction Watch, 4, 1:37.30, July 17, 2007
1 mile 70 yds: Western Pleaser, 4, 1:39.76, May 30, 2007
a1 mile 70 yds: Star of Sahm, 6, 1:40.66, September 8, 2007
1$\frac{1}{16}$ miles: Wooden Stone, 8, 1:41.68, June 23, 2007
a1$\frac{1}{16}$ miles: Speakthruthebridle, 3, 1:44.63, July 21, 2007
1$\frac{1}{8}$ miles: Perfect Arrival, 6, 1:50.87, August 4, 2007
a1$\frac{1}{8}$ miles: Fox the Hound, 4, 1:50.90, July 10, 2007
1$\frac{3}{8}$ miles: Raging Rapids, 6, 2:21.15, August 11, 2007
a2$\frac{1}{16}$ miles: John Law, 6, 3:42.32, July 28, 2007

Presque Isle Downs

The opening of Presque Isle Downs in September 2007 returned Thoroughbred racing to western Pennsylvania for the first time since Commodore Downs closed in 1988. Located in Erie, about 110 miles east of Cleveland and 90 miles west of Buffalo, Presque Isle is supported by a racino that houses 2,000 slots. Built with a Tapeta Footings racing surface, Presque Isle became the first track to use that type of artificial substance for racing.

Location: 8199 Perry Highway, P.O. Box 10728, Erie, Pa. 16514
Phone: (866) 374-3386
Website: *www.presqueisledowns.com*
E-Mail: pidracing@pidowns.com
Dates of Inaugural Meeting: September 1-September 29, 2007
Year Founded: 2007
Abbreviation: PID

Ownership

MTR Gaming

Officers

Chairman: Edson R. Arneault
President and Chief Executive Officer: Richard Knight
Vice President: Patrick Arneault
Secretary/Treasurer: Rose Mary Williams
Director of Racing: Debbie Howells
Director of Finance: Rita Smith
Director of Marketing: Jennifer See
Director of Facilities: William Syrek
Director of Slot Operations: Thomas Moore
Director of Security: Steven Planchon
Director of Internet Technology: J. R. Farrar
Racing Secretary: David Frizzell
Assistant Racing Secretary: James Cornes
Stewards: Stephen DeAngelis, Jeffrey Lloyd, Patrick Bovenzi
Track Superintendent: Pasquale Pontillo
Track Announcer: William Downes
Track Photographer: Coady Photography
Horsemen's Bookkeeper: Bev Deeb

Racing Dates

2007: September 1-September 29, 25 days
2008: May 9-September 27, 100 days

Track Layout

Main Circumference: 1 mile (Tapeta Footings)
Main Track Chute: 6$\frac{1}{2}$ furlongs and one-quarter mile
Main Width: 80 feet
Main Length of Stretch: 1,062 feet

Attendance

Total Attendance Recent Meeting: 37, 443, 2007
Average Daily Recent Meeting: 1,498, 2007
Highest Single-Day Recent Meeting: 3,447, September 1, 2007

Handle

Average All-Sources Recent Meeting: $585,665, 2007
Average On-Track Recent Meeting: $58,268, 2007
Total All-Sources Recent Meeting: $14,641,637, 2007
Total On-Track Recent Meeting: $ 1,456,691, 2007
Highest Single-Day Record Recent Meeting: $830,915, September 1, 2007

Leaders

Recent Meeting, Leading Jockey: Miguel Mena, 35, 2007
Recent Meeting, Leading Trainer: Tom Amoss, 12, 2007
Recent Meeting, Leading Owner: Loren G. Cox, 7, 2007
Recent Meeting, Leading Horse: Catonight, 3, 2007

Principal Races

Presque Isle Mile, Presque Isle Downs Masters Stakes

Fastest Times of 2007 (All Weather)

4$\frac{1}{2}$ furlongs: Blind River Fox, 5, :50.31, September 17, 2007
5 furlongs: Flaming Comet, 3, :57.74, September 9, 2007
5$\frac{1}{2}$ furlongs: Indian Chant, 4, 1:02.51, September 15, 2007
6 furlongs: Miss Macy Sue, 4, 1:08.21, September 15, 2007
6$\frac{1}{2}$ furlongs: Coyoteshighestcall, 5, 1:15.80, September 16, 2007
1 mile: Victory Pool, 5, 1:36.15, September 16, 2007

1 mile 70 yds: Vettriano (Ire), 7, 1:41.86, September 19, 2007
1 1/16 miles: Exterior, 6, 1:44.07, September 28, 2007
1 1/8 miles: One Eyed Joker, 9, 1:53.18, September 1, 2007
1 1/2 miles: Red Rock Creek, 6, 2:33.25, September 29, 2007

South Dakota

Brown County Fair

Location: Old Highway 10, Aberdeen, S.D. 57401
Phone: (605) 229-0013
Fax: (605) 229-0013
Website: *www.sdhorseracing.com*
E-Mail: mischmidt@nrctv.com
Year Founded: 1950
Abbreviation: BCF

Ownership
Brown County

Officers
President and General Manager: Mike Schmidt
Vice President: Randy Bonn
Racing Secretary: Harold Sanderson
Treasurer: Kent Larson
Director of Racing: Ray Sauerwein
Director of Operations: Joe Gauer
Director of Marketing: Hank Bowker
Director of Mutuels: Theresa Sauerwein
Director of Publicity: Kent Larson
Stewards: Lloyd Just, Dan Zinter, Walt Van Dyke
Track Announcer: Jay Kleinknecht
Track Photographer: Ron Krogman
Track Superintendent: Randy Bonn

Racing Dates
2007: May 12-May 28, 7 days
2008: May 10-May 26, 7 days

Attendance
Average Daily Recent Meeting: 828, 2007
Total Attendance Recent Meeting: 5,800, 2007

Handle
Average On-Track Recent Meeting: $28,142, 2007
Total On-Track Recent Meeting: $197,000, 2007

Leaders
Recent Meeting, Leading Jockey: Jacob Olesiak, 15, 2007
Recent Meeting, Leading Trainer: Bob Johnson, 15, 2007

Principal Races
South Dakota Bred Futurity, South Dakota Bred Derby, NAHR Sprint, Governor's H., Legion S.

Fort Pierre Horse Races

Location: P.O. Box 426, Fort Pierre, S.D. 57532-0426
Phone: (605) 223-2178
Website: *www.sdhorseracing.com*
Abbreviation: FtP

Officers
General Manager: Pat Sutley
Racing Secretary: Bill Floyd
Stewards: Lloyd Just, Walt Van Dyke, Dan Zinter

Racing Dates
2007: April 14-May 6, 8 days
2008: April 12-May 4, 8 days

Handle
Average On Track Recent Meeting: $18,026, 2007
Total On Track Recent Meeting: $144,211, 2007

Principal Races
Lucky Bendewald Memorial S., Thoroughbred Allowance S., Fort Pierre Thoroughbred Derby, Governor's H., South Dakota Thoroughbred Futurity Trials

Fastest Times of 2007 (Dirt)
5 furlongs: I Tell U What, 4, 1:02.80, April 14, 2007

Texas

Gillespie County Fairgrounds

Location: 530 Fair Dr., P.O. Box 526, Fredericksburg, Tx. 78624-0526
Phone: (830) 997-2359
Fax: (830) 997-4923
Website: *www.gillespiefair.com*
E-Mail: gcffa@ctesc.net
Year Founded: 1881
Abbreviation: Gil
Number of Stalls: 200
Seating Capacity: 3,000

Ownership
Gillespie County Fair and Festival Association

Officers
President: Edward Stroeher
Vice Presidents: Leon Welgehausen, Ruben Sagebiel Jr.
Director of Racing: Brian Roeder
Director of Operations: Mike Klein
Director of Publicity: Russell Hartmann
Racing Secretary: Scott Sherwood
Treasurer: Frederick Jung
Track Announcers: Dudley Althaus, Louis Rech
Track Photographer: Marc Bennett
Track Superintendent: Dorman Schmidt

Racing Dates
2007: July 7-August 26, 8 days
2008: July 4-August 24, 8 days

Track Layout
Main Circumference: 5 furlongs

Attendance
Average Daily Recent Meeting: 1,516, 2007
Total Attendance Recent Meeting: 12,132, 2007

Handle
Average On-Track Recent Meeting: $141,811, 2007
Total On-Track Recent Meeting: $1,134,495, 2007

Leaders
Recent Meeting, Leading Jockey: Santos Carrizales, 5, 2007
Recent Meeting, Leading Trainer: Bobby Needham Jr., 4, 2007

Principal Races
Texas Thoroughbred Breeders' S., Gillespie County Fair Association S.

Fastest Times of 2007 (Dirt)
5 1/2 furlongs: Appealing Air, 5, 1:06.08, July 7, 2007
6 furlongs: Aggies Rule, 4, 1:13.05, July 21, 2007
7 furlongs: General Naevus, 5, 1:25.63, August 26, 2007

Lone Star Park

One decade after Texas legalized pari-mutuel racing, Lone Star Park at Grand Prairie opened in 1997 and joined Sam Houston Race Park in Houston and Retama Park near San Antonio as the three major tracks in the state. Located in the Dallas-Fort Worth metropolitan area, Lone Star was built for $96-million by the Lone

Star Jockey Club, a group headed by real estate moguls Trammell Crow and his son, Harlan, of Trammell Crow Co. The track's sale to Magna Entertainment Corp. for $99-million, including assumption of debt, was completed in 2002. Lone Star was host to the Breeders' Cup World Championships in 2004. The Lone Star Millions program features six stakes with a combined value of $1.1-million.

Location: 1000 Lone Star Pkwy., Grand Prairie, Tx. 75050-7941
Phone: (972) 263-7223, (800) 795-7223
Fax: (972) 237-1155
Website: www.lonestarpark.com
E-Mail: feedback@lonestarpark.com
Dates of Inaugural Meeting: April 17, 1997
Abbreviation: LS
Acreage: 285
Number of Stalls: 1,594
Seating Capacity: 12,000

Ownership
Magna Entertainment Corp.

Officers
Chairman and Chief Executive Officer: Frank Stronach
President and General Manager: Drew Shubeck
Vice President and Assistant General Manager: G.W. Hail
Vice President and Assistant General Manager: Paula Newman
Director of Racing and Racing Secretary: Larry A. Craft
Director of Sales and Catering: Don Feneziani
Director of Operations: Harry Johnson
Director of Human Resources: Melody Johnson
Director of Track Maintenance: George McDermott
Director of Marketing: Kim Archie
Director of Security and Parking: Craig Randall
Director of Post Time Pavilion: John Records
Director of Mutuels: Melinda Tyler
Director of Communications: Dan Leary
Assistant Racing Secretary: Jeanette Hughes
Simulcasting Coordinator: Mindy Freeland
Horsemen's Liaison: Rainey Brookfield
Stewards: Jerry Burgess, Stephen O'Malley, Dennis Sidener
Track Announcer: John Lies
Track Photographer: Reed Palmer

Racing Dates
2007: April 12-July 29, 67 days
2008: April 10-July 27, 65 days

Track Layout
Main Circumference: 1 mile
Main Track Chute: 7 furlongs and 1⅛ miles
Main Width: 90 feet
Main Length of Stretch: 930 feet
Main Turf Circumference: 7 furlongs
Main Turf Chute: 1⅛ miles
Main Turf Width: 80 feet
Main Turf Length of Stretch: 900 feet

Attendance
Average Daily Recent Meeting: 7,100, 2007
Highest Single-Day Record: 53,717, October 30, 2004
Highest Single-Meeting Record: 715,900, 1998
Daily Average Single Meeting: 9,800, 1998; 9,800 Fall 2004
Total Attendance Recent Meeting: 475,000, 2007
Highest Single-Day Recent Meeting: 25,040, July 4, 2007

Handle
Average All-Sources Recent Meeting: $1,700,000, 2007
Average On-Track Recent Meeting: $423,000, 2007
Single-Day On-Track Handle: $13,326,726, October 30, 2004
Single-Day All-Sources Handle: $120,863,117, October 30, 2004
Total All-Sources Recent Meeting: $111,700,000, 2007
Total On-Track Recent Meeting: $28,400,000, 2007
Highest Single-Day All-Sources Recent Meeting: $2,897,829, May 28, 2007
Highest Single-Day On-Track Recent Meeting: $1,015,620, May 28, 2007

Mutuel Records
Highest Win: $231.40, Purse Stealer, May 26, 2001
Highest Exacta: $6,900, May 26, 2001
Highest Quinella: $4,871, May 12, 2001
Highest Trifecta: $58,544, May 26, 2001
Highest Superfecta: $107,388, October 30, 2004
Highest Daily Double: $3,016.80, July 18, 1998
Highest Pick Three: $16,825.50, May 28, 2001
Highest Pick Four: $46,791.20, October 30, 2004
Highest Pick Six: $39,891.80, April 26, 1998
Highest Other Exotics: $96.40, Place, June 26, 1997; $35.40, Show, June 12, 1997;
Highest Stakes Win: $114.00, Thatsusintheolbean, 1997 Alysheba Breeders' Cup

Leaders
Career, Leading Jockey by Titles: Corey Lanerie, 4
Career, Leading Owner by Titles: Tom Durant, 4
Career, Leading Trainer by Titles: Steve Asmussen, 9
Career, Leading Jockey by Stakes Wins: Eddie Martin Jr., 23
Career, Leading Owner by Stakes Wins: Heiligbrodt Racing Stable, 13
Career, Leading Trainer by Stakes Wins: Steve Asmussen, 58
Career, Leading Jockey by Wins: Cliff Berry, 530
Career, Leading Owner by Wins: Tom Durant, 135
Career, Leading Trainer by Wins: Steve Asmussen, 724
Career, Leading Horse by Wins: Hadenough, 10; Ski Bum, 10
Career, Leading Horse by Wins on Turf: Hadenough, 10
Career, Leading Horse by Stakes Wins: Cinemine, 4; Mocha Express, 4
Career, Leading Jockey by Earnings: Cliff Berry, $10,099,784
Career, Leading Owner by Earnings: Heiligbrodt Racing Stables, $2,861,164
Career, Leading Trainer by Earnings: Steve Asmussen, $17,233,021
Career, Leading Horse by Earnings: Mocha Express, $487,796
Recent Meeting, Leading Jockey: Ramsey Zimmerman, 82, 2007
Recent Meeting, Leading Owner: Heflin & Driver Racing, 30, 2007
Recent Meeting, Leading Trainer: Steve Asmussen, 73, 2007
Recent Meeting, Leading Horse: Moneyinmywranglers, 4, 2007; Valid Lil, 4, 2007

Records
Single-Day Jockey Wins: Ronald Ardoin, 6, July 17, 1997, Anthony Lovato, 6, July 3, 2001
Single-Day Trainer Wins: Steve Asmussen, 7, July 14, 2002
Single Meeting, Leading Jockey by Wins: Cliff Berry, 103, 2006
Single Meeting, Leading Owner by Wins: Heflin & Driver Racing, 30, 2007
Single Meeting, Leading Trainer by Wins: Cole Norman, 98, 2003
Single Meeting, Leading Horse by Wins: Saf Link, 5, 2005
Single Meeting, Leading Jockey by Stakes Wins: Eddie Martin Jr., 8, 2003; Quincy Hamilton, 8, 2006
Single Meeting, Leading Owner by Stakes Wins: Mt. Brilliant Stable, 4, 1999; Heiligbrodt Racing Stable, 4, 2000
Single Meeting, Leading Trainer by Stakes Wins: Steve Asmussen, 9, 2004
Single Meeting, Leading Horse by Stakes Wins: Heritage of Gold, 3, 1999; Desert Air, 3, 1999

Principal Races
Lone Star Park H. (G3), Ouija Board Distaff H. (G3), Lone Star Derby (G3), Dallas Turf Cup (G3)

Interesting Facts
Achievements/Milestones: Lone Star Park handled a daily average of $2.39-million during its inaugural 1997 meeting, which ranked number one among all U.S. racetracks built since '70. As an encore, Lone Star became the first racetrack in modern history to increase attendance in its second year of operation—from 712,673 customers during the 1997 Thoroughbred season to 715,995 in '98.

Notable Events
Lone Star Million Day

Track Records, Main Dirt
4½ furlongs: Miss Missile, :51.18, April 28, 2007
5 furlongs: Joyful Tune, :56.25, May 5, 2002
5½ furlongs: That Tat, 1:01.88, April 11, 2003

6 furlongs: Savorthetime, 1:07.82, May 31, 2004
6½ furlongs: Spiritbound, 1:14.16, May 3, 1997
7 furlongs: Yearly Report, 1:20.67, October 29, 2004
1 mile: Isitingood, 1:34.44, April 20, 1997
1 1/16 miles: Dixie Dot Com, 1:40.53, May 28, 2001
1 1/8 miles: Ashado, 1:48.26, October 30, 2004
1 3/16 miles: Moosekabear, 1:56.21, May 10, 1997
1 1/4 miles: Ghostzapper, 1:59.02, October, 30, 2004
1 1/2 miles: Tali Hai, 2:32.57, July 5, 1997
1 3/4 miles: Sir Moon Dancer, 3:00.46, July 19, 1998
Other: 2½ furlongs, Yes He Will, :26.53, November 7, 1997; 1 5/16 miles, Gabriel's Pat, 2:12.34, October 22, 2004

Track Records, Main Turf
5 furlongs: Joe Move, :55.13, July 15, 2007
7½ furlongs: Song Dancer, 1:27.90, July 16, 2006; P F Don D, 1:27.90, May 18, 2007
1 mile: Kiraday, 1:33.56, July 4, 1997
1 1/16 miles: Sharpest Image (Ire), 1:40.05, June 12, 1998
1 1/8 miles: Yaqthan (Ire), 1:45.54, May 25, 1998
1 3/8 miles: Rugged Bugger, 2:13.53, May 10, 1998
1½ miles: Final Val, 2:28.20, July 4, 1998

Fastest Times of 2007 (Dirt)
4½ furlongs: Miss Missile, 2, :51.18, April 28, 2007
5 furlongs: Mystery Classic, 4, :56.73, July 4, 2007
5½ furlongs: Gold Coyote, 2, 1:03.04, July 7, 2007
6 furlongs: Sumfun, 3, 1:09.21, July 28, 2007
6½ furlongs: Trouble Now, 6, 1:16.18, April 26, 2007
7 furlongs: Danish Dancer (Arg), 8, 1:24.11, June 21, 2007
1 mile: Silent Pleasure, 4, 1:35.39, April 28, 2007
1 1/16 miles: Service Hawk, 4, 1:44.74, July 5, 2007
1 1/8 miles: Red Rock Creek, 6, 1:51.75, June 16, 2007
1 9/16 miles: Red Rock Creek, 6, 2:12.59, July 6, 2007

Fastest Times of 2007 (Turf)
4 furlongs: Classy Cade, 6, :43.87, April 21, 2007
5 furlongs: Joe Move, 7, :55.13, July 15, 2007
7½ furlongs: P F Don D, 6, 1:27.90, May 18, 2007
1 mile: Brego, 5, 1:34.29, July 22, 2007
1 1/16 miles: D Fine Okie, 5, 1:41.26, July 14, 2007
1 1/8 miles: Embossed (Ire), 5, 1:52.68, May 28, 2007
1½ miles: Red Rock Creek, 6, 2:28.43, July 28, 2007

Manor Downs

Thoroughbred racing debuted in 2002 at Manor Downs, a small racetrack near Austin, that long had offered only straightaway Quarter Horse and Paint racing. Ordered by the Texas Racing Commission to improve its racetrack to accommodate Thoroughbred racing, Manor (pronounced May-ner) spent more than $4-million to expand its oval to 7½ furlongs and to renovate the barn area and other sections. Manor, which is owned by Frances Tapp, was among the tracks in Texas's far-flung non-pari-mutuel circuit that flourished before legislation allowing pari-mutuel wagering was passed in 1987.

Location: 9211 Hill Ln., Manor, Tx. 78653
Phone: (512) 272-5581
Fax: (512) 272-4403
Website: www.manordowns.com
Abbreviation: Man

Ownership
Frances Tapp

Officers
Director of Racing: Sammy J. Burton
Racing Secretary: Sammy Burton
Track Superintendent: Robert Allan Key

Racing Dates
2007: February 24-April 22, 18 days
2008: February 23-April 20, 18 days

Attendance
Average Daily Recent Meeting: 3,307, 2007
Total Attendance Recent Meeting: 59,539, 2007

Handle
Average On-Track Recent Meeting: $80,617, 2007
Total On-Track Recent Meeting: $1,451,110, 2007

Leaders
Recent Meeting, Leading Jockey: Santos Carrizales, 11, 2007; Salvatore Perez, 9, 2008
Recent Meeting, Leading Trainer: M. Shawn Finch, 6, 2007; Jaime Castellano, 3, 2008; J.R. Caldwell, 3, 2008; Charlotte Bronstad, 3, 2008; Bradley C. Bolen, 3, 2008; Glynn Winn, 3, 2008; Juan A. Martinez, 3, 2008
Recent Meeting, Leading Horse: Stalwart's Heir, 2, 2007; Suvu, 2, 2007; Our Resurrection, 2, 2007; Rusted Steel, 2, 2007; Madd Dogg Itt, 2, 2007; Tootallwoo, 2, 2008; Runnin Branch, 2, 2008; Mystardreamer, 2, 2008

Principal Races
Manor Downs Thoroughbred Distaff S., Tony Sanchez Memorial Mile S., Manor Downs Thoroughbred Futurity, Manor Downs Distance Cup S.

Fastest Times of 2007 (Dirt)
4½ furlongs: Luken Boss, 7, :52.58, March 4, 2007
5½ furlongs: Imaluckymemorie, 5, 1:05.60, March 4, 2007
6 furlongs: Cuz I Da Mon, 3, 1:12.57, March 31, 2007
7½ furlongs: Madd Dogg Itt, 4, 1:33.05, March 24, 2007
1 mile: Begborrowanddeal, 6, 1:37.91, April 21, 2007
1 1/16 miles: Moon Kid, 4, 1:44.80, April 1, 2007

Retama Park

One of the country's newest racing facilities, Retama Park opened in April 1995 in Selma, 15 minutes northeast of San Antonio. The racetrack is both uniquely named—for the green-limbed deciduous tree or shrub native to south and west Texas—and uniquely designed, with its mission-style, five-tiered grandstand featuring arched entranceways, food courts, the Terrace Dining Room, the Race Book and Sports Bar, and the Player's Club for Turf and Field Club members. The track's original investors hired well-known racing executive Robert J. Quigley to oversee construction of the $79-million plant and the track's opening, but the facility failed to meet even modest wagering projections. After failing to pay its bondholders, the track filed for bankruptcy protection in 1996 and was purchased by Call Now Inc. Retama serves as a year-round simulcast facility and also operates a Quarter Horse meeting from April through June.

Location: 1 Retama Pkwy., Selma, Tx. 78154-3808
Phone: (210) 651-7000
Fax: (210) 651-7055
Website: www.retamapark.com
E-Mail: run@retamapark.com
Year Founded: 1989
Dates of Inaugural Meeting: April 7, 1995
Abbreviation: Ret
Acreage: 226
Number of Stalls: 1,288
Seating Capacity: 6,543

Ownership
Retama Development Corp.

Officers
Chief Executive Officer: Bryan P. Brown
Chairman: Joe R. Straus Jr.
General Manager: Robert W. Pollock
Director of Racing: Larry A. Craft

Racing Secretary: James C. Leatherman
Chief Financial Officer: Lisa L. Medrano
Director of Marketing and Publicity: Doug Vair
Director of Mutuels: Jackie F. Hart
Director of Simulcasting: Steven M. Ross
Horsemen's Liaison: Wanda O'Bannan
Stewards: Donnie Walker, Ricky Walker, Fred Winch Jr.
Track Announcer: Tom Harris
Track Photographer: Coady Photography
Track Superintendent: Jesse L. Cardenas
Security: Richard L. Cole

Racing Dates
2007: September 7-November 17, 32 days
2008: August 29-November 15, 35, days

Track Layout
Main Circumference: 1 mile
Main Track Chute: 7 furlongs
Main Width: Homestretch: 110 feet; Backstretch: 90 feet
Main Length of Stretch: 990 feet
Main Turf Circumference: 7 furlongs
Main Turf Chute: 1 1/8 miles
Main Turf Width: 90 feet
Main Turf Length of Stretch: 990 feet

Attendance
Average Daily Recent Meeting: 2,997, 2007
Record Daily Average Single Meeting: 4,713, 1995
Highest Single-Day Record: 16,827, April 7, 1995
Highest Single-Day Recent Meeting: 6,985, November 17, 2007
Total Attendance Recent Meeting: 95,917, 2007
Highest Single-Meeting Record: 452,421, 1995

Handle
Average All-Sources Recent Meeting: $1,073,783, 2007
Average On-Track Recent Meeting: $292,122, 2007
Single-Day On-Track Handle: $705,712, April 7, 1995
Single-Day All-Sources Handle: $2,502,823, October 27, 2001
Total All-Sources Recent Meeting: $25,013,161, 2007
Total On-Track Recent Meeting: $9,347,905, 2007
Highest Single-Day All-Sources Recent Meeting: $1,233,388, November 17, 2007
Highest Single-Day On-Track Recent Meeting: $197,233, November 17, 2007

Mutuel Records
Highest Win: $136.40, Icy's Baba, August 15, 1999

Leaders
Recent Meeting, Leading Jockey: Eguard Tejera, 50, 2007
Recent Meeting, Leading Trainer: Dan Pish, 40, 2007
Recent Meeting, Leading Horse: Olmos Creek, 3, 2007

Records
Single Meeting, Leading Jockey by Wins: Corey Lanerie, 99, 1995, Ted Gondron, 99, 1996
Single Meeting, Leading Owner by Wins: Carolyn A. Crowly, 17, 1996
Single Meeting, Leading Trainer by Wins: Steve Asmussen, 48, 1995

Track Records, Main Dirt
4 1/2 furlongs: Raise a Tab, :51.06, August 1, 1998
5 furlongs: Teed Off, :56.20, August 20, 2000
5 1/2 furlongs: Bailando, 1:02.90, May 13, 1995
6 furlongs: Devil's Money, 1:08.78, August 25, 2006
6 1/2 furlongs: Heavily Armed, 1:15.30, August 30, 1997
7 furlongs: Bucharest, 1:22.05, May 24, 1995
1 mile: Mr. Pappion, 1:36.90, May 11, 1995
1 1/16 miles: Heavily Armed, 1:43.20, September 20, 1997
1 1/8 miles: Fletcher's Pride, 1:51.43, August 14, 1998
1 1/4 miles: Call Me Wild, 2:04.01, September 3, 1995
1 3/8 miles: Slews Minister, 2:19.95, October 28, 2000
Other: 2 1/2 furlongs, Texas Hope, :28.20, June 28, 1998; 1 5/16 miles, Opening Remark, 2:13.99, September 5, 1996

Track Records, Main Turf
5 furlongs: Rockin' Kate, :55.48, October 1, 2005
7 1/2 furlongs: Haveuseenthelight, 1:28.26, October 26, 2007
1 mile: Eagle Lake, 1:34.54, October 4, 2003

1 1/16 miles: General Charley, 1:40.65, October 13, 2007
1 1/8 miles: Untraceable, 1:48.13, August 10, 1996
1 3/8 miles: Bullet Crane, 2:16.88, November 4, 2006
Other: 1 13/16 miles, Misting Rain, 3:13.22, September 28, 1996

Fastest Times of 2007 (Dirt)
5 furlongs: Bering Sea, 2, :59.92, September 20, 2007
5 1/2 furlongs: War Bridle, 5, 1:03.71, September 7, 2007
6 furlongs: Mystery Classic, 4, 1:08.84, September 29, 2007
6 1/2 furlongs: Brother Norm, 2, 1:19.30, November 8, 2007
7 furlongs: Joe Henry, 5, 1:23.23, September 15, 2007
1 mile: Play the Chime, 5, 1:38.22, September 21, 2007

Fastest Times of 2007 (Turf)
5 furlongs: Temperamental Miss, 3, :55.64, October 13, 2007
7 1/2 furlongs: Haveuseenthelight, 3, 1:28.26, October 26, 2007
1 1/16 miles: General Charley, 5, 1:40.65, October 13, 2007
1 3/8 miles: Precision Strike, 5, 2:17.42, November 17, 2007

Sam Houston Race Park

In April 1994, Sam Houston Race Park opened as the first Class I racetrack in Texas, which had outlawed pari-mutuel wagering for more than 50 years. Built for $85-million and named for one of the state's founding fathers, the racetrack in northwest Houston is a part of the Class I Texas racing circuit that includes Lone Star Park in the Dallas-Fort Worth metroplex and Retama Park near San Antonio. Sam Houston, which conducts nighttime racing, holds a fall-winter-spring Thoroughbred meet and hosts Quarter Horse racing in the summer. The track's signature event is Texas Champions Day, which offers nine lucrative stakes races for state-breds. Sam Houston's majority owner is MAXXAM Inc., a Houston-based Fortune 500 company involved in forest products and real estate that is chaired by Texas native Charles Hurwitz. The track is the home of the Houston Equine Research Organization, a not-for-profit group that works to promote the welfare of racehorses through research and offers a successful racehorse adoption program.

Location: 7575 N. Sam Houston Pkwy. W., Houston, Tx. 77064-3417
Phone: (281) 807-8700
Fax: (281) 807-8777
Website: www.shrp.com
E-Mail: ask@shrp.com
Year Founded: 1994
Dates of Inaugural Meeting: April 29, 1994
Abbreviation: Hou
Acreage: 230
Number of Stalls: 1,250
Seating Capacity: 18,000

Ownership
MAXXAM Inc.

Officers
President and Chief Executive Officer: Shawn Hurwitz
Chief Operating Officer: Andrea Bouchey Young
Senior Vice President/Chief Sales and Marketing Officer: Wayne Hodes
Vice President of Finance: David Jackson
Vice President of Business Development: Eric Heacock
Vice President of Facility Operations: Dwight Berube
Vice President of Racing: Eric M. Johnston
Director of Marketing: Sandy Barton
Director of Mutuels: Kim Pomposelli
Director of Media Relations: Gina Rotolo
Stewards: Jerry Burgess, Steve O'Malley, J. David Rollinson
Track Announcer: Michael Chamberlain
Track Photographer: Coady Photography
Park Superintendent: Greg Johnson

Assistant Racing Secretary: Ronald Anthony
Horsemen's Bookkeeper: Doris Sims
Security: Donald Ahrens

Racing Dates
2007: November 17, 2006-April 7, 2007, 68 days
2008: November 23, 2007-April 5, 2008, 67 days; November 28-December 31, 19 days

Track Layout
Main Circumference: 1 mile
Main Track Chute: 7 furlongs and 1¼ miles
Main Width: 90 feet
Main Length of Stretch: 966 feet
Main Turf Circumference: 7 furlongs
Main Turf Chute: 1⅛ miles
Main Turf Width: 80 feet

Attendance
Highest Single-Day Record: 24,316, July 4, 2003
Average Daily Recent Meeting: 4,442, 2007/2008
Highest Single-Day Record: 24,316, July 4, 2003
Total Attendance Recent Meeting: 297,614, 2007/2008

Handle
Average All-Sources Recent Meeting: $1,622,982, 2007/2008
Average On-Track Recent Meeting: $101,485, 2007/2008
Single-Day On-Track Handle: $3,557,018, December 7, 2002
Single-Day All-Sources Handle: $5,740,955, December 7, 2002
Total All-Sources Recent Meeting: $108,739,794, 2007/2008
Total On-Track Recent Meeting: $6,799,516, 2007/2008

Leaders
Recent Meeting, Leading Jockey: Jorge Guzman, 65, 2007/2008
Recent Meeting, Leading Trainer: John G. Locke, 50, 2007/2008
Recent Meeting, Leading Horse: Supper Struggler, 5, 2007/2008; Gringa Vaya, 5, 2007/2008; I'm a Badman, 5, 2007/2008; Scrappy Roo, 5, 2007/2008

Records
Single-Day Jockey Wins: Austin Lovelace, 7, December 10, 1994
Single-Day Trainer Wins: Gilbert Ciavaglia, 5, February 23, 1997
Single Meeting, Leading Jockey by Wins: Steve Bourque, 120, 2000/2001
Single Meeting, Leading Owner by Wins: John Franks, 24, 1994/1995
Single Meeting, Leading Trainer by Wins: Steve Asmussen, 57, 2002/2003

Principal Races
John B. Connally Breeders' Cup Turf H., Maxxam Gold Cup H., Jim's Orbit S., Two Altazano S.

Interesting Facts
Trivia: First Class I racetrack in Texas.

Track Records, Main Dirt
4½ furlongs: Prime Time Man, :51.70, February 12, 2004
5 furlongs: Endofthestorm, :57.21, October 25, 2003
5½ furlongs: Bucharest, 1:02.92, April 13, 1996
6 furlongs: Bucharest, 1:08.91, May 11, 1994
6½ furlongs: Brass Jacks, 1:15.77, May 21, 1994
7 furlongs: Bucharest, 1:21.29, May 4, 1996
1 mile: Catalissa, 1:36.33, March 8, 2003
1 mile 70 yds: Capt. Tiff's Beau, 1:40.52, October 24, 1998
1 1/16 miles: Desert Air, 1:42.74, February 13, 1999
1⅛ miles: Lost Soldier, 1:48.75, May 3, 1997
1¼ miles: Sauvage Isn't Home, 2:04.75, December 29, 1995
1½ miles: Final Val, 2:32.99, February 20, 1998
1¾ miles: Final Val, 3:01.50, March 13, 1998
2 miles: Final Val, 3:31.29, April 3, 1998

Track Records, Main Turf
5 furlongs: Charming Socialite, :56.61, April 8, 2006
1 mile: Solo Attack, 1:36.16, March 17, 2001
1 1/16 miles: Luna Delight, 1:43.24, December 4, 1998
1⅛ miles: Chorwon, 1:47.65, March 6, 1999
1½ miles: Commander Calhoun, 2:32.56, October 3, 1996

Fastest Times of 2007 (Dirt)
5 furlongs: Greggo, 7, :58.16, January 14, 2007
5½ furlongs: Leeway, 4, 1:03.65, February 25, 2007
6 furlongs: Mystery Classic, 4, 1:09.55, December 1, 2007
6½ furlongs: Leeway, 4, 1:17.24, December 27, 2007
7 furlongs: Moneyinmywranglers, 3, 1:23.31, December 15, 2007
1 mile: Nine M. M., 3, 1:38.48, December 6, 2007
1 mile 70 yds: Gold Wonder, 3, 1:42.75, December 31, 2007; Regina's Mon, 6, 1:42.75, March 16, 2007
1 1/16 miles: Sandburr, 8, 1:44.53, December 1, 2007
1⅛ miles: Student Council, 5, 1:51.89, January 27, 2007
1½ miles: Regina's Mon, 6, 2:36.75, March 31, 2007

Fastest Times of 2007 (Turf)
5 furlongs: Cat Genius, 7, :58.17, April 7, 2007
1 mile: Chromedoll, 5, 1:38.26, March 29, 2007
1 1/16 miles: General Charley, 5, 1:43.94, February 24, 2007
1⅛ miles: Mending Fences, 5, 1:52.34, April 7, 2007

Virginia

Colonial Downs

Colonial Downs has featured a high standard of racing since its opening in 1997, and the facility has slowly built a local brand name and a national following for its simulcast signal. Constructed in New Kent County approximately 24 miles from Richmond, the track is the only facility to open in Virginia since pari-mutuel wagering was legalized in 1993. The track features seating for 6,000 in an attractive setting. Colonial's 1¼-mile dirt track is one of North America's largest, and its turf course has drawn praise. Colonial originally raced in late summer and early fall but switched to an early summer meeting in 2001. In mid-2001, principal investor Jeffrey Jacobs bought out the track's shareholders and transformed Colonial into a private company. In 2005, he bought out the Maryland Jockey Club's franchise to operate the track.

Location: 10515 Colonial Downs Pkwy., New Kent, Va. 23124
Phone: (804) 966-7223, (888) 482-8722
Fax: (804) 966-1565
Website: www.colonialdowns.com
E-Mail: info@colonialdowns.com
Year Founded: 1997
Dates of Inaugural Meeting: September 1-October 12, 1997
Abbreviation: Cnl
Acreage: 607.46
Number of Stalls: 1,050
Seating Capacity: 10,000

Ownership
Jacobs Entertainment

Officers
Chairman: Jeffrey P. Jacobs
President: Ian M. Stewart
Vice Presidents: Jeanna Bouzek, Tom Hamilton, Jerry Monahan, Iain F. Woolnough
General Manager: Iain F. Woolnough
Racing Secretary: Randy R. Wehrman
Assistant Racing Secretary: Wendy Pensivy
Treasurer: Tom Hamilton
Director of Marketing and Publicity: Darrell Wood
Director of Mutuels: Jeff Wingrove
Horsemen's Liaison: Alice Marcacci
Stewards: Stan Bowker, Jean Chalk, William Passmore
Track Announcer: Dave Rodman
Track Photographer: Jeff Coady
Track Superintendent: Wes Nadolin
Horsemen's Bookkeeper: Connie Collier
Security: Pat Kelleher

Racetracks — Washington

Racing Dates
2007: June 15-August 7, 40 days
2008: June 9-August 6, 45 days

Track Layout
Main Circumference: 1 1/4 miles
Main Track Chute: 1 1/8 miles
Main Width: 80 feet
Main Length of Stretch: 1,290.50 feet
Main Turf Circumference: 7 furlongs to 1 1/8 miles, depending on rail position
Main Turf Width: 180 feet
Main Turf Length of Stretch: 1,123.62 feet

Attendance
Average Daily Recent Meeting: 1,996, 2007
Highest Single-Day Record: 13,468, September 1, 1997
Highest Single-Meeting Record: 108,591, 1997
Record Daily Average Single Meeting: 3,620, 1997
Total Attendance Recent Meeting: 79,859, 2007

Handle
Average All-Sources Recent Meeting: $1,262,689, 2007
Average On-Track Recent Meeting: $164,557, 2007
Record Daily Average Single Meeting: $197,577, 2004
Single-Day On-Track Handle: $753,680.50, July 21, 2007
Single-Day All-Sources Handle: $4,537,507.80, July 21, 2007
Total All-Sources Recent Meeting: $50,507,580, 2007
Total On-Track Recent Meeting: $6,582,262, 2007
Highest Single-Day On-Track Recent Meeting: $753,680.50, July 21, 2007
Highest Single-Day All-Sources Recent Meeting: $4,537,507.80, July 21, 2007
Record Total All-Sources Single Meeting: $51,587,423, 2006
Record Total Single Meeting: $6,805,009, 2005

Leaders
Career, Leading Jockey by Titles: Mario Pino and Horacio Karamanos, 3
Career, Leading Trainer by Titles: A. Ferris Allen III, 6
Career, Leading Jockey by Wins: Horacio Karamanos, 292
Career, Leading Trainer by Wins: A. Ferris Allen III, 171
Recent Meeting, Leading Jockey: Horacio Karamanos, 62, 2007
Recent Meeting, Leading Owner: David A. Ross, 24, 2007
Recent Meeting, Leading Trainer: Hamilton A. Smith, 20, 2007
Recent Meeting, Leading Horse: Who's First, 3, 2007, Rolling Honor, 3, 2007, Limey, 3, 2007

Records
Single-Day Jockey Wins: Mario Pino, 7, July 7, 2002
Single Meeting, Leading Jockey by Wins: Horacio Karamanos, 66, 2005
Single Meeting, Leading Trainer by Wins: A. Ferris Allen III, 25, 1997

Principal Races
Virginia Derby (G2), All Along S. (G3), Colonial Turf Cup S. (G3), Virginia Oaks (G3)

Track Records, Main Dirt
5 furlongs: Timothy Mac, :55.74, July 1, 2003
5 1/2 furlongs: Love's Strong Hart, 1:02.53, July 7, 2006
6 furlongs: Satan's Code, 1:08.48, June 27, 2004
6 1/2 furlongs: Cool Ken Jane, 1:16.60, September 7, 1997
7 furlongs: Sky Watch, 1:20.87, September 1, 1997
1 mile: Mt. Carson, 1:35.07, June 26, 2004
1 1/16 miles: Gold Token, 1:41.09, September 13, 1998
1 1/8 miles: Our Toby, 1:48.95, October 4, 1997
1 1/4 miles: Macgyver, 2:03.54, September 1, 1997
1 1/2 miles: Lord Mendelson, 2:30.13, September 4, 2000

Track Records, Main Turf
5 furlongs: Tommie's Star, :55.27, July 4, 2006
5 1/2 furlongs: Dreaming of Anna, 1:01.63, July 29, 2006
6 furlongs: Tyaskin, 1:08.11, September 20, 1998
1 1/16 miles: Kona Blend, 1:41.03, August 5, 2007
1 1/8 miles: Film Maker, 1:46.58, June 24, 2006
1 3/16 miles: Showing Up, 1:52.98, June 24, 2006
1 1/4 miles: Go Between, 1:59.74, July 15, 2006
1 1/2 miles: Marsh Side, 2:30.98, July 15, 2006
1 5/8 miles: Beluga, 2:45.80, September 26, 1998

Track Records, Inner Turf
5 furlongs: Smart Sunny, :56.02, September 8, 2000
5 1/2 furlongs: Smart Sunny, 1:02.94, September 13, 1998
1 mile: La Reine's Terms, 1:34.24, September 17, 1998
1 1/16 miles: Grass Roots, 1:41.01, October 8, 1999
1 1/8 miles: Steak Scam, 1:48.71, September 25, 1999
1 1/4 miles: Franc, 2:03.02, September 9, 2000
1 1/2 miles: Winsox, 2:27.04, September 28, 1998
1 5/8 miles: Our Game, 2:44.82, September 24, 1999

Fastest Times of 2007 (Dirt)
5 1/2 furlongs: Mr. Madison, 3, 1:03.58, July 8, 2007; Rolling Honor, 4, 1:03.58, August 4, 2007
6 furlongs: Infatuated, 4, 1:09.06, July 9, 2007
7 furlongs: Unbridled Behavior, 4, 1:22.40, July 14, 2007
1 mile: Curry's Honor, 5, 1:36.17, July 3, 2007; Park Avenue Prince, 4, 1:36.17, July 8, 2007
1 1/16 miles: Sweetdownthelane, 4, 1:43.29, June 30, 2007; Wye, 3, 1:43.29, June 30, 2007

Fastest Times of 2007 (Turf)
5 furlongs: On the Prowl, 5, :56.48, July 27, 2007
5 1/2 furlongs: Hesa Big Star, 5, 1:01.99, June 25, 2007; Rudirudy, 12, 1:01.99, June 24, 2007
1 mile: Pass Play, 6, 1:35.05, July 7, 2007
1 1/16 miles: Kona Blend, 4, 1:41.03, August 5, 2007
1 1/8 miles: Dreaming of Anna, 3, 1:47.38, July 21, 2007; Dubai Cat, 8, 1:47.38, June 17, 2007
1 3/16 miles: El Viaje, 5, 1:55.41, June 24, 2007
1 1/4 miles: Red Giant, 3, 1:59.62, July 21, 2007
1 1/2 miles: Roi de Violette, 6, 2:31.02, July 28, 2007
2 1/4 miles: Moneytrain (Ger), 8, 4:01.63, July 15, 2007

Washington

Dayton Days

Location: P.O. Box 264, Dayton, Wa. 99328
Phone: (509) 382-2370
Year Founded: 1918
Abbreviation: Day

Officers
President: Norm Hansen
Vice President: Lanny Adams
Director of Racing and Racing Secretary: Billie Jean Brown
Treasurer: Melissa Hansen
Director of Marketing: Tim Donohue
Director of Mutuels: Norm Hansen
Stewards: Eddie Alves, Charlie Landel, Bob Lightfoot
Track Announcer: Zane Troester
Track Photographer: Roger Nielsen

Racing Dates
2007: May 26-May 27, 2 days
2008: May 24-May 25, 2 days

Handle
Average All-Sources Recent Meeting: $21,968, 2007
Total All-Sources Recent Meeting: $43,937, 2007

Leaders
Recent Meeting, Leading Jockey: Connie P. Doll, 2, 2007; Roger Butterfly, 2, 2007
Recent Meeting, Leading Trainer: Keith Duane Davis, 2, 2006

Principal Races
Queens Derby

Fastest Times of 2007 (Dirt)
5 furlongs: Roman Governor, 6, 1:03.20, May 27, 2007
6 1/2 furlongs: Zoolu Nights, 7, 1:27.60, May 26, 2007

Emerald Downs

Emerald Downs returned Thoroughbred racing to the Seattle area when it opened in 1996. Since the 1930s, the hub of Northwest racing had been Longacres, which was sold in '90 to aircraft manufacturer Boeing Co. After Longacres held its last season of racing in 1992, Yakima Meadows in Yakima became its short-term successor. A group of investors headed by Ron Crockett, who formerly was involved in an airline-related company, built Emerald for $83-million. The track, which offers racing from mid-April to late September, became the new host of the Northwest's most famous race when the Longacres Mile Handicap (G3) was first held at the track during its inaugural season. The Muckleshoot Indian Tribe purchased the 167-acre property on which the track is located for $73-million in 2002.

Location: 2300 Emerald Downs Dr., Auburn, Wa. 98001-1633
Phone: (253) 288-7000, (888) 931-8400
Website: www.emeralddowns.com
Year Founded: 1996
Abbreviation: EmD
Acreage: 167
Number of Stalls: 1,480

Ownership
Northwest Racing Associates LLP

Officers
President: Ron Crockett
Vice President: Jack E. Hodge Jr.
Vice President of Marketing: Susie Sourwine
Director of Racing: Bret Anderson
Director of Operations: Bob Fraser
Director of Broadcast Publicity: Joe Withee
Director of Media Relations: Vince Bruun
Track Announcer: Robert Geller
Track Photographer: Reed Palmer

Racing Dates
2008: April 18-September 28, 91 days

Track Layout
Main Circumference: 1 mile
Main Track Chute: 6½ furlongs and 1¼ miles
Main Width: 90 feet
Main Length of Stretch: 990 feet

Handle
Highest Single-Day All-Sources Recent Meeting:: $3,191,831, 2007
Average All-Sources Recent Meeting: $1,415,172, 2007
Highest Single-Day Record On-Track Recent Meeting: $3,191,831, August 19, 2007
Record Average All-Sources Single Meeting: $1,415,172, 2007
Record Total All-Sources Single Meeting: $139,493,888, 2005

Mutuel Records
Highest Win: $142.80, My Lady Boots, July 27, 1997
Lowest Win: $2.20, Victory Script, September 15, 2007
Highest Exacta: $2,317.80, October 28, 1998
Lowest Exacta: $2.40, June 1, 2003
Highest Trifecta: $27,356.90, July 3, 2002
Lowest Trifecta: $5.30, June 10, 2007
Highest Daily Double: $1,878.20, August 8, 2003
Lowest Daily Double: $4.40, August 24, 1997
Highest Pick Three: $7,479.90, July 9, 2000
Lowest Pick Three: $4.70, May 8, 1997
Highest Pick Six: $217,140, June 8, 1997
Lowest Pick Six: $146.20, August 31, 1997
Highest Other Exotics: $15,487.20, Superfecta, June 2, 2002
Lowest Other Exotics: $9.60, Superfecta, September 15, 2007
Highest Stakes Win: $122.00, No Giveaway, August 21, 2005, Longacres Mile
Highest Pick Four: $13,373.30, August 2, 2007

Leaders
Career, Leading Jockey by Stakes Wins: Gallyn Mitchell, 52
Career, Leading Owner by Stakes Wins: Northwest Farms, 20
Career, Leading Trainer by Stakes Wins: Bud Klokstad, 41
Career, Leading Jockey by Wins: Gallyn Mitchell, 966
Career, Leading Owner by Wins: Ron Crockett, Inc., 168
Career, Leading Trainer by Wins: Tim McCanna, 578
Recent Meeting, Leading Jockey: Ricky Frazier, 157, 2007
Recent Meeting, Leading Trainer: Tim McCanna, 50, 2007
Recent Meeting, Leading Horse: Victory Script, 7, 2007
Recent Meeting, Leading Owner: Ron Crockett, Inc., 21, 2007

Records
Single-Day Jockey Wins: Kevin Radke, 6, September 2, 2002
Single-Day Trainer Wins: Jim Penney, 5, September 6, 1998
Single Meeting, Leading Jockey by Wins: Ricky Frazierr, 157, 2007
Single Meeting, Leading Owner by Wins: West Ridge Ranch, 23, 2003
Single Meeting, Leading Trainer by Wins: Tim McCanna, 55, 1999; Tim McCanna, 55, 2003
Single Meeting, Leading Trainer by Stakes Wins: Doris Harwood, 12, 2007
Single Meeting, Leading Jockey by Stakes Wins: Gallyn Vick Mitchell, 13, 2000

Principal Races
Longacres Mile (G3), Washington Oaks, Emerald Distaff, Emerlad Downs Derby, Gottstein Futurity

Track Records, Main Dirt
4½ furlongs: Sea Speaker, :50, August 25, 2007
5 furlongs: Jazzy Mac, :55.40, August 20, 2000; Victor Slew, :55.40, August 24, 2003; Starbird Road, :55.40, October 1, 2006
5½ furlongs: Willie the Cat, 1:01.20, April 16, 2004; The Great Face, 1:01.20, April 20, 2007
6 furlongs: Starbird Road, 1:07.40, September 17, 2006
6½ furlongs: Sabertooth, 1:13, May 22, 2005
1 mile: Sky Jack, 1:33, August 24, 2003
1¹/₁₆ miles: Kid Katabatic, 1:39.60, July 26, 1998
1¼ miles: Flying Notes, 1:45.40, September 2, 2002
1½ miles: Itstufftobegood, 2:01, August 5, 2005
1½ miles: Military Deputy, 2:29, August 26, 2007
1¾ miles: Itstufftobegood, 3:02, September 18, 2005
2 miles: Horatio, 3:22.60, September 20, 2004
Other: 2 furlongs, Midnight Cruiser, :21.40, May 4, 2000; 2 furlongs, Adventure Man, :21.40, May 10, 2000

Fastest Times of 2007 (Dirt)
4½ furlongs: Sea Speaker, 5, :50, August 25, 2007
5 furlongs: Chickasaw Park, 5, :56, September 30, 2007
5½ furlongs: The Great Face, 5, 1:01.20, April 20, 2007
6 furlongs: Chickasaw Park, 5, 1:07.60, September 16, 2007; Izzacopy, 4, 1:07.60, May 12, 2007; Nationhood, 5, 1:07.60, September 3, 2007; Salt Grinder, 8, 1:07.60, May 19, 2007
6½ furlongs: Westsideclyde, 5, 1:13.40, May 28, 2007
1 mile: Random Memo, 6, 1:34.20, May 28, 2007; Sudden Departure, 5, 1:34.20, July 4, 2007; Westsideclyde, 5, 1:34.20, June 17, 2007
1¹/₁₆ miles: Shampoo, 3, 1:41, July 22, 2007
1¹/₁₆ miles: Mulcahy, 5, 1:47.20, September 3, 2007
1¼ miles: Military Deputy, 5, 2:01.60, August 3, 2007
1½ miles: Military Deputy, 5, 2:29, August 26, 2007
2 miles: Geririg, 7, 3:32.80, September 30, 2007

Sun Downs

Location: P.O. Box 6662, Kennewick, Wa. 99336-0639
Phone: (509) 582-5434
Fax: (509) 586-9780
Year Founded: 1969
Abbreviation: SuD
Number of Stalls: 365
Seating Capacity: 3,800

Ownership
Tri-City Horse Racing Association

Officers
President: Malon Cowgill
Vice President: William Henderson
General Manager and Treasurer: Nancy Sorick
Director of Racing: Nellie Schellinger
Racing Secretary: Shorty Martin
Director of Marketing and Publicity: Des Ritari
Director of Mutuels: Helen Lizotte
Track Announcer: Zane Torester
Track Superintendent: Jimmie McDonnell
Security: Benton-Franklin, Mounted Posse

Racing Dates
2007: April 7-May 6, 10 days
2008: April 5-May 4, 10 days

Track Layout
Main Circumference: 5 furlongs
Main Track Chute: 6½ furlongs

Handle
Average On-Track Recent Meeting: $51,938, 2007
Total On-Track Recent Meeting: $519,389, 2007

Leaders
Recent Meeting, Leading Jockey: Nikeela Renae Black, 11, 2007; J. Luis Torres, 16, 2008
Recent Meeting, Leading Trainer: Robert L. Lawrence, 8, 2007; Jerry Holifield, 13, 2008
Recent Meeting, Leading Horse: Schu True Sleeper, 3, 2007; Height of Summer, 3, 2007; Marie S., 2, 2008; I'm Rough N Ready, 2, 2008; Maid In Monroe, 2, 2008; Im Pure Country, 2, 2008; Easter Sonny Boy, 2, 2008; Baby Johnny, 2, 2008; Got No Socks, 2, 2008

Fastest Times of 2007 (Dirt)
4 furlongs: David Strike Back, 7, :46, May 6, 2007; Northern Ricky, 11, :46, May 6, 2007
6 furlongs: Roman Governor, 6, 1:14.60, April 28, 2007
6½ furlongs: Roman Governor, 6, 1:19.40, May 6, 2007
7 furlongs: Chuzz, 5, 1:25, May 6, 2007

Waitsburg Race Track

Location: P.O. Box 391, Waitsburg, Wa. 99361-0391
Phone: (509) 337-6241
Year Founded: 1911
Abbreviation: Wts

Officers
President: Terry Hofer
Racing Secretary: Shorty Martin
Secretary: Rose Englebrite

Racing Dates
2007: May 19-May 20, 2 days
2008: May 17-May 18, 2 days

Handle
Average On-Track Recent Meeting: $24,137, 2007
Total On-Track Recent Meeting: $48,275, 2007

Leaders
Recent Meeting, Leading Jockey: Troy Stillwell, 4, 2008
Recent Meeting, Leading Trainer: Bill D. Hoff, 2, 2008; Judi Yearout, 2, 2008; Wade Ross, 2, 2008

Fastest Times of 2007 (Dirt)
a5 furlongs: Ninetenthsofthelaw, 8, 1:05.40, May 19, 2007
6½ furlongs: Blazing Genius, 11, 1:25.60, May 19, 2007
1¹/₁₆ miles: Gassan Royal, 7, 1:48.20, May 20, 2007

Walla Walla

Location: P.O. Box G, Walla Walla, Wa. 99362-0036
Phone: (509) 527-3247
Fax: (509) 527-3259
Website: www.wallawallafairgrounds.com
E-Mail: wwfair@hscis.net

Year Founded: 1866
Abbreviation: WW
Number of Stalls: 180
Seating Capacity: 3,000

Ownership
Walla Walla County

Officers
Chairman: Dick Monahan
President: Dick Moeller
Vice President and Director of Mutuels: Bill Clemens
General Manager and Director of Marketing: Cory Hewitt
Directors of Racing: Bill Clemens, Dick Monahan
Racing Secretary: Debbie Delaney
Secretary and Director of Security: Barry Morgan
Horsemen's Liaison: Dick Monahan
Stewards: Charles Landells, Robert Lightfoot
Track Announcer: Pete O'Laughlin
Track Photographer: Roger Nielsen

Racing Dates
2007: May 12-May 13, 2 days; August 31-September 2, 3 days
2008: May 10-May 11, 2 days; August 29-September 1, 3 days

Track Layout
Main Circumference: 4 furlongs
Main Track Chute: 6 furlongs

Handle
Average On-Track Recent Meeting: $32,948, Spring 2007; $33,161, Summer 2007
Total On-Track Recent Meeting: $65,897, Spring 2007; $99,484, Summer 2007
Highest Single-Day On-Track Record Recent Meeting: $35,512, May 12, 2007; $45,737, September 1, 2007

Leaders
Recent Meeting, Leading Jockey: Ty Dangerfield, 6, Summer 2007
Recent Meeting, Leading Trainer: Emil Abrahamson, 3, Summer 2007

Fastest Times of 2007 (Dirt)
a5 furlongs: Height of Summer, 6, 1:02, September 1, 2007
7 furlongs: Looks Lika Fish, 7, 1:27, September 1, 2007
1¹/₈ miles: Tender Offer (Ire), 10, 2:00.40, May 13, 2007

West Virginia

Charles Town Races

Founded in 1933 by Albert Boyle, Charles Town Races in Charles Town has been wholly owned by Penn National Gaming Inc. since 2000. The company also owns Penn National Race Course in Pennsylvania as well as other gaming and resort facilities. Penn National Gaming bought a majority interest in Charles Town after local voters approved slot machines at the track in 1996. Charles Town Races has seen its fortunes improve dramatically since the slot machines were installed. Purses for horse racing receive a portion of revenues on slot-machine play at Charles Town, which has more than 3,800 machines at the track. The track's marquee event is the West Virginia Breeders' Classic, a series of races that showcase runners bred, sired, or raised in the state, and is highlighted by the $500,000 West Virginia Breeders' Classic Stakes. Charles Town completed a multimillion-dollar remodeling project, including a new racing surface, in August 2004.

Location: U.S. Route 340, P.O. Box 551, Charles Town, W.V. 25414-0551
Phone: (304) 725-7001, (800) 795-7001
Fax: (304) 724-4326
Website: www.ctownraces.com
Year Founded: 1933

Dates of Inaugural Meeting: December 2, 1933
Abbreviation: CT
Number of Stalls: 1,250
Seating Capacity: 6,000

Ownership
Penn National Gaming

Officers
Vice President of Regional Operations: John V. Finamore
General Manager: Albert T. Britton
General Manager of Racing: Richard L. Moore
Racing Secretary: Randy Wehrman
Assistant Racing Secretary: M. Michael Elliott
Director of Marketing: Dee Mara
Director of Mutuels: Joy Lushbaugh
Director of Publicity: Jeffrey Gilleas
Stewards: L. Robert Lotts, Larry Dupuy, Danny R. Wright
Track Announcer: Jeff Cernik
Track Photographer: Mike Montgomery
Track Superintendent: Douglas Bowling
Horsemen's Bookkeeper: W. C. Perry
Security: Michael Connor

Racing Dates
2007: January 1-December 31, 223 days
2008: January 1-December 31, 220, days

Track Layout
Main Circumference: 6 furlongs
Main Track Chute: 4½ furlongs and 1⁵⁄₁₆ miles
Main Length of Stretch: 660 feet

Attendance
Highest Single-Day Record: 21,480, September 17, 1981

Handle
Total All-Sources Recent Meeting: $200,133,675, 2007
Average All-Sources Recent Meeting: $873,946, 2007
Total On-Track Recent Meeting: $20,811,955, 2007
Average On-Track Recent Meeting: $90,882, 2007

Leaders
Recent Meeting, Leading Jockey: Arnaldo Bocachica, 210, 2007
Recent Meeting, Leading Trainer: Jeff Runco, 145, 2007
Recent Meeting: Leading Horse: Shes Appealing, 8, 2007

Records
Single-Day Jockey Wins: Travis Dunkelberger, 7, March 30, 2000

Principal Races
Charles Town Dash Invitational H., West Virginia Breeders' Classic S., "Cavada" West Virginia Breeders' Classic S.

Notable Events
Owners Day, West Virginia Breeders' Classics Day

Track Records, Main Dirt
4½ furlongs: Outcashem, :50.20, July 4, 2006
6½ furlongs: Jet Appeal, 1:17, January 6, 1976
7 furlongs: P. Kerney, 1:23.29, July 8, 2006
1¹⁄₁₆ miles: My Sister Pearl, 1:43.83, January 4, 2001
1⅛ miles: Cherokee's Boy, 1:49.88, October 9, 2005
1¼ miles: Belle d'Amour, 2:05⅗, June 28, 1941
1½ miles: Guasave Breeze, 2:34, June 9, 1972

Fastest Times of 2007 (Dirt)
4½ furlongs: Outcashem, 6, :50.94, October 19, 2007
6½ furlongs: Djembe, 4, 1:18.04, January 11, 2007
7 furlongs: Confucius Say, 9, 1:24.20, July 4, 2007
1⅛ miles: Researcher, 3, 1:50.54, December 29, 2007
1¼ miles: Abracapocus, 3, 2:10.99, December 31, 2007
1⅝ miles: E and D's Dreams, 5, 2:52.98, October 26, 2007

Mountaineer Casino Racetrack and Resort

Mountaineer Race Track in Chester was recognized in 2001 as one of the top small businesses in the United States when Forbes magazine ranked MTR Gaming Group Inc., which owns the track, seventh among the top 200 such enterprises. Much of Mountaineer's success resulted from the legalization of slot machines in 1993, which increased revenues and enabled the track to offer higher purses. In 2003, the track received approval for 500 additional slot machines, enabling it to operate a maximum of 3,500 slot machines. A special election in 2007 allowed it to add table games. MTR Gaming, headed by Edson "Ted" Arneault, also owns a golf course, hotel, spa, theater, and other entertainment facilities at the track's location. The track was known as Waterford Park when it was opened in 1951 by the Charles Town Jockey Club; the facility was renamed Mountaineer Park in '87 and Mountaineer Race Track in 2001. Mountaineer offers year-round racing four nights a week. The West Virginia Derby (G3), worth $750,000 in 2007, is the richest race to be run in West Virginia history. In 2003, MTR Gaming Group bought Scioto Downs, an Ohio Standardbred track, and opened Presque Isle Downs in Pennsylvania in '07.

Location: P.O. Box 358, Route 2 S., Chester, W.V. 26034-0358
Phone: (304) 387-8300, (800) 804-0468
Website: www.mtrgaming.com
E-Mail: info@mtrgaming.com
Year Founded: 1951
Dates of Inaugural Meeting: May 16, 1951
Abbreviation: Mnr
Acreage: 215
Number of Stalls: 1,234
Seating Capacity: 7,400

Ownership
MTR Gaming Group Inc.

Officers
Chairman and Chief Executive Officer: Edson R. Arneault
President: Edson R. Arneault
Vice President: Patrick J. Arneault
Director of Racing: Rose Mary Williams
Director of Finance: John Bittner
Director of Marketing: Dale Maurer
Director of Publicity: Tamara Cronin
Racing Secretary: Joseph J. Narcavish
Horsemen's Liaison: Rose Mary Williams
Stewards: Maureen Andrews, Steve Kourpas, James O'Brien
Track Announcer: Peter Berry
Track Photographer: Ethel Riser
Track Superintendent: Tom Trevor

Racing Dates
2007: January 20-December 30, 233 days
2008: January 19-December 30, 232 days

Track Layout
Main Circumference: 1 mile
Main Track Chute: 6 furlongs and 1¼ miles
Main Width: 76 feet
Main Length of Stretch: 900 feet
Main Turf Circumference: 7 furlongs
Main Turf Width: 88 feet
Main Turf Length of Stretch: 850 feet

Attendance
Highest Single-Day Record: 25,336, May 7, 2005

Attendance
Average Daily Recent Meeting: 5,773, 2007
Highest Single-Day Record: 25,336, May 7, 2005
Record Daily Average Single Meeting: 6,168, 2004
Highest Single-Meeting Record: 1,350,785, 2004
Total Attendance Recent Meeting: 1,287,445, 2007
Highest Single-Day Recent Meeting: 22,736, October 27, 2007

Handle

Average All-Sources Recent Meeting: $1,919,005, 2007
Average On-Track Recent Meeting: $42,077, 2007
Single-Day On-Track Handle: $966,508, May 8, 1973
Single-Day All-Sources Handle: $3,444,914 August 14, 2005
Total All-Sources Recent Meeting: $427,938,086, 2007
Total On-Track Recent Meeting: $27,411,213
Highest Single-Day Record Recent Meeting: $2,628,025 November 16, 2007
Record Average All-Sources Single Meeting: $1,919,005, 2007
Record Total All-Sources Single Meeting: $434,893,975, 2006

Leaders

Recent Meeting, Leading Jockey: Rex A. Stokes III, 263, 2007
Recent Meeting, Leading Owner: Dale Baird, 112, 2007
Recent Meeting, Leading Trainer: Dale Baird, 121, 2007
Recent Meeting, Leading Horse: Bernie Blue, 6, 2007

Principal Races

West Virginia Derby (G3), West Virginia Governor's S., Mountaineer Mile H., Harvey Arneault Memorial S., West Virginia Senate President's Breeders' Cup S.

Interesting Facts

Previous Names: Waterford Park

Track Records, Main Dirt

$4\frac{1}{2}$ furlongs: Ameri Brilliance, :50.16, August 7, 2004
5 furlongs: Mayor Steve, :55.92, August 31, 2003
$5\frac{1}{2}$ furlongs: The Dancer, 1:02.24, December 29, 2000
6 furlongs: Hustler, 1:07.81, August 11, 2001
1 mile: Find the Mine, 1:33,86, July 4, 2000
1 mile 40 yds: Ski Sez, 1:39.83, March 9, 1996
1 mile 70 yds: Mort, 1:38.81, April 1, 2000
$1\frac{1}{16}$ miles: Be Like Mike, 1:41.15, August 9, 2003
$1\frac{1}{8}$ miles: Soto, 1:46.29, August 9, 2003
$1\frac{3}{16}$ miles: Game Bird, 1:56.66, May 17, 2003
$1\frac{1}{4}$ miles: Georgie Porgie, 2:03.69, August 6, 1995
$1\frac{1}{2}$ miles: Pete's Skianno, 2:31.43, June 10, 2000
$1\frac{5}{8}$ miles: Prince Swivel, 2:45, September 8, 1973
$1\frac{3}{4}$ miles: Chased Again, 2:58$\frac{4}{5}$, July 18, 1959
2 miles: Sovereign M.D., 3:27.66, December 10, 2000
Other: 2 furlongs, Promised Cruise, :21, June 23, 1990; a1 mile, Mr. Pantop, 1:36$\frac{1}{5}$, June 26, 1970; a$1\frac{1}{4}$ miles, Grain, 2:08, May 29, 1974; a2 miles, Dark Ajax, 3:27$\frac{2}{5}$, June 9, 1973; $2\frac{1}{16}$ miles, Sovereign M.D., 3:28.40, December 30, 2000

Track Records, Main Turf

$4\frac{1}{2}$ furlongs: Jump for Joyeux, :49.69, May 29, 2006
5 furlongs: Fina Dur, :55.52, September 6, 1999
7 furlongs: On to Richmond, 1:21.40, June 16, 2002
$7\frac{1}{2}$ furlongs: Magical Madness, 1:27.48, May 22, 2002
1 mile: La Reine's Term, 1:33.49, September 2, 2002
1 mile 70yds: Fast and Friendly, 1:43, September 7, 1964; Poteau, 1:43, July 25, 1982
$1\frac{3}{8}$ miles: Sunset Party, 2:13.23, September 26, 1999
$1\frac{1}{2}$ miles: Guild Hall, 2:33$\frac{1}{5}$, June 20, 1969
$1\frac{3}{4}$ miles: Inaugural Address, 2:53.35, August 15, 2005
Other: a5 furlongs, Skindles Hotel, :55$\frac{1}{5}$, July 26, 1960; a$1\frac{1}{16}$ miles, Black Eye, 1:40$\frac{1}{5}$, June 28, 1958; a$1\frac{1}{4}$ miles, King Haigler, 2:09$\frac{3}{5}$, July 4, 1983; a$1\frac{5}{16}$ miles, Ruff Mack, 2:06, August 25, 1962; a$1\frac{1}{2}$ miles, Revenooer, 2:29, July 4, 1959; $1\frac{7}{8}$ miles, Code's Best, 3:08.23, September 4, 2000

Fastest Times of 2007 (Dirt)

$4\frac{1}{2}$ furlongs: Bernie Blue, 5, :52.40, August 4, 2007
5 furlongs: Fabulous Strike, 4, :57.18, May 5, 2007
$5\frac{1}{2}$ furlongs: Bernie Blue, 5, 1:03.27, August 20, 2007
6 furlongs: Thatsalottabull, 3, 1:09.44, February 19, 2007
1 mile: Lace Manzotti, 7, 1:37.40, January 27, 2007
1 mile 70 yds: Big Daddy Catty, 4, 1:42.45, February 19, 2007
$1\frac{1}{16}$ miles: D' Springs, 3, 1:44.50, December 7, 2007
$1\frac{1}{8}$ miles: M B Sea, 8, 1:51.46, October 2, 2007
$1\frac{3}{16}$ miles: Decoy Dan, 4, 2:01.61, May 19, 2007
$1\frac{1}{4}$ miles: Cryptolight, 3, 2:08.41, July 30, 2007
$1\frac{1}{2}$ miles: Humble Chris, 6, 2:36.58, June 9, 2007
$1\frac{5}{8}$ miles: Pleasant Company, 8, 2:53.77, October 30, 2007
$1\frac{3}{4}$ miles: Sir Dorset, 12, 3:08.86, November 18, 2007
2 miles: Dancer's Legacy, 3, 3:30.26, December 9, 2007
$2\frac{1}{16}$ miles: Dancer's Legacy, 3, 3:41.55, December 30, 2007

Fastest Times of 2007 (Turf)

$4\frac{1}{2}$ furlongs: Ima Hogg, 5, :50.37, May 28, 2007
5 furlongs: Ridge Runner (GB), 9, :56.32, June 11, 2007
7 furlongs: Muqbil, 7, 1:22.22, July 23, 2007
$7\frac{1}{2}$ furlongs: Sicilian Boy, 6, 1:28.17, July 16, 2007
1 mile: Puppeteer (GB), 7, 1:34.11, May 28, 2007
1 mile 70 yds: Beautiful Venue, 3, 1:38.14 , August 4, 2007
$1\frac{3}{8}$ miles: Jill's Cat, 5, 2:19.48, July 24, 2007
$1\frac{3}{4}$ miles: Pleasant Company, 8, 2:59.47, August 13, 2007

Wyoming

Wyoming Downs

Though it is one of North America's least-known Thoroughbred facilities, Wyoming Downs has been providing racing to southwestern Wyoming for nearly 20 years. Located just north of Evanston, Wyoming Downs offers Thoroughbred and Quarter Horse racing, with most emphasis on the latter. The track's top races are Quarter Horse events, the Silver Dollar and Diamond Classic Futurities, each with estimated purses of $100,000. For Thoroughbreds, the top event is the $4,000-added Bettie Bullock Memorial Derby for three-year-olds. Wyoming Downs, which races during the summer, also operates four off-track betting facilities that offer simulcast wagering year-round. In 2003, the track's OTB facilities added Instant Racing, an electronic pari-mutuel game developed at Oaklawn Park in Arkansas.

Location: 10180 Highway 89 N., P.O. Box 2970, Evanston, Wy. 82931
Phone: (307) 789-0511, (866) 681-7223
Fax: (307) 789-9439
Website: *www.wyomingdowns.com*
E-Mail: wydowns@wyent.net
Year Founded: 1985
Dates of Inaugural Meeting: May 25, 1985
Abbreviation: Wyo
Acreage: 200
Number of Stalls: 860
Seating Capacity: 2,100

Ownership

Wyoming Entertainment

Officers

Chief Executive Officer and President: Eric M. Spector
Chief Financial Officer: Harlyn Enholm
General Manager: Duayne Diderickson
Director of Racing and Racing Secretary: Shorty Martin
Director of Operations and Admissions: Ethellyn Sims
Directors of Marketing: T Pat Stubbs, Savannah Feehan
Directors of Mutuels: Jodi Lopez, Mike Fansler
Director of Simulcasting: Jodi Lopez
Track Announcer: John Petti
Track Photographer: Trident Media
Track Superintendent: Angel Lopez
Horsemen's Bookkeeper: Linda Fansler

Racing Dates

2007: June 30-August 19, 16 days
2008: June 28-August 17, 16 days

Track Layout

Main Circumference: $7\frac{1}{2}$ furlongs

Main Track Chute: 550 yards and 6½ furlongs
Main Length of Stretch: 1,050 feet

Attendance
Average Daily Recent Meeting: 1,583, 2007
Total Attendance Recent Meeting: 23,750, 2007
Highest Single-Day Recent Meeting: 1,904, June 30, 2007

Handle
Total All-Sources Recent Meeting: $1,513,117, 2007
Average All-Sources Recent Meeting: $100,874, 2007
Total On-Track Recent Meeting: $1,003,233, 2007
Average On-Track Recent Meeting: $66,882, 2007
Largest Single-Day All-Sources Recent Meeting: $327,375, August 11, 2007
Largest Single-Day On-Track Recent Meeting: $86,647, June 30, 2007

Leaders
Recent Meeting, Leading Jockey: Cam Colledge, 25, 2007
Recent Meeting, Leading Trainer: Mike Taylor, 17, 2007
Recent Meeting, Leading Owner: Stan Young, 17, 2007
Recent Meeting, Leading Horse: Smart Dawn, 3, 2007

Fastest Times of 2007 (Dirt)
4½ furlongs: Restrictions Apply, 7, :51, July 22, 2007
5 furlongs: Western Roar, 6, :56.30, July 28, 2007
5½ furlongs: Ockley Green, 4, 1:03.20, August 18, 2007
6 furlongs: Reef Shark, 4, 1:08.20, August 12, 2007
7½ furlongs: Cut Class, 8, 1:32.10, August 5, 2007; Row Row Man, 8, 1:32.10, July 1, 2007
1 mile: Lawn Mower, 8, 1:41.10, August 18, 2007

Canada

Alberta

Evergreen Park (Grand Prairie)

Location: Box 370, Grand Prairie, Ab. T8V 3A5
Phone: (780) 532-3279
Fax: (780) 539-0373
Website: www.evergreenpark.ca
E-Mail: brianc4@telus.net
Abbreviation: GPr
Acreage: 700
Number of Stalls: 700
Seating Capacity: 2,700

Officers
General Manager: Greg Suess
Director of Racing: Brian Cook

Racing Dates
2007: July 6-August 19, 22 days
2008: July 4-August 17, 22 days

Track Layout
Main Circumference: 5 furlongs

Leaders
Recent Meeting, Leading Jockey: Angelle Wilson, 17, 2007
Recent Meeting, Leading Trainer: Tom Rycroft, 12, 2007; Pete Dubois, 12, 2007
Recent Meeting, Leading Horse: George's Stick, 3, 2007

Fastest Times of 2007 (Dirt)
4 furlongs: No Holds Barred, 6, :45.80, July 6, 2007
5½ furlongs: Flying Lady Cue, 7, 1:06.40, July 14, 2007
6 furlongs: Art History, 5, 1:12.20, July 28, 2007; Kubwa, 4, 1:12.20, August 3, 2007; Lukin Awesome, 4, 1:12.20, July 15, 2007; Timetoteeitup, 5, 1:12.20, July 7, 2007
6½ furlongs: Ta Keel, 7, 1:18.80, August 11, 2007
7 furlongs: Rare Remark, 6, 1:25.20, July 13, 2007
1 mile: Past Time, 10, 1:41.20, July 22, 2007

Lethbridge

Location: 3401 Parkside Dr. S, Lethbridge, Ab. T1J 4R3
Phone: (403) 380-1900
Fax: (403) 380-1909
Website: www.rockymountainturfclub.com
E-Mail: racedot@telusplanet.net
Abbreviation: Lbg
Number of Stalls: 400
Seating Capacity: 3,000

Ownership
Rocky Mountain Turf Club

Officers
Chairman and President: Max Gibb
Director of Racing and Simulcasting: Dorothy Stein
Racing Secretary: Jim Ralph
Director of Marketing and Publicity: Rose Rossi
Director of Mutuels: Dorothy Stein
Stewards: D. G. Rees, Scott Dahl
Track Announcer: Dale Johnson
Track Photographer: Coady Photo

Racing Dates
2007: May 5-July 2, 24 days; September 1-October 28, 27 days
2008: May 3-June 29, 23 days; August 30-October 26, 27 days

Track Layout
Main Circumference: 4 furlongs

Leaders
Recent Meeting, Leading Jockey: Scott Sterr, 32, Fall 2007
Recent Meeting, Leading Trainer: Allen Fogle, 31, Fall 2007
Recent Meeting, Leading Horse: Lafleur, 5, Fall 2007

Principal Races
Autotote Derby, "B" Cup Classic S., Last Chance S., Alberta Bred S., Open S.

Notable Events
Chuckwagon Racing, Street Machine Weekend, Hot Rod 50's Weekend

Fastest Times of 2007 (Dirt)
5 furlongs: Hesademon, 2, 1:00, September 30, 2007
5½ furlongs: Lafleur, 8, 1:05.60, June 3, 2007
a5½ furlongs: Lafleur, 8, 1:06.60, September 3, 2007
6 furlongs: Regal Hit, 7, 1:11.80, May 26, 2007
a6 furlongs: Cool Synsation, 3, 1:08.40, September 16, 2007
7 furlongs: Lafleur, 8, 1:24, June 23, 2007
1 1/16 miles: Dr. Mo, 8, 1:46.60, September 16, 2007
1 1/8 miles: Lafleur, 8, 1:53.40, October 13, 2007
1 3/16 miles: Chief Joseph, 8, 2:03.20, October 21, 2007

Millarville Race Society

Location: General Delivery Box 68, Millarville, Ab. T0L 1K0
Phone: (403) 931-3411
Fax: (403) 931-3411
Website: www.millarville-ab.com
Abbreviation: Mil

Racing Dates
2007: July 1, 1 day
2008: July 1, 1 day

Fastest Times of 2007 (Dirt)
5 furlongs: Cowboy Auctioneer, 7, 1:06, July 1, 2007
7 furlongs: Tiz Handsome, 5, 1:31.20, July 1, 2007
1 1/8 miles: Tata Pantoja, 8, 2:08.60, July 1, 2007

Northlands Park

Like many Canadian racetracks, Northlands Park in Edmonton races both Thoroughbreds and Standardbreds. Both breeds enjoy richer purses due to the arrival of slot machines. In late December 2001, Northlands received 250 additional machines to double its original total as part of a $42-million racing rehabilitation project under Alberta Premier Ralph Klein, an amateur harness driver, former TV reporter, and former Calgary mayor. Opened in July 1925 as Edmonton Racetrack, the track was renamed Northlands Park in January '64. Northlands conducts Standardbred racing from early March through mid-June and Thoroughbred racing from late June through late October.

Location: Northlands Spectrum, P.O. Box 1480, Edmonton, Ab. T5J 2N5
Phone: (780) 471-7379
Fax: (403) 471-7134
Website: *www.thehorsesatnorthlands.com*
E-Mail: info@northlands.com
Year Founded: 1925
Dates of Inaugural Meeting: July 1925
Abbreviation: NP
Number of Stalls: 1,100
Seating Capacity: 4,500

Ownership

Edmonton Northlands

Officers

President: Dale Leschiutta
Vice Presidents: Jerry Bouma, Jim Campbell
General Manager of Racing and Gaming: Les Butler
Racing Manager: Kevin Behm
Racing Secretary: Fred Hilts
Treasurer: Mark Bamford
Director of Mutuels and Simulcasting: Glen Weir
Marketing Manager: Sandra Symbaluk
Public Relations Coordinator: Marilyn Mohr
Stewards: Al Lennox, Robert Noda, Wayne Armstrong
Track Announcer: Mike Dimoff
Track Photographer: Coady Photography
Track Superintendent: Ron Grift
Horsemen's Bookkeeper: Carey Blenkinsop

Racing Dates

2007: June 22-September 30, 61 days
2008: June 20-October 5, 60 days

Track Layout

Main Circumference: 5 furlongs
Main Track Chute: 6½ furlongs
Main Width: 70 feet
Main Length of Stretch: 625 feet

Attendance

Highest Single-Day Record: 15,922, August 25, 1973

Handle

Single-Day On-Track Handle: $1,652,940, August 16, 1990

Leaders

Recent Meeting, Leading Jockey: Ricky A. Walcott, 89, 2007
Recent Meeting, Leading Trainer: Ron K. Smith, 35, 2007
Recent Meeting, Leading Horse: Jekar, 4, 2007; Hurricane Tiki, 4, 2007; Beam Spirit, 4, 2007; Premium Gail, 4, 2007

Principal Races

Canadian Derby (Can-G3), Northlands Oaks, Sonoma S., Speed to Spare S., City of Edmonton Distaff H.

Track Records, Main Dirt

5½ furlongs: So Long Fellas, 1:04⅖, August 16, 1975
6 furlongs: Sageata, 1:09⅘, July 22, 1984; Lynn's Dream, 1:09.80, July 8, 2000
6½ furlongs: Timely Ruckus, 1:15.40, June 26, 1999
1 mile: Bagfull, 1:35⅘, May 16, 1981
1 1/16 miles: Chilcoton Blaze, 1:42⅗, August 4, 1984
1⅜ miles: Slyly Gifted, 2:15⅘, August 30, 1986
1⅝ miles: Dancers Nugget, 2:45.20, September 21, 2001
Other: 3½ furlongs, Steel Penny Black, :38⅕, June 14, 1984; 1 5/16 miles, Arctic Laur, 2:09, August 20, 1995

Fastest Times of 2007 (Dirt)

3½ furlongs: Just Call Me Duke, 2, :39.60, July 27, 2007
5½ furlongs: Native Wrangler, 2, 1:06.20, August 26, 2007
6 furlongs: Mocha John, 4, 1:11, September 9, 2007
6½ furlongs: Cool Synsation, 3, 1:16.60, September 29, 2007
1 mile: Footprint, 3, 1:36.40, July 14, 2007
1 1/16 miles: True Metropolitan, 5, 1:42.80, August 19, 2007
1 5/16 miles: Willy's Ruckus, 5, 2:15.20, August 10, 2007
1⅜ miles: True Metropolitan, 5, 2:17, September 8, 2007
1⅝ miles: Deputy Spy, 4, 2:51.80, September 15, 2007

Stampede Park

Though it is famous for its annual Calgary Stampede rodeo, Stampede Park was also a longtime part of the Thoroughbred racing scene in Alberta. Thoroughbred racing debuted at Stampede in 1974, with the facility offering racing on a five-furlong oval and stabling for 1,400 horses. Though the track's seating of 25,000 is snug during the Calgary Stampede in July, it has been more than adequate for racing; the track's record attendance is 6,167, set on August 15, 1981. Stampede conducts a spring Thoroughbred meet from early April through mid-June and a Standardbred meet in the summer and early fall. Its major Thoroughbred race is the $100,000 Alberta Derby (Can-G3). In 2004, a competing organization, United Horsemen of Alberta, was awarded the license to operate racing in the Calgary area from 2007 to '17, and the group will build an $80-million track to open in '10.

Location: 2300 Stampede Trail S.E., Calgary, Ab. T2G 2W1
Phone: (403) 261-0214
Fax: (403) 265-7009
Website: *www.stampede-park.com*
E-Mail: stpracing@calgarystampede.com
Year Founded: 1973 as Stampede Park
Dates of Inaugural Meeting: July 1925 (Victoria Park); June 20, 1974 (Stampede Park)
Abbreviation: StP
Number of Stalls: 1,300
Seating Capacity: 17,800

Ownership

Calgary Exhibition and Stampede

Officers

Chairman and President: Steve Allan
Vice Presidents: Mike Whittle, Gord Fache, Laurie Schild, Doug Armitage
Senior Manager of Racing: Keith Marrington
Racing Secretary: Russell Armstrong
Director of Operations: Gerry McHugh
Director of Marketing and Publicity: Patti Hunt
Director of Mutuels and Simulcasting: Sheri Holmes
Pari-Mutuels Supervisor: Cheri Finch
Group Sales Coordinator: Carole Slobodzian
Horsemen's Liaison: Carole Larson
Stewards: Wayne Armstrong, Al Lennox, Robert Noda
Track Announcer: Joe Carbury
Track Photographer: Coady Photography
Horsemen's Bookkeeper: Bob Tutt

Racing Dates
2007: March 23-June 17, 50 days
2008: March 21-June 15, 50 days

Track Layout
Main Circumference: 5 furlongs
Main Track Chute: 4 furlongs
Main Width: 70 feet
Main Length of Stretch: 660 feet

Attendance
Highest Single-Day Record: 6,167, August 15, 1981

Leaders
Recent Meeting, Leading Jockey: Quincy Welch, 73, 2008
Recent Meeting, Leading Trainer: Stuart Simon, 26, 2008
Recent Meeting, Leading Horse: Ghost Pirate, 4, 2008

Principal Races
Alberta Derby (Can-G3), Penny Ridge S., Duchess of York S., Herald Gold Plate H.

Interesting Facts
Previous Names and Dates: Victoria Park (1925-'72)

Fastest Times of 2007 (Dirt)
3$^1/_2$ furlongs: I Lost My Halo, 2, :39.80, May 30, 2007
4 furlongs: Steven O, 4, :44.20, March 30, 2007
6 furlongs: Calendar Girl, 3, 1:10, May 6, 2007; Frontier Express, 4, 1:10, May 9, 2007; Laketon, 7, 1:10, April 15, 2007; Teagues Fight, 4, 1:10, April 14, 2007
1 mile: Test Boy, 4, 1:35.80, May 19, 2007
1$^1/_{16}$ miles: Teagues Fight, 4, 1:43.60, June 10, 2007

British Columbia

Hastings Race Course

For more than 80 years, the racing scene in the Canadian province of British Columbia has focused on the tract of land where Hastings Race Course currently stands. From 1994 to 2002, the not-for-profit Pacific Racing Association managed racing at Hastings, which conducts Thoroughbred racing at the five-furlong facility usually from April through November. Woodbine Entertainment Group bought the facility in 2002, and in '04 sold it to Great Canadian Gaming Corp. for $15.7-million. First opened in 1920, Hastings reached its peak as a racing facility in the early 1980s, when the track sometimes drew crowds of 20,000 or more. The track also has appealed to Vancouver's expanding Asian population by offering simulcast wagering from Hong Kong.

Location: Hastings Racecourse, Vancouver, B.C. V5K 3N8
Phone: (604) 254-1631, (800) 677-7702
Fax: (604) 251-0411
Website: *www.hastingsracecourse.com*
E-Mail: info@hastingsracecourse.com
Year Founded: 1889 (Exhibition Park); 1994 (Hastings Race Course)
Abbreviation: Hst
Acreage: 45
Number of Stalls: 1,000
Seating Capacity: 5,600

Ownership
Great Canadian Gaming Corp.

Officers
Vice President: Chuck Keeling
General Manager: Michael Mackey
Racing Secretary: Lorne Mitchell

Director of Operations: Raj Mutti
Director of Marketing: Deborah Stetz
Director of Mutuels: George Akerman
Director of Simulcasting: Dan Jukich
Stewards: Wayne J. Russell, Douglas F. Scott, Keith G. Smith
Track Announcer: Dan Jukich
Track Photographer: Winner's Photography
Track Superintendent: Drew Levere
Horsemen's Bookkeeper: Merrilee Elliott
Security: Paul Bouchard

Racing Dates
2007: April 28-November 4, 68 days
2008: April 26-November 2, 71 days

Track Layout
Main Circumference: 5 furlongs, 208 feet
Main Track Chute: 6$^1/_2$ furlongs, 1$^1/_{16}$ miles, and 1$^1/_8$ miles
Main Width: 65 feet
Main Length of Stretch: 513 feet
Training Track: 4 furlongs

Attendance
Highest Single-Day Record: 21,156, July 9, 1982

Handle
Single-Day On-Track Handle: $2,612,316, July 9, 1982
Average On-Track Recent Meeting: $263,143, 2007
Average All-Sources Recent Meeting: $17,893,740, 2007
Total On-Track Recent Meeting: $17,893,740, 2007
Total All-Sources Recent Meeting: $49,725, 370, 2007

Mutuel Records
Highest Win: $508.10, 1953
Highest Exacta: $4,092, 1962
Highest Trifecta: $21,806.20, 1982
Highest Daily Double: $4,863.10, 1995
Highest Pick Three: $11,474, 1993
Highest Other Exotics: $920,411.70, Sweep 6, 1982; $63,526.70, Win 4, 1988; $42,946, Superfecta, June 13, 2004

Leaders
Career, Leading Jockey by Titles: Chris Loseth, 8
Career, Leading Trainer by Titles: Harold J. Barroby, 10
Career, Leading Jockey by Stakes Wins: Chris Loseth, 204
Career, Leading Jockey by Wins: Chris Loseth, 3,561
Recent Meeting, Leading Jockey: Mario Gutierrez, 134, 2007
Recent Meeting, Leading Trainer: Troy Taylor, 46, 2007

Records
Single-Day Jockey Wins: Chris Loseth, 8, April 9, 1984
Single-Day Trainer Wins: George Cummings, 5, November 8, 1992
Single Meet, Leading Jockey by Wins: Mark Patzer, 173, 1991
Single Meet, Leading Trainer by Wins: Lance Giesbrecht, 76, 1997

Principal Races
British Columbia Breeders' Cup Derby (Can-G3), British Columbia Breeders' Cup Oaks (Can-G3), Ballerina Breeders' Cup S. (Can-G3), British Columbia Premiers' H. (Can-G3), Ascot Graduation S.

Notable Events
British Columbia Cup Day

Track Records, Main Dirt
6 furlongs: Great Discretion, 1:10$^3/_5$, May 10, 1969; Humphrey Lad, 1:10$^3/_5$, April 13, 1988; Sir Khaled, 1:10$^3/_5$, April 15, 1988
6$^1/_2$ furlongs: Torque Converter, 1:15, July 1, 1996
1m 70 yds: Westbury Road, 1:40$^2/_5$, July 29, 1967
1$^1/_{16}$ miles: Coral Isle, 1:42$^1/_5$, July 28, 1973; No Time Flat, 1:42$^1/_5$, August 12, 1987; Timely Stitch, 1:42.20, July 6, 1996
1$^1/_8$ miles: Artic Son, 1:46.80, August 3, 1998
1$^3/_8$ miles: Irish Bear, 2:14$^2/_5$, October 17, 1987
1$^1/_2$ miles: Lucky Son, 2:29, August 25, 1995
1$^3/_4$ miles: Glen Gower, 2:59, September 23, 1987
Other: a3$^1/_2$ furlongs, Turn to Knight, :41$^1/_5$, May 27, 1990; 3$^1/_2$ furlongs, Wanabe Klassy, :38.97, October 29, 2006; a6 furlongs, Count the Green, 1:10$^4/_5$, April 17, 1971; 1$^7/_{16}$ miles, Who's in Command, 2:23, August 10, 1987; a1$^1/_2$ miles, Golden Gentry, 2:29$^2/_5$, September 20, 1987; 1$^{11}/_{16}$ miles, Glen Gower, 2:51$^1/_5$,

September 9, 1987; $1^3/_4$ miles, Glen Gower, 2:59, September 23, 1987; $2^1/_{16}$ miles, Laddie's Prince, 3:30, October 8, 1987; a$2^1/_{16}$ miles, High Hawk, 3:48, October 16, 1983; $2^1/_8$ miles, Mr. Chancellor, 3:38$^4/_5$, October 18, 1987

Fastest Times of 2007 (Dirt)

$3^1/_2$ furlongs: Cabron, 2, :39.48, June 9, 2007
6 furlongs: Krazy Koffee, 2, 1:11.05, October 14, 2007
$6^1/_2$ furlongs: Winter Warning, 4, 1:15.73, August 10, 2007
$1^1/_{16}$ miles: Sir Gallovic, 3, 1:43.23, September 2, 2007
$1^1/_8$ miles: Celtic Dreamin, 3, 1:49.50, September 23, 2007
$1^3/_8$ miles: Sir Gallovic, 3, 2:15.89, October 14, 2007
$1^1/_2$ miles: Cusack (NZ), 8, 2:33.73, September 15, 2007
$1^3/_4$ miles: Lord Vic, 4, 3:00.77, October 8, 2007
$2^1/_8$ miles: Afternoon Express, 5, 3:44.57, November 3, 2007

Kamloops

Location: 479 Chilcotin Rd., Kamloops, B.C. V2H 1G4
Phone: (250) 314-9645
Fax: (250) 828-0836
Website: *www.bcinteriorhorseracing.com*
Year Founded: 1895
Abbreviation: Kam
Number of Stalls: 310
Seating Capacity: 2,000

Ownership

Kamloops Exhibition Association

Officers

Chairman and President: Luigi Sale
Director of Racing: Luigi Sale
Racing Secretary: Jim Rogers
Vice President: Dave Carswell
Director of Publicity: Lugi Sale
Track Announcer: Keith Reid
Track Superintendent: Jim Larson

Racing Dates

2007: May 12-June 9, 4 days; August 11-August 18, 2 days
2008: May 24-June 21, 3 days; August 2-August 16, 3 days

Principal Races

HBPA/Sagebrush Derby

Fastest Times of 2008 (Dirt)

$4^1/_2$ furlongs: Libra Del Sol, 4, :51.95, May 12, 2007
a$4^1/_2$ furlongs: Kruisin Karen, 3, :48.20, August 18, 2007
$6^1/_2$ furlongs: Hopingandwishing, 4, 1:18.91, August 11, 2007
a1 mile: Dalton Green, 5, 1:37.63, August 18, 2007

Kin Park

Location: P.O. Box 682, Vernon, B.C. V2H 6M6
Website: *www.bcinteriorhorseracing.com*
Abbreviation: Kin

Officers

President: Ed Wooley

Racing Dates

2007: July 15-July 29, 3 days
2008: July 13-July 27, 3 days

Leaders

Recent Meeting, Leading Jockey: Caroline Stinn, 3, 2007; Paula Enns, 3, 2007
Recent Meeting, Leading Trainer: Vicki Pozzobon, 3, 2007
Recent Meeting, Leading Horse: Big'n'jazzy, 2, 2007

Principal Races

British Columbia Lottery Corp. Mile S.

Fastest Times of 2007 (Dirt)

a4 furlongs: Big'n'jazzy, 5, :44.72, July 15, 2007
a$6^1/_2$ furlongs: Dreamoneir, 7, 1:21.36, July 29, 2007
a7 furlongs: Funky Friends, 4, 1:24.42, July 15, 2007
a$1^1/_8$ miles: Lord Frederick, 5, 1:53.37, July 29, 2007

Sunflower Downs

Location: P.O. Box 1234, Princeton, B.C. V0X 1W0
Phone: (250) 295-3970
Website: *www.bcinteriorhorseracing.com*
Abbreviation: SnD

Officers

Chairman and President: John Bey
Vice President: Ed Vermette
General Manager and Director of Racing: John Bey
Racing Secretary: Carol Ruoss
Director of Operations: John Bey
Director of Marketing: Ed Vermette
Director of Mutuels: Carol Ruoss
Director of Publicity: Ed Vermette
Secretary: Carol Ruoss
Treasurer: Sandy Kinsey
Horsemen's Liaison: John Bey
Stewards: Nina Ferguson, Denise Rogers, Jim Rogers
Track Announcer: Keith Reid
Track Photographer: Ed Muckle
Track Superintendent: John Bey

Racing Dates

2007: June 29, 1 day
2008: June 27, 1 day

Principal Races

Similkameen Cup S., Bob Beale Memorial "Tulameen Cup" S., Luke Gibson Memorial S., Sunflower Derby

Fastest Times of 2007 (Dirt)

a$5^1/_2$ furlongs: Marquetry Rose, 4, 1:05.88, June 29, 2007
a7 furlongs: Funky Friends, 4, 1:25.36, June 29, 2007
a$1^1/_{16}$ miles: Crescent Remark, 8, 1:46.07, June 29, 2007

Manitoba

Assiniboia Downs

Assiniboia Downs continues a rich tradition of horse racing in Winnipeg, dating from the last quarter of the 19th century. Racing enthusiast and businessman Jack Hardy built Assiniboia, which opened in 1958 to replace Polo Park, a 30-year-old track located on property that became a shopping center. In 1974, Jim Wright bought the track and racing prospered under his leadership. By the early 1990s, however, competition from other gambling forms made the track unprofitable. In 1993, Assiniboia was sold to its current owners, the Manitoba Jockey Club, a not-for-profit organization that solidified its future by pouring profits from video lottery terminals and full-card simulcasting back into the facility. Assiniboia, which offers live racing from early May through September, was the first track in Canada to offer pick-six and telephone-account wagering. The track's richest race, the Manitoba Derby (now Can-G3), has been run at Assiniboia since 1960. In 1970, Queen Elizabeth II and Prince Philip attended the race as part of Manitoba's centennial year. The winner was Fanfreluche, a Northern Dancer filly who was that year's Canadian Horse of the Year as well as North America's champion three-year-old filly. Her son L'Enjoleur won the Manitoba Derby in 1975, the

year in which he earned his second Canadian Horse of the Year title.

Location: 3975 Portage Ave., Winnipeg, Mb. R3K 2E9
Phone: (204) 885-3330
Fax: (204) 831-5348
Website: www.assiniboiadowns.com
E-Mail: info@assiniboiadowns.com
Dates of Inaugural Meeting: 1958
Abbreviation: AsD
Number of Stalls: 936
Seating Capacity: 6,000

Ownership
Manitoba Jockey Club

Officers
President: Harvey Warner
Vice President: Norm Elder
General Manager: Sharon Gulyas
Director of Racing and Operations: Darren Dunn
Racing Secretary: Ray Miller
Assistant Racing Secretary: Dustin Davis
Secretary: Barry Anderson
Director of Finance: Kris Nancoo
Director of Marketing: Pat Tymkiw
Director of Publicity: Ernest Nairn
Director of Sales: Holly Klos
Director of Simulcasting: Sheri Flaman
Promotions and Media Coordinator: Allan Gray
Track Announcer: Darren Dunn
Track Photographer: Gerry Hart
Track Superintendent: Bob Timlick
Security: Tim McDonald
Horsemen's Bookkeeper: Louise Russell

Racing Dates
2007: May 5-September 23, 70 days
2008: May 2-September 21, 70 days

Track Layout
Main Circumference: 6½ furlongs
Main Track Chute: 6 furlongs and 1⅛ miles
Main Width: 80 feet
Main Length of Stretch: 990 feet
Training Track: 4 furlongs

Attendance
Highest Single-Day Record: 13,276, August 6, 1979

Handle
Single-Day On-Track Handle: $713,756, September 5, 1988
Average All-Sources Recent Meeting: $113,393, 2007
Total On-Track Recent Meeting: $5,586,141, 2007

Mutuel Records
Highest Win: $474.20, May 31, 1986
Highest Exacta: $3,514.80, May 16, 1998
Highest Trifecta: $40,026.60, May 18, 1981
Highest Daily Double: $4,235.50, July 23, 1971
Highest Pick Three: $3,269.40, June 28, 1998
Highest Pick Four: $14,584.95, September 1, 1986

Leaders
Career, Leading Jockey by Titles: Bobby Stewart, 5
Career, Leading Trainer by Titles: Clayton Gray, 7
Career, Leading Jockey by Wins: Ken Hendricks, 1,663
Career, Leading Trainer by Wins: Gary Danelson, 1,050
Recent Meeting, Leading Jockey: Alan Cuthbertson, 106, 2007
Recent Meeting, Leading Trainer: Martin Drexler, 43, 2007

Records
Single-Day Jockey Wins: Jim Sorenson, 7, June 23, 1976

Principal Races
Manitoba Derby (Can-G3), Gold Breeders' Cup, Matron Breeders' Cup, Winnipeg Futurity

Track Records, Main Dirt
4 furlongs: Northern Spike, :44^{2}/$_{5}$, April 23, 1982
4½ furlongs: Astral Moon, :50^{1}/$_{5}$, May 1, 1982
5 furlongs: Northern Spike, :56^{2}/$_{5}$, September 5, 1982
5½ furlongs: Sunny Famous, 1:02.80, September 19, 1992
6 furlongs: Mr. Quill, 1:09, October 10, 1981; Nephrite, 1:09, October 8, 1989
7 furlongs: Victor's Pride, 1:23^{1}/$_{5}$, August 16, 1978
1 mile: *Gladiatore II, 1:35^{4}/$_{5}$, July 7, 1972; Tower of Shan, 1:35.80, June 24, 1990
1^{1}/$_{16}$ miles: Goa, 1:41^{3}/$_{5}$, July 23, 1988
1^{1}/$_{8}$ miles: Overskate, 1:47^{3}/$_{5}$, September 9, 1978
1^{1}/$_{4}$ miles: Nifty (Fr), 2:05, September 20, 1986; Northern Debut, 2:05, October 3, 1993
1^{3}/$_{8}$ miles: Island Fling, 2:16^{4}/$_{5}$, October 29, 1977
1^{1}/$_{2}$ miles: Baron Hudec, 2:32, September 9, 1978
1^{5}/$_{8}$ miles: Northern Kip, 2:46^{4}/$_{5}$, October 30, 1978
1^{3}/$_{4}$ miles: Just As Sunny, 3:01^{2}/$_{5}$, October 14, 1989
Other: a3 furlongs, Apart, :29, May 8, 1972; a6 furlongs, Lone Spruce, 1:12, June 24, 1984; a7 furlongs, Proven Reserve, 1:23^{3}/$_{5}$, July 9, 1986; 1^{5}/$_{16}$ miles, Scarlet Rich, 2:15^{1}/$_{5}$, October 21, 1981; 1^{11}/$_{16}$ miles, Hi Executor, 2:56^{2}/$_{5}$, September 30, 1984; 2^{1}/$_{4}$ miles, Fremarcton, 3:58^{1}/$_{5}$, August 15, 1960

Fastest Times of 2007 (Dirt)
4½ furlongs: Sophisticated Sis, 2, :54, July 14, 2007
5 furlongs: Amelia True Heart, 5, :59, August 31, 2007; Benewin, 6, :59, July 29, 2007
5½ furlongs: Yankee Beauty, 5, 1:05, May 20, 2007
6 furlongs: Jade Beret, 3, 1:10.60, July 31, 2007
7½ furlongs: Shadow Rush, 4, 1:32.80, July 21, 2007
1 mile: Arthurlooksgood, 5, 1:38.60, August 6, 2007
1^{1}/$_{16}$ miles: Mancini's Man, 3, 1:45.60, August 10, 2007
1^{1}/$_{8}$ miles: Tejano Trouble, 4, 1:51.80, September 23, 2007

Ontario

Fort Erie

Founded in 1897, Fort Erie is one of Canada's oldest racetracks. Located in southern Ontario across the border from Buffalo, New York, the track began its premier event, the Prince of Wales Stakes, in 1959 with the help of prominent Ontario horseman E. P. Taylor. The race for three-year-old Canadian-breds now has become the second leg of Canada's Triple Crown. Taylor-bred Northern Dancer made his career debut at Fort Erie in August 1963. The following year, the Nearctic colt became the first Canadian-bred to win the Kentucky Derby. The track now is owned by Nordic Gaming Corp., which consists of three business interests from southern Ontario and two foreign investors. It underwent $30-million in renovations in 1999 to build a 75,000-square-foot gaming floor that features 1,200 slot machines, which help to support the racing operation.

Location: 230 Catherine St., P.O. Box 1130, Fort Erie, On. L2A 5N9
Phone: (905) 871-3200, (800) 295-3770
Fax: (905) 994-3629
Website: www.forterieracing.com
E-Mail: femedia@forterieracetrack.ca
Year Founded: 1897
Dates of Inaugural Meeting: June 16, 1897
Abbreviation: FE
Number of Stalls: 1,100
Seating Capacity: 4,000

Ownership
Nordic Gaming Corp.

Officers
Chief Executive Officer: Bonnie Loubert

Director of Racing and Operations: Herb McGirr Sr.
Racing Secretary: Thomas G. Gostlin
Director of Media and Communications: Daryl Wells Jr.
Director of Mutuels and Simulcasting: Chad Gates
Track Announcer: Pete Kyte
Track Photographer: Michael Burns
Track Superintendent: Alan Gouck

Racing Dates

2007: May 5-October 30, 84 days
2008: May 3-October 28, 80 days

Track Layout

Main Circumference: 1 mile
Main Track Chute: $6\frac{1}{2}$ furlongs and $1\frac{1}{4}$ miles
Main Width: 75 feet
Main Length of Stretch: 1,060 feet
Main Turf Circumference: 7 furlongs
Main Turf Length of Stretch: 930 feet

Handle

Average On-Track Recent Meeting: $80,418, 2007
Average All-Sources Recent Meeting: $882,550, 2007
Total On-Track Recent Meeting: $6,755,112, 2007
Total All-Sources Recent Meeting: $74,134,200, 2007

Leaders

Recent Meeting, Leading Jockey: Robert King Jr., 106, 2007
Recent Meeting, Leading Trainer: Mark Fournier, 46, 2007

Principal Races

Prince of Wales S., Rainbow Connection S., Daryl Wells Sr. Memorial S., Ernie Samuel Memorial S.

Track Records, Main Dirt

4 furlongs: Kirk's Dandy, :47$\frac{2}{5}$, May 2, 1957
$4\frac{1}{2}$ furlongs: Astral Moon, :50$\frac{4}{5}$, May 1, 1982
5 furlongs: Cool Shot, :56.60, July 15, 1995
$5\frac{1}{2}$ furlongs: Emotionally, 1:03.60, June 28, 1997; Just a Lord, 1:03.60, June 15, 1991
6 furlongs: High Blitz, 1:08.35, June 13, 2005
$6\frac{1}{2}$ furlongs: Muzledick, 1:15$\frac{4}{5}$, August 10, 1968; Souvenier Biz, 1:15.85, August 13, 2005
1 mile 70 yds: Myrtle Irene, 1:39.80, August 26, 1994
$1\frac{1}{16}$ miles: Goa, 1:41$\frac{3}{5}$, July 23, 1988
$1\frac{1}{8}$ miles: Lauries Dancer, 1:48, August 23, 1972
$1\frac{3}{16}$ miles: Bruce's Mill, 1:53.80, July 31, 1994
$1\frac{1}{4}$ miles: Do's Vigil, 2:03$\frac{2}{5}$, August 14, 1974; French Tambourine, 2:03$\frac{2}{5}$, August 10, 1975
$1\frac{1}{2}$ miles: Itshouldbesoeasy, 2:32.57, August 10, 1999
$1\frac{5}{8}$ miles: Gay Story, 2:48$\frac{3}{5}$, August 27, 1956
$1\frac{3}{4}$ miles: Brave Zappa, 2:59, July 9, 1984
Other: 2 furlongs, Leisure Road, :21.20, September 5, 1998; $1\frac{13}{16}$ miles, Captain Charisma, 3:09$\frac{2}{5}$, August 12, 1984; $1\frac{7}{8}$ miles, Frost Prince, 3:22.60, August 20, 1999; 2m 70 yds, Devils Gold, 3:33, October 6, 1997

Track Records, Main Turf

5 furlongs: Oh Mar, :56.99, September 9, 2002
1 mile: Fifth and a Jigger, 1:34.30, June 10, 1991
$1\frac{1}{16}$ miles: Road of War, 1:40.80, June 19, 1994
$1\frac{3}{8}$ miles: Lord Vancouver, 2:15, July 30, 1972
$1\frac{1}{2}$ miles: Norwick, 2:28, August 21, 1983
$1\frac{3}{4}$ miles: Ahead of the Best, 2:56.60, September 10, 1991
Other: a7 furlongs, National Hero, 1:21.96, June 3, 2007; a$1\frac{7}{8}$ miles, Regal Admiral, 3:19$\frac{4}{5}$, August 7, 1974; $1\frac{7}{8}$ miles, Medlaw, 3:16$\frac{1}{5}$, September 30, 1985

Fastest Times of 2007 (Dirt)

2 furlongs: Fast Trick, 3, :21.35, July 3, 2007
$4\frac{1}{2}$ furlongs: Souvenier Biz, 7, :51.70, May 5, 2007
5 furlongs: Trigone, 3, :57.01, September 17, 2007
6 furlongs: Starticus, 3, 1:09.32, October 22, 2007
$6\frac{1}{2}$ furlongs: Frezacon, 4, 1:15.93, August 21, 2007
1 mile 70 yds: Draven's Cross, 4, 1:40.90, September 16, 2007
$1\frac{1}{16}$ miles: Smiling Jordan, 5, 1:43.13, September 16, 2007
$1\frac{1}{8}$ miles: Smiling Jordan, 5, 1:51.93, October 16, 2007
$1\frac{3}{16}$ miles: Alezzandro, 3, 1:55.04, July 15, 2007
$1\frac{5}{8}$ miles: Lettherebejustice, 6, 2:46.39, October 7, 2007
2 miles 70 yds: Dancer's Legacy, 3, 3:33.75, October 30, 2007

Fastest Times of 2007 (Turf)

5 furlongs: Marco Be Good, 5, :57.04, July 15, 2007
a5 furlongs: Chemistry Class, 6, :58.13, July 3, 2007
a7 furlongs: National Hero, 5, 1:21.96, June 3, 2007
1 mile: Canadian Music, 5, 1:37.41, July 31, 2007
a1 mile: Silver Strip, 6, 1:38.12, July 8, 2007
a$1\frac{1}{2}$ miles: Saucy Vinny, 5, 3:06.42, September 18, 2007
$1\frac{1}{16}$ miles: Bunny Lake, 7, 1:43.89, July 16, 2007
a$1\frac{1}{16}$ miles: Tap Show, 4, 1:45.41, June 19, 2007

Woodbine

The addition of 1,700 slot machines in March 2000 substantially increased purses and made Canada's best-known racetrack into a financial success after years of operating under a burdensome debt load. After installing the slot machines, the organization that owns the track changed its name from the Ontario Jockey Club to the Woodbine Entertainment Group. Woodbine, located in the Toronto suburb of Rexdale, is home of the Queen's Plate Stakes, first run in 1860 and North America's oldest continually run stakes race. With a unique track arrangement on its 650 acres, Woodbine is the only track in North America to conduct Standardbred and Thoroughbred racing on the same day. Its $1\frac{1}{2}$-mile grass course, the E. P. Taylor Turf Course, features the longest stretch run in North America, 1,440 feet. Inside the turf course is the one-mile Polytrack synthetic racing surface, which was installed in 2006. Inside the main dirt track is a seven-furlong, 85-foot-wide Standardbred track. Woodbine's rich history dates to 1874, when the track opened on what was then the eastern outskirts of Toronto, which is now Toronto's downtown. That track's name was changed to Old Woodbine in 1956 and then renamed Greenwood Raceway in '63. The present Woodbine opened on June 12, 1956. In 1996, Woodbine became the first track outside the United States to host the Breeders' Cup World Championships, and it drew a record Woodbine crowd of 42,243. Besides the Queen's Plate, Woodbine hosts the Canadian International Stakes (Can-G1) and the Woodbine Mile Stakes (Can-G1), which has evolved into an important stakes for grass horses aiming for the Breeders' Cup Mile (G1).

Location: 555 Rexdale Blvd., Rexdale, On. M9W 5L2
Phone: (416) 675-7223, (888) 675-7223
Fax: (416) 213-2122
Website: *www.woodbineentertainment.com*
E-Mail: csd@woodbineentertainment.com
Year Founded: 1874 (Old Woodbine); 1956 (Woodbine)
Abbreviation: WO
Acreage: 850
Number of Stalls: 2,138
Seating Capacity: 13,500

Ownership

Woodbine Entertainment Group

Officers

Chairman and Chief Executive Officer: David S. Willmot
President: Nick R. Eaves
Senior Vice Presidents: Jamie Martin, Steve N. Mitchell
Vice President of Marketing and Communications: Andrew MacDonald
Vice President of Thoroughbred Racing: Steve Koch
Vice President of Wagering Services: Sean Pinsonneault
Vice President of Broadcasting: David Naylor
Director of Racing: Tom Cosgrove
Racing Secretary: Steven Lym
Assistant Racing Secretary: Sheryl McSwain

Treasurer: Robert Careless
Director of Operations: Ed Stutz
Director of Mutuels: Greg Martin
Director of Communications: Glenn Crouter
Director of Publicity: John Siscos
Stewards: Richard Grubb, Gunnar Lindberg, Fenton Platts
Track Announcer: Dan Loiselle
Track Photographer: Michael Burns
Track Superintendent: Irwin Driedger
Horsemen's Bookkeeper: F. Courtney

Racing Dates
2007: March 31-December 9, 167 days
2008: April 5-December 7, 167 days

Track Layout
Main Circumference: 1 mile (Polytrack)
Main Track Chute: 7 furlongs and 1 1/4 miles
Main Width: 85 feet
Main Length of Stretch: 975 feet
Main Turf Circumference: 1 1/2 miles
Main Turf Chute: 1 1/8 miles
Main Turf Width: Homestretch: 100 feet; Backstretch: 120 feet
Main Turf Length of Stretch: 1,440 feet
Inner Circumference: 7-furlong Standardbred track
Training Track: 1 mile (dirt); 7 furlongs (turf)

Attendance
Highest Single-Day Record: 42,243, October 26, 1996

Handle
Average All-Sources Recent Meeting: $2,032,500, 2006
Single-Day On-Track Handle: $6,884,357, October 26, 1996
Single-Day All-Sources Handle: $67,738,890, October 26, 1996
Total All-Sources Recent Meeting: $339,427,648, 2007

Mutuel Records
Highest Win: $794.20, Waverley Steps, June 24, 1968
Highest Exacta: $6,405, June 11, 1995
Lowest Exacta: $2.70, June 16, 1991
Highest Trifecta: $123,279, November 28, 1999
Lowest Trifecta: $11.60, August 11, 1998
Highest Daily Double: $5,497.50, June 16, 1978
Lowest Daily Double: $3.80, May 20, 1998
Highest Pick Three: $10,881.80, June 29, 1991
Lowest Pick Three: $1.80, July 28, 1991
Highest Other Exotics: $466,671.65, Super 7, July 1, 1989; $131,407.85, Superfecta, October 25, 2007
Lowest Other Exotics: $221.50, Super 7, May 10, 1997; $86.30, Superfecta, July 5, 2000
Highest Pick Four: $123,372.30, June 15, 1988
Lowest Pick Four: $21.75, April 29, 1995

Leaders
Career, Leading Jockey by Titles: Sandy Hawley, 19
Career, Leading Trainer by Titles: Frank Merrill, 30
Recent Meeting, Leading Jockey: Patrick Husbands, 149, 2007
Recent Meeting, Leading Owner: Stronach Stables, 29, 2007
Recent Meeting, Leading Trainer: Mark E. Casse, 84, 2006

Records
Single-Day Jockey Wins: Richard Grubb, 7, May 16, 1967; Sandy Hawley, 7, May 22, 1972; Sandy Hawley, 7, October 10, 1974
Single Meet, Leading Jockey by Wins: Mickey Walls, 221, 1991
Single Meet, Leading Trainer by Wins: Frank Passero, 89, 1995

Principal Races
Canadian International S. (Can-G1), Woodbine Mile S. (Can-G1), E. P. Taylor S. (Can-G1), Northern Dancer Turf S. (Can-G1), Queen's Plate S., Breeders' S., Woodbine Oaks

Interesting Facts
Previous Names and Dates: Ontario Jockey Club (1881-2001)
Achievements/Milestones: Hosted Arlington Million in 1988. Hosted first Breeders' Cup outside the U.S. in 1996.

Notable Events
In January 2004, Woodbine Entertainment launched hpibet.com, an Internet wagering site.

Track Records, Main All Weather
4 1/2 furlongs: Executrix, :51.88, June 2, 2007
6 furlongs: Financingavailable, 1:08.56, November 3, 2007
6 1/2 furlongs: Prince Atlantis, 1:14.94, November 24, 2007
7 furlongs: Verne's Baby, 1:20.54, September 20, 2006
1 mile 70 yds: Regal Courser, 1:39.60, August 8, 1998
1 1/16 miles: Palladio, 1:43.07, May 21, 2007
1 1/8 miles: Leonnatus Anteas, 1:49.55, October 13, 2007

Track Records, Main Turf
6 furlongs: Wild Zone, 1:07.60, July 7, 1996; Spring Barley, 1:07.63, September 5, 2001
6 1/2 furlongs: My Lucky Strike, 1:13.97, August 7, 2005
7 furlongs: Soaring Free, 1:19.38, July 24, 2004
1 mile: Royal Regalia, 1:31.84, July 1, 2004
1 1/16 miles: Jet Freighter, 1:39.20, June 4, 1995; Honolulu Gold, 1:39.20, July 11, 1996; Western Express, 1:39.20, July 12, 1998
1 1/8 miles: Bold Ruritana, 1:45.20, June 18, 1995
1 1/4 miles: Mrs. Lindsay, 2:00.68, October 21, 2007
1 3/8 miles: Shoal Water, 2:12.37, July 25, 2004
1 1/2 miles: Raintrap (GB), 2:25.60, October 16, 1994
Other: a 1 1/8 miles, Surging River, 1:42.87, August 8, 2004; a 1 1/4 miles, Desert Waves, 2:02.40, July 24, 1995; a 1 1/4 miles, Murad, 2:02.40, June 4, 1998; a 1 3/8 miles, Chief Bearhart, 2:16, July 25, 1996; a 1 1/2 miles, Mr. Lucky Junction, 2:29.60, July 26, 1996

Fastest Times of 2007 (All Weather)
2 furlongs: Bella Nevada, 2, :21.99, May 19, 2007
4 1/2 furlongs: Executrix, 2, :51.88, June 2, 2007
5 furlongs: Northern Netti, 2, :57.08, October 13, 2007
5 1/2 furlongs: Dawn Raid, 2, 1:03.37, September 27, 2007
6 furlongs: Financingavailable, 6, 1:08.56, November 3, 2007
6 1/2 furlongs: Prince Atlantis, 2, 1:14.94, November 24, 2007
7 furlongs: Cool Selection, 8, 1:21.19, November 25, 2007
1 mile 70 yds: Miner's Claim, 2, 1:41.79, November 2, 2007
1 1/16 miles: True Metropolitan, 5, 1:42.22, November 17, 2007
1 1/8 miles: Leonnatus Anteas, 3, 1:49.55, October 13, 2007
1 3/16 miles: Dancer's Flyer, 6, 2:01.54, August 11, 2007
1 1/4 miles: Like a Gem, 4, 2:03.51, November 10, 2007
1 1/2 miles: Pellegrino (Brz), 8, 2:30.71, November 16, 2007
1 3/4 miles: Torquay, 5, 3:01.08, December 9, 2007
1 7/8 miles: Benz Boy, 6, 3:13.79, December 9, 2007

Fastest Times of 2007 (Turf)
6 furlongs: Stradivinsky, 4, 1:07.90, June 1, 2007
6 1/2 furlongs: Ju Ju Beast, 5, 1:14.42, May 30, 2007
7 furlongs: Awesome Action, 7, 1:20.47, July 21, 2007
1 mile: Shakespeare, 3, 1:33.58, September 16, 2007
1 1/16 miles: Strike Softly, 4, 1:39.90, June 2, 2007
1 1/8 miles: Eccentric (GB), 6, 1:46.83, July 2, 2007
a 1 1/8 miles: Masseuse, 5, 1:45.55, July 22, 2007
1 1/2 miles: Sky Conqueror, 5, 2:27.45, July 22, 2007
1 1/4 miles: Mrs. Lindsay, 3, 2:00.68, October 21, 2007
1 3/8 miles: Cloudy's Knight, 7, 2:14.10, September 23, 2007

Saskatchewan

Marquis Downs

Marquis Downs in Saskatoon has offered live racing since 1969. With a five-furlong track and a grandstand capacity of 4,500, Marquis is part of the Saskatoon Prairieland Exhibition, a multipurpose facility that includes meeting and exhibition halls and a casino. Racing annually takes place from May through September.

Location: 503 Ruth St. W., P.O. Box 6010, Saskatoon, Sk. S7K 4E4
Phone: (306) 242-6100
Fax: (306) 242-6907
Website: www.marquisdowns.com
E-Mail: contactus@saskatoonex.com
Dates of Inaugural Meeting: August 18, 1969
Abbreviation: MD

Number of Stalls: 750
Seating Capacity: 3,027

Ownership
Saskatoon Prairieland Park Corp.

Officers
Chief Executive Officer: Mark Regier
President: Dennis Wiebe
Manager of Live Racing: Rick Fior
Treasurer: Dan Kemppainen
Director of Operations: Wayne Heiser
Director of Communications: Marlene Rochelle
Director of Marketing and Publicity: Maurice Neault
Director of Mutuels: Vel Colter
Director of Simulcasting: Doug King
Horsemen's Liaison: Rick Fior
Stewards: Terry Harkness, Zorka Fuentes, Doug Schneider, Margo Tutt
Track Announcer: Dave Paulsen
Track Photographer: Naomi Wilson
Track Superintendent: Dennis Paules
Horsemen's Bookkeeper: Shawn Irwin

Racing Dates
2007: May 25-September 8, 30 days
2008: May 23-September 6, 30 days

Track Layout
Main Circumference: 5 furlongs
Main Track Chute: 7 furlongs and 1 $^1/_8$ miles
Main Width: 90 feet
Main Length of Stretch: 660 feet

Handle
Average On-Track Recent Meeting: $29,300, 2007
Total On-Track Recent Meeting: $850,000, 2007

Leaders
Recent Meeting, Leading Jockey: Tim Moccasin, 48, 2007
Recent Meeting, Leading Trainer: Russell Gardipy, 31, 2007

Principal Races
Prairie Lily Sales S., Parkland Heritage S., Shortgrass Heritage S., Western Heritage S., Woodland Heritage S., Saskatchewan Derby

Interesting Facts
Trivia: Jockey Tim Moccasin rode 14 consecutive winners August 24 through September 1, 2001, believed to be a North American record.

Track Records, Main Dirt
4 furlongs: Zizzilin, :45, May 8, 1981
5$^1/_2$ furlongs: Mickey's Mark, 1:04$^2/_5$, July 28, 1980
6 furlongs: Shotgun Annie, 1:10$^2/_5$, August 7, 1981
6$^1/_2$ furlongs: Christmas Country, 1:18$^3/_5$, August 1, 1994
7 furlongs: Standoff, 1:23.35, July 21, 2007
1 mile: Three for You, 1:37$^1/_5$, June 12, 1981
1$^1/_{16}$ miles: Little Bo, 1:42, September 1, 1984
1$^1/_8$ miles: Zance, 1:49$^3/_5$, October 10, 1988
1$^3/_8$ miles: Secret Cipher, 2:18, October 15, 1983
1$^5/_8$ miles: Bright Bern, 2:48, July 31, 1976
1$^3/_4$ miles: Lloyd's Admiral, 3:01$^2/_5$, October 19, 1986
Other: 3$^1/_2$ furlongs, Kid Dynamo, :40$^2/_5$, June 20, 1977; a4 furlongs, Royal Alibi, :45$^1/_5$, May 20, 1978; a6$^1/_2$ furlongs, Shona Rae, 1:17$^4/_5$, June 11, 1992; a7 furlongs, Graceful Klinchit, 1:23$^3/_5$, August 31, 1991; a1$^1/_8$ miles, Easy Riser, 1:49$^2/_5$, August 25, 1980; 1$^5/_{16}$ miles, Extrapolate, 2:13, August 29, 1993; a1$^1/_2$ miles, Spring Sunsation, 2:35, September 26, 1993

Fastest Times of 2007 (Dirt)
4 furlongs: Jazzy Express, 6, :46.06, May 26, 2007
6 furlongs: Emblemofpower, 3, 1:11.50, July 6, 2007
6$^1/_2$ furlongs: Y. C. Rail, 2, 1:21.75, September 1, 2007
7 furlongs: Standoff, 6, 1:23.35, July 21, 2007
1 mile: Shewinagin, 4, 1:40.25, July 6, 2007
1$^1/_{16}$ miles: Standoff, 6, 1:45.47, September 7, 2007
1$^1/_8$ miles: Redflex, 7, 1:55.37, August 3, 2007
1$^1/_{16}$ miles: Bragger, 5, 2:16.37, August 24, 2007
1$^3/_8$ miles: Double Bid, 7, 2:21.28, September 7, 2007

Puerto Rico

Hipodromo Camarero

Located in Canovanas, Hipodromo Camarero—formerly known as El Comandante—has been the island's racing outlet for decades. To many racing fans, the track is probably best known for producing Bold Forbes and Mister Frisky. A dual classic winner and 1976 champion three-year-old male in the United States, Bold Forbes began his career in Puerto Rico. So did Mister Frisky, who started his unbeaten string there in 1989 before coming to the U.S. and going off as the favorite in the '90 Kentucky Derby (G1), in which he finished eighth. In recent years, the track has added a sophisticated network of off-track wagering outlets and a daily television racing report. Camarero Group bought the track out of bankruptcy for $73-million in early 2007 and renamed it for a legendary Puerto Rican horse who won 56 consecutive races from 1953-'55.

Location: P.O. Box 1643, Canóvanas, P.R. 00729-1643
Phone: (787) 641-6060
Fax: (787) 641-6085
Website: www.camareroracepr.com
E-Mail: webmaster@elcomandantepr.net
Year Founded: 1976 (El Comandante); 2007 (Hipodromo Camarero)
Abbreviation: Cmr
Acreage: 257
Number of Stalls: 1,500+

Ownership
Camarero Racetrack Corp.

Officers
President: Ervin Rodriquez
Senior Vice President: Lionel Muller
Vice President: Alejandro Fuentes Fernandez
Controller: Edwin Padovani
Director of CCTV System and Programming: Ricardo Alfaro
Director of Human Resources: Luis Figueroa
Communications: Nidnal Adrover
TV Production: Isabel Aybar

Racing Dates
2007: January 1-December 31, 260 days
2008: January 1-December 31, 260 days

Track Layout
Main Circumference: 1 mile
Main Track Chute: 7 furlongs

Principal Races
Derby Puertorriqueno, Copa Gobernador, Copa San Juan, Clasico Antonio Fernandez Castrillon, Clasico Internacional del Caribe

Track Records, Main Dirt
5 furlongs: Lozier Kaplan, :57$^2/_5$, April 16, 1978
5$^1/_2$ furlongs: Bandit Bomber, 1:02.60, May 3, 1996
6 furlongs: Bandit Bomber, 1:09, August 16, 1995
6$^1/_2$ furlongs: Bo Judged, 1:15$^1/_5$, May 14, 1989; Sonvida Red, 1:15.17, April 7, 2007
7 furlongs: Bandit Bomber, 1:21.40, October 1, 1995
1$^1/_{16}$ miles: Shake Shake Shake, 1:42$^3/_5$, June 25, 1978
1$^1/_8$ miles: Dr. Abraham, 1:48.80, July 20, 1996
1$^3/_{16}$ miles: Lightning Al, 1:55.40, February 17, 1997

Fastest Times of 2007 (Dirt)
2 furlongs: Dana My Love, :21.91, March 23, 2007
5$^1/_2$ furlongs: Tonadilla, 1:03.76, September 23, 2007
6 furlongs: Gold Gift, 1:09.13, December 17, 2007
6$^1/_2$ furlongs: Sonvida Red, 1:15.17, April 7, 2007
1 mile: Shewinagin, 4, 1:40.25, July 6, 2007
1$^1/_8$ miles: Soy Conquistador, 1:50.06, December 2, 2007
1$^1/_4$ miles: Gran Estefania, 2:02.30, December 1, 2007

North American Racetracks

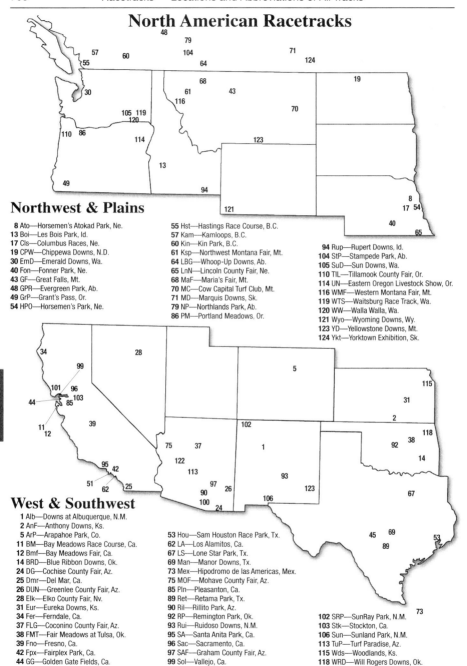

Northwest & Plains

8 Ato—Horsemen's Atokad Park, Ne.
13 Boi—Les Bois Park, Id.
17 Cls—Columbus Races, Ne.
19 CPW—Chippewa Downs, N.D.
30 EmD—Emerald Downs, Wa.
40 Fon—Fonner Park, Ne.
43 GF—Great Falls, Mt.
48 GPR—Evergreen Park, Ab.
49 GrP—Grant's Pass, Or.
54 HPO—Horsemen's Park, Ne.
55 Hst—Hastings Race Course, B.C.
57 Kam—Kamloops, B.C.
60 Kin—Kin Park, B.C.
61 Ksp—Northwest Montana Fair, Mt.
64 LBG—Whoop-Up Downs, Ab.
65 LnN—Lincoln County Fair, Ne.
68 MaF—Maria's Fair, Mt.
70 MC—Cow Capital Turf Club, Mt.
71 MD—Marquis Downs, Sk.
79 NP—Northlands Park, Ab.
86 PM—Portland Meadows, Or.
94 Rup—Rupert Downs, Id.
104 StP—Stampede Park, Ab.
105 SuD—Sun Downs, Wa.
110 TIL—Tillamook County Fair, Or.
114 UN—Eastern Oregon Livestock Show, Or.
116 WMF—Western Montana Fair, Mt.
119 WTS—Waitsburg Race Track, Wa.
120 WW—Walla Walla, Wa.
121 Wyo—Wyoming Downs, Wy.
123 YD—Yellowstone Downs, Mt.
124 Ykt—Yorktown Exhibition, Sk.

West & Southwest

1 Alb—Downs at Albuquerque, N.M.
2 AnF—Anthony Downs, Ks.
5 ArP—Arapahoe Park, Co.
11 BM—Bay Meadows Race Course, Ca.
12 Bmf—Bay Meadows Fair, Ca.
14 BRD—Blue Ribbon Downs, Ok.
24 DG—Cochise County Fair, Az.
25 Dmr—Del Mar, Ca.
26 DUN—Greenlee County Fair, Az.
28 Elk—Elko County Fair, Nv.
31 Eur—Eureka Downs, Ks.
34 Fer—Ferndale, Ca.
37 FLG—Coconino County Fair, Az.
38 FMT—Fair Meadows at Tulsa, Ok.
39 Fno—Fresno, Ca.
42 Fpx—Fairplex Park, Ca.
44 GG—Golden Gate Fields, Ca.
45 Gil—Gillespie County Fair, Tx.
51 Hol—Hollywood Park, Ca.
53 Hou—Sam Houston Race Park, Tx.
62 LA—Los Alamitos, Ca.
67 LS—Lone Star Park, Tx.
69 Man—Manor Downs, Tx.
73 Mex—Hipodromo de las Americas, Mex.
75 MOF—Mohave County Fair, Az.
85 Pln—Pleasanton, Ca.
89 Ret—Retama Park, Tx.
90 Ril—Rillito Park, Az.
92 RP—Remington Park, Ok.
93 Rui—Ruidoso Downs, N.M.
95 SA—Santa Anita Park, Ca.
96 Sac—Sacramento, Ca.
97 SAF—Graham County Fair, Az.
99 Sol—Vallejo, Ca.
100 SON—Santa Cruz County Fair, Az.
101 SR—Santa Rosa, Ca.
102 SRP—SunRay Park, N.M.
103 Stk—Stockton, Ca.
106 Sun—Sunland Park, N.M.
113 TuP—Turf Paradise, Az.
115 Wds—Woodlands, Ks.
118 WRD—Will Rogers Downs, Ok.
122 Yav—Yavapai Downs, Az.
123 Zia—Zia Park, NM

Abbreviations and Locations

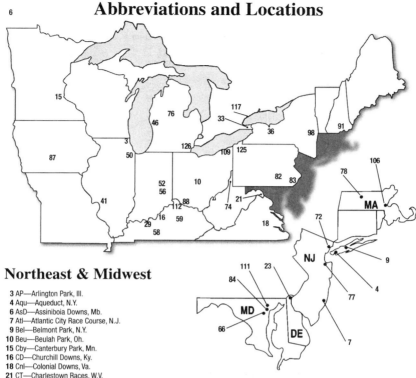

Northeast & Midwest

- 3 AP—Arlington Park, Ill.
- 4 Aqu—Aqueduct, N.Y.
- 6 AsD—Assiniboia Downs, Mb.
- 7 Atl—Atlantic City Race Course, N.J.
- 9 Bel—Belmont Park, N.Y.
- 10 Beu—Beulah Park, Oh.
- 15 Cby—Canterbury Park, Mn.
- 16 CD—Churchill Downs, Ky.
- 18 Cnl—Colonial Downs, Va.
- 21 CT—Charlestown Races, W.V.
- 23 Del—Delaware Park, De.
- 29 EIP—Ellis Park, Ky.
- 33 FE—Fort Erie, On.
- 36 FL—Finger Lakes, N.Y.
- 41 FP—Fairmount Park, Il.
- 46 GLD—Great Lakes Downs, Mi.
- 50 Haw—Hawthorne Park, Il.
- 52 Hoo—Hoosier Park, In.
- 56 Ind—Indiana Downs, In.
- 58 KD—Kentucky Downs, Ky.
- 59 Kee—Keeneland Race Course, Ky.
- 66 Lrl—Laurel Park, Md.
- 72 Med—Meadowlands, N.J.
- 74 Mnr—Mountaineer Race Track, W.V.
- 76 MPM—Mount Pleasant Meadows, Mi.
- 77 Mth—Monmouth Park, N.J.
- 78 Nmp—Northampton Fair, Ma.
- 82 Pen—Penn National Race Course, Pa.
- 83 Pha—Philadelphia Park, Pa.
- 125 PID—Presque Isle Downs, Pa.
- 84 Pim—Pimlico Race Course, Md.
- 126 PRC—Pinnacle Race Course, Mi.
- 87 PrM—Prairie Meadows Racetrack, Ia.
- 88 RD—River Downs, Oh.
- 91 Rkm—Rockingham Park, N.H.
- 98 Sar—Saratoga Race Course, N.Y.
- 106 Suf—Suffolk Downs, Ma.
- 109 Tdn—Thistledown, Oh.
- 111 Tim—Timonium, Md.
- 112 TP—Turfway Park, Ky.
- 117 WO—Woodbine, On.

Southeast

- 20 Crc—Calder Race Course, Fl.
- 22 DeD—Delta Downs, La.
- 27 Cmr—Hipodromo Camarero, P.R.
- 32 Evd—Evangeline Downs, La.
- 35 FG—Fair Grounds, La.
- 47 GP—Gulfstream Park, Fl.
- 63 LaD—Louisiana Downs, La.
- 80 OP—Oaklawn Park, Ar.
- 81 OTC—Ocala Training Center, Fl.
- 108 Tam—Tampa Bay Downs, Fl.

North American Purse Distribution by Year

Year	No. of Runners	No. of Races	Total Purses	Average Purse	Per Runner Average	Per Runner Median
2007	72,691	56,202	$1,251,579,551	$22,269	$17,218	$6,680
2006	72,445	56,730	1,189,277,214	20,964	16,416	6,520
2005	72,784	57,481	1,153,930,533	20,051	15,851	6,135
2004	73,915	58,686	1,177,769,795	20,069	15,934	5,877
2003	73,614	58,813	1,154,238,845	19,626	15,680	5,714
2002	72,504	59,712	1,170,169,267	19,597	16,139	6,003
2001	70,942	60,538	1,146,337,367	18,936	16,159	6,010
2000	69,230	60,579	1,093,661,241	18,053	15,798	5,796
1999	68,435	60,118	1,008,162,608	16,770	14,732	5,310
1998	68,419	61,141	968,366,929	15,838	14,153	4,939
1997	69,067	63,491	888,667,752	13,997	12,867	4,425
1996	70,371	64,263	845,916,706	13,163	12,021	3,937
1995	72,316	68,197	815,987,125	11,965	11,283	3,702
1994	74,939	70,617	770,426,193	10,910	10,280	3,314
1993	78,763	72,224	748,415,925	10,362	9,502	2,850
1992	83,468	77,711	771,136,296	9,989	9,238	2,731
1991	86,483	78,671	761,446,198	9,679	8,805	2,433
1990	89,722	79,971	775,006,519	9,691	8,637	2,376
1989	91,436	82,726	771,421,230	9,325	8,437	2,218
1988	90,482	79,589	736,698,230	9,256	8,142	2,127
1987	89,504	80,376	704,372,435	8,763	7,870	2,101
1986	86,022	77,732	661,826,092	8,514	7,694	2,070
1985	82,548	75,687	641,658,553	8,478	7,773	2,158
1984	78,253	74,396	599,348,425	8,056	7,659	2,345
1983	74,540	71,034	544,260,167	7,662	7,302	2,435
1982	69,505	71,515	526,587,096	7,363	7,576	2,703
1981	65,797	70,881	507,007,953	7,153	7,706	2,865
1980	64,499	68,236	449,631,322	6,589	6,971	2,524
1979	63,728	69,406	414,629,063	5,974	6,506	2,440
1978	62,937	69,498	367,163,242	5,283	5,834	n/a
1977	61,960	68,826	335,720,312	4,878	5,418	2,189
1976	61,084	69,480	318,680,094	4,587	5,217	2,100
1975	58,818	68,203	291,194,571	4,270	4,951	2,058
1974	56,524	65,288	262,942,547	4,027	4,652	1,904
1973	54,812	62,264	233,662,724	3,753	4,263	1,764
1972	52,561	59,417	210,435,265	3,542	4,004	1,647

Data reflect all Thoroughbred purses distributed to racehorses in North America, excluding Mexico and Puerto Rico, from Jockey Club Information Systems data. Steeplechase races are excluded.

Top 25 Race Meetings by Average Attendance in 2007

Rank	Meet	Racing Dates	Total Attendance	Average Attendance
1	Saratoga Race Course	36	958,574	26,627
2	Del Mar	43	718,923	16,719
3	Keeneland Race Course (Spring)	15	243,606	16,240
4	Horsemen's Atokad Park	3	48,000	16,000
5	Keeneland Race Course (Fall)	17	239,296	14,076
6	Oaklawn Park	52	618,284	11,890
7	Monmouth Park*	79	754,750	9,554
8	Santa Anita Park	85	785,167	9,237
9	Arlington Park	94	784,177	8,342
10	Pimlico Race Course	31	255,804	8,252
11	Oak Tree at Santa Anita	31	254,018	8,194
12	Fresno	11	86,498	7,863
13	Lone Star Park	67	475,000	7,090
14	Golden Gate Fields (Spring)	35	246,717	7,049
15	Hollywood Park (Spring)	59	405,922	6,880
16	Belmont Park (Spring)	59	380,495	6,449
17	Bay Meadows (Spring)	48	305,882	6,373
18	Golden Gate Fields (Winter)	31	196,258	6,331
19	Remington Park	69	402,109	5,828
20	Bay Meadows (Fall)	56	319,202	5,700
21	Fairplex Park	16	90,114	5,632
22	Mountaineer Race Track	233	1,287,445	5,526
23	Canterbury Park	68	372,358	5,476
24	Hollywood Park (Fall)	31	158,218	5,104
25	Belmont Park (Fall)	33	165,045	5,001

*Including Breeders' Cup World Championships day. Based on racetracks reporting attendance.

Top 25 Race Meetings by Average All-Sources Wagering in 2007

Rank	Meet	Racing Dates	Total All-Sources Wagering	Average All-Sources Wagering
1	Saratoga Race Course	36	$582,656,103	$16,184,892
2	Del Mar	43	601,356,177	13,985,027
3	Hollywood Park (Spring)	59	755,763,334	12,809,548
4	Belmont Park (Spring)	59	676,568,657	11,467,265
5	Hollywood Park (Fall)	31	350,733,340	11,313,979
6	Belmont Park (Fall)	33	338,599,297	10,260,585
7	Keeneland Race Course (Spring)	15	150,497,482	10,033,165
8	Santa Anita Park	85	785,396,063	9,239,954
9	Keeneland Race Course (Fall)	17	139,816,831	8,224,519
10	Oak Tree at Santa Anita	31	251,603,606	8,116,245
11	Aqueduct (Spring)	76	596,819,923	7,852,894
12	Pimlico Race Course	31	236,905,285	7,642,106
13	Aqueduct (Fall)	45	338,599,297	7,524,429
14	Monmouth Park*	79	420,603,300	5,324,092
15	Fairplex Park	16	74,785,157	4,674,072
16	Golden Gate Fields (Spring)	35	160,020,990	4,572,028
17	Golden Gate Fields (Winter)	31	135,222,922	4,362,030
18	Tampa Bay Downs	94	383,943,754	4,084,508
19	Oaklawn Park	52	193,366,592	3,718,588
20	Laurel Park (Winter)	75	210,433,200	2,805,776
21	Turfway Park (Holiday)	27	73,712,679	2,730,099
22	Turfway Park (Spring)	60	150,672,555	2,511,209
23	Hawthorne Park (Spring)	45	109,990,560	2,444,235
24	Turfway Park (Fall)	22	53,395,447	2,427,066
25	Hoosier Park	31	72,714,857	2,345,641

*Including Breeders' Cup World Championships day. Based on racetracks reporting pari-mutuel wagering.

Top 25 Race Meetings by Average On-Track Wagering in 2007

Rank	Meet	Racing Dates	Total On-Track Wagering	Average On-Track Wagering
1	Saratoga Race Course	36	$134,606,756	$3,739,077
2	Del Mar	43	104,800,659	2,437,225
3	Hollywood Park (Spring)	59	106,948,664	1,812,689
4	Santa Anita Park	85	126,436,574	1,487,489
5	Keeneland Race Course (Spring)	15	21,329,702	1,421,980
6	Monmouth Park*	79	112,069,988	1,418,607
7	Hollywood Park (Fall)	31	43,157,247	1,392,169
8	Oaklawn Park	52	65,778,477	1,264,971
9	Oak Tree at Santa Anita	31	39,048,838	1,259,640
10	Keeneland Race Course (Fall)	17	20,790,718	1,222,983
11	Belmont Park (Spring)	59	68,718,518	1,164,721
13	Belmont Park (Fall)	33	26,846,579	813,533
14	Bay Meadows (Spring)	48	31,739,002	661,229
15	Golden Gate Fields (Spring)	35	22,059,817	630,280
16	Pimlico Race Course (Spring)	31	19,108,805	616,413
17	Golden Gate Fields (Winter)	31	18,813,662	606,892
18	Aqueduct (Spring)	76	46,088,996	606,434
19	Aqueduct (Fall)	45	26,876,579	597,257
20	Arlington Park	94	54,600,942	580,861
21	Bay Meadows (Fall)	56	31,175,463	556,705
22	Fairplex Park	16	8,771,936	548,246
23	Canterbury Park	68	31,287,928	460,117
24	Lone Star Park	67	28,400,000	423,881
25	Ellis Park	46	14,632,037	318,088

*Including Breeders' Cup World Championships day. Based on racetracks reporting pari-mutuel wagering.

Revenues to States From Horse Racing

For a few decades, horse racing was the golden goose for state governments, as shown in the table of current-dollar revenues prepared by the Association of Racing Commissioners International. The revenues cover all forms of horse racing, but a substantial portion of the total is derived from Thoroughbred racing.

When the effects of inflation are removed from the figures using the United States Commerce Department's gross domestic product implicit price deflator, the peak period for state taxation of horse racing was from 1962 through '80, when inflation-adjusted state revenues exceeded $1.3-billion annually. State revenues topped out in 1975 at more than $2-billion in deflated dollars.

In both current and inflation-adjusted dollars, state revenues began a sharp decline in the 1980s as states reduced their pari-mutuel tax rates. By 1983, inflation-adjusted revenues had fallen below $1-billion, and by 1995 those revenues had slipped below $500-million. With two exceptions, 1990 and '95, current-dollar revenues to the state have declined from the preceding 12 months in every year since 1988.

Revenue to States from Horse Racing

Year	Current Dollars	Deflated Dollars
2005	$325,919,323	$288,424,180
2004	338,885,365	313,144,856
2003	343,588,382	325,152,249
2002	346,799,090	333,637,106
2001	351,511,182	343,363,174
2000	367,786,590	367,786,590
1999	392,201,085	400,744,968
1998	431,722,361	447,510,533
1997	441,768,972	463,002,255
1996	443,882,538	472,960,127
1995	455,764,292	494,825,844
1994	451,546,549	500,278,697
1993	471,735,474	533,752,135
1992	491,259,606	568,686,237
1991	523,249,392	619,640,699
1990	623,839,806	764,603,268
1989	584,888,183	744,549,344
1988	596,202,319	787,648,055
1987	608,351,461	831,126,648
1986	587,357,677	824,361,652
1985	625,159,697	896,762,006
1984	650,262,852	961,145,299
1983	641,387,176	983,617,060
1982	652,888,463	1,040,857,799
1981	680,199,584	1,150,560,030
1980	712,727,523	1,318,815,615
1979	680,919,798	1,374,262,933
1978	673,063,831	1,470,952,709
1977	700,239,986	1,637,911,644
1976	714,629,120	1,777,861,280
1975	780,081,431	2,052,737,832
1974	645,980,984	1,860,276,412
1973	585,201,524	1,837,425,112
1972	531,404,550	1,761,600,975
1971	512,838,417	1,773,852,226
1970	486,403,097	1,766,554,431
1969	461,498,886	1,764,881,586
1968	426,856,448	1,713,388,384
1967	394,381,913	1,650,616,971
1966	$388,452,125	$1,676,096,501
1965	369,892,036	1,641,411,298
1964	350,095,928	1,581,925,480
1963	316,570,791	1,452,292,830
1962	287,930,030	1,334,925,263
1961	264,853,077	1,244,727,310
1960	258,039,385	1,226,364,645
1959	243,388,655	1,172,900,848
1958	222,049,651	1,083,274,715
1957	216,747,621	1,081,682,907
1956	207,456,272	1,069,748,218
1955	186,989,588	997,650,259
1954	178,015,828	966,584,286
1953	167,426,465	917,757,304
1952	142,489,696	790,643,081
1951	117,250,564	661,759,589
1950	98,366,167	595,040,633
1949	95,327,053	582,968,768
1948	95,803,364	584,808,717
1947	97,926,984	631,542,525
1946	94,035,859	672,357,064
1945	65,265,405	522,541,273
1944	55,971,233	460,062,740
1943	38,194,727	321,342,142
1942	22,005,278	195,099,548
1941	21,128,173	201,893,674
1940	16,145,182	164,612,378
1939	10,369,807	106,960,361
1938	9,576,335	97,817,518
1937	8,434,792	83,653,595
1936	8,611,538	89,100,238
1935	8,386,255	87,740,688
1934	6,024,193	64,292,348

Minimum Age to Attend and Wager at U.S. Racetracks

State	Minimum Age	Legal Wagering Age
Arizona	None	18
Arkansas	Under 16 with adult	18
California	None	18
Colorado	None	18
Delaware	Under 18 with adult	18
Florida	Under 18 with adult	18
Idaho	None	18
Illinois	Under 17 with adult	17
Indiana	Under 17 with adult	18
Iowa	Under 18 with adult	21
Kansas	Under 18 with adult	18
Kentucky	None	18
Louisiana	6	21
Maryland	None	18
Massachusetts	None	18
Michigan	None	18
Minnesota	Under 18 with adult	18
Montana	None	18
Nebraska	Under 18 with adult	19
New Hampshire	Under 18 with adult	18
New Jersey	Under 18 with adult	18
New Mexico	Under 18 with adult	18
New York	Under 18 with adult	18
Ohio	Under 18 with adult	18
Oklahoma	6	18
Oregon	12 after 6 p.m.	18
Pennsylvania	None	18
Puerto Rico	None	18
Texas	Under 16 with adult	21
Virginia	None	18
Washington	None	18
West Virginia	None	18
Wyoming	None	19

PEOPLE
Leading Owners of 2007

Along with bettors, Thoroughbred owners are the primary source of the billions of dollars of investments that make the Thoroughbred industry the living, breathing, wonderful thing that it is.

Owners spend well over $1-billion annually purchasing Thoroughbreds of various descriptions at public auctions and by private contract, thus taking on the privilege and responsibility of paying further untold sums for their training, veterinary care, board, and other expenses. In return, owners in North America get a shot at more than $1-billion annually in purses each year.

Total purses are divided among thousands of owners but, in the natural order of things, some do better than others. The following lists document the accomplishments of owners in 2007 according to various criteria. Among those criteria are total purse money earned by the owners' runners, average earnings per starter, number of wins, and percent of stakes winners from starters.

Leading Owners by Earnings
North American Earnings Only

Year	Name	Wins	Earnings
2007	Stronach Stables	128	$7,076,134
2006	Darley Stable	63	6,449,822
2005	Michael J. Gill	371	6,397,180
2004	Michael J. Gill	486	10,811,211
2003	Michael J. Gill	425	9,236,530
2002	Stronach Stables	122	8,347,017
2001	Richard A. Englander	405	9,784,822
2000	Stronach Stables	162	11,133,785
1999	Stronach Stables	124	6,221,147
1998	Stronach Stables	91	7,221,416
1997	Allen E. Paulson	66	5,259,107
1996	Allen E. Paulson	88	6,686,629
1995	Allen E. Paulson	62	5,626,396
1994	Golden Eagle Farm	95	3,674,692
1993	Golden Eagle Farm	102	3,613,828
1992	Golden Eagle Farm	112	4,487,959
1991	Sam-Son Farm	29	3,613,473
1990	Kinghaven Farms	66	5,041,280
1989	Ogden Phipps	25	5,438,034
1988	Ogden Phipps	35	5,858,168
1987	Eugene V. Klein	81	4,904,247
1986	John Franks	250	4,463,115
1985	Hunter Farm	10	3,662,989
1984	John Franks	172	3,073,036
1983	John Franks	183	2,645,884

Leading Owners of 2007 by Total Earnings

A minimum of ten starters is required to be considered for inclusion. Names of owners are of individual property lines as reported by the Jockey Club. No attempt was made to consolidate names where a owner had more than one partnership or property line. Statistics are for North America only and for racing in 2007.

Owner	No. Strs	No. Wnrs	No. SWs	SWs/ Strs	No. GSWs	GSWs/ Strs	Total Earnings	Average Earnings/ Starter	Leading Earner	Earnings of Leading Earner
Stronach Stables	150	81	7	4.7%	3	2.0%	$7,076,134	$47,174	Ginger Punch	$1,827,060
Zayat Stables	123	70	14	11.4%	7	5.7%	6,180,916	50,251	Z Humor	543,700
Maggi Moss	220	124	5	2.3%	0	0.0%	4,230,837	19,231	Indian Chant	266,645
Ken and Sarah Ramsey	99	58	9	9.1%	2	2.0%	3,996,973	40,373	Precious Kitten	1,090,000
Melnyk Racing Stables	115	52	7	6.1%	4	3.5%	3,967,399	34,499	Sealy Hill	958,389
Live Oak Plantation	63	30	11	17.5%	4	6.4%	3,805,208	60,400	My Typhoon (Ire)	639,000
Heiligbrodt Racing Stable	106	58	13	12.3%	3	2.8%	3,792,466	35,778	Inca King	364,446
Fox Hill Farms	30	20	1	3.3%	1	3.3%	3,705,486	123,516	Hard Spun	2,572,500
James B. Tafel	22	9	2	9.1%	1	4.6%	3,655,913	166,178	Street Sense	3,205,000
Shadwell Stable	34	18	5	14.7%	5	14.7%	3,449,878	101,467	Lahudood (GB)	1,560,500
Four Roses Thoroughbreds	48	30	6	12.5%	5	10.4%	2,969,978	61,875	Diamond Stripes	588,645
Darley Stable	83	40	6	7.2%	4	4.8%	2,826,166	34,050	Marietta	292,759
Robert L. Cole Jr.	135	90	4	3.0%	0	0.0%	2,703,898	20,029	Coyoteshighestcall	110,890
Frank Carl Calabrese	149	85	3	2.0%	3	2.0%	2,654,225	17,814	Dreaming of Anna	391,932
Edward P. Evans	48	24	9	18.8%	5	10.4%	2,626,237	54,713	Christmas Kid	554,500
Stoneside Stable	55	24	9	16.4%	5	9.1%	2,460,053	44,728	Country Star	575,900
Jay Em Ess Stable	52	31	4	7.7%	1	1.9%	2,450,870	47,132	By the Light	451,815
Flying Zee Stables	76	38	3	4.0%	2	2.6%	2,443,408	32,150	Cosmonaut	658,563
J. Paul Reddam	36	16	5	13.9%	3	8.3%	2,432,177	67,560	Notional	460,000
West Point Thoroughbreds	40	28	4	10.0%	3	7.5%	2,424,923	60,623	Hurley Bull	635,063
Augustin Stable	71	37	8	11.3%	2	2.8%	2,400,805	33,814	Forever Together	176,540
Millennium Farms	33	17	5	15.2%	2	6.1%	2,309,726	69,992	Student Council	900,000
Robert V. LaPenta	37	16	2	5.4%	1	2.7%	2,209,380	59,713	War Pass	1,397,400
Robert D. Bone	107	65	3	2.8%	0	0.0%	2,191,960	20,486	Relato Del Gato	171,302
Sam-Son Farm	42	14	4	9.5%	1	2.4%	2,140,450	50,963	Strike Softly	305,775
Centennial Farms	16	13	4	25.0%	2	12.5%	2,138,205	133,638	Corinthian	1,174,173
Bear Stables Ltd.	68	24	4	5.9%	1	1.5%	2,042,466	30,036	Bear Now	747,517
Juddmonte Farms	29	11	5	17.2%	4	13.8%	1,988,847	68,581	Price Tag (GB)	232,560
Dale Baird	193	83	0	0.0%	0	0.0%	1,937,809	10,040	Market Force	66,687
Woodford Racing	30	14	5	16.7%	1	3.3%	1,900,642	63,355	Turf War	518,548

People — Leading Owners of 2007

Owner	No. Strs	No. Wnrs	No. SWs	SWs/ Strs	No. GSWs	GSWs/ Strs	Total Earnings	Average Earnings/ Starter	Leading Earner	Earnings of Leading Earner
Glencrest Farm	13	6	2	15.4%	2	15.4%	$1,891,685	$145,514	Panty Raid	$1,024,180
Mr. and Mrs. Jerome S. Moss	36	11	2	5.6%	1	2.8%	1,881,900	52,275	Tiago	1,234,750
Pam and Martin Wygod	24	9	2	8.3%	2	8.3%	1,879,465	78,311	Idiot Proof	803,136
Overbrook Farm	64	30	2	3.1%	1	1.6%	1,879,241	29,363	Fiery Pursuit	263,045
Pin Oak Stable	58	28	3	5.2%		0.0%	1,839,215	31,711	Brownie Points	152,700
Everest Stables Inc.	75	41	3	4.0%	1	1.3%	1,826,344	24,351	Plug Me In	125,908
Peachtree Stable Inc.	35	16	3	8.6%	1	2.9%	1,805,742	51,593	Red Giant	846,720
Vinery Stables	50	26	8	16.0%	2	4.0%	1,795,189	35,904	Kodiak Kowboy	204,825
Gumpster Stable	78	44		0.0%		0.0%	1,782,955	22,858	Harvest Lisa	134,030
Patti and Hal Earnhardt III	16	10	2	12.5%	1	6.3%	1,757,122	109,820	Indian Blessing	1,320,000
Winchell Thoroughbreds	16	7	1	6.3%	1	6.3%	1,749,897	109,369	Zanjero	1,060,977
Dogwood Stable	58	28	3	5.2%	1	1.7%	1,731,686	29,857	Cotton Blossom	366,607
Hobeau Farm	15	6	3	20.0%	3	20.0%	1,637,521	109,168	Miss Shop	787,408
K. K. Sangara	27	17	2	7.4%	1	3.7%	1,602,404	59,348	Financingavailable	451,151
Gary and Cecil Barber	60	32	2	3.3%		0.0%	1,598,419	26,640	Curiously Sweet	207,160
Tucci Stables	29	14	4	13.8%	1	3.5%	1,570,350	54,150	My List	213,187
Puglisi Racing and Steve Klesaris	29	17	4	13.8%	1	3.5%	1,564,842	53,960	Miraculous Miss	371,300
WinStar Farm	49	20	5	10.2%	2	4.1%	1,557,468	31,785	Court Vision	257,542
Jayeff "B" Stables	44	25	3	6.8%		0.0%	1,555,009	35,341	Awfully Smart	228,035
Aces Full Racing Stable	77	43	1	1.3%		0.0%	1,550,843	20,141	Truly Blushed	114,092
Stan E. Fulton	54	21	4	7.4%		0.0%	1,547,927	28,665	Some Ghost	262,051
Winning Move Stable	90	35	2	2.2%		0.0%	1,540,017	17,111	Americanus	105,210
Silverton Hill	39	24	1	2.6%	1	2.6%	1,496,409	38,369	Dominican	549,140
Tommy Town Thoroughbreds	99	48	3	3.0%		0.0%	1,467,723	14,825	You Are the Answer	145,391
Gary A. Tanaka	22	8	6	27.3%	3	13.6%	1,466,328	66,651	Eccentric (GB)	289,590
Bruno Schickedanz	135	70		0.0%		0.0%	1,459,422	10,811	Tatti Man	89,255
David A. Ross	79	42	2	2.5%		0.0%	1,438,718	18,212	Pass Play	157,185
Plumstead Stables	63	36		0.0%		0.0%	1,425,331	22,624	Emperor Fusaichi	102,060
William A. Sorokolit Sr.	22	10	2	9.1%	1	4.6%	1,411,759	64,171	Sky Conqueror	827,043
Patricia A. Generazio	41	22	3	7.3%	1	2.4%	1,408,843	34,362	Pure Disco	285,050
Starlight Stable and Donald Lucarelli	13	5	1	7.7%	1	7.7%	1,399,021	107,617	Octave	1,050,234
La Canada Stables	79	32	2	2.5%		0.0%	1,375,090	17,406	Epic Power	261,460
E. Paul Robsham Stables	33	19	1	3.0%	1	3.0%	1,359,368	41,193	Trippi's Storm	344,320
Bahadur Cheema	21	12	5	23.8%	2	9.5%	1,336,838	63,659	True Metropolitan	441,268
Carlos Oyola Stable	132	72		0.0%		0.0%	1,333,960	10,106	Cachetito Suave	84,559
Paul P. Pompa Jr.	41	21	2	4.9%		0.0%	1,325,667	32,333	Backseat Rhythm	316,760
Team Valor	21	6	3	14.3%	3	14.3%	1,325,564	63,122	Unbridled Belle	620,000
Stud TNT	17	5	3	17.7%	3	17.7%	1,320,671	77,687	Out of Control (Brz)	471,080
Pyrite Stables	40	29	5	12.5%		0.0%	1,313,553	32,839	Bernie Blue	305,021
Phipps Stable	23	11	3	13.0%	2	8.7%	1,305,417	56,757	Sightseeing	393,716
Paraneck Stables	59	25	2	3.4%		0.0%	1,303,667	22,096	Pink Viper	102,661
Amerman Racing Stables	31	12	2	6.5%	1	3.2%	1,295,042	41,776	Balance	448,332
Wertheimer & Frere	35	20	4	11.4%		0.0%	1,292,843	36,938	Quiet Royal	194,659
Kingfield Farms	10	3	1	10.0%	1	10.0%	1,290,039	129,004	Jambalaya	979,421
Louis D. O'Brien	132	102		0.0%		0.0%	1,276,203	9,668	Raving Rocket	59,026
Godolphin Racing	23	13	6	26.1%	2	8.7%	1,254,010	54,522	Discreet Cat	140,000
Knob Hill Stable/Estate of Steve Stavro	17	8	3	17.7%	2	11.8%	1,247,055	73,356	Alezzandro	551,550
B. Wayne Hughes	37	12	2	5.4%	1	2.7%	1,244,021	33,622	Into Mischief	448,800
Padua Stables	43	24	3	7.0%	1	2.3%	1,237,779	28,786	Electrify	295,530
Haras Santa Maria de Araras	31	12	4	12.9%	2	6.5%	1,230,385	39,690	Quite a Bride	297,125
Oxbow Racing	24	15	2	8.3%	2	8.3%	1,220,586	50,858	Ermine	439,052
Klaravich Stables and William Lawrence	23	9	2	8.7%	1	4.4%	1,216,987	52,912	Summer Doldrums	683,582
Joseph Allen	11	8	4	36.4%	4	36.4%	1,211,164	110,106	Political Force	520,747
D. Morgan Firestone	14	6	1	7.1%	1	7.1%	1,198,537	85,610	Mike Fox	657,431
Stonestreet Stables	37	17	2	5.4%	1	2.7%	1,194,503	32,284	Eyes On Eddy	212,477
Jerry Hollendorfer and George Todaro	78	40		0.0%		0.0%	1,178,390	15,108	Nottingham Forest	57,800
Roddy J. Valente	39	23	1	2.6%		0.0%	1,170,715	30,018	Callmetony	148,080
Monarch Stables Inc.	55	40	1	1.8%		0.0%	1,165,465	21,190	Blondie's Halos	77,760
Kinsman Stable	33	13	4	12.1%	3	9.1%	1,160,178	35,157	Sweet Fervor	237,308
Richard A. Englander	71	36		0.0%		0.0%	1,155,872	16,280	Wild Debutante	73,093
Curtis C. and Lila Lee Lanning	41	25	2	4.9%		0.0%	1,101,473	26,865	Gentle Charmer	215,978
W. S. Farish	38	16	3	7.9%		0.0%	1,097,475	28,881	Patriot Act	208,250
Elisabeth H. Alexander	17	13	3	17.7%	2	11.8%	1,093,954	64,350	Magna Graduate	500,255
Heflin Driver Racing	94	45		0.0%		0.0%	1,076,746	11,455	Davids Expectation	86,590
J D Farms	32	12	4	12.5%		0.0%	1,061,396	33,169	Wise Answer	458,300
Montesano Racing	74	43	2	2.7%		0.0%	1,060,640	14,333	Nonesuch Kiss	92,400
Peter Vegso	20	8	3	15.0%	2	10.0%	1,054,934	52,747	Go Between	386,040
Southern Equine Stable	67	25	2	3.0%	2	3.0%	1,023,657	15,278	Salute the Sarge	286,540
Triple B Farms	11	4	1	9.1%	1	9.1%	1,020,575	92,780	Shamdinan (Fr)	864,000
Establo Villa Real	61	41	3	4.9%	2	3.3%	999,107	16,379	Classical Concerto	85,779

Leading Owners by Average Earnings per Starter in 2007
(Minimum of 10 Starters)

Owner	No. Strs	No. Wnrs	Average Earnings per Starter
James Tafel	22	9	$166,178
Glencrest Farm	13	6	145,514
Centennial Farms	16	13	133,638
Kingfield Farms	10	3	129,004
Fox Hill Farms	30	20	123,516
Joseph Allen	11	8	110,106
Patti and Hal Earnhardt III	16	10	109,820
Winchell Thoroughbreds	16	7	109,369
Hobeau Farm	15	6	109,168
Starlight Stable and Donald J. Lucarelli	13	5	107,617
Shadwell Stable	34	18	101,467
Triple B Farms	11	4	92,780
D. Morgan Firestone	14	6	85,610
Harry J. Aleo	12	8	80,717
Pam and Martin Wygod	24	9	78,311
Stud TNT	17	5	77,687
Knob Hill Stable and Estate of Steve Stavro	17	8	73,356
Millennium Farms	33	17	69,992
Juddmonte Farms	29	11	68,581
J. Paul Reddam	36	16	67,560
Jon and Sarah Kelly	11	8	66,799
Gary A. Tanaka	22	8	66,651
Elisabeth H. Alexander	17	13	64,350
William A. Sorokolit Sr.	22	10	64,171
Bahadur Cheema	21	12	63,659
Woodford Racing	30	14	63,355
Bruce Lunsford	12	5	63,340
Team Valor	21	6	63,122
Four Roses Thoroughbreds	48	30	61,875
West Point Thoroughbreds	40	28	60,623
Victory Thoroughbreds	13	12	60,584
Live Oak Plantation	63	30	60,400
Centaur Farms Inc.	16	10	60,344
Robert LaPenta	37	16	59,713
K. K. Sangara	27	17	59,348
Joseph Lacombe Stable	13	4	59,316
Phipps Stable	23	11	56,757
H. Joseph Allen	12	6	56,240
Edward P. Evans	48	24	54,713
Godolphin Racing	23	13	54,522
Tucci Stables	29	14	54,150
Puglisi Racing & Steve Klesaris	29	17	53,960
Cathy and Bob Zollars	16	9	53,909

Leading Owners by Number of Stakes Winners in 2007

Owner	No. Strs	No. Wnrs	No. SWs
Zayat Stables	123	70	14
Heiligbrodt Racing Stable	106	58	13
Live Oak Plantation	63	30	11
Edward P. Evans	48	24	9
Ken and Sarah Ramsey	99	58	9
Stonerside Stable	55	24	9
Augustin Stable	71	37	8
Vinery Stables	50	26	8
Dennis E. Weir	38	27	8
Melnyk Racing Stables	115	52	7
Stronach Stables	150	81	7
Darley Stable	83	40	6
Four Roses Thoroughbreds	48	30	6
Godolphin Racing	23	13	6
Gary A. Tanaka	22	8	6
Camelia J. Casby	21	13	5
Bahadur Cheema	21	12	5
Establo Hermosura	32	22	5
Juddmonte Farms	29	11	5
K-5 Stable	20	9	5
Millennium Farms	33	17	5
Maggi Moss	220	124	5
Pyrite Stables	40	29	5
J. Paul Reddam	36	16	5
Shadwell Stable	34	18	5
Silent Stable Inc.	25	20	5
WinStar Farm	49	20	5
Woodford Racing	30	14	5
Harry J. Aleo	12	8	4
Joseph Allen	11	8	4
A & R Stables & Class Racing Stable	21	8	4
Bear Stables Ltd.	68	24	4
Centennial Farms	16	13	4
Robert L. Cole Jr.	135	90	4
Stan E. Fulton	54	21	4
Richard W. Galyen	11	8	4
Haras Santa Maria de Araras	31	12	4
Jay Em Ess Stable	52	31	4
J D Farms	32	12	4
Kinsman Stable	33	13	4
Puglisi Racing and Steve Klesaris	29	17	4
Sam-Son Farm	42	17	4
Tucci Stables	29	14	4
Wertheimer & Frere	35	20	4
West Point Thoroughbreds	40	28	4

Leading Owners by Number of Stakes Wins in 2007

Owner	No. Stakes Starts	No. Stakes Wins
Stronach Stables	74	20
Heiligbrodt Racing Stable	106	18
Live Oak Plantation	90	18
Bahadur Cheema	26	17
Edward P. Evans	59	15
Zayat Stables	104	15
Ken and Sarah Ramsey	43	14
Stonerside Stable	45	13
Melnyk Racing Stables	48	12
Vinery Stables	60	12
Pyrite Stables	45	11
Dennis E. Weir	45	11
Maggi Moss	38	10
Harry J. Aleo	19	9
Millennium Farms	48	9
J. Paul Reddam	44	9
Bear Stables	43	8
Aaron U. and Marie D. Jones	20	8
Northwest Farms	12	8
Gary A. Tanaka	59	8
Augustin Stable	39	7
Centennial Farms	16	7
Darley Stable	53	7
Four Roses Thoroughbreds	42	7
Patricia A. Generazio	26	7

Owner	No. Stakes Starts	No. Stakes Wins
Jay Em Ess Stable	32	7
Roll Reroll Stables	10	7
James T. Scatuorchio	23	7
Shadwell Stable	29	7
Peter Vegso	16	7
Woodford Racing	34	7
Joseph Allen	13	6
Chris Di Piero	32	6
Stan E. Fulton	30	6
Godolphin Racing	30	6
Haras Santa Maria de Araras	34	6
Hobeau Farm	31	6
J D Farms	29	6
Juddmonte Farms	44	6
Kinsman Stable	15	6
Padua Stables	45	6
Virginia Kraft Payson	8	6
Rolbea Thoroughbred Racing	22	6
Silent Stable	18	6
Victory Thoroughbreds	19	6
West Point Thoroughbreds	25	6
Warren B. Williamson	11	6
WinStar Farm	16	6
Pam and Martin Wygod	20	6

Leading Owners by Percent of Stakes Winners from Starters in 2007
(Minimum of 10 Starters)

Owner	No. Strs	No. SWs	SWs/Str
Joseph Allen	11	4	36.4%
Richard W. Galyen	11	4	36.4%
Harry J. Aleo	12	4	33.3%
Donald A. Adam	10	3	30.0%
Gary A. Tanaka	22	6	27.3%
Godolphin Racing	23	6	26.1%
Centennial Farms	16	4	25.0%
K-5 Stable	20	5	25.0%
Susan Magnier, Michael Tabor, and Derrick Smith	12	3	25.0%
Savorthetime Stables	12	3	25.0%
Camelia J. Casby	21	5	23.8%
Bahadur Cheema	21	5	23.8%
Northwest Farms	13	3	23.1%
Victory Thoroughbreds	13	3	23.1%
Dennis E. Weir	38	8	21.1%
George E. Coleman	10	2	20.0%
F. Daniel and S. Fifer Frost	10	2	20.0%
Dell Ridge Farm	10	2	20.0%
Hobeau Farm	15	3	20.0%
Dean Honrath	10	2	20.0%
Doug Oliver	10	2	20.0%
Sandra Hall Trust	10	2	20.0%
Edward A. Seltzer	10	2	20.0%
Silent Stable Inc.	25	5	20.0%
A & R Stables/Class Racing Stable	21	4	19.1%
Edward P. Evans	48	9	18.8%
Fox Ridge Farm	16	3	18.8%
Cathy and Bob Zollars	16	3	18.8%
Morris Bailey	11	2	18.2%
Shawn H. Davis	11	2	18.2%
Dunn Bar Ranch	11	2	18.2%
Jon and Sarah Kelly	11	2	18.2%
O'Sullivan Farms	11	2	18.2%
Richter Family Trust	11	2	18.2%
Elisabeth H. Alexander	17	3	17.6%
Edmund A. Gann	17	3	17.6%
Knob Hill Stable and Estate of Steve Stavro	17	3	17.6%
Stud TNT	17	3	17.6%
Live Oak Plantation	63	11	17.5%

Leading Owners by Number of Graded Stakes Winners in 2007

Owner	No. Strs	No. Wnrs	No. GSWs	GSWs/Strs
Zayat Stables	123	70	7	5.7%
Edward P. Evans	48	24	5	10.4%
Four Roses Thoroughbreds	48	30	5	10.4%
Shadwell Stable	34	18	5	14.7%
Stonerside Stable	55	24	5	9.1%
Joseph Allen	11	8	4	36.4%
Darley Stable	83	40	4	4.8%
Juddmonte Farms	29	11	4	13.8%
Live Oak Plantation	63	30	4	6.3%
Melnyk Racing Stables	115	52	4	3.5%
Frank Carl Calabrese	149	85	3	2.0%
Heiligbrodt Racing Stable	106	58	3	2.8%
Hobeau Farm	15	6	3	20.0%
Aaron U. and Marie D. Jones	8	7	3	37.5%
Kinsman Stable	33	13	3	9.1%
J. Paul Reddam	36	16	3	8.3%
James T. Scatuorchio	8	6	3	37.5%
Stronach Stables	150	81	3	2.0%
Stud TNT	17	5	3	17.6%
Gary A. Tanaka	22	8	3	13.6%
Team Valor Stables	21	6	3	14.3%
West Point Thoroughbreds	40	28	3	7.5%

Leading Owners by Graded Stakes Wins in 2007

Owner	No. Graded Stakes Starts	No. Graded Stakes Wins
Stronach Stables	44	12
Melnyk Racing Stables	33	8
Zayat Stables	63	8
Shadwell Stable	27	7
Edward P. Evans	22	6
Four Roses Thoroughbreds	25	6
Aaron U. and Marie D. Jones	14	6
Live Oak Plantation	48	6
James T. Scatuorchio	19	6
Stonerside Stable	15	6
Pam and Martin Wygod	10	6
Darley Stable	21	5
Virginia Kraft Payson	6	5
Stonestreet Stables, Padua Stables, George Bolton, and Midnight Cry Stables	8	5
Stud TNT	12	5
Michael B. Tabor and Derrick Smith	13	5
Elizabeth J. Valando	10	5
Joseph Allen	26	4
Arindel Farm	12	4
Fox Hill Farms	11	4
Glencrest Farm	11	4
Hobeau Farm	22	4
Juddmonte Farms	36	4
Millennium Farms	15	4
Monceaux Stable	10	4
Ken and Sarah Ramsey	14	4

People — Leading Owners of 2007

Owner	No. Graded Stakes Starts	No. Graded Stakes Wins
J. Paul Reddam	34	4
James Tafel	11	4
Gary A. Tanaka	48	4
West Point Thoroughbreds	16	4
Warren B. Williamson	7	4
Elisabeth H. Alexander	12	3
Bantry Farms, Paula Capestro, and Martin Racing Stable	3	3
Frank Carl Calabrese	11	3
Centennial Farms	9	3
Bahadur Cheema	7	3
Jeff Davenport, Tom Lenner, Jess Ravich, and Thomas Murray	3	3
Heiligbrodt Racing Stable	16	3
Kingfield Farms	6	3
Kinsman Stable	7	3
Mr. and Mrs. Jerome S. Moss	11	3
Martin S. Schwartz	10	3
S J Stables	8	3
Southern Equine Stable	8	3
Team Valor Stables	13	3
Peter Vegso	9	3
WinStar Farm	10	3
WinStar Farm and Padua Stables	7	3
Christopher Wright	5	3
Joyce B. Young and Gerald McManis	4	3

Leading Owners by Most Grade 1 Stakes Wins in 2007

Owner	No. G1 Starts	No. G1 Wins
Stronach Stables	13	5
Melnyk Racing Stables	14	4
Shadwell Stable	13	4
Michael Tabor and Derrick Smith	8	4
James T. Scatuorchio	10	3
Stonestreet Stables, Padua Stables, George Bolton, and Midnight Cry Stables	6	3
Pam and Martin Wygod	6	3
Patti and Hal J. Earnhardt III	3	2
Glencrest Farm	7	2
Hines Racing	4	2
Kingfield Farms	2	2
Robert V. LaPenta	5	2
Mr. and Mrs. Jerome S. Moss	5	2
Ken and Sarah Ramsey	6	2
Starlight Stable and Donald J. Lucarelli	8	2
STD Racing Stable and Jason Wood	4	2
Stonerside Stable	5	2
James Tafel	5	2
Watson & Weitman Performances and Pegram	3	2
West Point Thoroughbreds	8	2
West Point Thoroughbreds, Lewis Lakin, and John G. Sikura	3	2
Warren B. Williamson	3	2

Leading Owners by Most Grade 1 Stakes Winners in 2007

Owner	No. G1 Starters	No. G1 Winners
Shadwell Stable	7	3
Stronach Stables	5	3
Melnyk Racing Stables	5	2
West Point Thoroughbreds	3	2
Pam and Martin Wygod	3	2

Leading Owners by Number of Wins in 2007

Owner	No. Strs	No. Wnrs	No. Wins
Louis D. O'Brien	132	102	221
Maggi Moss	220	124	196
Robert L. Cole Jr.	135	90	159
Carlos Oyola Stable	132	72	150
Frank Carl Calabrese	149	85	134
Bruno Schickedanz	135	70	131
Stronach Stables	150	81	128
Dale Baird	193	83	123
Ken and Sarah Ramsey	99	58	106
Robert D. Bone	107	65	104
Zayat Stables	123	70	99
Heiligbrodt Racing Stable	106	58	95
Establo Villa Real	61	41	94
Aces Full Racing Stable	77	43	82
R & P Racing Stables Inc.	84	46	80
Gumpster Stable	78	44	79
Bridget Sipp	87	43	77
Monarch Stables Inc.	55	40	74
David A. Ross	79	42	73
Tommy Town Thoroughbreds	99	48	71
Jan Haynes	69	41	70
Plumstead Stables	63	36	70
Melnyk Racing Stables	115	52	69
Flying Zee Stables	76	38	66
Heflin Driver Racing	94	45	66
M. Y. Stables Inc.	52	37	66
Acclaimed Racing Stable	62	39	63
Jerry Hollendorfer and George Todaro	78	40	63
Montesano Racing	74	43	61
Richard A. Englander	71	36	59
Everest Stables Inc.	75	41	59
Pyrite Stables	40	29	59
Augustin Stable	71	37	57
Darley Stable	83	40	56
Poindexter Thoroughbreds	57	31	56
Thomas Vanderhyde	46	26	55
Steven M. Asmussen	59	32	54
Live Oak Plantation	63	30	54
Bar None Ranches Ltd.	62	32	52
Les Blake	67	37	52
Jay Em Ess Stable	52	31	51
Charles Lawson	47	30	51
Richard N. Averill	38	23	50
My Purple Haze Stables	63	34	50

Most Wins for an Owner on One Day in 2007

Wins	Owner	Date	Track(s)
5	Louis D. O'Brien	4/10/2007	FP
	Louis D. O'Brien	3/23/2007	FP, HAW
	Louis D. O'Brien	6/2/2007	FP, IND
	Louis D. O'Brien	3/6/2007	FP
4	Carlos Oyola Stable	4/21/2007	CMR
	Gabriel Road Stables	6/30/2007	MD
	Marvin A. Johnson	8/17/2007	CLS
	La Canada Stables	11/1/2007	BM, OSA
	Louis D. O'Brien	5/22/2007	FP
	Louis D. O'Brien	3/16/2007	FP, HAW, TP
	Brian Mundell	3/25/2007	SUN
	Gary Owens	3/12/2007	WRD
	Ken & Sarah Ramsey	3/22/2007	GP, OP, TP
	Stronach Stables	8/25/2007	MTH, WO
	Stronach Stables	5/28/2007	FE, HOL, MTH
	TradeWinds Stable	3/18/2007	GP, LRL

Most Wins for an Owner on One Program in 2007

Wins	Owner	Date	Track
5	Louis D. O'Brien	4/10/2007	FP
	Louis D. O'Brien	3/6/2007	FP
4	Carlos Oyola Stable	4/21/2007	CMR

Wins	Owner	Date	Track
	Gabriel Road Stables	6/30/2007	MD
	Marvin A. Johnson	8/17/2007	CLS
	Louis D. O'Brien	5/22/2007	FP
	Louis D. O'Brien	3/23/2007	FP
	Brian Mundell	3/25/2007	SUN
	Gary Owens	3/12/2007	WRD

Leading Owners by Earnings in a Year (1986-2007)

Owner	Year	Earnings	Leading Earner (Earnings)
Stronach Stables	2000	$11,133,785	Perfect Sting ($1,367,000)
Michael J. Gill	2004	10,811,211	Umpateedle ($216,160)
Richard A. Englander	2001	9,784,822	Elektraline ($222,383)
Michael J. Gill	2003	9,236,530	Highway Prospector ($290,397)
Stronach Stables	2002	8,347,017	Milwaukee Brew ($1,590,000)
The Thoroughbred Corp.	2001	8,000,763	Point Given ($3,350,000)
The Thoroughbred Corp.	2002	7,887,915	War Emblem ($3,125,000)
Someday Farm	2004	7,584,305	Smarty Jones ($7,563,535)
Richard A. Englander	2002	7,530,362	Boston Common ($303,177)
Stronach Stables	2003	7,289,114	Milwaukee Brew ($743,000)
Stronach Stables	1998	7,221,416	Awesome Again ($3,845,990)
Stronach Stables	2004	7,193,867	Ghostzapper ($2,590,000)
Stronach Stables	2007	7,076,134	Ginger Punch ($1,827,060)
Juddmonte Farms	2001	6,806,015	Aptitude ($1,410,000)
Allen E. Paulson	1996	6,686,629	Cigar ($2,510,000)
Stronach Stables	2001	6,539,481	Macho Uno ($563,400)
Darley Stable	2006	6,449,822	Bernardini ($3,060,480)
Michael J. Gill	2005	6,397,180	Umpateedle ($331,050)
Juddmonte Farms	2003	6,265,030	Empire Maker ($1,936,200)
Stronach Stables	1999	6,221,147	Golden Missile ($838,240)
Zayat Stables	2007	6,180,916	Z Humor ($543,700)
Overbrook Farm	1996	5,996,242	Boston Harbor ($1,906,325)
The Thoroughbred Corp.	2000	5,880,705	Spain ($1,979,500)
Melnyk Racing Stables	2005	5,875,007	Flower Alley ($2,435,200)
Ogden Phipps	1988	5,858,168	Seeking the Gold ($2,145,620)
Kenneth and Sarah Ramsey	2004	5,855,964	Roses in May ($1,723,277)
Edmund A. Gann	2003	5,848,681	Medaglia d'Oro ($1,990,000)
John Franks	1999	5,735,827	Littlebitlively ($868,303)
Michael J. Gill	2002	5,639,292	Rusty Spur ($180,610)
Golden Eagle Farm	1999	5,630,399	General Challenge ($1,658,100)
Allen E. Paulson	1995	5,626,396	Cigar ($3,670,000)
Golden Eagle Farm	1998	5,590,971	Excellent Meeting ($773,824)
Juddmonte Farms	2000	5,496,951	Chester House ($1,408,500)
Allen E. Paulson	1998	5,483,756	Escena ($2,032,425)
Ogden Phipps	1989	5,438,034	Easy Goer ($3,837,150)
Godolphin Racing	2001	5,359,804	Fantastic Light ($2,896,615)
Richard A. Englander	2003	5,347,231	My Cousin Matt ($237,500)
Live Oak Plantation	2006	5,263,594	Miesque's Approval ($1,906,405)
Allen E. Paulson	1997	5,259,107	Ajina ($979,175)
Juddmonte Farms	2002	5,172,287	Beat Hollow (GB) ($1,437,150)
John Franks	1998	5,145,343	Precocity ($868,630)
Michael E. Pegram	1999	5,128,905	Silverbulletday ($1,707,640)
Eugene V. Klein	1988	5,093,091	Winning Colors ($1,347,746)
Shadwell Stable	2006	5,084,218	Invasor (Arg) ($3,690,000)
Stonestreet Stables, Padua Stables, George Bolton, and Midnight Cry Stables	2007	5,080,000	Curlin ($5,102,800)
Overbrook Farm	1999	5,052,194	Cat Thief ($3,020,500)
Kinghaven Farms	1990	5,041,280	Izvestia ($2,486,667)
Richard A. Englander	2000	4,927,214	Watchman's Warning ($210,862)
Eugene V. Klein	1987	4,904,247	Success Express ($737,207)
Live Oak Plantation	2005	4,904,171	High Fly ($901,500)
Sam-Son Farm	2004	4,830,939	Soaring Free ($1,113,862)
Stronach Stables	2006	4,765,089	Spun Sugar ($487,200)
Sam-Son Farm	2000	4,698,712	Quiet Resolve ($967,871)
The Thoroughbred Corp.	1999	4,598,903	Anees ($609,200)
Gaillard-Hancock-Whittingham	1989	4,580,404	Sunday Silence ($4,578,454)
Golden Eagle Farm	1992	4,487,959	Best Pal ($955,000)
Edward P. Evans	2002	4,472,047	Summer Colony ($992,500)
John Franks	1986	4,463,115	Herat ($541,000)
Eugene and Laura Melnyk	2004	4,447,689	Speightstown ($1,045,556)
Golden Eagle Farm	1997	4,420,911	Career Collection ($482,005)
John Franks	1990	4,386,593	Beyond Perfection ($345,614)

Leading Breeders of 2007

While it can be fairly said that owners, trainers, and jockeys are essential to the Thoroughbred industry, breeders are truly indispensable participants. No breeder, no horse.

For all their importance, breeders rarely receive their due notice. When newspapers and general-interest magazines write about horses and horse races, the owner sometimes does not even get a mention, much less the breeder.

Horse people by necessity are very patient, and no one is more patient than the breeder. The breeder's involvement begins as soon as a broodmare is purchased or a filly is retired off the racetrack. When it is time to put the mare in production, the breeder must decide which stallion best fits the mare, both in terms of pedigree and economics.

The mare is bred, and then the breeder gets to wait, and wait some more. With good luck, the mare goes to full term and delivers a healthy foal. A weanling can be offered for sale within a few months, but, if the strategy is to sell the foal as a two-year-old in training or to retain it as a racing prospect, the wait can be more than two years. A lot can go wrong in that time period, and often does. This leads to the conclusion that breeders are mighty dedicated folks.

Breeders will tell you that the satisfactions are worth the wait. They often get to see that foal emerge from its dam and wobble to its feet for the first time. They have the opportunity to watch that foal grow from a gangly newborn to a sprightly youngster dancing and prancing in a field. And they carry the hope that someday they will see the horse that they bred and nurtured being led into a winner's circle somewhere. That is the ultimate satisfaction for the breeder, to produce a quality athlete.

Leading Breeders by Earnings

Year	Name	Wins	Earnings
2007	Adena Springs	527	$17,618,475
2006	Adena Springs	500	12,849,805
2005	Adena Springs	456	11,613,323
2004	Adena Springs	383	14,122,256
2003	Adena Springs	296	11,542,871
2002	Mockingbird Farm	516	11,175,975
2001	Mockingbird Farm	390	9,550,610
2000	Harry T. Mangurian Jr.	495	10,757,845
1999	Harry T. Mangurian Jr.	490	10,851,459
1998	Mr. and Mrs. John Mabee	270	8,221,982
1997	Allen E. Paulson	248	7,723,615

Leading Breeders of 2007 by Total Earnings

A minimum of ten starters is required to be considered for inclusion. Names of breeders are of individual property lines as reported by the Jockey Club. No attempt was made to consolidate names where a breeder had more than one partnership or property line. Statistics are for North America only and for racing in 2007.

Breeder	No. Strs	No. Wnrs	No. SWs	SWs/ Strs	No. GSWs	GSWs/ Strs	Total Earnings	Average Earnings/ Starter	Leading Earner	Earnings of Leading Earner
Adena Springs	558	310	21	3.8%	8	1.4%	$17,618,475	$31,574	Ginger Punch	$1,827,060
Sez Who Thoroughbreds	267	165	14	5.2%		0.0%	7,860,444	29,440	Premium Wine	311,700
Farnsworth Farms	325	185	7	2.2%	1	0.3%	6,329,979	19,477	Suave Jazz	266,076
Mr. and Mrs. Martin Wygod	138	82	14	10.1%	3	2.2%	6,318,155	45,784	Octave	1,050,234
Eugene Melnyk	163	100	6	3.7%	3	1.8%	5,862,903	35,963	Sealy Hill	958,389
Ken and Sarah Ramsey	141	90	9	6.4%	1	0.7%	5,175,051	36,702	Precious Kitten	1,090,000
Brereton C. Jones	222	111	6	2.7%	4	1.8%	4,661,097	20,996	Proud Spell	608,770
John Franks	250	118	3	1.2%	1	0.4%	3,985,679	15,943	Silent Pleasure	505,000
Arthur I. Appleton	131	76	4	3.1%	3	2.3%	3,688,366	28,155	Smokey Stover	471,000
Overbrook Farm	136	72	5	3.7%	1	0.7%	3,652,689	26,858	Fiery Pursuit	263,045
Edward P. Evans	116	63	9	7.8%	4	3.4%	3,625,642	31,256	Christmas Kid	554,500
Stonerside Stable	88	46	14	15.9%	7	8.0%	3,526,790	40,077	Country Star	575,900
Padua Stables	134	80	6	4.5%	2	1.5%	3,376,703	25,199	Electrify	295,530
ClassicStar	87	46	8	9.2%	3	3.4%	3,202,689	36,813	Bear Now	747,517
Live Oak Stud	86	42	9	10.5%	3	3.5%	3,154,824	36,684	Hesanoldsalt	247,200
Keene Ridge Farm	10	5	2	20.0%	1	10.0%	3,131,360	313,136	English Channel	2,640,000
Tommy Town Thoroughbreds	193	109	3	1.6%		0.0%	3,000,638	15,547	Topper Shopper	129,590
Gilbert G. Campbell	140	71	3	2.1%		0.0%	2,919,837	20,856	Ryan's for Real	139,055
WinStar Farm	87	48	5	5.7%	2	2.3%	2,866,380	32,947	Colonel John	255,300
Flying Zee Stables	105	54	3	2.9%		0.0%	2,788,201	26,554	Stunt Man	347,739
Everest Stables	119	68	3	2.5%	1	0.8%	2,711,569	22,786	Plug Me In	125,908
Juddmonte Farms	57	25	6	10.5%	4	7.0%	2,710,700	47,556	Price Tag (GB)	232,560
Center Hills Farm	42	23	1	2.4%	1	2.4%	2,606,309	62,055	Kip Deville	1,965,780
W. S. Farish	73	37	4	5.5%	1	1.4%	2,566,670	35,160	Student Council	1,041,755
Haras Santa Isabel	203	106	1	0.5%	1	0.5%	2,373,931	11,694	Cachetito Suave	84,559
Thomas & Lakin	94	45	5	5.3%		0.0%	2,210,748	23,519	Kadira	136,525
Darley	57	31	5	8.8%	3	5.3%	2,195,550	38,518	Marietta	292,759
Heiligbrodt Racing Stables	83	47	6	7.2%	1	1.2%	2,183,394	26,306	Rated Fiesty	204,291
Hobeau Farm	38	20	4	10.5%	3	7.9%	2,183,309	57,456	Miss Shop	787,408
Pin Oak Stud	77	45	3	3.9%		0.0%	2,128,796	27,647	Brownie Points	152,700

People — Leading Breeders of 2007

Breeder	No. Strs	No. Wnrs	No. SWs	SWs/ Strs	No. GSWs	GSWs/ Strs	Total Earnings	Average Earnings/ Starter	Leading Earner	Earnings of Leading Earner
James T. Hines Jr.	35	19	2	5.7%	2	5.7%	$2,120,509	$60,586	Lawyer Ron	$1,320,000
J D Farms	124	48	4	3.2%	1	0.8%	2,083,767	16,805	Wise Answer	458,300
Foxwood Plantation	71	44	4	5.6%		0.0%	2,068,976	29,141	St. Zarb	249,750
Jayeff B Stables	44	22	4	9.1%	3	6.8%	2,057,738	46,767	Z Humor	543,700
Charles Nuckols Jr. & Sons	96	45	2	2.1%		0.0%	2,039,651	21,246	Jazz Quest	218,369
Harris Farms	91	59	5	5.5%	1	1.1%	2,031,727	22,327	Now Victory	236,135
Cherry Valley Farm	12	5	3	25.0%	2	16.7%	1,948,291	162,358	War Pass	1,397,400
D. W. Frazier	90	58	5	5.6%		0.0%	1,900,967	21,122	Bernie Blue	305,021
Centaur Farms	35	22	4	11.4%	1	2.9%	1,893,442	54,098	Gottcha Gold	488,445
Donald R. Dizney	86	42	2	2.3%		0.0%	1,800,221	20,933	Joint Effort	275,000
Gulf Coast Farms Bloodstock	40	24	4	10.0%	3	7.5%	1,756,517	43,913	Cowtown Cat	510,500
Sam-Son Farm	36	16	2	5.6%	1	2.8%	1,752,893	48,691	Strike Softly	305,775
Wimborne Farm	26	15	3	11.5%	2	7.7%	1,749,320	67,282	Honey Ryder	740,850
Mr. and Mrs. Jerry S. Moss	30	9	2	6.7%	1	3.3%	1,699,173	56,639	Tiago	1,234,750
Wertheimer & Frere	44	23	5	11.4%	1	2.3%	1,662,892	37,793	Silent Name (Jpn)	311,000
Vessels Stallion Farm	38	22	4	10.5%	2	5.3%	1,638,162	43,110	River's Prayer	610,175
Kinghaven Farms	32	18	3	9.4%	1	3.1%	1,621,968	50,687	Twilight Meteor	348,816
Haras Santa Maria de Araras S.A.	44	24	2	4.5%	1	2.3%	1,619,768	36,813	Quite a Bride	297,125
Gustav Schickedanz	29	14	2	6.9%	2	6.9%	1,610,325	55,528	Jambalaya	979,421
George Strawbridge Jr.	41	24	2	4.9%		0.0%	1,570,774	38,312	Elkhart	140,784
Arthur B. Hancock III	60	34	2	3.3%	1	1.7%	1,563,914	26,065	Wanderin Boy	296,708
Kinsman Farm	58	29	4	6.9%	3	5.2%	1,559,157	26,882	Sweet Fervor	237,308
Gardiner Farms	58	26	1	1.7%		0.0%	1,552,220	26,762	Legal Move	222,728
Gainesway Thoroughbreds	56	33	3	5.4%	2	3.6%	1,518,237	27,111	Drilling for Oil	172,211
William Sorokolit	25	15	2	8.0%	1	4.0%	1,514,967	60,599	Sky Conqueror	827,043
John D. Murphy	61	31	2	3.3%	1	1.6%	1,492,522	24,468	Awfully Smart	228,035
Gaines-Gentry Thoroughbreds	58	30	4	6.9%	2	3.4%	1,437,508	24,785	Ashley's Kitty	190,958
Hargus and Sandra Sexton	79	40	2	2.5%		0.0%	1,413,388	17,891	Amazin Blue	151,660
Bruno Schickedanz	122	56		0.0%		0.0%	1,407,715	11,539	Tatti Man	89,255
Hermitage Farm	60	30	3	5.0%		0.0%	1,394,450	23,241	Strike Impact	137,014
Chester and Mary Broman	54	25	1	1.9%		0.0%	1,370,341	25,377	Spanky Fischbein	161,595
Racehorse Management	20	8	1	5.0%	1	5.0%	1,327,187	66,359	Any Given Saturday	994,320
Aaron and Marie Jones	38	22	2	5.3%	2	5.3%	1,317,114	34,661	Sunriver	415,014
E & D Enterprises	70	36	2	2.9%	1	1.4%	1,302,459	18,607	Arson Squad	264,000
Patricia Generazio	39	27	1	2.6%		0.0%	1,289,538	33,065	Pure Disco	285,050
Dell Ridge Farm	34	18	2	5.9%	1	2.9%	1,275,947	37,528	Shakespeare	629,640
J. Adcock	73	31	2	2.7%		0.0%	1,272,152	17,427	Leesa Lee	184,050
E Paul Robsham	27	17	1	3.7%	1	3.7%	1,258,660	46,617	Trippi's Storm	344,320
Stud TNT	12	5	3	25.0%	3	25.0%	1,245,721	103,810	Out of Control (Brz)	471,080
Liberation Farm & Oratis Thoroughbreds	62	30	1	1.6%		0.0%	1,235,576	19,929	Ketchikan	173,100
Claiborne Farm and Adele Dilschneider	25	15	2	8.0%	1	4.0%	1,211,228	48,449	Lattice	227,699
Hopewell Investments	73	33	3	4.1%		0.0%	1,192,062	16,330	Lady Marlboro	191,524
Ocala Stud Farm	66	33	1	1.5%		0.0%	1,174,323	17,793	Angelic Aura	105,411
Hidden Point Farm	60	37	1	1.7%		0.0%	1,166,684	19,445	Calico Bay	331,900
Ro Parra	70	42		0.0%		0.0%	1,145,294	16,361	Name in Lights	98,289
Gainsborough Farm	45	25	3	6.7%		0.0%	1,145,138	25,448	Angel Craft	112,060
Potrero Los Llanos	98	49	2	2.0%	2	2.0%	1,143,008	11,663	Batalladora	110,459
Joseph LaCombe Stables	24	11	2	8.3%	1	4.2%	1,141,186	47,549	Slew's Tizzy	500,872
Knob Hill Stable	19	9	2	10.5%	1	5.3%	1,125,064	59,214	Alezzandro	551,550
Frank Bertolino	34	23	2	5.9%	1	2.9%	1,122,500	33,015	True Metropolitan	441,268
Joseph Allen	13	9	3	23.1%	3	23.1%	1,105,693	85,053	Political Force	520,747
Michael C. Byrne	38	24	1	2.6%		0.0%	1,093,185	28,768	Backgammon	140,907
Gus Schoenborn Jr.	33	18	2	6.1%		0.0%	1,090,304	33,040	Tishmeister	167,516
Shadwell Farm	39	19	2	5.1%		0.0%	1,086,853	27,868	Mabadi	143,428
Franks Farms	49	29	3	6.1%		0.0%	1,066,815	21,772	Lost Etiquette	188,480
Payson Stud	32	14	1	3.1%	1	3.1%	1,066,620	33,332	Rutherienne	548,975
Clover Leaf Farms II	56	29	2	3.6%		0.0%	1,054,046	18,822	Check It Twice	144,500
John C. Oxley	46	22	3	6.5%		0.0%	1,054,013	22,913	Peak Maria's Way	215,229
Vegso Racing Stable	22	12	2	9.1%	2	9.1%	1,053,287	47,877	Go Between	386,040
Jacks or Better Farm	49	29	2	4.1%	1	2.0%	1,047,202	21,371	Bayou's Lassie	159,174
Marablue Farm	51	28	1	2.0%		0.0%	1,043,739	20,465	Country Diva	224,962
J. D. Squires	18	10	2	11.1%	2	11.1%	1,036,266	57,570	Cotton Blossom	366,607
Brylynn Farm	44	22	2	4.5%		0.0%	1,030,052	23,410	He's Eze	114,850
Mr. and Mrs. Samuel H. Rogers Jr.	28	15	2	7.1%	1	3.6%	1,020,122	36,433	Diamond Stripes	588,645
Thomas/Lakin/Kintz	33	21	2	6.1%		0.0%	1,008,237	30,553	Big Booster	223,260
Luis de Hechavarria	34	17	2	5.9%	1	2.9%	995,226	29,271	May Night	177,320
Calumet Farm	47	21	2	4.3%		0.0%	985,319	20,964	Princess Janie	135,020
Foxfield	49	26	2	4.1%		0.0%	984,183	20,085	Nite Light	165,280
Palides Investments N.V.	30	11	1	3.3%	1	3.3%	974,471	32,482	Lear's Princess	429,100
Brushwood Stable	18	8	2	11.1%	1	5.6%	959,472	53,304	Master Command	598,170

Leading Breeders by Average Earnings per Starter in 2007
(Minimum of 10 Starters)

Breeder	No. Strs	No. Wnrs	Average Earnings per Starter
Keene Ridge Farm	10	5	$313,136
Cherry Valley Farm	12	5	162,358
Stud TNT	12	5	103,810
Joseph Allen	13	9	85,053
Mel P. Lawson	10	5	84,017
Nicole Zitani & Ramon Rangel	12	10	68,527
Ogden Mills Phipps	10	7	67,390
Wimborne Farm	26	15	67,282
Racehorse Management	20	8	66,359
Allen E. Paulson Living Trust	13	6	63,822
Richard Giacopelli	11	7	63,380
Center Hills Farm	42	23	62,055
William Sorokolit	25	15	60,599
James T. Hines Jr.	35	19	60,586
Rustlewood Farm	14	9	59,215
Knob Hill Stable	19	9	59,214
Lothenbach Stables	16	11	58,294
J. D. Squires	18	10	57,570
Hobeau Farm	38	20	57,456
Mr. and Mrs. Jerry S. Moss	30	9	56,639
Gustav Schickedanz	29	14	55,528
RPM Thoroughbred Farm	11	10	55,317
Double Dam Farm	14	7	54,192
Centaur Farms	35	22	54,098
Asiel Stable	11	7	53,421
Brushwood Stable	18	8	53,304
Elizabeth R. Houghton	12	8	52,201
Chiefswood Stables	13	7	51,453
Kinghaven Farms	32	18	50,687
W. S. Farish and Kilroy Thoroughbred Partnership	17	10	50,675
William Wilmot and Joan Taylor	11	6	49,702
Sam-Son Farm	36	16	48,691
Claiborne Farm and Adele B. Dilschneider	25	15	48,449
Mr. and Mrs. Leverett S. Miller	15	5	47,896
Vegso Racing Stable	22	12	47,877
Carson Springs Farm	11	6	47,842
Juddmonte Farms	57	25	47,556
Joseph LaCombe Stables	24	11	47,549
F. E. Dixon Jr.	19	12	47,030
Jayeff "B" Stables	44	22	46,767
Mace & Samantha Siegel	16	10	46,683
E Paul Robsham	27	17	46,617
Dark Hollow Farm	12	6	46,274
William L. Pape and Jonathan E. Sheppard	10	7	46,109
Mr. and Mrs. Martin J. Wygod	138	82	45,784
Dr. and Mrs. Thomas Bowman	19	10	45,664
Patricia Staskowski Purdy	11	7	44,154
T/C Stable	11	10	44,094
Robert S. Evans	12	5	44,089
Gulf Coast Farms Bloodstock	40	24	43,913

Leading Breeders by Number of Stakes Wins in 2007

Breeder	Stakes Starts	Stakes Wins
Adena Springs	233	42
Stonerside Stable	76	21
Mr. and Mrs. Martin J. Wygod	122	21
Sez Who Thoroughbreds	145	19
Ken and Sarah Ramsey	69	15
ClassicStar	50	14
Edward P. Evans	73	14
Eugene Melnyk	52	14
Live Oak Stud	67	13
D. W. Frazier	52	11
Arthur I. Appleton	43	10
Padua Stables	69	10
Farnsworth Farms	87	9
Flying Zee Stables	45	9
Heiligbrodt Racing Stables	54	9
Juddmonte Farms	55	9
Vessels Stallion Farm	28	9
Dennis E. Weir	48	9
Gulf Coast Farms Bloodstock	28	8
Hobeau Farm	43	8
Lilley Ranch	15	8
Dede McGehee	16	8
Northwest Farms	17	8
Bent Tree Farm	20	7
Frank Bertolino	16	7
Dr. and Mrs. Thomas Bowman	18	7
Willard Burbach	32	7
Darley	48	7
W. S. Farish	37	7
Foxwood Plantation	42	7
John Franks	46	7
Harris Farms	33	7
J D Farms	34	7
Brereton C. Jones	62	7
WinStar Farm	34	7
Richard Brunacini and Kay Thurman	17	6
Jose Carro	28	6
Gatsas Thoroughbreds	16	6
Kinsman Farms	18	6
Mr. and Mrs. Jerome S. Moss	15	6
Payson Stud	13	6
Rolando Rodriguez and Rolbea Stables	15	6
Thomas & Lakin	31	6
Wertheimer & Frere	48	6
Williamson Racing	9	6
Phyllis Wood	13	6

Leading Breeders by Number of Stakes Winners in 2007

Breeder	No. Strs	No. Wnrs	No. SWs
Adena Springs	558	310	21
Sez Who Thoroughbreds	267	165	14
Stonerside Stable	88	46	14
Mr. and Mrs. Martin J. Wygod	138	82	14
Edward P. Evans	116	63	9
Live Oak Stud	86	42	9
Ken and Sarah Ramsey	141	90	9
ClassicStar	87	46	8
Farnsworth Farms	325	185	7
Dennis E. Weir	46	34	7
Jose Carro	50	32	6
Heiligbrodt Racing Stables	83	47	6
Brereton C. Jones	222	111	6
Juddmonte Farms	57	25	6
Eugene Melnyk	163	100	6
Padua Stables	134	80	6
Willard Burbach	20	13	5

People — Leading Breeders of 2007

Breeder	No. Strs	No. Wnrs	No. SWs
Darley	57	31	5
D. W. Frazier	90	58	5
Harris Farms	91	59	5
Overbrook Farm	136	72	5
Thomas & Lakin	94	45	5
Wertheimer & Frere	44	23	5
WinStar Farm	87	48	5
Arthur I. Appleton	131	76	4
Centaur Farms	35	22	4
W. S. Farish	73	37	4
Foxwood Plantation	71	44	4
Gaines-Gentry Thoroughbreds	58	30	4
Gulf Coast Farms Bloodstock	40	24	4
Haras Don Jorge	69	38	4
Hobeau Farm	38	20	4
Jayeff "B" Stables	44	22	4
J D Farms	124	48	4
K 5 Stables	19	10	4
Kinsman Farm	58	29	4
Vessels Stallion Farm	38	22	4

Leading Breeders by Graded Stakes Wins in 2007

Breeder	Graded Starts	Graded Wins
Adena Springs	86	18
Stonerside Stable	22	8
Mr. and Mrs. Martin J. Wygod	25	8
Eugene Melnyk	24	7
Alanesic Farm	5	5
Arthur I. Appleton	19	5
ClassicStar	23	5
Edward P. Evans	29	5
Fares Farm	8	5
Payson Stud	10	5
Stud TNT	10	5
Elizabeth Jones Valando	10	5
Vessels Stallion Farm	6	5
Jose Carro	23	4
Cherry Valley Farm	10	4
Darley	30	4
Gulf Coast Farms Bloodstock	16	4
James T. Hines Jr.	9	4
Hobeau Farm	25	4
Brereton C. Jones	14	4
Juddmonte Farms	39	4
Michael Moran and Brushwood Stable	9	4
James H. Petrey Jr.	5	4
Ken and Sarah Ramsey	22	4
Gustav Schickedanz	11	4
Shadwell Estate Co.	11	4
Skara Glen Stables	6	4
James Tafel	8	4
Williamson Racing	5	4
Joseph Allen	18	3
Dr. and Mrs. Thomas Bowman	6	3
Brushwood Stable	10	3
Frank C. Calabrese	10	3
Center Hills Farm	7	3
Heaven Trees Farm	6	3
Irish National Stud	3	3
Jayeff "B" Stables	31	3
Aaron U. and Marie D. Jones	19	3
Keene Ridge Farm	11	3
Kinsman Farm	9	3
Live Oak Stud	31	3
Mr. and Mrs. Jerry S. Moss	10	3
Newchance Farm	5	3
Padua Stables	12	3
Potrero Los Llanos	23	3
Racehorse Management	7	3
Jerrold Schwartz	8	3
Stratford Place Stud	7	3
Sunderland Holdings	7	3
Vegso Racing Stable	10	3
WinStar Farm	21	3
Bonner Young and Joyce B. Rowand	4	3

Leading Breeders by Graded Stakes Winners in 2007

Breeder	No. Strs	No. Wnrs	No. GSWs	GSWs/Str.
Adena Springs	558	310	8	1.4%
Stonerside Stable	88	46	7	8.0%
Jose Carro	50	32	4	8.0%
Edward P. Evans	116	63	4	3.5%
Brereton C. Jones	222	111	4	1.8%
Juddmonte Farms	57	25	4	7.0%
Joseph Allen	13	9	3	23.1%
Arthur I. Appleton	131	76	3	2.3%
Frank C. Calabrese	5	4	3	60.0%
ClassicStar	87	46	3	3.5%
Darley	57	31	3	5.3%
Gulf Coast Farms Bloodstock	40	24	3	7.5%
Hobeau Farm	38	20	3	7.9%
Jayeff "B" Stables	44	22	3	6.8%
Kinsman Farm	58	29	3	5.2%
Live Oak Stud	86	42	3	3.5%
Eugene Melnyk	163	100	3	1.8%
Shadwell Estate Co.	7	3	3	42.9%
Stud TNT	12	5	3	25.0%
Mr. & Mrs. Martin J. Wygod	138	82	3	2.2%
Buckram Oak Farm	21	15	2	9.5%
Cherry Valley Farm	12	5	2	16.7%
Fox Ridge Farm	14	5	2	14.3%
Gaines-Gentry Thoroughbreds	58	30	2	3.5%
Gainesway Thoroughbreds	56	33	2	3.6%
Richard Giacopelli	11	7	2	18.2%
Haras Don Jorge	69	38	2	2.9%
James T. Hines Jr.	35	19	2	5.7%
Aaron and Marie Jones	38	22	2	5.3%
Lothenbach Stables	16	11	2	12.5%
Padua Stables	134	80	2	1.5%
Potrero Los Llanos	98	49	2	2.0%
Gustav Schickedanz	29	14	2	6.9%
J. D. Squires	18	10	2	11.1%
Vegso Racing Stable	22	12	2	9.1%
Vessels Stallion Farm	38	22	2	5.3%
Wimborne Farm	26	15	2	7.7%
WinStar Farm	87	48	2	2.3%

Leading Breeders by Most Grade 1 Stakes Wins in 2007

Breeder	No. G1 Starts	No. G1 Wins
Adena Springs	22	6
Mr. and Mrs. Martin J. Wygod	13	5
Eugene Melnyk	12	4
Skara Glen Stables	5	4
Dr. and Mrs. Thomas Bowman	5	3
Fares Farm	6	3
James T. Hines Jr.	6	3

Leading Breeders by Most Grade 1 Stakes Winners in 2007

Breeder	No. G1 Starts	No. G1 Wins
Keene Ridge Farm	7	3
Lonnie Arterburn and Eve and Kim Kuhlmann	4	2
Center Hills Farm	4	2
Cherry Valley Farm	3	2
Patti and Hal Earnhardt III	3	2
Tom Evans, Macon Wilmil Equines, and Marjac Farms	3	2
Heaven Trees Farm	3	2
Mr. and Mrs. Jerry S. Moss	5	2
James H. Petrey Jr.	3	2
Ken and Sarah Ramsey	7	2
Ervin Rodriguez	3	2
Gustav Schickedanz	3	2
Shadwell Estate Co.	6	2
Stonerside Stable	4	2
James Tafel	5	2
Williamson Racing	3	2

Leading Breeders by Most Grade 1 Stakes Winners in 2007

Breeder	No. G1 Starters	No. G1 Winners
Adena Springs	13	4
Mr. and Mrs. Martin J. Wygod	5	3
James T. Hines Jr.	2	2
Eugene Melnyk	4	2

Leading Breeders by Number of Wins in 2007

Breeder	No. Strs	No. Wnrs	No. Wins
Adena Springs	558	310	527
Farnsworth Farms	325	185	356
Sez Who Thoroughbreds	267	165	292
Haras Santa Isabel	203	106	255
John Franks	250	118	214
Ken and Sarah Ramsey	141	90	182
Tommy Town Thoroughbreds	193	109	181
Brereton C. Jones	222	111	178
Eugene Melnyk	163	100	166
Mr. and Mrs. Martin J. Wygod	138	82	148
Arthur I. Appleton	131	76	143
Padua Stables	134	80	141
Gilbert G. Campbell	140	71	140
Overbrook Farm	136	72	129
Bruno Schickedanz	122	56	118
Edward P. Evans	116	63	117
Everest Stables	119	68	111
Flying Zee Stables	105	54	107
D. W. Frazier	90	58	104
Potrero Los Llanos	98	49	98
J D Farms	124	48	97
Heiligbrodt Racing Stables	83	47	93
WinStar Farm	87	48	93
Harris Farms	91	59	92
ClassicStar	87	46	82
Charles Nuckols Jr. & Sons	96	45	82
Stonerside Stable	88	46	82
Foxwood Plantation	71	44	77
Pin Oak Stud	77	45	75
Haras Don Jorge	69	38	74
Thomas & Lakin	94	45	74
Live Oak Stud	86	42	73
Donald R. Dizney	86	42	70
E & D Enterprises	70	36	70
Ro Parra	70	42	70
Triple AAA Ranch	56	32	69
Dennis E. Weir	46	34	68
W. S. Farish	73	37	66
Jose Carro	50	32	64
James and Marcia Arnold and Deborah Miley	54	34	60
John D. Murphy	61	31	60
Arthur B. Hancock III	60	34	59
Marilyn McMaster	47	27	59
Ocala Stud Farm	66	33	59
Hargus and Sandra Sexton	79	40	59
K. K. and V. Devi Jayaraman	54	28	58
Gaines-Gentry Thoroughbreds	58	30	57
Patricia Generazio	39	27	56
Potrero Luna	48	24	54
Francis McDonnell	40	23	53
South River Ranch	42	30	53
Gainesway Thoroughbreds	56	33	53
Hermitage Farm	60	30	53
Terry C. Lovingier	69	35	53
Foxfield	49	26	51
Marablue Farm	51	28	51
Meadowbrook Farms	53	28	51

Leading Breeders by Number of Winners in 2007

Breeder	No. Strs	No. Wnrs
Adena Springs	558	310
Farnsworth Farms	325	185
Sez Who Thoroughbreds	267	165
John Franks	250	118
Brereton C. Jones	222	111
Tommy Town Thoroughbreds	193	109
Haras Santa Isabel	203	106
Eugene Melnyk	163	100
Ken and Sarah Ramsey	141	90
Mr. and Mrs. Martin J. Wygod	138	82
Padua Stables	134	80
Arthur I. Appleton	131	76
Overbrook Farm	136	72
Gilbert G. Campbell	140	71
Everest Stables	119	68
Edward P. Evans	116	63
Harris Farms	91	59
D. W. Frazier	90	58
Bruno Schickedanz	122	56
Flying Zee Stables	105	54
Potrero Los Llanos	98	49
J D Farms	124	48
WinStar Farm	87	48
Heiligbrodt Racing Stables	83	47
ClassicStar	87	46
Stonerside Stable	88	46
Charles Nuckols Jr. & Sons	96	45
Pin Oak Stud	77	45
Thomas & Lakin	94	45
Foxwood Plantation	71	44
Donald R. Dizney	86	42
Live Oak Stud	86	42
Ro Parra	70	42
Hargus & Sandra Sexton	79	40
Haras Don Jorge	69	38
W. S. Farish	73	37
Hidden Point Farm	60	37
E & D Enterprises	70	36

Leading Trainers of 2007

Training Thoroughbred racehorses is a tough way to make a living. The days are long, and most trainers are on the job before the sun climbs over the stable area and are there when the last race is run. Increasingly, the job entails considerable travel and mastering the complexities of running a million-dollar business. Not only must the trainer understand the personalities of the owners—some of whom invariably will be more difficult to handle than others—but he or she also must devise and execute a plan of action that leads from the auction ring to the winner's circle.

Indeed, the hopes and aspirations of all trainers are focused on the winner's circle. To win is to please everyone—the owner, the breeder, the stallion manager, the jockey, and the stable staff. For the trainer, day money to train the horse yields a subsistence living at best, and getting to the winner's circle yields the greatest monetary reward. While the money is important, most trainers thrive on getting to the winner's circle.

The following tables recognize those who have succeeded at a tough job.

Leading Trainers by Earnings
North American Earnings Only

Year	Trainer	Wins	Earnings
2007	Todd Pletcher	488	$28,115,697
2006	Todd Pletcher	294	26,820,243
2005	Todd Pletcher	257	20,867,842
2004	Todd Pletcher	240	17,511,923
2003	Robert Frankel	114	19,143,289
2002	Robert Frankel	117	17,750,340
2001	Robert Frankel	101	14,607,446
2000	Bob Baffert	145	11,793,355
1999	Bob Baffert	169	16,842,332
1998	Bob Baffert	138	12,604,110
1997	D. Wayne Lukas	175	10,351,397
1996	D. Wayne Lukas	192	15,967,609
1995	D. Wayne Lukas	194	12,852,843
1994	D. Wayne Lukas	147	9,249,577
1993	Robert J. Frankel	78	8,928,602
1992	D. Wayne Lukas	246	10,061,240
1991	D. Wayne Lukas	289	15,953,757
1990	D. Wayne Lukas	267	14,508,871
1989	D. Wayne Lukas	305	16,103,998
1988	D. Wayne Lukas	318	17,842,358
1987	D. Wayne Lukas	343	17,502,110
1986	D. Wayne Lukas	259	12,344,520
1985	D. Wayne Lukas	218	11,155,188
1984	D. Wayne Lukas	131	5,838,221
1983	D. Wayne Lukas	78	4,267,261
1982	Charles Whittingham	62	4,586,077
1981	Charles Whittingham	74	3,991,877
1980	Lazaro Barrera	99	2,971,626

Leading Trainers of 2007 by Total Earnings

A minimum of ten starters is required to be considered for inclusion. Statistics are for North America only and for racing in 2007.

Trainer	No. Strs	No. Wnrs	No. SWs	SWs/ Strs	No. GSWs	GSWs/ Strs	Total Earnings	Average Earnings/ Starter	Leading Earner	Earnings of Leading Earner
Todd Pletcher	337	179	55	16.3%	33	9.8%	$28,115,697	$83,429	English Channel	$2,640,000
Steven Asmussen	538	295	51	9.5%	10	1.9%	23,899,544	44,423	Curlin	5,080,000
Robert Frankel	160	75	18	11.3%	13	8.1%	12,188,227	76,176	Ginger Punch	1,827,060
Doug O'Neill	306	110	17	5.6%	9	2.9%	10,160,141	33,203	Lava Man	1,410,000
William Mott	207	96	27	13.0%	16	7.7%	9,948,867	48,062	My Typhoon (Ire)	639,000
Scott Lake	500	278	9	1.8%		0.0%	9,724,556	19,449	Cantrel	133,890
Richard Dutrow Jr.	199	104	17	8.5%	8	4.0%	9,604,524	48,264	Kip Deville	1,965,780
Kiaran McLaughlin	151	75	18	11.9%	10	6.6%	9,277,203	61,438	Lahudood (GB)	1,560,500
Gary Contessa	296	126	13	4.4%	2	0.7%	7,597,713	25,668	Stunt Man	335,381
Jerry Hollendorfer	267	146	16	6.0%	4	1.5%	7,309,698	27,377	Hystericalady	984,438
Bob Baffert	116	52	11	9.5%	8	6.9%	7,156,672	61,697	Midnight Lute	1,368,000
H. Graham Motion	163	91	18	11.0%	7	4.3%	6,562,654	40,262	Better Talk Now	499,647
Anthony Dutrow	196	119	10	5.1%	3	1.5%	6,555,533	33,447	Premium Wine	311,700
Mark Casse	128	62	10	7.8%	5	3.9%	6,317,290	49,354	Sealy Hill	958,389
Larry Jones	80	44	7	8.8%	2	2.5%	5,931,956	74,149	Hard Spun	2,572,500
John Sadler	178	73	14	7.9%	6	3.4%	5,409,824	30,392	Crossing The Line (NZ)	245,400
Christophe Clement	115	55	13	11.3%	7	6.1%	5,318,976	46,252	Royal Highness (Ger)	559,500
Barclay Tagg	88	38	11	12.5%	6	6.8%	5,174,308	58,799	Nobiz Like Shobiz	1,318,330
Nicholas Zito	121	48	7	5.8%	4	3.3%	5,140,394	42,483	War Pass	1,397,400
Bruce Levine	183	93	7	3.8%		0.0%	4,756,338	25,991	Lila Paige	250,200
Thomas Amoss	196	106	5	2.6%		0.0%	4,503,190	22,975	Indian Chant	240,645
Dale Romans	151	60	9	6.0%	3	2.0%	4,498,453	29,791	Thorn Song	298,720
Patrick Biancone	98	39	11	11.2%	9	9.2%	4,491,030	45,827	Lady of Venice (Fr)	775,272
Carl Nafzger	17	8	2	11.8%	2	11.8%	4,378,855	257,580	Street Sense	3,205,000
W. Bret Calhoun	223	108	11	4.9%		0.0%	4,190,679	18,792	Valid Lil	150,358
Steve Klesaris	117	73	5	4.3%	1	0.9%	4,041,192	34,540	Miraculous Miss	371,300
Art Sherman	241	136	3	1.2%	1	0.4%	4,025,569	16,704	Lang Field	376,313
Mike Mitchell	94	46	7	7.5%	4	4.3%	3,831,637	40,762	On the Acorn (GB)	398,400
James Jerkens	57	30	9	15.8%	2	3.5%	3,809,641	66,836	Corinthian	1,174,173
Jeff Mullins	175	80	7	4.0%		0.0%	3,796,169	21,692	Scottsbluff	167,382

People — Leading Trainers of 2007

Trainer	No. Strs	No. Wnrs	No. SWs	SWs/ Strs	No. GSWs	GSWs/ Strs	Total Earnings	Average Earnings/ Starter	Leading Earner	Earnings of Leading Earner
Richard Violette Jr.	108	50	5	4.6%	3	2.8%	$3,776,863	$34,971	Summer Doldrums	$ 683,582
Reade Baker	118	37	8	6.8%	2	1.7%	3,752,824	31,804	Bear Now	747,517
Michael Trombetta	112	67	11	9.8%	3	2.7%	3,581,259	31,976	Sweetnorthernsaint	229,375
Craig Dollase	59	28	8	13.6%	3	5.1%	3,371,771	57,149	Awesome Gem	1,032,400
Sid Attard	69	38	5	7.3%	1	1.4%	3,229,189	46,800	Jiggs Coz	364,277
Patrick Mouton	107	52	11	10.3%		0.0%	3,210,220	30,002	Cort's P. B.	187,250
H. Allen Jerkens	54	26	7	13.0%	6	11.1%	3,206,478	59,379	Miss Shop	787,408
Patrick Gallagher	127	44	7	5.5%	1	0.8%	3,192,692	25,139	Valbenny (Ire)	380,410
Frank Kirby	126	50	1	0.8%	1	0.8%	3,105,423	24,646	Cloudy's Knight	1,526,868
Edward Plesa Jr.	121	55	5	4.1%	2	1.7%	3,011,536	24,889	Gottcha Gold	488,445
John Shirreffs	47	14	3	6.4%	2	4.3%	3,007,147	63,982	Tiago	1,234,750
Mark Hennig	100	37	10	10.0%	2	2.0%	2,897,246	28,972	Barcola	242,155
Kenneth McPeek	93	44	4	4.3%	1	1.1%	2,865,159	30,808	Old Man Buck	228,312
Claude McGaughey III	56	24	7	12.5%	4	7.1%	2,827,672	50,494	Sightseeing	393,716
Keith Bourgeois	179	98	1	0.6%		0.0%	2,794,342	15,611	Madison's Music	195,270
Donnie Von Hemel	97	48	8	8.3%	1	1.0%	2,789,448	28,757	Going Ballistic	690,140
Michael Gorham	114	54	3	2.6%	1	0.9%	2,779,016	24,377	Peak Maria's Way	215,229
Richard Mandella	74	24	4	5.4%	4	5.4%	2,704,144	36,542	The Tin Man	536,920
Timothy Ritchey	64	30	4	6.3%	1	1.6%	2,627,604	41,056	Moon Catcher	663,450
Mark Shuman	76	43	3	4.0%	1	1.3%	2,560,058	33,685	Xchanger	510,500
Michael Matz	90	37	6	6.7%	2	2.2%	2,539,756	28,220	Chelokee	319,525
Cody Autrey	204	89	1	0.5%		0.0%	2,525,507	12,380	Davids Expectation	104,890
Wayne Catalano	137	78	3	2.2%	3	2.2%	2,509,714	18,319	Dreaming of Anna	391,932
Ronny Werner	82	40	5	6.1%	2	2.4%	2,506,206	30,563	Ermine	439,052
Malcolm Pierce	58	26	4	6.9%	1	1.7%	2,495,254	43,022	She's Indy Money	252,131
Jonathan Sheppard	105	43	9	8.6%	1	1.0%	2,429,930	23,142	Forever Together	176,540
D. Wayne Lukas	85	35	4	4.7%	2	2.4%	2,424,503	28,524	Fiery Pursuit	263,045
Todd Beattie	86	59	2	2.3%	1	1.5%	2,401,046	27,919	Fabulous Strike	403,332
Jeff Runco	180	94	1	0.6%		0.0%	2,384,564	13,248	Hopewebreakeven	65,600
Roger Attfield	55	21	5	9.1%	2	3.6%	2,380,445	43,281	Eccentric (GB)	289,590
Samuel Breaux	148	87	2	1.4%		0.0%	2,377,857	16,067	Indigo Girl	173,800
Robert Tiller	74	29	2	2.7%		0.0%	2,357,793	31,862	Dancer's Bajan	268,181
Neil Drysdale	68	27	8	11.8%	5	7.4%	2,316,442	34,065	Obrigado (Fr)	188,770
Albert Stall Jr.	104	51	6	5.8%		0.0%	2,294,908	22,066	Raspberry Wine	299,560
Kelly Von Hemel	81	37	11	13.6%	1	1.2%	2,273,314	28,066	Miss Macy Sue	546,217
Thomas Proctor	96	50	4	4.2%	1	1.0%	2,269,236	23,638	Purim	496,450
Ian Black	28	15	3	10.7%	1	3.6%	2,266,270	80,938	Mike Fox	656,561
Rafael Becerra	80	33	4	5.0%	1	1.3%	2,250,348	28,129	Celtic Dreamin	321,463
Timothy Hills	104	46	4	3.9%		0.0%	2,239,825	21,537	Maddy's Heart	194,198
Linda Rice	112	44	1	0.9%		0.0%	2,237,617	19,979	Canadian Ballet	148,862
Henry Dominguez	155	67	5	3.2%		0.0%	2,227,578	14,371	Song of Navarone	312,180
David Hofmans	66	14	3	4.6%	3	4.5%	2,224,681	33,707	Greg's Gold	566,995
Michael Pino	144	63	4	2.8%		0.0%	2,219,871	15,416	Pass Play	157,185
Nicholas Gonzalez	80	41	7	8.8%		0.0%	2,217,493	27,719	Stuck in Traffic	246,929
Vladimir Cerin	71	26	1	1.4%	1	1.4%	2,196,384	30,935	Student Council	600,000
Josie Carroll	73	29	3	4.1%		0.0%	2,169,334	29,717	Authenicat	190,216
Mark Frostad	43	17	4	9.3%	1	2.3%	2,163,114	50,305	Strike Softly	305,775
John Kimmel	69	28	4	5.8%	2	2.9%	2,140,975	31,029	Timber Reserve	577,600
Dale Capuano	126	61	2	1.6%	1	0.8%	2,137,809	16,967	Heros Reward	515,826
Clifford Sise Jr.	66	28	3	4.6%	1	1.5%	2,128,998	32,258	Idiot Proof	803,136
Carla Gaines	53	19	2	3.8%	1	1.9%	2,114,481	39,896	Nashoba's Key	972,090
John Rigattieri	116	80	1	0.9%		0.0%	2,088,292	18,003	Saratoga Lulaby	152,311
Thomas Bush	78	33	5	6.4%		0.0%	2,073,996	26,590	A True Pussycat	176,624
William Morey	130	78				0.0%	2,053,594	15,797	Dangerous Devil	65,098
Charlton Baker	87	62	3	3.5%		0.0%	2,047,137	23,530	Talking Treasure	252,620
Kirk Ziadie	83	52	7	8.4%	1	1.2%	2,045,894	24,649	Paradise Dancer	255,800
Michael Maker	97	51	6	6.2%		0.0%	2,032,712	20,956	Miami Sunrise	179,130
Dale Baird	201	89				0.0%	2,030,982	10,104	Market Force	66,687
Randy Allen	105	59				0.0%	2,014,084	19,182	Flying Clipper	88,420
Michael Stidham	130	52	6	4.6%	1	0.8%	2,010,149	15,463	General Charley	162,645
Julio Canani	59	29	5	8.5%	2	3.4%	2,003,015	33,949	Kris' Sis	163,935
Michael De Paulo	58	28	3	5.2%		0.0%	1,999,377	34,472	Krz Exec	215,902
Dallas Stewart	93	37				0.0%	1,998,986	21,494	Smokeyjonessutton	131,177
Chris Hartman	125	72	5	4.0%		0.0%	1,985,318	15,883	Etoile de Dome	144,880
Neil Howard	41	18	2	4.9%		0.0%	1,967,499	47,988	Grasshopper	378,520
Jayne Vaders	103	61				0.0%	1,962,712	19,055	Thisonesforsam	104,420
George Arnold II	70	27	3	4.3%	1	1.4%	1,952,114	27,887	Wicked Style	445,000
Barry Abrams	48	18	3	6.3%	1	2.1%	1,941,897	40,456	Unusual Suspect	376,221
Michael Hushion	76	32	3	4.0%		0.0%	1,935,508	25,467	Southern Prince	174,370
Flint Stites	151	73	1	0.7%		0.0%	1,932,973	12,801	My Sister Sue	131,580

Leading Trainers by Average Earnings per Starter in 2007
(Minimum of 10 Starters)

Trainer	No. Strs	No. Wnrs	Average Earnings per Starter
Carl Nafzger	17	8	$257,580
Angel Penna Jr.	19	6	88,223
Todd Pletcher	337	179	83,429
Ian Black	28	15	80,938
Robert Frankel	160	75	76,176
Larry Jones	80	44	74,149
Kevin Attard	17	7	73,013
Lorne Richards	13	6	70,401
Francois Parisel	13	1	68,683
James Jerkens	57	30	66,836
Catherine Day Phillips	24	8	66,795
William Kaplan	23	10	64,157
John Shirreffs	47	14	63,982
Bob Baffert	116	52	61,697
Kiaran McLaughlin	151	75	61,438
Darwin Banach	27	13	61,177
H. Allen Jerkens	54	26	59,379
Barclay Tagg	88	38	58,799
Craig Dollase	59	28	57,149
Saeed bin Suroor	23	13	54,522
William Currin	16	3	51,055
Claude McGaughey III	56	24	50,494
Mark Frostad	43	17	50,305
Kevin Sleeter	23	13	49,384
Mark Casse	128	62	49,354
Richard Dutrow Jr.	199	104	48,264
William Mott	207	96	48,062
Neil Howard	41	18	47,988
Sid Attard	69	38	46,800
George Yetsook	11	6	46,656
Christophe Clement	115	55	46,252
Patrick Biancone	98	39	45,827
James Toner	21	7	44,764
Eric Coatrieux	16	8	44,630
Steve Asmussen	538	295	44,423
Cam Gambolati	13	6	43,606
Roger Attfield	55	21	43,281
Malcolm Pierce	58	26	43,022
Nicholas Zito	121	48	42,483
Gary Hartlage	16	9	42,466
Alan Goldberg	41	20	41,986
Timothy Ritchey	64	30	41,056
Stanley Hough	45	25	40,811
Mike Mitchell	94	46	40,762
Barry Abrams	48	18	40,456
H. Graham Motion	163	91	40,254
Michael McCarthy	17	6	40,262
Carla Gaines	53	19	39,896
Patrick Kelly	38	13	39,491
Robert Earl Barnett	20	7	39,091

Leading Trainers by Stakes Wins in 2007

Trainer	No. Stakes Starts	No. Stakes Wins
Todd Pletcher	427	94
Steve Asmussen	431	79
William Mott	199	45
Robert Frankel	182	37
Richard Dutrow Jr.	108	29
Christophe Clement	104	27
Jerry Hollendorfer	134	27
Doug O'Neill	166	25
Barclay Tagg	87	23
Kiaran McLaughlin	118	22
H. Graham Motion	131	22
Gary Contessa	171	19
Kelly Von Hemel	56	18
Terry Jordan	32	17
Bob Baffert	83	16
Mark Casse	88	16
Patrick Mouton	73	16
John Sadler	85	16
Anthony Dutrow	56	15
Mark Hennig	82	15
Michael Trombetta	66	15
W. Bret Calhoun	106	14
James Jerkens	60	14
Martin Wolfson	65	14
Reade Baker	72	13
Patrick Biancone	106	13
Doris Harwood	27	13
Dale Romans	89	13
Donnie Von Hemel	79	13
Larry Jones	57	12
Mike Mitchell	56	12
Miguel Feliciano	45	11
Scott Lake	54	11
Edward Plesa Jr.	103	11
Kirk Ziadie	41	11
Jon Arnett	44	10
Greg Gilchrist	24	10
H. Allen Jerkens	73	10
Jeff Mullins	59	10
Albert Stall Jr.	41	10
Michael Stidham	47	10
Craig Dollase	63	9
Christopher Grove	32	9
Claude McGaughey III	51	9
Timothy Ritchey	38	9
John Shirreffs	27	9
Richard Violette Jr.	47	9
Thomas Amoss	59	8
Robertino Diodoro	29	8
Neil Drysdale	58	8
Patrick Gallagher	84	8
Nicholas Gonzalez	36	8
Bart Hone	51	8
Christine Janks	52	8
Bruce Levine	34	8
Kevin Lewis	38	8
Michael Matz	63	8
Jamie Ness	18	8
McLean Robertson	37	8
Nicholas Zito	77	8

Leading Trainers by Number of Stakes Winners in 2007

Trainer	No. Strs	No. Wnrs	No. SWs
Todd Pletcher	337	179	55
Steve Asmussen	538	295	51
William Mott	207	96	27
Robert Frankel	160	75	18
Kiaran McLaughlin	151	75	18
H. Graham Motion	163	91	18
Richard Dutrow Jr.	199	104	17

Trainer	No. Strs	No. Wnrs	No. SWs
Doug O'Neill	306	110	17
Jerry Hollendorfer	267	146	16
John Sadler	178	73	14
Christophe Clement	115	55	13
Gary Contessa	296	126	13
Bob Baffert	116	52	11
Patrick Biancone	98	39	11
W. Bret Calhoun	223	108	11
Patrick Mouton	107	52	11
Barclay Tagg	88	38	11
Michael Trombetta	112	67	11
Kelly Von Hemel	81	37	11
Mark Casse	128	62	10
Anthony Dutrow	196	119	10
Mark Hennig	100	37	10
Martin Wolfson	57	31	10
James Jerkens	57	30	9
Scott Lake	500	278	9
Dale Romans	151	60	9
Jonathan Sheppard	105	43	9
Reade Baker	118	37	8
Craig Dollase	59	28	8
Neil Drysdale	68	27	8
Donnie Von Hemel	97	48	8
Jon Arnett	104	64	7
Patrick Gallagher	127	44	7
Nicholas Gonzalez	80	41	7
H. Allen Jerkens	54	26	7
Larry Jones	80	44	7
Bruce Levine	183	93	7
Kevin Lewis	62	40	7
Claude McGaughey III	56	24	7
Mike Mitchell	94	46	7
Jeff Mullins	175	80	7
McLean Robertson	84	55	7
Kirk Ziadie	83	52	7
Nicholas Zito	121	48	7
Jim Fergason	77	53	6
Jack O. Fisher	29	16	6
Bart G. Hone	107	46	6
Michael J. Maker	97	51	6
Michael R. Matz	90	37	6
Dan L. McFarlane	113	37	6
Albert M. Stall Jr.	104	51	6
Michael Stidham	130	52	6
Saeed bin Suroor	23	13	6

Trainer	No. Strs	No. Wnrs	No. SWs	SWs/Str
John Sadler	178	73	14	7.87%
Mark Casse	128	62	10	7.81%
Reade Baker	118	37	8	6.78%
Jon Arnett	104	64	7	6.73%
Jerry Hollendorfer	267	146	16	5.99%
Dale Romans	151	60	9	5.96%
Nicholas Zito	121	48	7	5.79%
Albert Stall Jr.	104	51	6	5.77%
Bart Hone	107	46	6	5.61%
Doug O'Neill	306	110	17	5.56%
Patrick Gallagher	127	44	7	5.51%
Dan McFarlane	113	37	6	5.31%
Anthony Dutrow	196	119	10	5.10%
W. Bret Calhoun	223	108	11	4.93%
Richard Violette Jr.	108	50	5	4.63%
Michael Stidham	130	52	6	4.62%
Keith Bennett	131	65	6	4.58%
Gary Contessa	296	126	13	4.39%
Steve Klesaris	117	73	5	4.27%
Edward Plesa Jr.	121	55	5	4.13%
Jeff Mullins	175	80	7	4.00%
Chris Hartman	125	72	5	4.00%
Timothy Hills	104	46	4	3.85%
Bruce Levine	183	93	7	3.83%
Jamie Ness	106	70	4	3.77%
Henry Dominguez	155	67	5	3.23%
Danny Pish	139	86	4	2.88%
Eddie Kenneally	105	33	3	2.86%
Michael Pino	144	63	4	2.78%
Michael Gorham	114	54	3	2.63%
Thomas Amoss	196	106	5	2.55%
Wayne Catalano	137	78	3	2.19%

Leading Trainers by Percent of Stakes Winners from Starters in 2007
(Minimum of 100 Starters)

Trainer	No. Strs	No. Wnrs	No. SWs	SWs/Str
Todd Pletcher	337	179	55	16.32%
William Mott	207	96	27	13.04%
Kiaran McLaughlin	151	75	18	11.92%
Christophe Clement	115	55	13	11.30%
Robert Frankel	160	75	18	11.25%
H. Graham Motion	163	91	18	11.04%
Patrick Mouton	107	52	11	10.28%
Mark Hennig	100	37	10	10.00%
Michael Trombetta	112	67	11	9.82%
Steve Asmussen	538	295	51	9.48%
Bob Baffert	116	52	11	9.48%
Jonathan Sheppard	105	43	9	8.57%
Richard Dutrow Jr.	199	104	17	8.54%

Leading Trainers by Graded Stakes Wins in 2007

Trainer	No. Graded Stakes Starts	No. Graded Stakes Wins
Todd Pletcher	251	56
Robert Frankel	134	27
William Mott	112	23
Steve Asmussen	106	18
Christophe Clement	52	13
Kiaran McLaughlin	69	13
Doug O'Neill	76	12
Barclay Tagg	36	12
Bob Baffert	54	11
Patrick Biancone	80	10
Richard Dutrow Jr.	47	10
Mark Casse	31	8
Allen Jerkens	45	8
H. Graham Motion	49	7
John Shirreffs	22	7
Carl Nafzger	13	6
John Sadler	42	6
Richard Violette Jr.	29	6
Neil Drysdale	41	5
David Hofmans	33	5
Jerry Hollendorfer	38	5
Larry Jones	18	5
Claude McGaughey III	31	5
Mike Mitchell	24	5
Nicholas Zito	55	5
Carla Gaines	8	4
Eoin Harty	17	4

Trainer	No. Graded Stakes Starts	No. Graded Stakes Wins
Dan Hendricks	19	4
James Jerkens	27	4
Richard Mandella	29	4
Michael McCarthy	10	4
Dale Romans	50	4
Roger Attfield	30	3
Reade Baker	22	3
Paula Capestro	6	3
Wayne Catalano	11	3
Ben Cecil	22	3
Catherine Day Phillips	6	3
Craig Dollase	38	3
Anthony Dutrow	14	3
Eric Guillot	10	3
Terry Jordan	9	3
Angel Penna Jr.	12	3
Edward Plesa Jr.	19	3
James Toner	11	3
Michael Trombetta	19	3

Trainer	No. G1 Starts	No. G1 Wins
Richard Dutrow Jr.	18	4
Doug O'Neill	30	4
John Shirreffs	12	4
Steve Asmussen	22	3
Christophe Clement	10	3
Richard Mandella	10	3
Carl Nafzger	9	3
Catherine Day Phillips	2	2
Carla Gaines	3	2
Allen Jerkens	16	2
James Jerkens	7	2
William Mott	21	2
Barclay Tagg	10	2
Richard Violette Jr.	9	2
Nicholas Zito	23	2

Leading Trainers by Most Grade 1 Stakes Winners in 2007

Trainer	No. G1 Starters	No. G1 Winners
Todd Pletcher	44	10
Kiaran McLaughlin	17	6
Bob Baffert	12	5
Robert Frankel	27	5
Christophe Clement	7	3
Richard Dutrow Jr.	8	3
Richard Mandella	7	3
Doug O'Neill	15	3
Mark Casse	4	2
H. Allen Jerkens	4	2
James Jerkens	4	2
William Mott	13	2
Carl Nafzger	2	2
John Shirreffs	4	2
Barclay Tagg	6	2

Leading Trainers by Number of Graded Stakes Winners in 2007

Trainer	No. Strs	No. Wnrs	No. GSWs	GSWs/Strs
Todd Pletcher	337	179	33	9.8%
William Mott	207	96	16	7.7%
Robert Frankel	160	75	13	8.1%
Steve Asmussen	538	295	10	1.9%
Kiaran McLaughlin	151	75	10	6.6%
Patrick Biancone	98	39	9	9.2%
Doug O'Neill	306	110	9	2.9%
Bob Baffert	116	52	8	6.9%
Richard E. Dutrow Jr.	199	104	8	4.0%
Christophe Clement	115	55	7	6.1%
H. Graham Motion	163	91	7	4.3%
H. Allen Jerkens	54	26	6	11.1%
John Sadler	178	73	6	3.4%
Barclay Tagg	88	38	6	6.8%
Mark Casse	128	62	5	3.9%
Neil Drysdale	68	27	5	7.4%
Jerry Hollendorfer	267	146	4	1.5%
Richard Mandella	74	24	4	5.4%
Michael McCarthy	17	6	4	23.5%
Claude McGaughey III	56	24	4	7.1%
Mike Mitchell	94	46	4	4.3%
Nicholas Zito	121	48	4	3.3%
Wayne Catalano	137	78	3	2.2%
Craig Dollase	59	28	3	5.1%
Anthony Dutrow	196	119	3	1.5%
Eoin Harty	61	27	3	4.9%
David Hofmans	66	14	3	4.5%
Dale Romans	151	60	3	2.0%
Michael Trombetta	112	67	3	2.7%
Richard Violette Jr.	108	50	3	2.8%

Leading Trainers by Most Grade 1 Stakes Wins in 2007

Trainer	No. G1 Starts	No. G1 Wins
Todd Pletcher	93	17
Robert Frankel	50	9
Bob Baffert	24	7
Kiaran McLaughlin	27	7
Mark Casse	10	4

Leading Trainers by Number of Wins in 2007

Trainer	No. Strs	No. Individual Wnrs	No. Wins
Steve Asmussen	538	295	438
Scott Lake	500	278	435
Todd Pletcher	337	179	289
Jerry Hollendorfer	267	146	244
Ralph Martinez	133	102	221
Art Sherman	241	136	207
W. Bret Calhoun	223	108	182
Anthony Dutrow	196	119	182
Gary Contessa	296	126	176
Maximo Gomez	197	91	176
Richard Dutrow Jr.	199	104	166
Keith Bourgeois	179	98	160
William Mott	207	96	156
Doug O'Neill	306	110	152
Chris Englehart	145	84	151
Thomas Amoss	196	106	149
Jeff Runco	180	94	146
H. Graham Motion	163	91	145
Jeffrey Radosevich	117	70	145
Arderson Santiago	149	68	145
Stephanie Beattie	131	88	143
Bruce Levine	183	93	141
John Rigattieri	116	80	138
Danny Pish	139	86	136

People — Leading Trainers of 2007

Trainer	No. Strs	No. Individual Wnrs	No. Wins
Cody Autrey	204	89	133
Dale Baird	201	89	132
Jamie Ness	106	70	132
Rodney Faulkner	143	77	131
Steven Miyadi	146	90	129
Robert Frankel	160	75	124
Murray Rojas	148	77	124
Samuel Breaux	148	87	123
Steve Klesaris	117	73	123
Jayne Vaders	103	61	122
Wayne Catalano	137	78	120
John Locke	171	80	120
Flint Stites	151	73	118
Kiaran McLaughlin	151	75	117
Jeff Mullins	175	80	117
William Morey	130	78	115
Gerald Bennett	87	53	114
Gaston Capote	86	47	113
John Sadler	178	73	113
Jon Arnett	104	64	111
Chris Hartman	125	72	110
Charlton Baker	87	62	106
Michael Trombetta	112	67	106
Keith Bennett	131	65	105
Jorge Lara	139	67	105
Kirk Ziadie	83	52	105

Most Wins for a Trainers on One Day in 2007

Wins	Trainer	Date	Track(s)
9	Steve Asmussen	6/16/2007	AP, CD, LS, MTH
8	Todd Pletcher	3/31/2007	AQU, GP, SA
7	Steve Asmussen	12/22/2007	DED, FG
6	Steve Asmussen	6/9/2007	CD, EVD, LS
	Steve Asmussen	1/26/2007	HOU, OP
	Steve Asmussen	4/7/2007	EVD, HOU, KEE, OP
	Scott Lake	9/19/2007	DEL, LRL, PID
	Scott Lake	4/19/2007	GP, PEN, PIM
	Todd Pletcher	3/3/2007	GP, SA
	Todd Pletcher	4/7/2007	AQU, HAW, OP, SA
5	Jon Arnett	5/28/2007	ARP
	Jon Arnett	5/26/2007	ARP
	Steve Asmussen	11/25/2007	AQU, FG, RP
	Steve Asmussen	12/6/2007	AQU, FG, HOU
	Steve Asmussen	3/1/2007	AQU, FG, OP
	Steve Asmussen	4/14/2007	OP
	Steve Asmussen	7/21/2007	CBY, LAD, LS
	Steve Asmussen	6/29/2007	AP, CD, LS
	Steve Asmussen	7/7/2007	CD, LS
	Steve Asmussen	7/28/2007	LS, MTH
	Steve Asmussen	9/29/2007	HAW, PID, TP
	Steve Asmussen	11/30/2007	FG, HOU, RP
	Steve Asmussen	8/4/2007	ELP, MNR, RP
	Dave Bernhardt	6/24/2007	CPW
	Richard Dutrow Jr.	6/16/2007	BEL, MTH
	Robert Frankel	6/30/2007	HOL, MTH
	Chris Hartman	3/25/2007	SUN
	Jerry Hollendorfer	11/24/2007	GG
	Scott Lake	6/9/2007	CT, DEL, MTH, PIM
	Scott Lake	4/17/2007	FL, PEN, PHA
	Scott Lake	9/11/2007	DEL, PEN
	Scott Lake	3/18/2007	GP, LRL
	Scott Lake	1/28/2007	CT, GP, LRL
	Scott Lake	11/20/2007	PEN, PHA
	Ralph Martinez	6/2/2007	FP, IND
	Ralph Martinez	3/23/2007	FP, HAW
	Ralph Martinez	4/10/2007	FP
	Ralph Martinez	3/6/2007	FP
	William Mott	4/7/2007	GP, TAM
	Todd Pletcher	3/10/2007	AQU, FG, GP, OP
	Todd Pletcher	11/23/2007	AQU, CD, HOL
	Todd Pletcher	11/24/2007	AQU, CD, HOL, LRL
	Todd Pletcher	5/26/2007	AP, BEL, MTH
	Murray Rojas	1/16/2007	PEN

Most Wins for a Trainers on One Program in 2007

Wins	Trainer	Date	Track
6	Steve Asmussen	12/22/2007	FG
5	Jon Arnett	5/28/2007	ARP
	Jon Arnett	5/26/2007	ARP
	Steve Asmussen	4/14/2007	OP
	Dave Bernhardt	6/24/2007	CPW
	Chris Hartman	3/25/2007	SUN
	Jerry Hollendorfer	11/24/2007	GG
	Ralph Martinez	4/10/2007	FP
	Ralph Martinez	3/6/2007	FP
	Todd Pletcher	3/3/2007	GP
	Todd Pletcher	3/31/2007	GP
	Murray Rojas	1/16/2007	PEN
4	Jon Arnett	6/11/2007	ARP
	Jon Arnett	7/1/2007	ARP
	Jon Arnett	7/16/2007	ARP
	Steve Asmussen	7/28/2007	LS
	Steve Asmussen	6/16/2007	CD
	Steve Asmussen	7/13/2007	LS
	Steve Asmussen	7/7/2007	CD
	Robert Baze	12/4/2007	PM
	Gerald Bennett	7/3/2007	GLD
	Gary Contessa	3/2/2007	AQU
	Jim Fergason	11/27/2007	PM
	Russell Gardipy	6/30/2007	MD
	Kenneth Gleason	6/4/2007	ARP
	Maximo Gomez	2/18/2007	ELC
	Michael Gorham	5/9/2007	DEL
	Chad Hassenpflug	3/30/2007	DED
	Jerry Hollendorfer	4/25/2007	GG
	Marvin Johnson	8/17/2007	CLS
	Scott Lake	11/20/2007	PEN
	Scott Lake	9/11/2007	DEL
	Scott Lake	3/18/2007	LRL
	Scott Lake	4/19/2007	PEN
	Martin Lozano	3/12/2007	WRD
	John Martin	10/28/2007	BM
	Ralph Martinez	5/22/2007	FP
	Ralph Martinez	3/23/2007	FP
	Barbara McBride	9/8/2007	HOO
	Jonathan Nance	3/20/2007	PM
	Doug O'Neill	3/3/2007	SA
	Danny Pish	11/16/2007	RET
	Michael Reavis	4/2/2007	HAW
	McLean Robertson	5/6/2007	CBY
	Murray Rojas	3/1/2007	PEN
	Jeff Runco	10/14/2007	CT
	Jeff Runco	9/2/2007	CT
	Art Sherman	8/12/2007	BMF
	Art Sherman	6/7/2007	GG
	Ronny Werner	12/1/2007	FG
	Kirk Ziadie	6/2/2007	CRC

Leading Trainers by Earnings in a Year (1985-2007)

Trainer	Year	Earnings	Leading Earner
Todd Pletcher	2007	$28,115,697	English Channel ($2,640,000)
Todd Pletcher	2006	26,908,915	Bluegrass Cat ($1,547,500)
Steve Asmussen	2007	23,899,544	Curlin ($5,080,000)
Todd Pletcher	2005	20,987,233	Flower Alley ($2,435,200)
Robert Frankel	2003	19,147,129	Medaglia d'Oro ($1,990,000)
D. Wayne Lukas	1988	17,842,358	Gulch ($1,360,840)
Robert Frankel	2002	17,750,340	Medaglia d'Oro ($2,245,000)
D. Wayne Lukas	1987	17,502,110	Tejano ($1,177,189)
Todd Pletcher	2004	17,481,923	Ashado ($2,259,640)
Bob Baffert	1999	16,842,332	Silverbulletday ($1,707,640)
D. Wayne Lukas	1989	16,103,998	Steinlen (GB) ($1,521,378)
D. Wayne Lukas	1996	15,967,609	Boston Harbor ($1,928,605)
D. Wayne Lukas	1991	15,953,757	Farma Way ($2,598,350)
Robert Frankel	2004	15,605,911	Ghostzapper ($2,590,000)
Robert Frankel	2001	14,607,446	Skimming ($1,330,000)
D. Wayne Lukas	1990	14,508,871	Criminal Type ($2,270,290)
Robert Frankel	2005	14,493,670	Leroidesanimaux (Brz) ($1,305,000)
Steve Asmussen	2004	14,003,445	Lady Tak ($439,412)
Steve Asmussen	2005	13,295,106	Summerly ($786,728)
D. Wayne Lukas	1995	12,852,843	Thunder Gulch ($2,644,080)
Bob Baffert	2001	12,761,034	Point Given ($3,350,000)
Bob Baffert	1998	12,608,670	Silver Charm ($2,296,506)
Todd Pletcher	2003	12,356,924	Balto Star ($907,500)
D. Wayne Lukas	1986	12,344,520	Lady's Secret ($1,871,053)
Robert Frankel	2007	12,188,227	Ginger Punch ($1,827,060)
D. Wayne Lukas	1999	12,070,460	Cat Thief ($3,020,500)
Bob Baffert	2002	12,029,115	War Emblem ($3,125,000)
Bob Baffert	2000	11,793,355	Captain Steve ($1,882,276)
William Mott	1995	11,789,625	Cigar ($4,819,800)
Steve Asmussen	2003	11,727,910	Lady Tak ($675,350)
William Mott	1996	11,703,723	Cigar ($2,510,000)
Charles Whittingham	1989	11,402,231	Sunday Silence ($4,578,454)
Doug O'Neill	2006	11,252,048	Lava Man ($2,770,000)
D. Wayne Lukas	1985	11,155,188	Lady's Secret ($994,349)
D. Wayne Lukas	2000	10,492,317	Spain ($1,925,500)
D. Wayne Lukas	1997	10,351,397	Marlin ($1,521,600)
Steve Asmussen	2002	10,248,260	Easyfromthegitgo ($606,905)
Robert Frankel	2000	10,209,071	Chester House ($1,408,500)
Doug O'Neill	2007	10,160,141	Lava Man ($1,410,000)
D. Wayne Lukas	1992	10,061,240	Mountain Cat ($1,460,627)
William Mott	1998	10,012,899	Escena ($2,032,425)
William Mott	2007	9,948,867	My Typhoon (Ire) ($639,000)
Richard Mandella	2003	9,871,468	Pleasantly Perfect ($2,470,000)
Robert Frankel	2006	9,815,673	Cacique (Ire) ($994,432)
Richard E. Dutrow Jr.	2005	9,798,106	Saint Liam ($3,183,600)
Scott Lake	2007	9,724,556	Cantrel ($133,890)
Richard Dutrow Jr.	2007	9,604,524	Kip Deville ($1,965,780)
Scott Lake	2006	9,565,656	Outcashem ($248,856)
Doug O'Neill	2005	9,478,263	Stevie Wonderboy ($1,028,940)
William Mott	1997	9,474,680	Ajina ($979,175)
Bob Baffert	2003	9,442,281	Congaree ($1,608,000)
William Mott	2001	9,418,657	Hap ($919,070)
Charles Whittingham	1987	9,415,097	Ferdinand ($2,185,150)
William Mott	2005	9,403,986	Gun Salute ($630,550)
Kiaran McLaughlin	2007	9,277,203	Lahudood (GB) ($1,560,500)
D. Wayne Lukas	1994	9,249,577	Tabasco Cat ($2,164,334)
Scott Lake	2003	9,164,949	Shake You Down ($814,640)
Scott Lake	2005	8,973,467	Don Six ($199,940)
Robert Frankel	1993	8,928,602	Bertrando ($2,217,800)
John Servis	2004	8,922,686	Smarty Jones ($7,563,535)
Bob Baffert	1997	8,867,128	Silver Charm ($1,638,750)
Charles Whittingham	1986	8,801,284	Estrapade ($1,184,800)
Todd Pletcher	2002	8,702,228	Left Bank ($626,146)
William Mott	2000	8,591,389	Snow Polina ($772,943)
Kiaran McLaughlin	2006	8,499,205	Invasor (ARG) ($3,690,000)
Richard E. Mandella	1997	8,432,774	Gentlemen (ARG) ($2,125,300)
Ronald L. McAnally	1991	8,388,214	Festin (ARG) ($2,003,250)
Scott A. Lake	2002	8,307,347	Thunderello ($355,600)
Claude R. McGaughey III	1989	8,306,888	Easy Goer ($3,837,150)
Nicholas P. Zito	2005	8,199,368	Sun King ($1,134,800)

Leading Jockeys of 2007

Jockeys have been described as pound for pound the strongest human athletes. Their task is formidable: balance by their toes on a half-ton of fury and navigate through a 35 mph stampede to the winner's circle. Often, they perform this feat seven or eight times a day. From the time they first show ability astride a horse, they are destined to pursue only this one calling—as long as they keep their weight under 112 pounds or so.

Hundreds of men and women possess the agility and ability to ride professionally and make a living as a jockey. Some transcend their peers and become leaders of their circuits or the sport. A very, very few achieve greatness.

Eddie Arcaro ruled the 1940s, and Bill Shoemaker was the little man with the gifted hands through the '60s. He passed the crown to Laffit Pincay Jr., who set a new standard of accomplishment, with more than 9,500 victories, until Russell Baze took over the top spot.

For a decade beginning in the mid-1990s, Jerry Bailey and Pat Day were leaders in a very talented colony of North American jockeys. As they and their contemporaries began to contemplate life after racing, a new generation emerged to assume the top spots.

Leading Jockeys by Earnings
North American Earnings Only

Year	Jockey	Wins	Earnings
2007	Garrett Gomez	265	$22,800,074
2006	Garrett Gomez	261	20,122,592
2005	John Velazquez	250	20,799,923
2004	John Velazquez	335	22,250,261
2003	Jerry Bailey	206	23,354,960
2002	Jerry Bailey	213	19,271,814
2001	Jerry Bailey	227	19,015,720
2000	Pat Day	267	17,481,863
1999	Pat Day	254	18,094,045
1998	Pat Day	276	17,380,569
1997	Jerry Bailey	272	15,920,743
1996	Jerry Bailey	297	17,815,376
1995	Jerry Bailey	287	16,315,288
1994	Mike Smith	316	15,974,592
1993	Mike Smith	342	14,017,365
1992	Kent Desormeaux	364	14,196,390
1991	Chris McCarron	265	14,437,083
1990	Gary Stevens	283	13,881,198
1989	Jose Santos	285	13,838,389
1988	Jose Santos	369	14,856,214
1987	Jose Santos	305	12,405,075
1986	Jose Santos	328	11,330,067
1985	Laffit Pincay Jr.	289	13,315,049
1984	Chris McCarron	355	11,997,588
1983	Angel Cordero Jr.	362	10,116,697
1982	Angel Cordero Jr.	397	9,675,040

Leading Jockeys of 2007 by Total Earnings

A minimum of 100 mounts is required to be considered for inclusion. Statistics are for North America only and for racing in 2007.

Jockey	No. Mounts	No. Wins	Wins/ Mounts	No. SW	Stakes Wins/ Mounts	No. GSWs	Total Earnings	Average Earnings/ Mount	Leading Earner	Earnings of Leading Earner
Garrett Gomez	1,259	265	21.0%	63	5.0%	35	$22,800,074	$18,110	Indian Blessing	$1,320,000
Robby Albarado	1,260	253	20.1%	31	2.5%	16	19,399,249	15,396	Curlin	5,080,000
John Velazquez	1,127	199	17.7%	42	3.7%	23	18,059,313	16,024	English Channel	2,640,000
Cornelio Velasquez	1,618	262	16.2%	24	1.5%	14	15,997,513	9,887	Kip Deville	1,614,280
Rafael Bejarano	1,468	240	16.4%	21	1.4%	15	15,882,988	10,819	Ginger Punch	1,767,060
Ramon Dominguez	1,337	318	23.8%	33	2.5%	14	15,560,486	11,638	Unbridled Belle	1,096,500
Eibar Coa	1,628	284	17.4%	29	1.8%	8	14,215,407	8,732	Dream Rush	452,085
Edgar Prado	1,116	207	18.6%	40	3.6%	26	13,655,623	12,236	Panty Raid	681,675
Javier Castellano	1,106	168	15.2%	29	2.6%	16	12,550,903	11,348	Timber Reserve	577,600
Julien Leparoux	1,407	262	18.6%	17	1.2%	12	12,205,775	8,675	Shamdinan (Fr)	855,000
Kent Desormeaux	1,091	206	18.9%	26	2.4%	10	11,922,428	10,928	Corinthian	933,000
Victor Espinoza	1,162	185	15.9%	23	2.0%	11	11,817,119	10,170	The Tin Man	536,920
Alan Garcia	1,439	235	16.3%	23	1.6%	10	11,806,322	8,205	Lahudood (GB)	1,553,000
Joseph Talamo	1,472	249	16.9%	20	1.4%	5	10,703,003	7,271	Nashoba's Key	820,290
David Flores	923	161	17.4%	23	2.5%	9	10,413,397	11,282	Awesome Gem	860,000
Eddie Castro	1,380	235	17.0%	22	1.6%	5	10,019,601	7,261	My Typhoon (Ire)	639,000
Calvin Borel	980	146	14.9%	11	1.1%	8	10,006,226	10,210	Street Sense	3,205,000
Michael Baze	1,306	218	16.7%	17	1.3%	8	9,372,717	7,177	Out of Control (Brz)	388,000
Jeremy Rose	1,183	288	24.3%	15	1.3%	7	9,147,449	7,732	Rosinka (Ire)	396,720
Patrick Husbands	729	150	20.6%	17	2.3%	6	9,012,632	12,363	Sealy Hill	949,259
Corey Nakatani	811	116	14.3%	21	2.6%	12	8,895,070	10,968	Lava Man	1,410,000
Emma-Jayne Wilson	1,216	154	12.7%	8	0.7%	2	8,628,499	7,096	Mike Fox	656,561
Elvis Trujillo	1,447	305	21.1%	19	1.3%	8	8,220,006	5,681	Maryfield	780,500
Mario Pino	961	183	19.0%	9	0.9%	2	7,967,128	8,290	Hard Spun	2,512,500
Shaun Bridgmohan	1,025	153	14.9%	17	1.7%	6	7,955,388	7,761	Zanjero	601,617
Richard Migliore	864	115	13.3%	14	1.6%	7	7,186,013	8,317	Student Council	900,000
Russell Baze	1,211	399	33.0%	17	1.4%	1	6,978,044	5,762	Bold Chieftain	268,350
Jose Lezcano	1,089	218	20.0%	12	1.1%	1	6,413,062	5,889	Summer Doldrums	510,000
Manoel Cruz	1,507	291	19.3%	10	0.7%	1	6,386,607	4,238	Calico Bay	331,300
Mike Smith	520	71	13.7%	12	2.3%	10	6,345,175	12,202	Tiago	1,205,950

People — Leading Jockeys of 2007

Jockey	No. Mounts	No. Wins	Wins/ Mounts	No. SW	Stakes Wins/ Mounts	No. GSWs	Total Earnings	Average Earnings/ Mount	Leading Earner	Earnings of Leading Earner
Joe Bravo	843	157	18.6%	15	1.8%	3	$6,313,321	7,489	Joey P.	$ 225,994
Michael Luzzi	1,014	128	12.6%	15	1.5%	6	6,195,295	6,110	Daaher	364,545
Rene Douglas	912	173	19.0%	14	1.5%	4	6,115,222	6,705	Royal Highness (Ger)	448,500
Ramsey Zimmerman	1,123	212	18.9%	11	1.0%	1	5,955,650	5,303	Cloudy's Knight	1,738,860
Alex Solis	630	81	12.9%	7	1.1%	4	5,940,641	9,430	After Market	686,280
Miguel Mena	1,452	215	14.8%	15	1.0%	1	5,858,759	4,035	Miami Sunrise	117,000
Stewart Elliott	972	147	15.1%	14	1.4%	3	5,805,506	5,973	Talkin About Love	286,175
Jamie Theriot	1,163	172	14.8%	11	1.0%	3	5,641,523	4,851	Purim	432,450
Aaron Gryder	889	102	11.5%	7	0.8%	3	5,569,147	6,265	Smokey Stover	449,000
Rajiv Maragh	1,271	165	13.0%	10	0.8%	2	5,535,031	4,355	Hotstufanthensome	129,000
Emile Ramsammy	813	124	15.3%	6	0.7%	3	5,476,002	6,736	Last Answer	226,278
Charles Lopez	924	138	14.9%	9	1.0%	1	5,447,998	5,896	Gottcha Gold	483,000
Corey Lanerie	959	129	13.5%	9	0.9%	1	5,439,142	5,672	Desert Wheat	158,820
Tyler Baze	1,033	135	13.1%	6	0.6%	2	5,374,737	5,203	Black Mamba (NZ)	175,800
Kendrick Carmouche	1,145	206	18.0%	9	0.8%		5,331,615	4,656	Barcola	182,170
Christopher Emigh	1,369	210	15.3%	5	0.4%		5,208,805	3,805	High Expectations	145,972
Tyler Pizarro	951	141	14.8%		0.0%		5,190,452	5,458	Executive Flight	170,361
Harry Vega	936	185	19.8%	6	0.6%		4,785,914	5,113	Premium Wine	157,500
James Graham	1,285	137	10.7%	8	0.6%	1	4,685,873	3,647	West Coast Swing	140,100
Channing Hill	1,172	103	8.8%	4	0.3%		4,652,396	3,970	Malibu Moonshine	151,671
Horacio Karamanos	967	185	19.1%	9	0.9%	1	4,500,586	4,654	Red Giant	600,000
Mark Guidry	575	77	13.4%	10	1.7%	5	4,473,957	7,781	Benny the Bull	257,960
Luis Quinonez	988	200	20.2%	11	1.1%		4,454,303	4,508	Valid Lilly	213,406
Luis Garcia	1,024	173	16.9%	7	0.7%		4,340,188	4,238	Xchanger	238,000
David Clark	527	89	16.9%	7	1.3%	1	4,315,047	8,188	Jiggs Coz	364,277
Martin Garcia	984	118	12.0%	2	0.2%	1	4,302,697	4,373	Stormin Away	129,553
Todd Kabel	342	51	14.9%	10	2.9%	3	4,236,558	12,388	Alezzandro	503,634
Martin Pedroza	855	118	13.8%	9	1.1%	1	4,148,771	4,852	Medici Code (GB)	372,718
J. D. Acosta	1,166	225	19.3%	7	0.6%		4,112,418	3,527	Five Steps	109,440
Jose Valdivia Jr.	648	79	12.2%	6	0.9%	2	4,079,799	6,296	Buzzards Bay	200,400
Dana Whitney	1,378	218	15.8%	5	0.4%		3,991,316	2,896	Bwana Bull	150,000
Jon Court	864	83	9.6%	4	0.5%	3	3,890,891	4,503	Lang Field	375,913
John Jacinto	952	173	18.2%	12	1.3%		3,889,446	4,086	Ahead of Her Time	194,000
Gerard Melancon	942	168	17.8%	4	0.4%		3,858,644	4,096	Golden Yank	190,000
Rex Stokes III	1,347	266	19.8%	4	0.3%		3,815,928	2,833	Country Diva	167,825
Frankie Pennington	943	182	19.3%		0.0%		3,807,169	4,037	Thisonesforsam	98,330
M. Clifton Berry	1,008	178	17.7%	8	0.8%	1	3,697,579	3,668	Going Ballistic	510,140
Jono C. Jones	506	58	11.5%	9	1.8%	3	3,662,783	7,239	Essential Edge	246,966
Eusebio Razo Jr.	854	122	14.3%	6	0.7%	1	3,603,244	4,219	Miss Macy Sue	478,717
Justin Stein	699	67	9.6%	1	0.1%		3,570,453	5,108	Saskawea	237,988
Terry Thompson	1,008	179	17.8%	13	1.3%		3,548,543	3,520	Red Hot N Gold	139.178
Eurico Rosa Da Silva	651	83	12.8%	4	0.6%		3,536,997	5,433	You Will Love Me	320,801
Brice Blanc	563	53	9.4%	7	1.2%	3	3,520,832	6,254	Jack's Wild	213,933
Eduardo Nunez	1,045	148	14.2%	7	0.7%	1	3,516,011	3,365	Finallymadeit	362,450
Eddie Martin Jr.	906	112	12.4%	4	0.4%		3,512,531	3,877	Landofopportunity	86,598
Chantal Sutherland	669	79	11.8%		0.0%		3,480,583	5,203	Red Raffles	151,875
Ken Tohill	899	197	21.9%	7	0.8%		3,477,423	3,868	Good Looker R F	165,600
Jose Luis Flores	1,029	144	14.0%	4	0.4%		3,472,429	3,375	Raging Rapids	206,100
Arnaldo Bocachica	1,120	216	19.3%	1	0.1%		3,375,954	3,014	On My Hip	60,783
Joel Rosario	1,024	154	15.0%	3	0.3%		3,323,006	3,245	Kalookan Year	103,440
Deshawn Parker	1,564	207	13.2%	2	0.1%		3,288,034	2,102	Bernie Blue	256,265
Alfredo Juarez Jr.	827	185	22.4%	11	1.3%		3,223,388	3,898	Romeos Wilson	176,769
Alonso Quinonez	1,171	158	13.5%	4	0.3%		3,184,459	2,719	Plug Me In	120,253
Curt Bourque	957	147	15.4%	2	0.2%		3,177,520	3,320	Star Guitar	84,000
Ryan Fogelsonger	689	90	13.1%	6	0.9%		3,159,870	4,586	Talent Search	499,480
Donnie Meche	953	108	11.3%	3	0.3%		3,159,474	3,315	Tensas Yucatan	202,000
Timothy Doocy	977	137	14.0%	4	0.4%		3,119,044	3,192	Going Ballistic	180,000
Jesse Campbell	793	90	11.4%	7	0.9%		3,106,054	3,917	Mi Isabella	130,800
Daniel Centeno	1,011	168	16.6%	4	0.4%		3,074,483	3,041	Lookinforthesecret	91,300
Christopher DeCarlo	363	68	18.7%	14	3.9%	2	3,069,075	8,455	Twilight Meteor	241,285
Carlos Gonzalez	864	159	18.4%	7	0.8%		3,067,258	3,550	St. Zarb	133,200
Quincy Hamilton	1,091	154	14.1%	8	0.7%	1	3,046,304	2,792	Mending Fences	128,400
Frank Alvarado	765	116	15.2%	6	0.8%	2	3,044,053	3,979	McCann's Mojave	736,600
Chad Phillip Schvaneveldt	668	145	21.7%	6	0.9%	1	3,041,770	4,554	Fantastic Spain	118,900
Eduardo Perez	801	126	15.7%	3	0.4%		2,994,002	3,738	Secret Kin	113,471
Roberto Alvarado Jr.	701	107	15.3%	4	0.6%		2,976,215	4,246	Lila Paige	211,000
Tracy Hebert	846	122	14.4%	4	0.5%	1	2,958,423	3,497	Silent Pleasure	439,400
Jesus Lopez Castanon	764	87	11.4%	3	0.4%		2,954,474	3,867	Junior College	114,046
Scott Spieth	1,082	223	20.6%	3	0.3%		2,954,472	2,731	All Bold	97,733
Gabriel Saez	476	76	16.0%	3	0.6%	1	2,924,747	6,144	Proud Spell	608,770

Leading Jockeys by Average Earnings per Starter in 2007
(Minimum of 10 Mounts)

Jockey	No. Mounts	No. Wins	Average Earnings per Starter
Garrett Gomez	1,259	265	$18,110
John Velazquez	1,127	199	16,024
Robby Albarado	1,260	253	15,396
Todd Kabel	342	51	12,388
Patrick Husbands	729	150	12,363
Edgar Prado	1,116	207	12,236
Mike Smith	520	71	12,206
Ramon Dominguez	1,337	318	11,638
Javier Castellano	1,106	168	11,348
David Flores	923	161	11,283
Corey Nakatani	811	116	10,968
Kent Desormeaux	1,091	206	10,928
Rafael Bejarano	1,468	240	10,819
Calvin Borel	980	146	10,210
Victor Espinoza	1,162	185	10,170
Cornelio Velasquez	1,618	262	9,887
Alex Solis	630	81	9,430
Eibar Coa	1,628	284	8,732
Julien Leparoux	1,407	262	8,675
James McAleney	256	37	8,656
Christopher DeCarlo	363	68	8,455
Richard Migliore	864	115	8,323
Mario Pino	961	183	8,290
Alan Garcia	1,439	235	8,205
David Clark	527	89	8,188
Mark Guidry	575	77	7,781
Shaun Bridgmohan	1,025	153	7,761
Jeremy Rose	1,183	288	7,732
Elvis Joseph Perrodin	283	49	7,602
Joe Bravo	843	157	7,489
Joseph Talamo	1,472	250	7,284
Eddie Castro	1,380	235	7,261
Jono Jones	506	58	7,239
Michael Baze	1,306	218	7,180
Emma-Jayne Wilson	1,216	154	7,096

Leading Jockeys by Number of Stakes Wins in 2007

Jockey	No. Mounts	No. Wins	No. Stakes Wins
Garrett Gomez	1,259	225	76
John Velazquez	1,127	155	55
Edgar Prado	1,116	181	47
Robby Albarado	1,260	213	41
Ramon Dominguez	1,337	264	41
Eibar Coa	1,628	242	36
Javier Castellano	1,106	144	34
Rafael Bejarano	1,468	207	32
Victor Espinoza	1,162	156	31
Elvis Trujillo	1,447	236	30
Cornelio Velasquez	1,618	212	30
David Romero Flores	923	126	29
Kent Desormeaux	1,091	176	28
Alan Garcia	1,439	196	25
Corey Nakatani	811	100	25
Joseph Talamo	1,472	204	25
Eddie Castro	1,380	207	24
Russell Baze	1,211	296	23
Patrick Husbands	729	109	22
Michael Baze	1,306	163	21
Shaun Bridgmohan	1,025	132	21
Julien Leparoux	1,407	225	21
Mike Smith	520	59	20
Paul Nolan	871	124	19
Calvin Borel	980	122	18
Glenn Corbett	815	140	18
Michael Luzzi	1,014	109	18
Jeremy Rose	1,183	225	18

Leading Jockeys by Number of Stakes Winners in 2007

Jockey	Stakes Mounts	Stakes Wnrs
Garrett Gomez	229	63
John Velazquez	167	42
Edgar Prado	154	40
Ramon Dominguez	145	33
Robby Albarado	134	31
Javier Castellano	124	29
Eibar Coa	163	29
Kent Desormeaux	145	26
Cornelio Velasquez	180	25
Victor Espinoza	133	23
David Flores	116	23
Alan Garcia	119	23
Eddie Castro	149	22
Rafael Bejarano	148	21
Corey Nakatani	103	21
Joseph Talamo	115	20
Elvis Trujillo	86	19
Michael Baze	104	17
Russell Baze	42	17
Shaun Bridgmohan	92	17
Patrick Husbands	58	17
Julien Leparoux	134	17
Joe Bravo	92	15
Glenn Corbett	56	15
Michael Luzzi	75	15
Miguel Mena	70	15
Paul Nolan	41	15
Jeremy Rose	69	15
Christopher DeCarlo	53	14
Rene Douglas	78	14
Stewart Elliott	80	14
Richard Migliore	83	14
Terry Thompson	53	13

Leading Jockeys by Percent of Stakes Wins from Mounts in 2007
(Minimum of 10 Mounts)

Jockey	No. Stakes Mounts	No. Stakes Wins	No. Stakes Wins	Stakes Wins/ Mounts
Pamela Peaker	12	4	1	8.3%
David Fowler-Wright	25	8	2	8.0%
April Friesen	27	7	2	7.4%
Nicholas Petro	27	13	2	7.4%
Nathan Condie	28	11	2	7.1%
Garrett Gomez	885	225	63	7.1%
Marcus Delorme	59	19	4	6.8%
Elvis Perrodin	109	33	7	6.4%
John Velazquez	683	155	42	6.1%
Carolyn Stinn	34	7	2	5.9%
Angelle Wilson	140	34	8	5.7%
Christopher DeCarlo	251	60	14	5.6%
Tony McNeil	55	25	3	5.5%

Jockey	No. Stakes Mounts	No. Stakes Wins	No. Stakes Wins	Stakes Wins/ Mounts
Gary Wade	38	6	2	5.3%
Edgar Prado	761	181	40	5.3%
Todd Kabel	195	47	10	5.1%
Patrick Husbands	333	109	17	5.1%
Julio Garcia	80	18	4	5.0%
Hugh Cade Huston	108	34	5	4.6%
Javier Castellano	636	144	29	4.6%
Octavio Vergara	22	1	1	4.5%
Brian Long	221	68	10	4.5%
David Flores	520	126	23	4.4%
Brooke Mellish	122	26	5	4.1%
Mike Smith	293	59	12	4.1%
Corey Nakatani	514	100	21	4.1%
Casey Lambert	150	28	6	4.0%
Zachary Sebreth	75	13	3	4.0%
Glenn Corbett	386	140	15	3.9%
Kent Desormeaux	672	176	26	3.9%

Leading Jockeys by Number of Graded Stakes Wins in 2007

Jockey	No. Starters	No. Wins	No. Graded Stakes Wins	Graded Wins/ Mounts
Garrett Gomez	1,259	265	42	3.3%
John Velazquez	1,127	199	31	2.8%
Edgar Prado	1,116	207	29	2.7%
Robby Albarado	1,260	253	22	1.7%
Rafael Bejarano	1,468	240	22	1.5%
Javier Castellano	1,106	168	19	1.7%
Cornelio Velasquez	1,618	262	18	1.1%
Ramon Dominguez	1,337	318	14	1.0%
Victor Espinoza	1,162	185	14	1.2%
David Flores	923	161	14	1.5%
Mike Smith	520	71	14	2.7%
Calvin Borel	980	146	13	1.3%
Julien Leparoux	1,407	262	13	0.9%
Corey Nakatani	811	116	13	1.6%
Alan Garcia	1,439	235	11	0.8%
Michael Baze	1,306	218	10	0.8%
Eibar Coa	1,628	284	10	0.6%
Kent Desormeaux	1,091	206	10	0.9%
Patrick Husbands	729	150	9	1.2%
Richard Migliore	864	115	9	1.0%
Elvis Trujillo	1,447	305	9	0.6%
Alex Solis	630	81	8	1.3%
Joseph Talamo	1,472	250	8	0.5%
Shaun Bridgmohan	1,025	153	7	0.7%
Eddie Castro	1,380	235	7	0.5%
Michael Luzzi	1,014	128	7	0.7%
Jeremy Rose	1,183	288	7	0.6%
Mark Guidry	575	77	6	1.0%
Mario Pino	961	183	6	0.6%
Rene Douglas	912	173	5	0.5%

Leading Jockeys by Number of Graded Stakes Winners in 2007

Jockey	No. Starters	No. Wnrs	No. Graded Stakes Wnrs	Graded Wnrs/ Mounts
Garrett Gomez	1,259	225	35	2.8%
Edgar Prado	1,116	181	26	2.3%
John Velazquez	1,127	155	23	2.0%
Robby Albarado	1,260	213	16	1.3%
Javier Castellano	1,106	144	16	1.4%
Rafael Bejarano	1,468	207	15	1.0%
Cornelio Velasquez	1,618	213	14	1.4%
Julien Leparoux	1,407	225	12	0.8%
Corey Nakatani	811	100	12	1.5%
Ramon Dominguez	1,337	264	11	0.8%
Victor Espinoza	1,162	156	11	0.9%
Kent Desormeaux	1,091	176	10	0.9%
Alan Garcia	1,439	196	10	0.7%
Mike Smith	520	59	10	1.9%
David Flores	923	126	9	1.0%
Michael Baze	1,306	163	8	0.6%
Calvin Borel	980	122	8	0.8%
Eibar Coa	1,628	242	8	0.5%
Elvis Trujillo	1,447	236	8	0.6%
Richard Migliore	864	93	7	0.8%
Jeremy Rose	1,183	225	7	1.0%
Shaun Bridgmohan	1,025	132	6	0.6%
Patrick Husbands	729	109	6	0.8%
Michael Luzzi	1,014	109	6	0.6%
Eddie Castro	1,380	207	5	0.4%
Mark Guidry	575	71	5	0.9%
Joseph Talamo	1,472	204	5	0.3%
E. T. Baird	532	87	4	0.8%
Rene Douglas	912	149	4	0.4%
Fernando Jara	470	36	4	0.9%
Alex Solis	630	64	4	0.6%
Brice Blanc	563	45	3	0.5%
Joe Bravo	843	131	3	0.4%
Jon Kenton Court	864	62	3	0.3%
Stewart Elliott	972	117	3	0.3%
Aaron Gryder	889	84	3	0.3%
Jono Jones	506	45	3	0.6%
Todd Kabel	342	47	3	0.9%
Larry Melancon	570	54	3	0.5%
Emile Ramsammy	813	92	3	0.4%
Jamie Theriot	1,163	158	3	0.3%

Leading Jockeys by Most Grade 1 Stakes Wins in 2007

Jockey	No. G1 Mounts	No. G1 Wins
Garrett Gomez	60	13
Rafael Bejarano	43	9
John Velazquez	46	9
Robby Albarado	24	6
Javier Castellano	37	5
Mike Smith	25	5
Cornelio Velasquez	34	5
Calvin Borel	16	4
Eibar Coa	25	4
Victor Espinoza	38	4
David Flores	40	4
Patrick Husbands	10	4
Corey Nakatani	35	4
Joseph Talamo	18	4
Ramon Dominguez	27	3
Richard Migliore	21	3
Edgar Prado	26	3
Shaun Bridgmohan	13	2
Eddie Castro	18	2
Rene Douglas	9	2
Alan Garcia	17	2
Julien Leparoux	37	2
Alex Solis	19	2

Leading Jockeys by Most Grade 1 Stakes Winners in 2007

Jockey	No. G1 Mounts	No. G1 Winners
Garrett Gomez	43	10
Rafael Bejarano	32	5
Javier Castellano	24	5
John Velazquez	30	5
Robby Albarado	18	4
Victor Espinoza	27	4
David Romero Flores	30	4
Mike E. Smith	17	4
Cornelio Velasquez	22	4
Calvin Borel	7	3
Eibar Coa	18	3
Ramon Dominguez	18	3
Richard Migliore	15	3
Corey Nakatani	24	3
Edgar Prado	22	3
Joseph Talamo	16	3
Shaun Bridgmohan	11	2
Eddie Castro	12	2
Rene Douglas	8	2
Patrick Husbands	4	2
Julien Leparoux	28	2

Leading Jockeys by Number of Wins in 2007

Jockey	No. Mounts	No. Wnrs	No. Wins
Russell Baze	1,211	296	399
Ramon Dominguez	1,337	264	318
Elvis Trujillo	1,447	236	305
Manoel Cruz	1,507	229	291
Jeremy Rose	1,183	225	288
Eibar Coa	1,628	242	284
Edgar Paucar	1,397	218	271
Rex Stokes III	1,347	214	266
Garrett Gomez	1,259	225	265
Julien Leparoux	1,407	225	262
Cornelio Velasquez	1,618	212	262
Robby Albarado	1,260	213	253
Joseph Talamo	1,472	204	250
Rafael Bejarano	1,468	207	240
Eddie Castro	1,380	207	235
Alan Garcia	1,439	196	235
Rodney Prescott	1,634	186	229
Victor Lebron	1,471	200	228
J. D. Acosta	1,166	186	225
Scott Spieth	1,082	149	223
Michael Baze	1,306	163	218
Jose Lezcano	1,089	191	218
Dana Whitney	1,378	192	218
Arnaldo Bocachica	1,120	176	216
Miguel Mena	1,452	190	215
Ramsey Zimmerman	1,123	176	212
Christopher Emigh	1,369	173	210
Orlando Mojica	1,214	169	207
Deshawn Parker	1,564	153	207
Edgar Prado	1,116	181	207
Kendrick Carmouche	1,145	161	206
Kent Desormeaux	1,091	176	206
Luis Quinonez	988	161	200
John Velazquez	1,127	155	199
Joe Crispin	842	155	198
Ken Tohill	899	154	198
Glenn Corbett	815	140	194
Luis Antonio Gonzalez	1,117	165	194

Leading Jockeys by Number of Winners in 2007

Jockey	No. Mounts	No. Wnrs
Russell Baze	1,211	296
Ramon Dominguez	1,337	264
Eibar Coa	1,628	242
Elvis Trujillo	1,447	236
Manoel Cruz	1,507	229
Garrett Gomez	1,259	225
Julien Leparoux	1,407	225
Jeremy Rose	1,183	225
Edgar Paucar	1,397	218
Rex Stokes III	1,347	214
Robby Albarado	1,260	213
Cornelio Velasquez	1,618	212
Rafael Bejarano	1,468	207
Eddie Castro	1,380	207
Joseph Talamo	1,472	204
Victor Lebron	1,471	200
Alan Garcia	1,439	196
Dana Whitney	1,378	192
Jose Lezcano	1,089	191
Miguel Mena	1,452	190
J. D. Acosta	1,166	186
Rodney Prescott	1,634	186
Edgar Prado	1,116	181
Arnaldo Bocachica	1,120	176
Kent Desormeaux	1,091	176
Ramsey Zimmerman	1,123	176
Christopher Emigh	1,369	173
Orlando Mojica	1,214	169
Luis Antonio Gonzalez	1,117	165
Michael Baze	1,306	163
Kendrick Carmouche	1,145	161
Luis Quinonez	988	161
Jamie Theriot	1,163	158
Victor Espinoza	1,162	156
Joe Crispin	842	155
John Velazquez	1,127	155
Ken Tohill	899	154

Leading Jockeys by Career Purses
Worldwide Earnings

Jockey	Career Purses
Jerry Bailey	$311,356,757
Pat Day	297,912,019
Chris McCarron	257,717,924
Gary Stevens	237,644,302
Laffit Pincay Jr.	237,157,192
Kent Desormeaux	232,669,509 +
Alex Solis	215,356,901 +
Edgar Prado	209,702,685 +
John Velazquez	209,519,267 +
Eddie Delahoussaye	192,469,869
Corey Nakatani	189,969,970 +
Mike Smith	189,457,810 +
Jose Santos	187,255,105
Jorge Chavez	155,993,172 +
Russell Baze	155,806,822 +
Richard Migliore	153,701,403 +
Patrick Valenzuela	150,805,200 +
Robby Albarado	141,559,604 +
David Flores	131,612,336 +
Garrett Gomez	131,296,163 +
Victor Espinoza	123,922,912 +
Shane Sellers	122,431,794
Robbie Davis	115,737,627

People — Leading Jockeys of 2007

Jockey	Career Purses
Eibar Coa	$108,528,091 +
Mario Pino	108,232,704 +
Craig Perret	104,802,090
Joe Bravo	104,433,072 +
Ramon Dominguez	102,034,911 +
Aaron Gryder	101,365,010 +
Mark Guidry	100,857,648 +
Todd Kabel	98,757,717 +
Jorge Velasquez	98,538,544
Javier Castellano	97,674,664
Rene Douglas	97,447,202 +
Cornelio Velasquez	95,672,280 +
Calvin Borel	94,724,956 +
Chris Antley	92,277,031
Jean-Luc Samyn	91,693,362 +
Eddie Maple	91,097,360
Julie Krone	90,125,644
Michael Luzzi	89,788,125 +
Patrick Husbands	79,607,548

+Active through June 24, 2008

Leading Jockeys by Career Wins
Worldwide Wins by North American Jockeys

Jockey	Career Wins
1. Russell Baze	10,182 +
2. Laffit Pincay Jr.	9,530
3. Bill Shoemaker	8,833
4. Pat Day	8,803
5. David Gall	7,396
6. Chris McCarron	7,141
7. Angel Cordero Jr.	7,057
8. Jorge Velasquez	6,795
9. Sandy Hawley	6,449
10. Earlie Fires	6,442 +
11. Larry Snyder	6,388
12. Eddie Delahoussaye	6,384
13. Carl Gambardella	6,349
14. Mario Pino	6,083 +
15. Edgar S. Prado	6,080 +
16. John Longden	6,032
17. Jerry Bailey	5,900
18. Jacinto Vasquez	5,231
19. Ronnie Ardoin	5,225
20. Kent Desormeaux	5,114 +
21. Anthony S. Black	5,109 +
22. Perry Ouzts	5,071 +
23. Mark Guidry	5,043
24. Gary Stevens	5,005
25. Robert Colton	4,979 +
26. Rick Wilson	4,934
27. Timothy Doocy	4,929 +
28. Rudy Baez	4,875
29. Eddie Arcaro	4,779
30. Mike Smith	4,692 +
31. Alex Solis	4,590 +
32. Don Brumfield	4,573
33. Calvin Borel	4,489 +
34. Steve Brooks	4,451
35. Craig Perret	4,413
36. Eddie Maple	4,398
37. Walter Blum	4,382
38. Richard Migliore	4,348 +
39. Jorge F. Chavez	4,335 +
40. Roberto M. Gonzalez	4,318
41. Randy Romero	4,294
42. Jeff Lloyd	4,276
43. Bill Hartack	4,272
44. Ray Sibille	4,264
45. R. D. Williams	4,252 +

Jockey	Career Wins
46. Joe Bravo	4,155 +
47. Nick Santagata	4,117 +
48. Jose Santos	4,083
49. Avelino Gomez	4,081
50. Shane Sellers	4,070

+Active jockeys; statistics through June 24, 2008

Female Jockeys With More Than 1,000 Wins

Jockey	Wins	Active Years
Julie Krone	3,704	1981-2004
Patti Cooksey	2,136	1979-2004
Rosemary Homeister Jr.	1,935	1992-2008
Cindy Noll Murphy	1,833	1990-2006
Jill Jellison	1,771	1982-2005
Vicky Aragon Baze	1,769	1985-2001
Dodie Cartier Duys	1,760	1983-2004
Tammi Piermarini	1,686	1985-2008
Vicki Warhol	1,634	1979-2007
Mary Randall Doser	1,535	1985-2008
Jerri Elizabeth Nichols	1,466	1988-2006
Lori Wydick	1,429	1984-2006
Lillian Kuykendall	1,419	1980-2001
Sandi Lee Gann	1,201	1987-2008
Donna Barton Brothers	1,130	1987-1998
Cynthia Herman Medina	1,116	1986-2004
Diane Nelson	1,095	1986-2007
Patti Barton	1,085	1969-1984

Through June 11, 2008

Most Wins by a Jockey on One Day in 2007

Wins	Jockey	Date	Track(s)
6	Russell Baze	2/23/2007	BM
	Russell Baze	10/18/2007	BM
	Calvin Borel	7/5/2007	CD
	Shaun Bridgmohan	12/22/2007	FG
	Dennis Collins	8/31/2007	CLS
	Joe Crispin	2/5/2007	PM
	Joe Crispin	1/23/2007	PM
	Joe Crispin	12/4/2007	PM
	Francisco Fuentes	11/3/2007	HST
	James Graham	5/24/2007	AP
	Robert King Jr.	8/21/2007	FE
	Julien Leparoux	6/27/2007	CD
	Orlando Mojica	7/7/2007	ELP
	Edgar Prado	3/31/2007	GP
	Ken Tohill	3/25/2007	SUN

Most Wins by a Jockey on One Program in 2007

Wins	Jockey	Date	Track
6	Russell Baze	10/18/2007	BM
	Russell Baze	2/23/2007	BM
	Calvin Borel	7/5/2007	CD
	Shaun Bridgmohan	12/22/2007	FG
	Dennis Collins	8/31/2007	CLS
	Joe Crispin	1/23/2007	PM
	Joe Crispin	12/4/2007	PM
	Joe Crispin	2/5/2007	PM
	Francisco Fuentes	11/3/2007	HST
	James Graham	5/24/2007	AP
	Robert King Jr.	8/21/2007	FE
	Julien Leparoux	6/27/2007	CD
	Orlando Mojica	7/7/2007	ELP
	Edgar Prado	3/31/2007	GP
	Ken Tohill	3/25/2007	SUN

Most Consecutive Wins by a Jockey in 2007

Wins	Jockey	Date(s)	Track(s)
9	Joe Crispin	1/23-1/28/2007	PM
6	J. D. Acosta	9/27-9/28/2007	LRL, CT
	Russell Baze	2/23/2007	BM
	Shaun Bridgmohan	12/22/2007	FG
	Kerwin Clark	8/9-8/11/2007	EVD
	Glenn Corbett	3/12-3/13/2007	TUP
	John Grabowski	5/5-5/6/2007	FL
	Tammi Piermarini	5/9-5/12/2007	SUF
	Chad Schvaneveldt	9/21-9/23/2007	BM

Most Consecutive Wins for a Jockeys Since 1976

Wins	Jockey	Dates	Track(s)
9	Russell Baze	8/17/2006-8/18/2006	BMF
	Joe Crispin	1/23/2007-1/28/2007	PM
8	Maureen Andrews	11/16/1997-11/17/1997	MNR
	Russell Baze	8/31/1984-9/1/1984	SAC, BMF
	Anthony Black	7/31/1992-8/1/1992	ATL, PHA
	Anthony Dlugopolski	4/28/1996-4/29/1996	MNR
	David Gall	9/25/1981-9/26/1981	FP
	D. Jin	3/22/1980-3/25/1980	IMP
	William Passmore	3/5/1976-3/6/1976	BOW
	Leroy. Tauzin	7/14/1978-7/15/1978	ELP
	John Velazquez	4/22/2005-4/24/2005	KEE, HAW
	Robert Williams	5/21/2004-5/22/2004	LNN

Wins	Jockey	Dates	Track(s)
7	Chris Antley	10/31/1987	Aqu, Med
	Russell Baze	8/21/1999-8/22/1999	Bmf, EmD
	Rick Bucholtz	9/21/1986-7/5/1987	MPM
	Perry Compton	4/13/1982-4/14/1982	Fon
	Wendy Dean	5/9/1999-5/16/1999	FtP, BCF
	Richard Depass	3/15/1980	FD
	Stewart Elliott	3/29/1985-3/30/1985	Suf
	Christopher Emigh	11/1/2006-11/2/2006	Haw
	H. F. Enriquez	1/26/1986	AC
	Earlie Fires	5/25/1987	AP
	David A. Gall	10/8/1989	FP
	T. D. Houghton	7/19/1999-7/20/1999	GLD
	Sebastian Madrid	6/15/1991-6/17/1991	Tdn, RD
	Chris McCarron	11/25/1983-11/26/1983	Hol
	Robert Messina	11/23/2001-11/24/2001	FL
	Paul Nicol Jr.	6/7/1983-6/8/1983	Pim
	Perry Ouzts	4/30/1979-5/2/1979	RD
	Mark Patzer	7/10/1981-7/11/1981	EP
	Laffit Pincay Jr.	3/13/1987-3/14/1987	SA
	Clinton Potts	2/7/2001-2/8/2001	Pen
	S. Rodriguez	5/15/1983-5/18/1983	AsD
	Michael Rowland	7/30/2001-8/1/2001	Mnr, Tdn
	Miguel Santiago	9/19/1997-9/20/1997	GBF
	Randy Schacht	8/29/1985-9/5/1985	Sac, Bmf
	Larry Snyder	8/19/1984-8/22/1984	LaD
	Scott Spieth	10/15/2005-10/16/2005	Tdn, Mnr
	Jack Wash	7/22/1993	MD

Leading Jockeys by Earnings in a Year (1994-2007)

Jockey	Year	Earnings	Leading Earner (Earnings)
Jerry Bailey	2003	$23,354,960	Medaglia d'Oro ($1,990,000)
Garrett Gomez	2007	22,800,074	Indian Blessing ($1,320,000)
John Velazquez	2004	22,220,261	Ashado ($1,829,640)
John Velazquez	2005	21,001,171	Flower Alley ($1,916,000)
Garrett Gomez	2006	20,145,988	Wait a While ($1,020,137)
Edgar Prado	2006	19,789,413	Barbaro ($2,203,200)
Robby Albarado	2007	19,399,249	Curlin ($5,080,000)
Jerry Bailey	2002	19,271,814	Medaglia d'Oro ($1,700,000)
Jerry Bailey	2001	19,015,720	Include ($1,210,000)
Edgar Prado	2005	18,624,933	Saint Liam ($963,360)
Edgar Prado	2003	18,477,832	Peace Rules ($1,650,000)
Edgar Prado	2004	18,342,230	Birdstone ($1,200,000)
Jerry Bailey	2005	18,337,384	Saint Liam ($2,733,600)
Pat Day	1999	18,094,045	Cat Thief ($2,585,500)
John Velazquez	2007	18,059,313	English Channel ($2,640,000)
Edgar Prado	2002	18,024,429	Harlan's Holiday ($1,415,000)
Jerry Bailey	1996	17,815,376	Cigar ($2,510,000)
Pat Day	2000	17,481,863	Surfside ($1,147,637)
Jerry Bailey	2000	17,468,690	Perfect Sting ($1,367,000)
Pat Day	1998	17,380,569	Awesome Again ($3,818,090)
Jerry Bailey	1999	17,150,705	Silverbulletday ($947,280)
Jerry Bailey	1998	17,083,428	Skip Away ($2,740,000)
Jorge Chavez	1999	17,013,337	Behrens ($1,735,000)
Gary Stevens	1998	16,708,840	Silver Charm ($2,296,506)
John Velazquez	2002	16,361,445	Storm Flag Flying ($967,000)
Jerry Bailey	1995	16,315,288	Cigar ($4,819,800)
Alex Solis	2003	16,309,490	Pleasantly Perfect ($2,470,000)
Victor Espinoza	2006	16,138,708	The Tin Man ($990,000)
Cornelio Velasquez	2007	15,997,513	Kip Deville ($1,614,280)
Mike Smith	1994	15,974,592	Holy Bull ($2,095,000)
Victor Espinoza	2004	15,931,157	Southern Image ($1,612,150)
Jerry Bailey	1997	15,920,743	Behrens ($894,000)
Pat Day	2002	15,904,396	With Anticipation ($1,498,500)
Rafael Bejarano	2007	15,882,988	Ginger Punch ($1,767,060)
Patrick Valenzuela	2003	15,699,752	Adoration ($1,160,750)
John Velazquez	2006	15,637,056	English Channel ($1,240,000)
Ramon Dominguez	2007	15,560,486	Unbridled Belle ($1,096,500)
John Velazquez	2003	15,463,963	Strong Hope ($582,360)
Gary Stevens	1997	15,380,137	Gentlemen (Arg) ($2,125,300)

Notable Names in Racing's Past

(Names of Racing Hall of Fame members are in boldface italics.)

As much as great horses are central to the sport, Thoroughbred racing and breeding would not exist without the important individuals of the past who worked to perfect the breed or sport and who performed with distinction within the industry. Here are outstanding individuals from racing's history, with members of the Racing Hall of Fame noted in boldface italics.

Adams, Frank D. "Dooley," 1927-2004. Jockey, trainer. Leading steeplechase jockey 1946, '49-'55; inducted into Racing Hall of Fame in '70. Rode 337 winners, including Neji, Elkridge, Oedipus, Refugio, and Floating Isle. Trained Subversive Chick.

Adams, John H., 1914-'95. Jockey, trainer. Leading jockey 1937, '42, '43; inducted into Racing Hall of Fame in '65; George Woolf Memorial Jockey Award in '56. Rode 3,270 winners, including *Kayak II, Hasty Road. Trained J. O. Tobin. Won 1954 Preakness Stakes aboard Hasty Road.

Aga Khan III, Sultan Sir Mahomed Shah, 1877-1957. Ismaili Muslim leader. Owner of Gilltown, Sheshoon, Ballymany, Sallymount, and Ongar Studs in Ireland; Haras de la Coquenne, Haras de Marly-la-Ville, Haras de Saint-Crespin in France. Leading owner in England 13 times; leading breeder in England eight times. Bred *Bahram, *Nasrullah, *Tulyar, *Mahmoud, *Alibhai, *Khaled, *Masaka; owned Mumtaz Mahal, *Blenheim II. Grandfather of current Aga Khan.

Alexander, Alexander J., 1824-1902. Iron works, farming. Owner of Woodburn Stud, Kentucky. Stood leading sire Lexington. Leading breeder. Bred Duke of Magenta, Spendthrift, Tom Bowling, Tom Ochiltree, Harry Bassett, Joe Daniels, Fellowcraft, Fonso, etc. Brother of Robert A. Alexander.

Alexander, Robert A., 1819-'67. Iron works, farming. Founder of Woodburn Stud, Kentucky. Stood leading sire Lexington. Leading breeder. Bred Norfolk, Asteroid, Maiden, Virgil, Preakness, etc. Brother of Alexander J. Alexander.

Annenberg, Moses L., 1878-1942. Publisher. Published *Daily Racing Form* 1922-'42, *Morning Telegraph.* Founded Triangle Publications.

Annenberg, Walter, 1908-2002. Former publisher, *Daily Racing Form.* Took control of his family's Triangle Publications Inc. in 1940 and built largest private publishing empire in the country; ambassador to Great Britain 1968-'74. Sold publishing enterprises by late 1980s. Son of publisher Moses Annenberg.

Appleton, Arthur, 1915-2008. Electrical manufacturing. Owner of Bridlewood Farm, Florida. Bred and owned Jolie's Halo, Wild Event. Owned Skip Trial.

Arcaro, Eddie, 1916-'97. Jockey. Inducted into Racing Hall of Fame in '58; George Woolf Memorial Jockey Award in '53. Rode 4,779 winners, including Whirlaway, Citation, Bold Ruler, Nashua. Won two Triple Crowns, five Kentucky Derbys, six Preakness Stakes, and six Belmont Stakes.

Archer, Fred, 1857-'86. Jockey. Winner of 12 consecutive riding titles in England (1874-'85) and rode 2,748 career winners, a record that stood for 57 years. Won 21 classic races, including five Epsom Derbys with Silvio, Bend Or, Iroquois, Melton, *Ormonde.

Atkinson, Ted F., 1916-2005. Jockey, racing official. Leading jockey by money won in 1944, '46; leading jockey by races won in 1944, '46; inducted into Racing Hall of Fame in '57; George Woolf Memorial Jockey Award in '57. Rode 3,795 winners, including Tom Fool, Gallorette, Devil Diver. Rode 1953 Horse of the Year Tom Fool to handicap triple crown; first jockey whose mounts earned more than $1-million in one year (1946).

Bacon, Mary, 1948-'91. Pioneer female jockey; rode 286 winners.

Baird, Dale, 1935-2007. Trainer. Leading American trainer by annual winners 15 times. On November 5, 2004, became the first trainer to saddle more than 9,000 career winners. Inducted into National HBPA Hall of Fame in 2001. Based at Mountaineer Racetrack in West Virginia. Special Eclipse Award in 2004.

Baldwin, Elias J. "Lucky," 1828-1909. Mining, investments. Owned Rancho el Santa Anita, California. Bred and owned Emperor of Norfolk, Volante, Rey El Santa Anita, Americus. Built original Santa Anita Park racetrack.

Barbee, George, ca. 1855-1941. Jockey. Inducted into Racing Hall of Fame in 1996. Rode Saxon, Survivor, Shirley, Jacobus. Won the first Preakness Stakes aboard Survivor in 1873; won two other Preakness Stakes and one Belmont Stakes.

Barrera, Lazaro, 1924-'91. Trainer. Eclipse Award trainer 1976-'79; leading trainer by money won in 1977-'80; inducted into Racing Hall of Fame in '79. Trained more than 140 stakes winners and six champions, including Affirmed, Bold Forbes.

Bassett, Carroll K., 1905-'72. Jockey. Inducted into Racing Hall of Fame in 1972. Rode more than 100 steeplechase winners, including Battleship, Peacock, Night Retired, Passive, Sable Muff. Rode Battleship to victory in the American Grand National and two National Steeplechase Hunt Cups.

Beard, Louis A., 1888-1954. Farm manager, racing executive. Managed Greentree Stud 1927-'48. Co-founder and president, Keeneland Race Course; co-founder, American Thoroughbred Breeders' Association; co-founder, Grayson Foundation.

Bedwell, H. Guy, 1876-1951. Trainer. Leading trainer by races won in 1909, '12-'17; leading trainer by money won in 1918-'19; inducted into Racing Hall of Fame in '71. Trained 2,160 winners, including Sir Barton, Billy Kelly. First trainer to saddle a Triple Crown winner (Sir Barton in 1919); won 16 races in 14 days in 1910.

Bell, John A. III, 1918-2007. Owner, breeder, bloodstock agent. Owned Jonabell Farm, Kentucky. Bred Battlefield, Aglimmer, One for All, Never Say Die. Owned Epitome. Former president of *The Blood-Horse* magazine; acquired half-interest in Cromwell Bloodstock Agency in 1950.

Belmont, August I, 1816-'90. Banker. President of American Jockey Club (Jerome Park) 1866-'86. Owner of Nursery Stud in New York and later in Kentucky. Leading owner. Bred and owned Woodbine, Potomac, Fides, Prince Royal; also owned Glenelg, Fenian, *The Ill-Used.

Belmont, August II, 1853-1924. Banker. First president of Belmont Park; chairman, Jockey Club 1895-1924; chairman, Belmont Park. Owned Nursery Stud, Kentucky. Leading breeder. Bred Man o' War, Fair Play, Tracery, Beldame; also owned *Hourless, Henry of Navarre.

Bieber, Isidor, 1887-1974. Restaurateur, gambler. Co-owner of Bieber-Jacobs Stable, Stymie Manor, Mary-

land. Leading breeder 1964-'67; co-breeder of Hail to Reason, Allez France, Affectionately, Straight Deal; also co-owned Stymie, Searching.

Bobinski, Kazimierz, 1905-'69. Russian-born pedigree authority. In collaboration with Stefan Zamoyski, authored the landmark *Family Tables of Racehorses, Volumes I & II*, which expanded on the work of Bruce Lowe and Hermann Goos.

Bostwick, George, 1909-'82. Jockey, trainer. Leading amateur steeplechase jockey 1928-'32, '41; leading steeplechase trainer 1940, '51, '55; inducted into Racing Hall of Fame in 1968. Rode 87 winners, including Chenango, Escapade, Sussex, Darkness. Trained Neji and Oedipus. Played on six United States championship polo teams.

Boussac, Marcel, 1889-1980. Textile tycoon. Leading French breeder 19 times, winner of the Prix du Jockey-Club (French Derby) 12 times. Bred notable racehorses or sires Tourbillon, Pharis, Djebel, *Goya II, and *Ambiorix. In 1950 became first foreign owner to lead English owners list, the year he won the Epsom Derby with Galcador. Also bred and owned two-time Prix de l'Arc de Triomphe winner Corrida.

Bowie, Oden, 1826-'94. Railways, politician. Maryland governor 1869-'72; first president of Pimlico Race Course in 1870. Owner of Fairview Plantation, Maryland. Bred Catesby, Crickmore.

Bradley, Edward R., 1859-1946. Gambler. Owner of Idle Hour Stock Farm, Kentucky. Bred and owned Blue Larkspur, Bimelech, Black Helen, Busher, Bubbling Over. Bred and owned four Kentucky Derby winners and imported foundation mare *La Troienne.

Brady, James Cox Jr., 1908-'71. Investments. Chairman of Jockey Club 1961-'69; chairman of New York Racing Association 1961-'69. Owner of Dixiana Farm, Kentucky, and Hamilton Stable. Bred Long Look, War Plumage, Jungle Cove. Co-founder of Monmouth Park, American Horse Council; oversaw rebuilding of Belmont Park. Father of Nicholas J. Brady, United States treasury secretary 1988-'93, and chairman of the Jockey Club 1976-'82.

Brooks, Steve, 1922-'79. Jockey. Leading jockey in 1949; inducted into Racing Hall of Fame in 1963; George Woolf Memorial Jockey Award in 1962. Rode 4,451 winners, including Two Lea, Citation, Round Table. Rode Ponder in 1949 Kentucky Derby.

Brown, Edward D. "Brown Dick," 1850-1906. Trainer, jockey. Inducted into Racing Hall of Fame in 1984. Trained Ben Brush, Plaudit, Spendthrift, Hindoo. Rode Asteroid to an undefeated 9-for-9 record in 1864-'65.

Brown, Harry D. "Curly," 1863-1930. Restaurateur, racetrack executive. Founder and first president of Arlington Park; built Laurel Park, Oriental Park. Owned Brown Shasta Farm, California.

Bruce, Benjamin G., 1827-'91. Publisher. Founder and editor of the *Livestock Record* 1875-'91 (predecessor of *The Thoroughbred Record*). Brother of Sanders D. Bruce.

Bruce, Sanders D., 1825-1902. Hotelier, publisher. Co-editor of *Turf, Field and Farm* 1865-1902. Compiler of first four volumes of *American Stud Book*. Brother of Benjamin G. Bruce.

Bull, Phil, 1910-'89. Handicapper, gambler, owner, breeder, publisher. In 1948 launched *Timeform*, a British Thoroughbred industry information service that annually assesses the individual merits of thousands of runners. Founded Hollins Stud; bred champion Romulus.

Burch, Preston, 1884-1978. Trainer, breeder, owner. Leading trainer in 1950; inducted into Racing Hall of Fame in 1963. Trained more than 70 stakes winners, including George Smith, Sailor, Flower Bowl, Bold. Bred Gallorette. Trained stakes winners in New York, Canada, Cuba, France, and Italy. Wrote influential book on training, *Training Thoroughbred Horses*. Son of William P. Burch; father of Racing Hall of Fame trainer J. Elliott Burch.

Burch, William P., 1846-1926. Trainer. Inducted into Racing Hall of Fame in 1955. Trained Grey Friar, My Own, Decanter. First of three generations of Hall of Fame trainers. Father of Preston Burch.

Burke, Carleton F., 1882-1962. Banker, farmer. First chairman of California Horse Racing Board 1933-'39.

Burlew, Fred, 1871-1927. Trainer. Inducted into Racing Hall of Fame in 1973. Trained 32 stakes winners and two champions, including Beldame, Morvich, Inchcape.

Burns, Tommy H., 1879-1913. Jockey. Leading jockey by races won in 1898-'99; inducted into Racing Hall of Fame in 1983. Rode 1,333 winners, including Broomstick, Imp, Caughnawaga. Set an American record in the 1¼-mile Brighton Beach Handicap aboard Broomstick.

Butler, James Sr., 1855-1934. Grocery-chain owner. Owner of Empire City racetrack. Owner of East View Farm, New York. Bred Questionnaire, Sting, Pebbles, Spur; owned Comely.

Butler, James II, 1891-1940. Grocery-chain owner. President of Empire City Racing Association. Owner of East View Farm, New York.

Butwell, James, 1896-1956. Jockey, racing official. Leading jockey in 1912; leading jockey by races won in '20; inducted into Racing Hall of Fame in '84. Rode 1,402 winners, including Roamer, Sweep, Hilarious, Maskette. Leading American jockey by number of wins at the time of his retirement.

Byers, J. Dallett "Dolly," 1898-1966. Jockey, trainer. Leading steeplechase jockey 1918, '21, '28; leading jockey by money won in '28; inducted into Racing Hall of Fame in '67. Rode 149 winners, including Jolly Roger, Fairmount. Trained Tea-Maker, Lovely Night, Invader. Won the Temple Gwathmey Steeplechase Handicap five years in a row.

Byrnes, Matthew, 1854-1933. Jockey, trainer. Rode Glenelg, Kingfisher; trained Racing Hall of Fame members Parole, Salvator, Firenze.

Caldwell, Thomas, 1928-2001. Auctioneer. Auctioneer and director of auctions for the Keeneland Association 1975-2001. Owned Gavel Ranch, Oregon.

Campbell, John B., 1876-1954. Racing executive. Racing secretary and handicapper at New York tracks 1935-'54. Handicapped three-way dead heat in 1944 Carter Handicap.

Capossela, Fred, 1903-'91. Famed race caller at New York racetracks 1943-'71.

Cassidy, Mars, 1862-1929. Racing executive. Legendary starter at New York racetracks 1902-'29. Father of Marshall Cassidy.

Cassidy, Marshall, 1892-1968. Racing executive. Executive secretary of Jockey Club. Developed first modern starting gate; developed modern photo-finish camera; instituted first film patrol and saliva tests; founded Jockey Club Round Table meetings. Son of Mars Cassidy.

Cella, Charles, 1875-1940. Hotelier, theater owner. Founder of Oaklawn Park; co-owner of Fort Erie racetrack.

Chenery, Christopher T., 1886-1973. Utilities. First president of Thoroughbred Owners and Breeders As-

sociation. Owner of Meadow Stud, Virginia. Bred Secretariat, Riva Ridge, Hill Prince, Cicada, First Landing, Sir Gaylord. Co-founder of New York Racing Association.

Childs, Frank E., 1886-1973. Trainer. Inducted into Racing Hall of Fame in 1968. Trained 23 stakes winners, including *Tomy Lee, Canina, Dinner Gong. Known for his ability to turn claiming horses into stakes winners.

Chinn, Philip T., 1874-1962. Horse trader. Owner of Himyar Stud, Kentucky. Bred 58 stakes winners, including Miss Merriment, Black Maria, In Memoriam, High Resolve. Leading consignor at Saratoga in 1920s; sold then-record $70,000 yearling in '27.

Clark, Henry S., 1904-'99. Trainer. Inducted into Racing Hall of Fame in 1982. Trained 37 stakes winners and one champion, including Tempted, Cyane, Endine, Obeah. Twice won back-to-back Delaware Handicaps.

Clark, John C., 1891-1974. Advertising executive. President of Hialeah Park 1940-'54; first president of Thoroughbred Racing Associations 1942-'43. Owned Sun Briar Court, New York. Bred Charlie McAdam, Accomplish.

Clark, John H. "Trader," 1919-'96. Horse trader, author. President, Thoroughbred Breeders of Kentucky. Author of *Trader Clark*.

Clark, Meriwether Lewis, 1846-'99. Racing executive. Founder and president of Louisville Jockey Club. Founder of Kentucky Derby in 1875. Established first uniform scale of weights in America.

Clay, Albert, 1917-2002. Farmer, burley warehousing. Breeder or co-breeder of at least 20 stakes winners, including Albert the Great, Seaside Attraction, Gorgeous, Pompeii, George Navonod; helped to found the American Horse Council and was instrumental in establishing the University of Kentucky's Maxwell H. Gluck Equine Research Center. Father of Three Chimneys Farm owner Robert Clay.

Clay, Ezekiel F., 1841-1920. Farmer, breeder. President, Kentucky Racing Association. Co-owner of Runnymede Farm, Kentucky. Chairman of Kentucky Racing Commission. Bred Hanover, Sir Dixon, Miss Woodford, Raceland.

Clay, Henry, 1777-1852. Lawyer, politician. Owner of Ashland Stud, Kentucky. Bred Heraldry. Father of John M. Clay.

Clay, John M., 1820-'87. Farmer, breeder. Owner of Ashland Stud, Kentucky. Bred Kentucky, Maggie B. B., Daniel Boone, Simon Kenton, Gilroy, Star Davis, Lodi, Day Star. Son of Henry Clay.

Cocks, W. Burling, 1915-'98. Trainer. Leading steeplechase trainer 1949, '65, '73, '80; inducted into Racing Hall of Fame in '85; F. Ambrose Clark Award in '73. Trained 49 stakes winners, including six American Grand National winners. Trained Zaccio, Down First.

Coe, William R., 1869-1955. Insurance, financier. Owner of Shoshone Farm, Kentucky. Bred and owned Pompey, Pompoon; owned Ladysman, Cleopatra, Black Maria, Pilate.

Cole, Ashley T., 1876-1965. New York industry leader. Chairman of the New York State Racing Commission 1945-'65; president of the National Association of State Racing Commissioners. Involved in organizing the not-for-profit New York Racing Association, in building the new Aqueduct Race Course, and in developing the New York breeders awards program.

Coltiletti, Frank, 1904-'87. Jockey, trainer, racing official. Inducted into Racing Hall of Fame in 1970. Rode 667 winners, including Mars, Crusader, Sun Beau. Won Preakness Stakes at age 17 aboard Broomspun in 1921.

Combs, Leslie II, 1901-'90. Breeder. Owner of Spendthrift Farm, Kentucky. Leading breeder in 1972. Chairman of Kentucky Racing Commission. Bred 247 stakes winners, including Majestic Prince, Myrtle Charm, Idun, Mr. Prospector. Originated modern stallion syndicates in 1950s.

Conway, James P., 1910-'84. Trainer. Inducted into Racing Hall of Fame in 1996. Trained 43 stakes winners and five champions, including Chateaugay, Primonetta, Grecian Queen. Won 1963 Kentucky Derby and Belmont Stakes with three-year-old champion colt Chateaugay.

Corrigan, Edward, 1854-1924. Railway investor. Founded Hawthorne Race Course. Raced *McGee.

Corum, M. W. "Bill," 1895-1958. President of Churchill Downs (1949-'58). Sports writer for the New York *Journal-American*. In 1925 coined the phrase "run for the roses" to describe the Kentucky Derby.

Cowdin, John E., 1859-1941. Silk merchant. President of Queens County Jockey Club (Aqueduct).

Crawford, Robert H. "Specs," 1897-1975. Jockey, trainer. Leading steeplechase jockey 1919-'20, '22, '26; inducted into Racing Hall of Fame in '73. Rode 139 winners, including Jolly Roger, Fairmount, Lytle, Erne II. Won four American Grand Nationals.

Croker, Richard "Boss," 1841-1922. Real estate, politician. Head of New York's Tammany Hall political machine. Owner of Glencairn Stud, Ireland. Bred Orby, Rhodora, Grand Parade.

Croll, Warren A. "Jimmy" Jr., 1920-2008. Trainer. Inducted into Racing Hall of Fame in 1994; United Thoroughbred Trainers of America Outstanding Trainer Award in '94; Big Sport of Turfdom Award in '95; Mr. Fitz Award in '95. Owned and trained Holy Bull. Trained Mr. Prospector, Bet Twice, Parka, Forward Gal, Housebuster.

Cromwell, Thomas B., 1871-1957. Publisher, bloodstock agent. Founded *The Blood-Horse*, Cromwell Bloodstock agency. Credited with refining past performance charts.

Crosby, H. L. "Bing," 1903-'77. Entertainer. First president of Del Mar Turf Club 1936-'46. Co-owner of Binglin Stock Farm, California. Owned *Meadow Court, *Ligaroti, *Don Bingo, *Blackie II.

Daingerfield, Algernon, 1867-1941. Racing executive. Executive secretary of Jockey Club. Son of Foxhall Daingerfield.

Daingerfield, Elizabeth, 1870-1951. Farm manager. Owner of Haylands Farm. Managed Wickliffe Stud, Faraway Farm. Managed leading sires Man o' War, High Time. Daughter of Foxhall Daingerfield.

Daingerfield, Foxhall A., ca. 1840-1913. Farm manager. Managed stud careers of Domino, Commando, Ben Brush, Kingston at Castleton Stud, Kentucky. Father of Algernon and Elizabeth Daingerfield.

Daingerfield, J. Keene, 1910-'93. Racing executive, author. Kentucky state steward 1973-'85. Eclipse Award of Merit in 1989. Author of *Training for Fun and Profit (Maybe)*. Grandson of Foxhall Daingerfield.

Daly, Marcus, 1842-1900. Mining. Owner of Bitter Root Stock Farm, Montana. Bred *Ogden, Tammany; owned Hamburg.

Daly, William C. "Father Bill," 1837-1931. Trainer. Famous mentor of Racing Hall of Fame jockeys James McLaughlin, Snapper Garrison, Winnie O'Connor, Danny Maher.

DeBartolo, Edward J., 1909-'94. Real estate developer. Owned Louisiana Downs, Thistledown, Remington Park. Special Eclipse Award in 1988.

De Francis, Frank, 1927-'89. Lawyer, racing executive. Owner of King of Mardi Gras, Hail Emperor. Led groups to buy Laurel Park in 1984 and Pimlico Race Course in '86, thus consolidating ownership of Maryland racetracks.

de Kwiatkowski, Henryk, 1924-2003. Aviation. Owner of Calumet Farm, Kentucky; Kennelot Stable. Joe Palmer Award in 1993. Owned Conquistador Cielo, De La Rose, Danzig, Stephan's Odyssey, Sabin. Bought bankrupt Calumet Farm for $17-million at public auction in 1992.

DeLancey, James, 1732-1801. Real estate. Owner of Bouwerie Farm, New York. Bred Maria Slamerkin, Bashaw. Imported *DeLancey's Cub mare (great American foundation mare), *Lath, *Wildair.

Delp, Grover G. "Bud," 1932-2006. Trainer. Eclipse Award trainer in 1980. Inducted into Racing Hall of Fame in 2002. Trained Spectacular Bid, Include, Timeless Native, Aspro, Silent King.

Dixon, F. Eugene, 1923-2006. Investments. Owner of Erdenheim Farm in Pennsylvania, formerly owned by his uncle George D. Widener. Chairman of the Pennsylvania Horse Racing Commission. Former owner of Philadelphia 76ers basketball team.

Donn, James Sr., 1887-1972. Landscaping contractor, nursery owner. Chairman of Gulfstream Park 1944-'72. Grandfather of former Gulfstream Park executive Douglas Donn.

Donoghue, Steve, 1884-1945. Jockey. Winner of ten consecutive riding titles in England (1914-'23). Rode six Epsom Derby winners: Humorist, Captain Cuttle, *Papyrus, Manna, Pommern, Gay Crusader. Rode 1,840 winners in a 33-year career.

Doswell, Thomas W., 1792-1890. Tobacco plantations. Owner of Bullfield Plantation. Bred Planet, Eolus, Algerine, Morello, Fanny Washington; owner of Knight of Ellerslie, Nina, Abd-el-Kader. Mentor and partner of Capt. Richard Hancock, who established Ellerslie Stud.

Dragone, Allan, 1926-2006. Racetrack and manufacturing executive. Former chairman of New York Racing Association. Owned Canadian champion Term Limits, Grade 1 winner Vergennes.

Drayton, Spencer, 1911-'94. FBI special agent who, upon recommendation of J. Edgar Hoover, in 1946 became the first head of the Thoroughbred Racing Protective Bureau. Served as TRPB president until his retirement in 1978. Inaugurated lip tattoos as a means of horse identification.

Duke, William, 1858-1926. Trainer. Inducted into Racing Hall of Fame in 1956. Trained Flying Ebony, Coventry. Won the 1924 French Derby with *Pot Au Feu; won '25 Kentucky Derby with Flying Ebony; won '25 Preakness Stakes with Coventry.

Dunn, Neville, 1904-'57. Publisher, editor. Editor of *The Thoroughbred Record* 1941-'57. Co-founder of Thoroughbred Club of America.

duPont, Allaire (Mrs. Richard C.), 1913-2006. Investments. Owner of Woodstock Farm, Maryland; Bohemia Stable, Maryland. Member of Jockey Club. Thoroughbred Owners and Breeders Association award for Maryland in 1984. Bred and owned Politely, Believe the Queen. Bred and raced Kelso, only five-time Horse of the Year (1960-'64); one of the first three women inducted into Jockey Club, in 1983.

duPont, William Jr., 1897-1966. Banker. Owner of Walnut Hall Farm, Virginia. Bred and owned Parlo, Berlo, Rosemont, Fairy Chant, Ficklebush; owned Fair Star, Dauber. Founder of Delaware Park.

Duryea, Herman B., 1862-1916. Investments. Owner of Haras du Gazon, France. Leading owner in 1904, when leasing W. C. Whitney's horses. Co-bred and owned *Durbar II, Banshee, *Sweeper; also co-owned Irish Lad.

Dwyer, Michael F., 1847-1906. Meat processor. Leading owner. Owned or co-owned Hindoo, Hanover, Miss Woodford, Kingston, Luke Blackburn, Bramble, Ben Brush, Tremont, etc. Brother of Philip J. Dwyer.

Dwyer, Philip J., 1843-1917. Meat processor. President of Brooklyn Jockey Club (Gravesend), Queens County Jockey Club (Aqueduct). Leading owner. Co-owned Hindoo, Hanover, Miss Woodford, Kingston, Luke Blackburn, Bramble, Tremont, etc. Brother of Michael F. Dwyer.

Easton, William, ca. 1850-1909. Auctioneer. American representative of Tattersalls; auctioneer for Fasig-Tipton Co. First great American auctioneer.

Ellis, James C., 1872-1956. Oilman, banker, Thoroughbred breeder, racetrack owner. In 1925 he acquired Dade Park racetrack in Henderson, Kentucky, at court auction. Thirty years later the track's name was changed to James C. Ellis Park.

Ellsworth, Rex, 1907-'97. Rancher. Owner of Ellsworth Farm, California. Leading owner and breeder 1962-'63. Bred and owned Swaps, Candy Spots, Olden Times, Prove It; owned *Prince Royal II; imported *Khaled.

Engelhard, Charles W., 1917-'71. Precious metals. Owner of Cragwood Stable. Leading owner in England in 1970. Owned Nijinsky II, *Hawaii, Assagai, Ribocco, Ribero, Halo, Mr. Leader, Indiana.

Ensor, Lavelle "Buddy," 1900-'47. Jockey. Inducted into Racing Hall of Fame in 1962. Rode 411 winners, including Exterminator, Grey Lag, Hannibal. Rode 33 winners in 11 days, including five of six races on one of those days, in 1919.

Estes, Joseph A., 1902-'70. Journalist. Editor of *The Blood-Horse* 1930-'63. Devised Average Earnings Index; established Jockey Club Statistical Bureau.

Evans, Thomas Mellon, 1910-'97. Mergers and acquisitions. Owner of Buckland Farm. Bred and owned Pleasant Colony, Pleasant Tap, Pleasant Stage.

Fairbairn, Robert A., 1867-1951. Financier. Owner of Fairholme Farm, Kentucky. Bred Gallahadion, Hoop, Jr. Co-owner of *Sir Gallahad III, *Blenheim II.

Fasig, William B., 1846-1902. Auctioneer. Co-founder of Fasig-Tipton Co. in 1898. Conducted first equine auctions in Madison Square Garden.

Fator, Laverne, 1900-'36. Jockey. Leading jockey 1925-'26; inducted into Racing Hall of Fame in '55. Rode 1,075 winners, including Grey Lag, Black Maria, Pompey, Scapa Flow. Won consecutive runnings of Belmont Futurity and Carter and Gazelle Handicaps.

Feustel, Louis, 1884-1970. Trainer. Leading trainer in 1920; inducted into Racing Hall of Fame in '64. Trained two champions and Man o' War, Rock View, Ordinance, Ladkin. Won 20 of 21 races with Man o' War.

Field, Marshall W. III, 1893-1956. Publisher, retailer. Bred High Quest, High Strung, Escutcheon, Clang, Eclair; owned Nimba, Stimulus.

Fink, Jule, 1913-'90. Thoroughbred owner-breeder and noted handicapper. Known as one of the "Speed Boys," his gambling success resulted in Jockey Club refusing to renew his owner's license in 1949. His subsequent suit against Jockey Club led to a significant reduction in the club's power over racing, but the New York State Racing and Wagering Board continued the

ban until 1967. He was a partner in 1966 Santa Anita Derby winner Boldnesian.

Finney, Humphrey S., 1903-'84. Auctioneer. Chairman of Fasig-Tipton Co. 1952-'84. Founded *Maryland Horse*; author of *A Stud Farm Diary, Fair Exchange*. Father of John M. S. Finney.

Finney, John M. S., 1934-'94. Auctioneer. President Fasig-Tipton Co. 1968-'89. Son of Humphrey Finney.

Fisher, Charles T., 1880-1964. Automobile manufacturer. Owner of Dixiana Farm, Kentucky. Bred Spy Song, Mata Hari, Sweep All, Star Reward.

Fitzsimmons, James E. "Sunny Jim," 1874-1966. Trainer. Leading trainer 1930, '32, '36, '39, '55; inducted into Racing Hall of Fame in '58. Trained 2,275 winners, 155 stakes winners, including Triple Crown winners Gallant Fox and Omaha, and eight champions, including Bold Ruler, Nashua, Granville.

Forrest, Henry, 1906-1975. Trainer. Conditioned runners for such clients as Claiborne and Calumet Farm during his 38-year career between 1937 and '75. Saddled Kentucky Derby-Preakness Stakes winners Kauai King in 1966 and Forward Pass in 1968. One of the all-time leading trainers at Churchill Downs (271 wins) and Keeneland Race Course (153). Inducted into the Racing Hall of Fame in 2007.

Franks, John, 1925-2004. Oil production. Owner of Franks Farms, Louisiana; Louisiana Stallions, Louisiana; Southland Farm, Florida. Co-owner of Heatherten Farm, Maryland. Leading owner by money won in 1983-'84, '86, '93; leading owner by races won in 1983-'84, '86-'89; leading breeder by races won in 1988-'93; Eclipse Award owner in 1983-'84, '93-'94. Bred and owned Answer Lively, Derby Wish, Kissin Kris. Bred Sharp Cat, Royal Anthem. Owned Heatherten, Dave's Friend, Top Avenger. Earned $3.1-million in 1984, then a single-season record for owners.

Fustok, Mahmoud, 1936-2006. Owner-breeder. Owner of the Buckram Oak. Raced Breeders' Cup Sprint (G1) winner Silver Train, champion Green Forest, classic winner In Fijar.

Gaines, John R., 1928-2005. Breeder. Former chairman, Breeders' Cup Ltd. Founder of Gainesway Farm, Kentucky. Eclipse Award of Merit in 1984; John W. Galbreath Award in '93. Bred Halo, Silent King, Time Limit. Owned Bold Bidder, Oil Royalty. Founder of Breeders' Cup, Kentucky Horse Park; assisted in developing the Maxwell H. Gluck Center for Equine Research at the University of Kentucky.

Galbreath, John W., 1897-1988. Real estate developer. Owned Darby Dan Farm, Kentucky and Ohio. Eclipse Award, Man of the Year in 1972. Bred and owned Roberto, Chateaugay, Primonetta, Little Current, Graustark, His Majesty, Proud Truth, Proud Clarion. Instrumental in rebuilding of Belmont Park and Aqueduct.

Garner, J. Mack, 1900-'36. Jockey. Leading jockey by races won in 1915; leading jockey by money won in '29; inducted into Racing Hall of Fame in '69. Rode 1,346 winners, including Cavalcade, Blue Larkspur. Won 1934 Kentucky Derby on Cavalcade.

Garrison, Edward R. "Snapper," 1868-1930. Jockey, stable agent, trainer, racing official. Inducted into Racing Hall of Fame in 1955. By his estimate, rode more than 700 winners, including Firenze, Tammany. His come-from-behind style immortalized as "Garrison finish."

Gaver, John M., 1900-'82. Trainer. Leading trainer 1942, '51; inducted into Racing Hall of Fame in '66. Trained 73 stakes winners and four champions, including Tom Fool, Capot, Stage Door Johnny, Devil Diver. Won the handicap triple crown with Tom Fool in 1953.

Genter, Frances S., 1898-1992. Household appliances manufacturer. Owned Frances S. Genter Stable. Eclipse Award owner in 1990. Bred and owned In Reality, Smile; owned Unbridled, My Dear Girl, Rough'n Tumble.

Gentry, Olin B., 1900-'90. Farm manager. Managed Idle Hour Stock Farm, Darby Dan Farm. Planned matings for 188 stakes winners, 20 champions, five Kentucky Derby winners. Father of Kentucky breeder Tom Gentry.

Gerry, Martha Farish, 1918-2007. Investments. Owner of Lazy F Ranch, Texas. Member of Jockey Club. Bred and owned Forego, Maid of France, Clef d'Argent, French Colonial. Bred and raced three-time Horse of the Year Forego, who earned nearly $2-million from 1973-'78. Aunt of William S. Farish.

Gluck, Maxwell F., 1899-1984. Apparel stores. Owner of Elmendorf Farm. Eclipse Award outstanding owner in 1977; leading owner '77, '81; leading breeder '73, '81. Bred and owned Protagonist, Talking Picture, Big Spruce, Hold Your Peace; owned Prince John. Donation endowed Maxwell F. Gluck Equine Research Center at University of Kentucky.

Gomez, Avelino, 1929-'80. Jockey. Leading Canadian jockey seven times; North American leading jockey in 1966; inducted into Racing Hall of Fame in '82. Rode 4,081 winners, including Ridan, Buckpasser, Affectionately.

Graham, Florence N. "Elizabeth Arden," 1885-1966. Cosmetics manufacturer. Owner of Maine Chance Farm, Kentucky. Leading owner in 1945. Bred Gun Bow, Jewel's Reward, Jet Action; owned Jet Pilot, Beaugay, Myrtle Charm, Star Pilot, Mr. Busher, Lord Boswell.

Grayson, Cary T., 1878-1938. Physician. Owner of Blue Ridge Farm, Virginia. Bred Insco, My Own, Happy Argo; also owned High Time. Co-founder of Grayson Foundation.

Griffin, Henry "Harry," 1876-1955. Jockey. Inducted into Racing Hall of Fame in 1956. Rode 569 winners, including The Butterflies, Henry of Navarre. One of the original investors in Hollywood Park.

Griffin, Merv, 1925-2007. Entertainment executive. Owner of Stevie Wonderboy, Eclipse Award for champion two-year-old male of 2005. Creator of multiple television shows, including "Jeopardy," "Wheel of Fortune," and "Merv Griffin Show."

Guerin, O. Eric, 1924-'93. Jockey. Leading apprentice jockey 1942; inducted into Racing Hall of Fame in '72. Rode 2,712 winners, including Native Dancer, Bed o' Roses, Jet Pilot. Rode Native Dancer in 20 of his 21 victories (in 22 starts).

Guest, Raymond R., 1907-'91. Investments. Owner of Powhatan Plantation, Virginia; Ballygoran Stud, Ireland. Bred and owned Tom Rolfe, Chieftain; bred Cascapedia; owned Sir Ivor, Larkspur.

Guggenheim, Harry F., 1890-1971. Publisher, mining. Owner of Cain Hoy Stable. Leading breeder in England in 1963. Bred and owned Never Bend, Bald Eagle, Ack Ack, Cherokee Rose, Red God; bred Ragusa, Crafty Admiral; owned Dark Star, *Turn-to. Co-founder of New York Racing Association.

Haggin, James Ben Ali, 1821-1914. Lawyer, mining. Owner of Elmendorf Farm, Kentucky; Rancho del Paso, California. Bred Firenze, Africander, Tyrant, Waterboy, Tournament; owned Salvator, Ben Ali.

Haggin, Louis L. II, 1913-'80. Real estate. Chairman of Keeneland Association 1970-'80; president of Thoroughbred Racing Associations 1967-'68; co-founder of Thoroughbred Breeders of Kentucky. Bred and owned Himalayan, Harbor Springs, Tingle. Great-grandson of James Ben Ali Haggin.

Hagyard, Charles W., 1901-'95. Veterinarian. Owner of Hagyard Farm, Kentucky. Breeder of Rough'n Tumble, Rising Market. Stood Hail to Reason, Promised Land. Co-founder of Hagyard-Davidson-McGee equine clinic.

Hancock, Arthur B. Jr. "Bull," 1910-'72. Breeder. President of American Thoroughbred Breeders' Association. Owner of Claiborne Farm, Kentucky, and Ellerslie Stud, Virginia. Leading breeder 1958-'59, '68-'69. Breeder of Round Table, Gamely, Apalachee, Moccasin, Doubledogdare, Bayou, Lamb Chop. Imported and syndicated *Nasrullah, *Ambiorix, *Herbager; stood Bold Ruler, Nijinsky II, *Princequillo, Round Table. Son of A. B. Hancock Sr.; father of Kentucky breeders Arthur B. Hancock III (Stone Farm) and Seth Hancock (Claiborne Farm).

Hancock, Arthur B. Sr., 1875-1957. Breeder. President of Breeders' Sales Co. Founder and owner of Claiborne Farm, Kentucky; owner of Ellerslie Stud, Virginia. Leading breeder 1935-'37, '39, '43. Breeder of Johnstown, Beaugay, Cleopatra, St. James, Jacola, Nimba, Jet Pilot. Imported and syndicated *Sir Gallahad III, *Blenheim II. Son of Richard J. Hancock, father of Arthur B. "Bull" Hancock Jr.

Hancock, Richard J., 1838-1912. Breeder. Founder of Ellerslie Stud, Virginia. Bred Knight of Ellerslie, Elkwood, Eon, Eole, Eolist. Father of A. B. Hancock Sr.

Hanes, John W., 1892-1988. Textiles, investments. Co-founder and first chairman of New York Racing Association; president of National Museum of Racing Hall of Fame. Bred Idun; owned Bold Bidder.

Harbut, Will, 1885-1947. Groom. Stud groom of Man o' War. Coined well-known phrase, "He was the mostest hoss."

Harding, William G., 1808-'86. Farming, railways. Owner of Belle Meade Stud, Tennessee. Bred Vandalite. Stood leading sires *Priam, Vandal, *Bonnie Scotland.

Harper, John, 1803-'74. Farmer. Owner of Nantura Stock Farm, Kentucky. Bred Longfellow, Ten Broeck, Rhynodyne, Fanny Holton.

Harriman, W. Averill, 1891-1986. Railways, politician. Owner of Arden Park Stable. Owned Chance Play, Ladkin, Mary Jane. As governor of New York (1955-'59) aided formation of New York Racing Association.

Hartack, William J., 1932-2007. Jockey, racing official. Leading jockey by races won in 1955-'57, '60; leading jockey by money won in 1956-'57; inducted into Racing Hall of Fame in '59. Rode 4,272 winners, including Northern Dancer, Tim Tam, Majestic Prince. First jockey to earn $3-million in one year (1957); won five Kentucky Derbys (aboard Iron Liege in 1957, Venetian Way in '60, Decidedly in '62, Northern Dancer in '64, and Majestic Prince in '69).

Haskell, Amory L., 1894-1966. Automobiles, safety glass. President of Monmouth Park 1946-'66; president of Thoroughbred Racing Associations 1954-'55. Owner of Blue Sparkler. Aided campaign to legalize pari-mutuel wagering in New Jersey.

Hatton, Charles W., 1906-'75. Journalist. President, New York Turf Writers Association. Eclipse Special Award in 1974. Popularized concept of American Triple Crown.

Hawkins, Abe, Birthdate unknown-1867. Jockey. A slave when he rode Lecomte to victory over Lexington in an 1854 match race, was perhaps the first African-American professional athlete to gain national and international prominence.

Headley, Duval A., 1910-'87. Horseman. President, Keeneland Race Course; president, Thoroughbred Club of America. Owner of Manchester Farm, Kentucky. Breeder of Tom Fool, Dark Mirage, Aunt Ginny. Trained 23 stakes winners, including champions Menow, Apogee. Nephew of Hal Price Headley.

Headley, Hal Petit, 1856-1921. Timber interests. Founder of Beaumont Farm, Kentucky. Bred and owned Ornament. Father of Hal Price Headley.

Headley, Hal Price, 1888-1962. Timber, burley. First president of Keeneland Race Course. Owner of Beaumont Farm, Kentucky. Bred and owned Menow, Alcibiades, Askmenow, Handy Mandy, Chacolet. Co-founder of Keeneland Association; co-founder of American Thoroughbred Breeders' Association. Father of Kentucky breeder Alice Headley Chandler (Mill Ridge Farm).

Healey, Thomas J., 1866-1944. Trainer, racing official. Inducted into Racing Hall of Fame in 1955. Trained three champions, Equipoise, Top Flight, Campfire. Won five Preakness Stakes.

Helis, William G., 1887-1950. Oil exploration. Co-owner of Fair Grounds. Owner of Helis Stock Farm, New Jersey. Owned Cosmic Bomb, Rippey, Salmagundi.

Hern, Maj. William Richard "Dick," 1921-2002. Trainer. Four-time leading British trainer; won 17 classics, including Epsom Derby three times; trained once-beaten Brigadier Gerard; trained for Queen Elizabeth II.

Hernandez, Joe, 1909-'72. Race caller at Santa Anita Park 1935-'72 and Hollywood Park.

Hertz, John D., 1879-1961 and **Frances,** 1881-1963. Taxis and rental cars. Co-owner of Arlington Park. Owner of Stoner Creek Stud, Kentucky; Leona Farm, Illinois. Bred and owned Count Fleet, Anita Peabody, Prince John, Fleet Nasrullah, Blue Banner, Count of Honor; owned Reigh Count.

Hervey, John L., 1870-1947. Journalist. Racing historian and author under pen name of "Salvator." Author of *Racing in America,* Vols. 1, 2, 4.

Hildreth, Samuel, 1866-1929. Trainer, owner. Leading trainer by money won nine times; leading trainer by races won in 1921, '27; leading owner by money won in 1909-'11; inducted into Racing Hall of Fame in '55. Trained Grey Lag, Zev. Trained ten champions, seven Belmont Stakes winners.

Hine, Hubert "Sonny," 1931-2000. Trainer. Elected to Racing Hall of Fame in 2003. Trained Skip Away, Guilty Conscience, Skip Trial, Technology.

Hirsch, Clement L., 1914-2000. Canned foods. Co-founder and president of Oak Tree Racing Association. Eclipse Award for distinguished service in 1999. Owner of *Figonero, June Darling, *Snow Sporting, Magical Mile, Magical Maiden.

Hirsch, Mary (Mrs. Charles McLennan), 1914-'63. Trainer. First licensed woman trainer in 1933. Trained (with Charles McLennan) of Cowpens Farm, Maryland. Trained stakes winner No Sir. Daughter of Max Hirsch.

Hirsch, Max, 1880-1969. Trainer, jockey, owner, breeder. Inducted into Racing Hall of Fame in 1959. Trained more than 100 stakes winners and six champions, including Assault, Sarazen, Middleground, Bold Venture, Gallant Bloom. Won 1946 Triple Crown with

Assault. Father of William J. "Buddy" Hirsch, Mary Hirsch.

Hirsch, William J. "Buddy," 1909-'97. Trainer. Inducted into Racing Hall of Fame in 1982. Trained 56 stakes winners and one champion, Gallant Bloom. Owned stakes winner Columbiana. Son of Max Hirsch.

Hitchcock, Thomas, 1861-1941. Trainer. Inducted into Racing Hall of Fame in 1973. Trained three champions: Good and Plenty, Salvidere, Annibal. Captained America's first international polo team.

Hollingsworth, Kent, 1930-'99. Journalist. Editor of *The Blood-Horse* 1963-'87; president of Thoroughbred Club of America 1974-'75; president of National Museum of Racing Hall of Fame 1982-'86.

Hoomes, John, 1755-1805. Stagecoaches. Founder of Virginia Jockey Club. Imported *Diomed, *Spread Eagle, *Buzzard.

Hooper, Fred W., 1898-2000. Highway construction. Owner of Hooper Farm, Florida. Eclipse Award outstanding breeder 1975, '82; Eclipse Award of Merit in '92. Bred and owned Susan's Girl, Precisionist, Crozier, Tri Jet, Copelan; owned Hoop, Jr., Olympia, Education. Brought Racing Hall of Fame jockeys Braulio Baeza, Laffit Pincay Jr., and Jorge Velasquez to United States.

Howard, Charles S., 1881-1950. Automobile dealer, real estate. Leading owner 1937, '40. Owner of Seabiscuit, *Noor, *Kayak II.

Hughes, Hollie, 1888-1981. Trainer. Inducted into Racing Hall of Fame in 1973. Trained more than 20 stakes winners, including, *Tourist II. Trained 1916 Kentucky Derby winner George Smith.

Hunter, John, 1833-1914. Real estate. First chairman of the Jockey Club 1894-'95; co-founder of Saratoga Race Course. Owner of Annieswood Stud, New York. Owner of Kentucky, Sultana; bred and owned Alarm, Olitipa, Rhadamanthus.

Hyland, John J., Birthdate unknown-1913. Trainer. Inducted into Racing Hall of Fame in 1956. Trained six champions, including Beldame, Henry of Navarre, His Highness, The Butterflies.

Isaacs, Harry Z., 1904-'90. Clothing manufacturer. Owner of Brookfield Farm, Maryland. Bred and owned Intentionally, Intent, Itsabet.

Iselin, Philip H., 1902-'76. Clothing manufacturer. President of Monmouth Park 1966-'77. Instrumental in consolidation of year-end polls into Eclipse Awards.

Jackson, James, 1782-1840. Merchant. Owner of Forks of Cypress Farm, Alabama. Bred Peytona, Reel. Imported *Glencoe, *Galopade, *Leviathan.

Jacobs, Hirsch, 1904-'70. Owner-breeder, trainer. Leading breeder by money won in 1964-'67; leading trainer by money won in 1946, '60, '65; leading trainer by races won in 1933-'39, '41-'44; inducted into Racing Hall of Fame in '58. Trained 3,596 winners and four champions. Bred Affectionately, Hail to Reason, Straight Deal, Personality. Co-owned and trained Hail to Reason, Stymie, Affectionately, Straight Deal.

Janney, Stuart S. Jr., 1907-'88. Lawyer, financier. Chairman, Maryland Racing Commission in 1947; president of Maryland Horse Breeders Association. Owner of Locust Hill Farm, Maryland. Bred and owned Ruffian, Icecapade, Buckfinder, Private Terms. Father of Maryland breeder Stuart S. Janney III.

Jeffords, Walter M. Sr., 1883-1960. Investments. President of Grayson Foundation; president of National Museum of Racing Hall of Fame 1954-'60. Owner of Faraway Farm, Kentucky. Bred and owned One Count, Pavot, Bateau, Kiss Me Kate, Scapa Flow, Snow Goose.

Jerome, Leonard W., 1817-'91. Financier. Built Jerome Park in 1866; president of Coney Island Jockey Club (Sheepshead Bay racetrack). Owned Kentucky, Fleetwing, Decoursey.

Johnson, Albert, 1900-'66. Jockey, trainer. Leading jockey by money won in 1922; inducted into Racing Hall of Fame in '71. Rode 503 winners, including Exterminator, American Flag, Crusader. Rode two Kentucky Derby winners.

Johnson, Phil G., 1925-2004. Trainer. Inducted into Racing Hall of Fame in 1997. Trained Quiet Little Table, *Amen II, Maplejinsky, Match the Hatch, Naskra, Nasty and Bold, Volponi.

Johnson, William Ransom, 1782-1849. Trainer. Inducted into Racing Hall of Fame in 1986. Trained more than 20 champions, including Boston, Sir Archy. First great American trainer, called the "Napoleon of the Turf;" won 61 of 63 races during a two-year period.

Johnston, Elwood B., 1909-'81. California industry leader. Established Old English Rancho in the 1930s. Founder of the HBPA's California division. North America's leading breeder of stakes winners in 1972, with 13; co-leader in '71 (nine). Breeder of more than 100 stakes winners, including Real Good Deal, Special Warmth, MacArthur Park, Impressive Style, June Darling, Fleet Treat, Admirably, Generous Portion. Bought and raced Fleet Nasrullah.

Jones, Ben A., 1882-1961. Trainer. Leading trainer by money won in 1941, '43-'44, '52; inducted into Racing Hall of Fame in '58. Trained 11 champions, including Whirlaway, Lawrin, Bewitch, Twilight Tear, Armed. Won record six Kentucky Derbys. Father of Horace A. "Jimmy" Jones.

Jones, Farrell W., 1922-2007. Trainer. Leading California-based trainer, topped Santa Anita Park standings eight times, Del Mar 11 times. Trained Santa Margarita Handicap winner Manta. Father of noted trainer Gary Jones.

Jones, Horace A. "Jimmy," 1906-2001. Trainer. Leading trainer by money won in 1947-'49, '57, '61; inducted into Racing Hall of Fame in '59. Trained 54 stakes winners and seven champions, including Citation, Armed, Coaltown, Tim Tam. First trainer to win more than $1-million in purses. Son of Ben Jones.

Jones, Richard I. G., 1938-2007. Lawyer, bloodstock agent. Co-founded Walnut Green Bloodstock with brother Russell B. Jones Jr.

Jones, Warner L., 1916-'94. Distiller, breeder. Chairman of Churchill Downs 1984-'92; president of Thoroughbred Breeders of Kentucky. Owner of Hermitage Farm, Kentucky. Eclipse Award of Merit in 1990. Breeder of Dark Star, Lomond, Is It True, Seattle Dancer, Northern Trick, Woodman, King's Bishop. Sold world-record $13.1-million yearling in 1984; co-founder of the American Horse Council.

Joyce, Joseph Jr., 1929-2006. Racetrack executive. President, chief executive officer of Arlington Park from 1976-1982, where in 1981 he launched the Arlington Million, the world's first million-dollar race. Co-winner of a Special Eclipse Award.

Joyner, Andrew Jackson, 1861-1943. Trainer. Leading trainer by races won in 1908; inducted into Racing Hall of Fame in '55. Trained five champions, including Ethelbert, St. James, Whisk Broom II.

Karches, Peter, 1951-2006. Industry executive. Co-chairman, New York Racing Association, 2005. Former co-chief operating officer, NYRA, 2003-'04. Former president and chief operating officer, Morgan Stanley Dean

Witter Securities Group. Campaigned graded stakes winners Dynevor, Statesmanship, Fast Decision.

Keck, Howard B., 1913-'96. Oil production. Bred Ferdinand; bred and owned Turkish Trousers, Bagdad, Fiddle Isle, Tell, etc.

Keene, Foxhall P., 1867-1941. Sportsman. Owner of Domino, Cap and Bells. Purchased Domino for $3,000 as a yearling. Son of James R. Keene.

Keene, James R., 1838-1913. Financier. Owner of Castleton Stud, Kentucky. Leading owner 1905-'08; leading breeder. Bred and owned Colin, Commando, Peter Pan, Sweep, Kingston, Sysonby, Cap and Bells; owned Domino, Spendthrift. Prime mover in formation of the Jockey Club in late 1893. Father of Foxhall P. Keene.

Kenner, Duncan F., 1813-'87. Sugar planter. President, Louisiana Jockey Club. Owner of Blue Bonnet. Owned slave jockey Abe Hawkins.

Kilmer, Willis Sharpe, 1868-1940. Patent-medicine distributor. Owner of Court Manor Stud, Virginia; Sun Briar Court, New York. Bred and owned Sun Beau, Sally's Alley, Chance Sun; owned Exterminator, *Sun Briar; bred Reigh Count.

Kilroe, Frank E. "Jimmy," 1912-'96. Racing executive. Racing secretary and handicapper at Santa Anita Park 1953-'90 and at New York tracks 1954-'59. Eclipse Award of Merit in 1979.

Kirkpatrick, Haden, 1911-'88. Publisher, journalist. Publisher, editor of *The Thoroughbred Record* 1941-'80.

Kleberg, Robert J., 1896-1974. Rancher, oilman. Owner of King Ranch, Kentucky and Texas. Leading owner in 1954. Bred and owned Assault, Middleground, Gallant Bloom, Dawn Play, Stymie, Miss Cavandish; owned High Gun, But Why Not, Bridal Flower.

Klein, Eugene V., 1921-'90. Automobile dealer. Leading owner 1985, '87; Eclipse Award owner 1985-'87. Owned Lady's Secret, Winning Colors, Capote, Life's Magic, Tank's Prospect, Open Mind, Family Style.

Knapp, Willie, 1888-1972. Jockey, trainer, racing official. Inducted into Racing Hall of Fame in 1969. Rode 649 winners, including Exterminator, Upset. Won 1919 Sanford Stakes aboard Upset, handing Man o' War his only loss.

Knight, Henry H., 1889-1959. Automobile dealer. Owner of Almahurst Farm and Coldstream Stud, Kentucky. Bred Nail, Cosmah, Stood leading sires *Bull Dog, *Heliopolis.

Kummer, Clarence, 1899-1930. Jockey. Leading jockey by money won in 1920; inducted into Racing Hall of Fame in '72. Rode 464 winners, including Man o' War, Sir Barton, Exterminator, Sarazen. Defeated French champion *Epinard by a head aboard Ladkin in 1924 International Special.

Kurtsinger, Charles F., 1906-'46. Jockey. Leading jockey by money won in 1931, '37; inducted into Racing Hall of Fame in '67. Rode 721 winners. Won 1931 Kentucky Derby with Twenty Grand; rode War Admiral to victory in 1937 Triple Crown.

Kyne, William P., 1887-1957. Racing executive. General manager of California Jockey Club (Bay Meadows Race Course) 1934-'57; owner of Portland Meadows racetrack 1946-'57. Promoted passage of California parimutuel law in 1933.

Lakeland, William, 1853-1914. Trainer. Trained Domino, Hamburg, *Ogden, Electioneer, Exile. Co-breeder and co-owner of Commando.

Laurin, Lucien, 1912-2000. Trainer, jockey. Eclipse Award trainer in 1972; inducted into Racing Hall of Fame in '77. Trained 36 stakes winners and three champions: Secretariat, Quill, Riva Ridge. Trained 1972-'73 Horse of the Year Secretariat to Triple Crown.

LeRoy, Mervyn, 1900-'87. Movie producer. President of Hollywood Park 1951-'85. Co-bred and owned Honeymoon, Stepfather, Honey's Alibi.

Lewis, J. Howard, 1862-1947. Trainer. Inducted into Racing Hall of Fame in 1969. Trained 14 steeplechase champions, including Bushranger, Fairmount.

Lewis, Robert, 1924-2006. Beer distributor. Eclipse Award of Merit in 1997; Big Sport of Turfdom Award in '95. Member of Jockey Club. Owned Silver Charm, Charismatic, Serena's Song, Timber Country, Hennessy. Won two-thirds of the Triple Crown in 1997 and '99 (with Silver Charm and Charismatic, respectively).

Lindheimer, Benjamin F., 1891-1960. Real-estate developer. Chairman of Arlington Park 1938-'60, Washington Park 1934-'60. Father of Marjorie Everett, former chief executive of Hollywood Park.

Loftus, Johnny, 1895-1976. Jockey, trainer. Leading jockey by money won in 1919; inducted into Racing Hall of Fame in '59. Rode 580 winners, including Man o' War, Sir Barton, Pan Zareta. First jockey to win the Triple Crown, aboard Sir Barton in 1919.

Longden, John, 1907-2003. Jockey, trainer. Leading jockey by races won in 1938, '47-'48; leading jockey by money won in 1943, '45; inducted into Racing Hall of Fame in '58; Special Eclipse Award in '94; George Woolf Memorial Jockey Award in '52; Avelino Gomez Memorial Award in '85. Rode then-record 6,032 winners, including Count Fleet, Busher, *Noor. Trained Majestic Prince, Jungle Savage, Baffle. Founded Jockeys' Guild with Eddie Arcaro and Sam Renick in 1940. Only man to both ride (Count Fleet) and train (Majestic Prince) a Kentucky Derby winner.

Lord Derby (Edward Stanley, 12th Earl of Derby), 1752-1834. A pillar of 18th-century British racing, he was responsible for founding the Epsom Oaks (1779) and Epsom Derby (1780), the latter bearing his family name after he won a coin toss with Sir Charles Bunbury. Won 1787 Derby with Sir Peter Teazle.

Lord Derby (Edward Stanley, 17th Earl of Derby), 1865-1948. Bred then-record 19 English classic winners, including Hyperion, Sansovino, Fairway, Swynford, Colorado, and *Watling Street. Also bred influential sires Phalaris, Pharos, *Sickle, and *Pharamond II. Generally acknowledged as one of the most successful owners-breeders in British Turf history.

Lorillard, George, 1843-'86. Tobacco sales. President of Monmouth Park. Owner of Westbrook Stable. Leading owner 1877-'80. Owned Tom Ochiltree, Spinaway, Duke of Magenta, Harold, Saunterer, Grenada.

Lorillard, Pierre, 1832-1901. Tobacco sales. Owner of Rancocas Stud, New Jersey. Bred and owned Wanda, Exile, Sibola, Dewdrop, Hiawasse; owned Iroquois, Parole, Saxon, Democrat. First American to win Epsom Derby, with Iroquois in 1881; inspired formation of the Board of Control (predecessor to the Jockey Club) in 1891.

Luro, Horatio, 1901-'91. Trainer. Inducted into Racing Hall of Fame in 1980. Trained 43 stakes winners, including Northern Dancer, *Kayak II, Decidedly, *Princequillo, *Miss Grillo.

Mabee, John C., 1921-2002. Grocery chain owner. Chairman, Del Mar Thoroughbred Club. Co-owner with wife Betty of Golden Eagle Farm, California. Eclipse Award breeder 1991, '97-'98. Bred and owned Best Pal, Event of the Year, General Challenge, Jeanne Jones, Worldly Manner. Founding member of the board of di-

rectors of Breeders' Cup Ltd.; Del Mar's largest growth occurred under his leadership.

MacBeth, Don, 1949-'87. Jockey. George Woolf Memorial Jockey Award in 1987. Rode Chief's Crown, Temperence Hill, Silver Buck, Half Iced. Inspired formation of injured jockey's fund that bears his name.

Macomber, A. Kingsley, 1876-1955. Banker, oilman. Important owner-breeder in California and France. Worked in 1920s to bring big-time horse racing to California; founder of the New Pacific Coast Jockey Club; also owned Haras du Quesnay in France, Mira Monte Stock Farm in California. Owned Parth, Rose Prince; imported *North Star III.

Madden, John E., 1856-1929. Trainer, owner, breeder. Owner of Hamburg Place. Leading breeder 1917-'27; leading trainer 1901-'03; inducted into Racing Hall of Fame in '83. Trained at least 38 stakes winners and eight champions. Bred Grey Lag, Sir Barton, Old Rosebud; owned Hamburg; trained Hamburg, Plaudit, Sir Martin. Bred five Kentucky Derby winners.

Maher, Danny, 1881-1916. Jockey. Leading jockey in U.S. in 1898; leading jockey in England 1908, '13; inducted into Racing Hall of Fame in '55. Rode 1,771 winners, including *Rock Sand, Spearmint, Cicero.

Maktoum, Sheikh Maktoum bin Rashid al, 1943-2006. Ruler of Dubai; vice president and prime minister of United Arab Emirates. Owner of Gainsborough Farm, Kentucky; Woodpark Stud, Ballysheehan Stud, Ireland; Gainsborough Stud, England. Owned Shareef Dancer, Touching Wood, Shadeed, Ma Biche. Partner in Godolphin Racing with brothers Mohammed and Hamdan.

Maloney, James W., 1909-'84. Trainer. Inducted into Racing Hall of Fame in 1989. Trained 42 stakes winners and two champions, including Gamely, Lamb Chop, Princessnesian.

Markey, Lucille P. (Wright), 1897-1982. Investments. Owner of Calumet Farm, Kentucky. Leading breeder 1950-'57, '61; leading owner 1952, '56-'58, '61. Bred and owned Alydar, Fabius, Tim Tam, Our Mims, Forward Pass, Davona Dale, Iron Liege, Barbizon, Before Dawn.

Mars, Ethel V., 1884-1945. Confectioner. Owner of Milky Way Farm, Tennessee. Leading owner in 1936. Owned Gallahadion, Forever Yours, Sky Larking, Case Ace, Reaping Reward.

Mayer, Louis B., 1885-1957. Movie producer. Owner of Louis B. Mayer Stock Farm, California. Bred Honeymoon, Your Host, On Trust, Clem, Lurline B.; imported *Alibhai, *Beau Pere.

McAtee, J. Linus "Pony," 1897-1963. Jockey. Leading jockey in 1928; inducted into Racing Hall of Fame in '56. Rode 930 winners, including Exterminator, Twenty Grand, Jack High. Won 1927, '28 Kentucky Derby.

McCabe, Frank, 1859-1924. Trainer. As trainer for the Dwyer Brothers stable beginning in 1884, saddled future Racing Hall of Fame members Hanover, Kingston, and Miss Woodford. Sent out three consecutive Belmont Stakes winners in Inspector B., Hanover, and Sir Dixon; also trained undefeated champion Tremont. Inducted into the Racing Hall of Fame in 2007.

McCaffery, Trudy, 1944-2007. Owner-breeder, industry leader. Co-owner of major West Coast stakes winners Free House, Came Home, and Pacific Squall.

McCarthy, Clem, 1883-1962. Sportscaster. First radio broadcast of Kentucky Derby in 1928; broadcast Derby from 1928-'50.

McCreary, Conn, 1921-'79. Jockey, trainer. Inducted into Racing Hall of Fame in 1975. Rode 1,263 winners, including Racing Hall of Fame members Stymie, Twilight Tear, Armed, Searching. Trained three stakes winners.

McDaniel, Henry, 1867-1948. Trainer. Co-leading trainer by races won in 1922; inducted into Racing Hall of Fame in '56. Trained 1,041 recorded winners and four champions, including Exterminator, Reigh Count, Sun Beau.

McDaniel, Robert H. "Red," 1911-'55. Trainer. Leading trainer by races won 1950-'54. Trained *Poona II, Blue Reading.

McGrath, H. Price, 1814-'81. Tailor, bookmaker. Owner of McGrathiana Stud, Kentucky. Bred first Kentucky Derby winner Aristides, Thora, Tom Bowling.

McKay, Jim (Jim McManus), 1921-2008. Broadcaster. Eclipse Award of Merit in 2000; Big Sport of Turfdom Award in 1987; Joe Palmer Award in 2000. Member of Jockey Club. Co-founder of Maryland Million; broadcast host of Triple Crown 1975-2000 on ABC.

McKinney, Rigan, 1908-'85. Jockey, trainer, breeder. Leading amateur steeplechase jockey 1933-'34, '36, '38; inducted into Racing Hall of Fame in '63. Rode 138 winners, including Green Cheese, Beacon Hill, Annibal. Trained Navigate, Drift, The Heir. Won American Grand National aboard Green Cheese in 1931.

McKnight, William L., 1888-1978. Industrialist. Chairman, Minnesota Mining and Manufacturing Co. 1949-'66. Co-founder of Calder Race Course. Owner of Tartan Farms, Florida. Eclipse Award, Man of the Year, in 1974. Leading breeder in 1990. Bred and owned Dr. Fager, Ta Wee, Dr. Patches; bred Unbridled.

McLaughlin, James, 1861-1927. Jockey. Leading jockey 1884-'87; inducted into Racing Hall of Fame in 1955. Rode Hindoo, Tecumseh, Tremont, Firenze. Won 1881 Kentucky Derby on Hindoo; won '85 Preakness Stakes aboard Tecumseh; won six Belmont Stakes.

McLennan, Joseph, 1868-1933. Racing executive. Racing secretary at Hialeah Park, Arlington Park.

Meadors, Joel C. "Skeets," 1896-1967. Photographer.

Mellon, Paul, 1908-'99. Investments, banking. Owner of Rokeby Stud, Virginia. Eclipse Award owner-breeder in 1971; breeder in '86; Award of Merit in '93. Bred and owned Mill Reef, Arts and Letters, Key to the Mint, Fort Marcy, Sea Hero, Quadrangle, Run the Gantlet, Java Gold; owned Fit to Fight, Summer Guest, Blue Banner.

Miller, Walter, 1890-1959. Jockey. Leading jockey 1906-'07; inducted into Racing Hall of Fame in '55. Rode 1,904 winners, including Colin, Ballot, Peter Pan, Whimsical. Won 388 races in 1906 (at age 16), a record that stood until Racing Hall of Fame jockey William Shoemaker tied the mark 44 years later in 1950 and broke it in '52.

Mills, James P., 1909-'87, and **Alice**, 1912-2000. Aviation. Owner of Hickory Tree Farm, Virginia. Bred and owned Committed, Believe It, Terpsichorist, Hagley; owned Devil's Bag, Gone West.

Mills, Ogden, 1884-1937. Investments. Co-owner of Wheatley Stable. Bred Seabiscuit, Edelweiss; owned Dice, Diavolo, Dark Secret. Brother of Gladys Phipps.

Molter, William, 1910-'60. Trainer. Leading trainer by races won in 1946-'49; leading trainer by money won 1954, '56, '58, '59; inducted into Racing Hall of Fame in '60. Trained 2,158 winners and 48 stakes winners, including Round Table, Determine, T. V. Lark.

Mori, Eugene, 1898-1975. Banker, real-estate developer. Builder and president of Garden State Park 1942-

'72; owned Hialeah Park 1954-'72. Owner of East Acres Farm, New Jersey. Bred Tosmah; owned Alma North, Cosmah. Promoted pari-mutuel wagering in New Jersey.

Morris, Francis, 1810-'86. Shipping. Owner of Morris Stud, New York. Bred and owned Ruthless, Relentless, Narragansett. Aided Leonard W. Jerome in founding of American Jockey Club and Jerome Park in 1866.

Morris, Green B., 1837-1920. Owner, trainer. Leading owner in 1902. Trained Apollo, Sir Dixon, Strathmeath, *Star Ruby.

Morris, John A., 1892-1985. Financier. President of Thoroughbred Racing Associations, Jamaica Racetrack. Eclipse Award, Man of the Year, in 1975. Bred and owned Missile Belle, Proudest Roman, L'Heureux; owned Missile. Great-grandson of Francis Morris.

Morrissey, John, 1831-'78. Prizefighter, gambler, politician. Co-founder of Saratoga Race Course in 1863.

Mulholland, W. F. "Bert," 1884-1968. Trainer. Inducted into Racing Hall of Fame in 1967. Trained 832 winners, 57 stakes winners, and five champions, including Jaipur, Eight Thirty, Lucky Draw, Battlefield. Trained for George D. Widener for more than 40 years.

Munnings, Sir Alfred, 1878-1959. Painter. Greatest English painter of horses of 20th century.

Murphy, Isaac, 1860-'96. Jockey, trainer, owner. Inducted into Racing Hall of Fame in 1955. Rode 530 recorded winners, including Falsetto, Firenze, Salvator, Emperor of Norfolk. First jockey to win three Kentucky Derbys; first jockey elected to Racing Hall of Fame. Won with 44% of his mounts.

Neloy, Eddie, 1921-'71. Trainer. Leading trainer by money won in 1966-'68; inducted into Racing Hall of Fame in '83. Trained 60 stakes winners and five champions, including Buckpasser, Bold Lad, Gun Bow.

Neves, Ralph, 1921-'95. Jockey. Inducted into Racing Hall of Fame in 1960; George Woolf Memorial Jockey Award in '54. Rode 3,771 winners, sixth all-time by wins at retirement; rode 173 stakes winners, including Round Table, Native Diver. Rode five winners at Bay Meadows after track announcer declared him "deceased" following an accident the previous day.

Newman, Neil, 1886-1951. Journalist. Wrote under the pen name of "Roamer." Author of *Famous Horses of the American Turf* series 1930-'32.

Niarchos, Stavros, 1909-'96. Shipping. Owner of Haras de Fresnay-le-Buffard, France; Oak Tree Farm, Kentucky. Bred and owned Miesque, Spinning World, Kingmambo, Hernando (Fr), Hector Protector, Machiavellian; owned Nureyev.

Niccolls, Richard, 1624-'72. Soldier, politician. Founded first American racecourse, Newmarket, at Salisbury Plain (near modern Hempstead), Long Island, New York.

Notter, Joe, 1890-1973. Jockey. Leading jockey by money won in 1908; inducted into Racing Hall of Fame in '63. Rode Regret, Whisk Broom II, Colin. First jockey to ride a filly, Regret, to victory in the Kentucky Derby (1915); first jockey to win handicap triple crown, on Whisk Broom II.

Nuckols, Charles Jr., 1922-2005. Breeder. Former president, Thoroughbred Club of America; director, Keeneland Association. Member of Jockey Club. Owner of Nuckols Farm, Kentucky. Bred Hidden Lake, Habitat, Decathlon, Typecast. Co-bred War Emblem. Co-authored the Kentucky Thoroughbred Development Fund legislation.

O'Connor, Winnie, 1884-1947. Jockey, trainer. Leading jockey in 1901; inducted into Racing Hall of Fame in '56. Rode 1,229 winners in United States and France, including Yankee, Reina. One of "Father Bill" Daly's "Five Aces."

Odom, George M., 1883-1964. Jockey, trainer. Inducted into Racing Hall of Fame in 1955. Rode 527 winners, including Broomstick, Delhi, Banastar. Trained Busher, Pasteurized. Won the Belmont Stakes as a jockey and later as a trainer.

O'Farrell, Joe, 1912-'82. Breeder. President, Florida Breeders' Sales Co. Owner of Ocala Stud, Florida. Bred Roman Brother, Office Queen, My Dear Girl. Stood Rough'n Tumble. Primary founder of Florida breeding industry.

Olin, John M., 1892-1982. Small-arms munitions. Bred and owned Cannonade; owned Bold Bidder, Northfields.

O'Neill, Frank, 1886-1960. Jockey. Inducted into Racing Hall of Fame in 1956. Rode Beldame, Roseben, *Prince Palatine, Spion Kop. Also successful jockey in France and England.

Palmer, Joe H., 1904-'52. Journalist. Author of *This Was Racing, American Racehorses* series 1944-'51.

Parke, Burley, 1905-'77. Trainer. Inducted into Racing Hall of Fame in 1986. Trained 37 stakes winners and three champions: Roman Brother, *Noor, Raise a Native. *Noor beat Citation in four consecutive stakes races. Brother of Ivan Parke.

Parke, Ivan, 1908-'95. Jockey, trainer. Leading jockey by races won in 1923, '24 (his first two years of racing); leading jockey by money won in '24; inducted into Racing Hall of Fame in '78. Rode 419 winners, including Backbone. Trained 27 stakes winners, including Exclusive Native, Hoop, Jr. Brother of Burley Parke.

Patrick, Gilbert "Gilpatrick," 1812-ca. 1880. Jockey. Inducted into Racing Hall of Fame in 1970. Rode Ruthless, Boston, Kentucky, Lexington. Rode first Belmont Stakes winner, Ruthless, in 1867.

Paulson, Allen E., 1922-2000. Aviation. Owner of Brookside Farm, Kentucky. Eclipse Award breeder in 1993; owner '95 and '96. Owned and bred Cigar, Ajina, Escena, Fraise; owned Theatrical (Ire), Strawberry Road (Aus), Blushing John, Arazi, Paradise Creek; bred Azeri.

Payson, Mrs. Charles S. (Joan Whitney), 1903-'75. Publisher, investments. Co-owner of Greentree Stud. Leading owner in 1951. Owned and bred Stage Door Johnny, Capot, Bowl Game, Late Bloomer, The Axe II, Cohoes, Stop the Music; owned Tom Fool. Daughter of Mr. and Mrs. Payne Whitney; sister of John Hay Whitney.

Pelleteri, Anthony, 1893-1952. Trainer, racing executive. Won the 1941 Santa Anita Handicap with 90-to-1 Bay View, and developed stakes winners Bull Reigh and Andy K. In 1941 Pelleteri organized a partnership that saved the historic Fair Grounds racetrack in New Orleans from being auctioned and subdivided; served as the track's executive vice president until his death.

Penna, Angel, 1923-'92. Trainer. Leading trainer in Argentina in 1952; leading trainer in Venezuela in '54; leading trainer in France in '74; inducted into Racing Hall of Fame in '88. Trained more than 250 stakes winners, including Allez France, Relaxing, San San, Private Account.

Perry, William Haggin, 1911-'93. Investments. Owner of Waterford Farm, Virginia. Co-owned and co-bred Gamely, Lure, Revidere, Coastal, Lamb Chop, Boldnesian.

Phipps, Mrs. Henry C. (Gladys Mills), 1883-1970.

Investments. Owner of Wheatley Stable. Leading owner in 1966. Bred and owned Bold Ruler, Bold Lad, Seabiscuit, High Voltage, Misty Morn, Queen Empress, Successor, Bold Bidder, Castle Forbes. Mother of leading owner-breeder Ogden Phipps; sister of Ogden Mills.

Phipps, Ogden, 1908-2002. Investments. Chairman, Jockey Club 1964-'74; former chairman New York Racing Association. Leading owner by money won 1988, '89; Eclipse Award breeder in '88; Eclipse Award owner 1988, '89; Eclipse Award of Merit 2002; Mr. Fitz Award in '89. Bred and owned Buckpasser, Easy Goer, Private Account. Bred and raced Personal Ensign, who was unbeaten in 13 starts.

Piatt, Thomas, 1877-1965. Farmer, tobacco. First president of Thoroughbred Club of America; president, Breeders' Sales Co. Owner of Brookdale Farm, Kentucky. Bred Alsab, Donau. Father of Thomas Carr Piatt.

Piatt, Thomas Carr, 1900-'53. Farmer, tobacco. President, Breeders' Sales Co. 1949-'53. Owner of Crestwood Farm, Kentucky. Co-breeder of Occupation, Occupy, Errard. Son of Thomas Piatt.

Pincus, Jacob, 1838-1918. Trainer, jockey. Leading trainer in 1869; inducted into Racing Hall of Fame in '88. Trained Glenelg, Eagle, Richmond. Trained Iroquois, first American winner of the Epsom Derby.

Pollard, John "Red," 1909-1981. Canadian-born jockey. Rode his first Thoroughbred winner in 1926. In mid-1930s began association with C. S. Howard, owner of Seabiscuit, whom he rode to many important victories—although not in the famed 1938 match against War Admiral. Retired after injury-plagued 30-year career. Later inducted into the Canadian Racing Hall of Fame.

Porter, William T., 1809-'58. Publisher. Founded *Spirit of the Times* magazine in 1831.

Price, Jack, 1908-'95. Trainer. Trained 1961 Kentucky Derby and Preakness Stakes winner Carry Back, whom he bred out of the $265 mare Joppy.

Purdy, Samuel, 1785-1836. Jockey. Inducted into Racing Hall of Fame in 1970. Semi-retired when pulled from the crowd to replace American Eclipse's jockey at the Union Course in 1823, winning the next two heats to win the match over Henry.

Rasmussen, Leon, 1915-2003. Journalist. "Bloodlines" columnist, *Daily Racing Form* 1950-'87. Walter Haight Award in 1987; Engelhard Award in '87. Bred and owned Apollo, Nanetta. Popularized Dr. Steven A. Roman's dosage system in his column.

Reiff, John, 1885-1974. Jockey. Leading jockey in France in 1902; inducted into Racing Hall of Fame in '56. Rode 1,016 winners, including Orby, Tagalie, Retz, Moia. Among the top ten jockeys for ten seasons in France; won two Epsom Derbys and one French Derby.

Rice, Daniel, 1896-1975, and **Ada L.,** 1899-1977. Stock and grain broker. Co-owners of Arlington Park 1940-'68. Owners of Danada Farm, Kentucky. Bred and owned Lucky Debonair, Pucker Up, Proud Delta, Delta Judge, Advocator.

Rice, Grantland, 1880-1954. Journalist. Covered most major sports for the New York *Herald Tribune*, but horse racing was a favorite. Among the great racing events he covered was the 1938 Seabiscuit-War Admiral match.

Richards, A. Keene, 1827-'81. Sugar and cotton planter. Owner of Blue Grass Park Stud, Kentucky. Owned *Australian, Starke, War Dance. Bred Fenian, Target, Eliza Davis, Ulrica.

Richards, Sir Gordon, 1904-'86. Jockey. Champion British flat jockey 26 times in 34 seasons of racing. First to ride more than 4,000 winners, he retired in 1954 with a then-world record 4,870 career victories. In 1953 he became the first professional jockey to be knighted.

Richards, Leonard P., Birthdate and date of death unknown. Chemical manufacturer. Second chairman of the Delaware Racing Commission.

Rickman, William Sr., 1924-2005. Racing executive, owner-breeder. Chairman of Delaware Park. Bought Delaware Park in 1983, reopened it after a one-year shutdown, and turned it into profitable enterprise. Introduced slots in 1995. Son William Rickman Jr. is president and chief executive. Also owns Ocean Downs harness track and holds license to build a new track in Allegany County, Maryland.

Riddle, Samuel D., 1862-1951. Textiles. Owner of Faraway Farm, Kentucky; Glen Riddle Stable. Leading owner in 1925. Owned Man o' War; bred and owned War Admiral, Crusader, American Flag, War Relic.

Riggs, William P., 1874-1936. Racetrack executive. Secretary of the Maryland Jockey Club; a driving force behind the revival of Pimlico Race Course and return of Preakness Stakes to Maryland in 1909.

Robertson, Alfred, 1911-'75. Jockey Inducted into Racing Hall of Fame in '71; New York Turf Writers Association's best jockey in 1942. Rode 1,856 winners, including Top Flight, Whirlaway, Riverland, Sky Larking. Twice rode six winners in a single day.

Robertson, William H. P., 1920-'82. Journalist. Editor of *The Thoroughbred Record* 1962-'78. Author of *History of Thoroughbred Racing in America, Hoofprints of the Century.*

Roebling, Joseph M., 1909-'80. Building contractor. Owner of Harbourton Stud, New Jersey. Bred and owned Blue Peter, Fall Aspen, Rainy Lake.

Rogers, John W., ca. 1850-1908. Trainer. Inducted into Racing Hall of Fame in 1955. Trained 11 champions, including Artful, Modesty. Trained Artful to win the 1904 Belmont Futurity, giving Sysonby the only defeat of his career.

Rolapp, R. Richards, 1941-'93. Lawyer. President of American Horse Council 1978-'93.

Ross, John K. L., 1876-1951. Railways. Leading owner 1918-'19. Owned Sir Barton, Billy Kelly, Cudgel.

Rous, Adm. Henry J., 1795-1877. English Jockey Club steward, Turf reformer, handicapper. Published *Handbook on the Laws of Racing,* which included the first standard scale of weights. Established and enforced strict standards and banned unsavory characters. Often referred to as the "Father of the Turf."

Rowan, Louis R., 1911-'88. Investments. Original shareholder in Santa Anita Racetrack; six-term president of the California Thoroughbred Breeders Association; conceived California Cup; founding director of Oak Tree Racing Association and Del Mar Thoroughbred Club. Founding chairman of the Winners Foundation.

Rowe, James Sr., 1857-1929. Trainer, jockey. Leading jockey 1871-'73; leading trainer 1908, '13, '15; inducted into Racing Hall of Fame in '55. Trained 34 horses regarded as champions, more than any other Hall of Fame trainer. Trained Colin, Miss Woodford, Regret, Luke Blackburn, Hindoo.

Rubin, Sam, 1914-2006. Eclipse Award-winning co-owner with wife Dorothy of two-time Horse of the Year and Racing Hall of Fame member John Henry, in the name of Dotsam Stable.

Runyon, Damon, 1884-1946. Journalist, sports columnist, author, humorist. Many of his short stories had to do with gambling and horse racing. Most famous for

writing *Guys and Dolls*, although probably best known in racing for the poem "Gimme a Handy Guy Like Sande," about jockey Earl Sande.

Ryan, Dr. Tony, 1936-2007. Airline executive. Owner and chairman, Castleton Lyons, Kentucky. Bred Antonius Pius and Naissance Royale (Ire).

Salman, Ahmed bin, 1958-2002. Publisher, Saudi royal family. Owner of The Thoroughbred Corp. Bred and owned Point Given, Spain. Owned Sharp Cat, Jewel Princess, Oath, Anees, Royal Anthem, War Emblem.

Salmon, Walter J., ca. 1880-1953. Real estate. Owner of Mereworth Farm. Leading breeder in 1946. Bred Discovery, Display, Dr. Freeland, Battleship (first American-bred and -owned winner of England's Grand National Steeplechase), Free For All; owned Vigil.

Samuel, Ernest, 1930-2000. Steel distribution. Owner of Sam-Son Farm, Ontario and Florida. Eclipse Award owner in 1991; leading owner and breeder '91. Bred and raced more than 100 stakes winners, including Dance Smartly, Sky Classic, Chief Bearhart.

Samuel-Balaz, Tammy, 1960-2008. Investments. Co-owner of Sam-Son Farm, Canada and Florida. Bred and owned Dancethruthedawn, Scatter the Gold, Catch the Ring, Mountain Angel, Quiet Resolve. Daughter of Ernest Samuel.

Sande, Earl, 1899-1968. Jockey, trainer. Leading jockey 1921, '23, '27; leading trainer in '38; inducted into Racing Hall of Fame in '55. Rode 968 winners, including Gallant Fox, Zev, Man o' War. Trained Stagehand, Sceneshifter. Won three Kentucky Derbys, five Belmont Stakes, and five Jockey Club Gold Cups.

Sanford, John, 1851-1939. Carpet mills, politician. Owner of Hurricane Stud, New York. Bred and raced *Affection, *Snob II, Sir John Johnson, *Donnacona; owned George Smith. Son of Stephen Sanford.

Sanford, Milton H., 1812-'83. Cotton mills. Owner of Preakness Stud, New Jersey; North Elkhorn Farm, Kentucky. Bred Vagrant, Vigil; also owned Preakness, Virgil, Monarchist. Stood leading sire Glenelg.

Sanford, Stephen, 1826-1913. Carpet mills. Owner of Hurricane Stud, New York. Raced only homebreds, which he gave Indian names, including Caughnawaga, Chuctununda, and Mohawk II. Stood Clifford, *Voter. Father of John Sanford.

Sangster, Robert, 1936-2004. Betting pools, investments. Co-owner of Coolmore Stud; owner of Swettenham Stud. Renowned owner-breeder who helped to fuel the 1980s boom at Thoroughbred yearling sales, with partners purchased a yearling for then-world-record $13.1-million in '85, campaigned more than 800 stakes winners, including champions The Minstrel, Alleged, Caerleon, and homebred Sadler's Wells; five-time leading owner in England.

Schapiro, John, 1914-2002. Racetrack executive. President of Laurel Park. Eclipse Award of Merit in 1980; *Sports Illustrated*'s Racing Man of the Year in 1960; Inaugurated the Washington, D.C., International at Laurel in 1952.

Schulhofer, Flint "Scotty," 1926-2006. Trainer, whose top runners included 1999 Belmont Stakes (G1) winner Lemon Drop Kid, champion sprinters Ta Wee, Smile, and Rubiano, male turf champion Mac Diarmida, and champion two-year-old male Fly So Free. Inducted into Racing Hall of Fame in 1992.

Scott, Marion duPont, 1891-1983. Investments. Owner of Montpelier Farm, Virginia. Bred more than 50 stakes winners, including Mongo, Parka, Neji, Soothsayer; owned Proud Delta, Battleship. Founded Carolina Cup Steeplechase in Camden, South Carolina. Member of syndicate that imported *Blenheim II.

Seagram, Joseph E., 1841-1919. Distiller. Member of Canadian Parliament. President of Ontario Jockey Club. Bred and raced Inferno, Belle Mahone. Won 15 King's (Queen's) Plates.

Shaffer, Charles B., 1859-1943. Oil production. Owner of Coldstream Stud, Kentucky. Bred Bull Lea, Occupation, Occupy, Star Pilot, Reaping Reward, Plucky Play. Stood leading sires *Bull Dog, *Heliopolis. Father of E. E. Dale Shaffer.

Shaffer, E. E. Dale, 1917-'74. Oil production. Founder of Detroit Race Course; chairman of Kentucky Racing Commission 1950-'51; president of Michigan Racing Association; president of Thoroughbred Racing Associations 1960-'61. Owner of Coldstream Stud, Kentucky. Leading breeder in 1945. Bred Sweet Patootie, Star Pilot, Johns Joy. Stood leading sires *Bull Dog, *Heliopolis. Son of Charles Shaffer.

Shilling, Carroll, 1882-1950. Jockey. Leading jockey in 1910; inducted into Racing Hall of Fame in '70. Rode 969 winners, including Colin, Sir Martin, Fitz Herbert, King James. Won 1912 Kentucky Derby aboard Worth.

Shoemaker, William, 1931-2003. Jockey, trainer. President, Jockeys' Guild in 1975-'90. Leading jockey by money won in 1958-'64; inducted into Racing Hall of Fame in '58; Special Eclipse Award in '76; Eclipse Award jockey in '81; Eclipse Award of Merit in '81; George Woolf Memorial Jockey Award in '51; Mike Venezia Award in '90. Rode then-record 8,833 winners and 1,009 stakes winners, including Swaps, Spectacular Bid, Round Table, Ack Ack, Forego, John Henry, Prove It, Olden Times, Sword Dancer. Trained Fire the Groom, Alcando (Ire). First jockey to reach $100-million in earnings; mounts earned more than $123-million in purses. Paralyzed in single-car accident April 8, 1991.

Simms, Edward F., 1870-1938. Oil production. Owner of Xalapa Farm, Kentucky. Bred Coventry; owned Eternal, My Play.

Simms, Willie, 1870-1927. Jockey. Leading jockey in 1894; inducted into Racing Hall of Fame in 1977. Rode 1,125 winners, including Henry of Navarre, Ben Brush, Plaudit, Commanche. Won back-to-back Belmont Stakes (1893-'94) aboard Commanche and Henry of Navarre.

Sinclair, Harry F., 1876-1956. Oil production. Owner of Rancocas Stud, New Jersey. Leading owner 1921-'23. Bred and owned Mad Play, Ariel; owned Zev, Grey Lag, Mad Hatter.

Skinner, John S., 1788-1851. Publisher. Founded *American Turf Register* in 1830.

Sloan, James F. "Tod," 1874-1933. Jockey. Inducted into Racing Hall of Fame in 1955. Rode Hamburg, Clifford. Credited with popularizing the use of shortened stirrups in United States and England.

Sloane, Isabel Dodge, 1898-1962. Automobile heiress. Owner of Brookmeade Stud, Virginia. First female leading owner 1934, '50. Bred and owned Sword Dancer, Bowl of Flowers, Bold, Sailor, Greek Ship; owned Cavalcade, High Quest.

Smith, George "Pittsburgh Phil," 1862-1905. Gambler. Most successful gambler of Victorian era, died a millionaire.

Smith, Robert A., 1869-1942. Trainer, owner. Leading trainer 1933-'34; inducted into Racing Hall of Fame in '76. Trained more than 27 stakes winners and three champions, including 1934 Horse of the Year Cavalcade, High Quest. Owned Articulate. Won 1934 Kentucky Derby with Cavalcade.

Smith, Tom "Silent Tom," 1879-1957. Trainer. Leading trainer 1940, '45; inducted into Racing Hall of Fame in 2001. Trained 29 stakes winners and six champions, including Seabiscuit, Jet Pilot, *Kayak II. Trained 1947 Kentucky Derby winner Jet Pilot.

Smithwick, Alfred "Paddy," 1927-'73. Jockey. Leading steeplechase jockey by races won 1956-'58, '62; inducted into Racing Hall of Fame in '73. Rode 398 winners, including Neji, Bon Nouvel, Elkridge. Won two American Grand Nationals aboard Neji. Trained two stakes winners.

Smithwick, D. M. "Mike," 1929-2006. Trainer. Inducted into Racing Hall of Fame in 1971. Trained 52 stakes winners and six champions. Trained Neji, Bon Nouvel, Ancestor, Mako, Top Bid, Straight and True. Trained Neji to championships in 1955, '57, '58; trained the first two winners (Top Bid and Inkslinger) of the Colonial Cup. Brother of Racing Hall of Fame jockey Paddy Smithwick.

Sommer, Sigmund, 1917-'79. Real estate. Leading owner 1971-'72. Owned 29 stakes winners, including Autobiography, Sham, Never Bow.

Spreckels, Adolph, 1857-1924. Sugar merchant. President of Pacific Coast Jockey Club. Owner of Napa Stock Farm, California. Bred Morvich; bred and owned Runstar.

Stanford, Leland, 1824-'93. Politician. Governor of California 1861-'63; United States senator '85-'93; founder of Stanford University. Developed Palo Alto Stock Farm. In 1872 hired photographer to prove that all of a horse's feet are off the ground at one point in the gallop.

Stavro, Steve, 1927-2006. Grocery stores. Under the name of Knob Hill Stable, campaigned more than 50 stakes winners, six Canadian champions, including Horses of the Year Benburb and Thornfield. Sovereign Award as Canada's outstanding owner-breeder. Inducted into Canadian Racing Hall of Fame in 2006.

Stephens, Woodford C. "Woody," 1913-'98. Trainer. Eclipse Award trainer in 1983; inducted into Racing Hall of Fame in '76. Trained 131 stakes winners and 11 champions, including Swale, Conquistador Cielo, Never Bend. Won five consecutive Belmont Stakes (1982-'86).

Stout, James, 1914-'76. Jockey, racing official. Inducted into Racing Hall of Fame in 1968. Rode Johnstown, Granville, Assault, Omaha, Stymie. Finished in the first triple win dead heat in a major stakes aboard Bousset in the 1944 Carter Handicap.

Strub, Charles H., 1884-1958. Baseball team owner, real estate, investments. Founder of Santa Anita Park. Father of Robert P. Strub.

Strub, Robert P., 1919-'93. Real estate. President of Los Angeles Turf Club (Santa Anita Park); chairman, Santa Anita Operating Co.; president of Thoroughbred Racing Associations 1963-'64. Eclipse Award of Merit in 1992. Son of Charles H. Strub.

Stull, Henry, 1851-1913. Noted American equine painter. First to accurately portray racehorses at a gallop. Owned Swarthmore.

Sutcliffe, Leonard S., 1880-1937. Photographer. Published photographic volumes *Thoroughbred Sires* and *Famous Mares in America*.

Swigert, Daniel, 1833-1912. Breeder. Founded Elmendorf Farm, Kentucky. Leading breeder. Bred Spendthrift, Hindoo, Salvator, Tremont, Baden-Baden. Managed Woodburn Stud. Father-in-law of Leslie Combs Sr.

Swinebroad, George W., 1901-'75. Auctioneer. Legendary auctioneer at Keeneland and Saratoga. Hammered down first $100,000 yearling in 1961.

Swope, Herbert Bayard, 1882-1958. Journalist, investments. Chairman of New York Racing Commission.

Taral, Fred, 1867-1925. Jockey, trainer. Inducted into Racing Hall of Fame in 1955. Rode 1,437 winners, including Domino, Henry of Navarre, Dr. Rice, Ramapo. Rode Domino to nine consecutive victories in 1893.

Tasker, Col. Benjamin Jr., 1720-'60. Planter. Prominent owner-breeder during Colonial era. Owner of Belair Stud, Maryland. Imported great racemare *Selima from England in 1750, notable sire *Othello; bred Pacolet, Selim.

Tayloe, John II, 1721-'79. Planter. Owner of Mount Airy Stud, Virginia. Bred Yorick, Ariel, Bellair; owned *Selima, Moreton's Traveller. Father of John Tayloe III.

Tayloe, John III, 1771-1828. Planter. Owner of Mount Airy Stud, Virginia. Bred American foundation sire Sir Archy, Lady Lightfoot, Grey Diomed, Calypso. Imported *Castianira, dam of Sir Archy. Son of John Tayloe II.

Taylor, Charles P. B., 1935-'97. Journalist, investments. Owner of Windfields Farm, Canada and Maryland; chairman, Canadian Jockey Club; vice president, Breeders' Cup Inc. Son of Edward P. Taylor.

Taylor, Edward P., 1901-'89. Brewing. President, Ontario Jockey Club and Canadian Thoroughbred Horse Society. Owner of Windfields Farm, Canada and Maryland. Leading breeder 1974-'80; Eclipse Award breeder 1977, '83. Bred and owned Northern Dancer, Nearctic, Victoria Park; bred Nijinsky II, El Gran Senor, Devil's Bag, The Minstrel, Secreto, Shareef Dancer, Storm Bird, Viceregal. Father of Charles P. B. Taylor.

Taylor, Joe, 1924-2003. Noted Kentucky horseman and author, whose sons founded Taylor Made Farm and Taylor Made Sales Agency, manager of Gainesway Farm 1950-'90.

Taylor, Shirley, 1923-2007. Industry leader, owner-breeder. Former president, Thoroughbred Owners and Breeders Association. Part-owner of European champion Alleged. Breeder of Grade 1 winner Scorpion.

Ten Broeck, Richard, 1809-'92. Gambler, sportsman. Owner of Metairie Race Course, Louisiana. Bred Umpire; owned Lexington, Lecompte, Prioress, *Eclipse, Starke. Conducted first successful invasion of England with American-breds in 1860s.

Tenney, Meshach, 1907-'93. Trainer. Leading trainer 1962-'63; inducted into Racing Hall of Fame in '91. Trained 36 stakes winners and one champion, including Swaps, Candy Spots, Olden Times, Prove It. Won 1955 Kentucky Derby with Swaps.

Tesio, Federico, 1869-1954. Breeder. Acclaimed Italian breeder of *Ribot, Nearco, Donatello II, Niccolo Dell'Arca. Bred and owned 20 Italian Derby winners. Author of *Breeding the Racehorse*.

Thomas, Barak G., 1826-1906. Planter, publisher. Noted owner-breeder in post-Civil War America. Founded Dixiana Farm, Kentucky. Bred and owned Himyar; bred Domino, Correction.

Thompson, Henry J. "Derby Dick," 1881-1937. Trainer. Inducted into Racing Hall of Fame in 1969. Trained 373 recorded winners and five champions, including Blue Larkspur, Burgoo King, Bubbling Over. First trainer to saddle four Kentucky Derby winners.

Tipton, Edward A., 1855-1930. Auctioneer. Co-founder of Fasig-Tipton Co. in 1898. Sold company to E. J. Tranter. Manager of Bitter Root Stud, Montana, 1896-1900.

Tranter, Enoch J., 1875-1938. Auctioneer. Owner of Fasig-Tipton Co. 1904-'38. Revolutionized Thoroughbred auction business in America. Launched annual yearling sale at Saratoga.

Travers, William R., 1819-'87. Stockbroker, raconteur. First president of Saratoga Association. Owned Kentucky, Alarm, Sultana.

Trotsek, Harry, 1912-'97. Trainer. Inducted into Racing Hall of Fame in 1984. Trained 96 stakes winners and two champions; trained Moccasin, Hasty Road, *Stan. Expert handler of imported horses; coached young jockeys at his jockey school in the 1940s.

Troye, Edward, 1808-'74. Painter. Prolific equine portraitist; his subjects included Lexington, Boston, and many of America's great mid-19th-century Thoroughbreds.

Tuckerman, Bayard J., 1889-1974. Jockey, breeder, owner. First president of Suffolk Downs. Inducted into Racing Hall of Fame in 1973. Rode Homestead. Bred Lavender Hill. Leading amateur jockey.

Turner, Nash, 1881-1937. Jockey, trainer, owner. Inducted into Racing Hall of Fame in 1955. Rode Imp, Flying Star, Goldsmith, Irish Lad. Rider of Imp, the first filly to win the Suburban Handicap in 1899; won 1906 Prix du Jockey-Club (French Derby).

Umphrey, Bob, 1952-2006. Racetrack executive. Racing secretary at Calder Race Course, Laurel, Arlington, and Hollywood Park.

Van Berg, Marion H., 1896-1971. Trainer, owner. Leading owner by money won in 1965, '68-'70; leading owner by races won in 1952, '54, '56, '60-'70; inducted into Racing Hall of Fame in '70. Trained more than 1,470 winners and six stakes winners, including *Estacion, Rose Bed. Father of Racing Hall of Fame trainer Jack Van Berg.

Vanderbilt, Alfred G., 1912-'99. Investments. Chairman, New York Racing Association; president, Belmont Park and Pimlico Race Course. Owner of Sagamore Farm, Maryland. Eclipse Award of Merit in 1994. Bred and owned Native Dancer, Next Move, Bed o' Roses, Now What, Petrify; owned Discovery; bred Conniver, Miss Disco.

Van Ranst, Cornelius W., Birthdate and date of death unknown. Owned American Eclipse, *Messenger.

Veitch, Sylvester, 1910-'96. Trainer. Inducted into Racing Hall of Fame in 1977. Trained 44 stakes winners and five champions, including Counterpoint, Career Boy. Trained Horse of the Year Counterpoint, who won the 1951 Belmont Stakes. Father of Racing Hall of Fame trainer John Veitch.

Vosburgh, Walter, 1855-1938. Handicapper, author. Racing secretary, Westchester Racing Association (Belmont Park) 1894-1934. Author of *Racing in America 1866-1921;* Turf editor of *Spirit of the Times*. Originated Experimental Free Handicap in 1933.

Waggoner, William T., 1852-1934. Oil production, rancher. Early 20th-century force in Texas racing. Owner of 3D's Stock Farm, Texas. Built Arlington Downs racetrack, Texas, in 1929.

Walden, R. Wyndham, Birthdate unknown-1905. Trainer. Inducted into Racing Hall of Fame in 1970. Trained 101 stakes winners, including Duke of Magenta, Grenada, Saunterer. Trained seven Preakness Stakes winners, five consecutively.

Walsh, Michael G., 1906-'93. Trainer. Leading steeplechase trainer by races won in 1953-'55; leading steeplechase trainer by money won in 1953-'54, '60; inducted into Racing Hall of Fame in '97; F. Ambrose Clark Award in '75. Trained 31 stakes winners.

Ward, Sherrill, 1911-'84. Trainer. Eclipse Award trainer in 1974; inducted into Racing Hall of Fame in '78. Trained 20 stakes winners and two champions, including Forego, Summer Tan, and Idun. Trained Forego to Horse of the Year honors in 1975 and '76.

Warfield, Elisha, 1781-1859. Physician. Co-founder of the Kentucky Association racetrack, Lexington. Owner of The Meadows Stud, Kentucky. Breeder of Lexington, Berthune, Alice Carneal. Known as the "Father of the Kentucky Turf."

Watters Jr., Sidney, 1917-2008. Trainer. Champion steeplechase trainer in 1951, '56, '61, and '63, co-leader by wins in '48 and '71. Leading steeplechase trainer by earnings in 1956, '63, and '71. Trained champions Amber Diver and Shadow Brook. On flat, trained 1970 champion two-year-old male Hoist the Flag and '83 three-year-old male Slew o' Gold. Inducted into Racing Hall of Fame as a steeplechase trainer in 2005.

Welch, Aristides J., 1811-'90. Owner of Erdenheim Stud, Pennsylvania. Bred Iroquois, Parole, Sensation, Harold, Spinaway. Stood leading sire *Leamington.

Wells, Thomas J., 1803-'62. Sugar planter. President of Metairie Race Course. Bred Lecomte, Prioress; owned Reel.

Werblin, David A. "Sonny," 1910-'91. Entertainment and sports executive. First president of New Jersey Sports and Exposition Authority (originally the Meadowlands and now including Monmouth Park). Owner of Silent Screen, Process Shot.

West, R. Smiser, 1909-2006. Owner-breeder. Co-owner with his wife Kathryn of Waterford Farm. Bred champions Chilukki, De La Rose and Grade 1 winner Lite Light in partnership with Racing Hall of Fame trainer MacKenzie Miller.

Westrope, Jack, 1918-'58. Jockey. Leading jockey in 1933 at age 15, when he rode 301 winners. Inducted into Racing Hall of Fame in 2002.

Wheeler, Robert L., 1920-'92. Trainer. Native of Crawford, Nebraska, worked for Woolford Farm and Louis B. Mayer before taking out his trainer's license in 1938. Trained 56 stakes winners; West Coast trainer for C. V. Whitney in the 1950s and '60s; trained Santa Anita Derby winners Tompion and Silver Spoon, who was co-champion three-year-old filly in 1959; also trained champion Track Robbery and The Axe II.

Whiteley, Frank Jr., 1915-2008. Trainer. Inducted into Racing Hall of Fame in 1978. Trained 35 stakes winners and four champions, including Damascus, Forego, Ruffian, Tom Rolfe.

Whitney, Cornelius V., 1899-1992. Investments. First president of National Museum of Racing Hall of Fame. Owner of C. V. Whitney Farm, Kentucky. Leading breeder 1933-'34, '38, '60; leading owner 1930-'33, '60. Bred more than 175 stakes winners. Bred and owned Counterpoint, Silver Spoon, Career Boy, First Flight; owned Equipoise, Top Flight. Son of Harry Payne Whitney.

Whitney, Harry Payne, 1872-1930. Investments. Owner of Brookdale Stud, New Jersey; Whitney Farm, Kentucky. Leading breeder 1926-'32; leading owner 1913, '20, '24, '26, '27, '29. Bred and owned Regret, Equipoise, Top Flight, Whisk Broom II, Whichone, Whiskery, Pennant, Upset, John P. Grier, Prudery. Father of C. V. Whitney.

Whitney, Mrs. Payne (Helen Hay), 1876-1944. Investments. "First Lady of the American Turf." Owner of Greentree Stud, Kentucky. Leading owner and breeder in 1942. Bred and owned Twenty Grand, Shut Out, Devil Diver, First Minstrel. Mother of John Hay Whitney and Joan Whitney (Mrs. Charles S.) Payson.

Whitney, John Hay "Jock," 1904-'82. Investments, publisher. Co-founder of American Thoroughbred Breed-

ers' Association. Co-owner of Greentree Stud, Kentucky; owner of Mare's Nest Farm, Kentucky. Leading owner in 1951. Bred and raced Stage Door Johnny, Capot, Late Bloomer, Bowl Game, The Axe II, Cohoes, Stop the Music; owned Tom Fool. Stood The Porter.

Whitney, W. Payne, 1875-1927. Investments. Owner of Greentree Stud, Kentucky. Son of William C. Whitney; brother of H. P. Whitney; father of John Hay Whitney and Joan Whitney (Mrs. Charles S.) Payson.

Whitney, William C., 1841-1904. Transportation, oil production. President of Saratoga Race Course. Owner of La Belle Stud, Kentucky. Leading owner 1901, '03. Owned Volodyovski, Plaudit, Artful, Endurance By Right, Nasturtium; bred Artful, Tanya. Father of Harry Payne and W. Payne Whitney.

Whittingham, Charles E., 1913-'99. Trainer. Leading trainer 1970-'73, '75, '81, '82; Eclipse Award trainer 1971, '82, '89; inducted into Racing Hall of Fame in '74. Trained 252 stakes winners and 11 champions, including Ack Ack, Sunday Silence, Ferdinand, Turkish Trousers. All-time leading trainer at Hollywood Park and Santa Anita Park; trained two Kentucky Derby winners.

Wickham, John, 1763-1839. Lawyer. Bred champion and leading sire Boston, Tuckahoe.

Widener, George D., 1889-1971. Investments. Chairman of the Jockey Club 1950-'64; president, National Museum of Racing; president, Belmont Park. Owner of Old Kenney Farm, Kentucky; Erdenheim Stud, Pennsylvania. Bred and owned more than 100 stakes winners, including Jaipur, Eight Thirty, What a Treat, Jamestown, High Fleet, Platter, Stefanita, Jester, Seven Thirty, Rare Treat. Nephew of Joseph E. Widener.

Widener, Joseph E., 1871-1943. Investments. President of Hialeah Park, Belmont Park. Owner of Elmendorf Farm, Kentucky. Leading breeder in 1940. Bred Polynesian, Peace Chance, Osmand; owned Chance Shot. Imported leading sire *Sickle. Father of P. A. B. Widener II; uncle of George D. Widener.

Widener, Peter A. B. II, 1896-1952. Investments. Owner of Elmendorf Farm, Kentucky. Son of Joseph E. Widener.

Williamson, Ansel, ca. 1806-'81. Trainer. Inducted into Racing Hall of Fame in 1998. Trained Aristides, Tom Bowling, Brown Dick, Virgil. Trained first Kentucky Derby winner, Aristides.

Willmot, Donald G., 1917-'94. Brewer, investments. Owner of Kinghaven Farm, Ontario. Leading owner in 1990. Bred and owned With Approval, Izvestia, Steady Growth, Candle Bright, Bayford, Play the King, Carotene; co-owner of Deputy Minister.

Winfrey, G. Carey, 1885-1962. Trainer, owner. Inducted into Racing Hall of Fame in 1975. Trained 16 stakes winners and one champion, including Dedicate, Squared Away, Bulwark, Martyr. Stepfather of William C. Winfrey.

Winfrey, William C., 1916-'94. Trainer. Leading trainer in 1964; inducted into Racing Hall of Fame in '71. Trained 38 stakes winners and seven champions, including Native Dancer, Bed o' Roses, Next Move, Bold Lad. Trained Native Dancer, who retired in 1954 with 21 wins in 22 starts. Stepson of G. Carey Winfrey.

Winkfield, Jimmy, 1882-1974. Jockey. Inducted into the Racing Hall of Fame in 2004. Won the 1901 and '02 Kentucky Derbys aboard His Eminence and Alan-a-Dale, respectively, becoming the last African-American rider to capture the Louisville classic. In 1904 became a leading rider in Russia; later competed in Poland, Romania, Germany, and France.

Winn, Col. Matt. G., 1861-1949. Racing executive. President of Louisville Jockey Club. Legendary racetrack promoter, developed Kentucky Derby into world-class event.

Winters, Theodore, 1823-'94. Mining. Owner of Rancho del Rio, California; Rancho del Sierra, Nevada. Bred Emperor of Norfolk, Yo Tambien, El Rio Rey, Rey del Rey, Thad Stevens; owned Norfolk.

Withers, David D., 1821-1972. Banker. President, Monmouth Park. Owner of Brookdale Farm, New Jersey. Bred Requital, Laggard, Kinglike.

Wolfson, Louis, 1912-2007. Investments. Owner of Harbor View Farm, Florida. Leading breeder in 1970-'71. Bred and owned Affirmed, Flawlessly, Exclusive Native, It's In the Air, Outstandingly. Owned Raise a Native. Bred and raced two-time Horse of the Year Affirmed, winner of the Triple Crown in 1978. Bred and owned Racing Hall of Fame Flawlessly. Wife Patrice Wolfson is daughter of Racing Hall of Fame trainer Hirsch Jacobs.

Wood, Eugene D., Birthdate unknown-1924. Racing executive. Treasurer of the Metropolitan Jockey Club (Jamaica). Namesake of Wood Memorial Stakes.

Woodford, Catesby, 1849-1923. President of Kentucky Racing Association. Owner of Raceland Farm, Kentucky. Co-owner of Runnymede Stud, Kentucky. Stood Hindoo, *Star Shoot. Co-breeder of Miss Woodford, Hanover, Sir Dixon.

Woodward, William Jr., 1920-'55. Banker, sportsman. Owner of Belair Stud. Owned Nashua.

Woodward, William Sr., 1876-1953. Banker. Chairman of the Jockey Club 1930-'50. Owner of Belair Stud, Maryland. Leading owner in 1939. Part of syndicate that imported *Sir Gallahad III. Bred and owned Gallant Fox, Omaha, Nashua, Granville, Vagrancy.

Woolf, George "The Iceman," 1910-'46. Jockey. Leading jockey by money won 1942, '44; inducted into Racing Hall of Fame in '55. Rode 721 winners, including Seabiscuit, Whirlaway, Challedon. Won the Belmont Futurity three straight years, the first running of the Santa Anita Derby, and the Preakness Stakes.

Workman, Raymond "Sonny," 1909-'66. Jockey. Leading jockey by races won in 1930, '33, '35; leading jockey by money won in 1930, '32; inducted into Racing Hall of Fame in '56. Rode 1,169 winners, including Equipoise, Top Flight, Discovery.

Wright, Warren, 1875-1950. Baking powder, investments. Owner of Calumet Farm, Kentucky. Leading breeder 1941, '44, '47-'50; leading owner 1941, '43-'44, '46-'49. Bred and owned Citation, Whirlaway, Pensive, Ponder, Coaltown, Bewitch, Hill Gail, Twilight Tear, Real Delight, Armed; owned Nellie Flag, Bull Lea. Stood leading sire Bull Lea, Sun Again, Chance Play.

Yoshida, Zenya, 1921-'93. Breeder. Owner of Shadai Farm, Japan; Fontainebleau Farm, Kentucky. Leading Japanese breeder 20 times. Bred Amber Shadai, Gallop Dyna, Dyna Gulliver, Vega; co-owned Wajima; stood Northern Taste, Sunday Silence.

Young, Col. Milton S., 1851-1918. Retail hardware, real estate. Chairman of Kentucky Racing Commission. Owner of McGrathiana Stud, Kentucky. Leading breeder in 1890. Bred Broomstick, Yankee; stood Hanover.

Young, William T., 1918-2004. Foods, storage. Owner of Overbrook Farm, Kentucky. Eclipse Award breeder in 1994. Bred and owned Storm Cat, Tabasco Cat, Cat Thief, Boston Harbor, Flanders, Surfside, Golden Attraction, Grindstone. Owned Editor's Note.

Contemporary Individuals in Racing and Breeding

(Names of Racing Hall of Fame members are in boldface italics.)

Abdullah, Khalid, 1942-. Investments. Owner of Juddmonte Farms, Kentucky and England. Eclipse Award breeder in 1995, 2001-'03; Eclipse Award owner in '92, 2003; P.A.B. Widener Trophy in '93; honorary member of Great Britain's Jockey Club in '83. Bred Ryafan, Wandesta (GB), Commander in Chief, Warning (GB), Banks Hill (GB), Empire Maker. Owned Known Fact, Dancing Brave, Rainbow Quest. Member of the ruling family of Saudi Arabia; first Arab owner to win a British classic (Two Thousand Guineas [Eng-G1] with Known Fact in 1980).

Abercrombie, Josephine, 1926-. Oil production, boxing promoter. Owner of Pin Oak Farm, Kentucky. Member of Jockey Club. Bred and owned Laugh and Be Merry, Peaks and Valleys. Co-owned Maria's Mon. Bred Elocutionist, Touching Wood.

Adam, Donald, 1935-. Former chairman and CEO, First American Bank. Owner, Courtlandt Farm, Ocala. Owned Film Maker, Commendation, Gourmet Girl, Pike Place Dancer, Adriano.

Aga Khan IV, Karim, 1936-. Investments, Ismaili Muslim leader. Owner of Gilltown Stud, Sheshoon Stud in Ireland; Haras de Bonneval in France. Bred and owned Shergar, Sinndar, Kahyasi, Daylami (Ire), Kalanisi (Ire), Dalakhani. Built Aiglemont training facility near Chantilly, France, in 1977; continued breeding operations begun by his grandfather, Aga Khan III, and his father, Aly Khan.

Aitcheson, Joe Jr., 1929-. Jockey. Leading steeplechase jockey 1961, '63-'64, '67-'70; inducted into Racing Hall of Fame in '78; first jockey to receive the F. Ambrose Clark Memorial Award, in '75. Rode 478 winners, including Amber Diver, Bon Nouvel, Tuscalee, Top Bid, Soothsayer, Inkslinger. Won eight Virginia Gold Cups, seven Carolina Cups, and two Colonial Cups.

Alexander, Helen, 1951-. Investments. Member of Jockey Club. President, Thoroughbred Club of America, 1989-'91. Owner of Middlebrook Farm, Kentucky. Bred Twining. Bred and owned Althea, Aishah, Aquilegia. Granddaughter of Robert J. Kleberg.

Allbritton, Joseph, 1924-. Publishing, banking, broadcasting, real estate. Owner of Lazy Lane Farms, Kentucky and Virginia. Member of Jockey Club. Owned Hansel, Secret Hello, Life At the Top, Kittiwake.

Amerman, John, 1932-. Owner, industry official. Chairman and chief executive officer of Mattel Inc., 1987-'97. Member and steward, Jockey Club. Owner of Amerman Racing Stable, California. Owned stakes winners Lido Palace (Chi), Happyanunoit (NZ), Valor Lady, Mash One (Chi), Adoration.

Anthony, John Ed, 1939-. Timber. Owner of Shortleaf Farm, Arkansas; president of Loblolly Stable. Member of Jockey Club. Bred and owned Temperence Hill, Vanlandingham, Prairie Bayou. Owned Cox's Ridge. Established the Exercise Induced Pulmonary Hemorrhage Fund after his Demons Begone bled during the 1987 Kentucky Derby (G1).

Arnold, Doug, 1954-. Breeder. Owner, Buck Pond Farm, Kentucky.

Asmussen, Cash, 1962-. Jockey. Leading jockey by money won in 1979; leading jockey in France 1985-'86, '88-'90; Eclipse Award apprentice jockey in '79. Rode Suave Dancer, Hector Protector, Mill Native, Northern Trick. Won inaugural Japan Cup aboard Mairzy Doates in 1981; three times won five races on a single card in New York. Brother of trainer Steve Asmussen.

Asmussen, Steven, 1965-. Trainer. Leading trainer by wins in 2002, '04-'05, and '07. Saddled record 555 winners in 2004. Trains 2007 Horse of the Year Curlin, other Grade 1 winners Cuvee, Dreams Gallore, Lady Tak. Brother of Cash Asmussen.

Avioli, Greg, 1964-. Lawyer, lobbyist. President, Breeders' Cup Ltd.; former NTRA president and deputy commissioner; chaired NTRA Wagering Systems Task Force. Formerly senior vice president, International Sports and Entertainment Strategies.

Bacharach, Burt, 1929-. Composer. Co-owner of Country Roads Farm, West Virginia. Thoroughbred Owners and Breeders Association Award for outstanding owner-breeder 1995-'96. Bred and owned Heartlight No. One, Afternoon Deelites, Soul of the Matter.

Baeza, Braulio, 1940-. Jockey, trainer. Leading jockey by money won in 1965-'68, '75; Eclipse Award jockey 1972, '75; inducted into Racing Hall of Fame in '76; George Woolf Memorial Jockey Award in '68. Rode 3,140 winners, including Buckpasser, Dr. Fager, Ack Ack, Gallant Bloom, Affectionately, Chateaugay. Trained Double Zeus. Rode Buckpasser to one-mile record in 1966 and then lowered it aboard Dr. Fager in '68.

Baffert, Bob, 1953-. Trainer. Leading trainer by money won, 1998-2001; Eclipse Award trainer 1997-'99; United Thoroughbred Trainers of America's trainer of the year in '98; Mr. Fitz Award in '97. Trained Chilukki, Real Quiet, Silverbulletday, Silver Charm, Point Given, War Emblem. Won a record 13 stakes at Del Mar in 2000; only trainer to win Kentucky Derby (G1) and Preakness Stakes (G1) in consecutive years (1997-'98).

Bailey, Jerry, 1957-. Jockey. President, Jockeys' Guild, 1990-'97. Leading jockey by money won in 1995-'98, 2001-'03; inducted into Racing Hall of Fame in 1995; Eclipse Award jockey 1995-'97, 2000-'03; George Woolf Memorial Jockey Award in 1992; Mike Venezia Award in '93. Rode Cigar, Fit to Fight, Black Tie Affair (Ire), Sea Hero. In 1996, rode Cigar to his 16th consecutive win; rode seven winners on Florida Derby (G1) day program in '95; successfully lobbied for protective vests to be worn by all jockeys; won handicap triple crown with Fit to Fight in '84. Retired in 2006 and now television racing analyst.

Bandoroff, Craig, 1955-. Farm owner, consignor. Owner of Denali Stud, Kentucky. One of country's leading consignors of yearlings, broodmares, and weanlings.

Barr, John, 1929-. Real estate. Owner, Los Amigos Thoroughbred Farm in Temecula, California; Member and steward, Jockey Club; director, Oak Tree Racing Association; secretary-treasurer, Richard Nixon Presidential Library. Races horses as Oakcrest Stable.

Barton, Patti, 1945-. Jockey. Helped break gender barrier when she became one of the first female jockeys in 1969. Retired in 1984 as world's winningest female rider, with 1,202 victories. Mother of former jockey and television personality Donna Barton Brothers and trainer Jerry Barton.

Bassett, James E. "Ted" III, 1921-. Racing executive. Former chairman, Keeneland Association; former president, Breeders' Cup Ltd.; also served as chairman, Equibase Co.; president, Thoroughbred Racing Associations; chairman, Kentucky Horse Park; pres-

ident, Thoroughbred Club of America. Co-owner of Lanark Farm, Kentucky. Eclipse Award of Merit in 1995; John W. Galbreath Award in '91; Turf and Field Club Award in '84; Joe Palmer Award in '86; John A. Morris Award in '97; Lord Derby Award in '98.

Baugh, Rollin, 1937-. Bloodstock agent. California-based agent maintains international trade, especially to Japan. Brokered sales of Forty Niner, Charismatic, Captain Steve, and Chief Bearhart to Japan. Member, Jockey Club. Director of Del Mar, Tranquility Farm Thoroughbred retirement facility.

Baze, Russell, 1958-. Jockey. All-time leading North American jockey; won his 9,531st race to surpass Laffit Pincay Jr. on December 1, 2006; leading jockey by races won in 1992-'96, 2002; inducted into Racing Hall of Fame in '99; Special Eclipse Award in '95; Isaac Murphy Award 1995-2003, '05-'07; George Woolf Memorial Jockey Award in '02. Rode Hawkster, Both Ends Burning, Itsallgreektome, Lost in the Fog. Won 400 races a year 11 times in 12 years.

Beasley, Rogers W. B., 1949-. Racing executive. Director of racing for Keeneland Association since 2001; previously director of sales for Keeneland for 19 years; led the initiative to introduce preferred sessions to the September sale and to inaugurate the April two-year-olds in training sales.

Beck, Antony, 1962-. Breeder. President, Gainesway, Kentucky. Director, the National Thoroughbred Racing Association's Horse Political Action Committee since 2006. Member of the board of directors of the Breeders' Cup since 2006.

Beck, Graham, 1929-. Mining, investments, vintner. Owner of Gainesway, Kentucky; Silvercrest Farm, Kentucky; Midway Farm, Kentucky; Highlands Farm, South Africa; Maine Chance Farm, South Africa; Noreen Stud, South Africa. Bred Pompeii, Real Cozzy, Irish Prize. Co-owned Timber Country.

Bell, Headley, 1954-. Bloodstock agent. Son of Mill Ridge Farm owner Alice Chandler; maternal grandson of Hal Price Headley, co-founder of Keeneland. Past board member, Thoroughbred Club of America, Sales Integrity Sales Force.

Bell, James, 1954-. Farm manager. President of Darley USA, member of Jockey Club. Son of John A. Bell III.

Bell, Reynolds Jr., 1952-. Bloodstock agent. Son of Mill Ridge Farm owner Alice Chandler; maternal grandson of Hal Price Headley, co-founder of Keeneland. Member, Jockey Club. Vice president, Thoroughbred Owners and Breeders Association. Former manager of Mill Ridge Farm. Past president, Thoroughbred Club of America.

Bellocq, Pierre "Peb," 1926-. Caricaturist. Special Eclipse Award in 1980; John Hervey Award 1965-'66, '68; Knights of Arts and Letters Award in '90; Golden Horseshoe Award in '91. Achieved international acclaim as *Daily Racing Form*'s caricaturist; has murals at Aqueduct, Churchill Downs, Oaklawn Park, and Arlington Park; founded the Amateur Riders Club of the Americas with son Remi Bellocq.

Bellocq, Remi, 1961-. Marketing, organization executive. Former marketing director at Turf Paradise and Santa Anita Park. Became executive director of the National Horsemen's Benevolent and Protective Association in 2001. Son of Pierre Bellocq.

Berube, Paul, 1941-. Retired president of the Thoroughbred Racing Protective Bureau. Background in military intelligence; TRPB agent and vice president 1965-'88.

Beyer, Andrew, 1943-. Handicapper, journalist. Horse racing columnist for the Washington *Post*, 1978-2004. Developed Beyer Speed Figures and wrote four books on handicapping.

Biancone, Patrick, 1952-. Trainer. Trained All Along (Fr) to North America Horse of the Year title in 1983 with sweep of three turf races carrying a $1-million bonus; All Along also won the Prix de l'Arc de Triomphe (Fr-G1) that year. Also won Arc in 1984 with Sagace (Fr). Trained champion Bikala, Strawberry Road (Aus), Triptych, Palace Music.

Biszantz, Gary, 1934-. Golf-club manufacturer. Former chairman of Thoroughbred Owners and Breeders Association. Jockey Club member. Owns 350-acre Cobra Farm in Lexington. Owned Old Trieste, Running Flame (Fr), Admise (Fr), Lord Grillo (Arg), homebred Cobra King. Co-founder of Cobra Golf, sold in 1996 to American Brands.

Blum, Walter, 1934-. Jockey, racing official. Former president, Jockeys' Guild. Leading jockey by races won in 1963-'64; inducted into Racing Hall of Fame in '87; George Woolf Memorial Jockey Award in '65. Rode 4,382 winners, including Affectionately, Gun Bow, Forego, Mr. Prospector, Pass Catcher, Summer Scandal, Boldnesian, Priceless Gem, Lady Pitt.

Boland, Bill, 1933-. Jockey. Won the 1950 Kentucky Derby and Belmont Stakes as an apprentice aboard Middleground. Also won the 1960 Belmont on Amberoid. Won a total of 1,980 races. Elected to the Racing Hall of Fame in 2006 by Historical Review Committee.

Bonnie, Edward S. "Ned," 1929-. Lawyer, steeplechase horseman. Member, Jockey Club, Kentucky Horse Racing Authority. With wife Nina, received 2002 First USA Bank/USA Equestrian Lifetime Achievement Award. Responsible for National Steeplechase and Kentucky protective helmet regulations for jockeys.

Boulmetis, Sam Sr., 1927-. Jockey, racing official. Inducted into Racing Hall of Fame in 1973. Rode 2,783 winners. Rode Tosmah, Helioscope, Dedicate. Long-time steward at New Jersey tracks.

Bowen, Edward L., 1942-. Industry executive, author. President, Grayson-Jockey Club Research Foundation. Editor-in-chief, *The Blood-Horse*, 1987-'92. Author of 15 books, including *The Jockey Club Illustrated History of Racing*, *Matriarchs*, and *Man o' War*.

Bowlinger, Paul, 1960-. Lawyer, industry executive. Vice president, Association of Racing Commissioners International. Former executive director, North American Pari-Mutuel Regulators Association and North Dakota Racing Commission.

Brady, Nicholas J., 1930-. Financier. Chairman, Jockey Club, 1974-'82; United States treasury secretary 1988-'93; Co-owner of Mill House Stable. Bred and owned Sensational, Furiously, Meritus. Son of James Cox Brady Jr.

Bramlage, Larry, 1952-. Veterinarian. President, American Association of Equine Practitioners in 2003-'04. Member, Jockey Club. Jockey Club Gold Medal in 1994; British Equine Veterinary Association's Special Award of Merit in '98. Developed and improved ways to repair serious bone fractures.

Brennan, Niall, 1961-. Bloodstock agent, pinhooker. Owner of Niall Brennan Stables, Florida. Leading two-year-old consignor in 2000-'04. Sold Ecton Park, Jersey Girl, Kurofune, Read the Footnotes, Whitmore's Conn, Yonaguska.

Broman, Chester, 1935-. Building contractor. President of Clifford Broman & Sons Inc. in Babylon, New

York. Trustee, New York Racing Association; New York Thoroughbred Breeders board of directors. Owner of Chestertown Farm, New York. With his wife, Mary, owned and bred Friends Lake.

Brumfield, Don, 1938-. Jockey, racing official. Inducted into Racing Hall of Fame in 1996; George Woolf Memorial Jockey Award in '88. Rode 4,573 winners, including Forward Pass, Alysheba, Gold Beauty, Our Mims, Old Hat. Retired in 1989 with the most wins in Churchill Downs's (925) and Keeneland Race Course's (716) history.

Brunetti, John, 1931-. President and owner of Hialeah Park, which he purchased in 1978; track has not conducted racing since 2001. Owner of Red Oak Farm, Florida; owned Strolling Belle.

Burch, J. Elliott, 1922-. Trainer. Leading trainer by money won in 1969; inducted into Racing Hall of Fame in '80. Trained more than 30 stakes winners and six champions, including Sword Dancer, Fort Marcy, Arts and Letters, Bowl of Flowers, Run the Gantlet, Key to the Mint. Son of Hall of Fame trainer Preston Burch; grandson of Hall of Fame trainer William Burch.

Burge, Doug, 1971-. Industry executive. Executive vice president and general manager, California Thoroughbred Breeders Association, 1997-.

Campbell Jr., Alex, 1928-. Thoroughbred owner-breeder, philanthropist. Member, Jockey Club. Director, Breeders' Cup Ltd. Retired from tobacco business in 1989. Helped to develop Thoroughbred Park in Lexington. Co-breeder, Grade 1 winner Goodbye Halo. Owner and breeder of Mr Purple.

Campbell, W. Cothran "Cot," 1927-. Advertising, racing syndicates. President of Dogwood Stable, South Carolina. Member, Jockey Club. John W. Galbreath Award in 1992. Owned Summer Squall, Storm Song, Dominion (GB). Popularized racing syndicates; wrote *Lightning in a Jar: Catching Racing Fever, Rascals and Racehorses*, and *Memoirs of a Longshot*.

Card, Keith E., 1927-. President of the California Thoroughbred Breeders Association, 2005. Founder and former president of board of directors, Las Tortugas Riding Organization.

Carey, Thomas, 1932-. Racing executive. President and general manager, Hawthorne Race Course. Inducted into Chicago Sports Hall of Fame in 1998. Instrumental in rebuilding Hawthorne after fire in 1978.

Casner, William, 1948-. Heavy equipment. Partner in WinStar Farm, Kentucky. Chairman, Thoroughbred Owners and Breeders Association. Board of advisers, The Race for Education scholarship foundation. Vice chairman and co-founder, Kentucky Equine Education Project. In WinStar name, bred Funny Cide, One Cool Cat. Owned Awesome Humor, Bet Me Best, Byzantium (Brz), and Pompeii..

Casse, Mark, 1961-. Trainer, consignor, bloodstock agent. Former private trainer and director of operations for Mockingbird Farm, Florida. Sovereign Award as leading Canadian trainer in 2006-'07. Trained Exciting Story, Dark Ending, Added Edge.

Cauthen, Steve, 1960-. Jockey. Leading jockey by races won in 1977; inducted into Racing Hall of Fame in '94; Eclipse Award apprentice jockey in '77; Eclipse Award jockey in '77; Eclipse Award of Merit in '77; George Woolf Memorial Jockey Award in '84. Rode 2,794 winners, including Affirmed, Oh So Sharp (Ire), Old Vic, Johnny D., Diminuendo, Indian Skimmer. Rode Affirmed to Triple Crown in 1978; only jockey to win the Kentucky, Epsom, Irish, French, and Italian Derbys; at 18, youngest jockey to win Kentucky Derby.

Cella, Charles, 1936-. Real estate, racing executive. President, Oaklawn Park; president, Thoroughbred Racing Associations 1975-'76. TRA's youngest president in 1975. Eclipse Award of Merit in 2004. Owned Northern Spur (Ire), Out of Hock, Crafty Shaw.

Chace, Baden P. "Buzz," 1941-. Bloodstock agent. Since 1983, buyer of racing prospects for various clients. Selected Breeders' Cup winners Unbridled's Song and champion Artax, Belmont Stakes (G1) winner Sarava, and numerous Grade 1 winners.

Chandler, Alice Headley, 1927-. Farm owner. Chairwoman, Maxwell F. Gluck Equine Research Center; former chairwoman, Kentucky Racing Commission; president, Kentucky Thoroughbred Owners and Breeders Association; former president, Kentucky Thoroughbred Associaton; director, Keeneland Association. Member of Jockey Club. Owner of Mill Ridge Farm, Kentucky. Bred and owned Keeper Hill. Bred Sir Ivor, Secret Hello, Ciao, Flemensfirth.

Chandler, John. Co-owner, Mill Ridge Farm. Trustee, Thoroughbred Owners and Breeders Association. Racing manager, Juddmonte Farms.

Chavez, Jorge, 1961-. Jockey. Leading jockey in New York 1994-'99; Eclipse Award jockey in '99. Rode Monarchos, Artax, Beautiful Pleasure, A P Valentine, Affirmed Success. Rode six winners on single card at Gulfstream Park in 1999.

Chenery, Helen "Penny," 1931-. Investments. President, Thoroughbred Owners and Breeders Association, 1976-'84. Former owner of Meadow Stud and Meadow Stable, Virginia. Bred Alada. Owned Secretariat, Riva Ridge. First woman to head a major national racing organization; one of the first three women inducted into Jockey Club, in 1983.

Chillingworth, Sherwood, 1926-. Executive vice president of Oak Tree Racing Association. Jockey Club member; vice chairman of Santa Anita Realty 1994-'96.

Clay, Robert N., 1946-. Farm owner. President, Thoroughbred Owners and Breeders Association, 1990-'93; past president, National Thoroughbred Association and Thoroughbred Club of America. Member, Jockey Club. Co-owner of Three Chimneys Farm, Kentucky. John W. Galbreath Award in 1995. Bred and owned Hidden Lake, Gorgeous. Bred Seaside Attraction, Subordination.

Combs II, Brownell, 1933-. Former president and chairman of Spendthrift Farm; former Kentucky Racing Commission chairman. Son of Leslie Combs II, renowned commercial horse salesman, stallion syndicator, and founder of Spendthrift Farm in 1930s. Pleaded guilty in 2001 to federal income tax fraud charges.

Cooksey, Patricia, 1958-. Jockey. Second all-time leading female jockey with more than 2,100 winners and purse earnings of $20-million. Captured four riding titles at Turfway Park. All-time leading female rider at Churchill Downs. In 1985 became first female to ride in the Preakness Stakes (G1) (sixth on Tajawa). Member of the Kentucky Athletic Hall of Fame; Mr. Fitz Award in 2004; Mike Venezia Memorial Award in 2004. Retired 2004.

Cordero, Angel Jr., 1942-. Jockey, jockey's agent. Leading jockey by money won 1976, '82-'83; leading jockey by races won in '68; inducted into Racing Hall of Fame in '88; Eclipse Award jockey 1982-'83; George Woolf Memorial Jockey Award in '72; Mike Venezia Award in '92. Rode 7,076 winners, including Seattle Slew, Slew o' Gold, All Along (Fr), Bold Forbes, Broad Brush. Won jockey's title at Saratoga 13 times, 11 consecutively. Agent for John Velazquez.

Couto, Drew, 1959-. Lawyer. President, Thoroughbred Owners of California. Former president, Thoroughbred Owners and Breeders Association.

Craig, Sidney, 1932- and **Craig, Jenny**, 1932-. Diet foods. Owners of Rancho del Rayo training center in California. Owned 1992-'93 champion older female Paseana (Arg), Exchange, Dr Devious (Ire), Alpride (Ire).

Crist, Steven. Journalist. Publisher, *Daily Racing Form* since 1998. Has published four books and co-authored two others. Founding editor, *Racing Times*.

Cruguet, Jean, 1939-. Jockey. Rider of 1977 Triple Crown winner Seattle Slew and other stakes winners, including Bold Reason, Hoist the Flag, Bailrullah. Leading rider at Deauville 1972-'73; second leading rider in France in '73; came to the United States in 1965. Was the first rider to win three stakes races in one day, Belmont Stakes (G1) day in 1984.

Day, Pat, 1953-. Jockey. President, Jockeys' Guild, 2000-'01. Leading jockey by races won in 1982-'84, '86, '90-'91; inducted into Racing Hall of Fame in '91; Eclipse Award jockey in 1984, '86-'87, '91; George Woolf Memorial Jockey Award in '85; Mike Venezia Award in '95; Mr. Fitz Award in 2000. Rode Wild Again, Flanders, Lady's Secret, Easy Goer, Summer Squall, Tank's Prospect, Louis Quatorze, Lil E. Tee, Dance Smartly. All-time leader by earnings among jockeys and third-highest number of winners; set a record for most stakes won (60) in a single season in 1991; rode seven winners in one day at Churchill Downs in '84; won on eight of nine mounts at Arlington Park in '89. Retired in 2005. Active in Racetrack Chaplaincy of America.

De Francis, Joseph, 1955-. Racing executive, lawyer. Former president, Maryland Jockey Club. Son of Frank De Francis.

Delahoussaye, Eddie, 1951-. Jockey. Leading jockey in 1978; inducted into Racing Hall of Fame in '93; George Woolf Memorial Jockey Award in '81. Rode A.P. Indy, Princess Rooney, Prized, Gato Del Sol, Sunny's Halo, Pleasant Stage, Thirty Slews, Gate Dancer. One of four jockeys to win consecutive Kentucky Derbys, in 1982-'83. Retired in early 2003.

Desormeaux, Kent, 1970-. Jockey. Leading jockey by races won in 1987-'89; leading jockey by money won in '92; inducted into Racing Hall of Fame in 2004; Eclipse Award apprentice jockey in '87; Eclipse Award jockey 1989, '92; George Woolf Memorial Jockey Award in '93. Rode Fusaichi Pegasus, Big Brown, Real Quiet, Kotashaan (Fr), Risen Star. Won record 598 races in 1989; won six races on a single card at Hollywood Park in 1992.

Dickinson, Michael, 1950-. Trainer. Inventor. Owner of Tapeta Farm, Maryland. Trained Da Hoss, Fleet Renee, Cetewayo, Tapit. Trained first five finishers in England's Cheltenham Gold Cup in 1983. Developer of Tapeta Footings synthetic race surface.

DiMauro, Steve Sr., 1932-. Trainer. Owner of DiMauro Farm, New York. Eclipse Award trainer in 1975. Bred Flip's Pleasure, Father Don Juan. Trained Wajima, Dearly Precious, Nagurski, Father Don Juan.

Dizney, Donald R., 1942-. Health care, banking. Founder and chairman, United Medical Corp. Owner of Double Diamond Farm in Ocala. President, Florida Thoroughbred Breeders' and Owners' Association. Member and steward of the Jockey Club. Bred and co-owned Grade 1 winner Wekiva Springs.

Donn, Douglas, 1947-. Racing executive. President of Gulfstream Park racetrack 1978-2000; chairman of the board '00-'04, after the track was purchased by Magna Entertainment Corp. Grandson of late Gulfstream owner James Donn Sr.

Dreyfus Jr., Jack J., 1913-. Financier. Chairman, New York Racing Association, in 1969 and '75. Owner Hobeau Farm, Florida. Member, Jockey Club. Leading owner by money won in 1967; Eclipse Award of Merit in '76. Bred and owned Beau Purple, Duck Dance, Never Bow, Step Nicely. Exacta introduced in New York betting under his direction; his Beau Purple upset Kelso three times.

Drysdale, Neil, 1947-. Trainer. Inducted into Racing Hall of Fame in 2000. Trained A.P. Indy, Fusaichi Pegasus, Princess Rooney, Tasso, Hollywood Wildcat, Fiji (GB), Bold 'n Determined.

Duchossois, Richard L., 1921-. Industrialist. Chairman, Arlington Park. Owner of Hill 'N Dale Farm, Illinois. Special Eclipse Award in 1989; Eclipse Award of Merit in 2004. Special Sovereign Award in 1988; Lord Derby Award in '88; Jockey Club Medal in '86; Jockey Agents' Benevolent Association's man of the year in '90. Member, Jockey Club. Bred Explosive Darling. Rebuilt Arlington Park after the track was destroyed by fire in 1985; under his leadership, Arlington received a Special Eclipse Award in '85, the first awarded to a racetrack.

Duncker, C. Stephen, 1958-. Industry executive. Chairman, New York Racing Association; Former co-chief operating officer, NYRA, 2003-'04. Member, Jockey Club. Trustee, Thoroughbred Owners and Breeders Association. Former managing director, Goldman Sachs. Bred and owned Grade 2 winner Middlesex Drive.

Dutrow Jr., Richard, 1959-. Trainer. Leading trainer by wins in New York in 2001-'02. One of only seven trainers to train two or more winners on a Breeders' Cup card; Saint Liam in the 2006 Breeders' Cup Classic (G1) and Silver Train in the Sprint (G1). Son of late trainer Richard Dutrow Sr. Also trained Big Brown, Cativa, Offlee Wild, Carson Hollow.

Englander, Richard, 1959-. Investments. Eclipse Award owner in 2001, when he led the nation with stable earnings of $9,784,822, and in '02.

Evans, Edward P. "Ned," 1942-. Publishing. Owner of Spring Hill Farm, Virginia. Member, Jockey Club. Bred and owned Minstrella, Prenup, Raging Fever, Fairy Garden, Colonial Minstrel. Bred Saint Liam. Brother of Robert S. Evans; son of Thomas Mellon Evans.

Evans, Robert L., 1952-. Racetrack executive. President and chief executive officer, Churchill Downs Inc. since 2006. Owner, Tenlane Farm, Versailles, Kentucky. Formerly associated with private equity firm in California; held executive positions with Caterpillar Inc., Mazda Motor of America Inc., and Accenture Ltd.

Evans, Robert S. "Shel," 1944-. Manufacturing. Owner of Winter Haven Farm, Florida; Courtland Farm, Maryland. Member, Jockey Club. Bred and owned Sewickley, Shared Interest. Bred Forestry, Cash Run. Brother of Edward P. Evans; son of Thomas Mellon Evans.

Everett, Marjorie L., 1921-. Racing executive. Former chairman and chief executive officer, Hollywood Park; former owner, Arlington Park; former owner, Washington Park. Undertook major improvements at Hollywood, including expanding the circumference of the track, building the Cary Grant Pavilion, and improving the backstretch; successfully lobbied for inaugural Breeders' Cup to be held at Hollywood in 1984.

Fabian, Franklin, 1952-. President, Thoroughbred Racing Protective Bureau since 2005. FBI agent and executive, 1985-2005. Received 1996 Director's Award for Excellence in Investigation.

Fabre, Andre, 1945-. Trainer. Champion French trainer 1987-2007. Won five Prix de l'Arc de Triomphes (Fr-G1), three Breeders' Cup events—the 1993 Classic (G1) with 134-to-1 Arcangues; '90 Turf (G1) with In the Wings (GB); and 2001 Filly and Mare Turf (G1) with Banks Hill (GB). Also trained Trempolino, Swain (Ire), Subotica (Fr), Sagamix (Fr), Zafonic.

Farish, William S., 1939-. Investments. Chairman, Churchill Downs, 1992-2001. Vice chairman of Jockey Club. President and owner of Lane's End, Kentucky. Eclipse Award breeder in 1992, '99; P.A.B. Widener Trophy in '92. Bred or co-bred A.P. Indy, Mineshaft, Law Society, Lemon Drop Kid, Charismatic, Summer Squall, Prospectors Delite. Owned Bee Bee Bee, Miss Brio (Chi), Sweet Revenge. Former chairman of the Breeders' Cup executive committee; United States ambassador to Great Britain and Northern Ireland, 2001-'04. Nephew of Martha Gerry.

Farish, William "Bill" Jr., 1964-. Business manager and sales director of Lane's End, Kentucky. Son of William S. Farish. Member of the Jockey Club. Chairman, Breeders' Cup Ltd.; member, Kentucky Thoroughbred Association board, Thoroughbred Owners and Breeders Association, Maxwell H. Gluck Equine Research Center. Former president, Thoroughbred Club of America. Owned and bred Grade 2 winner Shadow Cast and bred Grade 1 winner Burning Roma.

Farmer, Tracy, 1939-. Auto dealer. Owns Farmer Automotive Group Inc. in Louisville and has dealerships in Atlanta and Florida. University of Kentucky Board of Trustees, 1979-'91. Chairman, Kentucky Democratic Party, 1981. Owner of Shadowlawn Farm, Kentucky. Co-owned Hidden Lake, Joyeux Danseur; raced Albert the Great.

Fenwick Jr., Charles, 1948-. Auto dealer; steeplechase jockey, trainer. Trained and rode *Dosdi to two National Steeplechase Association Timber Horse of the Year titles. In 1980 rode *Ben Nevis II to victory in England's Grand National Steeplechase. Trained 1987 Eclipse Award-winning steeplechaser Inlander (GB) and timber champions Buck Jakes, Free Throw, Sugar Bee.

Ferguson, John, 1960-. Bloodstock agent, racing manager. Purchased Pentire, E Dubai, Dubai Destination, Essence of Dubai, Moon Ballad. Chief buying agent and racing manager for Sheikh Mohammed bin Rashid al Maktoum.

Fermin, Ingrid, 1942-. Executive director, California Horse Racing Board, 2005-'07. In 1981, became the first female steward in California.

Fick, Dan, 1948-. Industry executive. Executive vice president and executive director of the Jockey Club. Chairman of the Racing Medication and Testing Consortium. Former senior vice president of racing for the American Quarter Horse Association. Credited with revitalizing the Race Track Chaplaincy of America.

Finley, Terry, 1964-. Founder and president, West Point Thoroughbreds. Director, National Thoroughbred Racing Association's Political Action Committee since 2004. Member of the board of directors of the Breeders' Cup since 2006.

Fires, Earlie, 1947- Jockey. Leading apprentice jockey in 1965; inducted into Racing Hall of Fame in 2001; George Woolf Memorial Jockey Award in 1991. Rode In Reality, War Censor, Dike, Abe's Hope, Pattee Canyon, Woozem, Gallant Romeo. Won seven races from eight mounts in a single day at Arlington Park in 1983. Ninth all-time leading jockey with more than 6,450 wins.

Firestone, Bertram S., 1931-, and **Firestone, Diana,** 1932-. Real estate, investments. Owner, Calder Race Course and Gulfstream Park 1988-'91. Owner of Catoctin Stud, Virginia. Eclipse Award owner in 1980. Owned Racing Hall of Fame member Genuine Risk. Bred and owned Theatrical (Ire), Paradise Creek, April Run (Ire), Honest Pleasure, What a Summer.

Fishback, Jerry, 1947-. Jockey, bloodstock agent. Leading steeplechase jockey by races won in 1971, '73-'75, '77; leading steeplechase jockey by money won in '85; inducted into Racing Hall of Fame in '92. Rode 301 winners, including Cafe Prince, Flatterer. Won Temple Gwathmey Steeplechase six times; won four Carolina Cups and four International Gold Cups.

Ford, Gerald, 1944-. Banker and insurer. Chairman of Dallas-based First Acceptance Corp., formerly Liberte Investments Inc., of which he owns approximately 45%. In 2000, bought 815 acres of former Brookside Farm in Kentucky for approximately $11-million and renamed it Diamond A Farms. Also owns 120,000-acre Diamond A Ranch in New Mexico. Raced Pleasantly Perfect, winner of the 2003 Breeders' Cup Classic (G1) and '04 Dubai World Cup (UAE-G1). Also raced homebred Minister Eric.

Foreman, Alan, 1950-. Lawyer. Chairman and chief executive officer, Thoroughbred Horsemen's Association. Creator of Mid-Atlantic Thoroughbred Championship (MATCH) series; general counsel for the Maryland Thoroughbred Horsemen's Association.

Forsythe, John, 1918-. Actor. Director, Hollywood Park. Owner of Big Train Farm. Eclipse Award of Merit in 1988. Owned Targa. Longtime Eclipse Awards dinner host.

Francis, Dick, 1920-. Jockey, author. International best-selling author of 39 mystery novels about horse racing. England's champion steeplechase jockey of 1953-'54 when he rode for the Queen Mother. Published first novel—*Dead Cert*—in 1962. Winner of three Edgar Allen Poe Awards for best mystery novel.

Frankel, Robert, 1941-. Trainer. Leading trainer by money won in 1993, 2002-'03; inducted into Racing Hall of Fame in '95; Eclipse Award trainer in 1993, 2000-'03. Trained Bertrando, Possibly Perfect, Wandesta (GB), Marquetry, Squirtle Squirt, Empire Maker, Medaglia d'Oro, Ghostzapper. Once called the king of claimers for his ability to turn claiming horses into winners; won a record 60 races at Hollywood Park during his first year in California (1972). Established earnings record and mark for most Grade 1 victories in a year in 2003.

Fravel, Craig, 1958-. Lawyer, racetrack executive. Executive vice president, Del Mar Thoroughbred Club, 1990-. Director, NTRA; member, Equibase Management Committee.

Fuller, Peter S., 1923-. Automobile dealer. John A. Morris Award in 1985. Bred and owned Dancer's Image, Mom's Command, Shananie, Donna's Time.

Fulton, Stanley, 1931-. Owner of Sunland Park Racetrack and Casino, New Mexico; consultant, Anchor Gaming; Thoroughbred owner, philanthropist. Leading buyer at 2003 Fasig-Tipton Kentucky July sale of selected yearlings.

Gagliano, James L., 1965-. Executive vice president and chief administrative officer of the Jockey Club,

2005-. Formerly executive vice president of Maryland Racing Operations for Magna Entertainment Corp.

Gann, Edmund A., 1923-. Commercial fisheries, banking. Entered racing in 1960s when a fishing buddy offered him half-interest in a filly to settle a debt. Owned more than 35 stakes winners, including Pay the Butler, Al Mamoon, Medaglia d'Oro, Peace Rules, Midas Eyes, You.

Garland, Bruce, 1950-. Racing executive. Former senior executive vice president of racing for New Jersey Sports and Exposition Authority; vice chairman of Harness Tracks of America; served on board of the Thoroughbred Racing Associations and U.S. Trotting Association. Formerly executive director of New Jersey Racing Commission.

Gaylord, E. K. II, 1957-. Chairman and executive producer, Gaylord Films. Board of directors, Gaylord Entertainment Co. Member, Breeders' Cup board of directors. Director, National Cowboy & Western Heritage Center. Breeder, owner, owns Lazy E Ranch in Edmond, Oklahoma. Son of E. L. Gaylord, part-owner of 1980 Kentucky Derby (G1) runner-up Rumbo and graded stakes winner Cactus Road.

Gentry, Tom, 1937-. Bloodstock agent, breeder. Former owner of Tom Gentry Farm, Kentucky. Bred Royal Academy, Brazen, Marfa, Terlingua, Pancho Villa, Artichoke. Leading Keeneland consignor in 1970s, '80s. Son of Olin Gentry.

Gertmenian, L. Wayne, 1939-. Former president, Jockeys' Guild; president and chief executive officer, Matrix Capital Associates; professor of economics and management, Graziadio School of Business and Management, Pepperdine University.

Gill, Michael, 1956-. Mortgage banking. Led all owners in the United States by wins and earnings, 2003-'05; finished second among U.S. owners by wins in 2000 and '02. Broke records at Gulfstream and Monmouth Parks for wins in 2003. Eclipse Award owner in 2005.

Haire, Darrell, 1957-. Jockey, industry executive. Interim national manager, Jockeys' Guild, 2005-'06. Rode professionally, 1973-1990. Won 1980 Arkansas Derby (G2) with Temperence Hill.

Hamilton, Lucy Young, 1952-. Co-owner of Overbrook Farm in Lexington. Member, Jockey Club. Daughter of the late William T. Young and widow of trainer Francois Boutin.

Hancock, Arthur B. III, 1943-. Breeder. Owner of Stone Farm, Kentucky. Member, Jockey Club. Mr. Fitz Award in 1990. Bred and owned Sunday Silence, Gato Del Sol, Goodbye Halo. Co-bred Fusaichi Pegasus. Stood leading sire Halo. Brother of Seth Hancock; son of Arthur B. "Bull" Hancock Jr.

Hancock, Dell, 1952-. Co-owner of Claiborne Farm and spokesperson for the Paris, Kentucky, breeding operation. Member, Jockey Club; chairman, Grayson-Jockey Club Research Foundation. Daughter of the late A. B. "Bull" Hancock Jr.

Hancock, Richard E., 1940-. Industry executive. Executive vice president and chief executive officer for the Florida Thoroughbred Breeders' and Owners' Association since 1988. Board member, National Thoroughbred Retirement Foundation and the Florida Division of the Thoroughbred Retirement Foundation.

Hancock, Seth, 1949-. Breeder. Director, Keeneland Association. Member, Jockey Club. President, Claiborne Farm, Kentucky. Eclipse Award breeder in 1979, '84. Bred and owned Swale, Forty Niner, Lure. Bred Wajima, Nureyev, Caerleon. Organized a syndicate to acquire Secretariat for more than $6-million. Stood Mr. Prospector, Unbridled, Danzig. Stands Seeking the Gold. Brother of Arthur B. Hancock III and Dell Hancock; son of Arthur B. "Bull" Hancock Jr.

Hanford, Carl, 1916-. Trainer. Developed and conditioned five-time Horse of the Year Kelso (1960-'64). Saddled nearly 200 winners during a 23-year career, many of those while overseeing the private stable of Allaire duPont. Other top runners included major East Coast stakes winner La Corredora. Inducted into the Racing Hall of Fame in 2006.

Harper, Joseph, 1943-. Racing executive. President and chief executive officer, Del Mar Thoroughbred Club since 1990; president, Thoroughbred Racing Associations, 2003-'04. Member, Jockey Club; former executive vice president and general manager, Oak Tree Racing Association; grandson of Cecil B. DeMille.

Harris, John C., 1943-. Breeder, agricultural products. Past president, California Thoroughbred Breeders Association; director, Thoroughbred Owners of California. Member of Jockey Club. Owner of Harris Farms, California. Bred and owned Soviet Problem.

Handel, Harold G. "Hal," 1947-. Racing executive. Chief operating officer, New York Racing Association, 2007-. Chief executive officer, Greenwood Racing Inc. operator of Philadelphia Park, 1998-2007. President, the Thoroughbred Racing Associations, 1997-'98. Former executive vice president, New Jersey Sports and Exposition Authority, owner of the Meadowlands and Monmouth Park racetracks; former executive director and legal counsel, New Jersey Racing Commission.

Hawley, Sandy, 1949-. Jockey. Leading jockey by races won in 1970, '72-'73, '76; leading rider in Canada nine times; inducted into Racing Hall of Fame in '92; inducted into Canada's Hall of Fame in '86; Eclipse Award jockey in '76; George Woolf Memorial Jockey Award in '76; Sovereign Award in 1978, '88; Avelino Gomez Memorial Award in '86; Joe Palmer Award in '98. Rode 6,449 winners, including Youth, Desert Waves, Kiridashi, Smart Strike, Highland Vixen. First jockey to win more than 500 races in one season (1973).

Hayward, Charles, 1950-. Racetrack executive. President and chief executive officer, New York Racing Association since 2004. Former president and chief executive officer, *Daily Racing Form*. Member, NYRA board of trustees, 1995-'99.

Heiligbrodt, William, 1941-. Retired from banking, financial services, and funeral services. Campaigned more than 55 stakes winners. Board member, Texas Thoroughbred Association and Texas Horse Racing Hall of Fame. With wife, Corinne, raced 2003 Grade 1 winner Lady Tak and top sprinter Posse.

Hettinger, John, 1933-. Investments, real estate. Director, Breeders' Cup Ltd. Owner of Akindale Farm, New York. Member, Jockey Club. Special Eclipse Award in 2000. Bred and owned Warfie, Yestday's Kisses, Chase the Dream, Genuine Regret. Instrumental in founding the Racehorse Adoption Referral Program; chairman emeritus of the Grayson-Jockey Club Research Foundation; major shareholder, Fasig-Tipton Co. Activist for ending horse slaughter.

Hickey, Jay, 1944-. Lawyer, lobbyist. President, American Horse Council. Represented equine organizations, horse owners, and horse breeders during his time as a practicing lawyer.

Hirsch, Joe, 1929-. Journalist. Co-founder and first president, the National Turf Writers Association 1959-'60. Lord Derby Award in 1985; Jockey Club Medal in '89; Mr. Fitz Award in '98; Walter Haight Award in '84; Joe Palmer Award in '94; Eclipse Award of Merit in '92; Eclipse Award for outstanding newspaper writing in '79. Longtime executive columnist of *Daily Racing Form;* retired in late 2003.

Hollendorfer, Jerry, 1949-. Trainer. All-time leading trainer in Northern California. Trained more than 4,300 winners through mid-2005. Won Bay Meadows Race Course and Golden Gate Fields training titles more than 20 times consecutively; won Golden Gate title 22 consecutive times. Trained Lite Light, King Glorious, Pike Place Dancer, Event of the Year.

Hooper, Dave, 1935-. Executive director, Texas Thoroughbred Association.

Hubbard, R. D., 1935-. Glass manufacturing. Former chairman and chief executive officer, Hollywood Park; owner, Ruidoso Downs. Owner of Crystal Springs Farm, Kentucky; Frontera Farm, New Mexico. Owned Gentlemen (Arg), Talloires, Leger Cat (Arg), Fit to Lead, Invited Guest, Mistico (Chi).

Hughes, B. Wayne, 1933-. Warehousing, philanthropist. Founder and president, Public Storage, of which he and his family own 39%. Director, Thoroughbred Owners and Breeders Association. Founder, Parker Hughes Cancer Center in Minnesota. Bought Spendthrift Farm in 2004. Owner of Action This Day, Joyeux Danseur, Shake the Yoke (GB), Trishyde.

Humphrey, G. Watts Jr., 1944-. Investments, manufacturing. Vice president, Breeders' Cup; director, Keeneland Association; steward of Jockey Club. Owner of Shawnee Farm, Kentucky. Bred Creme Fraiche, Sacahuista. Owned Likely Exchange, Amherst Wayside, Noble Damsel, Sorbet.

Hunt, Nelson Bunker, 1926-. Oil production. Owned Bluegrass Farm, Kentucky. Eclipse Award breeder in 1976, '85, '87; P.A.B. Widener Trophy in '85-'87. Bred and owned Dahlia, Youth, Empery, Trillion, Estrapade. Owned *Vaguely Noble, Exceller, Glorious Song. Bred Dahlia, the first mare to earn more than $1-million.

Icahn, Carl, 1936-. Financier. Owner of Foxfield Thoroughbreds, Kentucky. John A. Morris Award in 1990. Bred Blushing K. D., Great Navigator, Vaudeville, Helmsman, Brave Tender. Owned Meadow Star, Rose's Cantina, Colonial Waters.

Jackson, Jess, 1930-. Vintner, owner-breeder. Founder and principal owner of Kendall-Jackson Wine Estates. Owner of Stonestreet Stables. Majority owner of Curlin.

Jackson, Roy, 1937- and **Gretchen,** 1937-. Owners-breeders. Shared 2006 Eclipse Award as outstanding owner; bred and raced Barbaro, winner of the 2006 Kentucky Derby Presented by Yum! Brands (G1) who broke down in the Preakness Stakes (G1); recipients, Eclipse Special Award for their efforts to save Barbaro's life; also campaigned graded stakes winner Showing Up and bred 2006 Stan James Two Thousand Guineas (Eng-G1) winner George Washington (Ire) in the name of their Lael Stables.

Janney, Stuart III, 1948-. Financier. Former chairman, Thoroughbred Owners and Breeders Association; steward, Jockey Club. Bred and owned Coronado's Quest, Warning Glance, Deputation, Mesabi Maiden. Aided in the formation of the National Thoroughbred Racing Association.

Jerkens, H. Allen, 1929-. Trainer. Leading trainer in New York in 1957, '62, '66, '69; inducted into Racing Hall of Fame in '75; Eclipse Award trainer in '73; Mr. Fitz Award in 2001. Trained more than 150 stakes winners, including Sky Beauty, Onion, Beau Purple, Duck Dance, Prove Out. Known as the "Giant Killer" for training horses who upset champions Secretariat, Kelso, Forego, and Buckpasser. Father of trainer Jimmy Jerkens.

Johnsen, Corey, 1955-. Racing executive. Co-owner, Kentucky Downs. Former Magna Entertainment Corp. vice president and president of Lone Star Park; former general manager, Remington Park; created the All-Star Jockey Championship in 1997; played a key role in the development, construction, and opening of Lone Star and Remington. Elected president of TRA in 2005.

Jolley, LeRoy, 1938-. Trainer. Inducted into Racing Hall of Fame in 1987. Trained Foolish Pleasure, Honest Pleasure, Genuine Risk, What a Summer, Manila, Meadow Star. Won the Kentucky Derby in 1980 with filly Genuine Risk. Son of trainer Moody Jolley.

Jones, Aaron U., 1921-. and **Marie.** Timber. Bred and owned Lemhi Gold, Western, Tiffany Lass. Owned Riboletta (Brz), Forestry, Plenty of Light. Bred Speightstown, Ashado.

Jones, Brereton C., 1939-. Breeder, politician. Director, Breeders' Cup Ltd.; past president and director, Thoroughbred Club of America. Owner of Airdrie Stud, Kentucky. Bred Desert Wine, Southjet, Formidable Lady, Dansil, Proud Spell. Owned By Land by Sea, Imp Society, Silver Medallion. Helped persuade Breeders' Cup to supplement purses at tracks around the country in addition to the Breeders' Cup day events; inaugurated Kentucky Thoroughbred Development Fund while governor of Kentucky, 1991-'95, co-founder of Kentucky Equine Education Project.

Jones, John T. L. Jr., 1935-. Breeder. Owner and general manager, Walmac International, Kentucky. One of the founding members of the Breeders' Cup Ltd.; stood Alleged, Nureyev, Phone Trick.

Jones, Russell B. Jr., 1935-. Bloodstock agent. President and chief operating officer, Walnut Green Bloodstock, which he co-founded with brother Richard I. G. Jones. Member, Jockey Club. General manager of Morven Stud, 1991-2000.

Kelly, Tommy J., 1919-. Trainer. Inducted into Racing Hall of Fame in 1993. Trained Plugged Nickle, Colonel Moran, Droll Role, Pet Bully, Globemaster. Co-owner of Evening Attire. Father of trainer Pat Kelly.

Kimmel, John, 1954-. Veterinarian, trainer. Conditioned 1997 champion Hidden Lake. In veterinary practice, 1980-'87. Has saddled more than 1,000 winners and the earners of more than $49-million. Father, Caesar Kimmel, owned racehorses for more than 30 years.

Krantz, Bryan, 1960-. Racing executive. Past president and general manager, Fair Grounds Race Course; owner, Jefferson Downs. Built new grandstand after a fire destroyed Fair Grounds's physical plant in 1993.

Krone, Julie, 1963-. Jockey. Inducted into Racing Hall of Fame in 2000. All-time leading female jockey with more than 3,700 victories. First woman to win a Triple Crown race (Colonial Affair, 1993 Belmont Stakes [G1]) and Breeders' Cup race (Halfbridled, 2003 Breeders' Cup Juvenile Fillies [G1]).

Lake, Scott, 1965-. Trainer. Manages a stable of approximately 150 horses, mostly claimers. Leading North American trainer by wins in 2001 with 406, in

'03 with 455, and '06 with 528. Trained former claimers Shake You Down and My Cousin Matt to Grade 2 victories.

Lavin, A. Gary, 1937-. Veterinarian. President, American Association of Equine Practitioners, 1994; AAEP's Lavin Cup, an annual award for commitment to horse welfare, in his honor. Founded Longfield Farm in Goshen, Kentucky, in 1979. Elected to Jockey Club in 1994, the first veterinarian chosen in 100 years. Past president, Kentucky Thoroughbred Association.

Levy, Robert P., 1931-. Chemical storage. Former owner, Atlantic City Race Course; former president, Thoroughbred Racing Associations. Owner of Muirfield East, Maryland. Owned Housebuster, Smoke Glacken, Bet Twice. Inaugurated full-card simulcasting in 1983.

Liebau, F. Jack, 1938-. Lawyer, racetrack executive. President, Bay Meadows Racing Assocation; former president, Santa Anita Park. Member, Jockey Club. Owner of Valley Creek Farm, California. Owned Yashgan (GB), Boo La Boo, Forzando (GB), Kadial (Ire).

Little, Donald, 1934-. Financial management. Owner of Centennial Farms, Virginia. Owned Colonial Affair, Rubiano, King Cugat. Past president of the United States Polo Association; organizes racing syndicates.

Lukas, D. Wayne, 1935-. Trainer. Leading trainer by money won in 1983-'92, '94-'97; leading trainer by races won in 1987-'90; leading trainer by stakes races won in 1985-'92; inducted into Racing Hall of Fame in '99; Eclipse Award trainer in 1985-'87, '94; John W. Galbreath Award in '98. Leading trainer of Eclipse Award winners. Trained Lady's Secret, Thunder Gulch, Timber Country, Gulch, Flanders, Tabasco Cat, Codex, Charismatic. First trainer to reach both $100-million and $200-million in earnings; first trainer to win two Breeders' Cup races in one day (in 1985) and three races in one day (in '88); transformed modern training with entrepreneurial methods.

Lyster, Wayne G. III, 1948-. Owner, Ashview Farm, Kentucky. Former chairman, Kentucky Racing Commission. Co-bred champion Johannesburg; bred stakes winners At the Half, Lu Ravi.

Mabee, Betty, 1921-. Owner of Golden Eagle Farm near Ramona, California. Along with late husband, John, who died in 2002, won Eclipse Award as outstanding breeder in 1991, '97, and '98. Campaigned $5-million winner Best Pal, $2-million earners General Challenge and Dramatic Gold, and millionaire Excellent Meeting.

Mack, Earle, 1939-. Real estate. Owner, Rising Son Stable. Member, board of trustees, New York Racing Association; member, Thoroughbred Owners and Breeders Association; chairman, New York State Racing Commission, 1983-'89. Established the New York Thoroughbred Owners Awards. Owned Peteski, 1993 Canadian Horse of the Year.

Madden, Preston, 1934- and **Anita**, 1933-. Real estate development. Owner of Hamburg Place, Kentucky. Bred Alysheba, Pink Pigeon, Miss Carmie, Romeo, Kentuckian. Owned T. V. Lark. Stood leading sire T. V. Lark; Anita Madden was the first female member of the Kentucky State Racing Commission.

Magnier, John, 1948-. Farm owner, breeder. Owner of Coolmore Stud, Ireland; Coolmore Stud, Australia; Ashford Stud, Kentucky; Creek View Farm, Kentucky. Bred Galileo (Ire), Sadler's Wells, Dr Devious (Ire). Originated shuttle-stallion concept; expanded mare books; stood Be My Guest, El Gran Senor, Danehill. Stands Sadler's Wells, Woodman.

Maktoum, Sheikh Hamdan bin Rashid al, 1945- Deputy ruler of Dubai; minister of finance and industry for United Arab Emirates; UAE representative to OPEC. Owns Shadwell Farm in Kentucky, Shadwell Estate, Nunnery Stud, England; Derrinstown Stud, Ireland. Leading owner in England, 1995. Owned 2006 Horse of the Year Invasor (Arg). Bred and owned Nashwan, Erhaab, Salsabil (Ire); partner with brothers Mohammed and Maktoum in Godolphin Racing.

Maktoum, Sheikh Mohammed bin Rashid al, 1949-. Ruler of Dubai. Shared Eclipse Award as outstanding owner in 2006. Owner of Raceland Farm, Kentucky; Darley at Jonabell, Kentucky; Dalham Hall Stud, England; Kildangan Stud, Ireland; Darley Australia, Australia. Bred and owned Dubai Millennium, Intrepidity (GB), In the Wings (GB), Swain (Ire), Bernardini. Owned Oh So Sharp (GB), Daylami (Ire), Pebbles (GB). Created Godolphin Racing, Dubai World Cup (UAE-G1).

Mandella, Richard, 1950-. Trainer. Inducted into Racing Hall of Fame in 2001. Trained Kotashaan (Fr), Phone Chatter, Dixie Union, Gentlemen (Arg), Halfbridled, Johar, Pleasantly Perfect, Wild Rush, and Dare and Go, who won the Pacific Classic (G1) in 1996, ending Cigar's 16-race winning streak. Won record four Breeders' Cup races in 2003.

Mangurian, Harry T. Jr., 1926-. Real estate development, construction. Former owner, Mockingbird Farm. Member, Jockey Club. Eclipse Award of Merit, 2002. Leading breeder in North America by earnings and races won in 1999-2002. First chairman of Ocala Breeders' Sales Co. Past director, Breeders' Cup Ltd., Florida Thoroughbred Breeders' and Owners' Association. Bred or owned more than 150 stakes winners, including Appealing Skier, Desert Vixen, Gilded Time, Successful Appeal, Valid Appeal. Former owner, Boston Celtics.

Maple, Edward, 1948-. Jockey. Began riding in Ohio and West Virginia, moved to New Jersey in 1970 and New York in '71. Rode champions Conquistador Cielo, Devil's Bag; won the Belmont Stakes (G1) with Temperence Hill and Creme Fraiche. Won 4,398 races and earned more than $105-million; rode Secretariat in champion's last career start, 1973 Canadian International. George Woolf Memorial Jockey Award in 1995; retired from racing in 1998 after receiving Mike Venezia Award.

Martin, Ed, 1954-. President, Association of Racing Commissioners International since 2005. Former executive director, New York State Racing and Wagering Board.

Martin, Frank "Pancho," 1925-. Trainer. Leading trainer by money won in 1974; leading trainer in New York for 1973-'82; inducted into Racing Hall of Fame in '81. Trained 51 stakes winners and two champions, including Autobiography, Outstandingly, Sham, Manassa Mauler, Rube the Great.

Marzelli, Alan, 1954-. Racing executive. President and chief operating officer of Jockey Club since January 1, 2003; chairman of Equibase Co. LLC since 1996. Joined Jockey Club in 1983 as chief financial officer and later became executive vice president.

Matz, Michael, 1951-. Trainer. Began training in late 1990s after successful career as a show rider, winning an Olympic team silver medal in '96; credited with saving four children in '89 crash of United Flight 232 in Sioux City, Iowa; trained Barbaro, winner of the 2006 Kentucky Derby Presented by Yum! Brands (G1); also trained '04 Arlington Million Stakes (G1) winner Kicken

Kris and '06 Emirates Airline Breeders' Cup Distaff (G1) winner Round Pond.

McAlpine, James R., 1946-. Former president and chief executive officer, Magna Entertainment Corp; vice chairman of corporate development for Magna.

McAnally, Ron, 1932-. Trainer. Inducted into Racing Hall of Fame in 1990; Eclipse Award trainer in 1981, '91-'92; Mr. Fitz Award in '92. Trained John Henry, Bayakoa (Arg), Tight Spot, Paseana (Arg), Northern Spur (Ire).

McCarron, Chris, 1955-. Jockey, racetrack executive. Leading jockey by races won in 1974-'75, '80; leading jockey by money won in 1980-'81, '84, '91; inducted into Racing Hall of Fame in '89; Eclipse Award apprentice jockey in '74; Eclipse Award jockey in '80; George Woolf Memorial Jockey Award in '80; Mike Venezia Award in '91. Rode Alysheba, John Henry, Lady's Secret, Sunday Silence, Tiznow. Retired in 2002 as leading earner among jockeys with $264-million; along with his wife, Judy, and comedian Tim Conway, created the Don MacBeth Memorial Fund for disabled jockeys. General manager of Santa Anita Park in 2003-'04. Founded North American Riding Academy.

McDonald, Reiley, 1957-. Bloodstock agent. Partner, Eaton Sales Inc. Kentucky. Owner, Indian Hills Farm and Athens-Woods Farm, Kentucky. Former vice president, Fasig-Tipton Co., former president, Stallion Access. Driving force behind development of Thoroughbred Retirement Foundation's Secretariat Center at Kentucky Horse Park. Board member, Keeneland Association, University of Kentucky's Maxwell H. Gluck Equine Research Center, Kentucky Horse Park. Sold Banshee Breeze, Grand Slam, Hawk Wing, High Yield, Victory Gallop, Yes It's True. Owned Nasty Storm.

McGaughey, Claude R. "Shug" III, 1951-. Trainer. Eclipse Award trainer in 1988; inducted into Racing Hall of Fame in 2004. Trained Easy Goer, Rhythm, Inside Information, Heavenly Prize, My Flag, Storm Flag Flying and Personal Ensign, unbeaten in 13 races; won five graded stakes at Belmont Park on Breeders' Cup preview day in 1993.

McKathan, J. B., 1966- and **Kevin**, 1968-. Bloodstock agents. Owners of McKathan Brothers Training Facility in Ocala; purchased for clients Silver Charm, Real Quiet, Silverbulletday, Captain Steve.

McLaughlin, Kiaran, 1960-. Trainer. Left University of Kentucky to pursue a career with horses; former assistant to trainer John Hennig, his father-in-law, and D. Wayne Lukas; trained privately for the Maktoum family, 1993-2003, in Dubai and New York before returning to the United States full time; trained 2006 Horse of the Year Invasor (Arg) and '06 Belmont Stakes (G1) winner Jazil for the Shadwell Stable of Sheikh Hamdan bin Rashid al Maktoum.

McMahon, Gerald F. "Jerry," 1950-. Sales company executive. President and general manager, Barretts Equine Sales Ltd.; former vice president, Fasig-Tipton California.

McNair, Robert, 1937-, and **Janice**, 1936-. Investments, NFL team owner. Owner of Stonerside Stable, Kentucky; training facilities in Aiken, South Carolina and Saratoga Springs, New York. Co-bred Fusaichi Pegasus; bred and owned Congaree. Owned Chilukki, Tuzla (Ire). Co-owned Coronado's Quest, Touch Gold. Robert is member of Jockey Club.

Meeker, Thomas, 1943-. Racing executive. Former president, Churchill Downs Inc.; president, Thoroughbred Racing Associations, 1991-'92. John W. Galbreath Award in 1999. Beginning in 1984, implemented a $25-million, five-year improvement plan for Churchill, including a $3.6-million turf course and a $2.8-million paddock. Undertook $121-million renovation of Churchill in 2002.

Melnyk, Eugene, 1959-. Pharmaceuticals. Owns Ottawa Senators of the National Hockey League. Owner, Winding Oaks Farm, Florida. Member, New York Racing Association board of trustees. Co-recipient of National Turf Writers Association 2002 Joe Palmer Award for contributions to racing. Campaigns horses with wife, Laura. Co-owned Archers Bay; owned Graeme Hall, Harmony Lodge, Marley Vale, Pico Teneriffe, Strong Hope, Tweedside, Speightstown, Sealy Hill.

Metzger, Dan, 1963-. Racing executive. President, Thoroughbred Owners and Breeders Association since 1999. Former director of marketing services and licensing, Breeders' Cup Ltd.

Meyerhoff, Robert, 1924-. Real estate development. Owner of Fitzhugh Farm, Maryland. Bred and owned Broad Brush, Concern, Include, Valley Crossing.

Meyocks, Terry, 1951-. Racing executive. National manager, Jockeys' Guild since 2007; former president and chief operating officer, New York Racing Association; former vice president of racing, NYRA; former racing secretary, Calder Race Course; director of racing at Gulfstream Park.

Migliore, Richard, 1964-. Jockey. Eclipse Award apprentice jockey in 1981. He has won more than 4,200 races. Mike Venezia Memorial Award and Thurman Munson Award in 2003. Has ridden more than 4,000 winners, including Funny Cide, Kazoo, Incorporatetime, Great Intentions.

Miller, Leverett, 1931-. Owner-breeder. With wife, Linda, owns and operates T-Square Stud in Fairfield, Florida. Campaigns in Eton blue silks of late uncle C.V. Whitney. Bred Silver Wagon. Member, Jockey Club. Board member, Breeders' Cup, Florida Thoroughbred Breeders' and Owners' Association. Former board member, Ocala Breeders' Sales Co.

Miller, MacKenzie "Mack," 1921-. Trainer, breeder. Inducted into Racing Hall of Fame in 1987; Mr. Fitz Award in '96. Member, Jockey Club. Trained 72 stakes winners, including champions Leallah, Assagai, Hawaii, and *Snow Knight. Trained Fit to Fight to New York handicap triple crown in 1984; trained Sea Hero to Kentucky Derby victory in 1993. Bred De La Rose, Lite Light, Chilukki.

Moran, Elizabeth "Betty," 1932-. Investments. Owner of Brushwood Stable, Pennsylvania. Bred Russian Rhythm, High Yield. Owned Creme Fraiche. Won English Grand National Steeplechase Handicap with Papillon in 2000.

Mott, William, 1953-. Trainer. Inducted into Racing Hall of Fame in 1998; Eclipse Award trainer in 1995-'96. Trained Cigar, Paradise Creek, Ajina, Theatrical (Ire), Geri, Escena, Wekiva Springs. Trained Cigar for 16 consecutive victories from 1994-'96.

Nafzger, Carl, 1941-. Trainer. Eclipse Award trainer in 1990; Big Sport of Turfdom Award in '90. Trained Unbridled, Street Sense, Banshee Breeze, Unshaded, Vicar, Solvig. Wrote *Traits of a Winner: The Formula for Developing Thoroughbred Racehorses* in 1994.

Nerud, John A., 1913-. Trainer, breeder. President of Tartan Farms, Florida, 1959-'89. Inducted into Racing Hall of Fame in 1972. Eclipse Award of Merit, 2006. Trained 27 stakes winners and five champions, including Dr. Fager, Ta Wee, Delegate, Intentionally, Dr.

Patches, *Gallant Man. Bred and owned Cozzene, Fappiano. Dr. Fager is the only horse to win four championships in one year.

Niarchos-Gouazé, Maria, Investments. Director, Breeders' Cup Ltd. Owner of Haras de Fresnay-le-Buffard, France. In partnership with her brothers, breeds under the name Flaxman Holdings Ltd. Bred and owned champion Aldebaran, Dream Well (Fr), Sulamani (Ire), Bago, Six Perfections (Fr), Divine Proportions. Daughter of shipping magnate Stavros Niarchos.

Nicholson, George "Nick," 1947-. Racing executive. President and chief executive officer, Keeneland Association; executive director, Jockey Club 1989-2000; former chief operating officer, National Thoroughbred Racing Association; president, Thoroughbred Club of America in '91. Jockey Club Gold Medal in 1998. Involved in the planning and development of the Kentucky Horse Park; played key role in formation of Equibase; helped to pull industry together to support the National Thoroughbred Racing Association.

Noe, Kenneth Jr. "Kenny," 1928-. Former racing executive. New York Racing Association chairman and chief executive officer 1995-2000. NYRA president, general manager 1994-'95; president, general manager, Calder Race Course 1979-'90. Member, Jockey Club.

O'Brien, Aidan, 1969-. Trainer. Won then-record 23 Grade/Group 1 races in 2001. Trains for Coolmore Stud and partners at Ballydoyle, Ireland. Won 2001-'02 Epsom Derby (Eng-G1) with Galileo (Ire) and High Chaparral (Ire), respectively. Trained Giant's Causeway, King of Kings (Ire), Milan (GB), Imagine (Ire), Stravinsky, Hawk Wing, Rock of Gibraltar (Ire), Ballingarry (Ire), Johannesburg, Footstepsinthesand.

O'Brien, Vincent, 1917-. Legendary Irish trainer. Founded Ballydoyle training center in Ireland; with John Magnier and Robert Sangster established Coolmore Stud in 1975. Trained winners of 27 Irish classics, 16 English classics, and in 1977 saddled then-record 22 Group 1 winners. Trained Nijinsky II, Roberto, Golden Fleece, Sir Ivor, The Minstrel, Alleged. In a 2003 *Racing Post* poll, he was voted the all-time most important figure in English racing.

O'Byrne, Dermot "Demi," 1944-. Bloodstock agent, veterinarian. Purchased Thunder Gulch, Honour and Glory, High Yield, Fasliyev, Stravinsky, King of Kings (Ire), Johannesburg. Chief talent spotter for Coolmore Stud-Michael Tabor partnerships.

O'Farrell, J. Michael Jr., 1948-. Breeder. First vice president, Florida Thoroughbred Breeders' and Owners' Association; member, Jockey Club; owner, Ocala Stud Farm, Florida. Bred Bolshoi Boy, Proudest Duke, Queen Alexandra. Son of Joe O'Farrell.

O'Neill, Doug F., 1968-. Trainer. Set single-meet training record of 48 wins at Santa Anita Park in 2005. Set an Oak Tree record for single-meet wins in 2003 with 22 wins. In 2003, was named the Cal-bred trainer of the year by the California Thoroughbred Breeders Association. Trained Lava Man, Whilly (Ire), Sharp Lisa, Sky Jack, Classy Cara, Stevie Wonderboy, Avanzado (Arg).

Oxley, John C., 1937-, and **Debbie**, 1951-. Oil production. John is steward of Jockey Club. Owner of Fawn Leap Farm, Kentucky. Bred and owned Pyramid Peak. Owned Monarchos, Beautiful Pleasure, Sky Mesa.

Pape, William L., 1930-. Auto dealership. Former president, National Steeplechase Association. Co-bred champions Flatterer and Martie's Anger; owned champion Athenian Idol.

Paragallo, Ernie, 1958-. Investment banking, computer software. In name of Paraneck Stable, raced 1999 champion sprinter Artax; also campaigned '95 Breeders' Cup Juvenile (G1) winner Unbridled's Song, '99 Wood Memorial Stakes (G2) winner Adonis.

Payson, Virginia Kraft, 1930-. Investments. Owner of Payson Stud, Kentucky. Bred and owned St. Jovite, L'Carriere. Owned Carr de Naskra. Bred 2002 champions Vindication and Farda Amiga. Owner and operator of Payson Park training center in Florida.

Pedersen, Pete, 1920-. Steward of the California Horse Racing Board, 1955-'05. National Turf Writers Association Joe Palmer Award for meritorious service to racing in 2005. Eclipse Award of Merit in 2001. Known for elevating professionalism of stewards.

Pegram, Mike, 1952-. Fast food franchises. Owned Real Quiet, Silverbulletday, Isitingood, Thirty Slews, Captain Steve.

Perret, Craig, 1951-. Jockey. Eclipse Award jockey in 1990; George Woolf Memorial Jockey Award in '98. Rode Unbridled, Housebuster, Safely Kept, Eillo, Rhythm, Alydeed, Bet Twice. Won a record-tying 57 stakes in 1990.

Phillips, John W., 1952-. Investments, lawyer. Member of Jockey Club. Managing partner of Darby Dan Farm, Kentucky. Bred and owned Memories of Silver, Sunshine Forever, Brian's Time, Soaring Softly. Grandson of John W. Galbreath.

Phipps, Ogden Mills "Dinny," 1940-. Investments. Chairman, Jockey Club; former chairman, New York Racing Association; director, Grayson-Jockey Club Research Foundation. Eclipse Award of Merit in 1978. Bred and owned Inside Information, Rhythm, Educated Risk, Storm Flag Flying, Smuggler. Co-bred and owned Successor. Son of Ogden Phipps.

Pickens, Madeleine Paulson, 1957-. Owner-breeder. Bred and co-owned stakes winner Rock Hard Ten and owned Fraise, winner of 1992 Breeders' Cup Turf (G1). Widow of Allen Paulson, owner of Brookside Farms and of eight Eclipse champions, including Cigar, Blushing John, Estrapade, Theatrical (Ire). Married to corporate investor T. Boone Pickens.

Piggott, Lester, 1936-. Retired jockey, trainer. Champion English jockey 11 times. Won more than 5,300 races, including record 30 English classics. Winner of the Epsom Derby record nine times; Ascot Gold Cup 11 times; Irish Derby five times; and the 1990 Breeders' Cup Mile (G1) at age 54. Rode Nijinsky II, Sir Ivor, Roberto, The Minstrel, Alleged. Imprisoned a year for tax evasion 1987-'88 before resuming his riding career.

Pincay, Laffit Jr., 1946-. Jockey. Leading jockey by money won in 1970-74, '79, '85; leading jockey by races won in '71; inducted into Racing Hall of Fame in '75; Eclipse Award jockey in 1971, '73-'74, '79, '85; Special Eclipse Award in '99; George Woolf Memorial Jockey Award in '70. Big Sport of Turfdom Award in '85. Rode Affirmed, John Henry, Gamely, Susan's Girl, Desert Vixen, Genuine Risk. Broke Bill Shoemaker's lifetime win record on December 10, 1999, with his 8,834th victory; first jockey to win seven races on a single card at Santa Anita Park, in '87; first jockey to win more than 9,000 races. Retired on April 29, 2003, with a record 9,530 victories and purse earnings of $237-million.

Pletcher, Todd, 1967-. Trainer. Established records in 2006 for earnings, stakes wins, and graded stakes wins, earnings record in 2007. Eclipse Award trainer

in 2004-'07. Son of horseman Jake Pletcher and a longtime assistant to Racing Hall of Fame trainer D. Wayne Lukas. Trained champions Ashado, Left Bank, Speightstown, Wait a While, Fleet Indian, English Channel, Rags to Riches, Lawyer Ron.

Polk, Hiram Jr., 1936-. Surgeon, breeder. Retired chair, University of Louisville School of Medicine surgery department. Member, Jockey Club. Breeder and co-owner of multiple stakes winner Mrs. Revere.

Pollard, Carl, 1938-. Health care executive. Chairman, Churchill Downs Inc.; president, Kentucky Derby Museum. Owner of Hermitage Farm, Kentucky. Owned Caressing, Sheepscot, Duck Trap, Take Me Out.

Powell, Lonny, 1959-. Racing executive. Former vice president of public affairs, Youbet.com Inc.; former president, Association of Racing Commissioners International; former president, Santa Anita Park.

Prado, Edgar, 1967-. Jockey. Eclipse Award jockey in 2006. Registered 6,000th career victory in 2008; won '06 Kentucky Derby (G1) with Barbaro; Belmont Stakes (G1) with Birdstone ('04) and Sarava ('02). Led all North American riders by victories with 536 in 1997, 474 in '98, and 402 in '99.

Ragozin, Leonard, 1928-. Handicapper. Founder of Ragozin Thoroughbred Data. Developed Ragozin speed figures also known as "the sheets." Author of the book, *The Odds Must Be Crazy.*

Ramsey, Kenneth L., 1935-. Cellular telephones. In 1990s, acquired cellular telephone franchises along Interstate 75 in northeastern Georgia and southeastern Kentucky. Acquired Almahurst Farm in 1994 and renamed it Ramsey Farm. With wife, Sarah, won Eclipse Award as outstanding owner in 2004. Owner of 2004 champion turf male Kitten's Joy, Grade 1 winner Roses in May.

Reddam, J. Paul, 1955-. Finance. Founder, Ditech.com, an Internet-based mortgage company that he sold in 1999 to General Motors. President, Cash Call, a consumer loan company. Former Standardbred syndicator claimed his first Thoroughbred in 1988. Owner, Metropolitan Handicap (G1) winner Swept Overboard, millionaire Elloluv, and 2004 Breeders' Cup Juvenile (G1) winner Wilko.

Reid, Mark, 1950-. Bloodstock agent. Prominent agent in private deals for owner Edmund Gann and trainer Bobby Frankel. Purchased Walnut Green bloodstock agency, 2005. All-time leading trainer at Garden State Park; sixth-leading trainer in U.S. in '91; won the fall-winter training title at Philadelphia Park in 1986.

Richardson, Dean W., 1953-. Veterinary surgeon. Charles W. Raker professor of surgery at the New Bolton Center of the University of Pennsylvania School of Veterinary Medicine. Performed life-saving surgery on Kentucky Derby Presented by Yum! Brands (G1) winner Barbaro after breakdown in the Preakness Stakes (G1); guided treatment until the Derby winner was euthanized due to effects of laminitis in January 2007. Recipient of the 2006 Joe Palmer Award of the National Turf Writers Association and '06 Big Sport of Turfdom Award of Turf Publicists of America.

Richardson, J. David, 1945-. Vascular surgeon. Member, Jockey Club; past president, Kentucky Thoroughbred Association; co-bred, raced Mrs. Revere.

Roark, John, 1940-. Lawyer. In private practice in Temple, Texas. Former president, National Horsemen's Benevolent and Protective Association; former president, Texas Thoroughbred Partnership.

Robertson, Walter, 1949-. Auctioneer. President, Fasig-Tipton Co.; former president, Thoroughbred Club of America. Auctioneer at the Calumet Farm sale in 1992.

Robbins, Jack K., 1921-. Veterinarian, racing executive. President, founding director of Oak Tree Racing Association; member, Jockey Club; director of Grayson-Jockey Club Research Foundation; distinguished life member of American Association of Equine Practitioners. Father of trainer Jay Robbins, Del Mar Director of Racing Tom Robbins, and former Hollywood Park President Don Robbins.

Robinson, J. Mack, 1923-. Financier, philanthropist. Member, Jockey Club. Family owns Rosehill Plantation in Thomasville, Georgia. Daughter Jill raced 1994 champion sprinter Cherokee Run. Honored as owner of the year by the Georgia Thoroughbred Owners and Breeders Association. Chief benefactor of J. Mack Robinson College of Business at Georgia State University.

Roman, Steve, 1943-. Researcher, theorist. Author of 53 United States agricultural and animal health chemical patents. Creator of the dosage index. Author of *Dosage: Pedigree and Performance*, published in 2003.

Romero, Randy, 1957-. Jockey. Father, Lloyd, was Quarter Horse trainer; film *Casey's Shadow* was based on his Louisiana family; won Breeders' Cup races with champions Sacahuista (1987 Distaff [G1]), Personal Ensign ('88 Distaff), and Go for Wand ('89 Juvenile Fillies [G1]). Sustained life-threatening burns in a 1983 accident in Oaklawn Park jockeys' room. Won 4,294 races, earned more than $75-million.

Rotz, John L., 1934-. Jockey, racing official. Leading jockey by stakes winners in 1968-'69; inducted into Racing Hall of Fame in '83; George Woolf Memorial Jockey Award in '73. Rode 2,908 winners. Rode Gallant Bloom, Ta Wee, Carry Back, Dr. Fager, Silent Screen.

Russell, Geoffrey, 1961-. Keeneland director of sales since 2001; former assistant director of sales, 1996-2001; also worked at Goffs Bloodstock Sales and Fasig-Tipton Co.

Sahadi, Jenine, 1963-. Trainer. First female to win a Breeders' Cup race on the flat, champion Lit de Justice in the 1996 Breeders' Cup Sprint (G1) and Elmhurst in the same race in 1997. First female to saddle a Santa Anita Derby (G1) winner, The Deputy (Ire) in 2000. Also trained stakes winners Grand Flotilla, and Creston. Daughter of Fred Sahadi, founder of Cardiff Stud.

Sampson, Curtis, 1933-. Telecommunications. Chairman of Canterbury Park Holding Corp.; bought closed track in 1994 with partners and reopened it in 1995. Entered racing in 1987 as an owner; among Minnesota's leading breeders.

Sams, Timothy H., 1944-. Breeder. Indiana Horse Racing Commission member, 1998-2002. Indiana Horse Racing Commission vice chairman, 2002. Member, Jockey Club. Former director, Breeders' Cup Ltd., Indiana Thoroughbred Breed Development Advisory Committee.

Samyn, Jean-Luc, 1956-. Jockey. Best known for riding ability on the turf. Leading apprentice at Keystone and Garden State Park. On November 20, 1985, was the first jockey to ride in two stakes races on different continents on the same day; Japan Cup (Jpn-G1) and Matriarch Stakes (G1), Hollywood Park.

Sanan, Satish, 1949-. Information technology. Owner with wife, Anne, of Padua Stables. Large investor in racing prospects starting in the late 1990s. Owner or co-owner of Horse of the Year Curlin, champion Vindication,

Grade 1 winners Cash Run, Cajun Beat, and Yes It's True.

Santos, Jose, 1961-. Jockey. Inducted into Racing Hall of Fame in 2007. Leading jockey by money won in 1986-'89; Eclipse Award jockey in '88; George Woolf Memorial Jockey Award in '99. Rode Lemon Drop Kid, Skip Away, Colonial Affair, Chief Bearhart, Volponi, Funny Cide. Led all jockeys by money won with a then-record $14.86-million in 1988; rode 13 winners in three days at Aqueduct in '88. Won 2003 Kentucky Derby (G1) and Preakness Stakes (G1) on Funny Cide. Retired in 2007.

Santulli, Richard, 1944-. Aviation. Co-owner of Jayeff B Stable. Member, Jockey Club. Bred and owned Ciro. Owned Safely Kept, Banshee Breeze, Korveya.

Savin, Scott, 1960-. Owner, executive. Former president, Gulfstream Park, Florida Horsemen's Benevolent and Protective Association. Owned Bet Big, Cheshire Kitten. Grandson of A. I. "Butch" Savin, owner of Mr. Prospector.

Scherf, Christopher, 1951-. Racing executive. Executive vice president of Thoroughbred Racing Associations since 1988; president of TRA Enterprises. Serves on the American Horse Council's Racing and Government Affairs committees. Former sportswriter for the Louisville *Courier-Journal* and United Press International; director of press relations for the New York Racing Association, 1978-'81.

Schickedanz, Gustav, 1929-. President and CEO of family construction and development company. Owner of Schonberg Farm in Ontario. Bred and owned 2003 Canadian Triple Crown winner and Canadian Horse of the Year Wando and 2004 Canadian champion Mobil. Also campaigned Sovereign Award winners Glanmire and Langfuhr.

Schiff, Peter G., 1952-. Financier. Trustee, New York Racing Association; member, Jockey Club; owner, Fox Ridge Farm. Owned Christiecat, Riskaverse, Token Dance, Wortheroatsingold. Son of John Schiff.

Schwartz, Barry, 1942-. Clothing executive. Former chairman and chief executive officer, New York Racing Association; member, Jockey Club; owner, Stonewall Farm, New York. Bred and owned Beru, Patricia J. K. Owned Three Ring.

Seitz, Fred, 1946-, Consignor, breeder. Former president, Thoroughbred Club of America and Kentucky Thoroughbred Association; director, Keeneland Association. Owner, Brookdale Farm, Kentucky, which stood Deputy Minister and stands Forest Wildcat, Silver Deputy. Bred Bluebird in partnership.

Sellers, John, 1937-. Jockey, bloodstock agent. America's leading rider in 1961 by number of winners, 328. Rode champion and Racing Hall of Fame member Carry Back to victories in the 1961 Kentucky Derby and Preakness Stakes, and won the '65 Belmont and Travers Stakes aboard Hail to All. Other top mounts included champions T. V. Lark and Straight Deal. Rode 2,797 winners for $18.4-million in purse money during a 23-season career spanning 1955-1977. Inducted into the Racing Hall of Fame in 2007.

Sexton, Steve, 1959-. Racetrack executive. President, Churchill Downs; former executive vice president of Arlington Park; former executive vice president and general manager, Lone Star Park; former general manager, Thistledown racetrack.

Sheppard, Jonathan, 1940-. Trainer, breeder. Owner of Ashwell Stables, Pennsylvania. Former president, National Steeplechase Association. Leading steeplechase trainer by money won in 1973-'90, '92-'95; inducted into Racing Hall of Fame in '90. Trained more than 120 stakes winners, including champions Cafe Prince, Flatterer, Athenian Idol, Martie's Anger, Jimmy Lorenzo (GB), Highland Bud. Also trained Storm Cat, With Anticipation. Co-bred Martie's Anger, Flatterer.

Sherman, Michael, 1940-. Breeder. Former owner of Farnsworth Farms, Florida. Leading breeder by stakes winners in 1994-'95; Eclipse Award breeder in '96. Bred Beautiful Pleasure, Jewel Princess, Mecke, Frisk Me Now, Once Wild.

Shields, Joseph V. Jr., 1938-. Investment manager, owner-breeder. Chairman and CEO of Shields & Co., brokerage and investment management firm. Vice chairman, New York Racing Association; member, Jockey Club; trustee, National Museum of Racing Hall of Fame, Thoroughbred Owners and Breeders Association; director, Grayson-Jockey Club Research Foundation. Owner-breeder of Wagon Limit, Passing Shot, House Party, Puzzlement, Limit Out.

Sikura, John G., 1958-. Thoroughbred owner and breeder. Owner of Hill 'n' Dale Farm and Hill 'n' Dale Sales Agency in Kentucky. Breeder or co-breeder of Grade 1-Group 1 winners Hawk Wing and Touch Gold. Son of Hill 'n' Dale founder John Sikura Jr.

Smith, Mike, 1965-. Jockey. Elected to Racing Hall of Fame in 2003. Leading jockey by races won in 1994; Eclipse Award jockey in 1993-'94; Mike Venezia Award in '94; George Woolf Memorial Jockey Award in 2000. Rode Holy Bull, Lure, Skip Away, Azeri, Unbridled's Song, Coronado's Quest, Vindicator, Giacomo. Won record 66 stakes in 1994. Through April 2008, won more than 4,600 races and earned more than $180-million.

Smith, Tim, 1948-. Racing executive. Former commissioner of National Thoroughbred Racing Association, 1998-2004. Helped increase national television exposure for horse racing. Former president, Friends of New York Racing.

Solis, Alex, 1964-. Jockey. Among top ten leading riders by career earnings. Panama native first rode in United States in 1982; recipient of the first Bill Shoemaker Award in 2003 for outstanding achievement on the Breeders' Cup program; rode two winners, Johar in Breeders' Cup Turf (G1) dead heat and Pleasantly Perfect in the Breeders' Cup Classic (G1). Also rode Pleasantly Perfect to win in 2004 Dubai World Cup (UAE-G1).

Sommer, Viola, 1921-. Real estate. Eclipse Award owner in '82. Member, Jockey Club. Bred and owned Bottled Water. Owned Sham, Ten Below, Tom Swift.

Steinbrenner, George, 1930-. Shipping. Director, Florida Thoroughbred Breeders' and Owners' Association; owner, Kinsman Farm, Florida. Bred and owned Concerto, Diligence, Eternal Prince; owned Bellamy Road. Former co-owner, Florida Downs (later Tampa Bay Downs); retired managing partner, New York Yankees.

Stevens, Gary, 1963-. Jockey. President, Jockeys' Guild, 1995-2000. Leading jockey by money won in 1990; inducted into Racing Hall of Fame in '97; Eclipse Award jockey in '98; George Woolf Memorial Jockey Award in '96. Rode more than 4,800 winners, including Point Given, Silver Charm, Winning Colors, Thunder Gulch, Hennessy, Broad Brush. Youngest rider to earn more than $100-million in purses, in 1993. Retired in 2005. Now television racing analyst.

Stoute, Sir Michael, 1945-. Trainer. Five-time champion trainer in England. Trained Epsom Derby (Eng-G1) winners Shergar (1981), Shahrastani ('86), Kris Kin (2003), North Light ('04), and Unite (Ire), stakes win-

ners Sonic Lady, Shareef Dancer, Melodist, Ivor's Image, Ajdal, Saddlers' Hall, Marwell (Ire), Zilzal, Opera House (GB), Ezzoud (Ire), Russian Rhythm, Islington (Ire).

Strauss, Robert S., 1918-. Lawyer, diplomat. Chairman of Del Mar Thoroughbred Club since 2002. Jockey Club member. Former FBI special agent; ambassador to the Soviet Union 1991-'92; President Carter's representative to the Middle East peace negotiations; winner of the Presidential Medal of Freedom '81; chairman of the Democratic National Committee 1973-'76. Bred Last Tycoon (Ire).

Strawbridge, George Jr., 1937-. Investments. Former president, National Steeplechase Association; member, Jockey Club; owner, Augustin Stables, Pennsylvania. F. Ambrose Clark Award in 1979. Bred and owned Tikkanen, Selkirk, Silver Fling, With Anticipation. Bred Treizieme, Turgeon. Owned Cafe Prince, Mo Bay.

Stronach, Frank, 1932-. Auto-parts manufacturer. Chairman, Magna International Corp., Magna Entertainment Corp. Owner of Adena Springs Farm, Kentucky; Adena Springs North, Ontario; Adena Springs South, Florida. Owner of Stronach Stable. Eclipse Award owner in 1998-2000; Eclipse Award breeder in 2000, '04-'07; nine Sovereign Awards as owner of year and six Sovereign Awards as breeder of year. Bred and owned Macho Uno, Perfect Sting, Ghostzapper. Co-owned Touch Gold, Glorious Song. Also bred and owned Awesome Again, richest Canadian-bred runner of all-time with $4,374,590. Through Magna Entertainment, purchased Thoroughbred racetracks Santa Anita Park, Gulfstream Park, Thistledown, Golden Gate Fields, Remington Park, Great Lakes Downs, Portland Meadows, Lone Star Park, Pimlico Race Course, and Laurel Park.

Stute, Melvin F., 1927-. Trainer. Trained two Eclipse Award winners in 1986, Preakness Stakes (G1) winner Snow Chief and Breeders' Cup Juvenile Fillies (G1) winner Brave Raj. Also trained Very Subtle, winner of the 1987 Breeders' Cup Sprint (G1). Brother of trainer Warren Stute.

Suroor, Saeed bin, 1967-. Trainer. Leading trainer in England by money won in 1995. Trained Dubai Millennium, Fantastic Light, Swain (Ire), E Dubai, Lammtarra, Mark of Esteem (Ire). Head trainer for Godolphin Racing; won the Emirates World Series in 1999 with Daylami (Ire), Fantastic Light (2000-'01), and Grandera in 2002.

Switzer, David, 1945-. Executive director, Kentucky Thoroughbred Association; board member, University of Kentucky-Gluck Research Foundation.

Tabor, Michael, 1941-. Former betting shop owner, investments. Owned or co-owned Thunder Gulch, Montjeu (Ire), Desert King, Honour and Glory, Johannesburg, Galileo (Ire), High Chaparral (Ire), Rags to Riches.

Tanaka, Gary, 1943-. Stockbroker, co-owner of Amerindo Investment Advisors Inc. Frequently bought proven horses in Europe and raced them in California. Owned User Friendly (GB), Dernier Empereur, Donna Viola (GB), Dreams Gallore, Golden Apples (Ire).

Taylor, Duncan, 1956-. Farm owner. Co-owner (with brothers Frank, Ben, and Mark) of Taylor Made Farm and Sales Agency, Kentucky. Sold more than $1-billion total value of horses at public auctions since 1978. Stands Unbridled's Song, Forestry. Son of Joe Taylor.

Taylor, Mickey, 1940-, and **Karen**, 1940-. Timber. Owned and bred Slew o' Gold, Slewpy. Co-owned Seattle Slew, who won 14 of 17 starts, including the Triple Crown in 1977, and earned $1.2-million.

Thomas, Becky, 1957-. Bloodstock agent. Co-founder of Lakland and Lakland North with partners Lewis and Brenda Lakin. Owns and operates Sequel Bloodstock, which consigns at two-year-old sales.

Threewitt, Noble, 1911-. Trainer. President, California Horsemen's Benevolent and Protective Association for six terms; president emeritus, California Thoroughbred Trainers Association. Recipient of Laffit Pincay Jr. Award in 2005. Trained more than 2,000 winners, including Correlation, Devoted Brass, Old Topper, Theresa's Tizzy.

Thompson, David, 1936-, **and Patricia**, 1940-. Owners, Cheveley Park Stud, Newmarket, England. Owned Red Bloom, Russian Rhythm.

Troutt, Kenny, 1948-. Telecommunications. Partner in WinStar Farm, Kentucky. Trustee, Thoroughbred Owners and Breeders Association; director, Breeders Cup Ltd. In WinStar name, bred Funny Cide, One Cool Cat. Owned Awesome Humor, Bet Me Best, Byzantium (Brz), and Pompeii. Co-owner of Ipi Tombe (Zim), Crimson Palace. Stands Tiznow, Distorted Humor, Victory Gallop. Stood Kris S.

Turcotte, Ron, 1941-. Jockey. Leading jockey by stakes won in 1972-'73; inducted into Racing Hall of Fame in '79; George Woolf Memorial Jockey Award in '79. Rode 3,032 winners, including Secretariat, Damascus, Northern Dancer, Riva Ridge, Shuvee, Dark Mirage, Fort Marcy. Won Triple Crown in 1973 aboard Secretariat. Paralyzed in 1978 spill.

Turner, William H. "Billy," 1941-. Trainer. Trained Seattle Slew through his three-year-old season to become the first undefeated American Triple Crown winner. Also trained Czaravich. Rode in steeplechase races from 1958-'62; assistant to Racing Hall of Fame trainer W. Burling Cocks before going on his own in 1966.

Ussery, Robert N., 1935-. Jockey. Inducted into Racing Hall of Fame in 1980. Rode 3,611 winners, including Hail to Reason, Bally Ache, Bramalea, Never Bow. Fifth by money won among jockeys at retirement; finished first in two consecutive Kentucky Derbys, aboard Proud Clarion (1967) and Dancer's Image ('68, disqualified, placed last).

Valenzuela, Ismael "Milo," 1934-. Jockey. Regular jockey of Kelso. Rode Tim Tam to Derby and Preakness victories in 1958. Uncle of jockey Patrick Valenzuela. Inducted into Racing Hall of Fame, 2008.

Valpredo, Don, 1939-. Agriculture. Director, Thoroughbred Owners of California, Breeders' Cup Ltd.; member, Jockey Club; president, Ridge Ginning Co.; director, Kern Ridge Growers, Arvin Edison Water Storage District. Son of John Valpredo.

Van Berg, Jack, 1936-. Trainer. Leading trainer by races won in 1968-'70, '72, '74, '76, '83-'84, '86; leading trainer by money won in '76; inducted into Racing Hall of Fame in '85; Eclipse Award trainer in '84; Big Sport of Turfdom Award in '87; Jockey Club Gold Medal in '87; Mr. Fitz Award in '88. Trained Alysheba, Gate Dancer. Holds record for most races won in a single year (496 in 1976); trained champion Alysheba, who retired with a then-record total earnings of $6,679,242; 6,000th career win in February 1995. Son of Racing Hall of Fame trainer Marion Van Berg.

Van Clief, Daniel G. Jr., 1948-. Racing executive. Former commissioner, National Thoroughbred Racing Assocation; former president, Breeders' Cup Ltd.; chairman, Fasig-Tipton Co.; member, Jockey Club. Co-owner of Nydrie Stud, Virginia. Eclipse Award of Merit in 1998; Jockey Club Medal in '84. Worked to put together Breed-

ers' Cup day of championship races; key figure in development of NTRA.

Van de Kamp, John, 1936-. Lawyer, association executive. Past president, Thoroughbred Owners of California; director, National Thoroughbred Racing Association. Gathered support in the TOC to pass account wagering bill; lobbied for horse industry tax relief measures in California.

VanMeter II, Tom, 1957-. Veterinarian, sales agent, owner-breeder. Co-owner with Reiley McDonald of Eaton Sales, Kentucky. Owner of Victory U. S. A., Be Gentle; raced Brahms; co-bred Mr. Mellon.

Varola, Francesco, 1922-. Author, bloodstock adviser. Author of *Typology of the Racehorse*; added to the dosage theory by creating aptitudinal classes in which he categorized each *chef-de-race* stallion.

Vasquez, Jacinto, 1944-. Jockey, trainer. Inducted into Racing Hall of Fame in 1998. Rode winners of 5,231 races, including Ruffian, Genuine Risk, Princess Rooney, Forego. Nation's 15th all-time winning jockey at his retirement in 1996; rode Ruffian to victory in the New York filly triple crown in '75.

Veitch, John, 1945-. Racing official, former trainer. Chief steward, Kentucky Horse Racing Authority. Inducted into Racing Hall of Fame in 2007. Trained Davona Dale, Our Mims, Before Dawn, Proud Truth. Trained Alydar, who finished second behind Affirmed in all three Triple Crown races in 1978. Son of Racing Hall of Fame trainer Sylvester Veitch.

Velasquez, Jorge, 1946-. Jockey. Leading jockey by races won in 1967; leading jockey by money won in '69; leading jockey by stakes races won in '85; inducted into Racing Hall of Fame in '90; George Woolf Memorial Jockey Award in '86. Rode 6,795 winners, including Alydar, Chris Evert, Davona Dale, Lady's Secret, Shuvee, Fort Marcy. Won the New York filly triple crown with Chris Evert in 1974 and Davona Dale in '79; first jockey to win six of six races in New York, in '81.

Velazquez, John R., 1971-. Jockey. Eclipse Award jockey, 2004-'05; North American leading rider by earnings in 2004 with $22.2-million; in '05 with $20.8-million. Rode winners of six Breeders' Cup races: Ashado, Speightstown, Da Hoss, Caressing, Starine, and Storm Flag Flying. Won 2007 Belmont with Rags to Riches.

Valenzuela, Patrick, 1962-. Jockey. Rode Sunday Silence to win 1989 Kentucky Derby (G1) and Preakness Stakes (G1). Winner of seven Breeders' Cup races.

Violette, Richard Jr., 1953-. Trainer. Chairman, New York Jockey Injury Compensation Fund since 1996; president, National Thoroughbred Horsemen's Association since 2000; director, New York Thoroughbred Horsemen's Association. Trained Citadeed, Read the Footnotes, Nijinsky's Gold.

von Stade, John, 1938-. President, National Museum of Racing, 1989-2005; chairman, National Museum of Racing since 2005. Instrumental in completion of a new wing and handicap-accessible areas at museum.

Waldrop, Alex, 1956-. Chief executive officer, National Thoroughbred Racing Association since 2006; former president, Churchill Downs.

Walsh, Thomas, 1940-. Jockey. Leading American steeplechase rider 1960, '66; fifth-ranked all-time American steeplechase jockey with 253 victories. Regular rider of champions Barnabys Bluff, Bon Nouvel, and Mako. Won American Grand National six times, five years in succession, 1959-'63. Inducted into Racing Hall of Fame in 2005.

Ward, John T. Jr., 1945-. Trainer. Owner of Sugar Grove Farm, Kentucky; John T. Ward Stables, Kentucky. Trained Monarchos, Beautiful Pleasure, Darling My Darling, Jambalaya Jazz, Pyramid Peak. Nephew of Racing Hall of Fame trainer Sherrill Ward.

Waterman, Scot, 1966-. Veterinarian, industry executive. Executive director, Racing Medication and Testing Consortium. Recipient of North American Pari-Mutuel Regulators Association's Winner's Circle Award in 2004. Thoroughbred owner and breeder.

Weber, Charlotte, 1942-. Investments. Member, Jockey Club; owner, Live Oak Stud, Florida. Bred and owned Miesque's Approval, Peaceful Union, Gnome Home, Medieval Man, Laser Light, Sultry Song, High Fly, Sultry Sun.

Weisbord, Barry, 1950-. Publisher. Joe Palmer Award in 1992. Co-owned Safely Kept. Created the American Championship Racing Series in 1991; created the Matchmaker Breeders' Exchange, the first centralized market for stallion seasons and shares.

Whitney, Marylou, 1926-. Investments. Owner of Whitney Farm, Kentucky; Blue Goose Stable, Kentucky. Bred and owned Silver Buck, Bird Town, Birdstone. Long known for her Derby Eve parties and for her parties in Saratoga Springs, New York. Widow of C. V. Whitney; married to John Hendrickson.

Willmot, David, 1950-. Breeder, investments. President, Woodbine Entertainment Group. Owner of Kinghaven Farms, Canada. John W. Galbreath Award in 2001; Sovereign Award in 1998. Bred and owned Talkin Man, Poetically, Alywow, Play the King, Summer Mood, With Approval. Successfully lobbied for legislation to add slot machines at Woodbine racetrack. Son of Donald Willmot.

Wygod, Martin, 1940-. Executive, owner-breeder. Chairman and chief executive of WebMD. Sold his Medco Containment Services Inc. to Merck & Co. for $6.5-billion in 1994. Owns River Edge Farm and 102-acre property in Rancho Santa Fe, both in California. Member of the Jockey Club. With wife, Pam, bred and owned champion Sweet Catomine.

Ycaza, Manuel, 1938-. Jockey. Inducted into Racing Hall of Fame in 1977. Rode 2,367 winners, including Ack Ack, Dr. Fager, Damascus, Sword Dancer, Gamely, Dark Mirage, Never Bend. Won first New York filly triple crown with Dark Mirage in 1968.

Yoshida, Teruya, 1947-. Breeder. Owner, president of Shadai Farm, founded by his late father, Zenya Yoshida. With brothers Haruya and Katsumi, owns Shadai Stallion Station, home to Japan's leading sire in 20 of the last 21 years, including ten-time leader Northern Taste and eight-time leader Sunday Silence. Vice chairman, Japanese Racing Horse Association.

Young, William Jr., 1948-. Managing owner, Overbrook Farm, Kentucky; member, Jockey Club; director, Keeneland Association, Kentucky Thoroughbred Owners and Breeders Association.

Zilber, Maurice, 1926-. Trainer. Ten times leading trainer during the 1950s in his native Egypt; leading trainer in France. Trained Racing Hall of Fame members Dahlia and Exceller, and Trillion, Youth, Argument (Fr), Hippodamia.

Zito, Nick, 1948-. Trainer. Elected to Racing Hall of Fame in 2005. Trained Kentucky Derby (G1) winners Go for Gin (1994) and Strike the Gold ('91), Preakness Stakes (G1) winner Louis Quatorze, Belmont Stakes (G1) winner Birdstone, plus A P Valentine, Thirty Six Red, Bird Town.

Industry Awards

Eric Beitia Memorial Award

Awarded by the New York Racing Association to the leading apprentice jockey at the NYRA tracks. Named for the leading apprentice of 1980 who died November 28, 1983, at age 21 of a gunshot wound a week earlier.

2007	Not awarded
2006	Pablo Morales
2005	Channing Hill
2004	Pablo Fragoso
2003	Pablo Fragoso
2002	Lorenzo Lezcano
2001	Lorenzo Lezcano
2000	Norberto Arroyo Jr.
1999	Ariel Smith
1998	Shaun Bridgmohan
1997	Phil Teator
1996	Jose Trejo
1995	Ramon Perez
1994	Dale Beckner
1993	Caesar Bisono
1992	Gerry Brocklebank
1991	Rafael Mojica Jr.
1990	Paul Toscano
1989	Jose Martinez
1988	Brian Peck
1987	David Nuesch
1986	David Nuesch, Edward Thomas Baird
1985	Wesley Ward
1984	Wesley Ward
1983	Declan Murphy

Big Sport of Turfdom

Sponsored by the Turf Publicists of America and awarded to the individual or individuals whose cooperation with the media enhances coverage and brings favorable attention to Thoroughbred racing.

2007	Carl Nafzger
2006	Dean Richardson, D.V.M.
2005	Pat Day
2004	John Servis
2003	Sackatoga Stable
2002	Ken and Sue McPeek
2001	Laura Hillenbrand
2000	Laffit Pincay Jr.
1999	D. Wayne Lukas
1998	Mike Pegram
1997	Bob Baffert
1996	Cigar, Allen Paulson, Bill Mott, Jerry Bailey
1995	Robert and Beverly Lewis
1994	Warren "Jimmy" Croll Jr.
1993	Chris McCarron
1992	Angel Cordero Jr.
1991	Hammer and Oaktown Stable
1990	Carl Nafzger
1989	Tim Conway
1988	Julie Krone
1987	Jack Van Berg
1986	Jim McKay
1985	Laffit Pincay Jr.
1984	John Henry
1983	Joe Hirsch
1982	Woody Stephens
1981	John Forsythe
1980	Jack Klugman
1979	Laz Barrera
1978	Ron Turcotte
1977	Steve Cauthen
1976	Telly Savalas
1975	Francis P. Dunne
1974	Eddie Arcaro
1973	Penny Chenery
1972	John Galbreath
1971	Burt Bacharach
1970	Saul Rosen
1969	Bill Shoemaker
1968	John Nerud
1967	Allaire duPont
1966	E. P. Taylor

F. Ambrose Clark Award

Presented periodically by the National Steeplechase Association to those who promote, improve, or encourage steeplechase racing. Named for a renowned steeplechase owner.

2007	Austin A. Brown
2006	Not awarded
2005	Not awarded
2004	Stephen P. Groat
2002	George A. Sloan
2001	John A. Wayt Jr.
1995	John T. von Stade
1991	Beverly Steinman
1988	William L. Pape
1982	Mrs. Miles Valentine
1980	Charles Fenwick Jr.
1979	George Strawbridge Jr.
1978	Morris H. Dixon
1977	Alfred M. Hunt
1976	Joseph Aitcheson Jr.
1975	Michael Walsh
1974	John Cooper
1973	W. Burling Cocks
1972	Russell M. Arundel
1971	Raymond G. Woolfe
1970	Raymond R. Guest
1969	Mrs. Odgen Phipps
1968	John W. Hanes
1967	S. Bryce Wing
1966	Crompton Smith Jr.
1965	Marion duPont Scott

Coman Humanitarian Award

Presented by Kentucky Thoroughbred Owners and Breeders for contributions to better human relations in the Thoroughbred industry. Named for KTOB Executive Director William C. Coman. No longer awarded.

2002	Alice Chandler
2001	Sheikh Mohammed bin Rashid al Maktoum
2000	Benjamin Roach, M.D.
1999	J. David Richardson, M.D.
1998	Gary Biszantz
1997	Dr. John T. Bryans
1996	Larry Weber
1994	Paul Mellon
1993	John A. Bell III
1992	Charles Nuckols Jr.
1991	William T. Young
1990	Carl Icahn
1989	Tim Conway
1988	Jim and Linda Ryan
1987	Jay Spurrier
1986	James E. "Ted" Bassett III
1985	Drs. Charles Hagyard, Arthur Davidson, and William McGee
1984	Keene Daingerfield
1983	Brownell Combs, Maxwell Gluck

Dogwood Dominion Award

Sponsored by Dogwood Stable and presented to the "unsung heroes" of racing, especially in the backstretch areas. Named for Dominion (GB), Dogwood's first graded stakes winner who raced from 1974 to '78.

2007	Phyllis Shetron
2006	Pete Lizazaburu
2005	Jo Anne Normile
2004	Pam Berg
2003	Neftali "Junior" Gutierrez
2002	Jim Greene and Shirley Edwards
2001	Julian "Buck" Wheat
2000	Katherine Todd Smith
1999	Danny Perlsweig
1998	Donald "Peanut Butter" Brown
1997	Nick Caras
1996	Grace Belcuore
1995	Peggy Sprinkles
1994	Howard "Gelo" Hall
1993	H. W. "Salty" Roberts

Charles W. Engelhard Award

Presented by Kentucky Thoroughbred Owners and Breeders for outstanding media coverage of the Thoroughbred industry.

2007	Randy Moss
2006	Ed Bowen
2005	Charlsie Cantey
2004	Seabiscuit
2003	Ercel Ellis Jr.
2002	Television Games Network
2001	John Henderson ("Thoroughbred Week")
2000	Ray Paulick (The Blood-Horse)
1999	Maryjean Wall (Lexington Herald-Leader)
1998	David Heckerman (The Blood-Horse)
1997	Jim Bolus
1996	Kenny Rice (WTVQ-TV)
1994	Jay Hovdey (The Blood-Horse)
	John Asher (WHAS Radio)
1993	Jennie Rees (Louisville Courier-Journal)
1992	Josh Pons (Country Life Diary)
1991	Cawood Ledford
1990	Jim McKay (ABC)
1989	Lewis Owens (Lexington Herald-Leader)
1988	Anheuser-Busch
1987	Jim Wilburn and Chris Lincoln (Winner Communications)
1986	Leon Rasmussen (Daily Racing Form)
1985	Dick Enberg (NBC)
1984	NBC Sports
1983	Cawood Ledford
1982	Tom Hammond
1981	The Thoroughbred Record
1980	Billy Reed (Louisville Courier-Journal)
1979	Logan Bailey (Daily Racing Form)
1978	Kent Hollingsworth (The Blood-Horse)
1977	Jim McKay (ABC)
1976	Heywood Hale Broun (CBS)
1975	Robert Wussler (CBS)
1974	Joe Hirsch (Daily Racing Form)
1973	Jack Whitaker (CBS)
1972	Hugh "Mickey" McGuire (Daily Racing Form)
1971	Red Smith (New York Times)
1970	Win Elliott (CBS Radio)

Jerry Frutkoff Preakness Photography Award

Sponsored by Pimlico Race Course and Nikon, for best Preakness Stakes (G1) photo from previous year. Renamed for longtime Maryland Jockey Club photographer who died in 2003.

2008	Brandon Benson (Mid-Atlantic Thoroughbred)
2007	Jim McCue (Maryland Jockey Club)
2006	Molly Riley (Reuters)
2005	Gary Hershorn (Reuters)
2004	Jeff Snyder (The Blood-Horse)
2003	Skip Dickstein (The Blood-Horse)
2002	Molly Riley (Reuters)

John W. Galbreath Award

Sponsored by the University of Louisville's Equine Industry Program, the award named for the Darby Dan Farm owner honors equine-industry entrepreneurs.

2007	R. D. Hubbard
2006	Carol Rose
2005	Brian Derrick Mehl
2004	Judith Forbis
2003	Frank "Scoop" Vessels
2002	William S. Morris III
2001	David Willmot
2000	Denny Gentry
1999	Tom Meeker
1998	D. Wayne Lukas
1997	John M. Lyons
1996	B. Thomas Joy
1995	Robert Clay
1994	Ami Shinitzky
1993	John Gaines
1992	W. Cothran "Cot" Campbell
1991	James E. "Ted" Bassett III
1990	John A. Bell III

Avelino Gomez Memorial Award

Sponsored by Woodbine, the award named for jockey Avelino "El Perfecto" Gomez is presented to the Canadian-born, -raised, or -based jockey who has made a significant contribution to Thoroughbred racing. North America's leading rider in 1966, Gomez died of injuries incurred in a three-horse spill in the Canadian Oaks on June 21, 1980.

2008	Jack Lauzon
2007	George HoSang
2006	John LeBlanc Sr.
2005	Sam Krasner
2004	Francine Villeneuve
2003	Robert Landry
2002	Richard Dos Ramos
2001	Chris Loseth
2000	Jim McKnight
1999	David Clark
1998	Irwin Driedger
1997	Richard Grubb
1996	David Gall
1995	Don Seymour
1994	Not awarded
1993	Larry Attard
1992	Robin Platts
1991	Hugo Dittfach
1990	Lloyd Duffy
1989	Jeff Fell
1988	Chris Rogers
1987	Don MacBeth
1986	Sandy Hawley
1985	John Longden
1984	Ron Turcotte

John K. Goodman Alumni Award

University of Arizona Race Track Industry Program

award for a program graduate who has achieved distinction in the racing industry. Named for one of the program's founders.

2007	Joe Osborne
2006	Michael Weiss
2005	Scot Waterman
2004	Phil O'Hara
2003	Patricia McQueen
2002	Todd Pletcher
2001	Luke Kruytbosch
2000	Ann McGovern
1999	Lonny Powell
1998	Dan Fick
1997	Bob Baffert

Walter Haight Award

Presented by the National Turf Writers Association for excellence in Turf writing. Named for Washington *Post* racing columnist and handicapper known for his humorous style.

2007	Dick Jerardi (Philadelphia *Daily News*)
2006	Steven Crist (*Daily Racing Form*)
2005	Jay Privman (*Daily Racing Form*)
2004	Steve Haskin (*The Blood-Horse*)
2003	Russ Harris (career excellence)
2002	Billy Reed (career excellence)
2001	Gary West (Dallas *Morning News*)
2000	Bill Christine (Los Angeles *Times*)
1999	Jennie Rees (Louisville *Courier-Journal*)
1998	Andrew Beyer (Washington *Post*)
1997	Jim Bolus
1996	Ed Schuyler Jr. (Associated Press)
1995	Jay Hovdey
1994	Ed Bowen
1993	Jack Mann (New York *Herald-Tribune*)
1992	Mike Barry (*Kentucky Irish American* and The Louisville *Times*)
	Bill Nack (*Sports Illustrated*)
1991	Bob Harding (Newark *Star-Ledger*)
1990	Kent Hollingsworth (*The Blood-Horse*)
1989	William Leggett (THOROUGHBRED TIMES)
1988	Leon Rasmussen (*Daily Racing Form*)
1987	Si Burick (Dayton *Daily News*)
1986	Ed Comerford (*Newsday*)
1985	Sam McCracken (Boston *Globe*)
1984	Joe Hirsch (*Daily Racing Form*)
1983	Fred Russell (Nashville *Banner*)
1982	Joe Agrella (Chicago *Sun-Times*)
1981	Bill Robertson (*The Thoroughbred Record*)
1980	Joe Nichols (New York *Times*)
1979	Barney Nagler (*Daily Racing Form*)
1978	Nelson Fisher (San Diego *Union*)
1977	Red Smith (New York *Times*)
1976	Saul Rosen (*Daily Racing Form*)
1975	Don Fair (*Daily Racing Form*)
1974	Raleigh Burroughs (*Turf and Sport Digest*)
1973	George Ryall (*The New Yorker*)
1972	Jimmy Doyle (Cleveland *Plain Dealer*)

Hardboot Award

Sponsored by Kentucky Thoroughbred Owners and Breeders.

2007	William O'Neill
2006	Carter Thornton, Dave Fishback
2005	Josephine Abercrombie
2004	Diane Perkins
2003	Henry White
2002	Charles Nuckols Jr., Virginia Kraft Payson
2001	Robert Courtney Sr.
2000	Carlos Perez
1999	Dr. and Mrs. R. Smiser West
	Mr. and Mrs. MacKenzie Miller

Joe Hirsch Breeders' Cup Newspaper Writing Award

Sponsored by Breeders' Cup Ltd. and the National Thoroughbred Racing Association, the award named for the longtime *Daily Racing Form* columnist honors excellence in newspaper coverage of the previous year's Breeders' Cup World Thoroughbred Championships.

2007	Not awarded
2006	Jay Privman
2005	Richard Edmondson
2004	Jay Privman
2003	Pat Forde
2002	Jay Privman
2001	Pat Forde
2000	Robert Edmondson
1999	Dick Jerardi
1998	Jennie Rees
1997	Pat Forde
1996	Dick Jerardi
1995	Jay Posner

Jockey Club Medal of Honor

Awarded periodically by the Jockey Club for meritorious service to the Thoroughbred industry.

2007	Louis Romanet
2003	Hans J. Stahl
1998	Nick Nicholson and Alan Marzelli
1994	Larry Bramlage, D.V.M.
1993	Kenny Noe Jr.
1992	R. Richards Rolapp
1991	Dr. Manuel Gilman
1990	Dr. Charles Randall
1989	Joe Hirsch
1988	Dennis Swanson
1987	Jack Van Berg
1986	Richard Duchossois
1985	Jean Romanet
1984	D. G. Van Clief Jr.

Lavin Cup

Sponsored by the American Association of Equine Practitioners and awarded to a nonveterinary individual or organization that has demonstrated exceptional compassion for horses or has developed and enforced guidelines for horses' welfare. Named for Kentucky veterinarian A. Gary Lavin, AAEP president in 1994.

2007	Finger Lakes Thoroughbred Adoption Program
2006	Not awarded
2005	Allan and Kathleen Schwartz
2004	Herb and Ellen Moelis
2003	Professional Rodeo Cowboys Association
2002	Dayton O. Hyde
1999	Tom Dorrance
1998	Thoroughbred Retirement Foundation
1997	American Quarter Horse Association
1996	California Horse Racing Board

Bill Leggett Breeders' Cup Magazine Writing Award

Sponsored by Breeders' Cup Ltd. and the National Thoroughbred Racing Association, award named for the late *Sports Illustrated* and THOROUGHBRED TIMES writer

honors excellence in magazine coverage of the previous year's Breeders' Cup World Thoroughbred Championships.

2007	Not awarded
2006	Ed DeRosa
2005	Tom Law
2004	Michele MacDonald
2003	Billy Reed
2002	Billy Reed
2001	Tom Law
2000	Bill Heller
1999	Tom LaMarra
1998	Robbie Henwood
1997	Glenye Cain
1996	Jay Hovdey
1994	Jay Hovdey

William H. May Award

Awarded by Association of Racing Commissioners International for distinguished service to racing. Named for a former president of National Association of State Racing Commissioners.

2007	American Greyhound Council
2006	Curtis Barrett, Ph.D.
2005	Lonny Powell
2004	Race Track Chaplaincy of America
2003	American Association of Equine Practitioners
2002	American Quarter Horse Association
2001	John R. Gaines
2000	R. D. Hubbard
1999	Bob and Beverly Lewis
1998	Fred Noe
1997	James E. "Ted" Bassett III
1996	Allen Paulson
1995	Paul Mellon
1994	Joe Hirsch
1993	Tony Chamblin
1992	Bill Shoemaker
1991	Jockey Club
1990	James P. Ryan
1989	Stanley Bergstein
1988	Daily Racing Form
1987	Breeders' Cup Ltd.
1986	Robert H. Strub

Mr. Fitz Award

Sponsored by National Turf Writers Association, award named for Racing Hall of Fame trainer James E. "Sunny Jim" Fitzsimmons honors individuals who typify the spirit of horse racing.

2007	Calvin Borel
2006	Team Barbaro
2005	Nick Zito
2004	Patti Cooksey
2003	Sackatoga Stable
2002	Chris McCarron
2001	H. Allen Jerkens
2000	Pat Day
1999	Bob and Beverly Lewis
1998	Joe Hirsch
1997	Bob Baffert
1996	MacKenzie Miller
1995	Warren "Jimmy" Croll
1994	Jeff Lukas
1993	Angel Cordero Jr.
1992	Ron McAnally
1991	Frances Genter
1990	Arthur B. Hancock III
1989	Ogden Phipps
1988	Jack Van Berg
1987	Laffit Pincay Jr.
1986	Arlington Park management
1985	John Henry
1984	Penny Chenery
1983	Fred Hooper
1982	Bill Shoemaker, Woody Stephens
1981	Jack Klugman

Isaac Murphy Award

Named for 19th-century black jockey who won with 44% of his career mounts, National Turf Writers Association award honors jockey with highest winning percentage for the year.

2005-2007	Russell Baze
2004	Ramon Dominguez
1995-2003	Russell Baze

Old Hilltop Award

Presented by Pimlico Race Course for distinction in Thoroughbred racing reporting. Name derives from Pimlico's nickname.

2008	Dick Jerardi (Philadelphia Daily News)
	Mike Pupo (Baltimore's WJZ-TV)
2007	Don Clippinger (THOROUGHBRED TIMES)
	Jerry Izenberg (Newark Star-Ledger)
2006	Kenny Mayne (ESPN)
	Lucy Acton (Mid-Atlantic Thoroughbred)
2005	Jay Privman (Daily Racing Form)
	Scott Garceau (WMAR-TV)
2004	Gary West (Dallas Morning News)
	Bruce Cunningham (WBFF-TV)
2003	John Patti (WBAL-AM)
	Steve Haskin (The Blood-Horse)
2002	Stan Charles (Baltimore radio)
	Michele MacDonald (THOROUGHBRED TIMES)
2001	Keith Mills (WMAR-TV)
	Jennie Rees (Louisville Courier-Journal)
2000	Marty Bass (WJZ-TV)
	Joe Kelly (Turf historian)
1999	Harry Kakel (WMAR-TV)
	Pohla Smith (Pittsburgh Post-Gazette)
1998	Ed Kiernan (WBAL Radio)
	Vinnie Perrone (Maryland Turf Writers)
1997	Reid Cherner (USA Today)
	Chris Lincoln (ESPN)
1996	Dan Farley (Racing Post)
	George Michael (WRC-TV)
1995	Charlsie Cantey (ABC Sports)
	Neil Milbert (Chicago Tribune)
1994	Ed Schuyler Jr. (Associated Press)
	Jim West (WBAL Radio)
1993	Jim Bolus (free-lance journalist)
	John Buren (WJZ TV)
1992	Dave Johnson (ABC Sports)
	Maryjean Wall (Lexington Herald-Leader)
1991	Sam Lacy (Baltimore Afro-American)
	Demmie Stathopolos (Sports Illustrated)
1990	Bill Tanton (Baltimore Evening Sun)
	Shelby Whitfield (ABC Radio)
1989	Bill Christine (Los Angeles Times)
	John Steadman (Baltimore Evening Sun)
1988	Ed Bowen (The Blood-Horse)
	Bill Nack (Sports Illustrated)
1987	Jack Dawson (WMAR-TV)
	Dave Feldman (Chicago Sun-Times)
1986	Vince Bagli (WBAL-TV)
	Shirley Povich (Washington Post)

People — Industry Awards 771

1985	Howard Cosell (ABC Sports)		1967	John Longden
	Sam McCracken (Boston *Globe*)		1966	Marshall Cassidy
1984	Jim McKay (ABC Sports)		1965	John Schapiro
	Billy Reed (Louisville *Courier-Journal*)		1964	Wathen Knebelkamp

1983 Jack Whitaker (ABC Sports)
 Dale Austin (Baltimore *Sun*)
1982 Russ Harris (New York *Daily News*)
 Kent Hollingsworth (*The Blood-Horse*)
1981 William Leggett (*Sports Illustrated*)
 Jack Mann (Baltimore *Evening Sun*)
1980 Edwin Pope (Miami *Herald*)
 Snowden Carter (*Maryland Horse*)
1979 Whitney Tower (*Sports Illustrated*)
 Joe Kelly (Washington *Star*)
1979 William C. Phillips (*Daily Racing Form*)
1978 Win Elliott (CBS)
 Joe Hirsch (*Daily Racing Form*)
 Bob Maisel (Baltimore *Sun*)
1977 William Boniface (Baltimore *Sun*)
 Barney Nagler (*Daily Racing Form*)
 Charles Lamb (*News American*)
1976 Red Smith (New York *Times*)
 Raoul Carlisle (Arkansas *Times Herald*)

Joe Palmer Award

National Turf Writers Association Award for meritorious service to racing. Named for New York *Herald-Tribune* Turf writer known for his overall appreciation of the sport.

2006 Larry Bramlage, D.V.M.
2006 Dean Richardson, D.V.M./New Bolton Center
2005 Pete Pedersen
2004 Noble Threewitt
2003 Laffit Pincay Jr.
2002 Richard Duchossois, Eugene Melnyk
2001 Shirley Day Smith
2000 Jim McKay
1999 Kent Hollingsworth
1998 Sandy Hawley
1997 Jim Bolus
1996 Allen Paulson
1995 Mark Kaufman
1994 Joe Hirsch
1993 Henryk de Kwiatkowski
1992 Barry Weisbord
1991 Joe Burnham
1990 James P. Ryan
1989 Claude "Shug" McGaughey III
1988 Charlie Whittingham
1987 Alfred Vanderbilt
1986 James E. "Ted" Bassett III
1985 John Gaines
1984 E. P. Taylor
1983 David "Sonny" Werblin
1982 Frank "Jimmy" Kilroe
1981 Keene Daingerfield, Marion duPont Scott
1980 Chick Lang Sr., Leo O'Donnell
1979 Laz Barrera
1978 Steve Cauthen
1977 Nelson Bunker Hunt
1976 Fred Hooper
1975 I. J. Collins
1974 Secretariat
1973 John Galbreath
1972 Paul Mellon
1971 Bill Shoemaker
1970 Warner Jones Jr.
1969 Raymond Guest
1968 Marion Van Berg

Joan F. Pew Award

Sponsored by the Association of Racing Commissioners International and awarded to racing commissioner who demonstrates vision and vitality. Named for first woman member of Pennsylvania Horse Racing Commission and first woman president of National Association of State Racing Commissioners.

2008 Michael Hoblock
2007 Connie Whitfield
2006 Richard Shapiro
2005 Lynda Tanaka
2004 Cecil Alexander
2003 Norman I. Barron
2002 Stan Sadinsky
2001 Basil Plasteras
2000 Timothy "Ted" Connors
1999 Robin Traywick Williams
1998 Jon McKinnie
1997 Arthur Khoury
1996 Not awarded
1995 Not awarded
1994 Gil Moutray
1993 Joe Neglia
1992 Joanne McAdam
1991 Dr. Glenn Blodgett
1990 Frank Drea
1989 Richard Corbisiero Jr.
1988 Dr. James Smith
1987 Eric Braun

Clay Puett Award

Sponsored by the University of Arizona Race Track Industry Program, for long-term, multifaceted, or far-reaching contributions to the racing industry. Named for creator of modern starting gate.

2007 Stan Bergstein
2006 Jay Hickey/American Horse Council
2005 WinStar Farm
2004 Trudy McCaffery
2003 W. Cothran "Cot" Campbell
2002 John and Betty Mabee and family
2001 Joe Hirsch
2000 John Gaines
1999 Vessels family
1998 Brady family
1997 Hancock family
1996 Phipps family
1995 Allen Paulson
1994 Clement Hirsch

Red Smith Award

Churchill Downs award for outstanding print coverage of the Kentucky Derby (G1) in four categories. Named for late New York *Times* columnist.

Feature Story

2007 William Nack (*The Blood-Horse*)
2006 Wright Thompson (Kansas City *Star*)
2005 Greg Hall (Louisville *Courier-Journal*)
2004 C. Ray Hall (Louisville *Courier-Journal*)
2003 Mike Kane ([Schenectady] *Daily Gazette*)
2002 Jennie Rees (Louisville *Courier-Journal*)
2001 Bill Christine (Los Angeles *Times*)
2000 Jerry Izenberg (Newark *Star-Ledger*)
1999 Jay Privman (*Daily Racing Form*)

1998	Matt Graves (Albany *Times Union*)
1997	Jennie Rees (Louisville *Courier-Journal*)
1996	Dave Koerner (Louisville *Courier-Journal*)
1995	Bob Fortus (New Orleans *Times-Picayune*)
1994	Rick Bozich (Louisville *Courier-Journal*)
1993	Rick Bozich (Louisville *Courier-Journal*)
1992	Tom Archdeacon (Dayton *Daily News*)
1991	Dave Koerner (Louisville *Courier-Journal*)
1990	Jim Wells (St. Paul *Pioneer-Press*)
1989	Steve Crist (New York *Times*)
1988	Bill Christine (Los Angeles *Times*)
1987	Hubert Mizell (St. Petersburg *Times*)
1986	Bill Christine (Los Angeles *Times*)
1985	Dick Fenlon (Columbus *Dispatch*)
1984	Stan Hochman (Philadelphia *Daily News*)
1983	Jim Bolus (Louisville *Times*)

Advance Story

2007	John Scheinman (Washington *Post*)
2006	Bob Ford (Philadelphia *Inquirer*)
2005	Dick Jerardi (Philadelphia *Daily News*)
2004	Richard Rosenblatt (Associated Press)
2003	Rick Bozich (Louisville *Courier-Journal*)
2002	Rick Bozich (Louisville *Courier-Journal*)
2001	Mike Kane ([Schenectady] *Daily Gazette*)
2000	Rick Bozich (Louisville *Courier-Journal*)
1999	Rick Bozich (Louisville *Courier-Journal*)
1998	Vic Ziegel (New York *Daily News*)
1997	Matt Graves (Albany *Times Union*)
1996	Steve Haskin (*Daily Racing Form*)
1995	Blackie Sherrod (Dallas *Morning News*)
1994	Billy Reed (Lexington *Herald-Leader*)
1993	Rick Bozich (Louisville *Courier-Journal*)
1992	Vic Ziegel (New York *Daily News*)
1991	Steve Woodward (*USA Today*)
1990	Jerry Izenberg (New York *Post*)
1989	Rick Bozich (Louisville *Courier-Journal*)
1988	Billy Reed (Lexington *Herald-Leader*)
1987	Billy Reed (Lexington *Herald-Leader*)
1986	Bob Harding (Newark *Star-Ledger*)
1985	Jack Patterson (Akron *Beacon-Journal*)
1984	Bill Christine (Los Angeles *Times*)
1983	Peter Finney (New Orleans *Times-Picayune*)

Sunday Wrap-Up

2007	Eric Crawford (Louisville *Courier-Journal*)
2006	Mike Jensen (Philadelphia *Inquirer*)
2005	Jennie Rees (Louisville *Courier-Journal*)
2004	Pat Forde (Louisville *Courier-Journal*)
2003	Richard Rosenblatt (*Associated Press*)
2002	Mike Kane ([Schenectady] *Daily Gazette*)
2001	Jennie Rees (Louisville *Courier-Journal*)
2000	Mike Kane ([Schenectady] *Daily Gazette*)
1999	Mike Kane ([Schenectady] *Daily Gazette*)
1998	Jay Privman (New York *Times*)
1997	Jay Privman (New York *Times*)
1996	Billy Reed (Lexington *Herald-Leader*)
1995	Chuck Culpepper (Lexington *Herald-Leader*)
1994	Tom Archdeacon (Dayton *Daily News*)
1993	Jennie Rees (Louisville *Courier-Journal*)
1992	Bill Christine (Los Angeles *Times*)
1991	Tom Archdeacon (Dayton *Daily News*)
1990	Billy Reed (Lexington *Herald-Leader*)
1989	Jay Privman (Los Angeles *Daily News*)
1988	Jay Privman (Los Angeles *Daily News*)
1987	Bill Christine (Los Angeles *Times*)
1986	Paul Moran ([Long Island] *Newsday*)
1985	Tom McEwen (Tampa *Tribune*)
1984	Billy Reed (Louisville *Courier-Journal*)
1983	Billy Reed (Louisville *Courier-Journal*)

Monday Wrap-Up

2007	Steve Haskin (*The Blood-Horse*)
2006	Dick Jerardi (Philadelphia *Daily News*)
2005	Steve Haskin (*The Blood-Horse*)
2004	Steve Haskin (*The Blood-Horse*)
2003	Tom Law (THOROUGHBRED TIMES)
2002	Lew Freedman (Chicago *Tribune*)
2001	John Harrell (THOROUGHBRED TIMES)
2000	Steve Haskin (*The Blood-Horse*)
1999	Steve Haskin (*The Blood-Horse*)
1998	Bill Nack (*Sports Illustrated*)
1997	Dick Jerardi (Philadelphia *Daily News*)
1996	Greg Boeck (*USA Today*)
1995	Bill Nack (*Sports Illustrated*)
1994	Chuck Culpepper (Lexington *Herald-Leader*)
1993	Jack Murray (Cincinnati *Enquirer*)
1992	Harry King (*Associated Press*)
1991	Dick Jerardi (Philadelphia *Daily News*)
1990	Rick Bozich (Louisville *Courier-Journal*)
1989	Tom Cushman (San Diego *Tribune*)
1988	Stan Hochman (Philadelphia *Daily News*)
1987	Dick Jerardi (Philadelphia *Daily News*)
1986	Stan Hochman (Philadelphia *Daily News*) Edwin Pope (Miami *Herald*)
1985	Stan Hochman (Philadelphia *Daily News*)
1984	Dave Anderson (New York *Times*)
1983	Tom Jackson (Washington *Times*)

University of Arizona Race Track Industry Program Distinguished Senior Award

2007	Jon Forbes
2006	Jason Egan, Jon Moss
2005	Heather Belmonte, Dorothee Kieckefer, Eric Yee
2004	Jon Hansen
2003	Heather Meacham
2002	Stacia Mumm
2001	Laura Plato
2000	Scot Waterman
1999	Sable Downs
1998	Mike Hummel
1997	Valora Kilby

University of Arizona Race Track Industry Program Distinguished Service Award

2007	Not awarded
2005	Hans Stahl
2004	Not awarded
2003	Fred Stone
2001	Bob Benoit
2000	Stan Bergstein
1999	*Daily Racing Form*
1998	Sherwood Chillingworth
1997	Bennett Liebman, Ronald Sultemeier
1996	Joe Harper
1995	Lonny Powell
1994	Rukin Jelks
1993	John Goodman, Dr. Darrel Metcalfe, Vessels family
1992	Dan Fick

UTTA Outstanding Trainer of the Year Award

No longer awarded.

2001	John T. Ward Jr.

2000	Bobby Frankel
1999	D. Wayne Lukas
1998	Bob Baffert
1997	Pat Byrne
1996	Hubert "Sonny" Hine
1995	Bill Mott
1994	Warren "Jimmy" Croll Jr.
1993	Claude R. "Shug" McGaughey III
1992	H. Allen Jerkens
1991	Frank Brothers

Alfred Gwynne Vanderbilt Award

New York Turf Writers Association award for individual or group that did the most for racing. Named for owner-breeder of Native Dancer; formerly known as the John A. Morris Award.

2007	IEAH Stables
2006	Team Barbaro
2005	Cash is King stable, Robert Lewis
2004	Team Smarty Jones
2003	Joe Hirsch
2002	Hans Stahl
2001	Barry K. Schwartz
2000	Kenny Noe Jr.
1999	Alfred Gwynne Vanderbilt
1998	Carolyn and Hubert "Sonny" Hine
1997	Skip Away
1996	James "Ted" Bassett
1995	Cigar
1994	Holy Bull
1993	Paul Mellon
1992	Allen Gutterman
1991	Barry Weisbord, American Championship Racing Series
1989	John Gaines, Whitney Tower
1988	Linda and Jim Ryan
1987	David "Sonny" Werblin
1986	ESPN/Thoroughbred Sports Television
1985	Peter Fuller, John Galbreath, Fred Hooper
1984	John Nerud
1983	Allaire duPont
1982	Helen "Penny" Chenery, Frank "Jimmy" Kilroe
1981	Sam Rubin
1980	Jack Klugman
1979	Louis and Patrice Wolfson
1978	Affirmed, Alydar
1977	Ogden Mills Phipps
1976	Marion duPont Scott
1975	Eddie Arcaro, Johnny Longden, Warren Mehrtens, William "Smokey" Saunders, Ron Turcotte, Jack Dreyfus Jr.
1974	Martha F. Gerry
1973	Secretariat
1972	John H. "Jack" Krumpe, Arthur B. "Bull" Hancock Jr.
1971	Jacques D. Wimpfheimer
1970	Charles W. Engelhard, Sen. Thomas Morton
1969	Raymond Guest
1968	John W. Hanes
1967	Robert J. Kleberg Jr.
1966	Jack Dreyfus
1965	James Cox Brady
1964	Allaire duPont
1963	Alfred Gwynne Vanderbilt
1962	Capt. Harry F. Guggenheim
1961	Francis Dunne
1960	Capt. Harry F. Guggenheim
1959	John W. Hanes
1958	Marshall Cassidy
1957	C. V. Whitney
1956	George Widener
1953	Walter Jeffords
1952	C. V. Whitney
1951	John Hay Whitney
1950	Saratoga Association
1949	Marshall Cassidy, George Widener
1948	Lou Smith
1947	Dr. Charles H. Strub
1946	John Blanks Campbell
1944	Harry Parr III
1943	Lincoln Plaut
1942	Herbert Bayard Swope
1941	Alfred Gwynne Vanderbilt
1940	Herbert Bayard Swope
1939	George H. Bull
1938	Alfred Gwynne Vanderbilt
1937	Mrs. Payne Whitney
1936	Alfred Gwynne Vanderbilt

Mike Venezia Memorial Award

Named for the popular New York jockey who was killed in an on-track accident on October 13, 1988, the Mike Venezia Memorial Award honors jockeys who exemplify extraordinary sportsmanship and citizenship.

2007	Not awarded
2006	Edgar Prado
2005	Not awarded
2004	Patti Cooksey
2003	Richard Migliore
2002	Dean Kutz
2001	Mike Luzzi
2000	Jorge Chavez
1999	Gary Stevens
1998	Eddie Maple
1997	Robbie Davis
1996	Laffit Pincay Jr.
1995	Pat Day
1994	Mike Smith
1993	Jerry Bailey
1992	Angel Cordero Jr.
1991	Chris McCarron
1990	Bill Shoemaker
1989	Mike Venezia

White Horse Award

Sponsored by the Race Track Chaplaincy of America to honor an industry member for a specific act of heroism.

2007	Johnny Arredondo Ponce
2006	Clinton Beck
2005	Louis Pomes
2004	John Woodley
2003	Leigh Grey

P.A.B. Widener II Trophy

Sponsored by Kentucky Thoroughbred Owners and Breeders and presented to breeder whose Kentucky-bred horses have performed the best based on a point system. Named for owner-breeder who raced under Elmendorf Farm.

2007	Stonerside Stable
2006	Darley

2005	Ogden Mills Phipps
2004	Aaron and Marie Jones
2003	Juddmonte Farms
2002	Allen Paulson
2001	Juddmonte Farms
2000	Adena Springs
1999	Overbrook Farm
1998	Mr. and Mrs. John C. Mabee
1997	Juddmonte Farms
1996	Juddmonte Farms
1995	Juddmonte Farms
1994	Overbrook Farm
1993	Juddmonte Farms
1992	William S. Farish and partners
1991	Verne Winchell
1990	Calumet Farm
1989	Ogden Phipps
1988	Ogden Phipps
1987	Nelson Bunker Hunt
1986	Nelson Bunker Hunt
1985	Nelson Bunker Hunt
1984	Hancock family
1983	Hancock family
1982	Fred Hooper
1981	Verna Lehmann
1980	Verna Lehmann
1979	Hancock family
1978	Randolph Weinsier
1977	Ben Castleman
1976	Ogden Mills Phipps
1975	Hancock family
1974	John Galbreath
1973	Maxwell H. Gluck
1972	Leslie Combs

David F. Woods Memorial Award

Presented by Pimlico Race Course for best Preakness Stakes (G1) story from previous year. Named for longtime racetrack publicist and Baltimore *Evening Sun* columnist.

2008	Sean Clancy (*Mid-Atlantic Thoroughbred*)
2007	Sean Clancy (*Mid-Atlantic Thoroughbred*)
2006	Mike Brunker (NBCSports.com)
2005	Dick Jerardi (Philadelphia *Daily News*)
2004	Sean Clancy (*Mid-Atlantic Thoroughbred*)
2003	Bill Finley (New York *Times*)
2002	Jay Privman (*Daily Racing Form*)
2001	Tom LaMarra (*The Blood-Horse*)
2000	Rick Snider (Washington *Times*)
1999	Bill Mooney (*The Backstretch*)
1998	Jay Hovdey (*Daily Racing Form*)
1997	Jay Hovdey (*Daily Racing Form*)
1996	Steve Haskin (*Daily Racing Form*)
1995	Bill Finley (New York *Daily News*)
1994	Jay Posner (San Diego *Union-Tribune*)
1993	Bill Mooney (*The Blood-Horse*)
1992	Jay Hovdey (*The Blood-Horse*)
1991	Bill Christine (Los Angeles *Times*)
1990	Bill Christine (Los Angeles *Times*)
1989	Larry Bortstein (Orange County *Register*)
1988	Don Clippinger (*The Thoroughbred Record*)
	Bob Roberts (Cleveland *Plain Dealer*)
1987	Billy Reed (Lexington *Herald-Leader*)
1986	Dave Kindred (Atlanta *Constitution-Journal*)
1985	George Vecsey (New York *Times*)
1984	Jack Murphy (Cincinnati *Enquirer*)
1983	John Schulian (Chicago *Sun-Times*)
1982	Billy Reed (Louisville *Courier-Journal*)

George Woolf Memorial Jockey Award

Sponsored by Santa Anita Park and awarded to jockey whose career and character earn esteem for themselves and Thoroughbred racing, based on a vote of their fellow jockeys. Named for Racing Hall of Fame jockey George "Iceman" Woolf, who died January 4, 1946, a day after incurring severe head injuries in a spill at Santa Anita.

2008	Richard Migliore
2007	Jon Court
2006	Mark Guidry
2005	Ray Sibille
2004	Robby Albarado
2003	Edgar Prado
2002	Russell Baze
2001	Dean Kutz
2000	Mike Smith
1999	Jose Santos
1998	Craig Perret
1997	Alex Solis
1996	Gary Stevens
1995	Eddie Maple
1994	Phil Grove
1993	Kent Desormeaux
1992	Jerry Bailey
1991	Earlie Fires
1990	John Lively
1989	Larry Snyder
1988	Don Brumfield
1987	Don MacBeth
1986	Jorge Velasquez
1985	Pat Day
1984	Steve Cauthen
1983	Marco Castaneda
1982	Patrick Valenzuela
1981	Eddie Delahoussaye
1980	Chris McCarron
1979	Ron Turcotte
1978	Darrel McHargue
1977	Frank Olivares
1976	Sandy Hawley
1975	Fernando Toro
1974	Alvaro Pineda
1973	John Rotz
1972	Angel Cordero Jr.
1971	Jerry Lambert
1970	Laffit Pincay Jr.
1969	John Sellers
1968	Braulio Baeza
1967	Donald Pierce
1966	Alex Maese
1965	Walter Blum
1964	Manuel Ycaza
1963	Ismael Valenzuela
1962	Steve Brooks
1961	Peter Moreno
1960	Bill Harmatz
1959	Bill Boland
1958	Merlin Volzke
1957	Ted Atkinson
1956	John Adams
1955	Ray York
1954	Ralph Neves
1953	Eddie Arcaro
1952	John Longden
1951	Bill Shoemaker
1950	Gordon Glisson

BREEDING
Development of Breeding Industry

Because the English aristocracy developed the Thoroughbred, the first harbingers of anything remotely resembling a Thoroughbred breeding industry necessarily appeared in England. Kings James I, Charles I, and especially Charles II were crucially important in importing Arabian stallions and broodmares in the 17th century.

When Charles I was deposed and beheaded by the Puritans in 1649, his stud at Tutbury was inventoried and dispersed, thus providing some of the earliest written records on the foundations of many modern pedigrees. Principal beneficiaries of that dispersal were members of Yorkshire's Darcy family, whose head, James Darcy Sr., was appointed Master of the Horse to Charles II. The Darcys, whose principal stud farm was at Sedbury in northern Yorkshire, were closely connected by marriage to other prominent early Yorkshire breeders: the Wyvil, Gascoigne, Hutton, and Villiers (the Dukes of Buckingham) families.

The Yorkshire land holdings of those families centered the early English breeding industry in that county, but Charles II chose the more southerly Suffolk village of Newmarket in East Anglia as his racing headquarters and established Newmarket racecourse in the 1660s. Newmarket's Rowley Mile, the course over which the Two Thousand Guineas (Eng-G1) and One Thousand Guineas (Eng-G1) are run, is named after Charles II, whose nickname in his more mature days was "Old Rowley."

The English lords who followed the royal family's lead in breeding racehorses owned estates all over the country, and each established their principal stud farms according to the location of their lands. For example, the various Earls of Derby's principal stud farms were at Knowsley, near Liverpool, while the Dukes of Newcastle's (and later Dukes of Portland's) stud was at Welbeck Abbey, near Newcastle. Newmarket's place as the headquarters of English racing eventually led to a cluster of breeding farms in the surrounding area, but English stud farms are still scattered throughout the country.

Printed Record

The early Yorkshire breeders often kept meticulous, handwritten records of their breeding activities in private stud books, some of which have survived. The earliest printed record that included pedigrees was John Cheney's *Racing Calendar*, an annual volume of race results that first appeared in 1727. After Cheney's death in 1751, competing calendars produced by John Pond, Reginald Heber, and William

Jersey Act

America's Thoroughbred industry was nearly destroyed between 1908 and '10 when antiwagering legislation swept the country—closing many racetracks, slashing purses to minuscule levels for those that remained open, and rendering American bloodstock all but worthless at home. Desperate breeders thus began to look abroad for racing opportunities and markets for their horses.

English breeders were disturbed by this sudden influx of foreign bloodstock onto European shores. They had long perceived themselves as the world's supplier of Thoroughbreds and feared that American horses for sale in great numbers would threaten the international demand for their own products. In 1913, England's Jockey Club, chaired by the seventh Earl of Jersey, sought to protect its breeders' interests by enacting a rule that effectively barred American bloodstock from the Thoroughbred canon, but not from racing.

Known as the Jersey Act, the rule designated as "half-bred" any horse that did not trace in every pedigree line "without flaw" to foundation stock recorded in the earliest volumes of England's *General Stud Book*, which much of the world accepted as an industry bible. The Jersey Act thus labeled as half-breds many American Thoroughbreds whose distant ancestors had been lost in the chaos of revolution and civil war. Although the rule was not retroactive, after 1913 horses carrying the blood of Lexington, Hanover, Domino, Spendthrift, Ben Brush, and other influential American progenitors no longer were admitted into the *General Stud Book*.

This discriminatory rule ultimately worked to America's advantage. For more than three decades and through two world wars, Americans imported top English bloodstock to enrich their breeding programs, while England could not look to America to do the same. While America acquired such horses as *Mahmoud, *Sir Gallahad III, and *Bull Dog, England had no access to Man o' War, Bull Lea, or Black Toney—half-breds one and all under the Jersey Act.

In June 1949, the Jersey Act was quietly repealed. Lady Wentworth, a respected British pedigree authority and historian, applauded the action as long overdue and described the Jersey Act as "a mistake that made us look rather foolish." Under the revised rule, admission to the *General Stud Book* required only eight or nine proven crosses of pure blood and "such performances of its immediate family on the Turf as to warrant the belief in the purity of its blood."

Pick appeared, and the competition continued until James Weatherby established his version of the *Racing Calendar* as the sole authority beginning in 1773.

Although Cheney included pedigree information on prominent runners in his annual volumes, it was Heber who first requested pedigree information from breeders in a standardized format. But no one attempted to collect this information into a separate book until Weatherby published Volume 1 of the *General Stud Book* in 1791. Based largely on private stud books and the various *Racing Calendars*, especially Pick's reconstruction of pre-Cheney races and pedigrees, Volume 1 of the *General Stud Book* was revised five times, with the final edition published in 1891.

The *Racing Calendar* and the *General Stud Book* gave the nascent Thoroughbred industry the kind of documentation required for expansion to other countries. Although records of racing in America extend back almost to the earliest English colonization, the first Thoroughbred recorded as imported to the New World in the *American Stud Book* is *Bulle (or Bully) Rock, by Darley Arabian, listed as imported to Virginia, "before the Revolution," specifically in 1730.

Virginia and Maryland became the first centers for breeding racehorses in America, led by the Tayloe family of Virginia and the Tasker family in Maryland. Given the primitive conditions of Colonial America, it is little wonder that many early records of imported Thoroughbreds and their produce in America were lost, and other records were reconstructed or fabricated at later dates.

As in England, early racing in America was the province of aristocratic families, and further progress by American breeders did not occur until the disruption caused by the American Revolution had thoroughly passed. The importation of *Diomed in 1799 proved pivotal because he established the first enduring American sire line through his son Sir Archy, great-grandsire of Lexington.

Commercial Beginnings

It was Lexington who cemented the transfer of the breeding industry west across the Appalachian Mountains to Kentucky. If any one man is the founder of the American commercial breeding industry, that person is Robert A.S.C. Alexander, who purchased Lexington for his Woodburn Stud near the city of Lexington in 1855. Lexington's success as 16-time leading sire and the many top racehorses that Alexander and his brother Alexander J. Alexander sold at Woodburn's annual yearling auctions enticed many other breeders to locate their stud farms in the Bluegrass.

The Alexanders also were among the sponsors of what became the definitive *American Stud Book*, after several false starts. George W. Jeffreys published the *Virginia Stud Book* in 1828, but the first comprehensive attempt at an American Stud Book was Patrick Nisbett Edgar's *American Race-Turf Register, Sportsman's Herald, and General Stud Book*, published in 1833.

Unfortunately, Edgar's work included a stunning number of obvious inaccuracies, some of which remain in the official record. As in England, several competitors, including John S. Skinner and William T. Porter, published versions of Racing Calendars or Stud Books before Sanders D. Bruce's *American Stud Book, Volume 1*, appeared in 1868.

Although Bruce's book retained some of Edgar's errors and created some of its own, it was a considerable advance on previous offerings. It rapidly became the official record and was purchased by the American Jockey Club in May 1897 for $35,000. That purchase was the first step toward the Jockey Club's current position as the breed registry and the keeper of the sport's records.

Early American race results were recorded primarily by periodicals such as Porter's *Spirit of the Times* and Bruce's *Turf, Field, and Farm*.

Designating Imported Horses

In its earliest years, the *American Stud Book* designated horses imported to North America for racing or breeding with "Imported" or "Imp." before the horse's name.

This practice changed in 1906 with publication of the *American Stud Book's* Volume 9. Its preface noted: "While the general features of this volume remain the same as Volume 8, it has been found necessary, in order to avoid a two-volume work, to condense the subject matter in every way possible, the most radical change being the substitution of an * in place of the word Imported wherever possible.

"The prefix Imported has been omitted from the following horses, they having been foaled in the United States, viz.: Bel Demonio, Donald A., Dundee, Flax Spinner, Glenelg, Keene, Loiterer, Pontiac, Paladin, Uncommon and Victory."

The asterisk, which preceded such notable names in American breeding history as *Nasrullah and *Ribot, was eliminated in 1975. An introductory note to the *American Stud Book, Foals of 1981*, states: "The practice of designating imported horses with an asterisk (*) was discontinued in 1975, and from that time forward, the country of origin is reflected in the suffix attached to the name. The asterisk or suffix is omitted in the cases of horses which were imported in utero."

Daily Racing Form and the *Morning Telegraph* took over these functions in the late 19th century, and the *Racing Form* became the de facto newspaper of record by the 1920s. In 1991, the Jockey Club and the Thoroughbred Racing Associations formed Equibase Co. to develop the official database of the Thoroughbred industry, and in '98 Equibase became the data provider to the *Racing Form* as well.

Key Figures

Key figures in the development of an American commercial breeding industry on the foundation laid by the Alexanders were John E. Madden, Arthur B. Hancock Sr. and his son Arthur B. "Bull" Hancock Jr., Leslie Combs II, and John R. Gaines. A hands-on horseman who bred and trained his own horses with a keen eye for profit, Madden bred five Kentucky Derby winners at Hamburg Place, named for his first great coup with the great racehorse and sire Hamburg.

Hancock Sr. founded Claiborne Farm near Paris, Kentucky, in 1908 and stood Celt, who became the first of 11 leading American sires who won 29 sire championships at Claiborne during the 20th century.

Combs modernized both the stallion-syndication process and yearling salesmanship at his Spendthrift Farm near Lexington. He stood leading sires Exclusive Native and Seattle Slew, but it was his recruitment of wealthy clients to the sales ring and the breeding industry that helped set the stage for the bloodstock boom of the 1970s and '80s.

Combs's success made clear that big money could be made by breeding and selling potential racehorses, but it was Gaines who developed the syndication of stallions into a highly lucrative enterprise. An innovative thinker, Gaines also created the concept of the Breeders' Cup, which came to fruition in 1984, and he was one of the founders of the National Thoroughbred Association, which was quickly subsumed by the industry-backed National Thoroughbred Racing Association in 1998.

From its beginnings as a passionate pursuit of a few aristocratic Englishmen, Thoroughbred racing and breeding have developed into a worldwide, multibillion-dollar industry. Though still primarily a business for the wealthy, Thoroughbreds are now produced in every condition from the brick palaces of the Bluegrass and Newmarket to, quite literally, suburban back yards.—*John P. Sparkman*

Registration Rules for Breeding
Copyright © 2008 The Jockey Club

History of Registration

The Jockey Club, an organization dedicated to improving Thoroughbred breeding and racing, registers more than 30,000 Thoroughbred foals each year, introducing them to the *American Stud Book* following a disciplined process of initiation that began more than 300 years ago.

Early in the 17th century, three stallions brought to England—the Darley Arabian, the Godolphin Arabian, and the Byerly Turk—became the foundation sires of the Thoroughbred industry. In 1791, James Weatherby published the first stud book, the *General Stud Book*. It listed the pedigrees of 387 mares that could each be traced to one of three descendants of the foundation sires: Eclipse, a direct descendant of the Darley Arabian; Matchem, a grandson of the Godolphin Arabian; and Herod, a great-great-grandson of the Byerly Turk.

In America, Patrick Edgar attempted to publish a national stud registry in 1833 but was unsuccessful. One year later, John Skinner reprinted the entire *General Stud Book* and added the existing pedigrees of American horses at the end. Following Skinner's effort, the pedigree section of *Mason's Farrier* was the only available resource until 1867, when John H. Wallace published *Wallace's American Stud Book*. Wallace soon abandoned the enterprise, which was a financial failure, and turned his attention to compiling the American Trotting Registry.

One year later, Col. Sanders D. Bruce published the *American Stud Book*. On May 17, 1897, the Jockey Club acquired the rights to Bruce's work for $35,000. Now, more than 100 years later, the Jockey Club continues to maintain the *American Stud Book* to ensure the integrity of the breed.

Today, registering a Thoroughbred is as simple as logging onto the Internet. Through Jockey Club Interactive Registration™ (*www.registry.jockeyclub.com*), owners and breeders can complete registration forms, submit digital photos, review a database of active names, and check the status of a registration. A goal of the Jockey Club is to provide a virtual foal certificate that will eliminate paper, which can be lost, destroyed, or illegally altered, while at the same time providing real-time access to all registry-related information.

How to Register

All requirements of the Principal Rules and Requirements of the *American Stud Book* must be met within one year of a foal's originally reported foaling date.

Step 1

For foals of 2001 and after, the foal's sire and dam must be genetically typed. For foals of 2000 and earlier, the foal's sire and dam must be blood-typed.

Step 2

Report of Mares Bred (Deadline: August 1 each year)
Stallion owners must file a report of all Thoroughbred mares bred to a stallion in a breeding season (February-July).

Step 3

Live Foal/No Foal Report (Deadline: Within 30 days after foaling)

1. The owner of record of each broodmare in the Jockey Club files will receive a preprinted Live Foal/No Foal Report. Note: All changes of mare ownership should be reported to the Jockey Club immediately.

2. The Live Foal/No Foal Report must be filed no later than 30 days following the birth of a foal, or in January if the mare was not bred. Note: The registration services department at the Jockey Club should be contacted immediately if a preprinted Live Foal/No Foal Report is not received by the time the foal is born.

Step 4

Genetic-Typing (Deadline: Within 45 days of receipt of genetic typing kit)

1. Within 180 days of the foaling date, a Registration and Genetic Typing Kit will be mailed to the address shown on the Live Foal/No Foal Report. Note: If genetic typing kit is not used within 45 days, the genetic typing process may have to be restarted at an additional fee.

2. Mane hairs pulled/blood drawn from the foal must be mailed to the laboratory shown on the preprinted mailer.

Notes:
Helpful hints for taking a DNA sample:
• Clean the mane comb thoroughly before pulling the mane.
• Grasp the mane close to the neck to help ensure you get roots.
• Do not try to pull a sample if the mane is wet.
Helpful hints for drawing blood:
• If, for some reason, a syringe must be used to draw blood, insert needle through stopper and depress plunger on syringe slowly.
• Do not remove stoppers or chemicals from tubes.
• Do not shake tubes; turn them end over end.
• Refrigerate blood if not mailing the same day. (Do not put tubes in Styrofoam container during refrigeration, and do not freeze the sample).
• Do not mail samples on the weekend or immediately before a holiday. (If samples are untestable on receipt by laboratory, another kit will be mailed and the process must be repeated.)

Step 5

Registration/Genetic Typing/Blood-Typing Form (Deadline: Send to the Jockey Club when DNA/blood sample is mailed to lab. Before sending to the Jockey Club, be certain that):

1. Both sides of form are completed, including:
   i) Written description of markings, indicating:
   • All white markings.
   • All flesh-colored markings.
   • All dark and chestnut markings on coronet.
   • All head and neck cowlicks (except cowlick at the very top of forehead).
   • Any other distinguishing characteristics.
   ii) Signature by foal's owner or authorized agent.
   iii) One to six name choices. (This could avoid additional naming fees.)

2. A set of four color photos is enclosed, clearly showing color and all markings from the front, back, and both sides. Note: Do not take photographs until the foal has shed its "baby hair."

3. The Stallion Service Certificate (acquired from the stallion owner) is attached.

4. Fee payment is enclosed.

How to Name a Horse

A. A name may be claimed on the Registration Application, on a Name Claiming Form, or through Interactive Registration™ at *www.registry.jockeyclub.com*. Name selections should be listed in order of preference. Names will be assigned based upon availability and compliance with the naming rules as stated herein. Names may not be claimed or reserved by telephone. When a foreign language name is submitted, an English translation must be furnished to the Jockey Club. An explanation must accompany "coined" or "made-up" names that have no apparent meaning. Horses born in the United States, Puerto Rico, or Canada and currently reside in another country must be named by the Jockey Club through the Stud Book Authority of their country of residence.

B. If a valid attempt to name a foal is submitted to the Jockey Club by February 1 of the foal's two-year-old year and such a name is determined not eligible for use, no fee is required for a subsequent claim of name for that foal. If a valid attempt to name a foal is not submitted to the Jockey Club by February 1 of the foal's two-year-old year, a fee is required to claim a name for such a foal.

C. A reserved name must be used within one year (365 days) from the day it was reserved. Reserved names cannot be used until written notification requesting the assignment of the name to a specific horse is received by the Registry Office. If the reserved name is not used within one year (365 days) from its reservation, it will become available for any horse. A fee is required to reserve a name.

D. A foal's name may be changed at any time prior to starting in its first race. Ordinarily, no name change will be permitted after a horse has started in its first race or has been used for breeding purposes. However, in the event a name must be changed after a horse has started in its first race, both the old and new names should be used until the horse has raced three times following the name change. The prescribed fee and the Certificate of Foal Registration must accompany any request to the Registry Office for a change of name.

E. Names of horses over ten years old may be eligible if they are not excluded and have not been used during the preceding five years either in breeding or racing.

Names of geldings and horses that were never used for breeding or racing may be available five years from the date of their death as reported.

F. The following classes of names are not eligible for use:

1. Names consisting of more than 18 letters (spaces and punctuation marks count as letters).

2. Initials such as C.O.D., F.O.B., etc.

3. Names ending in "filly," "colt," "stud," "mare," "stallion," or any similar horse-related term.

4. Names consisting entirely of numbers, except numbers above 30 may be used if they are spelled out.

5. Names ending with a numerical designation such as "2nd" or "3rd," whether or not such a designation is spelled out.

6. Names of persons unless written permission to use their name is on file with the Jockey Club.

7. Names of "famous" people no longer living unless approval is granted by the Board of Stewards of the Jockey Club.

8. Names of "notorious" people.
9. Names of racetracks or graded stakes races.
10. Recorded names such as assumed names or stable names.
11. Names clearly having commercial significance, such as trade names.
12. Copyrighted material, titles of books, plays, motion pictures, popular songs, etc., unless the applicant furnishes the Jockey Club with proof that the copyright has been abandoned or that such material has not been used within the past five years.
13. Names that are suggestive or have a vulgar or obscene meaning; names considered in poor taste; or names that may be offensive to religious, political, or ethnic groups.
14. Names that are currently active either in racing or breeding, and names similar in spelling or pronunciation to such names.
15. Permanent names and names similar in spelling or pronunciation to permanent names. The list of criteria to establish a permanent name is as follows:
  a. Horses in the Racing Hall of Fame;
  b. Horses that have been voted Horse of the Year;
  c. Horses that have won an Eclipse Award;
  d. Horses that have won a Sovereign Award (Canadian champions);
  e. Annual leading sire and broodmare sire by progeny earnings;
  f. Cumulative money winners of $2-million or more;
  g. Horses that have won the Kentucky Derby (G1), Preakness Stakes (G1), Belmont Stakes (G1), Jockey Club Gold Cup (G1), Breeders' Cup Classic (G1), or Breeders' Cup Turf (G1); and
  h. Horses included in the International List of Protected Names.
  G. In addition to the provisions of this rule, the Registrar of the Jockey Club reserves the right of approval on all name requests.

Age Definitions

Foal: A young horse of either sex in its first year of life.
Suckling: A foal of any sex in its first year of life while it is still nursing.
Weanling: A foal of any sex in its first year of life after being separated from its dam.
Yearling: A colt, filly, or gelding in its second calendar year of life (beginning January 1 of the year following its birth).
Two-Year-Old: A colt, filly, or gelding in its third calendar year of life (beginning January 1 of the year following its yearling year).

Color Definitions

The following colors are recognized by the Jockey Club:
Bay: The entire coat of the horse may vary from a yellow-tan to a bright auburn. The mane, tail, and lower portion of the legs are always black, unless white markings are present.
Black: The entire coat of the horse is black, including the muzzle, flanks, mane, tail, and legs, unless white markings are present.
Chestnut: The entire coat of the horse may vary from a red-yellow to a golden-yellow. The mane, tail, and legs are usually variations of coat color, unless white markings are present.
Dark Bay or Brown: The entire coat of the horse will vary from a brown, with areas of tan on the shoulders, head, and flanks, to a dark brown, with tan areas seen only in the flanks and/or muzzle. The mane, tail, and lower portion of the legs are always black, unless white markings are present.
Gray or Roan: The Jockey Club has combined these colors into one color category. This does not change the individual definitions of the colors for gray and roan and in no way impacts on the two-coat color inheritance principle as stated in a previous rule.
Gray: The majority of the coat of the horse is a mixture of black and white hairs. The mane, tail, and legs may be either black or gray, unless white markings are present.
Roan: The majority of the coat of the horse is a mixture of red and white hairs or brown and white hairs. The mane, tail, and legs may be black, chestnut, or roan, unless white markings are present.
Palomino: The entire coat of the horse is golden-yellow, unless white markings are present. The mane and tail are usually flaxen.
White: A rare color not to be confused with the colors gray or roan. The entire coat, including the mane, tail, and legs, is white and no other color should be present.

Breeding Terminology

Bred (Mated): Any filly or mare that has undergone the physical act of breeding (mating).
Bred (Area Foaled): The term "bred" is sometimes used to describe the location where a foal was born; i.e., Kentucky-bred, New York-bred, etc.
Breeder: The breeder of a foal is the owner of the dam at the time of foaling, unless the dam was under a lease or foal-sharing agreement at the time of foaling. In that case, the person(s) specified by the terms of the agreement is (are) the breeder of the foal.
Stallion: A male horse that is used to produce foals.
Sire: A male horse that has produced, or is producing, foals.
Broodmare: A filly or mare that has been bred (mated) and is used to produce foals.
Dam: A female horse that has produced, or is producing, foals.
Maiden: A filly or mare that has never been bred (mated).
In Foal (Pregnant) Broodmare: A filly or mare that was bred (mated), conceived, and is currently in foal (pregnant).
Aborted: A term used to describe a broodmare that has been pronounced in foal (pregnant) based on an examination of 42 days or more post breeding (mating) and lost her foal prematurely; or a broodmare from whom an aborted fetus has been observed.
Barren (Not Pregnant): A term used to describe a filly or mare, other than a maiden mare, that was bred (mated) and did not conceive during the last breeding season.
Breeding (Mating): The physical act of a stallion mounting a broodmare with intromission and ejaculation of semen into the reproductive tract.

Gender Terminology

Colt: An entire male horse four years old or younger.
Horse: When reference is made to gender, a "horse" is an entire male five years old or older.
Ridgling ("rig"): A lay term used to describe either a monorchid or cryptorchid.
Cryptorchid: A male horse of any age that has no testes in his scrotum but was never gelded (the testes are undescended).
Monorchid: A male horse of any age that has only one testicle in his scrotum (the other testicle was either removed or is undescended).
Gelding: A male horse of any age that is unsexed (had both testicles removed).
Filly: A female horse four years old or younger.
Mare: A female horse five years old or older.

Deadlines

Report of Mares Bred (Stallion Reports): This report must be filed no later than August 1 of the breeding year.
Live Foal/No Foal Report (Mare Reports):
- Reporting live foal information. This report must be filed within 30 days after the foaling date.
- Reporting no foal information. This report must be filed no later than 30 days after the intended foaling date or in January if the mare was not bred.

Foal Registration: All requirements must be completed by one year from the foaling date, including genetic typing, to avoid paying an additional fee.
Naming: Must be named by February 1 of two-year-old year to avoid paying a fee.
Death: Must be reported within 30 days after the death.
Export: Requirements must be met within 60 days after the horse's departure to avoid paying an additional fee.
Foreign Registration: All requirements must be met within 60 days after the horse's arrival to avoid paying an additional fee.
Geldings: Should be reported immediately.
Sold Without Pedigree: Should be reported within 60 days after the date of sale.

Fees

Foal Registration Fees: If all requirements are met within one calendar year from foaling date (includes genetic typing of the foal and parentage verification, as well as ownership transfers and corrections): $200
By December 31 of yearling year: $525
By December 31 of two-year-old year: $775
After December 31 of two-year-old year: $2,000
Reserved Names: $75
Foal-Naming Fee: After February 1 of the foal's two-year-old year. (Before this date, no fee is required): $75
Name-Change Fee: $100
Genetic Typing Fees:
Genetic typing, entry into the Ownership Registry: $80
Additional Genetic Typing: $80 (or retyping as required by the Jockey Club)
Duplicate Certificate Fee: $150
Corrected Certificate Fee (six months after original certificates issued): $50

Certificate of Exportation Fees:
If all requirements are completed within 60 days of the horse's departure from the United States, Canada, or Puerto Rico: $150
If all requirements are completed after 60 days of the horse's departure from the United States, Canada, or Puerto Rico: $400
Certificate of Foreign Registration Fees:
If all requirements are completed within 60 days of the horse's arrival in the United States, Canada, or Puerto Rico: $150
If all requirements are completed after 60 days and up until one year of the horse's arrival in the United States, Canada, or Puerto Rico: $400
If all requirements are not completed within one year of the horse's arrival in the United States, Canada, or Puerto Rico, and the horse is eligible for late registration: $750
Horses registered in the *American Stud Book* returning from a foreign country: $150
Thirty-day foreign racing permit fee:
If application is received within 30 days of the horse's arrival in the United States, Canada, or Puerto Rico: $150
Express handling fee: $100

How to Contact the Jockey Club:

Address: The Jockey Club, 821 Corporate Dr., Lexington, Ky. 40503-2794
Telephone: (859) 224-2700
Registration Services: (800) 444-8521
Fax: (859) 224-2710
Website: *www.jockeyclub.com*
Jockey Club Interactive Registration™ Website: *www.registry.jockeyclub.com*

Brief History of Foal Identification

When registering Thoroughbreds in North America, foal identification traditionally has been documented by markings, both narrative descriptions of the distinctive characteristics and diagrams of those markings.

For instance, the breeder would be required to describe any white markings and their locations, as well as any flesh-colored areas and markings on the coronet, when applicable. If the horse had a blaze, the breeder would include a diagram of the horse's head and the shape of the blaze.

Over time, photographs of the horse and any markings became a requirement of foal registration. This process occurred gradually, beginning when breeders would attach photographs of the markings with the registration application. The Jockey Club Registry began accepting digital photos in 2001.

Beginning with the foal crop of 1987, blood-typing for parentage verification was made a requirement for registration.

Advances in technology allowed the Jockey Club to begin DNA verification of parentage with the foal crop of 2001. Within 180 days of the foaling date, breeders receive a registration and genetic typing kit. The genetic typing kit, which contains instructions for pulling mane hairs and drawing blood, must be returned within 45 days.

Current registration practices still require breeders to include a narrative of all markings as well as four-color photographs of the foal from the front, back, and both sides to document the markings.

Foal Registration

Foal registration for all Thoroughbreds in North America—the United States, Canada, and Puerto Rico—is performed by the Jockey Club, which was founded in 1894 and is a not-for-profit organization dedicated to improving the Thoroughbred breed. To be registered in the *American Stud Book*, which is maintained by the Jockey Club, the parentage of all foals must be verified, a process that today includes DNA typing of all stallions, broodmares, and foals.

Registration of American Thoroughbreds was started by Col. Sanders D. Bruce, a Kentuckian who spent a lifetime researching pedigrees of American Thoroughbreds. He published the first volume of the *American Stud Book* in 1868, and he produced six volumes of the registry. In 1897, the Jockey Club purchased all rights to the *American Stud Book*.

Foal Registration by State in North America in 2006

State	#	State	#	State	#	State	#
Alabama	57	Kansas	81	New Jersey	308	Utah	95
Alaska	0	Kentucky	10,346	New Mexico	977	Vermont	2
Arizona	352	Louisiana	2,257	New York	1,815	Virgin Islands	2
Arkansas	294	Maine	2	North Carolina	26	Virginia	370
California	3,223	Maryland	839	North Dakota	47	Washington	685
Colorado	210	Massachusetts	25	Ohio	335	West Virginia	583
Connecticut	2	Michigan	275	Oklahoma	862	Wisconsin	9
Delaware	3	Minnesota	320	Oregon	223	Wyoming	7
Florida	4,296	Mississippi	22	Pennsylvania	1,187	**Total U.S.**	**33,548**
Georgia	51	Missouri	26	Rhode Island	1	**Total Canada**	**2,557**
Idaho	115	Montana	65	South Carolina	34	**Total Puerto Rico**	**541**
Illinois	865	Nebraska	155	South Dakota	50	**Total Crop**	**36,646**
Indiana	295	Nevada	8	Tennessee	42		
Iowa	340	New Hampshire	1	Texas	1,363		

Trend of Foal Registration in North America

Year	United States	Change	Canada	Change	Puerto Rico	Change	Total	Change
2008	34,350*	0.0%	2,650*	0.0%	500*	0.0%	37,500*	0.0%
2007	34,350*	0.4%	2,650*	1.9%	500*	0.0%	37,500*	0.5%
2006	34,200*	−1.4%	2,600*	0.0%	500*	0.0%	37,300*	−1.8%
2005	34,696	−0.1%	2,769	6.1%	525	−1.5%	37,990	0.3%
2004	34,745	2.3%	2,610	1.5%	533	3.5%	37,888	2.3%
2003	33,959	3.0%	2,572	4.2%	515	−1.7%	37,046	3.0%
2002	32,982	−5.0%	2,468	−4.7%	524	−11.2%	35,974	−5.1%
2001	34,720	0.0%	2,590	5.1%	590	5.0%	37,900	0.4%
2000	34,724	2.6%	2,464	1.2%	562	−13.5%	37,750	2.2%
1999	33,843	2.7%	2,435	4.1%	650	−11.4%	36,928	2.5%
1998	32,947	2.6%	2,340	2.5%	734	−0.8%	36,021	2.5%
1997	32,117	−0.4%	2,284	−4.7%	740	1.9%	35,141	−0.6%
1996	32,243	1.1%	2,397	−2.0%	726	11.2%	35,366	1.1%
1995	31,884	−0.7%	2,446	−5.6%	653	3.3%	34,983	−1.0%
1994	32,118	−5.0%	2,591	−4.5%	632	4.5%	35,341	−4.8%
1993	33,820	−3.5%	2,713	−2.3%	605	−0.8%	37,138	−3.4%
1992	35,051	−8.1%	2,777	−8.2%	610	−2.9%	38,438	−8.0%

*Estimated or incomplete

Annual Foal Registration in North America

Year	#	Year	#	Year	#	Year	#	Year	#
2008	37,500*	1985	50,433	1962	14,870	1939	6,316	1916	2,128
2007	37,500*	1984	49,247	1961	13,794	1938	5,696	1915	2,120
2006	37,300*	1983	47,237	1960	12,901	1937	5,535	1914	1,702
2005	37,990	1982	42,894	1959	12,240	1936	5,042	1913	1,722
2004	37,888	1981	38,669	1958	11,377	1935	5,038	1912	1,900
2003	37,046	1980	35,679	1957	10,832	1934	4,924	1911	2,040
2002	35,974	1979	32,904	1956	10,112	1933	5,158	1910	1,950
2001	37,900	1978	31,510	1955	9,610	1932	5,256	1909	2,340
2000	37,750	1977	30,036	1954	9,064	1931	5,266	1908	3,080
1999	36,928	1976	28,809	1953	9,040	1930	5,137	1907	3,780
1998	36,021	1975	28,271	1952	8,811	1929	4,903	1906	3,840
1997	35,141	1974	27,586	1951	8,944	1928	4,503	1905	3,800
1996	35,366	1973	26,811	1950	9,095	1927	4,182	1904	3,990
1995	34,983	1972	25,726	1949	8,770	1926	3,632	1903	3,440
1994	35,341	1971	24,301	1948	8,434	1925	3,272	1902	3,600
1993	37,138	1970	24,361	1947	7,705	1924	2,921	1901	3,784
1992	38,438	1969	23,848	1946	6,579	1923	2,763	1900	3,476
1991	41,803	1968	22,910	1945	5,819	1922	2,352	1899	3,080
1990	44,143	1967	21,876	1944	5,650	1921	2,035	1898	2,940
1989	48,235	1966	20,228	1943	5,923	1920	1,833	1897	2,992
1988	49,220	1965	18,846	1942	6,427	1919	1,665	1893-'96	5,940*
1987	50,917	1964	17,343	1941	6,805	1918	1,950	1803-'92	3,950*
1986	51,296	1963	15,917	1940	6,003	1917	1,680	*Estimated	

Evolution of the Breed

In genetic terms, the Thoroughbred is a hybrid, created by crossing two or possibly more breeds of horses to produce an animal with specific characteristics. One of those breeds was the Arabian horse, but the exact identities of other contributors are considerably less clear.

Early records do not identify most of the mares mated to the many Arabian, Barb, and Turk (all are varieties of Arabians) stallions imported to England after the Markham Arabian's acquisition by King James I. Although the Markham Arabian was the first Arabian whose importation was noted by history, no doubt others, both males and females, were transported from the Middle East over several centuries, beginning with the Crusades of the 12th and 13th centuries. However, many horses called Arabians or Barbs in the *General Stud Book* were certainly not purebreds.

These imports were crossed with native English stock over many generations. By the time the modern Thoroughbred was created, there were two varieties of pony-sized English and Irish racehorses known as Hobbies and Galloways, and Oriental imports of the time were not much larger. Both English breeds certainly carried Oriental blood, but no one knows how much. Before the Puritan revolution in 1649, the royal stud of King James I and his ill-fated son King Charles I probably included mares of both mixed English and Oriental blood and pure-bred Arabians. These mares came to be called "royal mares" and now stand as the earliest known female ancestors of several modern female families.

The surge of importations that began with the restoration of King Charles II in 1660 included both males and females. With King Charles leading the way, the English nobility engaged in fierce competition to produce better, faster racehorses, and they quickly learned that the more Arabian blood their stock could claim, the better chance they had.

Estimated Relationships of Some Important Horses to Modern Thoroughbreds

Horse (Year of Birth)	Percentage Relationship
Herod (1758)	17.2%
Eclipse (1764)	15.2%
Highflyer (1774)	12.8%
Godolphin Arabian (1724)	12.7%
Partner (1718)	11.4%
Regulus (1739)	9.4%
St. Simon (1881)	8.7%
Stockwell (1849)	8.7%
Curwen Bay Barb mare (1710)	8.4%
Birdcatcher (1833)	7.4%
Pocahontas (1837)	7.0%
Matchem (1748)	6.3%
Flying Childers (1715)	5.7%
Darley Arabian (ca. 1700)	5.3%
*Teddy (1913)	4.9%
Byerley Turk (ca. 1680)	4.6%
Curwen Bay Barb (ca. 1695)	4.4%
Hyperion (1930)	4.2%
*Nasrullah (1940)	4.2%
Bald Galloway (ca. 1700)	4.0%

Figures based on an unpublished statistical study. Percentages of horses born since about 1850 may change slightly.

Foundation Sires

The arrivals of the Byerley Turk, Place's White Turk, the Curwen Bay Barb, the Darley Arabian, and finally the Godolphin Arabian (around 1730) sharply accelerated the development of the breed. The Darley Arabian sired Flying Childers, generally recognized as the first great Thoroughbred, in 1714. Through Flying Childers's full brother Bartlett's Childers, the Darley Arabian

The Darley Arabian

Of the Thoroughbred's three male-line foundation sires, only the Darley Arabian was almost certainly a pure-bred Arabian. The Godolphin Arabian was probably a Turcoman-Arabian cross, while the Byerley Turk may have been born in England, sired by another Turcoman-Arabian cross horse whose identity is uncertain.

Probably born in what is now Syria in 1700, the Darley Arabian was purchased in Aleppo, then part of the Ottoman Empire, by English merchant Thomas Darley in '04 and shipped to his brother Richard Darley at Aldby Park near York, England. The Darley Arabian was said to be of the "keheilan" or "manicca" breed, the subset of Arabians then most prized by Bedouins. Ottoman law forbade the sale of any pure-bred Arabian to a foreigner, but Darley's merchant connections in Aleppo allowed him to spirit the horse out of the country.

The Darley Arabian mostly covered his owner's broodmares, but one of the few outside mares bred to him was Leonard Childers's Betty Leedes, by Careless, who produced Flying Childers in 1714 and his full brother Bartlett's Childers in '15. Flying Childers was unbeaten and considered by far the fastest horse until that time. Darley Arabian also sired the good racehorses Almanzor, Cupid, and Brisk.

Although Flying Childers was a successful sire, his brother Bartlett's Childers—unraced because he was a bleeder—carried on the line. He sired the good racehorse Squirt, who in turn sired Marske, sire of Eclipse (1764). Eclipse in turn founded the male l nes that lead to the modern lines of Phalaris (Northern Dancer, *Nasrullah, Native Dancer), St. Simon (*Ribot and *Princequillo), Hyperion, Domino, *Teddy, and Blandford.

established today's dominant male line, leading to Phalaris and his descendants.

The Godolphin Arabian was the most prepotent immediate influence among the three founding male-line sires, establishing the male line that leads to dual Breeders' Cup Classic (G1) winner Tiznow. Although the Godolphin Arabian male line is now far less prominent than that of the Darley Arabian, almost 13% of the genes of the modern Thoroughbred come from the Godolphin Arabian, according to modern statistical studies.

The male line tracing to the Byerley Turk achieved dominance in the late 18th century through his great-great-grandson Herod. By 1825, inbreeding to Herod had reached its limit, and his overall influence began to decline. Today, his male line appears to be headed for extinction, with tendrils hanging on in Europe through Ahonoora and in Australia through Century. Nevertheless, more than 17% of the genes of the modern Thoroughbred come from Herod.

Beneficiary of the intense early inbreeding to Godolphin Arabian and Herod was the Darley Arabian line. The line from Flying Childers was prominent for approximately 50 years, but descendants of his unraced full brother, the bleeder Bartlett's Childers, gained ascendance through his great-grandson Eclipse, foaled in 1764. Eclipse was the greatest of the four-milers, and during his stud career a shift began from the four-mile heat racing that had been popular since King Charles's era to "dash" racing over shorter distances, exemplified by the Epsom Derby, founded in 1780 and contested at one mile that year.

Eclipse and Herod surpassed all other stallions of their time in producing the speedier, more brilliant horse necessary for dash racing. Added together, Herod, Godolphin Arabian, and Eclipse account for 45% of the genes of the modern Thoroughbred.

In the same time period that surviving male lines were being whittled down to three, female lines descending from approximately 100 foundation mares listed in Volume 1 of the *General Stud Book* were cut in half. That, of course, does not mean that those additional foundation mares and stallions had no influence on the development of the breed. Indeed, their names persist, sometimes with great influence, in the nether reaches of pedigrees.

Exportation of the Thoroughbred to other countries, particularly to North America, Australia, and Argentina, inevitably resulted in the introduction of female lines not found in the *General Stud Book*. The chaotic circumstances of Colonial and Revolutionary America meant that

Averages for the Breed

Averages for the Breed statistics are designed to provide a baseline to evaluate the performances of contemporary racehorses, sires, and dams. Statistics shown in the column on the left below reflect the worldwide performances of all named foals born in North America between 1990-'99. Statistics in the column on the right reflect the same data for foals by the top 1% of all sires for the same decade. All statistics are based on data in the Jockey Club Information System's worldwide database. The Jockey Club database includes complete records for racing in the United States, Argentina, Australia, Brazil, Canada, England, France, Germany, Hong Kong, Ireland, Italy, Japan, Puerto Rico, Saudi Arabia, and United Arab Emirates for some, but not all, of the years covered by these statistics.

Statistics below are designed to give a snapshot of what an average "good" horse should accomplish.

	All foals 1990-'99	Foals by top 1% of sires
Starters/foals	71.0%	84.5%
Winners/foals (starters)	48.1% (67.8%)	65.2% (77.1%)
Repeat winners/foals (starters)	36.9% (51.9%)	52.6% (62.2%)
Stakes placed/foals (starters)	5.7% (8.1%)	11.3% (13.3%)
Stakes winners/foals (starters)	3.7% (5.2%)	8.6% (10.1%)
Graded SW/foals (starters)	0.8% (1.2%)	3.3% (3.9%)
Grade 1 SW/foals (starters)	0.2% (0.3%)	1.0% (1.2%)
Two-year-old starters/foals	34.7%	46.2%
Two-year-old winners/foals (2yo starters)	11.6% (33.6%)	18.0% (39.0%)
Two-year-old SW/foals (2yo starters)	1.1% (3.0%)	2.2% (4.8%)
Three-year-old starters/foals	61.0%	76.0%
Four-year-old starters/foals	46.8%	57.4%
Five-year-old and up starters/foals	30.2%	37.0%
Average career starts/foal	15	18
Average career starts/starter	21	21
Average winning distance in furlongs	6.80	7.16
Average winning turf distance in furlongs	8.13	8.27
Average earnings/starter	$41,475	$88,185
Average earnings/starter male (female)	$49,219 ($33,418)	$110,357 ($64,358)
Average earnings/start	$1,982	$4,186
Average earnings/start male (female)	$2,041 ($1,898)	$4,187 ($4,184)
Average Racing Index	1.15	2.14

records were lost on many legitimate members of the breed and invented for many who doubtless were not.

Such chaos inevitably led to controversy. When American racing collapsed early in the 20th century due to antigambling hysteria, England's Turf authority, the Jockey Club, essentially banned American-bred stock from the hallowed pages of the *General Stud Book* when American exports threatened to flood the market. Fortunately for the future of the breed, the Jersey Act of 1913 excluding American-breds included a provision that grandfathered in American-bred stock already included in earlier volumes.

Within 40 years, descendants of those acceptable American-breds—including such horses as Nearco and his son *Nasrullah—and descendants of French-bred Tourbillon (branded as a half-bred by the Jersey Act because of his American antecedents) dominated English racing, which forced the repeal of these exclusionary rules.

Changing Conditions

The descendants of Eclipse's great-grandson Whalebone through his great-great-grandson Stockwell proved especially adaptable to the pattern of English racing established by the five classic races (Two Thousand Guineas, One Thousand Guineas, Epsom Derby, Epsom Oaks, and St. Leger Stakes). Stockwell led the English sire list eight times and his great-grandson, unbeaten Triple Crown winner *Ormonde, is widely considered the best racehorse of the 19th century. The male line of *Ormonde lives on tenuously through the descendants of Damascus.

The inauguration of several valuable races outside the classic pattern in the 1890s changed the requirements of English racing at about the same time that an invasion of American jockeys changed race-riding. After American riders such as Tod Sloan and Danny Maher proved the virtues of setting a faster pace, male-line descendants of one stallion, Phalaris, gradually proved the most capable of adapting to the new conditions.

A top-class sprinter during World War I, Phalaris sired two sets of full brothers who established powerful male lines: Pharos and Fairway, and *Sickle and *Pharamond II. Pharos and his descendants generally sired heavier, more muscular horses with speed, while the Fairways tended toward taller, lighter individuals. Today the Fairway line hangs by the thread of Lord At War (Arg), while Pharos reigns supreme through descendants of his grandsons *Nasrullah, sire of Bold Ruler, and Nearctic, sire of Northern Dancer.

*Sickle led the U.S. sire list twice, and his brother *Pharamond II finished second to him in 1938. *Sickle's great-grandson Native Dancer, another heavy, powerful horse, established the second most dominant male line in modern pedigrees, that descending from his grandson Mr. Prospector.

In 300 years, the Thoroughbred breed has evolved from a small, relatively lightly made animal designed to gallop 3½ miles at a sedate pace and then sprint for a half-mile. It has become a much larger, heavier, proportionally shorter-legged animal designed primarily for high speeds from the start over distances up to 1¼ miles. Without much doubt, Flying Childers would hardly recognize his modern descendants.

—*John P. Sparkman*

Breeding Theories

Flying Childers was the first great racehorse who clearly could be defined as a Thoroughbred. Undoubtedly, his breeder, Leonard Childers, had a theory to explain why his greatest creation was so fast. In the three centuries since Flying Childers first saw daylight in 1714, it is certain that most breeders were equally sure they knew why their latest champion could run a hole in the wind.

Over time, however, breeders' ideas about why one horse runs faster than another have coalesced into a remarkably small set of concepts. Breeding theories range from vaguely generalized precepts such as "breed the best to the best and hope for the best" to highly specific constructs such as the many varieties of dosage theory.

Breed the Best to the Best

The logic behind the broadest of these ideas— breed the best to the best—is obvious. If speed in the racehorse is determined to a degree by inheritance, then it is logical to assume that the fastest horses—both male and female—have the best chances to pass on their abilities to their offspring.

The history of the breed has shown irrefutably that this assumption is true. In general, the horses that turn out to be the best sires are almost always high-class racehorses themselves. The correlation between racecourse ability and sire success is, of course, far from guaranteed but undeniably positive.

The case for the female of the species is less clear but still undeniable. On average, the best

racemares become more successful broodmares than those females that showed less ability on the racecourse. Thus, if a high-class racehorse is mated to a high-class racemare, the breeder theoretically increases the probability that another high-class racehorse will result.

Because probability is capricious, the odds are still against the breeder. The most successful stallions in history have sired only about 25% stakes winners. Individual broodmares may achieve higher percentages, but percentages based on the relatively small numbers of foals from those mares are meaningless in the larger picture.

So, breeding the best to the best certainly works, on average. However, it is far too general a precept to satisfy many Thoroughbred breeders—and of no use whatsoever to those who cannot afford to buy the best, most expensive racing prospects, both male and female.

Inbreeding

For the first 100 years or so of the Thoroughbred's existence as a distinct, definable breed, the number of horses bred each year was so small that inbreeding was inevitable.

Inbreeding, as most commonly used by Thoroughbred breeders, means the repetition of one or more names at least once on both the sire's and dam's side of a pedigree within the first four or five generations. In genetic terms, inbreeding reduces the number of different and distinct gene alleles available to appear in the genome of the new individual. Thus, it increases the chances that the offspring of that mating will display uniform and specific characteristics.

Inbreeding is therefore used in animal husbandry to fix type—that is, to create a more uniform subspecies, which is exactly what Thoroughbred breeders were doing in the 18th century.

The process of creating the Thoroughbred was largely one of inbreeding to certain prepotent stallions and mares—often very closely. For example, the third dam of Flying Childers is listed in the *General Stud Book*'s Volume 1—detailing the genesis of the Thoroughbred breed—as being by the excellent 17th-century racehorse and sire Spanker and out of Spanker's own dam, the Old Morocco mare. That's about as close as inbreeding can get.

The best racehorses of the 18th century and early 19th century were almost invariably closely inbred to a succession of great stallions, beginning with the Godolphin Arabian and continuing through Eclipse, Herod, and the latter's son Highflyer. By about 1825, the genes of those four stallions were so highly concentrated in the Thoroughbred that breeders were forced to seek outcrosses. Since that time, inbreeding has gone in and out of fashion, and a few great breeders, notably French breeder Marcel Boussac, have used its principles to create great racehorses, sires, and broodmares.

Inbreeding is described in contemporary industry texts by a shorthand method that denotes the name and location in the five-cross pedigree of the individual or individuals to which the subject horse is inbred. Thus "inbred 3x4 to Northern Dancer" means that the name of Northern Dancer appears in the third generation on the sire's side of the pedigree and in the fourth generation of the dam's side.

Some Famous Inbred Horses

Horse (Year of Birth)	Inbreeding	Accomplishment
Spanker mare (ca 1690)	2x1 Old Morocco mare	Third dam of Flying Childers
Rachel (1763)	2x3 Godolphin Arabian	Dam of Highflyer, undefeated, 13-time leading sire
Eclipse (1764)	3x4 Snake mare	Unbeaten champion, sire line founder
Prunella (1788)	3x3 Blank	Dam of three classic winners, grandam of seven others
Sir Archy (1802)	3x4 Herod	American foundation sire
Boston (1833)	3x3 *Diomed	Greatest American four-miler
Lexington (1850)	3x4 Sir Archy	16-time leading American sire
Galopin (1872)	3x3 Voltaire	Epsom Derby winner, sire of St. Simon
Americus (1892)	3x3 Lexington	Key horse in pedigree of *Nasrullah
Flying Fox (1896)	3x2 Galopin	English Triple Crown, grandsire of *Teddy
Bromus (1905)	2x3 Springfield	Dam of Phalaris
Bayardo (1906)	4x2 Galopin	English champion, sire of two Triple Crown winners
Havresac II (1915)	2x3 St. Simon	Leading Italian sire, broodmare sire of Nearco
***Ksar** (1918)	3x2 Omnium II	Prix de l'Arc de Triomphe winner, sire of Tourbillon
Pharos (1920)	4x3 St. Simon	Champion Stakes winner, sire of Nearco, Pharis
Hyperion (1930)	4x3 St. Simon	Epsom Derby winner, six-time leading sire
Coronation (1946)	2x2 Tourbillon	Prix de l'Arc de Triomphe winner
***Turn-to** (1951)	3x3 Pharos	Sire of sires Hail to Reason, Sir Gaylord, Cyane, Best Turn
Broad Brush (1983)	3x3 *Turn-to	Leading sire of 1995

A more accurate method would be to calculate the inbreeding coefficient, or percentage of inbreeding, to that individual. By that method, the inbreeding coefficient of a horse inbred 3x4 to Northern Dancer would be 1.56%.

Nicks

Thoroughbred breeding is of necessity both a retrospective and a predictive art. Early Thoroughbred breeders could not help but notice the efficacy of inbreeding to certain stallions and mares, and the repeated success of combining certain sires and broodmares also became apparent. For reasons that are now obscure, this pattern of combining a specific sire and broodmares sired by another stallion became known as a nick.

Perhaps the best early example of a nick was the combination of the immortal racehorse and great sire Eclipse and mares by the even-greater sire Herod. This direct cross produced 1784 Epsom Derby winner Serjeant. The reverse cross of Herod on an Eclipse mare produced 1783 St. Leger Stakes winner Phenomenom, but the real gold mine for breeders was in the innumerable crosses of sons of Eclipse on mares by Herod or his sons, and sons of Herod on mares by Eclipse or his sons. That more generalized nick was preserved in the breed most notably through 1793 Derby winner Waxy (by Eclipse's son Pot8O's out of a Herod mare), tail-male ancestor of the Phalaris male line.

Phalaris, a foal of 1913, contributed to the most famous 20th-century nick. The four current male lines tracing to Phalaris all descend from sons out of Chaucer mares. *Sickle (Raise a Native line) and *Pharamond II (Buckpasser line) were both foaled by Selene, by Chaucer, while Pharos (*Nasrullah and Northern Dancer lines) and Fairway (Lord At War [Arg] line) were both sons of Scapa Flow, by Chaucer.

Contemporary advocates of the nicking theory have compiled and marketed nicking information that evaluates various crosses according to percentage of stakes winners or graded winners produced by all exemplars of that cross. To accumulate sufficient numbers of exemplars of the cross to be statistically meaningful, these formulations frequently extend the concept to include grandsons or great-grandsons of a particular sire crossed on granddaughters or great-granddaughters of another sire.

At that point, such data are focusing on the hypothetical power of one individual in the third generation of a pedigree and another in the fourth while ignoring the rest of the pedigree. Even at the sire–broodmare sire level, statistical studies of some of the most famous nicks such as the *Nasrullah–*Princequillo cross have not been encouraging.

Still, the fact that certain crosses such as Phalaris–Chaucer have had extraordinary impact on the breed lends some credence to the concept.

Bruce Lowe Numbers

For the first 150 years of the Thoroughbred as a distinct breed, breeding theories focused almost entirely on the influence of stallions. Toward the end of the 19th century, however, an Australian, Bruce Lowe, and a German, Herman Goos, independently began to trace every mare in the *General Stud Book* back to the earliest female ancestor recorded in Volume 1. Both found that every mare traced to one of about 50 of approximately 100 original foundation mares recorded in Volume 1.

Goos published his results in *Family Tables of English Thoroughbred Stock*, a monumental work that was the foundation for the even more monumental *Family Tables of Racehorses* by Kazimierz Bobinski and Stefan Zamoyski in 1953. Goos noted that some female lines had been much more successful than others, but Lowe went several steps further. The Australian numbered each family according to the cumulative number of winners of the Epsom Derby, Epsom Oaks, and St. Leger Stakes each had produced up to his era. Thus, the female line tracing to Tregonwell's Natural Barb mare was named the Number 1 family, and that tracing to the Burton Barb mare was Number 2. In all, 49 families were numbered.

Based on their success rates, Lowe designated families 1 through 5 as his "running" families. He also designated families 3, 8, 11, 12, and 14 his "sire" families, based on his judgment that the highest number of successful sires occurred in those families. He called those family numbers "figures." He then developed several theories of breeding racehorses based on combinations of those families. His theories were published posthumously in 1895 in *Breeding Race Horses by the Figure System*.

Lowe's system ignored the fact that the primary reason families 1 through 5 produced the most classic winners was that they had produced the most foals in pretty much the same proportions. Numerical superiority, not innate hereditary superiority, accounted for the differences. His theories on breeding also ignored the fact that the original foundation mares were so many generations removed from contemporary horses that their genetic influences were statistically negligible.

Bruce Lowe's theories were promoted assiduously by his editor, English journalist and bloodstock agent William Allison. Lowe's theories were widely influential around the turn of the 20th century, especially in America, where Allison's purchases of broodmares formed the basis for James R. Keene's stud. Genetic science in the 20th century proved Lowe's theories were useless, but his numbering system of female lines has remained a valuable contribution.

Vuillier Dosage

The late 19th century was a remarkably fertile period for pedigree research. At about the same time Lowe and Goos were tracing their female lines, French cavalry officer Col. Jean-Joseph Vuillier overheard two men arguing over whether Eclipse or Herod was the more influential sire and set out to answer the question statistically. To do so, Vuillier compiled complete pedigrees of more than 650 high-class racehorses, mostly winners of the English classics that Lowe used.

Although he apparently had no knowledge of either theory, Vuillier correctly applied a modern Mendelian interpretation of Galton's Law of genetic inheritance, which states that each parent contributes 50% of the genetic material to their offspring on average. Extending his pedigrees to a minimum of 12 generations, he assigned a value of 1 to a name that appeared in the 12th generation, a value of 2 in the 11th, 4 in the tenth, 8 in the ninth, and on down to a value of 2,048 for first-generation parents.

To determine the percentage contribution of Eclipse and Herod, Vuillier added up the numbers for each occurrence in each generation. Vuillier found that when he averaged the results for his 650 pedigrees, Herod's average number was 750 while Eclipse's average was only 568. He also discovered that Herod's son Highflyer was almost as influential as Eclipse with an average of 543.

In pursuing his research over 15 years, Vuillier noticed that other, more recent ancestors also accumulated high numbers, and he compiled figures that he called "dosages" for 11 more stallions and one mare, Pocahontas. Vuillier's dosages are, in fact, remarkably accurate representations of the percentage of genetic influence on the classic Thoroughbred of the 15 horses in his classification.

Since classic winners were frequently the most successful sires of future generations, Vuillier reasoned that the breed as a whole would and should move in the same direction as the classic pedigree. Thus, he concluded the object of a breeding program should be to produce pedigrees with the same dosages as his classic pedigrees.

Vuillier Dosages

First Series

Horse	Dosage
Herod (1758)	750
Eclipse (1764)	568
Highflyer (1774)	543

Second Series

Birdcatcher (1833)	288
Touchstone (1831)	351
Pocahontas (1837)	313
Voltaire (1826)	186
Pantaloon (1824)	140
Melbourne (1834)	184
Bay Middleton (1833)	127
Gladiator (1833)	95

Third Series

Stockwell (1849)	340
Newminster (1848)	295

Fourth Series

St. Simon (1881)	420
Galopin (1872)	405
Isonomy (1875)	280
Hampton (1872)	260
Hermit (1864)	235
Bend Or (1877)	210

To facilitate this process, Vuillier devised the *ecart* system. *Ecart* is a French word that translates loosely to mean mathematical difference. For any potential mating using Vuillier's system, the breeder could calculate the dosages of the prospective foal. The difference between the prospective dosages and the ideal is the *ecart*. The object of Vuillier's system was to reduce the ecart as much as possible.

Vuillier published his findings privately in volumes 1 and 2 of *Les Croisements Rationnels* (Rational Breeding) in 1903 and '27. The Aga Khan hired him to manage his stud in 1925, but Vuillier died shortly thereafter. His widow took over and arranged the Aga Khan's matings for more than 30 years. During that period, the Aga Khan was the most successful and influential breeder in the world, with his stud producing such great racehorses and sires as *Bahram, *Mahmoud, and *Nasrullah. The Vuillier system, privately modernized and updated, is still in use by the current Aga Khan.

Varola Dosage

Vuillier's method was not widely available and

was difficult to execute because it required constructing 12-generation pedigrees and keeping track of mathematical data in an era long before computers. Italian journalist Francesco Varola built on Vuillier's work in his *Typology of the Racehorse*, published in 1974. Since Vuillier's published series of influential stallions extended only through the late 19th century, Varola updated and vastly expanded this list of influential stallions. His initial work identified 120 more horses, all born in the 20th century.

Unlike Vuillier, Varola did not utilize Galton's Law in his formulation, applying equal value to an appearance by a given stallion regardless of the generation of the pedigree in which he appeared. Recognizing that the modern Thoroughbred racehorse is much more specialized than in Vuillier's day, Varola divided his 120 stallions initially into five groups defined by his judgment of the type of influence they exerted on the breed.

His five categories—Brilliant, Intermediate, Classic, Stout, and Professional—were based partly on sociological concepts, partly on physical type and racecourse expression, and partly on inspiration. Varola eventually split the Brilliant group into Brilliant and Transbrilliant and Stout into Solid and Rough, but the original five categories quickly became associated in the public mind with varying degrees of stamina. Varola has consistently disavowed this interpretation.

Varola arranged the names of all his "*chefs-de-race*" in a "dosage diagram," dividing the names of each *chef-de-race* (chief of the breed) that occurs in a given pedigree into the five (or seven) categories and totaling the number of occurrences, regardless of generation. The resulting series of numbers offered breeders a thumbnail picture of the balance in a pedigree among all of Varola's different aptitudes.

Varola's chief contribution may be his insight into the increasing specialization of the Thoroughbred into sprinters, stayers, and middle-distance horses, among others, and his recognition that human sociology plays a role in determining the type of racehorse produced in different countries in different eras.

Roman Dosage

In the 1980s, Steve Roman, an American chemistry professor, developed a system combining some of the aspects of the Vuillier and Varola dosage systems. Considering only the first four generations of a pedigree, Roman assigned a numerical value of 16 to any *chef-de-race* that appeared in the first generation of a pedigree, eight to a second-generation *chef*, four for the third generation, and two for the fourth.

Roman interpreted Varola's five original categories strictly in terms of stamina, with Brilliant horses defined as those contributing extreme speed but little stamina, while Professional *chefs* contributed stamina but little speed. Applying the appropriate value according to generation for each occurrence of a *chef*'s name and adding those values up for each of Varola's five aptitudinal categories, Roman devised a "dosage profile" meant to give breeders insight into the relative stamina inherent in a given pedigree.

Roman invented the "dosage index," a single number that is calculated by dividing the total points in the Brilliant and Intermediate categories plus half the Classic points by the total of the points in the Stout and Professional categories plus the other half of the Classic points. The resultant figure is intended to predict a horse's ability to stay classic distances.

Applying his ideas to the history of the Kentucky Derby (G1), Roman found that almost all Derby winners since the 1930s had dosage indexes of 4.00 or less. Leon Rasmussen of *Daily Racing Form* popularized Roman's ideas in the 1980s and early '90s, and, although several Kentucky Derby winners have subsequently defied their Roman dosage, his theories remain popular.

Modern Genetics

The science of genetics, like the other physical sciences, made enormous strides during the 20th century. Though published earlier, Mendel's laws were virtually unknown at the turn of the 20th century, but early in the 21st century the complete human genome was mapped. Science had progressed from crossbreeding garden peas to cloning sheep and other large mammals.

None of this progress has significantly affected Thoroughbred breeding. An equine genome mapping project is under way, but even that should have no immediate effect on the breed because knowing the location of genes does not reveal the traits or characteristics they control. Even coat-color genetics, once thought to be a relatively simple dominance series consisting of gray, bay (or brown), and chestnut alleles, proved to be not so simple because white Thoroughbreds began to appear about 30 years ago.

The problem is that the traits that produce a successful racehorse are not governed by single genes. Factors such as speed, stamina, temperament, and soundness are each dependent on thousands of different genes working together with the environment to create outstanding racehorses.—*John P. Sparkman*

SIRES
Leading Sires by Progeny Earnings in 2007

Worldwide earnings for stallions who stand in North America or stood in North America if pensioned or dead.
♦ Denotes freshman sire.

Sire	Strs	Wnrs	SWs	Leading Earner (Earnings)	Total Earnings
Smart Strike, Ky.	214	102	16	Curlin ($5,102,800)	$14,477,651
Langfuhr, Ky.	350	174	15	Lawyer Ron ($1,320,000)	10,709,065
Distorted Humor, Ky.	269	127	20	Any Given Saturday ($994,320)	10,639,082
A.P. Indy, Ky.	172	80	18	Rags to Riches ($1,340,028)	10,028,967
Giant's Causeway, Ky.	294	124	15	Red Giant ($846,720)	9,717,748
Fusaichi Pegasus, Ky.	304	105	4	Floral Pegasus ($1,691,018)	8,945,533
Royal Academy, Ky.	348	147	20	Bullish Luck ($803,057)	8,423,171
Awesome Again, Ky.	159	79	11	Ginger Punch ($1,827,060)	7,557,131
Tale of the Cat, Ky.	327	158	12	Tale of Ekati ($313,200)	7,531,639
Mr. Greeley, Ky.	198	94	7	Finsceal Beo ($844,219)	7,166,342
Hennessy, Dead	216	94	12	Sunrise Bacchus ($1,625,032)	6,924,884
Dynaformer, Ky.	187	86	7	Lucarno ($1,033,373)	6,885,041
Unbridled's Song, Ky.	170	86	14	Octave ($1,050,234)	6,813,635
Street Cry (Ire), Ky.	127	47	11	Street Sense ($3,205,000)	6,785,085
Pulpit, Ky.	165	82	9	Corinthian ($1,174,173)	6,751,900
Grand Slam, Ky.	284	137	10	Fresh Vanilla ($280,704)	6,657,989
Stormy Atlantic, Ky.	246	130	13	Icy Atlantic ($367,110)	6,628,954
Cherokee Run, Ky.	179	105	9	War Pass ($1,397,400)	6,625,121
Victory Gallop, Tur	194	100	8	Eishin Dover ($1,107,208)	6,605,618
Lemon Drop Kid, Ky.	174	85	14	Citronnade ($701,405)	6,587,197
More Than Ready, Ky.	297	146	10	Ready's Image ($259,422)	6,470,753
Broken Vow, Ky.	180	109	6	Unbridled Belle ($1,116,500)	6,115,147
Kingmambo, Ky.	178	64	7	Student Council ($1,041,755)	6,072,950
Rahy, Ky.	159	76	9	Flying Apple ($561,195)	6,006,669
Storm Cat, Ky.	154	73	10	After Market ($686,725)	5,844,576
Silver Deputy, Ky.	184	103	11	Spring At Last ($722,000)	5,815,095
Not For Love, Md.	177	100	11	Talkin About Love ($375,875)	5,784,263
Mutakddim, Ky.	291	162	6	Ravalo ($201,655)	5,691,425
Catienus, Ky.	165	103	8	Precious Kitten ($1,090,000)	5,616,081
Thunder Gulch, Ky.	277	105	10	Recast ($620,193)	5,514,926
Yes It's True, Ky.	199	112	11	Takara True ($291,772)	5,402,187
Maria's Mon, Dead	191	99	9	Wait a While ($406,000)	5,394,914
Pleasant Tap, Ky.	121	59	7	Premium Tap ($1,234,920)	5,324,277
Touch Gold, Ky.	190	96	5	Ferrari Pisa ($687,115)	5,213,994
Forest Wildcat, Ky.	183	98	16	Wild Gams ($303,280)	5,207,569
Elusive Quality, Ky.	233	112	6	Maryfield ($896,330)	5,195,399
Carson City, Dead	186	104	8	Zenno Striker ($447,806)	5,124,234
Honour and Glory, Ky.	301	147	5	Chevronic ($454,711)	5,095,770
Tiznow, Ky.	159	79	6	Bear Now ($747,517)	5,067,896
Danzig, Dead	61	35	6	Hard Spun ($2,572,500)	5,052,654
Malibu Moon, Ky.	160	78	13	Moon Catcher ($663,450)	5,037,398
Johannesburg, Ky.	218	81	7	Scat Daddy ($826,500)	4,822,679
Indian Charlie, Ky.	140	82	9	Indian Blessing ($1,357,200)	4,817,290
Belong to Me, Ky	211	96	11	Bon Hoffa ($327,854)	4,796,552
Trippi, Ky.	142	83	5	Miss Macy Sue ($546,217)	4,672,183
Chester House, Dead	133	73	12	Deepwater Bay ($216,884)	4,630,871
Cozzene, Ky.	109	59	6	Robe Decollete ($1,376,264)	4,603,668
Anabaa, Fr	226	98	9	Loup Breton ($164,376)	4,534,120
Dixie Union, Ky.	162	80	4	Turf War ($518,548)	4,496,195
Holy Bull, Ky.	157	73	7	Flashy Bull ($635,063)	4,463,144
Forestry, Ky.	159	81	9	Hishi Aspen ($309,717)	4,441,933
Real Quiet, Pa.	152	75	4	Midnight Lute ($1,368,000)	4,437,148
Smoke Glacken, Ky.	196	96	9	Lady Marlboro ($191,524)	4,421,074
El Corredor, Ky.	164	82	5	Dominican ($549,140)	4,405,703
Gone West, Ky.	153	57	5	Istan ($380,992)	4,368,232
Bold Executive, On.	133	77	4	Legal Move ($222,728)	4,311,113
Bertrando, Ca.	159	92	8	Bilo ($327,780)	4,233,527
Lear Fan, Pens	93	43	5	Good Ba Ba ($1,943,291)	4,117,519
War Chant, Ky.	119	57	7	Top Diamante ($367,772)	4,110,389
Orientate, Ky.	139	71	7	Lady Joanne ($808,993)	4,105,297

Sires — Leading General Sires

Sire	Strs	Wnrs	SWs	Leading Earner (Earnings)	Total Earnings
Slew City Slew, Ky.	147	86	4	Lava Man ($1,410,000)	$4,072,164
Seeking the Gold, Ky.	130	67	8	Wanderin Boy ($296,708)	4,060,568
Include, Ky.	115	58	4	Panty Raid ($1,024,180)	3,922,292
Twining, Jpn	171	72	3	Fusaichi Assort ($354,839)	3,915,995
Cat Thief, Ky.	165	96	3	Sam P. ($235,058)	3,912,324
Gilded Time, Ab.	228	102	3	Getback Time ($200,330)	3,799,971
Deputy Commander, Ca.	179	81	5	Reporting for Duty ($288,810)	3,799,148
Gulch, Ky.	173	78	5	Court Vision ($257,542)	3,798,355
In Excess (Ire), Ca.	142	78	8	Notional ($460,000)	3,797,819
Stormin Fever, Ky.	180	92	6	Stormin Baghdad ($211,322)	3,783,837
Put It Back, Fl.	123	78	7	Black Bar Spin ($687,085)	3,698,907
Arch, Ky.	113	70	6	Arch Swing ($321,174)	3,689,294
El Prado (Ire), Ky.	155	59	6	Fort Prado ($264,421)	3,679,206
Northern Afleet, Ky.	161	107	3	Big City Man ($143,540)	3,601,034
Montbrook, Fl.	160	93	4	Bentrovhto ($159,020)	3,589,363
Point Given, Ky.	109	40	3	Sealy Hill ($958,389)	3,560,385
Unusual Heat, Ca.	115	59	5	Unusual Suspect ($376,221)	3,534,363
City Zip, Ky.	120	68	4	Tishmeister ($167,516)	3,525,903
Quiet American, Ky.	127	64	9	Folk ($341,438)	3,509,001
Songandaprayer, Ky.	93	54	6	Surplus Singer ($502,971)	3,491,929
Outflanker, Md.	133	82	7	Annabill ($238,680)	3,462,004
Storm Boot, Dead	176	100	6	Coco Belle ($223,250)	3,447,820
Dehere, Ky.	146	37	2	Fortune Word ($306,553)	3,424,908
Salt Lake, Ca.	225	122	5	Salt Track ($131,810)	3,410,843
Swiss Yodeler, Ca.	196	99	3	Yodelen Dan ($146,066)	3,398,539
Out of Place, Ky.	142	76	2	Brother Bobby ($239,101)	3,387,868
Stephen Got Even, Ky.	154	78	9	Steve's Double ($238,346)	3,372,827
Tactical Cat, Ky.	171	79	7	Like a Gem ($278,495)	3,356,705
Theatrical (Ire), Ky.	87	32	2	Mrs. Lindsay ($1,170,915)	3,256,589
Deputy Minister, Dead	106	53	3	Miss Shop ($787,408)	3,251,927
Yonaguska, Ky.	136	81	6	Cherokee Country ($226,110)	3,233,772
Forest Camp, Unknown	140	65	2	Timber Reserve ($577,600)	3,232,627
Mizzen Mast, Ky.	122	60	5	Tropical Light ($306,698)	3,218,106
Sea of Secrets, Ca.	154	92	5	Seiun Pleasure ($265,742)	3,212,683
Golden Missile, N.Y.	151	76	3	Cobalt Blue ($329,433)	3,204,018
Bernstein, Ky.	177	76	8	Goshawk Ken ($650,439)	3,191,612
Doneraile Court, Ky.	221	118	7	Noble Court ($157,918)	3,162,524
Louis Quatorze, Md.	181	110	4	Tap Dancing Mauk ($200,355)	3,139,562
Exchange Rate, Ky.	89	42	10	Xchanger ($510,500)	3,132,680
Lite the Fuse, Pa.	126	74	5	Going Ballistic ($690,140)	3,089,116
Devil His Due, Ky.	207	108	2	Southern Missile ($152,730)	3,077,572
Sky Classic, Ky.	125	62	2	Sky Conqueror ($827,043)	3,072,908
Officer, Ky.	101	55	10	Apollo Dolce ($444,277)	3,072,447
Cryptoclearance, Ky.	176	86	2	Lila Paige ($291,100)	3,067,708
Marquetry, Ky.	155	72	7	Double Brother ($257,573)	3,040,489
Notebook, Dead	99	63	4	Diamond Stripes ($588,645)	3,031,287
Concerto, Fl.	118	76	3	Finallymadeit ($362,450)	3,019,171
Double Honor, Fl.	133	80	4	Double Action ($188,335)	3,012,244
Leestown, La.	167	72	5	Ahead of Her Time ($254,000)	2,992,949
Benchmark, Ca.	132	63	5	Idiot Proof ($803,136)	2,977,199
Petionville, Ky.	158	79	2	Look Deep ($123,400)	2,946,300
Brahms, Ky.	159	76	3	Arson Squad ($264,000)	2,941,205
Aptitude, Ky.	164	70	2	Augment ($204,160)	2,908,332
Dance Brightly, Chi	163	77	6	Arden Belle ($262,522)	2,873,599
Albert the Great, Pa.	99	50	2	Nobiz Like Shobiz ($1,318,330)	2,849,580
Halo's Image, Fl.	145	77	3	Hal's My Hope ($125,250)	2,839,023
Crafty Prospector, Pens	120	72	3	Terano Force One ($169,211)	2,833,702
Runaway Groom, Dead	135	67	4	Joint Effort ($275,000)	2,803,073
Silver Hawk, Pens	45	23	4	Nashoba's Key ($972,090)	2,782,919
Partner's Hero, Pa.	118	63	3	Heros Reward ($515,826)	2,769,834
Horse Chestnut (SAf), Ky.	98	48	4	Smart Enough ($427,477)	2,767,039
Chief Seattle, N.Y.	139	87	5	Bold Chieftain ($283,950)	2,763,345
Two Punch, Md.	124	64	2	Grand Champion ($279,240)	2,736,761
Mt. Livermore, Dead	143	73	2	False Straight ($114,302)	2,735,594
Wild Event, Brz	140	74	2	Imawildandcrazyguy ($392,100)	2,718,248
King Cugat, N.Y.	119	49	4	Devil Moon ($607,269)	2,615,717
Pioneering, Ky.	124	62	8	Blue Pepsi Lodge ($143,360)	2,601,395
Mazel Trick, B.C.	127	71	3	Gantu ($186,846)	2,557,742
Alphabet Soup, Fl.	159	72	3	Silver Swallow ($185,478)	2,547,800
Gold Case, N.M.	138	80	3	Footprint ($303,107)	2,513,471

Sires — Leading General Sires

Sire	Strs	Wnrs	SWs	Leading Earner (Earnings)	Total Earnings
Jump Start, Ky.	105	57	4	Mrs. Began ($184,801)	$2,504,694
Monarchos, Ky.	92	50	3	Mr Monarchos ($275,743)	2,469,975
Lion Hearted, Md.	104	64	2	Maddy's Heart ($194,194)	2,463,857
Running Stag, Tx.	135	77	2	Chucker ($152,400)	2,456,501
Peaks and Valleys, On.	124	68	2	Meribel ($210,993)	2,430,746
E Dubai, Ky.	84	40	3	High Heels ($411,788)	2,427,632
Slew Gin Fizz, Arg	186	81	5	Dry Martini ($383,970)	2,425,855
Pure Prize, Ky.	110	61	8	Pure Clan ($316,209)	2,416,889
Kipling, Ky.	33	15	2	Kip Deville ($1,965,780)	2,400,506
Artax, N.Y.	133	66	4	Diabolical ($354,750)	2,398,195
Suave Prospect, N.M.	121	71	3	Suave Jazz ($266,076)	2,396,410
Valid Expectations, Tx.	141	77	5	Valid Lilly ($213,406)	2,346,764
Boundary, Pens	88	47	4	Eucharis ($204,048)	2,340,042
Skip Away, Ky.	119	68	2	Karakorum Starlet ($227,664)	2,334,812
Lord Carson, Dead	142	82	5	Camela Carson ($128,720)	2,311,947
Lost Soldier, Ky.	112	52	5	Soldier's Dancer ($424,760)	2,310,017
Yankee Victor, Unknown	106	56	3	Now a Victor ($186,140)	2,301,397
Valid Wager, Dead	152	80	2	My Redeemer ($144,688)	2,301,312
Broad Brush, Pens	67	35	2	A Shin Turbo ($257,623)	2,298,061
Successful Appeal, Ky.	88	46	4	Dawn After Dawn ($157,623)	2,294,040
Sweetsouthernsaint, Fl.	90	52	3	Sweetnorthernsaint ($229,375)	2,293,976
Patton, Pa.	68	35	2	Kelly's Landing ($1,313,000)	2,289,726
Game Plan, Ca.	96	55	5	Mistical Plan ($421,569)	2,286,938
Siphon (Brz), Pa.	116	56	4	Rio Samba City ($213,220)	2,263,813
Came Home, Jpn	84	47	4	C P West ($305,620)	2,262,928
Lord Avie, Pens	28	16	2	Cloudy's Knight ($1,762,868)	2,245,784
Woodman, Dead	150	50	3	Satono Throne ($341,767)	2,239,188
Bold n' Flashy, On.	97	56	2	Red Raffles ($165,239)	2,229,979
Evansville Slew, Ok.	104	56	7	Knocker ($205,050)	2,228,501
Allen's Prospect, Dead	146	73	0	All Giving ($101,835)	2,208,861
Freud, N.Y.	81	40	2	Karakorum Elektra ($111,993)	2,169,585
Kiridashi, Ab.	54	30	3	Financingavailable ($451,151)	2,165,995
Cee's Tizzy, Ca.	109	58	6	Tiz Elemental ($201,800)	2,149,978
Glitterman, Pens	134	73	2	Glitter Rox ($123,335)	2,147,631
Afternoon Deelites, La.	114	52	4	Zappa ($165,930)	2,129,954
Cape Canaveral, Ab.	108	58	5	Jilli's Cape ($129,420)	2,128,097
Straight Man, Fl.	121	56	2	Get Funky ($181,932)	2,125,454
Wheaton, Dead	80	56	2	Miami Sunrise ($187,773)	2,107,028
Service Stripe, Pa.	106	59	2	Joan's Rose ($107,215)	2,102,065
Memo (Chi), Ca.	80	43	4	McCann's Mojave ($736,600)	2,084,997
Formal Gold, Ca.	108	58	4	Snark Tiger ($137,755)	2,082,280
Good and Tough, La.	109	56	1	City in the Clouds ($140,836)	2,059,593
Western Expression, N.Y.	94	46	2	Stunt Man ($347,739)	2,053,210
Sefapiano, La.	68	37	5	Jonesboro ($382,030)	2,043,406
Lucky Lionel, Ok.	82	49	3	Benny the Bull ($420,460)	2,022,040
Regal Classic, Pens	128	59	2	Half Heaven ($158,065)	2,016,438
Honor Grades, Dead	58	39	2	Magna Graduate ($500,255)	2,007,515
Banker's Gold, Pa.	115	58	2	My List ($213,187)	1,996,660
Ide, La.	92	40	3	Tensas Yucatan ($284,877)	1,991,850
Black Tie Affair (Ire), W.V.	43	9	2	Fujino Wave ($722,180)	1,982,810
Saint Ballado, Dead	67	34	6	Sunriver ($415,014)	1,982,337
Phone Trick, Dead	106	58	1	Sort of Tricky ($82,430)	1,981,888
Diamond, Ok.	86	48	2	Silmaril ($405,820)	1,980,526
Three Wonders, Fl.	91	55	1	Calico Bay ($331,300)	1,975,047
Pine Bluff, Ar.	91	48	4	Raise the Bluff ($169,190)	1,970,035
Eltish, N.Y.	103	57	1	Silk Ridge ($369,240)	1,963,173
Lit de Justice, Ca.	94	56	1	La Salle Glory ($159,040)	1,955,120
Old Topper, Ca.	104	60	4	Topper Shopper ($129,590)	1,937,674
Capote, Ok.	89	48	3	Dance Away Capote ($188,968)	1,922,748
Crafty Friend, N.J.	110	57	2	Friendly Island ($490,000)	1,909,920
Old Trieste, Dead	75	40	3	Barcola ($242,155)	1,904,358
Concorde's Tune, Fl.	100	57	2	Tune of the Spirit ($95,160)	1,886,692
Zarbyev, La.	66	42	4	St. Zarb ($249,750)	1,882,575
Disco Rico, N.Y.	57	43	2	Pure Disco ($285,050)	1,852,797
Tour d'Or, Dead	94	48	3	Take D' Tour ($395,000)	1,843,221
Robyn Dancer, La.	132	61	2	Lord Robyn ($121,100)	1,832,841
Sahm, Dead	74	44	6	Red Moloney ($147,193)	1,823,698
Friendly Lover, Il.	94	48	1	Fusaichi Weed ($401,869)	1,816,955
Prime Timber, N.Y.	66	35	1	Premium Wine ($311,700)	1,815,886
West Acre, Fl.	70	40	3	Forty Acres ($137,620)	1,815,078

Leading Sires by Average Earnings per Starter in 2007
Minimum of 25 Starters

Sire	Strs	Wnrs	Average
Danzig, Dead	61	35	$82,830
Lord Avie, Pens	28	16	80,207
Kipling, Ky.	33	15	72,743
Smart Strike, Ky.	214	102	67,641
Silver Hawk, Pens	45	23	61,843
A.P. Indy, Ky.	172	80	58,308
Street Cry (Ire), Ky.	126	47	53,830
Awesome Again, Ky.	159	79	47,529
Black Tie Affair (Ire), W.V.	43	9	46,112
Pleasant Tap, Ky.	120	59	44,369
Lear Fan, Pens	93	43	44,274
Cozzene, Ky.	109	59	42,235
◆Posse, Ky.	42	23	41,757
Desert God, N.M.	28	17	41,696
◆Empire Maker, Ky.	25	8	41,277
Pulpit, Ky.	165	82	40,921
Kiridashi, Ab.	54	30	40,111
Unbridled's Song, Ky.	170	86	40,070
Distorted Humor, Ky.	269	127	39,516
Storm Cat, Ky.	154	73	37,952
Lemon Drop Kid, Ky.	174	85	37,857
Rahy, Ky.	159	76	37,778
Songandaprayer, Ky.	93	54	37,548
Theatrical (Ire), Ky.	87	32	37,432
Cherokee Run, Ky.	179	105	37,010
Dynaformer, Ky.	187	86	36,818
Mr. Greeley, Ky.	198	94	36,169
◆Macho Uno, Ky.	32	16	35,928
Exchange Rate, Ky.	89	42	35,199
Chester House, Dead	133	73	34,819
Honor Grades, Dead	58	39	34,612
War Chant, Ky.	119	57	34,528
Indian Charlie, Ky.	140	82	34,409
Broad Brush, Pens	67	35	34,299
Kingmambo, Ky.	178	64	34,118
Include, Ky.	115	58	34,107
Victory Gallop, Ky.	194	100	34,050
Catienus, Ky.	165	103	34,037
Broken Vow, Ky.	180	109	33,918
◆D'wildcat, Fl.	25	7	33,695
Patton, Pa.	68	35	33,672
Giant's Causeway, Ky.	293	123	33,031
Trippi, Fl.	142	83	32,895
Not For Love, Md.	177	100	32,679
Point Given, Ky.	109	40	32,664
Arch, Ky.	113	70	32,649

Leading Sires by Median Earnings per Starter in 2007
Minimum of 25 Starters

Sire	Strs	Wnrs	Median
Disco Rico, N.Y.	57	43	$23,220
Desert God, N.M.	28	17	21,330
Zarbyev, La.	66	42	20,488
Archers Bay, Dead	47	30	19,670
A.P. Indy, Ky.	172	80	18,990
Trippi, Fl.	142	83	18,006
Chester House, Dead	133	73	17,849
Not For Love, Md.	177	100	17,500
Citidancer, Pens	44	24	17,100
Raffie's Majesty, N.Y.	42	26	16,780
Broken Vow, Ky.	180	109	16,675
Honor Grades, Dead	58	39	16,640
Graeme Hall, Fl.	70	46	16,333
Songandaprayer, Ky.	93	54	16,082
Unbridled's Song, Ky.	170	86	15,880
Vision and Verse, Ky.	76	50	15,786
Joyeux Danseur, Dead	47	27	15,782
Quaker Ridge, Phi	66	41	15,701
Notebook, Dead	99	63	15,651
Cat Thief, Ky.	165	96	15,600
Yes It's True, Ky.	199	112	15,524
Wheaton, Dead	80	56	15,378

Sire	Strs	Wnrs	Median
Lemon Drop Kid, Ky.	174	85	$15,346
Prime Timber, N.Y.	66	35	15,223
Prospect Bay, W.V.	45	28	15,144
City Zip, Ky.	120	68	15,081
War Chant, Ky.	119	57	14,920
Northern Afleet, Ky.	161	107	14,868
Yonaguska, Ky.	136	81	14,802
Include, Ky.	115	58	14,793
Luftikus, W.V.	57	34	14,760
Concerto, Fl.	118	76	14,703
Freud, N.Y.	81	40	14,586
Hesabull, Ar.	25	14	14,564
Dynaformer, Ky.	187	86	14,235
Maria's Mon, Dead	191	99	14,124
Silver Hawk, Pens	45	23	14,058
Kiridashi, Ab.	54	30	14,009
Came Home, Jpn	84	47	13,916
Outflanker, Md.	133	82	13,841
Jump Start, Ky.	105	57	13,815
Dixie Brass, Dead	37	17	13,767
Storm Broker, Tx.	39	25	13,754
Catienus, Ky.	165	103	13,658
El Corredor, Ky.	164	82	13,598
Sejm, Dead	29	22	13,589
Successful Appeal, Ky.	88	46	13,541
Danzig, Dead	61	35	13,528
Crafty Prospector, Pens	120	72	13,412
Bold Executive, On.	133	77	13,393
◆Posse, Ky.	42	23	13,380
Silver Deputy, Ky.	184	103	13,375

Leading Sires by Number of Winners in 2007

Sire	Strs	Wnrs	Wnrs/Strs
Langfuhr, Ky.	347	173	49.9%
Mutakddim, Ky.	291	162	55.7%
Tale of the Cat, Ky.	322	157	48.8%
Honour and Glory, Ky.	299	147	49.2%
Royal Academy, Ky.	345	146	42.3%
More Than Ready, Ky.	295	145	49.2%
Grand Slam, Ky.	284	137	48.2%
Stormy Atlantic, Ky.	246	130	52.8%
Distorted Humor, Ky.	269	127	47.2%
Giant's Causeway, Ky.	293	123	42.0%
Salt Lake, Ca.	224	122	54.5%
Doneraile Court, Ky.	221	118	53.4%
Yes It's True, Ky.	199	112	56.3%
Elusive Quality, Ky.	231	110	47.6%
Louis Quatorze, Md.	181	110	60.8%
Broken Vow, Ky.	180	109	60.6%
Devil His Due, Ky.	207	108	52.2%
Northern Afleet, Ky.	161	107	66.5%
Cherokee Run, Ky.	179	105	58.7%
Fusaichi Pegasus, Ky.	304	105	34.5%
Thunder Gulch, Ky.	277	105	37.9%
Carson City, Dead	186	104	55.9%
Catienus, Ky.	165	103	62.4%
Silver Deputy, Ky.	184	103	56.0%
Gilded Time, Ab.	227	102	44.9%
Smart Strike, Ky.	214	102	47.7%
Not For Love, Md.	177	100	56.5%
Storm Boot, Dead	176	100	56.8%
Victory Gallop, Ky.	194	100	51.5%
Maria's Mon, Dead	191	99	51.8%
Swiss Yodeler, Ca.	196	99	50.5%
Forest Wildcat, Ky.	183	98	53.6%
Anabaa, Fr	226	96	42.5%
Cat Thief, Ky.	165	96	58.2%
Smoke Glacken, Ky.	196	96	49.0%
Touch Gold, Ky.	190	96	50.5%
Belong to Me, Ky.	209	94	45.0%
Mr. Greeley, Ky.	198	94	47.5%
Hennessy, Dead	215	93	43.3%
Montbrook, Fl.	160	93	58.1%
Sea of Secrets, Ca.	154	93	60.4%
Bertrando, Ca.	159	92	57.9%
Stormin Fever, Ky.	180	92	51.1%

Sires — Leading General Sires

Sire	Strs	Wnrs	Wnrs/Strs
Chief Seattle, N.Y.	139	87	62.6%
Cryptoclearance, Ky.	176	86	48.9%
Dynaformer, Ky.	187	86	46.0%
Slew City Slew, Ky.	147	86	58.5%
Unbridled's Song, Ky.	170	86	50.6%
Lemon Drop Kid, Ky.	174	85	48.9%
Trippi, Fl.	142	83	58.5%
El Corredor, Ky.	164	82	50.0%
Indian Charlie, Ky.	140	82	58.6%
Lord Carson, Dead	142	82	57.7%
Outflanker, Md.	133	82	61.7%
Pulpit, Ky.	165	82	49.7%

Leading Sires by Number of Wins in 2007

Sire	Strs	Wnrs	Wins
Langfuhr, Ky.	347	173	310
Mutakddim, Ky.	291	162	251
Honour and Glory, Ky.	299	147	239
Tale of the Cat, Ky.	322	157	230
Royal Academy, Ky.	345	146	227
Stormy Atlantic, Ky.	246	130	226
More Than Ready, Ky.	295	145	223
Catienus, Ky.	165	103	209
Grand Slam, Ky.	284	137	209
Louis Quatorze, Md.	181	110	203
Yes It's True, Ky.	199	112	199
Distorted Humor, Ky.	269	127	198
Doneraile Court, Ky.	221	118	196
Northern Afleet, Ky.	161	107	195
Giant's Causeway, Ky.	293	123	192
Swiss Yodeler, Ca.	196	99	191
Salt Lake, Ca.	224	122	189
Devil His Due, Ky.	207	108	182
Broken Vow, Ky.	180	109	179
Gilded Time, Ab.	227	102	176
Carson City, Dead	186	104	175
Storm Boot, Dead	176	100	175
Smoke Glacken, Ky.	196	96	174
Belong to Me, Ky.	209	94	173
Cat Thief, Ky.	165	96	173
Silver Deputy, Ky.	184	103	173
Not For Love, Md.	177	100	172
Montbrook, Fl.	160	93	171
Smart Strike, Ky.	214	102	170
Maria's Mon, Dead	191	99	168
Elusive Quality, Ky.	231	110	167
Mr. Greeley, Ky.	198	94	166
Cherokee Run, Ky.	179	105	162
Outflanker, Md.	133	82	162
Concerto, Fl.	118	76	161
Thunder Gulch, Ky.	277	105	160
Victory Gallop, Ky.	194	100	159
Stormin Fever, Ky.	180	92	158
Sea of Secrets, Ca.	154	93	156
Forest Wildcat, Ky.	183	98	155
Fusaichi Pegasus, Ky.	304	105	155

Leading Sires by Number of Stakes Winners in 2007

Sire	Strs	Wnrs	SWs	SWins
Distorted Humor, Ky.	269	127	20	28
Royal Academy, Ky.	345	146	20	27
A.P. Indy, Ky.	172	80	18	30
Forest Wildcat, Ky.	183	98	16	19
Smart Strike, Ky.	214	102	16	29
Giant's Causeway, Ky.	293	123	15	23
Langfuhr, Ky.	347	173	15	26
Lemon Drop Kid, Ky.	174	85	14	23
Unbridled's Song, Ky.	170	86	14	18
Malibu Moon, Ky.	160	78	13	20
Stormy Atlantic, Ky.	246	130	13	18
Chester House, Dead	133	73	12	15
Hennessy, Dead	215	93	12	17
Tale of the Cat, Ky.	322	157	12	13
Awesome Again, Ky.	159	79	11	21
Belong to Me, Ky.	209	94	11	16
Not For Love, Md.	177	100	11	17
Silver Deputy, Ky.	184	103	11	12
Street Cry (Ire), Ky.	126	47	11	19
Yes It's True, Ky.	199	112	11	15
Exchange Rate, Ky.	89	42	10	15
Grand Slam, Ky.	284	137	10	11
More Than Ready, Ky.	295	145	10	15
Officer, Ky.	101	55	10	12
Storm Cat, Ky.	154	73	10	16
Thunder Gulch, Ky.	277	105	10	12
Anabaa, Fr	226	96	9	10
Cherokee Run, Ky.	179	105	9	13
Forestry, Ky.	159	81	9	10
Indian Charlie, Ky.	140	82	9	11
Maria's Mon, Dead	191	99	9	13
Pulpit, Ky.	165	82	9	19
Quiet American, Ky.	127	64	9	15
Rahy, Ky.	159	76	9	14
Smoke Glacken, Ky.	196	96	9	9
Stephen Got Even, Ky.	154	78	9	14

Leading Sires by Number of Graded Stakes Winners in 2007

Sire	Strs	Wnrs	GSWs	GSWins
A.P. Indy, Ky.	172	80	10	17
Giant's Causeway, Ky.	293	123	9	14
Distorted Humor, Ky.	269	127	8	16
Royal Academy, Ky.	345	146	8	12
Smart Strike, Ky.	214	102	8	16
Street Cry (Ire), Ky.	126	47	8	14
Johannesburg, Ky.	215	81	6	8
Kingmambo, Ky.	178	64	6	8
Victory Gallop, Ky.	194	100	6	8
Awesome Again, Ky.	159	79	5	11
Hennessy, Dead	215	93	5	7
Langfuhr, Ky.	347	173	5	9
Pulpit, Ky.	165	82	5	10
Rahy, Ky.	159	76	5	7
Storm Cat, Ky.	154	73	5	9
Unbridled's Song, Ky.	170	86	5	6
War Chant, Ky.	119	57	5	5
Cherokee Run, Ky.	179	105	4	6
Danzig, Dead	61	35	4	7
Exchange Rate, Ky.	89	42	4	5
Forest Wildcat, Ky.	183	98	4	5
Lemon Drop Kid, Ky.	174	85	4	9
Maria's Mon, Dead	191	99	4	6
Put It Back, Fl.	122	75	4	7
Seeking the Gold, Ky.	130	67	4	4
Stormy Atlantic, Ky.	246	130	4	5
Stuka, Chi	120	68	4	9
◆Van Nistelrooy, Ky.	69	27	4	4

Leading Sires by Number of Grade 1 Stakes Winners in 2007

Sire	Strs	Wnrs	G1SWs	G1SWins
Honour and Glory, Ky.	313	154	4	5
Street Cry (Ire), Ky.	132	50	4	6
Awesome Again, Ky.	159	79	3	5
Bernstein, Ky.	187	84	3	4
Distorted Humor, Ky.	271	129	3	3
Kingmambo, Ky.	178	64	3	3
Langfuhr, Ky.	361	181	3	5
Roy, Dead	136	66	3	3
Smart Strike, Ky.	214	102	3	7
A.P. Indy, Ky.	172	80	2	5
Broken Vow, Ky.	180	109	2	2
Danzig, Dead	61	35	2	2
Dynaformer, Ky.	187	86	2	2
Elusive Quality, Ky.	244	116	2	2
Jules, Dead	76	39	2	2
Lemon Drop Kid, Ky.	174	85	2	2
Mr. Greeley, Ky.	198	94	2	4
Orientate, Ky.	142	71	2	2
Pulpit, Ky.	165	82	2	2
Put It Back, Fl.	131	81	2	2
Real Quiet, Pa.	158	76	2	3
Slew Gin Fizz, Arg	197	88	2	3
Theatrical (Ire), Ky.	87	32	2	3
Unbridled's Song, Ky.	171	86	2	3

Leading Juvenile Sires by Progeny Earnings in 2007

Worldwide earnings for stallions who stood in North America in year of conception of two-year-olds of 2007.
◆ Denotes freshman sire.

Sire	Strs	Wnrs	SWs	Leading Earner (Earnings)	Total Earnings
Cherokee Run, Ky.	44	19	2	War Pass ($1,397,400)	$2,200,756
Indian Charlie, Ky.	24	14	3	Indian Blessing ($1,357,200)	2,012,401
◆Posse, Ky.	42	23	7	Kodiak Kowboy ($544,825)	1,753,807
◆Harlan's Holiday, Ky.	54	23	5	Into Mischief ($448,800)	1,697,898
Tale of the Cat, Ky.	68	27	3	Tale of Ekati ($313,200)	1,535,071
◆Proud Citizen, Ky.	51	19	3	Proud Spell ($608,770)	1,430,219
Distorted Humor, Ky.	47	17	1	Z Humor ($543,700)	1,401,415
Pulpit, Ky.	53	16	2	Pyro ($516,718)	1,393,588
More Than Ready, Ky.	65	24	3	Ready's Image ($259,422)	1,372,334
Malibu Moon, Ky.	54	26	2	By the Light ($451,815)	1,345,769
◆Van Nistelrooy, Ky.	59	23	5	Strike the Deal ($267,665)	1,327,300
Fusaichi Pegasus, Ky.	73	20	1	Saki to Me ($114,000)	1,278,459
Mr. Greeley, Ky.	27	11	2	Saoirse Abu ($579,940)	1,247,193
Officer, Ky.	45	20	3	Apollo Dolce ($444,277)	1,228,231
◆Macho Uno, Ky.	32	16	2	Wicked Style ($445,000)	1,150,566
Dixie Union, Ky.	39	14	2	Turf War ($518,548)	1,146,317
Mizzen Mast, Ky.	54	23	3	C J's Leelee ($120,023)	1,106,235
◆Whywhywhy, Ky.	36	11	2	Nownownow ($641,950)	1,073,613
Bernstein, Ky.	33	13	1	Goshawk Ken ($650,439)	1,048,484
◆Empire Maker, Ky.	25	8	3	Country Star ($575,900)	1,031,923
Doneraile Court, Ky.	68	29	4	Doneraile Gem ($115,409)	1,023,394
Kingmambo, Ky.	40	10	3	Thewayyouare ($314,432)	988,215
◆Hold That Tiger, Vic.	75	23	2	Old Man Buck ($228,312)	984,271
Grand Slam, Ky.	59	20	1	Grand Minstrel ($101,350)	979,822
Storm Cat, Ky.	41	17	3	You'resothrilling ($208,740)	971,048
Hennessy, Dead	47	19	6	Mousse Au Chocolat ($111,791)	962,470
Trippi, Fl.	45	19	1	Sok Sok ($179,043)	953,061
◆Vindication, Ky.	53	19	1	More Happy ($129,300)	951,254
Smart Strike, Ky.	58	18	1	Smarty Deb ($171,055)	931,154
Yonaguska, Ky.	56	25	2	Yonagucci ($112,545)	925,715
Bold Executive, On.	27	11	2	Krz Exec ($215,902)	922,052
Stormy Atlantic, Ky.	58	20	3	Maya's Storm ($126,099)	892,244
Langfuhr, Ky.	45	17	1	Daiwa Mach One ($387,323)	887,352
◆Kafwain, Ky.	34	14	4	Massive Drama ($199,200)	866,768
A.P. Indy, Ky.	29	12	1	Majestic Warrior ($195,200)	865,246
Broken Vow, Ky.	56	25	0	Mighty Vow ($130,488)	859,748
Jump Start, Ky.	50	19	2	Mrs. Began ($184,801)	857,773
Thunder Gulch, Ky.	30	10	1	Iide Kenshin ($526,217)	855,301
El Corredor, Ky.	40	13	1	Backseat Rhythm ($316,760)	850,204
E Dubai, Ky.	43	17	1	Treadmill ($132,000)	847,825
◆D'wildcat, Fl.	25	7	2	Authenticat ($190,216)	842,377
Forest Wildcat, Ky.	37	12	3	Salute the Sarge ($286,540)	841,869
Tiznow, Ky.	47	14	1	Colonel John ($255,300)	836,567
Johannesburg, Ky.	76	21	1	Jupiter Pluvius ($84,199)	834,289
Exchange Rate, Ky.	36	12	3	Rated Fiesty ($204,291)	822,391
Carson City, Dead	40	13	3	Kesagami ($199,428)	810,735
Victory Gallop, Tur	42	14	3	Anak Nakal ($220,916)	807,103
Eltish, N.Y.	32	16	1	Silk Ridge ($369,240)	799,597
Three Wonders, Fl.	37	16	1	Calico Bay ($331,300)	789,048
Cat Thief, Ky.	51	18	1	A Shin Commander ($79,364)	782,820
City Zip, Ky.	32	16	1	Canadian Ballet ($148,862)	766,846
Smoke Glacken, Ky.	35	11	4	Irish Smoke ($187,200)	762,663
Giant's Causeway, Ky.	44	13	2	Giant Moon ($135,870)	759,499
◆Yankee Gentleman, Ky.	41	15	2	Golden Yank ($264,832)	719,602
Songandaprayer, Ky.	33	14	2	Preachin Man ($229,614)	718,106
◆Repent, Fl.	44	18	2	Check It Twice ($144,500)	714,181
Valid Expectations, Tx.	31	19	3	Valid Lilly ($213,406)	713,980
Silver Deputy, Ky.	34	13	2	Deputiformer ($208,486)	712,797
Menifee, Unknown	33	17	0	A to the Croft ($210,018)	711,899
Street Cry (Ire), Ky.	49	10	2	Cry and Catch Me ($191,000)	709,147
Yes It's True, Ky.	52	20	2	Asi Asi ($81,030)	705,606
Orientate, Ky.	41	18	2	Gipson Dessert ($132,799)	678,533
Montbrook, Fl.	33	14	2	Phantom Income ($153,200)	673,497
Rahy, Ky.	23	8	1	Rio de La Plata ($493,714)	641,171
◆Mineshaft, Ky.	26	9	1	La Mina ($147,601)	640,161

Leading Juvenile Sires by Average Earnings per Starter in 2007
Minimum of 10 Starters

Sire	Strs	Wnrs	Average
Indian Charlie, Ky.	24	14	$83,850
Wised Up, Fl.	10	4	58,165
Cherokee Run, Ky.	44	19	50,017
Mr. Greeley, Ky.	27	11	46,192
◆Posse, Ky.	42	23	41,757
◆Empire Maker, Ky.	25	8	41,277
◆Macho Uno, Ky.	32	16	35,955
Bold Executive, On.	27	11	34,150
◆D'wildcat, Fl.	25	7	33,695
War Chant, Ky.	16	5	32,777
Bernstein, Ky.	33	13	31,772
◆Harlan's Holiday, Ky.	54	23	31,443
Precise End, Jpn	19	8	30,065
In Excess (Ire), Ca.	17	6	30,003
A.P. Indy, Ky.	29	12	29,836
Bertrando, Ca.	18	10	29,828
◆Whywhywhy, Ky.	36	11	29,823
Distorted Humor, Ky.	47	17	29,817
Dixie Union, Ky.	39	14	29,393
Snow Ridge, Pa.	15	11	28,897
Tethra, On.	12	5	28,523

Leading Juvenile Sires by Median Earnings per Starter in 2007
Minimum of 10 Starters

Sire	Strs	Wnrs	Median
Snow Ridge, Pa.	15	11	$21,200
Cape Canaveral, Ab.	25	14	17,580
Indian Charlie, Ky.	24	14	16,294
Erlton, La.	14	8	16,008
Vision and Verse, Ky.	10	6	15,300
Maria's Mon, Dead	23	10	14,971
Ciano Cat, On.	15	6	14,797
Freud, N.Y.	23	8	13,984
Bertrando, Ca.	18	10	13,730
Tethra, On.	12	5	13,412
◆Posse, Ky.	42	23	13,380
Seeking the Gold, Ky.	26	14	13,094
Gibson County, Fl.	11	8	12,679
City Zip, Ky.	32	16	12,462
Sefapiano, La.	10	3	12,122
Meadowlake, Dead	11	7	12,000
Outflanker, Md.	26	13	11,927
Bold Executive, On.	27	11	11,819
Successful Appeal, Ky.	30	13	11,672
Catienus, Ky.	24	12	11,587
A.P. Indy, Ky.	29	12	11,498

Leading Juvenile Sires by Number of Winners in 2007

Sire	Strs	Wnrs	Wnrs/Strs
Doneraile Court, Ky.	68	29	42.6%
Tale of the Cat, Ky.	68	27	39.7%
Malibu Moon, Ky.	54	26	48.1%
Broken Vow, Ky.	56	25	44.6%
Yonaguska, Ky.	56	25	44.6%
More Than Ready, Ky.	65	24	36.9%
◆Harlan's Holiday, Ky.	54	23	42.6%
◆Hold That Tiger, Vic.	75	23	30.7%
Mizzen Mast, Ky.	54	23	42.6%
◆Posse, Ky.	42	23	54.8%
◆Van Nistelrooy, Ky.	59	23	39.0%
Johannesburg, Ky.	76	21	27.6%
◆Sunday Break (Jpn), Ky.	53	21	39.6%
Fusaichi Pegasus, Ky.	73	20	27.4%
Grand Slam, Ky.	59	20	33.9%
Officer, Ky.	45	20	44.4%
Stormy Atlantic, Ky.	58	20	34.5%
Yes It's True, Ky.	52	20	38.5%
Cherokee Run, Ky.	44	19	43.2%
Hennessy, Dead	47	19	40.4%
Jump Start, Ky.	50	19	38.0%
◆Proud Citizen, Ky.	51	19	37.3%
Trippi, Fl.	45	19	42.2%
Valid Expectations, Tx.	31	19	61.3%
◆Vindication, Ky.	53	19	35.8%

Leading Juvenile Sires by Number of Wins in 2007

Sire	Strs	Wnrs	Wins
Doneraile Court, Ky.	68	29	42
Malibu Moon, Ky.	54	26	39
◆Posse, Ky.	42	23	39
Tale of the Cat, Ky.	68	27	36
More Than Ready, Ky.	65	24	32
◆Van Nistelrooy, Ky.	59	23	32
Yonaguska, Ky.	56	25	31
◆Hold That Tiger, Vic.	75	23	30
Mizzen Mast, Ky.	54	23	30
Trippi, Fl.	45	19	30
◆Harlan's Holiday, Ky.	54	23	29
Broken Vow, Ky.	56	25	28
Officer, Ky.	45	20	28
Double Honor, Fl.	33	17	27
Hennessy, Dead	47	19	27
Cherokee Run, Ky.	44	19	26
Eltish, N.Y.	32	16	26
Johannesburg, Ky.	76	21	26
Stormy Atlantic, Ky.	58	20	26
◆Repent, Fl.	44	18	25
Valid Expectations, Tx.	31	19	25

Leading Juvenile Sires by Number of Stakes Winners in 2007

Sire	Strs	Wnrs	SWs	SWins
◆Posse, Ky.	42	23	7	11
Hennessy, Dead	47	19	6	6
◆Harlan's Holiday, Ky.	54	23	5	6
◆Van Nistelrooy, Ky.	59	23	5	5
Doneraile Court, Ky.	68	29	4	4
Evansville Slew, Ok.	17	10	4	4
◆Kafwain, Ky.	34	14	4	7
Smoke Glacken, Ky.	35	11	4	4
Carson City, Dead	40	13	3	3
Chimes Band, Dead	28	8	3	3
◆Empire Maker, Ky.	25	8	3	4
Exchange Rate, Ky.	36	12	3	5
Forest Wildcat, Ky.	37	12	3	4
Indian Charlie, Ky.	24	14	3	4
In Excess (Ire), Ca.	17	6	3	4
Kingmambo, Ky.	40	10	3	6
Marquetry, Ky.	17	7	3	3
Mizzen Mast, Ky.	54	23	3	3
More Than Ready, Ky.	65	24	3	5
Not For Love, Md.	29	8	3	4
Officer, Ky.	45	20	3	4
◆Proud Citizen, Ky.	51	19	3	4
Storm Cat, Ky.	41	17	3	5
Stormy Atlantic, Ky.	58	20	3	4
Tale of the Cat, Ky.	68	27	3	3
Valid Expectations, Tx.	31	19	3	4
Victory Gallop, Tur	42	14	3	3
◆Volponi, Unknown	25	12	3	3

Leading Juvenile Sires by Number of Graded Stakes Winners in 2007

Sire	Strs	Wnrs	GSWs	GSWins
◆Van Nistelrooy, Ky.	59	23	4	4
Kingmambo, Ky.	40	10	3	4
Dixie Union, Ky.	39	14	2	2
◆Empire Maker, Ky.	25	8	2	3
◆Harlan's Holiday, Ky.	54	23	2	2
◆Posse, Ky.	42	23	2	3
◆Proud Citizen, Ky.	51	19	2	2
Storm Cat, Ky.	41	17	2	3
Street Cry (Ire), Ky.	49	10	2	4
Victory Gallop, Tur	42	14	2	2
◆Volponi, Unknown	25	12	2	2
War Chant, Ky.	16	5	2	2

Leading Freshman Sires by Progeny Earnings in 2007

Worldwide earnings for stallions who stood in North America in year of conception of two-year-olds of 2007.
◆ Denotes freshman sire.

Sire	Strs	Wnrs	SWs	Leading Earner (Earnings)	Total Earnings
◆Posse, Ky.	42	23	7	Kodiak Kowboy ($544,825)	$1,753,807
◆Harlan's Holiday, Ky.	54	23	5	Into Mischief ($448,800)	1,697,898
◆Van Nistelrooy, Ky.	70	28	6	Strike the Deal ($267,665)	1,496,719
◆Proud Citizen, Ky.	51	19	3	Proud Spell ($608,770)	1,430,219
◆Macho Uno, Ky.	32	16	2	Wicked Style ($445,000)	1,150,566
◆Whywhywhy, Ky.	36	11	2	Nownownow ($641,950)	1,073,613
◆Empire Maker, Ky.	25	8	3	Country Star ($575,900)	1,031,923
◆Hold That Tiger, Vic.	75	23	2	Old Man Buck ($228,312)	984,271
◆Vindication, Ky.	53	19	1	More Happy ($129,300)	951,254
◆Kafwain, Ky.	34	14	4	Massive Drama ($199,200)	866,768
◆D'wildcat, Fl.	25	7	2	Authenicat ($190,216)	842,377
◆Yankee Gentleman, Ky.	41	15	2	Golden Yank ($264,832)	719,602
◆Repent, Fl.	44	18	2	Check It Twice ($144,500)	714,181
◆Mineshaft, Ky.	26	9	1	La Mina ($147,601)	640,161
◆Hook and Ladder, N.Y.	26	8	2	Spanky Fischbein ($161,595)	630,489
◆Sunday Break (Jpn), Ky.	53	21	0	Sunday Holiday ($98,356)	613,036
◆Flatter, Ky.	42	17	1	Indy's Alexandra ($88,100)	575,215
◆Cactus Ridge, Ky.	37	13	0	Senor ($105,443)	537,706
◆Volponi, Unknown	25	12	3	Clearly Foxy ($119,482)	527,734
◆Sky Mesa, Ky.	43	12	0	Cozy Mesa ($73,002)	515,932
◆Aldebaran, Ky.	25	9	0	Danon Go Go ($140,936)	482,336
◆Milwaukee Brew, Fl.	38	14	0	Salomea ($84,572)	468,543
◆Full Mandate, Fl.	46	12	1	Thoroughly ($58,725)	392,191
◆Drewman, Fl.	26	11	0	Cigar Man ($105,200)	373,281
◆Trust N Luck, Fl.	32	9	1	Wonderful Luck ($98,846)	370,440
◆Sligo Bay (Ire), Fl.	27	9	1	Wind in My Wings ($133,308)	363,869
◆Changeintheweather, Pa.	28	11	1	Cold Trial ($40,820)	325,054
◆Equality, Mi.	15	9	1	Equalitysdebutante ($118,086)	318,681
◆Early Flyer, Tx.	13	9	1	Ferdinand's Flyer ($95,200)	313,410
◆Decarchy, Ca.	17	7	1	Timehascometoday ($73,998)	289,243
◆Gulf Storm, Fl.	37	11	2	Ogygian's Storm ($52,191)	286,207
◆Zavata, Ky.	25	13	0	Good Direction ($34,442)	278,071
◆Polish Gift, Dead	9	3	1	Margo's Gift ($243,714)	269,885
◆Najran, Ky.	31	8	0	Sky Cape ($84,180)	264,699
◆Premeditation, N.M.	3	3	2	Run Like Fire ($190,092)	264,355
◆Smooth Jazz, N.Y.	17	9	0	Smooth Air ($75,500)	243,553
◆Greatness, Fl.	19	8	0	Immortal Eyes ($42,300)	242,044
◆Wiseman's Ferry, Ky.	31	6	0	Fort Drum ($50,943)	223,316
◆Finality, B.C.	13	5	2	Remarkable Miss ($79,691)	219,898
◆Awesome of Course, Fl.	5	3	1	Honey Honey Honey ($145,000)	212,918
◆Desert Warrior, N.Y.	13	7	0	Run Warrior Run ($68,550)	212,590
◆Sudden Thunder, P.R.	26	11	0	La Avispa Pica ($41,084)	196,452
◆Stormy Jack, Ca.	8	5	1	Bob Black Jack ($131,425)	193,270
◆Pure Precision, Fl.	18	9	0	Predate ($40,754)	192,407
◆Authenticate, La.	20	9	0	Dr. Nick ($57,127)	179,342
◆Shore Breeze, Ky.	15	6	0	Grand Obsession ($38,700)	169,480
◆Seeking Daylight, Md.	15	7	0	Pit Lizard ($48,374)	167,016
◆Indy King, Fl.	7	3	0	Indy O. ($74,721)	163,546
◆Mayakovsky, N.Y.	9	3	0	Alexandros ($56,400)	162,321
◆Best of the Rest, Fl.	7	6	0	Hidden Wish ($47,370)	150,580
◆Rock Slide, Md.	12	2	0	Happy Hailey ($56,320)	141,703
◆Essence of Dubai, Fl.	24	9	0	Stephaningrid ($21,875)	138,542
◆Capsized, Ca.	13	4	0	Maxie's Night Cap ($26,615)	125,921
◆Easyfromthegitgo, La.	9	3	0	Peachsfromthegitgo ($38,850)	125,578
◆Ghostly Minister, W.V.	5	1	1	Ghostly Thunder ($109,158)	124,708
◆Agnes Gold (Jpn), Fl.	7	0	0	Cosmo Zagaria ($36,070)	115,770
◆A. P. Delta, La.	7	1	1	Delta Vixen ($81,400)	115,206
◆David Copperfield, Ky.	8	4	0	Hunterbunter ($33,680)	111,913
◆Paynes Bay, On.	14	3	0	Corossol ($34,373)	111,641
◆Gotham City, Ca.	9	1	0	Commissioner Gordon ($55,102)	111,187
◆Lido Palace (Chi), Fl.	23	3	0	Delayed Start ($24,450)	110,252
◆Crafty C. T., Ca.	8	3	1	C. T. Phone Home ($41,400)	108,930
◆Lightnin N Thunder, Fl.	12	4	0	Always Enchanting ($54,600)	108,652
◆Father Steve, Ar.	7	4	0	Prince Steve ($30,990)	106,498
◆Century City (Ire), Ky.	14	2	0	Joannie Not Jo ($55,299)	99,524

Leading Freshman Sires by Average Earnings per Starter in 2007
Minimum of 10 Starters

Sire	Strs	Wnrs	Average
◆Posse, Ky.	42	23	$41,757
◆Empire Maker, Ky.	25	8	41,277
◆Macho Uno, Ky.	32	16	35,955
◆D'wildcat, Fl.	25	7	33,695
◆Harlan's Holiday, Ky.	54	23	31,443
◆Whywhywhy, Ky.	36	11	29,823
◆Proud Citizen, Ky.	51	19	28,044
◆Kafwain, Ky.	34	14	25,493
◆Mineshaft, Ky.	26	9	24,622
◆Hook and Ladder, N.Y.	26	8	24,250
◆Early Flyer, Tx.	13	9	24,108
◆Van Nistelrooy, Ky.	70	28	21,382
◆Equality, Mi.	15	9	21,245
◆Volponi, Unknown	25	12	21,109
◆Aldebaran, Ky.	25	9	19,293
◆Vindication, Ky.	53	19	17,948
◆Yankee Gentleman, Ky.	41	15	17,551
◆Decarchy, Ca.	17	7	17,014
◆Finality, B.C.	13	5	16,915
◆Desert Warrior, N.Y.	13	7	16,353
◆Repent, Fl.	44	18	16,231
◆Cactus Ridge, Ky.	37	13	14,533
◆Drewman, Fl.	26	11	14,357
◆Smooth Jazz, N.Y.	17	9	14,327
◆Flatter, Ky.	42	17	13,696
◆Sligo Bay (Ire), Fl.	27	9	13,477
◆Hold That Tiger, Vic.	75	23	13,124
◆Greatness, Fl.	19	8	12,739
◆Milwaukee Brew, Fl.	38	14	12,330

Leading Freshman Sires by Median Earnings per Starter in 2007
Minimum of 10 Starters

Sire	Strs	Wnrs	Median
◆Posse, Ky.	42	23	$13,380
◆Equality, Mi.	15	9	10,906
◆Macho Uno, Ky.	32	16	10,791
◆Desert Warrior, N.Y.	13	7	10,458
◆Early Flyer, Tx.	13	9	10,200
◆Harlan's Holiday, Ky.	54	23	10,000
◆Hook and Ladder, N.Y.	26	8	9,829
◆Greatness, Fl.	19	8	8,200
◆Zavata, Ky.	25	13	7,950
◆D'wildcat, Fl.	25	7	7,591
◆Volponi, Unknown	25	12	7,505
◆Changeintheweather, Pa.	28	11	7,450
◆Seeking Daylight, Md.	15	7	7,320
◆Pure Precision, Fl.	18	9	7,300
◆Repent, Fl.	44	18	6,955
◆Decarchy, Ca.	17	7	6,818
◆Drewman, Fl.	26	11	6,761
◆Vindication, Ky.	53	19	6,718
◆Flatter, Ky.	42	17	6,408
◆Shore Breeze, Ky.	15	6	6,245
◆Milwaukee Brew, Fl.	38	14	6,080
◆Capsized, Ca.	13	4	6,030
◆Sunday Break (Jpn), Ky.	53	21	5,890
◆Empire Maker, Ky.	25	8	5,600
◆Sudden Thunder, P.R.	26	11	5,583
◆Avanzado (Arg), Ca.	10	3	5,540

Leading Freshman Sires by Number of Winners in 2007

Sire	Strs	Wnrs	Wnrs/Strs
◆Van Nistelrooy, Ky.	70	28	40.0%
◆Harlan's Holiday, Ky.	54	23	42.6%
◆Hold That Tiger, Vic.	75	23	30.7%
◆Posse, Ky.	42	23	54.8%
◆Sunday Break (Jpn), Ky.	53	21	39.6%
◆Proud Citizen, Ky.	51	19	37.3%
◆Vindication, Ky.	53	19	35.8%
◆Repent, Fl.	44	18	40.9%
◆Flatter, Ky.	42	17	40.5%
◆Macho Uno, Ky.	32	16	50.0%
◆Yankee Gentleman, Ky.	41	15	36.6%
◆Kafwain, Ky.	34	14	41.2%
◆Milwaukee Brew, Fl.	38	14	36.8%
◆Cactus Ridge, Ky.	37	13	35.1%
◆Zavata, Ky.	25	13	52.0%
◆Full Mandate, Fl.	46	12	26.1%
◆Sky Mesa, Ky.	43	12	27.9%
◆Volponi, Unknown	25	12	48.0%
◆Changeintheweather, Pa.	28	11	39.3%
◆Drewman, Fl.	26	11	42.3%
◆Gulf Storm, Fl.	37	11	29.7%
◆Sudden Thunder, P.R.	26	11	42.3%
◆Whywhywhy, Ky.	36	11	30.6%

Leading Freshman Sires by Number of Wins in 2007

Sire	Strs	Wnrs	Wins
◆Posse, Ky.	42	23	39
◆Van Nistelrooy, Ky.	70	28	38
◆Hold That Tiger, Vic.	75	23	30
◆Harlan's Holiday, Ky.	54	23	29
◆Repent, Fl.	44	18	25
◆Sunday Break (Jpn), Ky.	53	21	24
◆Proud Citizen, Ky.	51	19	23
◆Kafwain, Ky.	34	14	22
◆Macho Uno, Ky.	32	16	22
◆Vindication, Ky.	53	19	22
◆Flatter, Ky.	42	17	21
◆Yankee Gentleman, Ky.	41	15	20
◆Full Mandate, Fl.	46	12	19
◆Volponi, Unknown	25	12	19
◆Cactus Ridge, Ky.	37	13	18
◆Gulf Storm, Fl.	37	11	18
◆Sudden Thunder, P.R.	26	11	18
◆Whywhywhy, Ky.	36	11	18
◆Milwaukee Brew, Fl.	38	14	15
◆Zavata, Ky.	25	13	15
◆Mineshaft, Ky.	26	9	14
◆Sky Mesa, Ky.	43	12	14
◆Pure Precision, Fl.	18	9	13
◆Sligo Bay (Ire), Fl.	27	9	13
◆Trust N Luck, Fl.	32	9	13

Leading Freshman Sires by Number of Stakes Winners in 2007

Sire	Strs	Wnrs	SWs	SWins
◆Posse, Ky.	42	23	7	11
◆Van Nistelrooy, Ky.	70	28	6	6
◆Harlan's Holiday, Ky.	54	23	5	6
◆Kafwain, Ky.	34	14	4	7
◆Empire Maker, Ky.	25	8	3	4
◆Proud Citizen, Ky.	51	19	3	4
◆Volponi, Unknown	25	12	3	3
◆D'wildcat, Fl.	25	7	2	2
◆Finality, B.C.	13	5	2	2
◆Gulf Storm, Fl.	37	11	2	2
◆Hold That Tiger, Vic.	75	23	2	3
◆Hook and Ladder, N.Y.	26	8	2	2
◆Macho Uno, Ky.	32	16	2	4
◆Premeditation, N.M.	3	3	2	3
◆Repent, Fl.	44	18	2	2
◆Whywhywhy, Ky.	36	11	2	5
◆Yankee Gentleman, Ky.	41	15	2	3

Leading Freshman Sires by Number of Graded Stakes Winners in 2007

Sire	Strs	Wnrs	GSWs	GSWins
◆Van Nistelrooy, Ky.	70	28	4	4
◆Empire Maker, Ky.	25	8	2	3
◆Harlan's Holiday, Ky.	54	23	2	2
◆Posse, Ky.	42	23	2	3
◆Proud Citizen, Ky.	51	19	2	2
◆Volponi, Unknown	25	12	2	2

Leading Broodmare Sires by Progeny Earnings in 2007

Worldwide earnings for broodmare sires who stand or last stood in North America or had 60 or more North American starters in 2007.

Sire	Strs	Wnrs	SWs	Leading Earner (Earnings)	Total Earnings
Woodman, Dead	689	268	20	Aston Machan ($1,307,902)	$19,724,483
Deputy Minister, Dead	427	215	18	Curlin ($5,102,800)	18,546,427
Mr. Prospector, Dead	492	203	19	War Pass ($1,397,400)	17,979,963
Storm Cat, Ky.	467	217	23	Nobiz Like Shobiz ($1,318,330)	17,343,572
Sadler's Wells, Ire	618	214	25	Youmzain ($1,545,300)	16,906,795
Dixieland Band, Ky.	458	221	22	Street Sense ($3,205,000)	16,598,734
Danzig, Dead	418	179	20	Daring Heart ($587,414)	15,013,988
Seeking the Gold, Ky.	329	158	18	Robe Decollete ($1,376,264)	13,681,802
Nureyev, Dead	375	162	12	Fusaichi Pandora ($1,100,132)	11,969,664
Miswaki, Dead	418	196	11	My Typhoon (Ire) ($639,000)	10,352,285
Kris S., Dead	366	164	9	Eishin Dover ($1,107,208)	10,228,465
A.P. Indy, Ky.	238	115	11	Zanjero ($1,060,977)	10,029,530
Forty Niner, Jpn	291	149	16	Lady of Venice (Fr) ($835,272)	9,933,684
Theatrical (Ire), Ky.	331	122	11	English Channel ($2,640,000)	9,779,817
Seattle Slew, Dead	383	169	13	Circuit Lady ($272,217)	9,469,536
Gulch, Ky.	303	134	9	Lawman ($1,538,005)	9,448,490
Diesis (GB), Dead	304	137	10	Dylan Thomas (Ire) ($4,116,100)	9,425,962
Royal Academy, Ky.	439	172	13	Finsceal Beo ($844,219)	9,207,676
Rahy, Ky.	337	172	11	After Market ($686,725)	8,924,571
Crafty Prospector, Pens	372	194	9	Agnes Jedi ($570,605)	8,537,238
Affirmed, Dead	337	157	6	Honey Ryder ($740,850)	8,236,665
Wild Again, Pens	356	174	14	Pyro ($516,718)	8,098,157
Storm Bird, Dead	337	160	12	Continent ($369,985)	8,007,159
Red Ransom, Eng	309	148	11	Marchfield ($371,524)	7,903,865
Capote, Dead	296	157	11	Ferrari Pisa ($687,115)	7,903,761
Gone West, Ky.	369	162	8	Pipedreamer ($356,076)	7,775,762
Valid Appeal, Dead	305	176	11	Vacare ($377,856)	7,657,558
Pleasant Colony, Dead	302	144	12	Kinshasa no Kiseki ($614,319)	7,520,997
Dynaformer, Ky.	272	139	16	Spring At Last ($722,000)	7,507,253
Conquistador Cielo, Dead	342	160	10	Sky Conqueror ($827,043)	7,472,369
Devil's Bag, Dead	346	167	7	Teuflesberg ($464,050)	7,246,877
Relaunch, Dead	325	173	17	Storm in May ($405,181)	7,233,773
Mt. Livermore, Dead	354	162	12	Flashy Bull ($635,063)	7,104,392
Silver Hawk, Pens	235	92	12	Tokai Trick ($1,131,478)	7,077,846
Broad Brush, Pens	282	146	9	Dreaming of Anna ($391,932)	7,072,993
Carson City, Dead	274	158	7	Eishin Lombard ($736,183)	7,056,910
Afleet, Jpn	293	114	3	Sachino Sweetie ($505,363)	7,048,445
Cure the Blues, Dead	340	174	5	Rolling Sea ($361,081)	6,990,128
Meadowlake, Dead	297	139	14	I'll Love Again ($842,865)	6,827,926
Private Account, Dead	264	121	6	Panty Raid ($1,024,180)	6,800,669
Kingmambo, Ky.	196	85	8	Red Giant ($846,720)	6,659,169
El Gran Senor, Dead	196	93	6	Ramonti ($2,574,626)	6,527,431
Unbridled, Dead	239	110	9	Lady Joanne ($808,993)	6,325,929
Lord At War (Arg), Dead	184	91	10	Citronnade ($701,405)	5,945,926
Silver Deputy, Ky.	266	153	7	Miraculous Miss ($371,300)	5,939,830
Dehere, Ky.	212	99	6	Midnight Lute ($1,368,000)	5,939,498
Cozzene, Ky.	234	118	9	River's Prayer ($610,175)	5,560,902
Irish River (Fr), Dead	323	121	9	Listen ($412,709)	5,557,161
Phone Trick, Dead	321	153	5	Silk Dragoon ($306,347)	5,545,624
Alydar, Dead	212	91	7	Asaka Defeat ($712,829)	5,515,325
Known Fact, Dead	239	98	6	Cockney Rebel ($736,490)	5,514,577
Clever Trick, Dead	340	146	10	Ready's Image ($259,422)	5,507,309
Black Tie Affair (Ire), W.V.	273	132	6	Takara True ($291,772)	5,460,850
With Approval, Eng	189	104	10	Twilight Meteor ($348,816)	5,165,401
Halo, Dead	269	110	2	Bwana Bull ($473,920)	5,136,222
Turkoman, Ca.	144	62	10	Hard Spun ($2,572,500)	5,112,724
Nijinsky II, Dead	179	69	5	Clean ($426,076)	5,059,381
Majestic Light, Dead	229	82	5	Excuse ($783,984)	4,995,782
Dayjur, Ky.	208	84	8	Diabolical ($354,750)	4,896,482
Regal Classic, Pens	221	113	11	Lila Paige ($291,100)	4,876,418
Ogygian, Pens	182	79	2	Sun Zeppelin ($937,128)	4,867,794
Bold Ruckus, Dead	234	112	8	Paradise Dancer ($255,800)	4,802,322
Vice Regent, Dead	212	94	5	Jambalaya ($979,421)	4,794,292
Chief's Crown, Dead	262	100	4	Hishikatsu Leader ($405,293)	4,780,841
Alysheba, KSA	169	67	6	Purple Moon ($1,044,903)	4,632,988

Leading Broodmare Sires by Average Earnings per Starter in 2007
Minimum of 25 Starters

Sire	Strs	Wnrs	Average
Thirty Six Red, Dead	72	39	$44,643
Deputy Minister, Dead	427	215	43,434
A.P. Indy, Ky.	238	115	42,141
French Deputy, Jpn	76	54	41,895
Seeking the Gold, Ky.	329	158	41,586
Pleasant Tap, Ky.	99	50	37,299
Storm Cat, Ky.	467	217	37,138
Mr. Prospector, Dead	492	203	36,545
Dixieland Band, Ky.	458	221	36,242
Danzig, Dead	418	179	35,919
Turkoman, Ca.	144	62	35,505
Baldski, Dead	87	41	34,989
Great Above, Dead	128	63	34,431
Forty Niner, Jpn	291	149	34,136
Kingmambo, Ky.	196	85	33,975
Boundary, Pens	94	51	33,414
El Gran Senor, Dead	196	93	33,303
Jolie's Halo, Dead	99	47	32,429
Lord At War (Arg), Dead	184	91	32,315
Nureyev, Dead	375	162	31,919
Gulch, Ky.	303	134	31,183
Polish Navy, Ky.	102	51	31,054
Diesis (GB), Dead	304	137	31,006
Silver Hawk, Pens	235	92	30,118
Theatrical (Ire), Ky.	331	122	29,546

Leading Broodmare Sires by Median Earnings per Starter in 2007
Minimum of 25 Starters

Sire	Strs	Wnrs	Median
French Deputy, Jpn	76	54	$16,527
A.P. Indy, Ky.	238	115	14,244
With Approval, Eng	189	104	13,732
Horatius, Dead	97	52	13,725
Boundary, Pens	94	51	13,606
Seeking the Gold, Ky.	329	158	13,501
Diablo, Jpn	97	55	12,327
Forty Niner, Jpn	291	149	12,300
Silver Deputy, Ky.	266	153	12,295
Country Pine, Dead	68	41	12,238
Broad Brush, Pens	282	146	12,121
Valid Appeal, Dead	305	176	12,044
Deputy Minister, Dead	427	215	12,030
Rubiano, Dead	170	90	11,890
Carson City, Dead	274	158	11,874
Olympio, Ca.	93	49	11,780
Lord At War (Arg), Dead	184	91	11,765
Storm Cat, Ky.	467	217	11,751
Waquoit, Dead	104	49	11,730
Hold Your Peace, Dead	62	36	11,633
Notebook, Dead	148	82	11,520
Rahy, Ky.	337	172	11,383
Kingmambo, Ky.	196	85	11,025
Eastern Echo, Dead	98	41	11,008

Leading Broodmare Sires by Number of Winners in 2007

Sire	Strs	Wnrs	Wnrs/Strs
Woodman, Dead	689	268	38.9%
Dixieland Band, Ky.	458	221	48.3%
Storm Cat, Ky.	467	217	46.5%
Deputy Minister, Dead	427	215	50.4%
Sadler's Wells, Ire	618	214	34.6%
Mr. Prospector, Dead	492	203	41.3%
Miswaki, Dead	418	196	46.9%
Crafty Prospector, Pens	372	194	52.2%
Danzig, Dead	418	179	42.8%
Valid Appeal, Dead	305	176	57.7%
Cure the Blues, Dead	340	174	51.2%
Wild Again, Pens	356	174	48.9%
Relaunch, Dead	325	173	53.2%
Rahy, Ky.	337	172	51.0%
Royal Academy, Ky.	439	172	39.2%
Seattle Slew, Dead	383	169	44.1%
Devil's Bag, Dead	346	167	48.3%
Southern Halo, Arg	353	166	47.0%
Kris S., Dead	366	164	44.8%
Gone West, Ky.	369	162	43.9%
Mt. Livermore, Dead	354	162	45.8%
Nureyev, Dead	375	162	43.2%
Conquistador Cielo, Dead	342	160	46.8%
Storm Bird, Dead	337	160	47.5%

Leading Broodmare Sires by Number of Wins in 2007

Sire	Strs	Wnrs	Wins
Woodman, Dead	689	268	439
Dixieland Band, Ky.	458	221	380
Deputy Minister, Dead	427	215	364
Storm Cat, Ky.	467	217	360
Crafty Prospector, Pens	372	194	340
Mr. Prospector, Dead	492	203	329
Sadler's Wells, Ire	618	214	320
Miswaki, Dead	418	196	310
Relaunch, Dead	325	173	305
Danzig, Dead	418	179	302
Valid Appeal, Dead	305	176	299
Cure the Blues, Dead	340	174	288
Conquistador Cielo, Dead	342	160	284
Devil's Bag, Dead	346	167	283
Storm Bird, Dead	337	160	283
Rahy, Ky.	337	172	282
Kris S., Dead	366	164	276
Seattle Slew, Dead	383	169	272
Carson City, Dead	274	158	267
Gone West, Ky.	369	162	263
Wild Again, Pens	356	174	263
Red Ransom, Eng	309	148	260
Phone Trick, Dead	321	153	259

Leading Broodmare Sires by Number of Stakes Winners in 2007

Sire	Strs	Wnrs	SWs	SWins
Sadler's Wells, Ire	618	214	25	38
Storm Cat, Ky.	467	217	23	36
Dixieland Band, Ky.	458	221	22	34
Danzig, Dead	418	179	20	27
Woodman, Dead	689	268	20	29
Mr. Prospector, Dead	492	203	19	26
Deputy Minister, Dead	427	215	18	30
Seeking the Gold, Ky.	329	158	18	22
Relaunch, Dead	325	173	17	22
Dynaformer, Ky.	272	139	16	24
Forty Niner, Jpn	291	149	16	26
Meadowlake, Dead	297	139	14	17
Wild Again, Pens	356	174	14	23
Royal Academy, Ky.	439	172	13	17
Seattle Slew, Dead	383	169	13	14

Leading Broodmare Sires by Number of Graded Stakes Winners in 2007

Sire	Strs	Wnrs	GSWs	GSWins
Sadler's Wells, Ire	618	214	15	25
Mr. Prospector, Dead	492	203	11	15
Woodman, Dead	689	268	10	16
Dixieland Band, Ky.	458	221	9	14
Deputy Minister, Dead	427	215	8	16
Seeking the Gold, Ky.	329	158	8	10
Storm Cat, Ky.	467	217	8	15
Forty Niner, Jpn	291	149	7	10
A.P. Indy, Ky.	238	115	6	10
Danzig, Dead	418	179	6	7
Royal Academy, Ky.	439	172	6	7
Storm Bird, Dead	337	160	6	7
Capote, Dead	296	157	5	5
Diesis (GB), Dead	304	137	5	8
Irish River (Fr), Dead	323	121	5	9
Rahy, Ky.	337	172	5	14
Relaunch, Dead	325	173	5	6
Southern Halo, Arg	353	166	5	10

Leading Sires by Progeny Earnings in North America in 2007

Earnings in North America only for stallions represented by at least one starter in North America in 2007, regardless of where the stallion stands or stood.

Sire	Strs	Wnrs	SWs	Leading Earner (Earnings)	Total Earnings
Smart Strike, Ky.	201	96	15	Curlin ($5,102,800)	$14,189,337
A.P. Indy, Ky.	157	76	18	Rags to Riches ($1,340,028)	9,542,341
Distorted Humor, Ky.	214	104	19	Any Given Saturday ($994,320)	9,415,269
Langfuhr, Ky.	223	131	15	Lawyer Ron ($1,320,000)	8,503,038
Awesome Again, Ky.	149	77	11	Ginger Punch ($1,827,060)	7,508,749
Giant's Causeway, Ky.	145	72	14	Red Giant ($846,720)	7,325,921
Stormy Atlantic, Ky.	242	126	13	Icy Atlantic ($367,110)	6,348,881
Pulpit, Ky.	144	76	9	Corinthian ($1,174,173)	6,327,064
Cherokee Run, Ky.	169	102	9	War Pass ($1,397,400)	6,327,009
Unbridled's Song, Ky.	146	79	13	Octave ($1,050,234)	6,222,342
Broken Vow, Ky.	176	107	6	Unbridled Belle ($1,116,500)	6,066,358
Street Cry (Ire), Ky.	69	30	9	Street Sense ($3,205,000)	5,996,722
Lemon Drop Kid, Ky.	142	73	14	Citronnade ($701,405)	5,915,870
Tale of the Cat, Ky.	224	123	11	Tale of Ekati ($313,200)	5,879,234
Not For Love, Md.	176	99	11	Talkin About Love ($375,875)	5,774,874
Catienus, Ky.	159	102	8	Precious Kitten ($1,090,000)	5,569,097
Maria's Mon, Dead	184	97	9	Wait a While ($406,000)	5,319,533
Royal Academy, Ky.	166	81	14	Molengao (Brz) ($470,000)	5,134,416
Mutakddim, Ky.	206	126	5	Ravalo ($201,655)	5,109,832
Malibu Moon, Ky.	154	76	13	Moon Catcher ($663,450)	5,014,946
Tiznow, Ky.	148	78	6	Bear Now ($747,517)	4,952,985
Yes It's True, Ky.	191	109	11	Off Duty ($214,295)	4,890,828
Silver Deputy, Ky.	175	95	10	Deputiformer ($208,486)	4,822,512
Grand Slam, Ky.	232	119	9	Ruby's Grand Slam ($152,910)	4,670,766
More Than Ready, Ky.	180	96	10	Ready's Image ($259,422)	4,604,679
Indian Charlie, Ky.	136	82	9	Indian Blessing ($1,357,200)	4,550,457
Dynaformer, Ky.	149	70	5	Purim ($496,450)	4,520,881
Victory Gallop, Tur	182	92	6	Kettleoneup ($548,462)	4,506,754
Mr. Greeley, Ky.	159	76	5	Miraculous Miss ($371,300)	4,480,954
Smoke Glacken, Ky.	189	94	9	Lady Marlboro ($191,524)	4,405,484
Carson City, Dead	173	99	6	Fiery Pursuit ($263,045)	4,392,361
Trippi, Fl.	138	80	5	Miss Macy Sue ($546,217)	4,382,492
Forest Wildcat, Ky.	160	82	15	Wild Gams ($303,280)	4,372,601
Bold Executive, On.	133	77	4	Legal Move ($222,728)	4,311,113
Storm Cat, Ky.	105	53	7	After Market ($686,725)	4,254,293
Bertrando, Ca.	159	92	8	Bilo ($327,780)	4,233,527
Holy Bull, Ky.	149	71	7	Flashy Bull ($635,063)	4,189,051
Real Quiet, Pa.	125	69	4	Midnight Lute ($1,368,000)	4,146,283
El Corredor, Ky.	156	78	5	Dominican ($549,140)	4,069,515
Slew City Slew, Ky.	146	85	4	Lava Man ($1,410,000)	4,067,179
Thunder Gulch, Ky.	183	76	9	Balance ($448,332)	4,061,354
Chester House, Dead	108	62	11	Sans Souci Island ($202,734)	4,036,258
Elusive Quality, Ky.	145	78	4	Maryfield ($896,330)	3,971,658
Touch Gold, Ky.	181	91	4	Sugar Swirl ($253,017)	3,930,541
Pleasant Tap, Ky.	108	55	6	Tiago ($1,234,750)	3,890,302
Dixie Union, Ky.	143	71	4	Turf War ($518,548)	3,872,088
Wild Rush, Jpn	112	70	8	Dream Rush ($570,800)	3,870,956
Include, Ky.	111	57	4	Panty Raid ($1,024,180)	3,811,364
Danzig, Dead	31	21	3	Hard Spun ($2,572,500)	3,804,776
In Excess (Ire), Ca.	142	78	8	Notional ($460,000)	3,797,819
High Yield, Dead	164	76	8	Alezzandro ($551,550)	3,782,690
Tiger Ridge, SAf	162	82	4	Storm in May ($405,181)	3,712,235
Forestry, Ky.	145	76	9	Kris' Sis ($163,935)	3,711,993
Deputy Commander, Ca.	171	78	5	Reporting for Duty ($288,810)	3,592,558
Honour and Glory, Ky.	196	107	3	Again and Again ($144,260)	3,580,640
Northern Afleet, Ky.	159	106	3	Big City Man ($143,540)	3,570,866
Cat Thief, Ky.	154	90	3	Sam P. ($235,058)	3,549,644
Unusual Heat, Ca.	115	59	5	Unusual Suspect ($376,221)	3,534,363
City Zip, Ky.	119	67	4	Tishmeister ($167,516)	3,510,497
Stormin Fever, Ky.	164	90	6	Stormin Baghdad ($211,322)	3,494,371
Montbrook, Fl.	157	92	4	Bentrovhto ($159,020)	3,486,582
Menifee, Unknown	123	75	4	Yolie ($214,821)	3,474,293
Johannesburg, Ky.	110	45	5	Scat Daddy ($826,500)	3,473,881
Rahy, Ky.	90	49	6	Dreaming of Anna ($391,932)	3,463,317
Outflanker, Md.	129	81	7	Annabill ($238,680)	3,447,107

Sires — Leading North American Sires

Leading Sires by Average Earnings per Starter in North America in 2007
Minimum of 25 Starters

Sire	Strs	Wnrs	Average
Danzig, Dead	31	21	$122,735
Street Cry (Ire), Ky.	69	30	86,909
Lord Avie, Pens	28	16	80,207
Kipling, Ky.	33	15	72,743
Smart Strike, Ky.	201	96	70,594
A.P. Indy, Ky.	157	76	60,779
Giant's Causeway, Ky.	145	72	50,524
Awesome Again, Ky.	149	77	50,394
Theatrical (Ire), Ky.	52	22	46,883
Distorted Humor, Ky.	214	104	43,997
Pulpit, Ky.	144	76	43,938
Lasting Approval, Arg	26	12	43,937
Unbridled's Song, Ky.	146	79	42,619
Posse, Ky.	42	23	41,757
Desert God, N.M.	28	17	41,696
Lemon Drop Kid, Ky.	142	73	41,661
Storm Cat, Ky.	105	53	40,517
Kiridashi, Ab.	54	30	40,111

Leading Sires by Median Earnings per Starter in North America in 2007
Minimum of 25 Starters

Sire	Strs	Wnrs	Median
Danzig, Dead	31	21	$35,620
Disco Rico, N.Y.	57	43	23,220
Desert God, N.M.	28	17	21,330
Honor Grades, Dead	52	37	20,663
Zarbyev, La.	66	42	20,488
Chester House, Dead	108	62	20,040
Wild Rush, Jpn	112	70	19,842
Archers Bay, Dead	47	30	19,670
Unbridled's Song, Ky.	146	79	18,851
A.P. Indy, Ky.	157	76	18,700
Seeking the Gold, Ky.	82	45	18,328
Menifee, Unknown	123	75	18,200
War Chant, Ky.	88	48	18,025
Trippi, Fl.	138	80	18,006
Not For Love, Md.	176	99	17,600
Quaker Ridge, Phi	64	41	17,599
Put It Back, Fl.	83	56	17,432
Citidancer, Pens	43	24	17,400
Rahy, Ky.	90	49	17,250

Leading Sires by Number of Winners in North America in 2007

Sire	Strs	Wnrs	Wnrs/Strs
Langfuhr, Ky.	223	131	58.7%
Mutakddim, Ky.	206	126	61.2%
Stormy Atlantic, Ky.	242	126	52.1%
Tale of the Cat, Ky.	224	123	54.9%
Grand Slam, Ky.	232	119	51.3%
Yes It's True, Ky.	191	109	57.1%
Broken Vow, Ky.	176	107	60.8%
Devil His Due, Ky.	205	107	52.2%
Honour and Glory, Ky.	196	107	54.6%
Northern Afleet, Ky.	159	106	66.7%
Distorted Humor, Ky.	214	104	48.6%
Catienus, Ky.	159	102	64.2%
Cherokee Run, Ky.	169	102	60.4%
Carson City, Dead	173	99	57.2%
Not For Love, Md.	176	99	56.3%
Swiss Yodeler, Ca.	195	99	50.8%
Storm Boot, Dead	173	98	56.6%
Maria's Mon, Dead	184	97	52.7%
More Than Ready, Ky.	180	96	53.3%
Smart Strike, Ky.	201	96	47.8%
Louis Quatorze, Md.	154	95	61.7%
Salt Lake, Ca.	160	95	59.4%
Silver Deputy, Ky.	175	95	54.3%

Leading Sires by Number of Wins in North America in 2007

Sire	Strs	Wnrs	Wins
Langfuhr, Ky.	223	131	243
Stormy Atlantic, Ky.	242	126	217
Catienus, Ky.	159	102	207
Mutakddim, Ky.	206	126	200
Tale of the Cat, Ky.	224	123	192
Swiss Yodeler, Ca.	195	99	191
Yes It's True, Ky.	191	109	191
Northern Afleet, Ky.	159	106	188
Grand Slam, Ky.	232	119	184
Devil His Due, Ky.	205	107	180
Honour and Glory, Ky.	196	107	179
Louis Quatorze, Md.	154	95	177
Broken Vow, Ky.	176	107	175
Storm Boot, Dead	173	98	173
Smoke Glacken, Ky.	189	94	172
Not For Love, Md.	176	99	171
Montbrook, Fl.	157	92	170

Leading Sires by Number of Stakes Winners in North America in 2007

Sire	Strs	Wnrs	SWs	SWins
Distorted Humor, Ky.	214	104	19	27
A.P. Indy, Ky.	157	76	18	30
Forest Wildcat, Ky.	160	82	15	18
Langfuhr, Ky.	223	131	15	26
Smart Strike, Ky.	201	96	15	27
Giant's Causeway, Ky.	145	72	14	22
Lemon Drop Kid, Ky.	142	73	14	23
Royal Academy, Ky.	166	81	14	20
Malibu Moon, Ky.	154	76	13	20
Stormy Atlantic, Ky.	242	126	13	18
Unbridled's Song, Ky.	146	79	13	17
Awesome Again, Ky.	149	77	11	21
Chester House, Dead	108	62	11	14
Not For Love, Md.	176	99	11	17
Tale of the Cat, Ky.	224	123	11	12
Yes It's True, Ky.	191	109	11	15
Exchange Rate, Ky.	89	42	10	15
More Than Ready, Ky.	180	96	10	15
Silver Deputy, Ky.	175	95	10	11

Leading Sires by Number of Graded Stakes Winners in North America in 2007

Sire	Strs	Wnrs	GSWs	GSWins
A.P. Indy, Ky.	157	76	10	17
Giant's Causeway, Ky.	145	72	9	12
Distorted Humor, Ky.	214	104	7	13
Smart Strike, Ky.	201	96	7	15
Street Cry (Ire), Ky.	69	30	6	9
Awesome Again, Ky.	149	77	5	11
Johannesburg, Ky.	110	45	5	7
Langfuhr, Ky.	223	131	5	9
Pulpit, Ky.	144	76	5	10
Royal Academy, Ky.	166	81	5	6
Unbridled's Song, Ky.	146	79	5	6
Cherokee Run, Ky.	169	102	4	6
Exchange Rate, Ky.	89	42	4	5
Forest Wildcat, Ky.	160	82	4	5
Hennessy, Dead	122	64	4	5
Lemon Drop Kid, Ky.	142	73	4	9
Maria's Mon, Dead	184	97	4	6
Seeking the Gold, Ky.	82	45	4	4
Storm Cat, Ky.	105	53	4	7
Stormy Atlantic, Ky.	242	126	4	5
Victory Gallop, Tur	182	92	4	5

Leading Sires by Number of Grade 1 Stakes Winners and Wins in North America in 2007

Sire	Strs	Wnrs	G1SWs	G1SWins
Awesome Again, Ky.	149	77	3	5
Distorted Humor, Ky.	214	104	3	3
Langfuhr, Ky.	223	131	3	5
Smart Strike, Ky.	201	96	3	7
A.P. Indy, Ky.	157	76	2	5
Broken Vow, Ky.	176	107	2	2
Lemon Drop Kid, Ky.	142	73	2	2
Pulpit, Ky.	144	76	2	2
Real Quiet, Pa.	125	69	2	3
Street Cry (Ire), Ky.	69	30	2	3
Theatrical (Ire), Ky.	52	22	2	2
Unbridled's Song, Ky.	146	79	2	3

Leading Juvenile Sires by Progeny Earnings in North America in 2007

Earnings in North America only for stallions represented by at least one starter in North America in 2007, regardless of where the stallion stands or stood. ♦ Denotes freshman sire.

Sire	Strs	Wnrs	SWs	Leading Earner (Earnings)	Total Earnings
Cherokee Run, Ky.	38	17	2	War Pass ($1,397,400)	$2,106,886
Indian Charlie, Ky.	24	14	3	Indian Blessing ($1,357,200)	2,012,401
♦Posse, Ky.	42	23	7	Kodiak Kowboy ($544,825)	1,753,807
♦Harlan's Holiday, Ky.	49	21	5	Into Mischief ($448,800)	1,637,125
Distorted Humor, Ky.	41	15	1	Z Humor ($543,700)	1,346,465
Malibu Moon, Ky.	49	25	2	By the Light ($451,815)	1,336,818
Tale of the Cat, Ky.	47	19	3	Tale of Ekati ($313,200)	1,286,008
♦Proud Citizen, Ky.	45	16	2	Proud Spell ($608,770)	1,275,389
Pulpit, Ky.	42	11	2	Pyro ($516,718)	1,174,411
♦Macho Uno, Ky.	30	14	2	Wicked Style ($445,000)	1,084,765
♦Whywhywhy, Ky.	36	11	2	Nownownow ($641,950)	1,073,613
Dixie Union, Ky.	32	11	2	Turf War ($518,548)	1,062,207
♦Empire Maker, Ky.	21	8	3	Country Star ($575,900)	1,028,065
♦Van Nistelrooy, Ky.	51	18	3	Set Play ($255,450)	1,016,159
More Than Ready, Ky.	46	16	3	Ready's Image ($259,422)	1,000,772
Fusaichi Pegasus, Ky.	53	15	1	Saki to Me ($114,000)	993,776
Trippi, Fl.	44	18	1	Sok Sok ($179,043)	947,871
♦Vindication, Ky.	49	19	1	More Happy ($129,300)	946,017
Doneraile Court, Ky.	64	25	4	Doneraile Gem ($115,409)	935,216
Yonaguska, Ky.	54	25	2	Yonagucci ($112,545)	925,139
Bold Executive, On.	27	11	2	Krz Exec ($215,902)	922,052
Smart Strike, Ky.	54	16	1	Smarty Deb ($171,055)	900,894
Stormy Atlantic, Ky.	57	19	3	Maya's Storm ($126,099)	884,234
♦Kafwain, Ky.	32	13	4	Massive Drama ($199,200)	860,881
Jump Start, Ky.	50	19	2	Mrs. Began ($184,801)	857,773
♦Hold That Tiger, Vic.	60	20	2	Old Man Buck ($228,312)	851,568
El Corredor, Ky.	38	12	1	Backseat Rhythm ($316,760)	844,297
♦D'wildcat, Fl.	25	7	2	Authenicat ($190,216)	842,377
Exchange Rate, Ky.	36	12	3	Rated Fiesty ($204,291)	822,391
Broken Vow, Ky.	55	24	0	Mighty Vow ($130,488)	815,962
Tiznow, Ky.	44	14	1	Colonel John ($255,300)	808,707
E Dubai, Ky.	39	16	1	Treadmill ($132,000)	800,713
Eltish, N.Y.	32	16	1	Silk Ridge ($369,240)	799,597
Mizzen Mast, Ky.	40	16	1	C J's Leelee ($120,023)	790,789
Three Wonders, Fl.	37	16	1	Calico Bay ($331,300)	789,048
Smoke Glacken, Ky.	33	11	4	Irish Smoke ($187,200)	761,400
Victory Gallop, Tur	38	12	3	Anak Nakal ($220,916)	758,114
Officer, Ky.	40	18	2	Officer Cherrie ($256,212)	757,583
City Zip, Ky.	31	15	1	Canadian Ballet ($148,862)	751,440
Valid Expectations, Tx.	31	19	3	Valid Lilly ($213,406)	713,980
♦Yankee Gentleman, Ky.	39	14	2	Golden Yank ($264,832)	708,530
Yes It's True, Ky.	51	20	2	Asi Asi ($81,030)	702,673
A.P. Indy, Ky.	26	10	1	Majestic Warrior ($195,200)	698,126
Silver Deputy, Ky.	32	11	2	Deputiformer ($208,486)	697,183
Forest Wildcat, Ky.	30	9	3	Salute the Sarge ($286,540)	692,476
Grand Slam, Ky.	41	14	1	Grand Minstrel ($101,350)	685,017
♦Repent, Fl.	42	17	2	Check It Twice ($144,500)	682,051
Menifee, Unknown	31	16	0	A to the Croft ($210,018)	677,540
Montbrook, Fl.	33	14	2	Phantom Income ($153,200)	673,497
Cat Thief, Ky.	43	15	1	Urn ($58,397)	638,453
♦Hook and Ladder, N.Y.	26	8	2	Spanky Fischbein ($161,595)	630,489
Not For Love, Md.	29	8	3	Love for Not ($149,273)	626,779
Hennessy, Dead	33	14	2	Remarkable Remy ($97,627)	620,993
Forestry, Ky.	37	14	1	Etched ($95,880)	620,918
Double Honor, Fl.	33	17	1	Ultimate Authority ($95,210)	604,353
Pure Prize, Ky.	25	11	2	Pure Clan ($316,209)	603,310
Tribal Rule, Ca.	22	10	2	Georgie Boy ($286,806)	602,056
Successful Appeal, Ky.	28	12	1	Barbazilla ($64,900)	600,784
Mutakddim, Ky.	37	17	1	Elocution ($97,600)	583,707
Wised Up, Fl.	10	4	2	Wise Answer ($458,300)	581,646
Carson City, Dead	35	10	2	Kesagami ($199,428)	577,705
Songandaprayer, Ky.	30	11	2	Preachin Man ($229,614)	574,703
Precise End, Jpn	19	8	2	Expect the End ($204,380)	571,234
♦Flatter, Ky.	40	17	1	Indy's Alexandra ($88,100)	569,119
Maria's Mon, Dead	22	9	1	Sky Mom ($174,841)	566,905

Sires — Leading North American Juvenile Sires

Leading Juvenile Sires by Average Earnings per Starter in North America in 2007
Minimum of 10 Starters

Sire	Strs	Wnrs	Average
Indian Charlie, Ky.	24	14	$83,850
Wised Up, Fl.	10	4	58,165
Cherokee Run, Ky.	38	17	55,444
◆Empire Maker, Ky.	21	8	48,955
◆Posse, Ky.	42	23	41,757
◆Macho Uno, Ky.	30	14	36,159
War Chant, Ky.	10	4	36,065
Bold Executive, On.	27	11	34,150
◆D'wildcat, Fl.	25	7	33,695
◆Harlan's Holiday, Ky.	49	21	33,411
Dixie Union, Ky.	32	11	33,194
Distorted Humor, Ky.	41	15	32,841
Seeking the Gold, Ky.	11	7	31,564
Precise End, Ky.	19	8	30,065
In Excess (Ire), Ca.	17	6	30,003
Bertrando, Ca.	18	10	29,828
◆Whywhywhy, Ky.	36	11	29,823
Tethra, On.	12	5	28,523
◆Proud Citizen, Ky.	45	16	28,342
Pulpit, Ky.	42	11	27,962
Street Cry (Ire), Ky.	19	5	27,800
Tribal Rule, Ca.	22	10	27,366
Tale of the Cat, Ky.	47	19	27,362
Malibu Moon, Ky.	49	25	27,282
Marquetry, Ky.	17	7	27,164
◆Kafwain, Ky.	32	13	26,903
A.P. Indy, Ky.	26	10	26,851
Mr. Greeley, Ky.	14	5	26,603

Leading Juvenile Sires by Median Earnings per Starter in North America in 2007
Minimum of 10 Starters

Sire	Strs	Wnrs	Median
Seeking the Gold, Ky.	11	7	$26,285
Snow Ridge, Pa.	14	10	20,470
Cape Canaveral, Ab.	25	14	17,580
Indian Charlie, Ky.	24	14	16,294
Erlton, La.	14	8	16,008
Vision and Verse, Ky.	10	6	15,300
Malibu Moon, Ky.	49	25	15,130
Ciano Cat, On.	15	6	14,797
Freud, N.Y.	23	8	13,984
El Prado (Ire), Ky.	15	6	13,760
Bertrando, Ca.	18	10	13,730
Tethra, On.	12	5	13,412
◆Posse, Ky.	42	23	13,380
Distorted Humor, Ky.	41	15	12,782
Gibson County, Fl.	11	8	12,679
Successful Appeal, Ky.	28	12	12,575
Catienus, Ky.	23	12	12,573
Put It Back, Fl.	27	15	12,125
Sefapiano, La.	10	3	12,122
War Chant, Ky.	10	4	12,071
Meadowlake, Dead	11	7	12,000
Outflanker, Md.	26	13	11,927
Bold Executive, On.	27	11	11,819
◆Empire Maker, Ky.	21	8	11,726
Hussonet, Aus	21	9	11,720
Mr. Greeley, Ky.	14	5	11,703
Evansville Slew, Ok.	17	10	11,475

Leading Juvenile Sires by Number of Winners in North America in 2007

Sire	Strs	Wnrs	Wnrs/Strs
Doneraile Court, Ky.	64	25	39.1%
Malibu Moon, Ky.	49	25	51.0%
Yonaguska, Ky.	54	25	46.3%
Broken Vow, Ky.	55	24	43.6%
◆Posse, Ky.	42	23	54.8%
◆Harlan's Holiday, Ky.	49	21	42.9%
◆Hold That Tiger, Vic.	60	20	33.3%
Yes It's True, Ky.	51	20	39.2%
Jump Start, Ky.	50	19	38.0%
Stormy Atlantic, Ky.	57	19	33.3%
Tale of the Cat, Ky.	47	19	40.4%
Valid Expectations, Tx.	31	19	61.3%
◆Vindication, Ky.	49	19	38.8%
Officer, Ky.	40	18	45.0%
Trippi, Fl.	44	18	40.9%
◆Van Nistelrooy, Ky.	51	18	35.3%
Cherokee Run, Ky.	38	17	44.7%
Double Honor, Fl.	33	17	51.5%
◆Flatter, Ky.	40	17	42.5%
Mutakddim, Ky.	37	17	45.9%
◆Repent, Fl.	42	17	40.5%
◆Sunday Break (Jpn), Ky.	49	17	34.7%

Leading Juvenile Sires by Number of Wins in North America in 2007

Sire	Strs	Wnrs	Wins
◆Posse, Ky.	42	23	39
Malibu Moon, Ky.	49	25	38
Doneraile Court, Ky.	64	25	35
Yonaguska, Ky.	54	25	31
Trippi, Fl.	44	18	29
Broken Vow, Ky.	55	24	27
Double Honor, Fl.	33	17	27
◆Harlan's Holiday, Ky.	49	21	27
◆Hold That Tiger, Vic.	60	20	27
Tale of the Cat, Ky.	47	19	27
Eltish, N.Y.	32	16	26
Officer, Ky.	40	18	25
Stormy Atlantic, Ky.	57	19	25
Valid Expectations, Tx.	31	19	25
◆Van Nistelrooy, Ky.	51	18	25
◆Repent, Fl.	42	17	24
Yes It's True, Ky.	51	20	24
Jump Start, Ky.	50	19	23
More Than Ready, Ky.	46	16	23
Cherokee Run, Ky.	38	17	22
◆Vindication, Ky.	49	19	22

Leading Juvenile Sires by Number of Stakes Winners in 2007

Sire	Strs	Wnrs	SWs	SWins
◆Posse, Ky.	42	23	7	11
◆Harlan's Holiday, Ky.	49	21	5	6
Doneraile Court, Ky.	64	25	4	4
Evansville Slew, Ok.	17	10	4	4
◆Kafwain, Ky.	32	13	4	7
Smoke Glacken, Ky.	33	11	4	4
Chimes Band, Dead	28	8	3	3
◆Empire Maker, Ky.	21	8	3	4
Exchange Rate, Ky.	36	12	3	5
Forest Wildcat, Ky.	30	9	3	4
Indian Charlie, Ky.	24	14	3	4
In Excess (Ire), Ca.	17	6	3	4
Marquetry, Ky.	17	7	3	3
More Than Ready, Ky.	46	16	3	5
Not For Love, Md.	29	8	3	4
Stormy Atlantic, Ky.	57	19	3	4
Tale of the Cat, Ky.	47	19	3	3
Valid Expectations, Tx.	31	19	3	4
◆Van Nistelrooy, Ky.	51	18	3	3
Victory Gallop, Tur	38	12	3	3

Leading Juvenile Sires by Number of Graded Stakes Winners in North America in 2007

Sire	Strs	Wnrs	GSWs	GSWins
Dixie Union, Ky.	32	11	2	2
◆Empire Maker, Ky.	21	8	2	3
◆Harlan's Holiday, Ky.	49	21	2	2
◆Posse, Ky.	42	23	2	3
Street Cry (Ire), Ky.	19	5	2	2
◆Van Nistelrooy, Ky.	51	18	2	2
Victory Gallop, Tur	38	12	2	2

Leading Freshman Sires by Progeny Earnings in North America in 2007

Earnings in North America only for stallions represented by at least one starter in North America in 2007, regardless of where the stallion stands or stood. ◆ Denotes freshman sire.

Sire	Strs	Wnrs	SWs	Leading Earner (Earnings)	Total Earnings
◆Posse, Ky.	42	23	7	Kodiak Kowboy ($544,825)	$1,753,807
◆Harlan's Holiday, Ky.	49	21	5	Into Mischief ($448,800)	1,637,125
◆Proud Citizen, Ky.	45	16	2	Proud Spell ($608,770)	1,275,389
◆Macho Uno, Ky.	30	14	2	Wicked Style ($445,000)	1,084,765
◆Whywhywhy, Ky.	36	11	2	Nownownow ($641,950)	1,073,613
◆Empire Maker, Ky.	21	8	3	Country Star ($575,900)	1,028,065
◆Van Nistelrooy, Ky.	51	18	3	Set Play ($255,450)	1,016,159
◆Vindication, Ky.	49	19	1	More Happy ($129,300)	946,017
◆Kafwain, Ky.	32	13	4	Massive Drama ($199,200)	860,881
◆Hold That Tiger, Vic.	60	20	2	Old Man Buck ($228,312)	851,568
◆D'wildcat, Fl.	25	7	2	Authenticat ($190,216)	842,377
◆Yankee Gentleman, Ky.	39	14	2	Golden Yank ($264,832)	708,530
◆Repent, Fl.	42	17	2	Check It Twice ($144,500)	682,051
◆Hook and Ladder, N.Y.	26	8	2	Spanky Fischbein ($161,595)	630,489
◆Flatter, Ky.	40	17	1	Indy's Alexandra ($88,100)	569,119
◆Sunday Break (Jpn), Ky.	49	17	0	Sunday Holiday ($98,356)	564,870
◆Mineshaft, Ky.	21	8	1	La Mina ($147,601)	541,952
◆Cactus Ridge, Ky.	37	13	0	Senor ($105,443)	537,706
◆Sky Mesa, Ky.	40	12	0	Cozy Mesa ($73,002)	508,974
◆Milwaukee Brew, Fl.	37	14	0	Salomea ($84,572)	456,448
◆Volponi, Unknown	24	11	2	Clearly Foxy ($119,482)	431,819
◆Full Mandate, Fl.	46	12	1	Thoroughly ($58,725)	392,191
◆Drewman, Fl.	26	11	0	Cigar Man ($105,200)	373,281
◆Trust N Luck, Fl.	32	9	1	Wonderful Luck ($98,846)	370,440
◆Sligo Bay (Ire), Fl.	26	8	1	Wind in My Wings ($133,308)	328,593
◆Changeintheweather, Pa.	28	11	1	Cold Trial ($40,820)	325,054
◆Equality, Mi.	15	9	1	Equalitysdebutante ($118,086)	318,681
◆Early Flyer, Tx.	13	9	1	Ferdinand's Flyer ($95,200)	313,410
◆Aldebaran, Ky.	19	6	0	Grace Anatomy ($97,160)	291,168
◆Decarchy, Ca.	17	7	1	Timehascometoday ($73,998)	289,243
◆Gulf Storm, Fl.	37	11	2	Ogygian's Storm ($52,191)	286,207
◆Zavata, Ky.	23	13	0	Good Direction ($34,442)	278,071
◆Polish Gift, Dead	9	3	1	Margo's Gift ($243,714)	269,885
◆Najran, Ky.	29	8	0	Sky Cape ($84,180)	264,699
◆Premeditation, N.M.	3	3	2	Run Like Fire ($190,092)	264,555
◆Greatness, Fl.	19	8	0	Immortal Eyes ($42,300)	242,044
◆Finality, B.C.	13	5	2	Remarkable Miss ($79,691)	219,898
◆Awesome of Course, Fl.	5	3	1	Honey Honey Honey ($145,000)	212,918
◆Desert Warrior, N.Y.	13	7	0	Run Warrior Run ($68,550)	212,590
◆Wiseman's Ferry, Ky.	29	5	0	Fort Drum ($50,943)	211,569
◆Sudden Thunder, P.R.	26	11	0	La Avispa Pica ($41,084)	196,452
◆Stormy Jack, Ca.	8	5	1	Bob Black Jack ($131,425)	193,270
◆Smooth Jazz, N.Y.	16	8	0	Smooth Air ($75,500)	192,460
◆Pure Precision, Fl.	18	9	0	Predate ($40,754)	192,407
◆Authenticate, La.	20	9	0	Dr. Nick ($57,127)	179,342
◆Shore Breeze, Ky.	15	6	0	Grand Obsession ($38,700)	169,480
◆Seeking Daylight, Md.	15	7	0	Pit Lizard ($48,374)	167,016
◆Indy King, Fl.	7	3	0	Indy O. ($74,721)	163,546
◆Mayakovsky, N.Y.	9	3	0	Alexandros ($56,400)	162,321
◆Best of the Rest, Fl.	7	6	0	Hidden Wish ($47,370)	150,580
◆Rock Slide, Md.	12	2	0	Happy Hailey ($56,320)	141,703
◆Essence of Dubai, Fl.	24	9	0	Stephaningrid ($21,875)	138,542
◆Capsized, Ca.	13	4	0	Maxie's Night Cap ($26,615)	125,921
◆Easyfromthegitgo, La.	9	3	0	Peachsfromthegitgo ($38,850)	125,578
◆Ghostly Minister, W.V.	5	1	1	Ghostly Thunder ($109,158)	124,708
◆A. P. Delta, La.	7	1	1	Delta Vixen ($81,400)	115,206
◆David Copperfield, Ky.	8	4	0	Hunterbunter ($33,680)	111,913
◆Paynes Bay, On.	14	3	0	Corossol ($34,373)	111,641
◆Gotham City, Ca.	9	1	0	Comissioner Gordon ($55,102)	111,344
◆Lido Palace (Chi), Fl.	23	3	0	Delayed Start ($24,450)	110,252
◆Crafty C. T., Ca.	8	3	1	C. T. Phone Home ($41,400)	108,930
◆Lightnin N Thunder, Fl.	11	4	0	Always Enchanting ($54,600)	108,652
◆Father Steve, Ar.	7	4	0	Prince Steve ($30,990)	106,498
◆Castle Gandolfo, Dead	14	3	0	Salt Castle ($39,122)	92,987
◆Storm Passage, La.	6	2	0	Little Thorn ($52,900)	92,465

Sires — Leading North American Freshman Sires

Leading Freshman Sires by Average Earnings per Starter in North America in 2007
Minimum of 10 Starters

Sire	Strs	Wnrs	Average
◆Empire Maker, Ky.	21	8	$48,955
◆Posse, Ky.	42	23	41,757
◆Macho Uno, Ky.	30	14	36,159
◆D'wildcat, Fl.	25	7	33,695
◆Harlan's Holiday, Ky.	49	21	33,411
◆Whywhywhy, Ky.	36	11	29,823
◆Proud Citizen, Ky.	45	16	28,342
◆Kafwain, Ky.	32	13	26,903
◆Mineshaft, Ky.	21	8	25,807
◆Hook and Ladder, N.Y.	26	8	24,250
◆Early Flyer, Tx.	13	9	24,108
◆Equality, Mi.	15	9	21,245
◆Van Nistelrooy, Ky.	51	18	19,925
◆Vindication, Ky.	49	19	19,306
◆Yankee Gentleman, Ky.	39	14	18,167
◆Volponi, Unknown	24	11	17,992
◆Decarchy, Ca.	17	7	17,014
◆Finality, B.C.	13	5	16,915
◆Desert Warrior, N.Y.	13	7	16,353
◆Repent, Fl.	42	17	16,239
◆Aldebaran, Ky.	19	6	15,325
◆Cactus Ridge, Ky.	37	13	14,533
◆Drewman, Fl.	26	11	14,357
◆Flatter, Ky.	40	17	14,228
◆Hold That Tiger, Vic.	60	20	14,193
◆Greatness, Fl.	19	8	12,739
◆Sky Mesa, Ky.	40	12	12,724

Leading Freshman Sires by Median Earnings per Starter in North America in 2007
Minimum of 10 Starters

Sire	Strs	Wnrs	Median
◆Posse, Ky.	42	23	$13,380
◆Empire Maker, Ky.	21	8	11,726
◆Equality, Mi.	15	9	10,906
◆Macho Uno, Ky.	30	14	10,791
◆Desert Warrior, N.Y.	13	7	10,458
◆Harlan's Holiday, Ky.	49	21	10,400
◆Early Flyer, Tx.	13	9	10,200
◆Hook and Ladder, N.Y.	26	8	9,829
◆Zavata, Ky.	23	13	9,345
◆Greatness, Fl.	19	8	8,200
◆D'wildcat, Fl.	25	7	7,591
◆Changeintheweather, Pa.	28	11	7,450
◆Vindication, Ky.	49	19	7,400
◆Volponi, Unknown	24	11	7,338
◆Seeking Daylight, Md.	15	7	7,320
◆Pure Precision, Fl.	18	9	7,300
◆Flatter, Ky.	40	17	6,946
◆Decarchy, Ca.	17	7	6,818
◆Drewman, Fl.	26	11	6,761
◆Shore Breeze, Ky.	15	6	6,245
◆Capsized, Ca.	13	4	6,030

Leading Freshman Sires by Number of Winners in North America in 2007

Sire	Strs	Wnrs	Wnrs/Strs
◆Posse, Ky.	42	23	54.8%
◆Harlan's Holiday, Ky.	49	21	42.9%
◆Hold That Tiger, Vic.	60	20	33.3%
◆Vindication, Ky.	49	19	38.8%
◆Van Nistelrooy, Ky.	51	18	35.3%
◆Flatter, Ky.	40	17	42.5%
◆Repent, Fl.	42	17	40.5%
◆Sunday Break (Jpn), Ky.	49	17	34.7%
◆Proud Citizen, Ky.	45	16	35.6%
◆Macho Uno, Ky.	30	14	46.7%
◆Milwaukee Brew, Fl.	37	14	37.8%
◆Yankee Gentleman, Ky.	39	14	35.9%
◆Cactus Ridge, Ky.	37	13	35.1%
◆Kafwain, Ky.	32	13	40.6%
◆Zavata, Ky.	23	13	56.5%
◆Full Mandate, Fl.	46	12	26.1%
◆Sky Mesa, Ky.	40	12	30.0%
◆Changeintheweather, Pa.	28	11	39.3%
◆Drewman, Fl.	26	11	42.3%
◆Gulf Storm, Fl.	37	11	29.7%
◆Sudden Thunder, P.R.	26	11	42.3%
◆Volponi, Unknown	24	11	45.8%
◆Whywhywhy, Ky.	36	11	30.6%
◆Authenticate, La.	20	9	45.0%
◆Early Flyer, Tx.	13	9	69.2%
◆Equality, Mi.	15	9	60.0%
◆Essence of Dubai, Fl.	24	9	37.5%
◆Pure Precision, Fl.	18	9	50.0%
◆Trust N Luck, Fl.	32	9	28.1%

Leading Freshman Sires by Number of Wins in North America in 2007

Sire	Strs	Wnrs	Wins
◆Posse, Ky.	42	23	39
◆Harlan's Holiday, Ky.	49	21	27
◆Hold That Tiger, Vic.	60	20	27
◆Van Nistelrooy, Ky.	51	18	25
◆Repent, Fl.	42	17	24
◆Vindication, Ky.	49	19	22
◆Flatter, Ky.	40	17	21
◆Kafwain, Ky.	32	13	21
◆Macho Uno, Ky.	30	14	20
◆Full Mandate, Fl.	46	12	19
◆Proud Citizen, Ky.	45	16	19
◆Sunday Break (Jpn), Ky.	49	17	19
◆Cactus Ridge, Ky.	37	13	18
◆Gulf Storm, Fl.	37	11	18
◆Sudden Thunder, P.R.	26	11	18
◆Whywhywhy, Ky.	36	11	18
◆Yankee Gentleman, Ky.	39	14	18
◆Volponi, Unknown	24	11	16
◆Milwaukee Brew, Fl.	37	14	15
◆Zavata, Ky.	23	13	15
◆Sky Mesa, Ky.	40	12	14
◆Mineshaft, Ky.	21	8	13
◆Pure Precision, Fl.	18	9	13
◆Trust N Luck, Fl.	32	9	13

Leading Freshman Sires by Number of Stakes Winners in North America in 2007

Sire	Strs	Wnrs	SWs	SWins
◆Posse, Ky.	42	23	7	11
◆Harlan's Holiday, Ky.	49	21	5	6
◆Kafwain, Ky.	32	13	4	7
◆Empire Maker, Ky.	21	8	3	4
◆Van Nistelrooy, Ky.	51	18	3	3
◆D'wildcat, Fl.	25	7	2	2
◆Finality, B.C.	13	5	2	2
◆Gulf Storm, Fl.	37	11	2	2
◆Hold That Tiger, Vic.	60	20	2	3
◆Hook and Ladder, N.Y.	26	8	2	2
◆Macho Uno, Ky.	30	14	2	4
◆Premeditation, N.M.	3	3	2	3
◆Proud Citizen, Ky.	45	16	2	3
◆Repent, Fl.	42	17	2	2
◆Volponi, Unknown	24	11	2	2
◆Whywhywhy, Ky.	36	11	2	5
◆Yankee Gentleman, Ky.	39	14	2	3

Leading Freshman Sires by Number of Graded Stakes Winners in North America in 2007

Sire	Strs	Wnrs	GSWs	GSWins
◆Empire Maker, Ky.	21	8	2	3
◆Harlan's Holiday, Ky.	49	21	2	2
◆Posse, Ky.	42	23	2	2
◆Van Nistelrooy, Ky.	51	18	2	2
◆Kafwain, Ky.	32	13	1	1
◆Macho Uno, Ky.	30	14	1	2
◆Proud Citizen, Ky.	45	16	1	1
◆Vindication, Ky.	49	19	1	1
◆Volponi, Unknown	24	11	1	1

Leading Broodmare Sires by Progeny Earnings in North America in 2007

Earnings in North America only for broodmare sires represented by at least one starter in North America in 2007, regardless of where the stallion stands or stood.

Sire	Strs	Wnrs	SWs	Leading Earner (Earnings)	Total Earnings
Deputy Minister, Dead	356	190	18	Curlin ($5,102,800)	$15,840,287
Dixieland Band, Ky.	379	193	18	Street Sense ($3,205,000)	13,214,480
Storm Cat, Ky.	322	157	21	Nobiz Like Shobiz ($1,318,330)	10,709,980
Mr. Prospector, Dead	239	119	11	War Pass ($1,397,400)	9,113,145
A.P. Indy, Ky.	172	90	10	Zanjero ($1,060,977)	7,449,328
Kris S., Dead	301	139	8	Student Council ($1,041,755)	7,350,077
Valid Appeal, Dead	289	172	11	Vacare ($377,856)	7,125,666
Theatrical (Ire), Ky.	213	95	10	English Channel ($2,640,000)	6,978,242
Rahy, Ky.	241	132	10	After Market ($686,725)	6,794,161
Seeking the Gold, Ky.	212	113	11	Excellent Art (GB) ($526,000)	6,733,858
Conquistador Cielo, Dead	305	151	10	Sky Conqueror ($827,043)	6,637,314
Crafty Prospector, Pens	318	179	7	Xchanger ($510,500)	6,612,437
Broad Brush, Pens	255	134	9	Dreaming of Anna ($391,932)	6,447,100
Wild Again, Pens	282	150	13	Pyro ($516,718)	6,370,863
Dynaformer, Ky.	237	125	15	C P West ($305,620)	6,329,537
Red Ransom, Eng	231	122	9	Marchfield ($371,524)	6,153,735
Pleasant Colony, Dead	253	126	11	Sightseeing ($401,716)	6,135,969
Woodman, Dead	265	123	6	Mrs. Lindsay ($621,240)	6,106,788
Storm Bird, Dead	227	126	11	Trippi's Storm ($344,320)	6,023,692
Forty Niner, Jpn	182	104	14	Lady of Venice (Fr) ($835,272)	5,944,725
Miswaki, Dead	261	141	8	My Typhoon (Ire) ($639,000)	5,929,515
Capote, Dead	245	137	10	Cosmonaut ($658,563)	5,911,987
Cure the Blues, Dead	288	156	4	Rolling Sea ($361,081)	5,906,435
Relaunch, Dead	284	153	15	Storm in May ($405,181)	5,866,586
Affirmed, Dead	262	125	6	Honey Ryder ($740,850)	5,805,361
Seattle Slew, Dead	255	133	10	Souvenir Slew ($199,715)	5,722,141
Devil's Bag, Dead	263	134	7	Teuflesberg ($464,050)	5,646,580
Lord At War (Arg), Dead	173	87	9	Citronnade ($701,405)	5,627,334
Mt. Livermore, Dead	307	144	10	Flashy Bull ($635,063)	5,558,515
Private Account, Dead	174	94	6	Panty Raid ($1,024,180)	5,476,748
Carson City, Dead	251	146	6	Lear's Princess ($429,100)	5,419,234
Meadowlake, Dead	266	132	13	Coco Belle ($223,250)	5,388,006
Unbridled, Dead	202	96	9	Lady Joanne ($808,993)	5,284,403
Danzig, Dead	195	104	14	Bold Hawk ($273,376)	5,241,477
Silver Deputy, Ky.	238	140	7	Miraculous Miss ($371,300)	5,225,045
Dehere, Ky.	138	81	6	Midnight Lute ($1,368,000)	4,872,013
Clever Trick, Dead	306	136	8	Ready's Image ($259,422)	4,788,232
Turkoman, Ca.	112	49	10	Hard Spun ($2,572,500)	4,610,335
Bold Ruckus, Dead	226	109	8	Paradise Dancer ($255,800)	4,602,639
Phone Trick, Dead	286	140	4	Forty Grams ($279,409)	4,546,729
Vice Regent, Dead	181	90	5	Jambalaya ($979,421)	4,501,292
Regal Classic, Pens	187	100	10	Lila Paige ($291,100)	4,473,568
With Approval, Eng	167	95	10	Twilight Meteor ($348,816)	4,428,382
Lost Code, Dead	220	120	6	Fabulous Strike ($403,332)	4,291,063
Gone West, Ky.	212	110	3	Jibboom ($229,700)	4,287,508
Fortunate Prospect, Pens	189	107	6	Fort Prado ($264,421)	4,279,872
Black Tie Affair (Ire), W.V.	233	119	6	Awfully Smart ($228,035)	4,278,392
Pentelicus, Dead	161	89	8	Awesome Gem ($1,032,400)	4,250,587
Lord Avie, Pens	174	93	2	Lawyer Ron ($1,320,000)	4,088,636
Allen's Prospect, Dead	221	115	4	S W Aly'svalentine ($161,770)	4,000,495
Salt Lake, Ca.	195	105	6	Who What Win ($245,830)	3,948,495
Polish Numbers, Dead	172	87	6	Smart Enough ($427,477)	3,873,601
Runaway Groom, Dead	245	122	5	You Go West Girl ($146,680)	3,812,473
Saratoga Six, Dead	181	93	8	Meribel ($210,993)	3,780,637
Cozzene, Ky.	177	93	6	River's Prayer ($610,175)	3,774,993
Time for a Change, Dead	157	79	6	Fairbanks ($322,675)	3,765,464
Smarten, Dead	150	71	4	Moon Catcher ($663,450)	3,658,840
Fit to Fight, Pens	208	109	5	Greg's Gold ($566,995)	3,642,331
Known Fact, Dead	182	78	5	Naughty New Yorker ($271,799)	3,619,407
Rubiano, Dead	151	84	6	Like a Gem ($278,495)	3,575,786
Gilded Time, Ab.	173	85	6	High Heels ($411,788)	3,566,786
Halo, Dead	210	93	2	Bwana Bull ($473,920)	3,530,473
Cryptoclearance, Ky.	230	114	7	Broadway Bully ($115,311)	3,491,506
Gulch, Ky.	167	86	5	Baroness Thatcher ($330,295)	3,472,293
Kingmambo, Ky.	103	51	8	Red Giant ($846,720)	3,397,853

Leading Broodmare Sires by Average Earnings per Starter in North America in 2007
Minimum of 25 Starters

Sire	Strs	Wnrs	Average
Deputy Minister, Dead	356	190	$44,495
A.P. Indy, Ky.	172	90	43,310
Turkoman, Ca.	112	49	41,164
French Deputy, Jpn	70	50	39,295
Mr. Prospector, Dead	239	119	38,130
Dehere, Ky.	138	81	35,304
Dixieland Band, Ky.	379	193	34,867
Storm Cat, Ky.	322	157	33,261
Kingmambo, Ky.	103	51	32,989
Theatrical (Ire), Ky.	213	95	32,762
Forty Niner, Jpn	182	104	32,663
Lord At War (Arg), Dead	173	87	32,528
Seeking the Gold, Ky.	212	113	31,763
Private Account, Dead	174	94	31,476
Pleasant Tap, Ky.	79	42	29,863
Jolie's Halo, Dead	74	40	29,711
Thirty Six Red, Dead	66	37	29,227
Dayjur, Ky.	104	53	29,002
Sadler's Wells, Ire	62	26	28,754
Rahy, Ky.	241	132	28,192
Olympio, Ca.	88	48	27,989
Desert Wine, Dead	84	39	27,868
Unbridled's Song, Ky.	66	36	27,513

Leading Broodmare Sires by Median Earnings per Starter in North America in 2007
Minimum of 25 Starters

Sire	Strs	Wnrs	Median
French Deputy, Jpn	70	50	$17,010
Seeking the Gold, Ky.	212	113	15,702
A.P. Indy, Ky.	172	90	15,355
Boundary, Pens	73	43	15,266
Southern Halo, Arg	103	66	15,238
Dehere, Ky.	138	81	15,175
Unbridled's Song, Ky.	66	36	14,510
Horatius, Dead	93	51	14,300
With Approval, Eng	167	95	13,970
Nureyev, Dead	116	59	13,925
Seattle Song, Dead	68	43	13,380
Deputy Minister, Dead	356	190	13,043
Silver Deputy, Ky.	238	140	12,785
Rahy, Ky.	241	132	12,700
Seattle Dancer, Dead	98	58	12,690
Rubiano, Dead	151	84	12,587
Danzig, Dead	195	104	12,581
Seattle Slew, Dead	255	133	12,500
Red Ransom, Eng	231	122	12,480
Valid Appeal, Dead	289	172	12,420
Lord At War (Arg), Dead	173	87	12,377
Diablo, Jpn	90	55	12,339
Forty Niner, Jpn	182	104	12,303

Leading Broodmare Sires by Number of Winners in North America in 2007

Sire	Strs	Wnrs	Wnrs/Strs
Dixieland Band, Ky.	379	193	50.9%
Deputy Minister, Dead	356	190	53.4%
Crafty Prospector, Pens	318	179	56.3%
Valid Appeal, Dead	289	172	59.5%
Storm Cat, Ky.	322	157	48.8%
Cure the Blues, Dead	288	156	54.2%
Relaunch, Dead	284	153	53.9%
Conquistador Cielo, Dead	305	151	49.5%
Wild Again, Pens	282	150	53.2%
Carson City, Dead	251	146	58.2%
Mt. Livermore, Dead	307	144	46.9%
Miswaki, Dead	261	141	54.0%
Phone Trick, Dead	286	140	49.0%
Silver Deputy, Ky.	238	140	58.8%
Kris S., Dead	301	139	46.2%
Capote, Dead	245	137	55.9%
Clever Trick, Dead	306	136	44.4%
Broad Brush, Pens	255	134	52.5%
Devil's Bag, Dead	263	134	51.0%
Seattle Slew, Dead	255	133	52.2%
Meadowlake, Dead	266	132	49.6%
Rahy, Ky.	241	132	54.8%
Pleasant Colony, Dead	253	126	49.8%
Storm Bird, Dead	227	126	55.5%

Leading Broodmare Sires by Number of Wins in North America in 2007

Sire	Strs	Wnrs	Wins
Dixieland Band, Ky.	379	193	336
Deputy Minister, Dead	356	190	333
Crafty Prospector, Pens	318	179	316
Valid Appeal, Dead	289	172	295
Relaunch, Dead	284	153	273
Storm Cat, Ky.	322	157	273
Conquistador Cielo, Dead	305	151	270
Cure the Blues, Dead	288	156	258
Carson City, Dead	251	146	246
Kris S., Dead	301	139	245
Phone Trick, Dead	286	140	238
Devil's Bag, Dead	263	134	236
Wild Again, Pens	282	150	231
Meadowlake, Dead	266	132	229
Mt. Livermore, Dead	307	144	228
Storm Bird, Dead	227	126	227
Clever Trick, Dead	306	136	226
Pleasant Colony, Dead	253	126	226
Red Ransom, Eng	231	122	226
Silver Deputy, Ky.	238	140	224
Capote, Dead	245	137	223
Seattle Slew, Dead	255	133	221
Woodman, Dead	265	123	221

Leading Broodmare Sires by Number of Stakes Winners in North America in 2007

Sire	Strs	Wnrs	SWs	SWins
Storm Cat, Ky.	322	157	21	33
Deputy Minister, Dead	356	190	18	30
Dixieland Band, Ky.	379	193	18	28
Dynaformer, Ky.	237	125	15	23
Relaunch, Dead	284	153	15	18
Danzig, Dead	195	104	14	16
Forty Niner, Jpn	182	104	14	21
Meadowlake, Dead	266	132	13	16
Wild Again, Pens	282	150	13	22
Mr. Prospector, Dead	239	119	11	17
Pleasant Colony, Dead	253	126	11	13
Seeking the Gold, Ky.	212	113	11	14
Storm Bird, Dead	227	126	11	14
Valid Appeal, Dead	289	172	11	16
A.P. Indy, Ky.	172	90	10	15
Capote, Dead	245	137	10	12
Conquistador Cielo, Dead	305	151	10	12
Mt. Livermore, Dead	307	144	10	12
Rahy, Ky.	241	132	10	21
Regal Classic, Pens	187	100	10	16
Seattle Slew, Dead	255	133	10	10
Theatrical (Ire), Ky.	213	95	10	13
Turkoman, Ca.	112	49	10	16
With Approval, Eng	167	95	10	14

Leading Broodmare Sires by Number of Graded Stakes Winners in North America in 2007

Sire	Strs	Wnrs	GSWs	GSWins
Deputy Minister, Dead	356	190	8	16
Dixieland Band, Ky.	379	193	7	10
Mr. Prospector, Dead	239	119	7	11
Storm Cat, Ky.	322	157	7	14
A.P. Indy, Ky.	172	90	6	10
Seeking the Gold, Ky.	212	113	6	7
Capote, Dead	245	137	5	5
Forty Niner, Jpn	182	104	5	9
Storm Bird, Dead	227	126	5	6
Rahy, Ky.	241	132	4	11
Unbridled, Dead	202	96	4	8

Leading Worldwide Sires by 2007 Earnings

Worldwide earnings for stallions represented by one starter in any of the following jurisdictions: United States, Argentina, Australia, Brazil, Canada, England, France, Germany, Hong Kong, Ireland, Italy, Japan, Puerto Rico, Saudi Arabia, and United Arab Emirates.

Sire, YOB, Sire	Loc	2007 Stud Fee	Strs	Wnrs	SWs/Stk Wins	Leading Earner (Earnings)	Progeny Earnings
SUNDAY SILENCE, 86, by Halo	Dead		260	82	17/27	=Daiwa Major (Jpn) ($2,825,603)	$34,382,456
AGNES TACHYON, 98, by Sunday Silence	Jpn	N/A	242	100	6/10	=Daiwa Scarlet (Jpn) ($3,985,857)	23,548,051
BRIAN'S TIME, 85, by Roberto	Jpn	N/A	200	81	9/12	=Victory (Jpn) ($1,398,976)	20,014,377
DANCE IN THE DARK, 93, by Sunday Silence	Jpn	N/A	280	79	6/6	=Jolly Dance (Jpn) ($1,241,072)	19,969,084
FUJI KISEKI, 92, by Sunday Silence	Jpn	N/A	303	96	9/11	=Yumeno Shirushi (Jpn) ($1,066,021)	19,127,506
DANEHILL, 86, by Danzig	Dead		280	113	19/32	Dylan Thomas (Ire) ($4,116,103)	17,886,052
FRENCH DEPUTY, 92, by Deputy Minister	Jpn	N/A	219	77	8/11	=Sans Adieu (Jpn) ($1,604,557)	17,252,618
SAKURA BAKUSHIN O, 89, by Sakura Yutaka O		N/A	228	81	3/3	=Kanoya Zakura (Jpn) ($670,924)	15,355,077
SPECIAL WEEK, 95, by Sunday Silence	Jpn	N/A	219	76	2/3	=Inti Raimi (Jpn) ($1,134,097)	15,126,431
SMART STRIKE, 92, by Mr. Prospector	Ky.	$75,000	214	102	16/29	Curlin ($5,102,800)	14,477,651
EL CONDOR PASA, 95, by Kingmambo	Dead		97	37	4/7	=Vermilion (Jpn) ($3,609,013)	14,312,025
END SWEEP, 91, by Forty Niner	Dead		155	45	1/4	=Admire Moon (Jpn) ($7,191,318)	13,203,950
KUROFUNE, 98, by French Deputy	Jpn	N/A	195	69	2/3	=White Melody (Jpn) ($694,759)	11,454,306
LANGFUHR, 92, by Danzig	Ky.	$25,000	350	174	15/26	Lawyer Ron ($1,320,000)	10,709,065
DISTORTED HUMOR, 93, by Forty Niner	Ky.	$225,000	269	127	20/28	Any Given Saturday ($994,320)	10,639,082
ADMIRE VEGA, 96, by Sunday Silence		N/A	185	42	1/1	=Al Nasrain (Jpn) ($874,145)	10,259,833
A.P. INDY, 89, by Seattle Slew	Ky.	$300,000	172	80	18/30	Rags to Riches ($1,340,028)	10,028,967
GIANT'S CAUSEWAY, 97, by Storm Cat	Ky.	(MF250,000)	294	124	15/23	Red Giant ($846,720)	9,717,748
ZABEEL, 86, by *Sir Tristram	NZ	$70,450	108	31	6/8	=Vengeance Of Rain (NZ) ($4,251,723)	9,573,813
GALILEO (IRE), 98, by Sadler's Wells	Ire	$198,015	243	96	11/19	=Soldier of Fortune (Ire) ($1,570,120)	9,370,472
MAYANO TOP GUN, 92, by Brian's Time	Jpn	N/A	138	35	2/4	=Meisho Tokon (Jpn) ($1,542,971)	9,080,371
GRASS WONDER, 95, by Silver Hawk	Jpn	N/A	182	45	3/4	=Silk Nexus (Jpn) ($913,866)	9,028,866
TAIKI SHUTTLE, 94, by Devil's Bag	Jpn	N/A	190	51	1/1	=Dear Chance (Jpn) ($665,966)	8,947,286
FUSAICHI PEGASUS, 97, by Mr. Prospector	Ky.	$75,000	304	105	4/6	=Floral Pegasus (Aus) ($1,691,018)	8,945,533
AFLEET, 84, by Mr. Prospector	Jpn	N/A	150	52	3/3	=Hasufel (Jpn) ($439,529)	8,537,760
ROYAL ACADEMY, 87, by Nijinsky II	Ky.	$15,000	348	147	20/27	Bullish Luck ($803,057)	8,423,171
KING HALO, 95, by Dancing Brave	Jpn	N/A	120	39	4/4	=Kikuno Arrow (Jpn) ($714,826)	8,349,781
DANEHILL DANCER, 93, by Danehill	Ire	$151,811	434	157	19/24	=Arapaho Miss (Aus) ($594,936)	8,268,152
TANINO GIMLET, 99, by Brian's Time		N/A	128	28	2/3	=Vodka (Jpn) ($2,980,561)	8,107,737
STRAVINSKY, 96, by Nureyev	Jpn	$21,098	284	119	12/17	=Kongo Rikishio (Ire) ($850,938)	8,085,160
MONTJEU (IRE), 96, by Sadler's Wells	Ire	$165,012	272	100	19/23	=Authorized (Ire) ($2,365,763)	8,073,212
OPERA HOUSE (GB), 88, by Sadler's Wells	Jpn	$12,605	83	22	1/3	=Meisho Samson (Jpn) ($3,894,358)	7,804,947
SADLER'S WELLS, 81, by Northern Dancer	Ire	N/A	222	87	18/30	=Yeats (Ire) ($634,581)	7,596,874
AWESOME AGAIN, 94, by Deputy Minister	Ky.	$125,000	159	79	11/21	Ginger Punch ($1,827,060)	7,557,131
TALE OF THE CAT, 94, by Storm Cat	Ky.	$37,500	327	158	12/13	Tale of Ekati ($313,200)	7,531,639
STAY GOLD, 94, by Sunday Silence		N/A	113	26	4/5	=Dream Journey (Jpn) ($820,422)	7,388,510
MR. GREELEY, 92, by Gone West	Ky.	$75,000	198	94	7/11	=Finsceal Beo (Ire) ($844,219)	7,166,342
WHITE MUZZLE (GB), 90, by Dancing Brave	Jpn	N/A	95	24	2/3	=Asakusa Kings (Jpn) ($2,459,998)	7,150,033
HENNESSY, 93, by Storm Cat	Dead		216	94	12/17	=Sunrise Bacchus (Jpn) ($1,625,032)	6,924,984
DYNAFORMER, 85, by Roberto	Ky.	$150,000	187	86	7/12	Lucarno ($1,033,373)	6,885,041
UNBRIDLED'S SONG, 93, by Unbridled	Ky.	$200,000	170	86	14/18	Octave ($1,050,234)	6,813,635
STREET CRY (IRE), 98, by Machiavellian	Ky.	$50,000	127	47	11/19	Street Sense ($3,205,000)	6,785,085
PULPIT, 94, by A.P. Indy	Ky.	$80,000	165	82	9/19	Corinthian ($1,174,173)	6,751,900
SINGSPIEL (IRE), 92, by In the Wings (GB)	Eng	$68,530	223	98	13/14	Lahudood (GB) ($1,560,500)	6,687,137
GRAND SLAM, 95, by Gone West	Ky.	$35,000	284	137	10/11	Fresh Vanilla ($280,704)	6,657,989
MANHATTAN CAFE, 98, by Sunday Silence	Jpn	N/A	159	43	2/2	=Meiner Kirov (Jpn) ($442,614)	6,640,663
STORMY ATLANTIC, 94, by Storm Cat	Ky.	$30,000	246	130	13/18	Icy Atlantic ($367,110)	6,628,954
CHEROKEE RUN, 90, by Runaway Groom	Ky.	$40,000	179	105	9/13	War Pass ($1,397,400)	6,625,121
VICTORY GALLOP, 95, by Cryptoclearance	Tur	$10,000	194	100	8/13	Eishin Dover ($1,107,208)	6,605,618
LEMON DROP KID, 96, by Kingmambo	Ky.	$20,000	174	85	14/23	Citronnade ($701,405)	6,587,197
MORE THAN READY, 97, by Southern Halo	Ky.	$40,000	297	146	10/15	Ready's Image ($259,422)	6,470,753
FORTY NINER, 85, by Mr. Prospector	Jpn	$37,814	117	35	1/1	=Sunrise Lexus (Jpn) ($382,547)	6,308,017
JUNGLE POCKET, 98, by Tony Bin	Jpn	N/A	88	29	5/5	=Tall Poppy (Jpn) ($654,983)	6,248,150
FUSAICHI CONCORDE, 93, by Caerleon	Jpn	N/A	141	29	2/3	=Blue Concorde (Jpn) ($1,693,107)	6,193,629
BROKEN VOW, 97, by Unbridled	Ky.	$25,000	180	109	6/10	Unbridled Belle ($1,116,500)	6,115,147
BUBBLE GUM FELLOW, 93, by Sunday Silence	Jpn	N/A	159	34	0/0	=Tosen the O (Jpn) ($482,899)	6,092,785
KINGMAMBO, 90, by Mr. Prospector	Ky.	(MF250,000)	178	64	7/13	Student Council (Jpn) ($1,041,755)	6,072,950
RAHY, 85, by Blushing Groom (Fr)	Ky.	$60,000	159	57	9/14	Flying Apple ($561,195)	6,006,669
MARVELOUS SUNDAY, 92, by Sunday Silence		N/A	111	30	1/2	=Never Bouchon (Jpn) ($1,142,389)	5,915,771
CHIEF BEARHART, 93, by Chief's Crown	Jpn	$10,924	100	30	2/2	=Toho Racer (Jpn) ($744,646)	5,908,112
STORM CAT, 83, by Storm Bird	Ky.	$500,000	154	73	10/16	After Market ($686,725)	5,844,576
SILVER DEPUTY, 85, by Deputy Minister	Ky.	$30,000	184	103	11/12	Spring At Last ($722,000)	5,815,095
NOT FOR LOVE, 90, by Mr. Prospector	Md.	$25,000	177	100	11/17	Talkin About Love ($375,875)	5,784,263
MUTAKDDIM, 91, by Seeking the Gold	Ky.	$12,500	292	163	6/8	Ravalo ($201,655)	5,702,040
MEINER LOVE, 95, by Seeking the Gold	Jpn	$10,084	111	27	0/0	=Love Heart (Jpn) ($485,801)	5,670,100

Leading General Sire by Year

Year	General Sire	Earnings	Year	General Sire	Earnings	Year	General Sire	Earnings
2007	Smart Strike	$14,475,153	1957	*Princequillo	$1,698,427	1907	Commando	$270,345
2006	A.P. Indy	9,830,318	1956	*Nasrullah	1,462,413	1906	*Meddler	151,243
2005	Saint Ballado	10,409,467	1955	*Nasrullah	1,433,660	1905	Hamburg	153,160
2004	Elusive Quality	10,865,792	1954	*Heliopolis	1,406,638	1904	*Meddler	222,555
2003	Kris S.	11,497,747	1953	Bull Lea	1,155,846	1903	*Ben Strome	106,965
2002	Dehere	9,337,302	1952	Bull Lea	1,630,847	1902	Hastings	113,865
2001	Danehill	13,542,612	1951	Count Fleet	1,160,847	1901	Sir Dixon	165,682
2000	Storm Cat	9,269,521	1950	*Heliopolis	852,292	1900	Kingston	116,368
1999	Storm Cat	10,383,259	1949	Bull Lea	991,842	1899	*Albert	95,975
1998	Deputy Minister	8,526,094	1948	Bull Lea	1,334,027	1898	Hanover	118,590
1997	Deputy Minister	8,581,511	1947	Bull Lea	1,259,718	1897	Hanover	122,374
1996	Palace Music	5,231,734	1946	*Mahmoud	638,025	1896	Hanover	86,853
1995	Sadler's Wells	5,862,410	1945	War Admiral	591,352	1895	Hanover	106,908
1994	Broad Brush	5,397,181	1944	Chance Play	431,100	1894	*Sir Modred	134,318
1993	Danzig	5,082,552	1943	*Bull Dog	372,706	1893	Himyar	249,502
1992	Danzig	6,932,569	1942	Equipoise	437,141	1892	Iroquois	183,026
1991	Danzig	6,997,402	1941	*Blenheim II	378,981	1891	Longfellow	189,334
1990	Alydar	6,661,455	1940	*Sir Gallahad III	305,610	1890	*St. Blaise	189,005
1989	Halo	7,525,638	1939	*Challenger II	316,281	1889	*Rayon d'Or	175,877
1988	Mr. Prospector	9,575,605	1938	*Sickle	327,822	1888	Glenelg	130,746
1987	Mr. Prospector	5,877,385	1937	The Porter	292,262	1887	Glenelg	120,031
1986	Lyphard	4,045,447	1936	*Sickle	209,800	1886	Glenelg	114,088
1985	Buckaroo	4,145,272	1935	Chance Play	191,465	1885	Virgil	73,235
1984	Seattle Slew	5,361,259	1934	*Sir Gallahad III	180,165	1884	Glenelg	98,862
1983	Halo	2,773,637	1933	*Sir Gallahad III	136,428	1883	*Billet	89,998
1982	His Majesty	2,675,823	1932	Chatterton	210,040	1882	*Bonnie Scotland	103,475
1981	Nodouble	2,499,946	1931	*St. Germans	315,585	1881	*Leamington	139,219
1980	Raja Baba	2,483,352	1930	*Sir Gallahad III	422,200	1880	*Bonnie Scotland	135,700
1979	Exclusive Native	2,872,605	1929	*Chicle	289,123	1879	*Leamington	70,837
1978	Exclusive Native	1,969,867	1928	High Time	307,631	1878	Lexington	50,198
1977	Dr. Fager	1,593,079	1927	Fair Play	361,518	1877	*Leamington	41,700
1976	What a Pleasure	1,622,159	1926	Man o' War	408,137	1876	Lexington	90,570
1975	What a Pleasure	2,011,878	1925	Sweep	237,564	1875	*Leamington	64,518
1974	T. V. Lark	1,242,000	1924	Fair Play	296,102	1874	Lexington	51,889
1973	Bold Ruler	1,488,622	1923	The Finn	285,759	1873	Lexington	71,565
1972	Round Table	1,199,933	1922	*McGee	222,491	1872	Lexington	71,515
1971	Northern Dancer	1,288,580	1921	Celt	206,167	1871	Lexington	109,095
1970	Hail to Reason	1,400,839	1920	Fair Play	269,102	1870	Lexington	120,360
1969	Bold Ruler	1,357,144	1919	*Star Shoot	197,233	1869	Lexington	56,375
1968	Bold Ruler	1,988,427	1918	Sweep	139,057	1868	Lexington	68,340
1967	Bold Ruler	2,249,272	1917	*Star Shoot	131,674	1867	Lexington	54,030
1966	Bold Ruler	2,306,523	1916	*Star Shoot	138,163	1866	Lexington	92,725
1965	Bold Ruler	1,091,924	1915	Broomstick	94,387	1865	Lexington	58,750
1964	Bold Ruler	1,457,156	1914	Broomstick	99,043	1864	Lexington	28,440
1963	Bold Ruler	917,531	1913	Broomstick	76,009	1863	Lexington	14,235
1962	*Nasrullah	1,474,831	1912	*Star Shoot	79,973	1862	Lexington	9,700
1961	*Ambiorix	936,976	1911	*Star Shoot	53,895	1861	Lexington	22,425
1960	*Nasrullah	1,419,683	1910	Kingston	85,220	1860	Revenue	49,450
1959	*Nasrullah	1,434,543	1909	Ben Brush	75,143			
1958	*Princequillo	1,394,540	1908	Hastings	154,061			

Leading Juvenile Sire by Year

Year	Juvenile Sire	Earnings	Year	Juvenile Sire	Earnings	Year	Juvenile Sire	Earnings
2007	Cherokee Run	$2,200,491	1985	Fappiano	$1,232,408	1963	Bold Ruler	$343,585
2006	Stormy Atlantic	2,150,146	1984	Danzig	2,146,530	1962	*Nasrullah	574,231
2005	Giant's Causeway	1,642,157	1983	Alydar	1,136,063	1961	Bryan G.	428,810
2004	Storm Cat	1,927,589	1982	Olden Times	948,900	1960	*My Babu	437,240
2003	Tale of the Cat	2,077,206	1981	Hoist the Flag	680,753	1959	Determine	413,765
2002	Storm Cat	2,540,238	1980	Raja Baba	807,335	1958	*Turn-to	463,280
2001	Hennessy	1,766,695	1979	Mr. Prospector	529,665	1957	Jet Jewel	360,402
2000	Honour and Glory	1,436,584	1978	Secretariat	600,617	1956	*Nasrullah	422,573
1999	Storm Cat	1,570,026	1977	In Reality	432,596	1955	*Nirgal	293,800
1998	Storm Cat	1,686,995	1976	Raja Baba	419,872	1954	*Nasrullah	625,692
1997	Phone Trick	1,737,764	1975	What a Pleasure	611,071	1953	Roman	550,966
1996	Capote	2,756,558	1974	What a Pleasure	387,748	1952	Polynesian	341,730
1995	Storm Cat	1,281,030	1973	Raise a Native	311,002	1951	Menow	274,700
1994	Woodman	1,303,362	1972	Bold Ruler	541,990	1950	War Relic	272,182
1993	Storm Cat	1,567,979	1971	First Landing	551,120	1949	Roman	227,604
1992	Storm Cat	1,729,366	1970	Hail to Reason	473,244	1948	War Admiral	346,260
1991	Blushing Groom (Fr)	1,295,629	1969	Prince John	418,183	1947	Bull Lea	420,940
1990	Woodman	1,310,633	1968	Bold Ruler	609,243	1946	*Mahmoud	283,983
1989	Mr. Prospector	1,514,223	1967	Bold Ruler	1,126,844	1945	*Sickle	183,510
1988	Seattle Slew	946,433	1966	Bold Ruler	941,493	1944	Case Ace	230,525
1987	Mr. Prospector	1,566,919	1965	Tom Fool	592,871	1943	*Bull Dog	178,344
1986	Rajab	950,335	1964	Bold Ruler	967,814	1942	*Bull Dog	221,332

Leading Freshman Sire by Year

Year	Freshman Sire	Earnings	Year	Freshman Sire	Earnings	Year	Freshman Sire	Earnings
2007	Posse	$1,753,807	1996	Salt Lake	$850,954	1985	Fappiano	$1,232,408
2006	Johannesburg	1,955,459	1995	Farma Way	818,043	1984	Danzig	2,146,530
2005	Tiznow	1,376,265	1994	Red Ransom	817,550	1983	Alydar	1,136,063
2004	Successful Appeal	1,727,557	1993	Seeking the Gold	939,642	1982	Seattle Slew	666,755
2003	Stravinsky	1,271,620	1992	Forty Niner	578,567	1981	Turn and Count	283,279
2002	Grand Slam	1,403,880	1991	Capote	1,185,886	1980	Foolish Pleasure	536,783
2001	Valid Expectations	1,397,911	1990	Woodman	1,310,633	1979	L'Enjoleur	201,116
2000	Honour and Glory	1,436,584	1989	Secreto	584,023	1978	Mr. Prospector	309,168
1999	Cherokee Run	1,369,126	1988	Chief's Crown	760,842	1977	Roberto	359,285
1998	End Sweep	947,013	1987	Crafty Prospector	349,405	1976	Raja Baba	419,872
1997	Gilded Time	730,106	1986	Sportin' Life	781,754	1975	Al Hattab	217,630

Leading Broodmare Sire by Year

Year	Broodmare Sire	Earnings	Year	Broodmare Sire	Earnings	Year	Broodmare Sire	Earnings
2007	Woodman	$19,699,202	1985	Speak John	$5,187,865	1963	Count Fleet	$1,866,809
2006	Mr. Prospector	19,617,716	1984	Buckpasser	5,111,391	1962	War Admiral	1,654,396
2005	Mr. Prospector	20,987,357	1983	Buckpasser	3,479,749	1961	Bull Lea	1,632,559
2004	Mr. Prospector	20,311,039	1982	Prince John	3,072,150	1960	Bull Lea	1,915,881
2003	Mr. Prospector	21,425,839	1981	Double Jay	3,453,131	1959	Bull Lea	1,481,291
2002	Mr. Prospector	9,725,924	1980	Prince John	3,423,135	1958	Bull Lea	1,646,812
2001	Mr. Prospector	11,430,437	1979	Prince John	2,856,004	1957	*Mahmoud	1,593,782
2000	Mr. Prospector	10,390,642	1978	Crafty Admiral	2,298,048	1956	*Bull Dog	1,683,908
1999	Mr. Prospector	11,124,523	1977	Double Jay	2,696,490	1955	*Sir Gallahad III	1,499,162
1998	Mr. Prospector	9,364,191	1976	*Princequillo	2,763,189	1954	*Bull Dog	1,780,267
1997	Mr. Prospector	9,829,817	1975	Double Jay	2,233,642	1953	*Bull Dog	1,941,345
1996	Seattle Slew	9,105,905	1974	Olympia	2,292,178	1952	*Sir Gallahad III	1,656,221
1995	Seattle Slew	8,291,630	1973	*Princequillo	3,079,810	1951	*Sir Gallahad III	1,707,823
1994	Nijinsky II	7,606,160	1972	*Princequillo	2,717,859	1950	*Sir Gallahac III	1,376,629
1993	Nijinsky II	7,179,266	1971	Double Jay	2,053,235	1949	*Sir Gallahad III	1,393,104
1992	Secretariat	7,345,089	1970	*Princequillo	2,451,785	1948	*Sir Gallahad III	1,468,648
1991	Northern Dancer	6,030,243	1969	*Princequillo	2,189,583	1947	*Sir Gallahad III	1,458,309
1990	*Grey Dawn II	6,211,259	1968	*Princequillo	2,104,439	1946	*Sir Gallahad III	1,529,393
1989	Buckpasser	10,111,605	1967	*Princequillo	2,302,065	1945	*Sir Gallahad III	1,020,235
1988	Buckpasser	7,593,450	1966	*Princequillo	2,007,184	1944	*Sir Gallahad III	1,024,290
1987	Hoist the Flag	5,516,181	1965	Roman	2,394,944	1943	*Sir Gallahad III	703,301
1986	Prince John	4,468,468	1964	War Admiral	2,028,459	1942	*Chicle	533,572

Most Times as Leading General Sire (1830-2007)
- 16 Lexington (1861-'74, '76, '78)
- 8 Bold Ruler (1963-'69, '73)
- *Glencoe (1847, '49-'50, '54-'58)
- 5 Bull Lea (1947-'49, '52-'53)
- *Leviathan (1837-'39, '43, '48)
- *Nasrullah (1955-'56, '59-'60, '62)
- Sir Charles (1830-'33, '36)
- *Star Shoot (1911-'12, '16-'17, '19)
- 4 Glenelg (1884, '86-'88)
- Hanover (1895-'98)
- *Leamington (1875, '77, '79, '81)
- *Priam (1842, '44-'46)
- *Sir Gallahad III (1930, '33-'34, '40)
- 3 Boston (1851-'53)
- Broomstick (1913-'15)
- Danzig (1991-'93)
- Fair Play (1920, '24, '27)

Before 1860, leading sire was determined by number of wins.

Most Times as Leading Juvenile Sire (1942-2007)
- 7 Storm Cat (1992-'93, '95, '98-'99, 2002, '04)
- 6 Bold Ruler (1963-'64, '66-'68, '72)
- 3 Mr. Prospector (1979, '87, '89)
- *Nasrullah (1954, '56, '62)
- Woodman (1990, '94, '98)
- 2 *Bull Dog (1942-'43)
- Raja Baba (1976, '80)
- What a Pleasure (1974-'75)

Most Times as Leading Broodmare Sire (1942-2007)
- 12 *Sir Gallahad III (1939, '43-'52, '55)
- 10 Mr. Prospector (1997-2006)
- 8 *Princequillo (1966-'70, '72-'73, '76)
- 4 Buckpasser (1983-'84, '88-'89)
- Bull Lea (1958-'61)
- Double Jay (1971, '75, '77, '81)
- Prince John (1979-'80, '82, '86)

Most Times as Leading General Sire in Consecutive Years (1830-2007)
- 14 Lexington (1861-'74)
- 7 Bold Ruler (1963-'69)
- 5 *Glencoe (1854-'58)
- 4 Hanover (1895-'98)
- Sir Charles (1830-'33)
- 3 Boston (1851-'53)
- Broomstick (1913-'15)
- Bull Lea (1947-'49)
- Danzig (1991-'93)
- Glenelg (1886-'88)
- *Leviathan (1837-'39)
- *Priam (1844-'46)
- 2 Bull Lea (1952-'53)
- Deputy Minister (1997-'98)
- Exclusive Native (1978-'79)
- *Glencoe (1849-'50)
- Mr. Prospector (1987-'88)
- *Nasrullah ('955-'56)
- *Nasrullah (1959-'60)
- *Princequillc (1957-'58)
- *Sir Gallahad III (1933-'34)
- *Star Shoot (1911-'12)
- *Star Shoot (1916-'17)

Before 1860, leading sire was determined by number of wins.

Most Times as Leading Juvenile Sire in Consecutive Years (1942-2007)
- 3 Bold Ruler (1966-'68)
- 2 Bold Ruler (1963-'64)
- *Bull Dog (1942-'43)
- Storm Cat (1992-'93)
- Storm Cat (1998-'99)
- What a Pleasure (1974-'75)

Most Times as Leading Broodmare Sire in Consecutive Years (1942-2007)
- 10 Mr. Prospector (1997-2006)
- Sir Gallahad III (1943-'52)
- 5 *Princequ llo (1966-'70)
- 4 Bull Lea (1958-'61)
- 2 Buckpasser (1983-'84)
- Buckpasser (1988-'89)
- *Bull Dog (1953-'54)
- Nijinsky II (1993-'94)
- Prince John (1979-'80)
- *Princequillo (1972-'73)
- Seattle S ew (1995-'96)

Profiles of Leading Sires

2007—SMART STRIKE, 1992 b. h., Mr. Prospector—Classy n' Smart, by Smarten. Bred in Ontario by Sam-Son Farm. Full brother to graded stakes winners Strike Smartly and Full of Wonder and half brother to 1991 Canadian Horse of the Year Dance Smartly. Trained by Mark Frostad. 8-6-1-0, $337,376. Won the Philip H. Iselin H. (G1) and the Salvator Mile H. (G3) as a four-year-old. Retired in 1997 to Lane's End. In 2007 set single-year earnings record for an American-based stallion ($14,475,153). Sired 2007 Horse of the Year and champion three-year-old male Curlin and '07 champion turf male English Channel. On September 30, 2007, made history when three of his progeny won Grade 1 races at Belmont Park: Curlin in the Jockey Club Gold Cup S. (G1), English Channel in the Joe Hirsch Turf Classic Invitational S. (G1), and Fabulous Strike in the Vosburgh S. (G1). Through 2007, sire of at least 51 stakes winners (8% of foals of racing age), with 26 graded stakes winners and nine champions. Other top runners include 2004 Canadian Horse of the Year Soaring Free and Canadian champions Eye of the Sphynx, Portcullis, and Gold Strike.

2006—A.P. INDY, 1989 dk. b. or br. h., Seattle Slew—Weekend Surprise, by Secretariat. Bred in Kentucky by William S. Farish and William S. Kilroy. Half brother to Summer Squall, Welcome Surprise, and Eavesdropper. Sold for $2.9-million at the 1990 Keeneland July sale of selected yearlings to British Bloodstock Agency (Ireland), agent for Tomonori Tsurumaki. An interest in him was sold to Farish, Kilroy, and Harold Goodman in the summer of 1992, and he was retired to Lane's End Farm at the end of that year. Trained by Neil Drysdale. 11-8-0-1, $2,979,815, Belmont S. (G1), Breeders' Cup Classic (G1), Santa Anita Derby (G1), Peter Pan S. (G2), San Rafael S. (G2), 1992 Horse of the Year and champion three-year-old male. Through 2007, sire of at least 107 stakes winners (11%), 64 graded stakes winners, and seven champions, with progeny earnings exceeding $90-million. In North America, sire of 2003 Horse of the Year Mineshaft, '07 champion three-year-old filly and Belmont S. (G1) winner Rags to Riches, '06 champion three-year-old male Bernardini, and '01 champion two-year-old filly Tempera.

2005—SAINT BALLADO, 1989 dk. b. or br. h., Halo—Ballade, by *Herbager. Bred in Ontario by Windfields Farm. Full brother to champions Devil's Bag and Glorious Song. Sold for $90,000 at the 1990 Keeneland September yearling sale to Tartan Farms. Owned by Steve Herold, Robert J. Lothenbach, and trainer Clint C. Goodrich. 9-4-2-0, $302,820. At three, stood the Arlington Classic S. (G2) and Sheridan S. (G3). Stood initially at Ocala Stud Farm in Florida and moved to Taylor Made Farm in Kentucky in 1998. Euthanized in 2002 due to effects of progressive cervical myelopathy. Through 2007, sire of at least 70 stakes winners (10%), 26 graded stakes winners, and three champions, with progeny earnings exceeding $50-million. Sire of 2005 Horse of the Year Saint Liam and '04 champion three-year-old filly and '05 champion older female Ashado.

2004—ELUSIVE QUALITY, 1993 b. h., Gone West—Touch of Greatness, by Hero's Honor. Bred in Kentucky by Silver Springs Stud Farm and Marie Costelloe. Raced in name of Sheikh Mohammed bin Rashid al Maktoum and his Darley operation. 20-9-3-2, $413,284. Half brother to stakes winner Rossini. Trained by Bill Mott, won 1998 Poker H. (G3), world record for mile on turf, 1:31.63; Jaipur H. (G3). Set seven-furlong track record at Gulfstream Park, 1:20.17, on dirt. Stands at Darley in Lexington after beginning stud duty at Gainsborough Stud and shuttled to Australia from 2003-'07. Through 2007, sire of at least 32 stakes winners (4%), including ten group or graded stakes winners, with progeny earnings exceeding $28-million. Sire of 2004 champion three-year-old male Smarty Jones; '07 champion female sprinter Maryfield; and Elusive City, '02 highweighted two-year-old on French Free Handicap. Substantial part of 2004 progeny earnings, $10,876,981, from Smarty Jones, who received a $5-million bonus from Oaklawn Park for winning the Rebel S., Arkansas Derby (G2), and Kentucky Derby (G1).

2003—KRIS S., 1977 dk. b. or br. h., Roberto—Sharp Queen, by *Princequillo. Bred in Florida by John Brunetti Jr.'s Red Oak Farm. Raced by estate of Lloyd Schunemann and partners. 5-3-1-0, $53,350. Won 1980 Bradbury S. Entered stud in 1982 at Joseph and Barbara LaCroix's Meadowbrook Farm in Florida; moved to Prestonwood Farm in Kentucky in '94; and was acquired by WinStar Farm when it purchased Prestonwood's assets. Through 2007, sire of 93 stakes winners (11%), including 43 graded stakes winners, with total progeny earnings exceeding $77-million. His four champions are: Symboli Kris S, 2002-'03 Horse of the Year in Japan; Hollywood Wildcat, 1993 champion three-year-old filly; Soaring Softly, '99 champion turf female; and Action This Day, 2003 champion two-year-old male. Also sire of Kris Kin, winner of the 2003 Epsom Derby (Eng-G1) and dual Grade 1 winner Rock Hard Ten. Sire of sires. Died in 2002.

2002—DEHERE, 1991 b. h., Deputy Minister—Sister Dot, by Secretariat. Bred in Kentucky by Robert E. Brennan's Due Process Stable. 9-6-2-0, $723,712. Champion two-year-old male in 1993. Trained by Reynaldo Nobles, swept Saratoga Race Course's three major juvenile races culminating with the Hopeful Stakes (G1); also won the Champagne Stakes (G1) at two. At three, won the Fountain of Youth Stakes (G2) but broke down before the Triple Crown races. Retired initially to Ashford Stud and sold to Japan in 1999. Returned to Ashford Stud in 2005. Through 2007, sire of at least 60 stakes winners (6%) and 26 graded stakes winners, including multiple Grade 1 winner Take Charge Lady, '00 Puerto Rican champion imported two-year-old colt Mi Amigo Guelo, and Belle Du Jour, highweighted two-year-old filly on the 1999 Australian Free Handicap.

2001—DANEHILL, 1986 b. h., Danzig—Razyana, by His Majesty. Bred in Kentucky by Juddmonte Farms. 9-4-1-2, $321,064. Highweighted sprinter at three on European Free Handicap. Retired to Coolmore Stud, Ireland, in 1990. From 1991 through 2001, shuttled annually to Coolmore Australia; in '02, covered mares on Southern Hemisphere schedule in Ireland. Stood in Japan in 1996. Leading sire in Australia eight times; leading sire in France 2001, '02, and '07; leading sire in Ireland '05-'07; leading sire in England '05 and '07. Through 2007, sire of at least 344 stakes winners (14%), 221 group or graded stakes winners, and 25 champions with earnings exceeding $263-million. Best runners: 2007 European Horse of the Year Dylan Thomas (Ire); '05 and '06 European champion male George Washington (Ire); North American champion turf females Intercontinental (GB) and Banks Hill (GB); European highweights Rock of Gibraltar (Ire), Desert King, Mozart (Ire), Tiger Hill; Hong Kong Horse of the Year Fairy King Prawn; and Australian champions Elvistroem, Dane Ripper, Danewin, Catbird, and Merlene. In 2001, set a single-season record with 48 stakes winners. Died May 13, 2003, at Coolmore, age 17.

2000, 1999—STORM CAT, 1983 dk. b. or br. h., Storm Bird—Terlingua, by Secretariat. Bred in Pennsylvania by W. T. Young Storage Inc., raced for W. T. Young. 8-4-3-0, $570,610. Won Young America Stakes (G1) and finished second by a nose to champion Tasso in 1985 Breeders' Cup Juvenile (G1). Entered stud in 1988 at Overbrook Farm in Kentucky for initial fee of $30,000; by 2002, stood for American high of $500,000. Through 2007, sire of at least 158 stakes winners (12%) and

97 graded stakes winners, including North American champion Storm Flag Flying, '00 European highweight and Horse of the Year Giant's Causeway, and major American winners Tabasco Cat, Cat Thief, Sharp Cat, and Bluegrass Cat. Led juvenile sire list a record seven times, 1992-'93, '95, '98-'99, 2002, '04. Pensioned in 2008.

1998, 1997—DEPUTY MINISTER, 1979 dk. b. or br. h., Vice Regent—Mint Copy, by Bunty's Flight. Bred in Canada by Mr. and Mrs. Morton Levy's Centurion Farms. 22-12-2-2, $696,964. Canadian Horse of the Year in 1981; Eclipse- and Sovereign Award-winning two-year-old male. Half-interest purchased by Kinghaven Farm midway through two-year-old season; purchased by Robert Brennan's Due Process Stable prior to 1982 season. Entered stud in 1984 at Windfields Farm Maryland; relocated in '88 to Brookdale Farm in Kentucky. Through 2007, sire of at least 89 stakes winners (8%), including 12 millionaires. Best include Racing Hall of Fame member Go for Wand; two-time champion and filly triple crown winner Open Mind; 1993 champion juvenile male and 2002 leading sire Dehere; 1998 Breeders' Cup Classic (G1) winner Awesome Again. Sire of sires. Broodmare sire of at least 148 stakes winners. Died September 10, 2004, at age 24.

1996—PALACE MUSIC, 1981 ch. h., The Minstrel—Come My Prince, by Prince John. Bred in Kentucky by Mereworth Farm. Sold for $130,000 to Nelson Bunker Hunt at 1982 Keeneland July sale of selected yearlings and raced for partnership of Hunt and Allen Paulson. 21-7-5-3, $918,700. Group 1 and Grade 1 turf stakes winner in England and North America. Stood one season at Hunt's Bluegrass Farm in Kentucky, then moved in 1988 to Paulson's Brookside Farm. Shuttled between Kentucky and New Zealand for several years before relocating permanently in 1991 to Australia, where he was pensioned in 2005. Was 1996 leading U.S. sire due to one horse—Cigar, a two-time Horse of the Year and leading American money winner ($9,999,815). Also sire of several important Australasian runners, including 1992 champion stayer Naturalism; also sire of South Africa two-year-old champion Palace Line. Through 2007, sire of at least 33 stakes winners (3%).

1995—SADLER'S WELLS, 1981 b. h., Northern Dancer—Fairy Bridge, by Bold Reason. Bred in Kentucky by Swettenham Stud and Partners. 11-6-3-0, $713,690. Winner of 1984 Irish Two Thousand Guineas (Ire-G1) and Eclipse Stakes (Eng-G1). Stands at Coolmore Stud in Ireland. Eleven-time leading sire on English-Irish list, four-time leading sire in France. Through 2007, sire of at least 292 stakes winners (14%), including 157 group or graded winners and 18 champions. Best include champions High Chaparral (Ire), Montjeu (Ire), Galileo (Ire), Northern Spur (Ire), Old Vic, Yeats, Barathea (Ire), Islington (Ire). Pensioned in 2008.

1994—BROAD BRUSH, 1983 b. h., Ack Ack—Hay Patcher, by Hoist the Flag. Bred in Maryland by Robert E. Meyerhoff and raced three seasons for Meyerhoff. 27-14-5-5, $2,656,793. Winner of Santa Anita Handicap (G1), Suburban Handicap (G1), etc. Syndicated and entered stud in 1988 at Gainesway Farm in Kentucky. Through 2007, sire of at least 93 stakes winners (14%), including '02 champion three-year-old filly Farda Amiga, 1994 Breeders' Cup Classic (G1) winner Concern, $4-million earner Broad Appeal (in Japan), and 2001 North American Grade 1 winners Include and Pompeii. Pensioned December 1, 2004.

1993, 1991-'92—DANZIG, 1977 b. h., Northern Dancer—Pas de Nom, by Admiral's Voyage. Bred in Pennsylvania by Derry Meeting Farm and William S. Farish. Sold for $310,000 to Henryk de Kwiatkowski at the 1978 Saratoga yearling sale. 3-3-0-0, $32,400. Undefeated New York allowance winner before injury ended his career. Entered stud in 1981 at Claiborne Farm. Through 2007, sire of at least 199 stakes winners (18%), including champions in U.S., Canada, Japan, England, France, Ireland, Spain, and United Arab Emirates. Best runners: 1991 Horse of the Year and Canadian Triple Crown winner Dance Smartly, '84 two-year-old male champion Chief's Crown, 2007 King's Bishop S. (G1) winner Hard Spun, two-time Breeders' Cup Mile (G1) winner Lure, 1990 English Horse of the Year Dayjur. Through 2007, broodmare sire of at least 153 stakes winners, including '00 Kentucky Derby (G1) winner Fusaichi Pegasus. Died at Claiborne Farm on January 3, 2006, at age 18.

1990—ALYDAR, 1975 ch. h, Raise a Native—Sweet Tooth, by On-and-On. Bred in Kentucky by Calumet Farm. 26-14-9-1, $957,195. Won 1978 Blue Grass Stakes (G1), Florida Derby (G1), etc.; second to Affirmed in all three '78 Triple Crown races. Entered stud in 1980 at Calumet Farm and became leading American freshman sire of '83. Sired 77 stakes winners (11%) in 11 crops, with career progeny earnings of more than $60-million. Best runners include Horses of the Year Alysheba (1988) and Criminal Type ('90), North American champions Easy Goer, Turkoman, and Althea, and '91 Kentucky Derby (G1) winner Strike the Gold. Broodmare sire of 150 stakes winners through 2007. Died at Calumet on November 15, 1990, following a leg injury of suspicious cause, at age 15.

1989, 1983—HALO, 1969 dk. b. or br. h., Hail to Reason—Cosmah, by Cosmic Bomb. Bred in Kentucky by John R. Gaines. Purchased for $100,000 by Charles Engelhard at 1970 Keeneland July yearling sale. 31-9-3-5, $259,553. Won 1974 United Nations Handicap (G1). Sold for $600,000 to stand in England, but sale fell through upon discovery he was a cribber. Syndicated for $30,000 per share and retired in 1974 to Windfields Farm Maryland. In 1984, was sold based on $36-million valuation and moved to Stone Farm in Kentucky. Sire of 63 stakes winners (9%), including champion and Racing Hall of Fame member Sunday Silence, all-time leading sire in Japan; 1983 Kentucky Derby winner Sunny's Halo; and champions Glorious Song and Devil's Bag. Broodmare sire of 147 stakes winners through 2007. Pensioned in 1997 and died at Stone Farm on November 28, 2000, at age 31.

1988, 1987—MR. PROSPECTOR, 1970 b. h., Raise a Native—Gold Digger, by Nashua. Bred in Kentucky by Leslie Combs II. Sold for a sale-topping $220,000 at 1971 Keeneland July sale to Abraham I. "Butch" Savin, for whom he won the Gravesend and Whirlaway Handicaps and set a Gulfstream Park track record, six furlongs in 1:07⅘, in '73. 14-7-4-2, $112,171. Retired in 1975 to Savin's Aisco Farm in Florida and was top freshman sire of '78. Moved to Claiborne Farm in Kentucky in 1981. Through 2007, sired 181 stakes winners (15%) and 16 champions, including Gulch, Forty Niner, Conquistador Cielo, and Woodman. Sire of 2007 leading sire Smart Strike. Broodmare sire of 339 stakes winners through 2007. Leading broodmare sire ten times. Died of peritonitis at Claiborne Farm on June 1, 1999, at age 29.

1986—LYPHARD, 1969 b. h., Northern Dancer—Goofed, by *Court Martial. Bred in Pennsylvania by Mrs. J. O. Burgwin. Sold for $35,000 as a weanling at 1969 Keeneland November sale; resold as a yearling in Ireland for $38,000. 12-6-1-0, $195,427. Became one of Europe's top milers, winning 1972 Prix de la Foret and Prix Jacques le Marois while racing for Mrs. Pierre Wertheimer. Retired in 1973 and stood five seasons in France, where he was twice leading sire and twice leading broodmare sire. For 1978 season, moved to Gainesway Farm in Kentucky and syndicated. Sired 115 stakes winners (14%) and eight champions, including Manila, Dancing Brave, and Three Troikas (Fr). Broodmare sire of 212 stakes winners through 2007. Pensioned in 1996, died on June 10, 2005.

1985—BUCKAROO, 1975 b. h., Buckpasser—Stepping High, by No Robbery. Bred in Kentucky by Greentree Stud. 18-5-

5-1, $138,604. Won 1978 Saranac (G2) and Peter Pan (G3) Stakes. Retired to Greentree in 1980. Sold privately in 1985 to Gary and Stephen Wolfson and moved to Happy Valley Farm in Florida. Relocated in 1991 to Florida Stallion Station and again in '92 to Bridlewood Farm near Ocala. Leading sire of 1985 due largely to Horse of the Year and Kentucky Derby (G1) winner Spend a Buck, who received a $2-million bonus for winning the Jersey Derby (G3). Also sired millionaires Roo Art and Lite the Fuse among 29 stakes winners from 17 crops. Died of kidney failure at the University of Florida School of Veterinary Medicine, on July 30, 1996, at age 21.

1984—SEATTLE SLEW, 1974 dk. b. or br. h., Bold Reasoning—My Charmer, by Poker. Bred in Kentucky by Ben Castleman. Sold at 1975 Fasig-Tipton Kentucky July sale for $17,500 to partnership of Mickey and Karen Taylor and Jim and Sally Hill. 17-14-2-0, $1,208,726. Champion at two, three, and four, Horse of the Year at three; in 1977, became first to win American Triple Crown while undefeated. Retired in 1979 to Spendthrift Farm in Kentucky but later relocated to Three Chimneys Farm; moved to Hill 'n' Dale Farms shortly before his death. Through 2007, sired 114 stakes winners (10%) including Horse of the Year and leading sire A.P. Indy, champions Slew o' Gold, Vindication, Surfside, Swale, Capote, and Landaluce. First to sire winners of $5-million in a single season (1984). Noted sire of sires. Broodmare sire of Cigar; twice leading broodmare sire; broodmare sire of 172 stakes winners, including 11 champions, through 2007. Died on May 7, 2002, at Hill 'n' Dale in Kentucky, at age 28.

1982—HIS MAJESTY, 1968 b. h., *Ribot—Flower Bowl, by *Alibhai. Bred in Kentucky by Mr. and Mrs. John W. Galbreath. Full brother to Graustark. 22-5-6-3, $99,430. Only stakes victory was 1971 Everglades Stakes. Syndicated for $2-million valuation and retired in 1974 to his birthplace, Darby Dan Farm, where he remained throughout a 23-season stud career. Sired 59 stakes winners (9%) and champions in U.S., Italy, Canada, Panama, and Mexico. Best include 1981 champion and dual classic winner Pleasant Colony, '91 grass champion Tight Spot, and $2-million earner Majesty's Prince. Maternal grandsire of leading international sire Danehill and 100 other stakes winners through 2007. Died at Darby Dan on September 21, 1995, at age 27.

1981—NODOUBLE, 1965 ch. h., *Noholme II—Abla-Jay, by Double Jay. Bred in Arkansas by Gene Goff. 42-13-11-5, $846,749. Two-time champion handicap horse, 1969-'70; known as "Arkansas Traveler" because he won stakes in seven states. Winner of 1969 Santa Anita Handicap, '70 Metropolitan Handicap, etc. Retired in 1971 and stood at four different farms from California to Florida before moving in '86 to Three Chimneys Farm in Kentucky. Sired 91 stakes winners (14%), including two-time Canadian Horse of the Year Overskate, Japan Cup (Jpn-G1) winner Mairzy Doates, and world record-setter Double Discount. Broodmare sire of 89 stakes winners to 2006. Pensioned in 1988. Died of colic at Three Chimneys on April 26, 1990, at age 25.

1980—RAJA BABA, 1968 b. h., Bold Ruler—Missy Baba, by *My Babu. Bred in Kentucky by Michael G. Phipps. 41-7-12-9, $123,287. Modest stakes winner retired in 1974 to Hermitage Farm in Kentucky and sired 62 stakes winners (10%), including '87 champion and Breeders' Cup Distaff (G1) winner Sacahuista, two-time Mexican Horse of the Year Gran Zar (Mex), and Canadian champion sprinter Summer Mood. Broodmare sire of more than 76 stakes winners of $69.4-million to 2006. Pensioned at Hermitage in 1987 and died on October 9, 2002, at age 34.

1979, 1978—EXCLUSIVE NATIVE, 1965 ch. h., Raise a Native—Exclusive, by Shut Out. Bred in Florida by Harbor View Farm. 13-4-4-3, $169,013. Won 1968 Arlington Classic Stakes but far better sire than racehorse. Entered stud in 1969 at Spendthrift Farm in Kentucky for a fee of $1,500. Sired 66 stakes winners (13%), including Racing Hall of Fame members Affirmed and Genuine Risk—the former an American Triple Crown winner, the latter only the second filly to win the Kentucky Derby (G1). Syndicated in 1972 for $1.8-million. Broodmare sire of 97 stakes winners. Died of cancer at Spendthrift Farm on April 21, 1983, at age 18.

1977—DR. FAGER, 1964 b. h., Rough'n Tumble—Aspidistra, by Better Self. Bred in Florida by William L. McKnight's Tartan Farms. 22-18-2-1, $1,002,642. Horse of the Year in 1968. Set world record mile of 1:32% at Arlington Park carrying 134 pounds. Syndicated for $3.2-million in 1968 and entered stud the next year at Tartan Farms in Florida, where he sired nine crops. His 35 stakes winners (13%) include 1978 champion sprinter Dr. Patches, '75 champion juvenile filly Dearly Precious, and '77 Canadian Horse of the Year L'Alezane. Broodmare sire of 98 stakes winners, including notable sires Fappiano and Quiet American. Inducted into the Racing Hall of Fame in 1971. Died at Tartan Farms from torsion of the large colon, on August 5, 1976, at age 12.

1976, 1975—WHAT A PLEASURE, 1965 ch. h., Bold Ruler—Grey Flight, by *Mahmoud. Bred in Kentucky by Wheatley Stable. 18-6-5-2, $164,935. Won Hopeful Stakes and was fourth on 1967 Experimental Free Handicap. Sold in 1968 to Howard Sams. Entered stud the following year at Sams's Waldemar Farm in Florida. Sired 50 stakes winners (10%), including Foolish Pleasure and Honest Pleasure, juvenile champions in 1974 and '75, respectively. Syndicated in 1976 for $8-million. Twice top juvenile sire by money won. Broodmare sire of 83 stakes winners, including champion juveniles Gilded Time and Tasso. Died of a heart attack at Waldemar Farm on March 13, 1983, at age 18.

1974—T. V. LARK, 1957 b. h., *Indian Hemp—Miss Larksfly, by Heelfly. Bred in California by Dr. Walter D. Lucas and raised in a half-acre paddock. Sold for $10,000 to Chase McCoy at 1958 Del Mar yearling sale. 72-19-13-6, $902,194. Champion grass horse of 1961 with victory over Kelso in Washington, D.C., International. Sold for $600,000 to syndicate headed by Preston Madden and retired in 1963 to Hamburg Place in Kentucky. First crop included world record-setter Pink Pigeon. Sired 53 stakes winners and 35% stakes horses from winners. Did not establish an enduring male line but became broodmare sire of Racing Hall of Fame filly Chris Evert. Died at Hamburg on March 6, 1975, at age 18.

1973, 1963-'69—BOLD RULER, 1954 dk. b. h., 1954, *Nasrullah—Miss Disco, by Discovery. Bred in Kentucky by Wheatley Stable. 33-23-4-2, $764,204. Racing Hall of Fame member, 1957 Horse of the Year. Retired to Claiborne Farm in 1959 and began his reign as perennial leading sire four years later. Became the dominant force in American breeding throughout the 1960s and '70s, leading by progeny earnings seven times in succession, eight times overall—more than any other 20th-century stallion. Also six times leading juvenile sire. Sired 43% stakes horses from starters, 82 stakes winners (22%), and 11 champions, among them Secretariat, Gamely, Wajima, and Bold Bidder. Broodmare sire of 119 stakes winners, although he never led in that category. Died of cancer at Claiborne on July 12, 1971, at age 17.

1972—ROUND TABLE, 1954 b. h., *Princequillo—*Knight's Daughter, by Sir Cosmo. Bred in Kentucky by Claiborne Farm. Sold privately in 1957 to Travis Kerr. 66-43-8-5-5, $1,749,869. Set or equaled 16 track, American, and world records. Horse of the Year in 1958, three-time champion grass horse, and world's leading money-earner at retirement. Entered stud in 1960 at Claiborne Farm. Made international impact, siring 83 stakes winners (21%) from 19 crops, including champions in England, Ireland, France, and Canada. Did not establish

significant male line, although several sons proved useful stallions. Broodmare sire of 125 stakes winners, including champions Outstandingly, De La Rose, and Bowl Game. Inducted into Racing Hall of Fame in 1972. Pensioned in 1978 and died at Claiborne on June 13, 1987, at age 33.

1971—NORTHERN DANCER, 1961 b. h., Nearctic—Natalma, by Native Dancer. Bred in Canada by E. P. Taylor. 18-14-2-2, $580,647. Champion in Canada and U.S., won 1964 Kentucky Derby, Preakness Stakes. Entered stud in 1965 at Windfields Farm in Canada but later relocated to Windfields's Maryland division. Syndicated in 1970 for $2.4-million. Became one of the most sought-after commercial stallions of all time, with numerous offspring selling at auction for $1-million and more. Leading sire in England four times. Leading U.S. broodmare sire in 1991. Former international leader by stakes winners, with 146—including 23 champions and noted sires Sadler's Wells, Nijinsky II, Danzig, Lyphard, Nureyev, and Storm Bird. Daughters produced 241 stakes winners (19 champions) to 2006. Inducted into Racing Hall of Fame in 1976. Died of colic at Windfields in Maryland on November 16, 1990, at age 29. Buried at Windfields, Canada.

1970—HAIL TO REASON, 1958 b. h., *Turn-to—Nothirdchance, by Blue Swords. Bred in Kentucky by Bieber-Jacobs Stable. 18-9-2-2, $328,434. Champion at two. Sesamoid injury forced retirement in 1961 to Hagyard Farm in Kentucky. Syndicated for $1,085,000. Leading sire and juvenile sire of 1970, and also among leading sires in England and France. Sired 43 stakes winners (13%), including 1970 co-Horse of the Year Personality and fillies Trillion, Straight Deal, and Regal Gleam. Several sons became top sires, including two-time American leader Halo and 1972 Epsom Derby winner Roberto, both of whom kept his male line alive. Daughters produced millionaires Allez France, Triptych, Royal Glint, Colonial Waters, and 110 additional stakes winners. Died at Hagyard on February 24, 1976, at age 18.

1962, 1959-'60, 1955-'56—*NASRULLAH, 1940 b. h., Nearco—Mumtaz Begum, by *Blenheim II. Bred in Ireland by the Aga Khan. 10-5-1-2, $15,259. Champion at two in England and classic-placed at three but generally a disappointment due to tendency to sulk before and during races. Entered stud in 1944 at Great Barton Stud in England; sold and relocated the next year to Brownstown Stud in Ireland. Purchased in 1950 for approximately $400,000 by A. B. Hancock on behalf of an American syndicate and sent to Claiborne Farm in Kentucky for '51 breeding season. Sired 93 international stakes winners (22%) and established an enduring male line through Racing Hall of Fame son Bold Ruler and Englishraced sons Red God and Grey Sovereign. Reigned five times as leading sire in America and once in England. Broodmare sire of 159 stakes winners. Suffered fatal heart attack at Claiborne on May 26, 1959, at age 19.

1961—*AMBIORIX, 1946 dk. b. h., Tourbillon—Lavendula, by Pharos. Bred in France by Marcel Boussac. 7-4-2-0, $25,165. Champion at two in France, winning Grand Criterium, and added the Prix Lupin at three before being narrowly beaten in the Prix du Jockey-Club (French Derby). Three-quarter brother to champion *My Babu. After failing to acquire *My Babu, A. B. Hancock purchased *Ambiorix in 1949 for syndication in America. Entered stud at Claiborne Farm in Kentucky the following year and ultimately sired 51 stakes winners (12%), including champion two- and three-year-old filly High Voltage. Leading sire of 1961 when runners included major winners Ambiopoise, Hitting Away, Make Sail, and Sarcastic. Also a successful broodmare sire, leading the list in England in 1963. Pensioned in 1972 and died at Claiborne on January 17, '75, at age 29.

1958, 1957—*PRINCEQUILLO, 1940 b. h., Prince Rose—*Cosquilla, by *Papyrus. Bred in England by American Laudy Lawrence. 33-12-5-7, $96,550. Imported to U.S. as a yearling, leased to Anthony Pelleteri at two, and claimed for $2,500 by future Racing Hall of Fame trainer Horatio Luro for Dimitri Djordjaze. Became a top stayer, with victories including the 1943 Jockey Club Gold Cup. Retired in 1945 to A. B. Hancock's Ellerslie Farm in Virginia for $250 fee. Moved two years later to Claiborne Farm in Kentucky. Hall of Fame members Round Table and Hill Prince were among his 65 stakes winners (13%), and *Princequillo arguably was one of America's greatest broodmare sires of the 20th century. Was eight times atop broodmare sire list; his daughters produced 170 stakes winners, including champions Secretariat, Mill Reef, Fort Marcy, Key to the Mint, and Bold Lad. Died at Claiborne on July 18, 1964, at age 24.

1954, 1950—*HELIOPOLIS, 1936 b. h., Hyperion—Drift, by Swynford. Bred in England by Lord Derby. 15-5-2-1, $71,216, stakes winner at two and three in England, third in 1939 Epsom Derby. Imported to America the following year by Charles B. Shaffer and finished last after sulking in his only U.S. start, an allowance race at Hialeah Park. Retired in 1941 to Shaffer's Coldstream Stud in Kentucky. Sold in 1951 to Henry Knight and relocated to Almahurst Farm. Among his 53 stakes winners (15%) were 1954 Belmont Stakes victor and champion High Gun, and champion fillies Grecian Queen, Parlo, Berlo, and Aunt Jinny. Died at Almahurst on April 2, 1959, at age 23.

1953, 1952, 1947-'49—BULL LEA, 1935 br. h., *Bull Dog—Rose Leaves, by Ballot. Bred in Kentucky by Coldstream Stud. 27-10-7-3, $94,825. Sold as a yearling for $14,000 to Calumet Farm. A moderately accomplished racehorse, he won the Widener Handicap and Blue Grass Stakes. Retired to Calumet in 1940 for a $750 fee and became one of the greatest American sires of all time. Sired 57 stakes winners (15%), including a record seven Racing Hall of Fame members—Citation, Armed, Coaltown, Bewitch, Two Lea, Real Delight, and Twilight Tear. In 1947, became first stallion with single-season progeny earnings of $1-million. Four-time leading broodmare sire of 105 stakes winners. Died and buried at Calumet on June 16, 1964, at age 29.

1951—COUNT FLEET, 1940 br. h., Reigh Count—Quickly, by Haste. Bred in Kentucky by Mrs. John D. Hertz. 21-16-4-1, $250,300. In the Hertz colors, won 1943 Triple Crown, taking Belmont Stakes by 25 lengths. Retired in 1945 to Stoner Creek Farm near Paris, Kentucky, where he remained for the next 30 years. Outstanding sire and even better broodmare sire, leading in the latter category in 1963 and in the top five ten times. Among his 39 stakes winners (9%) were back-to-back Horses of the Year and Belmont Stakes winners Counterpoint (1951) and One Count ('52). Daughters produced 118 stakes winners and seven champions, including Racing Hall of Fame member Kelso. Pensioned in 1966. Count Fleet was inducted into the Racing Hall of Fame in 1961. He died at Stoner Creek on December 3, 1973, at age 33.

1946—*MAHMOUD, 1933 gr. h., *Blenheim II—Mah Mahal, by Gainsborough. Bred in France by the Aga Khan. 11-4-2-3, $86,439. Champion at three in England in 1936 when he won the Epsom Derby in record time. Entered stud at Newmarket in 1937. Purchased in 1940 by C. V. Whitney for $85,000 and imported to stand at his Kentucky farm. Prior to his arrival, gray Thoroughbreds were spurned by many prominent American breeders, but *Mahmoud made the color acceptable. Sired 66 stakes winners, including U.S. champions Oil Capitol, The Axe II, and First Flight, and European champions *Majideh and Donatella. Leading broodmare sire of 1957 and among leaders throughout the '60s. Daughters produced 139 stakes winners, including Racing Hall of Fame members *Gallant Man and Silver Spoon. Died at C. V. Whitney Farm on September 18, 1962, at age 29.

1945—WAR ADMIRAL, 1934 br. h., Man o' War—Brushup, by Sweep. Bred in Kentucky by Samuel D. Riddle and raced

for Glen Riddle Stable. 26-21-3-1, $273,240. Racing Hall of Fame runner is generally acknowledged as Man o' War's best son, both on the track and in the stud. Won 1937 Triple Crown and stood alongside Man o' War at Faraway Farm in Kentucky. Sire of 40 stakes winners (11%), including 1945 Horse of the Year Busher, champion Blue Peter, and the great racemares-broodmares Searching and Busanda. Twice leading broodmare sire of 113 stakes winners, including champions Buckpasser, Hoist the Flag, and Affectionately. Died on October 30, 1959, at age 25 and buried next to Man o' War at Faraway. Remains were exhumed, along with his sire's, in the 1970s, and reinterred at Kentucky Horse Park.

1944, 1935—CHANCE PLAY, 1923 ch. h., Fair Play—*Quelle Chance, by Ethelbert. Bred in Kentucky by August Belmont II. 39-16-9-2, $137,946. A handsome horse who resembled his sire, he raced for W. Averill Harriman's Log Cabin Stable and was considered the best horse of the year in 1927. Retired in 1929, stood at farms from Kentucky to New York until purchased by Warren Wright, who made him one of first stallions to stand at Calumet Farm in Lexington. Sired 23 stakes winners (7%), including 1939 champion juvenile filly Now What and '45 Jockey Club Gold Cup winner Pot o' Luck. Pensioned in 1947 following heart attack. Euthanized at Calumet on July 6, 1950, at age 27 and buried in the farm's cemetery.

1943—*BULL DOG, 1927 b. or br. h., *Teddy—Plucky Liege, by Spearmint. Bred in France by Jefferson Davis Cohn. 8-2-1-0, $7,802. Stakes winner at three in France. Full brother to leading sire *Sir Gallahad III and half brother to top European sires Bois Roussel and Admiral Drake. Imported by Charles B. Shaffer in 1930 to stand at his Coldstream Stud in Kentucky. Top runners include champion two-year-olds Occupy and Our Boots and five-time leading American sire Bull Lea. Sired 52 stakes winners (15%) in 18 crops, and 27% of his starters were of stakes class. In 1953, he supplanted *Sir Gallahad III atop broodmare sire list and subsequently led that list three times. His daughters produced 89 stakes winners and four champions. Pensioned in 1948. Died at Coldstream on October 10, 1954, at age 27.

1942—EQUIPOISE, 1928 ch. h., Pennant—Swinging, by Broomstick. Bred in Kentucky by Harry Payne Whitney. 51-29-10-4, $338,610. First great racehorse to carry colors of Whitney's son, Cornelius Vanderbilt Whitney. Nicknamed the "Chocolate Soldier" because of his dark chestnut color and combative spirit, he was an American champion at ages two, four, and five. Entered stud at C. V. Whitney Farm in 1935. Sired just four crops and 74 foals, one of whom won stakes (12%), including 1940 champion juvenile filly Level Best and '42 Kentucky Derby and Belmont Stakes winner Shut Out. Broodmare sire of 1946 Triple Crown winner Assault. First foals were two-year-olds when he died of enteritis at age ten on August 4, 1938. Inducted into Racing Hall of Fame in 1957.

1941—*BLENHEIM II, 1927 br. h., Blandford—Malva, by Charles O'Malley. Bred in England by Lord Carnarvon. Sold as yearling from the Aga Khan for about $20,000. 10-5-3-0, $73,060. Injury forced retirement following victory in 1930 Epsom Derby. Stood in Europe for six seasons, siring 1936 Epsom Derby winner *Mahmoud, Italian champion Donatello II. Sold in 1936 for reported $250,000 to an American syndicate and sent to Claiborne Farm in Kentucky. Sire of more than 45 stakes winners, including 1941 American Triple Crown winner Whirlaway and '43 champion handicap mare Mar-Kell. Broodmare sire of more than 120 stakes winners, including *Nasrullah and Kentucky Derby winners Ponder, Hill Gail, and Kauai King. Died at Claiborne on May 26, 1958, at age 31.

1940, 1933-'34, 1930—*SIR GALLAHAD III, 1920 b. h., *Teddy—Plucky Liege, by Spearmint. Bred in France by Jefferson Davis Cohn. 24-11-3-3, $17,009, Poule d'Essai des Poulains (French Two Thousand Guineas), match with *Epinard, etc. Full brother to leading sire *Bull Dog, half brother to top European sires Bois Roussel and Admiral Drake. Stood 1925 season in France, then sold for $125,000 to U.S. syndicate headed by A. B. Hancock. First important American stallion syndication. Stood at Claiborne Farm in Kentucky for remainder of career. First U.S. crop included 1930 Triple Crown winner Gallant Fox, and with two crops racing he led general sire list for the first of four times. Sired 56 stakes winners (10%), including three Kentucky Derby victors and several champions. Not a notable sire of sires but an all-time great broodmare sire, leading in that category 12 times. Died and buried at Claiborne on July 8, 1949, at age 29.

1939—*CHALLENGER II, 1927 b. h., Swynford—Sword Play, by Great Sport. Bred in England by the National Stud. 2-2-0-0 $10,930, Richmond S., Clearwell S., ranked third on English Free Handicap, one pound above future leading American sire *Blenheim II. Classic engagements canceled upon death of owner Lord Dewar under the rules then in force. Sold for reported $100,000 to William L. Brann and Robert Castle and imported to U.S. but injured in paddock accident before he could race again. Stood 17 seasons at Brann's Glade Valley Farm in Maryland, the first leading sire to spend his entire career outside Kentucky since *Sir Modred in 1894. Sired 34 stakes winners (11%), including future Racing Hall of Fame members Challedon and Gallorette. Died at Glade Valley on December 23, 1948, at age 21.

1938, 1936—*SICKLE, 1924 br. h., Phalaris—Selene, by Chaucer. Bred in England by Lord Derby. 10-3-4-2, $23,629, stakes winner at two, third in the 1927 Two Thousand Guineas. Half brother to the great racehorse and sire Hyperion, full brother to *Pharamond II. Stood one season in England before being imported under a lease agreement in 1930 by Joseph E. Widener, who eventually purchased him for a reported $100,000. Sent to Widener's Elmendorf Farm in Kentucky, where he replaced deceased Fair Play as the stud's leading stallion. Sired 22% stakes horses from foals, with 41 stakes winners (14%), including champions Stagehand, Star Pilot, and *Gossip II. Broodmare sire of 57 stakes winners, including 1951 Horse of the Year Counterpoint. Died on December 26, 1943, at Elmendorf at age 19.

1937—THE PORTER, 1915 b. h., Sweep—Ballet Girl, by St. Leonards. Bred in Kentucky by David Stevenson. Raced for Samuel Ross and later Edward McLean. 52-26-10-8, $89,249, Annapolis Handicap, etc. Stood barely 15 foals. From 1922-'31 stood at McLean Stud in Virginia. At age 16, purchased for $27,000 at McLean's 1931 dispersal by Mrs. John Hay Whitney and sent to Kentucky. Sired 11% stakes winners from foals, with the best of his 34 stakes winners being 1937 Santa Anita Handicap winner Rosemont, '37 Suburban Handicap winner Aneroid, and the top juvenile Porter's Mite. Died at Mare's Nest Farm in Kentucky on October 23, 1944, at age 29.

1932—CHATTERTON, 1919 ch. h., Fair Play—Chit Chat, by *Rock Sand. Bred in Kentucky by August Belmont II. 32-15-5-4, $26,565. Bred like Man o' War, by Fair Play out of *Rock Sand mare. Sold privately and raced for Frank J. Kelley. Multiple stakes winner in Midwest, though not a top runner. Stood 1924 in California but after Kelley's death sent to Claiborne Farm in Kentucky. Remained there except for 1932 season when leased to Arrowbrook Farm in Illinois. His position atop list was due almost entirely to 1932 champion and Belmont Stakes winner Faireno. Also sired 1928 champion juvenile filly Current and nine other stakes winners. Died at Claiborne of kidney ailment on July 14, 1933, at age 14.

1931—*ST. GERMANS, 1921 b. h., Swynford—Hamoaze, by Torpoint. Bred in England by Lord Astor. 20-9-4-4, $44,793,

Coronation Cup, Doncaster Cup, etc., second in Epsom Derby. Imported by Payne Whitney to stand at his Greentree Stud. Advertised "for private use only" in early years. He suffered from low fertility and averaged fewer than ten foals per crop, but those were highly successful. Best of 23 stakes winners (13%) was Twenty Grand, winner of the Kentucky Derby and Belmont Stakes; two-time handicap champion Devil Diver; and 1936 Kentucky Derby-Preakness Stakes winner Bold Venture. Twenty Grand was sterile, and several prominent male-line descendants experienced fertility problems. Died at Greentree Stud on May 18, 1929, at age 18 following attack of enteritis.

1929—*CHICLE, 1913 b. h., Spearmint—Lady Hamburg II, by Hamburg. Bred in France by Harry Payne Whitney but raced in U.S. 4-7-6-0, $4,765. Had soundness problems but nonetheless won Champagne Stakes and Brooklyn Derby (now Dwyer Stakes). Entered stud in Kentucky at H. P. Whitney Farm for fee of $500. Fee later raised as high as $1,500. Bad tempered, kept muzzled as a stallion for safety of farm workers. Sired six stakes winners from first 13-foal crop and about 40 overall—including champion juveniles Whichone and Mother Goose. Leading broodmare sire of 1942. Died at C. V. Whitney Farm near Lexington on May 20, 1939, at age 26.

1928—HIGH TIME, 1916 ch. h., Ultimus—Noonday, by Domino. Bred in Kentucky by Wickliffe Stud of Corrigan and McKinney. 7-1-0-1, $3,950, Hudson S., Third Great American S. Highly inbred to Domino, with three crosses in first three generations. Beautiful physical specimen, sold at auction as two-year-old for $8,500. Career limited by throat problems. Won Aqueduct's Hudson Stakes in track-record time for five furlongs. Retired to Haylands Stud in 1919 but was not well received by Kentucky breeders. In later years, changed ownership several times before settling at Dixiana Farm in Kentucky. Sired about 40 stakes winners, including 1928 champion juvenile colt High Strung. Leading broodmare sire of 1940. Died at Dixiana on November 20, 1937, at age 21.

1927, 1924, 1920—FAIR PLAY, 1905 ch. h., Hastings—*Fairy Gold, by Bend Or. Bred in Kentucky by August Belmont II. 32-10-11-3, $86,950. Racing Hall of Fame runner had misfortune to come along in same crop as unbeatable Colin. Won 1908 Lawrence Realization. When betting was outlawed in New York, shipped to England, where heavy weight assignments and a deteriorating attitude led to a 6-0-0-0 record. Retired to Nursery Stud in 1910. When Belmont died in 1924, sold at age 20 on $100,000 bid to Joseph Widener. Renowned for producing stamina, the three-time leading sire got champions Chance Play and Mad Hatter but was immortalized as sire of Man o' War, through whom his male line survives today. Leading broodmare sire in 1931, '34, and '38. Died in paddock at Elmendorf Farm in Kentucky on December 16, 1929, at age 24.

1926—MAN O' WAR, 1917 ch. h., Fair Play—Mahubah, by *Rock Sand. Bred in Kentucky by August Belmont II. 21-20-1-0, $249,465. Sold at auction as yearling for $5,000 to Samuel Riddle. Became one of the greatest racehorses of all time, winning Preakness and Belmont Stakes. Retired in 1921 to Hinata Stock Farm but soon moved to Faraway Farm, both in Kentucky. Instant success, led general sire list with only three crops racing. Top runners include future Racing Hall of Fame members War Admiral and Crusader as well as six other American champions. Also a great broodmare sire. As Riddle's private stallion, did not receive the best mares but nonetheless sired 64 stakes winners, 17% of foals. Died at Faraway on November 1, 1947, at age 30. Thousands attended funeral, which was nationally broadcast on radio and filmed for newsreels. Grave and larger-than-life bronze statue relocated in late 1970s to Kentucky Horse Park.

1925, 1918—SWEEP, 1907 br. h., Ben Brush—Pink Domino, by Domino. Bred in Kentucky by James R. Keene. 13-9-2-2, $59,998, champion at two in 1909 when he won the Futurity Stakes and added the Belmont Stakes at three. Sold at 1913 Keene estate dispersal at Madison Square Garden for $17,500 to partnership of John Barbee, J. C. Carrick, and Andrew Stone. Led broodmare sire list twice and twice was leader by number of two-year-old winners. Sired more than 40 stakes winners. Top runners include 1918 champion juvenile Eternal and handicap star The Porter, leading sire of '37. Died from "indigestion" at Glen-Helen Stud in Kentucky on August 15, 1931, at age 24.

1923—THE FINN, 1912 bl. h., *Ogden—Livonia, by *Star Shoot. Bred in Kentucky by John E. Madden. 50-19-10-6, $38,965. Raced initially for Madden before being sold to H. C. Hallenbeck. Victories included Belmont and Withers Stakes as well as Metropolitan, Manhattan, and Havre de Grace Handicaps. Generally regarded as champion three-year-old colt of 1915. Madden later bought him back and in 1923 he was sold again, for $100,000, to W. R. Coe. Stood thereafter at Hinata Stock Farm in Kentucky. Sired Kentucky Derby winners Flying Ebony and Zev, the latter America's first racehorse to top $300,000 in earnings (1924). Died at Hinata on September 4, 1925, from "inflammation of the bowels," at age 13.

1922—*MCGEE, 1900 b. h., White Knight—Remorse, by Hermit. Bred in England by Lord Bradford. 53-24-14-5, $18,391, Fleetfoot H., etc. Only foal by an unraced stallion. Sold cheaply as yearling to Ed Corrigan and imported to U.S. Raced in Midwest, a minor stakes winner of 24 races. Primarily a sprinter—set American 5½-furlong record in 1903. Retired to Corrigan's Freeland Stud near Lexington, then sold in 1908 for $1,300 to Charles Moore. Relocated to nearby Mere Hill Stud where his 1909 fee was $50. Sired at least 20 stakes winners, most notably the great gelding Exterminator and Donerail, winner of 1913 Kentucky Derby at 91.45-to-1. His last foal was conceived in 1930 when *McGee was 30 years old. Prior to his death at Mere Hill on September 18, 1931, he was believed to be the oldest stallion in Kentucky.

1921—CELT, 1905 ch. h., Commando—*Maid Of Erin, by Amphion. Bred in Kentucky by James R. Keene. 6-4-1-1, $29,975. Lightly raced winner of 1908 Brooklyn Handicap, overshadowed by unbeaten stablemate Colin, another son of Commando. Stood initially at Castleton Stud, then leased for 1912 to stand at Hancock family's Ellerslie Stud in Virginia. Though lease expired in 1913, A. B. Hancock acquired him that fall for $20,000 at Keene's estate dispersal. Returned to Ellerslie to sire a total of at least 25 stakes winners. In 1930, was top broodmare sire when Gallant Fox swept the Triple Crown. Died in 1919, at age 14.

1919, 1916-'17, 1911-'12—*STAR SHOOT, 1898 ch. h., Isinglass—Astrology, by Hermit. Bred in England by Maj. Eustace Loder. 10-3-1-3, $34,747, National Breeders' Produce S., etc. A good two-year-old, developed wind problems at three and was unplaced in two starts that season. Because he was from a family not noted for producing good sires, he was sold to America and entered stud in 1902 at Runnymede Farm in Kentucky, where he was an immediate success. Purchased privately by John Madden in 1912 and relocated to Hamburg Place. One of the most influential American-based stallions of his time; his sons included future Racing Hall of Fame members Grey Lag and Sir Barton. In 1916, had record 27 juvenile winners. Died of pneumonia at Hamburg on November 19, 1919, at age 21.

1915, 1913-'14—BROOMSTICK, 1901 b. h., Ben Brush—*Elf, by Galliard. Bred in Kentucky by Col. Milton Young. 39-14-11-5, $74,730, Travers S., etc. Young acquired *Elf for

$250 in foal with Broomstick. Colt was sold privately to race for coal millionaire Samuel Brown. Racing Hall of Fame runner raced through age four. Retired in 1906 to Brown's Senorita Stud in Kentucky. Sold for $7,250 two years later at estate sale of his owner to H. P. Whitney. Eventually sired about 25% stakes winners from foals—nearly 60 in all—including the first New York handicap triple crown winner, Whisk Broom II; the first filly Kentucky Derby winner, Regret; 1911 Derby winner Meridian; and '12 Two Thousand Guineas winner *Sweeper. Died at C. V. Whitney Farm in Kentucky, on March 24, 1931, at age 30.

1910, 1900—KINGSTON, 1884 br. h., Spendthrift—*Kapanga, by Victorious. Bred in Kentucky by James R. Keene. 138-89-33-12, $140,195, First Special S., etc. Raced through age ten, primarily for Phil and Mike Dwyer. His 89 career victories remains an all-time record, and for about one year (1892-'93) he reigned as America's leading money earner. Entered stud in 1895 at Eugene Leigh's La Belle Farm in Kentucky for a $150 fee. Moved in a few years to Keene's Castleton Farm near Lexington, where he stood privately. Represented by Futurity Stakes winners Ballyhoo Bey (1900) and Novelty ('10) as well as '00 Belmont Stakes winner Ildrim. Died at Castleton on December 4, 1912, at age 28.

1909—BEN BRUSH, 1893 b. h., Bramble—Roseville, by Reform. Bred in Kentucky by Catesby Woodford and Ezekiel Clay. 40-25-5-5, $65,208. Small, plain, and tough, a superb racehorse, and Racing Hall of Fame member. Sold as yearling for $1,200 to Eugene Leigh and Ed Brown, and again at three for reported $25,000 to Mike Dwyer. Won 1896 Kentucky Derby and '97 Suburban Handicap. Sold to James R. Keene for stud duty at Castleton Farm in Kentucky. Following Keene's death in 1913, acquired for $10,000 by Kentucky Senator Johnson Camden and lived out his days at Camden's Hartland Stud near Versailles. Established noted male line that endured for decades. Best offspring include three-time leading American sire Broomstick and two-time leader Sweep. Died on June 8, 1918, at age 25.

1908, 1902—HASTINGS, 1893 br. h., Spendthrift—*Cinderella, by Tomahawk or Blue Ruin. Bred in Kentucky by Dr. J. D. Neet. 21-10-8-0, $16,340. Raced at two for Gideon and Daly. Upon dispersal of that stable in 1895, acquired for $37,000 by August Belmont II. Won 1896 Belmont Stakes, although generally not regarded as a top racehorse. Entered stud in 1898 at Belmont's Nursery Stud in Kentucky and was known for his savage disposition. Sire of champion filly Gunfire (1899), but by far his best was the 1905 colt Fair Play, the future sire of Man o' War. Died at Nursery Stud following an attack of paralysis in 1917, at age 24.

1907—COMMANDO, 1898 b. h., Domino—Emma C., by *Darebin. Bred in Kentucky by James R. Keene. 9-7-2-0, $58,196. Coarse and heavily muscled, he did not resemble his handsome sire but was at least his equal on the racecourse. In Keene's colors, won 1901 Belmont Stakes. The Racing Hall of Fame member retired to Keene's Castleton Stud in 1902 to take the place of Domino, who died at age six in 1897. Immediate success at stud but, like his sire, he died young. From three crops and 27 foals, sired ten stakes winners, among them Hall of Fame members Peter Pan and Colin and influential sires Celt and Ultimus. Died of tetanus at Castleton in early March 1905, at age seven.

1906, 1904—*MEDDLER, 1890 b. h., *St Gatien—Busybody, by Petrarch. Bred in England by George Abington Baird. 3-3-0-0, $16,689, Dewhurst S., etc. By an Epsom Derby winner and out of an Epsom Oaks winner. Unraced after two-year-old season following the death of his owner, which, under rules in force at the time, voided his nominations to the three-year-old classics. Sold in 1893 for $76,000 to American William Forbes, who stood him initially at Neponset Stud in Massachusetts. Upon Forbes's death in 1897, sold to W. C. Whitney for $49,000 and moved to La Belle Stud in Kentucky. Sold at 1904 Whitney estate dispersal for $51,000. Represented by champion fillies Trigger, Tangle, and Tanya (winner of 1905 Belmont Stakes). When American racing was decimated by 1909 antiwagering legislation, relocated to France, where he died at Haras de Fresnay-le-Buffard in Normandy on April 17, 1916, at age 26.

1905—HAMBURG, 1895 b. h., Hanover—Lady Reel, by Fellowcraft. Bred in Kentucky by C. J. Enright. Sold for $1,250 as yearling to John E. Madden, who later named his famous breeding farm, Hamburg Place, for the Racing Hall of Fame member. 21-16-3-2, $60,380, Lawrence Realization, etc. Sold privately for $40,001 to Marcus Daly in 1898. Stood two seasons at Daly's Bitter Root Stud in Montana. After Daly's death in 1900, sold for $60,000 to W. C. Whitney, who sent him to La Belle Stud in Kentucky. At 1904 Whitney dispersal, sold for $70,000 to Whitney's son Harry Payne Whitney, who took him to Brookdale Stud in New Jersey. Sired Racing Hall of Fame filly Artful, champions Borrow, Hamburg Belle, Burgomaster, and Rosie O'Grady, and foundation mare Frizette. Died at Brookdale on September 15, 1915, at age 20.

1903—*BEN STROME, 1886 b. h., Bend Or—Strathfleet, by The Scottish Chief. Bred in England by the Duke of Westminster. 35-3-6-6, $2,975. Big (16.2 hands tall), good-looking, and beautifully bred, but a poor racehorse in England. Entered stud in 1894 at Thomas J. Carson's Dixiana Farm in Kentucky. When his first foals were yearlings, Dixiana advertised that a limited number of approved mares would be accepted by special contract, which meant at no cost. By 1904, his fee had jumped to $300, one of the highest in the country. Most noted as sire of Racing Hall of Fame member Roseben, but offspring also included juvenile champions Eugenia Burch and Highball. Died at Dixiana in 1909, at age 23.

1901—SIR DIXON, 1885 br. h., *Billet—Jaconet, by *Leamington. Bred in Kentucky by Col. Ezekiel Clay. 29-10-7-7, $54,915. Sold for $1,125 as yearling to Green B. Morris, who resold him at three for $20,000 to Mike and Phil Dwyer. A high-strung, delicate type, he was unable to endure the tough campaigns favored by the Dwyers but nevertheless scored victories in the 1888 Belmont, Withers, and Travers Stakes. Stood his entire career at Clay's Runnymede Stud in Kentucky. Sired champions Butterflies, Blue Girl, Kilmarnock, and Running Water, and 1905 Kentucky Derby winner Agile. Died after breaking his right hip in a paddock accident on March 23, 1909, at age 14.

1899—*ALBERT, 1882 b. h., Albert Victor—Hawthorn Bloom, by Kettledrum. Bred in England by Sir Richard Jardine. 6-1-1-0, $2,547. A racehorse of modest talents, won a minor stakes at Newcastle as a two-year-old. Imported as a stallion by Alfred Withers. Later spent most of his breeding career at the Adelbert Stud of Williams and Radford near Hopkinsville, Kentucky. Advertised for a $100 fee in 1896, with a reference to him as "the most uniform sire of winners in America—they mature early and make great campaigners." Not an outstanding sire, his best was probably 1899 juvenile champion Mesmerist and the good filly Hatasoo, an ancestress of many top racehorses. Believed to have died in 1907, because his last five foals arrived the following spring.

1898, 1895-'97—HANOVER, 1884 ch. h., Hindoo—Bourbon Belle, by *Bonnie Scotland. Bred in Kentucky at Col. Ezekiel Clay's Runnymede Farm. 50-32-14-2, $118,887, champion three-year-old, 1887 Belmont Stakes, etc. Sold as a yearling for $1,350 to Phil and Mike Dwyer. Won 17 consecutive races at two and three and ultimately retired with American earnings record. One of America's better all-time stallions, his best by far was Racing Hall of Fame member and leading sire Hamburg. Hanover was valued at $100,000 when he died at McGrathiana Stud in Kentucky on March

23, 1899, at age 15. Cause of death was said to be blood poisoning caused by a leg injury. He was originally buried at McGrathiana, but his skeleton was later exhumed for research and display.

1894—*SIR MODRED, 1877 b. h., Traducer—Idalia, by Cambuscan. Bred in New Zealand by Middle Park Stud. Among the foremost racehorses of his day in New Zealand, with victories in the Canterbury Derby, Canterbury Cup, and Metropolitan Stakes. Imported to California in 1885 by James Ben Ali Haggin. In 1894, became the first California-based stallion to lead the American sire list when his offspring won 137 races and $134,318. Notable offspring include champion Tournament, 1893 Belmont Stakes winner Comanche, 1890 Travers Stakes winner Sir John, and the outstanding fillies Gloaming and Lucania. Stood at Haggin's 44,000-acre Rancho del Paso near Sacramento, where he was pensioned for several seasons prior to his death due to infirmities of old age in June 1904, at age 27.

1893—HIMYAR, 1875 b. h., Alarm—Hira, by Lexington. Bred in Kentucky by Maj. Barak Thomas. 27-14-6-2, $11,650, Phoenix Hotel Stakes, etc. Finished second in 1878 as one of the heaviest favorites ever for the Kentucky Derby. High-strung, nervous, and hard to train, considered primarily a speed horse. Entered stud in 1882 at Thomas's Dixiana Farm near Lexington and got, among others, immortal racehorse and sire Domino and '98 Kentucky Derby winner Plaudit. In 1893, due largely to Domino, he established a single-season progeny earnings record of $259,252, which stood for 24 years. Died on December 30, 1905, at age 30, and was buried at Dixiana under a tombstone that reads: "Speed springs eternal from his ashes."

1892—IROQUOIS, 1878 b. h., *Leamington—Maggie B.B., by *Australian. Bred by Aristides Welch at Erdenheim Stud in Pennsylvania. 26-12-4-3, $99,707. Sold as a yearling to tobacco magnate Pierre Lorillard, who sent him to race in England. First American-bred winner of Epsom Derby and St. Leger Stakes; finished second in the Two Thousand Guineas. Wall Street briefly halted trading to celebrate news of his Derby triumph. Returned to U.S., he raced three times without success, probably because of pulmonary bleeding. Retired to stud at W. H. Johnson's Belle Meade Farm, where he died in 1899, at age 21. His offspring included champion Tammany.

1891—LONGFELLOW, 1867 br. h., *Leamington—Nantura, by Brawner's Eclipse. Bred, owned, and trained by John Harper. 16-13-2-0, $11,200. Standing a towering 17 hands, he was named for his long legs and not for the noted poet. One of the great racehorses of the 1870s, an injury forced his retirement to Harper's Nantura Stud near Midway, Kentucky. Sired more than 40 stakes winners, including Kentucky Derby winners Leonatus and Riley, 1886 Preakness winner The Bard, and champions Thora and Freeland. A dominant bay, it was said that all his foals but one were bay or brown. Died at Nantura on November 5, 1893, and was buried with a marker that reads: "King of Racers and King of Stallions."

1890—*ST. BLAISE, 1880 ch. h., Hermit—Fusee, by Marsyas. Bred in England by Lord Alington. 16-7-2-1, $41,066. Won 1883 Epsom Derby. Imported for $30,000 in 1885 by August Belmont I to stand at his Nursery Stud in Kentucky. Following Belmont's death, sold at auction in 1891 by Tattersalls of New York for a then-world record $100,000. Purchased on a solitary bid by Charles Reed of Tennessee. Not successful for Reed, sold at auction again in 1902 for $8,300 to James Ben Ali Haggin of Elmendorf Farm, Kentucky, but subsequently purchased privately by August Belmont II. At age 22, he returned to Nursery Stud to live out his days. Best runners include 1890 Futurity Stakes winner Potomac and '96 Preakness Stakes winner Margrave. Died in October 1909, at age 29.

1889—*RAYON D'OR, 1876 ch. h., Flageolet—Araucaria, by Ambrose. Bred in France by Haras de Dangu. 32-18-7-5, $110,207. Won from five to 18 furlongs, including 1879 St. Leger, and carried up to 132 pounds to victory. Imported in 1883 by W. L. Scott, who paid nearly $40,000 for him and stood him initially at his Algeria Stud in Pennsylvania. When Algeria dispersed in 1892, purchased by August Belmont II and moved to Nursery Stud in Kentucky. Sired many top runners, including Brooklyn Handicap winner Tenny, Futurity Stakes winner Chaos, and Banquet, winner of 62 races and $118,872. Died from "fever" at Nursery Stud on July 15, 1896, at age 20.

1888, 1886-'87, 1884—GLENELG, 1866 b. h., Citadel—*Babta, by Kingston. Imported in utero by R. W. Cameron, who earlier had imported four-time leading sire *Leamington. Foaled at Cameron's Clifton Farm in New York. 18-10-5-2, $23,340. Purchased as a yearling by August Belmont I for $2,000. Big, bad-tempered, and prone to colic, he nonetheless won the 1869 Travers Stakes and other important races. After his racing days, he was sold to Milton H. Sanford for $10,000. His many outstanding runners include Racing Hall of Fame mare Firenze. Died at the farm of Tyree Bate in Castalian Springs, Tennessee on October 23, 1897, at age 31.

1885—VIRGIL, 1864 dk. b. h., Vandal—Hymenia, by *Yorkshire. Bred in Woodford County, Kentucky, by Hyman C. Gratz. 10-7-2-1, $2,950, Sequel S. three times, etc. A beautiful, nearly black horse, owned during his racing days by Milton Sanford, primarily a sprinter in an era that prized stamina (although he won once at two miles). Initially had few opportunities as a stallion and was even broken to harness and used to pull a carriage. Sold cheaply in 1874. When his son Vagrant won the 1876 Kentucky Derby, Virgil was repurchased by Sanford. He subsequently sired Racing Hall of Fame member Hindoo (also a great sire) and unbeaten Tremont. Died at Quindaro Stud in Kentucky in 1893, at age 29.

1883—*BILLET, 1865 br. h., Voltigeur—Calcutta, by Flatcatcher. Bred in England by James Smith. 18-5-3-1, $3,983. Insignificant racehorse in England, racing most often in selling races. Imported to America in 1869 and stood several seasons in Illinois. After son Elias Lawrence established a Saratoga three-mile record in 1878, was moved to Runnymede Stud in Paris, Kentucky, where he remained until his death on January 17, 1889, at age 24. Top runners include Racing Hall of Fame member Miss Woodford, the first American Thoroughbred to top $100,000 in earnings, and 1901 leading sire Sir Dixon.

1882, 1880—*BONNIE SCOTLAND, 1853 b. h., Iago—Queen Mary, by Gladiator. Bred in England by William I'Anson. 4-2-1-0, $6,308. Lightly raced and never truly sound because of an injury as a foal, won Liverpool St. Leger and Doncaster Stakes. Imported to America in 1857, believed to have stood originally in Ohio before relocating to Gen. W. G. Harding's famous Belle Meade Stud near Nashville, Tennessee. Offspring include Racing Hall of Fame member Luke Blackburn, 1883 Belmont Stakes winner George Kinney, and champion Bramble. Died in his paddock at Belle Meade on February 2, 1880, at age 27.

1881, 1879, 1877, 1875—*LEAMINGTON, 1853 br. h., Faugh-a-Ballagh—mare by Pantaloon. Bred in England by Mr. Halford. 24-8-3-3, $33,446, Goodwood S., Tradesmen's Plate twice, etc. Imported in 1865 by R. W. Cameron of New York after standing six seasons in England. In U.S., stood first at Bosque Bonita Stud in Kentucky, later at Cameron's Clifton Stud on Staten Island, and finally at Aristides Welch's Erdenheim Stud near Philadelphia. Sire of Racing Hall of Fame members Longfellow and Parole, inaugural Kentucky Derby winner Aristides, and Iroquois, first American-bred winner of the Epsom Derby. Many of his best offspring were

Sires — Profiles of Leading Sires

out of Lexington mares and were raced by the Lorillard brothers, George and Pierre, who dominated American racing during the 1870s and '80s. Died at Erdenheim on May 6, 1878, at age 25.

1878, 1876, 1861-'74—LEXINGTON, 1850 b. h., Boston—Alice Carneal, by *Sarpedon. Bred in Kentucky by Dr. Elisha Warfield. 7-6-1-0, $56,600, Great Post S., etc. Sold to Richard Ten Broeck as a three-year-old and in 1855 set an American four-mile record of 7:19¾. By then, he was going blind and was sold for $15,000 to R. A. Alexander of Woodburn Stud, Kentucky. He stood at that Midway farm his entire career except for an interlude in Illinois for his own safety during the Civil War. As with *Glencoe, a number of his offspring were utilized as Civil War mounts. His many outstanding runners include champions Kentucky, Asteroid, Norfolk, Duke of Magenta, Harry Bassett, Sultana, and Tom Bowling. Lexington's post-Civil War fee of $500 was unprecedented. His male-line survived into the 20th century, and numerous crosses of his name are still present in far branches of modern pedigrees. The 16-time leading sire died on July 1, 1875, at age 25. His skeleton is in the possession of the Smithsonian Institution in Washington, D.C.

1860—REVENUE, 1843 b. h., *Trustee—Rosalie Somers, by Sir Charles. Bred in Virginia by statesman John M. Botts. 21-16-5-0. Son of a leading sire and champion racemare. Stood at Botts's farm in Virginia, where he sired the great Planet, widely viewed as the best American racehorse in the era preceding the Civil War, compiling a 31-27-4-0 record and surpassing Peytona as America's top earner with $69,700, a mark that stood for 20 years. In 1860, Revenue became the first stallion to lead an American sire list based on earnings ($49,450) rather than races won (the previously recognized standard), although he led by wins as well. He died in Virginia in September 1868, at age 25.

1859—*ALBION, 1837 bl. h., Cain or Actaeon—Panthea, by Comus or Blacklock. Bred in England; reportedly was a successful racehorse in America during the early 1840s. A reliable sire of winners during pre-Civil War years and later an outstanding broodmare sire. Died in Sumner County, Tennessee, in 1859, at age 22.

1858, 1854-'57, 1849-'50, 1847—*GLENCOE, 1831 ch. h., Sultan—Trampoline, by Tramp. Bred in England by Lord Jersey. 10-8-1-1, $33,459. Winner of 1834 Two Thousand Guineas, third in Epsom Derby. Stood one season in England, getting legendary broodmare Pocahontas. Imported in 1836 by James Jackson, who reportedly paid $10,000 for him. Swaybacked but otherwise handsome, he was much admired by breeders of the day. Stood from 1837-'44 in Alabama; 1845-'48 in Tennessee; and 1849-'57 in Kentucky as property of A. Keene Richards, an ardent secessionist who allegedly turned over many of his offspring for use as Confederate mounts during the Civil War. Sired the great mares Reel and Peytona, the latter America's leading money winner from 1845-'61 ($62,400), as well as top sons Star Davis and Vandal. Died of "lung fever" on August 25, 1857, at Blue Grass Park in Georgetown, Kentucky.

1853, 1851-'52—BOSTON, 1833 b. h., Timoleon—Sister to Tuckahoe, by Ball's Florizel. Bred in Virginia by John Wickham. 45-40-2-1, $51,700. Sold at two for $800 to Nathaniel Rives to satisfy a gaming debt. Racing Hall of Fame member won 30 four-mile heat races. Nicknamed "Old White Nose" for his distinctively blazed face, his vicious temper struck fear into the hearts of his handlers. Sire of Racing Hall of Fame member Lexington and his great rival, Lecomte (also known as Lecompte), as well as the great racemare Nina, dam of Planet. Died at Col. E. M. Blackburn's farm in Woodford County, Kentucky, in 1850, at age 17.

1848 (co-leader), 1843, 1837-'39—*LEVIATHAN, 1823 ch. h., Muley—Coxcomb's dam, by Windle. Bred in England by Mr. Painter. 19-15-3-0, $11,096, Dee S., etc. At 16 hands, large for his time. Imported in 1830 by James Jackson of Alabama. Not well received at first because of his enormous size. In 1838, became America's first $100,000 sire when his progeny won 92 races. At one time, his $75 fee was the highest in America. Stood in Tennessee, managed by Col. George Elliott. Died from "inflammation of the bowels" in Gallatin, Tennessee, in 1846, at age 23.

1848 (co-leader)—*TRUSTEE, 1829 ch. h., Catton—Emma, by Whisker. 11-4-3-3, $7,446, Claret S., etc. Third in 1832 Epsom Derby in first career start. Brother to 1835 Epsom Derby winner Mundig, half brother to '43 Derby winner Cotherstone. Imported in 1835 by Commodore Robert Stockton, later senator from New Jersey. Not well received by American breeders and moved often during his stud career. Stood in New York between 1836-'41; Virginia in 1842; Kentucky in 1843-'44; Virginia in 1845-'46; and back to New York in 1847, where he remained until his death at age 27. Sire of Racing Hall of Fame filly Fashion, the great mare Levity, and leading 1860 American sire Revenue. Died at West Farms, Westchester County, New York, in 1856.

1846, 1844-'45, 1842—*PRIAM, 1827 b. h., Emilius—Cressida, by Whisker. Bred in England by Sir John Shelley. 16-14-1-1, $65,100. Winner of the 1830 Epsom Derby, Goodwood Cup. Considered the greatest English racehorse of his era. Imported in 1837 by Merritt and Co. for $15,000, then believed to be a record. Leading American sire four times. Sire of Epsom Oaks winners Crucifix, Miss Letty, and Industry before his importation. Sire in America of Margaret Wood, Little Trick, Lucy Long. Died in Tennessee in 1847, at age 20.

1841, 1840—MEDOC, 1829 ch. h., American Eclipse—Young Maid of the Oaks, by *Expedition. Bred in New York by James Bathgate. 5-4-1-0, $5,300. Greatest son of American Eclipse. Entered stud in Kentucky in 1835. His offspring won 61 races in 1840 and 51 races the following year. Sire of top four-milers Grey Medoc, Bob Letcher, Mary Morris, Picayune. Broke his near foreleg when he stepped in a hole during exercise in 1839 and died at age ten from the injury at Col. William Buford's farm in Woodford County, Kentucky.

1836, 1830-'33—SIR CHARLES, 1816 ch. h., Sir Archy—*Citizen mare, by *Citizen. Won 20 of 25 starts. Believed to have been bred in Virginia by W. R. Johnson. Ancestry of his dam questioned; some referred to her as a "cart mare" whose pedigree had been fabricated. Dominant in long heat races throughout the South. Beaten while lame in final start, 1822 match with American Eclipse for the national championship in Washington, D.C. Sired the great racemares Trifle, Bonnets o' Blue, and Rosalie Somers, and notable racehorse and sire Wagner. Died at George Johnson's Earnscliffe Plantation, Virginia, on June 7, 1833, at age 17.

1835—BERTRAND, 1821 b. h., Sir Archy—Eliza, by *Bedford. Bred in South Carolina by Col. John R. Spann. Won 13 of 16 starts. In 1826, he was sold to Hutchcraft and Co. and sent to Kentucky, where he stood his entire 12-season career, and was said to have covered between 175 and 200 mares per season. He is credited with vastly improving the Thoroughbred of the Bluegrass region. His best include John Bascombe, Richard Singleton, and Queen Mary. Died in Hopkinsville, Kentucky, in 1838, at age 17.

1834—MONSIEUR TONSON, 1822 b. h., Pacolet—Madam Tonson, by Top Gallant. Bred in Tennessee by Thomas Foxhall. Won 11 of 12 starts; only defeat was his first start as a two-year-old. William R. Johnson, the "Napoleon of the Turf" in America, bought him for $10,000. Stood initially in Virginia, later in North Carolina, and finally was sent to Kentucky, where he died. Sire of South Carolina champion Argyle and many other winners.

Note: Prior to 1860, leading sires were based on races won rather than progeny earnings.

All-Time Leading Sires

The sire lists on the following pages do not include steeplechase statistics.

All-Time Leading North American Sires by Total Worldwide Earnings
Through 2007

Sire, YOB, Sire	Where Stood	Earnings
Danzig, 1977, by Northern Dancer	U.S.	$110,977,411
Storm Cat, 1983, by Storm Bird	U.S.	110,649,125
Mr. Prospector, 1970, by Raise a Native	U.S.	97,910,212
Woodman, 1983, by Mr. Prospector	U.S., Aus.	95,267,592
Royal Academy, 1987, by Nijinsky II	Ire., Jpn., U.S., Aus.	91,552,321
Crafty Prospector, 1979, by Mr. Prospector	U.S.	90,274,158
A.P. Indy, 1989, by Seattle Slew	U.S.	89,196,907
Seattle Slew, 1974, by Bold Reasoning	U.S.	83,725,712
Seeking the Gold, 1985, by Mr. Prospector	U.S.	80,825,456
Deputy Minister, 1979, by Vice Regent	U.S.	80,164,273
Wild Again, 1980, by Icecapade	U.S.	79,657,592
Nureyev, 1977, by Northern Dancer	Fr., U.S.	78,740,091
Rahy, 1985, by Blushing Groom (Fr)	U.S.	78,242,668
Cozzene, 1980, by Caro (Ire)	U.S.	76,631,367
Kris S., 1977, by Roberto	U.S.	76,521,772
Kingmambo, 1990, by Mr. Prospector	U.S.	75,553,023
Dynaformer, 1985, by Roberto	U.S.	72,922,993
Gulch, 1984, by Mr. Prospector	U.S.	71,845,051
Dixieland Band, 1980, by Northern Dancer	U.S.	71,473,603
Miswaki, 1978, by Mr. Prospector	U.S.	70,888,880
Theatrical (Ire), by 1982, Nureyev	U.S.	70,527,950
Mt. Livermore, 1981, by Blushing Groom (Fr)	U.S.	69,076,121
Gone West, 1984, by Mr. Prospector	U.S.	68,720,106
Silver Deputy, 1985, by Deputy Minister	U.S.	68,508,053
Broad Brush, 1983, by Ack Ack	U.S.	66,795,461
Carson City, 1987, by Mr. Prospector	U.S.	66,474,709
Pleasant Colony, 1978, by His Majesty	U.S.	64,934,679
Conquistador Cielo, 1979, by Mr. Prospector	U.S.	63,268,521
Dehere, 1991 by, Deputy Minister	U.S., Jpn., Aus.	61,665,247
Alydar, 1975, by Raise a Native	U.S.	60,556,180
El Prado (Ire), 1989, by Sadler's Wells	U.S.	59,247,392
Thunder Gulch, 1992, by Gulch	U.S.	59,108,780
Runaway Groom, 1979, by Blushing Groom (Fr)	U.S.	56,675,501
Cure the Blues, 1978, by Stop the Music	U.S.	56,286,324
Hennessy, 1993, by Storm Cat	U.S.	56,131,324
Nijinsky II, 1967, by Northern Dancer	U.S.	55,220,808
Relaunch, 1976, by In Reality	U.S.	54,515,764
Affirmed, 1975, by Exclusive Native	U.S.	53,932,744
Silver Hawk, 1979, by Roberto	U.S.	53,381,214
Green Dancer, 1972, by Nijinsky II	U.S.	52,980,655
Phone Trick, 1982, by Clever Trick	U.S.	52,572,003
Black Tie Affair (Ire), 1986, by Miswaki	U.S., Jpn.	51,887,079
Allen's Prospect, 1982, by Mr. Prospector	U.S.	51,675,117
Saint Ballado, 1989, by Halo	U.S.	50,753,132
Lyphard, 1969, by Northern Dancer	Fr., U.S.	49,926,936
Devil's Bag, 1981, by Halo	U.S.	49,325,997
Valid Appeal, 1972, by In Reality	U.S.	48,690,733
Langfuhr, 1992, by Danzig	U.S.	48,668,121
Capote, 1984, by Seattle Slew	U.S.	48,227,749
Smart Strike, 1992, by Mr. Prospector	U.S.	48,107,767

All-Time Leading Sires by Number of Winners Worldwide
Through 2006

Sire, YOB, Sire	Where Stood	Wnrs
Danehill, 1986, by Danzig	Ire., Jpn., Aus.	1,543
Royal Academy, 1987, by Nijinsky II	Ire., Jpn., U.S., Aus.	1,044
Sadler's Wells, 1981, by Northern Dancer	Ire.	988
Woodman, 1983, by Mr. Prospector	U.S., Aus.	984
Sunday Silence, 1986, by Halo	Jpn.	950
Southern Halo, 1983, by Halo	Arg., U.S., Jpn.	863
Night Shift, 1980, by Northern Dancer	Eng., U.S., Ire.	839
Last Tycoon (Ire), 1983, by Try My Best	Ire., Aus., Jpn., N.Z.	769
Allen's Prospect, 1982, by Mr. Prospector	U.S.	759
Grand Lodge, 1991, by Chief's Crown	Ire.	759
Mr. Prospector, 1970, by Raise a Native	U.S.	753
Crafty Prospector, 1979, by Mr. Prospector	U.S.	727
Dixieland Band, 1980, by Northern Dancer	U.S.	721
Bluebird, 1984, by Storm Bird	Ire., Aus.	715
Miswaki, 1978, by Mr. Prospector	U.S.	700
Runaway Groom, 1979, by Blushing Groom (Fr)	U.S.	700
Alzao, 1980, by Lyphard	Ire., Aus.	697
Clever Trick, 1976, by Icecapade	U.S.	690
Red Ransom, 1987, by Roberto	Eng., U.S.	688
Danzig, 1977, by Northern Dancer	U.S.	670
Mr. Leader, 1966, by Hail to Reason	U.S.	669
Phone Trick, 1982, by Clever Trick	U.S.	669
Zabeel, 1986, by *Sir Tristram	N.Z.	662
Storm Cat, 1983, by Storm Bird	U.S.	658
Mt. Livermore, 1981, by Blushing Groom (Fr)	U.S.	641
Thunder Gulch, 1992, by Gulch	U.S., Jpn., Aus.	640
Cryptoclearance, 1984, by Fappiano	U.S.	638
Salt Lake, 1989, by Deputy Minister	U.S.	634
Wild Again, 1980, by Icecapade	U.S.	630
Danehill Dancer, 1993, by Danehill	Ire.	628
Carson City, 1987, by Mr. Prospector	U.S.	625
Green Dancer, 1972, by Nijinsky II	U.S.	602
Honour and Glory, 1993, by Relaunch	U.S.	597
Afleet, 1984, by Mr. Prospector	U.S., Jpn.	595
Geiger Counter, 1982, by Mr. Prospector	Can., U.S., Aus.	593
Green Desert, 1983, by Danzig	Eng.	593
Conquistador Cielo, 1979, by Mr. Prospector	U.S.	590
Be My Guest, 1974, by Northern Dancer	Ire.	586
Caerleon, 1980, by Nijinsky II	Ire.	586
Deputy Minister, 1979, by Vice Regent	U.S.	586
Regal Classic, 1985, by Vice Regent	U.S.	583
Scenic (Ire), 1986, by Sadler's Wells	Ire., Aus.	581
Two Punch, 1983, by Mr. Prospector	U.S.	573
Kris S., 1977, by Roberto	U.S.	568

All-Time Leading Sires of Stakes Winners Worldwide
Through 2007

Sire, YOB, Sire	Where Stood	SWs
Danehill, 1986, by Danzig	Ire., Jpn., Aus.	343
Sadler's Wells, 1981, by Northern Dancer	Ire.	270
Danzig, 1977, by Northern Dancer	U.S.	199
Mr. Prospector, 1970, by Raise a Native	U.S.	181
Sunday Silence, 1986, by Halo	Jpn.	168
Southern Halo, 1983, by Halo	Arg., U.S., Jpn.	160
Storm Cat, 1983, by Storm Bird	U.S.	158
Nijinsky II, 1967, by Northern Dancer	U.S.	153
Royal Academy, 1987, by Nijinsky II	U.S.	147
Northern Dancer, 1961, by Nearctic	Ire., Jpn., U.S., Aus.	146
Nureyev, 1977, by Northern Dancer	Fr., U.S.	137
Riverman, 1969, by Never Bend	Fr., U.S.	127
Roy, 1983, by Fappiano	Chi., U.S., Brz., Arg.	127
Caerleon, 1980, by Nijinsky II	Ire., Aus.	125
*Sir Tristram, 1971, by Sir Ivor	N.Z.	125
Dixieland Band, 1980, by Northern Dancer	U.S.	114
Lyphard, 1969, by Northern Dancer	U.S.	114
Seattle Slew, 1974, by Bold Reasoning	U.S.	114
Zabeel, 1986, by *Sir Tristram	N.Z.	111
A.P. Indy, 1989, by Seattle Slew	U.S.	106
Woodman, 1983, by Mr. Prospector	U.S., Aus.	106

Sires — All-Time Leading Sires

Sire, YOB, Sire	Where Stood	SWs
Vice Regent, 1967, by Northern Dancer	Can.	104
Miswaki, 1978, by Mr. Prospector	U.S.	98
Rainbow Quest, 1981, by Blushing Groom (Fr)	Eng.	98
Alleged, 1974, by Hoist the Flag	U.S.	94
Alzao, 1980, by Lyphard	Ire., Aus.	94
Carson City, 1987, by Mr. Prospector	U.S.	92
*Nasrullah, 1940, by Nearco	Ire., U.S.	92
Night Shift, 1980, by Northern Dancer	Eng., U.S., Ire.	92
Sir Ivor, 1965, by Sir Gaylord	Ire., U.S.	92
Blushing Groom (Fr), 1974, by Red God	U.S.	91
Broad Brush, 1983, by Ack Ack	U.S.	91
Kris S., 1977, by Roberto	U.S.	91
Crafty Prospector, 1979, by Mr. Prospector	U.S.	89
Darshaan, 1981, by Shirley Heights	Ire.	89
Deputy Minister, 1979, by Vice Regent	U.S.	89
Nodouble, 1965, by *Noholme II	U.S.	89

All-Time Leading Sires by Percentage of Stakes Winners Worldwide
Through 2007

Sire, YOB, Sire	Where Stood	% SWs
Northern Dancer, 1961, by Nearctic	Can., U.S.	22.6%
Bold Ruler, 1954, by *Nasrullah	U.S.	22.4%
*Nasrullah, 1940, by Nearco	Ire., U.S.	21.6%
Round Table, 1954, by *Princequillo	U.S.	20.5%
Hoist the Flag, 1968, by Tom Rolfe	U.S.	19.9%
*Sea-Bird, 1962, by Dan Cupid	U.S., Fr.	18.9%
Danzig, 1977, by Northern Dancer	U.S.	17.9%
Nijinsky II, 1967, by Northern Dancer	U.S.	17.7%
Blushing Groom (FR), 1974, by Red God	U.S.	17.4%
Nureyev, 1977, by Northern Dancer	Fr., U.S.	17.0%
*Mahmoud, 1933, by *Blenheim II	Eng., U.S.	16.6%
Never Bend, 1960, by *Nasrullah	U.S.	16.5%
Tentam, 1969, by Intentionally	U.S.	16.1%
*Court Martial, 1942, by Fair Trial	Eng., U.S.	16.0%
Philately, 1962, by *Princequillo	U.S.	16.0%
Roberto, 1969, by Hail to Reason	U.S.	16.0%
*Amerigo, 1955, by Nearco	U.S.	15.7%
Sea Aglo, 1971, by *Sea-Bird	U.S.	15.6%
*Heliopolis, 1936, by Hyperion	U.S.	15.3%
Bull Lea, 1935, by *Bull Dog	U.S.	15.2%
*Ribot, 1952, by Tenerani	Ity., Eng., U.S.	15.2%
Mr. Prospector, 1970, by Raise a Native	U.S.	15.1%
Nedayr, 1935, by Neddie	U.S.	15.1%
Vice Regent, 1967, by Northern Dancer	Can.	15.1%
Eight Thirty, 1936, by Pilate	U.S.	14.7%
*Herbager, 1956, by Vandale	Fr., U.S.	14.5%
Chop Chop, 1940, by Flares	Can.	14.4%
In Reality, 1964, by Intentionally	U.S.	14.4%
Native Dancer, 1950, by Polynesian	U.S.	14.4%
Nearctic, 1954, by Nearco	Can., U.S.	14.3%
Pelouse, 1951, by Pavot	U.S.	14.3%
Royal Charger, 1942, by Nearco	Ire., U.S.	14.2%

All-Time Leading Sires of Group or Graded Stakes Winners Worldwide
Through 2007

Sire, YOB, Sire	Where Stood	GSWs
Danehill, 1986, by Danzig	Ire., Jpn., Aus.	203
Sadler's Wells, 1981, by Northern Dancer	Ire.	153
Southern Halo, 1983, by Halo	Arg., U.S., Jpn.	115
Danzig, 1977, by Northern Dancer	U.S.	112
Mr. Prospector, 1970, by Raise a Native	U.S.	111
Roy, 1983, by Fappiano	Chi., U.S., Brz., Arg.	98
Nijinsky II, 1967, by Northern Dancer	U.S.	97
Storm Cat, 1983, by Storm Bird	U.S.	95
*Sir Tristram, 1971, by Sir Ivor	N.Z.	83
Zabeel, 1986, by *Sir Tristram	N.Z.	78
Northern Dancer, 1961, by Nearctic	Can., U.S.	77

Sire, YOB, Sire	Where Stood	GSWs
Nureyev, 1977, by Northern Dancer	Fr., U.S.	77
Royal Academy, 1987, by Nijinsky II	Ire., U.S., Jpn., Aus.	77
Caerleon, 1980, by Nijinsky II	Ire., Aus.	67
Riverman, 1969, by Never Bend	Fr., U.S.	67
Ghadeer, 1978, by Lyphard	Brz.	64
Lyphard, 1969, by Northern Dancer	U.S.	64
A.P. Indy, 1989, by Seattle Slew	U.S.	59
Seattle Slew, 1974, by Bold Reasoning	U.S.	59
Blushing Groom (Fr), 1974, by Red God	U.S.	58
Alleged, 1966, by Hoist the Flag	U.S.	57
Rainbow Quest, 1981, by Blushing Groom (Fr)	Eng.	57
Habitat, 1966, by Sir Gaylord	Ire.	55
Fitzcarraldo, 1981, by Cipayo	Arg.	52
Hussonet, 1991, by Mr. Prospector	Chi., U.S., Aus.	49
Cipayo, 1974, by Lacydon	Arg.	48
Lode, 1986, by Mr. Prospector	Brz.	48
Alydar, 1975, by Raise a Native	U.S.	46
Clackson, 1976, by I Say	Brz.	46
Sir Ivor, 1965, by Sir Gaylord	Ire., U.S.	44
Sunday Silence, 1986, by Halo	Jpn.	44
Theatrical (Ire), 1982, by Nureyev	U.S.	44
*Vaguely Noble, 1965, by Vienna	U.S.	44
Bluebird, 1984, by Storm Bird	Ire., Aus.	43
Candy Stripes, 1982, by Blushing Groom (Fr)	Arg., U.S.	43
Diesis (GB), 1980, by Sharpen Up (GB)	U.S.	43
Dixieland Band, 1980, by Northern Dancer	U.S.	43
Elliodor, 1977, by Lyphard	S. Af.	43
Gone West, 1984, by Mr. Prospector	U.S.	43
Green Dancer, 1972, by Nijinsky II	Fr., U.S.	43
Machiavellian, 1987, by Mr. Prospector	Eng.	43
Seeking the Gold, 1985, by Mr. Prospector	U.S.	43
Alzao, 1980, by Lyphard	Ire., Aus.	42
Darshaan, 1981, by Shirley Heights	Ire.	42
Roberto, 1969, by Hail to Reason	U.S.	42
Affirmed, 1975, by Exclusive Native	U.S.	41
Damascus, 1964, by Sword Dancer	U.S.	41
Deputy Minister, 1979, by Vice Regent	U.S.	41
Egg Toss, 1977, by Buckpasser	Arg.	41
Irish River (Fr), 1976, by Riverman	U.S.	41

All-Time Leading Sires of Group 1 or Grade 1 Stakes Winners Worldwide
Through 2007

Sire, YOB, Sire	Where Stood	G1Ws
Danehill, 1986, by Danzig	Ire..	80
Sadler's Wells, 1981, by Northern Dancer	Ire..	70
Southern Halo, 1983, by Halo	Arg.. U.S., Jpn..	54
Roy, 1983, by Fappiano	Chi., U.S., Brz., Arg.	53
Mr. Prospector, 1970, by Raise a Native	U.S.	48
Danzig, 1977, by Northern Dancer	U.S.	46
*Sir Tristram, 1971, by Sir Ivor	N.Z.	45
Zabeel, 1986, by *Sir Tristram	N.Z.	37
Nijinsky II, 1967, by Northern Dancer	U.S.	34
Storm Cat, 1983, by Storm Bird	U.S.	32
Nureyev, 1977, by Northern Dancer	U.S.	29
Seattle Slew, 1974, by Bold Reasoning	U.S.	27
Ghadeer, 1978, by Lyphard	Brz.	26
Northern Dancer, 1961, by Nearctic	Can., U.S.	26
Blushing Groom (Fr), 1974, by Red God	U.S.	25
Hussonet, 1991, by Mr. Prospector	Chi., Aus., U.S.	25
Lyphard, 1969, by Northern Dancer	Fr., U.S.	25
Lode, 1986, by Mr. Prospector	Arg.	24
Riverman, 1969, by Never Bend	Fr., U.S.	24
Sunday Silence, 1986, by Halo	Jpn.	23
*Vaguely Noble, 1965, by Vienna	U.S.	23
Alleged, 1974, by Hoist the Flag	U.S.	22
Candy Stripes, 1982, by Blushing Groom (Fr)	U.S., Arg., Brz.	22
Caerleon, 1980, by Nijinsky II	Ire., Aus.	22
Cipayo , 1974, by Lacydon	Arg.	21
Royal Academy, 1987, by Nijinsky II	U.S.	21
Alydar, 1975, by Raise a Native	U.S.	20
Fitzcarraldo , 1981, by Cipayo	Arg.	20

Sires — All-Time Leading Sires

Sire, YOB, Sire	Where Stood	G1Ws
Caro (Ire), 1967, by Fortino II	U.S.	19
Habitat, 1966, by Sir Gaylord	Ire.	19
Mill Reef, 1968, by Never Bend	Eng.	19
Rainbow Quest, 1981, by Blushing Groom (Fr)	Eng.	19
Theatrical (Ire), 1982, by Nureyev	U.S.	19

All-Time Leading Sires by Progeny Earnings Worldwide
Through 2007

Sire, YOB, Sire	Where Stood	Earnings
Sunday Silence, 1986, by Halo	Jpn.	$683,937,981
Danehill, 1986, by Danzig	Ire., Jpn., Aus.	259,177,979
Brian's Time, 1985, by Roberto	Jpn.	251,358,617
Tony Bin, 1983, by Kampala	Jpn.	191,538,308
Afleet, 1984, by Mr. Prospector	U.S., Jpn.	146,540,688
Fuji Kiseki, 1992, by Sunday Silence	Jpn.	138,511,359
Northern Taste, 1971, by Northern Dancer	Jpn.	132,995,738
Sadler's Wells, 1981, by Northern Dancer	Ire.	132,943,602
Forty Niner, 1985, by Mr. Prospector	Jpn.	113,163,636
Danzig, 1977, by Northern Dancer	U.S.	110,977,411
Jade Robbery, 1987, by Mr. Prospector	Jpn.	110,841,752
Storm Cat, 1983, by Storm Bird	U.S.	110,649,125
Real Shadai, 1979, by Roberto	Jpn.	106,622,303
End Sweep, 1991, by Forty Niner	Jpn.	102,781,027
Mr. Prospector, 1970, by Raise a Native	U.S.	97,910,212
Caerleon, 1980, by Nijinsky II	Ire., Aus.	95,868,544
Woodman, 1983, by Mr. Prospector	U.S., Aus.	95,267,592
Royal Academy, 1987, by Nijinsky II	Ire., Jpn., U.S., Aus.	91,553,919
Crafty Prospector, 1979, by Mr. Prospector	U.S.	90,274,158
Last Tycoon (Ire), 1983, by Try My Best	Jpn.	89,429,717
A.P. Indy, 1989, by Seattle Slew	U.S.	89,196,907
Seattle Slew, 1974, by Bold Reasoning	U.S.	83,725,712
Sakura Yutaka O, 1982, by Tesco Boy	Jpn.	83,365,879
Zabeel, 1986, by *Sir Tristram	N.Z.	82,129,364
Amber Shadai, 1977, by Northern Taste	Jpn.	81,891,714
Seeking the Gold, 1985, by Mr. Prospector	U.S.	80,825,456
Deputy Minister, 1979, by Vice Regent	U.S.	80,164,273
Wild Again, 1980, by Icecapade	U.S.	79,657,592
Nureyev, 1977, by Northern Dancer	Fr., U.S.	78,740,091
Rahy, 1985, by Blushing Groom (Fr)	U.S.	78,242,668
Cozzene, 1980, by Caro (Ire)	U.S.	76,631,367
Kris S., 1977, by Roberto	U.S.	76,521,772
Kingmambo, 1990, by Mr. Prospector	U.S.	75,553,023
Dynaformer, 1985, by Roberto	U.S.	72,922,993
Gulch, 1984, by Mr. Prospector	U.S.	71,845,051
Nihon Pillow Winner, 1980, by Steel Heart	Jpn.	71,700,582
French Deputy, 1992, by Deputy Minister	Jpn.	71,511,475
Dixieland Band, 1980, by Northern Dancer	U.S.	71,473,603
Tamamo Cross, 1984, by C B Cross	Jpn.	71,232,860
Miswaki, 1978, by Mr. Prospector	U.S.	70,888,880
Theatrical (Ire), 1982, by Nureyev	U.S.	70,527,950

All-Time Leading North American Broodmare Sires by Progeny Earnings Worldwide
Through 2007

Sire, YOB, Sire	Where Stood	Earnings
Mr. Prospector, 1970, by Raise a Native	U.S.	$275,606,326
Nijinsky II, 1967, by Northern Dancer	U.S.	209,221,063
Danzig, 1977, by Northern Dancer	U.S.	201,317,040
Lyphard, 1969, by Northern Dancer	Fr., U.S.	175,292,949
Nureyev, 1977, by Northern Dancer	Fr. U.S.	175,023,848
Northern Dancer, 1961, by Nearctic	Can., U.S.	163,922,032
Seattle Slew, 1974, by Bold Reasoning	U.S.	163,280,883
Alydar, 1975, by Raise a Native	U.S.	159,959,608

Sire, YOB, Sire	Where Stood	Earnings
Blushing Groom (Fr), 1974, by Red God	U.S.	$145,694,738
Secretariat, 1970, by Bold Ruler	U.S.	140,761,223
Halo, 1969, by Hail to Reason	U.S.	130,394,452
Vice Regent, 1967, by Northern Dancer	Can.	128,843,401
Riverman, 1969, by Never Bend	Fr., U.S.	127,905,720
Miswaki, 1978, by Mr. Prospector	U.S.	125,721,357
Affirmed, 1975, by Exclusive Native	U.S.	124,100,217
Deputy Minister, 1979, by Vice Regent	U.S.	114,009,278
Alleged, 1974, by Hoist the Flag	U.S.	109,393,768
Green Dancer, 1972, by Nijinsky II	U.S.	106,380,866
Woodman, 1983, by Mr. Prospector	Aus., U.S.	105,127,963
Dixieland Band, 1980, by Northern Dancer	U.S.	104,412,040
Damascus, 1964, by Sword Dancer	U.S.	103,636,030
Storm Bird, 1978, by Northern Dancer	U.S.	103,077,742
Roberto, 1969, by Hail to Reason	U.S.	102,744,053
Valid Appeal, 1972, by In Reality	U.S.	99,631,106
Raise a Native, 1961, by Native Dancer	Fr., U.S.	98,139,282
Storm Cat, 1983, by Storm Bird	U.S.	95,591,932
*Grey Dawn II, 1962, by *Herbager	U.S.	92,046,481
Irish River (Fr), 1976, by Riverman	Fr., U.S.	91,468,185
In Reality, 1964, by Intentionally	U.S.	90,876,991
Key to the Mint, 1969, by Graustark	U.S.	90,676,470
Fappiano, 1977, by Mr. Prospector	U.S.	89,367,318
Caro (Ire), 1967, by Fortino II	Fr., U.S.	87,895,249
Graustark, 1963, by *Ribot	U.S.	87,168,507
Sir Ivor, 1965, by Sir Gaylord	Ire., U.S.	85,962,052
*Vaguely Noble, 1965, by Vienna	U.S.	85,150,327
Relaunch, 1976, by In Reality	U.S.	84,270,442
Private Account, 1976, by Damascus	U.S.	83,086,279
Mr. Leader, 1966, by Hail to Reason	U.S.	80,490,637
Conquistador Cielo, 1979, by Mr. Prospector	U.S.	80,088,212
Stop the Music, 1970, by Hail to Reason	U.S.	78,312,755
The Minstrel, 1974, by Northern Dancer	U.S.	78,289,201
Tom Rolfe, 1962, by *Ribot	U.S.	78,200,764
Majestic Light, 1973, by Majestic Prince	U.S.	76,334,552
Clever Trick, 1976, by Icecapade	U.S.	73,348,674
Cox's Ridge, 1974, by Best Turn	U.S.	72,735,581

All-Time Leading Broodmare Sires by Progeny Earnings Worldwide
Through 2007

Sire, YOB, Sire	Where Stood	Earnings
Northern Taste, 1971, by Northern Dancer	Jpn.	$530,493,367
Mr. Prospector, 1970, by Raise a Native	U.S.	275,606,326
Nijinsky II, 1967, by Northern Dancer	U.S.	209,221,063
Danzig, 1977, by Northern Dancer	U.S.	201,317,040
Tosho Boy, 1973, by Tesco Boy	Jpn.	197,657,401
Lyphard, 1969, by Northern Dancer	Fr., U.S.	175,292,949
Nureyev, 1977, by Northern Dancer	Fr. U.S.	175,023,848
Northern Dancer, 1961, by Nearctic	Can., U.S.	163,922,032
Seattle Slew, 1974, by Bold Reasoning	U.S.	163,280,883
Alydar, 1975, by Raise a Native	U.S.	159,959,608
Sunday Silence, 1986, by Halo	Jpn.	148,585,928
Blushing Groom (Fr), 1974, by Red God	U.S.	145,694,738
Caerleon, 1980, by Nijinsky II	Ire., Aus.	145,339,991
Secretariat, 1970, by Bold Ruler	U.S.	140,761,223
Sadler's Wells, 1981, by Northern Dancer	Ire.	138,297,801
Halo, 1969, by Hail to Reason	U.S.	130,394,452
Bravest Roman, 1972, by Never Bend	Jpn.	128,881,569
Vice Regent, 1967, by Northern Dancer	Can.	128,845,055
Riverman, 1969, by Never Bend	Fr., U.S.	127,905,981
Miswaki, 1978, by Mr. Prospector	U.S.	125,721,753
Affirmed, 1975, by Exclusive Native	U.S.	124,078,727
Deputy Minister, 1979, by Vice Regent	U.S.	114,009,278
Alleged, 1974, by Hoist the Flag	U.S.	109,395,437
Green Dancer, 1972, by Nijinsky II	Fr., U.S.	106,381,322
Real Shadai, 1979, by Roberto	Jpn.	105,482,482
Woodman, 1983, by Mr. Prospector	Aus., U.S.	105,128,039
Mill George, 1975, by Mill Reef	Jpn.	104,932,257
Dixieland Band, 1980, by Northern Dancer	U.S.	104,412,520

Sire, YOB, Sire	Where Stood	Earnings
Damascus, 1964, by Sword Dancer	U.S.	$103,636,030
Storm Bird, 1978, by Northern Dancer	U.S.	103,077,742
Roberto, 1969, by Hail to Reason	U.S.	102,744,053
Tesco Boy, 1963, by Princely Gift	Jpn.	102,000,155
Valid Appeal, 1972, by In Reality	U.S.	99,631,106
Raise a Native ,1961, by Native Dancer	U.S.	98,139,282
Storm Cat, 1983, by Storm Bird	U.S.	95,591,932
*Grey Dawn II, 1962, by *Herbager	U.S.	92,046,481
Irish River (Fr), 1976, by Riverman	U.S.	91,471,393
Partholon, 1960, by Milesian	Jpn.	91,371,123
In Reality, 1964, by Intentionally	U.S.	90,877,294
Key to the Mint, 1969, by Graustark	U.S.	90,676,470
Fappiano, 1977, by Mr. Prospector	U.S.	89,367,318
Caro (Ire), 1967, by Fortino II	U.S.	87,895,249
Graustark,1963, by *Ribot	U.S.	87,168,507

All-Time Leading Broodmare Sires by Number of Stakes Winners Worldwide
Through 2007

Sire, YOB, Sire	Where Stood	SWs
Mr. Prospector, 1970, by Raise a Native	U.S.	337
Nijinsky II, 1967, by Northern Dancer	U.S.	241
Northern Dancer, 1961, by Nearctic	Can., U.S.	234
Habitat, 1966, by Sir Gaylord	Ire.	222
Lyphard, 1969, by Northern Dancer	Fr., U.S.	204
Raise a Native, 1961, by Native Dancer	U.S.	181
Sadler's Wells, 1981, by Northern Dancer	Ire.	177
Riverman, 1969, by Never Bend	Fr., U.S.	175
Hyperion, 1930, by Gainsborough	Eng.	172
*Princequillo, 1940, by Prince Rose	U.S.	170
Prince John, 1953, by *Princequillo	U.S.	169
Nureyev, 1977, by Northern Dancer	Fr., U.S.	168
*Sir Tristram, 1971, by Sir Ivor	N.Z.	168
Seattle Slew, 1974, by Bold Reasoning	U.S.	167
*Vaguely Noble, 1965, by Vienna	U.S.	167
Secretariat, 1970, by Bold Ruler	U.S.	165
Damascus, 1964, by Sword Dancer	U.S.	160
Green Dancer, 1972, by Nijinsky II	Fr., U.S.	159
*Nasrullah, 1940, by Nearco	Ire., U.S.	159
Northfields, 1968, by Northern Dancer	Aus.	159
Shirley Heights, 1975, by Mill Reef	Eng.	155
Nearco, 1935, by Pharos	Eng.	153
Alleged, 1974, by Hoist the Flag	U.S.	151
Danzig, 1977, by Northern Dancer	U.S.	150
*Sir Gallahad III, 1920, by *Teddy	Fr., U.S.	150
In Reality, 1964, by Intentionally	U.S.	149
Sir Ivor, 1965, by Sir Gaylord	Ire., U.S.	149
Blushing Groom (Fr), 1974, by Red God	U.S.	145
Fleet Nasrullah, 1955, by *Nasrullah	U.S.	145
Alydar, 1975, by Raise a Native	U.S.	144
Deputy Minister, 1979, by Vice Regent	U.S.	144
Halo, 1969, by Hail to Reason	U.S.	144
Graustark, 1963, by *Ribot	U.S.	143
Roberto, 1969, by Hail to Reason	U.S.	143
Buckpasser, 1963, by Tom Fool	U.S.	137
*Mahmoud, 1933, by *Blenheim II	Eng., U.S.	137
Miswaki, 1978, by Mr. Prospector	U.S.	135
*Grey Dawn II, 1962, by *Herbager	U.S.	130

All-Time Leading Broodmare Sires of Group or Graded Stakes Winners Worldwide
Through 2007

Sire, YOB, Sire	Where Stood	GSWs
Mr. Prospector, 1970, by Raise a Native	U.S.	152
Nijinsky II, 1967, by Northern Dancer	U.S.	113
Habitat, 1966, by Sir Gaylord	Ire.	104
Northern Dancer, 1961, by Nearctic	Can., U.S.	104
Northfields, 1968, by Northern Dancer	Ire., Aus., SAf	100
*Sir Tristram, 1971, by Sir Ivor	N.Z.	94
Lyphard, 1969, by Northern Dancer	Fr., U.S.	83
Riverman, 1969, by Never Bend	Fr., U.S.	83
Sadler's Wells, 1981, by Northern Dancer	Ire.	83
Nureyev, 1977, by Northern Dancer	Fr., U.S.	77
Seattle Slew, 1974, by Bold Reasoning	U.S.	77
Shirley Heights, 1975, by Mill Reef	Eng.	76
*Vaguely Noble, 1965, by Vienna	U.S.	76
Ghadeer, 1978, by Lyphard	Brz.	74
Roberto, 1969, by Hail to Reason	U.S.	69
Alydar, 1975, by Raise a Native	U.S.	68
Alleged, 1974, by Hoist the Flag	U.S.	67
Green Dancer, 1972, by Nijinsky II	Fr., U.S.	67
Prince John, 1953, by *Princequillo	U.S.	67
Blushing Groom (Fr), 1974, by Red God	U.S.	65
Sir Ivor, 1965, by Sir Gaylord	Ire., U.S.	65
Buckpasser, 1963, by Tom Fool	U.S.	64
Secretariat, 1970, by Bold Ruler	U.S.	64
Darshaan, 1981, by Shirley Heights	Ire.	63
Graustark, 1963, by *Ribot	U.S.	63
Mill Reef, 1968, by Never Bend	Eng.	60
Sovereign Edition, 1962, by Sovereign Path	N.Z.	59
Damascus, 1964, by Sword Dancer	U.S.	57
Raise a Native, 1961, by Native Dancer	U.S.	57
Round Table, 1954, by *Princequillo	U.S.	57
Caerleon, 1980, by Nijinsky II	Ire.	56
Vain, 1966, by Wilkes	Aus.	55
Key to the Mint, 1969, by Graustark	U.S.	53
Southern Halo, 1983, by Halo	Arg., Jpn.	53
Bletchingly, 1970, by Biscay	Aus.	51
Busted, 1963, by Crepello	Eng.	51
Irish River (Fr), 1976, by Riverman	Fr., U.S.	51
The Minstrel, 1974, by Northern Dancer	U.S.	51

All-Time Leading Broodmare Sires of Group 1 or Grade 1 Stakes Winners
Through 2007

Sire, YOB, Sire	Where Stood	G1Ws
Northfields, 1968, by Northern Dancer	Ire., Aus., SAf	45
Nijinsky II, 1967, by Northern Dancer	U.S.	42
Mr. Prospector, 1970, by Raise a Native	U.S.	40
Northern Dancer, 1961, by Nearctic	U.S.	40
Ghadeer, 1978, by Lyphard	Brz.	39
Riverman, 1969, by Never Bend	Fr., U.S.	31
Sadler's Wells, 1981, by Northern Dancer	Ire.	31
Lyphard, 1969, by Northern Dancer	Fr., U.S.	30
*Sir Tristram, 1971, by Sir Ivor	N.Z.	30
Buckpasser, 1963, by Tom Fool	U.S.	29
*Vaguely Noble, 1965, by Vienna	U.S.	29
Habitat, 1966, by Sir Gaylord	Ire.	27
Key to the Mint, 1969, by Graustark	U.S.	27
Sovereign Edition, 1962, by Sovereign Path	N.Z.	26
Nureyev, 1977, by Northern Dancer	Fr., U.S.	25
Logical, 1972, by Buckpasser	Arg.	24
Secretariat, 1970, by Bold Ruler	U.S.	24
Darshaan, 1981, by Shirley Heights	Ire.	23
Graustark, 1963, by *Ribot	U.S.	23
Seattle Slew, 1974, by Bold Reasoning	U.S.	23
Shirley Heights, 1975, by Mill Reef	Eng.	23
Green Dancer, 1972, by Nijinsky II	Fr., U.S.	22
Prince John, 1953, by *Princequillo	U.S.	22
Roberto, 1969, by Hail to Reason	U.S.	22
Sir Ivor, 1965, by Sir Gaylord	Ire., U.S.	22
Waldmeister, 1961, by Wild Risk	Brz.	22
Alydar, 1975, by Raise a Native	U.S.	21
Zamazaan, 1965, by Exbury	Aus.	21
High Top, 1969, by Derring-Do	Eng.	20
Irish River (Fr), 1976, by Riverman	U.S.	20
Marscay, 1979, by Biscay	Aus.	20
Round Table, 1954, by *Princequillo	U.S.	20
Stage Door Johnny, 1965, by Prince John	U.S.	20

All-Time Leading Sires With Only One Crop to Race Worldwide
Through 2007

Name, Location	Strs	Wnrs	SWs	Leading Earner (Earnings)	Total Lifetime Earnings
Mozart (Ire), Ire	84	53	8	=Amadeus Wolf (GB) ($718,985)	$4,019,655
=Alannon (Aus), Aus	55	39	2	=Falvelon (Aus) ($2,281,645)	3,470,105
Strolling Along, Ky.	54	38	3	Bio Master ($840,292)	3,433,878
=Dubai Millennium (GB), Eng	35	25	5	=Dubawi (Ire) ($1,256,932)	2,836,348
Pay the Butler, Jpn	16	6	1	=Pal Bright (Jpn) ($1,071,129)	2,022,186
Silver Survivor, Ar.	48	38	1	Stoney Jody ($384,813)	1,840,581
Owington (GB), Eng	28	22	3	Gateman (GB) ($788,466)	1,695,574
Ajdal, Eng	28	19	2	Cezanne (GB) ($449,734)	1,461,876
Gold Seam, N.Y.	17	12	2	Tailor's Thread ($502,545)	1,380,236
Sailor's Warning, N.J.	19	14	0	Highland Lass ($149,143)	962,084
Countertrade, Ven	5	3	3	Stillwater (Ven) ($480,125)	950,007
Woodchopper, Fl.	31	26	2	Lumber Bun ($276,156)	883,020
Festival of Light, Tx.	42	25	1	Mistycal Light ($88,314)	825,037
Regal Conquest, La.	13	8	1	Midge Too ($506,283)	726,263
Unduplicated, On.	15	14	1	Not to Be Copied ($170,685)	678,217
The Real McCoy, Fl.	19	17	0	Big McCoy ($230,340)	646,340
=Shergar (GB), Ire	30	14	5	Maysoon (GB) ($156,963)	592,423
Chilito, N.Y.	9	5	0	Toscani ($321,820)	575,134
=North Stoke (GB), Ire	37	16	5	Leccia (Ire) ($155,069)	545,777
Aljamin, Ky.	20	18	2	Sooner Cat ($68,351)	521,905
All the More, Il.	11	10	0	Quite Enough ($122,282)	483,779
Meadow Mint, Ire	28	17	6	Great Sound (Ire) ($214,148)	480,249
Mr. Pow Wow, Ky.	16	12	2	Noontime ($145,463)	478,670
One Magic Moment, SAf	14	8	0	Without Papers ($196,555)	451,060
Sir Rossel, Ky.	8	8	1	Royal Cape ($160,705)	447,685
Frere Basile (Fr), Fr	23	12	3	=Flic Story (Fr) ($96,979)	434,262
Turn of Coin, Ky.	16	13	1	Wishing Coin ($154,674)	426,179
Sickletoy, Oh.	2	2	1	Sickle's Image ($413,275)	418,000

All-Time Leading Sires by Number of Millionaires
Through 2007
(Names of Millionaires)

176 Sunday Silence (Admire Boss, Admire Groove, Admire Japan, Admire Kiss, Admire Main, Admire Max, Admire Vega, Agnes Arashi, Agnes Flight, Agnes Gold [Jpn], Agnes Partner, Agnes Special, Agnes Tachyon, Air Gang Star, Air Messiah, Air Shady, Air Shakur, Albireo, Alfajores, Azuma Sanders, Believe [Jpn], Beluga, Big Sunday, Black Cafe, Black Tide, Black Tuxedo, Born King, Bright Sunday, Bubble Gum Fellow, Chapel Concert, Cheerful Smile, Cheers Brightly, Cheers Grace, Cheers Message, Cheers Silence, Chokai Flight, Chokai Ryoga, Chunyi, Coin Toss, Croupier Star, Daitaku Surgeon, Dance del Cielo, Daiwa Major, Daiwa Raiders, Daiwa Rouge, Dance in the Dark, Dance in the Mood [Jpn], Dance Partner [Jpn], Daring Heart, Deep Impact, Dia de la Novia [Jpn], Diamond Biko, Divine Light, Durandal, Egao o Misete, Eishin Rudens [Jpn], Emerald Isle, Er Nova, Firenze, Fuji Kiseki, Fusaichi Airedale, Fusaichi Pandora, Fusaichi Run Heart, Fusaichi You Can, Genuine, Glorious Sunday, Gold Allure, Great Journey, Hallelujah Sunday, Happy Path, Hat Trick [Jpn], Heart's Cry, Heavenly Romance, Higher Game, Hustler, Iron Reality, Isao Heat, Ishino Sunday, Jo Big Bang, King of Daiya, King of Sunday, King's Trail, Kiss Me Tender, Kyowa Roaring, Les Clefs d'Or, Limitless Bid, Lincoln, Machikane Akatsuki, Machikane Aura, Machikane Kirara, Magic Kiss, Manhattan Cafe, Maruka Candy, Maruka Komachi, Maruka Shenck, Maruka Sieg, Marvelous Sunday, Matsurida Gogh, Meisho Domenica, Meisho Ho O, Meisho Odo, Meteor Burst, Millennium Bio, Miscast, Monopole, Mystic Age, Neo Universe, Noblesse Oblige, Not Seldom, Orange Peel, Orewa Matteruze, Otomeno Inori, Painted Black, Peace of World, Peer Gynt, Pisa no Patek, Ponderosa, Prime Stage, Quiet Day, Reportage, Rikiai Silence, Rosado, Rosebud, Rosen Kavalier, Rosenkreuz, Royal Cancer, Royal Touch, Saikyo Sunday, Sakura President, Seiko Academy, Shinin' Ruby, Shinko Singular, Silence Suzuka, Silent Cruise, Silent Deal, Silent Happiness, Silent Hunter, Silent Savior, Six Sense, Spartacus, Special Week, Starry Heaven, Stay Gold, Still in Love, Stinger [Jpn], Stormy Sunday, Stratagem, Sunday Branch, Sunday Kaiser, Sunday Sarah, Sun Place, Sunrise Pegasus, Super Chance, Suzuka Mambo, Suzuka Phoenix, Swift Current, Tagano Silence, Tayasu Meadow, Tayasu Tsuyoshi, Tiger Cafe, Time to Change, T.M.Sunday, T M Tenrai, Tokai Elite, Tokai Oza, Tokai Wild, To the Victory, Vita Rosa, Waltz Dancer, What a Reason, Win Duel, Win Marvelous, Win Radius, Yamanin Respect, Yukino Sun Royal, Zenno Rob Roy)

49 Danehill (Ace [Ire], Air Eminem, Air Smap, Aqua D'Amore, Aquareliste, Arena, Banks Hill [GB], Breaktime, Cacique [Ire], Catbird, Dane Ripper, Danewin, Desert King, Dr More, The Duke, Dylan Thomas [Ire], Elvstroem, Fairy King Prawn, Fastnet Rock, Fine Motion, Flying Spur, Gaily Flash, Gamble Rose, Generalist, George Washington [Ire], Green Treasure, Ha Ha, Intercontinental [GB], Jeune King Prawn, Johan Cruyff, Lord Flag, Lucky Owners, Machikane Jindaiko, Mayano Absolute, Merlene, Midtown [Ire], North Light [Ire], Nothin' Leica Dane, Oratorio [Ire], Peeping Fawn, Planet Ruler, Rock of Gibraltar [Ire], Scintillation, Tamamo Ruby King, Tiger Hill, Tsukuba Symphony, Uncle Super, Westerner, Zipping)

48 Tony Bin (Air Dublin, Air Groove, Air Thule, Bu O, Christmas Tree, Daddy's Dream, Derby Regno, Eighty Grow, Eishin One Schon, Emocion, Felicitar, Freeway Heart, Gemmy Dress, Happy Look, Inter Licence, Irish Dance, Island Oja, Jungle Pocket, Ken Tony O, Lady Pastel, Leningrad, Long Kaiun, Lord Cronos, Lord Platinum, Maquereau, Misuzu Chardon, My Joker, Narita Century, Nobori Yukio, North Flight, Offside Trap, Royce and Royce, Sakura Chitose O, Sakura Victoria, Sidewinder, Spring Coat, Tai Kalamoun, Tayasu Intime, Telegnosis, Tenzan Seiza, Tosen Tensho, Towa Treasure, Vega, Wedding Honey, Winning Ticket, Yuki Slugger, Yuki Vivace, Yu One Protect)

47 Brian's Time (Admire Gale, Al Dragon, Automatic, Big Don, Big Gold, Brilliant Road, Chokai Carol, Chokai Royal, Dantsu Flame, En Dehors, Erimo Brian, Erimo Dandy, Erimo Maxim, Furioso, Matikanemenimomiyo, Mayano Top Gun, Meine Nouvelle, Meiner Brian, Meiner Max, Meine Sorceress, M.I.Blanc, Narita Brian, Narita Luna Park, Nishino Con Safos, Nishino Due, No Reason, Osumi Stayer, Phalaenopsis, Port Brian's, Run to the Freeze, Sawano Brave, Seattle You, Silk Justice, Silk Prima Donna, Silky Lagoon, Spring Verbena, Sunny Brian, Tagano Guernica, Tanino Gimlet, Teruno Shingeki, Time Paradox, Toho Emperor, Toho Kelly, Toho Shiden, Tosen Bright, Treasure, Victory, Wild Wonder)

Leading 2007 Sires by State and Province Where Bred

Earnings of horses as reported bred in states and provinces, regardless of where sire stands or stood. Based on 2007 progeny earnings.

Alabama

Sire, YOB, Sire	Strs	Wnrs	Wins	SWs	Leading Runner (Earnings)	Total Earnings
Royal Empire, 1994, by Forty Niner	19	7	11	1	Comalagold ($48,050)	$197,805
Chief Persuasion, 1983, by Liege Lord	1	1	4	0	Chief Tudor ($47,065)	47,065
Magic Flagship, 1992, by Northern Flagship	2	1	3	1	Ack Magical ($45,507)	45,600
Special Coach, 1996, by Zafarrancho (Arg)	5	3	3	0	Batesee ($14,994)	43,849
Distorted Humor, 1993, by Forty Niner	1	1	1	0	Rose Data ($37,883)	37,883

Arizona

Sire, YOB, Sire	Strs	Wnrs	Wins	SWs	Leading Runner (Earnings)	Total Earnings
Benton Creek, 1993, by Septieme Ciel	54	28	43	4	Moores Bridge ($44,354)	$440,998
Chanate, 1995, by Storm Cat	49	24	41	1	Blackbird ($47,523)	351,958
Society Max, 1982, by Mr. Prospector	26	14	26	1	Komax ($110,140)	327,569
Midnight Royalty, 1995, by Danzig	29	15	19	3	Combo Royale ($57,058)	245,558
In Excess (Ire), 1987, by Siberian Express	4	3	6	2	Staten Island ($83,700)	172,214

Arkansas

Sire, YOB, Sire	Strs	Wnrs	Wins	SWs	Leading Runner (Earnings)	Total Earnings
Storm and a Half, 1997, by Storm Cat	59	32	47	1	Cat and a Half ($55,770)	$695,591
Etbauer, 1996, by Silver Deputy	16	11	27	2	Time for Etbauer ($130,668)	395,426
Smolderin Heart, 1995, by Two Punch	27	12	20	0	Heart Appeal ($50,770)	290,195
Idabel, 1986, by Mr. Prospector	28	12	25	1	Star of Idabel ($90,590)	286,081
Bold Anthony, 1990, by Bold Ruckus	35	8	15	0	All Bold ($97,733)	265,627

California

Sire, YOB, Sire	Strs	Wnrs	Wins	SWs	Leading Runner (Earnings)	Total Earnings
Bertrando, 1989, by Skywalker	152	91	145	8	Bilo ($327,780)	$4,007,802
Unusual Heat, 1990, by Nureyev	115	59	97	5	Unusual Suspect ($376,221)	3,521,521
In Excess (Ire), 1987, by Siberian Express	127	67	105	5	Notional ($460,000)	3,363,309
Swiss Yodeler, 1994, by Eastern Echo	185	93	178	2	Yodelen Dan ($146,066)	3,129,970
Benchmark, 1991, by Alydar	125	59	99	5	Idiot Proof ($803,136)	2,929,955

Colorado

Sire, YOB, Sire	Strs	Wnrs	Wins	SWs	Leading Runner (Earnings)	Total Earnings
Oliver's Twist, 1992, by Horatius	28	17	22	2	Menoken Moon ($21,317)	$175,335
Kennedy Factor, 1988, by Meadowlake	16	10	12	2	Meadow Dancer ($44,250)	145,051
Cash Deposit, 1994, by Deposit Ticket	32	14	17	0	Music Goes Round ($23,556)	141,834
Twining, 1991, by Forty Niner	1	1	4	1	Folsom ($92,891)	92,891
Distorted Humor, 1993, by Forty Niner	2	2	2	1	The Nth Degree ($79,062)	92,442

Connecticut

Sire, YOB, Sire	Strs	Wnrs	Wins	SWs	Leading Runner (Earnings)	Total Earnings
Lear Fan, 1981, by Roberto	1	0	0	0	Heart Broken ($4,415)	$4,415
Hook and Ladder, 1997, by Dixieland Band	1	0	0	0	Sabael ($2,280)	2,280

Delaware

Sire, YOB, Sire	Strs	Wnrs	Wins	SWs	Leading Runner (Earnings)	Total Earnings
Diamond, 1995, by Mr. Prospector	1	1	2	0	Zygomatic Smile ($20,506)	$20,506

Florida

Sire, YOB, Sire	Strs	Wnrs	Wins	SWs	Leading Runner (Earnings)	Total Earnings
Yes It's True, 1996, by Is It True	177	99	182	10	Takara True ($291,772)	$4,830,235
Trippi, 1997, by End Sweep	138	81	148	5	Miss Macy Sue ($546,217)	4,559,641
Tiger Ridge, 1996, by Storm Cat	142	77	141	4	Storm in May ($405,181)	3,574,597
Put It Back, 1998, by Honour and Glory	81	56	94	5	Black Bar Spin ($687,085)	3,502,361
Northern Afleet, 1993, by Afleet	144	99	178	3	Big City Man ($143,540)	3,403,992

Georgia

Sire, YOB, Sire	Strs	Wnrs	Wins	SWs	Leading Runner (Earnings)	Total Earnings
Roaring Camp, 1991, by Forty Niner	19	8	11	0	Jag Man ($24,300)	$120,857
Play Both Ends, 1992, by Fast Play	5	4	7	0	Plays Pops Choice ($37,959)	67,103
Kelly Kip, 1994, by Kipper Kelly	1	1	2	0	Kickstand Kelli ($46,793)	46,793
Roundup, 1999, by Deputy Minister	3	2	2	0	Veva E ($21,250)	32,425
Fitz, 1993, by Waquoit	3	1	2	0	Bama ($13,310)	23,764

Idaho

Sire, YOB, Sire	Strs	Wnrs	Wins	SWs	Leading Runner (Earnings)	Total Earnings
Suave Prospect, 1992, by Fortunate Prospect	1	1	4	1	Crypts Seeker ($94,884)	$94,884
T. U. Slew, 1990, by Seattle Slew	3	2	8	2	Petite Motion ($53,129)	76,408
Cobra King, 1993, by Farma Way	1	1	1	0	Bitter Bill ($64,249)	64,249
Renteria, 1994, by Incinorator	14	5	11	2	Bonk ($19,428)	61,474
Game Plan, 1993, by Danzig	5	4	8	0	Blazeisagamelady ($31,440)	61,033

Sires — Leading Sires by State in 2007

Illinois

Sire, YOB, Sire	Strs	Wnrs	Wins	SWs	Leading Runner (Earnings)	Total Earnings
Cartwright, 1990, by Forty Niner	106	58	102	4	Wiggins ($117,480)	$1,608,361
Classified Facts, 1993, by Seattle Slew	40	24	33	1	Turbulent Thinking ($82,984)	807,672
Unreal Zeal, 1980, by Mr. Prospector	63	32	54	1	River Bear ($109,499)	719,879
Alaskan Frost, 1988, by Copelan	48	25	43	0	Indigo Ice ($89,902)	523,095
Sefapiano, 1989, by Fappiano	6	4	15	1	Rolling Sea ($361,081)	491,598

Indiana

Sire, YOB, Sire	Strs	Wnrs	Wins	SWs	Leading Runner (Earnings)	Total Earnings
Crown Ambassador, 1994, by Storm Cat	48	27	45	3	Father John ($83,400)	$646,968
Moro Oro, 1993, by Moro	36	17	35	0	Mo Faster ($36,179)	354,449
Black Moonshine, 1987, by Mt. Livermore	17	10	25	1	Basin Banannie ($83,775)	353,197
Lil E. Tee, 1989, by At the Threshold	16	8	19	3	Lil E Rose ($85,414)	352,645
Presidential Order, 1993, by Danzig	29	12	21	0	Dollar for Dollar ($38,209)	225,013

Iowa

Sire, YOB, Sire	Strs	Wnrs	Wins	SWs	Leading Runner (Earnings)	Total Earnings
Sharkey, 1987, by Sharpen Up (GB)	47	25	37	1	Judy Faye ($84,002)	$601,052
Blumin Affair, 1991, by Dynaformer	26	13	29	0	Dynamic Affair ($42,348)	332,640
Mutakddim, 1991, by Seeking the Gold	7	7	12	1	Seekingthereinbow ($88,320)	323,803
Humming, 1996, by Summer Squall	22	12	16	0	Joggins ($67,269)	315,961
Mercedes Won, 1986, by Air Forbes Won	13	7	12	1	Won Won Wonder Why ($85,063)	269,685

Kansas

Sire, YOB, Sire	Strs	Wnrs	Wins	SWs	Leading Runner (Earnings)	Total Earnings
Gold Ruler, 1980, by Mr. Prospector	20	8	14	1	Nick Missed ($18,268)	$75,391
Exetera, 1993, by Forty Niner	1	1	3	1	Summer Recital ($72,040)	72,040
Grand On Dave, 1995, by Meadowlake	6	3	5	1	Manovan ($40,777)	50,899
Admiral Indy, 1994, by A.P. Indy	7	3	3	2	Dee Indy Go ($14,880)	43,519
Sabona, 1982, by Exclusive Native	4	2	2	0	Donnie O ($10,472)	22,322

Kentucky

Sire, YOB, Sire	Strs	Wnrs	Wins	SWs	Leading Runner (Earnings)	Total Earnings
Smart Strike, 1992, by Mr. Prospector	132	61	110	9	Curlin ($5,102,800)	$11,498,356
A.P. Indy, 1989, by Seattle Slew	154	71	129	15	Rags to Riches ($1,340,028)	8,018,844
Distorted Humor, 1993, by Forty Niner	171	80	131	13	Any Given Saturday ($994,320)	7,985,494
Unbridled's Song, 1993, by Unbridled	151	75	132	13	Octave ($1,050,234)	6,235,488
Cherokee Run, 1990, by Runaway Groom	147	87	140	9	War Pass ($1,397,400)	5,970,218

Louisiana

Sire, YOB, Sire	Strs	Wnrs	Wins	SWs	Leading Runner (Earnings)	Total Earnings
Leestown, 1994, by Seattle Slew	153	63	107	5	Ahead of Her Time ($254,000)	$2,816,764
Zarbyev, 1984, by Nureyev	64	41	76	4	St. Zarb ($249,750)	1,875,892
Ide, 1993, by Forty Niner	46	19	35	2	Tensas Yucatan ($284,877)	1,172,339
Gold Tribute, 1994, by Mr. Prospector	67	28	37	1	Tortuga Straits ($105,600)	961,506
Finest Hour, 1994, by Forty Niner	81	27	40	1	Arcatec ($86,110)	890,609

Maryland

Sire, YOB, Sire	Strs	Wnrs	Wins	SWs	Leading Runner (Earnings)	Total Earnings
Not For Love, 1990, by Mr. Prospector	91	48	72	5	Smart and Fancy ($297,513)	$2,383,762
Partner's Hero, 1994, by Danzig	64	36	66	3	Heros Reward ($515,826)	1,924,059
Malibu Moon, 1997, by A.P. Indy	45	22	39	4	Moon Catcher ($663,450)	1,751,655
Two Punch, 1983, by Mr. Prospector	69	35	59	2	Grand Champion ($279,240)	1,598,109
Allen's Prospect, 1982, by Mr. Prospector	82	44	80	0	All Giving ($101,835)	1,246,059

Massachusetts

Sire, YOB, Sire	Strs	Wnrs	Wins	SWs	Leading Runner (Earnings)	Total Earnings
Sundance Ridge, 1986, by Cox's Ridge	16	11	16	2	Sundance Richie ($58,417)	$247,906
Key Contender, 1988, by Fit to Fight	3	2	7	1	Ask Queenie ($146,195)	156,821
Senor Conquistador, 1991, by Conquistador Cielo	9	2	4	1	Senor St. Pat ($71,360)	125,124
Mesopotamia, 1993, by Deputy Minister	2	1	4	0	Mr. Meso ($104,426)	105,794
Disco Rico, 1997, by Citidancer	4	4	5	0	Disco Fox ($40,140)	95,132

Michigan

Sire, YOB, Sire	Strs	Wnrs	Wins	SWs	Leading Runner (Earnings)	Total Earnings
Demaloot Demashoot, 1990, by Bold Ruckus	55	34	62	6	Valley Loot ($170,000)	$852,185
Native Factor, 1987, by Foolish Pleasure	38	24	44	0	Scarlet Fact ($65,398)	521,679
Daylight Savings, 1994, by Sky Classic	17	9	21	2	Hot Chili ($152,680)	485,229
Matchlite, 1983, by Clever Trick	40	23	40	1	Clever Idea ($64,224)	478,129
Quiet Enjoyment, 1989, by Ogygian	33	21	42	1	Nell's Enjoyment ($114,180)	443,391

Minnesota

Sire, YOB, Sire	Strs	Wnrs	Wins	SWs	Leading Runner (Earnings)	Total Earnings
Ghazi, 1989, by Polish Navy	30	13	16	1	Run With Joy ($84,027)	$267,745
Evansville Slew, 1992, by Slew City Slew	7	6	12	3	Thanks for the Tip ($69,370)	234,585
Shot of Gold, 1995, by Jolie's Halo	26	13	17	0	Shot of Silver ($29,905)	214,761
Quick Cut, 1994, by Storm Cat	18	9	11	0	R K Bigshot ($22,633)	145,606
Demidoff, 1990, by Mr. Prospector	9	5	9	1	Vazandar ($30,550)	122,945

Sires — Leading Sires by State in 2007

Mississippi

Sire, YOB, Sire	Strs	Wnrs	Wins	SWs	Leading Runner (Earnings)	Total Earnings
Golden Omen, 1996, by Strike the Gold	4	2	6	0	Ceasars Pleaser ($31,120)	$59,420
Blushing Star, 1993, by Blushing John	5	2	2	0	Blushing Sugarplum ($18,250)	39,655
Evansville Slew, 1992, by Slew City Slew	1	0	0	0	Smalltown Slew ($38,411)	38,411
Moving Shoulder, 1992, by Gone West	1	1	3	0	Tredinock ($23,995)	23,995
Warlaunch, 1990, by Relaunch	1	1	2	0	Lowndes County ($16,740)	16,740

Missouri

Sire, YOB, Sire	Strs	Wnrs	Wins	SWs	Leading Runner (Earnings)	Total Earnings
Liginsky, 1989, by Nijinsky II	1	1	2	0	Samba G ($57,617)	$57,617
Victorious, 1980, by Explodent	3	3	5	0	Campinout ($44,640)	51,284
Wood Reply, 1992, by Woodman	2	2	3	0	Reply N Aces ($14,600)	26,480
Mocha Express, 1994, by Java Gold	1	1	1	0	Espresso Express ($17,190)	17,190
Isaypete, 1996, by Peteski	4	1	1	0	Dialing Pete ($14,958)	17,149

Montana

Sire, YOB, Sire	Strs	Wnrs	Wins	SWs	Leading Runner (Earnings)	Total Earnings
D'wildcat, 1998, by Forest Wildcat	1	1	1	1	The Golden Noodle ($144,380)	$144,380
Slewdledo, 1981, by Seattle Slew	5	5	7	0	Little Miss Jo ($38,035)	101,566
Global View, 1994, by Fly Till Dawn	1	1	1	0	Lord's View ($46,000)	46,000
Western Fame, 1992, by Gone West	1	1	1	0	Dream West ($44,250)	44,250
Black Mackee, 1976, by Captain Courageous	4	3	4	0	Dublin's Woodwin ($26,798)	35,526

Nebraska

Sire, YOB, Sire	Strs	Wnrs	Wins	SWs	Leading Runner (Earnings)	Total Earnings
Blumin Affair, 1991, by Dynaformer	20	10	21	6	Blumin Attitude ($48,122)	$237,839
Shawklit Player, 1994, by Fast Play	13	9	19	2	Plaer's Trump ($53,488)	192,115
Dazzling Falls, 1992, by Taylor's Falls	16	9	21	2	Bevys Dazzler ($57,702)	180,966
Silver Launch, 1995, by Relaunch	19	10	15	0	Carol's Tinkerbell ($19,591)	140,993
Miracle Heights, 1989, by Gate Dancer	19	10	12	0	Future Fun ($19,423)	131,727

Nevada

Sire, YOB, Sire	Strs	Wnrs	Wins	SWs	Leading Runner (Earnings)	Total Earnings
Presidents Summit, 1985, by Taylor's Falls	1	1	1	0	Hyatopthehills ($6,248)	$6,248
Jestic, 1987, by His Majesty	1	1	2	0	King's Option ($4,422)	4,422

New Hampshire

Sire, YOB, Sire	Strs	Wnrs	Wins	SWs	Leading Runner (Earnings)	Total Earnings
Senor Conquistador, 1991, by Conquistador Cielo	2	1	1	0	Highland Toreador ($6,810)	$7,665

New Jersey

Sire, YOB, Sire	Strs	Wnrs	Wins	SWs	Leading Runner (Earnings)	Total Earnings
Private Interview, 1992, by Nureyev	48	20	30	0	Corvo ($74,190)	$1,096,453
Defrere, 1992, by Deputy Minister	33	18	26	1	Carrots Only ($111,780)	903,021
Not For Love, 1990, by Mr. Prospector	15	11	18	2	Talkin About Love ($375,875)	861,174
Numerous, 1991, by Mr. Prospector	24	12	19	1	Sherunsforbilly ($151,681)	659,282
Disco Rico, 1997, by Citidancer	6	6	15	1	Pure Disco ($285,050)	567,923

New Mexico

Sire, YOB, Sire	Strs	Wnrs	Wins	SWs	Leading Runner (Earnings)	Total Earnings
Chimes Band, 1991, by Dixieland Band	86	39	63	3	Playingwithchimes ($118,545)	$1,514,746
Desert God, 1991, by Fappiano	25	15	35	3	Peppers Pride ($364,560)	1,134,615
Ghostly Moves, 1992, by Silver Ghost	68	30	48	1	Some Ghost ($262,051)	1,118,312
Dome, 1998, by Storm Cat	45	21	36	2	Z Z Dome ($219,716)	922,541
In Excessive Bull, 1994, by In Excess (Ire)	74	28	45	1	Hecamefromaclaim ($96,154)	815,365

New York

Sire, YOB, Sire	Strs	Wnrs	Wins	SWs	Leading Runner (Earnings)	Total Earnings
City Zip, 1998, by Carson City	101	56	92	4	Tishmeister ($167,516)	$2,967,954
Precise End, 1997, by End Sweep	78	43	75	5	Expect the End ($204,380)	2,381,134
Western Expression, 1996, by Gone West	94	45	88	0	Stunt Man ($347,739)	2,021,170
Freud, 1998, by Storm Cat	72	33	51	2	Karakorum Elektra ($111,993)	1,894,865
Prime Timber, 1996, by Sultry Song	52	28	57	1	Premium Wine ($311,700)	1,553,668

North Carolina

Sire, YOB, Sire	Strs	Wnrs	Wins	SWs	Leading Runner (Earnings)	Total Earnings
Chelsey Cat, 1998, by Storm Cat	24	15	25	0	Chelsey Gallop ($39,155)	$250,068
Mongoose, 1998, by Broad Brush	1	1	2	0	Steady Slew ($36,800)	36,800
One More Power, 1993, by Mt. Livermore	1	1	1	0	Carolina Power ($29,590)	29,590
You and I, 1991, by Kris S.	1	1	2	0	Hermotherandido ($21,734)	21,734
Friendly Lover, 1988, by Cutlass	1	1	1	0	Java's Lover ($14,380)	14,380

North Dakota

Sire, YOB, Sire	Strs	Wnrs	Wins	SWs	Leading Runner (Earnings)	Total Earnings
Codys Key, 1989, by Corridor Key	5	2	5	1	Aferds Code Red ($22,362)	$38,515
Aferd, 1976, by Hoist the Flag	3	2	4	1	Maddies Blues ($25,260)	31,878
Patriot Strike, 1989, by General Assembly	9	4	6	1	Liberty Reigns ($12,298)	31,868
Coordinator, 1992, by Deputy Minister	1	1	2	1	Givem Hell Harley ($20,169)	20,169
Free House, 1994, by Smokester	1	1	1	0	Miss Free House ($18,311)	18,311

Ohio

Sire, YOB, Sire	Strs	Wnrs	Wins	SWs	Leading Runner (Earnings)	Total Earnings
Mercer Mill, 1994, by Forty Niner	68	38	66	2	Magg's Choice ($107,300)	$746,946
Bernstein, 1997, by Storm Cat	5	3	8	2	Pay the Man ($180,660)	340,538
Parents' Reward, 1998, by Mr. Prospector	14	6	14	2	Mini Mom ($122,002)	339,208
Noble Cat, 1995, by Storm Cat	21	8	20	1	Catlaunch ($181,660)	324,508
Winthrop, 1996, by Storm Cat	27	11	27	0	Reckless Wind ($92,475)	302,298

Oklahoma

Sire, YOB, Sire	Strs	Wnrs	Wins	SWs	Leading Runner (Earnings)	Total Earnings
Kipling, 1996, by Gulch	13	5	9	1	Kip Deville ($1,965,780)	$2,016,248
Prospector's Music, 1989, by Mr. Prospector	37	13	29	2	Lauras Last Music ($122,013)	496,338
Here We Come, 1988, by Mr. Prospector	57	26	41	0	Here Comes Marv ($36,421)	490,467
King of Scat, 1996, by Eastern Echo	49	19	26	0	King Robert ($41,726)	346,880
Mi Selecto, 1985, by Explodent	46	16	24	0	Some Quick ($40,603)	329,879

Oregon

Sire, YOB, Sire	Strs	Wnrs	Wins	SWs	Leading Runner (Earnings)	Total Earnings
Baquero, 1995, by Forty Niner	33	20	39	3	Jimbos Fire Ant ($42,425)	$222,919
Ochoco, 1998, by Mr. Prospector	18	12	20	3	Ochoco Salmon ($47,443)	142,333
Cisco Road, 1990, by Northern Baby	19	12	27	4	Bagels Baby ($21,070)	141,242
True Confidence, 1997, by Storm Cat	33	14	26	1	Sexy Romance ($18,050)	124,668
Bagshot, 1994, by Smokester	11	5	14	2	Lady's Purse ($41,073)	103,612

Pennsylvania

Sire, YOB, Sire	Strs	Wnrs	Wins	SWs	Leading Runner (Earnings)	Total Earnings
Danzig, 1977, by Northern Dancer	3	2	5	1	Hard Spun ($2,572,500)	$2,581,502
Dynaformer, 1985, by Roberto	7	4	9	0	Lucarno ($1,033,373)	1,215,350
Theatrical (Ire), 1982, by Nureyev	2	1	4	1	Mrs. Lindsay ($1,170,915)	1,171,195
Not For Love, 1990, by Mr. Prospector	31	19	39	2	Obi Wan ($146,542)	1,153,110
Malibu Moon, 1997, by A.P. Indy	23	13	26	1	S W Aly'svalentine ($161,770)	809,474

South Carolina

Sire, YOB, Sire	Strs	Wnrs	Wins	SWs	Leading Runner (Earnings)	Total Earnings
Kokand, 1985, by Mr. Prospector	20	12	18	0	Socks Bishop ($46,244)	$251,381
Signal, 1993, by Forty Niner	8	4	6	0	Raise a Signal ($46,399)	109,094
East of Easy, 1995, by Trempolino	4	4	8	0	Put Step On It ($39,180)	83,410
Crush, 1997, by Gone West	4	3	8	0	Mr Perfect ($23,810)	62,906
Play Both Ends, 1992, by Fast Play	1	1	3	0	Taber's Tiger ($46,800)	46,800

South Dakota

Sire, YOB, Sire	Strs	Wnrs	Wins	SWs	Leading Runner (Earnings)	Total Earnings
Crowning Season (GB), 1990, by Danzig	3	3	6	0	Hat Trick ($21,168)	$28,149
Get Me Out, 1996, by Capote	3	1	1	0	Spitfire Flyer ($4,833)	7,905
Crafty Ridan, 1986, by Crafty Prospector	7	1	1	0	Flexible Type ($3,530)	5,768
Patton, 1991, by Lord At War (Arg)	1	1	1	0	Dakota Lighting ($3,779)	3,779
Mr. O. P., 1986, by Naskra	7	0	0	0	Champagns Holiday ($2,079)	3,571

Tennessee

Sire, YOB, Sire	Strs	Wnrs	Wins	SWs	Leading Runner (Earnings)	Total Earnings
Expanding Man, 1994, by Hermitage	1	1	3	0	Dark Contessa ($67,650)	$67,650
Dusty Screen, 1988, by Silent Screen	1	1	3	0	Crimson Slasher ($39,211)	39,211
With Approval, 1986, by Caro (Ire)	2	1	1	0	Approved by Dylan ($26,860)	27,760
Running Stag, 1994, by Cozzene	1	1	1	0	Bit of Attitude ($22,160)	22,160
Sahm, 1994, by Mr. Prospector	1	1	1	0	Sahm Psalm ($20,250)	20,250

Texas

Sire, YOB, Sire	Strs	Wnrs	Wins	SWs	Leading Runner (Earnings)	Total Earnings
Valid Expectations, 1993, by Valid Appeal	108	58	95	5	Valid Lilly ($213,406)	$1,619,711
Magic Cat, 1995, by Storm Cat	51	26	44	4	Banquo ($90,731)	783,699
Hadif, 1986, by Clever Trick	55	23	41	1	Austin Lights ($107,427)	643,824
Wild Zone, 1990, by Wild Again	50	28	49	0	Wild Series ($44,228)	613,756
Commanchero, 1995, by Unbridled	49	24	40	1	Real Soup ($75,532)	553,574

Utah

Sire, YOB, Sire	Strs	Wnrs	Wins	SWs	Leading Runner (Earnings)	Total Earnings
Four Seasons (GB), 1990, by Sadler's Wells	3	3	3	0	Steeleon Season ($11,747)	$26,701
Rhythm, 1987, by Mr. Prospector	1	1	3	0	Olympic Stride ($14,377)	14,377
Easy N Dirty, 1983, by Debussy	2	2	2	0	Boulder Chief ($8,289)	13,529
Crystal Gazer, 1994, by Slewpy	6	2	2	0	Slewpy G. D. ($4,030)	10,629
Stalwart Boy, 1990, by Stalwart	2	1	1	0	Gotztu ($5,061)	9,264

Virginia

Sire, YOB, Sire	Strs	Wnrs	Wins	SWs	Leading Runner (Earnings)	Total Earnings
Lemon Drop Kid, 1996, by Kingmambo	4	3	10	1	Christmas Kid ($554,500)	$718,397
Stormin Fever, 1994, by Storm Cat	29	11	22	2	Dorm Fever ($147,616)	664,666
Housebuster, 1987, by Mt. Livermore	36	15	29	0	Side Buster ($58,290)	400,238
Pulpit, 1994, by A.P. Indy	5	3	7	1	Mini Sermon ($256,100)	385,944
Malibu Moon, 1997, by A.P. Indy	10	7	11	2	Jenkin Jones ($98,420)	328,951

Sires — Leading Sires by Province in 2007

Washington

Sire, YOB, Sire	Strs	Wnrs	Wins	SWs	Leading Runner (Earnings)	Total Earnings
Cahill Road, 1988, by Fappiano	67	32	58	2	The Great Face ($292,875)	$967,282
Slewdledo, 1981, by Seattle Slew	106	46	77	1	Carrie's a Jewel ($84,170)	809,835
Free At Last, 1989, by Wild Again	65	29	47	4	Wild Cycle ($59,787)	480,065
Petersburg, 1986, by Danzig	47	23	42	0	Midwesterner ($84,900)	463,069
Tribunal, 1997, by Deputy Minister	31	16	28	1	Mulcahy ($142,259)	453,822

West Virginia

Sire, YOB, Sire	Strs	Wnrs	Wins	SWs	Leading Runner (Earnings)	Total Earnings
Luftikus, 1996, by Meadowlake	56	33	52	2	Love to Plunge ($127,410)	$1,192,809
Eastover Court, 1991, by Seattle Slew	37	17	35	3	Eastern Delite ($276,895)	1,167,810
Makin, 1990, by Danzig	51	16	24	0	Georgia Moon ($52,530)	481,859
My Boy Adam, 1987, by Encino	39	11	15	0	Smart Pace ($59,292)	326,137
Kokand, 1985, by Mr. Prospector	30	11	15	0	Glorious Appearing ($45,180)	301,394

Wisconsin

Sire, YOB, Sire	Strs	Wnrs	Wins	SWs	Leading Runner (Earnings)	Total Earnings
Armed Truce, 1981, by Bold Forbes	2	2	2	0	Solaratee ($9,525)	$15,885
Quick Cut, 1994, by Storm Cat	1	1	1	0	Snow Country Cat ($9,687)	9,687
Hacker, 1994, by Jade Hunter	1	0	0	0	R's Star ($7,330)	7,330

Wyoming

Sire, YOB, Sire	Strs	Wnrs	Wins	SWs	Leading Runner (Earnings)	Total Earnings
Cup Challenge, 1989, by Mr. Prospector	1	1	2	0	Bh Whata Challenge ($3,340)	$3,340

Puerto Rico

Sire, YOB, Sire	Strs	Wnrs	Wins	SWs	Leading Runner (Earnings)	Total Earnings
Eqtesaad, 1991, by Danzig	58	39	100	0	Bachatera ($79,707)	$775,293
Fappiano's Star, 1988, by Fappiano	57	22	51	1	Borrascoso ($102,862)	680,321
Sejm, 1987, by Danzig	29	22	51	2	El Enganado ($192,184)	649,910
Royal Merlot, 1993, by Forty Niner	50	23	49	1	Tonadilla ($131,393)	538,012
Just Typical, 1998, by A.P. Indy	36	25	46	0	Ojos Bellos ($61,161)	485,716

Alberta

Sire, YOB, Sire	Strs	Wnrs	Wins	SWs	Leading Runner (Earnings)	Total Earnings
Devonwood, 1994, by Woodman	40	21	39	5	Teagues Fight ($123,697)	$600,051
Regal Remark, 1982, by Vice Regent	30	20	35	3	Pat of Gold ($67,805)	461,904
Rosetti, 1999, by Seattle Slew	23	14	24	0	Slews the Standard ($38,525)	302,898
Desperately, 1990, by Greinton (GB)	17	12	22	4	Bear Nobility ($54,704)	291,590
Esteem, 1995, by Forty Niner	17	10	16	3	Just Call Me Duke ($61,248)	249,869

British Columbia

Sire, YOB, Sire	Strs	Wnrs	Wins	SWs	Leading Runner (Earnings)	Total Earnings
Vying Victor, 1989, by Flying Paster	93	47	71	1	Suva ($74,692)	$881,120
Millennium Allstar, 1998, by Meadowlake	24	17	29	3	Dancing Allstar ($299,428)	819,319
Stephanotis, 1993, by Regal Classic	56	39	72	2	Stephanson ($60,113)	708,044
Katahaula County, 1988, by Bold Ruckus	77	33	50	2	Cafe Tortoni ($52,795)	669,231
Mass Market, 1997, by Marquetry	47	25	42	1	Post Rio ($40,905)	413,412

Manitoba

Sire, YOB, Sire	Strs	Wnrs	Wins	SWs	Leading Runner (Earnings)	Total Earnings
Circulating, 1990, by Bold Ruckus	21	8	11	1	Miss Doubletrouble ($25,981)	$107,580
Langfuhr, 1992, by Danzig	2	1	3	0	Albarino ($103,028)	106,423
Forest Wildcat, 1991, by Storm Cat	1	1	2	1	La Wildcat ($92,110)	92,110
Battle Cat, 1998, by Storm Cat	13	4	4	1	Bella Mariella ($24,621)	79,081
Act Smart, 1992, by Smarten	7	3	4	0	Smart Miss ($26,690)	57,120

Ontario

Sire, YOB, Sire	Strs	Wnrs	Wins	SWs	Leading Runner (Earnings)	Total Earnings
Bold Executive, 1984, by Bold Ruckus	130	75	121	4	Legal Move ($222,728)	$4,281,801
Bold n' Flashy, 1989, by Bold Ruckus	94	56	93	2	Red Raffles ($165,239)	2,230,536
Kiridashi, 1992, by Bold Ruckus	50	28	57	3	Financingavailable ($451,151)	2,057,336
Langfuhr, 1992, by Danzig	39	20	27	0	Jambalaya ($979,421)	2,010,590
Tethra, 1992, by Cure the Blues	78	41	67	2	Don's Folly ($133,283)	1,592,139

Quebec

Sire, YOB, Sire	Strs	Wnrs	Wins	SWs	Leading Runner (Earnings)	Total Earnings
Silver Deputy, 1985, by Deputy Minister	2	2	3	0	Chest of Silver ($64,419)	$95,098
Cat Thief, 1996, by Storm Cat	1	1	2	0	Urn ($58,397)	58,397
Salt Lake, 1989, by Deputy Minister	1	1	2	0	Hot Spell ($43,550)	43,550
Chief Seattle, 1997, by Seattle Slew	1	0	0	0	Shillelagh Slew ($22,334)	22,334
Langfuhr, 1992, by Danzig	2	1	1	0	Maccabi ($13,295)	16,340

Saskatchewan

Sire, YOB, Sire	Strs	Wnrs	Wins	SWs	Leading Runner (Earnings)	Total Earnings
Shaheen, 1994, by Danzig	13	7	10	3	Time to Danze ($11,594)	$53,048
You've Got Action, 1994, by Son of Briartic	16	3	7	1	Brilliant Action ($18,714)	37,327
Stop the Stage, 1985, by Gold Stage	9	3	4	1	Dorothy Hazel ($11,648)	32,757
Royal Quiz, 1984, by Real Emperor	10	5	7	1	Royal Rust ($8,514)	29,916
A Fleets Dancer, 1995, by Afleet	1	1	1	0	Fleet Foot Fran ($27,268)	27,268

Stallion Syndications

In part because the definition of stallion syndication has changed over the decades, pinpointing the first syndication contract is difficult, if not impossible. However, the earliest syndication agreement comparable in form and intent to modern syndicates was that of Tracery in 1923. That agreement between the syndicators, the International Horse Agency and Exchange and a group of 30 subscribers, placed a value of $219,840 on the 1912 St. Leger winner, who was the sire of '23 Epsom Derby victor *Papyrus.

The principle behind that syndicate and all subsequent ones was to spread the risk of purchasing a very expensive breeding horse (and, in Tracery's case, returning him from Argentina). From the beginning of the Thoroughbred breeding industry in the late 17th century right up to the 20th century, Thoroughbred breeding was essentially a private affair, with rich aristocrats wholly owning stallions and breeding mostly their own mares to those sires.

As Thoroughbred breeding slowly became more commercial in the late 19th and early 20th centuries, a new method of financing was required, both to spread the risk of failure and to ensure that a stallion received an appropriate number and quality of mares. Syndication was the answer. In Tracery's case, spreading the risk was a wise strategy because the stallion died after only one season at stud in England.

In a modern syndicate agreement, individuals agree to purchase a specific percentage of ownership in a stallion—the percentage ownership is determined by the number of shares—with payment for that percentage interest usually spread in installments over several years. In return, the buyer of a syndicate share gains the right to breed one or more mares to that stallion each year without additional payments (except for agreed maintenance fees). The syndicate manager normally receives a specified number of free nominations each year as compensation.

The similarity to buying stock market shares is evident. The syndicate manager receives capital to pay for a major capital asset, and shareholders gain the possibility of dividends from the share through sale of the nomination or value of the produce. Shares also may be sold later to other investors at a profit (or loss), just as in the stock market, although syndication agreements may place restrictions on the transfer of the shares.

Although the first clearly identifiable syndicate was English, Americans soon became active syndicators. Arthur B. Hancock of Claiborne Farm formed a four-man partnership in 1926 to purchase the high-class French miler *Sir Gallahad III for $125,000. When *Sir Gallahad III sired Triple Crown winner Gallant Fox in his first crop, making him leading sire for the first of four times, the syndication process gained impetus in America. In 1936, Hancock syndicated another leading sire, *Blenheim II, for a record

Chronology of Record Stallion Syndications

Stallion	Year	Price	Farm	Seller	Share Price	No. Shares
Fusaichi Pegasus	2000	†$60,000,000	Ashford Stud (Ky.)	Fusao Sekiguchi	$1,500,000	40
Lammtarra	1996	42,000,000	Arrow Stud (Jpn)	Dalham Hall Stud	1,050,000	40
Shareef Dancer	1983	40,000,000	Dalham Hall Stud (Eng)	Aston Upthorpe Stud	1,000,000	40
Conquistador Cielo	1982	36,400,000	Claiborne Farm (Ky.)	Henryk de Kwiatkowski (retained 10 shares)	910,000	40
Storm Bird	1981	30,000,000	Ashford Stud (Ky.)	Robert Sangster, et al.	750,000	40
Spectacular Bid	1980	22,000,000	Claiborne Farm (Ky.)	Hawksworth Farm (retained 20 shares)	550,000	40
Troy	1979	16,500,000	Highclere Stud (Eng)	Sir Michael Sobell and Arnold Weinstock	412,500	40
Alleged	1978	16,000,000	Walmac-Warnerton Int'l. (Ky.)	Robert Sangster, et al.	400,000	40
Seattle Slew	1978	12,000,000	Spendthrift Farm (Ky.)	Wooden Horse Investments (retained 20 shares)	300,000	40
The Minstrel	1977	9,000,000	Windfields Farm (Md.)	Robert Sangster, et al.	250,000	36
What a Pleasure	1976	8,000,000	Waldemar Farm (Ky.)	Waldemar (retained 16 shares)	250,000	32
Wajima	1975	7,200,000	Spendthrift Farm (Ky.)	East-West Stable (retained 20 shares)	200,000	36
Secretariat	1973	6,080,000	Claiborne Farm (Ky.)	Meadow Stable	190,000	32
Nijinsky II	1970	5,440,000	Claiborne Farm (Ky.)	Charles W. Englehard (retained 10 shares)	170,000	32
*Vaguely Noble	1969	5,000,000	Gainesway (Ky.)	Nelson Bunker Hunt and Dr. Robert Franklyn	125,000	40
Buckpasser	1967	4,800,000	Claiborne Farm (Ky.)	Ogden Phipps (retained 16 shares)	150,000	32
Raise a Native	1967	2,625,000	Spendthrift Farm (Ky.)	Louis Wolfson and Leslie Combs	75,000	35
Graustark	1966	2,400,000	Darby Dan Farm (Ky.)	John W. Galbreath	60,000	40
Tom Fool	1960	1,750,000	Greentree Stud (Ky.)	Greentree Stud	50,000	35
Nashua	1955	1,251,200	Spendthrift Farm (Ky.)	Estate of William Woodward Jr.	39,200	32
*Tulyar	1952	697,500	Irish National Stud (Ire)	H. H. Aga Khan	17,438	40
The Phoenix	1948	619,920	Ballykisteen Stud (Ire)	Fred Myerscough	15,498	40
*Alibhai	1948	500,000	Spendthrift Farm (Ky.)	Louis B. Mayer	16,667	30
Stardust	1945	451,360	Gilltown Stud (Ire)	H. H. Aga Khan	11,284	40
Tehran	1945	403,000	Barton Stud (Eng)	Prince Aly Khan	10,075	40
*Blenheim II	1936	240,000	Claiborne Farm (Ky.)	H. H. Aga Khan	30,000	8
Tracery	1923	219,400	Cobham Stud (Eng)	Senor Unzue	5,485	40

†Estimated value

price, $240,000. In his first crop, *Blenheim II sired Triple Crown winner Whirlaway.

The record returned to England in 1945 when the good young sires Stardust and Tehran were syndicated in rapid succession, but the record price returned to America in '48 when Leslie Combs II purchased *Alibhai from Louis B. Mayer as a replacement for Combs's first syndicated horse, *Beau Pere.

Combs also syndicated Nashua, the first $1-million stallion, as a four-year-old in 1956. The record price remained in America until 1983 (except for a brief period in '79) when Sheikh Mohammed bin Rashid al Maktoum syndicated his Irish Derby (Ire-G1) winner, Shareef Dancer, for a reported $40-million.

That reported price signifies one of the problems with modern syndications. With values soaring to astronomical figures, stallion managers now often decline to publish the exact price per share or contract terms. Thus, the $60-million to $70-million figure for current record holder Fusaichi Pegasus is based on approximate figures released by the syndicate manager and private communications from syndicate members.

Most Expensive North American Stallion Syndications

Stallion	Year	Price	Farm	Seller	Share Price	No. Shares
Fusaichi Pegasus	2000	$60,000,000	Ashford Stud (Ky.)	Fusao Sekiguchi	†$1,500,000	40
Big Brown	2008	†50,000,000	Three Chimneys Farm (Ky.)	IEAH Stables and Paul Pompa Jr.	N/A	N/A
Point Given	2001	50,000,000	Three Chimneys Farm (Ky.)	The Thoroughbred Corp.	1,000,000	50
Smarty Jones	2004	39,000,000	Three Chimneys Farm (Ky.)	Someday Farm	650,000	60
Conquistador Cielo	1982	36,400,000	Claiborne Farm (Ky.)	Henryk de Kwiatkowski	910,000	40
Devil's Bag	1983	36,000,000	Claiborne Farm (Ky.)	Hickory Tree Farm	900,000	40
Halo	1984	36,000,000	Stone Farm (Ky.)	Windfields Farm	900,000	40
Storm Bird	1981	30,000,000	Ashford Stud (Ky.)	Robert Sangster, et al.	750,000	40
Lemon Drop Kid	2000	30,000,000	Lane's End (Ky.)	Jeanne Vance	750,000	40
Assert (Ire)	1982	25,000,000	Windfields Farm (Md.)	Robert Sangster	625,000	40
Cigar	1996	25,000,000	Ashford Stud (Ky.)	Allen Paulson	500,000	50
Spectacular Bid	1980	22,000,000	Claiborne Farm (Ky.)	Hawksworth Farm	550,000	40
Mr. Prospector	1980	20,000,000	Claiborne Farm (Ky.)	Aisco Farm	500,000	40
Chief's Crown	1984	20,000,000	Three Chimneys Farm (Ky.)	Star Crown Stable	500,000	40
Secreto	1984	20,000,000	Calumet Farm (Ky.)	Luigi Miglietti	500,000	40
Unbridled	1996	19,000,000	Claiborne Farm (Ky.)	Frances A. Genter	475,000	40
Aloma's Ruler	1982	18,880,000	Mare Haven Farm (Ky.)	Nathan Scherr	472,000	40
Riverman	1979	18,000,000	Gainesway (Ky.)	Haras du Quesnay	450,000	40
Skip Away	1998	18,000,000	Hopewell Farm (Ky.)	Carolyn Hine	400,000	45
Alleged	1978	16,000,000	Walmac-Warnerton Int.'l. (Ky.)	Robert Sangster, et al.	400,000	40
Saratoga Six	1984	16,000,000	North Ridge Farm (Ky.)	Eugene Klein, et al.	400,000	40
A P Valentine	2000	16,000,000	Ashford Stud (Ky.)	Celtic Pride Stable	N/A	N/A
Exceller	1979	15,000,000	Gainesway (Ky.)	Nelson Bunker Hunt	375,000	40
Northjet	1981	15,000,000	Airdrie Stud (Ky.)	Serge Fradkoff	375,000	40
Coronado's Quest	1998	15,000,000	Claiborne Farm (Ky.)	Stuart Janney and Stonerside Stable	300,000	50
Affirmed	1979	14,400,000	Spendthrift Farm (Ky.)	Harbor View Farm	400,000	36
Shahrastani	1986	14,400,000	Three Chimneys Farm (Ky.)	H. H. Aga Khan	400,000	36
Nureyev	1981	14,200,000	Walmac-Warnerton Int.'l. (Ky.)	Stavros Niarchos	355,000	40
Risen Star	1988	14,000,000	Walmac Int.'l. (Ky.)	Louis Roussell III and Ronnie Lamarque	350,000	40
Desert Wine	1984	13,000,000	Cardiff Stud Farms (Ca.)	Cardiff Stud Farms and T90 Ranch	325,000	40
L'Emigrant	1983	13,000,000	Gainesway (Ky.)	Stavros Niarchos	325,000	40
Seattle Slew	1978	12,000,000	Spendthrift Farm (Ky.)	Wooden Horse Investments	300,000	40
Fappiano	1981	12,000,000	Tartan Farms (Fl.)	John Nerud	300,000	40
Flying Paster	1981	12,000,000	Cardiff Stud Farms (Ca.)	B. J. Ridder	300,000	40
Pleasant Colony	1981	12,000,000	Buckland Farm (Ky.)	Thomas M. Evans	300,000	40
Bering (GB)	1986	12,000,000	Walmac Int.'l. (Ky.)	Alec Head	300,000	40
Aldebaran	2002	12,000,000	Darby Dan Farm (Ky.)	Niarchos Family	300,000	40
Tale of the Cat	1998	11,600,000	Ashford Stud (Ky.)	Phantom House Stable	290,000	40
Noble Nashua	1981	11,000,000	Schoenborn Brothers Farm (N.Y.)	Flying Zee Stable	275,000	40
Cure the Blues	1986	11,000,000	Pillar Stud (Ky.)	Gilltown Stud	275,000	40
General Assembly	1986	11,000,000	Pillar Stud (Ky.)	Gilltown Stud	275,000	40
Cresta Rider	1981	10,000,000	Gainesway (Ky.)	Stavros Niarchos	250,000	40
Lord Avie	1981	10,000,000	Lane's End (Ky.)	SKS Stable	250,000	40
Master Willie	1981	10,000,000	Windfields Farm (Md.)	William Barnett	250,000	40
A.P. Indy	1992	10,000,000	Lane's End (Ky.)	Tomonoru Tsurumaki	250,000	40
Kingmambo	1993	10,000,000	Lane's End (Ky.)	Niarchos Family	250,000	40
Lure	1994	10,000,000	Claiborne Farm (Ky.)	Claiborne Farm and Nicole Perry Gorman	250,000	40
Grand Slam	1998	10,000,000	Ashford Stud (Ky.)	Baker, Cornstein, and Mack	250,000	40
War Chant	2000	10,000,000	Three Chimneys Farm (Ky.)	Irving Cowan	200,000	50
Slew o' Gold	1983	9,600,000	Three Chimneys Farm (Ky.)	Equusequity Stable	240,000	40
The Minstrel	1977	9,000,000	Windfields Farm (Md.)	Robert Sangster, et al.	250,000	36

†Estimated value

Leading Stud Farms of 2007

Minimum of 200 starters in 2007, worldwide earnings. Includes all active stallions at each farm in 2007 and deceased or pensioned stallions that last stood at that farm. Order is based on total stallion progeny earnings.

Farm (State)	Stallion Earnings	Avg. Earnings	SWs/Strs	GSWs/Strs
Lane's End, Versailles, Ky.	$84,677,291	$32,656	4.97%	1.89%
Ashford Stud, Versailles, Ky.	71,881,626	23,046	3.66%	1.54%
Three Chimneys Farm, Midway, Ky.	31,337,322	31,718	4.35%	2.13%
Darley, Lexington, Ky.	30,435,392	31,836	5.33%	2.20%
Claiborne Farm, Paris, Ky.	30,001,635	31,781	4.77%	2.12%
Vinery Kentucky, Lexington, Ky.	27,213,485	21,277	3.36%	0.47%
Hill 'n' Dale Farms, Lexington, Ky.	25,537,791	22,781	3.30%	1.34%
Overbrook Farm, Lexington, Ky.	25,477,839	22,789	3.85%	0.89%
Gainesway, Lexington, Ky.	25,293,189	30,328	4.44%	0.96%
Airdrie Stud, Midway, Ky.	24,565,130	27,726	4.18%	1.02%
WinStar Farm, Versailles, Ky.	23,457,356	37,116	5.54%	2.85%
Adena Springs Kentucky, Paris, Ky.	22,433,752	27,225	3.40%	1.21%
Ocala Stud Farm, Ocala, Fl.	19,453,800	22,995	2.60%	0.71%
Taylor Made Stallions, Nicholasville, Ky.	17,933,184	29,789	5.81%	1.50%
Northview Stallion Station, Chesapeake City, Md.	14,969,984	24,785	3.31%	0.50%
Castleton Lyons, Lexington, Ky.	14,802,550	22,360	5.29%	1.36%
Pin Oak Lane Farm, New Freedom, Pa.	13,209,435	21,584	2.45%	0.65%
Brookdale Farm, Versailles, Ky.	13,179,760	28,283	6.22%	1.50%
Pin Oak Stud, Versailles, Ky.	11,299,074	28,605	2.53%	1.01%
Bridlewood Farm, Ocala, Fl.	11,137,006	19,607	2.82%	1.41%
Highcliff Farm, Delanson, N.Y.	10,888,163	21,224	2.92%	0.39%
Juddmonte Farms, Lexington, Ky.	10,437,880	24,618	4.25%	1.18%
Walmac Farm, Lexington, Ky.	9,993,055	21,630	2.60%	0.87%
Wintergreen Stallion Station, Midway, Ky.	9,346,568	17,213	2.21%	1.11%
Gardiner Farms, Caledon, On.	8,999,079	23,194	2.06%	0.00%
Margaux Farm, Midway, Ky.	8,939,714	16,050	1.08%	0.00%
River Edge Farm, Buellton, Ca.	8,793,833	25,788	5.28%	0.88%
Ballena Vista Farm, Ramona, Ca.	8,677,273	18,987	3.50%	0.22%
Crestwood Farm, Lexington, Ky.	8,235,997	18,384	2.01%	0.22%
Red River Farms, Coushatta, La.	7,965,815	14,225	1.79%	0.00%
Murmur Farm, Darlington, Md.	7,908,630	19,149	2.42%	0.00%
O'Sullivan Farms, Charles Town, W.V.	7,500,715	16,668	0.89%	0.22%
Clear Creek Stud, Folsom, La.	6,896,928	18,246	2.65%	0.00%
Rancho San Miguel, San Miguel, Ca.	6,790,045	13,635	1.81%	0.40%
Stonewall Farm Stallions, Versailles, Ky.	6,485,865	16,420	4.05%	1.01%
Windfields Farm, Oshawa, On.	6,437,782	18,084	1.40%	0.00%
Tommy Town Thoroughbreds, Santa Ynez, Ca.	6,086,796	17,243	3.12%	0.28%
Golden Eagle Farm, Ramona, Ca.	6,066,319	16,529	2.18%	0.82%
Padua Stables, Summerfield, Fl.	5,953,099	26,696	6.28%	2.69%
Lane's End Texas, Hempstead, Tx.	5,574,292	13,662	1.72%	0.00%
Old English Rancho, Sanger, Ca.	5,311,332	23,093	4.35%	0.43%
Shadwell Farm, Lexington, Ky.	5,179,188	17,093	3.63%	0.00%
Harris Farms, Coalinga, Ca.	5,155,016	15,073	3.22%	0.29%
Mill Ridge Farm, Lexington, Ky.	5,119,385	23,483	2.29%	0.46%
Maryland Stallion Station, Glyndon, Md.	4,591,755	22,182	3.38%	0.97%
Magali Farms, Santa Ynez, Ca.	4,580,017	17,154	1.50%	0.00%
El Dorado Farms, Enumclaw, Wa.	4,485,208	10,966	2.20%	0.24%
Sugar Maple Farm, Poughquag, N.Y.	4,358,377	16,324	1.12%	0.00%
Vessels Stallion Farm, Bonsall, Ca.	4,329,742	24,601	4.55%	1.14%
Rising Hill Farm, Ocala, Fl.	4,310,691	17,667	3.69%	0.41%

Leading Stud Farms of 2007

LANE'S END—Location: Versailles, Kentucky. **Founded:** 1979. **Principals:** William S. Farish and Bill Farish. **Acreage:** 3,000. **Stallions for 2008:** A.P. Indy, After Market, Aragorn (Ire), Belong to Me, Bowman's Band, City Zip, Dixieland Band, Dixie Union, Gulch, Kingmambo, Langfuhr, Lemon Drop Kid, Mineshaft, Mingun, Pleasant Tap, Pleasantly Perfect, Rock Hard Ten, Smart Strike, Stephen Got Even, Wando. **Graded or group stakes winners of 2007 by Lane's End stallions:** Alexandros, Alpine Garden, A. P. Arrow, Archipenko, Bel Air Beauty, Boca Grande, Bon Hoffa, Christmas Kid, Citronnade, Cosmonaut, Court Vision, Curlin, Devil Moon, Dixie Chatter, English Channel, Fabulous Strike, Forever Together, Henrythenavigator, Indian Vale, Jambalaya, Lang Field, Last Answer, Lawyer Ron, Light Shift, Majestic Warrior, Master Command, Most Distinguished, Paradise Dancer, Pleasant Hill, Pleasant Strike, Premium Tap, Rags to Riches, Sahara Heat, Saint Anddan, She's Indy Money, Solo Survivor, Steve's Double, Strike Softly, Student Council, Super Freaky, Teammate, That's Life, Thewayyouare, Tiago, Time to Get Even, Tungsten Strike, Turf War.

ASHFORD STUD—Location: Versailles, Kentucky. **Founded:** 1984. **Principals:** John Magnier and partners. **Acreage:** 2,500. **Stallions for 2008:** Chapel Royal, Dehere, Fusaichi Pegasus, Giant's Causeway, Grand Slam, Johannesburg, Lion Heart, Powerscourt (GB), Scat Daddy, Tale of the Cat, Thunder Gulch, Van Nistelrooy. **Graded or group stakes winners of 2007 by Ashford stallions:** Art Master, Ashley's Kitty, Balance,

Sires — Leading Stud Farms

Bantry Bay, Baroness Thatcher, Bridge Game, Charm the Giant (Ire), Circular Quay, Dance The Waves, Danzon, Deferential, Dream Impact, Drilling for Oil, Elusive Lady, Fairbanks, Fishy Advice, Floral Pegasus, Giant Wrecker, Haradasun, Heatseeker (Ire), Here De Angels, India, Jupiter Pluvius, Just Little (Fr), La Dancia, La Traviata, Liquor Cabinet (Ire), Marcavelly, Mary Delaney, Mike Fox, Molengao (Brz), Murjana, My Typhoon (Ire), Naissance Royale (Ire), Naughty Rafaela (Brz), Onward Royal, Oprah Winney, Our Giant, Pasikatera, Purrealist, Ravel, Raymi Coya, Red Giant, Scat Daddy, Seductively, Serious Speed, Set Play, Silver Tree, Strike the Deal, Sunrise Bacchus, Tale of Ekati, Teufelsberg, Tipungwuti, Top Hat, Yuro.

THREE CHIMNEYS FARM—Location: Midway, Kentucky. **Founded:** 1972. **Principal:** Robert N. Clay. **Acreage:** 1,500. **Stallions for 2008:** Dynaformer, Exchange Rate, Flower Alley, Good Reward, Point Given, Rahy, Sky Mesa, Smarty Jones, War Chant, Yes It's True. **Graded or group stakes winners of 2007 by Three Chimneys stallions:** Actin Good, Asperity, Classic Campaign, Dreaming of Anna, El Roblar, Go Between, Karen's Caper, Legerete, Lewis Michael, Lucarno, Masseuse, My Great Love, Nobiz Like Shobiz, Norman Invader, Off Duty, Purim, Rio de La Plata, Sea Chanter, Sealy Hill, Yes He's the Man.

DARLEY—Location: Lexington. **Founded:** 2001. **Principal:** Sheikh Mohammed bin Rashid al Maktoum. **Acreage:** 4,000. **Stallions for 2008:** Any Given Saturday, Bernardini, Cherokee Run, Consolidator, Discreet Cat, E Dubai, Elusive Quality, Hard Spun, Henny Hughes, Holy Bull, Kafwain, Offlee Wild, Quiet American, Rockport Harbor, Street Cry (Ire), Street Sense. **Graded or group stakes winners in 2007 by Darley stallions:** Bwana Bull, Camarilla, Chelokee, Cry and Catch Me, Desert Code, Flashy Bull, Globetrotter, High Heels, Indian Flare, Jade's Revenge, Majestic Roi, Maryfield, Massive Drama, Per Incanto, Raven's Pass, Street Magician, Street Sense, Street Sounds, Summer Doldrums, War Pass, Zanjero.

CLAIBORNE FARM—Location: Paris, Kentucky. **Founded:** 1910. **Principal:** Seth Hancock. **Acreage:** 3,000. **Stallions for 2008:** Arch, During, Easing Along, Eddington, First Samurai, Flatter, Horse Chestnut (SAf), Out of Place, Political Force, Pulpit, Seeking the Gold, Strong Hope, War Front. **Graded or group stakes winners of 2007 by Claiborne stallions:** Arch Swing, Bob and John, Corinthian, Duveen, Ecclesiastic, Lattice, Mini Sermon, Rutherienne, Sightseeing, Smart Enough, Society Hostess, Sweet Fervor, Wanderin Boy.

VINERY KENTUCKY—Location: Lexington. **Founded:** 1999. **Principal:** Thomas Simon. **Acreage:** 460. **Stallions for 2008:** Limehouse, More Than Ready, Posse, Pure Prize, Purge, Silver Train, Stormello, The Cliff's Edge, Yonaguska. **Graded or group stakes winners in 2007 by Vinery Kentucky stallions:** Arson Squad, Forbidden Prince, Kodiak Kowboy, Lantana Mob, Pure Clan, Ready's Image, Runaway Dancer.

HILL 'N' DALE FARMS—Location: Lexington. **Founded:** 1987. **Principal:** John G. Sikura. **Acreage:** 950. **Stallions for 2008:** Candy Ride (Arg), Closing Argument, El Corredor, Grand Reward, Mr. Sekiguchi, Mutakddim, Roman Ruler, Seeking the Best, Shakespeare, Stormy Atlantic, Theatrical (Ire), Vindication. **Graded or group stakes winners in 2007 by Hill 'n' Dale stallions:** Dicky's Cat, Dominican, Icy Atlantic, Jazzy (Arg), Leonnatus Anteas, Magnificience, Minion, More Happy, Mrs. Lindsay, Quite a Bride, Shakespeare, Storm Allied, Teamgeist, Tita Diquera.

OVERBROOK FARM—Location: Lexington.

Founded: 1972. **Principals:** Bill Young and Lucy Young Hamilton. **Acreage:** 2,400. **Stallions for 2008:** Cape Town, Cat Thief, Grindstone, Jump Start, Pioneering, Storm Cat, Tactical Cat. **Graded or group stakes winners in 2007 by Overbrook stallions:** After Market, Burmilla, Essential Edge, Huracan, Jump On In, The Leopard, Thethiefatmidnight, Triano, You'resothrilling.

GAINESWAY—Location: Lexington. **Founded:** 1989. **Principals:** Graham and Antony Beck. **Acreage:** 1,500. **Stallions for 2008:** Afleet Alex, Birdstone, Corinthian, Cozzene, Cuvee, Mr. Greeley, Orientate, Smoke Glacken, Strategic Mission, Tapit, Whywhywhy. **Graded or group stakes winners of 2007 by Gainesway stallions:** Finsceal Beo, Irish Smoke, Lady Joanne, Lady Sprinter, Saoirse Abu, Time's Mistress.

AIRDRIE STUD—Location: Midway, Kentucky. **Founded:** 1972. **Principals:** Brereton and Libby Jones. **Acreage:** 2,600. **Stallions for 2008:** Badge of Silver, Canadian Frontier, Flashy Bull, Forest Grove, Friends Lake, Harlan's Holiday, Include, Indian Charlie, Istan, Proud Citizen, Slew City Slew, Stevie Wonderboy, Stormin Fever, Yankee Gentleman. **Graded or group stakes winners of 2007 by Airdrie Stud stallions:** Indian Blessing, Into Mischief, Lava Man, Panty Raid, Proud Spell, River Proud, Tasha's Miracle, Timber Reserve.

WINSTAR FARM—Location: Versailles, Kentucky. **Founded:** 2000. **Principals:** Bill Casner and Kenny Troutt. **Acreage:** 1,450. **Stallions for 2008:** Bluegrass Cat, Distorted Humor, Sharp Humor, Speightstown, Tiznow. **Graded or group stakes winners of 2007 by WinStar stallions:** Anak Nakal, Any Given Saturday, Bear Now, Bit of Whimsy, Cowtown Cat, Don Dandy, Eishin Dover, Eishin Lombard, Fourty Niners Son, Hystericalady, Kettleoneup, Sir Gallovic, Slew's Tizzy, Texas Fever, The Nth Degree, Tough Tiz's Sis, Z Humor.

ADENA SPRINGS KENTUCKY—Location: Paris, Kentucky. **Founded:** 1989. **Principal:** Frank Stronach. **Acreage:** 2,000. **Stallions for 2008:** Awesome Again, Congaree, El Prado (Ire), Ghostzapper, Giacomo, Macho Uno, North Light, Silent Name (Jpn), Touch Gold. **Graded or group stakes winners in 2007 by Adena Springs Kentucky stallions:** Asi Siempre, Awesome Gem, Cobalt Blue, Daaher, Dreaming of Liz, Ginger Punch, Lord Admiral, Sharp Susan, Sugar Shake, Tessa Blue.

OCALA STUD FARM—Location: Ocala. **Founded:** 1958. **Principal:** J. Michael O'Farrell Jr. **Acreage:** 500. **Stallions for 2008:** Best of the Rest, Concerto, Concorde's Tune, Drewman, High Cotton, Mecke, Montbrook, Sweetsouthernsaint, Trippi. **Graded or group stakes winners in 2007 by Ocala Stud Farm stallions:** Miss Macy Sue, Trippi's Storm.

TAYLOR MADE STALLIONS—Location: Nicholasville, Kentucky. **Founded:** 1976. **Principals:** Duncan, Ben, Frank, and Mark Taylor. **Acreage:** 1,600. **Stallions for 2008:** Forest Danger, Forestry, Half Ours, Master Command, Northern Afleet, Officer, Southern Image, Unbridled's Song. **Graded or group stakes winners of 2007 by Taylor Made stallions:** Etched, Half Ours, Mending Fences, Octave, Officer Cherrie, Political Force, Silent Roar, Thorn Song, Woodlander.

NORTHVIEW STALLION STATION—Location: Chesapeake City, Maryland. **Founded:** 1989. **Principals:** Richard Golden and Tom Bowman. **Acreage:** 600. **Stallions for 2008:** Dance With Ravens, Deputy Storm, Domestic Dispute, Great Notion, Lion Hearted, Love of Money, Medallist, Not for Love, Two Punch. **Graded or group stakes winners of 2007 by Northview Stallion Station stallions:** Control System, Heros Reward, Talkin About Love.

Live Foal Report of 2007

Despite a 0.5% increase in reported foals by Kentucky stallions, live-foal numbers declined 2.5% in North America in 2007. Kentucky annually leads all states and provinces by Thoroughbred output, and Kentucky-based stallions accounted for 33.6% of the mares reported bred in North America in 2006 and 38.5% of live foals reported in '07. The 21,470 mares reported bred to 378 Kentucky stallions in 2006 produced 15,463 live foals, as reported to the Jockey Club through early March 2008. Kentucky obtained those increases despite no change in its stallion population of 378.

Other leading states ranked by number of state-sired live foals of 2007 were Florida, 4,426; California, 3,354; Louisiana, 2,266; Texas, 1,495; and New York, 1,423.

Several large breeding states experienced declines, including a 9.5% decline in Texas, a 7.7% drop in California, a 6.4% dip in Maryland, and a 1.1% decline in live foals by Florida stallions. The largest percentage loss was in Ohio, where the live-foal crop by Ohio sires plummeted 22.5% to 196. Despite new slots providing purse money, Oklahoma had a significant decline, by 14.3% to 767 live foals by its in-state stallions.

The biggest gainers were states that have added alternative gaming. Live foals by New Mexico stallions rose 9.3% to 1,184, and Louisiana grew 7.9% to 2,266.

Among individual stallions, Ashford Stud's Giant's Causeway sired the most live foals of 2007 with 169 reported. The top stallions by number of live reported foals are Giant's Causeway, Roman Ruler (157), El Corredor (156), Eurosilver (148), and Johannesburg (also at 148). Johannesburg stands at Ashford, Roman Ruler and El Corredor stand at Hill 'n' Dale Farms, and Eurosilver stands at Dromoland Farm, all in Central Kentucky.

Leading Stallions by 2007 Foals

Stallion	Mares Bred	Live Foals	Live Foal Rate	State
Giant's Causeway	192	169	88	Ky.
Roman Ruler	197	157	80	Ky.
El Corredor	195	156	80	Ky.
Eurosilver	179	148	83	Ky.
Johannesburg	183	148	81	Ky.
Maria's Mon	165	142	86	Ky.
Stormy Atlantic	191	142	74	Ky.
Afleet Alex	169	141	83	Ky.
Songandaprayer	186	140	75	Ky.
Grand Reward	187	139	74	Ky.
Purge	177	137	77	Ky.
Malibu Moon	157	126	80	Ky.
Buddha	172	125	73	Ky.
Wildcat Heir	173	125	72	Fl.
More Than Ready	152	124	82	Ky.
Mr. Greeley	162	120	74	Ky.
Elusive Quality	140	119	85	Ky.
City Zip	145	116	80	Ky.
Tale of the Cat	154	116	75	Ky.
Lion Heart	158	112	71	Ky.
Tiznow	131	111	85	Ky.
Pollard's Vision	133	110	83	Ky.
Smart Strike	133	110	83	Ky.
Unbridled's Song	141	110	78	Ky.
Vindication	136	110	81	Ky.
Kitten's Joy	127	109	86	Ky.
Value Plus	146	109	75	Ky.
Stephen Got Even	145	108	74	Ky.
Chapel Royal	165	107	65	Ky.
Consolidator	137	107	78	Ky.
Yonaguska	153	106	69	Ky.
Dixie Union	130	105	81	Ky.
Empire Maker	131	104	79	Ky.
Medaglia d'Oro	154	104	68	Ky.
Closing Argument	158	103	65	Fl.
Victory Gallop	138	103	75	Ky.
Even the Score	152	102	67	Ky.
Bernstein	123	101	82	Ky.
Fusaichi Pegasus	131	101	77	Ky.
Grand Slam	120	101	84	Ky.
Limehouse	141	101	72	Ky.
Roar of the Tiger	165	101	61	Fl.
Forestry	130	100	77	Ky.
Langfuhr	127	100	79	Ky.
Saint Liam	126	100	79	Ky.
Broken Vow	130	99	76	Ky.
Cuvee	136	99	73	Ky.
Five Star Day	143	97	68	Ky.
Posse	129	97	75	Ky.
Southern Image	132	97	73	Ky.
Thunder Gulch	140	97	69	Ky.
Distorted Humor	115	96	83	Ky.
Orientate	123	96	78	Ky.
Speightstown	126	96	76	Ky.
Candy Ride (Arg)	146	95	65	Ky.
Yes It's True	112	95	85	Ky.
Forest Camp	131	94	72	Ky.
Holy Bull	129	92	71	Ky.
Sky Mesa	115	92	80	Ky.
Indian Charlie	121	91	75	Ky.
Peace Rules	135	91	67	Fl.
Dance With Ravens	126	90	71	Md.
Ecton Park	130	90	69	Ky.
Eddington	121	90	74	Ky.
Domestic Dispute	127	89	70	Md.
Forest Danger	121	89	74	Ky.
Repent	126	89	71	Fl.
Omega Code	124	88	71	Fl.
Lion Hearted	125	87	70	Md.
Old Topper	111	87	78	Ca.
Strong Hope	105	87	83	Ky.
Trippi	127	87	69	Fl.
Wheelaway	128	87	68	N.Y.
Macho Uno	113	86	76	Fl.
Storm Cat	111	86	77	Ky.
Cactus Ridge	122	85	70	Ky.
Dynaformer	112	85	76	Ky.
Full Mandate	125	85	68	Fl.
Pioneering	125	85	68	Ky.
Royal Academy	107	85	79	Ky.

Live Foals by Stallions by State and Province in 2007

State	Stallions	Mares Bred	Live Foals	Live Foal Rate	State	Stallions	Mares Bred	Live Foals	Live Foal Rate
Alabama	21	120	42	35	North Dakota	19	145	70	48
Arizona	67	579	326	56	Ohio	78	455	196	43
Arkansas	63	560	281	50	Oklahoma	210	1,608	767	48
California	329	4,942	3,354	68	Oregon	54	457	266	58
Colorado	50	341	177	52	Pennsylvania	121	1,167	665	57
Connecticut	3	6	5	83	Puerto Rico	70	872	602	69
Delaware	1	2	2	100	Rhode Island	1	2	2	100
Florida	256	7,163	4,426	62	South Carolina	19	125	62	50
Georgia	16	78	37	47	South Dakota	15	128	49	38
Idaho	39	243	125	51	Tennessee	26	108	60	56
Illinois	108	1,027	499	49	Texas	336	2,701	1,495	55
Indiana	82	472	209	44	Utah	37	283	142	50
Iowa	41	425	230	54	Vermont	2	3	3	100
Kansas	25	138	61	44	Virginia	67	231	135	58
Kentucky	378	21,470	15,463	72	Washington	89	1,059	607	57
Louisiana	293	4,068	2,266	56	West Virginia	83	1,176	659	56
Maryland	69	1,642	1,078	66	Wisconsin	10	35	14	40
Massachusetts	9	29	15	52	Wyoming	8	20	10	50
Michigan	61	556	306	55					
Minnesota	39	375	200	53	**Province**				
Mississippi	11	46	17	37	Alberta	82	924	414	45
Missouri	16	63	23	37	British Columbia	61	780	462	59
Montana	36	164	78	48	Manitoba	24	155	62	40
Nebraska	38	367	189	51	New Brunswick	1	2	1	50
Nevada	6	12	8	67	Ontario	104	1,510	949	63
New Jersey	34	459	267	58	Saskatchewan	23	170	81	48
New Mexico	185	2,048	1,184	58					
New York	122	2,327	1,423	61	**Totals**	**3,976**	**63,961**	**40,126**	**63**
North Carolina	13	64	37	58					

Stallions With Live Foals in 2007
(Reported as of March 1, 2008; Minimum of Ten Mares Bred)

Stallion	Mares Bred	Fls	Live Foal Rate	Stallion	Mares Bred	Fls	Live Foal Rate	Stallion	Mares Bred	Fls	Live Foal Rate
Alabama				Glorious Bid	16	10	63	Decarchy	62	43	69
Casey On Deck	18	3	17	Goodbye Doeny	11	1	9	Defy Logic	21	16	76
Guaranteed	10	5	50	Joy's Report	16	13	81	Downtown Seattle	10	7	70
Royal Empire	29	13	45	Minister's Gold	10	1	10	Emerald Creme	14	14	100
Youngs Neck Arod	13	0	0	Proper Reality	10	9	90	Event of the Year	46	35	76
				Rinka Das	13	3	23	Extra	14	11	79
Arizona				Skeet	18	10	56	Faculty	18	11	61
Benton Creek	44	28	64	Southern Forest	12	4	33	Formal Gold	63	53	84
Big Sky Chester	10	8	80	Storm and a Half	105	63	60	For Really	17	10	59
Buck Strider	33	19	58	**California**				Freespool	84	59	70
Cromwell	13	5	38	Affirmative	19	14	74	Fruition	18	11	61
Ellusive Quest	10	8	80	All the Gears	11	9	82	Future Storm	29	16	55
Equinox	15	9	60	America's Storm	10	9	90	Game Plan	27	20	74
Gent	11	7	64	Ancient Art	34	25	74	General Gem	24	11	46
Hidden City	15	11	73	Atticus	89	69	78	Globalize	44	30	68
Individual Style	17	6	35	Avanzado (Arg)	24	20	83	Golden Gear	41	29	71
Jila (Ire)	11	9	82	Bartok (Ire)	30	20	67	Gotham City	51	37	73
Larrupin'	37	21	57	Beau Genius	27	22	81	Grey Memo	16	12	75
Midnight Royalty	16	10	63	Benchmark	112	84	75	High Brite	54	35	65
Odds On	11	4	36	Bertrando	62	54	87	High Demand	52	38	73
Red	13	8	62	Birdonthewire	20	8	40	Highland Gold	18	6	33
Red Sky's	61	40	66	Bonus Money (GB)	12	9	75	Illinois Storm	43	15	35
Rocky Bar	24	16	67	Boomerang	25	13	52	Indian Country	25	21	84
Sideburn	16	11	69	Bring the Heat	18	10	56	In Excess (Ire)	85	73	86
Slew Mood	20	7	35	Built for Pleasure	13	11	85	Iron Cat	32	25	78
Star of Halo	17	9	53	Capsized	30	16	53	Ironman Dehere	11	8	73
Top Hit	22	14	64	Caros Love	11	5	45	Jackpot	23	19	83
Arkansas				Cat Dreams	48	37	77	Kamsack	10	2	20
Bold Anthony	36	13	36	Cayoke (Fr)	30	14	47	Lake George	14	8	57
Cinnamon Creek	10	6	60	Cee's Tizzy	70	45	64	Laramie's Deputy	11	3	27
Cornish Snow	26	17	65	Comet Shine	11	5	45	Larry the Legend	17	10	59
District	29	8	28	Comic Strip	51	34	67	Lasersport	33	22	67
Explosive Truth	22	13	59	Commander's Flag	19	11	58	Latin American	12	7	58
Father Steve	56	32	57	Corslew	10	7	70	Lit de Justice	37	27	73
				Crafty C. T.	25	14	56	Madraar	32	26	81

Sires — Live Foal Report

Stallion	Mares Bred	Fls	Live Foal Rate
Marino Marini	90	75	83
Memo (Chi)	31	23	74
Michael's Flyer	15	11	73
Ministers Wild Cat	80	56	70
Momentum	66	55	83
Mongol Warrior	16	9	56
Monsignor Casale	10	6	60
Moscow Ballet	18	15	83
Mt. Bellewood	28	18	64
Mud Route	34	25	74
Muqtarib	35	22	63
Nineeleven	30	16	53
Northern Devil	11	8	73
Old Topper	111	87	78
Ole'	12	2	17
One Man Army	35	20	57
Our New Recruit	22	13	59
Perfect Mandate	30	25	83
Persian Turban (Ire)	15	8	53
Phonetics	16	6	38
Popular	19	15	79
Rainbow Blues (Ire)	10	8	80
Redattore (Brz)	50	42	84
Regent Act	14	9	64
Replicate	10	10	100
Rhythm	24	15	63
Richly Blended	46	33	72
Rio Verde	51	36	71
River Flyer	24	13	54
Roar	25	17	68
Robannier	27	21	78
Roman Dancer	19	12	63
Royal Cat	31	23	74
Royal Walk	17	12	71
Salt Lake	74	55	74
Sea of Secrets	30	23	77
Seattle Bound	13	9	69
Serve the Flag	17	9	53
Sharan (GB)	22	7	32
Siberian Summer	41	33	80
Singletary	56	48	86
Skimming	78	53	68
Sky Terrace	10	10	100
Slewvescent	23	15	65
Snow Blink	11	6	55
Soft Gold (Brz)	10	9	90
Sought After	16	10	63
Souvenir Copy	39	31	79
Spinelessjellyfish	15	10	67
Storm Creek	31	22	71
Stormed	15	7	47
Stormy Jack	23	15	65
Strive	60	30	50
Suances (GB)	34	22	65
Suggest	10	7	70
Swiss Yodeler	98	72	73
Takin It Deep	14	11	79
Tannersmyman	17	13	76
Temescal Ridge	17	7	41
The Good Life	10	3	30
Thisnearlywasmine	26	19	73
Tizbud	36	31	86
Trapper	10	9	90
Tribal Rule	43	26	60
Truckee	18	12	67
Truly Met	11	0	0
Turkoman	20	10	50
Unbridled Native	24	17	71
Unbridled's Love	12	6	50
Unusual Heat	72	53	74
Valid Wager	51	37	73
Vernon Castle	10	4	40
Via Lombardia (Ire)	16	10	63
Vronsky	25	19	76
Western Fame	43	26	60

Colorado

Stallion	Mares Bred	Fls	Live Foal Rate
Cash Deposit	14	8	57
Coverallbases	13	12	92
Crystal Class	15	9	60
Dash Ahead	13	9	69
Eishin Masamune (Jpn)	44	18	41
Ernie Tee	11	6	55
Frontier Gold	16	6	38
Majorbigtimesheet	18	12	67
Moon Spider	10	2	20
Oliver's Twist	35	28	80
The Rufus	11	6	55
Unbridled Vision	15	9	60

Florida

Stallion	Mares Bred	Fls	Live Foal Rate
Act of Duty	93	58	62
Adcat	30	15	50
Alajwad	58	29	50
Alex's Pal	42	25	60
Alke	102	66	65
Alysweep	25	19	76
American Spirit	19	8	42
Anasheed	32	14	44
Austinpower (Jpn)	11	4	36
Awesome Sword	22	13	59
Band Is Passing	15	5	33
Black Mambo	80	52	65
B L's Appeal	74	49	66
Boastful	13	7	54
Burning Roma	86	51	59
Bwana Charlie	70	48	69
Cashel Castle	30	22	73
Cimarron Secret	15	13	87
City Place	95	48	51
Classic Cat	21	8	38
Closing Argument	158	103	65
Cloud Hopping	18	9	50
Colony Light	35	21	60
Concerto	62	38	61
Concorde's Tune	59	40	68
Dance Master	41	26	63
Dark Kestrel	12	10	83
Delaware Township	60	33	55
Deputy Rokeby	11	6	55
Deputy Wild Cat	35	24	69
Diligence	19	11	58
Don Six	27	20	74
Double Honor	106	58	55
Drewman	86	49	57
D'wildcat	132	80	61
Eltish	10	7	70
Essence of Dubai	72	48	67
Exchange Rate	92	58	63
Express Tour	21	11	52
Fappie's Notebook	13	6	46
Fast 'n Royal	21	11	52
February Storm	37	20	54
First Tour	12	7	58
Flame Thrower	19	12	63
Forbidden Apple	28	10	36
Formal Dinner	51	24	47
Freefourinternet	53	34	64
French Envoy	33	19	58
Full Mandate	125	85	68
Gibson County	32	11	34
Gimmeawink	83	49	59
Gneiss	12	6	50
Graeme Hall	56	38	68
Greatness	55	35	64
Great Pyramid (Ire)	36	19	53
Gulf Storm	34	16	47
Hadrian's Wall	15	13	87
Halo's Image	44	28	64
Hear No Evil	15	13	87
Heckle	27	15	56
High Fly	29	19	66
Honor Glide	25	14	56
Indian Express	18	9	50
Indian Ocean	108	72	67
Indy King	60	38	63
Invisible Ink	25	17	68
Irish Road	27	15	56
Key Moment	16	10	63
Lexicon	30	17	57
Lido Palace (Chi)	48	39	81
Lightnin N Thunder	98	49	50
Macho Uno	113	86	76
Marciano	40	29	73
Marco Bay	12	5	42
Master Bill	15	8	53
Max's Pal	28	20	71
Mecke	18	10	56
Migrating Moon	16	9	56
Milwaukee Brew	102	83	81
Mongoose	29	19	66
Monsieur Cat	19	13	68
Montbrook	64	49	77
Mount McKinley	15	9	60
Mr. Livingston	66	43	65
Omega Code	124	88	71
One Nice Cat	61	41	67
Outofthebox	62	50	81
Parents' Reward	11	6	55
Peace Rules	135	91	67
Pico Central (Brz)	75	52	69
Proud Accolade	91	65	71
Proud and True	45	20	44
Pure Precision	38	20	53
Put It Back	72	37	51
Quick Action	14	8	57
Rationalexuberance	30	7	23
Recommended List	17	2	12
Red Bullet	37	21	57
Repent	126	89	71
Roar of the Tiger	165	101	61
Running Stag	29	21	72
Safe in the U S A	19	16	84
Safely's Mark	15	9	60
Saint Afleet	20	15	75
Salty Sea	26	13	50
Sarava	101	58	57
Scorpion	32	13	41
Skip to the Stone	29	17	59
Skip Trial	14	8	57
Sligo Bay (Ire)	81	62	77
Smooth Jazz	27	17	63
Snow Ridge	83	57	69
Snuck In	51	24	47
Spanish Steps	82	36	44
Straight Man	22	13	59
Sugar's Saint	30	17	57
Supah Blitz	31	15	48
Sweetsouthernsaint	120	71	59
Texas Glitter	42	20	48
Three Wonders	58	34	59
Tiger Ridge	98	68	69
Tiltam	12	7	58
Trippi	127	87	69
True Direction	21	14	67
Unbridled Affair	20	14	70
Unbridled's Image	42	24	57
Unbridled Time	61	35	57
Untuttable	32	27	84
U So Bad	10	6	60
Valid Reprized	13	3	23
Weekend Cruise	31	20	65
Wekiva Springs	63	25	40
Werblin	110	77	70
West Acre	37	21	57
Western Pride	57	35	61
Wildcat Heir	173	125	72
Wild Event	12	3	25
Winged Foot Willie	21	11	52
Wised Up	18	13	72

Georgia

Stallion	Mares Bred	Fls	Live Foal Rate
Muted	13	7	54
Prospector Street	12	6	50

Idaho

Stallion	Mares Bred	Fls	Live Foal Rate
Cause Ur Mine	44	31	70
Derby Drive	18	5	28
Kings Blood (Ire)	17	10	59
Pulzarr	14	1	7
Starmaniac	13	8	62

Illinois

Stallion	Mares Bred	Fls	Live Foal Rate
Alaskan Frost	32	19	59
Allen Charge	10	5	50

Sires — Live Foal Report

Stallion	Mares Bred	Fls	Live Foal Rate
Animo de Valeroso	27	12	44
Awesome Cat	28	12	43
Canyon Run	23	12	52
Cap'n Capote	41	14	34
Cat Creek Slew	11	1	9
Chicago Six	28	20	71
Classic Account	19	11	58
Company Approval	15	7	47
Conte Di Savoya	20	9	45
Denouncer	17	10	59
Devil Hunter	10	8	80
Diazo	12	9	75
Gogarty (Ire)	13	6	46
Goliard	17	4	24
He's a Tough Cat	25	14	56
Honour Attendant	25	12	48
Irgun	29	13	45
Kiri's Clown	10	3	30
Marte	12	5	42
Phoneforchampagne	11	3	27
Posh	19	13	68
Powerful Goer	19	11	58
Quaker Ridge	45	25	56
Regal Code	11	1	9
Sabona	19	8	42
Saint Ballistic	16	8	50
Southland Blues	13	10	77
Summer Cloud	16	2	13
Supeona	12	5	42
Theran	12	8	67
Time Chopper	10	1	10
Unbridled Success	14	4	29
Uncommon Valor	15	5	33
Unreal Zeal	24	11	46
Viareggio (Ire)	10	3	30
Western Outlaw	74	46	62

Indiana

Stallion	Mares Bred	Fls	Live Foal Rate
Arromanches	27	11	41
Assembly Dancer	11	7	64
Black Moonshine	24	14	58
Cat Doctor	12	6	50
Commemorate	13	10	77
Fast Ferdie	11	9	82
Glitter Code	16	7	44
Indy Mood	10	6	60
Plenty Chilly	12	2	17
Presidential Order	19	6	32
Sixto G	13	4	31
Unbridled Man	12	6	50
Valiant Style	20	5	25
Waki Warrior	10	1	10
Whitney Tower	10	6	60

Iowa

Stallion	Mares Bred	Fls	Live Foal Rate
Bravo Bull	11	9	82
Canaveral	11	4	36
Corporate Report	13	5	38
Deerhound	21	13	62
Deposit Ticket	13	5	38
Doug Fir	32	18	56
Friendly Lover	25	14	56
Governor Vasquez	18	9	50
Humming	18	10	56
Indian Territory	20	14	70
King of Scat	28	17	61
Mi Cielo	13	9	69
Rage	13	8	62
Sharkey	15	7	47
Wild Gold	26	16	62
Wild Invader	10	6	60
Winter Glitter	30	11	37

Kansas

Stallion	Mares Bred	Fls	Live Foal Rate
Admiral Indy	34	9	26
Polly's Comet	11	5	45
Prospector's Treat	11	8	73
So Ever Clever	12	9	75

Kentucky

Stallion	Mares Bred	Fls	Live Foal Rate
Action This Day	82	59	72
Afleet Alex	169	141	83
Albert the Great	45	34	76
Aldebaran	83	60	72
Aljabr	14	12	86
Alphabet Soup	59	45	76
A.P. Indy	109	82	75
Aptitude	71	53	75
Arch	82	62	76
Arthur's Ring	54	13	24
Awesome Again	99	76	77
Ballado's Devil	11	2	18
Barkerville	12	7	58
Bedivere	11	0	0
Behrens	13	9	69
Belong to Me	62	41	66
Ben Bulben	22	14	64
Bernstein	123	101	82
Big Country	30	18	60
Birdstone	69	44	64
Black Minnaloushe	47	33	70
Blazonry	31	13	42
Brahms	58	40	69
Bright Launch	25	17	68
Broken Vow	130	99	76
Buddha	172	125	73
Bull Market	22	14	64
Cactus Ridge	122	85	70
Came Home	85	67	79
Canadian Frontier	65	47	72
Candy Ride (Arg)	146	95	65
Cape Canaveral	27	18	67
Cape Town	32	19	59
Castledale (Ire)	51	23	45
Cat Ridge	21	10	48
Cat Thief	37	25	68
Century City (Ire)	36	20	56
Champali	81	62	77
Chapel Royal	165	107	65
Cherokee Run	101	70	69
City Zip	145	116	80
Colonial Colony	18	8	44
Congaree	90	59	66
Consolidator	137	107	78
Cozzene	53	36	68
Crafty Friend	32	19	59
Crafty Prospector	33	15	45
Crafty Shaw	44	30	68
Crimson Classic	43	17	40
Cryptoclearance	68	46	68
Cuvee	136	99	73
Dancing Missile	10	7	70
David Copperfield	48	29	60
Dayjur	25	18	72
Dehere	103	73	71
Deputy Commander	76	51	67
Devil His Due	110	77	70
Distant View	15	11	73
Distorted Humor	115	96	83
Dixieland Band	59	45	76
Dixie Union	130	105	81
Doneraile Court	56	36	64
Down the Aisle	38	20	53
Dumaani	20	8	40
During	64	44	69
Dynaformer	112	85	76
Eavesdropper	63	47	75
Ecton Park	130	90	69
Eddington	121	90	74
E Dubai	84	62	74
El Corredor	195	156	80
El Prado (Ire)	76	60	79
Elusive Quality	140	119	85
Empire Maker	131	104	79
Erewhon	18	12	67
Eurosilver	179	148	83
Evansville Slew	51	30	59
Even the Score	152	102	67
Explicit	48	22	46
Five Star Day	143	97	68
Flatter	57	46	81
Forest Camp	131	94	72
Forest Danger	121	89	74
Forestry	130	100	77
Forest Wildcat	112	83	74
Friends Lake	103	74	72
Fusaichi Pegasus	131	101	77
Ghostzapper	111	84	76
Giant's Causeway	192	169	88
Gilded Time	60	44	73
Gold Case	18	13	72
Golden Missile	74	57	77
Gone West	73	61	84
Grand Reward	187	139	74
Grand Slam	120	101	84
Greenwood Lake	19	7	37
Grindstone	42	18	43
Gulch	67	46	69
Hap	14	9	64
Harlan's Holiday	107	82	77
Hennessy	86	74	86
Hero's Tribute	33	18	55
Hold That Tiger	90	70	78
Holy Bull	129	92	71
Home At Last	10	5	50
Honour and Glory	107	78	73
Horse Chestnut (SAf)	29	12	41
Include	117	82	70
Indian Charlie	121	91	75
Intidab	15	12	80
Is It True	54	26	48
Jade Hunter	28	17	61
Johannesburg	183	148	81
Johar	41	32	78
Jump Start	77	55	71
Kafwain	133	82	62
Kayrawan	10	5	50
Kela	95	62	65
King Cugat	40	28	70
Kingmambo	65	49	75
Kissin Kris	15	10	67
Kitten's Joy	127	109	86
Kutsa	23	11	48
Langfuhr	127	100	79
Leelanau	42	31	74
Lemon Drop Kid	58	48	83
Leroidesanimaux (Brz)	110	75	68
Lil E. Tee	12	10	83
Limehouse	141	101	72
Lion Heart	158	112	71
Lost Soldier	70	43	61
Malabar Gold	58	36	62
Malibu Moon	157	126	80
Mancini	25	15	60
Margie's Wildcat	22	13	59
Maria's Mon	165	142	86
Marquetry	68	41	60
Matty G	31	20	65
Medaglia d'Oro	154	104	68
Medallist	81	60	74
Menifee	52	41	79
Midas Eyes	48	34	71
Military	79	58	73
Minardi	16	9	56
Mineshaft	106	81	76
Mingun	106	73	69
Mister Phone (Arg)	25	11	44
Mizzen Mast	69	49	71
Monarchos	65	52	80
Monashee Mountain	75	52	69
More Than Ready	152	124	82
Morluc	15	12	80
Mr. Greeley	162	120	74
Mutakddim	65	50	77
Najran	73	50	68
Newfoundland	57	39	68
Northern Afleet	104	82	79
Northern Spur (Ire)	12	5	42

Sires — Live Foal Report

Stallion	Mares Bred	Fls	Live Foal Rate	Stallion	Mares Bred	Fls	Live Foal Rate	Stallion	Mares Bred	Fls	Live Foal Rate
North Light (Ire)	92	69	75	Tenpins	74	57	77	Huff	17	6	35
Officer	111	76	68	Teton Forest	111	66	59	Ide	75	48	64
Offlee Wild	97	70	72	Theatrical (Ire)	50	35	70	In a Walk	29	22	76
Olmodavor	76	54	71	The Cliff's Edge	76	53	70	Island Born	14	6	43
Orientate	123	96	78	Thunder Gulch	140	97	69	Jaunatxo	11	9	82
Ouragan	24	18	75	Tiznow	131	111	85	Joe's Son Joey	13	10	77
Out of Place	43	30	70	Toccet	112	75	67	Jolie's Frolic	10	4	40
Pembroke	12	3	25	Touch Gold	89	74	83	Kadhaaf	11	1	9
Perfect Soul (Ire)	101	76	75	Tropical Storm	54	27	50	Keats	39	23	59
Petionville	76	50	66	Trust N Luck	38	30	79	Kimberlite Pipe	13	5	38
Pikepass	51	35	69	Unbridled's Song	141	110	78	Kingkiowa	23	17	74
Pine Bluff	19	7	37	Unforgettable Max	75	50	67	K One King	40	25	63
Pioneering	125	85	68	Value Plus	146	109	75	Laabity	18	15	83
Pleasantly Perfect	53	41	77	Van Nistelrooy	86	59	69	Lake Austin	79	36	46
Pleasant Tap	112	83	74	Vicar	75	53	71	Leestown	121	77	64
Point Given	78	58	74	Victory Gallop	138	103	75	Left Banker	12	9	75
Polish Navy	12	4	33	Vindication	136	110	81	Like a Soldier	20	8	40
Pollard's Vision	133	110	83	Vision and Verse	35	23	66	Littlebitlively	72	28	39
Posse	129	97	75	Wagon Limit	15	11	73	Lone Star Saint	16	4	25
Powerscourt (GB)	100	76	76	Wando	56	37	66	Lone Star Sky	33	22	67
Prince Nureyev	13	3	23	War Chant	59	48	81	Lunarpal	35	22	63
Private Terms	34	16	47	Whywhywhy	64	51	80	Lydgate	40	32	80
Proud Citizen	64	50	78	Wild and Wicked	32	27	84	Macabe	38	15	39
Pulpit	100	78	78	Wild Zone	52	27	52	Malibu Wesley	37	29	78
Pure Prize	77	50	65	Winning Bid	13	2	15	Man of the Night	11	7	64
Purge	177	137	77	Wiseman's Ferry	99	67	68	Mom's Little Guy	13	8	62
Quest	34	26	76	Woke Up Dreamin	91	60	66	Montana Dreamin'	14	6	43
Quiet American	90	62	69	Woodman	42	27	64	Mr. Baskets	32	15	47
Rahy	59	45	76	Yankee Gentleman	105	78	74	Mr. John	13	8	62
Regal Vision	10	4	40	Yes It's True	112	95	85	Mustang Jock	41	16	39
Repriced	18	7	39	Yonaguska	153	106	69	My Friend Max	37	24	65
Richter Scale	47	31	66	Zavata	91	62	68	My Mike	12	3	25
Rock Hard Ten	118	83	70					Native Regent	35	24	69
Rocking Trick (Arg)	13	5	38	**Louisiana**				Northern Niner	13	7	54
Roman Ruler	197	157	80	Abajo	41	22	54	On Target	16	10	63
Rossini	58	34	59	A Corking Limerick	20	6	30	Out of the Crisis	16	10	63
Royal Academy	107	85	79	Afternoon Deelites	52	9	17	Piccolino	13	9	69
Royal Anthem	35	19	54	Alyzig	16	9	56	Placid Fund	23	11	48
Runaway Groom	30	23	77	American Champ	15	8	53	Planet Earth	23	14	61
Saarland	104	61	59	Announce	33	19	58	Political Whit	15	10	67
Safado	19	14	74	A. P. Delta	35	15	43	Power and Peace	18	10	56
Sahm	33	26	79	Banderas	10	1	10	Prince of the Mt.	10	4	40
Saint Liam	126	100	79	Be Like Mike	42	24	57	Promissory	40	11	28
Scrimshaw	39	23	59	Broadway Show	18	16	89	Prospector's Gift	28	18	64
Seattle Fitz (Arg)	47	34	72	Buzzy's Gold	22	17	77	Puck	10	8	80
Seeking the Gold	61	44	72	Canboulay	11	3	27	Pulling Punches	13	7	54
Seinne (Chi)	40	27	68	Capitalimprovement	16	7	44	Rail	23	11	48
Service Stripe	33	22	67	Catastrophe	20	11	55	Rainmaker	28	19	68
Shore Breeze	18	15	83	Catniro	16	12	75	Reformer Rally	18	14	78
Silver Deputy	78	50	64	Choosing Choice	21	17	81	Rodeo	48	20	42
Silver Ghost	35	22	63	Classic Alliance	13	8	62	Royal Strand (Ire)	14	8	57
Sir Cherokee	36	24	67	Crowned King	10	3	30	Run Production	24	15	63
Skip Away	44	31	70	Cyclone	13	8	62	Secret Claim	10	1	10
Sky Classic	29	23	79	Daring Bid	19	17	89	Sefapiano	77	42	55
Sky Mesa	115	92	80	De Guerin	29	18	62	Shrubs	17	15	88
Slew City Slew	97	75	77	Direct Hit	28	17	61	Silky Sweep	39	14	36
Smart Strike	133	110	83	Dow Jones U S	12	1	8	Silver On Silver	10	6	60
Smarty Jones	112	80	71	Dream Tripper	19	9	47	Southern States	16	9	56
Smoke Glacken	69	54	78	Easyfromthegitgo	49	27	55	Space Shot	17	8	47
Songandaprayer	186	140	75	Entepreneur	31	21	68	Storm Day	109	68	62
Soto	73	33	45	Eriton	24	18	75	Storm Passage	21	14	67
Southern Image	132	97	73	Escrito	21	11	52	Supremo Secret	20	7	35
Speightstown	126	96	76	Esplanade Ridge	12	5	42	Taxicat	12	6	50
State City	55	33	60	Eugene's Third Son	27	16	59	Thank the Bank	12	6	50
Stephen Got Even	145	108	74	Evon's Bully	14	7	50	Time Bandit	44	32	73
Storm Boot	50	42	84	Finder's Gold	15	8	53	Toolighttoquit	27	18	67
Storm Cat	111	86	77	Finest Hour	57	32	56	Top Venture	19	7	37
Stormin Fever	97	71	73	Fly Cry	15	8	53	Tricky	22	10	45
Stormy Atlantic	191	142	74	Ford Every Stream	63	49	78	Twilight Agenda	12	6	50
Street Cry (Ire)	92	64	70	Free	10	6	60	Two Punch Sonny	14	8	57
Stroll	25	21	84	Global Mission	24	18	75	Undeniable	15	9	60
Strong Hope	105	87	83	Golden Slew	26	15	58	Upping the Ante	10	8	80
Successful Appeal	101	65	64	Gold Tribute	54	39	72	Valid Belfast	63	34	54
Sultry Song	56	22	39	Grand Appointment	24	17	71	Valid Bidder	47	31	66
Sunday Break (Jpn)	55	36	65	Green Raskal	11	3	27	Whambam	10	3	30
Syncline	25	15	60	Grim Reaper	12	9	75	Whiff of Indy	14	3	21
Tactical Cat	67	47	70	Groovy Jett	10	7	70	Wildcat Shoes	58	36	62
Tale of the Cat	154	116	75	Hervy	11	2	18	Wild West	37	20	54
Talk Is Money	10	5	50	High Cascade	80	48	60	Winthrop	18	12	67
Tapit	104	78	75	Hold Hands	12	3	25	Wire Me Collect	25	16	64
Taste of Paradise	67	49	73	Holy Sting	19	11	58	Zarbyev	29	16	55
Ten Most Wanted	51	39	76	House Burner	17	9	53				

Sires — Live Foal Report

Stallion	Mares Bred	Fls	Live Foal Rate
Maryland			
Bowman's Band	74	47	64
Crowd Pleaser	13	6	46
Cruisin' Dixie	10	5	50
Crypto Star	14	8	57
Dance With Ravens	126	90	71
Disco Rico	28	21	75
Domestic Dispute	127	89	70
Fantasticat	45	30	67
Fleet Foot	11	10	91
Gators N Bears	71	50	70
Go for Gin	30	19	63
Great Notion	56	35	63
Lion Hearted	125	87	70
Louis Quatorze	107	77	72
Meadow Monster	25	18	72
Mojave Moon	10	9	90
Mr. Shoplifter	15	9	60
No Armistice	35	16	46
Not For Love	76	56	74
Oratory	108	66	61
Outflanker	25	17	68
Parker's Storm Cat	58	36	62
Partner's Hero	45	29	64
Polish Miner	28	19	68
Purple Passion	13	8	62
Rock Slide	52	35	67
Seeking Daylight	21	15	71
St Averil	41	27	66
Two Punch	52	32	62
Unbridled Jet	11	7	64
Waquoit	19	13	68
Wayne County (Ire)	13	4	31
Yarrow Brae	35	24	69
Michigan			
Allie's Punch	12	7	58
Binalong	13	7	54
Career Best	13	10	77
Creative	12	9	75
Demaloot Demashoot	18	13	72
Elusive Hour	49	19	39
Equality	40	24	60
Fire Blitz	16	12	75
Georgia Crown	12	4	33
Island Storm	13	11	85
Meadow Prayer	34	23	68
Mr. Katowice	10	5	50
Native Factor	18	11	61
Override Battle	10	3	30
Perfect Circle	19	7	37
Research	19	11	58
Secret Romeo	32	18	56
Sky Approval	10	5	50
The Deputy (Ire)	55	32	58
Ulises	17	12	71
Minnesota			
Ballado Chieftan	19	11	58
Demidoff	32	22	69
Dixie Power	12	7	58
Dynomania	18	9	50
Frisk Me Now	38	17	45
Ghazi	26	15	58
Kyle's Our Man	14	9	64
Late Edition	18	13	72
Quaker Hill	11	6	55
Sam Lord's Castle	16	8	50
Shotiche	11	9	82
Shot of Gold	12	4	33
Silk Song	13	3	23
Supremo	22	18	82
Tahkodha Hills	27	13	48
Mississippi			
Minister Slew	12	5	42
Missouri			
Bananas	10	2	20

Stallion	Mares Bred	Fls	Live Foal Rate
Montana			
C Spot Go	13	7	54
Double Dewars	11	5	45
Gold Bayou T B	11	8	73
In the Zone	10	5	50
Son's Corona	16	5	31
White Tie Tryst	12	2	17
Nebraska			
A Trio of Devils	12	6	50
Blumin Affair	35	19	54
Box Buster	27	15	56
Dazzling Falls	17	9	53
Flannigan	14	7	50
Not So Fast	11	7	64
Quest of the King	12	10	83
Senor Speedy	24	10	42
Shadow Hawk	56	32	57
Shawklit Player	21	8	38
Silent Bluff	32	17	53
Still Be Smokin'	12	8	67
New Jersey			
Believe in Saints	22	17	77
Close Up	49	30	61
Contemplate	25	2	8
Defrere	82	54	66
Deputy Warlock	10	8	80
Fastness (Ire)	40	23	58
Funny Frolic	11	9	82
Gerosa	10	8	80
Hit the Trail	14	7	50
Iron Deputy	17	9	53
Mo Mon	42	23	55
Mr. Nugget	14	11	79
Mr. Sinatra	11	9	82
Private Interview	27	16	59
New Mexico			
Aeneas	32	19	59
Avenue of Flags	40	24	60
Bay Head King	31	15	48
Bestbandintheland	13	7	54
B. G.'s Drone	18	11	61
Caracal	15	9	60
Chopin	10	9	90
Claudius	14	4	29
Cold n Calculating	15	7	47
Comic Genius	41	30	73
Con Artist	15	9	60
Copelan's Pache	22	14	64
Dancin Rahy	20	7	35
Desert God	32	21	66
Devon Lane	94	59	63
Digging In	18	12	67
Dome	37	26	70
Dominique's Cat	13	11	85
Don Lux	10	6	60
Eishin Storm	24	14	58
Elegant Cat	12	6	50
El Sancho	18	13	72
Emerald Jig	13	10	77
Favorite Trick	32	27	84
Ghostly Moves	31	19	61
Golden Ransom	20	14	70
Gone Hollywood	26	20	77
Grand Champion Cat	10	5	50
Groomstick	10	9	90
Halory Hunter	30	22	73
Hit a Jackpot	11	2	18
Hot War	17	7	41
Houston Slue	11	6	55
Indies (GB)	16	8	50
In Excessive Bull	69	48	70
Isaypete	14	13	93
Istintaj	23	13	57
Joey the Student	12	6	50
King of the Hunt	38	16	42
K. O. Punch	19	11	58
Lazy Lode (Arg)	29	22	76
Le Grande Danseur	17	12	71

Stallion	Mares Bred	Fls	Live Foal Rate
Local Time	10	3	30
Newton's Law (Ire)	11	2	18
Not Tricky	18	4	22
Pallets	14	2	14
Precocity	40	24	60
Premeditation	11	9	82
Prospector Jones	38	29	76
Proud Irish	23	16	70
Quinton's Gold	21	10	48
Rancho Azul	13	4	31
Red's Honor	11	8	73
Reuben	17	7	41
Robyn Dancer	18	12	67
R. Payday	10	5	50
Sadler Slew	15	9	60
Sandia Slew	12	10	83
Saratoga Six	11	7	64
Scatmandu	46	15	33
Slew the Deputy	10	6	60
So Long Birdie	15	9	60
Source	14	8	57
Squall	13	5	38
Stagecoach	12	9	75
Storm of Goshen	15	10	67
Suave Prospect	28	19	68
Super Quercus (Fr)	10	7	70
Super Special	19	12	63
The Trader's Echo	21	11	52
Tin Can Sailor	10	7	70
To Teras	24	13	54
Touchdown Ky	12	9	75
Tricky Creek	20	16	80
Valet Man	10	5	50
Vulcan's Pulpit	21	8	38
Wild Deputy	10	6	60
Your Eminence	54	45	83
New York			
Adonis	22	6	27
A. P Jet	25	18	72
Artax	59	42	71
Badge	28	15	54
Best of Luck	19	8	42
Bright Beau	13	1	8
Cappuchino	19	13	68
Captain Red	16	11	69
Catienus	67	43	64
Chief Seattle	55	32	58
City Hall Slew	12	5	42
Comeonmom	24	16	67
Desert Warrior	94	62	66
Dream Run	43	23	53
Excellent Payback	10	0	0
Fast Decision	11	7	64
Fast Play	24	16	67
Freud	99	69	70
Gold Fever	30	14	47
Gold Token	44	25	57
Good and Tough	39	28	72
Griffinite	45	16	36
Here's Zealous	46	34	74
Hook and Ladder	80	59	74
Kalu	13	9	69
Kelly Kip	10	7	70
Legion Field	17	13	76
Lycius	31	19	61
Mayakovsky	37	21	57
Millennium Wind	65	46	71
Nunzio	10	8	80
Performing Magic	38	26	68
Prime Timber	101	65	64
Raffie's Majesty	19	13	68
Read the Footnotes	88	60	68
Regal Classic	38	16	42
River Keen (Ire)	14	8	57
Rizzi	13	7	54
Roaring Fever	88	57	65
Say Florida Sandy	103	58	56
Stanislavsky	16	10	63
Strategic Mission	86	49	57
Take Me Out	12	7	58
Tomorrows Cat	105	76	72

Sires — Live Foal Report

Stallion	Mares Bred	Fls	Live Foal Rate
Well Noted	28	20	71
Western Expression	47	33	70
Wheelaway	128	87	68

North Carolina

Stallion	Mares Bred	Fls	Live Foal Rate
Chelsey Cat	22	14	64
Dixie's Wild Again	11	3	27

North Dakota

Stallion	Mares Bred	Fls	Live Foal Rate
Academy	19	8	42
Beeper	10	3	30
Buzzer	15	5	33
Lyre	10	0	0
Paranoide (Arg)	15	7	47
Pen 'n Ink	10	3	30
Rock Climb	10	6	60
Win Lose Or Draw	15	11	73

Ohio

Stallion	Mares Bred	Fls	Live Foal Rate
Ago	13	4	31
Colony Key	24	7	29
Donthelumbertrader	17	8	47
Habayeb	40	22	55
King Tutta	14	8	57
Lovesthecowgirls	15	0	0
Pacific Waves	22	15	68
Political Folly	16	6	38
Pride of Burkaan	10	6	60
Ray of Gold	10	7	70
Runto the Mountain	11	3	27
The Badger's Comin	10	4	40
Waist Gunner John	11	5	45

Oklahoma

Stallion	Mares Bred	Fls	Live Foal Rate
Actor	11	3	27
Alybel	12	4	33
Apollo	10	4	40
Baltimore Gray	16	7	44
Board Member	55	15	27
Bonus Time Cat	17	10	59
Broadway Bullet	11	6	55
Burbank	12	6	50
Carr Tech	11	7	64
Concern	18	10	56
Confide	25	12	48
Country Be Gold	21	12	57
Dark Lightning	14	14	100
Deal an Ace	13	7	54
Deodar	15	13	87
Diamond	24	16	67
Distinction	34	19	56
Fashion Find	43	14	33
Ferrara	12	6	50
Fistfite	18	10	56
Flying Baron	15	10	67
Forestwood	19	12	63
Inca Chief	39	12	31
Indy Thunder	20	10	50
It'sallinthechase	11	7	64
Ivory Dreams	10	0	0
Jazzman's Prospect	11	8	73
Kipling	40	25	63
Lendell Ray	15	8	53
Lucky Lionel	15	11	73
Major Henry	17	7	41
Major Leaguer	18	7	39
May Day Warrior	14	5	36
Monarch's Maze	27	6	22
National Saint	24	16	67
New Way	19	13	68
Nicholas	12	7	58
Notable Beaux	10	6	60
Notable Cat	23	14	61
Ocean Terrace	15	8	53
Orange Power	14	4	29
Overview	26	10	38
Rare Brick	23	12	52
Reel On Reel	11	6	55
Riverside	13	10	77
Rojo Dinero	11	6	55
Run to Daylight	13	8	62

Stallion	Mares Bred	Fls	Live Foal Rate
Sasha's Prospect	26	14	54
Seeking Greatness	24	14	58
Semoran	12	8	67
Star of the Crop	15	8	53
Strategic Partner	33	17	52
Stromboli	13	6	46
Tarakam	13	7	54
Wee Thunder	13	3	23
Wood Reply	22	11	50
Worldly Manner	11	2	18
Zerotosixty	12	6	50

Oregon

Stallion	Mares Bred	Fls	Live Foal Rate
Baquero	22	16	73
Cascadian	47	20	43
Count Me In	19	12	63
Ex Marks the Cop	22	11	50
Harbor the Gold	43	24	56
Klinsman (Ire)	16	6	38
Prospected	19	16	84
Seattle Shamus	71	49	69
Tomorrow's Slew	18	7	39

Pennsylvania

Stallion	Mares Bred	Fls	Live Foal Rate
Activist	17	10	59
Aisle	11	8	73
Appealing Skier	13	6	46
Banker's Gold	10	8	80
Brian Is Golden	18	8	44
Buckle Down Ben	31	18	58
Caller I. D.	16	8	50
Cat's Career	19	10	53
Certain Storm	19	10	53
Cetewayo	30	22	73
Changeintheweather	32	22	69
Cocky	13	9	69
Congressionalhonor	86	42	49
Duckhorn	26	13	50
Flying Chevron	15	9	60
Harry the Hat	28	12	43
Lite the Fuse	49	31	63
Lord Ofthe Thunder	14	13	93
Lucky Clone	10	6	60
Mazel Trick	16	13	81
Middlesex Drive	11	9	82
Patton	17	8	47
Polish Rifle	17	7	41
Power by Far	14	7	50
Quarry	28	14	50
Real Quiet	68	34	50
Rimrod	22	14	64
Rubiyat	10	7	70
Siphon (Brz)	48	34	71
Smart Guy	16	9	56
Song of the Sword	20	10	50
Special Times	16	9	56
Stonecoldbroke	12	5	42
Storm Center	24	14	58
Turn West	20	10	50
Wheaton	41	26	63
Will's Way	24	12	50

Puerto Rico

Stallion	Mares Bred	Fls	Live Foal Rate
Balcony	35	24	69
Bargello	19	17	89
Be Frank	22	14	64
Billions	45	31	69
Cape Cod	28	25	89
Casanova Star	18	9	50
Cats Castle	30	26	87
D' Coach	13	8	62
Don Guido	23	18	78
Elusive Chris	12	9	75
Eqtesaad	41	29	71
Fappiano's Star	48	39	81
Figure of Speech	18	14	78
Galic Boy	14	10	71
Goldwater	23	18	78
Greedy	11	7	64
Johnny Jones	12	6	50

Stallion	Mares Bred	Fls	Live Foal Rate
Just Typical	20	16	80
King's Crown	16	8	50
Lightning Al	10	9	90
Marshall Greeley	15	12	80
Munasaaq	14	10	71
My Favorite Dream	11	10	91
Myfavorite Place	23	16	70
Ordway	11	4	36
Plato	19	10	53
Royal Merlot	12	7	58
Shawnee Warrior	22	13	59
Solari	26	14	54
Sudden Thunder	38	26	68
Tamhid	13	7	54
Virtua Cop	12	10	83
Wonder Bird	28	26	93

South Carolina

Stallion	Mares Bred	Fls	Live Foal Rate
Cat in Town	18	7	39
Lad	12	6	50
Ride the Storm	19	13	68

South Dakota

Stallion	Mares Bred	Fls	Live Foal Rate
Emailit	13	6	46
Finn McCool	15	11	73
Neff Lake	17	11	65
Storm of the Night	45	2	4

Tennessee

Stallion	Mares Bred	Fls	Live Foal Rate
Head West	12	4	33
Moro Oro	16	15	94
Take the Shot	10	3	30

Texas

Stallion	Mares Bred	Fls	Live Foal Rate
All Gone	11	4	36
A P Valentine	16	4	25
Authenticate	72	37	51
Blue Eyed Streaker	11	9	82
Boone's Mill	12	9	75
Byars	10	7	70
Capote's Prospect	17	12	71
Captain Countdown	36	18	50
City Street	58	40	69
Conroe	10	7	70
Dixieland Heat	27	13	48
Dove Hunt	18	13	72
Early Flyer	47	36	77
El Amante	10	8	80
El Leopardo	54	32	59
Excellent Secret	16	8	50
Finance the Cat	13	10	77
Flaming Quest (GB)	18	9	50
Flying Kris	13	7	54
Gen Stormin'norman	21	12	57
Gold Alert	35	24	69
Gold Legend	41	28	68
Gone East	10	1	10
Grande's Grandslam	10	9	90
Hadif	14	4	29
Hi Teck Man	20	12	60
Holzmeister	18	12	67
Imperial Cat	10	6	60
Intimidator	21	11	52
Irisheyesareflying	13	6	46
Itchetucknee	16	12	75
Itron	11	7	64
Jadacus	15	5	33
Joe Move	13	4	31
Karen's Cat	13	6	46
Littleexpectations	32	18	56
Magic Cat	21	12	57
Marked Tree	20	14	70
Maverick	21	19	90
Meacham	19	12	63
Midway Road	46	37	80
New Trieste	57	36	63
Northdrop	11	6	55
Olmos	10	6	60
Open Forum	14	7	50
Parade Ground	12	7	58
Pass the Peace	35	10	29

Sires — Live Foal Report

Stallion	Mares Bred	Fls	Live Foal Rate
Pepper M.	13	3	23
Porto Varas	18	11	61
Saints n' Sinners	11	4	36
Sand Ridge	29	15	52
Seattle Sleet	35	19	54
Seeking a Home	24	17	71
Seneca Jones	43	26	60
Sequoia Grove	11	8	73
Silent Picture	16	12	75
Sir Bedivere	20	9	45
Smoken Devine	13	3	23
Special Rate	33	20	61
Star Programmer	30	14	47
Statement	16	13	81
Struggler (GB)	10	7	70
Sudden Storm	12	4	33
Supreme Cat	13	11	85
Swamp	10	6	60
Thats Our Buck	20	15	75
Thorn Cat	45	20	44
Tinners Way	32	17	53
Top Gear	10	5	50
Touch Tone	21	5	24
Traffic Circle	12	7	58
Trancus	12	6	50
Truluck	40	25	63
Uncle Abbie	33	15	45
Valid Expectations	63	45	71
Western Power	18	4	22
Wild Horses	36	15	42
Wimbledon	64	47	73
Z Smart Prospect	18	11	61

Utah

Stallion	Mares Bred	Fls	Live Foal Rate
Classic Chrys	12	12	100
Joe Who (Brz)	49	26	53
Meet Me in Dixie	10	7	70
Rapid Thunder	14	7	50
Reciprocate	19	11	58
Regal Groom	11	6	55
Wild Escapade	83	37	45

Virginia

Stallion	Mares Bred	Fls	Live Foal Rate
Aaron's Gold	10	2	20
Ball's Bluff	10	6	60
Fred Astaire	10	5	50
Hay Halo	10	5	50
Mr. Executioner	11	9	82
Rock Point	10	5	50

Washington

Stallion	Mares Bred	Fls	Live Foal Rate
Cahill Road	43	28	65
Chumaree	26	17	65
Consigliere (GB)	11	8	73
Delineator	29	22	76
Free At Last	30	20	67
Hampton Bay	10	2	20
Heavenly Search	25	15	60
He's Tops	38	32	84
Ito the Hammer	10	8	80
Just Ruler	10	3	30
Kasparov	28	12	43
Katowice	12	10	83
Kentucky Lucky	23	9	39
Liberty Gold	50	31	62
Makors Mark	17	7	41
Matricule	50	31	62
Nacheezmo	19	9	47
Our Boy Harvey	14	3	21
Outing	12	7	58
Patriot Noise	10	5	50
Petersburg	27	15	56
Polish Gift	22	12	55
Private Gold	69	45	65
Slewdledo	17	12	71
Snowbound	76	33	43
Storm Blast	14	7	50
Sum Trick	10	0	0
Tamoured	13	0	0
Top Account	11	6	55
Tribunal	70	46	66
Tropic Lightning	14	10	71
Waiting Game	15	11	73
You and I	43	35	81

West Virginia

Stallion	Mares Bred	Fls	Live Foal Rate
Black Tie Affair (Ire)	58	39	67
Bop	42	22	52
Castine	15	8	53
Citislipper	10	8	80
Civilisation	37	23	62
Cowboy Carson	15	5	33
Dancinwiththedevil	11	6	55
Danish Gold	10	3	30
Deputy Rummy	12	7	58
Devon Deputy	23	12	52
Emancipator	15	7	47
Endeavouring	14	4	29
Family Calling	25	9	36
Garnered	18	13	72
Ghostly Minister	13	10	77
Green Fee	18	11	61
Gunnerside	22	15	68
Inner Harbour	22	13	59
Kokand	30	13	43
Limit Out	13	7	54
Luftikus	75	48	64
Make Your Mark	13	6	46
Medford	20	11	55
Mesopotamia	10	8	80
Native Slew	14	4	29
Ormsby	14	10	71
Our Valley View	20	7	35
Peak Dancer	13	8	62
Prints of Peace	32	23	72
Prized	60	36	60
Race On Green	31	18	58
Reparations	32	12	38
Robb	13	4	31
Run Softly	22	12	55
Sandlot Star	27	8	30
Spreebee	10	8	80
Standing On Edge	14	6	43
Stored	22	15	68
Strike Adduce	13	8	62
Stritzel	15	9	60
Valiant Nature	13	8	62
Wesham	19	6	32
Windsor Castle	51	36	71
Zizou	11	3	27

Wisconsin

Stallion	Mares Bred	Fls	Live Foal Rate
Gazebo	15	7	47

Alberta

Stallion	Mares Bred	Fls	Live Foal Rate
Alydeed	37	20	54
Brass Minister	19	5	26
Captain Bodgit	44	24	55
Cobra King	51	31	61
Commitisize	20	9	45
Desperately	12	9	75
Easy Climb	13	6	46
Esteem	19	8	42
General Royal	25	12	48
Highland Ruckus	28	14	50
Hurricane Center	17	6	35
Important Notice	13	6	46
Just a Cat	18	6	33
Kahuna Jack	19	13	68
Kiridashi	85	31	36
Linkage	10	4	40
Lost Canyon (GB)	14	6	43
Magic Prospect	16	8	50
Misnomer	28	12	43
Native Storm	10	5	50
Nicholas Ds	12	7	58
Othello	19	6	32
Real West	17	8	47
Rebmec	19	3	16
Rosetti	50	24	48
Smile Again	31	13	42
Tempered Appeal	19	11	58
Tiger Trap	41	27	66
Tossofthecoin	17	5	29

British Columbia

Stallion	Mares Bred	Fls	Live Foal Rate
Alfaari	20	11	55
Amaruk	21	12	57
Bright Valour	26	17	65
Catrail	14	2	14
Dramatic Show	12	9	75
Finality	29	21	72
Fisher Pond	39	16	41
Flaming West	18	13	72
Katahaula County	57	33	58
Light of Mine	14	10	71
Mass Market	62	49	79
Nightofthegaelics	13	0	0
Orchid's Devil	12	8	67
Regal Intention	43	31	72
Royal Albert Hall	13	9	69
Stephanotis	30	19	63
Storm Victory	38	21	55
Terrell	34	28	82
Vying Victor	84	51	61
Wandering	22	15	68
Western Trick	10	6	60
Yoonevano	30	16	53

Manitoba

Stallion	Mares Bred	Fls	Live Foal Rate
Battle Cat	28	16	57
Fabulous Champ	23	10	43
Going Commando	13	8	62
Slippery Gator	16	8	50

Ontario

Stallion	Mares Bred	Fls	Live Foal Rate
A Fleets Dancer	40	23	58
Ascot Knight	14	10	71
Bold Executive	66	47	71
Bold n' Flashy	38	22	58
Box Office Event	11	7	64
Cat's At Home	24	20	83
Ciano Cat	12	4	33
Compadre	34	20	59
Dance to Destiny	33	24	73
Domascan Dan	26	14	54
Foxtrail	29	19	66
Guaranteed Gold	12	12	100
Gun Power	15	10	67
Impeachment	31	17	55
Kinshasa	23	11	48
Mobil	75	57	76
Mr. Jester	51	27	53
One Way Love	117	81	69
Parisianprospector	14	8	57
Paynes Bay	17	10	59
Peaks and Valleys	90	61	68
Perigee Moon	40	19	48
Porto Foricos	15	10	67
Pride of New York	11	4	36
Salty Note	17	8	47
Solomon's Decree	15	12	80
Swampster	11	8	73
Tejabo	15	8	53
Tejano Run	52	28	54
Tempolake	10	9	90
Tethra	18	12	67
The Fed	10	6	60
Tomahawk	76	41	54
Trajectory	81	59	73
Union Place	12	9	75
Valid N Bold	19	14	74
Wake At Noon	13	9	69
Where's the Ring	82	47	57
Whiskey Wisdom	23	14	61

Saskatchewan

Stallion	Mares Bred	Fls	Live Foal Rate
Blowin de Turn	10	3	30
Dream Guide	12	0	0
Just Cash	17	9	53
Nation Wide News	13	3	23
Serious Business (Ire)	15	6	40
Shaheen	12	9	75
Striking Song	24	11	46
You've Got Action	13	8	62

Report of Mares Bred for 2007

With Thoroughbred racing and breeding under pressure in states such as Texas and Maryland that do not have alternative gaming, the 2007 Jockey Club Report of Mares Bred documented downward trends throughout North America. The number of mares reported bred in 2007 declined 3.1% to 60,188. Stallion numbers fell to 3,399 and continued a steady downward trend that has been occurring for at least the last decade and a half.

Fewer stallions are servicing more mares—the average stallion covered 17.7 mares in 2007, up from an average of 16 mares in 2006. The average book size also has been dropping steadily; in 1992, 6,753 stallions were bred to 63,766 mares, yielding an average book size of 9.4 mares.

The number of mares in production has remained relatively stable. Since 1992, the number of mares in production has declined by only 5.6%, and the mare census was above 63,000 as recently as 2004 and '05. In that 16-year period, the number of stallions in production declined by nearly half.

Through March 1, 2008, Kentucky led all states with 354 stallions and 21,911 mares bred to those stallions. As expected in a region with highly commercial sires, the average book was very high—nearly 62 mares per sire—up from 60 in the previous year. Florida, which also has a highly commercial industry, also boasted large books, with 233 stallions bred to 6,467 mares, an average book of 27.8 mares. However, Florida's average book was down from 31.4 in 2006, because it added seven stallions and bred 8.8% fewer mares to those Florida stallions.

California ranked third with 4,597 mares bred (down 4.4%), followed by Louisiana, whose 4,128 mares bred were up 5.3% from the previous year. Texas clung to fifth position with its 2,200 mares bred in 2007 less than 150 ahead of New York, with 2,051. The number of mares bred to Texas sires declined 14.2% from 2,564 in 2006. Maryland reported a similar trend, down 12.6% to 1,416 mares bred to Free State stallions.

In North America in 2007, 126 stallions were bred to at least 100 mares, equaling 2006 and two fewer than the record 128 stallions to do so in '05. Stormy Atlantic led all stallions with 199 mares bred.

Leading Stallions by Mares Bred
(Reported as of March 1, 2008)

Stallion, Location	Mares Bred	Stallion, Location	Mares Bred	Stallion, Location	Mares Bred	Stallion, Location	Mares Bred
Stormy Atlantic, Ky.	199	Rockport Harbor, Ky.	146	Aptitude, Ky.	123	Aragorn (Ire), Ky.	110
Johannesburg, Ky.	195	Exchange Rate, Fl.	145	Old Forester, On.	123	Johar, Ky.	110
Wildcat Heir, Fl.	177	E Dubai, Ky.	142	First Samurai, Ky.	122	Mingun, Ky.	109
With Distinction, Fl.	177	Pure Prize, Ky.	142	Forestry, Ky.	122	Perfect Soul (Ire), Ky.	109
Giant's Causeway, Ky.	176	Distorted Humor, Ky.	141	Sunday Break (Jpn), Ky.	122	War Front, Ky.	109
Tapit, Ky.	174	Candy Ride (Arg), Ky.	140	Trippi, Fl.	122	Kela, Ky.	108
Congrats, Fl.	172	Cactus Ridge, Ky.	139	Arch, Ky.	121	Limehouse, Ky.	108
Grand Slam, Ky.	172	Henny Hughes, Ky.	139	Broken Vow, Ky.	121	Unbridled's Song, Ky.	108
Orientate, Ky.	168	Artie Schiller, Ky.	138	Forest Wildcat, Ky.	121	Bernstein, Ky.	107
Chapel Royal, Ky.	166	Bellamy Road, Ky.	137	Suave, Ky.	121	Giacomo, Ky.	107
Lion Heart, Ky.	165	Holy Bull, Ky.	137	Afleet Alex, Ky.	120	Gibson County, Fl.	107
Include, Ky.	163	More Than Ready, Ky.	136	Ghostzapper, Ky.	118	Good Reward, Ky.	107
Bandini, Ky.	162	Consolidator, Ky.	135	Indian Charlie, Ky.	117	Leroidesanimaux (Brz), Ky.	107
Purge, Ky.	161	Indian Ocean, Fl.	134	Officer, Ky.	117	Forest Grove, Ky.	106
Songandaprayer, Ky.	159	Thunder Gulch, Ky.	134	Storm and a Half, Ar.	117	Mizzen Mast, Ky.	106
Whywhywhy, Ky.	159	Bernardini, Ky.	133	Kitten's Joy, Ky.	116	Put It Back, Fl.	105
Mr. Greeley, Ky.	158	Smart Strike, Ky.	133	Sky Mesa, Ky.	116	Belong to Me, Ky.	104
Tale of the Cat, Ky.	158	Speightstown, Ky.	133	El Corredor, Ky.	115	Bowman's Band, Ky.	104
Tiznow, Ky.	156	Tribal Rule, Ca.	132	Teton Forest, Ky.	115	Omega Code, Fl.	103
Malibu Moon, Ky.	154	Maria's Mon, Ky.	131	Flower Alley, Ky.	114	Benchmark, Ca.	102
Street Cry (Ire), Ky.	154	Empire Maker, Ky.	130	Kafwain, Ky.	114	Pollard's Vision, Ky.	102
Badge of Silver, Ky.	153	Touch Gold, Ky.	128	Mutakddim, Ky.	114	Successful Appeal, Ky.	102
Medaglia d'Oro, Ky.	153	Domestic Dispute, Md.	127	North Light (Ire), Ky.	114	Dixie Union, Ky.	101
Silver Train, Ky.	153	Posse, Ky.	127	Smarty Jones, Ky.	114	Forest Danger, Ky.	101
Hold That Tiger, Ky.	151	Vindication, Ky.	127	Powerscourt (GB), Ky.	113	Friends Lake, Ky.	101
Fusaichi Pegasus, Ky.	150	Harlan's Holiday, Ky.	126	Value Plus, Ky.	113	Grand Reward, Ky.	101
Lemon Drop Kid, Ky.	150	Awesome Again, Ky.	125	Alphabet Soup, Ky.	112	Momentum, Ca.	101
Pomeroy, Fl.	150	Dance With Ravens, Md.	124	Roman Ruler, Ky.	112	Rock Slide, Md.	101
Closing Argument, Fl.	149	Eddington, Ky.	124	Yes It's True, Ky.	112	Catienus, N.Y.	100
Bluegrass Cat, Ky.	148	Elusive Quality, Ky.	124	Dehere, Ky.	111	Lake Austin, La.	100
Sharp Humor, Ky.	148	Hook and Ladder, N.Y.	124	Roar of the Tiger, Fl.	111	Don't Get Mad, Ky.	99
Eurosilver, Ky.	147	Pleasant Tap, Ky.	124	Unbridled Energy, Ky.	111	Hennessy, Ky.	99

Sires — Report of Mares Bred

Stallion, Location	Mares Bred	Stallion, Location	Mares Bred	Stallion, Location	Mares Bred	Stallion, Location	Mares Bred
Jump Start, Ky.	99	Rock Hard Ten, Ky.	94	Victory Gallop, Ky.	87	Mass Media, Fl.	80
Strong Hope, Ky.	98	Royal Academy, Ky.	94	Freud, N.Y.	85	Perfect Mandate, Ca.	80
Tenpins, Ky.	98	In Excess (Ire), Ca.	93	Peace Rules, Fl.	85	Smoke Glacken, Ky.	80
Yankee Gentleman, Ky.	98	Swiss Yodeler, Ca.	93	Real Quiet, Pa.	85	Good and Tough, La.	79
Alluvial, Ky.	97	Alke, Fl.	92	City Zip, Ky.	84	Halo's Image, Fl.	79
Birdstone, Ky.	97	Langfuhr, Ky.	92	Freespool, Ca.	84	Mr. Livingston, Fl.	79
Leestown, La.	97	Offlee Wild, Ky.	92	Oratory, Md.	84	Pleasantly Perfect, Ky.	79
Mineshaft, Ky.	97	Shaniko, Ky.	92	Southern Image, Ky.	83	Full Mandate, Fl.	78
Pulpit, Ky.	97	Borrego, Ky.	91	Three Wonders, Fl.	83	Devil His Due, Ky.	77
Dynaformer, Ky.	96	Niigon, On.	91	Wiseman's Ferry, Ky.	83	Werblin, Fl.	77
Golden Missile, Ky.	96	Sea of Secrets, Ca.	91	Chief Seattle, N.Y.	82	Congaree, Ky.	76
Storm Cat, Ky.	96	Slew City Slew, Ky.	91	Flatter, Ky.	82	Not For Love, Md.	76
Congressionalhonor, Pa.	95	Aldebaran, Ky.	90	Proud Citizen, Ky.	82	Around the Cape, N.Y.	75
Cuvee, Ky.	95	Strong Contender, Ky.	90	Sweetsouthernsaint, Fl.	82	Lite the Fuse, Pa.	75
Macho Uno, Fl.	95	Lightnin N Thunder, Fl.	89	Da Stoops, Fl.	81	Old Topper, Ca.	75
Quiet American, Ky.	95	Best of the Bests (Ire), On.	88	Flame Thrower, Ca.	81	Spanish Steps, Fl.	75
A.P. Indy, Ky.	94	Sarava, Fl.	88	Forest Camp, Ky.	81	Eavesdropper, Ky.	74
Bertrando, Ca.	94	Desert Warrior, N.Y.	87	Good Journey, Ca.	81	Petionville, Ky.	74
Pioneering, Ky.	94	Five Star Day, Ky.	87	El Prado (Ire), Ky.	80		

Stallions and Mares Bred in the United States, Canada, and North America 1992-2007

Year	U.S. Stallions	U.S. Mares Bred	Avg. Book	Canada Stallions	Canada Mares Bred	Avg. Book	Total NA Stallions	Total NA Mares Bred	Avg. Book
2007	3,135	57,008	18.2	264	3,180	12.0	3,399	60,188	17.7
2006	3,581	58,597	16.4	303	3,488	11.5	3,884	62,085	16.0
2005	3,838	59,300	15.5	312	3,700	11.9	4,150	63,000	15.2
2004	3,964	59,210	14.9	325	3,810	11.7	4,289	63,020	14.7
2003	4,038	58,687	14.5	340	3,596	10.6	4,378	62,283	14.2
2002	4,094	59,452	14.5	347	3,562	10.3	4,441	63,014	14.2
2001	4,250	59,433	14.0	338	3,539	10.5	4,588	62,972	13.7
2000	4,329	59,887	13.8	352	3,462	9.8	4,681	63,349	13.5
1999	4,396	57,301	13.0	350	3,431	9.8	4,746	60,732	12.8
1998	4,513	55,914	12.4	386	3,544	9.2	4,899	59,458	12.1
1997	4,675	54,944	11.8	414	3,652	8.8	5,089	58,596	11.5
1996	4,882	54,571	11.2	427	3,700	8.7	5,309	58,271	11.0
1995	5,182	55,435	10.7	425	3,656	8.6	5,607	59,091	10.5
1994	5,365	55,275	10.3	430	3,730	8.7	5,795	59,005	10.2
1993	5,801	56,269	9.7	453	3,973	8.8	6,254	60,242	9.6
1992	6,263	59,607	9.5	490	4,159	8.5	6,753	63,766	9.4

Figures for 2007 complete through March 27, 2008.

Stallions and Mares Bred by State and Province
(Reported as of March 1, 2008)

State	Stallions	Mares Bred	State	Stallions	Mares Bred	State	Stallions	Mares Bred
Alabama	20	96	Mississippi	10	41	Utah	22	194
Arizona	49	458	Missouri	17	69	Vermont	1	1
Arkansas	63	603	Montana	28	108	Virginia	38	129
California	280	4,597	Nebraska	28	305	Washington	68	871
Colorado	46	290	Nevada	6	18	West Virginia	76	973
Connecticut	1	1	New Hampshire	1	4	Wisconsin	4	24
Delaware	1	1	New Jersey	24	370	Wyoming	4	7
Florida	233	6,467	New Mexico	166	1,918	Unknown	14	28
Georgia	13	83	New York	106	2,051			
Idaho	31	219	North Carolina	9	36	**Province**		
Illinois	88	840	North Dakota	20	134	Alberta	75	751
Indiana	69	552	Ohio	61	339	British Columbia	53	716
Iowa	37	411	Oklahoma	162	1,614	Manitoba	18	125
Kansas	23	133	Oregon	51	367	New Brunswick	1	1
Kentucky	354	21,911	Pennsylvania	88	1,076	Ontario	88	1,418
Louisiana	289	4,128	Puerto Rico	69	843	Prince Edward Island	2	4
Maryland	54	1,416	South Carolina	22	129	Quebec	3	5
Massachusetts	9	32	South Dakota	12	107	Saskatchewan	22	153
Michigan	52	415	Tennessee	19	86			
Minnesota	33	313	Texas	264	2,200	**Totals**	**3,397**	**60,181**

Stallions Bred to Five or More Mares in 2007
(Reported as of March 1, 2008)

Alabama

Stallion	Mares Bred
Casey On Deck	14
Gold Spring (Arg)	10
Mountain Legionair	6
Royal Empire	17
Special Coach	7
Storm Man	10

Arizona

Stallion	Mares Bred
Absolute Harmony	10
Al Ghazi	6
Benton Creek	37
Bierstadt	12
Buck Strider	25
Chief Planner	8
Cromwell	19
Deposit Ticket	23
Equinox	10
Gent	9
Hidden City	14
Individual Style	9
Jeep Shot	7
Jila (Ire)	7
Jonathan's Gold	9
Larrupin'	21
Louis Arthur	9
Midnight Royalty	20
Odds On	19
Perforce	8
Red Sky's	42
Rocky Bar	30
Sideburn	11
Tax Collection	7
Teddy Boy	13
Top Hit	15

Arkansas

Stallion	Mares Bred
Bob's Prospect	9
Cinnamon Creek	13
Cornish Snow	7
Croydon	9
District	26
Explosive Truth	9
Fan the Flame	11
Father Steve	30
Funontherun	16
Glorious Bid	14
Hesabull	31
Ile St. Louis (Chi)	14
Irish Regent	6
Lil Honcho	9
Mi Cielo	13
Oneofthejonesboys	12
Pine Bluff	26
Proper Ridge	7
Proudest Romeo	13
Rinka Das	41
Siberian Pine	8
Skeet	7
Southern Forest	25
Stauder	15
Storm and a Half	117

California

Stallion	Mares Bred
Acclaimed Honour	7
Alymagic	7
America's Storm	26
Ancient Art	15
Anziyan Royalty	22
Atticus	34
Avanzado (Arg)	21
Awesome Jet	10
Bartok (Ire)	13
Beau Genius	19
Beau Soleil	23
Benchmark	102
Bertrando	94
Best Minister	23
Birdonthewire	15
Blue Afleet	10
Boomerang	17
Brand Name	20
Bridle and Bit	6
Bring the Heat	24
Cactus Creole	14
Calkins Road	9
Capsized	34
Caros Love	8
Cat Dreams	30
Cayoke (Fr)	32
Cee's Tizzy	48
Cindago	14
Comet Shine	14
Comic Strip	23
Commander's Flag	11
Compelling Sound	7
Crafty C. T.	21
Cyclotron	15
Decarchy	63
Deep Fall	6
Defy Logic	10
Del Mar Show	10
Deputy Commander	30
Dismissed	6
Doc Gus	33
Downtown Seattle	7
Emerald Creme	10
Emeritus	7
Epic Honor	7
Event of the Year	17
Excessive Barb	12
Expressionist	21
Extra	26
Faculty	20
Fast Eclipse	6
Flame Thrower	81
Formal Gold	66
For Really	18
Freespool	84
Fullbridled	14
Fusaichi Accele	10
Future Storm	21
Game Plan	54
Globalize	42
Golden Gear	31
Good Journey	81
Gotham City	33
Grey Memo	14
Half Term	8
Helmsman	9
High Brite	33
High Demand	36
Highland Gold	11
Illinois Storm	30
Indian Country	19
In Excess (Ire)	93
Iron Cat	24
Ironman Dehere	8
Jackpot	23
King Excess	7
Kissin Kris	8
Lake George	15
Larry the Legend	13
Lasersport	26
Lit de Justice	17
Lost in Paradise	13
Lucky Pulpit	29
Madraar	10
Marino Marini	57
Market Forecast	6
Memo (Chi)	38
Michael's Flyer	13
Ministers Wild Cat	71
Momentum	101
Monsignor Casale	13
Moscow Ballet	21
Mt. Bellewood	24
Mud Route	17
Muqtarib	20
Naevus Star	7
Nineeleven	25
Northern Devil	23
Nosetothe	10
Old Topper	75
Olympio	24
Oly Ogy	8
Onebadshark	19
Our New Recruit	20
Peak a Bootrando	11
Peppered Cat	6
Perfect Mandate	80
Persian Turban (Ire)	8
Popular	20
Quick Action	16
Rainbow Blues (Ire)	10
Raz Lea	9
Redattore (Brz)	59
Regent Act	12
Replicate	10
Rhythm	10
Rio Verde	50
Roar	40
Robannier	8
Roman Dancer	19
Roots and Ropes	7
Royal Cat	10
Royal Legacy	11
Royal Walk	18
Salt Lake	70
Score Early	7
Score Quick	11
Sea of Secrets	91
Seattle Bound	14
Seattle Buddy	6
Seattle Proud	12
Serve the Flag	12
Siberian Summer	62
Silic (Fr)	15
Singletary	55
Skimming	33
Sky Terrace	16
Slewcious	7
Smooth Runner	14
Sought After	26
Soul of the Matter	6
Souvenir Copy	20
Spensive	8
Spinelessjellyfish	20
Storm Creek	19
Stormed	37
Stormy Jack	27
Suances (GB)	29
Suggest	10
Supah Blitz	6
Swiss Yodeler	93
Tactical Heir	6
Takin It Deep	17
Tale of the Hills	16
Tannersmyman	26
Taskmaster	10
Temescal Ridge	13
The Good Life	8
Thisnearlywasmine	13
Tizbud	57
Trapper	11
Tribal Rule	132
Truckee	23
Turkoman	13
Unbridled Man	8
Unbridled Native	20
Unbridled's Love	7
Uncle Denny	33
Unusual Heat	47
Valid Wager	13
Vernon Castle	11
Via Lombardia (Ire)	6
Vronsky	26
Western Fame	21

Colorado

Stallion	Mares Bred
Annual Tradition	7
Cash Deposit	14
Coverallbases	14
Eckelson	16
Eishin Masamune (Jpn)	39
Ernie Tee	13
Kennedy Factor	7
Leelanau	17
Majorbigtimesheet	23
Mauk Eight	7
Oliver's Twist	18
Prince of the Wild	7
Silver Saint	7
Unbridled Vision	17

Florida

Stallion	Mares Bred
Act of Duty	62
Agnes Gold (Jpn)	16
Alajwad	22
Alex's Pal	26
Alke	92
Alysweep	16
American Spirit	27
Aspen Ridge	12
Awesome of Course	10
Awesome Sword	10
Bachelor Blues	27
Black Mambo	66

Sires — Report of Mares Bred

Stallion	Mares Bred
Blowing Rock	9
B L's Appeal	30
Boastful	19
Burning Roma	59
Bwana Charlie	66
Cashel Castle	44
Celcius Slew	13
China Grind	13
Cimarron Secret	11
City Place	63
Closing Argument	149
Colony Light	23
Concerto	50
Concorde's Tune	34
Congrats	172
Conscience Clear	29
Copper Man	10
Dark Kestrel	11
Da Stoops	81
Delaware Township	18
Deputy Wild Cat	39
Diligence	6
Diplomatic Jet	7
Don Hector	7
Don Six	24
Dont Look N Laugh	7
Double Honor	59
Drewman	54
D'wildcat	66
Essence of Dubai	39
Exchange Rate	145
Express Tour	12
Fast 'n Royal	11
February Storm	15
Fire Slam	39
First Tour	13
Forbidden Apple	9
Formal Dinner	58
Freefourinternet	68
French Envoy	17
Frisco Star	17
Full Mandate	78
Gato Del Sur	6
Gemma's Star	7
Gibson County	107
Gimmeawink	42
Graeme Hall	73
Greatness	70
Great Pyramid (Ire)	30
Gulf Storm	68
Hadrian's Wall	7
Halifax	6
Halo's Image	79
Hear No Evil	14
High Fly	28
Holy Ground	25
Honor Glide	15
Im Millennium Man	7
Imperialism	72
Indian Express	18
Indian Ocean	134
Indy King	30
Invisible Ink	15
Irish Road	24
Key Moment	10
Leading the Parade	44
Lido Palace (Chi)	26
Lightnin N Thunder	89
Macho Uno	95
Marciano	23
Marco Bay	16
Mass Media	80
Master Bill	12
Max's Pal	19
Mecke	8
Milwaukee Brew	57
Mongoose	35
Montbrook	44
Mount McKinley	10
Mr. Livingston	79
Omega Code	103
One Nice Cat	50
Orchard Park	9
Outofthebox	15
Parents' Reward	9
Peace Rules	85
Pico Central (Brz)	35
Pomeroy	150
Proud Accolade	39
Proud and True	39
Pure Precision	11
Put It Back	105
Red Bullet	51
Repent	68
Rey de Cafe	66
Roar of the Tiger	111
Royal Providence	10
Sabre d'Argent	51
Safe in the U S A	23
Safely's Mark	11
Saint Afleet	22
Salty Note	15
Salty Sea	21
Sarava	88
Scorpion	32
Seize the Day	10
Shanawi (Ire)	8
Skip to the Stone	7
Skip Trial	13
Sligo Bay (Ire)	38
Smooth Jazz	14
Snow Ridge	17
Snuck In	14
Spanish Steps	75
Straight Man	33
Sugar's Saint	19
Sweetsouthernsaint	82
Tadreeb	12
Texas Glitter	14
The Daddy	70
The Kaiser	17
Three Wonders	83
Tiltam	15
Too Much Bling	39
Trippi	122
True Enough	10
Trust N Luck	33
Unbridled Affair	10
Unbridled's Image	32
Unbridled Time	30
Unforgettable Max	21
Untuttable	6
U So Bad	9
Weekend Cruise	12
Wekiva Springs	26
Werblin	77
West Acre	29
Western Pride	45
Wildcat Heir	177
Winged Foot Willie	34
Wised Up	13
With Distinction	177

Georgia

Stallion	Mares Bred
Monster Winner	9
Muted	14
Prospector Street	9
Slew the Slewor	6
Smokin' John	13

Idaho

Stallion	Mares Bred
Allover	7
All the Gears	6
Alymah	6
Bachelor of Arts (GB)	26
Cause Ur Mine	26
Classi Envoy	7
Collateral	6
Crescendo	12
Derby Drive	10
Fabulous Frolic	8
Gone Irish	12
Reversal	9
Smart Chip	6
Starmaniac	12
Tavasco	10
Vermont	11
Wanna Be Like Dad	10

Illinois

Stallion	Mares Bred
Alaskan Frost	13
Allen Charge	6
Animo de Valeroso	30
Awesome Cat	23
Battle Star	16
Brave 'n Away	11
Canyon Run	10
Cherokee Rap	29
Chicago Six	34
Classic Account	9
Company Approval	18
Composer	8
Conte Di Savoya	9
Dave and Busters	16
Denouncer	16
Elhayq (Ire)	18
Eloped Again	10
Fact Book	19
Friendly Lover	34
Garcon Rouge	9
Gogarty (Ire)	16
Goldminers Gold	50
He's a Tough Cat	11
Honour Attendant	20
Indy Snow (GB)	31
Magna	8
Posh	35
Powerful Goer	8
Roanoke	20
Rouse the Louse	6
Sam the Pettyjudge	6
Shadow Launcher	10
Silver Zipper	8
Southland Blues	7
Summer Cloud	15
Talkin Tough	6
The Bold Bruiser	11
Theran	8
Time Chopper	11
Tough Call	17
Tricky Victor	11
Unbridled Success	14
Viareggio (Ire)	9

Stallion	Mares Bred
Western Outlaw	48
Wild Gambler	10

Indiana

Stallion	Mares Bred
Armada	6
Arromanches	24
Assembly Dancer	19
Bartlettsunbridled	15
Black Moonshine	39
Cat Power	7
Commemorate	15
Devils Folly	7
Easy Scoop	6
Fast Ferdie	12
Glitter Code	16
Gold Search	15
Goods	19
Grand Chance	7
Green Stamp	7
Hunting Hard	31
Indy Mood	9
Judge Vonsteubon	8
Just Plain Joe	8
King Tiara	6
Latin Reign	12
Le Casque Gris	12
Moro Oro	9
Pass Rush	29
Philadream	7
Plenty Chilly	16
Presidential Order	22
Prince Giustino	8
Radio Daze	7
Ripsaw	8
Timeraker	22
Valiant Style	15
Waki Warrior	16
Whitney Tower	15

Iowa

Stallion	Mares Bred
Added Edge	51
Bravo Bull	7
Canaveral	9
Classic Cat	17
Connecticut	9
Deerhound	25
Doug Fir	30
General Thomas	11
Governor Vasquez	11
Humming	18
Indian Territory	29
King of Scat	38
Pin Stripe	12
Regency Park	7
Sharkey	14
Storm Catcher	8
Too Much Ice	8
Tucan	6
Wild Gold	33
Wild Invader	7
Winter Glitter	22

Kansas

Stallion	Mares Bred
Admiral Indy	23
Big Splash	6
Grand On Dave	6
Polly's Comet	15
Prospector's Treat	10
So Ever Clever	14
Testafly	7
Tricky Six	9
Winaprize	9

Sires — Report of Mares Bred

Stallion	Mares Bred	Stallion	Mares Bred	Stallion	Mares Bred	Stallion	Mares Bred
Kentucky		Don't Get Mad	99	Lion Heart	165	Shore Breeze	11
Action This Day	66	Down the Aisle	17	Littleexpectations	41	Silver Deputy	65
Adair Star	6	Dumaani	7	Lost Soldier	39	Silver Train	153
Afleet Alex	120	During	26	Malabar Gold	20	Sir Cherokee	23
Air to Apache	6	Dynaformer	96	Malibu Moon	154	Sir Shackleton	62
Albert the Great	67	Eavesdropper	74	Mancini	41	Skip Away	31
Aldebaran	90	Ecton Park	50	Margie's Wildcat	37	Sky Classic	50
Aljabr	7	Eddington	124	Maria's Mon	131	Sky Mesa	116
Alluvial	97	E Dubai	142	Marquetry	47	Slew City Slew	91
Alphabet Soup	112	El Corredor	115	Medaglia d'Oro	153	Smart Strike	133
American Patriot	14	El Prado (Ire)	80	Medallist	57	Smarty Jones	114
Anabaa	54	Elusive Quality	124	Military	44	Smoke Glacken	80
Andromeda's Hero	25	Empire Maker	130	Mineshaft	97	Songandaprayer	159
A.P. Indy	94	Eurosilver	147	Mingun	109	Soto	59
Aptitude	123	Even the Score	69	Mizzen Mast	106	Southern Image	83
A. P. Warrior	52	Explicit	15	Monarchos	31	Speightstown	133
Aragorn (Ire)	110	Eye of the Tiger	19	Monashee Mountain	28	Stage Colony	12
Arch	121	Fast Decision	14	More Than Ready	136	Star Dabbler	67
Arthur's Ring	22	First Samurai	122	Morluc	10	State City	24
Artie Schiller	138	Five Star Day	87	Mr. Greeley	158	Stephen Got Even	49
Awesome Again	125	Flatter	82	Mull of Kintyre	68	Storm Boot	39
Badge of Silver	153	Flower Alley	114	Mutakddim	114	Storm Brewing	7
Bandini	162	Forest Camp	81	Najran	59	Storm Cat	96
Bellamy Road	137	Forest Danger	101	Newfoundland	15	Stormin Fever	33
Belong to Me	104	Forest Grove	106	Northern Afleet	64	Stormy Atlantic	199
Ben Bulben	13	Forestry	122	Northern Spur (Ire)	6	Strategic Mission	61
Bernardini	133	Forest Wildcat	121	North Light (Ire)	114	Street Cry (Ire)	154
Bernstein	107	Friends Lake	101	Officer	117	Stroll	11
Birdstone	97	Fusaichi Pegasus	150	Offlee Wild	92	Strong Contender	90
Blazonry	12	Generous Rosi (GB)	7	Olmodavor	46	Strong Hope	98
Bluegrass Cat	148	Ghostzapper	118	Orientate	168	Suave	121
Bold Truth	13	Giacomo	107	Osidy	61	Successful Appeal	102
Borrego	91	Giant's Causeway	176	Ouragan	17	Summinitup	12
Bowman's Band	104	Gilded Time	54	Out of Place	53	Sunday Break (Jpn)	122
Brahms	57	Golden Missile	96	Perfect Soul (Ire)	109	Surachai	7
Bright Launch	21	Gone West	51	Personal First	21	Swain (Ire)	23
Broken Vow	121	Good Reward	107	Petionville	74	Syncline	6
Buddha	33	Grand Reward	101	Phone the King	9	Tactical Cat	18
Bull Market	11	Grand Slam	172	Pikepass	17	Tale of the Cat	158
Cactus Ridge	139	Grindstone	27	Pioneering	94	Tapit	174
Came Home	34	Gulch	49	Pleasantly Perfect	79	Taste of Paradise	41
Canadian Frontier	39	Hap	13	Pleasant Tap	124	Ten Centuries	24
Candy Ride (Arg)	140	Harlan's Holiday	126	Point Given	61	Tenpins	98
Cape Canaveral	16	Hennessy	99	Pollard's Vision	102	Teton Forest	115
Cape Town	27	Henny Hughes	139	Posse	127	Theatrical (Ire)	36
Castledale (Ire)	49	Hero's Tribute	11	Powerscourt (GB)	113	The Call of Duty	6
Cat Ridge	18	Hold for Gold	11	Proud Citizen	82	The Cliff's Edge	55
Cat Thief	44	Hold That Tiger	151	Pulpit	97	Thunderello	38
Century City (Ire)	29	Holy Bull	137	Pure Prize	142	Thunder Gulch	134
Champali	52	Home At Last	14	Purge	161	Tiznow	156
Chapel Royal	166	Honour and Glory	50	Quest	34	Toccet	66
Cherokee Run	61	Horse Chestnut (SAf)	47	Quick Cut	6	Touch Gold	128
City Zip	84	Inamorato	23	Quiet American	95	Tropical Storm	39
Colonial Colony	7	Include	163	Rahy	73	Two Chiefs	7
Congaree	76	Indian Charlie	117	Razor	7	Unbridled Energy	111
Consolidator	135	Intidab	23	Regal Vision	7	Unbridled's Song	108
Cozar	8	It's No Joke	53	Repriced	17	Valiant Halory	22
Cozzene	47	Johannesburg	195	Richter Scale	6	Value Plus	113
Crafty Shaw	27	Johar	110	Rock Hard Ten	94	Van Nistelrooy	71
Crimson Classic	19	Jump Start	99	Rocking Trick (Arg)	23	Victory Gallop	87
Cryptoclearance	39	Kafwain	114	Rockport Harbor	146	Vindication	127
Cuvee	95	Kayrawan	8	Roman Ruler	112	Vision and Verse	23
David Copperfield	22	Kela	108	Royal Academy	94	Wagon Limit	48
Dayjur	16	Kingmambo	65	Saarland	70	Wando	63
Dehere	111	Kitten's Joy	116	Scrimshaw	46	War Chant	51
Devil His Due	77	Kutsa	9	Seattle Fitz (Arg)	17	War Front	109
Distorted Humor	141	Langfuhr	92	Seeking the Gold	48	Whywhywhy	159
Dixieland Band	38	Lee's Badger	6	Seinne (Chi)	8	Wild and Wicked	20
Dixie Union	101	Lemon Drop Kid	150	Service Stripe	25	Wildman Joey	8
Doneraile Court	23	Leroidesanimaux (Brz)	107	Shaniko	92	Wild Zone	16
		Limehouse	108	Sharp Humor	148	Wiseman's Ferry	83

Sires — Report of Mares Bred

Stallion	Mares Bred
Woke Up Dreamin	62
Woodman	50
Yankee Gentleman	98
Yes It's True	112
Yonaguska	61
Zavata	67

Louisiana

Stallion	Mares Bred
A Corking Limerick	11
Afternoon Deelites	68
Aggie Southpaw	6
Almostashar	35
Aloha Bold	8
Announce	42
A. P. Delta	42
Authenticate	39
Bayou Hebert	10
Be Like Mike	35
Best Idea	19
Big Top Cat	43
Broadway Show	12
Buzzy's Gold	12
Canboulay	9
Capitalimprovement	10
Catastrophe	23
Catniro	9
Charleston Man	6
Cherokee Beau	7
Cherokee Tin	7
Chief Okie Dokie	6
Choosing Choice	23
Chop Chop	6
Classic Alliance	8
Counter Punch	14
Count the Time	32
Crowned King	13
Cyclone	16
Dancing Missile	18
Daring Bid	22
De Guerin	9
Direct Hit	35
Doctor Mike	8
Doeny Rain	9
Dow Jones U S	38
Dr. Best	6
Easyfromthegitgo	56
El Amante	11
Enteprenuer	15
Ents Dream	14
Erlton	26
Escrito	18
Esplanade Ridge	19
Etbauer	12
Eugene's Third Son	19
Eulogize	11
Evon's Bully	21
E Z Glory	16
Fiend	9
Finder's Gold	11
Finest Hour	52
Ford Every Stream	45
Forty Won	7
Full Moons Arisin	7
Fusaichi Rock Star	28
Gauguin	14
Global Mission	20
Gold Tribute	69
Good and Tough	79
Goodbye Doeny	23
Grand Appointment	11
Green Raskal	13
Groovy Jett	9
Groovy's Ghost	8
Halos and Horns	22
Harborage	23
Hat Trick X Three	7
Henriques	8
High Cascade	36
Holy Sting	22
Honorable Pic	15
House Burner	21
Huff	25
Ide	59
In a Walk	21
Island Born	12
Islander	6
Jaunatxo	6
Jolie's Frolic	10
Justa Red Bird	8
Keats	38
K One King	58
Laabity	16
Lake Austin	100
Lampedusa	21
Leestown	97
Left Banker	7
Like a Soldier	13
Lion Tamer	34
Littlebitlively	27
Lone Star Saint	16
Lone Star Sky	31
Lunarpal	35
Lydgate	44
Macabe	55
Malibu Wesley	23
Man of the Night	6
Many a Wish	25
Mauk Four	13
Midbar	7
Middlesex Drive	7
Mike's Little Man	12
Mister Herbert	9
Mom's Little Guy	9
Montana Dreamin'	10
Moonlight Dancer	7
Mr. Baskets	21
Mr. John	7
Mustang Jock	17
My Friend Max	73
My Mike	13
Native Regent	22
New York Prospect	8
Northern Niner	7
Ole Rebel	25
One More Power	9
On Target	7
Our Diablo	10
Our Shining Hour	11
Out of the Crisis	13
Parting Guest	7
Piccolino	8
Placid Fund	18
Planet Earth	9
Porto Foricos	31
Power and Peace	10
Prince of the Mt.	22
Prince T.	10
Promissory	29
Prospector's Gift	20
Puck	22
Pulling Punches	18
Rahy's Secret	16
Rail	17
Rainmaker	52
Reformer Rally	12
Regreta	7
Richburg	8
Road Rush	7
Roaring Camp	12
Robyn Dancer	19
Rodeo	27
Roger That	6
Rossini	20
Royal Strand (Ire)	27
Ruler's Court	26
Run Production	19
Safe Prospect	9
Saint's Honor	8
Satchmo's Band	13
Saxton	7
Seattle Sleet	19
Sefapiano	21
Sheryar	12
Sheryar Special	25
Sikorsky	7
Silky Sweep	38
Silver On Silver	9
Space Shot	8
Spritely Walker	7
Storm Day	46
Storm Passage	33
Supremo Secret	11
Swamp Rat	9
Tafaul	6
Thank the Bank	6
Time Bandit	29
Toolighttoquit	25
Top Venture	28
Tricky	12
Two Punch Sonny	6
Undeniable	9
Upping the Ante	6
Valid Belfast	21
Valid Bidder	54
Valid Virtue	12
Vic I Am	14
Virginia Carnival	10
War Eagle	14
Warp Speed Scottie	10
Whambam	18
Whiff of Indy	33
Wildcat Shoes	42
Wild West	27
Wire Me Collect	35
Zarbyev	17

Maryland

Stallion	Mares Bred
Ameri Valay	7
Cherokee's Boy	44
Cruisin' Dixie	11
Crypto Star	12
Dance With Ravens	124
Deputy Storm	42
Disco Rico	34
Domestic Dispute	127
Fantasticat	49
Fleet Foot	6
Gators N Bears	60
Go for Gin	39
Goldmember	7
Great Notion	30
Java Royal	6
La Reine's Terms	19
Lion Hearted	67
Louis Quatorze	50
Love of Money	52
Mojave Moon	6
No Armistice	37
Not For Love	76
Oratory	84
Outflanker	20
Parker's Storm Cat	29
Partner's Hero	20
Polish Miner	8
Port Vila (Fr)	14
Rock Slide	101
Seeking Daylight	27
St Averil	55
Two Punch	61
Waquoit	15
Yarrow Brae	19
Yoh May Kenta	14

Massachusetts

Stallion	Mares Bred
Sociano	9
Sundance Ridge	6

Michigan

Stallion	Mares Bred
Allie's Punch	12
Arctic Cielo	6
Awesome Cannonball	14
Binalong	10
Career Best	12
Comedy Show	14
Creative	11
Demaloot Demashoot	13
Elusive Hour	24
Equality	24
Fire Blitz	21
Gainango	20
Haslam	6
Man From Eldorado	10
Meadow Prayer	18
Mr. Katowice	12
Native Factor	17
Perfect Circle	19
Quiet Enjoyment	12
Secret Romeo	17
Sky Approval	7
The Deputy (Ire)	41
Ulises	7

Minnesota

Stallion	Mares Bred
Appealing Skier	17
Ariel Chief	8
Ballado Chieftan	15
Demidoff	22
Dixie Power	10
Dynomania	17
Ghazi	37
Green West	8
Hero's Pleasure	7
Late Edition	11
Polished Brass	9
Quaker Hill	6
Sam Lord's Castle	7
Seattle Syn	7
Shotiche	15
Shot of Gold	11
Silk Song	8
Supremo	18
Tahkodha Hills	34
Willo' Sweep	10

Sires — Report of Mares Bred

Stallion	Mares Bred	Stallion	Mares Bred	Stallion	Mares Bred	Stallion	Mares Bred
Mississippi		Corker	8	The Trader's Echo	11	Western Expression	14
Dark Prince	8	Cozy Drive	7	Ticketless	10	Wheelaway	61
Minister Slew	10	Dancin Rahy	7	Tin Can Sailor	10	**North Carolina**	
Valid Victorious	7	Desert God	57	To Teras	25	Chelsey Cat	19
Missouri		Devon Lane	71	Touchdown Ky	14	Programable	8
Bananas	14	Distinctive Cat	20	Tricky Creek	28	**North Dakota**	
Liginsky	9	Dome	39	Union Mills	6	Academy	21
Pulpit Music	8	Dominique's Cat	23	Weeping Willow	8	Beeper	8
Montana		Don Lux	6	Your Eminence	44	Cats and Dogs	7
C Spot Go	6	Eishin Seattle	8	**New York**		Corporate Report	10
Double Dewars	9	Eishin Storm	10	Adonis	25	Eddie B. Ready	6
Gold Bayou T B	9	Elegant Cat	6	Aggadan	27	Emigrant Peak	8
Khalsa	6	Elijah's Song	7	Anasheed	59	Lush	6
Letter of Marque	6	El Sancho	13	Around the Cape	75	Nick (Chi)	14
Montbretia	10	Elusive Jazz	23	Artax	35	Paranoide (Arg)	14
Son's Corona	16	Emerald Jig	15	Badge	16	Rock Climb	10
Nebraska		Ex Federali	6	Best of Luck	12	Skipper Kipper	6
A Trio of Devils	13	Expected Program	15	Catienus	100	**Ohio**	
Blumin Affair	39	Fusaichi Zenon (Jpn)	24	Chief Seattle	82	Canvas	8
Box Buster	20	Gen Stormin'norman	9	Comeonmom	19	Cherokee Park	7
Dazzling Falls	20	Ghostly Moves	41	Contante (Arg)	10	Colony Key	25
Drinkwiththedevil	17	Gold Case	45	Desert Warrior	87	De Hero	6
Fighting Fantasy	9	Golden Ransom	15	Dream Run	9	Destitute	9
Flannigan	14	Grand Champion Cat	7	Eltish	51	Extra Effort	8
March Time	14	Groomstick	8	Fast Play	21	Gnarler	9
Not So Fast	10	Halory Hunter	37	Freud	85	Habayeb	23
Quest of the King	11	Hot War	10	Gold Fever	19	Kentucky Dane	8
Rhythm Bound	7	Houston Slue	9	Gone for Real	9	King Tutta	13
Shadow Hawk	39	Imperial Cat	13	Greeley's Galaxy	58	Mahogany Hall	6
Shawklit Player	31	Indies (GB)	20	Griffinite	39	Mercer Mill	12
Silent Bluff	20	Insinger	9	Ground Storm	8	Pacific Waves	11
Nevada		Iron Halo (Arg)	10	Here's Zealous	63	Polish Spray	7
Captain's Rebel	6	Isaypete	14	Hook and Ladder	124	Political Folly	20
New Jersey		Istintaj	8	Jade Hunter	34	Railway Cat	7
Capture the Gold	6	Joey the Student	7	Kalu	10	Risk and Reward	14
Close Up	27	King Bull	6	Key Contender	8	Swift Crusader	11
Crafty Friend	36	King of the Hunt	10	Legion Field	16	The Badger's Comin	15
Defrere	70	K. O. Punch	25	Lycius	13	Waist Gunner John	7
Deputy Warlock	11	Lazy Lode (Arg)	13	Manlove	7	**Oklahoma**	
Fastness (Ire)	45	Le Grande Danseur	20	Mayakovsky	38	Actor	8
Gerosa	12	Minister Eric	26	Meadaaar	6	All Storm	7
Hit the Trail	13	Mr. Trieste	16	Michael's Temper	7	Apollo	11
Iron Deputy	11	Night Fright	20	Midas Eyes	73	Back Packer	7
Lord of Cat	8	Ole'	10	Millennium Wind	27	Baltimore Gray	8
Master Phone	7	Paradis	11	Millions	10	Board Member	12
Mo Mon	43	Parentheses	10	Ommadon	9	Broadway Bullet	14
Mr. Nugget	21	Patsyprospect	12	Orville N Wilbur's	19	Burbank	23
Mr. Sinatra	14	Precocity	24	Our Frankie	6	Charleys Gamble	7
Private Interview	10	Premeditation	14	Peruvian	16	City of Peace	16
Unbridled Jet	20	Proud Irish	22	Polish Pro	6	City Sharpster	12
New Mexico		Quinton's Gold	18	Prime Timber	27	Concern	12
Abajo	51	Randy's Moon	9	Quigley	14	Confide	10
Aeneas	31	Red's Honor	16	Raffie's Majesty	29	Country Be Gold	18
Anziyan	10	Regal Groom	7	Read the Footnotes	67	Crafty Song	6
Avenue of Flags	28	Reuben	14	Redskin Warrior	6	Dance Master	31
Awesome Dividend	11	Roll Hennessy Roll	49	Red Tail Hawk	6	Dark Lightning	24
Bay Head King	57	Sable's Boy	9	Regal Classic	9	Day Trader	19
Bestbandintheland	6	Sadler Slew	8	Rizzi	6	Deal an Ace	6
B. G.'s Drone	6	Sandia Slew	11	Roaring Fever	69	Diamond	32
Call Me Cat	10	Scatmandu	44	Say Florida Sandy	57	Distinction	28
Caracal	18	Silver Season	27	Slice of Reality	12	Douglas Fir	11
Chopin	13	Slew the Deputy	7	Smokin Mel	6	Evansville Slew	61
Chueco	8	So Long Birdie	14	Squall Warning	6	Fashion Find	17
Comic Genius	35	Source	29	Stanislavsky	30	Fistfite	15
Con Artist	25	Squall	15	Take Me Out	11	Flying Baron	10
Copelan's Pache	17	Stagecoach	12	Talk Is Money	7	Forestwood	24
		Star Programmer	8	Ten Most Wanted	37	Garbu	22
		Storm of Goshen	21	Tomorrows Cat	56	Gold Regent	20
		Suave Prospect	20	Trick Me	7	Harriman	8
		Super Quercus (Fr)	14	True Direction	23		
		Survivor Slew	13	Uncle Camie	15		
		Tailfromthecrypt	8	Well Noted	23		
		The Black Rocket	9				

Sires — Report of Mares Bred

Stallion	Mares Bred
Inca Chief	33
Indy Talent	14
Indy Thunder	14
It'sallinthechase	12
Jack Wilson	10
Jazzman's Prospect	14
Jomax	6
Karate Kick	6
Kipling	70
Lendell Ray	14
Lucky Lionel	40
Maghnatis	7
Major Henry	12
Major Leaguer	10
May Day Warrior	13
Mister Deville	7
Monarch's Maze	36
My Liege	9
National Saint	19
New Way	6
Nicholas	34
Niner Bush	7
Norfield	17
Notable Beaux	7
Notable Cat	35
Ocean Terrace	18
Orange Power	10
Overview	15
Prize Cat	32
Quebracho	7
Rage	12
Rare Brick	21
River Eagle	7
Riverside	6
Rojo Dinero	12
Sasha's Prospect	17
Scarlet Storm	6
Seeking Greatness	36
Semoran	24
Senor Speedy	13
Shoer of Power	6
Skip Skip	6
Slewship	9
Speak	15
Star of the Crop	11
State Craft	18
St. Dehere	10
Strategic Partner	27
Tarakam	16
Thorn Cat	14
Under David's Wing	10
Unome	6
Uptown Miami	6
Wee Thunder	17
Wild Horses	11
Wild Rex	8
Wood Reply	12
Zayzoom	8

Oregon

Stallion	Mares Bred
Airdrie Apache	9
Baquero	14
Cascadian	35
Count Me In	30
Dark Feather	7
Ex Marks the Cop	19
Harbor the Gold	53
Klinsman (Ire)	11
Malarkey Lane	7
Panoramic	8
Prospected	6
Seattle Shamus	53
Timber Legend	14
Tuxedo Suit	7
Unbridled's Comet	14

Pennsylvania

Stallion	Mares Bred
Activist	19
Aisle	10
Aquarian Prince	10
Banker's Gold	24
Basketball Court	7
Brian Is Golden	15
Buckle Down Ben	40
Certain Storm	23
Cetewayo	30
Changeintheweather	32
Coastal Storm	13
Cocky	7
Congressionalhonor	95
Digamist	9
Duckhorn	25
Eastern Daydream	7
Ecliptical	6
Harley Quinn	8
Harry the Hat	14
Kandaly	7
Kentucky Pride	8
Lite the Fuse	75
Lord At Law	8
Lord Ofthe Thunder	11
Lyracist	8
Nudge	8
Patton	26
Pies Prospect	14
Power by Far	20
Pretty Wild	31
Quarry	25
Real Quiet	85
Revival Song	9
Rimrod	30
Rubiyat	9
Show Tune	22
Silver Leader	15
Siphon (Brz)	36
Smart Guy	11
Song of the Sword	14
Sort It Out	7
Special Times	21
Spectaculardynasty	9
Super Victory	6
Tekken (Ire)	8
This Fleet Is Due	6
Tricky Mister	9
Valid Request	8
Will's Way	18

Puerto Rico

Stallion	Mares Bred
Alter Ego	6
Balcony	10
Bargello	12
Billions	41
Cape Cod	12
Casanova Star	20
Cats Castle	28
Crowd	11
D' Coach	11
Despreciado	13
Divac	10
Dixie Dynamo	17
Don Guido	55
Elshaan	18
Elusive Chris	13
Eqtesaad	31
Figure of Speech	16
Flamenco	15
Fort La Roca	11
Frisk Me Now	20
Fusaichi Ruler	27
Galic Boy	22
Greedy	24
Harbor Master	8
Hard Charger	6
Johnny Jones	9
Just Typical	38
King's Crown	23
Marshall Greeley	19
My Favorite Dream	18
Myfavorite Place	26
My Man Ryan	7
Ordway	7
Plato	26
Portentoso	10
Shawnee Warrior	10
Solari	12
Stake Procpect	9
Striking Lord	7
Sudden Thunder	49
Tamhid	11
Virtua Cop	22
Voice of Destiny	6
Wonder Bird	8

South Carolina

Stallion	Mares Bred
Arouse	9
Bias	7
Cat in Town	7
Crush	6
Dynamometer	10
East of Easy	10
Just a Miner	18
Lad	10
Lake Highlands	8
Ride the Storm	16

South Dakota

Stallion	Mares Bred
Emailit	6
Finn McCool	22
Neff Lake	10
Skye'n Thunder	8
Storm of the Night	37
Testimony	6

Tennessee

Stallion	Mares Bred
Allamystique	21
Forest Fire	7
Head West	15
Take the Shot	8

Texas

Stallion	Mares Bred
Al Sabin	10
A.p Jetter	6
A P Valentine	7
Awestruck	6
B L's Dixie Band	11
Banderas	6
Baron de Vaux	11
Blue Eyed Streaker	12
Boone's Mill	10
Byars	15
Captain Countdown	44
Cathode	6
Cat Strike	6
Chief Three Sox	15
Churchhill	7
City Street	17
Commanchero	10
Conroe	10
Count the Deposit	6
Crap Shooter	11
Day of the Cat	31
Devils Pulpit	7
Dixieland Heat	22
Dove Hunt	11
Dynameaux	8
Early Flyer	40
El Leopardo	32
Excellent Secret	6
Famous Forest	13
Flaming Quest (GB)	11
Flying Kris	8
Georgia Crown	14
Gold Alert	20
Gold Legend	30
Gone East	9
Grande's Grandslam	17
Grave Digger	9
Half Fast George	6
Heckle	23
High Estate (Ire)	9
Hi Teck Man	18
Improper Again	12
Inca Chief Sap	6
Indian Prospector (Fr)	7
In the Headlights	6
Intimidator	28
Irisheyesareflying	19
Itchetucknee	14
Jadacus	16
Karen's Cat	20
King of the Heap	12
Lil's Lad	23
Lots of Slew	8
Lucky So n' So	6
Magic Cat	24
Maverick	39
Memento	9
Menhal	24
Middle Man	9
Midway Road	41
Miguel Cervantes	15
Missouri Brave	7
New Trieste	46
Olmos	16
Open Forum	32
Orbit's Revenge	8
Parade Ground	7
Pass the Peace	6
Pete's Cat	6
Pink Duck	9
Pistareen	11
Porto Varas	10
Positively Gold	7
Power Storm	14
Primal Storm	37
Proud Halo	12
Ra Ra Superstar	16
Running Stag	47
Safado	10
Sam Again	7
Sand Ridge	27
Sawgrass	6
Seeking a Home	23
Seneca Jones	6
Senor Amigo	16
Sequoia Grove	15
Serazzo	6
Shaquin	12
Silent Picture	14
Sir Bedivere	20
Slew Gulch	8
Special Rate	37

Sires — Report of Mares Bred

Stallion	Mares Bred	Stallion	Mares Bred	Stallion	Mares Bred	Stallion	Mares Bred
Struggler (GB)	6	Top Account	15	Commitisize	8	**Ontario**	
Sudden Storm	6	Trail City	40	Deputy Country	18	Ascot Knight	13
Sunny's Irish	7	Tribunal	57	Desperately	12	Best of the Bests (Ire)	88
Supreme Cat	31	Tristaino	8	Dream Tripper	16	Bluesbreaker	6
Swamp	6	Tropic Lightning	11	Easy Climb	8	Bold Executive	48
Texas City	18	Waiting Game	19	Elusive Star	8	Bold n' Flashy	11
Thats Our Buck	21	You and I	34	Esteem	17	Brite Adam	6
The Prime Minister	12	**West Virginia**		Haus of Dehere	14	Cat's At Home	8
Tinners Way	20			Highland Ruckus	33	Compadre	9
Top Gear	9	Black Tie Affair (Ire)	40	Important Notice	9	Copper Karat	6
Touch Tone	8	Bop	44	Just a Cat	10	Dance to Destiny	14
Traffic Circle	11	Castine	6	Kahuna Jack	10	Devil Begone	20
Trancus	6	Civilisation	31	Kiridashi	60	Domasca Dan	22
Truluck	31	Classy E. T.	9	Lanciano (Ger)	10	Fort Chaffee	12
Uncle Abbie	54	Constant Escort	8	Lost Canyon (GB)	13	Foxtrail	7
Usedtobeaferrari	10	Country Only	22	Magic Prospect	7	Gone Fishin	16
Valid Expectations	57	Dancinwiththedevil	8	Mandolin Wind	10	Guaranteed Gold	15
Valid Flight	19	Danish Gold	10	Max Forever	9	Gun Power	14
Walesa	8	Deputy Rummy	15	Nicholas Ds	15	Hubba Hubba	11
War	7	Devon Deputy	11	Othello	15	Impeachment	27
Wild Eyed Cat	7	Dixie's Wild Again	7	Pike Place Gold	10	Iskandar Elakbar	8
Wimbledon	36	Emancipator	12	Real West	17	Kinshasa	12
Zap	16	Endeavouring	9	Rosetti	18	Line of Departure	15
Utah		Family Calling	26	Run to Victory	13	Lodge Hill	9
		Fear the Cape	12	Smile Again	25	Mobil	38
Blessed Trinity	11	Green Fee	18	Tempered Appeal	30	Mr. Jester	44
Brave Call	9	Gunnerside	18	The Key Rainbow (Ire)	6	Mr. Scotty	17
File Away	9	Inner Harbour	17	Tiger Trap	36	My Way Only	7
Holy Mountain	12	Kokand	38	Tossofthecoin	9	Niigon	91
Joe Who (Brz)	42	Limit Out	16	Zuppardo's Future	12	Old Forester	123
Nick of Time	8	Luftikus	42	**British Columbia**		One Way Love	38
Reciprocate	15	Make Your Mark	9			Parisianprospector	8
Wild Escapade	54	Makin	8	Acceptable	17	Paynes Bay	17
Virginia		Meadow Monster	48	Alfaari	16	Peaks and Valleys	47
		Medford	29	Amaruk	9	Philanthropist	60
Aaron's Gold	11	Mesopotamia	16	Bright Valour	10	Raj Waki	9
Ball's Bluff	6	Mike's Memory	7	Catrail	11	Russian Tsar	7
Mr. Executioner	13	My Boy Adam	15	Finality	41	Saffir	16
Split	6	Peak Dancer	12	Flaming West	12	Sambuca On Ice	17
Up Periscope	14	Prints of Peace	18	Flammabull	6	Sardegna	17
Zillionair	7	Prized	36	Joey Franco	24	Sato	6
Washington		Prospect Bay	21	Katahaula County	42	Shelter	8
		Race On Green	23	Light of Mine	12	Simple Faith	10
Basket Weave	12	Reparations	14	Mass Market	26	Single Remarque	6
Big Stan B	6	Rich Deeds	18	Mazel Trick	42	Solomon's Decree	13
Cahill Road	41	R. S. V. P. Please	10	New Advantage	7	Strut the Stage	33
Chumaree	30	Run Softly	12	Nightofthegaelics	12	Survivalist	70
Consigliere (GB)	9	Sandlot Star	18	Orchid's Devil	9	Swampster	15
Courageous King	12	San Mont Andreas	38	Perfect Score	7	Tejano Run	26
Delineator	53	Select Session	7	Persian Star	6	Tomahawk	35
Demon Warlock	12	Slew O'Quoit	7	Polish	11	Trajectory	63
Devine Cozzene	12	Spreebee	8	Quiet Cash	47	Union Place	12
Exit to Rio	7	Stored	14	Regal Intention	15	Valid N Bold	16
Free At Last	47	Stritzel	10	Royal Albert Hall	9	Where's the Ring	37
Go	7	Unbridled Mate	6	Silver Fox	7	Whiskey Wisdom	34
Hampton Bay	6	Valiant Nature	8	Stephanotis	33	**Saskatchewan**	
Heavenly Search	15	Weshaam	14	Storm Victory	41		
He's Tops	25	Windsor Castle	53	Terrell	52	Band Aight	6
Ito the Hammer	9	Zizou	8	The Lady's Groom	15	Blowin de Turn	8
Just Ruler	10	**Wisconsin**		Vying Victor	60	Bound by Honor	12
Kasparov	16			Wandering	28	Dream Guide	9
Katowice	25	Be Valiant	9	Western Trick	13	Favorite Affair	7
Kentucky Lucky	11	Gazebo	13	Yoonevano	22	Hell Roaring Creek	9
Liberty Gold	20	**Alberta**		**Manitoba**		Just Cash	6
Matricule	30					McCallister's Risk	6
Matty G	56	Alydeed	31	Battle Cat	14	Nation Wide News	12
Nacheezmo	18	Big E E	14	Best to Be King	8	Sea Wall	20
Outing	13	Birdzilla	17	Fabulous Champ	12	Serious Business (Ire)	7
Patriot Noise	7	Brunswick	12	Going Commando	23	Striking Song	12
Private Gold	33	Cappuchino	30	Hurricane Center	10	You've Got Action	10
Sirpa	6	Captain Bodgit	31	Quadrophonic Sound	6		
Stolen Gold	64	Castle Arms	6	Ran South	9		
Stormy Destiny	6	Cobra King	44	Slippery Gator	14		

BROODMARES
Broodmares of the Year
As awarded by the Kentucky Thoroughbred Owners and Breeders Association

2007—BETTER THAN HONOUR
1996 b. m. Deputy Minister—Blush With Pride, by Blushing Groom (Fr)
Breeder, Foxfield (Ky.). Owners, Southern Equine Stable and John G. Sikura.
Dam of 7 foals, 4 starters, 4 winners, including **RAGS TO RICHES**, 5 wins, $1,342,528, champion three-year-old filly, 2007 Belmont S. (G1), Kentucky Oaks (G1), etc.; **JAZIL**, 2 wins, $890,532, 2006 Belmont S. (G1); **CASINO DRIVE**, 2 wins, $185,282, Peter Pan S. (G2).

2006—CARA RAFAELA
1993 gr. or ro. m., Quiet American—Oil Fable, by Spectacular Bid
Breeder, Mike G. Rutherford Sr. (Ky.). Owner, Darley.
Dam of 8 foals, 5 starters, 3 winners, including **BERNARDINI**, 6 wins, $3,060,480, 2006 champion three-year-old male, 2006 Preakness S. (G1), etc.

2005—BABY ZIP
1991 b. m., Relaunch—Thirty Zip, by Tri Jet
Breeder, J. Robert Harris Jr. Owner, Frank Stronach.
Dam of 11 foals, 8 starters, 6 winners, including **GHOSTZAPPER**, 9 wins, $3,446,120, 2004 Horse of the Year, 2004 champion older male, 2004 Breeders' Cup Classic (G1), 2005 Metropolitan H. (G1), etc.; **CITY ZIP**, 9 wins, $818,225, 2000 Hopeful S. (G1), 2000 Saratoga Special S. (G2), etc.

2004—DEAR BIRDIE
1987 ch. m., Storm Bird—Hush Dear, by Silent Screen
Breeder, Echo Valley Horse Farm Inc. (Ky.). Owner, Marylou Whitney.
Dam of 13 foals, 11 starters, all winners, including **BIRD TOWN**, 4 wins, $871,251, 2003 champion three-year-old filly, 2003 Kentucky Oaks (G1), etc.; **BIRDSTONE**, 5 wins, $1,575,600, 2004 Belmont S. (G1), etc.

2003—PROSPECTORS DELITE
1989 ch. m., Mr. Prospector—Up the Flagpole, by Hoist the Flag
Breeder, W. S. Farish (Ky.). Owners, William S. Farish, James Elkins Jr., and W. Temple Webber Jr.
Dam of 5 foals, all winners, including **MINESHAFT**, 10 wins, $2,283,402, 2003 Horse of the Year, 2003 champion older male, 2003 Jockey Club Gold Cup S. (G1), etc.; **TOMISUE'S DELIGHT**, 7 wins, $1,207,537, 1998 Personal Ensign H. (G1), **ROCK SLIDE, MONASHEE MOUNTAIN, DELTA MUSIC**.

2002—TOUSSAUD
1989 dk. b. or br. m., El Gran Senor—Image of Reality, by In Reality
Breeder, Juddmonte Farms Inc. (Ky.). Owner, Juddmonte Farms
Dam of 10 foals, 7 starters, 6 winners, including **EMPIRE MAKER**, 4 wins, $1,985,800, 2003 Belmont S. (G1), etc.; **CHESTER HOUSE**, 6 wins, $1,944,545, 2000 Arlington Million S. (G1), etc.; **HONEST LADY**, 6 wins, $894,168, 2000 Santa Monica H. (G1); **CHISELLING**, 3 wins, $410,000, 2002 Secretariat S. (G1), etc.; **DECARCHY**, 6 wins, $703,862, 2002 Frank E. Kilroe Mile H. (G2), etc.

2001—TURKO'S TURN
1992 ch. m., Turkoman—Turbo Launch, by Relaunch
Breeder, John F. Dolan (Ky.). Owner, The Thoroughbred Corp.
Dam of 9 foals, 5 starters, 4 winners, including **POINT GIVEN**, 9 wins, $3,968,500, 2001 Horse of the Year, 2001 champion three-year-old male, 2001 Preakness S. (G1), etc.

2000—PRIMAL FORCE
1987 b. m., Blushing Groom (Fr)—Prime Prospect, by Mr. Prospector
Breeders, Mr. and Mrs. Bertram R. Firestone (Ky.). Owner, Frank Stronach.
Dam of 11 foals, 5 starters, all winners, including **MACHO UNO**, 6 wins, $1,851,803, 2000 champion two-year-old male, 2000 Breeders' Cup Juvenile (G1), etc.; **AWESOME AGAIN**, 9 wins, $4,374,590, 1998 Breeders' Cup Classic (G1), etc.

1999—ANNE CAMPBELL
1973 b. m., Never Bend—Repercussion, by *Tatan
Breeder, Mill House (Ky.). Owner, Arthur B. Hancock III.
Dam of 14 foals, 10 starters, 7 winners, including **MENIFEE**, 5 wins, $1,732,000, 1999 Haskell Invitational H. (G1), etc.; **DESERT WINE**, 8 wins, $1,618,043, 1984 Hollywood Gold Cup (G1), etc.

1998—IN NEON
1982 b. m., Ack Ack—Shamara, by Dewan
Breeder, Clairmont Farm (Ky.). Owner, John Franks.
Dam of 7 foals, all starters, 6 winners, including **SHARP CAT**, 15 wins, $2,032,575, 1998 Beldame S. (G1), etc.; **ROYAL ANTHEM**, 4 wins, $1,876,876, 1998 Canadian International S. (Can-G1), etc.; **STAR RECRUIT**, 5 wins, $807,200, 1991 Alysheba S. (G3), etc.

1997—SLIGHTLY DANGEROUS
1979 b. m., Roberto—Where You Lead, by Raise a Native
Breeder, Alan Clore (Ky.). Owner, Juddmonte Farms.
Dam of 13 foals, 11 starters, 10 winners, including **COMMANDER IN CHIEF**, 5 wins, $1,311,514, 1993 champion three-year-old male in Eur, 1993 Epsom Derby (Eng-G1), etc.; **WARNING (GB)**, 8 wins, $937,280, 1987 champion two-year-old male in Eng, 1988 champion three-year-old male in Eng, 1988 Queen Elizabeth II S. (Eng-G1), etc.; **YASHMAK**, 4 wins, $529,382, 1997 Flower Bowl Invitational H. (G1), etc.; **DUSHYANTOR**, 5 wins, $1,197,570, 1996 Great Voltigeur S. (Eng-G2), **JIBE**.

1996—PERSONAL ENSIGN
1984 b. m., Private Account—Grecian Banner, by Hoist the Flag
Breeder, Ogden Phipps (Ky.). Owner, Ogden Phipps, Phipps Stable.
Dam of 11 foals, 9 starters, 8 winners, including **MY FLAG**, 6 wins, $1,557,057, 1995 Breeders' Cup Juvenile Fillies (G1), etc.; **MINER'S MARK**, 6 wins, $967,170, 1993 Jockey Club Gold Cup (G1), etc.; **TRADITIONALLY**, 5 wins, $495,660, 2001 Oaklawn H. (G1).

Broodmares of the Year

Year	Broodmare	Year	Broodmare	Year	Broodmare	Year	Broodmare	Year	Broodmare
2007	Better Than Honour	1994	Fall Aspen	1981	Natashka	1968	Delta	1955	Iron Reward
2006	Cara Rafaela	1993	Glowing Tribute	1980	Key Bridge	1967	Kerala	1954	Traffic Court
2005	Baby Zip	1992	Weekend Surprise	1979	Smartaire	1966	Juliets Nurse	1953	Gaga
2004	Dear Birdie	1991	Toll Booth	1978	Primonetta	1965	Pocahontas	1952	Ace Card
2003	Prospectors Delite	1990	Kamar	1977	Sweet Tooth	1964	Maid of Flight	1951	*Alpenstock III
2002	Toussaud	1989	Relaxing	1976	*Gazala II	1963	Misty Morn	1950	Hildene
2001	Turko's Turn	1988	Grecian Banner	1975	Shenanigans	1962	Track Medal	1949	Easy Lass
2000	Primal Force	1987	Banja Luka	1974	Cosmah	1961	Striking	1948	Our Page
1999	Anne Campbell	1986	Too Bald	1973	Somethingroyal	1960	Siama	1947	Potheen
1998	In Neon	1985	Dunce Cap II	1972	*Moment of Truth II	1959	*Knight's Daughter	1946	Bloodroot
1997	Slightly Dangerous	1984	Hasty Queen II	1971	Iberia	1958	Miss Disco		
1996	Personal Ensign	1983	Courtly Dee	1970	Levee	1957	Belle Jeep		
1995	Northern Sunset (Ire)	1982	Best in Show	1969	All Beautiful	1956	Swoon		

Broodmares — Broodmares of the Year

1995—NORTHERN SUNSET (IRE)
1977 ch. m., Northfields—Moss Greine, by *Ballymoss
Breeder, Basil Brindly (Ire). **Owner**, Virginia Kraft Payson.
Dam of 13 foals, 12 starters, 11 winners, including **ST. JOVITE**, 6 wins, $1,604,439, 1992 Horse of the Year in Eur, 1991 champion two-year-old male in Ire, 1992 Irish Derby (Ire-G1), etc.; **SALEM DRIVE**, 13 wins, $1,046,065, 1987 Bougainvillea H. (G2), etc.; **LAC OUIMET**, 12 wins, $817,863, 1986 Jim Dandy S. (G2), etc.; **L'CARRIERE**, 8 wins, $1,726,175, 1996 Saratoga Cup H. (G3), etc.

1994—FALL ASPEN
1976 ch. m., Pretense—Change Water, by Swaps
Breeder, Joseph M. Roebling (Ky.). **Owner**, John Magnier.
Dam of 14 foals, 13 starters, 12 winners, including **TIMBER COUNTRY**, 5 wins, $1,560,400, 1994 champion two-year-old male, 1995 Preakness S. (G1), etc.; **BIANCONI**, 3 wins, $134,520, 1998 Diadem S. (Eng-G2); **FORT WOOD**, 3 wins, $359,995, 1993 Grand Prix de Paris (Fr-G1), etc.; **NORTHERN ASPEN**, 5 wins, $253,678, 1987 Gamely H. (G1), etc.; **HAMAS (IRE)**, 5 wins, $237,814, 1993 July Cup S. (Eng-G1), etc.; **COLORADO DANCER (IRE)**, 3 wins, $203,389, 1989 Prix de Pomone (Fr-G2), etc.; **ELLE SEULE**, 3 wins, $101,478, 1986 Prix d'Astarte (Fr-G2); **MAZZACANO (GB)**, 3 wins, $153,421, 1989 Goodwood Cup (Eng-G3); **PRINCE OF THIEVES**, 2 wins, $368,474.

1993—GLOWING TRIBUTE
1973 b. m., Graustark—Admiring, by Hail to Reason
Breeder, Paul Mellon (Va.). **Owner**, John R. Gaines.
Dam of 12 foals, 10 starters, 9 winners, including **SEA HERO**, 6 wins, $2,929,869, 1993 Kentucky Derby (G1), etc.; **HERO'S HONOR**, 7 wins, $499,025, 1984 Bowling Green H. (G1), etc.; **GLOWING HONOR**, 6 wins, $296,450, 1988, '89 Diana H. (G2), etc.; **WILD APPLAUSE**, 5 wins, $240,136, 1984 Diana H. (G2); **CORONATION CUP**, 3 wins, $172,181, 1994 Nijana S. (G3); **MACKIE**, 3 wins, $164,579, 1996 Busher S. (G3); **SEATTLE GLOW**, 4 wins, $69,023.

1992—WEEKEND SURPRISE
1980 b. m., Secretariat—Lassie Dear, by Buckpasser
Breeders, W. S. Farish III and W. S. Kilroy (Ky.). **Owners**, W. S. Farish III and W. S. Kilroy.
Dam of 14 foals, 12 starters, 9 winners, including **A.P. INDY**, 8 wins, $2,979,815, 1992 Horse of the Year, 1992 champion three-year-old male, 1992 Belmont S. (G1), etc.; **SUMMER SQUALL**, 13 wins, $1,844,282, 1990 Preakness S. (G1), etc.; **WELCOME SURPRISE**, 2 wins, $143,574, 2000 Dogwood S. (G3); **EAVESDROPPER**, 3 wins, $167,794.

1991—TOLL BOOTH
1971 b. m., Buckpasser—Missy Baba, by *My Babu
Breeder, John M. Schiff (Ky.). **Owner**, Lazy Lane Farms.
Dam of 13 foals, 12 starters, 11 winners, including **PLUGGED NICKLE**, 11 wins, $647,206, 1980 champion sprinter, 1980 Florida Derby (G1), etc.; **CHRISTIECAT**, 11 wins, $799,745, 1992 Flower Bowl H. (G1), etc.; **KEY TO THE BRIDGE**, 7 wins, $289,747, 1988 Beaugay H. (G3); **TOLL FEE**, 7 wins, $333,917; **TOLL KEY**, 9 wins, $290,218; **IDLE GOSSIP**, 5 wins, $101,721; **TOKENS ONLY**, 4 wins, $50,455.

1990—KAMAR
1976 b. m., Key to the Mint—Square Angel, by Quadrangle
Breeder, E. P. Taylor (Can). **Owner**, Heronwood Farm.
Dam of 9 foals, 8 starters, 7 winners, including **KEY TO THE MOON**, 13 wins, $714,536, 1984 champion three-year-old male in Can, 1984 Discovery H. (G3), etc.; **GORGEOUS**, 8 wins, $1,171,370, 1989 Ashland S. (G1), etc.; **SEASIDE ATTRACTION**, 4 wins, $272,541, 1990 Kentucky Oaks (G1); **HIAAM**, 3 wins, $48,081, 1986 Princess Margaret S. (Eng-G3), etc.

1989—RELAXING
1976 b. m., Buckpasser—Marking Time, by To Market
Breeder, Ogden Phipps (Ky.). **Owner**, Ogden Phipps.
Dam of 12 foals, 9 starters, all winners, including **EASY GOER**, 14 wins, $4,873,770, 1988 champion two-year-old male, 1989 Belmont S. (G1), etc.; **EASY NOW**, 4 wins, $359,466, 1992 Go for Wand S. (G1), etc.; **CADILLACING**, 7 wins, $268,137, 1988 Ballerina S. (G1), etc.

1988—GRECIAN BANNER
1974 dk. b. or br. m., Hoist the Flag—*Dorine, by Aristophanes
Breeder, Ogden Phipps (Ky.). **Owner**, Ogden Phipps.
Dam of 7 foals, 5 starters, all winners, including **PERSONAL ENSIGN**, 13 wins, $1,679,880, 1988 champion older female, 1996 Broodmare of the Year, 1988 Breeders' Cup Distaff (G1), etc.; **PERSONAL FLAG**, 8 wins, $1,258,924, 1988 Suburban H. (G1), etc.

1987—BANJA LUKA
1968 b. m., Double Jay—Legato, by Dark Star
Breeder, Howard B. Keck (Ky.). **Owner**, Howard B. Keck.
Dam of 9 foals, all starters, 7 winners, including **FERDINAND**, 8 wins, $3,777,978, 1987 Horse of the Year, 1987 champion older male, 1986 Kentucky Derby (G1), etc.; **DONNA INEZ**, 4 wins, $101,275; **JAYSTON**, 7 wins, $92,143; **DANCING**, 4 wins, $77,925; **ANCIENT ART**, 4 wins, $74,250; **PLINTH**, 3 wins, $65,980.

1986—TOO BALD
1964 dk. b. or br. m., Bald Eagle—Hidden Talent, by Dark Star
Breeder, H. F. Guggenheim (Ky.). **Owner**, North Ridge Farm.
Dam of 13 foals, 11 starters, all winners, including **CAPOTE**, 3 wins, $714,470, 1986 champion two-year-old male, 1986 Breeders' Cup Juvenile S. (G1), etc.; **EXCELLER**, 5 wins, $1,674,587, 1978 Jockey Club Gold Cup (G1), etc.; **VAGUELY HIDDEN**, 8 wins, $239,313, 1990 New Jersey Turf Classic S. (G3); **AMERICAN STANDARD**, 5 wins, $180,120; **BALDSKI**, 7 wins, $103,214.

1985—DUNCE CAP II
1960 dk. b. or br. m., Tom Fool—Bright Coronet, by Bull Lea
Breeder, Greentree Stud Inc. (Ky.). **Owner**, Greentree Stud Inc.
Dam of 11 foals, 8 starters, all winners, including **LATE BLOOMER**, 11 wins, $512,040, 1978 champion older female, 1978 Beldame S. (G1), etc.; **JOHNNY APPLESEED**, 4 wins, $91,910, 1976 Louisiana Derby (G2); **LATE ACT**, 9 wins, $661,089, 1985 Cliff Hanger H. (G3), etc.

1984—HASTY QUEEN II
1963 dk. b. or br. m., One Count—Queen Hopeful, by Roman
Breeder, A. E. Reuben (Ky.). **Owners**, Robert E. Courtney and Robert B. Congleton.
Dam of 16 foals, 14 starters, 12 winners, including **FIT TO FIGHT**, 14 wins, $1,042,075, 1984 Brooklyn H. (G1), etc.; **HASTY FLYER**, 10 wins, $293,663, 1974 Round Table H. (G3), etc.; **HASTY TAM**, 16 wins, $211,738; **PLAYFUL QUEEN**, 5 wins, $101,837; **MICHAEL NAVONOD**, 6 wins, $86,380; **HASTY CUTIE**, 8 wins, $63,639.

1983—COURTLY DEE
1968 dk. b. or br. m., Never Bend—Tulle, by War Admiral
Breeder, Donald Unger (Ky.). **Owners**, Helen Alexander, David Aykroyd, and Helen Groves.
Dam of 18 foals, 17 starters, 15 winners, including **ALTHEA**, 8 wins, $1,275,255, 1983 champion two-year-old filly, 1984 Arkansas Derby (G1), etc.; **ALI OOP**, 7 wins, $174,020, 1976 Sapling S. (G1); **KETOH**, 8 wins, $173,550, 1985 Cowdin S. (G1); **AQUILEGIA**, 8 wins, $446,081, 1993 New York H. (G2), etc.; **TWINING**, 5 wins, $238,140, 1994 Peter Pan S. (G2), etc.; **AISHAH**, 6 wins, $169,340, 1990 Rare Perfume S. (G2); **NATIVE COURIER**, 14 wins, $522,635, 1981 Bernard Baruch H. (G3), etc.; **PRINCESS OOLA**, 5 wins, $108,291.

1982—BEST IN SHOW
1965 ch. m., Traffic Judge—Stolen Hour, by Mr. Busher
Breeder, Philip Connors (Ky.). **Owners**, Mr. and Mrs. Darrell Brown.
Dam of 18 foals, 12 starters, 9 winners, including **MALINOWSKI**, 2 wins, 1975 champion two-year-old in Ire, 1976 Ladbroke Craven S. (Eng-G3); **BLUSH WITH PRIDE**, 6 wins, $536,807, 1982 Kentucky Oaks (G1), etc.; **GIELGUD**, 1 win, $56,635, 1980 Champagne S. (Eng-G2); **MONROE**, 3 wins, $34,422, 1980 Ballyogan S. (Ire-G3), etc.

1981—NATASHKA
1963 dk. b. or br. m., Dedicate—Natasha, by *Nasrullah
Breeder, Greentree Stud Inc. (Ky.). **Owner**, W. S. Farish III.
Dam of 9 foals, 7 starters, all winners, including **GREGORIAN**, 4 wins, $194,912, 1980 Joe McGrath Memorial S. (Ire-G1), etc.;

Broodmares — Broodmares of the Year

TRULY BOUND, 9 wins, $382,449, 1980 Arlington-Washington Lassie S. (G2), etc.; **IVORY WAND**, 5 wins, $97,452, 1976 Test S. (G3); **BLOOD ROYAL**, 4 wins, $28,870, 1975 Jockey Club Cup (Eng-G3), etc.; **ARKADINA**, 2 wins, $79,830, Athasi S. (Ire-G3), etc.

1980—KEY BRIDGE
1959 b. m., *Princequillo—Blue Banner, by War Admiral
Breeder, Paul Mellon (Va.). **Owner**, Paul Mellon.
Dam of 12 foals, 8 starters, 7 winners, including **FORT MARCY**, 21 wins, $1,109,791, 1970 Horse of the Year, 1967, '68, '70 champion turf male, 1970 champion older male, 1967, '70 Washington D.C. International S., etc.; **KEY TO THE MINT**, 14 wins, $576,015, 1972 champion three-year-old male, 1973 Suburban H. (G1), etc.; **KEY TO CONTENT**, 7 wins, $354,772, 1981 United Nations H. (G1), etc.; **KEY TO THE KINGDOM**, 7 wins, $109,590, 1974 Stymie H. (G3).

1979—SMARTAIRE
1962 dk. b. or br. m., *Quibu—Art Teacher, by Olympia
Breeder, F. W. Hooper (Al.). **Owners**, Mr. and Mrs. James P. Ryan.
Dam of 12 foals, all starters, 10 winners, including **SMART ANGLE**, 7 wins, $414,217, 1979 champion two-year-old filly, 1979 Frizette S. (G1), etc.; **SMARTEN**, 11 wins, $716,426, 1979 American Derby (G2), etc.; **QUADRATIC**, 6 wins, $233,941, 1977 Cowdin S. (G2); **SMART HEIRESS**, 6 wins, $154,999.

1978—PRIMONETTA
1958 ch. m., Swaps—Banquet Bell, by Polynesian
Breeder, John W. Galbreath (Ky.). **Owner**, John W. Galbreath.
Dam of 7 foals, 6 starters, all winners, including **CUM LAUDE LAURIE**, 8 wins, $405,207, 1977 Beldame S. (G1), etc.; **PRINCE THOU ART**, 3 wins, $167,902, 1975 Florida Derby (G1); **MAUD MULLER**, 3 wins, $138,383, 1974 Gazelle H. (G2), etc.; **GRENFALL**, 4 wins, $19,467, 1971 Gallinule S. (Ire-G2), etc.

1977—SWEET TOOTH
1965 b. m., On-and-On—Plum Cake, by Ponder
Breeder, Calumet Farm (Ky.). **Owner**, Calumet Farm.
Dam of 13 foals, 10 starters, 8 winners, including **OUR MIMS**, 6 wins, $368,034, 1977 champion three-year-old filly, 1977 Coaching Club American Oaks (G1), etc.; **ALYDAR**, 14 wins, $957,195, 1978 Blue Grass S. (G1), etc.; **SUGAR AND SPICE**, 5 wins, $257,046, 1980 Mother Goose S. (G1), etc.

1976—*GAZALA II
1964 dk. b. or br. m, Dark Star—*Belle Angevine, by L'Amiral
Breeder, Nelson Bunker Hunt (Fr). **Owner**, Nelson Bunker Hunt.
Dam of 10 foals, 8 starters, 7 winners, including **YOUTH**, 8 wins, $716,146, 1976 champion three-year-old in Fr, 1976 champion turf male, 1976 Prix du Jockey Club (Fr-G1), etc.; **MISSISSIPIAN**, 3 wins; $248,520, 1973 champion two-year-old in Fr, 1973 Grand Criterium (Fr-G1), etc.; **GONZALES**, 4 wins, $103,968, 1980 Irish St. Leger (Ire-G1), etc.; **SILKY BABY**, 2 wins, $51,351, 1981 Prix de Guiche (Fr-G3); **BEST OF BOTH**, 6 wins $242,150.

1975—SHENANIGANS
1963 gr. m., Native Dancer—Bold Irish, by Fighting Fox
Breeder, Stuart S. Janney Jr. (Md.). **Owner**, Locust Hill Farm.
Dam of 6 foals, all winners, including **RUFFIAN**, 10 wins, $313,428, 1974 champion two-year-old filly, 1975 champion three-year-old filly, 1975 Filly Triple Crown, 1975 Coaching Club American Oaks (G1), etc.; **ICECAPADE**, 13 wins, $256,468, 1973 William duPont Jr. H. (G2); **BUCKFINDER**, 9 wins, $230,513, 1978 William duPont Jr. H. (G2), etc.

1974—COSMAH
1953 b. m., Cosmic Bomb—Almahmoud, by *Mahmoud
Breeder, Henry H. Knight (Ky.). **Owner**, John R. Gaines.
Dam of 15 foals, 10 starters, 9 winners, including **TOSMAH**, 23 wins, $612,588, 1963 champion two-year-old filly, 1964 champion three-year-old filly, 1964 champion handicap female, 1964 Beldame S., etc.; **HALO**, 9 wins, $259,553, 1974 United Nations H. (G1), etc.; **FATHERS IMAGE**, 7 wins, $173,318; **MARIBEAU**, 4 wins, $20,925.

1973—SOMETHINGROYAL
1952 b. m., *Princequillo—Imperatrice, by Caruso
Breeder, Mr. C. T. Chenery (Va.). **Owner**, Meadow Stable.
Dam of 18 foals, 15 starters, 11 winners, including **SECRETARIAT**, 16 wins, $1,316,808, 1972, 1973 Horse of the Year, 1972 champion two-year-old male, 1973 champion three-year-old male, 1973 champion turf male, 1973 Triple Crown, 1973 Kentucky Derby (G1), etc.; **SIR GAYLORD**, 10 wins, $237,404, 1961 Sapling S., etc.; **FIRST FAMILY**, 7 wins, $188,040, 1966 Gulfstream Park H., etc.; **SYRIAN SEA**, 6 wins, $178,245, 1967 Selima S., etc.

1972—*MOMENT OF TRUTH II
1959 ch. m., Matador—Kingsworthy, by Kingstone
Breeder, Mrs. M. Clarke (GB). **Owner**, Cragwood Estates.
Dam of 9 foals, all winners, including **CONVENIENCE**, 15 wins, $648,933, 1973 Vanity H. (G1), etc.; **NIGHT ALERT**, 3 wins, $121,268, 1980 Prix Jean Prat (Fr-G2), etc.; **INDULTO**, 27 wins, $466,789, 1966 Withers S., etc.; **PROLIFERATION**, 7 wins, $66,680; **PUNTILLA**, 3 wins, $64,255.

1971—IBERIA
1954 ch. m., *Heliopolis—War East, by *Easton
Breeder, L. S. MacPhail (Md.). **Owner**, Meadow Stable.
Dam of 10 foals, all starters, 8 winners, including **RIVA RIDGE**, 17 wins, $1,111,497, 1971 champion two-year-old male, 1973 champion older male, 1972 Kentucky Derby, etc.; **HYDROLOGIST**, 10 wins, $277,958, 1970 Excelsior H., etc.; **POTOMAC**, 3 wins, $37,361.

1970—LEVEE
1953 ch. m., Hill Prince—Bourtai, by Stimulus
Breeder, Claiborne Farm (Ky.). **Owner**, Whitney Stone.
Dam of 11 foals, 9 starters, 7 winners, including **SHUVEE**, 16 wins, $890,445, 1970, 1971 champion handicap mare, 1969 Filly Triple Crown, 1969 Coaching Club American Oaks, etc.; **ROYAL GUNNER**, 6 wins, $334,650; **NALEE**, 8 wins, $141,631, 1963 Black-Eyed Susan S., etc.; **A. T'S OLIE**, 6 wins, $82,211.

1969—ALL BEAUTIFUL
1959 ch. m., Battlefield—Parlo, by *Heliopolis
Breeder, William duPont Jr. (Va.). **Owner**, Paul Mellon.
Dam of 13 foals, 11 starters, 9 winners, including **ARTS AND LETTERS**, 11 wins, $632,404, 1969 Horse of the Year, 1969 champion three-year-old male, 1969 champion handicap horse, 1969 Belmont S., etc.

1968—DELTA
1952 b. m., *Nasrullah—Bourtai, by Stimulus
Breeder, Claiborne Farm (Ky.). **Owner**, Claiborne Farm.
Dam of 10 foals, all starters, 9 winners, including **OKAVANGO**, 6 wins, $153,802, 1975 San Pasqual H. (G2), etc., **DIKE**, 7 wins, $351,274, 1969 Wood Memorial S., etc.; **CANAL**, 33 wins, $280,358; **CABILDO**, 22 wins, $267,265; **SHORE**, 6 wins, $62,357.

1967—KERALA
1958 b. m., *My Babu—Blade of Time, by *Sickle
Breeder, Greentree Stud Inc. (Ky.). **Owner**, Mrs. Thomas M. Bancroft.
Dam of 15 foals, 9 starters, 8 winners, including **DAMASCUS**, 21 wins, $1,176,781, 1967 Horse of the Year, 1967 champion three-year-old male, 1967 champion handicap male, 1967 Preakness S., etc.

1966—JULIETS NURSE
1948 dk. b. or br. m., Count Fleet—Nursemaid, by Luke McLuke
Breeder, Mrs. Roy Carruthers (Ky.). **Owner**, J. Graham Brown.
Dam of 13 foals, all starters, 11 winners, including **RUN FOR NURSE**, 22 wins, $253,145; **GALLANT ROMEO**, 15 wins, $202,401, 1966 Vosburgh H., etc.; **WOOZEM**, 7 wins, $163,083, 1966 Demoiselle S., etc.; **DUTIFUL**, 5 wins, $80,780.

1965—POCAHONTAS
1955 ch. or br. m., Roman—How, by *Princequillo
Breeder, H. B. Delman (Ky.). **Owner**, Raymond Guest.
Dam of 9 foals, 6 starters, 5 winners, including **TOM ROLFE**, 16 wins, $671,297, 1965 champion three-year-old male, 1965 Preakness S., etc.; **LADY REBECCA**, 2 wins, $26,434, 1974 Prix Vanteaux (Fr-G3); **CHIEFTAIN**, 13 wins, $405,256, 1964 Governor's Gold Cup, etc.; ***WENONA**, 3 wins, Blandford S. (Ire), etc.

1964—MAID OF FLIGHT
1951 dk. b. or br. m., Count Fleet—Maidoduntreath, by Man o' War
Breeder, Mrs. Silas B. Mason (Ky.). **Owner**, Mrs. Richard C. duPont.
Dam of 11 foals, 10 starters, 9 winners, including **KELSO**, 39 wins, $1,977,896, 1960, '61, '62, '63, '64 Horse of the Year, 1960 champion three-year-old male, 1961, '62, '63, '64 champion handicap horse, 1960, '61, '62, '63, '64 Jockey Club Gold Cup, etc.

1963—MISTY MORN
1952 b. m., *Princequillo—Grey Flight, by *Mahmoud
Breeder, Wheatley Stable (Ky.). **Owner**, Mrs. H. C. Phipps.
Dam of 10 foals, 8 starters, 7 winners, including **SUCCESSOR**, 7 wins, $532,254, 1966 champion two-year-old, 1966 Champagne S., etc.; **BOLD LAD**, 14 wins, $516,465, 1964 champion two-year-old, 1964 Champagne S., etc.; **SUNRISE FLIGHT**, 11 wins, $380,995, 1963 Gallant Fox H., etc.; **BEAUTIFUL DAY**, 7 wins, $160,007; **BOLD CONSORT**, 6 wins, $38,147.

1962—TRACK MEDAL
1950 dk. b. or br. m., *Khaled—Iron Reward, by *Beau Pere
Breeder, Rex C. Ellsworth (Ca.). **Owner**, Greentree Stud.
Dam of 11 foals, 8 starters, 6 winners, including **OUTING CLASS**, 6 wins, $229,759, 1962 Hopeful S., etc.; *O'HARA, 8 wins, $202,180, 1966 Sunset H.; **TUTANKHAMEN**, 12 wins, $157,530, 1962 Manhattan H.; **FOOL'S GOLD II**, 1 win, 1962 Musidora S. (Eng), etc.

1961—STRIKING
1947 b. m., War Admiral—Baby League, by Bubbling Over
Breeder, Ogden Phipps (Ky.). **Owner**, Ogden Phipps.
Dam of 15 foals, 12 starters, 11 winners, including **HITTING AWAY**, 13 wins, $309,079, 1961 Dwyer H., etc.; **BATTER UP**, 7 wins, $166,542, 1962 Black-Eyed Susan S., etc.; **MY BOSS LADY**, 4 wins, $64,174; **GLAMOUR**, 6 wins, $60,775; **BASES FULL**, 3 wins, $17,627.

1960—SIAMA
1947 b. m., Tiger—China Face, by Display
Breeder, E. K. Thomas (Ky.). **Owner**, Harry F. Guggenheim.
Dam of 9 foals, 5 starters, all winners, including **BALD EAGLE**, 12 wins, $692,946, 1960 champion handicap male, 1959, 1960 Washington D.C. International, etc.; **ONE-EYED KING**, 15 wins, $266,281, 1960 Arlington H., etc.; **DEAD AHEAD**, 8 wins, $73,645.

1959—*KNIGHT'S DAUGHTER
1941 b. m., Sir Cosmo—Feola, by Friar Marcus
Breeder, King George VI (GB). **Owner**, Claiborne Farm.
Dam of 8 foals, 7 starters, 6 winners, including **ROUND TABLE**, 43 wins, $1,749,869, 1958 Horse of the Year, 1958, 1959 '59 champion turf male, 1958, '59 champion older male, 1957 Hollywood Gold Cup, etc.; **MONARCHY**, 7 wins, $85,737; *LOVE GAME.

1958—MISS DISCO
1944 b. m., Discovery—Outdone, by Pompey
Breeder, Alfred G. Vanderbilt (Md.). **Owner**, Mrs. H. C. Phipps.
Dam of 11 foals, 7 starters, all winners, including **BOLD RULER**, 23 wins, $764,204, 1957 Horse of the Year, 1957 champion three-year-old male, 1958 champion sprinter, 1957 Preakness S., etc.; **INDEPENDENCE**, 12 wins, $132,088; **NASCO**, 7 wins, $71,930.

1957—BELLE JEEP
1949 b. m., War Jeep—Model Beauty, by *Blenheim II
Breeder, Maine Chance Farm (Ky.). **Owner**, Maine Chance Farm.
Dam of 15 foals, 12 starters, all winners, including **JEWEL'S REWARD**, 7 wins, $448,592, 1957 champion two-year-old male, 1957 Champagne S., etc.; **TRIPLE CROWN**, 4 wins, $128,874, 1974 San Jacinto S. (G2), etc.; **LORD JEEP**, 11 wins, $64,504; **EVASIVE ACTION**, 3 wins, $47,004.

1956—SWOON
1942 ch. m, Sweep Like—Sadie Greenock, by Greenock
Breeder, E. Gay Drake (Ky.). **Owner**, E. Gay Drake.
Dam of 10 foals, all starters, 8 winners, including **SWOON'S SON**, 30 wins, $970,605, 1956 American Derby, etc.; **DOGOON**, 28 wins, $220,360, 1954 Hawthorne Juvenile H., etc.

1955—IRON REWARD
1946 b. m., *Beau Pere—Iron Maiden, by War Admiral
Breeder, W. W. Naylor (Ca.). **Owner**, Rex Ellsworth.
Dam of 11 foals, 9 starters, 5 winners, including **SWAPS**, 19 wins, $848,900, 1956 Horse of the Year, 1956 champion handicap horse, 1955 Kentucky Derby, etc.; **THE SHOE**, 10 wins, $105,000, 1958 Cinema H., etc.; **LIKE MAGIC**, 10 wins, $87,372.

1954—TRAFFIC COURT
1938 dk. b. or br. m., Discovery—Traffic, by Broomstick
Breeder, C. V. Whitney (Ky.). **Owner**, Clifford Mooers.
Dam of 3 foals, all winners, including **HASTY ROAD**, 14 wins, $541,402, 1953 champion two-year-old male, 1954 Preakness S., etc.; **TRAFFIC JUDGE**, 13 wins, $432,450, 1957 Suburban H., etc.

1953—GAGA
1942 b. m., *Bull Dog—Alpoise, by Equipoise
Breeder, A. C. Ernst (Ky.). **Owner**, Duval Headley.
Dam of 5 foals, all winners, including **TOM FOOL**, 21 wins, $570,165, 1953 Horse of the Year, 1951 champion two-year-old male, 1953 champion sprinter, 1953 champion older male, 1953 Surburban H., etc., **AUNT JINNY**, 5 wins, $106,020, 1950 champion two-year-old filly, 1950 Demoiselle S., etc.

1952—ACE CARD
1942 b. m., Case Ace—Furlough, by Man o' War
Breeder, Walter M. Jeffords (Pa.). **Owner**, Mrs. Walter M. Jeffords.
Dam of 12 foals, all starters, 11 winners, including **ONE COUNT**, 9 wins, $245,625, 1952 Horse of the Year, 1952 champion three-year-old male, 1952 Belmont S., etc.; **POST CARD**, 14 wins, $170,525; **MY CARD**, 7 wins, $98,404, 1963 Selima S.; **YILDIZ**, 7 wins, $90,475, 1951 Flamingo S., etc.

1951—*ALPENSTOCK III
1936 dk. b. or br. m., Apelle—Plymstock, by Polymelus
Breeder, Cliveden Stud (GB). **Owner**, Mereworth Farm.
Dam of 13 foals, 10 starters, 8 winners, including **RUHE**, 11 wins, $294,490, 1951 Blue Grass S., etc.; **STURDY ONE**, 13 wins, $202,970, 1951 Tanforan H., etc.; **ALLADIER**, 9 wins, $61,712, 1951 Breeders' Futurity, etc.

1950—HILDENE
1938 b. m., Bubbling Over—Fancy Racket, by *Wrack
Breeder, Xalapa Farm (Ky.). **Owner**, Meadow Stable.
Dam of 13 foals, 12 starters, 9 winners, including **HILL PRINCE**, 17 wins, $422,140, 1950 Horse of the Year, 1949 champion two-year-old male, 1950 champion three-year-old male, 1951 champion older male, 1950 Preakness S., etc.; **FIRST LANDING**, 19 wins, $779,577, 1958 champion two-year-old male, 1958 Champagne S., etc.; **THIRD BROTHER**, 9 wins, $310,787; **MANGOHICK**, 23 wins, $115,115; **PRINCE HILL**, 8 wins, $98,300.

1949—EASY LASS
1940 bl. m., *Blenheim II—Slow and Easy, by Colin
Breeder, Calumet Farm (Ky.). **Owner**, Calumet Farm.
Dam of 7 foals, all starters, 6 winners, including **COALTOWN**, 23 wins, $415,675, 1949 Horse of the Year, 1948 champion sprinter, 1949 champion older male, 1949 Washington Park H., etc.; **WISTFUL**, 13 wins, $213,060, 1949 champion three-year-old filly, 1949 Coaching Club of America Oaks, etc.; **ROSEWOOD**, 9 wins, $92,950; **FANFARE**, 9 wins, $46,140.

1948—OUR PAGE
1940 b. m., Blue Larkspur—Occult, by *Dis Donc
Breeder, Woodvale Farm (Oh.). **Owner**, Royce C. Martin.
Dam of 5 foals, all winners, **BULL PAGE**, 9 wins, $25,730, 1951 Horse of the Year in Canada, 1951 champion older horse in Canada, 1951 Canadian Championship S.; **NAVY PAGE**, 21 wins, $127,322, 1953 Jerome H., etc.; **SPORT PAGE**, 4 wins, $79,175; **BROTHER TEX**, 8 wins, $77,633; **PAGE BOOTS**, 3 wins, $51,635.

1947—POTHEEN
1928 dk. b. or br. m., Wildair—Rosie O'Grady, by Hamburg
Breeder, H. P. Whitney (Ky.). **Owner**, Calumet Farm.
Dam of 12 foals, 11 starters, 9 winners, including **BEWITCH**, 20 wins, $462,605, 1947 champion two-year-old filly, 1949 champion older female, 1947 Washington Park Futurity, etc.; **POT O' LUCK**, 14 wins, $239,150, 1945 Jockey Club Gold Cup, etc.; **LOT O LUCK**, 9 wins, $46,950.

1946—BLOODROOT
1932 b. m., Blue Larkspur—*Knockany Bridge, by Bridge of Earn
Breeder, Idle Hour Stock Farm (Ky.). **Owner**, Ogden Phipps.
Dam of 13 foals, 11 starters, 8 winners, including **ANCESTOR**, 26 wins, $237,956, 1959 champion steeplechaser, 1952 Discovery H., etc.; **BE FAITHFUL**, 14 wins, $189,040, 1947 Hawthorne Gold Cup H., etc.; **BRIC A BAC**, 13 wins, $103,225, 1945 San Juan Capistrano H., etc.; **BIMLETTE**, 4 wins, $28,065, 1946 Frizette S.

Leading Broodmares by Progeny Earnings
Worldwide Leaders, 1930-May 20, 2008

Broodmare, YOB, Sire—Dam	Fls	Strs	Wnrs	SWs	Progeny Earnings	Leading Earner	Earnings
Dancing Key, 1983, Nijinsky II—Key Partner	14	14	10	4	$20,537,358	Dance Partner (Jpn)	$5,973,652
Once Wed, 1984, Blushing Groom (Fr)—Noura	12	10	7	1	18,431,882	T.M.Opera O	16,200,337
Pacificus, 1981, Northern Dancer—Pacific Princess	11	10	8	4	18,186,440	Narita Brian	9,296,552
Scarlet Bouquet, 1988, Northern Taste—Scarlet Ink	11	11	9	3	18,066,493	Daiwa Major	9,208,471
Wind in Her Hair (Ire), 1991, Alzao—Burghclere	10	10	7	4	16,246,523	Deep Impact	12,825,285
Vega, 1990, Tony Bin—Antique Value	4	4	4	3	11,867,874	Admire Don	7,712,841
Golden Sash, 1988, Dictus—Dyna Sash	12	11	6	2	11,671,096	Stay Gold	8,682,142
Katies (Ire), 1981, Nonoalco—Mortefontaine	14	13	10	5	11,357,150	Hishi Amazon	6,981,102
Mejiro Aurola, 1978, Remand—Mejiro Iris	11	6	5	2	11,174,759	Mejiro McQueen	7,875,326
Tugela, 1995, Riverman—Rambushka	5	4	3	2	11,045,833	Makybe Diva	10,767,186
Roamin Rachel, 1990, Mining—One Smart Lady	6	5	3	2	10,909,802	Zenno Rob Roy	10,483,242
Tokai Natural, 1982, Nice Dancer—Tokai Midori	13	12	10	2	10,849,208	Tokai Teio	4,698,139
Scarlet Lady, 1995, Sunday Silence—Scarlet Rose	4	4	4	2	10,712,518	Vermilion	6,638,142
Princess Reema, 1984, Affirmed—First Fling	16	15	12	3	10,673,702	Meisho Doto	8,088,202
Crafty Wife, 1985, Crafty Prospector—Wife Mistress	14	13	11	3	10,653,675	Big Shori	2,984,808
Floral Magic, 1985, Affirmed—Rare Lady	10	10	8	1	10,607,619	Narita Top Road	8,389,594
Happy Trails, 1984, Posse—Roycon (GB)	14	12	8	3	10,498,242	Shinko Lovely	4,596,546
All Dance, 1978, Northern Dancer—All Rainbows	12	11	8	3	10,439,595	Tap Dance City	9,586,479
My Katies, 1998, Sunday Silence—Katies First	4	3	2	1	10,400,940	Admire Moon	10,219,948
Ingot Way, 1981, Diplomat Way—Ingot	14	10	9	1	10,384,401	Skip Away	9,616,360
Solar Slew, 1982, Seattle Slew—Gold Sun (Arg)	11	7	7	2	10,363,980	Cigar	9,999,815
Irish Dance, 1990, Tony Bin—Buper Dance	7	6	3	1	10,176,223	Heart's Cry	8,054,175
Miyabi Sakurako, 1989, Northern Taste—Dyna Freeway	10	9	8	4	10,060,874	Win Marvelous	3,406,109
Jolie Zaza, 1991, Alzao—Bold Lady	7	7	4	1	9,851,225	Time Paradox	8,820,070
Cee's Song, 1986, Seattle Song—Lonely Dancer	14	12	8	4	9,834,740	Tiznow	6,427,830
Chancey Squaw, 1991, Chief's Crown—Alliacnce	9	6	4	3	9,738,572	Agnes Digital	8,095,160
Campaign Girl, 1987, Maruzensky—Lady Shiraoki	3	2	2	1	9,519,113	Special Week	9,346,435
Dream Vision, 1986, Northern Taste—Honey Dreamer	10	10	9	2	9,517,163	Utopia (Jpn)	4,913,585
Danelagh (Aus), 1995, Danehill—Palatious	4	4	4	3	9,486,310	Vengeance Of Rain	8,557,899
Dyna Carle, 1980, Northern Taste—Shadai Feather	9	9	8	1	9,368,616	Air Groove	6,832,242
Fairy Doll, 1991, Nureyev—Dream Deal	9	7	5	3	9,346,474	To the Victory	5,303,281
Tee Kay, 1991, Gold Meridian—Tri Argo	6	5	5	1	9,142,909	Symboli Kris S	8,401,282
Takeno Falcon, 1982, Philip of Spain—Cool Fair	9	8	5	1	9,125,759	Hokuto Vega	8,300,301
Sawayaka Princess, 1986, Northern Taste—Scotch Princess	10	10	9	2	9,071,597	Durandal	4,621,343
Tree of Knowledge (Ire), 1977, Sassafras (Fr)—Sensibility	10	7	5	2	9,019,381	Taiki Blizzard	5,523,549
Powerful Lady, 1981, Maruzensky—Roch Tesco	17	12	9	2	9,006,794	Winning Ticket	3,359,368
Mejiro Beauty, 1982, Partholon—Mejiro Nagasaki	9	9	8	2	8,917,477	Mejiro Dober	6,240,681
Sherriff's Deputy, 1994, Deputy Minister—Barbarika	5	5	3	1	8,912,285	Curlin	8,807,800
Reru du Temps, 1982, Maruzensky—Kei Tsunami	9	6	5	2	8,891,809	Mejiro Bright	6,848,423
Never Ichiban, 1971, Never Beat—Miss Nanba Ichiban	14	9	6	1	8,885,229	Daitaku Helios	5,193,625
Jood, 1989, Nijinsky II—Kamar	12	10	5	2	8,815,422	Fantastic Light	8,486,957
Croupier Lady, 1983, What Luck—Question d'Argent	12	11	7	1	8,799,433	Genuine	5,455,575
Sakura Clare, 1982, Northern Taste—Clare Bridge	13	9	5	2	8,742,526	Sakura Chitose O	5,178,760
Legacy of Strength, 1982, Affirmed—Katonka	15	14	9	2	8,706,044	Stinger (Jpn)	3,467,289

Leading Broodmares by 2007 Progeny Earnings in North America

Broodmare, YOB, Sire—Dam	2007 Earnings	Leading Earner (Earnings)
Sherriff's Deputy, 1994, Deputy Minister—Barbarika	$5,103,600	Curlin ($5,102,800)
Bedazzle, 1997, Dixieland Band—Majestic Legend	3,214,600	Street Sense ($3,205,000)
Belva, 1998, Theatrical (Ire)—Committed	2,875,765	English Channel ($2,640,000)
Turkish Tryst, 1991, Turkoman—Darbyvail	2,572,500	Hard Spun ($2,572,500)
Klondike Kaytie, 1988, Encino—Charming Dawn	1,965,780	Kip Deville ($1,965,780)
Nappelon, 1992, Bold Revenue—Sally Go Gray	1,829,908	Ginger Punch ($1,827,060)
Cloudy Spot, 1987, Solar City—Gladwewin	1,762,868	Cloudy's Knight ($1,762,868)
Rahayeb (GB), 1996, Arazi—Bashayer	1,560,500	Lahudood (GB) ($1,560,500)
Li'l Ms. Leonard, 1992, Nostalgia's Star—Pink Native	1,410,000	Lava Man ($1,410,000)
Candytuft, 1996, Dehere—Bolt From the Blue	1,402,775	Midnight Lute ($1,368,000)
Vue, 1989, Mr. Prospector—Harbor Flag	1,398,640	War Pass ($1,397,400)
Shameful, 1999, Flying Chevron—Lady's Legacy	1,363,446	Indian Blessing ($1,357,200)
Better Than Honour, 1996, Deputy Minister—Blush With Pride	1,358,343	Rags to Riches ($1,340,000)
Donation, 1995, Lord Avie—Reddy Change	1,343,674	Lawyer Ron ($1,320,000)
Nightstorm, 1994, Storm Cat—Halo's Daughter	1,318,330	Nobiz Like Shobiz ($1,318,330)
Multiply, 1992, Easy Goer—Add	1,278,879	Corinthian ($1,174,173)
Set Them Free, 1990, Stop the Music—Valseuse (Fr)	1,235,150	Tiago ($1,234,750)
Belle Nuit, 1990, Dr. Carter—Belle Noel	1,141,206	Octave ($1,050,234)
Little Bold Belle, 1993, Silver Buck—Bold Juana	1,117,670	Unbridled Belle ($1,116,500)

Broodmare, YOB, Sire—Dam	2007 Earnings	Leading Earner (Earnings)
Kitten's First, 1991, Lear Fan—That's My Hon	$1,090,330	Precious Kitten ($1,090,000)
Checkered Flag, 1998, A.P. Indy—Shawnee Creek	1,081,217	Zanjero ($1,060,977)
Class Kris, 1992, Kris S.—Classic Value	1,041,755	Student Council ($1,041,755)
Piano, 1995, Pentelicus—Thwack	1,036,824	Awesome Gem ($1,032,400)
Adventurous Di, 1990, Private Account—Tamaral	1,034,955	Panty Raid ($1,024,180)

Leading Broodmares by Most Group or Graded Stakes Winners
(1930-May 20, 2008)

8 **Fall Aspen** (1976, Pretense—Change Water, by Swaps). Broodmare of the Year. 14 foals, 13 starters, 12 winners, 9 stakes winners, 8 graded/group stakes winners, 2 champions (Fort Wood [Fr-G1], Hamas [Ire] [Eng-G1], Northern Aspen [G1], Timber Country [G1], Colorado Dancer [Ire] [Fr-G2], Elle Seule [Fr-G2], Bianconi [Eng-G2], Mazzacano [GB] [Eng-G3])

7 **Courtly Dee** (1968, Never Bend—Tulle, by War Admiral). Broodmare of the Year. 18 foals, 17 starters, 15 winners, 8 stakes winners, 7 graded/group stakes winners, 1 champion (Ali Oop [G1], Althea [G1], Ketoh [G1], Aishah [G2], Aquilegia [G2], Twining [G2], Native Courier [G2])

6 **Chaldee** (1978, Banner Sport—Gevar, by Right of Way). 13 foals, 9 starters, 8 winners, 6 stakes winners, 6 graded/group stakes winners, 2 champions (Potrichal [Arg] [Arg-G1], Potrinner [Arg] [Arg-G1], Potrizaris [Arg] [Arg-G1], Potridee [Arg] [G1], Potro Rex [Arg-G1], Sun Banner [Arg-G3])

Dahlia (1970, *Vaguely Noble—Charming Alibi, by Honeys Alibi). 13 foals, 11 starters, 8 winners, 6 stakes winners, 6 graded/group stakes winners (Dahar [G1], Dahlia's Dreamer [G1], Delegant [G1], Rivlia [G1], Wajd [Fr-G2], Llandaff [G2])

Glowing Tribute (1973, Graustark—Admiring, by Hail to Reason). Broodmare of the Year. 12 foals, 10 starters, 9 winners, 7 stakes winners, 6 graded/group stakes winners (Hero's Honor [G1], Sea Hero [G1], Glowing Honor [G2], Wild Applause [G2], Coronation Cup [G3], Mackie [G3])

Hasili (Ire) (1991, Kahyasi—Kerali, by High Line). Broodmare of the Year in Eng. 8 foals, 7 starters, 6 winners, 6 stakes winners, 6 graded/group stakes winners (Banks Hill [GB] [G1], Heat Haze [GB] [G1], Intercontinental [GB] [G1], Cacique [Ire] [Fr-G2], Champs Elysees (GB) [G2], Dansili [GB] [Fr-G2])

5 **Blessings (Fr)** (1971, Floribunda—*Marabelle, by Miralgo). 17 foals, 11 starters, 8 winners, 6 stakes winners, 5 graded/ group stakes winners (Bleding [Arg] [Arg-G1], Sings [Arg-G1], Blue Boss [Aus-G3], Blue Bles [Arg-G3], Flibless [Arg-G3])

Coup de Folie (1982, Halo—Raise the Standard, by Hoist the Flag). 12 foals, 10 starters, 7 winners, 5 stakes winners, 5 graded/group stakes winners, 2 champions (Coup de Genie [Fr-G1], Exit to Nowhere [Fr-G1], Machiavellian [Fr-G1], Hydro Calido [Fr-G2], Ocean of Wisdom [Fr-G3])

Eight Carat (1975, *Pieces of Eight II—Klairessa [GB], by *Klairon). Broodmare of the Year in Aus, NZ (3 times). 10 foals, 5 starters, 5 winners, 5 stakes winners, 5 graded/group stakes winners, 2 champions (Kaapstad [Aus-G1], Marquise [NZ-G1], Mouawad [Aus-G1], Octagonal [Aus-G1], Our Diamond Lover [NZ-G1])

Griffe de Paris (Brz) (1986, Telescopico—April In Paris, by Locris). 12 foals, 8 starters, 8 winners, 5 stakes winners, 5 graded/group stakes winners (Lady de Paris [Brz-G1], Genereux [Arg-G1], Global Hunter [Arg] [Arg-G2], House Of Lords [Brz-G2], King de Paris [Brz-G3])

Halory (1984, Halo—Cold Reply, by Northern Dancer). 14 foals, 12 starters, 10 winners, 5 stakes winners, 5 graded/group stakes winners (Van Nistelrooy [Ire-G2], Halory Hunter [G2], Brushed Halory [G3], Key Lory [G3], Prory [G3])

Hone (1974, Sharpen Up [GB]—Lucy, by Sheshoon). 10 foals, 8 starters, 7 winners, 5 stakes winners, 5 graded/group stakes winners, 2 champions (Balkan Prince [Fr] [Bel-G1], First Mate [Bel-G1], Hondo Mondo [Ger-G2], Quartz Stone [Bel-G2], Hondero [Ger-G3])

***Lupe II** (1967, Primera—Alcoa, by Alycidon). 10 foals, 9 starters, 8 winners, 5 stakes winners, 5 graded/group stakes winners (Lascaux [Fr-G2], Louveterie [Fr-G3], Legend of France [Eng-G3], Leonardo Da Vinci [Fr] [Eng-G3], L'Ile Du Reve [Eng-G3])

Princess Tracy (Ire) (1981, Ahonoora—Princess Ru, by Princely Gift). 10 foals, 9 starters, 7 winners, 5 stakes winners, 5 graded/group stakes winners, 1 champion (Tracy's Element [Aus] [SAf-G1], Danasinga [Aus-G1], Topasannah [SAf-G2], Cullen [Aus-G3], Towkay [Aus-G3])

Proflare (1984, Mr. Prospector—Flare Pass, by Buckpasser). 13 foals, 12 starters, 10 winners, 6 stakes winners, 5 graded/group stakes winners (Apple of Kent [G2], True Flare [G2], Capital Secret [Ger-G3], Set Alight [Fr-G3], War Zone [G3])

Summoned (1978, Crowned Prince—Sweet Life, by *Pardao). 16 foals, 16 starters, 13 winners, 5 stakes winners, 5 graded/group stakes winners, 1 champion (Zeditave [Aus-G1], Alannon [Aus-G3], Pampas Fire [Aus-G3], Square Deal [Aus-G3], Zedagal [Aus-G3])

Toussaint (1989, El Gran Senor—Image of Reality, by In Reality). Broodmare of the Year. 10 foals, 7 starters, 6 winners, 5 stakes winners, 5 graded/group stakes winners (Chester House [G1], Chiselling [G1], Empire Maker [G1], Honest Lady [G1], Decarchy [G2])

Urban Sea (1989, Miswaki—Allegretta [GB], by Lombard). Broodmare of the Year in Eng, Ire. 10 foals, 7 starters, 6 winners, 6 stakes winners, 5 graded/group stakes winners, 3 champions (Black Sam Bellamy [Ity-G1], Galileo [Ire] [Eng-G1], My Typhoon [Ire] [G1], All Too Beautiful [Ire] [Eng-G3], Urban Ocean [Ire-G3])

Most Stakes Winners for a Broodmare
(1930-2007)

9 **Fall Aspen** (1976, Pretense—Change Water, by Swaps) 14 foals, 13 starters, 12 winners, 9 stakes winners (Bianconi, Colorado Dancer [Ire], Elle Seule, Fort Wood, Hamas [Ire], Mazzacano [GB], Northern Aspen, Prince of Thieves, Timber Country)

Fallow (1957, *Worden—Galloway Queene, by Colombo) 16 foals, 12 starters, 12 winners, 9 stakes winners (Fact [Arg], Factory, Fairly [Arg], Fallowed, Far, *Farm, Farmer, Fazenda [Arg], *Fizz)

Grey Flight (1945, *Mahmoud—Planetoid, by Ariel) 15 foals, 15 starters, 14 winners, 9 stakes winners (Bold Princess, Bold Queen, Full Flight, Gray Phantom, Misty Day, Misty Flight, Misty Morn, Signore, What a Pleasure)

8 **Astronomie** (1932, Asterus —Likka, by Sardanapale) 10 foals, 9 starters, 8 winners, 8 stakes winners (Arbar, Arbele, *Asmena, Caracalla, Estremadur, Floriados, Marsyas II, Pharas)

8 Courtly Dee (1968, Never Bend—Tulle, by War Admiral) 18 foals, 17 starters, 15 winners, 8 stakes winners (Aishah, Ali Oop, Althea, Aquilegia, Ketoh, Native Courier, Princess Oola, Twining)
Retorica (1955, Snob—Rochelle, by Selim Hassan) 12 foals, 9 starters, 8 winners, 8 stakes winners (*Legent II, Leon II, Lioness, *Lirio, Llegador [Arg], Locomotor, *Lostalo, Ruizero [Arg])
7 Bold Pat (1975, Bold Destroyer—Bolerita, by Bolero) 14 foals, 14 starters, 13 winners, 7 stakes winners (A Bold Embrace, Arctic Pat, Bay Is O. K., Bold Fawn, Elegant Black, Milden's Girl, Pat's Bold Brat)
Dan's Dream (1961, Your Host—Rosella, by War Relic) 15 foals, 15 starters, 12 winners, 7 stakes winners (Costly Dream, Dream 'n Be Lucky, El Corazon, Go On Dreaming, Jesta Dream Away, Once Upon a Star, Royal Knightmare)
Donatella (1939, *Mahmoud—Delleana, by Clarissimus) 13 foals, 12 starters, 10 winners, 7 stakes winners (*Daumier, De Dreux, Delaroche, *Dominate II, *Donatellina II, Donna Lydia, Duccio)
Flying B. G. (1978, Barachois—Up Alone, by Solo Landing) 15 foals, 12 starters, 11 winners, 7 stakes winners (B. G.'s Drone, Burnone Gimmetwo, Draconic's B. G., Flying Drone, Soiree, Talent Connection, Texas Holdem)
Glowing Tribute (1973, Graustark—Admiring, by Hail to Reason) 12 foals, 10 starters, 9 winners, 7 stakes winners (Coronation Cup, Glowing Honor, Hero's Honor, Mackie, Sea Hero, Seattle Glow, Wild Applause)
Gwynedd II (1947, Owen Tudor —Ryswick, by Blandford) 9 foals, 8 starters, 8 winners, 7 stakes winners (Angers, Anne III, Fort Coulonge, Gaspesie, La Touques, Maintenon, Montigny)
Here's Lookn Adder (1983, Superbity—Sarah Blue Eyes, by Explodent) 15 foals, 12 starters, 12 winners, 7 stakes winners (Drumm Valley, Jessen, Just Lookn, Lookn At a Blurr, Lookn At Another, Peak Out, Takin It Deep)
Moccasin (1963, Nantallah—*Rough Shod II, by Gold Bridge) 9 foals, 8 starters, 7 winners, 7 stakes winners (Apalachee, Belted Earl, Brahms, Flippers, Indian, Nantequos, Scuff)
Modena (1983, Roberto—Mofida [GB], by Right Tack) 14 foals, 10 starters, 10 winners, 7 stakes winners (Elmaamul, High Walden, Modern Day, Modernise, Modesta, Novellara, Reams of Verse)
My Dear Girl (1957, Rough'n Tumble—Iltis, by War Relic) 15 foals, 14 starters, 13 winners, 7 stakes winners (Gentle Touch, In Reality, My Dear Lady, Really and Truly, Return to Reality, Superbity, Watchfulness)
Qui Royalty (1977, Native Royalty—Qui Blink, by Francis S.) 14 foals, 12 starters, 10 winners, 7 stakes winners (Appointed One, Bakharoff, Demonry, Emperor Jones, Majlood, Sum, Thyer)
Roar n' Honey (1965, Hezahoney—Rip 'n Roar, by Rippey) 14 foals, 12 starters, 11 winners, 7 stakes winners (Bar Tender, Dandy Man, My Favorite Gal, One That Got Away, Singh Honey, Sonny Says, St. Aubin)
Soumida (1953, Tehran —*Sou'wester, by Blue Peter) 10 foals, 9 starters, 9 winners, 7 stakes winners (Sarcelle, Senechal, Siska, Solidor, Solon, Sorana, *Soudard)
Toll Booth (1971, Buckpasser—Missy Baba, by *My Babu) 13 foals, 12 starters, 11 winners, 7 stakes winners (Christiecat, Idle Gossip, Key to the Bridge, Plugged Nickle, Tokens Only, Toll Fee, Toll Key)
Up the Flagpole (1978, Hoist the Flag—The Garden Club, by *Herbager) 11 foals, 10 starters, 10 winners, 7 stakes winners (Allied Flag, Flagbird, Fold the Flag, Long View, Prospectors Delite, Runup the Colors, Top Account)

Most Foals for a Broodmare
(1930-May 22, 2008)

Broodmare, YOB, Pedigree	Fls.	Strs.	Wnrs.	Wins	Earnings
*Betsy Ross II, 1939, *Mahmoud—*Celerina, by *Teddy	23	19	13	44	$ 153,124
Day Line, 1963, *Day Court—Fast Line, by Mr. Busher	21	17	14	42	421,940
Wayward Miss, 1936, Brumeux —Miss Contrary, by Cannobie	21	17	6	41	15,967
Alanette, 1962, Alarullah—Jaconet, by *Jacopo	20	18	9	33	128,897
Battle Creek Girl, 1977, His Majesty—Far Beyond, by Nijinsky II	20	18	15	80	4,259,718
Bold Bikini, 1969, Boldnesian—Ran-Tan, by Summer Tan	20	14	12	38	975,703
Bright Festive, 1966, Festive—Bright Cirrus, by Solferino	20	5	0	0	1,518
Capulet, 1977, Gallant Romeo—Indaba, by Sir Gaylord	20	17	10	55	601,360
Cequillo, 1956, *Princequillo—Boldness, by *Mahmoud	20	18	14	81	1,031,646
Delagoa (Fr) 1975, Targowice—Derna, by Sunny Boy	20	15	11	26	221,216
Feather Bed, 1961, Johns Joy—Silly Sara, by *Rustom Sirdar	20	17	13	64	400,354
Jettapart, 1979, Tri Jet—Annulment, by Manifesto	20	16	13	76	1,057,944
Such 'n Such, 1974, Ack Ack—Long Stemmed Rose, by Jacinto	20	16	11	46	735,875
Tie a Bow, 1979, Dance Spell—Bold Bikini, by Boldnesian	20	15	9	36	487,305
Wind in Her Sails, 1972, Mr. Leader—Bunch of Daisies, by Sir Gaylord	20	13	12	44	375,991
Wisp O'Will, 1964, New Policy—Miss Willow, by Oil Capitol	20	16	14	70	894,640

Most Consecutive Foals for a Broodmare
(1930-May 22, 2008)

Broodmare, YOB, Pedigree	Foals	Consecutive Foals
Bold Bikini, 1969, Boldnesian—Ran-Tan, by Summer Tan	20	19
Such 'n Such, 1974, Ack Ack—Long Stemmed Rose, by Jacinto	20	19
Photo Flash, 1965, *Match II—Picture Light, by *Court Martial	19	19
Sarasail, 1966, Hitting Away—*Sail Riona, by *Royal Charger	19	19
Council Rock, 1985, General Assembly—Dancing Rocks, by Green Dancer	18	18
Gallant Lady, 1930, *Sir Gallahad III—*Peroration, by Clarissimus	18	18
Maxencia (Fr), 1977, Tennyson—Matuschka, by *Orsini II	18	18
So What, 1978, Iron Ruler—Merry Mama, by Prince John	18	18
Trinity, 1978, Logical—Trinidad, by Make Tracks	18	18
Whitewood, 1960, *Worden—Solarist, by Supreme Court	18	18

Most Wins by Broodmare's Offspring
(1930-2007)

Broodmare, YOB, Sire—Dam	Foals	Starters	Winners	Starts	Wins	Earnings
Slow and Easy, 1922, Colin—*Shyness	15	14	11	962	182	$287,417
*Adorable II, 1925, Sardanapale—Incredule	15	13	12	1,175	181	164,936
Cotton Candy, 1945, Stimulus—Sugar Bird	13	12	12	1,109	178	359,502
Transit, 1926, *Chicle—*Traverse	10	10	10	1,169	178	308,632
*Clonaslee, 1922, Orpiment—Bullet Proof	18	17	16	1,170	176	258,219
Sag Rock, 1930, Rock Man—Atomin	13	12	11	981	170	237,689
Dame Mariechen, 1931, High Time—Carrie Hogan	14	14	14	1,149	167	254,771
Pevensea, 1935, Enoch—Truly Movin	13	13	13	1,177	166	167,298
Lady Excellent, 1932, Nocturnal—Falco	14	13	12	1,180	165	185,899
Ginogret, 1941, *Gino—Sunlygret	12	12	12	982	164	223,038
Alondra, 1947, War Admiral—Lady Lark	17	17	15	1,173	163	496,993
Doggerel, 1935, *Bull Dog—Shenanigan	10	9	9	1,113	163	200,484
Jemima Lee, 1929, General Lee—Miss Jemima	15	15	14	860	163	219,609
Sassaby, 1931, Broomstick—Saucy Sue	9	9	9	1,112	163	321,217
Agnes Ayres, 1923, King James—Sweet Mary	15	14	12	1,201	161	364,151
Lady Floyd, 1924, Sir Martin—Fruit Cake	13	11	10	1,015	159	151,435
Much Ado, 1921, Ed Crump	14	13	13	1,026	159	93,168
Vanrose, 1920, Vandergrift	13	10	9	993	159	123,744
Blame, 1921, *Wrack—Censure	11	10	9	1,153	157	132,321
Balking, 1935, Balko—Bodega	11	11	10	853	156	426,263
*Miss Turley, 1924, Bachelor's Jap—Raftonia	12	12	11	967	154	74,273
New Melody, 1952, Bimelech—Melodious	13	13	13	961	154	688,387
Mary Kelly, 1926, Ormondale—Starina	14	14	13	1,097	153	136,548
Kind Annie, 1938, Brilliant—*Chaucer Girl	12	11	10	992	152	273,962
Daunt, 1925, Lucullite—Dauntless	13	13	13	817	151	230,505
Knightess, 1929, *Bright Knight—Markiluna	13	13	10	1,005	151	175,222
Lucy T., 1933, Whichone—*Refugee III	13	11	9	1,092	151	254,071
Cariboo Lass, 1928, *Marcus—Mary Fuller	13	12	11	1,115	150	126,034
Softie, 1943, Flares—Sicklefeather	16	15	13	1,073	150	338,172

Most Winners for a Broodmare
(1930-May 23, 2008)

Broodmare, YOB, Sire—Dam	Foals	Starters	Winners	SWs	Earnings
Dear Guinevere, 1977, Fearless Knight—Brave and Free	19	18	17	1	$1,642,478
*Mindrum Maid, 1939, *Mahmoud—Imp	17	17	17	0	149,615
Miss Velocity, 1957, Spy Song—Fairy Dancer	18	17	17	0	560,219
Arizona Jubilee, 1964, Spotted Moon—The Frog Hook	18	17	16	1	271,893
*Clonaslee, 1922, Orpiment—Bullet Proof	18	17	16	3	258,219
Lady Ambassador, 1959, Hill Prince—Your Hostess	17	17	16	1	880,821
Northern Beauty, 1955, Borealis—Fleeting Beauty	18	16	16	2	267,724
Pia Mia, 1968, Pia Star—Surprise Lady	18	18	16	3	933,832
Pretty Sonnet, 1982, Stop the Music—Gay Sonnet	19	18	16	1	1,113,412
Sable Lady, 1927, *Waygood—Kolinsky	17	17	16	2	180,004
Admittance, 1946, Maeda—Stitches	15	15	15	0	208,098
Alondra, 1947, War Admiral—Lady Lark	17	17	15	2	496,993
Amazer, 1967, Mincio —*Alzara	17	17	15	2	1,916,353
Battle Creek Girl, 1977, His Majesty—Far Beyond	20	18	15	6	4,259,718
Blinking Owl, 1938, *Pharamond II—Baba Kenny	19	16	15	0	195,196
Bold Essence, 1977, Native Charger—Cologne	16	16	15	1	1,048,236
Bold Pythian, 1975, Bold Reason—Pythian	18	18	15	0	589,322
Bonnie Blade, 1976, Blade—Promised Princess	16	16	15	1	1,063,997
Cherry Lady, 1973, Bold Lad—Cherry Fool	16	15	15	1	773,746
Courtly Dee, 1968, Never Bend—Tulle	18	17	15	8	3,446,275
Dancing Liz, 1972, Northern Dancer—Crimson Queen	16	16	15	1	1,215,005
Day and a Half, 1972, Time Tested—Jolly	18	17	15	2	942,371
Dog Show, 1940, *Bull Dog—Pomp and Glory	16	15	15	1	361,952
Don't Honey Me, 1977, Triple Bend—Honey Deb	16	15	15	1	1,407,094
Dream Circle, 1977, Irish Ruler—Marian Z.	18	16	15	2	1,209,995
Fibber, 1981, No Robbery—Little True	18	15	15	5	1,376,791
Godzilla, 1972, Gyr—Gently	15	15	15	2	4,372,510
Grecian Coin, 1960, Royal Coinage—Greek Pillar	17	15	15	0	787,886
Kaylem Ho, 1978, Salem—Kay Ho	16	15	15	3	2,294,780
Lafayette's Lady, 1980, Young Commander—French Tout	15	15	15	1	1,391,874
Manhattan Gold, 1981, Quadratic—Golden Feathers	15	15	15	2	1,072,840
Maxencia (Fr), 1977, Tennyson—Matuschka	18	17	15	2	396,667
Mideau, 1942, *Bull Dog—Wild Waters	18	18	15	1	509,729
Miss Cotton, 1962, Swoon's Son—Always Movin	16	15	15	4	959,195
Newsun, 1973, Penowa Rullah—Sunshine Bright	16	16	15	2	1,273,538

Broodmares — Most Starts by Offspring

Broodmare, YOB, Sire—Dam	Foals	Starters	Winners	SWs	Earnings
Our Patty, 1933, Brown Bud—Perjury	17	15	15	0	$ 141,309
Pass the Mums, 1980, Inverness Drive—Mum	17	16	15	1	868,017
Patsy Dru, 1959, Alorter—Patsy	17	17	15	6	459,604
Peace Please, 1978, Hold Your Peace—Please Say Yes	16	16	15	1	856,818
Pines Lady, 1966, Pinebloom—Lady Peabody	15	15	15	0	497,559
Poker's Errand, 1974, Poker—Gallant Lesina	18	17	15	1	621,863
Proof Enough, 1969, Prove It—Theonia	16	16	15	3	910,495
Raw Sugar, 1977, Judger—Chic Valentino	15	15	15	3	766,801
Ribbon Duster, 1973, Dust Commander—First Ribbon	17	16	15	1	596,754
Stepping High, 1969, No Robbery—*Bebop II	17	17	15	2	1,395,683
Sweet Tulle, 1978, Tom Tulle—Little Divy	17	17	15	0	281,628
Tattooed Miss, 1960, Mark-Ye-Well—Mossy Number	18	18	15	2	375,182
Tweentzel Pie, 1966, Four-and-Twenty—Peachywillow	16	16	15	2	633,905
Wolf Hands, 1963, All Hands—Wolf Bait	16	16	15	3	462,595

Most Starts by Broodmare's Offspring
(1930-2007)

Broodmare, YOB, Sire—Dam	Foals	Starters	Winners	Starts	Earnings
Our Patty, 1933, Brown Bud—Perjury	17	15	15	**1,275**	$141,309
Mrs. Burke, 1923, *Berrilldon—Pinkie	12	11	11	**1,248**	104,588
Admittance, 1946, Maeda—Stitches	15	15	15	**1,217**	208,098
Mica, 1924, Fair Play—Malachite	9	8	8	**1,215**	106,918
Tabset, 1938, Upset Lad—McTab	12	12	12	**1,212**	194,434
Agnes Ayres, 1923, King James—Sweet Mary	15	14	12	**1,201**	364,151
Lina Clark, 1919, Delhi—Prism	13	13	11	**1,187**	115,562
Lady Excellent, 1932, Nocturnal—Falco	14	13	12	**1,180**	185,899
Dark Victory, 1929, *Traumer—Sun Vive	11	11	10	**1,179**	213,242
Pevensea, 1935, Enoch—Truly Movin	13	13	13	**1,177**	167,298
***Adorable II**, 1925, Sardanapale —Incredule	15	13	12	**1,175**	164,936
Miss Velocity, 1957, Spy Song—Fairy Dancer	18	17	17	**1,174**	560,219
Alondra, 1947, War Admiral—Lady Lark	17	17	15	**1,173**	496,993
***Clonaslee**, 1922, Orpiment—Bullet Proof	18	17	16	**1,170**	258,219
Transit, 1926, *Chicle—*Traverse	10	10	10	**1,169**	308,632
Brown Maiden, 1933, Brown Bud—Tailor Maid	10	10	10	**1,165**	202,886
***Valdina Spirea**, 1940, Canon Law —*Spiraea II	14	14	13	**1,157**	413,361
Blame, 1921, *Wrack—Censure	11	10	9	**1,153**	132,321
Respite, 1922, Hilarious—Lucinda	13	12	9	**1,151**	134,844
Dame Mariechen, 1931, High Time—Carrie Hogan	14	14	14	**1,149**	254,771
Galful, 1940, Hadagal—Armful	16	16	13	**1,136**	183,184
Hurry Home, 1921, *Omar Khayyam	14	13	10	**1,128**	105,900
Happy Seas, 1939, *Happy Argo—Golden Billows	12	10	9	**1,120**	188,979
Cariboo Lass, 1928, *Marcus—Mary Fuller	13	12	11	**1,115**	126,034
Doggerel, 1935, *Bull Dog—Shenanigan	10	9	9	**1,113**	200,484
Asianna, 1935, Wise Counsellor—Asia	13	11	10	**1,112**	185,443
Miss Dora, 1918, Jack Atkin	14	10	9	**1,112**	83,443
Sassaby, 1931, Broomstick—Saucy Sue	9	9	9	**1,112**	321,217
Cotton Candy, 1945, Stimulus—Sugar Bird	13	12	12	**1,109**	359,502
Drystone, 1929, Man o' War—*Keystone	12	12	11	**1,107**	189,932

Oldest Broodmares to Produce a Named Foal
(1930-2007)

Broodmare, YOB, Pedigree	Foals	Age Produced First Foal	Age Produced Last Foal
Mercian Queen, 1929, Mercian King—Cetus, by Joculator	12	7	**34**
Iceolita, 1968, Break the Ice—Jeff's Dream, by Break the Ice	8	9	**31**
Miss Jubilee, 1951, Cassis—Bacchante, by Questionnaire	5	16	**31**
***Betsy Ross II**, 1939, *Mahmoud—*Celerina, by *Teddy	23	4	**30**
Clay's Queen, 1937, Doc Horn—Hot Flash, by General Thatcher	11	8	**30**
Fancy's Dream, 1941, Somebody—Fancy Flight, by Infinite	11	11	**30**
Honey Doc, 1961, Martins Rullah—Fair Vision, by Gray Dream	14	8	**30**
Sumpinextra, 1952, Super Duper—Ariels Elite, by Ariel	10	13	**30**

Oldest Broodmares to Produce a Winner
(1930-2007)

Broodmare, YOB, Pedigree	Foals	1st Winner	Age Foaled Last Winner
Miss Jubilee, 1951, Cassis—Bacchante, by Questionnaire	5	31	**31**
Royal Fleur, 1973, Hasty Royalty—Fleurange, by Fulcrum	12	5	**30**
Sumpinextra, 1952, Super Duper—Ariels Elite, by Ariel	10	19	**30**
Faila Suit, 1957, Faila—Follow Suit, by Revoked	9	12	**28**

Oldest Broodmares to Produce a Stakes Winner
(1930-2007)

Broodmare, YOB, Pedigree	Fls.	1st SW	Age Foaled Last SW	Stakes Winner
Au Printemps, 1979, Dancing Champ—*Lorgnette II, by High Hat	16	6	26	Royal Hudson
Fantasy Miss, 1975, Dumpty's Cutter—Caminar, by Last Round	13	12	26	Fanteria
Mary's Fantasy, 1973, Olympian King—Fantasy Dream, by Everett Jr.	12	12	26	Perfect Fantasy
Beaconaire, 1974, *Vaguely Noble—Ole Liz, by Double Jay	14	6	25	Binya (Ger)
Brown Berry, 1960, Mount Marcy—Brown Baby, by Phalanx	19	8	25	Hours After
Conejo Bonita, 1949, Trace Call—Downy Pillow, by Morvich	10	25	25	Coneja's Con Man
Fairy Sprite, 1953, Papa Redbird—Fairy Fleet, by Broadside	11	15	25	Orphan Annye
Fire's Gem, 1961, *Royal Gem II—Fire Fire Fire, by Attention	13	22	25	Lassafras
Floral Victory, 1962, Victoria Park—La Belle Rose, by Le Lavandou	16	6	25	Floral Dancer
Green Finger, 1958, Better Self—Flower Bed, by *Beau Pere	17	12	25	Blandford Park
Heat of Holme, 1970, *Noholme II—Heat Lamp, by Better Self	18	4	25	Speed On Holme
Hill of Sheba, 1964, Federal Hill—Sheba S., by Errard King	13	17	25	Apart
Knightly Spritely, 1975, Knightly Dawn—Craim Check, by Terrang	17	11	25	Spritely Walker
Little Blush, 1968, *Day Court—Beaukiss, by *Mahmoud	14	7	25	Cartofel
Melanie's Girl, 1958, Nashua—*Nebroda, by Nearco	14	8	25	Hagley's Relic
Phanatam, 1941, Mokatam—Phantom Fairy, by *Negofol	12	25	25	Jacks Again
Sooni, 1970, Buckpasser—Missy Baba, by *My Babu	16	20	25	Black Cash
Sultry Sun, 1980, Buckfinder—Sunny Dame, by Damascus	16	7	25	El Sultry Sun
***Uvira II**, 1938, Umidwar—Lady Lawless, by Son-in-Law	13	6	25	Francis U.

Most Millionaires Produced by a Broodmare

No. Millionaires	Broodmare, YOB, Pedigree	Millionaires (Earnings)
5	**Dancing Key**, 1983, Nijinsky II—Key Partner, by Key to the Mint	Dance Partner (Jpn) ($5,973,652), Dance in the Mood (Jpn) ($5,456,107), Dance in the Dark ($3,459,758), Air Dublin ($3,401,386), Air Gang Star ($1,259,625)
	Miyabi Sakurako, 1989, Northern Taste—Dyna Freeway, by Dictus	Win Marvelous ($3,406,109), Royal Cancer ($1,637,674), Win Duel ($1,511,480), King of Sunday ($1,257,788), Freeway Heart ($1,114,742)
4	**Hasili (Ire)**, 1991, Kahyasi —Kerali, by High Line	Intercontinental (GB) ($2,052,463), Banks Hill (GB) ($1,824,008), Cacique (Ire) ($1,462,331), Heat Haze (GB) ($1,183,696)
	Millracer, 1983, *Le Fabuleux—Marston's Mill, by In Reality	Shinin' Racer ($1,915,140), Fuji Kiseki ($1,319,239), Super License ($1,214,916), Agnes Special ($1,104,196)
	Scarlet Bouquet, 1988, Northern Taste—Scarlet Ink, by Crimson Satan	Daiwa Major ($9,208,471), Daiwa Scarlet ($4,820,741), Daiwa Rouge ($1,097,647), Glorious Sunday ($1,081,040)
3	**Antique Value**, 1979, Northern Dancer—Moonscape, by Tom Fool	Vega ($2,105,918), News Value ($1,246,690), Maquereau ($1,245,865)
	Brilliant Very, 1990, Northern Taste—Crafty Wife, by Crafty Prospector	Company ($4,236,721), New Very ($2,024,497), Leningrad ($1,305,376)
	Certain Secret (GB), 1985, Known Fact—Freeze the Secret, by Nearctic	Taiki Enigma ($1,414,403), Taiki Python ($1,232,186), Kurofune Mystery ($1,009,342)
	Croupier Lady, 1983, What Luck—Question d'Argent, by Tentam	Genuine ($5,455,575), Croupier Star ($1,257,929), What a Reason ($1,074,212)
	Daring Danzig, 1990, Danzig—Impetuous Gal, by Briartic	Daring Heart ($2,451,059), Pit Fighter ($2,020,068), Ecton Park ($1,503,825)
	Eileen's Moment, 1982, For The Moment—Sailaway, by *Hawaii	Lil E. Tee ($1,437,506), Agnes Arashi ($1,108,588), Agnes Partner ($1,011,810)
	First Act, 1986, Sadler's Wells—Arkadina, by *Ribot	Heavenly Romance ($3,527,120), Reportage ($1,446,054), Mr Big Ben ($1,027,220)
	Happy Trails, 1984, Posse—Roycon (GB) by High Top	Shinko Lovely ($4,596,546), Happy Path ($2,117,320), Taiki Marshal ($1,910,894)
	Legacy of Strength, 1982, Affirmed—Katonka, by Minnesota Mac	Stinger (Jpn) ($3,467,289), Silent Happiness ($1,870,725), Legacy of Zelda ($1,256,666)
	National Flag, 1986, Dictus—Dyna World, by Huntercombe	Inter Flag ($2,498,883), Maruka Komachi ($1,672,369), Daiwa Geant ($1,117,364)
	Northern Sunset (Ire), 1977, Northfields—Moss Greine, by *Ballymoss	L'Carriere ($1,726,175), St. Jovite ($1,604,439), Salem Drive ($1,046,065)
	Powerful Lady, 1981, Maruzensky—Roch Tesco, by Tesco Boy	Winning Ticket ($3,359,368), Royal Touch ($2,795,933), Marubutsu Powerful ($1,100,278)
	Rosa Nay, 1988, Lyphard—Riviere Doree, by Secretariat	Rosado ($3,686,146), Vita Rosa ($2,849,240), Rose Colour ($1,044,385)
	Star Ballerina, 1990, Risen Star—Berliani, by Nureyev	En Dehors ($2,329,504), Spartacus ($1,215,814), Grand Pas de Deux ($1,084,664)
	Tokai Natural, 1982, Nice Dancer—Tokai Midori, by Faberge II	Tokai Teio ($4,698,139), Tokai Oza ($2,035,432), Tokai Elite ($1,526,365)
	Vega, 1990, Tony Bin—Antique Value, by Northern Dancer	Admire Don ($7,712,841), Admire Vega ($2,466,038), Admire Boss ($1,101,340)

Consecutive Generations of Producing Graded Stakes Winners
(Through May 30, 2008)

(5) OLE LIZ, 1963 m., Double Jay—Islay Mist, by Roman. 6 wins, $98,271, Bewitch S. (2nd Div.), etc. Dam of—
    KITTIWAKE, 1968 m., *Sea-Bird. 18 wins, $338,086, Columbiana H. (G2), etc. Dam of—
        LARIDA, 1979 m., Northern Dancer. 10 wins, $328,319, Orchid H. (G2), etc. Dam of—
            MAGIC OF LIFE, 1985 m., Seattle Slew. 4 wins, $254,841. Coronation S. (Eng-G1). Dam of—
                ENTHUSED, 1998 m., Seeking the Gold. 3 wins, $142,639, Peugeot Lowther S. (Eng-G2), etc. Dam of—
                      NORMAN INVADER, 2005 c., War Chant. 2 wins, $229,249, Go and Go Round Tower S. (Ire-G3), etc.
(4) FILLE D'ETOILE, 1971 m., Prince Bright—Ascalon, by Jekyll. Unraced. Dam of—
    EAU D'ETOILE, 1982 m., *Sir Tristram. 3 wins, Trumps Eulogy S. (NZ-G3), etc. Dam of—
        BINT MARSCAY (AUS), 1990 m., Marscay. 4 wins, $1,034,821, chp 2yo in Aus, Tooheys Golden Slipper S. (Aus-G1), etc. Dam of—
            MANNINGTON (AUS), 1997 m., Danehill. 3 wins, $232,302, Blue Diamond Prelude (Aus-G3), etc. Dam of—
                BENICIO (AUS), 2002 h., More Than Ready. 3 wins, $735,012, AAMI Victoria Derby (Aus-G1), etc.
(4) SWOON'S TUNE, 1962 m., Swoon's Son—Recess, by Count Fleet. 4 wins, $23,162, Junior Miss S. (1st Div.), etc. Dam of—
    BAG OF TUNES, 1970 m., *Herbager. 4 wins, $151,203, Kentucky Oaks (G2), etc. Dam of—
        ANDALEEB, 1985 m., Lyphard. 2 wins, $65,452, Lancashire Oaks (Eng-G3). Dam of—
            PROPHECY, 1991 m., Warning (GB). 3 wins, $138,990, Shadwell Stud Cheveley Park S. (Eng-G1), etc. Dam of—
                MODERN LOOK, 2005 f., Zamindar. 3 wins, $147,416. Prix Miesque (Fr-G3), etc.
(4) TEREUS, 1965 m., Major General—Pussywillow, by Star Kingdom. Winner. Dam of—
    CAP D'ANTIBES (AUS), 1971 m., Better Boy. 10 wins, $23,656, Marlboro Cup (Aus-G2), etc. Dam of—
        BREATH TAKING (FR), 1984 m., Nureyev. 3 wins, $68,167, Prix de Meautry (Fr-G3), etc. Dam of—
            BORODISLEW, 1990 m., Seattle Slew. 10 wins, $679,781, Chula Vista H. (G2), etc. Dam of—
                SEEKING SLEW, 2002 h., Seeking the Gold. 4 wins, $327,265, Kent Breeders' Cup S. (G3).
                CANADIAN FRONTIER, 1999 h., Gone West. 6 wins, $253,239, Bold Ruler H. (G3), etc.
(4) FLORIDE, 1960 m., Oise—Firenze, by Figaro. Unraced. Dam of—
    FIGURITA, 1976 m., El Califa. Winner, Premio Asociacion de Propietarios de Caballos de Carrera (Arg-G3). Dam of—
        FIJEZA, 1986 m., Pepenador. 6 wins, $271,232, Premio Los Haras (Arg-G2), etc. Dam of—
            FILARMONIA, 2003 m., Slew Gin Fizz. 6 wins, $137,857, Criadores (Arg-G1), etc.
            FIEREZE, 1995 m., Political Ambition. 3 wins, $85,096, Abril (Arg-G2). Dam of—
                FIESTA LADY (ARG), 2004 f., Southern Halo. 4 wins, $169,035. Argentine Oaks (Arg-G1), etc.
(4) JUANITA, 1962 m., Decathlon—Pavonia, by Pavot. 10 wins, $126,000, Delaware Oaks (G3). Dam of—
    WANIKA, 1970 m., Sadair. 8 wins, $84,167, Little Silver H. (G3), etc. Dam of—
        CINEGITA, 1977 m., Secretariat. 3 wins, $54,050, Railbird S. (G3), etc. Dam of—
            STORM STAR, 1983 m., Storm Bird. 2 wins, $47,931, Pritchard Services Cherry Hinton S. (Eng-G3), etc. Dam of—
                DODGE, 1988 h., No Pass No Sale. 3 wins, $93,768, Best Turn S. (G3), etc.
(4) LIKELY SWAP, 1962 m., Swaps—Most Likely, by *Heliopolis. 15 wins, $64,582, Great Lakes H., etc. Dam of—
    LIKELY EXCHANGE, 1974 m., Terrible Tiger. 23 wins, $475,140, Delaware H. (G1), etc. Dam of—
        DREAM DEAL, 1986 m., Sharpen Up (GB). 4 wins, $215,222, Monmouth Oaks (G1), etc. Dam of—
            CLEAR MANDATE, 1992 m., Deputy Minister. 10 wins, $1,085,588, Three Chimneys Spinster S. (G1), etc. Dam of—
                NEWFOUNDLAND, 2000 h., Storm Cat. 7 wins, $677,534, Canadian Turf H. (G3), etc.
            DREAM SCHEME, 1993 m., Danzig. 8 wins, $431,823, Churchill Downs Distaff H. (G2).
(4) MARGARETHEN, 1962 m., *Tulyar—Russ-Marie, by *Nasrullah. 16 wins, $162,933, Beverly H. (twice). Dam of—
    TRILLION, 1974 m., Hail to Reason. 9 wins, $957,413, chp older female in Fr (twice), Prix Ganay (Fr-G1), etc. Dam of—
        BARGER, 1983 m., Riverman. 2 wins, $60,562, Prix Vanteaux (Fr-G3). Dam of—
            NARRATIVE (IRE), 1998 h., Sadler's Wells. 4 wins, $277,840, hwt older male in Ity, 14 fur & up, Premio Carlo d'Alessio (Ity-G2), etc.
        BAYA, 1990 m., Nureyev. 2 wins, $202,393, Prix de La Grotte (Fr-G3), etc. Dam of—
            BIRTHSTONE, 2002 m., Machiavellian. 2 wins, $63,340, Prix d'Aumale (Fr-G3).
(4) REMEDIA, 1971 m., Dr. Fager—*Monade, by *Klairon. 4 wins, $34,020. Dam of—
    TOO CHIC, 1979 m., Blushing Groom (Fr). 4 wins, $136,270, Maskette S. (G1), etc. Dam of—
        QUEENA, 1986 m., Mr. Prospector. 10 wins, $565,024, chp older female, Maskette S. (G1), etc. Dam of—
            BRAHMS, 1997 h., Danzig. 5 wins, $843,050, Early Times Hollywood Derby (G1), etc.
            LA REINA, 2001 m., A.P. Indy. 4 wins, $350,062, Tempted S. (G3).
        CHIC SHIRINE, 1984 m., Mr. Prospector. 3 wins, $237,944, Ashland S. (G1), etc. Dam of—
            WALDOBORO, 1991 h., Lyphard. 6 wins, $204,877, True North H. (G2), etc.
            TARA ROMA, 1990 m., Lyhpard. 5 wins, $192,017, Ladies H. (G2). Dam of—
                SERRA LAKE, 1997 m., Seattle Slew. 7 wins, $486,760, Go for Wand H. (G1), etc.
                CAPPUCHINO, 1999 h., Capote. 8 wins, $509,220, Ack Ack H. (G3), etc.
(4) STICK TO BEAUTY, 1973 m., Illustrious—Hail to Beauty, by Hail to Reason. 3 wins, $41,924, Busanda S., etc. Dam of—
    GOLD BEAUTY, 1979 m., Mr. Prospector. 8 wins, $251,901, chp sprinter, Fall Highweight H. (G2), etc. Dam of—
        MAPLEJINSKY, 1985 m., Nijinsky II. 5 wins, $293,196, Alabama S. (G1), etc. Dam of—
            SKY BEAUTY, 1990 m., Blushing Groom (Fr). 15 wins, $1,336,000, chp older female, filly triple crown, Alabama S. (G1), etc. Dam of—
                HURRICANE CAT, 2003 h., Storm Cat. 2 wins, $73,640, San James Morris Hill S. (Eng-G3), etc.

Champions Who Produced Champions

Dam, YOB, Sire—Dam	Year Championship(s)	Progeny, YOB Sex, Sire, Year Championship(s)
Inside Information, 1991, Private Account—Pure Profit	1995 older female	**Smuggler**, 2002 f., Unbridled, 2005 3-year-old female
Flanders, 1992, Seeking the Gold—Starlet Storm	1994 2-year-old filly	**Surfside**, 1997 f., Seattle Slew, 2000 3-year-old filly
Glorious Song, 1976, Halo—Ballade	1980 older female	**Singspiel (Ire)**, 1992 c., In the Wings (GB), 1996 turf male
Relaxing, 1976, Buckpasser—Marking Time	1981 older female	**Easy Goer**, 1986 c., Alydar, 1988 2-year-old male
Affectionately, 1960, Swaps—Searching	1962 2-year-old filly, 1965 sprinter, '65 older female	**Personality**, 1967 c., Hail to Reason, 1970 Horse of the Year, 1970 3-year-old male
High Voltage, 1952, *Ambiorix—Dynamo	1954 2-year-old filly, 1955 3-year-old filly	**Impressive**, 1963 c., *Court Martial, 1966 sprinter
Misty Morn, 1952, *Princequillo—Grey Flight	1955 3-year-old filly, 1955 older female	**Bold Lad**, 1962 c., Bold Ruler, 1964 2-year-old male
Two Lea, 1946, Bull Lea—Two Bob	1949 3-year-old filly, 1950 older female	**Successor**, 1964 c., Bold Ruler, 1966 2-year-old male
		Tim Tam, 1955 c., Tom Fool, 1958 3-year-old male
Now What, 1937, Chance Play—That's That	1939 2-year-old filly	**Next Move**, 1947 f., Bull Lea, 1950 3-year-old filly, 1952 older female
Jacola, 1935, *Jacopo—La France	1937 2-year-old filly	**Phalanx**, 1944 c., Pilate, 1947 3-year-old male
Myrtlewood, 1932, Blue Larkspur—*Frizeur	1936 sprinter, '36 handicap female	**Durazna**, 1941 f., Bull Lea, 1943 2-year-old filly

AUCTIONS
History of Thoroughbred Auctions

By far the oldest brand name in Thoroughbred racing is Tattersalls, the English auction company founded by Richard Tattersall at London's Hyde Park Corner in 1766. Tattersalls (the appropriate apostrophe was lost at some point in its history) remains the preeminent European auction house and has served as the model for Thoroughbred sales companies throughout the world.

Richard Tattersall expanded his position as the leading seller of Thoroughbreds by providing a dining room for Jockey Club members, and his descendants (who remained in charge of the company for more than 200 years) transferred its headquarters to Newmarket in 1870.

The first American to attempt to emulate Tattersalls's success was English-educated William Easton, who served as Tattersalls's American representative for the last quarter of the 19th century and in 1879 established his own company, the American Horse Exchange, which he later merged with Tattersalls of New York. Easton was the auctioneer at the famous dispersal of August Belmont I's breeding stock in 1891, when Charles Reed made the first $100,000 bid at auction to acquire leading sire *St. Blaise.

Several competitors for Easton's company emerged in the 1890s, principally Powers-Hunter and the Fasig Co. William B. Fasig began auctioneering in his native Cleveland in the early 1890s, and Easton soon invited him to join Tattersalls. The English company chose to sell its American division after the financial panic of 1893, and Fasig took control. In 1898, he took on a partner, Edward A. Tipton, giving the company its now-familiar name, Fasig-Tipton.

Fasig's assistant Enoch J. Tranter took control of the company when Fasig abandoned ship after another panic in 1907, and Tranter established the Saratoga yearling sale in '17. Saratoga has remained the backbone of Fasig-Tipton ever since, through the stewardship of Humphrey S. Finney, his son John M. S. Finney, and D. G. Van Clief Jr. The company was sold in 2008 to Synergy Investments Ltd. of Dubai.

The commercial breeding industry began in both England and the U.S. around the middle of the 19th century. William Blenkiron's Middle Park Stud was the first famously successful commercial breeding operation in England, sending a long succession of high-priced horses to the annual Tattersalls October yearling sale.

Robert A.S.C. Alexander was the key figure in establishing Thoroughbred breeding as a viable commercial endeavor in the U.S. through the foundation of his Woodburn Stud near Lexington in the 1850s. Though hampered by the Civil War, Woodburn held annual yearling sales at the Kentucky farm until 1890. Those sales drew buyers from all over the U.S., and its success—plus the presence of 16-time leading sire Lexington at Woodburn—effectively concentrated the breeding industry in the Bluegrass.

Once Woodburn's star faded, buyers, predominantly from the East, rarely could be enticed to Kentucky to buy horses. Petroleum rationing during World War II prevented Kentucky breeders from shipping their horses to Saratoga in 1943, however, and Fasig-Tipton agreed to hold a sale in a tent on the grounds of Keeneland Race Course in Lexington. That sale included eventual 1945 Kentucky Derby winner Hoop, Jr.

Kentucky breeders liked the idea so much that by the next year they had formed their own cooperative company, Breeders' Sales Co., and purchased Fasig-Tipton's Lexington sales pavilion, which was dismantled and reconstructed at Keeneland. Breeders' Sales Co. merged with Keeneland in 1962 to become the sales division of the Keeneland Association.

Benefiting from the worldwide success of American-breds over the last 50 years, Keeneland has become the world's largest and most successful sales company. Keeneland sold the first $100,000 yearling, $130,000 Swapson in 1961; the first $1-million yearling, Canadian Bound at $1.5-million in '76; and the world-record-priced yearling, Seattle Dancer, at $13.1-million in '85.

Fasig-Tipton re-established itself in Kentucky in the 1970s, selling three Kentucky Derby (G1) winners in five years, including Triple Crown winner Seattle Slew, but its strategy differs from Keeneland's. While Keeneland's sales are based almost exclusively at its facility in Lexington, Fasig-Tipton spreads a wider net with sales at six locations in five states, often serving regional markets as well as national ones. Fasig-Tipton sold the most expensive horse offered at public auction, The Green Monkey, for $16-million at its 2006 Fasig-Tipton sale of selected two-year-olds in training at Calder Race Course.

As the breeding industry has grown, regional markets have also begun to support their own sales organizations, most notably Ocala Breeders' Sales Co. in Florida. OBSC, founded in 1974, grew out of the two-year-old sales industry that began in the late 1950s when one of the first Florida breeders, Carl Rose, started selling his two-year-olds to trainers at Hialeah Park.

In the late 1980s, Barretts Equine Ltd. was formed to build a sales pavilion and to conduct sales on the Los Angeles County Fair Grounds in Pomona. Barretts's two-year-old sales were particularly successful when Japanese buyers were active in the market in the early 1990s.—*John P. Sparkman*

Auction Review of 2007

Sheikh Mohammed bin Rashid al Maktoum spent about $19.4-million more in the international Thoroughbred public auction marketplace in 2007 than he did in '06, but how he distributed his purchases produced some surprising differences in the four major market segments.

In 2006, Sheikh Mohammed, who usually buys in the name of his principal bloodstock adviser, John Ferguson, spent approximately $83-million in the international yearling market, $2.6-million for weanlings, $11.1-million for two-year-olds in training, and $5.9-million on broodmares or broodmare prospects. In 2007, he reduced his spending on yearlings to $34.6-million, paid out about the same amount for weanlings ($2.9-million), increased his outlay for juveniles slightly to $14.1-million, and focused his attention on broodmares and broodmare prospects, spending $67.7-million for mares to breed to his burgeoning list of stallions.

All North American Thoroughbred Sales		
Year No. Sold (Chg)	Total Sales (Chg)	Average (Chg)
2007 29,584 (38.2%)	$1,234,601,872 (–2.6%)	$41,732 (–29.4%)
2006 21,407 (3.2%)	1,267,054,866 (11.3%)	59,189 (7.8%)
2005 20,739 (2.7%)	1,138,751,345 (8.0%)	54,909 (5.2%)
2004 20,196 (11.0%)	1,054,384,913 (2.3%)	52,207 (15.5%)
2003 18,916 (2.8%)	855,123,171 (11.5%)	45,206 (8.4%)
2002 18,397 (–4.1%)	767,048,402 (–9.4%)	41,694 (–5.5%)
2001 19,191 (–9.6%)	846,478,571 (–22.5%)	44,108 (–14.3%)
2000 21,225 (5.5%)	1,091,872,249 (9.0%)	51,443 (3.3%)
1999 20,117 (2.4%)	1,001,718,775 (20.9%)	49,795 (18.1%)
1998 19,653 (5.1%)	828,664,233 (18.3%)	42,165 (12.6%)
1997 18,698 (–0.9%)	700,362,250 (12.8%)	37,457 (13.9%)
1996 18,871 (1.9%)	620,712,382 (17.9%)	32,892 (15.7%)
1995 18,518 (3.0%)	526,647,938 (17.4%)	28,440 (13.9%)
1994 17,972 (8.2%)	448,685,293 (23.1%)	24,966 (13.7%)
1993 16,605 (–5.0%)	364,519,425 (4.5%)	21,952 (9.9%)
Highest figures in boldface.		

That is largely why broodmares were the only segment of the marketplace to show an increase in total receipts in 2007. Overall, the market could not quite match the record total of 2006, falling about $32-million short. Still, a $1.2-billion marketplace can hardly be considered anemic.

Overall average and median prices for a Thoroughbred remained relatively stable for the year, but averages fluctuated within the major segments, primarily due to the shifting pattern of Sheikh Mohammed's investments.

Yearlings

After average prices of auction juveniles declined 11.4%, and similar drops occurred at Fasig-Tipton's Kentucky July sale of selected yearlings and Saratoga sale of selected yearlings, it was easy to conclude that the yearling market for 2007 was down about 10%.

The first two days of the bellwether Keeneland September yearling sale, which feature selected yearlings, experienced an even larger dip, down 23.6%. To an extent, the September decline reflected the lack of bidding contests between Sheikh Mohammed and the Coolmore combine. As a result, top price in the North American yearling market declined from $11.7-million in 2006 to $3.7-million in '07.

Mostly ignored before Keeneland September, however, was the fact that average price had held steady at the Ocala Breeders' Sales Co. August yearling sale, the first certifiably middle-to-lower market yearling sale of the year. Over the 13 Keeneland September sale days immediately following Keeneland's selected sessions, it became obvious that the OBSC August results were a better indicator of the state of the yearling market as a whole than the glitzier sales that had grabbed far bigger headlines. In the end, the average price at the largest Thoroughbred sale in history was down 9.9%.

Buoyed by the positive results of the latter part of Keeneland September, subsequent North American yearling sales often posted gains, leading to some surprisingly strong overall figures for the year:

• Record 14,107 horses offered;
• 10,215 sold, one short of the number sold in 2006;
• Buy-back rate rose to 27.6%;
• Total proceeds declined 3% to $562,026,375;
• Average dipped 3% to $55,020;
• Median rose 7.1%, from $14,000 to a record $15,000; and
• Top price dropped from $11.7-million to $3.7-million.

As in the larger Thoroughbred marketplace, the changes at the top of the yearling market in 2007 can largely be ascribed to changes in the buying patterns of Sheikh Mohammed. For the first time since 1998, Ferguson was not the leading buyer at Keeneland September, and his $17.78-million in purchases were more than $42-million less than he signed for at the same sale in 2006.

North American Yearling Sales		
Year No. Sold (Chg)	Total Sales (Chg)	Average (Chg)
2007 10,215 (0.0%)	$562,026,375 (–3.0%)	$55,020 (–3.0%)
2006 10,216 (0.9%)	579,476,050 (4.6%)	56,722 (3.7%)
2005 10,130 (7.5%)	554,105,373 (11.5%)	54,699 (3.7%)
2004 9,421 (6.9%)	496,937,672 (17.0%)	52,748 (9.4%)
2003 8,812 (–1.3%)	424,854,888 (8.5%)	48,213 (10%)
2002 8,928 (–1.7%)	391,472,126 (–17.3%)	43,848 (–15.9%)
2001 9,081 (–4.7%)	473,487,556 (–8.9%)	52,140 (–4.4%)
2000 9,527 (9.4%)	519,775,432 (18.2%)	54,558 (8.0%)
1999 8,705 (5.4%)	439,800,627 (24.2%)	50,523 (17.8%)
1998 8,260 (2.5%)	354,191,040 (15.1%)	42,880 (12.3%)
1997 8,057 (0.4%)	307,689,262 (11.0%)	38,189 (10.6%)
1996 8,026 (1.8%)	277,221,538 (13.9%)	34,540 (11.9%)
1995 7,882 (1.8%)	243,392,908 (15.6%)	30,880 (13.6%)
1994 7,744 (3.8%)	210,460,233 (12.4%)	27,177 (8.3%)
1993 7,460 (–6.0%)	187,232,894 (5.9%)	25,098 (12.6%)
Highest figures in boldface.		

He signed for only three of the ten highest-priced yearlings internationally.

One huge factor in the latent strength at Keeneland September was the weakness of the dollar in currency markets, giving Europeans the upper hand in many midlevel bidding duels. That also helped the Tattersalls Ltd. October yearling sale provide the year's highest-priced yearling, a Sadler's Wells filly purchased by agent Charlie Gordon-Watson for $5,343,187, well above the top American price of $3.7-million for a colt by Unbridled's Song signed for by Demi O'Byrne for Coolmore.

Overall ratio of average price to stud fee was 2.59, just over the industry rule of thumb for profitability of 2.5-to-1. That was well below the 3.03 average ratio attained in 2006, and a sure sign that stud-fee inflation had outstripped any increases in demand in the marketplace.

As has become the rule, Taylor Made Sales Agency led all consignors by number of yearlings sold (536), with total sales of $73.7-million, less than $1-million below the record it set in 2006. After buying their products in a record weanling market in 2006, pinhookers found it difficult to make a profit when the yearling market failed to continue its steady climb in '07. After posting a marginal paper profit in 2006, pinhookers lost more than $10.7-million as a group in '07 before commissions and after-market sales.

Two-Year-Olds

When the top of a market declines by 84.4% from one year to the next, it is almost impossible to escape the statistical ramifications. Such was the case with the market for two-year-olds in training, which went from a season-best and world-record price of $16-million paid for The Green Monkey in 2006 to a season-best $2.5-million for The Leopard in '07.

That $13.5-million drop explains a good portion of the approximately $24-million decline in year-to-year total sales, but a deeper look at the numbers suggests it was only one of the factors that caused the juvenile market to retreat from the phenomenal results of 2006.

The statistics show:
• 4,591 horses were offered, up 7.1% from 2006;
• 3,123 horses were reported sold, up 0.4%; thus
• Buy-back rate increased from 27.4% in '06 to 32% in '07;
• Total sales declined 11% to $193,064,064;
• Average price slipped 11.4% to 61,820; and
• Median declined 16.7% to $20,000.

The Leopard, pinhooked by Hoby and Layna Kight after buying him for $1-million at the 2006 Keeneland September yearling sale, ended up as the most expensive two-year-old to sell at public auction in '07, and he got there without a bid from bloodstock agent John Ferguson, who was the leading buyer of two-year-olds at auction with 21 purchases for $14,143,635.

Total pinhooking returns for the year showed expenditures of $137,102,973 and resale of $127,205,038, a net loss of $9,897,935 after upkeep costs. That was a considerable turnaround from the $20,722,485 profit posted in 2006, but it follows the overall seesaw pattern of pinhooking net returns, which were down $13-million in '05, up $22.1-million in '04, and down $4.1-million in '03.

North American Two-Year-Old Sales			
Year	No. Sold (Chg)	Total Sales (Chg)	Average (Chg)
2007	3,123 (0.4%)	$193,064,064 (−11.0%)	$61,820 (−11.4%)
2006	3,111 (−0.7%)	**217,004,539** (13.7%)	**69,754** (14.5%)
2005	**3,133** (7.7%)	190,882,771 (11.4%)	60,927 (3.4%)
2004	2,908 (−3.7%)	171,333,601 (23.0%)	58,918 (27.7%)
2003	3,019 (11.6%)	139,296,135 (8.1%)	46,140 (−3.1%)
2002	2,706 (0.0%)	128,870,834 (1.4%)	47,624 (1.4%)
2001	2,705 (−11.1%)	127,056,203 (−17.9%)	46,971 (−7.7%)
2000	3,043 (5.0%)	154,807,648 (0.1%)	50,873 (−4.7%)
1999	2,897 (−2.9%)	154,648,585 (13.4%)	53,382 (16.9%)
1998	2,985 (12.3%)	136,318,616 (12.9%)	45,668 (0.5%)
1997	2,657 (−0.8%)	120,694,031 (2.9%)	45,425 (14.1%)
1996	2,946 (−0.5%)	117,263,901 (23.9%)	39,804 (24.5%)
1995	2,961 (−0.2%)	94,666,095 (23.1%)	31,971 (23.3%)
1994	2,966 (−0.3%)	76,905,149 (26.7%)	25,929 (27.1%)
1993	2,976 (0.1%)	60,716,936 (7.8%)	20,402 (7.7%)
Highest figures in boldface.			

The most profitable pinhooking price range was for yearlings that cost between $40,000 and $49,999, which produced a 17.5% profit.

The overall returns by stud fee ratio was 3.87 in 2007, down from a robust ratio of 4.46 in '06 but higher than the 3.72 of '05 and identical to '04. Niall Brennan Stables was leading consignor with 76 horses sold for $12,267,400. Brennan ranked first or second in total sales for eight consecutive years.

Weanlings

Buyers were faced with the second-largest number of weanlings ever offered on the North American market in 2007, but weanling-to-yearling pinhookers, still recovering from a $10-million overall loss on weanlings they purchased in 2006, were considerably more cautious in buying, resulting in the following disappointing overall figures for North American sales:
• 2,954 weanlings offered, up 3.8%, and the second-highest figure on record; but
• Only 1,955 sold, down 3.7%; which meant
• Buy-back rate rose from 28.7% to 33.8%;
• Total proceeds dipped 13.9% to $86,771,752;
• Average dropped 10.6% from the record level of 2006 to $44,385; but
• Median was unchanged at $17,000; and
• Top price declined from $2.7-million to $1.7-million.

As has become the norm, the year's most ex-

pensive weanling on the international market appeared at the Japan Race Horse Association July sale, where Riichi Kondo paid $2.4-million for a half brother to top Japanese runner Admire Moon sired by 2001 Japan Cup Dirt winner Kurofune (by French Deputy).

That was one of only six seven-figure weanlings sold in 2007 (compared with nine in '06), including the top-priced American weanling, a Pulpit filly out of Madcap Escapade, by Hennessy. Mike Moreno's Southern Equine Stable, represented by trainer Eric Guillot, bought out partners in the first foal of her Grade 1-winning dam, the top-priced mare at the previous year's Keeneland November breeding stock sale at $6-million.

North American Weanling Sales

Year	No. Sold (Chg)	Total Sales (Chg)	Average (Chg)
2007	1,955 (–3.7%)	$ 86,771,752 (–13.9%)	$44,385 (–10.6%)
2006	2,030 (11.5%)	100,734,475 (26.4%)	49,623 (13.3%)
2005	1,820 (–6.1%)	79,703,444 (11.1%)	43,793 (18.3%)
2004	1,938 (14.5%)	71,713,850 (5.7%)	37,004 (–7.7%)
2003	1,693 (8.7%)	67,866,478 (39.8%)	40,087 (28.6%)
2002	1,557 (–19.2%)	48,549,515 (–7.2%)	31,181 (14.9%)
2001	1,926 (–17.9%)	52,288,439 (–37.6%)	27,149 (–24.0%)
2000	**2,345** (2.4%)	83,755,053 (–14.6%)	35,716 (–16.7%)
1999	2,289 (0.5%)	98,087,172 (9.8%)	42,852 (9.3%)
1998	2,278 (9.0%)	89,303,995 (32.8%)	39,203 (21.8%)
1997	2,090 (–3.4%)	67,251,828 (10.1%)	32,178 (14.0%)
1996	2,164 (8.3%)	61,094,609 (17.0%)	28,232 (8.1%)
1995	1,999 (5.4%)	52,221,842 (26.2%)	26,124 (19.7%)
1994	1,896 (23.4%)	41,374,263 (14.2%)	21,822 (–7.5%)
1993	1,536 (2.3%)	36,233,360 (51.1%)	23,589 (47.8%)

Highest figures in boldface.

The top of the market experienced declines, but the middle ranks rose markedly, fueled by pinhookers trying to buy horses to resell at a lower investment level than in 2006. The down market was apparent in the overall average price to stud fee ratio of 2.34, with significantly lower returns at the highest stud fee levels.

Kingmambo, sire of the highest-priced weanling colt (out of Because [Ire], by Sadler's Wells) sold in North America at $950,000, led weanling sires with an average of $896,896 for three sold. Kingmambo also provided the second-highest-priced filly on the American market.

Consignor lists both by total proceeds and average are naturally dominated by the lucrative Japanese weanling market, with Katsumi Yoshida's Northern Farm leading his brother Teruya's Shadai Farm at the top of the list. Taylor Made Sales Agency and Hill 'n' Dale Sales Agency topped American consignors.

Broodmares

The broodmare segment of the market was the direct beneficiary of Sheikh Mohammed's shift of investment in 2007. Sheikh Mohammed's representative, John Ferguson, signed for about $61.8-million more—$33.5-million of that in North America—for broodmares on the international market in 2007 than he had in '06.

That led directly to the following seemingly astounding figures in North America:
- 7,455 broodmares were offered, down 1.9%;
- 5,531 sold, a 3.1% decline;
- A record $384,674,148 in receipts, 7.6% more than the previous record set in 2006;
- Average soared 11.1% to a record $69,549; while
- Median tied a record of $12,000, a 20% increase; and
- Playful Act (Ire) sold for a world-record $10.5-million; but
- Buy-back rate increased from 24.9% in 2006 to 25.8%.

Before the beginning of the Lexington fall breeding stock sales in November, it did not seem that anyone in the commercial market had thought through the implications of Sheikh Mohammed's purchases of a half-dozen stallion prospects during the 2007 racing season. The ruler of Dubai began buying expensive broodmares to breed to those new sires at the Fasig-Tipton Kentucky November selected mixed sale, and by the end of the second session of the Keeneland November breeding stock sale two days later, he had purchased eight mares for $35.2-million.

North American Broodmare Sales

Year	No. Sold (Chg)	Total Sales (Chg)	Average (Chg)
2007	5,531 (–3.1%)	**$384,674,148** (7.6%)	**$69,549** (11.1%)
2006	5,710 (6.6%)	357,509,948 (15.8%)	62,611 (8.7%)
2005	5,358 (0.1%)	308,602,769 (3.5%)	57,597 (3.4%)
2004	5,354 (7.5%)	298,240,342 (37.0%)	55,704 (27.5%)
2003	4,983 (5.1%)	217,672,620 (13.3%)	43,683 (7.8%)
2002	4,741 (–6.3%)	192,082,219 (2.1%)	40,515 (9.0%)
2001	5,059 (–12.7%)	188,107,111 (–40.7%)	37,183 (–32.1%)
2000	**5,797** (3.9%)	317,398,250 (6.4%)	54,752 (2.4%)
1999	5,582 (1.7%)	298,397,805 (24.4%)	53,457 (22.3%)
1998	5,489 (8.5%)	239,875,672 (25.1%)	43,701 (15.3%)
1997	5,058 (0.9%)	191,764,648 (22.7%)	37,913 (21.5%)
1996	5,011 (2.6%)	156,304,244 (24.2%)	31,192 (21.0%)
1995	4,883 (6.6%)	125,836,989 (12.8%)	25,770 (5.8%)
1994	4,579 (10.2%)	111,520,366 (46.9%)	24,355 (33.3%)
1993	4,154 (–2.8%)	75,910,215 (–1.4%)	18,274 (1.5%)

Highest figures in boldface.

That number included the record $10.5-million Ferguson bid for Playful Act, the high-weighted English two-year-old filly of 2004, a beautifully conformed and bred daughter of Sadler's Wells from the dispersal of the late Robert Sangster's Swettenham Stud. Playful Act was the most expensive of a record 52 broodmares or broodmare prospects sold for $1-million or more on the American market. Taylor Made Sales Agency led consignors by total sales, selling 315 horses for $55,186,100.

—*John P. Sparkman and Pete Denk*

Highest-Priced Yearlings of 2007

Horse	Consignor	Buyer	Sale	Price
F., by Sadler's Wells—Brigid	Oaks Farm Stables	Charles P. Gordon-Watson	Tatt Oct.	$5,343,187
C., by Unbridled's Song—Secret Status	Lane's End, agent	Demi O'Byrne	Kee Sept.	3,700,000
F., by Sadler's Wells—=Albanova (GB)	Staffordstown Stud	Demi O'Byrne	Goffs Orby	3,593,268
C., by Dynaformer—Preach	Claiborne Farm, agent	John Ferguson Bloodstock	Kee Sept.	2,900,000
C., by Unbridled's Song—Zing	Taylor Made Sales Agency, agent for Aaron and Marie Jones	Demi O'Byrne	Kee Sept.	2,600,000
C., by A.P. Indy—Denebola	Lane's End, agent	John Ferguson Bloodstock	Kee Sept.	2,400,000
C., by Mr. Greeley—Win My Heart	Gainesway, agent	Team Valor	F-T Saratoga	2,200,000
C., by =Dalakhani (Ire)—=Bella Lambada (GB)	Meon Valley Stud	Charles P. Gordon-Watson	Tatt Oct.	2,137,275
F., by Giant's Causeway—Ellen (Ire)	Marston Stud	Charles P. Gordon-Watson	Tatt Oct.	2,137,275
C., by Gone West—Myth to Reality (Fr)	Highclere Stud	John Ferguson Bloodstock	Tatt Oct.	2,137,275
C., by French Deputy—=My Katies (Jpn)	Northern Farm	Riichi Kondo	Japan July	2,024,291
C., by A.P. Indy—Blithe	Lane's End, agent	Demi O'Byrne	Kee Sept.	2,000,000
C., by A.P. Indy—Fire the Groom	Denali Stud, agent for Crystal Springs Farm	Demi O'Byrne	Kee Sept.	2,000,000
C., by =Dance in the Dark (Jpn)—=Air Groove (Jpn)	Northern Farm	Kaneko Makoto Holdings	Japan July	1,983,806
C., by Distorted Humor—Stormy Bear	Maynard Farm	John Ferguson Bloodstock	Kee Sept.	1,900,000
C., by Galileo (Ire)—=Clara Bow (Fr)	Haras d'Etreham	Demi O'Byrne	Deauville Aug.	1,878,240
C., by A.P. Indy—Desert Tigress	Three Chimneys Sales, agent	Three Chimneys Farm, agent	Kee Sept.	1,700,000
C., by Storm Cat—Mythomania	Eaton Sales, agent for Overbrook Farm	Demi O'Byrne	Kee Sept.	1,700,000
C., by Galileo (Ire)—Silver Colours	Stratford Place Stud	Demi O'Byrne	Tatt Oct.	1,602,956
F., by Seeking the Gold—Crystal Crossing (Ire)	Eaton Sales, agent	Demi O'Byrne	Kee Sept.	1,600,000
F., by Storm Cat—Welcome Surprise	Lane's End, agent	M.A.B. Agency	Kee Sept.	1,600,000
F., by Giant's Causeway—Mayville's Magic	Lane's End, agent	Chiefswood Stables Ltd.	Kee Sept.	1,550,000
F., by A.P. Indy—Wife for Life	Three Chimneys Sales, agent For Spendthrift Farm	My Meadowview Farm	Kee Sept.	1,500,000
F., by Giant's Causeway—Onaga	Lane's End, agent	Brushwood Stable	Kee Sept.	1,500,000
F., by Gone West—Silken Cat	Taylor Made Sales Agency, agent for Aaron and Marie Jones	Live Oak Plantation	Kee Sept.	1,500,000
F., by Storm Cat—Win Crafty Lady	Taylor Made Sales Agency, agent	Aaron Jones	Kee Sept.	1,500,000
F., by =Danehill Dancer (Ire)—Flawly (GB)	Newsells Park Stud	Simon Christian	Tatt Oct.	1,496,092
F., by Awesome Again—Maggy Hawk	Gainesway, agent for Stonestreet Thoroughbred Holdings	Clarence Scharbauer	Kee Sept.	1,400,000
C., by =Jungle Pocket (Jpn)—=Every Whisper (Jpn)	Northern Farm	Takaya Shimakawa	Japan July	1,376,518
F., by Rock of Gibraltar (Ire)—Spirit of Tara (Ire)	Kilcarn Stud	De Burgh Equine and Farrington Bloodstock	Goffs Orby	1,347,475
C., by Montjeu (Ire)—=Zivania (Ire)	Kildaragh Stud, Ireland	Demi O'Byrne	Tatt Oct.	1,282,365
C., by Dansili (GB)—=Abbatiale (Fr)	Haras de la Perelle	Margaret O'Toole Bloodstock	Deauville Aug.	1,274,520
C., by A.P. Indy—Arabis	Taylor Made Sales Agency, agent for Aaron and Marie Jones	John Ferguson Bloodstock	Kee Sept.	1,200,000
F., by Giant's Causeway—Win's Fair Lady	Taylor Made Sales Agency, agent	Hugo Merry Bloodstock	Kee Sept.	1,200,000
C., by Mineshaft—Casual Look	Lane's End, agent	My Meadowview LLC	Kee Sept.	1,200,000
F., by Storm Cat—Fashion Star	Lane's End, agent	Diamond A Racing Corp.	Kee Sept.	1,200,000
C., by Storm Cat—Spunoutacontrol	Lane's End, agent	Lukas Enterprises	Kee Sept.	1,200,000
F., by Sadler's Wells—Dedicated Lady (Ire)	Camas Park Stud, Ireland	Charles P. Gordon-Watson	Tatt Oct.	1,154,128
C., by Kurofune—=Fusaichi Airedale (Jpn)	Northern Farm	Rosehill Thoroughbred Mgmt.	Japan July	1,133,603
C., by Montjeu (Ire)—=Secret Dream (Ire)	Voute Sales LLC, agent	Demi O'Byrne	Tatt Oct.	1,111,383
F., by Dansili (GB)—Valleyrose (Ire)	Haras de la Reboursiere et de Montaig	Shadwell France	Deauville Aug.	1,073,280
C., by Montjeu (Ire)—Millennium Dash (GB)	Meon Valley Stud	Demi O'Byrne	Tatt Oct.	1,068,637
C., by Distorted Humor—Lots of Hope (Brz)	Lane's End, agent	Stud TNT	Kee Sept.	1,050,000
C., by Unbridled's Song—Bally Five	Lane's End, agent	John Moynihan, agent	Kee Sept.	1,050,000
C., by Unbridled's Song—Riboletta (Brz)	Taylor Made Sales Agency, agent	John Ferguson Bloodstock	F-T Saratoga	1,050,000
F., by Cape Cross (Ire)—=Zelding (Ire)	Kilfrush Stud	Robert Collet	Deauville Aug.	1,046,448
C., by =Dalakhani (Ire)—=Time Honoured (GB)	Jamie Railton, agent	John Ferguson Bloodstock	Tatt Oct.	1,025,892
F., by =Kyllachy (Ire)—Halland Park Lass (Ire)	Trickledown Stud	Blandford Bloodstock	Tatt Oct.	1,025,892
C., by Oasis Dream (GB)—=Wunders Dream (Ire)	Corduff Stud	John Magnier	Tatt Oct.	1,025,892
C., by =Pivotal (GB)—Miss Pinkerton (GB)	Hascombe Stud	Demi O'Byrne	Tatt Oct.	1,015,205
C., by A.P. Indy—House Party	Lane's End, agent	Demi O'Byrne	Kee Sept.	1,000,000
C., by Distorted Humor—Alchemist	Middlebrook Farm, agent	John Ferguson Bloodstock	Kee Sept.	1,000,000
C., by Distorted Humor—Santa Croce	Winter Quarter Farm, agent	WinStar Farm, agent	Kee Sept.	1,000,000
C., by Distorted Humor—Seattle Queen	Paramount Sales, agent for Swordlestown Stud	Shadwell Estate Co. Ltd.	Kee Sept.	1,000,000
C., by Johannesburg—American Jewel	Dromoland Farm, agent	Jacob J. Pletcher, agent	Kee Sept.	1,000,000
F., by Kingmambo—Mystery Trip	Lane's End, agent	Gasper Bloodstock, agent	Kee Sept.	1,000,000
F., by Storm Cat—She's a Winner	Taylor Made Sales Agency, agent	WinStar Farm, agent	Kee Sept.	1,000,000
F., by Vindication—Seinita (Arg)	Gainesway, agent	John Ferguson Bloodstock	Kee Sept.	1,000,000
C., by Galileo (Ire)—=Onereuse (GB)	Clare Castle	Demi O'Byrne	Goffs Orby	973,176
C., by Montjeu (Ire)—Maskaya (Ire)	Croom House Stud	Demi O'Byrne	Goffs Orby	973,176
C., by Galileo (Ire)—=Llia (GB)	Lavington Stud	John Warren Bloodstock	Tatt Oct.	961,773
C., by Distorted Humor—Bold Burst	Dromoland Farm, agent	John Ferguson Bloodstock	Kee Sept.	950,000
F., by Oasis Dream (GB)—=Sunset Cafe (Ire)	Lodge Park Stud	Margaret O'Toole	Tatt Oct.	919,028
C., by Oasis Dream (GB)—Rubies From Burma	Watership Down Stud	John Ferguson Bloodstock	Tatt Oct.	908,341
F., by A.P. Indy—Felicita	Taylor Made Sales Agency, agent	Century Ventures	Kee Sept.	900,000
C., by =Indian Ridge (Ire)—=Alleluia (GB)	Airlie Stud	Charles P. Gordon-Watson	Goffs Orby	898,317
C., by Distorted Humor—Queen of Money	Bluegrass T'bred. Services, agent	B. Wayne Hughes	F-T Saratoga	875,000
F., by Storm Cat—Blissful	Eaton Sales, agent	Lukas Enterprises	F-T Saratoga	875,000
C., by Montjeu (Ire)—=Park Crystal (Ire)	Castlemartin Stud	Demi O'Byrne	Goffs Orby	860,887
C., by =Medicean (GB)—=Complimentary Pass (GB)	Croom House Stud	Shadwell Estate Co. Ltd.	Tatt Oct.	854,910

Highest-Priced Weanlings of 2007

Horse	Consignor	Buyer	Sale	Price
C., by Kurofune—=My Katies (Jpn)	Northern Farm	Riichi Kondo	Japan July	$2,429,150
F., by Pulpit—Madcap Escapade	Hill 'n' Dale Sales Agency, agent	Southern Equine Stable	Kee Nov.	1,700,000
C., by =Agnes Tachyon (Jpn)—Rustic Belle	Northern Farm	Takaya Shimakawa	Japan July	1,255,061
C., by =King Kamehameha (Jpn)—=Must Be Loved (Jpn)	Northern Farm	Riichi Kondo	Japan July	1,255,061
C., by Kurofune—=Fusaichi Airedale (Jpn)	Northern Farm	Rosehill Thoroughbred Mgmt.	Japan July	1,093,117
C., by Galileo (Ire)—=Epping (GB)	Newtown Stud	Demi O'Byrne	Tatt Dec.	1,017,054
C., by =Monsun (Ger)—=Mandamou (Ger)	Hillwood Stud	Demi O'Byrne	Tatt Dec.	973,775
F., by =Agnes Tachyon (Jpn)—Manfath (Ire)	Northern Farm	Grandprix Co. Ltd.	Japan July	971,660
C., by Kingmambo—Because (Ire)	Eaton Sales, agent	John Ferguson Bloodstock	Kee Nov.	950,000
C., by Kingmambo—Bejoyfulandrejoyce	Northern Farm	Nobutaka Tada	Japan July	890,688
C., by =King Kamehameha (Jpn)—Roza Robata	Northern Farm	Danox Co. Ltd.	Japan July	874,494
C., by Oasis Dream (GB)—=Dominica (GB)	Stowell Hill Stud	John Ferguson Bloodstock	Tatt Dec.	865,578
F., by Kingmambo—Crystal Crossing (Ire)	Hill 'n' Dale Sales Agency, agent for Swettenham Stud	Gasper Bloodstock, agent	Kee Nov.	850,000
C., by =Manhattan Cafe (Jpn)—Daring Danzig	Shadai Farm	Takaya Shimakawa	Japan July	825,911
C., by Montjeu (Ire)—=Masskana (Ire)	West Blagdon Stud	Demi O'Byrne	Tatt Dec.	822,299
C., by =Zenno Rob Roy (Jpn)—Argentine Star (Arg)	Shadai Farm	Nobutaka Tada	Japan July	809,717
F., by Giant's Causeway—Fly North	Gainesway, agent	Demi O'Byrne	Kee Nov.	800,000
C., by Falbrav (Ire)—Ringlet (Jpn)	Northern Farm	Kaneko Makoto Holdings	Japan July	793,522
C., by =Agnes Tachyon (Jpn)—=Xua (Ire)	Shadai Farm	Globe Equine Management	Japan July	777,328
C., by Ghostzapper—Checkered Flag	Bluewater Sales, agent	Ronald L. Rhodes, agent	Kee Nov.	775,000
C., by =Fuji Kiseki (Jpn)—Tricky Code	Oiwake Farm	Kaneko Makoto Holdings	Japan July	744,939
C., by =Neo Universe (Jpn)—Good Game	Northern Farm	Riichi Kondo	Japan July	744,939
F., by Ghostzapper—Questress	Hill 'n' Dale Sales Agency, agent	Baden P. Chace, agent	Kee Nov.	735,000
C., by =Neo Universe (Jpn)—=Birthday Rose (Jpn)	Shadai Farm	Takaya Shimakawa	Japan July	728,745
F., by Dynaformer—Mandela (Ger)	Three Chimneys Sales, agent	John Ferguson Bloodstock	Kee Nov.	700,000
C., by Montjeu (Ire)—=Sweeten Up (GB)	John Troy, agent	Demi O'Byrne	Tatt Dec.	670,822
C., by =King Kamehameha (Jpn)—Lady Ballade (Ire)	K. I. Farm	Yasushi Tsumura	Japan July	655,870
C., by =Special Week (Jpn)—Taiki Dia	Paca Paca Farm	Kaneko Makoto Holdings	Japan July	631,579
C., by =Pivotal (GB)—Monnavanna (Ire)	John Troy, agent	John Ferguson Bloodstock	Tatt Dec.	627,544
C., by =Motivator (GB)—=Diagonale (Ire)	Darley Japan	RRA Co. Ltd.	Japan July	615,385
C., by =Pivotal (GB)—Fortune (Ire)	Darley Japan	Danox Co. Ltd.	Japan July	615,385
F., by Dynaformer—Prima Centauri	Eaton Sales, agent	Overbrook Farm	Kee Nov.	600,000
C., by Brian's Time—Lady Upstage (Ire)	Shiraoi Farm	Kaneko Makoto Holdings	Japan July	599,190
C., by Fusaichi Pegasus—Kournakova (Ire)	Northern Farm	RRA Co. Ltd.	Japan July	582,996
C., by Symboli Kris S—=Out of the Whim (Jpn)	Northern Farm	Grandprix Co. Ltd.	Japan July	582,996
C., by =Agnes Tachyon (Jpn)—=Stars In Her Eyes (Ire)	Yano Farm	Danox Co. Ltd.	Japan July	574,899
C., by =Durandal (Jpn)—=Miss Berbere (Fr)	Shadai Farm	Danox Co. Ltd.	Japan July	566,802
C., by Timber Country—Silent Prayer (Jpn)	Shadai Farm	Takaya Shimakawa	Japan July	558,704
C., by Symboli Kris S—=Relique Reine (Jpn)	Shadai Farm	Hiroyoshi Usuda	Japan July	550,607
C., by Fusaichi Pegasus—Butterfly Blue (Ire)	Michael C. Byrne, agent	Olin B. Gentry, agent	Kee Nov.	550,000
F., by Hennessy—Polar Bird (Ire)	Hill 'n' Dale Sales Agency, agent for Swettenham Stud	Frankfort Park Farm	Kee Nov.	550,000
C., by Galileo (Ire)—=Lady Karr (GB)	Castlebridge Consignment	T. Hyde	Tatt Dec.	540,986
C., by Brian's Time—Home Sweet Home	Chiyada Farm	Yasushi Tsumura	Japan July	534,413
C., by =Neo Universe (Jpn)—Indy Bold	Shadai Farm	Keiko Tahara	Japan July	534,413
C., by =Agnes Tachyon (Jpn)—Rubia	Northern Farm	Riichi Kondo	Japan July	526,316
F., by Green Desert—=Hotelgenie Dot Com (GB)	Catridge Farm Stud	Dwayne Woods	Tatt Dec.	519,346
C., by Green Desert—Lucky for Me	Cooneen Stud	Shadwell Estate Co. Ltd.	Tatt Dec.	519,346
C., by =Pivotal (GB)—=Tiriana (GB)	Mill House Stud, agent	John Ferguson Bloodstock	Tatt Dec.	519,346
C., by Singspiel (Ire)—=Josette (Ire)	Shadai Farm	RRA Co. Ltd.	Japan July	518,219
C., by Unbridled's Song—Ancho	Oiwake Farm	Danox Co. Ltd.	Japan July	510,121
C., by Harlan's Holiday—Elrose	Bluewater Sales, agent	B. Wayne Hughes	Kee Nov.	500,000
F., by Galileo (Ire)—=Mohican Princess (GB)	St. Simon Stud	Kennycourt Stud Farm	Tatt Dec.	497,707
C., by Montjeu (Ire)—Magnificent Style	Swettenham Stud	New Cross Bloodstock	Tatt Dec.	497,707
C., by =Durandal (Jpn)—=Western World (GB)	Northern Farm	Danox Co. Ltd.	Japan July	493,927
C., by Kurofune—=Fast Friend (Jpn)	Northern Farm	Yoshirou Kubota	Japan July	493,927
C., by Galileo (Ire)—=Dapprima (Ger)	Knocktoran Stud	Kennycourt Stud Farm	Tatt Dec.	476,067
F., by Galileo (Ire)—=Royal Fizz (Ire)	Norelands Stud	Charles P. Gordon-Watson	Tatt Dec.	476,067
C., by Unbridled's Song—Ashtabula	Taylor Made Sales Agency, agent	Gulf Coast Farms	Kee Nov.	475,000
C., by Broken Vow—Tango Passion	Blandford Stud, agent	Chesapeake Partners	Kee Nov.	460,000
F., by Sadler's Wells—Diali	Chevington Stud and Loughtown Stud	Margaret O'Toole	Tatt Dec.	454,428
C., by Falbrav (Ire)—=Spring a Mine (Jpn)	Shadai Farm	Hiroyoshi Usuda	Japan July	453,441
C., by =Tiger Hill (Ire)—=May Ball (GB)	Shadai Farm	Globe Equine Management	Japan July	453,441
C., by =Zenno Rob Roy (Jpn)—=Air Rag Doll (Jpn)	Shadai Farm	Kaneko Makoto Holdings	Japan July	445,344
C., by =Monsun (Ger)—Ailette (Jpn)	European Sales Management	T. Hyde	Tatt Dec.	443,608
C., by Kurofune—=Primrose Eve (Jpn)	Shadai Farm	Takushi Hirai	Japan July	437,247
C., by Dansili (GB)—=Bandanna (GB)	Stowell Hill Stud	Willie Browne	Tatt Dec.	432,789
C., by Montjeu (Ire)—=Delicieuse Lady (GB)	Knocktoran Stud	Glenvale Stud	Tatt Dec.	432,789
F., by Mr. Greeley—Civility Cat	Churchman House Stud	BBA (Ireland)	Tatt Dec.	432,789
C., by Noverre—=Radha Cindari (Ire)	Ballybin Stud	A. O. Nerses	Tatt Dec.	432,789
F., by Fantastic Light—Sharpwitted (GB)	Darley Japan	Takaya Shimakawa	Japan July	429,150
C., by =Sakura Bakushin O (Jpn)—=Toccoa (Jpn)	Northern Farm	Kaneko Makoto Holdings	Japan July	429,150
C., by Mr. Greeley—Jive Talk	Hunter Valley Farm, agent	Brushwood Stable	Kee Nov.	425,000
C., by =Agnes Tachyon (Jpn)—=Erimo Excel	Northern Farm	Riichi Kondo	Japan July	421,053
C., by Giant's Causeway—Saudia	Gracefield, agent	Grove Stud	Kee Nov.	420,000

Highest-Priced Two-Year-Olds of 2007

Horse, Sex, Sire—Dam	Consignor	Buyer	Sale	Price
The Leopard, c., by Storm Cat—Moon Safari	Hoby and Layna Kight, agent for Kight, Adams, Mattox, & Raymon	Demi O'Byrne	F-T Calder	$2,500,000
Patricia's Gem, f., by Mineshaft—Stylish Talent	Hartley/De Renzo Thoroughbreds	B. Wayne Hughes	Kee April	1,750,000
Wolgan Valley, c., by Mr. Greeley—Dancing Naturally	Wavertree Stables, agent	John Ferguson Bloodstock	F-T Calder	1,450,000
Noble Lad, c., by Officer—Rovie Wade	B.C.3 Thoroughbreds, agent	John Ferguson Bloodstock	Barretts March	1,400,000
Strike the Deal, c., by Van Nistelrooy—Countess Gold	Shalfleet Stables	Kerri Radcliffe	Tatt Dec.	1,038,693
Anewday, c., by Vindication—Charm a Gendarme	Scanlon Training Center, agent	RBTS, agent	F-T Calder	1,000,000
More Happy, f., by Vindication—Apelia	Eddie Woods, agent	Hill 'n' Dale Bloodstock	F-T Calder	1,000,000
Sebastian County, c., by Hennessy—Double Park (Fr)	Tony Bowling & Bobby Dodd, agent	Buzz Chace, agent	F-T Calder	1,000,000
Seventh Street, f., by Street Cry (Ire)—Holiday Runner	John D. Stephens	John Ferguson Bloodstock	F-T Calder	1,000,000
Silver Trigger, c., by Forestry—Unbridled Spirit	Four Roses Thoroughbreds	John Ferguson Bloodstock	F-T Calder	1,000,000
Benjamin Z, c., by Johannesburg—Decadent Designer	B.C.3 Thoroughbreds, agent	Zayat Stables	Barretts March	950,000
Forest Echoes, c., by Forest Wildcat—Whattacapote	Eisaman Equine Services	John Ferguson Bloodstock	OBS March	900,000
Heisman U, c., by Fusaichi Pegasus—Gera, by Capote	Scanlon Training Center, agent	B. Wayne Hughes	F-T Calder	900,000
Royal Estate, c., by Harlan's Holiday—Third Street	Murray Smith, agent	John Ferguson Bloodstock	F-T Calder	850,000
Blessing, f., by Pulpit—My Prayer	Niall Brennan Stables, agent	Robert Ogden	F-T Calder	800,000
Charming Hostess, f., by Cape Town—Charming Gal	B.C.3 Thoroughbreds, agent	John Ferguson Bloodstock	Barretts March	800,000
Rocky Engagement, c., by Stormy Atlantic—Corner the Groom	Scanlon Training Center, agent	John Ferguson Bloodstock	Barretts March	800,000
Verify, c., by Vindication—Twosies Answer	Hartley/De Renzo, agent	Stonestreet Stables LLC	F-T Calder	800,000
Unnamed, f., by Quiet American—Laiyl (Ire)	Kirkwood Stables	Gill Richardson Bloodstock	Tatt April	779,836
Irish Smoke, f., by Smoke Glacken—Added Time	Hill 'n' Dale Sales Agency, agent	IEAH Stables	F-T Ky. Nov.	750,000
Unnamed, f., by Tale of the Cat—Flashy Attraction	Robert J. Harris, agent	Demi O'Byrne	F-T Calder	725,000
A Shin Sun Star, c., by Sky Mesa—Sailing On	Kirkwood Stables, agent	Hirotsugu Hirai	F-T Calder	700,000
Freakstein, f., by Bernstein—Cometuseibella	B.C.3 Thoroughbreds, agent	Zayat Stables	Barretts March	700,000
Messias da Silva, f., by Tale of the Cat—Indy Power	Maurice W. Miller, agent	Robert Ogden	F-T Calder	700,000
That's OK, f., by Not For Love—My New Pal	Niall Brennan Stables, agent	John Ferguson Bloodstock	F-T Calder	700,000
Pont des Soupirs, c., by Harlan's Holiday—Flirted	Mocklershill Stables	John Ferguson Bloodstock	Tatt April	674,452
Without Prejudice, c., by Johannesburg—Awesome Strike	Bansha House Stables	Jamie McCalmont	Tatt April	653,376
Inner Light, c., by Songandaprayer—Pinta	B.C.3 Thoroughbreds, agent for John J. Brocklebank	Zayat Stables	F-T Calder	650,000
Square Deal, c., by Sky Mesa—Jaded	Sequel Bloodstock, agent	JMJ Racing Stables	Barretts May	650,000
Charming Assets, f., by Empire Maker—Storm Away	Jerry Bailey Sales Agency, agent	John Ferguson Bloodstock	Barretts March	600,000
Classic Aspiration, f., by Mr. Greeley—Crusie	Kirkwood Stables, agent	Centennial Farms	Kee April	600,000
Sign of the Four, c., by Forestry—Sez Fourty	H.T. Training, agent	Stonestreet Stables LLC	Barretts March	600,000
Vulcan, c., by Tiznow—Clear Destiny	Scanlon Training Center, agent	John W. Sadler	F-T Calder	600,000
Grand Vow, c., by Broken Vow—French Grand	Niall Brennan Stables, agent	Buzz Chace, agent	F-T Midlantic	575,000
Not for Gold, c., by Not For Love—Glacken's Grace	Scanlon Training Center, agent	B. Wayne Hughes	F-T Calder	550,000
Smoke'n Coal, c., by Smoke Glacken—Cherokyfrolicflash	Peacock Ridge, agent	Darley	OBS Feb.	550,000
Total Bull, c., by Fusaichi Pegasus—Pattern Step	Ricky Leppala, agent	Patti and Hal Earnhardt III	F-T Calder	550,000
Venetian Causeway, f., by Giant's Causeway—Alleged World	Kirkwood Stables, agent	Stewart L. Armstrong	F-T Calder	550,000
Sibi Saba, f., by Dixieland Band—Dancing Mirage	Mocklershill Stables	John Ferguson Bloodstock	Tatt April	547,992
Francesca D'Gorgio, f., by Proud Citizen—Betty's Solutions	Niall Brennan Stables, agent	Robert Ogden	F-T Calder	530,000
Sagaponack, c., by Hussonet—Reina Victoriosa (Arg)	Wavertree Stables, agent	Jerry Frankel	Kee April	525,000
Jumpin Charlie, c., by Indian Charlie—Misty Weave	Wavertree Stables, agent	John W. Sadler, agent	Barretts March	520,000
Kindasorta, f., by Yankee Gentleman—Aray	Excel Bloodstock, agent	John Ferguson Bloodstock	F-T Calder	510,000
Big Divot, c., by Distorted Humor—Ms Louisett	Don R. Graham	Stonestreet Stables LLC	F-T Calder	500,000
Cohen Thebarbarian, c., by Pulpit—Dama	Leprechaun Racing, agent	IEAH Stables	F-T Calder	500,000
County Storm, f., by Storm Cat—County Fair	Niall Brennan Stables, agent	Christopher S. Paasch	F-T Calder	500,000
Explosive Surge, c., by Mineshaft—Immerse	Sequel Bloodstock, agent	Dennis R. O'Neill	Kee April	500,000
Final Lap, c., by A.P. Indy—Golden Sonata	Casse Sales, agent	W. S. Farish	OBS March	500,000
Lindelaan, f., by Rahy—Crystal Symphony	Casse Sales, agent	John McCormack	F-T Calder	500,000
Perfect Saturday, c., by Empire Maker—Lady of Choice	Scanlon Training Center, agent	Michael J. Ryan, agent	F-T Calder	500,000
Phantom Wildcat, c., by Forest Wildcat—Valarone	Murray Smith, agent	Sierra Sunset	Barretts March	500,000
Rollers, c., by Stormy Atlantic—Elise'	Nick de Meric, agent	Lael Stables	OBS Feb.	500,000
That's Grand, c., by Grand Slam—Goodness	Leprechaun Racing, agent	John W. Sadler, agent	OBS March	500,000
Manofthewest, c., by Gone West—Twin Sails	Hoby and Layna Kight, agent	Eldon Farm Equine	F-T Calder	485,000
Yetholm, c., by Dynaformer—Gypsy	Bansha House Stables	Amanda J. Skiffington	Tatt April	484,762
Distorted Passion, f., by Distorted Humor—Arianna's Passion	Jerry Bailey Sales Agency, agent	Legacy Ranch	Barretts March	475,000
Pulpitina, f., by Pulpit—Double Sixes	Stephens Thoroughbreds, agent for Vision Sales	David E. Hager, agent	Kee April	475,000
Ikigail, c., by Whywhywhy—Contessa Halo	Wavertree Stables, agent	John W. Sadler, agent	Barretts March	470,000
Raw Silk, f., by Malibu Moon—Silken Sash (Ire)	Niall Brennan Stables, agent	John Ferguson Bloodstock	F-T Calder	460,000
British Columbia, c., by E Dubai—Courtney Lake	Eddie Woods, agent	John Ferguson Bloodstock	F-T Calder	450,000
Influenced, f., by Malibu Moon—Tsu Lou	Sequel Bloodstock, agent	JMJ Racing Stables	Barretts March	450,000
Magical Freedom, c., by El Corredor—Freedom's Magic	Jerry Bailey Sales Agency, agent	Southern Equine Stable	Barretts May	450,000
Overbid, c., by Pulpit—Critikola (Arg)	Jerry Bailey Sales Agency, agent	Southern Equine Stable	Kee April	450,000
Tanganyika, c., by Smart Strike—Valenza	H. T. Stables, agent for Montpelier Thoroughbreds Inc.	John P. Fort	F-T Calder	450,000
Tiz T'was, f., by Tiznow—French Satin	Eddie Woods, agent	Southern Equine Stable	Barretts May	450,000
Phantom Strike, c., by Elusive Quality—Light of the Moon	Niall Brennan Stables, agent	Al and Sandee Kirkwood	Kee April	440,000
Acclaimed, c., by Vindication—Statuette	Scanlon Training Center, agent	Michael J. Ryan, agent	F-T Calder	430,000
Kiss the Ring, f., by Touch Gold—Act Devoted	Hoby and Layna Kight, agent	Merry/Newmarket/Meehan	F-T Calder	430,000
Tribal Star, c., by Tribal Rule—Star of the Woods	Excel Bloodstock, agent	Marsha J. Naify	Barretts May	430,000
Ernie Owl, c., by Tale of the Cat—Capitol View	Welcome Gate Farm	B. Meehan/Newmarket Int'l.	OBS Feb.	425,000
Humboldt, c., by Forestry—Cozy Blues	Niall Brennan Stables, agent	W. K. Warren	Barretts March	425,000
M Biarritz, c., by Came Home—Big Fins	Kirkwood Stables, agent	Dennis R. O'Neill	F-T Calder	425,000
Processor's Turf, c., by Sky Mesa—Procession	Niall Brennan Stables, agent	John W. Sadler, agent	F-T Calder	425,000

Highest-Priced Broodmares and Broodmare Prospects of 2007

Horse (Covering Sire), Sex, Age	Consignor	Buyer	Sale	Price
Playful Act (Ire), m., 5	Hill 'n' Dale Sales Agency, agent for Swettenham Stud	John Ferguson Bloodstock	Kee Nov.	$10,500,000
Satwa Queen (Fr), m., 5	Jean de Roualle	John Ferguson Bloodstock	Tatt Dec.	7,357,413
Ocean Silk (=Pivotal [GB]), m., 7	Swettenham Stud	John Ferguson Bloodstock	Tatt Dec.	6,924,624
Sander Camillo, f., 3	Shalfleet Stables	John Ferguson Bloodstock	Tatt Dec.	6,924,624
Angara (GB) (Montjeu [Ire]), m., 6	Swettenham Stud	London Thoroughbred Services	Tatt Dec.	6,491,835
=Mandellicht (Ire), m., 13	Ronald Rauscher, agent	Richard O'Gorman Bloodstock	Tatt Dec.	6,491,835
Round Pond, m., 5	Taylor Made Sales Agency, agent for Fox Hill Farms	John Ferguson Bloodstock	F-T Nov.	5,750,000
Spun Sugar (A.P. Indy), m., 5	Hidden Brook Farm, agent for Adena Springs	Shadwell Estate Co. Ltd.	Kee Nov.	4,500,000
=Indian Ink (Ire), f., 3	East Everleigh Stables	Shadwell Estate Co. Ltd.	Tatt Dec.	4,327,890
Island Sand (A.P. Indy), m., 6	Maynard Farm, agent for B. A. Mann Inc.	Kern/Lillingston Association, agent	Kee Nov.	4,200,000
Octave, f., 3	Taylor Made Sales Agency	John Ferguson Bloodstock	F-T Nov.	4,000,000
Ama, f., 3	Haras de Fresnay Le Buffard	John Ferguson Bloodstock	Tatt Dec.	3,895,101
=Beta (GB), f., 3	Haras de Fresnay Le Buffard	John Ferguson Bloodstock	Tatt Dec.	3,678,706
Dream Rush, f., 3	Hill 'n' Dale Sales Agency, agent	Halsey Minor	F-T Nov.	3,300,000
Kamarinskaya (Kingmambo), f., 4	Lane's End, agent	Kern/Lillingston Association, agent	Kee Nov.	3,200,000
Adoration (Smart Strike), m., 8	Mill Ridge Sales, agent	Demi O'Byrne	Kee Nov.	3,100,000
=Galatee (Fr) (=Dalakhani [Ire]), f., 4	Ennistown Stud, Ireland	John Ferguson Bloodstock	Tatt Dec.	3,029,523
Asi Siempre, m., 5	Bluewater Sales, agent	John Ferguson Bloodstock	F-T Nov.	3,000,000
Indy Five Hundred (Kingmambo), m., 7	Lane's End, agent	John Ferguson Bloodstock	F-T Nov.	3,000,000
Evil (Bernardini), m., 9	Taylor Made Sales Agency, agent	John Ferguson Bloodstock	Kee Nov.	2,700,000
Lemons Forever, f., 4	Eaton Sales, agent	R. J. Bennett	Kee Nov.	2,500,000
=Sweet Stream (Ity) (=Monsun [Ger]), m., 7	European Sales Management	Charles P. Gordon-Watson	Tatt Dec.	2,380,339
Melhor Ainda (Maria's Mon), m., 5	Lane's End, agent	John Ferguson Bloodstock	Kee Nov.	2,300,000
Pussycat Doll, m., 5	Hill 'n' Dale Sales Agency, agent	Lael Stables	F-T Nov.	2,300,000
Rosa Parks (GB) (Kingmambo), m., 8	Three Chimneys Sales, agent for Eydon Hall Farm	John Ferguson Bloodstock	Kee Nov.	2,300,000
Sand Springs (Kingmambo), m., 7	Hill 'n' Dale Sales Agency, agent for Swettenham Stud	RBTS, agent	Kee Nov.	2,300,000
Amorama (Fr) (Ghostzapper), m., 6	Hidden Brook Farm, agent for Adena Springs	Cecil O. Seaman, agent	Kee Nov.	2,100,000
Megahertz (GB) (Bernardini), m., 8	Mill Ridge Sales, agent	Lael Stables and Nicoma Bloodstock, agent	Kee Nov.	2,100,000
Lovely Regina (A.P. Indy), m., 6	Lane's End, agent	Padua Stables	Kee Nov.	2,000,000
Leto (Galileo [Ire]), f., 4	Kiltinan Stud, Ireland	Charles P. Gordon-Watson	Tatt Dec.	1,947,550
Be My Queen (Ire) (Mr. Greeley), f., 4	Gainesway, agent	M L Bloodstock Ltd.	Kee Nov.	1,900,000
Cotton Blossom, f., 3	Three Chimneys Sales, agent for Dogwood Stable	Overbrook Farm	F-T Nov.	1,900,000
Lovely Rafaela (Forestry), m., 6	Lane's End, agent	Live Oak Plantation	Kee Nov.	1,900,000
Singhalese (GB) (Rahy), m., 5	Three Chimneys Sales, agent for Gould Family Trust	Katsumi Yoshida	Kee Nov.	1,900,000
Winds Of March (Ire) (Kingmambo), m., 6	Lane's End, agent	My Meadowview LLC	Kee Nov.	1,900,000
Bushfire, f., 4	Taylor Made Sales Agency, agent	Shadai Farm	Kee Nov.	1,850,000
Happy Tune (Storm Cat), m., 12	Taylor Made Sales Agency, agent	Stonestreet Thoroughbred Holdings	Kee Nov.	1,850,000
Point Ashley, f., 3	Hill 'n' Dale Sales Agency, agent	Hill 'n' Dale Bloodstock	Kee Jan.	1,800,000
=Distinctive Look (Ire) (Galileo [Ire]), f., 4	Swettenham Stud	John Warren Bloodstock	Tatt Dec.	1,785,254
Spoken Fur (Smart Strike), m., 7	Mill Ridge Sales, agent	Southern Equine Stable	Kee Nov.	1,650,000
Silverskaya (Galileo [Ire]), m., 6	European Sales Management	Charles P. Gordon-Watson	Tatt Dec.	1,622,958
Quiet Eclipse (A.P. Indy), m., 11	Taylor Made Sales Agency, agent	Stonestreet Thoroughbred Holdings	Kee Nov.	1,600,000
=Madura (Ger) (=Monsun [Ger]), f., 4	Kiltinan Stud, Ireland	Simon Christian	Tatt Dec.	1,536,400
=Indian Maiden (Ire) (Mr. Greeley), m., 7	Ballyhimikin Stud, Ireland	Cecil O. Seaman, agent	Tatt Dec.	1,514,761
Downthedustyroady, f., 4	Eaton Sales, agent	Fleetwood Bloodstock	Kee Jan.	1,500,000
Flaming Heart (Street Cry [Ire]), m., 6	Hidden Brook Farm, agent for Adena Springs	WinStar Farm	Kee Nov.	1,500,000
River's Prayer, f., 4	Taylor Made Sales Agency, agent	Stonestreet Thoroughbred Holdings	Kee Nov.	1,500,000
Buy The Sport (Unbridled's Song), m., 7	Hidden Brook Farm, agent for Adena Springs	Shadai Farm	Kee Nov.	1,400,000
Chaibia (Ire) (A.P. Indy), f., 4	Lane's End, agent	Skara Glen Stables	Kee Nov.	1,400,000
Golden Sonata (Bernardini), m., 6	Lane's End, agent	Sha-li Leasing Associates	Kee Nov.	1,400,000
Mandela (Ger) (Mr. Greeley), m., 7	Three Chimneys Sales, agent	Katsumi Yoshida	Kee Nov.	1,400,000
Reina Victoriosa (Arg) (Ghostzapper), m., 11	Vinery, agent	Stonestreet Thoroughbred Holdings	F-T Nov.	1,400,000
Magic America, f., 3	Christiane Head	London Thoroughbred Services	Tatt Dec.	1,352,465
Cassydora (GB) (Hennessy), m., 5	Matagorda Farm, agent	BBA (Ireland)	Kee Nov.	1,350,000
Real Expectations (Mr. Greeley), f., 4	Taylor Made Sales Agency, agent	Success Racing Team	Kee Nov.	1,350,000
=Jewel in the Sand (Ire) (Galileo [Ire]), m., 5	Lisieux Stud, Ireland	Epona Bloodstock	Tatt Dec.	1,341,645
=White Rose (Ger) (=Pivotal [GB]), m., 7	Haras de Bouquetot	Blandford Bloodstock	Tatt Dec.	1,341,645
Guilty Pleasure (Bernardini), m., 10	Burleson Farms, agent	Stonestreet Thoroughbred Holdings	Kee Nov.	1,300,000
Passageway (=Pivotal [GB]), m., 5	Castlebridge Consignment	BBA (Ireland)	Tatt Dec.	1,298,367
Elrose (Empire Maker), m., 8	Bluewater Sales, agent	Stonestreet Thoroughbred Holdings	Kee Nov.	1,250,000
Kushnarenkovo (GB) (Kingmambo), f., 4	Eaton Sales, agent	Hugo Merry Bloodstock	Kee Nov.	1,250,000
Maryfield, m., 6	Taylor Made Sales Agency, agent	Southern Equine Stable	F-T Nov.	1,250,000
Pleasant Dixie (A.P. Indy), m., 12	Hill 'n' Dale Sales Agency, agent for Bridlewood Farm	Stonestreet Thoroughbred Holdings	Kee Nov.	1,250,000
=Mont Etoile (Ire), f., 4	Voute Sales LLC, agent	John Ferguson Bloodstock	Tatt Dec.	1,244,268
Untouched Talent (Unbridled's Song), f., 3	Hill 'n' Dale Sales Agency, agent	Audley Farm	Kee Nov.	1,200,000
Valbenny (Ire), f., 3	Three Chimneys Sales, agent	Lael Stables	F-T Nov.	1,200,000
=Rachelle (Ire) (Cape Cross [Ire]), m., 9	Jamie Railton, agent	John Ferguson Bloodstock	Tatt Dec.	1,190,169
Promenade Girl, m., 5	Eaton Sales, agent	Thoroughbred Advisory Group	Kee Nov.	1,125,000

Chronological Review of 2007 Sales

Sale	Sold	Total	Change	Average	Change	Median	Change	Top Price
January								
Keeneland January horses of all ages	1,862	$72,868,200	0.7%	$39,134	−11.9%	$15,000	−6.3%	$1,800,000
Stemman's winter mixed	105	225,300	140.6%	2,146	28.3%	1,000	−4.8%	17,000
Ocala Breeders' Sales Co. winter mixed	531	6,921,100	−34.4%	13,034	−8.2%	5,500	−9.8%	260,000
Heritage Place winter mixed	138	343,050	−20.5%	2,486	−24.0%	1,100	−51.1%	22,000
Barretts winter mixed	438	4,180,400	20.1%	9,544	20.7%	4,500	28.6%	560,000
February								
Fasig-Tipton Midlantic winter mixed	45	253,200	−50.8%	5,627	27.9%	4,000	100.0%	20,000
Tattersalls February breeding stock, fillies, horses in training, and yearlings	191	4,691,288	31.0%	24,562	39.3%	11,376	48.1%	393,015
Fasig-Tipton Kentucky winter mixed	371	6,332,300	−18.5%	17,068	−2.5%	7,000	40.0%	295,000
Ocala Breeders' Sales Co. selected two-year-olds in training	96	12,831,000	−1.0%	133,656	−4.1%	100,000	−9.1%	550,000
March								
Fasig-Tipton Florida selected two-year-olds in training	124	43,622,000	−29.9%	351,790	−12.9%	250,000	25.0%	2,500,000
Goffs Bloodstock Sales Ltd. breeze-up	65	4,005,556		61,624		48,283		212,445
John Franks Memorial two-year-olds in training	158	1,432,700	27.0%	9,068	−11.6%	4,850	−28.1%	135,000
Barretts March selected two-year-olds in training	88	19,340,000	34.7%	219,773	42.3%	147,500	84.4%	1,400,000
Adena Springs two-year-olds in training	90	4,892,000	11.3%	54,356	−19.6%	40,000	−11.1%	220,000
Ocala Breeders' Sales Co. selected two-year-olds in training	253	26,541,000	−14.5%	104,905	−3.4%	80,000	6.7%	900,000
April								
Fasig-Tipton Texas two-year-olds in training	183	3,263,200	−27.1%	17,832	−23.1%	10,000	−28.6%	180,000
Louisiana Thoroughbred Breeders Sales Co. spring mixed	89	223,850	−36.0%	2,515	−19.5%	1,600	−20.0%	20,000
Keeneland April two-year-olds in training	82	16,637,000	−9.8%	202,890	−4.3%	155,000	3.3%	1,750,000
Tattersalls Craven breeze-up two-year-olds in training	120	18,536,847	−8.5%	154,474	12.9%	115,921	24.0%	779,836
Ocala Breeders' Sales Co. spring two-year-olds in training	786	22,698,400	−7.6%	28,878	−11.1%	17,000	0.0%	410,000
Illinois Thoroughbred Breeders and Owners Foundation two-year-olds in training and horses of racing age	28	368,200	4.4%	13,150	4.4%	9,600	20.0%	54,000
May								
Tattersalls Guineas breeze-up two-year-olds in training	76	4,444,051		58,474		48,010		187,866
Iowa Thoroughbred Breeders and Owners two-year-olds in training	15	112,500	−57.6%	7,500	−43.5%	3,000	−52.0%	30,000
Mountain Springs Horse Sales racing bred spring mixed	76	293,050		3,856		2,600		15,500
Barretts May two-year-olds in training	181	11,331,300	7.8%	62,604	19.1%	25,000	−7.4%	650,000
Fasig-Tipton Midlantic two-year-olds in training	350	19,498,700	−8.2%	55,711	−2.9%	34,500	15.0%	575,000
June								
Michigan Thoroughbred Owners and Breeders Association two-year-olds in training and unraced three-year-olds	8	12,100		1,513		1,400		2,700
Ocala Breeders' Sales Co. June two-year-olds in training and horses of racing age	316	6,860,700	23.2%	21,711	−0.6%	13,000	−7.1%	260,000
Heritage Place summer mixed	20	52,550	−32.0%	2,628	49.6%	1,150	0.0%	15,000
Fasig-Tipton Midlantic two-year-olds in training and horses of racing age	61	879,800	24.3%	14,423	38.6%	9,000	53.8%	60,000
Barretts summer two-year-olds in training & horses of racing age	89	1,680,200	48.1%	18,879	99.7%	4,700	−21.7%	525,000
July								
Japan Racing Horse Association's selected foals and yearlings	348	93,740,062	−8.5%	269,368	−13.3%	202,429	−3.0%	2,429,150
Tattersalls July mixed sale	593	23,126,220	−1.9%	38,999	3.1%	22,173	4.2%	527,940
Fasig-Tipton Kentucky select yearling	354	36,441,000	2.4%	102,941	−11.2%	80,000	−11.1%	450,000
August								
Minnesota Thoroughbred Association state-bred yearling	48	368,200	35.3%	7,671	9.9%	5,100	27.5%	33,000
Louisiana Thoroughbred Breeders Sales Co. summer mixed	108	469,500	−30.6%	4,347	1.6%	2,700	−11.5%	17,000
Fasig-Tipton Saratoga selected yearling	142	41,082,000	−2.4%	289,310	−10.6%	227,500	−7.1%	2,200,000
Fasig-Tipton New York Saratoga preferred yearling	113	5,831,500	10.1%	51,606	−1.6%	37,000	5.7%	265,000
Fasig-Tipton New York Saratoga open yearling	73	523,600	−23.1%	7,173	−26.2%	4,200	−21.5%	50,000
Ruidoso Thoroughbred yearling and mixed	193	1,233,250	−24.5%	6,390	−23.3%	3,000	−25.0%	42,000
L'Agence Francaise Deauville August yearling sale	382	50,246,221	31.5%	131,519	26.0%	80,486	10.1%	1,878,240
Carter Sales Co. Oklahoma City summer Thoroughbred yearling	40	334,400		8,360		4,250		50,000
Ocala Breeders' Sales Co. selected yearling	945	18,726,900	−4.2%	19,817	0.8%	9,500	5.6%	210,000
Indiana Thoroughbred Owners and Breeders Association yearling and horses of all ages	37	83,600	42.1%	2,259	−0.2%	1,000	0.0%	30,000
Iowa Thoroughbred Breeders and Owners Assoc. fall mixed	59	206,300	−22.6%	3,497	1.1%	1,400	−17.6%	28,000
Michigan Thoroughbred Owners and Breeders Assoc. yearling	20	85,900	−56.0%	4,295	−29.6%	2,350	−24.2%	16,000
Fasig-Tipton Texas summer yearling	241	3,283,200	1.7%	13,623	14.8%	6,000	9.1%	330,000
C.T.H.S. (Alberta division) summer yearling	112	1,178,101	−1.3%	10,519	4.8%	6,302	0.0%	57,294
September								
C.T.H.S. (Manitoba division) yearling	23	97,627	−23.7%	4,245	9.5%	1,899	−8.6%	14,247
Washington Thoroughbred Breeders Assoc. summer yearling	147	2,214,100	−7.9%	15,062	−1.6%	12,000	20.0%	80,000
C.T.H.S. (Ontario division) selected and open yearling	310	7,238,326	−3.4%	23,349	−6.2%	11,397	−15.9%	185,211
Mountain Springs Horse Sales racing bred fall mixed	59	140,775		2,386		1,500		10,100
Keeneland September yearling	3,799	385,018,600	−3.7%	101,347	−9.9%	42,000	−6.7%	3,700,000
C.T.H.S. (British Columbia division) yearling and mixed	102	1,072,877	−24.1%	10,518	2.7%	4,988	−6.8%	47,510

Auctions — Histories of Major Sales

Sale	Sold	Total	Change	Average	Change	Median	Change	Top Price
C.T.H.S. (Alberta division) fall mixed	84	$ 186,816	−27.2%	$ 2,224	−9.9%	$ 1,102	19.4%	$ 11,520
Charles Town Thoroughbred Horse Sales West Virginia fall mixed	44	78,050	−33.7%	1,774	−14.2%	1,200	−20.0%	12,200
C.T.B.A. Northern California yearling	154	899,200	−33.5%	5,839	−28.7%	4,000	0.0%	40,000
October								
Louisiana Thoroughbred Breeders' Sales Co. yearling	98	602,800		6,151		3,350		40,000
Goffs Bloodstock Sales Ltd. Million yearling	488	80,625,192	1.7%	165,216	6.5%	107,798	15.0%	3,593,268
Fasig-Tipton Midlantic Eastern fall yearling	574	13,331,400	−8.6%	23,225	4.8%	10,000	−13.0%	325,000
Barretts Equine and C.T.B.A. October yearling	169	3,369,600	−22.3%	19,938	−21.4%	11,000	−31.3%	150,000
Oregon Thoroughbred Breeders Association fall mixed	48	50,350	−50.1%	1,049	−27.3%	675	−37.2%	5,000
Ocala Breeders' Sales Co. fall mixed	669	9,841,600	−29.3%	14,711	−10.7%	7,500	−1.3%	185,000
Tattersalls October yearling sale part 1	510	138,755,951	27.2%	272,070	7.8%	170,982	5.2%	5,343,187
New York Breeders' Sales Co. Saratoga fall mixed	170	1,778,700	27.0%	10,463	36.7%	4,000	−20.0%	85,000
Breeders Sales Co. of Louisiana fall mixed	244	1,478,100	−28.9%	6,058	−24.6%	2,200	−37.1%	90,000
Tattersalls October yearling sale part 2	473	51,292,457	−5.6%	108,441	71.9%	75,091	66.5%	643,639
Arizona Thoroughbred Breeders Association fall mixed	153	802,450	−7.3%	5,245	−6.1%	2,200	−21.4%	60,000
Tattersalls October yearling sale part 3	367	7,964,056	254.6%	21,700	73.0%	15,500	123.1%	154,057
Fasig-Tipton Kentucky fall yearling	566	10,595,700	8.7%	18,720	22.0%	10,000	33.3%	320,000
Heritage Place fall mixed	81	146,150		1,804		1,100		11,500
Barretts fall mixed	392	3,818,200	86.1%	9,740	74.2%	3,500	29.6%	250,000
November								
Tattersalls October yearling sale part 4	94	1,070,891		11,392		7,021		54,852
Fasig-Tipton Kentucky fall selected mixed	208	53,762,000	−19.1%	258,471	0.4%	50,000	−47.1%	5,750,000
Keeneland November breeding stock	3,381	340,877,200	8.6%	100,821	1.1%	35,000	0.0%	10,500,000
Tattersalls December mixed sale	1,690	221,419,461	10.6%	131,017	17.7%	43,278	−13.0%	7,357,413
December								
C.T.H.S. (Ontario division) fall mixed	115	568,300	9.8%	4,942	19.4%	2,700	14.5%	35,000
Washington Thoroughbred Breeders Association winter mixed	139	460,500	−32.9%	3,313	−10.2%	1,000	−54.5%	24,000
Fasig-Tipton Midlantic December mixed	287	2,056,500	−23.2%	7,166	−9.6%	3,500	9.4%	62,000
Fasig-Tipton Texas mixed	125	574,700	6.2%	4,598	5.3%	2,100	−25.0%	35,000

Histories of Major Sales

Following are the histories of several prominent Thoroughbred auctions in North America. The sales are listed by type of sale, with the order within each category determined by total sales.

Keeneland September Yearlings

Year	Offered	Sold	Total Sales	Chg	Average	Chg	High Price
2007	4,901	3,799	$385,018,600	−3.7%	$101,347	−9.9%	$3,700,000
2006	4,560	3,556	**399,791,800**	4.0%	**112,427**	3.7%	**11,700,000**
2005	4,510	3,544	384,147,400	18.3%	108,450	12.5%	9,700,000
2004	4,359	3,370	324,904,300	18.6%	96,411	4.5%	8,000,000
2003	3,819	2,968	273,925,300	29.9%	92,293	28.5%	3,800,000
2002	3,840	2,934	210,809,000	−17.1%	71,850	−18.2%	2,500,000
2001	4,003	2,895	254,190,600	−12.9%	87,803	−0.3%	6,400,000
2000	4,302	3,313	291,827,100	25.2%	88,085	13.8%	6,800,000
1999	3,788	3,011	233,020,800	37.2%	77,390	30.3%	3,900,000
1998	3,528	2,860	169,811,800	9.8%	59,375	9.2%	2,100,000
1997	3,396	2,844	154,666,800	12.7%	54,384	16.3%	2,300,000
1996	3,649	2,936	137,233,800	5.5%	46,742	6.2%	1,400,000
1995	3,495	2,955	130,085,300	24.4%	44,022	18.4%	1,200,000
1994	3,264	2,812	104,552,900	19.8%	37,181	6.1%	625,000
1993	2,862	2,492	87,308,100	11.3%	35,035	23.0%	775,000
1992	3,188	2,754	78,427,400	1.2%	28,478	−4.0%	400,000
1991	3,065	2,612	77,511,000	−10.7%	29,675	−0.5%	900,000
1990	3,310	2,909	86,756,500	12.8%	29,823	−12.6%	535,000
1989	2,578	2,253	76,887,600	19.2%	34,127	20.7%	700,000
1988	2,752	2,281	64,500,600	−10.8%	28,277	−14.6%	625,000
1987	2,452	2,182	72,289,100	28.9%	33,130	11.3%	1,100,000
1986	2,175	1,884	56,097,000	−9.1%	29,775	−10.8%	525,000
1985	2,172	1,849	61,741,900	10.6%	33,392	5.1%	440,000
1984	2,173	1,757	55,803,400	−10.4%	31,761	−4.5%	675,000
1983	2,245	1,848	61,766,100	30.9%	33,423	1.0%	735,000
1982	1,644	1,426	47,202,800	−20.6%	33,102	18.6%	400,000
1981	2,442	2,131	59,486,500	19.2%	27,915	3.7%	600,000
1980	1,967	1,855	49,922,800	50.9%	26,913	40.9%	310,000
1979†	N/A	1,733	33,082,200	47.2%	19,098	35.6%	300,000
1978	N/A	1,596	22,474,000	21.2%	14,081	8.2%	142,000
1977	N/A	1,425	18,538,500	14.3%	13,009	21.1%	200,000
1976	N/A	1,510	16,216,400	38.7%	10,739	12.8%	200,000
1975	N/A	1,228	11,688,000	−5.1%	9,518	23.7%	110,000
1974	N/A	1,601	12,315,700	17.7%	7,693	−5.8%	100,000

First held in current format in 1960. From 1944 to '48, fall yearlings were part of a mixed sale format. In 1949, approximately half the yearlings were sold in a separate October sale and the remainder in a November breeding stock sale. In 1950, yearlings were in a separate session of breeding stock sale. In 1951, fall yearling sales were separated from breeding stock by a week. Selected sessions were inaugurated in 1989.
† Before 1980, gross sales include RNAs. N/A Not available.

Auctions — Histories of Major Sales

Keeneland July Selected Yearlings

Year	Offered	Sold	Total Sales	Chg	Average	Chg	High Price
2002	146	87	$ 42,385,000	−32.9%	$487,184	−31.4%	$3,100,000
2001	132	89	63,212,000	−21.7%	710,247	14.4%	4,000,000
2000	180	130	80,732,000	5.1%	621,015	6.7%	3,600,000
1999	181	132	76,815,000	6.8%	581,932	20.5%	3,000,000
1998	201	149	71,932,000	15.0%	482,765	35.0%	4,000,000
1997	236	175	62,565,000	7.1%	357,514	2.2%	1,500,000
1996	204	167	58,430,000	25.8%	349,880	41.6%	1,700,000
1995	225	188	46,450,000	2.6%	247,074	5.9%	1,250,000
1994	257	194	45,265,000	−8.3%	233,325	−1.2%	1,050,000
1993	251	209	49,350,000	4.7%	236,124	−9.3%	1,050,000
1992	266	181	47,120,000	−35.8%	260,331	−18.8%	1,700,000
1991	300	229	73,443,000	−21.0%	320,712	10.8%	2,600,000
1990	416	321	92,920,000	−19.9%	289,470	−4.7%	2,900,000
1989	**448**	**382**	115,978,000	18.5%	303,607	−17.5%	2,800,000
1988	323	266	97,845,000	−10.1%	367,838	−1.3%	3,500,000
1987	344	292	108,839,000	4.5%	372,736	−9.5%	3,700,000
1986	291	253	104,174,000	−24.2%	411,755	−23.3%	3,600,000
1985	292	256	137,505,000	−17.2%	537,129	−10.5%	**13,100,000**
1984	320	277	**166,155,000**	12.8%	599,838	14.0%	8,250,000
1983	301	280	147,330,000	53.4%	526,179	52.9%	10,200,000
1982	297	279	96,027,000	7.5%	344,183	32.5%	4,250,000
1981	369	344	89,342,000	55.3%	259,715	29.6%	3,500,000
1980	301	287	57,522,000	21.2%	200,425	28.8%	1,700,000
1979†	N/A	305	47,448,000	11.4%	155,567	27.9%	1,600,000
1978	N/A	350	42,579,000	54.0%	121,654	42.5%	1,300,000
1977	N/A	324	27,651,000	20.0%	85,343	28.2%	725,000
1976	N/A	346	23,035,000	25.6%	66,575	24.1%	1,500,000
1975	N/A	342	18,344,000	7.2%	53,637	0.3%	715,000
1974	N/A	320	17,116,500	−13.9%	53,489	−5.9%	625,000

First held in 1943; last held in 2002. †Before 1980, gross sales include RNAs. N/A Not available.

Fasig-Tipton Saratoga Selected Yearlings

Year	Offered	Sold	Total Sales	Chg	Average	Chg	High Price
2007	188	142	$41,082,000	−2.4%	$289,310	−10.6%	$2,200,000
2006	160	130	42,085,000	25.9%	323,731	−0.2%	1,600,000
2005	136	103	33,415,000	−26.9%	324,417	6.5%	3,100,000
2004	191	150	45,705,000	−5.3%	304,700	−2.8%	3,300,000
2003	196	154	48,257,000	36.9%	313,357	24.5%	2,700,000
2002	196	140	35,242,000	−43.5%	251,729	−34.7%	1,300,000
2001	201	162	62,412,000	49.0%	**385,259**	26.0%	3,300,000
2000	173	137	41,901,000	7.6%	305,847	17.0%	4,200,000
1999	201	149	38,957,000	13.8%	261,456	23.7%	3,000,000
1998	220	162	34,246,000	23.7%	211,395	15.3%	1,700,000
1997	205	151	27,691,000	1.4%	183,384	13.5%	1,400,000
1996	220	169	27,311,000	21.1%	161,604	26.2%	630,000
1995	207	176	22,545,000	21.4%	128,097	32.5%	440,000
1994	241	192	18,566,000	53.4%	96,698	3.9%	520,000
1993	162	130	12,101,000	0.5%	93,085	−4.2%	350,000
1992	152	124	12,046,000	−20.0%	97,145	−19.4%	525,000
1991	168	125	15,062,000	−54.3%	120,496	−42.5%	800,000
1990	219	157	32,923,000	3.7%	209,701	−12.8%	1,500,000
1989	170	132	31,745,000	−12.0%	240,492	19.4%	1,750,000
1988	259	179	36,054,000	−23.1%	201,419	−16.6%	1,500,000
1987	237	194	46,871,000	22.0%	241,603	29.0%	2,400,000
1986	253	205	38,407,000	−24.3%	187,351	−27.7%	1,625,000
1985	233	196	50,760,000	6.1%	258,980	4.0%	2,700,000
1984	235	192	47,825,000	10.9%	249,089	17.8%	**4,600,000**
1983	248	204	43,127,000	19.6%	211,407	19.6%	3,000,000
1982	243	204	36,053,000	−5.7%	176,730	10.0%	2,100,000
1981	**265**	**238**	38,222,000	47.6%	160,597	44.5%	1,200,000
1980	253	233	25,900,000	26.3%	111,159	13.3%	1,600,000
1979†	N/A	209	20,502,000	22.2%	98,096	22.2%	650,000
1978	N/A	209	16,771,500	39.4%	80,246	40.0%	800,000
1977	N/A	210	12,035,000	14.5%	57,310	29.2%	375,000
1976	N/A	237	10,510,700	23.3%	44,349	19.6%	550,000
1975	N/A	230	8,525,700	2.3%	37,068	−0.4%	260,000
1974	N/A	224	8,337,100	−13.6%	37,219	−12.9%	350,000

First held in 1917. Not held 1943-'45, because of World War II travel restrictions.
† Before 1980, gross sales include RNAs. N/A Not available.

Fasig-Tipton Kentucky July Selected Yearlings

Year	Offered	Sold	Total Sales	Chg	Average	Chg	High Price
2007	520	354	$36,441,000	2.4%	$102,941	−11.2%	$450,000
2006	407	307	35,598,000	−4.1%	**115,954**	15.0%	1,200,000
2005	**603**	368	37,106,000	−3.9%	100,832	−11.8%	650,000
2004	452	338	38,620,000	36.9%	114,260	22.8%	950,000
2003	425	303	28,202,000	−11.3%	93,076	−4.8%	800,000
2002	536	325	31,790,000	37.3%	97,815	0.1%	700,000

Year	Offered	Sold	Total Sales	Chg	Average	Chg	High Price
2001	381	237	$23,148,000	−11.6%	$97,671	25.7%	$625,000
2000	517	337	26,186,500	17.9%	77,705	3.6%	525,000
1999	361	296	22,211,000	58.2%	75,037	35.3%	525,000
1998	340	253	14,036,500	43.9%	55,480	5.3%	220,000
1997	238	185	9,751,000	−2.6%	52,708	36.3%	290,000
1996	393	259	10,013,500	52.2%	38,662	4.0%	300,000
1995	227	177	6,580,500	16.6%	37,178	18.5%	200,000
1994	245	180	5,645,000	24.1%	31,361	−0.8%	170,000
1993	173	144	4,550,500	95.2%	31,601	−6.5%	147,000
1992	97	69	2,331,000	−35.0%	33,783	−0.1%	115,000
1991	154	106	3,585,000	−28.8%	33,821	−16.8%	140,000
1990	143	124	5,038,500	−44.5%	40,633	−12.3%	140,000
1989	240	196	9,080,500	−34.2%	46,329	−27.8%	255,000
1988	296	215	13,795,500	0.0%	64,165	13.0%	475,000
1987	309	243	13,797,000	−35.7%	56,778	−29.1%	450,000
1986	365	268	21,465,500	−26.7%	80,095	−10.1%	400,000
1985	421	329	29,297,500	−17.8%	89,050	−13.6%	730,000
1984	428	346	35,648,000	−13.7%	103,029	−2.7%	900,000
1983	439	390	41,302,000	37.1%	105,903	35.0%	1,750,000
1982	459	384	30,118,000	−0.2%	78,432	11.7%	1,000,000
1981	502	430	30,186,000	43.7%	70,200	32.0%	1,300,000
1980	441	395	21,010,500	56.2%	53,191	31.7%	325,000
1979†	N/A	333	13,450,000	19.5%	40,390	23.7%	310,000
1978	N/A	353	11,258,500	57.4%	32,659	36.5%	205,000
1977	N/A	299	7,154,900	151.0%	23,929	50.3%	255,000
1976	N/A	179	2,850,100	84.0%	15,922	49.0%	75,000
1975	N/A	145	1,549,000	287.8%	10,683	12.3%	110,000
1974	N/A	42	399,400	−48.3%	9510	13.2%	30,000

First held in 1972. Held at Newtown Paddocks since 1975. †Before 1980, gross sales include RNAs. N/A Not available.

Fasig-Tipton Calder Selected Two-Year-Olds in Training

Year	Offered	Sold	Total Sales	Chg	Average	Chg	High Price
2008	171	102	$35,100,000	−19.5%	$344,118	−2.2%	$2,100,000
2007	209	124	43,622,000	−29.9%	351,790	−12.9%	2,500,000
2006	229	154	62,187,000	24.0%	403,812	18.4%	16,000,000
2005	267	147	50,132,000	20.6%	341,034	16.4%	5,200,000
2004	223	142	41,586,000	43%	292,859	40%	4,500,000
2003	246	139	29,077,000	−1.4%	209,187	−1.4%	1,400,000
2002	254	139	29,479,000	4.6%	212,079	2.3%	1,000,000
2001	237	136	28,186,000	−16.3%	207,250	−4.0%	1,000,000
2000	264	156	33,690,000	0.9%	215,962	17.1%	1,950,000
1999	296	181	33,386,000	26.9%	184,453	33.9%	1,100,000
1998	302	191	26,303,000	13.6%	137,712	14.2%	1,000,000
1997	297	192	23,162,000	1.7%	120,635	16.1%	780,000
1996	309	219	22,765,000	22.2%	103,950	11.1%	875,000
1995	306	199	18,624,000	39.0%	93,588	31.3%	550,000
1994	276	188	13,403,000	17.7%	71,293	25.2%	390,000
1993	318	200	11,386,000	−8.0%	56,930	−3.9%	450,000
1992	292	209	12,376,000	14.1%	59,215	−5.5%	350,000
1991	299	173	10,846,000	−24.6%	62,694	−17.2%	375,000
1990	269	190	14,383,000	36.0%	75,700	18.8%	625,000
1989	233	166	10,579,000	−13.1%	63,729	−1.1%	360,000
1988	296	189	12,175,500	4.4%	64,421	−2.3%	275,000
1987	243	177	11,666,000	21.0%	65,910	24.4%	315,000
1986	232	182	9,640,000	56.8%	52,967	25.8%	525,000
1985	208	146	6,146,000	8.2%	42,096	−11.0%	325,000
1984	179	120	5,678,000	−20.5%	47,317	−2.6%	360,000
1983	206	147	7,144,000	—	48,599	—	195,000

First held in 1983.

Keeneland April Two-Year-Olds in Training

Year	Offered	Sold	Total Sales	Chg	Average	Chg	High Price
2008	125	77	$16,299,000	−2.0%	$211,675	4.3%	$ 800,000
2007	155	82	16,637,000	−9.8%	202,890	−4.3%	1,750,000
2006	147	87	18,440,000	8.2%	211,954	30.6%	1,050,000
2005	176	105	17,040,500	−22.6%	162,290	−25.5%	800,000
2004	183	101	22,012,000	2.7%	217,941	30.1%	3,300,000
2003	198	128	21,440,000	20.8%	167,500	−3.7%	950,000
2002	178	102	17,749,500	19.1%	174,015	6.3%	850,000
2001	146	91	14,898,000	−19.2%	163,714	8.3%	775,000
2000	195	122	18,435,000	−0.7%	151,107	0.1%	825,000
1999	179	123	18,560,500	33.3%	150,894	0.8%	2,000,000
1998	125	93	13,925,000	−3.5%	149,731	52.6%	725,000
1997	210	147	14,427,000	0.9%	98,143	−14.9%	900,000
1996	195	124	14,305,500	20.6%	115,363	11.8%	400,000
1995	169	115	11,865,000	3.3%	103,174	41.0%	700,000
1994	219	157	11,491,500	69.0%	73,194	15.2%	400,000
1993	136	107	6,800,500	—	63,556	—	300,000

First held in 1993.

Ocala Breeders' Sales Co. February Two-Year-Olds in Training

Year	Offered	Sold	Total Sales	Chg	Average	Chg	High Price
2008	124	89	$14,030,000	9.3%	$157,640	17.9%	$520,000
2007	137	96	12,831,000	−1.0%	133,656	−4.1%	550,000
2006	138	93	12,967,000	−13.1%	139,430	1.9%	650,000
2005	158	109	14,921,000	−2.3%	136,890	0.4%	600,000
2004	169	112	15,266,000	19.9%	136,403	25.2%	1,600,000
2003	166	117	12,733,000	−2.4%	108,829	−4.9%	1,200,000
2002	175	114	13,041,000	−7.7%	114,395	10.2%	500,000
2001	188	136	14,124,000	−9.5%	103,853	−5.5%	900,000
2000	226	142	15,599,000	−5.2%	109,852	6.8%	550,000
1999	204	160	16,454,000	31.0%	102,838	25.2%	525,000
1998	193	153	12,564,000	20.5%	82,118	20.5%	430,000
1997	184	153	10,428,000	12.0%	68,157	16.4%	300,000
1996	218	159	9,314,000	19.5%	58,579	6.7%	275,000
1995	181	142	7,794,500	24.7%	54,891	24.7%	270,000
1994	202	142	6,248,500	9.4%	44,004	14.0%	350,000
1993	200	148	5,712,000	8.6%	38,595	2.7%	325,000
1992	182	140	5,261,000	−1.5%	37,579	2.7%	260,000
1991	218	146	5,341,000	−17.6%	36,582	−14.2%	135,000
1990	205	152	6,478,000	18.3%	42,618	23.0%	360,000
1989	209	158	5,474,500	−5.8%	34,649	−2.8%	302,000
1988	231	163	5,811,500	−20.4%	35,653	−13.5%	140,000
1987	232	177	7,298,500	0.1%	41,234	−3.3%	175,000
1986	207	171	7,290,500	71.6%	42,635	28.5%	250,000
1985	173	128	4,247,500	—	33,184	—	135,000

First held in 1985 at Hialeah Park; held at Calder Race Course from '86 to 2006; held at Ocala Breeders' Sales Co. complex in 2007.

Barretts Equine Ltd. Selected Two-Year-Olds in Training

Year	Offered	Sold	Total Sales	Chg	Average	Chg	High Price
2008	132	73	$12,996,000	−32.8%	$178,027	−19.0%	$800,000
2007	150	88	19,340,000	34.7%	219,773	42.3%	1,400,000
2006	139	93	14,361,000	0.0%	154,419	−5.4%	1,500,000
2005	145	88	14,360,500	4.6%	163,188	−6.1%	1,900,000
2004	128	79	13,728,000	12.3%	173,722	22%	2,000,000
2003	166	86	12,228,000	11.7%	142,186	−5.2%	2,700,000
2002	121	73	10,950,000	8.6%	150,000	5.6%	1,900,000
2001	130	71	10,085,000	−41.7%	142,042	−21.1%	750,000
2000	170	96	17,287,000	−21.4%	180,073	−20.6%	2,000,000
1999	172	97	21,995,000	−3.2%	226,753	30.8%	2,000,000
1998	200	131	22,711,000	−28.9%	173,366	−21.8%	1,000,000
1997	255	144	31,926,000	−3.3%	221,708	7.4%	1,100,000
1996	233	160	33,016,000	56.1%	206,350	56.1%	900,000
1995	274	160	21,148,000	57.4%	132,175	61.3%	900,000
1994	240	164	13,440,000	51.6%	81,951	39.6%	700,000
1993	237	151	8,863,400	−7.5%	58,698	−5.1%	430,000
1992	280	155	9,584,000	−33.0%	61,832	−20.1%	370,000
1991	317	185	14,313,000	−12.8%	77,368	−7.6%	600,000
1990	270	196	16,405,000	—	83,699	—	700,000

First held in 1990.

Keeneland November Breeding Stock

Year	Offered	Sold	Total Sales	Chg	Average	Chg	High Price
2007	4,343	3,381	$340,877,200	8.6%	$100,821	1.1%	$10,500,000
2006	4,088	3,147	313,843,800	8.4%	99,728	−2.9%	6,100,000
2005	3,713	2,819	289,606,400	3.5%	102,734	5.5%	9,000,000
2004	3,736	2,873	279,680,200	18.5%	97,348	7.8%	4,800,000
2003	3,337	2,614	236,070,900	26.1%	90,310	14.6%	7,100,000
2002	2,982	2,377	187,230,000	4.3%	78,767	9.9%	4,000,000
2001	3,383	2,506	179,568,600	−41.0%	71,655	−22.9%	4,000,000
2000	4,367	3,277	304,549,800	−4.1%	92,936	1.3%	4,900,000
1999	4,227	3,461	317,666,000	20.0%	91,784	17.2%	4,700,000
1998	4,312	3,379	264,657,700	23.7%	78,324	10.3%	7,000,000
1997	3,673	3,013	213,979,800	25.4%	71,019	17.6%	1,400,000
1996	3,451	2,826	170,691,800	21.2%	60,400	22.5%	2,600,000
1995	3,505	2,855	140,822,300	16.3%	49,325	1.6%	2,500,000
1994	2,932	2,494	121,056,900	32.5%	48,539	10.3%	2,700,000
1993	2,300	2,075	91,342,900	24.6%	44,021	16.6%	1,150,000
1992	2,324	1,942	73,337,200	−11.6%	37,764	−9.7%	1,100,000
1991	2,281	1,984	82,938,400	−18.0%	41,804	5.8%	1,400,000
1990	3,061	2,558	101,107,700	−34.8%	39,526	−43.1%	2,300,000
1989	2,518	2,235	155,161,300	36.7%	69,423	22.3%	4,600,000
1988	2,401	2,000	113,517,600	−4.1%	56,759	−15.8%	1,900,000
1987	1,999	1,756	118,358,900	−5.3%	67,403	−3.4%	2,600,000
1986	2,159	1,791	125,022,700	−22.0%	69,806	−27.3%	5,400,000
1985	2,076	1,668	160,207,100	5.1%	96,047	−7.7%	5,500,000
1984	1,915	1,465	152,373,200	−9.6%	104,009	−1.4%	4,600,000
1983	1,977	1,598	168,518,600	44.6%	105,456	42.8%	5,250,000
1982	1,989	1,578	116,538,700	−1.7%	73,852	28.4%	3,800,000
1981	2,491	2,060	118,494,900	26.4%	57,522	13.2%	2,150,000
1980	2,024	1,845	93,746,700	40.0%	50,811	44.4%	2,000,000

Auctions — All-Time Highest-Priced Horses

Year	Offered	Sold	Total Sales	Chg	Average	Chg	High Price
1979†	N/A	1,903	$66,968,300	50.6%	$35,191	23.6%	$1,600,000
1978	N/A	1,562	44,472,200	21.2%	28,471	11.6%	800,000
1977	N/A	1,439	36,699,400	33.2%	25,503	28.1%	575,000
1976	N/A	1,384	27,548,800	70.4%	19,905	35.8%	1,000,000
1975	N/A	1,103	16,163,700	-3.5%	14,654	30.8%	295,000
1974	N/A	1,495	16,751,200	-33.6%	11,205	-29.9%	385,000

First held in 1944. †Before 1980, gross sales include RNAs. N/A Not available.

Keeneland January Horses of All Ages

Year	Offered	Sold	Total Sales	Chg	Average	Chg	High Price
2008	1,965	1,493	$70,446,000	-3.3%	$47,184	20.6%	$2,700,000
2007	2,410	1,862	72,868,200	0.7%	39,134	-11.9%	1,800,000
2006	2,080	1,628	72,329,100	35.4%	44,428	13.2	1,000,000
2005	1,765	1,361	53,418,000	8.2%	39,249	0.2%	1,350,000
2004	1,602	1,260	49,362,600	58.3%	39,177	48.9%	850,000
2003	1,600	1,185	31,186,000	-10.1%	26,317	-28.9%	475,000
2002	1,135	937	34,689,200	-12.5%	37,022	12.7%	3,600,000
2001	1,667	1,207	39,657,700	-34.9%	32,856	-33.1%	1,700,000
2000	1,605	1,241	60,951,200	43.7%	**49,115**	39.3%	**5,000,000**
1999	1,452	1,203	42,410,900	-20.2%	35,254	-23.1%	3,250,000
1998	1,378	1,160	53,164,800	121.1%	45,832	91.2%	3,400,000
1997	1,156	1,003	24,042,300	-20.6%	23,970	-21.0%	710,000
1996	1,220	997	30,263,400	56.2%	30,354	61.2%	1,800,000
1995	1,195	1,029	19,377,700	29.5%	18,832	7.0%	375,000
1994	948	850	14,960,600	25.5%	17,601	24.0%	210,000
1993	1,018	840	11,918,600	-37.5%	14,189	-36.4%	210,000
1992	952	855	19,066,000	-14.2%	22,299	38.9%	650,000
1991	1,670	1,385	22,229,900	9.9%	16,050	-33.1%	685,000
1990	983	844	20,234,200	-1.8%	23,974	5.9%	2,100,000
1989	1,083	901	20,469,300	-66.7%	22,718	-53.1%	745,000
1988	1,382	1,268	61,450,100	291.4%	48,462	102.5%	2,500,000
1987	796	656	15,701,800	-23.1%	23,936	-22.5%	1,750,000
1986	836	661	20,411,100	0.5%	30,879	-10.8%	3,000,000
1985	754	587	20,317,400	-5.1%	34,612	-13.3%	1,250,000
1984	693	536	21,399,100	11.8%	39,924	-1.8%	2,500,000
1983	602	471	19,139,700	-15.4%	40,636	29.3%	825,000
1982	860	720	22,626,600	-4.3%	31,426	24.7%	1,000,000
1981	1,073	938	23,640,900	25.3%	25,204	3.9%	1,000,000
1980	856	778	18,874,000	115.6%	24,260	105.1%	850,000
1979†	N/A	740	8,753,000	18.7%	11,828	15.9%	145,000
1978	N/A	723	7,375,200	41.6%	10,201	15.0%	215,000
1977	N/A	587	5,208,500	5.0%	8,873	23.4%	310,000
1976	N/A	690	4,961,700	-1.8%	7,191	13.5%	295,000
1975	N/A	798	5,053,900	19.3%	6,333	1.3%	100,000
1974	N/A	678	4,238,000	10.1%	6,251	8.1%	122,000

First held in 1956. Not held 1958-'60. †Before 1980, gross sales include RNAs. N/A Not available.

Highest-Priced Horses of All Time
North American Top-Priced Yearlings
(With Subsequent Race Record)

$13,100,000   **SEATTLE DANCER**, 1984 c., Nijinsky II—My Charmer, by Poker. Consignor: Warner L. Jones Jr.; Buyer: BBA (England), agent for Robert Sangster and partners. 1985 Keeneland July. 5 starts, 2 wins, $152,413 in France and Ireland, SW, Ire-G2.

11,700,000   **MEYDAN CITY**, 2005 c., Kingmambo—Crown of Crimson, by Seattle Slew. Consignor: Burleson Farms, agent; Buyer: John Ferguson Bloodstock. 2006 Keeneland September. Unraced.

10,200,000   **SNAAFI DANCER**, 1982 c., Northern Dancer—My Bupers, by Bupers. Consignor: Crescent Farm; Buyer: Aston Upthorpe Stud, agent for Sheikh Mohammed bin Rashid al Maktoum. 1983 Keeneland July. Unraced.

9,700,000   **JALIL**, 2004 c., Storm Cat—Tranquility Lake, by Rahy. Consignor: Mill Ridge Sales, agent for Martin J. Wygod; Buyer: John Ferguson Bloodstock. 2005 Keeneland September. 8 starts, 4 wins, $327,188 in England and UAE, SW, UAE-G2.

9,200,000   **PLAVIUS**, 2005 c., Danzig—Sharp Minister, by Deputy Minister. Consignor: Monticule; Buyer: John Ferguson Bloodstock. 2006 Keeneland September. 1 start, unplaced in England.

8,250,000   **IMPERIAL FALCON**, 1984 c., Northern Dancer—Ballade, by *Herbager. Consignor: Windfields Farm; Buyer: BBA (England), agent for Robert Sangster and partners. 1984 Keeneland July. 3 starts, 2 wins, $13,395 in Ireland.

8,200,000   **ACT OF DIPLOMACY**, 2005 c., Storm Cat—Awesome Humor, by Distorted Humor. Consignor: Taylor Made Sales Agency, agent; Buyer: John Ferguson Bloodstock. 2006 Keeneland September. Unraced.

8,000,000   **MR. SEKIGUCHI**, 2003 c., Storm Cat—Welcome Surprise, by Seeking the Gold. Consignor: Lane's End, agent; Buyer: Hideyuki Mori. 2004 Keeneland September. 4 starts, 2 wins, $85,800.

7,100,000   **JAREER**, 1983 c., Northern Dancer—Fabuleux Jane, by *Le Fabuleux. Consignor: Bruce Hundley, agent for Ralph C. Wilson Jr.; Buyer: Darley Stud Management. 1984 Keeneland July. 9 starts, 1 win, $5,591 in England and France.

7,000,000   **LAA ETAAB**, 1984 c., Nijinsky II—Crimson Saint, by Crimson Satan. Consignor: Tom Gentry; Buyer: Gainsborough Farm. 1985 Keeneland July. Unraced.

6,800,000   **TASMANIAN TIGER**, 1999 c., Storm Cat—Hum Along, by Fappiano. Consignor: Lane's End, agent; Buyer: Demi O'Byrne. 2000 Keeneland September. 25 starts, 3 wins, $154,543 in Ireland and Hong Kong.

6,500,000   **AMJAAD**, 1983 c., Seattle Slew—Desiree, by Raise a Native. Consignor: Spendthrift Farm, agent for Mr. and Mrs. Louis E. Wolfson and Mrs. Ethel D. Jacobs; Buyer: Darley Stud Management. 1984 Keeneland July. 4 starts, unplaced in England, Ireland, and North America.

6,400,000   **VAN NISTELROOY**, 2000 c., Storm Cat—Halory, by Halo. Consignor: Lane's End, agent for Stonerside Stable; Buyer: Demi O'Byrne. 2001 Keeneland September. 6 starts, 3 wins, $229,980 in England, Ireland, and North America, SW, Ire-G2.

Auctions — All-Time Highest-Priced Horses

$6,300,000	OBJECTIVITY, 2004 c., Storm Cat—Secret Status, by A.P. Indy. Consignor: Lane's End, agent; Buyer: John Ferguson Bloodstock. 2005 Keeneland September. Unraced.
5,700,000	NAWAKHIDA, 2005 c., Mr. Greeley—Silvester Lady, Pivotal. Consignor: Vinery; Buyer: John Ferguson Bloodstock. 2006 Keeneland September. Unraced.
5,500,000	ALAJWAD, 2000, c., Storm Cat—La Affirmed, by Affirmed. Consignor: Eaton Sales, agent; Buyer: John Ferguson Bloodstock. 2001 Keeneland September. 6 starts, 2 wins, $77,445 in North America and UAE.
5,400,000	OBLIGATO, 1983 c., Northern Dancer—Truly Bound, by In Reality. Consignor: Windfields Farm; Buyer: BBA (Ireland), agent for Robert Sangster and partners. 1984 Keeneland July. 2 starts, unplaced in Ireland.
5,300,000	KING'S CONSUL, 1999 c., Kingmambo—Battle Creek Girl, by His Majesty. Consignor: Lane's End, agent; Buyer: John Ferguson Bloodstock. 2000 Keeneland September. 8 starts, 1 win, $40,759 in England and North America.
5,200,000	EGYPTIAN HERO, 2005 c., Danzig—Al Theraab, by Roberto. Consignor: Indian Creek (Dave C. Parrish Jr.), agent; Buyer: Demi O'Byrne. 2006 Keeneland September. Unraced.
5,100,000	**WASSL TOUCH**, 1983 c., Northern Dancer—Queen Sucree, by *Ribot. Consignor: North Ridge Farm; Buyer: Darley Stud Management. 1984 Keeneland July. 6 starts, 3 wins, $30,168 in England, SW.
4,600,000	PARLANDO, 1983 c., Northern Dancer—Bubbling, by Stage Door Johnny. Consignor: Wild Oak Plantation; Buyer: BBA (Ireland), agent for Robert Sangster and partners. 1984 Fasig-Tipton Saratoga. Unraced.
	PROFESSOR BLUE, 1983 c., Northern Dancer—Mississippi Mud, by Delta Judge. Consignor: Lane's End; Buyer: BBA (England), agent for Stavros Niarchos. 1984 Keeneland July. 7 starts, placed, $5,171 in France and North America.
	Maimonides, 2005 c., Vindication—Silvery Swan, by Silver Deputy. Consignor: Hill 'n' Dale Sales Agency, agent; Buyer: Zayat Stables. 2006 Keeneland September. 2 starts, 1 win, $62,200, spl, G1.
4,400,000	MOON'S WHISPER, 1999 f., Storm Cat—East of the Moon, by Private Account. Consignor: Lane's End; Buyer: Shadwell Estate Co. Ltd. 2000 Keeneland September. Unraced.
	Shah Jehan, 1999 c., Mr. Prospector—Voodoo Lily, by Baldski. Consignor: Lane's End; Buyer: Demi O'Byrne. 2000 Keeneland September. 30 starts, 6 starts, 3 wins, $238,238 in North America, England, and France, sp, G3.
4,250,000	**EMPIRE GLORY**, 1981 c., Nijinsky II—Spearfish, by Fleet Nasrullah. Consignor: Glencoe Farm; Buyer: BBA (Ireland). 1982 Keeneland July. 6 starts, 2 wins, $35,420 in Ireland, SW, Ire-G3.
	FOXBORO, 1982 c., Northern Dancer—Desert Vixen, by In Reality. Consignor: North Ridge Farm; Buyer: BBA (England), agent for Robert Sangster and partners. 1983 Keeneland July. 1 start, unplaced in Ireland.
4,200,000	DISTINCTION, 1999 c., Seattle Slew—Omi, by Wild Again. Consignor: Double Diamond Farm; Buyer: David J. Shimmon. 2000 Fasig-Tipton Saratoga. 21 starts, 3 wins, $78,058.
4,100,000	**GALLANT ARCHER**, 1982 c., Nijinsky II—Belle of Dodge Me, by Creme dela Creme. Consignor: E. A. Seltzer and Parlina; Buyer: Aston Upthorpe Stud, agent for Sheikh Mohammed bin Rashid al Maktoum. 1983 Keeneland July. 16 starts, 5 wins, $294,477 in England and North America, SW, G3.
4,000,000	**ELNAWAAGI**, 1983 c., Roberto—Gurkhas Band, by Lurullah. Consignor: Keswick Stables; Buyer: Darley Stud Management. 1984 Fasig-Tipton Saratoga. 11 starts, 4 wins, $23,607 in England and Germany, SW.
	FUSAICHI PEGASUS, 1997 c., Mr. Prospector—Angel Fever, by Danzig. Consignor: Stone Farm, agent; Buyer: Fusao Sekiguchi. 1998 Keeneland July. 9 starts, 6 wins, $1,994,400, SW, G1.
	SHOWLADY, 1999 f., Theatrical (Ire)—Claxton's Slew, by Seattle Slew. Consignor: Brookside Farms; Buyer: John Ferguson Bloodstock. 2000 Keeneland September. 6 starts, 2 wins, $158,640, SW, G3.
	WARHOL, 2000 c., Saint Ballado—Charm a Gendarme, by Batonnier. Consignor: Taylor Made Sales Agency, agent; Buyer: Demi O'Byrne. 2001 Keeneland July. 4 starts, 1 win, $18,809 in Ireland and England.

Key—Bold-faced caps: stakes winner. Bold-faced caps and lowercase: stakes-placed.

North American Top-Priced Two-Year-Olds

$16,000,000	THE GREEN MONKEY, 2004 c., Forestry—Magical Masquerade, by Unbridled. Consignor: Hartley/De Renzo Thoroughbreds, agent; Buyer: Demi O'Byrne. 2006 Fasig-Tipton Florida February. 3 starts, placed, $10,440.
5,200,000	EVER SHIFTING, 2003 c., Tale of the Cat—Carry All, by Devil's Bag. Consignor: Robert N. Scanlon, agent; Buyer: Darley. 2005 Fasig-Tipton Florida February. 2 starts, unplaced, $507.
4,500,000	FUSAICHI SAMURAI, 2002 c., Fusaichi Pegasus—Hidden Storm, by Storm Cat. Consignor: Kirkwood Stables, agent; Buyer: Fusao Sekiguchi. 2004 Fasig Tipton Florida February. 4 starts, 1 win, $22,200.
3,300,000	**Chekhov**, 2002 c., Pulpit—In My Cap, by Vice Regent. Consignor: Niall Brennan Stables, agent; Buyer: Demi O'Byrne. 2004 Keeneland April. 17 starts, 1 win, $194,296, spl, G3.
3,100,000	DUBAI DREAMER, 2002 c., Stephen Got Even—Blacktie Bid, by Black Tie Affair (Ire). Consignor: Niall Brennan Stables, agent; Buyer: John Ferguson Bloodstock. 2004 Fasig-Tipton Florida February. 14 starts, 1 win, $23,311 in England and UAE.
3,000,000	BARBADOS, 2003 c., Forestry—Rare Bird, by Rahy. Consignor: Tony Bowling and Bobby Dodd, agent; Buyer: Demi O'Byrne. 2005 Fasig-Tipton February. 10 starts, 1 win, $87,730.
	WILD FIT, 2003 f., Wild Wonder—Grannies Feather, by At Full Feather. Consignor: Eaton Sales, agent; Buyer: Demi O'Byrne. 2005 Fasig-Tipton Kentucky November. 10 starts, 2 wins, $555,079, SW, G1.
2,900,000	RONDO, 2003 c., Grand Slam—Dama, by Storm Cat. Consignor: Maurice W. Miller, agent; Buyer: Darley. 2005 Fasig-Tipton Florida February. 9 starts, 3 wins, $127,989.
2,700,000	DIAMOND FURY, 2001 g., Sea of Secrets—Swift Spirit, by Tasso. Consignor: Sequel Bloodstock, agent; Buyer: Charles Fipke. 2003 Barretts March. 16 starts, 3 wins, $135,000.
2,500,000	UNBRIDLED SLEW, 2004 c., Red Bullet—Sookloozy, by Avenue of Flags. Consignor: Wavertree Stables, agent; Buyer: Darley Stable. 2006 Barretts May. Unraced.
	THE LEOPARD, 2005 c., Storm Cat—Moon Safari, by Mr. Prospector. Consignor: Hoby and Layna Kight, agent for Kight/Adams/Mattox & Raymon; Buyer: Demi O'Byrne. 2007 Fasig-Tipton Florida February. 6 starts, 3 wins, $173,700, SW, G3.
2,200,000	POSITIVE FORCE, 2004 c., Storm Cat—Brushed Halory, by Broad Brush. Consignor: Hartley/de Renzo Thoroughbreds, agent; Buyer: Dale L. Romans. 2006 Fasig-Tipton Florida February. 2 starts, placed, $4,700.
2,100,000	DESERT PARTY, 2006 c., Street Cry (Ire)—Sage Cat, by Tabasco Cat. Consignor: Scanlon Training Center, agent; Buyer: John Ferguson Bloodstock. 2008 Fasig-Tipton Florida February. Unraced.
2,000,000	LA SALLE STREET, 1997 c., Not For Love—Three Grand, by Assert (Ire). Consignor: H. T. Stables, agent, for Cam Allard; Buyer: Demi O'Byrne. 1999 Keeneland April. 3 starts, placed, $3,420.
	MOROCCO, 1997 c., Brocco—Roll Over Baby, by Rollin On Over. Consignor: Sequel Bloodstock, agent; Buyer: The Thoroughbred Corp. 1999 Barretts March. 16 starts, 4 wins, $133,640.
	GOTHAM CITY, 1998 c., Saint Ballado—What a Reality, by In Reality. Consignor: Jerry Bailey Sales Agency; Buyer: David J. Shimmon. 2000 Barretts March. 2 starts, unplaced, $2,880.
	DUBAI ESCAPADE, 2002 f., Awesome Again—Sassy Pants, by Saratoga Six. Consignor: Jerry Bailey Sales Agency, agent; Buyer: John Ferguson Bloodstock. 2004 Barretts March. 8 starts, 6 wins, $427,050 in England, UAE and North America, SW, G1.
	MERCANTILE, 2004 c., Golden Missile—Silverdew, by Silver Deputy. Consignor: O & H Bloodstock, agent; Buyer: John Ferguson Bloodstock, agent. 2006 Fasig-Tipton Florida. 11 starts, 3 wins, $83,160.

Auctions — All-Time Highest-Priced Horses

$2,000,000	**BELGRAVIA**, 2004 c., Mr. Greeley—Peaks Mill, by Stalwart. Consignor: Nick de Meric, agent; Buyer: Demi O'Byrne. 2006 Fasig-Tipton Florida. 5 starts, 2 wins, $127,115, SW, G3.
1,950,000	**YONAGUSKA**, 1998 c., Cherokee Run—Marital Spook, by Silver Ghost. Consignor: Niall Brennan Stables, agent; Buyer: Demi O'Byrne. 2000 Fasig-Tipton Florida February. 18 starts, 6 wins, $536,355, SW, G1.
1,900,000	**ATLANTIC OCEAN**, 2000 f., Stormy Atlantic—Super Chef, by Seattle Slew. Consignor: Chapman Farms; Buyer: The Thoroughbred Corp. 2002 Barretts March. 19 starts, 5 wins, $678,210, SW, G3.
	WHAT A SONG, 2003 c., Songandaprayer—What a Knight, by Tough Knight. Consignor: Murray Smith, agent; Buyer: Robert B. Lewis and Beverly J. Lewis. 2005 Barretts March. 3 starts, 3 wins, $179,700, SW, G2.
1,800,000	**GARIFINE**, 2004 c., Belong to Me—Vassar, by Royal Academy. Consignor: Wavertree Stables, agent; Buyer: Buzz Chace, agent. 2006 Ocala Breeders' Sales Co. March. 4 starts, 1 win, $28,078.
1,750,000	**PATRICIA'S GEM**, 2005 f., Mineshaft—Stylish Talent, by Forty Niner. Consignor: Hartley/De Renzo Thoroughbreds; Buyer: B. Wayne Hughes. 2007 Keeneland April. 2 starts, placed, $10,320.
1,700,000	**MUNNINGS**, 2006 c., Speightstown—La Comete, by Holy Bull. Consignor: Leprechaun Racing, agent; Buyer: Demi O'Byrne. 2008 Fasig-Tipton Florida February. Unraced.
1,650,000	**HARMONY LODGE**, 1998 f., Hennessy—Win Crafty Lady, by Crafty Prospector. Consignor: Eddie Woods, agent; Buyer: Eugene Melnyk. 2000 Fasig-Tipton Florida February. 24 starts, 13 wins, $851,120, SW, G1.
1,600,000	**MUTANABI**, 2002 c., Wild Rush—Freudenau, by Meadowlake. Consignor: W. D. North, agent; Buyer: John Ferguson Bloodstock. 2004 Ocala Breeders' Sales Co. February. 2 starts, placed, $3,171 in England.
1,500,000	**TIMSAAH**, 2002 c., Rubiano—Magari, by Quack. Consignor: H. T. Inc., agent for Cam Allard; Buyer: John Ferguson Bloodstock. 2004 Fasig Tipton Florida February. 2 starts, unplaced in UAE.
	CLOSE SECRET, 2003 f., Storm Cat—Turbo Launch, by Relaunch. Consignor: Hartley/De Renzo Thoroughbreds LLC, agent; Buyer: Demi O'Byrne. 2005 Fasig-Tipton Florida February. 2 starts, placed, $5,000.
	GARIBALDI, 2003 c., Golden Missile—Ms. Copelan, by Copelan. Consignor: Wavertree Stables, agent; Buyer: Demi O'Byrne. 2005 Fasig-Tipton Florida February. 17 starts, 1 win, $100,679, SW.
	COWTOWN CAT, 2004 c., Distorted Humor—Tom's Cat, by Storm Cat. Consignor: Jerry Bailey Sales Agency, agent; Buyer: WinStar Farm. 2006 Barretts March. 12 starts, 4 wins, $544,293, SW, G2.
	ZOFZIG, 2004 f., Danzig—Zoftig, by Cozzene. Consignor: Taylor Made Sales Agency, agent for ClassicStar; Buyer: Stonerside Stable. 2006 Fasig-Tipton November. 2 starts, 2 wins, $62,489.
	MR MISTOFFELEES, 2006 c., Storm Cat—Country Romance, by Saint Ballado. Consignor: Ricky Leppala, agent; Buyer: Demi O'Byrne. 2008 Fasig-Tipton Florida February. 1 start, 1 win, $31,255.
1,450,000	**WOLGAN VALLEY**, 2005 c., Mr. Greeley—Dancing Naturally, by Fred Astaire. Consignor: Wavertree Stables, agent; Buyer: John Ferguson Bloodstock. 2007 Fasig-Tipton Florida February. 3 starts, placed, $6,513 in England.

North American Top-Priced Weanlings

$2,700,000	**AMOUR MALHEUREUX**, 2006 c., Montjeu (Ire)—Elbaaha (GB), by Arazi. Consignor: Indian Creek (Dave J. Parrish Jr.), agent; Buyer: Globe Equine Management Co. 2006 Keeneland November. Unraced.
2,500,000	**MAGIC OF LIFE**, 1985 f., Seattle Slew—Larida, by Northern Dancer. Consignor: Newstead Farm Trust; Buyer: British Bloodstock Agency (England). 1985 Newstead Farm Trust Dispersal. 9 starts, 4 wins, $254,841 in England, SW, Eng-G1.
2,400,000	**CARPOCRATES**, 2003 c., Storm Cat—Spain, by Thunder Gulch. Consignor: Three Chimneys Farm; Buyer: Dromoland Farm. 2003 Keeneland November. 3 starts, unplaced in Ireland.
	ISLA CANELA, 2006 f., Gone West—Islington (Ire), by Sadler's Wells. Consignor: Paramount Sales, agent for Ballymacoll Stud Farm; Buyer: M.A.B. Agency. 2006 Keeneland November. Unraced.
2,300,000	**GHASHTAH**, 1987 f., Nijinsky II—My Charmer, by Poker. Consignor: Hermitage Farm; Buyer: Shadwell Estate Co. Ltd. 1987 Warner L. Jones Jr. Dispersal. Unraced.
1,700,000	**UNNAMED**, 2007 f., Pulpit—Madcap Escapade, by Hennessy. Consignor: Hill 'n' Dale Sales Agency, agent; Buyer: Southern Equine Stable. 2007 Keeneland November.
	ZONG, 2005 c., Unbridled's Song—Zing, by Storm Cat. Consignor: Taylor Made Sales Agency, agent; Buyer: Aaron U. Jones and Marie D. Jones. 2005 Keeneland November. Unraced.
	LA SUENA, 2005 f., Storm Cat—Garden Secrets, by Time for a Change. Consignor: Lane's End, agent; Buyer: Courtlandt Farm. 2005 Keeneland November. 2 starts, unplaced, $800.
1,500,000	**KING CHARLEMAGNE**, 1998 c., Nureyev—Race the Wild Wind, by Sunny's Halo. Consignor: Ashford Stud, agent; Buyer: Demi O'Byrne. 1998 Keeneland November. 6 starts, 5 wins, $200,211 in England, France, and Ireland, SW, Fr-G1.
1,450,000	**Juniper**, 1998 c., Danzig—Montage, by Alydar. Consignor: Taylor Made Sales Agency, agent; Buyer: Demi O'Byrne. 1998 Keeneland November. 6 starts, 1 win, $37,214 in England and Ireland, spl, Eng-G2.
1,400,000	**WINTHROP**, 1996 c., Storm Cat—Tinnitus, by Restless Wind. Consignor: John R. Gaines Thoroughbreds; Buyer: Demi O'Byrne. 1996 Keeneland November. Unraced.
	RESTORATION, 1999 c., Sadler's Wells—Madame Est Sortie (Fr), by Longleat. Consignor: Eaton Sales, agent for Padua Stables; Buyer: M. W. Miller III, agent. 1999 Keeneland November. Unraced.
	SERENA'S CAT, 2003 f., Storm Cat—Serena's Tune, by Mr. Prospector. Consignor: Hill 'n' Dale Sales Agency, agent; Buyer: Dell Ridge Farm. 2003 Keeneland November. 12 starts, 4 wins, $131,391, SW.
	SECRET THYME, 2003 f., Storm Cat—Garden Secrets, by Time for a Change. Consignor: Eaton Sales, agent; Buyer: Brushwood Stable. 2003 Keeneland November. Unraced.
1,300,000	**NEW TRIESTE**, 1999 c., A.P. Indy—Lovlier Linda, by Vigors. Consignor: John R. Gaines Thoroughbreds; Buyer: Paul Shanahan. 1999 Keeneland November. 1 start, unplaced, $1,500.
1,200,000	**Net Dancer**, 1989 f., Nureyev—Doubles Partner, by Damascus. Consignor: Bruce Hundley, agent for Ralph C. Wilson Jr. and Oxford Stable; Buyer: E. Hudson. 1989 Keeneland November. 13 starts, 2 wins, $46,225, spl.
	TIDE CAT, 1998 f., Storm Cat—Maytide, by Naskra. Consignor: John R. Gaines Thoroughbreds; Buyer: Brad Martin, agent for 505 Farms. 1998 Keeneland November. Unraced.
	SHE'S A BEAUTY, 2000 f., Storm Cat—Now That's Funny, by Saratoga Six. Consignor: Gaines-Gentry Thoroughbreds; Buyer: Timothy Hyde. 2000 Keeneland November. 3 starts, placed, $1,772 in Ireland.
1,175,000	**RAZEEN**, 1987 c., Northern Dancer—Secret Asset, by Graustark. Consignor: Hermitage Farm; Buyer: Darley Stud Management. 1987 Warner L. Jones Jr. Dispersal. 9 starts, 3 wins, $106,665 in England and North America, SW.
1,150,000	**A. P. PETAL**, 2000 f., A.P. Indy—Golden Petal, by Mr. Prospector Consignor: Taylor Made Sales Agency, agent; Buyer: B. Wayne Hughes. 2000 Keeneland November. Unraced.
	Diamond Necklace, 2004 f., Unbridled's Song—Helsinki (GB), by Machiavellian. Consignor: Taylor Made Sales Agency, agent; Buyer: John Sikura. 2004 Keeneland November. 10 starts, placed, $13,428 in Ireland, spl.
1,100,000	**WOROOD**, 1985 f., *Vaguely Noble—Northern Dancer. Consignor: Newstead Farm Trust; Buyer: British Bloodstock Agency (England). 1985 Newstead Farm Trust Dispersal. 16 starts, 4 wins, $82,067 in France, SW.
	HOLD THAT TIGER, 2000 c., Storm Cat—Beware of the Cat, by Caveat. Consignor: Lane's End, agent for Ten Broeck Farm; Buyer: Demi O'Byrne. 2000 Keeneland November. 10 starts, 3 wins, $644,235 in England, France, Ireland and North America, SW, Fr-G1, Champion 2-year-old in Europe.

Auctions — All-Time Highest-Priced Horses

$1,050,000	**SEASIDE ATTRACTION**, 1987 f., Seattle Slew—Kamar, by Key to the Mint. Consignor: Hermitage Farm; Buyer: Monty Hinton. 1987 Warner L. Jones Jr. Dispersal. 12 starts, 4 wins, $272,541, SW, G1.
	WILDCAT QUEEN, 2000 f., Storm Cat—Jetapat, by Tri Jet. Consignor: Brereton C. Jones, agent; Buyer: Bradley and Bowden, agent. 2000 Keeneland November. 5 starts, 1 win, $33,595.
	UNNAMED, 2006 c., Giant's Causeway—Thorough Fair, by Quiet American; Consignor: Hill 'n' Dale Sales Agency, agent; Buyer: My Meadowview Farm. 2006 Keeneland November. Unraced.
1,000,000	**BLISSFUL**, 1996 f., Mr. Prospector—Angel Fever, by Danzig. Consignor: Stone Farm, agent; Buyer: J. B. & B. Stables. 1996 Keeneland November. 3 starts, unplaced, $3,240.
	LEMON TART, 1998 f., Deputy Minister—Lemon Dove, by Forty Niner. Consignor: Hill 'n' Dale Sales Agency, agent; Buyer: Brushwood Stable. 1998 Keeneland November. 4 starts, unplaced, $2,460.
	MALIBU KAREN, 1998 f., Seeking the Gold—Regent's Walk, by Vice Regent. Consignor: Claiborne Farm, agent for Edward A. Cox Jr; Buyer: B. Wayne Hughes. 1998 Keeneland November. 5 starts, placed, $18,490.
	PRINCESS ATOOSA, 1998 f., Gone West—Kooyonga (Ire), by Persian Bold. Consignor: Eaton Sales, agent; Buyer: Brushwood Stable. 1998 Keeneland November. Unraced.
	SWISS DESERT, 1989 c., Danzig—Strictly Raised, by Raise a Native. Consignor: Bruce Hundley, agent for Kentucky Select Bloodstock and Kentucky Heritage Thoroughbred Breeding Partners; Buyer: Gainsborough Farm. 1989 Keeneland November. Unraced.

North American Top-Priced Broodmares

$10,500,000	**PLAYFUL ACT (Ire)**, 2002, Sadler's Wells—Magnificient Style, by Silver Hawk. Consignor: Hill 'n' Dale Sales Agency, agent for Swettenham Stud; Buyer: John Ferguson Bloodstock. 2007 Keeneland November.
9,000,000	**ASHADO**, 2001, Saint Ballado—Goulash, by Mari's Book. Consignor: Taylor Made Sales Agency, agent; Buyer: John Ferguson Bloodstock. 2005 Keeneland November.
7,100,000	**CASH RUN**, 1997, Seeking the Gold—Shared Interest, by Pleasant Colony. (In foal to Storm Cat). Consignor: Taylor Made Sales Agency, agent; Buyer: John Magnier. 2003 Keeneland November.
7,000,000	**KORVEYA**, 1982, Riverman—Konafa, by Damascus. (Woodman). Consignor: Claiborne Farm, agent; Buyer: Reynolds Bell Jr., agent. 1998 Keeneland November.
	MISS OCEANA, 1981, Alydar—Kittiwake, by *Sea-Bird. (Northern Dancer). Consignor: Newstead Farm Trust; Buyer: Foxfield. 1985 Newstead Farm Trust reduced sale.
6,100,000	**WINDSHARP**, 1991, Lear Fan—Yes She's Sharp, by Sharpen Up (GB). (Gone West). Consignor: Mill Ridge Sales, agent; Buyer: John Ferguson Bloodstock. 2003 Keeneland November.
6,000,000	**PRICELESS FAME**, 1975, Irish Castle—Comely Nell, by Commodore M. (Seattle Slew). Consignor: Highclere, agent for Joseph O. Morrissey; Buyer: Darley Stud Management. 1984 Fasig-Tipton Kentucky November.
	MADCAP ESCAPADE, 2001, Hennessy—Sassy Pants, by Saratoga Six. (Pulpit). Consignor: Claiborne Farm, agent; Buyer: Hill 'n' Dale Bloodstock. 2006 Keeneland November.
5,750,000	**ROUND POND**, 2002, Awesome Again—Gift of Dance, by Trempolino. Consignor: Taylor Made Sales Agency, agent for Fox Hill Farms; Buyer: Ferguson Bloodstock. 2007 Fasig-Tipton Kentucky November.
5,500,000	**PRINCESS ROONEY**, 1980, Verbatim—Parrish Princess, by Drone. (Danzig). Consignor: Stone Farm agent; Buyer: Wichita Equine. 1985 Keeneland November.
5,400,000	**LADY'S SECRET**, 1982, Secretariat—Great Lady M., by Icecapade. Consignor: D. Wayne Lukas, agent for Eugene V. Klein; Buyer: Fasig-Tipton Bloodstock, agent. 1987 Night of the Stars, Fasig-Tipton Kentucky November.
	LIFE'S MAGIC, 1981, Cox's Ridge—Fire Water, by Tom Rolfe. (Mr. Prospector). Consignor: Mel Hatley Racing Stables, agent; Buyer: Eugene V. Klein. 1986 Keeneland November.
5,300,000	**SPAIN**, 1997, Thunder Gulch—Drina, by Regal and Royal. (Storm Cat). Consigner: Three Chimneys Sales, agent; Buyer: Dromoland Farm. 2003 Keeneland November.
5,250,000	**PRODUCER**, 1976, Nashua—*Marion, by Tantieme. (Northern Dancer). Consignor: Walnut Green, agent for Carelaine Stable; Buyer: BBA (England). 1983 Keeneland November.
5,000,000	**I'LL GET ALONG**, 1992, Smile—Dont Worry Bout Me, by Foolish Pleasure. (Elusive Quality).Consignor: Brent Fernung, agent for CloverLeaf Farms Ii; Buyer: Gaines-Gentry Thoroughbreds. 2004 Fasig-Tipton Kentucky November.
	MACKIE, 1993, Summer Squall—Glowing Tribute, by Graustark. (Mr. Prospector). Consignor: Eaton Sales, agent; Buyer: Britton House Stud. 2000 Keeneland January.
	RISKAVERSE, 1999, Dynaformer—The Bink, by Seeking the Gold. Consignor: Bluegrass Thoroughbred Services, agent for Fox Ridge Farm; Buyer: Eaton Sales, agent. 2005 Fasig-Tipton Kentucky November.
4,900,000	**JEWEL PRINCESS**, 1992, Key to the Mint—Jewell Ridge, by Melyno (Ire). (Storm Cat). Consignor: Lane's End, agent; Buyer: John Magnier. 2000 Keeneland November.
4,800,000	**SANTA CATARINA**, 2000, Unbridled—Purrfectly, by Storm Cat. (A.P. Indy). Consignor: Denali Stud, agent for Robert and Beverly Lewis; Buyer: Eaton Sales, agent. 2004 Keeneland November.
4,700,000	**CATCHASCATCHCAN (GB)**, 1995, Pursuit of Love—Catawba, by Mill Reef. (Danzig). Consignor: Claiborne Farm, agent; Buyer: Lyons Demesne. 2000 Keeneland November.
	DANCE DESIGN (Ire), 1993, Sadler's Well—Elegance in Design (Ire), by Habitat. (A.P. Indy). Consignor: Eaton Sales, agent for Padua Stables; Buyer: Hugo Lascelles, agent. 1998 Keeneland November.
4,600,000	**IT'S IN THE AIR**, 1976, Mr. Prospector—A Wind Is Rising, by Francis S. (Seattle Slew). Consignor: Hill 'n' Dale Sales Agency; Buyer: Darley Stud Management. 1984 Keeneland November.
	MYHRR, 1997, Mr. Prospector—Miesque, by Nureyev. Consignor: Lane's End, agent; Buyer: Reynolds Bell Jr., agent. 2000 Keeneland November.
	WINGLET, 1988, Alydar—Highest Trump, by Bold Bidder. (Storm Cat). Consignor: Lane's End, agent for Brookside Farms; Buyer: John Magnier. 1999 Keeneland November.
4,500,000	**ESTRAPADE**, 1980, *Vaguely Noble—Klepto, by No Robbery. Consignor: Blue Grass Farm, agent; Buyer: Allen E. Paulson. 1985 Keeneland November.
	SASSY PANTS, 1992, Saratoga Six—Special Portion, by Czaravich. (Storm Cat). Consignor: Dromoland Farm, agent; Buyer: Hill 'n' Dale Bloodstock. 2006 Keeneland November.
	SPUN SUGAR, 2002, Awesome Again—Irish Cherry, by Irish Open. (A.P. Indy). Consignor: Hidden Brook Farm, agent for Adena Springs; Buyer: Shadwell Estate Co. Ltd. 2007 Keeneland November.
4,400,000	**LIFE'S MAGIC**, 1981, Cox's Ridge—Fire Water, by Tom Rolfe. (Alydar). Consignor: D. Wayne Lukas, agent for Eugene V. Klein; Buyer: Shadwell Estate Co. Ltd. 1987 Night of the Stars, Fasig-Tipton Kentucky November.
	TWO RINGS, 1970, Round Table—Allofthem, by Bagdad. (Nijinsky II). Consignor: Mint Lane Farm, agent for Kinghaven Farms; Buyer: Due Process Stable. 1983 Keeneland November.
	UNBRIDLED ELAINE, 1998, Unbridled's Song—Carols Folly, by Taylor's Falls. (Forestry). Consignor: Taylor Made Sales Agency, agent; Buyer: John Ferguson Bloodstock. 2004 Keeneland November.

Highest Yearling Prices Through the Years

Public interest in record prices paid for Thoroughbreds at public auction soared in the 1970s and '80s, when the record price for a yearling racing prospect exceeded $1-million. Yet there has always been a record-priced yearling ever since the first yearling was sold. Just when that may have been, no one can say with certainty, but the first really famous record-priced yearling was Sceptre, a lovely brown filly foaled in 1899 at the Duke of Westminster's Eaton Stud in England. Breeder and owner of *Ormonde, the greatest racehorse of the 19th century, and his grandson Flying Fox, winner of the Triple Crown in the year of Sceptre's birth, the Duke died late in 1899, forcing the dispersal of his bloodstock.

Sceptre, by the great Persimmon out of *Ormonde's full sister Ornament, by Bend Or, and with the looks to match her purple pedigree, came up for sale in 1900 at the Tattersalls Newmarket July sale, then one of the two most important auctions in England. Victorian England was scandalized when the gambler Robert Sievier outbid the late Duke's son and heir to acquire Sceptre for 10,000 guineas ($51,133 at the contemporary exchange rate).

Sceptre proved more than worth the price, though her racing career was somewhat scarred by the roller-coaster fortunes of Sievier, who won and lost fortunes betting on horses and cards for the two years he owned her. Sometimes training the great filly himself, Sievier could not resist attempting betting coups with Sceptre, running her in inappropriate races, such as the Lincolnshire Handicap against older males in her first start at three. Sceptre overcame such abuse, winning four of the five English classics of 1902 (she finished fourth in the Epsom Derby), and is still acclaimed as one of the greatest racemares of all time.

Sceptre's successors as world-record-priced yearlings have never achieved quite the same level of fame or accomplishment, but overall the race records of the 21 successive record-priced yearlings have been quite good. Of the 21 listed in the accompanying chart, five (including Sceptre) have become champions or classic winners, and four more won recognized stakes races. Thus, nine of the 21 record-priced yearlings listed, or 42.9%, were stakes winners, which is far superior to the breed average of about 3%.

On the other hand, only two, Sceptre and Majestic Prince, recaptured their purchase price in purse money on the racecourse, and there were certainly some very expensive failures. Hustle On, who wrested the record away from the English (though he himself was American-bred only by virtue of his dam being imported while carrying him), never raced. His immediate successor, New Broom, could not win in nine starts, the same dismal record as the $1.6-million Hoist the King.

Perhaps the saddest tale of any record-priced yearling, though, is that of Colonel Payne, the Fairway colt out of Golden Hair, by Golden Sun, purchased for 15,000 guineas ($78,278) by Dorothy Paget at Tattersalls Doncaster yearling sale in 1936. An eccentric English-born granddaughter of William C. Whitney, founder of the Whitney family's bloodstock empire, Paget generally refused to grant her horses a name until they had won a race, a practice then permissible under English rules. Colts that failed to meet her standards, she habitually had shot.

The Golden Hair colt ran with promise in his only outing at two, finishing third in the National Breeders' Produce Stakes, then the richest two-year-old race in England. Unfortunately, he proved to be the victim of his owner's eccentricities and never reappeared on the racecourse or anywhere else.—*John P. Sparkman*

Progression of Top-Priced Yearlings

Price	Year	Horse, Sex, Breeding	Sale	Consignor	Buyer	Race Record
$13,100,000	1985	SEATTLE DANCER c., Nijinsky II—My Charmer	Keeneland July	Warner L. Jones Jr.	BBA England (agent for Robert Sangster)	5-2-1-1, $152,413 Gallinule S. (Ire-G2), etc.
10,200,000	1983	SNAAFI DANCER c., Northern Dancer—My Bupers	Keeneland July	Crescent Farm	Aston Upthorpe Stud (Sheikh Mohammed bin Rashid al Maktoum)	unraced
4,250,000	1982	EMPIRE GLORY c., Nijinsky II—Spearfish	Keeneland July	Glencoe Farm	BBA Ireland (agent for Robert Sangster)	6-2-2-2, $35,420, Royal Whip S. (Ire-G3), etc.
3,500,000	1981	BALLYDOYLE c., Northern Dancer—South Ocean	Keeneland July	Windfields Farm	BBA Ireland (agent for Robert Sangster)	4-1-1-0, $2,542
1,700,000	1980	LICHINE c., Lyphard—Stylish Genie	Keeneland July	Carelaine Farm, Getty, Riordan, Heerman, agent	BBA England (agent for Stavros Niarchos)	16-3-1-4, $71,527, Prix de Suresnes, etc.
1,600,000	1979	HOIST THE KING c., Hoist the Flag—Royal Dowry	Keeneland July	Tom Gentry	Kazuo Nakamura	9-0-1-1, $6,977
1,500,000	1976	CANADIAN BOUND c., Secretariat—Charming Alibi	Keeneland July	Bluegrass Farm	Blue Meadows Farm, agent (Ted Burnett, John Sikura, and partners)	4-0-1-0, $4,769
625,000	1974	KENTUCKY GOLD c., Raise a Native—Gold Digger	Keeneland July	Spendthrift Farm	Wallace A. Gilroy	7-1-0-3, $5,950
600,000	1973	WAJIMA c., Bold Ruler—*Iskra	Keeneland July	Claiborne Farm	James A. Scully (agent for Zenya Yoshida and partners)	16-9-5-0, $537,837, Champion 3-year-old male, Travers S. (G1), etc.
510,000	1970	CROWNED PRINCE c., Raise a Native—Gay Hostess	Keeneland July	Spendthrift Farm	Frank McMahon	4-2-0-0, $37,883, champion 2-year-old in England, Dewhurst S., etc.
250,000	1967	MAJESTIC PRINCE c., Raise a Native—Gay Hostess	Keeneland July	Spendthrift Farm	Frank McMahon	10-9-1-0, $414,200, Kentucky Derby, Preakness S., etc.

Auctions — Highest-Priced Yearlings by Year

Price	Year	Horse, Sex, Breeding	Sale	Consignor	Buyer	Race Record
$200,000	1966	BOLD DISCOVERY c., Bold Ruler—La Dauphine	Keeneland July	Spendthrift Farm	Frank McMahon	3-0-0-0, $0
170,000	1964	ONE BOLD BID c., Bold Ruler—Forgetmenow	Keeneland July	Warner L. Jones Jr.	Mrs. Velma Morrison	unraced
130,000	1961	SWAPSON c., Swaps—Obedient	Keeneland July	Spendthrift Farm	John M. Olin	31-8-3-5, $26,766
118,492 (28,000g)	1945	SAYAJIRAO c., Nearco—Rosy Legend	Tattersalls Doncaster	Sir Eric Ohlson	Gaekwar of Baroda	16-6-6-3, $96,647, champion 3-year-old in England,, St. Leger S., etc.
78,278 (15,000g)	1936	Colonel Payne c., Fairway—Golden Hair	Tattersalls Doncaster	Viscount Furness	Dorothy Paget	1-0-0-1, $494, 3rd National Breeders' Produce S.
75,000	1928	NEW BROOM c., Whisk Broom II—Payment	Fasig-Tipton Saratoga	Mrs. T. J. Regan	C.V.B. Cushman	9-0-2-1, $275
70,000	1927	HUSTLE ON c., Hurry On—*Fatima II	Fasig-Tipton Saratoga	Himyar Stud	W. R. Coe	unraced
55,724 (14,500g)	1920	BLUE ENSIGN c., The Tetrarch—Blue Tit	Tattersalls Doncaster	Sledmere Stud	Lord Glanely	1-0-0-0, $0
53,492 (11,500g)	1919	WESTWARD HO c., Swynford—Blue Tit	Tattersalls Doncaster	Sledmere Stud	Lord Glanely	6-2-0-0, $3,989, Great Yorkshire S., 3rd St. Leger S.
51,133 (10,000g)	1900	SCEPTRE f., Persimmon—Ornament	Tattersalls Newmarket July	Estate of Duke of Westminster	Robert Sevier	25-13-4-4, $192,544 champion 3-year-old, champion older horse, Epsom Oaks, etc.

Top-Priced Yearlings by Year

High-priced yearlings have a poor reputation in the Thoroughbred industry. Although statistics show that, on average, the higher the price paid for a yearling the better the racehorse, high-priced failures such as the $10.2-million Snaafi Dancer, who never raced, are remembered more readily than success stories such as the $2.9-million Horse of the Year A.P. Indy. Even the world's record-priced yearling, the $13.1-million Seattle Dancer, is regarded as a failure though he won a Group 2 race in Europe.

In the years since Fasig-Tipton first began selling yearlings at Saratoga, 24 of the 92 top-priced yearlings each year (there were six ties) have become stakes winners. That 26% strike rate is obviously far higher than the 3% average of stakes winners to foals for the breed.

Yearling buyers appear to have greatly improved their selection techniques over the last few decades. The record of top-priced yearlings for the first half of the 20th century was little better than that of the average horse. But in the 36 years since 1969 Kentucky Derby winner Majestic Prince sold for $250,000 at Keeneland July in 1967, 15 year-toppers have become stakes winners. —*John P. Sparkman*

Most Expensive North American Yearlings by Year

Year Sold	Horse	Sex, Sire—Dam	Price	Sale	Buyer	Race Record
2007	DUNKIRK	c., Unbridled's Song—Secret Status	$3,700,000	Kee Sept	Demi O'Byrne	Unraced
2006	MEYDAN CITY	c., Kingmambo—Crown of Crimson	11,700,000	Kee Sept	John Ferguson Bldstk.	Unraced
2005	JALIL	c., Storm Cat—Tranquility Lake	9,700,000	Kee Sept	John Ferguson Bldstk.	8-4-2-0, $327,188, Al Maktoum Challenge Round 3-Sakhee (UAE-G2)
2004	MR. SEKIGUCHI	c., Storm Cat—Welcome Surprise	8,000,000	Kee Sept	Hideyuki Mori	4-2-2-0, $85,800
2003	HASHIMIYA	f., Gone West—Touch of Greatness	3,800,000	Kee Sept	John Ferguson Bldstk.	2-0-0-0, $1,250
2002	ONE COOL CAT	c., Storm Cat—Tacha	3,100,000	Kee July	Demi O'Byrne	10-5-0-1, $568,086, Champion 2yo male in Europe, Hwt. at 3, 5-7 fur. in Eng, Ire, Phoenix S. (Ire-G1), etc.
2001	VAN NISTELROOY	c., Storm Cat—Halory	6,400,000	Kee Sept	Demi O'Byrne	6-3-1-1, $229,980, EBF Futurity S. (Ire-G2), etc.
2000	TASMANIAN TIGER	c., Storm Cat—Hum Along	6,800,000	Kee Sept	Demi O'Byrne	25-3-1-1, $154,543
1999	DUBAI TO DUBAI	c., Kris S.—Mr. P's Princess	3,900,000	Kee Sept	John Ferguson Bldstk.	11-3-1-2, $152,319
1998	FUSAICHI PEGASUS	c., Mr. Prospector—Angel Fever	4,000,000	Kee July	Fusao Sekiguchi	9-6-2-0, $1,994,400, Kentucky Derby (G1), etc.
1997	SASHA'S PROSPECT	c., Mr. Prospector—Missy's Mirage	2,300,000	Kee Sept	Padua Stables	10-1-0-0, $37,200
1996	PARGATA KING	c., Storm Cat—Alpargata	1,700,000	Kee July	Fusao Sekiguchi	1-0-0-0, $0
1995	CONSTANT WISH	f., Mr. Prospector—Daring Bidder	1,250,000	Kee July	Demi O'Byrne	Unraced
1994	Golden Colors	f., Mr. Prospector—Winning Colors	1,050,000	Kee July	Pegasus Bloodstock	10-3-1-0, $509,963, 2nd Daily Hai Queen Cup
1993	GOLDEN LEGEND	c., Mr. Prospector—Reminiscing	1,050,000	Kee July	John R. Gaines, agt.	6-0-0-0, $5,700
1992	NUMEROUS	c., Mr. Prospector—Number	1,700,000	Kee July	Finney Bloodstock, agt.	18-4-2-2, $255,348, Derby Trial S. (G3), etc.
1991	JEUNE HOMME	c., Nureyev—Alydariel	2,600,000	Kee July	Morio Sakurai	20-4-5-3, $431,724, Citation H. (G2), etc.
1990	A.P. INDY	c., Seattle Slew—Weekend Surprise	2,900,000	Kee July	BBA (Ire)	11-8-0-1, $2,979,815, Horse of the Year, champion 3yo male, Breeders' Cup Classic (G1), etc.
1989	NORTHERN PARK	c., Northern Dancer—Mrs. Penny	2,800,000	Kee July	Zenya Yoshida	30-4-7-4, $171,493, Grand Prix de Villeurbanne
1988	ROYAL ACADEMY	c., Nijinsky II—Crimson Saint	3,500,000	Kee July	Vincent O'Brien	7-4-2-0, $758,994, Hwt. at 3, 7-9½ fur. in Eur, Ire, Breeders' Cup Mile (G1), etc.

Auctions — Highest-Priced Yearlings by Year

Year Sold	Horse	Sex, Sire—Dam	Price	Sale	Buyer	Race Record
1987	WARRSHAN	c., Northern Dancer—Secret Asset	$3,700,000	Kee July	Darley Stud Mgt.	11-4-0-3, $125,928, Gordon S. (Eng-G3), etc.
1986	NORTHERN STATE	c., Northern Dancer—South Ocean	3,600,000	Kee July	Darley Stud Mgt.	4-1-0-0, $2,137
1985	SEATTLE DANCER	c., Nijinsky II—My Charmer	13,100,000	Kee July	BBA (Eng), agt. for Robert Sangster	5-2-1-1, $152,413, Gallinule S. (Ire-G2), etc.
1984	IMPERIAL FALCON	c., Northern Dancer—Ballade	8,250,000	Kee July	BBA (Eng)	3-2-0-0, $13,395
1983	SNAAFI DANCER	c., Northern Dancer—My Bupers	10,200,000	Kee July	Aston Upthorpe Stud	Unraced
1982	EMPIRE GLORY	c., Nijinsky II—Spearfish	4,250,000	Kee July	BBA (Ire), agt. for Robert Sangster	6-2-2-2, $35,420, Royal Whip S. (Ire-G3), etc.
1981	BALLYDOYLE	c., Northern Dancer—South Ocean	3,500,000	Kee July	BBA (Ire), agt. for Robert Sangster	4-1-1-0, $2,542
1980	LICHINE	c., Lyphard—Stylish Genie	1,700,000	Kee July	BBA (Eng), agt. for Stavros Niarchos	16-3-1-4, $71,527, Prix de Suresnes, etc.
1979	HOIST THE KING	c., Hoist the Flag—Royal Dowry	1,600,000	Kee July	Kazuo Nakamura	9-0-1-1, $6,977
1978	NUREYEV	c., Northern Dancer—Special	1,300,000	Kee July	BBA (Eng)	3-2-0-0, $42,522, champion miler in France, Prix Thomas Bryon (Fr-G3), etc.
1977	FOREIGN SECRETARY	c., Secretariat—Lady Victoria	725,000	Kee July	BBA (Ire)	11-3-1-1, $47,375
1976	CANADIAN BOUND	c., Secretariat—Charming Alibi	1,500,000	Kee July	Blue Meadows Farm, agt.	4-0-1-0, $4,769
1975	ELEGANT PRINCE	c., Raise a Native—Gay Hostess	715,000	Kee July	Franklin Groves	Unraced
1974	KENTUCKY GOLD	c., Raise a Native—Gold Digger	625,000	Kee July	Wallace A. Gilroy	7-1-0-3, $5,950
1973	WAJIMA	c., Bold Ruler—*Iskra	600,000	Kee July	James A. Scully, agt. for Zenya Yoshida and partners	16-9-5-0, $537,837, champion 3-year-old male, Travers S. (G1), etc.
1972	Riboquill	c., *Ribot—Quill	230,000	Kee July	Cromwell Bloodstock	11-3-1-1, $46,875, 3rd Grand Prix de Deauville (Fr-G2)
1971	PASS	c., Buckpasser—*Casaque Grise	235,000	FT Sara	Marion duPont Scott	Unraced
1970	CROWNED PRINCE	c., Raise a Native—Gay Hostess	510,000	Kee July	Frank McMahon	4-2-0-0, $37,883, champion two-year-old in Eng., Dewhurst S., etc.
1969	KNIGHTS HONOR	c., Round Table—Vestment	210,000	Kee July	Bert W. Martin	4-0-1-1, $1,670
1968	REINE ENCHANTEUR	f., *Sea-Bird—*Libra	405,000	Kee July	W. P. Rosso	7-1-1-5, $9,305
1967	MAJESTIC PRINCE	c., Raise a Native—Gay Hostess	250,000	Kee July	Frank McMahon	10-9-1-0, $414,200, Kentucky Derby, Preakness S., etc.
1966	BOLD DISCOVERY	c., Bold Ruler—La Dauphine	200,000	Kee July	Frank McMahon	3-0-0-0, $0
1965	ROYAL MATCH	f., *Turn-to—Cosmah	140,000	Kee July	Arnold Winick, agt.	Unraced
1964	ONE BOLD BID	c., Bold Ruler—Forgetmenow	170,000	Kee July	Mrs. Velma Morrison	Unraced
1963	LENSO	c., Swaps—*Blue Star II	85,000	Kee July	Leonard Sasso	5-0-0-1, $420
1962	GOLDEN GORSE	f., Swaps—*Auld Alliance	83,000	FT Sara	J. T. Skinner, agt.	2-0-0-2, $735
1961	SWAPSON	c., Swaps—Obedient	130,000	Kee July	John M. Olin	31-8-3-5, $26,766
1960	NASHOLIN	c., Nashua—*Pashmina	75,000	Kee July	N. McLeod	25-2-0-3, $7,955
1959	ROYAL DRAGOON	c., *Royal Charger—Grecian Queen	80,000	Kee July	C. G. Raible	9-1-2-1, $5,050
	GLOBEMASTER	c., *Heliopolis—No Strings	80,000	FT Sara	Penowa Farms	27-10-9-2, $355,423, Wood Memorial S., etc.
1958	PRINCE BLESSED	c., *Princequillo—Dog Blessed	77,000	Kee July	Kerr Stables	35-8-6-4, $255,805, Hollywood Gold Cup S., etc.
1957	LAW AND ORDER	c., *Nasrullah—In Bloom	65,000	Kee July	J. H. Rouse Farm, agt. for King Ranch	Unraced
1956	*RISE 'N SHINE	c., Hyperion—Deodara	$87,000	FT Sara	Mrs. M. E. Lunn	43-4-2-1, $17,515
1955	TULSAN	c., *Nasrullah—In Bloom	80,000	Kee July	Forrest Lindsay Farm	25-2-2-3, $8,050
1954	NALUR	c., *Nasrullah—Lurline B	86,000	Kee July	F. J. Adams Syndicate	20-2-1-0, $6,575
1953	ROMAN BOAT	f., Roman—Boat	59,000	Kee July	Duntreath Farm	4-1-0-0, $1,950
1952	LADYBREATH	f., Roman—Miss Brief	46,000	Kee July	Chester Gates, agt.	7-1-0-0, $2,100
1951	PERFECTION	f., Bull Lea—Lady Lark	60,000	Kee July	C. S. Jones	31-3-4-4, $30,600, Playa del Rey S., etc.
1950	FARAHAAN	f., *Mahmoud—Aphaona	35,000	FT Sara	William Post	3-0-0-1, $725
1949	Unification	c., War Admiral—Summer Time	37,000	Kee July	William Helis	80-6-11-14, $24,015, 3rd Dominion Day H.
	OLD ROWLEY	c., Menow—Risk	37,000	Kee July	Moody Jolley, agt.	9-2-1-1, $5,275
1948	DESTINO	c., *Beau Pere—Sun Lady	52,000	FT Sara	King Ranch	7-0-4-1, $3,400
1947	Spotted Bull	c., *Bull Dog—Spotted Beauty	45,000	Kee July	Jaclyn Stable	19-4-1-2, $12,850, 3rd Will Rogers H.
1946	LA CHICUELA	f., *Blenheim II—La Chica	54,000	Kee July	J. P. Smith	14-1-2-2, $4,100
	SILVER QUEEN	f., War Admiral—Danise M	54,000	Kee July	Maine Chance Farm	16-1-1-1, $3,650
1945	SIR GALLASCENE	c., *Sir Gallahad III—*Scenery II	46,000	Kee July	C. C. Tanner	54-1-5-3, $8,175
	BLUE FANTASY	f., Blue Larkspur—Risk	46,000	Kee July	Leslie Combs II, agt. for Elizabeth Nightingale Graham	Unraced
1944	COLONY BOY	c., Eight Thirty—Heritage	46,000	Kee July	Leslie Combs II, agt. for Elizabeth Arden (Graham)	17-5-0-3, $39,750, Walden S., etc.
1943	PERICLES	c., *Blenheim II—Risk	66,000	FT Kee	William Helis	5-2-0-1, $5,200
1942	BOY KNIGHT	c., *Sir Gallahad III—Heloise	9,000	FT Sara	Crispin Oglebay	36-5-2-10, $44,145, Wilmington H., etc.
1941	BULRUSHES	c., *Bull Dog—Spur Flower	10,000	FT Sara	Ogden Phipps	196-25-40-33, $24,232
1940	REAPER'S BLADE	c., *Sickle—Friendly Gal	18,000	FT Sara	Brookmeade Stable	15-3-2-2, $3,425
1939	TOM-TOM	c., *Sir Gallahad III—Percussion	20,000	FT Sara	Manhasset Stable	Unraced
	Lord Kitchener	c., *Blenheim II—Argosie	20,000	FT Sara	Samuel D. Riddle	38-4-5-7, $9,726, 3rd Travers S., etc.
1938	Romanov	c., *Ksar—Duration	$22,000	FT Sara	Brookmeade Stable	28-2-3-3, $4,756, 3rd Lawrence Realization H.

Auctions — Leading Buyers of 2007

Year Sold	Horse	Sex, Sire—Dam	Price	Sale	Buyer	Race Record
1937	TEMULAC	c., *Sir Gallahad III—Marching Along	$26,000	FT Sara	Calumet Farm	69-7-5-11, $6,732
1936	FARRELL	c., *Sir Gallahad III—Sari	18,000	FT Sara	Milky Way Farms	100-12-19-13, $9,999
1935	WINGED VICTORY	c., Victorian—Grief	13,000	FT Sara	Milky Way Farms	97-7-16-11, $7,130
1934	TEDDY BOY	c., *Teddy—Superstitious	11,500	FT Sara	Calumet Farm	32-1-3-5, $1,425
1933	CALUMET DICK	c., Gallant Fox—*Martha Snow	13,000	FT Sara	Calumet Farm	51-17-6-8, $72,515, Dixie H.
1932	THE TRIUMVIR	c., Pompey—Cowslip	14,500	FT Sara	Greentree Stable	176-12-15-15, $10,935
1931	CARRY THE NEWS	c., The Porter—Cypher Code	16,000	FT Sara	J. H. Whitney	20-1-3-6, $1,665
1930	TEXAS KNIGHT	c., *Sir Gallahad III—Fasnet	30,000	FT Sara	Three D's Stock Farm	82-8-5-11, $6,390
	GALA FLIGHT	f., *Sir Gallahad III—*Starflight	30,000	FT Sara	Griffin Watkins	25-3-0-4, $3,425
1929	War	c., Man o' War—Milky Way	45,000	FT Sara	Sagamore Stable	61-8-13-4, $8,280, 2nd Brookdale H.
1928	NEW BROOM	c., Whisk Broom II—Payment	75,000	FT Sara	C.V.B. Cushman	9-0-2-1, $275
1927	HUSTLE ON	c., Hurry On—*Fatima II	70,000	FT Sara	W. R. Coe	Unraced
1926	TUSKEGEE	c., Black Toney—Humanity	35,000	FT Sara	E. M. Byers	43-10-7-8, $11,925 Belgrade Claiming S.
1925	WAR FEATHERS	c., Man o' War—*Tuscan Red	50,500	FT Sara	Hamilton Farms	7-1-10, $1,350
1924	BLASISTA	c., Eternal—*Aquamarine	16,000	FT Sara	William Zeigler Jr.	5-0-0-0, $0
1923	FLYING EBONY	c., The Finn—Princess Mary	21,000	FT Sara	G. A. Cochran	13-6-1-2, $62,420, Kentucky Derby, etc.
1922	THE TRAMP	c., The Finn—Kate Adams	12,500	FT Sara	Montfort Jones	1-0-0-0, $0
1921	COEUR DE LION	c., Fair Play—*Couronne de Laurier	8,600	FT Sara	Rancocas Stable	288-48-50-43, $33,165
1920	PIRATE GOLD	c., Rock View—Gold	14,000	FT Sara	Greentree Stable	157-20-34-20, $23,258
1919	SUN TURRET	c., Sunstar—Marian Hood	25,000	FT Sara	J.K.L. Ross	103-6-5-11, $3,855
1918	Royal Jester	c., Black Jester—*Primula II	14,500	FT Sara	J.K.L. Ross	33-1-9-7, $4,381, 2nd Earl Grey H., etc.
1917	*HURON	c., *Sweeper—Zuna	4,000	FT Sara	Joseph E. Widener	105-28-20-14, $17,131, Windon H., etc.
	THE SAINT	c., Sain—Nannette	4,000	FT Sara	Samuel D. Riddle	Unraced

†† Through May 1, 2008

Leading Sires of Top-Priced Yearlings

Northern Dancer	7
*Sir Gallahad III	7
Mr. Prospector	6
Storm Cat	6
Raise a Native	4
*Blenheim II	3
*Nasrullah	3
Bold Ruler	3
Nijinsky II	3
Roman	3
Swaps	3

Leading Consignors of Top-Priced Yearlings

Arthur B. Hancock Sr.	12
Spendthrift Farm/ Leslie Combs II	9
Lane's End	7
Hermitage Farm/ Warner L. Jones	4
Windfields Farm	4
Claiborne Farm	3
Robert A. Fairbarn	3
Himyar Stud/Phil T. Chinn	3

Leading Buyers of Top-Priced Yearlings

†Sheikh Mohammed bin Rashid al Maktoum	7
Demi O'Byrne	5
British Bloodstock Agency (Eng)	4
British Bloodstock Agency (Ire)	4
Greentree Stud	4
Calumet Farm	3
Maine Chance Farm/ Elizabeth Arden	3
Frank McMahon	3
‡Fusao Sekiguchi	3

† Includes those bought in the name of Aston Upthorpe Stud, Darley Stud Management, and John Ferguson Bloodstock
‡ Includes horses bought for Fusao Sekiguchi by Hideyuki Mori

Leading Buyers by Total Purchases in 2007

Buyer	No. Horses Bought	Total Expenditure
John Ferguson Bloodstock	51	$68,150,000
Demi O'Byrne	22	27,060,000
Zayat Stables	83	19,359,000
Michael J. Ryan, agent	80	18,363,700
Shadwell Estate Co. Ltd.	31	17,795,000
Stonestreet Thoroughbred Holdings	20	17,580,000
B. Wayne Hughes	67	16,792,700
Southern Equine Stable	41	13,668,000
WinStar Farm, agent	31	12,225,000
RBTS, agent	34	11,615,000
BBA (Ireland)	60	11,014,000
My Meadowview LLC	42	10,854,000
Kern/Lillingston Association, agent	12	8,539,000
Baden P. "Buzz" Chace, agent	47	7,581,000
Shadai Farm	11	7,495,000
Hill 'n' Dale Bloodstock, agent	37	6,120,000
Katsumi Yoshida	11	6,050,000
Frankfort Park Farm	21	5,994,000
Ben Glass, agent	34	5,806,000
Nick de Meric, agent	46	5,661,000
Nicoma Bloodstock, agent for Lael Stables	3	5,600,000
Tom Gentry, agent	26	5,562,000
Kenneth G. McPeek, agent	50	5,091,000
Blandford Bloodstock	36	4,806,000
Ben Walden Jr., agent for Kelley Farms Racing	21	4,767,500
Padua Stables	7	4,750,000
Live Oak Plantation	7	4,725,000
Jay Em Ess Stable, agent	18	4,720,000
Dennis R. O'Neill	24	4,654,000
Cecil O. Seaman, agent	24	4,421,500
M L Bloodstock Ltd.	16	4,285,000
Bear Stables	38	4,249,323
Maverick Racing	20	4,210,000
R. J. Bennett	6	4,088,000
Dogwood Stable	28	4,075,000
Leprechaun Racing, agent	46	3,890,000
Todd Quast, agent for GoldMark Farm	24	3,845,000
Audley Farm	5	3,710,000
Lukas Enterprises	6	3,620,000
Epona Bloodstock	12	3,585,000
Heiligbrodt Racing Stable	56	3,553,500
Overbrook Farm	4	3,400,000
RBTS, agent for Sequoia Racing	12	3,390,000
Hugo Merry Bloodstock	8	3,381,000
Rabbah Bloodstock	15	3,345,000
Margaret O'Toole	32	3,343,000
Oxbow Racing	78	3,340,800

Leading Buyers by Yearling Purchases in 2007

Buyer	No. Yearlings Bought	Total Yearling Expenditures
John Ferguson Bloodstock	27	$21,680,000
Demi O'Byrne	16	19,375,000

Auctions — Leading Buyers of 2007

Buyer	No. Yearlings Bought	Total Yearling Expenditures
Zayat Stables	56	$12,124,000
Michael J. Ryan, agent	55	11,636,700
Shadwell Estate Co. Ltd.	21	10,790,000
Nick de Meric, agent	46	5,661,000
B. Wayne Hughes	24	5,654,500
RBTS, agent	22	5,580,000
Ben Glass, agent	27	5,167,000
Kenneth G. McPeek, agent	50	5,091,000
BBA (Ireland)	32	4,861,000
Jay Em Ess Stable, agent	17	4,620,000
Baden P. "Buzz" Chace, agent	32	4,235,000
Tom Gentry, agent	15	3,853,000
Todd Quast, agent for GoldMark Farm	24	3,845,000
Leprechaun Racing, agent	43	3,675,000
Lukas Enterprises	6	3,620,000
My Meadowview LLC	5	3,550,000
Blandford Bloodstock	24	3,469,000
Rabbah Bloodstock	15	3,345,000
M.A.B. Agency	16	3,204,000
Southern Equine Stable	13	3,110,000
Oxbow Racing	58	2,998,500
Team Valor	3	2,830,000
Live Oak Plantation	6	2,825,000
M.S.T.S.	25	2,763,500
Beverly J. Lewis	5	2,725,000
Tom McGreevy, agent	7	2,715,000
Clarence Scharbauer Jr.	3	2,700,000
Jacob J. Pletcher, agent	10	2,690,000
WinStar Farm, agent	6	2,690,000
Charles P. Gordon-Watson, agent	7	2,660,000
Starlight Stables	10	2,620,000
Maverick Racing	9	2,495,000
James S. Delahooke, agent	17	2,440,000
Jon Kelly	4	2,425,000
Chiefswood Stables Ltd.	2	2,350,000
McKeever-St. Lawrence	8	2,340,000
Dale L. Romans, agent	19	2,251,200
Brushwood Stable	3	2,210,000
G. Watts Humphrey Jr., agent	6	2,175,000
Three Chimneys Farm, agent	4	2,155,000

Leading Buyers by Weanling Purchases in 2007

Buyer	No. Weanlings Bought	Total Weanling Expenditures
Southern Equine Stable	4	$1,950,000
John Ferguson Bloodstock	2	1,650,000
Maverick Racing	10	1,615,000
Shadwell Estate Co. Ltd.	7	1,350,000
BG Stables	7	1,110,000
Margaret O'Toole	9	1,099,000
Baden P. "Buzz" Chace, agent	6	1,056,000
Olin B. Gentry, agent	3	1,050,000
Classic Oaks Farm	6	1,027,000
Chesapeake Partners	5	1,025,000
Ronald L. Rhodes, agent	2	955,000
Josham Farms, agent	9	920,000
Grove Stud	7	875,000
Stoney Lane Farm	10	872,000
Gasper Bloodstock, agent	1	850,000
Gulf Coast Farms	2	810,000
Demi O'Byrne	1	800,000
Dapple Bloodstock, agent	9	786,000
Tom Gentry, agent	6	782,000
Walnut Hill Racing	4	695,000
Meadowlands Stud	5	685,000
Zayat Stables	4	675,000
M L Bloodstock Ltd.	4	655,000
Overbrook Farm	1	600,000
Walnut Hill Stable	5	586,000
Ben Glass, agent	5	569,000
Sugar Valley Farm	7	566,000
White Church Farm	6	556,000
Frankfort Park Farm	1	550,000
J D R Farms	5	535,000
Blandford Bloodstock	5	530,000
Angus Glen Farm	3	$525,000
Hill 'n' Dale Bloodstock	4	523,000
B. Wayne Hughes	2	501,200
Ponder Hill Farm, agent	22	495,500
Ronald Rauscher, agent	2	490,000
Ten Broeck Farm	2	490,000
DOC Bloodstock	5	490,000
Wayne G. Lyster III	3	482,000
Thoroughbred Advisory Group	2	470,000
Tally-Ho Stud	2	462,000
Foxtale Farm	2	440,000

Leading Buyers by Juvenile Purchases in 2007

Buyer	No. Juveniles Bought	Total Juvenile Expenditures
John Ferguson Bloodstock	15	$11,820,000
Zayat Stables	22	5,760,000
Dennis R. O'Neill	24	4,654,000
B. Wayne Hughes	8	4,650,000
Demi O'Byrne	4	3,785,000
John W. Sadler, agent	9	3,135,000
Southern Equine Stable	14	2,558,000
Michael J. Ryan, agent	8	2,325,000
Baden P. "Buzz" Chace, agent	9	2,290,000
Bear Stables Ltd.	17	2,276,000
Stonestreet Thoroughbred Holdings	4	2,250,000
Dogwood Stable	16	2,210,000
Sir Robert Ogden	3	2,030,000
Christopher S. Paasch, agent	8	1,915,000
Tim Kegel, agent	13	1,885,000
West Point Thoroughbreds	12	1,820,000
RBTS, agent	5	1,725,000
Gary S. Broad	12	1,710,000
Merry/Newmarket/Meehan	5	1,430,000
JMJ Racing Stables	5	1,420,000
Brian J. Koriner, agent	12	1,402,000
Hirotsugu Hirai	3	1,340,000
Joseph Brocklebank, agent	18	1,334,000
IEAH Stables	3	1,325,000
Gary C. Contessa, agent	25	1,263,000
Elite Racing	7	1,217,000
Barry Berkelhammer, agent	13	1,137,000
Tom McCrocklin, agent for Marc Keller	8	1,135,000
Centennial Farms	3	1,075,000
Thomas Clark Bloodstock Ltd., agent	80	1,048,200
John P. Fort	3	1,035,000
Hill 'n' Dale Bloodstock	1	1,000,000
Felix G. Norat	19	990,000
Thor-bred Stables	7	925,000
Jerry Hollendorfer	10	924,000
Sierra Sunset	5	907,000
Klaravich Stables and William Lawrence	4	897,000
Katsumi Yoshida	3	870,000

Leading Buyers by Broodmare or Broodmare Prospect Purchases in 2007

Buyer	No. Broodmare or Broodmare Prospects Bought	Total Broodmare or Broodmare Prospect Expenditures
John Ferguson Bloodstock	8	$33,550,000
Stonestreet Thoroughbred Holdings	12	13,670,000
WinStar Farm	23	9,085,000
Kern/Lillingston Association, agent	6	7,717,000
Shadai Farm	11	7,495,000
My Meadowview LLC	36	6,904,000
Southern Equine Stable	10	6,050,000
B. Wayne Hughes	33	5,987,000
BBA (Ireland)	20	5,791,000
Ben P. Walden Jr., agent	25	5,707,500
Shadwell Farm	3	5,655,000

Buyer	No. Broodmare or Broodmare Prospects Bought	Total Broodmare or Broodmare Prospect Expenditures
Nicoma Bloodstock, agent for Lael Stables	3	$5,600,000
Katsumi Yoshida	5	4,575,000
RBTS, agent	7	4,310,000
R. J. Bennett	6	4,088,000
Padua Stables	4	4,050,000
Frankfort Park Farm	12	3,779,000
Audley Farm	5	3,710,000
Michael J. Ryan, agent	14	3,702,000
Hill 'n' Dale Bloodstock, agent	22	3,340,000
Debbie Easter, agent for Halsey Minor	1	3,300,000
Epona Bloodstock	8	3,160,000
Sha-li Leasing Associates	3	3,150,000
Demi O'Byrne	1	3,100,000
Cecil O. Seaman, agent	4	2,576,500
Woodford Thoroughbreds	5	2,345,000
M L Bloodstock Ltd.	3	2,250,000
Taylor Made Sales Agency, agent	14	2,208,700
Nofa Equestrian Resort	9	2,135,000
Omar Trevino, agent	6	2,099,000
Castleton Lyons	4	2,051,200
I T C International Thoroughbred	8	2,050,000

Leading Consignors and Consignor Agents by Total Receipts in 2007

Consignor	No. Offered	No. Sold	Total
Taylor Made Sales Agency	1,272	968	$137,603,700
Lane's End	467	401	83,129,600
Eaton Sales	681	552	71,982,700
Hill 'n' Dale Sales Agency	483	400	66,102,693
Three Chimneys Sales	464	365	46,691,900
Northern Farm	102	102	39,032,382
Gainesway	366	304	36,506,700
Hidden Brook Farm	328	292	27,147,800
Paramount Sales	567	408	25,795,900
Bluewater Sales	324	262	25,746,400
Mill Ridge Sales	234	190	23,360,400
Swettenham Stud	31	30	22,606,718
Denali Stud	305	227	22,501,900
Shadai Farm	83	77	20,663,155
Four Star Sales	442	351	19,870,900
Legacy Bloodstock	567	419	18,279,700
Warrendale Sales	358	269	16,983,600
Castlebridge Consignment	178	132	15,209,356
Brookdale Sales	177	150	15,006,400
Niall Brennan Stables	101	76	12,267,400
Oaks Farm Stables	47	39	12,257,668
Voute Sales	210	126	11,998,098
Haras de Fresnay Le Buffard	20	17	11,610,807
Summerfield	499	346	11,082,100
Highclere Stud	49	47	10,945,331
Indian Creek	167	128	10,742,500
Claiborne Farm	122	108	10,459,500
Jamie Railton	146	90	10,083,240
Dromoland Farm	92	67	9,989,200
Bluegrass Thoroughbred Services	132	101	9,828,600
Woods Edge Farm	88	66	8,843,100
Haras d'Etreham	53	44	8,831,200
Camas Park Stud	30	29	8,714,960
Hunter Valley Farm	155	111	8,581,594
Kirkwood Stables	81	58	8,521,093
Darby Dan Farm	188	148	8,496,300
Scanlon Training Center	68	39	8,390,000
Brereton C. Jones	156	121	8,346,800
Shalfleet Stables	15	12	8,293,366
Burleson Farms	95	78	8,269,800
Ashtown House Stud	24	24	8,219,878
Trickledown Stud	113	91	8,068,089
B.C.3 Thoroughbreds	98	71	7,953,100
James B. Keogh	204	146	7,948,400
Eddie Woods	99	74	7,911,500
Glenvale Stud	38	38	7,861,125

Leading Consignors by Yearling Receipts in 2007

Consignor	No. Yearlings Sold	Total Yearling Revenues
Taylor Made Sales Agency	536	$73,700,000
Eaton Sales	366	47,935,700
Lane's End	184	43,517,200
Gainesway	187	25,313,500
Three Chimneys Sales	147	18,220,000
Hill 'n' Dale Sales Agency	187	17,387,693
Paramount Sales	248	16,815,200
Denali Stud	148	16,398,900
Warrendale Sales	151	11,669,500
Legacy Bloodstock	249	11,667,500
Mill Ridge Sales	93	10,663,500
Four Star Sales	204	9,685,400
Dromoland Farm	51	9,176,500
Bluewater Sales	134	8,590,500
Woods Edge Farm	41	7,614,500
Summerfield	194	7,406,900
Darby Dan Farm	91	6,726,600
Brookdale Sales	71	5,858,700
Bluegrass Thoroughbred Services	64	5,732,400
Claiborne Farm	44	5,471,000
Indian Creek	66	5,053,100
Brereton C. Jones	78	4,719,800
Crossroads Sales Agency	75	4,634,300
Gracefield	34	3,757,000
Beth Bayer	182	3,687,800
Brandywine Farm	74	3,354,000
Robert E. Courtney	23	3,247,900
Burleson Farms	40	3,045,600
Walnut Green	40	2,940,200
Highclere Sales	79	2,809,900
Hunter Valley Farm	42	2,799,200
James B. Keogh	66	2,751,900
Middlebrook Farm	15	2,665,200
Trackside Farm	43	2,554,700
Hidden Brook Farm	51	2,496,800
James M. Herbener Jr.	37	2,468,900
Hopewell Farm	57	2,421,800
Stone Farm	26	2,363,500

Leading Consignors by Weanling Receipts in 2007

Consignor	No. Weanlings Sold	Total Weanling Revenues
Taylor Made Sales Agency	104	$8,397,900
Hill 'n' Dale Sales Agency	55	7,374,700
Eaton Sales	58	5,192,200
Three Chimneys Sales	55	3,955,400
Bluewater Sales	27	3,168,200
Lane's End	51	2,797,900
Gainesway	33	2,649,200
James B. Keogh	48	2,559,700
Paramount Sales	45	2,448,900
Brereton C. Jones	26	2,405,000
Legacy Bloodstock	64	2,040,300
Hunter Valley Farm	23	1,999,000
Summerfield	69	1,774,700
Indian Creek	20	1,755,500
Four Star Sales	33	1,677,400
Warrendale Sales	32	1,626,400
Pope McLean	18	1,237,700
Brookdale Sales	16	1,181,000
Bluegrass Thoroughbred Services	9	1,055,700
Gracefield	13	997,000
James M. Herbener Jr.	10	914,000
Highclere Sales	15	802,500
Trackside Farm	19	785,200
Blandford Stud	5	758,000
Denali Stud	18	707,300
Dapple Stud	7	683,000
Viking Stud	12	680,500
Hidden Brook Farm	24	659,900
Burleson Farms	13	623,200
Beth Bayer	28	605,400

Auctions — Leading Consignors of 2007

Consignor	No. Weanlings Sold	Total Weanling Revenues
Elm Tree Farm	7	$587,000
Kingswood Farm	12	581,700
Journeyman Bloodstock	23	566,200
Nardelli Sales	18	564,400
Michael C. Byrne	1	550,000
Occidental Thoroughbreds	11	515,700
Kaizen Sales	14	499,900
Susan H. Forrester	20	475,700
Longfield Farm	4	472,000
Nursery Place	7	453,800

Leading Consignors by Juvenile Receipts in 2007

Consignor	No. Juveniles Sold	Total Juvenile Revenues
Niall Brennan Stables	76	$12,267,400
Scanlon Training Center	39	8,390,000
Eddie Woods	74	7,911,500
B.C.3 Thoroughbreds	49	7,330,600
Wavertree Stables	43	7,261,000
Kirkwood Stables	49	6,542,000
Nick de Meric	63	6,088,000
Leprechaun Racing	56	5,831,000
Murray Smith	26	5,272,000
Hartley/De Renzo Thoroughbreds	27	5,153,500
Hoby and Layna Kight	14	5,100,000
Adena Springs	90	4,892,000
Sequel Bloodstock	32	4,887,000
Jerry Bailey Sales Agency	24	4,490,000
Eisaman Equine Services	66	4,330,500
O & H Bloodstock	31	3,848,500
M & H Training and Sales	93	3,570,500
Randall Miles	46	3,327,700
Tony Bowling and Bobby Dodd	18	3,000,500
Ocala Stud Farm	57	2,984,900
Crupi's New Castle Farm	27	2,639,500
Stephens Thoroughbreds	39	2,583,000
Robert J. Harris	18	2,523,500
Solitary Oak Farm	35	2,418,300
Off the Hook	20	2,380,500
Excel Bloodstock	14	2,307,500
Casse Sales	29	2,269,500
Shadybrook Farm	34	2,012,400
Paul Sharp	47	1,958,700
CloverLeaf Farms II and Brent Fernung	40	1,763,200
Halcyon Hammock Farm	36	1,486,200
Don R. Graham	10	1,478,500
Cary Frommer	16	1,450,500
Havens Bloodstock Agency	70	1,415,300
Four Roses Thoroughbreds	2	1,400,000
Bridlewood Farm	23	1,396,200
Ricky Leppala	12	1,296,800
John D. Stephens	2	1,280,000
True South	19	1,266,500
Maurice W. Miller III	3	1,200,000

Leading Consignors by Broodmare or Broodmare Prospect Receipts in 2007

Consignor	No. Broodmare or Broodmare Prospects Sold	Total Broodmare or Broodmare Prospect Revenues
Taylor Made Sales Agency	315	$55,186,100
Hill 'n' Dale Sales Agency	154	40,577,100
Lane's End	150	36,542,200
Three Chimneys Sales	161	24,445,000
Hidden Brook Farm	217	23,991,100
Eaton Sales	116	18,429,800
Bluewater Sales	99	13,935,700
Mill Ridge Sales	73	11,866,900
Gainesway	83	8,534,000
Four Star Sales	110	8,463,100
Brookdale Sales	63	7,966,700
Paramount Sales	105	6,406,800
Denali Stud	57	5,213,700
Claiborne Farm	54	4,679,500
Burleson Farms	25	4,601,000
Legacy Bloodstock	105	4,561,900
Nursery Place	31	4,323,700
Maynard Farm	1	4,200,000
Indian Creek	41	3,925,900
Vinery	15	3,863,000
Warrendale Sales	81	3,561,700
Anderson Farms	10	3,173,800
Bluegrass Thoroughbred Services	26	2,898,500
James B. Keogh	32	2,636,800
Walnut Green	33	2,536,000
Greenfield Farm	35	2,456,200
Havens Bloodstock Agency	58	2,085,400
Pope McLean	36	2,003,200
James M. Herbener Jr.	23	1,914,200
Hunter Valley Farm	36	1,871,700
Summerfield	80	1,863,500
Hopewell Farm	53	1,774,200
Charlton	41	1,734,200
Adena Springs	101	1,726,000
Darby Dan Farm	49	1,690,700
Grovendale Farm	32	1,599,500
Matagorda Farm	4	1,457,000
Hagyard Farm	6	1,375,000
Lantern Hill Farm	11	1,362,500
Richland Hills	12	1,330,200

Leading Consignors and Consignor Agents by Average
20 or more sold

Consignor	No. Offered	No. Sold	Average
Swettenham Stud	31	30	$753,557
Northern Farm	102	102	382,670
Ashtown House Stud	24	24	342,495
Meon Valley Stud	25	20	330,922
Oaks Farm Stables	47	39	314,299
Camas Park Stud	30	29	300,516
Croom House Stud	27	25	295,756
Watership Down Stud	27	25	273,054
Shadai Farm	83	77	268,353
Highclere Stud	49	47	232,879
Scanlon Training Center	68	39	215,128
Vinery	27	21	211,857
Lane's End	467	401	207,306
Glenvale Stud	38	38	206,872
Murray Smith	33	26	202,769
Haras d'Etreham	53	44	200,709
Corduff Stud	26	23	196,357
Hartley/De Renzo Thoroughbreds	31	27	190,870
Haras de Bouquetot	25	23	189,884
Ballylinch Stud	46	39	188,782
John Troy	56	40	188,291
Jerry Bailey Sales Agency	27	24	187,083
Lynn Lodge Stud	23	22	184,428
Haras de la Reboursiere et de Montaigu	28	21	174,216
Middlebrook Farm	26	23	170,574
Hill 'n' Dale Sales Agency	483	400	165,257
Wavertree Stables	71	44	165,023
Niall Brennan Stables	101	76	161,413
Haras des Capucines	47	37	157,076
Newsells Park Stud	39	35	152,852
Mocklershill Stables	45	35	151,571
Winter Quarter Farm	24	20	151,350
Dromoland Farm	92	67	149,093
Sequel Bloodstock	46	33	148,091
Hillwood Stud	51	43	147,788
Kirkwood Stables	81	58	146,915
Taylor Made Sales Agency	1,272	968	142,153
Woods Edge Farm	88	66	133,986

Consignor	No. Offered	No. Sold	Average
Yeomanstown Stud	51	44	$133,661
Haras du Quesnay	30	24	132,914
Haras du Mezeray	32	27	132,272
Eaton Sales	681	552	130,403
Kildaragh Stud	37	27	128,186
Three Chimneys Sales	464	365	127,923
Whatton Manor Stud	36	28	127,781
Bansha House Stables	44	28	126,102
Mill Ridge Sales	234	190	122,949
Rathbarry Stud	41	32	122,108
O & H Bloodstock	42	32	120,266
Gainesway	366	304	120,088

Leading Consignors and Consignor Agents by Percent Sold
20 or more sold

Consignor	No. Offered	No. Sold	Pct. Sold
Northern Farm	102	102	100.00%
Ashtown House Stud	24	24	100.00%
Glenvale Stud	38	38	100.00%
Juddmonte Farms	75	75	100.00%
WinStar Racing	21	21	100.00%
Pin Oak Lane Farm	44	44	100.00%
Swettenham Stud	31	30	96.77%
Camas Park Stud	30	29	96.67%
Golden Eagle Farm	89	86	96.63%
Shadwell Stud	28	27	96.43%
Highclere Stud	49	47	95.92%
Darley Stud Management	49	47	95.92%
McFadden Farm	24	23	95.83%
Red River Farms	69	66	95.65%
Lynn Lodge Stud	23	22	95.65%
Thornmar	21	20	95.24%
Paddockhurst Stables	30	28	93.33%
The National Stud	42	39	92.86%
Shadai Farm	83	77	92.77%
Croom House Stud	27	25	92.59%
Watership Down Stud	27	25	92.59%
Ocala Stud Farms	53	49	92.45%
Bruno DeBerdt	26	24	92.31%
Sequel Stallions New York	25	23	92.00%
Haras de Bouquetot	25	23	92.00%
Manton House Stables	24	22	91.67%
Kingswood Farm	24	22	91.67%
Kingsley House Stables	35	32	91.43%
New England Stud	57	52	91.23%
Chanceland Farm	22	20	90.91%
Miller Thoroughbred Farm	22	20	90.91%
Lantern Hill Farm	31	28	90.32%
Crupi's New Castle Farm	30	27	90.00%
Halcyon Hammock Farm	40	36	90.00%
Newsells Park Stud	39	35	89.74%
Robert E. Courtney	57	51	89.47%
Hidden Brook Farm	328	292	89.02%
Jerry Bailey Sales Agency	27	24	88.89%
Castle Park Farms	63	56	88.89%
Bar C Racing Stables	27	24	88.89%
Lynne Martin-Boutte	35	31	88.57%
Claiborne Farm	122	108	88.52%
Middlebrook Farm	26	23	88.46%
Corduff Stud	26	23	88.46%
Mount Coote Stud	26	23	88.46%

Sales Average of All Horses by Year

Year	Average	Change
2007	$41,732	−29.5%
2006	59,189	7.8%
2005	54,909	5.2%
2004	52,205	15.5%
2003	45,206	8.4%
2002	41,694	−5.5%
2001	44,108	−14.3%
2000	51,443	3.3%
1999	49,795	18.1%
1998	42,165	12.6%
1997	37,457	13.9%
1996	32,892	15.7%
1995	28,440	13.9%
1994	24,966	13.7%
1993	21,952	9.9%
1992	19,972	−5.5%
1991	21,136	−10.6%
1990	23,645	−11.3%
1989	26,648	−1.1%
1988	26,957	−6.0%

Two-Year-Olds in Training Sales Average by Year

Year	Average	Change
2007	$61,820	−11.4%
2006	69,754	14.5%
2005	60,927	3.4%
2004	58,918	27.7%
2003	46,140	−3.1%
2002	47,624	1.4%
2001	46,971	−7.7%
2000	50,873	−4.7%
1999	53,382	16.9%
1998	45,668	0.5%
1997	45,425	14.1%
1996	39,804	24.5%
1995	31,971	23.3%
1994	25,929	27.1%
1993	20,402	7.7%
1992	18,947	4.9%
1991	18,056	−11.5%
1990	20,403	30.0%
1989	15,690	−5.2%
1988	16,542	5.4%

Yearling Sales Average by Year

Year	Average	Change
2007	$55,020	−3.0%
2006	56,722	3.7%
2005	54,699	3.7%
2004	52,748	9.4%
2003	48,213	10.0%
2002	43,848	−15.9%
2001	52,140	−4.4%
2000	54,558	8.0%
1999	50,523	17.8%
1998	42,880	12.3%
1997	38,189	10.6%
1996	34,540	11.9%
1995	30,880	13.6%
1994	27,177	8.3%
1993	25,098	12.6%
1992	22,290	−14.8%
1991	26,157	−12.9%
1990	30,030	−6.4%
1989	32,097	−2.0%
1988	32,748	−7.3%

Weanling Sales Average by Year

Year	Average	Change
2007	$44,385	−10.6%
2006	49,623	13.3%
2005	43,796	18.4%
2004	36,986	−7.7%
2003	40,087	28.6%
2002	31,181	14.9%
2001	27,149	−24.0%
2000	35,716	−16.7%
1999	42,852	9.3%
1998	39,203	21.8%
1997	32,178	14.0%
1996	28,232	8.1%
1995	26,124	19.7%
1994	21,822	−7.5%
1993	23,589	47.8%
1992	15,962	−21.7%
1991	20,376	12.0%
1990	18,195	−23.0%

Auctions — Pinhooking

Year	Average	Change
1989	$23,635	50.1%
1988	15,743	-55.5%

Broodmare Sales Average by Year

Year	Average	Change
2007	$69,549	11.1%
2006	62,611	8.7%
2005	57,597	3.4%
2004	55,694	27.5%
2003	43,683	7.8%
2002	40,515	9.0%
2001	37,183	-32.1%
2000	54,752	2.4%
1999	53,457	22.3%
1998	43,701	15.3%
1997	37,913	21.5%
1996	31,192	21.0%
1995	25,770	5.8%
1994	24,355	33.3%
1993	18,274	1.5%
1992	18,009	2.3%
1991	17,604	-8.7%
1990	19,280	-29.4%
1989	27,291	-0.1%
1988	27,328	7.3%

Pinhooking in American Auctions

No one knows exactly how the terms pinhooking or pinhooker entered the English language—or at least Thoroughbred racing's esoteric subset of Shakespeare's tongue—but the practice and profession have become far more common, lucrative, and important to the industry since the early 1990s, when the market for two-year-olds exploded.

Pinhooking is a variation on the capitalist concept of wholesale versus retail. The pinhooker buys a horse—for example, a yearling at auction—with the express purpose of reselling that horse at a later auction, almost always a sale of two-year-olds in training. Thus, the pinhooker tries to purchase at a relatively low price (wholesale) and resell later at a higher price (retail). In between, the pinhooker makes further investments of time and money trying to improve the quality of the wholesale purchase in hopes of cashing in on a retail sale.

Pinhooking is a business with high risks and the potential for high rewards, as illustrated by the following tables, which detail the most successful and least successful pinhooks on record.

Most Successful Pinhooks by Total Gain (through June 11, 2008)
Yearling to Juvenile

$15,575,000 THE GREEN MONKEY, 2004 b. c., Forestry—Magical Masquerade, by Unbridled. **Yearling Purchase:** $425,000, 2005 Fasig-Tipton Kentucky July, by Hartley/De Renzo Thoroughbreds. **Juvenile Sale:** $16,000,000, 2006 Fasig-Tipton Calder February, consigned by Hartley/De Renzo Thoroughbreds, agent, purchased by Demi O'Byrne. 3,664.7% gain. [3-0-0-1, $10,440].

$4,230,000 FUSAICHI SAMURAI, 2002 dk. b. or br. h., Fusaichi Pegasus—Hidden Storm, by Storm Cat. **Yearling Purchase:** $270,000, 2003 Fasig-Tipton Saratoga selected, by White Horse Stables. **Juvenile Sale:** $4,500,000, 2004 Fasig-Tipton Calder February, consigned by Kirkwood Stables, agent, purchased by Fusao Sekiguchi. 1,566.7% gain. [4-1-0-0, $22,200].

$3,130,000 CHEKHOV, 2002 b. g., Pulpit—In My Cap, by Vice Regent. **Yearling Purchase:** $170,000, 2003 Keeneland September, by Michael J. Ryan, agent. **Juvenile Sale:** $3,300,000, 2004 Keeneland April, consigned by Niall Brennan Stables, agent, purchased by Demi O'Byrne. 1,841.2% gain. [17-1-4-2, spl, $194,296].

$2,943,000 DUBAI DREAMER, 2002 gr. or ro. h., Stephen Got Even—Blacktie Bid, by Black Tie Affair (Ire). **Yearling Purchase:** $157,000, 2003 Fasig-Tipton Kentucky July, by Michael J. Ryan, agent. **Juvenile Sale:** $3,100,000, 2004 Fasig-Tipton Calder February, consigned by Niall Brennan Stables, agent, purchased by John Ferguson. 1,874.5% gain. [14-1-1-1, $23,311].

$2,800,000 BARBADOS, 2003 b. c., Forestry—Rare Bird, by Rahy. **Yearling Purchase:** $200,000, 2004 Fasig-Tipton Kentucky July, by Tony Bowling and Bobby Dodd. **Juvenile Sale:** $3,000,000, 2005 Fasig-Tipton Calder February, consigned by Tony Bowling and Bobby Dodd, agent, purchased by Demi O'Byrne. 1,400% gain. [10-1-5-1, $87,730].

$2,670,000 DIAMOND FURY, 2001 ch. r., Sea of Secrets—Swift Spirit, by Tasso. **Yearling Purchase:** $30,000, 2002 Fasig-Tipton Kentucky July, by Becky Thomas. **Juvenile Sale:** $2,700,000, 2003 Barretts March, consigned by Sequel Bloodstock, agent, purchased by Charles Fipke. 8,900% gain. [16-3-3-3, $135,200].

$2,450,000 RONDO, 2003 b. c., Grand Slam—Dama, by Storm Cat. **Yearling Purchase:** $450,000, 2004 Fasig-Tipton Kentucky July, by Maurice W. Miller, agent. **Juvenile Sale:** $2,900,000, 2005 Fasig-Tipton Calder February, consigned by Maurice W. Miller, agent, purchased by Darley. 544.4% gain. [9-3-3-0, $127,989].

$2,310,000 UNBRIDLED SLEW, 2004 ch. c., Red Bullet—Sookloozy, by Avenue of Flags. **Yearling Purchase:** $190,000, 2005 Keeneland September, by Dapple Bloodstock. **Juvenile Sale:** $2,500,000, 2006 Barretts May, consigned by Wavertree Stables, agent, purchased by Darley Stable. 1,215.8% gain. Unraced.

$1,925,000 DUBAI ESCAPADE, 2002 b. m., Awesome Again—Sassy Pants, by Saratoga Six. **Yearling Purchase:** $75,000, 2003 Keeneland September, by Gulf Coast Farms. **Juvenile Sale:** $2,000,000, 2004 Barretts March, consigned by Jerry Bailey Sales Agency, agent, purchased by John Ferguson Bloodstock. 2,566.7% gain. [8-6-0-0, G1, $427,050].

$1,869,000 ATLANTIC OCEAN, 2000 dk. b. or br. m., Stormy Atlantic—Super Chef, by Seattle Slew. **Yearling Purchase:** $31,000, 2001 Keeneland September, by James K. Chapman. **Juvenile Sale:** $1,900,000, 2002 Barretts March, consigned by Chapman Farms, purchased by The Thoroughbred Corp. 6,029% gain. [19-5-3-2, G3, $678,210].

$1,825,000 MERCANTILE, 2004 b. c., Golden Missile—Silverdew, by Silver Deputy. **Yearling Purchase:** $175,000, 2005 Keeneland September, by O & H Bloodstock. **Juvenile Sale:** $2,000,000, 2006 Fasig-Tipton Calder February, consigned by O & H Bloodstock, agent, purchased by, agent. 1,042.9% gain. [11-3-2-2, $83,160].

$1,825,000 MOROCCO, 1997 ch. h., Brocco—Roll Over Baby, by Rollin On Over. **Yearling Purchase:** $175,000, 1998 Fasig-Tipton Saratoga selected, by Alfred T. Eldredge. **Juvenile Sale:** $2,000,000, 1999 Barretts March, consigned by Sequel Bloodstock, agent, purchased by The Thoroughbred Corp. 1,042.9% gain. [16-4-0-1, $133,640].

$1,820,000 BELGRAVIA, 2004 b. c., Mr. Greeley—Peaks Mill, by Stalwart. **Yearling Purchase:** $180,000, 2005 Keeneland September, by D & B Ventures. **Juvenile Sale:** $2,000,000, 2006 Fasig-Tipton Calder February, consigned by Nick de Meric, agent, purchased by Demi O'Byrne. 1,011.1% gain. [5-2-1-0, G3, $127,115].

$1,805,000 WHAT A SONG, 2003 dk. b. or br. c., Songandaprayer—What a Knight, by Tough Knight. **Yearling Purchase:** $95,000, 2004 Fasig-Tipton Kentucky July, by M.S.T.S. **Juvenile Sale:** $1,900,000, 2005 Barretts March, consigned by Murray Smith, agent, purchased by Robert and Beverly Lewis. 1,900% gain. [3-3-0-0, G2, $179,700].

$1,805,000 YONAGUSKA, 1998 dk. b. or br. h., Cherokee Runó-Marital Spook, by Silver Ghost. **Yearling Purchase:** $145,000, 1999 Keeneland September, by Michael J. Ryan, agent. **Juvenile Sale:** $1,950,000, 2000 Fasig-Tipton Calder February, consigned by Niall Brennan, agent, purchased by Demi O'Byrne. 1,244.8% gain. [18-6-1-5, G1, $536,355].

Most Successful Pinhooks by Percentage Gain (through June 11, 2008)
Yearling to Juvenile

8,900.0%   DIAMOND FURY, 2001 ch. r., Sea of Secrets—Swift Spirit, by Tasso. **Yearling Purchase:** $30,000, 2002 Fasig-Tipton Kentucky July, by Becky Thomas. **Juvenile Sale:** $2,700,000, 2003 Barretts March, consigned by Sequel Bloodstock, agent, purchased by Charles Fipke. [16-3-3-3, $135,200].

7,400.0%   COLONEL CHICK, 2004 b. c., West Acre—Telling Tales (Arg), by Ahmad. **Yearling Purchase:** $2,000, 2005 OBSC August, by Dagoberto Delgado. **Juvenile Sale:** $150,000, 2006 OBSC April, consigned by Double H Stables, agent, purchased by Mike House. $148,000 gain. [7-1-1-1, $47,640].

6,029.0%   ATLANTIC OCEAN, 2000 dk. b. or br. m., Stormy Atlantic—Super Chef, by Seattle Slew. **Yearling Purchase:** $31,000, 2001 Keeneland September, by James K. Chapman. **Juvenile Sale:** $1,900,000, 2002 Barretts March, consigned by Chapman Farms, purchased by The Thoroughbred Corp. $1,869,000 gain. [19-5-3-2, G3, $678,210].

5,700.0%   GATO GO WIN, 2006 dk. b. or br. c., City Place—Brooks N Boots, by Odyle. **Yearling Purchase:** $2,500, 2007 Fasig-Tipton Midlantic September, by H.H.T.S. **Juvenile Sale:** $145,000, 2008 Barretts May, consigned by Hartley/De Renzo Thoroughbreds, purchased by Jack Sims and Joey Platts. $142,500 gain. Unraced.

4,900.0%   AFTERNOON QUE, 2002 dk. b. or br. g., Afternoon Deelites—How 'bout Chris, by Unbridled. **Yearling Purchase:** $5,000, 2003 Fasig-Tipton Midlantic October, by M & H Training and Sales. **Juvenile Sale:** $250,000, 2004 OBSC March, consigned by M & H Training and Sales, agent, purchased by West Point Thoroughbreds. $245,000 gain. [7-2-0-1, $25,530].

4,687.2%   Major Adonis, 1997 b. g., Major Impact—Adonara, by Strawberry Road (Aus). **Yearling Purchase:** $4,700, 1998 Fasig-Tipton Kentucky October, by Bea and Robert H. Roberts. **Juvenile Sale:** $225,000, 1999 Keeneland November, consigned by Bea and Robert H. Roberts, purchased by Eugene N. Melnyk. $220,300 gain. [16-2-3-2, spl, $100,926].

3,900.0%   URBANE PROSPECT, 2005 dk. b. or br. c., Suave Prospect—Cody Zamorra, by Jeblar. **Yearling Purchase:** $3,000, 2006 OBSC August, by Michael H. Sherman. **Juvenile Sale:** $120,000, 2007 OBSC April, consigned by Sherman Family Thoroughbreds, purchased by William J. Condren. $117,000 gain. [5-1-1-0, $24,360].

3,664.7%   THE GREEN MONKEY, 2004 b. c., Forestry—Magical Masquerade, by Unbridled. **Yearling Purchase:** $425,000, 2005 Fasig-Tipton Kentucky July, by Hartley/De Renzo Thoroughbreds. **Juvenile Sale:** $16,000,000, 2006 Fasig-Tipton Calder February, consigned by Hartley/De Renzo Thoroughbreds, agent, purchased by Demi O'Byrne. $15,575,000 gain. [3-0-0-1, $10,440].

3,650.0%   HYPER NAKAYAMA, 1995 dk. b. or br. h., Well Decorated—Tea and Roses, by Fleet Nasrullah. **Yearling Purchase:** $8,000, 1996 Keeneland January, by Donna M. Wormser. **Juvenile Sale:** $300,000, 1997 OBSC February, consigned by Donna M. Wormser, agent, purchased by Heatherway, agent. $292,000 gain. [24-4-7-4, $1,002,590].

3,650.0%   IRREVOCABLE, 2001 b. m., Our Emblem—Northern Glance, by Nijinsky II. **Yearling Purchase:** $3,200, 2002 Keeneland January, by Burden Creek Farm. **Juvenile Sale:** $120,000, 2003 Keeneland April, consigned by American Equistock and Parrish Farms, purchased by John C. Kimmel. $116,800 gain. [11-3-3-0, $75,055].

3,455.6%   MUTANABI, 2002 b. h., Wild Rush—Freudenau, by Meadowlake. **Yearling Purchase:** $45,000, 2003 OBSC August, by Ricky Leppala. **Juvenile Sale:** $1,600,000, 2004 OBSC February, consigned by W. D. North, agent, purchased by John Ferguson. $1,555,000 gain. [2-0-1-1, $3,171].

Least Successful Pinhooks by Total Loss (through June 11, 2008)
Yearling to Juvenile

–$360,000   Unnamed, 2006 b. c., Distorted Humor—Mombasa, by Dynaformer. **Yearling Purchase:** $650,000, 2007 Keeneland September, by Jerry Bailey. **Juvenile Sale:** $290,000, 2008 Keeneland April, consigned by Jerry Bailey Sales Agency, agent, purchased by The Stallion Company, agent. –55.4% loss. Unraced.

–$300,000   EVIL MINISTER, 2002 ch. h., Deputy Minister—Evil's Pic, by Piccolino. **Yearling Purchase:** $500,000, 2003 Fasig-Tipton Saratoga selected, by Ventures Partnership. **Juvenile Sale:** $200,000, 2004 Fasig-Tipton Calder February, consigned by Kings Equine, agent, purchased by Namcook Stable. –60% loss. [11-2-0-2, G3, $126,000].

–$280,000   Acquileia, 2003 dk. b. or br. f., Arch—Questress, by Seeking the Gold. **Yearling Purchase:** $360,000, 2004 Keeneland September, by Whitehorse Stables. **Juvenile Sale:** $80,000, 2005 Fasig-Tipton Florida Calder February, consigned by Solitary Oak Farm, agent, purchased by Germania Farms. –77.8% loss. [11-1-3-4, spl, $51,380].

–$270,000   MON'S THE MAN, 2003 gr. or ro. c., Maria's Mon—City Gold, by Carson City. **Yearling Purchase:** $350,000, 2004 Keeneland September, by Gulf Coast Farms. **Juvenile Sale:** $80,000, 2005 Barretts May, consigned by Jerry Baily Sales Agency, agent, purchased by J D Thoroughbred Farm. –77.1% loss. [6-1-1-1, $45,740].

–$260,891   RAILBIRD (Ire), 1995 ch. h., Caerleon—My Lady's Key, by Key to the Mint. **Yearling Purchase:** $302,891, 1996 Goffs Orby, by Kenneth E. Ellenbery. **Juvenile Sale:** $42,000, 1997 Barretts March, consigned by Bailey-Ellenbery Select, purchased by Waldon Randall Welty. –86.1% loss. [16-1-3-3, $11,165].

–$250,000   RUSH TO DEFEND, 2000 b. g., Wild Rush—Mary Sloan, by Woodman. **Yearling Purchase:** $500,000, 2001 Fasig-Tipton Kentucky July, by Paul Collins, agent. **Juvenile Sale:** $250,000, 2002 Fasig-Tipton Calder February, consigned by Eddie Woods, agent, purchased by Chester Broman. –50% loss. [17-4-1-1, $37,865].

–$220,000   OVERVIEW, 1998 b. h., Kingmambo—Long View, by Damascus. **Yearling Purchase:** $300,000, 1999 Fasig-Tipton Saratoga selected, by Two Bucks Stable, agent. **Juvenile Sale:** $80,000, 2000 Keeneland April, consigned by Jerry Bailey Sales Agency, agent, purchased by John C. Oxley. –73.3% loss. [14-2-1-4, SW, $105,831].

–$220,000   COLONY STAR, 1995 dk. b. or br. m., Pleasant Colony—Star Glimmer, by General Assembly. **Yearling Purchase:** $250,000, 1996 Keeneland July, by Cam Allard. **Juvenile Sale:** $30,000, 1997 Keeneland April, consigned by H. T. Stables, agent, purchased by Henri Mastey. –88% loss. [1-0-0-0, $150].

–$220,000   TOY SOLDIER, 2005 dk. b. or br. c., Came Home—Luxuriously, by Danzig. **Yearling Purchase:** $275,000, 2006 Keeneland September, by Thornton Racing. **Juvenile Sale:** $55,000, 2007 OBSC March, consigned by Stephens Thoroughbreds, agent, purchased by Equine Analysis Systems Inc. –80% loss. [10-5-0-1, $68,656].

–$215,000   MT. GLITTERMORE, 2005 b. c., Orientate—Spanish Glitter, by Glitterman. **Yearling Purchase:** $250,000, 2006 Fasig-Tipton Saratoga selected, by Dapple Bloodstock. **Juvenile Sale:** $35,000, 2007 Fasig-Tipton Midlantic June, consigned by Wavertree Stables, agent, purchased by Joanne M. Hoover. –86.0% loss. [2-0-1-1, $12,400].

–$210,000   PLUNKIT, 2002 b. g., Lemon Drop Kid—April Starlight, by Storm Bird. **Yearling Purchase:** $500,000, 2003 Fasig-Tipton Kentucky July, by Jeanne G. Vance. **Juvenile Sale:** $290,000, 2004 Keeneland April, consigned by Jeanne G. Vance, purchased by Robert and Beverly Lewis Thoroughbred Racing. –42% loss. [28-3-3-5, $82,351].

–$203,000   JETTIN HIGH, 2002 ch. g., High Yield—Rhodesia, by Polish Navy. **Yearling Purchase:** $220,000, 2003 Keeneland September, by White Horse Stables. **Juvenile Sale:** $17,000, 2004 Keeneland April, consigned by Kirkwood Stables, agent, purchased by Gary Owens. –92.3% loss. [19-3-4-1, $25,465].

Least Successful Pinhooks by Percentage Loss (through June 11, 2008)
Yearling to Juvenile

-98.2%   PAID LEAVE, 2003 dk. b. or br. g., Exchange Rate—Timely Holiday, by Caveat. **Yearling Purchase:** $170,000, 2004 OBSC August, by Gulf Coast Bloodstock. **Juvenile Sale:** $3,000, 2005 Keeneland April, consigned by Jerry Bailey Sales Agency, agent, purchased by Harold Wheeler. –$167,000 loss. [13-1-0-1, $6,192].

-96.0%   FILL MY CUP, 2003 b. c., Belong to Me—Cup of Tricks, by Clever Trick. **Yearling Purchase:** $150,000, 2004 Keeneland September, by Gulf Coast Farms. **Juvenile Sale:** $6,000, 2005 OBSC June, consigned by Jerry Baily Sales Agency, agent, purchased by Narvick International. –$144,000 loss. [9-2-2-1].

-95.5%   DEPUTY PRIZE, 2005 dk. b. or br. c., Deputy Commander—Luminous Prize, by Prized. **Yearling Purchase:** $210,000, 2006 Fasig-Tipton Kentucky July, by William F. Andrews. **Juvenile Sale:** $9,500, 2007 Barretts May, consigned by B.C.3 Thoroughbreds, agent, purchased by Ronald A. Goldfarb. –$200,500 loss. [2-0-0-0, $800].

-92.5%   BEN'S QUEST, 2002 ch. g., Coronado's Quest—Donna Karan (Chi), by Roy. **Yearling Purchase:** $160,000, 2003 Keeneland September, by Becky Thomas. **Juvenile Sale:** $12,000, 2004 Keeneland April, consigned by Sequel Bloodstock, agent, purchased by Moneylane Farms. –$148,000 loss. [11-1-3-0, $13,823].

-92.5%   BOB'S CLOG BUSTER, 1996 b. h., Beau Genius—Told It All, by Told. **Yearling Purchase:** $200,000, 1997 Keeneland September, by Louie J. Roussel. **Juvenile Sale:** $15,000, 1998 Fasig-Tipton Calder February, consigned by Jockey Club Farm, agent, purchased by Ralph C. Sessa. –$185,000 loss. Unraced.

-92.4%   SPRING IN HIS STEP, 2003 b. c., Mr. Greeley—Fairy Song (Ire), by Fairy King. **Yearling Purchase:** $105,000, 2004 Keeneland September, by Kirkwood Stables, agent. **Juvenile Sale:** $8,000, 2005 Keeneland April, consigned by Kirkwood Stables, agent, purchased by Valentine Feerick. –$97,000 loss. [1-0-0-0].

-92.3%   JETTIN HIGH, 2002 ch. g., High Yield—Rhodesia, by Polish Navy. **Yearling Purchase:** $220,000, 2003 Keeneland September, by White Horse Stables. **Juvenile Sale:** $17,000, 2004 Keeneland April, consigned by Kirkwood Stables, agent, purchased by Gary Owens. –$203,000 loss. [19-3-4-1, $25,465].

-92.2%   TRIP CARD, 2004 b. g., Trippi—Sly Stylist, by Sovereign Dancer. **Yearling Purchase:** $115,000, 2005 Fasig-Tipton Kentucky July, by Leprechaun Racing, agent. **Juvenile Sale:** $9,000, 2006 Fasig-Tipton Midlantic May, consigned by Leprechaun Racing, agent, purchased by Roger C. Mattei. –$106,000 loss. [15-3-3-2, $52,540].

-92.2%   WHITE FLASH, 2006 gr. or ro. c., Smoke Glacken—Cho Cho San, by Deputy Minister. **Yearling Purchase:** $115,000, 2007 Keeneland September, by Jimmy Davis, agent. **Juvenile Sale:** $9,000, 2008 OBSC March, consigned by Harris Training Center, agent, purchased by Jaime Rivera. –$106,000 loss. Unraced.

-92.1%   GOTTA TEMPER, 1999 b. m., Pleasant Colony—Omnia, by Green Dancer. **Yearling Purchase:** $140,000, 2000 Keeneland September, by Murray Smith, agent. **Juvenile Sale:** $11,000, 2001 Keeneland April, consigned by Murray Smith, agent, purchased by Wheeler Racing. –$129,000 loss. [20-3-6-3, $63,806].

-91.9%   SCUBAI DUBAI, 2005 b. g., E Dubai—Lupe Valez, by Seattle Slew. **Yearling Purchase:** $210,000, 2006 Keeneland September, by Maurice W. Miller, agent. **Juvenile Sale:** $17,000, 2007 Fasig-Tipton Midlantic May, consigned by Scanlon Training Center, agent, purchased by Donald L. Brown. –$193,000 loss. [8-1-1-1, $15,478].

-91.9%   Cal's Baby, 1998 dk. b. or br. m., Smart Strike—Silver Dollar Kate, by Green Dancer. **Yearling Purchase:** $185,000, 1999 Keeneland September, by James Cassels. **Juvenile Sale:** $15,000, 2000 Keeneland April, consigned by Hartley/De Renzo Thoroughbreds, agent, purchased by Shah Stables. –$170,000 loss. [26-4-2-8, spl, $110,350].

-91.7%   HONOUR TOPPER, 2002 b. g., Honour and Glory—Chart Topper, by Groovy. **Yearling Purchase:** $120,000, 2003 Fasig-Tipton Kentucky July, by Michael J. Ryan, agent. **Juvenile Sale:** $10,000, 2004 Fasig-Tipton Midlantic May, consigned by Niall Brennan Stables, agent, purchased by John E. Salzman. –$110,000 loss. [11-3-2-0, $23,770].

Most Successful Pinhooks by Total Gain (through June 12, 2008)
Weanling to Yearling

$1,440,000   TIMES GONE BY, 2005 ch. c., Giant's Causeway—Happy Tune, by A.P. Indy. **Weanling Purchase:** $460,000, 2005 Keeneland November, by Eaton Sales. **Yearling Sale:** $1,900,000, 2006 Keeneland September, consigned by Eaton Sales, agent, purchased by B. Wayne Hughes. 313% gain. Unraced.

$1,180,000   DUBAI TOUCH, 1999 dk. b. or br. h., Saint Ballado—Jettin Diplomacy, by Roman Diplomat. **Weanling Purchase:** $220,000, 1999 Keeneland November, by B.M.K. Equine. **Yearling Sale:** $1,400,000, 2000 Keeneland July select, consigned by Hartwell Farm, agent, purchased by John Ferguson Bloodstock. 536.4% gain. [9-0-0-0, $3,868].

$1,100,000   SEEKING AN ALIBI, 2002 ch. h., Storm Cat—Seeking Regina, by Seeking the Gold. **Weanling Purchase:** $500,000, 2002 Keeneland November, by Bradley Thoroughbred Brokerage. **Yearling Sale:** $1,600,000, 2003 Keeneland September, consigned by Eaton Sales, agent, purchased by John Ferguson Bloodstock. 220% gain. [13-2-1-0, $18,799].

$1,015,000   TALK IS MONEY, 1998 ch. h., Deputy Minister—Isle Go West, by Gone West. **Weanling Purchase:** $785,000, 1998 Keeneland November, by Smithfield Investments. **Yearling Sale:** $1,800,000, 1999 Keeneland September, consigned by Dromoland Farm, agent, purchased by Buzz Chace, agent. 129.3% gain. [7-2-1-1, SW, $104,110].

$1,000,000   LIFESTYLE, 2000 b. h., Indian Charlie—Inlaw, by Gold Seam. **Weanling Purchase:** $100,000, 2000 Keeneland November, by Holiday Stables. **Yearling Sale:** $1,100,000, 2001 Keeneland September, consigned by Paternostro & Herbener, agent, purchased by The Thoroughbred Corp. 1,000% gain. [20-4-3-2, $139,950].

$938,000   WEATHERMAN, 1998 ch. h., Summer Squall—Plucky Maid, by Housebuster. **Weanling Purchase:** $62,000, 1998 Keeneland November, by Plaza Stud. **Yearling Sale:** $1,000,000, 1999 Keeneland September, consigned by Jann J. FitzGerald, agent, purchased by Stonerside Stable. 1,512.9% gain. [4-1-1-1, $38,280].

$900,000   Dubai Tiger, 1999 b. g., Storm Cat—Toga Toga Toga, by Saratoga Six. **Weanling Purchase:** $900,000, 1999 Keeneland November, by Tim Hyde. **Yearling Sale:** $1,800,000, 2000 Keeneland September, consigned by Eaton Sales, agent, purchased by John Ferguson Bloodstock. 100% gain. [8-2-1-1, spl, $106,510].

$900,000   ZINZAN, 2003 b. c., Grand Slam—Sheza Honey, by Honey Jay. **Weanling Purchase:** $400,000, 2003 Keeneland November, by Michael Byrne. **Yearling Sale:** $1,300,000, 2004 Keeneland September, consigned by Michael C. Byrne, agent, purchased by Demi O'Byrne. 225% gain. [5-1-2-0, $44,965].

$888,000   EALING PARK, 1999 dk. b. or br. g., Saint Ballado—Jeannie the Meanie, by Rare Performer. **Weanling Purchase:** $62,000, 1999 Keeneland November, by Phillip Frances McCarthy. **Yearling Sale:** $950,000, 2000 Keeneland September, consigned by Taylor Made Sales Agency, agent, purchased by Eugene N. Melnyk. 1,432.3% gain. [31-5-1-2, $38,566].

$850,000   STORMIN' HEAVEN, 1998 ch. h., Hennessy—Afleet Francais, by Afleet. **Weanling Purchase:** $350,000, 1998 Keeneland November, by Greenwood Farm. **Yearling Sale:** $1,200,000, 1999 Keeneland July, consigned by Eaton Sales, agent, purchased by Robert B. Hess, agent. 242.9% gain. [12-4-0-1, $124,224].

Most Successful Pinhooks by Percentage Gain (through June 12, 2008)
Weanling to Yearling

11,233.3%	TORTONI, 2000 dk. b. or br. h., Candy Stripes—Our Dani, by Homebuilder. **Weanling Purchase:** $1,500, 2000 Keeneland November, by Pasco Bloodstock. **Yearling Sale:** $170,000, 2001 OBSC August, consigned by Summerfield, agent, purchased by Journeyman Bloodstock, agent. $168,500 gain. [8-1-1-1, $25,880].	3,300.0%	select yearling sale at Newtown Paddocks, consigned by Clarkland Farm, agent, purchased by Buzz Chace, agent. $170,500 gain. Unraced. AIR TOUCH, 1996 ch. h., Phone Trick—Serna, by Cox's Ridge. **Weanling Purchase:** $5,000, 1996 Keeneland November, by Green Meadow Farm. **Yearling Sale:** $170,000, 1997 Keeneland September, consigned by Taylor Made Sales Agency, agent, purchased by Supervent Inc. $165,000 gain. [1-0-0-0].
8,048.1%	DUKE OF DESTINY, 2003 dk. b. or br. c., Pikepass—Dutch's Duchess, by Roy. **Weanling Purchase:** $2,700, 2003 Keeneland November, by Benedict A. Mohit. **Yearling Sale:** $220,000, 2004 OBSC August, consigned by Kaizen Sales, agent, purchased by Martin L. Cherry. $217,300 gain. [3-0-1-0, $7,076].	3,181.3%	LORD ADMIRAL, 1982 b. g., Topsider—Tumbling Dancer, by Dancer's Image. **Weanling Purchase:** $16,000, 1982 Keeneland November, by Charles St. George. **Yearling Sale:** $525,000, 1983 Keeneland September, consigned by Ashleigh Stud Farm, purchased by BBA (England). $509,000 gain. [1-0-0-0, $100].
6,566.7%	GOLDEN TONES, 2001 b. h., Seeking the Gold—Bethany, by Dayjur. **Weanling Purchase:** $6,000, 2001 Keeneland November, by Jay Rodgers. **Yearling Sale:** $400,000, 2002 Keeneland September, consigned by Taylor Made Sales Agency, agent, purchased by Robert and Beverly Lewis. $394,000 gain. [3-1-1-0, $35,720].	3,150.0%	WINDSOR COURT, 1998 dk. b. or br. g., Southern Halo—Her Grace, by Northern Flagship. **Weanling Purchase:** $8,000, 1998 Keeneland November, by Rachel Holden. **Yearling Sale:** $260,000, 1999 Keeneland September, consigned by Tri-County Farm, agent, purchased by James T. Scatuorchio. $252,000 gain. [43-3-10-3, $90,640].
6,566.7%	KING BRIDLE, 1998 b. h., Unbridled—Life's Magic, by Cox's Ridge. **Weanling Purchase:** $3,000, 1998 Keeneland November, by Lori Tanel. **Yearling Sale:** $200,000, 1999 Keeneland September, consigned by Susan Y. Foreman, agent, purchased by David and Jill Heerensperger. $197,000 gain. [23-1-1-1, $11,948].	2,600.0%	MR. AFTER HOURS, 2004 gr. or ro. c., Wild Wonder—Susie Do, by Talinum. **Weanling Purchase:** $10,000, 2004 Keeneland November, by Chad Johnson, agent. **Yearling Sale:** $270,000, 2005 Keeneland September, consigned by Taylor Made Sales Agency, agent, purchased by John J. Brocklebank. $260,000 gain. Unraced.
4,900.0%	UNTOLD STORY, 1995 b. h., Theatrical (Ire)—Committed Miss, by Key to Content. **Weanling Purchase:** $4,000, 1995 Keeneland November, by Bruce Hundley. **Yearling Sale:** $200,000, 1996 Keeneland September, consigned by James B. Keogh, agent, purchased by Newmarket International. $196,000 gain. [23-0-0-1, $1,654].	2,300.0%	Faah Emiss, 1998 b. h., Is It True—Change the Set, by Gold Stage. **Weanling Purchase:** $5,000, 1998 Keeneland November, by Barbara Crabtree. **Yearling Sale:** $120,000, 1999 OBSC August, consigned by Beth Bayer, agent, purchased by Cam Allard. $115,000 gain. [31-4-8-2, spl, $149,777].
3,788.9%	Unnamed, 1994 b. h., Lord At War (Arg)—Corking, by Sensitive Prince. **Weanling Purchase:** $4,500, 1994 Keeneland November, by Chad R. Schumer, agent. **Yearling Sale:** $175,000, 1995 Fasig-Tipton Kentucky		

Least Successful Pinhooks by Total Loss (through June 12, 2008)
Weanling to Yearling

–$800,000	NEW TRIESTE, 1999 ch. h., A.P. Indy—Lovlier Linda, by Vigors. **Weanling Purchase:** $1,300,000, 1999 Keeneland November, by Paul Shanahan. **Yearling Sale:** $500,000, 2000 Keeneland September, consigned by Eaton Sales, agent, purchased by Daniel M. Borislow. –61.5% loss. [1-0-0-0, $1,500].	–$270,000	SIR BEDIVERE, 1999 ch. h., Unbridled—Bold Windy, by Bold Tropic (SAf). **Weanling Purchase:** $400,000, 1999 Keeneland November, by Narvick International. **Yearling Sale:** $130,000, 2000 Keeneland November, consigned by 505 Farm, purchased by Leprechaun Racing, agent. –67.5% loss. [7-1-0-1, $12,630].
–$475,000	WISEMAN'S FERRY, 1999 ch. h., Hennessy—Emmaus, by Silver Deputy. **Weanling Purchase:** $775,000, 1999 Keeneland November, by Indian Hill Farm. **Yearling Sale:** $300,000, 2000 Keeneland September, consigned by Eaton Sales, agent, purchased by Hugo Merry Bloodstock. –61.3% loss. [16-4-3-2, G3, $825,266].	–$250,000	Truckle Feature, 2000 dk. b. or br. h., Saint Ballado—Magic Gleam, by Danzig. **Weanling Purchase:** $275,000, 2000 Keeneland November, by Indian Hill Farm. **Yearling Sale:** $25,000, 2001 Keeneland September, consigned by Eaton Sales, agent, purchased by Straightaway Farm, agent. –90.9% loss. [10-2-1-2, spl, $151,460].
–$416,000	HOSTILE, 2006 ch. g., Lion Heart—Shorewalk Drive, by Formal Gold. **Weanling Purchase:** $420,000, 2006 Keeneland November, by Wright Brothers Bloodstock. **Yearling Sale:** $4,000, 2007 Keeneland September, consigned by Dromoland Farm, agent, purchased by Linda Dixon. –99% loss. [1-1-0-0, $6,660].	–$240,000	SPINNING MISS, 1999 ch. m., Spinning World—Bemissed, by Nijinsky II. **Weanling Purchase:** $575,000, 1999 Keeneland November, by Narvick International. **Yearling Sale:** $335,000 2000 Keeneland September, consigned by 505 Farm, purchased by Brushwood Stable. –41.7% loss. [6-0-0-0, $300].
–$375,000	SPORTS HERO, 1999 dk. b. or br. h., Mr. Prospector—Alysoft, by Alydar. **Weanling Purchase:** $775,000, 1999 Keeneland November, by High Mills Farm. **Yearling Sale:** $400,000, 2000 Fasig-Tipton Saratoga selected, consigned by Lakland LLC, agent, purchased by Select Equine. –48.4% loss. [2-2-0-0, $26,890].	–$225,000	ELUSIVE BLUFF, 2006 b. c., Elusive Quality—Megans Bluff, by Pine Bluff. **Weanling Purchase:** $275,000, 2006 Keeneland November, by Robert E. Courtney, agent. **Yearling Sale:** $50,000, 2007 Keeneland September, consigned by Robert E. Courtney, agent, purchased by Horse Traders. –81.8% loss. Unraced.
–$350,000	Manhattan Skyline, 1999 b. or br. m., Spinning World—Crystal Cream, by Secretariat. **Weanling Purchase:** $550,000, 1999 Keeneland November, by Farfellow Farms. **Yearling Sale:** $200,000, 2000 Keeneland July, consigned by Taylor Made Sales Agency, agent, purchased by Jockey Club Farm. –63.6% loss. [11-4-5-0, spl, $141,255].	–$222,000	RED REDDING, 2005 ch. c., Hold That Tiger—Chicado, by Talkin Man. **Weanling Purchase:** $235,000, 2005 Keeneland November, by C.S. Stable. **Yearling Sale:** $13,000, 2006 Fasig-Tipton Kentucky October, consigned by Hunter Valley Farm, agent, purchased by Bowel Bloodstock. –94.5% loss. [6-1-1-0, $48,390].
–$325,000	CARELESS ALY, 1991 ch. m., Alydar—Careless Notion, by Jester. **Weanling Purchase:** $350,000, 1991 Keeneland November, by Mandysland Farm. **Yearling Sale:** $25,000, 1992 Keeneland September, consigned by Joe Riggs, agent, purchased by Helen C. Alexander, agent. –92.9% loss. Unraced.	–$200,000	AJMAAN, 1990 dk. b. or br. h., Arctic Tern—Melodina (GB), by *Tudor Melody. **Weanling Purchase:** $425,000, 1987 Keeneland July select, by James S. Delahooke. **Yearling Sale:** $225,000, 1991 Keeneland July select, consigned by Pegasus Stud, purchased by Darley Stud Management. –47.1% loss. [7-0-2-2, $4,752].

Auctions — Pinhooking   891

Least Successful Pinhooks by Percentage Loss (through June 12, 2008)
Weanling to Yearling

-99.0% HOSTILE, 2006 ch. g., Lion Heart—Shorewalk Drive, by Formal Gold. **Weanling Purchase:** $420,000, 2006 Keeneland November, by Wright Brothers Bloodstock. **Yearling Sale:** $4,000, 2007 Keeneland September, consigned by Dromoland Farm, agent, purchased by Linda Dixon. –$416,000 loss. [1-1-0-0, $6,660].

-97.5% BLACK MAGIC MAUKER, 2006 dk. b. or br. c., Include—Witness Post, by Gone West. **Weanling Purchase:** $140,000, 2006 Keeneland November, by BKG Ranch. **Yearling Sale:** $3,500, 2007 Keeneland September, consigned by Gainesway, agent, purchased by Fletcher Mauk and Small Batch Thoroughbred. –$136,500 loss. Unraced.

-96.3% BECKY MOSS, 2003 dk. b. or br. f., Red Ransom—British Columbia (GB), by Selkirk. **Weanling Purchase:** $190,000, 2003 Keeneland November, by Arosa Farms. **Yearling Sale:** $7,000, 2004 Keeneland September, consigned by Arosa Farms, purchased by John Collins. –$183,000 loss. [19-1-1-1, $28,671].

-94.5% RED REDDING, 2005 ch. c., Hold That Tiger—Chicado, by Talkin Man. **Weanling Purchase:** $235,000, 2005 Keeneland November, by C.S. Stable. **Yearling Sale:** $13,000, 2006 Fasig-Tipton Kentucky October, consigned by Hunter Valley Farm, agent, purchased by Bowel Bloodstock. –$222,000 loss. [6-1-1-0, $48,390].

-94.0% TRAVIS HARDIN, 2005 b. c., Harlan's Holiday—Cidacape, by Procida. **Weanling Purchase:** $100,000, 2005 Fasig-Tipton Kentucky November, by Ted Campion Stable. **Yearling Sale:** $6,000, 2006 Fasig-Tipton Kentucky October, consigned by Hunter Valley Farm, agent, purchased by Gregory D. Foley. –$94,000 loss. [1-0-0-0].

-93.8% RING DANG DO, 2000 b. h., Red Ransom—Laurentine, by Private Account. **Weanling Purchase:** $130,000, 2000 Keeneland November, by Bridlestown Stud. **Yearling Sale:** $8,000, 2001 Keeneland September, consigned by Dromoland Farm, agent, purchased by Kern/Lillingston Associates. –$122,000 loss. [23-1-2-4, $2,240].

-93.3% GRAND IMPACT, 2004 dk. b. or br. g., Grand Slam—Tojur, by Dayjur. **Weanling Purchase:** $150,000, 2004 Keeneland November, by Tthens Woods. **Yearling Sale:** $10,000, 2005 Keeneland September, consigned by Eaton Sales, agent, purchased by Straightaway Farm, agent. –$140,000 loss. [18-3-1-3, $32,366].

-93.0% BOOBOOLISCIOUS, 2005 dk. b. or br. c., Harlan's Holiday—Elaine's Booboo, by Pertsemlidis. **Weanling Purchase:** $100,000, 2005 Keeneland November, by Walnut Hill Racing. **Yearling Sale:** $7,000, 2006 Keeneland September, consigned by Woods Edge Farm, agent, purchased by Ted Bowman. –$93,000 loss. [5-1-1-0, $11,330].

-92.9% CARELESS ALY, 1991 ch. m., Alydar—Careless Notion, by Jester. **Weanling Purchase:** $350,000, 1991 Keeneland November, by Mandysland Farm. **Yearling Sale:** $25,000, 1992 Keeneland September, consigned by Joe Riggs, agent, purchased by Helen C. Alexander, agent. –$325,000 loss. Unraced.

-92.9% CUM LAUDE, 1999 dk. b. or br. g., Honor Grades—Jody G., by Roberto. **Weanling Purchase:** $175,000, 1999 Keeneland November, by Grade 1 Bloodstock. **Yearling Sale:** $12,500, 2000 Fasig-Tipton Kentucky October, consigned by Darby Dan Farm, agent, purchased by Kenneth Ayres. –$162,500 loss. [40-4-4-7, $46,621].

-92.9% ENDYMION, 2006 b. c., Tapit—Forever Young, by Shadeed. **Weanling Purchase:** $210,000, 2006 Keeneland November, by Blandford Stud, agent. **Yearling Sale:** $15,000, 2007 Fasig-Tipton Kentucky October, consigned by Hunter Valley Farm, agent, purchased by Gabriel Dixon. –$195,000 loss. Unraced.

-92.0% CATRINA ERINA, 1998 ch. m., Candy Stripes—Erina, by Slewpy. **Weanling Purchase:** $100,000, 1998 Keeneland November, by Green Hall Stud. **Yearling Sale:** $8,000, 1999 Fasig-Tipton Kentucky October, consigned by Taylor Made Sales Agency, agent, purchased by Ted Latour. –$92,000 loss. [18-4-2-4, $31,905].

Most Successful Pinhooks by Total Gain (through June 12, 2008)
Weanling to Juvenile

$860,000 Brave Quest, 1997 b. h., Miswaki—Cousin Margaret, by Topsider. **Weanling Purchase:** $90,000, 1997 Fasig-Tipton Kentucky November, by Richard Spoor. **Juvenile Sale:** $950,000, 1999 Fasig-Tipton Calder February, consigned by Robert N. Scanlon, agent, purchased by John C. Oxley. 955.6% gain. [7-4-1-1, spl, $164,502].

$815,000 SOMETHING ELSE, 1995 ch. m., Seeking the Gold—Rythmical, by Fappiano. **Weanling Purchase:** $185,000, 1995 Keeneland November, by BBA (England). **Juvenile Sale:** $1,000,000, 1997 Barretts March, consigned by Kirkwood Stables, agent, purchased by The Thoroughbred Corp. 440.5% gain. [3-0-2-0, $18,144].

$750,000 CINDAGO, 2003 b. c., Indian Charlie—Tupelo Belle, by Turkoman. **Weanling Purchase:** $150,000, 2003 Keeneland November, by Gage Hill Stable. **Juvenile Sale:** $900,000, 2005 Barretts March, consigned by H.T. Stables, agent, purchased by John W. Sadler, agent. 500% gain. [3-2-1-0, SW, $98,180].

$725,000 UNCOMMON VALOR, 1997 b. h., Kris S.—Patchiano, by Fappiano. **Weanling Purchase:** $75,000, 1997 Keeneland November, by Tom Reeves. **Juvenile Sale:** $800,000, 1999 Fasig-Tipton Florida Calder February, consigned by Robert J. Harris, agent, purchased by Team Valor. 966.7% gain. [5-3-1-0, $86,200].

$600,000 DEBIT ACCOUNT, 1996 b. m., Mr. Prospector—Awesome Account, by Lyphard. **Weanling Purchase:** $350,000, 1996 Keeneland November, by Cypress Farms. **Juvenile Sale:** $950,000, 1998 Barretts March, consigned by Bailey-Ellenberg Select, purchased by Demi O'Byrne. 171.4% gain. [9-3-0-0, $70,260].

$578,000 CLASSIC ASPIRATION, 2005 b. c., Mr. Greeley—Crusie, by Country Light. **Weanling Purchase:** $22,000, 2005 Keeneland November, by Bobby Rankin. **Juvenile Sale:** $600,000, 2007 Keeneland April, consigned by Kirkwood Stables, agent, purchased by Centennial Farms. 2,627.3% gain. Unraced.

$565,000 GOLDEN PENNY, 2000 b. m., Touch Gold—Penny's Growl, by Strike Gold. **Weanling Purchase:** $85,000, 2000 Keeneland November, by The Narrows. **Juvenile Sale:** $650,000, 2002 Keeneland April, consigned by Tony Bowling and Bobby Dodd, agent, purchased by Robert and Beverly Lewis. 664.7% gain. [18-2-3-3, $67,554].

$558,000 NASEMA'S SLAM, 2002 dk. b. or br. m., Grand Slam—Nasema, by Encino. **Weanling Purchase:** $42,000, 2002 Keeneland November, by Luann Baker. **Juvenile Sale:** $600,000, 2004 Fasig-Tipton Calder February, consigned by Equine Legacy Farm, agent, purchased by Fleetwood and NW Management. 1,328.6% gain. [9-2-3-1, $49,200].

$530,000 Swissle Stick, 2002 ch. h., Swiss Yodeler—Miss Soft Sell, by Siyah Kalem. **Weanling Purchase:** $70,000, 2002 Keeneland November, by Terry Oliver, agent. **Juvenile Sale:** $600,000, 2004 Barretts March, consigned by Wavertree Stables, agent, purchased by Robert and Beverly Lewis. 757.1% gain. [49-5-9-7, spl, $118,116].

$510,000 MEDIA CITY, 2004 ch. c., Forest Camp—Holy Love, by Holy Bull. **Weanling Purchase:** $140,000, 2004 Keeneland November, by Roy B. Smith and Bill Wilks. **Juvenile Sale:** $650,000, 2006 OBSC February, consigned by Wavertree Stables, agent, purchased by John Ferguson Bloodstock. 364.3% gain. [10-1-4-3, $76,848].

$490,000 GOLDEN BAND, 1999 ch. m., Dixieland Band—Honey Bee Gold, by Drone. **Weanling Purchase:** $285,000, 1999 Keeneland November, by Cam Allard. **Juvenile Sale:** $775,000, 2001 Keeneland April, consigned by H.T. Stables, agent, purchased by Bob Baffert, agent. 171.9% gain. [6-1-2-2, $61,240].

$480,000 SARANOIA, 2000 dk b/. h., Seattle Slew—Sharp Call, by Sharpen Up (GB). **Weanling Purchase:** $320,000, 2000 Keeneland November, by Chad Johnson, agent. **Juvenile Sale:** $800,000, 2002 Fasig-Tipton Calder February, consigned by Terry Oliver, agent, purchased by Michael Gill. 150.0% gain. [6-0-1-1, $12,970].

Most Successful Pinhooks by Percentage Gain (through June 12, 2008)
Weanling to Juvenile

6,900.0%   MR. ELUSIVE, 2000 dk. b. or br. g., Elusive Quality—Capote's Joy, by Capote. **Weanling Purchase:** $1,500, 2000 Keeneland November, by Silverwood, agent. **Juvenile Sale:** $105,000, 2002 Barretts May, Fairplex Park, consigned by Timber Creek, agent, purchased by Larry and Veralene Hillis. $103,500 gain. [48-13-6-3, $100,014].

5,900.0%   EISHIN GONZALES, 1997 b. h., Take Me Out—Aunt Mockey, by Our Native. **Weanling Purchase:** $4,500, 1997 Fasig-Tipton Kentucky November, by William D. Snyder. **Juvenile Sale:** $270,000, 1999 Fasig-Tipton Calder February, consigned by Sequel Bloodstock, agent, purchased by Silky Green. $265,500 gain. [19-3-1-0, $308,887].

5,500.0%   EXTINGUISH, 2006 dk. b. or br. c., Hook and Ladder—Mighty Emy, by Mighty Adversary. **Weanling Purchase:** $2,500, 2006 New York Breeders' Sales Co. Saratoga Fall mixed sale at Carousel Pavilion, Saratoga Race Course, by JMJ Racing Stables. **Juvenile Sale:** $140,000, 2008 OBSC March, consigned by Sequel Bloodstock, agent, purchased by North Shore Racing. $137,500 gain. Unraced.

5,455.6%   BIG BIG CASINO, 1998 dk. b. or br. h., Pioneering—Kelly's Super Pet, by Muscovite. **Weanling Purchase:** $1,800, 1998 Keeneland November, by Shari Kepsel. **Juvenile Sale:** $100,000, 2000 Barretts May, consigned by Jerry Bailey Sales Agency, agent, purchased by Bruno de Berdt, agent. $98,200 gain. [4-1-1-1, $25,520].

4,185.7%   OUR EMM, 2001 dk. b. or br. h., Our Emblem—Thoughts, by Seattle Slew. **Weanling Purchase:** $3,500, 2001 Keeneland November, by Clouston Farm. **Juvenile Sale:** $150,000, 2003 Keeneland April, consigned by American Equistock and Parrish Farms, purchased by International Equine Acquisitions. $146,500 gain. [5-2-2-0, $18,940].

3,488.2%   Mancari's Rose, 1996 b. m., Glitterman—Puddin Hill, by Afleet. **Weanling Purchase:** $8,500, 1996 Keeneland November, by Jockey Club Farm. **Juvenile Sale:** $305,000, 1998 OBSC March, consigned by Jockey Club Farm, agent, purchased by William Bronstad. $296,500 gain. [6-1-0-1, spl, $33,275].

2,627.3%   CLASSIC ASPIRATION, 2005 b. c., Mr. Greeley—Crusie, by Country Light. **Weanling Purchase:** $22,000, 2005 Keeneland November, by Bobby Rankin. **Juvenile Sale:** $600,000, 2007 Keeneland April, consigned by Kirkwood Stables, agent, purchased by Centennial Farms. $578,000 gain. Unraced.

2,578.6%   PRIME TIMBER, 1996 b. h., Sultry Song—Wine Taster, by Nodouble. **Weanling Purchase:** $14,000, 1996 Keeneland November, by Donna M. Wormser. **Juvenile Sale:** $375,000, 1998 OBSC February, consigned by Donna M. Wormser, agent, purchased by Aaron U. Jones. $361,000 gain. [17-4-4-0, G2, $621,238].

2,361.5%   King's Silver Son, 2005 gr. or ro. c., Mizzen Mast—River Dyna, by Dynaformer. **Weanling Purchase:** $13,000, 2005 Keeneland November, by Listen Here LLC. **Juvenile Sale:** $320,000, 2007 OBSC April, consigned by Paul Sharp, agent, purchased by Mike McCarty. $307,000 gain. [10-1-5-0, spl, $125,392].

2,087.5%   CHIEF BEAR, 2005 dk. b. or br. c., Chief Seattle—Sabreen, by Foolish Pleasure. **Weanling Purchase:** $16,000, 2005 Keeneland November, by Jessie and Stacy Longoria. **Juvenile Sale:** $350,000, 2007, consigned by Murray Smith, agent, purchased by Bear Stables Ltd. $334,000 gain. [4-0-2-0, $20,820].

2,000.0%   MAYAKOVSKY, 1999 dk. b. or br. h., Matty G—Joy to Raise, by Raise a Man. **Weanling Purchase:** $10,000, 1999 OBSC October, by Gold Circle Racing. **Juvenile Sale:** $210,000, 2001 OBSC April, consigned by Eisaman Equine Services, agent, purchased by Robert N. Scanlon, agent. $200,000 gain. [9-3-1-0, G3, $275,200].

Least Successful Pinhooks by Total Loss (through May 1, 2007)
Weanling to Juvenile

-$800,000   TIDE CAT, 1998 dk. b. or br. m., Storm Cat—Maytide, by Naskra. **Weanling Purchase:** $1,200,000, 1998 Keeneland November, by 505 Farm. **Juvenile Sale:** $400,000, 2000 Barretts July, consigned by 505 Farms, purchased by B. Wayne Hughes. -66.7% loss. Unraced.

-$360,000   SINCITY GLOW, 2005 b. r., Pulpit—Mississippi Lights, by Majestic Light. **Weanling Purchase:** $480,000, 2005 Keeneland November, by Cumberland Bloodstock. **Juvenile Sale:** $120,000, 2007 Barretts May, consigned by Hartley/De Renzo Thoroughbreds, agent, purchased by Class Racing Stable. -75% loss. [4-0-0-0, $1,600].

-$330,000   ZINNED, 1998 b. m., Silver Deputy ol'm in Celebration, by Copelan. **Weanling Purchase:** $500,000, 1998 Keeneland November, by Brad Martin. **Juvenile Sale:** $170,000, 2000 Barretts July, consigned by 505 Farms, purchased by C. Beau Greely, agent. -66% loss. Unraced.

-$325,000   NIJINSKY'S CROWN, 1999 ch. h., Gone West—Nijinsky's Lover, by Nijinsky II. **Weanling Purchase:** $725,000, 1999 Keeneland November, by R. A. Adkinson. **Juvenile Sale:** $400,000, 2001 Fasig-Tipton Calder February, consigned by Robert Scanlon, agent, purchased by B.T.A. Stable. -44.8% loss. [3-0-0-0].

-$245,000   Alive With Hope, 1991 ch. m., Alydar—Awesome Account, by Lyphard. **Weanling Purchase:** $400,000, 1991 Keeneland November, by Oaktown Stable. **Juvenile Sale:** $155,000, 1993 Keeneland November, consigned by Jonabell Farm, agent, purchased by Millhouse. -61.3% loss. [18-6-2-3, spl, $184,631].

-$211,000   VOODOO DOCTOR, 2006 b. c., Songandaprayer—Sweet Remedy, by Dr. Carter. **Weanling Purchase:** $220,000, 2006 Keeneland November, by Rambling Rose Stable. **Juvenile Sale:** $9,000, 2008 OBSC April, consigned by Niall Brennan Stables, agent, purchased by Whitechurch Bloodstock. -95.9% loss. Unraced.

-$210,000   HATSURATSU, 2000 ch. h., Pulpit—Afare, by Meadowlake. **Weanling Purchase:** $360,000, 2000 Keeneland November, by Bohanon-Walden LLC. **Juvenile Sale:** $150,000, 2002 Fasig-Tipton Calder February, consigned by Maurice W. Miller, agent, purchased by Everglades Stable. -58.3% loss. 8-3-2-0, $399,052 [15-3-3-0, $419,354].

-$195,000   PREACH TO ME, 2005 ch. c., Pulpit—Tajannub, by Dixieland Band. **Weanling Purchase:** $230,000, 2005 Keeneland November, by Maverick Racing. **Juvenile Sale:** $35,000, 2007 OBSC March, consigned by Hartley/De Renzo Thoroughbreds, agent, purchased by Nolan Hajal. -84.8% loss. [4-0-0-1].

-$193,000   SEGUIN, 1997 ch. h., Miswaki—Anytimeatall, by It's Freezing. **Weanling Purchase:** $195,000, 1997 Keeneland November, by Horse France. **Juvenile Sale:** $2,000, 1999 Keeneland April, consigned by Hartley/De Renzo Thoroughbreds, agent, purchased by Spring Farm. -99% loss. [13-1-1-3, $24,774].

-$180,000   A R RIO BRAVO, 2005 ch. c., Pulpit—Affirmative Choice, by Affirmed. **Weanling Purchase:** $200,000, 2005 Keeneland November, by Atwood-Wells. **Juvenile Sale:** $20,000, 2007 OBSC March, consigned by Woodside Ranch, agent, purchased by Bryon Rice. -90% loss. [6-0-0-0, $1,950].

-$179,000   GRAY EMBLEM, 2002 gr. or ro. m., Our Emblem—Lingquoit, by Waquoit. **Weanling Purchase:** $200,000, 2002 Keeneland November, by Venture One Partnership. **Juvenile Sale:** $21,000, 2004 OBSC April, consigned by SAB Training, agent, purchased by Gary Owens. -89.5% loss. [3-0-0-0].

-$175,000   PRICELY GEM, 2003 b. c., Honour and Glory—Thirty Six Carat, by Meadowlake. **Weanling Purchase:** $210,000, 2003 Keeneland November, by Jack Smith. **Juvenile Sale:** $35,000, 2005 Barretts March, consigned by Excel Bloodstock, agent, purchased by NJ Cal Breeders. -83.3% loss. [1-0-1-0, $8,000].

-$175,000   TALE OF THE BEAR, 2004 b. g., Tale of the Cat—Prosper, by Affirmed. **Weanling Purchase:** $260,000, 2004 Keeneland November, by DOC Bloodstock. **Juvenile Sale:** $85,000, 2006 OBSC February, consigned by Nick de Meric, agent, purchased by Bear Stable. -67.3% loss. [14-2-0-2, $14,831].

Least Successful Pinhooks by Percentage Loss (through June 12, 2008)
Weanling to Juvenile

-99.0%   SEGUIN, 1997 ch. h., Miswaki—Anytimeatall, by It's Freezing. **Weanling Purchase:** $195,000, 1997 Keeneland November, by Horse France. **Juvenile Sale:** $2,000, 1999 Keeneland April, consigned by Hartley/De Renzo Thoroughbreds, agent, purchased by Spring Farm. –$193,000 loss. [13-1-1-3, $24,774].

-97.5%   SILVER SILKS, 1999 ch. m., Silver Deputy—Roses n Silks, by Golden Choice. **Weanling Purchase:** $100,000, 1999 Keeneland November, by M.J. Guerin. **Juvenile Sale:** $2,500, 2001 Keeneland January, consigned by Hartwell Farm, agent, purchased by Beaver Rim Land and Cattle. –$97,500 loss. Unraced.

-95.9%   VOODOO DOCTOR, 2006 b. c., Songandaprayer—Sweet Remedy, by Dr. Carter. **Weanling Purchase:** $220,000, 2006 Keeneland November, by Rambling Rose Stable. **Juvenile Sale:** $9,000, 2008 OBSC April, consigned by Niall Brennan Stables, agent, purchased by Whitechurch Bloodstock. –$211,000 loss. Unraced.

-93.6%   Unnamed, 1998 ch. h., Forest Wildcat—Musical Precedent, by Seattle Song. **Weanling Purchase:** $140,000, 1998 Keeneland November, by A. Cafferrata. **Juvenile Sale:** $9,000, 2000 Fasig-Tipton Midlantic May, consigned by Eddie Woods, agent, purchased by Sean C. Magee, agent. –$131,000 loss. Unraced.

-93.0%   PYTCHLEY, 1993 b. h., Cryptoclearance—Cuca's Lady, by Great Above. **Weanling Purchase:** $150,000, 1993 Keeneland November, by Paul Mellon. **Juvenile Sale:** $10,500, 1995 Fasig-Tipton New York November, consigned by Rokeby Stables, purchased by H. Allen Jerkens. –$139,500 loss. [23-3-2-3, $46,203].

-92.9%   CHET, 2002 dk. b. or br. g., Chester House—King's Pact, by Slewacide. **Weanling Purchase:** $170,000, 2002 Keeneland November, by Dromoland Farm and Hartwell Farm. **Juvenile Sale:** $12,000, 2004 Keeneland April, consigned by Robert Scanlon, agent, purchased by Rosebud Stable. –$158,000 loss. [49-5-4-5, $49,464].

-92.5%   BASKET CASE, 2005 gr. or ro. g., Buddha—Pattyg, by Housebuster. **Weanling Purchase:** $140,000, 2005 Keeneland November, by B.T.A. Stable. **Juvenile Sale:** $10,500, 2007 OBSC April, consigned by Hartley/De Renzo Thoroughbreds, agent, purchased by Daniel Limongelli. –$129,500 loss. [2-0-0-0, $330].

-90.6%   PAPPA'S MONEY, 1996 ch. g., St. Jovite—Queen of Bronze, by Roberto. **Weanling Purchase:** $180,000, 1996 Keeneland November, by Cypress Farms. **Juvenile Sale:** $17,000, 1998 Barretts March, consigned by Bailey-Ellenberg Select, purchased by Dale V. Ray. –$163,000 loss. [10-1-0-0, $4,552].

-90.0%   A R RIO BRAVO, 2005 ch. c., Pulpit—Affirmative Choice, by Affirmed. **Weanling Purchase:** $200,000, 2005 Keeneland November, by Atwood-Wells. **Juvenile Sale:** $20,000, 2007 OBSC March, consigned by Woodside Ranch, agent, purchased by Bryon Rice. –$180,000 loss. [6-0-0-0, $1,950].

-90.0%   ROYAL TROMP'E, 2001 b. m., Cozzene—Attractive Crown, by Chief's Crown. **Weanling Purchase:** $100,000, 2001 Keeneland November, by Michael R. Duffy. **Juvenile Sale:** $10,000, 2003 Fasig-Tipton Midlantic May, consigned by Eddie Woods, agent, purchased by Kathleen P. Mongeon, agent. –$90,000 loss. [10-0-2-0, $20,324].

-89.5%   GRAY EMBLEM, 2002 gr. or ro. m., Our Emblem—Lingquoit, by Waquoit. **Weanling Purchase:** $200,000, 2002 Keeneland November, by Venture One Partnership. **Juvenile Sale:** $21,000, 2004 OBSC April, consigned by SAB Training, agent, purchased by Gary Owens. –$179,000 loss. [3-0-0-0].

-88.7%   MEADOWLAKE JOHN, 2000 b. g., Meadowlake—Flowers for M'lady, by Stage Door Johnny. **Weanling Purchase:** $115,000, 2000 Keeneland November, by Granite Hill. **Juvenile Sale:** $13,000, 2002 Fasig-Tipton Midlantic May, consigned by Eddie Woods, agent, purchased by Jeffrey Gasperini. –$102,000 loss. [15-2-1-1, $39,783].

Biggest Auction Bargains (Sold Since 1980)

Horse, YOB Sex, Sire	Year Sale, Sold As	Sale Price	Current Earnings	Difference
Skip Away, 1993 h., Skip Trial	1995 OBS Feb., 2-year-old	$ 30,000	$9,616,360	$9,586,360
Curlin, 2004 c., Smart Strike	2005 Kee Sept., yearling	57,000	9,396,800	9,339,800
Pleasantly Perfect, 1998 h., Pleasant Colony	1999 Kee Sept., yearling	725,000	7,789,880	7,064,880
Silver Charm, 1994 h., Silver Buck	1995 OBS Aug., yearling	16,500	6,944,369	6,927,869
Silver Charm, 1994 h., Silver Buck	1996 OBS April, 2-year-old	100,000	6,944,369	6,844,369
Captain Steve, 1997 h., Fly So Free	1997 Kee Nov., weanling	12,000	6,828,356	6,816,356
Captain Steve, 1997 h., Fly So Free	1998 FTK July, yearling	70,000	6,828,356	6,758,356
Alysheba, 1984 h., Alydar	1985 Kee July, yearling	500,000	6,679,242	6,179,242
Nobo True, 1996 h., Broad Brush	1997 Kee Sept., yearling	110,000	5,854,142	5,744,142
Grass Wonder, 1995 h., Silver Hawk	1996 Kee Sept., yearling	250,000	5,987,405	5,737,405
Nobo True, 1996 h., Broad Brush	1998 FTF Feb., 2-year-old	200,000	5,854,142	5,654,142
Black Hawk (GB), 1994 h., Nureyev	1995 Kee July, yearling	200,000	5,750,386	5,550,386
Roses in May, 2000 h., Devil His Due	2001 Kee Sept., yearling	19,000	5,490,187	5,471,187
Roses in May, 2000 h., Devil His Due	2002 OBS April, 2-year-old	115,000	5,490,187	5,375,187
Taiki Blizzard, 1991 h., Seattle Slew	1991 Kee Nov., weanling	210,000	5,523,549	5,313,549
English Channel, 2002 h., Smart Strike	2003 Kee Sept., yearling	50,000	5,319,028	5,269,028
Sunday Silence, 1986 h., Halo	1988 CTS March, 2-year-old	32,000	4,968,554	4,936,554
South Vigorous, 1996 h., End Sweep	1996 OBS Oct., yearling	17,000	4,596,196	4,579,196
Unbridled, 1987 h., Fappiano	1987 FTK Nov., weanling	70,000	4,489,475	4,419,475
Broad Appeal, 1994 m., Broad Brush	1995 Kee Sept., yearling	70,000	4,418,037	4,348,037
Behrens, 1994 h., Pleasant Colony	1995 Kee July, yearling	225,000	4,563,500	4,338,500
Saint Liam, 2000 h., Saint Ballado	2001 FTN Aug., yearling	130,000	4,456,995	4,326,995
Broad Appeal, 1994 m., Broad Brush	1996 Bar March, 2-year-old	280,000	4,418,037	4,138,037
Azeri, 1998 m., Jade Hunter	1999 Kee Sept., yearling	110,000	4,079,820	3,969,820
David Junior, 2002 h., Pleasant Tap	2004 FTF Feb., 2-year-old	175,000	4,116,358	3,941,358
Nobo Jack, 1997 h., French Deputy	1997 Kee Nov., weanling	115,000	4,033,400	3,918,400
Good Ba Ba, 2002 g., Lear Fan	2003 Kee April, 2-year-old	85,000	3,992,469	3,907,469
Devil His Due, 1989 h., Devil's Bag	1989 Kee Nov., weanling	25,000	3,920,405	3,895,405
Creme Fraiche, 1982 g., Rich Cream	1983 FTK July, yearling	160,000	4,024,727	3,864,727
Eagle Cafe, 1997 h., Gulch	1999 Bar March, 2-year-old	375,000	4,227,985	3,852,985
Nobo Jack, 1997 h., French Deputy	1999 FTF Feb., 2-year-old	250,000	4,033,400	3,783,400
Ashado, 2001 m., Saint Ballado	2002 Kee Sept., yearling	170,000	3,931,440	3,761,440
Le Mars Girl, 2000 m., Defrere	2002 Kee April, 2-year-old	260,000	3,881,187	3,621,187
Electronic Unicorn, 1996 h., Housebuster	1997 Kee Sept., yearling	200,000	3,784,844	3,584,844
Eishin Berlin, 1992 m., Cozzene	1992 Kee Nov., weanling	24,000	3,569,724	3,545,724
Harlan's Holiday, 1999 h., Harlan	2000 FTK July, yearling	97,000	3,632,664	3,535,664

Horse, YOB Sex, Sire	Year Sale, Sold As	Sale Price	Current Earnings	Difference
Spain, 1997 m., Thunder Gulch	1998 Kee Sept., yearling	$ 25,000	$3,540,542	$3,515,542
Funny Cide, 2000 g., Distorted Humor	2001 FTN Aug., yearling	22,000	3,529,412	3,507,412
Victory Gallop, 1995 h., Cryptoclearance	1996 Kee Sept., yearling	25,000	3,505,895	3,480,895
War Emblem, 1999 h., Our Emblem	2000 Kee Sept., yearling	20,000	3,491,000	3,471,000
Sugino Hayakaze, 1993 h., Diesis (GB)	1994 Kee July, yearling	75,000	3,497,619	3,422,619
American Boss, 1995 h., Kingmambo	1996 Kee July, yearling	250,000	3,660,979	3,410,979
Eishin Berlin, 1992 m., Cozzene	1994 FTF March, 2-year-old	170,000	3,569,724	3,399,724
Eishin Washington, 1991 h., Ogygian	1992 Kee July, yearling	50,000	3,418,206	3,368,206
Biko Pegasus, 1991 h., Danzig	1992 Kee Sept., yearling	48,000	3,411,349	3,363,349
Gold Tiara, 1996 m., Seeking the Gold	1998 FTF Feb., 2-year-old	200,000	3,548,991	3,348,991
Biko Pegasus, 1991 h., Danzig	1993 Bar March, 2-year-old	105,000	3,411,349	3,306,349
Sugino Hayakaze, 1993 h., Diesis (GB)	1995 Bar March, 2-year-old	200,000	3,497,619	3,297,619
Black Tie Affair (Ire), 1986 h., Miswaki	1987 FTN Aug., yearling	85,000	3,370,694	3,285,694
Eishin Washington, 1991 h., Ogygian	1991 Kee Nov., weanling	140,000	3,418,206	3,278,206
Star King Man, 1999 h., Kingmambo	1999 Kee Nov., weanling	350,000	3,610,470	3,260,470
Bet Twice, 1984 h., Sportin' Life	1985 Kee Sept., yearling	50,000	3,308,599	3,258,599
Real Quiet, 1995 h., Quiet American	1996 Kee Sept., yearling	17,000	3,271,802	3,254,802
Serena's Song, 1992 m., Rahy	1992 Kee Nov., weanling	42,000	3,283,388	3,241,388
Eishin Washington, 1991 h., Ogygian	1993 Bar March, 2-year-old	230,000	3,418,206	3,188,206
Cryptoclearance, 1984 h., Fappiano	1985 Kee Sept., yearling	190,000	3,376,327	3,186,327

Earnings are worldwide and through June 12, 2008.

Notable Dispersals

Because of their selective and exclusive nature, dispersals have long been noted for high prices and long-term influence on the breeding industry. Most frequently, dispersals occur when a major breeder dies or decides to retire. Historically, that has meant that high-class bloodlines previously unavailable are on the market, attracting the most ambitious and wealthy breeders of a younger generation.

The first notable American dispersal was in 1891 when the stud of the late August Belmont I totaled $515,150. A large chunk of the total receipts came from Charles Reed's astonishing record bid of $100,000 for that year's leading sire, *St. Blaise.

Marcus Daly was a buyer at Belmont's dispersal, and when Daly died nine years later, financiers W. C. Whitney and James R. Keene were buyers at the dispersal of Daly's Bitter Root Stud. Whitney's and Keene's dispersals a few years later provided the foundations for the studs of Whitney's descendants and other great American breeders, including E. R. Bradley's Idle Hour Stock Farm.

The current record is $46,912,800 set by the dispersal of Nelson Bunker Hunt's Bluegrass Farm in 1988.

Notable North American Bloodstock Dispersals

Year	Dispersal	No. Sold	Total	Avg.	Notable Horses	Sales Company
1998	Fares Farm (Issam Fares)	232	$26,805,400	$115,541	Lady's Secret, Miss Alleged, November Snow	Keeneland
1998	Claiborne Farm/Nicole Perry Gorman	34	21,205,000	623,676	Limit	Keeneland
1997	Buckland Farm (Thomas Mellon Evans)	124	12,563,000	101,315	Meteor Stage	Keeneland
1996	Windfields Farm (Charles Taylor)	68	7,238,000	106,441	Baltic Sea, La Lorgnette	Keeneland
1992	Rokeby Stable (Paul Mellon)	32	6,294,600	196,706	Glowing Tribute, Wild Applause	
1991	Calumet Farm	185	15,068,500	81,451	Stick to Beauty, Tis Juliet	Keeneland
1989	Oxford Stable (Ralph C. Wilson Jr.)	46	18,572,700	379,034	Arazi, Fabuleux Jane	Keeneland
1989	Eugene Klein	114	29,623,000	259,851	Open Mind, Winning Colors, Lady's Secret	Keeneland, Fasig-Tipton Co.
1988	Nelson Bunker Hunt	580	46,912,800	80,884	Dahlia, Sangue (Ire), Highest Trump	Keeneland
1987	Hermitage Farm (Warner L. Jones Jr.)	130	32,676,500	251,358	My Charmer, Kamar, Seaside Attraction	Keeneland
1987	Tartan Farms/John Nerud	194	25,634,000	132,134	Unbridled, Gana Facil, Funistrada	Fasig-Tipton Co.
1986	Spendthrift Farm	163	19,171,700	117,618	Lillian Russell, Anne Campbell	Keeneland
1985	Newstead Farm (Hardin family)	42	37,186,000	885,381	Miss Oceana, Magic of Life, White Star Line	Fasig-Tipton Co.
1972	George D. Widener	69	6,643,700	96,286	What a Treat, Patelin, Seven Thirty	Fasig-Tipton Co.
1972	A. B. Hancock Jr./W. H. Perry	35	2,580,000	73,714	Sham, Apalachee	Fasig-Tipton Co.
1969	Cain Hoy Stable (Harry F. Guggenheim)	137	4,751,200	34,688	Riverman, Bold Reason, Too Bald, San San	Keeneland, Fasig-Tipton Co.
1967	Charlton Stud	18	796,100	44,228	Rose Bower, Leallah	Keeneland
1967	Maine Chance Farm (Elizabeth Graham)	83	1,270,700	15,310	Ribbons and Bows	Keeneland
1966-'70	Bieber-Jacobs Stable	175	3,851,000	22,005	Admiring, Priceless Gem	Keeneland, Timonium, Saratoga, Ocala, Pomona
1965	William duPont Jr.	51	2,401,300	47,084	Berlo, Parlo, All Beautiful	Maryland Breeders Sales Co.
1958	Louis B. Mayer	59	821,000	13,915	Popularity	Fasig-Tipton
1955-'56	Belair Stud (William Woodward Jr.)	59	2,475,600	41,959	Segula, Vagrancy	Keeneland
1955	Almahurst Farm (Henry Knight)	68	1,035,800	15,232	Almahmoud	Fasig-Tipton Co.
1951	Coldstream Stud (C.B. Shaffer)	48	990,500	20,635	Be Faithful, Spotted Beauty	Keeneland
1947-'50	Louis B. Mayer	248	4,479,650	18,063	Busher, Your Host, Honeymoon	Fasig-Tipton Co.
1935	Shoshone Stud (W. R. Coe)	86	201,090	2,338	Pompey, Pilate	Fasig-Tipton Co.
1925	Nursery Stud (August Belmont II)	68	782,000	11,500	Fair Play, *Quelle Chance	Joseph E. Widener
1913	Castleton Stud (James R. Keene)	45	229,000	5,088	Peter Pan, Colin, Sweep, Ultimus	Kentucky Sales Co.
1905	Rancho del Paso (James B. A. Haggin)	401	405,325	1,010	*Watercress, Colonial	Fasig-Tipton Co.
1904	LaBelle Stud (W. C. Whitney)	91	463,650	5,095	Hamburg, *Meddler, Endurance by Right	Fasig-Tipton Co.
1901	Bitter Root Stud (Marcus Daly)	186	406,525	2,185	Hamburg, *Pastorella	Fasig-Tipton Co.
1891	Nursery Stud (August Belmont I)	102	515,150	5,050	*St. Blaise	Tattersalls of New York

ORGANIZATIONS
Jockey Club

The Jockey Club, one of the Thoroughbred industry's most powerful and influential organizations, derives much of its strength from its position as the registration agency for all North American Thoroughbreds and from a membership comprising most of the sport's leading breeders and owners. In its distant past, the Jockey Club also was a regulator of racing; today, it has utilized advancing computer technology to expand its role and influence.

The Jockey Club grew out of meetings in late 1893 in which leading owners addressed the question of how to reform an unruly and corrupt racing industry. Two years earlier, prominent owner Pierre Lorillard had founded the Board of Control, but it largely represented the interests of racetrack owners, many of whom also were leading owners of racehorses. Alarmed that the racetrack owners might reduce purses, James R. Keene and seven fellow owners and breeders met on December 23 and 27, 1893, in a New York hotel to form an organization that represented the interests of both racetracks and racehorse owners. The goals of the organization were "not only to encourage the development of the Thoroughbred horse, but to establish racing on such a footing that it may command the interests as well as the confidence and favorable position of the public."

The organization was formally incorporated on February 9, 1894, as the Jockey Club, taking its name from the foundation institution in England. John Hunter was the first chairman of the American organization.

Although the Jockey Club today maintains the *American Stud Book*, it did not set out in 1894 to fulfill that function. Since 1868, Col. Sanders D. Bruce had been publishing a stud book of American pedigrees, and the Jockey Club wrote to him that it "does not propose to publish a stud book, but to keep a record of foals in the interest and for the protection of racing." The parallel projects proved to be incompatible, however, and on May 17, 1897, the Jockey Club purchased the six volumes of the *American Stud Book* previously published by Bruce, plus all related works and copyrights, for $35,000.

One of the Jockey Club's original goals was to bring order to racing in New York and New Jersey, and it played a significant role in developing the rules of racing for the East Coast and eventually the entire United States. Its influence in that area waned as the system of state racing commissions developed in the 1930s, and it lost a court case involving Jule Fink in the '50s, but it remains the official registrar of racing silks in New York.

Maintaining the sport's integrity has been the thread that runs through the Jockey Club's history, and the organization has been at the forefront of precise identification of horses. The Jockey Club adopted the photographing of night eyes—the structure on the inside of the leg that in the horse is the equivalent of a fingerprint—as a method of identifying Thoroughbreds. In the 1970s, the Jockey Club adopted blood-typing as an identification tool, and, with the foal crop of 2001, began DNA testing as a definitive verification of parentage.

In July 1953, Jockey Club Chairman George D. Widener convened in New York a meeting of 18 owners, racing officials, and journalists to discuss a wide range of issues facing the industry. The following year, the meeting was moved to Saratoga Springs, New York, and now is known as the Jockey Club Round Table Conference on Matters Pertaining to Racing.

The Jockey Club has developed the world's most extensive database of race records and pedigrees of Thoroughbreds. It has complete information for all North American racing from 1930 to the present. In recent years it has been able to work with other countries' registrars to obtain complete racing information and pedigrees from the world's major racing countries. The Jockey Club also has utilized its technology to develop a family of subsidiaries and affiliated companies.

Lexington Office
821 Corporate Dr.
Lexington, Ky. 40503
Phone: (859) 224-2700
Fax: (859) 224-2710
Website: www.jockeyclub.com

New York Office
40 East 52nd St.
New York, N.Y. 10022
Phone: (212) 371-5970
Fax: (212) 371-6123

Officers
Chairman: Ogden Mills Phipps
Vice Chairman: William S. Farish
Secretary-Treasurer: James C. Brady
President: Alan Marzelli
Executive Vice President, Chief Administrative Officer: James L. Gagliano
Executive Vice President, Executive Director: Dan Fick
Executive Vice President, Chief Financial Officer: Laura Barillaro

Stewards

John W. Amerman
James C. Brady
William S. Farish
Stuart S. Janney III
Ogden Mills Phipps

Reynolds Bell Jr.
Donald Dizney
Ian D. Highet
John C. Oxley

Members

Prince Khalid bin Abdullah
Helen C. Alexander
John W. Amerman
William Backer
John Barr
James E. Bassett III
James G. Bell
Gary Biszantz
Frank A. Bonsal Jr.
Nicholas F. Brady
Michael C. Byrne
W. Cothran Campbell
Charles J. Cella
Helen B. Chenery
Robert N. Clay
Donald R. Dizney
Richard L. Duchossois
William duPont III
Robert S. Evans
William S. Farish Jr.

Josephine E. Abercrombie
Joseph L. Allbritton
John E. Anthony
Charles Baker
Ramona Seeligson Bass
Rollin Baugh
Reynolds Bell Jr.
Edward S. Bonnie
James C. Brady
Larry Bramlage, D.V.M.
Alexander G. Campbell Jr.
Thomas R. Capehart
Alice H. Chandler
Sherwood C. Chillingworth
Duke of Devonshire CBE
Jack J. Dreyfus Jr.
C. Steven Duncker
Edward P. Evans
William S. Farish
Tracy Farmer

Hugh A. Fitzsimons Jr.
Louis L. Haggin III
Arthur B. Hancock III
Seth W. Hancock
John C. Harris
Ian D. Highet
G. Watts Humphrey Jr.
Russell B. Jones Jr.
F. Jack Liebau
Sheikh Mohammed bin Rashid al Maktoum
J. W. Y. Martin Jr.
Robert E. Meyerhoff
MacKenzie Miller
Kenneth Noe Jr.
John C. Oxley
Ogden Mills Phipps
Carl Pollard
Reuben F. Richards
Jack K. Robbins, V.M.D.
J. Mack Robinson
Richard Santulli
Barry Schwartz
Mace Siegel
Robert S. Strauss
Stella Thayer
Donald J. Valpredo
Frank "Scoop" Vessels III
Charlotte C. Weber
David Willmot
William T. Young Jr.
John K. Goodman
Lucy Young Hamilton
Dell Hancock
Joseph W. Harper
John Hettinger
E. Edward Houghton
Stuart S. Janney III
Gary Lavin
William C. MacMillen Jr.
Harry T. Mangurian Jr.
Frank L. Mansell
Robert McNair
Leverett Miller
Nick Nicholson
J. Michael O'Farrell Jr.
John W. Phillips
Hiram C. Polk Jr., M.D.
David P. Reynolds
J. David Richardson, M.D.
Walter S. Robertson
Timothy H. Sams
Peter G. Schiff
Joseph V. Shields Jr.
Viola Sommer
George Strawbridge Jr.
Oakleigh B. Thorne
Daniel G. Van Clief Jr.
Joseph Walker Jr.
Wheelock Whitney
Martin Wygod

Jockey Club Chairmen

Chairman	Term
Ogden Mills Phipps	February 10, 1983—present
August Belmont IV	May 3, 1982—February 10, 1983
Nicholas F. Brady	January 12, 1974—April 19, 1982
Odgen Phipps	January 7, 1964—January 12, 1974
George D. Widener	January 12, 1950—January 7, 1964
William Woodward	November 3, 1930—January 12, 1950
Frank K. Sturgis	December 30, 1924—November 3, 1930
August Belmont II	January 24, 1895—December 10, 1924
John Hunter	March 1, 1894—January 24, 1895

Jockey Club Subsidiaries

Jockey Club Information Systems Inc.

The Jockey Club Information Systems Inc., incorporated in 1989, is a wholly owned subsidiary of Jockey Club Holdings Inc. All profits from its activities are reinvested in the Thoroughbred industry and help to finance industry projects. The organization has three divisions: Information Services, Cataloguing, and Software Sales and Consulting. In 2000, it launched equineline.com (*www.equineline.com*), an Internet-based information and communication network. Through *equineline.com*, the Jockey Club sells information—pedigrees of horses, race records, sire progeny records, produce records of dams, etc.—online to customers. Under the *equineline.com* banner, the Lexington-based organization has launched management programs for horse owners and breeders, trainers, and farms.

Phone: (859) 224-2800 or (800) 333-1778
Fax: (859) 224-2810
Website: www.tjcis.com

Chairman and President: Carl E. Hamilton
Secretary: Alan Marzelli
Treasurer: Laura Barillaro
Board Members: Reynolds Bell Jr., C. Steven Duncker, Robert S. Evans, Alan Marzelli, John Phillips, and Ogden Mills Phipps

InCompass

InCompass, a wholly owned subsidiary of Jockey Club Holdings Inc., was created in November 2001 and provides record keeping and operational assistance to racing offices and horsemen's bookkeepers. Through InCompass Financial Services, horsemen can access their account statements and balances online. Horsemen in eligible states are able to transfer money from their horsemen's bookkeeper accounts electronically among participating tracks or their personal bank accounts.

Phone: (859) 296-3000 or (800) 625-4664
Fax: (859) 296-3010
Website: www.incompass-solutions.com
Chairman: Alan Marzelli
President: David Haydon
Secretary-Treasurer: Laura Barillaro

Grayson-Jockey Club Research Foundation

Established in 1940 to raise funds for equine veterinary research, the Grayson Foundation was combined in '89 with the similarly chartered Jockey Club Research Foundation. The Lexington-based foundation, which solicits contributions from the Thoroughbred community, allocated $1,226,457 in research grants in 2008, raising its total contributions during the last 25 years to more than $15.5-million.

Phone: (859) 224-2850
Fax: (859) 224-2853
Website: www.grayson-jockeyclub.org
E-Mail: contactus@grayson-jockeyclub.org

Chairman: Dell Hancock
Vice Chairman: Gary Lavin, V.M.D.
President: Edward L. Bowen
Chairman Emeritus: John Hettinger
Director Emeritus: Jack Robbins, V.M.D.
Treasurer: Laura Barillaro
Vice President of Development: Nancy C. Kelly
Board Members: Josephine Abercrombie, Rick Arthur, D.V.M., William Backer, Larry Bramlage, D.V.M., Charlsie Cantey, Aisling Cross, Adele Dilschneider, Donald Dizney, William Farish Jr., John Goodman, Lucy Young Hamilton, Dell Hancock, Joseph W. Harper, John Hettinger, Gary Laviin, V.M.D., Eugene Melnyk, Leverett Miller, John M. B. O'Connor, John C. Oxley, Ogden Mills Phipps, Hiram Polk Jr., M.D., Jack Robbins, V.M.D., Geoffrey Russell, and Joseph V. Shields Jr.

The Jockey Club Foundation

Established in 1943, the Jockey Club Foundation provides confidential financial assistance to needy members of the Thoroughbred industry and their families. The New York-based foundation has distributed nearly $12-million since its inception.

Phone: (212) 371-5970
Fax: (212) 371-6123
Website: www.tjcfoundation.org

Trustees: John Hettinger, C. Steven Duncker, D. G. Van Clief Jr.
Secretary-Treasurer: Laura Barillaro
Executive Director: Nancy C. Kelly

National Thoroughbred Racing Association

With its founding in 1998, the National Thoroughbred Racing Association immediately became one of the industry's leading organizations. The NTRA originated in part from a "Guest Commentary" by Lexington advertising executive Fred Pope in the August 27, 1993, issue of THOROUGHBRED TIMES. Pope, an associate of Breeders' Cup founder John Gaines, suggested that horse owners pool their media rights—the images of their horses in races—and establish a major league of racing. With the funds generated from simulcasting the sport's leading races, the proposed owners' association—the National Thoroughbred Association—would market the sport to the American public.

The industry was not ready for Pope's idea in 1993, but three years later full-card simulcasting exploded across the nation and provided a new stream of revenue for racing. Former Carter White House aides Hamilton Jordan and Tim Smith were hired by Pope and Gaines to sell the NTA concept to the Thoroughbred industry. Although not accepted by the racetracks, Pope's idea—that the sport needed a national presence and national marketing—gained momentum, and in March 1997 four industry organizations—Breeders' Cup Ltd., the Jockey Club, Keeneland Association, and Oak Tree Racing Association—put up $1-million each as seed money for a new organization to market the sport. In a short time, the new entity was named the National Thoroughbred Racing Association, and the efforts of the NTA were effectively folded into it. (The NTA formally merged into the NTRA in August 1998, and Pope was compensated for his intellectual property.)

Even with the backing of industry leaders, the NTRA was not a sure bet to be supported by racetracks and national organizations. Breeders' Cup President D. G. Van Clief Jr., serving as the NTRA's interim chief executive, and Jockey Club Executive Director Nick Nicholson traveled throughout the country to sell the concept of a national office to market racing to industry participants. They gained sufficient backing, and a business plan was released in December 1997. The NTRA formally began operation on April 1, 1998. Its first commissioner and chief executive officer was Smith, who, after leaving the White House, had served as deputy commissioner of the Professional Golfers' Association Tour and had helped to reorganize the Association of Tennis Professionals Tour.

The NTRA's first priority was marketing, and it produced an edgy, attention-grabbing national television advertisement featuring actress Lori Petty. Industry members, however, panned the ad, and the NTRA could not replicate its success through subsequent marketing campaigns. In its first years, the NTRA ventured beyond marketing, opening subsidiary operations such as NTRA Services, NTRA Investments, NTRA Productions (for television production), and NTRA Charities. The NTRA became the producer of the Eclipse Awards, assuming a role formerly held by Thoroughbred Racing Associations.

By the end of 1999, several racetrack executives, including Magna Entertainment Corp.'s Frank Stronach and a group of Mid-Atlantic track owners, complained that the NTRA had veered away from its original marketing mandate and had entered business enterprises where it was in competition with tracks, notably by operating a telephone-wagering hub in Oregon for Television Games Network. Some of the Mid-Atlantic tracks pulled out of the NTRA but returned later, while Stronach was appeased when more racetrack representation was added to the NTRA board of directors, including a seat for a Stronach representative. Also that year, NTRA transferred operation of the Oregon hub to TVG.

NTRA's continuing budget deficits contributed to a decision in 2000 to merge many of its operations with Breeders' Cup Ltd., and the merger took place on January 1, 2001. Smith remained commissioner and Van Clief became the NTRA's vice chairman. By the end of 2001, many NTRA functions had been melded into the Breeders' Cup operation. Smith resigned in 2004, and Van Clief was named commissioner on an interim basis. His appointment became permanent in April 2005, but he resigned a year later. He was succeeded by Greg Avioli on an interim basis until Alex Waldrop was appointed as the organization's president and chief executive officer in late 2006.

In recent years, the NTRA has worked to build the sport's fan base through increased television exposure, consumer research, and promotion of the Breeders' Cup World Championships. The NTRA has increased its lobbying and group-purchasing efforts, and it has proved effective in crisis management.

2525 Harrodsburg Rd., Suite 400
Lexington, Ky. 40504
Phone: (859) 245-6872 or (800) 792-6872
Fax: (859) 223-3945
Website: www.ntra.com
E-Mail: ntra@ntra.com

President and Chief Executive Officer: Alex Waldrop
Senior Vice Presidents: Keith Chamblin, Peggy Hendershot, Terry McElfresh
Directors: Robert Clay, Robert Elliston, Robert L. Evans, Alan Foreman, Robert Green, Charles Hayward, L. William Heiligbrodt, G. Watts Humphrey Jr., F. Jack Liebau, Alan Marzelli, Jim McAlpine, Marsha Naify, Nick Nicholson, Joe Santanna

Thoroughbred Racing Associations

In January 1942, racing's representatives to the National Association of State Racing Commissioners convention perceived themselves to be in a war-related emergency and convened a meeting that March in Chicago. The object of the meeting initially was to pull together all elements of the industry into a single ruling organization.

The two-day meeting that began on March 19, 1942, would not yield an overall ruling body for the fractious and fragmented industry. However, 33 executives of 22 racetracks at that meeting formed the Thoroughbred Racing Associations of the United States, with Hialeah Park President John C. Clark as its first president. The organization was formally incorporated on May 22, 1942. (The name subsequently was changed to the Thoroughbred Racing Associations of North America when Canada's tracks joined the organization.)

Representatives to the March 1942 meeting realized that they could not conduct racing throughout the war strictly as an entertainment vehicle, and the Turf Committee of America was formed to raise funds to support the war effort.

New challenges awaited in the postwar years; chief among them was the integrity of the sport. In 1946, at the behest of Federal Bureau of Investigation Director J. Edgar Hoover (an avid racing fan), the TRA formed the Thoroughbred Racing Protective Bureau. A former FBI agent, Spencer J. Drayton, became the first director of the TRPB and instituted practices such as fingerprinting of all licensees, from grooms to owners.

Drayton became the TRA's executive vice president in 1960, and his appointment resulted in the resignation of five racetracks. He retired in 1974, and, since '76 the TRA has had only two executive vice presidents, J. B. Faulconer and Christopher N. Scherf (since '88).

In 1950, the TRA had begun to select its own end-of-year champions, which sometimes differed from those chosen by the *Daily Racing Form*, which established its poll in '36. Faulconer was given the task of unifying the championships in 1971. Then president of Turf Publicists of America, Faulconer brought together the TRA, *Daily Racing Form*, and the National Turf Writers Association to launch the Eclipse Awards that year. In 1999, the National Thoroughbred Racing Association supplanted the TRA as the industry's representative to the Eclipse Awards.

420 Fair Hill Dr., Suite 1
Elkton, Md. 21921-2573
Phone: (410) 392-9200
Fax: (410) 398-1366
Website: *www.tra-online.com*
E-Mail: info@tra-online.com

President: Robert L. Bork
Vice Presidents: C. Kenneth Dunn, Randall D. Sampson
Secretary: Sherwood Chillingworth
Treasurer: William I. Fasy
Executive Vice President: Christopher N. Scherf
Directors: Roy Arnold, William J. Bissett, Robert L. Bork, Tim Carey, Charles J. Cella, Sherwood C. Chillingworth, Steve Duncker, C. Kenneth Dunn, Robert N. Elliston, Ronald Geary, Robert Green, Harold G. Handel, Joseph W. Harper, Charles E. Hayward, Derron Heldt, Gregory C. Hosch, Corey S. Johnsen, Chuck Keeling, Robert Kulina, Brant Latta, Robert P. Levy, Jim McAlpine, Christopher McErlean, Mark Midland, Hugh M. Miner Jr., Jerry M. Monahan, Howard M. Mosner Jr., Nick Nicholson, Lou Raffetto Jr., William M. Rickman Jr., Charles J. Ruma, Randall D. Sampson, Christopher N. Scherf, Steve Sexton, Drew Shubeck, Randall E. Soth, Stella F. Thayer, Scott Wells, David S. Willmot

TRA Presidents

Term	President	Representing
2007-'08	Robert L. Bork	Sam Houston Race Park
2005-'06	Corey S. Johnsen	Lone Star Park
2003-'04	Joseph W. Harper	Del Mar
2001-'02	Bryan G. Krantz	Fair Grounds
1999-'00	Stella F. Thayer	Tampa Bay Downs
1997-'98	Harold G. Handel	New Jersey Sports and Exposition Authority
1995-'96	Clifford C. Goodrich	Santa Anita
1993-'94	David M. Vance	Remington
1991-'92	Thomas H. Meeker	Churchill Downs
1989-'90	Robert P. Levy	Atlantic City
1987-'88	Gerard J. McKeon	New York Racing Association
1985-'86	James E. Bassett III	Keeneland
1983-'84	Morris J. Alhadeff	Longacres
1981-'82	Lynn Stone	Churchill Downs
1979-'80	Robert S. Gunderson	Bay Meadows
1977-'78	Baird C. Brittingham	Delaware
1975-'76	Charles J. Cella	Oaklawn
1973-'75	Frank M. Basil	New York Racing Association
1971-'73	James E. Brock	Ak-Sar-Ben
1969-'70	John D. Schapiro	Laurel
1967-'68	Louis Lee Haggin II	Keeneland
1965-'66	Edward P. Taylor	Ontario Jockey Club
1963-'64	Robert P. Strub	Santa Anita
1961-'62	E. E. Dale Shaffer	Detroit Race Course
1959-'60	John G. Cella	Oaklawn
1957-'58	James D. Stewart	Hollywood
1955-'56	Amory L. Haskell	Monmouth
1953-'54	John A. Morris	Jamaica
1951-'52	Alfred G. Vanderbilt	Belmont
1949-'50	Donald P. Ross Sr.	Delaware
1947-'48	James E. Dooley	Narragansett
1944-'46	Henry A. Parr II	Pimlico
1942-'43	John C. Clark	Hialeah

Thoroughbred Racing Protective Bureau

Modeled after the Federal Bureau of Investigation and initially staffed by former FBI agents, the Thoroughbred Racing Protective Bureau is the investigative and security arm of the Thoroughbred Racing Associations of North America. The TRPB was founded in January 1946 to protect the integrity of the sport.

420 Fair Hill Dr., Suite 2
Elkton, Md. 21921-2573
Phone: (410) 398-2261
Fax: (410) 398-1499
Website: www.trpb.com
E-Mail: trpbinfo@trpb.com

President and Treasurer: Franklin J. Fabian
Vice President and Secretary: James P. Gowen
Chairman: John E. Mooney
Directors: Robert L. Bork, Charles J. Cella, Ron Charles, Sherwood Chillingworth, C. Kenneth Dunn, Franklin J. Fabian, Charles Hayward, Chris McErlean, Nick Nicholson, Jim Ormiston, Stella F. Thayer

American Horse Council

The American Horse Council, organized in 1969 to give horse-industry participants a voice in Congress, comprises organizations and individuals from every facet of the horse world. The AHC's mission is to promote and protect the equine industry by representing its interests to Congress and federal agencies, and to advise the government of the equine industry's important role in the United States economy. It also aims to unify the industry by serving as a forum for member organizations and individuals.

In 1965, when a tax proposal to disallow the expense of raising racehorses and performance horses first surfaced, a group of industry members—including John H. Clark, Warner Jones Jr., and Leslie Combs II—reestablished the Thoroughbred Breeders of Kentucky. The first meeting of the group discussed that threat, recent increases in farrier rates, and local horse transporters' recent application to the Kentucky Department of Transportation to be regulated, which the organizers contended would make it unlawful for a farm operator to transport any horses but his or her own. Clark was voted president for 1966.

In 1967, with founding member Jones as president, they began to work toward creating a lobby to prevent the detrimental parts of the Tax Reform Act of '69 from passing. They were successful and established the AHC as their lobby in Washington. Albert G. Clay, also a founder, was secretary of the organization from its formation through 1990. The AHC grew to represent 5.2-million horses and one-million horsemen by 1990.

Led since 1993 by President James Hickey Jr., the AHC has recently worked more closely with the National Thoroughbred Racing Association on issues involving the racing industry, notably the 2001 mare reproductive loss syndrome crisis in Kentucky, when the NTRA and the AHC met with federal officials to set up federal disaster relief for breeders who had lost a substantial number of foals. Also in 2001, the congressional Racing and Breeding Caucus was formed by the NTRA and the AHC. The NTRA increased its lobbying budget to $900,000, dramatically increasing the presence of the AHC in Congress. In 2002, the AHC joined the NTRA's Wagering Technology Working Group, which intends to improve the security of pari-mutuel wagering.

In 1996, the American Horse Council published the first National Economic Impact Study of the Horse Industry in the United States. Another study was conducted and published in 2005, and the figures from the study have been used to demonstrate the importance of the horse industry to the U.S. economy.

Other recent issues the AHC has tackled include lobbying to change immigration laws to allow seasonal foreign workers to remain in the U.S. without reapplying for a visa every year, which is especially important for the many trainers and owners who employ foreign workers in their barns. The organization also has lobbied to protect horse racing from restrictive Internet legislation. The AHC's goal has been to win passage of a prohibition bill with an exception for horse racing and legal pari-mutuel wagering.

1616 H St. NW
7th Floor
Washington, D.C. 20006
Phone: (202) 296-4031
Fax: (202) 296-1970
Website: www.horsecouncil.org
E-Mail: ahc@horsecouncil.org

President: James J. Hickey Jr.
Board of Trustees: Nick Nicholson (chairman), Russell C. Williams (vice chairman), Jerry Black (secretary), Jim Shoemake (treasurer), James Barton, Marvin Beeman, Jane Clark, Paul Fontaine, G. Watts Humphrey Jr., F. Philip Langley, Ken Mumy, David O'Connor, Charles J. Ruma, Eric Straus, Alex Waldrop

Association of Racing Commissioners International

In August 1934, racing commissioners from nine states met when it became apparent that, if racing was to grow as a sport, each state could not function in a vacuum, unmindful of other jurisdictions' rules and regulations. The commissioners aspired to form a national organization that would "encourage forceful and honest nationwide control of racing for the protection of the public" and launched the National Association of State Racing Commissioners (NASRC) to represent Thoroughbred racing.

The NASRC gradually broadened to include all forms of flat racing, harness racing, greyhound racing, and jai-alai and in 1988 became the Association of Racing Commissioners International (RCI) to give the organization a global identity.

In 1947, the NASRC created a national database in which all rulings were summarized. The database provided all jurisdictions with easy access to national files and ended the need for massive files of duplicate information.

RCI maintains a vision to create a cohesive regulatory structure for a financially viable pari-mutuel sports industry. In its mission statement, RCI states that it strives to "protect and uphold the integrity of the pari-mutuel sports of horse racing, dog racing, and jai-alai through an informed membership, by encouraging forceful and uniform regulation, by promoting the health and welfare of the industry through various programs and projects."

RCI serves as a repository and distribution center for all official rulings by stewards and racing commissioners and encourages reciprocity, under which rulings in one jurisdiction are recognized and enforced in all others. In addition, it works to develop uniform rules and racing practices.

The association also recommends rules and regulations to governmental boards and regulatory agencies for the effective conduct of race meetings, wagering, and related pursuits. RCI studies, researches, and discusses the needs and problems regarding regulation of racing and wagering.

In 1997, several racing commissions that were displeased with the governance of RCI broke away to form the North American Pari-Mutuel Regulators Association. After several changes were made in the RCI structure, including the recognition of professional regulators as full members, the organizations merged in December 2005.

2343 Alexandria Dr., Suite 200
Lexington, Ky. 40504
Phone: (859) 224-7070
Fax: (859) 224-7071
Website: *www.arci.com*

Chairman: Joe Gorajec
President and Chief Executive Officer: Edward J. Martin
Executive Vice President: Paul Bowlinger
Chair-Elect: Erin Owens
Secretary and Treasurer: Daniel Hogan
Immediate Past Chairman: Peter Burnett
Board of Directors: Richard Abbott, Jim Bowers, Pat Brennan, John Cansdale, Peter Cofrancesco III, Timothy Connors, Larry Eliason, Randy Evers, Eddie Fowler, Charles Gardiner, Dan Hartman, Darcy Hitesman, David Kangaloo, Charla Ann King, Doug King, Marc Laino, Bryan Mitchell, Rudolph Muir, W. Duncan Patterson, David Roberts, Richard Shapiro, Rod Seiling, Lisa Underwood, Christine White

Equibase

Equibase Co. LLC, a general partnership of the Thoroughbred Racing Associations of North America (TRA) and the Jockey Club, is the official source of all racehorse past performances and racing data in North America. It was founded in 1991 because the racetracks and racing authorities at that time did not possess their own database of racing performance, nor did they have free access to the information. Rather, an independent daily newspaper, *Daily Racing Form*, compiled and owned all racing records of horses starting in North America.

For decades previous, racetracks published an official program containing official betting numbers and such basic information as a horse's pedigree, owner, trainer, jockey, post position, morning-line betting odds, and colors of each owner's racing silks. Past performances were the exclusive province of the *Daily Racing Form*.

Equibase began operation in 1991 with its own chart callers for the purpose of creating past-performance lines that could be used in programs sold by racetracks. (The charts, a statistical description of a race and each horse's running position, are the raw materials of past-performance lines.) To help subsidize the start-up, each participating track pledged 25 cents from each program sold to be paid to Equibase. While some tracks began to publish magazine-sized official programs with Equibase past performances, a significant competitor to *Daily Racing Form* emerged when *Racing Times*, backed by England-based publishing magnate Robert Maxwell, began operation. *Racing Times* purchased its past-performance lines from Equibase. *Racing Times* was making inroads into the *Daily Racing Form*'s monopoly when Maxwell drowned off the Canary Islands in late 1991, and his empire collapsed.

The magazine-sized programs, which usually sell for about one-third the price of the *Daily Racing Form*, gradually became popular with racegoers, which sharply reduced *Daily Racing Form*'s circulation. In 1998, after years of negotiations between the two parties, Equibase became the sole data-collection agency, with *Daily Racing Form* dropping its collection efforts and thereafter purchasing its racing information from Equibase. Today, Equibase provides information to more than 100 tracks and 1,100 simulcast outlets, as well as to *Daily Racing Form*, *Sports-Eye*, several online resellers, and the industry's major interactive wagering services.

Since repaying all start-up costs in 1997, Equibase profits have been shared among the TRA and its limited-partner racetracks (66%) and the Jockey Club (33%) in the form of dividends. In 2005, Equibase distributed dividends of $2.7-million to its partners.

The company also serves the sport's fan base through its website, *www.equibase.com*, which offers a wide array of handicapping information and services geared toward every level of handicapper. Among the products available are race programs with handicapping information in easy-to-understand formats for new and existing fans. These pages were developed in conjunction with the National Thoroughbred Racing Association. The Equibase Virtual Stable, the exclusive notification service of the NTRA, delivers entry, workout, and result notices for horses that fans wish to follow. Virtual Stable also features a race series notification service that allows fans to monitor the progress of leading contenders for the Triple Crown and Breeders' Cup races in the months leading up to those events.

In July 2000, it purchased AXCIS Information Network Inc., a provider of electronic handicapping information, through its Track Master product. In April 2004, Equibase hired Philip O'Hara as its president and chief executive officer. In April 2007, Equibase named Hank Zeitlin as its president and chief operating officer when O'Hara resigned to pursue other interests in the Thoroughbred industry.

821 Corporate Dr.
Lexington, Ky. 40503-2794
Phone: (859) 224-2860 or (800) 333-2211
Fax: (859) 224-2811
Website: www.equibase.com

Chairman and Chief Executive Officer: Alan Marzelli
President and Chief Operating Officer: Hank Zeitlin
Secretary: Christopher N. Scherf
Treasurer: Laura Barillaro
Management Committee: Peter Berube, Sherwood Chillingworth, C. Steven Duncker, Craig Fravel, James Gagliano, Hal Handel, Jim McAlpine, Nick Nicholson, Ogden Mills Phipps, Steve Sexton, Michael Weiss

Jockeys' Guild

The Jockeys' Guild was established in 1940 to negotiate for insurance and media rights contracts on behalf of riders. Founding members included Eddie Arcaro, Sam Renick, Ray Workman, Johnny Longden, Alfred Robertson, Charlie Kurtsinger, Red Pollard, and Harry Richards, who was elected the Guild's first president. Another founding member, Nick Jemas, guided the Jockeys' Guild as national manager from 1967 to '86, effectively running the organization from the garage of his home in Haddonfield, New Jersey. During his tenure, he waged a state-by-state campaign to raise jockeys' mount fees.

Jemas was succeeded by John Giovanni, a former jockey in New England who had been a Guild regional representative. With the headquarters relocated to Lexington from a New York office that Jemas used only occasionally, Giovanni championed workers' compensation coverage for jockeys and was instrumental in putting together a workers' comp program in New York.

Rising costs of health insurance for jockeys and their families led to dissension within the leadership, and directors led by Chris McCarron ousted Giovanni and his staff in 2001. Installed to manage the Guild was Wayne Gertmenian, who was elected president. Gertmenian and his staff took a confrontational approach to the industry and Guild members who opposed him. When jockey Gary Birzer was paralyzed in a 2004 spill at Mountaineer Race Track, it was disclosed that a catastrophic-injury policy had been allowed to lapse. Congressional hearings in 2005 eventually led to the ouster of Gertmenian and his chief assistant, Albert Fiss, late in the year. The Guild was found to be in severe financial straits, and Darrell Haire, a former Guild representative under Gertmenian who became interim national manager, worked to shore up the organization's finances through 2006. A new Jockeys' Guild Senate and new officers were elected in 2006, and Dwight Manley became the the national manager. In September 2007, Manley resigned and was succeeded by Terry Meyocks. The organization filed for bankruptcy in 2007.

103 Wind Haven Drive, Suite 200
Nicholasville, Ky. 40356
Phone: (866) 465-6257
Website: www.jockeysguild.com

Chairman: John Velazquez
Vice Chairman: G. R. Carter
Secretary: Jon Court
Treasurer: Jerry LaSala
National Manager: Terry Meyocks

Keeneland Association

Keeneland Association, a not-for-profit organization, was founded in 1936 with a vision of presenting "Racing as it was meant to be" and is dedicated to perpetuating and improving the sport while symbolizing the tradition of Thoroughbred racing. Located six miles west of downtown Lexington, Keeneland Race Course provides a model racetrack at the center of Kentucky's Bluegrass region. Keeneland continues to carry out the initiative of its founders through its three principal business activities: live racing, simulcast racing, and sales.

Keeneland, started on the grounds first established by owner-breeder Jack Keene, held its inaugural race meeting in October 1936. It now annually hosts two short meets, one in April and one in October, which feature some of the highest purses in the country, aided by year-round simulcasting. Keeneland's 15-day race meeting in the spring is highlighted by the Blue Grass Stakes (G1), and its 16-day meeting in the fall features the Spinster Stakes (G1).

The first public auction of Thoroughbreds at Keeneland was held in a paddock sale on April 25, 1938, when 31 horses sold for an average of $803. The first yearling sale at Keeneland was held in the summer of 1943, when wartime restrictions on rail transport forced Kentucky breeders to keep their yearlings at home, rather than send them to the prestigious yearling sale in Saratoga Springs, New York. This led to a sale of yearlings under a tent in the Keeneland paddock conducted by Fasig-Tipton Co.

When Fasig-Tipton did not offer a sale in 1944, local breeders formed the Breeders' Sales Co. to sell yearlings at Keeneland, which launched what has become the most successful sales company in the world. In 1962, Breeders' Sales Co. was dissolved, and Keeneland Association took over the business of selling horses.

Keeneland added a September sale of yearlings and a November breeding stock sale in 1944, a January horses of all ages sale in '56, and an April two-year-olds in training sale in '93.

Future generations of horsemen may also remember Keeneland for advocating the installation of Polytrack. Keeneland spearheaded the introduction of the synthetic racing surface to North American racing; Turfway Park in Florence, Kentucky, became the first North American track to use Polytrack for pari-mutuel wagering on September 7, 2005. A 50% owner of Turfway Park with Harrah's Entertainment Inc. and the North American distributor of Polytrack for inventor Martin Collins, Keeneland introduced Polytrack on its training track in Lexington in September 2004 and installed the all-weather surface on its main track before its October '06 meeting.

4201 Versailles Rd.
P. O. Box 1690
Lexington, Ky. 40588-1690
Phone: (859) 254-3412 or (800) 456-3412
Fax: (859) 255-2484
Website: www.keeneland.com

President and Chief Executive Officer: Nick Nicholson
Director of Racing: W. B. Rogers Beasley
Vice President: Harvie Wilkinson
Director of Sales: Geoffrey Russell
Treasurer: Jessica A. Green
Racing Secretary: Ben Huffman
Senior Auctioneer: Ryan Mahan
Trustees: Robert N. Clay, William S. Farish, L. L. Haggin III

Thoroughbred Owners and Breeders Association

Since 1961, the Thoroughbred Owners and Breeders Association has worked to promote the interests of Thoroughbred owners and breeders. With a network that includes 41 states and chapters in Puerto Rico and Ontario, Lexington-based TOBA includes owners and breeders at all levels in the Thoroughbred industry. Membership dues fund the organization.

After becoming a founding member of the National Thoroughbred Racing Association in 2000, TOBA helped to launch *TheGreatestGame. com*, a website dedicated to recruiting and retaining owners. The site contains everything from a consultant directory to answers to such questions as how a horse can be purchased.

In 1973, TOBA formed the North American Graded Stakes Committee (now the United States Graded Stakes Committee), which meets annually to assign one of three grades to races, and is active in the International Cataloguing Standards Committee (ICSC) and the Society of International Thoroughbred Auctioneers (SITA). Established in 1981, ICSC sets black-type standards throughout the world. SITA was founded in 1983 and investigates and monitors

bloodstock matters related to auctions.

The National Racing Compact, which allows multijurisdictional licenses for racing participants, is also supported by TOBA, and the organization keeps tabs on the political environment as an influential voice in the American Horse Council.

TOBA spearheaded the development of the Horse Industry Economic Impact Study, which strives to improve the effectiveness of national and state racing and breeding associations in the legislative and regulatory processes.

TOBA also created or cosponsored such projects as the Claiming Crown (in association with the National Horsemen's Benevolent and Protective Association).

The organization's Equine Health Committee works closely with the U.S. Department of Agriculture and monitors the outbreak or transmission of equine diseases throughout the world.

TOBA also manages the Sales Integrity Program and Thoroughbred Charities of America, is a founding member of the Racing Medication and Testing Consortium, and represents the U.S. on the International Breeders' Secretariat, a forum of 17 racing and breeding countries that meets annually to discuss issues of global significance to the industry.

P.O. Box 910668
Lexington, Ky. 40591-0668
Phone: (859) 276-2291
Fax: (859) 276-2462
Website: *www.toba.org*
E-Mail: toba@toba.org

President: Dan Metzger
Director of Industry Relations and Development: Andrew Schweigardt
Controller: Carl Gough
Executive and Financial Assistant: Helen Proffitt
Director of Marketing and Communications: Erin Halliwell

National Horsemen's Benevolent and Protective Association

The National Horsemen's Benevolent and Protective Association is a not-for-profit organization that began in New England in 1940. While horsemen had always helped to provide for one another's needs, such as medical attention, burial services, and aid to families, they felt that something more was needed. A group of horsemen founded what became the HBPA with a common goal: the betterment of racing on all levels.

In 1996, a formal mission statement was created and adopted; it states that the association's mission is to provide insurance services to members, circulate information on industry issues to horsemen, promote reform in medication rules and research, provide a national voice for horsemen, assist individual members with problems, and promote the preservation of live racing in North America.

Today, the National HBPA has more than 35,000 owner and trainer members in 31 affiliate organizations in 26 states and Canada. Services provided by the National HBPA include liability insurance for owners and trainers and fire, disaster, and vanning insurance.

The organization's quarterly publication is *The Horsemen's Journal*, and the National HBPA also publishes documents on such industry topics as workers' compensation, economic trends, and drug policy.

Recently, the National HBPA has focused its attention on establishing industrywide thresholds for medication positives, and it is represented on the board of directors of the Racing Medication and Testing Consortium.

The HBPA also strives to find ways to reduce the number of unwanted horses and to improve their overall welfare.

In addition, it raised funds for horsemen affected by Hurricanes Katrina and Rita in 2005, and it has donated to the Permanently Disabled Jockeys Fund and numerous other industry organizations.

The National HBPA worked on setting up an offshore international betting hub beginning in 2004 in response to offshore operations taking business from United States tracks and thus reducing purse payments.

The effort never became viable, however, and President John Roark resigned in April 2006 to establish an international wagering hub in Curacao with two partners.

870 Corporate Drive, Suite 300
Lexington, Ky. 40503-5416
Phone: (859) 259-0451
Fax: (859) 259-0452
Website: *www.hbpa.org*
E-Mail: racing@hbpa.org

President and Chairman: Joe Santanna
Chief Executive Officer: Remi Bellocq
General Counsel: Doug McSwain
Director of Operations: Laura Plato

National Industry Organizations

**American Academy
of Equine Art**
c/o Kentucky Horse Park
4089 Iron Works Pkwy.
Lexington, Ky. 40511
Ph: (859) 281-6031
Fax: (859) 281-6043
E-Mail: shelleyh@aaea.net
Website: www.aaea.net
President: Werner Rentsch

**American Association
of Equine Practitioners**
4075 Iron Works Pkwy.
Lexington, Ky. 40511
Ph: (859) 233-0147
Fax: (859) 233-1968
E-Mail: aepoffice@aaep.org
Website: www.aaep.org
President: Eleanor Green, D.V.M.

American Farriers Assn.
4059 Iron Works Pkwy., Suite 1
Lexington, Ky. 40511
Ph: (859) 233-7411
Fax: (859) 231-7862
E-Mail: farriers@americanfarriers.org
Website: www.americanfarriers.org
President: Andrew Elsbree

American Horse Council
1616 H St. NW, 7th floor
Washington, D.C. 20006
Ph: (202) 296-4031
Fax: (202) 296-1970
E-Mail: ahc@horsecouncil.org
Website: www.horsecouncil.org
President: James J. Hickey Jr.

**American Horse Protection
Assn.**
1000 29th St. NW., Suite T-100
Washington, D.C. 20007
Ph: (202) 965-0500
Fax: (202) 965-9621

Animal Transportation Assn.
111 East Loop North
Houston, Tx. 77029
Ph: (713) 532-2177
Fax: (713) 532-2166
E-Mail: info@aata-animaltransport.org
Website: www.aata-animaltransport.
org

**Association of Racing
Commissioners International**
2343 Alexandria Dr., Suite 200
Lexington, Ky. 40504-3276
Ph: (859) 224-7070
Fax: (859) 224-7071
E-Mail: support@arci.com
Website: www.arci.com
Chairman: Joe Gorajec
President: Ed Martin

Breeders' Cup Ltd.
P.O. Box 4230
Lexington, Ky. 40544-4230
Ph: (859) 223-5444
Fax: (859) 223-3945
E-Mail: breederscup@breederscup.
com
Website: www.breederscup.com
President: Greg Avioli

**Canadian Veterinary Medical
Assoc.**
339 Booth St.
Ottawa, On. K1R 7K1 Canada
Ph: (613) 236-1162
Fax: (613) 236-9681
E-Mail: admin@cvma-acmv.org
Website: www.canadianveterinarians.
net

**Grayson-Jockey Club
Research Foundation**
821 Corporate Dr.
Lexington, Ky. 40503
Ph: (859) 224-2850
Fax: (859) 224-2853
E-Mail: contactus@grayson-jockey
club.org
Website: www.grayson-jockeyclub.org
President: Edward L. Bowen

**Horsemen's Benevolent and
Protective Assn. (National)**
870 Corporate Dr., Suite 300
Lexington, Ky. 40503-5416
Ph: (859) 259-0451
Fax: (859) 259-0452
E-Mail: racing@hbpa.org
Website: www.hbpa.org
President: Joe Santanna

The Jockey Club
40 E. 52nd St.
New York, N.Y. 10022
Ph: (212) 371-5970
Fax: (212) 371-6123
E-Mail: contactus@jockeyclub.com
Website: www.jockeyclub.com
Chairman: Ogden Mills Phipps
President: Alan Marzelli

Jockey Club of Canada
P.O. Box 66, Station B
Etobicoke, On. M9W 5K9 Canada
Ph: (416) 675-7756
Fax: (416) 675-6378
E-Mail: jockeyclub@bellnet.ca
Website: www.jockeyclubcanada.
com
Chairman: Richard Bonnycastle

Jockeys' Guild
P.O. Box 150
Monrovia, Ca. 91017
Ph: (866) 465-6257
E-Mail: info@jockeysguild.com
Website: www.jockeysguild.com
Chairman: John Velazquez

National Horse Carriers Assn.
Website: www.nationalhorsecarriers.
com
Chairman: William J. Barry

**National Museum of Racing
and Hall of Fame**
191 Union Ave.
Saratoga Springs, N.Y. 12866-3566
Ph: (518) 584-0400
Fax: (518) 584-4574
E-Mail: nmrmedia@racingmuseum.net
Website: www.racingmuseum.org
Director: Joe Aulisi

National Steeplechase Assn.
400 Fair Hill Dr.
Elkton, Md. 21921-2573
Ph: (410) 392-0700
Fax: (410) 392-0706
E-Mail: info@nationalsteeplechase.com
Website: www.nationalsteeplechase.
com
Chairman: Francis Abbott
Chief Executive: Lou Raffetto

**National Thoroughbred
Racing Assn.**
2525 Harrodsburg Rd., Suite 400
Lexington, Ky. 40504-3359
Ph: (859) 245-6872
Fax: (859) 245-6868
E-Mail: ntra@ntra.com
Website: www.ntra.com
Chief Executive Officer: Alex Waldrop

National Turf Writers Assn.
1255 Morning Side Drive
Lexington, Ky. 40509
Ph: (859) 797-5533
E-Mail: info@turfwriters.org
President: Tom Law

**Thoroughbred Club
of America**
P.O. Box 8098
Lexington, Ky. 40533-8098
Ph: (859) 254-4282
Fax: (859) 231-6131
Website: thoroughbredclubofamerica.
com
President: Michael T. Barnett

**Thoroughbred Owners
and Breeders Assn.**
P.O. Box 910668
Lexington, Ky. 40591
Ph: (859) 276-2291
Fax: (859) 276-2462
E-Mail: toba@toba.org
Website: www.toba.org
President: Dan Metzger

**Thoroughbred Racing Assns.
of North America**
420 Fair Hill Dr., Suite 1
Elkton, Md. 21921-2573
Ph: (410) 392-9200
Fax: (410) 398-1366
E-Mail: info@tra-online.com
Website: www.tra-online.com
President: Robert L. Bork
Executive Vice President: Chris Scherf

Organizations — State

Thoroughbred Racing Protective Bureau
420 Fair Hill Dr., Suite 2
Elkton, Md. 21921
Ph: (410) 398-2261
Fax: (410) 398-1499
E-Mail: trpbinfo@trpb.com
Website: www.trpb.com
President: Frank Fabian

Triple Crown Productions
700 Central Ave.
Louisville, Ky. 40208-1200
Ph: (502) 636-4400
Website: www.thetriplecrown challenge.com
President: Robert L. Evans
Executive Vice President: Edward Seigenfeld

Turf Publicists of America
900 Third Avenue, Suite 901
New York, N.Y. 10022
Ph: (212) 230-9511
E-Mail: ewing@ntra.com
Website: www.turfpublicists.com
President: Eric Wing

State and Provincial Racing Organizations

Alabama

Alabama Horsemen's Benevolent and Protective Association
1523 Indian Hills
Hartselle, Al. 35640
Ph: (256) 773-3592
Fax: (256) 773-5370
E-Mail: alahbpa@aol.com
President: Skip Drinkard

Birmingham Racing Commission
1000 John Rogers Dr., Suite 102
Birmingham, Al. 35201
Ph: (205) 838-7470
E-Mail: kipkeefer@birminghamracing commission.com
Website: www.birminghamracing commission.com
Executive Secretary: W. Kip Keefer

Arizona

Arizona Horsemen's Benevolent and Protective Association
P.O. Box 43636
Phoenix, Az. 85080
Ph: (602) 942-3336
Fax: (602) 866-3790
E-Mail: azhbpa@qwest.net
President: George Bango

Arizona Racing Commission
1110 W. Washington, Suite 260
Phoenix, Az. 85007
Ph: (602) 364-1700
Fax: (602) 364-1703
E-Mail: ador@azracing.gov
Website: www.azracing.gov
Executive Director: Geoffrey Gonsher
Chairman: Paul Ulan

Arizona Thoroughbred Breeders Association
P.O. Box 41774
Phoenix, Az. 85080
Ph: (602) 942-1310
Fax: (602) 942-8225
E-Mail: atba@worldnet.att.net
Website: www.atba.net
President: Michael Lester

University of Arizona Race Track Industry Program
845 N. Park Ave., Suite 370
Tucson, Az. 85721
Ph: (520) 621-5660

Fax: (520) 621-8239
E-Mail: bprewitt@ag.arizona.edu
Website: www.ua-rtip.org
Director: Douglas Reed

Arkansas

Arkansas Horse Council
P.O. Box 251
Kingston, Ar. 72742
Ph: (479) 665-2733
Website: www.arhorsecouncil.org
President: Betty Jones

Arkansas Horsemen's Benevolent and Protective Association
P.O. Box 1670
Hot Springs, Ar. 71902
Ph: (501) 623-7641
Fax: (501) 623-1350
E-Mail: arhbpa@aol.com
Website: www.arhbpa.com
President: Dr. Earl Bellamy

Arkansas Racing Commission
P.O. Box 3076, 1515 W. 7th St.
Little Rock, Ar. 72203
Ph: (501) 682-1467
Fax: (501) 682-5273
E-Mail: ron.oliver@dfa.state.ar.us
Website: www.accessarkansas.org/ dfa/racing
Chairman: Cecil Alexander

Arkansas Thoroughbred Breeders and Horsemen's Association
P.O. Box 21641
Hot Springs, Ar. 71903-1641
Ph: (501) 624-6328
Fax: (501) 623-5722
Website: www.atbha.com
President: Bill McDowell

California

California Horse Racing Board
1010 Hurley Wy., Suite 300
Sacramento, Ca. 95825
Ph: (916) 263-6000
Fax: (916) 263-6042
E-Mail: wendyv@chrb.ca.gov
Website: www.chrb.ca.gov
Executive Director: Kirk Breed
Chairman: Richard Shapiro

California Thoroughbred Breeders Association
P.O. Box 60018

Arcadia, Ca. 91066-6018
Ph: (951) 445-7800
Fax: (626) 574-0852
E-Mail: ctbanfo@ctba.com
Website: www.ctba.com
President: Leigh Ann Howard

California Thoroughbred Farm Managers Association
P.O. Box 876
Fallbrook, Ca. 92088-0876
Ph: (951) 683-2813
E-Mail: ctfma@yahoo.com
Website: www.thoroughbredinfo.com/ showcase/ctfma.htm
President: Jerry Murphy

California Thoroughbred Horsemen's Foundation
P.O. Box 660129
Arcadia, Ca. 91066-0129
Ph: (626) 446-0169
Fax: (626) 447-6251
Website: www.cthf.info

California Thoroughbred Trainers
285 West Huntington Dr.
Arcadia, Ca. 91007
Ph: (626) 447-2145
Fax: (626) 446-0270
E-Mail: contact@caltrainers.org
Website: www.caltrainers.org
Executive Director: Ed Moger Jr.

Thoroughbred Owners of California
285 W. Huntington Dr.
Arcadia, Ca. 91007
Ph: (626) 574-6620
Fax: (626) 821-1515
E-Mail: toc@toconline.com
Website: www.toconline.com
President: Drew Couto

Colorado

Colorado Racing Commission
1881 Pierce St., Suite 108
Lakewood, Co. 80214
Ph: (303) 205-2990
Fax: (303) 205-2950
E-Mail: racing@spike.dor.state.co.us
Division Director: Daniel J. Hartman
Chairman: David Lynn Hoffman

Colorado Thoroughbred Breeders Association
4701 Marion St., Suite 203
Denver, Co. 80216

Ph: (303) 294-0260
Fax: (303) 294-0260
Website: www.toba.org/state/coindex.html
President: F. A. Heckendorf

Delaware

Delaware Thoroughbred Racing Commission
2320 S. DuPont Hwy.
Dover, De. 19901
Ph: (302) 698-4599
Fax: (302) 697-4748
E-Mail: john.wayne@state.de.us
Website: www.dda.delaware.gov
Executive Director: John F. Wayne
Chairman: Bernard J. Daney

Delaware Thoroughbred Horsemen's Association
777 Delaware Park Blvd.
Wilmington, De. 19804
Ph: (302) 994-2521
Fax: (302) 994-3392
E-Mail: dpha@aol.com
Website: www.dtha.com
Executive Director: Bessie Gruwell

Florida

Florida Division of Pari-Mutuel Wagering
1940 N. Monroe St.
Tallahassee, Fl. 32399-1035
Ph: (850) 488-9130
Fax: (850) 488-0550
E-Mail: david.roberts@dbpr.state.fl.us
Website: www.myflorida.com
Director: David J. Roberts

Florida Horsemen's Benevolent and Protective Association
P.O. Box 1808
Opa Locka, Fl. 33055
Ph: (305) 625-4591
Fax: (305) 625-5259
E-Mail: fhbpa@bellsouth.net
Website: www.fhbpa.org
President: Samuel Gordon
Executive Director: Kent Stirling

Florida Thoroughbred Breeders' and Owners' Association
801 SW. 60th Ave.
Ocala, Fl. 34474-1827
Ph: (352) 629-2160
Fax: (352) 629-3603
E-Mail: info@ftboa.com
Website: www.ftboa.com
President: Gilbert Campbell
Executive Vice President: Richard E. Hancock

Florida Thoroughbred Farm Managers
6998 NW. Highway 27, Suite 106B
Ocala, Fl. 34482
Ph: (352) 401-3535
Fax: (352) 401-3533
E-Mail: fttfm@atlantic.net
Website: www.flfarmmanagers.com
President: Bobby Jones

Horse Protection Association of Florida
20690 NW. 130th Ave.
Micanopy, Fl. 32667
Ph: (352) 466-4366
E-Mail: hpaf@bellsouth.net
Website: www.hpaf.org
Executive Director: Morgan Silver

Sunshine State Horse Council
State Horse Council Inc.
P.O. Box 6663
Brandon, Fl. 33508-6011
Ph: (813) 651-5953
E-Mail: vicshadyl@aol.com
Website: www.sshc.org
President: Vicki Lawry

Georgia

Georgia Thoroughbred Owners and Breeders Association
P.O. Box 611
Buford, Ga. 30515
Ph: (866) 664-8622
Fax: (866) 728-8043
E-Mail: gtoba@bellsouth.net
Website: www.gtoba.com

Idaho

Idaho Horsemen's Benevolent and Protective Association
P.O. Box 140143
Boise, Id. 83714
Ph: (208) 939-0650
Fax: (208) 853-3605
President: Sam Stephenson

Idaho Racing Commission
P.O. Box 700
Meridian, Id. 83680
Ph: (208) 884-7080
Fax: (208) 884-7098
E-Mail: jack.baker@isp.idaho.gov
Website: www.isp.state.id.us/race
Executive Director: Dennis C. Jackson
Chairman: Tim Ridinger

Idaho Thoroughbred Association
3085 N. Cole Rd. Suite 113
Boise, Id. 83704
Ph: (208) 375-5930
Fax: (208) 375-5959
E-Mail: ita3@qwest.net
Website: www.idahothoroughbred.org
Executive Director: Kathryn Mooney

Illinois

Illinois Horsemen's Benevolent and Protective Association
P.O. Box 429
Caseyville, Il. 62232-0429
Ph: (618) 345-7724
Fax: (618) 344-9049
E-Mail: ilhbpa@aol.com
Website: www.ilhbpa.com
President: John Wainwright

Illinois Racing Board
100 W. Randolph St., Suite 7-701
Chicago, Il. 60601
Ph: (312) 814-2600
Fax: (312) 814-5062
E-Mail: racing board@irb.state.il.us
Website: www.state.il.us/agency/irb
Chairman: Joseph J. Sinopoli

Illinois Thoroughbred Breeders and Owners Foundation
P.O. Box 336
Caseyville, Il. 62232
Ph: (618) 344-3427
Fax: (618) 346-1051
E-Mail: itboffp@apci.net
Website: www.itbof.org
President: Gary Moore

Indiana

Indiana Horse Council
225 S. East St., Suite 738
Indianapolis, In. 46202
Ph: (317) 692-7141
Fax: (317) 692-7153
E-Mail: inhorsecouncil@aol.com
Website: www.indianahorsecouncil.org
President: Dave Howell

Indiana Horsemen's Benevolent and Protective Association
6348 Behner Reach
Indianapolis, In. 46250
Ph: (317) 796-9106
Fax: (317) 594-8953
E-Mail: fsstults@aol.com
President: Randy Klopp

Indiana Horse Racing Commission
150 W. Market St.
ISTA Center, Suite 530
Indianapolis, In. 46204
Ph: (317) 233-3119
Fax: (317) 233-4470
Website: www.in.gov/hrc
Executive Director: Joe Gorajec
Chairwoman: Sarah McNaught

Indiana Thoroughbred Owners and Breeders Association
P.O. Box 866
Crawfordsville, In. 47933
Ph: (800) 450-9895
Fax: (877) 486-2232
E-Mail: info@itoba.com
Website: www.itoba.com
President: Herb Likens

Iowa

Iowa Horsemen's Benevolent and Protective Association
P.O. Box 163
Altoona, Ia. 50009
Ph: (515) 967-4804
Fax: (515) 967-4963
E-Mail: iahbpa@aol.com
President: Leroy Gessman

Organizations — State

Iowa Racing Commission
717 E. Court Ave., Suite B
Des Moines, la. 50309 4934
Ph: (515) 281-7352
Fax: (515) 242-6560
E-Mail: irgc@iowa.gov
Website: www.state.ia.us/irgc
Chairman: Kate Cutler

Iowa Thoroughbred Breeders and Owners Association
1 Prairie Meadows Dr.
Altoona, la. 50009
Ph: (515) 957-3002
Fax: (515) 967-1368
E-Mail: itboa@msn.com
Website: www.iowathoroughbred.com
President: Sharon Vail

Kansas

Kansas Horse Council
8831 Quail Ln., Suite 201
Manhattan, Ks. 66502
Ph: (785) 776-0662
Fax: (785) 539-2928
E-Mail: office@kansashorsecouncil.com
Website: www.kansashorsecouncil.com

Kansas Racing and Gaming Commission
700 SW Harrison St., Suite 420
Topeka, Ks. 66603-3754
Ph: (785) 296-5800
Fax: (785) 296-0900
E-Mail: krgc@ksracing.org
Website: www.ksracing.org
Executive Director: Stephen L. Martino
Chairman: Carol Sader

Kansas Thoroughbred Association
15400 Rock Creek Rd.
Westmoreland, Ks. 66549
Ph: (785) 457-2863
E-Mail: pmdavis@vet.ksu.edu
Website: www.kansasthoroughbred.com
Executive Director: Pam Davis

Kentucky

Kentucky Equine Education Project
4047 Ironworks Pkwy.
Lexington, Ky. 40511
Ph: (859) 259-0007
Fax: (859) 259-0501
E-Mail: info@horseswork.com
Website: www.horseswork.com
Executive Director: Patrick Neely

Kentucky Horse Council
1500 Bull Lea Rd., Suite 214C
Lexington, Ky. 40511
Ph: (859) 367-0509
Fax: (866) 618-3837
E-Mail: info@kentuckyhorse.com
Website: www.kentuckyhorse.org
Executive Director: Ginny Grulke

Kentucky Horsemen's Benevolent and Protective Association
3733 S. Fourth St.
Louisville, Ky. 40214
Ph: (502) 363-1077
Fax: (502) 367-6800
E-Mail: kyhbpa@insightbb.com
Website: www.kyhbpa.org
President: Rick Hiles

Kentucky Horse Racing Authority
4063 Iron Works Pkwy., Bldg. B
Lexington, Ky. 40511-8434
Ph: (859) 246-2040
Fax: (859) 246-2039
E-Mail: lisa.underwood@ky.gov
Website: www.khra.ky.gov
Executive Director: Lisa Underwood

Kentucky Thoroughbred Association
4079 Iron Works Pkwy.
Lexington, Ky. 40511-8483
Ph: (859) 381-1414
Fax: (859) 233-9737
E-Mail: office@kta-ktob.com
Website: www.kta-ktob.com
Executive Director: David Switzer

Kentucky Thoroughbred Farm Managers' Club
828 Lane Allen Rd. #210
Lexington, Ky. 40504
Ph: (859) 948-7321
E-Mail: info@ktfmc.org
Website: www.ktfmc.org
President: Barry Robinette

Kentucky Thoroughbred Owners and Breeders
4079 Iron Works Pkwy.
Lexington, Ky. 40511-8483
Ph: (859) 259-1643
Fax: (859) 233-9737
E-Mail: office@kta-ktob.com
Website: www.kta-ktob.com
Executive Director: David Switzer

Louisiana

Louisiana Horsemen's Benevolent and Protective Association
1535 Gentilly Blvd.
New Orleans, La. 70119
Ph: (504) 945-1555
Fax: (504) 945-1579
E-Mail: lahbpa@lahbpa.com
Website: www.lahbpa.org
President: Sean Alfortish

Louisiana Racing Commission
320 N Carrollton Ave., Suite 2-B
New Orleans, La. 70119
Ph: (504) 483-4000
Fax: (504) 483-4898
E-Mail: cgardiner@lrc.state.la
Website: http://horseracing.la.gov/index.html
Executive Director: Charles Gardiner III
Chairman: Bob Wright

Louisiana Thoroughbred Breeders Association
P.O. Box 24650
New Orleans, La. 70184
Ph: (504) 947-4676
Fax: (504) 943-2149
E-Mail: ltba@louisianabred.com
Website: www.louisianabred.com
President: Warren Harang III

Maryland

Maryland Horse Breeders Association
P.O. Box 427
30 East Padonia Rd., Suite 303
Timonium, Md. 21094
Ph: (410) 252-2100
Fax: (410) 560-0503
E-Mail: info@marylandthoroughbred.com
Website: www.mdhorsebreeders.com
President: James B. Steele Jr.

Maryland Horse Council
P.O. Box 233
Lisbon, Md. 21765
Ph: (410) 489-7826
Fax: (410) 489-7828
E-Mail: secretary@mdhorsecouncil.org
Website: www.mdhorsecouncil.org

Maryland Million Ltd.
P.O. Box 365
Timonium, Md. 21094
Ph: (410) 252-2100
Fax: (410) 252-0503
E-Mail: info@marylandthoroughbred.com
Website: www.mdhorsebreeders.com/million
President: Wayne A. Harrison

Maryland Racing Commission
300 East Towsontowne Blvd.
Towson, Md. 21286
Ph: (410) 296-9682
Fax: (410) 853-1668
E-Mail: racing@dllr.state.md.us
Website: www.dllr.state.md.us/racing
Chairman: John B. Franzone

Maryland Thoroughbred Horsemen's Association
6314 Windsor Mill Rd.
Baltimore, Md. 21207
Ph: (410) 265-6842
Fax: (410) 265-6641
E-Mail: info@mdhorsemen.com
Website: www.mdhorsemen.com
President: Richard Hoffberger

Massachusetts

Massachusetts Racing Commission
1 Ashburton Pl., Rm. 1313
Boston, Ma. 02108
Ph: (617) 727-2581
Fax: (617) 227-6062
E-Mail: racing.commission@state.ma.us

Website: *www.state.ma.us/src*
Chairman: Walter Sullivan

Massachusetts Thoroughbred Breeders Association
4 Thomas St.
Burlington, Ma. 01803
Ph: (508) 252-3690
E-Mail: mtba@comcast.net
Website: *www.massbreds.com*
Chairman: George Brown

New England Horsemen's Benevolent and Protective Association
P.O. Box 388
Revere, Ma. 02151
Ph: (617) 568-3333
Fax: (617) 569-3857
E-Mail: nehbpa@aol.com
Website: *www.newenglandhbpa.com*
President: Al Balestra

Michigan

Michigan Horsemen's Benevolent and Protective Association
841 N. Latson
Howell, Mi. 48843
Ph: (231) 798-2250
Fax: (517) 552-0004
E-Mail: mihbpa@aol.com
Website: *www.mihbpa.com*
President: Douglas Barron

Michigan Racing Commission
Office of Racing Commissioner
525 W. Allegan St.
Lansing, Mi. 48909-8273
Ph: (517) 335-1420
Fax: (517) 241-3018
E-Mail: perroned9@michigan.gov
Website: *www.mi.gov/horseracing*
Commissioner: Christine C. White

Michigan Thoroughbred Owners and Breeders Association
P.O. Box 48
Grand Haven, Mi. 49417
Ph: (231) 798-7721
Fax: (231) 798-7612
E-Mail: mtoba@iserv.net
Website: *www.mtoba.com*
President: Patti M. Dickinson

Minnesota

Minnesota Horsemen's Benevolent and Protective Association
1100 Canterbury Rd.
Shakopee, Mn. 55379
Ph: (952) 496-6442
Fax: (952) 496-6443
E-Mail: mnhbpa@yahoo.com
President: Tom Metzen Sr.

Minnesota Racing Commission
P.O. Box 630
Shakopee, Mn. 55379
Ph: (952) 496-7950
Fax: (952) 496-7954
E-Mail: richard.krueger@state.mn.us
Website: *www.mnrace.commission. state.msn.us*
Executive Director: Richard Krueger

Minnesota Thoroughbred Association
1100 Canterbury Rd.
Shakopee, Mn. 55379
Ph: (952) 496-3770
Fax: (952) 496-3672
E-Mail: mtassoc@voyager.net
Website: *www.mtassoc.com*
President: Del Sand

Mississippi

Mississippi Thoroughbred Breeders and Owners Association
107 Sundown Rd.
Madison, Ms. 39110
Ph: (601) 856-8293
President: Bruns Myers Jr.

Missouri

Missouri Equine Council
P.O. Box 608
Fulton, Mo. 65251
Ph: (800) 313-3327
E-Mail: info@mo-equine.org
Website: *www.mo-equine.org*
President: Sharon Marohl

Missouri Racing Commission
3417 Knipp Drive
Jefferson City, Mo. 65109
Ph: (573) 526-4080
Fax: (573) 526-1999
E-Mail: Gene.McNary@mgc.dps.mo.gov
Executive Director: Gene McNary

Montana

Montana Board of Horse Racing
P.O. Box 200512
Helena, Mt. 59620-0512
Ph: (406) 444-4287
Fax: (406) 444-4305
E-Mail: livemail@mt.gov
Website: *http://mt.gov/liv/horseracing/index.asp*
Executive Director: Susan Austin

Montana Horsemen's Benevolent and Protective Association
139 New Dracut Hill Rd.
Vaughn, Mt. 59487
Ph: (406) 452-2135
President: R. C. Forster

Nebraska

Nebraska Horsemen's Benevolent and Protective Association
6406 South 150th St.
Omaha, Ne. 68137
Ph: (402) 290-8216
Fax: (402) 474-4901

E-Mail: nebrhbpa@radiks.net
President: Jerry Fudge

Nebraska Racing Commission
P.O. Box 95014
Lincoln, Ne. 68509-5014
Ph: (402) 471-4155
Fax: (402) 471-2339
E-Mail: diane.vandeun@racing.ne.gov
Website: *www.horseracing.state.ne.us*
Chairman: Dennis Lee

Nebraska Thoroughbred Breeders Association
P.O. Box 2215
Grand Island, Ne. 68802
Ph: (308) 384-4683
Fax: (308) 384-9172
E-Mail: ntba@nebraskathoroughbredbreeders.com
Website: *www.nebraskathoroughbredbreeders.com*
President: Roger Lubbe

New Hampshire

New Hampshire Horse Council
P.O. Box 81
Conway, N.H. 03818
Ph: (603) 651-8017
E-Mail: lawz@roadrunner.com
Website: *www.nhhorsecouncil.com*
President: Laurie Weir

New Hampshire Pari-Mutuel Commission
78 Regional Dr., Unit 3
Concord, N.H. 03301-8530
Ph: (603) 271-2158
Fax: (603) 271-3381
E-Mail: paul.kelley@racing.nh.gov
Website: *www.rnh.gov/parimutuel*
Executive Director: Paul M. Kelley
Chairman: Timothy J. Connors

New Jersey

New Jersey Racing Commission
P.O. Box 088
Trenton, N.J. 08625
Ph: (609) 292-0613
Fax: (609) 599-1785
Website: *www.njpublicsafety.org/racing*
Executive Director: Frank Zanzuccki
Chairman: John Tucker

Thoroughbred Breeders' Association of New Jersey
265 Hwy. 36, Suite 1R
West Long Branch, N.J. 07764
Ph: (732) 542-8880
Fax: (732) 542-8881
E-Mail: info@njbreds.com
Website: *www.njbreds.com*
President: Michael Harrison

New Mexico

New Mexico Horse Breeders' Association
P.O. Box 36869
Albuquerque, N.M. 87176-6869
Ph: (505) 262-0224
Fax: (505) 265-8009

E-Mail: nmhbpa@worldnet.att.net
Website: www.nmhorsebreeders.com
President: Q. Mike Cadotte

New Mexico Horse Council
P.O. Box 10206
Albuquerque, N.M. 87184-0206
Ph: (505) 345-8959
Fax: (505) 565-3223
E-Mail: rustycook4412@msn.com
Website: www.nmhorsecouncil.org
President: Rusty Cook

New Mexico Racing Commission
490 Alameda NE, Suite A
Albuquerque, N.M. 87113
Ph: (505) 222-0700
Fax: (505) 222-0713
E-Mail: rosemary.leeder@state.nm.us
Website: www.nmrc.state.nm.us
Chairman: Arnold Rael

New York
Finger Lakes Horsemen's Benevolent and Protective Association
P.O. Box 25250
Farmington, N.Y. 14425
Ph: (585) 924-3004
Fax: (585) 924-1433
E-Mail: fingerlakes.hbpa@yahoo.com
President: Dave Brown

Genesee Valley Breeders Association
P.O. Box 301
Shortsville, N.Y. 14548-0301
Ph: (585) 289-8524
Fax: (585) 289-8524
Website: www.nybreds.com/gvba

New York State Horse Council
44 Eggleston Ln.
Westport, N.Y. 12993
Ph: (518) 962-2316
E-Mail: kinggeo@westelcom.com
Website: www.nyshc.org
President: George King

New York State Racing and Wagering Board
1 Broadway Center, Suite 600
Schenectady, N.Y. 12305-2553
Ph: (518) 395-5400
E-Mail: info@racing.state.ny.us
Website: www.racing.state.ny.us
Chairman: Daniel Hogan

New York State Thoroughbred Breeding and Development
19 Roosevelt Dr., Suite 250
Saratoga Springs, N.Y. 12866
Ph: (518) 580-0100
Fax: (518) 580-0500
E-Mail: nybreds@nybreds.com
Website: www.nybreds.com
Executive Director: Martin G. Kinsella

New York Thoroughbred Breeders
57 Phila St., 2nd Fl.
Saratoga Springs, N.Y. 12866
Ph: (518) 587-0777

Fax: (518) 587-1551
E-Mail: office@nybreds.org
Website: www.nybreds.org

New York Thoroughbred Horsemen's Association
P.O. Box 170070
Jamaica, N.Y. 11417
Ph: (516) 488-2337
Fax: (516) 488-1698
Website: www.nytha.com
President: Richard Z. Violette Jr.

North Carolina
North Carolina Horse Council
4904 Waters Edge Dr., Suite 290
Raleigh, N.C. 27606
Ph: (919) 854-1990
Fax: (919) 854-1989
E-Mail: suegray@nchorsecouncil.com
Website: www.nchorsecouncil.com
President: Robert Sanford

North Carolina Thoroughbred Association
813 Moss Rd.
Zebulon, N.C. 27597
Ph: (800) 957-3490
E-Mail: info@ncthoroughbreds.com
Website: www.ncthoroughbreds.com
President: Tom Hendrickson

North Dakota
North Dakota Racing Commission
500 North 9th St.
Bismarck, N.D. 58501
Ph: (701) 328-4290
Fax: (701) 328-4280
E-Mail: rblaseg@nd.gov
Website: www.ndracingcommission.com
Director of Racing: Randy Blaseg

Ohio
Ohio Horsemen's Benevolent and Protective Association
3684 Park St.
Grove City, Oh. 43123
Ph: (614) 875-1269
Fax: (614) 875-0786
E-Mail: ohio-hbpa@rrohio.com
Website: www.ohio-hbpa.com
President: Jim Yeagel

Ohio Racing Commission
77 S. High St., 18th Fl.
Columbus, Oh. 43215-6108
Ph: (614) 466-2757
Fax: (614) 466-1900
E-Mail: marty.evans@rc.state.oh.us
Website: www.racing.ohio.gov
Chairman: William Koester

Ohio Thoroughbred Breeders and Owners Association
6024 Harrison Ave., Suite 13
Cincinnati, Oh. 45248
Ph: (513) 574-0440
Fax: (513) 574-2313
E-Mail: gb.otbo@fuse.net
Website: www.otbo.com
President: Tim Hamm

Oklahoma
Oklahoma Horsemen's Benevolent and Protective Association
1 Remington Pl.
Oklahoma City, Ok. 73111
Ph: (405) 427-8753
Fax: (405) 427-7099
E-Mail: okhbpa@earthlink.net
Website: www.okhbpa.com
President: Joe Lucas

Oklahoma Racing Commission
2401 NW 23rd St., Suite 78
Oklahoma City, Ok. 73107
Ph: (405) 943-6472
Fax: (405) 943-6474
E-Mail: ohrc@socket.net
Website: www.ohrc.org
Chairman: Gene Bledsoe

Oklahoma Thoroughbred Association
2000 SE. 15th St., Bldg. 450, Suite A
Edmond, Ok. 73013
Ph: (405) 330-1006
Fax: (405) 330-6206
E-Mail: info@otawins.com
Website: www.otawins.com
President: Dan Case

Oregon
Oregon Horsemen's Benevolent and Protective Association
10350 N. Vancouver Way, #351
Portland, Or. 97217
Ph: (503) 285-4941
Fax: (503) 285-4942
E-Mail: ohbpa@aol.com
Website: www.oregonhbpa.com
President: Jim Fergason

Oregon Racing Commission
800 NE Oregon St., Suite 310
Portland, Or. 97232
Ph: (971) 673-0207
Fax: (971) 673-0213
E-Mail: randy.evers@state.or.us
Website: http://racing.oregon.gov
Chairman: Kerry Johnson
Executive Director: Randy Evers

Oregon Thoroughbred Owners and Breeders Association
P.O. Box 17248
Portland, Or. 97217
Ph: (503) 285-0658
Fax: (503) 285-0659
E-Mail: info@oregontoba.com
Website: www.oregontoba.com
President: Gay Welliver

Pennsylvania
Pennsylvania Equine Council
P.O. Box 62
Huntington Mills, Pa. 18622-0062
Ph: (888) 304-0281
E-Mail: info@pennsylvaniaequine council.com

Website: *www.pennsylvaniaequine council.com*
President: Robert A. Hoffa

Pennsylvania Horse Breeders Association
701 E. Baltimore Pk., Suite E
Kennett Square, Pa. 19348
Ph: (610) 444-1050
Fax: (610) 444-1051
E-Mail: exsec@pabred.com
Website: *www.pabred.com*
President: Peter Giangiulio
Executive Secretary: Mark McDermott

Pennsylvania Horsemen's Benevolent and Protective Association
P.O. Box 88
Grantville, Pa.17028
Ph: (717) 652-5849
Fax: (717) 469-7714
E-Mail: pahbpa@hughes.net
Website: *www.pahbpa.com*
President: Joe Santanna

Pennsylvania Horse Racing Commission
2301 N. Cameron St., Rm. 304
Harrisburg, Pa. 17110
Ph: (717) 787-1942
Fax: (717) 346-1546
Chairman: Richard D. Abbott

Pennsylvania Thoroughbred Horsemen's Association
P.O. Box 300
Bensalem, Pa. 19020-0300
Ph: (215) 638-2012
Fax: (215) 638-2919
President: Donald Reeder

South Carolina
South Carolina Thoroughbred Owners and Breeders
P.O. Box 12850
Charleston, S.C. 29422
E-Mail: info@sctoba.org
Website: *www.sctoba.org*
President: Lee Christian

South Dakota
South Dakota Commission on Gaming
221 W. Capitol Ave., Suite 101
Pierre, S.D. 57501
Ph: (605) 773-6050
Fax: (605) 773-6053
E-Mail: gaminginfo@state.sd.us
Website: *www.state.sd.us/drr2/reg/ gaming*
Chairman: Ralph "Chip" Kemnitz

Texas
Texas Horsemen's Benevolent and Protective Association
8000 Centre Park Dr., Suite 100
Austin, Tx. 78754
Ph: (512) 467-9799
Fax: (512) 467-9790
E-Mail: tommyazopardi@ texashorsemen.com
Website: *www.texashorsemen.com*
Executive Director: Tommy Azopardi

Texas Racing Commission
P.O. Box 12080
Austin, Tx. 78711-2080
Ph: (512) 833-6699
Fax: (512) 833-6907
E-Mail: caking@txrc.state.tx.us
Website: *www.txrc.state.tx.us*
Executive Secretary: Charla Ann King
Chairman: Jesse R. Adams

Texas Thoroughbred Association
P.O. Box 14967
Austin, Tx. 78761
Ph: (512) 458-6133
Fax: (512) 453-5919
E-Mail: info@texasthoroughbred.com
Website: *www.texasthoroughbred.com*
Executive Director: David E. Hooper

Vermont
Vermont Horse Council
P.O. Box 392, 34 Mullen Rd.
Underhill, Vt. 05489
Ph: (802) 899-3928
E-Mail: goodhorsekeeping@ yahoo.com
Website: *www.vthorsecouncil.org*
President: Cindy Cross-Greenia

Virginia
Virginia Horsemen's Benevolent and Protective Association
38 Garrett St.
Warrenton, Va. 20186
Ph: (540) 347-0033
Fax: (540) 347-0034
E-Mail: race@vhpa.org
Website: *www.vhbpa.org*
President: Robin Richards

Virginia Racing Commission
10700 Horsemen's Rd.
New Kent, Va. 23124
Ph: (804) 966-7400
Fax: (804) 966-7418
E-Mail: kimberly.carter@vrc. virginia.gov
Website: *www.vrc.state.va.us*
Chairman: Peter C. Burnett

Virginia Thoroughbred Association
38 Garrett St.
Warrenton, Va. 20186-3107
Ph: (540) 347-4313
Fax: (540) 347-7314
E-Mail: vta@vabred.org
Website: *www.vabred.org*
President: Donna Dennehy

Washington
Washington Horsemen's Benevolent and Protective Association
3702 W. Valley Hwy. N., Suite 210
Auburn, Wa. 98001
Ph: (253) 804-6822
Fax: (253) 804-6899
E-Mail: contactus@washingtonhbpa. com
Website: *www.washingtonhbpa.com*
President: Frank McDonald

Washington Horse Racing Commission
6326 Martin Way, Suite 209
Olympia, Wa. 98516
Ph: (360) 459-6462
Fax: (360) 459-6461
E-Mail: whrc@whrc.state.wa.us
Website: *www.whrc.wa.gov*
Chairman: Carol Smith-Merkulov

Washington Thoroughbred Breeders Association
P.O. Box 1499
Auburn, Wa. 98071-1499
Ph: (253) 288-7878
Fax: (253) 288-7890
E-Mail: maindesk@washington thoroughbred.com
Website: *www.washington thoroughbred.com*
Executive Director: Duane Belvoir

Washington Thoroughbred Farm Managers Association
P.O. Box 857
Enumclaw, Wa. 98022
Ph: (253) 288-7897
Fax: (253) 288-7890
E-Mail: maindesk@washington thoroughbred.com
Website: *www.washingtonthorough bred.com/IndAddrs/WTFMA.htm*

West Virginia
Charles Town Horsemen's Benevolent and Protective Association
P.O. Box 581
Charles Town, W.V. 25414
Ph: (304) 725-1535
Fax: (304) 728-2113
E-Mail: cthbpa@cthbpa.com
Website: *www.cthbpa.com*
President: Randy Funkhouser

Mountaineer Park Horsemen's Benevolent and Protective Association
P. O. Box 358
Chester, W.V. 26034
Ph: (304) 387-9772
Fax: (304) 387-1925
E-Mail: hbpa@raex.com
President: Loren G. Cox

West Virginia Breeders Classics Ltd.
P.O. Box 1251
Charles Town, W.V. 25414
Ph: (304) 725-0709
Fax: (540) 687-6927
E-Mail: wvbcmbn@verizon.net
Website: *www.wvbc.com*
President: Sam Huff

West Virginia Racing Commission
106 Dee Dr.
Charleston, W.V. 25311
Ph: (304) 558-2150
Fax: (304) 558-6319
E-Mail: lacyl@wvnet.edu
Website: www.wvf.state.wv.us/racing
Chairman: Fred C. Peddicord

West Virginia Thoroughbred Breeders Association
P.O. Box 626
Charles Town, W.V. 25414
Ph: (304) 728-6868
Fax: (304) 723-7870
E-Mail: wvbreeders@gmail.com
Website: www.wvtba.net
President: Doug Allara, D.V.M.

Wyoming

Wyoming Pari-Mutuel Commission
2515 Warren Ave., Suite 301
Cheyenne, Wy. 82002
Ph: (307) 777-5928
Fax: (307) 777-3681
E-Mail: cmoore@state.wy.us
Website: http://parimutuel.state.wy.us
Executive Director: Charles Moore

Canada

Alberta Division, Canadian Thoroughbred Horse Society
225 17th Ave. SW. #401
Calgary, Ab. T2S 2T8 Canada
Ph: (403) 229-3609
Fax: (403) 244-6909
E-Mail: cthsalta@telusplanet.net
Website: www.cthsalta.com
Manager: Jean Kruse

Alberta Horse Racing
9707 110th St., #720
Edmonton, Ab. T5K 2L9 Canada
Ph: (780) 415-5432
Fax: (780) 488-5105
Website: www.thehorses.com
Chairman: Dr. David Reid

British Columbia Division, Canadian Thoroughbred Horse Society
17687 56A Ave.
Surrey, B.C. V3S 1G4 Canada
Ph: (604) 574-0145
Fax: (604) 574-5868
E-Mail: cthsbc@uniserve.com
Website: www.cthsbc.org

Canada Horsemen's Benevolent and Protective Association
609 W. Hastings St., No. 888
Vancouver, B.C. V6B 4W4 Canada
Ph: (604) 647-2211
Fax: (604) 647-0095
E-Mail: bmcafee@hastingsracecourse.com
President: Mel Snow

Division of Racing of British Columbia
4603 Kingsway, Suite 408
Burnaby, B.C. V5H 4M4 Canada
Ph: (604) 660-7400
Fax: (604) 660-7414
E-Mail: gaming.branch@gov.bc.ca
Website: www.pssg.gov.bc.ca/gaming
Director: Sam Hawkins

Eastern Canadian Thoroughbred Association
Longview Farm
RR 4, 159 Lowe Rd.
Ashton, On. K0A 1B0 Canada
Ph: (613) 257-5837
Fax: (613) 257-5837
E-Mail: kenne58@attglobal.net
Website: http://ecta.ncf.ca
President: MaryEllen Kennedy

Horse Council of British Columbia
27336 Fraser Hwy.
Aldergrove, B.C. V4W 3N5 Canada
Ph: (604) 856-4304
Fax: (604) 856-4302
E-Mail: administration@hcbc.ca
Website: www.hcbc.ca
President: Sarah Bradley

Manitoba Division, Canadian Thoroughbred Horse Society
Westdale Box 46152
Winnipeg, Mb. R2R 3S3 Canada
Ph: (204) 832-1702
Fax: (204) 831-6735
E-Mail: cthsmb@mts.net
Website: www.cthsmb.ca
President: Grant Watson

Manitoba Horse Council
200 Main St., Suite 207
Winnipeg, Mb. R3C 4M2 Canada
Ph: (204) 925-5718
Fax: (204) 925-5792
E-Mail: admin@manitobahorsecouncil.ca
Website: www.manitobahorsecouncil.ca
Executive Director: Sheilagh Antoniuk

Manitoba Racing Commission
P.O. Box 46086 RPO Westdale
Winnipeg, Mb. R3R 3S3 Canada
Ph: (204) 885-7770
Fax: (204) 831-0942
E-Mail: lhuber@manitobahorsecomm.org
Executive Director: Larry Huber
Chairman: David Miles

Ontario Division, Canadian Thoroughbred Horse Society
P.O. Box 172
Rexdale, On. M9W 5L1 Canada
Ph: (416) 675-3602
Fax: (416) 675-9405
E-Mail: cthsont@idirect.com
Website: www.cthsont.com

Ontario Equestrian Federation
9120 Leslie St., Suite 203
Richmond Hill, On. L4B 3J9 Canada
Ph: (905) 709-6545
Fax: (905) 709-1867
E-Mail: horse@horse.on.ca
Website: www.horse.on.ca

Ontario Horse Breeders Association
P.O. Box 520
Caledon, On. L0N IC0 Canada
Ph: (519) 942-3527
President: Nicole Alain

Ontario Horsemen's Benevolent and Protective Association
135 Queens Plate Dr., Suite 370
Toronto, On. M9W 6V1 Canada
Ph: (416) 747-5252
Fax: (416) 747-9606
E-Mail: general@hbpa.com
Website: www.hbpa.on.ca
President: Sue Lesile

Ontario Racing Commission
10 Carlson Ct., Suite 400
Toronto, On. M9W6L2 Canada
Ph: (416) 213-0520
Fax: (416) 213-7827
E-Mail: inquiry@ontarioracingcommission.ca
Website: www.ontarioracingcommission.ca
Chairman: Rod Seiling

Quebec Division, Canadian Thoroughbred Horse Society
11871 Cote Des Anges N.
Mirabel, Pq., J7N 2W3
Ph/Fax: (450) 475-8648
President: Martine Fournelle

Saskatchewan Horse Federation
2205 Victoria Ave.
Regina, Sk. S4P 0S4 Canada
Ph: (306) 780-9244
Fax: (306) 525-4009
Website: www.saskhorse.ca
President: Mary-Ann Olson

Mexico

Mexico Racing Commission
Fuente de Templanza No. 6, P. H.
Col. Tecamachalco,
Naucalpan, Edo. De Mexico
Mexico City 53950
Ph: 011(52) 5 293-0264
Fax: 011 (52) 5 294-7928
E-Mail: cnccg@aol.com

Puerto Rico

Puerto Rico Thoroughbred Breeders Association
Mercantile Plaza Building, Suite 503
San Juan, P.R. 00918
Ph: (809) 759-9991
E-Mail: criadores@icepr.com

Charitable Organizations
National

American Horse Defense Fund
1718 M Street N.W., Unit 191
Washington, D.C. 20036-4504
Ph: (202) 609-8198
E-Mail: president@ahdf.org
Website: *www.ahdf.org*
President: Shelley Sawhook

Blue Horse Charities
P.O. Box 13610
Lexington, Ky. 40583
Leslie McCammish
Ph: (859) 255-1555
Fax: (859) 254-0794
E-Mail: lmccammish@fasigtipton.com
Website: *www.bluehorsecharities.org*

CANTER
Ph: (810) 796-9239
E-Mail: nancyk@canterusa.org
Website: *www.canterusa.org*

Don MacBeth Memorial Jockey Fund
P.O. Box 18470
Encino, Ca. 91416
Ph: (310) 550-4542
Fax: (818) 981-6914
E-Mail: info@macbethfund.org
Website: *www.macbethfund.org*

Equine Advocates
P.O. Box 354
Chatham, N.Y. 12037
Ph: (518) 245-1599
Website: *www.equineadvocates.com*
President: Susan Wagner

Equine Protection Network
Christine Barry
Ph: (570) 345-6440
Website: *www.equineprotectionnetwork.com*

Grayson-Jockey Club Research Foundation
821 Corporate Dr.
Lexington, Ky. 40503
Ph: (859) 224-2850
Fax: (859) 224-2853
E-Mail: contactus@grayson-jockeyclub.org
Website: *www.grayson-jockeyclub.org*
President: Edward L. Bowen

HoofPAC.com
Brooks Johnson
E-Mail: savethehorse@earthlink.net
Website: *www.hoofpac.com*

Humane Society of U.S.
Ph: (202) 452-1100
Website: *www.hsus.org*

The Jockey Club Foundation
40 East 52nd St.
New York, N.Y. 10022
Phone: (212) 371-5970
Fax: (212) 371-6123
E-Mail: contactus@tjcfoundation.org
Website: *www.tjcfoundation.org*
Chairman: Ogden Mills Phipps

Kentucky Horse Park Foundation
4089 Iron Works Pk.
Lexington, Ky. 40511
Ph: (859) 255-5727
Fax: (859) 254-7121
E-Mail: foundation@khpfoundation.org
Website: *www.kyhorsepark.com/khp/foundation*

Maryland Horsemen's Assistance Fund
6314 Windsor Mill Rd.
Baltimore, Md. 21207
Ph: (410) 265-6842
Fax: (410) 265-6841
E-Mail: info@mdhorsemen.com
Website: *www.mdhorsemen.com*

National Horse Protection League
P.O. Box 318
Chappaqua, N.Y. 10514
Ph: (202) 293-0570
E-Mail: info@horse-protection.org
Website: *www.horse-protection.org*

Race Track Chaplaincy of America
P.O. Box 91640
Los Angeles, Ca. 90009
Ph: (310) 419-1640
Fax: (310) 419-1642
E-Mail: edonnally@racetrackchaplaincy.org
Website: *www.racetrackchaplaincy.org*
President: Waverly Parsons
Executive Director: Enrique Torres

ReRun
P.O. Box 113
Helmetta, N.J. 08828
Ph: (732) 521-1370
E-Mail: rerunnj@comcast.net
Website: *www.rerun.org*
President: Laurie Lane

Thoroughbred Charities of America
P.O. Box 3856
Midway, Ky. 40347
Ph: (859) 312-5531
E-Mail: liz@speedbeam.com
Website: *www.thoroughbredcharities.org*
President: Herb Moelis
Executive Director: Liz Harris

Thoroughbred Retirement Foundation
P.O. Box 3387
Saratoga Springs, N.Y. 12866
Ph: (518) 226-0028
Fax: (518) 226-0699
E-Mail: trf@trfinc.org
Website: *www.trfinc.org*
Executive Director: Diana Pikulski
Operations Director: Fred Winters
Adoption Coordinator: Nicole Smith

United Pegasus Foundation
102 S. First Ave.
Arcadia, Ca. 91006
Ph: (626) 279-1306
E-Mail: unitedpegasus@yahoo.com
Website: *www.unitedpegasus.com*
President: Helen Meredith

Winners Foundation
285 W. Huntington Dr.
Arcadia, Ca. 91007
Ph: (626) 574-6498
Fax: (626) 821-9091
E-Mail: robert.fletcher@santaanita.com
Executive Director: Bob Fletcher

Winners Federation
777 Delaware Park Blvd.
Wilmington, De. 19084
Ph: (302) 383-7233
E-Mail: winfed@gmail.com
Website: *www.winnersfederation.org*
President: G. Wesley Jones II

Thoroughbred Retirement and Rescue

Alabama

Alabama Equine Rescue
Ph: (205) 680-1862
E-Mail: aerescue2000@yahoo.com
Website: *www.aerescue.netfirms.com*

Foal Train
Liz Creamer
Ph: (251) 545-7980
E-Mail: liz@foaltrain.com
Website: *www.foaltrain.com*

Alaska

Alaska Equine Rescue
Ph: (888) 588-4677
E-Mail: aer@alaskaequinerescue.com
Website: *www.alaskaequinerescue.com*
President: Dave Wachsmuth

Arizona

Equine Encore Foundation
3225 North El Burrito Ave.
Tucson, Az. 85705
Ph: (520) 349-6008
E-Mail: rillitorunner@aol.com
Website: *www.equineencorefoundation.com*

Organizations — Thoroughbred Retirement

Hacienda de los Milagros
3731 North Rd. One West
Chino Valley, Az. 86323
Ph: (928) 636-5348
E-Mail: milagro@commspeed.net
Website: www.haciendadelos
milagros.org

**Horse Rescue of
North Scottsdale**
6631 E. Montgomery Rd.
Cave Creek, Az. 85331
Holly Marino
Ph: (602) 689-8825
E-Mail: holly@rescueahorse.com
Website: www.rescueahorse.com

**X-S Ranch Livestock Rescue
& Sanctuary**
E-Mail: donswendy@yahoo.com
Website: www.xs-ranch.20m.com

Arkansas

Ozland Horse Rescue
120 Phyllis Lane
Newark, Ar. 72562
Ph: (870) 799-2465
Website: http://myozland.tripod.com

Tiny Timbers Horse Rescue
Ph: (479) 451-8900
E-Mail: minihoss@tinytimbersrescue.org
Website: http://tinytimbersrescue.org

California

**California Equine Retirement
Foundation**
34033 Kooden Rd.
Winchester, Ca. 92596
Ph: (951) 926-4190
Fax: (951) 926-4181
E-Mail: cerf1@earthlink.net
Website: www.cerfhorses.org

Equus Sanctuary
Ph: (530) 260-0148
E-Mail: mustangsb@hughes.net
Website: www.equus.org

Exceller Fund to Rescue Horses
P.O. Box 33274
Granada Hills, Ca. 91394
Ph: (818) 368-2871
E-Mail: mail@excellerfund.org
Website: www.excellerfund.org

**Glen Ellen Vocational
Academy (GEVA)**
P.O. Box 2101
Glen Ellen, Ca. 95442
Pam Berg
Ph: (707) 527-8092
E-Mail: gef@vom.com
Website: www.glenellenfarms.com/
geva

**Jack Auchterlonie Memorial
Equine Sanctuary (JAMES)**
Ph: (760) 362-1357
E-Mail: james29palms@aol.com
Website: www.jamesrescue.com

Redwings Horse Sanctuary
Ph: (831) 386-1035
E-Mail: info@redwings.org
Website: www.redwings.org

Return to Freedom
Neda De Mayo
Ph: (805) 737-9246
E-Mail: admin@returntofreedom.org
Website: www.returntofreedom.org

Tranquility Farm
Priscilla Clark
Ph: (661) 823-0307
E-Mail: info@tranquilityfarmtbs.org
Website: www.tranquilityfarmtbs.org

True Innocents Equine Rescue
Ph: (951) 360-1464
E-Mail: info@tierrescue.org
Website: www.tierrescue.org

United Pegasus Foundation
Helen Meredith
Ph: (626) 279-1306
E-Mail: unitedpegasus@yahoo.com
Website: www.unitedpegasus.com

Colorado

Colorado Horse Rescue
Nan Millett
Ph: (720) 494-1414
E-Mail: info@chr.org
Website: www.chr.org

**Friends of Horses Rescue &
Adoption**
Ph: (303) 210-0552
E-Mail: info@getahorse.org
Website: www.getahorse.org

Lasso Horse Rescue
Ph: (970) 264-0095
E-Mail: lassohorserescue@hotmail.com
Website: www.lassohorserescue.org

Rocky Mountain Foal Rescue
Pam Pietsch
Ph: (719) 683-5880
E-Mail: rmfr@qwest.net

Connecticut

Citizens for Animal Protection
P.O. Box 1496
Litchfield, Ct. 06759
Ph: (860) 567-3422
E-Mail: capinc@usa.net
Website: www.geocities.com/
Petsburgh/Zoo/7966

Greener Pastures Rescue
Ph: (860) 886-8510
E-Mail: 4arescue@greenerpasturesrescue.org
Website: www.greenerpasturesrescue.org

**Phoenix Rising Equine
Rescue**
1 Pinewoods Rd.
North Stonington, Ct. 06359
Ph: (860) 599-0555
E-Mail: skreutter@comcast.net
Website: www.phoenixrisingequinerescue.com
President: Susan Kruetter

Delaware

**Tri State Equine
Adoption and Rescue**
Ph: (302) 492-0492
E-Mail: saveahorse@aol.com
Website: www.tristateequine.org

Florida

**Equine Rescue & Adoption
Foundation**
Ph: (772) 220-0150
E-Mail: eraf2000@gmail.com
Website: www.eraf.org

Friends of the EIA Horse
Lynne Mandry
Ph: (954) 916-9847
E-Mail: info@eiahorses.org
Website: www.eiahorses.org

**Heavenly Meadows Horse
Rescue**
Melissa Wyzard
Ph: (850) 773-9991
E-Mail: info@heavenlymeadows.org
Website: www.heavenlymeadows.org

Horse Protection Association
Bruce Volling
Ph: (352) 466-4366
E-Mail: hpaf@bellsouth.net
Website: www.hpaf.org

Retirement Home for Horses
Peter Gregory
Ph: (386) 462-1001
E-Mail: rhh@millcreekfarm.org
Website: www.millcreekfarm.org

Georgia

**Begin Again Farms Equine
Shelter**
Rhonda Jackson
E-Mail: beginagainfarm@aol.com
Website: www.beginagainfarms.com

**Horse Rescue, Relief, &
Retirement Fund**
Cheryl Flanagan
Ph: (770) 886-5419
E-Mail: horseinc@aol.com
Website: www.savethehorses.org

Idaho

Orphan Acres
Ph: (208) 882-9293
E-Mail: orphanacres@hotmail.com
Website: http://community.palouse.net/orphanacres

Illinois

CANTER
Ph: (630) 341-1582
Website: www.canterusa.org/illinois

Crosswinds Equine Rescue
Denise Fillo
Ph: (217) 649-7915
E-Mail: info@cwer.org
Website: www.crosswindseqresq.org

Hooved Animal Humane Society
Ph: (815) 337-5563
E-Mail: info@hahs.org
Website: www.hahs.org

Indiana

Indiana Horse Rescue
Anthony Caldwell
Ph: (812) 729-7697
E-Mail: inrescue@ccwave.net
Website: www.indianahorserescue.com

Kentucky

Casey Creek Horse Rescue and Adoption Inc.
Kenneth Holland
Ph: (270) 789-4198
E-Mail: desperado_55@yahoo.com

Old Friends
Michael Blowen
Ph: (502) 863-1775
E-Mail: contact@oldfriendsequine.com
Website: www.oldfriendsequine.org

ReRun
Shon Wylie
E-Mail: jerryshon@bellsouth.net
Website: www.rerun.org

Louisiana

Hopeful Haven Equine Rescue
Debra Barlow
Ph: (318) 286-3116
E-Mail: info@hopefulhaven.com
Website: www.hopefulhaven.com

Maine

Standardbred Pleasure Horse Organization
Deb Ricker
Ph: (207) 839-2027
Website: www.sphomaine.net

Maryland

Days End Farm Horse Rescue
Kathy Schwartz
Ph: (301) 854-5037
E-Mail: info@defhr.org
Website: www.defhr.org

Equine Rescue & Rehabilitation
Debbie Frank
Ph: (410) 343-2142
E-Mail: equinerescue_rehab@yahoo.com
Website: www.horserescue.com

Fox Shadow Foundation
Jeannie Meade
Ph: (410) 673-2634
E-Mail: foxshadow@dmv.com

Horse Lovers United
Ph: (410) 749-3599
E-Mail: horse@intercom.net
Website: www.horseloversunited.com

HorseNet Horse Rescue
Ph: (410) 984-0824
E-Mail: info@horsenethorserescue.org
Website: www.horsenethorserescue.org

The Keep at Andelain Farm
Wendy Moulton
Ph: (301) 271-0029
E-Mail: wendy@andelainfarm.com
Website: www.andelainfarm.com

MidAtlantic Horse Rescue
Beverly Strauss
Ph: (302) 376-7297
E-Mail: bev@midatlantichorserescue.org
Website: www.midatlantichorserescue.org

New Life Equine Rescue
Ph: (301) 305-0702
E-Mail: info@nler.org
Website: www.nler.org

Royal Equine Rescue & Sanctuary
Alyssa Taylor
Ph: (443) 417-0069
E-Mail: alyssa@rersi.org
Website: www.rersi.org

Massachusetts

Eye of the Storm Equine Rescue
Nina Arbella
Ph: (978) 897-8866
Website: www.equine-rescue.com

Suffolk Downs
Ph: (617) 567-3900
Website: www.suffolkdowns.com

Michigan

CANTER
Ph: (810) 796-9239
Website: www.canterusa.org/michigan

Horses' Haven
P.O. Box 166
Howell, Mi. 48844
Ph: (517) 548-4880
E-Mail: horseshaven@earthlink.net
Website: www.horseshaven.org

Hugs2Horses
E-Mail: support@hugs2horses.com
Website: www.hugs2horses.com

Second Chance Thoroughbred Adoption
Dale Berryhill
E-Mail: brryhlls@aol.com
Website: www.horsenetwork.com/secondchance/

Minnesota

Midwest Horse Adoption Program
E-Mail: mwhorseadoption@yahoo.com
Website: http://mhap.tripod.com/mhap/

Minnesota Hooved Animal Rescue Foundation
Ph: (763) 856-3119
E-Mail: info@mnhoovedanimalrescue.org
Website: www.mnhoovedanimalrescue.org

The Original Funny Farm
E-Mail: donkey@cpinternet.com
Website: www.geocities.com/originalfunnyfarm

Save Our Souls Equine Rescue
Ph: (218) 637-2168
E-Mail: rescue@soser.us
Website: www.soser.us

Missouri

D-D Farm, Animal Sanctuary
Deb Tolentino
Ph: (573) 446-0648
E-Mail: ddfarm@tranquility.net

Fableview Equine Rescue
Valerie O'Brien
Ph: (816) 674-6748
E-Mail: vhatfie@fableview.org

Pientka Horse Rescue
Cheryl Pientka
Ph: (816) 690-7442

Rainbow Ridge Ranch Horse Sanctuary
E-Mail: info@rainbowridgeranch.com

Montana

Angels Among Us Equine Rescue
E-Mail: angels_among_us_rescue@hotmail.com

Montana Large Animal Sanctuary
Ph: (406) 741-3823
E-Mail: info@mtanimalsanctuary.com
Website: www.mtanimalsanctuary.com

Nevada

Miracle Horse Rescue
Ph: (775) 751-1101
E-Mail: miraclehorserescue01@gmail.com
Website: www.miraclehorse.com

New Hampshire

Live and Let Live Farm
Teresa Paradise
Ph: (603) 798-5615
E-Mail: info@liveandletlivefarm.org
Website: www.liveandletlivefarm.org

New Hampshire Equine Humane Association
Ph: (603) 878-0821
E-Mail: horseadopter@yahoo.com

Turtle Rock Rescue
Ph: (603) 585-9995
E-Mail: turtlerockrescue@juno.com

New Jersey

Mylestone Equine Rescue
Susan Thompson
Ph: (908) 995-9300
E-Mail: mer@eclipse.net
Website: www.mylestone.org

ReRun
Laurlie Lane
Ph: (732) 521-1370
E-Mail: rerunnj@comcast.net
Website: www.rerun.org

New Mexico

The Horse Shelter
Jan Bandler
Ph: (505) 471-6179
E-Mail: info@thehorseshelter.org
Website: www.thehorseshelter.org

Perfect Harmony Animal Rescue
Marianne Bailey
Ph: (505) 824-2130
E-Mail: perfectharmony1@aol.com
Website: www.perfectharmony-nm.org

New York

Crane Mountain Valley Horse Rescue
Nancy Van Wie or Eddie Mrozik
Ph: (518) 962-8512
E-Mail: horses@cmvhr.org
Website: www.cmvhr.org

Equine Advocates
Susan Wagner
Ph: (518) 245-1599
Website: www.equineadvocates.com

Equine Rescue Resource
Colleen Segarra
Ph: (845) 744-1728
E-Mail: equinerescueresource@hotmail.com
Website: www.equinerescueresource.com

H.O.R.S.E. Rescue & Sanctuary
Chris Dodge
Ph: (585) 584-8210
E-Mail: rescue@rochester.rr.com
Website: www.hrsny.org

Little Brook Farm
Lynn Cross
Ph: (518) 794-8104
E-Mail: lynn@h-o-r-s-e.org
Website: www.h-o-r-s-e.org

New York Horse Rescue
Mona Kanciper
Ph: (631) 874-9420
E-Mail: mona@nyhr.org
Website: www.nyhr.org

ReRun
Sue Swart
Ph: (315) 440-6823
E-Mail: reruntb@yahoo.com
Website: www.rerun.org

Tender Mercy Equine Rescue
Ph: (716) 471-4796
E-Mail: cripleridge@wnyip.net
Website: www.tendermercyrescue.com

Western New York Equine Sanctuary
CarolAnn Piazza
Ph: (716) 438-0182
E-Mail: cpiazza912@aol.com

North Carolina

Hope for Horses
Ph: (828) 683-0160
E-Mail: hopeforhorses@aol.com
Website: http://hopeforhorses.org

Horse Protection Society of North Carolina Inc.
Joan Benson
Ph: (704) 855-2978
E-Mail: hps@horseprotection.org
Website: www.horseprotection.org

United States Equine Rescue League
Ph: (800) 650-8549
E-Mail: info@userl.org
Website: www.userl.org

Ohio

CANTER
Ph: (614) 226-3975
Website: www.canterusa.org/ohio

Happy Trails
Annette Fisher
Ph: (330) 296-5914
Website: www.happytrailsfarm.org

Last Chance Corral
Victoria Goss
Ph: (740) 594-4336
Website: www.lastchancecorral.org

Lost Acres Horse Rescue & Rehabilitation
Ph: (740) 779-6761
Website: www.geocities.com/sblahrr

New Vocations Racehorse Adoption Program
3293 Wright Rd.
Laura, Oh. 45337
Dot Morgan
Ph: (937) 947-4020
Fax: (937) 947-3201
E-Mail: dot@horseadoption.com
Website: www.horseadoption.com

West Wind Horse Rescue
3130 Township Rd. 200
Bellefontaine, Oh. 43311
Ph: (937) 592-4666
E-Mail: suzieholycross@hotmail.com
Website: www.westwindhorserescue.com

Oregon

Emerald Valley Equine Assistance
Ph: (541) 935-3906
E-Mail: eveahr@earthlink.net

Pennsylvania

Angel Acres Horse Haven Rescue
Jo Deibel
Ph: (717) 965-7901
Website: www.angelacreshorsehavenrescue.com

Back in the Saddle Horse Adoption (BITS)
1313 Youngs Rd.
Linden, Pa. 17744
Ph: (570) 974-1087
E-Mail: bitsinfo@comcast.net
Website: www.bitshorseadopt.com

Bright Futures Farm
44793 Harrison Rd.
Spartansburg, Pa. 16434
Ph: (814) 827-8270
Fax: (814) 827-8278
E-Mail: info@brightfuturesfarm.org
Website: www.brightfuturesfarm.org

CANTER
Ph: (717) 385-0169
Website: www.canterusa.org/pennsylvania

Hooved Animal Welfare Council
Ph: (814) 899-0960
E-Mail: majek25@hotmail.com

Last Chance Ranch
Lori Benetz
Ph: (215) 538-2510

E-Mail: fronto@lastchanceranch.org
Website: www.lastchanceranch.org

Lost & Found Horse Rescue
Kelly Young
Ph: (717) 428-9701
E-Mail: lostandfound@lfhr.org
Website: www.lfhr.org

Ryerss Farm for Aged Equines
Joseph Donahue
Ph: (610) 469-0533, (866) 469-0507
E-Mail: ryerssfarm@verizon.net
Website: www.ryerss.com

Wind Ridge Farm Equine Sanctuary
Ph: (717) 432-2959
E-Mail: qmccarthy@earthlink.net
Website: www.stlf.org/ntc/11/windridg.htm

South Carolina

South Carolina Awareness and Rescue for Equines
Ph: (803) 422-6585
E-Mail: scare@scequinerescue.org
Website: www.scequinerescue.org

South Dakota

Black Hills Wild Horse Sanctuary
Dayton Hyde
Ph: (800) 252-6652
E-Mail: iram@gwtc.net
Website: www.wildmustangs.com

Tennessee

Angel Rescue and Transport
Lena M. Frensley
Ph: (615) 740-0964
E-Mail: lenafrensley@angelrescue.org

Horse Haven of Tennessee
Nina Margetson
Ph: (865) 609-4030
E-Mail: hht@horsehavenoftn.com
Website: www.horsehavenoftn.com

Texas

Bluebonnet Equine Humane Society
Ph: (888) 542-5163
E-Mail: info@bluebonnetequine.org
Website: www.bluebonnetequine.org

Brighter Days Horse Refuge
Jeanie Weatherholz
Ph: (830) 510-6607
E-Mail: info@brighterdayshorserefuge.org
Website: www.brighterdayshorserefuge.org

Habitat For Horses
Ph: (866) 434-5737
E-Mail: admin@habitatforhorses.org
Website: www.habitatforhorses.org

Hope for Horses Equine Rescue
Ph: (972) 736-3207
E-Mail: info@hopeforhorses.com
Website: www.hopeforhorses.com

Humane Help Animal Rescue
Ph: (432) 229-4295
E-Mail: hhar@animallover.com.au
Website: www.freewebs.com/hhar

True Blue Animal Rescue
Ph: (936) 878-2349
E-Mail: help@t-bar.org
Website: www.t-bar.org

United States Equine Sanctuary & Rescue
Ph: (940) 399-9363
E-Mail: headquarters@usesr.org
Website: www.usesr.org

Vermont

Spring Hill Horse Rescue
Ph: (802) 775-1098
E-Mail: springhillrescue@aol.com
Website: www.springhillrescue.com

Virginia

Dream Catcher Farm Horse Sanctuary
Kitty and Bucky Sutphin
E-Mail: home4them@horsesanctuary.com
Website: www.horsesanctuary.com

Equine Rescue League
P.O. Box 4366
Leesburg, Va. 20177
Pat Rogers
Ph: (540) 822-4577
E-Mail: bubbasays2@aol.com
Website: www.equinerescueleague.org

The Laughing Horse Sanctuary
Tom and Julia Durfee
Ph: (434) 927-5297
E-Mail: tom@laughinghorse.org

Lost Fantasy Rescue
E-Mail: lostfantasystables@yahoo.com
Website: www.lostfantasystables.org

Roanoke Valley Horse Rescue
Ph: (540) 797-1999
E-Mail: info@rvhr.com
Website: www.rvhr.com

Washington

Broken Oaks Equine Retirement Center
Jean and Gary Pratt
Ph: (509) 767-1461
E-Mail: gpratt@gorge.net

Hooved Animal Rescue of Thurston County
Ph: (360) 455-6100
Website: www.har-otc.com

Hope For Horses
Ph: (360) 453-4040
E-Mail: info@hopeforhorses.net
Website: www.hopeforhorses.net

People Helping Horses
Ph: (360) 435-9393
E-Mail: info@peoplehelpinghorses.org
Website: www.peoplehelpinghorses.com

West Virginia

C & M Equine Rescue
Michelle Eddy
Ph: (304) 758-5186
E-Mail: meddy@rcvideo.com

Second Wind Adoption Program
Ph: (304) 873-3532
E-Mail: secondwindadopt@aol.com
Website: www.crossedsabers.com

Wisconsin

Midwest Horse Welfare Foundation
Scott Bayerl
Ph: (715) 884-2215
E-Mail: scott@equineadoption.com
Website: www.equineadoption.com

Canada

Heaven Can Wait (Ontario)
Claire Malcolm
Ph: (705) 359-3766
E-Mail: hcwequinerescue@simpatico.ca
Website: www.heavencanwaitequinerescue.org

LongRun Thoroughbred Retirement (Ontario)
Vicki Pappas
Ph: (416) 675-3993
E-Mail: info@longrunretirement.com
Website: www.longrunretirement.com

New Stride Thoroughbred Retirement (British Columbia)
Deborah Macintyre
Ph: (604) 856-1399
E-Mail: newstride@yahoo.ca
Website: www.newstride.com

Sasha's Legacy Equine Rescue (Ontario)
Ph: (613) 336-1804
E-Mail: sler@mazinaw.on.ca
Website: www.mazinaw.on.ca/sashaslegacy/

Sales Companies

Agence Francaise de Vente du Pur-Sang
32 Ave. Hocquart de Turtot No.51
Deauville, 14800 France
Ph: 33 2 31 81 81 00
Fax: 33 2 31 81 81 01
E-Mail: info@argana.com
Website: www.deauville-sales.com
President: Eric Hoyeau

Arizona Thoroughbred Breeders Assn.
P.O. Box 41774
Phoenix, Az. 85080
Ph: (602) 942-1310
Fax: (602) 942-8225
E-Mail: atba@worldnet.att.net
Website: www.atba.net
President: Mike Lester

Barretts Equine Ltd.
P.O. Box 2010
Pomona, Ca. 91769
Ph: (909) 629-3099
Fax: (909) 629-2155
E-Mail: info@barretts.com
Website: www.barretts.com
President: Gerald F. McMahon

Breeders Sales Co. of Louisiana
P.O. Box 24650
New Orleans, La. 70184
Ph: (504) 947-4676
Fax: (504) 943-7556
E-Mail: ltbsc@cox-internet.com
President: Warren Harang III

California Thoroughbred Breeders Association
P.O. Box 60018
Arcadia, Ca. 91066-6018
Ph: (626) 445-7800
Fax: (626) 574-0852
E-Mail: ctbasales@ctba.com
Website: www.ctba.com
Sales Coordinator: Frank Vessels

Canadian Thoroughbred Horse Society (Ontario Division)
P.O. Box 172
Rexdale, On. M9W 5L1 Canada
Ph: (416) 675-3602
Fax: (416) 675-9405
E-Mail: cthsont@idirect.com
Website: www.cthsont.com

Doncaster Bloodstock Sales
Auction Mart Offices, Hawick
Roxburghshire, TD9 9NW England
Ph: 440 (1450) 372222
Fax: 440 (1450) 378017
E-Mail: winners@dbsauctions.com
Website: www.dbsauctions.com
Chairman: Henry G. Beeby

Fasig-Tipton Co.
2400 Newtown Pk.
Lexington, Ky. 40583
Ph: (859) 255-1555
Fax: (859) 254-0794
E-Mail: info@fasigtipton.com
Website: www.fasigtipton.com
President: Walt Robertson
Executive Vice President and Chief Operating Officer: Boyd T. Browning Jr.

Fasig-Tipton Florida
3641 SE 22nd Ave.
Ocala, Fl. 34471
Ph: (352) 368-6623
Fax: (352) 368-6733
E-Mail: ppenny@fasigtipton.com
Website: www.fasigtipton.com
Director of Two-Year-Old Sales: Peter Penny

Fasig-Tipton Midlantic
356 Fair Hill Dr., Suite C
Elkton, Md. 21921
Ph: (410) 392-5555
Fax: (410) 392-5556
Website: www.fasigtipton.com
Sales Coordinator: Paget Bennett

Goffs Bloodstock Sales Ltd.
Kildare Paddocks Kill
County Kildare, Ireland
Ph: 353 (45) 886600
Fax: 353 (45) 877119
E-Mail: sales@goffs.ie
Website: www.goffs.com
Chairman: Eimear Mulhern
Managing Director: Matt Mitchell

Heritage Place Sales Co.
2829 S. MacArthur Blvd.
Oklahoma City, Ok. 73128
Ph: (405) 682-4551
Fax: (405) 686-1267
E-Mail: info@heritageplace.com
Website: www.heritageplace.com
General Manager: Jeff Tebow

Illinois Thoroughbred Breeders and Owners Foundation
P.O. Box 336
Caseyville, Il. 62232
Ph: (618) 344-3427
Fax: (618) 346-1051
E-Mail: itboffp@apci.net
Website: http://itbof.org
President: Gary L. Moore

Iowa Thoroughbred Breeders and Owners Assn.
1 Prairie Meadows Dr.
Altoona, Ia. 50009
Ph: (515) 957-3002
Fax: (515) 957-1368
E-Mail: itboa@msn.com
Website: www.iowathoroughbred.com
President: Sharon Vail

Japan Racing Horse Assn.
Northern Horse Park
114-7, Misawa
Tomakomai
Hokkaido, Japan
Ph: 81-144-58-2812
E-Mail: info@jrha.or.jp
Website: www.jrha.or.jp/eng

Keeneland Association
4201 Versailles Rd.
Lexington, Ky. 40592-1690
Ph: (859) 254-3412
Fax: (859) 288-4348
E-Mail: sales@keeneland.com
Website: www.keeneland.com
President: Nick Nicholson
Director of Sales: Geoffrey G. Russell

Magic Millions Sales
28 Ascot Ct.
Bundall, QLD 9726 Australia
Ph: 61 (7) 5504 1200
Fax: 61 (7) 5531 7082
E-Mail: info@magicmillions.com.au
Website: www.magicmillions.com.au
Chairman: Gerry Harvey

Michigan Thoroughbred Owners and Breeders Assn.
P.O. Box 48
Grand Haven, Mi. 49417
Ph: (231) 798-7721
Fax: (231) 798-7612
E-Mail: mtoba@iserv.net
Website: www.mtoba.com
President: Patti M. Dickinson

Ocala Breeders' Sales Co.
P.O. Box 99
Ocala, Fl. 34478
Ph: (352) 237-2154
Fax: (352) 237-3566
E-Mail: obs@obssales.com
Website: www.obssales.com
President: Tom Chiota
Director of Sales: Tom Ventura

Ohio Thoroughbred Breeders and Owners Assn.
6024 Harrison Ave., Suite 13
Cincinnati, Oh. 45248-1621
Ph: (513) 574-0440
Fax: (513) 574-2313
E-Mail: gb.otbo@fuse.net
Website: www.otbo.com
President: Tim Hamm

Oregon Thoroughbred Breeders Assn.
P.O. Box 17248
Portland, Or. 97217
Ph: (503) 285-0658
Fax: (503) 285-0659
E-Mail: info@oregontoba.com
Website: www.oregontoba.com
President: Gay Welliver

Puerto Rico Thoroughbred Breeders Association
Centro de Seguros Bldg., Suite 312
Ponce de Leon Ave., 701 Pda 11
Miramar, San Juan, P.R. 00907
Ph: (787) 725-8715

Ruidoso Horse Sales Co.
P.O. Box 909
Ruidoso Downs, N.M. 88346
Ph: (575) 378-4474
Fax: (575) 378-4788
E-Mail: ruihorse@zianet.com

Tattersalls Ltd.
Terrace House
Newmarket, Suffolk, CB8 9BT
Great Britain
Ph: 44 (1638) 665931
Fax: 44 (1638) 660850
E-Mail: sales@tattersalls.com
Website: www.tattersalls.com
Chairman: Edmond Mahony

Tattersalls (Ireland) Ltd.
Fairyhouse, Ratoath
County Meath, Ireland
Ph: 353 (1) 8864300
Fax: 353 (1) 8864303
E-Mail: info@tattersalls.ie
Website: www.tattersalls.ie
Chairman: Edmond Mahony

Thomas Sales Co.
10410 N. Yale Ave.
Sperry, Ok. 74073

Ph: (918) 288-7308
Fax: (918) 288-7330
E-Mail: horsemensracingbredsales@yahoo.com
President: Betty Thomas

Washington Thoroughbred Breeders Assn.
P.O. Box 1499
Auburn, Wa. 98071-1499
Ph: (253) 288-7878
Fax: (253) 288-7890
E-Mail: maindesk@washingtonthoroughbred.com
Website: www.washingtonthoroughbred.com
Sales Barn Manager: Joe Pirone

Publicly Owned Companies With Thoroughbred Industry Holdings

Boyd Gaming Corp.

A relative newcomer to the horse racing industry, Boyd Gaming hit a home run when it purchased Delta Downs in Vinton, Louisiana, in 2001. Purses and wagering have increased substantially since the Las Vegas-based company opened its Delta Downs slots pavilion in early 2002. With the Boyd family controlling more than 35% of the common stock, the company has 16 gaming properties in Nevada, Mississippi, Illinois, and Indiana, in addition to Louisiana. It owns 50% of the Borgata casino hotel in Atlantic City, New Jersey, with MGM Mirage. Boyd Gaming owns two adjacent properties in Tunica, Mississippi—Sam's Town and Isle of Capri. In 2004, it bought Harrah's Shreveport, Louisiana, casino for $190-million and Las Vegas-based Coast Casinos for $820-million. In 2007, it tore down its Stardust Resort and Casino in Las Vegas and on the site is developing Echelon Place, scheduled to open in '10.

Headquarters: 3883 Howard Hughes Pkwy., 9th Fl., Las Vegas, Nv. 89169
Phone: (702) 792-7200
Website: www.boydgaming.com
Executive Chairman: William S. Boyd
President: Keith E. Smith
Symbol, Exchange: BYD, New York Stock Exchange
Employees: 16,900
2007 Revenues: $2.08-billion
2007 Net Profit: $303.0-million

Canterbury Park Holding Corp.

Canterbury Downs opened in 1985 outside Minneapolis, and, like several other tracks debuting in that era, such as the Birmingham Turf Club and the rebuilt Garden State Park, it struggled for survival as it failed to meet expectations for pari-mutuel handle and attendance. Ladbroke Racing bought the track in 1990 but closed it two years later. In late 1993, investor Irwin Jacobs bought the property and sold it a few months later to a group headed by Curtis A. Sampson, owner of a successful Minnesota telecommunications company. Randall Sampson, his son and an investor in the track, became president of Canterbury. The elder Sampson spearheaded an initial public offering in 1994, and the track, with its name changed to Canterbury Park, reopened for live racing in '95. Boosted by full-card simulcasting, Canterbury posted its first profit in 1997 and showed further gains when its card club opened in 2000.

Headquarters: 1100 Canterbury Road, Shakopee, Mn. 55379
Phone: (952) 445-7223
Website: www.canterburypark.com
Chairman: Curtis A. Sampson
President and CEO: Randall D. Sampson
Symbol, Exchange: ECP, American Stock Exchange
Employees: 381
2007 Revenues: $52.9-million
2007 Net Profit: $2.6-million

Churchill Downs Inc.

For more than a half-century, Churchill Downs has been America's best-known racetrack, but financial difficulties in the early 1980s almost led to a takeover. Warner L. Jones Jr., a prominent breeder, stepped in and reorganized the company, bringing in lawyer Thomas Meeker as president and chief executive officer in 1984. Over the next two decades, Churchill Downs Inc. became a heavyweight within the racetrack industry, occupying top spots with Magna Entertainment Corp. and the New York Racing

Association. Churchill's expansion began rather modestly, building Hoosier Park as a controlling partner and buying Ellis Park in western Kentucky. But the pace accelerated after Magna's Frank Stronach began his acquisitions in 1998, and Churchill bought Calder Race Course, Hollywood Park, and Arlington Park. The Arlington purchase made Duchossois Industries the track's largest stockholder with approximately 25% of outstanding shares. In 2004, Churchill acquired Fair Grounds in New Orleans for $47-million, and in '05 it was authorized to install slot machines there, but Hurricane Katrina delayed the slots until late 2007. Churchill began dismantling its racetrack collection in 2005, when Hollywood was sold to the Bay Meadows Land Co. for $257.5-million; it had paid $140-million for the Inglewood, California, property in 1999. Churchill Downs Inc. sold Ellis in 2006 and liquidated its interest in Hoosier late that year. The Meeker era, marked by an extensive remodeling of the Louisville property between 2002 and '05, ended in August '06 when Robert L. Evans became president and chief executive officer. Shortly before the 2007 Kentucky Derby Presented by Yum! Brands (G1), the company launched its Internet wagering site, *www.twinspires.com*, and in June 2007 it bought AmericaTAB and Bloodstock Research Information Services to bolster its online presence.

Headquarters: 700 Central Ave., Louisville, Ky. 40208
Phone: (502) 636-4400
Website: *www.churchilldownsincorporated.com*
Chairman: Carl F. Pollard
President and CEO: Robert L. Evans
Employees: 1,000
Symbol, Exchange: CHDN, NASDAQ
2007 Revenues: $410.7-million
2007 Net Profit: $15.7-million

Harrah's Entertainment

The world's largest casino company, Harrah's Entertainment has been increasing its involvement in the pari-mutuel industry. By virtue of a loan to Turfway Park, Harrah's became a one-third owner of the Northern Kentucky track when the Keeneland Association led a buyout of Jerry Carroll and his partners in January 1999. When another partial owner, GTECH Corp., closed out its investment, the gaming company's ownership of the Florence track rose to 50% in 2005. In August 2002, Harrah's announced it was buying 95% of Louisiana Downs. The attraction was the arrival of slot machines at the Bossier City track in 2003, and a new slots casino opened there in '04. The company's total investment in Louisiana Downs, including the purchase price, was estimated at $183-million. In 2007, the company accepted a private-equity buyout offer valued at $17-billion, went private and no longer reports financial information.

Headquarters: One Harrah's Ct., Las Vegas, Nv. 89119
Phone: (702) 407-6000
Website: *www.harrahs.com*
Chairman, President, and CEO: Gary W. Loveman
Employees: 85,000
Symbol, Exchange: HET, New York Stock Exchange
2006 Revenues: $9,673.9-million
2006 Net Profit: $535.8-million

Macrovision Solutions Corp.

Television Games Network, popularly known as TVG, landed in the hands of a new owner in May 2008 when Gemstar-TV Guide International was acquired for $2.3-billion by Macrovision Corp., a Santa Clara, California, company specializing in home-based digital entertainment and commerce. The new home, renamed Macrovision Solutions Corp., may be temporary for TVG because Macrovision said before the sale that it might sell both the satellite- and cable-based racing channel and the print edition of *TV Guide*. The purchase of Gemstar-TV Guide was very much a case of the guppy swallowing the whale—Gemstar's 2007 revenues were roughly eight times those of Macrovision, but the deal had the blessing of Rupert Murdoch's News Corp., which owned 41% of Gemstar-TV Guide. The purchase price was a mere fraction of the $14.2-billion that Gemstar paid for TV Guide, including TVG, in 2000, but the merged company lost much of its value, in part because of accounting irregularities linked to former Gemstar executive Henry Yuen.

Headquarters: 2830 De La Cruz Blvd., Santa Clara, Ca. 95050
Phone: (408)562-8400
Website: *www.macrovision.com*
Chairman: John Ryan
President and CEO: Alfred J. "Fred" Amoroso
Employees: 450
Symbol, Exchange: MVSN, NASDAQ
2007 Revenues: $78.8-million
2007 Net Profit: $14.1-million

Magna Entertainment Corp.

Spun off from Frank Stronach-controlled Magna International in 1999, Magna Entertainment Corp. quickly became the biggest player in the racetrack industry, and its most troubled entity. Stronach's buying spree began with Santa Anita Park in 1998 and grew to 12 tracks. In addition to Santa Anita, Magna acquired another top-level track, Gulfstream Park in South Florida, and in 2002 completed its purchase of Lone Star Park in the Dallas-Fort Worth metroplex for $80-million and assumption of $20-million in debt. Also in 2002, Magna added a Triple Crown track to its portfolio when it acquired controlling interest in Pimlico Race Course and Laurel

Park. Magna rolled out its XpressBet system for phone wagering, and in early 2003 unveiled HorseRacing TV, a cable-television network featuring races from the Magna-owned or -affiliated tracks and 60 other racetracks. In 2007, Magna sold half of HorseRacing TV to Churchill Downs Inc. Magna Entertainment doubled its ownership share of AmTote in 2006 to 60% and announced its intention to buy the remainder of the Maryland-based totalizator company, whose client tracks traditionally have been on the East Coast. As its financial problems deepened, Magna abandoned plans to build new tracks in Northern California and Michigan. Through MI Developments, Stronach owns approximately 95% of the voting stock in the company.

Headquarters: 337 Magna Dr., Aurora, On. L4G 7K1, Canada
Phone: (905) 726-2462
Website: www.magnaent.com
Chairman and Acting CEO: Frank Stronach
Employees: 5,300
Symbol, Exchange: MECA, NASDAQ
2007 Revenues: $625.7-million
2007 Net Loss: $113.8-million

MAXXAM Inc.

A highly diversified company that has stirred controversy with its past acquisitions, MAXXAM Inc. offers a range of products from lumber to live horse racing. MAXXAM owns Pacific Lumber, which owns more than 2,000 acres of commercial timberlands in Humboldt County, California. In addition, MAXXAM owns commercial and residential properties in several states and Puerto Rico. It purchased an interest in Kaiser Aluminum in 1988 and was the majority owner until the company emerged from bankruptcy in 2006. Its Sam Houston Race Park investment has been hurt in recent years by slot machines at Delta Downs in Louisiana, a short distance from the Texas border. Chairman Charles Hurwitz owns approximately 80% of the company, and his son Shawn became president and chief executive officer of the racetrack in 2007.

Headquarters: 1330 Post Oak Blvd., Suite 2000, Houston, Tx. 77056
Phone: (713) 975-7600
Chairman and CEO: Charles E. Hurwitz
President: Shawn Hurwitz
Employees: 925
Symbol, Exchange: MXM, American Stock Exchange
2007 Revenues: $95.9-million
2007 Net Loss: $46.9-million

MTR Gaming Group

Edson R. "Ted" Arneault thought he was simply helping a friend sell woebegone Mountaineer Park in 1992, but he ended up in the middle of a campaign to legalize video lottery terminals at West Virginia's racetracks. The effort succeeded, and Mountaineer became a hot property. MTR, of which Arneault owns approximately 13%, changed the name of the Chester facility to Mountaineer Race Track and Gaming Resort to emphasize that it has both racing and more than 3,000 slot machines. In 2002, MTR opened a hotel on the site and hosted its first graded race, the West Virginia Derby (G3). It owns Scioto Downs, a Standardbred track near Columbus, Ohio, and it opened a new racetrack, Presque Isle Downs near Erie, Pennsylvania, in September 2007. Presque Isle's slots casino opened in early 2007. Also in 2007, MTR won voter approval to operate table games at Mountaineer. It also owns Ramada Inn and Speedway Casino in North Las Vegas. Arneault was scheduled to step down at the end of 2008.

Headquarters: Rte. 2 S., Chester, W.V. 26034
Phone: (304) 387-5712
Website: www.mtrgaming.com
Chairman, President, and CEO: Edson R. "Ted" Arneault
Employees: 3,300
Symbol, Exchange: MNTG, NASDAQ
2007 Revenues: $429.9-million
2007 Net Loss: $11.4-million

Penn National Gaming

From relatively modest beginnings as the owner of a regional racetrack near Harrisburg, Pennsylvania, Penn National Gaming has grown into the nation's seventh-largest gaming company. Under Chairman and Chief Executive Officer Peter M. Carlino, son of the racetrack's principal owner, the company made profitable investments in off-track betting facilities in Central Pennsylvania, bought Pocono Downs and its off-track facilities, and then moved into gaming with its purchase of Charles Town Races in 1996. With extensive remodeling and slot machines, Charles Town has prospered and so has Penn National Gaming. It owns several casino properties and in early 2008 opened a new racetrack and casino on its Grantville, Pennsylvania, site. Because it cannot own two Pennsylvania gaming facilities, Penn National sold Pocono Downs and its five off-track wagering sites to the Mohegan Tribal Gaming Authority for $280-million in 2005. In 2007, Penn National purchased Zia Park and its Black Gold Casino in Hobbs, New Mexico, for $200-million. Penn National was to go private in a $6.1-billion transaction, but the deal collapsed in 2008.

Headquarters: 825 Berkshire Blvd., Suite 200, Wyomissing, Pa. 19610
Phone: (610) 373-2400
Website: www.pngaming.com
Chairman and CEO: Peter M. Carlino
Employees: 15,289

Symbol, Exchange: PENN, NASDAQ
2007 Revenues: $2.437-billion
2007 Net Profit: $160.1-million

Scientific Games Corp.

Autotote Corp., a leading provider of pari-mutuel equipment and services, acquired Scientific Games Holdings Corp. in September 2000, and the combined company took the name Scientific Games Corp. A. Lorne Weill, who had been chairman and chief executive officer of Autotote since 1992, took over those positions in the new company. Scientific Games is a leading provider of instant lottery tickets, and Autotote controlled approximately 65% of the racetrack pari-mutuel market through 2002. In late 2002, the company gained wide attention when an employee and two of his friends conspired to fix a winning ticket, worth $3-million, for the Breeders' Cup Ultra Pick Six at Arlington Park. The three quickly were indicted and sentenced for wire fraud, and Autotote took steps to improve security in its pari-mutuel operations, including centralized wagering facilities that opened in 2006. MacAndrews & Forbes Holdings, the investing vehicle of financier Ronald Perelman, owns nearly 30% of Scientific Games.

Headquarters: 750 Lexington Ave., 25th Floor, New York, N.Y. 10022
Phone: (212) 754-2233
Website: www.scientificgames.com
Chairman and CEO: A. Lorne Weill
Employees: 6,000
Symbol, Exchange: SGMS, NASDAQ
2007 Revenues: $1.047-billion
2007 Net Profit: $65.4-million

Youbet.com Inc.

After a rocky start, interactive wagering company Youbet.com became a major player in racetrack wagering over the Internet. A membership service with an Oregon wagering hub, Youbet.com offers wagering on races in most states as well as Canada, Australia, South Africa, and Hong Kong. Charles F. "Chuck" Champion became Youbet.com's president in 2002 and put in place operational and management changes that resulted in the company's first profit in '04, $4.6-million on revenues of $65.2-million. It posted a $5.7-million profit in 2005 but slid into the red again in '06, and the loss increased in '07. The company bought United Tote in 2006. Champion left the company in late 2007.

Headquarters: 5901 De Soto Ave., Woodland Hills, Ca. 91367
Phone: (818) 668-2100
Website: www.youbet.com
President and CEO: Michael Brodsky
Employees: 338
Symbol, Exchange: UBET, NASDAQ
2007 Revenues: $138.2-million
2007 Net Loss: $27.4-million

Racing Companies' 2007 Profit or Loss (in Millions of Dollars)

Company (Symbol)	Revenues	Profit (Loss)	Year-End Stock Price
Boyd Gaming Corp. (BYD)	$2,080.3	$303.0	$34.07
Canterbury Park Holding Corp. (ECP)	52.9	2.6	12.00
Churchill Downs Inc. (CHDN)	410.7	15.7	53.97
Macrovision (MVSN)	78.8	14.1	18.33
Magna Entertainment Corp. (MECA)	625.7	(113.8)	0.97
MAXXAM Inc. (MXM)	95.9	(46.9)	28.05
MTR Gaming Group Inc. (MNTG)	429.9	(11.4)	6.79
Penn National Gaming Inc. (PENN)	2,436.8	160.1	59.55
Scientific Games Corp. (SGMS)	1,046.7	65.4	33.25
Youbet.com Inc. (UBET)	138.2	(27.4)	1.12

Racetrack Stock Closing Prices by Year

Company (Symbol)	2007	2006	2005	2004	2003	2002
Boyd Gaming Corp. (BYD)	$34.07	$45.31	$47.66	$41.65	$16.14	$14.05
Canterbury Park Holding Corp. (ECP)	12.00	13.69	13.85	20.20	16.95	13.27
Churchill Downs Inc. (CHDN)	53.97	42.74	36.73	44.70	36.37	38.18
Macrovision (MVSN)	18.33	28.26	16.73	25.72	22.59	16.04
Magna Entertainment Corp. (MECA)	0.97	4.51	7.14	6.02	5.05	6.20
MAXXAM Inc. (MXM)	28.05	29.07	35.05	32.80	18.95	9.30
MTR Gaming Group Inc. (MTRG)	6.79	12.22	10.41	10.56	10.30	7.96
Penn National Gaming Inc. (PENN)	59.55	41.62	32.95	60.55	23.12	15.86
Scientific Games Corp. (SGMS)	33.25	30.23	27.28	23.84	16.97	7.26
Youbet.com Inc. (UBET)	1.12	3.69	4.73	5.06	2.51	0.77

INTERNATIONAL
Review of the 2007 Racing Season

International racing in 2007 featured an array of compelling story lines that involved several of the most accomplished racehorses in recent history and encompassed the emotional spectrum from elation to heartbreak. The spring and summer months saw Manduro emerge as a world-class performer on turf against elite competition, while autumn marked both the triumph of Dylan Thomas (Ire) at Longchamp and the death of George Washington (Ire) on an ill-fated journey to America.

Baron Georg von Ullmann's Manduro entered 2007 as a consistent and willing group stakes winner who seemed destined to fall just short of the top level. Prior to 2007, the five-year-old Monsun horse had tallied one Group 2 win and two Group 3 wins yet had failed to break through in six Group 1 contests. Trained by France's legendary Andre Fabre, Manduro opened 2007 with an authoritative score in the Weatherbys Earl of Sefton Stakes (Eng-G3) and then reeled off three consecutive Group 1 wins by open lengths in the Prix d'Ispahan (Fr-G1), Prince of Wales's Stakes (Eng-G1), and Prix du Haras de Fresnay-le-Buffard Jacques le Marois (Fr-G1).

There was little doubt among European racing observers heading into the fall that Manduro's maturation over the preceding months enhanced his chances to win the Prix de l'Arc de Triomphe Lucien Barriere (Fr-G1) in October. Fabre entered Manduro (Fr) in the Prix Foy Gray d'Albion Barriere (Fr-G2) at Longchamp on September 16 to prep for the Arc, and Manduro extended his unblemished 2007 racing record with a seemingly effortless, 2½-length win over champion filly Mandesha (Fr). Shortly afterward, however, Manduro's connections discovered a fracture to his right hind cannon bone, apparently sustained during the race.

Von Ullmann decided to retire Manduro, cutting short what was shaping up to be a campaign for the ages. Manduro was designated the world's top Thoroughbred for 2007 by the International Federation of Horseracing Authorities with a rating of 131 pounds in the Turf Intermediate category, the highest since the rankings were first published in 2004. He also received the greatest of compliments from Fabre, who appraised Manduro as the best horse he ever trained.

With Manduro's departure, the buildup to the Prix de l'Arc de Triomphe refocused on Dylan Thomas, who had won both the Budweiser Irish Derby (Ire-G1) and the Bailey's Irish Champion Stakes (Ire-G1) in 2006. The Danehill colt began 2007 with two victories, including a romp in the Prix Ganay (Fr-G1) at Longchamp, before being edged by Notnowcato in the Tattersalls Gold Cup (Ire-G1). Dylan Thomas subsequently raced in four straight Group 1 contests, finishing second to Manduro and Authorized in the Prince of Wales's and Juddmonte International Stakes (Eng-G1), respectively, and winning the King George VI and Queen Elizabeth Stakes (Eng-G1) and the Tattersalls Million Irish Champion Stakes (Ire-G1), the latter for the second consecutive year.

Ridden by embattled champion jockey Kieren Fallon in the Arc, Dylan Thomas settled in midpack as the field of 12 navigated through Longchamp's sweeping turn. Fallon guided his horse to the outside entering the straight, and Dylan Thomas surged to the front with 200 meters remaining before veering right to the rail for the finish. Under energetic handling from Fallon, Dylan Thomas held off fast-closing 80-to-1 longshot Youmzain by a head and survived a stewards' inquiry to capture the 86th running of the Arc, passing the $4-million mark in earnings for 2007 in the process.

For his achievements, Dylan Thomas received both the 2007 Horse of the Year and champion older horse honors from the Cartier Racing Awards.

The second act of two-time champion George Washington's racing career came to an abrupt and shocking end in the Breeders' Cup Classic Powered by Dodge (G1). The Danehill colt had been retired to stud at Coolmore following his three-year-old season in 2006, only to be brought back into training after he proved to be subfertile. George Washington made a promising return to racing with a close fourth-place finish to the excellent miler Ramonti in the Queen Anne Stakes (Eng-G1) at Ascot. He then finished third in the Coral Eclipse Stakes (Eng-G1) at Sandown.

After another third-place effort in the Qatar Prix du Moulin de Longchamp (Fr-G1), George Washington traveled to New Jersey for the Breeders' Cup Classic. It became evident midway through Monmouth Park's backstretch that the champion was laboring on the sloppy surface, and he broke down in midstretch after suffering an open fracture to his right front cannon bone and was euthanized.

The three-year-old division in Europe saw Cockney Rebel garner accolades during the spring with back-to-back classic wins in the Stan James Two Thousand Guineas (Eng-G1) and the Boylesports Irish Two Thousand Guineas (Ire-G1). After fading to fifth behind Excellent Art (GB) in the St. James's Palace Stakes (Eng-G1) at Royal Ascot, Cockney Rebel suffered a leg injury during a morning gallop in September and was retired to stud.

Saleh al Homeizi's and Imad al Saga's Authorized scored two of the most visually impressive wins of 2007 over a three-week span in the Totesport.com Dante Stakes (Eng-G2) and the Vodafone Epsom Derby (Eng-G1).

Authorized ran second to Notnowcato in the Coral Eclipse before turning the tables on that foe and besting Dylan Thomas as well in the Juddmonte International Stakes. Despite a lackluster performance in the Arc as the even-money favorite, Authorized's year-end tally of two Group 1 wins and more than $2.3-million in earnings was enough to earn him the Cartier Award as champion three-year-old male.

Unraced as a juvenile, Michael Tabor's and Susan Magnier's Peeping Fawn started three times during spring 2007 before winning at Naas in May, but she then improved dramatically by finishing third and second in the Boylesports Irish One Thousand Guineas (Ire-G1) and the Vodafone Oaks Stakes (Eng-G1), respectively. Remaining in Group 1 company, the daughter of Danehill would not lose again during the year as she took the Audi Pretty Polly Stakes (Ire-G1), the Darley Irish Oaks (Ire-G1), the Blue Square Nassau Stakes (Eng-G1), and the Darley Yorkshire Oaks (Eng-G1).

Among two-year-olds, New Approach received the Cartier Award for champion two-year-old male by going undefeated. In 2008, he won the Epsom Derby. Front-running Natagora prevailed in three group races, including the Skybet.com Cheveley Park Stakes (Eng-G1) in October, to earn champion two-year-old filly honors from the Cartier judges.

Japanese racing swiftly rebounded from Deep Impact's retirement at the end of 2006 on the strength of several memorable campaigns. Admire Moon amassed more than $7.1-million in earnings in 2007, winning the Dubai Duty Free (UAE-G1) at Nad al Sheba and the Takarazuka Kinen (Jpn-G1) and the Japan Cup (Jpn-G1) in his home country. Japanese fans also witnessed a historical achievement in May when Vodka captured the Tokyo Yushun (Japanese Derby), becoming the first filly to win the event in 64 years. Vodka was outperformed overall by Queen Elizabeth II Commemorative Cup (Jpn-G1) winner Daiwa Scarlet, who earned nearly $4-million in 2007 and received champion three-year-old filly honors from the Japan Racing Association.

Admire Moon's triumph in the Dubai Duty Free on March 31 followed wins by Kelly's Landing in the Gulf News Dubai Golden Shaheen (UAE-G1) and Vengeance Of Rain in the Nakheel Dubai Sheema Classic (UAE-G1) and served as a precursor to what was heralded as a showdown between fraternal rivals in the Emirates Airline Dubai World Cup (UAE-G1). Sheikh Mohammed bin Rashid al Maktoum's Godolphin sent 2006 Hill 'n' Dale Cigar Mile (G1) winner Discreet Cat to challenge Invasor (Arg) in the World Cup in an attempt to wrest the international spotlight from the Candy Stripes horse, North America's Horse of the Year in 2006.

The anticipated duel failed to materialize, however, as Discreet Cat never reached contention and finished a desultory last in the seven-horse field. Invasor, meanwhile, overcame a valiant effort by pacesetting Premium Tap to take command midway through Nad al Sheba's formidable stretch and score a 1¾-length victory in the world's richest race.—*Patrick Reed*

Richest International Races of 2007

Race (Grade)	Purse	Track, Location	Distance	Date	Winner	1st Purse
Emirates Airline Dubai World Cup (UAE-G1)	$6,000,000	Nad al Sheba, United Arab Emirates	9.94f	3/31	Invasor (Arg)	$3,600,000
Dubai Duty Free (UAE-G1)	5,010,320	Nad al Sheba, United Arab Emirates	8.83fT	3/31	=Admire Moon (Jpn)	3,006,192
Nakheel Dubai Sheema Classic (UAE-G1)	5,010,320	Nad al Sheba, United Arab Emirates	11.93fT	3/31	=Vengeance Of Rain (NZ)	3,006,192
Japan Cup (Jpn-G1)	4,407,406	Tokyo, Japan	11.93fT	11/25	=Admire Moon (Jpn)	2,314,815
Emirates Melbourne Cup (Aus-G1)	3,797,062	Flemington, Australia	15.91fT	11/6	=Efficient (NZ)	2,761,500
Arima Kinen Grand Prix (Jpn-G1)	3,000,000	Nakayama, Japan	12.43fT	12/23	=Matsurida Gogh (Jpn)	1,578,947
Prix de l'Arc de Triomphe Lucien Barriere (Fr-G1)	2,827,000	Longchamp, France	11.93fT	10/7	Dylan Thomas (Ire)	1,615,348
Tokyo Yushun (Japanese Derby) (Jpn-G1)	2,820,210	Tokyo, Japan	11.93fT	5/27	=Vodka (Jpn)	1,561,754
Cathay Pacific Hong Kong Cup (HK-G1)	2,566,000	Sha Tin, Hong Kong	9.94fT	12/9	=Ramonti (Fr)	1,462,620
Vodafone Epsom Derby (Eng-G1)	2,440,457	Epsom, England	12.05fT	6/2	=Authorized (Ire)	1,407,079
AAMI Golden Slipper S. (Aus-G1)	2,370,956	Rosehill, Australia	5.97fT	3/31	=Forensics (Aus)	1,618,400
Kikuka Sho (Japanese St. Leger)	2,365,967	Kyoto, Japan	14.91fT	10/21	=Asakusa Kings (Jpn)	1,331,221
Japan Cup Dirt (Jpn-G1)	2,296,296	Tokyo, Japan	10.44f	11/24	=Vermilion (Jpn)	1,203,704
Tattersall's Cox Plate (Aus-G1)	2,293,664	Moonee Valley, Australia	10.14fT	10/27	=El Segundo (NZ)	1,687,652
Tenno Sho (Autumn) (Jpn-G1)	2,203,509	Tokyo, Japan	9.94fT	10/28	=Meisho Samson (Jpn)	1,157,895
Tenno Sho (Spring) (Jpn-G1)	2,093,334	Kyoto, Japan	15.91fT	4/29	=Meisho Samson (Jpn)	1,100,000
Pattison Canadian International S. (Can-G1)	2,073,698	Woodbine, Canada	12.00fT	10/21	Cloudy's Knight	1,242,480
Cathay Pacific Hong Kong Mile (HK-G1)	2,052,800	Sha Tin, Hong Kong	7.95fT	12/9	Good Ba Ba	1,170,096
Prix du Jockey-Club Mitsubishi Motors (Fr-G1)	2,017,051	Chantilly, France	10.44fT	6/3	=Lawman (Fr)	1,152,542
Takarazuka Kinen (Jpn-G1)	2,009,600	Hanshin, Japan	10.94fT	6/24	=Admire Moon (Jpn)	1,056,000
Gulf News Dubai Golden Shaheen (UAE-G1)	2,000,000	Nad al Sheba, United Arab Emirates	5.97f	3/31	Kelly's Landing	1,200,000
S&M Al Naboodah Group UAE Derby (UAE-G2)	2,000,000	Nad al Sheba, United Arab Emirates	8.95f	3/31	=Asiatic Boy (Arg)	1,200,000
Parknasilla Hotel Goffs Million	1,992,641	The Curragh, Ireland	7.00fT	9/14	=Luck Money (Ire)	1,367,771
Parknasilla Hotel Goffs Fillies Million	1,992,641	The Curragh, Ireland	7.00fT	9/14	=Lush Lashes (GB)	1,367,771
Satsuki Sho	1,974,570	Nakayama, Japan	9.94fT	4/15	=Victory (Jpn)	1,111,254
Budweiser Irish Derby (Ire-G1)	1,938,889	The Curragh, Ireland	12.00fT	6/1	=Soldier of Fortune (Ire)	1,147,091
Yushun Himba (Japanese Oaks) (Jpn-G1)	1,891,228	Tokyo, Japan	11.93fT	5/20	Robe Decollete	1,057,177

International — Major International Races

Race (Grade)	Purse	Track	Distance	Date	Winner	1st Purse
BMW Caulfield Cup (Aus-G1)	$1,849,448	Caulfield, Australia	11.93fT	10/20	=Master O'Reilly (NZ)	$1,336,950
Singapore Airlines International Cup (Sin-G1)	1,818,180	Singapore, Malaysia	9.94fT	5/20	=Shadow Gate (Jpn)	1,041,768
Cathay Pacific Hong Kong Vase (HK-G1)	1,796,200	Sha Tin, Hong Kong	11.93fT	12/9	Doctor Dino (Fr)	1,023,834
Audemars Piguet Queen Elizabeth II Cup (HK-G1)	1,789,200	Sha Tin, Hong Kong	9.94fT	4/29	=Comic Strip (GB)	1,022,400
Oka Sho	1,753,723	Hanshin, Japan	7.95fT	4/8	=Daiwa Scarlet (Jpn)	982,571
Mile Championship (Jpn-G1)	1,711,711	Kyoto, Japan	7.95fT	11/18	=Daiwa Major (Jpn)	900,901
Emirates Doncaster H. (Aus-G1)	1,632,820	Randwick, Australia	7.95fT	4/9	=Haradasun (Aus)	1,109,624
Sprinters S. (Jpn-G1)	1,569,566	Nakayama, Japan	5.97fT	9/30	=Aston Machan (Jpn)	826,087
Yasuda Kinen (Jpn-G1)	1,557,377	Tokyo, Japan	7.95fT	6/3	=Daiwa Major (Jpn)	819,672
Queen Elizabeth II Commemorative Cup (Jpn-G1)	1,549,549	Kyoto, Japan	10.94fT	11/11	=Daiwa Scarlet (Jpn)	810,811
Cathay Pacific Hong Kong Sprint (HK-G1)	1,539,600	Sha Tin, Hong Kong	5.97fT	12/9	=Sacred Kingdom (Aus)	877,572
Takamatsunomiya Kinen (Jpn-G1)	1,529,661	Chukyo, Japan	5.97fT	3/25	=Suzuka Phoenix (Jpn)	805,085
King George VI and Queen Elizabeth S. (Eng-G1)	1,519,050	Ascot Racecourse, England	11.93fT	7/28	Dylan Thomas (Ire)	866,365

Progression of Richest International Race, 1980-2007

Purse	Race	Track	Country	Year	Winner	1st Purse
$6,000,000	Dubai World Cup (UAE-G1)	Nad al Sheba	U.A.E.	2000	Dubai Millennium	$3,600,000
5,000,000	Dubai World Cup (UAE-G1)	Nad al Sheba	U.A.E.	1999	Almutawakel (GB)	3,000,000
4,689,920	Breeders' Cup Classic (G1)	Churchill Downs	U.S.	1998	Awesome Again	2,662,400
4,030,400	Breeders' Cup Classic (G1)	Hollywood Park	U.S.	1997	Skip Away	2,288,000
4,000,000	Dubai World Cup	Nad al Sheba	U.A.E.	1996	Cigar	2,400,000
3,389,470	Japan Cup (Jpn-G1)	Tokyo	Japan	1994	Marvelous Crown	1,784,713
2,748,000	Breeders' Cup Classic (G1)	Churchill Downs	U.S.	1991	Black Tie Affair (Ire)	1,560,000
2,739,000	Breeders' Cup Classic (G1)	Hollywood Park	U.S.	1984	Wild Again	1,350,000
1,049,725	Hollywood Futurity (G1)	Hollywood Park	U.S.	1983	Fali Time	549,849
1,000,000	Arlington Million Invitational	Arlington Park	U.S.	1981	John Henry	600,000
641,093	Derby S. (Eng-G1)	Epsom	England	1980	Henbit	387,439

Major International Races
Canada
Breeders' Stakes
Not graded, Woodbine, three-year-olds, Canadian-foaled, 1½ miles, turf. Held August 5, 2007, with a gross value of $475,617. First held in 1889.

Year	Winner	Jockey	Second	Third	Strs	Time	1st Purse
2007	Marchfield	P. Husbands	Twilight Meteor	It's Like This	9	2:29.50	$284,460
2006	Royal Challenger	P. Husbands	French Beret	Shillelagh Slew	10	2:28.66	265,890
2005	Jambalaya	J. Jones	Area Limits	See the Wind	9	2:27.86	246,690
2004	A Bit O'Gold	J. Jones	Burst of Fire	Silver Ticket	11	2:27.15	300,000
2003	Wando	P. Husbands	Shoal Water	Colorful Judgement	8	2:28.69	300,000
2002	Portcullis	S. Callaghan	El Soprano	Mountain Beacon	10	2:29.80	300,000
2001	†Sweetest Thing	J. S. McAleney	Flaming Sky	†Asia	6	2:29.90	300,000
2000	Lodge Hill	M. E. Smith	Master Stuart	Scatter the Gold	7	2:28.97	300,000
1999	†Free Vacation	L. L. Gulas	John the Drummer	American Falcon	13	2:28.45	195,000
1998	†Pinafore Park	R. C. Landry	Patriot Love	Comet Kris	9	2:30.20	180,000
1997	John the Magician	S. R. Bahen	†One Emotion	†Heaven to Earth	12	2:35.60	175,860
1996	Chief Bearhart	M. Walls	Firm Dancer	Sealaunch	9	2:28.60	171,120
1995	Charlie's Dewan	C. Perret	Mt. Sassafras	Dagda	13	2:26.40	182,700
1994	Basqueian	J. M. Lauzon	Pagagar	Testalino	5	2:47.80	149,739
1993	Peteski	C. Perret	Flashy Regent	English Toff	4	2:30.40	237,549
1992	Blitzer	D. J. Seymour	†Classic Reign	Rodin	11	2:35.60	180,000

Held at Fort Erie 1994. †Denotes female.

E. P. Taylor Stakes
Grade 1, Woodbine, three-year-olds and up, fillies and mares, 1¼ miles, turf. Held October 21, 2007, with a gross value of $1,052,484. First held in 1956.

Year	Winner	Jockey	Second	Third	Strs	Time	1st Purse
2007	Mrs. Lindsay, 3	J. Murtagh	Sealy Hill, 3	Barancella (Fr), 6	10	2:00.68	$621,240
2006	Arravale, 4	J. Valdivia Jr.	Barancella (Fr), 5	Naissance Royale (Ire), 4	10	2:10.34	533,280
2005	Honey Ryder, 4	J. Velazquez	Latice (Ire), 4	Ambitious Cat, 4	12	2:06.70	504,960
2004	Commercante (Fr), 4	J. Velazquez	Punctilious (GB), 3	Classic Stamp, 4	8	2:04.02	450,000
2003	Volga (Ire), 5	R. Migliore	Tigertail, 4	Hi Dubai (GB), 3	10	2:05.68	450,000
2002	Fraulein (GB), 3	K. Darley	Alasha (Ire), 3	Volga (Ire), 4	6	2:10.03	450,000
2001	Choc Ice (Ire), 3	J. P. Murtagh	Volga (Ire), 3	Spring Oak (GB), 3	13	2:03.01	300,000
2000	Fly for Avie, 5	T. Kabel	Lady Upstage (Ire), 3	Innuendo (Ire), 5	6	2:02.78	300,000
1999	Insight (Fr), 4	M. E. Smith	Cerulean Sky (Ire), 3	Midnight Line, 4	7	2:05.34	300,000
1998	Zomaradah (GB), 3	G. L. Stevens	Tresoriere, 4	Griselda, 3	8	2:02.40	273,600
1997	Kool Kat Katie (Ire), 3	O. Peslier	Mousse Glacee (Fr), 3	L'Annee Folle (Fr), 4	9	2:02.00	206,460
1996	Wandering Star, 3	W. H. McCauley	Flame Valley, 3	Carling (Fr), 4	8	2:04.60	204,120
1995	Timarida (Ire), 3	L. Dettori	Matiara, 3	Bold Ruritana, 5	13	2:03.60	213,120
1994	Truly a Dream (Ire), 3	C. J. McCarron	Bold Ruritana, 4	Hero's Love, 6	9	2:01.60	207,180
1993	Hero's Love, 5	E. Fires	Dance for Donna, 4	Lady Shirl, 6	7	2:14.40	204,300
1992	Hatoof, 3	W. R. Swinburn	Urban Sea, 3	Hero's Love, 4	12	2:07.80	210,960

Pattison Canadian International Stakes

Grade 1, Woodbine, three-year-olds and up, 1½ miles, turf. Held October 21, 2007, with a gross value of $2,073,699. First held in 1938.

Year	Winner	Jockey	Second	Third	Strs	Time	1st Purse
2007	Cloudy's Knight, 7	R. Zimmerman	Ask (GB), 4	Quijano (Ger), 5	12	2:27.71	$1,242,480
2006	Collier Hill (GB), 8	D. McKeown	Go Deputy, 6	Sky Conqueror, 4	10	2:37.34	1,066,560
2005	Relaxed Gesture (Ire), 4	C. Nakatani	Meteor Storm (GB), 6	Electrocutionist, 4	10	2:32.64	1,009,920
2004	Sulamani (Ire), 5	L. Dettori	Simonas (Ire), 5	Brian Boru (GB), 4	10	2:28.64	900,000
2003	Phoenix Reach (Ire), 3	M. Dwyer	Macaw (Ire), 4	Brian Boru (GB), 3	10	2:33.62	900,000
2002	Ballingarry (Ire), 3	M. J. Kinane	Falcon Flight (Fr), 6	Yavana's Pace (Ire), 10	8	2:31.68	900,000
2001	Mutamam (GB), 6	R. Hills	Paolini (Ger), 4	Lodge Hill, 4	12	2:28.46	900,000
2000	Mutafaweq, 4	L. Dettori	Williams News, 5	Daliapour (Ire), 4	12	2:27.62	900,000
1999	Thornfield, 5	R. A. Dos Ramos	Fruits of Love, 4	Courteous (GB), 4	9	2:32.39	936,000
1998	Royal Anthem, 3	G. L. Stevens	Chief Bearhart, 5	Parade Ground, 3	8	2:29.60	630,000
1997	Chief Bearhart, 4	J. A. Santos	Down the Aisle, 4	Romanov (Ire), 3	6	2:29.00	600,000
1996	Singspiel (Ire), 4	G. L. Stevens	Chief Bearhart, 3	Mecke, 4	7	2:33.20	600,000
1995	Lassigny, 4	P. Day	Mecke, 3	Hasten To Add, 5	15	2:29.80	653,250
1994	Raintrap (GB), 4	R. G. Davis	†Alywow, 3	Volochine (Ire), 3	9	2:25.60	606,900
1993	Husband, 3	C. B. Asmussen	Cozzene's Prince, 6	Regency (GB), 3	11	2:36.40	623,100
1992	‡Snurge, 5	R. T. R. Quinn	Ghazi, 3	Wiorno (GB), 4	14	2:39.00	636,000

Rothmans Ltd. International S. 1992-'95. ‡Wiorno (GB) finished first, DQ to third, 1992. †Denotes female.

Prince of Wales Stakes

Not graded, Fort Erie, three-year-olds, Canadian-foaled, 1 3/16 miles, dirt. Held July 15, 2007, with a gross value of $476,850. First held in 1929.

Year	Winner	Jockey	Second	Third	Strs	Time	1st Purse
2007	Alezzandro	T. Kabel	Jiggs Coz	Daaher	6	1:55.04	$286,110
2006	Shillelagh Slew	D. Luciani	Pipers Thunder	Royal Challenger	8	1:55.87	265,800
2005	Ablo	G. Olguin	Autumn Snow	Wild Desert	6	1:56.90	245,760
2004	A Bit O'Gold	J. Jones	Niigon	His Smoothness	7	1:57.69	300,000
2003	Wando	P. Husbands	Arco's Gold	Shoal Water	7	1:55.84	300,000
2002	Le Cinquieme Essai	B. T. Bochinski	Bravely	Anglian Prince	12	1:56.53	300,000
2001	Win City	C. Montpellier	†Dancethruthedawn	Brushing Bully	6	1:56.14	210,000
2000	Scatter the Gold	T. Kabel	For Our Sake	Cool N Collective	7	1:56.01	170,280
1999	†Gandria	C. Montpellier	Woodcarver	Euchre	6	1:56.23	155,700
1998	Archers Bay	R. C. Landry	Nite Dreamer	One Way Love	6	1:55.20	118,500
1997	Cryptocloser	W. Martinez	C. C. On Ice	Rabbit in a Hat	6	1:56.00	117,660
1996	Stephanotis	M. Walls	Firm Dancer	Kristy Krunch	6	1:55.20	121,620
1995	Kiridashi	L. Attard	Regal Discovery	Mt. Sassafras	6	1:55.00	121,800
1994	Bruce's Mill	C. Perret	Basqueian	Parental Pressure	4	1:53.20	87,296
1993	Peteski	D. Penna	Flashy Regent	Cheery Knight	8	1:54.40	72,203
1992	Benburb	L. Attard	Alydeed	Judge Carson	6	1:57.40	107,700

†Denotes female.

Queen's Plate Stakes

Not graded, Woodbine, three-year-olds, Canadian-foaled, 1¼ miles, Polytrack. Held June 24, 2007, with a gross value of $936,022. First held in 1860.

Year	Winner	Jockey	Second	Third	Strs	Time	1st Purse
2007	Mike Fox	E. Wilson	Alezzandro	Jiggs Coz	8	2:05.45	$560,940
2006	Edenwold	E. Ramsammy	Sterwins	Malakoff	13	2:05.30	534,000
2005	Wild Desert	P. Valenzuela	King of Jazz	Gold Strike	9	2:07.37	486,840
2004	Niigon	R. Landry	A Bit O'Gold	Will He Crow	13	2:04.72	600,000
2003	Wando	P. Husbands	Mobil	Rock Again	12	2:02.48	600,000
2002	T J's Lucky Moon	S. R. Bahen	Anglian Prince	Forever Grand	13	2:06.88	600,000
2001	†Dancethruthedawn	G. Boulanger	Win City	Brushing Bully	10	2:03.78	600,000
2000	Scatter the Gold	T. Kabel	I and I	For Our Sake	16	2:05.53	600,000
1999	Woodcarver	M. Walls	†Gandria	Euchre	17	2:03.13	300,000
1998	Archers Bay	K. J. Desormeaux	Brite Adam	Kinkennie	13	2:02.20	300,000
1997	Awesome Again	M. E. Smith	Cryptocloser	Sovereign Storm	14	2:04.20	255,420
1996	Victor Cooley	E. Ramsammy	Stephanotis	Kristy Krunch	13	2:03.80	255,480
1995	Regal Discovery	T. Kabel	Freedom Fleet	Mt. Sassafras	14	2:03.80	261,660
1994	Basqueian	J. M. Lauzon	Bruce's Mill	Parental Pressure	11	2:03.40	276,420
1993	Peteski	C. Perret	Cheery Knight	Janraffole	11	2:04.20	218,600
1992	Alydeed	C. Perret	Grand Hooley	Benburb	12	2:04.60	228,900

†Denotes female.

Woodbine Mile Stakes

Grade 1, Woodbine, three-year-olds and up, 1 mile, turf. Held September 16, 2007, with a gross value of $973,893 (previously Atto Mile Stakes). First held in 1997.

Year	Winner	Jockey	Second	Third	Strs	Time	1st Purse
2007	Shakespeare, 6	G. Gomez	Kip Deville, 4	Galantas, 4	14	1:33.58	$582,240
2006	Becrux, 4	P. Valenzuela	Rebel Rebel (Ire), 5	Ad Valorem, 4	13	1:33.99	536,160
2005	Leroidesanimaux (Brz), 5	J. Velazquez	Mobil, 5	Le Cinquieme Essai, 6	9	1:35.08	509,040

Year	Winner	Jockey	Second	Third	Strs	Time	1st Purse
2004	Soaring Free, 5	T. Kabel	Perfect Soul (Ire), 6	Royal Regalia, 6	11	1:32.72	$600,000
2003	Touch of the Blues (Fr), 6	K. J. Desormeaux	Soaring Free, 4	Perfect Soul (Ire), 5	11	1:33.39	600,000
2002	Good Journey, 6	P. Day	†Chopinina, 4	Nuclear Debate, 7	13	1:33.27	600,000
2001	Numerous Times, 4	P. Husbands	Affirmed Success, 7	Quiet Resolve, 6	14	1:32.79	600,000
2000	Riviera (Fr), 6	J. R. Velazquez	Arkadian Hero, 5	Affirmed Success, 6	13	1:33.18	600,000
1999	‡Quiet Resolve, 4	R. C. Landry	Rob 'n Gin, 5	Jim and Tonic (Fr), 5	15	1:33.19	630,000
1998	Labeeb (GB), 6	K. J. Desormeaux	Jim and Tonic (Fr), 4	Poteen, 4	11	1:33.00	450,000
1997	Geri, 5	C. W. Antley	Helmsman, 5	Crown Attorney, 4	12	1:36.20	300,000

‡Woodbine Mile S. 1997-'98. Hawksley Hill (Ire) finished first, DQ to fourth, 1999. †Denotes female.

England
Gold Cup

Group 1, Royal Ascot Racecourse, four-year-olds and up, about 2½ miles, turf. Held June 21, 2007, with a gross value of $441,746. First held in 1807.

Year	Winner	Jockey	Second	Third	Strs	Time	1st Purse
2007	Yeats, 6	M. Kinane	Geordieland, 6	Le Miracle, 6	14	4:20.70	$254,692
2006	Yeats, 5	K. Fallon	Reefscape, 5	Distinction, 7	12	4:20.40	252,678
2005	Westerner, 6	O. Peslier	Distinction, 6	Vinnie Roe, 7	17	4:19.49	237,693
2004	Papineau, 4	L. Dettori	Westerner, 5	Darasim, 6	13	4:20.90	256,905
2003	Mr Dinos, 4	K. Fallon	Persian Punch, 10	Pole Star, 5	12	4:20.15	233,581
2002	Royal Rebel, 6	J. P. Murtagh	Vinnie Roe, 4	Wareed, 4	15	4:25.64	199,184
2001	Royal Rebel, 5	J. P. Murtagh	Persian Punch, 8	Jardines Lookout, 4	12	4:18.90	172,432
2000	Kayf Tara, 6	M. J. Kinane	Far Cry, 5	Compton Ace, 4	11	4:24.53	184,308
1999	Enzeli, 4	J. P. Murtagh	Invermark, 5	Kayf Tara, 5	17	4:18.85	191,662
1998	Kayf Tara, 4	L. Dettori	Double Trigger, 7	Three Cheers, 4	16	4:32.36	198,132
1997	Celeric, 5	P. Eddery	Classic Cliche, 5	Election Day, 5	13	4:26.19	187,197
1996	Classic Cliche, 4	M. J. Kinane	Double Trigger, 5	Nononito, 5	7	4:23.20	182,980
1995	Double Trigger, 4	J. Weaver	Moonax, 4	Admiral's Well, 5	7	4:20.25	178,465
1994	Arcadian Heights, 6	M. Hills	Vintage Crop, 7	Sonus, 5	9	4:27.67	169,666
1993	Drum Taps, 7	L. Dettori	Assessor, 4	Turgeon, 7	10	4:32.57	166,410
1992	Drum Taps, 6	L. Dettori	Arcadian Heights, 4	Turgeon, 6		4:18.20	198,590

King George VI and Queen Elizabeth Stakes

Group 1, Ascot Racecourse, three-year-olds and up, about 1½ miles, turf. Held July 28, 2007, with a gross value of $1,519,050. First held in 1951.

Year	Winner	Jockey	Second	Third	Strs	Time	1st Purse
2007	Dylan Thomas (Ire), 4	J. Murtagh	Youmzain, 4	Maraahel, 6	7	2:31.10	$862,517
2006	Hurricane Run (Ire), 4	C. Soumillon	Electrocutionist, 5	Heart's Cry, 5	6	2:30.20	793,359
2005	Azamour (Ire), 4	M. Kinane	Norse Dancer, 5	Bago (Fr), 4	12	2:28.06	709,115
2004	Doyen, 4	L. Dettori	Hard Buck (Brz), 5	Sulamani (Ire), 5	11	2:33.18	797,094
2003	Alamshar, 3	J. P. Murtagh	Sulamani (Ire), 4	Kris Kin, 3	12	2:33.26	700,742
2002	Golan (Ire), 4	K. Fallon	Nayef, 4	Zindabad (Fr), 6	9	2:29.70	636,448
2001	Galileo (Ire), 3	M. J. Kinane	Fantastic Light, 5	Hightori, 4	12	2:27.71	619,745
2000	Montjeu (Ire), 4	M. J. Kinane	Fantastic Light, 4	Daliapour (Ire), 4	7	2:29.98	654,023
1999	Daylami (Ire), 5	L. Dettori	Nedawi, 4	Fruits of Love, 4	8	2:29.35	539,676
1998	Swain (Ire), 6	L. Dettori	High-Rise (Ire), 3	Royal Anthem, 3	8	2:29.60	587,463
1997	Swain (Ire), 5	J. A. Reid	Pilsudski (Ire), 5	Helissio, 4	8	2:36.45	490,509
1996	Pentire, 4	M. Hills	Classic Cliche, 4	Shaamit, 3	8	2:28.11	457,867
1995	Lammtarra, 3	L. Dettori	Pentire, 3	Strategic Choice, 4	7	2:31.01	445,877
1994	King's Theatre (Ire), 3	M. J. Kinane	White Muzzle (GB), 4	Wagon Master, 4	12	2:28.92	408,813
1993	Opera House (GB), 5	M. Roberts	White Muzzle (GB), 3	Commander in Chief, 3	10	2:33.94	409,307
1992	St. Jovite, 3	S. Craine	Saddlers' Hall (Ire), 4	Opera House (GB), 4	8	2:30.85	497,878

Ladbrokes St. Leger Stakes

Group 1, York Racecourse, three-year-olds, 1¾ miles and 132 yards, turf. Held September 15, 2007, with a gross value of $1,057,813. First held in 1776.

Year	Winner	Jockey	Second	Third	Strs	Time	1st Purse
2007	Lucarno	J. Fortune	Mahler	Honolulu	10	3:01.90	$609,897
2006	Sixties Icon	L. Dettori	The Last Drop	Red Rocks (Ire)	11	2:57.20	503,216
2005	Scorpion	L. Dettori	The Geezer	Tawqeet	6	3:19.01	480,083
2004	Rule of Law	K. McEvoy	†Quiff (GB)	Tycoon (GB)	9	3:06.29	431,136
2003	Brian Boru (GB)	J. P. Spencer	High Accolade	Phoenix Reach (Ire)	12	3:04.64	386,040
2002	Bollin Eric	K. Darley	Highest	Bandari	8	3:02.92	374,640
2001	Milan (GB)	M. J. Kinane	Demophilos	Mr Combustible	10	3:05.10	326,629
2000	Millenary	T. R. Quinn	Air Marshall	Chimes At Midnight	11	3:02.58	315,018
1999	Mutafaweq	R. Hills	†Ramruma	Adair	9	3:02.75	353,664
1998	Nedawi	J. A. Reid	†High and Low	Sunshine Street	9	3:05.61	335,898
1997	Silver Patriarch	P. Eddery	Vertical Speed	The Fly (GB)	10	3:06.92	295,420
1996	Shantou	L. Dettori	Dushyantor	Samraan	9	3:05.10	271,692
1995	Classic Cliche	L. Dettori	Minds Music	Istidaad	10	3:09.74	259,794

International — Major International Races 927

Year	Winner	Jockey	Second	Third	Strs	Time	1st Purse
1994	Moonax	P. Eddery	Broadway Flyer	Double Trigger	8	3:04.19	$236,950
1993	Bob's Return	P. Robinson	Armiger	Edbaysaan	9	3:07.85	292,567
1992	†User Friendly (GB)	G. Duffield	Sonus	Bonny Scot	7	3:05.48	323,139

†Denotes female.

Stanjamesuk.com One Thousand Guineas

Group 1, Newmarket, three-year-old fillies, 1 mile, turf. Held May 4, 2008, with a gross value of $739,988. First held in 1814.

Year	Winner	Jockey	Second	Third	Strs	Time	1st Purse
2008	Natagora	C. Lemaire	Spacious	Saoirse Abu	15	1:38.99	$421,978
2007	Finsceal Beo	K. Manning	Arch Swing	Simply Perfect	21	1:34.90	396,109
2006	Speciosa	M. Fenton	Confidential Lady	Nasheej	9	1:40.53	384,235
2005	Virginia Waters	K. Fallon	Maids Causeway	Vista Bella	20	1:36.50	378,865
2004	Attraction	K. Darley	Sundrop (Jpn)	Hathrah (Ire)	16	1:36.78	347,265
2003	Russian Rhythm	K. Fallon	Six Perfections (Fr)	Intercontinental (GB)	19	1:38.43	292,747
2002	Kazzia (Ger)	L. Dettori	Snowfire (GB)	Alasha	17	1:37.85	250,612
2001	Ameerat (GB)	P. Robinson	Muwakleh (GB)	Toroca	15	1:38.30	250,473
2000	Lahan (GB)	R. Hills	Princess Ellen (GB)	Petrushka (Ire)	18	1:36.38	221,517
1999	Wince	K. Fallon	Wannabe Grand (Ire)	Valentine Waltz (Ire)	22	1:37.91	206,757
1998	Cape Verdi (Ire)	L. Dettori	Shahtoush (Ire)	Exclusive	16	1:37.86	214,081
1997	Sleepytime (Ire)	K. Fallon	Oh Nellie	Dazzle	15	1:37.66	169,872
1996	Bosra Sham	P. Eddery	Matiya (Ire)	Bint Shadayid	13	1:37.75	151,461
1995	Harayir	R. Hills	Aqaarid	Moonshell (Ire)	14	1:36.72	178,983
1994	Las Meninas (Ire)	J. A. Reid	Balanchine	Coup de Genie	15	1:36.71	166,127
1993	Sayyedati (GB)	W. R. Swinburn	Niche	Ajfan	12	1:37.34	163,969
1992	Hatoof	W. R. Swinburn	Marling (Ire)	Kenbu (Fr)	14	1:39.45	192,254

Stanjamesuk.com Two Thousand Guineas

Group 1, Newmarket, three-year-olds, 1 mile, turf. Held May 3, 2008, with a gross value of $728,671. First held in 1809.

Year	Winner	Jockey	Second	Third	Strs	Time	1st Purse
2008	Henrythenavigator	J. Murtagh	New Approach	Stubbs Art	15	1:39.14	$420,092
2007	Cockney Rebel	O. Peslier	Vital Equine	Dutch Art	24	1:35.20	421,267
2006	George Washington	K. Fallon	Sir Percy	Olympian Odyssey	14	1:36.86	348,235
2005	Footstepsinthesand	K. Fallon	Rebel Rebel	Kandidate	19	1:36.10	353,976
2004	Haafhd	R. Hills	Snow Ridge	Azamour	14	1:36.74	322,787
2003	Refuse To Bend (Ire)	P. J. Smullen	Zafeen	Norse Dancer	20	1:37.98	292,747
2002	Rock of Gibraltar (Ire)	J. P. Murtagh	Hawk Wing	Redback	22	1:36.50	250,612
2001	Golan (Ire)	K. Fallon	Tamburlaine (Ire)	Frenchmans Bay	18	1:37.40	250,473
2000	King's Best	K. Fallon	Giant's Causeway	Barathea Guest	27	1:37.77	265,820
1999	Island Sands	L. Dettori	Enrique	Mujahid	16	1:37.14	276,426
1998	King of Kings (Ire)	M. J. Kinane	Lend a Hand (GB)	Border Arrow	18	1:39.25	286,219
1997	Entrepreneur	M. J. Kinane	Revoque	Poteen	16	1:35.64	213,832
1996	Mark of Esteem (Ire)	L. Dettori	Even Top (Ire)	Bijou d'Inde	13	1:37.59	184,212
1995	Pennekamp	T. Jarnet	Celtic Swing	Bahri	11	1:35.16	190,487
1994	Mister Baileys (GB)	J. Weaver	Grand Lodge	Colonel Collins	23	1:35.08	194,491
1993	Zafonic	P. Eddery	Barathea (Ire)	Bin Ajwaad	14	1:35.32	173,569
1992	Rodrigo de Triano	L. Piggott	Lucky Lindy	Pursuit of Love	16	1:38.37	203,189

Vodafone Derby Stakes

Group 1, Epsom, three-year-olds, 1½ miles and 10 yards, turf. Held June 7, 2008, with a gross value of $2,462,500. First held in 1780.

Year	Winner	Jockey	Second	Third	Strs	Time	1st Purse
2008	New Approach	K. Manning	Tartan Bearer	Casual Conquest	16	2:36.50	$1,580,813
2007	Authorized	L. Dettori	Eagle Mountain	Aqaleem	17	2:34.70	1,407,079
2006	Sir Percy	M. Dwyer	Dragon Dancer	Dylan Thomas	18	2:35.23	1,395,247
2005	Motivator	J. P. Murtagh	Walk In The Park	Dubawi	13	2:35.60	1,314,425
2004	North Light	K. Fallon	Rule of Law	Let The Lion Roar (GB)	14	2:33.72	1,491,719
2003	Kris Kin	K. Fallon	The Great Gatsby	Alamshar	20	2:33.35	1,373,453
2002	High Chaparral (Ire)	J. P. Murtagh	Hawk Wing	Moon Ballad (Ire)	12	2:39.45	1,249,424
2001	Galileo (Ire)	M. J. Kinane	Golan (Ire)	Tobougg (Ire)	12	2:33.20	800,342
2000	Sinndar	J. P. Murtagh	Sakhee	Beat Hollow (GB)	15	2:36.75	918,981
1999	Oath	K. Fallon	Daliapour (Ire)	Beat All	16	2:37.43	990,671
1998	High-Rise (Ire)	O. Peslier	City Honours	Border Arrow	15	2:33.88	978,679
1997	Benny the Dip	W. Ryan	Silver Patriarch	Romanov (Ire)	13	2:34.77	971,448
1996	Shaamit	M. Hills	Dushyantor	Shantou	20	2:35.05	804,894
1995	Lammtarra	W. R. Swinburn	Tamure (Ire)	Presenting	15	2:32.31	805,687
1994	Erhaab	W. Carson	King's Theatre (Ire)	Colonel Collins	25	2:34.16	717,662
1993	Commander in Chief	M. J. Kinane	Blue Judge	Blues Traveller (Ire)	16	2:34.51	693,078
1992	Dr Devious (Ire)	J. A. Reid	St. Jovite	Silver Wisp	18	2:36.19	649,473

Vodafone Oaks Stakes

Group 1, Epsom, three-year-old fillies, 1½ miles and 10 yards, turf. Held June 6, 2008, with a gross value of $685,685. First held in 1779.

Year	Winner	Jockey	Second	Third	Strs	Time	1st Purse
2008	Look Here	S. Sanders	Moonstone	Katiyra	16	2:36.89	$407,724

Year	Winner	Jockey	Second	Third	Strs	Time	1st Purse
2007	Light Shift	T. Durcan	Peeping Fawn	All My Loving	14	2:40.30	$440,275
2006	Alexandrova	K. Fallon	Rising Cross	Short Skirt	10	2:37.71	467,244
2005	Eswarah	R. Hills	Something Exciting	Pictavia	12	2:39.00	403,971
2004	Ouija Board (GB)	K. Fallon	All Too Beautiful	Punctilious	7	2:35.41	376,585
2003	Casual Look	M. Dwyer	Yesterday (Ire)	Summitville	15	2:38.07	387,744
2002	Kazzia (Ger)	L. Dettori	Quarter Moon (Ire)	Shadow Dancing	14	2:44.52	297,009
2001	Imagine	M. J. Kinane	Flight of Fancy	Relish The Thought (Ire)	14	2:36.70	292,125
2000	Love Divine	T. R. Quinn	Kalypso Katie (Ire)	Melikah (Ire)	16	2:43.11	288,823
1999	Ramruma	K. Fallon	Noushkey	Zahrat Dubai (GB)	10	2:38.72	286,775
1998	Shahtoush (Ire)	M. J. Kinane	Bahr (GB)	Midnight Line	8	2:38.23	289,342
1997	Reams of Verse	K. Fallon	Gazelle Royale	Crown of Light	12	2:35.59	297,432
1996	Lady Carla (GB)	P. Eddery	Pricket	Mezzogiorno	11	2:35.55	309,279
1995	Moonshell (Ire)	L. Dettori	Dance a Dream (GB)	Pure Grain (GB)	10	2:35.44	236,037
1994	Balanchine	L. Dettori	Wind in Her Hair (Ire)	Hawajiss	10	2:40.37	223,758
1993	Intrepidity (GB)	M. Roberts	Royal Ballerina (Ire)	Oakmead (Ire)	14	2:34.19	228,404
1992	User Friendly (GB)	G. Duffield	All At Sea	Pearl Angel (GB)	7	2:39.77	269,851

France

Poule d'Essai des Poulains (French Two Thousand Guineas)

Group 1, Longchamp, three-year-olds, colts, 1,600 meters (7.9536 furlongs), turf. Held on May 11, 2008, with a gross value of $619,320. First run in 1883.

Year	Winner	Jockey	Second	Third	Strs	Time	1st Purse
2008	Falco	O. Peslier	Rio de La Plata	River Proud	19	1:35.60	$353,879
2007	Astronomer Royal	C. O'Donoghue	Creachadoir	Honoured Guest	14	1:37.10	309,265
2006	Aussie Rules	K. Fallon	Marcus Adronicus	Stormy River	11	1:37.00	295,505
2005	Shamardal	L. Dettori	Indesatchel	Gharir	15	1:39.20	288,511
2004	American Post	R. Hughes	Diamond Green (Fr)	Byron	7	1:36.50	247,048
2003	Clodovil	C. Soumillon	Catcher In The Rye	Krataios	10	1:36.40	217,809
2002	‡Landseer (GB)	M. J. Kinane	Medecis (GB)	Bowman	13	1:36.80	176,111
2001	Vahorimix	C. Soumillon	Clearing	Denon	12	1:35.40	133,600
2000	Bachir	L. Dettori	Berine's Son	Valentino	7	1:39.40	140,100
1999	Sendawar	G. Mosse	Dansili (GB)	Kingsalsa	15	1:36.20	162,660
1998	Victory Note	J. A. Reid	Muhtathir (GB)	Desert Prince (Ire)	12	1:34.50	168,500
1997	Daylami (Ire)	G. Mosse	Loup Sauvage	Visionary (Fr)	6	1:42.60	175,700
1996	Ashkalani	G. Mosse	Spinning World	Tagula	10	1:37.60	193,200
1995	Vettori	L. Dettori	Atticus	Petit Poucet (GB)	8	1:40.40	210,920
1994	Green Tune	O. Doleuze	Turtle Island	Psychobabble (Ire)	7	1:37.40	177,230
1993	Kingmambo	C. B. Asmussen	Bin Ajwaad	Hudo	10	1:39.10	187,740
1992	Shanghai	F. Head	Rainbow Corner (GB)	Lion Cavern	9	1:38.20	180,800

‡Noverre finished first, DQ to 12th, 2002.

Poule d'Essai des Pouliches (French One Thousand Guineas)

Group 1, Longchamp, three-year-old fillies, 1,600 meters (7.9536 furlongs), turf. Held on May 11, 2008, with a gross value of $619,320. First held in 1883.

Year	Winner	Jockey	Second	Third	Strs	Time	1st Purse
2008	Zarkava	C. Soumillon	Goldikova	Halfway To Heaven	14	1:35.20	$353,879
2007	Darjina	C. Soumillon	Finsceal Beo	Rahiyah	13	1:37.20	309,265
2006	Tie Black	J. Eyquem	Impressionnante	Price Tag	13	1:36.60	295,505
2005	Divine Proportions	C. Lemaire	Toupie	Ysoldina	8	1:38.50	288,511
2004	Torrestrella (Ire)	O. Peslier	Grey Lilas	Miss Mambo	13	1:35.70	247,048
2003	Musical Chimes	C. Soumillon	Maiden Tower (GB)	Etoile Montante	12	1:36.00	217,809
2002	Zenda (GB)	R. Hughes	Firth of Lorne (Ire)	Sophisticat	17	1:37.30	176,111
2001	Rose Gypsy (GB)	M. J. Kinane	Banks Hill (GB)	Lethals Lady (GB)	15	1:36.70	133,600
2000	Bluemamba	T. Jarnet	Peony	Alshakr	11	1:40.20	140,100
1999	Valentine Waltz (Ire)	R. Cochrane	Karmifira (Fr)	Calando	14	1:36.00	162,660
1998	Zalaiyka	G. Mosse	Cortona	La Nuit Rose	14	1:35.70	168,500
1997	Always Loyal	F. Head	Seebe	Red Camellia	7	1:40.20	175,700
1996	Ta Rib	W. Carson	Shake the Yoke (GB)	Sagar Pride (Ire)	9	1:38.70	193,200
1995	Matiara	F. Head	Carling (Fr)	Shaanxi	16	1:42.40	210,920
1994	East of the Moon	C. B. Asmussen	Agathe	Belle Argentine	8	1:37.10	177,230
1993	Madeleine's Dream	C. B. Asmussen	Ski Paradise	Gold Splash	8	1:36.40	187,740
1992	Culture Vulture	T. R. Quinn	Hydro Calido	Guislaine (Fr)	9	1:37.00	180,800

Prix de Diane (French Oaks)

Group 1, Chantilly, three-year-olds, fillies, 2,100 meters (10.439 furlongs), turf. Held June 8, 2008, with a gross value of $1,261,520. First held in 1843.

Year	Winner	Jockey	Second	Third	Strs	Time	1st Purse
2008	Zarkava	C. Soumillon	Gagnoa	Goldikova	13	2:07.10	$720,833
2007	West Wind	L. Dettori	Mrs. Lindsay	Diyakalanie	14	2:06.30	611,124
2006	Confidential Lady	S. Sanders	Germance	Queen Cleopatra	16	2:05.90	577,891
2005	Divine Proportions	C. Lemaire	Argentina	Paita	10	2:06.30	554,121

International — Major International Races

Year	Winner	Jockey	Second	Third	Strs	Time	1st Purse
2004	Latice (Ire)	C. Soumillon	Millionaia	Grey Lilas	17	2:07.00	$352,925
2003	Nebraska Tornado	R. Hughes	Time Ahead	Musical Chimes	10	2:08.10	320,955
2002	Bright Sky (Ire)	D. Boeuf	Dance Routine	Ana Marie	15	2:07.60	260,302
2001	Aquarelliste	D. Boeuf	Nadia (GB)	Time Away	12	2:09.50	220,490
2000	Egyptband	O. Doleuze	Volvoreta (GB)	Goldamix (Ire)	14	2:08.50	203,420
1999	Daryaba	G. Mosse	Star of Akkar	Visionnaire (Fr)	14	2:16.10	224,700
1998	Zainta	G. Mosse	Abbatiale	Insight (Fr)	11	2:11.20	235,340
1997	Vereva	G. Mosse	Mousse Glacee (Fr)	Brilliance (Fr)	12	2:08.20	240,520
1996	Sil Sila	C. B. Asmussen	Miss Tahiti	Matiya (Ire)	12	2:07.30	269,080
1995	Carling (Fr)	T. Thulliez	Matiara	Tryphosa	12	2:07.70	282,240
1994	East of the Moon	C. B. Asmussen	Her Ladyship	Agathe	9	2:07.90	248,850
1993	Shemaka	G. Mosse	Baya	Dancienne (Fr)	14	2:16.00	260,582
1992	Jolypha	P. Eddery	Sheba Dancer (Fr)	Verveine	12	2:09.50	259,770

Prix de l'Arc de Triomphe Lucien Barriere

Group 1, Longchamp, three-year-olds and up, 2,400 meters (11.9303 furlongs), turf. Held October 7, 2007, with a gross value of $2,827,000. First held in 1920.

Year	Winner	Jockey	Second	Third	Strs	Time	1st Purse
2007	Dylan Thomas (Ire), 4	K. Fallon	Youmzain, 4	Sagara, 3	12	2:28.50	$1,615,348
2006	Rail Link, 3	S. Pasquier	Pride, 6	Hurricane Run (Ire), 4	8	2:26.30	1,449,185
2005	Hurricane Run (Ire), 3	K. Fallon	Westerner, 6	Bago (Fr), 4	15	2:27.40	1,236,384
2004	Bago (Fr), 3	T. Gillet	Cherry Mix (Fr), 3	†Ouija Board (GB), 3	19	2:25.00	1,134,755
2003	Dalakhani, 3	C. Soumillon	Mubtaker, 6	High Chaparral (Ire), 4	13	2:32.30	1,002,738
2002	Marienbard, 5	L. Dettori	Sulamani (Ire), 3	High Chaparral (Ire), 3	16	2:26.70	899,704
2001	Sakhee, 4	L. Dettori	†Aquarelliste, 3	Sagacity, 3	17	2:36.10	840,000
2000	Sinndar, 3	J. P. Murtagh	†Egyptband, 3	†Volvoreta (GB), 3	10	2:25.80	806,400
1999	Montjeu (Ire), 3	M. J. Kinane	El Condor Pasa, 4	Croco Rouge, 4	14	2:38.50	654,000
1998	Sagamix, 3	O. Peslier	†Leggera (Ire), 3	Tiger Hill, 3	14	2:34.50	724,000
1997	Peintre Celebre, 3	O. Peslier	Pilsudski (Ire), 5	†Borgia (Ger), 3	18	2:24.60	677,600
1996	Helissio, 3	O. Peslier	Pilsudski (Ire), 4	Oscar Schindler, 4	16	2:29.90	771,600
1995	Lammtarra, 3	L. Dettori	Freedom Cry (GB), 4	Swain (Ire), 3	16	2:31.80	811,600
1994	Carnegie (Ire), 3	T. Jarnet	Hernando (Fr), 4	Apple Tree (Fr), 5	20	2:31.10	754,440
1993	†Urban Sea, 4	E. Saint-Martin	White Muzzle (GB), 3	Opera House (GB), 5	23	2:37.90	879,050
1992	Subotica (Fr), 4	T. Jarnet	User Friendly (GB), 3	Vert Amande, 4	18	2:39.00	1,039,500

†Denotes female.

Prix du Jockey-Club (French Derby)

Group 1, Chantilly, three-year-olds, 2,100 meters (10.44 furlongs), turf. Held June 1, 2008, with a gross value of $2,333,550. First held in 1836.

Year	Winner	Jockey	Second	Third	Strs	Time	1st Purse
2008	Vision d'Etat	I. Mendizabal	Famous Name	Natagora	20	2:08.60	$1,333,390
2007	Lawman	L. Dettori	Literato	Shamdinan	20	2:05.90	1,152,542
2006	Darsi	C. Soumillon	Best Name	Arras	15	2:05.80	1,107,630
2005	Shamardal	L. Dettori	Hurricane Run	Rocamadour	17	2:09.00	1,047,805
2004	Blue Canari	T. Thulliez	Prospect Park	Valixir	15	2:25.20	776,435
2003	Dalakhani	C. Soumillon	Super Celebre	Coroner	7	2:26.70	706,102
2002	Sulamani (Ire)	T. Thulliez	Act One	Simeon (GB)	15	2:25.00	569,080
2001	Anabaa Blue	C. Soumillon	Chichicastenango	Grandera	14	2:27.90	517,200
2000	Holding Court	P. Robinson	Lord Flasheart	Circus Dance	14	2:31.80	359,750
1999	Montjeu (Ire)	C. B. Asmussen	Nowhere to Exit	Rhagaas	8	2:33.50	395,500
1998	Dream Well (Fr)	C. B. Asmussen	Croco Rouge	Sestino (Ire)	13	2:29.30	417,250
1997	Peintre Celebre	O. Peslier	Oscar	Astarabad	14	2:29.60	433,500
1996	Ragmar	G. Mosse	Polaris Flight	Le Destin	15	2:27.20	484,250
1995	Celtic Swing	K. Darley	Poliglote (GB)	Winged Love	11	2:32.80	504,000
1994	Celtic Arms (Fr)	G. Mosse	Solid Illusion	Alriffa	15	2:31.30	444,375
1993	Hernando (Fr)	C. B. Asmussen	Dernier Empereur	Hunting Hawk	11	2:27.20	465,325
1992	Polytain	L. Dettori	Marignan	Contested Bid	17	2:30.30	463,875

Prix Royal-Oak (French St. Leger)

Group 1, Longchamp, three-year-olds and up, 3,100 meters (15.41 furlongs), turf. Held October 28, 2007, with a gross value of $359,800.

Year	Winner	Jockey	Second	Third	Strs	Time	1st Purse
2007	†Allegretto, 4	R. Moore	†Macleya, 5	†Ponte Tresa, 4	11	3:15.50	$205,590
2006	Montare, 4	O. Peslier	Bellamy Cay, 4	Sergeant Cecil, 7	10	3:20.30	180,262
2005	Alcazar (Ire), 10	M. Fenton	Reefscape, 4	Shamdala, 3	11	3:27.30	136,553
2004	Westerner, 5	S. Pasquier	†Behkara, 4	Alcazar, 9	8	3:28.90	144,838
2003	Westerner, 4	D. Boeuf	Alcazar, 8	†Behkara, 3	14	3:31.20	94,007
2002	Mr Dinos, 3	D. Boeuf	†Sulk (Ire), 3	Clety, 6	7	3:38.50	84,347
2001	Vinnie Roe, 3	P. J. Smullen	Generic, 6	Germinis, 7	13	3:37.80	54,440
2000	Amilynx, 4	O. Peslier	San Sebastian, 6	Tajoun, 6	11	3:33.40	51,280
1999	Amilynx, 3	O. Peslier	Tajoun, 5	Northerntown, 3	7	3:40.60	65,200
1998	Tiraaz, 4	G. Mosse	†Erudite, 3	Asolo, 4	7	3:58.40	72,840
1997	†Ebadiyla, 3	G. Mosse	†Snow Princess, 5	Oscar Schindler, 5	11	3:26.50	67,160

International — Major International Races

Year	Winner	Jockey	Second	Third	Strs	Time	1st Purse
1996	†Red Roses Story (Fr), 4	V. Vion	Moonax, 5	†Helen of Spain, 4	5	3:38.40	$77,840
1995	Sunshack (GB), 4	T. Jarnet	Shrewd Idea (GB), 5	†Sunrise Song, 4	7	3:16.20	81,160
1994	Moonax, 3	P. Eddery	Always Earnest, 6	†Dalara, 3	7	3:28.90	75,444
1993	Raintrap (GB), 3	P. Eddery	Mashaallah, 5	Sonus, 4	8	3:45.80	70,324
1992	Assessor, 3	T. R. Quinn	†Always Friendly, 4	†Sought Out, 4	12	3:35.80	83,160

†Denotes female.

Ireland

Boylesports Irish One Thousand Guineas

Group 1, The Curragh, three-year-old fillies, 1 mile, turf. Held May 25, 2008, with a gross value of $593,140. First held in 1922.

Year	Winner	Jockey	Second	Third	Strs	Time	1st Purse
2008	Halfway To Heaven	J. Heffernan	Mad About You	Carribean Sunset	13	1:40.82	$359,670
2007	Finsceal Beo	K. Manning	Dimenticata	Peeping Fawn	11	1:39.30	301,885
2006	Nightime	P. J. Smullen	Ardbrae Lady	Queen Cleopatra	15	1:48.37	285,699
2005	Saoire	M. J. Kinane	Penkenna Princess	Luas Line (Ire)	18	1:41.50	282,874
2004	Attraction	K. Darley	Alexander Goldrun	Illustrious Miss	15	1:37.60	278,190
2003	Yesterday (Ire)	M. J. Kinane	Six Perfections (Fr)	Dimitrova	8	1:40.80	252,889
2002	Gossamer (GB)	J. P. Spencer	Quarter Moon (Ire)	Starbourne	15	1:45.50	198,135
2001	Imagine	J. A. Heffernan	Crystal Music	Toroca	16	1:41.10	138,443
2000	Crimplene (Ire)	P. Robinson	Amethyst (Ire)	Storm Dream (Ire)	13	1:39.80	133,195
1999	Hula Angel	M. Hills	Golden Silca (GB)	Dazzling Park	17	1:38.80	151,446
1998	Tarascon	J. P. Spencer	Kitza (Ire)	La Nuit Rose	13	1:38.40	120,461
1997	Classic Park	S. Craine	Strawberry Roan (Ire)	Caiseal Ros (Ire)	10	1:42.20	128,119
1996	Matiya (Ire)	W. Carson	Dance Design (Ire)	My Branch	12	1:39.80	131,497
1995	Ridgewood Pearl (GB)	C. Roche	Warning Shadows	Khaytada	10	1:43.90	137,791
1994	Mehthaaf	W. Carson	Las Meninas (Ire)	Relatively Special (GB)	10	1:49.00	127,067
1993	Nicer (Ire)	M. Hills	Goodnight Kiss	Danse Royale (Ire)	14	1:44.20	174,235
1992	Marling (Ire)	W. Swinburn	Market Booster	Tarwiya	9	1:41.10	196,988

Boylesports Irish Two Thousand Guineas

Group 1, The Curragh, three-year-olds, 1 mile, turf. Held May 24, 2008, with a gross value of $593,140. First held in 1921.

Year	Winner	Jockey	Second	Third	Strs	Time	1st Purse
2008	Henrythenavigator	J. Murtagh	New Approach	Stubbs Art	5	1:39.63	$359,670
2007	Cockney Rebel	O. Peslier	Creachadoir	He's A Decoy	12	1:36.10	301,885
2006	Araafa	A. Munro	George Washington (Ire)	Decado	11	1:49.85	285,699
2005	Dubawi	L. Dettori	Oratorio (Ire)	Democratic Deficit	8	1:41.60	287,898
2004	Bachelor Duke	S. Sanders	Azamour (Ire)	Grey Swallow (Ire)	8	1:40.00	288,072
2003	Indian Haven	J. F. Egan	France (GB)	Tout Seul	16	1:41.50	245,265
2002	Rock of Gibraltar (Ire)	M. J. Kinane	Century City (Ire)	Della Francesca	7	1:47.30	209,239
2001	Black Minnaloushe	J. P. Murtagh	Mozart (Ire)	Minardi	12	1:41.40	138,443
2000	Bachir	L. Dettori	Giant's Causeway	Cape Town	8	1:39.80	137,926
1999	Saffron Walden	O. Peslier	Enrique	Orpen	10	1:38.10	151,379
1998	Desert Prince (Ire)	O. Peslier	Fa-Eq	Second Empire (Ire)	7	1:35.80	169,717
1997	Desert King	C. Roche	Verglas (Ire)	Romanov (Ire)	12	1:38.30	171,383
1996	Spinning World	C. B. Asmussen	Rainbow Blues (Ire)	Beauchamp King	10	1:38.80	175,902
1995	Spectrum	J. A. Reid	Adjareli	Bahri	9	1:40.30	187,592
1994	Turtle Island	J. A. Reid	Guided Tour	Ridgewood Ben	9	1:50.10	169,989
1993	Barathea (Ire)	M. Roberts	Fatherland (Ire)	Massyar (Ire)	11	1:43.00	175,777
1992	Rodrigo de Triano	L. Piggott	Ezzoud (Ire)	Brief Truce	6	1:41.00	198,616

Budweiser Irish Derby

Group 1, The Curragh, three-year-olds, 1½ miles, turf. Held July 1, 2007, with a gross value of $1,873,921. First held in 1866.

Year	Winner	Jockey	Second	Third	Strs	Time	1st Purse
2007	Soldier of Fortune	J. Heffernan	Alexander of Hales	Eagle Mountain	11	2:36.00	$1,147,091
2006	Dylan Thomas (Ire)	K. Fallon	Gentlewave	Best Alibi	13	2:29:35	1,084,122
2005	Hurricane Run	K. Fallon	Scorpion	Shalapour	9	2:29.40	901,795
2004	Grey Swallow	P. Smullen	North Light	Tycoon (GB)	10	2:28.70	837,101
2003	Alamshar	J. P. Murtagh	Dalakhani	Roosevelt	9	2:28.20	837,101
2002	High Chaparral (Ire)	M. J. Kinane	Sholokhov	Ballingarry (Ire)	9	2:32.20	678,466
2001	Galileo (Ire)	M. J. Kinane	Morshdi	Golan (Ire)	12	2:27.10	551,571
2000	Sinndar	J. P. Murtagh	Glyndebourne (Ire)	Ciro	11	2:33.90	584,814
1999	Montjeu (Ire)	C. B. Asmussen	Daliapour (Ire)	Tchaikovsky	10	2:30.10	583,427
1998	Dream Well (Fr)	C. B. Asmussen	City Honours	Desert Fox	10	2:44.30	592,554
1997	Desert King	C. Roche	Dr Johnson	Loup Sauvage	10	2:32.50	601,322
1996	Zagreb	P. Shanahan	Polaris Flight	His Excellence	13	2:30.60	546,276
1995	Winged Love	O. Peslier	Definite Article (GB)	Annus Mirabilis (Fr)	13	2:30.10	556,247
1994	†Balanchine	L. Dettori	King's Theatre (Ire)	Colonel Collins	9	2:32.70	515,040
1993	Commander in Chief	P. Eddery	Hernando (Fr)	Foresee	11	2:31.20	524,676
1992	St. Jovite	C. Roche	Dr Devious (Ire)	Contested Bid	10	2:25.10	591,093

†Denotes female.

Darley Irish Oaks

Group 1, The Curragh, three-year-old fillies, 1½ miles, turf. Held July 15, 2007, with a gross value of $627,309. First run in 1895.

Year	Winner	Jockey	Second	Third	Strs	Time	1st Purse
2007	Peeping Fawn	J. Murtagh	Light Shift	All My Loving (Ire)	12	2:39.12	$386,725
2006	Alexandrova	K. Fallon	Scottish Stage	Rising Cross	6	2:29.60	304,208
2005	Shawanda	C. Soumillion	Playful Act (Ire)	Mona Lisa (GB)	13	2:27.10	271,208
2004	Ouija Board (GB)	K. Fallon	Punctilious	Hazarista	7	2:28.20	295,290
2003	Vintage Tipple	L. Dettori	L'Ancresse (Ire)	Casual Look	11	2:28.30	252,990
2002	Margarula	K. Manning	Quarter Moon (Ire)	Lady's Secret	12	2:37.40	204,023
2001	Lailani (GB)	L. Dettori	Mot Juste (GB)	Karsavina (Ire)	12	2:30.50	137,466
2000	Petrushka (Ire)	J. P. Murtagh	Melikah (Ire)	Inforapenny	10	2:31.20	133,775
1999	Ramruma	K. Fallon	Sunspangled	Sister Bella	7	2:33.00	153,443
1998	Winona (Ire)	J. P. Murtagh	Kitza (Ire)	Bahr (GB)	9	2:39.80	157,965
1997	Ebadiyla	J. P. Murtagh	Yashmak	Brilliance (Fr)	11	2:33.70	170,988
1996	Dance Design (Ire)	M. J. Kinane	Shamadara	Key Change	6	2:29.70	192,348
1995	Pure Grain (GB)	J. A. Reid	Russian Snows	Valley of Gold	10	2:33.60	185,279
1994	Bolas (GB)	P. Eddery	Hawajiss	Gothic Dream	10	2:37.60	171,295
1993	Wemyss Bight (GB)	P. Eddery	Royal Ballerina (Ire)	Oakmead (Ire)	11	2:35.00	162,573
1992	User Friendly (GB)	G. Duffield	Market Booster	Arrikala	9	2:33.10	212,040

Irish Field St. Leger Stakes

Group 1, The Curragh, three-year-olds and up, 1¾ miles, turf. Held September 15, 2007, with a gross value of $386,364. First held in 1915.

Year	Winner	Jockey	Second	Third	Strs	Time	1st Purse
2007	Yeats, 6	K. Fallon	Scorpion (Ire), 5	Mores Wells, 3	9	3:03.40	$238,146
2006	Kastoria, 5	M. Kinane	Yeats, 6	The Whistling Teal, 10	8	3:01:00	221,079
2005	Collier Hill, 7	D. McKeown	The Whistling Teal, 9	Vinnie Roe, 7	9	3:01.20	209,935
2004	Vinnie Roe, 6	P. J. Smullen	Brian Boru (GB), 4	First Charter, 5	13	3:03.90	205,389
2003	Vinnie Roe, 5	P. J. Smullen	Gamut, 4	Powerscourt (GB), 3	6	2:25.90	203,410
2002	Vinnie Roe, 4	P. J. Smullen	Pugin, 4	Ballingarry (Ire), 3	8	2:59.00	171,824
2001	Vinnie Roe, 3	P. J. Smullen	Millenary, 4	Marienbard, 4	8	2:58.40	153,159
2000	Arctic Owl, 6	D. Harrison	Yavana's Pace, 8	Mutafaweq, 4	8	3:02.20	110,412
1999	Kayf Tara, 5	L. Dettori	Yavana's Pace, 7	Silver Patriarch, 5	5	3:12.50	143,953
1998	Kayf Tara, 4	J. A. Reid	Silver Patriarch, 4	†Delilah (Ire), 4	7	3:05.70	131,690
1997	Oscar Schindler, 5	S. Craine	Persian Punch, 4	†Whitewater Affair, 4	7	3:06.40	132,223
1996	Oscar Schindler, 4	S. Craine	†Key Change, 3	Sacrament, 5	9	2:59.10	137,349
1995	Strategic Choice, 4	T. R. Quinn	Moonax, 4	Oscar Schindler, 3	7	3:00.90	141,290
1994	Vintage Crop, 7	M. J. Kinane	†Rayseka, 4	†Kithanga, 4	8	3:07.30	133,045
1993	Vintage Crop, 6	M. J. Kinane	Assessor, 4	Foresee, 3	8	3:06.70	123,262
1992	Mashaallah, 4	S. Cauthen	Snurge, 5	Drum Taps, 6	9	3:02.01	163,314

†Denotes female.

United Arab Emirates

Dubai Duty Free

Group 1, Nad al Sheba, three-year-olds and up, 1,800 meters (8.9477 furlongs), turf. Held on March 29, 2008, with a gross value of $5,000,000.

Year	Winner	Jockey	Second	Third	Strs	Time	1st Purse
2008	Jay Peg, 4	A. Marcus	†Darjina, 4	Archipenko, 4	16	1:46.20	$3,000,000
2007	Admire Moon, 4	Y. Take	Linngari, 5	Daiwa Major, 6	16	1:47.94	3,000,000
2006	David Junior, 4	J. Spencer	The Tin Man, 8	Seihali, 7	15	1:49.65	3,000,000
2005	Elvstroem, 4, 121	N. Rawiller	Whilly (Ire), 4	Right Approach, 6	14	1:50:54	1,200,000
2004	dh-Right Approach, 5	W. Marwing					
	dh-Paolini (Ger), 7	E. Pedroza		Nayyir, 4	11	1:49:36	800,000
2003	Ipi Tombe (Zim), 4	K. Shea	Paolini (Ger), 6	Royal Tryst, 6	12	1:47:61	1,200,000
2002	Terre A Terre, 5,	C. Soumillion	Noverre, 4	Hoeberg, 4	16	1:48:75	1,200,000

†Denotes female.

Emirates Airline Dubai World Cup

Group 1, Nad al Sheba, three-year-olds and up, 2,000 meters (9.9419 furlongs), dirt. Held on March 29, 2008, with a gross value of $6,000,000. First held in 1996.

Year	Winner	Jockey	Second	Third	Strs	Time	1st Purse
2008	Curlin, 4	R. Albarado	Asiatic Boy, 5	Well Armed, 5	12	2:00.15	$3,600,000
2007	Invasor (Arg), 5, 126	F. Jara	Premium Tap, 5	Bullish Luck, 8	7	1:59.97	3,600,000
2006	Electrocutionist, 5, 126	L. Dettori	Wilko, 4	Magna Graduate, 4	11	2:01.32	3,600,000
2005	Roses in May, 5, 126	J. Velazquez	Dynever	Choctaw Nation	12	2:02.17	3,600,000
2004	Pleasantly Perfect, 6, 126	A. Solis	Medaglia d'Oro, 5	Victory Moon, 5	10	2:00.24	3,600,000
2003	Moon Ballad (Ire), 4, 126	L. Dettori	Harlan's Holiday, 4	Nayef, 5	11	2:00.48	3,600,000
2002	Street Cry (Ire), 4, 126	J. D. Bailey	Sei Mi, 6	Sakhee, 5	11	2:01.18	3,600,000
2001	Captain Steve, 4, 126	J. D. Bailey	†To the Victory, 5	Hightori, 5	12	2:00.47	3,600,000
2000	Dubai Millennium, 4, 126	L. Dettori	Behrens, 6	Public Purse, 6	13	2:00.65	3,600,000
1999	Almutawakel (GB), 5, 126	R. Hills	Malek (Chi), 6	Victory Gallop, 4	8	2:00.65	3,000,000
1998	Silver Charm, 4, 126	G. L. Stevens	Swain (Ire), 6	Loup Sauvage, 4	9	2:04.29	2,400,000
1997	Singspiel (Ire), 5, 126	J. D. Bailey	Siphon (Brz), 6	Sandpit (Brz), 8	12	2:01.91	2,400,000
1996	Cigar, 6, 126	J. D. Bailey	Soul of the Matter, 5	L'Carriere, 5	11	2:03.84	2,400,000

1996-'97 listed race.

Gulf News Dubai Golden Shaheen

Group 1, Nad al Sheba, three-year-olds and up, 1,200 meters (5.9652 furlongs), dirt. Held on March 29, 2008, with a gross value of $2,000,000.

Year	Winner	Jockey	Second	Third	Strs	Time	1st Purse
2008	Benny the Bull, 5	E. Prado	Idiot Proof, 4	Star Crowned, 5	15	1:08.70	$1,200,000
2007	Kelly's Landing, 6	L. Dettori	Friendly Island, 6	Salaam Dubai, 6	16	1:10.34	1,200,000
2006	Proud Tower Too, 4	D. Cohen	Thor's Eco 4	Jet West, 5	15	1:09.86	1,200,000
2005	Saratoga County, 4	J. Castellano	Tropicar Star, 5	Botanical, 4	11	1:11:21	1,200,000
2004	Our New Recruit, 5	A. Solis	Alke, 4	Conroy, 6	12	1:10:30	1,200,000
2003	State City, 4	M. Hills	Avanzado (Arg), 5	Captain Squire, 4	12	1:09:95	1,200,000
2002	Caller One, 5	G. Stevens	Echo Eddie, 5	Xtra Heat, 4	13	1:09:91	1,200,000
2001	Caller One, 4	C. Nakatani	Men's Exclusive, 8	Bertolini, 5	15	1:08:38	1,200,000

Nakheel Dubai Sheema Classic

Group 1, three-year-olds and up, 2,400 meters (11.93 furlongs). Held on March 29, 2008, with a gross value of $5,000,000.

Year	Winner	Jockey	Second	Third	Strs	Time	1st Purse
2008	Sun Classique, 4	K. Shea	Viva Pataca, 6	Doctor Dino (Fr), 6	16	2:27.45	$3,000,000
2007	Vengeance Of Rain, 7	A. Delpech	Oracle West, 6	Youmzain, 4	14	2:31:03	3,000,000
2006	Heart's Cry, 5, 124	Y. Take	Collier Hill, 5	Falstaff, 4	14	2:31.89	3,000,000
2005	Phoenix Reach (Ire), 5	M. Dwyer	Razkalla, 7	Collier Hill, 7	11	2:30:54	1,200,000
2004	Polish Summer (GB), 7	G. Stevens	Hard Buck (Brz), 4	Scott's View, 5	13	2:31:09	1,200,000
2003	Sulamani, 4	L. Dettori	Ange Gabriel, 5	Ekraar, 6	16	2:27:67	1,200,000
2002	Nayef, 4	R. Hills	Helene Vitality, 5	Boreal, 4	15	2:29:64	1,200,000

English Triple Crown

Throughout its long history, the English Triple Crown has proved to be as elusive as its younger American cousin, and perhaps even more so. As it enters its third century, the English Triple Crown has been won only 15 times. Since Gainsborough became the 13th winner in 1918, only two more have followed: unbeaten *Bahram in 1935 and the brilliant Nijinsky II in '70.

The English Triple Crown for three-year-olds, dating from 1809, consists of the one-mile Two Thousand Guineas (Eng-G1) at Newmarket in May, the 1½-mile Epsom Derby (Eng-G1) at Epsom Downs in June, and the St. Leger Stakes (Eng-G1) at 1¾ miles and 127 yards at Doncaster Race Course in September. Over the years, there has been some variance in the distances of the three races, and alternative races were used during war years.

The St. Leger Stakes was named for the popular local sportsman Lt. Col. Anthony St. Leger. Alabaculia was the first winner of the St. Leger Stakes in 1776. Four years later, *Diomed, later imported to the United States, won the initial running of the Epsom Derby. The first Two Thousand Guineas was taken by Wizard in 1809, nine years after Champion became the first three-year-old to win both the Epsom Derby and the St. Leger Stakes. In 1813, Sir Charles Bunbury's Smolensko became the first to win the Two Thousand Guineas and the Epsom Derby.

Forty years later in 1853, West Australian became the first to win all three stakes. He was followed by Gladiateur (1865), Lord Lyon ('66), *Ormonde ('86), Common ('91), Isinglass ('93), Galtee More ('97), Flying Fox ('99), Diamond Jubilee (1900), *Rock Sand ('03), Pommern ('15), Gay Crusader ('17), Gainsborough ('18), *Bahram ('35), and Nijinsky II ('70).

In today's racing world, the English Triple Crown is a prize not pursued. The most recent horse with a chance to seize the crown, 1989 Two Thousand Guineas (Eng-G1) and Epsom Derby (Eng-G1) victor Nashwan, was withheld from the St. Leger Stakes (Eng-G1) by owner Sheikh Hamdan bin Rashid al Maktoum to point for the Prix de l'Arc de Triomphe (Fr-G1), in which he did not start because of injury.

Following are the 15 English Triple Crown winners:

WEST AUSTRALIAN—1850 b. h., Melbourne–Mowerina, by Touchstone. 10-9-1-0, $68,615. Known popularly as "the West," West Australian gave owner-breeder John Bowes his fourth and final Epsom Derby victory. Trained by John Scott, West Australian ran second in the Criterion Stakes to Speed the Plough and then beat his rival in the Glasgow Stakes as a two-year-old. At three, West Australian won the Two Thousand Guineas by a half-length over the Duke of Bedford's Sittingbourne and the Epsom Derby by a desperate neck over the same opponent. West Australian won the St. Leger easily, and at four won the Triennial Stakes and the Ascot Gold Cup. Though not widely regarded as a success at stud, he sired The Wizard, the 1860 Two Thousand Guineas winner, and his son *Australian sired Spendthrift, tail-male ancestor of the Man o' War male line that leads to Tiznow.

GLADIATEUR—1862 b. h., Monarque–Miss Gladiator, by Gladiator. 19-16-0-1, $236,537. French-bred and -owned Gladiateur shattered the notion that England's Thoroughbreds were superior when he won the 1865 Two Thousand Guineas, earning the gleeful nickname "Avenger of Waterloo" among the French. Trained at Newmarket by Tom Jennings, he added the Epsom Derby "in a canter" and the St. Leger. In between, he traveled to his native France and captured that country's greatest race at the time, the Grand Prix de Paris. At four, Gladiateur won the Gold Cup at Ascot by 40 lengths after reputedly trailing by 300 yards at one point. He was not a success at stud.

LORD LYON—1863 b. h., Stockwell–Paradigm, by Paragone. 19-15-3-1, $180,497. Leased to Richard Sutton, the second son of Sir Richard Sutton, and trained by James Dover, Lord Lyon dead-heated with Redan in the Champagne Stakes for two-year-olds at Doncaster and

then won the Criterion and Troy Stakes at Newmarket. After winning the Two Thousand Guineas by one length over Monarch of the Glen, Lord Lyon completed the Triple Crown by beating Savernake by a head in the Epsom Derby and the same rival by inches in the St. Leger. The following year, Lord Lyon won the Ascot Biennial and the Stockbridge Cup. His most famous offspring were *Ormonde's rival Minting, winner of the 1886 Grand Prix de Paris, and '77 Oaks winner Placida.

*ORMONDE—1883 b. h., Bend Or–Lily Agnes, by Macaroni. 16-16-0-0, $138,340. Considered by many as the finest Thoroughbred of the 19th century, the Duke of Westminster's *Ormonde was unbeaten in his 16-race career despite developing a wind infirmity. At four in the Hardwicke Stakes, he bested Grand Prix de Paris winner Minting. *Ormonde sired just seven foals in his first season at stud in England, but that crop included Orme, a multiple stakes winner and sire of 1899 Triple Crown winner Flying Fox. After a stint in Argentina, *Ormonde was purchased by William O'Brien Macdonough, an American, for $150,000 in 1893 and stood in California. From 1894 through 1905, *Ormonde sired just 17 foals, but 12 started his career including Ormondale, won stakes races.

COMMON—1888 br. h., Isonomy–Thistle, by Scottish Chief. 5-4-0-1, $77,567. Owned by his breeder, Lord Allington, and Sir Frederick Johnstone, Common was a colt with dubious joints and thus was not raced at two by trainer John Porter. Common made his debut in the 1891 Two Thousand Guineas, and his profuse sweating prompted Prince Soltykoff to remark, "He's very well named." Uncommon on the Newmarket course, Common won easily. He won the Epsom Derby by two lengths in a downpour and subsequently won the St. James's Palace Stakes before finishing third in the Eclipse Stakes. In the final start of his only racing season, Common completed the Triple Crown by winning the St. Leger by one length. Common's progeny included 1898 One Thousand Guineas winner Nun Nicer and Mushroom, who became a successful stallion in Belgium.

ISINGLASS—1890 b. h., Isonomy–Deadlock, by Wenlock. 12-11-1-0, $279,231. Despite soundness problems that he passed on to his progeny, Isinglass lost only once for his owner, Col. Harry McCalmont, in a four-year career. Isinglass suffered the only loss in his three-year-old campaign when he was defeated by Raeburn in the Lancashire Plate at Manchester, giving the winner ten pounds over an inadequate distance. At four, Isinglass captured the Princess of Wales's Stakes, Eclipse Stakes, and Jockey Club Stakes. As a five-year-old, he won the 1895 Ascot Gold Cup and retired as the sport's all-time money winner. Isinglass stood at his owner's Cheveley Park Stud near Newmarket and sired three British classic winners as well as *Star Shoot, who was North America's leading sire five times and leading broodmare sire five times.

GALTEE MORE—1894 b. h., Kendal–Morganette, by Springfield. 13-11-1-0, $131,312. Galtee More, named after a peak in the Galtee Mountains, was owned by John Gubbins, who used his inheritance from an uncle to open two stud farms, one of which housed Galtee More's sire, Kendal. Trained by Sam Darling, Galtee More won the Molecomb Stakes, the Rous Plate, and the Middle Park Plate as a two-year-old. At three in 1897, Galtee More completed the Triple Crown by taking the St. Leger by three-quarters of a length over the filly Chelandry. At the end of his racing career, Galtee More was sold by Gubbins to the Russian government, and the stallion subsequently was purchased by German interests. His most noteworthy progeny was Orchidee II, dam of Oleander, leading German sire in the 1930s and '40s. Galtee More's half brother Ard Patrick won the Epsom Derby in 1892.

FLYING FOX—1896 b. h., Orme–Vampire, by Galopin. 11-9-2-0, $194,867. A large colt with beautiful shoulders, Flying Fox became the Duke of Westminster's second Triple Crown winner despite a difficult temperament that most likely came from his aptly named dam. At two in 1898, Flying Fox won the New, Stockbridge Foal, and Criterion Stakes, and he finished second in the Imperial Produce Stakes and the Middle Park Plate. Flying Fox was unbeaten at three and ended his career with a four-length victory in the Jockey Club Stakes. Flying Fox sired French classic winner Val d'Or, and his grandson *Teddy (by French Derby winner Ajax) became an important influence on North American bloodlines through full brothers *Sir Gallahad III and *Bull Dog.

DIAMOND JUBILEE—1897 b. h., St. Simon–Perdita, by Hampton. 16-6-5-1, $142,131. Owned by the Prince of Wales, Diamond Jubilee was described as "ferocious, with a nature more befitting the bullring than the racecourse." He was found to be a cryptorchid (and thus spared from gelding) after finishing unplaced in his first two starts at two. Diamond Jubilee's trainer, Richard Marsh, gave Diamond Jubilee's groom, 18-year-old Herbert Jones, a chance to ride the ridgling, and Diamond Jubilee won the Two Thousand Guineas by four lengths. He won the Epsom Derby by a half-length and the St. Leger by one length. After standing at stud in England, he was sold in 1906 to Las Ortegas Stud in Argentina, where he was the leading sire from 1914 through '16. Diamond Jubilee was a full brother to the outstanding racehorse Persimmon, winner of the Epsom Derby and the St. Leger in 1896.

*ROCK SAND—1900 br. h., Sainfoin–Roquebrune, by St. Simon. 20-16-1-3, $221,703. Although he hobbled along at a trot and canter, *Rock Sand would fully extend himself at a gallop once warmed up and never finished unplaced in his career. He won six stakes races as a two-year-old in 1902, and at three he won the St. James's Palace and Bennington Stakes in addition to the Triple Crown contests. He won the Hardwicke, Princess of Wales's, Lingfield Park Plate, First Foal, and the Jockey Club Stakes at four. Best known for his success as a broodmare sire, *Rock Sand sired Mahubah, dam of Man o' War. *Rock Sand's other leading daughters included Hour Glass, dam of Blue Glass and *Hourless, and Tea Biscuit, dam of Hard Tack. *Rock Sand's most accomplished sons were Tracery, winner of the St. James's Palace and Eclipse Stakes and one of the leading sires in England for many years in the 1920s; Friar Rock, who won the 1916 Belmont Stakes and Suburban Handicap in the United States; and 1916 Preakness Stakes winner Damrosch.

POMMERN—1912 b. h., Polymelus–Merry Agnes, by St. Hilaire. 10-7-1-0, $75,165. A homebred of Solomon B. Joel, Pommern won the Richmond Stakes at Goodwood and the Imperial Produce Stakes at Kemptonat age two. Steve Donoghue was engaged to ride Pommern in his unusual three-year-old season. Pommern won the 1915 Two Thousand Guineas comfortably at Newmarket. With World War I raging across the English Channel in France, Epsom Downs was requisitioned by the military, and Pommern scored a two-length victory in the substitute for the Epsom Derby, the New Derby at 1½ miles on Newmarket's July Course. He then won the substitute for the St. Leger, the 1¾-mile September Stakes at Newmarket. In his only start at four, Pommern won the June Stakes at Newmarket. His best offspring were Adam's Apple, who won the 1927 Two Thousand Guineas; Pondoland, second in the '22 Two Thousand Guineas; and Glommen, who won the '26 Goodwood Cup.

GAY CRUSADER—1914 b. c., Bayardo–Gay Laura, by Beppo. 10-8-2-0, $53,530. Bred and owned by A. W. "Fairie" Cox, Gay Crusader was the first foal of his dam and from his sire's first crop. Trained by Alec Taylor, Gay Crusader was a small colt who developed sore shins in June of his two-year-old season. He made a late start that year, losing his debut before winning the Criterion Stakes. After finishing second in his three-year-old debut, Gay Crusader won the 1917 Two Thousand Guineas by a head over Magpie, who also was trained by Taylor. With Magpie exported to Australia, Gay Crusader won the Epsom Derby, which was delayed until July 31 because of World War I, by four lengths. He then won the September Stakes, the St. Leger substitute. Gay Crusader also won the Newmarket Gold Cup, Champion Stakes, and Lowther Stakes. A tendon injury ended his career before his first start as a four-year-old. At stud, his best were Hot Night, second in the 1927 Epsom Derby, and Hurstwood, third in the '24 Derby.

GAINSBOROUGH—1915 b. h., Bayardo–Rosedrop, by St. Frusquin. 9-5-2-1, $67,021. Lady Jane Douglas bred Gainsborough and became the first woman to own an Epsom Derby winner when the colt took the 1918 classic. Gainsborough gave his sire, Bayardo, a second straight Triple Crown winner. Gainsborough, who was twice champion sire, sired Hyperion, the 1933 Epsom Derby winner who went on to be England's leading sire six times. Gainsborough also sired 1932 Two Thousand Guineas winner Orwell and Solario, who was England's leading sire in 1937 and its leading broodmare sire in 1949 and '50. Gainsborough died in 1945 at the age of 30 and was buried at Gainsborough Stud, which was originally named Harwood Stud.

*BAHRAM—1932 br. h., Blandford–Friar's Daughter, by Friar Marcus. 9-9-0-0, $212,816. A large colt who grew to 16.2 hands, *Bahram was bred and raced in England by the Aga Khan. Unbeaten in nine career starts through his three-year-old season, *Bahram won the National Produce, Rous Memorial, Gimcrack, and Middle Park Stakes at two. In addition to sweeping the Triple Crown at three, he won the St. James's Palace Stakes. England's second-leading sire in 1940, he was sold for $160,000 to an American syndicate that included Alfred G. Vanderbilt, Walter P. Chrysler, James Cox Brady, and S. W. Labrot. *Bahram stood in Maryland and Virginia before being sold in 1945 to stand in Argentina. *Bahram's 25 stakes winners included 1940 St. Leger and Irish Derby winner Turkhan, '40 Irish Oaks winner Queen of Shiraz, and '42 Two Thousand Guineas winner Big Game, who became the leading sire in England in '48, and the excellent sire Persian Gulf, winner of the '44 Coronation Cup.

NIJINSKY II—1967 b. h., Northern Dancer–Flaming Page, by Bull Page. 13-11-2-0, $667,220. Bred in Canada by E. P. Taylor and owned by Charles W. Engelhard, Nijinsky II was Northern Dancer's first international champion. He was a powerful, sickle-hocked colt who more closely resembled his dam than his diminutive sire. Trained by Vincent O'Brien, Nijinsky II was a champion in England and Ireland at two in 1969. He won the Two Thousand Guineas at odds of 4-to-7, the Epsom Derby at 11-to-8 odds, and the St. Leger at 2-to-7 odds, all under Lester Piggott. That year, Nijinsky II also won the Irish Sweeps Derby and the King George VI and Queen Elizabeth Stakes. His only defeats were in his final two starts, the Prix de l'Arc de Triomphe and Champion Stakes. At stud at Claiborne Farm in Kentucky, he was England's leading sire in 1986 and North America's leading brood-

The Influence of England's Triple Crown Worldwide

Although England's Triple Crown is the original and perhaps most difficult Triple Crown in the world to win, historically it has served as a model for racing programs around the globe. Virtually every major racing country has its set of Guineas, Derbys, and St. Legers, or their equivalents. As in most aspects of Thoroughbred racing, England, the birthplace of the Thoroughbred, established the pattern that the rest of the world adapted for its own local purposes, and the idea of a series of classic tests for three-year-olds is universal.

The Triple Crown in the United States evolved into the familiar Kentucky Derby (G1), Preakness Stakes (G1), and Belmont Stakes (G1) early in the 20th century, but several American racing jurisdictions in the 19th century attempted to establish Triple Crown series more closely modeled on the English pattern. For example, the Withers, Belmont, and Lawrence Realization Stakes were originally intended to be New York's version of the English series.

Other former English colonies such as Australia and New Zealand likewise established Guineas-Derby-St. Leger series, and those races still exist in Antipodean lands, though it has been many years since they have been a serious objective as a series for owners and trainers. As racing throughout the world has become more specialized, winning a Triple Crown over a variety of distances as wide as that in England has become increasingly difficult.

Argentina, historically the most important South American racing country, established its own series, the Polla de Potrillos (Arg-G1), Gran Premio Jockey Club (Arg-G1), and Gran Premio Nacional (Arg-G1) over 1,600 meters, 2,000 meters, and 2,500 meters, respectively, but went one better than the English. The Argentines also required their best three-year-olds to beat older horses in the 2,400-meter Gran Premio Carlos Pellegrini (Arg-G1) to win their Quadruple Crown. Twenty three-year-olds have captured the Argentine Triple Crown since 1902, with Refinado Tom (Arg) in '96 the most recent winner. Only ten horses, the last being the great *Forli in 1966, have completed the Quadruple Crown.

English fillies have an opportunity to win their version of the Triple Crown, though no filly has ever completed the Two Thousand Guineas (Eng-G1), Epsom Derby (Eng-G1), St. Leger (Eng-G1) triple. Two fillies, however, have won four of the five English classics, failing only to capture the Derby. Formosa in 1868 dead-heated in the Two Thousand and won the One Thousand Guineas, Epsom Oaks, and St. Leger. Sceptre won the One Thousand, Two Thousand, Oaks, and St. Leger in 1902 but was beaten into fourth place in the Derby by Ard Patrick.

Nine fillies have won a "fillies Triple Crown" consisting of the One Thousand Guineas, Oaks, and St. Leger:

1985	**Oh So Sharp (GB)**, ch. f., Kris—Oh So Fair, by Graustark
1955	**Meld**, b. f., Alycidon—Daily Double, by Fair Trial
1942	**Sun Chariot**, b. f., Hyperion—Clarence, by Diligence
1904	**Pretty Polly**, ch. f., Gallinule—Admiration, by Saraband
1902	**Sceptre**, b. f., Persimmon—Ornament, by Bend Or
1892	**La Fleche**, br. f., St. Simon—Quiver, by Toxophilite
1874	**Apology**, ch. f., Adventurer—Mandragora, by Rataplan
1871	**Hannah**, b. f., King Tom—Mentmore Lass, by Melbourne
1868	**Formosa**, ch. f., Buccaneer—Eller, by Chanticleer

mare sire in '93 and '94. Nijinsky II at one time was the all-time leading sire of stakes winners with 155, surpassing the record of his sire. Nijinsky II sired 11 champions, including 1987 North American Horse of the Year Ferdinand, '83 French champion Caerleon, two-time English champion Ile de Bourbon, and two undefeated winners of the Epsom Derby, Golden Fleece and Lammtarra.

—Bill Heller

2007 World Thoroughbred Racehorse Rankings
European-Based Two-Year-Olds

Rating	Horse	YOB Sex	Pedigree	Trained	2007 Record, Earnings
126	New Approach	2005 c.	Galileo (Ire)—Park Express (Ire), by Ahonoora	Ire	5-5-0-0, $730,686
125	Fast Company	2005 c.	Danehill Dancer—Sheezalady, by Zafonic	GB	3-2-1-0, $171,317
122	Myboycharlie	2005 c.	Danetime—Dulceata, by Rousillon	Ire	4-3-0-1, $392,771
120	Raven's Pass	2005 c.	Elusive Quality—Ascutney, by Lord At War (Arg)	GB	4-3-0-1, $133,769
	Rio de La Plata	2005 c.	Rahy—Express Way (Arg), by Ahmad	GB	6-3-1-1, $493,714
119	Zarkava	2005 f.	Zamindar—Zarkasha, by Kahyasi	Fr	2-2-0-0, $256,758
118	Kingsgate Native	2005 c.	Mujadil—Native Force, by Indian Ridge	GB	4-1-3-0, $397,275
	Natagora	2005 f.	Divine Light—Reinamixa, by Linamix	Fr	7-5-2-0, $536,982
	Thewayyouare	2005 c.	Kingmambo—Maryinsky (Ire), by Sadler's Wells	Fr	5-4-0-0, $314,432
117	Fleeting Spirit	2005 f.	Invincible Spirit—Millennium Tale, by Distant Relative (Ire)	GB	5-3-2-0, $266,970
	Hello Morning	2005 c.	Poliglote (GB)—Hello Molly, by Sillery	Fr	4-2-2-0, $127,130
	Ibn Khaldun	2005 c.	Dubai Destination—Gossamer (GB), by Sadler's Wells	GB	5-4-0-0, $301,548
	Listen	2005 f.	Sadler's Wells—Brigid, by Irish River (Fr)	Ire	4-2-2-0, $412,709
116	Alexandros	2005 c.	Kingmambo—Arlette (Ire), by King of Kings (Ire)	Fr	5-3-1-1, $168,846
	Young Pretender	2005 c.	Oasis Dream (GB)—Silent Heir, by Sunday Silence	GB	3-2-0-0, $82,057
115	Curtain Call	2005 c.	Sadler's Wells—Apsara, by Darshaan	Ire	5-1-2-0, $162,686
	Declaration of War	2005 c.	Okawango—Date Mate, by Thorn Dance	GB	6-2-2-0, $193,217
	McCartney	2005 c.	In the Wings (GB)—Messina, by Dashing Blade	GB	5-3-0-1, $150,291
	Proviso	2005 f.	Dansili (GB)—Binche, by Woodman	Fr	3-2-1-0, $164,497
115	Shediak	2005 c.	Selkirk—Shemissa, by Fairy King	Fr	3-1-1-1, $102,007
114	Dark Angel	2005 c.	Acclamation—Midnight Angel, by Machiavellian	GB	9-4-1-0, $685,840
	Henrythenavigator	2005 c.	Kingmambo—Sequoyah (Ire), by Sadler's Wells	Ire	4-2-1-1, $200,330
	Laureldean Gale	2005 f.	Grand Slam—Ravnina, by Nureyev	GB	3-1-1-0, $41,307
	Pomellato	2005 c.	Big Shuffle—Passata, by Polar Falcon	Ger	4-3-0-0, $253,753
	Scintillo	2005 c.	Fantastic Light—Danseuse du Soir (Ire), by Thatching	GB	8-2-1-2, $215,668
	Winker Watson	2005 c.	Piccolo—Bonica, by Rousillon	GB	3-3-0-0, $173,026
113	Achill Island (Ire)	2005 c.	Sadler's Wells—Prawn Cocktail, by Artichoke	Ire	5-1-4-0, $288,488
	Conference Call	2005 f.	Anabaa—Phone West, by Gone West	Fr	3-2-1-0, $134,452
	Full of Gold	2005 c.	Gold Away (Ire)—Funny Feerie, by Sillery	Fr	4-2-1-0, $233,369
	Gladiatorus	2005 c.	Silic (Fr)—Gmaasha (Ire), by Kris	Ity	9-6-2-0, $266,048
	Hatta Fort	2005 c.	Cape Cross (Ire)—Oshiponga, by Barathea (Ire)	GB	6-2-0-1, $136,954
	Lizard Island	2005 c.	Danehill Dancer—Add, by Spectacular Bid	Ire	5-1-2-0, $158,747
	Luck Money	2005 c.	Indian Ridge—Dundel, by Machiavellian	GB	4-2-0-1, $1,408,391
112	Gagnoa	2005 f.	Sadler's Wells—Gwynn (Ire), by Darshaan	Fr	4-2-0-1, $84,563
	Savethisdanceforme	2005 f.	Danehill Dancer—Bex, by Explodent	Ire	6-2-0-1, $94,881
	Stem Opinion	2005 c.	Mizzen Mast—Helstra, by Nureyev	Fr	4-1-1-1, $73,763
	Strike the Deal	2005 c.	Van Nistelrooy—Countess Gold, by Mt. Livermore	GB	8-2-2-1, $267,665
111	Blue Chagall	2005 c.	Testa Rossa—Eloisey, by Pitskelly	Fr	4-2-1-0, $112,728
	Captain Gerrard	2005 c.	Oasis Dream (GB)—Delphinus, by Soviet Star	GB	10-5-1-2, $171,176
	City Leader	2005 c.	Fasliyev—Kanmary (Fr), by Kenmare	GB	4-2-2-0, $263,572
	Feared in Flight	2005 c.	Hawk Wing—Solar Crystal, by Alzao	GB	5-1-0-2, $73,471
	Precious Boy	2005 c.	Big Shuffle—Pretty Su, by Surumu	Ger	3-3-0-0, $161,823
	Saoirse Abu	2005 f.	Mr. Greeley—Out too Late, by Future Storm	Ire	8-3-1-3, $579,940
	Sir Gerry	2005 c.	Carson City—Incredulous (Fr), by Indian Ridge	GB	4-2-0-0, $159,680
	Starlit Sands	2005 f.	Oasis Dream (GB)—Shimmering Sea, by Slip Anchor	GB	6-3-1-0, $108,885
	Tajdeef	2005 c.	Aljabr—Tabheej (Ire), by Mujtahid	GB	3-1-0-1, $62,344
110	Alnadana	2005 f.	Danehill Dancer—Alnamara, by Linamix	Fr	2-1-1-0, $23,645
	Farrel	2005 c.	Fruits of Love—Folcungi, by Mukaddamah	Ity	6-5-0-1, $161,716
	Goldikova	2005 f.	Anabaa—Born Gold, by Blushing Groom (Fr)	Fr	2-2-0-0, $38,602
	Indian Daffodil	2005 c.	Hernando (Fr)—Danseuse Indienne, by Danehill	Fr	3-3-0-0, $55,116
	Liang Kay	2005 c.	Dai Jin—Linton Bay, by Funambule	Ger	2-1-1-0, $48,602
	Mad About You	2005 f.	Indian Ridge—Irresistible Jewel (Ire), by Danehill	Ire	4-1-1-2, $116,561
	Magritte	2005 f.	Modigliani—Star of Sligo, by Saratoga Six	Ity	4-3-1-0, $146,366
	Modern Look	2005 f.	Zamindar—Prophecy, by Warning (GB)	Fr	4-3-0-0, $94,642
	Nahoodh	2005 f.	Clodovil—Mise, by Indian Ridge	GB	3-1-0-1, $102,330
	Redolent	2005 c.	Redback—Esterlina, by Highest Honor (Fr)	Fr	5-1-2-1, $68,996
	River Proud	2005 c.	Proud Citizen—Da River Hoss, by River Special	GB	5-2-1-0, $111,575
	Spirit of Sharjah	2005 c.	Invincible Spirit—Rathbawn Realm, by Doulab	GB	7-2-1-1, $87,071

Long, Three and Up, Turf

Rating	Horse	YOB Sex	Pedigree	Trained	2007 Record, Earnings
129	Authorized	2004 c.	Montjeu (Ire)—Funsie, by Saumarez (GB)	GB	5-3-1-0, $2,365,763
	Dylan Thomas (Ire)	2003 h.	Danehill—Lagrion, by Diesis (GB)	Ire	10-5-3-0, $4,116,100
125	English Channel	2002 h.	Smart Strike—Belva, by Theatrical (Ire)	USA	7-4-2-0, $2,640,000
	Soldier of Fortune	2004 c.	Galileo (Ire)—Affianced (Ire), by Erins Isle (Ire)	Ire	6-4-0-0, $1,570,120
124	Youmzain	2003 h.	Sinndar—Sadima, by Sadler's Wells	GB	6-0-2-2, $1,545,300
122	Getaway	2003 h.	Monsun—Guernica, by Unfuwain	Fr	3-1-1-0, $283,595

International — 2007 World Thoroughbred Racehorse Rankings

Rating	Horse	YOB Sex	Pedigree	Trained	2007 Record, Earnings
122	Meisho Samson	2003 h.	Opera House (GB)—My Vivien, by Dancing Brave	Jpn	6-3-1-1, $3,894,358
	Peeping Fawn	2004 f.	Danehill—Maryinsky (Ire), by Sadler's Wells	Ire	10-5-2-3, $1,387,274
	Pop Rock	2001 h.	Helissio—Pops, by Sunday Silence	Jpn	8-1-3-1, $2,569,270
	Sagara	2004 c.	Sadler's Wells—Rangoon Ruby, by Kingmambo	Fr	7-1-2-2, $519,968
121	Matsurida Gogh	2003 h.	Sunday Silence—Paper Rain, by Bel Bolide	Jpn	7-3-0-1, $2,810,329
120	Scorpion (Ire)	2002 h.	Montjeu (Ire)—Ardmelody, by Law Society	Ire	5-1-3-0, $494,037
119	Adlerflug	2004 c.	In the Wings (GB)—Aiyana, by Last Tycoon (Ire)	Ger	5-3-1-0, $617,585
	Ask (GB)	2003 h.	Sadler's Wells—Request, by Rainbow Quest	GB	3-2-1-0, $556,546
	Better Talk Now	1999 g.	Talkin Man—Bendita, by Baldski	USA	4-1-0-1, $499,647
	Cloudy's Knight	2000 g.	Lord Avie—Cloudy Spot, by Solar City	USA	9-3-3-1, $1,762,868
	Doctor Dino (Fr)	2002 h.	Muhtathir (GB)—Logica, by Priolo	Fr	6-2-0-4, $1,752,717
	Mountain High	2002 h.	Danehill—Hellenic, by Darshaan	GB	5-2-0-1, $373,846
	Quijano (Ger)	2002 g.	Acatenango—Quila, by Unfuwain	Ger	9-5-1-1, $1,121,787
	Saddex	2003 h.	Sadler's Wells—Remote Romance, by Irish River (Fr)	Ger	5-3-0-0, $290,974
	Sixties Icon	2003 h.	Galileo (Ire)—Love Divine, by Diesis (GB)	GB	3-1-0-0, $101,857
	Delta Blues	2001 h.	Dance in the Dark—Dixie Splash, by Dixieland Band	Jpn	7-0-0-0, $370,303
	Mrs Lindsay	2004 f.	Theatrical (Ire)—Vole Vole Monamour, by Woodman	Fr	6-4-1-0, $1,170,915
	Sky Conqueror	2002 h.	Sky Classic—Heavenly Ballerina, by Conquistador Cielo	Can	7-2-1-1, $827,043
	Zambezi Sun	2004 c.	Dansili (GB)—Imbabala, by Zafonic	Fr	6-3-0-1, $639,941
117	Chosan	2002 h.	Dance in the Dark—Stay Young, by Soccer Boy	Jpn	8-2-1-1, $829,074
	Irish Wells	2003 h.	Poliglote (GB)—Sign of the Vine, by Kendor	Fr	6-1-1-1, $311,067
	Lahudood (GB)	2003 m.	Singspiel (Ire)—Rahayeb (GB), by Arazi	USA	5-3-1-0, $1,560,500
	Light Shift	2003 f.	Kingmambo—Lingerie (GB), by Shirley Heights	GB	6-3-1-1, $676,067
	Maraahel	2001 h.	Alzao—Nasanice, by Nashwan	GB	7-3-0-2, $530,129
	Schiaparelli	2003 h.	Monsun—Sacarina, by Old Vic	Ger	6-4-0-1, $512,787
	Sir Percy	2003 h.	Mark of Esteem (Ire)—Percy's Lass, by Blakeney	GB	3-0-0-0, $266,671
	Sunriver	2003 h.	Saint Ballado—Goulash, by Mari's Book	USA	6-3-1-0, $410,014
	Vodka	2004 f.	Tanino Gimlet—Tanino Sister, by Rousillon	Jpn	8-3-1-1, $2,980,561
116	Admire Fuji	2002 h.	Admire Vega—Admire Lapis, by Be My Guest	Jpn	7-0-0-0, $412,896
	Bussoni	2001 h.	Goofalik—Blumme (Chi), by Jadar	Ger	8-3-1-3, $810,310
	Grand Couturier (GB)	2003 h.	Grand Lodge—Lady Elgar, by Sadler's Wells	USA	5-1-0-2, $362,010
	Laverock	2001 h.	Octagonal—Sky Song (Ire), by Sadler's Wells	GB	10-0-2-2, $280,211
	Papal Bull	2003 h.	Montjeu (Ire)—Mialuna, by Zafonic	GB	6-2-0-1, $179,269
	Pressing (Ire)	2003 h.	Soviet Star—Rafif, by Riverman	Ity	9-5-2-0, $592,215
	Prince Flori	2003 h.	Lando (Ger)—Princess Liberte, by Nebos	Ger	6-1-0-2, $147,612
	Stream of Gold (Ire)	2001 g.	Rainbow Quest—River Dancer, by Irish River (Fr)	USA	8-0-5-0, $356,148
	West Wind	2004 f.	Machiavellian—Red Slippers, by Nureyev	Fr	6-2-2-2, $773,178
115	Asakusa Kings	2004 c.	White Muzzle (GB)—Croupier Star, by Sunday Silence	Jpn	7-2-2-0, $2,459,998
	Boscobel	2004 c.	Halling—Dunnes River, by Danzig	GB	5-2-1-0, $337,903
	Daiwa Scarlet	2004 f.	Agnes Tachyon—Scarlet Bouquet, by Northern Taste	Jpn	7-4-3-0, $3,985,857
	Halicarnassus	2004 c.	Cape Cross (Ire)—Launch Time, by Relaunch	GB	11-3-1-1, $194,884
	Honey Ryder	2001 m.	Lasting Approval—Cuando Quiere, by Affirmed	USA	6-1-3-0, $740,850
	Inti Raimi	2002 h.	Special Week—Andes Lady, by Northern Taste	Jpn	8-2-0-1, $1,134,097
	Lucarno	2004 c.	Dynaformer—Vignette, by Diesis (GB)	GB	7-3-2-0, $1,025,239
	Oracle West (SAf)	2001 g.	Western Winter—Noble Prophet, by Noble Ambition	UAE	7-0-3-1, $1,145,928
	Passage of Time (GB)	2004 f.	Dansili (GB)—Clepsydra, by Sadler's Wells	GB	4-1-0-2, $328,216
	Poet Laureate	2004 c.	Highest Honor (Fr)—Desired, by Rainbow Quest	Fr	3-2-1-0, $110,290
	Prospect Park (GB)	2001 h.	Sadler's Wells—Brooklyn's Dance (Fr), by Shirley Heights	USA	3-0-1-1, $75,660
	Roc de Cambes	2004 c.	Red Ransom—Fairy Lights, by Fairy King	Jpn	6-4-0-1, $1,485,570
	Shamdinan (Fr)	2004 c.	Dr Fong—Shamdara, by Dr Devious (Ire)	USA	8-2-2-1, $1,120,298
	Silkwood	2004 f.	Singspiel (Ire)—Wood Vine, by Woodman	GB	3-2-0-0, $173,275

Extended, Three and Up, Turf

Rating	Horse	YOB Sex	Pedigree	Trained	2007 Record, Earnings
122	Septimus	2003 h.	Sadler's Wells—Caladira, by Darshaan	GB	4-3-1-0, $442,463
121	Yeats	2001 h.	Sadler's Wells—Lyndonville, by Top Ville	Ire	5-4-0-1, $634,581
120	Scorpion (Ire)	2002 h.	Montjeu (Ire)—Ardmelody, by Law Society	Ire	5-1-3-0, $494,037
117	Geordieland	2001 h.	Johann Quatz (Fr)—Aerdee, by Highest Honor (Fr)	GB	6-0-4-0, $211,126
115	Asakusa Kings	2004 c.	White Muzzle (GB)—Croupier Star, by Sunday Silence	Jpn	7-2-2-0, $2,459,998
	Coastal Path	2004 c.	Halling—Coraline, by Sadler's Wells	Fr	4-2-0-0, $193,035
	Erimo Expire	2003 h.	Scatter the Gold—Erimo Brownie, by Commander in Chief	Jpn	3-0-2-0, $584,812
	Honolulu (Ire)	2004 c.	Montjeu (Ire)—Cerulean Sky (Ire), by Darshaan	GB	7-2-1-3, $263,802
	Lucarno	2004 c.	Dynaformer—Vignette, by Diesis (GB)	GB	7-3-2-0, $1,025,239
	Sergeant Cecil	1999 h.	King's Signet—Jadidh, by Touching Wood	GB	5-1-0-0, $189,315
	Tokai Trick	2002 h.	El Condor Pasa—Zoonaqua, by Silver Hawk	Jpn	8-1-2-2, $1,131,478

Intermediate, Three and Up, Turf

Rating	Horse	YOB Sex	Pedigree	Trained	2007 Record, Earnings
131	Manduro	2002 h.	Monsun—Mandellicht, by Be My Guest	Fr	5-5-0-0, $1,242,444
129	Authorized	2004 c.	Montjeu (Ire)—Funsie, by Saumarez (GB)	GB	5-3-1-0, $2,365,763
124	Literato	2004 c.	Kendor—La Cibeles, by Cardoun (Fr)	Fr	6-4-2-0, $1,141,527
123	Notnowcato	2002 h.	Inchinor—Rambling Rose, by Cadeaux Genereux	GB	6-2-0-2, $979,935
122	Eagle Mountain	2004 c.	Rock of Gibraltar (Ire)—Masskana, by Darshaan	Ire	7-1-3-1, $1,067,768
122	Lava Man	2001 g.	Slew City Slew—Li'l Ms. Leonard, by Nostalgia's Star	USA	4-1-1-0, $340,000
	Meisho Samson	2003 h.	Opera House (GB)—My Vivien, by Dancing Brave	Jpn	6-3-1-1, $3,894,358
	Peeping Fawn	2004 f.	Danehill—Maryinsky (Ire), by Sadler's Wells	Ire	10-5-2-3, $1,387,274

International — 2007 World Thoroughbred Racehorse Rankings

Rating	Horse	YOB	Sex	Pedigree	Trained	2007 Record, Earnings
120	Duke of Marmalade	2004	c.	Danehill—Love Me True, by Kingmambo	GB	6-0-2-1, $527,666
	Red Rocks (Ire)	2003	h.	Galileo (Ire)—Pharmacist, by Machiavellian	GB	6-1-0-1, $436,182
119	After Market	2003	h.	Storm Cat—Tranquility Lake, by Rahy	USA	8-4-1-0, $686,725
	Better Talk Now	1999	g.	Talkin Man—Bendita, by Baldski	USA	4-1-0-1, $499,647
	George Washington (Ire)	2003	h.	Danehill—Bordighera, by Alysheba	Ire	3-0-0-2, $190,417
118	Jambalaya	2002	g.	Langfuhr—Muskrat Suzie, by Vice Regent	Can	6-3-0-3, $979,421
	Mandesha	2003	m.	Desert Style—Mandalara, by Lahib	Fr	5-1-3-0, $350,371
	Soldier Hollow (GB)	2000	h.	In the Wings (GB)—Island Race, by Common Grounds	Ger	5-2-1-1, $264,844
117	Agnes Ark	2003	h.	Agnes Tachyon—Belle Saison, by Bellypha (Ire)	Jpn	9-2-3-1, $1,398,225
	Distant Way	2001	h.	Distant View—Grey Way, by Cozzene	Ity	5-2-0-0, $266,590
	Red Giant	2004	c.	Giant's Causeway—Beyond the Sun, by Kingmambo	USA	8-4-3-0, $846,720
	Vadapolina	2004	f.	Trempolino—Vadaza, by Zafonic	Fr	6-3-0-0, $132,100
	Yellowstone (Ire)	2004	c.	Rock of Gibraltar (Ire)—Love and Affection, by Exclusive Era	GB	10-1-2-1, $244,631
116	Company	2001	h.	Miracle Admire—Brilliant Very, by Northern Taste	Jpn	3-1-0-1, $736,161
	Nashoba's Key	2003	m.	Silver Hawk—Nashoba (Ire), by Caerleon	USA	5-4-0-0, $500,430
	Pressing	2003	h.	Soviet Star—Rafif, by Riverman	Ity	9-5-2-0, $592,215
	Royal Highness (Ger)	2002	m.	Monsun—Reem Dubai, by Nashwan	USA	5-2-1-0, $559,500
	Satwa Queen (Fr)	2002	m.	Muhtathir (GB)—Tolga, by Irish River (Fr)	Fr	4-2-2-0, $379,306
	Shadow Gate	2002	h.	White Muzzle (GB)—Fabulous Turn, by Sunday Silence	Jpn	7-2-1-0, $1,801,061
115	Irridescence (SAf)	2001	m.	Caesour—Meretricious, by Dancing Champ	UAE	4-0-2-1, $260,755
	Legerete	2004	f.	Rahy—Sea Hill, by Seattle Slew	Fr	6-2-0-1, $228,657
	Promising Lead	2004	f.	Danehill—Arrive, by Kahyasi	GB	5-2-2-0, $152,821
	Red Rock Canyon	2004	c.	Rock of Gibraltar (Ire)—Imagine (Ire), by Sadler's Wells	Ire	6-0-4-1, $154,043
	Sealy Hill	2004	f.	Point Given—Boston Twist, by Boston Harbor	Can	3-1-2-0, $426,632
	Shamdinan (Fr)	2004	c.	Dr Fong—Shamdara, by Dr Devious (Ire)	USA	8-2-2-1, $1,120,298
	Stage Gift	2003	g.	Cadeaux Genereux—Stage Struck, by Sadler's Wells	GB	5-2-0-0, $168,238
	Tashelka	2004	f.	Mujahid—Tashiriya, by Kenmare	Fr	7-4-0-1, $178,310

Mile, Three and Up, Turf

Rating	Horse	YOB	Sex	Pedigree	Trained	2007 Record, Earnings
131	Manduro	2002	h.	Monsun—Mandellicht, by Be My Guest	Fr	5-5-0-0, $1,242,444
125	Admire Moon	2003	h.	End Sweep—My Katies, by Sunday Silence	Jpn	6-4-0-1, $7,191,318
123	Ramonti	2002	h.	Martino Alonso—Fosca, by El Gran Senor	GB	6-4-2-0, $2,574,626
122	Darjina	2004	f.	Zamindar—Darinska, by Zilzal	Fr	7-4-0-2, $1,162,634
	Excellent Art (GB)	2004	c.	Pivotal—Obsessive, by Seeking the Gold	GB	6-1-3-0, $1,065,583
	Kip Deville	2003	h.	Kipling—Klondike Kaytie, by Encino	USA	7-3-1-1, $1,965,780
121	Daiwa Major	2001	h.	Sunday Silence—Scarlet Bouquet, by Northern Taste	Jpn	7-2-0-3, $2,825,606
	Indian Ink	2004	f.	Indian Ridge—Maid of Killeen, by Darshaan	GB	3-1-1-0, $322,283
120	Cesare	2001	g.	Machiavellian—Tromond, by Lomond	GB	6-2-1-0, $217,884
	Cockney Rebel	2004	c.	Val Royal (Fr)—Factice, by Known Fact	GB	3-2-0-0, $736,490
	Duke of Marmalade	2004	c.	Danehill—Love Me True, by Kingmambo	GB	6-0-2-1, $527,666
	Lawman	2004	c.	Invincible Spirit—Laramie, by Gulch	Fr	6-3-1-0, $1,538,005
119	After Market	2003	h.	Storm Cat—Tranquility Lake, by Rahy	USA	8-4-1-0, $686,725
	Finsceal Beo	2004	f.	Mr. Greeley—Musical Treat (Ire), by Royal Academy	GB	6-2-1-0, $844,219
	George Washington (Ire)	2003	h.	Danehill—Bordighera, by Alysheba	Ire	3-0-0-2, $190,417
	Kongo Rikishio	2002	h.	Stravinsky—Principium, by Hansel	Jpn	5-1-1-0, $850,938
	The Tin Man	1998	g.	Affirmed—Lizzie Rolfe, by Tom Rolfe	USA	4-1-3-0, $536,920
118	Astronomer Royal	2004	c.	Danzig—Sheepscot, by Easy Goer	Ire	6-1-0-1, $405,788
	Creachadoir	2004	c.	King's Best—Sadima, by Sadler's Wells	GB	10-3-3-1, $932,001
	Nobiz Like Shobiz	2004	c.	Albert the Great—Nightstorm, by Storm Cat	USA	5-3-0-0, $709,830
	Showing Up	2003	h.	Strategic Mission—Miss Alethia, by T. V. Commercial	USA	1-0-1-0, $50,000
	Soldier Hollow (GB)	2000	h.	In the Wings (GB)—Island Race, by Common Grounds	Ger	5-2-1-1, $264,844
	Super Hornet	2003	h.	Rodrigo de Triano—You Sun Polish, by El Senor	Jpn	8-4-1-0, $1,528,831
	Toylsome	1999	h.	Cadeaux Genereux—Treasure Trove, by The Minstrel	Ger	8-5-1-1, $338,601
117	Asiatic Boy	2003	h.	Not for Sale—S. S. Asiatic, by Polish Navy	UAE	2-0-0-0, $60,803
	Einstein (Brz)	2002	h.	Spend a Buck—Gay Charm, by Ghadeer	USA	5-1-0-1, $329,835
	Holocene	2004	c.	Lemon Drop Kid—Witching Hour (Fr), by Fairy King	Fr	5-0-2-1, $219,907
	Jeremy	2003	h.	Danehill Dancer—Glint in Her Eye, by Arazi	GB	6-1-1-1, $287,107
	Linngari	2002	h.	Indian Ridge—Lidakiya (Ire), by Kahyasi	Fr	6-2-1-0, $1,335,854
	Precious Kitten	2003	m.	Catienus—Kitten's First, by Lear Fan	USA	8-4-3-0, $1,050,000
	Price Tag (GB)	2003	m.	Dansili (GB)—Tarocchi, by Affirmed	USA	3-1-1-1, $232,560
	Remarkable News (Ven)	2002	h.	Chayim—Unreachable, by Alhajras	USA	6-3-0-0, $360,611
	Spirito Del Vento	2003	g.	Indian Lodge (Ire)—Heavenly Song, by Machiavellian	Fr	6-3-0-2, 205,958
	Suzuka Phoenix	2002	h.	Sunday Silence—Rose of Suzuka (Ire), by Fairy King	Jpn	8-3-0-2, $2,242,095
	Turtle Bowl	2002	h.	Dyhim Diamond (Ire)—Clara Bow, by Top Ville	Fr	7-1-3-2, $298,630
116	Cosmonaut	2002	h.	Lemon Drop Kid—Cosmic Fire, by Capote	USA	8-2-3-1, $658,563
	He's A Decoy	2004	c.	In the Wings (GB)—Allegheny River, by Lear Fan	GB	3-0-0-1, $54,471
	Majestic Roi	2004	f.	Street Cry (Ire)—L'Extra Honor, by Hero's Honor	GB	6-2-1-0, $313,731
	My Typhoon (Ire)	2002	m.	Giant's Causeway—Urban Sea, by Miswaki	USA	6-2-1-0, $515,000
	Passager	2003	g.	Anabaa—Passionnee, by Woodman	Fr	4-0-0-4, $93,247
	Purim	2002	h.	Dynaformer—Kirsteena, by Lord at War (Arg)	USA	6-3-0-1, $485,910
	Racinger	2003	h.	Spectrum—Dibenoise, by Kendor	Fr	5-2-1-0, $202,158
	Vital Equine	2004	c.	Danetime—Bayalika, by Selkirk	Ire	3-0-0-1, $165,714
	Wait a While	2003	m.	Maria's Mon—Flirtatious, by A.P. Indy	USA	5-2-2-1, $400,000
115	Bit of Whimsy	2004	f.	Distorted Humor—Kristi B, by El Prado (Ire)	USA	7-4-2-0, $551,533
	Citronnade	2003	m.	Lemon Drop Kid—Primarily, by Lord At War (Arg)	USA	7-5-1-0, $701,405

Rating	Horse	YOB Sex	Pedigree	Trained	2007 Record, Earnings
115	Daytona (Ire)	2004 g.	Indian Ridge—Kyka, by Blushing John	USA	7-4-0-1, $529,920
	Dreaming of Anna	2004 f.	Rahy—Justenuffheart, by Broad Brush	USA	5-3-2-0, $375,040
	Echelon	2002 m.	Danehill—Exclusive, by Polar Falcon	GB	7-4-0-1, $512,635
	Echo of Light (GB)	2002 h.	Dubai Millennium—Spirit of Tara (Ire), by Sadler's Wells	GB	5-2-0-1, $166,618
	Golden Titus	2004 c.	Titus Livius (Fr)—Oraplata, by Silver Hawk	Fr	5-2-1-1, $280,766
	Mi Emma	2004 f.	Silvano (Ger)—Mi Anna, by Lake Coniston (Ire)	Ger	6-4-1-0, $338,004
	Nannina	2003 m.	Medicean—Hill Hopper, by Danehill	GB	5-1-1-1, $260,549
	Red Evie	2003 m.	Intikhab—Malafemmena (Ire), by Nordico	GB	6-2-1-0, $385,350
	Rutherienne	2004 f.	Pulpit—Ruthian, by Rahy	USA	8-6-0-0, $548,975
	Shakespeare	2001 h.	Theatrical (Ire)—Lady Shirl, by That's a Nice	USA	2-2-0-0, $629,640
	Silent Name (Jpn)	2002 h.	Sunday Silence—Danzigaway, by Danehill	USA	3-0-0-1, $60,000
	Tariq	2004 c.	Kyllachy—Tatora, by Selkirk	GB	6-3-0-0, $289,000

Sprint, Three and Up, Turf

Rating	Horse	YOB Sex	Pedigree	Trained	2007 Record, Earnings
120	Miss Andretti	2001 m.	Ihtiram—Peggie's Bid, by Marooned	Aus	8-6-0-0, $1,526,943
	Sakhee's Secret	2004 c.	Sakhee—Palace Street, by Secreto	GB	5-4-0-0, $535,573
119	Benbaun	2001 g.	Stravinsky—Escape to Victory (GB), by Salse	Ire	6-4-0-0, $405,909
118	Dutch Art	2004 c.	Medicean—Halland Park Lass, by Spectrum	GB	6-0-3-1, $369,823
	Soldier's Tale	2001 h.	Stravinsky—Myrtle (GB), by Batshoof (Ire)	GB	3-1-0-2, $424,573
117	Marchand d'Or	2003 g.	Marchand de Sable—Fedora, by Kendor	Fr	7-2-1-1, $469,735
	Red Clubs	2003 h.	Red Ransom—Two Clubs (GB), by First Trump	GB	7-1-1-1, $551,066
	Takeover Target	1999 g.	Celtic Swing—Shady Stream, by Archregent	Aus	7-3-2-0, $707,814
116	Dandy Man	2003 h.	Mozart (Ire)—Lady Alexander, by Night Shift	GB	7-1-3-1, $239,574
115	Asset	2003 g.	Marju—Snow Peak, by Arazi	GB	7-1-2-1, $208,113
	Garnica	2003 h.	Linamix—Gueridia, by Night Shift	Fr	5-2-1-0, $150,106
	Magnus	2002 h.	Flying Spur—Scandinavia, by Snippets	Aus	7-1-1-2, $370,964

Long, Three and Up, Dirt

Rating	Horse	YOB Sex	Pedigree	Trained	2007 Record, Earnings
127	Curlin	2004 c.	Smart Strike—Sherriff's Deputy, by Deputy Minister	USA	9-6-1-2, $5,102,800
123	Rags to Riches	2004 f.	A.P. Indy—Better Than Honour, by Deputy Minister	USA	6-5-1-0, $1,340,028
118	Tiago	2004 c.	Pleasant Tap—Set Them Free, by Stop the Music	USA	8-4-0-1, $1,234,750

Intermediate, Three and Up, Dirt

Rating	Horse	YOB Sex	Pedigree	Trained	2007 Record, Earnings
127	Curlin	2004 c.	Smart Strike—Sherriff's Deputy, by Deputy Minister	USA	9-6-1-2, $5,102,800
129	Invasor (Arg)	2003 h.	Candy Stripes—Quendom (Arg), by Interprete	USA	2-2-0-0, $3,900,000
126	Street Sense	2004 c.	Street Cry (Ire)—Bedazzle, by Dixieland Band	USA	8-4-3-0, $3,205,000
122	Hard Spun	2004 c.	Danzig—Turkish Tryst, by Turkoman	USA	10-4-3-1, $2,572,500
	Lava Man	2001 g.	Slew City Slew—Li'l Ms. Leonard, by Nostalgia's Star	USA	4-2-0-0, $1,070,000
120	Grasshopper	2004 c.	Dixie Union—Grass Skirt, by Mr. Prospector	USA	5-2-2-1, $378,520
118	Vermilion	2002 h.	El Condor Pasa—Scarlet Lady, by Sunday Silence	Jpn	5-4-0-0, $3,609,013
117	Political Force	2004 h.	Unbridled's Song—Glitter Woman, by Glitterman	USA	8-3-1-3, $520,747
116	Lady Joanne	2004 f.	Orientate—Oatsee, by Unbridled	USA	7-4-2-0, $808,993
	Student Council	2002 h.	Kingmambo—Class Kris, by Kris S.	USA	9-4-2-1, $1,041,755
115	Awesome Gem	2003 g.	Awesome Again—Piano, by Pentelicus	USA	9-2-4-1, $1,032,400
	C P West	2004 c.	Came Home—Queen's Legend, by Dynaformer	USA	7-1-3-0, $305,620
	Field Rouge	2002 h.	Croco Rouge—Mejiro Romer, by Lindo Shaver	Jpn	7-3-1-0, $1,364,516
	Miss Shop	2003 m.	Deputy Minister—Shopping, by Private Account	USA	6-2-2-0, $497,000

Mile, Three and Up, Dirt

Rating	Horse	YOB Sex	Pedigree	Trained	2007 Record, Earnings
124	Any Given Saturday	2004 c.	Distorted Humor—Weekend in Indy, by A.P. Indy	USA	8-4-1-1, $994,320
	Lawyer Ron	2003 h.	Langfuhr—Donation, by Lord Avie	USA	8-4-2-1, $1,320,000
123	Rags to Riches	2004 f.	A.P. Indy—Better Than Honour, by Deputy Minister	USA	6-5-1-0, $1,340,624
122	Hard Spun	2004 c.	Danzig—Turkish Tryst, by Turkoman	USA	10-4-3-1, $2,572,500
120	Corinthian	2003 h.	Pulpit—Multiply, by Easy Goer	USA	7-4-0-0, $1,174,173
118	Ginger Punch	2003 m.	Awesome Again—Nappelon, by Bold Revenue	USA	8-5-2-1, $1,827,060
	Nobiz Like Shobiz	2004 c.	Albert the Great—Nightstorm, by Storm Cat	USA	5-2-1-1, $608,560
	Tiago	2004 c.	Pleasant Tap—Set Them Free, by Stop the Music	USA	8-4-0-1, $1,234,750
117	Hystericalady	2003 m.	Distorted Humor—Sacramentada (Chi), by Northair	USA	8-3-3-1, $984,438
	Scat Daddy	2004 c.	Johannesburg—Love Style, by Mr. Prospector	USA	4-2-0-1, $826,500
116	Daaher	2004 c.	Awesome Again—Irish Cherry, by Irish Orpen	USA	7-4-0-1, $447,039
	Lear's Princess	2004 f.	Lear Fan—Pretty City, by Carson City	USA	7-4-2-0, $429,100
	Molengao (Brz)	2001 h.	Royal Academy—Court Lady, by Locris	USA	4-2-1-0, $470,000
	Nashoba's Key	2003 m.	Silver Hawk—Nashoba, by Caerleon	USA	3-3-0-0, $471,660
	Octave	2004 f.	Unbridled's Song—Belle Nuit, by Dr. Carter	USA	8-2-4-2, $1,050,294
	Panty Raid	2004 f.	Include—Adventurous Di, by Private Account	USA	7-3-1-1, $574,180
	Sightseeing	2004 c.	Pulpit—Resort, by Pleasant Colony	USA	8-1-2-3, $401,716
	Spring at Last	2003 h.	Silver Deputy—Winter's Gone, by Dynaformer	USA	4-1-1-0, $680,000
	Tough Tiz's Sis	2004 f.	Tiznow—Leasehold, by Taylor's Falls	USA	10-4-2-1, $399,732
115	Arson Squad	2003 g.	Brahms—Majestic Fire, by Green Dancer	USA	6-1-0-0, $264,000
	Balance	2003 m.	Thunder Gulch—Vertigineux, by Kris S.	USA	7-2-1-2, $448,332
	Blue Concorde	2000 h.	Fusaichi Concorde—Ebisu Family, by Brian's Time	Jpn	8-2-2-1, $1,693,107
	Buzzard's Bay	2001 h.	Marco Bay—Lifes Lass, by Seneca Jones	USA	6-2-0-1, $200,400
	Circular Quay	2004 c.	Thunder Gulch—Circle of Life, by Belong to Me	USA	4-1-0-0, $396,000

International — Cartier Awards

Rating	Horse	YOB	Sex	Pedigree	Trained	2007 Record, Earnings
115	Dominican	2004	g.	El Corredor—First Violin, by Dixieland Band	USA	5-2-0-1, $549,140
	Master Command	2002	h.	A.P. Indy—Lady Lochivar, by Lord at War (Arg)	USA	5-3-0-0, $598,170
	Stormello	2004	c.	Stormy Atlantic—Wilshewed, by Carson City	USA	4-0-1-1, $155,000
	Sun Boat (GB)	2002	g.	Machiavellian—One So Wonderful, by Nashwan	USA	5-2-1-0, $272,000
	Sunrise Bacchus	2002	h.	Hennessy—Real Sapphire, by Real Shadai	Jpn	7-1-1-3, $1,625,032
	Take d'Tour	2001	m.	Tour d'Or—Cherry Flare, by Mr. Washington	USA	4-1-2-0, $395,000
	Unbridled Belle	2003	m.	Broken Vow—Little Bold Belle, by Silver Buck	USA	5-2-2-0, $1,116,500
	Wanderin Boy	2001	h.	Seeking the Gold—Vid Kid, by Pleasant Colony	USA	5-1-1-0, $296,708

Sprint, Three and Up, Dirt

Rating	Horse	YOB	Sex	Pedigree	Trained	2007 Record, Earnings
122	Hard Spun	2004	c.	Danzig—Turkish Tryst, by Turkoman	USA	10-4-3-1, $2,572,500
121	Midnight Lute	2003	h.	Real Quiet—Candytuft, by Dehere	USA	6-2-2-0, $1,368,000
120	Fabulous Strike	2003	g.	Smart Strike—Fabulous Find, by Lost Code	USA	4-3-0-0, $403,332
118	Smokey Stover	2003	g.	Put It Back—Milady's Halo, by Jolie's Halo	USA	7-5-0-1, $471,000
117	Surf Cat	2002	h.	Sir Cat—Trust Greta, by Centrust	USA	2-0-2-0, $120,000
116	Dream Rush	2004	f.	Wild Rush—Turbo Dream, by Unbridled	USA	7-4-2-0, $570,800
	Greg's Gold	2001	g.	Lake George—Lake Windermere, by Fit to Fight	USA	10-4-3-1, $566,995
	In Summation	2003	h.	Put It Back—Fiesta Baby, by Dayjur	USA	3-2-1-0, $259,600
115	Benny the Bull	2003	h.	Lucky Lionel—Comet Cat, by Birdonthewire	USA	8-3-1-1, $420,460
	Idiot Proof	2004	c.	Benchmark—Perfectly Pretty, by Bertrando	USA	8-4-2-1, $803,136
	Kelly's Landing	2001	g.	Patton—Best Game, by Great Above	USA	4-2-0-0, $1,313,000
	Silent Name (Jpn)	2002	h.	Sunday Silence—Danzigaway, by Danehill	USA	3-1-0-0, $251,000
	Silver Wagon	2001	h.	Wagon Limit—So Ritzy, by Darn That Alarm	USA	4-2-0-1, $483,000

Cartier Awards

Established in 1991, the Cartier Awards are European racing's closest equivalent to the Eclipse Awards. Winners are determined by points earned in pattern races and votes of racing experts and Daily Telegraph readers.

Award of Merit
2007 Niarchos family
2006 Peter Willett
2005 Henry Cecil
2004 David and Patricia Thompson
2003 Lord John Oaksey
2002 Khalid Abdullah
2001 John Magnier
2000 Aga Khan
1999 Peter Walwyn
1998 Head family
1997 Sir Peter O'Sullevan
1996 Frankie Dettori
1995 John Dunlop
1994 Lord Hartington
1993 Francois Boutin
1992 Lester Piggott
1991 Henri Chalhoub

Horse of the Year
2007 Dylan Thomas (Ire)
2006 Ouija Board (GB)
2005 Hurricane Run (Ire)
2004 Ouija Board (GB)
2003 Dalakhani
2002 Rock of Gibraltar (Ire)
2001 Fantastic Light
2000 Giant's Causeway
1999 Daylami (Ire)
1998 Dream Well (Fr)
1997 Peintre Celebre
1996 Helissio
1995 Ridgewood Pearl (GB)
1994 Barathea (Ire)
1993 Lochsong (GB)
1992 User Friendly (GB)
1991 Arazi

Two-Year-Old Filly
2007 Natagora
2006 Finsceal Beo
2005 Rumplestiltskin
2004 Divine Proportions
2003 Attraction
2002 Six Perfections (Fr)
2001 Queen's Logic (Ire)
2000 Superstar Leo
1999 Torgau (Ire)
1998 Bint Allayl
1997 Embassy (GB)
1996 Pas de Reponse
1995 Blue Duster
1994 Gay Gallanta
1993 Lemon Souffle (GB)
1992 Lyric Fantasy (Ire)
1991 Culture Vulture

Two-Year-Old Colt
2007 New Approach
2006 Teofilo
2005 George Washington (Ire)
2004 Shamardal
2003 One Cool Cat
2002 Hold That Tiger
2001 Johannesburg
2000 Tobougg (Ire)
1999 Fasliyev
1998 Aljabr
1997 Xaar
1996 Bahamian Bounty
1995 Alhaarth
1994 Celtic Swing
1993 First Trump
1992 Zafonic
1991 Arazi

Three-Year-Old Filly
2007 Peeping Fawn
2006 Mandesha
2005 Divine Proportions
2004 Ouija Board (GB)
2003 Russian Rhythm
2002 Kazzia (Ger)
2001 Banks Hill (GB)
2000 Petrushka (Ire)
1999 Ramruma
1998 Cape Verdi (Ire)
1997 Ryafan
1996 Bosra Sham
1995 Ridgewood Pearl (GB)
1994 Balanchine
1993 Intrepidity (GB)
1992 User Friendly (GB)
1991 Kooyonga (Ire)

Three-Year-Old Colt
2007 Authorized
2006 George Washington (Ire)
2005 Hurricane Run (Ire)
2004 Bago (Fr)
2003 Dalakhani
2002 Rock of Gibraltar (Ire)
2001 Galileo (Ire)
2000 Sinndar
1999 Montjeu (Ire)
1998 Dream Well (Fr)
1997 Peintre Celebre
1996 Helissio
1995 Lammtarra
1994 King's Theatre (Ire)
1993 Commander in Chief
1992 Rodrigo de Triano
1991 Suave Dancer

Stayer
2007 Yeats
2006 Yeats
2005 Westerner
2004 Westerner
2003 Persian Punch
2002 Vinnie Roe
2001 Persian Punch
2000 Kayf Tara
1999 Kayf Tara
1998 Kayf Tara
1997 Celeric
1996 Nononito
1995 Double Trigger
1994 Moonax
1993 Vintage Crop
1992 Drum Taps
1991 Turgeon

Sprinter
2007 Red Clubs
2006 Reverence
2005 Avonbridge
2004 Somnus
2003 Oasis Dream (GB)
2002 Continent
2001 Mozart (Ire)
2000 Nuclear Debate
1999 Stravinsky
1998 Tamarisk
1997 Royal Applause (GB)
1996 Anabaa (Ire)
1995 Hever Golf Rose (GB)
1994 Lochsong (GB)
1993 Lochsong (GB)
1992 Mr Brooks (GB)
1991 Sheikh Albadou (GB)

Older Horse
2007 Dylan Thomas (Ire)
2006 Ouija Board (GB)
2005 Azamour (Ire)
2004 Soviet Song
2003 Falbrav (Ire)
2002 Grandera
2001 Fantastic Light
2000 Kalanisi (Ire)
1999 Daylami (Ire)
1998 Swain (Ire)
1997 Pilsudski (Ire)
1996 Halling
1995 Further Flight
1994 Barathea (Ire)
1993 Opera House (GB)
1992 Mr Brooks (GB)
1991 Terimon

Special Award
2002 Tony McCoy
1994 Vincent O'Brien

Millennium Award of Merit
2000 Queen Elizabeth II

Lord Derby Awards

Presented by the British Horserace Writers and Photographers Association for overall excellence.

Service to International Racing

- 2003 Khalid Abdullah
- 2002 Nick Clarke
- 2001 Pam Blatz-Murff
- 2000 Aga Khan
- 1999 Michael Osborne
- 1998 James E. "Ted" Bassett III
- 1997 Geoffrey Gibbs
- 1996 Flying Grooms
- 1995 Maj. Gen. Guy Watkins
- 1994 Robert Sangster
- 1993 Francois Boutin Niarchos family
- 1992 Maktoum family
- 1991 John Dunlop
- 1990 Louis Romanet
- 1989 Michael Byrne
- 1988 Richard Duchossois
- 1987 Yves Saint-Martin
- 1986 John Gaines
- 1985 Lord Derby
- 1984 Ivan Straker
- 1983 Paul Mellon
- 1982 Jean Romanet
- 1981 Joe Hirsch

Outstanding Achievement Award
(George Ennor Trophy)

- 2007 Nigel Payne
- 2006 Ginger McCain
- 2005 Peter Sayer
- 2004 Peter Willett
- 2003 Pat Eddery
- 2002 Ian Balding
- 2001 Graham Rock
- 2000 Johnny Murtagh
- 1999 Peter Walwyn
- 1998 Capt. Tim Forster
- 1997 Sir Peter O'Sullevan
- 1996 Peter Easterby
- 1995 Lester Piggott
- 1994 Vincent O'Brien
- 1993 Dermot Weld

Outstanding Achievement Award
(President's Trophy)

- 2007 J. P. McNamara
- 2006 Martin Pipe
- 2005 Reg Hollinshead
- 2004 George Ennor
- 2003 Lord John Oaksey
- 2002 Not awarded
- 2001 John Reid
- 2000 Ray Cochrane
- 1999 Jack Berry
- 1998 Not awarded
- 1997 Maj. Dick Hern
- 1996 Not awarded
- 1995 Jim Old Stable staff

International Trainer of the Year

- 2007 Aidan O'Brien
- 2006 Brian Meehan
- 2005 Andrew Balding
- 2004 Ed Dunlop
- 2003 Pascal Bary
- 2002 Demot Weld
- 2001 Aidan O'Brien
- 2000 Saeed bin Suroor
- 1999 Saeed bin Suroor
- 1998 Saeed bin Suroor
- 1997 Sir Michael Stoute
- 1996 Sir Michael Stoute
- 1995 Peter Chapple-Hyam
- 1994 John Dunlop
- 1993 John Dunlop
- 1992 Paul Cole
- 1991 Paul Cole
- 1990 Paul Cole
- 1989 Henry Cecil
- 1988 Luca Cumani
- 1987 Paul Cole
- 1986 Michael Stoute
- 1985 Clive Brittain
- 1984 Ian Balding
- 1983 Luca Cumani
- 1982 John Dunlop
- 1981 Ian Balding

Owner of the Year

- 2007 Clive Smith
- 2006 Victoria and Anthony Pakenham
- 2005 Graham Wylie
- 2004 Lord Derby
- 2003 Jim Lewis
- 2002 Sir Alex Ferguson
- 2001 Susan Magnier and Michael Tabor
- 2000 Aga Khan
- 1999 Michael Tabor
- 1998 The Summit Partnership
- 1997 Peter Winfield
- 1996 Godolphin Racing
- 1995 Godolphin Racing
- 1994 Jeff Smith
- 1993 Robert Sangster
- 1992 Bill Gredley
- 1991 Prince Fahd Salman
- 1990 Sheikh Hamdan bin Rashid al Maktoum
- 1989 Sheikh Hamdan bin Rashid al Maktoum
- 1988 Jim Joel
- 1987 Louis Freedman
- 1986 Khalid Abdullah
- 1985 Lord Howard de Walden
- 1984 Eric Moller
- 1983 Robert Barnett
- 1982 Paul Mellon
- 1981 Aga Khan
- 1980 Pat Muldoon
- 1979 Snailwell Stud
- 1978 David McCall
- 1977 Queen Elizabeth II
- 1976 Daniel Wildenstein
- 1975 Carlo Vittadini
- 1974 Peter O'Sullevan
- 1973 Louis Freedman
- 1972 Lady Beaverbrook
- 1971 John and Jean Hislop
- 1970 Charles Engelhard and David McCall
- 1969 Earl of Rosebery
- 1968 Lord Allendale
- 1967 Jim Joel

Trainer of the Year

- 2007 Peter Chapple-Hyam
- 2006 Marcus Tregoning
- 2005 Michael Bell
- 2004 Saeed bin Suroor
- 2003 Sir Michael Stoute
- 2002 Mark Johnston
- 2001 Aidan O'Brien
- 2000 John Oxx
- 1999 Henry Cecil
- 1998 Saeed bin Suroor
- 1997 Sir Michael Stoute
- 1996 Henry Cecil
- 1995 John Dunlop
- 1994 Mark Johnston
- 1993 Richard Hannon
- 1992 Richard Hannon
- 1991 Paul Cole
- 1990 Jack Berry
- 1989 Maj. Dick Hern
- 1988 David Chapman
- 1987 Henry Cecil
- 1986 Sir Michael Stoute
- 1985 Henry Cecil
- 1984 Roy Sheather
- 1983 John Dunlop
- 1982 David Chapman
- 1981 Guy Harwood
- 1980 Maj. Dick Hern
- 1979 Henry Cecil
- 1978 Michael Stoute
- 1977 Vincent O'Brien
- 1976 Henry Cecil
- 1975 Maj. Dick Hern
- 1974 Peter Walwyn
- 1973 Arthur Budgett
- 1972 Bruce Hobbs
- 1971 Ian Balding
- 1970 Vincent O'Brien
- 1969 Harvey Leader
- 1968 Sir Cecil Boyd-Rochfort
- 1967 Sir Noel Murless

Jockey of the Year

- 2007 Seb Sanders
- 2006 Ryan Moore
- 2005 Jamie Spencer
- 2004 Frankie Dettori
- 2003 Kieren Fallon
- 2002 Richard Hughes
- 2001 Michael Kinane
- 2000 Kevin Darley
- 1999 Richard Quinn
- 1998 Kieren Fallon
- 1997 Kieren Fallon
- 1996 Frankie Dettori
- 1995 Frankie Dettori
- 1994 Frankie Dettori
- 1993 Kevin Darley
- 1992 Michael Roberts
- 1991 Alan Munro
- 1990 Frankie Dettori
- 1989 Willie Carson
- 1988 Michael Roberts
- 1987 Steve Cauthen
- 1986 Pat Eddery
- 1985 Steve Cauthen
- 1984 Steve Cauthen
- 1983 Willie Carson
- 1982 Lester Piggott
- 1981 Lester Piggott
- 1980 Lester Piggott
- 1979 Joe Mercer
- 1978 Greville Starkey
- 1977 Willie Carson
- 1976 Brian Taylor
- 1975 Joe Mercer
- 1974 Pat Eddery
- 1973 Tony Murray
- 1972 Edward Hide
- 1971 Willie Carson
- 1970 Lester Piggott
- 1969 Geoff Lewis
- 1968 Sandy Barclay
- 1967 Doug Smith

National Hunt Owner of the Year
(Awarded 1969-'73)

- 1973 Noel le Mare
- 1972 Mrs. John Rogerson
- 1971 Col. Bill Whitbread
- 1970 Bryan Jenks
- 1969 Edward Courage

National Hunt Trainer of the Year

- 2007 Paul Nicholls
- 2006 Paul Nicholls
- 2005 Paul Nicholls
- 2004 Henrietta Knight
- 2003 Philip Hobbs
- 2002 Henrietta Knight
- 2001 Martin Pipe
- 2000 Noel Chance
- 1999 Paul Nichols
- 1998 Martin Pipe
- 1997 Martin Pipe
- 1996 Jim Old
- 1995 Kim Bailey
- 1994 David Nicholson
- 1993 Nigel Twiston-Davies
- 1992 Mary Reveley
- 1991 Martin Pipe
- 1990 Martin Pipe
- 1989 Martin Pipe
- 1988 David Elsworth
- 1987 Nicky Henderson
- 1986 Nicky Henderson
- 1985 Capt. Tim Forster
- 1984 Jenny Pitman
- 1983 Michael Dickinson
- 1982 Michael Dickinson
- 1981 Peter Easterby
- 1980 Peter Easterby
- 1979 Peter Easterby
- 1978 Fred Winter
- 1977 Peter Easterby
- 1976 Tony Dickinson
- 1975 Gordon Richards
- 1974 Donald "Ginger" McCain
- 1973 Fulke Walwyn
- 1972 David Barons
- 1971 Fred Winter
- 1970 Arthur Stephenson
- 1969 Colin Davies
- 1968 Fred Rimell

National Hunt Jockey of the Year
- 2007 Ruby Walsh
- 2006 Tony McCoy
- 2005 Ruby Walsh
- 2004 Tony McCoy
- 2003 Tony McCoy
- 2002 Tony McCoy
- 2001 Tony McCoy
- 2000 Tony McCoy
- 1999 Tony McCoy
- 1998 Tony McCoy
- 1997 Tony McCoy
- 1996 Tony McCoy
- 1995 Norman Williamson
- 1994 Aidrian Maguire
- 1993 Richard Dunwoody
- 1992 Peter Niven
- 1991 Peter Scudamore
- 1990 Peter Scudamore
- 1989 Peter Scudamore
- 1988 Chris Grant
- 1987 Peter Scudamore
- 1986 Peter Scudamore
- 1985 John Francome
- 1984 John Francome
- 1983 John Francome
- 1982 Peter Scudamore
- 1981 Bob Champion
- 1980 Jonjo O'Neil
- 1979 Tommy Carmody
- 1978 Jonjo O'Neill
- 1977 Tommy Stack
- 1976 Jeff King
- 1975 Tommy Stack
- 1974 Richard Pitman
- 1973 Ron Barry
- 1972 Bob Davies
- 1971 Graham Thorner
- 1970 Terry Biddlecombe
- 1969 Stan Mellor
- 1968 Brian Fletcher
- 1967 Josh Gifford

Stable Staff of the Year
- 2007 Graham Gray
  Derek Wilmott
- 2006 Clifford Baker
  John Wilsoncroft
- 2005 Steve Kingstree
  Ernie Peterson
- 2004 Jock Brown
  Brian Clothworthy
  Ian Wilder
- 2003 Albert "Corky" Browne
  Johnny Worrall
  Dennis Wright
- 2002 Tom Townsend
  Dave Goodwin
- 2001 Rodney Boult
  Peter Maughan
  Jimmy Scott
- 2000 George Charlton
  John Smillie
- 1999 Rachel Hume
  Robynne Watton
- 1998 Michael Leaman
  Geoff Snook
- 1997 Jack Nelson
  Eddie Watt
- 1996 Harry Buckle
- 1996 Ian Willows
- 1995 Sidney Outen
  John Sayers
- 1994 Vicki Harris
  Ron Thomas
- 1993 John Cullen
  Geoff Thompson
- 1992 Jimmy East
  Bill Palmer
- 1991 Harvey Ewart
  Steven Rose
- 1990 Steve Fox
  Colin Nutter
- 1989 Brian Delaney
  Meg MacDonald
- 1988 Peter Heaney
  Kevin Murrell
- 1987 Alison Dean
- 1986 Glyn Foster
- 1985 Jimmy Swales
- 1984 Syd McGahey
- 1983 Raymond Campbell
- 1982 Linda McCauley
- 1981 Olga Nicholson
- 1980 Alan Welborne
- 1979 Jack Kidd
- 1978 Nigel Atkinson

- 1977 John Hallum
- 1976 Mervyn Heath
- 1975 John Vickers

Journalist of the Year (Clive Graham Trophy)
- 2007 Chris McGrath (freelance)
- 2006 Tim Richards (freelance)
- 2005 Richard Edmondson (*The Independent*)
- 2004 Alan Lee (*The Times*)
- 2003 Clare Balding (BBC and *Evening Standard*)
  Doug Moscrop (*Newcastle Journal*)
- 2002 Tom O'Ryan (*Racing Post*)
- 2001 Alan Lee (*The Times*)
- 2000 Alan Amies (Raceform)
- 1999 Alastair Down (*Racing Post*)
- 1998 Claude Duval (*The Sun*)
- 1997 Rodney Masters (*Racing Post*)
- 1996 David Ashforth (*Sporting Life*)
- 1995 Richard Evans (*The Times*)
- 1994 Alastair Down (*Sporting Life*)
- 1993 Paul Haigh (*Racing Post*)
- 1992 Jim McGrath (*Daily Telegraph*)
- 1991 John Sexton (Wolverhampton *Express and Star*)
- 1990 Tony Morris (*Racing Post*)
- 1989 Michael Seely (*The Times*)
- 1988 Geoff Lester (*Sporting Life*)
- 1987 Peter Goodall (Press Association)
- 1986 Peter O'Sullevan (BBC)
- 1985 Jim Stanford (*Daily Mail*)
- 1984 John Sharratt (Raceform)
- 1983 Bill Garland (Press Association)
- 1982 George Ennor (*Sporting Life*)
- 1981 Jonathan Powell (*Sunday People*)
- 1980 Michael Seely (*The Times*)
- 1979 Christopher Poole (*Evening Standard*)
- 1978 Tim Richards (*Daily Mirror*)
- 1977 Brough Scott (*Sunday Times*)
- 1976 Peter Willett (*Sporting Chronicle*)
- 1975 Peter Scott (*Daily Telegraph*)
- 1974 Tom Cosgrove (London *Evening News*)
- 1973 Richard Baerlein (*The Guardian/Observer*)
- 1972 Roger Mortimer (*Sunday Times*)
- 1971 Clive Graham and Peter O'Sullevan (*Daily Express*)
- 1970 George Stevens (*Birmingham Post & Mail*)
- 1969 Geoffrey Hamlyn (*Sporting Life*)
- 1968 John Lawrence (*Daily Telegraph*)
- 1967 Quintin Gilbey (*Sporting Chronicle*)

Photographer of the Year
- 2007 David Dew (*Racing Post*)
- 2006 Ed Whitaker (*Racing Post*)
- 2005 Bill Selwyn (freelance)
- 2004 Dan Abraham (freelance)
- 2003 Ed Whitaker (*Racing Post*)
- 2002 Ed Whitaker (*Racing Post*)
- 2001 Anne Grossick (freelance)
- 2000 John Grossick (freelance)
- 1999 Ed Whitaker (*Racing Post*)
- 1998 Alec Russell (freelance)
- 1997 Mark Cranham (freelance)

Broadcaster of the Year (Sir Peter O'Sullevan Trohy)
- 2007 Nick Luck
- 2006 Mike Cattermole (At The Races)
- 2005 Robert Cooper (Attheraces)
- 2004 Clare Balding (BBC)

Major International Racetracks

Argentina

Argentino de Palermo

Located in the Palermo district close to downtown Buenos Aires and familiarly known as Palermo, Hipodromo Argentino opened on May 7, 1876. Originally a Standardbred facility offering just one Thoroughbred race daily, the track changed to full-time Thoroughbred racing on August 18, 1883, and was the first racetrack in Argentina to feature a totalizator. A sales pavilion, veterinary hospital and laboratory, equine institute, and museum complement the racetrack, which is home of the Gran Premio Nacional (Arg-G1), Argentina's equivalent of the Kentucky Derby (G1) and third race of the Argentine Triple Crown. Two of its most famous winners were *Yatasto in 1951 and *Forli in '66. Another major stakes race is the Polla de Potrillos (Arg-G1) (Argentine Two Thousand Guineas), the first race of the Triple Crown, in September. Racing is held over a 2,410-meter,* left-handed track with three chutes. (*See conversion table from metric to English distances in Reference section.)

Location: Ave. Del Libertador 4101, Capital Federal, Buenos Aires
Phone: 54 (11) 4778-2800
Fax: 541 (47) 746-807
Website: www.palermo.com.ar
E-Mail: mail@palermo.com.ar
Abbreviation: HAr
Principal Races: Comparacion (Arg-G1), Criadores (Arg-G1), De Honor (Arg-G1), De las Americas-Internacional (Arg-G1), Jorge de Atucha (Arg-G1), Nacional (Arg-G1), Polla de Potrancas (Arg-G1), Polla de Potrillos (Arg-G1), Santiago Luro (Arg-G1), Seleccion (Arg-G1)

La Plata

The first racetrack in Argentina to hold evening race cards, Hipodromo de La Plata opened on September 14, 1884. Situated approximately 35 miles south of

Buenos Aires, the track is in the city of La Plata in the province of Buenos Aires. The track's proximity to a railway station makes it easily accessible by public transportation. The left-handed, elliptical dirt track is 2,000 meters with two chutes. As many as 145 racing dates are held annually.

Location: La Plata, Pica de Buenos Aires
Phone: 541 (21) 211-071
Fax: 541 (21) 42-390
Website: *www.loteria.gba.gov.ar/hplp*
Abbreviation: LP or LPX
Principal Races: Dardo Rocha Internacional (Arg-G1), Joachin V. Gonzalez Internacional (Arg-G1), Ciudad de La Plata Internacional (Arg-G1), Seleccion de Potrancas (Arg-G1)

San Isidro

Located 14 miles north of Buenos Aires on the edge of the Pampas, San Isidro Racecourse was founded on December 8, 1935, by the Jockey Club Argentino. San Isidro hosts the Gran Premio Carlos Pellegrini-Internacional (Arg-G1), the country's most important race, which is the final leg of the San Isidro Triple Crown. *Yatasto won the Carlos Pellegrini in 1952 before a record crowd of 104,810. *Forli accomplished the feat in 1966 and was then exported to the United States. A daily card consists of as many as 14 races, which begin in midafternoon and conclude at night under lights. Two overlapping, left-handed turf courses—the main one is 2,783 meters—have three chutes.

Location: 504 Avenue Marquez, San Isidro 1642
Phone: 54 (11) 4743-4010
Website: *www.hipodromosanisidro.com.ar*
E-Mail: hipodromosanisidro@jockeyclub.com.ar
Abbreviation: SI
Principal Races: 25 de Mayo (Arg-G1), Carlos Pellegrini-Internacional (Arg-G1), Copa de Oro (Arg-G1), De Potrancas (Arg-G1), Estrellas Sprint (Arg-G1), Estrellas Distaff (Arg-G1), Estrellas Junior Sprint (Arg-G1), Estrellas Juvenile Fillies (Arg-G1), Estrellas Sprint (Arg-G1), Felix de Alzaga Unzue-Internacional (Arg-G1), Gran Criterium (Arg-G1), Jockey Club (Arg-G1)

Australia
Ascot

Located along the Swan River in the heart of Perth, capital city of Western Australia, Ascot features the Perth Cup (Aus-G2), first contested in 1879. In 1982, the track underwent a major renovation. It has a left-handed course of 2,000 meters with a 300-meter straight. Three different chutes are used to start Ascot's three major races: the Perth Cup, the Western Australian Turf Club Derby (Aus-G1) at 2,400 meters, and the Railway Stakes (Aus-G1) at 1,600 meters.

Location: 70 Grandstand Road, Ascot, WA 6104
Phone: 61 (08) 9277-0777
Fax: 61 (08) 9277-0740
Website: *www.perthracing.com.au*
E-Mail: perthracing@perthracing.org.au
Abbreviation: AsR
Chairman: E. Van Heemst
Chief Executive: Alasdair Robertson
Principal Races: Railway S. (Aus-G1), West Australian Turf Club Derby (Aus-G1), Perth Cup (Aus-G2)

Canterbury

Canterbury Racecourse, located approximately seven miles southwest of Sydney's central business district, is easily accessible by public transportation and offers ample free parking. Its intimate, 1,600-meter track affords spectators a close view of the 34 race cards conducted annually by the Sydney Turf Club. Racing is usually held on Thursday evenings, with occasional Saturday-evening programs, including the beginning of the rich Autumn Golden Slipper Festival. Programs of eight to ten races are held on the right-handed turf course. In July 2002, Sydney Turf Club officials announced that the Canterbury facility would not be sold for development. The 1,800-meter Canterbury Guineas (Aus-G1) for three-year-olds is the track's top race.

Location: King Street, Canterbury, NSW 2193
Phone: 61 (02) 9930-4000
Fax: 61 (02) 9930-4099
Website: *www.stc.com.au*
E-Mail: sydturf@stc.com.au
Abbreviation: Cby
Chairman: Alan Brown
Vice Chairman: Bill Picken
Chief Executive: Michael T. Kenny
Track Supervisor: Greg Carmoody
Principal Races: Canterbury Guineas (Aus-G1)

Caulfield

Situated about five miles southeast of Melbourne, Caulfield Racecourse has a rich history that traces to August 5, 1876. In 1996, the Melbourne Racing Club (formerly the Victoria Amateur Turf Club) widened the track to 30 meters around the entire circumference and lengthened the straight by 43 meters. Affectionately known as "the Heath," Caulfield is home to the Caulfield Carnival each spring, which features three major stakes: the 2,400-meter Caulfield Cup (Aus-G1), the 1,600-meter Caulfield Guineas (Aus-G1) for three-year-olds, and the 1,600-meter Vinery Australia Thousand Guineas (Aus-G1) for three-year-old fillies. The Autumn Carnival offers Victoria's richest race for two-year-olds, the AAMI Blue Diamond Stakes (Aus-G1) at 1,200 meters. Caulfield stages 20 dates of racing during the year.

Location: P.O. Box 231, Caulfield East, Victoria 3145 or Station Street, Caulfield, Victoria
Phone: 61 (3) 9257-7200
Fax: 61 (3) 9257-7210
Website: *www.melbourneracingclub.net.au*
E-Mail: contact@melbourneracingclub.net.au
Abbreviation: Cau
Chairman: Peter Young
Chief Executive: Warran Brown
General Manager: Simon Gardner
Director of Racing: Jason Kerr
Director of Marketing: Mary Morton
Principal Races: Blue Diamond Stakes (Aus-G1), Caulfield Cup (Aus-G1), Caulfield Guineas (Aus-G1), Underwood Stakes (Aus-G1), Vinery Australia Thousand Guineas (Aus-G1)

Doomben

Doomben Track, formerly the Doomben Park Recreation Grounds Ltd., was opened in 1933 by the Brisbane Amateur Turf Club, which subsequently changed its name to the Brisbane Turf Club. Called the "Garden Racecourse," Doomben was used as a base by United States troops during World War II. The track underwent an extensive renovation in 1982 and now hosts 40 race dates, 25 of them on Saturdays, each year. Its major races include the Doomben 10,000 Stakes (Aus-G1), formerly the T. M. Ahern Memorial

Stakes, and the Doomben Cup (Aus-G1) at 2,200 meters. Another highlight is the six-day Winter Racing Carnival. Doomben is adjacent to Eagle Farm Racecourse, the principal track in Brisbane, Queensland's capital. The track is approximately four miles from Brisbane's central business district and a short distance from Brisbane Airport.

Location: P.O. Box 168, Hamilton Central, Queensland 4007
Phone: 61 (07) 3268-6800
Fax: 61 (07) 3868-1281
Website: *www.doomben.com*
E-Mail: admin@doomben.com
Abbreviation: Doo
Chairman: Ian McGrath
Chief Executive Officer: Sean Kelk
Principal Races: Doomben 10,000 Stakes (Aus-G1), Doomben Cup (Aus-G1)

Eagle Farm

Located on the northern side of Brisbane in Ascot, Eagle Farm boasts a long history and excellent equine facilities. Its racing started on August 14, 1865, under the Queensland Turf Club, which was founded in 1863 by a group of 53 sportsmen. The training facilities include two turf tracks, a wood-fiber track, a sand track, two exercise rings, and an equine swimming pool. The main turf track is approximately 2,026 meters with a single chute. Horses race clockwise and must navigate a slight uphill climb heading for the finish line. During World War II, Eagle Farm was used as a military base by both Australian and United States troops. For those five years, the Queensland Turf Club held race meetings at Albion Park.

Location: P.O. Box 21, Hamilton Central, Queensland 4007 or 230 Lancaster Road, Ascot, Queensland 4007
Phone: 61 (07) 3268-2171
Fax: 61 (07) 3868-2410
Website: *www.qtc.org*
E-Mail: info@qtc.org
Abbreviation: EF
Chairman: W. J. Sexton
Chief Executive: Stephen Ferguson
Racecourse Manager: Bill Shuck
Principal Races: Brisbane Cup (Aus-G1), Queensland Derby (Aus-G1), Queensland Oaks (Aus-G1), Sires' Produce S. (Aus-G1), Stradbroke H. (Aus-G1), The T. J. Smith S. (Aus-G1)

Flemington

A breathtaking course with Melbourne's skyline as a backdrop, Flemington has staged racing since 1840, and the Melbourne Cup (Aus-G1), its famed stakes race at about two miles on the first Tuesday of November, is regarded as a national holiday. On the morning of the Melbourne Cup, a service held at St. Francis's Church is followed by a carnival on Burke Street, Melbourne's central thoroughfare. Up to 100,000 spectators fill Flemington on Melbourne Cup day to celebrate the stakes first run in 1861. The winner of the first Melbourne Cup, Archer, was reported to have walked more than 500 miles from his stable in New South Wales to enter the race. In 1930, *Phar Lap won the race after surviving an attempt on his life while training at Flemington. He was hidden in the ensuing days, arrived at the track just minutes before post time, and won the race in a canter. The legendary runner is honored by a bronze statue outside an entrance to the track. Flemington also holds the Victoria Derby (Aus-G1), first run in 1855 and the oldest established race in Australia. The left-handed, 2,300-meter turf course has a 1,200-meter straight chute.

Location: 448 Epsom Road, Flemington, Victoria 3031
Phone: 61 (3) 8378-0747
Website: *www.vrc.net.au*
E-Mail: customerservice@vrc.net.au
Abbreviation: Fle
Chief Executive: Dale Monteith
Chairman: R. M. Fitzroy
Vice Chairman: Peter Barnett
Principal Races: Australian Cup (Aus-G1), Australian Guineas (Aus-G1), MacKinnon S. (Aus-G1), Lightning S. (Aus-G1), Melbourne Cup (Aus-G1), Sires' Produce S. (Aus-G1), Victoria Derby (Aus-G1)

Moonee Valley

Located less than four miles from central Melbourne, Moonee Valley was founded by William Samuel Cox in 1883. The Cox Plate (Aus-G1), Australia's most important weight-for-age race, is run at Moonee Valley one week before the Melbourne Cup at Flemington. First run in 1922, the Cox Plate was won by *Phar Lap in '30 and '31. In a historic running of the Cox Plate in 1986, Bonecrusher edged fellow New Zealand champion Our Waverley Star by a neck. Moonee Valley offers a wide range of amenities, including a 1,000-seat dining room, glass-enclosed dining boxes, 20 bars, and electronic gaming machines, which were added in 1992. The 1,800-meter, left-handed course is more rectangular than oval, with very sharp turns and short straights, putting a high premium on agility and speed. It is intersected by a diagonal straight course. Inside the main course are hurdle and steeplechase courses.

Location: McPherson Street, Moonee Ponds, Victoria 3039
Phone: 61 (30) 9373-2222
Fax: 61 (03) 9326-0090
Website: *www.mvrc.net.au*
E-Mail: customerservice@mvrc.net.au
Abbreviation: Moo
Acting Chief Executive Officer: Brian Masters
Track Manager: Greg Barker
Principal Races: Manikato S. (Aus-G1), W. S. Cox Plate (Aus-G1)

Morphettville

Located along the Anzac Highway in Adelaide, South Australia, Morphettville is operated by the South Australian Jockey Club. Founded in 1860, Morphettville holds its principal meet in May, when it stages the South Australian Derby (Aus-G1), the South Australian Oaks (Aus-G1), and the Adelaide Cup (Aus-G1). The 2,300-meter course has a short straight of nearly 400 meters. The track's grandstand was razed in 1976 and replaced by a modern facility, and a multimillion-dollar renovation of the course itself was completed in 2002.

Location: P. O. Box 707, Park Holme, SA 5043 or Morphett Road, Morphettville, SA
Phone: 61 (08) 8295-0111
Fax: 61 (08) 8295-0136
Website: *www.sajc.com.au*
E-Mail: enquiries@sajc.com.au
Abbreviation: Mor
Ownership: South Australian Jockey Club
Chief Executive: Steve Ploubidis
Chairman: John Naffine
Operations and Facilities Manager: Brenton Wilkinson

Principal Races: Adelaide Cup (Aus-G1), Goodwood Handicap (Aus-G1), Robert Sangster Stakes (Aus-G1), South Australian Derby (Aus-G1)

Rosehill Gardens

Located about 14 miles west of Sydney, Rosehill frequently is called Sydney's garden course and is home to Australia's premier race for two-year-olds, the 1,200-meter Golden Slipper Stakes (Aus-G1), first contested in 1957. The beautifully landscaped track was constructed on Australia's most historic agricultural property, Elizabeth Farm, and major festivals are held in both the spring and autumn. The about 2,000-meter course features a 400-meter straight. Races of 1,200 meters start in the center of the course and traverse a long bend into the straight. Training facilities include Equitrack, grass, sand, and cinder training tracks with stabling available adjacent to the track.

Location: James Ruse Drive, P.O. Box 21, Rosehill, NSW 2142
Phone: 61 (02) 9930-4000
Fax: 61 (02) 9930-4099
Website: www.stc.com.au
E-Mail: sydturf@stc.com.au
Abbreviation: Roh
Chairman: Alan Brown
Vice Chairman: Bill Picken
Chief Executive Officer: Michael T. Kenny
Track Supervisor: Chris Toogood
Principal Races: George Ryder S. (Aus-G1), Golden Slipper S. (Aus-G1), H. E. Tancred S. (Aus-G1), Rosehill Guineas (Aus-G1), Storm Queen/Arrowfield Stud S. (Aus-G1)

Royal Randwick

Home of the Australian Jockey Club, Randwick has conducted racing since 1860, when the club relocated from Homebush. The inaugural running of the Australian Jockey Club St. Leger (Aus-G2) was held in 1841 at Homebush but was moved to Randwick when the track opened. The first A.J.C. Derby (Aus-G1) was run in 1861. The Sydney Cup (Aus-G1) was first contested in April 1865. Randwick, which is close to Sydney, holds racing festivals in both the spring at the start of October and in the fall in April. The major stakes in the spring is the Metropolitan (Aus-G1) at 2,600 meters. The A.J.C. Derby, Doncaster Handicap (Aus-G1), and Queen Elizabeth Stakes (Aus-G1) are contested in the fall. Randwick's 2,218-meter course with four chutes circles an infield lake and is considered one of the most demanding in Australia.

Location: Alison Road, Randwick, NSW 2031
Phone: 61 (29) 9663-8400
Fax: 61 (29) 9662-6292
Website: www.ajc.org.au
E-Mail: ajcfeedback@ajc.org.au
Abbreviation: Ran
Chairman: Ross Smyth-Kirk
Vice Chairman: John Ingham
Executive Director, Racing Operations: Richard Freedman
Principal Races: A.J.C. Australian Derby (Aus-G1), A.J.C. Australian Oaks (Aus-G1), Champagne S. (Aus-G1), Doncaster H. (Aus-G1), Sires' Produce S. (Aus-G1), Spring Champion S. (Aus-G1), Sydney Cup (Aus-G1)

Warwick Farm

Warwick Farm Racecourse, operated by the Australian Jockey Club, is located about 18 miles from Sydney and is renowned for its picnic atmosphere. Racing is conducted on an oblong, 1,937-meter oval with a straight of just 326 meters. The track has a chute for races between 1,000 and 1,400 meters, and it also has two short chutes for 1,600-meter and 2,400-meter races. Front-runners tend to do well because of Warwick Farm's sharp turns, which can force late closers very wide. The track opened in 1925 and resumed racing in '52 after being closed through World War II. Its J.M.B. Carr Grandstand was built in 1982.

Location: Hume Highway, Warwick Farm, NSW 2170
Phone: 61 (29) 9602-6199
Fax: 61 (29) 9821-2150
Website: www.ajc.org.au
Abbreviation: WF
Chairman: Ross Smyth-Kirk
Vice Chairman: John Ingham
Executive Director, Racing Operations: Richard Freedman
Principal Races: Chipping Norton Stakes (Aus-G1), George Main Stakes (Aus-G1)

Brazil

Cidade Jardim

Just minutes from downtown Sao Paulo, Cidade Jardim offers year-round turf and dirt racing on left-handed courses. Cidade Jardim opened on January 25, 1941, after Brazilian racing officials decided that Mooca, the track in the center of Sao Paulo, was too small and too crowded. Today, Cidade Jardim is a sprawling facility that houses many important Brazilian racing authorities, including the Stud-Book Brasileiro. Cidade Jardim's main turf course is an about 2,000-meter oval with a dirt course of about 1,800 meters. Cidade Jardim also encompasses a training center with two dirt training tracks, a stud farm, and an exhibition center for cultural and scientific activities.

Location: Avenida Lineu de Paula Machado, Sao Paulo 1263
Phone: 55 (11) 2161-8300
Website: www.jockeysp.com.br
Abbreviation: CJD
Principal Races: Consagracao (Brz-G1), Derby Paulista (Brz-G1), Diana (Brz-G1), Jockey Club de Sao Paulo (Brz-G1), Organizacao Sulamericana de Fomento ao Puro Sangue de Corrida (Brz-G1), Oswaldo Aranha (Brz-G1), Presidente da Republica (Brz-G1), Sao Paulo (Brz-G1)

La Gavea

With the Statue of Christ the Redeemer atop Corcovado Mountain in Rio de Janeiro serving as a dramatic backdrop, La Gavea is located adjacent to Lake Rodrigo de Freitas. An outer, 2,120-meter turf course rings a 2,036-meter dirt track with two separate turns out of the home straight. Though racing was conducted in Brazil as early as 1825, betting was not allowed until 1872. In that year, the Jockey Club Brasileiro was formed, which led to the opening of La Gavea. La Gavea's spring season is October and November features the Gran Premio Linneo de Paula Machado (Brz-G1), among other stakes. Racing is held year-round on Saturdays and Sundays.

Location: Rio de Janeiro
Phone: 55 (21) 3534-9000
Website: www.jcb.com.br
E-Mail: internetjcb@jcb.com.br

Abbreviation: GVA
Principal Races: Proprietarios do Cavalo de Corrida (Brz-G1), Brasil (Brz-G1), Cruzeiro do Sul (Brz-G1), Diana (Brz-G1), Jockey Club Brasileiro (Brz-G1), Linneo de Paula Machado (Brz-G1), Presidente da Republica (Brz-G1)

Taruma

Located ten minutes from downtown Curitiba, a city of 2.3-million people that is the capital of the state of Parana, Taruma races year-round under the ownership of Jockey Club do Parana. Opened on December 2, 1873, Taruma has an 1,800-meter course. Its biggest race, the 2,400-meter Gran Premio International Parana (Brz-G1), is run in December.

Location: Avenue Victor Ferreira Do Amaral, Curitiba Parana
Phone: 55 (41) 366-2121
Abbreviation: TAR
Chairman: Cesar de Paula ou Alessandro Reichel
Principal Races: International Parana (Brz-G1)

Chile
Club Hipico de Santiago

Lush, beautiful, and close to the center of Santiago, Club Hipico de Santiago encompasses more than 200 acres and is full of gardens, lakes, tennis courts, and fountains. Members of the Chilean bourgeoisie created Club Hipico in 1869, and its first race was run on September 20, 1870. Club Hipico is home to the oldest stakes race in South America, the El Ensayo (Chi-G1), first run in 1873 for three-year-old colts and fillies. The track stages as many as 16 races a day, usually on Mondays and Thursdays in January, February, and March, and on Sundays during other months.

Location: Avenida Blanco Encalada, Santiago
Phone: 56 (2) 693-9600
Fax: 56 (2) 683-9612
Website: www.clubhipico.cl/index2.htm
Abbreviation: CHS
Principal Races: Club Hipico de Santiago (Chi-G1), El Ensayo (Chi-G1), Las Oaks (Chi-G1), Polla de Pontrancas (Chi-G1), Polla de Potrillos (Chi-G1)

Hipodromo Chile

Founded in 1904 by a group of 19 breeders, owners, and trainers, Hipodromo Chile is located ten minutes north of Santiago and near the Comodo Merino Benitez Airport. Racing is conducted on every other Wednesday and every Saturday year-round on a 1,645-meter, left-handed dirt track. A nearby sales complex, conducting two-year-olds in training sales in the spring and fall, complement the racing.

Location: 1715 Avenue Hipodromo Chile, Independencia, Santiago 02753
Phone: 56 (2) 270-9237
Fax: 56 (2) 777-2089
Website: www.hipodromo.cl
E-Mail: sugerencias@hipodromochile.cl
Abbreviation: HCH
President: Juan Cuneo Solari
General Manager: Luis I. Salas
Vice President: Orlando Mercado Labbe
Executive Director: Luis Solar Feuereisen
Principal Races: Dos Mil Guineas (Chi-G1), Gran Criterium (Chi-G1), Hipodromo Chile (Chi-G1), Mil Guineas (Chi-G1), St. Leger (Chi-G1)

Vina del Mar

Hipodromo de Vina del Mar is operated by the Valparaiso Sporting Club. Thirteen to 17 dates are held annually on Wednesdays and Fridays, and races range from 800 meters to 2,400 meters. The two main turf courses and dirt training track can accommodate 600 horses. El Derby (Chi-G1), the third race of the Chilean Triple Crown, is contested at 2,400 meters (11.93 furlongs) on turf.

Location: Los Castanos 404, Vina Del Mar
Phone: 56 (3) 265-5600
Fax: 56 (3) 265-5691
Website: www.sporting.cl
E-Mail: sporting@sporting.cl
Abbreviation: Val
Principal Races: Copa de Plata Italo Traverso (Chi-G1), El Derby (Chi-G1)

England
Aintree

Located a short distance from Liverpool, Aintree is home to the world's best-known steeplechase race, the Grand National, a 4½-mile marathon in early April over 30 tall, testing fences. The Grand National was first run at Aintree in 1839, when the striking bay Lottery won the third running of a race known then as the Grand Liverpool Steeplechase, which had been held at another site in its first two years.

In the 1990s, animal-rights protests forced the taming of the 2¼-mile Grand National course's more terrifying fences. Most notable was the filling of Becher's Brook, named for Captain Martin Becher, who fell at its tall fence and tumbled into the creek after his mount allegedly was impeded by Lottery. The Chair, one of two obstacles on the 16-fence course that are jumped only once, stands 5'2" tall, and its landing side is higher than the takeoff side. As many as 40 horses can start in the Grand National, but often only a handful of horses complete the race.

Location: Ormskirk Road, Aintree, Liverpool L9 5AS
Phone: 44 (151) 523-2600
Fax: 44 (151) 522-2920
Website: www.aintree.co.uk
E-Mail: aintree@jockeyclubracecourses.com
Abbreviation: Ain
Managing Director: Julian Thick
Operations Manager: Zoe Greenall
Principal Races: Grand National Steeplechase

Ascot

Host of the traditional Royal Meeting in June as well as racing throughout the year in both National Hunt and flat divisions, Ascot is owned by Queen Elizabeth II. Queen Anne marked out the course in Windsor Park, and racing began there in August 1711. The National Hunt course was added in 1965. The Royal Meeting begins with the Queen and her royal party driving down the straight mile in horse-drawn carriages to the applause of the crowd, with the men sporting top hats and morning suits and the women wearing elegant hats.

Traditionally, the first race is the Queen Anne Stakes (Eng-G1), and the races that follow offer a wide variety of competition from sprinters to stayers. No Ascot race is more demanding than the 2½-mile Ascot Gold Cup (Eng-G1), first run in 1807. The St. James's Palace Stakes (Eng-G1), the King George VI and Queen Elizabeth

Stakes (Eng-G1), the King Edward VII Stakes (Eng-G2), the Queen Elizabeth II Stakes (Eng-G1), the Coronation Stakes (Eng-G1) for fillies, and the Meon Valley Stud Fillies' Mile (Eng-G1) are among Ascot's most definitive events. The flat course at Ascot is a right-handed triangular oval of 1¾ miles with two one-mile chutes.

Ascot, which was previously held in a private trust, underwent a $347-million renovation beginning in 2002 and, after closing in September '04, reopened in '06.

Location: Ascot Racecourse, Berkshire SL5 7JX
Phone: 44 (870) 722-7227
Fax: 44 (870) 460-1248
Website: www.ascot.co.uk
E-Mail: enquiries@ascot.co.uk
Abbreviation: Asc
Chairman: Duke of Devonshire CBE
Chief Executive: Charles Barnett
Director of Operations: Ronnie Wilkie
Commercial and Finance Director: Janet Walker
Other Officials: Directors: Mark Davies, John Varley, Johnny Weatherby
Principal Races: Coronation S. (Eng-G1), Gold Cup S. (Eng-G1), King George VI and Queen Elizabeth S. (Eng-G1), Prince of Wales's S. (Eng-G1), Queen Elizabeth II S. (Eng-G1), St. James's Palace S. (Eng-G1)

Cheltenham

Located in the Cotswolds in west-central England, Cheltenham is a stunning racecourse that is host each March to the National Hunt Festival, which features the Cheltenham Gold Cup and Champion Hurdle Stakes, championship races for their respective divisions. The 2001 Cheltenham festival was canceled because of the foot-and-mouth disease outbreak that winter, but in most years the festival is standing-room only.

The first Gold Cup was held in 1819 as a three-mile flat race on Cleeve Hill, which overlooks the current course. When crowds grew to 50,000, a grandstand was constructed, but it was torn down when an anti-gambling sentiment swept the area in the 1820s. Racing was reestablished at the current site in Prestbury Park in 1831, but no racing was conducted there from the 1840s through the '90s. Barry Bingham purchased the course, refurbished it, built a new grandstand and running rails, and launched the festival in 1902 as a two-day event. A third day was added in 1923, and a fourth day was inaugurated in 2005. The Gold Cup was reinstituted in 1924, and three years later the Champion Hurdle was added. Cheltenham has separate left-handed steeplechase and hurdle courses, with a testing, uphill run to the finish post.

Among the heroes of Cheltenham are Dorothy Paget's Golden Miller, who won five consecutive runnings of the Gold Cup (1932-'36), and trainer Michael Dickinson, who saddled the first five finishers in the 1983 Gold Cup.

Location: Prestbury Park, Cheltenham, Gloucestershire GL50 4SH
Phone: 44 (124) 222-6226
Fax: 44 (124) 222-4227
Website: www.cheltenham.co.uk
E-Mail: cheltenham@jockeyclubracecourses.com
Abbreviation: Chm
Ownership: Racecourse Holdings Trust
Chairman: Lord Vestey
General Manager: Edward W. Gillespie
Principal Races: Champion Hurdle S., Cheltenham Gold Cup

Doncaster

Home of the final race of the English Triple Crown, the St. Leger Stakes (Eng-G1) in September, Doncaster has hosted racing since 1776. Doncaster runs flat and jump races on separate courses. The pear-shaped, left-handed main course is nearly two miles in circumference. The St. Leger meeting begins with the filly version of the St. Leger Stakes, the Park Hill Stakes (Eng-G3). The Doncaster Cup (Eng-G3)—first run in 1766 and the oldest race still run by the Jockey Club, the Champagne Stakes (Eng-G2), the May Hill Stakes (Eng-G3), and the Flying Childers Stakes (Eng-G2) for two-year-olds precede the St. Leger, the oldest of the English classics and named for popular local sportsman Lt. Col. Anthony St. Leger. Winners of the St. Leger Stakes include Hambletonian in 1795, Champion (the first horse to win the Epsom Derby and St. Leger Stakes) in 1800, and West Australian, who became the first Triple Crown winner 53 years later. Nijinsky II became the most recent English Triple Crown winner in 1970. The Racing Post Trophy Stakes (Eng-G1) is Doncaster's most significant juvenile race.

Location: The Grandstand, Leger Way, South Yorkshire, Doncaster DN2 6BB
Phone: 44 (130) 230-4200
Fax: 44 (130) 232-3271
Website: www.doncaster-racecourse.co.uk
E-Mail: info@doncasterracing.co.uk
Year Founded: 1776
Abbreviation: Don
Ownership: Doncaster Metropolitan Borough Council
Chairman: Councillor Bill Mordue
Principal Races: Racing Post Trophy S. (Eng-G1), St. Leger S. (Eng-G1), Champagne S. (Eng-G2)

Epsom Downs

Thoroughbreds have been racing at Epsom, 15 miles south of London in Surrey, for more than 350 years. In 1648, a party of Royalists held races there, and the first recorded race meet was in 1661 on Banstead Downs, which is part of Epsom Downs. The jewel of the racing year is the Epsom Derby (Eng-G1), which traditionally had been run on the first Wednesday in June but now has been moved successfully to the Saturday five weeks after the Two Thousand Guineas (Eng-G1) at Newmarket on the first Saturday of May or, less commonly, the last Saturday in April. First run in 1780, one year after the initial running of the Epsom Oaks (Eng-G1), the 1½-mile Derby is the middle leg of the English Triple Crown. Epsom has other important stakes during its season, with meets beginning in April and concluding in September of each year. The major races include the Coronation Cup (Eng-G1) and the Diomed Stakes (Eng-G3). The course features a downhill run to the final turn, the world-famous Tattenham Corner, and an uphill pull to the finish.

Location: The Racecourse, Epsom Downs, Surrey KT18 5LQ
Phone: 44 (137) 272-6311
Fax: 44 (137) 274-8253
Website: www.epsomdowns.co.uk
E-Mail: epsom@jockeyclubracecourses.com
Info on Track Renovation During 2008:
www.epsomdowns.co.uk/grandstandhub.ink
Abbreviation: Eps
General Manager: Nick Blofeld
Principal Races: Coronation Cup (Eng-G1), Epsom Derby (Eng-G1), Epsom Oaks (Eng-G1)

Goodwood

Located amid rolling countryside on Sussex Downs 60 miles southwest of London, Goodwood traces its history to the Duke of Richmond, who first hosted racing on his estate in 1802. The fifth Duke of Richmond improved the quality of racing at Goodwood by making it part of the English social circuit, a task made easier by the development of a railroad network to transport horses and racegoers to the estate. The about one-mile Sussex Stakes (Eng-G1), the about two-mile Goodwood Cup (Eng-G2), the six-furlong Richmond Stakes (Eng-G2), and the 1⅛-mile Nassau Stakes (Eng-G1) for fillies and mares are the major races of the annual July meeting, though racing is also held in May, June, August, and October. Goodwood also is host to the Celebration Mile Stakes (Eng-G2) at the end of August. Goodwood has a skewered figure-eight, right-handed course with a six-furlong straight that allows horses to finish in front of Goodwood's restaurant atop the grandstand.

Location: Goodwood, Chichester, West Sussex PO18 0PX
Phone: 44 (124) 375-5022
Fax: 44 (124) 375-5025
Website: www.goodwood.co.uk/horseracing
E-Mail: enquiry@goodwood.co.uk
Abbreviation: Goo
Ownership: Goodwood Estate Co. Ltd.
President: Duke of Richmond
General Manager: Rod Fabricius
Principal Races: Nassau S. (Eng-G1), Sussex S. (Eng-G1)

Haydock Park

Located north of Liverpool, Haydock Park Racecourse was created as a successor to the nearby Old Golborne Heath course, home of the Newton Races, which flourished in the 1750s. Haydock conducted its first race in 1899. Haydock's 1⅜-mile track has a tight turn at the end, and the Sprint Cup Stakes (Eng-G1) is staged each September. A new grandstand was completed in 1982.

Location: Newton-Le-Willows, Merseyside WA12 0HQ
Phone: 44 (194) 272-5963
Fax: 44 (194) 227-0879
Website: www.haydock-park.co.uk
E-Mail: haydockpark@jockeyclubracecourses.com
Abbreviation: Hay
Ownership: Jockey Club Racecourses
Chairman: Andrew Gould
Chief Executive: Adam Waterworth
Principal Races: Haydock Sprint Cup S. (Eng-G1)

Kempton Park

Located a 35-minute train ride from Waterloo Station, Kempton Park advertises itself as "London's Racecourse," and it is nine miles south of Heathrow Airport. Built by S. H. Hyde, Kempton Park conducted its first race meet in July 1878. During World War II, the track housed German prisoners of war, and racing resumed in 1947. The track's major race is the King George VI Chase on Boxing Day, December 26, each year, and it also stages flat race meets during the year. In 2006, Kempton transformed itself into a night-time all-weather track for flat racing while retaining its steeplechase fixtures on turf.

Location: Sunbury-on-Thames, Middlesex TW16 5AQ
Phone: 44 (193) 278-2292
Fax: 44 (193) 278-2044
Website: www.kempton.co.uk
E-Mail: kempton@jockeyclubracecourses.com
Abbreviation: Kem
Clerk of the Course: Barney Clifford

Lingfield Park

Set on 300 acres in the Surrey countryside south of London, Lingfield Park is one of Great Britain's most modern racetracks, featuring year-round flat racing on its all-weather artificial-surface track.

Owned by Arena Leisure, Lingfield was the first of England's all-weather tracks, but its Equitrack surface increasingly drew complaints. In late 2001, the racecourse replaced Equitrack with Polytrack, a synthetic surface composed of polypropylene, polyester, Lycra, silica sand, and rubber, covered by a wax coating. The surface, which cost $4.2-million, has been praised by jockeys and trainers. The all-weather track is 1¼ miles around, with a quarter-mile stretch and a quarter-mile chute for 1½-mile races. Lingfield also has a 1¼-mile, left-handed turf course with a 3½-furlong run-in and a 1⅝-mile steeplechase course.

Location: Lingfield Park Racecourse, Lingfield, Surrey RH7 6PQ
Phone: 44 (134) 283-4800
Fax: 44 (134) 283-5874
Website: www.lingfield-racecourse.co.uk
E-Mail: info@lingfieldpark.co.uk
Year Founded: 1890
Abbreviation: Lin
Ownership: Arena Leisure
Executive Director: Ian Renton
General Manager: Clive Stephens
Clerk of the Course: Neil MacKenzie Ross
Principal Races: Derby Trial S. (Eng-G3), Oaks Trial, Winter Derby, Spring Cup

Newbury

Located west of London, Newbury has its own railway station just yards from the attractive left-handed racecourse. The course measures more than 1¾ miles with a slightly undulating straight mile ideal for galloping.

Fifteen days of flat racing extend from April through October, and steeplechase meets are conducted during the colder months. Its major flat races include the one-mile Juddmonte Lockinge Stakes (Eng-G1), and its premier race over fences is the Hennessy Cognac Gold Cup.

Newbury, which opened in 1905, resulted from a chance meeting between well-known trainer John Porter and King Edward VII. It quickly became known as one of the country's best courses, but the course has been pressed into other duties during wartime. Newbury was requisitioned during World War I and was used for troops, supplies, tank testing and repair, and as a prisoner of war camp. In World War II, the track became a major American base and prisoner of war camp.

Racing resumed on April 1, 1949, and now features elegant surroundings, including a sky-lighted "Long Bar" overlooking the track on the first floor and 41 private boxes. The New Grandstand, which opened in 2000, features several exhibition spaces as well as conference rooms for up to 1,000 delegates. The course also features an 18-hole, par 71 golf course and a 20-bay driving range. A leisure center with a swimming pool and gymnasium also are on the property.

Location: The Racecourse, Newbury, Berkshire RG14 7NZ
Phone: 44 (16) 354-0015
Fax: 44 (163) 522-8354
Website: www.newbury-racecourse.co.uk
E-Mail: info@newbury-racecourse.co.uk

Abbreviation: Nby
Chairman: Sir David Sieff
General Manager: Mark Kershaw
Clerk of the Course: Richard Osgood
Principal Races: Juddmonte Lockinge S. (Eng-G1)

Newmarket

Newmarket is the headquarters of British racing, and its racecourse is a fitting complement to the training gallops to the east of the course. An observer once said: "Newmarket is one of the only places where a man can go racing; elsewhere he merely goes to the races, which isn't the same thing at all."

Racing has been held at Newmarket, a Suffolk town 60 miles northeast of London, for more than 350 years. Newmarket's racing spans the entire British flat season, with the spring season featuring the year's first classics—the Two Thousand Guineas (Eng-G1) and One Thousand Guineas (Eng-G1)—down its Rowley Mile Course, usually on the first weekend in May. In the fall, the Champion Stakes (Eng-G1), Cheveley Park Stakes (Eng-G1), Middle Park Stakes (Eng-G1), and Dewhurst Stakes (Eng-G1) are contested across the flat, a 1¼-mile straight that includes the Rowley course. Longer races, such as the rich Cesarewitch Handicap over 2¼ miles, require the use of a 1¼-mile extension of the Rowley Mile in a backward, L-shape configuration that extends through the ancient "Devil's Dike." Between those spring and fall events, racing is conducted on the July Course, a straight that connects to the Rowley course. The July Cup (Eng-G1) is the major July stakes.

Though Charles I decided Newmarket would be an ideal place to race his horses, his son, Charles II, created the course and the straight mile derives its name from his nickname, "Old Rowley." In 1665, he founded the Newmarket Town Plate, a race that is still contested in a different form. With its uphill finish and no turns, Newmarket provides a severe test of stamina.

Location: Westfield House, The Links, Newmarket, Suffolk CB8 0TG
Phone: 44 (163) 866-3482
Fax: 44 (163) 866-3044
Website: *www.newmarketracecourses.co.uk*
E-Mail: newmarket@rht.net
Year Founded: 1664
Abbreviation: New
Ownership: Jockey Club Racecourses
Chairman: Andrew Gould
Managing Director: Stephen Wallis
Director of Racing: Michael Prosser
Principal Races: Champion S. (Eng-G1), Cheveley Park S. (Eng-G1), Dewhurst S. (Eng-G1), July Cup S. (Eng-G1), One Thousand Guineas S. (Eng-G1), Two Thousand Guineas S. (Eng-G1)

Sandown Park

Only 14 miles south of central London, Sandown Park opened in 1875 and was the first totally enclosed racecourse in the country. The course was the brainchild of Lt. Col. Owen Williams, and his brother, Hwfa (pronounced "Hoofer"), was instrumental in Sandown Park's development, serving as chairman and clerk of the course for 50 years. The grandstand, rebuilt in 1973 for approximately $5-million, sits on a hill overlooking the racecourse.

The right-handed, 1⅜-mile course includes a downhill run to the back straight and a substantial uphill pull to the homestretch. A five-furlong, uphill straight course runs through the main course.

Sandown Park's major stakes race is the 1¼-mile Eclipse Stakes (Eng-G1) in July. It was first run in 1886 and, at the time, was the country's richest stakes race. In the spring, Sandown features the Whitbread Gold Cup, the National Hunt season's final major race over steeplechase fences. Flat racing is held in short meets from late April through the beginning of October. A $33.4-million renovation of the grandstand was completed in early 2002.

Location: Portsmouth Road, Esher, Surrey KT10 9AJ
Phone: 44 (137) 246-4348
Fax: 44 (137) 246-1334
Website: *www.sandown.co.uk*
E-Mail: sandown.events@jockeyclubracecourses.com
Abbreviation: San
Ownership: Jockey Club Racecourses
Chairman: Andrew Gould
General Manager: Steve Brice
Director of Racing/Clerk of the Course: Andrew Cooper
Principal Races: Eclipse S. (Eng-G1)

York

Referred to by many as England's Ascot of the North, York is home to the popular Ebor Festival in mid-August at the Knavesmire, common land 20 minutes from the city of York that has featured racing since 1731. The wide horseshoe-shaped, two-mile, unenclosed course has a 4½-furlong straight after a left-handed turn. Two separate chutes are used for sprints of six and seven furlongs.

York came to prominence in 1767 when came the Gimcrack Club was founded to honor the champion Gimcrack, who won 26 races between 1764 and '71. The club members organized the York meeting to attract the best horses to the North, and by the 1840s the August meeting featured the Ebor Handicap, Yorkshire Oaks (Eng-G1), and the Gimcrack Stakes (Eng-G2). The Nunthorpe Stakes (Eng-G1) was added in 1903. In 1851, one of the most famous match races in Turf history pitted Epsom Derby winners The Flying Dutchman and Voltigeur, who had inflicted the former's only loss the previous year in the Doncaster Cup. More than 100,000 fans turned out to see the rematch, won by The Flying Dutchman.

More than a century later, the Benson & Hedges Gold Cup (Eng-G1), now known as the Juddmonte International Stakes, was created to match two champions of the 1970s, Mill Reef and Brigadier Gerard. Mill Reef broke down before the race, but John Galbreath's Epsom Derby (Eng-G1) victor Roberto handed Brigadier Gerard his only career defeat and set a course record.

Location: York, North Yorkshire YO23 1EX
Phone: 44 (190) 462-0911
Fax: 44 (190) 461-1071
Website: *www.yorkracecourse.co.uk*
E-Mail: enquiries@yorkracecourse.co.uk
Abbreviation: Yor
Chairman: N.H.T. Wrigley
Chief Executive and Clerk of the Course: William Derby
Principal Races: Aston Upthorpe Yorkshire Oaks (Eng-G1), Juddmonte International S. (Eng-G1), Nunthorpe S. (Eng-G1), Gimcrack S. (Eng-G2)

France
Chantilly

Racing at Chantilly, a village approximately 20 miles north of Paris, is held every June in front of the palatial Les Grandes Ecuries (literally, "the big stables") and the Chateau de Chantilly. The palatial stables were

built by the Prince de Conde, who believed he would be reincarnated as a horse. The estate includes a lavish stable that can house 250 horses. Chantilly, surrounded by woods, lakes, and 250 acres of greenery, also serves as France's principal training center, with as many as 100 trainers and 3,000 horses using its sand, all-weather, and turf training tracks. Chantilly's premier races are the 2,100-meter Prix du Jockey-Club (Fr-G1), first run in 1836 and popularly known as the French Derby, for three-year-olds, and the 2,100-meter Prix de Diane (Fr-G1) (French Oaks) for three-year-old fillies, begun in '41.

Location: 16 Avenue du General Leclerc, BP 209, Chantilly 60500
Phone: 33 (34) 462-4400
Fax: 33 (34) 457-3489
Abbreviation: Chy
Chief Executive: Matthieu Vincent
Principal Races: Prix de Diane (Fr-G1), Prix du Jockey-Club (Fr-G1), Prix Jean Prat (Fr-G1)

Deauville

Deauville, sometimes referred to as the Saratoga of France, held its first meet in 1864, the same year as Saratoga Race Course's first meet. It runs a short meeting in August, as Saratoga did for decades, and also features a major sale of yearlings, as does Saratoga. Deauville was founded by the Duke of Morny to cater to Parisian society vacationing on the Normandy coast. The setting allows horses to gallop on the beach or in the surf. There is also polo in the afternoons and the casino in the evenings for entertainment, as well as several first-rate restaurants. Deauville offers a top-class, 1,600-meter stakes, the Prix du Haras de Fresnay-le-Buffard Jacques Le Marois (Fr-G1), and the 1,200-meter Prix Morny (Fr-G1) for two-year-olds. Deauville is a right-handed course of 2,200 meters with a 1,600-meter chute on one end and a short chute on the other. Another major stakes, the Grand Prix de Deauville (Fr-G2), is held on the last Sunday of the meeting.

Location: 45 Avenue Hocquart de Turtot, BP 43300, Deauville 14800
Phone: 33 (23) 114-2000
Fax: 33 (23) 114-2001
Abbreviation: Dea
Chief Executive: Yves Deshayes
Principal Races: Prix du Haras de Fresnay-le-Buffard Jacques le Marois (Fr-G1), Prix Maurice de Gheest (Fr-G1), Prix Morny (Fr-G1)

Longchamp

Emperor Napoleon III traveled by boat on the Seine River to attend Longchamp's first day of racing on April 27, 1857, and he was joined at the Paris track by nearly 10,000 countrymen. Finishing second in the first of five races that afternoon was Miss Gladiator, the dam of Gladiateur, who became a legend as the first French-bred horse to win the Epsom Derby. For Gladiateur's first start after the English classic, 150,000 racegoers turned out to watch him win the Grand Prix de Paris (now a Group 1 race) at Longchamp.

But the race for which Longchamp is best known is the Prix de l'Arc de Triomphe (Fr-G1), first contested in 1920. Horses from both England and Italy took on France's best, and the first winner was Comrade, owned and bred by Frenchman Evremond de Saint-Alary, trained in England by Peter Gilpin, and ridden by Australian jockey Frank Bullock. The 2,400-meter race on the first Sunday in October was an instant international success and became Europe's championship race.

Other Longchamp stakes have longer histories. The Grand Prix de Paris was inaugurated in 1863 and for a century was France's most important race for three-year-olds. Following the modern trend, its distance was reduced from 3,000 meters to 2,000 meters in 1987. It was lengthened again to 2,400 meters in 2005. The first classics of each year, the 1,600-meter Poule d'Essai des Poulains (Fr-G1) (French Two Thousand Guineas) and Poule d'Essai des Pouliches (Fr-G1) (French One Thousand Guineas) for three-year-olds and three-year-old fillies, respectively, are run in May. The Poule d'Essai des Poulains was first run in 1840, while the Poule d'Essai des Pouliches debuted in '83. Longchamp's right-handed course has a long and testing homestretch with a slightly uphill finish.

Location: Route des Tribunes, Bois de Boulogne, Paris 75116
Phone: 33 (14) 430-7500
Fax: 33 (14) 430-7599
Abbreviation: Lch
Chief Executive: Christian Delporte
Principal Races: Grand Prix de Paris (Fr-G1), Poule d'Essai des Poulains (Fr-G1), Poule d'Essai des Pouliches (Fr-G1), Prix de l'Arc de Triomphe (Fr-G1), Prix du Moulin de Longchamp (Fr-G1), Prix Ganay (Fr-G1), Prix Marcel Boussac (Fr-G1)

Maisons-Laffitte

Secluded near the Saint-Germain forest just west of Paris and home to some 1,800 Thoroughbreds conditioned by more than 80 trainers, Maisons-Laffitte offers one of Europe's most pleasant settings for Thoroughbred racing. Its 2,000-meter straight course, rivaled only by the Rowley Mile at Newmarket in England, is complemented by both right- and left-handed courses to accommodate 35 racing dates from the end of March until the end of July and from early September through early December.

The Prix Robert Papin (Fr-G2) is the first major stakes for two-year-olds each year, while other juvenile stakes, such as the Criterium de Maisons-Laffitte (Fr-G2), are run later in the meet. Among the course's top races for two-year-old fillies is the Prix Miesque (Fr-G3), named for the outstanding filly who won two North American championships with her triumphs in the 1987 and '88 Breeders' Cup Mile (G1).

Miesque won the Prix Imprudence at Maisons-Laffitte immediately before her victory in the 1987 One Thousand Guineas (Eng-G1). Among other champions who have raced at Maisons-Laffitte are *Sea-Bird, Nureyev, Arctic Tern, *Match II, Exbury, and Relko.

Set on more than 120 acres, Maisons-Laffitte is home to the Museum of the Racecourse, which was opened in 1990 and allows fans to review the history of racing by walking through magnificent rooms of an ancient castle.

Location: 1 Avenue de la Pelouse, Maisons-Laffitte 78600
Phone: 33 (13) 912-8170
Fax: 33 (13) 962-7608
Abbreviation: ML
Chief Executive: Martial de Rouffignac
Principal Races: Prix Robert Papin (Fr-G2), Prix Miesque (Fr-G3)

Saint-Cloud

The most frequently used Parisian track, Saint-Cloud hosts racing from February through July and from Sep-

tember through December. Its history extends to 1901, when the Societe du Demi-Sang was thrown out of Vincennes by the army and retreated to a strip of land owned by Edmond Blanc to continue racing. After World War I, the course was given to the Societe Sportive d'Encouragement, which supervised Thoroughbred racing at Maisons-Laffitte. The major stakes race at Saint-Cloud is the Grand Prix de Saint-Cloud (Fr-G1), which began in 1904 under the name Prix du President de la Republique. *Sea-Bird, fellow Arc winners Rheingold and Sagace (Fr), and Epsom Derby winners Relko and Teenoso all won races at Saint-Cloud, which also was the site of *Vaguely Noble's lone three-year-old defeat.

The 1,600-meter Criterium International (Fr-G1) was inaugurated in 2001 after the distance of the Grand Criterium (Fr-G1) at Longchamp was changed from 1,600 meters to 1,400 meters. Saint-Cloud's left-handed, 2,200-meter course is dissected by a 600-meter straight.

Location: 1 Rue du Camp Canadien, Saint-Cloud 92210
Phone: 33 (14) 771-6926
Fax: 33 (14) 771-3774
Abbreviation: StC
Chief Executive: Christian Leger
Principal Races: Criterium de Saint-Cloud (Fr-G1), Criterium International (Fr-G1), Grand Prix de Saint-Cloud (Fr-G1)

Germany
Baden-Baden

Set among the foothills of the Black Forest nine miles northwest of Baden-Baden, Baden-Baden Racecourse was the idea of Edouard Benazet, who offered visitors to the world-famous spa not only Thoroughbred racing but also a casino. When the casino closed in 1872, racing was taken over by the Internationale Club, which today supervises racing in short meets from May through June and from August through September. The nearby attractions include a casino, the vineyards of Rebland, Old Town, theaters, concerts, and elegant boutiques. Baden-Baden hosts the Grosser Preis von Baden (Ger-G1) and the Grosser Mercedes-Benz Preis (Ger-G2). The three overlapping, left-handed courses at Baden-Baden are named Old Course, New Course, and Straight Course.

Location: Lichtentaler Alley 8, Baden-Baden 76530
Phone: 49 (72) 291-870
Fax: 49 (72) 291-87344
Website: www.baden-galopp.de
E-Mail: club@baden-galopp.com
Abbreviation: Bad
Chairman: Hartmann Freiherr von Richthofen
Chief Executive: Wolfgang Stuber
Principal Races: Grosser Preis von Baden (Ger-G1)

Dusseldorf

Located in a hilly, wooded park on the edge of the Grafenberg Forest in Dusseldorf's Broich district, Dusseldorf Racecourse is the site of one of Germany's richest races, the Deutschland-Preis (Ger-G1), which is contested in late July. Other important stakes include the Henkel-Rennen (Ger-G2) (German One Thousand Guineas) in early May and the Grosser Preis von Dusseldorf (Ger-G3) in mid-October. The hilly, undulating, right-hand track features a sharp bend.

Location: Rennbahnstrasse 20, Dusseldorf 40629
Phone: 49 (21) 117-7260
Fax: 49 (21) 135-1752
Website: www.duesseldorf-galopp.de
E-Mail: info@duesseldorf-galopp.de
Abbreviation: Dus
Chairman: Peter Endres
General Manager: Bernd Koenemann
Principal Races: Deutschland-Preis (Ger-G1), Henkel-Rennen (Ger-G2), Grosser Preis von Dusseldorf (Ger-G3)

Hamburg

Hamburg is the home of the Deutsches Derby (Ger-G1), a 2,400-meter race for three-year-olds first contested in 1869 under the management of the Hamburger Renn-Club. Hamburg's other major stakes races are the Hansa-Preis (Ger-G2) at 2,100 meters, the Deutscher Herold-Preis (Ger-G3) at the same distance, and the 1,200-meter Holsten-Trophy (Ger-G3). The racetrack is about six miles from Hamburg and is accessible by the motorway from Berlin, subway, and bus. Racing is conducted from the end of June through early July on a right-handed turf course of approximately 2,000 meters.

Location: Rennbahnstrasse 96, Hamburg 22111
Phone: 49 (40) 651-8229
Fax: 49 (40) 655-6615
Website: www.galopp-derby.galopprennvereine.de
E-Mail: info@galopp-hamburg.de
Abbreviation: Hbg
Chairman: Eugen-Andreas Wahler
General Manager: Ilona Vollmers
Principal Races: Deutsches Derby (Ger-G1)

Koln

Situated in the Cologne neighborhood of Weidenpesch, Koln Racecourse is a flat, right-handed track with a 2½-furlong straight. Top stakes at Koln include the Europa-Preis (Ger-G1), the Gerling-Preis (Ger-G2), the Mehl-Mulhens-Rennen (Ger-G2) (German Two Thousand Guineas), and the Union-Rennen (Ger-G2).

Location: Rennbahnstrasse 152, Weidenpesch, Koln 50737
Phone: 49 (221) 974-5050
Fax: 49 (221) 974-5055
Website: www.koeln-galopp.de
E-Mail: kontakt@koeln-galopp.de
Abbreviation: Kol
Chairman: Baron Georg von Ullman
Chief Executive: Benedikt Fassbender
Principal Races: Europa-Preis (Ger-G1), Gerling-Preis (Ger-G2), Mehl-Mulhens-Rennen (Ger-G2) (German Two Thousand Guineas), and Union-Rennen (Ger-G2)

Mulheim

Located in western Germany, Mulheim is host to the country's longest flat race, the 3,400-meter Silbernes Band der Ruhr. Mulheim is a right-handed track with a 2½-furlong straight. The Preis der Diana-Deutsches Stuten-Derby (Ger-G1) (German Oaks) is contested in mid-June.

Location: Akazienallee 80-82, Mulheim Ruhr 45478
Website: www.muelheim-galopp.de
E-Mail: info@muelheim-galopp.de
Phone: 49 (20) 857-001
Fax: 49 (20) 857-005
Abbreviation: Mul
President: Hans-Martin Schlebusch
General Manager: Günther Gudert
Principal Races: Preis der Diana-Deutsches Stuten-Derby (Ger-G1)

Hong Kong
Happy Valley

Surrounded today by Hong Kong's skyscrapers, Happy Valley was built on reclaimed marshland and has held racing since 1846. Training horses is not easy on the 31-square-mile island, now under the control of the People's Republic of China, but the rich purses attract horsemen whose runners are housed in high-rise stables. Overshadowed by Sha Tin, Happy Valley conducts a 60-day racing season that lasts from September through June.

Location: 2 Sports Road, Hong Kong Island
Phone: 852 (2) 895-1523
Website: www.happyvalleyracecourse.com
Abbreviation: HV

Sha Tin

In 1959, Sir John Saunders, then chairman of the Royal Hong Kong Jockey Club, proposed creating a racetrack in Sha Tin Bay to alleviate overcrowding at Happy Valley. After three years of planning, the project of reclaiming 250 acres from the bay was begun. The soil needed for the project was taken from the top of one of the nearby mountains, which allowed development of that property and paid the track's construction costs.

Working round the clock on a tight, three-year schedule, Sha Tin opened as planned on October 7, 1978, with an expansive grandstand that encompasses 16½ acres. A 1,900-meter turf course encircles an all-weather dirt track. Sha Tin's major races are the Hong Kong Derby for four-year-olds, run every February at the start of the Chinese New Year since 1990, the Hong Kong Cup (HK-G1), the Hong Kong Vase (HK-G1), the Hong Kong Mile (HK-G1), and the Hong Kong Sprint (HK-G1).

Location: New Territories
Phone: 852 (2) 695-6223
Website: www.sha-tin.com
E-Mail: shatin@runhorse.com
Abbreviation: ST
Chief Executive: Lawrence T. Wong
Principal Races: Hong Kong Cup (HK-G1), Hong Kong Mile (HK-G1), Hong Kong Sprint (HK-G1), Hong Kong Vase (HK-G1), Queen Elizabeth II Cup (HK-G1)

Ireland
Leopardstown

Roughly six miles from Dublin, Leopardstown overcame a troubled past. Nine years after its opening in 1888, the five-furlong course was found to be only 4½ furlongs long. Capt. George Quin, who headed a syndicate that had purchased the course, constructed a new five-furlong course that was not well received. Finally, Richard "Boss" Croker, owner of 1907 Irish Derby and Epsom Derby winner Orby, purchased additional land and a larger course was constructed. Leopardstown was owned by Fred Clarke until he sold the track to the Irish Racing Board in 1967. Two years later, Leopardstown received an extensive face-lift, reopening in 1971 with a new grandstand, an enclosed betting hall, new dining and bar facilities, and a new stable area. Another renovation in 1988 extended the grandstand and added 16 private boxes. Race meets are held at Leopardstown from mid-March through mid-November over a left-handed turf course of about 2,800 meters. Leopardstown's premier race is the Irish Champion Stakes (Ire-G1).

Location: Leopardstown, Dublin 00018
Phone: 353 (1) 289-0500
Fax: 353 (1) 289-2634
Website: www.leopardstown.com
E-Mail: info@leopardstown.com
Abbreviation: Leo
Chairman: Ged Pierse
Principal Races: Irish Champion S. (Ire-G1)

The Curragh

According to legend, St. Bridget was offered as much of the Curragh plain as she could cover with her cloak. Unfurling the cloak from her shoulder, she threw it to cover the whole plain of Kildare. When she gathered up her cloak, the land was covered in the richest and deepest grass imaginable—ideal for training and racing Thoroughbreds. Match races have been held there for centuries. The first recorded one was in 1634 when the Earl of Ormond beat Lord Digby in a four-mile race.

The first race recorded at the Curragh was in 1741, and the first Irish Derby (Ire-G1) was held in 1866. By 1921, all five Irish classic stakes were contested at the Curragh. Joining the Derby were the Irish Oaks (Ire-G1), the Irish St. Leger (Ire-G1), the Irish Two Thousand Guineas (Ire-G1), and the Irish One Thousand Guineas (Ire-G1).

Located 30 miles west of Dublin, the Curragh offers race meets from mid-March to the beginning of November. The horseshoe-shaped, right-handed course is two miles in length with an uphill, straight run-in of three furlongs to the finish line.

Location: Tara Court, Dublin Road Naas, Co. Kildare
Phone: 353 (4) 544-1205
Fax: 353 (4) 544-1442
Website: www.curragh.ie
E-Mail: info@curragh.ie
Abbreviation: Cur
Chairman: John McStay
General Manager: Paul Hensey
Principal Races: Irish Derby (Ire-G1), Irish Oaks (Ire-G1), Irish One Thousand Guineas (Ire-G1), Irish St. Leger (Ire-G1), Irish Two Thousand Guineas (Ire-G1), Moyglare Stud S. (Ire-G1), National S. (Ire-G1), Phoenix S. (Ire-G1), Tattersalls Gold Cup (Ire-G1)

Italy
Roma Capannelle

Less than eight miles from the Colosseum in Rome, Capannelle opened in 1926. The grandstand, turf course, and interior dirt course are close to an ancient Roman aqueduct and are not far from St. Peter's Basilica in the Vatican. Race meets are held from March to mid-June and from September through November on right-handed turf and sand courses that are slightly uphill near the start and slightly downhill near the finish. National Hunt races also are conducted. Top stakes races include the Premio Presidente della Repubblica (Ity-G1) for four-year-olds and up, the Derby Italiano (Ity-G1) for three-year-olds, and the Premio Roma (Ity-G1) for three-year-olds and older. Capannelle's training facilities include 2,600-meter turf and dirt tracks, another turf course inside them, and a 1,200-meter sand track around the stabling area.

Location: Viaduct Appia Nuova 1255, Rome 00178
Phone: 39 (6) 716-771
Fax: 39 (6) 7167-7213
Website: www.capannelleippodromo.it
E-Mail: capannel@tin.it
Abbreviation: Rom
President: Enzo Mei

Chief Executive: Tomaso Grassi
Principal Races: Derby Italiano (Ity-G1), Premio Presidente della Repubblica (Ity-G1), Premio Roma (Ity-G1)

San Siro

Racing began at San Siro in 1888 on a racecourse designed by architect Giulio Valerio. In 1909, a training center was added to the facility located just north of downtown Milan. Today, approximately 200 acres of training grounds include two turf tracks, two sand tracks, and a nearby all-weather track. San Siro's racecourse consists of three right-handed, overlapping turf courses of 2,800, 2,000, and 1,800 meters.

Race meets are held from mid-March through July and from September to mid-November. Its premier races are the Oaks d'Italia (Ity-G1) for three-year-old fillies, the Gran Criterium (Ity-G1) for two-year-olds, and the Gran Premio di Milano (Ity-G1) and the Premio del Jockey Club (Ity-G1) for three-year-olds and up.

Location: Viaduct Ippodromo 100, Milan 20151
Phone: 39 (24) 821-6440
Fax: 39 (24) 820-1721
Website: www.ippodromimilano.it
Abbreviation: Mil
Chief Executive: Claudio Corradini
Principal Races: Gran Criterium (Ity-G1), Gran Premio di Milano (Ity-G1), Oaks d'Italia (Ity-G1), Premio di Capua V. (Ity-G1), Premio Jockey Club (Ity-G1)

Japan
Hanshin

The newest of the Japan Racing Association's four major tracks, Hanshin opened in 1949 and is about 12 miles from Osaka. Hanshin completed an extensive modernization in 1991 and races from March through June and in September and December. A lush, wide, right-handed turf course—slightly downhill in the backstretch and slightly uphill in the homestretch—encircles a dirt track.

On the second Sunday in April, Hanshin stages the 1,600-meter Oka Sho (Japan's equivalent of the one-mile One Thousand Guineas [Eng-G1]), named for the cherry blossoms in bloom at that time each year. Other major stakes include the all-age Grand Prix Takarazuka Kinen (Jpn-G1) in mid-June and the Hanshin Sansai Himba Stakes in early December for two-year-old fillies.

Location: 1-1 Komano-cho, Takarazuka-shi, Hyogo 665-0053
Phone: 81(79) 851-2000
Website: www.japanracing.jp/course/j04.html
Abbreviation: Hsn
Principal Races: Takarazuka Kinen (Jpn-G1), Oka Sho

Kyoto

Another of the major Japan Racing Association tracks, Kyoto Racecourse is located six miles south of Kyoto and stages racing in January, February, April, May, October, and November over a 1,900-meter, right-handed turf course that is uphill in the backstretch. Enclosed within the main course is a dirt course, an inner turf course, and a huge lake. A mammoth walking ring allows thousands of fans to see horses prepare for their races. The Spring Tenno Sho (Emperor's Cup) is a 3,200-meter endurance stakes for four-year-olds and older held on the last Sunday in April. In November, three major stakes are held on successive Sundays: the 3,000-meter Kikuka Sho (Japanese St. Leger) for three-year-olds, the final leg of the Japanese Triple Crown; the 2,400-meter Queen Elizabeth Cup, which is the concluding race of the Japanese filly triple crown; and the 1,600-meter Mile Championship.

Location: 32 Yoshijima, Watashibajima-sho, Fushimi-ku, Kyoto 612-8265
Phone: 81 (79) 633-2000
Website: www.japanracing.jp/course/j03.html
Abbreviation: Kyo
Principal Races: Kikuka Sho, Mile Championship, Queen Elizabeth Cup, Spring Tenno Sho

Nakayama

Located 12 miles east of Tokyo, Nakayama Racecourse features two broad turf courses and a dirt course inside them. The outer course is 1,840 meters, and the inner grass course 1,667 meters. The dirt course is 1,493 meters. All three courses have a modest uphill run over the last 200 meters to the finish line. The track also has a steeplechase course in its infield. Among the racecourse's major races are the Arima Kinen, the Sprinters Stakes, and Satsuki Sho, which is Japan's equivalent of the Two Thousand Guineas for three-year-olds.

Location: 1-1-1 Kosaku, Funabashi-shi, Chiba 273-0037
Phone: 81 (47) 334-2222
Fax: 81 (47) 332-3327
Website: www.japanracing.jp/course/j02.html
Abbreviation: Nak
Principal Races: Arima Kinen, Satsuki Sho, Sprinters Stakes

Tokyo

Home of Japan's premier race, the Japan Cup (Jpn-G1), Tokyo Racecourse at Fuchu, 15 miles west of Tokyo, was built in 1933. Its 1,878-meter interior dirt course is based on the design of American courses but is uniquely fine-tuned to handle Japan's heavier precipitation. The track is packed firmly with a layer of mountain sand and covered with loose river sand, giving horses a strong bottom underneath and a surface on top to absorb impact and ease stress on their legs. The undulating turf course is 2,116 meters. The Japan Cup, which is run left-handed on turf at 2,400 meters, begins on a 400-meter straight run that minimizes the impact of poor post position. On the same weekend, the $2-million Japan Cup Dirt is run. The course underwent extensive renovations in 2002.

Location: 1-1 Hiyoshi-cho, Fuchu-shi, Tokyo 183-0024
Phone: 81 (42) 363-3141
Fax: 81 (42) 340-7070
Website: www.japanracing.jp/course/j01.html
Abbreviation: Tok
Principal Races: Japan Cup (Jpn-G1), Japan Cup Dirt

New Zealand
Avondale

Operated by the Avondale Jockey Club, which was formed in 1889, Avondale is located near Auckland and hosts 14 racing dates each year. The original left-handed course was just under a mile in circumference. It was enlarged to 1⅛ miles and converted to a right-handed course a few years later.

Location: 2-48 Ash Street, Avondale, Auckland 1026
Phone: 64 (09) 828-3309
Fax: 64 (09) 828-3099
E-Mail: admin@ajc.co.nz
Abbreviation: Avo

Secretary: Jim Patterson
Principal Races: Avondale Gold Cup H. (NZ-G1), Avondale Guineas (NZ-G1)

Ellerslie

Several of New Zealand's Group 1 races are held at Ellerslie, including the New Zealand Derby (NZ-G1) and the Easter Handicap (NZ-G1). The track, approximately five miles from Auckland, New Zealand's largest city, boasts an elegant grandstand and beautifully maintained grounds. Racing was first conducted about one mile from Ellerslie on January 5, 1842, but the present site was not used until May 25, 1874, a national holiday to observe Queen Victoria's birthday.

Ellerslie's major stakes races are held from December 26 through January 2 and during the first week in June. The main track is a 1,870-meter, right-handed turf course with a finishing straight of 380 meters that is slightly downhill.

Location: 80 Ascot Avenue, Greenlane East, Auckland 1015
Phone: 64 (9) 524-4069
Fax: 64 (9) 524-8680
Website: www.ellerslie.co.nz
E-Mail: racing@ellerslie.co.nz
Abbreviation: Ell
Chairman: G. J. Clatworthy
Chief Executive: Chris Weaver
Director of Racing: Andrew Castles
Principal Races: Auckland Cup (NZ-G1), Easter H. (NZ-G1), Ellerslie Sires' Produce S. (NZ-G1), New Zealand Derby (NZ-G1)

Hawke's Bay

Racing dates back to 1845 at Hawke's Bay, located near the cities of Napier and Hastings on the eastern shore of New Zealand's northern island. The four racing clubs using the racetrack, however, did not unite until 1989. Now, 14 dates are conducted annually. The highlight of the year is the Spring Carnival, which is held over five weeks in August and September and features the Kelt Capital Stakes (NZ-G1), the richest weight-for-age race in New Zealand. The Hawke's Bay Cup Handicap (NZ-G2), the country's second-oldest race, was first contested in 1860.

Location: Prospect Road, Box 1046, Hastings 4122
Phone: 64 (6) 873-4545
Fax: 64 (6) 6876-6488
Website: www.hawkesbayracing.co.nz
E-Mail: info@hawkesbayracing.co.nz
Abbreviation: HB
Chairman: Peter Roebuck
General Manager: John McGifford
Racecourse Manager: Richard Fenwick
Principal Races: Kelt Capital S. (NZ-G1), Hawke's Bay Gold Cup (NZ-G2), Mudgway PartsWorld Stakes (NZ-G2), Hawke's Bay Guineas (NZ-G3)

Otaki

Otaki Racecourse, located at the north end of Otaki on Kapiti island, has an 1,800-meter, left-handed track and is home of the Otaki-Maori Racing Club. Organized racing has been held at Otaki since the 1850s, and the Otaki-Maori Racing Club dates from 1866. In September 2000, the Levin Racing Club, Wellington Race Club, and Masterson Racing Club joined with the Otaki Maori Racing Club to form Capital Racing. The four clubs, each of which had been facing financial difficulties before the 2000 agreement, combine to run 27 days a year at Otaki, which is easily accessible by railroad from Wellington, at the southern tip of New Zealand's northern island. The WFA Stakes (NZ-G1) is staged there.

Location: P.O. Box 13, Otaki, Kapiti Coast
Phone: 64 (6) 364-8078
Fax: 64 (6) 364-8079
Website: www.otakimaoriracing.co.nz
E-Mail: otakimaoriracing@xtra.co.nz
Abbreviation: Oki
President: Stephen Moffatt
Principal Races: WFA Stakes (NZ-G1)

Riccarton Park

The Canterbury Jockey Club was formed in 1854, and the following year began racing at Riccarton Park Racecourse, which is located ten minutes from the center of Christchurch, New Zealand's second-largest city, on the southern island. Among the races held at Riccarton are the New Zealand Two Thousand Guineas (NZ-G1), New Zealand One Thousand Guineas (NZ-G1), and the New Zealand Cup Handicap (NZ-G2).

Location: Racecourse Road, Riccarton, Christchurch
Phone: 64 (3) 336-0000
Fax: 64 (3) 342-6114
Website: www.riccartonpark.co.nz/cjc
E-Mail: enquiries@riccartonpark.co.nz
Abbreviation: Ric
Chief Executive: Tim Mills
Racing Manager: Jim Langan
Course Manager: Alan Chapman
Principal Races: New Zealand One Thousand Guineas (NZ-G1), New Zealand Two Thousand Guineas (NZ-G1), New Zealand Cup Handicap (NZ-G2)

Te Rapa

Located north of Hamilton on New Zealand's northern island, Te Rapa Racecourse is operated by the Waikato Racing Cup and conducts 18 days of racing annually. Flat racing is conducted on a left-handed, 1,800-meter track with two chutes. Te Rapa has an expansive galloping track, tree-lined paddocks, and a large grandstand. Among its major races are the Waikato Draught Sprint Stakes (NZ-G1), Whakanui Stud International Stakes (NZ-G1), and the Cambridge Stud Sir Tristram Fillies Classic Stakes (NZ-G2).

Location: P.O. Box 10050, Te Rapa, Hamilton
Phone: 64 (7) 849-2839
Fax: 64 (7) 849-1211
Website: www.waikatoracing.co.nz
E-Mail: info@teraparacing.co.nz
Abbreviation: TeR
Chairman: David Smith
Vice Chairman: Peter McCowan
General Manager: A. C. Enting
Course Manager: Neil Treewek
Principal Races: Waikato Draught Sprint Stakes (NZ-G1), Whakanui Stud International (NZ-G1), Cambridge Stud Sir Tristram Fillies Classic Stakes (NZ-G2)

Trentham

Located about 20 miles north of New Zealand's capital city, Wellington, Trentham was founded in 1870, not long after the city itself was built. Trentham's figure-eight steeplechase course is ringed by a wide, 2,000-meter turf course with a 450-meter home straight. Its major races include the Wellington Cup Handicap (NZ-

G1), the Telegraph Handicap (NZ-G1), and the New Zealand Oaks (NZ-G1). Trentham was home of the country's top yearling sale for more than six decades. In its second year in 1928, the sale included a chestnut colt bought for 160 guineas. Named *Phar Lap, he was sent to Australia and made racing history. In 1988, the sale was shifted north to place it closer to the major breeding operations in the country.

Location: P.O. Box 47-024, Trentham, Upper Hutt, or Racecourse Road, Trentham, Upper Hutt
Phone: 64 (4) 528-9611
Fax: 64 (4) 528-4166
Website: www.trentham.co.nz
E-Mail: info@trentham.co.nz
Abbreviation: Tre
President: Mike Brown
Chief Executive: David Jewell
Racing Operations Manager: Logan Fenwick
Principal Races: New Zealand Oaks (NZ-G1), Telegraph H. (NZ-G1), Thorndon Mile H. (NZ-G1), Wellington Cup H. (NZ-G1)

Peru
Monterrico

Racing in Peru was held in the 19th century at a small racetrack called Cancha Meiggs, and successively was conducted at Hipodromo de Santa Beatriz and San Felipe before the opening of the Monterrico Race Track in Lima on December 18, 1960. Racing is conducted year-round on Tuesday and Thursday evenings, Saturdays, and Sundays. The left-handed track has both a dirt track and a grass course.

On December 8, 1997, Panama native Laffit Pincay Jr. and Peruvian-born Edgar Prado, Jorge Chavez, and Julio Pezua represented the United States in an international riders competition at Monterrico. Juan Jose Paule of Argentina and Peruvian Edwin Talaverano tied for first place in the three-race event. Monterrico's premier races form the Quadruple Crown. All of Peru's more than 40 graded races are run at Monterrico.

Location: Avenue El Derby, Santiago De Surco, Lima
Phone: 51 (1) 610-3000
Website: www.monterricoenlared.com
Abbreviation: Mon
President: Herbert Moebius Castaneda
Principal Races: Derby Nacional (Per-G1), Jockey Club del Peru (Per-G1)

Singapore
Singapore Racecourse

Singapore Racecourse at Kranji in the northern part of Singapore is the host of the Singapore Airlines International Cup (Sin-G1). The stakes race is contested at 1¼ miles in May over the 2,000-meter, left-handed track. The race was canceled in 2003 because of the severe acute respiratory syndrome (SARS) outbreak. Another major stakes is the Singapore KrisFlyer Sprint.

With three training tracks, the track accommodates approximately 1,000 horses. Horses are stabled in either air-conditioned or naturally ventilated stalls in barns separated by large courtyards. The four-story grandstand can accommodate 30,000 people.

Location: 1 Turf Club Avenue, Kranji 738078
Phone: 65 (6) 879-1000
Fax: 65 (6) 879-1010
Website: www.turfclub.com.sg
Abbreviation: Sin
President: Yu Pang Fey
Principal Races: International Cup (Sin-G1)

South Africa
Clairwood

Clairwood, operated by the Gold Circle Racing and Gaming Group in Merebank, is host of the 2,000-meter Champions Cup (SAf-G1) in late July. A flat, left-handed track of approximately 2,500 meters in circumference, Clairwood features a 1,200-meter straight that is used for all sprints. The start for 1,400-meter races begins very close to the turn, often resulting in a scramble for good position early, especially in large fields.

Location: 89 Barrier Lane, Clairwood 4052 or P.O. Box 31014, Merebank, 4059
Phone: 27 (31) 469-1020
Fax: 27 (31) 469-0607
Website: www.goldcircle.co.za
E-Mail: info@goldcircle.co.za
Abbreviation: Cla
Ownership: Gold Circle Racing and Gaming Group
Chief Executive: M. J. L. Nairac
Principal Races: Champions Cup (SAf-G1), Gold Challenge S. (SAf-G1), Mercury Sprint Stakes (SAf-G1)

Greyville

Located in a complex that includes a championship golf course, Greyville has conducted racing just outside the city of Durban since 1844. In 1897, the Durban Turf Club took over the track's administration.

The 2,000-meter Durban July Handicap (SAf-G1), the country's most prestigious race, is held on the first Saturday of the month and attracts crowds of up to 60,000. Other major stakes are the South African Guineas (SAf-G1) in May, the South African Fillies Guineas (SAf-G1), and the Daily News Two Thousand (SAf-G1). The right-handed, pear-shaped turf course of about 2,800 meters features tight turns and a straight of nearly 500 meters.

Location: 150 Avondale Road, Greyville, 4001 or P.O. Box 924, Durban, 4000
Phone: 27 (31) 314-1651
Fax: 27 (31) 309-4149
Website: www.goldcircle.co.za
E-mail: infor@goldcircle.co.za
Abbreviation: Grv
Ownership: Gold Circle Racing and Gaming Group
Chief Executive: M. J. L. Nairac
Principal Races: Daily News Two Thousand (SAf-G1), Durban July H. (SAf-G1), Garden Province S. (SAf-G1), Gold Cup (SAf-G1), Premier's Champion S. (SAf-G1), South African Fillies Guineas (SAf-G1), South African Guineas (SAf-G1)

Kenilworth

Serving the Cape Town region, Kenilworth boasts three tracks. Its largest course is 2,800 meters with a 600-meter run-in. Known as the "new course," this left-handed oval is used primarily in summer and is regarded as one of the fairest in South Africa. A smaller, 2,700-meter, left-handed course has a 450-meter run-in and is utilized mostly in the winter months. In addition, a 1,200-meter straight course bisects the infield on a diagonal, and the three courses come together only in the galloping-out area. The straight course is one of the stiffest tests in South African racing, with a climb for

the first 200 meters and another rise in the final 200 meters.

Location: Gate 7, Rosmead Avenue, Kenilworth, 7700, or P.O. Box 53073, Kenilworth, 7745
Phone: 27 (21) 700-1600
Fax: 27 (21) 762-1919
Website: www.goldcircle.co.za
E-Mail: info@goldcircle.co.za
Abbreviation: Ken
Ownership: Gold Circle Racing and Gaming Group
Chief Executive: M. J. L. Nairac
Principal Races: Graham Beck Wines Cape Derby (SAf-G1), J & B Met S. (SAf-G1)

Scottsville

Located near Pietermaritzburg, Scottsville conducted its first race meet on April 3, 1886. Racing is held on 14 Saturdays, two holidays, and 17 weekdays throughout the year on a right-handed, oval turf course approximately 2,270 meters in circumference. Nearby training centers in Ashburton, Clairwood Park, and Summerveld accommodate 2,000 horses for approximately 50 trainers. Scottsville hosts the South African Fillies Sprint (SAf-G1) and the Golden Spur Stakes (SAf-G1). Like Clairwood and Kenilworth, it is owned by the Gold Circle Racing and Gaming Group.

Location: 45 New England Road, Scottsville, 3201 or P.O. Box 101064, Scottsville, 3209
Phone: 27 (33) 345-3405
Fax: 27 (33) 394-1141
Website: www.goldcircle.co.za
E-Mail: info@goldcircle.co.za
Abbreviation: Sco
Ownership: Gold Circle Racing and Gaming Group
Chief Executive: M. J. L. Nairac
Principal Races: Allan Robertson Fillies Championship (SAf-G1), Gold Medallion (SAF-G1), Golden Spur S. (SAf-G1), South African Fillies Sprint (SAf-G1)

Turffontein

Only two miles south of Johannesburg, Turffontein has been home to racing since 1887, just one year after the first Thoroughbred race was held in the city. While maintaining its traditions, including a Royal Box, Turffontein has been thoroughly modernized. The grandstand, rebuilt in the 1970s, allows a panoramic view of the course, and the Ascot Bar and Lounge, Caradoc Room, and Lawn Enclosure give fans many alternatives for enjoying their day at the races. The course has its own water source, which allows for beautiful lawns, numerous flower gardens, meticulously maintained trees and shrubs, and a bird sanctuary. Racing is conducted mostly on Saturdays on a testing, uphill, right-handed turf course of 2,658 meters. Its single chute allows for a 1,200-meter straight. Turffontein also has a 2,000-meter grass training track and four sand training tracks. The South Africa Derby (SAf-G1), Champion Stakes (SAf-G1), and Horse Chestnut 1,600 Stakes (SAf-G1), formerly the President's Cup, are three of Turffontein's biggest races.

Location: 14 Turf Club Street, Turffontein, 2190, or P. O. Box 82625, Southdale, 2135
Phone: 27 (11) 681-1500
Fax: 27 (11) 683-7116
Website: www.phumelela.com
E-mail: phumelela@phumelela.com
Abbreviation: Tff

Chief Executive Officer: James Satchwell Tennant
Principal Races: Champion S. (SAf-G1), Empress Club S. (SAf-G1), Gold Bowl (SAf-G1), Horse Chestnut 1,600 S. (SAf-G1), South Africa Derby (SAf-G1), South Africa Nursery (SAf-G1), Summer Cup (SAf-G1), Triple Crown 1,600 (SAf-G1), Triple Tiara 1,600 (SAf-G1)

United Arab Emirates
Nad al Sheba

Offering the world's richest race—the $6-million Dubai World Cup (UAE-G1)—and no betting on any of its races, Nad al Sheba Racecourse is located within the tiny sheikhdom of Dubai in the United Arab Emirates. First laid out in 1986 and resurfaced in '97 before the third running of the World Cup, the 2,200-meter, left-handed dirt course has three chutes. A left-handed turf course inside the dirt course is composed of Bermuda hybrid grass, which thrives in hot and humid climates. Two-time North American Horse of the Year Cigar won the inaugural Dubai World Cup in 1996 to give the stakes instant credibility. Also on the Dubai World Cup program are the Dubai Duty Free Stakes (UAE-G1), the Dubai Golden Shaheen (UAE-G1), the Dubai Sheema Classic (UAE-G1), the United Arab Emirates Derby (UAE-G2), and the Godolphin Mile (UAE-G2). The Dubai World Cup Committee pays a wide array of costs for visiting horses competing in Dubai, including roundtrip airfare.

Location: City Tower 1, 2nd Floor, Ste. 206, P. O. Box 9305, Dubai
Phone: 971 (4) 327-0077
Fax: 971 (4) 327-0049
Website: www.dubairacingclub.com
E-Mail: info@dubairacingclub.com
Abbreviation: Nad
Chairman: Saeed H. Al Tayer
Chief Executive Officer: Frank Gabriel Jr.
Principal Races: Dubai Duty Free S. (UAE-G1), Dubai Golden Shaheen (UAE-G1), Dubai Sheema Classic (UAE-G1), Dubai World Cup (UAE-G1), Godolphin Mile (UAE-G2), United Arab Emirates Derby (UAE-G2)

Uruguay
Maronas National Racetrack

Shuttered for 5½ years, historic Maronas National Racetrack reopened in June 2003 after a multimillion-dollar renovation by its lessees, Hipica Rioplatense and Lone Star Park, a Magna Entertainment Corp. property. The Montevideo track, which dates from the mid-1870s, is owned by the Republic of Uruguay, and the partnership holds a 30-year lease on the track and concessions. By its first anniversary, the track was offering an average of almost ten races a day and was attracting increasingly larger crowds and wagering. The track's reopening also was credited with stimulating the Uruguayan breeding industry. The track, which also has four off-track facilities with slot machines and 20 off-track betting sites, simulcasts its races around the world and began sending Group 1 races into the United States in early 2005.

Location: 3540 Jose Maria Guerra, Montevideo, 120000
Phone: 598 (2) 511-7777
Fax: 598 (2) 511-9961
Website: www.maronas.com.uy
E-Mail: info@maronas.com.uy
Abbreviation: Man
Principal Races: Jose Pedro Ramirez

International Sire Lists
Leading Sires by 2007 Earnings by Country
(By Racing Season for Southern Hemisphere Countries)

Argentina

Sire	Strs	Wnrs	SWs	Leading Earner (Earnings)	Total Earnings
Southern Halo	115	57	6	Fiesta Lady (Arg) ($99,102)	$1,151,297
Slew Gin Fizz	116	52	5	Latency ($275,114)	1,073,665
Incurable Optimist	135	54	3	Life of Victory ($118,399)	933,656
Roy	104	52	5	Arriba Baby ($102,556)	894,725
Interprete	119	55	3	Ithamar ($70,959)	826,984
Lucky Roberto	116	57	4	Misty Lady ($47,770)	781,262
Numerous	100	47	1	Mr. Cacht ($28,635)	744,071
Salt Lake	72	38	3	Don Julio A ($44,281)	735,243
Alpha Plus	104	46	2	Mariah Plus ($97,542)	726,606
Honour and Glory	72	32	3	Indio Glorioso ($103,044)	714,792

Australia

Sire	Strs	Wnrs	SWs	Leading Earner (Earnings)	Total Earnings
Encosta de Lago	285	104	12	Sirmione ($1,212,355)	$8,383,770
More Than Ready	115	50	4	Sebring ($2,365,522)	5,219,318
Flying Spur	194	73	9	Forensics ($950,333)	5,170,402
Zabeel	130	32	6	Efficient ($2,864,921)	4,921,567
Hussonet	66	27	4	Weekend Hussler ($2,190,552)	3,832,704
Scenic (Ire)	155	70	8	Marasco ($439,265)	3,666,744
Redoute's Choice	173	61	8	Miss Finland ($455,676)	3,638,035
O'Reilly	79	41	3	Master O'Reilly ($1,644,742)	3,557,908
Commands	188	83	8	Marching ($532,757)	3,472,619
Danehill Dancer	213	72	5	Arapaho Miss ($622,678)	3,232,741

Brazil

Sire	Strs	Wnrs	SWs	Leading Earner (Earnings)	Total Earnings
Dubai Dust	43	25	2	Plutao ($943,431)	$1,168,266
Vettori	85	54	8	Site Oficial ($195,740)	817,850
Roi Normand	197	72	5	Favorite Guest ($46,532)	721,895
Public Purse	93	47	5	Celtic Princess (Brz) ($50,529)	541,371
Fahim (GB)	52	21	1	Reclamante ($279,190)	470,406
Know Heights (Ire)	111	41	6	Indianette ($83,381)	458,378
Notation	75	42	5	Super Duda ($75,611)	450,584
Dodge	88	51	2	Eletro Nuclear (Brz) ($35,986)	437,058
Yagli	89	44	4	Jet ($65,815)	429,157
Choctaw Ridge	119	58	3	Blue Elf ($26,905)	413,594

Canada

Sire	Strs	Wnrs	SWs	Leading Earner (Earnings)	Total Earnings
Bold Executive	122	63	4	Legal Move ($222,728)	$4,029,997
Kiridashi	44	21	3	Financingavailable ($451,151)	1,993,669
Bold n' Flashy	82	40	2	Red Raffles ($165,239)	1,890,336
Langfuhr	57	27	2	Last Answer ($226,278)	1,606,620
Lord Avie	3	2	1	Cloudy's Knight ($1,479,360)	1,516,875
Smart Strike	39	21	3	Strike Softly ($305,775)	1,512,929
Ascot Knight	55	26	0	Knightly Attire ($148,659)	1,448,223
Whiskey Wisdom	58	28	2	Dave the Knave ($104,309)	1,424,610
Tethra	64	27	2	Don's Folly ($133,283)	1,378,597
One Way Love	69	25	1	You Will Love Me ($320,801)	1,361,647

England

Sire	Strs	Wnrs	SWs	Leading Earner (Earnings)	Total Earnings
Montjeu (Ire)	105	34	6	Authorized ($2,365,763)	$4,194,751
Danehill	78	31	9	Dylan Thomas (Ire) ($1,246,353)	4,085,192
Galileo (Ire)	78	37	9	Allegretto ($364,107)	2,503,939
Danehill Dancer	134	51	6	Lady Rangali ($307,904)	2,457,729
Pivotal	131	57	5	Excellent Art (GB) ($508,678)	2,416,836
Sadler's Wells	103	36	9	Septimus ($362,921)	2,389,369
Royal Applause (GB)	137	58	4	Third Set ($403,259)	1,840,494
Rock of Gibraltar (Ire)	68	24	5	Eagle Mountain ($769,705)	1,795,783
Dansili (GB)	101	51	7	Dansant ($159,441)	1,738,061
Acclamation	43	22	3	Dark Angel ($685,840)	1,642,365

England/Ireland

Sire	Strs	Wnrs	SWs	Leading Earner (Earnings)	Total Earnings
Danehill	113	54	12	Dylan Thomas (Ire) ($2,191,747)	$7,557,865

Sire	Strs	Wnrs	SWs	Leading Earner (Earnings)	Total Earnings
Galileo (Ire)	117	52	10	Lush Lashes ($1,367,771)	$5,940,897
Montjeu (Ire)	136	47	8	Authorized ($2,365,763)	4,753,142
Danehill Dancer	193	79	15	Lady Rangali ($307,904)	4,633,009
Sadler's Wells	158	58	13	Yeats ($594,190)	4,336,378
Pivotal	149	69	7	Excellent Art (GB) ($508,678)	3,066,276
Rock of Gibraltar (Ire)	97	37	8	Eagle Mountain ($1,067,768)	2,842,033
Indian Ridge	83	31	2	Luck Money ($1,408,391)	2,631,507
In the Wings (GB)	105	41	7	Hi Calypso ($199,937)	2,166,744
Acclamation	55	24	4	Dark Angel ($685,840)	2,143,932

France

Sire	Strs	Wnrs	SWs	Leading Earner (Earnings)	Total Earnings
Danehill	21	6	4	Dylan Thomas (Ire) ($1,849,353)	$2,827,912
Anabaa	101	48	4	Loup Breton ($164,376)	2,310,272
Monsun	27	12	5	Manduro ($765,395)	2,035,564
Zamindar	26	14	5	Darjina ($872,917)	1,846,959
Poliglote (GB)	89	40	3	Irish Wells ($310,653)	1,794,710
Kendor	67	33	2	Literato ($685,420)	1,767,002
Verglas (Ire)	128	37	2	Stormy River ($117,422)	1,757,600
Linamix	84	39	3	Garnica ($150,106)	1,747,755
Invincible Spirit	10	4	2	Lawman ($1,538,005)	1,699,985
Marchand de Sable	100	37	2	Marchand d'Or ($291,221)	1,628,204

Germany

Sire	Strs	Wnrs	SWs	Leading Earner (Earnings)	Total Earnings
Big Shuffle	113	47	6	Precious Boy ($161,823)	$1,293,527
Monsun	74	33	8	Schiaparelli ($359,665)	1,214,378
In the Wings (GB)	4	3	2	Adlerflug ($617,585)	829,619
Acatenango	56	31	4	Quijano ($201,835)	710,383
Silvano (Ger)	37	16	2	Mi Emma ($230,813)	549,903
Dashing Blade	94	37	2	Tumult ($37,852)	545,267
Lando (Ger)	44	23	3	Prince Flori ($86,041)	486,010
Goofalik	52	29	2	Bussoni ($88,206)	400,340
Tiger Hill	58	22	2	Touch My Soul (Fr) ($45,987)	364,146
Tertullian	28	13	2	Aviso ($152,226)	326,317

Hong Kong

Sire	Strs	Wnrs	SWs	Leading Earner (Earnings)	Total Earnings
Danehill	44	19	1	Scintillation ($633,352)	$4,221,882
Marju	17	9	1	Comic Strip ($2,730,778)	3,557,814
O'Reilly	34	18	0	Master Hunter ($369,726)	2,711,693
Fusaichi Pegasus	11	7	1	Floral Pegasus ($1,691,018)	2,372,471
Encosta de Lago	16	7	1	Sacred Kingdom ($1,571,449)	2,356,618
Zabeel	13	8	1	Vengeance Of Rain ($1,251,723)	2,207,429
Cape Cross (Ire)	21	8	2	Able One ($799,247)	1,993,398
Flying Spur	23	10	0	Lucky Hero ($375,313)	1,958,638
Lear Fan	1	1	1	Good Ba Ba ($1,943,291)	1,943,291
Danasinga	19	12	0	Safety First ($225,020)	1,495,414

Ireland

Sire	Strs	Wnrs	SWs	Leading Earner (Earnings)	Total Earnings
Danehill	47	26	6	Dylan Thomas (Ire) ($945,394)	$3,472,673
Galileo (Ire)	47	18	3	Lush Lashes ($1,367,771)	3,436,958
Danehill Dancer	71	30	11	Alexander Tango (Ire) ($194,779)	2,175,280
Sadler's Wells	70	26	7	Yeats ($339,498)	1,947,009
Indian Ridge	22	7	0	Luck Money ($1,367,771)	1,610,959
Rock of Gibraltar (Ire)	39	14	3	Eagle Mountain ($298,063)	1,046,250
Mr. Greeley	7	4	2	Saoirse Abu ($531,838)	900,695
Invincible Spirit	42	16	1	Campfire Glow ($172,157)	733,123
In the Wings (GB)	40	12	2	Fracas (Ire) ($181,536)	676,931
Pivotal	23	12	2	Thoughtless Moment ($154,445)	649,440

Italy

Sire	Strs	Wnrs	SWs	Leading Earner (Earnings)	Total Earnings
Dr Devious (Ire)	128	60	0	Bernheim ($65,092)	$1,337,350
Almutawakel (GB)	42	21	1	Awelmarduk ($460,520)	1,007,985
Orpen	65	34	1	White Snow ($103,723)	927,631
Desert Prince (Ire)	61	28	2	Ceprin ($111,349)	884,649
Shantou	79	36	0	Biff Tannen ($85,121)	881,316
Celtic Swing	42	21	1	Freemusic ($127,750)	837,322
Soviet Star	25	15	1	Pressing (Ire) ($404,312)	713,331
Docksider	26	20	2	Place in Line ($179,772)	683,008
Titus Livius (Fr)	34	20	1	Golden Titus ($218,472)	663,047
Blu Air Force (Ire)	40	19	1	Amaldi ($132,720)	639,020

Japan

Sire	Strs	Wnrs	SWs	Leading Earner (Earnings)	Total Earnings
Sunday Silence	250	75	16	Matsurida Gogh ($2,810,329)	$33,334,817
Agnes Tachyon	243	101	6	Daiwa Scarlet ($3,985,857)	23,556,212
Brian's Time	201	81	9	Victory ($1,398,976)	20,049,653
Dance in the Dark	280	79	6	Jolly Dance ($1,241,072)	19,961,780
Fuji Kiseki	246	81	9	Yumeno Shirushi ($1,066,021)	18,285,811
French Deputy	177	62	8	Sans Adieu ($1,604,557)	16,944,307
Sakura Bakushin O	229	82	3	Kanoya Zakura ($670,924)	15,361,851
Special Week	219	76	2	Inti Raimi ($1,134,097)	15,126,431
El Condor Pasa	98	37	4	Vermilion ($3,309,013)	14,012,025
Kurofune	193	69	2	White Melody ($694,759)	11,419,664

Puerto Rico

Sire	Strs	Wnrs	SWs	Leading Earner (Earnings)	Total Earnings
Eqtesaad	58	39	0	Bachatera ($79,707)	$775,293
Fappiano's Star	57	22	1	Borrascoso ($102,862)	680,321
Sejm	29	22	2	El Enganado ($192,184)	649,910
Royal Merlot	50	23	1	Tonadilla ($131,393)	538,012
Just Typical	36	25	0	Ojos Bellos ($61,161)	485,716
Billions	35	19	1	Constelacion ($67,368)	463,769
Concerto	17	13	2	Classical Concerto ($85,779)	365,354
Myfavorite Place	11	7	1	Defensora ($240,202)	334,327
Virtua Cop	26	16	1	Procurador ($76,200)	332,459
Goldwater	16	10	0	Gold Gift ($69,722)	290,129

Saudi Arabia

Sire	Strs	Wnrs	SWs	Leading Earner (Earnings)	Total Earnings
Torrey Canyon	52	27	2	Lahfat Lahoom ($49,914)	$494,581
Freequent	26	13	1	Jaa Yez ($36,133)	249,501
Nero Zilzal	7	4	0	Sahm Allayl ($179,766)	218,828
Addath	13	7	0	Almotawaazen ($103,016)	198,094
Voleris	35	10	1	Yastaa Hel ($34,720)	184,616
Delius	29	9	0	Baarqat Rodhwaan ($38,096)	176,454
Another Review	27	5	0	Taa Wee ($60,842)	173,801
Alysheba	20	5	0	Kaamen ($43,775)	160,203
Mujahid	3	2	0	Lama Alriyadh ($134,366)	159,097
Meet the Greek	29	3	0	Alfajree ($68,508)	126,148

United Arab Emirates

Sire	Strs	Wnrs	SWs	Leading Earner (Earnings)	Total Earnings
Candy Stripes	3	1	1	Invasor (Arg) ($3,600,000)	$3,649,397
End Sweep	1	1	1	Admire Moon ($3,000,000)	3,000,000
Zabeel	1	1	1	Vengeance Of Rain ($3,000,000)	3,000,000
Not for Sale	3	1	1	Asiatic Boy ($1,458,000)	1,638,000
Indian Ridge	11	5	1	Linngari ($1,150,000)	1,340,138
Pleasant Tap	2	0	0	Premium Tap ($1,200,000)	1,200,817
Patton	1	1	1	Kelly's Landing ($1,200,000)	1,200,000
Western Winter	6	1	0	Oracle West ($1,060,000)	1,184,600
Royal Academy	5	1	1	Bullish Luck ($600,000)	778,200

Leading Sires by Year

Argentina*

Year	Sire, YOB, Sire	Earnings
2007	Southern Halo, 1983, by Halo	$1,151,297
2006	Bernstein, 1997, by Storm Cat	827,969
2005	Mutakddim, 1991, by Seeking the Gold	770,135
2004	Roy, 1983, by Fappiano	667,102
2003	Roar, 1993, by Forty Niner	642,453
2002	Southern Halo, 1983, by Halo	553,695
2001	Roy, 1983, by Fappiano	818,389
2000	Southern Halo, 1983, by Halo	1,632,869
1999	Southern Halo, 1983, by Halo	1,490,119
1998	Southern Halo, 1983, by Halo	1,883,179
1997	Southern Halo, 1983, by Halo	2,010,382

Australia*

Year	Sire, YOB, Sire	Earnings
2007	Encosta de Lago, 1993, by Fairy King	$8,383,770
2006	Flying Spur, 1992, by Danehill	7,273,846
2005	Redoute's Choice, 1996, by Danehill	8,249,457

Year	Sire, YOB, Sire	Earnings
2004	Danehill, 1986, by Danzig	$8,663,083
2003	Danehill, 1986, by Danzig	5,723,877
2002	Danehill, 1986, by Danzig	4,033,932
2001	Danehill, 1986, by Danzig	4,033,288
2000	Danehill, 1986, by Danzig	4,080,825
1999	Danehill, 1986, by Danzig	4,952,018
1998	Zabeel, 1986, by *Sir Tristram	6,793,635
1997	Danehill, 1986, by Danzig	5,034,265

Brazil*

Year	Sire, YOB, Sire	Earnings
2007	Dubai Dust, 1994, by Broad Brush	$1,168,266
2006	Roi Normand, 1983, by Exclusive Native	595,058
2005	Roi Normand, 1983, by Exclusive Native	630,531
2004	Roi Normand, 1983, by Exclusive Native	550,724
2003	Fast Gold, 1979, by Mr. Prospector	419,187
2002	Fast Gold, 1979, by Mr. Prospector	427,914
2001	Choctaw Ridge, 1989, by Mr. Prospector	563,482

International — Leading Sires by Year

Year	Sire, YOB, Sire	Earnings
2000	Minstrel Glory, 1980, by The Minstrel	$530,018
1999	Roi Normand, 1983, by Exclusive Native	278,000
1998	Bright Again, 1987, by Wild Again	397,767
1997	Punk, 1984, by Ringaro	406,900

Canada

Year	Sire, YOB, Sire	Earnings
2007	Bold Executive, 1984, by Bold Ruckus	$4,029,997
2006	Bold Executive, 1984, by Bold Ruckus	3,441,628
2005	Archers Bay, 1995, by Silver Deputy	2,663,439
2004	Smart Strike, 1992, by Mr. Prospector	3,289,278
2003	Langfuhr, 1992, by Danzig	3,783,111
2002	Regal Classic, 1985, by Vice Regent	2,777,503
2001	Regal Classic, 1985, by Vice Regent	2,663,430
2000	Regal Classic, 1985, by Vice Regent	2,778,491
1999	Regal Classic, 1985, by Vice Regent	2,000,300
1998	Silver Deputy, 1985, by Deputy Minister	2,097,515
1997	Bold Ruckus, 1976, by Boldnesian	1,859,252

England

Year	Sire, YOB, Sire	Earnings
2007	Montjeu (Ire), 1996, by Sadler's Wells	$4,194,751
2006	Danehill, 1986, by Danzig	3,368,734
2005	Montjeu (Ire), 1996, by Sadler's Wells	3,307,291
2004	Sadler's Wells, 1981, by Northern Dancer	5,082,034
2003	Sadler's Wells, 1981, by Northern Dancer	3,023,899
2002	Sadler's Wells, 1981, by Northern Dancer	3,006,898
2001	Sadler's Wells, 1981, by Northern Dancer	3,977,732
2000	Sadler's Wells, 1981, by Northern Dancer	2,606,967
1999	Fairy King, 1982, by Northern Dancer	1,962,154
1998	Nashwan, 1986, by Blushing Groom (Fr)	1,524,720
1997	Silver Hawk, 1979, by Roberto	1,488,473

England and Ireland

Year	Sire, YOB, Sire	Earnings
2007	Danehill, 1986, by Danzig	$7,557,865
2006	Danehill, 1986, by Danzig	6,647,846
2005	Danehill, 1986, by Danzig	6,187,530
2004	Sadler's Wells, 1981, by Northern Dancer	7,251,454
2003	Sadler's Wells, 1981, by Northern Dancer	5,823,175
2002	Sadler's Wells, 1981, by Northern Dancer	5,562,690
2001	Sadler's Wells, 1981, by Northern Dancer	5,738,357
2000	Sadler's Wells, 1981, by Northern Dancer	3,676,717
1999	Sadler's Wells, 1981, by Northern Dancer	2,952,410
1998	Sadler's Wells, 1981, by Northern Dancer	2,626,355
1997	Sadler's Wells, 1981, by Northern Dancer	2,241,578

France

Year	Sire, YOB, Sire	Earnings
2007	Danehill, 1986, by Danzig	$2,827,912
2006	Dansili (GB), 1996, by Danehill	2,732,441
2005	Montjeu (Ire), 1996, by Sadler's Wells	2,978,783
2004	Linamix, 1987, by Mendez	3,163,044
2003	Darshaan, 1981, by Shirley Heights	2,433,602
2002	Danehill, 1986, by Danzig	1,952,836
2001	Danehill, 1986, by Danzig	1,630,129
2000	Highest Honor (Fr), 1983, by Kenmare	1,424,916
1999	Sadler's Wells, 1981, by Northern Dancer	2,155,310
1998	Linamix, 1987, by Mendez	1,929,005
1997	Nureyev, 1977, by Northern Dancer	2,139,852

Germany

Year	Sire, YOB, Sire	Earnings
2007	Big Shuffle, 1984, by Super Concorde	$1,293,527
2006	Monsun, 1990, by Konigsstuhl	1,373,516
2005	Big Shuffle, 1984, by Super Concorde	1,337,884
2004	Monsun, 1990, by Konigsstuhl	1,882,789
2003	Big Shuffle, 1984, by Super Concorde	1,341,355
2002	Monsun, 1990, by Konigsstuhl	1,278,658
2001	Big Shuffle, 1984, by Super Concorde	917,838
2000	Monsun, 1990, by Konigsstuhl	1,361,406
1999	Dashing Blade, 1987, by Elegant Air	1,223,849
1998	Big Shuffle, 1984, by Super Concorde	$1,040,915
1997	Acatenango, 1982, by Surumu	1,484,293

Hong Kong

Year	Sire, YOB, Sire	Earnings
2007	Danehill, 1986, by Danzig	$4,221,882
2006	Danehill, 1986, by Danzig	6,701,927
2005	Danehill, 1986, by Danzig	7,440,932
2004	Danehill, 1986, by Danzig	7,998,326
2003	Danehill, 1986, by Danzig	8,562,038
2002	Danehill, 1986, by Danzig	6,308,554
2001	Danehill, 1986, by Danzig	5,549,309
2000	Rahy, 1985, by Blushing Groom (Fr)	3,106,199
1999	Danehill, 1986, by Danzig	3,089,946
1998	Danehill, 1986, by Danzig	2,779,929
1997	Green Desert, 1983, by Danzig	850,035

Ireland

Year	Sire, YOB, Sire	Earnings
2007	Danehill, 1986, by Danzig	$3,472,673
2006	Danehill, 1986, by Danzig	3,279,112
2005	Danehill, 1986, by Danzig	2,974,862
2004	Sadler's Wells, 1981, by Northern Dancer	2,169,420
2003	Sadler's Wells, 1981, by Northern Dancer	2,799,276
2002	Sadler's Wells, 1981, by Northern Dancer	2,555,792
2001	Sadler's Wells, 1981, by Northern Dancer	1,760,625
2000	Sadler's Wells, 1981, by Northern Dancer	1,069,750
1999	Sadler's Wells, 1981, by Northern Dancer	1,710,136
1998	Sadler's Wells, 1981, by Northern Dancer	1,150,913
1997	Danehill, 1986, by Danzig	1,198,712

Italy

Year	Sire, YOB, Sire	Earnings
2007	Dr Devious (Ire), 1989, by Ahonoora	$1,337,350
2006	Dr Devious (Ire), 1989, by Ahonoora	1,089,715
2005	Sri Pekan, 1992, by Red Ransom	1,625,891
2004	Sri Pekan, 1992, by Red Ransom	1,876,488
2003	Sri Pekan, 1992, by Red Ransom	1,586,332
2002	Love the Groom, 1984, by Blushing Groom (Fr)	979,041
2001	Roi Danzig, 1986, by Danzig	908,189
2000	Roi Danzig, 1986, by Danzig	847,389
1999	Sikeston, 1986, by Lear Fan	800,283
1998	Love the Groom, 1984, by Blushing Groom (Fr)	1,250,469
1997	Love the Groom, 1984, by Blushing Groom (Fr)	1,490,432

Japan

Year	Sire, YOB, Sire	Earnings
2007	Sunday Silence, 1986, by Halo	$33,334,817
2006	Sunday Silence, 1986, by Halo	66,933,387
2005	Sunday Silence, 1986, by Halo	83,080,919
2004	Sunday Silence, 1986, by Halo	82,901,306
2003	Sunday Silence, 1986, by Halo	69,987,197
2002	Sunday Silence, 1986, by Halo	52,712,230
2001	Sunday Silence, 1986, by Halo	53,790,988
2000	Sunday Silence, 1986, by Halo	53,883,429
1999	Sunday Silence, 1986, by Halo	45,579,976
1998	Sunday Silence, 1986, by Halo	33,925,214
1997	Sunday Silence, 1986, by Halo	29,390,122

United Arab Emirates

Year	Sire, YOB, Sire	Earnings
2007	Candy Stripes, 1982, by Blushing Groom (Fr)	$3,649,397
2006	Red Ransom, 1987, by Roberto	3,841,166
2005	Devil His Due, 1989, by Devil's Bag	3,600,000
2004	Pleasant Colony, 1978, by His Majesty	3,717,378
2003	Singspiel (Ire), 1992, by In the Wings (GB)	4,155,117
2002	Machiavellian, 1987, by Mr. Prospector	4,082,712
2001	Fly So Free, 1988, by Time for a Change	3,600,000
2000	Seeking the Gold, 1985, by Mr. Prospector	3,675,318
1999	Machiavellian, 1987, by Mr. Prospector	3,165,733
1998	Silver Buck, 1978, by Buckpasser	2,400,000
1997	In the Wings (GB), 1986, by Sadler's Wells	2,420,558

*Southern Hemisphere seasons

Sovereign Awards

Toronto-born pharmaceutical tycoon Eugene Melnyk had had several notable accomplishments since becoming a Thoroughbred owner in the 1980s, including a Queen's Plate Stakes victory with Archers Bay in 1998 and a win in the 2004 Breeders' Cup Sprint (G1) with eventual champion sprinter Speightstown. Despite his successes, Melnyk had never received the Sovereign Award as leading owner until 2007, when his homebred Sealy Hill collected three Sovereign Awards, including Horse of the Year, and boosted Melnyk to a new career pinnacle.

Sealy Hill's sweep of Canada's inaugural triple tiara—the Labatt Woodbine Oaks, the Bison City Stakes, and the Wonder Where Stakes—earned her champion turf female and three-year-old filly statuettes in addition to the Horse of the Year honor from Sovereign judges. In addition to Melnyk's award as outstanding owner, Sealy Hill's trainer, Mark Casse, and her regular jockey, Patrick Husbands, each received Sovereign Awards in their respective categories. It was Casse's second straight award and Husbands's fifth overall honor.

After winning the Glorious Song Stakes at Woodbine as a juvenile, Sealy Hill began her three-year-old campaign in late January 2007 with a second-place effort in an allowance race on dirt at Gulfstream Park. She then traveled north to Turfway Park, and in her return to Polytrack won the Bourbonette Oaks (G3) on March 24 by a head over eventual dual Grade 1 winner Panty Raid. In her next start, Sealy Hill struggled over Churchill Downs's muddy main track while finishing 12th to Rags to Riches in the Kentucky Oaks (G1) before returning to Canada.

Sealy Hill responded to her homecoming with three consecutive wins in the inaugural Canadian triple tiara over the summer months, each by open lengths. Remaining at Woodbine through the fall, she finished a neck behind Essential Edge in the Canadian Stakes (Can-G2) and then led briefly in midstretch before yielding to European Group 1 winner Mrs. Lindsay in the E. P. Taylor Stakes (Can-G1). Adept on both turf and Polytrack and at a variety of distances, Sealy Hill finished 2007 with a record of four wins and three seconds in eight starts, with earnings of $958,389.

Among the year's other Sovereign Award win-

History of the Sovereign Awards

Year	E. P. Taylor Award of Merit†	Owner	Breeder	Trainer	Jockey	Apprentice Jockey
2007	Not awarded	Melnyk Racing Stable	Adena Springs	Mark Casse	Patrick Husbands	Tyler Pizarro
2006	Not awarded	Sam-Son Farm	Adena Springs	Mark Casse	Todd Kabel	Emma-Jayne Wilson
2005	Not awarded	Frank Stronach	Adena Springs	Reade Baker	Todd Kabel	Emma-Jayne Wilson
2004	Not awarded	Sam-Son Farm	Sam-Son Farm	Robert Tiller	Todd Kabel	Corey Fraser
2003	Not awarded	Stronach Stable	Sam-Son Farm	Robert Tiller	Todd Kabel	Julia Brimo
2002	Not awarded	Stronach Stable	Sam-Son Farm	Roger Attfield	Patrick Husbands	Chantal Sutherland
2001	Not awarded	Sam-Son Farm	Sam-Son Farm	Robert Tiller	Patrick Husbands	Chantal Sutherland
2000	Mike Harris	Sam-Son Farm	Sam-Son Farm	Mark Frostad	Patrick Husbands	Cory Clark
1999	George Hendrie	Stronach Stable	Frank Stronach	Mark Frostad	Patrick Husbands	Ben Russell
1998	David Willmot	Stronach Stable	Frank Stronach	Michael Wright Jr.	David Clark	Helen Vanek
1997	Not awarded	Frank Stronach	Frank Stronach	Mark Frostad	Emile Ramsammy	Rui Pimentel
1996	Not awarded	Minshall Farms	Minshall Farms	Barbara Minshall	Emile Ramsammy	Neil Poznansky
1995	Charles Taylor	Frank Stronach	Kinghaven Farms	Danny Vella	Todd Kabel	Dave Wilson
1994	Jack Kenney	Frank Stronach	Kinghaven Farms	Danny Vella	Robert Landry	Dave Wilson
1993	Not awarded	Frank Stronach	Kinghaven Farms	Roger Attfield	Robert Landry	Constant Montpellier
1992	Col. Charles Baker	Knob Hill Stable	Knob Hill Stable	Philip England	Todd Kabel	Stanley Bethley
1991	Ernest Samuel	Sam-Son Farm	Sam-Son Farm	Jim Day	Mickey Walls	Mickey Walls
1990	James Wright	Kinghaven Farms	Kinghaven Farms	Roger Attfield	Don Seymour	Mickey Walls
1989	George C. Frostad	Kinghaven Farms	Kinghaven Farms	Roger Attfield	Don Seymour	Maree Richards
1988	Sandy Hawley	Sam-Son Farm	Sam-Son Farm	Jim Day	Sandy Hawley	Jim McAleney
1987	Larry Regan	Kinghaven Farms	Kinghaven Farms	Roger Attfield	Don Seymour	Jim McAleney
1986	D. G. Willmot	D. G. Willmot	D. G. Willmot	Roger Attfield	Larry Attard	Todd Kabel
1985	George Gardiner	Ernest Samuel	E. P. Taylor	Jim Day	Don Seymour	Nancy Jumpsen
1984	Jim Coleman	Ernest Samuel	Frank Stronach	Mike Doyle	Chris Loseth	Robert King
1983	Joe Thomas	B. K. Yousif	Mr. and Mrs. Russell Bennett	Bill Marko	Larry Attard	Robert King
1982	Jean-Louis Levesque	D. G. Willmot	D. G. Willmot	Bill Marko	Lloyd Duffy	Richard Dos Ramos
1981	Jim Bentley	Dave Kapchinsky	Tom Webb	Ron Brock	Erwin Driedger	Richard Dos Ramos
1980	Jack Stafford	Ernest Samuel	Mr. and Mrs. Marvin Hamilton	Gerry Belanger	Gary Stahlbaum	Valerie Thompson
1979	George C. Hendrie	James Shields	D. G. Willmot	Jim Day	Robin Platts	Ray Creighton
1978	Ron Turcotte	Conn Smythe	Jean-Louis Levesque	F. H. Merrill	Sandy Hawley	Ron Hansen
1977	E. P. Taylor	Bory Margolus	Conn Smythe	Red Smith	Avelino Gomez	Brad Smythe
1976	Jack Diamond	George Gardiner	E. P. Taylor	Lou Cavalaris	Chris Rogers	Chris Loseth
1975	E. P. Taylor	Jack Stafford	Bory Margolus	Gil Rowntree	Hugo Dittfach	Jeff Fell

†Formerly known as Man of the Year

ners, both True Metropolitan and Financingavailable repeated as champion older male and champion older female, respectively, and Financingavailable was also honored as champion sprinter. True Metropolitan's 2007 campaign included stakes wins at Hastings Racecourse, Northlands Park, and Woodbine, where he captured both the Dominion Day Stakes (Can-G3) and the Autumn Stakes (Can-G3). Two of Financingavailable's four stakes wins in 2007 came at sprint distances, and she established a track record at Woodbine for six furlongs when she blazed to a career-capping victory in the Ontario Fashion Stakes in 1:08.56 on October 30.

Although based in the United States, Kodiak Kowboy made the minimum two starts in Canada required for two-year-olds to be eligible for Sovereign Award consideration. Trained by Steve Asmussen, the Posse colt dominated the Victoria Stakes in June at Woodbine before returning stateside and winning the Saratoga Special Stakes (G2) and Bashford Manor Stakes (G3).

Dancing Allstar, 2007's champion two-year-old filly, raced exclusively in her native country for the year and amassed four stakes wins, including the Fantasy Stakes and the My Dear Stakes. Among three-year-old males, Alezzandro edged out Leonnatus Anteas for champion honors on the basis of two strong performances in Canadian Triple Crown races. Alezzandro finished second to Mike Fox in the Queen's Plate in late June after making much of the pace, but he rebounded to win the Prince of Wales Stakes at Fort Erie three weeks later.

Chicago-based Cloudy's Knight arrived at Woodbine during July in the midst of a career year, and the seven-year-old Lord Avie gelding elevated his game with a close second in the Nijinsky Stakes (Can-G2) and a win in the Sky Classic Stakes (Can-G2) before grinding to an upset victory in the Pattison Canadian International Stakes (Can-G1) on October 21. His nose win over the outstanding European invader Ask (GB) provided one of 2007's most thrilling moments and locked up the Sovereign Award for champion turf male as well.

The Canadian division of Frank Stronach's Adena Springs won its third consecutive award as outstanding breeder. Adena North, based in Aurora, Ontario, produced nine stakes winners in 2007. Lover's Talk was honored as Broodmare of the Year based largely on the success of Lyrically, a Thunder Gulch filly bred by Kinghaven Farms who placed in three stakes and earned nearly $190,000. Tyler Pizarro received the Sovereign Award as outstanding apprentice jockey after establishing himself as a leading rider at Woodbine, where he won 13.9% of his 2007 races and accounted for more than $5-million in purse earnings.

History of the Sovereign Awards

Year	Horse of the Year	Two-Year-Old Filly	Two-Year-Old Male	Three-Year-Old Filly	Three-Year-Old Male
2007	Sealy Hill	Dancing Allstar	Kodiak Kowboy	Sealy Hill	Alezzandro
2006	Arravale	Catch the Thrill	Leonnatus Anteas	Kimchi	Shillelagh Slew
2005	A Bit O'Gold	Knights Templar	Edenwold	Gold Strike	Palladio
2004	Soaring Free	Simply Lovely	Wholelottabourbon	Eye of the Sphynx	A Bit O'Gold
2003	Wando	My Vintage Port	Judiths Wild Rush	Too Late Now	Wando
2002	Wake At Noon	Brusque	Added Edge	Lady Shari	Le Cinquieme Essai
2001	Win City	Ginger Gold	Rare Friends	Dancethruthedawn	Win City
2000	Quiet Resolve	Poetically	Highland Legacy	Catch the Ring	Kiss a Native
1999	Thornfield	Hello Seattle	Exciting Story	Gandria	Woodcarver
1998	Chief Bearhart	Fantasy Lake	Riddell's Creek	Kirby's Song	Archers Bay
1997	Chief Bearhart	Primaly	Dawson's Legacy	Cotton Carnival	Cryptocloser
1996	Mt. Sassafras	Larkwhistle	Cash Deposit	Silent Fleet	Victor Cooley
1995	Peaks and Valleys	Silken Cat	Gomtuu	Scotzanna	Peaks and Valleys
1994	Alywow	Honky Tonk Tune	Talkin Man	Alywow	Bruce's Mill
1993	Peteski	Term Limits	Comet Shine	Deputy Jane West	Peteski
1992	Benburb	Deputy Jane West	Truth of It All	Hope for a Breeze	Benburb
1991	Dance Smartly	Buckys Solution	Free At Last	Dance Smartly	Bolulight
1990	Izvestia	Dance Smartly	Rainbows for Life	Lubicon	Izvestia
1989	With Approval	Wavering Girl	Sky Classic	Blushing Katy	With Approval
1988	Play the King	Legarto	Mercedes Won	Tilt My Halo	Regal Intention
1987	Afleet	Phoenix Factor	Regal Classic	One From Heaven	Afleet
1986	Ruling Angel	Ruling Angel	Blue Finn	Carotene	Golden Choice
1985	Imperial Choice	Stage Flite	Grey Classic	La Lorgnette	Imperial Choice
1984	Dauphin Fabuleux	Deceit Dancer	Dauphin Fabuleux	Classy 'n Smart	Key to the Moon
1983	Travelling Victor	Ada Prospect	Prince Avatar	Northern Blossom	Bompago
1982	Frost King	Candle Bright	Sunny's Halo	Avowal	Runaway Groom
1981	Deputy Minister	Choral Group	Deputy Minister	Rainbow Connection	Frost King
1980	Glorious Song	Rainbow Connection	Bayford	Par Excellence	Ben Fab
1979	Overskate	Par Excellance	Allan Blue	Kamar	Steady Growth
1978	Overskate	Liz's Pride	Medaille d'Or	La Voyageuse	Overskate
1977	L'Alezane	L'Alezane	Overskate	Northernette	Dance in Time
1976	Norcliffe	Northernette	Sound Reason	Bye Bye Paris	Norcliffe
1975	L'Enjoleur	Seraphic	Proud Tobin	Momigi	L'Enjoleur

Horse of the Year
Turf Female
Three-Year-Old Filly
SEALY HILL, 2004 dk. b. or br. f., Point Given—Boston Twist, by Boston Harbor. 2007 record: 8-4-3-0, $958,389. Career through 2007: 11-6-3-1, $1,087,794. Breeder: Eugene Melnyk (On.). Owner: Melnyk Racing Stables. Trainer: Mark E. Casse. In 2007, won Bourbonette Oaks (G3), Labatt Woodbine Oaks, Wonder Where S., Bison City S., Glorious Song S.; 2nd E. P. Taylor S. (Can-G1), Canadian S. (Can-G2).

Two-Year-Old Male
KODIAK KOWBOY, 2005 b. c., Posse—Kokadrie, by Coronado's Quest. 2007 record: 7-4-1-1, $544,825. Breeder: Hartwell Farm (Ky.). Owner: Vinery Stables and Fox Hill Farm. Trainer: Steven M. Asmussen. In 2007, won Saratoga Special S. (G2), Bashford Manor S. (G3), Victoria S.; 2nd Futurity S. (G2); 3rd Bessemer Trust Breeders' Cup Juvenile (G1).

Two-Year-Old Filly
DANCING ALLSTAR, 2005 ch. f., Millennium Allstar—High On Believen, by Honor Grades. 2007 record: 7-5-2-0, $299,428. Breeder: Bent Tree Farm (BC). Owner: Bob Cheema. Trainer: Terry Jordan. In 2007, won My Dear S., Fantasy S., Sadie Diamond Futurity, Mount Royal H., C.T.H.S. Sales S.; 2nd Ontario Debutante S., Colin S.

Three-Year-Old Male
ALEZZANDRO, 2004 dk. b. or br. c., High Yield—Eseni, by Granacus. 2007 and career record: 6-2-2-1, $551,550. Breeder: Knob Hill Stable (On.). Owner: Knob Hill Stable and Estate of Steve Stavro. Trainer: Kevin Attard. In 2007, won Prince of Wales S.; 2nd Queen's Plate S., Ontario Derby; 3rd Plate Trial S.

Older Male
TRUE METROPOLITAN, 2002 dk. b. or br. g., Proud and True—Forest Dunes, by Green

History of the Sovereign Awards

Year	Older Female	Older Male	Turf Female†	Turf Male	Sprinter	Broodmare of the Year
2007	Financingavailable	True Metropolitan	Sealy Hill	Cloudy's Knight	Financingavailable	Lover's Talk
2006	Financingavailable	True Metropolitan	Arravale	Sky Conqueror	Judiths Wild Rush	Dream Smartly
2005	One for Rose	A Bit O'Gold	Ambitious Cat	A Bit O'Gold	Judiths Wild Rush	Native Rights
2004	One for Rose	Mobil	Soaring Free	Inish Glora	Blonde Executive	Annasan
2003	One for Rose	Phantom Light	Inish Glora	Perfect Soul (Ire)	Soaring Free	Radiant Ring
2002	Small Promises	Wake At Noon	Chopinina	Portcullis	Wake At Noon	First Class Gal
2001	Mountain Angel	A Fleets Dancer	Sweetest Thing	Numerous Times	Mr. Epperson	Dance Smartly
2000	Saoirse	One Way Love	Heliotrope	Quiet Resolve	One Way Love	Primarily
1999	Magic Code	Deputy Inxs	Free Vacation	Thornfield	Deputy Inxs	Sharpening Up
1998	Santa Amelia	Terremoto	Colorful Vices	Chief Bearhart	Deputy Inxs	Fleet Courage
1997	Woolloomooloo	Chief Bearhart	Woolloomooloo	Chief Bearhart	Glanmire	Charming Sassafras
1996	Windsharp	Mt. Sassafras	Windsharp	Chief Bearhart	Langfuhr	Amelia Bearhart
1995	Bold Ruritana	Basqueian	Bold Ruritana	Hasten To Add	Scotzanna	Sea Regent
1994	Pennyhill Park	King Ruckus		Alywow	King Ruckus	Rainbow Connection
1993	Dance for Donna	Cozzene's Prince		Hero's Love	Apelia	Bold Debra
1992	Wilderness Song	Rainbows for Life		Rainbows for Life	King Corrie	Ballade
1991	Avant's Gold	Sky Classic		Sky Classic	King Corrie	Classy 'n Smart
1990	Diva's Debut	Twist the Snow		Izvestia	Twist the Snow	Shy Spirit
1989	Proper Evidence	Steady Power		Charlie Barley	Mr. Hot Shot	Passing Mood
1988	Carotene	Play the King		Carotene	Play the King	Polite Lady
1987	Carotene	Play the King		Carotene	Play the King	Arctic Vixen
1986	Bessarabian	Let's Go Blue		Carotene	New Connection	Loudrangle
1985	Lake Country	Ten Gold Pots		Imperial Choice	Summer Mood	No Class
1984	Sintrillium	Canadian Factor		Bounding Away	Diapason	Friendly Ways
1983	Eternal Search	Travelling Victor		Kingsbridge	Fraud Squad	Two Rings
1982	Eternal Search	Frost King		Frost King	Avowal	Yonnie Girl
1981	Glorious Song	Driving Home		Ben Fab	Eternal Search	Native Flower
1980	Glorious Song	Overskate		Overskate	La Voyageuse	Hangin Round
1979	La Voyageuse	Overskate		Overskate		Fitz's Fancy
1978	Christy's Mount	Giboulee		Overskate		Fanfreluche
1977	Reasonable Win	Norcliffe		Momigi		Doris White
1976	Momigi	Victorian Prince		Victorian Prince		Northern Minx
1975	Victorian Queen	Rash Move		Victorian Queen		Reasonable Wife

†1995 marks the first year the award for turf horse to be divided into male and female categories.

Canadian Triple Crown Winners

Year	Winner	Owner	Trainer	Jockey(s)
2003	Wando	G. Schickedanz	M. Keogh	P. Husbands
1993	Peteski	E. I. Mack	R. Attfield	C. Perret, D. Penna
1991	Dance Smartly	Sam-Son Farm	J. E. Day	P. Day
1990	Izvestia	Kinghaven Farms	R. Attfield	D. J. Seymour
1989	With Approval	Kinghaven Farms	R. Attfield	D. J. Seymour
1963	Canebora	Windfields Farm	G. McCann	M. Ycaza, H. Dittfach
1959	New Providence	Windfields Farm	G. McCann	R. Ussery, A. Gomez

Forest. 2007 record: 10-7-1-1, $441,268. Career through 2007: 33-16-5-4, $853,688. Breeder: Frank Bertolino (Fl.). Owner: Bob Cheema. Trainer: Terry Jordan. In 2007, won Dominion Day S. (Can-G3), Autumn S. (Can-G3), Speed to Spare S., George Royal S., Sir Winston Churchill H., Westerner S., 2nd BC Premiers H. (Can-G3); 3rd Eclipse S. (Can-G3).

Older Female
Sprinter
FINANCING AVAILABLE, 2001 gr. or ro. m., Kiridashi—Fascigrant, by L'Emigrant. 2007 record: 7-5-2-0, $451,151. Career through 2007: 28-16-7-3, $1,257,832. Breeders: Michael C. Byrne and Helen Irving (On.). Owner: K. K. Sangara. Trainer: Lorne Richards. In 2007, won Ontario Fashion S., Ballade S., Classy 'n Smart S., Victoriana S.; 2nd Royal North S. (Can-G3), Seaway S. (Can-G3).

Turf Male
CLOUDY'S KNIGHT, 2000 ch. g., Lord Avie—Cloudy Spot, by Solar City. 2007 record: 9-3-3-1, $1,762,868. Career through 2007: 32-10-8-4, $2,070,503. Breeder: Jerrold Schwartz (Ky.). Owner: S J Stables. Trainer: Frank J. Kirby. In 2007, won Pattison Canadian International S. (Can-G1), Sky Classic S. (Can-G2), Fair Grounds Breeders' Cup H. (G3); 2nd Mervin H. Muniz Jr. Memorial H. (G2), Nijinsky S. (Can-G2), Stars and Stripes Turf H. (G3); 3rd Colonel E. R. Bradley H.

Broodmare of the Year
LOVER'S TALK, 1984 b. m., Vice Regent—Lover's Walk, by Never Bend. Race record: 3-1-0-0, $10,440. Breeder: E. P. Taylor (On.). Through 2007, dam of 14 foals of racing age, 13 starters, 11 winners, four stakes winners. Dam of stakes winners Love Grows (by Steady Growth), Barley Talk (Charlie Barley), Torrid Affair (Alydeed), and Wild Whiskey (Whiskey Wisdom). Dam of Lyrically (Thunder Gulch), who placed in three stakes in 2007.

Canadian Horse Racing Hall of Fame

Founded in 1976, the Canadian Horse Racing Hall of Fame recognizes the people and horses who have established the roots of Canadian racing. The Hall of Fame was originally a list of inductees until a permanent site was established in 1997 at the west entrance of Woodbine.

Horses, YOB (Year Inducted)
Ace Marine 1952 (2003)
Afleet 1984 (1992)
*Anita's Son 1956 (2005)
Arise 1946 (1983)
Awesome Again 1994 (2001)
Belle Geste 1968 (1990)
Bold Ruckus 1976 (2006)
Bull Page 1947 (1977)
Bunty Lawless 1935 (1976)
Canadiana 1950 (1978)
Canadian Champ 1953 (2007)
Casa Camara 1944 (2000)
Carotene 1983 (2003)
Chief Bearhart 1993 (2002)
Chop Chop 1940 (1977)
Ciboulette 1961 (1983)
Classy 'n Smart 1981 (2004)
Cool Reception 1964 (2005)
Dance Smartly 1988 (1995)
Deputy Minister 1979 (1988)
Duchess of York 1923 (1976)
E. Day 1960 (1989)
Fanfreluche 1967 (1981)
Flaming Page 1959 (1980)
Frost King 1978 (1986)
Gallant Kitty 1916 (1977)
George Royal 1961 (1976)
Glorious Song 1976 (1995)
He's a Smoothie 1963 (2003)
Horometer 1931 (1976)
Inferno 1902 (1976)
Izvestia 1987 (1999)
Jammed Lovely 1964 (2007)
Joey 1930 (1976)
Kennedy Road 1968 (2000)
Kingarvie 1943 (1976)
Langcrest 1961 (1984)
Langfuhr 1992 (2004)
La Prevoyante 1970 (1976)
Lauries Dancer 1968 (2006)
L'Enjoleur 1972 (2007)
Major Presto 1963 (1982)
Martimas 1896 (2001)
Mona Bell 1935 (2000)

Natalma 1957 (2007)
Nearctic 1954 (1977)
New Providence 1956 (1982)
Nijinsky II 1967 (1976)
No Class 1974 (1997)
Norcliffe 1973 (2005)
Northern Dancer 1961 (1976)
Northernette 1974 (1987)
Overskate 1975 (1993)
Queensway 1929 (2003)
Runaway Groom 1979 (2001)
Shepperton 1939 (1976)
Sir Barton 1916 (1976)
Sky Classic 1987 (1998)
South Shore 1918 (2000)
Sunny's Halo 1980 (1986)
Terror 1866 (1996)
The Minstrel 1974 (1979)
Vice Regent 1967 (1989)
Victoria Park 1957 (1976)
Windfields 1943 (2002)
With Approval 1986 (1993)
Wonder Where 1956 (2004)
Yellow Rose 1837 (1996)
Youville 1939 (1977)

Jockeys (Year Inducted)
Ted Atkinson (2002)
Larry Attard (2001)
Hugo Dittfach (1983)
Jeff Fell (1993)
Jim Fitzsimmons (1984)
Norman "Dude" Foden (2000)
David Gall (1993)
Avelino Gomez (1977)
Sandy Hawley (1986)
Charles "Chick" Lang (1990)
Herb Lindberg (1991)
Charles Littlefield (2000)
John Longden (1976)
Chris Loseth (2007)
Don MacBeth (1988)
Frank Mann (2000)
Richard "Dick" O'Leary (2000)
Robin Platts (1997)

John "Red" Pollard (1982)
Pat Remillard (1979)
Chris Rogers (1977)
William "Smokey" Saunders (1976)
Don Seymour (1999)
Ron Turcotte (1980)
R. B. "Bobby" Watson (1998)
Headley Woodhouse (1980)
George Woolf (1976)

Trainers (Year Inducted)
A. E. "Burt" Alexandra (2002)
Roger Attfield (1999)
Macdonald "Mac" Benson (2002)
James "Jim" Bentley (1981)
Charles Boyle (2001)
W. H. "Bill" Bringloe (2000)
Donald "Duke" Campbell (1984)
Lou Cavalaris Jr. (1995)
David Cross (2006)
Jim Day (2000)
John Dyment Jr. (2001)
Morris Fishman (2001)
Harry Giddings (1985)
R. K. "Doc" Hodgson (2001)
Gord Huntley (1998)
Roy Johnson (2003)
Lucien Laurin (1978)
Barry Littlefield (2000)
Edward "Ted" Mann (1982)
Gordon "Pete" McCann (1980)
Frank Merrill Jr. (1981)
J. C. "Jerry" Meyer (1999)
John Nixon (2002)
John Passero (2000)
Gil Rowntree (1997)
F. H. "Fred" Schelke (2002)
Ronald K. "Red" Smith (2004)
Joseph "Yonnie" Starr (1979)
Austin Irwin "Butch" Taylor (1987)
J. J. "Johnny" Thorpe (2002)
John R. Walker (2000)
Arthur Warner (1984)
James White (1996)
Ed Whyte (2001)

REFERENCE
Rules of Racing

The following model rules were developed by the Association of Racing Commissioners International and the North American Pari-Mutuel Regulators Association, which merged with RCI in 2005. Although individual states implement their own regulations for how racing is conducted in their jurisdictions, the model rules combine both time-tested concepts and new developments in the Thoroughbred sport. The following rules encompass the running of the race. Other model rules include such matters as racing officials, medications, and pari-mutuel wagering.

I. Entries and Nominations
A. Entering
No horse shall be qualified to start unless it has been and continues to be entered.
B. Procedure
1. Entries and nominations shall be made with the racing secretary and shall not be considered until received by the racing secretary, who shall maintain a record of time of receipt of them for a period of one year.

2. An entry shall be in the name of the horse's licensed owner and made by the owner, trainer, or a licensed designee of the owner or trainer.

3. Races printed in the condition book shall have preference over substitute and extra races.

4. An entry must be sent in writing, by telephone, or facsimile machine to the racing secretary. The entry must be confirmed in writing should the stewards or the racing secretary so request.

5. The person making an entry shall clearly designate the horse so entered.

6. No alteration may be made in any entry after the closing of entries, but an error may be corrected with permission of the stewards.

7. No horse may be entered in more than one race (with the exception of stakes races) to be run on the same day on which pari-mutuel wagering is conducted.

8. Any permitted medication or approved change of equipment must be declared at time of entry.

C. Limitation as to Spouses
No entry in any race shall be accepted for a horse owned wholly or in part by, or trained by, a person whose husband or wife is under license suspension at time of such entry; except that, if the license of a jockey has been suspended for a routine riding offense, the stewards may waive this rule.

D. Coupled Entries
1. Two or more horses entered in a race shall be joined as a mutuel entry and single betting interest if they are owned or leased in whole or in part by the same owner or are trained by a trainer who owns or leases any interest in any of the other horses in the race, except that entries may be uncoupled in stakes races.

2. No more than two horses having common ties through ownership or training may be entered in an overnight race. Under no circumstances may both horses of a coupled entry start to the exclusion of a single entry. When making a coupled entry, a preference for one of the horses must be made.

E. Nominations
1. Any nominator to a stakes race may transfer or declare such nomination prior to closing.

2. Joint nominations and entries may be made by any one of joint owners of a horse, and each such owner shall be jointly and severally liable for all payments due.

3. Death of a horse, or a mistake in its entry when such horse is eligible, does not release the nominator or transferee from liability for all stakes fees due. No fees paid in connection with a nomination to a stakes race that is run shall be refunded, except as otherwise stated in the conditions of a stakes race.

4. Death of a nominator to a stakes race shall not render void any subscription, entry, or right of entry. All rights, privileges, and obligations shall be attached to the legal heirs of the decedent or the successor owner of the horse.

5. When a horse is sold privately or at public auction or claimed, stakes engagements shall be transferred automatically to its new owner, except when the horse is transferred to a person whose license is suspended or who is otherwise unqualified to race or enter the horse; then such nomination shall be void as of the date of such transfer.

6. All stakes fees paid toward a stakes race shall be allocated to the winner unless otherwise provided by the conditions for the race. If a stakes race is not run for any reason, all such nomination fees paid shall be refunded.

F. Closings
1. Entries for purse races and nominations to stakes races shall close at the time designated by the association in previously published conditions for such races. No entry, nomination, or declaration shall be accepted after such closing time; except in the event of an emergency or if an overnight race fails to fill, the racing secretary may, with the approval of a steward, extend such closing time.

2. Except as otherwise provided in the conditions for a stakes race, the deadline for accepting nominations and declarations is midnight of the day of closing, provided they are received in time for compliance with every other condition of the race.

G. Number of Starters in a Race
The maximum number of starters in any race shall be limited to the number of starting positions afforded by the association starting gate and its extensions. The number of starters may be further limited by the number of horses that, in the opinion of the stewards, can be afforded a safe, fair, and equal start.

H. Split or Divided Races
1. In the event a race is canceled or declared off, the association may split any overnight race for which post positions have not been drawn.

2. Where an overnight race is split, forming two or more separate races, the racing secretary shall give notice of not less than 15 minutes before such races are closed to grant time for making additional entries to such split races.

I. Post Positions
Post positions for all races shall be determined by lot and shall be publicly drawn in the presence of a steward or steward designee.

J. Also-Eligible List

1. If the number of entries for a race exceeds the number of horses permitted to start, the racing secretary may create and post an also-eligible list.

2. If any horse is scratched from a race for which an also-eligible list was created, a replacement horse shall be drawn from the also-eligible list into the race in order of preference. If none is preferred, a horse shall be drawn into the race from the also-eligible list by public lot.

3. Any owner or trainer of a horse on the also-eligible list who does not wish to start the horse in such race shall so notify the racing secretary prior to scratch time for the race, thereby forfeiting any preference to which the horse may have been entitled.

4. A horse that draws into a straightaway race from the also-eligible list shall start from the post position vacated by the scratched horse. In the event more than one horse is scratched, post positions of horses drawing in from the also-eligible list shall be determined by public lot.

5. A horse that draws into a nonstraightaway race from the also-eligible list shall start from the outermost post position. In the event more than one horse is scratched, post positions of horses drawing in from the also-eligible list shall be determined by public lot.

K. Preferred List

The racing secretary shall maintain a list of entered horses eliminated from starting by a surplus of entries, and these horses shall constitute a preferred list and have preference. The manner in which the preferred list shall be maintained and all rules governing such list shall be the responsibility of the racing secretary. Such rules must be submitted to the racing commission 30 days prior to the commencement of the race meeting and are subject to the approval of the commission.

II. Declarations and Scratches

Declarations and scratches are irrevocable.

A. Declarations

1. A "declaration" is the act of withdrawing an entered horse from a race prior to the closing of entries.

2. The declaration of a horse before closing shall be made by the owner, trainer, or their licensed designee in the form and manner prescribed in these rules.

B. Scratches

1. A "scratch" is the act of withdrawing an entered horse from a contest after the closing of entries.

2. The scratch of a horse after closing shall be made by the owner, trainer, or their licensed designee, with permission from the stewards.

3. A horse may be scratched from a stakes race for any reason at any time up until 45 minutes prior to post time for that race.

4. No horse may be scratched from an overnight race without approval of the stewards.

5. In overnight races, horses that are physically disabled or sick shall be permitted to be scratched first. Should horses representing more than ten betting interests in the daily double or exotic wagering races, or horses representing more than eight betting interests in any other overnight race, remain in after horses with physical excuses have been scratched, then owners or trainers may be permitted at scratch time to scratch horses without physical excuses down to such respective minimum numbers for such races. This privilege shall be determined by lot if an excessive number of owners or trainers wish to scratch their horses.

6. Entry of any horse that has been scratched or excused from starting by the stewards because of a physical disability or sickness shall not be accepted until the expiration of three racing days after such horse was scratched or excused and the horse has been removed from the Veterinarian's List by the official veterinarian.

III. Weights

A. Allowances

1. Weight allowance must be claimed at time of entry and shall not be waived after the posting of entries, except by consent of the stewards.

2. A horse shall start with only the allowance of weight to which it is entitled at time of starting, regardless of its allowance at time of entry.

3. Horses not entitled to the first weight allowance in a race shall not be entitled to any subsequent allowance specified in the conditions.

4. Claim of weight allowance to which a horse is not entitled shall not disqualify it unless protest is made in writing and lodged with the stewards at least one hour before post time for that race.

5. A horse shall not be given a weight allowance for failure to finish second or lower in any race.

6. No horse shall receive allowance of weight nor be relieved extra weight for having been beaten in one or more races, but this rule shall not prohibit maiden allowances or allowances to horses that have not won a race within a specified period or a race of a specified value.

7. Except in handicap races that expressly provide otherwise, two-year-old fillies shall be allowed three pounds, and fillies and mares three years old and upward shall be allowed five pounds before September 1 and three pounds thereafter in races where competing against male horses.

B. Penalties

1. Weight penalties are obligatory.

2. Horses incurring weight penalties for a race shall not be entitled to any weight allowance for that race.

3. No horse shall incur a weight penalty or be barred from any race for having been placed second or lower in any race.

4. Penalties incurred and allowances due in steeplechase or hurdle races shall not apply to races on the flat, and vice versa.

5. The reports, records, and statistics as published by *Daily Racing Form*, Equibase, or other recognized publications shall be considered official in determining eligibility, allowances, and penalties, but may be corrected.

C. Weight Conversions

For the purpose of determining weight assignments and/or allowances for imported horses, the following weight conversions shall be used:

1. 1 kilogram equals 2¼ pounds
2. 1 Stone equals 14 pounds

IV. Workouts

A. Requirements

A horse shall not start unless it has participated in an official race or has an approved timed workout satisfactory to the stewards. The workout must have occurred at a pari-mutuel or commission-recognized facility within the previous 30 days. A horse that has not started for a period of 60 days or more shall be ineligible to race until it has completed a timed workout approved by the stewards prior to the day of the race in which the horse is entered. The association may impose more stringent workout requirements.

B. Identification

1. Unless otherwise prescribed by the stewards or the commission, the official lip tattoo must have been affixed to a horse's upper lip or other identification method approved by the appropriate breed registry and the commission applied prior to its participation in workouts from the gate, schooling races, or workouts required for removal from the Stewards' List, Starter's List, Veterinarian's List, or Bleeder List.

2. The trainer or exercise rider shall take each horse scheduled for an official workout to be identified by the clocker or clocker's assistant immediately prior to the workout.

3. A horse shall be properly identified by its lip tattoo or other identification method approved by the appropriate breed registry and the commission immediately prior to participating in an official timed workout.

4. The trainer or trainer's designee shall be required to identify the distance the horse is to be worked and the point on the track where the workout will start.

C. Information Dissemination

Information regarding a horse's approved timed workout or workouts shall be furnished to the public prior to the start of the race for which the horse has been entered.

D. Restrictions

A horse shall not be taken onto the track for training or a workout except during hours designated by the association.

V. Ineligible Horses

A horse is ineligible to start in a race when:

1. It is not stabled on the grounds of the association or present by the time established by the commission;

2. Its breed registration certificate is not on file with the racing secretary or horse identifier, unless the racing secretary has submitted the certificate to the appropriate breed registry for correction;

3. It is not fully identified and tattooed on the inside of the upper lip or identified by any other method approved by the appropriate breed registry and the commission;

4. It has been fraudulently entered or raced in any jurisdiction under a different name, with an altered registration certificate or altered lip tattoo or other identification method approved by the appropriate breed registry and the commission;

5. It is wholly or partially owned by a disqualified person or a horse is under the direct or indirect training or management of a disqualified person;

6. It is wholly or partially owned by the spouse of a disqualified person or a horse is under the direct or indirect management of the spouse of a disqualified person, in such cases, it being presumed that the disqualified person and spouse constitute a single financial entity with respect to the horse, which presumption may be rebutted;

7. The stakes or entrance money for the horse has not been paid in accordance with the conditions of the race;

8. The losing jockey mount fee is not on deposit with the horsemen's bookkeeper;

9. Its name appears on the Starter's List, Stewards' List, or Veterinarian's List;

10. It is a first-time starter and has not been approved to start by the starter;

11. It is owned in whole or in part by an undisclosed person or interest;

12. It lacks sufficient official published workouts or race past performance(s);

13. It has been entered in a stakes race and has subsequently been transferred with its engagements, unless the racing secretary has been notified of such prior to the start;

14. It is subject to a lien that has not been approved by the stewards and filed with the horsemen's bookkeeper;

15. It is subject to a lease not filed with the stewards;

16. It is not in sound racing condition;

17. It has had a surgical neurectomy performed on a heel nerve that has not been approved by the official veterinarian;

18. It has been trachea tubed to artificially assist breathing;

19. It has been blocked with alcohol or otherwise drugged or surgically denerved to desensitize the nerves above the ankle;

20. It has impaired eyesight in both eyes;

21. It is barred or suspended in any recognized jurisdiction;

22. It does not meet the eligibility conditions of the race;

23. Its owner or lessor is in arrears for any stakes fees, except with approval of the racing secretary;

24. Its owner(s), lessor(s), and/or trainer have not completed the licensing procedures required by the commission;

25. It is by an unknown sire or out of an unknown mare; or

26. There is no current negative test certificate for Equine Infectious Anemia attached to its breed registration certificate, as required by statute.

VI. Running of the Race

A. Equipment

1. No whip shall be used unless it has affixed to the end of it a looped leather "popper" not less than 1¼ inches in width and not over 3 inches in length, and is "feathered" above the "popper" with not less than three rows of leather "feathers," each "feather" not less than 1 inch in length. No whip shall exceed 31 inches in length. All whips are subject to inspection and approval by the stewards.

2. No bridle shall exceed two pounds.

3. A horse's tongue may be tied down with clean bandages, gauze, or tongue strap.

4. No licensee may add blinkers to a horse's equipment or discontinue their use without the prior approval of the starter, the paddock judge, and the stewards.

5. No licensee may change any equipment used on a horse in its last race in this jurisdiction without approval of the paddock judge.

B. Racing Numbers

1. Each horse shall carry a conspicuous saddlecloth number corresponding to the official number given that horse on the official program.

2. In the case of a coupled entry that includes more than one horse, each horse in the entry shall carry the same number, with a different distinguishing letter following the number. As an example, two horses in the same entry shall appear in the official program as 1 and 1A.

3. Each horse in the mutuel field shall carry a separate number or may carry the same number with a distinguishing letter following the number.

C. Jockey Requirements

1. Jockeys shall report to the jockeys' quarters at the time designated by the association. Jockeys shall report their engagements and any overweight to the clerk of scales. Jockeys shall not leave the jockeys' quarters except to ride in scheduled races until all of their riding engagements of the day have been fulfilled, except as approved by the stewards.

2. A jockey who has not fulfilled all riding engagements who desires to leave the jockeys' quarters must first receive the permission of the stewards and must be accompanied by an association security guard.

3. While in the jockeys' quarters, jockeys shall have no contact or communication with any person outside the jockeys' quarters other than commission personnel and officials, an owner or trainer for whom the jockey is riding, or a representative of the regular news media, except with the permission of the stewards. Any communication permitted by the stewards may be conducted only in the presence of the clerk of scales or other person designated by the stewards.

4. Jockeys shall be weighed out for their respective mounts by the clerk of scales not more than 30 minutes before post time for each race.

5. Only valets employed by the association shall assist jockeys in weighing out.

6. A jockey must wear a safety vest when riding in any official race. The safety vest shall weigh no more than two pounds and be designed to provide shock-absorbing protection to the upper body of at least a rating of five as defined by the British Equestrian Trade Association (BETA).

7. A jockey's weight shall include his or her clothing, boots, saddle and its attachments, and any other equipment except the whip, bridle, bit or reins, safety helmet, safety vest, blinkers, goggles, and number cloth.

8. Seven pounds is the limit of overweight any horse is permitted to carry.

9. Once jockeys have fulfilled their riding engagements for the day and have left the jockeys' quarters, they shall not be readmitted to the jockeys' quarters until after the entire racing program for that day has been completed, except with permission of the stewards.

D. Paddock to Post

1. Each horse shall carry the full weight assigned for that race from the paddock to the starting post, and shall parade past the stewards' stand, unless excused by the stewards. The post parade shall not exceed 12 minutes, unless otherwise ordered by the stewards. It shall be the duty of the stewards to ensure that the horses arrive at the starting gate as near to post time as possible.

2. After the horses enter the track, no jockey may dismount nor entrust his or her horse to the care of an attendant unless, because of accident occurring to the jockey, the horse, or the equipment, and with the prior consent of the starter. During any delay during which a jockey is permitted to dismount, all other jockeys may dismount and their horses may be attended by others. After the horses enter the track, only the jockey, an assistant starter, the official veterinarian, the racing veterinarian, or an outrider or pony rider may touch the horse before the start of the race.

3. If a jockey is injured on the way to the post, the horse shall be returned to the paddock or any other area designated by the stewards, resaddled with the appropriate weight, and remounted with a replacement jockey.

4. After passing the stewards' stand in parade, the horses may break formation and proceed to the post in any manner unless otherwise directed by the stewards. Once at the post, the horses shall be started without unnecessary delay.

5. Horses shall arrive at the starting post in post-position order.

6. In case of accident to a jockey or his or her mount or equipment, the stewards or the starter may permit the jockey to dismount and the horse to be cared for during the delay, and may permit all jockeys to dismount and all horses to be attended to during the delay.

7. If a horse throws its jockey on the way from the paddock to the post, the horse must be returned to the point where the jockey was thrown, where it shall be remounted and then proceed over the route of the parade to the post. The horse must carry its assigned weight from paddock to post and from post to finish.

8. If a horse leaves the course while moving from paddock to post, the horse shall be returned to the course at the nearest practical point to that at which it left the course, and shall complete its parade to the post from the point at which it left the course, unless ordered scratched by the stewards.

9. No person shall willfully delay the arrival of a horse at the post.

10. The starter shall load horses into the starting gate in any order deemed necessary to ensure a safe and fair start. Only the jockey, the racing veterinarian, the starter, or an assistant starter shall handle a horse at the post.

E. Post to Finish

1. The Start

a. The starter is responsible for assuring that each participant receives a fair start.

b. If, when the starter dispatches the field, any door at the front of the starting-gate stalls should not open properly due to a mechanical failure or malfunction or should any action by any starting personnel directly cause a horse to receive an unfair start, the stewards may declare such a horse a nonstarter.

c. Should a horse, not scratched prior to the start, not be in the starting-gate stall, thereby causing it to be left when the field is dispatched by the starter, the horse shall be declared a nonstarter by the stewards.

d. Should an accident or malfunction of the starting gate or other unforeseen event compromise the fairness of the race or the safety of race participants, the stewards may declare individual horses to be nonstarters, exclude individual horses from one or more pari-mutuel pools, or declare a "no contest" and refund all wagers except as otherwise provided in the rules involving multi-race wagers.

2. Interference, Jostling, or Striking

a. A jockey shall not ride carelessly or willfully so as to permit his or her mount to interfere with, impede, or intimidate any other horse in the race.

b. No jockey shall carelessly or willfully jostle, strike, or touch another jockey or another jockey's horse or equipment.

c. No jockey shall unnecessarily cause his or her horse to shorten its stride so as to give the appearance of having suffered a foul.

3. Maintaining a Straight Course

a. When the way is clear in a race, a horse may be ridden to any part of the course, but if any horse swerves or is ridden to either side so as to interfere with, impede, or intimidate any other horse, it is a foul.

b. The offending horse may be disqualified if, in the opinion of the stewards, the foul altered the finish of

the race, regardless of whether the foul was accidental, willful, or the result of careless riding.

c. If the stewards determine the foul was intentional or due to careless riding, the jockey may be held responsible.

d. In a straightaway race, every horse must maintain position as nearly as possible in the lane in which it starts. If a horse is ridden, drifts, or swerves out of its lane in such a manner that it interferes with, impedes, or intimidates another horse, it is a foul and may result in the disqualification of the offending horse.

4. Disqualification

a. When the stewards determine that a horse shall be disqualified for interference, they may place the offending horse behind such horses as in their judgment it interfered with, or they may place it last.

b. If a horse is disqualified for a foul, any horse or horses in the same race owned or trained by the same interests, whether coupled or uncoupled, may also be disqualified.

c. When a horse is disqualified for interference in a time-trial race, for the purposes of qualifying only, it shall receive the time of the horse it is placed behind plus one-hundredth of a second penalty or more exact measurement if photo-finish equipment permits, and shall be eligible to qualify for the finals or consolations of the race on the basis of the assigned time.

d. Possession of any electrical or mechanical stimulating or shocking device by a jockey, horse owner, trainer, or other person authorized to handle or attend to a horse shall be prima-facie evidence of a violation of these rules and is sufficient grounds for the stewards to scratch or disqualify the horse.

e. The stewards may determine that a horse shall be unplaced for the purpose of purse distribution and time-trial qualification.

5. Horses Shall Be Ridden Out

All horses shall be ridden out in every race. A jockey shall not ease up or coast to the finish without reasonable cause, even if the horse has no apparent chance to win prize money. A jockey shall give a best effort during a race, and each horse shall be ridden to win.

6. Use of Whips

a. Although the use of a whip is not required, any jockey who uses a whip during a race shall do so only in a manner consistent with exerting his or her best efforts to win.

b. In all races where a jockey will ride without a whip, an announcement of such fact shall be made over the public address system.

c. No electrical or mechanical device or other expedient designed to increase or retard the speed of a horse, other than the whip approved by the stewards, shall be possessed by anyone or applied by anyone to the horse at any time on the grounds of the association during the meeting, whether in a race or otherwise.

d. Whips shall not be used on two-year-old horses before April 1 of each year.

e. Prohibited use of the whip includes whipping a horse:

i. On the head, flanks, or on any other part of its body other than the shoulders or hindquarters except when necessary to control a horse;

ii. During the post parade or after the finish of the race except when necessary to control the horse;

iii. Excessively or brutally, causing welts or breaks in the skin;

iv. When the horse is clearly out of the race or has obtained its maximum placing;

v. Persistently even though the horse is showing no response under the whip; or

vi. Striking another rider or horse.

7. Horse Leaving the Racecourse

If a horse leaves the racecourse during a race, it must turn back and resume the race from the point at which it originally left the course.

8. Order of Finish

a. The official order of finish shall be decided by the stewards with the aid of the photo-finish camera, and in the absence of the photo-finish film strip, the video replay. The photo finish and video replay are only aids in the stewards' decision. The decision of the stewards shall be final in all cases.

b. The nose of the horse shall determine the placement of the horse in relationship to other horses in the race.

9. Returning After the Finish

a. After a race has been run, the jockey shall ride promptly to the place designated by the stewards, dismount, and report to the clerk of scales to be weighed in. Jockeys shall weigh in with all pieces of equipment with which they weighed out.

b. If a jockey is prevented from riding to the designated unsaddling area because of an accident or illness to the jockey or the horse, the jockey may walk or be transported to the scales or may be excused from weighing in by the stewards.

10. Unsaddling

a. Only persons authorized by the stewards may assist the jockey with unsaddling the horse after the race.

b. No one shall place a covering over a horse before it is unsaddled.

11. Weighing In

a. A jockey shall weigh in at least at the same weight at which he or she weighed out, and if under that weight by more than two pounds, his or her mount shall be disqualified from any portion of the purse money.

b. In the event of such disqualification, all money wagered on the horse shall be refunded unless the race has been declared official.

c. No jockey shall weigh in at more than two pounds over the proper or declared weight, excluding the weight attributed to inclement weather conditions and/or of health and safety equipment approved by the stewards.

12. Dead Heats

a. When two horses run a dead heat for first place, all purses or prizes to which first and second horses would have been entitled shall be divided equally between them; and this principle applies in dividing all purses or prizes whatever the number of horses running a dead heat and whatever places for which the dead heat is run.

b. In a dead heat for first place, each horse involved shall be deemed a winner and liable to penalty for the amount it shall receive.

c. When a dead heat is run for second place and an objection is made to the winner of the race and sustained, the horses that ran a dead heat shall be deemed to have run a dead heat for first place.

d. If the dividing owners cannot agree as to which of them is to have a cup or other prize that cannot be divided, the question shall be determined by lot by the stewards.

VII. Protests, Objections, and Inquiries

A. Stewards to Inquire

1. The stewards shall take cognizance of foul riding and, upon their own motion or that of any racing offi-

cial or person empowered by this chapter to object or complain, shall make diligent inquiry or investigation into such objection or complaint when properly received.

2. In determining the extent of disqualification, the stewards in their discretion may:

a. Declare null and void a track record set or equaled by a disqualified horse or any horses coupled with it as an entry;

b. Affirm the placing judges' order of finish and hold the jockey responsible if, in the stewards' opinion, the foul riding did not affect the order of finish; or

c. Disqualify the offending horse and hold the jockey blameless if in the stewards' opinion the interference to another horse in a race was not the result of an intentional foul or careless riding on the part of a jockey.

B. Race Objections

1. An objection to an incident alleged to have occurred during the running of a race shall be received only when lodged with the clerk of scales, the stewards, or their designees, by the owner, the authorized agent of the owner, the trainer, or the jockey of a horse engaged in the same race.

2. An objection following the running of any race must be filed before the race is declared official, whether all or some riders are required to weigh in or the use of a "fast official" procedure is permitted.

3. The stewards shall make all findings of fact as to all matters occurring during and incident to the running of a race, shall determine all objections and inquiries, and shall determine the extent of disqualification, if any, of horses in the race. Such findings of fact and determinations shall be final.

C. Prior Objections

1. Objections to the participation of a horse entered in any race shall be made to the stewards in writing, signed by the objector, and filed not later than one hour prior to post time for the first race on the day that the questioned horse is entered. Any such objection shall set forth the specific reason or grounds for the objection in such detail so as to establish probable cause for the objection. The stewards upon their own motion may consider an objection until such time as the horse becomes a starter.

2. An objection to a horse entered in a race may be made on, but not limited to, the following grounds or reasons:

a. A misstatement, error, or omission in the entry under which a horse is to run;

b. The horse entered to run is not the horse it is represented to be at the time of entry, or the age was erroneously given;

c. The horse is not qualified to enter under the conditions specified for the race, or the allowances are improperly claimed or not entitled the horse, or the weight to be carried is incorrect under the conditions of the race;

d. The horse is owned in whole or in part, or leased or trained by a person ineligible to participate in racing or otherwise ineligible to own a racehorse as provided in these rules; or

e. The horse was entered without regard to a lien filed previously with the racing secretary.

3. The stewards may scratch from the race any horse that is the subject of an objection if they have reasonable cause to believe that the objection is valid.

D. Protests

1. A protest against any horse that has started in a race shall be made to the stewards in writing, signed by the protestor, within 72 hours of the race exclusive of nonracing days. If the incident upon which the protest is based occurs within the last two days of the meeting, such protest may be filed with the commission within 72 hours exclusive of Saturdays, Sundays, or official holidays. Any such protest shall set forth the specific reason or reasons for the protest in such detail as to establish probable cause for the protest.

2. A protest may be made on any of the following grounds:

a. Any grounds for objection as set forth in this chapter;

b. The order of finish as officially determined by the stewards was incorrect due to oversight or errors in the numbers of the horses that started the race;

c. A jockey, trainer, owner, or lessor was ineligible to participate in racing as provided in this chapter;

d. The weight carried by a horse was improper by reason of fraud or willful misconduct; or

e. An unfair advantage was gained in violation of the rules.

3. Notwithstanding any other provision in this article, time limitation on the filing of protests shall not apply in any case in which fraud or willful misconduct is alleged, provided the stewards are satisfied that the allegations are bona fide and verifiable.

4. No person shall file any objection or protest knowing the same to be inaccurate, false, untruthful, or frivolous.

5. The stewards may order any purse, award, or prize for any race withheld from distribution pending the determination of any protest. In the event any purse, award, or prize has been distributed to an owner or for a horse that by reason of a protest or other reason is disqualified or determined to be not entitled to such purse, award, or prize, the stewards or the commission may order such purse, award, or prize returned and redistributed to the rightful owner or horse. Any person who fails to comply with an order to return any purse, award, or prize erroneously distributed shall be subject to fines and suspension.

Preference Date System

Racing secretaries long have struggled with two problems: Not enough horses for a race in the track's condition book, which details prospective races for the meet, and too many horses for a specific race.

When a race has too few entries, the racing-office staff must make calls to trainers and solicit them to enter horses in the race. This process is widely known as "hustling," and a starter that is entered for such a race is often referred to a "hustled horse."

A race with too many entrants presents a different set of problems. Often, the race can be split. When other overnight races on the card are slow to fill, a racing secretary may choose to split a popular race, a maiden special weight race for instance, into two or three or more separate races.

If splitting a race is not feasible, the racing secretary needs a system that determines the eligible horses that will get starting positions. Racing offices long used the "star system," under which a horse denied a starting place in an oversubscribed race was given a star. A

horse excluded twice from a race would get two stars. Under the star system, horses with the most stars received preference for the next race with the same conditions.

Many tracks now have changed to a "preference date system," which is similar to the star system but simpler to maintain. In the preference date system, the horses with the earliest preference date get into the race first.

As an example of how the preference date rules system is used, following are the preference date rules of Golden Gate Fields in Northern California:

Preference Date System

All horses whose foal certificates are registered with the racing secretary on the first day of entries will receive an entry date for that day. Thereafter, horses will receive entry dates for the day their foal certificates are registered with the racing secretary. Such entry dates will be good for any category.

1. In all races, winners are preferred.
2. Maidens will not be eligible to receive an entry date in any race until their papers are on file with the racing office at the time of the draw. Entry dates for maidens are good for any maiden race.
3. Horses drawn into races and horses on the also-eligible list that draw into races will receive a running date corresponding to the date on which they are to run, and lose all dates previously held.
4. Horses on the Veterinarian's, Stewards' or Starter's List cannot establish a date. They will not be permitted to enter until they have been approved to start. Horses placed on these lists will keep their dates if they ran in the particular race in which they made the list. Horses that are scratched and placed on a list will be given a scratch date for the day of that race.
5. In all cases, an entry date takes preference over a running date of the same day and a running date takes preference over a scratch date of the same day.
6. Horses drawn on the overnight (either in the race or on the also-eligible) and scratched will lose their date and acquire a scratch date corresponding to the day of the race, unless otherwise specified by the stewards.

Any horse on the also-eligible list that is declared will retain its preference date if the scratch is not activated. Other scratched horses will be treated in the following manner:

 a. Runaway in the paddock—Entry date for day of race.
 b. Runaway in the post parade—Entry date for day of race.
 c. Flip in the gate prior to the start—Scratch date for day of race.
 d. Scratched for insufficient works—Scratch date for day of race.
 e. Scratched because of incorrect markings—Scratch date for day of race.
 f. Ineligible to race in which drawn into—Scratch date for day of race.
 g. Scratched because of breakdown in transportation to the track—Retains original date.
 h. Scratched at the gate and not put on any list—Scratch date for day of race.
 i. Entered in the wrong race by delegated agent or trainer—Scratch date for day of race.
 j. Horse hurt in gate due to accident involving another horse—Retains original date.
 k. Horse left behind the gate—Retains original date.

7. Horses that have established a date at the current meeting will lose that preference date should they race elsewhere.
8. Stakes races are not considered in the preference date system.
9. In no way does the claiming, ownership transfer, or trainer transfer of a horse affect the preference date.
10. Maidens, when entered in a winners' race, will retain original date.
11. Horses entered will initially receive an entry date corresponding to the date on which they are entered.
12. A same-owner entry cannot exclude a single entry except when race preferences indicate otherwise. Trainers must declare at time of entry if he or she has a same-owner or different-owner entry in the race. All same-owner entries must have a declared first and second choice at entry time.

How Jockeys Are Paid

Leading jockeys often will be paid upfront fees when they travel to ride a horse in a stakes race, but most jockeys are compensated according to a table of fees based on race purse and finish position of the horse they ride. Model rules of the Association of Racing Commissioners International contain a suggested fee table, although fees vary from one track or state to another. Following is the model fee schedule as published in 2008.

In the absence of a written agreement, the following jockey mount fees apply:

Purse	Winning Mount	2nd-Place Mount	3rd-Place Mount	Losing Mount
$599 and Under	$33	$33	$33	$33
$600-699	$36	$33	$33	$33
$700-999	10% Win Purse	$33	$33	$33
$1,000-1,499	10% Win Purse	$33	$33	$33
$1,500-1,999	10% Win Purse	$35	$33	$33
$2,000-3,499	10% Win Purse	$45	$40	$38
$3,500-4,999	10% Win Purse	$55	$45	$40
$5,000-9,999	10% Win Purse	$65	$50	$45
$10,000-14,999	10% Win Purse	5% Place Purse	5% Show Purse	$50
$15,000-24,999	10% Win Purse	5% Place Purse	5% Show Purse	$55
$25,000-49,999	10% Win Purse	5% Place Purse	5% Show Purse	$65
$50,000-99,999	10% Win Purse	5% Place Purse	5% Show Purse	$80
$100,000 & Up	10% Win Purse	5% Place Purse	5% Show Purse	$105

How to Handicap a Race

Handicapping is perhaps the most underappreciated aspect of horse racing. Do it well and you will not only identify winning horses but also assert your superior skill in an intellectual challenge unlike any other in sports. Wagering on horse racing is pari-mutuel, which means you are wagering against other bettors. (See pari-mutuel wagering section later in this chapter.)

Handicapping is the inexact science of predicting the results of races that can have as many as 20 horses, each a high-strung, unpredictable Thoroughbred traveling as fast as 40 miles per hour while carrying more than 100 pounds on its back. It is truly amazing that horses can sometimes race as far as a mile and a half and be separated literally by inches at the finish line.

You are not going to predict the winner of every race. No one does. But there is no better feeling in the world than correctly handicapping a race. The feeling is even better if you have bet on your selection, which provides a tangible reward to accompany the bragging rights you have earned for being, at least in this one instance, smarter than your companions. And when you are wrong about a race, you can still gain from the experience by keeping an open mind, and, if the opportunity presents itself, gleaning a nugget of information that could serve you well when handicapping another race.

Handicapping is a skill that you can continue to hone with one important caveat: You will improve only if you do not believe you already have all the answers.

Where do you start? First, you need to have a realistic framework.

Framework of Reality

Year after year at every single racetrack in North America, betting favorites—the horses with the most money wagered on them to win—are victorious only 25% to 35% of the time. That means the betting public handicaps a race correctly once every three or four times. When the betting public is wrong, the payoffs are obviously higher. If you can establish which favorites are vulnerable for any of a myriad of reasons—such as poor post position, an unreliable rider, or no recent races or workouts—you can locate overlays, which are horses whose odds are higher than they should be. Their opposites are underlays, horses whose odds are shorter than they deserve. Most bettors try to find overlays. If they can find one or two winning overlays a day, they are likely to exit the track with more money than they brought with them. Remember, there are no rules at the track saying you must bet every race or even a single race.

It is important to understand the difference between handicapping, which is trying to logically predict the winner of a race, and wagering.

Track Condition Abbreviations

Thoroughbred racing is contested on dirt and turf, the latter also called grass. The abbreviations for track conditions:

Dirt	Turf
ft: fast	**hd:** hard
gd: good	**fm:** firm
sy: sloppy	**gd:** good
my: muddy	**yl:** yielding
wf: wet fast	**sf:** soft
s: sealed track	

Relatively speaking, handicapping is a breeze compared to wagering. Wagering used to be simple. There used to be just a handful of wagering options, betting to win (finish first), place (finish first or second), or show (finish first, second, or third) and a daily double (selecting the winners of two consecutive races). Now, racetrack bettors have a smorgasbord of wagering options and, with the advent of full-card simulcast wagering in the 1990s, dozens of racetracks on which to bet from one location. Selecting the amount and right type of bet takes an incredible amount of self-discipline and excellent money management. We will focus here on handicapping.

Reading Past-Performance Lines

You cannot handicap a race without being able to read past-performance lines, which are a statistical representation of a horse's performance in each of its starts. Past-performance lines can be found in *Daily Racing Form*, a daily newspaper in tabloid format, or a track program, which is the size of a magazine. *Daily Racing Form* provides more information in its past-performance lines and usually has more of them for each horse than a track program. Either one is sufficient.

Past-performance lines contain a multitude of abbreviations and terms that are explained in the accompanying boxes. While past-performance lines appear intimidating to the novice, understanding them is much easier than it appears.

The conditions for each race appear at the top of all the horses' past-performance lines and determine which horses are eligible. Races may be limited to horses of one age or one sex, horses bred in one state, or horses that have not won a certain number of races or amount of purse money. Claiming races are for horses that can be purchased for a designated price. That amount is indicated in the race conditions, and the past performances disclose the horses' claiming prices in previous races.

In *Daily Racing Form*, horses are listed in post-position order beginning with the horse closest to the rail. Track programs list horses by the numbers they will be wearing on their saddlecloths during the race. That is the number you will use when placing your bet.

2-5	**BIG BROWN** (L)		Owners: IEAH Stables and Paul P. Pompa Jr.	2008:	4	4	0	0	$2,676,700
1	b. c. 3 Boundary—Mien, by Nureyev		Trainer: Richard E. Dutrow Jr.	2007:	1	1	0	0	$37,800
		126	Jockey: Kent Desormeaux	Life:	5	5	0	0	$2,714,500
	Bred in Ky. by Monticule			Turf:	1	1	0	0	$37,800
	WHITE, BLUE STARS, red hoops on sleeves, white cap, blue stars			Off Dirt:	0	0	0	0	$0

17May08 Pim12 ft 1³⁄₁₆ :46.81 1:10.48 1:35.72 1:54.80 3 Preakness S. (G1)-1000k 114 6 3³ 3⁴ 3¹ 1⁵¹⁄² 1⁵¹⁄₄ DesormeauxK 126 *0.20 Big Brown126⁵¹⁄₄ Macho Again126⁵¹⁄₄ Icabad Crane126¹¹⁄₄   5w move, under wraps 12
03May08 CD10 ft 1¹⁄₄ :47.04 1:11.14 1:36.56 2:01.82 3 Kentucky Derby Presented 114 20 6²⁰⁄₇ 6³¹⁄₄ 1⁴ᵈ 1²⁰⁄₁ 1⁴³⁄₄ DesormeauxK 126 *2.40 Big Brown126⁴³⁄₄ Eight Belles121³⁰⁄₇ Denis of Cork126²¹⁄₄ wide, steady urging 20
                 by Yum! Brands (G1)-2000k
29Mar08 GP10 ft 1¹⁄₈ :45.83 1:10.08 1:35.18 1:48.16 3 Florida Derby (G2)-1000k 117 12 1¹ 1¹ 1¹¹⁄² 1³ 1⁵ DesormeauxK 122 *1.50 Big Brown122⁵ Smooth Air122⁷¹⁄₂ Tomcito122³¹⁄₄   drew away, greenly 12
05Mar08 GP7 ft 1m :45.31 1:09.87   1:35.66 3 Alw-41500new1/x 115 4 2¹⁄² 3¹ 2ʰᵈ 1⁶ 1¹²³⁄₄ DesormeauxK 118 *1.30 Big Brown118¹²³⁄₄ Heaven's Awesome118¹¹⁄₂ Deputiformer118⁹¹⁄₂ drew off, handily 5
03Sep07 Sar5 ft 1¹⁄₁₆ :47.54 1:11.84 1:34.46 1:40.33 3 MSW-63000 92 1 1¹¹⁄² 1³¹⁄₂ 1¹¹¹⁄₄ DesormeauxK 119 14.70 Big Brown119¹¹¹⁄₄ Doctor Cal119³³⁄₄ Wotan119¹¹⁄₄   ran away when roused 10

Workouts: • 3 June 08 Bel 5f ft 1:00.03 Breezing 1/7 • 17 May 08 Pim 2f ft :25.80 Breezing 1/1 • 1 May 08 CD 3f ft :35.40 Breezing 1/19 • 24 Apr 08 Pmm 5f ft :58.60 Handily 1/1

(L) - Treated with furosemide; (L*) - First time using furosemide; (O) Off of furosemide

If there is an entry, when a betting number covers more than one horse because of a common owner, trainer, or both, the horses will be designated 1 and 1A. The horse closest to the rail is the 1, and the other is 1A. If there is a third horse in one entry, it will be 1X. If there is a second entry in the same race, the horses will be identified as 2 and 2B. A single bet covers all horses in an entry.

A single bet can also encompass horses that do not have a common owner or trainer but are grouped together because the race attracted more runners than the tote system or the tote board can handle. This is called a pari-mutuel field and is increasingly rare because one of the few American races with more than the usual 14 maximum starters, the Kentucky Derby (G1), now offers wagering on each horse in the race.

Located just above the program numbers are the preliminary odds set by a track handicapping specialist to reflect how he or she believes the betting on that race will unfold. This is called the morning line or program line.

Now, let's examine a single past-performance line, that of 2008 Derby and Preakness Stakes (G1) winner Big Brown before he attempted (and failed) to win the Triple Crown in the Belmont Stakes (G1) on June 7. (These past performances are courtesy of Equibase LLC, which provides past-performance information to *Daily Racing Form*, track programs, and other outlets.)

At the far left is the number on Big Brown's saddlecloth, one, which was the post position he drew for the Belmont. Above the saddlecloth number is his morning-line odds as they appeared in the track program, 2-to-5 (0.40-to-1). He was a prohibitive favorite to become the 12th Triple Crown winner after his Derby and Preakness victories.

To the right is information specific to Big Brown. The (L) next to his name indicates that he was treated with the antibleeding medication furosemide, which now is sold under the trade name Salix but formerly was known as Lasix in its veterinary formulation. His owners are IEAH Stables and Paul Pompa Jr., his trainer is Richard Dutrow Jr., and his jockey is Kent Desormeaux.

Beneath the name is information that describes Big Brown. B. c. 3 tells us that he is a bay-colored colt who is three years old. The first name next to that description is his sire, Boundary, and the second name is his dam, Mien. The third name, Nureyev, is the sire of Mien. This stallion is known as the broodmare sire or dam sire. The next line tells us that Big Brown was bred in Kentucky by Monticule. The next line, in boldface type, describes the silks of IEAH Stables that Desormeaux wore: a white field with blue stars and red hoops on the sleeves. His cap is white with blue stars. The number to the right of this information, 126, is the weight that Big Brown carried in the Belmont, 126 pounds.

To the far right is a statistical summary of Big Brown's racing career. The top line is the current year; he had started four times and won all of them. The number at the end of that line is Big Brown's purse earnings for 2008, $2,676,700. The next line indicates that he started once in 2007 and also won that race, with earnings of $37,800. The next line is his cumulative record going into the Belmont: five starts, five wins, and earnings of $2,714,500. The next line, Turf, indicates that he made one start on grass, won, and earned $37,800. That was his first start at Saratoga Race Course on September 3, 2007. The final line of that column, with the heading Off Dirt, describes how he performed on dirt tracks that were not rated as fast. He had made no starts on off tracks.

Beneath Big Brown's statistical record are his past performances, with his grass race at Saratoga listed last since the past performances are in descending order by date. Each past-performance line is a numerical summary of the horse's position in that race.

The past-performance line can be split into thirds. Let's start with the left one-third of Big Brown's past-performance line for the Preakness.
17May08 Pim12 ft 1³⁄₁₆ :46.81 1:10.48 1:35.72 1:54.80 3 Preakness S. (G1)-1000k

At the far left is the date of his most recent race, May 17, 2008 (17May08); the racetrack, Pimlico Race Course (Pim); and the race number, the 12th race on that day's program (12); the track condition, which was fast (ft); and the distance of the race, 1³⁄₁₆ miles (1³⁄₁₆). Next appears the fractional times of the race leader at specified distances during the race. Those distances vary according to the length of the race, but for the Preakness the specified distances—also known as points of call—were a half-mile (:46.81), three-quarters of a mile (1:10.48), one mile (1:35.72), and the race distance of 1³⁄₁₆ miles (1:54.80).

The following number, 3, denotes that the race

was limited to three-year-olds. The next bit of information describes the race itself: it was the Preakness Stakes, it was a Grade 1 race (G1), and it carried a purse of $1-million (1000k).

You will note that the information in this section describes the race itself and not the winner, Big Brown. The middle portion describes how Big Brown ran in the Preakness:

114   6 3^3 3^4 3^1 $1^{51/2}$ $1^{51/4}$ Desormeaux K J   126   *0.20

The first figure in boldface type, 114, is Big Brown's speed figure as calculated by Equibase. Speed figures take into consideration factors other than how fast the horse runs. The speed figures also factor in such information as weather conditions, track condition, head winds, and how fast all horses had been racing over the racetrack that day. In theory, speed figures allow handicappers to compare horses that have raced on different tracks and on different days, but they are by no means infallible. Any speed figure above 90 is very good, and Big Brown's number shows that he is one of the best runners in the country. *Daily Racing Form* utilizes its own speed figures, which were devised by racing and wagering journalist Andrew Beyer, a columnist for the Washington *Post* and *Daily Racing Form*.

The next number, 6, was Big Brown's starting post position in the Preakness. The next numbers describe where he was located at various points in the race, corresponding in part to the fractional times listed in the left-hand portion of the past-performance line. After a quarter-mile, approaching the beginning of Pimlico's clubhouse turn, Big Brown was running third, three lengths behind the leader (3^3).

A quarter-mile later, after a half-mile, he was holding his position although a length farther behind the pacesetter (3^4). At this point in the race, Big Brown was in traffic, and his jockey was looking for an opportunity to move to the outside.

Against a field that was badly outclassed, Big Brown drew closer to the leader while remaining in third position at the six-furlong point (3^1). The next point of call—and the next to last one in every past performance—is one-eighth mile from the finish line, at the furlong pole in midstretch. Big Brown had exploded leaving Pimlico's far turn, and by midstretch the race was all but over as the Boundary colt led by 5½ lengths ($1^{51/2}$). Big Brown was under no pressure in the final sixteenth mile, but he nonetheless won by 5¼ lengths ($1^{51/4}$). In effect, Big Brown was still running as fast as the horses behind him even though he was under restraint for the last 100 yards.

His jockey for the Preakness was Kent Desormeaux (Desormeaux K J), he carried 126 pounds (126), and he went off as the prohibitive betting favorite at odds of 1-to-5, which means that a bettor has to risk five dollars to win one. The asterisk denotes that Big Brown was the Preakness betting favorite, and 0.20 expresses his odds to a dollar (*0.20).

The final one-third of the past-performance line presents the order of finish and a brief commentary on the subject horse's race.

Big Brown$^{51/4}$ Macho Again$^{1/2}$ Icabad Crane$^{3/4}$ 5w move, under wraps 12

As noted earlier, Big Brown won by 5¼ lengths, Macho Again finished second, a half-length ahead of the third finisher, Icabad Crane, who in turn was three-quarters of a length in front of the fourth-place finisher. The brief comment reveals that Big Brown rushed toward the lead while five horse widths off the rail (5w move) and was allowed to gallop home under restraint (under wraps). The final figure, 12, is the total number of starters in the Preakness.

The past-performance lines detail all of Big Brown's starts, going back to his maiden victory in the Saratoga turf race on September 3, 2007. Customarily, each past performance will have between five and ten of the subject horse's most recent races.

At the bottom of the past performances are the horse's recent workouts, with the most recent one at the left. A horse with delicate feet—he had a quarter crack patched before the Belmont—Big Brown had relatively few workouts during his Triple Crown campaign, and three of them were, for the 21st century, unusually close to the day of the race. For instance, his workout two days before the Derby was described as breezing—the rider was not pushing the colt for speed—and he completed three furlongs (3F) in :35.40. It was the fastest of 19 workouts at that

---

Types of Bets

Win Your horse must finish first to collect.
Place Your horse must finish first or second.
Show Your horse must finish first, second, or third.
Quinella You bet two horses and they must finish first and second in either order.
Exacta You bet two horses and they must finish first and second in exact order.
Exacta box A multiple bet in which you select two or more horses and bet all combinations of them finishing first and second.
Exacta wheel You bet one horse to win and every other horse in the field to finish second.
Trifecta or triple You bet three horses and they must finish first, second, and third in exact order.

Trifecta box or triple box A multiple bet in which you select three or more horses and they must finish first, second, and third in any order.
Superfecta You bet four horses and they must finish first, second, third, and fourth in exact order.
Superfecta box You bet four or more horses and they must finish first, second, third, and fourth in any order.
Daily (or instant, late, or middle) double You must pick the winners of two consecutive races.
Pick three or pick four You must pick the winners of three or four consecutive races.
Pick six You must pick the winners of six consecutive races. A consolation payoff for those who pick five winners usually is offered.

distance (1/19) that morning, and the typographical bullet before the workout information also denotes that it was the fastest.

His breeze for the Preakness was on the morning of the race—very unusual by American standards—and he went a quarter-mile (2F) in :25.80. He was the only horse to work that distance (1/1). With the quarter-crack problem, he breezed five furlongs (5F) at Belmont Park (Bel) on June 3, four days before his failed attempt to win the Triple Crown. He breezed five furlongs (5F) in 1:00.03, which again was a bullet workout and the fastest of seven at that distance.

Three Aspects of Handicapping

There is no single correct way to handicap. In fact, that is one of handicapping's charms: What is important to you may be completely dismissed by the person standing next to you. In general, handicapping focuses on three aspects of racing: class, form, and speed. Each asks a question. Class asks: How good is this horse, judging by its previous record and the quality of its competition? Form asks: How has this horse been performing recently, not only in races but also in workouts? Speed simply asks: How fast is this horse?

Class

Class measures not only a horse's previous record but also the level of its competition. Its previous record indicates its number of wins, seconds, and thirds and number of starts for not only this year but also for last year, lifetime, at this particular distance, and on this particular racing surface, dirt or turf. It is important to emphasize that dirt and turf racing should be treated as separate disciplines. If a horse in a turf race has a poor record on dirt but a superior record on grass, discount its dirt record completely. For example, in the first two starts of her career, a horse named Inca Is Calling raced on dirt, finishing sixth by 15¾ lengths and seventh by 13¾ lengths. Switched to grass for her next start, she finished second by three-quarters of a length. Her future was on grass.

It is extremely rare for a horse to be proficient on both turf and dirt. One notable exception was the great John Henry, the two-time Horse of the Year who won Grade 1 stakes, the highest competition in racing, on both dirt and turf.

Two good ways to gauge a horse's class is by its winning percentage and by its average earnings per start. Horses with poor winning percentages, say zero-for-10 (0%) or one-for-20 (5%), are chronic losers and should be avoided. They may eventually find a field weak enough to beat, but over a long period of time they are poor investments, race after race, particularly if they come close to winning and amass a high number of seconds and thirds. They always look as though they are going to win their next start but rarely do.

Average earnings per start reflect a horse's competition. If Horse A has made $80,000 in ten lifetime starts, an average of $8,000 per start, and Horse B has earned $100,000 in 40 lifetime starts, an average of $2,500 per start, Horse A has demonstrated considerably more class. There is an important caveat, however. Races restricted to horses bred in one state, be it California, Florida, Illinois, or New York, inflate a horse's earnings, presenting a distorted picture of a horse's class. Consider that factor only if a horse that has made a lot of money in state-bred races is taking on open (non-restricted) company.

Class is evidenced frequently in claiming races, where horses race for a specified price at which they can be purchased from that race. That is

Racing Terms and Comments

Here are some terms commonly used in racing news stories and chart footnotes. Additional terms can by found in the following section, Glossary of Common Racing and Breeding Terms.

Apprentice A rider at the beginning of his career. Horses with apprentice jockeys carry five, seven, or ten pounds less than their rivals.

Bolted The horse made a sharp, sudden move to the extreme outside.

Bore in or bore out Instead of racing in a straight line, the horse veered inside or outside.

Boxed in The horse was trapped with nowhere to move.

Brushed The horse made light contact with another horse.

Dogs Pylons or traffic cones put around a course to protect the area on the inside near the rail. Horses that work around dogs cover more distance on turns. The symbol (d) is used to denote dogs were up in a workout.

Driving The horse was all out to win.

Entry Two or more horses are coupled in the wagering because of common ownership too, in some jurisdictions, the same trainer. You bet on one and collect if either member of the entry wins.

Field Two or more horses coupled as one betting entity. Just as in an entry, you get more than one horse and collect if any horse in the betting field wins.

Furlong One-eighth of a mile.

Furosemide A diuretic commonly used in American Thoroughbred racing to prevent or limit pulmonary bleeding. Trade name is Salix (formerly Lasix).

Gamely The horse showed courage while racing.

Greenly The horse showed inexperience by racing erratically.

Handily The horse won comfortably.

Hung The horse made an apparent winning move but then failed to sustain it.

Ridden out The jockey continued to ride the winning horse to the wire without undo urging.

Route A race of one mile or longer.

Saved ground The horse raced on the inside, thereby taking a shorter route around the track.

Sprint A race shorter than one mile.

Steadied The jockey had to physically stop his riding motion because of traffic problems.

Taken up The jockey had to restrain his or her mount severely, usually because of traffic problems or interference.

Unruly The horse acted up before the start.

Used up The horse expended all its energy by contesting the pace early in the race.

Willingly The horse continued to run its best without urging.

why it is important to read past-performance lines from the bottom (least recent) to the top (most recent), as explained in "Five Ways to Improve Your Handicapping." Say a horse won its previous start in a $15,000 claiming race and is competing today in a $25,000 claimer. Its most recent races may have been at $15,000, but several starts back it might have competed for $25,000 or even higher. The horse's performances in those races are a valuable indicator of whether it is capable of doing well against better horses today. If it previously won a $30,000 claimer, it has already demonstrated enough class to win at $25,000. If you only glanced at its two or three most recent races, you missed an important indicator of class.

An interesting nuance of class is called back class. That is when a horse with high career earnings or a high career average earnings per start has been performing poorly. Because of its recent form, it may be dismissed by bettors at high odds. However, if it shows a sign of life—that is, an improved effort in its previous start, which often is an indicator of soundness—it may be ready to reassert its class, possibly at generous odds. The improved effort could be significant.

Form

Horses are flesh-and-blood athletes, not machines. Even the best horses are unable to maintain their top-level performance for an extended period of time. That is why two-time Horse of the Year Cigar's record-tying, 16-race win streak was so remarkable in the mid-1990s. All but five of those 16 victories were in stakes races and ten of them were Grade 1 stakes.

Racehorses tend to race in form cycles, meaning they are either moving forward or backward in their performances. This is especially evident in young horses beginning their careers. If a horse making only its second lifetime start shows improvement, it is likely to improve again in its third start. Frequently, horses also show improvement in their second start off of a long layoff. Horses that are idle more than a month may need a return race to get back into top condition.

Workouts can also indicate a horse's form. Fast workouts following a horse's top performance indicate that it is maintaining its best form.

Perhaps the most difficult handicapping decision is determining whether a horse that had been racing well had a legitimate excuse for a poor performance. Was the horse forced extremely wide on a turn? Did it run into traffic? If it normally races on the lead, was it involved in a suicidal speed duel? Going through all the horse's past-performance lines may provide clues. If a horse has raced wide in four or five previous starts, then it may have a bad habit rather than a good excuse for a poor performance. If a horse consistently starts slowly or routinely gets into trouble at the start, then it is apt to do so again. With the advent of race-replay centers at many racetracks, you can watch the videotape of that poor last performance and decide for yourself whether the horse had a legitimate excuse and handicap and wager accordingly.

You should expect young horses to improve, especially if they have shown a hint of ability in their first race or two. For example, catching a good price on a horse trained by Todd Pletcher and ridden by John Velazquez, who have dominated New York racing in recent years, seems impossible. Yet World Cat, a two-year-old colt, showed up in a seven-furlong maiden dirt race

---

Five Ways to Improve Your Handicapping

1. Bottom to top. Always read a horse's past-performance lines from the bottom (least recent race) to the top (most recent race). This strategy will give you an edge on handicappers who glance only at a horse's two or three most recent races. By starting at the bottom, you will discover some important items. Perhaps the horse you are considering has previously raced against several of his opponents today. Perhaps he demonstrated that he could win at a certain claiming level or that he had success coming off a layoff. You will also get a feel for how a horse is coming into today's race in the context of his entire career or a good portion of his career.

2. Use all the available information. There has been an information explosion in past-performance lines in the last decade, and you should take advantage of it. You decide which statistics or information is important for this particular race and handicap accordingly.

3. Watch as many races as you can. This means either live, on television replay shows, on satellite broadcasts such as Television Games Network, or in replay centers at racetracks. When you watch a race just once, you are almost always focused on the single horse you have picked or bet on. Without that emotional attachment, a second look at the same race allows you to follow another horse or horses in the same race. You will be amazed at how much you would have missed on that other horse had you not bothered to watch it again. Take notes if you want.

4. Practice, practice, practice. You can improve your handicapping and wagering easily in a matter of minutes. Ultimately as a bettor, you strive to get value for your investment. You are searching for that 2-to-1 horse that for some reason is going off at 6-to-1. How do you know? Simple. Before the betting begins for each race, write down what you think the final odds will be, and then evaluate how you did. Do it time after time and you will get a better understanding of your handicapping versus the handicapping of the betting public shown in the final odds. Do you want to improve your knowledge of turf racing or how horses will perform on wet tracks? Simply write down your predicted top three finishers in grass races or races on a wet track and see how you score. Then go back and look at the breeding of the winner. Do it daily and you will quickly improve your skills.

5. Identify key races. If you win with a horse that had finished a close second in his last race, pay attention when the third-place finisher from that race is out again. Try to maximize your correct handicapping decisions.—*Bill Heller*

for New York-breds on November 26, 2005. He had made two previous starts, finishing fifth by 10½ lengths in his debut on turf at odds of 4.30-to-1. In his second start, he made his dirt debut on a sloppy track, fought on the lead the entire way from the 12th post position, and finished second by a nose at 5.40-to-1. With the fourth position on November 26, he could have been a heavy favorite off that first dirt race, but was not, paying $9.40 after winning at odds of 3.70-to-1.

Speed

If the horse with the highest speed figure won every race, handicapping would be simple. It is not. The reality is that speed is an important part of the handicapping puzzle but far from the only factor. Speed must always be considered in context. If a horse has early speed—that is, it likes to be on the lead—is it likely to make the front easily, or are there other horses in the race with early speed that will put pressure on the front-running horse? Are the others as fast as this horse? If the race has three speed horses and one of them routinely gets a first quarter-mile in :22 and a half-mile in :45 and the others' fastest times are :23 and :46, their presence may not compromise the faster speed horse's chances. Either way, the other two speed horses should be discarded. They want the lead and will not get it.

For a front-running horse, there is a world of difference between racing loose on the lead without head-to-head pressure from other horses and being pressed hard early by one or two others. If there are three speed horses with comparable early speed in a race, can one of them be rated just off the lead? The answer may show up in each horse's past-performance lines. That is why it is so important to look at all the horse's past-performance lines rather than one or two. If a speed horse has rated just off the lead in a previous race, was it a ticket to success or failure?

It is extremely important to differentiate between speed in sprints, which are races under one mile, and in longer contests, which are widely known as route races. Say a horse wins a 1⅙-mile race on the lead the whole way after running an opening half-mile in :48. To be in front in a sprint, it may have to run :46 or faster. Has it ever done that?

Time is the most important factor in workouts. Almost every Thoroughbred can run one furlong, an eighth of a mile, in :12. Maintaining that pace becomes more difficult with each subsequent furlong. Most horses can run a quarter mile in :24, but not all can work three furlongs in :36 or less. Four furlongs in :48 or faster is outstanding, and five furlongs in 1:00 (one minute) or quicker is even better. If a horse has had a workout on a training track as opposed to the main track, give the workout extra credit. Times are almost always slower on training tracks.

One word of caution: when looking at a horse's workouts, consider only the ones that came after its most recent race.

Changes

Changes are extremely significant in handicapping, be it the addition or the removal of blinkers, switching jockeys or trainers, trying a different surface (turf or dirt), racing on a wet track, or shipping to another track. The most significant change, however, is the addition of the anti-bleeding diuretic furosemide, which now is marketed as Salix for veterinary uses but still is identified in past performances by a capital L. Horses treated with furosemide for the first or, sometimes, the second time, frequently show tremendous improvement.

Breezy Way showed up in a $40,000 maiden claimer at Aqueduct on November 3, 2005, and was adding Salix for the first time. He was fifth by 14 lengths on a sloppy track and fifth by 16¾ lengths on a fast track in his previous two starts, both at the same maiden claiming level. He had not finished in the money in seven career starts. With Salix, he finished third by 1¾ lengths.

In his second lifetime start, Northern Disco, racing without Salix, finished a tired fourth by 21¼ lengths in a six-furlong optional claiming race at Laurel Park at odds of 12.40-to-1 on September 15, 2005. In his next start, in the same class but stretching out to one mile on October 14 at Laurel with Salix, he finished third by one length at odds of 9.50-to-1. His Beyer speed figure jumped from 18 to 51.

Frequently, horses adding Salix for the first time are bet heavily. In his career debut on August 12, 2005, without Salix, Kwik Bullet finished a tired eighth by 20½ lengths in a six-furlong, $40,000 maiden claiming race at Calder Race Course at odds of 61.40-to-1. With Salix in his second start on September 9, he dropped slightly to a $25,000 maiden claiming race at Calder but stretched out to seven furlongs. He won by 1¾ lengths at odds of 5.60-to-1. In doing so, his Beyer speed figure leaped from 23 to 59. *Daily Racing Form* indicates a horse using Salix for the first time by highlighting the capital letter L in white on a black circle background.

The addition of blinkers helps a horse to focus better by limiting its vision, and almost all horses show more speed when blinkers are added. This may be evidenced in a horse's most recent workouts if they are faster than they usually are. Conversely, removing blinkers usually allows a horse to see more and be a bit more relaxed.

When looking through a horse's previous races, had blinkers been added or removed previously? Did it produce a much different performance, better or worse? Was it on the same surface as today? A horse entered in a turf race could have been racing on dirt without blinkers, had blinkers added, and shown no improvement. Its prior races on grass could have been poor,

but what if it had raced all of them before the addition of blinkers? Even though adding blinkers did not improve the horse's performance on dirt, their addition may improve it on grass. The same holds true with the addition of Salix. Do not assume that because first-time Salix did not improve a horse on dirt that the medication will have no effect when it races on grass.

Trainer changes happen every time a horse gets claimed. Statistics included in some past-performance lines now allow you to see how well a trainer does with a horse in its first start after a claim.

Jockey changes are significant only when there is a substantial difference in ability between the two jockeys. A rider change from Edgar Prado to John Velazquez, or vice versa, is insignificant. They are both among the world's best. But if a horse changes from Prado to a rider with a poor winning percentage, or if Prado assumes the mount from a less successful rider—take note. Substantial changes of jockeys are usually reflected in a horse's odds. A horse switching from a lesser rider to John Velazquez, for instance, will be played heavily by bettors almost every time.

Note, too, that jockeys and trainers, just like horses, have different abilities on dirt and grass. As a general guideline, apprentice jockeys, who are allowed to carry less weight until they win a specified number of races, are better on dirt than on grass.

Layoffs

Most horses that have been off more than a month require at least one race back to perform well, but the key word here is "most." Not all horses need that comeback race to reach sufficient fitness to race well, and trainers have a wide range of success getting layoff horses to win their first start back. In New York, nobody is better

---

Types of Races

allowance race A race for which eligibility and weight to be carried are determined by the specific conditions of the race, such as number of career wins, earnings, or time since previous win. The lowest-level allowance race is for horses that have not won one race other than maiden or claiming. At the highest level, allowance conditions are written for horses that have not won a specific amount of purse money in their careers or within a specified period of time, such as $100,000 in the previous 12 months, or, for example, nonwinners of two races worth $40,000 (usually referring to the purse to the winner) since March 15. Allowance races are generally the second-best type of race on a card, behind stakes races.

claiming race A race for horses that can be purchased (claimed) immediately from that race for the price specified at the time of entry. The claimed horse becomes the new owner's property as soon as the starting gate opens, regardless if the horse finishes, but the previous owner collects any purse money earned by the claimed horse from that race. Claims must be entered before the race, usually ten to 15 minutes before post time depending on the state rules, and they can be made only by a person who is eligible to make claims under state rules. If more than one owner puts in a claim for the same horse, the disposition of the horse is determined by lot by the stewards. Claiming races are generally of lower class than allowance races. The lower the claiming price, the lower the class, and also the lower the purse.

futurity A race, usually for two-year-olds, that is restricted to horses whose owners have made nomination payments shortly after the horse's birth and subsequently have made sustaining payments to maintain the horse's eligibility. As field sizes and quality of futurities dwindled in the 1980s, this type of race became relatively rare, and nominating conditions changed as a result. In 1972, for instance, the first payment for the Futurity Stakes (G1) at Belmont Park had to have been made by August 15, 1970, the year the horses were foaled. By 1990, the subscription deadline was May 1, 1990, for a race to be run in September 1990. Two years later, the Futurity became a stakes race, with nominations closing 17 days before the race.

handicap race A race, usually of stakes caliber, in which the racing secretary determines the amount of weight each horse will carry based on career record and current form. In theory, the handicapper seeks to assign weights so that all starters finish at the same time in a dead heat to win. Handicap races formerly placed high weight assignments on such champions as Kelso (won the 1964 Straight Face Handicap with 136 pounds) and Forego (won the 1977 Nassau County Handicap with 136 pounds), but few top-weight assignments now exceed 126 pounds.

maiden claiming race A race for nonwinning horses that can be purchased immediately from that race for a specified price (see claiming race).

maiden race A race for horses that have never won a race. Maiden races are either maiden special weight, with all horses assigned a specified weight, or maiden claiming. Additional conditions may apply, such as the race being restricted to state-breds.

optional claiming A race that is both a claiming race, for those horses entered to be claimed for a specific price, and an allowance race, for those whose owners do not enter them to be claimed.

overnight handicap A race where owners do not pay to enter their horses but are assigned weights by the racing secretary. These races generally offer some of the higher purses, on a par with the best allowance races but below stakes race purses.

restricted race A race whose starters are limited to those eligible under specified conditions, such as horses that were bred in the state where the race is held, were offered or sold at a specific sale, or by their previous winnings.

stakes race A race that is generally the highest quality race offered by a track. For stakes, owners pay a fee to nominate and enter their horses in the starting gate, with the track putting up added money to make up the difference in the total purse. Stakes races are generally the richest races run at each track and attract the best horses on the grounds, plus horses coming in from other tracks or states when the purse money is high enough to attract shippers.

starter allowance An allowance race for horses that have started for a specified minimum claiming price within a specified time. For example, some starter allowances are restricted to horses that have started for a claiming price of $10,000 or less in the previous year. Conditions of the race, meaning the weight carried, are determined by allowances.

starter handicap A race similar to a starter allowance, except the horses are assigned weights by the track racing secretary, based on current ability and form rather than allowance conditions.

than Bill Mott and Todd Pletcher. *Daily Racing Form* now includes in each horse's past performance their trainer's record with horses that have been off a specified number of days: 60 to 120, for example, or more than 180. This is valuable information you should use in handicapping, but more conclusive information may be found in a horse's past-performance lines. Starting at the bottom, check to see if this horse has ever raced off a similar layoff in its last 12 races. How it did then indicates how it is likely to perform today.

Significant gaps between a horse's races or its workouts are frequently a sign of trouble. A horse that has been racing regularly should be working out regularly in between starts in the same pattern the trainer had previously used with this horse.

Post Positions

Post positions can be crucial to a horse's success, especially in turf racing. Think about it. Since racetracks in the United States have their turf courses inside their dirt courses, they have a smaller circumference and much tighter turns, penalizing horses that are forced to race wide by outside post positions. That effect is even more pronounced on inner turf courses at tracks with two grass courses, such as Belmont Park and Saratoga Race Course. Virtually every track updates its winning post positions on all its courses daily, and that information is readily available. Use it. If a horse drew a highly disadvantageous outside post on the inner turf course and, though racing wide, was still competitive, it should improve significantly with a better post position in its next start. If a horse has been plagued by outside post positions in several turf races, cut it slack and be aware when it gets a better post.

Also take into account the length of the straightaway before the first turn in grass racing. Certain races give horses ample time to work their way closer to the rail before the turn; others do not.

On dirt, the rail at some tracks can be a slight disadvantage for races at seven furlongs or one mile, especially if a horse lacks early speed. Extreme outside posts can be a disadvantage if there is not a long run into the first turn. Again, check the numbers.

Trainer Patterns

Both *Daily Racing Form* and track programs now contain extensive and useful trainer statistics for practically every race. They show not only the trainer's current record but also his or her recent history in a wide array of categories, from first-time starters to first start off a claim, from long layoffs, to running a horse back within a week. More recently, these publications have added percentages for a trainer when he or she uses the same jockey who will be riding in this race for that trainer.

Not to be lost in the avalanche of statistics is the common-sense observation that certain trainers excel in certain types of races. Some are better with fillies; others are great with two-year-olds; a few rarely win a grass race. Use all of this in your handicapping. Take every edge you can find because, remember, you are literally betting against other bettors.

Two-Year-Olds

Handicapping races with proven, experienced horses is difficult enough. Handicapping two-year-old races full of horses making their first career starts is daunting but not impossible. Here, trainer statistics are extremely helpful. So is the horse-by-horse analysis found in *Daily Racing Form*, which often discloses relevant statistics about the horse's sire or dam. For handicapping, the dam is more important than the sire. Again, it is common sense. A sire may have many new foals every year with its genetic capabilities; a mare obviously has only one. If a dam has already produced several two-year-old winners, take note.

Gauging two-year-old workouts are easier if you become familiar with trainer patterns. Some trainers, such as Bob Baffert in California, always work their two-year-olds fast. Other trainers, such as Shug McGaughey in New York, seldom do. Also, be sure to notice if workouts have been done on a main track or on a slower training track.

A single fast workout—for example, four furlongs in :47—stands out. But steady, good works, such as three or four four-furlong works between :48 and :49.80, are a great barometer that the horse has good speed and is fit and ready to go.

Weight

If weight were not an important factor in racing, trainers around the country would not go bananas when an apprentice with even a modicum of ability starts winning races with a weight allowance of five, seven, or ten pounds.

Generally, weight is more important in distance races than in sprints. But context is important. If every horse in a race carries 126 pounds, there is obviously no advantage. If, however, one horse is carrying 122 and the others between 115 to 118, weight is a factor. Also, watch for a significant shift of weight between two horses. For instance, Horse A may have carried 125 pounds and narrowly beat Horse B carrying 118. If they run at equal weights in their next encounter, the outcome may be different.

Final Thought

You can bet license-plate or telephone numbers every time you go to the racetrack and do all right, but the experience is much more enjoyable if you handicap a race and deduce a winner or two. Remember, this is a skill that you can improve only as you watch and handicap more races. With the dramatic increase in handicapping tournaments, there has never been a better time to try handicapping. Good luck!

Handicapping a Sample Race

The Pimlico Special Handicap (G1) has deep historical roots even though it has long gaps when it was not held. In 1938, Seabiscuit defeated War Admiral in an edition of the Pimlico Special that attracted only the two champions. The 41st running of the Pimlico Special on May 16, 2008, did not boast that kind of talent, but it was instructive in many ways. It featured a well-balanced field, and it also illustrated how the scratch of a favorite can affect a race. Nine older horses were entered for the 1 3/16-mile race, with A. P. Arrow rated as the 5-to-2 morning-line favorite. But trainer Todd Pletcher withdrew the 2007 Clark Handicap (G2) winner from the race; in addition trainer Nick Zito scratched Wanderin Boy, reducing the field size to seven. (The scratched horses have been omitted from the accompanying past performances.)

Here are brief descriptions of the starters, listed by their program numbers:

1. Ryan's for Real. Trained by Dale Capuano, Ryan's for Real had proved he indeed was for real by winning Hawthorne Race Course's Bill Hartack Memorial Handicap (G3) in his previous start. The 1 1/8-mile Hartack was his first recent start beyond a mile, and he was on the pace before drawing away in the stretch. In his prior 2008 starts, he had been outclassed at seven furlongs and a mile. Capuano took over training duties before the gelding's seventh-place finish in the Carter Handicap (G1). Ryan's for Real presents two questions for the handicapper: Can he continue to improve over a slightly longer distance, and can he successfully step up in class to a Grade 1 race?

2. Gottcha Gold. A highly consistent and high-quality runner, the Coronado's Quest horse is coming off a graded stakes victory two months earlier in the Skip Away Handicap (G3) at Gulfstream Park. After a dismal run in the 2007 Skip Away, Gottcha Gold won two graded stakes races at Monmouth Park and then was a well-beaten second to Corinthian in the inaugural Breeders' Cup Dirt Mile on a sloppy Monmouth track. In his first 2008 start, he did not handle Santa Anita Park's troubled Cushion Track surface and finished ninth to Go Between in the Sunshine Millions Classic Stakes. His class is not in doubt; the question for handicappers is whether he can come back after a two-month break and win at the Grade 1 level.

3. Student Council. After being sold by Will Farish to Ro Parra's Millennium Farms the previous summer, the Kingmambo horse had blossomed, winning the Pacific Classic Stakes (G1) a few days later and then taking the Hawthorne Gold Cup Handicap (G2). Parra then sent him into the Japan Cup Dirt (Jpn-G1), and the wheels came off. After finishing eighth in that race, he had run fifth in the San Antonio Handicap (G2), sixth in the Santa Anita Handicap (G1), and then seventh in the John B. Connally Handicap (G3) at Sam Houston Race Park six weeks before the Pimlico Special. Several factors need to be considered when assessing Student Council. First is a change of scene. Parra employs both Steve Asmussen and Vladimir Cerin to train Millennium Farms's horses. Asmussen had assumed training duties after the Santa Anita Handicap, and sometimes a horse will respond favorably to a change of location. Before the Pimlico Special, Student Council had had a good workout at Churchill Downs for Asmussen, going a half-mile in :49.60 on a muddy track. Another factor is back class. Less than a year earlier, he had had the class to win a Grade 1 race. Could he jump up and do it again?

5. Xchanger. In the previous year, Xchanger had only two victories in ten starts, the Barbaro Stakes (G3) at Delaware Park and the Federico Tesio Stakes at Pimlico Race Course, but he had run in top company. He fell a neck short of winning the 2007 Pennsylvania Derby (G2), finished third in the Meadowlands Cup Handicap (G2) against older horses, and was fourth in the Hill 'n' Dale Cigar Mile Handicap (G1), though well beaten. His previous start, the Commonwealth Stakes (G2) on Keeneland Race Course's Polytrack, had been terrible. Trainer Mark Shuman sent him out for a bullet workout in :59.60 on Fair Hill Training Center's Tapeta Footing synthetic surface six days before the Pimlico Special. Handicappers face at least two questions: Should they throw out the Keeneland race because it was a different surface, and was Xchanger's workout too fast for him to rebound into top form for the Pimlico Special?

7. Grasshopper. With A. P. Arrow out of the race, Grasshopper became the likely favorite. He had been running well since catching the racing world's attention by finishing a strong second to Kentucky Derby Presented by Yum! Brands (G1) winner Street Sense in the Travers Stakes (G1) at Saratoga Race Course. He had won the Mineshaft Handicap (G3) at Fair Grounds and had been second to Divine Park in the Westchester Handicap (G3) less than three weeks earlier. Although nothing truly argues against him, Grasshopper had not broken through at either the Grade 1 or Grade 2 levels, and his large number of second-place finishes—half of all starts—hints at a horse that is all too content to finish second.

8. Sir Whimsey. Trained by veteran Jimmy Toner, Sir Whimsey has a discernable pattern in his past performances. He reaches peak form in races that he wins, backs off in subsequent races, and then returns to top form. Fourth in an optional claiming race in November 2007, he finished second in the Don Rickles Stakes at Aqueduct in December and then won two races at Gulfstream, culminating with the Gulfstream Park Handicap (G2) on March 1. He subsequently finished third on Keeneland's Polytrack in the Ben Ali Stakes (G3). Handicappers should ask: Is Sir Whimsey coming off top form, or did he not like the Polytrack?

9. Temporary Saint. Claimed for $50,000 by Maggi Moss in October 2007, Temporary Saint had more than paid for his purchase. Trainer Bruce Levine had stepped him up to a Grade 3 victory in Aqueduct's Excelsior Handicap (G3) in his previous start. The obvious question is whether he could come off a huge effort to win a Grade 1 race.

Analysis

Grasshopper and Gottcha Gold are the class of

Reference — Handicapping a Sample Race

This page reproduces a past-performance (Daily Racing Form style) chart for four horses in a sample race. The dense tabular race-record data is not reliably transcribable as clean markdown text; key identifying information for each entry is given below.

5 — **Xchanger (LA)** — 20-1
Circle Z Stables, Joseph Masone & Mark Shuman
SILVER, black circled "Z", silver circled "Z" & cuffs on black sleeves, black cap
Gr/ro. c. 4 Exchange Rate – Saragota by Crafty Prospector, FL — 115
Bred in FL by Oscar Martinez (Apr 24, 2004)
Garrett K. Gomez — Current Meet: (10-0-2-1)
Mark Shuman — Current Meet: (23-2-3-4)
2008: 0 0 0 0 $0
2007: 1 1 0 0 $510,500
Life: 10 2 1 1 $734,990
PiM: 4 0 0 0 $60,000
Class Rating: 95
Workouts: ●10 May 08 Fai ⊗ tr 5F ft :59.3b 1/29   W. S. Howard, Edward J. Hudson, Jr. & Inwood Stable

7 — **Grasshopper (L)** — 3-1
Dk B/ Br. c. 4 Dixie Union – Grass Skirt by Mr. Prospector, KY — 117
Bred in VA by W. S. Farish, E. J. Hudson & James Elkins (Apr 08, 2004)
Robby Albarado — Current Meet: (5-1-1-0)
Neil J. Howard — Current Meet: (2-0-0-0)
2008: 2 2 0 0 $211,820
2007: 4 3 1 0 $378,520
Life: 0 0 0 0 $630,352
PiM: 2 0 0 Class Rating: 106.6
Workouts: 10 Jun 08 CD 4F ft :49b 12/38   Turtle Bird Stable

8 — **Sir Whimsey (LA)** — 10-1
POWDER BLUE, white diamond, white diamond bars on sleeves, powder blue cap
Dk B/ Br. c. 4 Jump Start – Apogee by Star de Naskra, VA — 117
Bred in VA by Chance Farm (Mar 27, 2004)
Edgar Prado — Current Meet: (8-1-1-3)
James J. Toner — Current Meet: (1-0-0-1)
2008: 3 2 1 0 $251,100
2007: 14 4 0 0 $82,851
Life: 0 Distance: $0 $371,043
PiM: 0 Class Rating: 104.64
Workouts: 4 Jun 08 CD 6F gd 1:13.1b 2/2   Previously trained by Miceli Michael 2007 as of 05/26: (83 7 17 10 0 08)   Miceli Paul J. — Trainer

9 — **Temporary Saint (LA)** — 10-1
ROYAL BLUE, lime green sash, lime green cuffs on sleeves, blue cap
Gr/ro. g. 9 Awesome Again – No Foul Play by Great Gladiator, KY — 114
Bred in KY by Adena Springs (Mar 10, 2003)
John Velazquez — Current Meet: (6-2-1-0)
Bruce N. Levine — Current Meet: (1-0-0-0)
2008: 3 0 0 1 $115,264
2007: 4 2 6 0 $92,867
Life: 0 Distance: $223,959
PiM: 0 Class Rating: 106.85
Workouts: 6 Jun 08 Bel tr 5F ft 1:04.4b 22/23   Maggi Moss
Claimed from Limestone Stables for $50,000, McGee Paul J. — Trainer

L = Lasix; L1 = First Time Lasix; LX = Lasix Off; A = Lasix & Adjunct Bleeder Medication

Scratched from race: #4 A. P. Arrow and #6 Wanderin Boy.

Copyright © 2008 by Equibase Co. LLC

the race, although Grasshopper's tendency to finish second is worrisome. Sir Whimsey, Temporary Saint, and Ryan's for Real are all improving, but they have not won at Grade 1 level. In fact, the only horse showing a recent win at Grade 1 level is Student Council, but his recent starts have been unimpressive. Xchanger had a terrible start in 2008, and he may need weaker company.

How To Read a Race Chart

The race chart is a summary of the race, offering factual information as well as a numerical description of how each horse performed. As an example, we will examine the chart of the 2008 Maryland Lottery Pimlico Special Handicap (G1).

Let's start at the top, which tells you that the Pimlico Special was the tenth race at Pimlico Race Course on May 16, 2008. It was a handicap—meaning that weights were assigned to nominated horses based on their recent accomplishments—and the purse was $250,000 guaranteed. The race was limited to horses four years old and older, and the distance was 1 3/16 miles on dirt. The track condition that day was muddy, and the surface had been sealed by pulling over it a device known as a float.

Below that information is the division of the $250,000 purse. The value of the race may sometimes differ from the announced purse in cases of added money, such as nominating and starting fees going into the purse, which would increase the race's value. Small fields can result in a smaller purse if some lesser placings are not paid and the money reverts to the racetrack.

The chart lists the horses in the order in which they finished, so Student Council is first. Before his name is his program number (3). After his name is the weight he carried, 118 pounds, and the race-day medications with which he had been treated: furosemide (L) and an adjunct antibleeding medication (A). The following set of numbers describes how he ran in the race. He started from the third stall in the starting gate (3), and after a quarter-mile he was sixth, a head in front of the last-place horse, Grasshopper, in a field of seven. To determine how far behind the leader Student Council was running, you must add up the superscript numbers of the

Maryland Lottery Pimlico Special H. – Grade 1
Purse: $1-Million Guaranteed

TENTH RACE Stakes. Purse $250,000. For four-year-olds and upward. 1 3/16 miles on dirt.
Pimlico Track Record: Farma Way, 1:52.55, May 11, 1991.
May 16, 2008 Track: Muddy (Sealed).

Value of race: $250,000. Value to winner: $150,000; second: $50,000; third: $27,500; fourth: $15,000; fifth: $7,500.

P#	Horse	Wgt	M/Eqt	PP	Start	1/4	1/2	3/4	Str.	Fin.	Jockey	Odds
3	Student Council	118	LA	3	7	6^{hd}	7	6^4	$2^{1/2}$	1^{nk}	S. Bridgmohan	7.20
2	Gottcha Gold	118	L bf	2	2	1^1	$1^{1 1/2}$	1^1	$1^{2 1/2}$	$2^{5 3/4}$	C. Lopez	2.10
8	Sir Whimsey	117	LA	6	5	$5^{1/2}$	$4^{1/2}$	$5^{1 1/2}$	5^6	3^1	E. Prado	4.00
9	Temporary Saint	114	LA bfc	7	4	$3^{1/2}$	$3^{2 1/2}$	3^2	3^3	$4^{2 1/2}$	J. Velazquez	8.50
7	Grasshopper	117	L	5	6	7	$5^{1/2}$	4^{hd}	4^{hd}	$5^{8 1/2}$	R. Albarado	*2.00
1	Ryan's for Real	115	LA bc	1	3	4^2	$6^{1/2}$	7	7	$6^{10 3/4}$	E. Rodriguez	14.30
5	Xchanger	115	LA b	4	1	2^1	2^1	$2^{1/2}$	$6^{1 1/2}$	7	G. Gomez	12.00

Scratched: A. P. Arrow, Wanderin Boy

OFF AT 4:43. Start: Good for all. Weather: Clear.
Fractional Times—:23.87, :47.46, 1:11.39, 1:36.17, 1:54.87

Total W/P/S Pool: $504,535	$2 PICK 3 2/3/4-1-3	$274,00	Total Pool: $69,835
Mutuel Payoffs	$2 EXACTA 3-2	63.60	Total Pool: $357,111
3—**Student Council**..........$16.40 $6.60 $4.00	$2 TRIFECTA 3-2-8	302.80	Total Pool: $238,789
2—**Gottcha Gold** 4.00 3.00	$1 SUPERFECTA 3-2-8-9	731.10	Total Pool: $73,331
8—**Sir Whimsey** 3.40			

Winner: Student Council, b. h., by Kingmambo—Class Kris, by Kris S. Foaled May 28, 2002, in Kentucky. **Breeder:** W. S. Farish.

STUDENT COUNCIL, taken to rate off the rail, angled out five wide entering the lane, advanced under left-handed urging in upper stretch, responded well when put to right-handed urging inside the sixteenth pole, closed determinedly, and wore down GOTTCHA GOLD in the final yards. GOTTCHA GOLD cleared early, set the pace toward the inside, was nudged along leaving the far turn, widened in upper stretch, was put to the whip a sixteenth out, but could not hold off the winner. SIR WHIMSEY, patiently rated off the rail, swung out five to six wide leaving the three-sixteenths marker but could only muster a mild rally. TEMPORARY SAINT lost ground three wide stalking the pace, remained a solid presence to midstretch, then faded. GRASSHOPPER had a shoe repair in the paddock, raced three wide around the first turn, settled off the rail in mid pack down the backstretch, made a mild four-wide run midway on the final turn, then gave up in the drive. RYAN'S FOR REAL saved ground, failed to keep pace, and faltered leaving the far turn. XCHANGER prompted the pace two wide, was hustled along leaving the far turn, then faltered entering the lane.

Trainers: (3) Steven Asmussen; (2) Edward Plesa Jr.; (8) James Toner; (9) Bruce Levine; (7) Neil Howard; (1) Dale Capuano; (5) Mark Shuman

Owners: (3) Millennium Farms; (2) Centaur Farms; (8) Turtle Bird Stable; (9) Maggi Moss; (7) W. S. Farish, Edward J. Hudson Jr., and Inwood Stable; (1) Rob Ry Farm and Jayne Marie Slysz; (5) Circle Z Stable, Joseph Masone, and Mark Shuman

horses ahead of him at that point. Although sixth, Student Council was only five lengths behind the leader, Gottcha Gold.

After a half-mile, Student Council was last, but he was by no means out of contention, running 6½ lengths behind Gottcha Gold, who remained the leader. The half-mile statistics also reveal that Gottcha Gold had increased his lead slightly, to 1½ lengths over second-place Xchanger. The three-quarter-mile call, near the start of Pimlico's final turn, had Student Council still well back in sixth position but on the move; he was four lengths ahead of the last-place horse, Ryan's for Real (who already was tiring), and five lengths behind Gottcha Gold, who maintained a length lead on Xchanger.

The next column in the chart is the stretch call (Str). It is always one-eighth of a mile (one furlong, or 220 yards) from the finish line and is in the middle of the stretch on one-mile racetracks like Pimlico. That point of call reveals how much the complexion of the race had changed in five-sixteenths of a mile, on the final turn and into the stretch. Student Council had advanced into second place, and he now is 2½ lengths behind Gottcha Gold. Temporary Saint had maintained his position in third, a half-length behind the surging Student Council, and Grasshopper had moved into fourth position while Xchanger had fallen back sharply to sixth.

The finish, which is measured by a photo-finish camera, reveals that Student Council overtook Gottcha Gold and won by a neck, which is approximately one-quarter length. Sir Whimsey, who had been fifth at the furlong pole, closed for third, but he was 5¾ lengths behind Gottcha Gold. Grasshopper could not maintain his momentum and finished fifth, 9½ lengths behind the winner. The right-hand side of the chart contains the jockeys' names and the final wagering odds for each starter. Student Council and his back class clearly were overlooked in the Pimlico Special. He went off at 7.20-to-1 odds. Grasshopper was the 2-to-1 favorite, with Gottcha Gold a close second choice at 2.10-to-1.

Beneath the horses' running lines are the time of day when the race went off (4:43 p.m. EDT), a description of the start (Good for all), and the weather (Clear). The next line gives the fractional times of the race: :23.87 for the first quarter-mile; :47.46 for the half-mile; 1:11.39 for three-quarters of a mile; 1:36.17 for the mile; and a final time of 1:54.87 for 1 3/16 miles. Those numbers indicate that Gottcha Gold maintained a reasonable pace, but Student Council nonetheless was able to overhaul him in deep stretch. The next line gives the total win-place-show wagering pool for the Pimlico Special, $504,535. Next are the pari-mutuel payoffs for the multiple-horse wagers and the win, place, and show payouts for the first three finishers. Student Council paid $16.40 to win on a $2 bet, $6.60 to place, and $4 to show. The $2 exacta (the first two horses in order) paid $63.60, and the trifecta (first three finishers in order) paid $302.80 for a $2 bet. Total betting pools for those wagers also are listed.

Next is the breeding of the winner and the name of the winner's breeder, William S. Farish. Under that is a narrative describing how each horse ran in the race. At the bottom are the names of the horses' owners, in finishing order and with program numbers, followed by the trainers of those horses.

—*Don Clippinger*

How Pari-Mutuel Wagering Began

Virtually all betting on horse races in North America, as in most countries, is conducted using the pari-mutuel wagering system. Unlike a casino, where bettors play against the house, racehorse bettors bet against each other, with the track holding the bets and, after taking out money for the track, purses, state taxes, and other mandated deductions, returning the money bet to the winning patrons after each race is run.

Unlike most traditions in North American horse racing, pari-mutuel wagering came from France rather than England. The system was devised in the mid-1860s by Pierre Oller, a Paris perfume merchant who had become disenchanted with the city's bookmakers.

Oller developed a variation of the auction pool, in which betting interests in individual horses were sold. Because fairly large sums of money were required to buy the winning interest in a favorite in the auction pools, they were not widely used by small-scale bettors. Oller's system allowed small wagers on all horses and quickly came into wide use in France. He called his wagering system perier mutuel, which means to wager among ourselves. Adopted in England, it became known as Paris mutuals, and finally pari-mutuel.

New York tracks used the pari-mutuel system (known then as Paris pools) in the early 1870s. Col. M. Lewis Clark, the founder of Churchill Downs, observed the pari-mutuels in operation during a sojourn in Europe in the early 1870s and introduced the devices at his track in 1878. (Auction pools were used in 1875, 1876, and 1877, the first three years of Churchill's existence.)

Bookmakers soon made their appearance in both New York and Louisville, and the popularity of betting with bookmakers supplanted the pari-mutuel machines. Clark abandoned pari-mutuels in 1889 at the demand of bookmakers.

In 1908, however, anti-Churchill forces took over City Hall and banned bookmaking. Col. Matt Winn, then the track's general manager, rounded up six of the old pari-mutuel machines, refurbished them, and used them for betting on the 1908 Kentucky Derby. Pari-mutuel wagering on the Derby day program that year was $67,570 ($18,300 of that total on the Derby, won by Stone Street at 23.72-to-1 odds), with another $12,669 in auction pools.

The first machines sold only one denomination of ticket, $5 for the 1908 Derby program, but by 1911 Winn had commissioned new machines that offered $2, $5, and $10 tickets. By 1914, most American tracks had switched to the pari-mutuel system as anti-gambling sentiment led to bans against bookmaking.

Betting Odds and Payouts

Pari-mutuel betting odds are based on the percentage of the net wagering pool placed on each horse. For instance, a horse sent off at even money, or 1-to-1 odds, has attracted 50% of the net wagering pool.

The net wagering pool on which the odds are based is total wagering minus deductions broadly known as takeout—money taken out for state tax, horsemen's purses, the track's share, and other deductions. Total wagering is known as handle, which the track holds until after each race is run and then returns the net balance to winning bettors.

When devising a program betting line, a line maker generally will assign odds based on 125% of handle to account for takeout.

All tracks in North America show payouts after each race on their tote boards based on a $2 wager. To figure the exact odds, for instance, at which a horse went off in the win pool, subtract the $2 bet and divide by two. If a horse paid $4.70 to win, its winning odds were 1.35-to-1 ([$4.70-$2]/2=1.35).

Exact betting odds usually are rounded down to the nearest 10 cents, although some jurisdictions round to the next lowest 5 cents.

Pari-Mutuel Odds	Percentage of Net Pool	Payout
1-to-20	95.23%	$2.10
1-to-10	90.91%	2.20
1-to-5	83.33%	2.40
2-to-5	71.42%	2.80
1-to-2	66.66%	3.00
4-to-5	55.55%	3.60
Even (1-to-1)	50.00%	4.00
7-to-5	41.67%	4.80
9-to-5	35.71%	5.60
2-to-1	33.33%	6.00
5-to-2	28.57%	7.00
3-to-1	25.00%	8.00
7-to-2	22.23%	9.00
4-to-1	20.00%	10.00
9-to-2	18.19%	11.00
5-to-1	16.67%	12.00
10-to-1	9.09%	22.00
15-to-1	6.25%	32.00
20-to-1	4.76%	42.00
30-to-1	3.23%	62.00
50-to-1	1.96%	102.00
100-to-1	0.99%	202.00

Race Winners with Highest All-Time Odds

Odds	Horse, YOB Sex, Sire	Date	Track	Race Type
610.00-to-1	Able Belle, 1979 m., by Swordfish Able	May 1, 1982	Turf Paradise	MCl
600.60-to-1	Watermelon Ms, 1974 m., by *Cartujo	June 29, 1980	Balmoral	Alw
560.50-to-1	An Enemy of My Own, 1988 m., by Enemy Number One	Jan. 10, 1992	Albuquerque	Clm
560.00-to-1	Whispering Command, 1987 m., by Top Command	April 26, 1991	Detroit	MCl
553.92-to-1	New Dancer, 1979 h., by Gaelic Dancer	April 12, 1987	Sunland	Clm
544.64-to-1	Intentionally Blue, 1982 g., by Neater	Aug. 2, 1987	Penn National	Clm
540.00-to-1	Unreasonable D., 1979 m., by Prince of Reason	May 14, 1982	Centennial	Clm
533.92-to-1	Retrimmer, 1983 h., by Recitalist	Dec. 27, 1986	Tampa Bay	Clm
523.20-to-1	Blue Money, 1981 h., by Money Lender	March 27, 1984	Latonia	MCl
500.50-to-1	Corporal Trim, 1974 h., by Grey Eagle	July 27, 1978	Ferndale	Alw
499.28-to-1	Sweet Wheat, 1980 m., by Etonian's Heir	Feb. 2, 1983	Bay Meadows	MCl
495.00-to-1	Gift Package, 1987 m., by Holy Gift	July 28, 1991	Assiniboia	Clm
480.00-to-1	Diamonds Or Gold, 1986 g., by Brilliant Sandy	Feb. 20, 1992	Delta Downs	Clm
438.00-to-1	Gee's Echo, 1974 h., by *Tiroles	Aug. 26, 1976	River Downs	MCl
423.20-to-1	Bachie Behr, 1977 h., by Bhagavad	Sept. 16, 1982	Fairmount	Clm
420.00-to-1	Tronds Key, 1979 m., by Trondheim	May 7, 1982	Golden Gate	Clm
410.00-to-1	Cesar's Special, 1990 g., by Cesar T.	Feb. 6, 1993	Sunland	Alw
400.00-to-1	Easy Angel, 1975 h., by Easersaid	Jan. 21, 1982	Delta Downs	Clm
390.00-to-1	Jamee May, 1978 m., by Speak Quick	Jan. 15, 1982	Latonia	Clm
388.30-to-1	Spin a Happy, 1974 m., by Happy Trail	Nov. 1, 1976	Yakima Meadows	MCl
380.80-to-1	Silas Green, 1987 g., by All Kings	Nov. 13, 1992	Laurel	Clm
377.20-to-1	Righteous Glory, 1986 m., by Roving Glory	May 5, 1990	San Juan	Clm
370.00-to-1	Native Skirt, 1975 h., by Northern Native	Feb. 1, 1982	Turf Paradise	Clm
345.70-to-1	Sal's Needle, 1986 h., by Flip Sal	Feb. 10, 1989	Garden State	MCl
344.64-to-1	Cowboy Shoes, 1979 h., by Great Sun	June 27, 1984	Ak-sar-ben	Alw
335.00-to-1	Glentress, 1976 m., by North Rock	June 14, 1982	Regina	Clm
335.00-to-1	Majestic Drifter, 1987 g., by Majestic Max	Sept. 25, 1991	Assiniboia	Clm
311.20-to-1	Smoky Isle, 1975 h., by Fiddle Isle	Dec. 21, 1982	Bay Meadows	Clm
310.00-to-1	Prince of Norwich, 1977 h., by Mr. Brogann	March 31, 1982	Waterford	Clm
299.10-to-1	Viv's Quip, 1985 h., by Quip	Oct. 3, 1987	Birmingham	Clm
293.64-to-1	Oak Tree, 1979 h., by Tarleton Oak	Feb. 17, 1982	Keystone	MSW
282.00-to-1	Rose o' Luck, 1974 m., by Real Luck	Sept. 23, 1977	Pomona	MSW
281.00-to-1	Rainbow Quartz, 1986 g., by Bold Josh	July 1, 1992	Monmouth	Clm
280.00-to-1	My Eternal Hope, 1988 m., by Rexson's Hope	Jan. 10, 1992	Rockingham	Clm
279.50-to-1	West Washington, 1995 g., by Jolly Blade	Jan. 7, 2000	Mountaineer	MCl
273.09-to-1	Bold Dole, 1979 h., by Bold Dun-Cee	Oct. 2, 1982	Thistledown	Clm
259.20-to-1	Black Ticket, 1972 h., by Green for Go	March 10, 1977	Fonner	Clm
259.10-to-1	Shashi Kala, 1980 m., by Rushton's Corsair	May 27, 1985	Darby Downs	Clm

Distance Equivalents

Race distances are directly or indirectly derived from distances conventionally run in England, the cradle of Thoroughbred racing. Distances of English races are measured in the traditional English system of furlongs and miles. A furlong is 660 feet, or one-eighth of a mile, and a mile comprises eight furlongs.

France has used the metric system instituted by Napoleon since the inception of racing in that country. As racing countries around the world have adopted the metric system of measurement, racing distances often have been changed to metric equivalents.

The following table includes equivalent distances for both systems.

Furlongs to Meters

Furlongs	Miles	Approx. Meters	Exact Meters
1.00	⅛	200	201.168
2.00	¼	400	402.336
3.00	⅜	600	603.504
4.00	½	800	804.672
4.50	9⁄16	900	905.256
5.00	⅝	1,000	1,005.840
5.50	11⁄16	1,100	1,106.424
6.00	¾	1,200	1,207.008
6.50	13⁄16	1,300	1,307.592
7.00	⅞	1,400	1,408.176
7.50	15⁄16	1,500	1,508.760
8.00	1	1,600	1,609.344
8.32	1&70 yds.	1,670	1,673.717
8.50	1 1⁄16	1,700	1,709.928
9.00	1 ⅛	1,800	1,810.512
9.50	1 3⁄16	1,900	1,911.096
10.00	1 ¼	2,000	2,011.680
10.50	1 5⁄16	2,100	2,112.264
11.00	1 ⅜	2,200	2,212.848
11.50	1 7⁄16	2,300	2,313.432
12.00	1 ½	2,400	2,414.016
12.50	1 9⁄16	2,500	2,514.600
13.00	1 ⅝	2,600	2,615.184
13.50	1 11⁄16	2,700	2,715.768
14.00	1 ¾	2,800	2,816.352
14.50	1 13⁄16	2,900	2,916.936
15.00	1 ⅞	3,000	3,017.520
15.50	1 15⁄16	3,100	3,118.104
16.00	2	3,200	3,218.688
16.50	2 1⁄16	3,300	3,319.272
17.00	2 ⅛	3,400	3,419.856
18.00	2 ¼	3,600	3,621.024
19.00	2 ⅜	3,800	3,822.192
20.00	2 ½	4,000	4,023.360
21.00	2 ⅝	4,200	4,224.528
22.00	2 ¾	4,400	4,425.696
23.00	2 ⅞	4,600	4,626.864
24.00	3	4,800	4,828.032

Meters to Furlongs

Meters	Approx. Furlongs	Approx. Miles	Exact Furlongs	Exact Miles
200	1.00	⅛	0.9942	0.1243
400	2.00	¼	1.9884	0.2485
600	3.00	⅜	2.9826	0.3728
800	4.00	½	3.9768	0.4971
900	4.50	9⁄16	4.4739	0.5592
1,000	5.00	⅝	4.9710	0.6214
1,100	5.50	11⁄16	5.4681	0.6835
1,200	6.00	¾	5.9652	0.7456
1,300	6.50	13⁄16	6.4623	0.8078
1,400	7.00	⅞	6.9594	0.8699
1,500	7.50	15⁄16	7.4565	0.9321
1,600	8.00	1	7.9536	0.9942
1,670	8.32	1&70 yds.	7.9784	0.9973
1,700	8.50	1 1⁄16	8.4506	1.0563
1,800	9.00	1 ⅛	8.9477	1.1185
1,900	9.50	1 3⁄16	9.4448	1.1806
2,000	10.00	1 ¼	9.9419	1.2427
2,100	10.50	1 5⁄16	10.4390	1.3049
2,200	11.00	1 ⅜	10.9361	1.3670
2,300	11.50	1 7⁄16	11.4332	1.4292
2,400	12.00	1 ½	11.9303	1.4913
2,500	12.50	1 9⁄16	12.4274	1.5534
2,600	13.00	1 ⅝	12.9245	1.6156
2,700	13.50	1 11⁄16	13.4216	1.6777
2,800	14.00	1 ¾	13.9187	1.7398
2,900	14.50	1 13⁄16	14.4158	1.8020
3,000	15.00	1 ⅞	14.9129	1.8641
3,100	15.50	1 15⁄16	15.4100	1.9263
3,200	16.00	2	15.9071	1.9884
3,300	16.50	2 1⁄16	16.4042	2.0505
3,400	17.00	2 ⅛	16.9013	2.1127
3,500	17.50	2 3⁄16	17.3984	2.1748
3,600	18.00	2 ¼	17.8955	2.2369
3,700	18.50	2 5⁄16	18.3926	2.2991
3,800	19.00	2 ⅜	18.8897	2.3612
3,900	19.50	2 7⁄16	19.3868	2.4233
4,000	20.00	2 ½	19.8839	2.4855
4,100	20.50	2 9⁄16	20.3810	2.5476
4,200	21.00	2 ⅝	20.8781	2.6098
4,300	21.50	2 11⁄16	21.3752	2.6719
4,400	22.00	2 ¾	21.8723	2.7340
4,500	22.50	2 13⁄16	22.3694	2.7962
4,600	23.00	2 ⅞	22.8665	2.8583
4,700	23.50	2 15⁄16	23.3636	2.9204
4,800	24.00	3	23.8607	2.9826

Countries and Measurements Used

Argentina	furlongs and meters
Australia	meters
Brazil	meters
Canada	furlongs
Chile	meters
England	furlongs
France	meters
Germany	meters
Hong Kong	meters
Ireland	furlongs
Italy	meters
Japan	meters
New Zealand	meters
United Arab Emirates	meters
United States	furlongs

Glossary of Common Racing and Breeding Terms

account wagering Betting by phone, in which a bettor must open an account with a track or an off-track agency. A synonym: phone betting.

acey-deucy Uneven stirrups, popularized by Racing Hall of Fame jockey Eddie Arcaro, who rode with his left (inside) iron lower than his right to achieve better balance on turns.

across the board A bet on a horse to win, place, and show. If the horse wins, the player collects three ways; if second, two ways (place and show); and if third, one way (show).

action 1) A horse's manner of moving. 2) A vernacular term for wagering.

added money Money added to the purse of a race by the racing association, a breeding fund, or other source. The association's money is added to the amount paid by owners in nomination, eligibility, entry, and starting fees. Added-money stakes became less common in the 1990s as more tracks went to guaranteed purses.

agent A person empowered to transact business for a stable owner or a jockey, or one empowered to sell or buy horses for an owner or a breeder.

aired Won particularly easily by open lengths.

all-age race A race for two-year-olds and up.

all out When a horse extends itself to the utmost.

allowance race A race for which the racing secretary drafts certain conditions to determine weights to be carried based on the horse's age, sex, past performance, or a combination of all three.

allowances Reductions in weights to be carried, with the adjustments based on the conditions of the race or because an apprentice jockey is on a horse. Also, a weight reduction that female horses are entitled to when racing against males or that three-year-olds receive against older horses.

also-eligible A horse officially entered for a race but not permitted to start unless the field is reduced by scratches below a specified number.

also-ran A horse that does not finish first, second, or third.

American Horse Council A national association of individuals, organizations, and companies formed as a lobbying group to represent all breeds of the horse industry. Based in Washington, D.C., the AHC works on tax regulations, import and export rules, disease prevention and control, trails and recreation enhancement, and humane concerns. Founded in 1969 as an advocate for the entire American horse industry, the AHC was founded principally by Thoroughbred interests concerned about legislation being discussed in Congress that would have negatively affected racing and breeding.

American Stud Book Official book of foal registrations in North America maintained by the Jockey Club.

apprentice allowance Weight concession given to an apprentice rider; usually ten pounds until the fifth winner, seven pounds until the 35th winner, and five pounds for one calendar year from the 35th winner. More rarely, a three-pound allowance for a rider under contract to a specific stable or owner for two years from his or her first win. This rule varies from state to state. Apprentices do not receive a weight allowance when riding in a stakes race.

apprentice jockey Rider at the beginning of his career who has not ridden a certain number of winners within a specified period of time. Also known as a bug rider or bug boy, from the asterisk used in racing programs and past performances to denote the weight allowance such riders receive.

apron The (usually) paved area between the grandstand and the racing surface.

Association of Racing Commissioners International (RCI) Formerly the National Association of State Racing Commissioners (NASRC). Its office is based in Lexington.

asterisk Used with names of horses to denote they were imported into the United States. Practice preceded the use of country codes starting January 1, 1977.

auxiliary starting gate A second starting gate used when the number of horses in a race exceeds the capacity of the main starting gate.

average earnings index (AEI) A breeding statistic that compares racing earnings of a stallion's or mare's foals to those of all other foals racing at that time. An AEI of 1.00 is considered average, 2.00 is twice the average, 0.50 half the average, etc.

baby race A race for two-year-olds.

backstretch 1) Straight portion of the far side of the racing surface between the turns. 2) Generally, a racetrack's stable area, which often contains dormitories, a track kitchen, chapel, and recreation area for stable employees. It gained its name because most stable areas are located along the racetrack's backstretch.

bad doer A horse with a poor appetite, a condition that may be due to nervousness or other causes.

bandage Wrappings used on a horse's legs are three to six inches wide and are made of a variety of materials. In a race, they are used for support or protection against injury. Rundown bandages are used during a race to affix a pad under the fetlock to avoid injury due to abrasion when the fetlocks sink toward the ground during the weight-bearing portion of the gallop. A horse also may wear standing bandages, thick cotton wraps used during shipping and while in the stall to prevent swelling, injury, or both, or to apply medication.

bar shoe A horseshoe closed at the back to help support the frog and heel of the hoof. It is often worn by horses with quarter cracks or bruised feet.

base The portion of the track that lies under the thick top layer, or cushion. The base provides support and drainage.

battery A term for an illegal electrical device used by a jockey to stimulate a horse by electrical shock during a race. Also known as a machine or a joint.

bay A horse color that varies from a yellow tan to a bright auburn. The mane, tail, and lower portion of the legs are always black, except where white markings are present.

bearing in (or out) Deviating from a straight course. May be due to weariness, infirmity, inexperience, or the rider overusing the whip or reins to make a horse alter its course.

bell Signal sounded when the starter opens the gates or, at some tracks, to mark the close of betting.

Beyer number A handicapping tool, popularized by author Andrew Beyer, assigning a numerical value (speed figure) to each race run by a horse based on final time and track condition. This enables different horses running at different racetracks to be objectively compared.

bid in The act of buying back a horse that does not meet a minimum price at public auction. Synonym for buy-back, reserve not attained (RNA).

Big Red Refers to either of two famous chestnut-colored horses: Man o' War or Secretariat.

Bill Daly (on the) Taking a horse to the front at the start of a race and remaining there to the finish. Term stems from "Father Bill" Daly, a famous old-time horseman who developed many great jockeys.

birthdays All Thoroughbreds born in the Northern Hemisphere celebrate their birthday on January 1. In the Southern Hemisphere, all Thoroughbred birthdays are as follows: South America, July 1; South Africa, Australia, and New Zealand, August 1.

bit A stainless steel, rubber, or aluminum bar attached to the bridle; it is placed in the bar, the space between front and back teeth in the horse's mouth, and is one of the means by which a jockey exerts guidance and control. The most common racing bit is the D-bit, named because the rings extending from the bar are shaped like the letter D. Most racing bits are snaffled (snaffle bit), which means the metal bar is made up of two pieces, connected in the middle, which leaves it free to swivel. Other bits may be used to correct specific problems, such as bearing in or out.

black A horse color that includes the hair and the skin of the muzzle, flanks, mane, tail, and legs, unless white markings are present.

black type Boldface type, used in sales catalogs and stakes results, to distinguish horses that have won or placed in a stakes race. Sales companies today have eliminated the use of black type for stakes below a certain monetary level—$15,000 in 1985; $20,000 from 1986-'89; $25,000 beginning in 1990; $30,000 beginning in 2002; $35,000 beginning in 2003; and $40,000 beginning in 2004. If a horse's name appears in boldface capital letters in a catalog or stakes results, the horse has won at least one black-type event. If the name appears in boldface type with capital and lower-case letters, the horse was second or third in at least one black-type event but has not won a black-type race.

blaze A generic term describing a large, white vertical marking on a horse's face.

blind switch A circumstance in which a rider's actions cause his or her mount to be impeded during a race when moving into a space in which the horse and rider find themselves blocked.

blinkers A cup-shaped device to limit a horse's vision and thus prevent it from swerving from objects or other horses on either side while racing. Blinker cups come in a variety of sizes and shapes to allow as little or as much vision as the trainer feels is necessary and may be attached to a hood or bridle.

blister Counterirritant causing acute inflammation; used to increase blood supply and blood flow and to promote healing in the leg.

bloodstock Horses of Thoroughbred breeding, especially such horses used for or considered in relation to racing.

bloodstock agent A person who advises or represents a buyer or a seller of Thoroughbreds at a public auction or a private sale. A bloodstock agent usually works on commission, often 5% of the purchase or sale price, and may also prepare a horse for sale.

blood typing A method of verifying a horse's parentage. Blood typing was usually completed within the first year of a horse's life and was necessary before registration papers were issued by the Jockey Club. Beginning in 2001, the Jockey Club adopted DNA technology to verify horse's parentage.

blowout A short, timed workout, usually a day or two before a race, designed to sharpen a horse's speed. Usually three-eighths or one-half mile in distance.

blue hen Used to describe an outstanding broodmare, the producer of a number of stakes winners and whose daughters, granddaughters, and great-granddaughters in turn produced important winners.

board Short for tote board, on which odds, betting pools, and other information is displayed.

boat race Slang for a fixed race.

bobble A bad step away from the starting gate, usually caused by the track surface breaking away from under a horse's hooves, causing it to duck its head or nearly go to his knees.

bolt Sudden veering from a straight course, usually to the outside rail.

bomb(er) A winning horse sent off at extremely high odds.

book 1) The group of mares being bred to a stallion in a given year. If a stallion attracts the maximum number of mares allowed by the farm manager, he has a full book. 2) A term used to describe a jockey's riding commitments with his agent.

bookie Short for bookmaker.

bookmaker A person who books bets.

bottom 1) Stamina in a horse developed over a long period of time. 2) Subsurface of a racing strip.

bottom line A Thoroughbred's breeding on the female side most specifically applied to the tail-female line listed on the bottom line of a standard pedigree diagram.

bounce A poor race run immediately after a career-best or near-best performance.

box 1) A wagering term denoting a combination bet whereby all possible numeric combinations are covered for certain horses. 2) A disadvantageous position in a race, behind and between horses. 3) A horse's stall.

boxed (in) To be trapped between, behind, or inside other horses.

brace (or bracer) Rubdown liniment used on a horse after a race or workout.

break 1) To train a young horse to wear a bridle and saddle, carry a rider, and respond to a rider's commands. Most often done when the horse is a yearling. 2) To leave from the starting gate.

breakage In pari-mutuel payoffs, which are rounded down to a nickel or dime, the pennies that are left over. Breakage may be used for any of a number of purposes. Depending upon a state's rules of racing, the money goes to the state, the track, purses, or benevolence programs.

breather Easing off on a horse for a short distance in a race to permit it to conserve or renew its strength.

bred A horse is considered to have been bred in the state or country where it was foaled.

breed-back rule Restriction imposed in some jurisdictions that, for a mare's offspring to be eligible for state-bred bonuses, the mare, after foaling, must be bred to a stallion standing in that state.

breeder Owner of the dam at time of foaling unless the dam was under a lease or foal-sharing arrangement at the time of foaling. In that case, the person specified by the terms of the agreement is the breeder of the foal.

Breeders' Cup Thoroughbred racing's year-end championship. Known as Breeders' Cup day, Breeders' Cup championship day, from 2001 to '05 as World Thoroughbred Championships, or beginning in '06 as World Championships, it consists of eight races conducted on one day at one of several major North American racetracks each year. (See Breeders' Cup chapter.)

Breeders' Cup Ltd. Corporate entity that oversees the Breeders' Cup program. It is a not-for-profit organization based in Lexington.

breeding fund A state fund set up to provide bonuses for state-breds.

breeding right The right to breed one mare per year to a specific stallion. Breeding rights, as opposed to stallion shares, do not usually come with bonuses (money derived from extra seasons sold), nor are they assessed expenses.

breeze (breezing) Working a horse at a moderate speed; less effort than handily.

bridge jumper A person who wagers large amounts of money, usually on short-priced horses to show, hoping to realize a small but almost certain profit.

bridle A piece of equipment, usually made of leather or nylon, that fits on a horse's head; other equipment, such as a bit and the reins, are attached to it.

broken wind Abnormality of the upper or lower respiratory tract causing loss of normal air exchange, generally resulting in reduced performance.

broodmare A mare that has been bred and is used to produce foals.

broodmare sire The maternal sire; the sire of the dam.

Broodmare Sire Index The Broodmare Sire Index is an average of the Racing Index (RI) of all foals (that started at least three times) out of the sire's daughters. For BSI to be calculated, a broodmare sire must be represented by a minimum of 75 starters lifetime.

brush 1) During a race when two horses lightly touch each other. 2) Injury that occurs when one hoof strikes the inside of the opposite limb. 3) A type of obstacle used in steeplechase racing.

bullet work The best workout time for a particular distance on a given day at a track. Derived from the printer's bullet that precedes the time of the workout in listings. Also known as a black-letter work in some parts of the country.

bullring A small racetrack, usually less than one mile in circumference.

buy-back A horse put through a public auction that fails to reach a minimum (reserve) price set by the consignor and so is retained. The consignor must pay a fee to the auction company based on a percentage of the reserve to cover the auction company's marketing, advertising, and other costs. A synonym for reserve not attained (RNA).

calk A projection on the heels of a horseshoe, similar to a cleat, on the rear shoes of a horse to prevent slipping, especially on a wet track. Also known as a sticker.

(race) call Running position of horses in a race at various points.

cast A horse positioned on its side or back and wedged against a wall, fence, or other object in such a way that it cannot get up.

chalk Wagering favorite in a race. Term dates from the days when on-track bookmakers would write current odds on a chalkboard, and the horse that was bet the most used the most chalk.

chalk player Bettor who wagers on favorites.

champion Horse or individual determined to be the outstanding performer in his or her division in a specific year. In the United States, champions are determined by the Eclipse Awards balloting.

chart A statistical picture of a race (from which past performances are compiled) showing the position and margin of each horse at designated points of call (depending on the distance of the race), as well as the horse's age, weight carried, owner, trainer, jockey, and the race's purse, conditions, payoff prices, odds, time, and other data. Before 1991, all charts were compiled by *Daily Racing Form*. From 1991 to '98, charts were compiled by both *Daily Racing Form* and Equibase; since mid-1998, charts have been compiled exclusively by Equibase.

check(ed) When a jockey slows a horse due to other horses impeding its progress.

chestnut 1) A horse color that may vary from a red-yellow to golden-yellow. The mane, tail, and legs are usually variations of coat color, except where white markings are present. 2) Horny, irregular growths found on the inside of the legs. On the forelegs, they are just above the knees. On the hind legs, they are just below the hocks. No two horses have been found to have the same chestnuts, and so chestnuts may be used for identification. Also called night eyes.

chute Extension of backstretch or homestretch to permit a straight start in a race, as opposed to starting on or near a turn.

claiming Process by which a licensed person may purchase a horse entered in a designated race for a predetermined price. When a horse has been claimed, its new owner assumes title after the starting gate opens although the former owner is entitled to all purse money earned in that race. Sometimes called halter or haltered, for the act of putting a new halter on a claimed horse so that it can be led back to its new barn.

claiming box, claims box Box in which claims are deposited before the race.

claiming race A race in which each horse entered is eligible to be purchased at a set price. Claims must be made before the race and only by licensed owners or their agents who have a horse registered to race at that meeting or who have received a claim certificate from the stewards. A claiming race in which there is an option to have horses entered to be claimed for a stated price or not eligible to be claimed is an optional claiming race.

classic 1) A race of traditional importance, usually modeled on one of the five original English classic races, and often considered part of a triple crown. 2) Used to describe a distance. The American classic distance is 1¼ miles on dirt. The European classic distance is 1½ miles on turf.

clerk of scales An official whose chief duty is to weigh the riders before and after a race to ensure proper weight is or was carried.

climbing When a horse lifts its front legs abnormally high as it gallops, causing it to run inefficiently.

clocker Individual who times workouts and races.

closer A horse that runs best in the latter part of the race, coming from off the pace.

clubhouse turn Generally, the turn on a racing oval that is closest to the clubhouse facility; usually the first turn after the finish line.

colors (horse) Colors accepted by the Jockey Club are bay, black, chestnut, dark bay or brown, gray or roan, and white. In 1996, the Jockey Club started combining gray and roan, which had been separate colors previously.

colt An ungelded (entire) male horse four years old or younger.

commingle Combining mutuel pools from off-track sites with the host track.

company Class of horses in a race or the class of horses a runner usually keeps.

comparable index (CI) Indicates the average earnings of progeny produced from mares bred to one sire when these same mares are bred to other sires. A CI of 1.00 is considered average, 2.00 is twice the average, and 0.50 half the average.

condition book(s) A series of booklets issued by a track's racing secretary setting forth conditions of races to be run at that track.

conditioner 1) A trainer. 2) A workout or race to enable a horse to attain fitness.

conditions The requirements for being able to enter a horse in a particular race as written by the track's racing secretary. Conditions may include age, sex, money or races won, weight carried, and the distance of the race.

conformation The physical makeup and bodily proportions of a horse.

connections Persons identified with a horse, such as owner, trainer, rider, and stable employees.

consolation double A payoff to holders of daily double tickets combining the winning horse in the first race of the double with a scratched horse in the second.

cooling out Restoring a horse to its normal body temperature, usually by walking, after it has become overheated during exercise or racing.

coupled (entry) Two or more horses running as an entry in a single betting unit.

cover A single breeding of a stallion to a mare.

crop 1) The number of foals by a sire in a given year. 2) All horses collectively born in the same year. 3) A jockey's whip.

cup horse A term once used to describe horses competing at the highest level of the sport in races at a distance of two miles or more.

cuppy (track) A drying and loose racing surface that breaks away under a horse's hooves.

cushion Top portion of a racetrack.

cut down Horse suffering injuries from being struck by the shoes of another horse. Or, due to a faulty stride, a horse may cut itself down.

daily double Type of wager calling for the selection of winners of two consecutive races, usually the first and second.

Daily Racing Form A daily newspaper containing news, past performance data, and handicapping information. Founded in 1895, it is the successor to the *Morning Telegraph*. The *Morning Telegraph* was founded in 1833 and was closed during a strike by printers in 1972.

dam The female parent of a foal.

dam's sire (broodmare sire) The sire of a broodmare. Used in reference to the maternal grandsire of a foal.

dark day A day when there is no racing at the track.

dark bay or brown A horse color that ranges from brown with areas of tan on the shoulders, head, and flanks, to a dark brown, with tan areas seen only in the flanks, muzzle, or both. The mane, tail, and lower portions of the legs are always black unless white markings are present.

dark horse Probably a good horse whose full potential is unknown before a race.

dead heat Two or more horses finishing a race in a tie.

dead track Racing surface lacking resiliency.

declared In the United States, a horse withdrawn from a race in advance of scratch time. In Europe, a horse confirmed to start in a race.

deep stretch A position very close to the finish line in a race.

Derby A stakes event for three-year-olds, deriving its name from Lord Derby, and usually the most important race for three-year-olds at a given track.

disqualification Change in order of finish by officials for an infraction of the rules.

distaffer A female horse.

distaff race A race for female horses.

distanced Horse so far behind the rest of the field of runners that it is out of contact and unable to regain a position of contention. A horse beaten more than 40 lengths.

dogs Rubber traffic cones (or a barrier) placed at certain distances out from the inner rail when the track is wet, muddy, soft, yielding, or heavy to prevent horses during the workout period from churning the footing along the rail.

dope 1) Any illegal drug. 2) Slang term for past performances: Readers of past performances are said to dope out a race.

dosage Although other dosage theories exist, the term is most commonly associated with the one interpreted by Dr. Steven Roman. A variation of Dr. Franco Varola's work on pedigree analysis, the system identifies patterns of ability in horses based on a list of prepotent sires, each of whom is designated a *chef-de-race*. The dosage system puts these sires into one of five categories: brilliant, intermediate, classic, solid, or professional, which are subjective judgments of speed and stamina. Sires can be listed in up to two *chef-de-race* categories. Each generation of sires is worth 16 points, divided by the number of sires; i.e., the immediate sire is worth 16 points while the four sires four generations back are worth four points apiece.

dosage index (DI) A mathematical reduction of the dosage profile to a number reflecting a horse's potential for speed or stamina. The higher the number, the more likely the horse is suited to be a sprinter. The average dosage index of all horses is about 4.00. The dosage index (DI) is derived from the dosage profile to reflect the ratio of speed to stamina in a pedigree. This is calculated by adding points from the two speed categories (brilliant and intermediate), plus half of those from the classic (middle) category, and dividing that total by the points from the two stamina categories (solid and professional), plus the other half of the classic points. The higher the DI, the more speed is imputed to be present in the pedigree. A 4.00 DI is generally the cutoff where a horse is considered not likely to be competitive at the American classic distance of 1¼ miles.

driving A horse that is all out to win and under strong urging from its jockey.

drop down A horse meeting a lower class of rival than it had been running against previously.

dwelt Extremely late in breaking from the gate.

earmuffs Equipment that covers a horse's ears to prevent it from hearing distracting sounds.

eased A horse that is gently pulled up during a race.

easily Running or winning without being pressed by rider or opposition.

Eclipse Award Thoroughbred racing's year-end awards, honoring the top horses and people in several categories. Named for the great 18th-century racehorse and sire Eclipse, who was undefeated in 18 career starts and sired the winners of 344 races. The Eclipse Awards are sponsored by the National Thoroughbred Racing Association, *Daily Racing Form*, and National Turf Writers Association. They were first awarded in 1971; previously, separate year-end champions were named by *Daily Racing Form* (beginning in 1936) and the Thoroughbred Racing Associations (beginning in 1950).

eligible Qualified to start in a race, according to conditions.

engagement 1) Stakes nomination. 2) Riding commitment.

entire An ungelded horse. In Europe, where geldings are not permitted to enter certain races, the race conditions might read: Entire colts and fillies.

entry Two or more horses with common ownership (in some cases, trained by the same trainer) that are paired as a single betting unit in one race or are placed together by the racing secretary as part of a mutuel field. Rules on entries vary from state to state. Also known as a coupled entry.

entry fee Money paid by an owner to enter a horse in a stakes race—and is what usually defines a race as a stakes. Entry fees are not required for overnight races and some invitational stakes races.

Equibase Co. A partnership between the Jockey Club and the Thoroughbred Racing Associations to establish and maintain an industry-owned, central database of racing records. Equibase past-performance information is used in track programs across North America. Formed in 1990, Equibase first collected data in '91. In 1998, it began supplying past performance information to *Daily Racing Form* and became the sole collector of racing data.

estrus (heat) Associated with ovulation; a mare usually is receptive to breeding during estrus. Referred to as horsing.

euthanize To end a horse's life by lethal injection because of a catastrophic injury or critical illness and thus prevent further pain and suffering.

evenly Neither gaining nor losing position during a race.

exacta (or perfecta) A wager in which the first two finishers in a race, in exact order of finish, must be picked. Called an exactor in Canada.

exacta box A wager in which all possible combinations using a given number of horses are bet on.

exercise rider Individual who is licensed to exercise a horse during morning training hours.

exotic (wager) Any wager other than win, place, or show that requires multiple combinations. Examples of exotic wagers: trifecta, pick six, pick three.

Experimental Free Handicap A year-end assessment of the best North American two-year-olds of the season. It is put together by a panel of racing secretaries under the auspices of the Jockey Club and is based on performances in unrestricted races. Two lists are drawn up, one for males and one for females. Only the handicap for two-year-olds is called the Experimental Free Handicap; lists for older horses are free handicaps. First started by Walter Vosburgh in 1933. Race based on Experimental was run at Aqueduct from 1940 to '56 at six furlongs (Experimental Free Handicap No. 1) and another from 1946 to '52 at $1\frac{1}{16}$ miles (Experimental Free Handicap No. 2).

extended Running at top speed.

farrier Horseshoer.

fast (track) Footing that is dry, even, and resilient.

fault Weak points of a horse's conformation or its character as a racehorse.

feather Light weight. Usually refers to the weight a horse is assigned to carry in a race.

fee 1) Amount paid to a jockey for riding in a race. 2) The cost of nominating, entering, or starting a horse in a stakes race.

fetal sexing Use of ultrasonography to identify genitalia of a fetus. Optimum time to perform fetal sexing is between 60 and 75 days of gestation.

field The horses in a race.

field horse (or mutuel field) Two or more starters running as a single betting unit (entry), when there are more starters in a race than positions on the totalizator board.

filly Female horse four years old or younger.

firm A condition of a turf course corresponding to fast on a dirt track.

flag Signal manually held a short distance in front of the gate at the exact starting point of a race. In some jurisdictions, official timing starts when flag is dropped by the flagman to denote proper start.

flak jacket Similar to a jacket worn by football quarterbacks, the jockey's flak jacket protects the chest, ribs, kidneys, and back from injury.

flat race Contested over a course without obstacles to jump. Often used in the term, on the flat.

flatten out A very tired horse that slows considerably, dropping its head on a straight line with its body.

float 1) An equine dental procedure in which sharp points on the teeth are filed down. 2) The instrument with which the above procedure is performed. 3) To drag a flat plate over a wet track surface to aid in draining water.

floating Flat plate or wooden implement (float) dragged over the surface of a wet track to aid in draining water.

foal(ed) 1) A horse of either sex in its first year of life. 2) Can also denote the offspring of either a male or female parent. 3) To give birth.

Fontana safety rail An aluminum rail, in use since 1981, designed to help reduce injuries to horse and rider. It has more of an offset (slant) to provide greater clearance between the rail and the vertical posts as well as a protective cover to keep horse and rider from striking the posts.

foundation mare A mare whose descendants show high quality and have impact on the breed after many generations.

founding sires The Darley Arabian, Byerly Turk, and Godolphin Arabian. Every Thoroughbred traces its male-line parentage to one of the three founding sires.

fractional time Intermediate times recorded in a race, as at the quarter-mile, half-mile, three-quarters, etc.

free handicap A race in which no nomination fees are required. More recently, and more commonly, a ranking of horses three years old and up by weight for a theoretical race or as an intellectual challenge.

front-runner A horse whose running style is to attempt to get on or near the lead at the start of the race and to continue there as long as possible.

frozen (track) The condition of a racetrack where any moisture present is frozen.

full brother, full sister Horses that share both the same sire and dam.

furlong One-eighth of a mile, which is equal to 220 yards or 660 feet.

furosemide A medication used in the treatment of bleeders, commonly known by the trade name Salix, a diuretic. Although research has not determined definitively how furosemide reduces bleeding, it is widely believed that the diuretic effect reduces pressure within capillaries in the lungs.

futurity A race for two-year-olds in which the owners make a scheduled series of payments over a period of time to keep their horses eligible. Purses for these races vary but can be considerable.

gait The characteristic footfall pattern of a horse in motion. Thoroughbreds have four natural gaits: walk, trot, canter, and gallop. Thoroughbreds compete at a gallop.

gap An opening in the rail where horses enter and leave the course.

Garrison finish A close victory, usually from off the pace. Derived from Ed "Snapper" Garrison, a 19th-century rider known for his close finishes.

gate card A card, issued by the starter, stating that a horse is properly schooled in starting-gate procedures.

gelding A male horse of any age that has been neutered by having both testicles removed (gelded).

gentleman jockey Amateur rider, generally in steeplechases.

get Progeny of sire.

girth An elastic and leather band, sometimes covered with sheepskin, that passes under a horse's belly and is connected to both sides of the saddle.

good (track) A dirt track that is almost fast or a turf course slightly softer than firm.

grab a quarter Injury to the back of the hoof or foot caused by a horse stepping on itself (affects the front foot). Very common in racing, the injury is usually minor.

graded race Established in 1973 to classify select stakes races in North America, at the request of European racing authorities, who had set up group races two years earlier. Grading of races is performed by a committee under the direction of the Thoroughbred Owners and Breeders Association. See graded stakes section in Racing chapter.

grandam A horse's grandmother. Also known as second dam when referring to the female line.

grandsire The grandfather of a horse; father (sire) of the horse's dam or sire.

grass slip Used in some areas, permission to exercise a horse on the turf course. Also known as a turf card.

gray A horse color in which the majority of the coat is a mixture of black and white hairs. The mane, tail, and legs may be either black or gray unless white markings are present. Starting with foals of 1993, the color classifications gray and roan were combined as gray or roan.

Grayson-Jockey Club Research Foundation A privately financed charitable organization established in 1989, which combined the Grayson Foundation Inc. (begun in 1940) and the Jockey Club Research Foundation.

group race Designation of best races in countries outside North America. European authorities began designating races as Group 1, Group 2, and Group 3 in 1971. North American officials, under the direction of the Thoroughbred Owners and Breeders Association, began grading races in 1973.

guineas By definition, a guinea is 21 shillings, or in current usage a pound and a shilling. Thus, the guinea is equal to 1.05 pounds. Used by sales companies in England and Ireland to report sales since it includes the sales company's 5% commission.

half brother, half sister Horses out of the same dam but by different sires. Horses with the same sire and different dams are not considered half siblings in Thoroughbred racing.

halter Like a bridle, but lacking a bit and reins. Used to handle horses around the stable and when they are not being ridden.

hand Four inches. A horse's height is measured in hands and inches from the top of the shoulder (withers) to the ground; that is, 15.2 hands is 15 hands, 2 inches, or a total of 62 inches. Thoroughbreds typically range from 15 to 17 hands.

handicap 1) Race for which the track handicapper assigns the weights to be carried. 2) To make selections on the basis of past performances.

handicap horse A horse that competes in handicap races.

handicapper 1) A person, usually the racing secretary, who assigns weights to horses. 2) A bettor who is making selections based on information of horses' performances from previous starts.

handily 1) Working in the morning with a strong effort. 2) A horse racing well within itself, with little exertion, during a race.

handle Amount of money wagered in the pari-mutuels on a race, a program, during a meeting, or for a year.

hand ride Urging a horse with the hands and not using the whip.

hard A condition of a turf course where there is no resiliency to the surface.

hardboot A Kentucky horseman.

hard-knocker A tough horse that makes a lot of starts.

harrow Implement or unit with pulling teeth, or tines, used to rake and loosen the upper surface of a track.

head A margin between horses. One horse leading another by the length of its head.

head of the stretch Beginning of the straight run to the finish line.

head to head Running on even terms.

heat 1) A race decided by two or more individual races over the same distance and between the same horses on the same day. Not used in flat racing today, though it was common in the 19th century. Still used occasionally in harness racing. 2) A breeding term for estrus in a mare.

heavy Wettest possible condition of a turf course; not usually found in North America.

helmet A lightweight fiberglass cap worn by riders to prevent head injuries. It is required equipment and is not considered part of a jockey's riding weight.

high weight Refers to highest weight assigned or carried in a race.

highweight Horse assigned the highest weight on the Experimental Free Handicap, a division of the International Classifications, or one of several free handicaps in individual countries, and often viewed as the equivalent of a champion in the absence of official championships.

homebred A horse bred by its owner.

homestretch Long section of racetrack closest to the stands.

hood A covering, usually nylon, that goes over a horse's head; blinkers or earmuffs may be attached to it.
hopped A horse that has been illegally stimulated with a drug.
horse When reference is made to sex, an ungelded male five years old or older.
Horsemen's Benevolent and Protective Association A national organization of horsemen, largely composed of owners, that has divisions at many racetracks in North America to help owners and trainers negotiate purses and other issues with track management.
hot walker A person or automatic machine that walks horses to cool them out after workouts or races.
hung A horse that does not advance its position in a race when called upon by its jockey.
icing 1) A physical therapy procedure, properly known as cryotherapy. 2) When a horse's leg or legs are placed in a tub of ice or ice packs are applied to the legs to reduce inflammation or swelling.
impost Weight carried by a horse or assigned to a horse.
inbreeding The mating of closely related individuals, resulting in a pedigree with at least one common ancestor duplicated on both sire's and dam's side of the pedigree. In Thoroughbreds, horses with one or more duplicated ancestors within the first four or five generations are generally considered inbred, while duplications of ancestors in more distant generations are often referred to as "linebreeding."
infield Area enclosed by the inner rail of the racetrack.
in hand Running under moderate control, at less than top speed.
inquiry A review of the running of the race to check into a possible infraction of the rules, called by the stewards. Also, a sign flashed by officials on the tote board on such occasions. If lodged by a jockey, it is called an objection.
in the money A horse that finishes first, second, or third in a race.
Irish rail Movable rail.
isolation barn A facility used to separate horses to ensure that disease is not carried into the area.
jail Requirement that when a claimed horse runs within 30 days of being claimed, it must run for a claiming price at least 25% higher than the price at which it was claimed.
Jockey Club Organization dedicated to the improvement of Thoroughbred breeding and racing. Incorporated February 9, 1894, in New York City, the Jockey Club serves as North America's Thoroughbred registry, responsible for the maintenance of the *American Stud Book*, a register of all Thoroughbreds foaled in the United States, Puerto Rico, and Canada; and of all Thoroughbreds imported into those countries from jurisdictions that have a registry recognized by the Jockey Club and the International Stud Book Committee.
jockey fee Sum paid to rider for competing in a race.
Jockeys' Guild National organization of professional riders.
jockey's race A race whose outcome will hinge mostly on strategic thinking by the riders; one in which riders must pay close attention to pace to keep their horses fresh for a strong finish.
jog Slow, easy gait commonly called a trot.
joint 1) Point of juncture of two bones and usually composed of fibrous connective tissue and cartilage. 2) Slang for an illegal electrical stimulation device.

jumper Steeplechase or hurdle horse.
juvenile Two-year-old horse.
key horse A single horse used in multiple combinations in an exotic wager.
kilometer One thousand meters and equal to .6214 of a mile.
lame A deviation from a normal gait due to pain in a limb or its supporting structures.
Lasix See Salix.
late double A second daily double offered during the latter part of a race program.
lead Refers to the leading leg when a horse is racing in full stride. The lead leg is the one that reaches out the farthest and bears the full weight of the horse's impact. Horses usually race on the left, or inside, lead on the turn, and on the right, or outside, lead on straightaways. Changing leads refers to the horse's ability to switch from one leading leg to the other at the proper time.
leaky-roof circuit Minor tracks.
leg up 1) To help a jockey mount a horse. 2) To improve a horse's fitness through long, slow gallops.
length A measurement approximating the length of a horse and used to describe the distances between horses in a race. A length is approximately eight feet.
listed race A stakes race just below a group race or graded race in quality.
lock Slang for a sure winner.
longe 1) A long rope or line fastened to a horse's head and held by a trainer, who causes the horse to move around in a circle. 2) A method of exercising a horse on a tether (longe line).
lug (bearing in or lugging out) Deviating from a straight course. May be due to weariness, infirmity, inexperience, or the rider overusing the whip or reins to make a horse alter its course.
maiden 1) A horse or rider who has not won a race. 2) A female horse that has never been bred.
maiden race A race for nonwinners.
mare Female horse five years old or older. Also, any female that has been bred regardless of age.
mare's month September. In theory, mares that have not run well during the summer often perform better in September.
mash Soft, moist mixture, hot or cold, of grain and other feed that is easily digested by horses.
massage Rubbing of various parts of the anatomy to stimulate healing.
match race A race between two horses.
medication list A list kept by the track veterinarian and published by the track showing which horses have been treated with legally prescribed medications.
meter The basic unit of length in the metric system. It is equal to approximately 39.37 inches. It takes 100 centimeters to make a meter and 1,000 meters to make a kilometer. To convert to inches, multiply by 39.37 (5 meters x 39.37 inches = 196.85 inches). To convert to yards, multiply by 1.1 (5 meters x 1.1 = 5.5 yards). Most European races are expressed in meters. A mile is approximately 1,600 meters, the distance at which the classic Poule d'Essai des Pouliches (Fr-G1) and the Poule d'Essai des Poulains (Fr-G1) are run. The Prix de l'Arc de Triomphe (Fr-G1) is 2,400 meters, or approximately 1½ miles; the Prix Eugene Adam (Fr-G2) is 2,000 meters, or approximately 1¼ miles. See Distance Equivalents table in preceding section.
middle distance Broadly, from one mile to 1¼ miles.

minus pool A negative mutuel pool created when a horse is so heavily played that, after deductions of state tax and commission, not enough money remains to pay the legally prescribed minimum on each winning bet. The racing association usually makes up the difference.

money rider A rider who excels in rich races.

monkey on a stick Type of riding with short stirrups popularized by riding great James F. "Tod" Sloan shortly before 1900.

morning glory Horse that performs well in morning workouts but fails to reproduce that form in races.

morning line Probable odds on each horse in a race, as determined by a mathematical formula used by the track oddsmaker, who tries to gauge both the ability of the horse and the most likely final odds as determined by the bettors. Those odds now are known as the program-line odds because they appear in the track's official program.

mud calks Special cleats that help a horse gain traction on a muddy track.

muddy (track) Condition of a racetrack that is wet but has no standing water.

mudder Horse that races well on muddy tracks. Also known as a mudlark.

mutuel pool Short for pari-mutuel pool. Sum of the wagers on a race or event, such as the win pool, daily double pool, exacta pool, etc.

muzzle 1) Nose and lips of a horse. 2) A guard placed over a horse's mouth to prevent it from biting or eating.

name (of a Thoroughbred) Names of North American Thoroughbreds are registered by the Jockey Club. They can be no longer than 18 characters, including punctuation and spaces.

National Thoroughbred Association Started as concept of advertising agency executive Fred Pope in early 1990s, with backing from owner-breeder John R. Gaines. The NTA was based on the concept that owners possess rights to their horses' images for simulcasting purposes, with the owners banding together to form a major league of racing through the pooling of simulcasting rights. Hamilton Jordan and Tim Smith were brought in to help sell the concept in 1997, and the NTA initiative eventually led to a broader industry coalition, the formation of the National Thoroughbred Racing Association. NTA officially was folded into the NTRA in August 1998.

National Thoroughbred Racing Association A not-for-profit association created by a consensus of industry factions to market the sport. Founding members were Breeders' Cup Ltd., the Jockey Club, Keeneland Association, and Oak Tree Racing Association, with each putting up $1-million in seed money. Before officially launching the office, the National Thoroughbred Association became a founding member when it ceased its existence and was rolled into the NTRA. In 2000, the Thoroughbred Owners and Breeders Association retroactively became a founding member. The NTRA first proposed a business plan to the industry in August 1997. The NTRA officially opened for business on April 1, 1998. Its first commissioner was Tim Smith. The NTRA formally merged many of its administrative functions with Breeders' Cup Ltd. on January 1, 2001.

National Museum of Racing and Hall of Fame Building in Saratoga Springs, New York, that houses a museum and a Racing Hall of Fame. The National Museum of Racing was founded in 1950. It had its first home in the old Canfield Casino, Congress Park, Saratoga Springs. It moved to its present site in 1955, when the Racing Hall of Fame was created.

near side Left side of a horse. Side on which a horse is mounted.

neck Unit of measurement. About the length of a horse's neck; a little less than one-quarter length.

nod Lowering of head. To win by a nod, a horse extends its head with its nose crossing the finish line ahead of a close competitor.

nominator One who owns a horse at the time it is named to compete in a stakes race or makes it eligible to a stakes program such as the Breeders' Cup.

North American Pari-Mutuel Regulators Association Organization founded in 1997 as a splinter group from the Association of Racing Commissioners International (RCI) due to philosophical differences in practices and policies. NAPRA's original members were Alabama, Arizona, Florida, Idaho, Kansas, Minnesota, Oklahoma, Oregon, Saskatchewan, South Dakota, Wisconsin, and Wyoming. Joining the organization by June 2005 were the Alberta Racing Corp., British Columbia, Colorado, Iowa, Manitoba, Montana, Nevada, North Dakota, Pennsylvania, and Virginia. Merged with RCI to form a unified association in 2005.

nose Smallest advantage a horse can win by. Called a short head in Britain.

nose band A strap that goes over the bridge of a horse's nose to help secure the bridle and keep the mouth closed. A figure-eight nose band goes over the bridge of the nose and under the rings of the bit to help keep the horse's mouth closed. The figure-eight nose band keeps the tongue from sliding up over the bit and is used on horses that do not like having a tongue tie used.

Oaks A stakes event for three-year-old fillies loosely patterned after England's Epsom Oaks and usually the most important race for that sex and age group at a given track.

objection Claim of foul lodged by rider, patrol judge, or other official after the running of a race.

odds-on Odds of less than even money.

oddsmaker The individual who prepares the program line for a track.

official 1) Notice displayed when a race result is confirmed. 2) Used to denote a racing official.

off side Right side of horse.

off-track betting Wagering at legalized betting outlets usually run by the tracks, management companies specializing in pari-mutuel wagering, or, in New York, by independent corporations chartered by the state. Wagers at OTB sites are usually commingled with on-track betting pools.

on the bit When a horse is eager to run. Also known as in the bridle.

on the board Finishing among the first three.

on the muscle Denotes a fit and eager horse.

on the nose Betting a horse to win only.

optional claiming A claiming race in which there is an option to have horses entered to be claimed for a stated price or not eligible to be claimed.

outcross When a horse has no inbreeding, especially within the first five generations.

out of the money A horse that finishes worse than third.

overcheck A strap that holds the bit in place.

overgirth An elastic band that goes completely around a horse's midsection and over the saddle, to keep the saddle from slipping.

overland, overland route Racing wide throughout, outside other horses.

overlay A horse going off at higher odds than it appears to warrant based on its past performances.

overnight A sheet published by the racing secretary's office listing the entries for an upcoming racing card.

overnight race A race in which entries close in a specific number of hours before running (such as 48 hours) and does not require an entry fee, as opposed to a stakes race for which nominations close weeks and sometimes months in advance and usually requires a monetary payment for a horse to be eligible.

over-reaching Toe of hind shoe striking the foreleg or foreleg.

overweight Excess weight carried by a horse when the rider exceeds the designated weight assignment.

pacesetter The horse that is running in front (on the lead).

paddock 1) Area where horses are saddled and paraded before being taken onto the track. 2) Field on a breeding farm where horses are turned out to graze.

paddock judge Official in charge of paddock and saddling routine.

panel A slang term for a furlong.

pari-mutuel A form of wagering originated in mid-1860s by Frenchman Pierre Oller in which all money bet is distributed to those who have winning tickets after taxes, takeout, and other deductions are made. Oller called his system perier mutuel, meaning mutual stake or betting among ourselves. As this wagering method was adopted in England, it became known as Paris mutuals, and later as pari-mutuels.

parlay A multirace bet in which all winnings are subsequently wagered on a succeeding race.

part wheel Using a key horse or horses in different, but not all, possible exotic wagering combinations.

pasteboard track A lightning-fast racing surface.

past performances A horse's racing record, earnings, bloodlines, and other data, presented in composite form.

patrol judges Officials who observe the progress of a race from various vantage points around the track.

pattern race Synonym for a group race in Europe.

photo finish A result so close it is necessary to use the finish-line camera to determine the order of finish.

pick (six—or other number) A type of multirace wager in which the winners of all the included races must be selected. Pick three (sometimes called the daily triple), pick six, and pick nine are commonly used by tracks in the United States.

pill Small numbered ball used in a blind draw to decide post positions.

pinched back A horse forced back when racing in close quarters, particularly on turns.

pin firing Thermocautery intended to increase blood flow to the leg and thus to promote healing.

pinhooker A person who buys a racehorse prospect with the intention of reselling it at a profit. Examples are weanling-to-yearling pinhookers and yearling-to-juvenile pinhookers.

pipe-opener Exercise at a brisk speed.

place Second position at finish.

place bet Wager on a horse to finish first or second.

placing judge Official who posts the order of finish in a race.

plate(s) 1) A prize for a winner. Usually less valuable than a cup. 2) Generic term for lightweight horseshoes, usually made of aluminum, that are used during a race.

plater Vernacular for a claiming horse.

pocket A position in a race with horses in front and alongside.

pole(s) Markers at measured distances around the track designating the distance from the finish. The quarter pole, for instance, is one-quarter mile from the finish line, not from the start.

Polytrack An artificial racing surface composed of polypropylene fibers, recycled rubber, and silica sand with a wax coating. Developed by Martin Collins of England, the surface was first used for North American racing at Turfway Park in September 2005. It had been installed at the Keeneland training track prior to that time.

pony Any horse that leads the parade of the field from paddock to starting gate. A horse that accompanies a Thoroughbred to the starting gate. Also known as a lead pony.

post 1) Starting point for a race. 2) An abbreviated version of post position.

post parade Horses going from paddock to starting gate past the stands.

post position Position of stall in starting gate from which a horse starts.

preferred list Horses with prior rights to starting, usually because they have previously been entered in races that have not filled with the minimum number of starters or they have been excluded from races that drew an excess of entries.

prep (race) A workout (or race) used to prepare a horse for a future engagement.

program line Probable odds on each horse in a race, as determined by a mathematical formula used by the track oddsmaker, who tries to gauge both the ability of the horse and the likely final odds as determined by the bettors. These odds are published in the track's official program and formerly were known as the morning line.

prop When a horse suddenly stops moving by digging its front feet into the ground.

public trainer One whose services are not exclusively engaged by a single stable and who accepts horses from a number of owners.

pull up To stop or slow a horse during or after a race or workout.

purse The total monetary amount distributed after a race to the owners of the entrants finishing in the top positions, usually five. Some racing jurisdictions may pay purse money through other places.

quarantine barn 1) A United States Department of Agriculture structure used to isolate foreign horses for a short period of time to ensure they are not carrying a disease. The structure may be at a racetrack, an airport, or a specially designated facility. Horses must be cleared by a federal veterinarian before being released from quarantine. 2) Any facility used to keep infected horses away from the general equine population.

quarter crack A vertical crack of the hoof between the toe and heel, usually extending into the coronary band.

quinella Wager in which the first two finishers must be picked in either order.

rabbit A speed horse running as an entry with another, usually a come-from-behind horse.

Racing Index Racing Index (RI) is based on the average earnings per start for all runners in the United States, Canada, England, Ireland, France, Italy, Germany, Puerto Rico, and the United Arab Emirates. RI is determined by calculating the average earnings per start, divided into males and females, of all starters in each individual country, and the average for each individual year is by definition 1.00. Median RI is much lower.

racing secretary Official who drafts conditions of races and assigns weights for handicap events.

racino A racetrack with other forms of gambling, especially slot machines.

rail The barrier on either side of the racing strip. Sometimes referred to as the fence.

rail runner Horse that prefers to run next to the inside rail.

rank A horse that refuses to settle under a jockey's handling in a race, running in a headstrong manner without respect to pace.

receiving barn Racetrack structure used to house horses shipping in for a race on a specific day. Horses trained on farms or at training centers often will be placed in the receiving barn until their races.

redboard 1) Old-time method of declaring a race official by posting a red flag or board on the tote board. 2) A mildly derogatory phrase used to describe someone who claims to have selected the winner, but always after the race.

refuse 1) When a horse will not break from the gate. 2) In jumping races, balking at a jump.

reins Long straps, usually made of leather, that are connected to the bit and used by the jockey to control the horse.

reserve A minimum price, set by the consignor, for a horse in a public auction.

reserved 1) Held for a particular engagement or race. 2) Held off the pace.

reserve not attained A minimum price, or reserve, set by the consignor for a horse at a public auction that is not met by those who are bidding. RNA.

resorption Death of an embryo or fetus before fourth month of gestation, usually followed by dehydration of the conceptus and self-dissolution of the remaining solid tissue.

ridden out A horse that finishes a race under mild urging; not as severe as driving.

ride short Using short stirrup leathers.

ridgling (rig) A term describing either a cryptorchid (neither testicle descended) or a monorchid (one testicle descended into the scrotum).

roan A horse color in which the majority of the coat is a mixture of red and white hairs or brown and white hairs. The mane, tail, and legs may be black, chestnut, or roan unless white markings are present. Starting with foals of 1993, the color classifications of gray and roan were combined as gray or roan.

rogue Ill-tempered horse.

route A race of long distance; broadly, a race at a distance of 1⅛ miles or more in North America.

router Horse that performs well at longer distances.

run-out bit A specialty bit to prevent a horse from bearing out (or in).

saddle A Thoroughbred racing saddle is the lightest saddle used, weighing less than two pounds.

saddlecloth A cotton cloth that goes under the saddle to absorb sweat. It usually has the horse's program number on it and, often in major races, the horse's name.

saddlepad A piece of felt, sheepskin, or more usually, foam rubber, used as a base for the saddle.

Salix An antibleeder medication that had been named Lasix until the medication's manufacturer, Intervet, changed the name in 2001. Its generic name is furosemide, and it was first used in veterinary practice in 1967.

savage When a horse bites another horse or a person.

scale of weights Fixed weights to be carried by horses according to their age, sex, race distance, and time of year. See scale of weights table in the Racing chapter.

schooling Process of familiarizing a horse with the starting gate and teaching it racing practices. A horse also may be schooled in the paddock. In steeplechasing, to teach a horse to jump.

schooling list List of horses eligible to school at the starting gate before being permitted to race.

scratch To be taken out of a race before a horse starts. Trainers or owners usually scratch horses due to adverse track conditions or a horse's health. A track veterinarian can scratch a horse at any time.

second call A secondary mount of a jockey in a race in case his primary mount is scratched.

second dam Grandmother of a horse in direct female line. Also known as a grandam.

set A group of horses being exercised together.

set down 1) To be suspended, usually referring to a jockey. 2) When a jockey assumes a lower crouch in the saddle while urging the horse to pick up speed.

sex allowance Female horses (fillies and mares), according to their age and the time of year, are allowed to carry three to five pounds less when racing against males.

shadow roll A bulky piece of material, usually sheepskin or synthetic fabric, that is secured over the bridge of a horse's nose to keep it from seeing shadows on the track. Often used with horses that shy away from shadows on the track or jump them.

shank Rope or strap attached to a halter or bridle by which a horse is led.

shedrow Stable area; walking path within a barn.

sheets A handicapping tool assigning a numerical value to each race run by a horse to enable different horses running at different racetracks to be objectively compared. Two principal companies in this field are operated by Len Ragozin, the originator, and Jerry Brown.

short A horse in need of more workouts or racing to reach winning form.

show Third position at the finish.

show bet Wager on a horse to finish in the money; third or better.

shut off Unable to improve position due to being surrounded by other horses.

silks Jacket and cap worn by riders to designate the owner of the horse, or at some smaller tracks, to designate post positions (e.g., yellow for post position one, blue for two, etc.).

Silky Sullivan A term sometimes used for a horse that makes a big run from far back. Named for the horse Silky Sullivan, who once made up 41 lengths to win

a six-furlong race.
simulcast A simultaneous live television transmission of a race to other tracks, off-track betting facilities, or other outlets for the purpose of wagering.
sire 1) The male parent. 2) To beget foals. According to cataloging standards and standard usage, a stallion must sire a winner before he can be called a sire; he is a stallion until that time.
Sire Index (SI) Sire Index is an average of the Racing Index (RI) of all foals by a sire that have started at least three times. For SI to be calculated, a sire must be represented by a minimum of three crops and 25 starters lifetime.
slipped A breeding term meaning spontaneous abortion.
sloppy A racing strip that is saturated with water and has standing water visible.
slow A racing strip that is wet on both the surface and base.
snip Small patch of white hairs on the nose or lips of a horse.
socks Solid white markings extending from the top of the hoof to the knee or hock. Also called stockings.
soft Condition of a turf course with a large amount of moisture. Horses' hooves sink deeply into the surface.
sophomores Three-year-old horses.
speed figure A handicapping tool in which a numerical value is assigned to a horse's performance.
speedy cut Injury to the inside of the knee or hock caused by a strike from another foot.
spit box A generic term describing a barn or area to which horses are taken for post-race testing. Tests may include saliva, urine, and/or blood.
spit the bit Or spit out the bit. A term referring to a tired horse that begins to run less aggressively.
split(s) Fractional times in a race in increments of one-eighth of a mile.
sprint Short race, less than one mile.
stakes A race for which the owner usually must pay a fee to run a horse. The fees can be for nominating, maintaining eligibility, entering, and starting; the track adds additional money to make up the total purse. Some stakes races are by invitation and require no payment or fee.
stakes horse A horse whose level of competition includes mostly stakes races.
stakes-placed Finished second or third in a stakes race.
stallion A male horse used for breeding.
stallion season The right to breed one mare to a specific stallion during one breeding season.
stallion share A lifetime right to breed one mare to a specific stallion each breeding season. Although generally limited to one mare per season per share, larger stallion books have in some cases allowed share owners to breed more than one mare each year. Stallion share owners are usually assessed a proportionate share of expenses and also will share in any bonuses.
stall walker Horse that moves about its stall constantly and frets rather than resting.
star 1) Any of several white markings on the forehead. (The forehead is defined as being above an imaginary line connecting the tops of the eyes.) 2) A type of credit a horse receives from the racing secretary if it is excluded from an overfilled race, giving it priority in entering future races.
starter 1) An official responsible for ensuring a fair start to the race. The starter supervises the loading of horses into the starting gate by assistant starters who collectively are known as a gate crew. The starter also has control of opening the gate. 2) A horse that is in the starting gate when the race begins, whether it runs or not.
starter race An allowance or handicap race restricted to horses that have started for a specific claiming price or less.
starting gate Partitioned mechanical device having stalls in which the horses are confined until the starter releases the stalls' front doors to begin the race.
stayer A horse that can race long distances successfully.
steadied A horse being taken in hand by its rider, usually when in close quarters.
steeplechase A race in which horses are required to jump a series of obstacles on the course. Steeplechase races in the United States are run over National Fences (artificial brush fences), natural brush fences, and timber fences. In England and Ireland, jump races are over hurdles and steeplechase fences.
step up A horse moving up in class to meet better competition.
steward Official of the race meeting responsible for enforcing the rules of racing.
stick A jockey's whip.
stirrups Metal D-shaped rings into which a jockey places his or her feet. They can be raised or lowered by shortening or lengthening the leather straps that connect the stirrups to the saddle. Also known as irons.
stockings Solid white markings extending from the top of the hoof to the knee or hock. Also called socks.
stone English system of weights is based on stones. A stone is equal to 14 pounds; thus, 126 pounds is nine stone.
(home) stretch Final straight; portion of the racetrack from the end of the final turn to the finish line.
stretch call Position of horses at the eighth pole, or one-eighth mile from the finish.
stretch runner Horse that runs fastest, relative to the pacesetters, nearing the finish of a race.
stretch turn Bend of track into the final straightaway.
stride Manner of going. Also, distance covered between successive imprints of the same hoof.
stripe A white marking running down a horse's face, starting under an imaginary line connecting the tops of the eyes.
stud 1) Male horse used for breeding. 2) A breeding farm.
stud book Registry and genealogical record of Thoroughbreds, maintained by the Jockey Club or Turf authority of another country.
subscription Fee paid by owner to nominate a horse for a stakes race or to maintain eligibility for a stakes.
substitute race Alternate race used on overnight sheets to replace a regularly scheduled race that does not fill or is canceled.
suckling A foal in its first year of life, while it is still nursing.
sulk When a horse refuses to extend itself.
swayback Horse with a prominent concave shape of the backbone, usually just behind the withers (saddle area). Lordosis.
tack Rider's racing equipment. Also applied to stable gear.
tail-male (-female) A horse's ancestry from sire to grandsire to great-grandsire, etc., tracing back to one of the three sires (or along the female line from

dam to grandam to great-grandam, etc., back to the original foundation mares).

tail off Used to describe a fit horse losing its competitive edge, or, in an individual race, when a horse slows down and loses contact with the field.

taken up A horse pulled up sharply by its rider due to being in close quarters.

takeout Commission deducted from mutuel pools that is shared by the track, horsemen (in the form of purses), breeding and benevolence funds, and local and state governing bodies in the form of tax. Also called take.

tattoo A permanent, indelible mark on the inside of the upper lip used to identify the horse.

teaser A male horse used at breeding farms to determine whether a mare is ready to receive a stallion.

teletimer Electronic means to time races, including fractional times at various points of call. The lead horse trips an electronic beam of light and the clockings are transmitted instantly to the tote board.

Thoroughbred A horse that traces in all lines of its pedigree to horses registered in previous volumes of the world's Thoroughbred stud books for at least eight consecutive crosses. All modern Thoroughbreds trace in male line to one of the three founding sires—the Darley Arabian, Byerly Turk, and Godolphin Arabian. The horse also must have satisfied the rules and requirements of the Jockey Club for inclusion in the *American Stud Book*, or it is registered in a foreign stud book recognized by the Jockey Club and the International Stud Book Committee.

Thoroughbred Horsemen's Association A representative group organized on local levels primarily in Mid-Atlantic states to represent the interests of owners in negotiations with tracks on purses and other issues. Started as an alternative to the Horsemen's Benevolent and Protective Association.

Thoroughbred Racing Associations An industry group founded in 1942 and comprising about 50 racetracks in North America.

tight Vernacular for fit and ready to race.

tightener 1) A race used to give a horse a level of fitness that cannot be obtained through morning exercise alone. 2) A leg race.

timber topper Steeplechase horse racing over post-and-rail fences.

tongue tie Strip of cloth or cloth-like material used to stabilize a horse's tongue to prevent it from choking down in a race or workout or to keep the tongue from sliding up over the bit, rendering the horse uncontrollable. Also known as a tongue strap.

top line 1) A Thoroughbred's breeding on its sire's side. 2) The visual line presented by the horse's back.

totalizator An automated pari-mutuel system that dispenses and records betting tickets, calculates and displays odds and payoffs, and provides the mechanism for cashing winning tickets. Often shortened to tote.

tote board Structure in the racetrack infield where up-to-the-minute odds and other information are listed. It also may show the amounts wagered in each mutuel pool as well as information such as jockey and equipment changes. Also known as the board.

tout Person who professes to have, and sells, advance information on a race.

track bias A racing surface that favors a particular running style or position.

track condition Physical state of the racetrack surface.

trial In Thoroughbred racing, a preparatory race created in tandem with a subsequent, more important stakes race to be run a few days or weeks later. In Europe, a trial can refer to a vigorous morning workout with other horses under race-like conditions.

trifecta A wager in which the first three finishers must be selected in exact order. Called a triactor in Canada and a triple in some parts of the United States.

trifecta box A trifecta wager in which all possible combinations using a given number of horses are bet upon.

trip An individual horse's race, with specific reference to the difficulty (or lack of difficulty) the horse had during competition, such as whether the horse was repeatedly blocked or had an unobstructed run.

Triple Crown Used generically to denote a series of three important races. In the United States, the Kentucky Derby, Preakness Stakes, and Belmont Stakes make up the Triple Crown. In England, the Two Thousand Guineas, Epsom Derby, and St. Leger Stakes. In Canada, the Queen's Plate, Prince of Wales Stakes, and Breeders' Stakes.

turn down(s) Rear shoe that is turned down—from a half-inch to one inch at the ends—to provide better traction on an off-track. Illegal in most jurisdictions.

twitch A restraining device usually consisting of a stick with a loop of rope or chain at one end, which is placed around a horse's upper lip and twisted, releasing endorphins that relax a horse and curb its fractiousness while it is being handled.

underlay A horse at shorter odds than seem warranted by its past performances.

under wraps Horse under stout restraint in a race or workout to keep it from pulling away from the competition by too large a margin.

untried 1) Not raced or tested for speed. 2) A stallion that has not been bred.

unwind Gradually withdrawing a horse from intensive training.

valet A person employed by a racing association to clean and care for a jockey's tack and other riding equipment.

walkover A race in which only one horse competes.

washed out A horse that becomes so nervous that it sweats profusely. Also known as washy or lathered (up).

weanling A foal less than one-year-old that has been separated (weaned) from its dam.

weigh out (in) The certification by the clerk of scales of a rider's weight before (after) a race. A jockey weighs in fully dressed with all equipment except for his or her helmet, whip, and flak jacket.

weight for age An allowance condition in which each entrant is assigned a weight according to its age. Females usually receive a sex allowance as well.

wheel Betting all possible combinations in an exotic wager using at least one horse as the key.

white A horse color, extremely rare, in which all the hairs are white. The horse's eyes are brown.

wire The finish line of a race.

workout A fast gallop at a predetermined distance.

yearling A horse in its second calendar year of life, beginning January 1 of the year following its birth for horses born in the Northern Hemisphere.

yielding Condition of a turf course with considerable moisture. Horses feet sink into it noticeably.

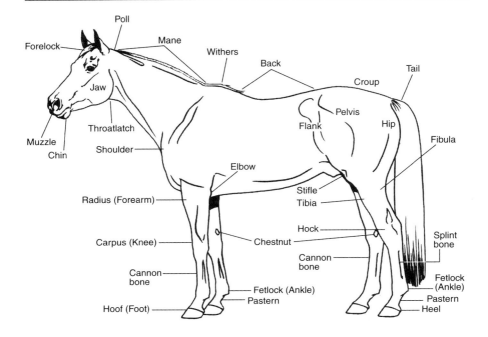

Conformation and Anatomy Terms

The following are words and expressions commonly used to describe Thoroughbred anatomy and conformation. This glossary contains many terms and definitions found in *The Media Guide to Equine Sport*, published by the American Association of Equine Practitioners.

angular limb deformity A limb that does not have correct conformation because of developmental problems in the angles of the joints.

anterior Toward the front.

back at the knee Conformation fault of foreleg. Upper leg is set back farther than lower leg, placing strain on tendons and ligaments. Synonym for calf knees.

cannon bone The third metacarpal (front leg) or metatarsal (rear leg), also referred to as the shin bone. The largest bone between the knee and ankle joints.

carpus A joint in the horse's front leg, more commonly referred to as the knee.

caudal Toward the tail.

cervical vertebrae Seven vertebrae that form the neck.

chestnut Horny growth on inside of each leg; located above the knee in the foreleg and below the hock in the hind leg. No two chestnuts are believed to be identical, and therefore were used for identification of horses in the registration process for many years. Also known as night eyes.

coccygeal vertebrae Eighteen vertebrae that form the tail in the Thoroughbred.

coffin bone The third phalanx (P3). The major bone within the confines of the hoof. Also called the pedal bone.

conformation The physical makeup and bodily proportions of a horse; how the horse is put together.

coronary band Where the hair meets the hoof. Also called the coronet.

cow hocks Abnormal conformation in which the points of the hocks turn in.

cranial Toward the head.

curb A thickening of the plantar ligament of the hock.

deep flexor tendon Present in all four legs, but injuries most commonly affect the front legs. Located on the back (posterior) of the front leg between the knee and the foot and between the hock and the foot on the rear leg. The function is to flex the digit (pastern) and knee (carpus) and to extend the elbow on the front leg and extend the hock on the rear leg. Functions in tandem with the superficial flexor tendon.

digital The part of the limb below the ankle (fetlock) joint. Includes the long and short pastern bones and the coffin bone.

digital cushion The area beneath the coffin bone in the back of the foot that separates it from the frog. The digital cushion serves as a shock absorber.

distal Away from a reference point. Usually refers to the limbs.

distal sesamoidean ligaments Attach to the bottom of the sesamoid bones, passing down and attaching to the long and short pastern bones.

Reference — Anatomy Terms

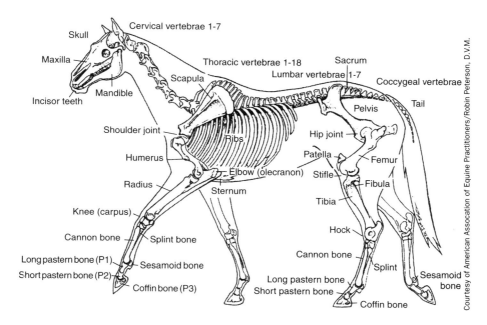

dorsal Up; toward the back or spine. Also used to describe the front of the lower limb below the knee (front) or hock (rear).

elbow (olecranon) Joint in forelimb that connects the humerus to the radius and ulna.

extensor tendon Extends the knee (carpus) joint, ankle joint, pastern, and foot and flexes the elbow. The muscles begin above the knee and attach to the coffin and pastern bones.

fault Weak points of a horse's conformation or its character as a racehorse.

femur Large bone of the hind limb that connects with the pelvis at the hip joint and the hind leg at the stifle joint.

fetlock Joint located between the cannon bone and the long pastern bone, also referred to as the ankle.

fibula Smaller bone in hind leg that extends half the length of the tibia and sits parallel to it. Taken together, the area from the stifle to the hock joint that includes the tibia and fibula is referred to as the gaskin.

frog The V-shaped, pliable support structure on the bottom of the foot.

hip joint Ball-and-socket joint in the hindquarters that accommodates the head of the femur.

hock A large joint just above the shin bone in the rear legs. Corresponds to the level of the knee of the front leg.

hoof The foot of the horse. Consists of several parts that play an integral role in supporting the weight of the horse.

humerus Long bone of the upper forearm that forms the point of the shoulder. The humerus connects the shoulder blade (scapula) to the radius and ulna, the two bones that compose the lower forearm.

inferior check ligament A direct continuation of the posterior (back) ligaments of the knee (carpus), located below the knee. Function is in support of the deep flexor tendon.

insensitive laminae The layer just under the wall of the hoof; similar to the human fingernail. It is an integral structure that helps attach the hoof wall to the underlying coffin bone.

joint Point of juncture of two bones and usually composed of fibrous connective tissue and cartilage.

joint capsule The sac-like structure that encloses the ends of bones in certain joints; contains synovial fluid.

ligament A band of fibrous tissue that connects bones, supports and strengthens joints, and limits the range of motion. Some ligaments support certain organs.

lumbar vertebrae Six vertebrae over the loin, immediately behind the rib cage.

mandible Lower jaw that contains teeth.

maxilla Upper jaw that contains teeth.

medial Pertaining to the middle in anatomy, nearer the median plane (the vertical plane that bisects the body into right and left halves).

metacarpal The cannon bone, located between the knee and the fetlock joint in the front leg. The cannon bone of the front leg is the third metacarpal.

metatarsal Cannon bone in the hind leg.

musculoskeletal system Consisting of the bones, muscles, ligaments, tendons, and joints of the head, vertebral column, and limbs, together with the associated muscles, tendons, ligaments, and joints.

muzzle Nose and lips of a horse.

navicular bone A small, flat bone within the confines of the hoof that helps, along with the short pastern bone and the coffin bone, to make up the coffin joint.

open knee A condition of young horses in which the physis of the knee has not closed; an immature knee. Often used to describe the status of the physis immediately above the knee and is an indicator of long-bone growth in two-year-olds.

over at the knee A leg that looks as though it has a forward arc with its center at the knee when viewed from the side.

palmer Pertaining to the back of the front limb from the knee down.

parrot mouth A horse with an extreme overbite.

pastern Bones in the area between the fetlock joint and the hoof. The joint between the long and short pastern bones is called the pastern joint. Can also be used to describe the area of the limb or to describe a specific bone: long pastern bone. Technically known as the P1 (long) and the P2 (short).

patella Bone in the stifle joint, similar to human knee cap. Ligaments attach it to the femur and the tibia.

pelvis Bone structure of the hindquarters that joins the spine around the sacrum, the fused bones of the spine. The largest structure of the pelvis is the os coxae, or hip bone.

physis The growth plate at the end of the long bones (such as the cannon bone) that lets the bone grow in length.

plantar Pertaining to the sole of the foot or back of the hind limb from the hock down.

plantar ligament The large ligament that is below and behind the hock joint.

poll The top of the head between the ears.

posterior Situated behind or toward the rear.

proximal Toward the body; the proximal cannon region is the upper portion of the cannon bone.

radius Long bone of the foreleg that extends from the elbow to the knee; principal bone of the lower forearm.

respiratory system Organ system responsible for gas exchange from nostrils to lungs.

sacral vertebrae Five fused vertebrae that make up the hip girdle.

scapula Shoulder blade in the foreleg.

sensitive laminae The area of the hoof that contains nerves and vessels.

sesamoid Two small bones (medial and lateral sesamoids) located above and at the back of the fetlock joint. Four common fractures of the sesamoids are apical (along the top of the bone), abaxial (the side of the sesamoid away from the ankle joint), midbody (sesamoid broken in half), and basilar (through the bottom) fractures. Fractures can be small chips or involve the entire bone. Surgical repair is often done by arthroscopy.

shoulder joint Ball-and-socket joint between the shoulder blade and humerus in the foreleg. Sometimes referred to as the scapulo-humeral joint.

sickle hocks Forward deviation of the lower hind leg, from the hocks to the hoof, producing the appearance of a sickle when viewed from the side. Also known as curby hocks.

splint Either of the two small bones that lie along the sides of the cannon bone.

stifle Hinge joint between the femur and tibia of the hind leg, similar to the human knee. It is the largest joint in the horse's body.

superficial flexor tendon Present in all four legs, but injuries most commonly affect the front legs. Located on the back (posterior) of the front leg between the knee and the foot and between the hock and the foot in the rear leg. Functions are to flex the digit (pastern) and knee (carpus), to extend the elbow on the front leg, and to extend the hock on the rear leg. Functions in tandem with the deep flexor tendon.

superior check ligament Fibrous band of tissue that originates above the knee and attaches to the superficial flexor tendon. Primary function is support of this tendon. Accessory ligament of the superficial flexor tendon.

suspensory ligament Originates at the back of the knee (front leg) and the back of the top part of the cannon bone (hind leg), attaching to the sesamoid bones. The lower portion of the ligament attaches the lower part of the sesamoid bones to the pastern bones. Its function is to support the fetlock. The lower ligaments that attach the sesamoid bone to the pastern bones are the distal sesamoidean ligaments.

synovial joint A movable joint that consists of articulating bone ends covered by articular cartilage held together with a joint capsule and ligaments and containing synovial fluid in the joint cavity.

synovial sheath The inner lining of a tendon sheath that produces synovial fluid. Allows ease of motion for the tendons as they cross joints.

tendon Cords of strong, white (collagen) elastic fibers that connect a muscle to a bone or other structure and transmit the forces generated by muscular contraction to the bones.

thoracic vertebrae Eighteen vertebrae in the horse's midsection that connect to the ribs.

throatlatch Point on underside of horse's head where it meets the neck.

tibia Larger of the two bones of the hind leg that extend from the stifle to the hock.

toe-in A conformation flaw in which the front of the foot angles inward and looks pigeon-toed, often causing the leg to swing outward during locomotion (paddling).

toe-out A conformation flaw in which the front of the foot faces out, often causing the leg to swing inward during locomotion (winging).

ventral Down; toward the belly.

vocal folds The membranes attached to the arytenoid cartilages in the larynx. Vibration produces vocalization.

white line When looking at the sole of the foot, the thin area between the insensitive outer hoof wall (insensitive laminae) and the inner sensitive laminae.

withers Area above the shoulder, where the neck meets the back.

Common Veterinary Terms

The following are commonly used veterinary terms. This glossary contains many terms and definitions found in the *Media Guide to Equine Sport*, published by the American Association of Equine Practitioners.

acupressure Utilizing stimulation on acupuncture points to treat an animal.

acupuncture A centuries-old therapy for treating an animal or human through the use of needles, electrical current, or moxibustion (heat and herbs) to stimulate or realign the body's electrical fields.

anhydrosis Inability to sweat in response to work output or increases in body temperature. Most commonly occurs when both temperature and humidity are high.

anterior enteritis Acute inflammation of the small intestine producing signs of abdominal distress, such as colic and diarrhea.

arthritis Inflammation of a joint. An increase in the amount of synovial fluid in the joint is a result of this inflammation.

arthroscope A thin tube containing a lens that is used for viewing areas inside a joint. Usually attached to a small video camera.

arthroscopic surgery Utilizing an arthroscope to perform surgery, eliminating the need to open the joint with a large incision to view the damaged area.

articular cartilage Cartilage that covers the ends of bones where they meet in a joint.

arytenoid cartilages Triangular cartilages in the upper part of the entrance to the larynx. Movements of the arytenoid cartilages control the diameter of the laryngeal opening.

ataxia Loss or failure of muscular coordination.

atrophy To waste away; usually used in describing muscles.

bleeder A horse that bleeds within its lungs when small capillaries that surround the lungs' air sacs (alveoli) rupture. The veterinary term is exercise-induced pulmonary hemorrhage. Blood may be seen coming out of the horse's nostrils, known as epistaxis, although it is typically discovered by an examination using a fiber-optic endoscope after exercise or racing. Hot, humid weather and cold conditions are known to exacerbate the problem. The most common preventive treatment currently available is the use of the diuretic furosemide (Salix). Less than one bleeder in 20 shows signs of epistaxis.

blister Counterirritant causing acute inflammation; used to increase blood supply and blood flow to promote healing in the leg.

bog spavin A filling with excess synovial fluid of the largest joint of the hock, called the tibial tarsal joint.

bone graft Utilizing bone taken from one part of the body to promote formation of bone in another region.

bone spavin Arthritis of the hock joint. A bone spavin that has progressed to the point that the arthritis can be seen externally is called a jack spavin.

bowed tendon A type of tendinitis. The most common injury to the tendon is a strain or bowed tendon, so named because of the appearance of a bow shape due to swelling. The most common site of injury is in the superficial flexor tendon between the knee and the ankle. Despite aggressive treatment with anti-inflammatory drugs, physical therapy, and rest, horses commonly reinjure the tendon when they return to strenuous training. Two surgeries are felt to aid horses to come back to racing: tendon splitting at the lesion site to release accumulated fluid and blood, and superior check ligament desmotomy. The latter surgery is designed to reduce forces on the tendon when the horse returns to training and racing.

breakdown When a horse suffers a potentially career-ending injury, usually to the leg.

broken wind Abnormality of the upper or lower respiratory tract causing loss of normal air exchange, generally resulting in reduced performance.

bronchodilator A drug that widens the airways in the lungs to improve breathing and to relieve muscle contraction or accumulation of mucus.

bucked shins Inflammation of the covering of the bone (periosteum) of the front surface of the cannon bone to which young horses are particularly susceptible. Usually a condition of the front legs.

bursa A sac containing synovial fluid (a natural lubricant). Its purpose is to pad or cushion and thus facilitate motion between soft tissue and bone, most commonly where tendons pass over bones.

bursitis Inflammation in a bursa that results in swelling due to accumulation of synovial fluid.

Bute Short for phenylbutazone, a nonsteroidal anti-inflammatory medication that is legal in many racing jurisdictions. Often known by the trade names Butazolidin and Butazone.

capillary refill time The amount of time it takes for blood to return to capillaries after it has been forced out, normally two seconds; usually assessed by pressing the thumb against the horse's gums. When the pressure is removed, the gum looks white but the normal pink color returns as blood flows into the capillaries.

capped elbow Inflammation of the bursa over the point of the elbow. Also known as a shoe boil.

capped hock Inflammation of the bursa over the point of the hock.

chiropractic The use of bone alignment to treat specific or general health problems.

chronic obstructive pulmonary disease Commonly known as COPD, a hyperallergenic response of the respiratory system that involves damage to the lung tissue, similar in many ways to human asthma. Affected horses may cough, develop a nasal discharge, and have a reduced tolerance for exercise. Respiratory rate is increased and lung elasticity is diminished.

chronic osselet Permanent buildup of synovial fluid in a joint, characterized by inflammation and thickening of the joint capsule over the damaged area. Usually accompanied by changes in the bone and cartilage.

clenbuterol A bronchodilator used for respiratory ailments. It is not permissible for use on race day.

closed knees A condition when the cartilaginous growth plate above the knee (distal radial physis) has turned to bone. Indicates completion of long bone growth and is one sign of maturity.

Coggins test Used to identify antigens or antibodies against equine infectious anemia.

colic Often used broadly to describe abdominal pain, it is the leading cause of death in horses. Its causes include obstruction in the large colon; a twist in the intestine that shuts off the food passageway and blocks the blood supply; or gastric ulcers.

comminuted A fracture with more than two fragments.

compound A fracture in which the damaged bone breaks through the skin. Also known as an open fracture.

condylar A fracture in the knuckle (condyle) of the lower (distal) end of a long bone such as the cannon bone or humerus (upper front limb).

congenital Present at birth.

contagious equine metritis A venereal disease. Mares may have a profuse vaginal discharge. No symptoms of CEM may be obvious in stallions.

corticosteroids Hormones (class of steroid) that are either naturally produced by the adrenal gland or man-made. They function as anti-inflammatory hormones or as hormones that regulate the chemical stability (homeostasis) of the body.

cough To expel air from the lungs in a spasmodic manner. Can be a result of inflammation or irritation to the upper airways (pharynx, larynx, or trachea) or may involve the lower airways of the lungs (deep cough).

cracked hoof A vertical split of the hoof wall. Cracks may extend upward from the bearing surface of the wall or downward from the coronary band, as the result of a defect in the band. Varying in degrees of severity, cracks can result from injuries or concussion. Hooves that are dry or thin (shelly) or improperly shod are susceptible to cracking upon concussion. Corrective trimming and shoeing may remedy mild cracks, but in severe cases, when the crack extends inward to the sensitive laminae, more extensive treatment is required, such as using screws and wires to stabilize the sides of the crack.

cribber A horse that clings to objects with its teeth and sucks air into its stomach. Also known as a wind sucker.

cryptorchid A unilateral cryptorchid is a male horse of any age that has one testicle undescended. A bilateral cryptorchid is a male horse of any age that has both testicles undescended. The Jockey Club defines cryptorchid as a male horse of any age that has both testicles undescended.

cup Refers to the irregular occlusal surface of the tooth (the surfaces that meet when a horse closes its mouth) and is used as a visual method of determining age in a horse.

curb A thickening of the plantar ligament of the hock.

degenerative joint disease Any joint problem that has progressive degeneration of joint cartilage and the underlying (subchondral) bone. Occurs most frequently in the joints below the radius in the foreleg and femur in the hind leg. Some of the more common causes include repeated trauma, conformation faults, blood disease, traumatic joint injury, subchondral bone defects, osteochondritis dissecans (OCD) lesions, and excessive intra-articular corticosteroid injections. Also known as osteoarthritis or as developmental orthopedic disease (DOD).

desmitis Inflammation of a ligament. Often a result of tearing of any number of ligament fibrils.

deworming The use of drugs (anthelmintics) to kill internal parasites, often performed by administration of oral paste or liquid or by passing a nasogastric tube into the horse's stomach.

digestible energy The amount of energy a horse is able to digest from its feed.

DMSO Dimethyl sulfoxide, a topical anti-inflammatory. Its chief characteristic is its ability to penetrate the skin and therefore act as a vehicle for medications.

dorsal displacement of the soft palate A condition in which the soft palate, located on the floor of the airway near the larynx, moves up into the airway. A minor displacement causes a gurgling sound during exercise, while in more serious cases the palate can block the airway. This is sometimes known as choking down, but the tongue does not actually block the airway. The base of the tongue is connected to the larynx, of which the epiglottis is a part. When the epiglottis is retracted, the soft palate can move up into the airway (dorsal displacement). This condition can sometimes be managed with equipment such as a figure-eight noseband or a tongue tie. In more extreme cases, surgery might be required, most commonly a myectomy.

drench Liquid administered through mouth.

Eastern equine encephalomyelitis One of several different types of encephalomyelitis that are extremely contagious, causing sickness and death in horses by affecting the central nervous system. EEE is spread by mosquitoes and can affect humans. Can be prevented by annual vaccination.

endoscope An instrument used for direct visual inspection of a hollow organ or body cavity such as the upper airway or stomach. A fiber-optic endoscope comprises a long, flexible tube that has a series of lenses and a light at the end to allow the veterinarian to view and photograph the respiratory system through the airway. Other internal organs may be viewed through a tiny surgical opening. A video endoscope has a small camera at its tip.

entrapped epiglottis A condition in which the thin membrane lying below the epiglottis moves up and covers the epiglottis. The abnormality may obstruct breathing. It is usually corrected by surgery to cut the membrane if it impairs respiratory function.

enzyme-linked immunosorbant assay A test, commonly referred to as the ELISA test, that is used after a race to detect the presence of drugs in racehorses. The post-race ELISA test was developed in the early 1990s by the University of Kentucky.

epiphysitis An inflammation in the growth plate (physis) at the ends of the long bones (such as the cannon bone). Symptoms include swelling, tenderness, and heat. Although the exact cause is unknown, contributing factors seem to be high caloric intake (either from grain or a heavily lactating mare) and a fast growth rate.

epistaxis Blood coming out of the horse's nostrils. See bleeder.

Epogen Genetically engineered form of the natural hormone erythopoietin (EPO) used to stimulate red blood cell production and thereby increase stamina. Abuse may cause fatal anemia. Banned by the Association of Racing Commissioners International as a Class 2 performance-enhancing drug.

equine protozoal myeloencephalitis Commonly called EPM. A neurological condition in a horse caused by a parasite that infects the horse's central nervous system. The cause of EPM is *Sarcocystis neurona*, a small protozoan organism that is slightly larger than a bacterium. The host necessary to complete the organism's life cycle is the opossum.

equine viral arteritis A highly contagious disease that is characterized by swelling in the legs of all horses and swelling in the scrotum of stallions. EVA can cause abortion in mares and can be shed in the semen of stallions for years after infection.

exercise-induced pulmonary hemorrhage (EIPH) See bleeder.

fissure Longitudinal crack through only one surface of a bone.

float An equine dental procedure in which sharp points on the teeth are filed down.

founder See laminitis.

fracture A break in a bone.

furosemide A medication used in the treatment of bleeders, commonly known by the trade name Salix, a diuretic.

gastric ulcers Ulceration of a horse's stomach. Often causes symptoms of abdominal distress (colic) and general unthriftiness.

gravel Infection of the hoof resulting from a crack in the white line (the border between the insensitive and sensitive laminae). An abscess usually forms in the sensitive structures and eventually breaks through at the coronet as a result of the infection.

green osselet In young horses, a swelling in the fetlock joint, particularly on the front of the joint where the cannon and long pastern bones meet. This swelling is a result of inflammation and reactive changes of the front edges of these two bones and adjacent cartilage. If the green osselet does not heal, a chronic osselet might develop with a permanent buildup of synovial fluid in the joint and inflammation and thickening of the joint capsule over the damaged area with secondary bone changes following the initial inflammation.

heaves Emphysema.

heel crack A crack on the heel of the hoof. Also called a sand crack.

hematoma A blood-filled area resulting from injury.

hyaluronic acid A normal component of joint fluid. Also can be a man-made intra-articular medication used to relieve joint inflammation.

impaction A type of colic caused by a blockage of the intestines by ingested materials (constipation).

intra-articular Within a joint.

intramuscular An injection given in a muscle.

intravenous An injection given in a vein.

ischemia Deficiency of blood supply, either temporary or permanent. Caused by the shutting down of blood vessels.

lactic acid Organic acid normally present in muscle tissue, produced by anaerobic muscle metabolism as a byproduct of exercise. An increase in lactic acid causes muscle fatigue, inflammation, and pain.

lame A deviation from a normal gait due to pain in a limb or its supporting structures.

laminitis An inflammation of the sensitive laminae of the foot. Many factors are involved, including changes in the blood flow through the capillaries of the foot. Many events can cause laminitis, including ingesting toxic levels of grain, eating lush grass, systemic disease problems, high temperature, toxemia, retained placenta, excessive weight-bearing as occurs when the opposite limb is injured, and the administration of some drugs. Laminitis usually manifests itself in the front feet, develops rapidly, and is life-threatening. In mild cases, however, a horse can resume a certain amount of athletic activity. Also known as founder.

magnetic therapy Physical therapy technique using magnetic fields. The low-energy electrical field created by the magnetic field causes dilation of the blood vessels (vasodilation) and tissue stimulation. Magnetic therapy may be used on soft tissue to treat such injuries as tendinitis or bony (skeletal) injuries such as bucked shins.

mare reproductive loss syndrome In the spring of 2001, a severe outbreak believed to have been caused by Eastern tent caterpillars caused the loss in Central Kentucky of more than 500 late-term fetuses and newborn foals and almost 5,000 early-term fetuses. The economic loss to Central Kentucky's Thoroughbred industry from MLRS was estimated at more than $300-million.

metacarpal (fracture) Usually refers to a fracture of the cannon bone, located between the knee and the fetlock joint in the front leg. Also may refer to a fracture of the splint bone. The cannon bone of the front leg is the third metacarpal.

monorchid A male horse of any age that has only one testicle in his scrotum; the other testicle was either removed or is undescended.

myectomy Surgery to treat horses that displace their soft palate or have an entrapped epiglottis while racing. Two strap muscles in the neck are cut to change the position of the larynx in the airway. Believed to release backward pressure on the larynx that may pull the epiglottis off the soft palate.

nasogastric tube A long, flexible tube that reaches from the nose to the stomach.

navicular disease A degenerative disease that affects the navicular bone (small bone in the back of the foot), navicular bursa, and deep flexor tendon. Generally considered a disease of the front feet.

neurectomy A surgical procedure in which the nerve supply to the navicular area is removed. The toe and remainder of the foot retain feeling. Sometimes referred to as posterior digital neurectomy or heel nerve. Also known as nerving.

nuclear scintigraphy Radioactive isotope tracer is injected into the horse, and its body is scanned with a specialized camera to produce an image that is interpreted by a computer. Concentration of the tracer is an indication of bone remodeling or inflammation and registers as a "hot spot"—a red area on the film; areas of diminished blood flow show up as "cold spots."

oblique Fracture at an angle.

oiling Administration of mineral oil by nasogastric tube to relieve gas or to break a blockage. Preventive procedure commonly used before long van rides to prevent impaction and subsequent colic.

open knee A condition of young horses in which the physis of the knee has not closed; an immature knee. Often used to describe the status of the physis immediately above the knee and is an indicator of long bone growth in two-year-olds.

osteoarthritis A permanent form of arthritis with progressive loss of the articular cartilage in a joint.

osteochondritis dissecans A cartilaginous or bony lesion that is the result of a fragment of cartilage and its underlying bone becoming detached from an articular surface. The OCD lesions occur commonly in the knee joint and are associated with a failure in bone development.

pastern Bones located between the fetlock joint and the hoof. The joint between the long and short pastern bones is called the pastern joint.

periostitis Inflammation of the tissue (periosteum) that overlies bone. Periostitis of the cannon bone is referred to as bucked shins, while periostitis of the splint bone is called a splint, which may be expressed as a popped splint.

phenylbutazone A nonsteroidal anti-inflammatory medication that is legal in many racing jurisdictions. Trade names are Butazolidin and Butazone.

physis The growth plate at the end of the long bones (such as the cannon bone) that lets the bone grow in length.

pin firing Thermocautery intended to increase blood flow to the leg and thus to promote healing.

pulled suspensory Suspensory ligament injury (suspensory desmitis) in which some fibers of the ligament have been disrupted and some loss of support of the distal limb may have occurred.

quarter crack A crack between the toe and heel, usually extending into the coronary band.

radiograph The picture or image on film or digital medium generated by X rays.

ring bone Osteoarthritis of joints between the pastern bones (high ring bone) or just above the coronet (low ring bone).

roaring (laryngeal hemiplegia) A whistling sound made by a horse during inhalation while exercising. The condition is caused by a partial or total paralysis of the nerves controlling the muscles that elevate the arytenoid cartilages and thereby open the larynx. In severe cases, a surgical procedure known as tie-back surgery (laryngoplasty) is performed, in which a suture is inserted through the cartilage to hold it out of the airway permanently. Paralysis almost exclusively occurs on the left side and most frequently in horses over 16 hands tall.

run down Abrasion of the heel during stride.

saucer Stress fracture of the front of the cannon bone; the fracture can be straight or curved.

screw fixation A procedure in which steel-alloy screws are surgically inserted to hold together a fractured bone.

sesamoid One of two small bones located above at the back of the fetlock joint. Fractures can be small chips or involve the entire bone. Surgical repair is often done by arthroscopy.

sesamoiditis Inflammation of the sesamoid bones.

shock-wave therapy Focus of high-energy sound waves on an affected body part to trigger natural repair mechanisms. Has been shown to stimulate bone formation and produce analgesia through numbness, which has potential for abuse.

simple A fracture along a single line that does not penetrate the skin.

slab A bone fracture in a joint that extends from one articular surface to another. Most often seen in the third carpal bone of the knee.

slipped Spontaneous abortion.

splint A condition in which calcification occurs on the splint bone and causes a bump. This condition can occur in response to a fracture or other irritation to the splint bone. A common injury is a popped splint.

stress A fracture created by the repetitive impact on a bone, most often in athletic training. Usually seen in the front of the cannon bone as a severe form of bucked shins. Also seen in the tibia and causes a hard-to-diagnose hind-limb lameness.

synchronous diaphragmatic flutter A contraction of the diaphragm in synchrony with the heartbeat after strenuous exercise, giving the appearance of hiccups. Affected horses have a noticeable twitch or spasm in the flank area that may cause an audible sound, often referred to as "thumps." Most commonly seen in electrolyte-depleted or exhausted horses. The condition resolves spontaneously with rest.

synovitis Inflammation of a synovial structure, typically a synovial sheath.

tendinitis Inflammation of a tendon.

thermography Diagnostic technique utilizing instrumentation that measures temperature differences. Records the surface temperature of a horse. Unusually hot or cold areas may be indicative of some underlying pathology (deviation from the normal).

thoroughpin Swelling of the synovial sheath of the deep flexor tendon above the hock.

tie-back surgery A procedure (laryngoplasty) used to suture the arytenoid cartilage out of the airway.

toe crack A crack near the front of the hoof.

torsion A twist in the intestine.

toxemia Poisoning sometimes caused by the absorption of bacterial products (endotoxins) that form at a local source of infection.

tubing Inserting a nasogastric tube through a horse's nostril into its stomach for the purpose of providing oral medication.

twitch A restraining device, usually consisting of a stick with a loop of rope or chain at one end, that is placed around a horse's upper lip and twisted, releasing endorphins that relax a horse and curb its fractiousness while it is being handled.

tying up Known as acute rhabdomyolysis, a form of muscle cramp that ranges in severity from mild stiffness to a life-threatening disorder. A generalized condition of muscle-fiber breakdown usually associated with exercise. The cause of the muscle-fiber breakdown is uncertain. Signs include sweating, reluctance to move, stiffness, and general distress.

ultrasound 1) Diagnostic ultrasound: A technique that uses ultrasonic waves to produce images of internal structures. 2) Therapeutic ultrasound: A therapy to create heat and stimulate healing.

Venezuelan equine encephalomyelitis A highly contagious disease affecting the central nervous system that can cause illness or death in horses and humans. Abbreviated as VEE.

Western equine encephalomyelitis A highly contagious disease spread by mosquitoes that affects the central nervous system. Can be prevented by annual vaccination.

West Nile virus Encephalitis first reported in North America in 1999. Virus is harbored in birds and spread by mosquitoes to other birds, horses, and humans. Not all horses bitten by infected mosquitoes develop clinical signs, but mortality rate is 38% in those that do. Can be prevented by seminannual vaccination.

wind puff Accumulation of synovial fluid in the fetlock-joint capsule. Also known as a wind gall.

wobbler syndrome Neurological disease clinically associated with general incoordination and muscle weakness. Can be caused by an injury to the spinal cord in the area of the cervical (neck) vertebrae or is associated with malformation or degeneration of the cervical vertebrae.

ABBREVIATIONS AND SYMBOLS

The following abbreviations and symbols are used throughout the *Racing Almanac*.

* See asterisk (*).
2yo Two-year-olds.
3yo Three-year-olds.
3yo & up Three-year-olds and up.
4yo Four-year-olds.
4yo & up Four-year-olds and up.
abt About.
Arg Country code for Argentina.
asterisk (*) In racing and breeding in North America, from 1906 through '74, an asterisk before a name indicates that the horse had been imported to North America in those years. For example: *Nasrullah, *Mahmoud, *Princequillo. Beginning in 1975, the asterisk was replaced by a country code, which designates the country in which the imported horse had been bred (see country code).
Aus Country code for Australia.
Avg. Average.
b. Bay coat color.
BHR Country code for Bahrain.
blk. Black coat color.
boldface type Typography that indicates a stakes winner, in boldface capital letters, or a stakes-placed horse, indicated by boldface capital and lowercase letters.
br. Brown coat color.
Brz Country code for Brazil.
c. Colt, an ungelded male horse from birth to age five.
c. & g. Colts and geldings.
ca. About, approximately.
Can Country code for Canada.
ch. Chestnut coat color.
Chi Country code for Chile.
Cond. Condition of track.
Corp. Corporation.
country code Beginning in 1975, the asterisk (*) (see above) was replaced by a country code, which designated the country in which the imported horse had been bred. For example: Black Tie Affair (Ire), Waya (Fr), Siphon (Brz). A horse whose name is followed by a country code has been imported to the United States.
CTHS California Thoroughbred Horse Society.
Dist. Distance of race.
Div. A stakes race split and run in divisions.
dk. b. or br. Dark bay or brown coat color.
DRF *Daily Racing Form.*
Eng England; an indication of where a race was run but not a country code for where a horse was bred. (see GB)
f Furlong.
f. A female horse from birth to age five.
f. & m. Fillies and mares.
Fr Country code for France.
g. A gelding of any age.
G1 Grade 1 or Group 1. Grade is used for North America; group is used everywhere else in the world.
G2 Grade 2 or Group 2. Grade is used for North America; group is used everywhere else in the world.
G3 Grade 3 or Group 3. Grade is used for North America; group is used everywhere else in the world.
GB Country code for Great Britain.
Ger Country code for Germany.
gr. Gray coat color.
gr. or ro. Gray or roan coat color.
GSWs Graded stakes winners (for sire references) or graded stakes wins (for runner references).
H. Handicap.
h. An ungelded male horse five years old or older.
HBPA Horsemen's Benevolent and Protective Association.
HK Country code for Hong Kong.
Imp. Imported. Used to designate horses imported to North America for racing or breeding prior to 1906.
Ind Country code for India.
Inc. Incorporated.
Ire Country code for Ireland.
Ity Country code for Italy.
Jpn Country code for Japan.
KSA Country code for Kingdom of Saudi Arabia.
L Listed race, a stakes race that is eligible for grading in the United States but is not graded.
Ltd. Limited.
m Mile.
m. A female horse five years old or older.
MRLS Mare reproductive loss syndrome (see veterinary terms section).
NTRA National Thoroughbred Racing Association.
NZ Country code for New Zealand.
OBSC Ocala Breeders' Sales Co.
OTB Off-track betting.
Pan Country code for Panama.
Per Country code for Peru.
Ph.D. Doctor of Philosophy.
Pol Country code for Poland.
PR Country code for Puerto Rico.
PRY Country code for Paraguay.
QA Country code for Qatar.
R A restricted race, such as for state-breds or horses sold at a specific sale.
rig. Ridgling, a lay term used to describe either a monorchid or a cryptorchid.
ro. Roan coat color.
Rus Country code for Russia.
S. Stakes.
SAf Country code for South Africa.
Sca Country code for Norway and Sweden.
Sin Country code for Singapore and Malaysia.
spl Stakes-placed.
Strs Starters.
St.Wns Stakes wins.
SWs Stakes winners or stakes wins.
T A stakes race run on turf.
TCP Triple Crown Productions.
TOBA Thoroughbred Owners and Breeders Association.
TRA Thoroughbred Racing Associations.
TVG Television Games Network.
UAE Country code for United Arab Emirates.
U.S. or USA Country code for United States.
Ven Country code for Venezuela.
Wnrs Winners.
Wnrs/Strs Percentage of winners from starters.
yds Yards.
yo Years old.
YOB Year of birth.

QUICK REFERENCE INDEX

Auctions	862
Belmont Stakes	167
Breeders' Cup	184
Breeding	775
Broodmares	851
Chronology of 2007 and 2008	33
Claiming, Claimers	599
Contemporary Individuals	753
Eclipse Awards	95
Glossary of Racing, Breeding Terms	986
Graded Stakes	244
Handicapping	971
History of Racing	57
International	922
Kentucky Derby	140
Key Dates in History	65
Leading Earners of All Time	552
Notable Horses in Racing	74
Notable Names of the Past	738
Obituaries, Horses	44
Obituaries, People	36
Organizations in Racing	895
People	713
Preakness Stakes	156
Purses by Track	23
Racetracks	613
Racing	236
Racing Hall of Fame	112
Reference	964
Rules of Racing	964
Sires, Leading	789
Sovereign Awards	960
Stakes Histories	244
Stakes Races of 2007	498
State of the Industry	1
Triple Crown	121
Year of 2007 in Review	28